P9-DBN-670

THE
ENCYCLOPEDIA
OF
SCIENCE
FICTION

THE
ENCYCLOPEDIA
OF
SCIENCE
FICTION

EDITED BY
JOHN CLUTE AND PETER NICHOLLS

Contributing editor
BRIAN STABLEFORD

Technical editor
JOHN GRANT

ST. MARTIN'S PRESS
New York

First published in the United States of America in 1993
Reprinted 1993, 1994

Typeset in Palatino by 🗡\Tek-Art, Croydon, Surrey, England
Printed in England by Butler & Tanner Ltd, Frome and London

Library of Congress Cataloging-in-Publication Data
The Encyclopedia of science fiction/edited by John Clute and Peter Nicholls;
    technical editor, John Grant; contributing editor, Brian Stableford
        ISBN 0-312-09618-6
        1. Science fiction – Dictionaries. I. Clute, John, 1940–
    II. Nicholls, Peter, 1939–
PN3433.4.E53 1993
809.3'8762'03 – dc20

92-47048
CIP

94-2725

CONTENTS

INTRODUCTION

The first edition of *The Encyclopedia of Science Fiction* won a Hugo Award as best nonfiction sf book of its year, and immediately became the standard one-volume reference in the field. However, as the years passed, its usefulness diminished as it fell slowly out of date. That first edition was completed, over 14 years ago, in June 1978, and published in 1979. This is its second edition, from new publishers. It has been not only updated but also wholly revised and almost wholly rewritten. In effect it is a new book, and we believe it is a better one. It is certainly very much bigger.

Excluding straightforward cross-reference entries, the first edition contained approximately 2800 entries; measured on the same basis, this new edition contains over 4360. The first edition was approximately 730,000 words long; this new edition is approximately 1,300,000 words long. In addition to the 4360+ entries, it contains around 2100 cross-reference entries.

The first edition was written faster than any of us were comfortable with (about 20 months); this edition took two years to write, a tight timetable, but manageable in part because of the technology of computer wordprocessing which allows cross-checking of data (by word search) in far shorter time than before. The book has been typeset from computer text generated by the editors. The three senior editors – John Clute, Peter Nicholls and Brian Stableford – were the same three who were primarily responsible for the first edition, and feel that our mutual familiarity made the task much easier this time round. Moreover, in the late 1970s the number of secondary sources available for cross-checking were comparatively few; now they are many ($\lozenge$ BIBLIOGRAPHIES). We continued to use primary sources whenever we could locate them, which we usually could, but it was a burden removed from our shoulders to have these secondary sources as a back-up. Our **Acknowledgements** section (page xxviii) lists some of those we found most useful.

On the other hand, the world of sf in 1992 is much more complex than it was in 1978. GENRE SF continues to grow and flourish, and its description remains our central task; but genre sf more and more occupies a world which, because of new category and marketing distinctions, is difficult to comprehend at a glance. Game worlds, film and tv spin-offs, shared worlds, graphic novels, franchises, young-adult fiction, choose-your-own-plot tales, technothrillers, survivalist fiction, sf horror novels, fantasy novels with sf centres, and so on – all contribute to a structure that hardly existed in the 1970s. The world of sf is also harder to describe now – not just because it has *become* more difficult, but because we have begun to discover that it *always was*. We entered on the first edition with joyful naïveté; we are older and wiser now, and we know that the secret history of sf, like the house in John Crowley's *Little Big* (**1981**), is bigger on the inside than the outside, and that the further in you go the bigger it gets. This is by way of apology: for every problem we have put right, two more have raised their heads; every discovery we (and others) make opens vistas which need to be explored. We know our book is neither perfect nor complete.

We have tried to cope with the expanding world of sf, and with our expanding perceptions of that world, by including many more theme and terminology entries with – we hope – a clarifying effect. There are, indeed, more entries in every category in this edition (details in **Contents of this Book** [page xi]), not just entries dealing with updatings over the past 14 years, but entries covering the whole body of the genre as we have found out more about it.

There is another difference between this edition and the last. The first time Peter Nicholls was where the buck stopped. This time John Clute, Nicholls's Associate Editor in the first edition, is a full and equal partner. There is no seniority on either side, and editorial differences of opinion have been remarkably few. The only problems have been the communications difficulties brought about by Clute working in London, UK, while Nicholls worked in Melbourne, Australia. To simplify matters when we began work (in August 1990) we agreed, like the ancient Romans, to split the Empire. Clute, who for several years has been updating a bibliographic data bank, took charge of author entries; Nicholls took charge of the rest. This system (which to a degree reflects what happened in practice on the first book, too) works out at about half the book each. Each of us, however, has written entries for the other's half, and each of us has checked the other's text. Brian Stableford has been our safety net, and a major contributor in his own right. We have commissioned many new writers (and received a gratifying number of volunteers), some for single and some for multiple entries, but none of these, this time around, has written as many entries as did, for the first edition, Malcolm Edwards – who was with Stableford then a Contributing Editor – John Brosnan and David Pringle; many of their entries survive in this edition, albeit in (almost always) modified form.

In this second edition, to a greater degree than in the first, most of the writing – perhaps 85% – is by Clute, Nicholls and Stableford, who despite small disagreements have displayed a critical consensus over a strikingly large range of issues. This means, for good or ill, that the book has a more unified tone of voice than most reference books (whose editors often write only a small proportion of the text themselves). We should point out, remembering charges of Anglophilia made of the first edition by a vocal minority, that only Stableford is English. Clute is Canadian and Nicholls Australian, and both have spent some years in the USA, whose culture they regard as adoptively an important part of what they are, and central to what sf is.

All entries are signed by initials. We do this to give credit where credit is due, and also to apportion responsibility for those cases where the reader may feel that the content of an entry has gone beyond the strictly factual into the judgemental. In the interest of liveliness and readability, we continue to allow, as we did in the first edition, a modicum of explicit critical comment. There is, anyway, no such thing as a purely objective reference work, since the very choice of what is discussed (and at what length) will suggest (to some readers) a value judgment. But here a cautionary note: the length of an entry depends on many factors; we cannot stress too strongly that conclusions drawn by readers about editorial preferences, on the basis of an entry's length, may well be wrong. To restate: opinion has been kept minimal, and in every case it is possible to identify, through the initials used, whose opinion it may be, though this second edition does contain many more examples of entries signed by two, three or even four initials than did the first. Some of this results from editorial modification of existing entries whose authors in many cases were not able to revise their own entries; some entries were collaborative from the first. The first initial given is generally that of the primary contributor. However, even though every entry is signed, there is a real sense in which this volume is a team effort, not least in that each entry has been scanned by at least four readers apart from its author, resulting often in the incorporation of uncredited suggestions and corrections.

We envisage our readership as ranging widely in age and background. Two specialist readerships, those belonging to the academic world and those belonging to organized fandom, will, we hope, find much to interest them; but this encyclopedia is not specifically aimed at either of these articulate lobby groups. (Though two of the editors have been university lecturers in the past, all are now full-time writers; the personal connections each of us has with sf fandom are enjoyable but peripheral.)

The final manuscript (on computer disk, not paper) of this encyclopedia was completed in mid-August 1992, though many subsequent modifications (and small factual additions relating to awards, deaths and so on) continued to be made up to the last possible moment. However, we claim double-checked consistency only for the period ending 31 December 1991, and we list almost no authors whose book publications commenced in 1992. Nevertheless, we do cite a great many 1992 publications and some 1992 films, tv shows, etc., though bibliographic and other information for the period after May 1992 is necessarily less secure than for the earlier part of the year. We have occasionally listed projected titles, in a format entirely distinct from that used for confirmed publications (◊ **How to Use this Book** [page xxxiii]). We cannot emphasize too strongly, however, that projected titles are *projected*: in strict bibliographic terms they are nothing but *guesses*.

This is intended as a book to be dipped into or read for pleasure, not merely as a reference source for data. Serendipity may bring curious and pleasing conjunctions of entries; an elaborate system of cross-references is designed to allow readers to weave zigzag trails from entry to entry, constructing interrelations – sometimes surprising – as they do so. We see this book as more than merely an encyclopedia of sf; it is a comprehensive history and analysis of the genre.

We intend to continue revising and updating our sf data with future editions – and new formats – in mind. As before, so now, we deeply appreciate all the help we can get. Letters can, of course, be sent via our publishers; or suggestions about and corrections of author entries can be sent directly to John Clute, 221 Camden High Street, London NW1 7BU, UK, and about all other entries to Peter Nicholls, 26A Wandsworth Road, Surrey Hills, Victoria 3127, Australia.

John Clute and Peter Nicholls, November 1992

CONTENTS OF THIS BOOK

In the first edition of this encyclopedia we laid out frankly what was included and what we had chosen to leave out. Let us do so again, by examining one at a time the various subcategories (authors, themes, magazines, films, etc.) into which, for administrative purposes, we have normally divided the book when discussing its structure.

1. Authors In the beginning it seemed very simple. In late 1976, as the first edition of this encyclopedia began to take shape, we decided that we would give an individual entry to any writer who published a book of sf in English before the beginning of 1978, as well as entries to some authors who had never published a book of their own. We had no idea how huge a task we had taken on, though it did not take us more than a couple of months to discover that our goals were unattainable.

Very soon we decided that, even with English-language book authors, we would have to exercise some discretion. We would have to exclude some authors of genre sf who seemed to have made no impact on the field in general; generally speaking these authors had published only one book and were not expected to publish any more (we did not treat authors who had only recently published a first book as one-book authors in this sense). And we would exercise a similar (though less easily defined) control over non-genre sf authors as well, especially those who wrote prior to the 20th century.

In the event, we were reasonably successful with writers of genre sf, missing only a few obvious names (Damien BRODERICK, Octavia BUTLER, John S. GLASBY, Jacqueline LICHTENBERG and Robert LORY were among our most visible omissions, none of them deliberate). But genre sf, by definition (◊ GENRE SF), had reasonably distinct boundaries, and we were able to be pretty sure (errors aside) that we had covered the territory. Non-genre sf was, however, another matter. Because many of the research aids we now take for granted (◊ BIBLIOGRAPHIES) had not yet been published in the mid-1970s, we only slowly discovered the hugeness of the world of non-genre sf (◊ FABULATION, HISTORY OF SF *and* MAINSTREAM WRITERS OF SF *for an overview*), and how remarkably difficult it was going to be to know when to stop looking for authors who merited inclusion. In fact we never did stop finding previously unsuspected sf books of interest by non-genre writers, and we probably never will. By the time we ceased adding entries to the first edition, we found that we had given as many entries to non-genre writers as to genre ones, although our central focus on genre sf meant of course that we paid far more attention to writers like Isaac ASIMOV and Robert A. HEINLEIN than to literary figures (some major, like Vladimir NABOKOV) who made occasional use of sf devices. In the end, taking Authors, Editors and Critics together, we had a total of 1817 entries on individual writers.

For the second edition we have eliminated about 50 of these writers, on several grounds, all of which apply also to more recent candidates for inclusion:

1. Because of the increasingly book-oriented nature of written sf, we have with reluctance decided not to give entries to writers who have not yet published a book of their own; individual stories by these writers will of course be referred to in the relevant Theme entries.
2. Some fantasy writers, we have come to feel, did not in fact have enough impact on the sf world to warrant an entry.
3. We no longer knowingly include writers whose books have been solely published by vanity presses.
4. We no longer give individual entries to authors none of whose books in other languages have been translated into English (these authors are of course treated in Country entries: ◊ **Science Fiction in Various Countries** [page xvi] *for a list of countries covered, and for an overall view of our very-much expanded coverage of non-English language sf*).
5. We eliminated a few routine one-book authors.

Having by these means reduced the total to below 1800, we then added more than 1100 new entries. The new total of Author entries is 2900+.

Some of the new entries are devoted to authors we missed the first time around:

some were culpably omitted, and some were authors neither we (nor anybody else then in print) had known were responsible for sf books, but most were authors of works in subgenres associated with sf, which we now cover more thoroughly (see below). However, more than half of the new entries are devoted to authors who published their first book after the beginning of 1978. Some writers whose impact has been negligible have been excluded deliberately, just as in 1979; and almost certainly there will be others who have been excluded in error. And we have had some new things to think about, too. There has been a huge growth, for instance, in ties of all sorts (◊ **How to Use this Book** *and* ◊ TIE *for what we mean when we say that a book is tied or untied*), including a large number of shared-world productions (◊ SHARED WORLDS). We have excluded very few sf authors who have solely written books tied to shared-world endeavours (like STAR WARS or STAR TREK), but we have excluded some authors solely of books tied (for instance) to films (novelizations), to fantasy role-playing games (◊ GAME WORLDS) and also choose-your-own-plot format game books (◊ GAMES AND TOYS). Although we do not feel it desirable (or possible) to give an entry to every writer of sf for children (◊ CHILDREN'S SF), we are now much more inclusive in our coverage, leaving out mainly (it is an area extremely difficult to define) authors of sf written specifically for younger children. Finally, although the number of entries for non-genre sf writers has grown very considerably, we remain very conscious of the impossibility of definitively covering an area whose boundaries cannot be defined (but see below for genres and subgenres which, although affiliated to sf, are not sf as we understand the term; *see also* DEFINITIONS OF SF). These caveats and exclusions are, we recognize, numerous enough to give us considerable latitude in our selection of authors to include or leave out. Within these terms, however, we have attempted to give an individual entry to every writer who has published an (inarguably) sf book in English – or had one translated into English – before the beginning of 1992.

In selecting FANTASY and supernatural-HORROR authors for inclusion, we have attempted to restrict our coverage to those authors whose works have had some significant influence on the complex webs that bind the three genres together, or whose work contains many elements of *rationalized* fantasy or horror. In the first category, it is obvious that, the earlier a writer is, the more likely it will be that his or her work has had time to affect the world (and the genres) around him; and we have therefore given entries to writers like Algernon BLACKWOOD, James Branch CABELL, Lord DUNSANY, E.R. EDDISON, Robert E. HOWARD, H.P. LOVECRAFT, George MacDONALD and J.R.R. TOLKIEN.

The second category is infinitely debatable, and it is here that subjective judgements have had to come into play. Much fantasy and horror makes use of idea-clusters (or tropes or motifs) that are also fundamental to sf. The four most important are perhaps ALTERNATE WORLDS, MONSTERS, PSI POWERS and TIME TRAVEL. These tropes are commonly used as magical facilitating devices or threats, but sometimes they are given sufficient logical cohesion and grounding as to be readable in sf terms (*see also* SCIENCE FANTASY); indeed, MAGIC itself – as often in John W. CAMPBELL's magazine UNKNOWN – can be treated like this. But we have entered the borderlands, where nothing can be finally and entirely clear. A particularly common feature of fantasy (for instance) is time travel accomplished by fantastic means, as in several tales by the significant children's author E. Nesbit; we do not regard such books as sf. At the same time we *do* regard Mark TWAIN's *A Connecti-*

cut Yankee in King Arthur's Court (**1889**), in which time travel is also accomplished by fantastic means, as an important sf text. We do not (for instance) give entries to such exemplary writers of horror fiction as Clive Barker, Ramsey Campbell, James Herbert, Thomas Ligotti or Peter Straub, even though we are aware that an occasional sf trope makes its way into their pages; we do give entries to Charles L. GRANT and Whitley STRIEBER, though primarily for their post-HOLOCAUST novels. Many popular fantasy writers, like Craig Shaw Gardner and Robert Jordan, have been left out; while others, like David GEMMELL and Barbara HAMBLY, have entries because we judge their work to be sufficiently akin to sf. When we have erred in making these decisions, we hope that we have done so on the side of inclusiveness.

In our treatment of authors (most of them dating from the late 19th and early 20th centuries) who specialized in subgenres associated with the development of genre sf (but not usefully defined as being themselves early sf), we do not pretend to be comprehensive. We do not attempt to provide entries for all authors of LOST-WORLD novels, FANTASTIC VOYAGES, prehistoric romances, future-WAR tales, occultist stories set on this or other worlds, stories of possession and split personality, tales of REINCARNATION and IMMORTALITY, *contes philosophiques* and UTOPIAS, especially utopias set in the present day. But the last decades have seen an enormous increase in the field's understanding of the intersecting genres that helped shape modern sf, and we now have a much better idea of the amount and variety of early sf and its siblings. We have therefore very considerably increased our author coverage in these areas.

In our treatment of authors (most of them writing after WWII) who make occasional use of sf devices (◊ McGUFFIN; TECHNOTHRILLER) to propel plots set in an undated NEAR

FUTURE, we have been highly selective, for most of these books are neither written nor read as sf, and do not reward any attempt to incorporate them as sf or sf-ish, though we have given entries to a few (e.g., Ian FLEMING). With political thrillers or SATIRES set in an undated near future, we have erred on the side of inclusiveness (Alan DRURY, for instance, is given an entry), and do so out of a genuine insecurity as to the sf nature of some political thought.

We regret that several factors have persuaded us to drop a feature from the first edition that we know some found useful: there, we listed all separate, uncollected short stories (when we could locate them) that belonged to a series, as well as all the books in the series. We still list all series books, but we no longer, normally, append uncollected short stories. The main factor is utility: it is now very uncommon for readers to have ready access to the sort of magazine collections that would allow them to find these stories; the shift away from magazine publication towards book publication of recent work – as well as the extensive republication of worthwhile early work in book form – also argues against the inclusion of this feature.

So far we have been speaking only about fiction writers. We have been moderately generous, but not comprehensive, in giving entries to editors of sf magazines and sf anthologies (and few editors of only one or two anthologies have been included). More often than not, of course, the issue of inclusion or exclusion does not arise on this score, because many – perhaps most – sf editors have also been sf writers.

For critics and scholars and other authors of relevant nonfiction, we have been highly selective. We divide nonfiction authors into two categories:

1. Authors about sf. The number of books, pamphlets, chapbooks and so on published about the field is now very large, and authors of only one book about sf may not receive an entry. Nonetheless, the number of "academic" and "bibliography" entries is considerable.

2. Authors whose ideas have fed so strongly into sf (for good or ill) that we thought a summary of their work would be useful to readers. They run all the way from PLATO to Erich VON DÄNIKEN, taking in Immanuel VELIKOVSKY and others *en route*. (◊ PROTO SCIENCE FICTION *for a discussion of just how recent the distinction between fiction and nonfiction historically is*.) We are not at all inclusive about this category. Many writers have been left out, with no imputation intended as to their stature. If the scientist Stephen W. Hawking does not appear while the scientist Freeman J. DYSON does, it is because the latter has given his surname to a concept used widely in modern sf (◊ DYSON SPHERE).

Author entries were written mostly by John Clute (about 2300, plus some in collaboration); Peter Nicholls wrote about 290 entries, and Brian Stableford also contributed many major entries. Neither Malcolm EDWARDS nor David PRINGLE had time to rework their numerous entries (although the latter was able to revise his 1979 J.G. BALLARD entry), and these have been updated by Clute and Stableford. John Eggeling was able to do some revision work on his entries. E.F. BLEILER and Neal Tringham each supplied several new entries. Other contributors of one or more author entries to either or both editions of this book are listed under **Checklist of Contributors** (page xxiii).

2. Themes The theme entries are the connective tissue of this encyclopedia and constitute a quarter of its length. Through them it is possible to derive a coherent sense of the HISTORY OF SF (itself a theme entry) and of what sf is all about. We are aware, too, of the usefulness of theme entries to teachers and academics, who may wish to use sf stories to throw light on contemporary issues but be at a loss to know which stories or novels would best be chosen for the task. Together, the theme entries form a very detailed lexicon of sf's main concerns, its subgenres, the genres to which it is most closely related, and the terms we use in talking about it. Entries range from ANTIMATTER and ATLANTIS through CONCEPTUAL BREAKTHROUGH, DYSTOPIAS and FUTUROLOGY, via NEAR FUTURE and ORIGIN OF MAN to VENUS, UNDER THE SEA and WEAPONS. For a complete list ⟡ **Checklist of Themes** (page xxix).

The theme entries were a major feature in the first edition, and loom even larger here. There is no clear distinction between a theme entry and a terminology entry (see below), but the theme entry is likely to be substantially longer (most over 1000 words, and some over 3000) and to give more examples from actual sf texts. However, many common items of sf terminology (ANDROIDS, ROBOTS, CRYONICS, MATTER TRANSMITTERS, TERRAFORMING and so on) are so important that they warrant a full theme entry.

Since the first edition we have upgraded some terminology entries to full theme entries, and reclassified some shorter theme entries as terminology entries. The upshot is that 169 theme entries, all updated, remain from 1979. Two of those that have been eliminated have become multiple entries. The original MUSIC AND OPERA has been broken into three: MUSIC #1: SF IN CLASSICAL MUSIC, #2: SF IN POPULAR AND ROCK MUSIC, and #3: MUSIC IN SF. The original WOMEN, originally written by a man (Nicholls), has become FEMINISM, WOMEN SF WRITERS and WOMEN AS PORTRAYED IN SCIENCE FICTION, all written by a woman (Lisa

TUTTLE). Counting these six, there are 43 new theme entries, making a total of 212 theme entries in all. Some new entries relate to recent developments in sf: BIG DUMB OBJECTS, CYBERPUNK, GAMES AND TOYS, GAME WORLDS, GRAPHIC NOVELS, NANOTECHNOLOGY, SHARED WORLDS, SURVIVALIST FICTION, VIRTUAL REALITY and so on; others could well have appeared in the first edition had we thought of them: APES AND CAVEMEN, AWARDS, BALLOONS, CLUB STORIES, GOLEM, HITLER WINS, HOLLOW EARTH, LIBERTARIAN SF, MONSTER MOVIES, POETRY, RURITANIA, SENSE OF WONDER, SLEEPER AWAKES, SMALL PRESSES AND LIMITED EDITIONS, SPACE HABITATS and SUPERHEROES are some of these. Some relate to genre criticism: EDISONADE, HORROR IN SF, PLANETARY ROMANCE, POCKET UNIVERSE, POSTMODERNISM AND SF, RECURSIVE SF and TECHNOTHRILLER are the main ones.

Brian Stableford wrote 78 of the original theme entries – this being where he has left his profoundest mark on the book – and Peter Nicholls 55, the remaining 36 being by other hands. Twelve contributors of theme entries to the first edition, including Brian W. ALDISS, David PRINGLE, Tom SHIPPEY and John SLADEK, were not able to update their entries for this edition. These entries have nevertheless (all but one, RADIO #1: U.S.) been revised and updated, mostly by Stableford (who also updated some of Nicholls's) and Nicholls, others by John Clute, Everett BLEILER, Professor I.F. CLARKE and others. Of the 43 new entries, 16 are primarily by Nicholls, 14 primarily by Clute, and 13 by other hands, including Damien BRODERICK, Robert FRAZIER and Neil GAIMAN.

3. Terminology A terminology entry is effectively a short theme entry. This edition retains 48 such entries from 1979, and adds a further 17. Most are terms often used in sf, but sometimes found obscure by new readers, like AI, BEM, CORPSICLE, GAS GIANT,

ION DRIVE, LAGRANGE POINT, PARSEC, RIM-WORLD and TELEKINESIS. Some are terms used in describing sf and associated genres, like BRAID, HEROIC FANTASY, MAGIC REALISM, OULIPO, ROBINSONADE, SCIENTIFICTION, SCI FI, SEMIPROZINE, SHARECROP, SLIPSTREAM, SPECULATIVE FICTION, SPLATTER MOVIES and TIE. There are also entries on certain movements allegedly connected to sf, such as GENERAL SEMANTICS and SCIENTOLOGY. For a full list of terminology entries ◊ TERMINO-LOGY. Most terminology entries are by Peter Nicholls, some are by John Clute, and two are by Scott BRADFIELD.

4. Science Fiction in Various Countries

It would be redundant to give separate entries for the USA and the UK, since sf from these areas dominates the book. We do, however, give entries to three other English-speaking countries, AUSTRALIA, CANADA and NEW ZEALAND. The entry for Canada is now divided into two sections: one for English-speaking Canada and one for French-speaking Canada.

This area of the book is, relatively, the most expanded, and was perhaps the most difficult to put together. Communications difficulties with parts of the world in considerable turmoil have left some entries with an occasional date or translation of title missing. We retain entries for BENELUX and SCANDINAVIA (with DENMARK and FINLAND now separate entries), but two other portmanteau entries from the first edition have been broken up, to a degree, into their component nations. There are no longer entries for "Eastern Europe" and "Spain, Portugal and South America" but, as the list below shows, some new portmanteau entries are now included. It should be noted that the YUGOSLAVIA entry was sent to us – in December 1990 – before that nation began to split into a group of smaller states with a Serbian rump still calling itself Yugoslavia. We decided for ease of reference not even to attempt to divide the Yugoslavia entry into its component nation-states of Croatia, Slovenia, etc.

The full list of 27 entries is as follows (new entries asterisked): ALBANIA*, ARABIC SF*, AUSTRALIA, AUSTRIA*, BENELUX (Belgium, Luxembourg, Netherlands), BLACK AFRICAN SF*, BULGARIA*, CANADA, CHINESE SF*, CZECH AND SLOVAK SF*, DENMARK*, FINLAND*, FRANCE, GERMANY, HUNGARY*, ISRAEL*, ITALY, JAPAN, LATIN AMERICAN SF* (primarily Argentina, Brazil, Cuba, Mexico), NEW ZEA-LAND*, POLAND*, ROMANIA*, RUSSIA, SCAN-DINAVIA (Sweden and Norway), SOVIET UNION* (more a note than an entry), SPAIN* and YUGOSLAVIA*. All but a handful of these have been written by experts from the areas or nations concerned. We have not attempted to contact scholars from every country. We apologize to Greece, India and all the many other countries where we know some sf exists, but where we did not have the necessary contacts to enable us to codify it. What was approximately 14,000 words in 1979 has been expanded to around 40,000, close to three times the length. The Anglo-American readership must be our first concern; they make up the vast majority of our audience. But we feel that, while we might not have done full justice to sf in non-English-speaking countries, then at least we have outlined, on a scale not previously attempted in an English-language sf reference work, the extraordinary scope of what has now become a truly international literature.

All authors – about 300 of them – who receive substantive treatment in the Country entries are cross-referred to there from the rest of the encyclopedia. On the other hand, when a Country entry mentions authors who are well known in English translation and therefore have their own entries, their names are given in SMALL CAPITALS, referring readers to those entries, with generally only a brief coverage in the

Country entry. Under FRANCE, therefore, there is not much about Jules VERNE, and in RUSSIA not much about the STRUGATSKI brothers.

5. Films Our coverage of films is thorough but not fully comprehensive. Depending on where you draw the boundaries, there may have been 2000 sf films made. We covered about 286 in the first edition (an exact count is difficult, since several entries covered more than one film); we have deleted 5 and added 263, making a total of 544. Of the 263 we have added, 38 belong to the period covered in the first edition (1901-77 for movies) – our original selection of 286 films was a little arbitrary, and had some notable omissions, including BRIDE OF FRANKENSTEIN – and 224 have been released since. Sf/fantasy/horror film-making, as readers will know, has become almost the dominant genre in the industry since at least the time of STAR WARS.

Dates of films are difficult to establish with certainty. Most written sources give the copyright date, some the date of first release (often a year later), and some appear simply to guess. An examination of the film itself will give only the copyright date, and we have where possible given date of first release, but there are a number of cases, especially with older films, where we cannot be certain of the category into which the date falls.

We have included representative films from the fringes of sf, such as near-future thrillers about, for example, a presidential assassination or a technological breakthrough. By far the most important of the fringe subgenres is the rationalized HORROR film or MONSTER MOVIE (there are many in this book) where the monster is provided with a scientific explanation, and, more importantly (as in the case of George A. ROMERO's zombie films), where the apparently supernatural threat is regarded with

a sciencefictional eye. (Can you train zombies? Do they have a society? What will their presence do to existing society?)

We count made-for-tv films as film entries rather than tv entries, in part because many US films made for tv have been given theatrical release abroad. Also (like ordinary theatrical movies) many are available on videotape, and not distinguished in the video shop from ordinary movies. There may be some apparent inconsistencies here, because we count tv miniseries as tv series rather than films, even though cut versions of miniseries sometimes turn up on videotape or on tv as if they were single films. Made-for-tv films are identified as such throughout. Because their standard is on average lower than that of theatrical films, we do not attempt in this area the same level of comprehensiveness.

A word about omissions: most (but not all) sf films exclusively for children or teenagers are out, hence few Disney films; most foreign-language films with little or no circulation outside their country of origin are out (though many foreign-language films remain in); most SUPERHERO films are out (e.g., *Spiderman*, *Batman*) unless there is a strong sf rationale (e.g., DARKMAN); horror movies and monster movies that effectively rely on the supernatural are out (e.g., *Wolfen*, *Nightwing*, *Gremlins*); time-travel accomplished by fantastic means is usually out (e.g., *Biggles*, *The Navigator: A Medieval Odyssey*, *Peggy Sue Got Married*, *Somewhere in Time*, *Time Bandits*); apart from the great originals, films about monsters made from body parts are out, especially if jokey (e.g., all post-war films in the FRANKENSTEIN series, *The Incredible Two-Headed Transplant*); most Bigfoot films are out (e.g., *Legend of Boggy Creek*); most ESP thrillers are out (e.g., *Eyes of Laura Mars*, *The Medusa Touch*); many future-gladiator, post MAD MAX films are out (e.g., *The New Barbarians*, *Steel Dawn*, *Turkey Shoot*, *The Salute of the Jugger* [vt *The Blood of*

Heroes]); many limp parodies are out (e.g., *Attack of the Killer Tomatoes*, *Class of Nuke 'Em High*); many mediocre sequels and remakes are out, or more probably, mentioned in passing (e.g., *Critters 2*, *The Stepford Children*). We hope we have given separate entries to all the better sequels and remakes.

Readers of sf in the written form, for whom this book is primarily designed, may justifiably feel that films are given undue prominence in this book. After all, we do not discuss individual novels in anything like the same detail given to individual films. On the other hand, the audience for sf cinema is massively greater than that for sf books, and in the light of the huge popular interest in sf films it seemed a thorough coverage was necessary, especially since we enjoy them ourselves. All the same, sf-cinema entries, including those on film-makers, constitute less than 10% of the entire text, though at at 110,000 words this makes the film section of this book one of the most comprehensive studies available.

All the original entries (John Brosnan was then the primary contributor in this area) have been thoroughly revised and in many cases wholly rewritten. New film entries are mostly by Peter Nicholls, quite a few by Kim Newman, some by other hands.

Theme entries about films are CINEMA, HORROR IN SF (in part), MONSTER MOVIES, SPLATTER MOVIES and SUPERHEROES (in part), all by Peter Nicholls. Relevant magazine entries are CINEFANTASTIQUE, STARBURST and STARLOG. We no longer give a checklist of all films receiving entries in this volume; the issue is confused by variant titles – which are of course cross-referred – and the fact that some films (usually sequels) are briefly discussed in the entries for other films. We decided therefore that the space consumed by a checklist would not be warranted by its utility.

6. Film-makers There were 19 film-maker entries in the first edition, or more if one counts such entries as those on Charles BEAUMONT, Michael CRICHTON and Richard MATHESON (and in this edition Alan BRENNERT and Glen A. LARSON) who would have received entries in any case on the basis of their sf work in written form. We have deleted one, and added 16 new film-maker entries (nearly all written by Kim Newman, who also updated some of the earlier ones) making 34 in all. The film-maker entries (including some whose work was primarily in television) are Irwin ALLEN, Gerry and Sylvia ANDERSON, Jack ARNOLD, John BADHAM, Charles BAND, James CAMERON, John CARPENTER, Larry COHEN, Roger CORMAN, David CRONENBERG, Joe DANTE, John FRANKENHEIMER, Ray HARRYHAUSEN, Byron HASKIN, Gale Anne HURD, Nigel KNEALE, Fritz LANG, Stanley KUBRICK, George LUCAS, Georges MÉLIÈS, George MILLER, Terry NATION, Willis O'BRIEN, George PAL, Gene RODDENBERRY, George A. ROMERO, John SAYLES, Ridley SCOTT, Rod SERLING, Curt SIODMAK, Steven SPIELBERG, Andrei TARKOVSKY, Peter WATKINS and Robert WISE.

7. Television As with films, we are thorough without being fully comprehensive. We have deleted two tv entries from the first edition, leaving 54 pre-existing entries, all revised, and have added 42 new entries, including ALIEN NATION, BATTLESTAR GALACTICA, BLAKE'S SEVEN, MAX HEADROOM, RED DWARF, SAPPHIRE AND STEEL, STAR TREK: THE NEXT GENERATION and WONDER WOMAN. This makes 96 tv entries in all, listed in the TELEVISION theme entry. Most of these entries are for tv series, some for tv miniseries and serials. (Made-for-tv movies we classify as films, as noted above.) We do not include animated tv series for children, such as *The Jetsons*, with the exception (by popular demand) of the various animated puppet series, like STINGRAY, made by Gerry and Sylvia ANDERSON. A fringe area, where we have made decisions which will certainly be seen by some as arbitrary, concerns tv series centring on a SUPERHERO whose powers (generally) stem from some sort of scientific disaster. Thus we do have an entry for *The* INCREDIBLE HULK, but no entry for *The Flash*, which we see as a crime show rather than sf. We have been rather niggardly about including serials and miniseries, concentrating primarily on those, like the four **Quatermass** stories and (much more recently) *The* CLONING OF JOANNA MAY, that have aroused much general interest or are of obviously high quality. We do tend to give entries in cases where there was a film spin-off, or a film of the same title, so as to clear up possible confusion, as with *The* TROLLENBERG TERROR and DAY OF THE TRIFFIDS. We believe there are no omissions at all of live-action tv series in the English language up to 1991 that lasted any length of time and are inarguably sf in content. We also give entries for famous fantasy series with occasional sf content, such as *The* TWILIGHT ZONE and AMAZING STORIES. Tv entries for the second edition have mostly been written by Peter Nicholls and Kim Newman; many surviving from the first edition are by John Brosnan.

8. Magazines We give entries to the most important pulp and other general-fiction magazines that printed sf before the advent of genre-sf magazines in 1926, such as *The* ARGOSY and *The* STRAND MAGAZINE; these are listed under MAGAZINES or PULP MAGAZINES. We include a number of the SUPERHERO and supervillain pulps of the 1930s, like CAPTAIN HAZZARD and DR. YEN SIN; these, too, will be found listed under PULP MAGAZINES. We count in the catch-all magazine category (as opposed to the specialized FANZINE category) maybe 10 critical journals about sf, some wholly academic, like SCIENCE-FICTION STUDIES, and some less so, like SCIENCE FICTION & FANTASY BOOK

REVIEW. We also include the most important sf-movie magazines: CINEFANTASTIQUE, STARBURST and STARLOG.

But the centrepiece of our magazine entries comprises the fiction magazines, whether fully professional or SEMIPROZINES. We attempt to give entries to *all* professional sf magazines and semiprozines in the English language, past and current, but will not tempt fate by claiming 100% success in this surprisingly difficult exercise; in the first edition we claimed (slightly incorrectly) to give entries also to "all fantasy magazines that regularly printed stories by sf authors", but we do not repeat that claim here: the borderland between FANTASY magazine and sf magazine is grey; and while we hope to have given entries to all fantasy magazines that extend clearly if occasionally into the sf area, and to some like UNKNOWN that rarely did but nevertheless featured largely in the ethos of the sf community, we have eliminated some entries, like *Coven 13*, *Mind Magic* and *Fantasy Tales*, where the distance from sf magazines proper seems too large. On the other hand, we have resuscitated some candidates not given entries first time around, like MAGAZINE OF HORROR, which have a genuine sf relevance, and generally we still include a great many magazines, like BIZARRE MYSTERY MAGAZINE, that were or are fantasy magazines primarily. The line has to be arbitrary, and we do not claim omniscience at generic diagnosis.

One feature of the Magazine entries in the first edition appeared under the rubric **Collectors should note:**. This was information mainly about irregularities in numeration and occasional skipped issues. Now that there are many more specialist publications catering for collectors' needs, we felt able to omit part of this information. We have moved the more important data of this sort to the main body of the text.

All magazines can be regarded as anthologies, and the distinction between the two is not nearly as clear as might be thought. In cases where original-anthology series announce themselves as periodicals by being numbered and dated (especially on the cover), and especially when they contain magazine features like letter columns, editorials and so on, they can be regarded as magazines, even if they physically resemble paperback or even hardcover books. Some announce themselves as such, PULP-HOUSE: THE HARDBACK MAGAZINE being one. Further borderline examples are AVON FANTASY READER (regarded by the fans of the time as a magazine, and so indexed in the standard magazine references by Donald DAY and Erwin STRAUSS), DESTINIES, FAR FRONTIERS and *New Destinies* – there are others. The main practical result of this policy is that we do not necessarily separately list every title in such series as we would have done if we regarded them as original-anthology series proper.

We no longer publish a checklist of all magazines given entries; it is space-consuming and of doubtful utility. We have deleted 12 fiction magazines and two critical journals from the first edition, which, not counting the 36 FANZINE entries (see below) leaves 192 entries from the first edition, to which 38 entries have been added, making a total of 230 fiction-magazine and critical-journal entries. Some of these single entries cover two magazines with identical titles, so about 240 magazines are given entries. We do not generally give entries to foreign-language magazines, though a good many of these are cross-referred to the relevant Country entry. Most magazine entries were written by Brian Stableford, Peter Nicholls, Frank Parnell and Malcolm Edwards. It is no longer the case that our encyclopedia gives the most comprehensive magazine coverage (see the reference book by Marshall TYMN and Mike ASHLEY), but it is certainly the most comprehensive in a book not exclusively devoted to the topic.

9. Fanzines There are 36 entries devoted to individual fanzines, this branch of amateur publishing being of central importance to the history of the sf community. (Data on an additional dozen or so titles are available by following up cross references, title changes being common in fanzine publishing.) However, we have been highly selective, concentrating on fanzines that have generally been quite long-running and which have as part of their content some serious comment on sf, as opposed to general news or gossip. Ten fanzine entries have been deleted from the first edition – we no longer include all HUGO-winning fanzines – and 13 added. There is a very thin line between fanzines and critical journals on the one hand, and fanzines and semiprozines on the other, so our count of 36 might be higher or lower than another's. For a full listing of these 36 titles ◊ FANZINES. Most of these entries were written by Peter Roberts (first edition), Rob Hansen and Peter Nicholls.

10. Comics Comic books and comic strips are taken more seriously by many more people now than was the case a decade ago, partly as a result of artistic developments in the field. We have reflected this widespread interest by expanding the size and number of entries dealing with both historical and contemporary sf comics. The two main theme entries dealing with comics are COMICS and GRAPHIC NOVELS; a third entry, SUPERHEROES, deals primarily with comics, films and tv. We have entries on three comic-book publishers, DC COMICS, EC COMICS and MARVEL COMICS. The entries on comics titles and comics characters are ALLEY OOP, AMERICAN FLAGG!, BARBARELLA, BRICK BRADFORD, BUCK ROGERS IN THE 25TH CENTURY, CAPTAIN MARVEL, CONNIE, DAN DARE – PILOT OF THE FUTURE, FLASH GORDON, GARTH, HEAVY METAL, JEFF HAWKE, JUDGE DREDD, LEGION OF SUPER-HEROES, LOVE AND

ROCKETS, MÉTAL HURLANT, MISTER X, NEXUS, SUPERMAN, SWAMP THING, TEENAGE MUTANT NINJA TURTLES, 2,000 A.D., WATCHMEN and X-MEN. Entries on writers and illustrators primarily associated with comics are Neal ADAMS, Enki BILAL, Vaughn BODÉ, Brian BOLLAND, Chester BROWN, Charles BURNS, Dick CALKINS, Howard CHAYKIN, Chris CLAREMONT, Richard CORBEN, Philippe DRUILLET, Dave GIBBONS, Jean GIRAUD (also known as Moebius), Frank HAMPSON, Jack KIRBY, Stan LEE, Winsor McCAY, Dave McKEAN, Lorenzo MATOTTI, Frank MILLER, Gray MORROW, Alan MOORE, Katsuhiro OTOMO, Alex RAYMOND, Bill SIENKEWICZ, Dave SIM, James STERANKO, Osamu TEZUKA and Wally WOOD. That makes 59 strongly comics-oriented entries, of which only 20 were present in the first edition. There are of course many further entries on artists we think of primarily as sf book and magazine illustrators, but who also worked in comics, such as Frank FRAZETTA. Many entries on writers and editors include discussion of their work in comics. These would include Alfred BESTER, Eando BINDER, James CAWTHORN, Gerard F. CONWAY, Gardner F. FOX, Neil GAIMAN, H.L. GOLD, Ron GOULART, Edmond HAMILTON, Harry HARRISON, Michael MOORCOCK, Philip Francis NOWLAN, Julius SCHWARTZ, Mort WEISINGER, Manly Wade WELLMAN.

The majority of comics entries were written by Ron Tiner and Steve Whitaker; but nine other contributors have also written some.

11. Illustrators We include no entries for "gallery" artists like John Martin (1789-1854) whose work occasionally (with hindsight) included sf themes: the END OF THE WORLD in Martin's case. We restrict ourselves to GENRE-SF artists whose sf illustrative work is most closely associated with magazines and books, though some have also worked in films, record covers or calendars. There is some cross-over between the SF-Illustrators category and the Comics category; several artists listed above under **Comics**, like Gray MORROW and Wally WOOD, worked also for the sf magazines. We have retained 44 artist entries from the first edition, all updated and revised. To these we have added a further 20, mostly from the modern period (e.g., Michael WHELAN, Jim BURNS) but some from the era of the PULP MAGAZINES (e.g., Margaret BRUNDAGE, Robert FUQUA). This makes a total of 64 entries in this category, aside from artists listed under **Comics** and occasional artists (e.g., Fred T. JANE, Keith ROBERTS) who would have appeared in this volume anyway for their fiction.

Nearly all Artist entries were written by Jon Gustafson, the majority in collaboration with Peter Nicholls.

The 64 SF-Illustrators entries are George BARR, Wayne BARLOWE, Earle K. BERGEY, Hannes BOK, Chesley BONESTELL, Howard V. BROWN, Margaret BRUNDAGE, Jim BURNS, Thomas CANTY, Edd CARTIER, David A. CHERRY, Mal DEAN, Roger DEAN, Vincent DI FATE, Leo and Diane DILLON, Elliott DOLD, Edmund EMSHWILLER, Stephen E. FABIAN, Virgil FINLAY, Christopher FOSS, Frank FRAZETTA, Frank Kelly FREAS, Robert FUQUA, Jack GAUGHAN, H.R. GIGER, Richard GLYN JONES, James GURNEY, David HARDY, Eddie JONES, Josh KIRBY, Roy G. KRENKEL, Paul LEHR, Brian LEWIS, A. LEYDENFROST, Angus McKIE, Don MAITZ, Rodney MATTHEWS, Ian MILLER, Leo MOREY, Paul ORBAN, Frank R. PAUL, Bruce PENNINGTON, Richard M. POWERS, Gerard A. QUINN, Anthony ROBERTS, Albert ROBIDA, Hubert ROGERS, ROWENA, Rod RUTH, J. Allen ST JOHN, Charles SCHNEEMAN Jr, John SCHOENHERR, Alex SCHOMBURG, Barclay SHAW, Rick STERNBACH, Lawrence Sterne STEVENS, Darrell SWEET, Karel THOLE, Ed VALIGURSKY, Boris VALLEJO, VAN DONGEN, H.W. WESSO, Michael WHELAN, Tim WHITE.

12. Book Publishers We have expanded our coverage of mass-market and general publishers with strong sf lines, while continuing our coverage of specialist sf publishers. The result, if these are read together with the PUBLISHING and SMALL PRESSES AND LIMITED EDITIONS theme entries, is a history (not comprehensive) of post-war publishing of sf books and also books about sf. Publisher entries are ACE BOOKS, ADVENT PUBLISHERS, ARKHAM HOUSE, ARNO PRESS, BADGER BOOKS, BALLANTINE BOOKS, BANTAM BOOKS, BLUEJAY, BORGO PRESS, CURTIS WARREN, DAW BOOKS, DEL REY BOOKS, DOUBLEDAY, ESSEX HOUSE, FANTASY PRESS, FANTASY PUBLISHING COMPANY INC., FAX COLLECTORS EDITIONS, GARLAND, GNOME PRESS, GOLLANCZ, GREENWOOD, GREGG PRESS, HADLEY PUBLISHING COMPANY, HYPERION PRESS, LASER BOOKS, MIRAGE PRESS, PRIME PRESS, ROBERT HALE LIMITED, SCIENCE FICTION BOOK CLUB, SHASTA PUBLISHERS, STARMONT HOUSE, TIMESCAPE, TOR BOOKS, UNDERWOOD-MILLER and MARK V. ZIESING. There are 35 entries in this selective list.

13. Original Anthologies The most important location, after the magazines, of sf short fiction – sf being one of the few forms of fiction where the short story and the novella are still very much alive – is in original anthologies (anthologies of stories not previously published). There are some hundreds of these, far too many to list individually. We do, however, give entries to English-language original-anthology *series* devoted to genre-sf stories, provided that the series contains three or more books. One or two such series may have slipped our net, but we believe we have caught most of them. We do not, however, give entries to SHARED-WORLD original-anthology series, though we make an exception for WILD CARDS and some more are listed under GAMES WORKSHOP. For a full listing of the 19 such entries ◊ ORIGINAL ANTHOLOGIES. When an original-anthology series like DESTINIES or PULPHOUSE: THE HARDBACK MAGAZINE describes itself as a magazine, even though it is in book form, then we list it under Magazines. The Original-Anthology entries were mostly written by Malcolm Edwards (first edition) and Peter Nicholls (second edition).

14. Awards There will always be argument as to the true significance (if any) of sf awards, but it is obviously necessary to give the most important, and to list all their winners. The general question of awards is discussed under AWARDS, which also lists the 11 major awards, notably the HUGO and the NEBULA, that receive their own entries.

15. Miscellaneous There remains a residue of bits and pieces, mostly about sf organizations (CLARION SCIENCE FICTION WRITER'S WORKSHOP, SCIENCE FICTION FOUNDATION, SCIENCE FICTION RESEARCH ASSOCIATION, WORLD SF and others), sf fandom (APA, CONVENTIONS, FANDOM, FAN LANGUAGE, FANZINE, FUTURIANS and others) sf COLLECTIONS (four of these), different publishing formats (BEDSHEET, DIGEST, etc.), and even a couple on characters like CAPTAIN JUSTICE. There are 30 miscellaneous entries, some of the fannish ones originally by Peter Roberts and revised by Rob Hansen, most of the rest by Nicholls.

CHECKLIST OF CONTRIBUTORS

Each contributor to this encyclopedia may be identified by his or her initials, as tabulated against his or her full name below. Rather more than half the contributors themselves receive entries in this book, and are listed below with their surnames capitalized. Data on other contributors appear below the list. Names asterisked once (*) are responsible only for material retained from the first edition; names asterisked twice (**) appear newly in this second edition. The remainder have worked on both editions.

**	Ivan ADAMOVIČ	IA	*	Thomas M. DISCH	TMD
*	Mark ADLARD	MA	**	Jane Donawerth	JD
**	Tim Adye	TA	*	Malcolm J. EDWARDS	MJE
*	Brian W. ALDISS	BWA		John Eggeling	JE
**	Hans Joachim ALPERS	HJA	**	Gregory FEELEY	GF
**	Mike ASHLEY	MA	**	Brian Forté	BF
**	Miquel BARCELÓ	MB	*	H. Bruce FRANKLIN	HBF
**	Zoran Bekric	ZB	**	Robert FRAZIER	RF
**	Matt Bishop	MB	**	Neil GAIMAN	NG
**	Russell BLACKFORD	RuB	**	Vladimir GAKOV	VG
**	Everett F. BLEILER	EFB	**	Bruce GILLESPIE	BG
**	Richard BLEILER	RB	**	John Grandidge	JoG
**	Scott BRADFIELD	SB	**	John Grant (Paul BARNETT)	JGr
**	Damien BRODERICK	DB	**	Colin GREENLAND	CG
*	John BROSNAN	JB		Jon Gustafson	JG
**	Stanislav Čermak	SČ	**	Rob Hansen	RH
**	Jacques Chambon	JCh	*	Jim HARMON	JH
**	I.F. CLARKE	IFC	**	Penny Heal	PH
	John CLUTE	JC		Steven Holland	SH
**	John Robert COLOMBO	JRC	**	John-Henri Holmberg	J-HH
**	Adrian Cox	AC	**	Jyrki IJÄS	JI
**	Niels DALGAARD	ND	*	Maxim JAKUBOWSKI	MJ
**	J.A. Dautzenberg	JAD	**	Colin A. Johnson	CJ
**	Hugh Davies	HD	**	Jörg Kastner	JK

**	Roz KAVENEY	RK		*	Peter Roberts	PR
	David KETTERER	DK		**	Roger ROBINSON	RR
**	Robert K.J. Killheffer	RKJK		**	Cornel ROBU	CR
**	Michael Klossner	MK			Franz ROTTENSTEINER	FR
**	David LANGFORD	DRL		**	Marcus Rowland	MR
**	Péter KUCZKA	PK		*	John Scarborough	JSc
**	Sam J. LUNDWALL	SJL		**	Mauricio-José SCHWARZ	M-JS
*	Robert Louit	RL			Takumi SHIBANO	TSh
**	Murray MacLachlan	MM		*	Tom SHIPPEY	TS
*	David I. MASSON	DIM		*	John SLADEK	JS
**	Charles Shaar Murray	CSM		**	Krzysztof SOKOŁOWSKI	KS
*	Alan Myers	AM			Brian STABLEFORD	BS
**	Kim NEWMAN	KN		*	Tony Sudbery	TSu
	Peter NICHOLLS	PN			Darko SUVIN	DS
**	Phil Nichols	PhN		**	Braulio TAVARES	BT
**	Patrick Nielsen Hayden	PNH		**	Sheldon TEITELBAUM	ST
**	Jaroslav OLŠA jr	JO		**	Ron Tiner	RT
**	Carlo PAGETTI	CP		**	Igor Tolokonnikov	IT
*	Frank H. Parnell	FHP		**	Neal Tringham	NT
**	Ellen Pedersen	EP		**	Lisa TUTTLE	LT
*	A.B. Perkins	ABP		**	Hermann Urbanek	HU
**	Luc POMERLEAU	LP		**	Janeen Webb	JW
**	Alexander POPOV	AP		**	Steve Whitaker	SW
	David PRINGLE	DP		**	Chris Williamson	CW
**	Phil Raines	PhR		**	Ralph Willingham	RW
**	Jenny Randles	JR		**	WU DINGBO	WD
**	Robert REGINALD	RoR		**	Zoran ŽIVKOVIĆ	ZŽ

Tim Adye is a member of the M.H. ZOOL group, members of which were collaboratively responsible for the *Bloomsbury Good Reading Guide to Science Fiction and Fantasy* (**1989**); several Zool group members made individual contributions here, and are identified below. **Zoran Bekric** and **Brian Forté** are freelance writers, based in South Australia, who have expertise in comics. **Matt Bishop** is with the Zool group. **Stanislav Čermak** is a Czech film critic and sf fan. **Jacques Chambon** is a French sf critic and publisher. **Adrian Cox** is with the Zool group. **J.A. Dautzenberg** is a Dutch college teacher and literary critic for a national newspaper, *De Volksrant*. **Hugh Davies** is a UK composer and musicologist. **Jane Donawerth** is a Professor of English at the University of Maryland at College Park, with a specialized interest in women's literature. **John Eggeling** is a UK antiquarian bookseller and expert in early sf publishing. **John Grandidge** is with the Zool group. **Jon Gustafson** is a US art and artbook appraiser, expert in sf art, who has had a column on the subject in *Pulphouse: The Hardback Magazine*. **Rob Hansen** is a UK fan, expert on the history of (in particular) UK fandom, as shown in his fanzine *Then*. **Patrick Nielsen Hayden** is a senior editor at Tor Books. **Penny Heal** and **Colin A. Johnson** are with the Zool group. **John-Henri Holmberg** is a Swedish editor and critic, author of several books on sf. **Jörg Kastner** is a German sf author and critic, whose criticism has appeared in *Science Fiction Times*. **Robert K.J. Killheffer** is Books Editor of *Omni* Magazine. **Michael Klossner** is a US critic with special interest in sf in film and tv, and a frequent contributor to *SFRA Review*. **Robert Louit** is a French critic, journalist and translator who has also been an sf book editor. **Murray MacLachlan** is a New Zealand freelance writer with a special interest in sf. **Charles Shaar Murray** is a UK rock-music critic and historian, author of *Shots from the Hip* (coll **1991**) and other books. **Alan Myers** is a UK teacher of Russian, and translator from the Russian. **Phil Nichols** is a video engineer and producer, for some time Information Officer of the BSFA. **Frank H. Parnell** is an authority on sf and fantasy magazines, compiler of *Monthly Terrors: An Index to the Weird Fantasy Magazines Published in the United States and Great Britain* (**1985**). **Ellen Pedersen** is a Danish critic and translator. **A.B. Perkins**, a UK researcher, has a special interest in UK boys' sf of the 1950s. **Phil Raines** is with the Zool group. **Jenny Randles** is an international researcher in ufology. **Peter Roberts** was for many years a fanzine editor in the UK. **Marcus Rowland** specializes in computers and games for a local education authority. **John Scarborough** is a US professor of medical history. **Tony Sudbery** is a lecturer in mathematics, and was for some time a regular sf critic in *Speculation* and elsewhere. **Ron Tiner** is a UK book and comics artist, and is author of *Figure Drawing without a Model* (**1992**). **Igor Tolokonnikov** is one half of the Russian literary agency Baziat. **Neal Tringham**, now with the Institut für Astronomie & Astrophysik in Munich, was also with Zool group. **Hermann Urbanek** is a German fan and sf critic, author of "SF in Germany", an occasional column in *Locus*. **Janeen Webb** is an Australian lecturer in literature, with a specialized interest in sf and fantasy, both for children and adults. **Steve Whitaker** is a comics historian, teacher, critic, strip cartoonist and colourist. **Chris Williamson** is with the Zool group. **Ralph Willingham** is the US author of a PhD dissertation, "Science Fiction and the Theatre".

ACKNOWLEDGEMENTS

We must first thank all the contributors, to both the first edition and the current edition. We thank especially our Contributing Editor, Brian Stableford, whose influence extended far beyond the 200,000 words signed with his initials, for his tasks included a severe examination of the entire text for errors of fact and critical blunders. We thank our Technical Editor, Paul Barnett, whose logistic and computer skills brought this book into publishable shape, and whose editing skills importantly influenced its language and form. We thank our proofreader, Lydia Darbyshire, a model of meticulousness whose examination of data for consistency was itself tantamount to a critical reading of the text. We thank also all those sf authors and critics who took the time to fill out a questionnaire or otherwise provided us with vital information. We also thank John Jarrold, the original commissioner of this volume.

It is not possible individually to thank all those who helped in other ways, for the list would contain some hundreds of names. It goes without saying that we remain grateful to all those we thanked in the preface to the first edition, and we do not repeat their names here. Of the large number who helped us with the current edition, there are some in particular whose extensive help we must comment on. Neil Barron, whose reference books were among those we most often consulted, provided us with much other information and with constant encouragement. Everett F. Bleiler, who read critically many parts of the encyclopedia that pertained to his areas of particular expertise, generously contributed to it – out of his deep love for the subject – several substantial entries on early sf and sf writers. His son, Richard Bleiler, also altruistically contributed advice and entries, as did Professor I.F. Clarke. Judith Clute kept John Clute alive, while painting in the next room. Clare Coney (Nicholls) provided not only support well beyond the call of wifely duty but also considerable editorial assistance. J. Fisher provided much biographical data on authors, along with other suggestions. Hal W. Hall generously provided research materials. Steve Holland helped us make sense of the bibliography of 1950s sf in the UK. Roz Kaveney commented on hundreds of author entries as they were drafted, and then read the manuscript. David Langford gave essential computer advice and help, made many suggestions throughout, and read the manuscript. Helen Nicholls understood her brother and her friend. Robert Reginald, author of the basic and essential checklist of sf literature from 1700 to 1974 (see below), made available successive drafts of his 1975-1991 supplement (now just published), and we supplied him in turn with final drafts of this encyclopedia. John Clute read and criticized the checklist; Reginald did the same for the encyclopedia. We are all hoping that both books show the benefits of this sharing of resources.

Others whose help was substantial (often in locating hard-to-find data, and in setting us right on first-edition errors) include Paul Alkon, Brian Ameringen, Mike Ashley, Nick Austin, John Betancourt, Jenny Blackford, Damien Broderick, John F. Carr, T.G. Cockcroft, Michael Rice Colpitts, Ian Covell, Richard Dalby, John Dallman, John Davey, Joyce Day, Jane Donawerth, Nann du Sautoy, John Eggeling, Alex Eisenstein, Alan C. Elms, Brian Forté, Andrew Fraknoi, D. Douglas Fratz, Neil Gaiman, Martin Gardner, C.N. Gilmore, Mark Goldberg, Paul Gravett, Scott Green, the Reverend Ron Grossman, Rob Hansen, David Hartwell, Patrick Nielsen Hayden, Richard J. Hooton, Maxim Jakubowski, Laurence M. Janifer, Don Keller, David Ketterer, Michael Klossner, Justin Knowles, Eleanor Lang, Anthony R. Lewis, Duncan Lunan, Kerzin Alexey Lvovich, Patrick McGuire, Murray MacLachlan, Sean McMullen, Barry N. Malzberg, Lee Mendham, Walter E. Meyers, Chris Morgan, Caroline Mullan, Alan Myers, Kim Newman, John C. Nine, Jaroslav Olša jr, Jan O'Nale, Bernie Peek, Dominique Petitfaux, Andrew Porter, David Pringle, Jenny Randles, Kim Stanley Robinson, Roger Robinson, Cornel Robu, Yvonne Rousseau, Darrell Schweitzer, the Science Fiction Foundation, A. Langley Searles, Efim Shur, Cyril Simsa, John Sladek, John B. Spencer, Phil Stephensen-Payne, Darko Suvin, Braulio Tavares, Sheldon Teitelbaum, Ron Tiner, Igor Tolokonnikov, Ian Watson, Bob Wayne, Janeen Webb, Andrew Wille, Madawc Williams, G. Peter Winnington, and Zoran Živkovíc.

In the first edition it was still possible to acknowledge individually the reference books that formed the basis of our research library. There are now too many, though perhaps we can select a few which were of special and continuous use: Neil Barron's *Anatomy of Wonder*, *Fantasy Literature* and *Horror Literature*; Everett F. Bleiler's *Science Fiction: The Early Years*; the annual sf/fantasy bibliographies edited by Charles N. Brown and William G. Contento for Locus Press; Thomas D. Clareson's *Science Fiction in America, 1870s-1930s*; the sf and fantasy book-review annuals compiled by Robert A. Collins and Robert Latham; William G. Contento's indexes to sf anthologies and collections; L.W. Currey's *Science Fiction and Fantasy Authors: A Bibliography of First Printings of their Fiction*; Donald B. Day's *Index to the Science Fiction Magazines 1926-50*; Hal W. Hall's various guides to sf book reviews and research papers; Phil Hardy's *The Aurum Film Encyclopedia: Science Fiction*; George Locke's *A Spectrum of Fantasy*; the NESFA sf-magazine indexes covering publications subsequent to 1965; Robert Reginald's *Science Fiction and Fantasy Literature: A Checklist, 1700-1974* and *Science Fiction and Fantasy Literature, 1975-1991*; Erwin S. Strauss's *Index to the S-F Magazines, 1951-65*; Darko Suvin's *Victorian Science Fiction in the UK*; Donald H. Tuck's *Encyclopedia of Science Fiction and Fantasy through 1968*; Marshall B. Tymn's and Mike Ashley's *Science Fiction, Fantasy and Weird Fiction Magazines*; the two volumes of Bill Warren's *Keep Watching the Skies*; Robert Weinberg's *A Biographical Dictionary of Science Fiction and Fantasy Artists*.

We end by issuing a conventional but heartfelt apology and thanks to all those others who have helped and have not appeared on the above lists.

John Clute and Peter Nicholls

CHECKLIST OF THEMES

Terminology entries can be regarded as short Theme entries. Readers who cannot find a Theme entry they hoped for in the list below are advised to turn to the list of Terminology entries to be found in this encyclopedia in the entry TERMINOLOGY.

ABSURDIST SF
ADAM AND EVE
ALIENS
ALTERNATE WORLDS
ANDROIDS
ANONYMOUS SF AUTHORS
ANTHOLOGIES
ANTHROPOLOGY
ANTIGRAVITY
ANTI-INTELLECTUALISM IN SF
ANTIMATTER
APES AND CAVEMEN (IN THE
   MODERN WORLD)
ARTS
ASTEROIDS
ASTRONOMY
ATLANTIS
AUTOMATION
AWARDS

BALLOONS
BIBLIOGRAPHIES
BIG DUMB OBJECTS
BIOLOGY
BLACK HOLES
BOYS' PAPERS

CHILDREN IN SF
CHILDREN'S SF

CINEMA
CITIES
CLICHÉS
CLONES
CLUB STORY
COLLECTIONS
COLONIZATION OF OTHER
   WORLDS
COMICS
COMMUNICATIONS
COMPUTERS
CONCEPTUAL BREAK-
   THROUGH
COSMOLOGY
CRIME AND PUNISHMENT
CRITICAL AND HISTORICAL
   WORKS ABOUT SF
CRYONICS
CYBERNETICS
CYBERPUNK
CYBORGS

DEFINITIONS OF SF
DEVOLUTION
DIME-NOVEL SF
DIMENSIONS
DISASTER
DISCOVERY AND INVENTION
DRUGS

DYSTOPIAS

ECOLOGY
ECONOMICS
EDISONADE
END OF THE WORLD
ENTROPY
ESCHATOLOGY
ESP
EVOLUTION

FABULATION
FANTASTIC VOYAGES
FANTASY
FAR FUTURE
FASTER THAN LIGHT
FEMINISM
FORCE FIELD
FUTUROLOGY

GALACTIC EMPIRES
GAMES AND SPORTS
GAMES AND TOYS
GAME-WORLDS
GENERATION STARSHIPS
GENETIC ENGINEERING
GENRE SF
GODS AND DEMONS
GOLDEN AGE OF SF

HOW TO USE THIS BOOK

In **Contents of this Book** (page xi) we briefly describe the principles governing the construction of this book, and the kinds of information which may be found here. We have tried throughout to present this material as clearly as possible, but some pointers may be helpful.

ALPHABETICAL ORDER

The main body of the encyclopedia is a single sequence of entries presented in strict alphabetical order. The alphabetization system used follows the convention whereby the whole of the principal entry heading, rather than just its first word, is taken into account – so that, for example, STARTLING STORIES precedes rather than succeeds STAR TREK. Subsidiary parts of the heading (e.g., forenames) are used for secondary sorting. Numbers are treated as if spelled out, as are contractions like SF (in the meaning "science fiction"), DR and ST; names beginning MC are treated as if they began MAC. On rare occasions common sense overrides alphabetization; for example, the STAR TREK movies are treated in numerical (and date) order rather than in the order V, IV, VI, III, II, as strict alphabetization would insist.

CROSS-REFERENCES

1. Approximately 2100 out of the 6460+ entries in the encyclopedia are cross-reference entries. Many simply cross-refer a term to the entry where it is covered, for example:

> **PERU** ◊ LATIN AMERICA.

When one name is simply cross-referred to a second, then the first name is a pseudonym of the second that has been used on a book, for example:

> **O'DONNELL, K.M.** ◊ Barry N. MALZBERG.

When one name is cross-referred to a second but with the addition of an [s], then the first name is a pseudonym of the second but has been used only for stories, for example:

> **SMITH, WOODROW WILSON** [s] ◊ Henry KUTTNER.

When one name is cross-referred to another entry but with the addition of an [r], then the first name is not a pseudonym of the second, for example:

SMITH, LAURA [r] ◊ Seth MCEVOY

SPITTEL, OLAF R. [r] ◊ GERMANY.

2. Within the text of entries, and in the **See also** sections attached to many of them, any word given in SMALL CAPITALS constitutes a cross-reference.

AUTHOR, CRITIC AND EDITOR ENTRIES

Names Each entry begins with the author's full real name, working name or pseudonym, whichever is best known. We step outside normal practice only with the concept of the working name, which we have defined as one which encompasses in easily recognizeable form a significant portion of a full name – as in the case of Connie WILLIS, which we treat as Constance Elaine Trimmer Willis's working name. For further discussion of working names and pseudonyms ◊ PSEUDONYMS, which also discusses floating pseudonyms and house names.

Titles For all authors writing in English we attempt to treat or to list every adult book with any significant sf content, to treat or (more commonly) simply to list all fantasy and horror books, and to at least list most children's books of genre interest; for foreign-language authors we do not claim to list all sf/horror/fantasy work not translated into English. We list most nonfiction works written by sf authors about the field or about other authors; we also list, sometimes selectively, nonfiction works of science or popular science by sf authors who also work in those fields. In author entries, each book is given a full ascription (see below for details); other kinds of entry (theme entries in particular) often identify titles in a briefer format. In our selection of titles we have tended to be extremely catholic; one may occasionally find – especially in the **Other works** list of titles at the foot of some entries – novels whose generic status is doubtful, and collections containing only a few relevant stories. This is deliberate: when we err, we prefer to do so through inclusion rather than exclusion.

We do not list all short stories by authors.

Story titles are given in normal face, within double quotes (" "), with dates in normal face. Book titles are given in *italics* with dates in **bold face**. Subtitles are sometimes omitted, though we do include them when appropriate. We do so for clarity's sake – there are, for instance, 3 Stanley G. WEINBAUM collections which can be distinguished only through subtitles: *A Martian Odyssey, and Others* (coll **1949**), *A Martian Odyssey, and Other Classics of Science Fiction* (coll **1962**) and *A Martian Odyssey, and Other Science Fiction Tales* (coll **1975**). And we list subtitles when they seem to be of inherent interest; for instance, Keith LAUMER's *Bolo: The Annals of the Dinochrome Brigade* (coll of linked stories **1976**). Series titles are given in **bold face**.

We generally give the titles of singletons – books which are not part of series – according to normal bibliographical practice by which the title as it appears on the title page (rather than on the cover or elsewhere) is deemed the true title. With books which are part of series, we have decided that normal bibliographical practice is of little use in helping sf readers through the often confusing tangle of conventions used to identify (and advertise) this category of title. Where there is no series identification, we list the title only as we would with a singleton, though in a context which makes clear its connection to its series-mates. Where series are accorded some form of ongoing title, wherever placed, we try to ascribe the first volume in full, but subsequently (as soon as individual volume titles can be clearly distinguished) we reduce that overall title to a number: as in David MELTZER's **Brain Plant** sequence, which we render as *Brain Plant #1: Lovely* (**1969**), *#2: Healer* (**1969**), *#3: Out* (**1969**) and *#4: Glue Factory* (**1969**).

Ghost titles and projected titles Books whose existence we doubt and books whose release we had not confirmed by press time we give in normal face between chevrons, giving their publication date in normal face; for example, Gene WOLFE's «Darkside the Long Sun» (1993).

Ties We define a TIE as any text whose contents take their substance from some prior inspiration, which may be a SHARED-WORLD bible, a film, a tv series, a role-playing or other form of game. All such novels, collections, anthologies and omnibuses are identified by an asterisk (*) placed immediately after the title, as with Donald F. GLUT's *The Empire Strikes Back* * (**1980**), which novelizes the film *The* EMPIRE STRIKES BACK.

Ascription data about titles is contained within brackets, and has been kept as simple as is consistent with our desire to provide as much information as we can, within the constraints of our encyclopedia format. We do not, for instance, normally provide full bibliographic data (i.e., city of publication, publisher, pagination, etc.); ◊ BIBLIOGRAHIES, where we discuss and recommend various sf and fantasy checklists. Most novels – i.e., Isaac ASIMOV's *The Gods Themselves* (**1972**) – therefore need no more than a simple date of publication; collections can be identified by the term "coll" placed directly before the date.

However, we use several further terms to describe books. Those given here in SMALL CAPITALS have individual entries, where they are more fully explained. Abbreviations placed before the date include:

> coll
> coll of linked stories
> FIXUP
> anth
> omni

A fixup – briefly – is a book composed of previously written stories which have been cemented together. An anth is an anthology, while an omni is an omnibus – a book that assembles previously published volumes.

Abbreviations placed after the date include:

> chap (◊ CHAPBOOK)
> DOS

"Chap" designates a book fewer than 100pp in length; "dos" designates two titles usually (but not always) bound back-to-back and upside down with respect to one another. We also indicate country of publication when a book was first published in a country other than its author's normal country of residence, as with Thomas M. DISCH's *334* (coll of linked stories **1972** UK).

When titles are published in two countries within a few weeks of one another we "follow the flag" and treat first publication as being in the author's country of residence.

We give variant titles, where they exist, for all books and films. A variant title may be identified by the abbreviation

> vt

placed initially, as in Daniel F. GALOUYE's *Counterfeit World* (**1964** UK; vt *Simulacron-3* 1964

US). We treat vts as variants of a main title, and therefore do not print their dates in boldface.

We designate revised editions of all books listed. However, we are not always able to specify the nature of the revision, in which case the revised edition will be identified by the abbreviation

> rev

placed initially, as in Marta RANDALL's *Islands* (**1976**; rev 1980); if we have further knowledge, we use such terms as

> cut
> exp
> much exp
> text restored

all of which are intended to be self-evident.

In the case of novels, we attempt to give magazine publication where it precedes book publication by three or more years, as with George Allen ENGLAND's *The Golden Blight* (1912 *Cavalier*; **1916**). We usually give the magazine title of a story when this differs from the book title, though we do so less consistently in cases where the story was published two years or less before the book version.

Translations Whenever possible we notate translated books according to the following example by Vladimir NABOKOV, *Priglashenie na kasn'* (**1938** France; trans Dmitri Nabokov and VN as *Invitation to a Beheading* **1959** US). As we treat translations as separate entities, we date them in **bold face**. We do not, however, necessarily list all variant translations, sometimes giving only the first. When untranslated books are mentioned, a rough English translation of the title appears in square brackets immediately after the original, as with Arno SCHMIDT's *Schwarze Spiegel* ["Black Mirrors"] (**1963**).

CHECKLIST OF ABBREVIATIONS

Abbreviations listed below in **bold face** are explained in **How to Use this Book** (page xxxi). Abbreviations in SMALL CAPITALS also have their own entries, where they are more fully explained.

« »	projected or ghost title (◊ page xxxiii)
◊	refer to (the entry thus indicated)
*	a tied title (◊ TIE)
#	number
AMZ	AMAZING STORIES
anth	anthology
ASF	ASTOUNDING SCIENCE FICTION/ANALOG
b/w	black and white
chap	under 100pp (◊ CHAPBOOK)
coll	collection
dir	directed/director
DOS	bound back-to-back
ed	edited/editor
edn	edition
exp	expanded
FIXUP	novel made up from stories
FSF	The MAGAZINE OF FANTASY AND SCIENCE FICTION
Gal	GALAXY SCIENCE FICTION
IASFM	ISAAC ASIMOV'S SCIENCE FICTION MAGAZINE
NW	NEW WORLDS
omni	omnibus
prod	produced/producer
[r]	not a pseudonym of the name to which it is cross-referred
rev	revised
[s]	pseudonym used only for short fiction
sf	science fiction
trans	translated

tv	television
TWS	THRILLING WONDER STORIES
var mags	published in various magazines
vol	volume
vt	variant title
WW	World War

ABBEY, EDWARD (1927-1989) US writer, perhaps best known for his numerous essays on the US West, in which he clearly expresses a scathing iconoclasm about human motives and their effects on the world. In *The Monkey-Wrench Gang* (**1975**; rev 1985) and its sequel, *Hayduke Lives!* (**1990**), this pessimism is countered by prescriptions for physically sabotaging the polluters of the West which, when put into practice, nearly displace normal reality. *Good Times* (fixup **1980**) is set in a balkanized USA after nuclear fallout has helped destroy civilization; an Indian shaman, along with other characters similar to those in *The Monkey-Wrench Gang*, fights back against tyranny. [JC]

ABBOTT, EDWIN A(BBOTT) (1839-1926) UK clergyman, academic and writer whose most noted work, published originally as by A Square, is *Flatland: A Romance of Many Dimensions* (**1884**). Narrated by Mr Square, the novel falls into two parts. The first is a highly entertaining description of the two-dimensional world of Flatland, in which inhabitants' shapes establish their (planar) hierarchical status. In the second part, Mr Square travels in a dream to the one-dimensional universe of Lineland, whose inhabitants are unable to conceive of a two-dimensional universe; he is in turn visited from Spaceland by a three-dimensional visitor – named Sphere because he is spherical – whom Mr Square cleverly persuades to believe in four-dimensional worlds as well. *Flatland* is a study in MATHEMATICS and PERCEPTION, and has stayed popular since its first publication. [JC]
See also: DIMENSIONS; HISTORY OF SF.

ABBOTT AND COSTELLO MEET THE INVISIBLE MAN ◊ *The* INVISIBLE MAN.

ABÉ, KOBO (1924-1993) Japanese novelist, active since 1948, several of whose later novels have been translated into English. He is known mainly for his work outside the sf field, like *Suna no Onna* (**1962**; trans E. Dale Saunders as *Woman in the Dunes* 1964 US), and has been deeply influenced by Western models from Franz KAFKA to Samuel Beckett (1906-1989); the intensely extreme conditions to which he subjects his alienated protagonists allow a dubious sf interpretation of novels like *Moetsukita Chizu* (**1967**; trans E. Dale Saunders as *The Ruined Map* 1969 US), or *Tanin no Kao* (**1964**; trans E. Dale Saunders as *The Face of Another* 1966 US). However, *Dai-Yon Kampyoki* (**1959**; trans E. Dale Saunders as *Inter Ice Age 4* 1970 US) is undoubtedly sf. It is a complex story set in a near-future Japan threatened by the melting of the polar icecaps. The protagonist, Professor Katsumi, has been in charge of developing a computer/information system capable of predicting human behaviour. This system, fatally for him, predicts his compulsive refusal to go along with his associates and his government in the creation of genetically engineered children, adapted for life in the rising seas. Most of the novel, narrated by Katsumi, deals with a philosophical confrontation between his deeply alienated refusal of the future and the computer's knowing representations of that refusal and the alternatives to it. The resulting psychodramas include a mysterious murder and the enlistment of his unborn child into the ranks of the mutated water-breathers. A later novel, *Hako-Otoko* (**1973**; trans E. Dale Saunders as *The Box Man* 1973 US) has some borderline sf elements; its protagonist walks about and lives in a large cardboard carton along with many other Tokyo residents who have refused a life of "normalcy". *Hakobune Sakura Maru* (trans Juliet Winter Carpenter as *The Ark Sakura* 1988 US) expands that basic metaphor in a tale about a man obsessively engaged with his bomb shelter. *Beyond the Curve* (coll trans Juliet Winters Carpenter **1991** US) collects sf short stories published in Japan 1949-66. [JC]
See also: DISASTER; GENETIC ENGINEERING; JAPAN; PSYCHOLOGY; UNDER THE SEA.

ABEL, R(ICHARD) COX [r] ◊ Charles BARREN.

ABLEMAN, PAUL (1927-) UK novelist known mainly for work outside the sf field, like his first book, *I Hear Voices* (**1958** France). *The Twilight of the Vilp* (**1969**) is not so much sf proper as an informed and sophisticated playing with the conventions of the genre in a FABULATION about the author of a work and his relation to its components. The eponymous Galaxy-spanning Vilp cannot, therefore, be taken literally. [JC]

ABORIGINAL SCIENCE FICTION US magazine published from Massachusetts by Absolute Entertainment Inc., ed Charles C. RYAN, first issue Oct 1986, 5 issues in both 1987 and 1988, then bimonthly; 30 issues to Dec 1991, quarterly from 1992, current. The original format was 24pp tabloid (11 x 17in; about 280 x 430mm), but changed to small BEDSHEET with #4 in 1987. A feature is the use of full-page, full-colour illustration throughout the magazine, which from #8 (1988) to #22 (1990) was printed entirely on slick paper: "cover art for every story", as the editor put it.

The title results from an ongoing but not very good joke about the publisher, envisaged as a "crazy alien", who produces the magazine for the aboriginals of Earth. The fiction has been reasonable but seldom excellent, with the work of little known writers like Robert A. Metzger mixed, very occasionally, with that of big names like Larry NIVEN. The regular book-review columns are by Darrell SCHWEITZER and Janice M. Eisen. Editor Ryan previously brought out the magazine GALILEO (1976-80), and continues, as he did then, to make most of his sales through subscription rather than newsstand purchases. At the end of 1991, with a hiatus in the bimonthly appearance, the future of this courageous but never very exciting magazine looked uncertain, with production and (increased) postage costs no longer covered by sales. A spin-off reprint anthology in magazine format is *Aboriginal Science Fiction, Tales of the Human Kind: 1988 Annual Anthology* (anth chap **1988**) ed Ryan. [PN]

ABOUT, EDMOND (FRANÇOIS VALENTIN) (1828-1885) French writer of much fiction, some of it sf, notably *L'homme à l'oreille cassée* (**1862**; trans Henry Holt as *The Man with the Broken Ear* **1867** US; vt *Colonel Fougas' Mistake* 1878 UK; vt "A New Lease of Life" 1880 UK), which is included in *A New Lease of Life, and Saving a Daughter's Dowry* (coll trans **1880** UK). In this tale a mummified military man is revived 46 years after his death and causes havoc with his Napoleonic jingoism. Another work in an English-language version is *The Nose of a Notary* (trans **1863** US; vt *The Notary's Nose* 1864; vt *The Lawyer's Nose* 1878 UK), which is included in *The Notary's Nose and Other Stories* (coll trans **1882** UK). [JC]
See also: MONEY.

ABRAMOV, ALEXANDER (1900-1985) **and SERGEI** (1944-   ) Russian authors of the sf adventure novel *Horsemen from Nowhere* (trans George Yankovsky **1969** Moscow). One of their short stories appears in *Vortex* (anth **1970**) ed C.G. Bearne. A later novel is *Journey across Three Worlds* (trans Gladys Evans with other stories as coll **1973** Moscow). [PN]

ABSENT MINDED PROFESSOR, THE Film (1961). Walt Disney. Dir Robert Stevenson, starring Fred MacMurray, Nancy Olson, Keenan Wynn. Screenplay Bill Walsh. 97 mins. B/w.

Historically important as the financially successful template for a great many lightweight, comparatively low-budget sf comedies from the Disney studio, though it was not their first live-action fantasy comedy (*The Shaggy Dog*, 1959). Subsequent movies in a similar vein include *The Computer Wore Tennis Shoes* (1969), *The Love Bug* (1969) and *The Cat from Outer Space* (1978); because these are largely assembly-belt products aimed at children, they do not receive entries in this volume. *TAMP*, perhaps the best, features MacMurray as a high-school science teacher who accidentally invents "flubber" (flying rubber), an ANTIGRAVITY substance he fits in a Model-T Ford. The flying scenes (matte work by Peter Ellenshaw) are astonishingly proficient for the period, but the science is puerile, the humour broad and the characters stereotyped. MacMurray gives one of his most charmingly deft performances.

The sequel was *Son of Flubber* (1963). [PN]
ABSOLUTE ENTERTAINMENT LTD ◊ ABORIGINAL SCIENCE FICTION.

ABSURDIST SF The word "absurdist" became fashionable as a literary term after its consistent use by the French novelist and essayist Albert Camus (1913-1960) to describe fictions set in worlds where we seem at the mercy of incomprehensible systems. These systems may work as metaphors of the human mind – outward manifestations of what J.G. BALLARD means when he uses the term INNER SPACE – or they may work as representations of a cruelly arbitrary external world, in which our expectations of rational coherence, whether from God or from human agencies, are doomed to frustration, as in the works of Franz KAFKA.

In this encyclopedia we cross-refer works of Absurdist sf to the blanket entry on FABULATION, but do not thereby wish to discount the usefulness of Absurdist sf as a separate concept, especially when we are thinking about some sf written between about 1950 and 1970. During this period Brian W. ALDISS, Ballard, David R. BUNCH, Jerzy KOSINSKI, Michael MOORCOCK, Robert SHECKLEY, John T. SLADEK, Kurt VONNEGUT Jr and many other writers tended to create metaphorical worlds shaped externally by a governing PARANOIA, and internally tortured by the psychic white noise of ENTROPY. Kafka haunted this work, of course – because Kafka can easily be transposed into terms that suggest a political protest. Most Absurdist writers were also indebted (a debt they tended freely to acknowledge) to the 19th-century Symbolist tradition, as exemplified by figures like Jean-Marie VILLIERS DE L'ISLE-ADAM, and to its 20th-century successors, from the 'pataphysics of Alfred JARRY to the Surrealism of André Breton (1896-1966) and many others. In the end, however, it might be suggested that Absurdist writers – as they did with Kafka – translated the

Symbolist and Surrealist traditions into political terms: in the end, Absurdist sf can be seen as a protest movement. The world – they said – should not be absurd. [PN/JC]

ABYSS, THE Film (1989). 20th Century-Fox. Dir James CAMERON, starring Ed Harris, Mary Elizabeth Mastrantonio, Todd Graff, Michael Biehn. Prod Gale Anne HURD. Screenplay Cameron. 139 mins. Colour.

Despite the largest budget of the period's undersea fantasies (◊ DEEPSTAR SIX; LEVIATHAN) at about $60 million, and despite director Cameron's impressive track record with sf, this was not a box-office smash. A nuclear-missile-armed US submarine crashes at the edge of the Cayman Trough and the crew of an experimental, submersible drilling rig are asked to help rescue any survivors. A hurricane cuts communications with the surface; the laid-back, jokey rig workers clash with a paranoid team of naval commandos who blame everything on the Russians; and ALIENS dwelling in the Trench (looking a little like angels, and therefore *good*) teasingly appear to some people but not others. The peace-lovers clash stereotypically with the "nuke the aliens" group, and mayhem is followed by transcendental First Contact. Cameron is good at the low-key establishment of team cameraderie among working people, but the cute-alien theme and the relationship between estranged husband and wife have traces of marshmallow softness. The moral-blackmail finale of an earlier version of the script (aliens threaten world with tidal waves if world peace is not restored) is replaced by something that looks more like divine intervention. The film's moralizing is attractive but simplistic. More interestingly, most of the miraculous technology on display is either actually possible today or plausible for the NEAR FUTURE. The novelization, whose author not unfairly calls it "a real novel", is *The Abyss* * (**1989**) by Orson Scott CARD. [PN]

See also: CINEMA; MONSTER MOVIES; UNDER THE SEA.

ACE BOOKS US paperback-publishing company founded by pulp-magazine publisher A.A. Wyn in 1953. Under editor Donald A. WOLLHEIM, Ace published a high proportion of sf, much of it in the "Ace Double" format of two titles bound together DOS-À-DOS. The series included the first or early novels of many writers who became famous, such as John BRUNNER, Samuel R. DELANY, Philip K. DICK, Gordon R. DICKSON, Thomas M. DISCH, R.A. LAFFERTY, Ursula K. LE GUIN, Robert SILVERBERG and Roger ZELAZNY. Terry CARR became an editor in 1964 and later began the **Ace Science Fiction Specials** series, which received considerable praise. Carr left the company in 1971, followed by Wollheim, who began his own imprint, DAW BOOKS, in 1972. Carr rejoined as freelance editor of a second series of **Ace Specials** in 1984, this time restricted to first novels; it included *Neuromancer* (**1984**) by William GIBSON, *The Wild Shore* (**1984**) by Kim Stanley ROBINSON, *Green Eyes* (**1984**) by Lucius SHEPARD, *In the Drift* (fixup **1985**) by Michael SWANWICK and *Them Bones* (**1984**) by Howard WALDROP. In-house editors Beth MEACHAM and Terri WINDLING and, for a longer period, Susan Allison, also ensured that some high-quality books continued to be published in the 1980s, although the emphasis remained on sf adventure. In 1975 Ace had been sold to Grosset & Dunlap; a new sale in July 1982 saw Ace absorbed by Berkley and ceasing to be an independent company, although it remained as an imprint. Ace had been publishing, prior to the sale, more sf than any other publisher; the Putnam/Berkley/Ace combination continued to dominate US sf publishing, in terms of number of books, until 1987, thereafter maintaining second place. [PN/MJE]

Further reading: There are several checklists of Ace sf publications, but none are complete. *Double your Pleasure: The Ace SF Double* (**1989** chap) by James A. Corrick is useful for doubles, while Dick Spelman's *Science Fiction and Fantasy Published by Ace Books (1953-1968)* (**1976** chap) covers the important years.

See also: HUGO.

ACKER, KATHY (1948-) US-born writer and playwright, in the UK for many years before returning to the USA in 1989. KA expresses an apocalyptic sense of the latterday world in works whose tortured absurdity (◊ FABULATION) sometimes catches the reader by surprise, or transfixes the spectator of one of her plays, which have been as a whole perhaps more telling than her prose. *The Birth of the Poet* (staged 1984 Rotterdam; in *Wordplays 5*, anth **1986**) runs a gamut from the nuclear HOLOCAUST of the first act to the picaresque jigs and jags of the second and third. Two novels – *Don Quixote* (**1986**), a surrealistic afterlife fantasy, and *Empire of the Senseless* (**1988**), which features the not-quite terminal coupling of fleshly beings and ROBOTS – are of some interest. Her use of sf icons and decor in this book resembles that of William S. BURROUGHS, especially in the homage to CYBERPUNK it contains, conveyed by cut-ups of text by William GIBSON. [JC]

ACKERMAN, FORREST J(AMES) (1916-) US editor, agent and collector. A reader of the sf magazines from their inception, he was an active member of sf FANDOM from his early teens, and as early as 1932 served as associate editor of *The Time Traveller*, the first FANZINE. For many decades thereafter he wrote stories and articles prolifically for fan journals – using his own name and a wide variety of elaborate pseudonyms, including Dr Acula, Jacques DeForest Erman, Alden Lorraine, Vespertina Torgosi, Hubert George Wells (cheekily), Weaver Wright and many others – and becoming known in fan circles as "Mr Science Fiction"; he won several awards for these activities, including a HUGO in 1953 for Number One Fan Personality. His first story was "A Trip to Mars" in 1929 for the *San Francisco Chronicle*, which won a prize for the best tale by a teenager; some of his more interesting work was assembled in *Science Fiction Worlds of Forrest J. Ackerman and Friends* (anth **1969**). He collected sf books and memorabilia from the very first, publishing in "*I Bequeath*" (*to the Fantasy Foundation*)

(**1946** chap) a bibliography of the first 1300 items, and eventually housing his 300,000-item library, which he called the Fantasy Foundation, in a 17-room house in Hollywood, the maintenance of which proved difficult to manage over the years. The library was further celebrated in *Souvenir Book of Mr Science Fiction's Fantasy Museum* (**1978** chap Japan). Disposals of collectable books have been made at times; and part of the library was auctioned in 1987, grossing over $550,000.

FJA was active as an editor for many years, though not deeply influential; he edited both the magazine *Famous Monsters of Filmland* (1958-82) and the US PERRY RHODAN series (1969-77), as well as several sf anthologies, including *The Frankenscience Monster* (anth **1969**), *Best Science Fiction for 1973* (anth **1973**), *Gosh! Wow! (Sense of Wonder)* (anth **1982**), *Mr Monster's Movie Gold* (anth **1982**) and *The Gernsback Awards, Vol 1: 1926* (anth **1982**). Notorious for his punning and use of simplified words, he is credited with introducing the term SCI FI in 1954. He was agent for a number of writers, notably A.E. VAN VOGT.

His wife, Wendayne Ackerman (1912-1990), was also a fan, and translated the STRUGATSKI brothers' *Trudno byt' bogom* (**1964**) as *Hard to be a God* (**1973** US). [MJE/JC]

Other works: *In Memoriam H.G. Wells 1866-1946* (**1946** chap) with Arthur Louis Jocquel II; *James Warren Presents the Best from Famous Monsters of Filmland* (anth **1964**); *James Warren Presents Famous Monsters of Filmland Strike Back!* (anth **1965**); *James Warren Presents Son of Famous Monsters of Filmland* (anth **1965**); *Close Encounters of the Third Kind* (**1977** chap), nonfiction; *J.R.R. Tolkien's The Lord of the Rings: A Fantasy Film* (**1979** chap), nonfiction; *A Reference Guide to American Science Fiction Films, Volume 1* (**1981**) with A.W. Strickland, only 1 vol published; *Lon of 1000 Faces* (**1983**), nonfiction; *Fantastic Movie Memories* (**1985**), nonfiction.

See also: COLLECTIONS.

ACKERMAN, WENDAYNE [r] ◊ Forrest J. ACKERMAN.

ACKROYD, PETER (1949-   ) UK author who began writing as a poet before turning to literary biographies of figures like T.S. Eliot and Charles DICKENS. His third novel, *Hawksmoor* (**1985**), interestingly conflates the occult geography of London constructed by an 18th-century architect – who closely resembles the historical Nicholas Hawksmoor (1661-1736) – with a series of 20th-century murders investigated by an Inspector Hawksmoor. As an alternate-world FABULATION, the book verges on sf. *First Light* (**1989**) invokes a similar sense of time-slippage, featuring a 20th-century neolithic dig over which appears a night sky whose star positions are those of neolithic times. [JC]

ACTION MAGAZINES ◊ FUTURE FICTION.

ACTON, [Sir] HAROLD (MARIO MITCHELL) (1904-   ) UK writer, long resident in Italy, best known for highly civilized reflections, in books like *Memoirs of an Aesthete* (**1948**), on his own style of life. His sf novel, *Cornelian* (**1928**), tells of a popular singer in a world which privileges old age. [JC]

ACULA, Dr [s] ◊ Forrest J. ACKERMAN.

ACWORTH, ANDREW (?   -?   ) UK writer – possibly, according to Darko SUVIN, a barrister named Andrew Oswald Acworth (?1857-?   ) – whose sf novel, *A New Eden* (**1896**), set 100 years in the future, features the escape of two depressed protagonists from the decaying republican UK to an egalitarian island UTOPIA which fails to cheer them up – despite electric factories, birth control and euthanasia. [JC]

ADAM AND EVE Brian W. ALDISS has given the name "Shaggy God stories" to stories which provide simple-minded sf frameworks for Biblical myths. A considerable fraction of the unsolicited material submitted to sf magazines is reputed to consist of stories of this kind, the plot most frequently represented being the one in which survivors of a space disaster land on a virgin world and reveal (in the final line) that their names are Adam and Eve. Understandably, these stories rarely see print, although A.E. VAN VOGT's "Ship of Darkness" (1947) was reprinted in *Fantastic* in 1961 as a "fantasy classic"; another example is *The Unknown Assassin* (**1956**) by Hank JANSON. Straightforward variants include "Another World Begins" (1942; vt "The Cunning of the Beast") by Nelson BOND (the most prolific writer of pulp Shaggy God stories), in which God is an ALIEN and Adam and Eve are experimental creatures who prove too clever for him; and "Evolution's End" (1941) by Robert Arthur, in which an old world lurches to its conclusion and Aydem and Ayveh survive to start the whole thing over again. Charles L. HARNESS's "The New Reality" (1950) goes to some lengths to set up a framework in which a new universe can be created around its hero, his faithful girlfriend, and the arch-villain (Dr Luce), and uses the idea to far better effect. More elaborate sf transfigurations of Biblical mythology include George Babcock's *Yezad* (**1922**) and Julian Jay SAVARIN's **Lemmus** trilogy (1972-7); a more subtle and sophisticated exercise along these lines can be found in *Shikasta* (**1977**) by Doris LESSING. Adam and Eve are, of course, frequently featured in allegorical fantasies, notably George MacDONALD's *Lilith* (**1895**), Mark TWAIN's *Extracts from Adam's Diary* (**1904**) and *Eve's Diary* (**1906**), George Bernard SHAW's *Back to Methuselah* (**1921**), John Erskine's *Adam and Eve* (**1927**), John CROWLEY's "The Nightingale Sings at Night" (1989) and Piero Scanziani's *The White Book* (**1969**; trans Linda Lappin **1991** UK).

The names Adam and Eve – particularly the former – are frequently deployed for their metaphorical significance. Adam is a natural name to give to the first ROBOT or ANDROID, and thus we find Eando BINDER writing a biography of *Adam Link, Robot* (1939-42; fixup **1965**), and William C. ANDERSON chronicling the career of *Adam M-1* (**1964**). Adam Link was provided with an Eve Link, but what they did together remains a matter for speculation. VILLIERS DE L'ISLE-ADAM had earlier described Thomas Alva Edison's creation of the perfect woman in *L'Ève future* (**1886**; trans Robert M. Adams as *Tomorrow's Eve* **1982**). The metaphor is found also in some SUPERMAN stories, including two novels entitled *The New Adam*, one by Noelle ROGER (**1924**; trans L.P.O. Crowhurst **1926** UK), the other by Stanley G. WEINBAUM (**1939**), and in prehistoric romances, most notably in *Intimations of Eve* (**1946**) and *Adam and the Serpent* (**1947**) by Vardis FISHER and in the final volume of George S. VIERECK and Paul ELDRIDGE's **Wandering Jew** trilogy, *The Invincible Adam* (**1932**), where much is made of the matter of the lost "rib". Alfred BESTER's last-man-alive story "Adam and No Eve" (1941) uses the names in an ironic vein.

More ambitious sf Creation myths of a vaguely Adamic kind can be found in stories in which human beings are enabled to play a part in cosmological processes of creation or re-creation (◊ COSMOLOGY). One example is van Vogt's "The Seesaw" (1941; integrated into *The Weapon Shops of Isher* fixup 1951); others are James BLISH's *The Triumph of Time* (**1958**; vt *A Clash of Cymbals*) and Charles Harness's *The Ring of Ritornel* (**1968**).

Shaggy God stories briefly became popular alternatives to orthodox history in the works of Immanuel VELIKOVSKY and Erich VON DÄNIKEN, and it is likely that they will continue to exert a magnetic attraction upon the naïve imagination. [BS]

See also: ANTHROPOLOGY; EVOLUTION; ORIGIN OF MAN; RELIGION.

ADAMOVIČ, IVAN (1967-) Czech translator and writer, an associate editor of the sf magazine *Ikurie* and a contributor to «Encyklopedie science fiction» ["Encyclopedia of Science Fiction"] (1992). His "Czech SF in the Last Forty Years" appeared in SCIENCE-FICTION STUDIES, Mar 1990. [PN]

ADAMS, DOUGLAS (NOEL) (1952-) UK scriptwriter and novelist who worked 1978-80 as an editor on the DR WHO tv series. He came to wide notice with his HITCH HIKER'S GUIDE TO THE GALAXY sequence, whose first incarnation was as two BBC RADIO series, the first in 1978, the second in 1980, totalling 12 parts in all, the last 2 scripted in collaboration with producer John Lloyd. Both series were assembled as *The Hitch Hiker's Guide to the Galaxy: The Original Radio Scripts* (coll **1985**) ed Geoffrey Perkins; the scripts as published here were modified for subsequent radio performances, and were also released on record albums in a format different from any of the radio incarnations. The second and third full reworkings of the sequence – as a tv series and as the first two volumes of a series of novels – seem to have been put together more or less simultaneously, and, although there are some differences between the two, it would be difficult to assign priority to any one version of the long and episodic plot. In novel form, the sequence comprises *The Hitch Hiker's Guide to the Galaxy* (**1979**), *The Restaurant at the End of the Universe* (**1980**), *Life, the Universe and Everything* (**1982**) and *So Long, and Thanks for All the Fish* (**1984**); the first three volumes were assembled as

The Hitchhiker's Trilogy (omni **1984** US), and all four were assembled as *The Hitch Hiker's Guide to the Galaxy: A Trilogy in Four Parts* (omni **1986**; vt *The Hitchhiker's Quartet* 1986 US; rev with "Young Zaphod Plays it Safe" added vt *The More than Complete Hitchhiker's Guide: Five Stories* 1987 US). One basic premise frames the various episodes contained in the differing versions of the sequence, though volumes three and four of the novel sequence carry on into new territory. A human-shaped ALIEN, on contract to revise the eponymous guide, has under the name Ford Prefect spent some time on Earth, where he befriends the protagonist of the series, Arthur Dent. On learning that Earth is to be demolished to make way for an interstellar bypass, Prefect escapes the doomed planet with Dent, and the two then hitchhike around the Galaxy, undergoing various adventures. Various satirical points are made, and, as the sequence moves ahead into the final episodes, DA's underlying corrosiveness of wit becomes more and more prominent. Earth proves to have been constructed eons earlier as a COMPUTER whose task it is to solve the meaning of life; but its demolition, only seconds before the answer is due, puts paid to any hope that any meaning will be found. For the millions of fans who listened to the radio version, watched the tv episodes, and laughed through the first two volumes of the book sequence, volumes three and four must have seemed punitively unamused by the human condition; and in *Mostly Harmless* (**1992**), a late addition to the sequence, the darkness only increases. But a satirist's intrinsic failure to be amused by pain did, in retrospect, underlie the most ebullient earlier moments.

A second sequence – *Dirk Gently's Holistic Detective Agency* (**1987**) and *The Long Dark Tea-Time of the Soul* (**1988**) – confirmed the dark bent of DA's talent. Though the tales inventively carry the eponymous detective through a wide range of sf experiences, this second series did not gain the extraordinary response of the first. In a sense that only time can test, it could be said that the **Hitch Hiker's Guide** has become folklore. [JC]

Other works: *The Meaning of Liff* (**1983**; rev vt *The Deeper Meaning of Liff* 1990) with John Lloyd, humour; *The Utterly Utterly Merry Comic Relief Christmas Book* (anth **1986**), ed (anon), charity fundraising book for Comic Relief; *Last Chance to See* (**1991**) with Mark Carwardine, nonfiction book promoting wildlife conservation, with text by DA to photographs by Carwardine.

About the author: *Don't Panic: The Official Hitch Hiker's Guide to the Galaxy Companion* (**1988**) by Neil GAIMAN.

See also: ANTI-INTELLECTUALISM IN SF; FANTASTIC VOYAGES; GAMES AND TOYS; GODS AND DEMONS; HUMOUR; MUSIC; MYTHOLOGY; ROBOTS; SATIRE; SPACE OPERA.

ADAMS, FREDERICK UPHAM (1859-1921) US writer whose two sf UTOPIAS – *President John Smith: The Story of a Peaceful Revolution (Written in 1920)* (**1897**) and *The*

Kidnapped Millionaires: A Tale of Wall Street and the Tropics (**1901**) – put into stiffly earnest narrative form the arguments that direct election of the US President would lead to a benevolent socialism and that the tycoons of Wall Street were a doomed race.   [JC]

ADAMS, HARRIET S(TRATEMEYER) (1892-1982) US writer and, after the death of her father Edward STRATEMEYER in 1930, editor of his publishing syndicate. Under a variety of house names, including Carolyn Keene, Franklin W. Dixon and Laura Lee Hope, she was herself responsible for writing approximately 170 of the Stratemeyer Syndicate novels about the **Bobbsey Twins**, the **Hardy Boys**, **Nancy Drew** and others; for further titles, she supplied plots and outlines. Under the house name Victor APPLETON she wrote the last in the first series of **Tom Swift** books, *Tom Swift and his Planet Stone* (**1935**), and successfully revived **Tom Swift**, or, to be more accurate, his son **Tom Swift, Jr.**, in a new series which began publication in 1954 (◊ TOM SWIFT for details).   [JC]

About the author: *Stratemeyer Pseudonyms and Series Books: An Annotated Checklist of Stratemeyer and Stratemeyer Syndicate Publications* (**1982**) ed Deirdre Johnson.

ADAMS, HUNTER ◊ Jim LAWRENCE.

ADAMS, JACK Collaborative pseudonym of US writers Alcanoan O. Grigsby (?   -?   ) and Mary P. Lowe (?   -?   ) whose *Nequa, or The Problem of the Ages* (**1900**) carries the character "Jack Adams" – in fact a wronged woman named Cassie – to polar regions, where she and her bigoted fiancé (who does not recognize her as Adams) are rescued by the inhabitants of Altruria (◊ William Dean HOWELLS, though there is no explicit connection between his utopias and this one). The Altrurians take them to their country, which lies inside a HOLLOW EARTH, demonstrate their flying machines and other marvels, and explain their sexually egalitarian, non-Christian culture (◊ FEMINISM). Nequa, as "Jack Adams" now calls herself, will marry her fiancé only if he attains some wisdom. *Nequa* is a surprisingly enjoyable salutary tale.   [JC]

ADAMS, JOHN ◊ John S. GLASBY.

ADAMS, LOUIS J.A. [s] ◊ Joe L. HENSLEY; Alexei PANSHIN.

ADAMS, NEAL (1941-   ) Influential and remarkably prolific US COMIC-strip artist specializing in the SUPERHERO genre, with a strong, gutsy yet sophisticated line style. His continued claim to fame probably rests largely on his ground-breaking personal reinterpretation of DC COMICS's **Batman**. He attended the School of Industrial Art in Manhattan, then worked for Archie Comics 1959-60 before establishing himself in syndicated newspaper strips with a strip version of the tv series *Ben Casey*, which he drew for dailies and Sundays 1962-6. He assisted on other newspaper strips including **Bat Masterson** (1961), **Peter Scratch** (1966), **Secret Agent Corrigan** (1967) and **Rip Kirby** (1968). He began working for National Periodical Publications (DC Comics) in 1967 drawing **Deadman**

(*Strange Adventures* #206-#216). Other characters to benefit from his innovative touch included **Spectre**, SUPERMAN, **Batman** (in *Detective Comics*, 9 issues between #369, Nov 1967, and #439, Mar 1974, and 9 issues in *Batman* between #219, Feb 1970, and #255, Apr 1974, as well as in other associated titles), **Flash**, **Green Lantern** and the X-MEN. He drew the team-up title **Green Lantern-Green Arrow** continuously from #76 (Apr 1970) to #89 (May 1972). #85 ("Snowbirds Don't Fly") and #86 ("They Say It'll Kill Me, But They Won't Say When") of this title featured a story about the drug scene and won an Academy of Comic-Book Art Award for NA and writer Denny O'Neill. His output for DC, MARVEL COMICS and other leading publishers was prolific throughout the 1970s and early 1980s; in addition he produced book covers, film posters, advertising art and the set and costume design for an unsuccessful sf play, *Warp* (1973; ◊ THEATRE). In 1987 he formed his own publishing company, Continuity Comics.

NA has also had a high profile as a campaigner for comics creators' rights, notably in connection with the financial recognition by DC of SUPERMAN's creators, Jerry SIEGEL and Joe Shuster. NA was involved in the setting-up of the Academy of Comic-Book Art (ACBA) in 1970.   [RT]

ADAMS, PAMELA CRIPPEN [r] ◊ Robert ADAMS.

ADAMS, (FRANKLIN) ROBERT (1932-1990) US soldier and writer who was best known for the post-HOLOCAUST **Horseclans** sequence of adventures set after AD2500 in a series of states occupying what was once the USA and dominated from behind the scenes by a strain of immortal MUTANTS, while an unsavoury group of human scientists opposes them from a secret base. Occasionally the reader gains sight of repulsive sects who decayedly parody 20th-century movements – ECOLOGY, for instance – that were *bêtes-noires* of the author, who was not averse to polemical intrusions. The sequence comprises *The Coming of the Horseclans* (**1975**; exp 1982), *Swords of the Horseclans* (**1977**) and *Revenge of the Horseclans* (**1977**) – all three being assembled as *Tales of the Horseclans* (omni **1985**) – *A Cat of Silvery Hue* (**1979**), *The Savage Mountains* (**1980**), *The Patrimony* (**1980**), *Horseclans Odyssey* (**1981**), *The Death of a Legend* (**1981**), *The Witch Goddess* (**1982**), *Bili the Axe* (**1982**) – which contained a background summary – *Champion of the Last Battle* (**1983**), *A Woman of the Horseclans* (**1983**), *Horses of the North* (**1985**), *A Man Called Milo Morai* (**1986**), *The Memories of Milo Morai* (**1986**), *Trumpets of War* (**1987**), *Madman's Army* (**1987**) and *The Clan of the Cats* (**1988**). Two SHARED-WORLD anthologies – *Friends of the Horseclans* (anth **1987**) and *Friends of the Horseclans II* (anth **1989**) – also appeared, both edited with his wife, Pamela Crippen Adams (1961-   ). A second series, the **Castaways in Time** alternate-history TIME-TRAVEL sequence, comprises *Castaways in Time* (**1980**), *The Seven Magical Jewels of Ireland* (**1985**), *Of Kings and Quests* (**1986**), *Of Chiefs and Champions* (**1987**), *Of Myths and Monsters* (**1988**) and *Of Beginnings and Endings*

(1989). Most of his remaining work, including another, unfinished series, was fantasy; some of his anthologies, however – including *Robert Adams' Book of Alternate Worlds* (anth **1987**) with Pamela Crippen Adams and Martin H. GREENBERG, *Robert Adams' Book of Soldiers* (anth **1988**) with P.C. Adams and Greenberg, and *Alternatives* (anth **1989**) with P.C. Adams – were of sf interest. [JC]

Other works: The **Stairway to Forever** sequence, comprising *The Stairway to Forever* (**1988**) and *Monsters and Magicians* (**1988**).

As editor: *Barbarians* (anth **1985**) with Martin H. Greenberg and Charles G. WAUGH and *Barbarians II* (anth **1988**) with P.C. Adams and Greenberg; the **Magic in Ithkar** sequence, with Andre NORTON, comprising *Magic in Ithkar* (anth **1985**), *#2* (anth **1985**), *#3* (anth **1986**) and *#4* (anth **1987**); *Hunger for Horror* (anth **1988**) with P.C. Adams and Greenberg; *Phantom Regiments* (anth **1990**) with P.C. Adams and Greenberg.

See also: ALTERNATE WORLDS; SWORD AND SORCERY.

ADAMS, SAMUEL HOPKINS (1871-1958) US writer, prolific and popular author of novels and screenplays, including that for the film *It Happened One Night* (1934). He wrote an sf novel with Stewart Edward WHITE (*whom see for details*), *The Mystery* (**1907**), about a ship found at sea with no crew aboard, and supplying an sf explanation for their disappearance: side-effects of a new radioactive element. The sequel, *The Sign at Six* (**1912**), also sf, is by White alone. SHA's solo sf books are *The Flying Death* (**1908**), an "impossible crime" tale in which Long Island, New York, is invaded by a pteranodon; and *The World Goes Smash* (**1938**), a NEAR-FUTURE story of a US civil war in which New York is devastated. [JC]

ADAMS, TERRY A. (? -   ) US writer whose **Sentience** sequence – *Sentience: A Novel of First Contact* (**1986**) and *The Master of Chaos* (**1989**) – begins in the conflict between "true" humans and D'Neerans, who are human telepaths (◊ ESP), and builds into a SPACE-OPERA sequence involving new races and challenges. They are told in a skittish but engaging style designed to give some sense of a telepath's way of thinking. [JC]

ADAMSKI, GEORGE [r] ◊ UFOS.

AD ASTRA UK magazine, small-BEDSHEET format, published by Rowlot Ltd, ed James Manning, 16 issues, bimonthly, Oct/Nov 1978-Sep/Oct 1981, only first 2 issues dated. Its subtitle, "Britain's First ScienceFact/ScienceFiction Magazine", contained the seeds of its eventual demise. It attempted to cover too many fields, most in no real depth. The fiction (about 2 stories an issue) – mainly from UK authors, including John BRUNNER, Garry KILWORTH, David LANGFORD and Ian WATSON – was supplemented by a mélange of film, book, games and theatre reviews, together with cartoon strips, sf news (from Langford), science articles, many about astronomy, and PSEUDO-SCIENCE articles. [RR]

ADDEO, EDMOND G. [r] ◊ Richard M. GARVIN.

ADDISON, HUGH Pseudonym used by UK author and journalist Harry Collinson Owen (1882-1956) for his future-WAR novel *The Battle of London* (**1923**), one of several contemporary works which warned of a communist revolution in the UK. It was given a slight twist by the inclusion of an advantageous German attack on London. [JE]

ADELER, MAX Principal pseudonym of US writer and businessman Charles Heber Clark (1841-1915), who wrote also as John Quill, under which name he published "The Women's Millennium" (1867), possibly the first sex-role-reversal DYSTOPIA. Set in an indeterminate future, and told from the perspective of an even later period when some balance has been achieved, it is a remarkably cutting demonstration of the foolishness of men's claims to natural superiority. As MA, he specialized in rather facetious tall tales, both sf and fantasy, many of which end in the perfunctory revelation that all was a dream. This convention aside, they remain of interest, especially "Professor Baffin's Adventures" (1880; vt "The Fortunate Island" 1882), a long lost-race tale (◊ LOST WORLDS) which first appeared in *Beeton's Christmas Annual* (anth **1880** UK) as centrepiece to "The Fortunate Island" – a linked assemblage of stories and sketches by various authors which made up the bulk of the volume – and was later published in *An Old Fogey and Other Stories* (coll **1881** UK; rev vt *The Fortunate Island and Other Stories* 1882 US). It is MA's story that almost certainly supplied Mark TWAIN with the basic premise and some of the actual plot of *A Connecticut Yankee in King Arthur's Court* (**1889**). When accused of plagiarism, Twain responded evasively. [JC]

Other works: *Random Shots* (coll **1878** UK); *Transformations* (coll **1883** UK); *By the Bend of the River* (coll **1914**).

About the author: "'Professor Baffin's Adventures' by Max Adeler: the Inspiration for *A Connecticut Yankee in King Arthur's Court?*" by David KETTERER in *Mark Twain Journal* #24 (Spr 1986); "'John Quill': The Women's Millennium", introduced by Ketterer in *Science Fiction Studies* #15 (1988); "Mark Twain's *A Connecticut Yankee*: Reconsiderations and Revisions", by Horst H. Kruse in *American Literature* 62, #3 (Sept 1990).

See also: SHARED WORLDS.

ADERCA, FELIX [r] ◊ ROMANIA.

ADLARD, MARK Working name used by UK writer Peter Marcus Adlard (1932-   ) for all his books. An arts graduate of Cambridge University, he was until his retirement in 1976 a manager in the steel industry. His knowledge of managerial and industrial problems plays a prominent role in his **Tcity** trilogy: *Interface* (**1971**), *Volteface* (**1972**) and *Multiface* (**1975**). The series is set in a CITY of the NEAR FUTURE. By calling it Tcity, MA plainly intended to confer on it a kind of regimented anonymity in the manner of Yevgeny ZAMIATIN; at the same time, he was probably making a pun on Teesside, the industrial conurbation in the northeast of England where he was raised (also, in some north-England dialects "t'city" means simply "the city"). With a rich but sometimes sour irony, and a real if distanced sympathy for the problems and frustrations of both management and workers, MA plays a set of variations, often comic, on AUTOMATION, hierarchical systems, the MEDIA LANDSCAPE, revolution, the difficulties of coping with LEISURE, class distinction according to INTELLIGENCE, fantasies of SEX and the stultifying pressures of conformity. *The Greenlander* (**1978**) is the first volume of a projected non-genre trilogy, further volumes of which have not appeared. His books are ambitious in scope and deserve to be more widely known. [PN]

About the author: "The Many Faces of Adlard" by Andy Darlington in *Arena 7*, March 1978.

ADLER, ALLEN A. (1916-1964) US writer, mostly for films, co-author of the story used as the basis for the film FORBIDDEN PLANET (1956), although he had nothing to do with the novelization by W.J. Stuart (Philip MacDONALD). AAA's only sf novel was an unremarkable adventure, also set on a planet threatened by a monster: *Mach 1: A Story of the Planet Ionus* (**1957**; vt *Terror on Planet Ionus* 1966). [JC]

ADOLPH, JOSÉ B. [r] ◊ LATIN AMERICA.

ADVENT: PUBLISHERS Chicago-based specialist publishing house, owned by sf fans, which publishes critical and bibliographical material. The first book was Damon KNIGHT's *In Search of Wonder* (**1956**); other notable volumes include James BLISH's two collections of critical essays (as William Atheling Jr) and, later, his posthumous *The Tale that Wags the God* (coll **1987**), as by Blish. A:P's most important scholarly publication has been Donald H. TUCK's *The Encyclopedia of Science Fiction and Fantasy through 1968* (vol 1 **1974**; vol 2 **1978**; vol 3 **1982**). [MJE]

See also: SMALL PRESSES AND LIMITED EDITIONS.

ADVENTURES OF BUCKAROO BANZAI ACROSS THE 8TH DIMENSION, THE Film (1984). Sherwood Productions. Dir W.D. Richter, starring Peter Weller, John Lithgow, Ellen Barkin, Jeff Goldblum, Christopher Lloyd. Screenplay Earl Mac Rauch. 103 mins. Colour.

The crazed but incoherent tale of rock-musician-neurosurgeon-particle-physicist Banzai (Weller), a kind of imaginary 1930s pulp hero with a distinctly 1980s ambience. In this episode Banzai defeats an alien INVASION which began in 1938 (as described by Orson Welles, who pretended it was fiction) led by frantically overacting John Lithgow. The film is ill directed and badly photographed, and appears to have been made by underground junk intellectuals who accidentally stumbled over a fairly big budget. REPO MAN, from the same year, is a wittier and better organized example of what might be called designer cult movies. [PN]

See also: ANDROIDS; WAR OF THE WORLDS.

ADVENTURES OF SUPERMAN, THE ◊ SUPERMAN.

ADVENTURES OF THE ROCKETEER ◊ *The* ROCKETEER.

ADYE, TIM [r] ◊ M.H. ZOOL.

A.E. or Æ Pseudonym used by Irish poet George William Russell (1867-1935) for all his writing. In 1886 he and William Butler Yeats (1865-1939) helped found the Dublin Lodge of the Theosophical Society, and much of his work reflects a mystical agenda – not very coherently in the supernatural tales assembled in *The Mask of Apollo, and Other Stories* (coll **1904**), but with very much more force in *The Interpreters* (**1922**), a philosophical fiction set in an idealized venue. More elegiacally and more concretely, in *The Avatars: A Futurist Fantasy* (**1932**), set in a future Ireland, this agenda comes to life in the form of two supernal beings who hauntingly invoke a vision of a world less abandoned to materialism, and thus draw the protagonists to "the margin of the Great Deep", as Monk Gibbon puts it in his long and informative essay on A.E.'s work which introduces *The Living Torch* (coll **1937**), a posthumous volume of nonfiction. [JC]

AELITA Film (1924). Mezhrabpom. Dir Yakov A. Protazanov, starring Nikolai M. Tseretelli, Igor Ilinski, Yulia Solntseva. Screenplay Fyodor Otzep, Alexei Faiko, based on *Aelita* (**1922**) by Alexei TOLSTOY. 78 mins cut from 120 mins. B/w.

This striking example of early sf cinema is a satiric comedy in which a group of Soviet astronauts travel to Mars, where they find the mass of the people living under an oppressive regime and spark off an abortive revolution; one of them teaches the lovely daughter of a Martian leader how to kiss. *A* is a very stylized silent film; its futuristic, Expressionistic sets, by Isaac Rabinovitch of the Kamerny Theatre, were to influence the design in FLASH GORDON. The sf elements in the story are vigorous and witty (though in the end it is revealed to be All a Dream), but occupy only a small part of the film. [PN/JB]

See also: CINEMA.

AELITA AWARD ◊ RUSSIA.

A FOR ANDROMEDA UK tv serial (1961). A BBC TV production. Prod Michael Hayes, Norman Jones, written John ELLIOT from a storyline by Fred HOYLE. 7 episodes, the first 6 45 mins, the last 50 mins. B/w. The cast included Peter Halliday, John Nettleton, Esmond Knight, Patricia Neale, Frank Windsor, Mary Morris, Julie Christie.

A radio signal transmitted from the Andromeda Galaxy proves, when decoded by maverick scientist Fleming (Halliday), to contain instructions for the building of a supercomputer. Once built by Earth scientists, the COMPUTER in turn provides instructions on how to create a living being. The final result is a beautiful young girl, named, naturally, Andromeda, mentally linked to the ever-more-powerful computer; her existence causes a great deal of controversy within the government. She helps Fleming wreck the computer, and is hurt and (seemingly) drowned. The story is intelligently presented despite its absurdities. The serial brought Julie Christie into the public eye for the first time. The novelization by Hoyle and Elliot is *A for Andromeda* (**1962**). The tv sequel was *The* ANDROMEDA BREAKTHROUGH (1962). [JB/PN]

AFRICA ◊ ARABIC SF; BLACK AFRICAN SF.

AGHILL, GORDON Pseudonym used collaboratively by Robert SILVERBERG and Randall GARRETT on two stories in 1956. [JC]

AGUILERA, JUAN MIGUEL [r] ◊ SPAIN.

AHERN, JERRY Working name of US author Jerome Morrell Ahern (1946-   ), most of whose output consists of violent post-HOLOCAUST novels, most notably in his **Survivalist** sequence, in which ex-CIA agent John Rourke attempts to preserve his family after a global nuclear conflict. Perhaps the most influential series in the subgenre of SURVIVALIST FICTION, it comprises *Survivalist #1: Total War* (**1981**), *#2: The Nightmare Begins* (**1981**), *#3: The Quest* (**1981**), *#4: The Doomsayer* (**1981**), *#5: The Web* (**1983**), *#6: The Savage Horde* (**1983**), *#7: The Prophet* (**1984**), *#8: The End is Coming* (**1984**), *#9: Earth Fire* (**1984**), *#10: The Awakening* (**1984**), *#11: The Reprisal* (**1985**), *#12: The Rebellion* (**1985**), *#13: Pursuit* (**1986**), *#14: The Terror* (**1987**), *#15: Overlord* (**1987**), *#16: The Arsenal* (**1988**), *#17: The Ordeal* (**1988**), *#18: Mid-Wake* (**1988**), *#19: Struggle* (**1989**), *#20: Final Rain* (**1989**), *#21: Firestorm* (**1990**) and *#22: To End All War* (**1990**). The continuation, beginning with *#23: The Legend* (**1991**) and *#24: Call to Battle* (**1992**), takes place after the Earth's atmosphere has been destroyed by a catastrophic fire, and Rourke has saved his family and himself by entering cryogenic sleep, emerging after 500 years to find a world deserted except for the personnel of the Eden Project – fresh from 500 years of hibernation aboard a fleet of space shuttles – and surviving groups of Nazis (*sic*) and fanatical communists.

A second but similar sequence, the **Defender** series, comprises *The Defender #1: The Battle Begins* (**1988**), *#2: The Killing Wedge* (**1988**), *#3: Out of Control* (**1988**), *#4: Decision Time* (**1989**), *#5: Entrapment* (**1989**), *#6: Escape* (**1989**), *#7: Vengeance* (**1989**), *#8: Justice Denied* (**1989**), *#9: Death Grip* (**1990**), *#10: The Good Fight* (**1990**), *#11: The Challenge* (**1990**) and *#12: No Survivors* (**1990**). With his wife, Sharan A(nn) Ahern (1948-   ), whose contributions were sometimes anonymous, he wrote the short **Takers** sequence, comprising *The Takers* (**1984**) and *River of Gold* (**1985**), as well as some singletons. He also contributed *Deathlight* (**1982**) to the long-running **Nick Carter** sequence, writing as Nick CARTER. [NT]

Other works: *The Freeman* (**1986**), *Miamigrad* (**1987**), *WerewolveSS* (**1990**) and *The Kamikaze Legacy* (**1990**), all with Sharon A. Ahern.

See also: SOCIAL DARWINISM.

AHERN, SHARON A. [r] ◊ Jerry AHERN.

AH! NANA ◊ MÉTAL HURLANT.

AHONEN, ERKKI [r] ◊ FINLAND.

AI The commonly used acronym for Artificial Intelligence, an item of terminology used increasingly often in information science, and hence in sf, since the late 1970s. Most writers would agree that for a COMPUTER or other MACHINE of some sort to qualify as an AI it must be self-aware. There are as yet none such in the real world. [PN]

See also: CYBERNETICS; CYBERSPACE.

AIKEN, JOAN (DELANO) [r] ◊ John AIKEN; ALTERNATE WORLDS.

AIKEN, JOHN (KEMPTON) (1913-1990) US-born UK writer, son of Conrad Aiken (1889-1973) and brother of Joan Aiken (1924-   ) and Jane Aiken Hodge (1917-   ). JA published his first sf story, "Dragon's Teeth", with *NW* in 1946, but did not remain active in the field. His only novel, *World Well Lost* (fixup **1970** as John Paget; as JA 1971 US), based on his 1940s *NW* stories, was published by ROBERT HALE LIMITED. It describes with some energy a conflict between a totalitarian Earth and free-minded colonists in the system of Alpha Centauri. *Conrad Aiken, Our Father* (**1989**) with Joan Aiken and Jane Aiken Hodge, is a revealing memoir. [JC]

AIKIN, JIM Working name of US writer James Douglas Aikin (1948-   ), whose sf novel, *Walk the Moons Road* (**1985**), gave operatic colour to a moderately intricate PLANETARY ROMANCE featuring aliens, humans, seas, politics and sex on a planet which is not Earth. [JC]

AINSBURY, RAY ◊ A. Hyatt VERRILL.

AINSWORTHY, RAY ◊ Lauran Bosworth PAINE.

AIRSHIPS ◊ TRANSPORTATION.

AIR WONDER STORIES US BEDSHEET-size PULP MAGAZINE, 11 issues, July 1929-May 1930, published by Stellar Publishing Corp., ed Hugo GERNSBACK, managing editor David Lasser.

This was a prompt comeback by Gernsback after the filing of bankruptcy proceedings against his Experimenter Publishing Co., with which he had founded AMAZING STORIES. *AWS* announced itself in its first editorial as presenting "solely flying stories of the future, strictly along scientific-mechanical-technical lines . . . to prevent gross scientific-aviation misinformation from reaching our readers". To this end Gernsback hired three professors and one Air Corps Reserve major, whose names appeared prominently on the masthead. The stories were by the foremost pulp writers of the day, including Edmond HAMILTON, David KELLER, Victor MacCLURE, Ed Earl REPP, Harl VINCENT and Jack WILLIAMSON; Raymond Z. GALLUN published his first story here. The cover designs for all issues were by Frank R. PAUL, who had previously worked on *AMZ*. A sister magazine, SCIENCE WONDER STORIES, began one month earlier, in June 1929. In 1930 Gernsback merged them into WONDER STORIES. [PN]

AITMATOV, CHINGIZ (TOREKULOVICH) (1928-   ) Formerly Soviet (now Kyrgyzstanian) writer and diplomat, known mostly for his mainstream fiction (for which he has been a Nobel candidate), which poetically depicts Man-Nature relations. His one venture into sf is *I Dol'she Veka Dlitsia Den'* (**1980**; trans John French as *The Day Lasts Longer than a Hundred Years* **1983** UK): part of this novel realistically depicts life in a small Kirghiz town near a secret Soviet cosmodrome, and part comprises a NEAR-FUTURE thriller set on board the Soviet-US carrier

Parity, which encounters ALIENS. Written before *perestroika*, the novel raised controversy due to its obvious pacifist mood. [VG]

AKERS, ALAN BURT ◊ Kenneth BULMER.

AKERS, FLOYD ◊ L. Frank BAUM.

AKI, TANUKI [s] ◊ Charles DE LINT.

AKIRA Animated film (1987). Akira Committee. Dir Katsuhiro OTOMO, from a screenplay by Otomo and Izo Hashimoto, based on the graphic epic *Akira* (begun 1982) by Otomo. Animation studio: Asahi. Chief animator: Takashi Nakamura. 124 mins. Colour.

A is the most successful attempt yet to transfer sophisticated, state-of-the-art comic-book graphics to the screen. Story-boarded in great detail by the comic's own creator, it is set in the teeming edginess of Neo-Tokyo in 2019. The convoluted story deals with two ex-orphanage kids in a biker gang, one tough and one a loser; the "weaker" one, Tetsuo, develops PSI POWERS, discovers the remnants of super-being "Akira" stored at Absolute Zero below the Olympic Stadium, metamorphoses, and becomes (along with others with whom he melds) the seed of a new cosmos. The link between persecution, adolescent *angst* and psychic power seems to come straight from Theodore STURGEON's *More than Human* (1953), and the opportunistic plotting draws also on Philip K. DICK, Ridley SCOTT's BLADE RUNNER and many other sources. Though *A* oscillates too extremely between bloody violence, sardonic cynicism (about scientists, the military, religious cults, politicians, terrorists) and dewy-eyed sentiment, and though the novelistic narrative – which despite weepy moments is rather low on human feeling – is unfolded awkwardly and at too great a length, much can be forgiven. Its sheer spectacle and the density and stylish choreography of its apocalyptic, CYBERPUNK ambience are unparalleled in cartoon films. [PN]

See also: CINEMA; COMICS; JAPAN.

AKSYONOV, VASSILY (PAVLOVICH) (1932-   ) Russian MAINSTREAM WRITER, one of those whose careers began in the Khrushchev Thaw and who responded to the subsequent chill by emigrating to the USA, where he became a citizen. His sf novel, *Ostrov Krym* (**1981** US; trans anon as *The Island of Crimea* **1984** US) is a powerful PARALLEL-WORLD story set in a Crimea which is an ISLAND (not, as in this world, a peninsula) where pre-revolutionary "Old Russia" is preserved; the real-life model is obviously China/Taiwan. The Soviet Union soon invades. [VG]

ALBANIA There has been some sf in Albanian since the late 1960s, but not until 1978 was the first sf book published there. By 1991 there had been about a dozen, of which five were by Thanas Qerama, a prolific writer and also an editor of juvenile science magazines; examples are *Roboti i pabindur* ["Disobedient Robot"] (coll **1981**), *Një javë në vitin 2044* ["One Week in the Year 2044"] (**1982**) and *Misteri i tempullit të lashtë* ["Mystery of the Old Church"] (**1987**). The following authors have written at least one sf book each: A. Bishqemi, N. Deda, B. Dedja, Vangjel Dilo, Dh. Konomi, Flamur Topi and B. Xhano. [JO]

ALBANO, PETER (?1940-   ) US writer known mainly for the **Seventh Carrier** sequence of military-sf adventures about a WWII Japanese aircraft carrier which has been unthawed decades later from polar ice to do good: *The Seventh Carrier* (**1983**), *The Second Voyage of the Seventh Carrier* (**1986**), *Return of the Seventh Carrier* (**1987**), *Attack of the Seventh Carrier* (**1989**), *Trial of the Seventh Carrier* (**1990**) and *Revenge of the Seventh Carrier* (**1992**). His other novels, *Waves of Glory* (**1989**) and *Tides of Valor* (**1990**), are unremarkable. [JC]

ALBING PUBLICATIONS ◊ COSMIC STORIES; STIRRING SCIENCE STORIES.

ALBRECHT, JOHANN FRIEDRICH ERNST [r] ◊ GERMANY.

ALDANI, LINO [r] ◊ ITALY.

ALDERMAN, GILL Working name of UK writer Gillian Alderman (1941-   ), who worked in microelectronics research until 1984. She began publishing sf with the first two volumes of her **Guna** sequence – *The Archivist: A Black Romance* (**1989**) and *The Land Beyond: A Fable* (**1990**) – which established her very rapidly as a figure of interest in the field. As usual in the PLANETARY ROMANCE, the world in which the tales are set (Guna) is heavily foregrounded throughout both volumes. Quite similar to Earth – with which its more technologically advanced civilizations have had concourse for many centuries – Guna is perhaps most remarkable for the wide range of relationships found there between the sexes, running from the complex matriarchy depicted in the first volume through Earth-like patterns of repressive patriarchy hinted at broadly in the second. Although it is clearly GA's intent, dexterously achieved, to make some FEMINIST points about male hierarchical thinking, she abstains from creating characters whose consciousnesses reflect these issues. The homosexual male protagonists of *The Archivist*, for instance, whose long love affair and estrangement provide much of the immediate action of the book, exhibit no "normal" resentment at the dominant role of women; and the political revolution fomented by the elder lover has little or nothing to do with sexual politics in any Earthly sense. The long timespan of *The Archivist*, the Grand Tour evocations of landscape which make up much of its bulk, and its distanced narrative voice mark a contemplative sf fantasist of the first order. *The Land Beyond*, a chill book set in a cold part of the planet, is less engaging; but GA is clearly a writer to welcome. [JC]

ALDISS, BRIAN W(ILSON) (1925-   ) UK writer, anthologist and critic, educated at private schools, which he disliked. He served in the Royal Signals in Burma and Sumatra, was demobilized in 1948 and became an assistant in an Oxford bookshop. BWA began his writing career by contributing fictionalized sketches about bookselling to the trade magazine *The*

Bookseller; these were later assembled as his first book, *The Brightfount Diaries* (**1955**).

BWA began publishing sf with "Criminal Record" for *Science Fantasy* in 1954. There followed such notable tales as "Outside" (1955), "Not for an Age" (1955), which was a prizewinner in an *Observer* sf competition), "There is a Tide" (1956) and "Psyclops" (1956), all of which appeared in BWA's first sf volume, *Space, Time and Nathaniel (Presciences)* (coll **1957**). *No Time Like Tomorrow* (coll **1959** US) reprints 6 stories from the 14 in *Space, Time and Nathaniel* and adds another 6. These early stories were ingenious and lyrical but dark in mood. BWA remains a prolific writer of short stories (his total exceeded 300 by 1992), almost all under his own name, though he has used the pseudonyms C.C. Shackleton, Jael Cracken and John Runciman for a few items. "All the World's Tears" (1957), "Poor Little Warrior" (1958), "But Who Can Replace a Man?" (1958), "Old Hundredth" (1960) and "A Kind of Artistry" (1962) are among the most memorable stories collected in *The Canopy of Time* (coll of linked stories **1959**); of the stories listed, only "All the World's Tears" and "But Who Can Replace a Man?" appear, with expository passages that make the book into a loose future HISTORY, in the substantially different *Galaxies like Grains of Sand* (coll of linked stories **1960** US; with 1 story added rev 1979 UK). *The Airs of Earth* (coll **1963**; with 2 stories omitted and 2 stories added, rev vt *Starswarm* 1964 US) and *Best Science Fiction Stories of Brian W. Aldiss* (coll **1965**; rev 1971; vt *Who Can Replace a Man?* 1966 US) also assemble early work. BWA received a 1959 award at the World SF CONVENTION as most promising new author, but his work was less well received in certain quarters where his emphasis on style and imagery, and his lack of an engineering mentality, were regarded with suspicion.

His first novel, *Non-Stop* (**1958**; cut vt *Starship* 1959 US), is a brilliant treatment of the GENERATION STARSHIP and also the theme of CONCEPTUAL BREAKTHROUGH; it has become accepted as a classic of the field. *Vanguard from Alpha* (**1959** dos US; with "Segregation" added, rev as coll vt *Equator: A Human Time Bomb from the Moon!* 1961 UK) – which became part of *The Year Before Yesterday* (1958-65; fixup **1987** US; rev vt *Cracken at Critical: A Novel in Three Acts* 1987 UK) – and *Bow Down to Nul* (**1960** US dos; text restored vt *The Interpreter* 1961 UK) are much less successful, but *The Primal Urge* (**1961** US) is an amusing treatment of SEX as an sf theme. Always ebullient in his approach to sexual morality, BWA was one of the authors who changed the attitudes of sf editors and publishers in this area during the 1960s. *The Long Afternoon of Earth* (fixup **1962** US; exp vt *Hothouse* 1962 UK) won him a 1962 HUGO award for its original appearance as a series of novelettes. It is one of his finest works. Set in the FAR FUTURE, when the Earth has ceased rotating, it involves the adventures of humanity's remnants, who live in the branches of a giant, continent-spanning tree (◊

DEVOLUTION). Criticized for scientific implausibility by James BLISH and others, *Hothouse* (BWA's preferred title) nevertheless displays all his linguistic, comic and inventive talents. It also illustrates BWA's main thematic concerns, namely the conflict between fecundity and ENTROPY, between the rich variety of life and the silence of death.

The Dark Light Years (**1964**) is a lesser work, though notable for the irony of its central dilemma – how one comes to terms with intelligent ALIENS who are physically disgusting. *Greybeard* (cut **1964** US; full version 1964 UK) is perhaps BWA's finest sf novel. It deals with a future in which humanity has become sterile due to an accident involving biological weapons. Almost all the characters are old people, and their reactions to the incipient death of the human race are well portrayed. Both a celebration of human life and a critique of civilization, it has been underrated, particularly in the USA. *Earthworks* (**1965**; rev 1966 US) is a minor novel about OVERPOPULATION. *An Age* (**1967**; vt *Cryptozoic!* 1968 US) is an odd and original treatment of TIME TRAVEL, which sees time as running backwards with a consequent reversal of cause and effect, comparable but superior to Philip K. DICK's *Counter-Clock World* (**1967**), published in the same year.

During the latter half of the 1960s BWA was closely identified with NEW-WAVE sf, and in particular with the innovative magazine NEW WORLDS, for which he helped obtain an Arts Council grant in 1967. Here BWA published increasingly unconventional fiction, notably his novel *Report on Probability A* (**1968**; written 1962 but unpublishable until the times changed), an sf transposition of the techniques of the French "antinovelists" into a Surrealist story of enigmatic voyeurism, and his **Acid-Head War** stories, collected as *Barefoot in the Head: A European Fantasia* (fixup **1969**). Set in the aftermath of a European war in which psychedelic drugs have been used as weapons, the latter is written in a dense, punning style reminiscent of James Joyce's *Finnegans Wake* (**1939**); it is an extraordinary *tour de force*.

The novella *The Saliva Tree* (1965 *FSF*; **1988** chap dos US) won a NEBULA and featured in *The Saliva Tree and Other Strange Growths* (coll **1966**). It is an entertaining tribute to H.G. WELLS, though the plot is reminiscent of "The Colour out of Space" (1927) by H.P. LOVECRAFT. Further volumes of short stories include *Intangibles Inc.* (coll **1969**; with 2 stories omitted and 1 added, rev vt *Neanderthal Planet* 1970 US), *The Moment of Eclipse* (coll **1970**), which won the BRITISH SCIENCE FICTION AWARD in 1972, and *The Book of Brian Aldiss* (coll **1972** US; vt *Comic Inferno* 1973 UK). Novels of this period include *Frankenstein Unbound* (**1973**), a time-travel fantasia which has Mary SHELLEY as a major character and presents in fictional form the myth-of-origin for sf he advocated in his history of the genre, *Billion Year Spree* (**1973**; rev and exp with David WINGROVE as *Trillion Year Spree* **1986**, which won a Hugo); and *The Eighty-Minute Hour: A Space*

Opera (**1974** US), a comedy in which BWA's penchant for puns and extravagant invention is thought by some critics to be overindulged. His long fantasy novel *The Malacia Tapestry* (**1976**) is a much more balanced work. Set in a mysterious, never-changing CITY, it is a love story with fantastic elements. Beautifully imagined, it is a restatement of BWA's obsessions with entropy, fecundity and the role of the artist, and was perhaps his best novel since *Greybeard*. *Brothers of the Head* (**1977**), about Siamese-twin rock stars and their third, dormant head, was a minor exercise in Grand Guignol; with an additional story, it was also assembled as *Brothers of the Head, and Where the Lines Converge* (coll **1979**). *Enemies of the System: A Tale of Homo Uniformis* (**1978**) was a somewhat disgruntled DYSTOPIAN novella. *Moreau's Other Island* (**1980**; vt *An Island Called Moreau* 1981 US) plays fruitfully with themes from H.G. Wells: during a nuclear war a US official discovers that bioengineering experiments performed on a deserted island are a secret project run by his own department. Stories collected in *Last Orders and Other Stories* (coll **1977**; vt *Last Orders* 1989 US), *New Arrivals, Old Encounters* (coll **1979**) and *Seasons in Flight* (coll **1984**) were unwearied, though sometimes hasty.

The 1970s also saw BWA beginning to publish non-sf fictions more substantial than his previous two, *The Brightfount Diaries* and *The Male Response* (**1961** US). He gained his first bestseller and some notoriety with *The Hand-Reared Boy* (**1970**). This, with its two sequels, *A Soldier Erect* (**1971**) and *A Rude Awakening* (**1978**), deals with the education, growth to maturity and war experiences in Burma of a young man whose circumstances often recall the early life of the author; the three were assembled as *The Horatio Stubbs Saga* (omni **1985**). *Forgotten Life* (**1988**) and its sequel «Remembrance Day» (**1992**) address similar wartime experiences in fictional retrospect, and even *Life in the West* (**1980**) – listed by Anthony BURGESS in his *Ninety-Nine Novels: The Best in English Since 1939* (**1984**) – flirts brusquely with autobiography. A novella, *Ruins* (**1987** chap), also explores contemporary material.

Some years had passed since his last popular success as an sf novelist when BWA suddenly reasserted his eminence in the field with the publication of the Helliconia books – *Helliconia Spring* (**1982**), which won the 1983 JOHN W. CAMPBELL MEMORIAL AWARD, *Helliconia Summer* (**1983**) and *Helliconia Winter* (**1985**) – three massive, thoroughly researched, deeply through-composed tales set on a planet whose primary sun is in an eccentric orbit around another star, so that the planet experiences both small seasons and an eon-long Great Year, during the course of which radical changes afflict the human-like inhabitants. Cultures are born in spring, flourish over the summer, and die with the onset of the generations-long winter. A team from an exhausted Terran civilization observes the spectacle from orbit. Throughout all three volumes, BWA pays homage to various high moments of pulp sf, rewriting several

classic action climaxes into a dark idiom that befits Helliconia. As an exercise in world-building, the Helliconia books lie unassailably at the heart of modern sf; as a demonstration of the complexities inherent in the mode of the PLANETARY ROMANCE when taken seriously, they are exemplary; as a Heraclitean revery upon the implications of the Great Year for human pretensions, they are (as is usual with BWA's work) heterodox.

Dracula Unbound (**1991**) continues through a similar time-travel plot the explorations of *Frankenstein Unbound*, although this time in a lighter vein. Two summary collections – *Best SF Stories of Brian W. Aldiss* (coll **1988**; vt *Man in his Time: Best SF Stories* 1989), not to be confused with the similarly titled 1965 collection, and *A Romance of the Equator: Best Fantasy Stories* (coll **1989**), not to be confused with *A Romance of the Equator* (**1980** chap), which publishes the title story only – closed off the 1980s, along with *Science Fiction Blues* (coll **1988**). This latter collects materials used by BWA in Dickensian stage readings he began to give in the 1980s at conventions and other venues; these readings have reflected something of the vast, exuberant, melancholy, protean corpus of one of the sf field's two or three most prolific authors of substance, and perhaps its most exploratory. Similarly, *Kindred Blood in Kensington Gore* (**1992** chap), a short play, gave BWA the opportunity to conduct on stage an imaginary conversation with the posthumous Philip K. DICK.

BWA has been an indefatigable anthologist and critic of sf. His anthologies (most of which contain stimulating introductions and other matter) include *Penguin Science Fiction* (anth **1961**), *Best Fantasy Stories* (anth **1962**), *More Penguin Science Fiction* (anth **1963**), *Introducing SF* (anth **1964**), *Yet More Penguin Science Fiction* (anth **1964**) and *The Penguin World Omnibus of Science Fiction* (anth **1986**) with Sam J. LUNDWALL. *The Book of Mini-Sagas I* (anth **1985**) and *The Book of Mini-Sagas II* (anth **1988**) are associational collections of 50-word stories. The **Space Opera** series of anthologies comprises *Space Opera* (anth **1974**), *Space Odysseys* (anth **1975**), *Evil Earths* (anth **1975**), *Galactic Empires* (anth in 2 vols 1976) and *Perilous Planets* (anth **1978**). Anthologies ed in collaboration with Harry HARRISON are: *Nebula Award Stories II* (**1967**); the **Year's Best SF** series comprising *Best SF: 1967* (**1968** US; vt *The Year's Best Science Fiction No 1* 1968 UK), *The Year's Best Science Fiction No 2* (anth **1969**; exp vt *Best SF: 1968* 1969 US), *The Year's Best Science Fiction No 3* (anth **1970**; vt *Best SF: 1969* 1970 US), *The Year's Best Science Fiction No 4* (anth **1971**; vt *Best SF: 1970* 1971 US), *The Year's Best Science Fiction No 5* (anth **1972**; vt *Best SF: 1971* 1972 US), *Best SF: 1972* (anth **1973** US; vt *The Year's Best Science Fiction No 6* 1973 UK), *Best SF: 1973* (anth **1974** US; cut vt *The Year's Best Science Fiction No 7* 1974 UK), *Best SF 1974* (anth **1975** US; cut vt *The Year's Best Science Fiction No 8* 1975 UK) and *The Year's Best Science Fiction No 9* (anth **1976**; vt *Best SF: 1975* 1976 US); *Venus* (anth **1968** US; exp vt *Farewell,*

Fantastic Venus! 1968 UK); *The Astounding-Analog Reader* (anth in 2 vols **1972-3** US; UK paperback of 1973 divided Vol 1 into 2 vols, and Vol 2 did not appear at all from this publisher); and the **Decade** series comprising *Decade: The 1940s* (**1975**), *The 1950s* (**1976**) and *The 1960s* (**1977**). Also with Harrison, with whom BWA has had a long and, considering the wide gulf between their two styles of fiction, amazingly successful working relationship, he edited two issues of *SF Horizons* (1964-5), a short-lived but excellent critical journal, and *Hell's Cartographers* (anth **1975**), a collection of six autobiographical essays by sf writers, including the two editors.

Most of BWA's nonfiction has a critical relation to the genre, though *Cities and Stones: A Traveller's Jugoslavia* (**1966**) is a travel book. *The Shape of Further Things* (**1970**) is autobiography-cum-criticism. *Billion Year Spree* (**1973**), a large and enthusiastic survey of sf, is BWA's most important nonfiction work (◊ HISTORY OF SF); its argument that sf is a child of the intersection of Gothic romance with the Industrial Revolution gives profound pleasure as a myth of origin, though it fails circumstantially to be altogether convincing; the book was much expanded and, perhaps inevitably, somewhat diluted in effect as *Trillion Year Spree* (**1986**) with David WINGROVE. *Science Fiction Art* (**1975**) is an attractively produced selection of sf ILLUSTRATION with commentary, mostly from the years of the PULP MAGAZINES, and *Science Fiction Art* (**1976**) – note identical title – presents a portfolio of Chris FOSS's art. *Science Fiction as Science Fiction* (**1978** chap), *This World and Nearer Ones* (coll **1979**), *The Pale Shadow of Science* (coll **1985** US) and *. . . And the Lurid Glare of the Comet* (coll **1986** US) assemble some of his reviews and speculative essays. As literary editor of the *Oxford Mail* for many years, BWA reviewed hundreds of sf books; his later reviews have appeared in the *Times Literary Supplement*, the *Guardian*, the *Washington Post* and elsewhere. BWA is a regular attender of sf conventions all over the world, a passionate supporter of internationalism in sf and all other spheres of life, and a consistent attacker of UK-US parochialism. Like Harlan ELLISON in the USA, BWA is an energetic and charismatic speaker and lecturer. He was guest of honour at the 23rd World SF Convention in 1965 (and at several since) and received the BSFA vote for "Britain's most popular sf writer" in 1969. In 1977 he won the first James Blish Award (◊ AWARDS) and in 1978 a PILGRIM AWARD, both for excellence in SF criticism. He was a founding Trustee of WORLD SF in 1982, and its president from 1983. *Bury My Heart at W.H. Smith's: A Writing Life* (**1990**; trade edition cut by 6 chapters 1990), a memoir, reflects on the public life of a man of letters in the modern world. [DP/JC]

Other works: *A Brian Aldiss Omnibus* (omni **1969**); *Brian Aldiss Omnibus 2* (omni **1971**); *Pile: Petals from St Klaed's Computer* (graph **1979**) with Mike Wilks, an illustrated narrative poem; *Foreign Bodies* (coll **1981** Singapore); *Farewell to a Child* (**1982** chap), poem;

Science Fiction Quiz (**1983**); *Best of Aldiss* (coll **1983** chap); *My Country 'Tis Not Only of Thee* (**1986** chap); *The Magic of the Past* (coll **1987** chap); *Sex and the Black Machine* (**1990** chap), a collaged *jeu d'esprit*; *Bodily Functions: Stories, Poems, and a Letter on the Subject of Bowel Movement Addressed to Sam J. Lundwall on the Occasion of His Birthday February 24th, A.D. 1991* (coll **1991**); *Journey to the Goat Star* (1982 *The Quarto* as "The Captain's Analysis"; **1991** chap US).

About the author: *Aldiss Unbound: The Science Fiction of Brian W. Aldiss* (**1977**) by Richard Matthews; *The Entropy Exhibition: Michael Moorcock and the British "New Wave" in Science Fiction* (**1983**) by Colin GREENLAND; *Apertures: A Study of the Writings of Brian Aldiss* (**1984**) by Brian GRIFFIN and David Wingrove; *Brian W. Aldiss* (**1986**) by M.R. COLLINGS; *Brian Wilson Aldiss: A Working Bibliography* (**1988** chap) by Phil STEPHENSEN-PAYNE; *A is for Brian* (anth **1990**) edited by Frank Hatherley, a 65th-birthday tribute; *The Work of Brian W. Aldiss: An Annotated Bibliography and Guide* (**1992**) by Margaret Aldiss (1933-   ).

See also: ABSURDIST SF; ADAM AND EVE; ANTHOLOGIES; ANTI-INTELLECTUALISM IN SF; ASTOUNDING SCIENCE-FICTION; BLACK HOLES; BOYS' PAPERS; BRITISH SCIENCE FICTION ASSOCIATION; CLICHÉS; COSY CATASTROPHE; CRITICAL AND HISTORICAL WORKS ABOUT SF; DEFINITIONS OF SF; DISASTER; ECOLOGY; ESP; EVOLUTION; FANTASTIC VOYAGES; GENETIC ENGINEERING; GODS AND DEMONS; GOLDEN AGE OF SF; GOTHIC SF; HIVE MINDS; HOLOCAUST AND AFTER; HORROR IN SF; IMMORTALITY; ISLANDS; *The* MAGAZINE OF FANTASY AND SCIENCE FICTION; METAPHYSICS; MUSIC; NEW WRITINGS IN SF; OPTIMISM AND PESSIMISM; PARALLEL WORLDS; PASTORAL; PERCEPTION; POCKET UNIVERSE; POETRY; PROTO SCIENCE FICTION; PSYCHOLOGY; RADIO; RECURSIVE SF; ROBOTS; SOCIOLOGY; SPACE HABITATS.

ALDRICH, THOMAS BAILEY (1836-1907) US writer responsible for *Pansy's Wish: A Christmas Fantasy* (**1869**). *The Queen of Sheba* (**1877**) is an early example of the marginal subgenre of sf in which contemporary explorations in PSYCHOLOGY suggest storylines ranging from amnesia to metempsychosis (and ultimately, it might be added, channelling). [JC]

ALEXANDER, DAVID (?   -   ) US author of the **Soldiers of War** Western sequence as by William Reed; of the **Phoenix** sequence of post-HOLOCAUST military-sf adventures, comprising *Dark Messiah* (**1987**), *Ground Zero* (**1987**), *Metalstorm* (**1988**) and *Whirlwind* (**1988**); and of vols 9-12 of the **C.A.D.S.** post-holocaust military sequence under the house name Jan Sievert (◊ Ryder SYVERTSON). DA is not to be confused with David M. ALEXANDER. [JC]

ALEXANDER, DAVID M(ICHAEL) (1945-   ) US lawyer and writer whose first sf novel, *The Chocolate Spy* (**1978**), concerns the creation of an organic COMPUTER using cloned braincells (◊ CLONES), and whose second, *Fane* (**1981**), set on a planet whose electromagnetic configurations permit the controlled use of MAGIC, describes an inimical attempt to augment these powers. DMA is not to be confused with David ALEXANDER. [JC]

ALEXANDER, JAMES B(RADUN) (1831-?) US writer whose sf fantasmagoria, *The Lunarian Professor and his Remarkable Revelations Concerning the Earth, the Moon and Mars; Together with an Account of the Cruise of the Sally Ann* (**1909**), might have been excluded from this encyclopedia – on the grounds that the insectoid Lunarian pedagogue and all that he surveys turn out to be a dream – were it not that JBA's imagination, though patently influenced by H.G. WELLS, is too vivid to be ignored. The altruistic three-sexed Lunarians, the future HISTORY of Earth (derived from mathematical models, which the professor passes on to the narrator), the TERRAFORMING of Mars, the journeys made possible through ANTIGRAVITY devices – all are of strong sf interest. [JC]

ALEXANDER, ROBERT W(ILLIAMS) (1905-1980) Irish author of several thrillers in the late 1920s and early 1930s under his own name before he adopted the pseudonym Joan Butler for 41 humorous novels. These latter, written in a very distinctive style, have resonances of Thorne Smith (1892-1934) and P.G. WODEHOUSE. *Cloudy Weather* (**1940**) and *Deep Freeze* (**1951**) centre on the resurrection of Egyptian mummies by scientific means. *Space to Let* (**1955**) features the building of a Venus rocket. *Home Run* (**1958**) is about the invention of pocket-size atom bombs. ESP plays a prominent part in *The Old Firm* (**1956**), while *Bed and Breakfast* (**1933**), *Low Spirits* (**1945**), *Full House* (**1947**) and *Sheet Lightning* (**1950**) focus on the super-natural.

RWA used his own name for two further sf novels, still written in his well established humorous style; both are set in the future and reflect on the aspirations of youth. In *Mariner's Rest* (**1943**) a group of children shipwrecked on a South Sea island during WWII are discovered some 10 years later running their own community. *Back To Nature* (**1945**) describes how young people abandon the comforts of a 21st-century city for the rigours of a more natural lifestyle. [JE]

Other works: *Ground Bait* (**1941**); *Sun Spots* (**1942**).

ALF US tv series (1986-90). Warner Bros TV for NBC. Created by Paul Fusco and Ed Weinberger. Prod Tom Patchett. Writers include Fusco, Patchett. Dirs include Fusco, Patchett, Peter Bonerz. 25 mins per episode. Colour.

ALF, an "alien life form" – in the line of extraterrestrial descent from MY FAVORITE MARTIAN and Mork in MORK AND MINDY, though also influenced heavily by E.T.: THE EXTRA-TERRESTRIAL (1982), EXPLORERS (1985) and the success of the Muppets – moves in with the Tanner family, a sitcom collection of typical Americans, after his spaceship crashlands in their garage. A furry puppet, somewhere between cute and obnoxious, voiced and operated by series creator Paul Fusco, ALF mainly sits in the middle of the living room insulting people, plotting to eat the family cat, making tv-style smart-ass remarks and dispensing reassuring sentiment. The sf premise aside, ALF is basically one of those stereotype sitcom characters –

like Benson (Robert Guillaume) in *Soap* or Sophia (Estelle Getty) in *The Golden Girls* – whose otherness (extraterrestrial, racial, social or mental) provides an excuse for them to comment rudely, satirically and smugly on the foibles of everyone else. The regular cast includes Max Wright, Anne Schedeen, Andrea Elson and Benji Gregory, as the Tanners, and John LaMotta and Liz Sheridan, as the nosy neighbours straight from *I Love Lucy* and *Bewitched*. [KN]

See also: SATIRE.

ALFVÉN, HANNES [r] ◊ Olof JOHANNESSON.

ALGOL US SEMIPROZINE (1963-84) ed from New York by Andrew PORTER, subtitled "The Magazine about Science Fiction". *A* began as a duplicated FANZINE but in the 1970s became an attractive printed magazine in small-BEDSHEET format, published four times a year. With #34, Spring 1979, it changed its name to *Starship*; it ceased publication with #44, Winter/Spring 1984, its 20th-anniversary issue.

A ran articles on sf and sf publishing, interviews with authors, and reviews and texts of speeches. Regular columnists included Vincent DI FATE (on sf artwork), Richard A. LUPOFF (on books), Frederik POHL, and Susan WOOD (on fanzines and books). Occasional contributors included Brian W. ALDISS, Alfred BESTER, Ursula K. LE GUIN, Robert SILVERBERG, Ted WHITE and Jack WILLIAMSON. *A*, which shared the HUGO for Best Fanzine in 1974, was much more interesting than its sister publication, the monthly news magazine SF CHRONICLE, also ed Porter. The latter still continues; the economics of magazine publishing meant that it was the more ambitious and expensive publication that had to go. [PN/PR]

ALGOZIN, BRUCE [r] ◊ Nick CARTER.

al-HAKĪM, TAWFĪQ [r] ◊ Tawfiq al-HAKĪM.

ALIEN Film (1979). 20th Century-Fox. Dir Ridley SCOTT, starring Sigourney Weaver, Tom Skerritt, Harry Dean Stanton, John Hurt, Ian Holm, Yaphet Kotto, Veronica Cartwright. Alien design H.R. GIGER. Screenplay Dan O'Bannon, from a story by O'Bannon and Ronald Shusett, with uncredited input from prods Walter Hill and David Giler. 117 mins. Colour.

One of the most influential sf films ever made, *A* is actually much closer to HORROR in its adherence to genre conventions. The merchant spaceship *Nostromo*, on a routine voyage, visits a planet where one of the crew is attacked by a crablike creature in an abandoned ALIEN spacecraft. Back aboard the *Nostromo* this metamorphoses, partly inside the crewman's body, into an almost invulnerable, rapidly growing, intelligent carnivore. Science officer Ash (Holm), who unknown to the crew is a ROBOT instructed to keep the alien alive for possible commercial exploitation, attacks Ripley (Weaver); he is messily dismantled. The alien picks off, piecemeal, all the remaining crew but Ripley.

Giger's powerful alien design, inorganic sleekness blended with curved, phallic, organic forms, renders the horror sequences extremely vivid, but for all their force they are plotted along deeply conventional lines. Considerably more original is the sense – achieved through design, terse dialogue and excellent direction – that this is a real working spaceship with a real, blue-collar, working crew, the future unglamorized and taken for granted. Also good sf are the scenes on the alien spacecraft (Giger's design again) which project a genuine sense of "otherness". Tough, pragmatic Ripley (contrasted with the "womanly" ineffectiveness of Cartwright as Lambert) is the first sf movie heroine to reflect cultural changes in the real world, where by 1979 FEMINISM was causing some men and many women to think again about the claustrophobia of traditional female roles.

A, which was made in the UK, was a huge success. It had precursors. Many viewers noticed plot similarities with IT! THE TERROR FROM BEYOND SPACE (1958) and with A.E. VAN VOGT's "Discord in Scarlet" (1939); a legal case about the latter resemblance was settled out of court for $50,000.

The sequels were ALIENS (1986) and ALIEN³ (1992). The novelization is *Alien* * (**1979**) by Alan Dean FOSTER.   [PN]

See also: CINEMA; HUGO; MONSTER MOVIES; TERRORE NELLO SPAZIO.

ALIEN CONTAMINATION ◊ CONTAMINATION: ALIEN ARRIVA SULLA TERRA.

ALIEN CRITIC, THE US FANZINE ed from Portland, Oregon, by Richard E. GEIS. For its first 3 issues, *AC* was an informal magazine written entirely by the editor and titled *Richard E. Geis*. With the title-change in 1973, the magazine's contents began to diversify, featuring regular columns by John BRUNNER and Ted WHITE as well as a variety of articles and a series of interviews with sf authors and artists, although its characteristic flavour still derived from the editor's own outspoken reviews and commentary. With #12 in 1975 the title changed to *Science Fiction Review*, a title used also by Geis for his previous fanzine PSYCHOTIC. *TAC/Science Fiction Review* won HUGOS for Best Fanzine in 1974 (shared), 1975, 1977 and 1979. *TAC*'s circulation became quite wide, and it effectively became a SEMIPROZINE. In pain from arthritis, Geis cancelled the magazine after #61, Nov 1986, though he continued to publish shorter, more personal fanzines under other titles.

Science Fiction Review was revived as a semiprozine in 1989, with some fiction added to the old *SFR* mix; 7 issues to Feb 1992, ed Elton Elliott. The schedule changed from quarterly to monthly with #5, Dec 1991, at which point the magazine also began to be sold at newsstands. This looks like a brave attempt at making this SMALL-PRESS publication fully professional.   [MJE/PN]

ALIEN NATION 1. Film (1988). 20th Century-Fox. Dir Graham Baker, starring James Caan, Mandy Patinkin, Terence Stamp. Prod Gale Anne HURD, Richard Kobritz. Screenplay Rockne S. O'Bannon. 90 mins. Colour.

Los Angeles, 1991. The Newcomers, or "Slags", are 300,000 humanoid ALIENS, genetically engineered for hard labour, survivors of a crashlanded slave ship, grudgingly accepted but disliked by humans, and ghettoized. Working in partnership with a human (Caan), Sam Francisco (Patinkin) becomes the first alien police detective in LA. There are murders related to the use of alien drugs. A stereotyped buddy-cop story follows (uneasy relationship between races deepens as tolerance is learned). This is an efficient, unambitious adventure film whose observations of racial bigotry towards cultural strangers – effectively "boat people" – are good-humoured but seldom rise above cliché. The novelization is *Alien Nation* * (**1988**) by Alan Dean FOSTER.   [PN]

2. US tv series (1989-90). Kenneth Johnson Productions for Fox Television. Starring Gary Graham and Eric Pierpoint. 100min pilot episode dir and written Johnson, plus 21 50min episodes.

The short-lived tv series that followed the film combined routine crime stories with mild SATIRE of NEAR-FUTURE Los Angeles and lessons about civil rights. The bizarre-looking but adaptable Newcomers act and talk exactly like humans, portraying housewives, teenagers, used-car salesmen, criminals, police and other stereotypes. The exception is George (no longer Sam) Francisco, whose earnest, humourless approach and precise speech recall Spock of STAR TREK. A few episodes involve the pregnancy of the male Newcomer hero. Johnson also produced the much harder-edged *"V"*.   [MK]

ALIENS Visitors to other worlds in stories of the 17th and 18th centuries met no genuine alien beings; instead they found men and animals, sometimes wearing strange forms but always filling readily recognizable roles. The pattern of life on Earth was reproduced with minor amendments: UTOPIAN improvement or satirical (◊ SATIRE) exaggeration. The concept of a differently determined pattern of life, and thus of a lifeform quite alien to Earthly habits of thought, did not emerge until the late 19th century, as a natural consequence of the notions of EVOLUTION and of the process of adaptation to available environments promulgated by Lamarck and later by Darwin.

The idea of alien beings was first popularized by Camille FLAMMARION in his nonfictional *Real and Imaginary Worlds* (**1864**; trans **1865** US) and in *Lumen* (**1887**; trans with some new material **1897** UK). These accounts of LIFE ON OTHER WORLDS describe sentient plants, species for which respiration and alimentation are aspects of the same process, etc. The idea that divinely created souls could experience serial REINCARNATION in an infinite variety of physical forms is featured in Flammarion's *Urania* (**1889**; trans **1891** US). Aliens also appear in the work of another major French writer, J.H. ROSNY aîné: mineral lifeforms are featured in "The Shapes" (1887; trans 1968) and "The Death of the World" (1910; trans 1928). Like Flammarion, Rosny took a positive attitude to alien beings: *Les navigateurs de l'infini* ["The Navigators of Infinity"] (**1925**) features a love affair between a human and a six-eyed tripedal Martian. In the tradition of the

French evolutionary philosophers Lamarck and Henri Bergson, these early French sf writers fitted both humans and aliens into a great evolutionary scheme.

In the UK, evolutionary philosophy was dominated by the Darwinian idea of the survival of the fittest. Perhaps inevitably, UK writers imagined the alien as a Darwinian competitor, a natural enemy of mankind. H.G. WELLS in *The War of the Worlds* (1898) cast the alien as a genocidal invader – a would-be conqueror and colonist of Earth (◊ INVASION). This role rapidly became a CLICHÉ. The same novel set the pattern by which alien beings are frequently imagined as loathsome MONSTERS. Wells went on to produce an elaborate description of an alien society in *The First Men in the Moon* (1901), based on the model of the ant-nest (◊ HIVE-MINDS), thus instituting another significant cliché.

Early US PULP-MAGAZINE sf in the vein of Edgar Rice BURROUGHS usually populated other worlds with quasihuman inhabitants – almost invariably including beautiful women for the heroes to fall in love with – but frequently, for melodramatic purposes, placed such races under threat from predatory monsters. The specialist sf magazines inherited this tradition in combination with the Wellsian exemplars, and made copious use of monstrous alien invaders; the climaxes of such stories were often genocidal. Edmond HAMILTON was a prolific author of stories in this vein. In the early SPACE OPERAS meek and benevolent aliens usually had assorted mammalian and avian characteristics, while the physical characteristics of nasty aliens were borrowed from reptiles, arthropods and molluscs (especially octopuses). Sentient plants and entities of "pure energy" were morally more versatile. In extreme cases, alien allies and enemies became straightforwardly symbolic of Good and Evil: E.E. "Doc" SMITH's Arisians and Eddorians of the **Lensman** series are secular equivalents of angels and demons.

Occasionally early pulp-sf writers were willing to invert their Darwinian assumptions and put humans in the role of alien invaders – significant early examples are Hamilton's "Conquest of Two Worlds" (1932) and P. Schuyler MILLER's "Forgotten Man of Space" (1933) – but stories focusing on the exoticism of alien beings tended to take their inspiration from the works of A. MERRITT, who had described a fascinating mineral life-system in *The Metal Monster* (1920; **1946**) and had transcended conventional biological chauvinism in his portrayal of "The Snake-Mother" (1930; incorporated in *The Face in the Abyss* **1931**). Jack WILLIAMSON clearly showed Merritt's influence in "The Alien Intelligence" (1929) and "The Moon Era" (1932).

A significant advance in the representation of aliens was achieved by Stanley G. WEINBAUM, whose "A Martian Odyssey" (1934) made a deep impression on readers. Weinbaum followed it up with other accounts of relatively complex alien biospheres (◊

ECOLOGY). Another popular story which directly challenged vulgarized Darwinian assumptions was Raymond Z. GALLUN's "Old Faithful" (1934), in which humans and a Martian set aside their extreme biological differences and acknowledge intellectual kinship. This spirit was echoed in "Liquid Life" (1936) by Ralph Milne FARLEY, which proposed that a man was bound to keep his word of honour, even to a filterable virus. Some of the more interesting and adventurous alien stories written in the 1930s ran foul of editorial TABOOS: *The Creator* (1935; **1946** chap) by Clifford D. SIMAK, which suggested that our world and others might be the creation of a godlike alien (the first of the author's many sf considerations of pseudo-theological themes – ◊ GODS AND DEMONS; RELIGION), was considered dangerously close to blasphemy and ended up in the semiprofessional MARVEL TALES, which also began serialization of P. Schuyler Miller's "The Titan" (1934-5), whose description of a Martian ruling class sustained by vampiric cannibalism was considered too erotic, and which eventually appeared as the title story of *The Titan* (coll **1952**). The influence of these taboos in limiting the potential the alien being offered writers of this period, and thereby in stunting the evolution of alien roles within sf, should not be overlooked.

Despite the Wellsian precedents, aliens were much less widely featured in the UK SCIENTIFIC ROMANCES. Eden PHILLPOTTS used aliens as "objective observers" to examine and criticize the human world in *Saurus* (**1938**) and *Address Unknown* (**1949**), but the latter novel explicitly challenges the validity of any such criticism. Olaf STAPLEDON's *Star Maker* (**1937**) built humans and aliens into a cosmic scheme akin to that envisaged by Rosny and Flammarion. Stapledon also employed the alien as a standard of comparison in one of his most bitter attacks on contemporary humanity, in *The Flames* (**1947**).

The alien-menace story remained dominant in sf for many years; its popularity did not begin to wane until the outbreak of WWII, and it has never been in danger of dying out. Such xenophobia eventually became unfashionable in the more reputable magazines, but monstrous aliens maintained their popularity in less sophisticated outlets. The CINEMA lagged behind written sf in this respect, producing a host of cheap MONSTER MOVIES during the 1950s and 1960s, although there was a belated boom in innocent and altruistic aliens in films of the 1970s.

While pulp sf writers continued to invent nastier and more horrific alien monsters during the late 1930s and 1940s – notable examples include John W. CAMPBELL Jr's "Who Goes There?" (1938), as Don A. Stuart, and A.E. VAN VOGT's "Black Destroyer" (1939) and "Discord in Scarlet" (1939) – the emphasis shifted towards the problems of establishing fruitful COMMUNICATION with alien races. During the WWII years human/alien relationships were often represented as complex, delicate and uneasy. In van Vogt's "Cooperate or Else!" (1942) a man and a bizarre alien are castaways in a harsh alien environment during an interstellar war, and must join forces in order to survive. In "First Contact" (1945) by Murray LEINSTER two spaceships meet in the void, and each crew is determined to give away no information and make no move which could possibly give the other race a political or military advantage – a practical problem which they ultimately solve. Another Leinster story, "The Ethical Equations" (1945), assumes that a "correct" decision regarding mankind's first actions on contact with aliens will be very difficult to achieve, but that priority should definitely be given to the attempt to establish friendly relationships; by contrast, "Arena" (1944) by Fredric BROWN bleakly assumes that the meeting of Man and alien might still be a test of their ability to destroy one another. (Significantly, an adaptation of "Arena" for the tv series STAR TREK changed the ending of the story to bring it into line with later attitudes.)

Attempts to present more credibly unhuman aliens became gradually more sophisticated in the late 1940s and 1950s, particularly in the work of Hal CLEMENT, but writers devoted to the design of peculiar aliens adapted to extraordinary environments tended to find it hard to embed such speculations in engaging stories – a problem constantly faced by Clement and by more recent workers in the same tradition, notably Robert L. FORWARD. Much more effective in purely literary terms are stories which juxtapose human and alien in order to construct parables criticizing various attitudes and values. Despite John W. Campbell Jr's editorial enthusiasm for human chauvinism – reflected in such stories as Arthur C. CLARKE's "Rescue Party" (1946) and L. Ron HUBBARD's Return to Tomorrow (1954) – many stories produced in the post-WWII years use aliens as contrasting exemplars to expose and dramatize human follies. Militarism is attacked in Clifford D. Simak's "You'll Never Go Home Again" (1951) and Eric Frank RUSSELL's "The Waitabits" (1955). Sexual prejudices are questioned in Theodore STURGEON's "The World Well Lost" (1953). Racialism is attacked in "Dumb Martian" by John WYNDHAM (1952) and Leigh BRACKETT's "All the Colours of the Rainbow" (1957). The politics of colonialism (◊ COLONIZATION OF OTHER WORLDS) are examined in "The Helping Hand" (1950) by Poul ANDERSON, Invaders From Earth (1958 dos) by Robert SILVERBERG and Little Fuzzy (1962) by H. Beam PIPER. The bubble of human vanity is pricked in Simak's "Immigrant" (1954) and Anderson's "The Martyr" (1960). The general human condition has been subject to increasingly rigorous scrutiny through metaphors of alien contact in such stories as A Mirror for Observers (1954) by Edgar PANGBORN, "Rule Golden" (1954) by Damon KNIGHT, What Rough Beast? (1980) by William Jon WATKINS and The Alien Upstairs (1983) by Pamela SARGENT. Sharp SATIRES on human vanity and prejudice include Brian W. ALDISS's The Dark Light Years (1964) and Thomas M. DISCH's The Genocides (1965) and Mankind Under the Leash (1966 dos).

The most remarkable redeployment of alien beings in sf of the 1950s and 1960s was in connection with pseudo-theological themes (◊ RELIGION). Some images of the inhabitants of other worlds had been governed by theological notions long before the advent of sf – interplanetary romances of the 19th century often featured spirits or angels – and the tradition had been revived outside the sf magazines by C.S. LEWIS in his Christian allegories Out of the Silent Planet (1938) and Perelandra (1943; vt Voyage to Venus). Within sf itself, however, the religious imagination had previously been echoed only in a few Shaggy God stories (◊ ADAM AND EVE). In sf of the 1950s, though, aliens appear in all kinds of transcendental roles. Aliens are spiritual tutors in "Dear Devil" (1950) by Eric Frank Russell and "Guardian Angel" (1950) by Arthur C. Clarke, in each case wearing diabolical physical form ironically to emphasize their angelic role. Edgar Pangborn's "Angel's Egg" (1951) and Paul J. MCAULEY's Eternal Light (1991) are less coy. Raymond F. JONES's The Alien (1951) is ambitious to be a god, and the alien in Philip José FARMER's "Father" (1955) really is one. In Clifford D. Simak's Time and Again (1951: vt First He Died) every living creature, ANDROIDS included, has an immortal alien "commensal", an sf substitute for the soul. In James BLISH's classic A Case of Conscience (1953; exp 1958) alien beings without knowledge of God appear to a Jesuit to be creations of the Devil. Other churchmen achieve spiritual enlightenment by means of contact with aliens in "The Fire Balloons" (1951; vt "In this Sign") by Ray BRADBURY, "Unhuman Sacrifice" (1958) by Katherine MACLEAN, and "Prometheus" (1961) by Philip José Farmer. In Lester DEL REY's "For I Am a Jealous People" (1954) alien invaders of Earth turn out to have made a new covenant with God, who is no longer on our side. Religious imagery is at its most extreme in stories which deal with literal kinds of salvation obtained by humans who adopt alien ways, including Robert Silverberg's Downward to the Earth (1970) and George R.R. MARTIN's "A Song for Lya" (1974).

The evolution of alien roles in Eastern European sf seems to have been very different. The alien-menace story typical of early US-UK sf is absent from contemporary Russian sf, and the ideological calculation behind this absence is made clear by Ivan YEFREMOV in "Cor Serpentis" (trans 1962; vt "The Heart of the Serpent"), which is explicitly represented as a reply to Leinster's "First Contact". Yefremov argues that, by the time humans are sufficiently advanced to build interstellar ships, their society will have matured beyond the suspicious militaristic attitudes of Leinster's humans, and will be able to assume that aliens are similarly mature.

UK-US sf has never become that confident – although similar ideological replies to earlier work are not unknown in US sf. Ted WHITE's By Furies Possessed (1970), in which mankind finds a useful symbiotic relationship with rather ugly aliens, is a reply to The

Puppet Masters (**1951**) by Robert A. HEINLEIN, which was one of the most extreme post-WWII alien-menace stories, while Joe HALDEMAN's *The Forever War* (**1974**) similarly responds to the xenophobic tendencies of Heinlein's *Starship Troopers* (**1959**), and Barry B. LONGYEAR's "Enemy Mine" (1979) can be seen as either a reprise of van Vogt's "Co-operate – or Else!" or a reply to Brown's "Arena"; Orson Scott CARD took the unusual step of producing an ideological counterweight to one of his own stories when he followed the novel version of the genocidal fantasy *Ender's Game* (1977; exp **1985**) with the expiatory *Speaker for the Dead* (**1986**). This is not to say that alien-invasion stories are not still being produced – Larry NIVEN's and Jerry POURNELLE's *Footfall* (**1985**) is a notable example – and stories of war between humans and aliens have understandably retained their melodramatic appeal. The recent fashionability of militaristic sf (◊ WAR) has helped to keep the tradition very much alive; examples include the **Demu** trilogy (1973-5; coll **1980**) by F.M. BUSBY, *The Uplift War* (**1987**) by David BRIN and the shared-world anthology series **The Man-Kzin Wars** (**1988-90**) based on a scenario created by Larry Niven. Anxiety has also been maintained by stories which answer the question "If we are not alone, where are they?" with speculative accounts of a Universe dominated by predatory and destructive aliens; notable examples include Gregory BENFORD's *Across the Sea of Suns* (**1984**), Jack Williamson's *Lifeburst* (**1984**) and David Brin's "Lungfish" (1986).

Stories dealing soberly and thoughtfully with problems arising out of cultural and biological differences between human and alien have become very numerous. This is a constant and continuing theme in the work of several writers, notably Jack VANCE, Poul Anderson, David LAKE, Michael BISHOP and C.J. CHERRYH. Cherryh's novels – including her **Faded Sun** trilogy (1978-9), *Serpent's Reach* (**1980**), the **Chanur** series (1982-6) and *Cuckoo's Egg* (**1985**) – present a particularly elaborate series of accounts of problematic human/alien relationships. Such relationships have become further complicated by virtue of the fact that the gradual decay of editorial taboos from the 1950s onwards permitted more adventurous and explicit exploration of sexual and psychological themes (◊ PSYCHOLOGY). This work was begun by Philip José Farmer, in such stories as *The Lovers* (1952; exp **1961**), "Open to Me, My Sister" (1960) and "Mother" (1953), and has been carried forward by others. Sexual relationships between human and alien have become much more complex and problematic in recent times: *Strangers* (1974; exp **1978**) by Gardner R. DOZOIS is a more sophisticated reprise of *The Lovers*, and other accounts of human/alien love affairs can be found in Jayge CARR's *Leviathan's Deep* (**1979**), Linda STEELE's *Ibis* (**1985**) and Robert THURSTON's *Q Colony* (**1985**). "And I Awoke and Found Me Here on the Cold Hill's Side" (1971) by James TIPTREE Jr displays human fear and loathing of the alien curiously alloyed with self-destructive erotic fascination, and

the **Xenogenesis** trilogy (1987-9) by Octavia BUTLER takes human/alien intimacy to its uncomfortable limit.

The greatest difficulty sf writers face with respect to the alien is that of depicting something authentically strange. It is common to find that aliens which are physically bizarre are entirely human in their modes of thought and speech. Bids to tell a story from an alien viewpoint are rarely convincing, although heroic efforts are made in such stories as Stanley SCHMIDT's *The Sins of the Fathers* (**1976**), John BRUNNER's *The Crucible of Time* (**1984**) and Brian HERBERT's *Sudanna, Sudanna* (**1985**). Impressive attempts to present the alien not merely as unfamiliar but also as unknowable include Damon KNIGHT's "Stranger Station" (1956), several novels by Philip K. DICK – including *The Game-Players of Titan* (**1963**), *Galactic Pot-Healer* (**1969**) and *Our Friends From Frolix-8* (**1970**) – Stanisław LEM's *Solaris* (1961; trans **1970**) and Phillip MANN's *The Eye of the Queen* (**1982**). Such contacts as these threaten the sanity of the contactees, as does the initial meeting of minds between human and alien intelligence in Fred HOYLE's *The Black Cloud* (**1957**), but here – as in most such stories – the assumption is made that common intellectual ground of some sort must and *can* be found. Faith in the universality of reason, and hence in the fundamental similarity of all intelligent beings, is strongly evident in many accounts of physically exotic aliens, including those featured in Isaac ASIMOV's *The Gods Themselves* (**1972**).

This faith is at its most passionate in many stories in which first contact with aliens is achieved via radio telescopes; these frequently endow such an event with quasitranscendental significance. Stories which are sceptical of the benefits of such contact – examples are Fred HOYLE's and John ELLIOT's *A for Andromeda* (**1962**) and Stanisław Lem's *His Master's Voice* (1968; trans **1983**) – have been superseded by stories like James E. GUNN's *The Listeners* (fixup **1972**), Robert Silverberg's *Tower of Glass* (**1970**), Ben BOVA's *Voyagers* (**1981**), Jeffrey CARVER's *The Infinity Link* (**1984**), Carl SAGAN's *Contact* (**1985**), and Frederick FICHMAN's *SETI* (**1990**), whose optimism is extravagant. Where once the notion of the alien being was inherently fearful, sf now manifests an eager determination to meet and establish significant contact with aliens. Despite continued exploitation of the melodramatic potential of alien invasions and interstellar wars, the predominant anxiety in modern sf is that we might prove to be unworthy of such communion.

Anthologies of stories dealing with particular alien themes include: *From off this World* (anth 1949) ed Leo MARGULIES and Oscar J. FRIEND; *Invaders of Earth* (anth **1952**) ed Groff CONKLIN; *Contact* (anth **1963**) ed Noel Keyes; *The Alien Condition* (anth 1973) ed Stephen GOLDIN; and the **Starhunters** series "created by" David A. DRAKE (3 anths 1988-90). [BS]

ALIENS Film (1986). Brandywine/20th Century-Fox. Prod Gale Anne HURD, dir James CAMERON, starring

Sigourney Weaver, Paul Reiser, Carrie Henn, William Hope, Michael Biehn, Lance Henriksen, Jenette Goldstein. Screenplay Cameron, based on a story by Cameron, David Giler, Walter Hill. 137 mins. Colour.

This formidable sequel to ALIEN is more an action than a HORROR movie, reminiscent of all those war films and Westerns about beleaguered groups fighting to the end. Ripley (Weaver, in a fine performance), the sole survivor at the end of *Alien*, is sent off again with a troop of marines to the planet (now colonized) where the original alien was found. The colony has been wiped out by aliens (lots of them this time); the marines, at first sceptical, are also almost wiped out. Ripley saves a small girl (Henn), the sole colonist survivor, and finally confronts the Queen alien.

A is conventional in its disapproval of corporate greed; less conventional is its demonstration of the inadequacy of the *machismo* expressed by all the marines, women and men. A peculiar subtext has to do with the fierce protectiveness of motherhood (Ripley and the little girl, the Queen and her eggs). This is a film unusually sophisticated in its use of sf tropes and is arguably even better than its predecessor. The novelization is *Aliens* * (**1986**) by Alan Dean FOSTER. [PN]

See also: HUGO.

ALIEN³ Film (1992). A Brandywine Production/20th Century-Fox. Dir David Fincher, starring Sigourney Weaver, Charles Dance, Charles S. Dutton, Lance Henriksen, Paul McGann, Brian Glover. Screenplay David Giler, Walter Hill, Larry Ferguson, based on a story by Vincent Ward. 110 mins. Colour.

One of Hollywood's occasional, strange films so unmitigatedly uncommercial that it is impossible to work out why they were ever made. The film had an unusually troubled development history, previous screenwriters having included William GIBSON and Eric Red, and previous directors Renny Harlin and Vincent Ward (director of *The Navigator: A Medieval Odyssey* [1988]); some of Ward's story ideas were retained, and the final script was reworked by producers Hill and Giler. The latter has said that he sees a subtext about the AIDS virus in this film, and the film itself supports this. The final director, Fincher, had previously been known primarily for his inventive rock videos.

Ripley (Weaver, who also has a credit as producer), having twice survived alien apocalypse (◊ ALIEN; ALIENS) crashlands on a prison planet occupied by a displeasing men-only group of double-Y-chromosomed mass murderers and rapists, who have now adopted a form of Christian fundamentalism, as well as three variously psychopathic minders. Her companions on the ship are dead, but she brings (unknown to her) an alien parasite within her and an external larva hiding in her ship. The latter grows, kills, grows again, lurks, and wipes out most of the base (as before). But the – again female – alien seems somehow unimportant this time; the film's twin

centres are the awfulness of the prison, explicitly and repeatedly compared to a cosmic anus, and the pared-to-the-bone Ripley, head shaven, face anguished, torso skinny, sister and mirror image of Alien herself: her *sole* function is as victim. Even the ongoing feminist joke (Ripley is as ever the one with metaphoric balls) is submerged in the bewildering, monochrome intensity of pain and dereliction, photographed in claustrophobic close-up throughout, that is *the whole* of this film. All else – including narrative tension and indeed the very idea of story – is subjugated to this grim motif. This (probably bad) film is almost admirable in its refusal to give the audience any solace or entertainment at all. At the end, Ripley immolates herself for the greater good, falling out of life as an alien bursts from her chest; she cradles it like a blood-covered baby as she falls away and away into the fires of purgatory. [PN]

ALIEN WORLDS UK DIGEST-size magazine. 1 undated issue, cJuly 1966, published and ed Charles Partington and Harry Nadler, some colour illustrations, stories by Kenneth BULMER, J.R. (Ramsey) Campbell and Harry HARRISON; articles on film were also included. *AW* grew from the FANZINE *Alien* (16 issues, 1963-6), which had also published stories and film articles. Its publishers lacked the distribution strength to make it work as a professional magazine. [FHP/PN]

ALKON, PAUL K(ENT) (1935-) Professor of English Literature at the University of Southern California and author of *Origins of Futuristic Fiction* (**1987**), a vigorous study of the idea of the future that developed in the late 18th and early 19th centuries, as reflected in the fiction and literary theory of the time. PA resuscitated the almost forgotten figure of Félix Bodin, arguably the first to provide (in 1834) an aesthetics of sf, his theories – appropriately futuristic – antedating their subject matter. [PN]

al-KUWAYRI, YUSUF [r] ◊ ARABIC SF.

ALLABY, (JOHN) MICHAEL (1933-) UK writer. Most of his books are nonfiction studies in fields like ECOLOGY, but his *The Greening of Mars* (**1984**) with James (Ephraim) Lovelock (1919-), though basically a nonfiction study of how that planet might be settled, is told as a fictionalized narrative whose tone is upliftingly UTOPIAN. [JC]

ALLBEURY, TED Working name of UK spy-fiction writer Theodore Edward le Bouthillier Allbeury (1917-), some of whose NEAR-FUTURE thrillers, like *Palomino Blonde* (**1975**; vt *OMEGA-MINUS* 1976 US), *The Alpha List* (**1979**) and *The Consequences of Fear* (**1979**), edge sf-wards. *All our Tomorrows* (**1982**) depicts a Russian-occupied UK and the resistance movement that soon takes shape. [JC]

ALLEN, F.M. Pseudonym of Irish-born UK writer and publisher Edmund Downey (1856-1937), whose short DISASTER sequence, set in Ireland – *The Voyage of the Ark, as Related by Dan Banim* (**1888**) and *The Round Tower of Babel* (**1891**) – conflates hyperbolic comedy and sf instruments, ending in a visionary plan to build a great tower for profit. *A House of Tears* (**1888** US), as by Edmund Downey, is fantasy, as are *Brayhard: The Strange Adventures of One Ass and Seven Champions* (**1890**) and *The Little Green Man* (**1895**). *The Peril of London* (**1891** chap as by FMA; vt *London's Peril* **1900** chap as Downey), set in the NEAR FUTURE, warns against a Channel Tunnel being constructed by the nefarious French. [JC]

ALLEN, (CHARLES) GRANT (BLAIRFINDIE) (1848-1899) UK writer, born in Canada, known primarily for his work outside the sf field, including the notorious *The Woman who Did* (**1895**), which attacked contemporary sexual mores. He was professor of logic and principal of Queen's College, Jamaica, before moving to the UK. He wrote a series of books based on EVOLUTION theory before turning for commercial reasons to fiction. After the success of *The Woman who Did* he published a self-indulgent novel of social criticism, *The British Barbarians* (**1895**), in which a time-travelling social scientist of the future is scathing about tribalism and taboo in Victorian society. GA's interest in ANTHROPOLOGY is manifest also in the novel *The Great Taboo* (**1890**) and in many of the short stories assembled in *Strange Stories* (coll **1884**); this collection includes two sf stories originally published under the pseudonym J. Arbuthnot Wilson: "Pausodyne" (1881), an early story about SUS-PENDED ANIMATION, and "A Child of the Phalanstery" (1884), about a future society's eugenic practices. (The former is also to be found in *The Desire of the Eyes and Other Stories* [coll **1895**] the latter in *Twelve Tales, with a Headpiece, a Tailpiece and an Intermezzo* [coll **1899**].) GA's other borderline-sf stories are "The Dead Man Speaks" (1895) and "The Thames Valley Catastrophe" (1897). The above-mentioned collections also feature a handful of fantasy stories. *The Devil's Die* (**1897**) is a mundane melodrama which includes an account of a bacteriological research project. GA's early "shilling shocker" *Kalee's Shrine* (**1886**), written with May Cotes (not credited in some US reprint editions), is a fantasy of mesmerism with some sf elements. [BS]

See also: CANADA; SATIRE; SOCIOLOGY; TABOOS; TIME TRAVEL.

ALLEN, HENRY WILSON (1912-1991) US author, as Will Henry, of many Westerns, including *MacKenna's Gold* (**1963**), later filmed. His sf novel, *Genesis Five* (**1968**), narrated by a resident Mongol, depicts the Soviet creation of a dubious SUPERMAN in Siberia. [JC]

ALLEN, IRWIN (1916-1991) US film-maker long associated with sf subjects. He worked in radio during the 1940s; later, with the arrival of tv, he created the first celebrity panel show. In 1951 he began producing films for RKO, and in 1953 won an Academy Award for *The Sea Around Us*, a pseudo-documentary which he wrote and directed. He then made a similar film for Warner Brothers, *The Animal World* (**1956**), which contained dinosaur sequences animated by Willis H. O'BRIEN and Ray HARRYHAUSEN. In 1957 he made *The Story of Mankind*, a bizarre potted history with a

fantasy framework, and then turned to sf subjects: a bland remake of *The* LOST WORLD (1960), VOYAGE TO THE BOTTOM OF THE SEA (1961) and *Five Weeks in a Balloon* (1962).

In 1964 he returned to tv and produced a series, VOYAGE TO THE BOTTOM OF THE SEA (1964-8), based on the movie. Other sf tv series followed: LOST IN SPACE (1965-8), *The* TIME TUNNEL (1966-7) and LAND OF THE GIANTS (1968-70). A further tv project, CITY BENEATH THE SEA, failed to generate the necessary interest and was abandoned, the pilot episode being released as a feature film (vt *One Hour to Doomsday*) in 1970.

Ever resilient, IA switched back to films. In 1972 he made the highly successful *The Poseidon Adventure*, which began the "disaster film" cycle of the 1970s, followed by the even more successful *The Towering Inferno* (1974). Theatrically, IA's fortunes with disaster films began to founder with *The Swarm* (1978), based on the 1974 novel by Arthur HERZOG about killer bees attacking Houston. *Beyond the Poseidon Adventure* (1979) and *When Time Ran Out . . .* (1980; vt *Earth's Final Fury*) were similar to *The Swarm* in their absurdity and their parade of embarrassed star cameos; their box-office failure contributed significantly to the petering out of the borderline-sf disaster movie cycle. However, IA had already transferred the essential formula – B-movie dramatics, spectacular (often secondhand) devastation footage, large casts – of the disaster movie to tv with *Flood!* (1976), followed by the diminishing returns of *Fire!* (1977) and *Cave-In* (1979, transmitted 1983). Another made-for-tv movie by IA (pilot for an unsold tv series planned as a return to the themes of *The Time Tunnel*) was *Time Travelers* (1976), based on an unpublished story by Rod SERLING; its use of stock footage as the story's centrepiece – here the fire from *In Old Chicago* (1938) – is an IA trademark. Subsequently his sf/fantasy work for tv has included *The Return of Captain Nemo* (1978), a three-part miniseries (based on Jules VERNE's characters and themes recycled from *Voyage to the Bottom of the Sea*) which was edited into a feature film for release outside the USA, and a two-part *Alice in Wonderland* (1985) with second-string stars.

Throughout his career IA has reworked a limited repertoire of basic formulae – the Verne/DOYLE "expedition" drama, the juvenile sf-series format, the disaster scenario – invariably setting groups of lazily stereotyped characters against colourful, threatening, bizarre but somehow cheap backdrops. His productions are wholly contemptuous (or ignorant) of scientific accuracy or even plausibility. The only variation in tone and effect has been strictly budgetary, with Michael Caine and Paul Newman essentially no different from David Hedison and Gary Conway, and even the most earth-shattering cataclysm failing to disturb the tidy complacency of IA's Poverty-Row worldview. In the end, his most interesting work might just have been *The Story of Mankind*, in which Harpo Marx played Isaac Newton. [JB/KN/PN]

See also: DISASTER; TELEVISION.

ALLEN, JOHANNES (1916-1973) Danish journalist and author of popular fiction and film scripts. Among his few sf titles the best known is *Data for din dod* (**1970**; trans Marianne Helweg as *Data for Death* **1971** UK), which tells of a criminal organization whose acquisition of advanced computer techniques permits it to blackmail people with information about their time of death. [ND]

ALLEN, ROGER MacBRIDE (1957-) US writer who began writing with a SPACE-OPERA series, *The Torch of Honor* (**1985**) and *Rogue Powers* (**1986**), whose considerable impact may seem excessive to anyone familiar only with the books in synopsis, as neither might have appeared to offer anything new. *The Torch of Honor* begins with a scene all too evocative of Robert A. HEINLEIN's sf juveniles from three decades earlier, as a batch of space cadets graduates from academy into interstellar hot water after learning – in a scene which any viewer of John Ford's Cavalry Westerns would also recognize – of the death of many of their fellows in a space encounter. But RMA, while clearly making no secret of his allegiance to outmoded narrative conventions, remained very much a writer of the 1980s in the physical complexity and moral dubiety of the Galaxy his crew enters, fighting and judging and having a fairly good time in the task of saving planets. The second novel, which features a no-nonsense female protagonist and a lovingly described ALIEN culture, builds on the strengths of the first while disengaging to some degree from the debilitating simplicities of military sf.

Orphan of Creation (**1988**), a singleton, demonstrates with greater clarity than the series the clarity and scientific numeracy of RMA's mind and narrative strategies. The story of a Black anthropologist who discovers in the USA the bones of some Australopithecines who had been transported there by slave traders, the novel gives an impressive accounting of the nature of ANTHROPOLOGY as a science, and mounts a welcome attack on the strange 1980s vogue for Creationism. *Farside Cannon* (**1988**), in which the NEAR-FUTURE Solar System witnesses political upheaval on time-tested grounds, and *The War Machine* * (**1989**) with David A. DRAKE, part of the latter's **Crisis of Empire** sequence, were sufficiently competent to keep interest in RMA alive. *Supernova* (**1991**), with Eric KOTANI, relates, again with scientific verisimilitude, the process involved in discovering that a nearby star is due to go supernova and flood Earth with hard radiation. *The Modular Man* (**1992**) deals complexly with the implications of a ROBOT technology sufficiently advanced for humans to transfer their consciousnesses into machines.

But potentially more interesting than any of these titles is the **Hunted Earth** sequence, though only one volume, *The Ring of Charon* (**1991**), has yet appeared. After the passing of a beam of phased gravity-waves – a new human invention – has awakened a long dormant semi-autonomous being embedded deep within the Moon, the Earth is shunted via wormhole to a new solar system dominated by a multifaceted culture occupying a DYSON SPHERE. The remnants of humanity must work out where Earth is while countering, or coming to terms with, the attempted demolition of the Solar System to make a new sphere. Although the human cultures described in the first volume are unimaginatively presented, the exuberance of RMA's large-scale plotting (and thinking) makes it seem possible that **Hunted Earth** will become one of the touchstone galactic epics of the 1990s. [JC]

See also: ASTEROIDS; BLACK HOLES; MOON; OUTER PLANETS; WEAPONS.

ALLEY OOP US COMIC strip, created and drawn by V(incent) T. Hamlin (1900-) from 1933 until his retirement in 1971, when it was taken over by other artists. Drawn in a style more comically exaggerated than usual in adventure strips, though with clear affection, Oop is a tough and likeable Neanderthal warrior, half Popeye, half Buck Rogers. His adventures were initially restricted to his home territory of Moo (the echo of Mu clearly being deliberate) but he soon began to visit various human eras – and the Moon – via Professor Wonmug's TIME-TRAVEL device. Some of these extended tales appear in Hamlin's *Alley Oop: The Adventures of a Time-Traveling Caveman: Daily Strips from July 20, 1946 to June 20, 1947* (graph coll **1990**). [JC]

ALLHOFF, FRED (1904-1988) US journalist and writer known in the sf field for *Lightning in the Night* (**1940** *Liberty*; **1979**), a future-WAR tale which, when serialized, caused considerable stir because of its defence of the arguments of General Billy Mitchell (1879-1936) about the primacy of air power in any future conflict, for its portrayal of a semi-defeated USA in 1945 as she recoups her moral and physical forces and begins to thrust back the Axis invaders, and for its presentation of a vast and successful US effort to develop the atomic bomb before Hitler can, and to use the threat of dropping it to end the war (◊ HITLER WINS). [JC]

ALLIGATOR Film (1980). Alligator Associates/Group 1. Dir Lewis Teague, starring Robert Forster, Robin Riker, Michael Gazzo, Dean Jagger. Screenplay John SAYLES, based on a story by Sayles and Frank Ray Perilli. 91 mins cut to 89 mins. Colour.

A pet baby alligator is flushed down the toilet, and it or another grows into a monster, aided by hormone-experiment waste materials illicitly dumped in the sewers. A policeman investigates the increasingly violent and bizarre alligator attacks, climaxing in the destruction of a wedding party held by (of course) the wicked polluter. *A* is funny and well made. Sayles has remarked that "my original idea was that the alligator eats its way through the whole socio-economic system". Many 1970s and 1980s MONSTER MOVIES, including this one, have been deliberately subversive of comfortable social norms. [PN]

ALLIGHAM, GARRY (1898-?) South African writer whose imaginary history, written as from the year

1987, *Verwoerd – The End: A Lookback from the Future* (**1961**), argues for a benevolently administered apartheid. [JC]

See also: POLITICS.

ALLOTT, KENNETH (1912-1973) UK writer best known for his distinguished and melancholy poetry, which was assembled In *Collected Poems* (coll **1975**). *The Rhubarb Tree* (**1937**), with Stephen Tait, is one of several 1930s novels predicting a fascist government in the UK. *Jules Verne* (**1940**) is a fluent study, free of the usual literary condescensions. [JC]

ALLPORT, ARTHUR [s] ◊ Raymond Z. GALLUN.

ALL-STORY, THE US PULP MAGAZINE published by the Frank A. MUNSEY Corp.; ed Robert Hobard Davis. *AS* appeared monthly Jan 1905-Mar 1914, weekly from 7 Mar 1914 (as *All-Story Weekly*), incorporated *Cavalier Weekly* (◊ *The* CAVALIER) to form *All-Story Cavalier Weekly* from 16 May 1914, and reverted to *All-Story Weekly* 15 May 1915-17 July 1920, when it merged with *Argosy Weekly* to form *Argosy All-Story Weekly* (◊ *The* ARGOSY).

TAS was the most prolific publisher of sf among the pre-1926 pulp magazines; it became important through its editor's discovery of several major authors. Foremost of these in popularity were Edgar Rice BURROUGHS, who was represented with 16 serials and novelettes 1912-20, Ray CUMMINGS, notably with *The Girl in the Golden Atom* (1919-20; fixup **1921**), and A. MERRITT. Other authors who contributed sf to *TAS* included Douglas DOLD, George Allan ENGLAND, Homer Eon FLINT, J.U. GIESY, Victor ROUSSEAU, Garrett P. SERVISS, Francis STEVENS and Charles B. STILSON. Many of *TAS*'s stories were reprinted in FAMOUS FANTASTIC MYSTERIES and FANTASTIC NOVELS. [JE]

Further reading: *Under the Moons of Mars: A History and Anthology of the Scientific Romances in the Munsey Magazines 1912-1920* (anth **1970**) ed Sam MOSKOWITZ.

ALL-STORY CAVALIER WEEKLY ◊ *The* ALL-STORY.

ALL-STORY WEEKLY ◊ *The* ALL-STORY.

ALMEDINGEN, E.M. Working name of Russian-born writer Martha Edith von Almedingen (1898-1971), who emigrated to the UK in 1923. Of her children's fictions, which made up about half her total works, several are of fantasy interest. Her only title of clear sf import is *Stand Fast, Beloved City* (**1954**), about a DYSTOPIAN tyranny. [JC]

ALPERS, HANS JOACHIM (1943-   ) German sf editor, critic, SMALL-PRESS publisher, literary agent and author, sometimes as Jurgen Andreas; editor 1978-80 of **Knaur SF** and 1980-86 of the **Moewig SF** list. With Ronald M. Hahn (1948-   ) he edited the first anthology of native German sf (◊ GERMANY), *Science Fiction aus Deutschland* ["Science Fiction from Germany"] (anth **1974**), and he was a co-editor of *Lexicon der Science Fiction Literatur* (2 vols **1980**; rev 1988; new edn projected 1993), an important sf encyclopedia covering almost all authors with German editions of their work. Further lexicons, of weird fiction and fantasy, are projected for 1993-4. With Hahn again and Werner Fuchs, HJA edited *Reclams*

Science Fiction Führer (**1982**), an annotated survey of sf novels with listings by author. With Fuchs HJA edited for Hohenheim six anthologies of sf stories (**1981-4**) covering sf history by the decades 1940s, 1950s and 1960s, with 2 vols for each, and has edited the **Kopernikus** sf anthologies for Moewig (15 vols **1980 88**). Also for Moewig he edited a German paperback edition of *Analog* (◊ ASTOUNDING SCIENCE-FICTION) (8 vols 1981-4) and a series of sf almanacs and year books – **Science Fiction Jahrbuch** (1981-7) and **Science Fiction Almanach** (1982-7) – containing sf data, stories and essays, the Almanac concentrating on the German scene. He wrote the GERMANY entry in this encyclopedia. [PN]

ALPHAVILLE (vt *Une Étrange Aventure de Lemmy Caution*) Pathé-contemporary/Chaumiane-Film Studio. Dir Jean-Luc Godard, starring Eddie Constantine, Anna Karina, Howard Vernon, Akim Tamiroff. Screenplay Godard. 100 mins. B/w.

In this archetypal French New Wave film, intergalactic secret agent Lemmy Caution (Constantine) arrives at the planet Alphaville to deal with Alpha 60, the computer used to impose conformity on the inhabitants. He succeeds, meeting the computer's logic with his own illogic, and at the same time wins the affections of the ruler's daughter (Karina). A typical pulp-sf plot is transformed into an allegory of feeling versus technology, the past versus the present: Alphaville itself is an undisguised (but selectively seen) Paris of the 1960s; Caution (a tough guy from the 1940s, hero of many novels by UK thriller writer Peter Cheyney [1896-1951]) does not use a spaceship to get there, but simply drives his own Ford car through "intersidereal space" – an ordinary road. *A* is filmed in high contrast, deep shadows and glaring light. It is a not always accessible maze of allusions culled from a wide variety of sources: semantic theory, the myth of Orpheus and Eurydice, Hollywood B-movies, comic books and pulp sf. The latter, like the other components of *A*, is used by Godard as a means of playfully imaging philosophical debate. [JB/PN]

See also: CINEMA.

ALRAUNE (vt *Unholy Love*; vt *Daughter of Destiny*) Film (1928). Ama Film. Dir Henrik Galeen, starring Brigitte Helm, Paul Wegener, Ivan Petrovich. Screenplay Galeen, from *Alraune* (1911; trans **1929**) by Hanns Heinz EWERS. 125 mins. B/w.

A professor of genetics (Wegener) conducts a cold-blooded experiment into the Nature-versus-nurture controversy. Using the semen of a hanged man to fertilize a whore, he creates life – a girl baby called Alraune – by artificial insemination in the laboratory. After this sciencefictional beginning, *A* becomes, like *Frankenstein* (**1818**) by Mary SHELLEY, a fantastic GOTHIC melodrama of retribution for a crime against Nature; nevertheless, in its distrust of the scientist, *A* is wholly central to the development of sf. Alraune (Helm), who is named after and compared throughout with the mythic mandrake root that grows where a hanged man's seed falls, appears to have no soul, and when, as a young woman, she learns of her dark origins, she revenges herself against her "father", the professor – although at the end there is hope she will be heartless no longer. Usually spoken of as a great classic of the German silent cinema, *A* is actually more of an early exploitation movie, stylish but prurient, with more than a whiff of incest in the theme. Helm's eroticism, which we are to deplore, was in fact the reason for the film's commercial success. However, Galeen considerably softened the portrait of Alraune rendered in Ewers' sensationalist novel: whereas in the book she is a monster of depravity, causing illness and suicide wherever she goes, in the film she merely causes mayhem and a little pain. This is generally agreed to be the best of the five film versions of the 1911 book, the others being from 1918 (twice – Germany and Hungary – the latter being directed by Mihaly Kèrtesz, who became Michael Curtiz, the director of *Casablanca*, 1942), 1930 (Germany, again starring Helm) and 1952 (Germany, starring Hildegard Knef and Erich von Stroheim). [PN]

See also: CINEMA; SEX.

ALTERED STATES Film (1980). Warner Bros. Dir Ken Russell, starring William Hurt, Blair Brown, Bob Balaban, Charles Haid. Screenplay Sidney Aaron (Paddy CHAYEFSKY), based on *Altered States* (**1978**) by Chayefsky. 102 mins. Colour.

Research scientist Jessup (Hurt) experiments with altered states of consciousness, with drugs, and with a sensory-deprivation tank. The alterations allow the primitive DNA in his genes to express itself (◊ DEVOLUTION and METAPHYSICS for why this is lunatic); he devolves into an apeman (◊ APES AND CAVEMEN), and later spends some time as primordial ooze. This is bad for his marriage. In this hearty blend of New Age mysticism and old-fashioned Jekyll-and-Hyde horror, director Russell has great fun with hallucinatory psychedelic trips and serious-sounding (but strictly bogus) scientific talk. The seriousness is skin-deep, and so is the film. However, even Russell's bad films – some claim there is no other category – are watchable. [PN]

ALTERNATE HISTORIES ◊ ALTERNATE WORLDS; HISTORY IN SF.

ALTERNATE WORLDS An alternate world – some writers and commentators prefer the designation "alternative world" on grammatical grounds – is an account of Earth as it might have become in consequence of some hypothetical alteration in history. Many sf stories use PARALLEL WORLDS as a frame in which many alternate worlds can be simultaneously held, sometimes interacting with one another.

Hypothetical exercises of this kind have long been popular with historians (◊ HISTORY IN SF) and their virtue was proclaimed by Isaac d'Israeli in *The Curiosities of Literature* (coll **1791-1823**). A classic collection of such essays, ed J.C. Squire, *If It had Happened Otherwise* (anth **1931**; vt *If, or History*

Rewritten; exp 1972) took its inspiration from G.M. Trevelyan's essay "If Napoleon had Won the Battle of Waterloo" (1907); its contributors included G.K. CHESTERTON, André MAUROIS, Hilaire BELLOC, A.J.P. Taylor and Winston Churchill. The most common preoccupations of modern speculative historians were exhibited in two essays written for *Look: If the South had Won the Civil War* (1960; **1961**) by MacKinlay KANTOR and "If Hitler had Won World War II" (1961), by William L. Shirer. The tradition has been continued in the MAINSTREAM by the film IT HAPPENED HERE (1963), Frederic MULLALLY's *Hitler Has Won* (**1975**) and Len DEIGHTON's *SS-GB* (**1978**). Another event seen today as historically pivotal, the invention of the atom bomb, is the basis of two novels by Ronald W. CLARK: *Queen Victoria's Bomb* (**1967**), in which the atom bomb is developed much earlier in history, and *The Bomb that Failed* (**1969**; vt *The Last Year of the Old World* UK), in which its appearance on the historical scene is delayed. Alternative histories are used satirically by non-genre writers in R. Egerton Swartout's *It Might Have Happened* (**1934**) and Marghanita LASKI's *Tory Heaven* (**1948**), and the notion is given a more philosophical twist in Guy DENT's *Emperor of the If* (**1926**). The continuing popularity of alternative histories with mainstream writers is further illustrated by John HERSEY's *White Lotus* (**1965**), Vladimir NABOKOV's *Ada* (**1969**), Martin Cruz SMITH's *The Indians Won* (**1970**), Guido Morselli's *Past Conditional* (**1975**; trans **1981**) and Douglas Jones's *The Court Martial of George Armstrong Custer* (**1976**).

Murray LEINSTER introduced the idea of alternate worlds to GENRE SF in "Sidewise in Time" (1934), and Stanley G. WEINBAUM used it in a light comedy, "The Worlds of If" (1935); but the first serious attempt to construct an alternative history in sf was L. Sprague DE CAMP's *Lest Darkness Fall* (1939; **1941**), in which a man slips back through time and sets out to remould history by preventing or ameliorating the Dark Ages. This story is set entirely in the distant past, but in "The Wheels of If" (1940) de Camp displayed a contemporary USA which might have resulted from 10th-century colonization by Norsemen. Most subsequent sf stories in this vein have tended to skip lightly over the detailed process of historical development to examine alternative presents, but sf writers with a keen interest in history often devote loving care to the development of imaginary pasts; a recent enterprise very much in the tradition of *Lest Darkness Fall* is Harry TURTLEDOVE's *Agent of Byzantium* (coll of linked stories **1986**).

The extraordinary melodramatic potential inherent in the idea of alternate worlds was further revealed by Jack WILLIAMSON's *The Legion of Time* (1938; **1952**), which features alternative futures at war for their very existence, with crucial battles spilling into the past and present. The idea of worlds battling for survival by attempting to maintain their own histories was further developed by Fritz LEIBER in *Destiny Times Three* (1945; **1957**) and in the **Change War** series, which includes *The Big Time* (1958; **1961**). Such stories gained rapidly in extravagance: *The Fall of Chronopolis* (**1974**) by Barrington J. BAYLEY features a time-spanning Empire trying to maintain its reality against the alternative versions which its adversaries are imposing upon it. Attempts by possible futures to influence the present by friendly persuasion were presented by C.L. MOORE in "Greater than Gods" (**1939**) and by Ross ROCKLYNNE in "The Diversifal" (**1951**).

The notion of competing alternative histories is further recomplicated in TIME-TRAVEL stories in which the heroes range across a vast series of parallel worlds, each featuring a different alternative history (alternate universes are often created wholesale, though usually ephemerally, in tricky time-travel stories; *see also* TIME PARADOXES). The policing of time-tracks – either singly, as in Isaac ASIMOV's *The End of Eternity* (**1955**), which features the totalitarian control of history by social engineers, or in great profusion – has remained a consistently popular theme in sf. One of the earliest such police forces is featured in Sam MERWIN's *House of Many Worlds* (**1951**) and *Three Faces of Time* (**1955**); the exploits of others are depicted in H. Beam PIPER's **Paratime** series, begun with "Time Crime" (**1955**), in Poul ANDERSON's **Time Patrol** series, whose early stories are in *Guardians of Time* (coll **1960**), in John BRUNNER's *Times without Number* (fixup **1962** dos), and – less earnestly – in Simon Hawke's **Time Wars** series (◊ Nicholas YERMAKOV), begun with *The Ivanhoe Gambit* (**1984**). Keith LAUMER's *Worlds of the Imperium* (**1962** dos) and sequels, Avram DAVIDSON's *Masters of the Maze* (**1965**), Jack L. CHALKER's *Downtiming the Night Side* (**1985**), Frederik POHL's *The Coming of the Quantum Cats* (**1986**), Mike MCQUAY's *Memories* (**1987**) and Michael P. KUBE-MCDOWELL's *Alternities* (**1988**) are convoluted adventure stories of an essentially similar kind. John CROWLEY's "Great Work of Time" (**1989**) is a more thoughtful work about a conspiracy which attempts to use time travel to take charge of history.

Early genre-sf stories of conflict between alternate worlds tend to assume that our world is better than most of the alternatives. This assumption owes much to our conviction that the "right" side won both the American Civil War and WWII. Ward MOORE's classic *Bring the Jubilee* (**1953**) paints a relatively grim portrait of a USA in which the South won the Civil War; and images of worlds in which the Nazis triumphed (◊ HITLER WINS) tend to be nightmarish – notable examples include "Two Dooms" (**1958**) by C.M. KORN-BLUTH, *The Sound of His Horn* (**1952**) by SARBAN, *The Man in the High Castle* (**1962**) by Philip K. DICK, *The Proteus Operation* (**1985**) by James P. HOGAN, and *Moon of Ice* (**1988**) by Brad LINAWEAVER. An interesting exception is *Budspy* (**1987**) by David DVORKIN, where a successful Third Reich is presented more evenhandedly. Other turning-points in which our world is held to have gone the "right" way include the Reformation and the Industrial Revolution –

whose suppression produces technologically primitive worlds in Keith ROBERTS's excellent *Pavane* (fixup **1968**), Kingsley AMIS's *The Alteration* (**1976**), Martin GREEN's *The Earth Again Redeemed* (**1978**), Phyllis EISENSTEIN's *Shadow of Earth* (**1979**) and John Whitbourn's *A Dangerous Energy* (**1992**) – and the Black Death, which aborts the rise of the West in Robert SILVERBERG's *The Gate of Worlds* (**1967**) and L. Neil SMITH's *The Crystal Empire* (**1986**). The idea that our world might have turned out far better than it has is more often displayed by ironic satires, including: Harry HARRISON's *Tunnel Through the Deeps* (**1972**; vt *A Transatlantic Tunnel, Hurrah!* UK), in which the American colonies never rebelled and the British Empire remains supreme; D.R. BENSEN's *And Having Writ . . .* (**1978**), in which the aliens whose crashing starship is assumed to have caused the Tunguska explosion survive to interfere in the course of progress; S.P. SOMTOW's *The Aquiliad* (fixup **1983**), in which the Roman Empire conquered the Americas; and William GIBSON's and Bruce STERLING's *The Difference Engine* (**1990**), in which Babbage's calculating machine precipitates an information-technology revolution in Victorian England. More earnest examples are fewer in number, but they include "The Lucky Strike" (**1984**) by Kim Stanley ROBINSON, in which a US pilot refuses to drop the atom bomb on Hiroshima, and *Elleander Morning* (**1984**) by Jerry YULSMAN, which imagines a world where Hitler was assassinated before starting WWII.

More philosophically inclined uses of the alternate-worlds theme, involving the worldviews of individual characters rather than diverted histories, were pioneered in genre sf by Philip K. Dick in such novels as *Eye in the Sky* (**1957**), *Now Wait for Last Year* (**1967**) and *Flow My Tears, the Policeman Said* (**1974**). Intriguing homage is paid to Dick's distinctive use of the theme by Michael BISHOP's *The Secret Ascension* (**1987**; vt *Philip K. Dick is Dead, Alas*). Other novels which use alternate worlds to explore personal problems and questions of identity include Bob SHAW's *The Two-Timers* (**1968**), Gordon EKLUND's *All Times Possible* (**1974**), Sheila FINCH's *Infinity's Web* (**1985**), Josephine SAXTON's *Queen of the States* (**1986**), Ken Grimwood's *Replay* (**1986**) and Thomas BERGER's *Changing the Past* (**1989**).

Radical alternative histories, which explore the consequences of fundamental shifts in biological evolution, include Harry Harrison's series about the survival of the dinosaurs, begun with *West of Eden* (**1984**); Harry Turtledove's *A Different Flesh* (fixup **1988**), in which *Homo erectus* survives in the Americas until 1492; and Brian M. STABLEFORD's *The Empire of Fear* (**1988**), in which 17th-century Europe and Africa are ruled by "vampires". More radical still are novels which portray universes where the laws of physics are different. Some of these are described in George GAMOW's series of educative parables *Mr Tompkins in Wonderland* (coll **1939**), and the "many worlds" interpretation of quantum theory has encouraged their use in more recent sf, a notable example being *The Singers of Time* (**1990**) by Frederik Pohl and Jack Williamson.

Worlds of Maybe: Seven Stories of Science Fiction (anth **1970**) ed Robert Silverberg contains further work on the theme by Poul Anderson, Philip José FARMER, Larry NIVEN and Silverberg, as well as the Murray Leinster story cited above. In addition to further stories, including the de Camp story mentioned above, *Alternative Histories: Eleven Stories of the World as it Might have Been* (anth **1986**) ed Martin H. GREENBERG and Charles G. WAUGH includes the definitive version of Barton C. Hacker's and Gordon B. Chamberlain's invaluable bibliography of the theme, "Pasts that Might Have Been, II"; the first version appeared in EXTRAPOLATION in 1981. *Alternatives* (anth **1989**), ed Robert ADAMS and Pamela Crippen Adams, presented original stories told from LIBERTARIAN perspectives. *Alternate Presidents* (anth **1992**) ed Michael RESNICK examines a particular aspect "from Benjamin Franklin to Michael Dukakis"; the same editor's *Alternate Kennedys* (anth **1992**) narrows the focus yet further. [BS]

See also: PARANOIA; STEAMPUNK.

ALTMAN, ROBERT ◊ COUNTDOWN; QUINTET.

ALTOV, GENRIKH Pseudonym of Russian writer and sf critic Henrikh (Saulovich) Altschuller (1926-   ); a trained engineer, he has registered dozens of patents. His unpublished "Altov's Register" is a mammoth catalogue of sf ideas, topics and situations. His three collections of sf stories, some written with his wife Valentina Zhuravlyova, *Legendy O Zviozdnykh Kapitanakh* ["Legends of the Star Captains"] (coll **1961**), *Opaliaiuschii Razum* ["The Scorching Mind"] (coll **1968**) and *Sozdan Dlia Buri* ["Created for Thunder"] (coll **1970**), represent the best of the Soviet style of brainstorming HARD SF. Some of these tales were assembled in *Ballad of the Stars* (anth trans Roger DeGaris **1982** US), which GA ed with Zhuravlyova. [VG]

ALVAREZ, JOHN [s] ◊ Lester DEL REY.

AMAZING ADULT FANTASY ◊ MARVEL COMICS.

AMAZING COLOSSAL MAN, THE Film (1957). Malibu/AIP. Prod and dir Bert I. Gordon, starring Glenn Langan, Cathy Downs, William Hudson. Screenplay Mark Hanna and Gordon, from a story by Gordon. 81 mins. B/w.

An attempt to duplicate the commercially successful pathos of The INCREDIBLE SHRINKING MAN (1957) by reversing its procedure, *TACM* has an army officer exposed to the radiation from a "plutonium bomb" and consequently growing to 60ft (18m) tall. Poignant dialogues take place between the colossal man (Langan) and his fiancée (Downs): "At high school I was voted the guy most likely to reach the top." He goes mad and is shot, falling into the Hoover Dam. The poorly matted special effects allow people standing behind the colossal man to be seen through his body. Often regarded as schlock producer Gordon's best film, it raises the question of what his worst must

look like: the sequel, *War of the Colossal Beast* (1958; vt *The Terror Strikes*), would be a good candidate.   [PN]

See also: FOOD OF THE GODS; GREAT AND SMALL; MONSTER MOVIES.

AMAZING DETECTIVE TALES ◊ SCIENTIFIC DETECTIVE MONTHLY.

AMAZING SCIENCE FICTION ◊ AMAZING STORIES.

AMAZING SCIENCE FICTION STORIES ◊ AMAZING STORIES.

AMAZING SCIENCE STORIES UK PULP MAGAZINE published in Manchester by Pembertons in 1951. Two unmemorable issues appeared, largely reprints from #2 and #3 of the Australian THRILLS, INCORPORATED, but also 2 stories reprinted from SUPER SCIENCE STORIES, a UK edition of which had been published by Pembertons. [BS/PN]

AMAZING STORIES 1. "The magazine of scientifiction", with whose founding Hugo GERNSBACK announced the existence of sf as a distinct literary species. It was a BEDSHEET-sized PULP MAGAZINE issued monthly by Gernsback's Experimenter Publishing Co. as a companion to SCIENCE AND INVENTION; #1 was dated Apr 1926. The title survives to the present day – having been more than once modified in the interim – but the magazine has seen great changes.

Gernsback lost control of Experimenter in 1929 and it was acquired by B.A. Mackinnon and H.K. Fly, who were almost certainly operating as front-men for Bernarr MACFADDEN. The name of the company was modified more than once, then changed to Radio-Science Publications in 1930, then to Teck Publications in 1931; but these name changes were cosmetic, at least some of the new publishers being in fact Macfadden employees, and Macfadden was himself listed as publisher and owner in December 1931; he did not interfere with his editors. Arthur H. Lynch was named as editor of the May-Oct issues, but Gernsback's assistant T. O'Conor SLOANE, who had stayed with the magazine, soon (Nov 1929) assumed full editorship. The magazine reverted to standard pulp format with the Oct 1933 issue. The title was sold in 1938 to ZIFF-DAVIS, who installed Raymond A. PALMER as editor (June 1938). Palmer adopted a radically different editorial policy, concentrating on action-adventure fiction, much of it "mass-produced" by a stable of authors using house names. Howard BROWNE became editor in Jan 1950 and the magazine became a DIGEST with the Apr-May 1953 issue. After a brief period with Paul W. FAIRMAN as editor (June 1956-Nov 1958) – during which time the title was changed to *Amazing Science Fiction* (Mar 1958) and then *Amazing Science Fiction Stories* (May 1958) – Cele GOLDSMITH took over (Dec 1958), using her married name of Cele Lalli from Aug 1964; she ran the magazine until June 1965, when the title, which had changed back to *Amazing Stories* in Oct 1960, was sold to Sol Cohen's Ultimate Publishing Co. For some years thereafter the bulk of the magazine's contents consisted of reprints, with Joseph ROSS acting as managing editor (from Aug 1965). Harry HARRISON became editor in Dec 1967, but a period of confusion followed as he handed over to Barry N. MALZBERG in Nov 1968, who was in turn soon replaced by Ted WHITE in May 1969. White eliminated the reprints and remained editor until Oct 1978, when Sol Cohen sold his interest in the magazine to his partner Arthur Bernhard; White's last issue was Feb 1979. Elinor Mavor, using the pseudonym "Omar Gohagen" (May 1979-Aug 1980) and then her own name, became editor until the Sep 1982 issue. But in March 1982 – by which time it had again become *Amazing Science Fiction Stories* and had been combined with its long-time companion FANTASTIC (from the Nov 1980 issue) – the title was sold to TSR Hobbies, the marketers of the *Dungeons & Dragons* role-playing game (◊ GAMES AND TOYS), who installed George SCITHERS as editor, his first issue being Nov 1982. Scithers was replaced in Sep 1986 by Patrick Lucien Price. *AMZ*'s circulation hit an all-time low in 1984 and recovery was slow, but a surge in sales in 1990 prepared the ground for the magazine to be relaunched in May 1991 in a large-sized slick format, with the original masthead restored. Kim Mohan took over as editor at the time of the image-change, and *AMZ* once again became monthly rather than bimonthly.

In its earliest days *AMZ* used a great many reprints of stories by H.G. WELLS, Jules VERNE and Edgar Allan POE (considered by Gernsback to be the founding fathers of sf) alongside more recent pulp stories by Garrett P. SERVISS, A. MERRITT and Murray LEINSTER. The artwork of Frank R. PAUL was a distinctive feature of the magazine in this period. Original material began to appear in greater quantity in 1928, in which year Miles J. BREUER, David H. KELLER and Jack WILLIAMSON published their first stories in *AMZ*. SPACE OPERA made a spectacular advent when the first BUCK ROGERS IN THE 25TH CENTURY story, *Armageddon 2419 A.D.* (1928; **1962**) by Philip Francis NOWLAN appeared in the same issue (Aug 1928) that E.E. "Doc" SMITH's *The Skylark of Space* (1928: **1946**) began serialization. Sloane maintained Gernsback's policy of favouring didactic material that was sometimes rather stilted by pulp-fiction standards, but extravagant serial novels – notably Smith's *Skylark Three* (1930; **1948**), Edmond HAMILTON's "The Universe Wreckers" (1930) and Jack Williamson's *The Green Girl* (1930; **1950**) – maintained the balance. From 1930 *AMZ* faced strong competition from ASTOUNDING STORIES, whose higher rates of pay secured its dominance of the market.

When Ray Palmer took over the ailing *AMZ* in 1938 he attempted to boost circulation in several ways. He aimed at a younger audience, obtaining several stories from Edgar Rice BURROUGHS, and ultimately (in the mid-1940s) elected to support a series of PARANOID fantasies by the obsessive Richard S. SHAVER with insinuations that Shaver's theories about evil subterranean forces dominating the world by superscientific means were actually true. However, the bulk of *AMZ*'s contents in the Palmer era consisted of lurid formulaic material by such writers as Don WILCOX, David Wright O'BRIEN and William P. McGivern (1922-1982); Palmer was probably a frequent pseudonymous contributor himself. The fiction-factory system operated by ZIFF-DAVIS reached its height in the mid-1950s when the contents of several of their magazines were produced on a regular basis by a small group of writers including sometime *AMZ* editor Paul Fairman, Robert SILVERBERG, Randall GARRETT, Harlan ELLISON and Henry SLESAR. This system resulted in some confusion with regard to the correct attribution of several "floating PSEUDONYMS", especially Ivar JORGENSEN. Few stories of note appeared under the first three Ziff-Davis editors, although Edmond Hamilton, Nelson BOND and Walter M. MILLER were occasional contributors.

Under Cele Goldsmith's editorship *AMZ* improved dramatically, publishing good work by many leading authors. Notable contributions included Marion Zimmer BRADLEY's first **Darkover** novella, *The Planet Savers* (Nov 1958; **1962** dos), Harlan Ellison's first sf novel, "The Sound of the Scythe" (Oct 1959; rev as *The Man with Nine Lives* **1960** dos), and Roger ZELAZNY's NEBULA-winning "He Who Shapes" (Jan-Feb 1964; exp as *The Dream Master* **1966**). Zelazny was one of several writers whose careers were aided in their early stages by Goldsmith; others include Ben BOVA (who did a series of science articles), David R. BUNCH, Thomas M. DISCH, Ursula K. LE GUIN and Robert F. YOUNG. When Ted White became editor he renewed the attempt to maintain a consistent standard of quality; although handicapped by having to offer a word-rate payment considerably less than that of his competitors, he achieved some degree of success. The special 50th-anniversary issue which he compiled appeared two months late (it bears the date June 1976) owing to scheduling difficulties.

AMZ's continued survival during the next 15 years was something of a surprise, given its poor sales, though Scithers in particular made considerable efforts to maintain its literary quality. Patrick Lucien Price published good work, too, by such writers as Gregory BENFORD and Paul J. MCAULEY, and also new writers like Paul Di Filippo, but the magazine seemed to receive almost no promotion. The new packaging is much more attractive than any of *AMZ*'s previous incarnations, and arguably the most attractive of any current (1992) sf magazine; time will tell whether it can attract the fresh readers needed if it is to become commercially viable.

AMZ had three UK reprint editions, 1946 (1 undated issue, pulp), 1950-53 (24 undated issues, pulp) and 1953-4 (8 undated issues, digest). Anthologies based on *AMZ* stories include *The Best of Amazing* (anth **1967**) ed Joseph Ross, *The Best from Amazing Stories* (anth **1973**) ed Ted White, *Amazing Stories: 60 Years of the Best Science Fiction* (anth **1985**) ed Isaac ASIMOV and Martin H. GREENBERG, *Amazing Stories: Vision of Other Worlds* (anth **1986**) ed Greenberg, and a number of others ed Greenberg.   [BS]

2. US tv series (vt *Steven Spielberg's Amazing Stories*) (1985-7). Amblin/Universal for NBC. Created by Steven SPIELBERG. Producers included Joshua Brand, John Falsey, David E. Vogel. Writers included Spielberg, Frank Deese, Richard Christian MATHESON, Mick Garris, Joseph Minion, Menno Meyjes, Michael McDowell, Paul Bartel. Directors included Spielberg, Robert Zemeckis, Peter Hyams, Burt Reynolds, Clint Eastwood, Joe DANTE, Martin Scorsese, Paul Bartel, Irvin Kershner, Danny DeVito, Tom Holland, Tobe Hooper. Two seasons, each of 22 25min episodes.

An ambitious attempt to revive the 1950s-60s anthology format – which came at the same time as actual revivals of *The* TWILIGHT ZONE (1985-7) and *Alfred Hitchcock Presents* (1985-6), and a few competitors like *The Hitch Hiker* (1983-6) and *Tales from the Darkside* (1984-7) – this was less an sf series than its pulp-derived title suggested, more often going for the blend of fantasy and sentiment found in the less scary episodes of the original *Twilight Zone*. Kept afloat for two years through NBC having committed themselves – astonishingly – to 44 episodes from the very beginning, *AS*, despite its large budget and the unusually strong directing talent Spielberg was able to attract (Eastwood, Zemeckis, Scorsese, Bartel, etc.), was unsuccessful. Many disappointed viewers and critics felt that Spielberg had stretched himself too thin, as had Rod SERLING with *Twilight Zone*, by generating the often fragile storylines for the bulk of the episodes (16 out of 22 in the first season); one such projected episode looked even more fragile when expanded into a feature, * BATTERIES NOT INCLUDED (1987). Too many of the stories, despite good special effects and performances, led nowhere.

Typical of *AS*'s uneven tone was the extended Spielberg-directed episode "The Mission", a 50min WWII-bomber anecdote presciently cast (Kevin Costner, Kiefer Sutherland) and suspensefully directed, but sinking limply into a ludicrous and irritating fantasy finale. *AS* did have surprises – the gritty cartoon episode "The Family Dog", designed by Tim Burton, being perhaps the overall highlight – but mainly it expressed the diminishing-return whimsy that was beginning to affect even Spielberg's big-screen work. Three episodes – "The Mission", "Mummy, Daddy" and "Go to the Head of the Class" – were released together as a feature film, *Amazing Stories* (1987), outside the USA, and many other episodes have been released in groups of three on videotape. Tie versions of individual episodes are collected in *Steven Spielberg's Amazing Stories* (anth **1986**) and *Volume II of Steven Spielberg's Amazing Stories* (anth **1986**), both ed Steven Bauer. [KN]

AMAZING STORIES ANNUAL US BEDSHEET-size 128pp PULP MAGAZINE published by Hugo GERNSBACK's Experimenter Publishing Co. Its only issue (1927) ran the first publication of *The Master Mind of Mars* (1927; **1928**) by Edgar Rice BURROUGHS. A successor, AMAZING STORIES QUARTERLY, resulted from the success of *ASA*. [BS]

AMAZING STORIES QUARTERLY US BEDSHEET-size PULP MAGAZINE, companion to AMAZING STORIES (but twice as fat) and successor to AMAZING STORIES ANNUAL. 22 issues, Winter 1928-Fall 1934, first under the aegis of Hugo GERNSBACK's Experimenter Publishing Co. and later (1929-34), ed T. O'Conor SLOANE after Gernsback had lost control, under several publishers. In addition to short stories it featured a complete novel in every issue, beginning with H.G. WELLS's *When the Sleeper Wakes* (**1899**) but thereafter using mainly original material. It published many of the most important early pulp sf novels: "White Lily" (Winter 1930; as *The Crystal Horde* **1952**) and *Seeds of Life* (Fall 1931; **1951**), both assembled as *Seeds of Life & White Lily* (omni **1966**), by John TAINE; *The Black Star Passes* (Fall 1930; **1953**) and *Invaders from the Infinite* (Spring/Summer 1932; **1961**) by John W. CAMPBELL Jr; "Paradise and Iron" (Summer 1930) and *The Birth of a New Republic* (Winter 1930; **1981**) by Miles J. BREUER (the latter with Jack WILLIAMSON); *The Sunken World* (Summer 1928 and Fall 1934; **1949**) by Stanton A. COBLENTZ; and *The Bridge of Light* (Fall 1929; **1950**) by A. Hyatt VERRILL. Gernsback's own *Ralph 124C 41+* (1911 *Modern Electrics*; **1925**; *ASQ* Winter 1929) was reprinted.

Some rebound issues of *AMZ* were re-released, three to a volume, in 1940-43 (13 issues) and 1947-51 (15 issues) as *Amazing Stories Quarterly*. [BS]

AMAZING STORIES SCIENCE FICTION NOVEL US DIGEST-size magazine. One undated issue, June 1957, published by ZIFF-DAVIS; ed (uncredited) Paul W. FAIRMAN. This was to be a quarterly magazine printing book-length novels in imitation of GALAXY SCIENCE FICTION NOVELS. The only novel was Henry SLESAR's routine novelization of the film 20 MILLION MILES TO EARTH (1957). [FHP]

AMAZON WOMEN ON THE MOON ◊ Joe DANTE; FEMINISM.

AMERICAN FICTION UK numbered pocketbook series which could be regarded (being numbered) as either an anthology series or a magazine. 12 issues known, most 36pp, numbered only from #2. Published by Utopian Publications, London; ed Benson HERBERT and Walter GILLINGS (who jointly owned the company). Irregular, Sep 1944-Jan 1946. *AF* was a reprint publication. All issues featured quasi-erotic covers, with the title story often being an already known sf or fantasy work under a racy new name. Thus S.P. MEEK's "Gates of Light" became *Arctic Bride* (**1944** chap), Edmond HAMILTON's "Six Sleepers" (1935) became *Tiger Girl* (*c***1945** chap), John Beynon Harris's (◊ John WYNDHAM) "The Wanderers of Time" (1933) became *Love in Time* (**1945** chap), Jack WILLIAMSON's "Wizard's Isle" (1934) became *Lady in Danger* (*c***1945** chap) and Stanton A. COBLENTZ's "Planet of Youth" (1932) became *Youth Madness* (**1945** chap). Other featured authors were Ralph Milne FARLEY and Robert BLOCH. All but #1 and #6 in the series contained short stories as well as the featured novella, hence their usual listing in indexes as if they constituted separate book publication of a single novella is technically incorrect. The emphasis was on weird fiction rather than sf, though stories from other genres were also used. [PN/FHP]

AMERICAN FLAGG! US COMIC-book series (1983-9, 63 issues), published by First Comics, created by writer/artist Howard V. CHAYKIN. Generally considered one of the best sf COMICS of the 1980s, *AF!* is set in a media-saturated USA reduced to Third-World status, and stars Reuben Flagg, drafted into the Plexus Rangers in Chicago in the 2030s (Plexus being a Mars-based mega-cartel planning to sell off the USA piece by piece). *AF!* is sophisticated fun, featuring cynically humorous writing and male and female characters with large sexual appetites. Except for #27, written by Alan MOORE, Chaykin wrote the first 30 issues and drew all but two of the first 26. The post-Chaykin issues of *AF!* were not well received, and First Comics took the unprecedented step of making #46 an apology for these. Chaykin returned with #47 and continued to #50, the end of the first series. In 1988 a second series, now called *Howard Chaykin's American Flagg!*, sent Flagg to the USSR; it had 12 issues, with Chaykin editing, writing (with John Moore) and providing art direction. There was also a one-off *American Flagg Special* in 1986. The first 9 issues of *AF!* have been collected as First Comics Graphic Novels #3, #12 and #20. [RH/ZB/BNF]

AMERICAN SCIENCE FICTION MAGAZINE Australian monthly pocketbook magazine, a companion to SELECTED SCIENCE FICTION. 41 issues, June 1952-Dec 1955, unnumbered and undated 32pp booklets. Published by Malian Press, Sydney; no editor named. The first 24 issues did not carry the word "magazine" on the cover, and it has been suggested that the publishers had bought book rights rather than serial rights to stories, which would explain the coyness about its being a regular periodical. *ASFM* contained reprints from US magazines of quite a good standard, including stories by James BLISH, John W. CAMPBELL Jr and Robert A. HEINLEIN. [PN/FHP]

A. MERRITT'S FANTASY MAGAZINE US PULP MAGAZINE. 5 issues, Dec 1949-Oct 1950, published by Popular Publications; no ed listed – it may have been Mary GNAEDINGER. *AMFM* was a companion magazine to FAMOUS FANTASTIC MYSTERIES and FANTASTIC NOVELS, and was begun in response to the considerable enthusiasm engendered by the reprinting of A. MERRITT's fiction in those magazines and elsewhere. Until the appearance in 1954 of VARGO STATTEN SCIENCE FICTION MAGAZINE, and then in 1977 of ISAAC ASIMOV'S SCIENCE FICTION MAGAZINE, *AMFM* was the only sf magazine which attempted to build its appeal on the popularity of a single author – even though Merritt himself had died in 1943 and much of his fiction was available elsewhere. In any event, the magazine failed to establish itself. *AMFM* also published reprints of stories by other authors. There was a Canadian reprint edition. [MJE/PN]

AMERY, CARL [r] ◊ GERMANY.

AMES, CLINTON [s] ◊ Rog PHILLIPS.

AMES, MILDRED (1919-) US writer of novels for older children. Of sf interest is *Is There Life on a Plastic Planet?* (**1975**), which effectively transforms the PARANOID theme of substitution – in this case a shop contains dolls identical to the young women its owner attempts to suborn – into a resonant tale of adolescence and identity. Questions of identity also lie at the heart of *Anna to the Infinite Power* (**1981**), whose protagonist sees another girl in her mirror image, eventually uncovering an experiment in cloning (◊ CLONES). Other novels, like *The Silver Link, the Silken Tie* (**1984**) and *Conjuring Summer In* (**1986**), are fantasy. [JC]

AMIS, KINGSLEY (WILLIAM) (1922-) UK novelist, poet and critic; father of Martin AMIS. He took his MA at Oxford, and was a lecturer in English at Swansea 1949-61 and Fellow of Peterhouse, Cambridge, 1961-3. Though KA is best known for such social comedies as his first novel, *Lucky Jim* (**1954**), which won him the sobriquet "Angry Young Man", in the catch-phrase of the time, he has also been closely connected with sf throughout his professional life. He delivered a series of lectures on sf in 1959 at Princeton University, probably to their surprise since sf was presumably not the context in which he was invited to speak. Revised, these were published as a book, *New Maps of Hell* (**1960** US), which was certainly the most influential critical work on sf up to that time, although not the most scholarly. It strongly emphasized the DYSTOPIAN elements of sf. KA, himself a satirist and debunker of note, saw sf as an ideal medium for satirical and sociological extrapolation; hitherto, most writing on sf had regarded it as primarily a literature of TECHNOLOGY. As a survey the book was one-sided and by no means thorough, but it was witty, perceptive and quietly revolutionary.

KA went on to edit a memorable series of ANTHOLOGIES, *Spectrum*, with Robert CONQUEST (like KA a novelist, poet, political commentator and sf fan). They were *Spectrum* (anth **1961**), *Spectrum II* (anth **1962**), *Spectrum III* (anth **1963**), *Spectrum IV* (anth **1965**) and *Spectrum V* (anth **1966**). These, too, were influential in popularizing sf in the UK and to some extent in rendering it respectable. The last of these volumes is selected almost entirely from *ASF*, a reflection, perhaps, of KA's increasing conservatism about HARD SF (and in his politics) which went along with a dislike for stories of the NEW WAVE, also evident in *The Golden Age of Science Fiction* (anth **1981**) ed KA alone.

As a writer, too, KA was influenced by sf. He wrote several sf short stories including "Something Strange" (1960), a minor *tour de force* about appearance and reality and about psychological conditioning. His short sf can mostly be found in *My Enemy's Enemy* (coll **1962**) and later in *Collected Short Stories* (coll **1980**; exp **1987**). *The Anti-Death League* (**1966**) is an extravagant spy story featuring miniaturized nuclear devices. The **James Bond** pastiche *Colonel*

Sun: A James Bond Adventure (**1968**) as by Robert Markham contains occasional sf elements. The fantasy *The Green Man* (**1969**), one of KA's best works, blends satirical social comedy with Gothic HORROR; it was dramatized as a miniseries by BBC TV in 1991. KA's major full-scale sf work is *The Alteration* (**1976**), set in an ALTERNATE WORLD in which the Reformation has not taken place and Roman Catholic domination has continued to the present. It won the JOHN W. CAMPBELL MEMORIAL AWARD for best sf novel in 1977. *Russian Hide-and-Seek* (**1980**) is a blackly amusing, pessimistic story about the vulnerability of English culture, set in a future England that has for decades been subject to the USSR. KA's controversial artistic evolution from supposed radical to national institution (during which he remained always his own man) was neatly summed up by his receipt of a knighthood in 1990. An autobiographical work is *Memoirs* (**1991**). [PN]

See also: CHILDREN IN SF; CRITICAL AND HISTORICAL WORKS ABOUT SF; DEFINITIONS OF SF; FEMINISM; *The* MAGAZINE OF FANTASY AND SCIENCE FICTION; RELIGION; SATIRE; SF IN THE CLASSROOM.

AMIS, MARTIN (LOUIS) (1949-   ) UK writer, son of Kingsley AMIS. From the first his novels have threatened and distressed their protagonists – and their readers – with narrative displacements that gnaw away at consensual reality, so that moments of normality in his work are, like as not, intended to reveal themselves as forms of entrapment. His interest in sf-like (and sf-mocking) venues dates back to his second novel, *Dead Babies* (**1975**), set in an indistinct NEAR FUTURE and featuring a protagonist who has made his pile by working at a local abortion factory. MA was responsible for the screenplay for SATURN 3 (**1980**), though Steve GALLAGHER wrote the book tie. *Other People: A Mystery Story* (**1981**) – which took its title from Jean-Paul Sartre's definition of Hell, in *Huis Clos* (**1945**; trans Stuart Gilbert as *In Camera* **1946** UK), as being other people – is an afterlife fantasy. *Einstein's Monsters* (coll **1987**) assembles several sf stories variously concerned with the decay of the world into HOLOCAUSTS, nuclear and otherwise. *London Fields* (**1989**) is set in 1999 in a world approaching a dread millennium. *Time's Arrow* (**1991**) – which begins, as does *Other People*, at the moment at which its protagonist "awakens" into a radically displaced world – is a full and genuine sf novel, based on the premise that the arrow of time has been reversed (MA's acknowledged sf sources for this premise run from Philip K. DICK's *Counter-Clock World* [**1967**] to Kurt VONNEGUT Jr's *Slaughterhouse-Five*, [**1969**]), but very much complexifies the implications of the conceit by making the protagonist an old Nazi, whose involvement in the death camps now becomes a hymn to life. Throughout the book, the reversal of the 20th century reads as a reprieve. It is a tale whose joys encode ironies so grim that the "happier" moments of return and redemption are impossible to read without considerable pain. *Time's Arrow* was,

inevitably, received as a FABULATION; at the same time, it reads with all the clarity of reportage.   [JC]

See also: PERCEPTION; TIME TRAVEL.

AMOSOV, N(ICOLAI MIKHAILOVITCH) (1913-   ) Russian engineer and writer. In his sf novel *Zapiski iz budushchego* (**1967**; trans George St George as *Notes from the Future* **1970** US as by N. Amosoff) a frozen sleeper awakens to 1991, where he is cured of leukaemia and reflects somewhat heavily upon the nature of the world he has come into.   [JC]

See also: CRYONICS.

AMRA ◊ George H. SCITHERS.

ANALOG ◊ ASTOUNDING SCIENCE-FICTION.

ANANIA, GEORGE [r] ◊ ROMANIA.

ANDERSEN, HANS CHRISTIAN [r] ◊ DENMARK

ANDERSON, ADRIENNE [r] ◊ ROBERT HALE LIMITED.

ANDERSON, ANDY [s] ◊ William C. ANDERSON.

ANDERSON, CHESTER (VALENTINE JOHN) (1932-1991) US novelist and poet, member of the Beat Generation, editor of underground journals on both coasts, and of Paul WILLIAMS's *Crawdaddy*, a rock'n'roll magazine, during the 1980s; he wrote poetry as c v j anderson. His sf was written in association with Michael KURLAND. *Ten Years to Doomsday* (**1964**), a straight collaboration, is a lightly written INVASION tale with a good deal of activity in space and on other planets. *The Butterfly Kid* (**1967**) was written by CA alone, but stands as the first volume of a comically surrealistic SHARED-WORLD trilogy set in Greenwich Village, the second instalment being *The Unicorn Girl* (**1969**) by Kurland and the third *The Probability Pad* (**1970**) by T A WATERS. The trilogy stars all three authors (◊ RECURSIVE SF), who become involved in the attempts of a pop group to fight off a more than merely psychedelic invasion menace: Greenwich Village is being threatened by a pill which actualizes people's fantasies.   [JC]

Other works: *Fox & Hare* (**1980**), a fictionalized memoir of the real lives behind the trilogy.

See also: PERCEPTION.

ANDERSON, COLIN (1904-   ) UK writer whose novel *Magellan* (**1970**) depicts a post-HOLOCAUST Earth dominated by a single city, and the somewhat metaphysical apotheosis afforded its inhabitants. [JC]

See also: CITIES.

ANDERSON, DAVID [s] ◊ Raymond F. JONES.

ANDERSON, GERRY (1929-   ) **and SYLVIA** (?   -   ) UK tv producers and writers; GA was also an animator and SA a voice artist. They will forever be remembered for a succession of 1960s children's puppet adventure shows on tv that occasionally dealt with sf themes on a far more extensive scale than contemporary adult programming. GA's first two series, *The Adventures of Twizzle* (1958) and *Torchy the Battery Boy* (1959), were fairly conventional 15min puppet shows, albeit featuring characters whose gimmicks (extensible arms, electrical powers) were notionally scientific. The Western series *Four Feather Falls* (1960) began his run of "SuperMarionation" shows, its magical feathers giving it a fantastical touch. With the half-hour series SUPERCAR (1961-2) GA was joined by his wife SA – who would provide female voices for and write for subsequent series – and came up with the format that continued for eight years in FIREBALL XL5 (1962-3), STINGRAY (1964-5), THUNDERBIRDS (1965-6) and CAPTAIN SCARLET AND THE MYSTERONS (1967-8). All these feature a wonderful vehicle from the 21st century, an ongoing struggle with evil forces, a catchy score suitable for spin-off records, impressively designed miniature sets, a quasi-military organization of good guys, and a family-like regular cast with a square-jawed hero, a stammering boffin, a non-weedy girl, a crusty chief and a sidekick, and usually a mysterious master villain with a bumbling accomplice.

Stingray was the first in colour, and introduced marginally more adult characterizations: Mike Mercury and Steve Zodiac, the heroes of *Supercar* and *Fireball XL5*, were never as bad-tempered as Troy Tempest in *Stingray* could be, and they would certainly never have been caught up in a three-way romance. *Thunderbirds* experimented with a 50min running time and a less confrontational plot premise – the Tracy family were rescuing innocents, not fighting ALIENS as Troy Tempest had done and Captain Scarlet would do – and became perhaps the highlight of the As' career, spinning off two feature films, *Thunderbirds are Go* (1966) and *Thunderbird Six* (1968), and creating a set of characters – Lady Penelope, Parker, the Hood, Brains and Jeff Tracy and his sons – who would remain identifiable enough to crop up in tv commercials as late as the early 1990s, when the series was also rerun on UK tv by the BBC. *Captain Scarlet*, returning to the half-hour format, tried for a more realistic approach by scaling down the exaggerated features of the puppets and adding a premise – spun off from *Thunderbirds are Go* – about a war between Earth and the Mysterons of Mars that was less clear-cut than previous conflicts insofar as Earth (admittedly by accident) was the initial aggressor. Also, the device of resurrecting dead personnel and equipment for use in battle raised the level of violence beyond the cosy destructiveness of the earlier shows.

Captain Scarlet was as far as the As' format could be stretched, and their subsequent puppet shows – JOE 90 (1968-9) and *The Secret Service* (1969) – were far less successful. The first, focusing on a boy genius, appeared childish to audiences who had become used to the increasing maturity of each new show – who had in effect grown up with SuperMarionation. The second, using live actors alongside puppets, was seen by few and cancelled mid-season.

The As had already produced a live-action film, DOPPELGANGER (1969; vt *Journey to the Far Side of the Sun*), by the time they determined to abandon tv puppets altogether and marry their skills with miniature effects to real-life actors – who, unfortunately, were almost always accused of being as wooden as their predecessors – in UFO (1970-73). This was a

marginally more realistic rerun of *Captain Scarlet* with elements also of *The* INVADERS (1967-8), in which a secret organization tried to fight off a plague of flying saucers.

After a nondescript non-sf series, *The Protectors* (1972-4), the As launched on their most elaborate venture yet, SPACE 1999 (1975-7), an internationally cast and impressively mounted attempt to produce a show with both mass and cult appeal along the lines of STAR TREK. It is frequently and not entirely without justification remembered as the worst sf series ever aired. During its run the As divorced, and GA, who remained on the series, gradually lost control to his varied UK and US backers. Subsequently GA went back to puppetry with TERRAHAWKS (1983-6), a feeble imitation of his 1960s triumphs, and worked extensively in commercials, some re-using characters from his earlier shows.

In their heyday, the SuperMarionation shows – which overlapped to a degree, creating a detailed 21st-century Universe as a backdrop – gave birth to *TV 21*, a successful and well drawn COMIC, along with toys, games, annuals, books and other now-valued ephemera. [KN]

See also: TELEVISION.

ANDERSON, KAREN [r] ◊ Poul ANDERSON.

ANDERSON, KEVIN J(AMES) (1962-) US technical writer and author who began publishing sf with "Luck of the Draw" in *Space & Time* #63 in 1982, and who gradually became a prolific contributor of short fiction and articles to various sf journals, over 100 items having been published by 1992. His first novel, *Resurrection, Inc.* (**1988**), combines elements of the usual sf near-future DYSTOPIA with elements of the horror novel, reanimated bodies serving a corrupt society as a worker-class. There followed the **Gamearth** trilogy – *Gamearth* (**1989**), *Gameplay* (**1989**) and *Game's End* (**1990**) – which treats with some verve a GAME-WORLD crisis involved the coming to life of game-bound personas who (or which) refuse to be cancelled. More interestingly, *Lifeline* (**1990**) with Doug BEASON sets up and solves a technically complex sequence of problems in space after a nuclear HOLOCAUST (the result of a USSR-US contretemps of the sort which, unluckily for the authors, had in the months before publication abruptly become much less likely) has stripped four habitats of all Earth support; the Filipino station boasts a GENETIC-ENGINEERING genius who can feed everyone, a US station has the eponymous monofilament, and so on. Some of the protagonists carrying on the quadripartite storyline are of interest in their own right. If one puts aside the whiplashes of Earth's realtime history, the book stands as a fine example of HARD SF and a gripping portrayal of the complexities of near space. *The Trinity Paradox* (**1991**), also with Beason, treats the now-standard sf TIME-PARADOX tale with overdue seriousness, suggesting that untoward moral consequences attend the sudden capacity of its protagonist – who has been accidentally timeslipped back to

Los Alamos in 1943 – to stop nuclear testing in its tracks.   [JC]

See also: MEDICINE; NUCLEAR POWER; REINCARNATION.

ANDERSON, MARY (1872-1964) UK writer whose novel, *A Son of Noah* (**1893**), features many of the conventions of prehistoric sf with the added spice of pterodactyl-worship on the part of a speciously advanced race. But the Flood will soon clear the air.   [JC]

ANDERSON, OLOF W. (?   -?   ) Untraced author of a routinely occult novel with sf elements, *The Treasure Vault of Atlantis* (**1925** US), with a 70-word subtitle; revived Atlanteans bring ancient knowledge to bear on contemporary problems.   [JC]

See also: SUSPENDED ANIMATION.

ANDERSON, POUL (WILLIAM) (1926-   ) US writer born in Pennsylvania of Scandinavian parents; he lived in Denmark briefly before the outbreak of WWII. In 1948 PA gained a degree in physics from the University of Minnesota. His knowledge of Scandinavian languages and literature and his scientific literacy have fed each other fruitfully through a long and successful career. He is Greg BEAR's father-in-law.

PA's first years as a writer were spent in Minnesota, where after WWII he joined the Minneapolis Fantasy Society (later the MFS) and associated with such writers as Clifford D. SIMAK and Gordon R. DICKSON, both of whom shared with him an attachment to semi-rural (often wooded) settings peopled by solid, canny stock (frequently, in PA's case, of Scandinavian descent) whose politics and social views often register as conservative, especially among readers from the urban East and the UK, although perhaps this cultural style could more fruitfully be regarded as a form of romantic, Midwestern, LIBERTARIAN individualism.

Although he is perhaps sf's most prolific writer of any consistent quality, PA began quite slowly, starting to publish sf with "Tomorrow's Children", with F.N. Waldrop, for *ASF* in 1947, but not publishing with any frequency until about 1950 – a selection of eloquent early tales appears in *Alight in the Void* (coll **1991**) – when he also released his first novel, a post-HOLOCAUST juvenile, *Vault of the Ages* (**1952**).

In 1953 PA seemed to come afire: in addition to 19 stories, he published magazine versions of three novels, *Brain Wave* (1953 *Space Science Fiction* as "The Escape", first instalment only before magazine ceased publication; **1954**), *Three Hearts and Three Lions* (1953 *FSF*; exp **1961**) and *War of Two Worlds* (1953 *Two Complete Science-Adventure Books* as "Silent Victory"; **1959** dos). The last of these is one of PA's many well told but routine adventures, in this case involving a betrayed Earth, alien overlords and plucky humans; but the other two are successful, mature novels, each in a separate genre. In *Three Hearts and Three Lions*, an ALTERNATE-WORLD fantasy, an Earthman is translated from the middle of WWII into a SWORD-AND-SORCERY

venue where he fights the forces of Chaos in a tale whose humour is laced with the slightly gloomy "Nordic twilight" colours that have become increasingly characteristic of PA's work (noticeably in *Three Hearts*'s sequel, *Midsummer Tempest* [**1974**]). *Brain Wave*, perhaps PA's most famous single novel, remains very nearly his finest. Its premise is simple: for millions of years the part of the Galaxy containing our Solar System has been moving through a vast forcefield whose effect has been to inhibit "certain electromagnetic and electrochemical processes", and thus certain neuronic functions. When Earth escapes the inhibiting field, synapse-speed immediately increases, causing a rise in INTELLIGENCE; after the book has traced various absorbing consequences of this transformation, a transfigured humanity reaches for the stars, leaving behind former mental defectives and bright animals to inherit the planet.

After *Brain Wave* PA seemed content for several years to produce competent but unambitious stories – in such great numbers that it was not until many years had passed that they were adequately assembled in volumes like *Explorations* (coll **1981**) and its stablemates – and SPACE OPERAS with titles like *No World of Their Own* (**1955** dos; with restored text vt *The Long Way Home* 1975 UK); he occasionally wrote under the pseudonyms A.A. Craig and Winston P. Sanders, and (according to one source) in the mid-1960s as Michael Karageorge, although PA does not admit to this. It was during these years, however, that he began to formulate and write the many stories and novels making up the complex **Technic History** series, in reality two separate sequences. The first centres on **Nicholas van Rijn**, a dominant merchant prince of the Polesotechnic League, an interstellar group of traders who dominate a *laissez-faire* Galaxy of scattered planets. Anderson has been widely criticized for the conservative implications it is possible (though with some effort) to draw from these stories, whose philosophical implications he modestly curtails. The second sequence properly begins about 300 years later, after the first flowering of a post-League Terran Empire, which, increasingly decadent and corrupt, is under constant threat from other empires. Most of the sequence features **Dominic Flandry**, a Terran agent who – sophisticated, pessimistic and tough – gradually becomes a figure of stature as Anderson fills in and expands his story, begun in 1951. The internal chronology of the double sequence is not secure, but the following list is close. **Van Rijn**: *War of the Wing-Men* (**1958** dos; with restored text and new introduction vt *The Man who Counts* 1978); *Trader to the Stars* (coll **1964**; with 1 story cut 1964 UK); *The Trouble Twisters* (coll **1966**); *Satan's World* (**1969**); *Mirkheim* (**1977**); *The Earth Book of Stormgate* (coll **1978**; in 3 vols 1980-81 UK); *The People of the Wind* (**1973**). **Flandry**: *Ensign Flandry* (**1966**); *A Circus of Hells* (**1970**); *The Rebel Worlds* (**1969**; vt *Commander Flandry* 1978 UK); *The Day of Their Return* (**1973**), also assembled with *The People of the Wind* as

The Day of Their Return/The People of the Wind (omni **1982**); *Mayday Orbit* (**1961** dos) and *Earthman, Go Home!* (**1960** dos), which are both assembled with revisions as *Flandry of Terra* (omni **1965**); *We Claim These Stars* (**1959** dos), which is included in *Agent of the Terran Empire* (coll **1965**); *A Knight of Ghosts and Shadows* (**1974**; vt *Knight Flandry* 1980 UK), assembled with *The Rebel Worlds* as *The Rebel Worlds/A Knight of Ghosts and Shadows* (omni **1982**); *A Stone in Heaven* (**1979**); *The Game of Empire* (**1985**), featuring Flandry's daughter, and pointing the way to two post-Flandry tales: *Let the Spacemen Beware* (1960 *Fantastic Universe* as "A Twelvemonth and a Day"; **1963** chap dos; with new introduction vt *The Night Face* 1978), also included in a separate collection, *The Night Face and Other Stories* (coll **1978**); and *The Long Night* (coll **1983**). Stories written later tend to moodier, darker textures.

A somewhat smaller sequence, the **Psychotechnic League** stories, traces the gradual movement of Man into the Solar System and eventually the Galaxy itself. There is a good deal of action-debate about AUTOMATION, the maintenance of freedom in an expanded polity, and so forth. The sequence comprises, by rough internal chronology: *The Psychotechnic League* (coll **1981**), *Cold Victory* (coll **1982**), *Starship* (coll **1982**), *The Snows of Ganymede* (1955 *Startling Stories* **1958** dos), *Virgin Planet* (**1959**), and *Star Ways* (**1956**; vt with new introduction *The Peregrine* 1978).

There are several further series. The early **Time Patrol** stories (◊ ALTERNATE WORLDS) are contained in *Guardians of Time* (coll **1960**; with 2 stories added vt *The Guardians of Time* 1981) and *Time Patrolman* (coll of linked novellas **1983**), both assembled as *Annals of the Time Patrol* (omni **1984**); subsequently, early and later material was rearranged as *The Shield of Time* (coll of linked stories **1990**) and *The Time Patrol* (omni/coll **1991**), which re-sorted long stories from the first volumes along with a new novel, "Star of the Sea", plus *The Year of the Ransom* (**1988**) and other new material. The **History of Rustum** sequence, mainly concerned with the establishing on *laissez-faire* lines of a human colony on a planet in the Epsilon Eridani system, includes *Orbit Unlimited* (coll of linked stories **1961**) and *New America* (coll of linked stories **1982**). With Gordon R. Dickson, PA wrote the **Hoka** series about furry aliens who cannot understand nonliteral language (i.e., metaphors, fictions) and so take everything as truth, with results intended as comic: *Earthman's Burden* (coll of linked stories **1957**), *Star Prince Charlie* (**1975**) and *Hoka!* (coll of linked stories **1984**). The **Last Viking** sequence – *The Golden Horn* (**1980**), *The Road of the Sea Horse* (**1980**) and *The Sign of the Raven* (**1980**) – is fantasy, as are the **King of Ys** novels, written with PA's wife Karen Anderson (1932–): *Roma Mater* (**1986**), *Gallicenae* (**1987**), *Dahut* (**1988**) and *The Dog and the Wolf* (**1988**).

Although many of the novels and stories listed as linked to series can be read as singletons, there seems little doubt that the interlinked complexity of reference and storyline in PA's fiction has somewhat muffled its effect in the marketplace. This situation has not been helped by a marked lack of focus in its publication, so that the interested reader will find considerable difficulty tracing both the items in a series and their intended relation to one another. With dozens of novels and hundreds of stories to his credit – all written with a resolute professionalism and widening range, though also with a marked disparity between copious storytelling skills and a certain banality in the creation of characters – PA is still not as well defined a figure in the pantheon of US sf as writers (like Isaac ASIMOV from the GOLDEN AGE OF SF and Frank HERBERT from a decade later) of about the same age and certainly no greater skill. Nonetheless he has been repeatedly honoured by the sf community, serving as SCIENCE FICTION WRITERS OF AMERICA President for 1972-3, and receiving 7 HUGOS for sf in shorter forms: in 1961 for "The Longest Voyage" (Best Short Story); in 1964 for "No Truce With Kings" (Best Short Story); in 1969 for "The Sharing of Flesh" (Best Novelette); in 1972 for "The Queen of Air and Darkness" (Best Novella), which also won a NEBULA; in 1973 for "Goat Song" (Best Novelette), which also won a Nebula; in 1979 for "Hunter's Moon" (Best Novelette); and in 1982 for "The Saturn Game" (Best Novella), which also won a Nebula. PA also won the Gandalf (Grand Master) Award for 1977.

Out of the welter of remaining titles, four singletons can be mentioned as outstanding. *The High Crusade* (**1960**) is a delightful wish-fulfilment conception; an alien SPACESHIP lands in medieval Europe where it is taken over by quick-thinking Baron Roger and his feudal colleagues who, when the ship takes them to the stars, soon trick, cajole, outfight and outbreed all the spacefaring races they can find, and found their own empire on feudal lines. It is PA's most joyful moment. *Tau Zero* (1967 *Gal* as "To Outlive Eternity"; exp **1970**) is less successful as fiction, though its speculations on COSMOLOGY are fascinating, and the hypothesis it embodies is strikingly well conceived. A spaceship from Earth, intended to fly near the speed of light so that humans can reach the stars without dying of old age (as a consequence of the time-dilatation described by the Lorentz-Fitzgerald equations), uncontrolledly continues to accelerate at a constant one gravity after reaching its intended terminal velocity, so that the disparity between ship-time and external time becomes ever greater: eons hurtle by outside, until eventually the Universe contracts to form a monobloc. After a new Big Bang the ship begins to slow gradually and the crew plans to settle a new planet in the universe that has succeeded our own. The felt scope of the narrative is convincingly sustained throughout, though the characters tend to soap opera. In *The Avatar* (**1978**) a solitary figure typical of PA's later work searches the Galaxy for an alien race sufficiently sophisticated to provide him with the means to confound a non-libertarian Earth government. *The Boat of a Million*

Years (**1989**) ambitiously follows the long lives of a group of immortals, whose growing disaffection with the recent course of Earth history again points up the sense of disenchantment noticeable in the later PA, along with a feeling that, in an inevitably decaying Universe, the tough thing (and the worthy thing) is to endure. [JC]

Other works: *The Broken Sword* (**1954**; rev **1971**); *Planet of No Return* (**1956** dos; vt *Question and Answer* **1978**); *The Enemy Stars* (**1959**; with one story added exp as coll **1987**); *Perish by the Sword* (**1959**) and *The Golden Slave* (**1960**; rev **1980**) and *Murder in Black Letter* (**1960**) and *Rogue Sword* (**1960**) and *Murder Bound* (**1962**), all associational; *Twilight World* (2 stories *ASF* 1947 including "Tomorrow's Children" with F.N. Waldrop; fixup **1961**); *Strangers from Earth* (coll **1961**); *Un-Man and Other Novellas* (coll **1962** dos); *After Doomsday* (**1962**); *The Makeshift Rocket* (**1958** *ASF* as "A Bicycle Built for Brew"; **1962** chap dos); *Shield* (**1963**); *Three Worlds to Conquer* (**1964**); *Time and Stars* (coll **1964**; with 1 story cut **1964** UK); *The Corridors of Time* (**1965**); *The Star Fox* (fixup **1965**); *The Fox, the Dog and the Griffin: A Folk Tale Adapted from the Danish of C. Molbeck* (**1966**), a juvenile fantasy; *World without Stars* (**1967**); *The Horn of Time* (coll **1968**); *Seven Conquests* (coll **1969**; vt *Conquests* **1981** UK); *Beyond the Beyond* (coll **1969**; with 1 story cut **1970** UK); *Tales of the Flying Mountains* (**1963-5** *ASF* as by Winston P. Sanders; fixup **1970**); *The Byworlder* (**1971**); *Operation Chaos* (coll of linked stories **1971**); *The Dancer from Atlantis* (**1971**) and *There Will Be Time* (**1972**), later assembled together as *There Will Be Time, and The Dancer from Atlantis* (omni **1982**); *Hrolf Kraki's Saga* (**1973**), a retelling of one of the greatest Icelandic sagas, associational; *The Queen of Air and Darkness and Other Stories* (coll **1973**); *Fire Time* (**1974**); *Inheritors of Earth* (**1974**) with Gordon EKLUND – the novel was in fact written by Eklund, based on a 1951 PA story published in *Future*; *The Many Worlds of Poul Anderson* (coll **1974**; vt *The Book of Poul Anderson* **1975**), not the same as *The Worlds of Poul Anderson* (omni **1974**), which assembles *Planet of No Return*, *The War of Two Worlds* and *World without Stars*; *Homeward and Beyond* (coll **1975**); *The Winter of the World* (**1975**), later assembled with *The Queen of Air and Darkness* as *The Winter of the World, and The Queen of Air and Darkness* (omni **1982**); *Homebrew* (coll **1976** chap), containing essays as well as stories; *The Best of Poul Anderson* (coll **1976**); *Two Worlds* (omni **1978**), which assembles *World without Stars* and *Planet of No Return*; *The Merman's Children* (**1979**); *The Demon of Scattery* (**1979**) with Mildred Downey Broxon (**1944-**); *Conan the Rebel* * (**1980**); *The Devil's Game* (**1980**); *Winners* (coll **1981**), a collection of PA's Hugo winners; *Fantasy* (coll **1981**); *The Dark between the Stars* (coll **1982**); the **Maurai** series comprising *Maurai and Kith* (coll **1982**), tales of post-catastrophe life, and *Orion Shall Rise* (**1983**), a pro-technology sequel, in which humanity once again aspires to the stars; *The Gods Laughed* (coll **1982**); *Conflict* (coll **1983**); *The Unicorn Trade* (coll **1984**) with Karen Anderson; *Past Times* (coll

1984); *Dialogue with Darkness* (coll **1985**); *No Truce with Kings* (**1963** *FSF*; **1989** chap dos); *Space Folk* (coll **1989**); *The Saturn Game* (**1981** *ASF*; **1989** chap dos); *Inconstant Star* * (coll **1991**), stories set in Larry NIVEN's **Man-Kzin** universe; *The Longest Voyage* (**1960** *ASF*; **1991** chap dos); *Losers' Night* (**1991** chap); *Kinship with the Stars* (coll **1991**); *How to Build a Planet* (**1991** chap), nonfiction; *The Armies of Elfland* (coll **1992**).

As editor: *West by One and by One* (anth **1965** chap); *Nebula Award Stories No 4* (anth **1969**); *The Day the Sun Stood Still* (anth **1972**), a common-theme anthology with Gordon R. Dickson and Robert SILVERBERG; *A World Named Cleopatra* (anth **1977**) ed Roger ELWOOD, a SHARED-WORLD anthology built around the title story and concept supplied by PA; 4 titles ed with Martin H. GREENBERG and Charles G. WAUGH, *Mercenaries of Tomorrow* (anth **1985**), *Terrorists of Tomorrow* (anth **1985**), *Time Wars* (anth **1986**) and *Space Wars* (anth **1988**); *The Night Fantastic* (anth **1991**) with Karen Anderson and (anon) Greenberg.

About the author: *Against Time's Arrow: The High Crusade of Poul Anderson* (**1978** chap) by Sandra MIESEL; *Poul Anderson: Myth-Maker and Wonder-Weaver: A Working Bibliography* (latest edition **1989** in 2 vols, each chap) by Gordon BENSON Jr and Phil STEPHENSEN-PAYNE.

See also: ALIENS; ANTHROPOLOGY; ASTEROIDS; ATLANTIS; BLACK HOLES; CLONES; COLONIZATION OF OTHER WORLDS; CRIME AND PUNISHMENT; CYBORGS; DESTINIES; ECOLOGY; ECONOMICS; END OF THE WORLD; ESCHATOLOGY; FANTASTIC VOYAGES; FANTASY; FASTER THAN LIGHT; FORCE FIELD; GALACTIC EMPIRES; GALAXY SCIENCE FICTION; GAMES AND SPORTS; GENETIC ENGINEERING; GODS AND DEMONS; GRAVITY; HEROES; HISTORY IN SF; HUMOUR; IMMORTALITY; JUPITER; *The* MAGAZINE OF FANTASY AND SCIENCE FICTION; MAGIC; MATTER TRANSMISSION; MUTANTS; MYTHOLOGY; NUCLEAR POWER; PLANETARY ROMANCE; POLITICS; PSI POWERS; PSYCHOLOGY; RELIGION; ROBERT HALE LIMITED; ROBOTS; SCIENTIFIC ERRORS; SENSE OF WONDER; SOCIAL DARWINISM; SOCIOLOGY; SPACE FLIGHT; STARS; SUN; SUPERMAN; TECHNOLOGY; TERRAFORMING; TIME PARADOXES; UNDER THE SEA; UTOPIAS; VENUS; WAR; WEAPONS.

ANDERSON, WILLIAM C(HARLES) (**1920-**)
USAF pilot and writer in various genres who published his first sf, *The Valley of the Gods* (**1957**) as Andy Anderson. Like his *Pandemonium on the Potomac* (**1966**), it features a father and daughter: in the former book they philosophize about the extinction of mankind; in the latter they act on their anxiety about Man's imminent self-destruction, blowing up a US city as a Dreadful Warning. *Penelope* (**1963**) and *Adam M-1* (**1964**) are further sf comedies, the former concerned with a communicating porpoise – which appears also in *Penelope, the Damp Detective* (**1974**) – and the latter with an ANDROID, the first Astrodynamically Designed Aerospace Man. [JC]

Other works: *Five, Four, Three, Two, One – Pffff* (**1960**); *The Gooney Bird* (**1968**); *The Apoplectic Palm Tree* (**1969**).

See also: ADAM AND EVE.

ANDOM, R. Pseudonym of UK writer Alfred Walter

Barrett (1869-1920), who remains best known for *We Three and Troddles: A Tale of London Life* (**1894**) and other light fiction in the mode of popular figures like Jerome K. Jerome (1859-1927). His sf and fantasy were similarly derivative; titles of interest include *The Strange Adventure of Roger Wilkins and Other Stories* (coll **1895**), *The Identity Exchange: A Story of Some Odd Transformations* (**1902**; vt *The Marvellous Adventures of Me* 1904), *The Enchanted Ship: A Story of Mystery with a Lot of Imagination* (**1908**) and *The Magic Bowl, and the Blue-Stone Ring: Oriental Tales with Occi(or Acci)dental Fittings* (coll **1909**), all exhibiting an uneasy *fin de siècle* flippancy characteristic of F. ANSTEY but with less weight. *In Fear of a Throne* (**1911**) is a RURITANIAN fantasy. [JC]

ANDRE, ALIX ◊ Gail KIMBERLY.

ANDREAS, JURGEN ◊ Hans Joachim ALPERS.

ANDREISSEN, DAVID ◊ David C. POYER.

ANDREWS, FELICIA ◊ Charles L. GRANT.

ANDREWS, KEITH WILLIAM Technically a house name, though all titles here listed are in fact by US writer William H(enry) Keith Jr (1950-   ). The **Freedom's Rangers** sequence of military-sf adventures, whose heroes roam into various epochs to combat the KGB, comprises *Freedom's Rangers* (**1989**), *Freedom's Rangers #2: Raiders of the Revolution* (**1989**), *#3: Search and Destroy* (**1990**), *#4: Treason in Time* (**1990**), *#5: Sink the Armada* (**1990**) and *#6: Snow Kill* (**1991**). The first volume features a commando raid through time to kill Hitler; as some of the titles indicate, the targets thereafter vary. It may be that the course of real history has determined the progress of the series.

Under his own name Keith has written two **Battletech** game ties (◊ GAMES AND TOYS): *Mercenary's Star*∗ (**1987**) and *The Price of Glory*∗ (**1987**); *Renegades Honor*∗ (**1988**) is another game novelization. [JC]

ANDROID Film (1982). New World. Dir Aaron Lipstadt, starring Klaus Kinski, Brie Howard, Norbert Weisser, Crofton Hardester, Don Opper. Screenplay James Reigle and Opper, based on a story by Will Reigle. 80 mins. Colour.

The co-scriptwriter, Don Opper, plays Max, the innocent ANDROID (part flesh, part metal) who does imitations of James Stewart and works for mad Dr Daniel (Kinski) in a space laboratory, soon invaded by three criminals. He experiences sex ("Max, you're a doll!"), is programmed to become a ruthless killer just as we were accepting him as human, participates in the awakening of a female android, learns Daniel's true nature (a plot twist stolen from ALIEN) and gets the girl. *A* is made with skill and panache, is good on android politics (for which one might read "working-class politics"), and is one of the most confident sf movies yet made, despite its low budget. The scriptwriters are infinitely more at home with the themes of written sf than is usual in sf cinema. Lipstadt's subsequent sf movie, CITY LIMITS (1984), was disappointing. [PN]

ANDROIDS The term "android", which means "manlike", was not commonly used in sf until the 1940s.

The first modern use seems to have been in Jack WILLIAMSON's *The Cometeers* (1936; **1950**). The word was initially used of automata, and the form "androides" first appeared in English in 1727 in reference to supposed attempts by the alchemist Albertus Magnus (*c*1200-1280) to create an artificial man. In contemporary usage "android" usually denotes an artificial human of organic substance, although it is sometimes applied to manlike machines, just as the term ROBOT is still occasionally applied (as by its originator Karel ČAPEK) to organic entities. The conventional distinction was first popularized by Edmond HAMILTON in his CAPTAIN FUTURE series, where Captain Future's sidekicks were a robot, an android and a brain in a box. The most important modern exceptions to the conventional rule are to be found in the works of Philip K. DICK.

The notion of artificial humans is an old one, embracing the GOLEM of Jewish mythology as well as alchemical homunculi. Until the 19th century, though, it was widely believed that organic compounds could not be synthesized, and that humanoid creatures of flesh and blood would therefore have to be created either by magical means or, as in Mary SHELLEY's *Frankenstein* (**1818**), by the gruesome process of assembly. Even after the discovery that organic molecules could be synthesized, some time passed before, in *R.U.R.* (**1920**; trans **1923**), Čapek imagined androids "grown" in vats as mass-produced slaves; these "robots" were made so artfully as to acquire souls, and eventually conquered their makers.

There was some imaginative resistance to the idea of the android because it seemed a more outrageous breach of divine prerogative than the building of humanoid automata. Several authors toyed with the idea but did not carry it through: the androids in *The Uncreated Man* (**1912**) by Austin Fryers and in *The Chemical Baby* (**1924**) by J. Storer CLOUSTON prove to be hoaxes. Edgar Rice BURROUGHS played a similar trick in *The Monster Men* (1913; **1929**), but did include some authentic artificial men as well, as he did also in *Synthetic Men of Mars* (**1940**).

In the early sf PULP MAGAZINES androids were rare, authors concentrating almost exclusively on mechanical contrivances. It was not until after WWII that Clifford SIMAK wrote the influential *Time and Again* (**1951**; vt *First He Died* 1953), the first of many stories in which androids seek emancipation from slavery; here they are assisted in their cause by the discovery that, in common with all living creatures, they have ALIEN "commensals" – sf substitutes for souls. Sf writers almost invariably take the side of the androids against their human masters, sometimes eloquently: the emancipation of the biologically engineered Underpeople is a key theme in Cordwainer SMITH's **Instrumentality** series; a Millennarian android religion is memorably featured in Robert SILVERBERG's *Tower of Glass* (**1970**); and androids whose personalities are based on literary models are effectively featured in *Port Eternity* (**1982**) by C.J. CHERRYH. Cherryh's *Cyteen* (**1988**) is one of the few novels to attempt to present a society into which androids are fully integrated. Other pleas for emancipation are featured in "Down among the Dead Men" (1954) by William TENN, *Slavers of Space* (**1960** dos; rev as *Into the Slave Nebula* 1968) by John BRUNNER and *Birthright* (**1975**) by Kathleen SKY, but the liberated androids in Charles L. GRANT's *The Shadow of Alpha* (**1976**) and its sequels are treated far more ambivalently. An android is used as an innocent observer of human follies in Charles PLATT's comedy *Less than Human* (**1986**), and to more sharply satirical effect in Stephen FINE's *Molly Dear: The Autobiography of an Android, or How I Came to my Senses, Was Repaired, Escaped my Master, and Was Educated in the Ways of the World* (**1988**).

Androids also feature, inevitably, in stories which hinge on the confusion of real and ersatz, including "Made in USA" (1953) by J.T. MCINTOSH, "Synth" (1966) by Keith ROBERTS, the murder mystery "Fondly Fahrenheit" (1954) by Alfred BESTER, and *Replica* (**1987**) by Richard BOWKER. The confusion between real and synthetic is central to the work of Philip K. Dick, who tends to use the terms "android" and "robot" interchangeably; he discusses the importance this theme had for him in his essays "The Android and the Human" (1972) and "Man, Android and Machine" (1976), both of which are reprinted in *The Dark-Haired Girl* (coll **1988**). His most notable novels dealing with the subject are *Do Androids Dream of Electric Sheep?* (**1968**) and *We Can Build You* (**1972**).

Stories featuring androids designed specifically for use at least in part as sexual partners have become commonplace as editorial taboos have relaxed; examples include *The Silver Metal Lover* (**1982**) by Tanith LEE and *The Hormone Jungle* (**1988**) by Robert REED.

Science Fiction Thinking Machines (anth **1954**) ed Groff CONKLIN has a brief section featuring android stories; *The Pseudo-People* (anth **1965** vt *Almost Human: Androids in Science Fiction*) ed William F. NOLAN mostly consists of stories of robots capable of imitating men. [BS]

ANDROMEDA BREAKTHROUGH, THE UK tv serial (1962). A BBC TV production. Prod John ELLIOT, written Fred HOYLE, Elliot. 6 episodes, 5 at 45 mins, the 6th 50 mins. B/w. The cast included Peter Halliday, Mary Morris, Barry Linehan, John Hollis, Susan Hampshire.

In this sequel to A FOR ANDROMEDA the android woman built according to instructions from the stars is played by Susan Hampshire, not Julie Christie; she has not drowned, as previously thought. She is kidnapped along with scientist Fleming (Halliday) by a Middle Eastern oil state where a new COMPUTER has been built according to plans stolen from the Scottish original. This is used by an international cartel in an attempt at world domination. The plot becomes ever more melodramatic. World weather is changed by the influence of computer-designed bacteria on the

oceans. The extraterrestrial beings who sent the original computer instructions are not, we are implausibly told, just malicious: they are merely undertaking social engineering on other worlds by administering salutary shocks. (It seems that yellow-star races tend to wipe themselves out using nuclear weapons or other devices.) This was a less powerful serial than its memorable predecessor. The noveliza-tion is *The Andromeda Breakthrough* * (**1964**) by Fred Hoyle and John Elliot. [PN]

ANDROMEDA NEBULA, THE ◊ TUMANNOST ANDRO-MEDY.

ANDROMEDA STRAIN, THE Film (1971). Universal. Dir Robert WISE, starring Arthur Hill, David Wayne, James Olson, Kate Reid. Screenplay Nelson Gidding, based on *The Andromeda Strain* (**1969**) by Michael CRICHTON. 130 mins. Colour.

This film, whose director had in 1951 made the classic sf film *The* DAY THE EARTH STOOD STILL, concerns a microscopic organism, inadvertently brought to Earth on a returning space probe, which causes the instant death of everyone in the vicinity of the probe's landing (near a small town) with the excep-tion of a baby and the town drunk. These two are isolated in a vast underground laboratory complex, where a group of scientists attempts to establish the nature of the alien organism. The real enemy seems to be not the Andromeda virus but technology itself: it is mankind's technology that brings the virus to Earth, and the scientists in the laboratory sequences – most of the film – are made to seem puny and fallible compared to the gleaming electronic marvels that surround them; they have, in effect, become unwanted organisms within a superior body. (Wise deliberately avoided using famous actors in order to get the muted performances he wished to juxtapose with the assertive machinery.) The celebration of technology is only apparent – the film, despite its implausible but exciting ending, is coldly ironic, and rather pessimistic. [PN]

ANDROMEDA THE MYSTERIOUS ◊ TUMANNOST ANDROMEDY.

ANDY WARHOL'S FRANKENSTEIN ◊ FRANKEN-STEIN.

ANESTIN, VICTOR [r] ◊ ROMANIA.

ANET, CLAUDE Pseudonym of Swiss writer Jean Schopfer (1868-1931). His sf novel *La fin d'un monde* (**1925**; trans Jeffery E. Jeffery as *The End of a World* **1927** US; vt *Abyss*) describes the cultural destruction of a prehistoric Ice Age people by a more advanced culture. [JC]

See also: ORIGIN OF MAN.

ANIMAL FARM ◊ George ORWELL.

ANMAR, FRANK [s] ◊ William F. NOLAN.

ANNA LIVIA Working name of Irish-born UK writer and editor Anna Livia Julian Brawn (1955-), a lesbian feminist of radical views, which she has advanced in tales of considerable wit, though at book length her effects become uneasy. Her second novel, *Accommodation Offered* (**1985**), invokes a spirit world which has a ring of fantasy. Her third, *Bulldozer Rising* (1988), is an sf DYSTOPIA which depicts a culture rigidly dominated by young males in which "old" women, unpersoned and unperceived from the age of 40, represent the only remaining human potential, the only hope for revolt. About half the stories assembled in *Saccharin Cyanide* (coll 1990) present similar lessons in sf terms. [JC]

Other works: *Minimax* (1992), a feminist vampire novel.

ANONYMOUS SF AUTHORS This rubric covers the authors of works which, in their first edition, appeared with no indication of authorship whatsoever, and any in which authorship is indicated only by a row of asterisks or some similar symbol. Works attributed to "the author of . . ." are considered only if the work referred to is itself anonymous. Cases where subsequent editions reveal authorship are not excluded. All other attributions are regarded as PSEUDONYMS. Anonymously edited sf ANTHOLOGIES are not particularly common, unlike the case with ghost and horror stories.

Before the 20th century literary anonymity was prevalent. Though this was most notable among the numerous works of Grub-Street fictional journalism of the early 19th century, many novels of a higher status likewise hid their authorship. On some occasions the practice was adopted by well known writers – e.g., Lord LYTTON – when the content of a novel differed radically from their earlier writings; although such works are "anonymous" in a bibliographic sense (and so within our purview), their authorship was often widely known at the time of publication.

Other authors used anonymity because their work was controversial, an attribute common in early sf. Such was the case with UTOPIAN novels, where the depiction of an ideal state highlighted faults the writer saw in his (or, rarely, her) own society. Falling into this category is *The Reign of George VI, 1900-1925* (1763), the earliest known example of the future-WAR novel. Showing the forceful George VI becoming master of Europe following his successes in the European War of 1917-20, the anonymous UK author gave no consideration to possible change in society, technology or military strategy, his depicted future being very similar to contemporary reality. Of more importance in the HISTORY OF SF is *L'an deux mille quatre cent quarante* (1771 France; trans W. Hooper as *Memoirs of the Year Two Thousand Five Hundred* 1772 UK) (by L.-S. MERCIER), the first futuristic novel to show change as an inevitable process. It was widely translated and reprinted, inspiring many imitators. Also anonymous, but set in an imaginary country, was the first US utopian work, *Equality, or A History of Lithconia* (1802 *The Temple of Reason* as "Equality: A Political Romance"; 1837), which depicted a communal economy in a society where conurbations had been rejected in favour of an equal distribution of houses.

Other anonymous utopian works, some of consid-

erable importance, appeared throughout the 19th century. Probably the most influential was Lytton's *The Coming Race* (1871). Of similar importance is W.H. HUDSON's *A Crystal Age* (1887), whose Darwinian extrapolation, although obscured by the author's animistic view of the world, shows humankind evolved towards a hive structure (◊ HIVE-MINDS) and living in perfect harmony with Nature. Another noteworthy Darwinian novel was *Colymbia* (1873) (by Robert Ellis DUDGEON, a friend of and physician to Samuel BUTLER), which describes a remote archipelago where humans have evolved into amphibious beings. Integral to this gentle SATIRE is a scene in which the country's leading philosophers debate their common origins with the seal family. Particular mention should also be made of Ellis James Davis (?1847-1935), author of the highly imaginative and carefully detailed novels *Pyrna, a Commune, or Under the Ice* (1875) and *Etymonia* (1875) – both utopias, the first located under a glacier, the second on an ISLAND – and of *Coralia: A Plaint of Futurity* (1876), a supernatural fantasy.

Other anonymous sf authors eschewed the utopian format for a more direct attack on aspects of contemporary society. Following the build-up in power by Germany in the early 1870s there appeared *The Battle of Dorking; Reminiscences of a Volunteer* (1871 chap) (by Sir George T. CHESNEY), the most socially influential sf novel of all time. Advocating a restructuring of the UK military system to meet a conceived INVASION, it provoked a storm in Parliament and enjoyed numerous reprints and translations throughout the world; it inspired many anonymous refutations.

Many other anonymous sf works, by contrast, enjoyed only rapid obscurity, in some case to the detriment of sf's development. Perhaps the three most important of these are: *Annals of the Twenty-ninth Century, or The Autobiography of the Tenth President of the World Republic* (1874) (by Andrew BLAIR), a massive work describing the step-by-step COLONIZATION of our Solar System; *In the Future: A Sketch in Ten Chapters* (1875 chap), the story of a struggle for religious tolerance in a future European empire; and *Thoth: A Romance* (1888) (by J.S. Nicholson [1850-1927]), an impressive LOST-WORLD novel set in Hellenic times and depicting a scientifically advanced race using airships in the North African desert.

Among the diversity of ideas expressed by anonymous sf authors were the stress inflicted upon an ape (◊APES AND CAVEMEN) when taught to speak, in *The Curse of Intellect* (1895), the emancipation of women, in the futuristic satire *The Revolt of Man* (1882) (by Sir Walter BESANT) and, in *Man Abroad: A Yarn of Some Other Century* (1887), the notion that humankind will take its international disputes into space.

The Checklist of Fantastic Literature (1948) by Everett F. BLEILER lists 127 anonymous works (though many are fantasy rather than sf). A number of anonymous authors whose identities are now known receive entries in this volume, the most famous being Mary

SHELLEY, author of *Frankenstein, or The Modern Prometheus* (**1818**). Others are too numerous and their works too slight to merit mention. *The Supplemental Checklist of Fantastic Literature* (**1963**) by Bradford M. DAY adds a further 27 titles to Bleiler's total, and there are certainly more waiting to be found – such as *The History of Benjamin Kennicott* (**1932**).

Anonymous sf authors are still with us today, particularly in the COMICS and in BOYS' PAPERS, often retaining their role as social critics or outrageous prognosticators. However, most modern authors, when seeking to retain their privacy, make use of PSEUDONYMS. Very few anonymous books – except for anthologies (which are often released without crediting the compiler) and erotica – are published today. [JE]

ANOTHER FLIP FOR DOMINICK ◊ *The* FLIPSIDE OF DOMINICK HIDE.

ANSIBLE 1. The imaginary device invented by Ursula K. LE GUIN for instantaneous communication between two points, regardless of the distance between them. The physics which led to its invention is described in *The Dispossessed* (**1974**), but the device is mentioned in a number of the **Hainish** series of stories written before *The Dispossessed*, and indeed is central to their rationale. It compares interestingly with James BLISH's DIRAC COMMUNICATOR. (◊ FASTER THAN LIGHT *and* COMMUNICATION *for further discussion of both.*) The ansible has since been adopted as a useful device by several other writers. [PN]

2. Fanzine (1979-87 and 1991 onwards), first sequence being 50 issues, quarto, 4-10pp, ed from Reading, UK, by David LANGFORD. *A* is a "newszine", a fanzine that carries news on sf and FANDOM. It replaced the earlier UK newszine *Checkpoint* (1971-9, 100 issues) ed Peter Roberts (briefly ed Ian Maule and ed Darroll Pardoe), which in turn had replaced *Skyrack* (1959-71, 96 issues) ed Ron Bennett. *A*'s news items were given sparkle by Langford's witty delivery. *A* was initially monthly, but latterly gaps between its issues grew ever longer. In 1987, at the time of but not due to the appearance of a later newszine, CRITICAL WAVE, Langford – who had long expressed weariness with the labour of producing *A* – folded it. However, he revived *A* in 1991, the second sequence being an approximately monthly A4 2pp newssheet with occasional extra issues (given ½ numbers), beginning with #51. *A* won a HUGO in 1987, and its editor won Hugos as Best Fan Writer in 1985, 1987, 1989, 1990, 1991 and 1992. [RH]

ANSON, AUGUST (? -) UK writer whose *When Woman Reigns* (**1938**) transports its protagonist to first the 26th and then the 36th century. Author and hero take a rather dim view of these two periods, because in both men are subservient to women. [JC]

ANSON, CAPTAIN (CHARLES VERNON) (1841-?) UK writer, in the Royal Navy 1859-96. His future-WAR tale, *The Great Anglo-American War of 1900* (**1896** chap), warrants modest interest for the worldwide scope of the conflict and for the UK's use of a new invention to destroy San Francisco and win the war. For verisimilitude, the tale should perhaps have been set many years further into the future. [JC]

ANSTEY, F. Pseudonym of Thomas Anstey Guthrie (1856-1934), UK writer and humorist, best known for his many contributions to the magazine *Punch* and for his classic satirical fantasies, most of which follow the pattern of introducing some magical item into contemporary society, with chaotic consequences. These were widely imitated by many writers, including R. ANDOM, W.D. Darlington (1890-1979) and Richard Marsh (1857-1915), and thus became the archetypes of a distinctive subgenre of "Ansteyan fantasies". In his most successful work, *Vice Versa, or A Lesson to Fathers* (**1882**; rev **1883**), a Victorian gentleman and his schoolboy son exchange personalities; the novel has to date been twice filmed and at least twice adapted as a tv serial. In *The Tinted Venus* (**1885**) a young man accidentally revives the Roman goddess of love, and in *A Fallen Idol* (**1886**) an oriental deity exerts a sinister influence on a young artist. The protagonist of *The Brass Bottle* (**1900**) acquires the services of a djinn; a stage version is *The Brass Bottle: A Farcical Fantastic Play* (**1911**). In *Brief Authority* (**1915**) reverses the pattern, with a Victorian matron established as queen of the Brothers Grimm's Märchenland. FA's work comes closest to sf in *Tourmalin's Time Cheques* (**1891**; vt *The Time Bargain*), one of the earliest TIME-PARADOX stories. The anonymously published *The Statement of Stella Maberley, Written by Herself* (**1896**) is an interesting story of abnormal PSYCHOLOGY. [BS]

Other works: *The Black Poodle and Other Tales* (coll **1884**); *The Talking Horse* (coll **1891**); *Paleface and Redskin, and Other Stories for Girls and Boys* (coll **1898**); *Only Toys!* (**1903**), for children; *Salted Almonds* (coll **1906**); *Percy and Others* (coll **1915**), the first 5 stories in which feature the adventures of a bee; *The Last Load* (coll **1928**); *Humour and Fantasy* (coll **1931**).

ANTHOLOGIES Before the late 1940s, sf short stories, novellas and novelettes (◊ HUGO *for definitions*) were largely restricted to MAGAZINES. (Magazines are, of course, a form of anthology, but they are not so counted in this encyclopedia.) Since then, increasingly, many readers have been introduced to sf through stories collected in books. Books are less fragile, kept in print longer, available in libraries and (especially for young readers in the days of the lurid PULP MAGAZINES) more acceptable to parents. The history of sf's ever-increasing respectability over the past half century has been in part the history of the gradual displacement of magazines by books, especially paperback books – although many anthology series have been given their initial publication in hardcover.

Much sf was anthologized in book form from quite early on, in a variety of fantasy and weird-fiction collections, but none of these was exclusively sf, although *The Moon Terror and Other Stories* (anth **1927**) ed A.G. Birch, a collection of four stories from WEIRD TALES, came close to it. The earliest sf anthology could more properly be described as an anthology of PROTO SCIENCE FICTION. It is *Popular Romances* (anth **1812**) ed Henry Weber, and contains *Gulliver's Travels* (**1726**) by Jonathan SWIFT, *Journey to the World Underground* (**1741**) by Ludwig HOLBERG, *Peter Wilkins* (**1751**) by Robert PALTOCK, *Robinson Crusoe* (**1719**) by Daniel DEFOE and *The History of Automathes* (**1745**) by John Kirkby; the latter is a lost-race (◊ LOST WORLDS) story set in the Pacific Ocean.

The usually accepted candidate as first sf anthology is *Adventures to Come* (anth **1937**) ed J. Berg Esenwein. It was also sf's first ORIGINAL ANTHOLOGY – i.e., its stories were all previously unpublished – but they were by unknowns, and it seems the anthology had no influence at all. Much more important was *The Other Worlds* (anth **1941**) ed Phil STONG, a hardcover publication reprinting stories by Harry BATES, Lester DEL REY, Henry KUTTNER, Theodore STURGEON and many other well known writers from the sf magazines. The first notable paperback anthology was *The Pocket Book of Science-Fiction* (anth **1943**) ed Donald A. WOLLHEIM, 8 of whose 10 stories are still well remembered, an extraordinarily high batting average considering that half a century has since elapsed.

The year that presaged the advancing flood was 1946, when two respectable hardcover publishers commissioned huge anthologies, both milestones. In Feb 1946 came *The Best of Science Fiction* (anth **1946**) ed Groff CONKLIN, containing 40 stories in 785pp, and in Aug came *Adventures in Time and Space* (anth **1946**) ed Raymond J. HEALY and J. Francis MCCOMAS, containing 35 stories in 997pp. The latter was the superior work and even today reads like a roll of honour, as all the great names of the first two decades of GENRE SF parade past. But Conklin's book is not to be despised, including as it does Sturgeon's "Killdozer" (1944), Robert A. HEINLEIN's "Universe" (1941) and Murray LEINSTER's "First Contact" (1945).

Both Conklin and Healy went on to do further pioneering work with anthologies. Conklin specialized in thematic anthologies, of which two of the earliest were his *Invaders of Earth* (anth **1952**) and *Science Fiction Thinking Machines* (anth **1954**). The thematic anthology has since become an important part of sf publishing, and many such books are listed in this volume at the end of the relevant theme entries.

Healy did not invent the original sf anthology, but he was one of the first to edit one successfully. His *New Tales of Space and Time* (anth **1951**) contains such well remembered stories as "Bettyann" by Kris NEVILLE, "Here There Be Tygers" by Ray BRADBURY and "The Quest for Saint Aquin" by Anthony BOUCHER. Kendell Foster CROSSEN was not slow to take the hint, and half of his compilation *Future Tense* (anth **1953**) consists of original stories, including "Beanstalk" by James BLISH. Wollheim had produced (anonymously) an original anthology, too: *The Girl with the Hungry Eyes and Other Stories* (anth **1949**), the title story being by Fritz LEIBER.

Until the 1970s the original anthology went from strength to strength, becoming an important alternative market to the sf magazines. The STAR SCIENCE FICTION STORIES series (1953-9) ed Frederik POHL, of which there were 6 vols in all, was its next important landmark. John CARNELL followed, in the UK, with his NEW WRITINGS IN SF series (1964-78; ed Kenneth BULMER from #22), with 30 vols in all. This was followed rather more dramatically in the USA by Damon KNIGHT, whose policy was more experimental and literary than Carnell's, with his ORBIT series (1965-80), which published 21 vols. Since then the most influential original anthology series have been Harlan ELLISON's two DANGEROUS VISIONS anthologies (**1968** and **1972**), Robert SILVERBERG's NEW DIMENSIONS series (1971-81), 10 vols in all, and Terry CARR's UNIVERSE series (1971-87), 17 vols in all. The zenith of influence of the original anthologies was probably the early to mid-1970s; they became a less important component of sf PUBLISHING in the 1980s. Nonetheless, the 1970s saw a remarkable number of HUGO and NEBULA nominees drawn from the ranks of the original anthologies, including a good few winners, and this is a measure of the change of emphasis from magazines to books. Other original anthologies which, like the above, receive separate entries in this volume are BERKLEY SHOWCASE, CHRYSALIS, DESTINIES, FULL SPECTRUM, INFINITY, L. RON HUBBARD PRESENTS WRITERS OF THE FUTURE, NEW VOICES, NOVA, OTHER EDENS, PULPHOUSE: THE HARDBACK MAGAZINE, QUARK, STELLAR and SYNERGY; *New Worlds Quarterly* (◊ NEW WORLDS) was also in book format. This list is not fully comprehensive, but contains most of the sf original anthology series that ran for three or more numbers.

Another original anthology series is WILD CARDS, ed George R.R. MARTIN, which is also an interesting representative of a kind of volume that began to flourish only in the 1980s, the SHARED-WORLD anthology. The majority of these are fantasy rather than sf.

Sf has been one of the few areas of literature to have kept alive the art of the short story. It is therefore unfortunate that, as sf-magazine circulations dropped further in the 1980s, so did the popularity of original anthologies. Nevertheless, as of the early 1990s, the quality of the best sf short-story writing remains high, and fears expressed about the imminent death of sf short fiction caused by shrinking markets seem premature.

The general standard of reprint anthologies has dropped since the mid-1960s, probably because the vast backlog of sf magazines had been mined and remined for gold and not much was left, though obviously new collectable stories are published every year. In terms of numbers of anthologies published, however, there has been no very perceptible falling off. Two extraordinarily prolific anthologists have been Roger ELWOOD, from 1964 to 1977, and Martin Harry GREENBERG, from 1974 to date, both of them often in partnership with others and both specializing in thematic anthologies. Greenberg, who has edited more anthologies than anyone else in sf, maintains the higher standard.

The other two important categories of anthology are the several "Best" series, and the various series devoted to award-winning stories. The "Best" concept was introduced to sf by Everett F. BLEILER and T.E. DIKTY, who between them edited 6 annual vols, beginning with *The Best Science-Fiction Stories 1949* (anth **1949**); Dikty went on to edit a further 3 vols alone in 1955, 1956 and 1958 (1957 was omitted). Judith MERRIL's record was long and distinguished, with 12 annual vols (1967 was omitted) beginning with *SF: The Year's Greatest Science-Fiction and Fantasy Stories and Novelettes* (anth **1956**) and ending with *SF 12* (anth **1968**; vt *The Best of Sci-Fi 12* UK 1970). Merril's anthologies were always lively, with an emphasis on stories of wit and literacy, and certainly helped to improve standards in sf generally. The editors of the major magazines, notably *ASF*, *FSF*, *Gal* and *NW*, published "Best" anthologies of one kind or another from their own pages, most consistently and influentially in the case of *FSF*.

Anthologies had a great deal to do with finding a new audience for sf in the UK. Here the important date was 1955, when Edmund CRISPIN launched his **Best SF** series (1955-70), 7 vols in all. Among the finest anthologies produced, always gracefully introduced, they were not selected on an annual basis and are thus not directly comparable to Merril's books. Later important anthologists in the UK were Kingsley AMIS and Robert CONQUEST with their **Spectrum** series (1961-6), 5 vols in all, and Brian W. ALDISS with the **Penguin Science Fiction** series (1961-4), 3 vols in all. Aldiss remained an active anthologist for some time, and with Harry HARRISON he edited 9 **Best SF** books annually 1967-75, beginning with *Best SF: 1967* (anth **1968** US; vt *The Year's Best Science Fiction No 1* UK).

More recent "Best" series have been edited by Lester DEL REY (1971-5), starting with *Best Science Fiction Stories of the Year (1971)* (anth **1972**), from E.P. Dutton & Co., Del Rey's successor as editor of this series being Gardner DOZOIS (1976-81); by Donald A. Wollheim with Terry Carr (1965-71) from ACE BOOKS starting with *World's Best Science Fiction: 1965* (anth **1965**); by Wollheim alone (1972-81) and with Arthur W. SAHA (1982-90) for DAW BOOKS, starting with *The 1972 Annual World's Best SF* (anth **1972**); by Carr alone (1972-87), first for BALLANTINE, later various publishers, UK edition from GOLLANCZ, beginning with *The Best Science Fiction of the Year* (anth **1972**); by Gardner Dozois alone (1984 to date), beginning with *The Year's Best Science Fiction, First Annual Collection* (anth **1984**), from BLUEJAY BOOKS to 1986, then from St Martin's (with UK reprint from Robinson) starting with *Year's Best Science Fiction, Fourth Annual Collection* (anth **1987**; vt *The Mammoth Book of Best New Science Fiction* UK) and *Year's Best Science Fiction, Fifth Annual Collection* (anth **1988**; vt *Best New SF 2* UK); and by David S. GARNETT in the UK (1988-90), in a short-lived but interesting series starting with *The Orbit Science*

Fiction Yearbook (anth **1988**). Tastes in these matters are subjective, but the critical consensus is clearly that Terry Carr's selection was on the whole the most reliable through to the mid-1980s, and that his mantle has passed to Gardner Dozois, whose selection is now both the biggest and the best. Carr's and Dozois's "Year's Best" collections are required reading for anybody seriously interested in sf in short forms.

Anthologies consisting of award-winning stories, of course, are of an especially high standard. Hugo-winning short fiction has been collected in a series of anthologies ed Isaac ASIMOV (*whom see for details*). Nebula-winning short fiction has been regularly anthologized along with some runners up, and also winners of the Rhysling Award for POETRY; the **Science Fiction Hall of Fame** stories, which like the Nebulas are judged by members of the SCIENCE FICTION WRITERS OF AMERICA, have also been anthologized (*for details of both these anthology series see* NEBULA).

A number of anthologies from the 1970s onwards have been specifically designed for teaching SF IN THE CLASSROOM, and some are discussed in that entry. Also important have been various anthologies characterizing particular historical periods of sf through reprinting their most interesting stories. Sam MOSKO-WITZ has been an important editor in this area, as have been Mike ASHLEY, Brian W. Aldiss and Harry Harrison, and Isaac Asimov and Martin Harry Greenberg with a series in which each book reprints stories all from a single year, beginning with *Isaac Asimov Presents the Great SF Stories Volume 1, 1939* (anth **1979**), from DAW Books, complete in 24 vols.

Aside from those mentioned above, notable anthologists have included Michael BISHOP, Anthony BOUCHER, Jack DANN, Ellen DATLOW, August DERLETH, Thomas M. DISCH, James E. GUNN, David HARTWELL, Richard LUPOFF and Barry N. MALZBERG. There have been many others.

A problem for all sf readers is the location in book collections or anthologies of short stories that have been recommended to them. Early indexes to sf anthologies, by Walter R. COLE and Frederick Siemon, have been superseded by a series of books by William G. CONTENTO, which are essential tools of reference for the serious sf researcher (*see also* BIBLIOGRAPHIES), beginning with *Index to Science Fiction Anthologies and Collections* (**1978**) and *Index to Science Fiction Anthologies and Collections: 1977-1983* (**1984**). After that, researchers need to turn to the annual compilations produced by Contento with Charles N. BROWN and published by LOCUS Press (◊ CONTENTO *for details*). [PN]

ANTHONY, PIERS Working name of US writer Piers Anthony Dillingham Jacob (1934-   ) for all his published work. Born in England, he was educated in the USA and took out US citizenship in 1958. He began publishing short stories with "Possible to Rue" for *Fantastic* in 1963, and for the next decade appeared fairly frequently in the magazines, though he has more and more concentrated on longer forms; his early work is fairly represented in *Anthonology* (coll **1985**). His two most ambitious novels came early in his career. *Chthon* (**1967**), his first, is a complexly structured adventure of self-discovery partially set in a vast underground prison, and making ambitious though sometimes over-baroque use of PASTORAL and other parallels; its sequel, *Phthor* (**1975**), is less far-reaching, less irritating, but also less involving. PA's second genuinely ambitious novel is the extremely long *Macroscope* (**1969**; cut 1972 UK), whose complicated SPACE-OPERA plot combines astrology with old-fashioned SENSE-OF-WONDER concepts like the use of the planet Neptune as a spaceship. In constructing a series of sf devices in this book to carry across his concern with representing the unity of all phenomena, microscopic to macroscopic, PA evokes themes from SUPERMAN to COSMOLOGY and Jungian PSYCHOLOGY; of all his works, this novel alone manages to seem adequately structured to convey the burden of a sometimes mercilessly hasty imagination.

The allegorical implications of *Macroscope* received more expansive – but less sustained or intense – treatment in two later series. In the **Tarot** series – *God of Tarot* (**1979**), *Vision of Tarot* (**1980**) and *Faith of Tarot* (**1980**), all recast as *Tarot* (omni **1987**) – various protagonists engage in a quest for the meaning of an emblem-choked Universe. The **Incarnations of Immortality** series – *On a Pale Horse* (**1983**), *Bearing an Hourglass* (**1984**), *With a Tangled Skein* (**1985**), *Wielding a Red Sword* (**1986**), *Being a Green Mother* (**1987**), *For Love of Evil* (**1988**) and *And Eternity* (**1990**) – features protagonists who are themselves embodiments of a meaningful Universe, representing in their very being aspects of the Universe like Death and Fate. The final volume involves a search to replace an increasingly indifferent God.

In distinct contrast to complex works like these lies the post-HOLOCAUST sequence comprising *Sos the Rope* (**1968**), winner of the $5000 award from Pyramid Books, FSF and Kent Productions, *Var the Stick* (**1972** UK; cut 1973 US) and *Neq the Sword* (**1975**), a combat-oriented trilogy assembled as *Battle Circle* (omni **1978**). Here and in other novels PA resorts to stripped-down protagonists with monosyllabic and/or generic names, like Sos or Neq, or like Cal, Veg and Aquilon, whose adventures on various planets make up his second trilogy, *Omnivore* (**1968**), *Orn* (**1971**) and *Ox* (**1976**), assembled as *Of Man and Manta* (omni **1986** UK): humanity turns out to be the omnivore. Both these series use action scenarios with thinly drawn backgrounds and linear plots not comfortably capable of sustaining the weight of significance the author requires of them. Perhaps the most successful of such books is *Steppe* (**1976** UK), a singleton featuring Alp, whose single-minded career playing Genghis Khan in a future dominated by a world-spanning computer-operated game (◊ GAMES AND SPORTS) is refreshingly unadulterated with any attempts at significance.

Prostho Plus (1967-8 *If*; fixup **1971**) and *Triple Detente* (1968 *ASF*; exp **1974**) are both interstellar epics, the former comic and featuring a dentist, the latter concentrating on an OVERPOPULATION theme and its solution through culling by INVASION. Far more ambitious – though again by no means more assured – are two series in the same vein. The **Cluster** series, comprising *Cluster* (**1977**; vt *Vicinity Cluster* 1979 UK), *Chaining the Lady* (**1978**), *Kirlian Quest* (**1978**), *Thousandstar* (**1980**) and *Viscous Circle* (**1982**), is an elaborate space opera; it relates to **Tarot** in its use of Kirlian auras and other similar material in a Universe ultimately obedient to occult commands. The **Bio of a Space Tyrant** sequence – *Refugee* (**1983**), *Mercenary* (**1984**), *Politician* (**1985**), *Executive* (**1985**) and *Statesman* (**1986**) – slowly but surely embroils its initially ruthless protagonist in a world whose complexities demand of him a moral (and therefore self-limiting) response.

PA is a writer capable of sweepingly intricate fiction, though his tendency to produce less demanding work may obscure this ambitiousness of purview. He is fluent and extremely popular, though his great success has done little to modify the truculent and solitary tone of his utterances on a variety of subjects. The critical apparatus surrounding the republication of *But What of Earth?* (**1976** Canada; text restored 1989 US) with Robert COULSON serves as an extraordinary (and, with the original Laser Books edition not in print, not easily testable) exercise in special pleading; and his autobiography, *Bio of an Ogre* (**1988**), similarly reveals a man unreconciled, unforgiving. It might be added, too, that few of PA's numerous fantasies (listed below) seem built to last. When he is helter-skelter – and much of even his better work is marred by hasty-seeming digressions – PA is of merely marginal interest; it is only when he embraces a complex mythologizing vision of the meaningfulness of things that he becomes fierce. [JC]

Other works: *The Ring* (**1968**) with Robert E. MARGROFF; *The E.S.P. Worm* (**1970**) with Margroff; *Race Against Time* (**1973**), a juvenile; *Rings of Ice* (**1974**), a DISASTER novel based on Isaac Newton Vail's Annular Theory (◊ PSEUDO-SCIENCE); a series of martial arts fantasies, all with Roberto Fuentes (1934-   ), comprising *Kiai!* (**1974**), *Mistress of Death* (**1974**), *The Bamboo Bloodbath* (**1974**), *Ninja's Revenge* (**1975**) and *Amazon Slaughter* (**1976**); the **Xanth** series of fantasies comprising *A Spell for Chameleon* (**1977**), *The Source of Magic* (**1979**) and *Castle Roogna* (**1979**), all three assembled as *The Magic of Xanth* (omni **1981**), and *Centaur Aisle* (**1982**), *Ogre, Ogre* (**1982**), *Night Mare* (**1983**), *Dragon on a Pedestal* (**1983**), *Crewel Lye: A Caustic Yarn* (**1984**), *Golem in the Gears* (**1986**), *Vale of the Vole* (**1987**), *Heaven Cent* (**1988**), *Man from Mundania* (**1989**), *Isle of View* (**1990**) and *Question Quest* (**1991**), plus *Piers Anthony's Visual Guide to Xanth* (**1989**) with Jody Lynn Nye; *Hasan* (1969-70 *Fantastic*; exp **1977**; exp **1986**); *Pretender* (**1979**) with Frances Hall (1914-   );

the **Apprentice Adept** sequence comprising *Split Infinity* (**1980**), *Blue Adept* (**1981**) and *Juxtaposition* (**1982**), all three assembled as *Double Exposure* (omni **1982**), and *Out of Phaze* (**1987**), *Robot Adept* (**1988**), *Unicorn Point* (**1989**) and *Phaze Doubt* (**1990**); *Mute* (**1981**); *Ghost* (**1986**); *Shade of the Tree* (**1986**); the **Dragon** series of fantasies with Robert E. Margroff comprising *Dragon's Gold* (**1987**), *Serpent's Silver* (**1988**) and *Chimaera's Copper* (**1990**); *Total Recall* ∗ (**1989**), a novelization of the film TOTAL RECALL (**1990**), itself based on Philip K. DICK's "We Can Remember It for You Wholesale" (**1966**); *Through the Ice* (**1989**) with Robert Kornwise (?1971-1987), a collaborative gesture to a dead teenage writer; *Pornucopia* (**1989**), a pornographic fantasy; *Hard Sell* (**1990**), humorous sf; *Dead Morn* (**1990**) with Roberto Fuentes, a TIME-TRAVEL tale of a visit from the 25th century to a revolutionary Cuba familiar to the book's co-author; *Firefly* (**1991**), horror; *Balook* (**1991**), young-adult sf; the **Mode** fantasy series, beginning with *Virtual Mode* (**1991**) and *Fractal Mode* (**1992**); *The Tatham Mound* (**1991**), a fantasy based on Amerindian material; *Mer-Cycle* (**1991**), an sf singleton.

As editor: *Uncollected Stars* (anth **1986**) with Barry N. MALZBERG, Martin H. GREENBERG and Charles G. WAUGH.

About the author: *Piers Anthony* (**1983** chap) by Michael R. COLLINGS; *Piers Anthony: Biblio of an Ogre: A Working Bibliography* (**1990** chap) by Phil STEPHENSEN-PAYNE.

See also: ASTRONOMY; CRIME AND PUNISHMENT; DEL REY BOOKS; ECOLOGY; GODS AND DEMONS; HUMOUR; *The* MAGAZINE OF FANTASY AND SCIENCE FICTION; MEDICINE; MUSIC; UNDER THE SEA.

ANTHROPOLOGY Anthropology is the scientific study of the genus *Homo*, especially its species *H. sapiens*. Physical anthropology deals with the history of *H. sapiens* and its immediate evolutionary precursors (some of which in fact coexisted with *H. sapiens*); cultural anthropology (ethnology) deals with the contemporary diversity of human cultures (*see also* SOCIOLOGY). The founding fathers of the science – Sir Edward Tylor (1832-1917) and Sir James Frazer (1854-1941) among them – made the dubious assumption that, by studying the diversity of contemporary societies and describing a "hierarchy" extending from the most "primitive" to the most "highly developed", they could discover a single evolutionary pattern; this assumption is built into much early anthropological sf. Modern anthropologists take care to avoid this kind of thinking, and tend to refer to "pre-literate", "tribal", "traditional" or "non-technological" societies, rather than "primitive" ones, in order to emphasize that there is no single path of progress which all societies must tread.

Anthropological speculations feature in sf in a number of different ways, representing various approaches to the two dimensions of inquiry. There is a subgenre of stories dealing directly with the issues surrounding the physical EVOLUTION of humans from bestial ancestors and with the cultural evolution of human societies in the distant past (◊ ORIGIN OF MAN *for discussion of such stories*); these are speculative fictions that owe their inspiration to scientific theory and discovery but, as they participate hardly at all in the characteristic vocabulary of ideas and imaginative apparatus of sf, they are often seen as "borderline" sf at best, although the evocation of ideas drawn from physical anthropology in such works as *No Enemy but Time* (**1982**) and *Ancient of Days* (**1985**) by Michael BISHOP is entirely science-fictional. The species of fantasy which straightforwardly represents the other dimension of the anthropological spectrum by dealing in the imaginary construction of contemporary societies is also borderline; most such stories are "lost-race" fantasies (◊ LOST WORLDS) that usually make little use of scientific anthropology in the design of their hypothetical cultures.

Some prehistoric fantasies are pure romantic adventure stories – e.g., Edgar Rice BURROUGHS's *The Eternal Lover* (**1925**; vt *The Eternal Savage*) – but the subgenre includes a considerable number of thoughtful analytical works: J.H. ROSNY aîné's *La guerre du feu* (**1909**; trans as *Quest for Fire* **1967**), the first 4 vols of Johannes V. JENSEN's *Den Lange Rejse* (**1908-22**; vols 1 and 2 trans as *The Long Journey: Fire and Ice* **1922**; vols 3 and 4 trans as *The Cimbrians: The Long Journey II* **1923**), J. Leslie MITCHELL's *Three Go Back* (**1932**), William GOLDING's *The Inheritors* (**1955**) and Björn KURTÉN's *Den svarta tigern* (**1978**; trans by the author as *Dance of the Tiger* **1978**) are the most outstanding.

There were also anthropological speculations in travellers' tales, but they were mostly too early to be informed by any genuinely scientific ideas. One of the most notable of such proto-anthropological speculations is to be found in Denis Diderot's "Supplement to Bougainville's Voyage" (**1796**), which masquerades as an addendum to a real travelogue in order to present a debate between a Tahitian and a ship's chaplain on the advantages of the state of Nature versus those of civilization. Benjamin DISRAELI's *Adventures of Captain Popanilla* (**1828**) also features a confrontation between the innocent and happy life of an imaginary South-Sea-island culture and the principles of Benthamite Utilitarianism. The earliest stories of this kind which embody speculations drawn from actual scientific thought include some of the items in Andrew LANG's *In the Wrong Paradise and Other Stories* (coll **1886**) and a handful of stories by Grant ALLEN, including *The Great Taboo* (**1890**) and some of his *Strange Stories* (coll **1884**). Allen was also the first writer to bring a hypothetical anthropologist from another culture to study tribalism and taboo in Victorian society, in *The British Barbarians* (**1895**). Another SATIRE in a similar vein is H.G. WELLS's *Mr Blettsworthy on Rampole Island* (**1928**), in which a deranged young man sees the inhabitants of New York as a brutal and primitive ISLAND culture. Recent sf stories which submit humans to the clinical eyes of alien anthropologists include *Mallworld* (**1981**) by S.P. SOMTOW, *Cards of Grief* (**1986**) by Jane YOLEN and (although they are FAR-FUTURE humans) *An Alien Light* (**1988**) by Nancy KRESS.

The failings of the lost-race story as anthropological sf lie not so much in the ambitions of writers as in limitations of the form. These limitations have occasionally been transcended in more recent times. In *You Shall Know Them* (**1952**; vt *Borderline*; vt *The Murder of the Missing Link*) by VERCORS a species of primate is discovered which fits in the margin of all our definitions of "humanity"; it becomes the focal point of a speculative attempt to specify exactly what we mean – or ought to mean – by "Man". *Brother Esau* (**1982**) by Douglas Orgill and John GRIBBIN, *Father to the Man* (**1989**) by Gribbin alone and *Birthright* (**1990**) by Michael STEWART develop similar premises in more-or-less conventional thriller formats, while Maureen DUFFY's *Gor Saga* (**1981**) uses a "half-human" protagonist as an instrument of clever satire (◊ APES AND CAVEMEN). *Providence Island* (**1959**) by Jacquetta HAWKES is a painstaking analysis of a society which has given priority to the development of the mind rather than technological control of the environment, thus calling into question the propriety of such terms as "primitive" and "advanced". Aldous HUXLEY's *Island* (**1962**) is somewhat similar, and a pulp sf story with the same fundamental message is "Forgetfulness" (**1937**) by John W. CAMPBELL Jr (writing as Don A. Stuart), though this latter skips over any actual analysis of the culture described.

The demise of the lost-race fantasy as an effective vehicle for anthropological speculation has led to a curiously paradoxical situation, in that the format has been recast in modern sf by use of non-technological ALIEN societies on other worlds in place of non-technological human societies on Earth. Ideas derived from the scientific study of humankind are widely – and sometimes very effectively – applied to the designing of cultures which are by definition *non*human. So, while most sf aliens have always been surrogate humans, this has not necessarily been just through idleness or lack of imagination on the part of writers: there is a good deal of sf in which alien beings are quite calculatedly and intelligently deployed as substitutes for mankind. Post-WWII sf has managed to ameliorate the paradoxicality of the situation by developing a convention which allows a more straightforward revival of the lost-race format: the "lost colony" scenario in which long-lost human colonists on an alien world have reverted to barbarism, often following the fall of a GALACTIC EMPIRE.

The anthropologist and sf writer Chad OLIVER has written a great many stories which deal with the confrontation between protagonists whose viewpoints are similar to ours and non-technological alien societies or human colonies. Notable are "Rite of Passage" (**1954**), "Field Expedient" (**1955**) and "Between the Thunder and the Sun" (**1957**). Like Grant Allen, Oliver has also attempted the more ambitious project of imagining the situation in reverse, with alien anthropologists studying our culture, in *Shadows in the Sun* (**1954**). Other impressive sf stories which use "alien" societies in this way are "Mine Own Ways" (1960) by Richard MCKENNA, *A Far Sunset* (**1967**) by Edmund COOPER, "The Sharing of Flesh" (**1968**) by Poul ANDERSON, *Beyond Another Sun* (**1971**) by Tom GODWIN, *The Word for World is Forest* (1972; **1976**) by Ursula K. LE GUIN (daughter of anthropologist Alfred Kroeber) and "Death and Designation Among the Asadi" (1973; exp vt *Transfigurations* **1979**) by Michael Bishop. Works which use the lost-colony format to model non-technological human societies include several interesting novels by Jack VANCE, notably *The Blue World* (**1966**), Le Guin's *Rocannon's World* (**1966**) and *Planet of Exile* (**1966**), Joanna RUSS's *And Chaos Died* (**1970**), Cherry WILDER's *Second Nature* (**1982**) and Donald KINGSBURY's *Courtship Rite* (**1982**; vt *Geta*). These human societies are often more different from non-technological human societies than are the alien examples, and the injection of some crucial distinguishing feature – usually PSI POWERS – is common. This tends to move the stories away from strictly anthropological speculation toward a more general hypothetical SOCIOLOGY. This convergence of the roles of aliens and technologically unsophisticated humans is shown off to its greatest advantage in Ian WATSON's *The Embedding* (**1973**), which juxtaposes an examination of a South American tribe who have a strange language and a correspondingly strange worldview with the arrival in Earth's neighbourhood of an equally enigmatic alien race. This is one of the very few stories to reflect the current state of anthropological science and its intimate links with modern linguistics and semiology; many sf writers prefer to take their inspiration from the scholarly fantasies of such mock-anthropological studies as Robert GRAVES's *The White Goddess* (**1948**); a notable example is Joan VINGE's *The Snow Queen* (**1980**).

Another much-used narrative framework for the establishment of hypothetical human societies is the post-disaster scenario (◊ DISASTER; HOLOCAUST AND AFTER; SOCIOLOGY). Most fictions in this area deal with the destruction and reconstitution of society, and are perhaps of more general sociological interest. Where they bear upon anthropology is not so much in their envisaging different states of social organization but in their embodiment of assumptions regarding social evolution. Interesting speculations are to be found in such novels as William GOLDING's *Lord of the Flies* (**1954**), Angela CARTER's *Heroes and Villains* (**1969**) and Russell HOBAN's *Riddley Walker* (**1980**), and in the **Pelbar** series by Paul O. WILLIAMS, begun with *The Breaking of Northwall* (**1981**). By far the most richly detailed of such accounts of technologically primitive future societies is Le Guin's *tour de force* of speculative anthropology, *Always Coming Home* (**1985**), which describes the tribal culture of the Kesh, inhabitants of a post-industrial California.

It is ironic that in the real world cultural anthropology's field of study is rapidly being eroded. No other science suffers so dramatically from Heisenberg's Uncertainty Principle: the effect the process of observation has on the subject of that observation. Cultural anthropology may soon become a largely speculative discipline, looking forward to a possible future rebirth if and when the possibilities mapped out in sf are realized; this point is neatly made by Robert SILVERBERG's story "Schwartz Between the Galaxies" (1974).

There is, of course, a much broader sense in which a great deal of sf may be said to embody anthropological perspectives. Sf must always attempt to put human individuals, human societies and the entire human species into new contexts. Sf writers aspire – or at least pretend – to a kind of objectivity in their examination of the human condition. Such an attitude is by no means unknown in mainstream fiction, but it is not typical. The attitude and method of sf writers are easily comparable to the difficult but fundamental task facing anthropologists, who must detach themselves from the inherited attitudes of their own society and immerse themselves in the life of an alien culture without ever losing their ability to stand back from their experience and take the measure of that culture as objectively as possible. Because of this, workers in the human sciences might find much to interest them in the study of sf. It is not surprising that the first sf anthology compiled as a teaching aid in a scientific subject (◊ SF IN THE CLASSROOM) was the anthropological *Apeman, Spaceman* (anth **1968**) ed Leon E. STOVER and Harry HARRISON; a more recent example is *Anthropology through Science Fiction* (anth **1974**) ed Carol Mason, Martin H. GREENBERG and Patricia WARRICK. A collection of critical essays on the theme is *Aliens: The Anthropology of Science Fiction* (anth **1987**) ed Eric S. RABKIN and George Edgar SLUSSER.

Further to the last point, it is worth taking note of the fairly considerable body of sf which represents a "speculative anthropology" with no analogue in the science itself, dealing with *H. sapiens* not as it is or has been but as it might be or might become. The ultimate example is, of course, Olaf STAPLEDON's *Last and First Men* (**1930**), which describes the entire evolutionary history of the human race and its lineal descendants, but there are many other works which deal with the possibilities of future developments in human nature. Now that the advent of GENETIC ENGINEERING promises to deliver control of our future EVOLUTION into our own hands, discussions of the physical anthropology of the future have acquired a new practical relevance. This point was first made by J.B.S. HALDANE in his prophetic essay *Daedalus, or Science and the Future* (**1924**); it is elaborately extrapolated in Brian M. STABLEFORD's and David LANGFORD's future history *The Third Millennium* (**1985**) and in many other works which wonder how human beings might remake their own nature, once they have the

power to do so. [BS]

See also: PASTORAL; SUPERMAN.

ANTIGRAVITY The idea of somehow counteracting GRAVITY is one of the great sf dreams: it is gravity that kept us earthbound for so long, and even now the force required to escape the gravity well of Earth or any other celestial body is the main factor that makes spaceflight so difficult and expensive. The theme of antigravity appeared early in sf, a typical 19th-century example being "apergy", an antigravity principle used to propel a spacecraft from Earth to Mars in Percy GREG's *Across the Zodiac* (**1880**) and borrowed for the same purpose by John Jacob ASTOR in *A Journey in Other Worlds* (**1894**). C.C. DAIL's *Willmoth the Wanderer, or The Man from Saturn* (**1890**) uses a convenient antigravity ointment to smear on the wanderer's space vehicle. More famously, in *The First Men in the Moon* (**1901**) H.G. WELLS used movable shutters made of "Cavorite", a metal that shields against gravity, to navigate a spacecraft to the Moon.

Other unexplained antigravity devices remained popular for a long time, especially in juvenile sf, as in the flying belt used by BUCK ROGERS or the antigravitic "flubber", flying rubber, in the film *The ABSENT-MINDED PROFESSOR* (1961). In two notable short stories of the 1950s about the discovery of antigravity, however – "Noise Level" (1952) by Raymond F. JONES and "Mother of Invention" (1953) by Tom GODWIN – there are (not very convincing) attempts to give it a scientific rationale. Much more famous (and more convincing – although still wrong) is James BLISH's explanation of the antigravity effect used by his SPINDIZZIES, the devices that enable whole cities to cross the Galaxy in the series of stories and novels collected as *Cities in Flight* (omni **1970**): in one, "Bridge" (1952), he invokes physicists Paul Dirac (1902-1984) and P.M.S. Blackett (1987-1974) in several pages of formulae purporting to show that "both magnetism *and* gravity are phenomena of rotation".

The term "antigravity" is scorned by physicists. Einstein's General Theory of Relativity sees a gravitational field as equivalent to a curving of spacetime. Thus an antigravity device could work only by locally rebuilding the basic framework of the Universe itself; antigravity would require negative mass, a concept conceivable only in a universe of "negative space" which could not co-exist with our own. Charles Eric MAINE confronted Einstein head-on when, in *Count-Down* (**1959**; vt *Fire Past the Future* US), he proposed that, if gravity were curved space, all that was necessary to permit antigravity – he made it sound easy – was to "simply bend space the other way".

The proliferation in the 1970s and 1980s of bestselling popularizing books about modern physics may have something to do with the fact that antigravity, for so long a popular theme, is now seldom used by sf writers. [PN/TSu]

See also: IMAGINARY SCIENCE; POWER SOURCES.

ANTIHEROES ◊ HEROES.

ANTI-INTELLECTUALISM IN SF Anti-intellectualism takes two forms in sf: a persistent if minor theme appears in stories in which the intellect is distrusted; more common are stories about future DYSTOPIAS in which society at large distrusts the intellect although the authors, themselves intellectuals, do not.

In stories of the first sort, INTELLIGENCE is usually seen to be sterile if unmodified by intuition, feeling or compassion – a familiar theme in literature generally. *That Hideous Strength* (**1945**) by C.S. LEWIS attacks a government-backed scientific organization for its thoughtlessness and smugness about the consequences for humanity of scientific development; one of the villains, a vulgar journalist, is clearly modelled on H.G. WELLS. The symbol of the sterile intellect is a disembodied head, cold and evil, in a bottle. In GENRE SF, too, brains in bottles – or at least in dome-shaped heads attached to merely vestigial bodies – have been among the commonest CLICHÉS, especially in the 1930s. The archetype here is "Alas, All Thinking!" (1935) by Harry BATES, in which the EVOLUTION of mankind is shown to culminate in just such a figure, rendered in a memorable image; the horrified protagonist, an intelligent man from the present, resolves to start spending less time on intellectual activities.

The theme of intelligence as insufficient on its own frequently takes the form of mankind learning to adapt harmoniously to an Eden-like world (◊ LIFE ON OTHER WORLDS) to which individuals somehow come to belong organically and transcendentally, a process that bypasses the intellect and proves impossible to humans whose minds outweigh their hearts. Such an evolution occurs towards the end of Michael SWANWICK's *Stations of the Tide* (**1991**) and is central to J.G. BALLARD's *The Drowned World* (**1962** US). Significantly, in both books – as in many others – the union with the non-intellectual world is envisaged as a return to water: back to the bloodstream, so to speak.

Anti-intellectual sf stories were given some impetus by the bombing of Hiroshima: a distrust of SCIENTISTS and of the potentially awesome results of irresponsibly wielded scientific knowledge became quite widespread. These moral issues were often quite responsibly examined in sf stories, but sf CINEMA tended to take a more simplistic line. The mid-1950s saw a procession of MONSTER MOVIES in which very often the monsters were the products of scientific irresponsibility; commonly a religiose voice, impressively baritone, would intone on the sound-track: "There are some things Man was not meant to know."

A new twist on the anti-intellectual theme became quite common in the pessimistic 1980s: the uselessness of the intellect in the face of cosmic indifference and boundless ENTROPY. It has even been suggested, in both sf and science fact, that intelligence may one day prove to have been a non-viable mutation, a mere comma in the long, mindless sentence of our Universe. Bruce STERLING's "Swarm" (1982) has a clever superhuman outmanoeuvred by an alien HIVE-MIND which has intelligence genetically available for special

circumstances, but most of the time repudiates it as being an antisurvival trait. The theme is seldom spelled out as clearly as this, but it appears – by implication, as a subtext – in all sorts of surprising places, as in Douglas ADAMS's HITCH HIKER'S GUIDE TO THE GALAXY books, which are generally thought of as being funny but in which any intellectual activity at all is seen as hubris – to be instantly, in Brian W. ALDISS's phrase, "clobbered by nemesis". Indeed, the evanescence of the life of the mind has long been a wistful theme of Aldiss's own, all the way from *The Long Afternoon of Earth* (**1962** US; rev vt *Hothouse* 1962 UK) to his **Helliconia** series of the 1980s. It is an implied theme, too, of Richard GRANT's *Rumours of Spring* (**1987**). Books like this are not anti-intellectual as such; they merely suggest that, in the evolutionary race, it is an error to bet too heavily on the brain.

In written sf, however, we more commonly find the opposite tack taken: that the life of the intellect is strong and precious, but needs constantly to be guarded from philistines and rednecks; that the prejudices of an ill-informed population against scientists and intellectuals might in the short term result in acts of violence against thinking people and, in the long term, lead to the stifling of all progress. One of the commonest themes in sf is the static society (◊ CONCEPTUAL BREAKTHROUGH; DYSTOPIAS; POLITICS; UTOPIAS). Wells, who was attacked by Lewis for a narrow and unfeeling "humanism", feared this, and he did indeed believe that the world would be better off if governed by a technocracy of trained, literate and numerate experts rather than by a hereditary ruling class or by demagogues elected through manipulation of an uninformed democracy. These ideas are expressed in *A Modern Utopia* (**1905**) and many of Wells's later works, but he had already given them dramatic expression in *The Food of the Gods, and How it Came to Earth* (**1904**), in which the anti-intellectual stupidity and fear of the general population are contrasted bitterly with the splendour of the new race of giants unencumbered by medieval prejudice. On the other hand, in *The Time Machine* (**1895** US; rev 1895 UK) Wells had rather implied, in giving the beauty to the Eloi and the brains to the Morlocks, that neither part of the equation was much good on its own. Many years later Fred HOYLE was to take up the theme of *A Modern Utopia*, notably in *The Black Cloud* (**1957**) and *Ossian's Ride* (**1959**), where he argues for an intellectual elite of scientists and technologists and proposes that traditionally arts-educated intellectuals are in reality anti-intellectual in that, being innumerate, they distrust and misunderstand science.

SATIRE against anti-intellectualism came to prominence in sf with the generation of the 1950s, especially among those writers associated with GALAXY SCIENCE FICTION, prominently C.M. KORNBLUTH, Frederik POHL and Robert SHECKLEY. H. Beam PIPER wrote a satirical plea for thought in "Day of the Moron" (1951 *ASF*), but better known is Kornbluth's "The Marching

Morons" (1951 *Gal*), in which a small coterie of future intellectuals secretly manipulates the vast anti-intellectual, moronic majority. Damon KNIGHT and James BLISH were two other writers who satirically defended "eggheads" (a newly fashionable word) against philistine attack. Fritz LEIBER's *The Silver Eggheads* (1958 *FSF*; **1961**) presents an appalling if amusing anti-intellectual future in which only ROBOTS are in the habit of constructive thought. The 1950s were the era of McCarthyism: it was a common fear of US writers and artists that to be viewed as a smart aleck might be a preliminary to being attacked as a homosexual and thence, by a curious progression, as a communist – that is, to be an intellectual implied that one was suspicious and unreliable. It is therefore not surprising that satires of the type noted above should be so densely clustered during this period.

Anti-intellectualism is commonly presented in connection with two of sf's main themes. One is that of the SUPERMAN who, through mutation (◊ MUTANTS) or for some other reason, develops unusually high intelligence. Two such books are *Mutant* (1945-53 *ASF*; fixup **1953**) by Henry KUTTNER and *Children of the Atom* (1948-50 *ASF*; fixup **1953**) by Wilmar H. SHIRAS; in both, superior intelligence incurs the anger of normals, and even persecution by them. The second relevant theme concerns stories set after the HOLOCAUST. In these the survivors, often living in a state of tribalism or medieval feudalism, are – in a very popular variant of the story – deeply suspicious of intellectuals, fearing that the renewal of technology will lead to another disaster. Three good novels of just such a kind are *The Long Tomorrow* (**1955**) by Leigh BRACKETT, *A Canticle for Leibowitz* (**1960**) by Walter M. MILLER, and *Re-Birth* (**1955** US; rev vt *The Chrysalids* 1955 UK) by John WYNDHAM.

Surprisingly few full-length works have taken anti-intellectualism as their overriding central theme. One such is *The Burning* (**1972**) by James E. GUNN, in which violent anti-intellectualism leads to the destruction of scientists; the return of science is via witchcraft, a theme that owes something to Robert A. HEINLEIN's *Sixth Column* (1941 *ASF* as by Anson MacDonald; **1949**) and Leiber's *Gather Darkness* (1943 *ASF*; **1950**). Ursula K. LE GUIN's early sf story, "The Masters" (1963), deals movingly with a similar theme in a story of a world dominated by religion in which independent thought is a heresy punishable by burning at the stake. But the classic novel of the intellect at bay is of course Ray BRADBURY's *Fahrenheit 451* (**1953**), set in a not-too-distant future where reading books is a crime. [PN]

ANTIMATTER The concept in PHYSICS that forms of matter may exist composed of antiparticles, opposite in all properties to the particles which compose ordinary matter, has a special appeal to sf writers. The idea itself was first formulated by the physicist Paul Dirac (1902-1984) in 1930; the confirmation of the existence of such particles came soon, with the discovery of the positron (the anti-electron) in 1932.

However, although antiparticles can be and are created in the laboratory, this has never been done in sufficient quantity (less than one trillionth of a gram to date) to form what we would think of as antimatter. It is a concept that must at the moment remain theoretical; aside from isolated particles (low-energy antiprotons have been detected in high-altitude balloon experiments), there may be little or no natural antimatter anywhere in the Universe. Antimatter cannot easily exist in our world, since it would combine explosively with conventional matter, mutually annihilating 100% of both forms of matter to create energy, a point basic to the plot of Paul DAVIES's *Fireball* (**1987**). Thus antimatter would make a fine power source if only we knew how to store it: no problem it seems for Scottie, the engineer in STAR TREK, since the starship *Enterprise* is fuelled by it. An early sf view of antimatter's potential usefulness appears in Jack WILLIAMSON's *Seetee Ship* (1942-43 *ASF*; **1951**) and its sequel *Seetee Shock* (1949 *ASF*; **1950**), originally published as by Will Stewart. ("Seetee" stands for "CT", which in turn stands for ContraTerrene matter, an old sf term for antimatter.)

Antimatter galaxies, or even an entire antimatter universe created in the Big Bang at the same time as our matter universe, have been postulated by physicists, with the enthusiastic support of the sf community. A.E. VAN VOGT was one of the first to use this idea, which has since become a CLICHÉ of pulp sf; it is dealt with more sophisticatedly in Ian WATSON's *The Jonah Kit* (**1975**). [PN]

ANTON, LUDWIG (1872-?) German novelist whose Anglophobe novel *Brücken über den Weltraum* (**1922**; trans by Konrad Schmidt as "Interplanetary Bridges" 1933 *Wonder Stories Quarterly*) describes the colonization of VENUS. [JC]

Other works: *Die japanische Pest* ["The Japanese Plague"] (**1922**); *Der Mann im Schatten* ["Man in the Shadows"] (**1926**).

ANTROBUS, JOHN [r] ◊ *The* BED-SITTING ROOM; Spike MILLIGAN.

ANVIL, CHRISTOPHER Pseudonym of US writer Harry C. Crosby Jr (? -   ), whose two earliest stories were published under his own name in *Imagination* in 1952 and 1953, the first being "Cinderella, Inc.". CA has been popularly identified with *ASF* since his initial appearance in that magazine with "The Prisoner" in 1956. He soon followed with the first of the stories making up the **Centra** series: *Pandora's Planet* (1956 *ASF*; exp **1972**), "Pandora's Envoy" (1961), "The Toughest Opponent" (1962), "Sweet Reason" (1966) and "Trap" (1969). His prolific fiction has been noted from the beginning for its vein of comic ethnocentricity, a vein much in keeping with the expressed feelings of John W. CAMPBELL Jr who, in his later years at least, felt it philosophically necessary for humans to win in any significant encounter with ALIENS. CA supplied this sort of story effortlessly, though his first novel, *The Day the Machines Stopped* (**1964**), is a DISASTER story in which a

Soviet experiment permanently cuts off all electrical impulses in the world. Chaos results, but Americans are soon making do again with steam engines and reconstructing a more rural civilization. Most of CA's stories take place in a consistent future galactic federation ($ GALACTIC EMPIRES), and quite a number deal with COLONIZATION OF OTHER WORLDS. Within this larger pattern are a number of lesser series, most of whose individual stories were published (usually in *ASF*) in magazine form only. Archaic, simplistic, insistently readable, *Warlord's World* (**1975**) and *Strangers in Paradise* (fixup **1969**) are representative of this material; *The Steel, the Mist, and the Blazing Sun* (**1980**), which depicts a Soviet-US war 200 years hence, is similar. Only the occasional non-*ASF* story, like "Mind Partners" (1960) from *Gal*, hints at the supple author who remained content within the cage of Campbell's expectations. Since Campbell's death, CA has been less active as a writer. What he might have offered has long been missed. [JC]

See also: ASTOUNDING SCIENCE-FICTION; WAR.

APA An acronym taken from National Amateur Press Association, an organization founded in 1869 to coordinate the distribution of its members' writings. An apa is a collection of individually produced contributions which have been sent to a central editor, who has then collated them and distributed the assembled result to all contributors. Apas – the term was most often found used in the plural, and was pronounced as a word – were common in the late 19th century, and became of genre significance with productions like *The Recluse*, published in the 1920s by W. Paul Cook (1881-1948), which distributed the work of H.P. LOVECRAFT and his circle. Figures involved in apas like *The Recluse* soon turned to more formal publishing ($ SMALL PRESSES AND LIMITED EDITIONS), but younger fans came into the scene. In 1937, Donald A. WOLLHEIM founded the Fantasy Amateur Press Association, which produced in FAPA the first sf apa proper. Many others followed, and apas remained for many decades an important device within FANDOM for maintaining affinities and circulating fiction by young writers. In recent years, computer bulletin boards have tended to supplant the apa as a forum; but many remain active. [JC]

APES AND CAVEMEN (IN THE HUMAN WORLD) The heading for this entry should be seen as no more than a rough short-hand designation for a subject whose nature is diffuse. As "apes" we include the great apes, chimpanzees, orang-utans and monkeys; by "cavemen" we mean to designate proto-human races, including Neanderthals, but without taking a particular stand in the debate on the evolutionary tree (or grove). We do not, however, refer here to Neanderthals or other cavemen in their natural habitat, which is the distant past (*for which see* ANTHROPOLOGY; ORIGIN OF MAN): our interest here is in survivors, Neanderthals thawed out of ice-floes or surviving in lost garden enclaves of our fallen world (like Bigfoot, the Yeti and other legendary humanoid

creatures, who are also relevant to the discussion) or even immortal. Our reason for conflating apes and cavemen is simple enough: insofar as sf writers take them both to embody the same set of metaphors – whether as innocent Candide-like observers of our corrupt mores or funhouse mirrors of humanity to whom we respond with horror – apes and cavemen have almost identical functions in the literature of the 19th and early 20th centuries.

For there to have been a sustained imaginative interest in, and use for, apes and cavemen as observers or mirrors of the human condition, two conditions were probably necessary. The first is obvious: the human condition itself must have become an issue for discourse. Though the pre-18th-century literatures of the world are full of animal doubles, monsters and prodigies, the degree of kinship to us of these creations has nothing to do with any attempt to define *Homo sapiens* as a species; and, in the absence of any sense (or hope) that we are a species distinct *as a species* from other species, there is in traditional literatures an absence of any propaganda intended to distinguish between us and those others – except, perhaps, discourse designed to argue the presence or absence of a soul. Hierarchies of living things in earlier literature are various, and principles of exclusion and inclusion tend to cross species, but, before taxonomical thinking emerged in the 18th century, beings tended to be thought of as human (or not human) according to their location, actual and symbolic. It is because he is a cusp figure, a Janus monster facing the deep past and the exposed future, that the Caliban of Shakespeare's *The Tempest* (*c*1612) – who reappears as a kind of ape in *Mrs Caliban* (**1982**) by Rachel Ingalls (1941-   ) – is so terribly difficult to reduce to a stereotype.

The second necessary circumstance was of course Time, or Progress. Moderns instinctively think of beasts and monsters as being *prior*. For there to have been an 18th-century Primitivist vision of the Noble Savage there must have been a sense that we had advanced – or retreated – from some earlier state. So it is no surprise that the first apes-as-human texts of interest to an sf reader are probably two works by a Primitivist philosopher, James Burnett, Lord Monboddo (1714-1799), whose *Of the Origin and Progress of Language* (**1773-92**) and *Ancient Metaphysics* (**1779-99**) contrast humanity's corrupt nature with that of the pacific orang-utan, a vegetarian flautist who may not have learned to speak but who was otherwise capable of human attainments. Monboddo's orang-utan was a potent and poignant figure, and soon entered fiction in Thomas Love Peacock's *Melincourt, or Sir Oran Haut-ton* (**1817**), where he saves a young maiden from rape, enters Parliament, and gazes wisely upon the human spectacle. But Peacock was an author of disquisitional SATIRES, a form of fiction soon swamped in the 19th century by the mimetic novel, where avatars of Sir Oran Haut-ton could not comfortably abide. *The Monikins* (**1835**) by James Fenimore COOPER features several captured specimens of an articulate monkey civilization who come from an Antarctic LOST WORLD; but they relate far more closely to that form of the imaginary-voyage satire brought into focus by Jonathan SWIFT in *Gulliver's Travels* (**1726**; rev 1735). The use of apes or yahoos or houyhnhnms as exemplary inhabitants of a UTOPIA or DYSTOPIA represents a very different – and ultimately more significant – tradition than the use of apes as illustrative examples *embedded* into our own human world.

Indeed, it would not be until the publication of Charles Darwin's *Origin of Species* (**1859**) that the apes-as-human topic became sufficiently ambiguous or threatening (◊ EVOLUTION) to be of widespread imaginative use (the ape in Edgar Allan POE's "The Murders in the Rue Morgue" [1841] is more or less a trained animal). But now that humans and other primates – as well as the Neanderthals whose existence soon entered public consciousness – could all seem members of one family, then the observer became a mirror. Apes-as-human could be seen as literal parodies of our species (and the reverse); in an uncomfortably intimate sense, they could represent the brother or sister we locked in the cellar for their protection, or to prevent them from shaming us. The terror Thomas De Quincey (1785-1859) felt whenever he envisioned the East (which he never in fact saw, but whose imagined inhabitants clearly represented a psychopathic self-image) turned into opium nightmares of being surrounded by apes. Mr Hyde, in Robert Louis STEVENSON's *Strange Case of Dr. Jekyll and Mr. Hyde* (**1886**), may not be a literal ape-as-human, but he surely fulfils the symbolic function of the brother-within-the-skin whom it is death to recognize. A perfectly understandable dis-ease therefore afflicted late-19th-century versions of the theme, from the frivolousness of Bill Nye's "Personal Experiences in Monkey Language" (1893) to the pathos and parodic horrificness of the animal victims of H.G. WELLS's *The Island of Dr Moreau* (**1896**). Further examples are Haydon Perry's "The Upper Hand" in *Contraptions* (anth **1895**), Frank Challice Constable's *The Curse of Intellect* (**1895**), and Don Mark Lemon's "The Gorilla" (**1905**).

The 20th century saw a flourishing, and a routinization, of the apes-as-human tale, though it never attained the popularity of its close cousin, the *enfant-sauvage*-as-Noble-Savage genre, which featured intensely readable wish-fulfilment tales like Rudyard KIPLING's **Mowgli** stories (which mostly appeared in *The Jungle Book* [coll **1894**] and *The Second Jungle Book* [coll **1895**]) and the **Tarzan** books of Edgar Rice BURROUGHS (from **1914**). Apes-as-human (or Neanderthals-as-human) appeared, variously emblematic, in the anonymous *The Curse of Intellect* (**1895**), in *Dwala: A Romance* (**1904**) by George Calderon (1868-1915), in James Elroy FLECKER's *The Last Generation* (**1908** chap), in Gaston LEROUX's *Balaoo* (**1912**; trans **1913**), in Max BRAND's "That Receding Brow" (**1919**), in Clement FEZANDIE's "The Secret of the Talking

Ape" (**1923**), in Erle Stanley GARDNER's "Monkey Eyes" (**1929**), in Sean M'Guire's *Beast or Man* (**1930**), in "Mogglesby" (1930 *Adventure*) by T(homas) S(igismund) Stribling (1881-1965), in John COLLIER's brilliant *His Monkey Wife* (**1930**), in an evolutionary pas-de-deux with the Second Men in Olaf STAPLEDON's *Last and First Men* (**1930**), in G.E. Trevelyan's *Appius and Virginia* (**1932**), in Alder Martin-Magog's *Man or Ape?* (**1933**), in L. Sprague DE CAMP's "The Gnarly Man" (**1939**), in Thor Swan's *Furfooze* (**1939**), in Aldous HUXLEY's *After Many a Summer Dies the Swan* (**1939**; vt *After Many a Summer* 1939 UK) (*see also* DEVOLUTION), in Justin ATHOLL's *The Grey Beast* (**1944** chap), in David V. REED's *The Whispering Gorilla* (**1950**), in *Hackenfeller's Ape* (**1953**) by Brigid Brophy (1929-), in Philip José FARMER's "The Alley Man" (**1959**; in *The Alley God* coll **1962**), in Robert NATHAN's *The Mallott Diaries* (**1965**), and elsewhere. Towards the end of this sequence, something of a new note could be perhaps detected – in De Camp's fine tale, or in Stephen GILBERT's *Monkeyface* (**1948**) – a lessening of the sense of latent or explicit menace, perhaps because the process of evolution no longer seemed quite so insulting to the race which was inflicting WWII upon itself and upon its cousins. But, in general, ironies or horror or condescension governed the presentation of the theme.

It is possible to detect two very broad tendencies in more recent years. Articulate and wise apes-as-humans (streetwise Candides) can be used, as in Roger PRICE's *J.G., the Upright Ape* (**1960**), to present, more or less straightforwardly, a satiric vision of the contemporary world; other examples would be *The Right Honourable Chimpanzee* (**1978**) by David ST GEORGE and Hans Werner Henze's opera, *Der junge Lord* ["The Young Lord"] (**1965**). However, work of this sort tends not to be created by anyone deeply immersed in sf, where the concept now tends to be treated with troubled complexity; the ironic distance has been lost. No longer is it sufficient merely to posit an articulate cousin who looks us in the eyes: the contemporary sf writer is much more interested in the moral and speculative consequences (◊ GENETIC ENGINEERING) of our capacity actually to implement the process of transformation. Stories like Joseph H. DELANEY's "Brainchild" (**1982**), Leigh KENNEDY's "Her Monkey Face" (**1983**), Judith MOFFETT's "Surviving" (**1986**) and Pat MURPHY's *Rachel in Love* (**1987** *IASFM*; **1992** chap) are dark fables of that transformation, the last three importing a FEMINIST agenda through metaphorical identifications of caged primates and women. Further tales with similar burdens include *Deutsche Suite* (**1972**; trans Arnold Pomerans as *German Suite* 1979 UK) by Herbert Rosendorfer (1934-), Ian MCEWAN's "Reflections of a Kept Ape" (**1978**), Paddy CHAYEFSKY's *Altered States* (**1978**), Michael CRICHTON's *Congo* (**1980**), Maureen DUFFY's *Gor Saga* (**1981**), Stephen GALLAGHER's *Chimera* (**1982**), Douglas Orgill's and John GRIBBIN's *Brother Esau* (**1982**), Bernard MALAMUD's *God's Grace* (**1982**), Peter VAN

GREENAWAY's *Manrissa Man* (**1982**), Michael BISHOP's *Ancient of Days* (**1985**), L. Neil SMITH's **North American Confederacy** series (1986-8) (intermittently), Justin LEIBER's *Beyond Humanity* (**1987**), Peter DICKINSON's *Eva* (**1988**), Harry TURTLEDOVE's *A Different Flesh* (fixup **1988**), Michael STEWART's *Monkey Shines* (**1983**), about the genetic transformation of a monkey (the film version is discussed below), and the same author's less sophisticated *Birthright* (**1990**), about the exploitation of a Neanderthal survival, Ardath MAYHAR's and Ron Fortier's *Monkey Station* ∗ (**1989**), Isaac ASIMOV's and Robert SILVERBERG's *Child of Time* (**1991**), and Daniel QUINN's Turner Fellowship Award-winning novel, *Ishmael* (**1992**), whose searching simplicity of idiom returns us all the way back to Peacock.

Generally less seriously, perhaps, the cinema has always been fond of the theme, at least since the archetype of ape-as-innocent-in-the-human-world appeared in KING KONG (1933) and again in MIGHTY JOE YOUNG (1949). One aspect of the theme perhaps more nakedly apparent in films than in books is the religious subtext of ape/caveman/Yeti/Bigfoot as, even if savage and dangerous, untainted by the Fall of Man. Such innocents discovered by a corrupt humanity, and usually envisaged sentimentally, are the Neanderthal survivors in TROG (1970), SCHLOCK (1973) – a parody of *Trog* – and ICEMAN (1984), the Yeti in *The Abominable Snowman of the Himalayas* (1957), and the Bigfoot in many low-budget films and one rather good big-budget film, HARRY AND THE HENDERSONS (1987). Something rather different seems to be happening in *A* COLD NIGHT'S DEATH (1975), in which experimental apes experiment on scientists; in *Link* (1985), in which an experimental ape becomes homicidal; and in MONKEY SHINES (1988), based on Michael Stewart's 1983 novel, in which an experimental ape injected with human genetic material gets more lethal the more human it becomes. However, in all these films, although the apes are a source of horror, it is suggested that it is human contact that has infected them; only in PROJECT X (1987) do the experimental apes remain decent, despite attempts by the military to teach them to fly nuclear bombers. It is also, indeed, an increase in INTELLIGENCE, catalysed by an alien monolith, that teaches the apemen of 2001: A SPACE ODYSSEY (1968) how to use weapons. While most of these films show apes behaving like humans, a persistent subgenre going back to Stevenson's *The Strange Case of Dr. Jekyll and Mr. Hyde* shows humans becoming apes (◊ DEVOLUTION). Such, with cod seriousness, is the theme of ALTERED STATES (1980) and, a great deal more amusingly, James Ivory's *Savages* (1972), in which primitive Mud People become human guests at a sophisticated country-house party only to revert again, and Howard Hawks's MONKEY BUSINESS (1952), the only sf movie to star Cary Grant, Ginger Rogers and Marilyn Monroe.

PLANET OF THE APES (1968) and its sequels have apes replacing humans, initially to complex satirical effect, eventually – with ever increasing simplemindedness

– as a metaphorical stick with which to beat people; however, because they are set deep into the future, they escape the natural confines of this entry, as did L. Sprague de Camp's and P. Schuyler MILLER's *Genus Homo* (1941; rev **1950**) in an earlier generation, and as does David BRIN's **Uplift** sequence more recently. Similarly, Robert Silverberg's *At Winter's End* (**1988**) and *The Queen of Springtime* (**1989** UK; vt *The New Springtime* 1990 US) place into the FAR FUTURE the revelation that the surviving inhabitants of Earth are in fact transformed primates. But none of us has survived in that world. The ape-as-human story, at its heart, is a tale of siblings.   [JC/PN]

APHELION Australian magazine, Summer 1985/6 to Summer 1986/7, 5 issues, ed Peter McNamara from Adelaide, BEDSHEET-format. One of many short-lived, quixotic Australian attempts to produce a viable sf magazine in a country with a population too small to support one, *A* soon failed, but honourably. Good stories by George TURNER, Greg EGAN, Rosaleen LOVE and, most often, Terry DOWLING, were among the better work published in an uneven magazine. McNamara has gone on to publish well produced sf books by Australian writers under his SMALL-PRESS imprint, Aphelion Publications.   [PN]

APOCALYPSE ◊ DISASTER; END OF THE WORLD; ESCHATOLOGY; HOLOCAUST AND AFTER; RELIGION.

APOSTOLIDES, ALEX [r] ◊ Mark CLIFTON.

APPEARANCE VERSUS REALITY ◊ CONCEPTUAL BREAKTHROUGH; METAPHYSICS; PERCEPTION.

APPEL, ALLEN (?1946-   ) US writer whose **Alex Balfour** TIME-TRAVEL sequence – *Time after Time* (**1985**), *Twice Upon a Time* (**1988**) and *Till the End of Time* (**1990**) – hovers, as do so many tales of this sort, between sf and fantasy. The protagonist's visits, first to the Russian Revolution, then to the time of Mark Twain and General Custer, and finally to Hiroshima, are without sf explanation; but Balfour's opportunity to intervene in the 1945 catastrophe engages him potentially in the sort of time-track manipulation generally conceded to be an sf trope. What distinguishes the books from many others is their intense focus on the ethical dilemmas that must face any adult protagonist given the chance to manipulate time-tracks, to kill a butterfly and change the world.   [JC/RK]

APPEL, BENJAMIN (1907-1977) US writer, long and variously active, known mainly for such work outside the sf field as *The Raw Edge* (**1958**). In his sf novel, *The Funhouse* (**1959**; vt *The Death Master* 1974), satirical (◊ SATIRE) and LINGUISTIC sideshows sometimes illuminate the story of two UTOPIAS as the Chief of Police from the anti-technological Reservation is called upon to save a future USA (the computer dominated Funhouse) from atomic demolition.   [JC]

Other works: *The Devil and W. Kaspar* (**1977**).

Nonfiction: *The Fantastic Mirror: Science Fiction across the Ages* (**1969**), not so much a critical study as a series of excerpts linked by commentary.

APPLEBY, KEN Working name of US writer Kenneth Philip Appleby (1953-   ). His first sf novel, *The*

Voice of Cepheus (**1989**), presents a clear-voiced, optimistic vision of the consequences of First Contact with an ALIEN species whose signals have been detected by the young female protagonist and her astronomer boss. [JC]

APPLETON, VICTOR House name of the US Stratemeyer Syndicate, used mainly on the two **Tom Swift** series. Howard R. GARIS wrote the first 35 of the first series, which stopped at #38. The second series, which deals with **Tom Swift, Jr.**, was initially the work of Harriet S. ADAMS, Edward STRATEMEYER's daughter; she generally upgraded the scientific side of the enterprise, though some of the flavour of the early **Tom Swifts** was lost. The third series, now with Byron PREISS as packager, began in 1991. The first novel of the first series is *Tom Swift and his Motor Cycle* (**1910**), which is modest enough; but very soon, as in *Tom Swift and his Giant Cannon* (**1913**), the mundane world is left far behind. The second series begins with *Tom Swift and his Flying Lab* (**1954**) and mounts to titles like *Tom Swift and his Repelatron Skyway* (**1963**). The third series begins with *Tom Swift #1: The Black Dragon* (**1991**) [by Bill McCay]; other writers involved include Debra Doyle and James D. Macdonald in collaboration, Steven Grant, Gwynplaine MacIntyre and Mike MCQUAY. (*For further information see* TOM SWIFT.) [JC]
See also: CHILDREN'S SF.

ARABIC SF There are, of course, many fantastic motifs in medieval Arabic literature, as in the collection of stories of various genres *Alf layla wa layla* ["One Thousand and One Nights"] (standard text 15th century; trans by Sir Richard Burton as *The Arabian Nights*, 16 vols, **1885-8**). In this, the stories of The City of Brass and The Ebony Horse could be regarded as PROTO SCIENCE FICTION. A few UTOPIAS were written, too, including al-Fārābī's *Risāla fi mabādi' ārā' ahl al-madīna al-fādila* (first half of 10th century; trans by Richard Walzer as *Al-Farabi on the Perfect State* **1985**).

The first real sf stories were published in the late 1940s by the famous mainstream Egyptian writer Tawfiq Al-HAKĪM, but are not considered genre sf by Arabic critics, who nominate Mustafā MAHMŪD (often transcribed Mahmoud) as the "Father of Arabic sf". Both of these authors have been translated into English.

Although there have been a lot of sf stories published in Arabic since the 1960s, few authors could be described as sf specialists. Among them, the most important is probably Imrān Tālib, a Syrian, author of seven sf novels and short-story collections to date. The most interesting of these are the three collections, *Kawkab al-ahlām* ["Planet of Dreams"] (coll **1978**), *Laysa fī al-qamar fuqarā'* ["There are No Poor on the Moon"] (coll **1983**) and *Asrār min madīna al-hukma* ["Secrets of the Town of Wisdom"] (coll **1988**), and the novel *Khalfa hājiz az-zaman* ["Beyond the Barrier of Time"] (**1985**). Tālib is also the author of the sole theoretical study of sf in Arabic: *Fī al-khayāl al-ilmī* ["About Science Fiction"] (**1980**).

Sf is written in practically all Arab countries. In Libya, for example, Yūsuf al-Kuwayrī has published the novel *Min mudhakkirāt rajul lam yūlad* ["From the Diary of a Man Not Yet Born"] (**1971**), which gives an optimistic view of life in Libya in the 32nd century. Mysterious ALIENS affect the life and work of the hero, a Palestinian living in the occupied territories, in Palestinian Amil Habībī's popular mainstream sf novel *Al-waqā' al-gharība fī ikhtifā' Said Abū an-Nahs al-Mutashā'il* (**1974**; trans as *The Secret Life of Saeed, the Ill-Fated Pessoptimist: A Palestinian who Became a Citizen of Israel* **1982**). Various other mainstream writers have written occasional sf stories, as in *Qisas* ["Short Stories"] (coll) by the Syrian Walīd Ikhlāsī and *Khurāfāt* ["Legends"] (coll **1968**) by the Tunisian Izzaddīn al-Madanī. The Algerian Hacène Farouk Zéhar, who writes in French, has published *Peloton de tête* ["Top Platoon"] (coll **1966**).

The role of drama in the Arab world is more important than in the West, and plays are very often published; some are of sf interest. The famous Egyptian dramatist Yūsuf Idrīs wrote *Al-jins ath-thālith* ["The Third Sex"] (**1971**), in which the protagonist, a scientist called Adam, attempts to discover the enzymes of life and death and travels to the Fantastic World. Another Egyptian, Alī Sālim, a satirist who writes in colloquial Arabic, has written several sf plays. In *En-nās ellī fī es-samā' et-tamna* ["People from the Eighth Heaven"] (**1965**) a protagonist called Dr Mideo struggles against the bureaucratic Academy of Sciences of the Universe. Fantastic discoveries and excavations are the main topic of Alī Sālim's other sf plays, *Barrīma aw bi'r el-qamh* ["Brace, or the Well of Wheat"] (**1968**), *Er-rāgel ellī dihik el-malā'ika* ["A Man who Laughed at Angels"] (**1968**) and *Afārīt Masr el-gadīda* ["Satan from Heliopolis"] (**1972**). [JO]

ARACHNOPHOBIA Film (1990). Hollywood Pictures/Amblin/Tangled Web. Executive prods Steven SPIELBERG, Frank Marshall. Dir Marshall, starring Jeff Daniels, Harley Jane Kozak, John Goodman, Julian Sands, Henry Jones. Screenplay by Don Jakoby, Wesley Strick, from a story by Jakoby and Al Williams. 109 mins. Colour.

Frank Marshall, a longtime colleague of Spielberg as a producer, here made his directorial début with an almost perfectly choreographed MONSTER MOVIE. The sf element in this social comedy is a large, male, hitherto-unknown variety of lethal Venezuelan spider which, accidentally carried in the coffin of its first victim to a small Californian town, mates with a local female to produce hordes of smaller but still lethal offspring, fortunately incapable of reproduction. Aimed at adults rather than teenagers, the film is as much about the horrors of small-town life – seen from the perspective of the new (arachnophobic) doctor in town – as it is about the horrors of killer spiders. The science is mystifying; nobody who sees the film understands the explanation of how a sterile male fathers a large family. Goodman's role as the local exterminator is a *tour de force* of bizarre comedy.

Sophisticated, tartly observed and more than adequately scary, *A* is certainly the best spider-invasion film ever made. [PN]

ARANGO, ANGEL [r] ◊ LATIN AMERICA

ARBES, JAKUB [r] ◊ CZECH AND SLOVAK SF.

ARCH, E.L. The pseudonym under which Rachel Ruth Cosgrove Payes (1922-), originally a research biologist, publishes her sf, though her first novel, a juvenile, *Hidden Valley of Oz* (**1951**), appeared as by Rachel Cosgrove. Her sf, from *Bridge to Yesterday* (**1963**) onwards, has been efficient but routine. [JC]
Other works: *The Deathstones* (**1964**); *Planet of Death* (**1964**); *The First Immortals* (**1965**); *The Double-Minded Man* (**1966**); *The Man with Three Eyes* (**1967**).

ARCHER, LEE ZIFF-DAVIS house name used 1956-7 on 3 stories in *AMZ* and *Fantastic*. "Escape Route" (1957 *AMZ*) is by Harlan ELLISON. The authors of the others have not been identified. [PN]

ARCHER, RON ◊ Ted WHITE.

ARCHETTE, GUY [s] ◊ Chester S. GEIER.

ARCHETYPES ◊ MYTHOLOGY.

ARDREY, ROBERT (1908-1980) US playwright, novelist and speculative journalist known mainly for his work outside the sf field, formerly for such plays as *Thunder Rock* (**1941**), which was filmed (1942) by the Boulting Brothers, latterly for his series of sociobiological speculations, beginning with *African Genesis* (**1961**), commercially the most successful. As the implications of his biological determinism have sunk in on advocates of FEMINISM and others, he has seemed increasingly isolated as an ethological popularizer. The uncomfortable nature of his speculative attempts may be found in his sf novel, *World's Beginning* (**1944**), where US society is benevolently rationalized by a chemicals company. [JC]
See also: ECONOMICS; METAPHYSICS.

ARGENTINA ◊ LATIN AMERICA.

ARGOSY, THE The US PULP MAGAZINE published by the Frank A. MUNSEY Corp.; ed Matthew White Jr (from 1886 to 1928) and others. It appeared weekly from 9 Dec 1882 as *The Golden Argosy*, became *The Argosy* from 1 Dec 1888, went monthly Apr 1894-Sep 1917, then weekly, as *Argosy Weekly*, 6 Oct 1917-17 July 1920. It combined with *All-Story Weekly* (◊ The ALL-STORY) to become *Argosy All-Story Weekly* 24 July 1920-28 Sep 1929. It then combined with MUNSEY'S MAGAZINE to form two magazines, *Argosy Weekly* and *All-Story Love Tales*, the former continuing as a weekly 5 Oct 1929-4 Oct 1941; it went biweekly from 1 Nov 1941, monthly from July 1942, and became a men's adventure magazine in Oct 1943, publishing its last sf in the July 1943 issue.

Of the general-fiction pulp magazines, *TA* was one of the most consistent and prolific publishers of sf. Prior to 1910 it had featured sf and fantasy serials and short stories by Frank AUBREY, James Branch CABELL, William Wallace COOK, Howard R. GARIS, George GRIFFITH and others. Its sf output slackened during the first half of the next decade, a period in which it published sf by Garrett P. SERVISS and Garret SMITH,

as well as stories in the **Hawkins** series by Edgar FRANKLIN, but picked up on becoming a weekly. It discovered a major author on publishing "The Runaway Skyscraper" (1919) by Murray LEINSTER (whose memorable "The Mad Planet" appeared in 1920) and published novels by Francis STEVENS before the merger with *All-Story Weekly*. Following this, White retained the editorship and continued publishing sf with many works by authors later to appear in the SF MAGAZINES, notably Edgar Rice BURROUGHS, Ray CUMMINGS, Ralph Milne FARLEY, Otis Adelbert KLINE, and A. MERRITT. Even in the 1930s such sf and weird-magazine authors as Eando BINDER, Donald WANDREI, Manly Wade WELLMAN, Jack WILLIAMSON and Arthur Leo ZAGAT were still appearing in its pages. Its last serialization was *Earth's Last Citadel* 1943; **1964**) by C.L. MOORE and Henry KUTTNER. Many of *TA*'s stories were reprinted in FAMOUS FANTASTIC MYSTERIES and FANTASTIC NOVELS.

The US *TA* should not be confused with UK magazines of the same name. There were two of these. *The Argosy*, pulp-size, Dec 1865-Sep 1901, ed Mrs Henry Wood (1814-1887), published occasional stories of the supernatural but was not known for sf. *The Argosy*, pulp-size, June 1926-Jan 1940, became a DIGEST in Feb 1940, retitled *Argosy of Complete Stories*. In both its pulp and digest forms this magazine primarily published reprints in many genres. Early on it serialized Mary SHELLEY's *Frankenstein* (**1818**; rev 1831) and Bram STOKER's *Dracula* (**1897**), and published stories by Lord DUNSANY. Later, in its digest form, it published many stories by Ray BRADBURY. It lasted into the 1960s. [JE]
Further reading: *Under the Moons of Mars: A History and Anthology of the Scientific Romances in the Munsey Magazines 1912-1920* (anth **1970**) ed Sam MOSKOWITZ.

ARGOSY ALL-STORY WEEKLY ◊ The ARGOSY.

ARGOSY WEEKLY ◊ The ARGOSY.

ARIEL: THE BOOK OF FANTASY Large-BEDSHEET-size US magazine (9 x 12in; about 230 x 305mm); 4 issues (Autumn 1976, 1977, Apr and Oct 1978), published by Morning Star Press; ed Thomas Durwood. *A:TBOF* was lavishly produced on glossy paper, emphasizing fantastic art and HEROIC FANTASY, including episodes of the COMIC strip **Den** by Richard CORBEN and a feature on Frank FRAZETTA. Critical and historical articles were interspersed with fiction by Harlan ELLISON, Michael MOORCOCK, Keith ROBERTS, Roger ZELAZNY and others. In the main *A: TBOF* can be said to have been a triumph of form (good) over content (generally indifferent). [PN]

ARIOSTO, LUDOVICO [r] ◊ ITALY.

ARISS, BRUCE (WALLACE) (1911-) US writer and illustrator. He published "Dreadful Secret of Jonas Harper" as early as 1948 in *What's Doing? Magazine*. *Full Circle* (**1963**), his sf novel about a post-HOLOCAUST conflict between Amerindians and other survivors after the War of Poisoned Lightning, appeared much later. He has also done a good deal of scriptwriting, has served in tv and films as an art director, and did the illustrations for Reginald BRET-NOR's *Through Time and Space with Ferdinand Feghoot* (coll **1962**) as Grendel Briarton. [JC]

ARKHAM COLLECTOR, THE ◊ ARKHAM SAMPLER.

ARKHAM HOUSE US SMALL PRESS founded in Sauk City, Wisconsin, by August DERLETH and Donald WANDREI in order to produce a collection of H.P. LOVECRAFT's stories, *The Outsider and Others* (coll **1939**). Although this was not initially a success, the imprint continued (Derleth bought out Wandrei in 1943) and published a variety of weird, fantasy and horror collections by Lovecraft, Robert E. HOWARD, Frank Belknap LONG, Clark Ashton SMITH and many others, later including original stories and novels; it produced the first books of Ray BRADBURY, Fritz LEIBER and A.E. VAN VOGT. By the mid-1940s it was becoming a legend, and an example to other small presses. In 1948-9 it published a magazine, ARKHAM SAMPLER. Lovecraft remained a main interest of the company, but after Derleth's death in 1971, AH (later under James Turner) began to change direction, publishing among other things some excellent collections by sf writers (sf previously having been a rather minor part of the company's output). These were not conservative choices: they included books from the cutting edge of sf by, for example, Greg BEAR, Michael BISHOP, John KESSEL and Joanna RUSS. AH remains a power in sf publishing, with books like *Gravity's Angels* (coll **1991**) by Michael SWANWICK; and with the memorial and definitive *Her Smoke Rose up Forever* (coll **1990**) AH did for James TIPTREE JR. what half a century earlier it had done for Lovecraft and Smith. Its early Lovecraft and Smith collections are among the most valuable collectors' items in the field. Two useful books about AH are *Thirty Years of Arkham House 1939-1969* (**1970**) by Derleth, and *Horrors and Unpleasantries: A Bibliographical History and Collectors' Guide to Arkham House* (**1983**; exp vt *The Arkham House Companion* 1989) by Sheldon JAFFERY. The GRAPHIC NOVEL *Arkham Asylum: A Serious House on Serious Earth* (graph **1989**) by Grant Morrison (writer) and Dave McKEAN (artist), published by DC COMICS, is a sort of tribute. [PN/MJE]

ARKHAM SAMPLER US magazine, intermediate format (6 x 9in; about 150 x 230mm), quarterly, 8 issues, Winter 1948-Autumn 1949, published by ARKHAM HOUSE, ed August DERLETH. An offshoot of Arkham House's book-publishing activities, *AS* was largely a fantasy magazine based on reprints – for example, H.P. LOVECRAFT's *The Dream Quest of Unknown Kadath* (1943; Winter-Fall 1948; **1955**). The Winter 1949 issue was devoted to sf, containing stories by Ray BRADBURY, A.E. VAN VOGT and others. At $1.00 *AS* was rather expensive, which may have contributed to the shortness of its life. A later Arkham House periodical was *The Arkham Collector*, in booklet format, 10 issues Summer 1967-Summer 1971, which mixed publishing news with some fiction, mostly fantasy and horror. [MJE]

ARLEN, MICHAEL (1895-1956) UK-Armenian writer, born Dikran Kouyoumidjian, who is mainly remembered for *The Green Hat* (**1924**) and other novels of fashionable London life.

His supernatural fiction is to be found in *These Charming People* (coll **1923**) and *May Fair* (coll **1924**); *Ghost Stories* (coll **1927**) assembles the supernatural stories from the previous volumes. MA's sf novel, *Man's Mortality* (**1933**) – although derivative of Rudyard KIPLING's *pax aeronautica* tale *With the Night Mail* (1905; **1909** chap US) – vividly depicts the collapse of International Aircraft and Airways in 1987 after 50 years of oligarchy; the melodramatic story carries some moral bite. *Hell! Said the Duchess* (**1934**) is set in 1938, with Winston Churchill as premier. A succubus is impersonating the duchess, who is accused of being a "Jane the Ripper" but is eventually exonerated. [JC]

About the author: *Michael Arlen* (**1975**) by Harry Keyishian.

See also: TRANSPORTATION.

ARMSTRONG, ANTHONY Working name of UK author and journalist George Anthony Armstrong Willis (1897-1976), a regular contributor to the magazine *Punch*. AA began writing as a novelist with two historical fantasies, *Lure of the Past* (**1920**) and *The Love of Prince Raameses* (**1921**), which were linked by the common theme of REINCARNATION. The historical framework was again used in his LOST-WORLD adventure *Wine of Death* (**1925**), a bloodthirsty novel about a surviving community of Atlanteans. *When the Bells Rang* (**1943**), with Bruce Graeme, is a morale-boosting alternate-history tale of a 1940 INVASION of the UK by the Nazis, and of their subsequent defeat (◊ HITLER WINS).

AA's short stories are, by comparison, slight, and are generally humorous. Of note are his two early Edgar Rice BURROUGHS parodies, "The Visit to Mars" and "The Battlechief of Mars" (1926 *Gaiety*) which briefly outline the extraordinary exploits of John Waggoner; they have yet to be reprinted. [JE]

Other works: *The Prince Who Hiccupped and Other Tales* (coll **1932**); *The Pack of Pieces* (**1942**; vt *The Naughty Princess* 1945); *The Strange Case of Mr Pelham* (**1957**).

See also: ALTERNATE WORLDS; HITLER WINS.

ARMSTRONG, CHARLES WICKSTEED (1871-?)
UK writer, still alive in 1951, whose first sf novel, *The Yorl of the Northmen, or The Fate of the English Race: Being the Romance of a Monarchical Utopia* (**1892**) as by Charles Strongi'th'arm, envisions a feudal and eugenics-dominated world partially modelled on the works of William MORRIS. CWA's second novel, *Paradise Found, or Where the Sex Problem Has Been Solved* (**1936**), uncovers once again a UTOPIA founded on eugenic principles, this time in South America. [JC]

ARMSTRONG, GEOFFREY [s] ◊ John Russell FEARN.

ARMSTRONG, MICHAEL (ALLAN) (1956-) US writer who began publishing sf with "Going after Arviq" in *Afterwar* (anth **1985**) ed Janet MORRIS; this story was expanded (with the name respelled) into his second novel, *Agviq: The Whale* (**1990**), a post-

HOLOCAUST tale set in Alaska and featuring a woman anthropologist whose book-knowledge of the ancient ways of the Eskimo usefully sophisticates the vitality of the tribal survivors.

MA's first novel, *After the Zap* (**1987**), is likewise set in Alaska, in this case in a People's Republic which has survived the phenomenon of the title, a pulse that, down south, has scrambled brains and computers alike. [JC]

ARMSTRONG, T.I.F. [r] ◊ John GAWSWORTH.

ARMYTAGE, W(ALTER) H(ARRY) G(REEN) (1915-) South-African born UK writer and professor of education. Of interest to sf readers among WHGA's 14 books is *Yesterday's Tomorrows: A Historical Survey of Future Societies* (**1967**). Primarily concerned with literary versions of the shape the future may take, it assembles its materials mainly from the 19th and 20th centuries, sometimes from books not well known to sf readers. It is not a critical work, and the material in its wide range seems sometimes to be merely cited rather than digested; it is, nevertheless, a useful work of scholarship. [PN]

See also: CRITICAL AND HISTORICAL WORKS ABOUT SF; UTOPIAS.

ARNASON, ELEANOR (ATWOOD) (1942-) US writer who began to publish sf with "A Clear Day in the Motor City" for *New Worlds Quarterly #6* (anth **1973**) ed Michael MOORCOCK and Charles PLATT. She has since published stories and poems with some regularity. Her first novel, *The Sword Smith* (**1978**), is a fantasy notable for the spare elegance of its narrative, which focuses with modest intensity upon its young protagonist's slow grasp of life's meaning. *To the Resurrection Station* (**1986**), which is sf with touches of GOTHIC imagery, brings a wide range of characters together in contexts which wittily embody FEMINIST readings of the world. *Daughter of the Bear King* (**1987**) is another fantasy. With *A Woman of the Iron People* (**1991**; vt in 2 vols as *In the Light of Sigma Draconis* 1992 and *Changing Women* 1992) EA came suddenly to wider notice. The long tale is set on a complicated stage: on the planet of Sigma Draconis II, inhabited by an ALIEN race seemingly in thrall – as is frequently the case in 1980s sf – to the imperatives of a sexually coercive biology (◊ SEX), a party of Terrans is attempting to come to some understanding of this species. The plot, in true PLANETARY-ROMANCE fashion, takes two humans and two aliens on a trek through the various domains and landscapes of the world, and lessons not unlike those taught in *The Sword Smith* – though far more complexly put – are shared by all about sexual dimorphism, the nature of violence and the intrinsic value of individual persons; and evidence is presented that *Homo sapiens* may have learned some wisdom from the DISASTERS which, prior to the novel's timespan, have almost destroyed Earth. [JC]

Other work: *Time Gum* (anth **1988** chap) ed with Terry A. Garey, sf POETRY.

ARNAUD, G.-J. [r] ◊ FRANCE.

ARNETT, JACK ◊ Mike MCQUAY.

ARNETTE, ROBERT A ZIFF-DAVIS house name used in *AMZ*, *Fantastic Adventures* and *Fantastic* by Robert SILVERBERG and Roger P. Graham (Rog PHILLIPS) for 1 identified story each and by unidentified authors for 6 stories 1951-7. [PN]

ARNO, ELROY [s] ◊ Leroy YERXA.

ARNOLD, EDWIN LESTER (1857-1935) UK writer, son of Sir Edwin Arnold (1832-1904), Victorian poet and popularizer of Buddhism. His fantasies include two REINCARNATION tales, *The Wonderful Adventures of Phra the Phoenician* (**1890** US; vt *Phra the Phoenician* 1910 UK) and *Lepidus the Centurion: A Roman of Today* (**1901**). His best-known novel is *Lieut. Gullivar Jones: His Vacation* (**1905**; vt *Gulliver of Mars* 1964 US), in which Jones tells the story of his brief disgruntlement with the US Navy, his trip by flying carpet to MARS, his rescue of a princess, his witnessing of the destruction of her domain, their adventures together, and his return to a trustful fiancée and promotion. In the preface to the retitled 1964 edition Richard A. LUPOFF claims this story as a source for Edgar Rice BURROUGHS's **Barsoom**. The provenance is visible in hindsight. [JC]

Other work: *The Story of Ulla and Other Tales* (coll **1895**), in which 1 story, "Rutherford the Twice-Born", is fantasy.

See also: HISTORY OF SF.

ARNOLD, FRANK EDWARD (1914-1987) UK writer, active in WWII; in the 1930s he was an early member of UK FANDOM. Four of his pulp sf stories from this period are collected in *Wings Across Time* (coll **1946**), published in the short-lived **Pendulum "Popular" Spacetime Series**, of which he was editor. They are strong on action. [JC]

ARNOLD, JACK (1916-1992) US film-maker who made a number of sf films during the 1950s. In WWII, while in the Army Signal Corps, which was producing training films, JA found himself working with the great documentary-maker Robert Flaherty and received an invaluable crash course in film-making. After WWII he made several successful documentaries. This led to an offer from Universal Studios to direct feature films, beginning with *Girls in the Night* (1953). In 1953 he directed his first sf film, IT CAME FROM OUTER SPACE, based on a treatment by Ray BRADBURY. His other relevant films are CREATURE FROM THE BLACK LAGOON (1954), REVENGE OF THE CREATURE (1955), TARANTULA (1956), *The* INCREDIBLE SHRINKING MAN (1957), MONSTER ON THE CAMPUS (1958) and *The* SPACE CHILDREN (1958). In 1959 he made the Peter Sellers comedy *The Mouse that Roared*, the last of his sf-oriented films. His MONSTER MOVIES, several of which make excellent, moody use of their cheap desert locations, have often moments of beauty, as in the underwater ballet of *Creature from the Black Lagoon*, when the Creature mimics the movements of the woman swimmer, unseen by her, with a curious, alien eroticism. His sf masterwork is *The Incredible Shrinking Man*, a surreal classic of sf cinema, with its tragic, suburban hero going mad, like some King Lear on the blasted heath of his own menacing cellar. JA was a genius of B-movies. [PN/JB]

Further reading: *Directed by Jack Arnold* (**1988**) by Dana M. Reemes.

See also: CINEMA.

ARNO PRESS US publisher specializing in facsimile reprint series. In 1975 Arno published a series of 62 sf titles (49 fiction and 13 nonfiction) ed R. REGINALD and Douglas MENVILLE. The fiction titles date mostly from the period 1885-1925; the nonfiction includes useful reprints of various bibliographic and critical works originally published in very small editions. In 1976 Arno produced a companion series of 63 supernatural and occult volumes, also ed Reginald and Menville, and including several anthologies assembled by them. [MJE]

ARONICA, LOU (1958-) US publisher and editor, Vice President and Publisher since 1989 of BANTAM BOOKS's mass-market division, and also editor of the **Foundation** sf programme until it was merged into the Bantam list. As editor in his own right, he produced *The Bantam Spectra Sampler* (anth **1985** chap) and, more importantly, edited the FULL SPECTRUM original anthology series: *Full Spectrum* (anth **1988**) with Shawna MCCARTHY; *#2* (anth **1989**) with Pat Lobrutto, McCarthy and Amy Stout; *#3* (anth **1991**) with Betsy Mitchell and Stout. As a knowledgeable reader of sf and fantasy, and as a senior figure in the publishing world, LA has for much of the past decade exercised considerable influence on the shape of the sf market. [JC]

AROUND THE WORLD UNDER THE SEA Film (1966). Ivan Tors Productions/MGM. Dir Andrew Marton, starring Lloyd Bridges, Shirley Eaton, David McCallum. Screenplay Arthur Weiss, Art Arthur. 120 mins. Colour.

This routine melodrama was produced by Ivan Tors, best known for such marine tv series as *Flipper*. After tidal waves, underwater experts use a futuristic submarine to plant a series of earthquake-warning devices along a fault that encircles the world. The characters, dialogue and giant eel are hackneyed, and the special effects cheap. The underwater sequences – not bad – were directed by Ricou Browning. [JB]

ARROW, WILLIAM House name used by BALLANTINE BOOKS. ◊ Donald PFEIL; PLANET OF THE APES; William ROTSLER.

ART *For art in sf* ◊ ARTS; *for sf artists* ◊ COMICS, ILLUSTRATION *and entries on individual artists.*

ARTHUR, PETER [s] ◊ Arthur PORGES.

ARTHUR C. CLARKE AWARD This award is given to the best sf novel whose UK first edition was published during the previous calendar year, and consists of an inscribed plaque and a cheque for £1000 from a grant donated by Arthur C. CLARKE. The winner is chosen by a jury, whose membership varies from year to year, and the award is administered by the SCIENCE FICTION FOUNDATION (of which Clarke is Patron), the BRITISH SCIENCE FICTION ASSOCIATION and

the International Science Policy Foundation. Each organization provides two jurors. Clarke's generosity is all the more notable, in hindsight, in that the award has generally gone to rather non-Clarkean books; the first award, for novels published during 1986, interestingly went to a non-genre novel. The awards are listed below by date of announcement. [PN]

Winners:

1987: Margaret ATWOOD, *The Handmaid's Tale*

1988: George TURNER, *The Sea and Summer* (vt *Drowning Towers*)

1989: Rachel POLLACK, *Unquenchable Fire*

1990: Geoff RYMAN, *The Child Garden*

1991: Colin GREENLAND, *Take Back Plenty*

1992: Pat CADIGAN, *Synners*

ARTIFICIAL INTELLIGENCE ◊ AI; COMPUTERS; CYBERNETICS; CYBERPUNK.

ARTS By virtue of its nature, sf has one foot firmly set in each of C.P. Snow's "two cultures", and sf stories occasionally exhibit an exaggerated awareness of that divide. Charles L. HARNESS's notable novella "The Rose" (1953) takes the reconciliation of an assumed antagonism between art and science as its theme, the author adopting the view that the emotional richness of art is necessary to temper and redeem the cold objectivity of science. Most sf writers argue along similar lines; even when they cannot celebrate the triumph of art they lament its defeat. The decline of theatrical artistry in the face of mechanical expertise is the theme of Walter M. MILLER's HUGO-winning novelette "The Darfsteller" (1955), and there are similar stories dealing with other arts: sculpture in C.M. KORNBLUTH's "With These Hands" (1951), fiction in Clifford D. SIMAK's "So Bright the Vision" (1956), even COMIC-book illustration in Harry HARRISON's "Portrait of the Artist" (1964).

The concern of sf writers with the arts is almost entirely a post-WWII phenomenon; early PULP-MAGAZINE sf writers and writers of scientific romance paid them little heed. Some 19th-century stories about artists may be considered to be marginal sf because of the remarkable nature of the particular enterprises featured therein: Nathaniel HAWTHORNE's "Artist of the Beautiful" (1844) concerns the making of a wondrous mechanical butterfly, and Robert W. CHAMBERS's "The Mask" (1895) is about a "sculptor" who makes statues by chemically turning living things to stone; but these are allegories rather than speculations. Scrupulous attention to the arts is paid by many UTOPIAN novels, although some utopians overtly or covertly accept PLATO's (ironic) claim in *The Republic* that artists comprise a socially disruptive force and ought to be banished from a perfect society. This thesis is dramatically extrapolated in Damon KNIGHT's "The Country of the Kind" (1956), where the world's only artist is an antisocial psychotic and is necessarily expelled from social life. Karl Marx's related dictum that in the socialist utopia there would be no painters but only men who paint is similarly dramatized in Robert SILVERBERG's "The Man with

Talent" (1955). Most utopians find the idea of abundant LEISURE without art nonsensical, but they have sometimes been hard-pressed to find material appropriate to fill the gap. The enthusiasm of Edward BELLAMY's *Looking Backward, 2000-1887* (**1888**) for the wonders of mechanically reproduced music reminds us how dramatically our relationship with the arts has been transformed by technology, and the treatment of arts and crafts in such novels as William MORRIS's *News from Nowhere* (**1890**) now seems irredeemably quaint, despite being echoed in such more recent works as Robert M. Pirsig's *Zen and the Art of Motorcycle Maintenance* (**1974**). More ambitious attempts to represent the artistic life of the future are featured in Herman HESSE's *Magister Ludi* (**1943**; trans **1949**; retrans as *The Glass Bead Game* **1960**), in which the life of society's elite is dominated by the aesthetics of a "game", and in Franz WERFEL's ironic *Stern der Ungeborenen* (**1946**; trans as *Star of the Unborn* **1946** US). The aesthetic life and its possible elevation to a universal *modus vivendi* are, however, mercilessly treated in some utopian satires – notably in Alexandr MOSZKOWSKI's account of the island of Helikonda in *Die Insel der Weisheit* (**1922**; trans as *The Isles of Wisdom* **1924**) and André MAUROIS's *Voyage aux pays des Articoles* (**1927**; trans as *A Voyage to the Island of the Articoles* **1928**). An early sf novel which deals satirically with the arts is Fritz LEIBER's *The Silver Eggheads* (**1961**), in which human literateurs use "wordmills" and authored fiction is strictly for the ROBOTS.

In *The Return of William Shakespeare* (**1929**) Hugh KINGSMILL used an sf framework for a commentary on Shakespeare, audaciously crediting his interpretations to the revivified bard himself. Isaac ASIMOV used a similar idea for a brief joke, "The Immortal Bard" (1954), in which a time-travelling Shakespeare fails a college course in his own works. More earnest stories of scientifically resurrected artists include Ray BRADBURY's "Forever and the Earth" (1950), which features Thomas Wolfe, and James BLISH's "A Work of Art" (1956), in which the resurrection of Richard Strauss into the brain of another man is hailed as a work of art in its own right, although Strauss discovers that rebirth has failed to re-ignite his creative powers. TIME-TRAVEL stories featuring the great artists of the past include Manly Wade WELLMAN's *Twice in Time* (**1940**; **1957**), whose hero becomes Leonardo da Vinci, Barry N. MALZBERG's *Chorale* (**1978**), whose hero becomes Beethoven, and Lisa GOLDSTEIN's *The Dream Years* (**1976**), which features the pioneers of the Surrealist movement.

Sf writers who have a considerable personal interest in one or other of the arts often reflect this in their work. Fritz Leiber's theatrical background is less obvious in his sf than in his fantasy, though it is manifest in "No Great Magic" (1963) and – obliquely – in *The Big Time* (**1961**). Samuel R. DELANY is one sf writer in whose works artists play prominent and significant parts; their aesthetic performances, especially their music, are sufficiently central to shape the

meanings of the stories – a method taken to its extreme in *Dhalgren* (**1975**). Another is Alexander JABLOKOV, who makes much of the cultural significance of artistry in "The Death Artist" (1990) and *Carve the Sky* (**1991**).

Music is the art most commonly featured in sf, as discussed under MUSIC IN SF. Theatre is also widely featured, and much easier to deploy convincingly. Sf novels which use theatrical backgrounds for various different purposes include *Doomsday Morning* (**1957**) by C.L. MOORE, John BRUNNER's *The Productions of Time* (**1967**) and *Showboat World* (**1975**) by Jack Vance, while the hero of Robert A. HEINLEIN's *Double Star* (**1956**) is an actor. The single work of art most often featured in sf stories is the Mona Lisa, which receives respectful treatment in Ray Bradbury's "The Smile" (1952) and disrespectful treatment in Bob SHAW's "The Gioconda Caper" (1976); but the most extravagant use of a work of pictorial art as an anchor for an sf story is in Ian WATSON's Bosch-inspired *The Gardens of Delight* (**1980**).

When it comes to inventing new arts, sf writers are understandably tentative. The aesthetics of time-tourism are elegantly developed in C.L. Moore's "Vintage Season" (1946), but the mask-making art of Jack Vance's "The Moon Moth" (1961), the holographic sculpture of William ROTSLER's *Patron of the Arts* (**1973**; exp **1974**) and Ian Watson's *The Martian Inca* (**1977**), the music-and-light linkages of John Brunner's *The Whole Man* (**1958-9**; fixup **1964** US; vt *Telepathist* 1965 UK), the sartorial art of Barrington J. BAYLEY's *The Garments of Caean* (**1976** US), the psychosculpture of Robert Silverberg's *The Second Trip* (**1972**) and the laser-based artform of J. Neil SCHULMAN's *The Rainbow Cadenza* (**1983**) are all fairly modest extrapolations of extant arts.

The most commonly depicted class of new artform in modern sf involves the recording of dreams. An early use of this notion was Isaac Asimov's "Dreaming is a Private Thing" (1955); more recent and much more elaborate explorations of the idea are *Hyacinths* (**1983**) by Chelsea Quinn Yarbro and *The Continent of Lies* (**1984**) by James MORROW.

The aesthetic uses of GENETIC-ENGINEERING techniques are featured in several stories by Brian M. STABLEFORD, including "Cinderella's Sisters" (1989) and "Skin Deep" (1991).

There have been several notable attempts by sf writers to portray the artists' colonies of the future, many of them imitative of J.G. BALLARD's lushly ironic stories of *Vermilion Sands* (coll **1971** US), which includes a story about the novel art of cloud-sculpting, "The Cloud-Sculptors of Coral D" (1967). Lee KILLOUGH's *Aventine* (coll **1982**) is the most blatant exercise in *Vermilion Sands* pastiche; more obliquely influenced items are Michael CONEY's *The Girl with a Symphony in her Fingers* (fixup **1975**; vt *The Jaws that Bite, the Claws that Catch*) and several stories by Eric BROWN, including "The Girl who Died for Art and Lived" (1987). Pat MURPHY's *The City, Not Long After*

(**1989**) is more original and more interesting.

Anthologies of sf stories about the arts include *New Dreams this Morning* (**1966**) ed James Blish and *The Arts and Beyond: Visions of Man's Aesthetic Future* (anth **1977**) ed Thomas F. MONTELEONE. In *Pictures at an Exhibition* (anth **1981**) ed Ian WATSON writers base their stories on selected works of art.   [BS]

See also: GAMES AND SPORTS.

ARZHAK, NIKOLAI [r] ◊ Yuli DANIEL.

ASCHER, EUGENE Pseudonym of UK writer Harold Ernest Kelly (?   -   ), author of *Uncanny Adventures* (coll **1944** chap) and the **Lucian Carolus** sequence: *The Grim Caretaker* (**1944** chap) and *There Were no Asper Ladies* (**1944**; vt *To Kill a Corpse* 1959).   [JC]

ASH, ALAN (1908-?   ) UK writer in whose routine sf adventure, *Conditioned for Space* (**1955**), a SLEEPER AWAKES, having been encased in a block of ice, to find himself in the front line of Earth defence in a space war.   [JC]

ASH, BRIAN (1936-   ) UK writer, scientific journalist and editor. His *Faces of the Future: The Lessons of Science Fiction* (**1975**) assumes that its readers might be ignorant of sf, which leads to more plot summarizing than is palatable for sf readers. BA's *Who's Who in Science Fiction* (**1976**; rev 1977) was well received by the general press, but heavily attacked in the sf specialist press for omissions and errors. The revised edition corrected many of the inaccuracies. BA then edited the thematically arranged *The Visual Encyclopedia of Science Fiction* (**1978**), whose coverage is not in fact truly encyclopedic, consisting for the most part of largely unsigned essays and compilations, by various contributors (listed in the prelims), arranged in chapters which trace the development of the major sf themes. A handsome volume, illustrated in colour, it did not work well as a reference work for people interested in particular writers, and was widely regarded as a "coffee-table" book. On the other hand, *Who's Who in H.G. Wells* (**1979**) is a useful guide which encompasses all the fiction, not only the well known early works.   [PN]

ASH, FENTON ◊ Frank AUBREY.

ASHE, GORDON ◊ John CREASEY.

ASHLEY, FRED ◊ Frank AUBREY.

ASHLEY, MIKE Working name of UK editor and researcher Michael Raymond Donald Ashley (1948-   ), who has a special expertise in the history of magazine sf, fantasy and weird fiction. MA's first major work as an anthology editor was the 4-vol *The History of the Science Fiction Magazines*: *Part 1 1926-35* (anth **1974**), *Part 2 1936-45* (anth **1975**), *Part 3 1946-55* (anth **1976**) and *Part 4 1956-65* (anth **1978**). The long introductions to the stories are packed with information, much of it unfamiliar, and there are useful bibliographical appendices. MA's other anthologies are *Souls in Metal* (anth **1977**), *Weird Legacies* (anth **1977**), *SF Choice 77* (anth **1977**), *The Best of British SF* (anth in 2 vols **1977**), *The Mammoth Book of Short Horror Novels* (anth **1988**) and *The Pendragon Chronicles: Heroic Fantasy from the Time of King Arthur* (anth **1990**) and its

sequel, *The Camelot Chronicles* (anth **1992**); he edited *Mrs Gaskell's Tales of Mystery and Horror* (coll **1978**), and 2 collections of Algernon BLACKWOOD stories.

MA's work has also resulted in a number of nonfiction books, the first being *Who's Who in Horror and Fantasy Fiction* (**1977**), which is markedly superior to its companion volume dealing with sf, ed Brian ASH, and draws interestingly on original research; it covers some 400 writers. Two useful indexes, showing increasing evidence of MA's thoroughness, are *Fantasy Readers' Guide: A Complete Index and Annotated Commentary to the John Spencer Fantasy Publications (1950-66)* (**1979**) and *The Complete Index to Astounding/ Analog* (**1981** US), the latter with Terry Jeeves. *The Illustrated Book of Science Fiction Lists* (**1982**; vt *The Illustrated Science Fiction Book of Lists* US) is well organized and fun for trivia buffs. But MA's main contribution to sf scholarship lies in his next three books. *Monthly Terrors: An Index to the Weird Fantasy Magazines Published in the United States and Great Britain* (**1985** US), compiled by Frank H. Parnell with the assistance of MA, gives proper professional coverage to an area indexed previously, if at all, mainly in mimeographed fan publications. *Algernon Blackwood: A Bio-Bibliography* (**1987** US) is an admirable work, around 300pp of scrupulous bibliography with a 34pp biographical preface. MA's masterwork, however, may be the 970pp *Science Fiction, Fantasy and Weird Fiction Magazines* (**1985** US), ed MA and Marshall B. TYMN. This book (which is not an index) dramatically superseded – in number of magazines discussed and in detail – the first edition of *The Encyclopedia of Science Fiction* (**1979**) ed Peter NICHOLLS as the most comprehensive account of this difficult area of publishing, and is interestingly written, much of it by MA himself. The book has uneven sections, but is generally a triumph.   [PN]

Other works: *Fantasy Readers' Guide to Ramsey Campbell* (chap **1980**)

See also: ANTHOLOGIES; ASTOUNDING SCIENCE-FICTION; BIBLIOGRAPHIES; SF MAGAZINES.

ASHTON, FRANCIS LESLIE (1904-?   ) UK writer whose first sf novel, *The Breaking of the Seals* (**1946**), sets a psychic time-traveller into a prehistoric world where primitive society ends in chaos with the breaking up of Bahste, Earth's then moon; a Deluge follows. Its thematic sequel, *Alas, That Great City* (**1948**), set in ATLANTIS, propounds a similar catastrophe, with a new planet arriving to become the Earth's moon and sinking the continent. *Wrong Side of the Moon* (**1952**), written with Stephen Ashton, deals more mundanely with an attempt at space travel.   [JC]

ASHTON, MARVIN ◊ Dennis HUGHES.

ASIMOV, ISAAC (1920-1992) US writer whose second marriage, in 1973, was to fellow writer J.O. Jeppson (who now signs herself Janet ASIMOV). IA, born in Russia, was brought to the USA by his family in 1923, and became a US citizen in 1928. He discovered sf through the magazines sold in his father's candy store; and, although he was not strongly involved in sf FANDOM, he was for a while associated with the FUTURIANS, one of whose members, Frederik POHL, later published several of IA's early stories in his magazines ASTONISHING STORIES and SUPER SCIENCE STORIES. Intellectually precocious, IA obtained his undergraduate degree from Columbia University in 1939, majoring in chemistry, and proceeded to take his MA in 1941 and PhD in 1948, after a wartime hiatus which he mostly spent working in the US Naval Air Experimental Station alongside L. Sprague DE CAMP and Robert A. HEINLEIN. In 1949 he joined the Boston University School of Medicine, where he became associate professor of biochemistry, a position he resigned in 1958 (although he retained the title) in order to write full-time. IA's fame as an sf writer grew steadily from 1940, and next to Heinlein he was the most influential US sf writer of his era. His life story is told in two volumes of memoirs – *In Memory Yet Green: The Autobiography of Isaac Asimov (1920-1954)* (**1979**) and *In Joy Still Felt: The Autobiography of Isaac Asimov (1954-1978)* (**1980**) – plus a late volume of anecdotes, *Asimov Laughs Again* (**1992**), the three together comprising the most extensive autobiographical record yet supplied by any sf figure.

IA began publishing sf with "Marooned off Vesta" for AMAZING STORIES in 1939, and, although his first stories did not attract the immediate attention accorded to contemporaries like Heinlein and A.E. VAN VOGT, he very soon developed a strong relationship with John W. CAMPBELL Jr, editor of ASTOUNDING SCIENCE-FICTION, who encouraged him, advised him, and eventually began to publish him. His tutelage was astonishingly fruitful, as the comments woven into *The Early Asimov, or Eleven Years of Trying* (coll **1972**; vt in 2 vols *The Early Asimov, Book One* 1974 and *Book Two* 1974; vt in 3 vols *The Early Asimov, or Eleven Years of Trying #1* 1973 UK, *#2* 1974 UK and *#3* 1974 UK) exhaustively demonstrate. The apprenticeship was, in fact, short. By 1942 the young IA, barely out of his teens, had already written or had clearly embarked upon the three works or sequences with which his name would be most associated for the following half century: first, "Strange Playfellow" (1940 *Super Science Stories*; vt "Robbie" in all later appearances from 1950), the first story in the **Robot** series, during the course of which he articulated the Three Laws of Robotics; second, "Nightfall" (1941 *ASF*), his most famous story and probably the single most famous US sf story of all time; and, third, "Foundation" (1942), the first instalment of the celebrated **Foundation** series, during the course of which IA established the GALACTIC EMPIRE as a template for almost every future HISTORY generated in the field from 1940 onwards.

As the **Robot** and **Foundation** sequences dominated IA's career into the 1990s, it is perhaps best to describe "Nightfall" first. Its success has been astonishing. Poll after poll, including one conducted by the SCIENCE FICTION WRITERS OF AMERICA, has found it considered the best sf short story of all time. The original idea – as was often the case in the GOLDEN AGE OF SF – was largely Campbell's. Emerson had said that, if the stars were visible only once in a thousand years, "how men would believe and adore"; but Campbell suggested to IA that something else would happen. "Nightfall" is set upon a world which complexly orbits six suns, at least one of which is always shining, except for one night of universal eclipse every two millennia. As the night approaches once again, scientists and others begin to sense that the psychological effects (◊ PSYCHOLOGY) of utter darkness may explain the fact that civilization on this world is cyclical, and every 2000 years the race must start again from scratch. Darkness falls. But it is not the darkness that finally deranges everyone. It is the thousands of suddenly and overwhelmingly visible stars. A novel version, *Nightfall* (**1990** UK) with Robert SILVERBERG, opens out the original story but in so doing fatally flattens the poetic intensity and SENSE OF WONDER felt by so many readers at the moment when the stars are seen.

It was the third story of the **Robot** series, *Liar!* (1941 *ASF*; rev **1977** chap), that saw the introduction of the Three Laws of Robotics, whose formulation IA credited essentially to Campbell, but which Campbell credited essentially to IA. (The laws are detailed in the entry on ROBOTS.) That the constraints engendered by these laws were matters of jurisprudence rather than scientific principle could have been no secret to IA, who almost certainly promulgated them for reasons that had nothing to do with science. In the first instance, the Laws helped put paid to the increasingly worn-out PULP-MAGAZINE convention that the robot was an inimical metal monster; they allowed IA to create a plausible alternative for the 1940s in his POSITRONIC ROBOTS; and – in lawyerly fashion – they generated a large number of stories which probed and exploited various loopholes. The early stories in the sequence tend, as a consequence, to treat the history of the robot as a series of conundrums to be solved; these early tales were assembled as *I, Robot* (coll of linked stories **1950**; cut 1958 UK), a title which included *Liar!* and *Little Lost Robot* (1947 *ASF*; rev **1977** chap). In his two robot novels of the 1950s – *The Caves of Steel* (**1954**) and *The Naked Sun* (**1957**) – IA definitively articulated the problem-solving nature of the series, creating in the human detective Lije Baley and his robot colleague R. Daneel Olivaw two characters far more memorable than usually found in his work. The two novels – his best of the 1950s – are set in a future in which the crowded inhabitants of Earth have moved underground (◊ OVERPOPULATION) while their cultural descendants and rivals, the Spacers, glory in naked suns. The conflict between the two contrasting versions of humanity's proper course forward would fuel the **Robot** novels (*see below*) of IA's second career as a fiction writer; his first came near to its close with the Baley/Olivaw books, which were assembled in

The Rest of the Robots (omni **1964**), along with some hitherto uncollected stories, these latter being separately republished as *Eight Stories from the Rest of the Robots* (coll **1966**), while the two novels were also assembled without the stories as *The Robot Novels* (omni **1971**).

The **Foundation** tales were from the first conceived on a different scale, and were set sufficiently far into the future so that IA need experience none of the difficulties of verisimilitude he faced in the **Robot** sequence, where his plumping for a robot-dominated NEAR FUTURE came to seem dangerously parochial as COMPUTERS increasingly came into actual being. The first **Foundation** sequence, set thousands of years hence in the closing centuries of a vast Galactic Empire, comprises *Foundation* (1942-4 *ASF*; fixup **1951**; cut vt *The 1,000 Year Plan* 1955 dos), *Foundation and Empire* (1945 *ASF*; fixup **1952**; vt *The Man who Upset the Universe* 1955) and *Second Foundation* (1948-50 *ASF*; fixup **1953**; vt *2nd Foundation: Galactic Empire* 1958), with all 3 vols being assembled as *The Foundation Trilogy* (**1963**; vt *An Isaac Asimov Omnibus* 1966 UK). Deriving background elements from an earlier story, "Black Friar of the Flame" (1942), the series was originally conceived by IA as a single extended tale, the fall of the Roman Empire rewritten as sf; it evolved into a much larger undertaking through consultation with Campbell, whose refusal to accept in *ASF* the presence of ALIENS superior to humanity was responsible for IA's decision not to introduce any aliens at all into his future history. Grandiose in conception, although suffering in overall design through having been written piecemeal over a period of years, the first **Foundation** trilogy was nevertheless a landmark, winning a HUGO for 1965 as "Best All-Time Series". Like its model, the Galactic Empire is entering a long senescence; but the hidden protagonist of the series, Hari Seldon, inventor of the IMAGINARY SCIENCE of PSYCHOHISTORY, has established two Foundations to shorten the period of interregnum between the fall and a new galactic order. The first Foundation, which is public, is given the explicit task of responding creatively to the historic impulses predicted by psychohistory; the second Foundation, which is secret, copes with the unknown, as in later tales represented by the Mule, a MUTANT, the effect of whose paranormal powers on history Seldon could not have anticipated. The first trilogy closes open to the future.

IA's first three published novels – *Pebble in the Sky* (**1950**), *The Stars, Like Dust* (**1951**; cut vt *The Rebellious Stars* 1954 dos) and *The Currents of Space* (**1952**), all three assembled as *Triangle* (omni **1961**; vt *A Second Isaac Asimov Omnibus* 1969 UK) – are set earlier in the galactic empire of the **Foundation** stories, but have no direct connection with them; they are relatively minor. Before 1958, when he closed off his first career as a fiction writer, IA wrote only one completely separate singleton, *The End of Eternity* (**1955**), a complex story of TIME TRAVEL and TIME PARADOXES

considered by some critics to be his best work. As Paul French, he produced the **Lucky Starr** CHILDREN'S SF sequence: *David Starr, Space Ranger* (**1952**; vt *Space Ranger* 1973 UK), *Lucky Starr and the Pirates of the Asteroids* (**1953**; vt *Pirates of the Asteroids* 1973 UK), *Lucky Starr and the Oceans of Venus* (**1954**; vt *The Oceans of Venus* 1974 UK), *Lucky Starr and the Big Sun of Mercury* (**1956**; vt *The Big Sun of Mercury* 1974 UK), *Lucky Starr and the Moons of Jupiter* (**1957**; vt *The Moons of Jupiter* 1974 UK) and *Lucky Starr and the Rings of Saturn* (**1958**; vt *The Rings of Saturn* 1974 UK). The sequence was assembled in the UK as *An Isaac Asimov Double* (omni **1972** UK), *A Second Isaac Asimov Double* (omni **1973** UK) and *A Third Isaac Asimov Double* (omni **1973** UK); and in the USA the first three titles were assembled as *The Adventures of Lucky Starr* (omni **1985**). Most of the best of his short stories – like "The Martian Way" (1952), "Dreaming is a Private Thing" (1955), "The Dead Past" (1956) and *The Ugly Little Boy* (1958 *Gal*; **1989** chap dos) – also came from the 1950s; his short work, very frequently reprinted in the 1980s, was initially assembled in a series of impressive volumes, including *The Martian Way, and Other Stories* (coll **1955**), *Earth is Room Enough* (coll **1957**) and *Nine Tomorrows: Tales of the Near Future* (coll **1959**). But then he stopped.

In 1958, there was every sense that the **Robot** and **Foundation** sequences were complete, and no sense that they could in any plausible sense be related to one another. IA himself, having abandoned fiction, plunged first into the writing of a popular-science column in *The* MAGAZINE OF FANTASY AND SCIENCE FICTION, which began in November 1958 and appeared continuously, for 399 unbroken issues, until mounting illness prevented his completing the 400th essay late in 1991; it won IA a special Hugo in 1963 for "adding science to science fiction". More significantly, he also began to produce an extraordinary stream of nonfiction titles, many of them very substantial, on all aspects of science and literature and – more or less – anything else. The triumphant *Opus 100* (coll **1969**) was followed by *Opus 200* (coll **1979**), both being assembled as *Opus* (omni **1980** UK); and these two were followed in turn by *Opus 300* (coll **1984**). By the time of his death in 1992, IA's total of published works had long passed the 400 mark.

During the years from 1958 to about 1980, however, little sf appeared, and what did varied widely in quality. A film tie, *Fantastic Voyage* * (**1966**) – which much later was not so much sequelled as recast in *Fantastic Voyage II: Destination Brain* (**1987**) – did his name no good; but *The Gods Themselves* (**1972**), which was only the second genuine singleton of his career and which won both Hugo and NEBULA awards, proved to be his finest single creation, a complex tale involving catastrophic energy transfers between alternate universes (◊ ALTERNATE WORLDS) and – rarely for him – intriguing alien beings. Two collections, *Buy Jupiter, and Other Stories* (coll **1975**; vt *Buy Jupiter!*) – which incorporated *Have You Seen These* (coll **1974** chap) – and *The Bicentennial Man* (coll **1976**), contained both desultory fillers and, in the title story of the second volume, his finest single **Robot** tale. His presence in the sf world may have been intermittent, but his reputation continued to grow, and in Spring 1977 IA was involved in founding the first successful new US sf magazine since 1950, ISAAC ASIMOV'S SCIENCE FICTION MAGAZINE, which soon became – and remains – one of the two or three dominant journals in the field.

In the 1980s, to the relief of his very numerous readers and to the trepidation of critics, he returned to the sf field as a fully active writer. Never in fact prolific as an author of fiction, IA began at this time to produce large novels at intervals of a year or less, most of them comprising an ambitious attempt to amalgamate the **Robot** and **Foundation** sequences into one overarching series, a task not made easier by the total absence of robots from the Galactic Empire. The bridging premise is simple: the Galactic Empire (and Hari Seldon's own career) are the consequences of a robot plot – based on their by-now enormously sophisticated reading of the Three Laws, by which they argue that the First Law requires robots to protect the human race as a whole – to ensure the survival of humanity among the stars. In terms of internal chronology, the new series comprises *The Robots of Dawn* (**1983**), *Robots and Empire* (**1985**), *Prelude to Foundation* (**1988**), *Foundation's Edge* (**1982**), which won a Hugo, and *Foundation and Earth* (**1986**). Apparently more or less completed in draft form just before his death, «Forward the Foundation» is projected to advance the sequence further into the future, tying up the remaining loose ends. Each tale was longer than anything IA had ever written before and sold enormously well, but disappointed some readers because of the undue relaxedness of the new style, the ponderousness of the action, and the memorial sense that was given off by the entire enterprise. Meanwhile, earlier material was assiduously intermixed with the new. *The Robot Collection* (omni **1983**) assembled *The Robot Novels* and *The Complete Robot* (coll **1982**), the latter title containing all the robot stories barring the novels; and *The Robot Novels*, in its original 1971 form an omnibus containing the Bayley/Olivaw tales, now reappeared as *The Robot Novels* (omni **1988**) incorporating *The Robots of Dawn* as well. *Robot Dreams* (coll **1986**) and *Robot Visions* (coll **1990**), both ed anon by Martin H. GREENBERG, while re-sorting much old material, also contained new short stories.

With Janet ASIMOV (*whom see for titles*) IA began a new robot series, the **Norby** books for children. Further singletons arrived, including *Azazel* (coll of linked stories **1988**), *Nemesis* (**1989**) and *Child of Time* (1958 *Gal* as "The Ugly Little Boy" by IA alone; exp **1991**) with Robert Silverberg. New stories were assembled in *The Winds of Change* (coll **1986**), and the entire career was memorialized in *The Asimov Chronicles: Fifty Years of Isaac Asimov* (coll **1989**; vt in 6 vols

as *The Asimov Chronicles* #1 1990, #2 1990, #3 1990, #4 1991, #5 1991 and #6 1991) ed Martin H. Greenberg; while at the same time there appeared *The Complete Stories, Volume One* (omni **1990**), comprising the contents of *Earth is Room Enough, Nine Tomorrows* and *Nightfall*, and *The Complete Stories, Volume Two* (coll **1992**), assembling work from 1941 through 1976. A cascade of anthologies (see listing below) appeared during this decade; the **Isaac Asimov's Robot City** series of TIES by various writers were issued regularly. During the last two decades of his life, IA's name seemed ubiquitous; he was given a Nebula Grand Master Award for 1986. It remained the case, however, that for younger generations it had become hard to see the forest for the trees. Their best course might well be to stick to the **Robots** and the **Foundation**, to *The Gods Themselves*, and to *The Asimov Chronicles*. There they would hear the clear unerring voice of the rational man, and the tales he told about solving the true world. For 50 years it was IA's tone of address that all the other voices of sf obeyed, or shifted from – sometimes with an eloquence he could not himself have achieved. It may indeed be said that he lacked poetry; but for five decades his was the voice to which sf came down in the end. His was the *default* voice of sf.   [JC/MJE]

Other works: *The Death Dealers* (**1958**; vt *A Whiff of Death* 1968), associational; *Through A Glass, Clearly* (coll **1967** UK); *Asimov's Mysteries* (coll **1968**), associational; *Nightfall and Other Stories* (coll **1969**; vt in 2 vols *Nightfall One* 1971 UK and *Nightfall Two* 1971 UK); *The Best New Thing* (**1971**), a juvenile; *The Best of Isaac Asimov* (coll **1973** UK) ed anon Martin H. Greenberg; the **Black Widowers** sequence of associational detective tales comprising *Tales of the Black Widowers* (coll **1974**), *More Tales of the Black Widowers* (coll **1976**), *Casebook of the Black Widowers* (coll **1980**), *Banquets of the Black Widowers* (coll **1984**) and *Puzzles of the Black Widowers* (coll **1990**); *The Heavenly Host* (**1975**), a juvenile; "The Dream," "Benjamin's Dream" and "Benjamin's Bicentennial Blast": *Three Short Stories* (coll **1976** chap); *Good Taste* (**1976** chap); *Murder at the ABA* (**1976**; vt *Authorized Murder* 1976 UK), a detection with RECURSIVE elements; *The Key Word and Other Mysteries* (coll **1977**), associational; *The Far Ends of Time and Earth* (omni **1979**) assembling *Pebble in the Sky, Earth is Room Enough* and *The End of Eternity*; *Prisoners of the Stars* (omni **1979**), assembling *The Stars Like Dust* and *The Martian Way*; *3 by Asimov* (coll **1981** chap); *The Union Club Mysteries* (coll **1983**), associational; *The Alternate Asimovs* (coll **1985**), ed anon Greenberg, containing early versions of *Pebble in the Sky, The End of Eternity* and "Belief" (1953); *The Edge of Tomorrow* (coll **1985**), part nonfiction; *The Best Mysteries of Isaac Asimov* (coll **1986**); *The Best Science Fiction of Isaac Asimov* (coll **1986**); *Other Worlds of Isaac Asimov* (omni **1987**) assembling *The Gods Themselves, The End of Eternity* and *The Martian Way*; *The Ugly Little Boy* (1958 *Gal*; **1989** chap dos); *Cal* (**1991** chap).

As editor: Because of the huge number of IA

anthologies, we omit those that are not of genre interest and also break our listing into two main divisions: **Miscellaneous** and **Series**. "Greenberg" is understood always to refer to Martin H. GREENBERG as collaborator, "Waugh" to Charles G. WAUGH as collaborator, and "Olander" to Joseph D. OLANDER as collaborator.

Miscellaneous titles

Soviet Science Fiction (anth **1962**) and *More Soviet Science Fiction* (anth **1962**); *Fifty Short Science Fiction Tales* (anth **1963**) with Groff CONKLIN; *Tomorrow's Children* (anth **1966**); *Where Do We Go from Here?* (anth **1971**; vt in 2 vols *Where Do We Go from Here? Book 1* 1974 UK and *Book 2* 1974 UK); *Nebula Award Stories 8* (anth **1973**); *Before the Golden Age* (anth **1974**; paperback edn split into 3 vols in the USA, 4 in the UK); *100 Great Science Fiction Short-Short Stories* (anth **1978**) with Greenberg and Olander; *The 13 Crimes of Science Fiction* (anth **1979**) with Greenberg and Waugh; *Microcosmic Tales* (anth **1980**) with Greenberg and Olander; *Space Mail* (anth **1980**) with Greenberg and Olander; *The Future in Question* (anth **1980**) with Greenberg and Olander; *The Seven Deadly Sins of Science Fiction* (anth **1980**) with Greenberg and Waugh; *Isaac Asimov's Science Fiction Treasury* (anth **1981**); *The Future I* (anth **1981**) with Greenberg and Olander; *Catastrophes!* (anth **1981**) with Greenberg and Waugh; *The Seven Cardinal Virtues of Science Fiction* (anth **1981**) with Greenberg and Waugh; *Space Mail, Volume II* (anth **1982**) with Greenberg and Olander; *TV: 2000* (anth **1982**), all with Greenberg and Waugh; *Laughing Space* (anth **1982**) with J.O. Jeppson (Janet ASIMOV); *Speculations* (anth **1982**) with Alice Laurance; *Flying Saucers* (anth **1982**) with Greenberg and Waugh; *Dragon Tales* (anth **1982**) with Greenberg and Waugh; *The Last Man on Earth* (anth **1982**) with Greenberg and Waugh; *Science Fiction A to Z* (anth **1982**) with Greenberg and Waugh; *Caught in the Organ Draft: Biology in Science Fiction* (anth **1983**) with Greenberg and Waugh; *Hallucination Orbit: Psychology in Science Fiction* (anth **1983**) with Greenberg and Waugh; *Starships* (anth **1983**) with Greenberg and Waugh; *The Science Fiction Weight-Loss Book* (anth **1983**) with Greenberg and George R.R. MARTIN; *Creations: The Quest for Origins in Story and Science* (anth **1983**) with Greenberg and George ZEBROWSKI; *100 Great Fantasy Short Short Stories* (anth **1984**) with Terry CARR and Greenberg; *Machines that Think: The Best Science Fiction Stories about Robots & Computers* (anth **1984**) with Greenberg and Patricia S. WARRICK; *Isaac Asimov Presents the Best Science Fiction Firsts* (anth **1984**) with Greenberg and Waugh; *Computer Crimes & Capers* (anth **1984**) with Greenberg and Waugh; *Sherlock Holmes through Time and Space* (anth **1984**) with Greenberg and Waugh; *Election Day 2084: Science Fiction Stories about the Future of Politics* (anth **1984**) with Greenberg; *Great Science Fiction Stories by the World's Greatest Scientists* (anth **1985**) with Greenberg and Waugh; *Amazing Stories: 60 Years of the Best Science Fiction* (anth **1985**) with Greenberg; *Science Fiction Masterpieces* (anth **1986**); *The Twelve Frights of Christmas* (anth **1986**) with Greenberg and Carol-Lynn Rössel Waugh; *Young Star Travelers* (anth **1986**) with Greenberg and Waugh; *Hound Dunnit* (anth **1987**) with Greenberg and Carol-Lynn Rössel Waugh; *Encounters* (anth **1988**); *Tales of the Occult* (anth **1989**) with Greenberg and Waugh; *Visions of Fantasy: Tales from the Masters* (anth **1989**).

Series titles

Hugo Winners: *The Hugo Winners* (anth **1962**); *The Hugo Winners, Vol II* (anth **1971**; vt in 2 vols *Stories from The Hugo Winners* 1973 and *More Stories from The Hugo Winners* 1973; vt in 2 vols *The Hugo Winners, Volume One, 1963-1967* 1973 UK and *Volume Two, 1968-1970* 1973 UK); *The Hugo Winners, Vol III* (anth **1977**); *The Hugo Winners, Vol IV: 1976-1979* (anth **1985**; vt in 2 vols *Beyond the Stars* 1987 UK and *The Dark Void* 1987 UK); *The Hugo Winners, Vol V: 1980-1982* (anth **1986**); *The New Hugo Winners: Award-Winning Science Fiction Stories* (anth **1989**) with Martin H. Greenberg; *The New Hugo Winners Volume 2* (anth **1992**) with Greenberg. *The Hugo Winners* and *The Hugo Winners, Vol II* were assembled as *The Hugo Winners, Volumes One and Two* (omni **1972**).

The **Great SF Stories**, all ed with Greenberg: *Isaac Asimov Presents the Great SF Stories 1 (1939)* (anth **1979**); *#2 (1940)* (anth **1979**); *#3 (1941)* (anth **1980**); *#4 (1942)* (anth **1980**); *#5 (1943)* (anth **1981**); *#6 (1944)* (anth **1982**); *#7 (1945)* (anth **1982**); *#8 (1946)* (anth **1982**); *#9 (1947)* (anth **1983**); *#10 (1948)* (anth **1983**); *#11 (1949)* (anth **1984**); *#12 (1950)* (anth **1984**); *#13 (1951)* (anth **1985**); *#14 (1952)* (anth **1985**); *#15 (1953)* (anth **1986**); *#16 (1954)* (anth **1987**); *#17 (1955)* (anth **1987**); *#18 (1956)* (anth **1988**); *#19 (1957)* (anth **1989**); *#20 (1958)* (anth **1990**); *#21 (1959)* (anth **1990**); *#22 (1960)* (anth **1991**); *#23 (1961)* (anth **1991**); *#24 (1962)* (anth **1992**), at which point the series ended. #1 and #2 of the above were assembled as *The Golden Years of Science Fiction #1* (omni **1982**); #3 and #4 as #2 (omni **1983**); #5 and #6 as #3 (omni **1984**); #7 and #8 as #4 (omni **1984**); #9 and #10 as #5 (omni **1986**) and #11 and #12 as #6 (omni **1988**).

The **Science Fiction Shorts**, all ed with Greenberg and Waugh: *After the End* (anth **1982** chap); *Earth Invaded* (anth **1982** chap); *Mad Scientists* (anth **1982** chap); *Mutants* (anth **1982** chap); *Thinking Machines* (anth **1982** chap); *Tomorrow's TV* (anth **1982** chap); *Travels through Time* (anth **1982** chap) and *Wild Inventions* (anth **1982** chap).

The **Nineteenth Century** series, all ed with Greenberg and Waugh: *Isaac Asimov Presents the Best Science Fiction of the Nineteenth Century* (anth **1981**); *Isaac Asimov Presents the Best Fantasy of the 19th Century* (anth **1982**) and *Isaac Asimov Presents the Best Horror and Supernatural of the 19th Century* (anth **1983**).

The **Magical Worlds of Fantasy**, all ed with Greenberg and Waugh: *Isaac Asimov's Magical Worlds of Fantasy #1: Wizards* (anth **1983**); *#2: Witches* (anth **1984**); *#3: Cosmic Knights* (anth **1985**); *#4: Spells* (anth **1985**); *#5: Giants* (anth **1985**); *#6: Mythical Beasties* (anth

1986; vt *Mythic Beasts* 1988 UK); *#7: Magical Wishes* (anth **1986**); *#8: Devils* (anth **1987**; vt *Devils* 1989); *#9: Atlantis* (anth **1987**); *#10: Ghosts* (anth **1988**; vt *Ghosts* 1989); *#11: Curses* (anth **1989**) and *#12: Faeries* (anth **1991**). Numbers 1 and 2 of the above were assembled as *Isaac Asimov's Magical Worlds of Fantasy: Witches & Wizards* (omni **1985**).

The **Wonderful Worlds of Science Fiction**, all ed with Greenberg and Waugh: *Isaac Asimov's Wonderful Worlds of Science Fiction 1: Intergalactic Empires* (anth **1983**); *#2: The Science Fictional Olympics* (anth **1984**); *#3: Supermen* (anth **1984**); *#4: Comets* (anth **1984**); *#5: Tin Stars* (anth **1986**); *#6: Neanderthals* (anth **1987**); *#7: Space Shuttles* (anth **1986**); *#8: Monsters* (anth **1988**; vt *Monsters* 1989); *#9: Robots* (anth **1989**) and *#10: Invasions* (anth **1990**).

The **Young** series, all ed with Greenberg and Waugh: *Young Extraterrestrials* (anth **1984**; vt *Asimov's Extraterrestrials* 1986; vt *Extraterrestrials* 1988); *Young Mutants* (anth **1984**; vt *Asimov's Mutants* 1986; vt *Mutants* 1988); *Young Ghosts* (anth **1985**; vt *Asimov's Ghosts* 1986) and *Young Monsters* (anth **1985**; vt *Asimov's Monsters* 1986) – both assembled as *Asimov's Ghosts & Monsters* (omni **1988** UK) – and *Young Witches & Warlocks* (anth **1987**).

The **Mammoth** books, all ed with Greenberg and Waugh: *Baker's Dozen: 13 Short Fantasy Novels* (anth **1985**; vt *The Mammoth Book of Short Fantasy Novels* 1988 UK); *The Mammoth Book of Short Science Fiction Novels* (anth **1986** UK); *The Mammoth Book of Classic Science Fiction: Short Novels of the 1930s* (anth **1988** UK; cut vt *Great Tales of Classic Science Fiction* 1990 US); *The Mammoth Book of Golden Age Science Fiction: Short Novels of the 1940s* (anth **1989** UK); *The Mammoth Book of Vintage Science Fiction: Short Novels of the 1950s* (anth **1990** UK); *The Mammoth Book of New World Science Fiction: Great Short Novels of the 1960s* (anth **1991**); *The Mammoth Book of Fantastic Science Fiction: Short Novels of the 1970s* (anth **1992**).

Nonfiction: We make no attempt to list IA's enormous nonfiction output; however, of the hundreds of titles published since *Biochemistry and Human Metabolism* (**1952**; rev 1954; rev 1957) with Burnham Walker and William C. Boyd, more than half are likely to be of interest to sf readers for their lucid and comprehensive popularizations of all forms of science. *Only a Trillion* (coll **1957**) contains three SATIRES. IA's *FSF* science columns have been regularly assembled, in many volumes, from *Fact and Fancy* (coll **1962**) on. Recent non-popular-science titles of interest include: *Isaac Asimov on Science Fiction* (coll **1981**); *Futuredays: A 19th-Century Vision of the Year 2000* (**1986**); *How to Enjoy Writing: A Book of Aid and Comfort* (**1987**) with Janet Asimov; *Asimov's Galaxy: Reflections on Science Fiction* (coll **1989**); *Frontiers* (coll **1990**); *Our Angry Earth* (**1991**) with Frederik POHL.

Nonfiction as editor: *Robots: Machines in Man's Image* (anth **1985**) with Karen A. Frenkel; *Cosmic Critique: How and Why Ten Science Fiction Stories Work* (anth **1990**) with Greenberg.

About the author: *FSF* Oct 1966, "Special Isaac Asimov Issue"; *The Science Fiction of Isaac Asimov* by Joseph F. Patrouch Jr (**1974**); *Asimov Analysed* (**1972**) by Neil GOBLE; *Isaac Asimov* (anth of critical articles **1977**) ed Joseph D. Olander and Martin H. Greenberg; *Isaac Asimov: The Foundations of Science Fiction Success* (**1982**) by James E. GUNN.

See also: ANTHOLOGIES; APES AND CAVEMEN (IN THE HUMAN WORLD); ARTS; ASTEROIDS; BIOLOGY; CHILDREN IN SF; CITIES; CLICHÉS; CLUB STORY; COLONIZATION OF OTHER WORLDS; CONCEPTUAL BREAKTHROUGH; CRIME AND PUNISHMENT; CYBERNETICS; DEVOLUTION; DIMENSIONS; DISCOVERY AND INVENTION; ENTROPY; FANTASY; FUTUROLOGY; GALAXY SCIENCE FICTION; HISTORY OF SF; JUPITER; JUVENILE SERIES; LONGEVITY (IN WRITERS AND PUBLICATIONS); MEDIA LANDSCAPE; MERCURY; MUSIC; OUTER PLANETS; PARALLEL WORLDS; PHYSICS; PLANETARY ROMANCE; POLITICS; PSEUDO-SCIENCE; PUBLISHING; RADIO; RELIGION; SF MAGAZINES; SCIENTISTS; SERIES; SEX; SHARED WORLDS; SOCIOLOGY; SPACE OPERA; STARS; TECHNOLOGY; TRANSPORTATION; UNDER THE SEA; UTOPIAS; VENUS; VILLAINS.

ASIMOV, JANET (OPAL JEPPSON) (1926-   ) US psychoanalyst and writer, married to Isaac ASIMOV from 1973 until his death in 1992; she signed her early books J.O. Jeppson. She began to publish sf, most of it for children, with *The Second Experiment* (**1974**) as Jeppson, as were *The Last Immortal* (**1980**) and *The Mysterious Cure, and Other Stories of Pshrinks Anonymous* (coll **1985**), the latter comprising comical tales of psychiatry. As JA, and in collaboration with Isaac Asimov, she wrote the **Norby Chronicles**, a sequence of tales for younger readers about a ROBOT and the scrapes it gets into: *Norby, the Mixed-Up Robot* (**1983**) and *Norby's Other Secret* (**1984**), both assembled as *The Norby Chronicles* (omni **1986**); plus *Norby and the Lost Princess* (**1985**) and *Norby and the Invaders* (**1985**), both assembled as *Norby: Robot for Hire* (omni **1987**); plus *Norby and the Queen's Necklace* (**1986**) and *Norby Finds a Villain* (**1987**), both assembled as *Norby through Time and Space* (omni **1988**); plus *Norby Down to Earth* (**1988**), *Norby and Yobo's Great Adventure* (**1989**), *Norby and the Oldest Dragon* (**1990**) and *Norby and the Court Jester* (**1991**). Of greater general interest is her third solo novel, *Mind Transfer* (**1988**) as JA, which carries over her interest in robots into an adult tale involving the proposal to gift them with brain structures so sophisticated that human minds can be transferred into the matrix provided. Sex, aliens and interstellar travel supervene, and the nature of human identity is explored with some panache.   [JC]

Other works: *Laughing Space: Funny Science Fiction Chuckled Over* (anth **1982**) as Jeppson with Isaac Asimov; *How to Enjoy Writing: A Book of Aid and Comfort* (**1987**) with Isaac Asimov.

ASIMOV'S SCIENCE FICTION ◊ ISAAC ASIMOV'S SCIENCE FICTION MAGAZINE.

ASNIN, SCOTT (?   -   ) US writer known exclusively for *A Cold Wind from Orion* (**1980**), one of several near-future DISASTER novels published around 1980, and not the least effective of them. The falling object in this case is a satellite. [JC]

ASPRIN, ROBERT LYNN (1946-) US writer who began publishing sf with his first novel, *The Cold Cash War* (**1977**), which alarmingly conflates GAME-WORLD antics (like fake wars between mercenaries representing rival corporations on rented turf – Brazil, for instance, being visualized mainly as an arena for world-dominating firms to play games in) and a political rationale to legitimize the corporate control of Earth. RLA's later novels continued to chafe against similar real-life constraints, and it was not until the invention of the **Thieves' World** universe that he came into his own. The individual volumes in the sequence – a SHARED-WORLD fantasy enterpise crafted by a number of writers – were designed by RLA to comprise a number of stories written (or edited) so that they read as BRAIDS; he may have been the first sf or fantasy editor to create a significant braided anthology or novel. The sequence comprises *Thieves' World* * (anth **1979**), *Tales from the Vulgar Unicorn* * (anth **1980**) and *Shadows of Sanctuary* * (anth **1981**) – these three being assembled as *Sanctuary* * (omni **1982**) – *Storm Season* * (anth **1982**), *The Face of Chaos* * (anth **1983**), with Lynn Abbey (1948-) and *Wings of Omen* * (anth **1984**) with Abbey – these three being assembled as *Cross-Currents* * (omni **1985**) – *The Dead of Winter* * (anth **1985**), *Soul of the City* * (anth **1985**) and *Blood Ties* * (anth **1986**) – these three all with Abbey and assembled as *The Shattered Sphere* * (omni **1986**) – and *Aftermath* * (anth **1987**), *Uneasy Alliances* * (anth **1989**) and *Stealer's Sky* * (anth **1989**) these three all with Abbey and assembled as *The Price of Victory* * (omni **1990**). GRAPHIC-NOVEL versions of material from the sequence were published, all with Abbey and Tim Sale, as *Thieves' World Graphics 1* (graph **1985**), *#2* (graph **1986**) and *#3* (graph **1986**).

Since 1979 almost all of RLA's work has been fantasy, mostly comic, though his **Phule's Company** sequence – *Phule's Company* (**1990**) and *#2: Phule's Paradise* (**1992**) – deploys the eponymous passel of ragbag soldiers in a SPACE-OPERA Universe. His reputation lies mainly in the ingenuity of his braiding activities as editor, but his comic fiction is craftsmanlike. [JC]

Other works: The **Myth** sequence of fantasy adventures in an Arabian Nights universe, comprising *Another Fine Myth . . .* (**1978**), *Myth Conceptions* (**1980**), *Myth Directions* (**1982**), *Hit or Myth* (**1983**) – all 4 being assembled as *Myth Adventures* (omni **1984**) – and *Myth-ing Persons* (**1984**), *Little Myth Marker* (**1985**), *M.Y.T.H. Inc. Link* (**1986**), *Myth-Nomers and Impervections* (**1987**) and *M.Y.T.H. Inc in Action* (**1990**), along with *Myth Adventures One* (graph coll **1985**) with Phil Foglio, which assembled a comics version; *Mirror Friend, Mirror Foe* (**1979**) with George TAKEI; *The Bug Wars* (**1979**); *Tambu* (**1979**); the **Duncan and Mallory** sequence of graphic novels, all with Mel White, comprising *Duncan and Mallory* (graph **1986**), *The Bar-None Ranch* (graph **1987**), and *The Raiders* (graph **1988**); *For King and Country* (**1991**) with Davydd ab

Hugh (1960-).

As editor: Some of the **Elfquest** series of braided anthologies, based on the fantasy sequence created by Richard Pini, RLA's contributions being *The Blood of Ten Chiefs* * (anth **1986**) with Lynn Abbey and Richard Pini and *#2: Wolfsong* * (anth **1988**) with Pini. **See also:** HUMOUR.

ASTEROIDS The asteroids (or minor planets) mostly lie between the orbits of Mars and Jupiter. The first to be discovered was Ceres, identified by Giuseppe Piazzi (1746-1826) in 1801; three more, including Vesta and Pallas, were discovered in the same decade, and more than 2000 have now been catalogued. Only a few are over 150km (100 miles) in diameter, the largest (Ceres) being some 700km (435 miles) across. A once popular but now unfashionable theory originated by Heinrich Olbers (1755-1840) holds that the asteroids may be the debris of a planet torn asunder in some long-ago cosmic disaster. A few moral tales of the 1950s – and works of PSEUDO-SCIENCE to this day – suggested that atomic WAR might have been responsible. The theory features prominently in James BLISH's thriller *The Frozen Year* (**1957**; vt *Fallen Star*), while the hypothetical war transcends time to continue in the mind of a human astronaut in "Asleep in Armageddon" (1948) by Ray BRADBURY. Some asteroids have extremely eccentric orbits which take them inside – in some cases well inside – the orbit of Mars or even that of the Earth. One such is featured in Arthur C. CLARKE's "Summertime on Icarus" (1960), and the climax of James Blish's and Norman L. KNIGHT's *A Torrent of Faces* (**1967**) involves a collision between Earth and asteroid Flavia.

In primitive SPACE OPERAS the asteroid belt tended to figure as a hazard for all ships venturing beyond Mars. Near misses and actual collisions were common; Isaac ASIMOV's "Marooned off Vesta" (1939) begins with one such. Modern writers, however, generally realize both that the matter in the asteroid belt is very thinly distributed and that, as the asteroids all lie roughly in the plane of the ecliptic, it is easy to fly "over" or "under" them *en route* to the outer planets.

The asteroids figure most frequently in sf in connection with mining. In early pulp sf they became an analogue of the Klondike, where men were men and mules were second-hand spaceships. Notable examples of this species of sub-Western space opera include Clifford D. SIMAK's "The Asteroid of Gold" (1932), Stanton COBLENTZ's "The Golden Planetoid" (1935), Malcolm JAMESON's "Prospectors of Space" (1940) and Jack WILLIAMSON's *Seetee Ship* (**1942-3**; fixup **1951**; magazine stories and early editions as by Will Stewart). The analogy between the asteroid belt and the Wild West was soon extended, so that the lawless asteroids became the perfect place for interplanetary skulduggery, and they featured frequently in space-piracy stories of the kind popularized by PLANET STORIES; examples are "Asteroid Pirates" (1938) by Royal W. Heckman and "The Prison of the Stars"

(1953) by Stanley MULLEN. The mythology was co-opted into juvenile sf by Asimov in *Lucky Starr and the Pirates of the Asteroids* (**1953** as by Paul French; vt *The Pirates of the Asteroids*).

The use of the asteroids as alien worlds in their own right or as places fit for COLONIZATION has been understandably limited, they are too small to offer much scope. Clark Ashton SMITH's "The Master of the Asteroid" (1932) and Edmond HAMILTON's "The Horror on the Asteroid" (1933) feature humans being marooned as a result of unfortunate collisions and meeting unpleasantly strange fates. The creature in Eden PHILLPOTTS's *Saurus* (**1938**) was dispatched to Earth from the asteroid Hermes but, as he was still an egg at the time, he was unable later to give much of an account of life there. Asteroidal Shangri-Las are featured in Fox B. Holden's "The Death Star" (1951) and Poul ANDERSON's "Garden in the Void" (1952), but in general the most interesting sf asteroids are those which turn out to be SPACESHIPS in disguise, like the one in Murray LEINSTER's *The Wailing Asteroid* (**1961**). The asteroid/spaceship in Greg BEAR's *Eon* (1985) turns out to be pregnant with all manner of astonishing possibilities. Jack VANCE's "I'll Build Your Dream Castle" (1947) depicts a series of asteroidal real-estate deals, but the feats of TERRAFORMING involved stretch the reader's credulity. Charles PLATT's *Garbage World* (**1967**) features an asteroid which serves as the dumping-ground for interplanetary pleasure resorts, but this is not to be taken too seriously. A scattered, tough-minded asteroid-belt society, the Belters, plays an important role in Larry NIVEN's **Tales of Known Space** series. Niven, in traditional fashion, sees the Belters as miners similar in spirit to the colonists of the Old West. One major work on this theme is Poul Anderson's *Tales of the Flying Mountains* (1963-5 *ASF* as by Winston P. Sanders; fixup **1970**), an episodic novel tracing the development of the asteroid culture from its inception to its declaration of independence. (An earlier Sanders story set in the asteroid belt was "Barnacle Bull" [1960].) A more up-to-date image of life on the belt frontier is offered in "Mother in the Sky with Diamonds" (1971) by James TIPTREE Jr, and a notable modern HARD-SF story partly set on an unusual asteroid is *Starfire* (**1988**) by Paul PREUSS. Stories in which asteroids are removed from their natural orbits include Bob SHAW's melodramatic *The Ceres Solution* (**1981**), in which Ceres is used to destroy the MOON, and *Farside Cannon* (**1988**) by Roger McBride ALLEN, in which a similar but less desirable collision is averted.

The asteroids have become less significant as action-adventure sf has moved out into the greater galactic wilderness, but the idea that colonization of the Solar System might involve the construction of purpose-built SPACE HABITATS rather than descents into hostile gravity-wells has suggested to some writers that hollowed-out asteroids might have their uses; the most extravagant extrapolation of this notion can be found in George ZEBROWSKI's *Macrolife* (**1979**). [BS]

ASTONISHING STORIES US PULP MAGAZINE, 16 issues Feb 1940-Apr 1943, mostly bimonthly, published by Fictioneers, Inc., Chicago; ed Feb 1940-Sep 1941 Frederik POHL and Nov 1941-Apr 1943 Alden H. Norton.

Fictioneers, Inc. was a subsidiary of Popular Publications. After the success of this magazine and its sister publication, SUPER SCIENCE STORIES, both ed by the 19-year-old Pohl, Popular Publications went on to acquire various of the Frank A. MUNSEY magazines, including *The* ARGOSY, FAMOUS FANTASTIC MYSTERIES and FANTASTIC NOVELS, and put Alden H. Norton in overall control of their sf, including the two being edited by Pohl. *AS* was a lively and successful magazine under Pohl and his successor, publishing mainly short stories while *Super Science Stories* emphasized novels. Although *AS* was in part a training ground for writers who would become famous later, its stories were surprisingly good considering how little was paid for them: the total budget per issue was $405. *AS* was also, with a cover price of 10 cents, the cheapest sf magazine on the market. It featured stories by, among others, Isaac ASIMOV, Alfred BESTER, Ray CUMMINGS, Neil R. JONES (several **Professor Jameson** stories), Henry KUTTNER, Clifford D. SIMAK and, under pseudonyms, various FUTURIANS (including Pohl himself and C.M. KORNBLUTH). A Canadian reprint edition published 3 issues in 1942. [PN]

ASTOR, JOHN JACOB (1864-1912) US writer, descendant of the celebrated fur trader; he died on the *Titanic*. His *A Journey in Other Worlds: A Romance of the Future* (**1894**) features an ANTIGRAVITY device – "apergy", borrowed from Percy GREG's *Across the Zodiac* (**1880**) – that powers a craft in a tour of the Solar System in AD2000. Earth itself is a conventional UTOPIA; JUPITER is Edenic; Saturn is a kind of Heaven. There is much mystical speculation, the journey having as much to do with theological allegory as with scientific prophecy or the theory of parallel EVOLUTION. [JC]

See also: OUTER PLANETS; POWER SOURCES; RELIGION.

ASTOUNDING SF (Ultimate Reprint Co. magazine) ◊ ASTOUNDING STORIES YEARBOOK.

ASTOUNDING SCIENCE-FICTION US magazine, pulp-size Jan 1930-Dec 1941, BEDSHEET-size Jan 1942-Apr 1943, pulp size May 1943-Oct 1943, DIGEST-size Nov 1943-Feb 1963, bedsheet-size Mar 1963-Mar 1965, digest-size Apr 1965 to date. Published by Publisher's Fiscal Corporation (which later became Clayton Magazines) Jan 1930-Mar 1933, STREET & SMITH Oct 1933-Jan 1961, Condé Nast Feb 1961-Aug 1980, Davis Publications Sep 1980-1992; ed Harry BATES Jan 1930-Mar 1933, F. Orlin TREMAINE Oct 1933-Nov 1937, John W. CAMPBELL Jr Dec 1937-Dec 1971, Ben BOVA Jan 1972-Nov 1978, Stanley SCHMIDT Dec 1978-current. *ASF* was sold to Dell Magazines, part of the BANTAM/DOUBLEDAY/Dell publishing group, early in 1992; the first redesigned *ASF* under the new management is projected to be Nov 1992.

ASF was brought into being when the PULP-MAGAZINE publisher William Clayton suggested to one of his editors, Harry Bates, the idea of a new monthly magazine of period-adventure stories, largely in order to fill a blank space on the sheet on which all the covers of his pulp magazines were simultaneously printed. Bates counterproposed a magazine to be called *Astounding Stories of Super-Science*. The idea was accepted, and the first issue appeared in Jan 1930 under that title. Bates was editor, with assistant editor Desmond W. HALL and consulting editor Douglas M. DOLD (who in 1931 became editor of the short-lived MIRACLE SCIENCE AND FANTASY STORIES). Where its predecessors AIR WONDER STORIES, AMAZING STORIES and SCIENCE WONDER STORIES were larger than the ordinary pulp magazines and attempted a more austere respectability, in response to Hugo GERNSBACK's proselytizing desire to communicate an interest in science through SCIENTIFIC-TION, ASF was unashamedly an action-adventure pulp magazine where "science" was present only to add a veneer of plausibility to its outrageous melodramas. The flavour is suggested by the following editorial blurb (for "The Pirate Planet" by Charles W. Diffin, Feb 1931): "From Earth & Sub-Venus Converge a Titanic Offensive of Justice on the Unspeakable Man-Things of Torg." The covers of the Clayton ASF, all the work of Hans Waldemar Wessolowski (H.W. WESSO), show, typically, men (or women) menaced by giant insects or – anticipating KING KONG (1933) – giant apes. Regular contributors included such names as Ray CUMMINGS, Paul ERNST, Francis FLAGG, S.P. MEEK and Victor ROUSSEAU. One of the most popular authors was Anthony GILMORE (the collaborative pseudonym of Bates and Hall), whose **Hawk Carse** series epitomized ASF-style SPACE OPERA.

In Feb 1931 the title was abbreviated to *Astounding Stories*; the full title was resumed in Jan 1933. During late 1932 the magazine became irregular as the Clayton chain encountered financial problems. In Mar 1933 Clayton went out of business and ASF ceased publication. Although the vast majority of the stories in its first incarnation (1930-33) are deservedly forgotten, ASF was a robust and reasonably successful magazine and, because its rates were so much better than those of its competitors (two cents a word on acceptance instead of half a cent a word on publication or later), it had attracted such authors as Murray LEINSTER and Jack WILLIAMSON.

The magazine's title was bought by STREET & SMITH, a well established pulp chain publisher, and after a six-month gap it reappeared in Oct 1933, restored to a monthly schedule which it has ever since maintained or improved upon (it has been four-weekly since 1981) – a record which no other magazine, even AMZ, can approach. Desmond Hall remained on the editorial staff for a time, but the new editor was F. Orlin TREMAINE. The first two Tremaine issues were an uneasy balance of sf, occult and straight adventure

but, with the Dec 1933 issue, ASF became re-established as an sf magazine (with the Street & Smith takeover the name had once again become *Astounding Stories*). In that issue Tremaine announced the formulation of his "thought-variant" policy: each issue of ASF would carry a story developing an idea which, as he put it, "has been slurred over or passed by in many, many stories". The first such story was "Ancestral Voices" by Nat SCHACHNER.

Although the thought-variant policy can be seen as a publicity gimmick rather than as a coherent intellectual design for the magazine, during 1934 Tremaine and Hall together raised ASF to an indisputably pre-eminent position in its small field. The magazine's payment rates were only half what they had been, but they were still twice as much as their competitors' and were paid promptly. ASF solicited material from leading authors: in 1934 it featured Donald WANDREI's "Colossus" (Jan), Williamson's "Born of the Sun" (Mar) and *The Legion of Space* (Apr-Sep; **1947**), Leinster's "Sidewise in Time" (June), E.E. "Doc" SMITH's *Skylark of Valeron* (Aug 1934-Feb 1935; **1949**), C.L. MOORE's "The Bright Illusion" (Oct), John W. Campbell Jr's first Don A. Stuart story, "Twilight" (Nov), Raymond Z. GALLUN's "Old Faithful" (Dec) and Campbell's *The Mightiest Machine* (Dec 1934-Apr 1935; **1947**). Furthermore, Charles FORT's nonfiction *Lo!* (**1931**) was serialized (Apr-Nov) and ASF's covers featured some startling work by Howard V. BROWN. Also during 1934 the magazine's wordage increased twice, first by adding more pages, then by reducing the size of type. ASF continued to dominate the field in the following years. Superscience epics in the Campbell style were largely phased out as the moodier stories of "Stuart" became popular. Stanley G. WEINBAUM was a regular contributor during 1935 (the year of his death); H.P. LOVECRAFT's fiction appeared in 1936. Tremaine's intention (announced in Jan 1935) to publish ASF twice a month did not materialize, but the magazine prospered and in Feb 1936 made the important symbolic step of adopting trimmed edges to its pages, which at a stroke made its appearance far smarter than those of its ragged competitors. Other artists who began to appear in ASF included Elliott DOLD and Charles SCHNEEMAN. Campbell and Willy LEY contributed articles; L. Sprague DE CAMP and Eric Frank RUSSELL had their first stories published. At the same time, ASF's competitors were ailing: both AMZ and WONDER STORIES switched from monthly to bimonthly in 1935; *Wonder Stories* was sold in the following year (becoming THRILLING WONDER STORIES), and AMZ suffered the same fate in 1938. When Tremaine became editorial director at Street & Smith late in 1937 and appointed John W. CAMPBELL Jr as his successor, he handed over a healthy and successful concern.

For his first 18 months as editor Campbell did not develop the magazine significantly, although in 1938 he published the first sf stories of Lester DEL REY and L. Ron HUBBARD and reintroduced Clifford D. SIMAK.

In Mar 1938 he altered the title to *Astounding Science-Fiction*. His intention was to phase out the word "Astounding", which he disliked, and to retitle the magazine *Science Fiction*; however, the appearance in 1939 of a magazine with that title (◊ SCIENCE FICTION) prevented him from doing so. He toyed briefly with "thought-variant" adaptations. "Mutant" issues (which would show significant changes in the direction of *ASF*'s evolution – and that of sf generally) and "Nova" stories (which would be "unusual in manner of presentation rather than basic theme"). Such gimmicks were soon forgotten. In Mar 1939 he began *ASF*'s successful fantasy companion, UNKNOWN.

The beginning of Campbell's particular GOLDEN AGE OF SF can be pinpointed as the summer of 1939. The July *ASF* (later reproduced as *Astounding Science Fiction, July, 1939* [anth **1981**] ed Campbell and Martin H. GREENBERG) contained A.E. VAN VOGT's first sf story, "Black Destroyer", and Isaac ASIMOV's "Trends" (not his first story, but the first he had managed to sell to Campbell); the Aug issue had Robert A. HEINLEIN's début, "Life-Line"; in the Sep issue Theodore STURGEON's first sf story, "Ether Breather", appeared. During the same period Hubert ROGERS became established as *ASF*'s major cover artist. The authors that he published have frequently attested to Campbell's dynamic editorial personality. Certainly he fed them ideas, but it was the coincidental appearance of a number of prolific and imaginative writers which gave *ASF* its remarkable domination of the genre-sf field during the WWII years – when, to begin with, a boom in sf-magazine publishing meant there was more competition than ever before. The key figure in 1940 and 1941 was Heinlein. His stories alone would have made the magazine notable, as a partial listing will indicate. In 1940 there were "Requiem" (Jan), "If This Goes On – " (Feb-Mar), "The Roads Must Roll" (June), "Coventry" (July) and "Blowups Happen" (Sep); in 1941 *Sixth Column* (Jan-Mar; **1949**), "And He Built A Crooked House" (Feb), "Logic of Empire" (Mar), "Universe" (May), "Solution Unsatisfactory" (May), *Methuselah's Children* (July-Sep; **1958**), "By His Bootstraps" (Oct), "Common Sense" (Oct). At the same time there were a number of stories by van Vogt, notably *Slan* (Sep-Dec 1940; **1946**; rev 1951), and by Asimov, including "Nightfall" (Sep 1941) and the early ROBOT series. Although Campbell lost Heinlein to war work in 1942, he gained Anthony BOUCHER, Fritz LEIBER and "Lewis Padgett" (Henry KUTTNER and C.L. MOORE). In Jan 1942 the magazine switched to bedsheet size – which gave more wordage while saving paper – but it reverted to pulp size in 1943 for a few months before becoming the first digest-size sf magazine in Nov 1943 as paper shortages (which killed off *Unknown*) became more acute. William Timmins replaced Rogers as *ASF*'s regular cover artist.

ASF's leadership of the field continued through the 1940s. Most of its regular authors had popular series to reinforce their appeal: Asimov's **Robot** and **Found-**ation stories; van Vogt's **Weapon Shops** tales and his two **Null-A** novels; George O. SMITH's **Venus Equila-teral** stories; Jack Williamson's **Seetee** stories (as by Will Stewart); "Padgett's" **Gallegher** stories; and E.E. Smith's epic **Lensman** series, the last two novels of which marked the last throes of the superscience epic in *ASF*. The only serious challenge to *ASF*'s superiority came from Sam MERWIN Jr's vastly improved STARTLING STORIES, which by 1948 was publishing much good material. However, *Startling Stories* was a particularly garish-looking pulp while *ASF* became more sober and serious in appearance as the decade went on; the covers featuring Chesley BONESTELL's astronomical art contributed to this effect. The word "Astounding" was reduced to a small-size italic script, often coloured so as to be virtually invisible. At a casual glance it looked as if Campbell had achieved his ambition of retitling the magazine.

But, with the appearance of *The* MAGAZINE OF FANTASY AND SCIENCE FICTION in 1949 and GALAXY SCIENCE FICTION in 1950, *ASF*'s leadership was successfully challenged. It continued on an even, respectable keel, but the exciting new authors of the 1950s, by and large, made their mark elsewhere. The May 1950 issue of *ASF* featured Hubbard's first article on DIANETICS, which launched the PSEUDO-SCIENCE that would later become SCIENTOLOGY. This was symptomatic of Campbell's growing wish to see the ideas of sf made real, a wish that led him into a fruitless championing of backyard inventors' space drives and PSIONIC machines. His editorials – idiosyncratic, deliberately needling, dogmatic, sometimes uncomfortably elitist and near-racist – absorbed much of the energy which had previously gone into the feeding of ideas to his authors. Many of the notions propounded in the editorials were duly reworked into fiction by a stable of unexceptional regular authors such as Randall GARRETT and Raymond F. JONES. *ASF*'s new contributors included Poul ANDERSON, James BLISH, Gordon R. DICKSON, Robert SILVERBERG and many others, and its new artists included, notably, Ed EMSHWILLER (Emsh), Frank Kelly FREAS and H.R. VAN DONGEN. It had settled into respectable middle age. Still popular with sf fans, it won HUGO awards in 1953, 1955, 1956 and 1957.

During 1960 the magazine's title was gradually altered to *Analog Science Fact ⚛ Science Fiction*, "Astounding" fading down as "Analog" became more visible. "That little symbol . . . is a home-invented one," wrote Campbell (Jan 1964): "In all mathematics, etcetera, there [is] . . . no symbol meaning 'is analogous to'. We invented one . . . We do not expect our readers to enunciate our title as clearly as 'ANALOG Science Fact is analogous to Science Fiction' but we thought you might be interested in why we did not use the traditional ampersand – &." (With the Apr 1965 issue the order of the two elements changed, without explanation, so that it became sf analogous to science fact.)

Street & Smith expired and the magazine was taken

over by Condé Nast in Feb 1962. This was an important change, because it assured *ASF* of excellent distribution (as one of a group which included such titles as *Good Housekeeping*) at a time when its rivals faced increasing difficulties in getting distributed and displayed. In Mar 1963 the magazine adopted a very elegant bedsheet-size format but, lacking the advertising support such an expensive production required, it reverted to digest size in Apr 1965. The large issues are most notable for Frank HERBERT's first two **Dune** serials: "Dune World" (Dec 1963-Feb 1964) and "The Prophet of Dune" (Jan-May 1965), combined as *Dune* (fixup **1965**); both were superbly illustrated by John SCHOENHERR, who became one of the magazine's regular artists of the 1960s. Other authors who became frequent contributors included Christopher ANVIL, Harry HARRISON and Mack REYNOLDS.

The magazine won further Hugos in 1961, 1962, 1964 and 1965. Although it maintained a circulation above 100,000 (nearly twice that of its nearest rival) it continued on a slow decline into predictability. Campbell died in July 1971, being replaced as editor by Ben BOVA (the first issue credited to Bova was that for Jan 1972). Not surprisingly, the magazine gained considerably in vitality through having a new editor after nearly 34 years. Authors such as Roger ZELAZNY, who would not readily have fitted into Campbell's magazine, began to appear. While the editorial policy remained oriented towards traditional sf, a more liberal attitude prevailed, leading to some reader protest over stories by Joe HALDEMAN and Frederik POHL, which, though mild by contemporary standards, were not what some old-time readers expected to find in *ASF*. New writers like Haldeman and George R.R. MARTIN established themselves. The range of artists was widened with the addition of Jack GAUGHAN and the discovery of Rick STERNBACH and Vincent DI FATE. A first for *ASF* was the special women's issue (June 1977), which contained a HUGO winner, "Eyes of Amber" by Joan D. VINGE, and a NEBULA winner, "The Screwfly Solution", by Raccoona Sheldon (better known as James TIPTREE Jr). Bova won the Hugo for Best Editor (which had replaced the award for Best Magazine) every year 1973-7 and again in 1979. The magazine's circulation remained extremely healthy.

Bova resigned in 1978, soon afterwards joining OMNI as fiction editor. His replacement, Stanley SCHMIDT, was a HARD-SF writer whose début had been in *ASF* in 1968 with "A Flash of Darkness". His editing style is quieter and more modest than Campbell's and Bova's, but he has continued the magazine with dignity. Magazine publishing, however, was becoming a less important component of the sf-publishing business (◊ ANTHOLOGIES; SF MAGAZINES), and, while subscription sales continued to hold up through the 1970s and 1980s, newsstand sales were dropping. In 1980 Condé Nast decided *ASF* no longer fitted their list, but they had no trouble finding a buyer. Davis Publications (whose owner, Joel Davis, was son of B.G. Davis, a partner in ZIFF-DAVIS, publisher of *AMZ*) had already begun publishing sf digest periodicals in 1977 with ISAAC ASIMOV'S SCIENCE FICTION MAGAZINE. In 1980 Davis bought *ASF*, and soon changed the publication schedule from 12 to 13 issues a year, presumably in a bid to gain more newsstand space.

Increasingly during the 1980s there was a feeling that *ASF*, with its image as the last magazine bastion of the hard-sf "problem" story, was becoming a dinosaur: a still formidable anachronism, but an anachronism nevertheless. The paid circulation oscillated, but the general direction was down, from 104,000 in 1980 to 83,000 in 1990; newsstand sales dropped from 45,000 to 15,000 during the same period. In 1990 *ASF* nevertheless retained the highest circulation of the pure sf magazines. Though fewer of its stories were now appearing in "Best of the Year" anthologies and lists of award winners, it still produced occasional very good work: award winners during the 1980s included "The Cloak and the Staff" (1980) by Gordon R. Dickson, "The Saturn Game" (1981) by Poul Anderson, "Melancholy Elephants" (1982) by Spider ROBINSON, "Cascade Point" (1983) by Timothy ZAHN, "Blood Music" (1983) by Greg BEAR, "The Crystal Spheres" (1984) by David BRIN and "The Mountains of Mourning" (1989) by Lois McMaster BUJOLD. A Nebula-winning novel first serialized in *ASF* was *Falling Free* (1987-8 *ASF*; **1988**) by Bujold, one of *ASF*'s most popular writers in recent years. Other writers often associated with *ASF* in the 1980s (and after) include Michael FLYNN, Charles SHEFFIELD and Harry TURTLEDOVE.

Campbell, Bova and Schmidt all edited a number of anthologies drawn from *ASF* (*see their entries for further details*). Many other anthologies have drawn extensively on the magazine; indeed, of the 35 stories contained in the first major sf anthology, *Adventures in Time and Space* (**1946**) ed Raymond J. HEALY and J. Francis MCCOMAS, all but three were from *ASF*. The 2 vols of *The Astounding-Analog Reader* (anths **1972** and **1973**) ed Harry HARRISON and Brian W. ALDISS provide an informative chronological survey of *ASF*'s history. The flavour of *ASF*'s first two decades is nostalgically, if uncritically, captured in Alva ROGERS's *A Requiem for Astounding* (**1964**). A useful index is *The Complete Index to Astounding/Analog* (**1981** US) by Mike ASHLEY.

The UK edition, published by Atlas, appeared Aug 1939-Aug 1963. The contents were severely truncated during the 1940s, and the magazine did not appear regularly, adopting a variable bimonthly schedule. It became monthly from Feb 1952; from Nov 1953, when it changed from pulp to digest, it was practically a full reprint (four months behind in cover date) of the US edition, although some stories and departments were omitted. [MJE/PN]

ASTOUNDING STORIES ◊ ASTOUNDING SCIENCE-FICTION.

ASTOUNDING STORIES OF SUPER-SCIENCE ◊

ASTOUNDING SCIENCE-FICTION.

ASTOUNDING STORIES YEARBOOK One of the many reprint DIGEST magazines published by Sol Cohen's Ultimate Reprint Co. 2 issues were released in 1970, the second under the title *Astounding SF*. Cohen's use of such a celebrated magazine title was thought by fans to be cheeky. [BS/PN]

ASTROBOY ◊ JAPAN; Osamu TEZUKA.

ASTROGATION Literally, guidance by the stars. In sf TERMINOLOGY this is the space equivalent of navigation, and the astrogator is conventionally one of the most important officers on a SPACESHIP. After a jump through HYPERSPACE, perhaps, it is necessary, although less frequently now than in the GOLDEN AGE OF SF, for the astrogator to identify several stars, usually through spectroscopy, to confirm the craft's position by triangulation. [PN]

ASTRONOMY Astronomers played the key role in developing the cosmic perspective that lies at the heart of sf. Their science gave birth (not without difficulty, given the public reluctance of the Medieval Church to accept non-geocentric cosmologies) to an understanding of the true size and nature of the Universe. To his astronomical treatise *The Discovery of a New World* (3rd edn **1640**) John WILKINS appended a "Discourse Concerning the Possibility of a Passage Thither", and took the notion of lunar travel out of the realms of pure fantasy into those of legitimate speculation. Johannes KEPLER's *Somnium* (**1634**) was developed from an essay intended to popularize the Copernican theory. The literary image of the astronomer as it developed in the 18th century was, however, by no means entirely complimentary. "The Elephant in the Moon" (1759) by Samuel "Hudibras" Butler (1613-1680) has a group of observers witnessing what they take to be tremendous events on the Moon, but which subsequently turn out to be the activities of a mouse and a swarm of insects on the objective lens of their telescope. Jonathan SWIFT's *Gulliver's Travels* (**1726**) includes a sharply parodic account of the astronomers of Laputa. Samuel JOHNSON's *Rasselas* (**1759**) features a comically mad astronomer.

The revelations of astronomy inspired 19th-century writers, including Edgar Allan POE, whose rhapsodic "poem" *Eureka* (**1848**) draws heavily upon contemporary work. They also encouraged hoaxers like Richard Adams LOCKE, who foisted his imaginary descriptions of lunar life on the unwary readers of the *New York Sun* in 1835. The development of sf in France was led by the nation's foremost astronomer, Camille FLAMMARION, who was also one of the first popularizers of the science. His *Lumen* (**1887**; trans **1897**) is a remarkable semi-fictional vehicle for conveying the astronomer's particular sense of wonder and awe. One of the first popularizers of astronomy in the USA, Garrett P. SERVISS – author of *Curiosities of the Sky* (**1909**) – also became an early writer of scientific romances; his most notable was *A Columbus of Space* (**1911**). The affinity between astronomy and

sf is eloquently identified by Serviss in *Curiosities of the Sky*: "What Froude says of history is true also of astronomy: it is the most impressive when it transcends explanation. It is not the mathematics, but the wonder and mystery that seize upon the imagination . . . All [of the things described in the book] possess the fascination of whatever is strange, marvellous, obscure or mysterious, magnified, in this case, by the portentous scale of the phenomena." Sf is the ideal medium for the communication of this kind of feeling, but it can also accommodate cautionary tales against the hubris that may come from the illusion of close acquaintance with cosmic mysteries.

Astronomical discoveries concerning the MOON were rapidly adopted into sf – Jules VERNE's *Autour de la lune* (**1870**; trans **1873**) is particularly rich in astronomical detail – and observations of MARS by Giovanni Schiaparelli (1835-1910) and Percival Lowell (1855-1916), which seemed to reveal the notorious "canals", were a powerful stimulus to the sf imagination. Many 20th-century discoveries in astronomy have been inconvenient for sf writers, revealing as they do the awful inhospitability of our nearest neighbours in space. It was astronomers who banished Earth-clone worlds to other solar systems and made much early pulp melodrama seem ludicrous. Intriguing and momentous discoveries in the Universe beyond the Solar System have, however, provided rich imaginative compensation (◊ COSMOLOGY). One of the best-known and least theoretically orthodox contemporary astronomers, Sir Fred HOYLE, has written a good deal of sf drawing on his expertise, including the classic *The Black Cloud* (1957) and, in collaboration with his son Geoffrey, *The Inferno* (1973); unkind critics remark that Hoyle's more recent speculative nonfiction, written in collaboration with Chandra Wickramasinghe – including *Lifecloud* (**1978**), *Diseases from Space* (**1979**) and *Evolution from Space* (**1981**) – seems even more fanciful than his fiction. The US astronomer Robert S. Richardson has also been an occasional contributor to sf magazines under the name Philip LATHAM, and some of his stories are particularly clever in dramatizing the work of the astronomer and its imaginative implications. Examples include "To Explain Mrs Thompson" (1951), "Disturbing Sun" (1959) and "The Dimple in Draco" (1967).

Modern observational astronomy has become far more abstruse as it has diversified into radio, X-ray and other frequencies, and its visionary implications have become increasingly peculiar as its practitioners have found explanations for such enigmatic discoveries as quasars and empirical evidence for the existence of theoretically predicted entities like BLACK HOLES and NEUTRON STARS. Notable sf stories featuring peculiar discoveries by astronomers include Gregory BENFORD's *Timescape* (**1980**) and Robert L. FORWARD's *Dragon's Egg* (**1980**). The advent of radio astronomy has made a considerable impact on post-WWII sf in connection with the possibility of picking up signals from an ALIEN intelligence (◊ COMMUNICATIONS), a theme developed in sf novels ranging from Eden PHILLPOTTS's cautionary *Address Unknown* (**1949**) through James E. GUNN's enthusiastic *The Listeners* (fixup **1972**) to Carl SAGAN's over-the-top *Contact* (**1985**) and Jack McDEVITT's *The Hercules Text* (**1986**). In the real world, various projects connected with SETI (Search for Extra-Terrestrial Intelligence) have been mounted or mooted, and many stories have proposed that the receipt of such a message would be *the* crucial event in the history of mankind. A satirical dissent from this view can be found in Stanisław LEM's novel *His Master's Voice* (**1968**; trans **1983**), and there is also a PARANOID school of thought which suggests that aliens whose own SETI discovers us might easily turn out to be very unfriendly; our radio telescopes nearly become the agents of our destruction in Frank CRISP's *The Ape of London* (**1959**) and the tv serial A FOR ANDROMEDA (**1961**).

Astronomy is sometimes confused by the ignorant with astrology. Although sf has been remarkably tolerant of some other pseudo-sciences, it has rarely tolerated astrology. An exception is Piers ANTHONY's *Macroscope* (**1969**), which features a hypothetical astrological device of awesome power. Two writers outside the genre have, however, written satirical novels based on the hypothesis that astrology might be made absolutely accurate: Edward HYAMS with *The Astrologer* (**1950**) and John CAMERON with (again) *The Astrologer* (**1972**).   [BS]

See also: JUPITER; MERCURY; OUTER PLANETS; STARS; SUN; VENUS.

ATHELING, WILLIAM Jr ◊ James BLISH.

ATHERTON, GERTRUDE (FRANKLYN) (1857-1948) US novelist, biographer and historian. In a long career that extended from 1888 to 1946 she published about 50 books in a multitude of genres, her best-known fiction being *The Californians* (**1898**; rev **1935**) and her sf novel *Black Oxen* (**1923**). In this book, whose sexual implications caused a scandal, women (only) are rejuvenated by X-rays directed to the gonads. Though her explicitness and exuberance would not be remarked upon today in a woman, she achieved some notoriety in her prime as an erotic writer; she was also a campaigning (though ambivalent) feminist. *The Bell in the Fog, and Other Stories* (coll **1905**) and *The Foghorn* (coll **1934**) both contain fantasy stories.   [JC]

Other works: *What Dreams May Come* (1888) as by Frank Lin; *The White Morning: A Novel of the Power of German Women in Wartime* (**1918**).

ATHOLL, JUSTIN (? -) UK writer whose several very short sf novels appeared obscurely but nevertheless are of some interest. *The Man who Tilted the Earth* (**1943** chap) does not go quite so far as the title hints, though an atomic disintegrator comes close to ending life on the planet. *Death in the Green Fields* (**1944** chap) features a death-dealing fungus. *Land of Hidden Death* (**1944** chap) is a LOST-WORLD tale. *The Oasis of Sleep* (**1944** chap) invokes SUSPENDED

ANIMATION. The main story in *The Grey Beast* (coll **1944** chap) features an apeman (◊ APES AND CAVEMEN).   [JC]

Other works: *The Trackless Thing* (**1944** chap); *There Goes his Ghost* (**1944** chap).

ATKINS, FRANK [r] ◊ Frank AUBREY.

ATKINS, JOHN (ALFRED) (1916-) UK writer. His *The Diary of William Carpenter* (**1943**) is a psychological fantasy inspired by Luigi Pirandello (1867-1936). *Tomorrow Revealed* (**1955**) is an imaginary future HISTORY reconstructed in AD5000 from a library containing the works of such writers as H.G. WELLS and C.S. LEWIS. The material assembled, often taken from the works of GENRE-SF writers as well, builds a picture of history directed towards a theological goal. *A Land Fit for 'Eros* (**1957**) with J.B. Pick (1921-) is fantasy.   [JC/BS]

ATLANTIDE, L' ◊ Die HERRIN VON ATLANTIS.

ATLANTIS The legend of Atlantis, an advanced civilization on a continent in the middle of the Atlantic which was overwhelmed by some geological cataclysm, has its earliest extant source in PLATO's dialogues *Timaeus* and *Critias* (*c*350BC). The legend can be seen as a parable of the Fall of Man, and writers who have since embroidered the story have generally shown less interest in the cataclysm itself than in the attributes of the prelapsarian Atlanteans, who have often been given moral and scientific powers surpassing those of mere modern humans. Francis BACON's *The New Atlantis* (**1627**; **1629**) portrays Atlantean survivors as the founders of a scientific utopia in North America. However, it was not until Ignatius DONNELLY published his *Atlantis: The Antediluvian World* (**1882**) that the lost continent became a great popular myth. Donnelly's monomaniacal work contained much impressive learning and professed to be nonfiction. Unlike Plato and Bacon, who had treated Atlantis as an exemplary parable, Donnelly was convinced that the continent had existed and had been the source of all civilization. In fact, Donnelly's was a mythopoeic book of considerable power, arguably ancestral to all the PSEUDO-SCIENCE texts of the 20th century, and the inspiration for many works of fiction.

Atlantis had already been used in sf by Jules VERNE. His *Twenty Thousand Leagues Under the Sea* (**1870**; trans **1873**) contains a brief but effective scene in which Captain Nemo and the narrator explore the tumbled ruins of an Atlantean city. Some of the fiction inspired by the theories of the Theosophists and spiritualists was less restrained – e.g., *A Dweller on Two Planets* (**1894**) by Phylos the Thibetan (Frederick Spencer Oliver [1866-1899]), in which the hero "remembers" his previous incarnation as a ruler of Atlantis. Other writers used Atlantis more as a setting for rousing adventure, one of the best examples being *The Lost Continent* (**1900**) by C.J. Cutcliffe HYNE, a first-person narrative "framed" by the discovery of an ancient manuscript in the Canaries. David M. PARRY's *The Scarlet Empire* (**1906**), on the other hand, is set in the present (it depicts Atlantis preserved under a huge watertight dome, an image which has since become a comic-strip cliché) and intended as a SATIRE of socialism. (Other stories about a surviving Atlantis are listed in UNDER THE SEA.)

One of the most successful of all Atlantean romances, filmed four times (◊ Die HERRIN VON ATLANTIS), was Pierre BENOIT's *L'Atlantide* (**1919**; trans as *Atlantida* **1920**; vt *The Queen of Atlantis* UK) which concerns the present-day discovery of Atlantis in the Sahara. Benoit was accused of plagiarizing H. Rider HAGGARD's *The Yellow God* (**1908**) for many of the details of his story. In fact, the latter was not an Atlantean romance, and nor was Haggard's *When the World Shook* (**1919**), set in Polynesia, although it has been so described. Arthur Conan DOYLE produced one Atlantis story, "The Maracot Deep", to be found in *The Maracot Deep* (coll **1929**), which is marred as sf by a large admixture of spiritualism. Stanton A. COBLENTZ's *The Sunken World* (1928 *Amazing Stories Quarterly*; rev **1949**) has much in common with Parry's *The Scarlet Empire*: it involves the contemporary discovery of a domed undersea city, and the purpose of the story is largely satirical. Dennis WHEATLEY's *They Found Atlantis* (**1936**) contains more of the same, but without the satire.

The heyday of Atlantean fiction was 1885-1930. Often a subgenre of the LOST-WORLD story, sometimes of the UTOPIAN story, sometimes both, it was perhaps most often the vehicle for occultist speculation about spiritual powers, and therefore only marginally sf.

Incidental use of the Atlantis motif by S.P. MEEK and many others became common in US MAGAZINE sf. Many stories are set in other mythical lands cognate with Atlantis – Mu, Lemuria, Hyperborea, Ultima Thule, etc. Fantasy writers who have used such settings include Lin CARTER, Avram DAVIDSON, L. Sprague DE CAMP, Robert E. HOWARD, Henry KUTTNER and Clark Ashton SMITH. Two sf/historical novels, *Stonehenge* (**1972**) by Harry HARRISON and Leon STOVER and *The Dancer from Atlantis* (**1971**) by Poul ANDERSON, fit Atlantis into the Mycenean Greek world.

Several UK writers continued the pursuit of Atlantis. Francis ASHTON's *The Breaking of the Seals* (**1946**) and its follow-up, *Alas, That Great City* (**1948**), are old-fashioned romances in which the heroes are cast backwards in time by mystical means. Pelham GROOM's *The Purple Twilight* (**1948**) finds that Martians destroyed Atlantis in self-defence, later almost destroying themselves by nuclear WAR. John Cowper POWYS's *Atlantis* (**1954**) is an eccentric philosophical novel in which the aged Odysseus visits the drowned Atlantis *en route* from Ithaca to the USA.

However, for post-WWII readers Atlantis seems to have lost its spell-binding quality, and the films in which it has appeared, like ATLANTIS: THE LOST CONTINENT (1960) and *Warlords of Atlantis* (1978) have had little to recommend them – though more than the dire tv series *The* MAN FROM ATLANTIS (1977), which features a hero with webbed hands. An Atlantean series by Jane GASKELL, colourful and inventive, but written in

a gushing prose, is the **Cija** sequence: *The Serpent* (**1963**; vt in 2 vols *The Serpent* **1975** and *The Dragon* **1975**), *Atlan* (**1965**), *The City* (**1966**) and *Some Summer Lands* (**1977**). These form the autobiography of a princess of Atlantis, contain a considerable amount of sexual fantasy, and are closer to popular romance than to sf proper. Taylor CALDWELL's *The Romance of Atlantis* (**1975**; published version written with Jess Stearn), is based, she claimed, on childhood dreams of her previous incarnation as an Atlantean empress. A very symbolic Atlantis arises again from the waves in Ursula K. LE GUIN's "The New Atlantis" (**1975**) as a dystopian USA begins to sink.

Where Le Guin's story gave new metaphoric life to Atlantis, most of the sunken continent's few appearances in the 1980s were romantic melodramas whose view of Atlantis was on the whole traditional. One of these was Marion Zimmer BRADLEY's **Atlantis Chronicles**: *Web of Light* (**1982**) and *Web of Darkness* (**1984**), both assembled as *Web of Darkness* (omni **1985** UK; vt *The Fall of Atlantis* **1987** US). These fantasies about Atlantean conflicts between forces of light and darkness had their origin in a long, unpublished romance Bradley wrote as a teenager, and indeed their subject matter seems more appropriate to the 1940s than the 1980s. David GEMMELL's lively post-HOLOCAUST **Sipstrassi** series of science-fantasy novels features stones of healing and/or destruction whose source is Atlantis; Atlantis itself plays a prominent role (through gateways between past and future) in the fourth of the series, *The Last Guardian* (**1989**) – a complex plan to save its destruction through changing history comes to nothing, though it does produce Noah.

A good nonfiction work on the subject is *Lost Continents: The Atlantis Theme in History, Science and Literature* (**1954**; rev 1970) by L. Sprague de Camp. Henry M. Eichner's *Atlantean Chronicles* (**1971**) is a bibliography with level-headed annotations. Other rational books on the subject are few and far between, but *The End of Atlantis* (**1969**) by J.V. Luce and *The Search for Lost Worlds* (**1975**) by James Wellard are useful and entertaining. [DP/PN]

See also: PARANOIA.

ATLANTIS, THE LOST CONTINENT Film (1961). Galaxy/MGM. Dir and prod George PAL, starring Anthony Hall, Joyce Taylor, Ed Platt, John Dall. Screenplay Daniel Mainwaring, based on *Atalanta* (1949), a play by Sir Gerald Hargreaves (1881-1972). 90 mins. Colour.

A young Greek fisherman becomes involved with a castaway who says she is a princess from Atlantis. A large, fish-shaped submarine surfaces and they are both taken there. He is enslaved and witnesses the evils of the Atlantean culture, which include crimes against God and Nature. These lead to the eventual destruction and sinking of Atlantis by (a) a destructive ray generated from a giant crystal and (b) an erupting volcano. The scope of the special effects was obviously affected by the low budget, but A. Arnold

Gillespie and his team achieved some colourful spectacles. However, the performances are wooden and the story strictly pulp. Pal was a better producer than director; this is one of his weakest films. [JB/PN]

ATLAS PUBLICATIONS ◊ SCIENCE FICTION MONTHLY.

ATOMCRACKER, BUZZ-BOLT ◊ Don WILCOX.

ATOMIC MAN, THE ◊ TIMESLIP.

ATOM MAN VS. SUPERMAN ◊ SUPERMAN.

ATOROX AWARD ◊ AWARDS; FINLAND.

ATTACK OF THE CRAB MONSTERS Film (1957). Los Altos/Allied Artists. Dir Roger CORMAN, starring Richard Garland, Pamela Duncan, Russell Johnson, Leslie Bradley. Screenplay Charles B. Griffith. 70 mins cut to 64 mins. B/w.

Two giant crabs, mutations caused by radiation from an H-bomb test on an island, scuttle out of the sea and destroy all of one and most of another expedition to the island. Eerily, they take over the minds (and voices) of their victims; it is disturbing when a crab the size of a van speaks to you in the voice of your recently deceased best friend. Vintage Corman: fast, absurd, intelligently scripted, made on a shoestring. One of the more memorable MONSTER MOVIES of the 1950s boom. [PN]

ATTACK OF THE GIANT LEECHES ◊ Roger CORMAN.

ATTACK OF THE MONSTERS ◊ DAIKAIJU GAMERA.

ATTANASIO, A(LFRED) A(NGELO) (1951-) US writer, BA (biochemistry), MFA (creative writing), MA (linguistics). He began publishing sf with "Once More, the Dream" as aa Attanasio for *New Worlds Quarterly #7* (anth **1974**) ed Hilary BAILEY and Charles PLATT; this tale, in its experimental heat and dark extravagance, proved typical of his short fiction in general. Not particularly attractive to the magazine markets, most of his shorter works appeared for the first time in *Beastmarks* (coll **1985**). AAA came to wide notice with the publication of his first novel, *Radix* (**1981**), the first volume of the **Radix Tetrad** sequence, which continues with *In Other Worlds* (**1984**), *Arc of the Dream* (**1986**) and *The Last Legends of Earth* (**1989**). As a whole, the sequence works as a complex meditation on metamorphosis couched in SPACE-OPERA terms, so that densely ambitious moments of poetic aspiration alternate with episodes out of the rag-and-bone shop of PULP-MAGAZINE fiction. After losing her radiation shield, which guards her against the full nakedness of the Universe, Earth begins to mutate savagely, a transformation articulated clearly in *Radix* itself through the story of a mutant SUPERMAN, who undergoes the same transcendental jumpstart that jolts his planet through terrors and DIMENSIONS. By the time *The Last Legends of Earth* has come to a close, long after Earth itself has become an inordinately complicated memory, human beings are strange creatures, resurrected out of dream, half-persona, half-godling. At the same time, however, a protagonist engages in a revenge fight with spiderlike ALIENS. It could not be said that AAA is a tempered writer; but the splurge and dance of his prose can be, at times, enormously enlivening. His next epic is awaited with alarmed admiration.

Of his other novels, *Wyvern* (**1988**) is a pirate-punk historical, with little or no fantasy content, *Hunting the Ghost Dancer* (**1991**) is an extremely late, and rather heated, example of prehistoric sf (◊ ANTHROPOLOGY) in which a last Neanderthal is pitted against several of us, and *Kingdom of the Grail* (**1992**) is an Arthurian tale. [JC]

See also: MUTANTS.

ATTERLEY, JOSEPH Pseudonym of George Tucker (1775-1861), Chairman of the Faculty of the University of Virginia while Edgar Allan POE was a student there, and an influence on him. JA's *A Voyage to the Moon with Some Account of the Manners and Customs, Science and Philosophy, of the People of Morosofia, and Other Lunarians* (**1827**) describes a trip to eccentric lunar societies, including one UTOPIA. The spacecraft is coated with the first antigravitic metal in literature, a forerunner of H.G. WELLS's Cavorite (◊ ANTIGRAVITY). The book is true sf, including much scientific speculation. It was reprinted in 1975 – including a review of 1828 and an introduction by David G. HARTWELL – as by George Tucker. Another sf work, dealing with OVERPOPULATION, was *A Century Hence, or A Romance of 1941* (**1977**), as by George Tucker, ed from his manuscript. [JC/PN]

See also: FANTASTIC VOYAGES; HISTORY OF SF; MOON.

AT THE EARTH'S CORE Film (1976). Amicus/AIP. Dir Kevin Connor, starring Doug McClure, Peter Cushing, Caroline Munro. Screenplay Milton Subotsky, based on *At the Earth's Core* (**1922**) by Edgar Rice BURROUGHS. 89 mins. Colour.

The success of Amicus's *The* LAND THAT TIME FORGOT (also based on a Burroughs novel) inspired the making of this lightweight film, in which genially routine adventures take place inside a vast cavern visited by a hero and a scientist in a mechanical mole. There are dinosaurs and ape-things. The wonders of Burroughs's fascinating, if illogical, HOLLOW-EARTH world-within-a-world (Pellucidar) are barely hinted at. [JB/PN]

ATWOOD, MARGARET (ELEANOR) (1939-) Canadian poet and novelist, some of whose poetry, like *Speeches for Doctor Frankenstein* (**1966** chap US), hints at sf content; but her interest as a prose writer in the form was minimal until the publication of *The Handmaid's Tale* (**1985**), which won the Governor General's Award in Canada and the first ARTHUR C. CLARKE AWARD in 1986. The 1990 film version (◊ *The* HANDMAID's TALE) stiffly travestied the book, treating it as an improbable but ideologically "correct" DYSTOPIA, rather than as a fluid nightmare requiem in the vein of George ORWELL's *Nineteen Eighty-four* (**1949**). The tale of Offred the Handmaid, contextually placed as it is within a frame dated 200 years later, reads overwhelmingly as a personal tragedy. The venue is dystopian – a sudden loss of fertility has occasioned a pre-emptive NEAR-FUTURE coup against all remaining fertile women by a fundamentalist New England, to keep them from power – and the lessons taught throughout have a sharp FEMINIST saliency. But Offred's liquid telling of her tale, and her ambivalent disappearance into death or liberation as the book closes, make for a novel whose context leads, liberatingly, out of nightmare into the pacific Inuit culture of the frame. Despite the occasional infelicity – MA's attempts at the language of GENRE SF are not unembarrassing – *The Handmaid's Tale* soon gained a reputation as the best sf novel ever produced by a Canadian. [JC]

See also: CANADA; SATIRE; WOMEN SF WRITERS.

ATWOOD, SAM [s] ◊ Thomas A. EASTON.

AUBREY, FRANK The first and main pseudonym of UK writer Francis Henry Atkins (1840-1927). A contributor to the pre-sf PULP MAGAZINESS, he wrote three LOST-WORLD novels. The first and most successful was *Devil-Tree of El Dorado: A Romance of British Guiana* (**1896**), which capitalized on the contemporary interest in the Roraima Plateau. Weird themes continued in FA's writings but sf elements became more prominent: *A Queen of Atlantis: A Romance of the Caribbean* (**1898**) related the discovery of a telepathic race living in the Sargasso Sea; and *King of the Dead: A Weird Romance* (**1903**) showed remnants of Earth's oldest civilization employing advanced science to resurrect the dead of untold generations in a bid to regain their lost empire. The first two of these loosely connected novels are linked by the appearance in both of Monella, a Wandering-Jew character.

Little is known about FA. There is evidence that he was involved in a scandal at the turn of the century; following a three-year hiatus, he began to write again, now as Fenton Ash. Publisher's files indicate that his son, Frank Atkins Jr (?   -1921) – who wrote many popular nature stories as F. St Mars – also used this name, perhaps in collaboration. Stylistic analysis indicates that a later story as by FA, "Caught by a Comet" (1910), may have been written exclusively by Frank Atkins Jr. Many sf stories as by Fenton Ash, all characterized by vividly imaginative but less than fully realized ideas, appeared in the BOYS' PAPERS. The majority are lost-world adventures; e.g., "The Sunken Island" (1904), "The Sacred Mountain" (1904), *The Radium Seekers, or The Wonderful Black Nugget* (**1905**), *The Temple of Fire, or The Mysterious Island* (**1905**) as Fred Ashley, "The Hermit of the Mountains" (1906-7), *By Airship to Ophir* (**1910**), *The Black Opal: A Romance of Thrilling Adventure* (1906 *The Big Budget*; **1915**), "In Polar Seas" (1915-16) and *The Island of Gold* (1915 *The Marvel*; **1918**). In two further works, "A Son of the Stars" (1907-8) and "A King of Mars" (1907 *The Sunday Circle*; vt *A Trip to Mars* 1909), the lost-world setting shifted to a war-torn Mars, preceding Edgar Rice BURROUGHS's use of the same idea by some years.

In his chosen market FA was extremely successful and influential. Although contributing little to the sophistication of sf, he played an important role in the HISTORY OF SF. [JE]

AUEL, JEAN M(ARIE) (1936-   ) US writer who is known solely for her enormously successful **Earth's Children** sequence of prehistoric-sf novels (◊ ANTHROPOLOGY; ORIGIN OF MAN): *The Clan of the Cave Bear* (**1980**), *The Valley of Horses* (**1982**), *The Mammoth Hunters* (**1985**) and *The Plains of Passage* (**1990**). It could not be suggested that the sequence is very effective as sf, or that, indeed, it is intended to be read as sf; but most of the events recounted – as the young Cro-Magnon protagonist grows up in the Neanderthal community which has adopted her, and begins to effect transformations in her world – are legitimate anthropological extrapolations pastwards. The greatest displacement from what might fairly be called romantic realism – the plots themselves have novelettish moments – lies in the growing capacity of the main characters to commune with animals. In any case, generic definitions aside, JMA's control over masses of detail, and her compulsive storytelling style, put the **Earth's Children** books on a level far above most of their very numerous predecessors. [JC]

See also: WOMEN SF WRITERS.

AUGUSTUS, ALBERT Jr ◊ Charles NUETZEL.

AUMBRY, ALAN [s] ◊ Barrington J. BAYLEY.

AUREALIS Australian SEMIPROZINE, subtitled "The Australian Magazine of Fantasy and Science Fiction", quarterly, A5 format, published by Chimaera Publications, Melbourne, ed Stephen Higgins and Dirk Strasser, dated by year only. Sep 1990-current, 5 issues to Sep 1991.

Yet another brave attempt by an Australian SMALL PRESS to publish an sf magazine in a market that has repeatedly proven itself too small to sustain one, though an initial print run of 10,000 was claimed. Some stories have been promising, few have risen to excellence. Mostly new writers mix with a sprinkling of better established names like Damien BRODERICK, Terry DOWLING, Leanne Frahm and Rosaleen LOVE. [PN]

AURORA ◊ AWARDS; CANADA.

AURORA Fanzine. ◊ JANUS/AURORA.

AUSTER, PAUL (1947-   ) US writer who came to sudden attention – after years of work – with a series of FABULATIONS playing on detective genres and the French *nouveau roman*. *City of Glass* (**1985**), *Ghosts* (**1986**) and *The Locked Room* (**1986**), assembled as *The New York Trilogy* (omni **1987** UK), are not sf; but *Moon Palace* (**1989**) comes very close to a literal reading of its lunar metaphorical structure. *In the Country of the Last Things* (**1987**), however, is sufficiently firm about its future New York setting and the nightmarish landscape its protagonist must traverse, to rest comfortably within the genre's increasingly commodious fringe. [JC]

AUSTIN, F(REDERICK) BRITTEN (1885-1941) UK writer and WWII army captain, most noted for his collections of stories illustrating problems for UK military security arising in future WARS from new weaponry and tactics: *In Action: Studies of War* (coll **1913**) and *The War-God Walks Again* (coll **1926**). The latter volume is occasionally eloquent. FBA also wrote several volumes of linked stories, each comprising a kind of anthropological romance telling the development of a significant aspect of Man's history through the ages; examples are *A Saga of the Sea* (coll of linked stories **1929**), where a ship's history is told, and *A Saga of the Sword* (coll of linked stories **1928**). The first and last stories of each of these collections tend to infringe upon sf material and concerns.   [JC]

Other works, some marginal sf: *Battlewrack* (coll **1917**); *According to Orders* (coll **1918**); *On the Borderland* (coll **1922**); *Under the Lens* (coll **1924**); *Thirteen* (coll **1925**); *When Mankind was Young* (coll of linked stories **1930**); *Tomorrow* (coll c**1930**) *The Red Flag* (coll of linked stories **1932**), the final tale of which is set in 1977.

See also: ORIGIN OF MAN.

AUSTIN, RICHARD ◊ Victor MILÁN.

AUSTRALIA Much early Australian sf falls into subgenres which can be described as sf only controversially: lost-race romances, UTOPIAN novels and NEAR-FUTURE political thrillers about racial invasion.

Works of utopian speculation began appearing in Australia about the middle of the 19th century and were set, appropriately for a new society in a largely unexplored land, either in the FAR FUTURE or in Australia's deep interior (indeed, Australia's remoteness encouraged UK and US writers to make similar use of the land as a venue for utopian speculation). Among early utopias by Australians are Joseph Fraser's *Melbourne and Mars: My Mysterious Life on Two Planets* (**1889**) and G. McIVER's *Neuroomia: A New Continent* (**1894**). The lost-race (◊ LOST WORLDS) theme was more romantically handled in novels such as Fergus HUME's *The Expedition of Captain Flick* (**1896** UK) and G. Firth Scott's *The Last Lemurian* (**1896** *The Golden Penny*; exp **1898** UK).

A FEMINIST perspective on social criticism is shown in *A Woman of Mars, or Australia's Enfranchised Woman* (**1901**) by Mary Ann Moore-Bentley (pseudonym of Mrs H.H. Ling). This depicts an ideal society on Mars in strongly Christian terms, and deals with an attempt to reform Earth in conformity with the Martian model. Of more merit is an earlier novel, C.H. SPENCE's feminist utopia *Handfasted* (written c**1879**; **1984**), which depicts a community distinguished by its advocacy of "handfasting" – a system of year-long "trial marriage" by contract. The book is unusual in that it explores the ways in which its central utopian idea might actually be adopted within the real-world community.

From the time of the mid-19th-century gold rushes, Australian society was marred by racial antagonism. By the end of the century, fears of Asian hordes had found their way into sf in such novels as *The Yellow Wave: A Romance of the Asiatic Invasion of Australia* (**1895** UK) by Kenneth MacKAY, *The Coloured Conquest* (**1904**) by "Rata" (Thomas Roydhouse) and *The Australian Crisis* (**1909**) by C.H. Kirmess. Novels of this kind, though less vitriolic and racist, have persisted up to the present: see John Hooker's *The*

Bush Soldiers (**1984**) and Eric Willmot's *Up the Line* (**1991**). INVASION by aliens of a more sciencefictional kind is found in Robert POTTER's *The Germ Growers* (**1892**), one of the earliest books with this theme. However, although it features space-dwelling shape-changers setting up beachheads in the Australian outback, and thereby looks forward to GENRE SF, it is also religious allegory.

The various early traditions achieved their apotheosis in Erle COX's *Out of the Silence* (**1919** *Argus*; **1925**; rev **1947**), in many ways a modern-seeming and sophisticated work of sf. A gentleman farmer in the outback discovers an ancient time-vault containing, in SUSPENDED ANIMATION, a beautiful and powerful woman, Earani. She is one of the last survivors of an early species of humanity which, although more highly developed than *Homo sapiens*, was ruthless: one of its cultural heroes purified the race by inventing a "Death Ray" to destroy its lower (i.e., coloured) racial strains. What is disturbing to the modern reader is the way the novel takes racialist thinking seriously. Though it finally rejects the Nazi-like utopia it depicts, this rejection has to be earned through layers of irony and complex narrative, in all of which Earani's attitudes are given what today seems more than their due. Indeed, she is depicted as morally cleaner than many of the 20th-century people she meets.

Little Australian sf of importance was published during the 1930s and 1940s, though the interplanetary thrillers of J.M. WALSH, such as *Vandals of the Void* (**1931** UK), should be noted. The next real milestone is *Tomorrow and Tomorrow* (cut **1947**; full text **1983** as *Tomorrow and Tomorrow and Tomorrow*) by M. Barnard ELDERSHAW. Framed by a story set in the 24th century, it sophisticatedly tells, through a novel supposedly written by one of the characters, of the tumultuous events occurring in Australian society during the late 20th century. It was cut by the censor at the time of first publication because of its supposedly subversive tendencies.

Professional commercial sf is the most international of literary forms – although much of it has internalized distinctive US values, its strength is in imaginative extrapolation rather than in the depiction of any local experience – and so UK and US sf, requiring no translation and readily available, has tended to be sufficient to meet the needs of Australian readers. Thus the indigenous sf industry has never achieved critical mass in the way it has in some other countries. Nonetheless, since the 1950s there has always been interest in genre sf among Australian writers and publishers.

There was a flurry of local magazine publishing around the 1950s, with THRILLS, INCORPORATED (1950-51), FUTURE SCIENCE FICTION (1953-5), POPULAR SCIENCE FICTION (1953-4) and SCIENCE FICTION MONTHLY (1955-7). Also during the 1950s, stories by Australian sf writers began to appear in the US and UK magazines. The work of Frank Bryning, Wynne WHITEFORD and

A. Bertram CHANDLER (whose magazine publishing began in the 1940s) represented a first consolidation of genre sf by writers in Australia. These authors expanded from their beachhead in the 1960s and thereafter, being joined during the 1960s by John BAXTER, Damien BRODERICK, Lee HARDING, David ROME and Jack WODHAMS.

The Australian-UK magazine VISION OF TOMORROW (1969-70) contained many stories by Australians, perhaps most notably Harding and Broderick. Harding developed into a thoughtful writer of sf, mainly for adolescents, whose doubts and alienation he has captured in a series of powerful metaphors. His most successful work is *Displaced Person* (**1979**; vt *Misplaced Persons* US), in which the characters find themselves lost in a bewildering limbo after they start becoming invisible to others. Other important sf for younger readers has been produced by Gillian RUBINSTEIN, notably *Space Demons* (**1986**) and *Beyond the Labyrinth* (**1988**), and by Victor KELLEHER, such as *Taronga* (**1986**); his *The Beast of Heaven* (**1984**) is sf for adults.

At the end of the 1960s John Baxter began a trend by editing two anthologies of Australian sf, *The Pacific Book of Australian Science Fiction* (anth **1968**; vt *Australian Science Fiction 1*) and *The Second Pacific Book of Australian Science Fiction* (anth **1971**; vt *Australian Science Fiction 2*). Lee Harding's anthology *Beyond Tomorrow* (anth **1976**) brought together stories by Australian and overseas writers, as did his further state-of-the-art anthology, *Rooms of Paradise* (anth **1978** UK). Several other one-off anthologies of Australian sf were published in Australia in the 1970s and 1980s, most notably those edited by Broderick: *The Zeitgeist Machine* (anth **1977**), *Strange Attractors* (anth **1985**) and *Matilda at the Speed of Light* (anth **1988**).

In 1975 Paul COLLINS began the magazine VOID (1975-81), which published original stories by Australian writers. He expanded this operation in 1980 into the publishing house Cory and Collins (partnered by Rowena Cory). For some years this firm produced anthologies of sf and fantasy edited by Collins (as if they were numbers of *Void*) as well as novels and collections by David LAKE (who has also published quite widely overseas), Wodhams, Whiteford and others. Collins himself is a prolific writer of short stories. A number of other SMALL PRESSES have attempted to produce either magazines or books containing sf by Australian writers, and some still do. However, this has not generally proved to be commercially viable.

Currently George TURNER is probably the most prominent Australian sf writer, having earlier established a reputation as a mainstream novelist and as a critic. Turner has written several very serious near-future novels containing detailed social and scientific extrapolation. His most ambitious work, *The Sea and Summer* (**1987** UK; vt *Drowning Towers* US), is a relentless extrapolation of social divisions, factoring in the consequences of the greenhouse effect. The novel borrows the frame-story technique of *Tomorrow and Tomorrow*, as if to state that Turner deliberately casts himself as M. Barnard Eldershaw's successor.

Damien Broderick continues to publish fiction notable for its innovation and humour, such as *The Dreaming Dragons* (**1980**) and the comic *Striped Holes* (**1988** US). Wynne Whiteford has gone from strength to strength in writing traditional sf. Australia has some claim upon the New Zealand-born Cherry WILDER, who now lives in Germany but who was in Australia for many years. Keith Taylor (1946-   ) is a major fantasy writer. Philippa Maddern (1952-   ), Leanne Frahm and Lucy SUSSEX have written some successful stories. Rosaleen LOVE's neat sf fables have been collected in *The Total Devotion Machine and Other Stories* (coll **1989** UK). Of the newer writers, the most exciting are Terry DOWLING and Greg EGAN. Most significant writers since the 1950s have aimed their work predominantly at international markets.

While there has been little success in establishing Australian sf publishing, Australia has been more notable for its efforts in two other areas, namely serious writing about sf and, perhaps unexpectedly, film. In the former category Donald H. TUCK's *The Encyclopedia of Science Fiction and Fantasy Through 1968* (vol 1 **1974** US; vol 2 **1978** US; vol 3 **1982** US) deserves special mention. Magazines such as John Bangsund's AUSTRALIAN SF REVIEW (1966-9) and its successor, AUSTRALIAN SCIENCE FICTION REVIEW: SECOND SERIES (1986-91), published by a small collective of sf fans, Bruce GILLESPIE's SF COMMENTARY (1969-current), and SCIENCE FICTION: A REVIEW OF SPECULATIVE LITERATURE (1977-current) ed Van Ikin (1951-   ) have all achieved international respect.

In regard to film, sf had its share in the renaissance in the Australian movie industry which began in the mid-1970s and continued until about 1983, with some successes still being produced. The three post-HOLOCAUST **Mad Max** films – MAD MAX (1979), MAD MAX 2 (1981; vt *The Road Warrior* US) and MAD MAX BEYOND THUNDERDOME (1985) – have been particularly well received. Unfortunately, some more recent ambitious (but uneven) movies such as *The Time Guardian* (1987) and *As Time Goes By* (1987) have flopped, and the future of sf cinema in Australia is doubtful, with the film industry as a whole having been in decline for several years. One recent sf film of note, a hit in Australia and quite successful abroad, is the comedy YOUNG EINSTEIN (1988).

Australian sf CONVENTIONS have been held regularly since 1952. The 1975 and 1985 World Science Fiction Conventions (Aussiecon and Aussiecon II) were held in Melbourne.   [RB]

AUSTRALIAN SF REVIEW Australian FANZINE (1966-9) ed John Bangsund (1939-   ). *ASFR* was one of the most literate and eclectic of the serious sf fanzines and, despite its relative isolation, was able to attract articles from such writers as Brian W. ALDISS, James BLISH and Harry HARRISON. *ASFR* also served as a focal point for renewed interest in sf and FANDOM in

Australia, and brought attention to Australian sf critics such as John BAXTER, John Foyster, Bruce GILLESPIE, Lee HARDING and George TURNER. *ASFR* was twice nominated for a HUGO, and won a Ditmar AWARD in 1969. [PR]

AUSTRALIAN SCIENCE FICTION REVIEW: SECOND SERIES Australian FANZINE (Mar 1986-Autumn 1991), ed "The Science Fiction Collective" (at first Jenny Blackford (1957-   ), Russell BLACKFORD, John Foyster, Yvonne Rousseau and Lucy SUSSEX; Janeen Webb joined and Sussex left in 1987). This worthy successor to the defunct AUSTRALIAN SF REVIEW was effectively though not officially an academic critical journal, of variable but often high quality, fannishly enlivened at times by name-calling. Spirited and regular, it had 27 issues before the collective collapsed from exhaustion. The most consistent Australian sf journal of its period, it won little support from local FANDOM who saw it as elitist, but received a farewell Ditmar AWARD in 1991. [PN]

AUSTRIA Austrian literature must be considered a part of the larger German literature (◊ GERMANY), although with a distinct voice; Austrian writers have always been published more by German publishing houses than by Austrian ones.

At the turn of the century, Vienna was a veritable laboratory for many of the ideas of modern times, from psychoanalysis and logical positivism to music, the arts and literature: here were found Freud, Wittgenstein, Mahler, Schoenberg, Klimt, Schiele, Schnitzler, Karl Kraus and so on. But, while the former Austro-Hungarian Empire produced many writers important in fantastic literature (notably Gustav MEYRINK, Herzmanovsky-Orlando and Leo PERUTZ), its contribution to sf has been rather modest. True, there is the one UTOPIA that became true: the Zionism of Theodor Herzl (1860-1904) and his desire for the foundation of a home country for the Jews found a literary expression in *Altneuland* (**1902**; trans as *Old-New Land* **1947**). A utopia of a more parochial sociopolitical character is *Osterreich im Jahre 2020* ["Austria in 2020 AD"] (**1893**) by Joseph Ritter von Neupauer. The utopias *Freiland* (**1890**; trans as *Free-land* **1891**) and its sequel *Eine Reise nach Freiland* (**1893**; trans as *A Visit to Freeland* **1894**) by the economist Theodor HERTZKA were internationally successful, although the utopias of the first woman winner (1905) of the Nobel Peace Prize, Bertha von Suttner (1843-1914), such as *Der Menschheit Hochgedanken* ["The Exalted Thoughts of Mankind"] (**1911**), found little resonance. Under the pseudonym Ludwig Hevesi, Ludwig Hirsch (1843-1910) wrote *MacEck's sonderbare Reise zwischen Konstantinopel und San Francisco* ["MacEck's Curious Journey between Constantinople and San Francisco"] (**1901**) as well as humorous sketches of Jules VERNE's adventures in Heaven and Hell in his collection *Die fünfte Dimension* ["The Fifth Dimension"] (coll **1906**). Hevesi was a collector of utopian literature, and upon his death his library was catalogued as "Bibiotheca Utopistica" (reprinted

Munich 1977) by an antiquarian bookstore, the first such listing in the German language. In *Im Reiche der Homunkuliden* ["In the Empire of the Homunculids"] (**1910**), Rudolf Hawel (1860-1923), another humorist, has his protagonist Professor Voraus ["Ahead"] sleep into the year 3907, where he encounters a world of asexual ROBOTS.

A curious future-WAR story is the anonymous *Unser letzter Kampf* ["Our Last Battle"] (**1907**), presented as the "legacy of an old imperial soldier" who describes how the Austro-Hungarian Empire perishes in a heroic fight against Serbs, Italians and Russians. There is the occasional sf story among the writings of K.H. Strobl (1877-1946) and Gustav Meyrink. Strobl's big, sprawling novel *Eleagabal Kuperus* (**1910**) is an apocalyptic vision of a fight between good and evil principles that involves a sciencefictional attempt by the villain to deprive humanity of oxygen; his *Gespenster im Sumpf* ["Ghosts in the Swamp"] (**1920**) is a nationalistic, anti-socialist and antisemitic account of the doom of Vienna, and is certainly closer to sf than is the visionary novel of the great illustrator Alfred Kubin (1877-1959), *Die andere Seite* ["The Other Side"] (**1909**).

At this time important work was being done at the fringes of sf. Highly ranked in world literature are the metaphysical parables of Franz KAFKA, one of a group of Jewish writers from Prague writing in German who included also Max Brod (1884-1968), Leo Perutz and Franz WERFEL, who wrote his spiritual utopia *Stern der Ungeborenen* (**1946**; trans as *Star of the Unborn* **1946**) during his US exile. Kafka's texts combine a total lucidity of prose with a sense of the equally total impenetrability of the world as a whole, usually seen as having a totalitarian-bureaucratic character, as in *Der Prozess* (**1925**; trans as *The Trial* **1935**). The story "In der Strafkolonie" (1919; trans 1933 as "In the Penal Settlement") might be considered an anticipation of the Nazi concentration camps. Also of note is the expressionist writer Robert Müller (1887-1924), whose *Camera Obscura* (**1921**) is a many-levelled futuristic mystery novel. Two of the fantastic novels of the great writer Leo Perutz could be considered as psychedelic sf: *Der Meister des Jüngsten Tages* (**1923**; trans as *The Master of the Day of Judgement* **1930**) **and** *St Petri Schnee* (**1933**; trans as *The Virgin's Brand* **1934** UK). Both involve consciousness-altering drugs. The books have a hallucinatory quality, and currently Perutz is undergoing a revival.

An acquaintance of Perutz was Oswald Levett (1889-?   ), a Viennese Jewish lawyer who probably perished in a German concentration camp. His two sf novels have recently been reprinted. *Verirrt in den Zeiten* ["Lost in Time"] (**1933**) is a TIME-TRAVEL novel of a journey back to the Thirty Years' War and an unsuccessful attempt to change history; as in Perutz's works, the harder the heroes try to change their fate, the more they are stuck with it. *Papilio Mariposa* (**1935**) can be read as a fantastic allegory of the fate of the Jews: an ugly and strange individual is changed into a vampiric butterfly; feelings of inferiority and the desire for a fantastic harmony with an inimical environment result in tragedy. In *Die Stadt ohne Juden* ["The City without Jews"] (**1925**) by another Jewish writer, Hugo Bettauer (1877-1925; he was murdered), the expelled Jews are finally recalled to restore the prosperity of the city. Otto Soyka (1882-1955), a best-selling mystery novelist in his day but now forgotten, wrote a novel about a chemical substance that influences people's dreams: *Die Traumpeitsche* ["The Dream Whip"] (**1921**).

After WWII, Erich Dolezal (1902-1960) wrote a series of a dozen successful, although stiffly didactic and boring, juveniles about rocketry, starting with *RS 11 schweigt* ["RS 11 Doesn't Answer"] (**1953**). Somewhat better are 2 books by the chemist Friedrich Hecht (1903-   ) which combine space travel with discoveries about ATLANTIS and a civilization on an exploded planet between Mars and Jupiter (◊ ASTEROIDS): *Das Reich im Mond* ["Empire in the Moon"] (**1951**) and its sequel *Im Banne des Alpha Centauri* ["Under the Spell of Alpha Centauri"] (**1955**). But the best Austrian sf juvenile is the anti-utopian *Tötet ihn* ["Kill Him!"] (**1967**) by Winfried Bruckner. *Der U-Boot-Pirat* (1951-2), *Yuma* (1951), *Star Utopia* (1958) and *Uranus* (1958) were all short-lived JUVENILE SERIES. Ernst Vlcek (1941-   ), a professional writer since 1970, wrote hundreds of novels in the field, especially for the PERRY RHODAN series.

The physicist Herbert W. FRANKE, considered the most important living sf writer in the German language, is also Austrian. He began his career with a collection of 65 short-short stories, *Der grüne Komet* ["The Green Comet"] (coll **1960**), in the Goldmann SF series which he at the time edited. His first novel was *Das Gedankennetz* (**1961**; trans as *The Mind Net* **1974** US). Two other novels that have been translated into English are *Der Orchideenkafig* (**1961**; trans as *The Orchid Cage* **1973** US) and *Zone Null* (**1970**; trans **1974** US). Franke has written more than a dozen sf novels, collections and radio plays, and has edited a number of international sf anthologies.

Among younger writers are: the physicist Peter Schattschneider (1950-   ), author of the two collections *Zeitstopp* ["Time Stop"] (coll **1982**) and *Singularitäten* ["Singularities"] (coll **1984**); Marianne Gruber, author of many short stories and two anti-utopian novels, *Die gläserne Kugel* ["The Glass Sphere"] (**1981**) and *Zwischenstation* ["Inter-Station"] (**1986**); Barbara Neuwirth (1958-   ), who writes brooding fantasy tales, sometimes with sf elements, her first collection, *In den Gärten der Nacht* ["In the Gardens of Night"] (coll **1990**), being one of the best to appear in many years; and Ernst Petz (1947-   ) and Kurt Bracharz (1947-   ), who are both writers of satirical stories.

Austria's most important (and most curious) contribution to sf cinema is a propagandist effort called *1 April 2000* (1952; vt *April 1st, 2000*), dir Wolfgang Liebeneiner. In AD2000 Austria is still occupied by the USA, the USSR, France and the UK. When, on 1st April, she declares her independence she is accused of breaking the peace. Forces of the world police, equipped with death-rays, descend upon her, and in a public trial she has to defend her right to exist. This is a charmingly naïve period piece, sponsored by the Austrian Government and with a high-class cast, including the Spanish Riding School and the Vienna Philharmonic Orchestra. [FR]

AUTHENTIC SCIENCE FICTION UK magazine. 85 issues, 1 Jan 1951-Oct 1957, published by Hamilton & Co., Stafford, fortnightly to #8 then monthly, issues numbered consecutively, no vol numbers; ed L.G. Holmes (Gordon Landsborough) (Jan 1951-Nov 1952), H.J. CAMPBELL (Dec 1952-Jan 1956) and E.C. TUBB (Feb 1956-Oct 1957). Pocketbook-size Jan 1951-Feb 1957, DIGEST-size Mar-Oct 1957. #1 and #2 were entitled *Authentic Science Fiction Series*, #3-#8 *Science Fiction Fortnightly*, #9-#12 *Science Fiction Monthly*, #13-#28 *Authentic Science Fiction*, #29-#68 *Authentic Science Fiction Monthly*, #69-#77 *Authentic Science Fiction* again, and finally *Authentic Science Fiction Monthly* #78-#85.

This magazine began as a numbered book series, with each number containing one novel, but a serial was begun in #26 and short stories appeared from #29. H.J. Campbell, under whose editorship the magazine considerably improved, included numerous science articles during his tenure, but E.C. Tubb gradually eliminated most of the nonfiction. The proportion of original stories relative to reprints increased. Full-length novels were phased out and transferred to Hamilton's new paperbook line, Panther Books. The covers got off to a bad start, but from #35 many fine covers by "Davis" (art editor John Richards) and others appeared featuring space flight and astronomy.

Authentic's rates of payment (£1 per 1000 words) were low even for the time, and although the magazine sold well it seldom published stories of the first rank; an exception was "The Rose" (Mar 1953) by Charles L. HARNESS. House pseudonyms were common and included Jon J. DEEGAN and Roy SHELDON. The mainstay contributors, under their own names and pseudonyms, were Bryan BERRY, Sydney J. BOUNDS, H.K. BULMER, William F. TEMPLE and Tubb. [FHP/PN]

AUTHENTIC SCIENCE FICTION MONTHLY ◊ AUTHENTIC SCIENCE FICTION.

AUTHENTIC SCIENCE FICTION SERIES ◊ AUTHENTIC SCIENCE FICTION.

AUTOMAN ◊ Glen A. LARSON.

AUTOMATION The idea that mechanical production processes might one day free mankind from the burden of labour is a common utopian dream, exemplified by Edward BELLAMY's *Looking Backward, 2000-1887* (**1888**) and its modern counterpart, Mack REYNOLDS's *Looking Backward from the Year 2000* (**1973**). But the dream has its nightmarish aspects: work can be seen as the way in which people justify their existence, and the spectres of unemployment and redundancy, historically associated with poverty and misery, have haunted the developed countries since the days of the Industrial Revolution. The utopian dream must be set alongside the memory of the Luddite riots and the Great Depression, and sociologists such as Jacques Ellul and Lewis Mumford have waxed eloquent upon the dangers of automation. Thus it is hardly surprising that an entirely negative view of the prospect of automation can be found in such works as *Les condamnés à mort* (**1920**; trans as *Useless Hands* **1926**) by Claude FARRÈRE. Indeed, the history of modern utopian thought (◊ DYSTOPIAS; UTOPIAS) is very largely the history of a loss of faith in utopia-through-automation and the growth of various fears: fear that MACHINES may destroy the world by using up its resources, poisoning it with waste, or simply by making available the means of self-destruction; fear that we may be "enslaved" by our machines, becoming "automated" ourselves through reliance upon them; and fear that total dependence on automated production might render us helpless were the machines ever to break down. The last anxiety is the basis of one of the most famous MAINSTREAM-sf stories, "The Machine Stops" (1909) by E.M. FORSTER, produced in response to the optimistic futurological writings of H.G. WELLS.

The wonders of automation were extensively celebrated by Hugo GERNSBACK, and much is made of the mechanical provision of the necessities of life in his *Ralph 124C 41+* (**1911**; **1925**). Even in the early sf PULP MAGAZINES, however, reservations were apparent in the works of such writers as David H. KELLER (e.g., "The Threat of the Robot" [1929]) and Miles J. BREUER (e.g., "Paradise and Iron" [1930]). Laurence MANNING's and Fletcher PRATT's "City of the Living Dead" (1930) offers a striking image of the people of the future living entirely encased in silver wires, all of their experience as well as all their needs being provided synthetically. The theme played a highly significant part in the work of John W. CAMPBELL Jr, who wrote several stories allegorizing mankind's relationship with machinery. In "The Last Evolution" (1932) and the linked Don A. Stuart stories "Twilight" (1934) and "Night" (1935), machines outlive their builders, but in the series begun with "The Machine" (1935) mankind breaks free of the benevolent bonds of mechanical cornucopia. Powerful images of people enslaved and automated by machines were offered in the classic film METROPOLIS (1926; novelization by Thea VON HARBOU **1926**; trans **1927**). The notion of the leisurely, machine-supported life was ruthlessly satirized in *The Isles of Wisdom* (**1924**) by Alexandr MOSZKOWSKI and *Brave New World* (**1932**) by Aldous HUXLEY.

One of the most significant advances in the automation of labour was anticipated in sf, and now bears the name of the story in which it appeared: Robert A. HEINLEIN's "Waldo" (1942) (◊ WALDO). Much attention has been devoted to ROBOTS, automatic workers which have received a good deal more careful and sympathetic consideration in GENRE SF than in the

moral tale which coined the word: Karel ČAPEK's *R.U.R* (**1920**; trans **1923**). Fully automated factories are featured in several of Philip K. DICK's stories, most notably "Autofac" (1955), and Dick extended this line of thought to consider the effects of the automation of production on the business of warfare in "Second Variety" (1953). Automated warfare is also featured in "Dr Southport Vulpes's Nightmare" (1954) by Bertrand RUSSELL and in "War with the Robots" (1962) by Harry HARRISON. The automation of the home has been taken to its logical extreme in a number of ironic sf stories, including "The Twonky" (1942) by Lewis Padgett (Henry KUTTNER and C.L. MOORE), filmed as *The* TWONKY (1952), "The House Dutiful" (1948) by William TENN and "Nor Custom Stale" (1959) by Joanna RUSS. Automated CITIES are the central figures in Greg BEAR's *Strength of Stones* (fixup **1981**), and one, Bellwether – the automated city as Jewish mother – appears satirically in *Dimension of Miracles* (**1968**) by Robert SHECKLEY. The automation of information storage and recovery systems and calculating functions is a theme of considerable importance in its own right (◊ COMPUTERS).

The grimmer imagery of the automated future became more extensive in the 1950s. Kurt VONNEGUT Jr's *Player Piano* (**1952**) tells of a hopeless revolution against the automation of human life and the human spirit. Several writers working under John W. CAMPBELL Jr's tutelage, however, produced stories which argued passionately that robots and computers would be a tremendous asset to human life if only we could learn to use them responsibly; rhetorically powerful examples include Jack WILLIAMSON's *The Humanoids* (**1949**) – whose ending decisively overturned the moral of its classic predecessor, his own "With Folded Hands . . ." (1947) – and Mark CLIFTON's and Frank RILEY's *They'd Rather Be Right* (**1954**; **1957**; vt *The Forever Machine*). Despite this stubborn defence, the encroachment of the machine upon the most essential and sacred areas of human activity and endeavour became a common theme in post-WWII sf. Artists find themselves replaced by machines in numerous stories (◊ ARTS), most notably Walter M. MILLER's "The Darfsteller" (1954), and ANDROIDS or robots often find a place in the most intimate of human relationships.

The basic idea of Campbell's "The Last Evolution" – that automation might be the prelude to the establishment of a self-sustaining, independently evolving mechanical life-system – was first considered in Samuel BUTLER's *Erewhon* (**1872**) and has been a constant preoccupation of sf writers; other early examples include Laurence Manning's "Call of the Mech-Men" (1933) and Eric Frank RUSSELL's "Mechanistra" (1942). More recent developments of the theme include Stanisław LEM's *The Invincible* (**1964**; trans **1973**) and James P. HOGAN's *Code of the Lifemaker* (**1983**), and such pointed SATIRES as John T. SLADEK's *The Reproductive System* (**1968** UK; vt *Mechasm* US) and Olaf JOHANNESSON's *Sagan om den stora datamaskinin*

(1966; trans as *The Tale of the Big Computer* **1968**; vt *The Great Computer*; vt *The End of Man?*). The sinister twist added by stories dealing with evolving systems of war-machines was adapted to an interstellar stage in Fred SABERHAGEN's **Berserker** series, whose early stories were assembled in *Berserker* (coll of linked stories **1967**), and the idea of a Universe-wide conflict between biological and mechanical systems has been further developed by Gregory BENFORD in *Great Sky River* (**1987**) and its sequels.

The dangers of automation comprise one of the fundamental themes of modern dystopian fiction; different variations can be found in Frederik POHL's "The Midas Plague" (1954) and its sequels (collected in *Midas World* [fixup **1983**]), Harlan ELLISON's "'Repent, Harlequin!' said the Ticktockman" (1966), Michael FRAYN's *A Very Private Life* (**1968**) and Gwyneth JONES's *Escape Plans* (**1986**). At a more intimate level, the notion of the automatization of the human psyche was a key theme in the later work of Philip K. Dick, displayed in such novels as *Do Androids Dream of Electric Sheep?* (**1968**) and explained in two notable essays: "The Android and the Human" (1972) and "Man, Android and Machine" (1976). The notion of an intimate hybridization of human and machine is carried forward in many stories featuring CYBORGS. [BS]

See also: CYBERNETICS; SOCIOLOGY; TECHNOLOGY.

AVALLONE, MICHAEL (ANGELO Jr) (1924-) US writer active since the early 1950s under a number of names in various genres. Although he began publishing genre fiction in 1953 with "The Man who Walked on Air" in *Weird Tales*, and though some stories of mild interest appear in *Tales of the Frightened* (coll **1963**; vt *Boris Karloff Presents Tales of the Frightened* 1973) as by Sidney Stuart, his sf is comparatively limited in amount and extremely borderline in nature, usually being restricted to such film or tv link-ups as his two **Girl from U.N.C.L.E.** ties, *The Birds of a Feather Affair* * (**1966**) and *The Blazing Affair* * (**1966**); his novelization of Robert BLOCH's script for the horror film of the same name, *The Night Walker* * (**1965**) as by Sidney Stuart; the first **Man from U.N.C.L.E.** novel, *The Thousand Coffins Affair* * (**1965**); and the film novelization *Beneath the Planet of the Apes* * (**1970**). Only the latter is wholehearted sf. MA's best known pseudonym has probably been Ed Noon, as whom he wrote thrillers; he has also written as Nick CARTER, Troy Conway, Priscilla Dalton, Mark Dane, Steve Michaels, Dorothea Nile, Edwina Noone and probably several other names. Of the **Coxeman** soft-porn thrillers as by Troy Conway, only a few are sf: *The Big Broad Jump* (**1968**), *Had Any Lately?* (**1979**), *The Blow-your-Mind Job* (**1970**), *The Cunning Linguist* (**1970**) and *A Stiff Proposition* (**1971**). *The Craghold Legacy* (**1971**), *The Craghold Curse* (**1972**), *The Craghold Creatures* (**1972**) and *The Craghold Crypt* (**1973**), all as by Edwina Noone, are marginal horror novels; as Noone he also edited *Edwina Noone's Gothic Sampler* (anth **1967**). [JC]

Other works: *The Man from Avon* (**1967**); *The Vampire Cameo* (**1968**) as by Dorothea Nile; *Missing!* (**1969**); *One More Time* * (**1970**), a film tie; *The Beast with the Red Hands* (**1973**) as by Sidney Stuart; *Where Monsters Walk: Terror Tales for People Afraid of the Dark and the Unknown* (coll **1978**); *Friday the 13th, Part 3, 3-D* * (**1982**), a film tie.

AVENGERS, THE UK tv series (1961-9). ABC TV for Thames. Created Sydney Newman. Prods Leonard White (seasons 1 and 2), John Bryce (seasons 2 and 3), Julian Wintle (season 4), Albert Fennell and Brian Clemens (seasons 5-7). Writers included Clemens, Terence Feely, Dennis Spooner, Malcolm Hulke and Terrance Dicks, Eric Paice, Philip Levene, Roger Marshall, Terry NATION. Dirs included Don Leaver, Peter Hammond, Roy Baker, Sidney Hayers, Gordon Flemyng, John Moxey, Robert Day, Robert Fuest, Charles Crichton, Don Chaffey, Don Sharp, John Hough. 7 seasons, 161 50min episodes. B/w 1961-6, colour 1967-9.

This series' precursor, *Police Surgeon*, began in 1960; prod and written by Julian Bond, it starred Ian Hendry as a compassionate police surgeon who spent his time helping people and solving cases. In 1961 Newman, later to be the BBC's head of drama, changed the format (making it less realistic), title (to *The Avengers*) and running time (from 25 to 50 mins); most importantly, he introduced Patrick Macnee as the new protagonist, secret agent John Steed, a cool, well dressed, absurdly posh gentleman. 1962 saw the departure of Hendry and the arrival of Honor Blackman as leather-clad Cathy Gale, judo expert; at first she alternated with Julie Stevens as Venus Smith, nightclub singer, who appeared in only 6 episodes.

The series, now far removed from its original format, became ever more popular as Steed and Mrs Gale battled increasingly bizarre enemies of the Crown.

TA peaked in 1965, becoming more lavish, coincident with its sale to US tv and Blackman's replacement as sidekick by Diana Rigg (strong-minded, intelligent, cynical and beautiful) as Emma Peel. The scripts became ever more baroque, not to say rococo. There had been occasional sf episodes from early on (nuclear blackmail, terrorism using bubonic plague); now sf plots became the norm, involving everything from invisible men and carnivorous plants to "Cybernauts" (killer ROBOTS), ANDROIDS, mind-control rays and TIME MACHINES, mostly connected with plots to take over the UK or the world. *TA* had become perhaps the archetypal 1960s tv series, in its snobbery about the upper class, its stylish decadence, its high-camp and its sometimes surreal visual ambience. Robert Fuest, who later made *The* FINAL PROGRAMME (1974; vt *The Last Days of Man on Earth*), directed many of the later episodes; so did other mildly distinguished film-makers such as Roy Baker, John Hough and Don Sharp. The writer most associated with the series, and responsible for much of its new look and lunatic plotting, was Brian Clemens, who became coproducer of the last 3 series. The last season (1968-9) had Linda Thorson (playing Tara King) replacing Diana Rigg as female sidekick, and also introduced Steed's grossly fat boss, Mother, played by Patrick Newell.

At least 9 original novels were based on or around *TA*, #5, #6 and #7 being by Keith LAUMER: *The Afrit Affair* * (**1968**), *The Drowned Queen* * (**1968**) and *The Gold Bomb* * (**1968**). *The Complete Avengers* (**1988**) by Dave Rogers is a book about the series.

Although *TA* belonged spiritually to the 1960s, Albert Fenell and Brian Clemens revived the series in 1976, with French financial backing, as *The New Avengers*, again starring Patrick Macnee, with Joanna Lumley as female sidekick Purdey and Gareth Hunt as kung-fu expert Mike Gambit. The series was made by Avengers (Film and TV) Enterprises/IDTV TV Productions, Paris; 2 seasons, 1976-7, 26 50min episodes, colour. The stories lacked the ease and panache of the 1960s version, and the sf ingredients became fewer and less inventive; the Cybernauts returned in one episode. John Steed's visible ageing must have acted as a kind of *memento mori* to nostalgic but dissatisfied viewers. In 1977 the entire production company moved to Canada, where the final episodes were set. [PN/JB]

AVENUE VICTOR HUGO ◊ GALILEO.

AVERY, RICHARD ◊ Edmund COOPER.

AVON FANTASY READER US DIGEST-size magazine published by Avon Books, ed Donald A. WOLLHEIM, who considered it an anthology series, although it resembled a magazine. Magazine bibliographers consider it a magazine; book bibliographers think of it as a series of books. The **Avon Fantasy Reader** sequence was primarily devoted to reprints, although it contained also 11 original stories. With WEIRD TALES as its chief source, it presented work by such authors as Robert E. HOWARD, H.P. LOVECRAFT, C.L. MOORE and Clark Ashton SMITH. It was numbered rather than dated, and appeared irregularly: 5 in 1947; 3 per year 1948-51; 1 in 1952. It was partnered by the **Avon Science Fiction Reader** sequence. When Wollheim left Avon in 1952, both runs were terminated. Nearly two decades later, with George Ernsberger, Wollheim briefly attempted a kind of successor series, the titles in which can be treated as anthologies: *The Avon Fantasy Reader* (anth **1969**) and *The 2nd Avon Fantasy Reader* (anth **1969**). [JC/MJE]

AVON PERIODICALS ◊ OUT OF THIS WORLD ADVENTURES.

AVON SCIENCE FICTION AND FANTASY READER US DIGEST-size magazine, 2 issues in 1953, published by Avon Books; ed Sol Cohen. A hybrid successor to the AVON FANTASY READER and AVON SCIENCE FICTION READER, the **Avon Science Fiction and Fantasy Reader** series started a year after those had ceased publication and had a different policy, concentrating on original stories rather than reprints. Both titles contained stories by John CHRISTOPHER, Arthur C. CLARKE and Milton LESSER. [JC/MJE]

AVON SCIENCE FICTION READER US DIGEST-size magazine, published by Avon Books, ed Donald A. WOLLHEIM, and – as with its companion series, AVON FANTASY READER – treated by Wollheim as an anthology series but by contemporary readers as a magazine. It had a policy similar to that of its companion, but featured sf – mostly of routine pulp quality – rather than fantasy reprints. There were 3 issues, 2 in 1951 and 1 in 1952. Both magazines were terminated when Wollheim left Avon Books in 1952. [JC/MJE]

AWARDS The following 11 English-language awards receive individual entries in this volume: ARTHUR C. CLARKE AWARD; BRITISH SCIENCE FICTION AWARD; HUGO; INTERNATIONAL FANTASY AWARD; JOHN W. CAMPBELL AWARD; JOHN W. CAMPBELL MEMORIAL AWARD; NEBULA; PHILIP K. DICK AWARD; PILGRIM AWARD; THEODORE STURGEON MEMORIAL AWARD; and WRITERS OF THE FUTURE CONTEST. Awards given exclusively for fantasy or horror, such as the August Derleth, Bram Stoker, British Fantasy, Crawford, Gandalf, Gryphon, Mythopoeic and World Fantasy awards do not receive entries, and nor generally do awards based in countries other than the UK and USA: the sheer proliferation of awards has necessitated this chauvinist ruling.

Thus we do not list individually the Ditmar (an Australian award given to novels, stories, fanzines), the William Atheling Jr Award (Australian award given to criticism), the Prix Jules Verne (French award given to novels in the spirit of Jules VERNE; discontinued in 1980), the Prix Apollo (French award given since 1972 to best sf novel published in France, regardless of whether it is French or translated), the Prix Rosny aîné (best sf in French), the Seiun (Japanese award for novels and stories, both Japanese and foreign), the Aurora (known until 1991 as the Casper; Canadian sf in both English and French), the Gigamesh (award given by Spanish bookshops for sf in Spanish and translation), European Science Fiction Award (given at annual Eurocon), Kurd Lasswitz Award (German equivalent of the Nebula), SFCD-Literaturpreis (given by large German fan club), Nova Science Fiction (Italian), Atorox (Finnish) and many others.

Other awards, such as the Balrog, the James Blish and the Jupiter, have not received the necessary administrative and/or public support and have been short-lived.

There are many fan awards largely given to professionals, like the HUGO. There are others given by fans to fans; those that most strikingly demonstrate fannish generosity are awards like DUFF and TAFF (Down Under Fan Fund and Trans Atlantic Fan Fund) for which it actually costs money to vote. The winner has his or her expenses paid to a foreign CONVENTION each year, from Australia to the USA or *vice versa* (DUFF) and from Europe (usually the UK) to the USA or *vice versa* (TAFF).

The most important awards not given a full entry

are the Locus Awards, winners of a poll in 13 categories announced each September by LOCUS and voted on by about 1000 presumably well informed readers. This represents a constituency of voters about the same size as that for the Hugos (sometimes bigger). The overlap between Locus voting and Hugo voting a month later is large, which is why we do not list the lesser-known award separately. Where the awards differ, it is often thought that the Locus assessment is the more accurate reflection of general reading tastes. The Locus Award is good for vanity and sales, but no scroll, plaque, letter or cash is given to mark the occasion.

Among the remaining awards, the following are too specialist, recent or small-scale to warrant full entries: Big Heart (sponsored by Forrest J. ACKERMAN for services to FANDOM), Chesley Award (sf artwork, given by the Association of Science Fiction and Fantasy Artists), Compton Crook/Stephen Tall Memorial Award (Baltimore-based award for best first novel), Davis Awards (voted on by readers of *Analog* and ISAAC ASIMOV'S SCIENCE FICTION MAGAZINE), First Fandom Awards (retrospective awards for services to sf prior to institution of the Hugos), James Tiptree Jr Award (from March 1992, given at Wiscon, the Wisconsin convention, for best FEMINIST sf or fantasy), J. Lloyd Eaton Award (from 1979, for a work of sf criticism), Pioneer Award (given by the SCIENCE FICTION RESEARCH ASSOCIATION from 1990 for best critical essay of the year about sf), Prometheus Award (sponsored by the Libertarian Futurist Society for best "libertarian" sf), Readercon Small Press Awards (inaugurated 1989 for best work in various sf categories published by small presses), Rhysling Award (sf POETRY), SFBC Award (chosen by members of the US SCIENCE FICTION BOOK CLUB), Saturn Awards (sf/fantasy film and tv work, given by the Academy of Science Fiction, Fantasy and Horror Films) and the Turner Tomorrow Award. This last is a literary competition with an unbelievable $500,000 first prize sponsored by broadcasting magnate Ted Turner, for best original sf-novel manuscript to be published in hardcover by Turner Publishing and containing practical solutions to world problems; when the winner, Daniel QUINN, was announced in June 1991, three of the judges, including novelist William Styron, declared their dismay at so huge a sum going to the winner of a contest in which none of the place-getters was, in their view, especially distinguished.

The best reference on the subject is *Reginald's Science Fiction and Fantasy Awards: A Comprehensive Guide to the Awards and their Winners* (**1991**) by Daryl F. MALLETT and Robert REGINALD. [PN]

AXLER, JAMES ◊ Laurence JAMES.

AXTON, DAVID ◊ Dean R. KOONTZ.

AYES, ANTHONY or WILLIAM [s] ◊ William SAMBROT.

AYLESWORTH, JOHN B. (1938-   ) Canadian-born US writer whose sf novel, *Fee, Fei, Fo, Fum* (**1963**), is a comic story in which a pill enlarges a man to Brobdingnagian proportions. [JC]

AYMÉ, MARCEL (ANDRÉ) (1902-1967) French novelist and dramatist, not generally thought of as a contributor to the sf field, though several of his best-known novels, such as *La jument verte* (**1933**; appalling anonymous trans as *The Green Mare* **1938** UK; retrans N. Denny 1955), are fantasies, usually with a satirical point to make about provincial French life. *La belle image* (**1941**; trans as *The Second Face* **1951** UK) comes close to sf nightmare in its rendering of the effect of being given a second, more attractive face. *La vouivre* (**1943**; trans as *The Fable and the Flesh* **1949** UK) is again a fantasy, its satirical targets again provincial. *Across Paris and Other Stories* (coll trans **1957** UK; vt *The Walker through Walls* 1962 US) assembles fantasy and the occasional sf tale. *Pastorale* (**1931** France) is a regressive UTOPIA that makes more articulate than is perhaps entirely comfortable the nostalgia that lies beneath MA's urbane "Gallic" style. [JC]

Other works: *Clérambard* (**1950**; trans N. Denny **1952** UK), a play; two children's fantasies, *The Wonderful Farm* (**1951** US) and *Return to the Wonderful Farm* (**1954** UK; vt *The Magic Pictures* 1954 US).

See also: PSYCHOLOGY.

AYRE, THORNTON [s] ◊ John Russell FEARN.

AYRTON, ELISABETH (WALSHE) (1910-1991) UK writer, best known for books on cooking, married first to Nigel BALCHIN, then to Michael AYRTON. Her sf novel, *Day Eight* (**1978**), portrays a NEAR-FUTURE UK in ecological *extremis*, to which Gaia responds through a sudden acceleration in the EVOLUTION of species other than humanity. [JC]

AYRTON, MICHAEL (1921-1975) UK painter and writer, married to Elisabeth AYRTON until his death. He was much respected as an illustrator, stage designer, painter and sculptor; through much of this work recurred images of the Minotaur and of Daedalus, the maker of the Labyrinth. Although little of this was in evidence in his first book of genre interest, *Tittivulus, or The Verbiage Collector* (**1953**), which was a SATIRICAL fantasy, *The Testament of Daedalus* (**1962** chap) presents in prose, verse and illustration the eponymous fabricator's reflections on the problem of flight. *The Maze Maker* (**1967**) is a biography of Daedalus in novel form. Some of the FABULATIONS assembled in *Fabrications* (coll **1972**) are of sf interest. [JC]

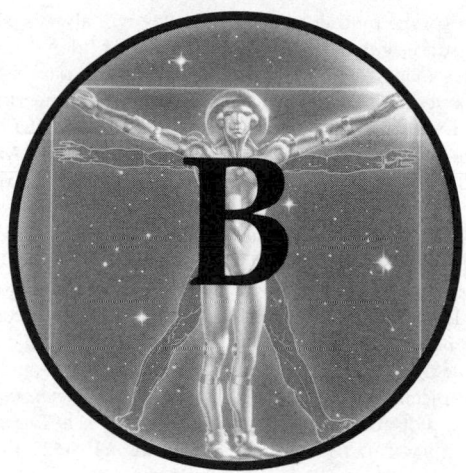

BABBAGE, CHARLES (1792-1871) UK mathematician and inventor, a founder of the Analytical Society in 1812, and a Fellow of the Royal Society from 1816. His recognition of the necessity for accurate calculation of mathematical tables, as used in navigation and astronomy, led in 1820-22 to his designing and building a calculating machine, using which he soon generated a table of logarithms for the positive integers up to 108,000. He then worked on a far more sophisticated machine, a full-size Difference Engine, intended to use punched cards in the computation and printing of mathematical tables. Impatient and not unduly practical, he abandoned this device before it was completed in favour of the far more ambitious Analytical Engine which, if built, would have been the world's first COMPUTER. It was this machine for which Ada, Countess Lovelace, wrote programs, as described in *Ada: The Enchantress of Numbers – A Selection from the Letters of Lord Byron's Daughter and her Description of the First Computer* (**1992**) ed Betty A. Toole. (Much later the computer language Ada was so-named in her honour.) CB spent decades on the project, deriving many of the basic principles of the digital computer, but 19th-century technology restricted him to mechanical rather than electronic components, and consequently the machine was never finished – indeed, it was probably by definition unfinishable. The Difference Engine remains on view in the Science Museum, London. Writers who have extrapolated a full-blown success of Babbage's machines into alternate histories (◊ ALTERNATE WORLDS; STEAMPUNK) include Michael F. FLYNN, in *In the Country of the Blind* (**1990**), and William GIBSON and Bruce STERLING, in *The Difference Engine* (**1990** UK), which transfers Ada's interest to the earlier machine. [JC]

BABITS, MIHÁLY (1883-1941) Hungarian editor, translator (from English and German) and writer, best known for his poetry, the finest example of which is probably the autobiographical *Jonas könyve* ["The Book of Jonah"] (**1938**). His sf novel, *Gólyakalifa* (**1916**; trans as *King's Stork* **1948** Hungary; retrans anon as *The Nightmare* **1966**), is of interest in its depiction of a split personality. A utopian novel, *Elza pilóta avagy a tökéletes társadalom* ["The Pilot Elza, or The Perfect Society"] (**1933**), remains untranslated. [JC]

See also: HUNGARY.

BACHMAN, RICHARD ◊ Stephen KING.

BACK BRAIN RECLUSE UK SEMIPROZINE, from June 1984, current, 18 issues to Mar 1991, A4 format, ed Chris Reed. Originally an A5-format xeroxed FANZINE, *BBR* developed into a professionally printed magazine, with bold design, able to attract fiction from writers such as Michael MOORCOCK, Bob SHAW, Ian WATSON and Garry KILWORTH. *BBR* is regarded as one of the more impressive semiprozines to emerge from the UK in the 1980s. [RH]

BACK TO THE FUTURE Film (1985). Amblin Entertainment/Universal. Dir Robert Zemeckis, Steven SPIELBERG among the executive prods, starring Michael J. Fox, Christopher Lloyd, Lea Thompson, Crispin Glover, Thomas F. Wilson. Screenplay Zemeckis, Bob Gale. 116 mins. Colour.

One of the major sf hits of the 1980s, *BTTF* is a disarming, calculated and intelligent comedy about TIME TRAVEL. Teenage guitar-playing Marty (Fox), son of a tacky and ineffectual mother and father (Thompson and Glover), is interrupted by Libyan terrorists while helping mad scientist Emmett Brown (Lloyd) test a TIME MACHINE mounted in a DeLorean car, and escapes to 1955. There he seeks out the young Dr Brown, but is disturbed to find his (now teenaged) mother strongly sexually attracted to him. The oedipal and culture-clash themes are deftly worked out with great good humour and something falling mercifully short of complete good taste. After demonstrating the power of rock'n'roll and convincing his teenage father to stand up to Biff the bully, he returns with the young Dr Brown's assistance to find a changed 1985, complete with a spruce mother and a confident father who is now a successful sf writer.

One of the few sf blockbusters made by a director wholly comfortable with the conventions of GENRE SF, *BTTF* deserved its success and won a HUGO. There was a four-year wait for its two sequels, BACK TO THE FUTURE PART II and BACK TO THE FUTURE PART III. [PN]

See also: CINEMA.

BACK TO THE FUTURE PART II Film (1989). Amblin Entertainment/Universal. Dir Robert Zemeckis, with Steven SPIELBERG among the executive prods. Starring Michael J. Fox, Christopher Lloyd, Lea Thompson, Thomas F. Wilson. Screenplay Bob Gale, based on a story by Zemeckis and Gale. 108 mins. Colour.

Panned by many critics as a typically disappointing follow-up, in part because its plot remains unresolved at the end, this film and BACK TO THE FUTURE PART III can properly be seen as two halves of a single film, and indeed were shot simultaneously. In fact it is perhaps the most sophisticated TIME-TRAVEL film ever made; what was supposed by critics unfamiliar with the genre to be an incoherence of plot was in large part the perfectly well realized convolutions of a TIME-PARADOX tale. The story, involving Marty and Brown's trip to the future, where the older Marty is interestingly a failure and his son a potential hoodlum, is too complex for synopsis. A trip back to 1955 generates a DYSTOPIAN 1985, an ALTERNATE WORLD run by Biff, the bully of the previous film. The scenario is dark; the acting suffers from Fox's tv sit-com mannerisms and Lloyd's hamming; but the story, ambitious and intellectually complex for a popular movie, is a joy. The good aspects of the film were perhaps ahead of their time, demanding a knowledge in the audience that not enough of them had. [PN]

BACK TO THE FUTURE PART III Film (1989). Credits as for Part II, but also starring Mary Steenburgen. 119 mins. Colour.

Made with Part II and released soon after, this is a hammy but enjoyable resolution of the story. Where Part II emphasizes change and darkness, this emphasizes continuity and reconciliation. Marty digs the damaged time machine out of a cave where it was buried in the past by Dr Brown, who is "now" stranded in the Wild West town which was Hill Valley, and, to judge from a nearby gravestone, will be shot in the back on 7 September 1885. Marty returns to that year on 2 September dressed in Western kitsch and adopting the pseudonym Clint Eastwood. He finds a rough town on the verge of transition into a decent community, and demonstrates his irrelevant, suburban 1985 values to the 1885 avatar of Biff the bully while learning some new ones himself. There is something pleasantly narcissistic and self-referential about the *BTTF* series embracing the past history of its own small-town Californian setting so passionately, like a communal version of wooing your own mother, the Freudian threat of the original film. If Marty and Brown make love to their own history the right way, it is intimated, then Hill Valley will always be a comfortable, limited, tranquil Garden of Eden. The overall vision of the three films is of a static paradise poised dangerously above the dark abyss of uncertainty and change. [PN]

BACON, FRANCIS, VISCOUNT ST ALBANS AND BARON VERULAM (1561-1626) English statesman, philosopher and writer who practised as a barrister before embarking on a political career which ended in 1621 with his dismissal, for taking bribes, from the post of Lord High Chancellor of England. Early in life he planned a vast work, *The Instauration of the Sciences*, a review and encyclopedia of all knowledge; the project was never completed, but FB's reputation as a philosopher rests largely on the first two parts: *De Augmentis Scientiarum* (**1623** in Latin, based on *The Advancement of Learning* [**1605**]) and *Novum Organum Scientiarum* (**1620** in Latin). The latter book championed observation, experiment and inductive theorizing, arguing that the object of scientific inquiry is to discover patterns of causation. His important contribution to PROTO SCIENCE FICTION, the posthumously published fragment *The New Atlantis* (with *Sylva Sylvarum* 1627; **1629**), is a speculative account of possible technological progress, probably written as an advertisement for a Royal College of Science which he hoped to persuade James VI & I to endow. Though little more than a catalogue, it is a remarkably accurate assessment of the potential of the scientific renaissance. [BS]

About the author: *Francis Bacon* (**1961** chap) by J. Max Patrick; *Francis Bacon* (**1978** chap) by Brian Vickers.

See also: ATLANTIS; BIOLOGY; FANTASTIC VOYAGES; FUTUROLOGY; MACHINES; MUSIC; UTOPIAS; WEAPONS.

BACON, WALTER [r] ◊ ROBERT HALE LIMITED.

BADGER BOOKS The main imprint of John Spencer & Co., used by that firm on almost all their books from about the beginning of 1955 through 1967, when the imprint was terminated. John Spencer & Co. itself was founded in 1947 and still exists; like several other UK firms (e.g., CURTIS WARREN), it specialized in the production of purpose-written paperback originals in various popular genres, though the early 1950s saw some emphasis on magazines (in small-DIGEST and pocketbook formats), including *Out of this World* and *Supernatural Stories*, both being amalgamated under the latter title in 1955. Some sf novels had been published, none distinguished, before the BB imprint was created; but in 1954-67 several dozen issues of *Supernatural Stories* were released, some consisting of a number of stories by a single author under various pseudonyms, and 37 issues comprising single novels (both categories are treated in this encyclopedia as books). More significantly, in 1958 BB began an sf series which ran until 1966 and consisted of 117 novels, almost all originals.

One single author, R.L. FANTHORPE, is popularly identified with BB; but although he did write most of the titles, both sf and supernatural, he did not write them all. John S. GLASBY also wrote a number, and other writers like A.A. GLYNN produced one or two each, almost invariably under pseudonyms (*for which see authors' individual entries*) or house names. For sf and supernatural titles, BB house names included Victor LA SALLE, John E. MULLER and Karl ZEIGFREID. Writers for BB worked for hire, and technically all BB books are SHARECROPS, though the publishers exercised control only over length (very rigidly), with content being a matter of some indifference.

It is understood that some sf readers have trawled the BB list for gems. Steve HOLLAND suggests that the Glasby novels written as by A.J. Merak are of some interest. [JC]

Further reading: *Fantasy Readers Guide 1: A Complete Index and Annotated Commentary to the John Spencer Fantasy Publications* (**1979** chap) by Mike ASHLEY; *John Spencer and Badger Books: 1948-1967* (**1985** chap) by Stephen Holland.

BADHAM, JOHN (1939-) US film-maker who showed a penchant for sf as far back as his early tv work on ROD SERLING'S NIGHT GALLERY (1970-72), for which he directed adaptations of stories by Basil Copper ("Camera Obscura") and Fritz LEIBER ("The Girl with the Hungry Eyes"). For the portmanteau tv film *Three Faces of Love* he directed Kurt VONNEGUT Jr's "Epicac", a forerunner of JB's big-screen involvement with COMPUTERS and ROBOTS which develop human characteristics. His first feature-length genre piece was *Isn't it Shocking?* (1973), a well done made-for-tv movie about a gadget-wielding murderer preying on the elderly.

JB's first theatrical feature was *The Bingo Long Traveling All Stars and Motor Kings* (1976). He followed up the enormous success of *Saturday Night Fever* (1977) with a lush, romantic, somewhat shallow version of *Dracula* (1979) and the soapy *Who's Life Is It Anyway?* (1981). Then in the 1980s JB turned out a commercially successful trilogy of borderline sf films on mechanist themes: BLUE THUNDER (1983), WARGAMES (1983) and SHORT CIRCUIT (1986). All three deal with superweapons – a police helicopter, a vast military computer and a military robot – that turn against violence, through, respectively, human intervention, logical reasoning and a divine lightning bolt. These are MACHINE movies, dependent on the glamour of robotry while distrustful of technology without a "heart", suffused with impeccable liberal sentiment of an increasingly stereotypical and less thoughtful variety. This is indicated by the change from the hard-edged *Blue Thunder*, a paranoid conspiracy movie, to the childish *Short Circuit*, which is essentially a reworking of Disney's *The Love Bug* (1969) with a robot instead of a Volkswagen. Subsequently JB has directed professional, impersonal thrillers like *Stakeout* (1967), *Bird on a Wire* (1990) and *The Hard Way* (1991). [KN]

See also: CINEMA; VILLAINS.

BAD TASTE Film (1987). WingNut. Prod, dir, ed, screenplay and special effects Peter Jackson, starring Jackson, Terry Potter, Pete O'Herne, Mike Minett, Doug Wren. 92 mins cut to 91 mins. Colour.

ALIENS invade a small town to kill humans and use them as a meat-source in a new galactic fast-food franchise, but the INVASION is defeated, in this deliberately tasteless (hence the title) low-budget New Zealand parody of sf and SPLATTER MOVIES. It is in the same undergraduate, disgusting vein as BIG MEAT EATER (1982) and *The Evil Dead* (horror, 1982) – drinking vomit, eating live brains – but made much later and less proficiently. *BT* is amateurish (made over four years at weekends), derivative and only occasionally funny. [PN]

BAEN, JIM Working name of US editor James Patrick Baen (1943-) from the beginning of his career in US publishing in 1972, when he became Gothics editor at ACE BOOKS, though he nevertheless sometimes signed himself James Baen. He moved to GALAXY SCIENCE FICTION in 1973 as managing editor, taking over the editorship in 1974 of both *Gal* and IF from Ejler JAKOBSSON. These magazines were then in a crisis, which resulted in their amalgamation (as *Gal*) in January 1975. JB soon showed himself to be a capable editor, and over the next two years turned *Gal* into one of the liveliest current magazines, introducing popular columns by Jerry POURNELLE (science fact), Spider ROBINSON (book reviews) and Richard E. GEIS (general comment). *Gal* also began regularly to feature the much acclaimed stories of John VARLEY, and serialized novels by Frank HERBERT, Larry NIVEN, Frederik POHL, Roger ZELAZNY and others. In 1977 JB returned to Ace Books as sf editor, becoming executive editor and vice-president before leaving in 1980 to join Tom Doherty's newly founded TOR BOOKS as editorial director. He retained this post until his departure in 1983 to form Baen Books, a firm which, though it distributes its publications through Simon & Schuster, has maintained itself as a full and genuine publisher, generally specializing in military sf, though the range of authors it publishes is fairly wide, including Lois McMaster BUJOLD, John DALMAS, David A. DRAKE, Elizabeth MOON, Niven, Pournelle, S.M. STIRLING and Timothy ZAHN.

As an editor of books in his own right, JB produced some anthologies of reprints from *Gal* and *If*, including *The Best from Galaxy III* (anth **1975**) and *#IV* (anth **1976**), *The Best from If III* (anth **1976**) and *Galaxy: The Best of My Years* (anth **1980**). He then produced, in **Destinies**, **Far Frontiers** (with Pournelle) and **New Destinies**, a sequence of magazine/anthologies printing original material. The DESTINIES sequence includes *Destinies: The Paperback Magazine of Science Fiction and Speculative Fact, Volume One* (in 4 successive "issues", anths **1979**), *Volume Two* (in 4 successive "issues", anths **1980**), *The Best of Destinies* (anth **1980**) and *Volume Three* (in 2 successive "issues", anths **1981**). The FAR FRONTIERS sequence, each co-edited with Pournelle (and, uncredited, John F. CARR), includes *Far Frontiers* (anth **1985**), *#2* (anth **1985**), *#3* (anth **1985**), *#4* (anth **1986**), *#5* (anth **1986**), *#6* (anth **1986**) and *#7* (anth **1986**). The third sequence, **New Destinies**, following on directly from the second, includes *New Destinies #1* (anth **1987**), *#2* (anth **1987**), *#3* (anth **1988**), *#4* (anth **1988**), *#6* (anth **1988**), which comprises a special tribute to Robert A. HEINLEIN (there is no *#5*), *#7* (anth **1989**), *#8* (anth **1989**), *#9* (anth **1990**) and *#10* (anth **1992**). He also edited *The Science Fiction Yearbook* (anth **1985**) with Carr and Pournelle.

With Barney COHEN, JB has written one novel, *The Taking of Satcom Station* (**1982**). [JC/MJE]

See also: HISTORY OF SF; SF MAGAZINES.

BAEN BOOKS ◊ Jim BAEN.

BAERLEIN, ANTHONY (? -) UK writer whose sf novel, *Daze, the Magician* (**1936**), features crimes committed through the use of MATTER TRANS- MISSION. [JC]

BAGNALL, R.D. (1945-) UK research chemist and writer. *The Fourth Connection* (coll of linked stories **1975**) presents a series of dramatized speculations on the fourth DIMENSION, and describes the scientific community's response to the challenges opened up. [JC]

BAHL, FRANKLIN [s] ◊ Rog PHILLIPS.

BAHNSON, AGNEW H. Jr (1915-c1964) US writer, inventor and textile-machinery manufacturer whose NEAR-FUTURE political thriller, *The Stars are too High* (**1959**), features hoax aliens with a real GRAVITY-driven ship who try to bring peace to the world. [JC/PN]

BAILEY, ANDREW J(ACKSON) (1840-1927) Writer, apparently UK despite his given names, in whose *The Martian-Emperor President* (**1932**) Earth is visited by a large spaceship containing a delegation from Mars. [JC]

BAILEY, CHARLES W(ALDO) (1929-) US writer and journalist who collaborated with Fletcher KNEBEL (*whom see for details*) on *Seven Days in May* (**1962**). [JC]

BAILEY, DENNIS B. [r] ◊ David F. BISCHOFF.

BAILEY, HILARY (1936-) UK writer and editor, married to Michael MOORCOCK 1962-78. She has written about 15 sf and fantasy stories, including "The Fall of Frenchy Steiner" (1964) and "Everything Blowing Up: An Adventure of Una Persson, Heroine of Time and Space" (1980), and was uncredited co-author with Moorcock of *The Black Corridor* (**1969**). When Moorcock's NEW WORLDS died as a magazine but continued for a while in quarterly paperback book format, she joined Charles PLATT as co-editor of *New Worlds Quarterly 7* (anth **1974**; vt *New Worlds 6* 1975 US), and was sole editor of *#8* (anth **1975**), *#9* (anth **1975**) and *#10* (anth **1976**). Most of her writing is mainstream fiction with occasional sf elements, as in *All the Days of my Life* (**1984**), her almost successful bid for the bestseller market, which is essentially an updated *Moll Flanders* (by Daniel DEFOE [**1722**]); it begins in 1941 and ends in 1996. Also set in the very NEAR FUTURE (1991) is *A Stranger to Herself* (**1989**). *Hannie Richards, or The Intrepid Adventures of a Restless Wife* (**1985**) has fantastic elements. [PN]

See also: HITLER WINS; SUSPENDED ANIMATION.

BAILEY, J(AMES) O(SLER) (1903-1979) US scholar, professor of literature at the University of North Carolina. His *Pilgrims through Space and Time* (**1947**) was the first academic study of sf, which it analyses primarily on a thematic basis. Only a small amount of its subject matter is taken from sf magazines, which is less surprising when one realizes that the work was based on JOB's 1934 doctoral dissertation. JOB had much trouble finding an academic publisher who would consider sf worthy of serious study; the book represents the first trickle of the great torrent of SF IN THE CLASSROOM. He was honoured when the SCIENCE FICTION RESEARCH ASSOCIATION'S PILGRIM AWARD (given annually for contributions to sf scholarship) was named after his book, and he himself was the first recipient (1970). JOB edited the 1965 edn of the HOLLOW-EARTH novel *Symzonia* (**1820**) by Adam SEABORN. [PN]

See also: CRITICAL AND HISTORICAL WORKS ABOUT SF; DEFINITIONS OF SF.

BAILEY, PAUL (DAYTON) (1906-1987) US osteopath, publisher and editor whose *Deliver Me From Eva* (**1946**) deals with the complications ensuing from the hero's father-in-law's capacity to increase INTELLI- GENCE artificially. [JC]

BAIR, PATRICK (? -) UK writer whose *Faster! Faster!* (**1950**) is a DYSTOPIAN fable with an sf flavour in which representatives of three classes, caught on a train which goes on for ever, must work out their destinies. *The Tribunal* (**1970**) satirizes a NEAR-FUTURE revolution in Italy. As David Gurney, he has written tales with a more popular slant, like *The "F" Certificate* (**1968**), which treats of a violent UK to come. [JC]

Other works as Gurney: *The Necrophiles* (**1969**); the **Conjurers** sequence comprising *The Conjurers* (**1972**; vt *The Demonists* 1977 US) and *The Devil in the Atlas* (**1976**); *The Evil Under the Water* (**1977**).

BAJLA, JÁN [r] ◊ CZECH AND SLOVAK SF.

BAKER, SCOTT (1947-) US-born writer, long resi- dent in France, whose novels are fantasy and horror with the exception of his first, *Symbiote's Crown* (**1978**), a slyly intelligent though uneasily metaphysi- cal SPACE OPERA. [JC]

Other works: *Nightchild* (**1979**; rev 1983); *Dhampire* (**1982**); the **Firedance** sequence comprising *Firedance* (**1986**) and *Drink the Fire from the Flames* (**1987**); *Webs* (**1989**).

BAKER, SHARON (1938-1991) US author of 3 PLANET- ARY ROMANCES – all set on the planet **Naphar** – whose richly layered FANTASY surface conceals much sf underpinning: Naphar's poisonous environment has an sf explanation; the planet has been colonized by humans who interbred with the native race; and contacts with galactic civilization remain active. *Quarreling, They Met the Dragon* (**1984**) describes the coming to adulthood of an escaped slave. *Journey to Membliar* (**1987**) and its immediate sequel *Burning Tears of Sassurum* (**1988**) comprise a quest tale culmi- nating in dynastic revelations in the capital city. [JC]

BAKER, W(ILLIAM ARTHUR) HOWARD (1925-1991) Irish journalist, editor and author, in the UK after WWII. After working as an editor of Panther Books he began to write for the **Sexton Blake Library** in

1955, soon taking over as editor of the series for Amalgamated Press, writing many titles under various names, and in 1965 taking the series to Mayflower Books, where it flourished briefly. He then set up his own publishing imprint, which continued to publish **Sexton Blake** books (among others). His stable of **Sexton Blake** writers included Wilfred MCNEILLY, whose claims (*see his entry*) to have written most of WHB's titles are false, and Jack Trevor STORY. His work was brisk and brash, and he did not waste much time seeking quality, though his war novels were of some interest; his sf – as editor and as author – rarely ventured beyond the routine. It is impossible to distinguish much of what he wrote from what he commissioned and what he doctored, under his own name and others. Of sf/fantasy interest, he wrote some books under the Peter SAXON house name, including 2 **Guardians** psychic investigator tales with McNeilly – *Dark Ways to Death* * (**1968**) and *The Haunting of Alan Mais* * (**1969**) – and one solo: *The Killing Bone* * (**1969**). Other titles with McNeilly included *The Darkest Night* (**1966**) and *The Torturer* (**1966**). With Stephen FRANCES (both as Saxon) he wrote *The Disorientated Man* (**1966**; vt *Scream and Scream Again* 1967 US), which was filmed as SCREAM AND SCREAM AGAIN (**1969**), and solo he wrote *Black Honey* (**1968**) and *Vampire's Moon* (**1970** US), both as Saxon. [JC]

About the author: "W. Howard Baker" by Jack Adrian, in *Million 3* (**1991**).

BALCH, FRANK (1880-1937) US writer whose sf novel, *A Submarine Tour* (**1905**) features, in its painfully Vernean progress, visits to more than one LOST WORLD, including ATLANTIS, in a submarine which hits 80 knots. All ends safely. [JC]

BALCHIN, NIGEL (MARLIN) (1908-1970) UK writer, industrialist and wartime scientific adviser to the Army Council; married for a time to Elisabeth AYRTON. From the beginning of WWII his fictions specialized in the creation of psychologically and physically crippled "competent men", as in *The Small Back Room* (**1943**), and were plotted around scientific problems at the verge of sf. Though *No Sky* (**1934**) is of marginal genre interest, his only sf novel proper is *Kings of Infinite Space* (**1967**), a rather weak NEAR-FUTURE look at the US space programme. [JC]

See also: SPACE FLIGHT.

BALDWIN, BEE Working name of New Zealand writer Beatrice Baldwin (? -). Her sf novel *The Red Dust* (**1965**), set in her native land, deals with a typical Antipodean theme (cf Nevil SHUTE's *On the Beach* [**1957**]): the far-reaching DISASTER whose consequences eventually embroil Southern climes. This time it is red dust. [JC]

BALDWIN, BILL Working name of US writer Merl William Baldwin Jr (1935-), known mainly for the efficient **Helmsman** adventure-sf sequence, whose plots are deployed on a galactic scale: *The Helmsman* (**1985** as Merl Baldwin; as BB 1990), *Galactic Convoy* (**1987**), *The Trophy* (**1990**) and *The Mercenaries* (**1991**). [JC]

BALDWIN, MERL ◊ Bill BALDWIN.

BALFORT, NEIL [s] ◊ R.L. FANTHORPE.

BALL, BRIAN N(EVILLE) (1932-) UK writer, until 1965 a teacher and lecturer, subsequently freelance. He began publishing sf with "The Pioneer" for *NW* in 1962, edited a juvenile anthology, *Tales of Science Fiction* (anth **1964**), soon after, and the next year published his first novel, *Sundog* (**1965**), one of his better books, in which – though restricted by ALIENS to the Solar System – mankind, in the person of space-pilot Dod, transcends its limitations.

There followed a trilogy involving an ancient Galactic Federation, its relics, TIME TRAVEL, and rebirth: *Timepiece* (**1968**), *Timepivot* (**1970** US) and *Timepit* (**1971**). A second series, *The Probability Man* (**1972** US) and *Planet Probability* (**1973** US), follows the exploits of Frame-Director Spingarn in his heterodox construction of reality-spaces (frames) for the delectation (and voluntary destruction) of billions of bored citizens. Though he sometimes aspires to the more metaphysical side of the sf tropes he utilizes, BNB's style tends to reduce these implications to routine action-adventure plots, competently executed. [JC]

Other works: *Lesson for the Damned* (**1971**); *Devil's Peak* (**1972**); *Night of the Robots* (**1972**; vt *The Regiments of Night* **1972** US); *Singularity Station* (**1973** US); *The Space Guardians* * (**1975**), a SPACE 1999 tie; *The Venomous Serpent* (**1974**; vt *The Night Creature* 1974 US); the two **Keegan** books: *The No-Option Contract* (**1975**) and *The One-Way Deal* (**1976**); the **Witchfinder** series, comprising *The Mark of the Beast* (**1976**) and *The Evil at Montaine* (**1977**).

For children: *Princess Priscilla* (**1975**); the **Jackson** books, comprising *Jackson's House* (**1975**), *Jackson's Friend* (**1975**), *Jackson's Holiday* (**1977**) and *Jackson and the Magpies* (**1978**); *The Witch in our Attic* (**1979**); *Young Person's Guide to UFOs* (**1979**), nonfiction; *Dennis and the Flying Saucer* (**1980**); *The Starbuggy* (**1983**); *The Doomship of Drax* (**1985**); *Truant from Space* (**1985** chap); *Stone Age Magic* (**1988**); *The Quest for Queenie* (**1988** chap).

BALL, JOHN (DUDLEY Jr) (1911-1988) US commercial pilot and writer, much better known for work in other genres – like *In the Heat of the Night* (**1965**) – than for his sf novels, the first of which, *Operation Springboard* (**1958**; vt *Operation Space* 1960 UK), is a juvenile about a space race to Venus. [JC]

Other works: *Spacemaster 1* (**1960**); *The First Team* (**1972**).

BALLANTINE BOOKS US publishing company founded in 1952 by Ian Ballantine, who had previously helped found BANTAM BOOKS, and Betty Ballantine; for the first six months BB operated from their apartment. Although it was a general publisher, an important priority was the prestigious sf list, the first of its kind in paperback, with many original works which were, initially, published simultaneously as hardbacks. BB's first sf novel was *The Space Merchants* (**1953**) by Frederik POHL and C.M.

KORNBLUTH. Pohl edited BB's STAR series of ANTHOLOGIES. The list of regular authors resembles an sf roll of honour: it included Arthur C. CLARKE, Larry NIVEN and many others. Almost 100 early Ballantine covers featured artwork by Richard POWERS, much of it semi-abstract; meant to emphasize the modernity and innovative quality of the fiction, the effect was wider than that: it was as if sf had suddenly grown up. The Powers covers were one of the symbols of sf's growth to maturity.

Ballantine became a division of Random House in 1973, and the two Ballantines left in 1974. Judy-Lynn DEL REY became sf editor, and in 1976 her husband Lester DEL REY took over the fantasy list initiated by Lin CARTER. In 1977 the sf/fantasy imprint was renamed DEL REY BOOKS. Since that time some sf has been published under the original Ballantine imprint, but this has mostly been borderline sf or sometimes, as with novels by Michael CRICHTON, sf books for which a substantial mainstream sale is expected. In 1990 the combined imprints of Ballantine, Del Rey and Fawcett, all under the same ownership, were running fifth in the USA in terms of the number of sf/fantasy/horror titles published.   [PN/MJE]

Further reading: *Ballantine Books: The First Decade: A Bibliographical History & Guide of the Publisher's Early Years* (**1987**) by David Aronovitz.

See also: HUGO.

BALLARD, J(AMES) G(RAHAM) (1930-   ) UK writer, born in Shanghai and as a child interned in a Japanese civilian POW camp during WWII. He first came to the UK in 1946. He later read medicine at King's College, Cambridge, but left without taking a degree.

JGB discovered sf while in Canada during his period of RAF service in the early 1950s. His first stories, "Escapement" and "Prima Belladonna", were published in E.J. CARNELL's NEW WORLDS and SCIENCE FANTASY, respectively, in 1956. His writing was influenced by the Surrealist painters and the early Pop artists. From the start, he opened a new prospect in sf; his interest in PSYCHOLOGY and in the emotional significance of deserted landscapes and wrecked TECHNOLOGY soon became apparent in such stories as "Build-Up" (1957; vt "The Concentration City"), "Manhole 69" (1957), "The Waiting Grounds" (1959), "The Sound-Sweep" (1960) and "Chronopolis" (1960). On the whole, he eschewed such sf themes as space travel, time travel, aliens and ESP, concentrating instead on NEAR-FUTURE decadence and DISASTER. In 1962 he began using the term INNER SPACE to describe the area of his obsessions, and stated that "the only truly alien planet is Earth". "The Voices of Time" (1960) is his most important early story, an apocalyptic view of a terrible new EVOLUTION (or DEVOLUTION) faced by the human race. As with much of his work, its impressive quality is a result of JGB's painterly eye, as shown in his moody descriptions of landscapes.

With "Studio 5, the Stars" (1961) JGB returned to the setting of "Prima Belladonna": a decaying resort, Vermilion Sands, where poets, artists and actresses pursue perverse whims. He subsequently wrote seven more stories against this background, and the series, which constitutes one of his most popular works, was collected as *Vermilion Sands* (coll **1971** US; with 1 story added rev 1973 UK). JGB's first novel, *The Wind from Nowhere* (**1962** US), was written in a fortnight, and the money that he earned from it enabled him to become a full-time writer. It is his only work of formula sf, the formula being that of John WYNDHAM's disaster novels. In *The Drowned World* (**1962** US) JGB inverted the pattern, creating a hero who conspires with rather than fights against the disaster that is overtaking his world. It was this novel, with its brilliant descriptions of an inundated London and an ECOLOGY reverting to the Triassic, which gained JGB acceptance as a major author. However, the self-immolating tendency of his characters drew adverse criticism; some readers, particularly devotees of GENRE SF, wrote JGB off, rather simplistically, as a pessimist and a life-hater. Certainly his next two novels, *The Burning World* (**1964** US; rev vt *The Drought* 1965 UK) and *The Crystal World* (fixup **1966**), served further to polarize opinion. Each contains a lovingly described cataclysm towards which the protagonist holds ambiguous attitudes. Some commentators – e.g., Kingsley AMIS and Michael MOORCOCK – praised these works very highly.

JGB is regarded by some as a better short-story writer than novelist, however, and his 1960s stories drew an enthusiastic audience. "Deep End" (1961), "Billenium" (1961) (spelt thus on its first appearance, and sometimes thereafter), "The Garden of Time" (1962), "The Cage of Sand" (1962) and "The Watch-Towers" (1962) are among the excellent stories reprinted in his collections *The Voices of Time and Other Stories* (coll **1962** US), *Billenium* (coll **1962** US) and *The Four-Dimensional Nightmare* (coll **1963**; rev 1974; vt *The Voices of Time* 1984); a third collection entitled *The Voices of Time* (coll **1985**) differs from all others. "The Subliminal Man", "A Question of Re-Entry" and "The Time-Tombs" (all 1963) are masterpieces of desolation and melancholy, as is "The Terminal Beach" (1964), which shows JGB beginning to move in a new direction, towards greater compression of imagery and nonlinearity of plot. All these stories contain "properties", described objects, which have become JGB's trademarks: wrecked spacecraft, sand-dunes, concrete deserts, broken juke-boxes, abandoned nightclubs, and military and industrial detritus in general. Sympathetic readers regard JGB's unique "properties" and landscapes as being very appropriate to the contemporary world: they constitute a "true" dream vision of our times. (In an essay – "Myth-Maker of the 20th Century", *NW* #142, 1964 – JGB has himself acknowledged similar qualities in the work of William S. BURROUGHS.)

Perhaps JGB's strongest single collection of stories

is *The Terminal Beach* (coll **1964** UK), not to be confused with *Terminal Beach* (coll **1964** US): the titles have only 2 stories in common. (The earlier US collections of JGB's short stories are quite different from the contemporaneous UK editions, and normally have different titles. Most of the earlier short stories appear in at least two collections.) Other collections, all containing much good material, are *Passport to Eternity* (coll **1963** US), *The Impossible Man* (coll **1966** US) and *The Disaster Area* (coll **1967**). One story, "The Drowned Giant" (1964; vt "Souvenir"), was nominated for a NEBULA, although the fact that JGB has never won an sf AWARD is indicative of his unpopularity with HARD-SF fans. He did, however, become a figurehead of the NEW WAVE of the later 1960s: younger UK writers such as Charles PLATT and M. John HARRISON show his influence directly.

"You and Me and the Continuum" (1966) inaugurated a series of stories – "condensed novels", as JGB has called them – in which he explored the MEDIA LANDSCAPE of advertising, broadcasting, POLITICS and WAR. Collected as *The Atrocity Exhibition* (coll **1970**; vt *Love and Napalm: Export USA* 1972 US; rev 1990 US), these are JGB's most "difficult" works, and they provoked more hostility than anything that had gone before; the collection's intended 1970 US edition, from DOUBLEDAY, was printed but, on the instructions of a panicking executive, pulped just before publication. The hostility was partly due to the fact that JGB uses real people such as Marilyn Monroe, the Kennedys and Ronald Reagan as "characters".

In the novel *Crash* (**1973**) JGB took his obsession with automobile accidents to a logical conclusion. Perhaps the best example of "pornographic" sf, it explores the psychological satisfactions of danger, mutilation and death on the roads; it is also an examination of the interface between modern humanity and its MACHINES. Brightly lit and powerfully written, it is a work with which it is difficult for many readers to come to terms; one publisher's reader wrote of the manuscript: "The author of this book is beyond psychiatric help." *Concrete Island* (**1974**) and *High-Rise* (**1975**) are also urban disaster novels set in the present, the one concerning a driver marooned on a traffic island between motorway embankments, the other focusing on the breakdown of social life in a multistorey apartment block. All three of these novels are about the ways in which the technological landscape may be fulfilling and reflecting our own ambiguously "worst" desires.

In the mid-1970s JGB returned to the short-story form, in which he still excelled. Such pieces as "The Air Disaster" (1975), "The Smile" (1976) and "The Dead Time" (1977) are outstanding psychological horror stories on the fringes of sf. The collection *Low-Flying Aircraft* (coll **1976**) contains an excellent original novella, "The Ultimate City", which projects JGB's urban obsessions of the 1970s into the future. Later volumes of stories are *Myths of the Near Future* (coll **1982**), *Memories of the Space Age* (coll **1988** US) and *War*

Fever (coll **1990**), all of which contain a good deal of sf mixed with psychological fantasy.

The Unlimited Dream Company (**1979**), JGB's first fully fledged fantasy novel, concerns a young man who crashes a stolen light aircraft into the River Thames, apparently dies and is reborn, finding himself trapped in the riverside town of Shepperton (where JGB in reality makes his home). The hero discovers the ability to change himself into various beasts and birds, and to transform the sleepy suburb around him into a vivid garden of exotic flowers. More sinisterly, he is able to "absorb" human beings into his body – before expelling them again, in the apocalyptic climax to the novel. The book is a remarkable fantasy of self-aggrandizement, colourfully and compellingly told. It was followed by JGB's most conventional sf novel in some years, *Hello America* (**1981**), a comparatively light work about the rediscovery of an abandoned 22nd-century USA.

JGB moved away from sf again for his most commercially successful novel to date, *Empire of the Sun* (**1984**). Based on his childhood experiences in Lunghua POW camp near Japanese-occupied Shanghai, it gained him a vast new readership. The book has great merit as a psychological war novel, but for the sf reader part of its interest lies in its apparent revelation of the "sources" of many of JGB's recurring images and "properties" (those drained swimming pools, abandoned buildings, low-flying aircraft, drowned landscapes – they are all here). Although it is not at all an sf or fantasy work, it has much in common with all JGB's earlier fiction. The novel was filmed in 1987 by Steven SPIELBERG, and JGB wrote a sequel, *The Kindness of Women* (**1991**). This latter is told in the first person – *Empire of the Sun* is told in the third – and covers a 50-year timespan: heavily autobiographical, it is an intriguing work for anyone interested in JGB's career, but contains little direct reference to sf.

Earlier JGB had written another psychological adventure novel, *The Day of Creation* (**1987**). Set in an imaginary African country, it is less overtly fantastic than *The Unlimited Dream Company* but resembles that novel in terms of theme and imagery. The narrator inadvertently causes a new river to well up from the parched earth, transforming a barren war zone into a luxuriant, although short-lived, jungle. Like all Ballard's novels it contains extraordinary descriptive passages embedded in a fairly simple plot peopled by perverse characters of some psychological complexity. This book was followed by an acute and entertaining novella, *Running Wild* (**1988** chap), a Thames Valley murder mystery of marginal sf interest.

Although most of his longer work of the past decade has been outside the field, the originality and appropriateness of his vision continue to ensure JGB's standing as one of the most important writers ever to have emerged from sf. [DP]

Other works: *The Drowned World and The Wind from Nowhere* (omni 1965 US); *By Day Fantastic Birds Flew* *through the Petrified Forest* (**1967**), wall-poster incorporating text from *The Crystal World*, sometimes wrongly included in JGB bibliographies as a book or chap; *The Day of Forever* (coll **1967**; rev 1971); *The Overloaded Man* (coll **1967**; rev vt *The Venus Hunters* 1980); *Why I Want to Fuck Ronald Reagan* (**1968** chap); *Chronopolis and Other Stories* (coll **1971** US); *The Best of J.G. Ballard* (coll **1977**); *The Best Short Stories of J.G. Ballard* (coll **1978** US); *News from the Sun* (**1982** chap); *The Crystal World; Crash; Concrete Island* (omni **1991** US).

About the author: *J.G. Ballard: The First Twenty Years* (**1976**) ed James Goddard and David PRINGLE; *Earth is the Alien Planet: J.G. Ballard's Four-Dimensional Nightmare* (**1979** US) by David Pringle; *J.G. Ballard: A Primary and Secondary Bibliography* (**1984** US) by David Pringle; *Re/Search 8/9: J.G. Ballard* (**1984** US) ed Vale and Andrea Juno; *J.G. Ballard: Starmont Reader's Guide 26* (**1985** US) by Peter Brigg; *Out of the Night and Into the Dream: A Thematic Study of J.G. Ballard* (**1991**) by Gregory Stephenson.

See also: ABSURDIST SF; ANTI-INTELLECTUALISM IN SF; ARTS; BRITISH SCIENCE FICTION AWARD; CITIES; CONCEPTUAL BREAKTHROUGH; CRIME AND PUNISHMENT; CYBERPUNK; DEFINITIONS OF SF; ECONOMICS; ENTROPY; FANTASTIC VOYAGES; FRANCE; GREAT AND SMALL; HISTORY OF SF; HOLOCAUST AND AFTER; ISLANDS; LEISURE; MARS; MEDICINE; MESSIAHS; MUSIC; MUTANTS; OPTIMISM AND PESSIMISM; OVERPOPULATION; PERCEPTION; SEX; SPACE FLIGHT; TIME TRAVEL; UFOS.

BALLINGER, BILL S. ◊ William S. BALLINGER.

BALLINGER, W.A. ◊ Wilfred Glassford MCNEILLY.

BALLINGER, WILLIAM S(ANBORN) (1912-1980) US screenwriter and novelist who has also signed his books Bill S. Ballinger. His work in radio and film was successful (he won an Edgar Award in 1960), but his sf is comparatively obscure, and some listed titles are dubious. We feel secure about listing *The 49 Days of Death* (**1969**) and *The Ultimate Warrior* ✳ (**1975**), which novelizes *The* ULTIMATE WARRIOR (1975). Other titles which have been ascribed to WSB, but which we cannot feel secure about, include *The Fourth of Forever* (**1963**) and *The Doom Maker* (**1959**) as by B.X. Sanborn, the latter being more widely credited to WSB than the former. He was perhaps best known for his detective novels under the name Frederic Freyer. [JC]

BALLOONS For some six months in 1783 Paris was the Cape Canaveral of the 18th century as Parisians watched a succession of extraordinary ascents by hot-air balloons. The first successful manned trip took place on 21 Nov, as reported by Benjamin Franklin, and it started off a long series of speculations about the conquest of the air. Thomas Jefferson was certain that balloon TRANSPORTATION would lead to the discovery of the north pole "which is but one day's journey in a balloon, from where the ice has hitherto stopped adventurers". Franklin was certain that the new balloons would revolutionize warfare; and L.S. MERCIER added a new chapter to the 1786 edition of his *L'an deux mille quatre cent quarante* (**1771**; rev 1786; trans as *Memoirs of the Year Two Thousand Five Hundred*

1772) to show how the "aerostats" were destined to link remote Pekin to Paris in a system of world communications. When the inhabitants of major European cities watched the new balloons drifting above, they thought they saw the beginning of a profound change in human affairs: the assurance of a growing mastery of Nature.

For a brief period there were plays, poems and stories about balloon travel – even a space operetta, *Die Luftschiffer*, performed before Catherine II in the Imperial Court Theatre at St Petersburg. Expectations about the future carried over into occasional stories like *The Aerostatic Spy* (**1785**), published anon, the first of the round-the-world stories that ran their course up to Jules VERNE's *Cinq semaines en ballon* (**1863**; trans as *Five Weeks in a Balloon* 1869). The balloon proved a most useful marker of the future (as the ROCKET was to do in a later period), and was used by early sf writers as a convincing way of establishing the more advanced circumstances of their future worlds. Balloons were also the source of the first visual fantasies of the future: there were engravings of balloon battles, vast transport balloons crossing the Atlantic and airborne troops crossing the Channel. By the 1870s, however, experiments with heavier-than-air flying machines had turned popular attention towards airships and aircraft of the future. [IFC]

BALMER, EDWIN (1883-1959) US writer and editor, trained as an engineer, who wrote in a variety of genres and edited (1927-49) the magazine *Red Book*, which occasionally published sf. With his brother-in-law William MacHarg (1872-1951) he wrote *The Achievements of Luther Trant* (coll **1910**), a series of 9 detective stories with borderline sf elements, notably the accurate forecasting of the lie detector; some were reprinted in Hugo GERNSBACK's AMAZING STORIES. EB is best known for his collaborations with Philip WYLIE, *When Worlds Collide* (**1933**), filmed as WHEN WORLDS COLLIDE (1951), and the inferior *After Worlds Collide* (**1934**). In the first, Earth is destroyed in a collision with the planet Bronson Beta; in the second, escapees settle on the new planet, fight off some Asiatic communists, and prosper. EB's solo sf novel was *Flying Death* (**1927**). [JC]

Other works: *The Golden Hoard* (**1934**) with Philip Wylie, a mystery thriller.

See also: COMICS; CRIME AND PUNISHMENT; DISASTER; END OF THE WORLD; HOLOCAUST AND AFTER; PREDICTION; SPACESHIPS.

BALROG AWARD ◊ AWARDS.

BALSDON, (JOHN PERCY VYVIAN) DACRE (1901-1977) UK historian and author; Fellow of Exeter College, Oxford 1927-69. His three sf novels are humorous satires on contemporary mores, little allowance being made for technological, social or behavioural change. The most imaginative, *Sell England?* (**1936**), is a DYSTOPIA set 1000 years hence. The UK is inhabited solely by a decadent aristocracy, the other echelons of society living in Africa under a totalitarian dictatorship. *Have a New Master* (**1935**) and

The Day They Burned Miss Termag (1957 as "Mr Botteaux's Story" in the coll *Oxford Life*; exp **1961**) are set, respectively, in a school 30 years hence and in an Oxford of the immediate future. They have had little influence. [JE]

Other works: *The Pheasant Shoots Back* (**1949**), a fantasy juvenile.

BALZAC, HONORÉ de (1799-1850) French writer best known for **La comédie humaine** ["The Human Comedy"], an immense series of novels into which his PROTO-SCIENCE-FICTION story, *La recherche de l'absolu* (**1834**; trans as *The Philosopher's Stone* **1844** US; vt *Balthazar, or Science & Love* 1859; vt *The Alchemist* 1861; vt *The Alkahest* 1887; vt *The Quest of the Absolute* 1895 UK; vt *The Tragedy of a Genius* 1912) fits somewhat dissonantly. Balthazar Claes invests everything into his search for a kind of universal element that lies at the base of all other elements, but fails. [JC]

Other works: HdB is, like Jules VERNE, a bibliographer's nightmare. Of his numerous early sensational novels, few translations seem to exist, and his later supernatural fiction appears in very various and chameleon guises. But some titles are of genre interest: *Le Centenaire: ou les deux Behringelds* (**1822** as by Horace de Saint-Aubin; trans George Edgar SLUSSER as *The Centenarian, or The Two Behringelds* **1976** US), a horror novel; *La Peau de chagrin* (**1831**; first trans as *Luck and Leather* **1843** US; first vt *The Magic Skin* 1888; many other vts), a fantasy; "Séraphita" (**1834**; trans in coll *Seraphita* **1897** UK), an occult romance; "Melmoth Reconcilé" (**1835**; trans in coll *The Unknown Masterpiece* **1896** UK), a sequel to *Melmoth the Wanderer* (**1820**) by Charles MATURIN.

About the author: *Balzac* (**1973**) by V.S. Pritchett.

See also: MONEY; SCIENTISTS.

BAMBER, GEORGE (1932-) US writer whose sf novel, *The Sea is Boiling Hot* (**1971**), deals with a large number of themes, including ECOLOGY: nuclear pollution has set the seas to boiling; mankind lives in huge domed CITIES; COMPUTERS do the work and provide sophisticated entertainment; many citizens opt out for lobotomized relief from a boring world. The protagonist discovers how to reverse the effects of POLLUTION by reconstituting pollutants into their original states; DISASTER routinely threatens and breaks. [JC]

BANCROFT, LAURA ◊ L. Frank BAUM.

BAND, CHARLES (1952-) US film producer, director and entrepreneur, his ambitions often undone by underbudgeting, but responsible for a vigorous burst of sf/fantasy/horror exploitation movies in the mid-1980s. His best works indicate a lively mind and a bizarre B-movie sensibility that has led to comparison with the Roger CORMAN of the 1950s. Son of exploitation film-maker Albert Band (*I Bury the Living* [1956] and others) and brother of prolific film composer Richard Band, CB produced his first film, *Mansion of the Doomed* (1976) – a mad-SCIENTIST picture modelled on Georges Franju's *Les YEUX SANS VISAGE* (1959) – at the age of 21, and directed his first, *Crash!* (1977), a

year later. With the healthy profits from a pair of derivative 3-D sf efforts that he produced and directed – *Parasite* (1982), a MONSTER MOVIE, and METALSTORM: THE DESTRUCTION OF JARED-SYN (1983) – CB set up Empire International, a prolific grindhouse outfit that flourished 1984-8. When Empire had financial problems, CB sold out to Irwin Yablans, who had produced for the company, and established a less ambitious production house, Full Moon International.

Other sf films, many of them marginal sf/horror, with which CB was involved as a producer (sometimes simply because Empire provided funding, sometimes with fuller creative participation) include *End of the World* (1977), *Tourist Trap* (1978), *The Day Time Ended* (1978; vt *Timewarp*; vt *Vortex*), LASERBLAST (1978), *Swordkill* (1984; vt *Ghost Warrior*), *The Dungeonmaster* (1984; vt *RageWar*; vt *Digital Knights*), RE-ANIMATOR (1985; CB uncredited), ZONE TROOPERS (1985), ELIMINATORS (1986), TERRORVISION (1986), *Mutant Hunt* (1986), *Breeders* (1986), FROM BEYOND (1986), *The Caller* (1987), *Arena* (1988), *ShadowZone* (1989), ROBOT JOX (1990), *Crash and Burn* (1990) and *Doctor Mordrid* (1992), the last codirected with his father.

While CB has certainly unleashed a torrent of middling-to-terrible product – often featuring cheap ROBOTS or small puppet demons – he deserves credit for fostering such talent as director Stuart Gordon, producer Brian Yuzna, special-effects-men-turned-directors David Allen and John Carl Buechler, and writers Danny Bilson and Paul DeMeo. TRANCERS (1984; vt *Future Cop*), dir CB from a snappy script by Bilson and DeMeo, is one of the best sf films of the decade, an imaginative TIME-TRAVEL adventure that beat *The TERMINATOR* to several punches and features as many ideas in its brief running time as an Alfred BESTER novel. CB also dir the disappointing sequel, *Trancers 2* (1991; vt *Future Cop 2*). [KN]

See also: HORROR IN SF.

BANGS, JOHN KENDRICK (1862-1922) Extremely prolific US writer under many names, most of whose books of interest were humorous fantasies, not sf. However, one of them (his most famous), *A House-Boat on the Styx: Being Some Account of the Divers Doings of the Associated Shades* (**1896**), provides a model for many stories featuring the famous dead as posthumous protagonists in venues that usually have an Arcadian glow. From it a suggestive line of association can be drawn through William Dean HOWELLS's *The Seen and Unseen at Stratford-on-Avon* (**1914**) and the works of Thorne Smith (1892-1934) down to the various **Riverworld** tales and novels of Philip José FARMER. The sequel is *The Pursuit of the House-Boat* (**1897**). [JC]

Other works: *Roger Camerden: A Strange Story* (**1887**); *New Waggings of Old Tales* (coll **1888**) with Frank Dempster Sherman; *Toppleton's Client, or A Spirit in Exile* (**1893**); *The Water Ghost* (coll **1894**); *A Rebellious Heroine* (**1896**); *Mr Bonaparte of Corsica* (**1895**); *Ghosts I* *have Met and Some Others* (coll **1898**); *The Enchanted Typewriter* (**1899**); *Mr Munchausen* (**1901**); *Over the Plum-Pudding* (coll **1901**); *Bikey the Skicycle and Other Tales of Jimmie-Boy* (coll **1902**), some stories being sf; *Embleland* (**1902**) with Charles R. Macauley, a desert-island fantasy; *Olympian Nights* (**1902**); *Alice in Blunderland: An Iridescent Dream* (**1907**); *The Autobiography of Methuselah* (**1909**); *Jack and the Check Book* (**1911**); *Shylock Homes: His Posthumous Memoirs* (coll **1973**).

BANISTER, MANLY (MILES) (1914-   ) US novelist and short-story writer. *Conquest of Earth* (**1957**) is a SPACE OPERA in which a resurgent mankind learns how to conquer the ALIEN Trisz. Other sf novels have been published in magazine form only.   [JC]

Other works: *Eegoboo: A Fantasy Satire* (**1957** chap).

See also: RECURSIVE SF.

BANKS, IAIN M(ENZIES) (1954-   ) Scottish writer who distinguishes between his fiction published for a general market and that aimed more directly at sf readers by signing the former books Iain Banks and the latter Iain M. Banks; although differences in register and venue can be detected in the two categories – as in the case of Graham Greene's "Entertainments" – those categories tend to merge. IB's first published novel, *The Wasp Factory* (**1984**), is a case in point: the familial intensities brought to light as the 17-year-old protagonist awaits the return home of his crazy older brother are psychologically probing in an entirely mimetic sense, while at the same time his dreams and behaviour are rendered in terms displaced into the surrealistic realms of modern horror. IB's second novel, *Walking on Glass* (**1985**), even more radically engages a mixture of genres – a mimetic rendering of an adolescent's coming of age, a paranoid's displaced and displacing conviction that he is a warrior from the stars, and the entrapment of a "genuine" set of characters from an sf war – in something like internecine warfare. *The Bridge* (**1986**), perhaps IB's finest single novel, once again conflates the literal with displacements of metaphor which are given the weight of reality, as a comatose man relives (or anticipates) his own life, which is represented in matrix form as an enormous bridge, among the interstices of which he engages in a rather hilarious parody of SWORD-AND-SORCERY conventions. Of later IB novels, *Canal Dreams* (**1989**) also stretches the nature of the MAINSTREAM novel by being set in AD2000.

The IMB novels (some of which were written, at least in an early form, before *The Wasp Factory*) are conspicuously more holiday in spirit and open in texture, seeming at first glance to occupy their space-opera venues without much thought for the morrow. It is a deceptive impression, though the exuberance is genuine enough. The four IMB novels published so far – *Consider Phlebas* (**1987**), *The Player of Games* (**1988**), *The State of the Art* (**1989** US), which was assembled with other stories, some of them **Culture** tales (see below), as *The State of the Art* (coll **1991**), and *Use of Weapons* (**1990**) – comprise loose-connected segments of a sequence devoted to a portrayal of a vast, interstellar, ship-based **Culture**. The underlying premises IMB uses to shape this Culture stand as a direct challenge to those underlying most future HISTORIES. Most importantly, and most unusually for SPACE OPERA, the Culture is genuinely post-scarcity. In other words, it boasts no hierarchies maintaining power through control of limited resources. There are no Empires in the Culture, no tentacled Corporations, no Enclave whose hidden knowledge gives its inhabitants a vital edge in their attempts to maintain independence against the military hardware of the far-off Czar at the apex of the pyramid of power. Even more remarkably, IMB represents the inhabitants of the Culture – they are most often met monitoring and exploring the Universe in the vast AI-run ships which comprise the ganglia of the colossal enterprise – as energetic volunteers at living in the UTOPIA that has, in a sense, been created for them.

The novels themselves, perhaps understandably, shy clear of any undue focus on this complex, free-form, secular paradise, concentrating on wars between the Culture and its occasional enemies. The protagonist of *Consider Phlebas* is a mercenary who has chosen the wrong side; in his battles against the Culture he exposes the reader to a number of sly ironies, because the doomed civilization for which he is fighting is remarkably similar to the standard backdrop GALACTIC EMPIRE found in routine space opera. *The Player of Games*, though more economically told than its bulbous predecessor, less challengingly pits its protagonist against a savage game-based civilization, which he causes to crumble. The novel *The State of the Art* contrasts contemporary Earth with a Culture mission, allowing a variety of satirical points to be made about the seamy, agonistic, death-obsessed mortals of our planet. *Use of Weapons*, constructed with some of the savage inhibiting intricacy of *Walking on Glass*, does finally address the question of Culture guilt for its manipulation of races not yet free of scarcity-bound behaviour; its portrayal of the relationship between a Culture woman and the mercenary in her employ is tough-minded, and provides no easy answers.

For many readers and critics, IB/IMB was the major new UK sf writer of the 1980s.   [JC]

Other works: *Cleaning Up* (**1987** chap) as IMB; *Espedair Street* (**1987**) as IB, associational; *The Crow Road* (**1992**) as IB, associational.

See also: OPTIMISM AND PESSIMISM; PSYCHOLOGY.

BANKS, MICHAEL A. (1951-   ) US writer and editor who began publishing sf with "Lost & Found", with George Wagner, for *IASFM* in 1978, and who has since published at least 45 stories, some as by Alan Gould. His first books of sf interest were the nonfiction *Understanding Science Fiction* (**1982**), a primer for teachers unfamiliar with the field, and *Ultraheroes* (**1983**), an sf interactive text for juveniles. His first sf novel as such was *The Odysseus Solution* (**1986**) with Dean R(odney) Lambe (1943-   ), an adventure tale involving ALIENS; he remains best known perhaps for his "collaborations" with the late Mack REYNOLDS (*whom see for details*), in which he edited or worked up material by Reynolds into *Joe Mauser: Mercenary from Tomorrow* (**1986**) and *Sweet Dreams, Sweet Princes* (**1986**). Other activities included the associate editorship of *New Destinies* (◊ DESTINIES) in 1986-7. Much of his nonfiction treats material of interest to sf writers and readers.   [JC]

Other works: MAB's nonfiction includes several computer product-training and applications texts, as well as *DELPHI: The Official Guide* (**1987**); *The Modem Reference* (**1988**); *Word Processing Secrets for Writers* (**1989**) with Ansen Dibel; and *Pournelle's Guide to PC Communications* (**1991**) with Jerry POURNELLE.

BANNERMAN, GENE [s] ◊ Thomas P. KELLEY.

BANNISTER, JO [r] ◊ ROBERT HALE LIMITED.

BANNON, MARK ◊ Paul CONRAD.

BANTAM BOOKS Large US publishing house, a general publisher, mainly of paperbacks, rather than an sf specialist. It was founded in 1945 by Ian Ballantine, but he left in 1952 to form BALLANTINE BOOKS because he wanted to publish paperback originals, whereas BB's list was almost entirely of reprints – although one early sf paperback original (but not published as sf) from BB was *Shot in the Dark* (anth **1950**) ed Judith MERRIL. In the 1950s and 1960s BB published some sf, including original collections by Fredric BROWN, but generally were not major players in sf publishing. Their sf line was expanded when Frederik POHL was hired as sf consultant in 1975; *inter alia* he introduced Samuel R. DELANY to the list, with *Dhalgren* (**1975**). Pohl was followed as sf editor by Sydny Weinberg, who was in turn succeeded in 1980 by Karen Haas. By 1981 BB was publishing over 20 sf/fantasy paperback originals a year, including such authors as David BRIN and John CROWLEY.

Lou ARONICA took over the sf line in 1982, with considerable success, his list coming to include Thomas M. DISCH, Richard GRANT, Harry HARRISON, Robert SILVERBERG and Norman SPINRAD, and introducing Pat CADIGAN, Sheila FINCH, R.A. MACAVOY and Robert Charles WILSON. By 1985 BB had become one of the top five sf publishers in terms of number of books published, and in that year launched the new **Bantam Spectra** imprint for sf, which emphasized original publications rather than reprints and also published some hardcovers. Shawna MCCARTHY joined BB as sf editor in 1985, working for Aronica, now Publishing Director. Soon BB authors included Karen Joy FOWLER, William GIBSON, Lisa GOLDSTEIN, Ian MCDONALD, Lewis SHINER and Connie WILLIS. McCarthy left in 1988. By the late 1980s BB had one of the most prestigious lines in sf publishing. Its anthology lines included WILD CARDS and FULL SPECTRUM.

In 1986 the German company Bertelsmann, which already owned BB, bought DOUBLEDAY. As a result, since 1987 Doubleday's new hardcover imprint, **Doubleday Foundation**, was closely associated with **Bantam Spectra**. In 1989 Aronica became vice-president and publisher of all BB mass-market books, while retaining his direct control of **Bantam Spectra**. It appears (1991) that much of the **Doubleday Foundation** list will be returned to **Bantam Spectra**.

The UK Transworld Publishers, which publishes sf and fantasy under the Corgi Books imprint, is a subsidiary of BB.   [PN]

BARBARELLA 1. COMIC strip created by French artist Jean-Claude Forest (1930-   ) for *V. Magazine* in 1962. The interplanetary SEX adventures of the scantily clad blonde astronaut were collected as *Barbarella* (graph coll **1964**; trans **1966** US). Despite its humorous attitudes, *B* incurred the wrath of French censorship. This row and the subsequent film version have tended to obscure the elegance and inventive sf content of the strip. Forest's later attempts to revive it, reducing the sex and increasing the sf elements, were less successful. Among his later, lesser known comic books is the witty *La revanche d'Hypocrite* ["The Revenge of Hypocrite"] (graph **1977**).

2. Film (1968). De Laurentiis-Marianne/Paramount. Dir Roger Vadim, starring Jane Fonda, John Phillip Law, Milo O'Shea, David Hemmings, Anita Pallenberg. Screenplay Terry Southern, Jean-Claude Forest, Vadim, Vittorio Bonicelli, Brian Degas, Claude Brule, Tudor Gates, Clement Biddle Wood, based on the comic strip by Forest. 98 mins. Colour.

Like Forest's strip, this Italian-French coproduction parodies the conventions of PULP-MAGAZINE sf as typified by FLASH GORDON but, where Forest's work was spare, Vadim's is lush, and it loses some of Forest's sharpness. The film is sometimes funny but seldom witty, despite the presence of Southern among the multinational crowd of eight scriptwriters. Barbarella (Fonda), agent of the Earth government, is sexually and culturally innocent in the manner of VOLTAIRE's Candide. Her search for a missing scientist on the planet Sogo results in an ever more baroque series of (mostly sexual) encounters: with sadistic children and their carnivorous dolls, with a blind angel (Law), with an inadequate revolutionary (Hemmings), with a pleasure machine and with the decadent lesbian Black Queen (Pallenberg), among others. Fonda – whose clothes look as if designed by Earle K. BERGEY – is memorable for her attractively wide-eyed air, combining eroticism with bafflement. FEMINIST critics were outraged at Vadim's exploitation of his real-life wife's sexuality in so voyeuristic a manner – he had done it before with Brigitte Bardot – though his evocation of the decadence he so obviously enjoys appears adolescent rather than corrupt. The exoticism with which the planet Sogo is created is what makes *B* a distinguished sf film; a real, if intermittent, SENSE OF WONDER is created by the sheer alienness of Mario Garbuglia's production design and Enrico Fea's art direction, all glowingly photographed by Claude Renoir.   [MJ/PN]

BARBARY, JAMES ◊ Jack BEECHING.

BARBEE, PHILLIPS [s] ◊ Robert SHECKLEY.

BARBET, PIERRE Pseudonym of Dr Claude Pierre Marie Avice (1925-   ), French writer; under his real name he is a pharmacist and an expert on bionics. He has also used the pseudonyms David Maine and Olivier Sprigel. A highly prolific if derivative popular writer of sf from 1962, PB has published over 35 novels, some of which have been translated into English: *Les grognards d'Éridan* (**1970**; trans Stanley Hochman as *The Napoleons of Eridanus* **1976** US) and its sequel *L'Empereur d'Éridan* (trans Stanley Hochman as *The Emperor of Eridanus* **1983** US), which make up a series of SPACE OPERAS based on **Napoleon**; the PARALLEL-WORLDS story *L'empire du Baphomet* (**1971**; trans Bernard Kay as *Baphomet's Meteor* **1972** US) and assembled with *Croisade Stellaire* (**1974**; trans C.J. CHERRYH as "Stellar Crusade" in *Cosmic Crusaders* [omni **1980** US]); *Liane de Noldaz* (**1973**; trans Stanley Hochman as *The Joan-of-Arc Replay* **1978** US); *A quoi songent les psyborgs?* (**1971**; trans Wendayne Ackerman as *Games Psyborgs Play* **1973** US); *La planète enchantée* (**1973**; trans C.J. Richards as *The Enchanted Planet* **1975** US). [MJ]

BARBOUR, DOUGLAS (FLEMING) (1940-   ) Canadian academic, a professor of English at the University of Alberta, whose "Patterns of Meaning in the SF Novels of Ursula K. Le Guin, Joanna Russ and Samuel R. Delany, 1962-1972", accepted by Queen's University in 1976, was the first Canadian doctoral dissertation in the field of sf. Two competent published studies were spun-off from this volume: *An Opening in the Field: The SF Novels of Joanna Russ* (**1978** US), a necessary study of Joanna RUSS, and *Worlds Out of Words: The SF Novels of Samuel R. Delany* (**1979** UK). Several shorter essays, specifically those on Samuel R. DELANY and Ursula K. LE GUIN, have demonstrated DB's adhesion to a high-road view of the genre, although he has published a short piece on *The Witches of Karres* (**1966**) by James H. SCHMITZ and has reviewed with some liberality of grasp. [JC]

See also: CANADA.

BĂRBULESCU, ROMULUS [r] ◊ ROMANIA.

BARBUSSE, HENRI (1874-1935) French writer, best known for his strongly realistic fiction, especially that concerning WWI. *Les enchaînements* (**1925**; trans as *Chains* in 2 vols **1925** US) attempts – like many novels from the first third of the century – to present a panoramic vision of mankind's prehistory and history, in this case through the transcendental experiences of a single protagonist who is struck by his significant visions while in the middle of a staircase. [JC]

See also: ORIGIN OF MAN.

BARCELÓ, ELIA [r] ◊ SPAIN.

BARCELÓ, MIQUEL (1948-   ) Spanish (Catalan) computer-systems professor and sf/fantasy book editor with Ediciones B. Having been publisher of the sf FANZINE *Kandama* from 1980, MB became a professional editor in 1986, and is author of *Ciencia ficción: Guía de lectura* ["Science Fiction Reader's Guide"]

(**1990**). He revised the SPAIN entry in this volume. [PN]

BARCLAY, ALAN Pseudonym of UK writer and civil engineer George B. Tait (1910-   ), who wrote some stories for *Science Fantasy*, beginning with "Enemy in their Midst" in 1952, and the **Jacko** series – mostly for *NW*, beginning with "Only an Echo" (**1954**) and ending with "The Thing in Common" (**1956**). Parts of this series became his sf novel *Of Earth and Fire* (fixup **1974**), which pits Earth's space service against ALIEN intruders. He wrote his novels exclusively for ROBERT HALE LIMITED. [JC]

Other works: *The City and the Desert* (**1976**); *No Magic Carpet* (**1976**); *The Cruel Years of Winter* (**1978**); *The Guardian at Sunset* (dated **1979** but **1980**).

BARCLAY, BILL or WILLIAM ◊ Michael MOORCOCK.

BARCLAY, GABRIEL House pseudonym used in 1940 for 2 stories in *Astonishing Stories* and *Super Science Stories*, 1 by Manly Wade WELLMAN and 1 by C.M. KORNBLUTH.

BARFIELD, (ARTHUR) OWEN (1898-   ) UK writer and philologist whose first book, *The Silver Trumpet* (**1925**), was a fantasy. He was long involved with the Anthroposophical philosophy of Rudolf Steiner (1861-1925). A member of the Inklings group and a long-time associate of C.S. LEWIS, OB contributed to *Essays Presented to Charles Williams* (anth **1947**), which Lewis had organized. As G.A.L. Burgeon he wrote an sf novel, *This Ever Diverse Pair* (**1950**). Later works include *Worlds Apart* (**1963**), described as "A Dialogue of the 1960s", and *Unancestral Voice* (**1968**). [JC]

About the author: "C.S. Lewis, Owen Barfield and the Modern Myth" by W.D. Norwood Jr in *Midwest Quarterly* 4(2) (1967).

BARGONE, FRÉDÉRIC CHARLES PIERRE ÉDOUARD [r] ◊ Claude FARRÈRE.

BARJAVEL, RENÉ (1911-1985) French novelist, active in later life as a screenwriter and journalist. His first novel to be translated, *Ravage* (**1943**; trans Damon KNIGHT as *Ashes, Ashes* **1967** US), describes a post-HOLOCAUST France driven inwards into rural quiescence by the sudden disappearance of electricity from the world; the corrupting effects of technology are described scathingly. The next sf work from this important early period is *Le voyageur imprudent* (**1944**; with postscript 1958; trans anon as *Future Times Three* **1970** US), a rather pessimistic TIME-TRAVEL story with the usual paradoxes, partly set in the same future world as the previous novel. Several novels have not been translated: *L'homme fort* ["The Strong Man"] (**1946**), about a self-created SUPERMAN whose efforts to bring happiness to humanity are doomed; and *Le diable l'emporte* ["The Devil Takes All"] (**1948**) and its sequel *Colomb de la Lune* ["Columbus of the Moon"] (**1962**), about the consequences of a future WAR. The epigraph to *Le diable l'emporte* reads, in translation, "To our grandfathers and grandchildren, the cavemen."

RB's later work decreases in intensity and is less interestingly (though almost unvaryingly) gloomy about humanity's prospects. Typical is *La nuit des temps* (**1968**; trans Charles Lam Markmann as *The Ice People* **1970** UK), a ramblingly told morality tale in which two long-frozen humans – survivors of an eons-prior nuclear war – revive into a disaster-bound present age. [JC/PN]

Other works: *Les enfants de l'hombre* ["Children of the Shadows"] (coll **1946**; exp vt *Le prince blessé* ["The Wounded Prince"] 1974); *Le grand secret* (**1973**; trans as *The Immortals* **1974** US); *Jour de feu* ["Day of Fire"] (**1974**); *Une Rose au Paradis* ["A Rose from Paradise"] (**1981**); *La Tempête* ["The Tempest"] (**1982**).

See also: FRANCE.

BARKER, D.A. [r] ◊ ROBERT HALE LIMITED.

BARLOW, JAMES (1921-1973) UK novelist, known mainly for such work outside the sf field as the anti-communist thriller *The Hour of Maximum Danger* (**1962**). His sf novel, *One Half of the World* (**1957**), presents a UK ruled by a totalitarian leftist regime. The protagonist, finding God again, conflicts with the powers-that-be. [JC]

BARLOW, JAMES WILLIAM (1826-1913) UK cleric and writer whose sf novel, *History of a World of Immortals without a God* (**1891** Ireland as by Antares Skorpios; vt *The Immortals' Great Quest* 1909 UK as JWB), presents in note form its protagonist's record of his trip to VENUS, where a large population has resided in a state of happy non-Christian socialism for many thousands of years. The inhabitants of the first continent visited by the misogynist narrator find themselves, after death, reincarnated (◊ REINCARNA-TION) on a second continent far to the south, where they continue their Great Quest for an explanatory principle, or God. [JC]

BARLOWE, WAYNE DOUGLAS (1958-) US illustrator whose successful *Barlowe's Guide to Extra-terrestrials* (**1979**), in collaboration with Ian Summers (who wrote the text), was published when he was 21, only two years after he had made his first sale, a cover for *Cosmos*. The book featured WDB's excellent paintings of many of sf's best-known ALIENS. The son of natural-history artists Sy and Dorothea Barlowe, WDB has a talent for creating believable surface textures, important in creating aliens – his attention to detail is reminiscent of Wyeth and Pyle. He works in acrylics and has done book covers, also magazine covers for *ASF* and *IASFM*, to whose ex-editor, Shawna MCCARTHY, he is married. *Expedition: Being an Account in Words and Artwork of the 2358 A.D. Voyage to Darwin IV* (**1990**), written and illustrated by WDB, is an interesting work of speculative XENOBIOLOGY, illustrating and describing the physiology of lifeforms on an imaginary planet. [JG/PN]

BARNARD, MARJORIE FAITH [r] ◊ M. Barnard ELDERSHAW.

BARNARD-ELDERSHAW, M. ◊ M. Barnard ELDER-SHAW.

BARNE, LEO [s] ◊ L.P. DAVIES.

BARNES, ARTHUR K(ELVIN) (1911-1969) US pulp writer known also for his works outside the sf field.

He was intermittently active in sf until 1946, his first story being published in 1931. His **Gerry Carlyle** series of stories, in which Miss Carlyle and a sidekick hunt down various alien prey, appeared originally in *TWS*. His *Interplanetary Hunter* (1937-46 *TWS*; fixup **1956**) combines 5 of these stories, omitting "The Dual World" (1938) and "The Energy Eaters" (1939). The latter story – and "The Seven Sleepers" (1940), worked into the fixup – were written with Henry KUTTNER, and used his character Tony Quade. AKB sometimes used the pseudonym Kelvin KENT, both alone and with Kuttner. [JC]

See also: GAMES AND SPORTS; OUTER PLANETS; THRILLING WONDER STORIES.

BARNES, JOHN (1957-) US writer who began publishing sf with "Finalities Besides the Grave" for *AMZ* in 1985, and who made some impact on the field with his first novel, *The Man who Pulled Down the Sky* (**1987**), an effective drama involving highly coloured political conflicts throughout the Solar System. His second, *Sin of Origin* (**1988**), rather more ambitiously attempts to combine SPACE OPERA, RELI-GION and SOCIOLOGY in a tale set on a planet (which humans call Randall) whose species enjoyed an extremely complex tripartite form of symbiosis before the arrival of two human sects – Christians and communists – who variously, and fatally, come to "understand" what is happening. As the tripartite symbiosis breaks down, the surviving singles begin to replicate human forms of behaviour – slavery becomes rife – and the novel continues to darken. The final conclusion is that DNA, found in all sentient species, reproduces by causing its bearers to destroy themselves and their planets violently in terminal HOLOCAUSTS, so that DNA spores are blown to new stars. JB's third novel, *Orbital Resonance* (**1991**), a juvenile, rather implausibly at times – though always with panache – shows adult humans deciding that their children are better equipped to handle the challenges of the new in space. [JC]

Other works: *How to Build a Future* (**1991** chap), nonfiction.

BARNES, JULIAN (PATRICK) (1946-) UK writer who has published detective novels as by Dan Kavanaugh. His most famous single novel is *Flaubert's Parrot* (**1984**). He has written two books of sf interest. *Staring at the Sun* (**1986**) carries its protagonist from her birth in 1922 into an exiguous future 98 years later, but closes movingly at a moment when, still archaically alive to the real world, she gazes at the unfaded reality of the Sun. *A History of the World in 10½ Chapters* (coll of linked stories **1989**) begins with Noah's Ark and gradually assembles a vision of history itself as a *Narrenschiff*, or Ship of Fools, or Ark, whose message is nothing without human love. [JC]

BARNES, MYRA EDWARDS (1933-) US author of *Linguistics and Language in Science Fiction-Fantasy* (**1975**), a reprint of her 1971 PhD dissertation. This is a useful introduction to the subject (◊ LINGUISTICS), although not as comprehensive as *Aliens and Linguists: Language Study and Science Fiction* (**1980**) by Walter E. MEYERS. [PN]

BARNES, (KEITH) RORY [r] ◊ Damien BRODERICK.

BARNES, STEVEN (EMORY) (1952-   ) US writer who began publishing with "Moonglow" in *Vampires, Werewolves and Other Monsters* (anth **1974**) ed Roger ELWOOD, and whose career has been associated since its early days with Larry NIVEN, SB's collaborator on most of his novels, including the first, *Dream Park* (**1981**). The **Dream Park** sequence – the eponymous venue in which it is set houses a wide variety of high-tech role-playing games (◊ GAME-WORLDS; VIRTUAL REALITY) – continues with *The Barsoom Project* (**1989**) and *Dream Park: The Voodoo Game* (**1991** UK; vt *The California Voodoo Game* 1992 US), both also with Niven, and has moments of relatively light-hearted agility, especially perhaps in the second volume, in which a terraformed MARS (*see also* TERRAFORMING) is advertised, although the action does not leave Earth. Further collaborations include *The Descent of Anansi* (**1982**) with Niven, *The Legacy of Heorot* (**1987** UK) with Niven and Jerry POURNELLE, a tale of planet-exploitation based on *Beowulf* and reflecting many of Pournelle's convictions, and *Achilles' Choice* (**1991**) with Niven alone, which returns to a game-world atmosphere, though not it seems advertently, in a tale set at a time when athletes can aspire to join the planet-dominating corporate elite by winning at competitions, the catch being that they must "Boost" to achieve stardom, and that only the winners are saved through real-time computer monitoring of the effects of doing so.

SB's solo work has been perhaps less infected by hi-tech gloss. *Streetlethal* (**1983**) and its sequel *Gorgon Child* (**1989**), set in post-earthquake Los Angeles, are moderately down-to-earth adventure tales set in the kind of CYBERPUNK urban venue that is always said to be gritty, with an abundance of sf instruments involved in keeping the action moving. *The Kundalini Equation* (**1986**) invokes its author's long interest in martial arts. It might be said that SB has acquired a good amount of skill and gear, but has yet to speak in his own voice. [JC]

See also: LEISURE; SPACESHIPS.

BARNETT, PAUL (LE PAGE) (1949-   ) Scottish writer and editor, resident in England, who has used the pseudonym John Grant for all his published work except some short stories and a nonfiction book as by Eve Devereux and a handful of essays and reviews and a nonfiction book translation under his own name. He entered the field through editing *Aries 1* (anth **1979**), which contains the first and so far only sf short story by Colin WILSON, with whom PB later edited the nonfiction *The Book of Time* (**1980**) and *The Directory of Possibilities* (**1981**). The solo *A Directory of Discarded Ideas* (**1981**), largely on PSEUDO-SCIENCE, led directly to his book-length fiction, *Sex Secrets of Ancient Atlantis* (**1985**), a parody of pseudo-science in general and ATLANTIS studies in particular. His first

novel, *The Truth about the Flaming Ghoulies* (**1984**), a comedy, describes in epistolary form a NEAR-FUTURE rock band whose members prove to be ANDROIDS. *Earthdoom!* (**1987**) with David LANGFORD is a perhaps overly broad parody of the DISASTER-novel genre. *Albion* (**1991**) is a fantasy novel about a POCKET UNIVERSE, the first of a projected tetralogy, the second of which, *The World* (**1992**), is more overtly science-fictional, depicting the fusion of two alternate universes to form a third. By training a publisher's editor, he has served as Technical Editor for the 2nd edn of this encyclopedia. [JC/JGr]

Other works: The **Legends of Lone Wolf** series of ties, SWORD-AND-SORCERY novels based on gamebooks by Joe Dever (1956-   ) and published as co-authorships: *Eclipse of the Kai* * (**1989**), *The Dark Door Opens* * (**1989**) – these 2 assembled as *Legends of Lone Wolf Omnibus* * (**1992**) – *The Sword of the Sun* * (**1989**; rev in 2 vols vt *The Tides of Treachery* * 1991 US and *The Sword of the Sun* * 1991 US), *Hunting Wolf* * (**1990**), *The Claws of Helgedad* * (**1991**), *The Sacrifice of Ruanon* * (cut **1991**), *The Birthplace* * (**1992**) and *The Book of the Magnakai* (**1992**), with 4 further vols projected; much nonfiction, including *Dreamers: A Geography of Dreamland* (**1984**) and *Encyclopedia of Walt Disney's Animated Characters* (**1987** US; «2nd edn» 1993 US).

See also: COSMOLOGY; GAMES AND SPORTS; MUSIC.

BARNEY, JOHN STEWART (1868-1925) US writer whose sf novel, *L.P.M.: The End of the Great War* (**1915**), is an unusually authoritarian EDISONADE in which an impatiently triumphal US scientist – in this case his name is Edestone – uses the futuristic weaponry he has invented to defeat the warring nations of Europe and introduce to the world a government ruled by an "Aristocracy of Intelligence". [JC]

BARNWELL, WILLIAM (CURTIS) (1943-   ) US author whose brief but interesting foray into the sf/fantasy genre was his well written **Blessing Trilogy**, consisting of *The Blessing Papers* (**1980**), *Imram* (**1981**) and *The Sigma Curve* (**1981**). This complex quest through a post-HOLOCAUST world, where some sort of grand design by mysterious powers is operating, at first appears lively but conventional SCIENCE FANTASY. In fact, the intellectual structure of the work is both demanding and very eccentric: a METAPHYSICAL allegory about free will and predestination. The holocaust was deliberately brought about to short-circuit humanity's DEVOLUTION as the left and right hemispheres of the brain lost contact due to corrupting visual imagery replacing the purity of the spoken word. This may be the only apocalyptic fiction where Earth's "Falling" was directly, it appears, due to tv programming rather than Original Sin. The books read as if produced by a member of a PSEUDO-SCIENCE cult, but it is not clear which one. [PN]

BARON, OTHELLO [s] ◊ R.L. FANTHORPE.

BARR, DENSIL NEVE Pseudonym of UK writer Douglas Norton Buttrey (1918-   ), whose sf novel, *The Man with Only One Head* (**1955**), develops the theme of novels like Pat FRANK's *Mr Adam* (**1946**). Only one man is left fertile; the subsequent moralistic World Federation set up to deal with the crisis is riddled with dissension. [JC]

BARR, DONALD (1921-) US writer and academic, former assistant dean of the Engineering School of Columbia University, and author of several non-fiction works for children as well as *Who Pushed Humpty Dumpty, or The Education of a Headmaster* (**1971**), on US education. His sf novel, *Space Relations: A Slightly Gothic Interplanetary Tale* (**1973**), is a SPACE OPERA interlaced amusingly with "literary" analogues to its tale of a space diplomat, sold into slavery, who is sexually excited by fear, thus enticing a princess, and who also finds out grim secrets about an alien INVASION of Earth. *A Planet in Arms* (**1981**) is noticeably less elated. [JC]

BARR, GEORGE (1937-) US sf illustrator. One of the most meticulous of sf/fantasy artists, he is also one of the least appreciated – at least for his professional work. GB started by illustrating sf FANZINES and was nominated five times for the HUGO as Best Fan Artist, winning in 1968 and 1969. However, he had by then already sold his first professional illustration to FANTASTIC, the cover for Mar 1961. He continued with some magazine work, but is perhaps best known for his paperback covers for ACE BOOKS, DAW BOOKS and others. His often delicate, sometimes whimsical, artwork is influenced by his appreciation of the work of Arthur Rackham (1867-1939) and Hannes BOK. GB works primarily in colour, laying watercolour washes over ball-point lines. In a field that emphasizes brightness, his pastel shades are almost unique. More recently he has done many interior illustrations for ISAAC ASIMOV'S SCIENCE FICTION MAGAZINE. A showcase for his work is *Upon the Winds of Yesterday, and Other Explorations* (**1976**). [JG/PN]

BARR, ROBERT (1850-1912) Scottish editor and a popular and prolific writer. His early catastrophe story in *The* IDLER (which he edited), "The Doom of London" (1892), deals with fog and POLLUTION. It was reprinted in *The Face & the Mask* (coll **1894**), which contains several other sf and fantasy stories, as does *In a Steamer Chair and Other Shipboard Stories* (coll **1892**). [JC]
Other works: *From whose Bourne* (**1893**); *Revenge!* (coll **1896**); *Tekla: A Romance of Love and War* (**1898** Canada; vt *The Countess Tekla* 1899 UK).
See also: CANADA.

BARR, TYRONE C. (? -?) UK writer. His sf novel, *Split Worlds* (**1959**; vt *The Last Fourteen* 1960 US), sees 14 crew members of a space station survive the extermination of everyone on Earth. Eventually they must land and breed and start again, though quarrelling furiously, in a fantastically transformed world. [JC]

BARREDO, EDUARDO [r] ◊ LATIN AMERICA.

BARREN, CHARLES (1913-) UK teacher and writer, best known for historical romances and co-

author with R(ichard) Cox Abel of *Trivana 1* (**1966**), in which an overpopulated Earth establishes a VENUS colony. He was chairman of the SCIENCE FICTION FOUNDATION from its inception in 1970 until his retirement in 1980, subsequently serving as its Honorary Administrator 1980-84. [JC]

BARRETT, GEOFFREY JOHN (1928-) UK writer who has also published thrillers as Cole Rickard and Westerns as Bill Wade; his sf novels, written for ROBERT HALE LIMITED under his own name and as Edward Leighton, Dennis Summers and James Wallace, are consistently routine. [JC]
Works: As GJB: *The Brain of Graphicon* (**1973**); *The Lost Fleet of Astranides* (**1974**); *The Tomorrow Stairs* (**1974**); *Overself* (**1975**); *The Paradise Zone* (**1975**); *City of the First Time* (**1975**); *Slaver from the Stars* (**1975**); *The Bodysnatchers of Lethe* (**1976**); *The Night of the Deathship* (**1976**); *Timeship to Thebes* (**1976**); *The Hall of the Evolvulus* (**1977**); *The Other Side of Red* (**1977**); *Robotria* (**1977**); *Earth Watch* (**1978**).
As Edward Leighton: *Out of Earth's Deep* (**1976**); *A Light from Tomorrow* (**1977**); *Lord of the Lightning* (**1977**).
As Dennis Summers: *A Madness from Mars* (**1976**); *Stalker of the Worlds* (**1976**); *The Robot in the Glass* (**1977**); *The Muster of Ghosts* (**1977**).
As James Wallace: *A Man from Tomorrow* (**1976**); *Plague of the Golden Rat* (**1976**); *The Guardian of Krandor* (**1977**) [JC]

BARRETT, NEAL Jr (1929-) US writer who began publishing sf with "To Tell the Truth" for *Gal* in 1960 and who has contributed with some regularity to the sf magazines. Though he has never been prolific in shorter forms, some of his later stories, like "Hero" (1979), "A Day at the Fair" (1982), "Trading Post" (1986), "Sallie C" (1987), "Perpetuity Blues" (1987), "Diner" (1987), "Stairs" (1988) and "Tony Red Dog" (1989), have caused considerable stir for the dark bravura of the vision they sometimes expose of a savaged USA. NB's first novels did not seem urgently to foretell the ambitious author of the 1980s, and titles like *Kelwin* (**1970**), whose eponymous hero has stirring adventures in a post-HOLOCAUST venue, the equally rambunctious *The Gates of Time* (**1970**), and the alternate-history (◊ ALTERNATE WORLDS) tale, *The Leaves of Time* (**1971**) – despite the title, not connected to the earlier volume – seemed little more than amusing and competently told routine fare, with twists.

Stress Pattern (**1974**), a densely constructed fable set on an alien planet whose profligate alienness is at points reminiscent of the worlds of Stanisław LEM, was clearly more ambitious, and NB followed this striking work with the **Aldair** series – *Aldair in Albion* (**1976**), *Aldair, Master of Ships* (**1977**), *Aldair, Across the Misty Sea* (**1980**) and *Aldair: The Legion of Beasts* (**1982**) – whose baroque surface tends to disguise the alarming implications of the tale, for the hero is a genetically engineered humanoid pig, the FAR-FUTURE Earth he travels lacks real solace, and his discovery of humans on another planet grants him no peace, for they themselves have been enslaved by a race of ALIENS. In retrospect, then, *Through Darkest America* (**1987**) and its sequel, *Dawn's Uncertain Light* (**1989**), which have gained NB considerable attention 30 years into his career, are a logical development of his earlier work. Their protagonists' hegira through a most terrifyingly bleak and terminally scarred USA, though told with an exhilarating and genre-sensitive competence, conveys a sense of grieved, embedded, millennial pessimism impossible to sidestep; and even *The Hereafter Gang* (**1991**), which less savagely focuses this vision on the churning psyche of a middle-aged man in crisis, turns into a sharp and garish parody of a sentimentalized small-town past over which it is easy, but dangerous, to pine – posthumously, as it were. NB seems a writer who has come into his times. [JC]

Other works: *Highwood* (**1972** dos); *The Karma Corps* (**1984**).

See also: ECOLOGY; EVOLUTION; LIVING WORLDS.

BARRETT, WILLIAM E(DMUND) (1900-1986) US writer who began publishing short stories with "The Music of Madness" for *Weird Tales* in 1926. He wrote *Flight from Youth* (**1939**) before WWII, later incorporating it into *The Edge of Things* (coll **1960**), whose 3 stories all relate in some way to flying. His sf novel, *The Fools of Time* (**1963**), unconvincingly posits an IMMORTALITY drug based on cancer. [JC]

BARRETTON, GRANDALL [s] ◊ Randall GARRETT.

BARRINGTON, MICHAEL Collaborative pseudonym of Michael MOORCOCK and Barrington J. BAYLEY on 1 story, "Peace on Earth" (1959). [JC]

BARRON, D(ONALD) G(ABRIEL) (1922-   ) UK architect and writer. In *The Zilov Bombs* (**1962**), unilateral UK nuclear disarmament has led to Soviet domination of all Europe; after five years (by 1973) the underground is putting pressure on characters like the narrator, who ultimately solves his moral anxieties by detonating an A-bomb. [JC]

Other works: *The Man who was There* (**1969**).

BARRON, (RICHARD) NEIL (1934-   ) US bibliographer and book editor, trained as a librarian, who has produced some of the liveliest and most readable scholarship in sf, notably in the three well researched editions of *Anatomy of Wonder: A Critical Guide to Science Fiction* (**1976**; exp 1981; further exp 1987), which he edited and to which he contributed. These volumes discuss many individual books, both fiction (including foreign-language) and secondary literature; the 3rd edn, with over 2600 entries, is by far the most thorough work of its kind. Companion vols ed NB are *Fantasy Literature: A Reader's Guide* (**1990**) and *Horror Literature: A Reader's Guide* (**1990**). NB founded and edited SCIENCE FICTION & FANTASY BOOK REVIEW 1979-80, and edited the same journal when it was revived by the SCIENCE FICTION RESEARCH ASSOCIATION in 1982-3. It merged with FANTASY NEWSLETTER in 1984 to form the newly titled FANTASY REVIEW (very briefly known at first as *SF & Fantasy Review*), for which NB was review editor Jan 1984-Apr 1985. He is a regular

contributor to the SFRA NEWSLETTER. NB received the 1982 PILGRIM AWARD for his contributions to sf scholarship. [PN]

See also: BIBLIOGRAPHIES; COLLECTIONS; CRITICAL AND HISTORICAL WORKS ABOUT SF.

BARRY, RAY ◊ Dennis HUGHES.

BARTH, JOHN (SIMMONS) (1930-   ) US novelist. One of the leading fabulists (◊ FABULATION) of his generation of writers, he is probably best known for his epic mock-picaresque *The Sot-Weed Factor* (**1960**; rev 1967). *Giles Goat-Boy, or The Revised New Syllabus* (**1966**), which derives its language in part from Vladimir NABOKOV and its central metaphor of the university as the world in part from Jorge Luis BORGES, can, by taking the metaphor literally, be read as sf. The hero is rendered literally as goat-horned. The novel itself is a complex SATIRE on education, human nature and knowledge, and also a remarkable *Bildungsroman*. Some of JB's later short fiction, as assembled in *Lost in the Funhouse: Fiction for Print, Tape, Live Voice* (coll **1968**; exp 1969), contains some intensely academic FANTASY, and *Chimera* (coll of linked stories **1972**) hovers at the edge of the fantastic in its literalization in narrative form of the powers of mythopoeisis.

Other works: *Letters* (**1979**); *The Last Voyage of Somebody the Sailor* (**1991**). [JC]

BARTHELME, DONALD (1933-1989) US writer known primarily as a surrealist and black-humorist. His novels are all FABULATIONS: *Snow White* (**1967**), an absurdist dissection of the fairy tale; *The Dead Father* (**1975**), in which the giant figure of a moribund Father is escorted with trauma and ritual to its final resting place; and *The King* (**1990**), which transports King Arthur and his knights to WWII. DB's early collections especially – like *Come Back, Dr Caligari* (coll **1964**), *Unspeakable Practices, Unnatural Acts* (coll **1968**) and *City Life* (coll **1970**) – present in the form of discontinuous spoofs and iconoclasms a number of ideas and themes taken from MYTHOLOGY, fantasy and sf. Many of these stories have been reprinted in sf anthologies. His work as a whole is conveniently assembled in *Sixty Stories* (coll **1981**) and *Forty Stories* (coll **1988**). [PR/JC]

Other works: *The Slightly Irregular Fire Engine* (**1971** chap); *Sadness* (coll **1972**); *Guilty Pleasures* (coll **1974**); *Amateurs* (coll **1976**); *Great Days* (coll **1979**); *Overnight to Many Distant Cities* (coll **1983**).

About the author: *Donald Barthelme's Fiction: The Ironist Saved from Drowning* (**1982**) by Charles Molesworth.

BARTHOLOMEW, BARBARA (1941-   ) US writer whose **Timeways Trilogy** for young adult readers – *The Time Keeper* (**1985**), *Child of Tomorrow* (**1985**) and *When Dreamers Cease to Dream* (**1985**) – traverses familiar TIME-TRAVEL themes without undue stress. Other books for younger readers include *The Cereal Box Adventures* (**1981**), *Flight into the Unknown* (**1982**) and *The Great Gradepoint Mystery* (**1983**). [JC]

BARTLETT, VERNON (OLDFIELD) (1894-1983) UK

broadcaster, politician and writer, whose *If I Were Dictator* (**1935** chap) reflected his centrist politics – he was an Independent MP 1938-50 – in its reformist agenda. His sf novel proper, *Tomorrow Always Comes* (**1943**), describes in fictional terms the task of reconstructing a defeated Germany after the end of WWII. [JC]

BARTON, ERLE ◊ R.L. FANTHORPE.

BARTON, JAMES (? -) Writer, apparently US, whose post-HOLOCAUST **Wasteworld** series – *Wasteworld #1: Aftermath* (**1983** UK), *#2: Resurrection* (**1984** UK), *#3: Angels* (**1984** UK) and *#4: My Way* (**1984**) – takes its military hero through the US South and elsewhere, fighting bigots and MUTANTS and winning an Apache lass. [JC]

BARTON, LEE ◊ R.L. FANTHORPE.

BARTON, SAMUEL (? -?) US writer who also published as A.B. Roker. His sf novel, *The Battle of the Swash and the Capture of Canada* (**1888**), thought by Thomas D. CLARESON to be the first US future-WAR tale, was written to show the defencelessness of the US coasts (and incidentally the vulnerability of Canada) as the USA and UK come to blows, a conflict eventually won by the USA through the invention of self-destructing torpedo boats. He has been claimed as a US Congressman, Samuel Barton (1785-1858), but it is extremely unlikely that *The Battle of the Swash* could have been conceived 30+ years before its publication. [JC]

BARTON, S.W. [r] ◊ Michael KURLAND.

BARTON, WILLIAM R(ENALD) III) (1950-) US writer whose sf novel, *Hunting on Kunderer* (**1973**), confronts humans with ALIEN natives on a dangerous new planet, and whose *A Plague of All Cowards* (**1976**) was also an sf adventure. Of much greater interest was *Iris* (**1990**) with Michael CAPOBIANCO, in which a group of artists, en route to Triton, encounters the eponymous GAS GIANT, which has drifted, with moons, into the Solar System. Alien artefacts are found and epiphanies are experienced; but the novel is primarily striking for the intense directness of the prose and for the capacity of the authors to address in that prose both matters of science (which might be expected in a HARD-SF novel) and matters of character, for the cast is deeply memorable. *Fellow Traveler* (**1991**), also with Capobianco, is perhaps more straightforward, but again shows a remarkable grasp of the human shape of experience, in this case a NEAR-FUTURE Soviet attempt to harness an asteroid for industrial purposes. Given the current state of the US space program, this novel is one of the very few of those caught out by the political transformation of the USSR to make one feel that there have been losses as well as gains. *Dark Sky Legion: An Ahrimanic Novel* (**1992**) is an ambitious, Galaxy-spanning, metaphysical, highly readable SPACE OPERA which provides some engrossing speculations about a universe in which FASTER-THAN-LIGHT travel is impossible and over which a conservative human hegemony exercises control, ruthlessly braking the tendency of isolated colonies

to vary too far from the declared norm; there are echoes of *Wolfbane* (**1959**) by C.M. KORNBLUTH and Frederic POHL. WB treats this use of power with due though occasionally rather moody ambiguity. [JC]

BARZMAN, BEN (1912-1989) Canadian-born US writer and film-writer whose sf novel *Out of this World* (**1960** UK; vt *Twinkle, Twinkle, Little Star* 1960 US; vt *Echo X* 1962 US) ambitiously portrays twin Earths and tells a love story involving people transported between them. [JC]

BASIL, OTTO (1901-1983) Austrian writer. His sf novel, *Wenn das der Führer wüsste* (**1966**; cut trans Thomas Weyr as *The Twilight Men* **1968** US), is set in an ALTERNATE WORLD in which HITLER WINS in 1945 through the use of atomic weapons; after Hitler dies, a battle for power ensues. [JC]

See also: GERMANY.

BASS, T.J. Working name of US writer Thomas J. Bassler (1932-), who began publishing sf with "Star Seeder" for *If* in 1969. He is almost exclusively associated with the series that comprises his only book publications, *Half Past Human* (1969-70 *Gal* and *If*; fixup **1971**) and *The Godwhale* (**1974**), itself expanded from an earlier story, "Rorqual Maru" (1972 *Gal*). Through a network of intricately interlinked stories, the first novel depicts a densely overcrowded Earth where problems of OVERPOPULATION have been dealt with by settling four-toed evolved human stock called Nebishes in vast underground silos (◊ CITIES) under the control of a COMPUTER net. Outside these hives, unevolved humans eke out savage existences; but an ancient sentient starship named Olga (◊ CYBORGS) plans to seed the stars with her beloved, five-toed, normal humans, and eventually succeeds, though the Earth society of the Nebishes continues, oblivious to any threat. In *The Godwhale*, a complexly structured SLEEPER-AWAKES tale, Larry Dever, a human from our own near future, is mutilated in an accident and decides to enter SUSPENDED ANIMATION to await a time when nerve regeneration is possible. However, he is found to be still incurable when awoken millennia later into an Earth society some time after the events of the previous volume. A great long-dormant cyborg whale has registered life in the desolate ocean and has reactivated herself, longing to serve mankind and harvest the seas for him; she soon comes across humans evolved into Benthics capable of living under water, and accepts them as human. Larry Dever escapes servitude in the silos and joins the Godwhale; the seas are alive with Benthics and lower forms of life – quite evidently, Olga has seeded the planet. Mankind begins to inhabit the archipelagos and the Earth will once again bear fruit.

In these two books, TJB demonstrates a thorough command of biological extrapolation and a sustained delight in the creation of a witty, acronym-choked language suitable for the description of this new environment. Though his control over the overall structure of a novel-length fiction is insecure, the abundance of his invention conveyed to readers of the 1970s a sense of TJB's potential importance as an sf writer. He has, however, fallen silent, his series incomplete. [JC]

See also: EVOLUTION; HIVE-MINDS; UNDER THE SEA.

BATCHELOR, JOHN CALVIN (1948-) US author. His first two novels, *The Further Adventures of Halley's Comet* (**1981**) and *The Birth of the People's Republic of Antarctica* (**1983**), are borderline fantasy and sf respectively. He has also published two mainstream novels, *American Falls* (**1985**) and *Gordon Liddy is My Muse, by Tommy "Tip" Paine* (**1990**). With John R. Hamilton he wrote *Thunder in the Dust: Images of Western Movies* (**1987**).

JCB's novels have a gravity and consistency which mark him as a significant contemporary writer; they confront such themes as the morality of terror, the justice of ends and means, and the construction of history by its victors. *Halley's Comet* is an extended Pop-GOTHIC exercise. It presents a satirically and grotesquely distorted picture of Western capitalism, whose distribution of wealth and power appears as a weird latter-day version of feudalism. *People's Republic* begins with similar Pop grotesquerie, but transforms into an unremittingly stark NEAR-FUTURE Viking saga, its narrator a kind of doomed and bloody seawolf. There is a vast backdrop of the collapse of civilization across Europe and massive worldwide dislocation, apparently in response to WAR in the Middle East and the virtual end of oil production. As suppressed racial and other hatreds become rampant, and the seas fill up with refugees on an uncontemplated scale, the so-called "fleet of the damned" drifts towards the Antarctic, refused succour on any populated shore. What are left of the civilized nations carry out a massive programme of relief and resettlement, but we are led to understand that the effort is half-hearted and serves the interests more of the donors than of the disenfranchised and dispossessed hordes on the ice. The narrative is heightened by awesome descriptions of both natural and socially engendered cataclysm. [RB]

See also: DISASTER.

BATEMAN, ROBERT (MOYES CARRUTHERS) (1922-1973) UK writer, primarily involved in radio and tv work. His sf novel, *When the Whites Went* (**1963**), is set in an England where only Blacks survive a disease to which all others fall victim. [JC]

See also: POLITICS.

BATES, HARRY Working name of US editor and writer Hiram Gilmore Bates III (1900-1981), who began his career with the Clayton chain of PULP MAGAZINES in the 1920s, working as editor of an adventure magazine. When William Clayton, the owner, suggested that HB initiate a period-adventure companion to it, he successfully counterproposed a magazine to be called *Astounding Stories of Super-Science*, which would compete with AMAZING STORIES. HB edited the magazine – whose title was soon abbreviated to *Astounding Stories* (◊ ASTOUNDING

SCIENCE-FICTION) – for 34 issues, Jan 1930-Mar 1933. (He later started a companion magazine, STRANGE TALES – intended as a rival to WEIRD TALES – which lasted for 7 issues, Sept 1931-Jan 1933.) His was the first true sf pulp magazine, paying four times as well as its competitors and impatient with the static passages of PSEUDO-SCIENCE characteristic of Hugo GERNSBACK's magazines. As Jack WILLIAMSON put it in *The Early Williamson* (coll **1975**): "Bates was professional . . . [he] wanted well constructed action stories about strong, successful heroes. The 'super-science' had to be exciting and more-or-less plausible, but it couldn't take much space." HB contributed stories to *ASF* in collaboration with his assistant editor, Desmond W. HALL, the two sometimes writing together as H.B. Winter but more famously as Anthony GILMORE, under which name they produced the popular **Hawk Carse** series, which reached book form as *Space Hawk* (coll of linked stories **1952**); the first of these stories, "Hawk Carse" (**1931**), was HB's first publication.

After the Clayton group went bankrupt in 1933, *Strange Tales* ceased publication and *ASF* was bought by the STREET & SMITH chain, which appointed F. Orlin TREMAINE editor. This ended HB's editorial connection with sf, though over the next 20 years he wrote a few short stories. Although he used the pseudonym A.R. Holmes on occasion, it was mainly under his own name that he published such notable stories as "A Matter of Size" (**1934**), a story on the then popular GREAT-AND-SMALL theme, and "Alas, All Thinking" (**1935**). "Farewell to the Master" (**1940**) was later filmed as *The* DAY THE EARTH STOOD STILL (**1951**), although the film lost the story's ironic twist, which demonstrated the pitfalls of interpreting nonhuman relationships in human terms – in this instance, the relationship between a huge ROBOT and its ALIEN "master". HB died in unfortunate obscurity. [MJE]

See also: ANTI-INTELLECTUALISM IN SF; EVOLUTION; SF MAGAZINES.

BATMAN ◊ Neal ADAMS; Brian BOLLAND; DC COMICS; Frank MILLER; Alan MOORE.

*BATTERIES NOT INCLUDED** Film (1987). Amblin/Universal. Executive Prod Steven SPIELBERG. Dir Matthew Robbins, starring Hume Cronyn, Jessica Tandy, Frank McCrae, Elizabeth Pena, Michael Carmine. Screenplay Brad Bird, Robbins, Brent Maddock, S.S. Wilson, based on a story by Mick Garris. 106 mins. Colour.

Originally intended as an episode of the tv series AMAZING STORIES, this film betrays its small-screen origins in its slightness of plot. A run-down rooming house with diner, which occupies land desired by a property speculator, is visited by tiny saucer-shaped aliens, who help out the residents and two elderly owners, eventually (with their new offspring and other saucers) rebuilding the blown-up premises. Escapist fantasy at best, this has no relationship other than the dubious aliens to genuine sf. The novelization is *batteries not included* (**1987**) (lower-case letters are *sic*) by Wayland DREW.   [PN]

See also: CINEMA.

BATTLE BEYOND THE STARS Film (1980). New World. Executive prod Roger CORMAN. Dir Jimmy T. Murakami, starring Richard Thomas, Robert Vaughn, John Saxon, George Peppard, Sybil Danning, Morgan Woodward, Steve Davis. Screenplay John SAYLES, based on a story by Sayles, Anne Dyer. 103 mins. Colour.

New World, never slow to capitalize on a trend, hoped – with partial success – to woo the STAR WARS market with this space-opera replay of *The Magnificent Seven* (1960). It follows the pattern of its Western original right down to Robert Vaughn's reprise of his role as a world-weary gunslinger. Sayles's script is entertaining, as are Danning as the huge-breasted Valkyrie, Woodward as the reptilian mercenary, and the heat-eating twin "Kelvin", but the emphasis is on space battles which, while better than expected, leave the story treatment perfunctory. Murakami's heavy direction muffles the lightness of the script. The special effects were recycled in the Corman-produced *Space Raiders* (1983), of which they are the *raison d'être*.   [PN]

BATTLE BEYOND THE SUN ◊ Roger CORMAN.

BATTLE FOR THE PLANET OF THE APES Film (1973). Apjac/20th Century-Fox. Dir J. Lee Thompson, starring Roddy McDowall, Claude Akins, Natalie Trundy, Lew Ayres, John Huston. Screenplay John William Corrington, Joyce Hooper Corrington, based on a story by Paul Dehn. 86 mins. Colour.

The fifth and last of the series beginning with PLANET OF THE APES (to which this is a "prequel") and the most disappointing. Established in their own Ape City after the near destruction of mankind in WWIII, the social-democrat chimpanzee people, still led by Caesar (from ESCAPE FROM THE PLANET OF THE APES), become involved in a three-way struggle with a community of radiation-scarred human survivors and the militant gorilla people. There is a feeling of pointlessness about this simplistic film's attempt to squeeze a few more dollars from the series. The novelization is *Battle for the Planet of the Apes* * (**1973**) by David GERROLD.   [PN/JB]

BATTLE OF THE ASTROS ◊ GOJIRA; RADON.

BATTLE OF THE WORLDS ◊ *Il* PIANETA DEGLI UOMINI SPENTI.

BATTLESTAR GALACTICA 1. US tv series (1978). Universal Television/ABC-TV. Created by Glen A. LARSON, also executive prod. Prods included John Dykstra and Don Bellisario; main writers Larson and Bellisario; dirs included Christian Nyby II and Dan Haller. 1 season only, beginning with a 150min pilot, followed by 19 50min episodes, including 3 2-episode stories, plus one 100min episode. Colour.

Perhaps the least likable of all tv sf in its ineptness, its cynicism, its sentimentality and its contempt for and ignorance of science, *BG* was devised by Larson (who went on to do a similar job on BUCK ROGERS IN THE 25TH CENTURY) in the wake of the successful film STAR WARS, which it resembles closely in many respects; moreover, John Dykstra, who initially did the special effects for *BG* (he soon pulled out), had supervised the miniature photography on that film. The series tells of humans (related to us according to a VON DÄNIKEN-derived narration) elsewhere in the Galaxy being largely wiped out by the robotic Cylons. A group of survivors, including the crew of a military craft, the *Battlestar*, search for the legendary human colony of Earth. Space battles, the *raison d'être* of *BG*, were carried out by planes apparently designed for flying in atmosphere, with fiery exhausts which, Larson is quoted as saying, "make Space more acceptable to the Midwest".

The casting of Western star Lorne Green as the patriarchal leader, Adama, emphasized the obvious subtext of wagon trains rolling west under constant attack by Indians. Other regular cast members were Dirk Benedict as Starbuck (né Solo), Richard Hatch as Apollo (né Skywalker), Maren Jensen as Athena and Noah Hathaway as the cute boy, Boxer, whose nauseating robot dog (né R2D2) may have been the low point. Ratings began well but soon fell off and, since each episode cost three times as much as a conventional one-hour drama, the series was terminated. An attempt to resuscitate it in altered form was GALACTICA: 1980. (◊ Glen A. LARSON for a listing of the 14 spin-off *BG* books 1978-87, all, according to the covers, co-authored by Larson, mostly with Robert THURSTON.)

2. Film (1978). Universal. Dir Richard A. Colla, starring the regular cast plus Ray Milland, Lew Ayres. Screenplay Glen A. Larson. 122 mins, cut to 117 mins. Colour.

To recoup production costs on the tv series, Universal gave theatrical release to the (edited) pilot episode. This militaristic film (all politicians seeking peace are self-deluded weaklings) begins the *BG* story with a battle against the Cylons, the round-up of survivors, the beginning of the long trek to Earth, a visit to a pleasure-filled but corrupt planet where they nearly get eaten, and a second battle against the Cylons (close relatives of *Star Wars*'s stormtroopers) – clearly a near thing: "The Cylon fleet is five microns away and closing." The film is poor. Another two-part episode from the tv series was theatrically released as *Mission Galactica: The Cylon Attack* (1979); it is more cardboard still.   [PN]

See also: SCIENTIFIC ERRORS.

BAUM, L(YMAN) FRANK (1856-1919) US writer of children's stories, who wrote also as Floyd Akers, Laura Bancroft, John Estes Cooke, Hugh Fitzgerald, Schuyler Staunton and Edith Van Dyne. He remains famous for his long series of tales set in the land of **Oz**, beginning with *The Wonderful Wizard of Oz* (**1900**; vt *The New Wizard of Oz* 1903), which served as the main source for the famous film version of 1939. The series continues with: *Ozma of Oz* (**1907**; vt *Princess Ozma of Oz* 1942 UK); *Dorothy and the Wizard of Oz* (**1908**); *The Road to Oz* (**1909**); *The Emerald City of Oz*

(1910); *The Patchwork Girl of Oz* (1913); *The Scarecrow of Oz* (1915); *Rinkitink in Oz* (1916); *The Lost Princess of Oz* (1917); *The Tin Woodman of Oz* (1918), the eponymous lumberjack of which is *not* a robot; *The Magic of Oz* (1919); *Glinda of Oz* (1920); later titles were from other hands. *Ozma of Oz* includes the first appearance of Tik-Tok, an intelligent clockwork man, one of the first ROBOTS in fiction; the tale was reworked as *The Tik-Tok Man of Oz*, a 1913 musical play, itself then rewritten as the novel *Tik-Tok of Oz* (1914), which features a TRANSPORTATION tube through the Earth. LFB's juvenile sf novel *The Master Key: An Electrical Fairy Tale Founded on the Mysteries of Electricity and the Optimism of its Devotees. It was Written for Boys, but Others May Read It* (1901), is an EDISONADE described rather fully by its title; the child tinkerer-hero, though his electrical gun and ANTIGRAVITY device are supplied magically, finds scientific explanations for everything he experiences. A story in *American Fairy Tales* (coll 1901; rev with 3 more stories 1908) describes the freezing of time in a US city. Some of LFB's other work, which was produced very rapidly (only a sample is listed below), was fantasy. Among a wide range of authors influenced by LFB, recent examples include Gene WOLFE in "The Eyeflash Miracles" (1976) and *Free Live Free* (1984), and Geoff RYMAN, whose non-fantastic novel *"Was . . ."* (1992; vt *Was* 1992 US), partly set in 19th-century Kansas, constitutes a thorough examination of the roots of **Oz**. [JC]

Other works: *A New Wonderland* (1900; vt *The Surprising Adventures of the Magical Monarch of Mo* 1903); *The Life and Adventures of Santa Claus* (1902); *John Dough and the Cherub* (1906); *The Sea Fairies* (1911) and its sequel *Sky Island* (1912); *The Purple Dragon and Other Fantasies* (1897-1905 various mags; coll 1976); *Animal Fairy Tales* (1905 *The Delineator*; coll 1989).

About the author: *Wizard of Oz and Who He Was* (1957) by Martin GARDNER and R.B. Nye; *The Oz Scrapbook* (1977) by David L. Greene and Dick Martin.

See also: CHILDREN'S SF; DIME-NOVEL SF; MACHINES.

BAX, MARTIN (1933-   ) UK doctor of medicine, current (1992) editor of the literary magazine *Ambit* and writer. In his sf novel, *The Hospital Ship* (1976), which has more than a passing resemblance to the *Narrenschiff* or Ship of Fools, a group of experimental doctors sail the world's oceans after a HOLOCAUST, curing those they can cure, stashing those they definitely cannot in the ship's mortuary, and applying a variety of techniques, many sexual, to the in-betweens. [JC]

BAXTER, JOHN (1939-   ) Australian writer, who has also lived and worked in the UK and USA. He began publishing sf with "Vendetta's End" for *Science Fiction Adventures* in 1962, and for the next four years appeared primarily in *New Worlds*; he wrote some stories with Ron Smith (1936-   ) under the joint pseudonym Martin Loran. His sf novel, *The Off-Worlders* (1966 dos US; vt *The God Killers* 1968 Aus) portrays the superstition-ridden ex-colony planet of Merryland and a search for the lost knowledge it

contains. *The Hermes Fall* (1978 US) depicts with some vigour the DISASTER created when an asteroid strikes the Earth. Increasingly, JB has concentrated on writing on the cinema, his work in this genre including the informative, though not always accurate, *Science Fiction in the Cinema* (1970), and 11 titles unconnected with sf. *The Fire Came By* (1976), written with Thomas A. Atkins, a science-fact book containing some almost-sf speculations, tells of the great Siberian explosion of 1908. As editor JB produced *The Pacific Book of Australian Science Fiction* (anth 1968; vt *Australian Science Fiction 1* 1969) and *The Second Pacific Book of Australian Science Fiction* (anth 1971; vt *Australian Science Fiction 2* 1971). [JC/PN]

Other works: *The Black Yacht* (1982 US); *Torched* (1986) with John BROSNAN, both writing as James Blackstone, a horror novel about spontaneous combustion.

See also: CINEMA.

BAXTER, STEPHEN (M.) (1957-   ) UK writer who has also signed his name Steve Baxter and S.M. Baxter. He began publishing sf with "The Xeelee Flower" for *Interzone* in 1987, and his short work has consistently espoused the kind of good-tempered, thoroughly worked-out HARD-SF venue that made his first novel, *Raft* (1991), an effective example of its category. Though the tale labours under the strain of an ineptly conceived protagonist, its presentation of a high-gravity universe, and of the consequences to migrant humans of living there, is of sustained interest. [JC]

See also: CLICHÉS; GRAVITY; IMAGINARY SCIENCE; INTERZONE.

BAYLEY, BARRINGTON J(OHN) (1937-   ) UK writer, active as a freelance under various names for many years, author of juvenile stories, picture-strips and features as well as sf, which he began to publish with "Combat's End" for *Vargo Statten Science Fiction Magazine* in 1954. His sf pseudonyms include P.F. Woods (at least 10 stories), Alan Aumbry (1 story), John Diamond (1 story), and (with Michael MOORCOCK) Michael BARRINGTON (1 story). Some early tales appear in *The Seed of Evil* (coll 1979). All his sf novels have been as BJB, beginning with *Star Virus* (1964 NW; exp 1970 dos US). This complex and somewhat gloomy space epic, along with some of its successors, has had a strong though not broadly recognized influence on such UK sf writers as M. John HARRISON; perhaps because BJB's style is sometimes laboured and his lack of cheerful endings is alien to the expectations of readers of conventional SPACE OPERA, he has yet to receive due recognition for the hard-edged control he exercises over plots whose intricate dealings in TIME PARADOXES and insistent metaphysical drive make them some of the most formidable works of their type. Though *Annihilation Factor* (1964 as "The Patch" NW as by Peter Woods; exp 1972 dos US), *Empire of Two Worlds* (1972 US) and *Collision Course* (1973 US; vt *Collision with Chronos* 1977 UK) – which utilizes the time theories of J.W. DUNNE – are all variously successful, probably the most fully realized time-paradox space opera from his pen is *The Fall of Chronopolis* (**1974** US; vt *Chronopolis* 1979 UK), in which the Chronotic Empire jousts against a terrifying adversary in doomed attempts to maintain a stable reality; at the crux of the book it becomes evident that the conflict is eternal, and that the same forces will oppose one another through time forever (*see also* ALTERNATE WORLDS).

The Soul of the Robot (**1974** US; rev 1976 UK), along with its sequel *The Rod of Light* (**1985**), marked a change of pace in its treatment of such ROBOT themes as the nature of self-consciousness; the book makes complex play with a number of philosophical paradoxes, though BJB's touch here is uncharacteristically light. *The Garments of Caean* (**1976** US; text restored 1978 UK) utilizes some fairly sophisticated cultural ANTHROPOLOGY in a space-opera tale of sentient clothing which owns the man. But perhaps the most significant work BJB produced in the 1970s was in short fiction, most of it collected in *The Knights of the Limits* (coll **1978**), a remarkable (though astonishingly bleak) assembly of experiments in the carrying of story ideas to the end of their tether. Later space operas – *The Grand Wheel* (**1977**), *Star Winds* (**1978** US), *The Pillars of Eternity* (**1982** US), *The Zen Gun* (**1983** US) and *The Forest of Peldain* (**1985** US) – continued to take an orrery joy in the galaxies. BJB continues to be seriously underestimated, perhaps because of his almost total restriction to pulp formats.   [JC]

Other works: *The Pillars of Eternity and The Garments of Caean* (omni **1989**); *The Fall of Chronopolis and Collision with Chronos* (omni **1989**).

About the author: "Knight Without Limit: An Overview of the Work of Barrington Bayley" by Andy Darlington in *Arena 10* (1980); *The Writings of Barrington J. Bayley* (**1981** chap) by Mike ASHLEY.

See also: ARTS; COSMOLOGY; CYBORGS; ECONOMICS; EVOLUTION; GALACTIC EMPIRES; HIVE-MINDS; INTERZONE; MEDIA LANDSCAPE; METAPHYSICS; MUSIC; NEW WAVE; NEW WORLDS.

BEACH, LYNN ◊ Kathryn LANCE.

BEACHCOMBER ◊ J.B. MORTON.

BEACON MAGAZINES ◊ Ned L. PINES; THRILLING WONDER STORIES.

BEALE, CHARLES WILLING (1845-1932) US writer in whose *The Secret of the Earth* (**1899**) aeronauts find a hole in the planet and penetrate a routine HOLLOW EARTH inhabited by a lost race (◊ LOST WORLDS), which they fail to contact.   [JC]

Other works: *The Ghost of Guir House* (**1897**).

BEAN, NORMAN [s] ◊ Edgar Rice BURROUGHS.

BEAR, GREG Working name of US writer Gregory Dale Bear (1951-   ), son-in-law of Poul ANDERSON. He began publishing sf with "Destroyers" for *Famous Science Fiction* in 1967, and began to write full-time in 1975. His first stories and novels were auspicious but not remarkably so, and he gave no immediate signs of becoming one of the dominant writers of the 1980s. Between 1985 and 1990, however, he published six novels whose importance to the realm of HARD SF –

and to the world of sf in general – it would be hard to overrate; he also served as President of the SCIENCE FICTION WRITERS OF AMERICA 1988-90. Other new writers in that period, like Lucius SHEPARD, had perhaps a greater grasp of the aesthetic trials and challenges of the art of fiction; still others, like Kim Stanley ROBINSON, might conceive a richer world; some, like David BRIN, might be handier with galaxies; and William GIBSON, by giving CYBERPUNK a habitation, gave Bruce STERLING a home. But only Orson Scott CARD could legitimately and centrally stand with GB and manifest the voice of US GENRE SF.

It would be a long trek from *Hegira* (**1979**; rev 1987 UK), GB's first novel, a PLANETARY-ROMANCE quest tale whose venue, a huge artificial hollow world comically called Hegira, turns out itself to be questing through space at the end of time, accompanied by a vast conglomeration of similar planets which constitute *en masse* a singularity capable of surviving the end of the Universe, and whose task it is to carry the burden of life into the subsequent reality. Even in the extensively revised version of 1987, the narrative is top-heavy with explanations pumped for SENSE OF WONDER. Though the variegations of cast and scenery are typical of later GB creations – and though the biological imperatives (◊ BIOLOGY), and the transcendental COSMOLOGY at novel's close, would be reiterated time and again in his work – *Hegira* seemed to show ambition far beyond the reach of talent. It was an impression only slowly to be modified by the far-reaching (but frequently lame) books which followed, like *Psychlone* (**1979**; vt *Lost Souls* 1982), though *Beyond Heaven's River* (**1980**) – a tale which carries a Japanese fighter pilot from WWII into a morally complex galactic venue 400 years hence – manages both to create a plausible protagonist and to match his understanding of the larger picture with ours. Set in a universe which shares some features with the one in that book are *Strength of Stones* (fixup **1981**; rev 1988 UK) and some of the stories assembled in *The Wind from a Burning Woman* (coll **1983**; with 2 stories added, rev vt *The Venging* 1992 UK) and *Tangents* (coll **1989**) – whose title story won both HUGO and NEBULA awards. These tales depict with some confidence venues created by a human civilization faced with the need to balance its nearly infinite capacity to transform the Universe against ancient moral imperatives. The title story of the first collection, for instance, evokes a conflict between environmentalist Naderites and technophilic Geshels which would echo down the aisles of *Eon* (**1985**); and "Sisters", in the second collection, brilliantly affirms a broad-church definition of the human family.

It was not, however, until the publication of *Blood Music* (**1985**) that GB began to show his true strength, which might be defined as the capacity to incorporate the hardest and most cognitively demanding of hard-sf premises and plot-logics into tales whose protagonists display far greater complexity than anything unliving. It can be argued that the singular failure of

almost all hard-sf writers to create noteworthy literature lies in their assumption that it is more difficult
to understand – say – plasma physics than to
understand human beings. The significance of GB's
later 1980s novels lies in the fact that his human
beings are more difficult to describe than his physics.
(It might be added that his political views – like most
hard-sf writers he constantly expresses them – are
also graced by a lack of dreadful simplicity.) In *Blood
Music* – the 1983 novella version won both Hugo and
Nebula – the hard science is GENETIC ENGINEERING, and
the character who ignites the plot is a humanly
ineffectual scientist who illicitly uses biochip technology to tranform DNA molecules into living computers; these join together into *Gestalts* which themselves combine into a single transcendental higher
consciousness incorporating all of life upon the
planet into one externally homogeneous biosphere.
The close of the book, as the new consciousness
enters into rapport with the true Universe, has been
appropriately likened to the climax of Arthur C.
CLARKE's *Childhood's End* (**1953**).

GB's other 1985 novel *Eon*, along with its sequel
Eternity (**1988**), is both more conventional and more
enthralling. The conventionality lies in a partial
return to the large-scale enterprises of cosmological
SPACE OPERA, accompanied by a marked retreat from
the nearly religious transcendentalism evoked in GB
by any application of information theory. The grip of
the sequence lies in the remarkable fertility of the
concepts presented: the hollowed-out asteroid, from
an alternate timeline, whose final chamber is literally
endless; the extraordinary architectonics of GB's
demonstration of the nature of this phenomenon; the
enormously complex COMPUTER-run culture partway
up the infinite corridor; the relentless expansion of
perspective, in a series of CONCEPTUAL BREAK-
THROUGHS, as the ordering and end of the entire
Universe come into question in the second volume.
In the final analysis, this relentlessness works
perhaps best in the earlier portions of the tale – *Eon*
itself is perhaps the best-constructed epic of cosmology yet written in the field – but the two volumes
together amply demonstrate GB's control over scale
and cognition.

In something like the same spirit, *The Forge of God*
(**1987**) tackles the END OF THE WORLD by confronting
NEAR-FUTURE humanity with a sequence of ALIEN
intrusions, one of which proves utterly and implacably fatal to the existence of the planet. The bulldog
inexorability with which GB presents this scenario is
darkly exhilarating, and seemed at the time a welcome prophylactic to the assumption embedded in
most hard-sf novels that catastrophes, no matter how
grave, will be sidestepped by the fit: a sequel,
however, *Anvil of Stars* (**1992** UK), somewhat softens
the blow of the first volume by carrying a few human
survivors in an alien ship on a revenge mission
directed against the apparent makers of the autonomous weapons which destroyed Earth. Ultimately

more interesting, though told with a complexity that
some readers have found congested, was *Queen of
Angels* (**1990**), which embodies a wide range of
speculations about the effects of recent theories about
NANOTECHNOLOGY. Set mainly in a Los Angeles
transformed into a kind of beehive of human and
para-human activity, the book tells several kinds of
story, in several venues: a formal tale of detection
(told from the complex viewpoint of a biotransformed
female cop); a prose-poem leading into voodoo; a tale
of VIRTUAL REALITY entrapments, and a narrative of the
coming to consciousness of an AI. Throughout,
sustaining these strands of story, is a boding sense of
transcendental transformation, a sense that *Queen of
Angels* is perhaps a snapshot of one moment in an
epic which will end in the total victory of information
that GB described in *Blood Music*. A short novel, *Heads*
(**1990** UK), set in something like the same Universe,
concisely conflates a Moon-based search for the
Absolute Zero of temperature and the threat that a
cryogenically preserved head might turn out to be
that of a 20th-century guru whose manipulative sect
generations earlier proved particularly attractive in
some sf circles.

It is not easy to say what might come next; it can
be expected that whatever GB writes will continue to
bring sf and the world together, relentlessly.   [JC]
Other works: *The Speculative Poetry Review #1* (anth
1977 chap), an anthology in magazine form; a STAR
TREK tie, *Corona* * (**1984**); the **Michael Perrin** fantasy
sequence comprising *The Infinity Concerto* (**1984**) and
The Serpent Mage (**1986**); *Sleepside Story* (**1988** chap);
Early Harvest (coll **1988**), containing also some nonfic-
tion; *Hardfought* (**1983** *IASFM*; **1988** chap dos), reprint-
ing the Nebula-winning story.
See also: ARKHAM HOUSE; ASTEROIDS; ASTOUNDING
SCIENCE-FICTION; AUTOMATION; BIG DUMB OBJECTS; CHIL-
DREN IN SF; CITIES; CYBERNETICS; DEVOLUTION; DISASTER;
DISCOVERY AND INVENTION; EVOLUTION; FANTASY; GALAC-
TIC EMPIRES; GODS AND DEMONS; INTELLIGENCE; INTER-
ZONE; ISAAC ASIMOV'S SCIENCE FICTION MAGAZINE; MACHI-
NES; MATHEMATICS; MEDICINE; METAPHYSICS; MUTANTS;
OMNI; OPTIMISM AND PESSIMISM; PSYCHOLOGY; SPACE
HABITATS; WOMEN AS PORTRAYED IN SCIENCE FICTION.

BEASON, DOUG (1953-   ) USAF officer with a PhD
in physics who began publishing sf with "The Man
I'll Never Be" for *AMZ* in 1987. *Return to Honor* (**1989**),
Assault on Alpha Base (**1990**) and *Strike Eagle* (**1991**) are
TECHNOTHRILLERS, but *Lifeline* (**1990**) with Kevin J.
ANDERSON is of sf interest, and marked both writers
as names to watch. A second novel with Anderson
(*whom see for further details of both books*), *The Trinity
Paradox* (**1991**), interestingly plumbs the moral perils
of TIME TRAVEL.   [JC]
See also: NUCLEAR POWER.

BEAST FROM HAUNTED CAVE ◊ Roger CORMAN.

BEAST FROM 20,000 FATHOMS, THE Film (**1953**).
Mutual Pictures/Warner Bros. Dir Eugène Lourié,
starring Paul Christian, Paula Raymond, Cecil Kell-
away, Kenneth Tobey. Screenplay Lou Morheim,

Fred Freiberger, based on "The Fog Horn" (1951) by Ray BRADBURY. 80 mins. B/w.

This was the second of the 1950s MONSTER MOVIES – the first being *The* THING (1951) – and the one that established the basic formula for most of those that followed. An atomic test in the Arctic wakes a dinosaur frozen in the ice. It swims to its ancestral breeding-grounds – an area now covered by the city of New York. It is finally trapped and killed in an amusement park. This is the first film on which model animator Ray HARRYHAUSEN had full control over the special effects, though these are not remarkable. Nor is the film, though it looks good: Lourié usually worked as an art director on mostly non-sf films, including some of Jean Renoir's most distinguished; his other sf films are BEHEMOTH, THE SEA MONSTER (1958), *The* COLOSSUS OF NEW YORK (1958) and GORGO (1959). [JB]

BEAST WITH A MILLION EYES ◊ Roger CORMAN.

BEAUJON, PAUL Pseudonym of UK writer Beatrice Lamberton Warde (1900-1969), whose sf novella, *The Shelter in Bedlem* (**1937** chap; rev vt *Peace Under Earth: Dialogues from the Year 1946* 1938 chap), expressed a grim view of the DYSTOPIA which would follow the end of conflict. [JC]

BEAUMONT, CHARLES The pseudonym by which US story- and scriptwriter Charles Nutt (1929-1967) is best known, though he wrote some non-sf under other names. He began publishing his blend of horror and sf with "The Devil, You Say?" for *AMZ* in 1951. Most of his work is collected in *The Hunger* (coll **1957**; with title story cut vt *Shadow Play* 1964 UK), *Yonder* (coll **1958**), *Night Ride and Other Journeys* (coll **1960**), *The Magic Man* (coll **1965**) and *The Edge* (coll **1966** UK), which reassembles *Yonder* and *Night Ride*; posthumously, this material was re-sorted and added to in *Best of Beaumont* (coll **1982**) and *Charles Beaumont: Selected Stories* (**1988**; vt *The Howling Man* 1992). CB's work combines humour and horror in a slick style extremely effective in underlining the grimness of his basic inspiration. As a writer of sf, fantasy and horror movies, he scripted or coscripted *Queen of Outer Space* (1958), *The Premature Burial* (1962), *Burn, Witch, Burn* (1962; vt *The Night of the Eagle*) – based on *Conjure Wife* (1943; **1953**) by Fritz LEIBER – *The Wonderful World of the Brothers Grimm* (1962), *The Haunted Palace* (1963), *The Seven Faces of Dr Lao* (1964), *The Masque of the Red Death* (1964) and BRAIN DEAD (1989). Several of these were directed by Roger CORMAN. His numerous tv scripts include around 19 for *The* TWILIGHT ZONE. He also collaborated with Chad OLIVER on the brief **Claude Adams** series (*FSF* 1955-6) and edited a horror anthology, *The Fiend in You* (anth **1962**). He was struck in 1964 by a savage illness which ravaged and eventually killed him. [JC]
About the author: *The Work of Charles Beaumont* (2nd edn **1990** chap) by William F. NOLAN.
See also: HORROR IN SF; INVISIBILITY.

BEAUMONT, ROGER [r] ◊ ROBERT HALE LIMITED.
BEAUTIFUL WOMEN AND THE HYDROGEN MAN

◊ BIJO TO EKITAI NINGEN.

BEAUTY AND THE BEAST US tv series (1987-90). A Witt-Tomas Production for CBS. Created Ron Koslow. Prods Paul Junger Witt, Tony Thomas, Koslow. Writers included George R.R. MARTIN, Koslow, Shelly Moore, Linda Campanelli. Dirs included Richard Franklin, Gus Trikonis, Ron Perlman. 3 seasons, totalling 55 50 min episodes. Colour.

An urban fairytale, inspired in its make-up design if not in its commitment to magic by Jean Cocteau's film *La Belle et la Bête* (1946), *BATB* centres on the relationship between Catherine (Linda Hamilton), a chic Manhattan district attorney, and Vincent (Ron Perlman), a poeticizing, romantic, MUTANT lion-man who lives with his adopted father (Roy Dotrice) in a world of derelicts in tunnels deep beneath the city. He has a telepathic link with his ladylove. Despite the involvement of distinguished sf writer George R.R. Martin as story editor, the show was a combination of soap opera and crime thriller rather than a real sf/fantasy offering, though the idea of a fantastic city beneath the real one is interesting. The unorthodox team normally righted wrongs that could as easily have served as springboards for episodes of any other action adventure, while for two seasons Catherine and Vincent merely pussy-footed around their relationship. The show's fragile charm being almost exhausted, the format underwent severe changes in its final season, first with the consummation of the central relationship, then with the casual killing-off of the heroine and several other supporting cast members, motivating Vincent's character change from mutant Care Bear to raging vigilante. Catherine was replaced briefly by Diana Bennett (Jo Anderson), a police officer, but the show never regained the – largely female – fan following its earlier, more wistful episodes had picked up. A novelization, largely of the first episode, is *Beauty and the Beast* ∗ (**1989**) by Barbara HAMBLY. [KN/PN]
See also: SUPERHEROES.

BECHDOLT, JACK Working name of US writer John Ernest Bechdolt (1884-1954) for his fiction, though he used his full name for other writing. *The Lost Vikings* (**1931**) features juveniles who discover a lost race (◊ LOST WORLDS) of Vikings in Alaska. *The Torch* (1920 *Argosy*; **1948**) is a post-HOLOCAUST story set in the New York of AD3000; the torch is the Statue of Liberty's. [JC]
See also: CITIES.

BECK, CHRISTOPHER ◊ T.C. BRIDGES.
BEDFORD, JOHN [r] ◊ ROBERT HALE LIMITED.
BEDFORD-JONES, H(ENRY JAMES O'BRIEN) (1887-1949) Canadian author, later a naturalized US citizen, who was one of the most prolific and popular pulp writers; of his more than 100 novels, a few – e.g., *The Star Woman* (**1924**) – were sf adventures. His works appeared in the PULP MAGAZINES – *The Magic Carpet*, *Golden Fleece*, *All-Story Weekly* and numerous others – under at least 15 pseudonyms. His fictions were primarily historical and adventure, sometimes having

sf or weird elements as a basic framework. Among his earliest fantasies are the LOST-WORLD adventures of his **John Solomon** series (in magazine form as by HBJ, in book form as by Allan Hawkwood): *Solomon's Quest* (**1915**); *Gentleman Solomon* (**1915**), about an unknown Middle Eastern pygmy race; *Solomon's Carpet* (**1915**); *The Seal of Solomon* (1915 *Argosy*; **1924** UK), about a community established by Crusaders in the Arabian desert; *John Solomon* (**1916**); *John Solomon Retired* (**1917**); *Solomon's Son* (**1918**); *John Solomon, Supercargo* (**1924** UK); *John Solomon, Incognito* (**1925** UK); *The Shawl of Solomon* (**1925** UK); *The Wizard of the Atlas* (**1928** UK). In similar vein are *Splendour of the Gods* (**1924**) and, in collaboration with W.C. Robertson, *The Temple of the Ten* (1921; **1973**), both of which appeared under his own name.

More germane to the genre were the several series that later appeared in *The* BLUE BOOK MAGAZINE. The first of these was the **Trumpets from Oblivion** series, 11 stories running from "The Stagnant Death" (1938) to "The Serpent People" (1939). In these tales a device capable of recording sounds and images from the past is used to establish a rational origin for various myths and legends. A similar gadget is employed in the nine **Counterclockwise** stories, running from "Counterclockwise" (1943) to "The Gods do not Forget" (1944). Also in *The Blue Book Magazine* appeared two futuristic series (as by Gordon Keyne) dealing, respectively, with the struggle to maintain peace in the post-WWII years and with a post-WWII Bureau of Missing Persons. The first, **Tomorrow's Men**, comprised "Peace Hath her Victories" (1943), "The Battle for France" (1943), "Sahara Doom" (1943) and "Tomorrow in Egypt" (1943). The second series was **Quest, Inc.**, with 12 stories from "The Affair of the Drifting Face" (1943) to "The Final Hoard" (1945). Other series included **The Adventures of a Professional Corpse** (1940-41 WEIRD TALES), **Carson's Folly** (1945-6 *Blue Book Magazine*) and **The Sphinx Emerald** (1946-7 *Blue Book Magazine*), which last traces the malign influence of a gem throughout history.   [JE]
See also: CANADA; MYTHOLOGY.

BEDSHEET A term used to describe a magazine format, in contrast to pulp and DIGEST. The bedsheet format – sometimes called large pulp format – is the largest of the three; it varies slightly but approximates 8.5 x 11.75in (216 x 298mm) – i.e., close to A4 (210 x 297mm). It was used by some of the more prestigious PULP MAGAZINES in the 1920s and 1930s and, in a slightly narrower version, became popular again in the late 1960s with such magazines as NEW WORLDS and VISION OF TOMORROW; these, having fewer pages than the earlier bedsheet magazines, were stapled rather than glued. Magazines of this type, when printed on coated paper, are often called slicks; although the term "slick" refers to paper quality rather than size, slicks (e.g., OMNI) are normally in a smallish bedsheet format.   [PN]
See also: SF MAGAZINES.

BED-SITTING ROOM, THE Film (1969). Oscar

Lewenstein/United Artists. Dir Richard Lester, starring Rita Tushingham, Mona Washbourne, Arthur Lowe, Ralph Richardson, Spike MILLIGAN, Michael Hordern, Roy Kinnear, Peter Cook, Dudley Moore. Screenplay John Antrobus from the play by Antrobus Milligan. 91 mins. Colour.

BSR is a FABULATION, a black comedy set in England after WWIII, where dazed survivors wander about pretending that nothing has happened, even when some of them mutate into wardrobes, bed-sitting rooms and parrots. The original play was a much-improvised piece of slapstick, and what remains of it clashes awkwardly with chillingly bleak settings showing the realistic aftermath of an atomic war: the shattered dome of St Paul's Cathedral protruding from a swamp, a line of wrecked cars along a disembodied length of motorway, a grim landscape dominated by great piles of sludge and heaps of discarded boots, broken plates and false teeth. The film effectively has no plot, and its disjointedness, while pleasantly surreal, gives it an inconsequential air.   [JB/PN]

BEEBEE, CHRIS (?   -   ) UK writer known exclusively for his **Cipola** sequence, set in the 21st century on Earth and in a SPACE HABITAT: *The Hub* (**1987**) and *The Main Event* (**1989**). The world of the sequence is dominated by COMPUTERS, and trouble brews when the GRAIL programs go missing; the protagonist tries to cope.   [JC]

BEECHING, JACK (1922-   ) UK writer, mostly of poetry, and (with his first wife) of juveniles as James Barbary. His novel *The Dakota Project* (**1968**) is a TECHNOTHRILLER whose eponymous government project contains top secrets of borderline sf interest.   [JC]

BEEDING, FRANCIS Joint pseudonym of UK writers John Leslie Palmer (1885-1944) and Hilary Saunders (1898-1951) for numerous works in various genres, mainly detective novels and thrillers; their sf novels are near-future political thrillers. In *The Seven Sleepers* (**1925** US) villainous Germans are kept from starting a second world war. In its sequel, *The Hidden Kingdom* (**1927**), Outer Mongolia is threatened with enslavement. *The One Sane Man* (**1934**) features a man's attempt to enforce world peace by threatening disaster, in this case via weather control.   [JC]
See also: CRIME AND PUNISHMENT.

BEERE, PETER (?   -   ) UK writer whose **Trauma 2020** sequence of 21st-century action thrillers – *Trauma 2020: Urban Prey* (**1984**), *#2: The Crucifixion Squad* (**1984**) and *#3: Silent Slaughter* (**1985**) – has some efficient moments.   [JC]

BEESE, P.J. (1946-   ) US writer whose sf novel, *The Guardsman* (**1988**), with Todd Cameron Hamilton, is an unremarkable example of interstellar-empire adventure sf; its nomination for the 1989 HUGO caused some stir, and there was evidence of block voting. When made aware of this, the authors requested that their novel be withdrawn from the ballot.   [JC]

BEGBIE, (EDWARD) HAROLD (1871-1929) UK writer and journalist, author of *The Day that Changed the*

World (**1912**), as by "The Man who Was Warned", a religious fantasy in which humankind's spiritual development is sharply uplifted by divine intervention. HB also wrote *On the Side of the Angels* (**1915**), a reply to Arthur MACHEN's *The Bowmen* (coll 1915; rev with 2 additional stories, **1915**), and two political satires, *Clara In Blunderland* (**1902**) and *Lost in Blunderland* (**1903**), both written with M.H. Temple and J. Stafford Ransome under the collaborative pseudonym Caroline Lewis. [JE]

BEGOUEN, MAX French prehistorian and author of three prehistoric novels, of which only *Les bisons d'argile* (**1925**; trans as *Bison of Clay* **1926**) has been translated into English. His entry for the Prix Jules Verne (◊ AWARDS), *Quand le mammouth ressuscita* ["When the Mammoth Revives"] (**1928**), although placed only second, was deemed of sufficient merit to warrant publication. [JE]

Other works: *Tisik et Katé, aventures de deux enfants à l'époque du renne* ["Tisik and Katé: The Adventures of Two Children in the Time of the Reindeer"] (**1946**).

See also: ORIGIN OF MAN.

BEHEMOTH, THE SEA MONSTER (vt *The Giant Behemoth* US) Film (1959). Diamond/Allied Artists. Dir Douglas Hickox, Eugène Lourié, starring Gene Evans, André Morell, Jack MacGowran, Leigh Madison. Screenplay Lourié. 80 mins, cut to 72 mins. B/w.

Lourié made several MONSTER MOVIES during his career, including *The* BEAST FROM 20,000 FATHOMS (1953), of which *BTSM* – his least successful – is a partial remake. The story is the usual one – a prehistoric reptile is revived by atomic radiation and immediately sets out to demolish the nearest city, in this case London. There is a good build-up of suspense in some sequences but, despite the presence of the elderly Willis H. O'BRIEN (designer of the original KING KONG) on the team, the very low budget severely restricted the scope of the effects. [JB]

BĚHOUNEK, FRANTIŠEK [r] ◊ CZECH AND SLOVAK SF.

BEKSICS, GUSZTÁV [r] ◊ HUNGARY.

BELAYEV, A. [r] ◊ Alexander BELYAEV.

"BELCAMPO" ◊ BENELUX.

BELDEN, DAVID (CORDEROY) (1949-) Swiss-born UK writer, in the USA from 1982, whose **Galactic Collectivity** sequence – *Children of Arable* (**1986**) and *To Warm the Earth* (**1988**) – depicts with clearly felt didactic urgency a FAR-FUTURE Earth trapped in sterile stasis, with a stagnant galactic civilization impotently observing the dying of the mother planet. In the first volume a woman gives birth to a child, and this has a rejuvenating effect (the novel is rich in feminist and religious discourse); in the second novel of the sequence, another female protagonist looks to a Collectivity satellite for a dubious technological fix. [JC]

BELGIUM ◊ BENELUX.

BELIAEV, ALEXANDER [r] ◊ Alexander BELYAEV.

BELIAYEV, ALEXANDER [r] ◊ Alexander BELYAEV.

BELL, CLARE (LOUISE) (1952-) UK-born writer, in the USA from 1957; a test-equipment engineer for a computer firm 1978-90. She began publishing sf with *Ratha's Creature* (**1983**), the first volume of the **Ratha Ya** sequence of juveniles – continued with *Clan Ground* (**1984**) and *Ratha and Thistle-Chaser* (**1990**) – which delineates the lives of an ALTERNATE-WORLD tribe of intelligent cougar-like felines, concentrating on Ratha, a rebel who becomes necessary for the survival of her people. *Tomorrow's Sphinx* (**1986**), also an sf juvenile but this time about an intelligent cheetah, is set on an Earth abandoned by the humans who have devastated it. In *People of the Sky* (**1989**), for adults, an Amerindian star-pilot discovers a planet inhabited by Pueblos; their relationship to the indigenous insect ALIENS, which they ride like horses, and the puzzle of their existence generate sufficient mystery to keep the competent narrative on the move. CB might choose to inhabit the consciousnesses of sentient animals or of a member of a culture foreign to her own (such as an Amerindian), but the true "aliens" in her imaginative world are the (human) representatives of technological society. In collaboration with M. Coleman EASTON, with whom she lives, some titles are projected under a joint pseudonym, Clare Coleman. [JC]

BELL, ERIC TEMPLE [r] ◊ John TAINE.

BELL, NEIL Pseudonym of UK writer Stephen Southwold (1887-1964), used on his early poetry and most of his later novels. Born Stephen Henry Critten, he took the name Southwold (from his birthplace) because he despised his father, for reasons made clear in the semi-autobiographical chapters which recur in many of his novels, including *Precious Porcelain* (**1931**) and *The Lord of Life* (**1933**). He wrote juveniles and a few biographical novels under his adopted name, and also used the pseudonyms Stephen Green, S.H. Lambert, Paul Martens and Miles. His first sf novel, *The Seventh Bowl* (**1930** as by Miles; reprinted 1934 as by NB), is a bitter future HISTORY in which the deployment of a technology of IMMORTALITY by corrupt politicians sets in train a chain of events leading to the END OF THE WORLD. His second, *The Gas War of 1940* (**1931** as by Miles; vt *Valiant Clay* 1934 as by NB), gives a more detailed account of an incident – the use of poison gas in war – from the same future history. The caustic outlook of these works is displayed also in the apocalyptic black comedy *The Lord of Life* and in the stories in his first and best collection, *Mixed Pickles: Short Stories* (coll **1935**); these include the sf stories "The Mouse" and "The Evanescence of Adrian Fulk" and the sarcastic messianic fantasy (◊ MESSIAHS) "The Facts About Benjamin Crede" (also in *Ten Short Stories*, coll **1948**).

Precious Porcelain, The Disturbing Affair of Noel Blake (**1932**) and *Life Comes to Seathorpe* (**1946**) are three similarly structured mystery stories in which peculiar happenings are ultimately revealed to have an sf explanation. *Death Rocks the Cradle* (**1933** as by Martens) is a hallucinatory fantasy about a UTOPIA populated by covert sadists. *One Came Back* (**1938**) is an interesting realistic novel which extends into the NEAR FUTURE in describing the founding of a new RELIGION following an apparent miracle. Occasional sf or fantasy stories crop up in NB's later collections, most significantly the first of the three horror novellas in *Who Walk in Fear* (coll **1954**) and several items in *Alpha and Omega* (coll **1946**); the latter collection includes an introduction descriptive of his working methods. His quirky studies in abnormal psychology, including *Portrait of Gideon Power* (**1944** as by Lambert; reprinted 1962 as by NB) and *The Dark Page* (**1951**), are of marginal interest. [BS/JC]

Other works: *Ten-Minute Tales* (coll **1927** as by Southwold), children's fantasy stories; *The Tales of Joe Egg* (coll **1936** as by Southwold), a non-sf juvenile story sequence narrated by a ROBOT; *The Smallways Rub Along* (coll **1938**) has 1 sf story; *Forty Stories* (coll **1948**) has 2 sf stories; *Three Pair of Heels* (coll **1951**); *The House at the Crossroads* (**1966**); *The Ninth Earl of Whitby* (coll **1966**) has 1 sf story.

About the author: *My Writing Life* (**1955**), autobiography.

See also: BIOLOGY; CRIME AND PUNISHMENT; MEDICINE; PSI POWERS; WAR; WEAPONS.

BELL, THORNTON ◊ R.L. FANTHORPE.

BELLAMY, EDWARD (1850-1898) US author and journalist, the latter from 1871, when he abandoned the practice of law before having properly begun it; no lawyers exist in the AD2000 of his most famous work, the UTOPIA *Looking Backward, 2000-1887* (**1888**) and its sequel, *Equality* (**1897**), whose influence in the 19th century was enormous. His early works of fiction were Gothic; though sentimental and labouredly influenced by Nathaniel HAWTHORNE, they are nevertheless strangely moving. They do not, however, show any great hint of the direction his work would take. *Dr Heidenhoff's Process* (**1880**), although not sf, interestingly prefigures some of the tactics of his later work; the doctor's process claims to mechanically wipe out diseased memories from those who wish for a new start. The protagonist's girl, who has been seduced by a rival, is persuaded to try the process, and is transformed until the last pages of the novel, when it turns out that Heidenhoff and his process have simply been dreamt by the protagonist, who awakens to find that his disgraced lover has committed suicide.

The emotional exorbitance and Gothic extremity of this tale are transformed in *Looking Backward* into a vision of a utopian society whose equally exorbitant realization is achieved while the protagonist, whose confusion upon his arrival into the world of the future is one of the best things in this uneasy work of fiction, has been in hypnotized sleep (◊ SLEEPER AWAKES). The people of AD2000 are devoid of irrational passions and their highly communalized society reflects a reasonableness so radically opposed to common sense that one is tempted to posit an impulse of deep violence behind EB's creation of such a world. William MORRIS was so appalled by the

bureaucratic and machine-like nature of EB's utopia that he was instantly driven to retort with *News from Nowhere* (**1890** US), which described an ideal world of a very different sort. EB's book has nonetheless been extraordinarily popular, especially in the USA, which suggests a greater receptivity to communist thought in that country than is generally recognized, and has been treated as a serious model for the positing of future societies by many thinkers and writers, including Mack REYNOLDS. The sequel, an uninspired sequence of fictionalized essays, did little to damage the effect of the earlier book. EB is more important to the history of utopian thought than he is as a writer of PROTO SCIENCE FICTION. His influence on the world of GENRE SF, except on didactic writers like Hugo GERNSBACK, has been indirect and diffuse. [JC]

Other works: *Miss Ludington's Sister: A Romance of Immortality* (**1884**); *The Blindman's World and Other Stories* (coll **1898**), especially the title story (written 1885).

About the author: *Utopian Novel in America, 1886-1896: The Politics of Form* (**1985**) by Jean Pfaelzer.

See also: ARTS; AUTOMATION; ECONOMICS; HISTORY OF SF; MACHINES; MUSIC; NEAR FUTURE; POLITICS; PSYCHOLOGY; SUSPENDED ANIMATION; TECHNOLOGY.

BELLAMY, FRANCIS RUFUS (1886-1972) US editor and writer. In his sf novel *Atta* (**1953**) a man is struck by lightning and, after shrinking until ½ in (12mm) tall, combines forces with a warrior ant by the name of Atta. [JC]

See also: NEAR FUTURE.

BELLOC, (JOSEPH) HILAIRE (PETER) (1870-1953) French-born UK writer, known for his poetry – notably his *Cautionary Tales* (coll **1907**) for children – his anti-Semitism, his Roman Catholic apologetics, and his novels. Most of his fiction was written either to argue a political case or to potboil, and his habit of displacing his venues from consensual reality served both motives, for his politics are fantastical and his commercial work tends to commit acts of vengeance against the *hoi polloi. Mr Clutterbuck's Election* (**1908**), *A Change in the Cabinet* (**1909**) and *Pongo and the Bull* (**1910**) together make up a NEAR-FUTURE assault on Edwardian politics in a 1920s UK. Of the several novels for which his friend and colleague G.K. CHESTERTON provided illustrations, *But Soft – We Are Observed!* (**1928**; vt *Shadowed!* 1929 US) is genuine sf, a satirical tale of suspense set in the USA and Europe in 1979, the main target once again being the parliamentary form of government. Other novels by HB of genre interest and illustrated by Chesterton are *Mr Petre* (**1925**), *The Emerald of Catherine the Great* (**1926**; vt *The Emerald* US), *The Haunted House* (**1928**), *The Man who Made Gold* (**1930**) and *The Postmaster-General* (**1932**). Packed with energy though formally negligent, HB's fiction awaits a modest revival. [JC]

About the author: *Hilaire Belloc* (**1945**) by Robert Hamilton.

See also: ALTERNATE WORLDS; POLITICS; TIME TRAVEL.

BELLOW, SAUL (1915-   ) Canadian-born US novelist.

Winner of the 1976 Nobel Prize for Literature, SB is perhaps the premier MAINSTREAM novelist of his generation in the USA today. Some of his books distantly resemble sf, specifically *Henderson the Rain King* (**1959**), a picaresque partly set in a quasimythical African kingdom. *Mr Sammler's Planet* (**1970**) has been wrongly annexed as sf by several commentators, who perhaps relied on the title alone; in the novel mankind's reaching of the Moon and establishment there of a utopia are matters which occur only in conversation. [JC]

BELL PUBLICATIONS ◊ UNIVERSE SCIENCE FICTION.

BELOT, ADOLPHE (1829-1890) French writer. Of the tales collected in English in *A Parisian Sultana* (coll trans H. Mainwaring Dunstan in 3 vols **1879** UK), one features a superhuman female explorer in Africa and another a LOST WORLD of Amazons. [JC]

BELYAEV, ALEXANDER (ROMANOVICH) (1884-?1942) Russian writer whose surname has been variously transliterated; further spellings include Beliaev, Beliayev and Belyayev. His death-date is likewise insecure: he died during the German occupation of the city of Pushkin and, while his body was discovered in January 1942, it is possible that his death was in fact in late 1941. As one of the originators of the sf genre in Soviet literature, AB's WELLS- and VERNE-influenced writings dominated the field between the wars, providing models for most other Soviet practitioners of the time. His first story, *Golova Professora Douellia* (1925 in story form; **1937**; trans Antonina W. Bouis as *Professor Dowell's Head* **1980** US), is both a prophetic story about organ transplantation and a dramatic account of life without motion – the affect of the latter focus being intensified by the author's own invalid status due to incurable illness. After dealing with traditional themes, such as that of ATLANTIS in *Poslednii Tchelovek Iz Atlantidy* ["The Last Man from Atlantis"] (**1927**), AB tackled space exploration in *Bor'ba V Efire* (**1927**; trans Albert Parry as *The Struggle in Space: Red Dream; Soviet-American War* **1965** US); he returned to this theme in *Pryzhok V Nichto* ["Jump into Nowhere"] (**1933**) and *Zvezda KETZ* ["The KET Star"] (**1940**), the latter promulgating the ideas of Russian space pioneer Konstantin TSIOLKOVSKY.

Though the literary style and themes of AB's sf had standard pulp limitations, a personal note resounded through his otherwise orthodox representations of potential SUPERMEN, a theme seemingly encouraged by his own miserable condition. In *Tchelovek-Amfibia* (**1929**; trans L. Kolesnikov as *The Amphibian* **1959** Russia), the protagonist – a boy with transplanted shark's gills – is totally uncomfortable in the society of "normal people"; in *Vlastelin Mira* ["The Master of the World"] (**1929**) a morally wicked but ingenious biophysicist tries to control people through the use of telepathy; and in *Ariel* (**1941**) the same dramatic incompatibility afflicts a levitating boy, the victim of another mad scientist's enthusiasms. Despite the manifest ideological content and frequent clichés in

AB's work, his books remain permanently in print, maintaining his status as the first Soviet sf "classic". [PN/VG/JC]

See also: RUSSIA; UNDER THE SEA.

BEM A common item of sf TERMINOLOGY, being an acronym of "bug-eyed monster" and referring to the type of ALIEN being, usually menacing, regularly pictured on the covers of SF MAGAZINES in the 1930s and 1940s.

See also: MONSTERS.

BEMMANN, HANS [r] ◊ GERMANY.

BENEATH THE PLANET OF THE APES Film (1969). Apjac/20th Century-Fox. Dir Ted Post, starring James Franciscus, Charlton Heston, Linda Harrison, Kim Hunter. Screenplay Paul Dehn, Mort Abrahams, based on characters created by Pierre BOULLE. 95 mins. Colour.

In this first and best of four sequels to PLANET OF THE APES another time-warped astronaut (Franciscus) crashlands on the ape world. Like his predecessor he is captured, befriended by the sympathetic chimpanzee Zira (Hunter), and meets the girl savage (Harrison). But when he escapes with her underground and discovers the remains of New York City the film goes off in a blacker direction: he finds a race of deformed, telepathic MUTANTS who worship a nuclear Doomsday Bomb, and meets the astronaut hero (Heston) of the previous film, now half-crazed and venomous, who ultimately detonates the bomb and brings about a HOLOCAUST, wiping out apes, mutants and humans alike. In its replacement of whimsical SATIRE by an altogether harsher judgement about the prospects for intelligent life on Earth, this film is arguably stronger than its original. The novelization is *Beneath the Planet of the Apes* * (**1970**) by Michael AVALLONE. [JB/PN]

BENELUX The Benelux consists of three nations: the Netherlands (Holland), Belgium and Luxembourg. The Dutch language is spoken in the Netherlands and in the northern part of Belgium, called Flanders. The French-speaking southern and eastern part of Belgium is called Wallonia. In the field of literature Flanders and the Netherlands are one domain, and the same can be said for Wallonia and France. Flemish (from Flanders) and Walloon (from Wallonia) authors are mostly published, respectively, in the Netherlands (Amsterdam) and in France (Paris), for reasons of prestige and because of the small number of Flemish and Walloon publishers.

Dutch and Flemish sf took shape in the 1960s, when several publishers began series of translated sf, FANDOM was organized and some Dutch and Flemish authors began to write sf novels. Before the 1960s there were isolated works (original or translated), but no real tradition of sf. Even during those periods when the fantastic was flowering everywhere in Western literature (as in the Romantic era, and at the turn of the century), the quantity of Dutch and Flemish sf was very small and all of it has been almost totally forgotten, even by the most comprehensive histories of Dutch and Flemish sf.

The sf boom begun in the 1960s did not last very long. In the 1980s the market declined to the figures of the early 1960s. In the late 1970s, for instance, the established sf publishers together published almost 100 books a year (mostly translations); in the early 1990s this had declined to some 25 books. Most publishers discontinued their sf lines, and by 1992 only two – Meulenhoff and Luitingh – were really active on the sf market. So one can say that the old situation has been restored: sf (and fantasy and horror) as genres consist of only isolated works scattered over the whole literary field.

During the early stage of the Romantic era, when the influence of the Enlightenment was still very strong, several writers produced, mostly in the form of IMAGINARY VOYAGES, descriptions of a future Holland. This genre of utopian literature continued during the 19th century. In the 1890s the Dutch publisher Elsevier produced a famous complete edition in 65 volumes of the work of Jules VERNE, which was widely sold but apparently had no real influence on Dutch literature (except the juvenile market).

In the first half of the 20th century only a few original sf works appeared, and only one of them is still in print, being considered a masterpiece of Dutch literature: *Blokken* ["Blocks"] (**1931**) by F. Bordewijk (1884-1965). This short novel is set in a NEAR-FUTURE Russia that has at the same time communist and fascist characteristics. In part it is a pure description of the State and its Ruling Council, in part a story about an unsuccessful revolt. A group of dissidents is mercilessly slaughtered, but at the end it is suggested that the upheavals will continue until the State is destroyed. It is a warning not so much against communism or fascism as against every sort of totalitarian government. Bordewijk also wrote a few sf short stories, most of which are to be found in his collection *Vertellingen van generzijds* ["Tales from the Other Side"] (coll **1951**). Not included in this collection is the remarkable "Einde der mensheid" ["End of Mankind"] (1959), a fictional essay in the manner of Jorge Luis BORGES about a Universe that consists of layers of "positiva, neutra, and negativa" in an endless continuation. Mankind is but an unimportant phenomenon in one of the uncountable layers, and will eventually disappear, leaving no trace at all.

A writer of short fantasies and some sf stories was "Belcampo" (pseudonym of H.P. Schönfeld Wichers [1902-1990]), whose clever and witty tales are still popular. Of his sf stories the best are the ROBOT tale "Voorland" ["Foreland"] (1935) and "Het verhaal van Oosterhuis" ["The Tale of Oosterhuis"] (1946), a curious blend of imaginary voyage, UTOPIA, DYSTOPIA and LOST WORLD.

In the 1960s and 1970s some MAINSTREAM novelists wrote one or two sf novels. *Het reservaat* (**1964**; trans as *The Reservation* **1978** UK) by the Fleming Ward Ruyslinck (1929-   ) is a bitter dystopian novel about a near-future Belgium where all dissidents are put away in reservations disguised as psychiatric clinics. The Belgian government is depicted as right-wing and as corrupted by the political imperialism of the USA. However, the reservations are more reminiscent of repression in the former USSR. As with Bordewijk's novella, the novel is essentially an attack on repressive societies of all kinds.

Hugo Raes (1929-   ), also from Flanders, wrote two imaginary voyages with sf elements, *De lotgevallen* ["The Events"] (**1968**) and *Reizigers in de anti-tijd* ["Voyagers in Anti-Time"] (**1971**). His *De verwoesting van Hyperion* ["The Destruction of Hyperion"] (**1978**) is straightforward sf, a post-HOLOCAUST novel about the nearly immortal descendants of mankind and their fight with evolved rats. Raes wrote some fine sf short stories, most of which are collected in *Bankroet van een charmeur* ["Bankruptcy of a Charmer"] (coll **1967**).

De toekomst van gisteren ["The Future of Yesterday"] (**1972**) by the Dutchman Harry Mulisch (1927-   ) is not a novel but a book-length essay in which the author explains that he has not in fact written a projected novel of that title. Had he done so, that novel would have presented an ALTERNATE WORLD in which the Germans had won WWII (*see also* HITLER WINS). Within that alternate world the protagonist is writing a novel about a world alternate to his, in which the Germans lost the war. So far the concept shows a remarkable resemblance to Philip K. DICK's *The Man in the High Castle* (**1962**), but – unlike Dick's – the second novel had to be fully reproduced within the text of the first. What interested Mulisch was the difference between the real world in which the Germans lost WWII and a world in which, although the same thing has happened, the present is as imagined by a writer who has grown up in a fascist world state. In his essay Mulisch demonstrates that the combination of alternate-world novel and novel-within-a-novel is rendered theoretically impossible by narrative restrictions. The book should be obligatory reading for alternate-world authors.

Other relevant modern Dutch authors include Rein Blijstra (1901-1975), whose 10 humorous stories about all kinds of sf CLICHÉS are collected as *Het planetarium van Otze Otzinga* ["The Orrery of Otze Otzinga"] (coll **1962**). The novelist and playwright Manuel van Loggem (1916-   ) has written interesting FANTASY with slight sf leanings; his best collection is *Het liefdeleven der Priargen* ["The Love Life of the Priargs"] (coll **1968**). The novelist and computer expert Gerrit Krol (1934-   ) wrote *De man achter het raam* ["The Man behind the Window"] (**1982**), the rather difficult story of Adam, a thinking COMPUTER, who contemplates the problem of what a human being really is. When he has developed into a full human being, he undergoes the fate of all mankind and dies. It is not so much sf as a novel of ideas, or even a study (disguised as fiction) of problems of identity and consciousness.

In the late 1950s and especially in the 1970s, some

authors came to the fore who can be considered true sf writers. The Dutch physicist Dionijs BURGER wrote *Bolland* (**1957**; trans as *Sphereland* **1965** US), a continuation and expansion of Edwin A. ABBOTT's famous *Flatland* (**1884**). As Abbott tried to demonstrate four-dimensional geometry by means of a story about two-dimensional creatures, Burger tries to explain Einstein's theories about curved space and the expanding Universe. His story takes place two generations after the events described by Abbott; the narrator is a grandson of Abbott's A Square. Abbott's book may be of higher literary quality, but Burger's is more inventive and humorous. The book has become a minor classic in the sf world.

Sam of de Pluterdag (**1968**; trans as *Where Were You Last Pluterday?* **1973** US), by the Flemish author Paul VAN HERCK, is a funny satirical novel about a society in which the higher social levels have access to an additional eighth day of the week, the "Pluterday". In 1972 it won the first Europa Award.

The two most prolific sf writers are the Dutchman Felix Thijssen (1933-) and the Fleming Eddy Bertin (1944-). Thijssen, originally a writer of adventure fiction for the juvenile market, started to write sf in 1971 when the first volume of the so-called **Mark Stevens** cycle appeared. This is a run-of-the-mill SPACE-OPERA series, whose first volumes seemed aimed at young adults, but which gradually became more mature. The series ended with a good eighth volume, *De poorten van het paradijs* ["The Gates of Paradise"] (**1974**). Later Thijssen wrote several rather more serious novels, the best of which is *Emmarg* (**1976**), a sad story about a pregnant female ALIEN abandoned on Earth. Eddy Bertin has some reputation in the English-speaking world, thanks to his own translations of several of his stories. The **Membrane Universe** series can be called his best work; it is collected in three volumes: *Eenzame bloedvogel* ["Lonely Blood-Bird"] (coll **1976**), *De sluimerende stranden van de geest* ["The Slumbering Beaches of the Mind"] (**1981**) and *Het blinde doofstomme beest op de kale berg* ["The Blind Deaf-Mute Beast on the Bare Mountain"] (**1983**). The stories are interspersed with lyrics, fake documents, comments, timetables and so on. Together, they form a future HISTORY from 1970 to AD3666. Bertin is an active fan who has been editing his own FANZINE, *SF Gids* ["SF Guide"] since 1973, and an ardent bibliographer. In addition to sf, he has written numerous horror stories, which are perhaps the better part of his opus.

A remarkable Dutch début was *De eersten van Rissan* ["The First of Rissan"] (**1980**) by Wim Gijsen (1893-1990), a lost-colony novel about the descendants of mankind on the planet Rissan. In the sequel, *De koningen van weleer* ["The Kings of Old"] (**1981**), it is discovered that the mysterious First of Rissan are the descendants of the kings of ATLANTIS. Both novels hold their own with the better US novels of this type. His later novels are all young-adult fantasy.

The most noteworthy forum for original sf stories in the Dutch language may have been the **Vlaamsche Filmkens** ["Flemish Movies"] sequence of booklets written for a young-adult audience; more than 2000 volumes have been produced in the series, which began in 1930 and continues. Of this total perhaps 200 have been sf, and many more have been fantasies. The author involved most centrally was the pseudonymous John Flanders (? -1964), who also wrote as Jean Ray; other contributors included Eddy C. Bertin, Dries Nieuwland, Paul Van Herck and John Vermeulen.

The same can be said about Walloon sf as about its Dutch/Flemish counterpart: only in the 1970s has there been a (small) sf boom; before and after it, sf consisted of only some individual works by writers whose output was primarily non-sf. The most prolific early author was J.H. ROSNY aîné, most of whose work was reprinted in France in the 1970s. He is best known for his prehistoric romances; sf proper is but a small part of his output. In 1973 his sf stories were collected as *Récits de science-fiction* ["SF Narratives"] (coll **1973** France); included is his famous novella about aliens, *Les Xipéhuz* (**1887**), his first published work. Other authors from before WWII are François Léonard with *Le triomphe de l'homme* ["The Triumph of Man"] (**1911**), a Verne-like novel in which Earth is accidentally propelled from the Solar System and drifts away into the Universe until its final destruction; Henri-Jacques Proumen with *Le sceptre est volé aux hommes* [The Sceptre is Stolen from the People"] (**1930**), about a race of MUTANTS who enslave the population of a Pacific island; and the poet Marcel Thiry (1897-1977), who wrote the alternate-world novel *Echec au temps* ["Set-Back in Time"] (written 1938; **1945**), in which Napoleon won the Battle of Waterloo.

Only one author from the 1950s and 1960s could be considered an sf writer: Jacques STERNBERG (1923-). He is influenced by prewar Surrealism and postwar Absurdism. His best novel is perhaps *La sortie est au fond de l'espace* ["The Exit is at the Bottom of Space"] (**1956**): the last remaining humans leave a bacteria-infested Earth only to discover that deep space is even more dangerous and that mankind has no real meaning in the Universe. A good story collection, available in English, is *Futurs sans avenir* (coll **1971**; cut trans as *Future without Future* **1974** US).

In the 1970s a small group of young sf writers (Vincent Goffart, Paul Hanost and Yves Varende, among others) formed around the paperback publisher Marabout, and for a while it looked as if a sort of sf tradition might be beginning. However, after the collapse of Marabout, the only sf publisher in Wallonia, most authors moved to other fields of writing.

Virtually nothing is known about sf in tiny Luxembourg, the third country which forms the Benelux – except that it was the homeland of Hugo GERNSBACK, who in a sense started it all. [JAD]

BENÉT, STEPHEN VINCENT (1898-1943) US writer, mainly of poetry and stories, much published in the *Saturday Evening Post*. He is best known for a single poem, "American Names" (whose last line, "Bury my heart at Wounded Knee", gained a peculiar and singular resonance in the campaign for Amerindian rights), and for two fantasy stories, *The Devil and Daniel Webster* (**1937** chap), also published with other fantasies in *Thirteen O'Clock: Stories of Several Worlds* (coll **1937**), and *Johnny Pye and the Fool-Killer* (**1938** chap), also included with other fantasies in *Tales Before Midnight* (coll **1939**). These collections were brought together to make up *Twenty-Five Short Stories* (coll **1943**), though most of their contents had already appeared in the 2-vol *Selected Works of Stephen Vincent Benét* (coll **1942**; cut vt *The Stephen Vincent Benét Pocket Book* 1946). Several of SVB's stories are of genre interest, his best-known being "By the Waters of Babylon" (1937), a clever post-HOLOCAUST story about a tribal adolescent boy who discovers the ruins of a great destroyed city (◊ CITIES). It was a main source of material for what became, after WWII, a clichéd subgenre in the field.   [JC/PN]

BENFORD, GREGORY (1941-   ) US physicist and writer who graduated from the University of Oklahoma 1963 and gained his PhD from the University of California, San Diego, 1967; in 1979 he was appointed Professor of Physics at the University of California, Irvine. One of a pair of identical twins, he has written some stories in collaboration with his brother James. He edited a notable FANZINE, *Void*, with various co-editors including Ted WHITE and Terry CARR. His first published story was "Stand-In" (1965), which won second place in a contest organized by *The* MAGAZINE OF FANTASY AND SCIENCE FICTION. He wrote regular articles on **The Science in SF** for AMAZING STORIES in collaboration with David Book 1969-72, continuing the series solo, somewhat less regularly, until 1976.

GB early established himself as a leading writer of HARD SF, although much of his writing also has a lyrical aspect reminiscent of the work of Poul ANDERSON. Some of his early work was with Gordon EKLUND, including the stories combined in *If The Stars are Gods* (fixup **1977**), the title-piece of which won a NEBULA in 1975, and the less impressive *Find the Changeling* (**1980**). His DISASTER novel *Shiva Descending* (**1980**) with William ROTSLER also fails to convey the imaginative and cognitive energy of his solo work. However, *Heart of the Comet* (**1986**) with David BRIN has moments of shared power. He also undertook a curious "collaboration" with Arthur C. CLARKE: *Beyond the Fall of Night* ∗ (omni **1990**; vt *Against the Fall of Night and Beyond the Fall of Night* 1991 UK), an "authorised sequel" by GB alone to Clarke's *Against the Fall of Night* (1948; **1953**); both versions of the tie include reprints of the earlier story. GB's sequel ignores Clarke's own subsequent revision of his novel as *The City and the Stars* (**1956**).

GB's first solo novel was *Deeper than the Darkness* (**1970**; rev vt *The Stars in Shroud* 1978), one of many stories in which humanity's confrontation with ALIENS proves deeply disturbing, and which in its revised form became an integral part of the **Ocean** sequence. Another patchwork novel, *In the Ocean of Night* (fixup **1977**), became the foundation-stone of an extending series of novels whose titles all contain metaphorical references to water. The central character of *In the Ocean of Night*, astronaut Nigel Walmsley, reappears in *Across the Sea of Suns* (**1984**; rev 1987), which introduces the theme of a Universe-wide struggle between organic and inorganic "lifeforms" in which self-replicating MACHINES appear to have the upper hand; this scenario is further developed in a trilogy begun by *Great Sky River* (**1987**) and continued in *Tides of Light* (**1989**).

GB achieved something of a breakthrough with *Timescape* (**1980**), which won both the Nebula and the JOHN W. CAMPBELL MEMORIAL AWARD. In its description of an attempt to change history by transmitting a tachyonic message across time it offers one of the best ever fictional descriptions of scientists at work. Another NEAR-FUTURE, almost MAINSTREAM novel is *Artifact* (**1985**), in which archaeologists discover evidence of an alien visitation with almost catastrophic consequences. *Against Infinity* (**1983**) is pure sf in terms of its plot, which involves the search for an enigmatic alien on Ganymede, but its structure is strongly reminiscent of William Faulkner's novella "The Bear"; and the novella "To the Storming Gulf" (1985) contains strong echoes of Faulkner's *As I Lay Dying*. Comments on these parallels by critic Gary K. WOLFE caused some controversy.

The best of GB's short fiction is collected in *In Alien Flesh* (coll **1986**), although there is more than enough material available to fill a second collection of equal merit. He has co-edited a number of anthologies with Martin Harry GREENBERG: *Hitler Victorious* (anth **1986**) (◊ HITLER WINS), *Nuclear War* (anth **1988**), *What Might Have Been? Vol I: Alternate Empires* (anth **1989**), *Vol II: Alternate Heroes* (anth **1989**) – these two assembled as *What Might Have Been, Volumes I and II* (omni **1990**) – and *Vol III: Alternate Wars* (anth **1991**). All but the second feature stories of ALTERNATE WORLDS.   [BS]

Other works: *Jupiter Project* (**1975**; rev vt *The Jupiter Project* 1980), an intelligent Robert A. HEINLEIN-esque juvenile; *Time's Rub* (**1984** chap); *Of Space/Time and the River* (**1985** chap); *At the Double Solstice* (**1986** chap); *We Could Do Worse* (**1988** chap); *Iceborn* (1989 *Synergy 3* as "Proserpina's Daughter" by GB alone; **1989** chap dos) with Paul A. CARTER; *Centigrade 233* (**1990** chap); *Matter's End* (**1991** chap).

See also: ASTRONOMY; AUTOMATION; BLACK HOLES; BRITISH SCIENCE FICTION AWARD; COMMUNICATIONS; CRYONICS; END OF THE WORLD; ESCHATOLOGY; EVOLUTION; GODS AND DEMONS; INVASION; JUPITER; LIVING WORLDS; MONSTERS; NEUTRON STARS; NEW WAVE; OUTER PLANETS; PHYSICS; PSYCHOLOGY; RELIGION; SCIENTISTS; STARS; SUN; TACHYONS; TECHNOLOGY; TERRAFORMING; TIMESCAPE BOOKS; WEAPONS; WRITERS OF THE FUTURE CONTEST.

BEN-NER, YITZHAK [r] ◊ ISRAEL.

BENNET, ROBERT AMES (1870-1954) US writer, more often than not of Westerns, and author of three sf novels. *Thyra: A Romance of the Polar Pit* (**1901**) is set in a clement LOST WORLD, hidden near the North Pole and full of prehistoric beasts, clairvoyant priestesses and unusually tall socialists whose lives are based on memories of old Scandinavia. The lost world of *The Forest Maiden* (**1913**) as by Lee Robinet features a flawed SUPERMAN who uses his PSI POWERS to create a new Eden, whose involuntary Eve is saved only when, while walking on water in search of her, he slips and sinks. *The Bowl of Baal* (**1916-17** *All Around Magazine*; **1975**) locates the lost world of Baal, where dinosaurs survive, in Arabia. [JC]

BENNETT, ALFRED GORDON (1901-1962) UK writer, documentary film-maker and founder of Pharos Books, through which he published a fantasy, *Whom the Gods Destroy* (**1946**). His sf novel *The Demigods* (**1939**) depicts a world menaced by giant ants, who derive their abilities from a central controlling brain. His father was Arthur BENNETT. [JC]
Other works: *The Forest of Fear* (**1924**); *The Sea of Sleep* (**1926**; vt *The Sea of Dreams* 1926 US).
See also: HIVE-MINDS.

BENNETT, ARTHUR (1862-1931) UK writer, father of Alfred Gordon BENNETT. His *A Dream of an Englishman* (**1893**) describes in inadequately fictionalized terms the history of the world in the 20th century; SPACE FLIGHT is mooted. *The Dream of a Warringtonian* (**1900**), self-published in Warrington, UK, describes a similar period as it applies to Warrington. [JC]

BENNETT, MARCIA J(OANNE) (1945-) US writer whose **Ni-Lach** sequence of PLANETARY ROMANCES includes *Where the Ni-Lach* (**1983**), *Shadow Singer* (**1984**), *Beyond the Draak's Teeth* (**1986**) and *Seeking the Dream Brother* (**1989**). The local-colour quotient is high, but the sequence itself is unremarkable. *Yaril's Children* (**1988**), a singleton, is set on a planet inhabited by human and MUTANT stock, and deals with the inevitable problems which ensue. [JC]

BENNETT, MARGOT (1912-1980) UK writer, from 1945 mostly of detective novels, in a subtle and atmospheric style. A fantasy story, "An Old-Fashioned Poker for My Uncle's Head" (1946), was reprinted in *FSF* in 1954. Her first sf novel, *The Long Way Back* (**1954**), has become well known. Long after a 1984 nuclear HOLOCAUST has ended European civilization, a reindustrialized and regimented African state sends a colonizing expedition to legendary Great Britain, where they find White people living in caves. The denouement uneasily combines love interests, satire and adventure. [JC]
Other works: *The Furious Masters* (**1968**).
See also: POLITICS.

BENNETT, RICHARD M. [r] ◊ Granville HICKS.

BENNI, STEFANO (1947-) Italian journalist and writer who published several nonfiction books before releasing his first novel, *Terra!* (**1983**; trans Annapaola Cancogni **1985** US), set in a post-HOLOCAUST world racked by nuclear winter; the action moves from the underground city of Paris to a race through space to occupy a new and Edenic planet. Governing the

farcical tone is a genuinely satirical assault on human mores. SB has been likened to Robert SHECKLEY. [JC]

BENOIST, ELIZABETH S(MITH) (1901-) US writer in whose sf novel, *Doomsday Clock* (**1975**), a passel of disparate characters takes refuge from nuclear HOLOCAUST in a very deep and luxurious bomb shelter, where they tell each other tales and prepare to die. [JC]

BENOIT, (FERDINAND MARIE) PIERRE (1886-1962) French writer remembered almost exclusively for *L'Atlantide* (**1919**; trans Mary C. Tongue and Mary Ross as *The Queen of Atlantis* 1920 UK; vt *Atlantida* 1920 US), a rather heated romance. Two French Foreign Legion officers discover, in North Africa, a lost race of Atlantean survivors whose queen has a rough way with ex-lovers. The novel has several times been filmed (◊ *Die* HERRIN VON ATLANTIS). [JC]
See also: ATLANTIS.

BENSEN, D(ONALD) R(OYNALD) (1927-) US editor and author, his novels being usually pseudonymous. The two anthologies he has edited, *The Unknown* (anth **1963**) and *The Unknown Five* (anth **1964**), are both fantasy and (all but one story) compiled from UNKNOWN. He was more important within the sf field for his editorship of Pyramid Books 1957-67, a period during which that firm became a significant producer of sf novels in reprint and original forms. In 1968 he became executive editor of Berkley Books. He moved to Dial Press in 1975, directing their **Quantum** sf programme, and he has also acted as consulting editor for Dell Books's sf since 1977. He wrote, in *And Having Writ . . .* (**1978**), a smoothly humorous sf novel set in an ALTERNATE WORLD engendered by the survival of the ALIENS whose crash-landing caused the Siberian Tunguska explosion of 1908. Thomas Alva Edison and H.G. WELLS make appearances. [JC]
See also: HISTORY IN SF.

BENSON, A(RTHUR) C(HRISTOPHER) (1862-1925) UK essayist, poet and novelist, elder brother of E.F. BENSON and Robert Hugh BENSON. Much of his short fiction was fantasy, and can be found in *The Hill of Trouble and Other Stories* (coll **1903**) and *The Isles of Sunset* (coll **1904**) – the two books being assembled as *Paul the Minstrel and Other Stories* (omni **1911**) – and in *Basil Netherby* (coll **1926**). *The Child of the Dawn* (**1912**) is an IMMORTALITY tale, religiously sententious but occasionally moving. [JC]

BENSON, E(DWARD) F(REDERICK) (1867-1940) UK novelist, brother of A.C. BENSON and Robert Hugh BENSON and by far the most prolific of them, with dozens of attractive, realistic novels and romances to his credit. His fantasy stories are well known, and some verge on sf: they can be found in *The Room in the Tower and Other Stories* (coll **1912**), *The Countess of Lowndes Square and Other Stories* (coll **1920**), *Visible and Invisible* (coll **1923**), *Spook Stories* (coll **1928**) and *More Spook Stories* (coll **1934**). *The Tale of an Empty House* (coll **1986**) is a convenient posthumous collection, while *The Flint Knife* (coll **1986**) ed Jack Adrian (1945-) assembles mostly uncollected material, including "Sir Roger de Coverley" (1927), an sf tale which reflects the time theories of J.W. DUNNE. [JC]

Other works: *The Luck of the Vails* (1901); *The Valkyries* (1903); *The Image in the Sand* (1905); *The Angel of Pain* (1905 US); *The House of Defense* (1906 Canada); *David Blaize and the Blue Door* (1918); *Across the Stream* (1919); *"And the Dead Spake – "* and *The Horror-Horn* (coll 1923 chap US); *Colin* (1923) and *Colin II* (1925); *The Inheritor* (1930), in which Pan and Dionysius cause conniptions in Cornwall; *Ravens' Blood* (1934).

BENSON, GORDON Jr (1936-) US bookseller, publisher and bibliographer. GB released the first of many solo BIBLIOGRAPHIES of sf figures in 1980, and moved into partnership with UK bibliographer Phil STEPHENSEN-PAYNE (*whom see for authors treated in collaboration*) in 1983. By the late 1980s GB had become relatively less active, although he continued to participate with Stephensen-Payne in many projects. His earlier bibliographies were sometimes technically deficient in their presentation of data, but the material presented was scrupulously trustworthy, and later editions of early publications, as well as projects dating from about the mid-1980s, are far more user-friendly. GB's solo bibliographical work covers the following authors (*whom see for titles*): Leigh BRACKETT, A. Bertram CHANDLER, Hal CLEMENT, Edmond HAMILTON, Harry HARRISON, Edgar PANGBORN, H. Beam PIPER, Margaret ST CLAIR, William TENN, Wilson TUCKER, Manly Wade WELLMAN, James WHITE and Jack WILLIAMSON. [JC]

BENSON, ROBERT HUGH (1871-1914) UK writer; third son of Archbishop Benson and brother of the writers A.C. BENSON and E.F. BENSON. He was ordained in the Church of England but later converted to Catholicism. His fiction is intensely propagandistic; many of his short stories – including the fantasies featured in *A Mirror of Shalott, Composed of Tales Told at a Symposium* (coll 1907) – use Catholic priests as central characters. In his remarkable apocalyptic novel, *Lord of the World* (1907), the Antichrist woos the world with socialism and humanism, and the remnants of the Papal hierarchy go into hiding. *The Dawn of All* (1911) shows the alternative as Benson saw it – a future of utopian Papal rule. [BS]

Other works: *The Light Invisible* (coll 1903); *The Conventionalist* (1908); *The Necromancers* (1909).

See also: DYSTOPIAS; END OF THE WORLD; RELIGION.

BENTLEY, PETER [r] ◊ ROBERT HALE LIMITED.

BERESFORD, J(OHN) D(AVYS) (1873-1947) UK writer. Son of a clergyman, he was crippled in infancy by polio; both facts were influential in forming his worldview. A determined but defensive agnosticism normally guides the development of his futuristic and metaphysical speculations, but occasionally he allowed a strong wish-fulfilment element into his work, as in *The Camberwell Miracle* (1933), in which a crippled girl is cured by a faith-healer; like Arthur Conan DOYLE he could adopt either an extremely hard-headed rationalism or a naïve mysticism. JDB's

first sf novel was the classic *The Hampdenshire Wonder* (1911; vt *The Wonder* 1917 US), a biographical account of a freak superchild born out of his time; the theme was recapitulated in Olaf STAPLEDON's *Odd John* (1935). His second, *Goslings* (1913; vt *A World of Women* 1913 US), is the first attempt to depict an all-female society which treats the issue seriously and with a degree of sympathy. Many of his early speculative short stories were collected in *Nineteen Impressions* (coll 1918) and *Signs and Wonders* (coll 1921). Some are allegories born of religious doubt, such as "A Negligible Experiment", in which the impending destruction of Earth is taken as evidence that God has become indifferent to mankind; others are visionary fantasies, such as "The Cage", in which a man is telepathically linked to a prehistoric ancestor for a few seconds; and yet others are studies in abnormal PSYCHOLOGY – an interest which also inspired the non-sf novel *Peckover* (1934). *Revolution* (1921) is a determinedly objective analysis of a socialist revolution in the UK.

JDB began a second phase of speculative work in 1941. *"What Dreams May Come . . ."* (1941) is a powerful novel about a young man drawn into a utopian future he has experienced in his dreams, and then returned, altered in body and mind, to a hopeless messianic quest in the war-torn present. *A Common Enemy* (1942) is reminiscent of much of the work of H.G. WELLS, showing the destruction of society by natural DISASTER as a prelude to utopian reform. *The Riddle of the Tower* (1944), written with Esmé Wynne-Tyson, is another wartime vision story following a future history in which utopian prospects are lost and society evolves towards "automatism", resulting in a hivelike social organization in which individuality – and ultimately humanity – are lost.

There are notable similarities between the methods and outlook of JDB and Wells (JDB's *H.G. Wells*, 1915, was the first critical study of Wells's early work), but JDB never achieved the critical acclaim he deserved, either for his mainstream fiction or for his sf. [BS]

Other works: *All or Nothing* (1928) and *The Gift* (1946, with Wynne-Tyson) are borderline fantasies about would-be MESSIAHS; *Real People* (1929) has a subplot involving ESP; there is 1 sf story, "The Man who Hated Flies", in *The Meeting Place* (coll 1929).

See also: BIOLOGY; CHILDREN IN SF; DYSTOPIAS; ECOLOGY; END OF THE WORLD; ESP; EVOLUTION; HISTORY OF SF; HIVE-MINDS; INTELLIGENCE; POLITICS; RELIGION; SOCIOLOGY; SUPERMAN.

BERESFORD, LEIGH [r] ◊ ROBERT HALE LIMITED.

BERESFORD, LESLIE (?1891-?1937) UK author who entered the genre with *The Second Rising* (1910), a future-WAR novel about the Second Indian Mutiny, and continued with two UTOPIAN novels published under the pseudonym Pan: *The Kingdom Of Content* (1918) and *The Great Image* (1921). Reverting to his own name, he wrote a novel about international air piracy, *Mr Appleton Awakes* (1924; cut 1932), and a humorous novel about a sensuous ALIEN with supranormal powers, *The Venus Girl* (**1925**; cut **1933**). LB was quite prolific in the magazine market, contributing "War of Revenge" (**1921**), "The Purple Planet" (**1922**) and "The People Of The Ice" (**1922**) – respectively future-war, interplanetary and LOST-WORLD adventures – to the BOYS' PAPERS, and "The Octopus Orchid" (**1921**) and "The Stranger from Somewhere" (**1922**), among others, to the pre-sf PULP MAGAZINES. [JE]

Other works: *The Last Woman* (**1922**); *The Invasion of the Iron-Clad Army* (**1928**); *The Flying Fish* (**1931**).

BERGER, THOMAS (LOUIS) (1924-   ) US writer best known for his work outside the sf field like the Western epic *Little Big Man* (**1964**), which combines farce and FABULATION, and was notably filmed in 1970. *Regiment of Women* (**1973**), which is sf, presents a world about a century hence where the roles of men and women have been completely reversed, direly for the men; the book is a blackly comic and chastening argument from premise, and in this prefigures most of TB's recent work, either outside the field, like the terrifying *Neighbors* (**1980**), or chillingly within, like *Nowhere* (**1986**), a yawningly vacuous Erewhonian spoof, *Being Invisible* (**1987**) and *Changing the Past* (**1989**), in which the laws of human nature, operating like theorems, show that all lives, even those we would aspire to could we ourselves enter a changed past, are lived in bondage to the march of inalterable law. [JC]

Other works: *Arthur Rex: A Legendary Novel* (**1978**), a fine fantasy.

See also: ALTERNATE WORLDS; INVISIBILITY; SOCIOLOGY; TIME TRAVEL.

BERGER, YVES (1936-   ) French novelist, editor and literary journalist. His ALTERNATE-WORLD novel, *Le sud* (**1962**; trans as *The Garden* **1963**), is set in an antebellum Virginia. [JC]

BERGEY, EARLE K(ULP) (1901-1952) US illustrator known to fans as the "inventor of the brass brassière". For just over a decade, starting with the Aug 1939 cover of STRANGE STORIES, EKB painted covers for some of the less sophisticated and more lurid PULP MAGAZINES, especially those published by Standard Magazines: 58 covers for *Startling Stories*, 59 covers for *TWS* and 13 covers for *Captain Future*, among others. These, often featuring half-dressed pin-up girls in peril, represent the pulp style at its most typical and thus were singled out for ridicule by non-sf readers, and helped give the SF MAGAZINES a rubbishy reputation. In fact EKB was a skilled commercial artist, painted faces well, and was by no means restricted to the subject matter that made him famous. He helped to change the emphasis of cover art, in which he specialized, from gadgetry to people. [PN/JG]

See also: THRILLING WONDER STORIES.

BERGSØE, VILHELM [r] ◊ DENMARK.

BERGSTRESSER, MARTA [s] ◊ Marta RANDALL.

BERK, HOWARD (1926-   ) US writer in whose interesting sf novel, *The Sun Grows Cold* (**1971**), a man whose brain has been tampered with and whose previous lives were disastrous reawakens (◊ SLEEPER AWAKES) in a terrifying future world. He asks to be restored to his amnesia. HB has published in other genres. [JC]

BERKLEY SHOWCASE, THE Original anthology series from Berkley Books, consisting of *The Berkley Showcase: Vol 1: New Writings in Science Fiction and Fantasy* (anth **1980**), *Vol 2* (anth **1980**), *Vol 3* (anth **1981**), *Vol 4* (anth **1981**), all ed Victoria Schochet and John SILBERSACK, and *Vol 5* (anth **1982**), ed Schochet and Melissa Singer. This shortlived but lively series published stories by up-and-comers (Pat CADIGAN, Orson Scott CARD, John KESSEL, Howard WALDROP, Connie WILLIS), established sf gurus (Thomas M. DISCH, R.A. LAFFERTY), and a few surprises from almost outside the ballpark (Marge PIERCY, Eric VAN LUSTBADER). Indeed, some of its work may have been too close to sf's leading edge to be commercial. It was announced in the first issue, unusually, that this "house" anthology did not expect to make money. [PN]

BERLYN, MICHAEL (STEVEN) (1949-   ) US writer and computer-game designer whose first novel, the sf adventure *Crystal Phoenix* (**1980**), received some adverse comment for the amount of female torture it contains. *The Integrated Man* (**1980**) projects a DYSTOPIAN future for urbanized humanity, with a plot based on the shunting of human consciousness into COMPUTER chips, reminiscent in this of John T. SLADEK's *The Müller-Fokker Effect* (**1970**). *Blight* (**1981**), as by Mark Sonders, is an sf/horror novel featuring mutated killer moths. During most of the 1980s, MB restricted himself to the creation of interactive fictions for computers (◊ GAME-WORLDS), including "Oo-Topos" (**1982**), "Cyborg" (**1982**), "Suspended" (**1983**), "Infidel" (**1984**), "Cutthroats" (**1984**), two titles in collaboration with his wife, Muffy McClung Berlyn – "Tass Times in Tonetown" (**1986**) and "Dr Dumont's Wild P.A.R.T.I." (**1988**) – and "Altered Destiny" (**1990**). He then returned to book sf with *The Eternal Enemy* (**1990**), a tale whose dystopian undercurrents are reminiscent of his second novel. Here an ALIEN race, almost magically facile in its use of GENETIC-ENGINEERING techniques to change its members at will, takes a moribund human and transforms him into a being who can breed with them, and perhaps also carry over humanity's inbred capacities as a killing-machine so that the aliens can defend themselves against an insatiable enemy. As with many serious-minded sf writers, MB has some tendency to hamper his effects through the use of generic plotting not well designed to bear the burden of contemplation; but muscle may be felt in his work, and greater focus hoped for. [JC]

See also: ESCHATOLOGY; REINCARNATION.

BERNARD, JOHN Pseudonym of UK writer Anna O'Meara de Vic Beamish (1883-?   ), whose *The New Race of Devils* (**1921**) describes a NEAR-FUTURE German plan to create a new race through artificial insemination. *The King's Missal* (**1934**) as by Noel de Vic

Beamish is a fantasy. [JC]

BERNARD, RAFE (? -?) UK writer whose first sf novel was *The Wheel in the Sky* (**1954**), which datedly concerns itself with the construction of a pre-NASA-style, privately financed space station. He also wrote a *The* INVADERS tie, *The Halo Highway* ∗ (**1967**; vt *Army of the Undead* 1967 US). [JC]

BERNAU, GEORGE (B.) (1945-) US writer whose two sf novels are both ALTERNATE-HISTORY thrillers. In *Promises to Keep* (**1988**) John F. Kennedy recovers from the attempt to assassinate him, and in *Candle in the Wind* (**1990**) Marilyn Monroe survives her semi-accidental overdose. [JC]

BERRY, ADRIAN (1937-) UK science journalist (often in the London *Daily Telegraph*) and occasional sf writer. His sf novels *Koyama's Diamond* (**1982**) and its sequel *Labyrinth of Lies* (**1984**), set in a FAR-FUTURE planetary system with much political intrigue, have some interesting ideas and plot turns, but are written in a lurid style reminiscent of 1930s PULP MAGAZINES. His more important service to sf has been the publication of a number of nonfiction science books about the future (◊ FUTUROLOGY), including the bestselling *The Next Ten Thousand Years: A Vision of Man's Future in the Universe* (**1974**) as well as *The Iron Sun: Crossing the Universe through Black Holes* (**1977**) and *From Apes to Astronauts* (coll **1980**). The topics discussed in these books – mostly to do with physics and speculative technology – are among those much exploited by HARD-SF writers in the 1970s and since. [PN]

See also: BLACK HOLES; TERRAFORMING.

BERRY, BRYAN (1930-1955) UK author who was active for only a few years. Along with such writers as John Russell FEARN, E.C. TUBB and Kenneth BULMER, he contributed many PULP-MAGAZINE-style sf novels to obscure paperback houses, most notably the **Venus** trilogy as by Rolf Garner. *And the Stars Remain* (**1952**) confronts men and Martians with a superior force. *Born in Captivity* (**1952**) presents a rigid post-WWIII society. Other novels include *Return to Earth* (**1951**), *Dread Visitor* (**1952**) and *The Venom Seekers* (**1953**). The **Venus** trilogy – *Resurgent Dust* (**1953**), *The Immortals* (**1953**) and *The Indestructible* (**1954**) – portrays in bold strokes mankind's fate on VENUS after the destruction of life on Earth: the man who eventually eliminates tyranny becomes Lord Kennet of Gryllaar. BB was closely associated with AUTHENTIC SCIENCE FICTION and also with TWO COMPLETE SCIENCE-ADVENTURE BOOKS, both of which published some of his novel-length fiction. "Aftermath" (1952) in the former became "Mission to Marakee" (1953) in the latter; as in the first case the story occupied the space allotted to fiction for an entire issue, it might better be listed as *Aftermath* (**1952**). [JC]

BERRY, JAMES R. (? -) US writer most noted for juveniles, beginning with *Dar Tellum: Stranger from a Distant Planet* (**1973**) for younger children, in which the eponymous ALIEN cures Earth of carbon-dioxide poisoning. *The Galactic Invaders* (**1976** Canada)

and *Quas Starbrite* (**1981**) are sf-adventure novels, and *Magicians of Erianne* (**1988**) is an Arthurian fantasy for older children. [JC]

BERRY, STEPHEN AMES (1947-) US writer whose **John Harrison** sequence of space-WAR adventures comprises *The Biofab War* (**1984**), *The Battle for Terra Two* (**1986**), *The AI War* (**1987**) and *Final Assault* (**1988**); military engagements predominate throughout. [JC]

BERRYMAN, JOHN (*c*1919-1988) US writer and engineer, author of many stories in *ASF* and elsewhere from the late 1930s to the mid-1980s. As Walter Bupp he also wrote a series of linked telekinesis tales (◊ ESP) for *ASF* in the early 1960s. JB is not the poet John Berryman (1914-1972), and Walter Bupp is not a pseudonym for Randall GARRETT, as often listed. [JC]

See also: LINGUISTICS.

BERTIN, EDDY [r] ◊ BENELUX.

BERTIN, JACK Pseudonym of Italian-born writer Giovanni Bertignono (1904-1963), who early moved to the USA and who published frequently from the late 1920s in various PULP MAGAZINES. His only sf novel, *Brood of Helios* (**1966**), is an unremarkable adventure. *The Pyramids from Space* (**1970**) and *The Interplanetary Adventurers* (**1970**), both signed JB and both likewise unremarkable, were in fact written by the executor of his estate, Peter B. Germano. [JC]

BERTRAM, NOEL [s] ◊ R.L. FANTHORPE.

BESANT, Sir WALTER (1836-1901) UK writer known primarily for his work outside the sf field; founder member of the Society of Authors; knighted 1895. His early novels were written in collaboration with James Rice (1843-1882); their *The Case of Mr Lucraft and Other Tales* (coll **1876**) contains several fantasies, including the bizarre title story about a man who leases out his appetite. *The Revolt of Man* (**1882** anon; 1897 as WB) is an anti-suffragette novel depicting a female-dominated society of the future; it exemplifies the sexual attitudes and imagination of the Victorian gentleman in a fashion which modern readers might find unwittingly funny. *The Inner House* (**1888**) is a significant early DYSTOPIA in which a technology of IMMORTALITY results in social stagnation. *The Doubts of Dives* (**1889**; reprinted in *Verbena Camellia Stephanotis* coll **1892**) is an earnest identity-exchange fantasy. *Uncle Jack etc.* (coll **1886**) includes "Sir Jocelyn's Cap", an F. ANSTEY-esque fantasy novella written in collaboration with Walter Herries Pollock. *A Five Years' Tryst* (coll **1902**) includes the sf story "The Memory Cell". WB's abiding interests in social reform and abnormal psychology bring a few of his other novels close to the sf borderline, most notably the dual-personality story *The Ivory Gate* (**1892**); his credulity concerning ESP is responsible for the introduction of (very minor) fantastic elements into several others. [BS]

See also: ANONYMOUS SF AUTHORS; PSYCHOLOGY; SOCIOLOGY.

BESSENYEI, GYÖRGY [r] ◊ HUNGARY.

BES SHAHAR, ELUKI (1956-) US writer who began publishing work of genre interest with "Casablanca" for *Hydrospanner Zero* in 1981; the tale became part of her first novel, *Hellflower* (fixup **1991**), featuring **Butterfly St Cyr**, a female space pilot whose smuggling activities embroil her in an interstellar plot involving dynasties and a young prince. The second novel in the sequence, *Darktraders* (**1992**), is less energetic. [JC]

BEST, (OSWALD) HERBERT (1894-1981) UK author of an sf novel, *The Twenty-Fifth Hour* (**1940**), in which, after a 1965 DISASTER, two survivors – a North American female and a European male – come together to participate in a UTOPIA founded in Alexandria, Egypt. [JC]

See also: WAR.

BESTER, ALFRED (1913-1987) US writer and editor, born into a Jewish family in New York, a city with which he was always closely associated. Educated in both humanities and sciences – including PSYCHOLOGY, perhaps the most important "science" in his sf – at the University of Pennsylvania, AB entered sf when he submitted a story to THRILLING WONDER STORIES. Mort WEISINGER, the editor, helped AB to polish it, and then suggested he submit it for an amateur story competition that *TWS* was running. AB did so and won. The story was "The Broken Axiom" (Apr 1939 *TWS*).

AB published another 13 sf stories to 1942, and then followed his friend Weisinger, along with Otto BINDER, Manly Wade WELLMAN and others, into the field of COMIC books, working on such DC COMICS titles as SUPERMAN, *The Green Lantern* and *Batman*. He worked successfully for four years on comics outlines and dialogue, later working on CAPTAIN MARVEL, and then moved into radio, scripting for such serials as *Charlie Chan* and *The Shadow*. After the intensive course in action plotting this career had given him, AB returned (part-time) to the sf magazines in 1950, by now more mature as a writer. (His main job at the time was scripting the new tv series TOM CORBETT: SPACE CADET.) There ensued over the next six years a series of stories and novels which are considered to be among the greatest creations of genre sf.

AB was never prolific in sf, which was more of a hobby than a career for him, publishing only 13 more short stories – mostly in *FSF* – before 1960. (One of the five "Quintets" in *FSF* Sep 1959 was by AB writing as Sonny Powell.) But these alone would have secured him a place in the sf pantheon. Most of his stories were originally issued in book form in two collections, *Starburst* (coll **1958**) and *The Dark Side of the Earth* (coll **1964**). These collections were reassembled with 6 stories dropped, and one older novella – "Hell is Forever" – and 3 quite recent stories added along with the amusing autobiographical essay "My Affair with Science Fiction" (1975), in two further collections, *The Light Fantastic* (coll **1976**) and *Star Light, Star Bright* (coll **1976**), which were in turn reissued as an omnibus volume, *Starlight: The Great Short Fiction of Alfred Bester* (omni **1976**). This last is the best available collection.

AB's talents were evident from the beginning. At least three stories from his 1939-42 period are memorable: "Adam and No Eve" (1941) (◊ ADAM AND EVE; END OF THE WORLD), "The Push of a Finger" (1942) and "Hell is Forever" (1942). The latter, a long novella for UNKNOWN, exhibits in a slightly sophomoric way the qualities for which AB would later be celebrated: it is cynical, baroque and aggressive, produces hard, bright images in quick succession, and deals with obsessive states of mind. The most notable later story is "Fondly Fahrenheit" (1954), a breathless story of a man and his ANDROID servant whose personalities intermesh in a homicidal *folie à deux*. Also memorable are "Of Time and Third Avenue" (1951), "Disappearing Act" (1953) and "The Men who Murdered Mohammed" (1958), which is perhaps the most concentratedly witty twist on the TIME-PARADOX story ever written. At about the time of this story AB addressed an sf symposium at the University of Chicago; his paper is one of the four reprinted in the anonymously edited *The Science Fiction Novel: Imagination and Social Criticism* (anth **1959**; intro by Basil DAVENPORT).

AB's first two sf novels, *The Demolished Man* (**1953**) and *Tiger! Tiger!* (**1956** UK; rev vt *The Stars My Destination* 1957 US), are among the few genuine classics of genre sf. They are the sf equivalent of the Jacobean revenge drama: both feature malcontent figures, outsiders from society bitterly cognizant of its corruption, but themselves partly ruined by it, just as in *The Revenger's Tragedy* or *The Duchess of Malfi*; like them, too, AB's novels blaze with a sardonic imagery, mingling symbols of decay and new life – rebirth is a recurrent theme of AB's – with a creative profligacy.

The Demolished Man, which won the first HUGO for Best Novel in 1953, tells a story which in synopsis is straightforward: industrialist Ben Reich commits murder (in a society where murder is almost unknown because telepathic ESPERS can detect the idea before the act is carried out), almost gets away with it, is ultimately caught by Esper detective Linc Powell, and is committed to curative brainwashing, "demolition" (◊ CRIME AND PUNISHMENT). It is the pace, the staccato style, the passion and the pyrotechnics that make the novel extraordinary. The future society is evoked in marvellously hard-edged details; the hero is a driven, resourceful man whose obsessions are explained in Freudian terms that might seem too glib if they were given straight, but are evoked with the same New Yorker's painful, ironic scepticism that informs the whole novel. AB's mainstream novel *Who He?* (**1953**; vt *The Rat Race* 1956), about the tv and advertising businesses, sheds some light on the milieu of *The Demolished Man*.

Tiger! Tiger! tells the story of the now legendary Gully Foyle, whose passion for revenge transforms him from an illiterate outcast to a transcendent, ambiguous, quasi-SUPERMAN in "an age of freaks, monsters and grotesques". Like the first novel, this one lives as much through the incidentals of the setting – in a lurid, crumbling, 25th-century world – as in the plot itself, which AB confesses, too modestly, was borrowed from Alexandre Dumas's *The Count of Monte Cristo* (**1844-5**). The first vol of a GRAPHIC-NOVEL version by Howard V. CHAYKIN (adaptation by Byron PREISS), was *The Stars My Destination Vol 1* (graph **1979**); the second vol, though widely bruited, was not in fact published until it appeared, with the first, in *The Stars My Destination* (**1992**).

In the late 1950s AB was taken on by *Holiday* magazine as a feature writer, ultimately becoming senior literary editor, a post he held until the magazine ceased publication in the 1970s, at which time he returned to sf. "The Four-Hour Fugue" (1974) shows the old extraordinary assurance and inventiveness, and just a trace of over-facility. Two decades after his last, his new novel, *The Computer Connection* (1974 *ASF* as "The Indian Giver"; **1975**; vt *Extro* UK), while full of incidental felicities, did not quite recapture the old drive in its ornate story of a group of immortals and an omniscient COMPUTER; perhaps it lacked a natural "Besterman" as focus. The pace and complexity were still there, but somehow looking like self-parody.

The next book, *Golem¹⁰⁰* (**1980**), was more ambitious, had a more authentic Bester flavour, and was regarded by AB as his best novel. It expands "The Four-Hour Fugue" into an extraordinary but overheated tale of the jungle of New York in AD2175, with diabolism, depth psychology (a Monster from the Id), bee superwomen, pheromones, perverse sex, and overall a miasma of death. But the 1960s-style radicalism now looked a little out of date, and what used to be spare and sinewy in his work had begun to seem prolix; the craziness looked like ornamentation rather than what it once was, structural. His last sf novel was *The Deceivers* (**1981**), which features a Synergist hero who can perceive patterns; sadly, but interestingly in the light of AB's fame, the sf press almost unanimously failed to review this, presumably out of respect for his feelings. It is not good. When he died six years later, after a long period of ill health, he willed his house and literary estate to his bartender. The posthumously published *Tender Loving Rage* (**1991**), written more than 20 years earlier, is a mainstream novel set in 1959, and appropriately features a scientist adopted by the New York advertising/tv people.

AB's innovative, ferocious, magpie (his word) talent has certainly been influential in GENRE SF, on writers as disparate as James BLISH, Samuel R. DELANY and Michael MOORCOCK. In many respects his work was a forerunner of CYBERPUNK. He is one of the very few genre-sf writers to have bridged the chasm between the old and the NEW WAVE, by becoming a legendary figure for both – perhaps because in his sf imagery he conjured up, with bravura, both outer and INNER SPACE. [PN]

See also: CONCEPTUAL BREAKTHROUGH; ESP; GALAXY SCIENCE FICTION; GOLDEN AGE OF SF; GOTHIC SF; HISTORY OF SF; HUMOUR; IMAGINARY SCIENCE; LINGUISTICS; *The* MAGAZINE OF FANTASY AND SCIENCE FICTION; NEBULA; OPTIMISM AND PESSIMISM; OUTER PLANETS; PERCEPTION; PSI POWERS; SF IN THE CLASSROOM; SUPERNATURAL CREATURES; TRANSPORTATION; VILLAINS.

BETANCOURT, JOHN GREGORY (1963-   ) US editor and writer who became involved in SMALL-PRESS publishing in his teens, his first professional sf sale – "Vernon's Dragon" for *100 Great Fantasy Short-Short Stories* (anth **1984**) ed Isaac ASIMOV, Terry CARR and Martin H. GREENBERG – being a reprint from a fan magazine. In the early 1980s he worked with editor George SCITHERS at *AMZ*, soon founding a literary agency with Scithers and Darrell SCHWEITZER; in 1987 the three of them relaunched WEIRD TALES. In 1989 JGB became an editor for Byron PREISS Visual Publications, Inc., an important sf packager. His first novel, *Starskimmer* * (**1986**), is a game tie. *Rogue Pirate* (**1987**) is fantasy, as is the more impressive *The Blind Archer* (**1988**), in whose ornate venue the stories assembled in *Slab's Tavern and Other Uncanny Places* (coll **1991** chap) are also set. His first book of direct sf interest, *Johnny Zed* (**1988**), embeds a somewhat desultory political analysis of revolutionary movements in a portrait of a NEAR-FUTURE USA whose Congress has become a hereditary gift of the rich, and whose populace has become lassitudinous. The sf devices of his second novel of interest, *Rememory* (**1990**), include brain-scans and the bio-engineering of humans into animal shapes, but the mystery plot that sends the cat-person protagonist down the mean streets of a corrupt government does not, in itself, generate much interest. JGB seems an author of very ample skill but limited perspective – a sense of his career which, given his clear intelligence and ambition, could change overnight. [JC]

Other works: A tied instalment in the **Dr Bones** enterprise, *Dr Bones #4: The Dragons of Komako* * (**1989**); *Letters of the Alien Publisher* (coll **1991**) with Charles C. RYAN.

As editor: Issues of *Weird Tales*, all with George Scithers and Darrell Schweitzer, are *Weird Tales: Spring 1988*, *Weird Tales #291* (1988) and *Weird Tales #292* (1988); *The Ultimate Frankenstein* (anth **1991**) and *The Ultimate Werewolf* (anth **1991**), both with David Keller, Megan Miller and Byron PREISS.

As Jeremy Kingston: A tied contribution to the **Time Tours** sequence, *Robert Silverberg's Time Tours #6: Caesar's Time Legions* * (**1991**).

As Victor Appleton (house name): *Tom Swift and the Undersea Raiders* * (**1992**).

BETHKE, BRUCE (1955-   ) US writer best known for his short stories, in particular his first professional publication, "Cyberpunk" (1983), which appeared in *AMZ* after circulating in manuscript and almost certainly inspiring Gardner DOZOIS's use of the term CYBERPUNK to designate the new movement. A novel based on this story is projected under the title «Def Cyberpunk» but BB's only book to date is a SHARECROP: *Isaac Asimov's Robot City: Robots and Aliens 5: Maverick* * (**1990**). [JC]

BETHLEN, T.D. [s] ◊ Robert SILVERBERG.

BETTAUER, HUGO [r] ◊ AUSTRIA.

BETTER PUBLICATIONS ◊ CAPTAIN FUTURE; Ned L. PINES; STARTLING STORIES; STRANGE STORIES; THRILLING WONDER STORIES.

BEVAN, ALISTAIR [s] ◊ Keith ROBERTS.

BEVERLEY, BARRINGTON (?   -?   ) UK writer in whose sf novel *The Space Raiders* (**1936**) the League of Nations defends the world from an alien invasion. [JC]
Other work: *The Air Devil* (**1934**).

BEVIS, H(ERBERT) U(RLIN) (1902-   ) US house-painter, author of a series of unremarkable sf adventures including *Space Stadium* (**1970**), which features wargames in space, *The Time Winder* (**1970**), whose protagonists escape killer ROBOTS by TIME TRAVEL, *The Star Rovers* (**1970**), *To Luna with Love* (**1971**) and *The Alien Abductors* (**1972**). [JC]

BEWARE THE BLOB ◊ The BLOB.

BEYER, W(ILLIAM) G(RAY) (?   -?   ) US writer, active before WWII in only one magazine, *The Argosy*, where he published all his novels. *Minions of the Moon* (1939 *Argosy*; **1950**), along with three further serials, "Minions of Mars" (1940), "Minions of Mercury" (1940), and "Minions of the Shadow" (1941), make up the **Minions** series of interplanetary SPACE-OPERA adventures involving humans and aliens. [JC]

BEYNON, JOHN ◊ John WYNDHAM.

BEYOND FANTASY FICTION US DIGEST-size magazine. 10 issues, July 1953-Jan 1955, published by Galaxy Publishing Corp., ed H.L. GOLD.

A companion magazine to GALAXY SCIENCE FICTION, *BFF* was a fantasy magazine conceived in the same spirit as UNKNOWN (to which Gold had contributed). It began promisingly, its first issue featuring such stories as Theodore STURGEON's ". . . And My Fear is Great" and Damon KNIGHT's "Babel II", but could maintain this standard only fitfully. #2 contained Theodore R. COGSWELL's classic "The Wall Around the World". Notable later stories included "The Watchful Poker Chip" by Ray BRADBURY (1954) and "The Green Magician", a **Harold Shea** story by L. Sprague DE CAMP and Fletcher PRATT (1954). The first 8 issues were bimonthly and dated; the last 2, undated, were titled *Beyond Fiction*. *BFF* was drab in appearance with uninspired cover paintings. *Beyond* (anth **1963**), no editor named, reprinted 9 stories. An abridged UK edition of the first 4 issues was published by Strato Publications, 1953-4. [MJE]

BEYOND FICTION ◊ BEYOND FANTASY FICTION.

BEYOND INFINITY US DIGEST-size magazine. 1 issue, Dec 1967, published by I.D. Publications, Hollywood; ed Doug Stapleton. The fantasy element was stronger than the sf in this rapidly aborted and not very strong magazine. [FHP]

BEYOND WESTWORLD ◊ WESTWORLD.

BIAGI, L.D. Pseudonym of US writer Lottie F. Ambrose (?   -?   ), whose sf novel *The Centaurians* (**1911**) amiably mixes SPACE FLIGHT and lost races (◊ LOST WORLDS) at the North Pole. [JC]

About the author: *A Spectrum of Fantasy* (**1980**) by George LOCKE (p33).

"BIBLES" ◊ SHARED WORLDS.

BIBLIOGRAPHIES Until the academic acceptance of sf there was no profit in bibliographies. Compiling them was a labour of love, very often carried out by fans or sometimes by book and magazine dealers. Until recent decades, few academically trained bibliographers paid any attention to fantastic literature; it was only the proliferation of work from about 1975 onwards that justified the publication of *Reference Guide to Science Fiction, Fantasy, and Horror* (**1992**) by Michael Burgess (Robert REGINALD), which annotates and comments upon more than 550 relevant studies.

The Checklist of Fantastic Literature: A Bibliography of Fantasy, Weird and Science Fiction Books Published in the English Language (**1948**) by Everett F. BLEILER, the earliest important bibliography in the field, made no distinction between sf and fantasy, was incomplete and had errors, and contained no information on contents. It was nevertheless invaluable for researchers from the first, although to look at it in 1992 is to contemplate the distance traversed since, both by the field as a whole and, in particular, by its author – who has since concentrated on more specialized bibliographical work (see below). For many years the only comparable effort was *333: A Bibliography of the Science-Fantasy Novel* (**1953** chap) by Joseph H. Crawford Jr (1932-   ) assisted by James J. Donahue and the publisher Donald M. Grant (1927-   ); this, though restricted to the titular total, provided valuable synopses of the 333 selected books. Bleiler's *Checklist* was first added to by Bradford M. DAY in his *The Supplemental Checklist of Fantastic Literature* (**1963**), which contained 3000 additional titles; Bleiler himself then thoroughly reworked his original research, publishing the result as *The Checklist of Science-Fiction and Supernatural Fiction (1800-1948)* (**1978**), which presented, alongside the corrected list, a useful category coding for most books included. But Bleiler's interest had by this point shifted to more specialized studies, and his checklist had in any case been superseded.

Research in a field like sf, the basic texts of which are often elusive, depends initially on the existence of one central tool: the comprehensive checklist. Bleiler's selective version served well for nearly three decades, and Marshall B. TYMN, in *American Fantasy & Science Fiction: Toward a Bibliography of Works Published in the United States, 1948-1973* (**1979**), gave selective coverage up to 1973. In the same year, however, the definitive work was published: this was Reginald's 2-vol *Science Fiction and Fantasy Literature: A Checklist, 1700-1974, with Contemporary Science Fiction Authors II* (**1979**), which listed, according to fairly strict criteria of eligibility, three times the number of titles Bleiler covered and included a biographical dictionary based on Reginald's earlier *Stella Nova: The Contemporary Science Fiction Authors* (**1970**) and *Contemporary Science Fiction Authors* (**1974**). Later Reginald

supplemented the checklist portion of this work in
«Science Fiction & Fantasy Literature: A Bibliography,
1975-1991» (1992) with Mary Wickizer Burgess and
Daryl F. MALLETT, which takes into account some
errors (very few) and omissions from the 1979
volumes while adding almost 22,000 new titles –
more new titles in 17 years, it might be noted, than
had appeared in the previous 250. Although – unlike
Bleiler's later work – the Reginald checklists do not
code cited texts according to the genres and subgenres contained within the broad field of the
fantastic, they are (1992) the central bibliographical
resource for any sf/fantasy library.

Also at the end of the 1970s appeared L.W. CURREY's
*Science Fiction and Fantasy Authors: A Bibliography of
First Printings of their Fiction* (1979), a genuine first-
edition bibliography which covered about 200 of the
principal genre writers (a second volume is projected)
and intensified Reginald's coverage; and George
LOCKE's remarkably accurate (and intriguingly anecdotal) *A Spectrum of Fantasy: The Bibliography and
Biography of a Collection of Fantastic Literature* (1980),
which suggested *en passant* several titles that plausibly supplemented the Reginald *Checklist* (a second
volume of Locke's work is also projected).

Other forms of extensive coverage were of varying
use. The *Dictionary Catalog of the J. Lloyd Eaton
Collection of Science Fiction and Fantasy Literature* (1982)
in 3 vols is a photographic record of the 37,500 cards
recording the 20,000 items then in the J. LLOYD EATON
COLLECTION (it is now badly out of date). From the
beginning of 1988, Kurt Baty has been producing a
comprehensive index in loose-leaf form entitled *The
Whole Science Fiction Data Base Quarterly*; by the end of
1991 about a third of the alphabet had been traversed,
though only in draft form, with very many titles
omitted or only partially ascribed, and it remained to
be seen whether the completed project would in fact
come to pass.

After gaining some control over the field as a
whole, the sf researcher would then find her/himself
needing more specialized aids as well. Sf was for
many years a genre dominated, in the USA at least,
by the MAGAZINES, and magazine indexes are an
essential tool. The publication of an exhaustive index
from Stephen T. Miller and William G. CONTENTO is
projected; but partial indexes do exist, and have
served well. They include: *Index to the Science Fiction
Magazines 1926-50* (1952) by Donald B. DAY; *The Index
of Science Fiction Magazines 1951-1965* (1968) by Norman METCALF or, for the same period, *The MIT Science
Fiction Society's Index to the S-F Magazines* (1966) by
Erwin S. STRAUSS; *Index to the Science Fiction Magazines
1966-70* (1971) by the New England Science Fiction
Association; and *The N.E.S.F.A. Index to the Science
Fiction Magazines and Original Anthologies 1971-1972*
(1973). Since then N.E.S.F.A. has brought out magazine indexes usually on an annual basis and usually
compiled by Anthony R. LEWIS, either alone or in
collaboration. More specialized productions include

*Monthly Terrors: An Index to the Weird Fantasy Maga-
zines Published in the United States and Great Britain*
(1985) by Mike ASHLEY and Frank H. Parnell. Indexes
to individual magazines – like *The Complete Index to
Astounding/Analog* (1981) by Ashley and Terry Jeeves
– are cited in this encyclopedia in the relevant
magazine entries.

Of course stories are not published solely in
magazines. In an ongoing project complementary to
his projected story index, Contento has produced, in
Index to Science Fiction Anthologies and Collections (1978)
and *Index to Science Fiction Anthologies and Collections,
1977-1983* (1984), a highly usable reference source
which, in addition to listing stories not initially
published in magazine form, also covers those
published originally in magazines and for one reason
or another thought worthy of being made more
generally available in book form. His *Indexes*, therefore, are an aid to the researcher, as the stories they
catalogue are both valued and available; but Contento
should be used with caution in this regard. He does
not himself make any qualitative claims about the
stories he lists in this format, nor is he complete
within his declared remit, and no researcher should
assume that unlisted stories are necessarily less
rewarding. Contento's indexes for coverage of the
years after 1983 appear in the LOCUS annuals (see
below).

From yet another angle of approach, Jack L.
CHALKER and Mark OWINGS (1945-   ), in *The Index to
the Science-Fantasy Publishers* (1966; rev vt *Index to the
SF Publishers* 1979; very much exp vt *The Science-
Fantasy Publishers: A Critical and Bibliographic History*
1991), provides a checklist of (and anecdotal commentary on) almost every title released by the
specialist sf houses, arranged by publisher. The 1991
version, 10 times the size of the first edition, gives its
users an invaluable grasp of the shape – though it is
less secure on the detail – of sf PUBLISHING through the
20th century; inconveniently, that first edition has
been several times revised in successive small
unmarked reprintings, with the result that readers
cannot know the status of the volume they have in
front of them.

Two ongoing index series by Hal W. HALL are also
essential. The first, the *Science Fiction Book Review
Index, 1923-1973* (1975), *1974-1979* (1981) and *1980-
1984* (1985), along with its annual supplements –
covering, as of the volume published in 1991, the
years up to 1987 – functions as an accurate if
incomplete bibliography of sf criticism. And Hall's 2-
vol *Science Fiction and Fantasy Reference Index, 1878-
1985* (1987), which incorporates early reference
guides, covers non-review research and criticism in
the field; it was supplemented by *Science Fiction and
Fantasy Research Index, Volume 7* (1987), covering 1986,
and *Volume 8* (1990), covering 1987.

In the late 1980s, perhaps following Contento's
lead, Hall made a significant publishing decision.
Although his *Book Review Index* remained a separate

production, he incorporated his *Reference Index* into Charles N. BROWN's and Contento's ongoing *Locus* annual **Science Fiction, Fantasy, & Horror** series, from the 1988 volume (published **1989**) onwards. The Brown/Contento production – each annual volume being subtitled *A Comprehensive Bibliography of Books and Short Fiction Published in the English Language* – extends from coverage year 1984, and in 1992 seems set to continue indefinitely. Although it does not precisely replace comprehensive bibliographies like Reginald's (see above), it has served to supply sf readers and researchers with an enormous amount of information. Its main deficiency as a research resource lay for several years in the fact that it was based on a localized books-received (rather than a books-published) basis, only books received for review by Brown's *Locus* magazine during a particular calendar year tending to be entered in the Brown/Contento volume for that year. As there is a very considerable difference between books *received* during a year by one magazine and books actually *published* during that year, early volumes of the series needed some getting used to. It is, however, clear that in recent years a considerable effort has been made to search out books not actually received for review, and, once the researcher understands this gradual change for the better through successive volumes, Brown/Contento begins to seem even more irreplaceable.

Moving from comprehensive bibliographies whose remit is to encompass the field rather than to evaluate it, we come to research aids which are designed to provide a critical commentary. *The Encyclopedia of Science Fiction and Fantasy through 1968* in 3 vols (**1974, 1978, 1982**) by Donald H. TUCK engagingly annotated a wide variety of texts, but its author frequently cross-referred readers to Bleiler for fuller listings. The first edition of the *Encyclopedia of Science Fiction* (**1979**) ed Peter NICHOLLS attempted to list or mention all sf or fantasy books published by the approximately 1700 fiction authors treated, but the ascriptions in that edition and in this second edition (which treats about 3000 authors) are not arranged in checklist form, and are not intended primarily for bibliographical reference. *Twentieth-Century Science-Fiction Writers* (**1981**; rev 1986; rev 1991), first 2 edns ed Curtis C. SMITH, 3rd edn ed Paul E. Schellinger (1962-   ) and Noelle Watson (1958-   ), though valuable for its biographical and critical sections, could not be recommended for its checklists, which were eccentrically conceived, inaccurate, and left complacently uncorrected from one edition to the next. *The New Encyclopedia of Science Fiction* (**1988**) ed James E. GUNN lists without bibliographic detail selected titles by those authors (about 500) given entries.

Broadest in scope of the non-encyclopedic projects are the three volumes ed Neil BARRON. The most relevant of these is *Anatomy of Wonder: A Critical Guide to Science Fiction* (**1976**; exp 1981; further exp 1987), which is a selective (but very broad) bibliography of the field, complete with critical annotations on each volume chosen. The other Barron productions, *Fantasy Literature: A Reader's Guide* (**1990**) and *Horror Literature: A Reader's Guide* (**1990**), are smaller and less definitive; but, it can be presumed, will also grow. Bibliography-based studies of particular periods have begun to appear, to date concentrating – very appropriately, considering the sf field's state of ignorance a decade ago about its earlier years – on the 19th and early 20th centuries. Darko SUVIN's *Victorian Science Fiction in the UK: The Discourses of Knowledge and of Power* (**1983**) and Thomas D. CLARESON's *Science Fiction in America, 1870s-1930s: An Annotated Bibliography of Primary Sources* (**1984**) supply complementary coverages from widely differing critical perspectives. And Everett F. Bleiler, in his enormous *Science-Fiction: The Early Years* (dated 1990 but **1991**) provides what may be a definitive coverage of the period up to 1930 in the form of story synopses.

Some thematic bibliographies had begun to appear before the end of the 1970s, including *Atlantean Chronicles* (**1971**) by Henry M. Eichner, *Voyages in Space: A Bibliography of Interplanetary Fiction 1801-1914* (**1975**) by George Locke, and *Tale of the Future* (**1961**; exp 1972; further exp 1978) by I.F. CLARKE. More appeared in the 1980s, including Paul Brians's *Nuclear Holocaust: Atomic War in Fiction, 1895-1984* (**1987**) and Lyman Tower SARGENT's *British and American Utopian Literature, 1516-1985* (**1988**). But there remains room for much further work of this sort.

Specialized bibliographies of individual authors have proliferated since the late 1970s (many are cited at the foot of the relevant author entries in this encyclopedia), often being published by sf houses like BORGO PRESS and STARMONT HOUSE, or by individuals like Phil STEPHENSEN-PAYNE in collaboration with Gordon BENSON Jr and like Chris DRUMM, or by academic presses like GARLAND, G.K. Hall and Meckler. Several pseudonym guides specifically devoted to sf and fantasy writers have also appeared, including James A. Rock's not entirely reliable but intriguing *Who Goes There* (**1979**) and Roger ROBINSON's fuller *Who's Hugh?* (**1987**). Interestingly, although the fan bibliographers in general exhibit a wide variety of ascription techniques (some of these being of Rube Goldbergian complexity), they have often accomplished the most interesting work, and their productions are very much more likely to be up-to-date than those which appear, sometimes years after completion, from the staider firms.

No volume like this encyclopedia could be properly written without the benefit of original research on the part of its authors. But, equally, no volume like this encyclopedia could hope to exist without the constant support and reassurance of every book mentioned above, and of 10 times again as many. The editors of this book are in debt to them all; specific acknowledgements can be found in the Introduction. [JC/PN]

BICKHAM, JACK M(ILES) (1930-   ) US writer who began publishing sf with *Kane's Odyssey* (**1976**

Canada) as by Jeff Clinton, and who later wrote two sf novels under his own name. *ARIEL* (**1984**) posits a COMPUTER whose AI is both alarming and charming. *Day Seven* (**1988**) is a TECHNOTHRILLER. [JC]

BIEMILLER, CARL L(UDWIG Jr) (1912-1979) US businessman, journalist and writer, of sf interest for his two series of novels for older children: the **Jonny** sequence comprising *The Magic Ball from Mars* (**1953**) and *Starboy* (**1956**); and, more interestingly, the post-HOLOCAUST **Hydronauts** sequence – *The Hydronauts* (**1970**), *Follow the Whales: The Hydronauts Meet the Otter People* (**1973**) and *Escape from the Crater* (**1974**) – focusing on the aquatic adventures of a group of trainees in the Ranger Service, which controls oceanic food production after radiation has devastated land-based farming. [JC]

BIERBOWER, AUSTIN (1844-1913) US writer whose anthropological (◊ ANTHROPOLOGY) sf novel, *From Monkey to Man, or Society in the Tertiary Age: A Story of the Missing Link* (**1894**), suggests the Ice Age as the effective cause of the Missing Link's expulsion from the Garden of Eden, and struggles with snakes as the basis for the symbol of the Serpent as evil. [JC]

See also: EVOLUTION; ORIGIN OF MAN.

BIERCE, AMBROSE (GWINETT) (1842-*c*1914) US journalist and writer of short stories and SATIRES, deeply affected by his experiences in the American Civil War (he was breveted major for bravery and wounded twice). Like Bret Harte (1836-1902), he went to California and became a journalist, and also like Harte he soon went abroad, spending 1872-6 in the UK, publishing several volumes of sketches as Dod Grile, most notably the savage little fables assembled as *Cobwebs from an Empty Skull* (coll dated 1874 but **1873** UK; vt *Cobwebs: Being the Fables of Zambri, the Parsee c*1873 UK); but afterwards – unlike Harte, who had permanently departed the thin cultural pickings there – he returned to California. At the close of 1913, after a hectic career and some notably intemperate journalism, he disappeared into Mexico, then in the middle of its own civil war. He is perhaps best known for *The Cynic's Word Book* (coll **1906**; vt *The Devil's Dictionary* 1911; exp vt *The Enlarged Devil's Dictionary* 1967), a collection of brilliantly cynical word "definitions". His numerous sketches and stories far more closely approach the canons of FANTASY than of sf, though, like Mark TWAIN's similar efforts, the speculative environment they create is often sufficiently displaced to encourage the interest of sf readers. AB's single most famous tale, "An Occurrence at Owl Creek Bridge", in which a condemned spy believes he has escaped the rope and returned to his wife the instant after his fall from the bridge and before the noose tightens, appears in *Tales of Soldiers and Civilians* (coll **1891**; vt *In the Midst of Life* 1892 UK; exp under first title 1898 US). The early ROBOT story "Moxon's Master", perhaps the closest thing to genuine sf he ever wrote, in which a SCIENTIST's death is apparently caused by a chess-playing automaton, appears in *Can Such Things Be?* (coll **1893**). The same

volume contains the notable story of monstrous INVISIBILITY, "The Damned Thing", which offers a scientific explanation of the phenomenon, and "Charles Ashmore's Trail", the story of a man who vanishes, much as AB seemed to do himself, into another DIMENSION. This and such similar volumes as *Fantastic Fables* (coll **1899**) have since been republished in a number of forms. *The Collected Writings of Ambrose Bierce* (coll **1946**) is valuable, though not complete; *Ghost and Horror Stories of Ambrose Bierce* (coll **1964**, ed Everett F. BLEILER) is probably the best single assemblage of his works of interest to the reader of sf or fantasy. *The Collected Short Stories* (coll **1970**) and *The Devil's Advocate: An Ambrose Bierce Reader* (coll **1987**) are also of value. [JC/PN]

Other works: *The Fiend's Delight* (coll **1873** UK) and *Nuggets and Dust Panned Out in California* (coll **1873** UK), both as Dod Grile.

About the author: *Ambrose Bierce, the Devil's Lexicographer* (**1951**) by Paul Fatout; *Ambrose Bierce* (**1970**) by M.C. Grenander.

See also: GOTHIC SF; HORROR IN SF; HUMOUR; PARANOIA.

BIG DUMB OBJECTS An unfailingly popular theme in sf is the discovery, usually by humans, of vast enigmatic objects in space or on other planets. These have normally been built by a mysterious, now-disappeared race of ALIEN intellectual giants, and humans can only guess at their purpose, though the very fact of being confronted by such artefacts regularly modifies or confounds their mental programming and brings them that much closer to a CONCEPTUAL BREAKTHROUGH into a more transcendent state of intellectual awareness (*see also* SENSE OF WONDER).

The enormous constructs described in the titles and contents of Larry NIVEN's *Ringworld* (**1970**) and Bob SHAW's *Orbitsville* (**1975**) are typical: artificial biospheres orbiting alien suns (Shaw's is a DYSON SPHERE) and having a surface area millions of times that of Earth. Not so big but every bit as enigmatic is the derelict SPACESHIP Rama, a still-functioning technological artefact hugely in advance of anything we could build, in Arthur C. CLARKE's *Rendezvous with Rama* (**1973**). More recently Greg BEAR topped this with another space habitat, bigger on the inside than the outside, one section of which is infinite in extent, projecting through time as well as space, in *Eon* (**1985**) and *Eternity* (**1988**); exhausted by the sheer problems of scale he paused in the hiatus between these books to write *The Forge of God* (**1987**) in which we are visited by alien spacecraft modestly disguised as very small mountains.

John VARLEY's **Gaean** trilogy – *Titan* (**1979**), *Wizard* (**1980**) and *Demon* (**1984**) – is also set in a space habitat, this one as large as a medium-sized moon, containing a whole set of lesser, but still biggish, dumb objects within, including the convenient staircases attached to its 600km (375-mile) spokes and at one point a 15m (50ft) Marilyn Monroe. The habitat is owned by, and in effect is an extension of the body of, a "goddess", Gaea, herself a construct (makers unknown) but sentient (◊ GODS AND DEMONS). This makes her a LIVING WORLD and hence not truly dumb. Self-awareness in BDOs, Varley correctly calculated, was the next logical step.

BDOs go back a long way in the history of written sf: the sun and planets within the Earth in Ludvig HOLBERG's *Nicolai Klimii iter Subterraneum* (**1741** in Latin; trans as *A Journey to the World Under-Ground by Nicolas Klimius*, **1742**), not actually artificial but still awesome, are proto-BDOs.

BDOs have proved surprisingly difficult to create in film. The difficulty is one of scale: the screen itself is not huge, so tiny humans have to be superimposed on BDOs in order to create the apparent enormity through contrast. Surprisingly, given the expertise of special-effects crews through the 1980s and the nearly universal use of the wide-screen format, one of the very best BDOs preceded all this (in a smaller format) by decades. This was the enigmatic machinery of the Krel in FORBIDDEN PLANET (1956), extending in a perspective to the vanishing point.

BDOs can also be plural in nature, and not restricted to orbiting a solitary star. There are many of these, a good example, demonstrating the recent popularity of grand-scale sentience, being "the swarm of the ten thousand moon-brains of the Solid State Entity" in David ZINDELL's *Neverness* (**1988**). (Many BDOs, as here, have been built by quasi-gods.) Charles SHEFFIELD's dubious strategy in *Summertide: Book One of the Heritage Universe* (**1990**), whose title gives fair warning, is to have 1200 or so gigantic artefacts scattered through our spiral arm of the Galaxy, necessitating a number of quotes from the *"Lang Universal Artifact Catalog* Fourth Edition". This comes close to BDO self-parody. To be fair, Sheffield concentrates on only one, a mildly spectacular bridge connecting the two worlds of a double-planet system.

The most endearing aspect of BDO stories is the disjunction between the gigantic scale of the BDO and the comparatively trite fictional events taking place on, in or about it. The sf imagination usually, if charmingly, falls short at this point, and many BDOs become backdrops for soap operas. For all that, they retain an archetypal power, no matter what crudenesses they may encompass. Sf's much vaunted SENSE OF WONDER is seldom more potently evoked than in a good BDO story. The mystery, only to be explained by a new Carl Gustav Jung, is why, even when these tales are awash with a bathetic failure to live up to their own heroic ambitions, they nearly always work.

The BDO story has certainly become a new sub-genre within sf, its parameters already clearly defined. Newspaper critics of sf, in the face of the stupendous, have shown a shameful failure of creativity in not having found an adequate neologism to describe the BDO genre in a single, terse word. It is not wholly certain which critic first used the phrase "Big Dumb Object" to describe the subject of these tales – it may have been Roz KAVENEY in "Science Fiction in the 1970s" in FOUNDATION #22, 1981 – but the term is now commonplace in describing megalotropic sf. [PN]

BIGFOOT AND THE HENDERSONS ◊ HARRY AND THE HENDERSONS.

BIGGLE, LLOYD Jr (1923-) US author and musicologist, with a PhD in musicology from the University of Michigan. His interest in MUSIC and the other ARTS, perhaps watered down more than necessary in an effort to make such concerns palatable to his readers, appears throughout his sf, which began to appear in 1956 with "Gypped", on a music theme, in *Gal*. His first novel, *The Angry Espers* (1959 *AMZ* as "A Taste of Fire"; rev with cuts restored **1961** dos), features an Earthman involved in complicated adventures on an alien planet, and sets the tone for much of his subsequent work in the field. The **Jan Darzek** sequence – *All the Colors of Darkness* (**1963**), *Watchers of the Dark* (**1966**), *This Darkening Universe* (**1975**), *Silence is Deadly* (**1977**) and *The Whirligig of Time* (**1979**) – recounts the adventures of a late-20th-century private eye who moves from investigating aliens to governing the Council of the Supreme, which itself governs the home Galaxy; by the third volume he is pitted against the inimical Udef, a Dark Force destroying civilization after civilization in the Smaller Magellanic Cloud. A similarly palatable Galaxy (LB's clearest affinity in his novels is to writers like Murray LEINSTER) provides a backdrop and sounding board for the **Cultural Survey** featured in *The Still, Small Voice of Trumpets* (1961 *ASF* as "Still Small Voice; exp **1968**) and *The World Menders* (**1971**). *Monument* (1962 *ASF*; exp **1974**) is an effective (though ultimately amiable) space-opera parable about imperialism. Selections of his stories, most of which are competent but undemanding, appear in *The Rule of the Door and Other Fanciful Regulations* (coll **1967**; vt *Out of the Silent Sky* 1977; vt *The Silent Sky* 1979 UK), *The Metallic Muse* (coll **1972**), which contains some of his best arts-related tales, and *A Galaxy of Strangers* (coll **1976**). As a writer of SPACE OPERA, LB is seldom less than relaxed and entertaining; it may be intellectual snobbery to ask for anything more, but his stories often convey the sense of an unrealized greater potential, and Orson Scott CARD argues his merits in his introduction to *The Tunesmith* (1957 *Gal*; **1991** chap dos). LB has been an active member of the SCIENCE FICTION WRITERS OF AMERICA, and edited *Nebula Award Stories Seven* (anth **1972**). [JC]

Other works: *The Fury Out of Time* (**1965**); *The Light that Never Was* (**1972**); *Alien Main* (**1985**) with T.L. SHERRED (*whom see for details*); two **Sherlock Holmes** pastiches – *The Quailsford Inheritance: A Memoir of Sherlock Holmes from the Papers of Edward Porter Jones, his Late Assistant* * (**1986**) and *The Glendower Conspiracy: A Memoir of Sherlock Holmes from the Papers of Edward Porter Jones, his Late Assistant* * (**1990**); *Interface for Murder* (**1987**) and *A Hazard of Losers* (**1991**), detective novels.

See also: ESP EVOLUTION; MATTER TRANSMISSION; NEBULA; PASTORAL; SOCIAL DARWINISM.

BIG HEART AWARD ◊ AWARDS.

BIG MEAT EATER Film (1982). BCD Entertainment. Dir Chris Windsor, starring George Dawson, Big Miller, Howard Taylor, Andrew Gillies. Screenplay Windsor, Laurence Keane. 82 mins. Colour.

This Canadian musical pastiche of sf and horror films – a sort of designer midnight movie about an INVASION by two ALIENS of a small town in the 1950s – waves its low budget like a flag and, despite incoherences, is cheerfully enjoyable. The aliens are played by toy robots. The plot, which defies description, involves a tank of disgusting waste from the butcher's shop in which is being formed radioactive baloneum (much desired by the aliens), a huge, murderous butcher's assistant who sings jolly songs like "Bagdad Boogie", the reanimated corpse of Mayor Rigatoni, a universal language, a car turned into a SPACESHIP, and other absurdities. The target audience appears similar to that for The ROCKY HORROR PICTURE SHOW. Everyone in the film seems to be having a very good time. [PN]

See also: MUSIC.

BIG MESS, THE ◊ *Der* GROSSE VERHAU.

BIG PULL, THE UK tv serial (1962). BBC. Prod Terence Dudley. Written Robert Gould. Starring William Dexter, June Tobin, Susan Purdie, Frederick Treves. 6 30-min episodes. B/w.

This fondly remembered thriller about alien INVASION, quite generously budgeted, has an astronaut returning to Earth after contamination by something strange in the Van Allen belts. There follow a series of strange "fusions" in which pairs of humans, one "dead" and one disappeared, return as single, altered individuals. [PN]

BIJO TO EKITAI NINGEN (vt *The H-Man;* vt *Beautiful Women and the Hydrogen Man)* Film (1958). Toho. Dir Inoshiro Honda, starring Yumi Shirakawa, Kenji Sahara, Akihiko Hirata, Koreya Senda. Screenplay Takeshi Kimura, based on a story by Hideo Kaijo. 87 mins, cut to 79 mins. Colour.

This Japanese film is, coincidentally, similar to *The* BLOB (also 1958) but is more ingenious and sinister. Fishermen examining a drifting freighter find only empty suits of clothing – empty except for the captain's uniform, from which a pool of green slime emerges and immediately runs up the leg of the nearest fisherman to dissolve him on the spot. The freighter has entered a cloud of fallout from an H-bomb and the crew has been transformed into a group organism. The monster reaches Tokyo but, unlike Toho's typical prehistoric MONSTERS (also awakened by radiation; ◊ GOJIRA), does not knock over buildings; instead it slithers in and out of drains, under doors and through windows, dissolving and absorbing anyone it can catch. There are good special effects by Eiji Tsuburaya, moody photography in the sewers, and rather too much attention paid to a subplot involving gangsters; all in all, a good, slightly

surreal *film noir.* [JB]

BILAL, ENKI (1951-) Yugoslav/French illustrator, a very distinctive, innovative and original creator of sensuous, decadent futures. EB was born in Belgrade, moving with his family to France in 1961. He attended the Académie des Beaux Arts briefly in the early 1970s. In 1971 he won a competition to create an sf COMIC-strip story run by the magazine *Pilote,* in which he subsequently published a number of strips later collected in book form as *L'appel des étoiles* ["The Call of the Stars"] (graph coll **1974**; vt *Le bol maudit* ["The Cursed Bowl"] 1982). A further collection was *Mémoires d'outre espace* (graph coll **1978**; trans as *Outer States* **1990** US). In 1973 he met and teamed up with sf writer Pierre Christin (1938-) to produce 5 graphic novels: *La croisière des oubliés* (graph **1975**; trans in *Heavy Metal* Apr-Nov 1982 as "The Voyage of Those Forgotten"), *Le vaisseau de pierre* (graph **1976**; trans in *Heavy Metal* July-Nov 1980 as "Progress"), *La ville qui n'existait pas* (graph **1977**; trans in *Heavy Metal* Mar-Sep 1983 as "The City that Didn't Exist"), *Les phalanges de l'ordre noir* (graph **1979**; trans as *The Ranks of the Black Order* **1989** US) and *Partie de chasse* (graph **1982**; trans in *Heavy Metal* June 1984-Mar 1985 as "The Hunting Party"). He collaborated with writer Pierre Dionnet to produce *Exterminateur 17* (graph **1979**; trans in *Heavy Metal* Oct 1977-Mar 1978 as *Exterminator 17;* **1986**). In 1981 he began to write and draw an as yet unfinished trilogy, so far consisting of *La foire aux immortels* (graph **1983**; trans as *Gods in Chaos* **1985**) and *La femme piegé* (graph **1986**; trans as *The Woman Trap* **1986**). In 1989-90 he collaborated with Christin on a series of reportage fictions from five different cities, under the series title **Coeurs sanglants** ["Bleeding Hearts"], for which his illustrations comprised photographs with additional features drawn or painted in. Since then (until mid-1992) he has published only a series of limited-edition prints.

EB has collaborated with French film-maker Alain Resnais, providing set designs for *La vie est un roman* (1983; vt *Life is a Bed of Roses*), and contributed design work to Michael Mann's film *The Keep* (1983) and to the film version of *The Name of the Rose* (1986), based on the novel by Umberto ECO. He also directed the sf movie *Bunker Palace Hotel* (1990), a thriller set in the future and involving ROBOTS. [RT]

See also: HEAVY METAL; ILLUSTRATION; MÉTAL HURLANT.

BILDERDIJK, WILLEM (1756-1831) Dutch writer of poetry and nonfiction on many subjects. His one work of fiction was the novella *Kort verhaal van eene aanmerklijke luchtreis en nieuwe planeetokdekking* (**1813** anon; trans Paul Vincent as *A Short Account of a Remarkable Aerial Voyage and Discovery of a New Planet* **1989** UK), in which a balloonist is cast away on a small satellite orbiting within the Earth's atmosphere. Its flora and fauna are described, and he finds the remains of an earlier castaway before undertaking a perilous homeward journey. The text acknowledges a debt to the satirical tradition of FANTASTIC VOYAGES, but is authentic sf, and has good claims to be considered the first such work. [BS]

BILENKIN, DMITRI (ALEKSANDROVICH) (1933-1987) Russian geologist and author of both fiction and popular-science books. For most of his career he concentrated on short stories – assembled as *Marsianskii Priboi* ["The Surf of Mars"] (coll 1967), *Notch Kontrabandoi* ["Night of Contraband"] (coll 1971), *Proverka NA Razumonst'* ["Test for a Reason"] (coll 1974), *Snega Olimpa* ["The Snows of Olympus"] (coll 1980), *Litso V Tolpe* ["A Face in the Crowd"] (coll 1985) and *Sila sil'nykh* ["The Power of Power"] (coll 1986) – which were generally more scientific than fictional but never boring or ill written. Some of his typical work was assembled as *The Uncertainty Principle* (coll trans Antonina W. Bouis 1978 US); some stories also appeared in *World's Spring* (anth 1981 US) ed Vladimir GAKOV. DB's longer works are *Pustynia Zhizni* ["The Life Desert"] (1984), a provoking comparison of different historical/cultural human types on a future Earth transformed by mysterious "timequakes", and an intellectual SPACE OPERA, *Prikliuchenia Polynova* ["Polynov's Adventures"] (1986). [VG]

BILL & TED'S BOGUS JOURNEY ◊ BILL & TED'S EXCELLENT ADVENTURE.

BILL & TED'S EXCELLENT ADVENTURE Film (1989). Interscope Communications/Soisson-Murphey/De Laurentiis. Dir Stephen Herek, starring Keanu Reeves, Alex Winter and George Carlin. Screenplay Chris Matheson (Richard Christian MATHESON), Ed Solomon. 89 mins. Colour.

Because the tranquillity of future life depends on the cultural changes brought about by a late-20th-century rock band, Wyld Stallyns, a TIME MACHINE is sent back to help the two teenaged future bandleaders pass their history test, thus ensuring their continuing partnership. The boys successfully collect Abraham Lincoln, Genghis Khan, Joan of Arc, Napoleon, etc., to give colour to their history presentation. This charming, silly film, made by a relative newcomer who had previously directed CRITTERS (1986), does not strain for credibility, but within its own relaxed, adolescent terms is done with great conviction. The running joke is linguistic: the boys speak a Southern Californian argot, "Valley Speak", so that, for example, bad things are "heinous" and "egregious", good things "excellent" and "bodacious". Their innocence (and ignorance) enables them, with a simple "Party on, dudes", to survive perilous situations. There is a bodacious new twist on the TIME PARADOX, and a splendid scene where Napoleon discovers the joys of water slides.

The sequel, *Bill and Ted's Bogus Journey* (1991), dir Pete Hewitt but with the same screenwriters, has the two boys visiting Hell and Heaven and outwitting the Grim Reaper (William Sadler) and a megalomaniac leader (Joss Ackland). Though amusing, it lacks the freshness of its predecessor. [PN]

See also: CINEMA.

BILLIAS, STEPHEN (?   -) US writer whose first novel, *The American Book of the Dead* (1987), makes use

of Zen points of view to approach an understanding of holocaust. *Quest for the 36* (1988) rather similarly convokes the 36 just men from Jewish folklore to see if, together again, they can save the world from fantasy-tinged chaos. SB's third and fourth novels were ties: *Deryni Challenge: A Crossroads Adventure in the World of Katherine Kurtz's Deryni* * (1988), and *Rune Sword #4: Horrible Humes* * (1991). [JC]

BINDER, EANDO Most famous of the joint pseudonyms used by the brothers Earl Andrew Binder (1904-1965) and Otto Oscar Binder (1911-1975), though they both used other pseudonyms as well; after about 1940, when Earl became inactive as a writer, Otto continued to sign himself EB, so that some EB books are collaborative and some by Otto alone. Together, the brothers also wrote 11 stories as John Coleridge and one as Dean D. O'Brien. Alone, Otto also wrote as Gordon A. Giles and, later, as Ione Frances (or Ian Francis) Turek, did some work under the house name Will GARTH, and finally published a couple of novels under his own name. A third brother, Jack, an illustrator, did much of the early drawing on CAPTAIN MARVEL, which was regularly scripted by Otto.

The two brothers' best-known works were all published as by EB, beginning with "The First Martian" for *AMZ* in 1932. The **Adam Link** series, by Otto alone, is EB's most important work in the sf field: Adam Link, a sentient ROBOT, narrates his own tales, quite feelingly. Most of his story appears in *Adam Link – Robot* (1939-42 *AMZ*; fixup 1965); uncollected stories, also from *AMZ*, are "Adam Link Fights a War" (1940), *Adam Link in the Past* (1941 *AMZ*; 1950 chap Australia) and "Adam Link Faces a Revolt" (1941). Link is highly anthropomorphic; though Isaac ASIMOV's somewhat more austere sense of the nature of robots and robotics was soon to establish itself in the sf field as an almost unbreakable convention, the **Adam Link** sequence is an important predecessor, significantly treating its robot hero (and his wife, Eve Link) with sympathy. The brothers' other main series, the **Anton York** tales, all collected in book form as *Anton York, Immortal* (1937-40 *TWS*; fixup 1965), tells how Anton and his wife achieve IMMORTALITY and live with it. Also as EB, the brothers published less interesting magazine serials in the 1930s which were only gradually to see book publication. Notable among them are *Enslaved Brains* (1934 *Wonder Stories*; rev 1951 *Fantastic Story Quarterly*; 1965) and *Lords of Creation* (1939 *Argosy*; 1949); in the latter, Overlords rule Earth but are resisted with ultimate success. As Gordon A. Giles, Otto wrote a series for *TWS* 1937-42 (the last story as by EB) in which a spaceship from Earth explores the Solar System, finding Martian pyramids on each planet; known as the **Via** series (after their individual titles, which always begin with "Via"), these stories were assembled as *Puzzle of the Space Pyramids* (fixup 1971) as by EB. Alone and in collaboration, Otto wrote a large number of additional stories that were not part of any sequence; appearing in the PULP MAGAZINES 1933-42, these were typical of the field before the revolution in quality symbolized (and in part caused) by the arrival of John W. CAMPBELL Jr at *ASF*. After 1940, Otto did script work on both **Captain Marvel** and SUPERMAN comics, and late in life he published under his own name a graphic-novel version of Jules VERNE's *The Mysterious Island* (graph **1974**). Though his fiction production decreased, he did considerable nonfiction work as well as taking on editorial tasks. He became interested in UFOS. He began publishing sf stories again, briefly, 1953-4, but a significant proportion of the books published in the 1960s and 1970s contain material from before WWII. [JC]

Other works: *The Cancer Machine* (**1940** chap); *Martian Martyrs* (*c*1942 chap) and *The New Life* (*c*1942 chap), both as by John Coleridge; *The Three Eternals* (**1939** *TWS*; **1949** chap Australia); *Where Eternity Ends* (**1939** *Science Fiction*; **1950** chap Australia); *Dracula* * (graph **1966**) with Craig Tennis; *The Avengers Battle the Earth-Wrecker* * (**1967**) as OOB; the **Saucer** series comprising *Menace of the Saucers* (**1969**) and *Night of the Saucers* (**1971**); *The Impossible World* (**1939** *Startling Stories*; **1970**); *Five Steps to Tomorrow* (**1940** *Startling Stories*; **1970**); *The Double Man* (**1971**); *Get Off My World* (**1971**); *Secret of the Red Spot* (**1971**); *Terror in the Bay* (**1971**) as Ione Frances Turek; *The Mind from Outer Space* (**1972**); *The Forgotten Colony* (**1972**) as OOB; *The Hospital Horror* (**1973**) as OOB; *The Frontier's Secret* (**1973**) as Ian Francis Turek, associational.

See also: ADAM AND EVE; COMICS; DC COMICS; EC COMICS; THRILLING WONDER STORIES; TIME PARADOXES.

BINDER, EARL ANDREW [r] ◊ Eando BINDER.

BINDER, JACK [r] ◊ Eando BINDER.

BINDER, OTTO O. [r] ◊ Eando BINDER.

BING, JON [r] ◊ SCANDINAVIA.

BINGHAM, CARTER Pseudonym of Bruce Bingham Cassiday (1920-   ), US editor and writer, who worked as editor with various PULP MAGAZINE publishers before going freelance in 1954. His three sf works are ties: *Gorgo* * (**1960**), *Flash Gordon 4: The Time Trap of Ming XIII* * (**1974**), as by Con STEFFANSON, and *Flash Gordon 5: The Witch Queen of Mongo* * (**1974**). The first, based on the film GORGO (1959), is notable for the added sex scenes, a custom of Monarch's film adaptations. [PN]

See also: FLASH GORDON; Dean OWEN.

BIOLOGICAL ENGINEERING ◊ GENETIC ENGINEERING.

BIOLOGY The growth of knowledge in the biological sciences has lagged behind that in the physical sciences; Newton's synthesis of PHYSICS and ASTRONOMY anticipated the linking of biology and chemistry by 200 years. The age of mechanical inventions began in the early 19th century, that of biological inventions is only just beginning, in the wake of the elucidation (during the 1960s) of the "genetic code" which controls naturally occurring biological processes of manufacture. Writers of speculative fiction have always been interested in biological hypotheses

but, while the fundamentals of the science still remained mysterious, their handling of them was of necessity markedly different from their deployment of ideas borrowed from physical science. It is only in the last 20-30 years that sf writers have begun thinking seriously about bio*technology* (◊ TECHNOLOGY), and the prospect of a usurpation of those mechanisms of organic production previously the sole prerogative of natural species has not been universally welcomed. As speculative writers have awakened to the awesome possibilities inherent in the notion of GENETIC ENGINEERING there has been a compensating investment of concepts like ECOLOGY and the biosphere with a quasireligious significance. James Lovelock's observations regarding the existence of long-term homeostatic mechanisms in the biosphere have helped to re-personify the biosphere as "Gaia", whose suitability as an object of worship seems to be taken seriously by many. There is in modern sf an evident dialectical tension between opposing trends towards the demystification and remystification of biological ideas.

Early works of PROTO SCIENCE FICTION which feature biological speculations include Johannes KEPLER's *Somnium* (**1634**), which concludes with an interesting attempt to design a lunar biology, and Francis BACON's *New Atlantis* (**1629**), which foresees significant advances in MEDICINE and agronomy. The positive outlook of the latter was, however, rarely found in works more obviously fictional. Even the anticipation of progress in medicine was capable of generating a particularly intimate kind of anxiety. Where experiments in physical science tended to be seen, even by cynics who thought no good could come of them, as perfectly legitimate adventures of human inquiry, those in human biology frequently seemed blasphemous. The undeniable fascination which many writers found in the possibilities of biological science is characteristically tinged with a sense of threat, if not an attitude of horror. This is very evident in Mary SHELLEY's *Frankenstein* (**1818**), whose eponymous hero is led to despair and destruction by the monster he creates, and in several of Nathaniel HAWTHORNE's allegorical stories, particularly "The Birthmark" (1843) and "Rappaccini's Daughter" (1844), where experiments on people have tragic results. Later examples of the same reactionary response include Robert Louis STEVENSON's *Strange Case of Dr Jekyll and Mr Hyde* (**1886**) and Harriet STARK's *The Bacillus of Beauty* (**1900**). This suggestion of blasphemy is one of the reasons why envisaged technologies that produce such at least superficially desirable effects as IMMORTALITY get such a bad press in fiction.

The biological idea most widely discussed in the late 19th century was, of course, EVOLUTION, and the conflict of ideas provoked by that subject was an important stimulus to the development of sf. The response to the controversy took several forms. Evolutionary speculation turned towards both the

FAR FUTURE and the distant past (◊ ANTHROPOLOGY; ORIGIN OF MAN). The notion of evolution as an adaptive process inspired several attempts to imagine life adapted to circumstances different from those on Earth (◊ ALIENS; LIFE ON OTHER WORLDS). A rather more modest version of this same inspiration encouraged a number of fantasies about exotic Earthly creatures, of which the most notable are the sea stories of William Hope HODGSON and the stories in *In Search of the Unknown* (coll **1904**) by Robert W. CHAMBERS. Exotic survivals from prehistory (usually dinosaurs) became a common feature of exploratory melodramas, most notably in Jules VERNE's *Voyage au centre de la terre* (**1864**; trans as *Journey to the Centre of the Earth* **1872**) and Arthur Conan DOYLE's *The Lost World* (**1912**). Other early sf writers who made prolific use of biological speculations in their work include H.G. WELLS, J.H. ROSNY aîné and J.D. BERESFORD.

Evolutionary fantasy remained the dominant species of biological sf for many years, overshadowing fiction dealing with experimental biology. Speculations related to medical science tended to engage increasingly well defined CLICHÉS: new plagues and cures for all diseases. The notion of biological engineering did appear in such novels as Wells's *The Island of Dr Moreau* (**1896**), but the methods involved were either crude or very vague. One real-world development which provoked a considerable response was the discovery of the mutagenic properties of radiation. The idea of mutation was implicitly intriguing (◊ MUTANTS), and was made important by its crucial role in evolutionary theory. Sf writers were already entranced with "rays" for a variety of melodramatic reasons (◊ POWER SOURCES; WEAPONS) and their recruitment to biological speculation resulted in the swift growth of the "mutagenic romance". John TAINE was a prolific author of such romances.

Few of the early pulp-sf writers had any knowledge of the biological sciences, and for the most part they handled biological ideas – when they did at all – in a careless and cavalier fashion. The principal exceptions were Taine, Stanley G. WEINBAUM, who employed his expertise mainly in connection with designing exotic life-systems for alien worlds, and David H. KELLER, a doctor who became a psychiatrist yet whose medical training did nothing to render his accounts of biological experiments – including the graphic eugenic fantasy "Stenographer's Hands" (**1928**) – less negative. AMAZING STORIES reprinted "The Tissue-Culture King" (**1927**) by biologist Julian Huxley (1887-1975), but biological sf in the pulps very rarely transcended the deployment of standardized clichés: loathsome alien invaders, man-eating plants, people driven horribly mad by attempts to save them from death via brain-transplantation. Contemporary UK material, though much more sober in tone and serious in intent, was hardly less negative. The ideas in J.B.S. HALDANE's prophetic manifesto for biotechnology, *Daedalus, or Science and the Future* (**1924**) were

transformed by Aldous HUXLEY into the nightmarishly satirical substance of *Brave New World* (**1932**), and there are several horrific stories of the "no good will come of it all" school in S. Fowler WRIGHT's *The New Gods Lead* (coll **1932**). Neil BELL and John GLOAG also dealt extensively with biological inventions in their sf, but their approach was determinedly cautionary. UK scientific romance from the period between the wars could find hope for the future only in a radical transformation of human nature, but even Wells had lost whatever faith he had had in the ability of 20th-century mankind to begin the work of remaking its own nature in a planned and profitable manner. In the eyes of the sf writers of the 1930s the real SUPERMAN-to-come was destined to be a freak of benevolent nature; his time was not yet, and attempts to hurry it by scientific endeavour were invariably disastrous.

GENRE SF's handling of biological ideas improved dramatically after WWII. Several new writers of the 1940s were trained in biology, most notably Isaac ASIMOV, who held an academic post in biochemistry, and (although he did not begin to publish prolifically until the 1950s) James BLISH, who had studied zoology at college and worked for a while as a medical technician. Blish was the first genre-sf writer to import biological ideas on a considerable scale and apply them with real ingenuity. A significant early attempt was "There Shall Be No Darkness" (**1950**), about a kind of werewolf, one of a group of stories which attempted to recruit biological ideas to the rationalization of symbols borrowed from the supernatural imagination (◊ SUPERNATURAL CREATURES); other examples include Jack WILLIAMSON's *Darker than You Think* (**1940**; exp **1948**) – more lycanthropy – and Richard MATHESON's *I am Legend* (**1954**), about vampires. It was Blish's PANTROPY series, ultimately collected in *The Seedling Stars* (fixup **1957**), which first treated the idea of man-remade-by-Man seriously and sympathetically.

As genre sf matured in the 1950s there was a gradual increase in the sophistication of biological analogies. ALIEN beings were still characteristically described and defined by reference to the diversity of Earthly lifeforms, but the subtlety with which this was done increased dramatically in the 1950s. Many stories appeared which used the strange reproductive habits of the lower organisms as models for the construction of exotic situations involving humans and aliens. Authors who made fruitful use of this kind of analogy included Philip José FARMER, notably in *The Lovers* (**1952**; exp **1961**), "Open to Me, My Sister" (**1960**; vt "My Sister's Brother") and "Strange Compulsion" (**1953**), and Theodore STURGEON, especially in "The Perfect Host" (**1948**), "The Sex Opposite" (**1952**) and "The Wages of Synergy" (**1953**). More recent users of the same strategy include James TIPTREE Jr, in "Your Haploid Heart" (**1969**) and "A Momentary Taste of Being" (**1975**). This kind of analogical device illustrates the manner in which biological ideas are usually deployed in sf. In all these stories exotic biological relationships are transformed into metaphors applicable to social relationships (or *vice versa*), relationships between humans and other intelligent beings or even, in a psychological sense, relationships between humans and their environment. This is, of course, a totally unscientific use of scientific ideas, but it can be very effective as a literary device. It is applied not only to such hypothetical biological ideas as LIVING WORLDS but also to such concepts as HIVE-MINDS, ECOLOGY (*see also* COLONIZATION OF OTHER WORLDS) and PARASITISM AND SYMBIOSIS. Thus, for example, the hive-mind becomes in sf not so much a mode of social organization pertaining to insect species as a metaphor for considering possible states of human society. Similarly, symbiosis becomes symbolic of an idealized relationship between humans, or between human and other beings. This misapplication of ideas extends into the real world where, in common usage as in much sf, terms like "ecology" have come to be symbolic of some abstract and quasimetaphysical notion of harmony between humanity and environment.

This constant quest to find biological metaphors has always tended to sidetrack or pervert realistic speculation about likely developments in the biological sciences. Symbolism, metaphor and crude analogical thinking dominate exploration in sf of such notions as ANDROIDS, CLONES, CYBORGS, GENETIC ENGINEERING, IMMORTALITY and SEX. Although much contemporary sf seems to be intimately concerned with current trends in biology, hardly any of this speculation can be said to be extrapolative in a purely rational fashion. These observations should not be taken as altogether pejorative: this method of using ideas is certainly not uninteresting and is often applied with considerable artistry. But one can certainly argue that sf's enduring inability to get to grips with the real possibilities of biotechnology, and to explore those possibilities in a reasonably scrupulous fashion, is a lamentable failure of the sciencefictional imagination. The last decade has produced a number of attempts to be more positive about the possible rewards of biotechnology (many are noted in the entry on IMMORTALITY), but there remains an excessive reliance on the benevolence of chance. Such works as Greg BEAR's *Blood Music* (**1985**), in which the apocalyptic consequences of a biotechnologist's recklessness are declared by the author to be happy ones (though many readers remain unconvinced), cannot reasonably be said to constitute sensible apologias. Paul PREUSS's *Human Error* (**1985**) and Charles SHEFFIELD's *Sight of Proteus* (fixup **1978**) and *Proteus Unbound* (**1989**) are other works which rely heavily on unplanned ecocatastrophes to generate optimistic outcomes. Even an enthusiastic propagandist for biotechnology like Brian M. STABLEFORD finds it easier to produce sarcastic fantasies of biotechnological experiments gone awry than utopian accounts of future humanity redeemed by careful effort, as evidenced by *Sexual Chemistry: Sardonic Tales of the Genetic Revolution* (coll 1991); and even a calculatedly optimistic writer like David BRIN awards a minor and relatively ineffectual role to biological science in describing responses to ecological crisis in his bold and extravagant novel *Earth* (**1990**).

The recent boom in HORROR fiction has involved a massive borrowing of ideas from sf, many of which involve extrapolations of biological science; writers like Robin COOK and Dean R. KOONTZ have produced very effective thrillers in this vein. The overwhelmingly negative image of biological experimentation conveyed by such fiction is only to be expected; it is the task of horror writers to horrify. It is perhaps surprising, though, that so little genre sf counterbalances that negative image with a more evenhanded investigation of the possible benefits of such experiments. One horror novel which regards its depicted biotechnological breakthrough – a potential cure for AIDS using a virus found in vampires' blood – with optimism is Dan SIMMONS's *Children of the Night* (**1992**).

The use of biological ideas as metaphors to apply to specifically human situations is inevitable, and the particular anxiety which attends speculation about experiments in human biology is entirely appropriate, but a too-ready acceptance of the horrified conviction that all biological experimentation is a sin against God or Gaia which will inevitably be punished by dire misfortune is a kind of intellectual cowardice. In its handling of biological ideas, then, sf has not yet attained a true maturity. [BS]

BIONICS ◊ CYBERNETICS; CYBORGS.

BIONIC WOMAN, THE US tv series (1976-8). Harve Bennett Productions and Universal for ABC. Created and prod Kenneth Johnson, starring Lindsay Wagner. 3 seasons, 57 50 min episodes. Colour.

In this spinoff from the successful series *The* SIX MILLION DOLLAR MAN – its first episode being Part 2 of a story begun in the parent series – Jaime Sommers is the former childhood sweetheart of the bionic man, Steve Austin. After a serious accident she, too, has part of her body artificially rebuilt and works for Oscar Goldman (Richard Anderson), head of a government intelligence agency. Unlike Steve Austin, who has a bionic eye, she has a bionic ear with which she can eavesdrop from a mile away. There is a bionic dog called Max. Several episodes involve ALIENS. The acting of the lead role is notably superior to that in the parent series. Two book ties were published: *The Bionic Woman #1: Welcome Home Jaime* * (**1976** by Eileen LOTTMAN; vt *Double Identity* 1976 UK as by Maud Willis) and #2: *Extracurricular Activities* * (**1977** by Lottman; vt *A Question of Life* 1977 UK as by Willis). [JB/PN]

BIOY CASARES, ADOLFO (1914-) Argentine writer, noted from his first book, *Prólogo* ["Prologue"] (**1929**), for the surreal displacements of his work, which uses sf or detective forms in an abstract, parodic fashion, and is generally metaphysical in intent. *La invención de Morel* (**1940**; trans Ruth I.C. Simms in *The Invention of Morel and Other Stories* **1964** US), tells in this fashion of its protagonist's eventually successful search through appearances and realities for IMMORTALITY; it was filmed in Italy as *L'Invenzione di Morel*, dir Emidio Greco, in 1974. *Plan de evasión* (**1945**; trans Suzanne Jill Levine as *A Plan for Escape* **1975** US) had close thematic links with the earlier novel. ABC's "El Perjurio de la Nieve" was filmed by Leopoldo Torre Nilsson as *El Crimen de Oribe* (1950), and features a house whose occupants are caught in a time-loop. ABC's most substantial novel, *El sueño del los héroes* (**1954**; trans Diana Thorold as *The Dream of the Heroes* **1987** US), features the saving of a workman from death by a mysterious figure, possibly supernatural, and the repetition of the same events years later, but without any intervention. *Dormir al sol* (**1973**; trans Suzanne Jill Levine as *Asleep in the Sun* **1978** US), which has soul-transplants, conflates the transformations of psycho-surgery with totalitarianism.

ABC met Jorge Luis BORGES in 1932. They became close literary friends, and under the shared pseudonym H. Bustos Domecq published *Seis problemas para Don Isidro Parodi* (coll **1942**; trans Norman Thomas di Giovanni as *Six Problems for Don Isidro Parodi* 1981 US), a set of introvertive detections. Both authors, with ABC's wife Silvina Ocampo, collaborated in the editing of a fantasy collection, *Antologia de la Literatura Fantástica* (anth **1940**; rev 1976; trans as *The Book of Fantasy* **1976** US). If ABC has for some years lived in the shadow of his famous friend, the continuing translation of his work may rectify a misprision. [JC]

See also: ISLANDS; LATIN AMERICA; PARALLEL WORLDS.

BIRD, CORDWAINER [s] ◊ Harlan ELLISON.

BIRD, WILLIAM HENRY FLEMING (1896-1971) UK art lecturer and writer who published some magazine sf in the 1950s under his own name, beginning with "Critical Age" for *Futurist Science Stories* in 1953, and also as John Toucan and John Eagle, a house name under which two novels almost certainly by WHFB appeared, *Reckless Journey* (**1947** chap) and *Brief Interlude* (c**1947** chap); his later work was almost exclusively written for the firm of CURTIS WARREN and was also released under house names: *War of Argos* (**1952**) as by Rand LE PAGE; *Two Worlds* (**1952**) as by Paul LORRAINE; *Operation Orbit* (**1953**) as by Kris LUNA; *Cosmic Conquest* (**1953**) as by Adrian Blair and *The Third Mutant* (**1953**) as by Lee ELLIOT. Most featured interstellar espionage agents fighting revolutionary MUTANTS. The later *Blast-off into Space* (**1966**) – not a Curtis Warren title – was written under a personal pseudonym, Harry Fleming, and exhibits more character. [JC]

BIRDS, THE Film (1963). Universal. Dir Alfred Hitchcock, starring Rod Taylor, Tippi Hedren, Jessica Tandy, Suzanne Pleshette. Screenplay Evan HUNTER, based on "The Birds" (1952) by Daphne DU MAURIER. 119 mins. Colour.

Ordinary birds in a small seaside town suddenly and without explanation launch a series of murderous attacks on people. The appearance of menace out of a clear sky is paralleled, symbolically, by the eruption of strong feeling in the too-perfectly groomed heroine of the Freudian love story that runs through the film. It is the arrival of this woman which apparently precipitates the bird attacks, and she herself is later imaged as a bird in a cage. The attacks are set-pieces, and carry considerable conviction, achieved with skilled editing and through use of a combination of real birds, models and process work by the veteran animator Ub Iwerks (1900-1971), an early colleague of Walt Disney and co-creator of Mickey Mouse. Although very much more sophisticated than usual, this famous film belongs formally and classically to the MONSTER-MOVIE genre, where the fragility of human hegemony over Nature and the world is conventionally imaged by a tranquil landscape ravaged without warning by some monstrous, inexplicable fury. The film is not strictly sf, since interestingly it neither seeks nor provides any rational explanation for its furies in terms of scientific meddling, atomic radiation or anything else. But not only is its central metaphor of human control vs natural disorder central to sf, historically it was a focal point of the genre as the catalyst for a whole series of revenge-of-Nature films over the next two decades. [PN]

See also: CINEMA.

BISCHOFF, DAVID F(REDRICK) (1951-) US writer who began publishing sf with "The Sky's an Oyster; The Stars are Pearls" in 1975, and who quickly established himself as a versatile and adaptable novelist, though his practice of working in collaboration has tended to muffle any sense that he has, in his own right, either a distinctive style or concerns which could be thought of as personal. His first novel, *The Seeker* (**1976** Canada) with Chris LAMPTON, is in a sense, therefore, typical, for there is nothing in particular to remember about this competent sf adventure featuring a fugitive ALIEN on Earth and a chase. *Forbidden World* (fixup **1978**) with Ted WHITE is, in the same way, efficiently anonymous; and the **Dragonstar** sequence – *Day of the Dragonstar* (**1983**), *Night of the Dragonstar* (**1985**) and *Dragonstar Destiny* (**1989**), all with Thomas F. MONTELEONE – explores with impersonal ingenuity a giant artificial-world-cum-zoo in space (see BIG DUMB OBJECTS) full of escaped menaces and a hidden agenda or two. The most memorable of his collaborations are *Tin Woodman* (**1979**) with Dennis R. Bailey – a complex adventure involving a telepathic human, a living alien starship, a convincingly psychopathic villain, and a galactic chase – and *The Selkie* (**1982**) with Charles SHEFFIELD, a fantasy.

Much the same impression of a genial but impersonal skilfulness is generated by some of DFB's solo fiction, too, although *Nightworld* (**1979**) interestingly combines elements of RECURSIVE SF – in the shape of an ancient ANDROID who replicates the physique and personality of H.G. WELLS – and SCIENCE FANTASY as the protagonist, Wells and a girl who must grow up combine to brave the COMPUTER-generated vampires of the forgotten colony planet of Styx; but the sequel, *The Vampires of Nightworld* (**1981**), merely exploits the already-established venue. Set on a starship with a cosmic troubleshooting mission, the **Star Fall** books – *Star Fall: A Space Fantasy* (**1980**) and *Star Spring: A Space Operetta* (**1982**) – show an uneasy lightness of tone, though the VIRTUAL-REALITY-like shuffling of pulp venues at its heart is enjoyable. The **Star Hounds** sequence – *The Infinite Battle* (**1985**), *Galactic Warriors* (**1985**) and *The Macrocosmic Conflict* (**1986**) – drifts dangerously close to the routine. On the other hand the **UFO Conspiracy** sequence – *Abduction: The UFO Conspiracy* (**1990**), *Deception* (**1991**) and *Revelation* (**1991**) – is a gripping excursion into camp PARANOIA. Companionable and chameleon, DFB seems at the time of writing (1992) to be a jack-of-all-trades who might well, one day, speak out on his own. [JC]

Other works: *Quest* (anth **1977** chap); *Strange Encounters* (anth **1977** chap); *The Phantom of the Opera* * (**1977**), a juvenile version; *Mandala* (1983 in *Chrysalis 10*, anth ed Roy Torgeson as "The Warmth of the Stars"; exp **1983**); *WarGames* * (**1983**), a film tie; a **Time Machine** tie, *Time Machine #2: Search for Dinosaurs* * (**1984**); *The Crunch Bunch* (**1985**); the **Gaming Magi** fantasy sequence, comprising *The Destiny Dice* (**1985**), *Wraith Board* (**1985**) and *The Unicorn Gambit* (**1986**); *A Personal Demon* (fixup **1985**) with Rich Brown (1942-   ) and Linda Richardson (1944-   ), comprising several stories published in *Fantastic* as by Michael F.X. Milhaus; *The Manhattan Project* * (**1986**), a film tie; *Some Kind of Wonderer* (**1987**); *The Blob* * (**1988**), a film tie; *Gremlins 2: The New Batch* * (**1990**), a film tie; two contributions to the sequence of **Bill, the Galactic Hero** tied sequels, *Bill, the Galactic Hero on the Planet of Tasteless Pleasures* * (**1991**) and *Bill, the Galactic Hero on the Planet of Ten Thousand Bars* * (**1991**; vt *Bill, the Galactic Hero on the Planet of the Hippies from Hell* 1992 UK), both with Harry HARRISON; the **Mutants Amok** sequence, comprising *Mutants Amok* (**1991**), *#2: Mutant Hell* (**1991**), *#3: Rebel Attack* (**1991**), *#4: Holocaust Horror* (**1991**) and *#5: Mutants Amok at Christmastime* (**1992**), all as by Mark Grant; *Daniel M. Pinkwater's Melvinge of the Megaverse #1: Night of the Living Shark!* * (**1991**) (◊ Daniel M. PINKWATER).

See also: MONSTERS; UFOS.

BISHOP, MATTHEW [r] ◊ M.H. ZOOL.

BISHOP, MICHAEL (1945-   ) US writer, much travelled in childhood, with an MA in English from the University of Georgia, where he did a thesis on the poetry of Dylan Thomas. He began publishing sf with "Piñon Fall" for *Gal* in 1970, and in a short period established himself as one of the significant new writers of the 1970s. Though his early stories and novels display considerable intellectual complexity, and do not shirk the downbeat implications of their anthropological (◊ ANTHROPOLOGY) treatment of ALIENS and alienating milieux, there remained a sense in which MB could not be treated as one of those writers, like Edward BRYANT, whose primary influences could be seen as the US NEW WAVE of the 1960s combined with the liberating influence of the numerous writing workshops of the succeeding decade. MB's first novel, for instance, *A Funeral for the Eyes of Fire* (**1975**; rev vt *Eyes of Fire* 1980; under original title with revs retained and new introduction 1989 UK), is written ostensibly within the terms of HARD SF, though laced with splashy Gothicisms (most of them removed as part of the extensive revision): on an alien planet, the protagonist must perform wonders or be sent back to a despotic Earth. But, *inter alia*, MB mounts the first of his complex and sometimes moving analyses of alien cultures. The finest of these anthropology-based interrogatory tales is *Transfigurations* (1973 *Worlds of If* as "Death and Designation among the Asadi"; fixup **1979**), where the colonizing impact of a "superior" culture upon less technologically advanced natives is complexly contrasted – in a story which owes much to Joseph CONRAD – with the recursive unknowableness of the Other. *And Strange at Ecbatan the Trees* (**1976**; vt *Beneath the Shattered Moons* 1977; vt as coll *Beneath the Shattered Moons and The White Otters of Childhood* 1978 UK), is a somewhat less convincing FAR-FUTURE tale dealing with a world most of whose people, long ago genetically engineered (◊ GENETIC ENGINEERING) into stoicism, are now apparently incapable of aggression or any other display of emotion. *Stolen Faces* (**1977**), again set on an alien planet, darkly offers a culture so diseased that its inhabitants must designate themselves through gross mutilations.

However, while publishing these novels and many of the stories collected in *Blooded on Arachne* (coll **1982**) and *One Winter in Eden* (coll **1984**), MB was increasingly focusing his sharp, earnest, exploratory vision upon the eerier provinces of the US South. In *A Little Knowledge* (**1977**) and its sequel, *Catacomb Years* (fixup **1979**), a theocratic regime repressively dominates a NEAR-FUTURE Atlanta, Georgia, until the conversion of some apparent aliens begins to destabilize society; the vision of Atlanta as a domed city whose various levels and intersections literally map the new social order may be cognitively daring, but it thins out in the mind's eye when described. However, MB's most public success soon followed. *No Enemy But Time* (**1982**), which won a NEBULA, intensified the movement of his imagination to a local habitat, and for the first time introduced a protagonist of sufficient racial (and mental) complexity to carry a storyline immured in the particular and haunted by the exotic. In this case, dogged by dreams of the Pleistocene, the new MB protagonist – who is not dissimilar to the Habiline who later featured in the less successful and overextended tale of Atlanta and Haiti, *Ancient of Days* (**1985**) (◊ APES AND CAVEMEN) – is enlisted into a TIME-TRAVEL project, returns to the Africa of his vision, fathers a child in the dawn of time, and returns with her to the battering world.

Through the 1980s, MB continued to strive for an adequate form to engage his humanist sympathies, the sociological (and anthropological) eye which found in the South perhaps all too much material, the lurking humorist within the preacher. *Who Made Stevie Crye?* (**1984**) is a strangely unengaged horror novel, with laughs; *The Secret Ascension* (**1987**; vt *Philip K. Dick is Dead, Alas* 1988 UK), set in an ALTERNATE-WORLDS USA, homages and stars DICK (*see also* RECURSIVE SF); *Unicorn Mountain* (**1988**), once again set partly in Atlanta, is a fantasy in which the dying of unicorns from another dimension and the problem of AIDS in this world intersect encouragingly; and *Count Geiger's Blues* (**1992**), another fantasy – set in the Atlanta-like Salonika, capital of the imaginary southern state of Oconee – was similarly told in MB's uneasily humorous, highly individual voice. Though full of energy and strongly willed, these novels do not feel entirely comfortably in focus. MB still gives the impression of a strong mind looking for a strong world to illuminate.

It seems unlikely he will fail.   [JC]

Other works: *Windows & Mirrors: A Chapbook of Poetry to Deep South Con XV* (coll **1977** chap); *Under Heaven's Bridge* (dated 1980 but **1981** UK) with Ian WATSON; *Close Encounters with the Deity* (coll **1986**); *To a Chimp Held Captive for Purposes of Research* (**1986** broadsheet); *Within the Walls of Tyre* (1978 *Weirdbook 13*; rev as screenplay **1989** chap UK); *Apartheid, Superstrings, and Mordecai Thubana* (**1989** chap); *Emphatically Not Sf, Almost* (coll **1991**); *The Quickening* (1981 *Universe 11*; **1991** chap), which won a Nebula for 1981.

As editor: *Changes: Stories of Metamorphosis* (anth **1983**) with Ian Watson; *Light Years and Dark* (anth **1984**); *Nebula Awards 23* (anth **1989**); *Nebula Awards 24* (anth **1990**); *Nebula Awards 25* (anth **1991**).

About the author: *Michael Bishop: A Working Bibliography* (**1988** chap) by Gordon BENSON Jr.

See also: APES AND CAVEMEN (IN THE HUMAN WORLD); ARKHAM HOUSE; BIG DUMB OBJECTS; COSMOLOGY; DEVOLUTION; ORIGIN OF MAN; POETRY; RECURSIVE SF; SEX; SOCIOLOGY; SUPERHEROES; TIMESCAPE BOOKS.

BISSON, TERRY (BALLANTINE) (1942-) US author who has also worked as a New York advertising copy-writer. His first novel, the fantasy *Wyrldmaker* (**1981**), though intermittently vivid and exceedingly intelligent, fails to cohere. It was only with his second, *Talking Man* (**1986**), that he came into his full powers as a novelist whose narrative voice was urgently and lucidly that of a teller of tales. The figure at the heart of *Talking Man* – who does not talk – seems at the story's beginning to be nothing more than a bemusedly eccentric rural Kentuckian who has a knack for repairing motors; as the novel develops into a quest west and then north across a USA more and more radically transformed the further the search proceeds, the talking man takes on qualities of Trickster and Redeemer, and eventually seems to

contain the world's reality in his hands. The tale closes back home, but home is now an American South changed magically into a clement UTOPIA. In *Fire on the Mountain* (**1988**), which is in no ostensible sense a sequel, this same utopia proves to be an ALTERNATE WORLD born from a different course of US history. The enslaved Blacks of the Southern states successfully revolted during the course of the Civil War, founded an independent Southern country, and by the late 20th century have established an unracist, beneficent, courteous, livable comity. Those parts of the tale set during this period are perhaps less convincing – and certainly less moving – than the central passages of the book, which represent the reminiscences of one of the Black revolutionaries; his descriptions of the successful campaign to free his people intensely invokes the haunted heartlands of the Civil War upriver from Washington, though subtly and upliftingly transformed.

TB's fourth novel, *Voyage to the Red Planet* (**1990**), complicatedly combines spoof and elegy. In the 21st century the USA has declined severely, and the *Mary Poppins*, an umbrella-shaped spaceship once destined to take humanity to Mars, is in a mothball orbit. But an entrepreneur decides that a good film could be made of an actual trip to Mars, using the original ageing crew; and this is done. The portrait of a spineless, privatized USA is scathing; but the ship and the voyage – both described with considerable versimilitude – evoke a powerful sense of genuine but wasted opportunity, while generating at the same time a sense that humanity's dream of travelling outwards was not yet, perhaps, over. TB wrote no stories during the 1980s, beginning in 1990. "Bears Discover Fire" (1990), which won a NEBULA, a HUGO and a THEODORE STURGEON MEMORIAL AWARD, again elegizes the land, the loss of the dream of America; it is also very funny. Fluent and moral and wry, TB has become one of the writers whose sf speaks to the world.   [JC]

See also: DISCOVERY AND INVENTION; EVOLUTION; FANTASY; ISAAC ASIMOV'S SCIENCE FICTION MAGAZINE; MARS.

BIXBY, (DREXEL) JEROME (LEWIS) (1923-) US writer and editor; an extremely prolific story-writer, though relatively little of his work is sf. Pseudonyms used on magazine stories include Jay B. Drexel, Harry Neal and Alger ROME, the last in collaboration with Algis BUDRYS. His stories include many Westerns; he has also written sf and horror screenplays and teleplays, including IT! THE TERROR FROM BEYOND SPACE (1958), *Curse of the Faceless Man* (1958), the original script, later rewritten, for FANTASTIC VOYAGE (1966), and several episodes of STAR TREK. He edited PLANET STORIES Summer 1950-July 1951 and initiated its companion magazine, TWO COMPLETE SCIENCE-ADVENTURE BOOKS, editing its first 3 issues; he also worked on GALAXY SCIENCE FICTION, THRILLING WONDER STORIES, STARTLING STORIES and several comics. He began publishing sf with "Tubemonkey" for *Planet*

Stories in 1949, and collected much of his output in this genre in *Space by the Tale* (coll **1964**). *Devil's Scrapbook* (coll **1964**; vt *Call for an Exorcist* 1974) is horror and fantasy. His widely anthologized and best-known story is sf/horror: "It's a *Good* Life" (1953), about a malignant superchild with PSI POWERS (*see also* CHILDREN IN SF); it was dramatized on tv in *The* TWILIGHT ZONE, and later as an episode, directed by Joe DANTE, of *Twilight Zone: The Movie* (1983). His work is professional, as evidenced by his perfectly competent **Star Trek** novel, *Day of the Dove* * (**1978**), but not of great significance in the field.   [JC]
See also: MUSIC; PSYCHOLOGY; SUPERMAN.

BIZARRE US SEMIPROZINE. 1 issue (Jan 1941), ed Walter E. Marconette and J. Chapman Miske, effectively a continuation of Marconette's earlier FANZINE *Scienti-Snaps*. Professional in appearance, with a colour cover by Hannes BOK, it is remembered mainly for publishing for the first time the original but previously unused ending of A. MERRITT's novel *Dwellers in the Mirage* (1932; rev 1953), which ending has been in use ever since. *B* also ran a discussion by John W. CAMPBELL Jr about writing styles.   [PN/FHP]

BIZARRE! MYSTERY MAGAZINE US DIGEST-size magazine. 3 issues (Oct and Nov 1965, Jan 1966), published by Pamar Enterprises, ed John Poe. *B!MM* had a strong horror/sf element overriding the ostensible mystery content, and included reprint work by Pierre BOULLE and new stories by Thomas M. DISCH, Avram DAVIDSON, James H. SCHMITZ and Arthur C. CLARKE.   [FHP/PN]

BJAŽIĆ, MLADEN [r] ◊ YUGOSLAVIA.

BLACK, LADBROKE (LIONEL DAY) (1877-1940) UK writer of much boys' fiction, often as Lionel Day or Paul Urquhart. He began publishing novels in 1902. *The Buried World* (**1928**), as by Lionel Day, is a LOST-WORLD juvenile; the head in *The Gorgon's Head* (**1932**) turns modern Britons to stone for a while; and *The Poison War* (**1933**) is a future-WAR novel in which the UK is attacked by chemical weapons. LB was not an innovative writer.   [JC]
Other works: *The Wager* (**1927**), a RURITANIAN tale.

BLACK, ROBERT ◊ Robert P. HOLDSTOCK.

BLACK AFRICAN SF Only a small amount of sf is published in the Black African nations. What follows is more a sampler than a full survey, since very few researchers have even looked at the topic.

Much of what is published is in English, and most of that is juvenile. Typical are the novelette *Journey to Space* (**1980** chap), by the Nigerian Flora Nwapa, and a novel about a scientist who discovers ANTIGRAVITY, *The Adventures of Kapapa* (**1976**) by the Ghanaian J.O. Eshun. One of the rare sf books for adults, a play, is *The Chosen Ones* (**1969**) by Azize Asgarally of Mauritius; it is set partly in the 30th century.

More common are adventure and spy novels for adults containing sf elements, much in the style of the **James Bond** movies based on Ian FLEMING's books. Such is *The Mark of Cobra* (**1980**), by Valentine Alily of Nigeria, in which a secret agent fights against

a multimillionaire seeking world domination by use of a "solar weapon". David G. Maillu of Kenya is a prolific writer of adventure novels, of which some are sf; in his *The Equatorial Assignment* (**1980**), for example, a secret agent penetrates a criminal conspiracy which is trying to control the whole of Africa by the use of fantastic weapons. More sf can be found in the so-called Onitsha market literature; a typical example is the Nigerian adaptation of George ORWELL's *Nineteen Eighty-four* (**1949**) done by Bala Abdullahi Funtua in the mid-1970s.

Sf in other languages is rare. Sony Labou Tansi is Congolese; his NEAR-FUTURE sf novel, set in a fictitious African country in 1995, is in French: *Conscience de tracteur* ["Consciousness of the Tractor"] (**1979**). Another adaptation of Orwell, this time of *Animal Farm* (**1945**), is *Pitso ea liphoofolo tsa hae* ["The Meeting of the Domestic Animals"] (**1956**); this, by Libakeng Maile, was published in the Southern Sotho language. A children's sf book written in Hausa, one of the languages of Nigeria, is *Tauraruwa mai wutsiya* ["The Comet"] (**1969**) by Umaru A. Dembo; it tells of the travels in space of a small boy, and of his encounter with a friendly ALIEN.   [JO]

BLACKBURN, JOHN (FENWICK) (1923-   ) UK writer and antiquarian book dealer, author of many novels whose ambience of HORROR derives from a calculated use of material from several genres, including sf. His early books, such as his first, *A Scent of New-Mown Hay* (**1958**; a reported vt *The Reluctant Spy* 1966 US, is possibly a ghost title), *A Sour Apple Tree* (**1958**), *Broken Boy* (**1959**) and *A Ring of Roses* (**1965**; vt *A Wreath of Roses* 1965 US) tended to use themes from espionage and thriller fiction to buttress and ultimately provide explanations for tales whose effects were fundamentally GOTHIC horror and fantasy. Ex-Nazis often cropped up in these books, as in the first, where a German scientist spreads around the world a mutated plague-bearing fungus with the eponymous aroma. Even in later stories, like *The Face of the Lion* (**1976**), which again (characteristically) deals with abominable disease, loathsome though by now rather elderly SS officers make their dutiful bows. JFB's use of sf is usually borderline, though not in *Children of the Night* (**1966**), one of his better works, where an underground lost race (◊ LOST WORLDS) in northern England kills by telepathic powers. Often what seem to be sf plot devices on introduction are satisfactorily explained in terms of contemporary science by the story's close, or are MCGUFFINS or red herrings like the atom-bomb conspiracy in *The Face of the Lion*. Though his use of sf situations is often ingenious, and though even his most straightforward novels are prone to internal generic mutations from one form to another, it would be unduly stretching matters to describe JFB as a genuine sf writer.   [JC]
Other works: *Dead Man Running* (**1960**); *The Gaunt Woman* (**1962**); *Blue Octavo* (**1963**; vt *Bound to Kill* 1963 US); *Colonel Bogus* (**1964**; vt *Packed for Murder* 1964 US); *The Winds of Midnight* (**1964**; vt *Murder at Midnight*

1964 US); *The Young Man from Lima* (**1968**); *Nothing But the Night* (**1968**); *Bury Him Darkly* (**1969**); *Blow the House Down* (**1970**); *The Household Traitors* (**1971**); *For Fear of Little Men* (**1972**); *Devil Daddy* (**1972**); a series comprising *Deep among the Dead Men* (**1973**), *Mister Brown's Bodies* (**1975**) and *The Cyclops Goblet* (**1977**); *Our Lady of Pain* (**1974**); *Dead Man's Handle* (**1978**); *The Sins of the Father* (**1979**); *A Beastly Business* (**1982**); *A Book of the Dead* (**1984**) and *The Bad Penny* (**1985**).

See also: GOTHIC SF; MYTHOLOGY.

BLACKFORD, RUSSELL (KENNETH) (1954-   ) Australian industrial advocate, writer and critic. The best of his small output of sf may be "Glass Reptile Breakout" (**1985**), the title story of *Glass Reptile Breakout* (anth **1990**) ed Van Ikin, a CYBERPUNK tale of self-healing teenagers. His only novel, *The Tempting of the Witch King* (**1983**), is ironic fantasy. Co-editor of AUSTRALIAN SCIENCE FICTION REVIEW: SECOND SERIES, RB has two William Atheling Jr AWARDS for criticism. With David King he edited *Urban Fantasies* (anth **1985**), sf and fantasy stories, and, with Jenny Blackford, Lucy Sussex and Norman Talbot, *Contrary Modes* (anth **1985**), essays on sf.   [PN]

BLACK HOLE, THE Film (1979). Walt Disney. Dir Gary Nelson, starring Maximilian Schell, Anthony Perkins, Robert Forster, Joseph Bottoms, Yvette Mimieux, Ernest Borgnine. Screenplay Jeb Rose-Brook, Gerry Day, based on a story by Rosebrook, Bob Barbash, Richard Landau. 98 mins. Colour.

The disappointment of its year in sf movies, this was a ludicrous though expensive reprise in space of Disney's 20,000 LEAGUES UNDER THE SEA (1954). Astronauts enter a derelict survey vessel orbiting a BLACK HOLE (painted red so that we can see it better); they find a Captain-Nemo-like figure (Schell) served by a killer ROBOT and ANDROID henchmen, who turn out to be the original crew evilly transformed by the mad SCIENTIST. His desire is to venture within the hole. After adventures involving two post-STAR WARS cute robots and a strike by a meteor (although the size of a house, it fails to bring about the decompression of the spacecraft), all enter the hole, which appears to Schell like DANTE ALIGHIERI's Inferno and to the good guys like a kitschy cathedral. The screenwriters, who appear to have no knowledge of science even to primary-school level, give all the fanatical oratory to Schell, leaving the remainder of the cast quite wooden. The novelization is *The Black Hole* * (**1979**) by Alan Dean FOSTER.   [PN]

BLACK HOLES Item of sf TERMINOLOGY borrowed from COSMOLOGY. The term was coined by physicist John Wheeler (1911-   ) in 1969 and adopted immediately and enthusiastically by sf writers. The concept of the black hole is quite complex, and is best approached by the layman through a reliable book of scientific popularization such as *A Brief History of Time: From the Big Bang to Black Holes* (**1988**) by Stephen W. Hawking (1942-   ), one of the theoretical physicists to have done fundamental work on the concept. The scientific element of the present discussion has been much simplified.

The possibility that a lump of matter might be compressible to the point at which its surface gravity would be so powerful that not even light could escape from it was first pointed out in the late 18th century by John Michell (c1724-1793) and then by Pierre Simon, Marquis de Laplace (1749-1827). It was resuscitated in the 20th century when the implications of General Relativity became clear. It was not until the 1960s, however, that physicists began to speculate as to whether a collapsing star of sufficient mass, about three times that of the Sun, might pass beyond even the NEUTRON-STAR state of collapsed matter to become a black hole of this kind, centred on a singularity (a point where infinite gravity crushed matter and energy entirely out of existence) and bounded by an event horizon (defined by the distance from the singularity at which the escape velocity is that of light; the name "event horizon" derives from the fact that it is of course impossible to observe from outside any events occurring closer to the singularity than this).

Many early sf stories dealing with the theme seized upon the extreme relativistic time-dilatation effect associated with objects falling towards the event horizons of such holes; examples include Poul ANDERSON's "Kyrie" (1968), Brian W. ALDISS's "The Dark Soul of the Night" (1976) and Frederik POHL's *Gateway* (**1977**). These stories make interesting metaphorical connections between physics and psychology, perhaps helping to cast some light on the intriguing question of why the black-hole concept has become one of the most charismatic ideas in contemporary physics. Few other notions have had such an immediate imaginative impact, or spawned so many exercises in lyrical quasi-scientific philosophizing. John Taylor's *Black Holes: The End of the Universe?* (**1973**), one of several books which helped to popularize the notion in the 1970s, is a rather eccentric ideative rhapsody built on the supposition that "the black hole requires a complete rethinking of our attitudes to life".

Further tense psychological melodramas using black holes to develop analogies between extraordinary physics and mental processes include Robert SILVERBERG's "To the Dark Star" (1968), Barry N. MALZBERG's *Galaxies* (**1975**) and John VARLEY's "Lollipop and the Tar Baby" (1977) – which features an intelligent black hole – but stories of this kind soon petered out. Familiarity bred contentment if not contempt, and the black hole was soon domesticated by sf writers into a standard image of no great moment. The idea proved, however, to be surprisingly adaptable. At first it seemed that anything falling into a black hole was destined for certain destruction, but this narrative inconvenience was frequently sidestepped. It was independently and for different reasons hypothesized by cosmologists and sf writers alike that – supposing one *could* travel through a black hole – the point of emergence might be far removed from the point of entry. Because this property of black holes offered an apparent means of dodging the relativistic limitations on getting around the Universe at FASTER-THAN-LIGHT speeds, they quickly began to crop up as "star gates" – rapid transit systems – as in Joan D. VINGE's *The Snow Queen* (**1980**). Early examples of stories in which they perform this function tend, in order to obscure the fundamental problem, to use fudge-names for them: George R.R. MARTIN's "The Second Kind of Loneliness" (1972) speaks of a "nullspace vortex" while Joe HALDEMAN's *The Forever War* (**1974**) refers to "collapsars". Obliging physicists soon began to speculate about the possibility of avoiding destruction within a black hole. According to some theoretical physicists, some solutions of the equations of General Relativity as they apply to rotating (rather than static) black holes offer the slim possibility that a spacecraft that entered such a hole might be able to avoid the naked singularity and so, rather than being crushed out of existence, might instantaneously re-emerge elsewhere in the Universe (travelling via a hypothetical bridge or tunnel known as a wormhole) – the word "elsewhere" referring to some other place, some other time (which would create havoc with the principle of causality), or both. Some physicists went further, proposing that the re-emergence might be into a *different* universe. Sf writers gladly accepted the imaginative warrant provided by these ideas, which were popularized by such bold works of "speculative nonfiction" as Adrian BERRY's *The Iron Sun: Crossing the Universe through Black Holes* (**1977**). Stories in which starships simply dived into black holes and passed through wormholes to distant parts of the Universe or to other universes began to appear in some profusion. The popularity of the theme was further boosted by the film *The* BLACK HOLE (**1979**), and quickly became so routine that recent writers have had to work hard to sustain the melodramatic potential of the notion. A notable example of conscientious work of this kind is Paul J. MCAULEY's *Eternal Light* (**1991**), while a more casual approach is manifest in Roger MacBride ALLEN's *The Ring of Charon* (**1991**), in which the Earth is kidnapped through a wormhole. The idea of a return journey from a black hole is more ingeniously deployed in Ian WALLACE's *Heller's Leap* (**1979**).

Although black holes formed through stellar collapse would have to be at least three times the mass of the Sun, the concept of miniature black holes emerged in the early 1970s, first in technical papers and then in sf. They were featured in "The Hole Man" (1973) by Larry NIVEN and adapted for use in a SPACESHIP drive in Arthur C. CLARKE's *Imperial Earth* (**1975**), but they really came into their own when theorists attempting to figure out the mechanics of the Big Bang decided that vast numbers of tiny black holes might have been created at that time (along with even more peculiar black-hole-like entities called cosmic strings). However, it was soon theorized

mathematically (Hawking described some of this work in a seminar in 1973) that mini black holes would be unstable, slowly decaying as a result of "quantum leakage" of radiation. (Such leakage would affect all black holes, of course, but only in the case of mini black holes would it be significant.) Any primordial black hole whose initial mass was less than about a billion tons would already have disappeared, although more massive (but still mini) primordial black holes might still exist. However, sf writers have had little difficulty in imagining accessory stabilizing methods, such as the one featured in Gregory BENFORD's thriller *Artifact* (**1985**). David BRIN's *Earth* (**1990**) simply ties neat knots in cosmic strings in order to make them available for mind-boggling high jinks of various kinds; the knotting of cosmic strings had earlier been examined less reverently by Rudy RUCKER in "The Man who was a Cosmic String" (1987).

Brin's *Earth* mentions an idea encountered elsewhere: that even tiny black holes might qualify as entire universes in their own right (thus, perhaps, reopening some potential for the kind of microcosmic romance that Ray CUMMINGS used to write; ◊ GREAT AND SMALL). Pohl, having introduced black holes into *Gateway*, continued to explore their potential in subsequent volumes of his **Heechee** series; the mysterious Heechee turn out to be hiding inside one in *Beyond the Blue Event Horizon* (**1980**) and venture forth again in *Heechee Rendezvous* (**1984**). Pohl's fascination with the notion is further extended in *The Singers of Time* (**1991**), with Jack WILLIAMSON, which involves interuniversal travel via wormholes and includes a series of rhapsodic infodump chapters celebrating the wonders of modern theoretical physics.

A series of theoretical papers in the 1970s suggested that for every black hole there must somewhere else (perhaps at the end of a wormhole) be a corresponding white hole gushing energy out into the Universe in the same way that a black hole would suck it in. The idea was popularized by John GRIBBIN in his "speculative nonfiction" *White Holes: Cosmic Gushers in the Universe* (**1977**), but suffered from the disadvantage that, although white holes should be by definition among the most visible objects in the Universe, none had (or has) been detected. One pleasing notion, however, equated the Big Bang with a white hole. The white-hole idea never had quite the same success in sf as its black-hole counterpart, but the New Sun in Gene Wolfe's **Book of the New Sun** series appears to be a white hole.

Yet another variant on the black-hole theme is based on the concept that a low-density black hole of enormous mass – perhaps 100,000 times greater than that of the Sun – might commonly occur at the centre of galaxies, our own included; there is considerable astronomical evidence that this is indeed the case. The physics constraining the properties of such low-density black holes seems to admit the possibility that whole stars and planets could go on existing inside them. Even more massive black holes, of perhaps 100,000,000 times solar mass, might exist at the heart of those incredibly distant, highly energetic galaxies known to astronomers as Seyfert galaxies and quasars. (The term quasar derives from their earlier description as "quasi-stellar radio sources".) The immense black hole at the galactic core has become almost a CLICHÉ of contemporary SPACE OPERA.

Other uses of black holes continue to be found. They become ultimate weapons in David LANGFORD's *The Space Eater* (**1982**) and others, and Gregory Benford, in *Beyond the Fall of Night* (**1990**), his sequel to Arthur C. Clarke's classic *Against the Fall of Night* (1948; **1953**), uses one as a prison for the Mad Mind from the earlier novel. It remains to be seen whether the changes have now been comprehensively rung, or whether there is further narrative colour yet to be discovered in the notion.

It is disappointing to learn that, while there is strong empirical and overwhelming theoretical evidence, there is as yet no concrete proof that even a single black hole exists anywhere in the real Universe. It is difficult to explain such phenomena as Seyfert galaxies and quasars without invoking black holes, and the existence of black holes seems inevitable in the light of our current understanding of the ways in which matter/energy behaves, but such theorizing is no substitute for proof. It is generally supposed by astronomers, however, that by far the likeliest explanation for certain intense periodic X-ray sources in our Galaxy (the first discovered being Cygnus X-1, in 1971) is that the X-rays are being emitted from particles falling towards a black hole which is in orbital partnership with a supergiant star. It is known that the objects concerned are too massive to be white dwarfs or neutron stars, and they seem to be invisible. [BS/PN]

BLACK MOON RISING ◊ John CARPENTER.

BLACK SCORPION, THE Film (1957). Warner Bros. Dir Edward Ludwig, starring Richard Denning, Mara Corday. Screenplay David DUNCAN, Robert Blees. 88 mins. B/w.

Giant scorpions and a rather good spider emerge from a cavern under the Mexican desert in this slow-moving, low-budget MONSTER MOVIE obviously inspired by THEM! (1954). The stop-motion animation of the scorpions, supervised by Willis H. O'BRIEN at the age of 70, is vivid but does not really redeem the wooden performances and routine direction. [JB/PN]

BLACKS IN SF ◊ POLITICS.

BLACKSTONE, JAMES ◊ John BAXTER; John BROSNAN.

BLACK SUN, THE ◊ TEMNÉ SLUNCE.

BLACKWOOD, ALGERNON (1869-1951) UK writer who spent a decade in Canada and the USA from the age of 20. His work is essentially fantasy, though his tales of occult pantheism – best exemplified in *The Centaur* (**1911**), which builds on the theories of Gustav Fechner (1801-1887) in its projections of a sentient Mother Earth – tend to argue a logic of history which

might seem sufficiently rational for his work to count as sf. His novels tend to the ponderous; his very numerous short stories, beginning with *A Mysterious House* (1889 *Belgravia*; **1987** chap ed Richard Dalby), are his best work and, though frequently overlong, often reach heights of morose lyricism. It is in his short stories, too, that AB most often became explicitly sciencefictional in his treatment of the concepts of time and of PARALLEL WORLDS. He was a friend of J.W. DUNNE, whose theories about the Serial Universe he espoused in stories like "The Willows" (1907), "Wayfarers" (1912), "The Pikestaffe Case" (1923), "The Man who was Milligan" (1923), "Full Circle" (1925) and "The Man who Lived Backwards" (1930). His short work is collected in *The Empty House and Other Ghost Stories* (coll **1906**), *The Listener and Other Stories* (coll **1907**), *The Lost Valley and Other Stories* (coll **1910**), *Pan's Garden: A Volume of Nature Stories* (coll **1910**), *Incredible Adventures* (coll **1914**), *Ten Minute Stories* (coll **1914**), *Day and Night Stories* (coll **1917**), *The Wolves of God and Other Fey Stories* (coll **1921**), with Wilfred Wilson, and *Tongues of Fire, and Other Sketches* (coll **1924**). With the exception of *The Doll and One Other* (coll **1946** US), later collections rearranged earlier material (though AB in fact continued to produce new work until the year before his death); the best of these are *Strange Stories* (coll **1929**), *The Tales of Algernon Blackwood* (coll **1938**) and *Tales of the Uncanny and Supernatural* (coll **1949**). In later years, AB enjoyed a rebirth of fame on UK RADIO and tv. His occult detective **John Silence**, some of whose adventures are collected in *John Silence, Physician Extraordinary* (coll **1908**), uses some PSEUDO-SCIENTIFIC techniques. The recurrent theme of REINCARNATION is developed most notably in *Julius Le Vallon: An Episode* (**1916**) and its sequel *The Bright Messenger* (**1921**) and in *The Wave: An Egyptian Aftermath* (**1916**) and *Karma: A Reincarnation Play* (**1918**) with Violet Pearn. [JC/MA]

Other works: *The Education of Uncle Paul* (**1909**) and its sequel, *A Prisoner in Fairyland* (**1913**); *Jimbo* (**1909**); *The Human Chord* (**1910**); *The Extra Day* (**1915**); *The Garden of Survival* (**1918**); *The Promise of Air* (**1919**); *Dudley and Gilderoy* (**1928**); *The Fruit Stoners* (**1934**); *Tales of the Supernatural* (coll **1983**) and *The Magic Mirror: Lost Tales and Mysteries* (coll **1989**), both ed Mike ASHLEY.

About the author: *Algernon Blackwood: A Bio-Bibliography* (**1987**) by Mike Ashley.

See also: DIMENSIONS; HORROR IN SF.

BLADE, ALEXANDER One of the longest-lasting ZIFF-DAVIS house names, originally the personal pseudonym of David Vern (David V. REED), whose contributions under the name have not been identified, though probably "The Strange Adventure of Victor MacLeigh" (1941 *AMZ*) is by him. The name was later used by Howard BROWNE, Millen Cooke, Chester S. GEIER, Randall GARRETT with Robert SILVERBERG (who also wrote solo under the name), Roger P. Graham (Rog PHILLIPS), Edmond HAMILTON, Heinrich Hauser, Berkeley LIVINGSTON, Herb Livingston,

William P. McGivern, David Wright O'BRIEN, Louis H. Sampliner, Richard S. SHAVER, Don WILCOX and Leroy YERXA. Approximately 50 stories were published as by AB, most in *AMZ* and *Fantastic Adventures* and some in *Imagination*, *Imaginative Tales* and *Science Fiction Adventures*. [JC]

BLADE RUNNER Film (1982). Blade Runner Partnership-Ladd Co.-Sir Run Run Shaw/Warner. Dir Ridley SCOTT, starring Harrison Ford, Rutger Hauer, Sean Young, Daryl Hannah, William Sanderson. Screenplay Hampton Fancher, David Peoples, based on *Do Androids Dream of Electric Sheep?* (**1968**) by Philip K. DICK. 117 mins (US). Colour.

In a future Los Angeles, Rick Deckard (Ford), whose job it is to destroy renegade "replicants" (ANDROIDS), has to hunt down a particularly dangerous group of advanced androids designed as slaves; their anger against humanity is all the greater because they have been given only a very limited lifespan.

The screenplay and the film itself went through a number of stages, with Peoples radically rewriting Fancher's original script only to see much of his filling-out material lost. The first US cut released (preview audiences only) was much longer than the 117min final US cut, and then for the UK/Europe distribution the film was hardened again with some of the more brutal sequences restored. Some important themes from Dick's book survive in a mystifying way: it is never explained in the film that most healthy humans have emigrated off a pollution-ridden Earth – though the prematurely ageing robotics expert, Sebastian (Sanderson), is meant to be one of the sick ones that stayed home; nor is the destruction of nearly all animal life explained – most surviving animals being artificial – though references to it are made throughout, notably in the android empathy test, where lack of sensitivity to animal life is a key clue to the androids' supposed lack of real feeling. Strangest of all, the possibility that Deckard himself may be a "replicant" exists in the final cut only as a subtext, unmistakable once pointed out, but missed by almost all audiences except, Ridley Scott has said, the French. Scott's own "director's cut" of *BR*, released in 1992, makes the subtext much clearer and deletes the voice-over narration.

BR has many narrative flaws, including a happy ending tacked on allegedly against the director's wishes, but remains one of the most important sf movies made. The density of information given right across the screen in the future setting (production designer Lawrence Paull, visual consultant Syd Mead, special-photographic-effects supervisor Douglas Trumbull, with Scott himself being primarily responsible for the look of the film) is extraordinary, showing almost for the first time – though fans had spent years hoping – how visually sophisticated sf in film form can be. *BR*'s *film-noir mise-en-scène*, with its ubiquitous advertisements (and rain), its Los Angeles dominated by an oriental population, its punk female android (Hannah), its high-tech traffic alongside bicycles, its steam and smoke, its shabbiness and glitter cheek-by-jowl, is film's first (and still best) precursor of the movement we now call CYBERPUNK. *BR* is even better, and much more ambitious, than Scott's previous sf film, ALIEN, and is especially interesting in its treatment of the central theme: whether "humanity" is something innate or whether it can be "programmed" in – or, indeed, out. [PN]

See also: CINEMA; HOLOCAUST AND AFTER; HUGO; MUSIC.

BLAINE, JOHN Pseudonym of US writer Harold Leland Goodwin (1914-1990) who specialized in sf-adventure novels for teenage readers. His books tended to emphasize the nuts and bolts of science and technology, and were more carefully written than most series books for teens. As Blake Savage he also wrote an sf novel for teens, *Rip Foster Rides the Gray Planet* (**1952**; vt *Assignment in Space with Rip Foster* 1958; vt *Rip Foster in Ride the Gray Planet* 1969). Under his own name, Goodwin wrote some popular-science texts, including *The Real Book About Stars* (**1951**), *The Science Book of Space Travel* (**1955**) and *Space: Frontier Unlimited* (**1962**). He remains best known for the long **Rick Brant Science Adventure** sequence, all as JB, a series of tales – some incorporating EDISONADE elements – which feature a teenage inventor on and off the planet: *The Rocket's Shadow* (**1947**) with Peter J. Harkins writing together as JB; *The Lost City* (**1947**) with Harkins; *Sea Gold* (**1947**) with Harkins; *100 Fathoms Under* (**1947**); *The Whispering Box Mystery* (**1948**); *The Phantom Shark* (**1949**); *Smuggler's Reef* (**1950**); *The Caves of Fear* (**1951**); *Stairway to Danger* (**1952**); *The Golden Skull* (**1954**); *The Wailing Octopus* (**1956**); *The Electronic Mind Reader* (**1957**); *The Scarlet Lake Mystery* (**1957**); *The Pirates of Shan* (**1958**) (not to be confused with Murray LEINSTER's *The Pirates of Zan*; **1959** dos); *The Blue Ghost Mystery* (**1960**); *The Egyptian Cat Mystery* (**1961**); *The Flaming Mountain* (**1963**); *The Flying Stingaree* (**1963**); *The Ruby Ray Mystery* (**1964**); *The Veiled Raiders* (**1965**); *The Rocket Jumper* (**1966**); *The Deadly Dutchman* (**1967**); *Danger Below!* (**1968**) with Philip Harkins (who may have been the same as Peter J. Harkins, above) writing together as JB; *The Magic Talisman* (written 1969; **1990**). [JC]

BLAIR, ANDREW (? -1885) Scottish medical doctor and writer whose *Annals of the Twenty-Ninth Century, or The Autobiography of the Tenth President of the World-Republic* (**1874**) celebrates, at times ponderously, Earth-boring, the complete ecospheric control of the planet, and interplanetary travels during which the protagonist visits several worlds whose human inhabitants demonstrate various levels of spiritual perfection. [BS/JC]

See also: ANONYMOUS SF AUTHORS; COLONIZATION OF OTHER WORLDS.

BLAIR, HAMISH Pseudonym of Andrew James Frazer Blair (1872-1935), Scottish author, journalist and editor, resident in India for many years. In *1957* (**1930**) he described how air power overcomes the Second Indian Mutiny. In its sequel, *Governor Hardy* (**1931**), he focused on the ensuing international intrigues and WAR. A third futuristic novel, *The Great Gesture* (**1931**), optimistically depicts the events leading to the founding in 1941 of a United States of Europe. [JE]

BLAIR, JOHN (M.) (1961-   ) US writer and poet who began publishing sf with *A Landscape of Darkness* (**1990**), an sf adventure in which a mercenary on a colony planet must pit himself against an ALIEN who wears the guise of a Japanese warrior. Though a plot of this sort offers many opportunities for action routines, JB generally avoids the temptation. His second novel, *Bright Angel* (**1992**), similarly concentrates upon the complex psychology of a central figure invested with human responses and a planet-shaking burden; in this case the protagonist must attempt to uncover a possible correlation between his unwilled, sudden awakening in a DYSTOPIAN Earth after surviving the onset of a fierce Ice Age on a colony planet and the beginning of similar conditions in the Antarctic. At times, JB has demonstrated a virtuoso control over complicated plot-lines and their implications. [JC]

BLAKE, KEN ◊ Kenneth BULMER; Robert P. HOLDSTOCK.

BLAKE, ROBERT [s] ◊ L.P. DAVIES.

BLAKENEY, JAY D. Pseudonym of US writer Deborah A. Chester (1957-   ), whose **Anthi** sequence – *The Children of Anthi* (**1985**) and *Requiem for Anthi* (**1990**) – aroused some interest. It is a far-reaching and moderately complex vision of humanity's future EVOLUTION, guided by the eponymous AI, into a form that is half-flesh and half-electronics. Set on a heavily populated galactic stage, the sequence demonstrates JDB's sensitivity to the potential differentness from 1990 of so multifarious a venue. Two singletons, *The Omcri Matrix* (**1987**) and *The Goda War* (**1989**), are less remarkable. JDB seemed to be a writer to watch with some interest, but the **Operation StarHawks** sf adventures, all written as by Sean Dalton, were not engrossing: *Operation StarHawks #1: Space Hawks* (**1990**), *#2: Code Name Peregrine* (**1990**), *#3: Beyond the Void* (**1991**), *#4: The Rostma Lure* (**1991**), *#5: Destination: Mutiny* (**1991**) and *#6: The Salukan Gambit* (**1992**). A new sequence began with *Time-Trap* (**1992**), with a man from the future trapped in 14th-century Greece. [JC]

BLAKE'S SEVEN UK tv series (1978-81). BBC TV. Created by Terry NATION. Prods David Maloney (seasons 1-3), Vere Lorrimer (season 4). Script editor Chris Boucher. Writers included Nation (all episodes in the first season), Boucher, James FOLLETT, Robert Holmes, Tanith LEE. Starring Gareth Thomas (Blake), Paul Darrow (Avon), Michael Keating (Vila), Jan Chappell (Cally), Jacqueline Pearce (Servalan), Stephen Grief (Travis, season 1), Brian Croucher (Travis, season 2), Steven Pacey (Tarrant). 52 50min episodes. Colour.

The series began rather crudely with some hoary sf CLICHÉS (political rebels against the totalitarian Federation are sent to a prison planet) but picked up considerably in later episodes of the first season,

where Blake and his allies take part in spirited SPACE-OPERA adventures in a miraculous spaceship (later to be operated by an ill tempered computer called Orac) which they find conveniently abandoned in space. Although free-spirited-rebels-vs-oppressive-empire is a theme straight from STAR WARS – coincidentally, since the UK premiere of both was on the same day – the feeling is very different. Blake's crew are quarrelsome, depressive, pessimistic and – especially Avon – cynical. Blake himself disappeared at the end of the second season, to reappear, apparently now on the wrong side, only at the very end. After the first season *BS* degenerated into sub-*DR WHO* tackiness, with much popping off of ray-guns in extraterrestrial quarries and poaching of secondhand plots (*The Picture of Dorian Gray*, etc.). The fourth season wound up on a depressing note as the bulk of the somewhat-changed cast were killed off by the villains. Despite this falling off, the series was addictive, and notable for the sense of doomed helplessness with which the rebels managed to inflict mere pinpricks on the seemingly indestructible Federation – no doubt a reflection of the times, and seemingly not too off-putting for the audience, for *BS* developed a large and passionate fan following, which it still retains. [PN/KN]

BLANCHARD, H(ENRY) PERCY (1862-1939) US writer whose sf novel, *After the Cataclysm: A Romance of the Age to Come* (**1909**), features a SLEEPER AWAKENING into 1934 to find the world become an electricity-run UTOPIA, founded after the near passage of a small planet in 1914 destroyed socialism and ended a world war caused by Zionists. [JC]

BLASTER In sf TERMINOLOGY, the hand-gun that blasts had an early place of honour along with the DEATH RAY, ray-gun and DISINTEGRATOR. Blasters were standard-issue WEAPONS in early SPACE OPERA, like six-guns in Westerns. [PN]

BLAYLOCK, JAMES P. (1950-   ) US writer, based in California, whose first published sf was "The Red Planet" (**1977**) in UNEARTH #3. JPB's first books were two fantasies in his **Elfin** series, *The Elfin Ship* (**1982**) and *The Disappearing Dwarf* (**1983**). The series, which includes the later and more assured *The Stone Giant* (**1989**), is remarkable for its geniality and quirkiness, and the general likeability of most of the characters, even the unreliable ones. Though dwarfs and elves are featured, it is difficult to imagine a fantasy series less like J.R.R. TOLKIEN's in tone.

A similar tone continued in JPB's next two books, which more closely resemble sf: *The Digging Leviathan* (**1984**) and *Homunculus* (**1986**), the latter being the winner of the PHILIP K. DICK AWARD for best paperback original (coincidentally appropriate, since JPB was a friend of Philip K. DICK during Dick's last years). It was by now clear that JPB's talent was strong, but sufficiently weird and literary as to be unlikely to attract a mass-market readership. Among his obvious and acknowledged influences are Laurence Sterne's *Tristram Shandy* (9 vols **1759-67**), Robert Louis

STEVENSON and Charles DICKENS. His books feature grotesques and eccentrics viewed with whimsical affection. These people often have crotchets and obsessions, and live in mutable worlds subject to curiosities and wonders whose explications – while sometimes earnestly scientific – are seen as hopelessly inadequate in the face of their absolute strangeness. The events of JPB's books fall into odd patterns rather than linear plots, though the later works have a stronger narrative drive. *The Digging Leviathan* is set in a modern Los Angeles, beneath which is a giant underground sea, and some of whose inhabitants hope to penetrate the centre of the HOLLOW EARTH. *Homunculus*, a kind of prequel to the previous work, is set in a Dickensian 19th-century London, and likewise features the spirit of scientific or alchemical inquiry, along with space vehicles, zombies and the possibility of IMMORTALITY through essence of carp; *Lord Kelvin's Machine* (**1992**), a sequel, carries on in the same vein. These spirited concoctions are reminiscent of the work of JPB's good friend Tim POWERS, though even more lunatic; they both write at times (as do others) a sort of sf set in the 19th century, featuring knowing pastiche – or at least reconstruction – of all sorts of early pulp-sf stereotypes. This has been a sufficiently marked phenomenon that the neologism STEAMPUNK has been coined for it. (JPB's books, in fact, could be regarded as belonging to the same metaseries as Powers's; they feature certain characters in common, including the 19th-century poet William Ashbless, who apparently originated as a pseudonym used by JPB and Powers for poetry they published while at college.) Like many of his POSTMODERNIST generation of writers, including Powers and another of his friends, K.W. JETER, JPB has no interest at all in generic purity, mixing tropes from FANTASY, HORROR, sf, magic realism, adventure fiction and MAINSTREAM literature with great aplomb, as if it were the most natural thing in the world. One could call his stories FABULATIONS.

JPB's next novel, *Land of Dreams* (**1987**), again mingles fantasy and sf tropes (mostly fantasy) with something of a dying fall, as does the more cheerful *The Last Coin* (**1988**), which features an ex-travelling salesman who turns out to be the Wandering Jew, and is anxious that the 30 pieces of silver used to betray Christ should be kept from the hands of a Mr Pennyman, who will use them for apocalyptic purposes. *Land of Dreams* is set in the same fantastic northern-Californian coastal setting as JPB's excellent short story *Paper Dragons* (1985 in anth *Imaginary Lands* ed Robin McKinley; **1992** chap), which won a World Fantasy AWARD. *The Paper Grail* (**1991**) is a quest novel, also set in northern California, mingling Arthurian Legend, Hokusai paintings, preRaphaelites and goodness knows what else. A children's book, *The Magic Spectacles* (**1991** UK), containing a magic window, an ALTERNATE WORLD and goblins, is less successfully childlike than some of his work for adults. It may be that JPB's unquenchable

relish for sheer oddity will inhibit his artistic growth, but meanwhile he is among the most enjoyable genre writers to have emerged from the 1980s. [PN]

Other works: *The Shadow on the Doorstep* (1986 *IASFM*; **1987** chap dos with short stories by Edward BRYANT).

See also: DEL REY BOOKS; GOTHIC SF; GREAT AND SMALL.

BLAYNE, HUGO ◊ John Russell FEARN.

BLAYRE, CHRISTOPHER Pseudonym of UK biologist and author Edward Heron-Allen (1861-1943) who, under his own name, wrote *The Princess Daphne* (**1885**), a novel of psychic vampirism, and *A Fatal Fiddle* (coll **1890**), which includes a story centred on telepathy (◊ ESP). After a long period away from fiction he returned as CB with a series of short weird and sf stories set in the NEAR FUTURE in the University of Cosmopoli. They appeared in *The Purple Sapphire* (coll **1921**; vt with other stories added *The Strange Papers of Dr Blayre* 1932), *The Cheetah-Girl* (**1923**) (a story deleted from the previous volume), and *Some Women of the University* (coll **1932**), the latter two titles being privately published. All are of high quality, but they have had little influence.

Similarities in style, content and sense of humour have led to speculation that CB was responsible for the weird fantasies appearing under the pseudonyms DRYASDUST and M.Y. HALIDOM. Hard evidence is, however, lacking. [JE]

BLEILER, EVERETT F(RANKLIN) (1920-   ) US editor and bibliographer who for many years remained best known as the compiler of *The Checklist of Fantastic Literature: A Bibliography of Fantasy, Weird and Science Fiction Books Published in the English Language* (**1948**; rev vt *The Checklist of Science-Fiction and Supernatural Fiction* 1978), which SHASTA PUBLISHERS was formed to produce, and which soon became recognized as the cornerstone of modern sf BIBLIOGRAPHY. The fact that other works – like R. REGINALD's *Science Fiction and Fantasy Literature* (**1979** edn) – have hugely expanded on its coverage (5000 books listed from the period 1800-1948) does not diminish the significance of EFB's original work. In two further books he has himself expanded upon that work: *The Guide to Supernatural Fiction* (**1983**), solo, and *Science Fiction: The Early Years* (dated 1990 but **1991**), with the assistance of his son, Richard BLEILER, bibliographies of the categories designated, are both annotated with an extraordinary thoroughness; they are essential reference sources for any student of the field; any otherwise unsourced quotations from EFB to be found in this encyclopedia – to which he has also contributed several entries – come from these two volumes. Two large edited studies – *Science Fiction Writers: Critical Studies of the Major Authors from the Early Nineteenth Century to the Present Day* (anth **1982**) and *Supernatural Fiction Writers: Fantasy and Horror* (anth in 2 vols **1985**) – cover much the same area, again thoroughly.

In collaboration with T.E. DIKTY, EFB produced in the late 1940s the first series of best-of-the-year ANTHOLOGIES: *The Best Science Fiction Stories, 1949* (anth **1949**) and *The Best Science Fiction Stories, 1950* (anth **1950**; cut vt *The Best Science Fiction Stories* 1951 UK), both being assembled as *Science Fiction Omnibus* (omni **1952**); *The Best Science Fiction Stories, 1951* (anth **1951**; cut vt *The Best Science Fiction Stories, Second Series* 1952 UK; further cut vt *The Mindworm* 1967 UK); *The Best Science-Fiction Stories, 1952* (anth **1952**; cut vt *The Best Science Fiction Stories, Third Series* 1953 UK); *The Best Science-Fiction Stories, 1953* (anth **1953**; cut vt *The Best Science Fiction Stories, Fourth Series* 1955 UK) and *The Best Science Fiction Stories, 1954* (anth **1954**; cut vt *The Best Science Fiction Stories, Fifth Series* 1956 UK) (the varying hyphenation of the titles is *sic*). *Frontiers in Space* (anth **1955**) presented a selection from the second, third and fourth volumes. A second series presented a selection of longer stories: *Year's Best Science Fiction Novels, 1952* (anth **1952**; cut vt *Year's Best Science Fiction Novels* 1953 UK); *Year's Best Science Fiction Novels, 1953* (anth **1953**; cut vt *Category Phoenix* 1955 UK) and *Year's Best Science Fiction Novels, 1954* (anth **1954**; cut vt *Year's Best Science Fiction Novels, Second Series* 1955 UK).

EFB joined Dover Publications in 1955, rising to Executive Vice-President in 1967, and retiring in 1977. Beginning with *Ghost and Horror Stories of Ambrose Bierce* (coll **1964**), he edited for the firm a series of well produced, cogently introduced and sometimes revelatory editions and anthologies of a wide range of fantasy writers, some of whom had been forgotten. The anthologies *per se* included *Three Gothic Novels* (omni **1960**), *Five Victorian Ghost Novels* (omni **1971**), *Three Supernatural Novels of the Victorian Period* (omni **1975**) and *A Treasury of Victorian Ghost Stories* (omni **1981**). Of more original importance than any of these, perhaps, was EFB's edition of *The Frank Reade Library* (omni **1979-86**) in 10 vols, which reprinted the complete sequence (◊ FRANK READE LIBRARY; Luis SENARENS). He has also translated works from Danish, Dutch, French, German, Italian, Latin, Polish and Swedish; his *Prophecies and Enigmas of Nostradamus* (trans **1979** US) as by Liberte E. LeVert (an anagram of Everett Bleiler) was of some genre interest. EFB won the PILGRIM AWARD in 1984. [JC]

Other works: *Imagination Unlimited* (anth **1952**) ed with T.E. Dikty; editions of the work of Algernon BLACKWOOD, P. Busson, Robert W. CHAMBERS, Arthur Conan DOYLE, Lord DUNSANY, M.R. James, Sheridan Le Fanu, H.P. LOVECRAFT, G. MEYRINK, G.M.W. Reynolds, Mrs J.H. Riddell and H.G. WELLS.

See also: ANONYMOUS SF AUTHORS; CRITICAL AND HISTORICAL WORKS ABOUT SF; DISCOVERY AND INVENTION; HISTORY OF SF; LOST WORLDS; NEW ZEALAND; PREDICTION; SLEEPER AWAKES.

BLEILER, RICHARD (JAMES) (1959-   ) US bibliographer whose *The Index to Adventure Magazine* (2 vols **1990**) and *The Annotated Index to The Thrill Book* (**1991**) are invaluable explorations into rich sources of pulp literature hitherto left generally unexamined. Of more direct sf interest is his collaboration with his father, Everett F. BLEILER (*whom see for details*), on the definitive *Science Fiction: The Early Years* (dated 1990

but **1991**). RB has contributed several entries to this encyclopedia. [JC]

BLIJSTRA, REIN [r] ◊ BENELUX.

BLIPVERTS ◊ MAX HEADROOM.

BLISH, JAMES (BENJAMIN) (1921-1975) US writer. JB's early career in sf followed the usual pattern. He was a fan during the 1930s. His first short story, "Emergency Refueling" (1940), was published in SUPER SCIENCE STORIES. He belonged to the well known New York fan group the FUTURIANS, where he became friendly with such writers as Damon KNIGHT and C.M. KORNBLUTH. He studied microbiology at Rutgers, graduating in 1942, and was then drafted, serving as a medical laboratory technician in the US Army. In 1945-6 he carried out postgraduate work in zoology at Columbia University, abandoning this to become a writer. He was married to Virginia KIDD 1947-63 and then, from 1964 until his death, to Judith Ann LAWRENCE. Three of his early short stories, two of them collaborations, were written under the pseudonyms Donald LAVERTY, John MacDOUGAL and Arthur Merlyn.

JB worked hard to develop his craft, but not until 1950, when the first of his **Okie** stories appeared in ASTOUNDING SCIENCE-FICTION, did it become clear that he could become an sf writer of unusual depth. The **Okie** stories featured flying CITIES, powered by ANTIGRAVITY devices called SPINDIZZIES, moving through the Galaxy looking for work, much as the Okies did in the 1930s when they escaped from the dustbowl. The first **Okie** book, a coherent if episodic novel, was *Earthman, Come Home* (1950-53 var mags; fixup **1955**; cut paperback 1958 US). Three more followed: *They Shall Have Stars* (1952-4 *ASF*; fixup **1956**; rev vt *Year 2018!* 1957 US), *The Triumph of Time* (**1958**; vt *A Clash of Cymbals* UK) and *A Life for the Stars* (**1962**). These four books were finally brought together in a single volume, *Cities in Flight* (omni **1970**), where they appeared in the order of their internal chronology: *They Shall Have Stars*, *A Life for the Stars*, *Earthman, Come Home* and *The Triumph of Time*. Underpinning the pulp-style plotting of much of this series is a serious and pessimistic interest in the cyclic nature of HISTORY, partly derived from JB's reading of Oswald Spengler (1880-1936), especially *The Decline of the West* (**1918-22**). The cycle is carried, at the end of *The Triumph of Time*, from the death of our Universe to the birth of the next, in a memorable passage where Mayor Amalfi becomes, literally, the deep structure of the new Universe.

The years 1950-58 were extraordinarily productive for JB, and many of his best short stories were published in this period, including "Beanstalk" (1952), "Surface Tension" (1952), "Common Time" (1953), which is probably his most praised story, "Beep" (1954) and "A Work of Art" (1956). Several appear in his first collection, *Galactic Cluster* (coll **1959**; with 3 stories cut and "Beanstalk" added, rev 1960 UK). JB's own choice was published as *Best Science Fiction Stories of James Blish* (coll **1965**; with 1 story cut and 2 added, rev 1973; rev vt *The Testament of Andros*). 6 of the 8 stories in this collection, along with an introduction by Robert A.W. LOWNDES, appear with 6 new stories in the posthumous *The Best of James Blish* (coll **1979** US).

These years also saw the publication of his first novel in book form, *Jack of Eagles* (*TWS* 1949 as "Let the Finder Beware"; rev **1952**; cut paperback 1953 US; full text vt *ESP-er* 1958 US). It was followed by *The Warriors of Day* (1951 *Two Complete Science Adventure Books* as "Sword of Xota"; **1953**), *The Seedling Stars* (1952-6 var mags; coll of linked stories **1957**), *The Frozen Year* (**1957**; vt *Fallen Star* UK), *A Case of Conscience* (part 1 in *If*, 1953; **1958**) and *VOR* (part 1949 *TWS* with Damon Knight; exp **1958**). *Jack of Eagles* contains one of the few attempts in sf to give a scientific rationale for telepathy. *A Case of Conscience*, which won the 1959 HUGO for Best Novel, was one of the first serious attempts to deal with RELIGION in sf, and remains one of the most sophisticated in its tale of a priest faced with a planet whose inhabitants seem free of the concept of Original Sin. In *The Seedling Stars* and other stories of the period, JB introduced biological themes (◊ BIOLOGY). This area of science had previously been rather neglected in sf in favour of the "harder" sciences – physics, astronomy, technology, etc. *The Seedling Stars* is an important roadmarker in the early development of sf about GENETIC ENGINEERING.

JB was interested in METAPHYSICS, and some critics regard as his most important work the trilogy **After Such Knowledge**: *A Case of Conscience*, *Doctor Mirabilis* (**1964**; rev 1971 US), and *Black Easter* (**1968**) and *The Day after Judgment* (**1971**); he regarded the last two books as one novel, and indeed they were so published in *Black Easter and The Day After Judgement* (omni **1980**; vt *The Devil's Day* 1990) – hence his use of the term "trilogy". **After Such Knowledge** poses a question once expressed by JB: "Is the desire for secular knowledge, let alone the acquisition and use of it, a misuse of the mind, and perhaps even actively evil?" This is one of the fundamental themes of sf, and is painstakingly explored in *Doctor Mirabilis*, an historical novel which treats the life of the 13th-century scientist and theologian Roger Bacon (*c*1214-1292). It deals with the archetypal sf theme of CONCEPTUAL BREAKTHROUGH from one intellectual model of the Universe to another, more sophisticated model. *Black Easter*, a better and more unified work than its sequel *The Day After Judgment*, is a strong fantasy in which black MAGIC – treated here as a science or, as JB has it, a "scholium" – releases Satan into the world again; Satan rules Heaven in the sequel. The four books were collected in *After Such Knowledge* (omni **1991** UK).

As a writer, JB was thrifty – to the point of parsimony in his later years. He returned to many of his best stories to revise and expand them, sometimes into novel form. Apart from those already mentioned, he also used this treatment on an early short

story, "Sunken Universe" (1942 as by Arthur Merlyn), and built it into another story, "Surface Tension" (1952 *Gal*), which revised again became part of *The Seedling Stars*; "Surface Tension" was his most popular and most anthologized story. Other examples are *Titan's Daughter* (1952, in *Future Tense*, ed Kendell Foster CROSSEN, as "Beanstalk"; vt "Giants in the Earth" in *The Original Science Fiction Stories* 1956; exp **1961**) and *The Quincunx of Time* (1954 *Gal* as "Beep"; exp **1973**).

JB wrote two not very successful sf novels in collaboration: *The Duplicated Man* (1953 *Dynamic SF*; **1959**) with Robert A.W. LOWNDES and *A Torrent of Faces* (fixup **1967**) with Norman L. KNIGHT. The latter is a tale of Earth suffering from, but to a degree coping with, OVERPOPULATION.

JB's later years were much preoccupied with the STAR TREK books. These are *Star Trek* * (coll **1967**), *Star Trek 2* * (coll **1968**), *#3* * (coll **1969**), *#4* * (coll **1971**), *#5* * (coll **1972**), *#6* * (coll **1972**), *#7* * (coll **1972**), *#8* * (coll **1972**), *#9* * (coll **1973**), *#10* * (coll **1974**) and *#11* * (coll **1975**). They are based on the original tv scripts, and hence are in fact collaborations, but *Spock Must Die* * (**1970**) is an original work, the first original **Star Trek** novel. The posthumous *Star Trek 12* (coll **1977**) contained two adaptations (out of five) completed by Judith Ann Lawrence, who also completed some of the work in *#11*. Omnibus editions include: *The Star Trek Reader* * (omni **1976**), containing *#2*, *#3* and *#8*; *The Star Trek Reader II* * (omni **1977**), containing *#1*, *#4* and *#9*; *The Star Trek Reader III* * (omni **1977**), containing *#5*, *#6* and *#7*; *The Star Trek Reader IV* * (omni **1978**), containing *#10*, *#12* and *Spock Must Die*. Re-sorted in order of tv appearance, they were reassembled as *Star Trek: The Classic Episodes #1* * (coll **1991**) with J.A. Lawrence, 27 first-season episodes, *Star Trek: The Classic Episodes #2* * (coll **1991**), 25 second-season episodes, and *Star Trek: The Classic Episodes #3* * (coll **1991**) with J.A. Lawrence, 24 third-season episodes.

Aside from *Spock Must Die* and *A Life for the Stars* (**1962**), the fourth of the **Okie** books, JB wrote four more juvenile novels, none very successful. These are a short and rather didactic series – *The Star Dwellers* (**1961**) and *Mission to the Heart Stars* (**1965**) – along with *Welcome to Mars!* (**1967**) and, the weakest of them, *The Vanished Jet* (**1968**).

JB's output remained fairly steady during the 1960s and 1970s, but the overall standard of his work had dropped, although his penultimate serious work was interesting. This was *Midsummer Century* (**1972**; with 2 stories added, as coll 1974), in which the disembodied consciousness of a scientist is cast forward into a FAR FUTURE where it meets different forms of AI and intervenes in an evolutionary struggle. It is hard to read this story of active mental life cut off from the physical world without thinking of the frail JB's last years. He had a successful operation for throat cancer in the 1960s but died from lung cancer in 1975, characteristically turning out an essay on Spengler and sf on his deathbed – its DEFINITION OF SF is "the internal (intracultural) form taken by syncretism in the West".

JB was also one of the earliest and most influential of sf critics, under the pseudonym William Atheling Jr. Much of his criticism was collected in two books, *The Issue at Hand* (coll **1964**) and *More Issues at Hand* (coll **1970**). It is notably stern in many cases, often pedantic, but intelligent and written from a much wider perspective than was usual for fan criticism of his era. Further essays, including that on Spengler noted above, appear in the posthumous, curate's egg collection *The Tale that Wags the God* (coll **1987**; published as by JB), ed Cy Chauvin. As anthologist, JB edited *New Dreams this Morning* (anth **1966**), *Nebula Award Stories 5* (anth **1970**) and *Thirteen O'Clock* (coll **1972**), a collection of short stories by C.M. Kornbluth. He also edited the only issue of the sf magazine VANGUARD SCIENCE FICTION (June 1958).

JB did much to encourage younger writers, and was one of the founders of the MILFORD SCIENCE FICTION WRITERS' CONFERENCE (he and J.A. Lawrence also founded the UK Milford workshop), and an active charter member of the SCIENCE FICTION WRITERS OF AMERICA. He also became, in 1970, one of the founder members of the SCIENCE FICTION FOUNDATION in the UK. The latter organization named the James Blish AWARD for excellence in sf criticism in honour of him after his death. The first award went in 1977 to Brian W. ALDISS, but it then lapsed for lack of funds.

His dominant intellectual passions, which often recur in his writing, were, aside from Spengler, the works of Ezra Pound, James Joyce (he published papers on both of them) and James Branch CABELL (he edited the Cabell Society magazine *Kalki*), the music of Richard Strauss, and relativistic physics. JB was an interesting example of a writer with an enquiring mind and a strong literary bent – with some of the crotchets of the autodidact – who turned his attention to fundamentally pulp GENRE-SF materials and in so doing transformed them. His part in the transformation of pulp sf to something bigger is historically of the first importance. Nonetheless, he was not a naturally easy or harmonious writer; his style was often awkward, and in its sometimes anomalous displays of erudition it could appear cold. On the other hand, there was a visionary, romantic side to JB which, though carefully controlled, is often visible below the surface.

JB had a scholastic temperament, and in 1969 emigrated to England to be close to Oxford, where he is buried. His manuscripts and papers are in the Bodleian Library. These include several unpublished works of both mainstream fiction and sf.   [PN]

Other works: *So Close to Home* (coll **1961**); *The Night Shapes* (**1962**); *Anywhen* (coll **1970**; with 1 story added, rev **1971** UK); *. . . And All the Stars a Stage* (**1960** *AMZ*; exp **1971**); *Get Out of My Sky, and There Shall Be No Darkness* (coll **1980** UK); *The Seedling Stars/Galactic Cluster* (omni **1983**).

About the author: By far the most complete critical and biographical account is *Imprisoned in a Tesseract: The Life and Work of James Blish* (**1988**) by David KETTERER; also essential is *A Clash of Cymbals: The Triumph of James Blish* (chap **1979**) by Brian M. STABLEFORD; relevant are "*After Such Knowledge:* James Blish's Tetralogy" by Bob Rickard in *A Multitude of Visions* (anth **1975**) ed Cy Chauvin, and the special Blish issue of *FSF* (April 1972).

See also: ADAM AND EVE; ALIENS; ANTI-INTELLECTUALISM IN SF; ARTS; ASTEROIDS; CHILDREN'S SF; COLONIZATION OF OTHER WORLDS; COMMUNICATIONS; COMPUTERS; COSMOLOGY; CRITICAL AND HISTORICAL WORKS ABOUT SF; DISCOVERY AND INVENTION; END OF THE WORLD; EVOLUTION; FANTASTIC VOYAGES; FASTER THAN LIGHT; GALACTIC EMPIRES; GENERATION STARSHIPS; GOLDEN AGE OF SF; GOTHIC SF; GRAVITY; GREAT AND SMALL; HISTORY OF SF; IMAGINARY SCIENCE; IMMORTALITY; JUPITER; LONGEVITY (IN WRITERS AND PUBLICATIONS); *The* MAGAZINE OF FANTASY AND SCIENCE FICTION; MARS; MATHEMATICS; MESSIAHS; MONSTERS; MUSIC; ORIGIN OF MAN; PANTROPY; PARANOIA; PERCEPTION; PHYSICS; POLITICS; POLLUTION; REINCARNATION; SHARED WORLDS; SOCIOLOGY; SPACE FLIGHT; SPACE OPERA; SUPERMAN; SUPERNATURAL CREATURES; TERRAFORMING; THRILLING WONDER STORIES; TRANSPORTATION; UNDER THE SEA; UTOPIAS; WEAPONS.

BLISS, REGINALD ◊ H.G. WELLS.

BLOB, THE 1. Film (1958). Tonylyn/Paramount. Dir Irvin S. Yeaworth Jr, starring Steve McQueen, Aneta Corseaut, Earl Rowe. Screenplay Theodore Simonson, Kate Phillips. 85 mins. Colour.

An ALIEN Blob which grows by absorbing flesh reaches Earth in a hollow meteorite and begins to consume the inhabitants of a small US town. Constantly enlarging, it is finally defeated by a young man who discovers that extreme cold renders it harmless. The special effects are by Barton Sloane. Simple, moderately well made, *TB* is now affectionately remembered as one of the definitive MONSTER MOVIES of the period. A 1971 sequel, *Beware the Blob* (vt *Son of Blob* US), was dir Larry Hagman, better known as J.R. of the tv soap opera *Dallas*. A black-comedy spoof, it is only mildly amusing.

2. Film (1988). Palisades California/TriStar. Dir Chuck Russell, starring Shawnee Smith, Kevin Dillon, Donovan Leitch, Del Close. Screenplay Russell, Frank Darabont. 95 mins. Colour.

This remake, which nowhere credits its 1958 predecessor, follows the original story quite closely. Proficient and exciting, with good and expensive state-of-the-art horror special effects (imploding faces, a man sucked down a plughole) and a spunky heroine (Smith), it is nonetheless rigidly formulaic. All the main changes (the Blob is now the result of a US Government experiment in biological warfare) are derived from other films, notably *The* CRAZIES (1973). Distance may have lent too much charm to the original; this has none at all. The novelization is *The Blob* * (**1988**) by David BISCHOFF.   [PN]

See also: CINEMA.

BLOCH, ROBERT (1917-   ) US writer of FANTASY, HORROR, thrillers and a relatively small amount of sf. Born in Chicago, RB was extremely active from 1935 in his several areas of specialization, but is best known for *Psycho* (**1959**), from which Alfred Hitchcock made the famous film (1960), and to which RB wrote two sequels, *Psycho II* (**1982**) – not related to the 1983 film sequel of the same name – and *Psycho House* (**1990**).

RB began as a devotee of the work of H.P. LOVECRAFT, who treated him with kindness. His first published story was "Lilies" (1934) in the semi-professional MARVEL TALES; his first important sale, "The Secret of the Tomb" (1935), appeared in *Weird Tales*, the magazine which, along with *Fantastic Adventures*, published most of the over 100 stories he wrote in the first decade of his career. Towards the end of this period he contributed the 22 **Lefty Feep** fantasy stories to *Fantastic Adventures* (1942-6); they were later assembled as *Lost in Time and Space with Lefty Feep* (coll **1987**). He published a booklet in the AMERICAN FICTION series, *Sea-Kissed* (coll **1945** chap UK), the title story of which was originally "The Black Kiss" (1937) by RB and Henry KUTTNER; but his first book-length volume, collecting much of his best early fantasy and horror and published by ARKHAM HOUSE, was *The Opener of the Way* (coll **1945**; in 2 vols as *The Opener of the Way* 1976 UK and *House of the Hatchet* 1976 UK); confusingly, a US compilation volume was published with a very similar UK vt, *Yours Truly, Jack the Ripper* (coll **1962**; vt *The House of the Hatchet, and Other Tales of Horror* 1965 UK), extracting a different mix of stories from *The Opener of the Way* plus some from the later *Pleasant Dreams – Nightmares* (coll **1960**; cut vt *Nightmares* 1961; with fewer cuts and some additions vt *Pleasant Dreams* 1979); *Yours Truly, Jack the Ripper* was accompanied by *More Nightmares* (coll **1962**), selected from the same sources. These titles have fortunately been superseded as overviews of his career by *The Selected Stories of Robert Bloch* (coll **1988** in 3 vols: *Final Reckonings* – which single volume is misleadingly vt *The Complete Stories of Robert Bloch, Volume 1: Final Reckonings* 1990 – *Bitter Ends* and *Last Rites*). During this period and afterwards, RB remained an active sf and fantasy fan; a collection of fanzine articles, *The Eighth Stage of Fandom* (coll **1962**), ed Earl KEMP, was assembled for the 1962 World Science Fiction CONVENTION. It is quite likely that his use of the term INNER SPACE, in his 1948 World Science Fiction Convention speech, was the first formulation of the concept later articulated by J.B. PRIESTLEY and J.G. BALLARD (the speech has not apparently seen print). In the first decade of his career RB also turned to radio work: *Stay Tuned for Horror* (1945), a 39-episode syndicated programme of adapted RB stories, became popular. RB sometimes used the pseudonym Tarleton Fiske during this period, and also contributed work to sf and horror magazines under various house names, including E.K. JARVIS and later Will Folke, Wilson KANE and John Sheldon.

His best-known story from this time was "Yours Truly, Jack the Ripper" (1943); much later he amplified his treatment of the fog-shrouded phenomenon of 1888 in *The Night of the Ripper* (**1984**). Since the 1940s he has continued to produce a wide variety of material, though less prolifically than before. Much of his later work, after the success of *Psycho*, was in Hollywood. His numerous collections published from 1960 combine old and new work, so that much of his pre-WWII work has become available.

His output of sf proper has been comparatively slender; the stories assembled in *Atoms and Evil* (coll **1962**) are representative. He is a witty, polished craftsman, and laces his horror with a wry humour which only occasionally slips into whimsy. He has for half a century been active as an sf fan and patron, and his writing shows complete professional control over sf themes when the need arises. He was awarded a 1959 HUGO for Best Short Story for "That Hell-Bound Train" (1958), though strictly speaking it is fantasy, not sf; and was given a Special Award in 1984. [JC]

Other works: *Terror in the Night and Other Stories* (coll **1958**); *Blood Runs Cold* (coll **1961**; with 4 stories cut 1963 UK); *Horror-7* (coll **1963**); *Bogey Men* (coll **1963**); *Tales in a Jugular Vein* (coll **1965**); *The Skull of the Marquis de Sade* (coll **1965**), the title story of which was filmed as *The Skull* (1965); *Chamber of Horrors* (coll **1966**); *The Living Demons* (coll **1967**); *This Crowded Earth* (1958 *AMZ*; **1968** dos) and *Ladies' Day* (**1968** dos), bound together; *Dragons and Nightmares* (coll **1968**), humorous fantasies; *Bloch and Bradbury* (anth **1969**; vt *Fever Dream and Other Fantasies* 1970 UK); *Fear Today, Gone Tomorrow* (coll **1971**); *It's All in Your Mind* (1955 *Imaginative Tales* as "The Big Binge"; **1971**); *Sneak Preview* (1959 *AMZ*; **1971**); *The King of Terrors* (coll **1977**); *Cold Chills* (coll **1977**); *The Best of Robert Bloch* (coll **1977**); *Strange Eons* (**1978**); *Out of the Mouths of Graves* (coll **1978**); *Such Stuff as Screams are Made Of* (coll **1979**); *Mysteries of the Worm: All the Cthulhu Mythos Stories of Robert Bloch* (coll **1981**); *The Twilight Zone: The Movie* * (coll of linked stories **1983**), screenplay adaptations; *Out of my Head* (coll **1986**); *Midnight Pleasures* (coll **1987**); *Fear and Trembling* (coll **1989**); *Lori* (**1989**), horror; *The Jekyll Legacy* * (**1990**) with Andre NORTON, a sequel to the Robert Louis STEVENSON novella; *Psycho-Paths* (anth **1991**) with (anon) Martin Harry GREENBERG.

Associational: Two omnibuses conveniently assemble RB's most interesting non-genre novels: *Unholy Trinity: Three Novels of Suspense* (omni **1986**), which contains *The Scarf* (**1947**; vt *The Scarf of Passion* 1949; rev 1966), *The Deadbeat* (**1960**) and *The Couch* * (**1962**), from the 1962 film; and *Screams: Three Novels of Terror* (omni **1989**), which contains *The Will to Kill* (**1954**), *Firebug* (**1961**) and *The Star Stalker* (**1968**). Further associational titles of interest include *The Kidnapper* (**1954**), *Spiderweb* (**1954**), *Shooting Star* (**1958** dos), *Terror* (**1962**), *The Todd Dossier* (**1969**) as by Collier Young, *Night-World* (**1972**), *American Gothic* (**1974**),

There is a Serpent in Eden (**1979**; vt *The Cunning* 1981). **About the author:** "Robert Bloch" in *Seekers of Tomorrow* (**1966**) by Sam MOSKOWITZ; *The Complete Robert Bloch: An Illustrated, Comprehensive Bibliography* (**1987**) by Randall D. Larson.

See also: FANTASY; MACHINES; *The* MAGAZINE OF FANTASY AND SCIENCE FICTION; RELIGION; ROBOTS; SF IN THE CLASSROOM; SEX; SOCIOLOGY.

BLOCK, THOMAS H(ARRIS) (1945-   ) US writer whose novels are often borderline TECHNOTHRILLERS, especially *Mayday* (**1980**) and the NEAR-FUTURE *Orbit* (**1982**), in which a 3900mph (6275kph) airliner is gimmicked by saboteurs into flying into orbit. *Airship Nine* (**1984**) is a full-fledged post-HOLOCAUST tale, with soldiers in Antarctica fending off nuclear winter and preparing to repopulate the planet.   [JC]

BLOOD BEAST FROM OUTER SPACE ◊ *The* NIGHT CALLER.

BLOODSTONE, JOHN ◊ J. Stuart BYRNE.

BLOOM, HAROLD (1930-   ) US academic and writer, best known for his Freudian analysis of the relationship between strong male authors and predecessor authors over the last several centuries of Western literature; *The Anxiety of Influence* (**1973**) and its several increasingly talmudic sequels have become central critical texts. His only novel, *The Flight to Lucifer* (**1979**), was described as a Gnostic fantasy, accurately. Of the many anthologies of critical pieces ed HB, several are of sf interest: *Mary Shelley* (anth **1985**), *Edgar Allan Poe* (anth **1985**), *Ursula K. Le Guin* (anth **1986**) and *Ursula K. Le Guin's The Left Hand of Darkness* (anth **1987**), *Doris Lessing* (anth **1986**), and *George Orwell* (anth **1987**) and *George Orwell's 1984* (anth **1987**).   [JC]

BLOT, THOMAS Pseudonym of US writer William Simpson (?   -?   ). In his sf novel *The Man from Mars: His Morals, Politics and Religion* (**1891**) the eponymous telepathic traveller tells of his UTOPIAN world. Unfortunately – if his desire was to communicate widely – the human he contacts is a hermit.   [JC]

BLUE BOOK MAGAZINE, THE US PULP MAGAZINE published by the Story-Press Corporation; ed Donald Kennicott, Maxwell Hamilton and others. It first appeared May 1905 as *The Monthly Story Magazine*, became *The Monthly Story Blue Book Magazine* Sep 1906, *The Blue Book Magazine* May 1907, and *Bluebook* Feb 1952. Later issues had no sf content.

This general-fiction pulp, a major competitor of the Frank A. MUNSEY group, had a long history of publishing sf and fantasy, with works by George Allan ENGLAND, William Hope HODGSON and others appearing in its opening years. Its heyday came in the late 1920s and early 1930s, when it published serializations of many novels by Edgar Rice BURROUGHS as well as others by Edwin BALMER and Philip WYLIE, James Francis DWYER and Edgar JEPSON, with additional short stories from Ray CUMMINGS. Later Nelson BOND came into prominence with his **Square-deal Sam** (1943-51) and **Pat Pending** (1942-8) series.   [JE]

BLUEJAY BOOKS US publishing house founded by James R. FRENKEL, who had previously been the editor of Dell's sf line. BB began publishing in 1983, their books being distributed by St Martin's Press. Among their titles were Gardner DOZOIS's best-of-the-year anthologies (◊ ANTHOLOGIES), books by Frenkel's wife Joan D. VINGE, Dan SIMMONS's first novel *The Song of Kali* (**1985**), Patti Perret's book of photographic studies *The Faces of Science Fiction* (**1984**) and Greg BEAR's *Eon* (**1985**). Other authors included Jack DANN, K.W. JETER, Nancy KRESS, Rudy RUCKER, Theodore STURGEON, Vernor VINGE, Connie WILLIS and Timothy ZAHN. It was a strong list, concentrating on hardcovers and trade paperbacks, with over 50 new sf, fantasy and horror titles as well as a number of reprints published during the company's short life; but this attempt of a small specialist publisher to enter the mass-marketing field, traditionally difficult especially as regards distribution, was apparently undercapitalized. BB ceased trading in 1986.   [PN]

BLUE RIBBON MAGAZINES ◊ FUTURE FICTION; SCIENCE FICTION.

BLUE SUNSHINE Film (1977). Ellanby/Blue Sunshine Co. Written and dir Jeff Lieberman, starring Zalman King, Deborah Winters, Mark Goddard, Robert Walden. 95 mins. Colour.

Lieberman's first film was a witty (if disgusting) MONSTER MOVIE, *Squirm* * (1976) – the last word on killer worms; its novelization was *Squirm* (**1976**) by Richard A. CURTIS. *BS*, Lieberman's second feature, is also unusually sharp and amusing for a low-budget exploitation movie. Middle-class ex-hippies inexplicably lose their hair and turn homicidal. The culprit turns out to be Blue Sunshine, an LSD variant – the bad acid they dropped a decade earlier has taken its toll on their chromosomes. As Kim NEWMAN puts it in *Nightmare Movies* (**1984**; rev 1988), "the flower children have become the Living Dead". The dialogue is good, the metaphor potent. *BS* is as pointed a film of sf social commentary as any that appeared in its decade, though its theme of human metamorphosis through corrupt TECHNOLOGY perhaps owes something to David CRONENBERG.   [PN]

BLUE THUNDER Film (1983). Rastar/Gordon Carroll Productions. Dir John BADHAM, starring Roy Scheider, Warren Oates, Candy Clark, Daniel Stern, Malcolm McDowell. Screenplay Dan O'Bannon, Don Jakoby. 110 mins. Colour.

Borderline sf set in a very NEAR-FUTURE Los Angeles, *BT* tells the story of Murphy (Scheider), a helicopter-based police officer, asked to try out a new super-copter: it can see through walls, fire missiles, fly at 200 knots and hear conversations from far away. Murphy gradually unravels a government conspiracy to create rioting among Blacks and Chicanos as a justification for the introduction of new, draconian police methods of surveillance and riot control. The post-Watergate, post-Vietnam PARANOIA of the plot is rather unconvincing, in part because of McDowell's overacting as a right-wing extremist, and there is much moral confusion between the overt theme – the dangers of using new TECHNOLOGY as an instrument of oppression – and the subtext, which says that this same technology is exciting and beautiful. *BT* is well made, suspenseful and meretricious, and owes altogether too much to FIREFOX. Columbia TV produced a disappointing tv series of the same title, *Blue Thunder*, starring James Farentino, which ran briefly for 11 episodes in 1984; in it the same supercopter becomes merely a useful aid for stereotypical police work. [PN]

See also: CINEMA.

BLUM, RALPH (1932-   ) US writer involved in early drug research, which is reflected in his sf novel, *The Simultaneous Man* (**1970**). A convict's mind is erased and the memories and identity of a research scientist are substituted, rather as in Robert SILVERBERG's *The Second Trip* (**1972**). The relationship between the scientist and his "twin" is complex, and ends tragically for him in the USSR, where he himself becomes a subject for experimentation. Of borderline interest is *Old Glory and the Real-Time Freaks* (**1972**). *The Book of Runes* (**1982**) is nonfiction. [JC]

BLUMENFELD, F. YORICK (1932-   ) UK writer whose *Jenny Ewing: My Diary* (**1981** chap; vt *Jenny: My Diary* 1982 chap US) offers an exceedingly grim vision of the UK after a nuclear HOLOCAUST, as seen by the reluctant survivor whose journal, written in a shelter, makes up the text. The book was first published as by Jenny herself. [JC]

BLUMLEIN, MICHAEL (1948-   ) US medical doctor and writer whose output in the latter capacity, though still restricted to two published books, has had considerable impact on the field. His first published story was "Tissue Ablation and Variant Regeneration: A Case Report" for *Interzone* in 1984. This tale remains one of the most astonishingly savage political assaults ever published. The target is Ronald Reagan, whose living body is eviscerated without anaesthetic by a team of doctors, partly to punish him for the evils he has allowed to flourish in the world and partly to make amends for those evils through the biologically engineered growth and transformation of the ablated tissues into foodstuffs and other goods ultimately derived from the flesh, which are then sent to the impoverished of the Earth. "Tissue Ablation" and other remarkable tales including "The Brains of Rats" (1986) and "The Wet Suit" (1989) were assembled as *The Brains of Rats* (coll **1989**), a publication that demonstrates the very considerable thematic and stylistic range of modern sf, and shows how very far from reassuring it can be.

MB's only published novel, *The Movement of Mountains* (**1987**), is told in a more immediately accessible style than some of his short FABULATIONS, though at moments the narrative form of the text – related by a doctor in the form of a confessional memoir – and some of the ornate chill of the narrator's mind are reminiscent of the darker tales of Gene WOLFE. The tale begins in a familiar, congested NEAR-FUTURE

California, moves to a colony planet mined by "mountainous", biologically engineered, short-lived slaves – whom the doctor helps liberate while at the same time analysing the plague which has killed his lover – and finally returns to Earth, where the doctor, having discovered that the plague has the effect of transforming humans into gestalt configurations, disseminates it in secret in order to bring down a repressive government.

At his best, MB writes tales in which, with an air of remote sang-froid, he makes unrelenting assaults on public issues (and figures). He writes as though his aesthetic demands justice; as though, in other words, beauty demands truth. [JC]

See also: INTERZONE; MEDICINE.

BLYTH, JAMES (1864-1933) UK writer, a fairly prolific author of popular fiction who is best remembered in the field for *The Tyranny* (**1907**), a NEAR-FUTURE tale of a UK dominated by a tyrant and at war with Germany. *Ichabod* (**1910**), which is defaced by an antisemitism that seemed "robust" even for the UK of 1910, grants victory to the UK against an unholy alliance of Jews and Germans through a MATTER TRANSMITTER and a machine which reads malign thoughts. *The Shadow of the Unseen* (**1907**) with Barry PAIN, a tale of the supernatural, was infused with JB's love of the motor car. [JC]

Other works: *With a View to Matrimony and Other Stories* (coll **1904**); *The Aerial Burglars* (**1906**), in which thieves use a flying motor car for nefarious purposes; *The Swoop of the Vulture* (**1909**); *A Haunted Inheritance* (**1910**); *My Haunted Home* (**1914**); *The Weird Sisters* (**1919**).

BOARDMAN, TOM Working name of UK publisher and editor Thomas Volney Boardman (1930-   ), who went to work for the family publishing company, T.V. Boardman, in 1949, and stayed on as managing director when the company changed ownership in 1954. The company published primarily mysteries, with some sf. TB was sf adviser, successively, to GOLLANCZ, Four Square Books, Macdonald and New English Library. He was business manager of *SF Horizons*. He edited the anthologies *Connoisseur's Science Fiction* (anth **1964**), *The Unfriendly Future* (anth **1965**), *An ABC of Science Fiction* (anth **1966**), *Science Fiction Horizons 1* (anth **1968**) and *Science Fiction Stories* (anth **1979**), the latter for children. He then worked in educational publishing. [MJE]

BODÉ, VAUGHN (FREDERICK) (1941-1975) US COMICS artist and writer with a bold, loose line who created a world of charming and whimsical – if somewhat cutesy – fantasy characters; the most famous of these were Cheech Wizard – a strange figure almost entirely engulfed in a star-spangled hat – a bevy of little busty sexpots and a number of almost indistinguishable reptilian characters. VB began by providing amateur material for FANZINES, and in 1969 won a HUGO for Best Fan Artist. From 1970 until his premature death he worked professionally for *Cavalier* and *National Lampoon*, and published his own comic book, *Junkwaffel* (1972-4), creating a number of oddball joke strips and short stories, plus a few longer ones. He won a Yellow Kid Award in 1975. His sf creations – apart from 14 covers for sf magazines (1967 onward), such as *If* and *Gal* – included the strips **Zooks** (1983), **Sunpot** (1984; *see also* GALAXY SCIENCE FICTION) and **Cobalt 60**, the latter being continued after VB's death, rather poorly, by his son Mark Bodé in *Epic*. [RT]

See also: COMICS; HEAVY METAL; MÉTAL HURLANT.

BODELSEN, ANDERS (1937-) Danish writer and journalist, author of several novels of suspense. *Villa Sunset* ["Villa Sunset"] (**1964**) is a NEAR-FUTURE tale of Fimbul-Winter and glacial transformation. *Frysepunktet* (**1969**; trans Joan Tate as *Freezing Point* **1971** UK; vt *Freezing Down* **1971** US) is also sf. Its protagonist is incurably sick, and is frozen until he can be cured (◊ CRYONICS). The world to which he awakens, complexly and satirically described in AB's intense manner, offers him ambivalent (and restricted) choices between an idle life (with death inevitable) and a life of drudgery (with access to spare parts). It is a dark story, told urgently, using a wide range of literary techniques. [JC]

See also: DENMARK; IMMORTALITY.

BODIN, FÉLIX [r] ◊ P.K. ALKON; FRANCE; FUTUROLOGY.

BOEHM, HERB [s] ◊ John VARLEY.

BOETZEL, ERIC [r] ◊ Herbert CLOCK.

BOGÁTI, PÉTER [r] ◊ HUNGARY.

BOGDANOV, ALEXANDER Pseudonym of Russian writer and political thinker Alexander (Alexandrovich) Malinovsky (1873-1928); he survived criticism from Vladimir Lenin only to die in a blood-transfusion experiment. He is remembered for a UTOPIAN sequence – *Krasnaia Zvezda* ["The Red Star"] (**1908**) and *Inzhener Menni* ["Engineer Menni"] (**1913**), both assembled with a 1924 poem as *The Red Star: The First Bolsehvik Utopia* (omni trans Charles Rougle **1984** US) – depicting the flight of its protagonist, a Russian revolutionary, to Mars where a technocratic utopia, based on principles of "rational management" is built. The first volume was reprinted just after the Socialist Revolution in 1917, and perhaps for that reason was thought of as the first authentic example of "Soviet" sf; however, it was not again reprinted until 1977, when it was purged of episodes describing "free love" in the utopia. The second volume includes interesting speculations that adumbrated the relationship of CYBERNETICS to modern management and also anticipated the need for a COMPUTER on SPACE-SHIPS, describing the ship itself as being driven by atomic energy. [VG]

See also: RUSSIA.

BOGORAS, WALDEMAR ◊ Vladimir Germanovitch BOGORAZ.

BOGORAZ, VLADIMIR GERMANOVITCH (1865-1936) Soviet anthropologist whose novel *Sons of the Mammoth* (trans Stephen Graham **1929** as by Waldemar Bogoras) reflects his professional concerns in a prehistoric tale in which Neanderthals encounter rising human stock and a "mysterious" beast that turns out to be natural. [JC]

See also: ORIGIN OF MAN.

BOISGILBERT, EDMUND ◊ Ignatius DONNELLY.

BOK, HANNES (1914-1964) US illustrator, author and astrologer, born Wayne Woodard. Sf ILLUSTRATION has had very few mavericks: HB was possibly the most famous. He did not let editors and publishers dictate the way he designed his work, and thereby lost hundreds of commissions. He was a master of the macabre, a stylist *par excellence*. He painted many covers and did hundreds of black-and-white illustrations for such magazines as COSMIC STORIES, FAMOUS FANTASTIC MYSTERIES, FANTASTIC UNIVERSE, FUTURE FICTION, IMAGINATION, PLANET STORIES, STIRRING SCIENCE STORIES, SUPER SCIENCE STORIES and, especially, 7 covers for WEIRD TALES. He also did book-jackets for ARKHAM HOUSE, FANTASY PRESS, GNOME PRESS and SHASTA PUBLISHERS, among others. His style was unique, though the colours and techniques he used were heavily influenced by Maxfield Parrish (1870-1966); his black-and-white illustrations are highly stylized, his human figures angular and almost Byzantine. HB was much stronger illustrating fantasy and horror than sf.

HB was also a writer. Two of his colourful, moralizing fantasy novels were published in book form after his death: *The Sorcerer's Ship* (1942 *Unknown*; **1969**) and *Beyond the Golden Stair* (1948 *Startling Stories* as "The Blue Flamingo"; rev **1970**); his other novel was "Starstone World" (1942 *Science Fiction Quarterly*). He also wrote several short stories. An admirer of A. MERRITT, he completed and illustrated two of the latter's novels after Merritt's death in 1943 – *The Black Wheel* (**1947**) and *The Fox Woman and The Blue Pagoda* (**1946**) – being credited in both books. "The Blue Pagoda" was an episode written by Bok to complete *The Fox Woman*, on which Merritt had worked sporadically for 20 years before his death.

HB did little illustration after about 1952, turning to astrology, about which he wrote 13 articles for *Mystic Magazine* (retitled *Search* in 1956). With Ed EMSHWILLER he shared the first HUGO in 1953 for Best Cover Artist. After his death, his friend Emil PETAJA became chairman of the Bokanalia Foundation, founded 1967. This group has published folios of HB's artwork, some of his poetry, and *And Flights of Angels: The Life and Legend of Hannes Bok* (**1968**) by Petaja. [JG/PN]

See also: FANTASY; FUTURIANS.

BOLAND, (BERTRAM) JOHN (1913-1976) UK author and journalist, a prolific story producer, although rarely of sf. His sf novels, *White August* (**1955**) and *No Refuge* (**1956**), are both set in frigid conditions. The first is a DISASTER tale, dealing with the dire effects of a botched attempt at weather control. *No Refuge* depicts an Arctic UTOPIA into which two criminals accidentally irrupt; after a good deal of discussion they are dealt with properly. *Holocaust* (**1974**) has a solar-cell satellite running amuck, spraying heat-rays, and being lusted after by the great powers as a weapon. A further novel, *Operation Red Carpet* (**1959**), has some borderline sf components. [JC]

BOLDIZSÁR, IVÁN [r] ◊ HUNGARY.

BOLLAND, BRIAN (JOHN) (1951-   ) UK COMIC-book artist highly regarded for his smooth line and meticulous, sculptural drawing style. His first strip work appeared in the underground magazine *Oz* in 1971. In 1975-7 he drew **Powerman**, a Black SUPERHERO, for the Nigerian market, his episodes alternating with those by Dave GIBBONS, and then he began producing covers for 2,000 AD. His most lasting contribution to date has been his development of JUDGE DREDD: BB's first **Judge Dredd** strip appeared in *2,000 AD* #40 (26 Nov 1977), and in all he drew 40, the last appearing in #244 (26 Dec 1981); he also provided a run of 40 covers for Eagle Comics's *2,000 AD* and *Judge Dredd* reprints 1983-6.

He began to produce cover artwork for DC COMICS with *Green Lantern* #127 (Apr 1980). For DC he also drew a number of short sf strips as well as a 12-issue series, *Camelot 3,000*, Dec 1982-Apr 1985. He produced *Batman – The Killing Joke* (graph **1988**), a very successful 48pp quality comic book written by Alan MOORE. Since then he has concentrated on artwork for covers, including 48 (to early 1992) for *Animal Man* and those for the Titan Books editions of the WILD CARDS graphic novels in 1991.

He has also written and drawn 48 12-panel strips featuring **Mr Mamoulian**, a mournful middle-aged man with a hangdog expression who seems to be permanently seated on a park bench. These have been published in the UK in *Escape* as well as in Spain (*Cimoc*), Sweden (*Pox*) and the USA (*Cheval Noir*). Of his other strip, *The Actress and the Bishop*, written in rhyme, only two sections have appeared (in *A1*). [RT]
See also: ILLUSTRATION.

BOLTON, CHARLES E. (1841-1901) US writer whose posthumously published sf novel, *The Harris-Ingram Experiment* (**1905**), conflates capitalist accomplishments, romantic love, a genius inventor and UTOPIAN experiments. [JC]

BOLTON, JOHANNA M. (?   -   ) US writer whose first novel, *The Alien Within* (**1988**), carries its revenge-seeking female protagonist through a crumbling Galactic Federation, introducing her to a variety of ALIEN empires. JMB's second novel, *Mission: Tori* (**1990**), also featuring a bereaved female protagonist, addresses but does not solve the mysteries surrounding the mineral-rich and much desired planet of Tori. [JC]

BONANATE, UGO [r] ◊ ITALY.

BONANNO, MARGARET WANDER (1950-   ) US writer whose first books were volumes of poetry, beginning with *A Certain Slant of Light* (coll **1979**), and who began writing sf with a highly successful **Star Trek** tie, *Dwellers in the Crucible* * (**1985**). Two others followed – *Strangers from the Sky* * (**1987**) and *Probe* * (**1992**), which latter she claimed had been extensively rewritten, and disavowed – but MWB's main achievement lay in **The Others**, a PLANETARY-ROMANCE

sequence comprising *The Others* (**1990**) and *Otherwhere* (**1991**), in which the eponymous aliens, stranded on an Earthlike world, must attempt, through telepathy and intermittent bouts of interracial breeding, to survive the onslaughts of jealous, inferior humanlike natives. [JC]

BOND, J. HARVEY ◊ Russ R. WINTERBOTHAM.

BOND, NELSON S(LADE) (1908-   ) US writer and in later years philatelist, publishing works in that field. He began his career in public relations, coming to sf in 1937 with "Down the Dimensions" for *ASF*. Later in that year he published "Mr Mergenthwirker's Lobblies" in *Scribner's Magazine*, a fantasy which became a radio series, was made into a tv play (**1957**), and in its original form was collected in *Mr Mergenthwirker's Lobblies and Other Fantastic Tales* (coll **1946**). It served as a model for the "nutty" fiction that NSB wrote for *Fantastic Adventures* in the early 1940s, comic tales involving implausible inventions and various pixillated doings, sometimes with an effect of excessive coyness. He wrote only two stories under pseudonyms, one as George Danzell (1940) and one as Hubert Mavity (1939).

NSB's active career in the magazines extended into the 1950s; his markets were not restricted to the sf PULP MAGAZINES, and he became strongly associated with *The* BLUE BOOK MAGAZINE for stories and series usually combining sf and fantasy elements, often featuring trick endings reminiscent of O. Henry. Further collections, assembling most of his best work, are *The 31st of February* (coll **1949**), *No Time Like the Future* (coll **1954**) and *Nightmares and Daydreams* (coll **1968**). Since the early 1950s he has been relatively inactive as a writer.

His most famous single series, the **Lancelot Biggs** stories concerning an eccentric space traveller, appeared 1939-43 in various magazines; it was published, with most stories revised, as *The Remarkable Exploits of Lancelot Biggs, Spaceman* (coll of linked stories **1950**). A similar series, about **Pat Pending** and his peculiar inventions, appeared 1942-57, all but the last in *Bluebook*; it remains uncollected. The **Square-deal Sam McGhee** stories, also in *Bluebook* (1943-51), are tall tales, not sf. A series of three stories about **Meg the Priestess**, a young girl who comes to lead a post-HOLOCAUST tribe, appeared in various magazines, 1939-42; they remain uncollected, as do the four **Hank Horse-Sense** stories, which appeared in *AMZ* 1940-42.

NSB's only novel in book form, *Exiles of Time* (1940 *Blue Book Magazine*; **1949**) is a darkly told story about the end of things in Mu (◊ DISASTER), told in a sometimes allegorical fashion. Perhaps because of the number of his markets, NSB established a less secure reputation in the sf/fantasy world than less versatile writers; not dissimilar in his wit and fantasticality to Robert BLOCH or Fredric BROWN, he is considerably less well known than either, though his work is attractive and often memorable. [JC]
Other works: *The Monster* (coll **1953** chap Australia);

State of Mind: A Comedy in Three Acts (**1958** chap), a comic fantasy play; *Animal Farm: A Fable in Two Acts* (**1964** chap), a play based on the 1945 novel by George ORWELL; *James Branch Cabell: A Complete Bibliography* (**1974**).

See also: ADAM AND EVE; AMAZING STORIES; DISCOVERY AND INVENTION; LIVING WORLDS.

BONE, J(ESSE) F(RANKLIN) (1916-   ) US writer and professor of veterinary medicine who began publishing sf with "Survival Type" for *Gal* in 1957. His first sf novel, *The Lani People* (**1962**), is his most memorable, later works being routine. It deals with an ALIEN people whose suffering from human exploitation is graphically related. His short fiction – about 30 stories in all – remains uncollected.   [JC]

Other works: *Legacy* (**1976**); *The Meddlers* (**1976**); *Gift of the Manti* (**1977**) with Ray Myers (an almost certainly unintended pseudonym for Roy MEYERS); *Confederation Matador* (**1978**).

See also: ARTS.

BONESTELL, CHESLEY (1888-1986) US astronomical illustrator. CB studied as an architect in San Francisco, his birthplace, but never graduated; he was employed by many architectural firms and aided in the design of the Golden Gate Bridge. He worked as a matte artist to produce special effects and background paintings for 14 films, including *Citizen Kane* (1941), DESTINATION MOON (1950), WHEN WORLDS COLLIDE (1951), WAR OF THE WORLDS (1953) and *The CONQUEST OF SPACE* (1955). In the early 1940s he began astronomical painting on a major scale, much of his work being used in *Life* magazine, and during 1949-72 completed astronomical artwork for 10 books, including the classic science-fact book *The Conquest of Space* (**1949**), with text by Willy LEY. In 1950-51 CB painted for the Boston Museum of Science a 10 x 40ft (about 3 x 12m) mural; it was transferred to the National Air and Space Museum of the Smithsonian Institution in 1976. His space paintings were used as cover illustrations for *ASF* (12 covers) and *FSF* (38 covers) from 1947 onwards; he became a favourite of sf fans in this period. His style was a photographic realism, showing great attention to correctness of perspective and scale in conformity with the scientific knowledge of the day, and some of his Moon paintings, for example, were truly prophetic in their accuracy. But, more than that, his work held great beauty and drama in its stillness and depth. Many book lovers of the post-WWII generation can trace back their fascination for space exploration as much to CB's paintings as to their reading of either science or sf. The recipient of many awards, he earned a Special Achievement HUGO in 1974.   [JG/PN]

See also: ASTOUNDING SCIENCE-FICTION.

BONFIGLIOLI, KYRIL [r] ◊ SCIENCE FANTASY.

BONHAM, FRANK (1914-1988) US writer, most of whose adult novels were Westerns, and who wrote in various modes for younger readers. *The Missing Persons League* (**1976**), set in a starving DYSTOPIAN USA, presents its young protagonist with the chance

to find a better world. *The Forever Formula* (**1979**) is a strong sf tale in which a young man awakens from SUSPENDED ANIMATION to find himself torn between opposing factions: those who wish for his father's IMMORTALITY formula, to which he has the secret, and those who wish for normal mortality. *Premonitions* (**1984**) is a fantasy.   [JC]

BOOTH, IRWIN [s] ◊ Edward D. HOCH.

BOOTHBY, GUY (NEWELL) (1867-1905) Australian-born writer, permanently in the UK from 1894, who remains best known for his **Dr Nikola** sequence: *A Bid for Fortune* (**1895**; rev vt *Dr Nikola's Vendetta* 1908 US), *Doctor Nikola* (**1896**), *Dr Nikola's Experiment* (**1899**) and *"Farewell, Nikola"* (**1901**). The heart of the series is devoted to the Doctor's convoluted search for a Tibetan process that will resuscitate the dead and ensure IMMORTALITY in the living, and there are some hints that – unhampered by compunctions, armed with PSI POWERS, and blessed with a powerful experimental intellect – he may have reached his goal. Of GB's 50 or so novels, several further titles were of fantasy interest.   [JC]

Other works: *The Lust of Hate* (**1898**); *Pharos, the Egyptian* (**1899**); *The Curse of the Snake* (**1902**); *Uncle Joe's Legacy, and Other Stories* (coll **1902**); *The Lady of the Island* (coll **1904**); *A Crime of the Under-Seas* (**1905**), a fantastic-invention tale.

BORDEN, MARY (1886-1968) US-born writer and journalist, in the UK for the last half-century of her life. After funding and running a field hospital in WWI, she began to write novels and nonfiction, some of the latter being of FEMINIST interest. Her sf novel, *Jehovah's Day* (**1928**), is a fable about the emergence of humanity, carrying its narrative from the earliest times to a NEAR-FUTURE catastrophe which destroys London. Throughout, the mysterious figure of Eryops the Mud Puppy makes emblematic appearances.   [JC]

BORDEWIJK, F. [r] ◊ BENELUX.

BORGES, JORGE LUIS (1899-1986) Argentine short-story writer, poet, essayist and university professor, known primarily for his work outside the sf field. Though much of his fiction is local and drawn from Argentine history and events, Borges is best known in the English-speaking world for his short fantasies. *Ficciones* (coll **1944**; rev 1961; trans Anthony Kerrigan **1962** US) and *El Aleph* (coll **1949**; rev 1952) contain his most important short stories, including most of those considered closest to sf. Most of the contents of these books, with some additional material, can be found in English in *Labyrinths* (coll trans **1962**; rev 1964). Another translated collection – the author collaborating on the translation – is *The Aleph and Other Stories 1933-1969* (coll trans with Norman Thomas di Giovanni **1970** US), which is not a translation of *El Aleph*, containing a quite different selection of stories.

JLB has argued that "the compilation of vast books is a laborious and impoverishing extravagance" and claims to have read few novels himself – and then only out of a "sense of duty". His stories are accordingly brief, but contain a bewildering number of ideas. Many are technically interesting, exploiting such forms as fictional reviews and biographies to summarize complex and equally fictional books and characters, or using the precise styles of the fable or the detective story to encapsulate involved ideas.

Among his most famous fantasies are: "The Library of Babel" (1941), which describes a vast library or Universe of books containing all possible combinations of the alphabet, and thus all possible gibberish alongside all possible wisdom; "The Garden of Forking Paths" (1941), which examines the potentials of ALTERNATE WORLDS; "The Babylon Lottery", which details the history of a game of chance that gradually becomes so complex and universal that it is indistinguishable from real life; "Tlön, Uqbar, Orbis Tertius" (1941), which chronicles the emergence in and takeover of everyday life by an entirely fictional and fabricated world; "The Circular Ruins", which portrays a character dreaming and giving life to a man, only to realize that he in turn is another man's dream; and "Funes, the Memorious" (1942), which describes a man with such perfect memory that the past is as accessible to him as the present. (All the above appear in *Ficciones*.) The profound influence of these – and other stories – on Gene WOLFE is reflected in *The Book of the New Sun* (1980-83), where they are all made use of.

JLB's interest in METAPHYSICS is apparent in these stories, and his examination, through FANTASY, of the nature of reality associates his fiction with that of many modern US authors, such as Philip K. DICK, Thomas PYNCHON and Kurt VONNEGUT Jr. He is an important influence on the more sophisticated recent sf writers, especially those dealing with ABSURDIST themes and paradoxes of PERCEPTION. His interest in puzzles and labyrinths is another stimulus that has led him to fantasy and the detective story as media for expressing his ideas in fiction.

JLB has published other collections of stories and sketches, some on the borderline of fantasy, as well as a fantastic bestiary, *Manual de zoologia fantastica* (1957 Mexico; exp vt *El libro do los seres imaginarios* 1967; the latter trans Norman Thomas di Giovanni and JLB as *The Book of Imaginary Beings* 1969 US). With Silvina Ocampo (1906-   ) and Adolfo BIOY CASARES he also edited a fantasy collection, *Antología de la Literatura Fantástica* (1940; rev 1965; further rev 1976; trans as *The Book of Fantasy* 1976 US; rev 1988 with intro by Ursula K. LE GUIN), and revealed a first-hand (if inaccurate) knowledge of sf by including H.P. LOVECRAFT, Robert A. HEINLEIN, A.E. VAN VOGT and Ray BRADBURY in his *Introduction to American Literature* (1967; trans Keating and Evans 1971). Translation of JLB's work into English is complex, and there is no definitive collection. A number of his early works have been reprinted in sf anthologies. [PR]

Other works: *Historia universal de la infamia* (coll **1935**; trans Norman Thomas di Giovanni as *A Universal History of Infamy* **1972** US); *Seis problemas para Don Isidro Parodi* (coll **1942**; trans Norman Thomas di Giovanni as *Six Problems for Don Isidro Parodi* **1981** US) with Adolfo Bioy Casares; *Crónicos de Busto Domecq* (coll **1967**; trans Norman Thomas di Giovanni as *Chronicles of Bustos Domecq* **1976** US) with Bioy Casares; *El hacedor* (coll **1960**; trans M. Boyer and H. Morland as *Dreamtigers* **1964** US); *Antología personal* (coll **1961**; trans Anthony Kerrigan as *A Personal Anthology* **1961** US); *El informe sobre Brodie* (coll **1970**; trans Norman Thomas di Giovanni as *Doctor Brodie's Report* **1972**), his last collection of original work; *El libro del arena* (coll **1975**; trans Norman Thomas di Giovanni as *The Book of Sand* **1977** US; exp **1979** UK); *Borges: A Reader* (coll **1981**); *Atlas* (coll **1984**; trans Anthony Kerrigan **1985** US).

About the author: *Jorge Luis Borges* (**1970**) by M.S. Stabb; *Jorge Luis Borges: An Annotated Primary and Secondary Bibliography* (**1984**) by D.W. Foster; *A Dictionary of Borges* (**1990**) by Evelyn Fishburn and Psiche Hughes.

See also: LATIN AMERICA.

BORGO PRESS US publishing house, a SMALL PRESS with a fairly extensive list, based in California, founded in 1975 by R. REGINALD, who is its publisher and editor. BP has several specialist publishing lines, including books and booklets about sf as well as on health, genealogy, politics, etc. BP's **The Milford Series: Popular Writers of Today**, which began with *Robert A. Heinlein: Stranger in his Own Land* (**1976** chap; rev 1977) by George Edgar SLUSSER, is a series of mostly short critical booklets – more recently *c*70,000 words – largely though not exclusively devoted to sf writers. BP announced a new series in 1988, **Bibliographies of Modern Authors**, many of them to be sf and fantasy authors, of which #1 was *The Work of Colin Wilson: An Annotated Bibliography and Guide* (**1989**) by Colin Stanley. As with many small presses, BP's books are often published much later than announced. BP has published, to 1991, around 130 books, of which more than 90 are of sf relevance. [PN]

See also: SF IN THE CLASSROOM.

BORIS ◊ Boris VALLEJO.

BORN IN FLAMES Film (1983). Lizzie Borden/Jerome Foundation/CAPS/Young Filmmakers. Written, prod, ed and dir Lizzie Borden, starring Honey, Adele Bertei, Jeanne Satterfield, Flo Kennedy, Kathryn Bigelow. 80 mins. Colour.

This underground movie, made over five years on 16mm film and video, was deservedly given quite wide distribution. 10 years after a peaceful social-democratic revolution in the USA, the Party is in power, the position of women in society is still not much improved, and unemployment (especially of women) is widespread. Radical FEMINIST groups (whose differing political positions are shown with a sort of cartoon clarity) are at first at odds; as disenchantment with the Party builds up they are drawn together and a new revolution begins. Stereotyped conceptions of feminists as humourless refugees from the middle classes are shaken (on several grounds) by this pleasing and lively film, whose near-future DYSTOPIA was imaginatively shot (out of low-budget necessity, a little as with ALPHAVILLE) in contemporary New York. [PN]

BORODIN, GEORGE Pseudonym of USSR-born surgeon and writer, George Alexis Milkomanovich Milkomane (1903-   ), who lived in the UK for many years from 1932; one of his pseudonyms, George Alexis Bankoff, was for some time thought to be his real name, but he himself has asserted the contrary. Other pseudonyms include George Braddon, Peter Conway, Alec Redwood and – best known – George Sava, under which name he wrote *The Healing Knife* (**1938**), a bestseller about his profession, and many novels, none of sf interest, for ROBERT HALE LIMITED. As GB he wrote a political tract, *Peace in Nobody's Time* (**1944**), *The Book of Joanna: A Fantasy Based on Historical Legend* (**1947**), in which a heavenly conclave attempts to determine the truth about the legend of the 9th-century Pope Joan, and *Spurious Sun* (**1948**; vt *The Threatened People* undated), a ponderously told but cogently meditated tale about the effects of a nuclear explosion in Scotland; against the odds, world peace comes closer. [JC]

BOSTON, BRUCE (1943-   ) US poet (◊ POETRY) and short-story writer whose early work tended to the surreal, but who began – with stories like "Break" for *New Worlds 7* (anth **1974**) ed Hilary BAILEY and Charles PLATT – to invoke fantasy and sf themes. His early poetry – much of it not genre at all, and almost all of it couched in a classically lucid voice – can most easily be approached through *The Bruce Boston Omnibus* (omni **1987**), which assembles various early chapbooks; titles of interest include *Jackbird: Tales of Illusion & Identity* (coll **1976** chap). Later poetry appears in *The Nightmare Collector* (coll **1989** chap) and *Faces of the Beast* (coll **1990** chap). Because his prose fictions tend to the densely surreal and to FABULATION, it is not easy to know when his work first began to merge with FANTASY and sf, though "Break" (noted above) may come close to being his first of genre interest. Collections and prose works include *She Comes when You're Leaving & Other Stories* (coll **1982** chap), *Skin Trades* (coll **1988** chap), *Hypertales & Metafictions* (coll **1990** chap) and *Short Circuits* (coll **1990** chap dos); independent tales include *Der Flüsternde Spiegel* (**1985** chap Germany; trans and rev as *After Magic* **1990** chap) and *All the Clocks are Melting* (**1991** chap). [JC]

BOUCHER, ANTHONY Generally used pseudonym of US editor and writer William Anthony Parker White (1911-1968), who began to publish stories of genre interest with "Snulbug" for UNKNOWN in 1941; he soon became a regular contributor to this magazine and to ASTOUNDING SCIENCE-FICTION. Most of his 1940s tales were humorous in approach (◊ HUMOUR); many are included in *The Compleat Werewolf* (coll **1969**), although *Far and Away* (coll **1955**) provides a better sense of his range. A notable TIME-TRAVEL story is "Barrier" (**1942**). AB also used the pseudonym

H.H. Holmes, publishing under this name the non-sf detection *Rocket to the Morgue* (**1942**), in which several sf authors, thinly disguised, appear in RECURSIVE roles; he went on to write several more detective novels. In 1949 he became founding editor, with J. Francis MCCOMAS, of *The* MAGAZINE OF FANTASY AND SCIENCE FICTION, which from its inception showed a more sophisticated literary outlook than any previous sf magazine. After McComas left, AB was sole editor from 1954 until his retirement, through ill health, in 1958; he won the HUGO for Best Professional Magazine for the years 1957 and 1958. AB occasionally published verse in *FSF* under the pseudonym Herman W. Mudgett. (Mudgett was the real name and Holmes the *nom de guerre* of the USA's first convicted serial murderer, hanged in 1896 after torture-murdering at least 27, possibly 200, young women.) AB wrote little sf after 1952. "The Quest for Saint Aquin" (1951), on a theme of RELIGION, is generally considered his best sf work. He was also a distinguished book reviewer, writing sf columns for both the *New York Times* (as AB) and the *New York Herald Tribune* (as Holmes); and he was influential in gaining for sf a certain measure of respectability. He edited an annual anthology of stories from *FSF*, beginning with *The Best from Fantasy and Science Fiction* (anth **1952**) with J. Francis McComas; he also produced the notable 2-vol *A Treasury of Great Science Fiction* (anth **1959**). An able and perceptive editor, AB did much to help raise the literary standards of sf in the 1950s. [MJE]

Other works: *Exeunt Murderers: The Best Mystery Stories of Anthony Boucher* (coll **1983**), with bibliography; *Anthony Boucher* (omni **1984** UK), collecting 4 of AB's detective novels, including *Rocket to the Morgue*, with intro by David LANGFORD.

As editor: Remaining volumes of the **Best from Fantasy and Science Fiction** sequence were *The Best from Fantasy and Science Fiction, Second Series* (anth **1953**) and *Third Series* (anth **1954**), both with J. Francis McComas, *Fourth Series* (anth **1955**), *Fifth Series* (anth **1956**), *Sixth Series* (anth **1957**), *Seventh Series* (anth **1958**) and *Eighth Series* (anth **1959**).

About the author: *A Boucher Bibliography* (**1969** chap) by J.R. Christopher, D.W. Dickensheet and R.E. Briney, bound with *A Boucher Portrait* (anth **1969** chap) ed Lenore Glen Offord.

See also: EC COMICS; GODS AND DEMONS; LINGUISTICS; ROBOTS.

BOULLE, PIERRE (1912-   ) French writer who trained as an electrical engineer and spent eight years in Malaysia as a planter and soldier. His experience of the Orient permeated much of his early work (generally not sf); *Le pont sur la rivière Kwai* (**1952**; trans as *The Bridge on the River Kwai* **1954** US) remains his best-known novel. PB uses moral fable to pinpoint human absurdities, and his relatively large body of work in the sf genre is a good illustration of this method. *La planète des singes* (**1963**; trans Xan Fielding as *Planet of the Apes* **1963** US; vt *Monkey Planet*

1964 UK) is a witty, philosophical tale *à la* VOLTAIRE, full of irony and compassion, quite unlike the later film adaptation, PLANET OF THE APES (1968), which used only the book's initial premise. [MJ]

Other works: *Contes de l'absurde* (coll **1953** France); *E = mc2* (coll **1957** France) (stories from these collections trans Xan Fielding as *Time Out of Mind* **1966** UK); *Le jardin de Kanashima* (**1964**; trans Xan Fielding as *Garden on the Moon* **1965** US); *Histoires charitables* ["Charitable Tales"] (coll **1965**); *Quia absurdum* (coll **1970**).

See also: COMPUTERS; DEVOLUTION; FRANCE; MOON; ROCKETS; SCIENTISTS.

BOULT, S. KYE ◊ William E. COCHRANE.

BOUNDS, SYDNEY J(AMES) (1920-   ) UK writer, active in various fields from the late 1940s, publishing his first HORROR fantasy, "Strange Portrait", for *Outlands* in 1946. He built a considerable (and well respected) oeuvre of short fiction in various genres, though he has never published a collection. Since the beginning of the 1970s he has concentrated on horror. Under at least nine pseudonyms (and house names like Peter SAXON, which he used for a **Sexton Blake** tale), SJB has published over 30 novels, mostly Westerns. His sf includes *The Moon Raiders* (**1955**), which features stolen U-235, human agents shanghaied to the Moon, and alien invaders, and *The World Wrecker* (**1956**), which stars a mad SCIENTIST who blows up cities by placing phase-shifted rocks under them and returning these rocks to normal spacetime, with calamitous effects. Of his numerous COMIC strips, "Jeff Curtiss and the V3 Menace" (*Combat Library #44* **1960**) is typical. [JC]

Other works: *Dimension of Horror* (**1953**); *The Robot Brains* (**1956**).

BOUSSENARD, LOUIS (1847-1910) French writer. His popular scientific romances, which have some speculative content, often appeared in *Journal des Voyages*. He is best known for *Les secrets de Monsieur Synthèse* ["The Secrets of Mr Synthesis"] (**1888-9**), and *Dix mille ans dans un bloc de glace* (**1889**; trans John Paret as *10,000 Years in a Block of Ice* **1898** US), a SLEEPER-AWAKES tale in which the hero discovers a unified world-UTOPIA peopled by small men – Cerebrals – who are descended from Chinese and black Africans and can fly by the power of thought. [JC]

Other works: *Les français au pôle nord* ["The French at the North Pole"] (**1893**); *L'île en feu* ["Island Ablaze"] (**1898**).

See also: CRYONICS; FRANCE.

BOUVÉ, EDWARD T(RACY) (?   -?   ) US writer. His sf novel, *Centuries Apart* (**1894**), deals with the discovery of lost-race-like UK and French colonies in the verdant heart of Antarctica. [JC]

BOVA, BEN(JAMIN WILLIAM) (1932-   ) US writer and editor. He worked as technical editor for Project Vanguard 1956-8 and science writer for Avco Everett Research Laboratory 1960-71 before being appointed editor of *Analog* (◊ ASTOUNDING SCIENCE-FICTION) following the death of John W. CAMPBELL Jr in 1971.

When he took over at *ASF* it was a moribund magazine; although commercially healthy, it had stagnated in the later years of Campbell's editorship. BB maintained its orientation towards technophilic sf but considerably broadened the magazine's horizons. In doing so he alienated some readers, who shared Campbell's puritanism – such stories as "The Gold at the Starbow's End" (1972) by Frederik POHL and "Hero" (1972) by Joe W. HALDEMAN, inoffensive though they might seem in the outside world, brought strong protests – but he revitalized the magazine. In recognition of this, he received the HUGO for Best Editor every year 1973-7; although he missed out in 1978 he gained it again in 1979 for his work during 1978, his final year as editor. BB also involved the magazine's name in other activities, producing *Analog Annual* (anth **1976**) – an original anthology intended as a 13th issue of the magazine – initiating a series of records and inaugurating a book-publishing programme. In 1978-82 he was editor of OMNI. From both journals he extracted several anthologies (see listing below).

BB was active as a writer for many years before his stint at *ASF*, his first published sf being a children's novel, *The Star Conquerors* (**1959**). Considerable work in shorter forms followed over the next decades, the best of it being assembled as *Forward in Time* (coll **1973**), *Viewpoint* (coll **1977**), *Maxwell's Demons* (coll **1979**), *Escape Plus* (coll **1984**), *The Astral Mirror* (coll **1985**), partly nonfiction, *Prometheans* (coll **1986**) and *Battle Station* (coll **1987**). His best-known stories, those about Chet Kinsman, an astronaut during the latter years of the 20th century, were assimilated into the **Kinsman Saga**, whose internal ordering is *Kinsman* (fixup **1979**) and *Millennium* (**1976**), the two volumes being assembled as *The Kinsman Saga* (omni **1987**); *Millennium*, his best novel, is a tale of power-POLITICS in the face of impending nuclear HOLOCAUST as the century ends. *Colony* (**1978**), set in the same Universe, carries the story – and humanity – further towards the stars, embodying the outward-looking stance BB has held throughout his writing life, and about the necessity for which he has been unfailingly eloquent. An earlier sequence, the **Exiles** series – *Exiled from Earth* (**1971**), *Flight of Exiles* (**1972**) and *End of Exile* (**1975**), all three being assembled as *The Exiles Trilogy* (omni **1980**) – is children's sf, as were all his novels before *THX 1138 * (**1971**), based on the George LUCAS filmscript. Other novels of interest include *The Starcrossed* (**1975**), a humorous example of RECURSIVE SF whose protagonist is a thinly disguised Harlan ELLISON (◊ *The* STARLOST), *The Multiple Man* (**1976**), a suspense-thriller built on the concept of CLONES, and *Privateers* (**1985**), which succumbs to an assumption common to US sf: that governments will sooner or later fail to conquer space, and that individual entrepreneurs (vast multinational corporations exercising Japanese foresight need not apply) will take up the slack.

More tellingly, the **Voyagers** sequence – *Voyagers*

(1981), *Voyagers II: The Alien Within* (1982) and *Voyagers III: Star Brothers* (1990) – treats humanity's expansion within a framework of SPACE-OPERA romance, with technology-dispensing ALIENS establishing First Contact with emergent humans, star-crossed lovers, biochips and a great deal more. The **Orion** sequence – *Orion* (1984), *Vengeance of Orion* (1988) and *Orion in the Dying Time* (1990) – puts into fantasy idiom a similar expansive message. In his nonfiction and fiction alike, BB is making it clear that survival for the race lies elsewhere than on this planet alone, a thesis underlined in *Mars* (1992) by the lovingly detailed verisimilitude with which he describes the first manned flight to that planet. BB was president of the SCIENCE FICTION WRITERS OF AMERICA 1990-92. [MJE/JC]

Other works: *Star Watchman* (1964); *The Weathermakers* (1967); *Out of the Sun* (1968), which was assembled with the nonfiction *The Amazing Laser* (1971) as *Out of the Sun* (omni 1984); *The Dueling Machine* (1963 *ASF* in collaboration with Myron R. Lewis; exp 1969); *Escape!* (1970); *As on a Darkling Plain* (fixup 1972); *The Winds of Altair* (1973; rev 1983); *When the Sky Burned* (1973; rev vt *Test of Fire* 1982); *Gremlins, Go Home!* (1974) with Gordon R. DICKSON; *City of Darkness* (1976); *The Peacekeepers* (1988; vt *Peacekeepers* 1989 UK); *Cyberbooks* (1989); *Future Crime* (coll 1990), made up of *City of Darkness* and a number of short stories; *The Trikon Deception* (1992) with Bill Pogue (1930-   ); *Sam Gunn, Unlimited* (fixup 1992).

As editor: *The Many Worlds of Science Fiction* (anth 1971); *Analog 9* (anth 1973); *The Science Fiction Hall of Fame vols 2A and 2B* (anths 1973; vol 2B designated vol 3 in UK); *The Analog Science Fact Reader* (anth 1974); *Closeup: New Worlds* (anth 1977) with Trudy E. Bell; *Analog Yearbook* (anth 1978); *The Best of Analog* (anth 1978); *The Best of Omni* (anth 1980) with Don Myrus, and its sequels, all with Myrus, *The Best of Omni Science Fiction #2* (anth 1981), *#3* (anth 1982) and *#4* (anth 1982); *Vision of the Future: The Art of Robert McCall* (anth 1982); *The Best of the Nebulas* (anth 1989); *First Contact: The Search for Extraterrestrial Intelligence* (anth 1990) with Byron PREISS, containing fiction and nonfiction.

Nonfiction: *The Uses of Space* (1965); *In Quest of Quasars* (1970); *The New Astronomies* (1972); *Starflight and Other Improbabilities* (1973); *Workshops in Space* (1974); *Through the Eyes of Wonder: Science Fiction and Science* (1975); *Notes to a Science Fiction Writer* (coll 1975; rev 1981); *The Seeds of Tomorrow* (1977); *The High Road* (1981), on the space programme; *Assured Survival: Putting the Star Defense Wars in Perspective* (1984); *Welcome to Moonbase* (1987).

See also: AMAZING STORIES; CHILDREN'S SF; ECONOMICS; HISTORY IN SF; JUPITER; MOON; NEBULA; OUTER PLANETS; SF MAGAZINES; SPACE FLIGHT; WRITERS OF THE FUTURE CONTEST.

BOWEN, JOHN (GRIFFITH) (1924-   ) UK novelist and playwright active in tv and radio; he often derives his novels from his plays, some of which, like the Year-King fantasy "Robin Redbreast" (produced by the BBC 1970; in *The Television Dramatist* [anth 1973] ed Robert Muller), are of strong genre interest. Such was the case with his first, also a fantasy, *The Truth Will not Help Us* (1956), in which an 18th-century piracy trial is depicted, with much anachronistic verisimilitude, as an example of McCarthyism, and with his sf novel proper, *After the Rain* (1958), in which a lunatic inventor starts a second Flood. Most of the novel takes place on a satirically convenient raft of fools, where survivors of the DISASTER act out their humanness and win through in the end only because of the dour fanaticism of one person. The stage version was later published as *After the Rain: A Play in Three Acts* (1967 chap). JB is a supple, subtle, sometimes profound writer. [JC]

Other works: *Pegasus* (1957) and *The Mermaid and the Boy* (1958), both juvenile fantasies.

See also: HOLOCAUST AND AFTER; McGUFFIN.

BOWEN, ROBERT SIDNEY (1900-1977) US author of the **Dusty Ayres** sf-adventure series: *Black Lightning* (1966), *Crimson Doom* (1966), *Purple Tornado* (1966), *The Telsa Raiders* (1966) and *Black Invaders vs. the Battle Birds* (1966). [JC]

BOWERS, R.L. ◊ John S. GLASBY.

BOWES, RICHARD (DIRRANE) (1944-   ) US writer whose novels evoke a congested, magically altered New York. *Warchild* (1986) and its sequel, *Goblin Market* (1988), set in an ALTERNATE-WORLD version of the city, follow the growth and adventures of a telepathic teenager who finds himself involved in time wars with a variety of exorbitant friends and foes. *Feral Cell* (1987), set at the end of the 20th century, carries its ageing hero into a millennial conflict between Good and Evil, seen in fantasy terms that evoke the New York of writers like John CROWLEY and Mark HELPRIN. RB's first books are, perhaps, insufficiently well organized; more are awaited. [JC]

BOWKER, RICHARD (JOHN) (1950   ) US writer who began publishing sf with "Side Effect" for *Unearth* in 1977. His first novel, *Forbidden Sanctuary* (1982), treats a ticklish theological problem – whether an ALIEN whose possession of a soul is moot can claim sanctuary in a church – with due regard for the likely Roman Catholic view on the issue (◊ RELIGION). *Replica* (1986), a political thriller also set in the NEAR FUTURE, is less engaging, but *Marlborough Street* (1987), a FANTASY about a man with PSI POWERS, is of considerably greater interest, and *Dover Beach* (1987), set in Boston and the UK a generation or so after a nuclear HOLOCAUST, is yet more substantial. The protagonist of the book – that he is a detective obsessed by genre thrillers from before the holocaust does not seriously detract from the tale – serves as an effective mirror of our state, reflecting the new world complexly and with wit. The title – it is that of Matthew Arnold's 1867 poem about the loss of faith and a world which continues – strikes an appropriate note. There is some sense that RB's liking for thriller

modes – his next novel, *Summit* (**1989**), is an espion-age thriller involving yet another psychic – consorts uneasily with his gift for the elegiac anatomy of individuals and their worlds; at the time of writing it is not certain which direction he will next take. [JC]
See also: ANDROIDS.

BOYAJIAN, JERRY Working name of US biblio-grapher Jerel Michael Boyajian (1953-), whose main work has been the *Index to the Science Fiction Magazines 1977* (**1982** chap) and its sequels through coverage year 1983, all with Ken JOHNSON (*whom see for details*). JB produced solo *A John Schoenherr SF Checklist* (**1977** chap) and, with Anthony R. LEWIS and Andrew A. Whyte, *The N.E.S.F.A. Index: Science Fiction Magazines and Original Anthologies, 1976* (**1977** chap). [JC]

BOY AND HIS DOG, A Film (1975). LQJaf Produc-tions. Dir L.Q. Jones, starring Don Johnson, Susanne Benton, Jason Robards, Alvy Moore, Tim McIntire (as the dog's voice). Screenplay Jones, based on "A Boy and his Dog" (1969) by Harlan ELLISON. 89 mins. Colour.

Set in AD2024, post-HOLOCAUST, this brutally prag-matic film concerns two survivors, a young man and his dog; the latter has high intelligence and the ability to communicate telepathically with his partner. They move through a desolate landscape, inhabited by dangerous scavengers, and find a girl from an underground society. She lures the youth below to her home society, which is a venomous parody of middle-class, small-town US values; here he is expected to become, in effect, a convenient sperm bank to be mechanically milked. He rejects this regimented existence and escapes back to the surface with the girl. Finding his dog starving, he kills the girl to provide food, and the two walk off into the menacing sunset, thus resolving an unusual love triangle. The underground sequences are perhaps too stagey and share the film uneasily with the gritty realism of the surface ones. Jones (character-actor turned director) adapted the Ellison story honestly and unfussily. This is one of the better small-budget sf films (it was the recipient of a HUGO), once again showing small independent producers taking risks that would horrify the big studios. [JB/PN]

BOYCE, CHRIS Working name of (Joseph) Chris-topher Boyce (1943-), Scottish writer and news-paper research librarian who published his first sf, "Autodestruct", in STORYTELLER #3 in 1964. In the mid-1960s he contributed to *SF Impulse*, but his most important work to date is the sf novel *Catchworld* (**1975**), joint winner (with Charles LOGAN's *Shipwreck*) of the GOLLANCZ/*Sunday Times* SF Novel Award. *Catchworld* is an ornate, sometimes overcomplicated tale combining sophisticated brain-computer inter-faces (◊ COMPUTERS; CYBORGS) and SPACE OPERA; the transcendental bravura of the book's climax is memorable. In *Brainfix* (**1980**), a cautionary tale about social disorder in the UK, CB had the misfortune of predicting a rise in unemployment to an unheard-of

three million in a fiction published just months before, in the harsh reality of the first Thatcher recession, it actually reached *four* million. [JC]
Other work: *Extraterrestrial Encounter* (**1979**), a speculative inquiry into XENOBIOLOGY and the search for extraterrestrial INTELLIGENCE (SETI).
See also: CYBERNETICS; GODS AND DEMONS.

BOYD, FELIX [s] ◊ Harry HARRISON.

BOYD, JOHN Pseudonym of Boyd Bradfield Upchurch (1919-), US sf writer active in the field for only a decade following publication of his first novel, *The Last Starship from Earth* (**1968**), which received considerable critical acclaim; it remains his most highly regarded work. A complex tale told with baroque vigour, a DYSTOPIA, an ALTERNATE-WORLDS story, a SPACE OPERA with TIME-TRAVEL components making it impossible to say which of various space-ships actually is the last to leave Earth, and in what sense "last" is intended, the book is a bravura and knowing traversal of sf protocols. The protagonist, sent from a stratified dystopian Earth to the prison planet Hell for machiavellian reasons, ends up travel-ling through time, making sure Jesus terminates his career this time at the age of 33, which will eliminate the dystopia by changing the future into ours; he becomes, in the end, the Wandering Jew. None of JB's subsequent novels, some of which are abundantly inventive, have made anything like the impression of this first effort, though they are not inconsiderable. *The Rakehells of Heaven* (**1969**), *The Pollinators of Eden* (**1969**) and *Sex and the High Command* (**1970**) all deal amusingly and variously with sexual matters (◊ SEX), and are full of rewarding hypotheses about the cultural forms human nature might find itself involved in. Some later novels, like *Andromeda Gun* (**1974**), a perfunctory comic novel involving a parasitic alien in the Old West, show a reduction of creative energy, though *Barnard's Planet* (**1975**) evinces a partial recovery, dealing with some of the same issues as his first novel and with some of the same verve. The feeling remains that JB has a larger talent than he allowed himself to reveal in his relatively short career, and that carelessness about quality sometimes badly muffled the effect of his wide inventiveness. [JC]
Other works: *The Slave Stealer* (**1968**), an historical novel under his real name; *The Organ Bank Farm* (**1970**); *The IQ Merchant* (**1972**); *The Gorgon Festival* (**1972**); *The Doomsday Gene* (**1973**); *Scarborough Hall* (**1976**), associational, under his real name; *The Girl with the Jade Green Eyes* (**1978**; rev 1979 UK).
See also: ECOLOGY; UNDER THE SEA.

BOYE, KARIN (1900-1941) Swedish writer known in translation for her DYSTOPIA, *Kallocain* (**1940**; trans Gustav Lannestock **1966** US), a savagely introspective narrative of a scientist who invents the eponymous truth drug, and who suffers the consequences in his own being. [JC]

BOYER, ROBERT H. [r] ◊ Marshall B. TYMN.

BOYETT, STEVEN R. (1960-) US writer whose first

novel, *Ariel* (**1983**), is a fantasy, but whose second, *The Architect of Sleep* (**1986**), is an sf tale set in a PARALLEL WORLD occupied by an intricately and plausibly depicted species which has evolved (◊ EVOLUTION) from raccoons. After crossing into this world from a cavern in ours, the protagonist becomes involved in a complex plot which is left incomplete, suggesting that sequels were intended or indeed written. Their publication is still awaited. [JC]

BOYS FROM BRAZIL, THE Film (1978). Producer Circle. Dir Franklin J. Schaffner, starring Gregory Peck, Laurence Olivier, James Mason, Jeremy Black. Screenplay Heywood Gould, based on *The Boys from Brazil* (**1976**) by Ira LEVIN. 125 mins. Colour.

Like the novel on which it is based, this is an absurd but entertaining concoction of pulp-thriller conventions with some rather interesting scientific conjecture about environment and heredity. Joseph Mengele (Peck), the notorious Nazi doctor, is discovered to be alive in the Brazilian jungle, where he is manufacturing CLONES of Adolf Hitler. Each of these is to be adopted by a family as close as possible to Hitler's own – which means, among other things, the necessity of engineering the deaths of 94 male civil servants as close as possible to their 65th birthday – in the hope that Der Führer will come again. Jewish Nazi-hunter Lieberman (Olivier) slowly uncovers the truth. A main interest of the film is that the arrow of narrative (genetic determinism) is turned aside at the last minute, when the twitching young Adolf-clone turns out to be his own man – or boy. [PN]

BOYS' PAPERS Although boys' papers could easily be dismissed as being of negligible literary value, perhaps unjustly since Upton SINCLAIR and other eminent writers found their footing there, they played an important role in the HISTORY OF SF in the last three decades of the 19th century and the early years of the 20th century by creating a potential readership for the SF MAGAZINES and by anticipating many GENRE-SF themes.

The prevailing style of US boys' papers was largely set in the 1870s and after by periodicals such as *The Boys of New York* and *Golden Hours*, which published serialized novels similar and often identical to those in dime-novel format (that is, one single short novel per issue); these are discussed in detail under DIME-NOVEL SF. Since US boys' papers were rare after WWI – *American Boy* was an exception (◊ Carl CLAUDY) – the current discussion is UK-oriented.

Some sf did appear quite early in UK boys' papers. W.S. HAYWARD's novel *Up in the Air and Down in the Sea* (**1865**) was serialized *c*1863-5 in Henry Vickers's *Boy's Journal*, as were its sequels. Nonetheless, the major impetus towards boys' sf in the UK came from abroad. Jules VERNE appeared in UK periodicals with *Hector Servadac* (trans 1877 *Good Things*; **1878**), *The Steam House* (trans 1880-81 *Union Jack*; **1881**) and 16 other serializations in *The Boys' Own Paper*. André LAURIE was represented with "A Marvellous Conquest: A Tale of the Bayouda" (**1888**; trans 1889 *The Boys' Own Paper*; vt *The Conquest of the Moon: A Story of the Bayouda*, **1889**), and US dime novels from the FRANK READE LIBRARY were reprinted in **The Aldine Romance of Invention, Travel and Adventure Library**.

UK authors soon followed this lead with a variety of themes. Several interplanetary adventures appeared in the mid-1890s in *The Marvel* and elsewhere; e.g., "In Trackless Space" (1902 *The Union Jack*) by George C. WALLIS, later a contributor to the sf pulps. LOST WORLDS were prominent, notably Sidney Drew's *Wings of Gold* (1903-4 *The Boy's Herald*; **1908**) and the works of Fenton Ash (◊ Frank AUBREY). World DISASTER appeared in "Doom" (1912 *The Dreadnought*), a vehicle capable of travel through the Earth in "Kiss, Kiss, the Beetle" (1913, *Fun and Fiction*), and an early SUPERMAN in "Vengeance of Mars" (1912 *Illustrated Chips*).

Overriding all these themes was the future-WAR story, previously a minor genre – and remaining so in US boys' fiction – but encouraged obsessively in the UK by Lord Northcliffe, head of Amalgamated Press. Between 1901 and the outbreak of WWI in 1914, numerous warnings of imminent INVASION were published, foremost among them the works of John Tregellis, who contributed *Britain Invaded* (1906 *The Boy's Friend*; **1910**), *Britain at Bay* (1906-7 *The Boy's Friend*; **1910**), *Kaiser or King?* (1912 *The Boy's Friend*; **1913**) and others.

When WWI did finally break out, many papers folded, but they were replaced shortly after the Armistice by new periodicals firmly rooted in the 20th century. Among these was *Pluck*; subtitled "The Boy's Wireless Adventure Weekly", it published several sf stories linked by the common theme of radio. Among its stories were Lester Bidston's *The Radio Planet* (1923; **1926**) and the first UK publication (1923) of Edgar Rice BURROUGHS's *At the Earth's Core* (1914 *All-Story Weekly*; **1922**); the latter contributed to the publication of Edgar WALLACE's *Planetoid 127* (1924 *The Mechanical Boy*; **1929**) and adaptations of various stories in Sax ROHMER's **Fu Manchu** series (1923-4 *Chums*). Notable among the many other stories published were Leslie BERESFORD's "War of Revenge" (1922 *The Champion*), an account of a German attack on the UK in 1956 using guided missiles, Frank H. Shaw's world-catastrophe novel "When the Sea Rose Up" (1923-4 *Chums*) and Eric Wood's DYSTOPIA *The Jungle Men: A Tale of 2923 AD* (1923-4 *The Boy's Friend*; **1927**).

Most popular of all were the SPACE OPERAS then appearing in *Boy's Magazine* (first published 1922). Typical was Raymond Quiex's "The War in Space" (1926), which was very reminiscent of the 1930s PULP MAGAZINES with its story of ASTEROIDS drawn from orbit and hurled as missiles towards Earth, manmade webs of metal hanging in space, domed cities on strange planets and giant insects stalking the surface of hostile worlds. Many similar stories appeared: time machines, androids, titanic war machines, robot armies and matter transmitters became commonplace.

When *Boy's Magazine* folded in 1934, its place was taken three weeks later by SCOOPS, the first UK all-sf periodical. In spite of its capable editor, Hadyn Dimmock, and contributions by John Russell FEARN, Maurice Hugi and A.M. LOW, *Scoops* folded after only 20 issues.

Adult sf magazines were available in the UK, both native and reprint, to fill the temporary gap left by the demise of *Scoops* – and COMIC books made their appearance in the later 1930s – but boys' papers continued to introduce young readers to sf concepts: *Modern Boy* with the CAPTAIN JUSTICE series that influenced a youthful Brian W. ALDISS, *Modern Wonder* with serializations of John WYNDHAM and W.J. Passingham, and **The Sexton Blake Library**, with pseudonymous contributions by E.C. TUBB and Michael MOORCOCK, are among the titles of the next few decades.

Sf continued until more recently to play a role in boys' papers, with content modified to suit the times. In 1976, for example, an anonymous adaptation – as "Kids Rule, OK" – in *Action* of Dave WALLIS's *Only Lovers Left Alive* (**1964**) proved so violent that public outcry led to temporary suspension of the paper; in retrospect, the adaptation can be seen as a forerunner to such modern favourites as JUDGE DREDD. [JE]

BPVP ◊ Byron PREISS.

BRACK, VEKTIS House name used on three sf novels by unidentified authors for Gannet Press. *The "X" People* (**1953**) concerns an alien invasion, *Castaway from Space* (**1953**) an alien crashlanding, and *Odyssey in Space* (**1953**) (insecurely identified as being by Leslie Humphrys, who also wrote as Bruno G. CONDRAY) space stations. [SH]

BRACKETT, LEIGH (DOUGLASS) (1915-1978) US writer, for most of her career deeply involved in the writing of fantasy and sf, for which she remains best known, though her detective novels and her film scenarios have been justly praised. The latter range from *The Vampire's Ghost* (1945) to *The Long Goodbye* (1973), with memorable scripts for Howard Hawks, including *The Big Sleep* (1946) and *Rio Bravo* (1958); her last effort, for *The* EMPIRE STRIKES BACK (1979), for which she received posthumously a 1980 HUGO, was not typical of her work in this form.

She began publishing sf stories in 1940 with "Martian Quest" for *ASF*, and although her first novel, *No Good from a Corpse* (**1944**) was a detection the 1940s were her period of greatest activity in the sf magazines; she appeared mostly in PLANET STORIES, THRILLING WONDER STORIES and others that offered space for what rapidly became her speciality: swashbuckling but literate PLANETARY ROMANCES, usually set on MARS, though there is no series continuity joining her Martian venues.

In 1946 she married sf author Edmond HAMILTON, and may well have influenced his writing, which improved sharply after WWII; but she continued to use the name LB for her sf, for her other books, and for her film work. Some of her work from this period can be found in *The Coming of the Terrans* (coll of linked stories **1967**) and *The Halfling and Other Stories* (coll **1973**). She approached all she wrote with economy and vigour: everything about her early stories – their colour, their narrative speed, the brooding forthrightness of their protagonists – made them an ideal and fertile blend of traditional SPACE OPERA and SWORD AND SORCERY. She was a marked influence upon the next generation of writers. One novelette, "Lorelei of the Red Mist" (*Planet Stories* 1946), was written in collaboration with Ray BRADBURY.

From the mid-1940s LB tended to move into somewhat longer forms, setting on her favourite neo-BURROUGHS Mars the first part of her **Eric John Stark** series: *The Secret of Sinharat* (1949 *Planet Stories* as "Queen of the Martian Catacombs"; rev **1964** dos), *People of the Talisman* (1951 *Planet Stories* as "Black Amazon of Mars"; rev **1964** dos) – both reportedly expanded for book publication by Edmond Hamilton, and both later assembled as *Eric John Stark: Outlaw of Mars* (omni **1982**) – and "Enchantress of Venus" (1949; vt "City of the Lost Ones"), the last being collected in *The Halfling*. Stark concentrates all the virtues of the sword-and-sorcery hero in his lean figure; along with Robert E. HOWARD's **Conan**, he has helped spawn dozens of snarling, indomitable mesomorphs, though his attitude to women is somewhat less utilitarian than that of his many successors. In the 1970s the series was restarted, having been conveniently transferred to an interstellar venue (as Mars and VENUS were no longer readily usable for the sf-adventure writer), with *The Ginger Star* (**1974**), *The Hounds of Skaith* (**1974**) and *The Reavers of Skaith* (**1976**), all three being assembled as *The Book of Skaith* (omni **1976**). Other novels involving Mars were *Shadow Over Mars* (1944 *Startling Stories*; **1951** UK; vt *The Nemesis from Terra* 1961 dos US) and, perhaps the finest of them all, *The Sword of Rhiannon* (1949 *TWS* as "Sea-Kings of Mars"; **1953** dos), which is connected to "Sorcerer of Rhiannon" (1942); it admirably combines adventure with a strongly romantic vision of an ancient sea-girt Martian civilization. Where Burroughs's Mars had been characterized by naïve barbaric energy, LB's represents the last gasp of a decadence endlessly nostalgic for the even more remote past.

By the 1950s, LB was beginning to concentrate more on interstellar space operas, including *The Starmen* (**1952**; cut vt *The Galactic Breed* 1955 dos; text restored vt *The Starmen of Llyrdis* 1976), *The Big Jump* (**1955** dos) and *Alpha Centauri or Die!* (1953 *Planet Stories* as "Ark of Mars"; fixup **1963** dos). All three are efficient but seem somewhat routine when set beside LB's best single work, *The Long Tomorrow* (**1955**), which is set in a strictly controlled post-HOLOCAUST USA, many years after the destruction of the CITIES and of the TECHNOLOGY that brought mankind to ruin. It is the slow, impressively warm and detailed epic of two boys and their finally successful attempts to find Bartorstown, where people are secretly reestablishing science and technology. After 20 years, readers of the book may be less hopeful than its author about Bartorstown's aspirations, but on its own terms the novel is a glowing success.

After 1955, LB generally preferred to work in films and tv. She was a highly professional writer, working with extreme competence within generic moulds that did not always, perhaps, sufficiently stretch her. *The Long Tomorrow* and her film scripts for Howard Hawks – whose positive attitude toward the creation of Competent Women must have been a blessing to her for decades – did suggest broader horizons for her work; but she declined to explore them fully. A summatory collection, edited by her husband, *The Best of Leigh Brackett* (coll **1977**), confirms the muscular panache of her work and its refusal to transcend competence. [JC]

Other works: *Stranger at Home* (**1946**) as by the actor George Sanders, *An Eye for an Eye* (**1957**), *The Tiger Among Us* (**1957**; vt *Fear No Evil* **1960** UK; vt *13 West Street* **1962**) and *Silent Partner* (**1969**), all crime novels; *Rio Bravo* * (**1959**), from the Hawks film, and *Follow the Free Wind* (**1963**) are Westerns; *The Jewel of Bas* (**1944**; **1990** chap dos).

As editor: *The Best of Planet Stories No 1* (anth **1974**); *The Best of Edmund Hamilton* (coll **1977**).

About the author: *Leigh Brackett, Marion Zimmer Bradley, Anne McCaffrey: A Primary and Secondary Bibliography* (**1982**) by Rosemarie Arbur; *Leigh Brackett: American Writer* (**1986** chap) by J.L. Carr; *Leigh Douglass Brackett and Edmond Hamilton: A Working Bibliography* (**1986** chap) by Gordon BENSON Jr.

See also: ALIENS; ANTI-INTELLECTUALISM IN SF; COLONIZATION OF OTHER WORLDS; FANTASY; GALACTIC EMPIRES; GENERATION STARSHIPS; JUPITER; MERCURY; MYTHOLOGY; PASTORAL; SPACESHIPS; WOMEN SF WRITERS.

BRADBURY, EDWARD P. ◊ Michael MOORCOCK.

BRADBURY, RAY(MOND) (DOUGLAS) (1920–   ) US writer, born in Waukegan, Illinois; in 1934 his father, a power lineman who was having trouble gaining employment during the Depression, moved with the family to Los Angeles, but images of the small-town Midwest always remained important in RB's stories. RB discovered sf FANDOM in 1937, meeting Ray HARRYHAUSEN, Forrest J. ACKERMAN and Henry KUTT-NER, and began publishing his FANZINE *Futuria Fantasia* in 1939. His first professional sale was "Pendulum" with Henry HASSE for *Super Science Stories* in Nov 1941. In that year he met a number of sf professionals, including Leigh BRACKETT, who generously coached him in writing techniques. He later collaborated with her, completing her "Lorelei of the Red Mist" (**1946** *Planet Stories*).

By 1943 RB's style was beginning to jell: poetic, evocative, consciously symbolic, with strong nostalgic elements and a leaning towards the macabre – his work has always been more FANTASY and HORROR

than sf. Many of RB's early stories, mostly written 1943-7, were collected in his first book, *Dark Carnival* (coll **1947**; cut **1948** UK; cut vt *The Small Assassin* **1962** UK); quite a few of them had originally appeared in WEIRD TALES. All but 4 of the stories in the later *The October Country* (coll **1955**; **1956** UK edition drops 7 stories and adds "The Traveller") had already appeared in *Dark Carnival*, but many were revised for this new book. Although some of these stories had sf elements, they could more accurately be described as weird fiction. RB used occasional pseudonyms in those early years; in non-sf magazines he appeared as Edward Banks, William Elliott, D.R. Banat, Leonard Douglas and Leonard Spaulding, and he wrote one story, "Referent" (1948), in *TWS* under the house name Brett STERLING. Much of his early sf was colourful SPACE OPERA, and appeared in *TWS* and PLANET STORIES.

One of these latter stories was "The Million Year Picnic" (1946). Later it was to appear in his second book, which remains RB's greatest work, *The Martian Chronicles* (coll of linked stories **1950**; with "Usher II" cut and "The Fire Balloons" added, rev vt *The Silver Locusts* **1951** UK; with "The Wilderness" added as well, rev **1953** UK). This book, which could be regarded as an episodic novel, made RB's reputation. Almost at once he found a new market for short stories in the "slicks", magazines such as *Esquire*, *Saturday Evening Post*, *McCall's* and COLLIER'S WEEKLY. Of the more than 300 stories he has published since, only a handful originally appeared in SF MAGAZINES. This was one of the most significant breakthroughs into the general market made by any GENRE-SF writer.

The Martian Chronicles is an amazing work. Its closely interwoven stories, linked by recurrent images and themes, tell of the repeated attempts by humans to colonize Mars, of the way they bring their old prejudices with them, and of their repeated, ambiguous meetings with the shape-changing Martians. Despite the sf scenario, there is no hard technology. The mood is of loneliness and nostalgia; a pensive regret suffuses the book. Colonists find, in "The Third Expedition", a perfect Midwest township waiting for them in the Martian desert; throughout the book appearance and reality slip, dreamlike, from the one to the other; desires and fantasy are reified but turn out to be tainted. At the beginning, in a typical RB image, the warmth of rocket jets brings a springlike thaw to the frozen Ohio landscape; at the end, human children look into the canal to see the Martians, and find them in their own reflections. All the RB themes that were later to be repeated, sometimes too often, find their earliest shapes here: the anti-technological bias, the celebration of simplicity and innocence as imaged in small-town life, the sense of loss as youth changes to adulthood, and the danger and attraction of masks, be they Hallowe'en, carnival or, as here, alien mimicry. The book was dramatized as a tv miniseries, *The* MARTIAN CHRONICLES (1980).

For the next few years the evocative versatility of RB's imagery kept a freshness and an ebullience unspoiled by occasional overwriting; what later came to look like a too cosy heartland sentiment was generally redeemed by the precision and strangeness of its expression. RB's talents are very clear in the first of his few novels, *Fahrenheit 451* (1951 *Gal* as "The Fireman"; with 2 short stories as coll **1953**; most later editions omit the short stories; rev 1979 with coda; rev 1982 with afterword). In its DYSTOPIAN future, in which books are burned because ideas are dangerous, we follow the painful spiritual growth of its renegade hero, a book-burning "fireman" and secret reader who finally flees, pursued by a Mechanical Hound attuned to his body chemistry, to a pastoral society of book "memorizers". François Truffaut's interesting film version, FAHRENHEIT 451 (1966), has as much of Truffaut as of Bradbury.

Two other books published as novels, neither of them sf, are *Dandelion Wine* (1950-57 various mags; fixup **1957**), in which an adolescent life is recorded in terms of a single summer in a small town in a series of vignettes, and *Something Wicked This Way Comes* (**1962**), an episodic, rather heavily symbolic tale of GOTHIC transformations in a small town, possibly written in homage to Charles G. FINNEY's *The Circus of Dr Lao* (**1935**), which RB had already anthologized in *The Circus of Dr Lao and other Improbable Stories* (anth **1956**), a collection of fantasies.

RB's vintage years are normally thought to be 1946-55; his other short-story collections of that period are certainly superior to those he produced later. They began with *The Illustrated Man* (coll **1951**; with 2 stories added and 4 deleted, rev 1952 UK), in which the tales are given a linking framework; they are all seen as magical tattoos which, springing from the body of the protagonist, become living stories. Three were filmed as *The* ILLUSTRATED MAN by Jack Smight in 1968. Later collections are *The Golden Apples of the Sun* (coll **1953**; with 2 stories deleted 1953 UK) and *A Medicine for Melancholy* (coll **1959**; vt with 4 stories removed and 5 added *The Day it Rained Forever* 1959 UK). These last two books were combined as *Twice Twenty Two* (omni **1966**). No later RB collection approaches the above in quality. The other important collection of early stories, drawing from many of the books already listed, is *The Vintage Bradbury* (coll **1965**), which has now been superseded by the massive retrospective *The Stories of Ray Bradbury* (coll **1980**; UK paperback in 2 vols 1983).

Yet in the late 1950s and 1960s RB's mainstream reputation continued to grow. He has appeared in well over 800 anthologies. In the USA, at least, he is regarded by many critics as a major literary talent. Sf as a genre can take little credit for this: RB's themes are traditionally US and, although early on he often chose to render them in sf imagery, it would be mistaken to see RB as basically an sf writer. He is, in effect, a fantasist, both whimsical and sombre, in an older, pastoral tradition. The high regard in which he

is held can indeed be justified on the basis of a handful of works, with *The Martian Chronicles*, *Fahrenheit 451*, and many stories from the late 1940s and the 1950s among them; it is here, too, that RB's small but very influential contribution to sf is located, which had much to do with sf's ceasing to be regarded as belonging to a genre ghetto.

RB is a reasonably prolific writer, but some have found his work from 1960s onwards to be increasingly disappointing, especially his plays and poetry, which have often been described as both stiltedly rhetorical and oversentimental. On the other hand, some of his theatrical work has been well received (◊ THEATRE). Those of his subsequent collections to include a substantial amount of previously uncollected work are *The Machineries of Joy* (coll **1964**; with 1 story cut, 1964 UK), *I Sing the Body Electric* (coll **1969**) and *The Toynbee Convector* (coll **1988**); it was the middle one of these that received the most adverse criticism for its alleged soft-centredness.

Just as it had come to seem, in the 1980s, that RB was content to become a grand old man (he won the NEBULA Grandmaster Award in 1989 for his lifetime achievements), his career took a new turn. Like many sf writers in the 1940s he had published some crime fiction in the mystery pulps – some collected in *A Memory of Murder* (coll **1984**) – and now in the 1980s he turned to crime fiction again. *Death is a Lonely Business* (**1985**) and its sequel *A Graveyard for Lunatics* (**1990**) are his strongest work for many years. Some of the old density and power return in their almost surreal conflations of appearance and reality. They are of strong associational interest for readers of his sf and fantasy (deliberately returning to many of the key metaphors of his work in these fields, with the canals of Venice, Los Angeles, standing perhaps for those of Mars), and are good examples of RECURSIVE fiction, in that both are to a degree *romans à clef*, with recognizable sf characters in them, not least a 1950s version of RB himself. Ray HARRYHAUSEN, for example, appears thinly disguised in the second, which revolves around the film world.

RB's work in film has been interesting. Two important early sf B-movies were loosely based on short stories by him: IT CAME FROM OUTER SPACE (1953) and *The* BEAST FROM 20,000 FATHOMS (1953). Neither, however, has any perceptible Bradbury quality. By far his best screenplay was that for *Moby Dick* (1956); RB shared credit on this with John Huston. The 18min animated film *Icarus Montgolfier Wright* (1962) was based on an RB story and screenplay, as was the made-for-tv film *Picasso Summer* (1972), based on RB's "In a Season of Calm Weather" (1957), on which he received a screenplay credit as Douglas Spaulding. Several Russian films (◊ RUSSIA) have been based on Bradbury stories, including VEL'D (1987), based on "The Veldt" (1950). Tv adaptations of his work have appeared in *The* TWILIGHT ZONE (both series) and, notably, on RAY BRADBURY THEATRE (1985-6). Many of RB's stories have also received COMIC book adaptation. 16 can be found in two books: *The Autumn People* (graph coll **1965**) and *Tomorrow Midnight* (graph coll **1966**). (◊ EC COMICS.)

A touching symbol of the high regard in which many of RB's peers hold him is the interesting anthology of stories in Bradbury settings, *The Bradbury Chronicles: Stories in Honor of Ray Bradbury* (anth **1991**), ed William F. NOLAN and Martin H. GREENBERG. [PN]

Other works: *Switch on the Night* (**1955**), a juvenile; *Sun and Shadow* (1953 *Reporter*; **1957** chap); *The Essence of Creative Writing* (**1962**), nonfiction; *R is for Rocket* (coll **1962**), all but 2 stories having appeared in earlier collections; *The Anthem Sprinters, and Other Antics* (coll **1963**), short plays; *The Pedestrian* (1952 *FSF*; **1964** chap); *The Day it Rained Forever: A Comedy in One Act* (**1966**), a play, not to be confused with the UK collection of the same title; *The Pedestrian: A Fantasy in One Act* (**1966**), a play; *S is for Space* (coll **1966**), all but 4 stories having appeared in earlier collections; *Bloch and Bradbury* (anth **1969**; vt *Fever Dream and Other Fantasies* 1970 UK), collecting stories by RB and Robert BLOCH; *Old Ahab's Friend, and Friend to Noah, Speak his Piece* (**1971**), verse; *The Wonderful Ice Cream Suit and other Plays* (coll **1972**); *Madrigals for the Space Age* (coll **1972**), words with music by Lalo Schifrin; *The Halloween Tree* (**1972**), juvenile; *Zen and the Art of Writing* (coll **1973**; exp vt *Zen in the Art of Writing* 1990), nonfiction essays; *When Elephants Last in the Dooryard Bloomed* (coll **1973**), collected verse; *Ray Bradbury* (coll **1975** UK), retrospective collection; *Pillar of Fire, and Other Plays for Today, Tomorrow and Beyond Tomorrow* (coll **1975**), plays; *Long After Midnight* (coll **1976**), retrospective collection; *Where Robot Mice and Robot Men Run Round in Robot Towns* (coll **1977**), verse; *The Mummies of Guanajuato* (**1978**), illustrated version with photos by Archie Lieberman of "The Next in Line" (1947); *The Ghosts of Forever* (coll **1981**), a large-format illustrated book with essays, stories, verse; *The Haunted Computer and the Android Pope* (coll **1981**), verse; *The Complete Poems of Ray Bradbury* (coll **1982**); *Dinosaur Tales* (coll **1983**); *Fahrenheit 451/The Illustrated Man/Dandelion Wine/The Golden Apples of the Sun/The Martian Chronicles* (omni **1987** UK); *Fever Dream* (1948 *Startling Stories*; **1987** chap), juvenile illustrated by Darrel Anderson; *Classic Stories 1* (coll **1990**), reprint anthology containing all but 5 stories from *The Golden Apples of the Sun* and *R is for Rocket*; *Classic Stories 2* (coll **1990**), reprinting most of *A Medicine for Melancholy* and *S is for Space*, with 4 of the 5 stories omitted from *Classic Stories 1*; *On Stage: A Chrestomathy of His Plays* (coll **1991**), 10 one-act plays, being effectively an omnibus of *The Anthem Sprinters*, *The Wonderful Ice Cream Suit* and *Pillar of Fire*.

As editor: *Timeless Stories for Today and Tomorrow* (anth **1952**).

About the author: *The Ray Bradbury Companion: A Life and Career History, Photolog, and Comprehensive Checklist of Writings* (**1975**) by William F. Nolan, supplemented by *Bradbury Bits & Pieces: The Ray Bradbury Bibliography: 1974-1988* (**1991**) by Donn Albright; *The Bradbury Chronicles* (**1977** chap) by George Edgar SLUSSER; *Ray Bradbury* (anth **1980**) ed Martin H. Greenberg and J.D. OLANDER; *Ray Bradbury and the Poetics of Reverie* (**1984**) and *Ray Bradbury* (**1989**), both by William F. Touponce.

See also: ALIENS; ANTI-INTELLECTUALISM IN SF; ARKHAM HOUSE; ARTS; ASTEROIDS; CHILDREN IN SF; CLICHÉS; COLONIZATION OF OTHER WORLDS; CRIME AND PUNISHMENT; END OF THE WORLD; ESCHATOLOGY; FANZINE; GALAXY SCIENCE FICTION; GOLDEN AGE OF SF; INVASION; LIVING WORLDS; LONGEVITY (IN WRITERS AND PUBLICATIONS); *The* MAGAZINE OF FANTASY AND SCIENCE FICTION; MARS; MEDIA LANDSCAPE; MESSIAHS; MUSIC; MYTHOLOGY; PASTORAL; POETRY; POLITICS; PSYCHOLOGY; RADIO; RADIO (USA); REINCARNATION; RELIGION; ROBOTS; ROCKETS; SEX; SPACE FLIGHT; SUPERNATURAL CREATURES; TELEVISION; TERRAFORMING; THRILLING WONDER STORIES; TIME PARADOXES; TIME TRAVEL; TRANSPORTATION; VENUS.

BRADDON, RUSSELL (1921-   ) Australian writer of biographies, many novels and some other work; he is interested in experiments on ESP. He was imprisoned by the Japanese in Changi, Singapore, during WWII. His first sf novel, *The Year of the Angry Rabbit* (**1964**), unsurprisingly in view of his nationality, is sensitive about the threat posed by giant rabbits to civilization as we know it; by the end of the book, only a few Aborigines remain, and they start a second Flood. A film, NIGHT OF THE LEPUS (1972), was made of it. *The Inseparables* (**1968**) and *When the Enemy is Tired* (**1968**) are also sf. [JC]

BRADFIELD, SCOTT (MICHAEL) (1955-   ) US writer and academic who has taught for the University of Connecticut since 1989. His first sf story, the orthodox "What Makes a Cage? Jamie Knows", published in *Protostars* (anth **1971**) ed David GERROLD, significantly fails to prefigure his mature works, the best of which appear in *The Secret Life of Houses* (coll **1988** UK; with 4 stories added vt *Dream of the Wolf* 1990 US), where they apply the torque of FABULATION to Southern Californian venues whose haunted inmates are trapped just this side of the Pacific Rim. His first novel, *The History of Luminous Motion* (**1989** UK), trawls in the same waters, though without the use of sf protocols. He wrote the entries on MAGIC REALISM and OULIPO in this encyclopedia. [JC]

See also: INTERZONE.

BRADFORD, J.S. (?   -?   ) UK author of *Even a Worm* (**1936**), a novel similar in content to Arthur MACHEN's *The Terror: A Fantasy* (1917; rev 1927): the animal kingdom revolts against humanity's rule. What merit it has is diminished by the concluding rationalization of the story as being just a game-hunter's nightmare. [JE]

BRADFORD, MATTHEW C. ◊ John W. JENNISON.

BRADLEY, MARION ZIMMER (1930-   ) US writer, initially of action sf with a good deal of swashbuckling, often nearing SWORD AND SORCERY, though always with a recognizably sf rationale; and of other routine work. But with the increasing substance of her **Darkover** series, which she began in 1958, and the great success of an Arthurian fantasy in 1983 (see below), she became a major figure in the genre. She began publishing short stories professionally in 1953 with "Women Only" and "Keyhole" for *Vortex Science Fiction #2*; several are collected in *The Dark Intruder and Other Stories* (coll **1964** dos). Her first novel, *The Door through Space* (1957 *Venture* as "Bird of Prey"; exp **1961** dos), is SPACE OPERA, as is *Seven From the Stars* (**1962** dos), an intriguingly told adventure involving seven interstellar castaways on Earth.

This early work pales beside **Darkover**, a sequence of novels (and latterly stories by MZB and others) set on the fringes of an Earth-dominated GALACTIC EMPIRE and comprising perhaps the most significant PLANETARY-ROMANCE sequence in modern sf. Darkover's inhabitants – partially bred from human colonists of a previous age – successfully resist the Empire's various attempts to integrate them into a political and economic union. Darkovans have a complex though loosely described anti-technological culture dominated by sects of telepaths conjoined in potent "matrices" around which much of the action of the series is focused. Increasingly, questions of sexual politics began significantly to shape the sequence, and to cast an ambivalent light upon the gender distortions forced primarily upon women (and the androgyny required by all aspirants to a higher state) through the strange exigencies of the Darkovan culture. It may be that some of these distortions are embedded in the history of the series itself, which by 1990 had been developing for more than 30 years; certainly several early volumes are highly discordant, and have been excluded from later versions of the internal chronology of Darkover. In order to make some sense of a most complex situation, the individual volumes of the series are here listed first in order of publication and then according to the "official" internal chronology established in the 1980s.

In publication order (to date): *The Sword of Aldones* (**1962** dos) and *The Planet Savers* (1958 *AMZ*; **1962** dos; with "The Waterfall" added as coll 1976), both assembled as *The Planet Savers; The Sword of Aldones* (omni **1980**); *The Bloody Sun* (**1964**; rev, with "To Keep the Oath" added, as coll 1979); *Star of Danger* (**1965**); *The Winds of Darkover* (**1970**); *The World Wreckers* (**1971**); *Darkover Landfall* (**1972**); *The Spell Sword* (**1974**); *The Heritage of Hastur* (**1975**); *The Shattered Chain* (**1976**); *The Forbidden Tower* (**1977**); *Stormqueen!* (**1978**); *The Keeper's Price* * (anth **1980**); *Two to Conquer* (**1980**); *Shaara's Exile* (fixup **1981**), which incorporates, very much modified, *The Sword of Aldones* plus other material; *Sword of Chaos* * (anth **1982**); *Hawkmistress!* (**1982**); *Thendara House* (**1983**); *City of Sorcery* (**1984**); *Free Amazons of Darkover* * (anth **1985**); *The Other Side of the Mirror* * (anth **1987**); *Red Sun of Darkover* * (anth **1987**); *Four Moons of Darkover* * (anth **1988**); *The Heirs of Hammerfell* (**1989**), *Domains of Darkover* * (anth **1990**), *Renunciates of Darkover* * (anth **1991**) and *Leroni of*

Darkover (anth **1991**). MZB's first novel, *The Door through Space* (**1961**), and *Falcons of Narabedla* (1957 *Other Worlds*; **1964** dos) – a pastiche of *The Dark World* (**1965**) by Henry KUTTNER and C.L. MOORE – are also marginally linked to the series.

The internal sequence is very different, beginning with *Darkover Landfall* (**1972**), which describes the initial landing of Terran colonists. The sequence then jumps an eon into the feudal turmoil of *Stormqueen!* (**1978**) and *Hawkmistress!* (**1982**); balkanization and the growth of order in *Two to Conquer* (**1980**) and *The Heirs of Hammerfell* (**1989**) finally evolve – after *The Shattered Chain* (**1976**) and *Thendara House* (**1983**), both assembled as *Oath of the Renunciates* (omni **1984**), and *City of Sorcery* (**1984**) set up a dubiously feminist Amazon sisterhood – into a sophisticated conflict with the returning Terrans in *The Spell Sword* (**1974**), *The Forbidden Tower* (**1977**), *The Heritage of Hastur* (**1975**) and *Shaara's Exile* (**1981**), the last two of which are also assembled as *Children of Hastur* (omni **1982**). The various group anthologies are deemed to infill.

Shadowy, complex, confused, the world of Darkover is increasingly a house of many mansions; a few (either writers or readers) seem to feel unwelcome.

Many other singletons and some series surround this central sequence; but *The Mists of Avalon* (**1983**) far outstripped any other title in its success in the marketplace and significance as a convincing revision of the Arthurian cycle. In this book the Matter of Britain revolves around a conflict between the sane but dying paganism of Morgan le Fay and the patriarchal ascetics of ascendant Christianity, whose victory in the war ensures eons of repression for women and the vital principles they espouse. It is a rousing assault, and less governed by genre demands than **Darkover**. There is, perhaps, something vulgar in MZB's edgy progress into an eccentric FEMINISM, but her work has had an electrifying effect on a very large readership; and at her best she speaks with the rare transparency of the true storyteller.   [JC]

Other works: *The Colors of Space* (**1963**; text restored 1983), a juvenile; *The Brass Dragon* (**1969**); the **Survivors** sequence comprising *Hunters of the Red Moon* (**1973**) and *The Survivors* (**1979**), the latter with Paul Edwin ZIMMER; *The Jewel of Arwen* (**1974** chap) and its partner, *The Parting of Arwen* (**1974** chap); *Endless Voyage* (**1975**; rev vt *Endless Universe* 1979); *Drums of Darkness: An Astrological Gothic Novel* (**1976**); *The Maenads* (**1978** chap), a poem on Greek myths; *The Ruins of Isis* (**1978**); *The Catch Trap* (**1979**), a circus novel about (male) homosexuals; *The House Between the Worlds* (**1980**; rev 1981); *Survey Ship* (**1980**); the **Atlantis Chronicles**, comprising *Web of Light* (**1982**) and *Web of Darkness* (**1984**), both assembled as *Web of Darkness* (omni **1985** UK; vt *The Fall of Atlantis* 1987 US); *The Inheritor* (**1984**) and its sequel, *Witch Hill* (**1972** as by Valerie Graves; rev 1990); *Night's Daughter* (**1985**); *Warrior Woman* (**1985**); *The Best of Marion Zimmer Bradley* (coll **1985**; rev 1988) ed Martin H.

GREENBERG; *Lythande* (coll **1986**), with 1 story by Vonda N. MCINTYRE; *The Firebrand* (**1987**); *Black Trillium* (**1990**) with Julian MAY and Andre NORTON.

Non-genre fiction: Many titles, including *I am a Lesbian* (**1962**) as by Lee Chapman; others as by John Dexter, Miriam Gardner, Valerie Graves, Morgan Ives; *Bluebeard's Daughter* (**1968**).

Nonfiction: *Men, Halflings and Hero-Worship* (**1973**); *The Necessity for Beauty: Robert W. Chambers and the Romantic Tradition* (**1974**); *Experiment Perilous: Three Essays on Science Fiction* (anth **1976**) with Norman SPINRAD and Alfred BESTER.

As editor: *Greyhaven* (anth **1983**); the **Sword and Sorceress** series, comprising *Sword and Sorceress I* (anth **1984**), *II* (anth **1985**), *III* (anth **1986**), *IV* (anth **1987**), *V* (anth **1988**), *VI* (anth **1990**), *VII* (anth **1990**), *VIII* (anth **1991**) and *IX* (anth **1992**); *Spells of Wonder* (anth **1989**).

About the author: *The Darkover Dilemma: Problems of the Darkover Series* (**1976**) by S. Wise; *The Darkover Concordance: A Reader's Guide* (**1979**) by Walter Breen, MZB's husband; *Leigh Brackett, Marion Zimmer Bradley, Anne McCaffrey: A Primary and Secondary Bibliography* (**1982**) by Rosemarie Arbur; *Marion Zimmer Bradley* (**1985**) by Rosemarie Arbur; *Marion Zimmer Bradley, Mistress of Magic: A Working Bibliography* (**1991** chap) by Gordon BENSON Jr and Phil STEPHENSEN-PAYNE.

See also: AMAZING STORIES; ATLANTIS; COLONIZATION OF OTHER WORLDS; DAW BOOKS; ESP; FANTASY; MAGIC; OPEN UNIVERSE; PLANETARY ROMANCE; SCIENCE FANTASY; SEX; SHARED WORLDS; WOMEN SF WRITERS.

BRADLEY, WILL ◊ Brad STRICKLAND.

BRADSHAW, WILLIAM R. (1851-1927) US writer whose *The Goddess of Atvatabar: Being the History of the Discovery of the Interior World and Conquest of Atvatabar* (**1892**) is set in a Symmesian HOLLOW EARTH with an interior sun. The chthonic culture includes a love cult whose devotees regard mild sex without orgasm as leading to perpetual youth. Catastrophic melodrama soon leads to trade relations with the surface (◊ ANTHROPOLOGY; LOST WORLDS). The book is heavily illustrated. [JC]

BRAID or BRAIDED Term used to designate a SHARED-WORLD anthology or book-length tale whose individual parts, written by different hands, are edited – generally by the proprietor/editor of the shared world – so that their beginnings and ends weave (or braid) into one another, and the whole tells a unified story. When done properly, braids can generate a chronicle-like sense in the reader – an effect attained also by successful FIXUPS, which can in this sense be defined as one-handed braids. It is probable that Robert Lynn ASPRIN created the first full-scale braid in sf or fantasy with his **Thieves' World** sequence from 1979. A further example of a braided anthology is the **Merovingen Nights** sequence created and presided over by C.J. CHERRYH. [JC]

BRAIN, THE ◊ VENGEANCE.

BRAIN DEAD Film (1989). Concorde/New Horizons. Dir Adam Simon, starring Bill Pullman, Bill Paxton, Patricia Charbonneau, Bud Cort, George Kennedy, Nicholas Pryor. Screenplay Charles BEAUMONT. 81 mins. Colour.

A neurosurgeon (Pullman) is asked to examine a genius (Cort) who has gone mad and killed his family. The surgeon soon finds that his own identity is being alarmingly eaten away, his friends, colleagues and wife supporting the process, gradually convincing him that he is the patient who needs brain surgery; the boundaries between the sane neurosurgeon and insane mathematician are gradually erased. Written for Roger CORMAN by Beaumont in 1963, this was filmed 22 years after Beaumont's death. The surprise is that so much of the writer's distinctive plotting – a mix of panicky humour and PARANOIA – has survived rewrites which, for example, update him by tapping into the species of gory medical humour exemplified by RE-ANIMATOR (1985). Where recent horror films like the **Nightmare on Elm Street** sequence domesticate the dream/reality uncertainty for irrelevant shock scenes, *BD* allows the ambiguity itself to fragment and take over the film. [KN]

BRAINSTORM Film (1983). A JF Production/MGM/UA. Dir Douglas Trumbull, starring Christopher Walken, Natalie Wood, Louise Fletcher, Cliff Robertson. Screenplay Robert Stitzel, Philip Frank Messina, based on a story by Bruce Joel Rubin. 106 mins. Colour.

A VIRTUAL-REALITY device is invented which faithfully records human experiences (including the accompanying emotions) and allows them to be re-experienced by another person. This promising notion is frittered away – first because, despite Trumbull's special-effects expertise, the cinematic equivalent of these experiences is just like old-fashioned Cinerama and has no emotional content at all (obviously); second because the device is largely used to reconcile husband and wife by replaying the one's banal romantic feelings for the other; third because, after the wife dies, thoughtfully recording her death experience *en passant*, we get to share her experience. This playback, supposedly almost lethal to the viewer, shows that the last great journey consists of cute bubbles with pictures inside them. Natalie Wood, who plays the wife, drowned while filming was still in progress, which necessitated a few last-minute rewrites that do not work. Rubin, writer of the original story, was obviously obsessed by afterlife experiences, and went on to script, among others, *Ghost* (1990) and *Jacob's Ladder* (1991). [PN]

BRAMAH, ERNEST Working name of UK writer Ernest Bramah Smith (1868-1942) for all his writing. His series of tales in which the Chinese **Kai Lung** tells stories to stave off punishment, like Scheherazade, contains some fantasy elements. The **Kai Lung** series includes: *The Wallet of Kai Lung* (coll **1900**), the first story in which was republished as *The Transmutation of Ling* (**1911** chap); *Kai Lung's Golden Hours* (coll **1922**) with intro by Hilaire BELLOC; *Kai Lung Unrolls his Mat* (coll **1928**); *The Story of Wan and the Remarkable Shrub and The Story of Ching-Kwei and the Destinies* (coll **1927** chap US), offering 2 stories from the previous volume, another story from which appeared as *Kin Weng and the Miraculous Tusk* **1941** chap); *The Moon of Much Gladness* (coll **1932**; vt *The Return of Kai Lung* 1937 US) and *Kai Lung Beneath the Mulberry Tree* (coll **1940**). The first three titles were assembled as *The Kai Lung Omnibus* (omni **1936**); *The Celestial Omnibus* (coll **1963**) is a selection; *Kai Lung: Six* (coll **1974**) assembles tales EB did not himself collect. Of sf interest is *What Might Have Been* (**1907** anon; with new preface vt *The Secret of the League* 1909 as by EB), a somewhat tedious anti-socialist melodrama, involving flight with belted-on mechanical wings; the sequel, a future-WAR tale called "The War Hawks" (1908), appeared in *The Specimen Case* (coll **1924**). [JC]

Other works: *The Mirror of Kong Ho* (**1905**); the associational **Max Carrados** books about a blind detective, comprising *Max Carrados* (coll **1914**), *The Eyes of Max Carrados* (coll **1923**) and *Max Carrados Mysteries* (coll **1927**); *Ernest Bramah* (coll **1929**).

BRAND, MAX Best-known pseudonym of US writer Frederick (Schiller) Faust (1892-1944), who from before 1920 used many names and produced innumerable tales and filmscripts in many genres, including the Western classic *Destry Rides Again* (**1930**), famously filmed in 1939. The psychic contortions that attend the discovery of a Missing Link in Africa (◊ APES AND CAVEMEN) impart a lurid glow to "That Receding Brow" (1919 *All-Story Magazine*), which may be his first tale of genre interest. MB began publishing books in volume form with *The Untamed* (**1919**), the first volume of the **Dan Barry** sequence of Westerns, whose protagonist, a "Pan of the desert" and werewolf, enjoys a strangely intimate rapport with wild animals; the series continued with *The Night Horseman* (**1920**), *The Seventh Man* (**1921**) and *Dan Barry's Daughter* (**1923**). *The Garden of Eden* (**1922**) is a LOST-WORLD tale, and *The Smoking Land* (1937 *Argosy* as by George Challis; **1980**) stereotypically discloses another lost world, in the Arctic, complete with futuristic aircraft and rumbustious action. Throughout MB's work, illuminating the most pulp-like plots, can be discerned the voice of a slyly civilized writer. [JC]

About the author: *Max Brand: Western Giant* (anth **1986**) ed William F. NOLAN.

BRANDON, FRANK [s] ◊ Kenneth BULMER.

BRAUN, JOHANNA [r] **and GÜNTER** [r] ◊ GERMANY.

BRAUTIGAN, RICHARD (1935-1984) US writer and poet, known primarily for his work outside the sf field. Most of his whimsically surreal fiction lies on the borderline of FANTASY. *The Hawkline Monster: A Gothic Western* (**1974**), which is sf, plays amusingly with the Frankenstein theme. *In Watermelon Sugar* (**1968**), set in an indeterminate hippie-pastoral setting, echoes the post-HOLOCAUST novels of conventional sf. RB committed suicide. [PR/JC]

See also: UTOPIAS.

BRAX, COLEMAN [s] ◊ M. Coleman EASTON.

BRAY, JOHN FRANCIS (1809-1897) US writer, mostly of (sometimes radical) economic tracts. He was in the UK 1822-42 and there produced, among other works, *A Voyage from Utopia* (written 1841; **1957** UK), which anticipated William Dean HOWELLS's technique of presenting the views of a visitor *from* the UTOPIA. In JFB's book the visitor's responses to the labour conditions and abiding hypocrisies characteristic of the UK and USA are republican, satirical (◊ SATIRE) and outraged. JFB rightly thought the work unpublishable in his time. [JC]

BRAZIL ◊ LATIN AMERICA.

BRAZIL Film (1985). Brazil/20th Century-Fox/Universal. Dir Terry Gilliam, starring Jonathan Pryce, Robert De Niro, Katherine Helmond, Bob Hoskins, Peter Vaughan, Ian Holm, Michael Palin, Kim Greist. Screenplay Gilliam, Tom Stoppard, Charles McKeown. 142 mins. Colour.

The US print of *B* was initially cut by Universal because it was too long and depressing, but, following a highly publicized squabble with Gilliam, Universal backed down when the film won three LA Film Critics Awards. Universal's commercial instincts, though condemned as philistine, were correct: the film is indeed self-indulgently long, and has never won mass acceptance, though gaining high cult status.

This black comedy pits a shy, romantic file clerk against a faceless, sinister, bureaucratic, all-powerful Ministry of Information in an imaginary present derived equally from George ORWELL and Franz KAFKA. Director Gilliam began his career as animation director of the classic tv series *Monty Python's Flying Circus* (1969-71), and *B*'s great strength is its stunning visual appearance, both in the prolonged and surreal dream sequences (showing freedom and heroic action) and in the slightly more realistic city of the main action, where industrial-Victorian gloom (ducts and pneumatic tubes everywhere) overshadows the futuristic (paste meals). The performances are unusually good, especially Palin's yuppie torturer, but Pryce's one-note, hysterical performance is tiringly unattractive. The satire veers arbitrarily in its objects between the trivial and the horrible, plastic surgery and paper-shuffling on the one hand, night raids by secret police and state-endorsed murder on the other. The bitterness of the film's plea for (unreachable) freedom is partly lost in the intellectual kitsch of its designer DYSTOPIA. Gilliam's obsessive relationship to a cruelty he seems to regard as inescapable has always been ambiguous: he both fears and uses it, which here produces an involuntary but pervasive subtext of collaboration with the torturers. [PN]

BREBNER, WINSTON (1924?-   ) US writer whose sf novel *Doubting Thomas* (**1956**) depicts a computer-ruled DYSTOPIA. [JC]

BREGGIN, PETER (ROGER) (1936-   ) US writer whose sf DYSTOPIA, *After the Good War: A Love Story*

(**1972**), excoriates meaningless SEX.   [JC]

BRENNERT, ALAN (MICHAEL) (1954-   ) US tv producer and scriptwriter, and also author, essentially of
fantasy and horror. His first genre publication was
"Jamie's Smile" for *The Ides of Tomorrow* (anth **1976**)
ed Terry CARR. In his first novel, *City of Masques*
(**1978**), actors scientifically programmed to become
their roles run amok. *Time and Chance* (**1990**) is a kind
of sf/horror tale in which two ALTERNATE WORLDS
intersect, allowing two versions of the same person
to switch roles: the consequences of the switch are
depicted with acumen and passion. The title story of
Her Pilgrim Soul and Other Stories (coll **1990**) is also sf,
and the title story of *Ma Qui and Other Phantoms* (coll
1991) won a 1992 NEBULA award for Best Short Story;
but much of AB's genre work lies in media other than
the written word.

He is very active in tv, his sf/fantasy scripts
including some for BUCK ROGERS IN THE 25TH CENTURY
(1979-81) and WONDER WOMAN (1978-9), and more
recently 11 scripts for the second series of *The*
TWILIGHT ZONE (1985-7). He is probably best known to
the world at large as a writer for, and producer of,
the top-rating tv series *LA Law*.

AB has written occasionally for COMICS, mostly
Batman, through the 1980s; his small but impressive
body of work in this medium also makes much use
of the PARALLEL-WORLDS concept. Some of these pieces
appear in DC COMICS's *The Greatest Batman Stories Ever
Told* (**1989**).   [JC/PN]

Other work: *Kindred Spirits* (**1984**), a juvenile.

BRETNOR, (ALFRED) REGINALD (1911-1992) US
writer and anthologist, born in Vladivostok, Siberia,
but resident in the USA since 1919; active since WWII
in a number of genres as an author of both fiction and
nonfiction. His interest in military theory, which first
generated articles and *Decisive Warfare* (**1969**), later
inspired the **The Future at War** series of anthologies:
Thor's Hammer (anth **1979**), *The Spear of Mars* (anth
1980) and *Orion's Sword* (anth **1980**).

RB began publishing sf with "Maybe Just a Little
One" for *Harper's Magazine* in 1947, and many of his
later stories appeared in the slick magazines. His
single most famous story is probably the hilarious
"The Gnurrs Come from the Voodvork Out" (1950),
a tale that, on its first publication in *FSF*, epitomized
for many the wit and literacy of that magazine's new
broom. This was the first of a protracted series of
stories about **Papa Schimmelhorn**, assembled as *The
Schimmelhorn File* (coll **1979**) and followed by *Schimmelhorn's Gold* (**1986**), a comic tale of alchemy which
brews sf and fantasy tropes in a pot of hornswog-
gling. The three critical symposia he edited on sf –
Modern Science Fiction, Its Meaning and Its Future (anth
1953; slightly exp 1979), *Science Fiction, Today and
Tomorrow* (anth **1974**) and *The Craft of Science Fiction*
(anth **1976**) – have proved among the most substantial nonfiction contributions to the field. Each contains articles by well known sf writers: the only critics
represented are those who also write sf. «One Man's

BEM: Thoughts on Science Fiction» (1992) vividly
represents his own views.

As Grendel Briarton, RB from 1956 contributed to
FSF a series of joke vignettes whose punch-lines are
as a rule distorted or punning catch-phrases. They
have become known, from Ferdinand Feghoot, their
continuing protagonist, as **Feghoots**, and can be
found assembled in *Through Time and Space with
Ferdinand Feghoot* (coll **1962**; exp vt *The Compleat
Feghoot* 1975; further exp vt *The (Even) More Compleat
Feghoot* 1980; final exp vt *The Collected Feghoot* 1992).
RB was also a translator and lecturer.   [JC]

Other works: *A Killing in Swords* (**1978**), associational,
featuring RB's detective hero, **Alastair Timoroff**;
Gilpin's Space (1983 *ASF* as "Owl's Flight"; exp **1986**);
«Of Force, Violence, and Other Imponderables:
Essays on War, Politics, and Government» (coll 1992).

About the author: *The Work of Reginald Bretnor: An
Annotated Bibliography & Guide* (**1989**) by Scott Alan
Burgess.

See also: CORPSICLE; CRITICAL AND HISTORICAL WORKS
ABOUT SF; DEFINITIONS OF SF; HUMOUR; *The* MAGAZINE OF
FANTASY AND SCIENCE FICTION; WAR.

BRETT, LEO ◊ R.L. FANTHORPE.

BREUER, MILES J(OHN) (1889-1947) US writer and
physician who began publishing sf with "The Man
with the Strange Head" for *AMZ* in 1927. He
published a number of notable stories until about
1942. His solo work has not been collected in book
form, which makes it difficult now to find such
stories as "The Appendix and the Spectacles" (1928),
"The Gostak and the Doshes" (1930), both in *AMZ*
and both since anthologized, and "Paradise and Iron"
(1930 *AMZ Quarterly*), a novel which strikes an early
(for US GENRE SF) warning note about the perils of the
UTOPIAN technological fix. His only works to have
reached book form are *The Girl from Mars* (**1929** chap)
with Jack WILLIAMSON and *The Birth of a New Republic*
(1930 *AMZ Quarterly*; **1981** chap, but at 2000 words
per page), also with Williamson, on whom MJB had
a formative influence; the latter tale is a political
melodrama in which the working residents of the
Moon rebel against Earth. An intelligent though
somewhat crude writer, MJB was particularly strong
in his articulation of fresh ideas.   [JC]

See also: AMAZING STORIES; AUTOMATION; COLONIZATION
OF OTHER WORLDS; COMPUTERS; DIMENSIONS; DYSTOPIAS;
HISTORY IN SF; LEISURE; MATHEMATICS; MEDICINE; MOON;
POLITICS; WAR.

BRIARTON, GRENDEL [s] ◊ Reginald BRETNOR.

BRICK BRADFORD US COMIC strip created by author
William Ritt and artist Clarence Gray for King
Features Syndicate. *BB* appeared in 1933 as a Sunday
page and daily strip, with the Sunday strip the more
fantastic and futuristic. Gray's clean, economical
style, together with Ritt's imaginative, purple prose,
made *BB* more than just an imitation of BUCK ROGERS
IN THE 25TH CENTURY, which probably inspired it. Ritt
was fired in 1948 for failing to keep deadlines, and
Gray developed cancer in the 1950s. Artist Paul

Norris took over the daily strip in 1952, and the Sunday page in 1957, writing as well as illustrating.

Bradford was a red-haired hero with a lovely sidekick, April Southern. The poetic imagery of *BB* was pure SPACE OPERA (futuristic cities rise out of lush jungles, flying ships battle with giant butterflies, etc.), while the scenarios were just as exotic as the contemporary sf appearing in the magazines: the discovery of lost races, a descent into the microcosmic universe within a coin, a journey by drilling vehicle to the Earth's interior world, and travels through time and space in the Time Top or "Chronosphere".

BB appeared as a serial film (Columbia, 1947, 15 episodes, starring Kane Richmond), an sf comic book and a **Big Little Book** (◊ JUVENILE SERIES). [JE/PN]

BRIDE, THE ◊ *The* BRIDE OF FRANKENSTEIN.

BRIDE OF FRANKENSTEIN, THE Film (1935). Universal. Dir James Whale, starring Boris Karloff, Colin Clive, Elsa Lanchester, Ernest Thesiger. Screenplay John Balderston, William Hurlbut. 80 mins. B/w.

This sequel to the 1931 FRANKENSTEIN, also dir Whale, is the greatest of the many **Frankenstein** movies and one of the greatest sf movies. Some watchers feel that the horror and pathos of the story are a little overwhelmed by Whale's morbid sense of comedy, seen here particularly in the bizarre figure of the gin-drinking, vain Dr Praetorious, creator of homunculi, who blackmails Frankenstein into constructing an artificial bride for the Monster. We learn immediately from the prologue – in which Mary SHELLEY ("frightened of thunder, fearful of the dark"), played by Lanchester, talks to Percy Shelley and Byron – that the Monster was not killed at the end of the previous film after all; later we see the Monster floundering through the forest, captured by villagers, breaking free, and befriended by a blind hermit where, in a scene of justly celebrated pathos, he is taught to smoke a cigarette. But nothing prepares one for the extraordinary, protracted finale, the most stylized scene in a stylized film, choreographed to perfection. Here the Bride (Lanchester again, thus making a clear and interesting identification of Mary Shelley with her sad, monstrous creation) comes to life – as electrical equipment splutters and sparks – lurches not ungracefully across the room, a white streak in her wild coiffure, screams at her first sight of the Monster, shrinks from him, and finally with a hiss like a maddened cat pulls the lever that will destroy herself and all the rest. It is an unforgettable tableau.

Whale was too theatrical for tragedy and perhaps too sceptical for true horror, with as much of Oscar Wilde as Shakespeare in his sensibility. But nevertheless his conservatism, his sophisticated, deeply un-American sense of irony, and his bold sense of symbolism make this one of the strongest cinematic statements ever made about, paradoxically, both the potency and the impotence of science.

A rather different story, although with deliberate parallels, is told in the much later *The Bride* (1985) dir Franc Roddam, starring Sting, Jennifer Beals, Clancy Brown, David Rappaport, Alexei Sayle. 118 mins. Colour. Here the Bride (Beals) is initially repelled by the Monster (Brown), who flees in dismay to wander afar in the company of a dwarf (Rappaport). Frankenstein (a wooden Sting) becomes obsessed with the Bride to the point of attempted rape; she is saved by the returned Monster, whose love she now reciprocates. In one of the deliberately humorous scenes the fleeing Monster encounters a blind man, who fondly touches his face and then triumphantly yells "I've *found* him!" to the pursuing mob. [PN/JGr]

BRIDE OF RE-ANIMATOR ◊ RE-ANIMATOR.

BRIDE OF THE INCREDIBLE HULK ◊ *The* INCREDIBLE HULK.

BRIDGEMAN, RICHARD [s] ◊ L.P. DAVIES.

BRIDGES, T(HOMAS) C(HARLES) (1868-1944) French-born UK writer, often in Florida. A prolific author of boys' fiction from about 1902, he wrote some sf tales for the oldest segment of his audience. Of greatest interest are *Martin Crusoe: A Boy's Adventure on Wizard Island* (**1920**), which takes young Martin Vaile to the eponymous island, a relic of ATLANTIS, and *The Death Star* (**1940**), a rather grim tale set on a depopulated Earth. [JC]
Other works: *Men of the Mist* (**1923**); *The Hidden City* (**1923**); *The City of No Escape* (**1925**).
As Christopher Beck: *The Crimson Airplane* (**1913**); *The Brigand of the Air* (**1920**); *The People of the Chasm* (**1924**).

BRIGGS, RAYMOND (REDVERS) (1934-   ) UK illustrator and writer, active in both capacities from about 1958, and best known for several tales told in COMIC- book format, including *Fungus the Bogeyman* (graph **1977**) and *Fungus the Bogeyman Plop-Up Book* (graph **1982**), both borderline sf, in which the meticulously worked-out topsy-turvy world of the underground Bogeys, opposite to humans in every way, serves to illuminate life on the surface, and *The Snowman* (graph **1978**), a fantasy. *When the Wind Blows* (graph **1982**) is a singularly unrelenting SATIRE on the true worth of civil defence in any genuine nuclear HOLOCAUST. The two protagonists, naïve and trusting "ordinary" people, follow the instructions to the letter, as though it were the Battle of Britain once again, and die slowly in horror and bewilderment. [JC]

BRIN, (GLEN) DAVID (1950-   ) US writer with a BS in astronomy and an MS in applied physics, who began publishing sf with his first novel, *Sundiver* (**1980**), which is also the first volume in the ongoing **Uplift** sequence, for which he remains best known: it continued with *Startide Rising* (**1983**; rev **1985**) and *The Uplift War* (**1987**), the two being assembled as *Earthclan* (omni **1987**); further volumes are projected. *Startide Rising* won both the HUGO and the NEBULA awards for best novel; *The Uplift War* won a Hugo. As a whole, the series established DB as the most popular and – with the exception of Greg BEAR – the most important author of HARD SF to appear in the 1980s.

However, despite their both being fairly characterized as hard-sf writers, DB and Bear demonstrate through their fundamental differences of approach something of the range of work which can be subsumed under that rubric. Some exponents of hard sf speak as though it were a kind of writing which adhered to rigorous models of scientific explanation and extrapolation, eschewing both the doubletalk of SPACE OPERA "science" and the psychobabble of "soft" disciplines like sociology; and it might be argued that Bear attempts to convey in his work a sense that he is carrying that form of discipline to its uttermost, and beyond. Not so with DB. Despite his professional competence as a physicist – a level of scientific qualification not shared by Bear – he writes tales in which the physical constraints governing the knowable Universe are flouted with high-handed panache, with the effect that – for instance – the **Uplift** books are as compulsive reading as anything ever published in the genre. The basic premise of the sequence is simple enough, though its workings-out are increasingly complicated. All thinking life in the Universe – or at least throughout the Five Galaxies encompassed in the three books so far – takes part in a vast hierarchical drama of evolutionary uplift, at the pinnacle of which are the Progenitors who – eons before humanity's entry into the scene – established laws to govern the creation and interaction of species. The Progenitors are now long gone – the intergalactic search for relics of their presence shapes much of the sequence – but before their departure they established five Patron Lines, races which govern individual galaxies. On achieving Contact with the local Patron Line, *Homo sapiens* (which uniquely among known races does not belong to the family tree that descends from the Progenitors) then replicates in small – by uplifting dolphins and chimpanzees to full sentience and partnership – a central imperative of the galactic ancestors. But problems arise.

The secondary premise of the sequence – one that breeds true from the GOLDEN-AGE assumptions that have tended to govern space opera on this scale – generates most of the action. The human race, according to this premise, is a kind of sport, more ambitious and energetic and fast-moving than other galactic peoples. The local Patron Line has become corrupt, and its rulers hope to batten on human vitality; moreover, the Galactic Library Institute, supposedly autonomous, has itself been corrupted, and the human race has begun to learn caution about the technological data and other lessons supposedly passed down from the Progenitors via this source. *Sundiver* plunges into the heart of all this. A human expedition penetrates the Sun, where lifeforms are found which impart secrets about the Universe and the Library. In *Startide Rising*, one of the most rousing space operas yet written, a starship crewed by uplifted dolphins and a GENETICALLY ENGINEERED human find an ancient fleet and an ancient cadaver, and must contrive somehow to escape an assortment

of Patron-led foes and get their prize of knowledge and power back to Earth. *The Uplift War*, seemingly an interlude, transfers the action to a planet occupied by Earth humans and neo-chimps who may have some clue as to the location of the Progenitors. The sequence is clearly intended to extend into further volumes.

Insofar as DB's singletons stay closer to home, they are less successful. *The Practice Effect* (**1984**) reworks in fantasy terms the oddly Lamarckian principles (◊ EVOLUTION) espoused in the space operas. *The Postman* (**1985**), set in a worryingly PASTORAL post-HOLOCAUST USA, eulogizes Yankee decencies without much analysing the hugely complex cultural matrix that shaped them. *Heart of the Comet* (**1986**) with Gregory BENFORD is an uneasy marriage of two very different hard-sf writers, Benford caught as usual in the coils of Stapledonian *Sehnsucht* (◊ Olaf STAPLEDON) and DB resolutely uplifting. In *Earth* (**1990**), a novel of very considerable ambition about the NEAR-FUTURE death of the planet for all the usual (and quite possibly valid) reasons, Gaia is rescued at the last moment from a gnawing BLACK HOLE and other threats by an infusion of PULP-MAGAZINE plotting that consorts ill with the pressing seriousness of the issues raised. This is not to say that DB fails to raise those issues: more than any of his earlier novels, *Earth* demonstrates his very considerable cognitive grasp of issues, his omnivorousness as a researcher, and the reasoning that lies behind his stubborn optimism. Like E.E. "Doc" SMITH before him, DB gives joy and imparts a SENSE OF WONDER; but he also thinks about the near world. It is to be hoped that he continues to do both. [JC]

Other works: *The River of Time* (coll **1986**), which contains the Hugo-winning "The Crystal Tears" (**1984**); *Dr Pak's Preschool* (**1988** chap); *Project Solar Sail* (anth **1990**) with Arthur C. CLARKE; *Piecework* (**1991** chap).

See also: ALIENS; APES AND CAVEMEN (IN THE HUMAN WORLD); ASTOUNDING SCIENCE-FICTION; BIOLOGY; DISASTER; ECOLOGY; GAMES AND TOYS; JOHN W. CAMPBELL MEMORIAL AWARD; LINGUISTICS; LIVING WORLDS; MERCURY; MONSTERS; OPTIMISM AND PESSIMISM; POLLUTION; SCIENTISTS; SOCIAL DARWINISM; SUN; UNDER THE SEA.

BRINGSVAERD, TOR ÅGE [r] ◊ SCANDINAVIA.

BRINTON, HENRY (1901-1977) UK writer, variously engaged in social and political work, whose sf novel *Purple-6* (**1962**) describes a world at the verge of atomic HOLOCAUST. [JC]

BRITAIN, DAN ◊ Don PENDLETON.

BRITISH FANTASY SOCIETY The BFS was formed in 1971 (as the British Weird Fantasy Society) for "all devotees of fantasy, horror, and the supernatural". Catering now in the main for horror fans, this active society – which sponsors an annual CONVENTION, Fantasycon (1975-current) – has no direct relevance to sf other than a substantial crossover of membership with sf groups. However, an earlier British Fantasy Society (1942-6) was sf-based (◊ BRITISH SCIENCE

FICTION ASSOCIATION *for further details*).   [PR]

BRITISH SCIENCE FICTION ASSOCIATION

(BSFA) Despite their names, the British Science Literary Association (1931), organized by Walter GILLINGS, and the first British Science Fiction Association (1933-5), organized by the Hayes SF Club, failed to become much more than local groups. The UK's first truly national organizations – the Science Fiction Association (1937-9), the first BRITISH FANTASY SOCIETY (1942-6) and the Science Fantasy Society (1948-51) – were short-lived. The BSFA was established at Easter 1958 in order to counteract a decline in UK FANDOM by providing a central organization of interest to casual sf readers. The association's principal attraction was (and is) its journal, VECTOR, published intermittently since 1958. The BSFA library has since the mid-1970s been held on indefinite loan as part of the SCIENCE FICTION FOUNDATION's collection. The BSFA sponsored the annual UK Easter sf CONVENTIONS 1959-67 and also initiated the British Fantasy Award (first presented 1966; changed 1970 to the BRITISH SCIENCE FICTION AWARD). Brian W. ALDISS was the BSFA's first president 1960-64, being followed by Edmund CRISPIN, who retained the position until the BSFA became a limited company in 1967.

Other periodicals published by the BSFA are *Matrix* (sf/fan news), *Paperback Inferno* (before 1980 titled *Paperback Parlour*; paperback book reviews) and *Focus* (articles on writing and selling sf). *Paperback Inferno* was merged into *Vector* in late 1992 (from *Vector #* 169). Membership has been substantial for the past decade. Despite occasional administrative slumps and only lukewarm support from established fandom, the BSFA has a useful function in introducing new fans to sf discussions and controversies, and in pointing them towards specific local fan organizations.   [RH/PR/PN]

BRITISH SCIENCE FICTION AWARD

This award developed from the British Fantasy Award, which was sponsored by the BRITISH SCIENCE FICTION ASSOCIATION and made to a writer: John BRUNNER won the first in 1966. It became the British Science Fiction Award in 1970, and thereafter was for a book. From 1979 the number of categories was increased. The eligibility rules have occasionally changed; most early versions required UK authorship, but later only UK publication was required. The Best Artist award is normally given for a specific cover rather than for a body of work. In recent years the BSFA Awards, as they are often known, have been voted on by BSFA members and members of the UK national Easter CONVENTION, Eastercon, although often not by very many of them; in some early years the adjudication was done by a small judging panel. They are announced at Eastercon. Because the award has not been well publicized and has a narrow voting base, it has never had the hoped-for effect of acting as a counterweight to the US-dominated HUGOS and NEBULAS. Although usually named for the year in which works became eligible, the awards are listed below according to the year in which they were actually made (i.e., the following year):

1970: *Stand on Zanzibar* by John Brunner

1971: *The Jagged Orbit* by John Brunner

1972: *The Moment of Eclipse* by Brian W. ALDISS

1973: No award (insufficient votes)

1974: *Rendezvous with Rama* by Arthur C. CLARKE; special award to Brian W. Aldiss for *Billion Year Spree*

1975: *Inverted World* by Christopher PRIEST

1976: *Orbitsville* by Bob SHAW

1977: *Brontomek!* by Michael G. CONEY; special award to David A. KYLE for *A Pictorial History of Science Fiction*

1978: *The Jonah Kit* by Ian WATSON

1979: novel *A Scanner Darkly* by Philip K. DICK; collection *Deathbird Stories* by Harlan ELLISON; media *The* HITCH HIKER'S GUIDE TO THE GALAXY

1980: novel *The Unlimited Dream Company* by J.G. BALLARD; short fiction "Palely Loitering" by Christopher Priest; media *The Hitch Hiker's Guide to the Galaxy* record; artist Jim BURNS

1981: novel *Timescape* by Gregory BENFORD; short fiction "The Brave Little Toaster" by Thomas M. DISCH; media *The Hitch Hiker's Guide to the Galaxy* 2nd series; artist Peter Jones

1982: novel *The Shadow of the Torturer* by Gene WOLFE; short fiction "Mythago Wood" by Robert P. HOLDSTOCK; media *Time Bandits*; artist Bruce PENNINGTON

1983: novel *Helliconia Spring* by Brian W. Aldiss; short fiction "Kitemaster" by Keith ROBERTS; media BLADE RUNNER; artist Tim WHITE

1984: novel *Tik-Tok* by John T. SLADEK; short fiction "After Images" by Malcolm EDWARDS; media ANDROID; artist Bruce Pennington

1985: novel *Mythago Wood* by Robert P. Holdstock; short fiction "The Unconquered Country" by Geoff RYMAN; media *The Company of Wolves*; artist Jim Burns

1986: novel *Helliconia Winter* by Brian W. Aldiss; short fiction "Cube Root" by David LANGFORD; media BRAZIL; artist Jim Burns

1987: novel *The Ragged Astronauts* by Bob Shaw; short fiction "Kaeti and the Hangman" by Keith Roberts; media ALIENS; artist Keith Roberts

1988: novel *Grainne* by Keith Roberts; short fiction "Love Sickness" by Geoff Ryman; media STAR COPS; artist Jim Burns

1989: novel *Lavondyss* by Robert P. Holdstock; short fiction "Dark Night in Toyland" by Bob Shaw; media *Who Framed Roger Rabbit*; artist Alan Lee

1990: novel *Pyramids* by Terry PRATCHETT; short fiction "In Translation" by Lisa TUTTLE; media RED DWARF; artist Jim Burns

1991: novel *Take Back Plenty* by Colin GREENLAND; short fiction "The Original Doctor Shade" by Kim NEWMAN; media *Twin Peaks*; artist Ian MILLER

1992: novel *The Fall of Hyperion* by Dan SIMMONS; short fiction "Bad Timing" by Molly Brown; media TERMINATOR 2: JUDGEMENT DAY; best artwork Mark Harrison   [PN]

BRITISH SCIENCE FICTION MAGAZINE ◊ VARGO

STATTEN SCIENCE FICTION MAGAZINE.

BRITISH SPACE FICTION MAGAZINE ◊ VARGO STATTEN SCIENCE FICTION MAGAZINE.

BRITTON, DAVID (1945-) UK publisher and writer, founder with Michael BUTTERWORTH of Savoy Books, whose list included works by Michael MOOR-COCK, Charles PLATT and Jack Trevor STORY. With Butterworth, he edited *The Savoy Book* (anth **1978**) and *Savoy Dreams* (anth **1984**), which attempted with some success to demonstrate the anti-establishment ethos of the house, an ethos that brought both DB and Butterworth into conflict with the UK obscenity laws, as applied by the local police. Copies of DB's first novel, *Lord Horror* (**1989**), a scatological examination of Nazism and the UK traitor Lord Haw-Haw which made use of pornographic imagery upsetting to the Manchester police, were seized. A GRAPHIC NOVEL version of some of the same material, *Lord Horror* (graph in 5 parts **1990-91**), was also produced. The novel – which depicts the survival in Burma of Hitler and Lord Haw-Haw – was clearly, if very offensively, a SATIRE; and the destruction order on remaining copies of the text was duly and properly lifted by a UK court in July 1992 – although the graphic novel remained banned. [JC]

BRITTON, LIONEL (ERSKINE NIMMO) (1887-1971) UK writer who gained some prominence between the two world wars for works of speculative political philosophy, the premises of which were transformed into *Brain: A Play of the Whole Earth* (**1930**), a drama in which a giant AI is set up in the Sahara to run human affairs, which it does until nearly the end of time, when a wandering star collides with the planet. *Spacetime Inn* (**1932**), also a play, expounds a vision of things derived in part from the theories of J.W. DUNNE. [JC]

BROCKLEY, FENTON ◊ Donald Sydney ROWLAND.

BROCKWAY, (ARCHIBALD) FENNER (1888-1988) UK writer long active in socialist politics – he was made a life peer in 1964 – and long respected for his humane views. His sf novel *Purple Plague: A Tale of Love and Revolution* (**1935**) uses a liner stranded at sea by a mysterious plague as a venue for egalitarian reversals of the status quo. [JC]

BRODERICK, DAMIEN (FRANCIS) (1944-) Australian writer, editor and critic; he has a PhD in the semiotics of fiction, science and sf with special reference to the work of Samuel R. DELANY. He has edited three anthologies of Australian sf: *The Zeitgeist Machine* (anth **1976**), *Strange Attractors* (anth **1985**) and *Matilda at the Speed of Light* (anth **1988**).

DB's first professionally published sf, "The Sea's Farthest End" in *New Writings in SF 1* (anth **1964**) ed John CARNELL, can be found in his early collection *A Man Returned* (coll **1965**), and he has written short stories intermittently ever since, some to be found in *The Dark Between the Stars* (coll **1991**). His first novel was *Sorcerer's World* (**1970** US); however, he hit his stride only with his second, *The Dreaming Dragons* (**1980**), followed by *The Judas Mandala* (**1982** US; rev **1990** Australia). Both books are crammed with ideas,

and like *The Black Grail* (**1986** US) – a far more complex and sophisticated rewrite of *Sorcerer's World* – depend upon elaborate plotting involving alternative time-lines and temporal paradoxes. His work is indebted to structural LINGUISTICS, and Noam Chomsky – apparently venerated by DB as a political radical and a universal grammarian – is offered explicit homage when DB names a future language in *The Judas Mandala* and a planet in *Valencies* (**1983**, with Rory Barnes) after him. *The Judas Mandala* is more explicitly influenced by French structuralism. DB has since shown a cautious interest in literary deconstruction, most obviously in his criticism and in his one mainstream novel, *Transmitters* (**1984**), a formidable but surprisingly funny book about sf fans (◊ RECURSIVE SF). *Striped Holes* (**1988**) reads like a comic version of *The Dreaming Dragons* or *The Judas Mandala*, with familiar temporal paradoxes and embedded plotting, but the style is classic sf comedy in the vein of Robert SHECKLEY or, perhaps, Kurt VONNEGUT Jr in a good mood. [RB]

See also: COMPUTERS; GENERATION STARSHIPS; INTELLIGENCE; VIRTUAL REALITY.

BRONX WARRIORS ◊ 1990: I GUERRIERI DEL BRONX.

BRONX WARRIORS 2 ◊ 1990: I GUERRIERI DEL BRONX.

BROOD, THE Film (1979). Mutual Productions/Elgin International. Written and dir David CRONENBERG, starring Oliver Reed, Samantha Eggar, Art Hindle, Cindy Hinds. 91 mins. Colour.

In this Canadian film, the Somafree Institute of Psychoplasmics's pop psychologist Raglan (Reed), author of *The Shape of Rage*, is regarded with suspicion by Carveth (Hindle), whose wife Nola (Eggar) is a patient there. Gathering evidence against Raglan, Carveth finds dreadful physical changes taking place in Raglan's ex-patients. Meanwhile, Nola's parents are murdered by monsters shaped like deformed children; these later kidnap Carveth's young daughter (Hinds). Confronting Raglan, Carveth learns that, through bodily metamorphosis, monsters of the mind are given literal shape as Raglan's therapy takes effect on his patients. In the final sequence Carveth witnesses yet another of his wife's "brood", the creatures of her rage, being born from a yolk sac extruded close to her vagina. It takes an extraordinarily confident film-maker to direct a farrago like this without faltering, but Cronenberg's use of the body as metaphor – psychobabble made flesh – is carried off with conviction and wit, and even, where lesser directors would be content with evoking disgust, a compassion for the monstrous as being, after all, only human. There is a subtext about children as victims, suffering a pain transmitted through generations. All the events are viewed with the unblinking, innocent gaze – itself childlike – that characterizes Cronenberg's surreal style. [PN]

See also: CINEMA; MONSTER MOVIES; SEX.

BROOKE, (BERNARD) JOCELYN (1908-1966) UK writer, most noted for psychological fantasias like *The Scapegoat* (**1949**) and *The Goose Cathedral* (**1950**). *The*

Image of a Drawn Sword (**1950**) uses borderline sf devices to convey the dreamlike horror of its protagonist's recruitment into a merciless army. *The Crisis in Bulgaria, or Ibsen to the Rescue!* (**1956**), with the author's own collage illustrations, combines Victorian fantasy and parody. [JC]

BROOKE, KEITH (1966-   ) UK writer who began publishing sf with "Adrenotropic Man" for *Interzone* in 1989, and whose first novel, *Keepers of the Peace* (**1990**), depicts in singularly gloomy terms the slow evisceration of a group of soldiers sent down from near space to police a fragmented USA. The **Expatria** sequence – *Expatria* (**1991**) and *Expatria Incorporated* (**1992**) – has elements of the PLANETARY ROMANCE in that its story takes place upon, although it does not materially affect, the eponymous colony planet; in the first volume, the young protagonist must both defend himself against the charge that he has murdered his father and attempt to prevent his fellow colonists from descending into barbarism, while at the same time awaiting a rescue ship (upon whose approach turns the plot of the second volume). KB has already demonstrated ample talent and energy, but has yet to focus them. [JC]

BROOKE-ROSE, CHRISTINE (1923-   ) UK novelist and academic, born in Switzerland, resident in the UK in the 1950s and 1960s, thereafter lecturer and then professor of American literature at the University of Paris VIII (Vincennes) from 1969 until her retirement in 1988. She was married 1968-75 to Jerzy PETERKIEWICZ. CB-R is widely known for critical works like *A Grammar of Metaphor* (**1958**) and *A Rhetoric of the Unreal* (**1981**), which formally assimilates the narrative strategies of sf and fantasy into those of metafiction (◊ FABULATION) in terms compatible with Tzvetan TODOROV's theory of the fantastic. As a novelist, she is perhaps best known for early works outside the field like *The Dear Deceit* (**1958**), but has increasingly produced texts whose displacements are more than linguistic.

The Middlemen: A Satire (**1961**) is a fantasticated NEAR-FUTURE assault on the worlds of public relations. *Out* (**1964**), an sf novel, is set in a post-HOLOCAUST Afro-Eurasia in which the colour barrier has been reversed, ostensibly for medical reasons, as the "Colourless" seem to be fatally ill. *Such* (**1966**) reanimates the dead astronomer Lazarus, who tells of his experiences during death, interrogating the nature of language as he does so. *Out* and *Such* were assembled with two non-genre novels, *Between* (**1968**) and *Thru* (**1975**), as *The Christine Brooke-Rose Omnibus* (omni **1986**). Some fantasies, including the title story, were assembled in *Go when You See the Green Man Walking* (coll **1969**). *Amalgamemnon* (**1984**) addresses the future through words which cannot be believed, as they come from Cassandra (who also speaks as a woman). *Xorandor* (**1986**) and its sequel *Verbivore* (**1990**), which make up a series designed ostensibly for older children, feature a sentient rock, with a computer-like mentality, awakened by the information-

noise of humans; in the second volume Xorandor's children – chips off the old block – shut down human communications systems to keep sane. And *Textermination* (**1991**) is a discourse on textuality, in which a large number of characters from famous novels come together in a campaign to transcend their "texts" and become "real". CB-R, with dry cunning, writes sf *nouveaux romans*, and challenges the genre to talk back. [JC]

See also: WOMEN SF WRITERS.

BROOKS, SAMUEL I. ◊ George S. SCHUYLER.

BROSNAN, JOHN (1947-   ) Australian writer and journalist, resident for many years in the UK, a onetime prominent member of RATFANDOM. He was known for his writing on genre films some time before he began publishing sf in any quantity. His five books on CINEMA are *James Bond in the Cinema* (**1972**), *Movie Magic: The Story of Special Effects in the Cinema* (**1974**), *The Horror People* (**1976**), *Future Tense: The Cinema of Science Fiction* (**1978**) and *The Primal Screen: A History of Science Fiction Film* (**1991**); the first three relate peripherally to sf, and the fifth is in effect a light-hearted update and rewrite of the fourth. JB wrote most of the film entries in the first edition of this volume; he has also contributed film columns to SCIENCE FICTION MONTHLY and STARBURST and was for some time the lead book reviewer for the UK horror magazine *The Dark Side*.

JB's first sf was "Conversation on a Starship in Warp-Drive" in *Antigrav* (anth **1975**) ed Philip STRICK. His books under his own name begin with the adventure novels *Skyship* (**1981**) and *The Midas Deep* (**1983**). He then went on to publish the first of his pseudonymous novels, most written in partnership with Leroy Kettle (1949-   ); these written equivalents of exploitation movies are slightly self-mocking but quite exciting as sf horror; all are variants on the humans-being-destroyed-by-monstrous-things theme. Those as by Harry Adam Knight include *Slimer* (**1983**), *Carnosaur* (**1984**) by JB alone, *The Fungus* (**1985**; vt *Death Spore* US) and *Bedlam* (**1992**); those as by Simon Ian Childer are *Tendrils* (**1986**) and, by JB alone, *Worm* (**1987**). The initials of the pseudonyms were no accident. *Torched* (**1986**) with John BAXTER, both writing as James Blackstone, is about spontaneous combustion.

JB reserved his own name for a more ambitious work, the **Sky Lords** trilogy: *The Sky Lords* (**1988**), *War of the Sky Lords* (**1989**) and *The Fall of the Sky Lords* (**1991**). These consist of fast-moving adventure in a post-HOLOCAUST society (after the Gene Wars), remorselessly evoking another sf trope every time the action flags – everything from mile-long dirigibles to computer guardians of ancient civilizations. [PN]

See also: DISASTER.

BROSTER, D(OROTHY) K(ATHLEEN) (1877-1950) UK writer of historical and weird fiction, noted within the fantasy genre for *Couching at the Door* (coll **1942**) and for "Clairvoyance" in *A Fire of Driftwood* (coll **1932**). Her evocatively titled *World under Snow* (**1935**) with G. Forester is not sf, although sometimes listed as such, but a murder mystery with a winter setting. [JE]

BROTHER FROM ANOTHER PLANET, THE Film (1984). A-Train Films. Dir John SAYLES, starring Joe Morton, Tom Wright, Caroline Aaron, Dee Dee Bridgewater. Screenplay Sayles. 108 mins. Colour.

Where Sayles's exploitation-movie scripts are cynical and hard-edged, the films he directs himself are gentler and also more overtly political. *TBFAP* is the only sf film he has written and directed, and to a degree it gets the best of both worlds, though it has a sentimental streak. The Brother is an ALIEN, indistinguishable in appearance from a Black American – apart from his clawed, three-toed feet and a detachable eye – who arrives at deserted Ellis Island, traditional gateway for immigrants to the USA, and goes to Harlem. There he is the clever innocent abroad, unable to speak but understanding a lot, sharply observing social attitudes of both Blacks and Whites, fixing machines (he is a healer), getting tough with a drug trafficker, and being pursued by alien bounty-hunters (one played by Sayles). Like a surprising amount of sf, this is a "to see ourselves as others see us" social comedy. Morton is excellent as an alien among the alienated; the meandering, episodic plot of this low-budget movie is fun. [PN]

BROTHER THEODORE [s] ◊ Marvin KAYE.

BROWN, ALEC (JOHN CHARLES) (1900-1962) UK writer in whose sf novel, *Angelo's Moon* (**1955**), set in an underground city in Africa called Hypolitania, a White scientist offers some hope of countering the degeneration of our species. [JC]

BROWN, CARTER ◊ Alan YATES.

BROWN, CHARLES N(IKKI) (1937-   ) US publisher and editor, an sf fan who began his involvement in the field in the 1950s and who remains best known for founding the sf news magazine LOCUS in 1968, and bringing it to pre-eminence: dispensing news, reviews, bibliographical updates, interviews, obituaries, convention data and reports, and some gossip, *Locus* is the central information forum of the sf world, and has won 16 HUGO awards in its category. In 1992, as the journal approaches its 400th issue, CNB remains both editor and publisher. In collaboration with William G. CONTENTO he began in the mid-1980s to compile yearly bibliographical volumes which covered the field with some thoroughness, though their dependence on the monthly Books Received columns in *Locus* – initially compiled from books received for review – somewhat constricted their coverage (◊ BIBLIOGRAPHIES). But the editing of the sequence grew in sophistication from year to year – Hal W. HALL's ongoing Research Index from the 1988 volume onwards was a significant addition – and later volumes were very nearly comprehensive. In chronological order, the sequence comprises *Science Fiction, Fantasy, & Horror: 1984* (**1990**), *Science Fiction in Print: 1985* (**1986**), *Science Fiction, Fantasy, &*

Horror: 1986 (**1987**), *Science Fiction, Fantasy, & Horror: 1987* (**1988**), *Science Fiction, Fantasy, & Horror: 1988* (**1989**), *Science Fiction, Fantasy, & Horror: 1989* (**1990**), *Science Fiction, Fantasy, & Horror: 1990* (**1991**) and *Science Fiction, Fantasy, & Horror: 1991* (**1992**). [JC]

Other works: *Far Travelers: Three Science Fiction Novellas* (anth **1976**); *Alien Worlds: Three Novellas of Science Fiction by Award Winning Authors* (anth **1976**); *Locus, the Newspaper of the Science Fiction Field* (anth in 2 vols **1978**), reprinting the first decade's issues.

See also: ANTHOLOGIES; SMALL PRESSES AND LIMITED EDITIONS.

BROWN, CHESTER (?1960-   ) Canadian creator of *Yummy Fur*, a fantasy comic whose stories lurch from one comics TABOO to another: religion, homosexuality, vampires, zombies, masturbation and a full spectrum of bodily excretions. *Yummy Fur* began life as a series of tiny (A6) self-published pamphlets in the early 1980s. CB was eventually approached by Vortex Comics in 1986 to produce a regular *Yummy Fur*. The first 3 issues of this reprinted all the minicomics and included characters and stories that were to feature in the 15 issues that followed, notably "Adventures in Science" (1985), "The Man who Couldn't Stop" (1985) and "Ed the Happy Clown" (1986); this last story involved ghosts, pygmy cannibalism, a frightening religious interpretation of vampirism, a gateway from another DIMENSION, and Ronald Reagan's head on the end of a clown's penis. Inevitably the comic suffered censorship, and distributors and retailers refused to stock it. The first 9 chapters plus relevant mini-comics stories were published as *Ed the Happy Clown* (graph **1989**). Issues of *Yummy Fur* (currently published by Drawn & Quarterly) since #18 lack sf references. [SW/RT]

See also: GRAPHIC NOVEL.

BROWN, ERIC (1960-   ) UK writer who began publishing sf – after a children's play, *Noel's Ark* (**1982** chap) – with "Krash-Bangg Joe and the Pineal-Zen Equation" for *Interzone* in 1987; like several further tales assembled in *The Time-Lapsed Man and Other Stories* (coll **1990**), it is set in a future world dominated by the effects of bio-engineering and dense with information. This marriage of Cordwainer SMITH to CYBERPUNK, though not in itself original, has considerable potential as a focus for a complex vision of things to come, as demonstrated in his first novel, *Meridian Days* (**1992**), set on a planet dominated by artists. [JC]

See also: ARTS; INTERZONE; PERCEPTION; TIME TRAVEL.

BROWN, FREDRIC (WILLIAM) (1906-1972) US writer of detective novels and much sf, and for many years active in journalism. He is perhaps best known for such detective novels as *The Fabulous Clipjoint* (**1947**), but is also highly regarded for his sf, which is noted for its elegance and HUMOUR, and for a polished slickness not generally found in the field in 1941, the year he published his first sf story, "Not Yet the End" for *Captain Future*. Many of his shorter works are vignettes and extended jokes: of the 47 pieces collected in *Nightmares and Geezenstacks* (coll **1961**), 38 are vignettes of the sort he specialized in (they feature sudden joke climaxes whose ironies are often cruel); this collection was assembled with another, *Honeymoon in Hell* (coll **1958**), as *And the Gods Laughed* (omni **1987**). Typical of somewhat longer works utilizing the same professional economies of effect are "Placet is a Crazy Place" (1946), "Etaoin Shrdlu" (1942) and "Arena" (1944). The latter was among the sf stories selected by the SCIENCE FICTION WRITERS OF AMERICA for inclusion in *Science Fiction Hall of Fame* (anth **1970**) ed Robert SILVERBERG. It tells of the settling of an interstellar WAR through single combat between a human and an ALIEN. FB is possibly at his best in these shorter forms, where his elegant and seemingly comfortable wit, its iconoclasm carefully directed at targets whose defacing sf readers would appreciate, had greatest scope.

FB's sf novels are by no means without merit, however. His first and most famous, *What Mad Universe* (**1946**), is a cleverly complex ALTERNATE-WORLDS story in which various sf conventions turn out, absurdly, to be true history. *The Lights in the Sky are Stars* (**1953**; vt *Project Jupiter* 1954 UK) depicts mankind at the turn of the 21st century and on the verge of star travel; the true subject of the tale might, movingly, be thought to be the SENSE OF WONDER itself. *Martians, Go Home* (**1955**) describes the infestation of Earth by little green men who drive everyone nearly crazy, until the sf writer who has perhaps imagined them into existence imagines them gone again; however, he is himself a figment of a larger imagination, so that in the end it is reality itself that dissolves. In *The Mind Thing* (**1961**) a stranded alien attempts to get back home using its ability to ride human minds piggyback, even though the experience is fatal for those possessed.

None of these novels is negligible, but it is perhaps the case, at least in his sf writing, that his short stories, with their natty momentum and the sudden flushes of humane emotion that transfigure so many of them, have proved more successful in the long run. The recent publication of a very large number of previously uncollected stories (see below) may intensify this sense of FB's central accomplishment. [JC]

Other works: *Space on my Hands* (coll **1951**); *Angels and Spaceships* (coll **1954**; vt *Star Shine* 1956); *Rogue in Space* (1949 *Super Science Stories*; 1950 *AMZ*; fixup **1957**); *Daymares* (coll **1968**); *Mitkey Astromouse* (**1971**), a juvenile; *Paradox Lost* (coll **1973**); *The Best of Fredric Brown* (coll **1977**); *The Best Short Stories of Fredric Brown* (coll **1982** UK); the **Detective Pulps** series of collections, most of which contain some sf and fantasy, comprehensively surveying FB's career and comprising *Homicide Sanitarium* (coll **1984**), *Before She Kills* (coll **1984**), *Madman's Holiday* (coll **1984**), *The Case of the Dancing Sandwiches* (coll **1985**), *The Freak Show Murders* (coll **1985**), *Thirty Corpses Every Thursday* (coll **1986**), *Pardon my Ghoulish Laughter* (coll **1986**), *Red is the Hue of Hell* (coll **1986**), *Brother Monster* (coll **1987**), *Sex Life on the Planet Mars* (coll **1986**), *Nightmare in Darkness*

(coll **1987**), *Who Was that Blonde I Saw You Kill Last Night?* (coll **1988**), *Three-Corpse Parlay* (coll **1988**), *Selling Death Short* (coll **1988**), *Whispering Death* (coll **1989**), *Happy Ending* (coll **1990**), *The Water-Walker* (coll **1990**), *The Gibbering Night* (coll **1991**) and *The Pickled Punks* (coll **1991**), which closed the series.

As editor: *Science Fiction Carnival* (anth **1953**) with Mack REYNOLDS.

About the author: *A Key to Fredric Brown's Wonderland: A Study and an Annotated Bibliographical Checklist* (**1981** chap) by N.D. Baird.

See also: COMPUTERS; EC COMICS; FASTER THAN LIGHT; GAMES AND SPORTS; HIVE-MINDS; INVASION; MEDIA LANDSCAPE; NUCLEAR POWER; PARANOIA; PASTORAL; PHYSICS; RECURSIVE SF; RELIGION; SPACE FLIGHT; STARS.

BROWN, HARRISON (SCOTT) (1917-1986) US scientist and writer whose nonfiction *The Challenge of Man's Future* (**1954**) combines demographical, ecological and energy concerns in a pioneering work of great admonitory influence. His sf novel, *The Cassiopeia Affair* (**1968**) with Chloe ZERWICK, treats fictionally the same problems through a story about a possibly bogus message from the stars that may keep mankind from destroying itself in a terminal conflagration.

Other nonfiction: *The Next Hundred Years* (**1957**) with James Bonner and John Weir.

BROWN, HOWARD V(ACHEL) (1878-1945) US illustrator. Born in Lexington, Kentucky, HVB studied at the Chicago Art Institute and became based in New York. He was cover artist for *Scientific American* c1913-31, typically showing human figures dwarfed by gigantic technological projects. His first cover for an SF MAGAZINE proper was for *ASF* Oct 1933, although he had earlier (1919 on) painted almost 50 covers for SCIENCE AND INVENTION. One of the Big Four sf illustrators in the 1930s (with Leo MOREY, Frank R. PAUL and H.W. WESSO), he helped soften the colours that appeared on magazine covers. Starting with a simple, almost primitive style, HB rapidly developed into one of the most dramatic cover illustrators of that era. Most closely associated with *ASF*, he also appeared in *Thrilling Wonder Stories* and *Startling Stories*, for which he did his best work. He specialized in BEMs, which he depicted with exciting vigour. He painted 90 sf covers in all to 1940, even though he was in his late 50s before he started. [JG/PN]

See also: ASTOUNDING SCIENCE-FICTION; THRILLING WONDER STORIES.

BROWN, JAMES COOKE (1921-   ) US writer in whose sf novel, *The Troika Incident: A Tetralogue in Two Parts* (**1970**), astronauts from the USA, France and the USSR are shot forward by a century. There they discover a UTOPIA – built on lines hinted at by Edward BELLAMY – before returning to a disbelieving present day. [JC]

BROWN, JERRY EARL (1940-   ) US writer in whose first sf novel, *Under the City of Angels* (**1981**), a sunken California is delved by the haunted protagonist, who finds powerful corporations and ALIENS at the root of things. *Darkhold* (**1985**) depicts the consequences of cloning one's own lovers (◊ CLONES). *Earthfall* (**1990**) unremarkably shows an Earth overrun by MUTANTS hungry for flesh. [JC]

BROWN, JOHN MacMILLAN [r] ◊ Godfrey SWEVEN.

BROWN, JOHN YOUNG [r] ◊ SMALL PRESSES AND LIMITED EDITIONS.

BROWN, PETER C(URRELL) (1940?-   ) UK writer whose first novel, *Smallcreep's Day* (**1965**), set in an indeterminate future, is an extremely effective ABSURDIST quest into the heart of a vast, palpably allegorical factory. The result of the quest for meaning is another assembly line. [JC]

BROWN, RICH [r] ◊ David F. BISCHOFF.

BROWN, ROSEL GEORGE (1926-1967) US writer with an advanced degree in ancient Greek; for three years she was a welfare visitor in Louisiana. She began publishing stories in 1958 with "From an Unseen Censor" for *Gal*; some of her stories were interplanetary, some more typical of "women's" fiction. *A Handful of Time* (coll **1963**) assembles much of her early work. Her **Sibyl Sue Blue** series – *Sibyl Sue Blue* (**1966**; vt *Galactic Sibyl Sue Blue* 1968) and *The Waters of Centaurus* (**1970**) – features a tough female cop who, with a teenage daughter, engages in various interstellar adventures; she is more than once required to defend herself (which she does more than adequately) against aggressive males. With Keith LAUMER, RGB wrote an expansive SPACE OPERA, *Earthblood* (**1966**), in which a lost Terran boy (rather like the protagonist of Robert A. HEINLEIN's *Citizen of the Galaxy* [**1957**]) searches through the stars for his heritage; the Earth he finds is a dire disappointment, and he sets out, successfully, to upset the applecart. RGB's career was taking off when she died at the early age of 41. [JC]

See also: CRIME AND PUNISHMENT; ECONOMICS.

BROWN, WENZEL (1912-   ) US writer, mostly of mysteries, who published some sf in magazines, most notably "Murderer's Chain" for *Fantastic Universe* in 1960. His one novel, *Possess and Conquer* (**1975**), is a modestly competent sf adventure. [JC]

BROWNE, GEORGE SHELDON ◊ Dennis HUGHES.

BROWNE, HOWARD (1908-   ) US author and editor who worked 1942-7 for ZIFF-DAVIS where, among other responsibilities, he was managing editor of AMAZING STORIES and FANTASTIC ADVENTURES, then under Raymond A. PALMER's editorship. He contributed stories to the magazines, two serials about the prehistoric adventurer **Tharn** being published also in book form as *Warrior of the Dawn* (**1943**) and *The Return of Tharn* (1948 *AMZ*; **1956**). His work appeared under a variety of pseudonyms and Ziff-Davis house names including Alexander BLADE, Lawrence Chandler, Ivar JORGENSEN (stories only) and Lee Francis. After a period in Hollywood, HB became in 1950 editor of *AMZ* – where he rejected a mass of material by Richard S. SHAVER – and *Fantastic Adventures*. He presided over *AMZ*'s change from PULP to DIGEST format, and over the demise of *Fantastic Adventures* in favour of the digest-sized FANTASTIC. He returned to

Hollywood in 1956. Primarily a mystery writer – his work in that field being signed John Evans – HB is reported to have detested sf. [MJE]

See also: POLITICS.

BROWNING, CRAIG [s] ◊ Rog PHILLIPS.

BROWNING, JOHN S. [s] ◊ Robert Moore WILLIAMS.

BROWNJOHN, ALAN (CHARLES) (1931-   ) UK poet and anthologist, active from the early 1950s. In *The Way You Tell Them: A Yarn of the Nineties* (**1990**), his first novel, the UK of 1999 is rendered as a Tory-dominated DYSTOPIA whose rulers have learned well how to subvert and co-opt those who still retain their integrity, political or artistic. [JC]

BROXON, MILDRED DOWNEY [r] ◊ Poul ANDERSON.

BRÜCKNER, KARL (1906-   ) German writer whose *Nur zwei Roboter?* (**1963**; trans anon as *The Hour of the Robots* **1964** UK) depicts the pacifying effects of robot-love on a quarrelling humanity. [JC]

BRUCKNER, WINFRIED [r] ◊ AUSTRIA.

BRUMMELS, J.V. (?   -   ) US writer, Poet-in-Residence at Wayne State College, and author of *Deus ex Machina* (**1989**), a complexly literate rendering in CYBERPUNK-influenced terms of an urban USA facing the death of the Sun. There is a choice, for some, of escaping into space; but it is an option JVB offers without any exuberance. [JC]

BRUNDAGE, MARGARET (JOHNSON) (1900-1976) US illustrator, resident in Chicago. Best-known for her erotic pastel covers for WEIRD TALES, MB was, as far as is known, the first woman artist to work in the sf/FANTASY field, and the first of either sex whose covers featured nudes; they were generally of the damsel-in-distress variety. Her first cover was for *Weird Tales* editor Farnsworth WRIGHT's other magazine, *Oriental Stories*. The positive response was immediate, proving once again that sex sells; MB was main cover artist for *Weird Tales* from late 1932 to 1938, doing occasional further covers to 1945. MB's soft colours were attractive, but her drawing of faces and bodies only so-so. [JG/PN]

BRUNNER, JOHN (KILIAN HOUSTON) (1934-   ) UK writer, mostly of sf, though he has published several thrillers, contemporary novels and volumes of poetry (see listing below). He began very early to submit sf stories to periodicals, and when he was 17 published his first novel, *Galactic Storm* (**1951**) under the house name Gill HUNT. Even in a field noted for its early starters, his precocity was remarkable. His first US sale, "Thou Good and Faithful" as by John Loxmith, was featured in *ASF* in early 1953, and in the same year he published in a US magazine the first novel he would later choose to acknowledge; it was eventually to appear in book form as *The Space-Time Juggler* (1953 *Two Complete Science-Adventure Books* as "The Wanton of Argus" as by Kilian Houston Brunner; **1963** chap dos US) which, with its sequel, *The Altar on Asconel* (**1965** dos US), plus an article on SPACE OPERA and "The Man from the Big Dark" (1958), was much later assembled as *Interstellar Empire* (omni **1976** US). This **Interstellar Empire** sequence takes place in the twilight of a Galactic Empire – a time rather favoured by JB in his space operas – when barbarism is general, though the Rimworlds (◊ GALACTIC LENS) hold some hope for adventurers and mutants, who may eventually rebuild civilization. But the series terminates abruptly, before its various protagonists are able to begin their renaissance, almost certainly reflecting JB's ultimate lack of interest in such stories, which he has since registered in print – though certainly he subsequently revised many of them, not necessarily to their betterment as "naïve" adventures.

In any case, this lessening of interest evinced itself only after very extensive publication of stories and novels describable as literate space opera. From 1953 to about 1957 JB's activity was intermittent, mainly through difficulty in making a living from full-time writing, a problem about which he has always been bitterly articulate. In the mid-1950s he was working full-time with a publishing house and elsewhere, writing only occasionally. In 1955 he published one story under the pseudonym Trevor Staines. A little later he sold two novels, again first to magazines: *Threshold of Eternity* (**1959** dos US) and *The Hundredth Millennium* (**1959** dos US; rev vt *Catch a Falling Star* 1968 US); they are two of the first novels he placed with ACE BOOKS. With the signing of the contract for the first, JB took up full-time freelancing once again.

Over the next six years he published under his own name and as Keith Woodcott a total of 27 novels with Ace Books, in addition to work with other publishers. For some readers, this spate of HARD-SF adventure stories still represents JB's most relaxed and fluent work as a writer. Two from 1960 are typical of the storytelling enjoyment he was able to create by applying to "modest" goals the formidable craft he had developed. *The Atlantic Abomination* (**1960** dos US) is a genuinely terrifying story about a monstrous ALIEN, long buried beneath the Atlantic, who survives by mentally enslaving "inferior" species, rather like the thrint in Larry NIVEN's *World of Ptavvs* (**1966**). *Sanctuary in the Sky* (**1960** dos US) is a short and simple SENSE-OF-WONDER tale, set in the FAR FUTURE in a star cluster very distant from Earth. Various conflicting planetary cultures (all human) can meet in peace only on the mysterious Waystation, which is a synthetic world. A ship full of squabbling passengers docks; with them is a mild-mannered stranger who immediately disappears. Soon it turns out that he's an Earthman, that Waystation is a colony ship owned by Earth, and that he's come to retrieve it. Mankind needs the ship: though this Galaxy is full, "there are other galaxies". Decades later, JB would rework the thematic concerns of this short novel at much greater length in *A Maze of Stars* (**1991** US).

The mass of Ace novels contains a second series, also truncated, though its structure is more open-ended than that of the earlier one. The **Zarathustra Refugee Planets** sequence, made up of *Castaways' World* (**1963** dos US; rev vt *Polymath* 1974 US), *Secret*

Agent of Terra (**1962** dos US; rev vt *The Avengers of Carrig* 1969 US) and *The Repairmen of Cyclops* (**1965** dos US; rev 1981 US), all later assembled as *Victims of the Nova* (omni **1989**), deals over a long timescale with the survivors of human-colonized Zarathustra; when the planet's sun goes nova, 3000 spaceships carry a few million survivors into exile on a variety of uninhabited worlds. 700 years later, the Corps Galactic has the job of maintaining the isolation of these various cultures, so that, having reverted to barbarism, they can develop naturally; their separate histories constitute an experiment in cultural evolution. Despite these two series, and in contrast to some of his older peers, JB has only rarely attempted to link individual items into series or fixups. Both his space operas and his later, more ambitious works are generally initially conceived in the versions which the reader sees on book publication. Further Ace titles of interest include *The Rites of Ohe* (**1963** dos US), *To Conquer Chaos* (**1964** US; rev 1981 US) and *Day of the Star Cities* (**1965** US; rev vt *Age of Miracles* 1973 US).

As the 1960s progressed, more space operas appeared as well as several story collections, including *Out of My Mind* (coll **1967** US; the UK coll with the same name is a different selection, **1968**) and *Not Before Time* (coll **1968**), which include outstanding items like "The Last Lonely Man" (1964) and "The Totally Rich" (1963). JB's stories are generally free in form, sometimes experimental. By 1965, with the publication of *The Whole Man* (1958-9 *Science Fantasy*; fixup **1964** US; vt *Telepathist* 1965 UK) and *The Squares of the City* (**1965** US), it was evident that JB would not be content to go on indefinitely writing the sf entertainments of which he had become master, and that he was determined to transform his sf habitat. *The Whole Man*, comprising fundamentally rewritten magazine stories and much new material, and generally considered to be one of JB's most successful novels, is an attempt to draw a psychological portrait of a deformed human with telepathic powers (◊ ESP) who gradually learns how to use these powers in psychiatrically curative ways (for to communicate is to be human). *The Squares of the City* is a respectable try at a chess novel in which a chosen venue (in this case a city) serves as the board and characters as the various players. The stiffness of the resulting story may have been inevitable.

JB's *magnum opus*, *Stand on Zanzibar* (**1968** US), perhaps the longest GENRE-SF novel to that date, came as the climax of the decade. The dystopian vision of this complex novel rests on the assumption that Earth's population will continue to expand uncontrollably; the intersecting stories of Norman House, a Black executive on a mission to the Third World to facilitate further economic penetration, and of Donald Hogan, a White "synthesist" and government agent, whose mission involves gaining control of a eugenics discovery, provide dominant strands in an assemblage of narrative techniques whose function of providing a social and cultural context points up their resemblance to the similar techniques used by John Dos Passos in *USA* (**1930-36**), but which (as John P. Brennan has noted) fail to conceal the underlying storytelling orthodoxy of the tale. It is perhaps for this reason that the resulting vision has a cumulative, sometimes overpowering effect, while at the same time the triumphalist logic of its pulp plotting (which descends from HOMER) urgently conveys a sense that answers will be forthcoming, and that the protagonists will win through. Through its density of reference, and through JB's admirable (though sometimes insecure) grasp of US idiom, the book's anti-Americanism has a satisfyingly US ring to it, so that its tirades do not seem smug; it won the 1968 HUGO and the 1970 BRITISH SCIENCE FICTION AWARD, and its French translation won the Prix Apollo ($\Diamond$ AWARDS) in 1973.

Three further novels, all with some of the the same pace and intensity, make together a kind of thematic series of DYSTOPIAS. *The Jagged Orbit* (**1969** US) conflates medical and military industrial complexes with the Mafia in a rather too tightly plotted, though occasionally powerful, narrative. *The Sheep Look Up* (**1972** US), perhaps the most unrelenting and convincing dystopia of the four, and depressingly well documented, deals scarifyingly with POLLUTION in a plot whose relative looseness allows for an almost essayist exposition of the horrors in store for us. *The Shockwave Rider* (**1975** US) employs similar reportage techniques in a story about a world enmeshed in a COMMUNICATIONS explosion. Unsurprisingly (with hindsight), though these novels received considerable critical attention, they in no way made JB's fortune. He has always been extremely open about his finances and his hopes for the future, and has made no secret of the let-down he felt on discovering himself, after these culminating efforts, still in the position of being forced to produce commercially to survive.

In his decreasingly frequent publications since 1972, JB has tended to return to a somewhat more flamboyant version of the space-opera idiom he had used earlier. For some years his health remained uncertain, with a consequent severe slowing down of his once formidable writing speed. The relative lack of fluency and enthusiasm of novels like *Total Eclipse* (**1974** US), *The Infinitive of Go* (**1980** US) and *Children of the Thunder* (**1989**) cannot easily be denied. There is a sense in these novels that skill wars with convictions, and that, as a consequence, JB cannot any longer *allow* himself the orthodox delights of pure storytelling. Even *The Great Steamboat Race* (**1983**), an associational novel, set on the Mississippi River, which he devoted years to writing, shows some signs of a nagging dis-ease. But JB has undeniably made significant contributions to the sf space-opera redoubt, and has written several intellectually formidable tract-novels about the state of the world. The opinions extractable from these works are closer to left-wing than usual with US sf writers of his generation (these opinions, which he has articulated publicly many times, may be in part responsible for his failure to acquire a secure US marketing niche, as well as contributing to his loss of belief in the naïve victories endemic to generic fiction), and in the end he may claim to have constituted a significant dissenting voice in the West's increasingly urgent debate about humanity's condition as the 20th century draws to a close. [JC]

Other works: *The Brink* (**1959**); *Echo in the Skull* (**1959** chap dos US; rev vt *Give Warning to the World* 1974 US); *The World Swappers* (**1959**); *The Skynappers* (**1960** dos US); *Slavers of Space* (**1960** dos US; rev vt *Into the Slave Nebula* 1968 US); *Meeting at Infinity* (**1961** dos US); *The Super Barbarians* (**1962** US); *Times without Number* (fixup **1962** dos US; rev 1969 US); *No Future in It* (coll **1962**); *The Astronauts Must Not Land* (**1963** dos US; rev vt *More Things in Heaven* 1973 US); *The Dreaming Earth* (**1963** US); *Listen! The Stars!* (**1963** chap dos US; rev vt *The Stardroppers* 1972 US); *Endless Shadow* (**1964** chap dos US; rev vt *Manshape* 1982 US); *Enigma from Tantalus* (**1965** dos US); *The Long Result* (**1965**); *Now Then* (coll **1965**); *A Planet of Your Own* (**1966** chap dos US); *No Other Gods but Me* (coll **1966**); *Born under Mars* (**1967** US); *The Productions of Time* (**1967** US; text restored 1977 US); *Quicksand* (**1967** US); *Bedlam Planet* (**1968** US); *Father of Lies* (1962 *Science Fantasy*; **1968** chap dos US); *Not Before Time* (coll **1968**); *Double, Double* (**1969** US); *Timescoop* (**1969** US); *The Evil that Men Do* (1966 NW; **1969** chap dos US); *The Gaudy Shadows* (1960 *Science Fantasy*; exp **1970**), a fantasy; *The Dramaturges of Yan* (**1972** US); *The Wrong End of Time* (**1971** US); *The Traveler in Black* (coll of linked stories **1971** US; with 1 story added vt *The Compleat Traveler in Black* 1986 US), his best fantasy; *Entry to Elsewhen* (coll **1972** US); *From this Day Forward* (coll **1972**); *Time-Jump* (coll **1973** US); *The Stone that Never Came Down* (**1973** US); *Web of Everywhere* (**1974** US); *The Book of John Brunner* (coll **1976** US); *Foreign Constellations* (coll **1980** US); *Players at the Game of People* (**1980** US); *While There's Hope* (**1982** chap); a series comprising *The Crucible of Time* (fixup **1983** US) and *The Tides of Time* (**1984** US); *The Shift Key* (**1987**); *The Best of John Brunner* (coll **1988** US); *A Case of Painter's Ear* (1987 in *Tales from the Forbidden Planet* anth ed Roz KAVENEY; **1991** chap US).

As Keith Woodcott: *I Speak for Earth* (**1961** dos US); *The Ladder in the Sky* (**1962** dos US); *The Psionic Menace* (**1963** dos US); *The Martian Sphinx* (**1965** dos US).

Non-genre novels: Of most interest are perhaps *The Crutch of Memory* (**1964**), *A Plague on Both your Causes* (**1969**; vt *Blacklash* 1969 US), *Black is the Color* (1956 as "This Rough Magic"; rev **1969** US), which is a thriller involving black MAGIC, *The Devil's Work* (**1970**), and *Honky in the Woodpile* (**1971**).

Poetry: *Trip: A Cycle of Poems* (coll **1966** chap; rev 1971 chap); *Life in an Explosive Forming Press* (coll **1970** chap); *A Hastily Thrown-together Bit of Zork* (coll **1974** chap); *Tomorrow May be Even Worse* (coll **1978** chap US), an "alphabet" of sf CLICHÉS; *A New Settlement of*

Old Scores (coll **1983** chap US).

About the author: *The Happening Worlds of John Brunner* (critical anth **1975**) ed Joseph W. de Bolt; *John Brunner, Shockwave Writer: A Working Bibliography* (latest edn **1989** chap) Gordon BENSON Jr and Phil STEPHENSEN-PAYNE.

See also: ALTERNATE WORLDS; ANDROIDS; ARTS; COLONIZATION OF OTHER WORLDS; COMPUTERS; CYBERPUNK; DISASTER; FUTUROLOGY; GALACTIC EMPIRES; GAMES AND SPORTS; GENERATION STARSHIPS; INVASION; MATTER TRANSMISSION; MONEY; NEW WAVE; NEW WORLDS; OVERPOPULATION; POLITICS; PSEUDO-SCIENCE; PSI POWERS; PSYCHOLOGY; SUPERMAN; TIME PARADOXES; TRANSPORTATION.

BRUNNGRABER, RUDOLF (1901-1960) German writer, active for many years. His sf novel *Radium* (**1936**; trans anon **1937**) features a near-contemporary corner on the radium market causing troubles in a hospital which is using it to cure cancer. [JC]

Other works: *Die Engel in Atlantis* ["The Angel in Atlantis"] (**1938**); *Karl und das 20 Jahrhundert* (**1933**; trans anon as *Karl and the Twentieth Century* **1933**).

BRUNT, SAMUEL [r] ◊ MONEY; MOON.

BRUSSOLO, SERGE [r] ◊ FRANCE.

BRUST, STEVEN (KARL ZOLTÁN) (1955-) US writer, almost exclusively of fantasy, mentioned here for *Cowboy Feng's Space Bar and Grille* (**1990**), an intermittently comic spoof about a saloon which dodges atomic HOLOCAUSTS by leaping through time and space to other planets, where a mysterious enemy awaits. Some of SB's novels, like *The Sun, the Moon, and the Stars* (**1987**), are more FABULATION than fantasy. [JC]

Other works: The **Vlad Taltos** fantasy series, comprising *Jhereg* (**1983**), *Yendi* (**1984**) and *Teckla* (**1986**) – all three assembled as *Taltos the Assassin* (omni **1991** UK) – *Taltos* (**1988**; vt *Taltos and the Paths of the Dead* 1991 UK) and *Phoenix* (**1990**), plus *The Phoenix Guards* (**1991**), set earlier in the **Vlad Taltos** universe; *To Reign in Hell* (**1984**); *Brokedown Palace* (**1986**).

BRYANT, ADRIAN ◊ Adrian COLE.

BRYANT, EDWARD (WINSLOW Jr) (1945-) US writer, almost exclusively of short stories, beginning with "They Come Only in Dreams" for *Adam* in 1970, since when he has made his living as a freelance writer. EB was raised in Wyoming (and graduated with an MA in English from the University of Wyoming in 1968), a circumstance to which he pays his respects in *Wyoming Sun* (coll **1980**), which assembles fictions affected by that visually superb region. His early career was assisted by Harlan ELLISON, whom he met at the CLARION SCIENCE FICTION WRITERS' WORKSHOP in 1968 and 1969. His first book, *Among the Dead and Other Events Leading up to the Apocalypse* (coll **1973**; rev 1974), made a considerable stir for the wide variety of stories included and the technical facility they display. His conversational, apparently casual style sometimes conceals the tight construction and density of his best work, like "Shark" (1973), a complexly told love story whose darker implications are brought to focus in the girl's

decision to have her brain transplanted into a shark's body, ostensibly as part of a research project; in the story, symbol and surface reality mesh impeccably. The setting for many of the stories in this collection is a California transmuted by sf devices and milieux into an image, sometimes scarifying, sometimes joyful, of the culmination of the American Dream, an image further developed and intensified in *Cinnabar* (coll of linked stories **1976**), whose eponymous CITY of the FAR FUTURE is a dreamlike re-enactment of an essentialized DYING-EARTH California. The earlier stories of the sequence intricately develop a strangely moving vision of the rococo, many-shaped life by which mankind is ultimately destined to explicate itself (*see also* LEISURE), though the end of the book presents stories with a somewhat reductive plottiness. Later stories – collected in *Particle Theory* (coll **1981**), *Trilobyte* (coll **1987** chap) and *Neon Twilight* (coll **1990**) – continue slyly to urge sf into fable, horror and myth. EB suggests that the face the genre should expect to see in the mirror is the Minotaur's.

With Ellison, EB began a GENERATION-STARSHIP series with *Phoenix without Ashes* (**1975**), which works into novel form the pilot for the abortive Ellison tv series *The Starlost*; the book is short and perfunctory. Future volumes, long projected, have not appeared. EB has also published stories as Lawrence Talbot. He is the editor of an anthology of original stories and some poems, *2076: The American Tricentennial* (anth **1977**; rev 1977). [JC]

Other works: *The Man of the Future* (**1990** chap); *The Cutter* (**1988** *Silver Scream*; **1991** chap); *Fetish* (**1991**), horror; *The Thermals of August* (**1981** *FSF*; **1992** chap).

See also: *The* MAGAZINE OF FANTASY AND SCIENCE FICTION; MESSIAHS; NEBULA; PERCEPTION; WILD CARDS.

BRYANT, PETER ◊ Peter GEORGE.

BSFA ◊ BRITISH SCIENCE FICTION ASSOCIATION.

BSFA AWARD ◊ BRITISH SCIENCE FICTION AWARD.

BUCHANAN, ROBERT WILLIAMS (1848-1901) UK man of letters whose sf novel, *The Rev. Annabel Lee: A Tale of To-Morrow* (**1898**), posits a 21st-century society whose rationalist ideals leave a void in the bosom of the Christian Rev. Lee, who violates eugenic taboos and by so doing manages to create in her banned choice of husband a martyr to the new supernaturalism. [JC]

BUCKLEY, KATHLEEN [r] ◊ Sharon JARVIS.

BUCKNER, BRADNOR [s] ◊ Ed Earl REPP.

BUCK ROGERS ◊ BUCK ROGERS IN THE 25TH CENTURY.

BUCK ROGERS IN THE 25TH CENTURY 1. US COMIC strip conceived by John Flint Dille for the National Newspaper Syndicate Inc., written by Philip Francis NOWLAN, based on his novel *Armageddon 2419 AD* (1928-29 *AMZ*; fixup **1962**). *BR* appeared first in 1929 in daily newspapers, illustrated by Dick CALKINS, and in March 1930 the Sunday version began, signed by Calkins although the actual illustrator was Russell Keaton (to 1933) and then Rick Yager (who also took over the daily strip in 1951). Calkins – whose illustration was embarrassingly inferior to that of his colleagues – was removed from the strip in 1947; Murphy Anderson drew the daily strip 1947-9, followed by Leonard Dworkins 1949-59, Yager 1951-8, and George Tuska, who took over both strips in 1958 when Yager resigned. After Nowlan's death in 1940 various writers worked on continuity, including Calkins, Bob Barton and Yager, with contributions after 1958 by Fritz LEIBER and Judith MERRIL. The Sunday strip ended in June 1965, the daily in June 1967.

BR was the first US sf comic strip with a moderately adult and sophisticated storyline, though both dialogue and artwork were crude and naïve by comparison with such imitators as BRICK BRADFORD and FLASH GORDON. Nonetheless, it remained extremely popular for many years. Its scenario is archetypal SPACE OPERA. Buck, a lieutenant in the USAF, is inadvertently transported 500 years into the future, where he finds the USA overrun by hordes of "Red Mongols". Accompanied by his perennial girl-friend, Wilma Deering, Buck is constantly engaged in battle, on land and sea and in space, with his mortal enemy Killer Kane. (The Sunday version, which was much better drawn, also featured Wilma's younger brother Buddy and Princess Alura of Mars.) All the standard accoutrements of space opera are used: ANTIGRAVITY belts, DEATH RAYS, DISINTEGRATORS, domed cities and space rockets. The strip became more sophisticated after 1958, with some real sf writers brought in to spice things up.

Although *BR* contributed little to the artistic evolution of the comic strip, its storyline was very influential. It was successfully translated into other media: in addition to those discussed below, it appeared as a popular RADIO serial, beginning 1932, and as a **Big Little Book** (◊ JUVENILE SERIES). Some of Buck Rogers's adventures have been reissued in book form, including *The Collected Works of Buck Rogers in the 25th Century* (**1969**; rev 1977) ed Robert C. Dille, which is in fact only a selection. [PN/JE]

2. Serial film (1939), titled simply *Buck Rogers*. Universal. Dir Ford Beebe, Saul A Goodkind, starring Larry ("Buster") Crabbe, Constance Moore, C. Montague Shaw, Jack Moran, Anthony Warde. Screenplay Norman S. Hall, Ray Trampe, based on the comic strip. 12 episodes. B/w.

After their success with FLASH GORDON, also played by Crabbe, in two serials (1936 and 1938), Universal cast him as Buck Rogers, the other famous SPACE-OPERA hero of the newspaper comic strips. This serial, not as lavish or baroque as the first **Flash Gordon** serial, concerns Buck's waking after a 500-year sleep (in the Arctic) to discover that the Zuggs from Saturn have invaded Earth aided by the villainous Killer Kane (Warde). He teams up with Wilma (Moore) and Dr Huer (Shaw). The remaining episodes deal with their travels to Saturn to face the Zuggs on their home ground, and their efforts to avoid the usual hazards of crashing spaceships, ray-guns, robots and mind-control devices. Edited episodes were later cobbled

together as a feature film, *Planet Outlaws* (1953), re-edited as *Destination Saturn* (1965). [JB/PN]

3. US tv serial (1950-51), titled simply *Buck Rogers*. ABC TV. Prod and dir Babette Henry, starring Ken Dibbs (replaced after several months by Robert Pastene) as Buck, Lou Prentis as Wilma, Harry Sothern as Dr Huer. Written by Gene Wyckoff, based on the comic strip. One season. 25 mins per episode. B/w.

BR was one of the earliest of many space-opera juvenile tv serials in the early 1950s. Its style was that of the Saturday matinée cinema serials, but restrictions imposed by tv production necessitated its being shot live on a cramped interior set, with the result that the cinema serials seemed visually extravagant by comparison. Buck and his pals fight against evil and tyranny from a base hidden behind Niagara Falls. [JB]

4. US tv series (1979-81). Glen A. Larson/Universal/NBC. Developed for tv by Glen A. LARSON and Leslie Stevens. Prod Larson (season 1), John MANTLEY (season 2). Dirs included Daniel Haller, Sig Neufeld, Larry Stewart, Jack ARNOLD, Vincent McEveety. Writers included Alan BRENNERT, Anne Collins. Starring Gil Gerard as Buck, Erin Gray as Wilma, Tim O'Connor as Dr Huer, Felix Silla as Twiki, Thom Christopher as Hawk, Wilfred Hyde-White as Dr Goodfellow. Two seasons. 100min pilot, 1 100min episode, 33 50min episodes. Colour.

In the year of his 50th anniversary a second **Buck Rogers** tv series began, the brainchild of Glen A. Larson, whose BATTLESTAR GALACTICA had aired the previous year. Buck is now a US astronaut who has been frozen in a space-probe for 500 years. After the success of *Batman* (1966-8), film and tv producers persisted for many years in believing, against all evidence, that sf and fantastic genre material did best when spoofed. *BR* was played rather too much for laughs, and the irritating STAR WARS-derived robot Twiki was no help. The stories were very weak and nobody much cared for Buck as a cocky, wise-cracking lout. The show improved in the second season, with better scripts and a new alien character called Hawk, but it was too late.

5. Film (1979). Dir Daniel Haller, screenplay Glen A. Larson, Leslie Stevens. Other credits as for tv series above, plus Pamela Hensley. 89 mins. Colour.

This is simply the pilot episode of the tv series, edited down and given theatrical release. It is not too bad in a frothy way. Buck returns to a post-HOLOCAUST Earth where a semi-military sanctuary, once Chicago, exists in the MUTANT-haunted wreckage of his old homeland. He is wooed by wicked princess Ardala (pretty dresses; Pamela Hensley) and by Wilma (white jumpsuit and lipgloss; Erin Gray), and is suspected of being a spy. Many conventions of the genre are parodied. [PN]

See also: AUSTRIA; CINEMA; GAMES AND TOYS.

BUDRYS, ALGIS Working name of writer and editor Algirdas Jonas Budrys (1931-   ); the surname is also apparently a shortening of a Lithuanian original. He was born in East Prussia, but has been in the USA since 1936. He early worked as an assistant to his father, who was the US representative of the government-in-exile of Lithuania, an experience which has arguably shaped some of AB's fiction. He began publishing sf in 1952 with "The High Purpose" for *ASF*, and very rapidly gained a reputation as a leader of the 1950s sf generation, along with Philip K. DICK, Robert SHECKLEY and others, all of whom brought new literacy, mordancy and grace to the field; since 1965 he has written regular, incisive book reviews for *Gal* and latterly for *FSF*, but relatively little fiction.

During his first decade as a writer AB used a number of pseudonyms on magazine stories: David C. Hodgkins, Ivan Janvier, Paul Janvier, Robert Marner, William Scarff, John A. Sentry, Albert Stroud and (in collaboration with Jerome BIXBY) Alger ROME. He wrote few series, though "The High Purpose" had two sequels: "A.I.D." (1954) and "The War is Over" (1957), both in *ASF*. The **Gus** stories, as by Paul Janvier, are "Nobody Bothers Gus" (1955) and "And Then She Found Him" (1957).

AB's first novel has a complex history. As *False Night* (**1954**) it was published in a form abridged from the manuscript version; this manuscript served as the basis for a reinstated text which, with additional new material, was published as *Some Will Not Die* (**1961**; rev 1978). In both versions a post-HOLOCAUST story is set in a plague-decimated USA and, through the lives of a series of protagonists, a half century or so of upheaval and recovery is described. *Some Will Not Die* is a much more coherent (and rather grimmer) novel than its predecessor.

His second novel, *Who?* (**1958**), filmed as WHO? (1974), not quite successfully grafts an abstract vision of the existential extremity of mankind's condition onto an ostensibly orthodox sf plot, in which it must be determined whether or not a prosthetically rebuilt and impenetrably masked man (◊ CYBORGS) is in fact the scientist, vital to the US defence effort, whom he claims to be. As AB is in part trying to write an existential thriller about identity (rather similar to the later work of Kobo ABÉ), not an sf novel about the perils of prosthesis, some of the subsequent detective work seems a little misplaced; however, the seriousness of purpose is never in doubt. Similarly, *The Falling Torch* (1957-9 various mags; fixup **1959**; text restored vt *Falling Torch* 1991) presents a story which on the surface is straight sf, describing an Earth, several centuries hence, dominated by an ALIEN oppressor; the son of an exiled president returns to his own planet to liaise with the underground. But the novel can also be read as an allegory of the Cold War in its effects upon Eastern Europe (less awkward but more discursive in the restored text), and therefore, like *Who?*, asks of its generic structure rather more significance than generic structures of this kind have perhaps been designed to bear.

Much more thoroughly successful is AB's next novel, *Rogue Moon* (**1960**), now something of an sf classic. A good deal has been written about the highly integrated symbolic structure of this story, whose perfectly competent surface narration deals with a HARD-SF solution to the problem of an alien labyrinth, discovered on the MOON, which kills anyone who tries to pass through it. At one level, the novel's description of attempts to thread the labyrinth from Earth via MATTER TRANSMISSION makes for excellent traditional sf; at another, it is a sustained *rite de passage*, a doppelgänger conundrum about the mind-body split, a death-paean. There is no doubt that AB intends that both levels of reading register, however any interpretation might run; in this novel the two levels interact fruitfully.

After some years away from fiction, AB returned in the late 1970s with his most humanly complex and fully realized novel to date. *Michaelmas* (**1977**) describes in considerable detail a NEAR-FUTURE world whose information media have become even more sophisticated and creative of news than at present – as depicted in Sidney Lumet's film *Network* (1976) and as represented by such figures as CBS broadcaster Walter Cronkite. Like Cronkite, though to a much greater extent, the Michaelmas of the title is a moulder of news. Unusually, however, the book does not attack this condition. Michaelmas is a highly adult, responsible, complex individual, who with some cause feels himself to be the world's Chief Executive; beyond his own talents, he is aided in this task by an immensely sophisticated COMPUTER program named Domino, with which he is in constant contact, and which itself (as in books like Alfred BESTER's *The Computer Connection* [**1975**; vt *Extro* UK]) accesses all the computers in the world-net. Although the plot – Michaelmas must confront and defeat mysterious aliens who are manipulating mankind from behind the scenes – is straight out of PULP-MAGAZINE fiction, *Michaelmas* is a sustained, involving and peculiarly realistic novel.

AB is that rarity, an intellectual genre writer, as is also demonstrated by his three collections of short stories, *The Unexpected Dimension* (coll **1960**), *Budrys's Inferno* (coll **1963**; vt *The Furious Future* 1964 UK) and *Blood and Burning* (coll **1978**). From his genre origins stem both his strengths – incisiveness, exemplary concision of effect – and his weaknesses – mainly the habit, which he may have mastered, of overloading genre material with mainstream resonances. His sf criticism, especially that from before the mid-1980s, is almost unfailingly perceptive, and promulgates with a convert's grim élan a view of the essential nature of the genre that ferociously privileged the US magazine tradition. *Non-Literary Influences on Science Fiction (An Essay)* (**1983** chap) eloquently represents this view, as do, more relaxedly, the reviews collected in *Benchmarks: Galaxy Bookshelf* (coll **1985**).

In the 1980s, AB controversially associated himself with a programme for new writers initiated (or at least inspired) by L. Ron HUBBARD, arousing fears that Hubbard's Church of SCIENTOLOGY might itself be the source for the apparent affluence of L. RON HUBBARD'S WRITERS OF THE FUTURE. It was, nevertheless, evident by their participation that many sf writers felt these worries to be trivial, and the programme can claim to have introduced several authors of note (like Karen Joy FOWLER and David ZINDELL) to the field. In pieces like *Writing Science Fiction and Fantasy* (**1990** chap), composed originally for the enterprise, AB projected a detailed sense of what it meant to be a professional. The Hubbard school absorbed most of his energies for the remainder of the decade, although in 1991 he announced his semi-retirement from Writers of the Future. [JC]

Other works: *Man of Earth* (1955 *Satellite*; rev **1958**); *The Amsirs and the Iron Thorn* (**1967**; vt *The Iron Thorn* 1968 UK); *Cerberus* (1967 *FSF*; **1989** chap).

As editor: The **L. Ron Hubbard Presents Writers of the Future** series: *L. Ron Hubbard Presents Writers of the Future* (anth **1985**; vt without title reference to Hubbard 1986 UK); *Vol II* (anth **1986**); *Vol III* (anth **1987**); *Vol IV* (anth **1988**); *Vol V* (anth **1989**); *Vol VI* (anth **1990**); *Vol VII* (anth **1991**).

About the author: *More Issues at Hand* (coll **1970**) by William Atheling Jr (James BLISH), Chapter V; "Rite de Passage: A Reading of *Rogue Moon*" by David KETTERER in FOUNDATION 5, 1974; *Visions of Tomorrow: Six Journeys from Outer to Inner Space* (**1975**) by David N. SAMUELSON; *An Algis Budrys Checklist* (**1983** chap) by Chris DRUMM; *Conspiracy Theories* (anth **1987** chap) ed Christopher EVANS, providing a range of views on the Writers of the Future/Scientology dispute and on AJB's role.

See also: CHILDREN IN SF; COMMUNICATIONS; CONCEPTUAL BREAKTHROUGH; CRITICAL AND HISTORICAL WORKS ABOUT SF; DISASTER; GALAXY SCIENCE FICTION; GOTHIC SF; INVASION; INVISIBILITY; *The* MAGAZINE OF FANTASY AND SCIENCE FICTION; MARS; MEDIA LANDSCAPE; METAPHYSICS; NEW WAVE; OPTIMISM AND PESSIMISM; OUTER PLANETS; PANTROPY; PARANOIA; PHILIP K. DICK AWARD; PSYCHOLOGY; REINCARNATION; ROBOTS; SCIENTISTS; WRITERS OF THE FUTURE CONTEST.

BUFFALO BOOK CO. ◊ HADLEY PUBLISHING COMPANY.

BUFFERY, JUDITH (1943-) UK writer known exclusively for her SPACE-OPERA **Star Lord Saga**: *The Sheeg* (**1979**), *Saffron* (**1979**), *The Iron Clog* (dated 1979 but **1980**) and *Gringol Weed* (**1980**). [JC]

BUG Film (1975). Paramount. Dir Jeannot Szwarc, starring Bradford Dillman, Joanna Miles, Richard Gilliland. Screenplay William Castle (also prod), Thomas PAGE, based on *The Hephaestus Plague* (**1973**) by Page. 100 mins. Colour.

After an earthquake near a small US town, strange insects appear out of a fissure. Capable of producing fire by rubbing their rear appendages together, they ignite countryside, cars, people and a cat. A scientist whose wife has fallen victim to their incendiary activities becomes bug-obsessed. Mating them with roaches, he produces a new carnivorous species

which can communicate, spelling out words by grouping themselves in patterns. Finally, in the traditional Faustian manner, he falls in flames into the fissure which conveniently closes behind him and the bugs. *B*, like its source novel, appears unclear about what it is trying to be – a straight MONSTER MOVIE or some kind of allegorical revenge-of-Nature warning to mankind. The insect photography, by Ken Middleham, is good. [JB]

See also: PHASE IV.

BUG-EYED MONSTERS Often known by their acronym, BEMs. ◊ BEM; MONSTERS.

BUJOLD, LOIS McMASTER (1949-) US writer who began publishing sf with "Barter" for *Twilight Zone* in 1985. Almost all her published work is part of a loose series of humorous adventures set in a future of feuding galactic colonies connected by FASTER-THAN-LIGHT "wormhole jumps". Most of these stories feature members of the **Vorkosigan** family, part of an elite military caste from the planet Barrayar, recently rediscovered by galactic civilization after regressing into semifeudalism. *Shards of Honor* (**1986**) and its immediate sequel *Barrayar* (**1991**) which won a 1992 HUGO, deal with the romance between Lord Aral Vorkosigan and a supremely off-worlder; the child of their marriage is **Miles Vorkosigan**, born with severe physical handicaps due to a politically inspired attempt to poison his father. Miles grows up to become a supremely charismatic, witty, compulsively driven military genius who triumphantly transcends the difficulties caused by his brittle bones and 4ft 9in (1.45m) stature. His complicated double life in the Barrayaran Navy (as an ensign) and the Dendarii Mercenaries (of which he accidentally becomes the founder and admiral) is followed, in order of internal chronology, in *The Warrior's Apprentice* (**1986**) – assembled with *Shards of Honor* as *Test of Honor* (omni **1987**) – *The Vor Game* (**1990**), which won a 1991 Hugo, and *Brothers in Arms* (**1989**). The short stories in *The Borders of Infinity* (coll **1989**) – assembled with *The Vor Game* as *Vorkosigan's Game* (omni **1990**) – including the Hugo- and NEBULA-winning "The Mountains of Mourning" (1989), feature Miles at various points in his career. *Ethan of Athos* (**1986**), set after *The Vor Game*, focuses on Elli Quinn, who eventually becomes Miles's lover. *Falling Free* (**1988**), LMMB's best known single novel and winner of the 1988 Nebula, is set 200 years before the start of the **Vorkosigan** tales and tells the story of a rebellion – by humans genetically engineered to live in zero GRAVITY – against the company which has created them and plans, once their commercial value has expired, to dump them on a planetary surface.

LMMB is a writer whose books are both funny and humane. Her characters have strong feeling for each other and, when compared to similar military figures in the work of such male writers as Jerry POURNELLE, are often remarkably (and perhaps unrealistically) gentle. Though the ideas content in her work is generally low, her novels and stories succeed on their own terms. [NT]

See also: ASTOUNDING SCIENCE-FICTION; COLONIZATION OF OTHER WORLDS; GENETIC ENGINEERING; SPACE OPERA; WAR.

BULGAKOV, MIKHAIL (1891-1940) Soviet playwright and novelist whose fame in the West has come only with the posthumous publication in translation of most of his fiction, including *Belaya gvardiya* (**1925**; trans Michael Glenny as *The White Guard* **1971** UK) and *Cherny sneg* (written late 1930s; trans Michael Glenny as *Black Snow* **1967** UK), neither of which are sf/fantasy. A collection of short stories, *Dyaboliada* (coll **1925**; trans Carl R. Proffer as *Diaboliad and Other Stories* **1972** US), includes "The Crimson Island: A Novel by Comrade Jules Verne Translated from the French into the Aesopian" (1924 Germany), a Jules VERNE-like fable made into a play (performed 1928) with the same title, and "The Fatal Eggs" (1924), whose indictment of the mechanizing hubris of science reflects the influence of H.G. WELLS's *The Food of the Gods* (**1904**). A similar analysis shapes *Sobacheye Serdste* (written 1925; trans Michael Glenny from the manuscript as *Heart of a Dog* **1968** UK and by Mirra GINSBURG **1968** US), a short sf novel in which a scientist transforms a dog into a sort-of-man who proves incapable of the fundamental transformation to civilized behaviour; eventually, the scientist is forced to change him back into a dog (or allegorical peasant) again. The tale reappeared in *The Heart of a Dog and Other Stories* (coll trans Kathleen Cook-Horujy and Avril Pyman **1990** Russia), along with other stories. *Master i Margarita* (written 1938; **1966-7** US; complete text trans Michael Glenny as *The Master and Margarita* **1967** UK; cut text trans Mirra Ginsburg **1967** US) is a fantasy in which the Devil appears in modern Moscow, and Christ's crucifixion is re-enacted. It was filmed in 1972 and adapted as a serial on BBC radio in 1992; the play within the novel was made into a Polish film (English title *Pilate and the Others*) in 1971. In "The Crimson Island" (written 1927), which appears in *The Early Plays* (coll trans Carl R. Proffer and Ellendea Proffer **1972** US), and in "Adam and Eve" (written 1931), "Bliss" (written 1934) and "Ivan Vasilievich" (written 1935), MB mounted a series of profound assaults upon the reality-distortions of ideology. MB was a powerful, often extremely funny, ultimately very serious writer whose use of sf and fantasy forms was tightly linked to the messages he laboured to produce about the state of the SOVIET UNION, whose apparatchiks criticized him severely during his life. [JC]

See also: RUSSIA; THEATRE.

BULGARIA The roots of Bulgarian sf can be found in the 1920s, when Svetoslav MINKOV published three unusual collections of short stories: *Siniata Hrizantema* ["The Blue Chrysanthemum"] (coll **1921**), *Tshasovnik* ["Clock"] (coll **1924**) and *Ognena Ptitza* ["The Fire Bird"] (coll **1927**). Minkov's work noticeably resembles that of Edgar Allan POE, H.P. LOVECRAFT and the German decadents of his period, and may be

closer to the "diabolic" fantasy of the German Romantics than to the main current of sf. A collection in English of Minkov's work is *The Lady with the X-Ray Eyes* (coll trans **1965** Bulgaria). Perhaps Georgi Iliev, author of the novels *O-Korse* (**1930**) and *Teut se Bountuva* ["Teut Rebels"] (**1933**), should be regarded as the real founding father of Bulgarian sf. These two books, intended as serious works for serious readers, deal with cosmic DISASTERS on the grand scale: the dying of the Sun; the cessation of our planet's rotation.

The promise of these early years was not followed up. No further sf or fantasy works were published until about 10 years after WWII, when Bulgarian sf's second period began. To understand the many paradoxes of Bulgarian socialist publishing 1946-89 one should remember that all publishing houses and printers were state property and poorly organized; that there was a chronic shortage of paper and printing presses; and that the whole publishing system was under strong ideological control. The soil for raising Bulgarian sf was, therefore, less than fertile – certainly in the 1950s – and much sf of the period was limited to tedious imitations of the Soviet model, dealing with a bright, happy communist future and the imminent destruction of all that capitalism stood for. Books of this period are *Zemiata Pred Gibel* ["Earth on the Verge of Destruction"] (**1957**) by Tsvetan Angelov, *Raketata ne Otgovaria* ["No Reply from the Rocketship"] (**1958**) by Dimitar Peev, *Gush-terat ot Ledovete* ["The Lizard from the Land of Ice"] (**1958**) by Petar Bobev and *Atomniat Tshovek* ["The Atomic Man"] (**1958**) by Ljuben Dilov.

In the 1960s, when the winds of change were detectable, a third and more interesting period began. The breakthrough was made by Georgi Markov (◊ David ST GEORGE) – later assassinated in London – with his important novel *Pobeditelite na Aiax* ["The Conquerors of Ajax"] (**1960**), a space story about the meeting of three races who are at different stages of cultural development. In 1962 the first Bulgarian sf club, "Friends of the Future", was founded in Sofia. The most active sf writer has been Ljuben Dilov (1927-   ), whose *Atomniat Tshovek* is mentioned above. His later works – often satirical – include *Mnogoto Imena na Straha* ["The Many Names of Fear"] (**1967**), *Tejesta na Skafandara* ["The Burden of the Spacesuit"] (**1969**), about ALIENS, *Moiat Stranen Priatel – Astronomat* ["My Strange Friend the Astronomer"] (coll **1971**), *Patiat na Ikar* ["The Way of Icarus"] (**1974**), about a GENERATION STARSHIP, *Da Nahranish Orela* ["To Feed the Eagle"] (coll **1977**), and *Jestokiat Eksperiment* ["Cruel Experiment"] (**1985**) about SEX. Other authors include Haim Oliver with *Heliopolis* (**1968**), Emil Manov with *Galacticheska Balada* ["Galactic Ballad"] (**1971**) and *Patuvane do Uibrobia* ["Journey to Wibrobia"] (**1976**) – the latter a continuation of Jonathan SWIFT's *Gulliver's Travels* (**1726**; rev 1735) – Svetoslav Slavshtev, Ljubomir Peevsky, and Pavel Vejinov with *Sinite Peperudi* ["Blue Butterflies"] (coll **1968**), *Beliat Gushter* ["The White Lizard"] (coll **1977**) and *Barierata* ["Barrier"] (coll **1977**); Dimitar Peev and Petar Bobev continue to publish.

In the 1980s many more new sf authors appeared, writing on the same – not outstanding – level. But things began to look promising in the late 1980s. In 1988 the first specialist sf magazine, *F.E.P.*, was launched; the title has since been changed to *Fantastika*. The great hope for Bulgarian sf came in 1989 with the removal of the ban on privately owned publishing companies. A new sf publishing house is Gemini, whose fortnightly sf magazine, *Drugi Svetove* ["Other Worlds"], began publication in 1991. The most active sf/fantasy publishing house is Orphia. Other publishers, too, are intending to publish sf, whose future in Bulgaria looks brighter.   [AP]

BULL, EMMA (1954-) US writer who began as an author of fantasies, her first being "Rending Dark" in *Sword and Sorceress* (anth **1984**) ed Marion Zimmer BRADLEY, and her best known being her first novel, *War for the Oaks* (**1987**). Her second novel, *Falcon* (**1989**), is a remarkably well constructed sf tale whose protagonist moves from the PLANETARY-ROMANCE setting of the first half of the book into the hi-tech SPACE-OPERA environment that dominates the second, where he has become an ace starship pilot; eventually everything fits together in an extremely well ordered climax. The subtitle of her third novel, *Bone Dance: A Fantasy for Technophiles* (**1991**), neatly demonstrates the difficulty – it is not uncommon for writers of the 1980s to pose the problem – of generic placement, though this particular book, which depicts a post-HOLOCAUST search for an ancient weapon, is sufficiently sf-like not to distress taxonomists. With her husband, the fantasy writer Will Shetterly (1955-), EB has edited the **Liavek** sequence of SHARED-WORLD fantasy anthologies: *Liavek* * (anth **1985**), *The Players of Luck* * (anth **1986**), *Wizard's Row* * (anth **1987**), *Spells of Binding* * (anth **1988**) and *Grand Festival* * (anth **1990**).   [JC]

See also: FASTER THAN LIGHT; PHILIP K. DICK AWARD.

BULMER, H.K. [r] ◊ Kenneth BULMER.

BULMER, KENNETH (1921-) UK writer, who also signs himself H.K. Bulmer, as well as using a number of pseudonyms for his books, including Alan Burt Akers, Ken Blake (not sf), Ernest Corley (not sf), Arthur Frazier (not sf), Adam Hardy (for his successful **Hornblower**-like novels of the sea) Philip Kent, Bruno Krauss (not sf), Neil Langholm (not sf), Manning Norvil, Charles R. Pike (not sf), Dray Prescot, Andrew Quiller, Richard Silver (not sf), Tully Zetford, the collaborative pseudonym Kenneth JOHNS (with John Newman) and the house name Karl Maras, under which he wrote two novels; there have also been several names restricted to magazine stories. After a career as an active fan dating from before WWII (editing various fanzines from 1941), KB began publishing sf with *Space Treason* (**1952**) and *Cybernetic Controller* (**1952**), both with A.V. Clarke, and *Encounter in Space* (**1952**), and was soon involved

in producing material for *NW*, *Authentic* and *Nebula*, the three major magazines among those proliferating in the volatile UK sf scene of the first post-WWII decade, though he sold few stories to US magazines. His first solo novels, like *Space Treason* (**1952**) and *Zhorani (Master of the Universe)* (**1953** as by Karl Maras), and much of his ensuing work were either SPACE OPERAS or adventure plots laid on simplified versions of·future Earths. Notable among these were several novels published in the USA from 1957, including *City Under the Sea* (**1957** dos US), *The Secret of ZI* (**1958** dos US; vt *The Patient Dark* 1969 UK), *The Earth Gods are Coming* (**1960** dos US; vt with one story added as coll *Of Earth Foretold* 1961 UK), *The Wizard of Starship Poseidon* (**1963** dos US), *Demons' World* (**1964** dos US; vt *The Demons* 1965 UK), *Worlds for the Taking* (**1966** US), possibly the best of them, a relatively sustained and dark-toned portrait of the costs of being a "competent man" in an environment of interstellar corporate intrigue, and *The Doomsday Men* (**1965** If; exp **1968** US).

In the period of his most interesting work, approximately 1955-68, KB was notable for the adept use he made of a wide range of sf themes, from underwater CITIES (◊ UNDER THE SEA) to giant ALIEN invaders (◊ GREAT AND SMALL) to TIME TRAVEL and MONSTERS – in *Cycle of Nemesis* (**1967** US) – to PARALLEL WORLDS. The latter theme is the sustaining conceit of the **Keys to the Dimensions** series: *Land Beyond the Map* (1961 *Science Fantasy* as "The Map Country"; **1965**); "The Seventh Stair" (1961 *Science Fantasy*) and "Perilous Portal" (1962 *Science Fantasy*), both as by Frank Brandon; *The Key to Irunium* (**1967** US); *The Key to Venudine* (**1968** US); *The Wizards of Senchuria* (**1969** US); *The Ships of Durostorum* (**1970** US); *The Hunters of Jundagai* (**1971** US), *The Chariots of Ra* (**1972** US) and *The Diamond Contessa* (**1983** US). Much of KB's later fiction under his own name has seemed to flounder somewhat in attempts to handle a more "contemporary" style and subject matter, as in *The Ulcer Culture* (**1969**; vt *Stained-Glass World* 1976), *On the Symb-Socket Circuit* (**1972**) and *Roller Coaster World* (**1972** US). As the **Dray Prescot** series would show, KB's forte lies in the transparency of the pulp tale truly told.

It was with the **Dray Prescot** sequence of Edgar Rice BURROUGHS pastiches – set in a SCIENCE-FANTASY interstellar venue and written either as by Alan Burt Akers or as told to Akers by Dray Prescot – that KB reached his largest and most faithful audience. To date the series comprises: *Transit to Scorpio* (**1972** US), *The Suns of Scorpio* (**1973** US), *Warrior of Scorpio* (**1973** US), *Swordships of Scorpio* (**1973** US), *Prince of Scorpio* (**1974** US), *Manhounds of Antares* (**1974** US), *Arena of Antares* (**1974** US), *Fliers of Antares* (**1975** US), *Bladesmen of Antares* (**1975** US), *Avenger of Antares* (**1975** US), *Armada of Antares* (**1975** US), *The Tides of Kregen* (**1976** US), *Renegades of Kregen* (**1976** US), *Krozair of Kregen* (**1977** US), *Secret Scorpio* (**1977** US), *Savage Scorpio* (**1977** US), *Captive Scorpio* (**1977** US), *Golden Scorpio* (**1978** US), *A Life for Kregen* (**1979** US), *A Fortune for*

Kregen (**1979** US), *A Victory for Kregen* (**1979** US), *Beasts of Antares* (**1980** US), *Rebel of Antares* (**1980** US), *Legions of Antares* (**1981** US), *Allies of Antares* (**1981** US), *Mazes of Scorpio* (**1981** US), *Delia of Vallia* (**1982** US), *Fires of Scorpio* (**1983** US), *Talons of Scorpio* (**1983** US), *Masks of Scorpio* (**1984** US), *Seg the Bowman* (**1984** US), *Werewolves of Kregen* (**1985** US), *Witches of Kregen* (**1985** US), *Storm over Vallia* (**1985** US), *Omens of Kregen* (**1985** US) and *Warlord of Antares* (**1988** US). The books are unfailing in their delivery.

With John CARNELL's death in 1972, KB took over the long-running anthology series NEW WRITINGS IN SF from #22 (anth **1973**), producing in short order #23 (anth **1973**), #24 (anth **1974**), #25 (anth **1975**), #26 (anth **1975**), #27 (anth **1975**), #28 (anth **1976**) and #29 (anth **1976**) before the series was terminated, and maintaining the generally traditionalist content of the books; some of the volumes under his editorship were later assembled as *New Writings in SF Special (1)* (omni **1975**), which included #21 (ed Carnell), #22 and #23, *New Writings in SF Special (2)* (omni **1978**), which included #26 and #29, and *New Writings in SF (3)* (omni **1978**), which included #27 and #28. As fan, writer and editor, KB has been one of the mainstays of UK sf for more than four decades; he served as a council member of the SCIENCE FICTION FOUNDATION from its inception to 1988. Though much of his work is routine, especially that written under pseudonyms, he has consistently shown himself to be one of the most competent, though not perhaps the most original, workers in the field. [JC]

Other works: *Empire of Chaos* (**1953**); *Galactic Intrigue* (**1953**); *Space Salvage* (**1953**); *The Stars are Ours* (**1953**); *Challenge* (**1954**); *World Aflame* (**1954**); *The Changeling Worlds* (**1959** dos US); *Beyond the Silver Sky* (**1961** dos US); *No Man's World* (**1961** dos US; vt with 1 story added as coll *Earth's Long Shadow* 1962 UK); *The Fatal Fire* (**1962**); *The Wind of Liberty* (coll **1962**); *Defiance* (coll of linked stories **1963**); *The Million Year Hunt* (fixup **1964** dos US); *Behold the Stars* (**1965** dos US); *To Outrun Doomsday* (**1967** US); *Kandar* (**1969** US); *The Star Venturers* (**1969** dos US); *Quench the Burning Stars* (**1970**; exp vt *Blazon* 1970 US); *Star Trove* (**1970**); *Sword of the Barbarians* (**1970**); *The Electric Sword-Swallowers* (**1971** dos US); *The Insane City* (**1971** US).

As Philip Kent: *Mission to the Stars* (**1953** chap); *Vassals of Venus* (**1953** chap); *Home is the Martian* (**1954** chap); *Slaves of the Spectrum* (**1954** chap).

As Karl Maras: *Peril from Space* (**1954**).

As Manning Norvil: A series starring **Odan the Half-God** and comprising *Dream Chariots* (**1977** US), *Whetted Bronze* (**1978** US) and *Crown of the Sword God* (**1980**).

As Tully Zetford: The **Hook** sequence comprising *Whirlpool of Stars* (**1974**), *The Boosted Man* (**1974**), *Star City* (**1975**) and *The Virility Gene* (**1975**).

About the author: *The Writings of Henry Kenneth Bulmer* (2nd edn **1984** chap) by Roger ROBINSON.

See also: ANTHOLOGIES; COMICS; DAW BOOKS; FASTER THAN LIGHT; GALACTIC EMPIRES; NEW WORLDS.

BULWER, EDWARD [r] ◊ First Baron LYTTON.

BULWER-LYTTON, Sir EDWARD [r] ◊ First Baron LYTTON.

BULYCHEV, KIR(ILL) Pseudonym of Russian historian and writer Igor (Vsevolodovich) Mozheiko (1934-   ), known also for books of popular science. He first gained popularity through his light and intelligent stories, assembled in volumes like *Tchudesa v Gusliaro* (coll **1972**; trans Roger DeGaris, with differing contents, as *Gusliar Wonders* 1983 US), *Liudi Kak Liudi* ["Men Who Are Like Men"] (coll **1975**), *Letneie Utro* ["A Summer Morning"] (coll **1979**) and *Pereval* ["The Pass"] (coll **1983**). Some of these stories were assembled as *Half a Life* (coll trans Helen Saltz Jacobson **1977** US). In the humorous **Gusliar** cycle, the eponymous old Russian town is a place where miracles occur on a routine basis – ALIENS land, for example, and fairy-tale Golden Fishes, which grant wishes, are a sell-out in the local pet-store. KB's only adult novel of note, *Posledniaia Voina* ["The Final War"] (**1970**), depicts a long-dead post-HOLOCAUST planet which is visited by Earthmen who have the technical means to resurrect it. A prolific writer of CHILDREN'S SF, KB may become best known as the author of a very long sequence of **Alice** tales about a futuristic young heroine, beginning with *Devotchka S Zemli* ["Girl From Earth"] (**1974**). Juvenile singletons include *Sto Let Tomu Vpered* ["One Hundred Years Ahead"] (**1978**), *Million Prikliuchenii* ["A Million Adventures"] (**1982**) and *Neposeda* ["Fidget"] (**1985**), which was successfully adapted for the screen. [VG]

BUNCH, CHRIS [r] ◊ Allan COLE.

BUNCH, DAVID R(OOSEVELT) (?   -   ) US writer of poetry and sf. He graduated as Bachelor of Science at Central Missouri State College and as MA in English at Washington University, worked as a civilian cartographer for the US Air Force 1954-73, and began publishing sf with "Routine Emergency" for *If* in 1957; before that he had published about 200 non-sf stories. Much of his sf work was assembled as *Moderan* (coll of linked stories **1971**), a series of short, narratively deranged, fable-like tales which describe in satirical terms (◊ SATIRE) a radically technologized future world where, after a nuclear HOLOCAUST, humans have been transformed into CYBORGS, the surface of the world is plastic, and thought and action are both solipsistic and deeply melancholy. The book's portrait of a manufactured humanity works as an arraignment of the late-20th-century slide into speed-lined rootlessness, and demonstrate his heterodoxy in the world of sf. Some of his poetry was assembled as *We Have a Nervous Job* (coll **1983** chap). Of the many non-**Moderan** stories, "That High-Up Blue Day that Saw the Black Sky-Train Come Spinning" (1968) has been described as an outstanding conflation of moral seriousness and Grand Guignol. The relentlessness of his vision and the "zany" extremity of his rendering of it ensure DRB's market inconspicuousness, but suggest that, for his readers, he will remain a vivid influence; and it may well be that, with the release of «The Best of David R. Bunch» (coll 1993), his considerable stature will be more widely understood. [JC]

See also: ABSURDIST SF; AMAZING STORIES; CYBERNETICS.

BUPP, WALTER [s] ◊ John BERRYMAN.

BURDEKIN, KATHARINE P(ENELOPE) (1896-1963) UK writer, some of whose 1920s books were signed Kay Burdekin; in the 1930s she wrote as Murray Constantine. Her early work in particular took the guise of FANTASY to express increasingly explicit FEMINIST interests. *The Burning Ring* (**1927**) is a TIME-TRAVEL fantasy in which a self-centred young man, having been given magic powers, visits various epochs in various disguises, learning more about real life than he at first wished. The 12th-century protagonist of *The Rebel Passion* (**1929**) is transported in a vision from his monastery to a 21st-century UK where women are equal, eugenic sterilization of the unfit is normal, and the Western world – after a futuristic war with Asia – gradually turns to a William MORRIS-style medievalism. *Proud Man* (**1934**), as Murray Constantine, subjects a sample of contemporary humanity to the searching interrogation of a visitor from the future whose hermaphroditism stands as a reproach to our local muddle. *The Devil, Poor Devil!* (**1934**), as Constantine, confronts the Devil with a killing spirit of secular sanity, against which He is helpless. KB's last published novels were the most explicitly didactic. *Swastika Night* (**1937** as Constantine; **1985** as KB), her best known novel, examines a Nazi-dominated Europe 500 years hence through the eyes of the young German protagonist, who begins to understand that something is perhaps awry in a world where women are breeding-animals and Hitler is deified (◊ HITLER WINS). The posthumous publication of KB's feminist UTOPIA, *The End of This Day's Business* (**1990**), apparently written before *Swastika Night*, further helped to disinter from pseudonymous obscurity a writer of considerable interest. Her work is at times surreptitiously couched, and her message is too often found embedded in romance-fiction plotting, but KB can now be seen as a figure of contemporary interest. [JC]

See also: DYSTOPIAS; GENRE SF; POLITICS.

BURDICK, EUGENE L(EONARD) (1918-1965) US writer of several extremely popular novels, both alone and in collaboration. His sf novel, *Fail-Safe* (**1962**) with Harvey WHEELER, presents a NEAR-FUTURE US attack in error on the USSR, and the horrifying tit-for-tat (the destruction of New York City) which the US President is forced to offer. The book was filmed as FAIL SAFE (1964). [JC]

BURGEON, G.A.L. ◊ Arthur Owen BARFIELD.

BURGER, DIONYS The Anglicized form of the name of Dutch physicist lecturer and author Dionijs Burger (1923-). His *Bolland: Een roman van gekromde ruimten en uitdijend heelal* (**1957**; trans Cornelia J. Rheinboldt as *Sphereland: A Fantasy about Curved Spaces and an Expanded Universe* **1965** US) is a MATHE-MATICAL fable written as a sequel to *Flatland* (**1884**) by

Edwin A. ABBOTT. [PN]
See also: BENELUX.

BURGESS, ANTHONY Working name of UK writer and composer John Anthony Burgess Wilson (1917-), known primarily for his work outside the sf field; as a composer he has worked under his full name. Trained in English literature and phonetics, AB taught at home and in Malaysia 1946-60, then returned to the UK (though he has since moved to Monaco) and became a full-time Protean man of letters, novelist, musician, composer and specialist in Shakespeare and James Joyce. *Devil of a State* (**1961**), set in an imaginary caliphate, skirts sf displacement, and several subsequent novels engage in linguistic flirtations with modes of FABULATION, but AB remains best known in the sf field for *A Clockwork Orange* (**1962**; with final chapter cut 1963 US), which was filmed by Stanley KUBRICK as A CLOCKWORK ORANGE (1971). A compelling and often comic vision of the way violence comes to dominate the mind, the novel is set in a future London and is told in a curious but readable Russified argot by a juvenile delinquent whose brainwashing by the authorities has destroyed not only his murderous aggression but also a deeper-seated sense of humanity (typified by his compulsive love for the music of Beethoven). It is an ironic novel in the tradition of Yevgeny ZAMIATIN's and George ORWELL's anti-UTOPIAS; much later, AB adapted the book as a play to be accompanied by his own music, publishing the result as *A Clockwork Orange* (**1987** chap). His other early sf novel is *The Wanting Seed* (**1962**), a DYSTOPIAN investigation of the dilemmas facing men who wish to curb the population explosion by every means possible (◊ OVERPOPULATION).

The Eve of Saint Venus (**1964**), perhaps inspired by F. ANSTEY's *The Tinted Venus* (**1885**), sympathetically brings the eponymous goddess back to life. "The Muse" (**1968**), a story of altered PERCEPTION and TIME TRAVEL, offers an alarming explanation for Shakespeare's never having blotted a line. *Beard's Roman Women* (**1976** US), a fantasy, is the melancholy tale of a widowed writer haunted in Rome by the supernatural presence (and insistent telephone calls) of his deceased wife. Two genuine sf novels followed: *1985* (**1978**), which is divided into a competent essay on Orwell's *Nineteen Eighty-four* (**1949**) and a blustering sf tale set in a 1985 dominated by Arabs and left-wing unions; and *The End of the World News* (**1983**), again a book divided but this time in three, with a short life of Sigmund Freud jostling a Broadway musical (without the music) about Leon Trotsky, both tales being filmed and viewed long afterwards aboard a spaceship which – in the third segment of the main narrative – has escaped the END OF THE WORLD just before a wandering planet strikes the rest of us dead. These novels both give off a sense of underlying sarcasm which has, perhaps, as much to do with AB's disdain for sf as with the tales' ostensible targets. *Any Old Iron* (**1989**), a treatment of Arthurian material in a contemporary context, was similarly distempered.

AB has written little short fiction; some of the stories in his first collection, *The Devil's Work* (coll **1989**), are of genre interest. [MJ/JC]

Other works: *A Long Trip to Teatime* (**1976**).

About the author: *The Clockwork Universe of Anthony Burgess* (**1978** chap) by Richard Mathews; *Anthony Burgess. An Enumerative Bibliography* (**1980**) by Jeutonne Brewer; *Anthony Burgess* (**1981**) by Samuel Coale.

See also: LINGUISTICS; MUSIC; PSYCHOLOGY; QUEST FOR FIRE.

BURGESS, ERIC (ALEXANDER) (1912-   ) UK author, in collaboration with A(rthur Henry) Friggens (1920-   ), of several sf novels for ROBERT HALE LIMITED. Though none are remarkable in content, the **Mortorio** sequence – *Mortorio* (**1973**) and *Mortorio Two* (**1975**) – stand out from the crowd. [JC]

Other works: *Anti-Zota* (**1973**); *Mants of Myrmedon* (**1977**); *Hounds of Heaven* (**1979**).

BURGESS, MARY WICKIZER [r] ◊ Daryl F. MALLETT; Robert REGINALD.

BURGESS, MICHAEL [r] ◊ Robert REGINALD.

BURKE, JONATHAN Working name of UK writer and editor John Frederick Burke (1922-   ) – who had been active in FANDOM in the 1930s (◊*The* FUTURIAN) – for much of the sf he published in UK magazines in the mid-1950s, beginning with "Chessboard" for *NW* in 1953, and for his earlier sf novels, which are all routine; he also wrote several thrillers as JB. His first novel, *Swift Summer* (**1949**) as by J.F. Burke, is a marginal fantasy of some slight interest. His sf deals with a variety of themes, from PARALLEL WORLDS in *The Echoing Worlds* (**1954**) to EVOLUTION in *Twilight of Reason* (**1954**), though without excessive energy; *Deep Freeze* (**1955**) faces an all-female world with the return of the male. He has also written as Robert Miall (see listing below). In more recent years, almost always as John Burke, he has edited horror anthologies and novelized film and tv productions. [JC]

Other works: *The Dark Gateway* (**1953**); *Hotel Cosmos* (**1954**); *Pattern of Shadows* (**1954**); *Alien Landscapes* (coll **1955**), much of whose contents, under different titles, were also assembled as *Exodus from Elysium* (coll **1965** Australia); *Revolt of the Humans* (**1955**); *Pursuit through Time* (**1956**); *Dr Terror's House of Horrors* * (**1965**) as John Burke, novelizing the film; *The Hammer Horror Omnibus* * (coll **1966**) and *The Second Hammer Horror Film Omnibus* * (coll **1967**), both as John Burke, stories from films; *Chitty Chitty Bang Bang* * (**1968**) as John Burke, novelizing the film of Ian FLEMING's tale; *Moon Zero Two* * (**1969**) as John Burke, novelizing the film MOON ZERO TWO (1969); *Expo 80* (**1972**) as John Burke; the **Dr Caspian, psychic investigator** series comprising *The Devil's Footsteps* (**1976**), *The Black Charade* (**1977**) and *Ladygrove* (**1978**); *Privilege* * (**1967**), novelizing PRIVILEGE. **As Robert Miall:** *UFO* * (**1970**; vt *UFO-1: Flesh Hunters* 1973 US) and *UFO 2* * (**1971**; vt *UFO-2: Sporting Blood* 1973 US), novelizations of the tv series UFO. **As editor:** *Tales of Unease* (anth **1966**), *More Tales of Unease* (anth **1969**) and *New Tales of Unease* (anth

1976), all as John Burke.

BURKE, RALPH Pseudonym used primarily by Robert SILVERBERG alone, but three times in collaboration with Randall GARRETT, in 1956-7. [JC]

BURKETT, WILLIAM R(AY) Jr (1943-   ) US author and journalist. His only published sf work, *Sleeping Planet* (1964 *ASF*; **1965**), very competently tells a hard-edged tale of conflict between the small Terran Federation and the huge Llralan Empire. The Llralans, having undeserved access to a toxic dust, spray the Earth, putting all but a few humans to sleep (◊ INVASION); in the best *ASF* manner – the book's resemblance to the work of Eric Frank RUSSELL is striking – they are ultimately sent packing. [JC]

BURKHOLZ, HERBERT [r] ◊ ESP.

BURKS, ARTHUR J. (1898-1974) US military man and writer who, after some years in the US Army, began publishing fantasy with "Thus Spake the Prophetess" for *Weird Tales* in 1924 and sf with "Monsters of Moyen" for *ASF* in 1930. After two decades of high productivity, he remained intermittently active into the 1960s, with time out for further service in WWII. Only one of his sf novels, *The Great Mirror* (1942 *Science Fiction Quarterly*; **1952**), has been reprinted in book form. The others included "Earth, the Marauder" (1930 *ASF*), "The Mind Master" (1932 *ASF*), "Jason Sows Again" (1938 *ASF*), "Survival" and its sequel "Exodus" (both 1938 *Marvel Science Stories*) and "The Far Detour" (1942 *Science Fiction Quarterly*). Much of his best work was fantasy, including *The Great Amen* (**1938**), *Look Behind You!* (coll **1954** chap), *Black Medicine* (coll **1966**) and *The Casket* (**1973**). AJB was one of the most prolific of all PULP-MAGAZINE writers: his sf and fantasy constitute only a small fraction of his prodigious output. [JC/MJE]

BURLAND, HARRIS ◊ J.B. HARRIS-BURLAND.

BURNS, ALAN (1929-   ) UK writer and academic long resident in the USA. Some of his FABULATIONS, like *Europe After the Rain* (**1965**), *Babel* (**1969**) and *Dreamerika!* (**1972**), utilize sf instruments to grapple with a surreal vision of a modern world toppling jaggedly into chaos. His techniques on occasion resemble those adopted by J.G. BALLARD during the 1960s. [JC]

BURNS, CHARLES (1955-   ) US COMIC-strip artist and writer, born in Washington DC and now based in Philadelphia. The drawing of his FABULATIONS displays a strange, heavily stylized vision; his work has been widely published in Italy (notably in *Vanity*), Spain (*El Vibora*) and France (MÉTAL HURLANT) as well as in his native USA (*Heavy Metal*, *Village Voice*, *National Lampoon*, *Face* and *Death Rattle*). His famous **El Borbah** strips, collected as *El Borbah* (graph coll **1985**) and as *Hard-Boiled Defective Stories* (graph coll **1988**), feature an eponymous private eye who is not so much hard-boiled as rock-hard-boiled. El Borbah has a black metal head with only rudimentary features, and wears only a black shiny leotard and black boots; his surreal adventures often contain sf elements. The series shows the influence of Chester Gould (of **Dick Tracy** fame) in its heavy-line style and its bizarre characters. Here, as in his serial *Big Baby* (collected as *Big Baby: Curse of the Molemen* graph coll **1986**) and his continuing self-syndicated strip distributed to freesheets and street-level papers throughout the USA, CB creates a world peopled by the inhabitants and served by the machinery of US 1950s B-movies. [RT/SW]

Other work: *Teen Plague* (graph **1989**), epic horror story; «Skin Deep» (graph 1992).

BURNS, JIM (1948-   ) Welsh illustrator, primarily of sf, born in Cardiff, with a diploma from St Martin's School of Art, London. During 1973-9 his work was exclusively for UK publishers, notably Sphere Books, and he was not really known in the USA until publication of his illustrated book *Planet Story* (**1979**), with story by Harry HARRISON. Since 1980 much of his book-cover work has been for US publishers, including BANTAM BOOKS, ACE BOOKS, Berkley and Byron PREISS, including the interior black-and-white illustrations for the latter's *Eye* (coll **1985**) by Frank HERBERT. JB's work (in many media, but mostly acrylics) is realistic, subtly textured, well known for its attractive women (sometimes attacked as sexist) and constantly inventive, and gives ample evidence in its detail that JB – somewhat unusually in this field – actually reads the books that he illustrates. His work is spectacularly commercial (but not merely so) and, along with that of Don MAITZ and Michael WHELAN, perhaps the most proficient currently (1992) being produced in the field. More than 100 of his covers may be seen in *Lightship* (coll **1985**), with text by Christopher EVANS. In 1987 JB became the first and so far only non-US winner of a HUGO for Best Professional Artist. [PN]

See also: BRITISH SCIENCE FICTION AWARD; ILLUSTRATION; TECHNOLOGY.

BURROUGHS, EDGAR RICE (1875-1950) US writer. Educated at Michigan Military Academy, ERB served briefly in the US Cavalry. His early life was marked by numerous false starts and failures – at the time he started writing, aged 36, he was a pencil-sharpener salesman – but it would seem that the impulse to create psychically charged SCIENCE-FANTASY environments was deep-set and powerful, for he began with a great rush of energy, and within two years had initiated three of his four most important series.

A Princess of Mars (1912 *All-Story Magazine* as "Under the Moons of Mars" as by Norman Bean; **1917**), a fantastic solution to mid-life frustrations, opens the long **Barsoom** sequence of novels set on MARS (Barsoom), which established that planet as a venue for dream-like and interminable sagas in which sf and fantasy protocols mix indiscriminately as a sort of enabling gear. *The Gods of Mars* (1913 *All-Story*; **1918**) and *The Warlord of Mars* (1913-14 *All-Story*; **1919**) further recount the exploits of John Carter as he battles with various green, yellow and black men and wins the hand of the red-skinned (and oviparous) princess Dejah Thoris. Starring different central characters, the series continued in *Thuvia, Maid of Mars* (1916 *All-Story Weekly*; **1920**), *The Chessmen of Mars* (**1922**), *The Master Mind of Mars* (**1928**), *A Fighting Man of Mars* (**1931**), *Swords of Mars* (**1936**), *Synthetic Men of Mars* (**1940**), *Llana of Gathol* (1941 *AMZ*; fixup **1948**) and *John Carter of Mars* (1941-3 *AMZ*; coll **1964**). "John Carter and the Giant of Mars", in the last volume, was originally written as a juvenile tale with ERB's son, John Coleman BURROUGHS, and was later expanded by ERB. The standard of storytelling and invention is high in the **Barsoom** books, *Chessmen* and *Swords* being particularly fine; but critics tend not to accept the series as good sf. Although Carter's adventures take place on another planet, he travels there by magical means, and Barsoom itself is inconsistent and scientifically implausible. It is clear, however, that ERB's immense popularity has nothing to do with conventional sf virtues, for it depends on storylines and venues as malleable as dreams, exotic and dangerous and unending.

The **Tarzan** saga is just as much sf (or non-sf) as the **Barsoom** series. Much influenced by H. Rider HAGGARD, ERB did not imitate one of that writer's prime virtues: his sense of reality. Tarzan's Africa is far removed from Allan Quatermain's, and has to be accepted as sheer fantasy, no more governed by the reality principle than Barsoom. *Tarzan of the Apes* (1912 *All-Story*; **1914**), the story of an English aristocrat's son raised in the jungle by "great apes" (of a nonexistent species), was immensely popular from the beginning, and ERB continued producing sequels to the end of his career. In most of them Tarzan has unashamedly fantastic adventures – discovering lost cities and live dinosaurs, being reduced to 18in (46cm) in height, visiting the Earth's core, etc. The early *The Return of Tarzan* (1913 *New Story*; **1915**), *The Beasts of Tarzan* (1914 *All-Story Cavalier*; **1916**), *The Son of Tarzan* (1915 *All-Story Cavalier*; **1917**) and *Tarzan and the Jewels of Opar* (1916 *All-Story Cavalier*; **1918**) are not among the best in the series, although *Jungle Tales of Tarzan* (coll **1919**; vt *Tarzan's Jungle Tales* 1961 UK) is cleverly reminiscent of Rudyard KIPLING's two *Jungle Books* (**1894**, **1895**). The best **Tarzan** novels came in the middle period: *Tarzan the Untamed* (coll of linked stories **1920**), *Tarzan the Terrible* (**1921**), *Tarzan and the Golden Lion* (**1923**), *Tarzan and the Ant Men* (**1924**; rev 1924), *Tarzan, Lord of the Jungle* (**1928**), *Tarzan and the Lost Empire* (**1929**) and *Tarzan at the Earth's Core* (**1930**). Later the series deteriorated, becoming ever more repetitive: *Tarzan the Invincible* (**1931**), *Tarzan Triumphant* (**1932**), *Tarzan and the City of Gold* (1931 *Argosy*; **1933**; cut 1952), *Tarzan and the Lion Man* (**1934**), *Tarzan and the Leopard Men* (**1935**), *Tarzan's Quest* (**1936**), *Tarzan and the Forbidden City* (**1938**; cut vt *Tarzan in the Forbidden City* 1940), *Tarzan the Magnificent* (fixup **1939**) and *Tarzan and the Foreign Legion* (**1947**). Two posthumous books are *Tarzan and the Madman* (**1964**) and *Tarzan and the Castaways* (1939-41 various mags; coll **1965**), neither of much merit. Two mildly interesting offshoots of the main series were *The Tarzan Twins* (**1927**; cut 1935; rev by other hands vt *Tarzan and the Tarzan Twins in the*

Jungle 1938) and its sequel, *Tarzan and the Tarzan Twins with Jad-Bal-Ja, the Golden Lion* (**1936**), both being assembled as *Tarzan and the Tarzan Twins* (omni **1963**). Despite ERB's overproduction, Tarzan is a remarkable creation, and possibly the best-known fictional character of the century. Part of Tarzan's fame is due to the many film adaptations, particularly those of the 1930s starring Johnny Weissmuller; none of these are very faithful to the books.

ERB's third major series, the **Pellucidar** novels based on the HOLLOW-EARTH theory of John Cleves SYMMES, began with *At the Earth's Core* (1914 *All-Story Weekly*; **1922**) and continued in *Pellucidar* (1915 *All-Story*; **1923**), *Tanar of Pellucidar* (**1930**), *Tarzan at the Earth's Core* (a notable "overlap" volume), *Back to the Stone Age* (**1937**), *Land of Terror* (**1944**) and *Savage Pellucidar* (1942 *AMZ*; fixup, incorporating 1 previously unpublished story, **1963**). Pellucidar is perhaps the best of ERB's locales – a world without time where dinosaurs and beast-men roam circularly forever – and is a perfect setting for bloodthirsty romantic adventure. The first of the series was filmed disappointingly as AT THE EARTH'S CORE (1976).

A fourth series, the **Venus** sequence – created much later in ERB's career – concerns the exploits of spaceman Carson Napier on VENUS, and consists of *Pirates of Venus* (1932 *Argosy*; **1934**), *Lost on Venus* (**1935**), *Carson of Venus* (**1939**) and *Escape on Venus* (1941-2 *Fantastic Adventures*; fixup **1946**). These books are not as stirring and vivid as the **Barsoom** series. A posthumous story, "The Wizard of Venus", was published in *Tales of Three Planets* (coll **1964**) and subsequently as the title story of a separate paperback, *The Wizard of Venus* (coll **1970**; vt *The Wizard of Venus and Pirate Blood* 1984). Two of the stories from *Tales of Three Planets*, "Beyond the Farthest Star" (1942) and the posthumous "Tangor Returns", form the opening of a fifth series which ERB abandoned. They are of interest because they are his only tales with an interstellar setting. The two stories were subsequently republished as a paperback entitled *Beyond the Farthest Star* (coll **1965**).

Of ERB's non-series tales, perhaps the finest is *The Land that Time Forgot* (1918 *Blue Book* in 3 parts; fixup **1924**; vt in 3 vols under original part-titles: *The Land that Time Forgot* 1982, *The People that Time Forgot* 1982 and *Out of Time's Abyss* 1982), set in the lost world of Caspak near the South Pole, and cunningly presenting in literal form – for animals here metamorphose through evolutionary stages – the dictum that ontogeny recapitulates phylogeny. The book was loosely adapted into two films, *The* LAND THAT TIME FORGOT (1975) and *The* PEOPLE THAT TIME FORGOT (1977). Also of interest is *The Moon Maid* (1923-25 *Argosy All-Story Weekly* as "The Moon Maid", "The Moon Men" and "The Red Hawk"; cut fixup 1926; vt *The Moon Men* 1962; vt in 2 vols and with text restored as *The Moon Maid* 1962 and *The Moon Men* 1962), which describes a civilization in the hollow interior of the MOON and a future INVASION of the Earth.

Among ERB's other books, those which can be claimed as sf are: *The Eternal Lover* (1914-15 *All-Story Weekly*; fixup **1925**; vt *The Eternal Savage* 1963), a prehistoric adventure involving TIME TRAVEL and featuring a character, Barney Custer, who reappears in the RURITANIAN *The Mad King* (1914-15 *All-Story Weekly*; fixup **1926**); *The Monster Men* (1913 *All-Story* as "A Man without a Soul"; **1929**), a reworking of the FRANKENSTEIN theme which should not be confused with *The Man without a Soul* (1916 *All-Story Weekly* as "The Return of the Mucker"; **1922** UK; vt *The Return of the Mucker* 1974 US), which is not fantasy or sf; *Jungle Girl* (**1932**; vt *Land of Hidden Men* 1963), about a lost civilization in Cambodia; *The Cave Girl* (1913-17 *All-Story Weekly*; fixup **1925**), another prehistoric romance; and *Beyond Thirty* (1916 *All Around Magazine*; **1957**; vt *The Lost Continent* 1963), a story set in the 22nd century after the collapse of European civilization.

It has often been said that ERB's works have small literary or intellectual merit. Nevertheless, because their lack of realistic referents frees them from time, because their efficient narrative style helps to compensate for their prudery and racism, and because ERB had a genius for the literalization of the dream, they have endured. His "rediscovery" during the 1960s was an astonishing publishing phenomenon, with the majority of his books being reprinted regularly. ERB has probably had more imitators than any other sf writer, ranging from Otis Adlebert KLINE in the 1930s to Kenneth BULMER (writing as Alan Burt Akers) in the 1970s, with even a much later writer like Terry BISSON homaging him in *Voyage to the Red Planet* (**1990**). There have been no "official" continuations of his series, however, with the exception of *Tarzan and the Valley of Gold* * (**1966**) by Fritz LEIBER and *Tarzan, King of the Apes* * (**1983**) by Joan D. VINGE, the latter being more accurately described as a rewriting. When some UK paperback firms, like CURTIS WARREN with **Azan the Apeman** (◊ Marco GARRON), attempted to capitalize on **Tarzan**, the ERB estate obtained injunctions halting publication. Later US attempts at similar series, like the **New Tarzan** books (1964-5) by Barton WERPER and *Tarzan at Mars' Core* (**1977**) by Edward Hirschman (1950-   ), were similarly dealt with. Serious sf writers who owe a debt to ERB include Leigh BRACKETT, Ray BRADBURY, Michael MOORCOCK (as Edward P. Bradbury) and, above all, Philip José FARMER, whose **Lord Grandrith** and **Ancient Opar** novels are among the most enjoyable latter-day Burroughsiana. [DP/JC]

About the author: *Golden Anniversary Bibliography of Edgar Rice Burroughs* (**1962**; rev 1964) by H.H. Heins; *Edgar Rice Burroughs: Master of Adventure* (**1965**; rev 1968) by Richard A. LUPOFF; *The Big Swingers* (**1967**) by Robert W. Fenton; "The Undisciplined Imagination: Edgar Rice Burroughs and Lowellian Mars" by R.D. MULLEN in *SF: The Other Side of Realism* (**1971**) ed Thomas D. CLARESON; *Tarzan Alive* (**1972**) by Philip José Farmer; *Edgar Rice Burroughs: The Man who*

Created Tarzan (**1975**) by Irwin Porges; *A Guide to Barsoom* (**1976**) by J.F. Roy; *Tarzan and Tradition: Classical Myth in Popular Literature* (**1981**) by E.B. Holtsmark.

See also: ALIENS; AMAZING STORIES; ANDROIDS; ANTHROPOLOGY; APES AND CAVEMEN (IN THE HUMAN WORLD); BOYS' PAPERS; COLLECTIONS; COMICS; CRYONICS; DIME-NOVEL SF; ECOLOGY; EVOLUTION; FANTASTIC VOYAGES; FANTASY; GAMES AND SPORTS; GAMES AND TOYS; HEROES; HISTORY OF SF; ISLANDS; JUPITER; LOST WORLDS; MUSIC; ORIGIN OF MAN; PARALLEL WORLDS; PASTORAL; PLANETARY ROMANCE; PULP MAGAZINES; RECURSIVE SF; SCIENTIFIC ERRORS; SENSE OF WONDER; SERIES; SEX; SPACESHIPS; SUSPENDED ANIMATION; SWORD AND SORCERY; TERRAFORMING; TRANSPORTATION; WAR; WEAPONS.

BURROUGHS, JOHN COLEMAN (1913-1979) US illustrator and writer, the younger son of Edgar Rice BURROUGHS and actively involved in his father's productions. He illustrated 13 of ERB's titles, and drew the weekly comic strip **John Carter of Mars** from Dec 1941 to its termination in 1943. This strip has been reproduced as *John Carter of Mars* (graph coll **1970**). JCB's sf novel, *Treasure of the Black Falcon* (**1967**), features undersea adventures and ALIEN contact. [JC]

BURROUGHS, WILLIAM S(EWARD) (1914-   ) US writer. Born into a successful business family, WSB was a Harvard graduate in English literature in 1936. A drop-out thereafter, he lived in Mexico, North Africa and the UK, and for many years was a heroin addict. He began writing in the late 1930s, but had no success until the early 1950s when he wrote two confessional books: *Junky* (**1953** as by William Lee; rev vt as by WSB *Junkie* 1977) and *Queer* (written 1950s; **1985**), which were respectively about drug-addiction and homosexuality, themes that have continued to dominate WSB's work. Although largely unpublished, WSB was immensely influential among the Beat writers of the 1950s – notably Jack Kerouac and Allen Ginsberg – and already had an underground reputation before the appearance of his first important book, *The Naked Lunch* (**1959** France; vt *Naked Lunch* 1962 US). This nightmarish SATIRE, first published by the daring and influential Olympia Press in Paris, contains large elements of sf – e.g., the DYSTOPIAS of "Freeland" and "Interzone", and some *outré* biological fantasy. Brilliantly written, funny and scatological, it is accepted as a modern classic; an inventive adaptation was filmed as *Naked Lunch* (1991) by David CRONENBERG. WSB's writings since are a bibliographer's despair, and no attempt can be made here to list all the pamphlets issued by various underground publishers. His major novels of this period, however, are *The Soft Machine* (**1961** France; rev 1966 US), *The Ticket that Exploded* (**1962** France; rev 1967 US), *Nova Express* (**1964**), *The Wild Boys: A Book of the Dead* (**1971**; rev 1979 UK) and *Exterminator!* (**1973**). In these works, WSB experimented with "cut-up" techniques, the importance of which has been overemphasized. More significant is the vividness of the imagery and the urgency of the subject matter.

Much concerned with the abuses of power, WSB uses addiction as an all-embracing metaphor for the ways in which our lives are controlled. He has also brought into luridly exemplary perspective many sf metaphors; e.g., the "Nova Mob", galactic gangsters who are taking over our planet. Images of space travel and "biomorphic horror" (J.G. Ballard's phrase) abound.

Later work has retained the corrosiveness of the worldview, but in narrations that verge, with some irony, towards the conventional. *Port of Saints* (**1973** Switzerland; rev 1980 US), *Cities of the Red Night* (**1981**) and *The Place of Dead Roads* (**1984**) can together be thought of as a kind of trilogy in which the genres of the West miscegenate, breed, and descry the road ahead. *Interzone* (coll **1989**) contains some surreal matter.

WSB has borrowed ideas from all areas of popular culture – films, COMICS, Westerns, sf – and the resulting powerful *mélange* has analogies with Pop Art. His influence can be detected in the sf of J.G. BALLARD, Michael MOORCOCK, John T. SLADEK, Norman SPINRAD and others. Overt pastiches of his work by sf writers include Barrington J. BAYLEY's "The Four-Colour Problem" (1971) and Philip José FARMER's "The Jungle Rot Kid on the Nod" (1968), the latter a **Tarzan** story in the manner of WSB rather than Edgar Rice BURROUGHS. [DP/JC]

Other works: *Dead Fingers Talk* (**1963** UK), a kind of alternative version of *The Naked Lunch*; *The Last Words of Dutch Schultz* (**1970** UK), a play; *Bladerunner: A Movie* (chap **1979**), nothing to do with the 1982 film BLADE RUNNER.

About the author: "Myth-Maker of the 20th Century" by J.G. Ballard in *NW* 142, 1964; "The Paris Review Interview" in *Writers at Work* (**1968**) ed George Plimpton; *The Job: Interview with William Burroughs* (**1969**) by Daniel Odier (trans **1970**); "Rub Out the Word" in *City of Words* (**1971**) by Tony Tanner; *Descriptive Catalogue of the WSB Archive* (**1973**) compiled by Miles Associates; *William Burroughs: The Algebra of Need* (**1977**) by Eric Mottram; *Literary Outlaw: The Life and Times of William S. Burroughs* (**1989**) by Ted Morgan.

See also: CYBERPUNK; MEDIA LANDSCAPE; MUSIC.

BUSBY, F(RANCIS) M(ARION) (1921-   ) US writer and long-time sf fan, co-editor with his wife Elinor Busby of the HUGO-winning FANZINE *Cry*, producing some of his early work as by Renfrew Pemberton. He began publishing sf stories with "A Gun for Grandfather" for *Future Science Fiction* in 1957, which appears in *Getting Home* (coll **1987**). He did not write any novels until much later, after attending the CLARION SCIENCE FICTION WRITERS' WORKSHOP in 1972, at which point he went freelance as a writer. His books began with the SPACE-OPERA **Demu** series about a hijacked human, Barton, and his war against the ALIEN Demu: *Cage a Man* (**1974**) and *The Proud Enemy* (**1975**), both assembled with the book-length "End of the Line" plus "The Learning of Eeshta" (1973) as *The*

Demu Trilogy (omni **1980**). The first, superior, instalment is particularly effective in its depiction of Barton's imprisonment and eventual escape. FMB's second sequence, which has shifted tone and protagonists over the years, began with *Rissa Kerguelen* (**1976**) and *The Long View* (**1976**), which two were actually a single extremely long novel and were republished as such, reset but apparently unaltered, as *Rissa Kerguelen* (**1977**; vt in 3 vols as *Young Rissa* [**1984**], *Rissa and Tregare* [**1984**] and the original second volume, *The Long View* [**1984**]). Ambitious, and featuring a rather diffuse character portrait of its female protagonist to justify its length, the **Rissa Kerguelen** story is, in essence, a stylistically awkward tale of bureaucratic oppression on Earth, flight to the stars, interstellar conflict and eventual revenge. The rhythm picks up somewhat but the portents of significance tend to fade in later volumes, which sooner or later connect with the earlier tale: *Zelde M'Tana* (**1980**), which is something of an offshoot, and the **Bran Tregare** novels, about Rissa's eventual husband: *The Star Rebel* (**1984**) and *Alien Debt* (**1984**), both assembled as *The Rebel Dynasty, Volume I* (omni **1987**); and *Rebel's Quest* (**1985**) and *Rebel's Seed* (**1986**), both assembled as *The Rebel Dynasty, Volume II* (omni **1988**). [JC]

Other works: *All These Earths* (fixup **1978**); *The Breeds of Man* (**1988**), about AIDS; *Slow Freight* (**1991**); *If This is Winnetka, You Must be Judy* (**1974** in *Universe 5* ed Terry CARR; **1992** chap).

See also: MEDICINE.

BUTLER, DAVID (1941-   ) UK writer whose first novel, *The Man who Mastered Time* (**1986**), rather ponderously confronts its protagonist, via TIME TRAVEL, with some revelations about the poetry of Samuel Taylor Coleridge. [JC]

BUTLER, JACK (1944-   ) US writer and college administrator. Most of JB's fiction – like his first novel, *Jujitsu for Christ* (**1986**) – has dealt with his native US South, but his second, *Nightshade* (**1989**), is a bravura and literate sf novel combining an effective presentation of human settlements on MARS with a scientific rationale for vampires – plus an examination of AI. Although the book shows a sophisticated knowledge of contemporary sf, JB's publishers marketed it for a non-genre audience. [GF]

BUTLER, JOAN ◊ Robert W. ALEXANDER.

BUTLER, NATHAN ◊ Jerry SOHL.

BUTLER, OCTAVIA E(STELLE) (1947-   ) US writer who began publishing sf with "Crossover" in *Clarion* (anth **1971**) ed Robin Scott WILSON, but who made no impact on the sf field until the first appearance of tales in the **Patternist** series: *Patternmaster* (**1976**), *Mind of my Mind* (**1977**), *Survivor* (**1978**), *Wild Seed* (**1980**) and *Clay's Ark* (**1984**). The order of publication has little to do with internal chronology; indeed, the first volume published stands last in a sequence that runs from the late 17th century into the FAR FUTURE. *Wild Seed*, which begins in 1690, demonstrates the very considerable strength of OEB's imagination in

being a prequel manifestly more interesting than much of the material it adumbrates. The setting is Africa. A 4000-year-old body-changer, Doro, who has been long engaged on a breeding programme designed to produce a race of superior humans with whom he can feel at home, selects for this purpose the "wild seed" shape-changer Anwanyu; their graphically ambivalent relationship is described in terms which potently evoke reflections on everything from family romance and SEX and FEMINISM to slavery itself (OEB is herself Black, and several of her novels directly and tellingly conflate this range of issues). Doro and his son both breed with Anwanyu, and found with her a sanctuary in New England and later in Louisiana where her MUTANT children can grow to adulthood. *Mind of my Mind*, set in contemporary California, focuses on the formal founding of the Patternist gestalt community, which begins to articulate itself into the hierarchical social organism of the final (though first-written) tale. *Survivor* takes place in a moderately distant future when Earth has become dominated by Patternists, whose hierarchies conflate family ties and a range of PSI POWERS into a complex whole. The novel depicts a conflict between star-travelling "mutes" – normal humans – and the ALIEN inhabitants of the planet to which, in a kind of missionary endeavour, they have been sent. *Clay's Ark*, set on Earth, depicts a conflict between those humans who have been transfigured by an extraterrestrial virus into intensely aggressive monsters and those, Patternist and mute, who have not been infected; an odour of plague invests the extraordinarily savage telling of this tale. In *Patternmaster*, Clayarks and Patternists continue what has become an age-long conflict, now brought to a head by a family dispute as to the proper inheritor of the role of Patternmaster: the one who wins will exercise paranormal control over the entire scene, making a Heaven or a Hell with his or her one voice. The strength of the **Patternist** books lies not in the sometimes routine premises laid down in the first published volume but in OEB's capacity to inhabit her venues with characters whose often anguished lives strike the reader as anything but frivolous.

One singleton appeared while the larger series was being published, and did not fail to be similarly harrowing. In *Kindred* (**1979**) a contemporary Black woman suffers a transition, by TIME TRAVEL, to the 19th-century South, where she becomes a slave: the nightmarishness of the concept alone is intensely educative in effect; the telling of the tale is just as effective. OEB has written few shorter stories, but those she has published are impressive. They include "Speech Sounds" (**1983**), which won a HUGO, "Bloodchild" (**1984**), which won a NEBULA, and *The Evening and the Morning and the Night* (**1987** Omni; **1991** chap).

Her main work of the 1980s was contained in a second sequence, the **Xenogenesis** books: *Dawn* (**1987**), *Adulthood Rites* (**1987**) and *Imago* (**1989**), all three being assembled as *Xenogenesis* (omni **1989**).

Thematic likenesses with the previous series – once again the human race is subjected to an intense breeding programme – are evident, but prove of little importance, for the **Xenogenesis** books are very differently told. The human race has managed to almost entirely destroy itself and its planet, and only a few relics have survived in SUSPENDED ANIMATION aboard the great interstellar ship of the visiting three-sexed, exogamous, gene-trading Oankali, who reawake selected humans in order to breed with them. Much of the plot takes place on a rehabilitated segment of Earth, but the action there is arguably peripheral to the exposition of the central concept: the presentation of a convincingly alien species, and the marriage of that species to those humans who can abandon the territoriality/aggression knot which has proven to be a fatal evolutionary dead-end.

At times OEB tends to succumb to the exigencies of GENRE-SF plotting, but again and again, in both her main series and in her shorter work, clarity burns through. [JC]

See also: IMMORTALITY; ISAAC ASIMOV'S SCIENCE FICTION MAGAZINE; MEDICINE; PARASITISM AND SYMBIOSIS.

BUTLER, SAMUEL (1835-1902) UK writer, educated at Cambridge, never married, emigrated to live in New Zealand 1859-64, best known for his posthumously published autobiographical novel, *The Way of all Flesh* (**1903**), which describes the conflict between SB and his minister father, the conflict that also provided much of the force of the SATIRE on RELIGION in his two UTOPIAS, *Erewhon, or Over the Range* (**1872**; rev 1872; rev 1901) and *Erewhon Revisited* (**1901**), in which the Musical Banks closely resemble the 19th-century Established Church. *Erewhon* and its sequel are set in a New Zealand utopia where MACHINES have been banned for many years, because (in a harsh parody of Darwin's theory of EVOLUTION, which SB disliked) of human fears that machines, in their rapid evolutionary progress, would soon supplant Man. The visitor to this utopia – which mixes DYSTOPIAN elements freely with its more attractive aspects – is named Higgs, and his eventual escape from Erewhon in a balloon triggers a new religion in that country, Sunchildism. The sequel is devoted mainly to this faith and Higgs's effect upon it on his return, in an analogical satire on Christianity's origins and growth and the legend of the Second Coming. SB was a compulsive speculator in and chivvier at ideas, and his two utopias are densely packed with parodic commentary on all aspects of 19th-century civilization. The calibre of his mind is indicated by his suggested modification to Darwin's theory – that more than chance was required to explain the variations that make for survival. In this he prefigured some of Darwin's own later thought, though generally his anti-Darwinian propaganda displayed a cavalier attitude to scientific evidence. [JC/DIM]

See also: ANONYMOUS SF AUTHORS; AUTOMATION; HISTORY OF SF; HUMOUR; MUSIC; NEW ZEALAND; PROTO SCIENCE FICTION; TECHNOLOGY.

BUTLER, WILLIAM (1929-) US author best known for non-genre novels. *The Butterfly Revolution* (**1962**), which is sf, depicts a 1960s-based nightmare of what happens to the world in the absence of adults. [JC]

Other works: *The House at Akiya* (**1963**), a ghost story; *Mr Three* (**1964**).

BUTOR, MICHEL (1926-) French critic and novelist, principally known as a leading exponent of the *nouveau roman*. MB was one of the first mainstream and academic critics to consider sf seriously according to the same standards as general literature. He published an invigorating analysis of Jules VERNE as early as 1949, and examined the dilemmas and future potential of the field in his penetrating study, "La crise de croissance de la SF" (1953); this was first trans by Richard Howard as "SF: The Crisis of its Growth" for *Partisan Review* in 1967, and, as "The Crisis in the Growth of Science Fiction", appeared along with "The Golden Age in Jules Verne" (trans by Patricia Dreyfus for *Repertoire* [coll **1960**]) in *Inventory* (coll trans **1968** US). MB has served on the jury panel of the Prix Apollo (◊ AWARDS). [MJ]

See also: CRITICAL AND HISTORICAL WORKS ABOUT SF.

BUTTERWORTH, MICHAEL (1947-) UK writer, editor – in the latter capacity initially of the semi-professional underground magazine *Corridors*, later called *Wordworks* – and cofounder and codirector with David BRITTON of Savoy Books. He began publishing sf with "Girl" for *NW* in 1966, and contributed regularly to the magazine for the rest of its existence. He began publishing novels with the first of the **Hawklords** sequence, *The Time of the Hawklords* (**1976**), with Michael MOORCOCK credited on the title-page and cover as co-author, though the "List of Credits" at the end of the volume lists Moorcock as Producer/Director and MB as Writer; MB was fundamentally responsible for the book, as well as for its sequel, *Queens of Deliria* (**1977**), with Moorcock also credited (this time unwillingly). The sequence, based on the real-life rock group Hawkwind, focuses on an electronic instrument that allays all pain and tension. With Britton, MB co-edited two defiant anthologies drawn from the world of Savoy Books, a firm which more than once suffered in the Manchester police force's battle against "obscenity": *The Savoy Book* (anth **1978**) and *Savoy Dreams* (anth **1984**). [JC]

Other works: A sequence tied to the second season of SPACE 1999, comprising: *Planets of Peril* ∗ (**1977**), *Mind-Breaks of Space* ∗ (**1977**) with Jeff Jones, *The Space-Jackers* ∗ (**1977**), *The Psychomorph* ∗ (**1977**), *The Time Fighters* ∗ (**1977**) and *The Edge of the Infinite* ∗ (**1977**).

BUZZATI, DINO (1906-1972) Italian writer and journalist. From his first unsettling children's stories in the 1930s he was noted for the KAFKA-like anxiety riddling his apparently simple plots. *Catastrophe* (original stories 1949-58; coll trans Judith Landry and Cynthia Jolly **1965** UK) is perhaps the most fully successful volume issued during his life; many of its stories are surrealist fables, always with a parable-like moral edge. Later selections, which intensify a sense of the claustrophobia of worlds about to collapse like eggshells into chaos, are *Restless Nights: Selected Stories* (coll trans Lawrence Venuti **1983** US) and *The Siren: A Selection* (coll trans Lawrence Venuti **1984** US). In *Il Grande Ritratto* (**1960**; trans Henry Reed as *Larger than Life* **1962** UK), a full-length novel and rather less successful, a not very convincingly described COMPUTER complex is programmed with the personality of a woman. [JC]

Other works: *Il Deserto dei Tartari* (**1940**; trans S.C. Hood as *The Tartar Steppe* **1952** UK).

See also: ITALY.

BYRNE, STUART J(AMES) (1913-   ) US writer who began publishing sf with "Music of the Spheres" for *AMZ* in 1935. He was intermittently active after WWII in the magazines, sometimes writing as John Bloodstone, a name he used also for some routine sf adventures, including *The Golden Gods* (**1957**), *Children of the Chronotron* (**1966**), *Godman!* (**1970**) and *Thundar, Man of Two Worlds* (**1971**). As SJB he wrote *The Metamorphs* (**1959**), *Starman* (**1969**), *The Alpha Trap* (**1976**) and *Star Man: The Universe Builder* (coll of linked stories **1980**). [JC]

BY ROCKET TO THE MOON ◊ *Die* FRAU IM MOND.

BYRON PREISS VISUAL PUBLICATIONS INC ◊ Byron PREISS.

BYWATER, HECTOR CHARLES (1884-1940) US writer of works on the nature and history of sea-power, and of a future-WAR novel on the same theme, *The Great Pacific War: A History of the American-Japanese Campaign of 1931-1933* (**1925**), which quite remarkably underestimates the Japanese. In his *Bywater: The Man who Invented the Pacific War* (**1990**), William H. Honan suggests that Admiral Yamamoto read *The Great Pacific War* in the 1920s and used it as a blueprint for his eventual attack on Pearl Harbor. [JC]

CABELL, JAMES BRANCH (1879-1958) US writer, mostly of mannered, witty and in later life sometimes rather enervated ALTERNATE-WORLD fantasies, a large number of which he assimilated, in some cases long after they were first published, as episodes in the **Biography of the Life of Manuel**. The imaginary kingdom of Poictesme is a central thread running through the more than 20 volumes of the series, and ties the whole – however arbitrarily – into a consistent purview. The stated (but not chronologically consistent) proper ordering of the sequence is: *Beyond Life* (**1919**), *Figures of Earth* (**1921**); *The Silver Stallion* (**1926**); *The Music from Behind the Moon* (**1926**) and *The White Robe* (**1928**), both assembled along with *The Way of Ecben* (**1928**) as *The Witch-Woman* (omni **1948**); *The Soul of Melicent* (**1913**; rev vt *Domnei* 1920); *Chivalry* (**1909**; rev 1921); *Jurgen* (**1919**); *The Line of Love* (coll of linked stories **1905**; rev 1921); *The High Place* (**1923**); *Gallantry* (**1907**; rev 1928); *Something about Eve* (**1927**); *The Certain Hour* (**1916**); *The Cords of Vanity* (**1909**; rev 1920); *From the Hidden Way* (**1916**; rev 1924); *The Jewel Merchants* (**1921**); *The Rivet in Grandfather's Neck* (**1915**); *The Eagle's Shadow* (**1904**; rev 1923); *The Cream of the Jest* (**1917**); *The Lineage of Lichfield* (**1922**); *Straws and Prayer-Books* (**1924**). A second series – *Smirt* (**1934**), *Smith* (**1935**) and *Smire* (**1937**), assembled as *The Nightmare has Triplets* (omni **1972**) – carries the eponym (who is three in one) ever downwards, through universes and incarnations: the effect is ironical.

JBC suffered from over-attention after the prosecution of *Jurgen* (most implausibly) for obscenity, and after his subsequent fame and neglect his more recent advocates – like James BLISH, who was for some time editor of the Cabell Society journal *Kalki* – perhaps argued too strenuously for his rehabilitation. By now, however, his place in US fiction is secure though not central. His relevance to sf proper derives from his engagingly haughty use of sf tropes – alternate worlds, DYSTOPIAS and UTOPIAS, TIME TRAVEL, and even the building of planets.   [JC]

Other works: *Taboo* (**1921** chap); *These Restless Heads* (**1932**); *The King was in his Counting House* (**1938**); *Hamlet had an Uncle* (**1940**); *The First Gentleman of America* (**1942**); *There Were Two Pirates* (**1946**) and a linked tale, *The Devil's Own Dear Son* (**1949**).

About the author: *James Branch Cabell* (**1962**) by Joe Lee Davis; *James Branch Cabell: A Complete Bibliography* (**1974**) by James N. Hall; *James Branch Cabell: Centennial Essays* (anth **1983**) ed M. Thomas Inge and Edgar E. MacDonald.

See also: FANTASY; GODS AND DEMONS; SWORD AND SORCERY.

CABOT, JOHN YORK [s] ◊ David Wright O'BRIEN.

CADIGAN, PAT Working name of US writer Patricia K. Cadigan (1953-   ), who began publishing sf with "Death from Exposure" for SHAYOL in 1978; this SEMIPROZINE, which she edited throughout its existence (1977-85), was remarkable both for the quality of stories it published and for its production values. She later assembled much of her best shorter work in *Patterns* (coll **1989**), where its cumulative effect is very considerable. From the beginning, PC has been a writer who makes use of her venues – usually NEAR-FUTURE, usually urban, and usually Californian – as highly charged gauntlets which her protagonists do not so much run as cling to, surviving somehow. It was an effect also to be found in the stories assembled in *Letters from Home* (coll **1991** UK) with Karen Joy FOWLER and Pat MURPHY, each contributing her own tales.

Unfortunately PC's first novel, *Mindplayers* (fixup **1987**), failed to sustain the intensity of her shorter work, treating in simplistic fashion a vision of the human mind as constituted of sequences of internal psychodramas into which a healer may literally enter, given the proper tools. The idea, which had been intensely and punishingly examined by Roger ZELAZNY in *The Dream Master* (**1966**), is not in any sense sophisticated by the can-do METAPHYSIC underlying the premise as PC described it 20 years later.

Her next novel, *Synners* (**1991**), on the other hand, takes full advantage of its considerable length to translate the street-wise, CYBERPUNK involvedness of her best short fiction into a comprehensive vision – racingly told, linguistically acute, simultaneously pell-mell and precise in its detailing – of a world dominated by the intricacies of the human/COMPUTER interface. The plot, which is extremely complicated, deals mainly with a disease of the interface, where computer viruses which pass for AIS are beginning to cause numerous human deaths. Like William GIBSON's cyberpunk novels – and unlike Bruce STERLING's – *Synners* offers no sense that the CONCEPTUAL BREAKTHROUGHS that proliferate throughout the text will in any significant sense transform the overwhelming urbanized world, though there is some hint that the system may begin to fail through its own internal imbalances. But at the heart of *Synners* is the burning presence of the future. One of the most acutely intelligent of 1980s writers, PC currently seems to be learning from everything. [JC]

Other works: *My Brother's Keeper* (**1988** *IASFM*; **1992** chap).

See also: MACHINES; PSYCHOLOGY.

CADY, JACK (**1932-**   ) US writer, almost exclusively of horror, although one novel, *The Man who Could Make Things Vanish* (**1982**), is a genuine sf DYSTOPIA set in a very bleakly conceived NEAR-FUTURE right-wing USA. [JC]

Other works: *The Well* (**1980**); *The Jonah Watch* (**1981**); *McDowell's Ghost* (**1981**).

CAIDIN, MARTIN (**1927-**   ) US writer, pilot and aerospace specialist, who has written over 80 nonfiction books, some for the juvenile market, mostly on aviation and space exploration, beginning with *Jets, Rockets and Guided Missiles* (**1950**; rev vt *Rockets and Missiles* 1954) with David C. Cooke and continuing with texts like *War for the Moon* (**1959**; vt *Race for the Moon* 1960 UK) and *I am Eagle* (**1962**) with G.S. Titov, the Soviet astronaut. MC's own firm, Martin Caidin Associates, was designed to provide information and other services to radio and tv in the areas of his special knowledge; he founded the American Astronautical Society in 1953. He began publishing sf with *The Long Night* (**1956**), in which a US city is firebombed, and gained considerable success with *Marooned* (**1964**), later filmed as MAROONED (1969) with Gregory Peck. Like much of his fiction, *Marooned* deals with realistically depicted NEAR-FUTURE crises in space, in this case the need to rescue astronauts trapped in orbit; it has been credited with inspiring the 1975 US-USSR Apollo-Soyuz joint mission. *Four Came Back* (**1968**) deals with human difficulties (and a mysterious plague) aboard a space platform. A series of CYBORG adventures – *Cyborg* (**1972**), *Operation Nuke* (**1973**), *High Crystal* * (**1974**) and *Cyborg IV* (**1975**) – served as inspiration and basis for the successful tv series *The* SIX MILLION DOLLAR MAN and its spin-off *The* BIONIC WOMAN; a later story, *ManFac* (**1981**) also presents an enforced intimacy between human and machine in unambiguously positive terms. MC's stories combine considerable storytelling drive with expertly integrated technical information, and tend to be rather more convincing, therefore, than the tv and film derivations they have inspired. [JC]

Other works: *No Man's World* (**1967**); *The Last Fathom* (**1967**); *The God Machine* (**1968**); *The Mendelov Conspiracy* (**1969**; vt *Encounter Three* 1978); *Anytime, Anywhere* (**1969**); *The Cape* (**1971**); *Almost Midnight* (**1971**); *Maryjane Tonight at Angels Twelve* (**1972**); *Destination Mars* (**1972**); *When War Comes* (**1972**); *Three Corners to Nowhere* (**1975**); *Whip* (**1976**); *Aquarius Mission* (**1978**); *Jericho 52* (**1979**); *Star Bright* (**1980**); *Killer Station* (**1985**); *The Messiah Stone* (**1986**) and its sequel, *Dark Messiah* (**1990**); *Zoboa* (**1986**); *Exit Earth* (**1987**); *Prison Ship* (**1989**); *Beamriders!* (**1989**; vt *Beamriders* 1990 UK).

See also: COMPUTERS; CYBERNETICS; UFOS; UNDER THE SEA.

CAINE, [Sir] (THOMAS HENRY) HALL (1853-1931) UK writer of what were enormously bestselling novels in the late 19th century but were almost forgotten by his death. *The Mahdi, or Love and Race* (**1894**) depicts a NEAR-FUTURE uprising at the behest of the eponymous leader of the faithful. *The Eternal City* (**1901**), printed in a first edition of 100,000, sets a complex near-future intrigue alight in a Pope-dominated Rome. *The White Prophet* (**1909**), again marginally displaced into the future, is set in Egypt, where intrigue is rife. A play, *The Prime Minister* (written c1911; **1918**), set in the future, depicts romance threatening policy. [JC]

CALDWELL, (JANET MIRIAM) TAYLOR (HOLLAND) (1900-1985) US popular novelist whose first sf novel, *The Devil's Advocate* (**1952**), though set in 1970, is in effect a right-wing denunciation of the New Deal of the 1930s. Her second effort, *Your Sins and Mine* (**1955**), is fundamentally FANTASY, in that the devastating drought inflicted by the Lord upon the world for its sins can be removed by assiduous prayer. She was also responsible for fantasies like *The Listener* (**1960**) and its sequel, *No One Hears but Him* (**1966**), and *Dialogues with the Devil* (**1967**). *The Romance of Atlantis* (**1975**), with Jess Stearn, is based on a novel she first wrote when aged 12; TC claimed that it in turn was based on her childhood dreams of her previous incarnation (◊ REINCARNATION) as an empress in ATLANTIS. [JC]

CALISHER, HORTENSE (**1911-**   ) US writer of several MAINSTREAM novels set mostly on the US East Coast. After an sf allegory, "In the Absence of Angels" (**1951**), which associates the military occupation of the USA with a poet's own imprisonment, came her sf novel *Journal from Ellipsia* (**1965**), which depicts a somewhat metaphysical ALTERNATE WORLD where everything – as in E.M. FORSTER's famous dictum – connects with everything, especially the transcendental sex that permeates the narrative. [JC]

Other work: *Mysteries of Motion* (**1983**).

CALKINS, DICK (1895-1962) US COMIC-strip illustrator from Grand Rapids who studied at the Art Institute in Chicago. In 1929 Philip NOWLAN scripted and DC illustrated BUCK ROGERS IN THE 25TH CENTURY, a comic strip based on Nowlan's "Armageddon: 2419 AD" (1928 *AMZ*) and "The Airlords of Han" (1929 *AMZ*), later published together as *Armageddon – 2419 AD* (**1962**). Though DC's style was stiff and amateurish by today's standards, the strip was extremely popular in the 1930s and 1940s. Its quality improved when Rick Yager joined him in some of the chores from the 1930s; Yager succeeded DC at his retirement in 1948. The artwork was never sophisticated, but DC's strong, simple lines were well suited to fast-paced narrative. A selection of **Buck Rogers** adventures has been reissued as *The Collected Works of Buck Rogers in the 25th Century* (coll **1969**; rev 1977) ed Robert C. Dille. [JG/PN]

See also: ILLUSTRATION; RADIO.

CALLAHAN, WILLIAM ◊ Raymond Z. GALLUN.

CALLENBACH, ERNEST (1929-   ) US environmentalist and writer whose own Banyan Tree Books published his first novel, *Ecotopia: The Notebooks and Reports of William Weston* (1974 *American Review* as "First Days in Ecotopia"; exp **1975**), after it had been refused by several professional houses; it was reported in the mid-1980s to have sold more than 300,000 copies, which should come as no surprise given the reasoned seductiveness of the UTOPIA premised in its pages. As of 1999, Washington, Oregon and Northern California have been in secession from the rest of the USA for almost two decades. The reporter William Weston is allowed within the borders to make contact with (and if possible to subvert) the Ecotopians. He finds irresistible the balance of life there, the manner in which the new state has tamed the juggernaut of TECHNOLOGY, and the refusal of its citizens to cost the world more than they give the world; and he, too, becomes an Ecotopian. *Ecotopia Emerging* (**1981**) is both a prequel and a kind of sequel to the previous book – a prequel in its long and persuasively detailed presentation of the Ecotopian route to secession, and the enormous power engendered by the (sf-like) discovery of a cheap solar-energy catalyst; but a "sequel" by virtue of treating the earlier book as being itself the inspiration for the emergence, in our world, of a "real" Ecotopia. Unfortunately for what may be guessed to have been EC's real-life hopes, a decade has passed since his second attempt at arousal.

Nonfiction texts which elaborate on some of the procedures and theories of the fiction include *The Ecotopian Encyclopedia for the 80s: A Survival Guide for the Age of Inflation* (**1980**) and *A Citizen Legislature* (**1985**). [JC]

CALVERT, THOMAS [s] ◊ Thomas Calvert MCCLARY.

CALVINO, ITALO (1923-1985) Italian novelist, born in Cuba, active since the end of WWII, at first with realist works but soon with GOTHIC, surrealist romances of great vigour and impact like *Il Visconte dimezzato* (**1952**) and *Il Cavaliere inesistente* (**1959**) – trans together by A. Colquhoun as *The Non-Existent Knight and The Cloven Viscount* **1962** UK) – and *Il Barone rampante* (**1957**; trans A. Colquhoun as *Baron of the Trees* **1959** UK), three thematically linked fables later assembled as *I nostri antenati* (omni **1960**; in the Colquhoun trans as *Our Ancestors* 1980 US). A more recent venture in the same idiom is *Il Castello dei Destini incrociati* (coll of linked stories **1973**; trans William Weaver as *The Castle of Crossed Destinies* **1977** US). Beneath the FABULATION-drenched protocols of these stories – the nonexistent knight, for instance, being an empty suit of armour with a "passion" for the formalities and ceremonies that keeps it "alive" – lies a concern for fundamental problems of being. IC's works closest to sf are the two linked volumes *Le Cosmicomiche* (coll of linked stories **1965**; trans William Weaver as *Cosmicomics* **1968** US) and *Ti con zero* (coll of linked stories **1967**; trans William Weaver as *t zero* **1969** US; vt *Time and the Hunter* 1970 UK); both volumes feature and are told by the presence called Qfwfq, who is the same age as the Universe. The various stories express in emblematic form speculations and fables about the nature of life, EVOLUTION, reality and so forth; they are witty, moving and, after their strange fashion, effectively didactic. One of the stories in *The Watcher and Other Stories* (1952-63; coll trans William Weaver **1971** US), "Smog" (1958), a remarkable POLLUTION tale, is sf. *Le città invisibili* (**1972**; trans William Weaver as *Invisible Cities* **1974** US) frames fragmented versions of Marco Polo's narrative of his voyages with a remarkable set of meditations ostensibly triggered by the distant, surrealistic CITIES he visits. *Se una notte d'inverno un viaggiatore* (**1979**; trans William Weaver as *If on a Winter's Night a Traveler* **1981** US) stunningly transfigures the conventions and momentums of narrative into a Buñuelesque labyrinth. IC's powers of invention were formally ingenious; at the same time he was an extremely lucid writer. His use of sf subjects and their intermixing with a whole array of contemporary literary devices made him a figure of considerable interest for the future of the genre. [JC]

See also: COSMOLOGY; ITALY; ORIGIN OF MAN; OULIPO.

CAMERON, BERL House name used for sf novels published by CURTIS WARREN and written by John S. GLASBY, Brian HOLLOWAY, Dennis HUGHES, David O'BRIEN and Arthur ROBERTS. [JC]

CAMERON, ELEANOR (BUTLER) (1912-   ) Canadian-born US writer whose career has been exclusively devoted to children's literature, and who received the National Book Award in 1974 for one of her finer fantasies, *The Court of the Stone Children* (**1973**); its sequel was *To the Green Mountains* (**1975**). She remains perhaps best known for the sf **Mushroom Planet** sequence with which she began her career: *The Wonderful Flight to the Mushroom Planet* (**1954**), *Stowaway to the Mushroom Planet* (**1956**), *Mr Bass's Planetoid* (**1958**), *A Mystery for Mr Bass* (**1960**) and *Time and Mr Bass* (**1967**). At the heart of the series is Mr Bass, whose mysterious filter permits his young friends – who have built him a SPACESHIP for the purpose of travelling there – to perceive the planet Basidium. Though perhaps slightly wholesome, the adventures of Bass and his companions on Basidium became, with justice, extremely popular. [JC]

Other works: *The Terrible Churnadryne* (**1959**); *The Mysterious Christmas Shell* (**1961**); *The Beast with the Magical Horn* (**1963**); *A Spell is Cast* (**1964**); *Beyond Silence* (**1980**), a timeslip fantasy.

CAMERON, IAN Pseudonym of UK writer Donald Gordon Payne (1924-   ), author of *The Lost Ones* (**1961**; vt *The Island at the Top of the World* 1974 US) and *The Mountains at the Bottom of the World* (**1972** US; vt *Devil Country* 1976 UK). The former, under what became as a result the later UK vt, was filmed by Disney in 1973. The mechanics of IC's plots derive from LOST-WORLD conventions generally – and, in the case of the second novel, from Conan DOYLE specifically. *Star-Raker* (**1962**), as by Donald Gordon, is a straightforward adventure. With George Erskine, he wrote two **Counter Force** tales, *Beware the Tektrons* (**1988**) and *Find the Tektrons* (**1988**). Payne has also written mainstream fiction as James Vance Marshall. [JC/PN]

Other work: *The White Ship* (**1975**).

CAMERON, JAMES (1956-   ) US film-maker. Originally a special-effects man and art director with Roger CORMAN's New World – where he worked on BATTLE BEYOND THE STARS (1980), ANDROID (1982) and several others including ESCAPE FROM NEW YORK (1981) for which New World did the special effects – JC made an inauspicious début as director with *Piranha II: Flying Killers* (1981; vt *Piranha II: The Spawning*; ◊ PIRANHA). However, he made a major impression with his second film, The TERMINATOR (1984), a TIME-TRAVEL thriller with a killer ROBOT. This low-budget success secured JC – and his then wife and producer-writer partner Gale Anne HURD – the plum assignment of ALIENS (1986), the follow-up to Ridley SCOTT's ALIEN (1979). Having improved on the original – especially in his 150min director's cut, later released on video – with this humanistic action movie of alien warfare, JC achieved a free hand with The ABYSS (1989), the most expensive of several underwater sf movies released at that time, and managed four-fifths of an excellent film before fumbling with a climactic deep-sea close encounter; it was a box-office disappointment. Following this JC separated personally from Hurd – who had in the meantime produced ALIEN NATION (1988) and TREMORS (1990) – although the couple stayed together to direct and produce TERMINATOR 2: JUDGMENT DAY (1991), a huge-budgeted box-office success, perhaps the most violent pacifist movie ever made. [KN/PN]

See also: CINEMA; HORROR IN SF.

CAMERON, J.D. A house name used by BPVP (◊ Byron PREISS) for the **Omega Sub** sequence of post-HOLOCAUST military-sf adventures about the crew of a nuclear sub which survives the final war. The series comprises *Omega Sub #1: Omega Sub* * (**1991**) by Mike JAHN, *#2: Command Decision* * (**1991**) by David ROBBINS,

#3: City of Fear * (**1991**) by Jahn, *#4: Blood Tide* * (**1991**) and *#5: Death Dive* * (**1992**), both by Robbins. [JC]

CAMERON, JOHN (1927-   ) US writer. His borderline sf novel, *The Astrologer* (**1972**), like *The Child* (**1976**) by John Symonds (1914-   ), deals with a new Virgin Mary and a new Virgin Birth, in this case discovered via astrological means (◊ ASTRONOMY; MESSIAHS). [JC]

See also: PSEUDO-SCIENCE; RELIGION.

CAMERON, JULIE ◊ Lou CAMERON.

CAMERON, LOU (1924-   ) US illustrator and writer, active in comic books in the 1950s. His sf, which was unremarkable, included two **Swinging Spy** tales – *The Spy with the Blue Kazoo* (**1967**) and *The Sky who Came in from the Copa* (**1967**) – as by Dagmar, and *Cybernia* (**1972**), as LC, which expresses COMPUTER paranoia through the tale of a town in the grips of a mad brain. *The Darklings* (**1975**), as by Julie Cameron, is fantasy. [JC]

CAMPANELLA, TOMMASO (1568-1639) Italian philosopher, admitted into the Dominican order at the age of 15. Like Francis BACON he attacked the reliance of contemporary science on the authority of Aristotle, advocating observation and experiment as the proper routes to knowledge in *Philosophia Sensibus Demonstrata* (**1591**; in Latin). His important UTOPIA, *Civitas Solis* (1st MS 1602; 2nd MS 1612; **1623** in Latin; 3rd MS 1637; cut trans Henry Morley as *The City of the Sun* in *Ideal Commonwealths*, coll **1885**, ed Morley) was written while he was imprisoned by the Spanish Inquisition, accused of having led a revolt in his native Calabria, then under Spanish rule. The book describes a city with seven concentric circular walls which is ruled by a philosopher-king, the *Hoh* or *Metaphysicus*; property is held in common and the elements of science are inscribed on the walls for educational purposes; flying machines and ships without sails are mentioned in passing. [BS]

See also: CITIES; FANTASTIC VOYAGES; ITALY.

CAMPBELL, CLYDE CRANE [s] ◊ H.L. GOLD.

CAMPBELL, DAVID [s] ◊ Leonard G. FISH.

CAMPBELL, H(ERBERT) J. (1925-   ) UK research chemist, writer and editor. He was active during the early 1950s as a fan. After writing some science articles he gradually branched out into the world of sf, as well as selling line drawings to many magazines, including *Amateur Photographer* and *Television Weekly*. He scripted the *Daily Herald* cartoon series **Captain Universe** and served as technical editor and then editor 1952-6 of AUTHENTIC SCIENCE FICTION, contributing many scientific articles to the magazine, which in general improved under his editorship. He also edited *Tomorrow's Universe* (anth **1953**), *Sprague de Camp's New Anthology* (coll **1953** UK) and *Authentic Book of Space* (anth **1954**), which last was a mixture of articles and stories. Increased pressure of research work forced him to leave the field in 1956; he gained a PhD in Chemistry in 1957, and from that point concentrated on writing textbooks.

His own fiction was not, perhaps, of substantial

interest, but his work was never incompetent. Novels published under his own name include *The Last Mutation* (**1951**), *The Moon is Heaven* (**1951**), a RECURSIVE tale which includes a portrait of Arthur C. CLARKE, *World in a Test Tube* (**1951**), *Beyond the Visible* (**1952**), *Chaos in Miniature* (**1952**), *Mice – Or Machines* (**1952**), *Another Space – Another Time* (**1953**), *Brain Ultimate* (**1953**), *The Red Planet* (**1953**) and *Once Upon a Space* (**1954**). Under the house name Roy SHELDON he wrote the **Magdah** sequence – *Mammoth Man* (**1952**), *Two Days of Terror* (**1952**), *Moment out of Time* (**1952**) and *The Menacing Sleep* (**1952**) – and the **Shiny Spear** sequence – *Atoms in Action* (**1953**) and *House of Entropy* (**1953**). It is probable, though not certain, that he also wrote most or all of the remaining Roy Sheldon novels (with the exception of *The Metal Eater*, **1954**, which was by E.C. TUBB): *Gold Men of Aureus* (**1951**), *Phantom Moon* (**1951**), *Energy Alive* (**1951**), *Beam of Terror* (**1951**), *Spacewarp* (**1952**) and *The Plastic Peril* (**1952**). [SH/MJE]

See also: ENTROPY; GREAT AND SMALL.

CAMPBELL, JOHN W(OOD) Jr (1910-1971) US writer and editor who took a degree in physics in 1932 from MIT and Duke University. JWC was a devotee of the SF MAGAZINES from their inception, and sold his first stories while still a teenager, beginning with "Invaders from the Infinite" to AMAZING STORIES; however, the manuscript was lost by editor T. O'Conor SLOANE, so it was his second sale, "When the Atoms Failed" (1930), that became his first published story.

In the early 1930s JWC quickly built a reputation as E.E. "Doc" SMITH's chief rival in writing galactic epics of superscience. The most popular of these was the **Arcot, Morey and Wade** series, in which the heroes faced a succession of battles of ever-increasing size fought with a succession of wonderful weapons of ever-decreasing likelihood. Initially published in various magazines from 1930, they were put into book form as *The Black Star Passes* (fixup **1953**), *Islands of Space* (1931 *Amazing Stories Quarterly*; **1957**) and *Invaders from the Infinite* (not his first, lost story) (1932 *Amazing Stories Quarterly*; **1961**); all were assembled as *A John W. Campbell Anthology* (omni **1973**). Also well received was *The Mightiest Machine* (1934 *ASF*; **1947**), but three sequels featuring its hero **Aarn Munro** were rejected by *ASF*'s editor F. Orlin TREMAINE, eventually appearing in *The Incredible Planet* (coll **1949**).

The second phase of JWC's career as a writer began with "Twilight" (1934), a tale of the FAR FUTURE written in a moody, "poetic" style, the first of a number of stories, far more literary in tone and varied in mood, published under the pseudonym Don A. Stuart. From now on, JWC wrote little sf under his own name, preferring to concentrate on the highly popular Stuart stories; exceptions included the **Penton and Blake** series published in *TWS* in 1936-8 and collected in *The Planeteers* (coll **1966** dos), and, on one occasion, the use of the name Karl Van Campen for a story in an issue of *ASF* that already contained a Stuart story

and part of a JWC novel. He was by now becoming closely identified with Tremaine's *ASF*, where all the Stuart stories appeared; these included the **Machine** series: "The Machine", "The Invaders" and "Rebellion" (all 1935). In 1936 he began, under his own name, a series of 18 monthly articles on the Solar System, and from 1937 he also published a number of articles as Arthur McCann. The climax of his popularity came with a Stuart effort, *The Thing from Another World* (1938 *ASF* as "Who Goes There?"; **1952** chap Australia), a classic sf horror story about an Antarctic research station menaced by a shape-changing ALIEN invader, which was first filmed, without the shape-changing, as *The* THING (1951), and later, also as *The* THING (1982), with the basic premise restored. Far more famous under its original title than under the film-influenced book retitling, "Who Goes There?" was not only the climax of his writing career but also effectively marked its end. Two collections were assembled to take advantage of that fame: *Who Goes There?* (coll **1948**; vt *The Thing and Other Stories* 1952 UK; vt *The Thing from Outer Space* 1966 UK) and – with differing contents – *Who Goes There?* (coll **1955**). In September 1937 JWC was appointed editor of *Astounding Stories*, a post he would retain until his death (the magazine being retitled ASTOUNDING SCIENCE-FICTION in 1938 and *Analog* in 1960); henceforth he wrote almost no fiction.

JWC brought to his editorial post the fertility of ideas on which his writing success as both JWC and Don A. Stuart had been based, together with a determination to raise the standards of writing and thinking in MAGAZINE sf. New writers were encouraged and fed with ideas, with remarkable success. By 1939, JWC had discovered Isaac ASIMOV, Lester DEL REY, Robert A. HEINLEIN, Theodore STURGEON and A.E. VAN VOGT, though the two latter writers had already been publishing for some time in other genres. L. Sprague DE CAMP, L. Ron HUBBARD, Clifford D. SIMAK and Jack WILLIAMSON, already established sf writers, soon became part of JWC's "stable". Henry KUTTNER and C.L. MOORE became regular contributors from 1942. These were the authors at the core of JWC's "GOLDEN AGE OF SF" – a period corresponding roughly to WWII – when *ASF* dominated the genre in a way no magazine before or since could match. Most of these authors, and many others, acknowledged the profound influence JWC had on their careers, and the number of acknowledged sf classics which originated in ideas suggested by him would be impossible to assess. Asimov persistently credited JWC with at least co-creating the articulation of the Three Laws of Robotics (◊ Isaac ASIMOV; ROBOTS). A startling example of the pervasiveness of his influence can be found in *The Space Beyond* (coll **1976**); it contains a hitherto unpublished JWC novella, "All", which forms the basis of Robert A. Heinlein's *Sixth Column* (**1949**).

In addition to editing *ASF*, JWC initiated the fantasy magazine UNKNOWN, which from its birth in 1939 to its premature death (caused by paper shortages) in

1943 was equally influential in its field.

Although the writing had been on the wall ever since about 1945, the period of *ASF*'s dominance can be said to have ended, quite abruptly, with the appearance of *The* MAGAZINE OF FANTASY AND SCIENCE FICTION in 1949 and GALAXY SCIENCE FICTION in 1950. By this time JWC's domineering editorial presence had become restricting rather than stimulating and several of his central authors had left the stable (sometimes acrimoniously); comparatively few major writers after 1950 began their careers in his magazine. Nevertheless, between 1952 and 1964 he won 8 HUGO awards for Best Editor. Much of his interest and energy became focused in his editorials, many of which showed an essentially right-wing political stance. Some are reprinted in *Collected Editorials from Analog* (coll **1966**) ed Harry HARRISON; and the characteristic flavour of his mind comes across, perhaps even more clearly, in *The John W. Campbell Letters, Volume 1* (anth **1986**) assembled by Perry A. CHAPDELAINE, Tony Chapedelaine and George HAY. He flirted with various kinds of PSEUDO-SCIENCE, notably Hubbard's DIANETICS, which was loosed on an unsuspecting world through an article in *ASF*. The bellicose appetite for knowledge of his early years, and the revelation that Competent Men might be able to figure the world's plumbing, narrowed into an incapacity to brook dissent. However, the magazine remained popular and commercially successful, winning 7 HUGO awards under JWC's editorship. His death in 1971 was marked by an unprecedented wave of commemorative activity: two awards were founded bearing his name (the JOHN W. CAMPBELL AWARD and the JOHN W. CAMPBELL MEMORIAL AWARD), a memorial anthology was published – *Astounding: John W. Campbell Memorial Anthology* (anth **1974**) ed Harry Harrison – and an Australian symposium about him – *John W. Campbell: An Australian Tribute* (anth dated **1974** but **1972**) ed John Bangsund – appeared. Such a response was justified; although in later years he had turned his back on most developments in sf, during the first two decades of his career he had created two significant writing reputations under two separate names, and had come to bestride the field as an editor. More than any other individual, he helped to shape modern sf.   [MJE]

Other works: *The Moon is Hell!* (coll **1951**; later UK edns contain only the title story); *Cloak of Aesir* (coll **1952**); *The Ultimate Weapon* (**1936** *ASF* as "Uncertainty"; **1966** dos); *The Best of John W. Campbell* (coll **1973** UK) and – with different contents – *The Best of John W. Campbell* (coll **1976**).

As editor: *From Unknown Worlds* (anth **1948**); *The Astounding Science Fiction Anthology* (anth **1952**; with 8 stories cut, vt in 2 vols as *The First Astounding Science Fiction Anthology* 1954 UK and *The Second Astounding Science Fiction Anthology* 1954 UK, these 2 vols being reissued with all cuts restored, 1964 and 1965 UK; with 15 stories cut 1956 US, this version being reissued, vt *Selections from the Astounding Science*

Fiction Anthology 1967; with 15 stories and an article cut, vt *Astounding Tales of Space and Time* 1957 US); *Prologue to Analog* (anth **1962**), *Analog 1* (anth **1963**) and *Analog 2* (anth **1964**), all three assembled as *Analog Anthology* (omni **1965** UK); *Analog 3* (anth **1965**; vt *A World by the Tale* 1970); *Analog 4* (anth **1966**; vt *The Permanent Implosion* 1970); *Analog 5* (anth **1967**; vt *Countercommandment and Other Stories* 1970); *Analog 6* (anth **1968**); *Analog 7* (anth **1969**); *Analog 8* (anth **1971**).

See also: ANTHROPOLOGY; AUTOMATION; COMPUTERS; CRIME AND PUNISHMENT; DEFINITIONS OF SF; DISASTER; DISCOVERY AND INVENTION; ECONOMICS; EDISONADE; END OF THE WORLD; ESP; EVOLUTION; FASTER THAN LIGHT; HEROES; HISTORY OF SF; HYPERSPACE; INVASION; JUPITER; MACHINES; MARS; MONSTERS; MOON; NEAR FUTURE; NEW WORLDS; NUCLEAR POWER; OPTIMISM AND PESSIMISM; OUTER PLANETS; PARANOIA; POLITICS; PSI POWERS; RELIGION; SF MAGAZINES; SCIENTIFIC ERRORS; SEX; SOCIAL DARWINISM; SOCIOLOGY; SPACE OPERA; STARS; STREET & SMITH; SUPERMAN; TABOOS; TECHNOLOGY; THRILLING WONDER STORIES; UTOPIAS; VENUS; WAR; WEAPONS.

CANADA 1. Sf in English. The first serious Canadian sf work was James DE MILLE's posthumously published *A Strange Manuscript Found in a Copper Cylinder* (**1888** US). In this UTOPIAN satire, set in a LOST WORLD, Western values are inverted (criminals are regarded as diseased, the ill are imprisoned, dying is deemed more desirable than living). Successors of De Mille were Grant ALLEN and Robert BARR (the latter Scottish-born), expatriate Canadian writers who published early sf in London and New York rather than in Montreal or Toronto.

Many major Canadian literary figures have written some fantasy or sf. Sir Charles G.D. ROBERTS was the author of *In the Morning of Time* (**1919** UK), a well presented prehistoric romance. In "The Great Feud", assembled in *Titans, and Other Epics of the Pliocene* (coll **1926** UK), E.J. Pratt (1882-1964) created a long narrative poem set in prehistoric Australasia. The popular humorist Stephen LEACOCK included short sf SATIRES in *The Iron Man and the Tin Woman, with Other Such Futurities* (coll **1929** US) and *Afternoons in Utopia* (coll **1932** US). A curious and powerful critique of modern society by Prairie novelist Frederick Philip GROVE is *Consider Her Ways* (written 1913-23; **1947**), which describes the march of 10,000 worker ants across the North American continent, including how they spend their last winter in the poetry section of the New York Public Library.

Among Canadian contributors to US PULP MAGAZINES were H. BEDFORD-JONES, John L. Chapman, Leslie A. Croutch (1915-1969), Chester D. Cuthbert, Francis FLAGG, Thomas P. KELLEY and Cyril G. Wates. Import restrictions during WWII created a climate for the so-called CanPulps – original and reprint pulp magazines with idiosyncratic editorial features. A.E. VAN VOGT, the Manitoba-born mainstay of the GOLDEN AGE OF SF, wrote 600,000 words of sf (notably "Black Destroyer", the **Weapon Shops** stories and *Slan*) in Canada before moving to Los Angeles in 1944. Other notable expatriates are Laurence MANNING and Gordon R. DICKSON.

Contemporary MAINSTREAM authors have contributed fantastic literature. Irish-born Brian MOORE published sf in *Catholics* (**1972** UK), fantasy in *The Great Victorian Collection* (**1975**) and supernatural horror in *The Mangan Inheritance* (**1979**). William Weintraub dramatized the plight of Montreal's Anglophone minority in a sovereign Francophone Québec in his biting satire *The Underdogs* (**1979**). Hugh MacLENNAN's *Voices in Time* (**1980**) is an ambitious, impressive, multi-levelled study of social breakdown in post-HOLOCAUST Montreal. DISASTER remains the sole theme of Richard ROHMER, lawyer, commissioner, general and author of fast-moving novels about near-future threats to national sovereignty, ecology, etc.

Gwendolyn MacEwen (1941-1987), Margaret ATWOOD and Phyllis GOTLIEB, in addition to writing memorable prose, have composed vivid sf poems (◊ POETRY) tinged with fantasy and horror; in particular, MacEwen's poetry collection *The Armies of the Moon* (coll **1972**) deserves an international readership, as do her stories assembled in *Noman* (coll **1972**) and *Noman's Land* (coll **1985**). Atwood's *The Handmaid's Tale* (**1985**), diffidently filmed by director Volker Schlöndorff in 1990 (◊ *The* HANDMAID'S TALE), is the most influential and internationally known sf novel written by a Canadian. But "Canada's premier sf novelist" during the 1960-80 formative period in the genre's growth, according to critic David KETTERER, was Phyllis Gotlieb. Her first novel, *Sunburst* (**1964** US), appears on high-school curricula, and mainstream anthologists have reprinted her short fictions, notably those in *Son of the Morning and Other Stories* (coll **1983** US); yet she remains better known at home as a poet. One reason is that her prose is demanding, intricate and psychologically probing; it frequently focuses on the problems of telepathic beings and intelligent animals.

High artistic and professional standards were set in the 1970s by immigrants to Canada: Michael G. CONEY, Monica HUGHES and Edward LLEWELLYN from the UK, and William GIBSON, Crawford KILIAN, Donald KINGSBURY, Judith MERRIL, Spider ROBINSON and Robert Charles WILSON from the USA. Merril, the country's leading "sf personality", has been active in promoting FEMINISM (a sense of gender) and sf (a SENSE OF WONDER) among mainstream writers and educators (*see also* MERRIL COLLECTION OF SCIENCE FICTION, SPECULATION AND FANTASY).

The first national sf anthology was *Other Canadas* (anth **1979**) ed John Robert COLOMBO; it gives historical representation to stories, novel excerpts, poems, film scripts and criticism. John Bell and Lesley Choyce anthologized past and present fiction from the Atlantic region in *Visions from the Edge* (anth **1981**). Merril edited *Tesseracts* (anth **1985**), the first collection of current Canadian sf writing in English with some translations from French; Phyllis Gotlieb and Douglas BARBOUR compiled *Tesseracts²* (anth **1987**), and Candas Jane DORSEY and Gerry Truscott *Tesseracts³* (anth **1990**). In the main, Canadian sf in English is more literary, concerned with COMMUNICATION, and less high-tech than most US sf. Characters and settings specifically identified as Canadian began to appear in genre fiction in the 1980s, a development notable in the novels of fantasists like Charles DE LINT, Guy Gavriel Kay and Tanya Huff. The Bunch of Seven, a Toronto-based group including Huff and expanded to nine writers in all, is most notable for the fiction, including SHARED-WORLDS fiction, of Shirley Meier, Karen Wehrstein and S.M. STIRLING. Among the Toronto (and Ontario) sf writers of achievement are Wayland DREW, Terence M. GREEN, Robert J. SAWYER and Andrew WEINER. Especially active in Alberta are Candas Jane Dorsey and J. Brian Clarke. Among the critics in Montreal who contribute to SCIENCE-FICTION STUDIES are Darko SUVIN, David Ketterer, Robert M. PHILMUS and Marc Angenot. Other influential critics include Douglas Barbour of Edmonton, the late Susan WOOD of Vancouver and the expatriate John CLUTE.

Toronto has hosted two world sf CONVENTIONS, in 1948 and 1973. Each year the designated national convention hosts the Canadian Science Fiction and Fantasy Achievement Awards, known as Caspers 1980-90 but then retitled the Auroras to avoid further association with Casper the Friendly Ghost, a US cartoon character. The first Casper – nicknamed the Coeurl because of its catlike appearance – was awarded to A.E. van Vogt, in whose "Black Destroyer" (1939) the original Coeurl appeared. The Speculative Writers Association of Canada, founded by Dorsey and others in Edmonton in 1989, issues a bimonthly newsletter called *SWACCESS*. Ketterer's *Canadian Science Fiction and Fantasy* (**1992** US) surveys the field as a whole, covering both French- and English-language literatures. In it he estimated that there were in all about 1200 works of Canadian sf and fantasy. [JRC]

2. Sf in French. The great majority of Francophone sf authors live in Québec; there are very few in other provinces. Québec sf can be divided into two periods. Before 1974 there was no sf published under that label, although Jules-Paul TARDIVEL's *Pour la Patrie* (**1895**; trans as *For My Country* **1975**) was a UTOPIA set in a 1945 Québec. Some established MAINSTREAM authors (like Yves Thériault [1915-] and Michel Tremblay [1942-]) occasionally touched on the themes of GENRE SF and FANTASY. Such works ranged from 19th-century *voyages extraordinaires* in the Jules-VERNE tradition to adventure novels with sf trappings; some juvenile sf was also published in the 1950s and 1960s. Despite these, no true sf tradition existed and no lasting sf FANDOM had been established.

In 1974 Norbert Spehner began publishing the FANZINE *Requiem*, which rapidly grew into a literary magazine centred on sf and fantasy, publishing fiction as well as essays and reviews and becoming the focus for a nascent sf milieu. In 1979 *Requiem* became *Solaris*, while another important magazine, *imagine . . .*, was created by Jean-Marc Gouanvic, followed as editor by Catherine Saouter, Gouanvic again and, in 1990, Marc Lemaire. Meanwhile, in 1983, Spehner had passed *Solaris* on to a collective led by Élisabeth VONARBURG as editor until Luc POMERLEAU took over in 1986. However, fanzines and fandom are not as central a tradition in Québec sf as in Anglophone North America – although some fanzines created towards the end of the 1980s (*Samizdat*, *CSF* and *Temps Tôt*) are doing good work in discovering new authors. Original ANTHOLOGIES were a driving force of Québec sf in the 1980s, but in 1991 only one specialist line remains.

In addition to the usual prejudices against sf, Québec authors have to cope with the circumstances of the Québec publishing industry, a small boat adrift between the Anglophone and Francophone oceans. Despite this, many authors have made their mark, largely through the efforts of *imagine . . .* and *Solaris*. Some, like Esther ROCHON, Élisabeth Vonarburg, Jean-Pierre April and Daniel SERNINE have published a substantial body of work. They have all written novels, including Rochon's *Coquillage* (**1986**; trans David Lobdell as *The Shell* **1990**), a strangely erotic story of the union between a sea-creature and a human; Sernine's *Les méandres du temps* ["The Meanders of Time"] (**1983**), about TIME TRAVEL and changing history; and April's *Berlin-Bangkok* (**1990**), set in a drug-infested world dominated and corrupted by multinationals.

Although Québec sf is young, already a second generation of authors is making itself known, including Joël Champetier, Claude-Michel Prévost, Yves Meynard and Francine Pelletier; the latter's forcefulness and sensitivity are shown in her collection *Le temps des migrations* ["The Time of the Migrations"] (coll **1987**). CHILDREN'S SF continues to account for many of the books published. One such is Champetier's *La mer au fond du monde* ["The Sea at the Bottom of the World"] (**1990**), which deals with interspecies contact in a refreshingly unromantic way.

Thematically, Québec sf has tended towards SOFT SF, although some (Champetier, Vonarburg and Meynard, for example) are more rigorous in creating a scientific background. The relative absence of the landscape of Québec in Québec sf – which often adopts a neutral US or international setting – is surprising; with the notable exception of April, Québec settings have been used mostly by immigrant authors like Prévost and Vonarburg. [LP]

CANDAR PUBLISHING CO. ◊ SATURN.

CANNING, VICTOR (1911-1986) UK writer, two of whose many thrillers are borderline sf. In *The Finger of Saturn* (**1973**) a group of individuals who claim to have come from space attempt to return there. *The Doomsday Carrier* (**1976**) features an escaped chimpanzee infected with an artificially induced contagion. The **Crimson Chalice**, an Arthurian FANTASY sequence, comprises *The Crimson Chalice* (**1976**), *The Circle of the*

Gods (**1977**) and *The Immortal Wound* (**1978**), all assembled as *The Crimson Chalice* (omni **1980**). [JC]

CANTWELL, ASTON ◊ Charles PLATT.

CANTY, THOMAS (? -) US illustrator known for his pale, delicate style, for the Art-Nouveau-inspired, ethereal women he often paints, and for his use of stylized costume details. His fame is out of proportion to the amount of work (mostly book covers) he has published, though he works also under pseudonyms. Although he has often been nominated for the HUGO and regularly scores highly in the LOCUS poll, his work is almost exclusively FANTASY. [PN/JG]

See also: ILLUSTRATION.

ČAPEK, JOSEF [r] ◊ Karel ČAPEK.

ČAPEK, KAREL (1890-1938) Czech writer whose copious production included plays, novels, stories, imaginative travel books and at least two volumes written to publicize President Tomáš Masaryk (1850-1937) of Czechoslovakia in his formidable old age. After publishing several volumes of stories (not all translated), including *Trapné povídky* (coll **1921**; trans by several hands as *Money and Other Stories* **1929** UK), he began to produce the plays for which he remains perhaps best known, in particular *R.U.R.* (**1920**; trans as *R.U.R. (Rossum's Universal Robots): A Fantastic Melodrama* by Paul Selver with Nigel Playfair **1923** UK; US trans Paul Selver alone 1923 differs) and, with his painter/writer brother Josef (who died in Belsen in 1945), *Že života hmyzu* (**1921**; trans Paul Selver as *And So Ad Infinitum (The World of the Insects)* 1923 UK; selected vt trans Owen Davis as *The World We Live In* 1933 US; most commonly known as *The Insect Play*). *R.U.R.* introduced the word ROBOT (at Josef's suggestion) to the world. In Czech it means something like "serf labour", and in the play it applies not to robots made of metal, as we have come to think of them, but to a worker-class of persecuted ANDROIDS. The play itself, if understood as a lurchingly hilarious vaudeville, can nearly transcend its portentous symbolism and the neo-Tolstoyan bathos of its life-affirming conclusion. In *The Insect Play*, which is far more adroit, various arthropods go through vaudeville routines explicitly related to cognate activities on the part of humans, to scathing effect. But it is only with the new translation by Tatian Firkusny and Robert T. Jones of Act Two in unexpurgated form – in *Toward the Radical Center: A Karel Čapek Reader* (coll **1990** US) ed Peter Kussi – that the reader can begin to assess the full impact of this extraordinary work.

A further play, *Věc Makropulos* (**1922**; unauthorized trans Randal C. Burrell as *The Makropoulos Secret* **1925** US; authorized trans Paul Selver *The Macropoulos Secret* **1927** UK), similarly cloaks in comic routines the terrifying story of the alluring, world-weary, 300-year-old protagonist, the secret of her longevity, and her ambivalently conceived death (a new translation, by Robert T. Jones and Yveta Synek Graff, also in *Toward the Radical Center*, does something to reveal the frightening pace of the play). The work is most familiar as the basis of an opera by Leoš Janáček (1854-1928). A later collaboration with Josef, *Adam stvořitel* (**1927**; trans Dora Round as *Adam the Creator* **1927** UK), was less successful; and *Bílá nemoc* (**1937**; trans Paul Selver and Ralph Neale as *Power and Glory* **1938** UK; new trans Michael Henry Heim as "The White Plague" in *Cross Currents 7*, 1988 US) has been available to an English-speaking readership in anything like its original form only since 1988.

Of greater interest to the sf reader was the first of KČ's sf novels, *Továrna na absolutno* (**1922**; trans Šárka B. Hrbková as *The Absolute at Large* **1927** UK/US), like most of his fiction a deceptively light-toned SATIRE. A scientist invents the Karburator, an atomic device which produces almost free power through the absolute conversion of energy, a process which unfortunately also releases the essence of God, causing a spate of miracles and other effects; ultimately there is a devastating religious WAR. Its immediate successor, *Krakatit* (**1924**; trans Lawrence Hyde **1925** UK; vt *An Atomic Phantasy: Krakatit* 1948), hearkens back to the fever-ridden brio of his stories and plays from the early 1920s, and serves to culminate this first – and in some ways most energetically dark – period of KČ's creative life. Krakatit is both a quasi-atomic explosive and – by analogy – the sexual abyss into which its inventor, Prokop, topples. Neither the world nor Prokop emerges unscathed from the consequent acid bath of reality – reality-to-excess. These novels are set in middle Europe, and the teasing of apocalypse so conspicuous in them works to transmit some sense of KČ's sensitive political consciousness, identifiably Central European in its inherent assumptions about the precariousness of institutions and the dubiousness of their claimed benevolence.

This almost allergenic awareness of the fragility of 20th-century civilization is perhaps best summed up in KČ's last sf novel, *Válka s Mloky* (**1936**; trans M. and R. Weatherall as *War With the Newts* **1937** UK; new trans Ewald Osers 1985 UK), in which a strange, apparently exploitable sea-dwelling race of "newts" is discovered in the South Pacific – where Rossum's robots also "lived". The newts are immediately enslaved by human entrepreneurs; but the resulting dramas of class struggle and social injustice are rendered with a high ashen ambivalence, for the newts, having gained the necessary human characteristics and a "newt Hitler" to guide them, turn against their masters and flood the continents in order to acquire lebensraum. It is the end for *Homo sapiens*. The book, told in the form of a chatty, typographically experimental feuilleton, chills with its seeming levity (and with its prefigurations of the end of Czechoslovakia two years later).

In the end, KČ is perhaps less memorable for his sf innovations – they are indeed slender – than for the heightened humaneness that so illuminates his tales of displaced and ending worlds.   [JC]

Other works: Though it has been listed as sf, *Povětroň* (**1934**; trans as *Meteor* **1935** UK), is neither sf nor fantasy, and *Tales from Two Pockets* (coll trans **1932** UK) selects only non-genre stories from the 2 vols originally published as *Povïdky z jedné kapsy* ["Tales from One Pocket"] (coll **1929**) and *Povïdky z druhé kapsy* ["Tales from the Other Pocket"] (coll **1929**). Further stories are collected in *Devatero Pohádek* (coll **1932**; trans as *Fairy Tales* **1933** UK), for older children, and *Kniha apokryfů* (coll **1945**; trans Dora Round as *Apocryphal Stories* **1949** UK).

About the author: *Karel Čapek* (**1962**) by William E. Harkins.

See also: AUTOMATION; CZECH AND SLOVAK SF; HISTORY OF SF; IMMORTALITY; MACHINES; MUSIC; POWER SOURCES.

CAPOBIANCO, MICHAEL (1950-   ) US writer whose most significant work has been in collaboration with William BARTON (*whom see for details*). His solo novel, *Burster* (**1990**), examines the stresses afflicting those aboard a GENERATION STARSHIP which has left an Earth that was possibly at the brink of destruction.   [JC]

CAPON, (HARRY) PAUL (1911-1969) UK writer who also worked for many years as an editor and administrator in film and tv production, ending his career as head of the Film Department of Independent Television News. From 1942 he wrote fairly copiously in various genres, including detective stories. His first sf was the **Antigeos** trilogy – *The Other Side of the Sun* (**1950**), *The Other Half of the Planet* (**1952**) and *Down to Earth* (**1954**) – some parts of which were serialized on BBC RADIO. The sequence deals with the discovery of an Earth-like planet, hidden directly behind the Sun, whose UTOPIAN life leaves itself open to exploitation by villainous humans. *Into the Tenth Millennium* (**1956**) concerns three people who travel into the future utilizing a drug which slows down body metabolism; they emerge into a utopian world of great charm and interest – Capon's utopias are less stuffy and preachy than most – but the woman cannot make the necessary psychological adjustment. Most of PC's sf was for children, including *The World at Bay* (**1953**), *The Wonderbolt* (**1955**), *Phobos, the Robot Planet* (**1955**; vt *Lost, a Moon* 1956 US) and *Flight of Time* (**1960**). PC wrote well and created unusually solid future worlds.   [PN]

See also: CHILDREN'S SF; PHYSICS

CAPRICORN ONE Film (1977). Capricorn One Associates/Associated General/ITC. Dir Peter Hyams, starring Elliott Gould, James Brolin, Brenda Vaccaro, Sam Waterston, O.J. Simpson, Hal Holbrook. Screenplay Hyams. 124 mins. Colour.

The premise of this PARANOIA movie – made at a time, in the wake of Watergate, when secret-political-conspiracy films had become commonplace – is that a supposedly manned mission to Mars cannot carry a crew because of a malfunction in the life-support system. Fearing a public-relations disaster and a cut in funding, NASA decides to fake the mission: an unmanned craft is sent and a remote film-set is used in place of Mars, the "astronauts" being blackmailed into taking part in the deception. But, after the real spacecraft burns up in the atmosphere on its return to Earth, the astronauts are officially "dead", and will probably be murdered to keep them quiet. Escapes, desert chases and confusions follow. The provocative theme of appearance vs reality in a media-dominated world could have been interesting, but Hyams raises the issue only to ignore it in favour of routine spectacle. That NASA should have cooperated in making the film is mystifying. Unusually, the film was novelized twice: in the USA as *Capricorn One* ∗ (**1977**) by Ron GOULART, and in the UK as *Capricorn One* ∗ (**1978**) by Bernard L. Ross (Ken FOLLETT). [JB/PN]

CAPTAIN FUTURE US PULP MAGAZINE, 17 issues Winter 1940-Spring 1944, quarterly (but Fall 1943 missing). Published by Better Publications; ed Leo MARGULIES with Mort WEISINGER (1940-41) and Oscar J. FRIEND (1941-4). A companion magazine to STARTLING STORIES and THRILLING WONDER STORIES, *CF* was an attempt to establish a SPACE-OPERA equivalent to the popular SUPERHERO pulps (DOC SAVAGE MAGAZINE and the like). Each issue ran a complete novel about tall, cheerful, red-headed Curt Newton, alias Captain Future, "Wizard of Science" or "Man of Tomorrow" according to the magazine's successive subtitles. With his trio of assistants, "Grag, the giant, metal robot; Otho, the man-made, synthetic android; and aged Simon Wright, the living Brain", he thwarted a succession of evil (and, more often than not, green) foes. All but two of the novels were written by Edmond HAMILTON (*whom see for details*), twice under the house name Brett STERLING. They were later reprinted in paperback form. After *CF* had become a casualty of WWII paper shortages, the character continued to appear intermittently in *Startling Stories* to 1946, and again 1950-51. *CF* also serialized some abridged reprints from WONDER STORIES and published a few short stories, including Fredric BROWN's début, "Not Yet the End" (1941). Like its companion magazines at that period, *CF* was unabashedly juvenile in its appeal. [MJE/PN]

CAPTAIN HAZZARD US PULP MAGAZINE; 1 issue, May 1938, published by Ace Magazines; no editor named. The (short) novel contained in this issue, "Python-Men of the Lost City", was by Chester Hawks. Hazzard, an imitation of Doc Savage (◊ DOC SAVAGE MAGAZINE) with great mental powers and a similar group of assistants, combats a master criminal. The lead novel was reprinted in facsimile in 1974 by Robert E. WEINBERG. [FHP]

CAPTAIN JUSTICE The hero of a long-running series of boy's stories (◊ BOY'S PAPERS) written by Murray Roberts (the pseudonym of Robert Murray Graydon) and published in *Modern Boy*, a weekly magazine published by Amalgamated Press through the 1930s. Very British, CJ wore white ducks, smoked cigars and worked out of Titanic Tower in the mid-Atlantic. In the course of battling for good he survived robots, giant insects, runaway planets and an Earth plunged into darkness. His exploits deeply affected the impressionable mind of a young Brian W. ALDISS, among others of that generation. Some CJ stories, including *The World in Darkness* (**1935**), were republished as issues of the **Boys' Friend Library**. [PN]

CAPTAIN MARVEL US COMIC-book character. Created and initially drawn by C.C. Beck, *CM* first appeared in 1940 in Fawcett's *Whiz Comics* (1940-53) and then contemporaneously in Fawcett's *Captain Marvel Adventures* (1941-53); Jack KIRBY and Mac Raboy were among its many illustrators. Foremost among its scriptwriters was Otto Binder (◊ Eando BINDER), who developed *CM*'s distinctive whimsical humour. Newsboy Billy Batson, on speaking the magic word "Shazam!" – an acronym for Solomon, Hercules, Atlas, Zeus, Achilles, Mercury – becomes CM, an invincible SUPERHERO. CM was successful enough in the late 1940s to be given a whole Marvel Family, including CM Jr, Mary Marvel (CM's sister), Uncle Marvel and even Hoppy the Marvel Bunny.

CM bore some resemblance to SUPERMAN, and thus became the subject of a lawsuit brought by National Periodical Publications (later DC COMICS); this was contested until, for financial reasons, Fawcett capitulated in 1953. In the UK the reprints of *CM* published by L. Miller had been sufficiently successful to warrant continued independent publication under a new name, *Marvelman* (346 issues, 1954-63), drawn by Mick Anglo Studios; the hero had a new crew-cut hairstyle and a new magic word, "Kimota!" ("Atomik!" backwards). Artists included Don Lawrence, Ron Embleton and George Stokes. Under this new name, the character much later ran into difficulties when Quality Communications obtained permission to resurrect him in *Warrior*, with an adult script by Alan MOORE (1984). MARVEL COMICS threatened legal action because of the use of the word "Marvel" in the title. So Marvelman was renamed Miracleman, otherwise continuing unchanged and subsequently appearing in the USA from Eclipse, for whom he is currently (1991) scripted by Neil GAIMAN.

Earlier a small company called Lightning Comics had tried to revive the original CM character but, owing to National's assumed ownership of the copyright, had found it necessary to rework the concept, first as *Todd Holton, Super Green-Beret* (1967; magic word turns boy into soldier) and then, more amazingly, as *Fatman the Human Flying Saucer* (1967; magic word turns boy into UFO), this latter being drawn by C.C. Beck, who had created the original CM. Neither character lasted long; however, the incident served to apprise both DC National and Marvel that there was a dilemma. Marvel quickly created another Captain Marvel in *Marvel Superheroes* #12 (1968); this was a more conventional superhero. As long as Marvel continued to publish the exploits of this character, Marvel reasoned, DC could not revive their own 1940s CM without causing an undesirable confusion. However, this prospect did not deter DC, who resurrected the original CM in a comic called *Shazam!* (1972-8), later continued as

Shazam: The New Beginning (1987). Nevertheless, Marvel Comics continue to maintain a token CM simply in order to stop DC publishing a comic book with the word "Marvel" in the title; thus, even though Marvel's CM was killed off in the GRAPHIC NOVEL *The Death of Captain Marvel* (graph **1982**) written and drawn by Jim Starlin, yet another CM was created to replace him.

There was, very briefly, a further CM. *Captain Marvel Presents the Terrible 5* (MF Enterprises 1966) was one of the worst comics of all time. This CM's magic word was "Split!", the saying of which caused a part of his body to detach itself. Needless to say, writs flew. [RT]

CAPTAIN MIDNIGHT (vt *Jet Jackson, Flying Commando*) US tv series (1954-6). Screen Gems/CBS. Prod George Bilson. Pilot episode dir D. Ross Lederman, written Dana Slade. 25 mins per episode. B/w.

Richard Webb played Captain Midnight (or Jet Jackson, depending on where the series was shown) in this early children's tv series; Sid Melton played his bumbling assistant, Ikky; Olan Soule played his scientist friend Tut. Midnight was a super-scientific crime-fighter who each week would zoom in his sleek jetplane from his mountaintop HQ to combat a new evil. The first episode concerned the theft of a powerful radioactive element by foreign agents; they are spotted by a member of Midnight's network of juvenile helpers, the Secret Squadron, and he tracks them down using a Geiger counter. The scripts were poor even by the juvenile standards of the mid-1950s, and *CM* was visually ludicrous. Storylines often featured atomic weapons and radioactivity, this being very much a product of the Cold-War period. *CM* is not to be confused with the 15-episode 1942 Columbia film serial (based on a RADIO serial) of the same name; this too had sf elements. [JB]

CAPTAIN MORS *See Der* LUFTPIRAT UND SEIN LENKBARES LUFTSCHIFF.

CAPTAIN NEMO AND THE UNDERWATER CITY Film (1969). Omnia/MGM. Dir James Hill, starring Robert Ryan, Chuck Connors, Nanette Newman, Luciana Paluzzi. Screenplay Pip and Jane Baker, R. Wright Campbell, based on the character created by Jules VERNE. 106 mins. Colour.

Towards the end of the 19th century a ship sinks in a violent storm. A few survivors find themselves on board a mysterious underwater vessel, the *Nautilus*, under the command of the legendary Captain Nemo. They are taken to Nemo's underwater city (likeably Victorian in design), where his oxygen-creator transmutes rocks into gold as a side-effect. A morality tale about greed ensues. This UK film is distinctly inferior to Disney's 20,000 LEAGUES UNDER THE SEA (1954). [PN/JB]

CAPTAIN SCARLET AND THE MYSTERONS UK tv series (1967-68). A Century 21 Production for ITC. Created Gerry and Sylvia ANDERSON. Prod Reg Hill. Script ed Tony Barwick. Writers included Barwick (most episodes), Shane Rimmer. Dirs included Brian Burgess, Ken Turner, Alan Perry, Bob Lynn. One season, 32 25min episodes. Colour.

This was the 5th sf tv series made by Gerry and Sylvia Anderson in SuperMarionation – i.e., with puppets. Not quite as good as THUNDERBIRDS, report people who were 11 years old at the time, but pretty exciting all the same, and the most sophisticated of all in terms of both narrative and special-effects techniques. Captain Scarlet and his colour-coded Spectrum agents fought against the Martian Mysterons, who could kill and then resuscitate people as Martian agents. Captain Scarlet himself had, as a result of an early brush with Mysterons, developed the ability to regenerate after death. *CSATM* is rather darker than other Anderson series because of the need to work a death into the plot each week. Eight episodes were cobbled together to make two made-for-tv feature films, *Captain Scarlet vs The Mysterons* (1967) and *Revenge of the Mysterons from Mars* (1981). [PN]

CAPTAIN VIDEO 1. US tv serial (1949-53 and 1955-6). DuMont. Prod Larry Menkin. DuMont was a New York tv company; in the early years of tv many programmes came from New York. *CV*, a 30min children's programme that went out 5 nights a week, was the first sf on tv. Written by Maurice Brockhauser, it starred Richard Coogan (replaced in 1950 by Al Hodge) as Captain Video, who 300 years from now, with the aid of his Video Rangers, battled various threats from outer space. Many early scripts were written by Damon KNIGHT, C.M. KORNBLUTH and Robert SHECKLEY.

CV was shot live in a small studio and on a low budget, with the result that much of the spectacle had to be provided by the imaginations of young viewers; it also incorporated filmed material, such as short Westerns and cartoons, which were introduced by the Captain himself. In 1953 the serial format was dropped; *CV* was retitled *The Secret Files of Captain Video* and became a weekly adventure with self-contained stories, but it folded that same year. In 1955 Hodge returned as Captain Video in a weekly 60min children's show, which he also produced. Though still wearing his uniform, which looked like a cross between a marine's and a bus driver's, he merely acted as the show's host, introducing stock adventure-film footage and undemanding shorts of an "educational" nature which he would then discuss with the studio audience of children. In 1956 CV ended his career with *Captain Video's Cartoons*, the Master of Time and Space reduced to announcing the funnies. There was a comic book based on *CV*.

2. In 1951 Sam Katzman produced a cinema serial of 15 parts based on the tv serial. Dir Spencer Bennet, Wallace A. Grissell, written by Royal K. Cole, Sherman L. Lowe, Joseph F. Poland, George H. Plympton, it starred Judd Holdren in the title role and contained robots. [JB]

CAPTAIN ZERO US PULP MAGAZINE; 3 bimonthly issues, Nov 1949-Mar 1950, published by Recreational Reading Corp., Indiana, ed anon Alden H. Norton.

Each issue contained a novel written by prolific pulp author G.T. Fleming-Roberts. As a result of a radiation overdose, Captain Zero (alias "The Master of Midnight") becomes involuntarily invisible at night; he uses his unwanted gift to operate against the underworld. When invisible he speaks in italics. This, the last of the hero pulps, was closer to detective fiction than sf. An almost identical edition was published simultaneously in Canada. [FHP/MJE]

CARAKER, MARY (? -) US writer who began writing sf with, for *ASF* in 1983, "The Vampires who Loved Beowulf", a story which makes up part of her first novel, *Seven Worlds* (fixup **1986**), whose protagonist, a tough female Space Exploratory Forces agent, is entrusted with the task of improving COMMUNICATIONS between humans and other species. The sequel, *The Snows of Jaspre* (**1989**), written for young adults, places that protagonist into a political and ecological crisis on the eponymous planet. *Water Song* (**1987**) and *The Faces of Ceti* (**1991**), singletons, likewise examine planets in crisis. *I Remember, I Remember* (**1991** chap), a novella, recounts the sensations of a woman who awakens on a "coldship" without any memory of how she entered SUSPENDED ANIMATION. [JC]

CARAVAN OF COURAGE ◊ *The* EWOK ADVENTURE.

CARD, ORSON SCOTT (1951-) US writer who exploded onto the sf scene with his first published story, "Ender's Game" for *ASF* in 1977; it was nominated for a HUGO and served as the germ for the **Ender** series, the first two volumes of which, published 1985 and 1986, each won both Hugo and NEBULA, the first time the two major prizes had been swept in successive years by one author. After a highly promising start at the end of the 1970s – he won the 1978 JOHN W. CAMPBELL AWARD – he entered a period during the early 1980s when his career seemed to be drifting; but by the end of 1986 he had clearly established himself as one of the two or three dominant figures of recent sf. That dominance remains (1992) unshaken.

No secret lies behind this success, for OSC has always been entirely explicit about the two factors which have shaped his career. The first is Mormonism. The gift of faith, in his case, has been a complex offering. Born and raised as a Mormon, OSC came to adulthood in a family-oriented, tight-knit community whose sense of historical uniqueness was confirmed in various ways: by recurrent persecution from without, while being intermittently threatened by scandal within; by *The Book of Mormon*, a holy book constructed as a nest of mythopoeic, justificatory narratives through which are expounded a pattern of truly unusual historical hypotheses rich in storytelling potential, not least among these the belief that Native Americans are the Lost Tribes of Israel; and by a tradition – both written and oral – dominated by messiah-like figures of great charisma who lead their people from exile into a promised land. It is perhaps not surprising, then, that OSC's tales have concerned

themselves from the first with matters of family and community in narratives constructed so as to unfold a mythic density at their hearts, and featuring lonely and manipulative MESSIAH-figures who – if they die – die sacrificially. The second factor behind OSC's career is the compulsion to tell stories. If he has a genius, it is for that. (And, if he has a fatal flaw, it resides in that compulsion.) Like Stephen KING, whose capacity for hard work he shares, he is a maker of tales.

Unlike King, however, OSC did not begin as a natural writer of novels, most of his pre-sf work being in the form of short plays for Mormon audiences and much of his early work at book length being expansions of short stories. "Ender's Game" and the other stories assembled in *Unaccompanied Sonata* (coll **1981**) – not to be confused with the release of the title story alone as *Unaccompanied Sonata* (1979 *Omni*; **1992** chap) – demonstrate a compulsive rightness of length (though at times the chill cruelty of the telling unveils a sadism over which the author seemed to have little control), but the first novels were incoherently told, if absorbing in parts. Because of OSC's habitual reworking of his early work, the bibliography of his first sequence, the **Worthing Chronicle**, is complex. Some of the stories in *Capitol: The Worthing Chronicle* (coll of linked stories **1979**) are journeyman work, and appear only in that first volume; both *Capitol* and its companion, *Hot Sleep* (fixup **1979**), were withdrawn from circulation only a few years later in order to make market room for *The Worthing Chronicle* (**1983**), a text which reworked beyond recognition the earlier material. Finally, in *The Worthing Saga* (omni **1990**), *The Worthing Chronicle* (apparently unchanged) was assembled along with 6 of the 11 stories originally published in *Capitol* plus 3 previously uncollected tales. Of all these versions, the most unified is very clearly the 1983 novel, which presents the long epic of Jason Worthing as a sequence of dreams – or scriptures – transmitted by Jason himself to young Lared, who transcribes them for his fellow colonists on a planet which, ages before, their ancestors settled under Worthing's guidance. These dreams – which are in fact some of the contents of the earlier versions of the long tale, here contoured and condensed into myth-like parables – tell Lared of Jason Worthing's pain-racked and interminable life as messiah and godling. Lared also learns why Jason removed all capacity to experience deep pain from his "children", and why, now, he has given them pain once more. Compact, multi-layered, mythopoeic and ultimately very strange, *The Worthing Chronicle* of 1983 remains one of OSC's finest and most revealing works.

A Planet Called Treason (**1979**; rev vt *Treason* **1988**) is a much inferior singleton, though its protagonist is illuminatingly similar to Jason Worthing; but *Songmaster* (fixup **1980**) is a fine rite-of-passage tale whose protagonist, a typical OSC child, is alienated from his family, is blessed with an extraordinary talent (in this case MUSIC), and grows into a messianic role for which he seems preordained.

OSC's career then seemed to drift. *Hart's Hope* (**1983**) was a FANTASY, obscurely published; *The Worthing Chronicle* appeared without much notice; and *A Woman of Destiny* (**1984**; text restored vt *Saints* 1988) was a historical novel about the founding of Mormonism which, in the cut 1984 version, seemed misshapen. Finally, however, the **Ender** books began to appear. The series comprises *Ender's Game* (1977 *ASF*; much exp **1985**), *Speaker for the Dead* (**1986**), both volumes being assembled as *Ender's War* (omni **1986**), plus *Xenocide* (**1991**), with a fourth volume projected. As the sequence begins, Ender Wiggin is a young boy who, along with his siblings, is the result of an experiment in eugenics (◊ GENETIC ENGINEERING) authorized by the government of Earth, which is apprehensive that the ALIEN Buggers will return from interstellar space and continue what seems a xenocidal assault upon humanity, and is convinced that only humans with superior abilities will be capable of defeating the foe. Ender is taken to a military academy, where he is subjected in the Battle Room to an escalating sequence of challenges to his extraordinary tactical and strategic abilities; eventually, at what seems to be a final game (the tale does here prefigure much of the VIRTUAL-REALITY imagery brought to the fore in the 1980s by writers under the influence of CYBERPUNK), Ender defeats the "imaginary" foe only to find that he has in fact been guiding genuine human space-fleets into enemy territory, and that by winning absolutely he has committed xenocide on behalf of the human race.

When it is discovered that the Buggers had long comprehended that humans were sentient beings and had had no intention of continuing any conflict, the grounds for *Speaker for the Dead* are laid. In the company of his chaste sister (his demagogic brother meanwhile takes over the government of Earth), and carrying a cocooned Bugger Hive Queen (the last of all her race), Ender travels from star to star for thousands of planetary years (except in *Xenocide* OSC, unusually, obeys Einsteinian constraints on interstellar travel) as a Speaker for the Dead, a person who sums up a dead person's life in a terminal ceremony, and by so doing heals the community of his or her death. The action takes place on the planet Lusitania, and concentrates upon the local alien race, the Pequeninos, whose strange BIOLOGY is not yet understood – its unravelling of which is fascinatingly prolonged. The novel concludes with the Pequeninos seemingly understood, the Hive Queen happy in a cave where she will breed Buggers, and Ender seeming to have expiated xenocide and become a messiah; but the human Galactic Federation is preparing to destroy Lusitania for fear of a deadly plague. *Xenocide* carries the plot onwards, though not to a conclusion, introducing many new characters, including a talkative AI in love with Ender. The plot of these two novels is much complicated by OSC's attempt, not fully successful, to envision a complex

Lusitanian family for Ender to transform, and has frequent recourse to PULP-MAGAZINE-style highlighting of eccentricities to distinguish one sibling from another; nor is his depiction of a Chinese world – run by MUTANTS dominated by artificially induced obsessive-compulsive disorders – fully convincing. But even incomplete, and despite its not infrequent dependence upon trivializing tricks of plot, the **Ender** saga stands as one of the very few serious moral tales set among the stars. It is also enthrallingly readable.

OSC's third sequence – the **Tales of Alvin Maker** comprising *Seventh Son* (**1987**), *Red Prophet* (**1988**) and *Prentice Alvin* (**1989**), all assembled as *Hatrack River* (omni **1989**), and with at least three further volumes projected – returns to Earth, to an ALTERNATE-WORLD version of the USA. On the basis of the first three volumes, it seems to come as close as humanly possible to the telling of an sf tale as Mormon parable, for the life of Alvin Maker clearly encodes the life of Joseph Smith (1805-1844), the founder of the Mormon Church. The early 19th-century USA in which he grows up has never experienced a Revolution; certain forms of MAGIC are efficacious; and Alvin may become a Maker, one who can delve to the heart of things and transform them. As the sequence progresses, the Indian Nations set up a demarcation line, which is observed, along the Mississippi; and Alvin seems due to become a Maker. Of greater sf relevance are *Wyrms* (**1987**), another rite-of-passage tale about the assumption of role and set on a planet of some interest, *The Folk of the Fringe* (coll of linked stories **1989**), a moderately heterodox vision of a Mormon post-HOLOCAUST civilization; *The Abyss* * (**1989**), which very effectively novelizes *The* ABYSS (1989); and *The Memory of Earth* (**1992**) and «The Call of Earth» (1993), the first volumes of the projected 5-vol **Homecoming** sequence, OSC's fourth series (he was writing three simultaneously). In its use of religious motifs to characterize the start of its protagonists' return to Earth, this latter is a tale whose Mormon subtext extends very close to the surface. Later stories are collected in *Cardography* (coll **1987**), and almost all OSC's independent short work, some of it written as Byron Walley, is assembled in *Maps in a Mirror: The Short Fiction of Orson Scott Card* (coll **1990**; with the 5th section cut, vt in 2 vols *Maps in a Mirror: Volume One* 1992 UK vt *The Changed Man* 1992 US, and *Maps in a Mirror: Volume Two* 1992 UK).

In a little over a decade, OSC has written enough work for a lifetime, has transformed pulp idioms into religious myth with an intensity not previously witnessed in the sf field, and has created a dozen worlds it would be impossible for any reader to forget. If he has had a significant failing – beyond a cruel insistence upon the moral strictures of his faith, writing at one point that adultery and homosexuality were equal (and dreadful) sins – it resides in his strengths. The surety of faith, the muscle of a honed storytelling urgency which has led him to write at times as though he genuinely believed that clarity and truth were identical, the bruising triumphalism of sf as a mode of knowing: all have led this extraordinarily talented author to sound, on occasion, as though he thought the fictions he wrote were scooped from the mouth of a higher being.　　[JC]

Other works: *Eye for Eye* (1987 *IASFM*; **1991** chapdos).

As editor: *Dragons of Light* (anth **1980**); *Dragons of Darkness* (anth **1981**); *Future on Fire* (anth **1991**) with (anon) Martin H. GREENBERG.

Nonfiction: *Characters and Viewpoints* (**1988**); *How to Write Science Fiction and Fantasy* (**1990**) – winner of the 1991 Hugo for Best Nonfiction Book.

About the author: *In the Image of God: Theme, Characterization and Landscape in the Fiction of Orson Scott Card* (**1990**) and «The Work of Orson Scott Card: An Annotated Bibliography & Guide» (**1993**), both by Michael R. COLLINGS.

See also: ARTS; CHILDREN IN SF; CRIME AND PUNISHMENT; DESTINIES; GAMES AND SPORTS; HEROES; HIVE-MINDS; ISAAC ASIMOV'S SCIENCE FICTION MAGAZINE; OPTIMISM AND PESSIMISM; PARANOIA; SLEEPER AWAKES; SUSPENDED ANIMATION; UNDER THE SEA; WRITERS OF THE FUTURE CONTEST.

CAREY, DIANE (L.) (1954-　　) US author of several STAR TREK ties including *Dreadnought!* * (**1986**) and its direct sequel *Battlestations!* * (**1986**), *Final Frontier* * (**1988**) and *Star Trek, the Next Generation: Ghost Ship* * (**1988**).　　[JC]

CAREY, PETER (1943-　　) Australian writer, once in advertising, an experience that pervades his work. PC's high reputation is mainly for mainstream novels like *Oscar and Lucinda* (**1988**), which won the Booker Prize. However, a streak of ironic FANTASY has run through his work from the beginning, occasionally taking the form of sf. *Bliss* (**1981**) and *Illywhacker* (**1985**) can both be regarded as fantasies (if you believe their unreliable narrators), the first about a man who dies and goes to Hell (much like Earth), the second a funny and touching picaresque which, although it is told by a liar, may in part be true; he practises INVISIBILITY and claims to span a century of Australian history, bits of which he recounts. PC's sf FABULATIONS, droll, morbid and scarifying by turns, are contained in two early collections, *The Fat Man in History* (coll **1974**) and *War Crimes* (coll **1979**); a selection from both was published, confusingly, as *The Fat Man in History* (coll **1980** UK; vt *Exotic Pleasures* 1981 UK). Among them, "Do You Love Me?" has a world subject to reality leakages, "The Chance" features a "Genetic Lottery" in which humans can get new bodies while keeping their memories, and "Exotic Pleasures" has ALIEN birdlife which transmits pleasure when touched and may destroy us all.　　[PN]

CARLSEN, CHRIS ◊ Robert P. HOLDSTOCK.

CARLSON, WILLIAM K. (?　　-　　) US writer who began publishing sf with "Dinner at Helen's" in *Strange Bed Fellows* (anth **1972**) ed Thomas N. SCORTIA. His first sf novel, *Sunrise West* (**1981**), features an attempt by multispecies commune-dwellers to survive in a post-HOLOCAUST USA. *Elysium* (**1982**), set

thousands of years later, expounds a moderately LIBERTARIAN view of the perils of allowing ECOLOGY-minded liberals too long a hegemony.　　[JC]

CARLTON, ROGER ◊ Donald Sydney ROWLAND.

CARMODY, ISOBELLE (1958-　　) Australian author of sf for adolescents. Her novels are set in post-HOLOCAUST venues. The first two belong to the still unfolding **Obernewtyn Chronicles**: *Obernewtyn* (**1987**) and *The Farseekers* (**1990**). The third and most challenging is separate from this series: *Scatterlings* (**1991**). IC writes vigorously and colourfully, but the sf ideas are all very familiar: teenaged misfit heroines with PSI POWERS learn about themselves while pitted against unfeeling, dictatorial societies. Each story revolves around a CONCEPTUAL BREAKTHROUGH as the true nature of the world unfolds.　　[PN]

See also: CHILDREN'S SF; PASTORAL.

CARNAC, LEVIN [s] ◊ George GRIFFITH.

CARNEIRO, ANDRÉ [r] ◊ LATIN AMERICA.

CARNELL, (EDWARD) JOHN (1912-1972) UK editor, anthologist and literary agent who worked usually as John Carnell and sometimes as E.J. Carnell; he was known to his friends as Ted. A prominent member of UK FANDOM, JC took over the editorship of NOVAE TERRAE, an early FANZINE, in 1939, retitling his issues (#29-#33) *New Worlds*. He began his professional career as editor in 1946 when NEW WORLDS was revived as a professional SF MAGAZINE. After only 3 issues the publisher failed, but JC with help from fandom was able to renew the title in 1949 with his own company, Nova Publications; he also took over from Walter GILLINGS as editor of the Nova Publications title SCIENCE FANTASY from #3 onwards. The third Nova Publications title, also ed JC, was the UK reprint edition of Larry SHAW's SCIENCE FICTION ADVENTURES. The first 5 UK issues of this, Mar-Nov 1958, were all US reprints, but from the Jan 1959 issue it became an original UK magazine. It ceased publication with the May 1963 issue, but the other two titles continued under JC until mid-1964, when they were taken over by Roberts & Vinter under new editors. JC then established a series of original ANTHOLOGIES, NEW WRITINGS IN SF, comprising *New Writings in SF 1* (anth **1964**), *#2* (anth **1964**), *#3* (anth **1965**), *#4* (anth **1965**), *#5* (anth **1965**), *#6* (anth **1965**), *#7* (anth **1966**), *#8* (anth **1966**), *#9* (anth **1966**), *#10* (anth **1967**), *#11* (anth **1967**), *#12* (anth **1968**), *#13* (anth **1968**), *#14* (anth **1969**), *#15* (anth **1969**), *#16* (anth **1970**), *#17* (anth **1970**), *#18* (anth **1971**), *#19* (anth **1971**), *#20* (anth **1972**), and *#21* (anth **1972**), the last being published after his death. Nine volumes of this series, with contents differing from those in the UK numeration, were published in the USA by BANTAM BOOKS 1966-72. JC, who formally set up the E.J. Carnell Literary Agency in 1964, was agent for most UK sf writers. He was cofounder of the INTERNATIONAL FANTASY AWARD. He was scrupulous, worked hard and profited little. His contribution to UK sf was enormous. For over a quarter of a century he was an early and often first publisher of an entire generation of UK and Irish sf writers. Although his own preference was for conservative HARD SF and sf adventure – he published a lot of it by writers such as John CHRISTOPHER and later Kenneth BULMER and E.C. TUBB – he also gave active encouragement to many of the writers who were later to become strongly associated with Michael MOORCOCK's *NW*, writers of the NEW WAVE including Brian W. ALDISS, J.G. BALLARD, John BRUNNER and Moorcock himself, whose succession to the editorship of *NW* JC supported. JC also edited a handful of reprint anthologies: *Jinn and Jitters* (anth **1946**), *No Place Like Earth* (anth **1952**), *Gateway to Tomorrow* (anth **1954**), *Gateway to the Stars* (anth **1955**), *The Best from New Worlds Science Fiction* (anth **1955**), *Lambda 1 & Other Stories* (anth **1964** US; with 1 story dropped and 2 added 1965 UK), *Weird Shadows from Beyond* (anth **1965**) and *Best of New Writings in SF* (anth **1971**). [PN]

CARNE PER FRANKENSTEIN ◊ FRANKENSTEIN.

CARO, DENNIS R. (1944-) US writer who began publishing sf with "Cantaloupes and Kangaroos" in *Clarion III* (anth **1973**) ed Robin Scott WILSON. His first sf novel, *The Man in the Darksuit: A Futuristic Mystery* (**1980**), depicts with concise and surrealistic hilarity a mean-streets urban future and a mystery concerning the owner of the eponymous INVISIBILITY-conferring outfit. *Devine War* (**1986**), set on a colony planet, even more complicatedly spends considerable energy on interstellar POLITICS and on a malevolent AI called Heathcliffe, as the eponymous female agent tries to bring her husband's killer to justice. DRC is an author who does not deserve obscurity, though the edgy, foregrounded cleverness of his work may continue to limit his success. [JC]

CARPELAN, BO [r] ◊ FINLAND.

CARPENTER, CHRISTOPHER ◊ Christopher EVANS.

CARPENTER, ELMER J. (?   -   ) US writer in whose *Moonspin* (**1967**) a foreign power gains control of Earth's weather. An earlier novel, *Nile Fever* (**1959**), is not sf. [JC]

CARPENTER, JOHN (1948-) US film-maker. At USC Film School JC collaborated with writer-actor-director Dan O'Bannon on DARK STAR (1974), a student effort expanded successfully into a feature that attracted attention for its ABSURDIST humour and classical suspense, following the adventures of a spaceship crewed by near-insane astronauts and dangerously unstable sentient bombs. That calling card enabled JC to make *Assault on Precinct 13* (1976), a very accomplished "urban Western", and to sell his (eventually rewritten) script for *The Eyes of Laura Mars* (1978); this in turn won him an assignment to write and direct *Halloween* (1978), an enormously influential "stalk and slash" movie. JC is usually classed as a HORROR director, his supernatural work including *The Fog* (1980), *Christine* (1983) from Stephen KING's novel, and *Big Trouble in Little China* (1986), but – perhaps influenced by Nigel KNEALE, who wrote HALLOWEEN III: SEASON OF THE WITCH for JC – he often mixes elaborate sf concepts with GOTHIC horror.

JC's sf films as a director include: ESCAPE FROM NEW YORK (1981), a cynical futuristic adventure; *The* THING (1982), a remake of the 1951 Howard Hawks production that returns to John W. CAMPBELL's paranoid original story for its creature-clogged theme; STARMAN (1984), a mellow and impersonal mix of *The Sugarland Express* (1973) with *The* MAN WHO FELL TO EARTH (1976), Jeff Bridges starring as a benign ALIEN visitor; PRINCE OF DARKNESS (1978), a horror movie cross-breeding quantum physics and demonology, whose credits acknowledge Kneale; THEY LIVE (1989), a witty and socially conscious pastiche of 1950s alien-invader motifs; and MEMOIRS OF AN INVISIBLE MAN (1992), from the 1987 novel by H.F. SAINT, a bland comedy thriller in the mould of *Starman*, distinguished by state-of-the-art INVISIBILITY effects. He is credited with contributions to *The* PHILADELPHIA EXPERIMENT (1984) and *Black Moon Rising* (1986), both based on scripts he wrote in the 1970s. A composer, JC has worked on the scores for most of his films, some of them rather good. [KN]

Further reading: *Order in the Universe: The Films of John Carpenter* (1990) by Robert C. Cumbow.

See also: CINEMA; MEDIA LANDSCAPE; MONSTER MOVIES.

CARR, CHARLES (?   -?   ) UK writer whose *Colonists in Space* (**1954**) and its sequel, *Salamander War* (**1955**), routinely deal with colonizing humans and their conflicts with the original salamander inhabitants of the planet Bel. [JC]

CARR, JAYGE Pseudonym of US writer Marj Krueger (1941-), a former nuclear physicist for NASA who began to publish sf with "Alienation" for *ASF* in 1976, and whose major work to date is probably her first novel, *Leviathan's Deep* (**1979**), in which star-travelling Terrans (much like 1950s Americans, particularly in their sexual politics) confront a female from a technologically primitive but culturally sophisticated humanoid race whose males are genuinely inferior. The ALIEN protagonist, in whose voice the tale is told, is depicted with flair, sympathy and a sense of her real differences from a human woman (◊ WOMEN AS PORTRAYED IN SCIENCE FICTION). The **Rabelais** sequence – *Navigator's Sindrome* (**1983**), *The Treasure in the Heart of the Maze* (**1985**) and *Rabelaisian Reprise* (**1988**), with a fourth volume, «Knight of a Thousand Eyes», projected – begins with a mildly humorous adventure, with added moral bite, about the search for a female interstellar Navigator lost on the planet Rabelais, where the powerful play out decadent fantasies on quasi-slaves bound to them by "contractual obligation". The series continues in much the same vein. In the late 1980s, JC began to appear occasionally in best-of-the-year collections with such stories as "Chimera" (1989), a hard-edged tale of revenge and genetic manipulation set in a nightmarish future heavily influenced by CYBERPUNK. While she is not the most inventive of recent writers, JC's stories are solidly crafted, well characterized and readable. [NT]

CARR, JOHN DICKSON (1906-1977) US writer, for long periods resident in the UK, where many of his famous early detective novels, such as *The Three*

Coffins (**1935** US; vt *The Hollow Man* 1935 UK), *Death Watch* (**1935**) and *The Ten Teacups* (**1937**) as by Carter Dickson, and others are evocatively set (although a number of his noteworthy early borderline-fantasy detections, such as *The Waxworks Murder* [**1932**], are set in France). After his inspiration regarding intricate locked-room mysteries and the like began to flag, and after a pious biography of DOYLE, *The Life of Sir Arthur Conan Doyle* (**1949**), JDC began to write mysteries of a fantastic coloration, in several of which modern detectives are transferred (by a form of TIME TRAVEL) into the England of an earlier era, where they are involved in murders. These books are *The Devil in Velvet* (**1951**), set in the 17th century, *Fear is the Same* (**1956**) as by Carter Dickson, set in the 18th, and *Fire, Burn!* (**1956**), set in the 19th. An earlier novel, *The Burning Court* (**1937** UK), does not entirely rationalize the supposition that reincarnated beings lie at the heart of the mystery. Some of the tales in *The Department of Queer Complaints* (coll **1940**) and *The Door to Doom* (coll **1980**) are fantasies.   [JC]

CARR, JOHN F(RANCIS) (1944-   ) US writer who began publishing sf with *The Ophidian Conspiracy* (**1976**), an unpretentious SPACE OPERA which demonstrated considerable imagination but a stylistic gaucheness; both characteristics mark his subsequent novels, *The Pain Gain* (**1977**) and *Carnifax Mardi Gras* (1982 *Fantasy Book* as "Dance of the Dwarfs"; exp **1982**), though the latter shows a saving exuberance. Memorial work on H. Beam PIPER resulted in his editing *The Worlds of H. Beam Piper* (coll **1983**) and writing a continuation in novel form of Piper's **Paratime Police/Lord Kalvan** sequence, *Great King's War* * (**1985**) with Roland J. GREEN.

From the beginning of the 1980s, most frequently in association with Jerry POURNELLE, JFC has been most active as an editor. With Pournelle, he edited (not always with title-page credit) *Black Holes* (anth **1978**); the **Endless Frontier** sequence, comprising *The Endless Frontier* (anth **1979**), *Volume 2* (anth **1985**) and *Cities in Space* (anth **1991**); *The Survival of Freedom* (anth **1981**); the **There Will Be War** sequence of military ANTHOLOGIES, comprising *There Will Be War* (anth **1983**), *Vol II: Men of War* (anth **1984**), *Vol III: Blood and Iron* (anth **1984**), *Vol IV: Day of the Tyrant* (anth **1985**), *Vol V: Warrior* (anth **1986**), *Vol VI: Guns of Darkness* (anth **1987**), *Vol VII: Call to Battle* (anth **1988**), *Vol VIII: Armageddon!* (anth **1989**) and *Vol IX: After Armageddon* (anth **1990**); *The Science Fiction Yearbook* (anth **1985**) with Jim BAEN and Pournelle; the **Far Frontiers** original anthology series, with Baen and Pournelle (JFC uncredited), comprising *Far Frontiers* (anth **1985**), *#2* (anth **1985**), *#3* (anth **1985**), *#4* (anth **1986**), *#5* (anth **1986**), *#6* (anth **1986**) and *#7* (anth **1986**); and the **Imperial Stars** reprint anthologies, *Imperial Stars, Vol 1: The Stars at War* (anth **1986**), *Vol 2: Republic and Empire* (anth **1987**) and *Vol 3: the Crash of Empire* (anth **1989**).

Also with Pournelle, JFC created and edited the **War World** sequence of SHARED-WORLD anthologies:

War World, Volume 1: The Burning Eye * (anth **1988**) with Roland J. Green, *Volume 2: Death's Head Rebellion* * (anth **1990**) with Green, and *Volume 3: Sauron Dominion* * (anth **1991**); *Codominium: Revolt on War World* * (anth **1992**) is set prior to the main sequence. These volumes, which carry Pournelle's **CoDominium** sequence into broader waters, have proved one of the more effective examples of a shared-world enterprise. As editor of the SFWA BULLETIN (1978-80), JFC devoted an entire issue (vol 14, #3) to a series of studies of "Science-Fiction Future Histories".   [JC]

See also: HISTORY IN SF; WAR.

CARR, ROBERT SPENCER (1909-   ) US writer, brother of John Dickson CARR. His first (teenage) stories appeared in *Weird Tales*, beginning with "The Composite Brain" (1925), which is sf. He is the author of one fantasy novel filled with an erotic nostalgia for death, *The Room Beyond* (**1948**), and of *Beyond Infinity* (coll **1951**), four warmly realized stories set on Earth in the mid-20th century but with sf content.   [JC]

CARR, TERRY (GENE) (1937-1987) US writer and editor. He became an sf fan in 1949 and, throughout the 1950s (and later), enjoyed a long and prolific career as such; one of his fanzines, FANAC, co-edited with Ron ELLIK, won a HUGO in 1959, and TC eventually won his second Hugo as Best Fan Writer in 1973. Some of this writing was assembled as *Fandom Harvest* (coll **1986**) and *Between Two Worlds* (coll **1986** chap dos), the latter being published with similar material by Bob SHAW.

In the early 1960s TC began to work as an editor and to write fiction, his first story being "Who Sups with the Devil" in 1962 for *FSF*, where most of his early stories appeared; most of it was assembled in *The Light at the End of the Universe* (coll **1976**). He was never prolific as a fiction writer, but the stories in that collection are thoughtful and distinctive. They include "Brown Robert" (1962), a neat TIME-TRAVEL variant, "The Dance of the Changer and the Three" (1968), an ambitious attempt to render an ALIEN culture by telling one of its myths, and "Ozymandias" (1972), which draws an effective parallel between modern CRYONICS techniques and the funeral practices of ancient Egypt. There were also two minor novels – *Invasion from 2500* (**1964**) with Ted WHITE under the joint pseudonym Norman EDWARDS, and *Warlord of Kor* (**1963** chap dos) – as well as one ambitious and substantial work, *Cirque* (**1977**), a religious allegory, elegiac in mood, set in the FAR FUTURE. Because he was not very prolific, TC's writing is in general somewhat undervalued.

It was as an editor that he became and remained best known. In 1964-71 he worked with Donald A. WOLLHEIM at ACE BOOKS, where he was responsible for the highly successful **Ace Special** series, whose most famous original publications were probably R.A. LAFFERTY's *Past Master* (**1968**) and Ursula K. LE GUIN's *The Left Hand of Darkness* (**1969**), and which included several further titles of strong merit. He co-edited seven annual best-of-the-year ANTHOLOGIES with Wollheim (*whom see for titles*), beginning with *World's Best Science Fiction: 1965* (anth **1965**; vt *World's Best Science Fiction: First Series* 1970 UK), and initiated the UNIVERSE series of original anthologies (see listing below) with *Universe 1* (anth **1971**). After leaving Ace and becoming a freelance editor, TC continued to produce a best-of-the-year anthology on his own in competition with Wollheim's, commencing with *The Best Science Fiction of the Year* (anth **1972**) and continuing through 1987 (see listing below); during its run, this series was generally regarded as the best of the annual compilations. *Universe* continued, although it changed publishers more than once; and with *The Year's Finest Fantasy* (anth **1978**) TC started a FANTASY annual (see listing below), which was less successful. Of a wide variety of reprint and original anthologies, the most notable was perhaps *The Ides of Tomorrow* (anth **1976**), with fine stories by Brian W. ALDISS, George R.R. MARTIN and others.

In the 1980s TC returned to Ace Books on a freelance basis to edit a second series of **Ace Specials**, this time restricted to first novels. The impact of this sequence was perhaps even greater than the first, for it included in its first 18 months William GIBSON's *Neuromancer* (**1984**), Kim Stanley ROBINSON's *The Wild Shore* (**1984**), Carter SCHOLZ's and Glenn Harcourt's *Palimpsests* (**1984**), Lucius SHEPARD's *Green Eyes* (**1984**), Michael SWANWICK's *In the Drift* (**1985**) and Howard WALDROP's *Them Bones* (**1984**). In 1985-6 he won his third and fourth Hugos, both as Best Editor. What perhaps marked TC most distinctively was his quite extraordinary capacity to commission or purchase work which, once published, seemed inevitable. His authors seemed to speak to the heart of their times. [MJE/JC]

Other works as editor: *Science Fiction for People who Hate Science Fiction* (anth **1966**); *The Others* (anth **1969**); *On Our Way to the Future* (anth **1970**); *This Side of Infinity* (anth **1972**); *An Exaltation of Stars* (anth **1973**); *Into the Unknown* (anth **1973**); *Worlds Near and Far* (anth **1974**); *The Fellowship of the Stars* (anth **1974**); *Creatures from Beyond* (anth **1975**); *Planets of Wonder* (anth **1976**); *Infinite Arena* (anth **1977**); *To Follow a Star: Nine Science Fiction Stories about Christmas* (anth **1977**); *Classic Science Fiction: The First Golden Age* (anth **1978**); *Beyond Reality* (anth **1979**); *Dream's Edge* (anth **1980**); *A Treasury of Modern Fantasy* (anth **1981**) with Martin H. GREENBERG; *100 Great Fantasy Short Short Stories* (anth **1984**) with Isaac ASIMOV and Greenberg; *The Science Fiction Hall of Fame, Volume 4* (anth **1986**).

New Worlds of Fantasy: *New Worlds of Fantasy* (anth **1967**; vt *Step Outside Your Mind* 1969 UK); *#2* (anth **1970**); *#3* (anth **1971**).

Universe: The sequence continued with *Universe 2* (anth **1972**), *#3* (anth **1973**), *#4* (anth **1974**), *#5* (anth **1975**), *#6* (anth **1976**), *#7* (anth **1977**), *#8* (anth **1978**), *#9* (anth **1979**), *#10* (anth **1980**), *#11* (anth **1981**), *#12* (anth **1982**), *#13* (anth **1983**), *#14* (anth **1984**), *#15* (anth **1985**), *#16* (anth **1986**) and *#17* (anth **1987**), plus *The Best from Universe* (anth **1984**).

Best Science Fiction of the Year: The sequence continued with *The Best Science Fiction of the Year 2* (anth **1973**), *#3* (anth **1974**), *#4* (anth **1975**), *#5* (anth **1976**), *#6* (anth **1977**), *#7* (anth **1978**), *#8* (anth **1979**), *#9* (anth **1980**), *#10* (anth **1981**), *#11* (anth **1982**), *#12* (anth **1983**), *#13* (anth **1984**; cut vt *Best SF of the Year #13* 1984 UK), *Terry Carr's Best Science Fiction of the Year #14* (anth **1985**; vt *Best SF of the Year #14* 1985 UK), *Terry Carr's Best Science Fiction of the Year #15* (anth **1986**; vt *Best SF of the Year #15* 1986 UK) and *#16* (anth **1987**; vt *Best SF of the Year #16* 1987 UK).

Finest Fantasy: The sequence continued with *The Year's Finest Fantasy #2* (anth **1979**), *#3* (anth **1981**), *#4* (anth **1981**) and *#5* (anth **1982**).

Best SF Novellas: *The Best Science Fiction Novellas of the Year #1* (anth **1979**) and *#2* (anth **1980**).

See also: CITIES; INVASION; LINGUISTICS; MILFORD SCIENCE FICTION WRITERS' CONFERENCE; MYTHOLOGY; RELIGION; SCI FI.

CARREL, FREDERIC (1869-?   ) UK writer, active as late as 1929. *Paul le Maistre* (**1901**) is not sf, the invention at the heart of the book being an improved plough, but *2010* (**1914**) is a racist and reactionary UTOPIA with high technologies (amply described), a comet, a sterility-inducing plague and a future WAR in which Oriental invaders are defeated when the plague is redirected at their women. It was published anonymously. [JC]

CARREL, MARK ◊ Lauran Bosworth PAINE.

CARRIE Film (1976). Red Bank/United Artists. Dir Brian De Palma, starring Sissy Spacek, Piper Laurie, John Travolta, Amy Irving, Nancy Allen. Screenplay Lawrence D. Cohen, based on *Carrie* (**1974**) by Stephen KING. 98 mins. Colour.

This was the breakthrough film for a director who had worked with fantastic subjects before, notably with *Sisters* (1972) and *Phantom of the Paradise* (1974). Only borderline sf, more centrally a HORROR film, *C* tells of a repressed and innocent child (Spacek), just entering puberty, whose powers of TELEKINESIS awaken partly in response to the dreadful religious bigotry of her mother and specifically to brutal teasing at high school. Widely praised and commercially successful, *C* is pyrotechnically directed, especially in those scenes where Carrie strikes back at her tormentors. Undoubtedly impressive, the film is, however, more simplistic about its fantasy of impotent-victim-becoming-potent-avenger than was its source novel. De Palma went on to make another film about PSI POWERS, *The* FURY (1978). [PN]

See also: CINEMA.

CARRIGAN, RICHARD (1932-?   ) **and NANCY** (1933-?   ) US writing team in whose sf novel, *The Siren Stars* (**1971**), the first intelligent messages from another star present a dire challenge. Rather ponderously, a clean-cut team of Earth scientists deals with the problem. [JC]

See also: CYBERNETICS.

CARRINGTON, GRANT (1938-   ) US writer who began publishing sf with "Night-Eyed Prayer" for

AMZ in 1971, though his later "After You've Stood on the Log at the Center of the Universe, What is There Left To Do?" (1974) was more notable. *Time's Fool* (**1981**) is an unremarkable though moderately appealing sf adventure. [JC]

CARROLL, LEWIS Pseudonym of UK mathematician and writer Charles Lutwidge Dodgson (1832-1898), whose famous children's stories, *Alice's Adventures in Wonderland* (**1865**) and *Through the Looking Glass and What Alice Found There* (**1871**), an early example of the novel whose "moves" are based on a game of chess, have had a profound impact on a wide range of writers. It has been argued by Brian W. ALDISS, among others, that the underlying logic of these "nonsense" adventures has provided a significant model for much of sf's typical reorderings of reality – certainly in most sf novels whose heroes' PARANOIA about reality turns out to be justified. Both novels were assembled much later, and very usefully, as *The Annotated Alice: Alice's Adventures in Wonderland and Through the Looking Glass* (omni **1960** US) ed Martin GARDNER. A series of "continuations" of the **Alice** novels was started by Gilbert Adair with *Alice Through the Needle's Eye* ∗ (**1984**). LC's mathematical and logical fantasies, as found in *A Tangled Tale* (**1886**), have also had repercussions in sf. [JC]

Other works include: *Phantasmagoria and Other Poems* (coll **1869**); *The Hunting of the Snark: An Agony in Eight Fits* (**1876** chap), *Sylvie and Bruno* (1867 *Aunt Judy's Magazine* as "Bruno's Revenge"; exp **1889**) and its sequel (also derived from the story), *Sylvie and Bruno Concluded* (**1893**); *The Wasp in a Wig* (**1977** chap), a portion of *Through the Looking-Glass* cut at proof stage and lost until 1977.

About the author: *The Life and Letters of Lewis Carroll* (**1898**) by Stuart Dodgson Collingwood; *Victoria through the Looking-Glass* (**1945**; vt *Lewis Carroll* 1954 UK) by Derek Hudson; *Aspects of Alice* (**1971**) ed Robert Phillips.

See also: FANTASTIC VOYAGES; HOLLOW EARTH; MATHEMATICS; VIRTUAL REALITY.

CARS THAT ATE PARIS, THE Film (1974). Salt Pan/Australian Film Development Corp/Royce Smeal. Written and dir Peter Weir, starring Terry Camilleri, John Meillon, Kevin Miles. 88 mins. Colour.

From a director who later made several impressive fantasy films, including *Picnic at Hanging Rock* (1975) and *The Last Wave* (1977), both of which edge close to sf at points, *TCTAP* is an idiosyncratic exploitation movie about a small town in which young people drive murderously redesigned cars (some covered in spikes) up and down the roads at high speed, rapidly disposing of any visitors via crashes and then cannibalizing the wreckage; any survivors are turned over to the local mad doctor who uses them as experimental subjects. An air of automotive apocalypse is produced, as in Jean-Luc Godard's otherwise very different WEEKEND (1967). In *TCTAP*, a witty, smaller-scale work, the town that lives by the car dies by the car. *TCTAP* points forward to the MAD MAX movies, also Australian, which similarly feature killer cars, gladiatorial sports and diseased societies. [PN]

CARTER, ANGELA (OLIVE STALKER) (1940-1992) UK writer best known for her work outside the sf field, though all her novels and tales are characterized by an expressionist freedom of reference to everyday "reality" which often emerges as fantasy. She won the John Llewelyn Rhys Memorial Prize for her second novel, *The Magic Toyshop* (**1967**), and the Somerset Maugham Award for *Several Perceptions* (**1968**). Her first tale to engage in a recognizably sf displacement of reality, *Heroes and Villains* (**1969**), does so with a similar freedom, for AC was one of the few UK writers of genuine FABULATIONS, of POSTMODERNIST works in which storytelling conventions are mixed and examined, and in which the style of telling is strongly language-oriented. *Heroes and Villains* is set in a post-HOLOCAUST England inhabited by (a) dwellers in the ruins of cities, whose society is rigidly stratified into Professors and the Soldiers who guard them and, (b) Barbarians who live in the surreal mutated forests that cover the land. Like much of her work, the novel uses GOTHIC images and conventions to examine and to parody the concerns of its protagonists and the desolate world they inhabit. In the story of Marianne, a Professor's daughter, who leaves the ruined city for a Barbarian life where she undergoes a violent erotic awakening, AC definitively entangles sex and decadence (or female freedom).

Erotic complexities, shamans and deliquescent urban landscapes proliferate in such later novels as *The Infernal Desire Machines of Doctor Hoffman* (**1972**; vt *The War of Dreams* 1974 US), which is a quest into dream, *The Passion of New Eve* (**1977**), which is a baroque picaresque through a holocaust-enflamed USA, and *Nights at the Circus* (**1984**), in which a grandly fabulated, densely conceived phantasmagorical world surrounds the tale of a "deformed" woman performer whose wings are real, whose womanhood is no deformity. AC's stories were collected as: *Fireworks* (coll **1974**; rev 1987), assembled with the non-genre *Love* (**1971**; rev 1987) as *Artificial Fire* (omni **1988** Canada); *The Bloody Chamber* (coll **1979**), a series of *contes* dissective of female sexuality; and *Black Venus* (coll **1985**; rev vt *Saints and Strangers* 1986 US), which includes *Black Venus's Tale* (**1980** chap). Though she was never associated with the sf NEW WAVE, it was perhaps through the widening of the gates of perception due to that movement that readers of sf were induced to treat AC's difficult but rewarding work as being of interest to a genre audience. She died very much too young. [JC]

Other works: *Moonshadow* (**1982** chap) with Justin Todd, a juvenile; *Come unto These Yellow Sands: Four Radio Plays* (coll **1985**); *The Virago Book of Fairy Tales* (anth **1990**; vt *The Old Wives' Fairy Tale Book* 1990 US).

As translator: *The Fairy Tales of Charles Perrault* (trans **1977**); *Sleeping Beauty and Other Favourite Fairy Tales* (trans and ed **1982**).

See also: ANTHROPOLOGY; DISASTER; FANTASTIC VOYAGES; FANTASY; HISTORY OF SF; MYTHOLOGY; PERCEPTION; PSYCHOLOGY; SUPERNATURAL CREATURES; WOMEN SF WRITERS.

CARTER, BRUCE Pseudonym of UK military historian, novelist and editor Richard (Alexander) Hough (1922-   ) for his stories and nonfiction books for juveniles, beginning with an sf title, *The Perilous Descent into a Strange Lost World* (**1952**; vt *Into a Strange Lost World* 1953 US). Other sf novels for older children have included *The Deadly Freeze* (**1976**) and *Buzzbugs* (**1977**). *Nightworld* (**1987**) is an animal fantasy. [JC]

CARTER, CARMEN (1954-   ) US writer who has been primarily associated with STAR TREK, writing one solo tie for **Star Trek** itself, *Dreams of the Raven* ∗ (**1987**), and two for **Star Trek, the Next Generation**, *The Children of Hamelin* ∗ (**1988**) and, with Michael Jan FRIEDMAN, Peter DAVID and Robert Greenberger, *Doomsday World* ∗ (**1990**). Earlier she published a short fantasy fable, *The Shy Beast* (**1984** chap). [JC]

CARTER, DEE ◊ Dennis HUGHES.

CARTER, LIN Working name of US writer and editor Linwood Vrooman Carter (1930-1988), most of whose work of any significance was done in the field of HEROIC FANTASY, an area of concentration he went some way to define in his critical study of relevant texts and techniques, *Imaginary Worlds* (**1973**). Much of his own heroic fantasy derives, sometimes too mechanically, from the precepts about its writing which he aired in this book. As an editor, he was most active about 1969-72, when as consultant for BALLANTINE BOOKS he conceived their adult FANTASY list and presented many titles under that aegis, bringing to the contemporary paperback market writers such as James Branch CABELL, Lord DUNSANY and Clark Ashton SMITH. With Cabell, he merely reprinted some titles; but with H.P. LOVECRAFT, Dunsany and Smith he reassembled material under his own titles *(for details see their entries)*. Most of his criticism has been closely linked to his strong interest in fantasy of this sort; it includes *Tolkien: A Look Behind "The Lord of the Rings"* (**1969**) and *Lovecraft: A Look Behind the "Cthulhu Mythos"* (**1972**). LC began publishing sf with "Masters of the Metropolis" for *FSF* in 1957 with Randall GARRETT; and with L. Sprague de Camp he adapted and expanded many stories, especially **Conan** infills, like *Conan the Swordsman* ∗ (**1978**) and *Conan the Liberator* ∗ (**1979**), which Robert E. Howard had left unpublished or unrealized, and created others *(for further details* ◊ L. Sprague DE CAMP; Robert E. HOWARD).

As an author in his own right, LC tended to concentrate on pastiches of the kind of heroic fantasy to which he was devoted. His first novel, *The Wizard of Lemuria* (**1965**; rev vt *Thongor and the Wizard of Lemuria* 1969), begins a long and (as it turned out) typical series of fantasies about the exploits of **Thongor** in various venues, continuing with *Thongor of Lemuria* (**1966**; rev vt *Thongor and the Dragon City* 1970), *Thongor Against the Gods* (**1967**), *Thongor in the City of Magicians* (**1968**), *Thongor at the End of Time* (**1968**) and *Thongor Fights the Pirates of Tarakus* (**1970**). Like succeeding series (see listing below), the **Thongor** tales represent a swift though somewhat exiguous fantasizing of routine pulp protocols. Though these fantasies were often set (like Edgar Rice BURROUGHS's) on various florid worlds, and could be thought of as PLANETARY ROMANCES, they were not in any committed sense sf in tone; LC's output of sf proper is relatively scant. The **Great Imperium** sequence – *The Star Magicians* (**1966** dos), *The Man without a Planet* (**1966** dos), *Tower of the Medusa* (**1969**), *Star Rogue* (**1970**) and *Outworlder* (**1971**) – comes attractively closer; and the **Mars** series – *The Man who Loved Mars* (**1973**), *The Valley where Time Stood Still* (**1974**), *The City Outside the World* (**1977**) and *Down to a Sunless Sea* (**1984**) – has moments of poignance where sf and SCIENCE FANTASY grant perspectives by overlapping. Overproduction blurred LC's image (though illness slowed him down considerably in later years), giving weight to the feeling that he sometimes paid inadequate attention to the quality of his products or to assuring their individuality. His work as an editor eclipses his own writings in importance. [JC]

Other works:

Series: The **Thoth** sequence, comprising *The Thief of Thoth* (**1968** chap) and *The Purloined Planet* (**1969** chap dos), which is sf; the **Chronicles of Kylix**, comprising *The Quest of Kadji* (**1971**) and *The Wizard of Zao* (**1978**); the **Gondwana Epic**, comprising *The Warrior of World's End*, (**1974**), *The Enchantress of World's End* (**1975**), *The Immortal of World's End* (**1976**), *The Barbarian of World's End* (**1977**), *The Pirate of World's End* (**1978**) and, first published but the concluding volume, *Giant of World's End* (**1969**); the **Callisto** sequence, comprising *Jandar of Callisto* (**1972**), *Black Legion of Callisto* (**1972**), *Sky Pirates of Callisto* (**1973**), *Mad Empress of Callisto* (**1975**), *Mind Wizards of Callisto* (**1975**), *Lankar of Callisto* (**1975**), *Ylana of Callisto* (**1977**) and *Renegade of Callisto* (**1978**); the **Green Star Rises** sequence, comprising *Under the Green Star* (**1972**), *When the Green Star Calls* (**1973**), *By the Light of the Green Star* (**1974**), *As the Green Star Rises* (**1975**), *In the Green Star's Glow* (**1976**) and *As the Green Star Rises* (**1983**); the DOC SAVAGE-like **Zarkon** sequence, comprising *Zarkon, Lord of the Unknown, in The Nemesis of Evil* (**1975**; vt *The Nemesis of Evil* 1978), *Zarkon, Lord of the Unknown, in Invisible Death* (**1975**; vt *Zarkon, Lord of the Unknown and his Omega Crew: Invisible Death* 1978), *Zarkon, Lord of the Unknown, in The Volcano Ogre* (**1976**; vt *Zarkon, Lord of the Unknown and his Omega Crew: The Volcano Ogre* 1978), *Zarkon, Lord of the Unknown, in The Earth-Shaker* (**1982**) and *Horror Wears Blue* (**1987**); the **Zanthodon** sequence, comprising *Journey to the Underground World* (**1979**), *Zanthodon* (**1980**), *Hurok of the Stone Age* (**1981**), *Darya of the Stone Age* (**1981**) and *Eric of Zanthodon* (**1982**); the **Terra Magica** sequence, comprising *Kesrick* (**1982**), *Dragon-*

rouge (**1984**), *Mandricardo* (**1986**) and *Callipygia* (**1988**).
Singletons: *Destination Saturn* (**1967**) with David Grinnell (Donald A. WOLLHEIM); *The Flame of Iridar* (**1967** chap dos); *Tower at the Edge of Time* (**1968**); *Beyond the Gates of Dream* (coll **1969**); *Lost World of Time* (**1969**); *Outworlder* (**1971**); *The Black Star* (**1973**); *Time War* (**1974**); *Dreams from R'lyeh* (coll **1975** chap), poetry; *Tara of the Twilight* (**1979**); *Lost Worlds* (coll **1980**); *Kellory the Warlock* (**1984**); *Found Wanting* (**1985**).
As editor: *Dragons, Elves and Heroes* (anth **1969**); *The Young Magicians* (anth **1969**); *The Magic of Atlantis* (anth **1970**); *Golden Cities, Far* (anth **1970**); *The Spawn of Cthulhu* (anth **1971**); *New Worlds for Old* (anth **1971**); *Discoveries in Fantasy* (anth **1972**); *Great Short Novels of Adult Fantasy* (anth **1972**) and *Great Short Novels of Adult Fantasy II* (anth **1973**); the **Flashing Swords** series, comprising *Flashing Swords 1* (anth **1973**), *#2* (anth **1973**), *#3: Warriors and Wizards* (anth **1976**), *#4: Barbarians and Black Magicians* (anth **1977**) and *#5: Demons and Daggers* (anth **1981**); the **Year's Best Fantasy series, comprising** *The Year's Best Fantasy Stories 1* (anth **1975**), *#2* (anth **1976**), *#3* (anth **1977**), *#4* (anth **1978**), *#5* (anth **1980**) and *#6* (anth **1980**); *Kingdoms of Sorcery* (anth **1976**); *Realms of Wizardry* (anth **1976**); the **Weird Tales** series, comprising *Weird Tales 1* (anth **1980**), *#2* (anth **1980**), *#3* (anth **1981**) and *#4* (anth **1983**).
Nonfiction: *Royal Armies of the Hyborean Age: A Wargamer's Guide to the Age of Conan* (**1975** chap) both with Scott Bizar; *Middle-Earth: The World of Tolkien* (**1977**) with David Wenzel (1950-   ), pictures with captions.
See also: ATLANTIS; DAW BOOKS; SWORD AND SORCERY.

CARTER, NICK Fictional sleuth, and house name for many of the titles in which he appears. Created by John Russell Coryell (1848-1924) in *The Old Detective's Pupil, or The Mysterious Crime at Madison Square Garden* (**1886**) on the model of Allan Pinkerton (1819-1884), founder of the famous detective agency, NC featured in many subsqent US dime novels, including several of sf interest (◊ DIME-NOVEL SF) by Frederick Van Rensselaer Dey (1861-1922) writing as Chickering Carter – the name of one of Carter's numerous assistants – published in the *New Nick Carter Weekly* in 1907, the most notable being "The Index of Seven Stars, or Nick Carter Finds the Hidden City", "An Amazonian Queen, or Nick Carter Becomes a Gladiator" and "The Seven-Headed Monster, or Nick Carter's Midnight Caller". Other authors of **Nick Carter** tales before WWII included John Chambliss, Philip Clark, William Wallace COOK, Frederick William Davis, George Charles Jenks (1850-1929), whose normal pseudonym was W.B. Lawson, Johnston McCulley (1883-1958) and Eugene Taylor Sawyer. Magazines such as the *Nick Carter Detective Library* were supplemented by radio, film and tv incarnations, over the course of which Carter himself became noticeably tougher and more murderous, his resemblance to Sexton Blake being correspondingly less marked in more recent years. The **Nick Carter** series

of soft-porn thrillers from the 1960s rarely slipped into sf, and never with much point; typical of titles verging on sf were (all as by Nick Carter) *The Human Time Bomb: A Killmaster Spy Chiller* (**1969**), *Living Death* (**1969**) by Jon Messmann, *Operation Moon Rocket* (**1970**) and *The Death Strain* (**1971**). It is understood that among the authors about this time were, in addition to Messmann, Michael AVALLONE, Dennis LYNDS, Martin Cruz SMITH and Richard WORMSER. A decade later, a further batch of sf titles was produced, again all as by NC, including *The Doomsday Spore* (**1979**) by George Warren, *The Q-Man* (**1981**) by John Stevenson, *The Solar Menace* (**1981**) and *Doctor DNA* (**1982**), both by Robert E. VARDEMAN, *The Last Samurai* (**1982**) by Bruce Algozin and *Deathlight* (**1982**) by Jerry AHERN. [JC]

CARTER, PAUL A(LLEN) (1926-   ) US social historian and writer who began publishing sf with "The Last Objective" for *ASF* in 1946. His occasional stories over the next decades showed that, had he wished, he could have made writing his primary career. In *The Creation of Tomorrow: Fifty Years of Magazine Science Fiction* (anth **1977**) he demonstrated an intimate and sophisticated knowledge of the field. With Gregory BENFORD he has published a short novel, *Iceborn* (**1989** in *Synergy 3* ed George ZEBROWSKI, as "Proserpina's Daughter"; exp **1989** chap dos). [JC]
See also: POLITICS.

CARTER, R.M.H. [r] ◊ ROBERT HALE LIMITED.

CARTIER, EDD Working name of US illustrator Edward Daniel Cartier (1914-   ). After graduation in 1936 from the Pratt Institute in Brooklyn, New York, EC was hired by STREET & SMITH to work on their PULP MAGAZINES, notably *The Shadow*. His skills were noticed by John W. CAMPBELL Jr, who began using him in the new magazine UNKNOWN, for which EC did many black-and-white interiors from #1 onwards and, from Dec 1939, five covers. For many readers EC's combination of whimsy and menace summed up the quality of that magazine. He quickly became very popular, perhaps because the humorous feel of his work was then so unusual in sf ILLUSTRATION. He left in 1941 to fight in WWII, was wounded in the Battle of the Bulge, and returned to illustration in 1946. Thereafter his main markets were ASTOUNDING SCIENCE-FICTION, DOC SAVAGE MAGAZINE, OTHER WORLDS and the SMALL PRESSES, like FANTASY PRESS and GNOME PRESS, which often reprinted *ASF* material in book form. EC later went back to college, graduated in fine arts, and left sf illustration around 1954 to work in graphic design. He will be remembered for the wit and boldness of his black-and-white work for the Street & Smith magazines. [JG/PN]
See also: COMICS; FANTASY.

CARTMILL, CLEVE (1908-1964) US author and journalist; co-inventor of the Blackmill system of high-speed typography. His early work appeared in *Unknown*, including his first story, "Oscar" (**1941**), and several short FANTASY novels; one of these, "Hell Hath Fury" (**1943**), was featured in the George HAY anthology of the same title (1963). During the 1940s he was also active in US sf magazines, publishing in all about 40 stories, including the **Space Salvage** series in *TWS*, later collected as *The Space Scavengers* (coll of linked stories 1975). He is remembered for a famous story in *ASF*, "Deadline" (1944), which described the atomic bomb a year before it was dropped. US Security subsequently descended on *ASF* but was persuaded (truthfully) by John W. CAMPBELL Jr that CC had used for his research only material available in public libraries. CC's prediction made sf fans enormously proud, and the story was made a prime exhibit in the arguments about PREDIC-TION in sf. In this NEAR-FUTURE fable the evil Sixa (i.e., Axis) forces are prevented from dropping the Bomb, and the Seilla (Allies) decline to do so, justly fearing its dread potential.   [JC]

About the author: "The Manhattan Project's Confrontation with Science Fiction" (1984 *ASF*) by Albert Berger.

See also: NUCLEAR POWER; RELIGION.

CARVER, JEFFREY A(LLAN) (1949-   ) US writer who began publishing sf with ". . . Of No Return" for *Fiction Magazine* in 1974. His first novel, *Seas of Ernathe* (1976 Canada), showed early signs of a love of plot and thematic complexity which would take him some time, and several novels, to control. *Star Rigger's Way* (1978), for instance, combines quest routines, new starflight technologies, various planets and transcendental ALIENS in a tale whose final effect is incoherent, though promising; nor is *Panglor* (1980) significantly better behaved. But *The Infinity Link* (1984) is a large and ambitious recasting of his abiding material – space epic venues, striving human protagonists in transcendental communion with aliens or AIS – into the tale of a human woman telepathically linked with a passing interstellar race. *The Rapture Effect* (1987) brought the ARTS into the mix, suggesting in the end that a secret war between a human-built AI and its distant alien counterpart might be resolved, finally, through the mediation of some ambitious human artists. And in the **Starstream** sequence – *From a Changeling Star* (1989), *Down the Stream of Stars* (1990) and *Dragons in the Stars* (1992) – JAC created at last a galactic environment of sufficient richness to contain a still somewhat overexuberant imagination. In the first volume, a "starstream" has opened up between Earth space and the centre of the Galaxy, allowing for intercourse and settlement; the plot, which is extremely complicated, involves its protagonist in a quest inwards to regions where stars are numerous, by the end of which, killed and rekilled and reborn, he is saved by the overseeing AI which narrates the second volume. NANOTECHNOLOGIES are described; poetries and epiphanies and space wars proliferate. JAC seems to be thoroughly enjoying his worlds.   [JC]

Other work: *Roger Zelazny's Alien Speedway #1: Clypsis* (1987).

See also: MUSIC.

CASANOVA DE SEINGALT, GIACOMO (1725-1798)

Venetian writer, variously employed; best known for his *Mémoires* (posthumously published in 12 vols 1826-38), the single-mindedness of which caused his name to pass into the language . He wrote primarily in French, the language of his FANTASTIC-VOYAGE novel, *Icosameron, ou Histoire d'Édouard et d'Élizabeth Qui Passèrent Quatre-Vingte Un Ans chez les Mégamicres Habitans Aborigènes du Protocosme dans l'Intérieur de Notre Globe* (1788; cut trans Rachel Zurer as *Casanova's "Icosameron" or the Story of Edward and Elizabeth who Spent Eighty-One Years in the Land of the Megamicres, Original Inhabitants of Protocosmos in the Interior of the Globe* 1986 US). The protagonists spend 81 years in a world in the HOLLOW EARTH inhabited by the androgynous and oviparous Mégamicres ("big/littles" – small in stature and large in spirit), who have been there from before the Fall – this land being an analogue of Eden – avoiding Original Sin, but soulless (cf James BLISH's *A Case of Conscience*, 1958). They describe their society to the two shipwrecked wanderers at some length (the novel occupies 5 vols, each 350pp or more), and the wanderers (brother and sister, though they mate in the Eden they discover) in turn tell their tale, in dialogue form, to a group of English aristocrats; they have left millions of descendants inside the Earth, and transformed society there. The book is quite realistic in tone, and contains a great deal of scientific speculation and anticipation, notably about electricity, and a fair amount of social SATIRE. It was probably influenced by VOLTAIRE's *Micromégas* (France 1752), and more directly by Ludvig HOLBERG's *Nicolaii Klimii Iter Subterraneum* (1741 in Latin; trans as *A Journey to the World Underground* 1742).   [JC/PN]

See also: FRANCE; ITALY.

CASARES, ADOLFO BIOY [r] ◊ Adolfo BIOY CASARES.

CASE, JOSEPHINE YOUNG (1907-1990) US writer of a remarkable book-length sf poem, *At Midnight on the 31st of March* (1938), set in a New England village suddenly isolated by some unidentified DISASTER from the rest of the USA, and consequently cast upon its own closely observed resources. What seemed, on its 1990 republication, to read as tocsin nostalgia for an impossible rapport with mythic roots may have read in 1938 as a clarion call.   [JC]

CASEWIT, CURTIS W(ERNER) (1922-   ) US writer born in Germany and educated in different countries (hence multilingual), resident in the USA from 1948. He has published in various fields, his first sf story, "The Mask" (1952), appearing in *Weird Tales*. His sf novel, *The Peacemakers* (1960), depicts conflicting societies after WWIII; a former soldier tries to become dictator.   [JC]

CASEY, RICHARD House name used on the ZIFF-DAVIS magazines 1943-8 by Leroy YERXA and others.

CASPER ◊ AWARDS; CANADA.

CASPER, SUSAN (1947-   ) US editor and writer, married to Gardner DOZOIS. She began publishing sf with "Spring-Fingered Jack" for *Fears* (anth 1983) ed Charles GRANT. Her fiction in collaboration with Dozois was assembled in *Slow Dancing through Time* (coll **1990**), which includes a collaboration with both Dozois and Jack M. DANN. Also with Dozois, she edited *Ripper!* (anth **1988**; vt *Jack the Ripper* 1988 UK).　　　　　　　　　　　　　　　　　　　[JC]

See also: CRIME AND PUNISHMENT.

CASSUTT, MICHAEL (1954-　) US writer who began publishing sf with "A Second Death" for *AMZ* in 1974, and whose numerous tv credits include serving as staff writer for *The* TWILIGHT ZONE in 1986 and story editor for MAX HEADROOM in 1987. His sf novel, *Star Country* (**1986**), set in a balkanized post-HOLOCAUST USA, competently dovetails two stories, one concerning an escaped ALIEN, the other a commune which has attempted to turn its collective back on the world. His *Who's Who in Space: The First 25 Years* (**1987**) provides biographies of a wide range of people involved in the first years of humanity's move off-planet. *Sacred Visions* (anth **1991**) with Andrew M. GREELEY is an anthology, by no means pious, of sf about and/or reflecting RELIGION.　　　　[JC]

Other works: *Dragon Season* (**1991**), a fantasy.

CASTERET, NORBERT (1897-　) French speleologist and writer whose sf novel, *Mission centre terre* (**1964**; trans Antonia Ridge and rev as *Mission Underground* **1968** UK), sends explorers several miles into the Earth in a specially designed craft.　　　　　　　[JC]

Other works: *La terre ardente* (**1950**); *Muta fille des cavernes* (**1965**).

CASTILLO, GABRIEL BERMÚDEZ [r] ◊ SPAIN.

CASTLE, DAMON ◊ Richard REINSMITH.

CASTLE, J(EFFERY) LLOYD (1898-　) UK writer whose first sf novel, *Satellite E One* (**1954**), deals awkwardly with the scientific details surrounding the construction of a space satellite. His second, *Vanguard to Venus* (**1957**), identifies UFOS as the ships of descendants of spacefaring ancient Egyptians.　　[JC]

CASTLE, ROBERT [s] ◊ Edmond HAMILTON.

CATASTROPHE ◊ DISASTER; END OF THE WORLD; HOLOCAUST AND AFTER.

CAVALIER, THE US general-fiction PULP MAGAZINE published by the Frank A. MUNSEY Co., ed Robert H. Davis. It evolved from *The* SCRAP BOOK and appeared monthly Oct 1908-Jan 1912, became *The Cavalier Weekly*, 6 Jan 1912-9 May 1914, then merged with *All-Story Weekly* to form *All Story Cavalier Weekly* (◊ *The* ALL-STORY). Although comparatively short-lived, *TC* published two celebrated sf works: Garrett P. SERVISS's *The Second Deluge* (1911-12; **1912**) and George Allan ENGLAND's *Darkness and Dawn* (1912-13 as 3 separate novels; fixup **1914**; in 5 vols with editorial changes **1964-77**). Among the numerous short stories were works by Edgar FRANKLIN, J.U. GIESY (with Junius B. Smith) and John D. Swain. Several stories from *TC* were reprinted in FAMOUS FANTASTIC MYSTERIES and FANTASTIC NOVELS.　　　　　　　　[JE]

CAVALIER WEEKLY ◊ *The* CAVALIER.

CAWTHORN, JAMES (1929-　) UK illustrator, critic and writer. He entered sf around 1954, early becoming friendly with Michael MOORCOCK through a shared interest in Edgar Rice BURROUGHS, and working with him on *Tarzan Adventures*, a COMIC book ed Moorcock. As Philip James he wrote *The Distant Suns* (1969 *The Illustrated Weekly of India*; exp **1975**) with Moorcock. As JC he wrote book reviews for *NW*, but was best known as an illustrator, his work appearing often in *NW* but also in comics and on occasional book covers. At his best his naïve, rough lines work vividly; sometimes they simply seem too crude. His SWORD-AND-SORCERY illustration is uneven. Books in GRAPHIC-NOVEL form are *Stormbringer* (graph **1975**), *The Jewel in the Skull* (graph **1978**), *The Crystal and the Amulet* (graph **1986**), all existing works by Moorcock adapted by JC, the latter based on *Sorcerer's Amulet* (**1968**; rev 1977; vt *The Mad God's Amulet*), the second of the **Runestaff** books. He co-scripted with Moorcock the 1975 film *The* LAND THAT TIME FORGOT. The critical book *Fantasy: The 100 Best Books* (**1988**) by JC and Moorcock is, according to Moorcock's Introduction, mostly by JC, and is notable for the heavy emphasis it places on early FANTASY, only 24 of the 100 works discussed being post-1955.　　　　　[PN]

CAXTON [s] ◊ W.H. RHODES.

ČECH, SVATOPLUK [r] ◊ CZECH AND SLOVAK SF.

CHABER, M.E. ◊ Kendell Foster CROSSEN.

CHADWICK, P(HILIP) G(EORGE) (1893-1955) UK author whose only novel, *The Death Guard* (**1939**), was virtually forgotten until its 1992 reissue. It describes the development of the "Flesh Guard", a race of laboratory-created vegetal humanoids, at the time of the emergence of a fascist dictatorship in the UK, and depicts a future WAR as the Earth's major nations react to the horror of such an army in the hands of an extremist government. The book contains several themes later developed by L. Ron HUBBARD and James BLISH, and is at times reminiscent of William Hope HODGSON.　　　　　[JE]

See also: POLITICS.

CHAIRMAN, THE ◊ *The* MOST DANGEROUS MAN IN THE WORLD.

CHALKER, JACK L(AURENCE) (1944-　) US writer and editor, though now very much better known for his fiction. He was active as a fan from an early age, and producer of a successful FANZINE, *Mirage*. As editor, he founded and edited the MIRAGE PRESS, which specialized in sf scholarship. His own work in that area began with *The New H.P. Lovecraft Bibliography* (**1962** chap; rev vt *The Revised H. P. Lovecraft Bibliography* 1974 chap with Mark OWINGS) and *In Memoriam: Clark Ashton Smith* (anth **1963** chap), continuing with some studies and guides with Owings, who is sometimes listed as a pseudonym of JLC, a confusion arising from his sole crediting for *The Necronomicon: A Study* (**1967** chap), which was in fact collaborative. They also worked together on *Mirage on Lovecraft* (**1965** chap) and *The Index to the Science Fantasy Publishers* (**1966** chap; rev vt *Index to the SF Publishers* 1979 chap). After the solo *An Informal Biography of $crooge McDuck* (1971 *Markings*; **1974** chap), JLC moved his attention to fiction, only returning to his earlier interest 20 years later with a new edition of his 1979 *Index*, which though technically a revision of the earlier work was in fact 10 times its length, and can logically be treated as either a vt or a new title: *The Science-Fantasy Publishers: A Critical and Bibliographic History* (**1991**), still with Owings (*see also* BIBLIOGRAPHIES).

His first novel, an ambitious singleton SPACE OPERA, *A Jungle of Stars* (**1976**), proved typical in that its opposing aliens (who are both ex-gods) represent in their conflict a form of populist argument about alternative utopian worldviews, and in that its plot concentrates on members of mortal races who have been recruited to do the superbeings' fighting for them in a kind of world-arena. This underlying articulacy and the plot-device of recruitment also mark his most successful single novel, *Dancers in the Afterglow* (**1978**), a complex and melancholy tale of oppression and enforced metamorphosis on a conquered colony planet, in which questions of power and morality are again asked with some ease, and the human need for freedom is answered (and at the same time deeply assaulted) by transformation tropes out of SCIENCE FANTASY and nightmare. *Dancers* contains in embryo almost all of the next decade or so of JLC's prolific career, most of which has been given over to the construction of large series. The first, the **Well World** sequence, begins with his second fiction title, *Midnight at the Well of Souls* (**1977**), and continues with *The Wars of the Well* – in 2 vols: *Exiles at the Well of Souls* (**1978**) and *Quest for the Well of Souls* (**1978**) – *The Return of Nathan Brazil* (**1980**) and *Twilight at the Well of Souls: The Legacy of Nathan Brazil* (**1980**). In this series the dominant pattern of the JLC multi-volume tale can be seen. Into a world which reveals itself in the shape of a game-board disguised as a DYSTOPIA, recruited and metamorphosed mortals are introduced to find their way, usually stark-naked, to the heart of the labyrinth, where wait the godlings, and, perhaps, as a reward, the true form they have always secretly wished to assume. It is a pattern open to facile abuse (several of JLC's fantasy series, as listed below, exhibit a strange monotony) but which remains exhilarating and innovative in his other major sf series, **The Four Lords of the Diamond** (omni **1983**), which assembles *Lilith: A Snake in the Grass* (**1981**), *Cerberus: A Wolf in the Fold* (**1982**), *Charon: A Dragon at the Gate* (**1982**) and *Medusa: A Tiger by the Tail* (**1983**). The **Quintara Marathon** sf series – *Demons at Rainbow Bridge* (**1989**), *The Run to Chaos Keep* (**1991**) and *The Ninety Trillion Fausts* (**1991**) – further rehearses this material. Of JLC's infrequent singletons, *The Identity Matrix* (**1982**) and *Downtiming the Night Side* (**1985**) perhaps stand out; his short fiction, also infrequent, is represented by *Dance Band on the Titanic* (coll **1988**). JLC is a novelist of considerable flair, with an ear acutely attuned to the secret dreams of freedom mortals tend to dream, but is prone to gross and compulsively repetitive overproduction. He will not be remembered for his second thoughts. [JC]

Other works: The **Soul Rider** science-fantasy

sequence, comprising *Spirits of Flux and Anchor* (**1984**), *Empires of Flux and Anchor* (**1984**), *Masters of Flux and Anchor* (**1985**), *The Birth of Flux and Anchor* (**1985**) – an sf prequel – and *Children of Flux and Anchor* (**1986**); the **Dancing Gods** sequence, comprising *The River of Dancing Gods* (**1984**), *Demons of the Dancing Gods* (**1984**), *Vengeance of the Dancing Gods* (**1985**) and *Songs of the Dancing Gods* (**1990**); the **Rings of the Master** sequence, comprising *Lords of the Middle Dark* (**1986**), *Pirates of the Thunder* (**1987**), *Warriors of the Storm* (**1987**) and *Masks of the Martyrs* (**1988**); the **Changewinds** fantasy sequence, comprising *When the Changewinds Blow* (**1987**), *Riders of the Winds* (**1988**) and *War of the Maelstrom* (**1988**), which JLC claims make up a single long novel; an ALTERNATE-WORLDS detective series, **G.O.D. Inc**, comprising *The Labyrinth of Dreams* (**1987**), *The Shadow Dancers* (**1987**) and *The Maze in the Mirror* (**1989**).

Singletons: *The Web of the Chozen* (**1978**); *A War of Shadows* (**1979**); *And the Devil Will Drag You Under* (**1979**); *The Devil's Voyage* (**1981**), mainly about the ship that carried the A-bomb used on Hiroshima to its rendezvous and which was subsequently sunk and its crew eaten by sharks, but also about the security scare caused by Cleve CARTMILL's "Deadline", published in 1944 in John W. CAMPBELL's *ASF*; *The Messiah Choice* (**1985**); *The Red Tape War: A Round-Robin Science Fiction Novel* (**1991**) with Michael RESNICK and George Alec EFFINGER.

See also: GODS AND DEMONS; INVASION; PARANOIA; POCKET UNIVERSE; SMALL PRESSES AND LIMITED EDITIONS; TIME TRAVEL; VIRTUAL REALITY.

CHALLENGE ◊ GAMES AND TOYS.

CHALLIS, GEORGE ◊ Max BRAND.

CHALMERS, GARET [r] ◊ ROBERT HALE LIMITED.

CHAMBERLAIN, HENRY RICHARDSON (1859-1911) US writer and newspaper editor of considerable political sophistication, which shows itself in the conclusion to his sf novel, *6,000 Tons of Gold* (**1894**). After the eponymous treasure trove has unbalanced the world's finances, and only dubiously assisted the needy, a cabal of the wise decides to dump it into the deep sea. [JC]

See also: MONEY.

CHAMBERLAIN, WILLIAM (1903-?   ) US writer whose two borderline sf novels, *Red January* (**1964**) and *China Strike* (**1967**), both feature US pre-emptive strikes against the enemy – in the first case Cuba, about to blackmail the USA, and in the second China, on the verge of dropping a cobalt bomb on her. Neither gets away with it. [JC]

CHAMBERS, ROBERT W(ILLIAM) (1865-1933) Popular US writer, author of over 70 novels in various genres, for the first decade or so of his career mostly fantasies, thereafter mainly historical and romantic works. His first successful work was *The King in Yellow* (coll **1895**; cut vt *The Mask* **1929**). The eponymous "King in Yellow" is not a person but a verse play in book form, which (not unlike several much discussed works of recent sf) drives its readers to despair, madness and even suicide (◊ PSYCHOLOGY). Of the four **King in Yellow** tales in the book, "The Repairer of Reputations" is of particular sf interest, being set in 1920, after a war, in a USA that has legalized suicide. Several other volumes featuring connected stories followed, including *The Maker of Moons* (coll **1896**; title story only **1954** chap) and two sf collections, *In Search of the Unknown* (coll of linked stories **1904**) and its thematic sequel, *Police!!!* (coll of linked stories **1915**), in each of which a philandering zoologist searches for unknown beasts (◊ BIOLOGY), finds them and loses them, along with various girls. *The Gay Rebellion* (1911 *Hampden Magazine*; coll of linked stories **1913**) consists of comical SATIRES in which women revolt but reform and marry properly. RWC's use of sf material is slick and casual, though nightmares sometimes intrude; a teasing, tamed decadence that had marked RWC from the beginning became routinized in his later work, which was presented with professional polish but little conviction. [JC]

Other works: *The Mystery of Choice* (coll **1897**); *The Tracer of Lost Persons* (coll of linked stories **1906**); *The Tree of Heaven* (coll **1907**); *Some Ladies in Haste* (**1908**); *The Green Mouse* (**1910**); *The Hidden Children* (**1914**); *Quick Action* (**1914**) and its sequel, *Athalie* (**1915**); *The Dark Star* (**1917**); *The Slayer of Souls* (**1920**); *The Talkers* (**1923**); *The King in Yellow and Other Horror Stories* (coll **1970**) ed with intro by E.F. BLEILER.

See also: ARTS; SUSPENDED ANIMATION.

CHANCE, JOHN NEWTON [r] ◊ John LYMINGTON.

CHANCE, JONATHAN ◊ John LYMINGTON.

CHANDLER, A(RTHUR) BERTRAM (1912-1984) UK-born writer who served in the Merchant Navy from 1928; in 1956 he emigrated to Australia, where he commanded merchant ships under Australian and New Zealand flags until his retirement in 1975. This long professional experience permeated his writing, and many of his novels feature SPACESHIPS and flotillas whose command structures are decidedly naval. ABC began publishing stories in *ASF* in 1944, on John W. CAMPBELL's invitation, with "This Means War", and concentrated on short fiction for almost two decades, often under the pseudonym George Whitley (in the USA and the UK), less frequently as Andrew Dunstan and S.H.M. (both only in Australia). But he published no books during this time, and maybe for that reason he was until the 1960s less well known than he perhaps deserved, even though some of his best stories date from this period. For some time he was known mainly as the author of "Giant Killer" (1945), a POCKET-UNIVERSE tale which dominates the work posthumously assembled in *From Sea to Shining Star* (coll **1990**), and whose solitary prominence suggests that – although he published nearly 200 stories – ABC was not entirely comfortable in shorter forms.

After reaching the rank of chief officer, ABC stopped writing for some time. He began again with a spate of tales in the late 1950s, and finally published his first novel at the beginning of the new decade. Thereafter he concentrated on full-length, albeit short, books, most of which have dealt, directly or indirectly, with his central venue, the various Rim Worlds set like isolated islands along the edge of the Galaxy (◊ GALACTIC LENS; RIMWORLD) during a period of human expansion. Not all these novels are serially connected, though all have a common background (which includes terminology and a set of frequently mentioned planets, like Thule and Faraway); John Grimes, the protagonist of the central sequence, appears also in some non-series novels. The two **Derek Calver** books – *The Rim of Space* (**1961** US), ABC's first novel, and *The Ship from Outside* (1959 *ASF* as "Familiar Pattern" by George Whitley; exp **1963** dos US) – make up a kind of trailer for the more numerous stories grouped about the figure of Grimes. In these books, Calver, following something like the same course Grimes will, comes to the Rim Worlds, eventually becomes captain of his own starship, *Lorn Lady*, loses her, sails on other star tramps, and engages in far-flung adventures.

Grimes is mentioned in this short series, and the **John Grimes/Rim World** series massively expands upon a very similar career and life. Grimes himself dominates two main sequences. The first chronologically (though most of it was written later) traces his career in the Federation Survey Service up to and beyond the point that he shifts loyalties to the Rim. Their internal order is as follows: *The Road to the Rim* (**1967** dos US); *To Prime the Pump* (**1971** US); *The Hard Way Up* (coll **1972** dos US), which also appears with the first novel as *The Road to the Rim* (omni **1979** US); *False Fatherland* (**1968**; vt *Spartan Planet* 1969 US); *The Inheritors* (**1972** dos US), which involves GENETIC ENGINEERING; *The Broken Cycle* (**1975** UK); *The Big Black Mark* (**1975** US); *The Far Traveller* (**1977** UK); *Star Courier* (**1977** US); *To Keep the Ship* (**1978** UK); *Matilda's Stepchildren* (**1979** UK); *Star Loot* (**1980** US); *The Anarch Lords* (**1981** US); *The Last Amazon* (**1984** US); *The Wild Ones* (**1984**); *Catch the Star Winds* (coll of 1 novel and 1 story **1969** US). The second sequence advances Grimes further into his second career with the Rim Runners and the Rim Worlds Naval Reserve. Begun earlier and not written with any internal order in mind, it includes, in order of publication: *Into the Alternate Universe* (**1964** dos US) and *Contraband from Other-Space* (**1967** dos US), both assembled as *Into the Alternate Universe* (omni **1979** US); *The Rim Gods* (coll of linked stories **1969** dos US) and *The Dark Dimensions* (**1971** dos US), both assembled as *The Dark Dimensions* (omni **1978** US); *Alternate Orbits* (coll **1971** dos US), assembled with *False Fatherland* as *The Commodore at Sea* (omni **1979** US); *The Gateway to Never* (**1972** dos US) – crudely reassembled out of sequence as *The Inheritors* (omni **1978** US), having been originally published *dos-à-dos* with the novel of that title – and *The Way Back* (**1976** UK). Through these books Grimes's somewhat melancholy temperament and consistent ingenuity often remind one of C.S. FORESTER's

Horatio Hornblower, an influence ABC acknowledged (though Grimes's sexual forthrightness strikes a new note); but it is of course more than Hornblower's character that is drawn from the earlier genre. The **Grimes/Rim World** sequence is very clearly a transposition – much more directly than is usually the case – of ships into spaceships, seas into the blackness between the stars, and ports into home-planets. Much of the warmth and detail of ABC's work derives from this direct translation of venues, and Grimes himself establishes a loyalty in his readers rather similar to that felt by readers of Hornblower. Indeed, ABC's SPACE OPERAS are among the most likeable and well constructed in the genre, and his vision of the Rim Worlds – cold, poor, at the antipodean edge of intergalactic darkness, but full of all the pioneer virtues – are the genre's homiest characterization of that corner of space opera's galactic arena.

Two singletons merit some notice. *The Bitter Pill* (**1974**) sourly depicts a totalitarian DYSTOPIA on Earth, and the ultimately successful attempts its leading characters make to wrest Mars free of oppression; and *Kelly Country* (1976 *Void*; exp **1983**) places a war for Australian independence in a PARALLEL-WORLDS setting.

ABC received the Australian Ditmar (◊ AWARDS) in 1969, 1971, 1974 and 1976. [JC]
Other works: *Bring Back Yesterday* (**1961** dos US); *Rendezvous on a Lost World* (**1961** dos US; vt *When the Dream Dies* 1981 UK); *The Hamelin Plague* (**1963** US); *Beyond the Galactic Rim* (coll **1963** dos US); the **Christopher Wilkinson** novels, comprising *The Coils of Time* (**1964** dos US) and *The Alternate Martians* (**1965** dos US); *Glory Planet* (**1964** US); *The Deep Reaches of Space* (**1946** *ASF* as "Special Knowledge"; rev **1964** UK), whose protagonist is ABC's main pseudonym, George Whitley; the **Empress** series of space operas, placed in an ALTERNATE-WORLDS universe similar to Grimes's and comprising *Empress of Outer Space* (**1965** dos US), *Space Mercenaries* (**1965** dos US) and *Nebula Alert* (**1967** dos US); *The Sea Beasts* (**1971** US); *Up to the Sky in Ships* (coll **1982** chap dos US); *To Rule the Refugees* (**1983** Japan); *Frontier of the Dark* (**1984** US); *Find the Lady* (**1984** Japan).
About the author: *Arthur Bertram Chandler, Master Navigator of Space: A Working Bibliography* (latest edn **1989** chap) by Gordon BENSON Jr.
See also: AUSTRALIA; COLONIZATION OF OTHER WORLDS; FASTER THAN LIGHT; GALACTIC EMPIRES; GREAT AND SMALL; ROBERT HALE LIMITED.

CHAPBOOK In the early 19th century this term described a pamphlet on any of a wide range of subjects – from sermons to sensational tales, often illustrated with woodcuts – sold not through bookshops but by "chapmen", who hawked their wares. In the later 19th century, the term began to acquire a contrived antiquarian air, and was used to designate a small book or pamphlet produced for collectors. Although the fake antiquarianism attached to the term has since faded, chapbooks in the sf field are usually produced by SMALL PRESSES as limited editions containing a short story or novella – although the short stories produced as individual volumes by PULPHOUSE PUBLISHING are clearly intended to appeal to a readership beyond merely collectors. In this encyclopedia (◊ How to Use this Book [*pages xxxi-xxxiv*] *for further details*) we have arbitrarily and for the sake of convenience used the abbreviation "chap" to designate any book of fewer than 100 pages. [JC]

CHAPDELAINE, PERRY A(NTHONY) (1925-) US writer, mathematician, research psychologist and director of an author's publishing co-op. His first published sf was "To Serve the Masters" for *If* in 1967. His first sf novel, *Swampworld West* (**1974**), routinely explores a COLONIZATION scenario involving problems between native ALIENS and Earth colonists. His more recent books, *The Laughing Terran* (**1977** UK) and *Spork of the Ayor* (1969 *If*; fixup **1978** UK), like their predecessor, suffer from awkward prose and sf stereotypes. In the 1980s he began with George HAY an enormous project in **The John W. Campbell Letters**; published to date is *The John W. Campbell Letters, Volume 1* (coll **1986**). [JC/PN]
See also: DIANETICS.

CHAPIN, PAUL [s] ◊ Philip José FARMER.

CHAPMAN, SAMUEL (? -?) US writer whose sf novel, *Doctor Jones' Picnic* (**1898**), published in San Francisco, takes the doctor on a BALLOON trip to the North Pole; en route he cures cancer. [JC]
See also: DISCOVERY AND INVENTION.

CHARBONNEAU, LOUIS (HENRY) (1924-) US writer and journalist who, after writing some radio plays at the end of the 1940s, took an MA at the University of Detroit and taught there for some years before beginning to publish sf novels with *No Place on Earth* (**1958**), about a coercive DYSTOPIA. He produced sf for several years thereafter, publishing: *Corpus Earthling* (**1960**), about invading telepathic Martian parasites who eventually pass on their ESP powers to mankind; *The Sentinel Stars* (**1963**), another dystopia, this time about doomed revolts in a regimented future; *Psychedelic-40* (**1965**; vt *The Specials* 1965 UK); and *Antic Earth* (**1967** UK; vt *Down to Earth* 1967 US).

In all these novels LC tends towards claustrophobic situations in which his rather conventional protagonists explore themselves through action scenarios. LC has written novels in other genres, including Westerns (as Carter Travis Young) and mysteries. [JC]
Other works: *The Sensitives* * (**1968**), from the filmscript by Deane ROMANO; *Barrier World* (**1970**); *Embryo* * (**1976**), novelizing EMBRYO (1976); *Intruder* (**1979**), marginal sf.

CHARBY, JAY [s] ◊ Harlan ELLISON.

CHARKIN, PAUL (SAMUEL) (1907-) UK writer, variously employed for many years before writing his three routine sf novels, *Light of Mars* (**1959**), *The Other*

Side of Night (**1960**) and *The Living Gem* (**1963**). [JC]

CHARLES, NEIL House name used by CURTIS WARREN for sf novels written by Brian HOLLOWAY, Dennis HUGHES and John W. JENNISON. [JC]

CHARLES, ROBERT ◊ Robert Charles SMITH.

CHARLES, STEVEN ◊ Charles L. GRANT.

CHARLY Film (1968). Selmur and Robertson Associates. Dir Ralph Nelson, starring Cliff Robertson, Claire Bloom, Lilia Skala, Dick van Patten. Screenplay Stirling Silliphant, based on *Flowers for Algernon* (**1966**) by Daniel KEYES. 106 mins. Colour.

Enthused with the idea of playing a character who goes from subnormality to super-genius and then back again, Cliff Robertson formed his own production company and, after setbacks, made *C* and won an Academy Award for his excellent performance. Much of the pathos of the original is evoked in 30-year-old Charly's progression, after experimental surgery, from amiable idiocy to high INTELLIGENCE, his falling in love with his teacher (Bloom), his further development to genius, and the horror of his final regression. But it is a sentimental story to start with, and Nelson milks it for all it is worth, both happiness (glamorized like a tv commercial) and sadness, and Charly's genius phase is severely marred by the platitudes about society that Silliphant's script requires him to speak. Nonetheless, *C* seriously addresses ideas about intelligence and feeling, and is more ambitious than most sf films of its time. [JB/PN]

CHARNAS, SUZY McKEE (1939-) US writer and former teacher, with an MA in that field. She began publishing sf with a series later assembled as *Walk to the End of the World, and Motherlines* (omni **1989** UK): *Walk to the End of the World* (**1974**) and *Motherlines* (**1978**). The first volume presents an elaborately structured, neurotic, urban, post-HOLOCAUST, misogynist DYSTOPIA in which women ("fems") serve as scapegoats for humanity's near self-destruction. The second offers a feminist (◊ FEMINISM) alternative beyond the CITY, a matriarchal high-plains world where women on horseback ride free and scapegrace. The books aroused considerable interest for the extreme clarity of the positions argued. This extremity, it soon became clear, stemmed from an habitual failure to repeat herself which perhaps cost SMC some market security, though her next book was extremely successful: *Vampire Tapestry* (coll of linked stories **1980**) recounts the life and thoughts of a vampire anthropologist whose experiences, in the end, lie within the human range; the first story thus assembled, "Unicorn Tapestry", won the 1980 NEBULA award. *Dorothea Dreams* (**1986**) is a ghost story in which modern Albuquerque, New Mexico (where SMC lives), intersects with Revolutionary France, bringing its protagonist sharply into an awareness of her human obligations to the world. The **Sorcery Hill** trilogy – *The Bronze King* (**1985**), *The Silver Glove* (**1988**) and *The Golden Thread* (**1989**) – features juvenile protagonists banded together to protect mundane reality from the malefic otherworld; it is a traditional theme, but crisply told, and further underlines the clear lines of thought – and moral persuasiveness – permeating her work. A short story, "Boobs", won the HUGO for 1989. [JC]

Other works: *Listening to Brahms* (1986 *Omni*; **1991** chap); *Moonstone and Tiger Eye* (coll **1992** chap).

About the author: "Utopia at the End of a Male Chauvinist Dystopian World" by Marleen Barr in *Women and Utopia* (anth **1983**) ed Barr; *Suzy McKee Charnas; Octavia Butler; Joan D. Vinge* (**1986**) by Marleen Barr.

See also: ISAAC ASIMOV'S SCIENCE FICTION MAGAZINE; MONSTERS; SUPERNATURAL CREATURES; UTOPIAS; WOMEN AS PORTRAYED IN SCIENCE FICTION; WOMEN SF WRITERS.

CHARTERIS, LESLIE (1907-) US writer born as Leslie Charles Bowyer Yin in Singapore, educated in the UK, legally changed his name to LC in 1928, and became a US citizen in 1946. He remains known almost exclusively for the **Saint** novels featuring Simon Templar, a long series which began – after a few previous heroes had been discarded – with *Meet the Tiger* (**1928** UK; vt *The Saint Meets the Tiger* 1940 US). Of these only *The Last Hero* (**1930** UK; vt *The Saint Closes the Case* 1941 US) features any device or displacement of an sf nature, though several short stories featuring Templar are sf; these have been assembled as *The Fantastic Saint* (coll **1982**) ed Martin Harry GREENBERG and Charles G. WAUGH. LC edited *The Saint's Choice of Impossible Crime* (anth **1945**). [JC]

CHARYN, JEROME (1937-) US writer who was born and educated in New York, which city he has gradually transformed in his fiction into a MAGIC-REALIST venue whose mythopoeic resonances and exorbitant happenings hover at the edge of generic displacements (and beyond), and strongly prefigure the fabulated New Yorks of writers like John CROWLEY and Mark HELPRIN. Few of his 20 or so books are actually fantasy or sf, though most are FABULATIONS; but *Darlin' Bill* (**1980**) creates an almost totally imaginary West and *Pinocchio's Nose* (**1983**) carries its stymied protagonist into the 21st century, where he finally learns to relax, though the world itself is battered. [JC]

Other works: *The Magician's Wife* (graph **1986** Belgium; first English version **1987** US) with François Boucq, a fantasy in GRAPHIC-NOVEL form; *Billy Budd, K.G.B.* (graph trans Elizabeth Bell **1991**) with Boucq.

CHASE, ADAM Pseudonym used usually by Milton LESSER alone, but once in collaboration with Paul W. FAIRMAN on *The Golden Ape* (**1959**), based on "The Quest of the Golden Ape" (1957 *AMZ*) as by Adam Chase and Ivar JORGENSEN, the latter being a house name associated in that spelling with Fairman. [JC]

CHASE, ROBERT R(EYNOLDS) (1948-) US writer initially associated with *ASF* for stories like his first, "Seven Scenes from the Ultimate Monster Movie" in 1984. He began to publish novels with the **Game** sequence of sf adventures set in a feudalized interplanetary venue: *The Game of Fox and Lion* (**1986**) and *Crucible* (**1991**). Intrigues, GENETIC ENGINEERING, and a dash of RELIGION generate a moderately engaging narrative. *Shapers* (**1989**), about an amnesia victim who awakens in a strange world, also invokes sf tradition. [JC]

CHAUCER, DANIEL ◊ Ford Madox FORD.

CHAVIANO, DAÍNA [r] ◊ LATIN AMERICA

CHAYEFSKY, PADDY Working name of US writer Sidney Aaron Chayefsky (1923-1981), most famous for his work as a tv dramatist; *Marty* (produced 1953) marks for many a culmination (and a sign of the passing) of the Golden Age of US tv drama. *The Tenth Man* (theatrical production, 1959) was a Dybbuk fantasy. His sf novel, *Altered States* (**1978**) (◊ METAPHYSICS), propounds the highly dubious Lamarckian concept (◊ EVOLUTION; PSEUDO-SCIENCE) that a person's altered consciousness would alter her/his genetic makeup, in this case re-invoking an inward primordial being (*see also* APES AND CAVEMEN); it was filmed in 1980 as ALTERED STATES. [JC]

See also: DEVOLUTION.

CHAYKIN, HOWARD V(ICTOR) (1950-) US writer/illustrator, mainly of COMICS. HC's first professional work (1973) was the art for MARVEL COMICS's *War of the Worlds* (a sequel to H.G. WELLS's novel!) and DC COMICS's *Sword of Sorcery* (which featured Fritz LEIBER's Fafhrd and the Gray Mouser). Much of his work has been sf. He was writer/artist on *Cody Starbuck* and *Iron Wolf* before drawing the bestselling adaptation of STAR WARS for Marvel in 1976. HC teamed up with Samuel R. DELANY to produce the GRAPHIC NOVEL *Empire* (graph **1978**), and the following year he worked with Michael MOORCOCK on *The Swords of Heaven, the Flowers of Hell* (graph **1979**), a story in Moorcock's **Eternal Champion** series. The first vol of his graphic-novel version (adaptation by Byron PREISS) of Alfred BESTER's *Tiger! Tiger!* (**1956**; vt *The Stars My Destination* US) appeared as *The Stars My Destination Vol 1* (graph **1979**); the second vol, though advertised, was not in fact published until it appeared, with the contents of the first, in *The Stars My Destination* (graph **1992**). After working on Marvel's *Micronauts*, HC painted a number of covers for sf and fantasy paperbacks, returning to comics in 1983 as writer/artist for First Comics's AMERICAN FLAGG! – perhaps his major work – and later on *Time*². He revitalized *The Shadow* for DC (some critics, such as Harlan ELLISON, disapproving of his innovations) in 1986 and *Blackhawk* in 1988. After the pornographic *Black Kiss* (1988-9) HC increasingly concentrated on writing, as in *Twilight* for DC and *Fafhrd and the Gray Mouser* for Marvel. Moorcock speaks of HC's "considerable intelligence and . . . excellent eye". [RH]

See also: HEAVY METAL.

CHEREZ TERNII – K ZVYOZDAM (vt *Per Aspera ad Astra*) Film (1980). Maxim Gorki Studio. Dir Richard Viktorov, starring Elena Metyolkina, Vadim Ledogorov, Uldis Lieldidzh, Vatzlav Dvorzhetsky. Screenplay Kir BULYCHEV, Viktorov. In 2 parts, 40 min and 78 min. Colour.

This pretentious, rather naïve, Soviet young-adult

sf movie typifies many of Bulychev's themes and approaches. It begins well, with a "space Mowgli" – the alien girl Niia – being found by an Earth expedition on a derelict space station; she is unexpectedly well played by a nonprofessional, Metyolkina, a fashion model. Later we have the grim story of her planet, Dessa, where ecological catastrophe has taken place. The capitalist tyranny on the polluted planet is contrasted with a future communist paradise on Earth, which sends a mission of help at the request of Dessa's "progressive forces": the Ecological Space Ambulance team, very specifically not an armed "brotherly" intervention, but peaceful. The high points of the film are its relaxed humour, something Bulychev is good at, and the impressively devastated landscapes of Dessa. [VG]

See also: RUSSIA.

CHERRY, DAVID A. (1949-) US part-time lawyer, part-time illustrator, raised in Oklahoma, brother of sf writer C.J. CHERRYH. Largely self-taught, DAC is a classic realist, working with acrylics and alkyds. He has done a number of book covers, especially for DAW BOOKS, including covers for his sister's work; his art is regularly displayed at sf CONVENTIONS. In 1988 he became President of the Association of Science Fiction/Fantasy Artists (ASFA), and was instrumental in strengthening that struggling organization. He has several times been nominated for a HUGO. A book of his work is *Imagination: The Art & Technique of David A. Cherry* (**1987**). [JG]

CHERRYH, C.J. Working name of US writer Carolyn Janice Cherry (1942-), who taught for some years (1965-76), during which period she published several sf stories, beginning with "The Mind Reader" for *ASF* in 1968; she is the sister of David A. CHERRY. Since becoming a full-time writer in 1976 – and winning the JOHN W. CAMPBELL AWARD for most promising writer for that year – she has produced more novels than stories. The first was *Gate of Ivrel* (**1976**), initiating the **Morgaine** series – continued in *Well of Shiuan* (**1978**) and *Fires of Azeroth* (**1979**), the trilogy being assembled as *The Book of Morgaine* (omni **1979**; vt *The Chronicles of Morgaine* 1985 UK), and the much later *Exile's Gate* (**1988**) – a romantic HEROIC-FANTASY quest epic whose interplanetary venue and underlying rationality prophetically underpin a hectic and perhaps rather florid imagination.

In all her work – which runs a gamut from SHARED-WORLD fantasies to HARD SF – an almost unfailingly creative tension can be sensed between argument and fantastication; and her underlying instinct for construction has been confirmed in the late 1980s by a retroactive and ongoing coordination of more and more of her work – singletons and series both – under the aegis of her sf-grounded **Union-Alliance** Future HISTORY, which embraces most of the home Galaxy through the third and fourth millennia, during which period the Alliance, structured around the Merchanter cultures which operate the huge interstellar freighters necessary for trade, manages to survive at the heart of the more ruthless, expansionist Union. A third force whose influence is felt throughout human space is Earth itself, hugely populous, dominated by aggressive supra-planetary corporations, still the heartland of *Homo sapiens*. Unusually, the sequence is not planet-based, much of the significant action of the central texts taking place in artificial environments, including a wide variety of spaceships, Merchanter freighters (each huge vessel housing an autonomous culture), satellites, waystations and self-sufficient habitats. The "Gehenna Doctrine", which prohibits the cultural contamination of newly discovered planets and therefore serves as a vital structuring device for the series, justifies the focus of those central texts while at the same time – for the Doctrine is often honoured in the breach – providing an enormously malleable frame: thus highly disparate tales may be fitted into the overarching sequence – almost to the point where singletons with no apparent connection to the sequence, including some PLANETARY ROMANCES, might still be thought to belong within the whole because their isolation from any other book proves that the Gehenna Doctrine is working.

The Union-Alliance structure, rough at the edges as it might be, serves primarily to hold and sort background material – a necessary aid for an author whose better work almost invariably offers too much material, too many ALIEN races intersecting too complexly for easy comprehension, a stricture true even of early novels like *Hunter of Worlds* (1977), in which three cultures express themselves in harrowing detail in too few pages; a sense of bustling, impatient cognition pervades the otherwise garish tale of an alien mercenary race fatally involved with *Homo sapiens*. But with her second series – *Kesrith* (1978), *Shon'jir* (1978) and *Kutath* (1979), all three assembled as *The Faded Sun Trilogy* (omni 1987 UK) – the Union-Alliance dichotomy, here presented late in its history when the antipathetic Union has begun to seem more attractive, works to order the profusion of material. Unlike the great majority of sf writers, the most consistent complaint about her work must be that individual stories are too *short*, though the **Merchanter** novels perhaps most central to the overall series use their galactic space-based venues with considerable skill to articulate busy narrative lines. Along with *Heavy Time* (1991) and *Hellburner* (1992), a 24th-century pre-**Alliance** series that currently, in terms of internal chronology, kicks the entire sequence off, these novels – *Serpent's Reach* (1980), *Downbelow Station* (1981), which won the 1981 HUGO, *Merchanter's Luck* (1982), *Cyteen* (1988; vt in 3 vols as *The Betrayal* 1989, *The Rebirth* 1989 and *The Vindication* 1989), which won the 1988 Hugo, and *Rimrunners* (1989) – are perhaps her best and most central work, generating a remarkable sense of the living density of space-born life. *Cyteen* is a book of enormous girth set on the intricate Union home planet and dense with speculative plays on genetics (◊ CLONES), identity,

family and power; while *Rimrunners*, unusually for CJC, fits into its normal length a shapely closet drama about life and survival below decks on an armed spaceship.

Closely associated with these books in tone and hard-edged complexity are **Union-Alliance** novels like *Hestia* (**1979**), *Wave without a Shore* (1981), *Port Eternity* (**1982**), *Forty Thousand in Gehenna* (1983) and *Voyager in Night* (**1984**). The **Chanur Saga**, made up of *The Pride of Chanur* (1982; text restored 1987), *Chanur's Venture* (**1984**), *The Kif Strike Back* (**1985**), *Chanur's Homecoming* (**1986**) and *Chanur's Legacy* (**1992**), another deft and crowded depiction of alien psyches in a complexly threatened interstellar venue, has also been fitted into the overall series. As the years have passed, individual stories within the structure have tended, very roughly, to shift their concern from honour (a focus typical of the "shame cultures" found in preliterate societies on Earth and endemic to much SPACE OPERA) to the responsibilities of power (a problem central to literate "guilt cultures").

The lineaments of the **Union-Alliance** series remain unclear, but the sense grows that for CJC the Universe, and everything imaginable within its parti-coloured quadrants, is both evanescent and full of marvel; and that sentient species must revere whatever habitats remain to them after the terrible years of species growth and species destruction hinted at in those books set early in the Universe. It is a vision which, after so many busy books, will take some time to settle, though within terms she has already cued us to anticipate. [JC]

Other works:
Series: The **Arafel** books, comprising *Ealdwood* (1981; rev vt *The Dreamstone* 1983) and *The Tree of Swords and Jewels* (**1983**), both assembled as *Arafel's Saga* (omni 1983; vt *Ealdwood* 1991 UK); the **Merovingen Nights** BRAIDED series (several titles being shared-world BRAIDED anthologies ed CJC, and all remotely connected to the **Union-Alliance** overview), comprising *Angel with the Sword* (**1985**), *Merovingen Nights #1: Festival Moon* * (anth **1987**), *#2: Fever Season* * (anth 1987), *#3: Troubled Waters* * (anth **1988**), *#4: Smuggler's Gold* * (anth **1988**), *#5: Divine Right* * (anth **1989**), *#6: Floodtide* * (anth 1990) and *#7: Endgame* * (anth **1991**); the **Heroes in Hell** SHARED-WORLD enterprise, co-created with Janet E. MORRIS and comprising *Heroes in Hell* * (anth **1985**), *The Gates of Hell* * (**1986**) and *Kings in Hell* * (**1987**), both with Morris, and *Legions of Hell* * (fixup 1987); the **Sword of Knowledge** shared-world enterprise (all vols in fact written by the various "collaborators"), comprising *A Dirge for Sabis* (**1989**) with Leslie Fish, *Wizard Spawn* (**1989**) with Nancy Asire (1945-   ) and *Reap the Whirlwind* (**1989**) with Mercedes Lackey; the **Rusalka** sequence, comprising *Rusalka* (**1989**), *Chernevog* (1990) and *Yvgenie* (1991).
Singletons: *Brothers of Earth* (**1976**); *Sunfall* (coll of linked stories 1981); *Cuckoo's Egg* (**1985**); *Visible Light* (coll **1986**), which contains the 1978 Hugo-winning

"Cassandra"; *Glass and Amber* (coll **1987**); *The Paladin* (**1988**).

About the author: *C.J. Cherryh: A Working Bibliography* (**1992** chap) by Phil STEPHENSEN-PAYNE.

See also: ANDROIDS; CITIES; DAW BOOKS; ESP; GALACTIC EMPIRES; GENETIC ENGINEERING; HIVE-MINDS; LINGUISTICS; *The* MAGAZINE OF FANTASY AND SCIENCE FICTION; MONSTERS; WOMEN SF WRITERS.

CHESLEY AWARDS ◊ AWARDS.

CHESNEY, Lt-Col. Sir GEORGE T(OMKYNS) (1830-1895) UK officer, founder in 1868 of the Royal Indian Civil Engineering College at Staines, Member of Parliament from 1892, and author of some fiction, including the famous *The Battle of Dorking* (**1871** chap; principal vt *The Fall of England? The Battle of Dorking: Reminiscences of a Volunteer* 1871 chap US) published anon. After great success in *Blackwood's Magazine*, and publication as a small book the same year, this tale virtually founded the future-WAR/INVASION genre of stories which attained great popularity in the UK as she neared the height of her insecure Empire in the latter years of the 19th century – an earlier and inferior tale, Alfred Bate RICHARDS's *The Invasion of England (A Possible Tale of Future Times)* (**1870** chap, privately printed), had had little effect. GTC's story warns against UK military complacency and incompetence in its bleak narrative of confusion and folly at home while the German army mounts an efficient invasion by surprise attack. *The Battle of Dorking* was remarkably successful, being immediately reprinted in Canada and the USA, and translated into several European languages, including German, each European nation soon developing its own version of the invasion theme – which saw its greatest popularity, understandably, in the years immediately preceding WWI. A second tale, *The New Ordeal* (**1879**), which posited the obsolescence of war through innovations in weaponry and its replacement by tournaments, proved less popular. [JC]

About the author: *Voices Prophesying War 1763-1984* (**1966**) by I.F. CLARKE (Chapter 2).

See also: ANONYMOUS SF AUTHORS; GAMES AND SPORTS; HISTORY OF SF; NEAR FUTURE; PROTO SCIENCE FICTION; WEAPONS.

CHESNEY, WEATHERBY ◊ C.J. Cutcliffe HYNE.

CHESTER, GEORGE RANDOLPH (1869-1924) US writer whose *The Jingo* (**1912**) satirizes simultaneously the lost-race (◊ LOST WORLDS) story and US know-how in a tale about a salesman selling his modern products to an obscure Antarctic civilization. [PN]

Other works: *The Cash Intrigue: A Fantastic Melodrama of Modern Finance* (**1909**); *The Ball of Fire* (**1914**) with Lillian Chester.

CHESTER, WILLIAM L. (1907-?) US writer known for his series about **Kioga**, a Tarzan-like Native American raised by bears on an island within the Arctic Circle: *Hawk of the Wilderness* (1935 *Blue Book*; **1936**); *Kioga of the Wilderness* (1936-7 *Blue Book*; **1976**); *One Against a Wilderness* (1937 *Blue Book*; coll of linked stories **1977**) and *Kioga of the Unknown Land*

(1938 *Blue Book*; **1978**). [JC]

CHESTERTON, G(ILBERT) K(EITH) (1874-1936) UK writer and illustrator of his own books and many by Hilaire BELLOC – with whom he was long associated, to use George Bernard SHAW's nickname, as The Chesterbelloc. A posthumous collection, *Daylight and Nightmare* (coll **1986**), which assembles fantasy and some sf stories from 1897 through 1931, may demonstrate the range of his emblem-haunted imagination as a teller of tales, but most of his numerous works fall into various other categories – GKC in general exemplified the Edwardian man of letters and wrote on almost everything, in every conceivable form, from poetry through the famous **Father Brown** detective stories to Catholic polemics on to "weekend" essays and literary criticism and history. His first novel, *The Napoleon of Notting Hill* (**1904**), sets the nostalgic, medievalizing, anti-Wellsian, surreally Merrie-Englande tone of most of his sf novels, which tended, in one way or another, to idealize a dreamlike England; in their arguments about its desirability they comprise a series of UTOPIAS, though often only by implication.

His finest novel, *The Man who was Thursday: A Nightmare* (**1908**), is a fantasy set in the Babylon-like London so alluring to writers of the *fin de siècle*: various secret agents disguised as anarchists are shown to have been recruited to man the frontiers of the world by their greatest foe, who turns out to be not only their legitimate boss but in fact God. The book – dramatized by his brother's widow, Mrs Cecil Chesterton, and Ralph Neale as *The Man Who Was Thursday* (**1926**) – has been an acknowledged influence upon such Catholic writers as R.A. LAFFERTY and Gene WOLFE; and the magic-carpet London so lovingly created by GKC and his confrères arguably marks a significant stepping-stone – along with Robert Louis STEVENSON's *New Arabian Nights* (coll **1882**) – between the world of Charles DICKENS and that of STEAMPUNK. [JC]

Other works: *The Ball and the Cross* (**1909** US); *The Flying Inn* (**1914**), featuring a Turkish conspiracy to impose Prohibition on England, attended by a Turkish INVASION; *The Man who Knew too Much* (coll **1922**); *The Return of Don Quixote* (**1927**); *Tales of the Long Bow* (coll of linked stories **1925**), which culminates in a NEAR-FUTURE revolution; a RURITANIAN novella, "The Loyal Traitor", in *Four Faultless Felons* (coll **1930**); "The Three Horsemen of Apocalypse", in *The Paradoxes of Mr. Pond* (coll **1937**), which Jorge Luis BORGES admired; *The Surprise* (written *c*1930; **1952**), a play.

About the author: The literature on GKC is very extensive. A bibliography is *G.K. Chesterton: A Bibliography* (**1958**) by John Sullivan; a recent study is *Gilbert: The Man who was G.K. Chesterton* (**1990**) by Michael G. Coren.

See also: ALTERNATE WORLDS; CLUB STORY; GODS AND DEMONS; TIME TRAVEL.

CHETWODE, R.D. (? -?) UK writer active at the end of the 19th century. *The Marble City: Being the*

Strange Adventures of Three Boys (**1895**) features a South Pacific LOST WORLD whose inhabitants boast high attainments. Nevertheless the three heroes soon make their escape, enriched. [JC]

CHETWYND, BRIDGET (1910-?) UK writer in whose *Future Imperfect* (**1946**) women run the world, leaving men behind, though romantic elements intervene. [JC]

CHEVALIER, HAAKON (MAURICE) (1902-1985) US writer and translator from the French of many works. *The Man who Would be God* (**1959**), meant as a self-defence against the accusation (1953) that he had committed treason with Robert Oppenheimer (1904-1967), the "father of the atomic bomb", almost inadvertently addresses the unfortunate megalomania of a nuclear physicist who wishes to save the world from itself. [JC]

CHIANG, TED [r] ◊ NEBULA; PERCEPTION.

CHIKYU BOEIGUN (vt *The Mysterians*; vt *Earth Defense Force*) Film (1957). Toho/MGM. Dir Inoshiro Honda, starring Kenji Sahara, Akihiko Hirata, Yumi Shirakawa. Screenplay Takeshi Kimura, based on a story by Jojiro Okami. 89 mins. Colour.

This Japanese sf pulp epic is about ALIEN invaders, their own planet destroyed by nuclear holocaust, who land in Japan seeking women for breeding purposes. Its memorable images, best observed at midnight in a drive-in cinema, include a giant birdlike robot crashing out of a mountainside, flying saucers, and lethal rays shooting in all directions. The special-effects extravaganza is by Eiji Tsuburaya, creator of the eponymous monster of GOJIRA (vt *Godzilla*). The story makes very little sense. As Bill WARREN points out in *Keep Watching the Skies! Volume II* (**1986**), Japanese special effects are not *meant* to be realistic, and they certainly are not here, but in their lurid theatricality they are a satisfying introduction to the world of SPACE OPERA. This was the first Japanese sf film not to be a MONSTER MOVIE. [JB/PN]

See also: CINEMA.

CHIKYU SAIDAI NO KESSAN ◊ GOJIRA; RADON.

CHILDER, SIMON IAN ◊ John BROSNAN.

CHILDERS, (ROBERT) ERSKINE (1870-1922) Irish nationalist, military theoretican and author of *The Riddle of the Sands* (**1903**), which describes an exploratory sea journey along the German coast and the uncovering of the secret plans for a German INVASION of the UK. The novel spawned many imitations, none meeting the power of the original, and was made into a lacklustre film in 1979. His warnings to the UK Government were continued later in two nonfiction works which exposed the folly of reliance on cavalry as an effective force against machine guns. EC was executed for treason (he was almost certainly guiltless) by the fledgling Irish Free State. [JE]

See also: WAR.

CHILDREN IN SF In his essay "The Embarrassments of Science Fiction" (in *Science Fiction at Large* ed Peter NICHOLLS anth **1976**; vt *Explorations of the Marvellous*) Thomas M. DISCH asserts, tongue only partly in

cheek, that sf is a branch of children's literature – because most lovers of the genre begin reading it in their early teens, and because many sf stories are *about* children. Whether or not sf is essentially juvenile in its appeal, there is no doubt that many of its writers are fascinated by childhood and its thematic corollaries: innocence and potentiality.

There are many types of sf story about children, but four particularly popular variants are of special interest. The first is the story of children with benign PSI POWERS. Examples are: A.E. VAN VOGT's *Slan* (1940 *ASF*; **1946**), about a nascent community of telepathic SUPERMEN; Theodore STURGEON's *The Dreaming Jewels* (**1950**; vt *The Synthetic Man*), about a strange boy adopted by a carnival, and *More Than Human* (**1953**), about a gestalt consciousness composed of children; Wilmar H. SHIRAS's *Children of the Atom* (fixup **1953**); John WYNDHAM's *The Chrysalids* (**1955**; vt *Re-Birth* US), about telepathic MUTANT children after an atomic war; and such later works in a similar vein as Richard COWPER's *Kuldesak* (**1972**) and "The Piper at the Gates of Dawn" (1976). The abilities of these children seem benign because the stories are usually narrated from the child's point of view. The societies depicted in these tales may persecute the children, but the latter generally win through and constitute their own, "higher" societies, with the reader's approval.

The second type is the reverse of the first: the story of monstrous children, frequently with malign psychic powers. Examples are: Ray BRADBURY's "The Small Assassin" (1946), about a baby which murders its parents; Richard MATHESON's "Born of Man and Woman" (1950), about a hideously mutated boy; and Jerome BIXBY's "It's a *Good* Life" (1953), about an infant who terrorizes a whole community with his awesome paranormal abilities. J.D. BERESFORD's *The Hampdenshire Wonder* (**1911**; vt *The Wonder* US) is an early example of this sort of story, in that the child prodigy is seen entirely from the outside and thus takes on a frightening aspect. In tales of this type, society is usually threatened by the child and the reader is encouraged to take society's side. *Brain Child* (**1991** US) by George TURNER is difficult to characterize, as its superchildren, created by an INTELLIGENCE-enhancing experiment in biological and psychological engineering, appear as both appalling and attractive. The purely monstrous child became a CLICHÉ of HORROR fiction, especially in the 1980s, a decade when, perhaps for some as-yet-undiagnosed sociological reason, sf itself showed a distinct falling off in the number of stories devoted to superchildren.

The third type, which overlaps the first two, concerns children in league with aliens, to good or ill effect. Examples include Henry KUTTNER's "Mimsy Were the Borogoves" (1943), in which alien educational toys provide two children with an escape route from their parents; Ray Bradbury's "Zero Hour" (1947), in which children side with alien invaders; Arthur C. CLARKE's *Childhood's End* (**1953**), in which the alien "Overlords" supervise the growth of a new generation, whose capacities are unknowable by ordinary humans and may be exercised among the stars; Edgar PANGBORN's *A Mirror for Observers* (**1954**), in which Martians compete for control of a child's mind; and John Wyndham's *The Midwich Cuckoos* (**1957**; vt *Village of the Damned* 1960 US), about the alien impregnation of Earthwomen and the terrifying powers of the amoral children they bear, and his later novel *Chocky* (1963 *AMZ*; exp **1968**), about a boy with an alien "brother" living in his head. Zenna HENDERSON's stories about the **People**, most of which are collected in *Pilgrimage* (coll **1961**) and *The People: No Different Flesh* (coll **1966**), belong here since they are largely concerned with sympathetic aliens who appear to be normal human children (their alien parents usually make only fleeting appearances). Jack WILLIAMSON's *The Moon Children* (**1972**) and Gardner DOZOIS's "Chains of the Sea" (1973) also belong in this category. Greg BEAR's *Anvil of Stars* (**1992**) features a community of adolescent children – but no adults – on a starship, undergoing tuition by aliens for making war against genocidal superbeings. This novel is interesting in its creation of an all-adolescent culture.

The fourth type of story is concerned not so much with a conflict between the child and adult society as with the child's attempts to prove himself worthy of joining that society. Much of Robert A. HEINLEIN's relevant work falls into this "initiation" category – e.g., his early story "Misfit" (1939), about a boy whose prodigious mathematical ability enables him to save the spaceship in which he is a very junior crew member. Most of Heinlein's teenage novels, from *Rocket Ship Galileo* (**1947**) to *Have Space-Suit – Will Travel* (**1958**), fit this pattern, as does the later *Podkayne of Mars* (**1963**). Precocious children, adults before their time, also feature in James H. SCHMITZ's **Telzey** stories, such as "Novice" (1962), in Alexei PANSHIN's *Rite of Passage* (**1968**), and in much of Samuel R. DELANY's work. Delany's novels – e.g., *Nova* (**1968**) – are characteristically, in Algis BUDRYS's words, about "the progress of the Magic Kid . . . the divine innocent whose naïve grace and intuitive deftness attract the close attention of all". The "Magic Kid", who gains the acceptance of adult society through sheer charm (rather than discipline in the manner of Heinlein), has appeared in the work of other writers, as in John VARLEY's "In the Bowl" (1975). More in the Heinlein tradition are a number of 1980s novels by Orson Scott CARD, whose stories regularly feature the transition from a troubled adolescence to a maturity forced by circumstance, most famously in *Ender's Game* (1978; exp **1985**) and again in *The Memory of Earth* (**1992**). However, many of the books listed above in this category feature post-pubertal teenagers rather than children proper. Such protagonists are so common in sf, their rite of passage being one of sf's basic themes, that there is little point in prolonging the list, although it is worth mentioning Doris PISERCHIA, who in books like *Earthchild*

(1977) seems to use sf imagery precisely because it provides objective correlatives for pubertal anguish.

As in literature generally, the child's point of view has frequently been used by sf writers because it is a convenient angle from which to see the world anew. Thus, Kingsley AMIS makes good use of his choirboy hero in the ALTERNATE-WORLD novel *The Alteration* (**1976**). Ray Bradbury transmutes his own childhood experience into the nostalgic and horrific FANTASY of *The Martian Chronicles* (**1950**; vt *The Silver Locusts* 1951 UK) and *Something Wicked This Way Comes* (**1962**). Gene WOLFE repeatedly uses a child's-eye view to haunting effect in such tales as "The Island of Dr Death and Other Stories" (1970), "The Fifth Head of Cerberus" (1972) and "The Death of Dr Island" (1973), and childhood memories haunt and shape the memoir structure of several of his novels such as *Peace* (**1975**) and **The Book of the New Sun** (**1980-3**). Harlan ELLISON's fantasy "Jeffty is Five" (1977), about a boy who is perpetually five years old, uses the child's viewpoint to make a statement about the apparent decline in quality of US popular culture. William GIBSON's *Mona Lisa Overdrive* (**1988**) is at its most successful and moving when filtering the bewildering events of its voodoo-in-CYBERSPACE story through the consciousness of the one of its four protagonists who is an actual child, the Japanese girl Kumiko. There are numerous other examples.

An interesting subgenre is the story that opposes a world of childhood and a world of adulthood as if they were, anthropologically, two different cultures whose clash is bound to cause pain. This is the fundamental strategy of much of Stephen KING's horror fiction and also his sf. It forms a particularly grim element in James Patrick KELLY's "Home Front" (1988), in which kids interact, eat hamburgers, and get drafted for an endless, meaningless war occurring offstage.

Although sf about children was not especially common in the 1980s in book form, it was popular in the cinema. Obviously relevant films include E.T.: THE EXTRATERRESTRIAL (1982), EXPLORERS (1985), D.A.R.Y.L. (1985), FLIGHT OF THE NAVIGATOR (1986) and a variety of "teen" movies, a number of which are listed in the CINEMA entry.

Anthologies devoted entirely to stories about children include *Children of Wonder* (anth **1953**; vt *Outsiders: Children of Wonder* 1954) ed William TENN, *Tomorrow's Children* (anth **1966**) ed Isaac ASIMOV, *Demon Kind* (anth **1973**) and *Children of Infinity* (anth **1973**) ed Roger ELWOOD, *Analog Anthology Number 3: Children of the Future* (anth **1982**; vt *Analog's Children of the Future*) ed Stanley SCHMIDT, and *Children of the Future* (anth **1984**) ed Asimov, Martin Harry GREENBERG and Charles G. WAUGH. [DP/PN]

CHILDREN OF THE DAMNED (vt *Horror!*) Film (1963). MGM. Dir Anton M. Leader, starring Ian Hendry, Alan Badel, Barbara Ferris, Bessie Love. Screenplay Jack Briley, based on *The Midwich Cuckoos* (**1957**) by John WYNDHAM. 90 mins. B/w.

This UK film is not a sequel to the successful VILLAGE OF THE DAMNED (1960); it is a remake, though much more remotely based on Wyndham's novel. This time the setting is urban. Once again, children are born with mysterious powers. They are gathered in London for investigation from different parts of the world. Where in the first film the children were malevolent, here they are treated more sympathetically; they remain children despite their superhuman qualities, and their destruction is a consequence of human fear and ignorance, not any hostile actions of their own. Moody use is made of the shadowy, ruined church where much of the action takes place. Though low-key and made with almost too much UK restraint, *COTD* is sadder and more pungent than its predecessor in its story of (literal) alienation. [JB/PN]

CHILDREN'S SF Sf written with a specifically juvenile audience in mind is almost as old as the genre itself. The **Voyages extraordinaires** of Jules VERNE, over 60 novels published between 1863 and 1920, were largely marketed as for adolescent boys, though they found an adult readership also. Contemporaneous with Verne's works were the early DIME NOVELS in the USA, also in the main written for children, and it was not long before BOYS' PAPERS with a strong sf content came along, followed by such JUVENILE SERIES as Victor APPLETON's TOM SWIFT stories. The juvenile series written under the floating pseudonym Roy ROCK-WOOD, **The Great Marvel Series**, published much sf between 1906 and 1935. These topics are discussed in greater detail under separate entries in this encyclopedia, as is children's sf written for the COMICS.

From 1890 to 1920 at least, and to some extent later on, most children's sf was aimed at boys rather than girls and was largely dedicated to the themes of the LOST WORLD, future WAR and DISCOVERY AND INVENTION (*see also* EDISONADE). L. Frank BAUM, writer of the celebrated **Oz** books, wrote an early work in the latter category – *The Master Key: An Electrical Fairy Tale* (**1901**) – but of course fantastic inventions had already played an important role in the stories featuring Frank Reade, Jr (◊ FRANK READE LIBRARY).

Children's sf has been and is written for a variety of age groups. Here we generally regard sf written for children of 11 and under as outside our range, although nostalgic reference must be made to the following: the splendidly bizarre *Doctor Dolittle in the Moon* (**1928**) by Hugh Lofting; the **Professor Brane-stawm** books by Norman HUNTER, beginning with *The Incredible Adventures of Professor Branestawm* (**1933**), all featuring the ridiculous adventures of the eponymous eccentric scientist; the minor children's classic *My Friend Mr Leakey* (coll of linked stories **1937**) by the biologist J.B.S. HALDANE, a fantasy combining elements of magic and sf; a better known classic series for younger children, the seven **Narnia** books by C.S. LEWIS, beginning with *The Lion, the Witch and the Wardrobe* (**1950**) and ending with *The Last Battle* (**1956**) – these stories are basically religious allegory cum FANTASY, but contain such sf elements as PARALLEL

WORLDS and TIME TRAVEL; and *The Twenty-One Balloons* (**1946**) by William Pène DU BOIS, an amusing Pacific-island scientific UTOPIA.

As noted, the above are primarily for younger children, but they point up a difficulty which exists also in sf stories for older children: the fact that there is little generic purity in children's literature. Much children's fantasy contains sf elements, and conversely much children's sf is written with a disregard for scientific accuracy, whether from hauteur or from ignorance, which effectively renders it fantasy. Time travel, for example, has long been an important theme in children's literature, going back at least as far as *The Cuckoo Clock* (**1877**) by Mrs Mary Molesworth (1839-1921), and continuing to the present day, through *A Traveller in Time* (**1939**) by Alison Uttley (1884-1976), several of the **Green Knowe** stories by Lucy Boston (1892-1990) and, perhaps the greatest of such novels, *Tom's Midnight Garden* (**1958**) by Philippa Pearce (1920-   ); this latter is the moving and subtle story of a boy who travels back in time, always to slightly more recent periods, to find the 19th-century child with whom he falls in love growing older, and away from him; finally, in an overwhelming surprise ending, she meets him in the present day. But in all these examples the time travel is an essentially magic device used in the service of fantasy.

Indeed, sadly for sf purists, most sf works of distinction since the 1960s have been at the fantastic end of the sf spectrum. A fine piece of such peripheral sf is *Earthfasts* (**1966**) by William MAYNE, one of the best children's writers of the period, in which an 18th-century drummer boy emerges from the ground to be met by a sceptical, scientifically inclined present-day youth.

There may be a sociological reason for the comparative scarcity of good HARD SF for children in the recent period, or it may be simply the arbitrary preference of the handful of writers who led the renaissance of juvenile fiction that has taken place since the 1960s. Certainly their creative imagination has fed as fiercely on MYTHOLOGY as on 20th-century breakthroughs in scientific understanding – breakthroughs that in the period of the Cold War, with the ever-present threat of nuclear DISASTER, seemed equivocal in their results. Signs of the renaissance are many: children's books generally and books for adolescents specifically are less patronizing; they more commonly contain a sardonic or even ironic realism; they have become, overall, more subtle, more evocative, more various, more original and more ready to confront problems of pain, or loss, or even sexual love. The new realism is evident even with those writers of HEROIC FANTASY who have followed in the footsteps of J.R.R. TOLKIEN; notable among them are Joy Chant (1945-   ) and especially Patricia MCKILLIP, although the latter, whose spectacular début years were devoted to fantasy, seems to write better the further she keeps her distance from sf.

The key theme in children's sf is MAGIC, and several

important children's works are discussed in that entry. Sometimes the magic is given a kind of pseudo-scientific rationale, with talk of dimensional gates and so on, as in Andre NORTON's many **Witch World** books, some of which are among her best work; e.g., *Warlock of the Witch World* (**1967**). (Norton has also written many colourful books for adolescents which are towards the hard-sf end of the spectrum, sometimes dealing with relations between ALIENS and humans.) Ursula K. LE GUIN's **Earthsea** books, beginning with *The Wizard of Earthsea* (**1968**), have combined sf and fantasy by making her magic obey such rigorous laws that it may be seen as a kind of IMAGINARY SCIENCE; it adheres, for example, to the law of conservation of energy.

Many critics regard the **Earthsea** books as the finest sf work for children of the postwar period. Some of Alan GARNER's novels would also rank very high. Apart from using teenage protagonists, Garner's *Red Shift* (**1973**) is an adult book in every respect, narrating a battle against intellectual and physical impotence considerably more demanding than would be found in most supposedly adult romances. It qualifies as marginal sf through its consistent use, from the title onwards, of scientific metaphor and because it depends structurally on a form of psychic time travel (focused on a neolithic stone axe).

More recently the work of Diana Wynne JONES has also been consistently distinguished, more playful than Le Guin's and more ebullient than Garner's, but as fully aware as either of the difficulties of life both for children and for grown ups. Much of her work, which treats generic boundaries with disdain, is more fantasy than sf. The more sciencefictional books include *The Homeward Bounders* (**1981**), *Archer's Goon* (**1984**) and *A Tale of Time City* (**1987**), which, with varying degrees of sciencefictional rigour, all revolve around causal paradoxes and problems created by travel through time or between alternate worlds, and often with more narrative sophistication than is common in sf for adults. The lunacies of book marketing have never been more clear than in the consignment of such distinguished works as the above, and many others, to what Le Guin has called "the kiddylit ghetto". The paradox is visible in the fact that occasionally US editions of UK children's books have been marketed as for adults, and vice versa.

Other important children's sf writers at the fantasy end of the spectrum whose works are discussed in greater detail under their own entries are Susan COOPER, Peter DICKINSON, Tanith LEE, Madeleine L'ENGLE and T.H. WHITE. Australia seems to produce such writers more liberally than it does their counterparts for adults: interesting work has been produced by Isobelle CARMODY, Lee HARDING, Victor KELLEHER and Gillian RUBINSTEIN. Most Kelleher novels are impossible to pigeonhole with any confidence as either sf or fantasy; they have elements of both, and do not appear to suffer as a result. Rubinstein's tone

falters – it is a sadly common symptom of writers of sf/fantasy for adolescents – when she approaches pure sf motifs, such as the visiting ALIEN in *Beyond the Labyrinth* (**1988**), but her books remain hard-edged and angry.

When we turn to hard sf, most work for children has been less distinguished. Carl CLAUDY wrote some exciting books in the 1930s. More recent writers of some quality whose production has been in significant part for children are Paul CAPON, John CHRISTOPHER, John Keir CROSS, Tom DE HAVEN, Sylvia Louise ENGDAHL, Nicholas FISK, Douglas HILL, H.M. HOOVER, Monica HUGHES, Philip LATHAM, Alice LIGHTNER, M.E. PATCHETT, Luděk PEŠEK, Donald SUDDABY, Jean and Jeff SUTTON, Hugh WALTERS, Robert WESTALL, Leonard WIBBERLY and Cherry WILDER. Between them even these more recent writers span close to 40 years of hard-sf adventure writing for children. Christopher, Engdahl, Fisk, Hoover, Pešek, Westall and Wilder are probably the most important names here, along with Andre Norton. Between them they have written much thoughtful and stimulating work, but the extent of the list is disappointing when set alongside the quantity, range and variety of adult sf from the same period. The difficulty is, of course, that the intellectual level of a book is not necessarily expressed by a marketing label. Much adult sf – the works of E.E. "Doc" SMITH or Isaac ASIMOV, for example – is of great appeal to older children, and is to some extent directed at them. To the degree that older children are able to enjoy adult sf that is well within their reading capacity, the size of the potential market in sf specifically labelled as juvenile obviously dwindles.

By far the most celebrated case of the unreal distinction between "juvenile" and "adult" concerns Robert A. HEINLEIN, almost half of whose novels were originally marketed for children. They have been re-released for many years now as if for adults. There are 13 in all, among the best being *Starman Jones* (**1953**), *The Star Beast* (**1954**) and *Citizen of the Galaxy* (**1957**). Heinlein's direct style, his solid science, the naturalness and ease with which he creates a societal background with just a few strokes, all help to make his juveniles among his best works; but their basic strength comes from the repeated theme of the rite of passage, the initiation ceremony, the growing into adulthood through the taking of decisions and the assumption of a burden of moral responsibility. This theme Heinlein made peculiarly and at times brilliantly his own; his is the most consistently distinguished of all hard sf written for young readers.

Heinlein is exceptional in that there was no falling-off in quality when he wrote for children. Other sf writers could not quite manage the trick. Isaac Asimov's **Lucky Starr** books are well below his best; James BLISH's juveniles are generally disappointing, with the exception of *A Life for the Stars* (**1962**), the second of the **Cities in Flight** tetralogy; Ben BOVA, Arthur C. CLARKE, Gordon R. DICKSON, Harry HARRISON,

Evan HUNTER and Robert SILVERBERG all write better for grown-ups, although Hunter's children's books are unusual and interesting. Alan E. NOURSE, on the other hand, seems more relaxed when writing for younger people, and some of his best work is in his future-MEDICINE books.

A more recent writer, Robert C. O'BRIEN, wrote two distinguished sf works for children. The witty and sympathetic *Mrs Frisby and the Rats of NIMH* (**1971**), about experimental rats which have developed super-INTELLIGENCE, is for younger children, and in the talking-animal line is preferred by some *aficionados* to Richard Adams's more celebrated *Watership Down* (**1972**). O'Brien's *Z for Zachariah* (**1975**) is a post-HOLOCAUST novel for older children; humane, touching and sometimes frightening. Also excellent, and very funny, is the **Book of the Nomes** trilogy by Terry PRATCHETT, beginning with *Truckers* (**1989**), about aliens trying to live invisibly in a human world.

Certain sf themes crop up again and again in recent sf for adolescents. Post-holocaust stories and stories of rebellion against totalitarian societies (which often practise degrading forms of social engineering) are both very common, as in the work of John Christopher, whose sf for children deservedly won him a new readership when he ceased writing sf DISASTER novels for adults. Stories about contact between humans and aliens are often used to impress on children an attitude of cultural open-mindedness which has a clear bearing on problems of racism, sexism and other isms of the real world. Cherry Wilder's **Torin** series is of this kind, but Wilder knows better than to preach. This is more than can be said of much modern juvenile sf, which has perhaps become, from the mid-1970s, the most ethically intransigent and propagandist since the juvenile fiction of the Victorian era. The familiar voice of the children's author calling for universal harmony can, paradoxically, come to seem hectoring; the list of "antis" is often and easily extended by many children's authors – nostalgically looking back to the seemingly more self-reliant lifestyles of a past age – to include anti-technology and anti-science (◊ ANTI-INTELLECTUALISM IN SF).

The theme of PSI POWERS is often found in conjunction with work of this sort. It appeals strongly to children, whose sense of weakness and entrapment in a world where they are by and large subject to adult control, whether wisely or not, can be eased by intimations of an inner superiority – and sensitivity – that may be available to them. Typically psi powers (from within) are seen as opposed, and morally preferable, to scientific and technological powers (from without). Isobelle Carmody's *Scatterlings* (**1991**), for example, has an urban scientific elite, remnants of those who polluted and nearly destroyed Earth through greed, opposed to the rural, tribalized but radiation-resistant and honest folk descended from the greenies and working-class outcasts the original scientists exploited. ECOLOGY-conscious people

versus corrupted technocrats; country versus town; psi powers versus science: these had, by 1990, become the dominant themes of adolescent sf as a whole. The ecology theme now appears almost as a religious motif in sf, and indeed, in the Gaea-worshipping form it sometimes takes, it has already become a secular religion in the real world.

An important commercial area of sf publishing for juveniles is series books, often based on films or tv shows. The STAR TREK books and the DR WHO books are two of the longest-running and most successful (the former series is not specifically marketed for children, but the latter is); they contain less hackwork than most of their competition in this sort of area.

Some distinguished writers of juvenile fiction, like Philippa Pearce, are not given separate entries in this volume, even though their work may contain some sf imagery: we do not have the space to give comprehensive coverage to children's writers, and our emphasis is on sf rather than fantasy. But many writers of sf for adolescents do receive entries, often because they have also written sf for adults or because, like Alan Garner, their work is likely to have repercussions in adult sf.   [PN]

CHILE ◊ LATIN AMERICA.

CHILSON, ROB Working name of US writer Robert Dean Chilson (1945-   ). His first sf story was "The Mind Reader" (1968) in *ASF*. Of his novels, which generally fail to step beyond the routine, *As the Curtain Falls* (**1974**) is a FAR-FUTURE adventure with some highly coloured moments, *The Star-Crowned Kings* (**1975**) is a SPACE OPERA about a member of a subject race who has latent ESP powers, and *Rounded with Sleep* (**1990**) confronts its hero with an Earth in the guise – and under the computerized control – of a fantasy-role-playing game (◊ GAMES AND TOYS). *The Shores of Kansas* (**1976**), perhaps (along with his first) RC's most interesting work, tells of a man with a natural, consciously controlled talent for TIME TRAVEL and his resulting psychological problems.   [JC/PN]

Other works: *Isaac Asimov's Robot City, Book 5: Refuge* * (**1988**); *Men like Rats* (**1989**).

CHILTON, CHARLES (FREDERICK WILLIAM) (1927-   ) UK RADIO producer and scriptwriter whose three sf novels comprise a juvenile trilogy based on his BBC radio serials about **Jet Morgan** and his companions as they protect Earth against Martians and other menaces ; the books are *Journey Into Space* * (**1954**), *The Red Planet* * (**1956**) and *The World in Peril* * (**1960**). He also wrote further **Jet Morgan** adventures for a COMIC strip in *Express Weekly* 1956-7.   [JC]

See also: MOON; RADIO; SPACE FLIGHT.

CHILTON, H(ENRY) HERMAN (1863-?   ) Belgian-born UK writer, apparently active as late as 1943. His first sf novel, *Woman Unsexed* (**1892**), melodramatically depicts a 1925 world ruined by women's right to work. *The Lost Children* (**1931**) visits the LOST WORLD to which the children of Hamelin followed the Pied Piper; there they have founded a UTOPIA. *Talking Totem* (**1938**) is a fantasy.   [JC]

CHINA SYNDROME, THE Film (1979). IPC Films. Dir James Bridges, starring Jane Fonda, Jack Lemmon, Michael Douglas, Wilford Brimley. Screenplay Mike Gray, T.S. Cook, Bridges. 122 mins. Colour.

Made by the production company with which Jane Fonda was associated (Indochina Peace Campaign), this is the first of two crusading borderline-sf films starring her, the other being ROLLOVER (1981). Here she plays a tv reporter hoping to do more "hard" news stories who stumbles across an "event" (crisis) caused by cost-cutting engineering in a nuclear power plant; this could (and almost does) lead to meltdown and the radioactive pollution of Southern California. Corporate bosses attempt, violently, to suppress the potential exposé. What looked at first like mere science fiction looked a lot more like science fact only weeks later, with the nuclear disaster at Three Mile Island – an apposite if unfortunate coincidence that made *TCS* a commercial hit. The subgenre of the near-future technological-disaster film (see, for example, ENDANGERED SPECIES and WARGAMES) is a kind of fringe sf, though usually made in the manner of the conspiracy thriller. *TCS* is well crafted and well acted. [PN]

CHINESE SF Chinese literature has a long tradition of the fantastic that prepared the way for, and leads up to, modern Chinese sf. It is believed that the earliest actual sf publication in China was the serialization in 1904 in the magazine *Portrait Fiction* of "Yueqiu zhimindi xiaoshuo" ["Tales of Moon Colonization"] by Huangjiang Diaosuo. Around 130,000 Chinese words long, this novel describes a group of Earthlings settling on the Moon. Another important sf work of the early period is Xu Nianci's "Xinfalu xiansheng tan" ["New Tales of Mr Absurdity"] (1905), which deals with the separation of body and soul. Lao She's *Maocheng ji* ["Cat Country"] (**1933**; reprinted 1947) remains one of the most significant Chinese sf novels; this DYSTOPIA about catlike Martians is in fact a biting satire of the Old China under its reactionary rule. Lao She wrote this novel without being aware of the genre, but at much the same time Gu Junzheng was consciously writing sf, even acknowledging the influence of Jules VERNE and H.G. WELLS. His *Heping de meng* ["Dream of Peace"] (coll **1940**) prints four of his sf short stories. Like Hugo GERNSBACK, Gu Junzheng advocated the popularization of science through sf, and all his stories try to stimulate readers' interest in science and technology.

The People's Republic of China was founded in 1949. Soon after that, Soviet sf works were translated into Chinese in great numbers. Also as a result of Soviet influence, the Chinese Youth Press systematically published selections of Verne's sf throughout the 1950s and into the 1960s. From 1949 through the 1960s, almost all Chinese sf stories were for juvenile readers. Representative works include Zheng Wenguang's "Cong Diqiu dao Huxing" ["From Earth to Mars"] (1954), Yu Zhi's "Shizong de gege" ["The Missing Elder Brother"] (1957), Xiao Jianheng's "Buke

de qiyu" ["Pup Buke's Adventures"] (1962) and Liu Xinshi's "Beifang de yun" ["Northern Clouds"] (1962).

During the 10 years of the notorious "Cultural Revolution" not a trace of sf could be found in China. However, 1978-83 saw a remarkable resurgence of sf creation. Among nearly 1000 titles are Jin Tao's "Yueguangdao" ["The Moonlit Island"] (1980), Tong Enzheng's "Shanhudao shang de siguang" ["Death Ray on a Coral Island"] (1978), Zheng Wenguang's *Feixiang Renmazuo* ["Forward to Sagittarius"] (**1979**), Meng Weizai's *Fangwen shizongzhe* ["Calling on the Missing People"] (**1981**), Wang Xiaoda's "Shenmi de bo" ["The Mysterious Wave"] (1980), Wei Yahua's "Wenrou zhixiang de meng" ["Conjugal Happiness in the Arms of Morpheus"] (1981) and Ye Yonglie's *Heiying* ["The Black Shadow"] (**1981**).

Sf during this period also found expression in other media, such as films, tv, radio broadcasts and comic books. In films, *Shanhudao shang de siguang* ["Death Ray on a Coral Island"], based on Tong Enzheng's story, was released in 1980, and Ji Hongxu's *Qianying* ["The Hidden Shadow"] in 1982. On tv, "Zuihou yige aizheng sizhe" [The Last Man who Dies of Cancer"] by Zhou Yongnian, Zhang Fengjiang and Jia Wanchao and "Yinxing ren" ["The Invisible Man"] by Wu Boze were both dramatized in 1980. *Xiongmao jihua* ["The Panda Project"] by Ye Yonglie was dramatized on tv in 1983. The same author's *An dou* ["Veiled Strife"] (**1981**) and *Mimi zhongdui* ["The Secret Column"] (**1981**) were broadcast on radio daily as serials in 1981. And in comic books, Ye Yonglie's sf detective series, 12 booklets with 8 million copies printed, was published by Popular Science Press in 1982 under the series title **The Scientific Sherlock Holmes**.

1978-83 also saw widespread publication of foreign sf in China. Among the famous sf writers from many parts of the world who were introduced to the Chinese reading public were Mary SHELLEY, Robert A. HEINLEIN, Isaac ASIMOV, Jack WILLIAMSON, Poul ANDERSON, Michael CRICHTON, Clifford D. SIMAK, Frederik POHL, Arthur C. CLARKE, Brian W. ALDISS, Alexander BELYAEV and Sakyo KOMATSU.

However, the 1983 political drive against "spiritual pollution" hurt sf writers so badly that their already small contingent quickly shrank. Since then Chinese sf has developed only slowly. There is just one mainland magazine devoted to sf, *Kehuan Shijia* ["SF World"]. In Taiwan there is the sf magazine *Huanxiang* ["Mirage"], ed and published by Dr Zhang Xiguo, a computer specialist who teaches at the University of Pittsburgh in the USA but shows much concern about the development of Chinese sf; there are about a dozen titles under his name. Another major sf writer in Taiwan is Huang Hai, best known for his high literary quality and for his scientific speculation. His first publication, "Hangxiang wuya de lucheng" ["A Boundless Voyage"], appeared in 1968. His best works are reckoned to be *10101* ["The Year 10101"] (**1969**) and *Xinshiji zhelu* ["Voyage to a

New Era"] (**1972**).

The most productive sf writer in Hong Kong is Ni Kuang, who often writes under the pseudonym Wei Shili. His sf works number about 25 titles, but most are marginal, being SWORD AND SORCERY – indeed, some critics doubt if his works belong to the sf genre at all.

There are 15 Chinese members of WORLD SF, whose 1991 annual meeting was held in Chengdu. An introduction to Chinese sf for English readers is *Science Fiction from China* (anth **1989** US) ed WU DINGBO and Patrick Murphy, which contains several of the stories mentioned above. [WD]

CHOSEN SURVIVORS Film (1974). Alpine-Churubusco/Metromedia. Dir Sutton Roley, starring Jackie Cooper, Richard Jaeckel, Alex Cord, Bradford Dillman. Screenplay H.B. Cross, Joe Reb Moffly, based on a story by Cross. 99 mins. Colour.

This US/Mexico coproduction is a small-scale, inventive little exploitation movie whose plot-line is purest PARANOIA. In a government test on stress reactions, 11 people are hoaxed into believing that nuclear war is devastating the world. These "chosen survivors" are forced by the army into an elaborate bomb-shelter deep beneath the desert. Once locked in, they learn – this seems not to be part of the experiment – that lethal vampire bats have been trapped inside with them. Character conflicts and bat attacks ensue in an unpretentious piece from a director more commonly associated with tv. [PN/JB]

CHOWN, MARCUS (1959-   ) UK writer, currently reviews editor for *New Scientist*, whose sf novels, both in collaboration with John GRIBBIN, are *Double Planet* (**1988**), a competent HARD-SF tale about a conflict of political interests over a comet which may or may not be about to strike the Earth, and its remote sequel, *Reunion* (**1991**), set 1000 years later, in which the lunar population has come under the influence of a cult claiming to hold the secret of how to replenish the MOON's atmosphere: the book is the story of a woman's fight against this church. [MB]

Other works: *Stars and Planets* (**1987**), a children's book on astronomy.

CHRISTOPHER, JOHN Working name of UK writer Christopher Samuel Youd (1922-   ); his first novel, *The Winter Swan* (**1949**), a fantasy, was published as by Christopher Youd. He was active as an sf fan before WWII, in which he served, and began publishing sf proper with "Christmas Story" for *ASF* in 1949, again writing as Christopher Youd. His first sf book, *The Twenty-Second Century* (coll **1954**; with 1 story dropped and 1 added, rev 1962 US) as JC, assembles his early work; but, after the success of his first sf novel, *The Year of the Comet* (**1955**; vt *Planet in Peril* 1959 US), and the even greater impact of his second, *The Death of Grass* (**1956**; vt *No Blade of Grass* 1957 US), he concentrated for some years on adult novels, soon becoming perceived as John WYNDHAM's rival and successor as the premier writer of the post-WWII UK DISASTER novel in the decade 1955-65.

The disaster which changes the face of England (and of the world) in *The Death of Grass* (filmed in 1970 by Cornel Wilde as NO BLADE OF GRASS) is, as the title makes clear, an upset in the balance of Nature which causes the extinction of all grass and related food plants, with catastrophic effects. Where Wyndham's novels featured protagonists whose middle-class indomitability signalled to the reader that the crisis would somehow come out right in the end, JC's characters – as witness John Custance's gradual hardening and deterioration of personality in this novel – inhabit and respond to a darker, less secure universe. It is a harshness of perspective characteristic of most of his work at this time: *The World in Winter* (**1962**; vt *The Long Winter* 1962 US), *A Wrinkle in the Skin* (**1965**; vt *The Ragged Edge* 1966 US) and *Pendulum* (**1968** US) all deal decks similarly stacked against political or environmental complacency, and their protagonists concentrate on the grim business of staying alive and making a life fit to live in a post-HOLOCAUST world stripped of culture and security.

When JC turned to other kinds of stories his touch was less assured, though *Sweeney's Island* (**1964** US; vt *Cloud on Silver* 1964 UK) plausibly updates the traditional ISLAND theme as the eponymous tycoon creates a DYSTOPIAN microcosm under stress. However, in 1967 JC successfully inaugurated a fresh phase of his sf career, this time in the juvenile market, with the **Tripods** sequence: *The White Mountains* (**1967**), *The City of Gold and Lead* (**1967**) and *The Pool of Fire* (**1968**), assembled as *The Tripods Trilogy* (omni **1980** US); a prequel, *When the Tripods Came* (**1988** US), followed much later. In these books, the alien tripods control all adults. However, the young protagonists avoid their thrall, discover their secret and save Earth (whose adults revert to their distressing old ways). Other juveniles followed: *The Lotus Caves* (**1969**), *The Guardians* (**1970**) – which appropriately won the *Guardian* award for best children's book of the year – *Dom and Va* (**1973**), much expanded from *In the Beginning* (**1972** chap), a tale for smaller children, *Wild Jack* (**1974** US), *Empty World* (**1977**) and the **Fireball** trilogy – *Fireball* (**1981**), *New Found Land* (**1983**) and *Dragon Dance* (**1986**) – set in a PARALLEL-WORLD version of Roman Britain and elsewhere. *The Prince in Waiting* (**1970**), *Beyond the Burning Lands* (**1971**) and *The Sword of the Spirits* (**1972**), assembled as *The Swords of the Spirits Trilogy* (omni **1980** US; vt *The Prince in Waiting Trilogy* 1983 UK), is FANTASY. As with his adult sf, most of JC's juveniles are set in a post-DISASTER situation, in which the romantic individualism of young protagonists finds itself pitted against some kind of conformist or even brainwashed system, sometimes symbolized as a struggle between the country and the CITY. They have been remarkably and deservedly popular. [JC/PN]

Other works: *The Caves of Night* (**1958** US), marginal; *The Long Voyage* (**1960**; vt *The White Voyage* 1961 US), a juvenile; *The Possessors* (**1964** US); *The Little People* (**1966** US).

About the author: *Christopher Samuel Youd, Master of All Genres: A Working Bibliography* (**1990** chap) by Phil STEPHENSEN-PAYNE.

See also: CHILDREN'S SF; ECOLOGY; GREAT AND SMALL; PASTORAL; PUBLISHING; RADIO; SUPERNATURAL CREATURES.

CHRYSALIS US original anthology series, 1977-83, 10 vols, ed Roy TORGESON. The first 7 were paperback originals from Zebra Books; the remaining 3 had hardcover first editions from DOUBLEDAY. They were *Chrysalis 1* (anth **1977**), *#2* (anth **1978**), *#3* (anth **1978**), *#4* (anth **1979**), *#5* (anth **1979**), *#6* (anth **1980**), *#7* (anth **1980**), *#8* (anth **1980**), *#9* (anth **1981**) and *#10* (anth **1983**). Torgeson's editorial policy was eclectic, perhaps too much so; he published sf, fantasy and horror by a mixture of new and established writers. The series title was intended to suggest something developing and changing and about to give birth to beauty. Although C published a number of interesting stories, including four each by Orson Scott CARD and Australian writer Leanne Frahm, it never developed a very strong personality, and it is perhaps surprising (though admirable) that it lasted as long as it did. [PN]

CHURCHILL, JOYCE [s] ◊ M. John HARRISON.

CHURCHILL, R(EGINALD) C(HARLES) (1916-   ) UK writer whose *A Short History of the Future* (**1955**), like John ATKINS's *Tomorrow Revealed* (**1955**), is an imaginary HISTORY, in this case set about AD7000, and similarly draws on genuine contemporary sources, mainly George ORWELL, into an unusually witty accounting of the course of history; in RCC's version, history comes in great cycles. [JC]

CICELLIS, KAY (1926-   ) French-born writer of Greek descent who writes in English. Her sf novel *The Day The Fish Came Out* * (**1967**), which novelizes *The* DAY THE FISH CAME OUT (1967), is about an H-bomb and the consequences of its loss off a Greek island; it is not up to the standard of her serious work. [JC]

CIDONCHA, CARLOS SAIZ [r] ◊ SPAIN.

CINEFANTASTIQUE US film magazine, specializing in sf, fantasy and horror CINEMA, and occasionally tv; published and ed Frederick S. Clarke from Illinois. Fall 1970-current. Slick BEDSHEET format, well illustrated in both colour and b/w. The production schedule has varied from 4 to 6 numbers a year, currently bimonthly. This is by far the most useful US fantastic-cinema magazine, being less juvenile in orientation and (apparently) less dependent on the studios for pictorial material, and thus more independent in its judgments, than magazines like STARLOG. Critical standards range from merely eccentric to excellent. Coverage is good on films with wide theatrical release, but patchy on films that go straight to video release and on tv programmes. Features range from interviews through articles on production problems and on how special effects are worked to occasional retrospectives (usually good) on famous genre movies of the past. [PN]

CINEMA The basis on which films and film-makers have been selected for inclusion in this volume is discussed in the Introduction.

From the outset, the cinema specialized in illusion to a degree that had been impossible on the stage. Sf itself takes as its subject matter that which does not exist, now, in the real world (though it might one day), so it has a natural affinity with the cinema: the illusory qualities of film are ideal for presenting fictions about things that are not yet real. The first sf film-maker of any consequence – indeed, one of the very first film-makers – was Georges MÉLIÈS, who used trick photography to take his viewers to the Moon in *Le* VOYAGE DANS LA LUNE (1902; vt *A Trip to the Moon*). What they saw there – chorus girls and lobster-clawed Selenites – was not exactly high art, but it was, for the time, wonderful. The ability of sf cinema to evoke wonders, for which it is often criticized as being a modern equivalent of a carnival freak show, is also its strength. Wonders themselves may pall, or be dismissed as childish, but nevertheless they are at the heart of sf; sf, no matter how sophisticated, by definition must feature something new, some alteration from the world as we know it (though of course newness can easily become mere novelty). Film, from this viewpoint, is sf's ideal medium.

But from another point of view film is *far from* the ideal medium. Sf as literature is analytic and deals with ideas; film is the opposite of analytic, and has trouble with ideas. The way film deals with ideas is to give them visual shape, as images which may carry a metaphoric charge, but metaphors are tricky things, and, while the ideas of sf cinema may be potent, they are seldom precise. Also, film is a popular artform which, its producers often believe, is unlikely to lose money by underestimating the intelligence of the public. So, on its surface, sf cinema has often been simplistic, even though complex currents may trouble the depths where its subtexts glide.

In fact, sf cinema in the silent period did become surprisingly sophisticated, though to the modern eye, which prefers the illusion of photographic realism, the theatrical Expressionism of much early sf cinema – especially in Russia and Germany – is as strange a convention as having people talk in blank verse. Two important early sf films came from those countries and that convention, AELITA (1924) from Russia and METROPOLIS (1926) from Germany. Nonetheless, *Metropolis* – the first indubitable classic of sf cinema – is, for all the apparent triteness of its story, striking even today, with its towering CITY of the future, its cowed lines of shuffling workers, its chillingly lovely female ROBOT. Fritz LANG, who made it, also made one of the first space movies, *Die* FRAU IM MOND (1929; vt *The Woman in the Moon*). The début film of René Clair (1898-1981), one day to be a very famous director, was also sf: PARIS QUI DORT (1923; vt *The Crazy Ray*), but this was an altogether lighter piece, a charming story of Parisians frozen in time.

Many people remember the sf-movie booms of the

1950s and the late 1970s, but the first sf boom, that of the 1930s, is often forgotten. Though some sf films were made in Europe at this time, it was in the USA that the most influential were produced: JUST IMAGINE (1930), FRANKENSTEIN (1931), ISLAND OF LOST SOULS (1932), DR JEKYLL AND MR HYDE (1932), KING KONG (1933), DELUGE (1933), The INVISIBLE MAN (1933), The BRIDE OF FRANKENSTEIN (1935), Mad Love (1935; ◊ ORLACS HÄNDE) and LOST HORIZON (1936). Just Imagine is a forgotten futuristic musical, and Deluge is a DISASTER movie which, like the earlier French La FIN DU MONDE (1931; vt The End of the World), is primarily interested in the effect of apocalypse on human morals. King Kong is of course an early and classic monster movie, with a sympathetic monster. Similarly, Lost Horizon is the most famous LOST-WORLD film, though the theme has never been very important in sf movies.

It is interesting that the remainder – all six of them good films, and mostly well remembered – have in common the over-reaching scientist destroyed by his own creation. This theme, which could be called the Promethean theme (after the hero who stole fire from the Gods – a literal parallel in the case of the **Frankenstein** films, where scientists steal lightning to create new life), remains a central theme in sf cinema today; it is a familiar paradox that much sf cinema is anti-science, even anti-intellectual (◊ ANTI-INTELLECTUALISM IN SF), and (especially in the 1930s) cast in the GOTHIC mode, which typically sees the limitation of science as being its reliance on Reason in a world of mysteries not susceptible to rational analysis – indeed, most of the SCIENTISTS who appear in the above films are seen as literally mad. This is true also of several European films of the time, including the archetypally Gothic German film ALRAUNE (1930; vt Daughter of Evil). It is, of course, a CLICHÉ of early sf generally and of sf in the cinema especially that scientists are mad, so much so that we seldom pause to analyse the oddness of this. It is as if these films were telling us that the brain, the seat of reason, is so delicate an instrument that its overuse leads to the very opposite, unreason. Although all these films are undeniably sf, they are generally and rightly categorized as HORROR. Also archetypal of the sf cinema is their clear Luddite subtext: the results of science are terrifying. This pessimistic view gave way to OPTIMISM later in the 1930s, but returned with new vigour when the real-world results of scientific advance – the bombing of Hiroshima and Nagasaki – proved to be so terrifying. The Bomb was the image that was to loom behind the MONSTER MOVIES of the 1950s, especially – not surprisingly – those made in JAPAN.

In the later 1930s few sf films were made, the most obvious new theme being SPACE OPERA, though this was mainly confined to cheerful juvenile serials such as FLASH GORDON (1936, with sequels in 1938 and 1940) and BUCK ROGERS IN THE 25TH CENTURY (1939). The one adult film made about the conquest of space, the hifalutin', rhetorical and romantic THINGS TO COME (1936), was from the UK; although it flopped, with hindsight we can see it as a milestone of sf film-making. While ultimately optimistic, its vision of the future has many dark aspects, and in this respect the movie is the inheritor of the DYSTOPIAN theme of Metropolis.

The 1940s, by contrast, were empty years for sf cinema, though they started well with the sinister DR CYCLOPS (1940), whose villain shrank people. Medical sf/horror was well represented by The LADY AND THE MONSTER (1944), about a sinister excised brain kept alive by science. More typical was comic sf, mostly weak, as in the ever more slapstick sequels to the **Frankenstein** and **Invisible Man** movies, both unnatural beings winding up as co-stars, in 1948 and 1951 respectively, with Bud Abbott and Lou Costello. The PERFECT WOMAN (1949) is a UK comedy interesting in its exploitation of sf to sexist ends: its underclothes fetishism would have been unthinkable had its robot heroine, played by a real woman, been a real woman. Prehistoric fantasy, which continues as a minor genre today, had a good start with ONE MILLION B.C. (1940). There was not much else.

The sf-movie boom of the 1950s, which figures largely in our cultural nostalgia today – even among viewers too young to have seen the originals when they first came out – was largely made up of MONSTER MOVIES (which see for details), but the theme of space exploration hit the screens even earlier and was also popular. (There were few monster movies before 1954, the first being The THING in 1951.) The first 1950s space film to be released was ROCKETSHIP X-M, which was rushed out in 1950 to capitalize on the pre-publicity for DESTINATION MOON; it was the latter, however, that was successful. It was followed by such spacecraft-oriented films as The DAY THE EARTH STOOD STILL (1951), WHEN WORLDS COLLIDE (1951), INVADERS FROM MARS (1953), IT CAME FROM OUTER SPACE (1953), WAR OF THE WORLDS (1953), RIDERS TO THE STARS (1954), The CONQUEST OF SPACE (1955), THIS ISLAND EARTH (1955), The QUATERMASS XPERIMENT (1955), FORBIDDEN PLANET (1956), and EARTH VS. THE FLYING SAUCERS (1956). In six of these, probably more for budgetary than for ideological reasons, the spacecraft bring ALIENS to Earth; all are monstrous except for the Christlike alien in The Day the Earth Stood Still, who dies and rises again before (in a manner more appropriate to the Old Testament than the New) threatening Earth with destruction if it does not repent its sins. In the remainder the urge for the conquest of space is apparent (as it was coming to be in the real world, with the first orbital satellite, Sputnik 1, launched in 1957), although the religious subtext of much 1950s sf cinema is found also in When Worlds Collide (a Noah's space-ark is used to save a remnant of humanity from God's wrath made manifest as cataclysm) and The Conquest of Space (the captain of a spacecraft goes mad because he believes space travel is an intrusion into the sphere of God).

The only full-blooded space operas of the period appeared moderately late on, with *This Island Earth* and *Forbidden Planet*, but even in these tales the central image is of the destruction that can be wrought by science.

One of the most memorable sf films of the 1950s boom is at first glance not sf at all: the **Mickey Spillane** *film noir* KISS ME DEADLY (1955), dir Robert Aldrich (1918-1983), in which the central object is a box which, when opened, emits a fiery light and unleashes destruction on the world. The film effortlessly and pessimistically links by metaphor the petty spites and bestialities that disfigure individuals with the greater capacity for destruction symbolized by the Pandora's Box which, in this case, appears to unbind, like the Bomb, a cleansing radioactivity to greet the fallen world.

The monster movie, of course, is even more obviously fearful of science: its text is "science breeds monsters". Political PARANOIA, a quite different theme (and one to be developed further in the 1960s) also found a niche in much 1950s sf, especially in those films in which creatures that look just like us on the outside turn out on the inside to be monsters or alien puppets (often identifiable as metaphoric stand-ins for such other secret worms in the apple of Western society as communist agents). *Invaders from Mars* (1953), one of the earliest and best of these (◊ MONSTER MOVIES and PARANOIA for other films on this theme), added a touch of Freudian fear to the paranoid brew by making Mummy and Daddy among the first humans to be rendered monstrous and emotionless by alien control. The most famous example is INVASION OF THE BODY SNATCHERS (1956), in which, as in most of its kind, the slightly diagrammatic fear of communism is surely secondary to the fear of the loss of affect: the monstrous quasi-humans have no emotions; they are like cogs in a remorseless machine. It is interesting that, although with hindsight we see the Eisenhower years precisely as years of conformity, it was fear of that very conformity that played so prominent a role in the US popular culture of those years.

Where in the 1940s only a handful of sf films were made, in the 1950s there were 150 to 200, their numbers increasing in inverse proportion to their quality: although the years 1957-9 had more sf movies than the years 1950-56, they were mostly B-movies from "Poverty Row", which, despite the fact that they include such old favourites as ATTACK OF THE CRAB MONSTERS, *The* INCREDIBLE SHRINKING MAN, QUATERMASS II and *The* MONOLITH MONSTERS (all 1957) and *The* FLY, *The* BLOB and I MARRIED A MONSTER FROM OUTER SPACE (all 1958), leave an overall impression of sf cinema as both sensationalist and tacky. The year 1959, however, while producing genre movies that were mostly forgettable exploitation material, also produced three films which, while obviously intended for a mainstream audience, had an sf theme: JOURNEY TO THE CENTER OF THE EARTH, *The* WORLD, THE FLESH AND THE DEVIL and ON THE BEACH. At last some sf themes (LOST WORLDS, the HOLOCAUST AND AFTER and the END OF THE WORLD), it seemed, were sufficiently familiar to general audiences to risk the involvement of big-name stars: James Mason, Harry Belafonte and Gregory Peck. None of these films was especially good, but as sociological signposts each has some importance.

Another phenomenon of the 1950s was the rise of Japanese sf cinema, built largely on the success of GOJIRA (1954; vt *Godzilla*), a monster movie. Many further monster movies followed, nearly all from Toho studios, which began working in the space-opera and alien-invasion genres later, as with CHIKYU BOIEGUN (1957; vt *The Mysterians*).

By the later 1950s the major studios were abandoning genre sf, and most memorable productions of the period were made by such low-budget independent producers as Roger CORMAN; the earlier 1950s, by contrast, had been dominated by studios like Universal, Warner Bros. and Paramount, which had sometimes used specialist producers like George PAL or even, in the case of Universal, developed their own specialist sf director, Jack ARNOLD. For the decades since then it has been arguable that much of the inventive energy of sf cinema has continued to bubble up from the marshes of "Poverty Row".

Sf films were quite numerous through most of the 1960s, without many clear lines of evolution being visible, although individual films sometimes showed real creativity (but see below for developments in the cinema of paranoia, and for the new wave of DYSTOPIAN films). Hollywood remained fairly uneventful so far as sf was concerned through the years 1960-67, with silly, colourful films like *The* TIME MACHINE (1960), *The* ABSENT-MINDED PROFESSOR (1961) and FANTASTIC VOYAGE (1966). Jerry Lewis made a surprisingly effective sf campus comedy out of the Jekyll and Hyde theme, *The* NUTTY PROFESSOR (1963). Roger Corman's low-budget, independent sf features became less common, but one of the last was one of the best: X – THE MAN WITH THE X-RAY EYES (1963). By far the best commercial movie in the genre belonged to it only marginally: Alfred Hitchcock's *The* BIRDS (1963). A revenge-of-Nature film which began a whole trend, this is a particularly surreal monster movie whose paranoid element – intimate sharers of our own world becoming the monsters – showed that the paranoia theme was continuing strongly in sf cinema, as it has ever since, but with a shift in emphasis. In the 1950s the monster movie had been comparatively innocent, and – not surprisingly with the Cold War being at its height and Hollywood itself about to become subject to investigations designed to weed out left-wingers – regularly featured monsters from outside normal experience; foreigners, so to speak. These films often opened with scenes of tranquillity – children playing, farmers hoeing, lovers strolling. The subsequent violence was almost a metaphor for the irrational forces which peaceful US citizens feared might enter their lives, forces beyond their control, such as (in real life) the Bomb or invasion. By contrast, the subtext of *The Birds* can, with hindsight, be seen as changing the focus of unease away from the alien monster towards the domestic monster. In the 1960s, elements of decay and division in Western society, especially US society, were becoming more obvious, and 1960s sf reflected this. Working like Hitchcock on the margins of sf cinema, John FRANKENHEIMER was perhaps the most distinguished Hollywood director of 1960s politically paranoid sf, with *The* MANCHURIAN CANDIDATE (1962), *Seven Days in May* (1964) and SECONDS (1966). Conspiracy-theory paranoia of the most extreme kind is the occasion for black comedy in Theodore Flicker's *The* PRESIDENT'S ANALYST (1967), in which the Telephone Company is out to rule the world. Even George Pal, of all people, had a very effective exercise in paranoia with *The* POWER (1967), a story of amoral superhumans disguised as ordinary people. Stanley KUBRICK, working outside the Hollywood system, made his memorably black and funny sf début with DR STRANGELOVE OR: HOW I LEARNED TO STOP WORRYING AND LOVE THE BOMB (1964), and Hollywood exile Joseph Losey made his nightmare of alienation and radioactivity, *The* DAMNED (1961), in the UK. In all of these, it is our own society that is frightening, not some alien import.

The 1960s were, famously, a decade of radicalism and social change, but the English-speaking cinema was slow to reflect this, being more interested in the miniskirt than in, say, the growing power of young people as a political force. Movies of youth revolution like PRIVILEGE [1967], WILD IN THE STREETS [1968] and GAS-S-S-S [1970] came only at the end of the decade, in a perhaps cynical attempt to cash in on the flower-power phenomenon, and there were never many of them. Spy movies were immensely popular – a phenomenon perhaps reflecting the idea of a society riddled with secrets and conspiracies – but there is nothing remotely radical or even modern about the **James Bond** series of films inaugurated with DR NO (1962) and going on to include many other borderline-sf films like YOU ONLY LIVE TWICE (1967); indeed, their central image of mad SCIENTISTS out to rule the world derives from the pulp sf of the 1920s and 1930s (*see also* CRIME AND PUNISHMENT). In Europe, however, especially in France, the so-called New Wave cinema was indeed revolutionizing the medium with lasting effect. Many New Wave directors made marginal sf films, typically incorporating sf tropes into a supposedly future but apparently contemporary setting. These included Chris Marker with *La* JETÉE (1963), Jean-Luc Godard with ALPHAVILLE (1965) and WEEKEND (1968), François Truffaut with FAHRENHEIT 451 (1966) and Alain Resnais with JE T'AIME, JE T'AIME (1967), all eccentric and interesting; Truffaut was perhaps the odd man out, as the director least comfortable with future scenarios. The exploitation cinema in Italy had no critical agenda of

reform like the New Wave in France, but it had plenty of intelligence and inventiveness, though the results were often extremely uneven; much of the Italian work was HORROR, but this often overlapped with sf, as in Mario Bava's TERRORE NELLO SPAZIO (1965; vt *Planet of the Vampires*). Further east, both RUSSIA and Czechoslovakia (◊ CZECH AND SLOVAK SF) made quite a few sf films, including Russia's PLANETA BUR (1962; vt *Planet of Storms*) and Czechoslovakia's IKARIE XB-1 (1963). The sf business in the UK was normally a matter of low-budget B-movies, but some respectable films emerged – e.g., *The* DAY THE EARTH CAUGHT FIRE (1961), CHILDREN OF THE DAMNED (1963), QUATERMASS AND THE PIT (1967) and Peter WATKINS's *The* WAR GAME (1965). This last was made for tv but banned from tv for giving too realistic a picture of nuclear HOLOCAUST; even today it comes across at least as powerfully as *The* DAY AFTER (1983), made for US tv two decades later.

The single most important year in the history of sf cinema is 1968. Before then sf was not taken very seriously either artistically or commercially; since then it has remained, much of the time, one of the most popular film genres, and has produced many more good films. Simply to list the main sf films of 1968 gives some idea of the year's significance: BARBARELLA, CHARLY, NIGHT OF THE LIVING DEAD, PLANET OF THE APES and 2001: A SPACE ODYSSEY. (Less important were COUNTDOWN, *The* ILLUSTRATED MAN, *The* LOST CONTINENT and *The* MONITORS.) George A. ROMERO's *Night of the Living Dead* is the exception here in being a low-budget, independent production, but, while it was seen by some contemporaries as being merely another milestone in making the cinema of horror more luridly graphic and disgusting – a key moment in the evolution of the SPLATTER MOVIE – its image of humans reduced to deranged, cannibalistic zombies has an undeniable metaphoric power and even a dark poetry, and it was revolutionary in its discomforting refusal to offer any solace throughout, nor any happy ending. The other four films were commercially reputable products, and interesting for different reasons. *Barbarella* is second-generation, spoof sf, the sort of film that can be made only when genre materials have already been thoroughly absorbed into the cultural fabric. *Charly* won its financier and star, Cliff Robertson, the first Oscar for Best Actor given to a performance in an sf movie, a good measure of sf's increasing respectability; the film was based on Daniel KEYES's *Flowers for Algernon* (1959 *FSF*; exp **1966**). *Planet of the Apes* and *2001: A Space Odyssey* are good films – the latter arguably one of the great classics of the genre – both notable for their commercial success and for their use of nonpatronizing screenplays that demanded thought from the audience. Though there were plenty of bad films still to come, sf cinema now had to be taken seriously, definitely by the money-men and to a degree by the critics.

To jump ahead for a moment, it would be another

decade before the commercial potential of sf cinema was thoroughly confirmed, partly in response to the technical developments in special effects that took place during that period. In 1977 STAR WARS, a smash hit, inaugurated a new boom in space-opera movies, and in the same year CLOSE ENCOUNTERS OF THE THIRD KIND also did very well with its blend of sentiment and UFO mysticism, inaugurating the friendly-ALIEN theme which the film's director, Steven SPIELBERG, was to exploit with even greater effect in E.T.: THE EXTRATERRESTRIAL (1982). Another money-maker that began a trend was SUPERMAN (1978), which led to a succession of ever-more-disappointing SUPERHERO movies. These films remain among the most financially successful ever made. In 1971 the cinema of the fantastic (sf, horror, fantasy, surrealism) accounted for about 5 per cent of US box-office takings; by 1982 this figure had risen amazingly to approach 50 per cent, and it remained as high as about 30 per cent in 1990.

Though special effects were to usher in a period of sf cinema whose spectacle was more overwhelming than its intelligence, in the late 1960s no vast teenage audience had as yet accumulated to drag down the genre with the commercial demand that it should remain always suitable for kids. A majority of the sf films of 1969-79 were downbeat and even gloomy, and even in the adventure films their heroes were hard pressed just to survive, let alone survive cheerfully. The three main themes were the dystopian, the Luddite and the post-HOLOCAUST.

Luddite films included practically everything made or written by Michael CRICHTON, notably WESTWORLD (1973), The TERMINAL MAN (1974) and COMA (1978). He has a gift for cinematic narrative, but his tireless replaying of the theme made him seem something of a one-note director. (John BADHAM, in the 1980s, would be another director to make a career out of Luddite sf movies, with WARGAMES [1983], BLUE THUNDER [1983] and SHORT CIRCUIT [1986].) Other films about the triumph of technology and the subsequent enslavement of humanity (whether actual or metaphorical) included: COLOSSUS, THE FORBIN PROJECT (1969), computer takes over; SLEEPER (1973), machines run amok; KILLDOZER (1974), a bulldozer goes mad; FUTUREWORLD (1976), robots take over; DEMON SEED (1977), computer as rapist and voyeur; The CHINA SYNDROME (1979), nuclear power station almost blows up; La MORT EN DIRECT (1979), intrusive journalist whose eyes are cameras. In DARK STAR (1974), the feature-film début of John CARPENTER and one of the wittiest sf films yet made, a computerized bomb undertakes phenomenological arguments with the crew of a starship.

Dystopian films ranged from the terrible – SILENT RUNNING (1971), we've destroyed all plant life; ROLLERBALL (1975), sport is the opium of the people; LOGAN'S RUN (1976), everyone over 30 is killed – through the interesting if exaggerated – SOYLENT GREEN (1973), overpopulation; The STEPFORD WIVES (1974), robot

wives replace human wives – to the excellent – THX 1138 (1970), the début of George LUCAS; A CLOCKWORK ORANGE (1971), brainwashing; The MAN WHO FELL TO EARTH (1976), the corrupting influence of human society on an alien; STALKER (1979 Russia), alien leavings turn out to be fairy gold in a trash-heap world.

Life after the holocaust had been an occasional theme in sf cinema for some time. Stories of survivors and the detritus they live among were becoming more numerous by the 1970s; the iconography of disaster cinema regularly includes a few rusting or ivy-clad ruins of 20th-century civilization, as in GLEN AND RANDA (1971), Logan's Run (1976) or, with more bravura, A BOY AND HIS DOG (1975). The ULTIMATE WARRIOR (1975) fights in the rubble, and BENEATH THE PLANET OF THE APES (1970) mutants live in it. In ZARDOZ (1974) the greater part of the population has reverted to superstitious barbarism. We see this reversion taking place in MAD MAX (1979) and its two entertaining designer-barbarism sequels. Other examples from the 1970s include The BED-SITTING ROOM (1969), NO BLADE OF GRASS (1970), The OMEGA MAN (1971) and DAMNATION ALLEY (1977). This is a theme that suits low-budget movies, which nearly all these are, since the real world produces settings of extraordinary dereliction in profusion.

In the 1970s the low-budget, independent exploitation-movie end of the film business was quite busy making sf movies of other kinds, too, usually borderline-sf/HORROR, including SCREAM AND SCREAM AGAIN (1969), DEATH LINE (1972; vt RAW MEAT), George A. Romero's The CRAZIES (1973), BLUE SUNSHINE (1977), PIRANHA (1978) – a witty partnership between screenwriter John SAYLES and director Joe DANTE – and PHANTASM (1979). But the two outstanding independent directors of exploitation sf in the 1970s (and after) were Larry COHEN and David CRONENBERG. The deeply eccentric social satirist Cohen is the inventor of the monster baby, in IT'S ALIVE (1973), where it is played by a doll pulled along by a string, and the Christ-figure, in GOD TOLD ME TO (1976; vt DEMON), who is an alien-fathered hermaphrodite. Cronenberg, whose biological metamorphoses almost constitute a new cinematic genre, has become perhaps the most important director associated with sf cinema; his work of the 1970s consists of chaotic, horrific comedies, including The PARASITE MURDERS (1974; vt They Came from Within; vt Shivers), RABID (1976) and The BROOD (1979).

One of the most complex and moving sf films to date is SOLARIS (1972), the first sf film of Andrei TARKOVSKY, with its delicate meshing of images from inner and outer space. Other films of the decade that at least stimulated discussion – none is outstanding – are SLAUGHTERHOUSE 5 (1972), The DAY OF THE DOLPHIN (1973), The ROCKY HORROR PICTURE SHOW (1975), The BOYS FROM BRAZIL (1978) and STAR TREK: THE MOTION PICTURE (1979). More influential than any of these was the very successful and much imitated ALIEN (1979), the first sf feature by Ridley SCOTT, but this was part of the big-budget sf-feature boom of the late 1970s, discussed above, and belongs in spirit more to the 1980s than the 1970s.

An interesting film of 1978, INVASION OF THE BODY SNATCHERS, was a successful remake of the classic 1956 film. Along with KING KONG (1976) this introduced a series of sf remakes in the 1980s which, contrary to cliché, contain a good deal of interesting work. The time was ripe for remakes because, in the post *Star Wars* period, sf was proving such a hot area of Hollywood movie-making. If you've had a success once, what more natural than to try to repeat it? The two best remakes were probably John Carpenter's *The* THING (1982) and David Cronenberg's *The* FLY (1986). Also better than expected were *The* BLOB (1988) and *The* FLY II (1989). Others, mostly poor, were BUCK ROGERS IN THE 25TH CENTURY (1979), FLASH GORDON (1980), GOJIRA 1985 (1985; vt *Godzilla 1985*), INVADERS FROM MARS (1986), LORD OF THE FLIES (1990), NIGHT OF THE LIVING DEAD (1990) and NOT OF THIS EARTH (1988).

A less welcome phenomenon of the 1980s was the number of successful films to which sequels were made almost as a matter of course, almost never as good as their originals, an observation that spans a variety of films including *Critters 2: The Main Course, It's Alive III: Island of the Alive,* HIGHLANDER II: THE QUICKENING, *Bronx Warriors II, 2010, Phantasm II, Re-Animator 2, Robocop 2, Short Circuit 2, Toxic Avenger 2* and *Future Cop 2*. Indeed, the list includes the most expensive film ever made, TERMINATOR 2: JUDGMENT DAY (1991), which, though quite good, is less uncompromising than its predecessor. Two sequels better than their originals are MAD MAX 2 (1981; vt *The Road Warrior*) and PREDATOR 2 (1990). As of 1992 there have been five **Planet of the Apes** films, six **Star Trek** films and four **Superman** films (plus SUPERGIRL, etc.) in the cycle begun by *Superman* (1978). The Japanese, however, probably have the record with their endless **Gojira** and **Gamera** films, two series that began in the 1950s (◊ GOJIRA; DAIKAIJU GAMERA).

The disappointment of the 1980s and the early 1990s was that, sf boom or no sf boom, many spectacular productions were the filmic equivalent of fast food, offering no lasting satisfaction. Also, too much US product seemed to more astringent foreign tastes to be suffused with an oversweet sentimentality, especially following the success of Spielberg's *E.T.* Films tainted in this way, some of them otherwise quite good, included RETURN OF THE JEDI (1983), with its Ewoks, STARMAN (1984), with its Christlike alien, COCOON (1985), with its rejuvenated oldies, EXPLORERS (1985), with its cute alien kids, INNERSPACE (1987), with a wimp finding true manhood with the help of a miniaturized macho astronaut, * BATTERIES NOT INCLUDED (1987), with nauseating baby flying saucers, STAR TREK V: THE FINAL FRONTIER (1989), the nadir of the geriatric-buddy movie, and *The* ABYSS (1989), whose threatening aliens turn out to be real friendly Tinker Bells.

At the very beginning of the 1980s, films of some interest included ALTERED STATES (1980), BATTLE BEYOND THE STARS (1980), especially *The* EMPIRE STRIKES BACK (1980), ESCAPE FROM NEW YORK (1981), OUTLAND (1981) and MEMOIRS OF A SURVIVOR (1981). But by far the most influential sf film was the superbly designed BLADE RUNNER (1982), Ridley Scott's second sf feature, whose shabby, lively, media-saturated city of the near future was an early manifestation of CYBERPUNK; a more knowing Japanese version of the cyberpunk ethos – by then almost an sf CLICHÉ – would be found years later in the animated film AKIRA (1990). Curiously, not many commercial films between these two partook full-bloodedly of cyberpunk thinking, though several small independent productions (see below), including VIDEODROME (1982) and HARDWARE (1990), did so. However, the cyberpunk theme of VIRTUAL REALITY – the notion of consensual hallucination, or of humans entering CYBERNETIC systems and reading their networks (or being read by them) not just as maps but as the territory itself – became quite popular in cinema. A far from comprehensive list includes the made-for-tv movie *The* LATHE OF HEAVEN (1980; based on the 1971 novel by Ursula LE GUIN), TRON (1982), BRAINSTORM (1983), DREAMSCAPE (1984) and *The* LAST STARFIGHTER (1984).

There are many other examples of thematic clusters in the 1980s. Hollywood (and other film centres) had seldom been so narcissistically absorbed – often stupidly – by its own previous productions, with each box-office breakthrough spawning multiple imitations. Hundreds of films featured a slow camera track along a giant spaceship (*2001, Star Wars*) or an alien parasite bursting bloodily from a human body (*Alien*).

A big hit, starting at the beginning of the decade with SATURN 3 (1980), ANDROID (1982) and RUNAWAY (1984), was the killer-robot movie, mostly after the success of ROBOCOP (1987); examples are *Hardware* (1990), CLASS OF 1999 (1990), ROBOCOP 2 (1990), ROBOT JOX (1990) and EVE OF DESTRUCTION (1991), but the best by far was *The* TERMINATOR (1984), which in turn spawned *Terminator 2: Judgement Day* (1991).

More seriously gruesome, but not without soap-opera elements, was the spate of nuclear-death films beginning with *The* DAY AFTER, SPECIAL BULLETIN and TESTAMENT (all 1983), the first two made for tv. They were followed by, among others, THREADS (1985), also made for tv, and the cartoon feature WHEN THE WIND BLOWS (1986).

A subgenre of the 1980s was a bastard form, the teen-sf movie, of which the three best were probably REAL GENIUS (1985), BILL & TED'S EXCELLENT ADVENTURE (1988) and EARTH GIRLS ARE EASY (1988), along with the **Back to the Future** series (see below). Others were DEAD KIDS (1981), CITY LIMITS (1984), NIGHT OF THE COMET (1984), MY SCIENCE PROJECT (1985), WEIRD SCIENCE (1985), FLIGHT OF THE NAVIGATOR (1986), SPACE CAMP (1986), YOUNG EINSTEIN (1988), MY STEPMOTHER IS AN ALIEN (1988), HONEY, I SHRUNK THE KIDS (1989) and SPACED INVADERS (1989).

TIME-TRAVEL movies made a big comeback in the 1980s, many of them (◊ Introduction) being not technically sf since their means of time travel was fantastic. Among the genuine sf the best are BACK TO THE FUTURE (1985) and its two sequels, all directed by Robert Zemeckis. *Bill & Ted's Excellent Adventure* (1988) and its sequel, *Bill & Ted's Bogus Journey* (1991), are both charming. Others are the entertaining *The* PHILADELPHIA EXPERIMENT (1984) and two disappointments, *The* FINAL COUNTDOWN (1980) and MILLENNIUM (1989).

After the success of CARRIE (1976), based on Stephen KING's 1974 novel about a persecuted schoolgirl with PSI POWERS, films about paranormal abilities, though never becoming overwhelmingly popular, nevertheless remained as a persistent subgenre. The best is probably Cronenberg's remorseless SCANNERS (1980). Others include *The* FURY (1978), *The* SENDER (1982), *The* DEAD ZONE (1983), also directed by Cronenberg, and the dire FIRESTARTER (1984).

The oddest subgenre was probably the alien-human buddy movie. ENEMY MINE (1985), one of the earlier ones, is set on another planet, but many examples are set on Earth. Not just two but *four* of them feature partnerships between alien and Earth police: ALIEN NATION (1988), *The* HIDDEN (1988), SOMETHING IS OUT THERE (1988; a tv miniseries released on videotape as a feature film) and I COME IN PEACE (1989; vt *Dark Angel*).

Other 1980s and 1990s films of interest but not fitting neatly into any of the above categories were HALLOWEEN III: SEASON OF THE WITCH (1983), STRANGE INVADERS (1983), DUNE (1984), BRAZIL (1985), ALIENS (1986), PREDATOR (1987), MONKEY SHINES (1988), TOTAL RECALL (1990) and *The* ROCKETEER (1991). *Aliens* and *Brazil* are the most distinguished of these, the former directed by James CAMERON, the most important sf director to emerge during the 1980s, the latter a perhaps too lovingly designed dystopia. *Monkey Shines*, also memorable, showed that George A. Romero was still a director of real power.

Once again, however, the lesson of the 1970s was in the main repeated. If you want to see what the commercial cinema will be doing next decade, take a good close look at what the low-budget cinema, even the exploitation cinema, is doing right now. For every film as inventive as *Blade Runner* produced by companies with access to very large sums of money, there are half a dozen thrown up by the shoestring independents. In the latter category, the 1980s produced *Scanners* (1980), ALLIGATOR (1981), *Android* (1982), LIQUID SKY (1982), *Videodrome* (1982), *Der* LIFT (1983), *The* BROTHER FROM ANOTHER PLANET (1984), *The Terminator*, REPO MAN (1984), TRANCERS (1984), *The* STUFF (1985), RE-ANIMATOR (1985), FROM BEYOND (1986), MAKING MR RIGHT (1987), THEY LIVE (1988) and SOCIETY (1989). If sf cinema were represented by these films alone it would have to be diagnosed as in vigorous health, though somewhat disreputable and threatening in appearance.

But, alas, by the late 1980s the increasingly floundering commercial film industries of the USA and the UK seemed caught in a desperate spiral of attempting to recapture past splendours by dint of colourful (and expensive) violence while giving ideological offence to none. Thus even death and destruction become anodyne. By 1990 the commercial sf cinema – especially in the USA – seemed to have lost not just whatever integrity it had had but also its common sense. As grave financial problems began to spread through Hollywood, it seemed possible to predict that 1991 might prove to have been the last year of insanely inflated film budgets. [PN]

Further reading: The following reading list is highly selective. An early but still useful reference work on sf cinema is the 3-vol *Reference Guide to Fantastic Films: Science Fiction, Fantasy & Horror 1* (vol 1 **1972**, vol 2 **1973**, vol 3 **1974**) compiled by Walt LEE. There is much information, with some rather brief and disappointing capsule comments, in *Horror and Science Fiction Films: A Checklist* (**1972**), *Vol II* (**1982**) and *Vol III* (**1984**) by Donald C. Willis. Although it does not cover as many titles as these two, *The Aurum Film Encyclopedia: Science Fiction* (**1984**; rev 1991) ed Phil HARDY is far more than a listing with credits; the best 1-vol guide, it is the fullest coverage of sf cinema to contain detailed description and critical analysis (generally very good), and, with upwards of 1400 films described in the revised edition, covers at least twice as many sf movies as any other critical book on the subject. Even more useful to the researcher is a run of the journal *Monthly Film Bulletin*, published by the British Film Institute, which gives (even after its incorporation during 1991 into its sister journal, *Sight and Sound*) full credits for all films it covers (all films released in the UK), and normally more complete critical discussion than anything available in book form; its sf critics include Kim NEWMAN, Philip STRICK and Tom Milne. This was the secondary source most consulted for films from the 1960s onwards in the compilation of this encyclopedia; its critical appreciations of sf films from earlier periods are briefer and far more conservative, and it does not cover the silent period (Hardy's book does). One other reference work extraordinarily useful for its period is *Keep Watching the Skies! American Science Fiction of the Fifties: Volume I 1950-57* (**1982**) and *Volume II 1958-62* (**1986**) by Bill WARREN.

The quality of most general discussions of sf cinema in books is not high; many are coffee-table books of little value, or are aimed at a juvenile fan market. An early study of some interest (despite irritating factual errors) is the pioneering *Science Fiction in the Cinema* (**1970**) by John BAXTER, the first book to attempt some kind of critical sorting of its subject matter. *Science Fiction Movies* (**1976**) by Philip Strick is witty, well informed and critically astute, but does not linger long enough on individual films. John BROSNAN's *Future Tense: The Cinema of Science Fiction* (**1978**; rev vt *The Primal Screen: A History of Science Fiction Film* **1991**) contains judgments, albeit at greater length, that will already be familiar to readers of the first edition of this volume, for which Brosnan wrote many of the film entries. Peter NICHOLLS's *Fantastic Cinema* (**1984** UK; vt *The World of Fantastic Films* US) is an illustrated survey, only partially devoted to sf, which attempts to establish a critical canon for fantastic films. *Omni's Screen Flights/Screen Fantasies: The Future According to Science Fiction Cinema* (anth **1984**) ed Danny Peary is probably the best collection of essays and interviews on sf cinema. *Harlan Ellison's Watching* (coll **1989**) by Harlan ELLISON collects most of his film criticism from 1965 on, much of it about sf movies. Academic and theoretical books on sf cinema – there are not many – have generally disappointed, and occasionally been crippled by a technical jargon that is the reverse of precise, as in some of the essays in *Alien Zone: Cultural Theory and Contemporary Science Fiction Cinema* (coll **1990**) ed Annette Kuhn; a rather more accessible collection of critical essays is *Shadows of the Magic Lamp: Fantasy and Science Fiction in Film* (coll **1985**) ed George E. SLUSSER and Eric S. RABKIN. But of these academic books the most challenging may be Vivian SOBCHACK's *Screening Space: The American Science Fiction Film* (**1986**), a radical expansion of her earlier *The Limits of Infinity* (**1980**); it is worth persevering with, jargon and all, for the intellectual strength it brings to bear in its attempt to define sf cinema in a POSTMODERNIST context. Finally *An Illustrated History of the Horror Film* (**1967**) by Carlos Clarens and *Nightmare Movies* (**1984**; rev vt *Nightmare Movies: A Critical History of the Horror Film, 1968-88*) by Kim Newman are two stimulating books that have a good deal to say, *en passant*, about sf films.

CITIES The city is the focal point of our civilization, and images of the city of the future bring into sharp relief the expectations and fears with which we imagine the future of civilization. Disenchantment with metropolitan life was evident even while UTO-PIAN optimism remained strong, and became remarkably exaggerated in DYSTOPIAN images of the future. The growth of the cities during the Industrial Revolution created filthy slums where crime, ill-health and vice flourished, and a new kind of poverty reigned; thus even the most devoted disciples of progress can and do lament the state of the industrial city, which has little in common with such utopian city-states as Tommaso CAMPANELLA's *City of the Sun* (**1637**) or the cities of L.S. MERCIER's *Memoirs of the Year Two Thousand Five Hundred* (**1771**; trans **1772**). Speculative thinkers who were not utopians found the evolution of the great cities a powerful argument against progress – a view strongly advanced in *After London* (**1885**) by Richard JEFFERIES, in which the cities have died but their remains still poison the Earth.

In much early sf the city is the same place of contrasts that it was in reality, with the rich and poor living in close but separate worlds, architectural grandeur masking squalor. This is evident in *Caesar's Column* (**1890**) by Ignatius DONNELLY, in "A Story of the Days to Come" (1897) and *When the Sleeper Wakes* (**1899**) by H.G. WELLS, and in Fritz LANG's film METROPOLIS (1926). Wells, the most determined prophet of technological supercivilization, frequently imagined the destruction of the present-day cities as a prelude to utopian rebuilding. (Many of the real-life urban utopian schemes of the late 19th century demanded that cities be built anew, cleansed of their manifest evils.) However, the splendid vision of the city as an architectural miracle which had inspired early utopians was a vision ever-present in early PULP MAGAZINE sf, thanks largely to the artwork of Frank R. PAUL, who was far better at drawing wonderful cities than human beings; his distinctive images contributed much to the flavour of Gernsbackian sf.

Modern sf has made extravagant use of three stereotyped images of the future city: one exaggerates the contrast between the city and a surrounding wilderness, often enclosing the city in a huge plastic dome, polarizing the opposition between city life and rural life; a second displays once-proud cities fallen into ruins, decaying and dying; and the third presents a vivid characterization of the future-city environment in which humans move in the shadow of awesomely impersonal and implicitly hostile artefacts.

The theme of stories of the first kind – for which E.M. FORSTER's "The Machine Stops" (1909) provided a prototype – is usually that of *escape* from the claustrophobic, initiative-killing comfort to the wilderness, which offers evolutionary opportunity through the struggle to survive. Simple expositions of the theme include *The Hothouse World* (1931; **1965**) by Fred MACISAAC, *The Adventure of Wyndham Smith* (**1938**) by S. Fowler WRIGHT, *Beyond the Sealed World* (**1965**) by Rena VALE, *From Carthage then I Came* (**1966**; vt *Eight against Utopia*) by Douglas R. MASON, *Magellan* (**1970**) by Colin ANDERSON, *Wild Jack* (**1974**) by John CHRISTOPHER, *The Crack in the Sky* (**1976**) by Richard LUPOFF and *Terrarium* (**1985**) by Scott Russell SANDERS. More sophisticated variants include *The City and the Stars* (**1956**; exp from *Against the Fall of Night* [1948; **1953**]) by Arthur C. CLARKE, *The World Inside* (**1971**) by Robert SILVERBERG, *The Eye of the Heron* (1978; **1982**) by Ursula K. LE GUIN and *Out on Blue Six* (**1989**) by Ian MCDONALD. Interesting inversions of the schema can be found in Harlan ELLISON's "A Boy and His Dog" (1969) and Greg BEAR's *Strength of Stones* (fixup **1981**).

Images of the ruined city are often remarkable for their exaggerated romanticism. Early examples include Jefferies's *After London*, George Allan ENGLAND's *Darkness and Dawn* (**1914**) and Stephen Vincent BENÉT's "By the Waters of Babylon" (1937). The ruins themselves may become charismatic and symbolic, as exemplified by the torch of the Statue of Liberty in *The Torch* (1920; **1948**) by Jack BECHDOLT. There is a surprisingly strong vein of similar romanticism in GENRE SF. Much of Clifford D. SIMAK's work – especially the episodic *City* (1944-51; fixup **1952**) – rejoices in the decline and decay of cities, as do

Theodore STURGEON's "The Touch of Your Hand" (1953), J.G. BALLARD's "Chronopolis" (1960) and "The Ultimate City" (1976), Charles PLATT's *The City Dwellers* (**1970** UK; vt *Twilight of the City* 1977 US) and Samuel R. DELANY's *Dhalgren* (**1975**). This rejoicing is not usually based on any naïve glorification of living wild and free; more often it reflects a hope that human beings will some day outgrow the need for cities. The probable inescapability of city life is, however, ironically reflected in two curious stories of nomadic cultures which must carry their cities with them: Christopher PRIEST's *Inverted World* (**1974**) and Drew MENDELSON's *Pilgrimage* (**1981**).

The third stereotype involves not merely the representation of city life as unpleasant or alienating but a strategic exaggeration of the city's form and aspects to stress its frightening and claustrophobic qualities. The "caves" of Isaac ASIMOV's *The Caves of Steel* (**1954**) are literally as well as metaphorically claustrophobic. Cities which cover the entire surface of planets are commonplace: Asimov's Trantor, in the **Foundation** trilogy (1942-50; **1951-3**), set an important example. The impersonality of the megalopolis is ingeniously exaggerated in such stories as J.G. Ballard's "Build-Up" (1957; vt "The Concentration City") and R.A. LAFFERTY's "The World as Will and Wallpaper" (1973), and stories in this vein are often outrightly surreal – examples are Fritz LEIBER's "You're All Alone" (1950; exp vt *The Sinful Ones* 1953) and Ted WHITE's "It Could Be Anywhere" (1969). In extreme cases the city may become personalized, as in Robert Abernathy's "Single Combat" (1955), Robert SHECKLEY's "Street of Dreams, Feet of Clay" (1968), Harlan Ellison's "The Whimper of Whipped Dogs" (1973) and John SHIRLEY's *City Come a-Walkin'* (**1980**).

The stress of life in a crowded environment is the subject of many stories of OVERPOPULATION, notably Thomas M. DISCH's *334* (fixup **1972** UK) and Felix C. GOTSCHALK's *Growing Up in Tier 3000* (**1975**). Such novels tend to visualize the city of the future as a conglomerate of vast tower-blocks. Silverberg dubs these urbmons; Philip K. DICK calls them conapts; more recently the term "arcology" has become widespread. Some writers, however, preserve a more optimistic view of life in such edifices, notably Mack REYNOLDS in *The Towers of Utopia* (**1975**) and Larry NIVEN and Jerry POURNELLE in *Oath of Fealty* (**1981**).

Outside the GENRE-SF establishment, attempts to characterize the city and identify its alienating forces are mostly grimly realistic, but some tend to the fabular; examples include *Le città invisibili* (**1972**; trans as *Invisible Cities* 1974) by Italo CALVINO, in which Marco Polo offers Kublai Khan an account of the great range of the possible products of civilization, *Les géants* (**1973**; trans as *The Giants* 1975) by J.M. LE CLÉZIO, in which the central image is that of the great shopping-centre Hyperbolis, and Alasdair GRAY's stories "The Start of the Axletree" (1979; vt "The Origin of the Axletree") and "The End of the Axletree" (1983).

One striking exception – in which the city becomes the symbol of escape and freedom rather than the oppressive environment to be escaped – is in the novels making up James BLISH's **Cities in Flight** series (omni **1970**), in which ANTIGRAVITY devices, SPINDIZZIES, lift whole cities from the Earth's surface to roam the Universe (although even this dream comes to a dead end in one section of *Earthman Come Home* [fixup **1955**], the part first published in 1953 as "Sargasso of Lost Cities"). And the charismatic quality of cities is paid adequate homage in sf stories which celebrate the sleazy decadent grandeur of various imaginary cities. These include: the eponymous cities of Edward BRYANT's *Cinnabar* (coll **1976**) and Terry CARR's *Cirque* (**1977**); M. John HARRISON's fabulous city of Viriconium, first glimpsed in *The Pastel City* (**1971**) but far more elaborately portrayed in *A Storm of Wings* (**1980**), *In Viriconium* (**1982**; vt *The Floating Gods*) and *Viriconium Nights* (coll **1985**); and C.J. CHERRYH's Merovingen, displayed in *Angel with the Sword* (**1985**). Brian W. ALDISS's *The Malacia Tapestry* (**1976**) is similarly ambivalent about the splendour and sickness of cities.

The possible futures of specific real cities are sometimes tracked by sf writers with interest and respect; examples include the Chicago of *The Time-Swept City* (**1977**) by Thomas F. MONTELEONE and the New York of Frederik POHL's *Years of the City* (**1984**). C.J. Cherryh's *Sunfall* (coll **1981**) sets stories in far-futuristic versions of six major cities. Michael MOORCOCK's work – including his non-sf – uses many different images of London.

In both sf writing and sf art, the city is one of the most important recurrent images, and carries with it one of the richest, densest clusters of associations to be found in the whole sf iconography. Relevant theme anthologies include *Cities of Wonder* (anth **1966**) ed Damon KNIGHT, *Future City* (anth **1973**) ed Roger ELWOOD, and *The City: 2000 A.D.* (anth **1976**) ed Ralph Clem, Martin Harry GREENBERG and Joseph OLANDER. [BS]

See also: AUTOMATION; SOCIOLOGY.

CITY BENEATH THE SEA (vt *One Hour to Doomsday*
1. Made-for-tv film (1970). 20th Century-Fox TV Productions for NBC TV. Dir Irwin ALLEN, starring Stuart Whitman, Robert Wagner, Joseph Cotton, Rosemary Forsyth, Richard Basehart, Robert Colbert, Sugar Ray Robinson. Screenplay John Meredyth Lucas from a story by Allen. 100 mins, cut to 93 mins. Colour.

Released outside the USA as a feature film called *One Hour to Doomsday*, this was a pilot for a tv series that was never made. In an incoherent jumble of over-familiar sf situations, the citizens of 21st-century Pacifica have to contend with a super-H-bomb to be exploded somewhere within their underwater city, invasion by an "unfriendly foreign power", a sea monster, rebellion, the theft of a shipment of gold from Fort Knox, and imminent destruction by the impact of a planetoid approaching Earth. This is

Irwin-Allen plotting at its most typical, foretelling the DISASTER movies which would become his speciality. All ends happily.

2. UK tv serial for children (1962). ABC TV. Written John Lucarotti. Prod Guy Verney. 7 25min episodes. B/w. This told of a reporter and his young sidekick kidnapped to the underwater base of a mad scientist intent on world control. [JB/PN]

CITY LIMITS Film (1984). Sho Films/Videoform/Island Alive. Dir Aaron Lipstadt, starring John Stockwell, Darrell Larson, Kim Cattrall, Rae Dawn Chong. Screenplay Don Opper, from a story by Lipstadt and James Reigle. 85 mins. Colour.

Disappointing exploitation movie from the writer and director of the first-rate ANDROID (1982). Fifteen years after the USA has been almost wiped out by plague, two biker gangs in the sort of trendy post-HOLOCAUST fashions associated with the MAD MAX movies live in the City, basing their culture on comic books. A manipulative quasigovernmental agency attempts to murder the whole of one gang and conscript the other (the sociology of this being wholly unbelievable), but the kids win out with the help of kind old Black man James Earl Jones, so that the City is left safe in the hands of comics-reading Youth. [PN]

CLAGETT, JOHN (HENRY) (1916-   ) US writer whose first sf novel, *A World Unknown* (**1975**), is of some interest for its portrayal of an ALTERNATE-WORLD USA dominated by a Latin civilization that has never been influenced by Christianity – Jesus having never existed. [JC]

Other work: *The Orange R* (**1978**).

CLAREMONT, CHRIS Working name of US writer Christopher Simon Claremont (1950-   ). He first became known through his revitalization from 1975 of MARVEL COMICS's X-MEN, a title which had been temporarily retired but now became the bestselling comic in the field; CC is still (1992) scripting the title. The series deals with a constantly expanding group of mutant SUPERHEROES, several female, whose relationships and conflicts are densely complicated, and who inspire sympathy both because they are adolescents with typical family problems and because society tends to reject them. CC's style, though consistent with the Marvel Group's experimental house-style, is often rather clumsy, and manifestly represents an earlier phase in the rapid evolution of the comic book than that of GRAPHIC-NOVEL writers like Frank MILLER and Alan MOORE. *God Loves, Man Kills* (graph **1982**) was an original tale; *The Uncanny X-Men* (graph **1987**) was assembled from the comic. The two **Nicole Shea** novels – *FirstFlight* (**1987**) and *Grounded!* (**1991**; vt *Grounded* 1991 UK), both assembled as «High Frontier» (omni **1992**) – cover much of the same emotional and stylistic territory, tracing the adventures of a NASA astronaut in a NEAR-FUTURE Solar System. [NT/JC]

Other works: As with many writers and illustrators involved in the fast-moving and hectic world of comics publishing, CC's bibliography is anything but

easy to fix; the following titles have been confirmed: *Wolverine* (1985; graph coll **1988**) with Frank MILLER; *The Savage Land* (graph **1990**); and various **X-Men** graphic presentations, including *X-Men: Asgardian Wars* (graph **1990**); *X-Men: From the Ashes* (graph **1990**).

CLARESON, THOMAS D(EAN) (1926-   ) US editor, critic and professor of English. By the time he took his PhD at the University of Pennsylvania, (1956) he had published his first sf criticism (*Science Fiction Quarterly* 1954). He is perhaps best known for editing EXTRAPOLATION continuously from its founding in Dec 1959 to Winter 1989, at which point he handed over the reins to his then co-editor, Donald M. HASSLER; the rare first 10 years' issues of this journal, the oldest established academic journal about sf, were reprinted in *Extrapolation, A Science Fiction Newsletter, Vols 1-10* (anth **1978**) ed TDC. He was also a pioneer in editing ANTHOLOGIES of sf criticism in book form: *SF: The Other Side of Realism* (anth **1971**); *Voices for the Future: Essays on Major Science Fiction Writers Vol 1* (anth **1976**) and its sequels *Vol 2* (anth **1979**) and *Vol 3* (anth **1983**), the latter with Thomas L. Wymer; and *Many Futures, Many Worlds: Theme and Form in Science Fiction* (anth **1977**). His *SF Criticism: An Annotated Checklist* (**1972**) began a specialist research series which would be continued by Marshall B. TYMN and Roger SCHLOBIN. TDC also edited a story anthology with notes, intended to be used in education: *A Spectrum of Worlds* (anth **1972**).

TDC's most important research has been in early US sf. He wrote the chapter "The Emergence of the Scientific Romance" in Neil BARRON's *Anatomy of Wonder: Science Fiction* (**1976**; rev 1981; rev 1987), revised in later editions as "The Emergence of Science Fiction: The Beginnings to the 1920s". He was general editor of GREENWOOD PRESS's (somewhat incomplete) microfilm reprint series of sf PULP MAGAZINES and, also from Greenwood, the large, wide-ranging collection *Early Science Fiction Novels: A Microfiche Collection* (coll **1984**). Perhaps his two most important works are *Science Fiction in America, 1870s-1930s: An Annotated Bibliography of Primary Sources* (**1984**) and *Some Kind of Paradise: The Emergence of American Science Fiction* (dated 1985 but **1986**). The latter – a historical and thematic survey rather than a critical study – is a breakthrough book in an area that was previously codified poorly and erratically; one of TDC's strategies, perhaps necessary in so little known a field, is the inclusion of much plot synopsis. This is precisely the strength of the former book, too, whose annotations are of real use to researchers who may find copies of the original works difficult to locate. In TDC's more recent book, *Understanding American Science Fiction: The Formative Period, 1926 1970* (**1990**), the subject matter is much more familiar.

TDC was chairman of the first Modern Language Association Seminar on sf in 1958, and first President of the SCIENCE FICTION RESEARCH ASSOCIATION, 1970-76. In recognition of his services to the academic study of sf he received the PILGRIM AWARD in 1977. [PN]

Other works: *SF: A Dream of Other Worlds* (chap **1973**); *Robert Silverberg* (chap **1983**); *Robert Silverberg: A Primary and Secondary Bibliography* (**1983**); *Frederik Pohl* (**1987**).

See also: BIBLIOGRAPHIES; CONCEPTUAL BREAKTHROUGH; CRITICAL AND HISTORICAL WORKS ABOUT SF; FRANCE; HISTORY OF SF; LOST WORLDS.

CLARION SCIENCE FICTION WRITERS' WORKSHOP This long-standing workshop enrols beginning writers who are interested in writing sf. It consists of intensive writing and discussion sessions under the direction of known sf writers, who have included Orson Scott CARD, Terry CARR, Samuel DELANY, Thomas M. DISCH, Harlan ELLISON, Karen Joy FOWLER, John KESSEL, Damon KNIGHT, Ursula K. LE GUIN, Tim POWERS, Lewis SHINER and Kate WILHELM. The first three sessions were held at Clarion State College in Pennsylvania in the summers of 1968-70. In 1971 "Clarion East" was held in Tulane University and "Clarion West" in Seattle. Clarion West soon folded, but was later re-established in Seattle (8 sessions to 1991). In 1972 Clarion East moved to Michigan State University, where it remains (as just Clarion; 24 sessions to 1991). Clarion has been more successful than many writers' workshops and has produced notable alumni, including Ed BRYANT, F.M. BUSBY, Octavia E. BUTLER, Gerard F. CONWAY, George Alec EFFINGER, Vonda N. MCINTYRE, Kim Stanley ROBINSON, Lucius SHEPARD and Lisa TUTTLE. The original director of Clarion was Robin Scott WILSON, who also edited the first three anthologies of students' and teachers' work: *Clarion* (anth **1971**), *#II* (anth **1972**) and *#III* (anth **1973**). *Clarion SF* (anth **1977**) was ed Kate Wilhelm; *The Clarion Awards* (anth **1984**) ed Damon Knight covers the previous six years of Clarion. [PN]

CLARK, CURT ◊ Donald E. WESTLAKE.

CLARK, RONALD W(ILLIAM) (1916-1987) UK writer and journalist, active mainly with nonfiction since before WWII. He began publishing sf with "The Man who Went Back" for the London *Evening Standard* in 1949, but has not been a prolific contributor to the genre. His first sf novel, *Queen Victoria's Bomb: The Disclosures of Professor Franklin Huxtable, MA, Cantab.* (**1967**), achieved some success, and was one of the numerous contributions to the subgenre of sf works that exhibit nostalgia for a previous generation's view of the future; it could be regarded as a precursor to STEAMPUNK. *The Bomb that Failed* (**1969**; vt *The Last Year of the Old World* 1970 UK) is a kind of sequel, in which a failed nuclear test at Alamagordo changes history. [JC]

Other works (nonfiction): *The Huxleys* (**1968**); *J.B.S.: The Life and Work of J.B.S. Haldane* (**1968**); *Einstein: The Life and Times* (**1971**); *The Life of Bertrand Russell* (**1975**), all nonfiction.

See also: ALTERNATE WORLDS; NUCLEAR POWER.

CLARKE, ARTHUR C(HARLES) (1917-) UK author, resident since 1956 in Sri Lanka. Born in Minehead, Somerset, after leaving school ACC came to London in 1936 to work as a civil-servant auditor with HM Exchequer. He was active in fan circles before WWII, in which he served (1941-6) as a radar instructor with the RAF, rising to the rank of flight-lieutenant. After WWII he entered King's College, London, in 1948 taking his BSc with first-class honours in physics and mathematics.

ACC's strong interest in the frontiers of science was evident early. He was chairman of the British Interplanetary Society 1946-7, and again 1950-53. His first professionally published sf story was "Loophole" for *ASF* in Apr 1946, though his first sale was "Rescue Party", which appeared in *ASF* in May 1946. In his early years as a writer he three times used the pseudonym Charles Willis, and wrote once as E.G. O'Brien. These four stories all appeared in UK magazines 1947-51. Four of ACC's early stories, written for FANZINES (1937-42), were reprinted in *The Best of Arthur C. Clarke 1937-71* (coll **1973** UK; reissued in 2 vols, **1977**, the first being inaccurately titled *1932-1955*) ed Angus WELLS; a 1930s poem and essay appear in *The Fantastic Muse* (coll **1992** chap). ACC also worked as adviser for the comic DAN DARE – PILOT OF THE FUTURE for its first six months in 1950.

ACC's early stories are very much GENRE SF, neatly constructed, usually turning on a single scientific point, often ending with a sting in the tail. Some are rather ponderously humorous. His first two novels were published in 1951: *Prelude to Space* (**1951** US; rev 1951 UK; rev 1954 US; vt *Master of Space* 1961 US; vt *The Space Dreamers* 1969 US), being GALAXY SCIENCE FICTION NOVEL #3, and *The Sands of Mars* (**1951**). Both suffer from the rather wooden prose which ACC later fashioned into a more flexible instrument, though he was never able to escape an occasional stiffness in his writing. They are, in effect, works of optimistic propaganda for science (◊ OPTIMISM AND PESSIMISM), with human problems rather mechanically worked out against a background of scientific discovery. It was with the science that ACC's imagination flared into life. *Islands in the Sky* (**1952** US) followed the same pattern; it is a juvenile about a boy in an orbital space station.

A new note appeared in *Expedition to Earth* (coll **1953** US). This includes the short story "The Sentinel", which had appeared in *10 Story Fantasy* in 1951 as "Sentinel of Eternity". A simple but haunting story, it tells of the discovery of an ALIEN artefact, created by an advanced race millions of years earlier, standing enigmatically on top of a mountain on the Moon. Many years later this story became the basis of 2001: A SPACE ODYSSEY (1968), for which ACC wrote the script with Stanley KUBRICK. The novelization, *2001: A Space Odyssey* * (**1968** US; with 2 related stories added, rev as coll 1990 UK), was written by ACC alone on the basis of the script after the film had been made. An account of ACC's connection with the film can be found in his *The Lost Worlds of 2001* (**1972** US), which also prints alternative script versions of key scenes.

With "The Sentinel" came the first clear appearance of the ACC paradox: the man who of all sf writers is most closely identified with knowledgeable, technological HARD SF is strongly attracted to the metaphysical, even to the mystical; the man who in sf is often seen as standing for the boundless optimism of the soaring human spirit, and for the idea (strongly presented in John W. CAMPBELL Jr's *ASF*) that there is nothing humanity cannot accomplish, is best remembered for the image of mankind being as children next to the ancient, inscrutable wisdom of alien races. There is something attractive, even moving, in what can be seen in Freudian terms as an unhappy mankind crying out for a lost father; certainly it is the closest thing sf has yet produced to an analogy for RELIGION, and the longing for God.

Although this theme is well seen in "The Sentinel", and even better seen in the iconography of the film *2001: A Space Odyssey*, at the end of which mankind is seen literally as a foetus, ACC gave it its most potent literary expression in two more books from 1953 which are still considered by many critics to be his finest, and in which he comes closest to continuing the tradition of the UK SCIENTIFIC ROMANCE. They are *Against the Fall of Night* (1948 *Startling Stories*; **1953** US; exp and much rev vt *The City and the Stars* **1956** US) – also assembled with "The Lion of Comarre" (1949 *TWS*) as *The Lion of Comarre and Against the Fall of Night* (coll **1968** US) – and *Childhood's End* (1950 *NW* as "Guardian Angel"; exp **1953** US; rev 1990 UK).

Both the original and the longer versions of *Against the Fall of Night* are readily available. Indeed, the shorter version was republished in *Beyond the Fall of Night* (omni **1990** US misleadingly credited – since it appears from the cover to be a single novel – to ACC and Gregory Benford; vt *Arthur C Clarke – Against the Fall of Night/Gregory Benford – Beyond the Fall of Night* UK 1991), along with a sequel, very different in tone and theme, by Gregory BENFORD. The longer version, *The City and the Stars*, is one of the strongest tales of CONCEPTUAL BREAKTHROUGH in genre sf. Alvin, a young man in the enclosed utopian CITY of Diaspar, on Earth in the FAR FUTURE, becomes impatient at the TECHNOLOGY-mediated stasis of the perfect life, and after many adventures makes his way outside the city to Lys, another UTOPIA but of a different kind, which stresses closeness to Nature. Ultimately Alvin finds an alien spaceship left behind millennia ago, visits the stars, and finally discovers the true nature of the cosmic perspective which has been hidden from both Lys and Diaspar. The final passages blend a sense of loss and of transcendence with an almost mystical intensity. ACC began working on this story as early as 1937, and it is clearly central to all his thinking and feeling; it is perhaps his most memorable work, and distinctly superior to the more awkward earlier version. It owes something to the evolutionary perspective of Olaf STAPLEDON, whose works ACC greatly admired, as does *Childhood's End*, in which mankind reaches transcendence under the tutelage of satanic-seeming aliens, eventually to fuse with a cosmic overmind which is an apotheosis forever to be denied both to their parents, who are ordinary humans, and to the alien tutors.

ACC continued to publish sf with some frequency over the next decade, with *Earthlight* (1951 *TWS*; exp **1955** US), *Reach for Tomorrow* (coll **1956** US), *The Deep Range* (1954 *Star SF #3*; exp **1957** US), *Tales from the White Hart* (coll of linked stories **1957** US), *The Other Side of the Sky* (coll **1958** US), *A Fall of Moondust* (**1961** US), *Tales of Ten Worlds* (coll **1962** US), *Dolphin Island* (**1963** US), a juvenile, and *Glide Path* (**1963** US), ACC's only non-sf novel, about the development of radar. The most interesting of these are *The Deep Range*, about NEAR-FUTURE farming UNDER THE SEA, containing some of ACC's most evocative writing, and *A Fall of Moondust*, a realistic account – in the light of theories about the Moon's surface now known to have been mistaken – of an accident to a surface transport on a lightly colonized Moon. ACC's "The Star" (1955), a short story of great pathos describing the discovery that the star put in the sky by God to prefigure the Birth at Bethlehem was a supernova that destroyed an entire alien race, won a HUGO.

By the 1960s most of ACC's creative energies had gone into writing nonfiction books and articles, many of them – not listed here – about undersea exploration; he was an enthusiastic skin-diver himself, one reason for his residence in Sri Lanka. His popularizations of science, which won him the UNESCO Kalinga Prize in 1962, are closely related to his fiction, in that the stories often fictionalize specific ideas discussed in the factual pieces. His most important nonfiction works, interesting still though some are rather out-of-date, are: *Interplanetary Flight* (**1950**; rev 1960), *The Exploration of Space* (**1951**; rev 1959; original text with new intro 1979), *The Exploration of the Moon* (**1954**), *The Young Traveller in Space* (**1954**; vt *Going into Space* US; vt *The Scottie Book of Space Travel* UK; rev with Robert SILVERBERG vt *Into Space* 1971 US), *The Making of a Moon: The Story of the Earth Satellite Programme* (**1957**; rev 1958 US), *Voice Across the Sea* (coll **1958** UK; rev 1974 UK; much rev, vt *How the World was One: Beyond the Global Village* 1992 UK), *The Challenge of the Space Ship* (coll **1959** US), *Profiles of the Future* (coll **1962**; rev 1973; rev 1984), *Man and Space* (**1964**; with the Editors of *Life*), *Voices From the Sky* (coll **1965** US), *The Promise of Space* (**1968**), *Beyond Jupiter: The Worlds of Tomorrow* (**1972** US; with Chesley BONESTELL), *Report on Planet 3 and other Speculations* (coll **1972**), *The View from Serendip* (coll **1977** US), *1984: Spring: A Choice of Futures* (coll **1984** US) and *Ascent to Orbit: A Scientific Autobiography: The Technical Writings of Arthur C. Clarke* (coll **1984** US). ACC's early professional experience as assistant editor of *Science Abstracts* 1949-50, before he became a full-time writer, has amply paid off. *The Exploration of Space* won a nonfiction INTERNATIONAL FANTASY AWARD in 1972. His science writing is lucid and interesting; his only rival as an sf writer of significance who is also of importance as a scientific journalist is Isaac ASIMOV. ACC became well known all over the world when he appeared as commentator on CBS TV for the Apollo 11, 12 and 15 Moon missions.

A good retrospective collection of stories, all but one reprinted from collections listed above, is *The Nine Billion Names of God* (coll **1967** US). Since 1962 only a small amount of fiction by ACC has appeared in sf magazines, though two of his most interesting stories date from this period: "Sunjammer" (1965; vt "The Wind from the Sun"), which is about the SOLAR WIND, and *A Meeting with Medusa* (1971 *Playboy*; **1988** chap dos US), winner of a NEBULA in 1972 for Best Novella, the story of a CYBORG explorer meeting ALIEN life in the atmosphere of JUPITER. Both stories are reprinted in *The Wind from the Sun* (coll **1972** US; with 3 vignettes added rev 1987 US), his sixth and most recent collection (not counting reprint volumes). The most comprehensive, though by no means complete, selection of ACC's short fiction is the misleadingly titled *More than One Universe: The Collected Stories of Arthur C. Clarke* (omni **1991** US), collecting *Tales of Ten Worlds*, *The Other Side of the Sky*, *The Nine Billion Names of God* and *The Wind from the Sun*, with several stories dropped.

After the success of *2001: A Space Odyssey*, ACC became perhaps the best-known sf writer in the world, and in the USA by far and away the most popular foreign sf writer. A few years later he signed a contract, for a sum of money larger than anything previously paid in sf publishing, to write three further novels. These turned out to be *Rendezvous with Rama* (**1973** UK), *Imperial Earth: A Fantasy of Love and Discord* (cut **1975**; with 10,000 words restored 1976 US) and *The Fountains of Paradise* (**1979** UK; with exp afterword 1989). All were bestsellers; all had a mixed critical reception, though *Rendezvous with Rama* scooped the awards: the Hugo, Nebula, JOHN W. CAMPBELL MEMORIAL AWARD and BRITISH SCIENCE FICTION AWARD. To what extent the book deserved it, and to what extent the awards merely celebrated the return of a much loved figure to the field after many years' comparative silence is unclear. All the old ACC themes are there in the story of a huge, apparently derelict alien spaceship which enters the Solar System, and its exploration by a party of humans. As an artefact, the spaceship is a symbol of almost mythic significance, enigmatic, powerful and fascinating (◊ BIG DUMB OBJECTS; DISCOVERY AND INVENTION), and the book derives considerable power from its description. The human characterization, on the other hand, is rather reminiscent of boys' fiction from an earlier era. *Imperial Earth* tells of relations between Earth and the OUTER PLANETS, and contains a rather meandering intrigue involving CLONES; there are some interesting speculations about BLACK HOLES. *Fountains of Paradise*, a much better book than *Imperial Earth* – it won the 1980 Hugo for Best Novel – tells of the construction on Earth of a space elevator 36,000km high, and

combines ACC's favourite themes of technological evolution and mankind's apotheosis with moving directness; it is the most considerable work of the latter part of ACC's career.

The 1980s and 1990s provided an astonishing coda to all of this. They have – in terms of the number of books appearing with ACC's name on the cover – been unexpectedly productive, unexpectedly because ACC was well into his 60s, and had previously announced that *Fountains of Paradise* would be his last work of fiction. However, soon there appeared *2010: Odyssey Two* (**1982** US), a sequel to *2001: A Space Odyssey*. This was made into a film directed by Peter Hyams, 2010 (1984). Neither book nor film is as distinguished as the original, but the book is better than the film. It was followed by *2061: Odyssey Three* (**1988** UK), which being open-ended suggests that the **Odyssey** saga of alien intervention may not yet be complete. A little earlier ACC had published *The Songs of Distant Earth* (**1986** US), which greatly expands on the story of the same title published in *If* in 1958. Quietly and without much action it recounts the meeting of an isolated human colony on a remote planet with one of the last spaceships to leave a doomed Earth, and the cultural clashes that follow.

In the mid-1980s ACC had developed a debilitating and continuing illness affecting the nervous system, but despite this he maintained considerable literary activity. His illness meant that much of his work was necessarily collaborative. While some of this was found disappointing by the critics, and even reviled, there is considerable gallantry in his having made the effort at all, more especially as the profit, it has been said, is intended to shore up various charitable enterprises ACC has founded, in order to render them financially secure after his death. The collaborative enterprises have included *Cradle* (**1988** UK) with Gentry LEE and, also with Lee, two sequels to *Rendezvous with Rama*, with a third projected; the sequels in the **Rama** series to date are *Rama II* (**1989** UK) and *The Garden of Rama* (**1991** US). Most of the writing seems to have been Lee's, whose style is less compact and more stereotyped than ACC's. All these books have moments of embarrassing prose reminiscent of popular romance, though they are progressively more confidently written. A more interesting partnership was that between Gregory Benford and Clarke, the former (as noted above) writing a sequel to the latter's 1948 novella *Against the Fall of Night*. ACC has also franchised out (◊ SHARED WORLDS) the **Venus Prime** series to Paul PREUSS (*whom see for titles*), each novel having some basis in an ACC short story. The series begins with *Arthur C. Clarke's Venus Prime, Volume 1: Breaking Strain* (**1987**), based on ACC's "Breaking Strain" (*TWS* 1949). The fact-and-fiction anthology *Project Solar Sail* (anth **1990** US) has a cover which says it is ed ACC, but a reading of the title page suggests the true ed, here "Managing Editor", was David BRIN.

During the period since 1988 there have been,

moreover, two books by ACC alone. The first is *Astounding Days: A Science Fictional Autobiography* (**1989**), consisting of enjoyable reminiscences of his own literary life, with a good amount of material on other writers, both these topics being often seen in relation to the magazine ASTOUNDING SCIENCE-FICTION. The second, somewhat surprisingly after all the collaborations, was another solo novel, *The Ghost from the Grand Banks* (**1990** UK), an interesting tale of an attempt to raise the *Titanic* in the early 21st century; it is indubitably Clarkean, though itself a little ghostlike, much of the story pared to the bone, though typically containing a technical (and neatly symbolic) diversion into the mathematics of the Mandelbrot set.

ACC is patron of the SCIENCE FICTION FOUNDATION. He has received many awards, including the Association of Space Explorers' Special Achievement Award. He has presented a number of tv programmes, including the series *Arthur C. Clarke's Mysterious World* at the beginning of the 1980s. He received a Nebula Grand Master Award in 1986.

For many readers ACC is the very personification of sf. Never a "literary" author, he nonetheless writes always with lucidity and candour, often with grace, sometimes with a cold, sharp evocativeness that has produced some of the most memorable images in sf. He is deservedly seen as a central figure in the development of post-WWII sf, especially in his liberal, optimistic view of the possible benefits of technology (though one that is by no means unaware of its dangers), and in his development of the Stapledonian theme of cosmic perspective, in which mankind is seen as reaching out like a child to an alien Universe which may treat us as a godlike father would, or may respond with cool indifference. [PN]

Other works: *Across the Sea of Stars* (omni **1959** US of 18 short stories from previous colls and the novels *Childhood's End* and *Earthlight*); *From the Ocean, From the Stars* (omni **1961** US of *The Deep Range*, *The Other Side of the Sky* and *The City and the Stars*); *Prelude to Mars* (omni **1965** US of 16 stories from previous collections plus *Prelude to Space* and *The Sands of Mars*); *An Arthur C. Clarke Omnibus* (omni **1965** UK of *Childhood's End*, *Prelude to Space* and *Expedition to Earth*); *An Arthur C. Clarke Second Omnibus* (omni **1968** UK of *A Fall of Moondust*, *Earthlight* and *The Sands of Mars*); *Of Time and Stars* (coll **1972** UK), a collection for children, all reprinted from previous collections; *Four Great SF Novels* (omni **1978** UK); *The Sentinel* (coll **1983** US), reprints; *Tales From Planet Earth* (coll **1989** UK) ed anon by Martin H. GREENBERG, the only previously uncollected story being "On Golden Seas" (**1987** *Omni*).

Nonfiction: *Arthur C. Clarke's Mysterious World* (**1980**) and *Arthur C. Clarke's World of Strange Powers* (**1985**), both with Simon Welfare and John Fairley, both tv-series spin-offs largely written by Welfare and Fairley; *The Odyssey File* (**1985** UK) with Peter Hyams, communications exchanged between author and director about the making of the film *2010*; *Arthur C. Clarke's July 20, 2019: A Day in the Life of the 21st Century* (**1986** US), illustrated; *Arthur C. Clarke's Chronicles of the Strange and Mysterious* (**1987**), again with Welfare and Fairley.

As editor: *Time Probe* (anth **1966** US); *The Coming of the Space Age* (anth of nonfiction pieces **1967**); *Science Fiction Hall of Fame, Vol 4* (anth **1981** as ed by ACC; vt *Science Fiction Hall of Fame, Vol III: Nebula Winners 1965-69* US 1981 as ed by ACC with Geo W. PROCTOR – Proctor did the actual editing).

About the author: *Arthur C. Clarke* (anth **1977**) ed Joseph D. OLANDER and Martin Harry GREENBERG; *Arthur C. Clarke: Starmont Readers' Guide No 1* (chap **1979**) by Eric S. RABKIN; *Arthur C. Clarke: A Primary and Secondary Bibliography* (**1984**) by David N. SAMUELSON; *The Odyssey of Arthur C. Clarke: An Authorized Biography* (**1992**) by Neil McAleer.

See also: ARTHUR C. CLARKE AWARD; ASTEROIDS; CHILDREN IN SF; CHILDREN'S SF; CITIES; CLUB STORY; COLONIZATION OF OTHER WORLDS; COMPUTERS; DEL REY BOOKS; DIMENSIONS; END OF THE WORLD; ESCHATOLOGY; EVOLUTION; FANTASTIC VOYAGES; FANTASY; FUTUROLOGY; GENERATION STARSHIPS; GODS AND DEMONS; GOLDEN AGE OF SF; GRAVITY; HISTORY OF SF; HIVE-MINDS; HUMOUR; INVASION; LEISURE; LONGEVITY (IN WRITERS AND PUBLICATIONS); MAGIC; MARS; MATHEMATICS; MEDIA LANDSCAPE; METAPHYSICS; MOON; MUSIC; MYTHOLOGY; PASTORAL; PERCEPTION; PHYSICS; POWER SOURCES; PREDICTION; PSI POWERS; RADIO; ROCKETS; SCIENTISTS; SPACE FLIGHT; SPACE HABITATS; SPACESHIPS; STARS; SUN; SUPERMAN; TERRAFORMING; TIME TRAVEL; TRANSPORTATION; VIRTUAL REALITY.

CLARKE, A(UBREY) V(INCENT) [r] ◊ Kenneth BULMER.

CLARKE, BODEN ◊ Robert REGINALD.

CLARKE, I(GNATIUS) F(REDERIC) (1918-) Intelligence officer and code-cracker during WWII, and retired Professor of English (from 1964) at the University of Strathclyde in Glasgow. His first major publication was the BIBLIOGRAPHY *The Tale of the Future: From the Beginning to the Present Day: A Checklist of those Satires, Ideal States, Imaginary Wars and Invasions, Political Warnings and Forecasts, Interplanetary Voyages and Scientific Romances – All Located in an Imaginary Future Period – that have been Published in the UK between 1644 and 1960* (**1961**; rev 1972; rev 1978); the third edition carries the story to 1976. This work is very useful but not always reliable, being occasionally weak on variant titles and plot summaries, and is far from comprehensive. These weaknesses lie primarily in the period from 1940 on, and IFC – whose work in the earlier period was pioneering – has since publicly regretted the fact that he did not stop at the year 1939.

IFC's next important contribution to sf studies was *Voices Prophesying War 1763-1984* (**1966**; rev edn projected), by a long way the most comprehensive account of the future-WAR story. This was followed by *The Pattern of Expectation: 1644-2001* (**1979**), which ranges widely through the literature of the future from its earliest days to the most recent forecasts of FUTUROLOGY, and takes in much work which tends to be ignored by historians of genre sf. This book broke new ground in the history and sociology of ideas, focusing on the interrelation between differing expectations and PREDICTIONS of the future in different historical periods and the characteristic future images they yielded, in pictures as well as in words. In most respects it supersedes W.H.G. ARMYTAGE's *Yesterday's Tomorrows* (**1967**). [PN]

See also: CRITICAL AND HISTORICAL WORKS ABOUT SF; DYSTOPIAS; HISTORY OF SF; INVASION; NEAR FUTURE; PILGRIM AWARD; PROTO SCIENCE FICTION.

CLARKE, ROBERT ◊ Charles PLATT.

CLARK PUBLISHING CO. ◊ IMAGINATION; OTHER WORLDS SCIENCE STORIES.

CLARKSON, HELEN Pseudonym of Helen (Worrell Clarkson) McCloy (1904-), most of whose works are detective novels written as Helen McCloy. Her sole sf work, *The Last Day: A Novel of the Day After Tomorrow* (**1959**), tellingly describes a nuclear HOLOCAUST from the viewpoint of an isolated woman, whose island retreat proves in the end no refuge against the consequences of final war. [JC]

CLASS OF 1999 Film (1990). Lightning/Original/Vestron. Prod and dir Mark L. Lester, starring Bradley Gregg, Traci Lin, John P. Ryan, Pam Grier, Patrick Kilpatrick, Stacy Keach, Malcolm McDowell. Screenplay C. Courtney Joyner, based on a story by Lester. 98 mins. Colour.

In the USA of 1999 most CITIES have no-go "Free Fire" zones ruled by teenage gangs, and many schools are closed. As an experiment, the Department of Educational Defense uses ex-military ANDROIDS for teachers, re-opening a school in Seattle. The androids – even the attractive Black "chemistry teacher from Hell" (Grier) – revert to military conditioning and run amok with disciplinary measures against the drug-taking, gang-warring students, killing many. This violent, amusingly over-the-top exploitation movie features every killer-ROBOT cliché found in movies from WESTWORLD (1973) to *The* TERMINATOR (1984), but for a low-budget film Eric Allard's mechanical effects are good, and the direction is capable. [PN]

CLAUDY, CARL H(ARRY) (1879-1957) US author of some 20 sf stories, all for the magazine *American Boy*. Four were revised and expanded into a series of juvenile novels with the general heading **Adventures in the Unknown**: *The Mystery Men of Mars* (**1933**), *A Thousand Years a Minute* (**1933**), *The Land of No Shadow* (**1933**) and *The Blue Grotto Terror* (**1934**). This was probably the most vigorous and imaginative juvenile sf book series up to that time. Two of these stories in their original magazine form, together with "Tongue of the Beast" (1939), appeared in *The Year after Tomorrow* (anth **1954**) ed Lester DEL REY, Carl Carmer (1893-1976) and Cécile Matschat. [JE]

See also: BOYS' PAPERS; CHILDREN'S SF; JUVENILE SERIES.

CLAYTON, (PATRICIA) JO (1939-) US writer, most of whose work consists of a long series of science-fantasy SPACE OPERAS of extended quests in highly coloured venues. The sequence divides into the **Diadem** books – *Diadem from the Stars* (**1977**), which romantically sets out the epic adventures of a young girl electronically attached to the power-bestowing diadem of the title, *Lamarchos* (**1978**), *Irsud* (**1978**), *Maeve* (**1979**), *Star Hunters* (**1980**), *The Nowhere Hunt* (**1981**), *Ghosthunt* (**1983**), *The Snares of Ibex* (**1984**) and *Quester's Endgame* (**1986**) – and the volumes dedicated to **Shadith's Quest**: *Shadowplay* (**1990**), *Shadowspeer* (**1990** and *Shadowkill* (**1991**). The speculative element in these titles does not significantly figure; but the differing venues, reminiscent of the worlds of Leigh BRACKETT, are depicted with some richness. *Shadow of the Warmaster* (**1988**) is an sf novel with thriller elements. [JC]

Other works: The **Duel of Sorcery** books, comprising *Moongather* (**1982**), *Moonscatter* (**1983**) and *Changer's Moon* (**1985**); *A Bait of Dreams* (fixup **1985**); the **Skeen** sequence, comprising *Skeen's Leap* (**1986**), *Skeen's Return* (**1987**) and *Skeen's Search* (**1987**); *Drinker of Souls* (**1986**), *Blue Magic* (**1988**) and *A Gathering of Stones* (**1989**), these three assembled as *The Soul Drinker* (omni **1989**).

CLAYTON MAGAZINES ◊ ASTOUNDING SCIENCE-FICTION.

CLEMENS, BRIAN [r] ◊ *The* AVENGERS.

CLEMENS, SAMUEL L. [r] ◊ Mark TWAIN.

CLEMENT, HAL Working name used for his sf by US writer Harry Clement Stubbs (1922-); he uses his surname for science articles and paints as George Richard. He holds degrees in astronomy, chemistry and education, and was long employed as a high-school science teacher. From the beginning of his career HC was associated with *ASF*, where his first story, "Proof", appeared in 1942, at the peak of the GOLDEN AGE OF SF. His work has from the first been characterized by the complexity and compelling interest of the scientific (or at any rate scientifically literate) ideas which dominate each story. He is not noted as a stylist, nor is his interest in character depiction very strong. Many of his books can for pages read like a dramatized exposition of ideas, absorbing though at times disconcerting for the novel reader. This is certainly the case with *Needle* (1949 *ASF*; exp **1950**; vt *From Outer Space* 1957), his first novel, a rather ponderous alien-INVASION story with detection elements and a juvenile protagonist in a tale where the invader is a police-parasite chasing another (malign) parasite that has possessed the boy's father; the boy, with the good alien in tow, helps to drive the bad alien from his Dad. It is a highly loaded theme, but is told without any of the necessary resonance, nor does its sequel, *Through the Eye of a Needle* (**1978**), written as a juvenile, manage to cope any better with the human implications of its material.

HC's most famous – and far better – work is

contained in his main series, a loose sequence consisting of *Mission of Gravity* (*ASF* 1953; cut **1954**; text restored with additions and 1 added story, as coll 1978), *Close to Critical* (1958 *ASF*; **1964**) and *Star Light* (**1971**). The third volume is a direct sequel to the first, while some of the characters in the second appear in the third as well, Elise ("Easy") Rich in *Close to Critical* being the "Easy" Hoffman of *Star Light*, 25 years older. *Mission of Gravity*, one of the best loved novels in sf, is set on the intriguingly plausible high-gravity planet of Mesklin, inhabited by HC's most interesting ALIENS. The plot concerns the efforts of the Mesklinite Captain Barlennan and his crew to assist a human team in extracting a vital component from a crashed space probe; the humans cannot perform the feat, because Mesklin's GRAVITY varies from an equatorial 3g to a polar 700g. Barlennan's arduous trek is inherently fascinating, but perhaps even more engaging is HC's presentation of the captain as a kind of Competent Man *in extremis*, a born engineer, a lover of knowledge. These characteristics permeate the texts of everything that HC writes, even those stories whose protagonists are no more than pretexts for the unfolding of the genuine text – which is the physical Universe itself.

HC's most successful novels apply the basic plot of *Mission of Gravity* to fundamentally similar basic storylines – a character, usually human, must cope with an alien environment, with or without the help of natives, as in *Iceworld* (**1953**), *Cycle of Fire* (**1957**) and the stories assembled in *Natives of Space* (coll **1965**) and *Small Changes* (coll **1969**; vt *Space Lash* 1969). HC's only collaboration, "Planet for Plunder" (1957) with Sam MERWIN Jr, demonstrates his fascination with alien environments and viewpoints, as he initially wrote the story entirely from a nonhuman standpoint; Merwin, acting for *Satellite Magazine*, where it appeared, wrote an additional 10,000 words from a human standpoint.

HC brought a new seriousness to the extrapolative HARD-SF physical-sciences story, and his vividness of imagination – his sense that the Universe is wonderful – has generally overcome the awkwardness of his narrative technique. He is a figure of importance to the genre.   [JC]
Other works: *Ranger Boys in Space* (**1956**), a juvenile; *Some Notes on XI Boötis* (**1960** chap), a lecture; *First Flights to the Moon* (anth **1970**), nonfiction; *Ocean on Top* (1967 *If*; **1973**); *The Best of Hal Clement* (coll **1979**); *The Nitrogen Fix* (**1980**); *Intuit* (coll of linked stories **1987**), four **Laird Cunningham** tales; *Still River* (**1987**).
About the author: *Hal Clement* (**1982**) by Donald M. HASSLER; *Hal Clement, Scientist with a Mission: A Working Bibliography* (**1989** chap) by Gordon BENSON Jr.
See also: CONCEPTUAL BREAKTHROUGH; CRIME AND PUNISHMENT; ECOLOGY; FANTASTIC VOYAGES; PARASITISM AND SYMBIOSIS; ROBERT HALE LIMITED; SCIENTIFIC ERRORS; STARS; SUN; UNDER THE SEA.

CLEMENTS, DAVID [r] ◊ ROBERT HALE LIMITED.

CLEVE, JOHN Pseudonym used mainly by Andrew J.

OFFUTT for several erotic sf novels and for the first 6 vols of the 19-vol **Spaceways** sequence; most of the rest were jointly authored. Offutt's collaborators included C.G. EDMONDSON, Roland GREEN, Jack C. HALDEMAN, Robin Kincaid, Victor KOMAN, Geo W. PROCTOR and Dwight V. SWAIN.

CLICHÉS Sf clichés have developed, perhaps, partly out of a need for identification of stories as genuine sf – readers know where they are with a time-space warp – but mainly out of the lazy and parsimonious recycling of ideas at every level. The most obvious are cliché gadgets (BLASTER, ANDROID, HYPERSPACE drive, CYBORG, TIME MACHINE, brain suspended in aquarium, FORCE FIELD, food pill, ANTIGRAVITY shield, translating machine, judiciary COMPUTER), but major sf cliché themes are also old friends (daring conquest of the Galaxy; scientist goes too far; witch-hunt for telepaths; post-HOLOCAUST barbarism; triumph of Yankee knowhow). A list of sf cliché characters might begin with mad SCIENTISTS (Frankenstein to Dr Strangelove), though scientists may also be either young, muscular and idealistic or else elderly, absentminded and eccentric. Cliché WOMEN AS PORTRAYED IN SF normally have no character above the neck (◊ SEX). Some are sexy and helpless (often lab assistants or daughters of elderly scientists, rescued from danger by young scientists), break into hysterical laughter and need a slap, faint during critical fight scenes, and twist their fragile ankles during the flight through the jungle. Others are sexy and threatening (Amazon Queens from *She* to *Wonder Woman*) or sexy but ignorant tomboys (as in FORBIDDEN PLANET). Since the advent of FEMINISM, however, women are less commonly weak ("She flexed her mighty thews"). Cliché CHILDREN IN SF are hardly more variable: some are MUTANT geniuses, possess magical or PSI POWERS, or prove mankind's only link with alien invaders by virtue of their innocence. With "The Small Assassin" (1946), Ray BRADBURY began a new line of sf cliché kids who, after menacing mankind in many of his stories, turned up to menace again in John WYNDHAM's *The Midwich Cuckoos* (**1957**; vt *Village of the Damned*) and in the film IT'S ALIVE! Sf cliché MACHINE characters must be comic (in many Isaac ASIMOV stories), horrifying (from the GOLEM to the DALEKS) or sometimes both (from Nathaniel HAWTHORNE's dancing partner in "The Artist of the Beautiful" [1844] to HAL in *2001: A SPACE ODYSSEY* [1968]); they are seldom allowed as much thought or emotion as even BEMS or other minatory extraterrestrials. Among MONSTERS, giantism, dwarfism, scales, hair, slime, claws and tentacles prevail. H.G. WELLS first used octopuses in "The Sea Raiders" (1897); other writers kept the loathsome tentacles waving for half a century, up to and beyond IT CAME FROM BENEATH THE SEA [1955].

Sf cliché plots and plot devices are so numerous that any list must be incomplete. We have the feeble old nightwatchman left to guard the smouldering meteorite crater overnight ("I'll be all right, yessirree");

the doomed society of lotus-eaters; civilization's future depending upon the outcome of a chess game, the answer to a riddle, or the discovery of a simple formula ("a one-in-a-million chance, but so crazy it just might work!"); shapeshifting aliens ("one of us aboard this ship is not human"); invincible aliens ("the billion-megaton blast had no more effect than the bite of a Sirian flea"); alien invaders finally stopped by ordinary water (as in films of both *The* DAY OF THE TRIFFIDS [1963] and *The Wizard of Oz* [1939]); the ANDROID spouse who cuts a finger and bleeds machine-oil; the spouse possessed or hypnotized by aliens ("darling, you've been acting so strangely since your trip to Ganymede"); the disguised alien sniffed out by "his" pet dog, who never acted this way before; destruction of giant computer brain by a simple paradox ("when is a door not a door?"); robot rebellion ("yes, 'Master'"); a *Doppelgänger* in the corridors of time ("it was – *himself!*"); Montagues and Capulets living in PARALLEL WORLDS; evil Master of the World stopping to smirk before killing hero; everyone controlled by alien mind-rays *except one man*; Oedipus kills great-great-grandad; world is saved by instant technology ("it may have looked like just a hunk of breadboard, a few widgets and wires – but wow!"); a youth elixir – but at what terrible price?; thick-headed scientist tampers unwittingly with elemental forces better left in the hands of the Deity; IMMORTAL-ITY tempts Nature to a terrible revenge; monster destroys its creator; dying alien race must breed with earthling models and actresses; superior aliens step in to save mankind from self-destruction (through H-bombs, POLLUTION, fluoridation, decadence); Dr X's laboratory (ISLAND, planet) goes up in flames ...

Pulp can always be recycled.

But, then again, it is always possible to add new pulp to old, as happened in the 1980s, when new clichés appeared while most of the old ones con-tinued. They were mostly found in films, but some were in books, too: kids playing with computers start or wage actual wars without knowing it; Japanese advertising appears everywhere from posters to retinas; GENETIC ENGINEERING produces warring sub-cultures; expanding BLACK HOLES at the galactic centre are the legacy of wars between superbeings; kids TIME-TRAVEL into the past and invent rock'n'roll; alien cops buddy up with Earth cops to nab alien criminals; unemotional teachers and scientists turn out to be killer android/robots; vast alien artefacts prove to have extensions infinite in time and/or space or to lead somewhere else (◊ BIG DUMB OBJECTS); future people obsessed with 1950s rock'n'roll (Stephen KING, Allen STEELE); God is an AI; an alien virus turns us all into cannibalistic zombies; transplant technology leads to sex orgies (severed heads have cunnilingus, penis grafts increase libido). An old cliché that returns more regularly than Halley's Comet, but especially at around the same time, has gigantic objects in space impacting with Earth. Two promising new clichés that could not have been predicted are

spacefaring trees (Stephen BAXTER, Larry NIVEN, Dan SIMMONS) and romantic poets such as Keats, Byron and Shelley meeting either separately or together with monsters, AIs and so on (Brian W. ALDISS, William GIBSON, Tim POWERS, Dan Simmons and others). [JS/PN]

CLIFTON, MARK (1906-1963) US writer and business-man, for many years occupied in personnel work, putting together many thousands of case histories from which he extrapolated conclusions after the fashion of Kinsey and Sheldon; these conclusions MC reportedly used to shape the arguments of his sf, most of which was published in *ASF*, beginning with "What Have I Done?" (1952).

Much of his fiction is comprised of two series. The **Bossy** sequence – "Crazy Joey" (1953) with Alex Apostolides (1924-   ), "Hide! Hide! Witch!" (1953) with Apostolides, and *They'd Rather be Right* (1954 *ASF*; edited version **1957**; vt *The Forever Machine* 1958; text restored under original title 1982) with Frank RILEY – concerns an advanced COMPUTER named Bossy who is almost made ineffective by the fears of mankind about her, even though she is capable of conferring IMMORTALITY. *They'd Rather be Right* won the 1955 HUGO award for Best Novel. MC's second series, the **Ralph Kennedy** sequence – "What Thin Partitions" (1953) with Alex Apostolides, "Sense from Thought Divide" (1955), "How Allied" (1957), "Remembrance and Reflection" (1958) and *When They Come from Space* (**1962**) – is rather lighter in tone, focusing initially on Kennedy's dealings with psi phenomena (◊ PSI POWERS) in his role as investigator for a cybernetics firm, and moving on in the novel which concludes the series to deal with a typical *ASF* target, inflated Federal bureaucracy. The long-suffering Kennedy is appointed "extraterrestrial psychologist" and is forced to cope with a team of aliens which is mounting hoax INVASIONS.

MC's only out-of-series novel is *Eight Keys to Eden* (**1960**), in which an E-man, or Extrapolator, is sent to the colony planet of Eden to extricate it from an apparently insuperable problem: the problem turns out to be normal human civilization, not the paradise. Despite a slightly awkward prose style and an occasionally heavy wit, MC's novels and stories – a convenient selection is *The Science Fiction of Mark Clifton* (coll **1980**) under the editorship and advocacy of Barry N. MALZBERG – convey a comfortable lucidity and optimism about the relation between technology and progress; his attempts to apply the tone of HARD SF to subjects derived from the SOFT SCIENCES reflect *ASF*'s philosophical bent in the 1950s under John W. CAMPBELL Jr's editorial guidance. [JC]

See also: AUTOMATION; COLONIZATION OF OTHER WORLDS; DIMENSIONS; ECOLOGY; INTELLIGENCE; PAST-ORAL.

CLINE, C(HARLES) TERRY, Jr (1935-   ) US writer of, among others, three borderline-sf novels – *Damon* (**1975**), about MUTANT superchildren, *Death Knell* (**1977**), which deals interestingly with REINCARNATION, and *Cross Current* (**1979**), and one sf tale, *Mindreader* (**1981**), whose protagonist, while in hiding, unremarkably uses ESP to save the rest of us.   [JC]

See also: REINCARNATION.

CLINGERMAN, MILDRED (McELROY) (1918-   )
US writer and book-collector who has never worked as a full-time author. Since beginning to publish her shapely stories in 1952 with "Minister without Portfolio" for *FSF* she has been as strongly associated with that magazine as has Zenna HENDERSON. *A Cupful of Space* (coll **1961**) reflects this association in the frequency of stories included which wed a literate tone to a sometimes sentimental cuteness.   [JC]

See also: WOMEN SF WRITERS.

CLINTON, DIRK [s] ◊ Robert SILVERBERG.

CLINTON, JEFF ◊ Jack M. BICKHAM.

CLIVE, DENNIS ◊ John Russell FEARN.

CLOCK, HERBERT (1890-1979) US writer, apparently the senior collaborator with Eric Boetzel on *The Light in the Sky* (**1929**), an sf tale set in a LOST WORLD under Mexico, where Aztecs retreated after the genocidal onslaught of the Spanish and have constructed, over the centuries, a culture dominated by high science, telepathy, and – apparently – human sacrifice. The immortal Aztec genius behind the throne is in fact benevolent, and plans to benefit humankind; but the usual terminal DISASTER puts an end to this.   [JC]

CLOCKWORK ORANGE, A Film (1971). Polaris/Warner Bros. Dir Stanley KUBRICK, starring Malcolm McDowell, Patrick Magee, Warren Clarke, Michael Bates, Aubrey Morris. Screenplay Kubrick, based on *A Clockwork Orange* (**1962**) by Anthony BURGESS. 137 mins. Colour.

This controversial adaptation of Burgess's novel about mind control tells of Alex (McDowell), a teenage thug in a tawdry NEAR FUTURE – dehumanizing and luridly presented – who is cured of his violent ways by a sadistic form of aversion therapy. It was the (arguable) glamorizing of Alex's anarchic sex and violence (in contrast to the book) that provoked so much angry reaction in the media, though otherwise Kubrick's adaptation is moderately faithful. The film is not in fact amoral, though its moral is controversial: *ACO* is a religious allegory with a FRANKENSTEIN theme – it warns humankind not to try to compete with God – but Burgess reverses the theme, showing it to be as evil to unmake a monster, by removing his free will, as to make one. *ACO* is an intensely visual *tour de force*, deploying clinically a spectrum of powerful cinematic effects. As in Kubrick's 2001: A SPACE ODYSSEY, some sequences were rendered even more disturbing by the use of MUSIC contrasting wildly with the visual content, most famously in Alex's rendition of "Singing in the Rain" while kicking in the ribs of a woman he is about to rape.

ACO received the 1972 HUGO for Best Dramatic Presentation.   [JB/PN]

CLONES A clone is a group of individuals comprising the asexually produced offspring of a single individual. A pair of identical twins is a clone because the twin cells are produced by the asexual fission of the fertilized ovum. Asexual reproduction is very common among protozoa and some groups of invertebrates, but is much rarer in vertebrates. The possibility of cloning humans by transplanting the nucleus of a somatic cell from a donor into an ovum which can then be replaced in a host womb has attracted much attention, although no such operation has yet been performed in the real world.

Clones of various kinds have long been common in sf, though not always recognized or labelled as such. The replication of individuals by matter-duplicator (◊ MATTER TRANSMISSION), as in William F. TEMPLE's *Four-Sided Triangle* (**1949**), Fletcher PRATT's *Double Jeopardy* (**1952**) and Primo LEVI's "Some Applications of the Mimer" (1966; trans 1990), is a kind of cloning, as is replication via TIME PARADOX, as in Robert A. HEINLEIN's "By His Bootstraps" (1941) and David GERROLD's *The Man who Folded Himself* (**1973**). The mechanism by which Gilbert Gosseyn was given so many genetically identical bodies in A.E. VAN VOGT's *The World of Ā* (1945; **1948**; vt *The World of Null-A*) is unclear, but a series of clone members is the result. All-female societies whose members reproduce by parthenogenesis, as in Poul ANDERSON's *Virgin Planet* (**1959**) and Charles Eric MAINE's *World without Men* (**1958**; rev vt *Alph* 1972), also consist of clones. Ironically, the first sf story prominently to display the term – *The Clone* (**1965**) by Theodore L. THOMAS and Kate WILHELM – is irrelevant to the theme, the eponymous monster being an all-consuming cellmass produced by pollution-induced mutation.

Long before the word "clone" became popular, sf writers had considered the possibility of duplicating people for eugenic purposes. Poul Anderson's "UN-Man" (1953) refers to its cloning process as "exogenesis". Here and in John Russell FEARN's *The Multi-Man* (**1954** as by Vargo Statten) the idea is used as a gimmick, and the possible consequences of such technological development are left unexplored. A more ambitious application of the notion is found in "When You Care, When You Love" (1962) by Theodore STURGEON, in which a rich woman attempts to reproduce her dead lover by growing him anew from one of the cancer cells which have destroyed him. Among the nonfiction books that popularized the term was Gordon Rattray Taylor's *The Biological Time-Bomb* (**1968**), which commented on the implications of experiments carried out by F.C. Steward in the early 1960s on the cloning of plants: "It is not mere sensationalism to ask whether the members of human clones may feel particularly united, and be able to cooperate better, even if they are not in actual supersensory communication with one another." This possibility has been widely explored in such stories as Ursula K. LE GUIN's "Nine Lives" (1969), Pamela SARGENT's *Cloned Lives* (**1976**), Kate Wilhelm's *Where Late the Sweet Birds Sang* (**1976**) and Fay WELDON's *The Cloning of Joanna May* (**1989**), in which intimate human relations are explored in depth and with some sensitivity. Stories of this kind often exaggerate the probable psychological effects of growing up as one of a clone (after all, identical twins have been doing it for centuries!). Even though clones are genetically identical, each member inhabits from the moment of implantation an environment subtly different from its fellows; it is a very naïve kind of genetic determinism that leads writers occasionally to argue that an adult donor and his or her environmentally differentiated clone-offspring may be reckoned "identical". One of the few sf novels fully to recognize this is Ira LEVIN's *The Boys from Brazil* (1976), in which neo-Nazis raise a batch of clones derived from Hitler but can make only absurdly inadequate attempts to reproduce the kind of environment that made Hitler what he was.

The concept of clone-identity in the stories cited above is best considered as a metaphor, enabling the authors to pose questions about the nature of individuality and the narcissistic aspects of intimate relationships. Other works which employ the notion in such a fashion include Gene WOLFE's *The Fifth Head of Cerberus* (1972), Jeremy LEVEN's *Creator* (1980) and C.J. CHERRYH's extraordinarily elaborate *Cyteen* (1988). This kind of theme seems to be particularly attractive to female writers; others to have written significant clone stories include Naomi MITCHISON, author of the DYSTOPIAN *Solution Three* (1975), Nancy FREEDMAN, whose *Joshua, Son of None* (1973) is about the cloning of John F. Kennedy, and Anna Wilson, whose *Hatching Stones* (1991) suggests that human males might lose all interest in ordinary sexual reproduction if they were able to raise clone-duplicates of themselves instead.

Male authors have tended to use cloning in more conventional action-adventure stories, exploiting its potential for establishing dramatic confrontations. Richard COWPER's *Clone* (1972) is a satirical account of events following a child's recovery of his memory of being one of a batch of superpowered clones. In Norman SPINRAD's *The Iron Dream* (1972) the narcissistic aspect of clonal reproduction is recruited by Hitler in his sf power-fantasy "Lord of the Swastika"; as the Earth dies, ships blast off for the stars to populate the Galaxy with duplicates of the pure-bred Aryan members of the SS. Cloning is used in Arthur C. CLARKE's *Imperial Earth* (1975) to perpetuate a dynasty of space pioneers. Ben BOVA's *The Multiple Man* (1976) is a thriller in which the clonal duplicates of the US President keep turning up dead – a murder mystery recalling Maurice RENARD's and Albert Jean's *Le singe* (1925; trans as *Blind Circle* 1928). John VARLEY's "The Phantom of Kansas" (1976) is another clone-based murder mystery; his *The Ophiuchi Hotline* (1977) deploys the idea more ingeniously. Michael WEAVER's *Mercedes Nights* (1987) features a conspiracy devoted to the cloning of a famous sex-object; the conspirators in Wolfgang JESCHKE's *Midas* (trans 1990) stick mostly to cloning famous scientists.

The idea of another self – an *alter ego* or *Doppelgänger*

– has always been a profoundly fascinating one, and recurs insistently in occult FANTASY and PSYCHOLOGY. Recent speculation about the cloning of humans has made the notion available to sf writers for detailed and intensive examination, and the stories thus inspired are of considerable psychological interest.   [BS]

See also: BIOLOGY; CHILDREN IN SF; GENETIC ENGINEERING; MEDICINE.

CLONING OF JOANNA MAY, THE UK tv miniseries (1991). Granada/ITV. Prod Gub Neal, dir Philip Saville, screenplay Ted Whitehead, from *The Cloning of Joanna May* (1989) by Fay WELDON. Starring Patricia Hodge as Joanna May, Brian Cox as Carl May, Billie Whitelaw as Mavis, Siri Neal as Bethany, and Emma Hardy, Helen Adie and Laura Eddy as the three clones.

Weldon's comic-romantic melodrama about an obsessive business tycoon who effectively clones his wife, then repudiates her when she is unfaithful – with the aim of taking one of the three clones as his new wife when they have grown up – is already painted in broad strokes. The three-hour tv dramatization is even broader, though not unwitty, with finely over-the-top performances all round.   [PN]

CLOSED UNIVERSE This term is in no sense a synonym for POCKET UNIVERSE, a literary term which describes a particular kind of story; nor is it here used in its cosmological sense. A closed universe is a work or series whose characters and venues remain strictly under its author's control, and which is not open to fans or others to make uncopyrighted use of in FANZINES. In this sense, a SHARED-WORLD enterprise may still be a closed universe, if its owners restrict its use to other professionals on a contractual basis – indeed, most are. It should perhaps be assumed by sf readers that any work of art is a closed universe unless otherwise signposted.   [JC]

See also: OPEN UNIVERSE.

CLOSE ENCOUNTERS OF THE THIRD KIND Film (1977). Columbia. Dir Steven SPIELBERG, starring Richard Dreyfuss, François Truffaut, Teri Garr, Melinda Dillon, Gary Guffey, Bob Balaban. Screenplay Spielberg. 135 mins. Colour.

After STAR WARS came the second major sf film production of 1977, at over twice the cost but with a story which, while lacking the comic-book appeal of *Star Wars*, perhaps cuts deeper in its evocation, rare in sf CINEMA, of a SENSE OF WONDER. A power company technician (Dreyfuss) witnesses a series of UFO appearances and develops an obsession with them which is almost religious in its nature and intensity. He becomes convinced that aliens plan to land one of their craft on an oddly shaped mountain in Wyoming. A parallel plot concerns a secret group of scientific and military experts also engaged in uncovering the secret of the UFOs. The film ends in a barrage of special effects when the spacecraft arrives; communication between the two species is achieved by means of bursts of light and music. The hero enters the mother ship, much as Tam Lin once entered the Fairy Mound, and is taken to the Heavens in a glowing apotheosis; the elfishness of the slim aliens supports a reading in which UFO occupants are mythically equivalent to fairies. *CEOTTK* has flaws, but remains an intensely evocative work, certainly one of the half dozen best sf films to date. Despite the pressure from Columbia to produce a financial blockbuster, Spielberg did not take the easy way out but made an intelligent and relatively complex film, maintaining the high standards he had set himself in *Duel* (1971) and *Jaws* (1978). The special effects are excellent. A different version, CLOSE ENCOUNTERS OF THE THIRD KIND – THE SPECIAL EDITION, was released in 1980.

The novelization, *Close Encounters of the Third Kind* * (**1977**), is as by Spielberg. [JB]

See also: HISTORY OF SF; LINGUISTICS; MUSIC.

CLOSE ENCOUNTERS OF THE THIRD KIND – THE SPECIAL EDITION Film (1980). Credits as for CLOSE ENCOUNTERS OF THE THIRD KIND. 132 mins.

This slightly shorter, re-edited version of SPIELBERG's huge 1977 success, which contains some new footage, represents a curious piece of cinematic history. Many critics saw it as inferior to the original, though the idea was that Spielberg now had so much commercial clout that he could, at last, release the film exactly as he had always wanted it. New material includes a scene where Neary, the UFO-obsessed power worker, makes his family hysterical; a surrealistic shot of an ocean liner left stranded by puckish aliens in the Gobi Desert; and a sequence inside the mother ship (so-so special effects) with an ill-judged soundtrack of "When You Wish Upon a Star" from Walt Disney's *Pinocchio* (1940). The new Neary sequences darken the film; the new ending, in contrast, lightens it by emphasizing its fairy-tale aspect. Whatever, the new version, which is the one now normally shown, made a lot of money. [PN]

CLOUD OF ANDROMEDA, THE ◊ TUMANNOST ANDROMEDY.

CLOUSTON, J(OSEPH) STORER (1870-1944) Scottish magistrate and usually humorous author. JSC began writing works of genre interest with *Tales of King Fido* (coll **1909**), a Graustarkian fantasy (◊ RURITANIA). His books of genre interest include *Two's Two* (**1916**), an F. ANSTEY-like fantasy about an embodied *alter ego*; *Button Brains* (**1933**), about a ROBOT that is taken for the human upon which it was modelled, with comic consequences; *The Chemical Baby* (**1934**), marginal as the baby turns out to be natural; *Not Since Genesis* (**1938**), a satirical look at the European nations faced by a meteoritic DISASTER; and *The Man in Steel* (**1939**), a TIME-TRAVEL tale. [JE/JC]

See also: ANDROIDS; HUMOUR.

CLUB STORY It is almost certainly no coincidence that volumes of club stories should have become popular in the UK towards the end of the 19th century. The classic club story may be described as a tall tale told by one man to other men in a sanctum restricted to those of similar outlook, who agree to believe in the story for their mutual comfort; and it was precisely during the decades before WWI that the great march of history began to seem problematical to socially dominant white UK males, whose sense of reality now began to fray under the assault of women, and Darwin, and dark rumours of Freud, and Marx, and Zola, and Flaubert . . . and Henry James. Though it is no more a true club story than Joseph CONRAD's "Heart of Darkness" (1902) or *Chance* (**1914**), James's "The Turn of the Screw" (1898) is indeed a tale told at a club, and it is indeed a tall tale. But James uses the convention of the story told within a frame to underline the unreliability of his narrator, and to make forever problematical the "true" reading of his tale; "The Turn of the Screw" is a preview of the epistemological insecurities of the dawning new world. The conventional club story, on the other hand, by foregrounding the security of the sanctum itself, sidesteps the question of the believability of the tall tale (and sidesteps most of the 20th century as well). In the conventional club story, that tale is accepted by the males to whom it is addressed not for its intrinsic plausibility but as part of a shared conspiracy to maintain an inward-looking, mutually supportive consensus.

The great counterexample to this model is – perhaps inevitably – the work of H.G. WELLS, who often imitated popular modes of storytelling in his early writings, but almost always to subversive effect. *The Time Machine* (**1895** USA; exp 1895 UK) does certainly exhibit some club-story features – a group of men gather together to hear the Time Traveller tell his tall tale – but in this case the ambience is far from consolatory, and the Traveller's dark report from the future seems all the darker when it is evident that his hearers may be *forced* to believe it. Some of Wells's early short stories, too, are club tales – notably "The Truth about Pyecraft" (1903) – though in name only. It should come as no surprise that the most typical club stories were composed by men of a very different cast of mind than Wells's, and that most club stories are conservative in both style and content. Though precursors to the convention can be adduced almost indefinitely – from Chaucer's *Canterbury Tales* and Boccaccio's *Decameron* to Charles Dickens's *Master Humphrey's Clock* (**1840-41**) – the first collection to express the ambience of the genuine club story is perhaps Robert Louis STEVENSON's *New Arabian Nights* (coll **1882** in 2 vols; 1st vol only vt *The Suicide Club, and The Rajah's Diamond* 1894) and its successor, *More New Arabian Nights: The Dynamiter* (coll **1885**; with Fanny Van de Grift Stevenson). As early a work as Jerome K. Jerome's *After Supper Ghost Stories* (coll **1891**), although set not in a club but around the table after Christmas Eve dinner, parodies the club-story format and the tales told therein. Some of the exploits recounted in Andrew LANG's *The Disentanglers* (coll of linked stories **1902**) are of sf interest, though more frequently – as in G.K. CHESTERTON's *The*

Club of Queer Trades (coll **1905**) – early examples of the form read more like lubricated SATIRE than fantasy. Alfred NOYES's *Tales of the Mermaid Tavern* (coll **1914**) is a set of narrative poems told in Shakespeare's pub; while sequences like P.G. WODEHOUSE's **Mulliner** books (from 1927) heavily emphasize the tall-tale element, and *The Salzburg Tales* (coll **1934**) by Christina Stead (1902-1983) evoke Boccaccio. Of greater genre interest are SAKI's *The Chronicles of Clovis* (coll **1907**), John Buchan's *The Runagates' Club* (coll **1928**), the five **Jorkens** books by Lord DUNSANY, beginning with *The Travel Tales of Mr Joseph Jorkens* (coll **1931**) and continuing for two decades, and T.H. WHITE's *Gone to Ground* (coll of linked stories **1935**), which – as these tales are told by survivors of a final HOLOCAUST – stretches to its limit the capacity of the form to comfort.

In "Sites for Sore Souls: Some Science-Fictional Saloons" (1991 *Extrapolation*), Fred Erisman suggests that sf club stories – or in his terms saloon stories – respond to a human need for venues in which an "informal public life" can be led. Although Erisman assumes that the paucity of such venues in the USA is reflected in the UK, and therefore significantly undervalues the unspoken but clearly felt ambience of the pub in Arthur C. CLARKE's cosily RECURSIVE *Tales from the White Hart* (coll **1957** US), his comments are clearly helpful in understanding the persistence of the club story in US sf. Beginning with L. Sprague DE CAMP's and Fletcher PRATT's *Tales from Gavagan's Bar* (coll **1953**; exp 1978), it has been a feature of magazine sf for nearly half a century – perhaps partly because imaginary US saloons and the genuine affinity groups that generate and consume US sf are similar kinds of informal public space. Further examples of the club story in the USA are assembled in Isaac ASIMOV's several volumes of **Black Widowers** tales, starting with *Tales of the Black Widowers* (coll **1974**), Sterling LANIER's *The Peculiar Exploits of Brigadier Ffellowes* (coll **1972**) and *The Curious Quests of Brigadier Ffellowes* (coll **1986**), Larry NIVEN's **Draco Tavern** tales, which appear mostly in *Convergent Series* (coll **1979**) and *Limits* (coll **1985**), and Spider ROBINSON's **Callahan** books, starting with *Callahan's Crosstime Saloon* (coll **1977**). There are many others; some individual stories are assembled in Darrell SCHWEITZER's and George SCITHERS's *Tales from the Spaceport Bar* (anth **1987**) and *Another Round at the Spaceport Bar* (anth **1989**). [JC]

CLUTE, JOHN (FREDERICK) (1940-   ) Canadian novelist and sf critic; in the UK from 1969. His first professional publication, a long sf-tinged poem called "Carcajou Lament", appeared in *Triquarterly* in 1959. He began publishing sf proper with "A Man Must Die" for *NW* (1966), where much of his earlier criticism also appeared; further criticism and reviews have appeared in *FSF*, *Washington Post*, *Omni*, *Times Literary Supplement*, *New York Times*, NEW YORK REVIEW OF SCIENCE FICTION, INTERZONE, *Los Angeles Times*, *Observer* and elsewhere. A selection from this work

appears in *Strokes: Essays and Reviews 1966-1986* (coll **1988** US). In 1960 he was Associate Editor of *Collage*, an ill fated Chicago-based "slick" magazine which in its 2 issues did manage to publish early work by Harlan ELLISON and R.A. LAFFERTY. He served as Reviews Editor of FOUNDATION 1980-90, and was a founder of *Interzone* in 1982; he remains Advisory Editor of that magazine and since 1986 has contributed a review column. JC's criticism, despite some studiously flamboyant obscurities, remains essentially practical; it has appeared mostly in the form of reviews, some of considerable length. He was the Associate Editor of the first edition of this encyclopedia (**1979**) and is Co-Editor of the current version. His novel, *The Disinheriting Party* (1973 *NW*; exp **1977**), is not sf. [JC]

Other works as editor: *The Aspen Poetry Handbill* (portfolio **1965** chap US), associational; *Interzone: The 1st Anthology* (anth **1985**) with Colin GREENLAND and David PRINGLE; *Interzone: The 2nd Anthology* (anth **1987**) with Greenland and Pringle; *Interzone: The 3rd Anthology* (anth **1988**) with Pringle and Simon Ounsley; *Interzone: The 4th Anthology* (anth **1989**) with Pringle and Simon Ounsley; *Interzone V* (anth **1991**) with Lee Montgomerie and Pringle.

See also: CANADA; COLLECTIONS; CRITICAL AND HISTORICAL WORKS ABOUT SF; DEFINITIONS OF SF; HISTORY OF SF; MUSIC; NEW WORLDS; SENSE OF WONDER.

COATES, ROBERT M(YRON) (1897-1973) US writer, primarily associated throughout his career with the *New Yorker*, on which he worked, and to which he contributed many stories. He is primarily of interest to the sf field for his first novel, *The Eater of Darkness* (**1926** France), which, written before he had fully assimilated the sometimes restrictive urbanity of *New Yorker* style, quite brilliantly applies a wide arsenal of literary devices, some of them surrealistic, to the exaggeratedly spoof-like tale of a master criminal and his absurd super-WEAPON, which sees through solids and applies remote-control heat to kill people invisibly; beneath the spoofing and the cosmopolitan style lies a sense of horror. *The Hour after Westerly and Other Stories* (coll **1957**) contains some fantasy of interest, though in general his later work lacks some of the fire of his first book. [JC]

Other works: *The Farther Shore* (**1955**).

See also: MATHEMATICS.

COBB, WELDON J. (?   -?   ) US businessman and writer who specialized in dime novels (◊ DIME-NOVEL SF), working mainly *c*1866-*c*1902. Tales of sf interest include *A Wonder Worker, or The Search for the Splendid City* (1894 *Golden Hours*; **1907**), which combines travel and invention after a fashion typical of the genre, and two EDISONADES, *At War With Mars, or The Boys who Won* (**1897**), and *To Mars With Tesla, or The Mystery of Hidden Worlds* (**1901**), the latter featuring, in place of Thomas Alva Edison, his great rival Nikola Tesla (1856-1943). Amusingly, the lad who carries most of the action goes by the name of Young Edison. [EFB/JC]

COBBAN, J(AMES) MacLAREN (1849-1903) UK writer, of some interest for *Master of his Fate* (**1890**), whose protagonist, tortured by the need to drain the life energy of others to maintain his own IMMORTALITY, confesses all to an expert in the field of animal magnetism; and then kills himself. *The Tyrants of Kool-Sim* (**1896**) is a LOST-WORLD tale featuring dwarfs with poisonous blood and brave British lads who prevail. [JC]

COBLENTZ, STANTON A(RTHUR) (1896-1982) US novelist and polemically traditionalist poet. He began his career in the early 1920s, after gaining an MA in English literature, with book reviews for New York papers and a volume of poems, *The Thinker and Other Poems* (coll **1923**); he also wrote considerable nonfiction. He began publishing sf with *The Sunken World* (1928 *AMZ Quarterly*; **1948**), a UTOPIA set in a glass-domed ATLANTIS, in which satirical points are made against both the egalitarian Atlanteans and the contemporary USA, though the obtuse narrator (of the sort found in most utopias) tends to blur some of these issues. SAC was never a smooth stylist, nor an imaginative plotter, as all his five novels for *AMZ Quarterly* tend to show, though at the same time he had a strong gift for the description of ingeniously conceived ALIEN environments, so that he was often regarded as one of the writers best capable of conveying the SENSE OF WONDER so rightly valued by the readers of US PULP-MAGAZINE sf between the two world wars. *The Sunken World* was followed by *After 12,000 Years* (1929 *AMZ Quarterly*; **1950**), "Reclaimers of the Ice" (1930 *AMZ Quarterly*), *The Blue Barbarians* (1931 *AMZ Quarterly*; **1958**) and "The Man from Tomorrow" (1933 *AMZ Quarterly*). Other novels from the same general period, like *The Wonder Stick* (**1929**), a prehistoric tale, and *Hidden World* (1935 *Wonder Stories* as "In Caverns Below"; **1957**; vt *In Caverns Below* 1975), share similar virtues and faults. *Hidden World*, for instance, is another SATIRE, set in an underground venue, with fascinating descriptions but cardboard characters. Later novels, like *Under the Triple Suns* (**1955**), failed to show much stylistic development, and were not successful. [JC]

Other works: *The Pageant of Man* (**1936**); *Youth Madness* (c**1944** chap); *When the Birds Fly South* (**1945**); *Into Plutonian Depths* (1931 *Wonder Stories Quarterly*; **1950**); *The Planet of Youth* (1932 *Wonder Stories*; **1952** chap); *Next Door to the Sun* (**1960**); *The Runaway World* (**1961**); *The Moon People* (**1964**) and its sequel, *The Crimson Capsule* (**1967**; rev vt *The Animal People* 1970); *The Last of the Great Race* (**1964**) and *The Lost Comet* (1930 *AMZ* as "Reclaimers of the Ice"; cut **1964**), both apparently severely edited; *The Lizard Lords* (**1964**); *Lord of Tranerica* (1939 *Dynamic Science Stories*; **1966**); *The Day the World Stopped* (**1968**); *The Island People* (**1971**).

See also: ASTEROIDS; FANTASTIC VOYAGES; LOST WORLDS; OUTER PLANETS; POLITICS; SOCIOLOGY; UNDER THE SEA; VENUS.

COCHRAN, MOLLY [r] ◊ Warren B. MURPHY.

COCHRANE, WILLIAM E(UGENE) (1926-   ) US writer who began publishing sf with "How High on the Ladder" for *Fantasy Book* in 1950, writing as Leo Paige. As S. Kye Boult from 1971, and also under his own name from 1973, he began to publish in *Analog* the hard-edged sf adventures, like "Whalekiller Grey" (1973) as WEC, for which he became known. After *Solo Kill* (1972 *Analog*; exp **1977**) as by Boult, he used his own name exclusively. *Class Six Climb* (**1980**), told from the viewpoint of a giant god-tree, is perhaps his most sustained effort. He was inactive during the 1980s, but new work is (1992) projected. [JC]

COCOON Film (1985). Fox-Zanuck-Brown. Dir Ron Howard, starring Don Ameche, Wilford Brimley, Hume Cronyn, Jack Gilford, Steve Guttenberg, Maureen Stapleton, Jessica Tandy, Gwen Verdon, Tahnee Welch. Screenplay Tom Benedek from a story by David Saperstein. 117 mins. Colour.

ALIENS disguised as humans come to Earth to revive their kinfolk who were abandoned millennia ago in cocoons on the ocean floor; the swimming pool prepared for their revival is discovered and used by occupants of a neighbouring old people's home, who are (to a degree) rejuvenated by it. Some leave Earth for a new life with the aliens. *C* was aptly described by critic Tom Milne as "*Peter Pan* for the senior citizen". Directed with intermittent panache, it oscillates between the whimsical, the genuinely touching and the merely vulgar. A saccharine sequel with a soap-opera plot, *Cocoon: The Return* (1988), dir Daniel Petrie, is dispiriting. [PN]

COCOON: THE RETURN ◊ COCOON.

CODE NAME TRIXIE ◊ *The* CRAZIES.

COEURL AWARD ◊ CANADA.

COFFEY, BRIAN ◊ Dean R. KOONTZ.

COGSWELL, THEODORE R(OSE) (1918-1987) US writer and academic, an ambulance driver on the Republican side in the Spanish Civil War. He began publishing sf in 1952 with what proved to be one of his most successful stories, "The Specter General" for *ASF*. In this long, amusing tale – much in the vein Keith LAUMER was later to make his own – a long-forgotten maintenance division of the Galactic Protectorate reinvigorates a decadent Space Navy. TRC's two volumes of stories, *The Wall around the World* (coll **1962**) and *The Third Eye* (coll **1968**), contain most of his fiction; his work is polished, enjoyable and, though it sticks closely to fantasy and sf genre formats, gives off a sense that it was written for pleasure. "The Wall around the World" (1953) was one of TRC's most popular stories; the tale of a boy who lives in a place where MAGIC seems to work, and discovers the true, POCKET-UNIVERSE nature of his world, is an archetypal rendering of the experience of CONCEPTUAL BREAKTHROUGH. [JC/PN]

Other works: *Spock, Messiah!* * (**1976**) with Charles A. Spano, a STAR TREK novel.

See also: SHARED WORLDS.

COHEN, BARNEY (?   -   ) US writer whose first

novel of genre interest was *The Night of the Toy Dragons* (**1977**). His *The Taking of Satcon Station* (**1982**) with Jim BAEN is an engagingly over-the-top application of private-eye idioms and plots (Dashiell Hammett's *The Maltese Falcon* [**1930**] being much in evidence) to the NEAR FUTURE and near space, the eponymous satellite being the focus for the climax. *Blood on the Moon* (**1984**) is similar but grimmer.　　[JC]

COHEN, LARRY (1938-　　) US film-maker. A cult figure as much for the wildness of his ideas as for the sporadic brilliance of his direction, LC has never tried to graduate to the mainstream in the way contemporaries like David CRONENBERG or Brian De Palma have, and turns out as many curate's eggs as low-budget masterpieces. Originally a tv writer, he early discovered PARANOIA in his creation of the Western show *Branded* (1965-6) and the sf show *The* INVADERS (1967-8), both featuring on-the-run protagonists, perhaps modelled on *The Fugitive* (1963-7). He continued to write for tv, including prestigious series like *The Defenders* and *Columbo*, turning also to film writing with Westerns and suspense dramas. He made his directorial début with the ABSURDIST thriller *Bone* (1972; vt *Dial Rat for Terror*; vt *Beverly Hills Nightmare*). Nearly all his films are written, prod and dir by LC and made by his own production company, Larco, which he founded in 1965.

He made the superior Black action movies *Black Caesar* (1973; vt *The Godfather of Harlem*) and *Hell up in Harlem* (1973) before discovering the sf MONSTER MOVIE with IT'S ALIVE (1974), a compound of ecological, familial and 1950s sf ideas about a mutant killer baby on the loose in Los Angeles. LC has subsequently developed the theme in two sequels, IT LIVES AGAIN (1978; vt *It's Alive II*) and *It's Alive III: Island of the Alive* (1986), and alternated between sf, HORROR and suspense in a series of gritty, oddball pictures: GOD TOLD ME TO (1976; vt *Demon*), in which a modern "Jesus" is shown to have been a hermaphrodite homicidal maniac from outer space; *The Private Files of J. Edgar Hoover* (1976), a fascinating political-psychological autopsy of Hoover's USA; *Full Moon High* (1982), a werewolf comedy; Q (1983; vt *The Winged Serpent*; vt *Q: The Winged Serpent*), an ingenious different take on the giant-monster theme; *Blind Alley* (1984), a Hitchcockian thriller; *Special Effects* (1984), a psycho-horror drama in a film milieu; *The* STUFF (1985), a sloppy but amiable parody of *The* BLOB (1958) in which the formless monster disguises itself as an addictive fast food; *Return to Salem's Lot* (1987), a clever variant on the village-of-vampires concept; *Wicked Stepmother* (1989), a farcical witch story; and *The Ambulance* (1990), a striking slice of medical paranoia and urban nightmare.

Energetic and often lopsided, LC's films benefit from unusual characterizations, wayward plotting, cleverly cast familiar faces and a determination not to do things the accepted way.　　[KN]

See also: CINEMA; HUMOUR.

COHEN, MATT Working name of Canadian novelist Matthew Cohen (1942-　　), best known for short stories and novels set among disturbed urban dwellers in contemporary Ontario. *Too Bad Galahad* (**1972** chap), however, is an Arthurian FABULATION, and several of the stories assembled in *Columbus and the Fat Lady* (coll **1972**) and *Night Flights* (coll **1978**) are fantasy. *The Colours of War* (**1977**) is a NEAR-FUTURE tale of civil strife for which the Ontario countryside serves as a not ungrim backdrop.　　[JC]

COLD NIGHT'S DEATH, A Made-for-tv film (1973). Spelling Goldberg/ABC. Dir Jerrold Freedman, starring Eli Wallach, Robert Culp. Teleplay Christopher Knopf. 73 mins. Colour.

Interesting, atmospheric but ponderous yarn with a bizarre premise about two quarrelsome scientists, one emotional (Wallach) and one dispassionately rational (Culp), in a remote Arctic station. Their experimental chimpanzees (◊ APES AND CAVEMEN) turn the tables and start conducting stress tests on the scientists themselves.　　[PN]

COLE, ADRIAN (CHRISTOPHER SYNNOT) (1949-　　) UK writer, most of whose books lace fantasy and horror venues with sf devices, but which in the final analysis read essentially as fantasies. He began publishing work of genre interest with "Wired Tales" for *Dark Horizons* in 1973, and several stories soon followed about a not entirely unusual Cursed Warrior named **The Voidal**, culminating perhaps in *The Coming of the Voidal* (**1977** chap). The quasi-sf **Dream Lords** FANTASY sequence – *A Plague of Nightmares* (**1975** US), *Lord of the Nightmares* (**1975** US) and *Bane of Nightmares* (**1976** US) – was followed by the fantasy **Omaran Saga** – *A Place among the Fallen* (**1986**), *Throne of Fools* (**1987**), *The King of Light and Shadows* (**1988**) and *The Gods in Anger* (**1988**). The **Star Requiem** sequence, which is sf – *Mother of Storms* (**1989**), *Thief of Dreams* (**1989**), *Warlord of Heaven* (**1990**) and *Labyrinth of Worlds* (**1990**) – demonstrates in a PLANETARY-ROMANCE setting AC's moderate familiarity with sf tropes (like the flight of a remnant of humanity from genocide, and the relentless search for that remnant by genocidal aliens) and a smooth style broken by intermittent moments of inattention. For collaborative stories he has also signed himself Adrian Bryant.　　[JC]

Other works: *Madness Emerging* (**1976**), which combines sf and horror, as does *Paths in Darkness* (**1977**); *Longborn the Inexhaustible* (**1978** chap); *The* LUCIFER *Experiment* (**1981**); *Wargods of Ludorbis* (**1981**); *Moorstones* (**1982**) and *The Sleep of Giants* (**1983**), both juveniles.

See also: ROBERT HALE LIMITED.

COLE, ALLAN (1943-　　) US tv scriptwriter and journalist. His sf sequence featuring **Sten**, a rebel who becomes a military hero in the defence of a GALACTIC EMPIRE under threat, comprises *Sten* (**1982**), *The Wolf Worlds* (**1984**), *Court of a Thousand Suns* (**1985**), *Fleet of the Damned* (**1988**), *Revenge of the Damned* (**1989**) and *The Return of the Emperor* (**1990**), all written with Chris Bunch.　　[JC]

COLE, BURT Pseudonym of US writer Thomas Dixon

(1930-   ), author of *The Funco File* (**1969**), in which a world-dominating COMPUTER is pitted against anarchic opposing forces. His other titles of genre interest are *Subi: The Volcano* (**1957**), a savage tale set in an Asia dominated by a WAR much like that in Vietnam a decade later, and *Blood Knot* (**1980**). *The Quick* (**1989**) is an extremely expert and iconoclastic exercise in military sf. [JC]

COLE, CYRUS (?   -?   ) US author. In his eccentrically interesting *The Auroraphone: A Romance* (**1890**), messages from Saturn are received on the eponymous instrument; life there is UTOPIAN in many ways, although a ROBOT revolt is under way. A later message includes recordings, for the benefit of the enthralled terrestrial listeners, of famous events on Earth, including the Battle of Gettysburg. [PN]

COLE, EVERETT B. (1910-   ) US writer, formerly a professional soldier. He began publishing sf in 1951 with the first of a series, "Philosophical Corps", in *ASF*, which concluded there in 1956. *The Philosophical Corps* (1951-5 *ASF*: fixup **1961**) is based on the first story and two others; the remaining stories are "These Shall Not Be Lost" (1953), "Exile" (1954), "Millennium" (1955), "Final Weapon" (1955) and "The Missionaries" (1956). The philosopher protagonist of the series, Commander A-Riman, brooks no nonsense from aliens and the like, whom he re-educates in course of his SPACE-OPERA adventures. A second novel, "The Best Made Plans" (*ASF* 1959), has not reached book form. [JC]

COLE, ROBERT W(ILLIAM) (?   -?   ) UK author. His first novel, *The Struggle for Empire: A Story of the Year 2236* (**1900**), took the future-WAR novel to its logical conclusion. In a UTOPIAN future the Anglo-Saxon Federation has expanded into other solar systems when interstellar warfare breaks out between Earth and a superior race from the Sirius system. The descriptions of space battles, and of an Earth surrounded by a barrage of space torpedoes and mines while scientists struggle to perfect the ultimate weapon, make it the equal of many of the SPACE-OPERA stories of the 1930s. RWC's later novels are anticlimactic. *His Other Self* (**1906**) is a mildly humorous tale of a physical *alter ego*; *The Death Trap* (**1907**) is a mundane though harsh account of an invasion of the UK; *The Artificial Girl* (**1908**) is not of genre interest. [JC]

See also: COLONIZATION OF OTHER WORLDS; FANTASTIC VOYAGES; GALACTIC EMPIRES; STARS.

COLE, WALTER R(ANDALL) (1933-   ) US sf fan and bibliographer, compiler of *A Checklist of Science-Fiction Anthologies* (**1964**), reissued in facsimile – it was originally stencilled – by ARNO PRESS in 1975. It has now been superseded and updated by William CONTENTO's indexes of ANTHOLOGIES. [PN]

COLEMAN, CLARE ◊ Clare BELL.

COLEMAN, JAMES NELSON (?   -?   ) US writer of two sf novels, *Seeker from the Stars* (**1967**) and *The Null-Frequency Impulser* (**1969**), both routine adventure stories with ALIENS and superscience providing much of the action. [JC]

COLERIDGE, JOHN ◊ Eando BINDER.

COLEY, ROBERT [s] ◊ Donald WANDREI.

COLLAPSARS ◊ BLACK HOLES; NEUTRON STARS.

COLLAZO, MIGUEL [r] ◊ LATIN AMERICA

COLLECTIONS With sf/fantasy now a subject for academic study, especially in the USA, many major institutional collections have been built up, a process which has supplemented but in no sense supplanted the large number of private collections amassed by fans and scholars. From the first, GENRE SF has tended to be published in formats significantly (and foolishly) slighted in the accession policies of every category of institutional library – from university libraries to libraries of record like the Library of Congress and the British Library; and without private collections much of the research undertaken in recent years would have been impossible to conduct successfully. Some private collections – notably those of Forrest J. ACKERMAN in Los Angeles and Sam MOSKOWITZ in Newark – are extremely well known, extremely large, and accessible to visitors, but they tend not to be thoroughly catalogued. Individual researchers in sf and fantasy almost invariably maintain their own store of material, on a scale rather larger than probably necessary in cognate fields. Entirely typical of such research collections are those held, for instance, by the editors of this volume: John CLUTE with 10,000 items, Peter NICHOLLS with 7000 items, and Associate Editor Brian STABLEFORD with 15,000 items.

The strongest library collection in the USA is the J. LLOYD EATON COLLECTION. For important library holdings in other countries, ◊ MAISON D'AILLEURS (Switzerland, extremely strong on French sf), MERRIL COLLECTION OF SCIENCE FICTION, SPECULATION AND FANTASY, formerly the Spaced Out Library (Canada), SCIENCE FICTION FOUNDATION (UK) and UNIVERSITY OF SYDNEY LIBRARY (Australia). A number of other large institutional collections exist. In the USA these include: the University of Arizona Library; California State University Library at Fullerton (which holds important research material on Philip K. DICK); Dallas Public Library; Louisiana State University Library; University of Louisville Library (very large Edgar Rice BURROUGHS collection); MIT Science Fiction Society Library at the Massachusetts Institute of Technology; San Francisco Academy of Comic Art Library; Texas A & M University Library.

Also important to sf researchers are the great libraries of record, such as the US Library of Congress (which, shortsightedly, does not normally catalogue its separately warehoused, inaccessible mass-market paperback fiction) and, in the UK, the British Library and the Bodleian Library. These, however, tend to be weak on ephemera (fanzines, comics, pulp magazines); in some cases their book and magazine collections have suffered depredation through theft.

Further data on large sf collections can be found in *Anatomy of Wonder: A Critical Guide to Science Fiction:*

Third Edition (**1987**) ed Neil BARRON and in *Science/ Fiction Collections: Fantasy, Supernatural and Weird Tales* (**1983**) ed Hal W. HALL. [PN/JC]

COLLIER, JOHN (HENRY NOYES) (1901-1980) UK novelist, poet and short-story writer who also spent time in the USA writing filmscripts. He was known mainly for his sophisticated though sometimes rather precious short stories, generally featuring acerbic snap endings; many of these stories have strong elements of fantasy or sf, in particular *No Traveller Returns* (**1931** chap), whose protagonist visits a DYSTO-PIAN future, and *The Devil and All* (coll **1934**), whose contents are exclusively FANTASY. His best-known title, *Fancies and Goodnights* (coll **1951** US; cut vt *Of Demons and Darkness* 1965 UK), assembles new material plus a selection of tales from *Presenting Moonshine* (coll **1941**) and *The Touch of Nutmeg* (coll **1943** US) – itself a compendium drawn from the previous volume and from *The Devil and All*; until the release of *The John Collier Reader* (coll **1972** US; cut vt *The Best of John Collier* 1975 US), *Fancies and Goodnights* remained the handiest presentation of the kind of short fiction with which JC has been identified: highly polished magazine stories, adroit, world-weary, waspish, often insubstantial. It won the first INTERNATIONAL FANTASY AWARD.

Radically dissimilar to his most familiar work is *Tom's A-Cold* (**1933**; vt *Full Circle* 1933 US), a remarkably effective post-HOLOCAUST novel set in the 1990s, long after an unexplained disaster has decimated England's (and presumably the world's) population and thrust mankind back into rural barbarism, a condition out of which the eldest survivors, who remember civilization, are trying to educate the young third generation. The simple plot plays no tricks on the reader: the young protagonist, a born leader, rises through raids and conflict to the chieftainship, undergoes a tragedy, and reconciles himself at the novel's close to the burdens of a government which will improve the lot of his people. Throughout the novel, very movingly, JC renders the reborn, circumambient natural world with a hallucinatory visual intensity found nowhere else in his work. Along with Alun LLEWELLYN's *The Strange Invaders* (**1934**), *Tom's A-Cold* can be seen, in its atmosphere of almost loving conviction, as a genuine successor to Richard JEFFERIES's *After London* (**1885**); and it contrasts markedly with JC's earlier *No Traveller Returns* (**1931** chap), a harsh dystopian novella set in a deadened world. [JC]

Other works: *His Monkey Wife, or Married to a Chimp* (**1930**), a fantasy; *Green Thoughts* (**1932** chap) and *Variation on a Theme* (**1935** chap), both assembled with other stories in *Green Thoughts and Other Strange Tales* (coll **1943** US); *Witch's Money* (**1940** chap US); *Pictures in the Fire* (coll **1958**); *Milton's "Paradise Lost": Screenplay for Cinema of the Mind* ∗ (**1973**).

See also: APES AND CAVEMEN (IN THE HUMAN WORLD); DISASTER; EC COMICS; HISTORY OF SF; HUMOUR; SATIRE.

COLLIER'S WEEKLY US "slick" magazine published by Crowell-Collier Publishing Co, ed William L. Chenery, Walter Davenport and others. Weekly from 28 Apr 1888 as *Collier's Once A Week*, became *CW* in Dec 1904, continuing weekly to 25 Jul 1953, then biweekly to 4 Jan 1957.

CW published sf – e.g., H.G. WELLS's "A Moonlight Fable" (1909) and George Allan ENGLAND's "June 6, 2016" (1916) – only intermittently until the 1920s and 1930s, when numerous serializations of works by Sax ROHMER appeared. Later well remembered sf publications were: "There Will Come Soft Rains" (1950), "A Sound of Thunder" (1952) and other stories by Ray BRADBURY; *The Day of the Triffids* (**1951**) by John WYNDHAM; and many early stories by Jack FINNEY from 1951, including his most famous novel *The Body Snatchers* (1954 Collier's; **1955**; vt *Invasion of the Body Snatchers*). [JE/PN]

COLLINGS, MICHAEL R(OBERT) (1947-) US poet, story writer and author of a number of nonfiction studies of sf and fantasy writers, including several on various aspects of the work of Stephen KING. In *Naked to the Sun: Dark Visions of Apocalypse* (coll **1986** chap) and *Dark Transformations: Deadly Visions of Change* (coll **1990** chap), he published POETRY which tended to use sf and fantasy motifs as premises for metamorphic brooding. His nonfiction includes *Piers Anthony* (**1984** chap), *Brian W. Aldiss* (**1986**) and *In the Image of God: Theme, Characterization, and Landscape in the Fiction of Orson Scott Card* (**1990**), plus the various books on King: *Stephen King as Richard Bachman* (**1985**), *The Shorter Works of Stephen King* (**1985**) with David Engebretson, *The Many Facets of Stephen King* (**1986**), *The Films of Stephen King* (**1986**), *The Stephen King Phenomenon* (**1987**) and «The Work of Stephen King: An Annotated Bibliography and Guide» (1992). His criticism tends to be theme-oriented. He edited *Reflections on the Fantastic: Selected Essays from the Fourth International Conference on the Fantastic in the Arts* (anth **1987**). [JC]

COLLINGWOOD, HARRY Pseudonym of UK writer William Joseph Cosens Lancaster (1851-1922), most of whose fiction was for boys and featured nautical settings. He remains best known for his **"Flying Fish"** sequence of sf tales: *The Log of the "Flying Fish": A Story of Aerial and Submarine Peril and Adventure* (**1887**), *With Airship and Submarine* (**1907**) and *The Cruise of the "Flying Fish": The Air-Ship-Submarine* (**1924**). The eponymous vehicle is a ship which operates in the air, on the surface and UNDER THE SEA, and which takes the tales' protagonists back and forth across the Earth, leading them to a LOST WORLD, to inner Africa and elsewhere. The third volume, in which a dreadnought successor to the ship fails to be built in time to affect WWI, is anticlimactic. Other HC tales include *Geoffrey Harrington's Adventures* (**1907**), *Harry Escombe: A Tale of Adventure in Peru* (**1910**) and *A Pair of Adventurers in Search of El Dorado* (**1915**; vt *In Search of El Dorado* 1925). [JC]

COLLINS, CLARK [s] ◊ Mack REYNOLDS.

COLLINS, GILBERT (1900-?) UK writer in various

genres, whose two LOST-WORLD novels are of sf interest. *The Valley of Eyes Unseen* (**1923**) finds a Tibetan hidden valley inhabited by scientifically advanced descendants of Alexander the Great's Greeks, from whom the protagonist eventually escapes using purloined mechanical wings. In *The Starkenden Quest* (**1925**) the valley is located in Indochina, the primordial dwarf inhabitants are enthralled by an immortal blonde priestess (who nevertheless dies), and a great flood ends the tale.   [JC]

Other works: *Flower of Asia: A Novel of Nihon* (**1922**), a fantasy of Japan.

COLLINS, HUNT ◊ Evan HUNTER.

COLLINS, MICHAEL ◊ Dennis LYNDS.

COLLINS, PAUL (1954-   ) Australian editor, publisher, writer and bookseller. At an early age he began publishing and editing a SEMIPROZINE, VOID SCIENCE FICTION AND FANTASY (1975-81), which in due course transmuted into a series of original ANTHOLOGIES. His début novel, *Hot Lead – Cold Sweat* (**1975**), not sf, was published by his own SMALL PRESS, Void Publications. With Peter Wilfert he edited *Sf aus Australien* ["Australian SF"] (anth **1982** Germany). In 1980 he set up a second small press, Cory & Collins, in partnership with Rowena Cory. Despite execrable production standards, this was of some importance in providing a platform for Australian sf and fantasy novelists – authors included Russell BLACKFORD, A. Bertram CHANDLER, David LAKE, Wynne N. WHITEFORD and Jack WODHAMS – but the venture ceased in 1985 after 14 books. PC's sf-writing career began with "The Test" for *Weirdbook* 12 in 1977, and he has since been remarkably prolific, with over 50 sf stories published, mostly in Australia but some overseas, though even in Australia he has not made the impression on sf readers that his craftsmanlike work may at its best deserve.   [PN]

See also: AUSTRALIA.

COLOMBIA ◊ LATIN AMERICA.

COLOMBO, JOHN ROBERT (1936-   ) Canadian author and editor of over 80 books, notably anthologies of Canadiana and works of popular reference. Books with sf relevance include: *CDN SF&F: A Bibliography of Canadian Science Fiction and Fantasy* (**1979** chap) with Michael Richardson, Alexandre L. Amprimoz and John Bell; *Blackwood's Books: A Bibliography* (**1981**); *Years of Light* (**1982**), about Canadian fandom; and *Mostly Monsters* (coll **1977**), fantastic POETRY. *Other Canadas* (anth **1979**) was the first anthology of Canadian sf, and *Not to be Taken at Night* (anth **1981**) likewise for Canadian HORROR fiction.   [PN]

Other works as editor: *Friendly Aliens* (anth **1981**); *Windigo* (anth **1982**).

Nonfiction: *Colombo's Book of Marvels* (**1979**; exp vt *Mysterious Canada* **1988**); *Extraordinary Experiences* (**1989**); *Mysterious Encounters* (**1990**); *Mackenzie King's Ghost* (**1991**); *UFOs over Canada* (**1991**).

See also: CANADA.

COLONIZATION OF OTHER WORLDS The idea of colonizing the other worlds of the Solar System has had an uncertain history because the optimism of sf writers has constantly been subverted and contradicted by the discoveries of ASTRONOMY. The attractions of the idea have, however, always overridden cautionary pessimism, and the reluctant acceptance of the inhospitability of local planets has served only to increase interest in colonizing the worlds of other stars (◊ GALACTIC EMPIRES).

The example of the British Empire was insufficient to inspire many early UK sf writers to speculate about its extension into space. The most important of those who did was Andrew BLAIR, whose *Annals of the Twenty-Ninth Century* (**1874**) was the most extravagant of early future HISTORIES. H.G. WELLS used the example of the UK's colonial history as an analogy for the Martians' conduct in *The War of the Worlds* (**1898**) but never considered the idea of mankind's colonizing MARS, although Robert W. COLE did in *The Struggle for Empire* (**1900**). Later writers of SCIENTIFIC ROMANCE were almost completely uninterested in the conquest of space; both J.B.S. HALDANE in "The Last Judgement" (1927) and Olaf STAPLEDON in *Last and First Men* (**1930**) imagined mankind migrating to other worlds but only under extreme duress, as Earth became uninhabitable. The avoidance of the notion may be connected with a sense of shame about the methods employed in colonizing terrestrial lands; the parallel which Wells drew between the European invasion of Tasmania and the Martian invasion of Earth is a harsh one, and the brutality of the POLITICS of colonization has always been a key issue in sf stories, even in the US PULP-MAGAZINE sf that made the conquest of space its central myth. Early cautionary allegories include Edmond HAMILTON's "Conquest of Two Worlds" (1932) and Robert A. HEINLEIN's grim "Logic of Empire" (1941), although it was not until the 1950s that such lurid polemics as Avram DAVIDSON's "Now Let Us Sleep" (1957) and Robert SILVERBERG's *Invaders from Earth* (**1958** dos) could be published, and not until the 1970s that mature and effective moral tales like Silverberg's *Downward to the Earth* (**1970**) and Ursula K. LE GUIN's *The Word for World is Forest* (1972; **1976**) became commonplace. These stories of genocide, slavery and exploitation are the harshest critiques of human behaviour found in US sf; they often embody a strong sense of guilt regarding the fate of the inhabitants of pre-Columbian North America. Mike RESNICK's bitter study of spoliation in *Paradise* (**1989**) is an effective transfiguration of the history of Kenya.

Political issues are at the heart of another recurrent colonization theme, which deals with the relationship between colonies and the mother world. Here history provides – at least for US writers – much more attractive parallels, and the War of Independence has frequently been refought, from the early "Birth of a New Republic" (1930) by Miles J. BREUER and Jack WILLIAMSON to Isaac ASIMOV's "The Martian Way" (1952), Robert A. Heinlein's *The Moon is a Harsh*

Mistress (**1966**) and Poul ANDERSON's *Tales of the Flying Mountains* (coll **1970**). UK writers have been less enthusiastic about the notion of colonial defection, and sometimes develop images of a very uneasy relationship between Earth and its colonies; examples include Arthur C. CLARKE's *The Songs of Distant Earth* (**1986**) and Paul J. MCAULEY's *Of the Fall* (**1989**; vt *Secret Harmonies*).

The pioneer spirit is something much celebrated in sf at all levels. The mythology of the conquest of the Old West is often transcribed into sf so literally that even the covered wagon is retained. AMAZING STORIES once published a novel – "Outlaw in the Sky" (**1953**) by Guy Archette (Chester S. GEIER) – in which only half a dozen words had been modified in making the transposition from Western to sf; a more recent example is the "pioneer" sequence of Heinlein's *Time Enough for Love* (**1973**). Celebrations of the heroism of colonists fighting tremendous odds to tame hostile environments include Henry KUTTNER's *Fury* (**1950**; vt *Destination: Infinity*), Walter M. MILLER's "Crucifixus Etiam" (**1953**), E.C. TUBB's *Alien Dust* (**1955**) and Harry HARRISON's *Deathworld* (**1960**). It is often difficult to offer a convincing motivation for the colonists, and so various reasons are commonly devised to compel colonization, as in *The Survivors* (**1958**; vt *Space Prison*) by Tom GODWIN, *Orbit Unlimited* (coll **1961**) by Poul Anderson, *Mutiny in Space* (**1964**) by Avram Davidson, *Castaways' World* (**1963** dos; rev as *Polymath* **1974**) by John BRUNNER and *Farewell, Earth's Bliss* (**1966**) by D.G. COMPTON. A frequent subtheme deals with native populations that resist colonization, sometimes consciously and sometimes by virtue of the fact that the ECOLOGY of the planet has no suitable niche for the colonists. Many stories by Poul Anderson fall into this category, as do "You'll Never Go Home Again" (**1951**; vt "Beachhead") and "Drop Dead" (**1956**) by Clifford D. SIMAK and "Colony" (**1953**) by Philip K. DICK.

One of the most significant uses which sf writers have found for human colonies on alien worlds is in building distorted societies, sometimes for SATIRE and sometimes for thought experiments in SOCIOLOGY. Notable satirical exercises include *Search the Sky* (**1954**) by Frederik POHL and C.M. KORNBLUTH, *The Perfect Planet* (**1962**) by Evelyn E. SMITH, *A Planet for Texans* (**1958**) by H. Beam PIPER and John J. MCGUIRE, and many short stories by Eric Frank RUSSELL, including the justly celebrated ". . . And Then There Were None" (**1951**). More straightforward sociological treatments include Poul Anderson's *Virgin Planet* (**1959**), John JAKES's *Mask of Chaos* (**1970**), Harry Harrison's *Planet of the Damned* (**1962**; vt *Sense of Obligation*) and such remarkable novels as *The Left Hand of Darkness* (**1969**) by Ursula K. Le Guin, *The Fifth Head of Cerberus* (**1972**) by Gene WOLFE and *And Chaos Died* (**1970**) by Joanna RUSS. In many of these stories the colonies are isolated worlds within a GALACTIC EMPIRE. The notion of an extended chain of remote colony worlds is used in A. Bertram CHANDLER's **Rim**

Worlds novels and Murray LEINSTER's **Med Ship** stories.

Two fundamental classes of colonization story can be easily distinguished: the "romantic" and the "realistic". The first derives from a tradition which makes much of the exotic qualities of alien environments. Here the alien worlds are exotic Earths, little different from the distant lands of travellers' tales. Human and humanoid alien co-exist. The politics of exploitation is not the focal point of the story but may serve to turn the wheels of the plot as the hero, alienated from his or her own kind, champions the downtrodden natives against the horrors of vulgar commercialism. Women writers have been particularly prolific in this vein: Leigh BRACKETT often used it, as has Marion Zimmer BRADLEY in her **Darkover** novels. Anne MCCAFFREY's **Pern** novels likewise belong to the romantic school, and Jack VANCE has written many novels featuring a less stylized romanticism. Some of the most impressive works in the romantic vein are Cordwainer SMITH's stories of Old North Australia and his *Quest of the Three Worlds* (fixup **1966**). Recent examples often emphasize quasimystical processes of adaptation to the alien environment: a reharmonization of mankind and nature that often covertly echoes the Eden myth ($\lozenge$ ECOLOGY; LIFE ON OTHER WORLDS; PASTORAL). A simple example is *Outpost Mars* (**1952**; vt *Sin in Space*) by Cyril Judd (C.M. Kornbluth and Judith MERRIL); a more complex one is *Eight Keys to Eden* (**1960**) by Mark CLIFTON. The archetype of the species is Ray BRADBURY's "The Million-Year Picnic" (**1946**). The image of a lost Eden plays an important part in many of the otherwise realistic colonization novels of Michael G. CONEY, tingeing them with a peculiar nostalgia; examples include *Mirror Image* (**1972**), *Syzygy* (**1973**) and *Brontomek!* (**1976**).

The "realistic" school, whose authors concentrate on blood, sweat and tears rather than glamorous exotica, developed in the post-WWII era, although Edmond Hamilton's archetypal "What's it Like out There?" (**1952**) was written in the 1930s. This school won its early successes outside the sf magazines, being extensively developed by Heinlein and Arthur C. Clarke in stories published in general-fiction magazines and in (often juvenile) novels. Heinlein's contributions include *Red Planet* (**1949**), *Farmer in the Sky* (**1950**) and many of the stories in *The Green Hills of Earth* (coll **1951**). Clarke's include the **Venture to the Moon** series of vignettes in the London *Evening Standard* and the novels *The Sands of Mars* (**1951**) and *Earthlight* (**1955**). Patrick MOORE's series of juveniles, including *Domes of Mars* (**1956**) and *Voices of Mars* (**1957**), also belongs to this tradition. These juvenile novels take great pains to achieve some kind of authenticity, but "realism" in the magazines was much more a matter of literary posturing, consisting mainly of ultra-tough novels with a strong seasoning of cynicism: *Police Your Planet* (**1956** as by Erik van Lhin; rev **1975**) by Lester DEL REY is a cardinal example. Realistic treatment of colonization methods remains a common theme in sf; it plays a subsidiary but important role in, for example, *Mindbridge* (**1976**) by Joe HALDEMAN and *Gateway* (**1977**) by Frederik Pohl. The realistic school has suffered somewhat where it has conscientiously remained within the boundaries of a Solar System whose hostility has become increasingly apparent, but it has been saved from extinction not only by the idea of domed colonies with self-enclosed ecologies but also by the notion of TERRAFORMING, significantly treated in such works as Kim Stanley ROBINSON's *Red Mars* (**1992** UK), Pamela SARGENT's *Venus of Dreams* (**1986**) and *Venus of Shadows* (**1988**), and Ian MCDONALD's *Desolation Road* (**1988**), which features a remarkable juxtaposition of the ultra-romantic and cynically realistic modes. Other writers have favoured the idea that colonists need not bother with worlds at all; Konstantin TSIOLKOVSKY, the pioneer of ROCKET research, proposed that we might build artificial satellites to contain orbital colonies, and this notion of SPACE HABITATS has been sophisticated in recent times by such nonfiction writers as Gerard K. O'Neill. Sf stories displaying such ideas include a series of novels by Mack Reynolds begun with *Lagrange Five* (**1979**; later novels in the series are ed Dean ING), Lois McMaster BUJOLD's *Falling Free* (**1988**), and the satellite-tv soap opera *Jupiter Moon* (1990).

Terraforming adapts worlds to colonists, but one might logically expect it to be much easier to adapt colonists to worlds. Relatively little attention has been given to this approach. Biological-engineering methods were applied to the business of colonization by James BLISH in the stories making up *The Seedling Stars* (fixup **1957**) (◊ PANTROPY) and by Poul Anderson in "Call Me Joe" (1957), and were investigated in more detail by Frederik Pohl in *Man Plus* (**1976**), but increasing interest in GENETIC ENGINEERING has yet to bring forth prolific speculation in this vein.

Theme anthologies concerning colonization include *The Petrified Planet* (anth **1952**) ed anon Fletcher PRATT and *Medea: Harlan's World* (anth **1985**) ed Harlan ELLISON. [BS]

See also: GENERATION STARSHIPS; LIVING WORLDS.

COLOSSUS OF NEW YORK, THE Film (1958). William Alland Productions/Paramount. Dir Eugène Lourié, starring John Baragrey, Mala Powers, Otto Kruger, Charles Herbert, Ed Wolff. Screenplay Thelma Schnee, based on a story by Willis Goldbeck. 70 mins. B/w.

A curious little film about a man killed in an accident whose brain is transferred by his scientist father into an 8ft (2.4m) ROBOT body. Without a human body his mind both loses all compassion and resents it in others; hence he decides to destroy good guys at the UN. But his lingering humanity asserts itself and he asks his son (who doesn't know who he is) to turn him off. TCONY has been praised, but most see it as a routine potboiler. Shooting took eight days, and its director claims he can barely remember

making it. [PN]

COLOSSUS, THE FORBIN PROJECT (vt *The Forbin Project*) Film (1969). Universal. Dir Joseph Sargent, starring Eric Braeden, Susan Clark, Gordon Pinsent, William Schallert. Screenplay James Bridges, based on *Colossus* (**1966**) by D.F. JONES. 100 mins. Colour.

A supercomputer, Colossus, is designed by Dr Forbin to take control of the US defence network but, once activated, develops ambitions of its own and ignores all commands. Unlike the neurotic HAL in 2001: A SPACE ODYSSEY (1968), Colossus is a COMPUTER of the old school – emotionless, arrogant and practically omnipotent. It forms an alliance with its Russian equivalent and the film ends with the two computers in charge and likely to stay that way. The subtext is the usual one: better to be human and idiotic, even at the risk of nuclear WAR, than to surrender our autonomy to machines. The scenes showing Colossus in vast caverns beneath the Rocky Mountains have a powerful admonitory charge. This is a neat, well made film. [JB/PN]

COLUMBIA PUBLICATIONS ◊ DYNAMIC SCIENCE FICTION; FUTURE FICTION; ORIGINAL SCIENCE FICTION STORIES; SCIENCE FICTION; SCIENCE FICTION QUARTERLY.

COLVIN, IAN (1912-1975) UK writer and journalist whose sf novel is *Domesday Village* (**1948**), set in a NEAR-FUTURE UK with a socialist regime. [JC]

COLVIN, JAMES House name used primarily by Michael MOORCOCK for book reviews and stories in *NW* (and for one independent collection of stories), and occasionally by others for book reviews. Moorcock has also written at least one story as Warwick Colvin Jr, who is identified as JC's nephew. [JC]

COLVIN, WARWICK Jr [s] ◊ James COLVIN.

COMA Film (1978). MGM. Dir Michael CRICHTON, starring Genevieve Bujold, Michael Douglas, Rip Torn, Richard Widmark. Screenplay Crichton, based on *Coma* (**1977**) by Robin COOK. 113 mins. Colour.

Crichton's most commercially successful film, C is a present-day thriller with one sf element: the use of hospital patients, deliberately put into irreversible coma by using poisoned anaesthetic, as living repositories of body parts which are profitably sold for use in transplant surgery – a scheme, it has been alleged, that by the 1980s had real-life counterparts. Bujold is good as the resourceful young woman doctor – the film was praised at the time by the Women's Movement – who uncovers the plot in this stylish but wholly implausible paranoid melodrama. Crude but effective visual symbolism equates medicine with the meat trade, which cannot have pleased those of Dr Crichton's old colleagues still in practice. [PN]

See also: CINEMA.

COMET US PULP MAGAZINE; 5 issues, Dec 1940-July 1941, bimonthly after Jan 1941. Published by H-K Publications; ed F. Orlin TREMAINE. Tremaine, former editor of *ASF*, made a brief and undistinguished return to sf-magazine editing with this title. Contributors included Eando BINDER, Frank Belknap LONG and Harl VINCENT. The last issue contained "The

Vortex Blaster", the first story of E.E. SMITH's series of that name. A continuing feature was "The Spacean", an imaginary future newspaper which betrayed the magazine's juvenile slant. *C* had little visual appeal; its cover layout was particularly ungainly. [MJE]

COMFORT, ALEX(ANDER) (1920-   ) UK writer and medical doctor who has published significant popular work in the fields of sexology and gerontology, being perhaps best known for *The Joy of Sex* (**1972**). Before WWII he established an extremely precocious reputation for poetry, fiction and a pacifism he espoused rigorously during the years of conflict. One early novel, *No Such Liberty* (**1941**), edges into parable in its description of the wartime internment of Germans; *Cities of the Plain* (**1943**) is an anti-capitalist DYSTOPIAN play; *Tetrarch* (**1980** US), a fantasy, takes its protagonists magically into a political and sexual UTOPIA named Los, where they must find their true shapes; and *Imperial Patient* (**1987**) infuses a tale of the emperor Nero with mythical elements. His first genuine sf novel, *Come Out to Play* (**1961**), is a near-future SATIRE on scientism narrated by a smug sexologist. *The Philosophers* (**1989**), set in a NEAR-FUTURE UK, savages a decrepit Tory hegemony. [JC]

COMICS This rubric covers the comic strip in daily and Sunday newspapers, European comic papers and the US-style comic book; it does not cover the GRAPHIC NOVEL *per se*, although clearly there is overlap between the two categories. Strip-cartoon stories use some interaction of text and picture, as opposed to the established "storybook" use of words plus illustrations of the words. Design, drawing style, caption and word-balloon continuity all serve to make the strip cartoon a medium with its own syntax and frame of reference.

Like the history of sf, the history of the comic strip is far more complex, and extends much further into the past, than had been assumed until recent decades, when researchers (see **Further Reading** list below) began properly to examine the record, and to establish a continuity between the graphic work of the 18th century and the comic papers and Sunday newspaper supplements which flourished so conspicuously in the USA a century later. Sf comic strips as such, however, were slow to develop. By the end of the 19th century, though the comic strip had achieved very considerable sophistication and was capable of treating very widely varied subject matter, there was virtually no sf presented in a credible manner, nor would there be for another 30 years. Prior to this, the emphasis on humour in the comic strips had relegated sf to the realms of fantasy, as in *Our Office Boy's Fairy Tales* (1895 *The Funny Wonder*), an anonymous UK series depicting a family on Mars facing totally impossible hardships and jubilations. More mature in its approach was Winsor MCCAY's fantasy *Little Nemo in Slumberland* (1st series 1905-11 *New York Herald*), which depicted the dream adventures of a young boy and an ever-increasing array of characters from the court of King Morpheus. McCay's manipulation of the size, shape and position of each panel, together with his use of perspective, gave added emphasis to the narrative and indicated how artistic technique could augment the text. (This attribute of the comic strip was sometimes itself used to create the fantasy element, as in *Krazy Kat* [1911-44] by George Herriman [1880-1944], where the scenic background, changing from panel to panel, created a surrealistically alien environment, or in *Felix The Cat* [1923 onwards] by Otto Messmer [1892-1983], where the eponymous feline gave substance to his imagination by treating the contents of his thought balloons as physical realities.) McCay's fantasies were perhaps topped only by the expressionist whimsy of his contemporary, Lyonel Feininger (1871-1956), in *Wee Willy Winky's World* and *The Kin-Der Kids*.

In the 1920s, when economic depression brought about a change in public outlook, a demand was created for action-adventure strips, making publication of outright sf comic strips feasible. The transition came with BUCK ROGERS IN THE 25TH CENTURY (1929-67), an adult comic strip inspired by a novel in AMAZING STORIES; it spawned several rivals, among them BRICK BRADFORD (1933 onwards), FLASH GORDON (1934 onwards), *Speed Spaulding* (1939), adapted from Edwin BALMER's and Philip WYLIE's *When Worlds Collide* (**1933**) and illustrated by Marvin Bradley, and not forgetting Frank Godwin's CONNIE (1927-44), which in the mid-1930s abandoned its everyday terrestrial setting for outer-space intrigue. These all drew their plots extensively from the epics of classical literature, modernized by the inclusion of SPACESHIPS and ray-guns, and distanced from reality by being located in the far future or remote past.

Similar innovations occurred in Europe following the reprintings there of the major US comic strips. High points were the appearances of: in France, *Futuropolis* (1937-8 *Junior*) and *Electropolis* (1939 *Jean-Pierre*), both written and illustrated by René Pellos; in Italy, *Saturno Contro la Terra* (1937-43), written by F. Pedrocchi and illustrated by G. Scolari; and, in the UK, GARTH (1943 onwards).

The growth in the number of sf comic strips was, however, largely a reflection of the increased number of comic strips in general; they were now so popular in the USA that new methods of packaging them were being explored. Out of this experimentation developed the comic book. Initially comic books contained merely reprints of the newspaper strips – e.g., *Buck Rogers* in *Famous Funnies* (1934-55) and *Flash Gordon* and *Brick Bradford* in *King Comics* (1936-51) – but soon the available existing strips were used up, and comic books featuring original strips were the inevitable second stage. In the first issue of one of these new titles, *Action Comics* (1938 onwards; ◊ DC COMICS), SUPERMAN appeared. Featuring a larger-than-life figure, omnipotent (mostly) in the face of all adversity, *Superman* (1939 onwards) proved so popular that numerous imitation SUPERHEROES appeared, from Batman through CAPTAIN MARVEL to the many heroes featured by the modern MARVEL COMICS group, all being variations on the same basic theme.

In many of these comic books a central sf story was backed up by strips from outside the genre, but some comics were entirely devoted to sf. The first sf comic book was *Amazing Mystery Funnies* (1938-40), which contained a pot-pourri of superhero and SPACE-OPERA strips, its artists including Bill Everett (1917-1973), Will Eisner (1917-   ) and Basil Wolverton (1909-1979). Hugo GERNSBACK briefly entered the field with *Superworld Comics* (1939). *Buck Rogers* (1940-43) and *Flash Gordon* (intermittently 1943-53) also appeared as titles. Most successful was *Planet Comics* (1940-54), a companion to PLANET STORIES, which featured *Star Pirate* by Murphy Anderson (1926-   ), *Lost World* by George Evans (1920-   ), *Auro, Lord of Jupiter* by Graham Ingels (1915-   ) and other memorable strips.

In such a competitive market it was inevitable that publishers would turn to the sf PULP MAGAZINES for help. National Periodicals (DC Comics) offered Mort WEISINGER, then editor of THRILLING WONDER STORIES, an editorial post. Accepting it, he worked initially on *Superman*, using authors of the calibre of Alfred BESTER, Edmond HAMILTON, Henry KUTTNER and Manly Wade WELLMAN to help compete with the rival publication, *Captain Marvel*, scripted by Otto Binder (◊ Eando BINDER). Well known artists from the sf magazines were also used. Alex SCHOMBURG appeared in *Startling Comics* (1940-51), Edd CARTIER in *Shadow Comics* (1940-50) and *Red Dragon*, 2nd series (1947-8), and Virgil FINLAY in *Real Fact Comics* (1946-9). Similarly, in the UK Serge Drigin, artist on SCOOPS and FANTASY, illustrated *Space Police* (1940 *Everyday Novels and Comics*).

By the early 1950s numerous sf comic books were appearing, among them: *Lars of Mars* (1951) and *Space Patrol* (1952), both issued by ZIFF-DAVIS, publishers of AMAZING STORIES and FANTASTIC ADVENTURES; and *Rocket to the Moon* (1951) and *An Earthman on Venus* (1952), both published by Avon and featuring adaptations of, respectively, Otis Adelbert KLINE's *Maza of the Moon* (**1930**) and Ralph Milne FARLEY's *The Radio Man* (1924 *Argosy All-Story Weekly*; **1948**; vt *An Earthman on Venus* 1950); and an anti-communist propaganda sf comic book, *Is This Tomorrow?* (1947). More durable were *Mystery in Space* (1951-66) and *Strange Adventures* (1950-73), both from DC, *Harvey's Race for the Moon* (1956) and Richard E. Hughes's *Forbidden Worlds* (1951-67), all of which managed some consistency, albeit of a distinctly juvenile nature. Distinguished artwork came from the likes of Sid Greene, Carmine Infantino, Gil Kane (1926-   ), Jack KIRBY, Mike Sekowsky, Al Williamson and sometime *Buck Rogers* illustrator Murphy Anderson. All the while, new sf comic strips were appearing in newspapers, two of the better titles being *Beyond Mars* (1951-3 *New York Sunday News*), scripted by Jack WILLIAMSON from his two novels *Seetee Shock* (**1950**) and *Seetee Ship* (**1951**), with illustrations by Lee Elias

(1920-   ), and *Twin Earths* (1951-4), a counter-Earth story created and written by Oskar Lebeck illustrated by Alden McWilliams (1916-   ) – not to forget *Sky Masters* (1959-61), drawn by Kirby and written by Bob and Dick Wood, doing their best to second-guess a space programme that still lay 10 years in the future.

The most important of this period, however, were the sf comic books published by EC COMICS. Appearing initially at the suggestion of Harry HARRISON, who had been working in comics as artist and scriptwriter since 1946, *Weird Science* (1950-53) and *Weird Fantasy* (1950-53) – which later merged to form *Weird Science Fantasy* (1953-5) before being finally renamed *Incredible Science Fiction* (1955-6) – published the most sophisticated sf stories yet to appear in the comic books, often featuring wry endings in the manner of Philip K. DICK. Illustrated by such well known sf artists as George Evans, Frank FRAZETTA, Roy G. KRENKEL, Bernard Krigstein (1919-1990), Al Williamson and Wallace WOOD, they often included adaptations of stories by popular sf authors, in particular Ray BRADBURY. With the imposition of the Comics Code in 1955, these and many other titles ceased, and comics then went through a period of restraint and unoriginality.

A similar boom in sf comic books was taking place in Europe. Included in these titles were *Super Science Thrills* (1945), *Tit-Bits Science Fiction Comics* (1953) and *The Jet Comic* (1953), a companion to AUTHENTIC SCIENCE FICTION, which appeared in the UK, and *Espace* (1953-54) and *L'An 2,000* (1953-4), in France. Also of interest was *Tarzan Adventures* (1953-9) which, under Michael MOORCOCK's editorship from 1957, published several sf comic strips, including James CAWTHORN's *Peril Planet*. It was in the weekly comic papers, however, that the best-drawn and -plotted sf comic strips were to appear. Foremost was DAN DARE (1950-67 *Eagle*). With its clean linework by Frank HAMPSON, this became the UK's most influential sf comic strip, inspiring several rivals – including JEFF HAWKE, *Captain Condor* (1952-5 *Lion*), at one time illustrated by Brian LEWIS (who also did many NEW WORLDS covers), and *Jet-Ace Logan* (1956-9 *Comet*; 1959-60 *Tiger*), written by Frank S. Pepper (1910-1988) and, later, by Moorcock (who also scripted *Rick Random, Space Ace*, drawn by Rowland [Ron] Turner (1922-   ) for **Thriller Picture Library**). Equally notable was *Rocket* (1956), an sf comic paper which featured US reprints and others, including *Escape from Earth*, *Seabed Citadel* and *Captain Falcon*; it ran to 32 issues. More successful was *Boy's World* (1963-4) which, prior to its merger with *Eagle*, published *Wrath of the Gods*, initially written by Moorcock and illustrated by Ron Embleton (1930-1988), then by John M. Burns (1938-   ), *Ghost World*, illustrated by Frank Bellamy (1917-1976), and *The Angry Planet*, an adaptation of Harry Harrison's *Deathworld* (**1960**) plotted by Harrison and scripted by Kenneth BULMER. Mention should also be made of *TV Century 21* (1965-9), which published material based on Gerry ANDERSON's tv puppet shows

STINGRAY, FIREBALL XL5, THUNDERBIRDS and CAPTAIN SCARLET AND THE MYSTERONS and on Terry NATION's horrors, the DALEKS. In 1977 the first truly UK sf comic arrived in the shape of 2,000 AD, starring the quasi-fascist supercop JUDGE DREDD.

A turning point was the publication by MARVEL COMICS – which had published innumerable horror, fantasy and sf anthology titles throughout the 1950s and early 1960s – of *The Fantastic Four* (1961 onwards), whose success heralded a new wave of superhero comics, starring new characters and heroes (like Captain America and Sub-Mariner) resuscitated from Marvel productions of the period during and immediately after WWII. National Periodicals (DC Comics), publishers of *Superman*, was already in the process of expanding its superhero list, so DC and Marvel very soon became established as the "Big Two" in the field. Another trend was the growing number of adaptations of sf TELEVISION series, notably STAR TREK and DR WHO, which both appeared in a variety of publications. Innovations appeared in the "underground" comics, where sf supplied an ideal framework for scatological examinations of society's neuroses and phobias; original artistic styles were developed by Richard CORBEN, Vaughn BODÉ and others. Roger ELWOOD edited *Starstream Comics* (1976) in an attempt to introduce adaptations of work by Poul ANDERSON, Larry NIVEN, Robert SILVERBERG and others, but this venture apparently failed to attract any substantial readership. A similar fate befell a slightly earlier series, *Unknown Worlds of Science Fiction* (1975) ed Roy Thomas, which adapted stories by Moorcock, Bob SHAW, Stanley G. WEINBAUM and others. Published by the Marvel Comics group and with the byline "Stan Lee Presents" (◊ Stan LEE), it ran for 6 issues in 1975. Several other sf comics appeared in the mid-1970s, notably Charlton Comics's *Space 1999 Magazine* (a companion to the Gerry Anderson tv series SPACE 1999), the apocalyptic colour comic *Doomsday Plus 1* (recently reprinted, due to the popularity of artist John Byrne [1950-], by Fantagraphics) and Marvel's *Planet of the Apes* magazine (based on the 1968 movie PLANET OF THE APES and its sequels), which was immensely popular in the UK in 1975. Mike Friedrich's titles *Star Reach* (1975-8) and *Imagine* (1976-8), which graduated in 1977 from underground comics to small-magazine format, had a heavy sf and fantasy bias. Friedrich's list of contributors reads like a who's who of comics experimenters and stars: Howard V. CHAYKIN, Michael T. Gilbert, Lee Marrs, P. Craig Russell (well remembered for his work on Marvel's *Killraven* space opera – see below – which ran in *Amazing Adventures* 1975-6 and was republished as a graphic novella, **1983**), Jim Starlin . . . the list is a long one. Mention should also be made of Marvel's 1977 adaptation of the 1968 film 2001: A SPACE ODYSSEY, done by Jack Kirby, who also had a 100pp novella, *The Silver Surfer* (graph **1977**), co-authored with Stan LEE, published in that year.

In the UK interest in *Jeff Hawke* had waned suffi-ciently for the London *Daily Express*, the national newspaper in which it had appeared, to discontinue the strip – although the *Express*'s sister newspaper, the *Scottish Daily Record*, missed *Jeff Hawke* enough that it commissioned a new and exceptionally similar strip from Sidney Jordan: this was *Lance McLane*, which ran from 1976 until the mid-1980s. Earlier, in 1973, writer Richard O'Neill and artist John M. Burns had created a Philip José FARMER-style fantasy, *Danielle* (1973-4; brief revival in 1978; graph coll as *Danielle* **1984**), for the *London Evening News*. In the USA Gil Kane and Ron GOULART embarked on a daily space-adventure strip, *Star Hawks* (1977-81), cleverly jumping in before the release, later that year, of the movie space opera STAR WARS.

With the success of that film came a renewed interest in sf proper, rather than the fringe-sf of the superhero adventure. The 1970s had seen their fair share of interesting though often short-lived features, such as: Mike Kaluta's elegant adaptation of Edgar Rice BURROUGHS's **Carson of Venus** adventures in *Korak* (1972-4); *Killraven* (*Amazing Adventures* 1973-6) by Don MacGregor, initially drawn by Howard V. Chaykin and after 1975 by Russell, which was an attempt at a sequel to H.G. WELLS's *The War of the Worlds* (**1898**); *Monark Starstalker* by Chaykin; *Deathlok*; *Star Hunters*; *Warlock* and CAPTAIN MARVEL, both these latter by Jim Starlin; *Guardians of the Galaxy* (written by Steve Gerber); *Starfire* and *The Eternals* (inspired by the notions of Erich von DÄNIKEN) – as well as the many excellent stories published by James Warren in his black-and-white magazines *Eerie* (1965-83), *Creepy* (1965-83), *1984* (1978-80) and *Comix International* (1974-7). Baronet Books issued *The Illustrated Roger Zelazny* (graph **1978**) by Gray MORROW and followed up with *The Illustrated Harlan Ellison*. HEAVY METAL – a US avatar of France's MÉTAL HURLANT – opened many eyes to European comics stars such as Moebius (Jean GIRAUD), later creator of *The Airtight Garage* (graph coll trans **1987**), and Philippe DRUILLET, with *Lone Sloane* (graph **1967**) and *Delirius* (graph **1973**). *Star Wars* and, to a lesser extent, LOGAN'S RUN (1976) began the deluge of late 1970s/early 1980s sf on film and tv. ALIEN, BATTLESTAR GALACTICA, BLADE RUNNER, BUCK ROGERS IN THE 25TH CENTURY, OUTLAND, 2010 and UFO all had comics adaptations. *Star Wars*'s own comic series ran for 10 years (1977-86); and, despite its having to change publishers several times, there has been a *Star Trek* comic book running continuously right through the 1970s and 1980s to today's *Star Trek: The Next Generation*. In the UK at this time it was the tv-related magazines that produced the best comic-strip sf. *Countdown* (later renamed *TV Action* 1970-74) ran a **Dr Who** strip and another based loosely on *2001: A Space Odyssey*, and *Look In* had some excellent stories ranging from *The* TOMORROW PEOPLE through **Buck Rogers in the 25th Century** to *The* SIX MILLION DOLLAR MAN.

Smaller independent companies like First Comics brought us items such as: *Mars* (1984) by Marc

Hempel and Mark Wheatley, a tale of Earth science and colonists versus Martian Mother Nature; NEXUS (1981-91) by Mike Baron and Steve Rude, possibly the ultimate mixture of HARD SF and superhero genres; AMERICAN FLAGG! (1983-8; 2nd series 1988-9), Chaykin's DYSTOPIAN masterpiece (there were 3 collections: *Hard Times* [graph **1984**], *Southern Comfort* [graph **1986**] and *State of the Union* [graph **1987**]), followed by his two stylish **Time²** novellas, *The Epiphany* (graph **1986**) and *The Satisfaction of Black Mariah* (graph **1987**). First Comics also continued the comics adaptations of Michael Moorcock's **Elric** books after Pacific Comics had expired – *Elric of Melniboné* (1984), *Sailor on the Seas of Fate* (1985-6), *Weird of the White Wolf* (1986-7), *The Vanishing Tower* (1987-8) and *Bane of the Black Sword* (1988-9) – as well as initiating further Moorcock series: *Hawkmoon* (5 series, 1986-9) and *Corum* (1987-9). Marvel Comics brought out a glossy magazine in the *Heavy Metal* mould called *Epic Illustrated* (1980-86; rev 1992), and this led Marvel to set up in 1984 a separate imprint, Epic Comics, which has put out some excellent material: *Starstruck* (1985-6; graph exp vt *Starstruck: The Expanding Universe* **1990-91**); also adapted as a stage play) by Elaine Lee and Mike Kaluta; *Void Indigo* (1984-5) by Steve Gerber, which dealt with a few too many TABOOS and was left unfinished; *Alien Legion* (1984-current); and *Plastic Forks* (1990), a Philip K. Dick-style adventure by Ted McKeever. Epic Comics is currently publishing McKeever's apocalyptic story *Metropōl* (1991-current). Other items of interest include: Frank MILLER Inc.'s story *Ronin* (1983-4; graph coll **1987**), a fascinating mixture in which post-HOLOCAUST techno-principality (New York) meets Samurai drama; and comics's answer to Fritz LANG's METROPOLIS (1926), MR X (1984-91) by Dean Motter and Paul Rivoche, issued by Canadian publisher Vortex and produced briefly by the LOVE AND ROCKETS creators Gilbert, Jaime and Mario Hernandez, with a collection published as *The Return of Mr X* (graph coll **1985**).

JAPAN – home of martial-arts epics, GOJIRA and gargantuan ROBOTS – deserves special discussion. The robots usually have an initial *manga* (comic-strip) incarnation. The ancestor of them all is Osamu TEZUKA's *Tetsuwan Atom* (vt *Astroboy*). This diminutive hero's comic-strip adventures date back to 1952, and his tv cartoon show, first aired in 1963, marked the birth of tv animation in Japan. As well as robo-colossi such as *Mazinger X* and *The Shogun Warriors*, space operas like *Space Cruiser Yamato* and *Galaxy Express 999* and the space piracy of *Captain Harlock* (all created by Reiji Matsumoto) were very popular in 1970s *manga* and on tv. More recently speculative *manga* have been given a chance to diversify a little as evidenced by *Mai the Psychic Girl* (trans graph coll **1990** UK); Rumiko Takahashi's *Lum* (1989-90), a sort of sf farce; the serene HARD SF of Yukinobu Hoshino's *2001 Nights* (trans graph **1990**); Masamune Shirow's *Appleseed* (trans graph coll, vol 1 **1990**, vol 2 **1991**, vol 3

1992); and Katsuhiro OTOMO's phenomenally successful *Akira* (1982 onwards), filmed as AKIRA (1987), whose nearly 2000 pages are being published in colour in English by Epic Comics (1989 onwards).

In the 1990s the "adult" cartoon strip has finally begun to find its way into bookshops and away from the "funnies" sections of the newspapers. Reading *V for Vendetta* (graph **1990**) by Alan MOORE and artist David Lloyd is not the simple, lowest-common-denominator entertainment that was once the norm for comic books; reading Bryan Talbot's **Luther Arkwright** trilogy (graph coll **1989**) involves an understanding of the language of comics, especially in layout; reading Matthias Schultheiss's *Bell's Theorem* (graph in 3 vols **1989**) really does hinge on an understanding of the eponym. Of course, there is no shortage of trashy adventure comics and fatuous newspaper strips, just like 50 years ago. The difference is that now there are intelligent comic strips, comic books and graphic novels as well.

For a list of all comics and comics-related entries ◊ Introduction.   [JE/SW/SH/JC]

Further reading: The best studies of the comic strip before the end of the 19th century are, both by David Kunzle, *The Early Comic Strip* (**1974**) and *The History of the Comic Strips: The 19th Century* (**1992**), the first 2 vols of an extended and intensive overview. For later periods, see *The Comics* (**1947**; reissued 1990) by Coulton Waugh; *The Penguin Book of Comics* (**1967**; rev 1971; rev 1990) by George Perry and Alan Aldridge; *A History of the Comic Strip* (**1968**) by P. Couperie and Maurice Horn; *The World Encyclopedia of Comics* (**1967**) by Maurice Horn; *The Adventurous Decade: Comic Strips in the Thirties* (**1976**) by Ron GOULART; *The World Encyclopedia of Comics* (**1976**) ed M. Horn; *Smithsonian Collection of Newspaper Comics* (**1977**) ed Bill Blackbeard and Martin Williams; *Smithsonian Book of Comic Book Comics* (**1979**) ed Blackbeard; *The International Book of Comics* (**1984**) by Denis Gifford; *Encyclopedia of Comic Characters* (**1987**) by Denis Gifford; *The Encyclopedia of Comic Books* (**1991**) by Ron Goulart; «The New Penguin Book of Comics» (1993) by Paul Gravett; the important annual bibliography *The Overstreet Comic Book Price Guide* by B. Overstreet.

COMMANDO CODY – SKY MARSHAL OF THE UNIVERSE US tv series (1955). Republic Studios/Hollywood Television Service for NBC TV. Prod Mel Tucker, Franklyn Adreon, dir Fred Bannon, Harry Keller. Written by Ronald Davidson, Barry Shipman. Weekly. 25 mins per episode. B/w.

Despite the title, the hero of this short-lived children's tv series was more likely to be found riding in a four-door sedan than travelling around the Universe. A cross between the Lone Ranger and Captain Midnight (his rival crime-fighter on CBS), Cody wore a costume that looked as if its previous owner had been in the German High Command and a mask whose function was unclear. Cody (here played by Judd Holdren) and his sidekick Joan (Aline Towne) had previously appeared in two Republic

Studios film serials, *Radar Men from the Moon* (1952; 12 episodes), in which Cody was played by George Wallace, and *Commando Cody* (1953; 12 episodes), starring Holdren. Equipped with several secret laboratories, a spaceship and an ordinary revolver, Cody fought conventional gangsters and, occasionally, the Ruler, an evil genius from outer space. Unsurprisingly reminiscent of the absurdities of the movie serials, *CC* was more entertaining than the slicker CAPTAIN MIDNIGHT. [JB/PN]

COMMUNICATIONS Many aspects of communication in sf are dealt with under separate entries in this volume. The most familiar form of communication is through language, for a discussion of which ◊ LINGUISTICS. Direct mental communication, or telepathy, is discussed under ESP. For communication in the sense of travel ◊ MATTER TRANSMISSION and TRANSPORTATION. For communications networks ◊ COMPUTERS, CYBERPUNK and MEDIA LANDSCAPE.

Once the implications of Relativity were absorbed by GENRE SF it was realized that most SPACE OPERAS and any story involving a GALACTIC EMPIRE faced the problem that messages from one star system to another might take many lifetimes to deliver. The issues raised here are discussed under FASTER THAN LIGHT (*see also* HYPERSPACE), and two of the best known sf devices invented by writers to cope with it are discussed under ANSIBLE and DIRAC COMMUNICATOR. Communication within our Solar System has been dealt with in many stories, mostly earlier, notably those collected in *Venus Equilateral* (coll of linked stories 1947) by George O. SMITH.

Messages can be sent forwards in time using time capsules. Sending them backwards in time is trickier, but the apparent prohibition against sending such messages implied by Relativity may be sidestepped by using the (theoretical) elementary particle called the TACHYON, which can travel only faster than light. Sending messages to the past in this way (*see also* TIME TRAVEL) is central to *Timescape* (1980) by Gregory BENFORD. Indeed, messages from the future to the past are not uncommon in sf, a recent example, with bewilderingly rococo detail, being provided by Dan SIMMONS's **Hyperion** books, *Hyperion* (1989) and *The Fall of Hyperion* (1990), in which a titanic struggle across the ages by different but ultimate AIs involves such sometimes contradictory time messages as the lethal Shrike (a God of Pain), mysterious Time Tombs, and Moneta, the goddess of backwards memory who lives backwards in time, along with what appears to be reversed predestination where the future determines the past. All such stories worryingly violate the Principle of Causality which states, to put it simply, that causes precede effects.

The most common communications scenario in sf – often but not always linguistic – involves the meeting of humans with ALIENS. These are often called first-contact stories, and perhaps the best known of them is "First Contact" (1945) by Murray LEINSTER; an anthology of such stories is *First Contact* (anth 1971)

ed Damon KNIGHT. Among some of the alien-contact stories most relevant to communication are "A Martian Odyssey" (1934) by Stanley G. WEINBAUM, "The Big Front Yard" (1958) by Clifford D. SIMAK and *The Mote in God's Eye* (1974) by Larry NIVEN and Jerry POURNELLE.

Aside from the areas of communications which are dealt with in greater detail elsewhere in this volume, there remains that of nonlinguistic communication, though the distinction is merely semantic, in that many writers would take linguistics to include, for example, mathematical symbology and sign language (◊ MATHEMATICS). In many nonfiction works – an early example, for the lay reader, being *We Are Not Alone* (1964) by Walter Sullivan – there is discussion of the possibility of using universal mathematical symbols to communicate with aliens, and this idea is by no means restricted to sf: it was used, for example, as the basis for the symbols inscribed on the first space capsule whose course would take it outside the Solar System. The best of all stories about talking to aliens via mathematics may be *Neverness* (1988) by David ZINDELL, in which the Solid State Entity, a godlike consciousness formed by an ordering of space and matter comprehending thousands of star systems, is talked to – at length and very convincingly, even movingly – in this manner.

There was not much emphasis on communication problems in early sf. Most nonlinguistic communication stories are post-WWII, by which time there had already been much discussion of information theory, especially in the context of CYBERNETICS. Any message consists of coded information: whether in the form of words, mathematical symbols, signs, modulated electromagnetic waves, intermittent laser beams or even the chemical pheromones used for communication by animals. A number of sf communication stories, then, have been in effect code-cracking stories. In James BLISH's *VOR* (1958) an alien communicates by changing the colours of a patch on his head (VOR stands for violet, orange, red). Jack VANCE's "The Gift of the Gab" (1955) turns on whether a squid-like alien creature is intelligent; his intelligence is proven when he learns to use a semaphore language – invented for the purpose – by waving his tentacles. Vance's stories persistently invent new communication systems, usually linked with the nature of alien cultures. Messages in various of his stories are passed by masks, music, smells, colours or signs. (A number of stories of this general type are discussed under ANTHROPOLOGY.) Suzette Haden ELGIN is another writer whose stories blend cultural anthropology with communication problems; she has a PhD in linguistics. Naomi MITCHISON has written a notable book in this area, *Memoirs of a Spacewoman* (1962), centred on a research worker whose job it is to understand and if possible communicate with alien species; Mitchison's aliens are more vivid and convincing than usual, perhaps because of her background in BIOLOGY. Communication with aliens is, of course, a popular theme in sf, and many books, such as *Conscience Interplanetary* (**1972**) by Joseph GREEN, have dealt with it at a less demanding level.

Fred HOYLE has several times tackled the problem of decoding alien messages, most interestingly in *The Black Cloud* (**1957**) but also in *A for Andromeda* (**1962**), written with John ELLIOT. The latter story tells of the cracking of a binary code picked up on a radio telescope and its interpretation as instructions for building an artificial person. One of the purest stories of this kind is James E. GUNN's *The Listeners* (**1972**), which concentrates on the motivation behind attempts to pick up messages from the stars, and brings in many questions of human communication as well. Decoding alien communication also occurs in Michael P. KUBE-MCDOWELL's début novel *Emprise* (**1985**), a first-contact story, in Carl SAGAN's bestselling *Contact* (**1985**) and in Jack MCDEVITT's *The Hercules Text* (**1986**). Sagan's book has some good detail on the physics of communication and contains the entertaining notion that hidden within the number pi, with its endless succession of apparently random numbers after the decimal point, is a message from the original geometers of the Universe. This outdoes Kurt VONNEGUT Jr who, in *The Sirens of Titan* (**1959**), reports the discovery that many great human events and artefacts are in fact coded messages from the alien Tralfamadorians. Stonehenge, when viewed from above and decoded, means "Replacement part being rushed with all possible speed".

Much closer to home, a popular theme has been attempts to communicate with species on our own planet, notably in *The Day of the Dolphin* (**1967**; trans **1969**) by Robert MERLE and *Clickwhistle* (**1973**) by William Jon WATKINS. Both of these owe much to the well known work carried out by the scientist John Cunningham Lilly, author of *The Mind of the Dolphin: A Nonhuman Intelligence* (**1968**). Ian WATSON adopts a rather different method of cetacean communication in *The Jonah Kit* (**1975**) – indeed, most of Watson's books dramatize methods of transcending the limitations of spoken human communication.

There are plenty of communication problems in our own society, even without aliens. D.G. COMPTON makes one of the best uses of a familiar idea in *Synthajoy* (**1968**), a well written and serious story about what happens when a machine is built which records emotional experiences and can be plugged into other minds. And, of course, there are many stories, both in the mainstream and in sf – too many to list here – about the effect of DRUGS in assisting (or militating against) genuine human communication.

Some of the most interesting sf communication stories are those which stress the ambiguity that may be involved in interspecies communication. Three particularly enigmatic novels on this theme are *Rogue Moon* (**1960**) by Algis BUDRYS, *Solaris* (**1961** Poland; trans **1970**) by Stanisław LEM and *Whipping Star* (**1970**) by Frank HERBERT. The Stanley KUBRICK film 2001: A SPACE ODYSSEY (**1968**) also comes into this group. In *Rogue Moon* a labyrinthine artefact, apparently meaningful, is found on the Moon's surface. However, those who walk through it, some penetrating further than others, have all died. These slaughters may in one sense be acts of communication also; they are given a number of human analogies by Budrys, who seems to see all communication as fraught with difficulty. (Alien-artefact stories are further discussed under BIG DUMB OBJECTS and DISCOVERY AND INVENTION.) Lem's *Solaris* tells of the living planet of Solaris; humans in an orbital laboratory hope to communicate with the (hypothetical) planetary intelligence; when communication arrives it takes the form of replicating figures from the scientists' subconscious minds. All efforts at communication are thwarted by the anthropomorphism of the observers, and the novel asks the pessimistic question: will it *ever* be possible to transcend our human-centred view of the Universe, or is communication with the alien a contradiction in terms? Herbert's *Whipping Star* is frivolous by comparison, but its ingenious array of semantic confusions – as humans attempt to communicate with entities whose corporeal form, it turns out, is as stars – poses some sharp questions. Kubrick ducked the question altogether in what has become the most famous sequence in sf CINEMA; when the mysterious alien intelligence of *2001* does communicate, the audience is given only an enigmatic and incomprehensible collage of lights, fragmentary landscapes, an unexpected 18th-century room and a foetus. We are given to understand that communication is achieved, but we receive only the static that surrounds it. CLOSE ENCOUNTERS OF THE THIRD KIND (**1977**) is another film which ends on a comparable note, the communication here being between humans and the occupants of a UFO by means of lights and musical notes; the climax is a kaleidoscope of colour and sound. [PN]

COMPTON, D(AVID) G(UY) (1930-) UK writer, born of parents who were both in the theatre; he has lived in the USA since 1981. DGC's novels are almost always set in the NEAR FUTURE, and each presents a moral dilemma. The future is used as a device for bringing contemporary trends into a clearer focus. Most of the interest lies in personal relationships and the behaviour of people under stress; minor characters are observed with humour which frequently arises from class differences. Endings are ambiguous or deliberately inconclusive. Later novels have varying modes of narrative technique. DGC's rare public utterances confirm the impression that he is not interested in the staple concerns of GENRE SF.

DGC's first sf novel was *The Quality of Mercy* (**1965**; rev 1970 US), concerning a genocidal plot, using a biological weapon, to combat OVERPOPULATION. In *The Silent Multitude* (**1967**) the crumbling of a cathedral city reflects a disintegration in the human spirit. *Farewell, Earth's Bliss* (**1966**; rev 1971 US) shows the plight of social misfits transported to MARS. *Synthajoy* (**1968**), a more complex novel, brought DGC wider notice, particularly in the USA. A surgeon and an electronics engineer develop tapes which enable unremarkable people to enjoy the experiences of those who are more gifted or fortunate. This basic idea is a premise for the exploration of a moral problem and the observation of human beings in extreme situations. *The Steel Crocodile* (**1970** US; vt *The Electric Crocodile* 1970 UK) presents the danger of new knowledge and its application. *Chronocules* (**1970**; vt *Hot Wireless Sets, Aspirin Tablets, the Sandpaper Sides of Used Matchboxes, and Something that Might have been Castor Oil* 1971 UK; a further apparent vt, as *Chronicules* 1976 UK, is almost certainly a publisher's misspelling) is a TIME-TRAVEL story. *The Missionaries* (**1972** US) describes the efforts of some evangelizing aliens with a good deal of social comedy.

DGC's strengths as a writer are all displayed in the much admired *The Continuous Katherine Mortenhoe* (**1974**; edited version vt *The Unsleeping Eye* 1974 US; vt *Death Watch* 1981 UK). A woman in her 40s is given four weeks to live. A reporter with eyes replaced by tv cameras has the job of watching her decline for the entertainment of a pain-starved public in a world where illness is almost unknown. The reporter sees one of the transmissions and realizes that the camera cannot tell the truth; the recorded film is without mind and therefore without compassion. The sequel, *Windows* (**1979** US), depicts the consequences of the reporter's decision to opt for the oxymoron of literal blindness; neither character in the end is allowed to escape into solitude. The former novel was filmed as *La* MORT EN DIRECT (1979). In DGC's most recent solo novel of real interest, *Ascendencies* (**1980** US), manna-like free energy begins to fall from space, but the side-effects include profound displacements, both physical and in the domestic psyches whose traumas have always inspired his best work. *Ragnarok* (**1991**) with John GRIBBIN shows DGC's grasp of character depiction, but its near-future plot – a scientist brings on a nuclear winter in an attempt to enforce disarmament – owes much to his collaborator's grasp of scientific process. [MA/JC]

Other works: *The Palace* (**1969**); *A Dangerous Malice* (**1978**) as by Frances Lynch; *A Usual Lunacy* (**1978** US); *Scudder's Game* (**1985** Germany, in German; English text **1988**); *Radio Plays* (coll **1988** chap).

See also: COLONIZATION OF OTHER WORLDS; COMMUNICATIONS; COMPUTERS; CYBERNETICS; CYBORGS; DISASTER; MEDIA LANDSCAPE; OVERPOPULATION; POWER SOURCES; PSYCHOLOGY; RELIGION; SCIENTISTS.

COMPTON CROOK/STEPHEN TALL MEMORIAL AWARD ◊ AWARDS.

COMPTON-RICKETT, Sir JOSEPH ◊ Joseph Compton RICKETT.

COMPUTERS The computer revolution in the real world has been so recent and so rapid that sf has had to struggle hard to keep up with actual developments. Although Charles BABBAGE's attempts to develop a mechanical computer have lately attracted attention in such STEAMPUNK novels as *The Difference Engine* (**1990** UK) by William GIBSON and Bruce

STERLING, they failed to inspire the 19th-century literary imagination. In fiction the notion of "mechanical brains" first evolved as a corollary to that of mechanical men (◊ ROBOTS) – an early one is featured in Edward Page MITCHELL's "The Ablest Man in the World" (1879) – but this tacit acceptance of the notion of powerful skull-sized computers contrasts oddly with the tendency to imagine advanced computers as huge machines the size of buildings, cities or even planets. Sf writers who had been awakened to the advent of computers by the building of ENIAC in the late 1940s failed utterly to foresee the eventual development of the microprocessor. A partial exception is Howard FAST's "The Martian Shop" (1959), which features a computer that fits into a 6in (15cm) cube; however, the point made is that such tininess (which anyway does not seem so tiny today) could not be achieved using foreseeable human technology.

In the early sf PULP MAGAZINES, artificial brains, like robots, showed a distinct tendency to go mad and turn against their creators; examples include "The Metal Giants" (1928) by Edmond HAMILTON and "Paradise and Iron" (1930) by Miles J. BREUER. But clever machines featured in more sympathetic roles in several stories by John W. CAMPBELL Jr, who went on from "The Metal Horde" (1930) to write such stories as the series begun with "The Machine" (1935 as by Don A. Stuart), in which a benevolently inclined machine intelligence finally bids farewell to the human race in order to prevent mankind from stagnating through dependence upon its generosity. Revolutions against a mechanical mind which rules society more-or-less benignly have long been commonplace in sf; examples include Francis G. RAYER's *Tomorrow Sometimes Comes* (**1951**), Philip K. DICK's *Vulcan's Hammer* (**1960** dos) and Ira LEVIN's *This Perfect Day* (**1970**). The *New York Times* commissioned Isaac ASIMOV's satirical explication of the theme, "The Life and Times of MULTIVAC" (1975), which questions whether such a rebellion would be desirable or necessary; Asimov had been consistently favourable towards the idea of a machine-run society ever since his early advocacy in "The Evitable Conflict" (1950). Another strongly pro-computer story from the 1950s, redolent of the conflict and confrontation typical of the period, is *They'd Rather Be Right* (**1957**; vt *The Forever Machine*) by Mark CLIFTON and Frank RILEY. Hysterical fear of computers is satirized in "The Man who Hated Machines" (1957) by Pierre BOULLE.

The idea that machine intelligence might be reckoned the logical end product of EVOLUTION on Earth has a long history in sf, extending from Campbell's "The Last Evolution" (1930) to *Sagan om den stora datamaskinin* (**1966**; trans as *The Tale of the Big Computer* **1968**; vt *The Great Computer*; vt *The End of Man?*) by Olof JOHANNESSON. The notion of computers evolving to become literally Godlike is featured in Fredric BROWN's "Answer" (1954), Isaac Asimov's "The Last Question" (1956), Dino BUZZATI's *Il Grande Ritratto* (**1960**; trans as *Larger than Life* **1962**) and Frank

HERBERT's *Destination: Void* (**1966**). Other accounts of huge computers with delusions of grandeur and the power to back them up include *The God Machine* (**1968**) by Martin CAIDIN, *Colossus* (**1966**) and its sequels by D.F. JONES, *Mayflies* (**1979**) by Kevin O'DONNELL Jr, *The Judas Mandala* (**1982**) by Damien BRODERICK and *The Venetian Court* (**1984**) by Charles L. HARNESS. The computer incarnation of the Father of Lies in Jeremy LEVEN's *Satan* (**1982**) is, by contrast, humble and unassuming. The notion that the computer might be the answer to all our problems is ironically encapsulated in Arthur C. CLARKE's fantasy "The Nine Billion Names of God" (1953), in which a computer rapidly and easily completes the task for which God created mankind.

The idea that computers might one day be endowed with – or spontaneously evolve – self-awareness has generated a whole series of speculative exercises in machine existentialism, which inevitably tend to the anthropocentric. Notable examples include "Mike" in *The Moon is a Harsh Mistress* (**1966**) by Robert A. HEINLEIN and the central characters of *When Harlie was One* (**1972**) by David GERROLD, *The Adolescence of P-1* by Thomas J. RYAN (**1977**), and *Valentina: Soul in Sapphire* (**1984**) by Joseph H. DELANEY and Marc STIEGLER. In recent years the notion has become so commonplace as to be intensively recomplicated in such novels as Rudy RUCKER's *Software* (**1982**) and *Wetware* (**1988**), although Rucker earlier treated the notion sceptically in *Spacetime Donuts* (**1981**). William Gibson's eponymous *Neuromancer* (**1984**) kicked off a new trend in sentient software, carried forward by other CYBERPUNK writers and fellow-travellers, including Kim NEWMAN in *The Night Mayor* (**1989**). Autobiographical statements are offered by nascently sentient machines in "Going Down Smooth" (**1968**) by Robert SILVERBERG, *Arrive at Easterwine* (**1971**) by R.A. LAFFERTY and – most impressively – *Queen of Angels* (**1990**) by Greg BEAR.

The fear of computers "taking over" our lives remains a powerful influence, manifest across a broad spectrum of story types. These range from straightforward foul-up stories – e.g., "Computers Don't Argue" (1965) by Gordon R. DICKSON – to surreal extravaganzas like "I Have No Mouth, and I Must Scream" (1967) by Harlan ELLISON. D.G. COMPTON's *The Steel Crocodile* (**1970**; vt *The Electric Crocodile*) and John BRUNNER's *The Shockwave Rider* (**1975**) offer striking examples of computers being used, with good intentions but repressively, by NEAR-FUTURE politico-technocratic elites. On the other hand, *Man Plus* (**1976**) by Frederik POHL presents a secret computer take-over as not necessarily a bad thing, and *Michaelmas* (**1977**) by Algis BUDRYS proposes that the dictatorship of the machine-based system might in the end be benevolent. A metaphysical (◊ METAPHYSICS) species of take-over is displayed in stories in which computers literally absorb human personalities. Interesting examples are *The Ring of Ritornel* (**1968**) by Charles L. HARNESS, *Midsummer*

Century (**1972**) by James BLISH and *Catchworld* (**1975**) by Chris BOYCE. In recent years the idea of "downloading" human personalities into machinery has been used very promiscuously indeed, being one of the key corollaries of the notion of "cyberspace"; it is featured in Vernor VINGE's proto-cyberpunk story *True Names* (1981; **1981** dos), and had become a virtual cliché by the time Frederik Pohl's *Heechee Rendezvous* (**1984**) and Greg BEAR's *Eon* (**1985**) proposed that software afterlives might one day be universally on offer. The attractions of this possibility are obvious, if slightly dubious.

Real-world developments in computer games have had a considerable influence on sf (◊ GAMES AND SPORTS; GAMES AND TOYS); Rob SWIGART's novel *Portal: A Dataspace Retrieval* (**1988**) is eccentrically modelled on such a game. Computer SCIENTISTS are nowadays common characters in sf stories and, despite the late start made by sf writers in getting in on the computer boom, it now seems that ideas developed by William Gibson and those who have followed his example are proving a significant inspiration to real computer scientists.

Relevant theme anthologies include *Science Fiction Thinking Machines* (anth **1954**) ed Groff CONKLIN; *Computers, Computers, Computers: In Fiction and in Verse* (anth **1977**) ed D. Van Tassel; *Machines that Think* (anth **1984**) ed Isaac Asimov, Patricia S. WARRICK and Martin H. GREENBERG; *Computer Crimes and Capers* (anth **1985**) ed Asimov, Greenberg and Charles G. WAUGH; *Microworlds: SF Stories of the Computer Age* (anth **1984**) ed Thomas F. MONTELEONE; and *Digital Dreams* (anth **1990**) ed David V. Barrett. [BS]
See also: AUTOMATION; CYBERNETICS; CYBORGS; INTELLIGENCE.

COMYNS, BARBARA Working name of UK writer Barbara Comyns-Carr (1909-1992), whose style's transfixed *faux-naïve* simplicity urged much of her work into a tone of pregnant magic realism (◊ FABULATION). *The Vet's Daughter* (**1959**) describes the emotional distress of its doomed narrator, Alice Rowlands, in such a deadpan fashion that the violent scene of fatal levitation which culminates the tale seems totally unfantasticated. *The Juniper Tree* (**1985**) is a retelling, in hallucinated modern garb, of a fable from the Brothers Grimm. [JC]

CONCEPTUAL BREAKTHROUGH The legends of Prometheus and of Dr Faustus contain a central image which is still vigorous in sf: the hero in his lust for knowledge goes against the will of God and, though he succeeds in his quest, he is finally punished for his overweening pride and disobedience. Adam eating the forbidden apple is another version of the legend. Its reverberations resonate throughout the whole of literature.

Of all the forms which the quest for knowledge takes in modern sf, by far the most important, in terms of both the quality and the quantity of the work that dramatizes it, is conceptual breakthrough. It is amazing that the importance and centrality of this idea in sf has had so little in the way of critical recognition, though an essay by Gary K. WOLFE, "The Known and the Unknown: Structure and Image in Science Fiction" (in *Many Futures, Many Worlds* [anth **1977**] ed Thomas D. CLARESON), points towards it.

Conceptual breakthrough can best be explained in terms of "paradigms", as that term is used by philosophers of science. A paradigm is a generally held way of looking at and interpreting the world; it consists of a set of often unspoken and unargued assumptions – for example, before Nicolas Copernicus (1473-1543) the paradigm saw Earth as the centre of the Universe. All the most exciting scientific revolutions have taken the form of breaking down a paradigm and substituting another. Often the old paradigm is eroded slowly at first, through discovery of lots of little puzzling anomalies, before the new paradigm can take over. Such an altered perception of the world, sometimes in terms of science and sometimes in terms of society, is what sf is most commonly about, and few sf stories do not have at least some element of conceptual breakthrough.

An important subset of conceptual-breakthrough stories consists of those in which the world is not what it seems. The structure of such stories is often that of a quest in which an intellectual nonconformist questions apparent certainties. Quite a number have been stories in which the world turns out to be a GENERATION STARSHIP, as in "Universe" (1941) by Robert A. HEINLEIN, *Non-Stop* (**1958**; vt *Starship* US – the US title giving the game away) by Brian W. ALDISS, and *Captive Universe* (**1969**) by Harry HARRISON. In "The Pit" (1975) by D. West the world turns out to be inside an artificial asteroid. In "Outside" (1955), by Aldiss, a suburban house turns out to be an experimental laboratory in which shape-changing aliens are incarcerated. In several stories the world is artificial, either literally or because its inhabitants have been brainwashed into seeing it wrongly, as in *Time out of Joint* (**1959**) by Philip K. DICK. Philip José FARMER's **Riverworld** books deal throughout with conceptual breakthrough; the first breakthrough is the realization that, despite all the resurrected dead who populate it, Riverworld is not Heaven; the second is the recognition that the inhabitants are being manipulated. There is a touch of PARANOIA here ("we are property"), quite common in conceptual-breakthrough stories, as in those where the world turns out to be a construct to aid market research; e.g., "The Tunnel Under the World" (1955) by Frederik POHL and *Counterfeit World* (**1964**; vt *Simulacron-3* US) by Daniel F. GALOUYE.

Closely allied to the above are stories where information about the world turns out to be not so much wrong as incomplete. The classic example here is "Nightfall" (1941) by Isaac ASIMOV, in which the constant presence of suns in the sky of another planet has prevented knowledge of the stars, and everyone panics every 21,049 years when five suns set and the sixth is eclipsed. Arthur C. CLARKE's *The City and the Stars* (**1956**) has two breakthroughs, the first out of a beautiful but static utopian city into the greater world, and the second into a knowledge of civilizations in the stars. Another post-WWII classic is "Surface Tension" (1952) by Blish, in which the hero breaks out of his underwater microcosm to discover a great world arching over his puddle. (Blish always recognized the shift from one paradigm to another as the essence of sf, and said as much in "The Science in Science Fiction" [1971; reprinted in *The Tale that Wags the God* coll **1987** ed Cy Chauvin]. His novel about Roger Bacon, *Doctor Mirabilis* [**1964**], which takes conceptual breakthrough as its theme, has, therefore, the flavour of sf even though based on historical fact.) Daniel F. Galouye's *Dark Universe* (**1961**) is perhaps the best of many stories in which an underground community has lost its memory of the surface. In *Lord of Light* (**1967**) by Roger ZELAZNY the breakthrough is into an understanding of the true nature of an artificial heaven.

All stories where the apparently complete world of the story's beginning, whether a generation starship or an underground community, turns out to be only part of a greater whole can be termed pocket-universe stories. (◊ POCKET UNIVERSE, where the case is made that many conceptual-breakthrough stories of this sort can be linked with the passage from the constrictions of childhood to the freedoms of adulthood.) The archetype of all such stories is *The History of Rasselas* (**1759**) by Samuel JOHNSON, in which the hero, walled into a tranquil Abyssinian valley by mountains, finds his yearning for knowledge of the outside world obsessing him, not letting him enjoy the happiness he sees all around him. He escapes; the world outside is less happy than his own, but it is interesting. *Rasselas* provides the template for the whole subgenre; moreover, the intellectual discontent and formless yearnings of its hero are among the commonest qualities of sf HEROES, and Johnson's mild pessimism – which recognizes that, even though the new world-picture may be uglier than the old, we need to know about it – captures exactly the accepting tone which was to permeate so much sf. It is a romantic, if often melancholy, form of striving, and sf never reveals its romantic origins more clearly than when it uses the tropes of conceptual breakthrough.

Sometimes the breakthrough is transcendent, and can be given to the reader only by analogy, inasmuch as the new state cannot be described in a terminology which itself belongs to the old paradigm. Such a state is commonly attained by the heroes of A.E. VAN VOGT and Alfred BESTER, and more recently those of Ian WATSON, all of whose works centre on a conceptual breakthrough of some kind. Such, too, are the end of the film 2001: A SPACE ODYSSEY (1968), where kaleidoscopic imagery of hypnagogic intensity is an emblem of the incomprehensible, and the vastly superior INTELLIGENCE attained by the hero of *Camp Concentration* (**1968**) by Thomas M. DISCH, a book which alludes with some subtlety to every celebrated literary variant of the Faust myth. In Algis BUDRYS's extraordinary novel *Rogue Moon* (**1960**) conceptual breakthrough (in the attempt to understand a labyrinthine artefact on the Moon) seems invariably accompanied by death, and this too recalls the Faustian theme, transcendence being linked to mortality. A similar consequence occurs in *The Black Cloud* (**1957**) by Fred HOYLE.

Sometimes conceptual breakthrough is ambiguous: the objective nature of the new paradigm cannot be understood because of the subjective nature of PERCEPTION. A joke version of this occurs in "The Yellow Pill" (**1958**) by Rog PHILLIPS, where one character believes himself to be in a room, the other in a spaceship, and both are tempted to break down the other's version of reality; one walks, fatally, through what he believes to be a door. Paradoxes of this kind were enjoyed by Philip K. Dick, as in "Impostor" (**1953**) – where a man who believes himself unjustly persecuted as a machine breaks through to the realization that he is indeed a robot with a bomb in his belly – and also in, among others, *Eye in the Sky* (**1957**), *Martian Time-Slip* (**1964**), *Ubik* (**1969**) and *A Maze of Death* (**1970**). A subjective, disturbing form of conceptual breakthrough is the basis for many of J.G. BALLARD's stories, such as "Build-Up" (**1957**; vt "The Concentration City"), "Manhole 69" (**1959**), "Thirteen to Centaurus" (**1962**) and even "The Drowned Giant" (**1964**; vt "Souvenir"). One of the most remarkable conceptual-breakthrough stories of recent years – whose author, Christopher PRIEST, saw the work as in part a homage to Aldiss's *Non-Stop* – is *Inverted World* (**1974**). In this book a city is constantly and painfully pushed forward on rails because the world-picture of its inhabitants is of a hyperboloid where time and space are progressively distorted both north and south of an always moving optimum line. The probable truth turns out to be very different. As in many such stories, the breakthrough is inner as well as outer; the book adopts the Berkeleyan view that the world is what we see it as being; changes in objective truth are changes in perception; there is no such thing as pure scientific truth.

The forms taken by conceptual breakthrough in sf are almost impossible to enumerate. David LINDSAY's *A Voyage to Arcturus* (**1920**) is structurally an ironic series of such breakthroughs, with each new truth seen in turn to be as inadequate as the previous one, until the grim, rather nihilistic and ultimate reality is revealed at the end. John FOWLES's *The Magus* (**1965**; rev 1977) achieves a similar effect in a non-sf context. C.S. LEWIS's *Perelandra* (**1944**; vt *Voyage to Venus*) has some moments of startling beauty when the hero tries to accommodate his perceptions to the alien configurations of Venus. William GOLDING's *The Inheritors* (**1955**) has the breakthrough symbolized in the confrontation between Neanderthal and Cro-Magnon. Many of Ray CUMMINGS's PULP-MAGAZINE stories deal with the realization (based, ironically, on a now discredited paradigm) that an infinite series of

worlds can exist, each within the atoms of the next higher in the series. Various conceptual leaps take place in most of Samuel R. DELANY's stories, notably "The Star Pit" (1967) and *Babel-17* (**1966**). In the latter story the breakthrough, ultimately conceptual, is initially LINGUISTIC. Delany sees paradigms as actually existing within, and created by, language itself, a common view in linguistic sf and one found also in Ian Watson's *The Embedding* (**1973**). In Theodore STURGEON's "Who?" (1955; vt "Bulkhead") a spaceship pilot, frightened of the unknown outside his ship, is cheered by the voice of his unreachable companion beyond the bulkhead; only at the end does he find that the other crewman is a mental projection of his own younger self, and that the bulkhead is, metaphorically, in his own mind. Hal CLEMENT's *Mission of Gravity* (**1954**) takes place on a high-gravity planet whose natives are forced to understand their world through human eyes, and vice versa. The SWORD-AND-SORCERY milieu of John CROWLEY's *The Deep* (**1975**), accepted by the reader as a literary convention, turns out to have a quite different explanation, necessitating a wrench to the reader's view of the novel as well as the hero's view of his world. Ursula K. LE GUIN's *The Dispossessed* (**1974**) is structured around parallel breakthroughs in political understanding and fundamental physics; the crossing of walls is the book's central image. The hero of Daniel KEYES's *Flowers for Algernon* (1959 *FSF*; exp **1966**) begins as a moron, comes to understand the nature of the world as no other human can, then tragically has the gift of intelligence taken away. The breakthrough in "Strangers" (1974) by Gardner DOZOIS is in cultural understanding, and is accomplished only after the death of the protagonist's alien lover. The breakthrough at the end of *Orbitsville* (**1975**) by Bob SHAW takes place in an almost unimaginably huge DYSON SPHERE, whose nature puts human evolutionary struggle into a new perspective.

Examples could be multiplied endlessly, and have been given extensively to demonstrate how all-pervasive the theme is in sf; no adequate DEFINITION OF SF can be formulated that does not somehow take it into account. It is present, regardless of the usual boundaries, in old wave and NEW WAVE, HEROIC FANTASY and HARD SF, GENRE SF and sf by MAINSTREAM writers. It recurs so compulsively, and so much of the feeling and passion of sf is generated by it, that it must be seen as springing from a deep-rooted human need: to reach out, escape mental traps, prefer movement to stasis; to understand. Sf is pre-eminently the literature of the intellectually discontented, those who need to feel there must be more to life than this; and therein lies its maturity, which by a paradox can be seen as a perpetual adolescent yearning.

The breakthrough is often merely implicit in the text, and sometimes easy enough to miss. In these cases it is the readers themselves whose perceptions are shifted through their reading of clues. An extreme case is that of Gene WOLFE, whose **Book of the New Sun** series is set in a quasimedieval-seeming heroic-fantasy milieu, but the readers' genre expectations are rudely broken as they realize that the book is pure sf, not fantasy; that the time is the far future, not the distant past; that the tower in which apprentice torturers are educated is in fact a derelict spaceship. Wolfe enjoys such coded jolts, as in *The Fifth Head of Cerberus* (**1972**), in which the narrator who at the outset was a human anthropologist has towards the end been supplanted by a shape-shifting native of the planet. The exact textual point of the breakthrough can be identified, but only by a careful reader. Thus conceptual breakthrough is not just the subject of much sf: it is also, quite often, its designed effect.

Conceptual breakthrough remained as popular a theme as ever in the 1980s and 1990s, though seldom provoking quite the same shock of surprise. The breakthrough in recent sf is often catalysed by confrontation with alien artefacts (◊ BIG DUMB OBJECTS; DISCOVERY AND INVENTION). The pre-eminent conceptual-breakthrough writer of the 1980s is Greg BEAR, notably in *Blood Music* (**1985**), a story of evolutionary transcendence mediated by a new form of microorganism. Nancy KRESS's *An Alien Light* (**1988**) contains a whole string of conceptual breakthroughs as two rival human cultures and one alien culture make a series of discoveries about each other's initially incomprehensible modes of thinking and patterns of behaviour.

Robert SILVERBERG is an interesting case of a writer who – often – no sooner evokes a conceptual breakthrough than he morosely contemplates its drawbacks for people who just want to be ordinary human beings. Such is his *The Face of the Waters* (**1991**), in which the revelation that all native life on a planet is linked in a single, godlike, transcendent organism is followed by *angst* on the part of the humans who may be allowed to join it. One feels that had Silverberg overheard Galileo muttering "Eppur si muove" ["And yet it moves"] he would have responded: "Yes, I agree, but I wish it didn't." [PN]

CONDÉ NAST ◊ ASTOUNDING SCIENCE-FICTION.

CONDON, RICHARD (THOMAS) (1915-) US writer, formerly in advertising, best-known for works outside the sf field such as *Money is Love* (**1975**), a rococo fantasy, though many, including most notably *The Manchurian Candidate* (**1959**), employ some sf elements in the complex generic mix characteristic of his fiction. Later made into a well known film, *The* MANCHURIAN CANDIDATE (**1962**), this novel combines a superior kind of brainwashing and elements of the political thriller (◊ POLITICS) in a story of the attempted assassination of the US President. So extreme is RC's rendering (and rending) of the US political scene that it is fair to think of much of his work as occupying a series of ALTERNATE WORLDS, as in the savage *Winter Kills* (**1974**), which features the assassination of a JFK-like US President at the behest of his own father; in *Mile High* (**1969**), which argues the

premise that Prohibition was created as the Mafia's answer to market insecurity; in *The Star Spangled Crunch* (**1974**), in which a 142-year-old tycoon manipulates the world through oil crises; in *The Whisper of the Axe* (**1976**), which augurs a successful overturning of the US Government, as does *The Emperor of America* (**1990**); in *Death of a Politician* (**1978**), which castigates unto death with Swiftian (◊ Jonathan SWIFT) vigour a Nixon-like figure; and in *The Final Addiction* (**1991**), which is set in a grotesquely corrupt NEAR FUTURE. All presume a USA subtly but distinctly other than our own. In all of RC's work, an almost magic-realist intensity of attention to the turns of plot combines with an unerring eye for the hypnotic surface of things to gloss over his profound cynicism about the human animal. But the abyss beneath never shelves. [JC]

About the author: "Fantastic Non-Fantastic: Richard Condon's Waking Nightmares" by Joe Sanders, *Extrapolation* 25.2 (1984).

See also: FANTASY; PARANOIA.

CONDRAY, BRUNO G. Pseudonym of UK writer Leslie George Humphrys (1921-), known only as the possible author of *Odyssey in Space* (**1953**), as by Vektis BRACK, and of *The Dissentizens* (**1954** chap) and *Exile from Jupiter* (**1955** chap). [JC]

CONEY, MICHAEL G(REATREX) (1932-) UK-born writer, resident in Canada since 1973, working for the British Columbia Forest Service until his retirement in 1989. He was the manager of the Jabberwock Hotel in Antigua when he published his first story, "Sixth Sense" for *Visions of Tomorrow* in 1969; several more followed rapidly. His first novel, *Mirror Image* (**1972** US) features ALIEN "amorphs" who can so perfectly mimic humans that, when they have done so, they believe themselves to be in fact human; the amorphs reappear in *Brontomek!* (**1976** UK), which won the BRITISH SCIENCE FICTION AWARD. The ecological (◊ ECOLOGY) puzzle story *Syzygy* (**1973** US) is set on the same world. Another novel loosely connected to these is *Charisma* (**1975** UK), a PARALLEL-WORLDS story whose chief locale is a Cornish fishing village; similar seaside towns, often transplanted to other planets, commonly feature in his work. *The Hero of Downways* (**1973** US) is a more stereotyped action-adventure story, but *Friends Come in Boxes* (fixup **1973** US; rev **1974** UK) is a fascinatingly grim account of an unorthodox solution to the problem of OVERPOPULATION. Perhaps the best of his early books are *Winter's Children* (**1974** UK), a post-HOLOCAUST novel, and *Hello Summer, Goodbye* (**1975** UK; vt *Rax* 1975 US; vt *Pallahaxi Tide* 1990 Canada), a wistful story of adolescent love in an alien environment. A series of stories somewhat reminiscent in their setting of J.G. BALLARD's **Vermilion Sands** includes several which were amalgamated into *The Girl with a Symphony in her Fingers* (fixup **1975** UK; vt *The Jaws that Bite, the Claws that Catch* 1975 US).

After *Brontomek!* there was a considerable gap in MGC's writing career, the two books published during the hiatus, the DYSTOPIAN *The Ultimate Jungle* (**1979** UK) and the UNDER-THE-SEA adventure *Neptune's Children* (**1981** US), being books written earlier that had not sold on first submission. His more recent work is bound together by a FAR-FUTURE background developed in the two-decker novel **The Song of Earth**: *The Celestial Steam Locomotive* (**1983** US) and *Gods of the Greataway* (**1984** US). Here humans co-exist with other humanoid species, living out a kind of languid dream thanks to the manipulation by a COMPUTER, Rainbow, of the Ifalong (a multiverse of ALTERNATE WORLDS) despite the interference of the godlike alien Starquin. Publication of this was preceded by the spinoff novel *Cat Karina* (**1982** US). MGC then employed the highly flexible metaphysical context to frame two eccentric Arthurian fantasies, *Fang the Gnome* (**1988** US) and its sequel *King of the Scepter'd Isle* (**1989** US). [MJE/BS]

Other works: *Monitor Found in Orbit* (coll **1974** US); *A Tomcat Called Sabrina* (**1992**), a fantasy.

See also: ARTS; COLONIZATION OF OTHER WORLDS; GAMES AND SPORTS; PLANETARY ROMANCE; REINCARNATION; UNDER THE SEA.

CONKLIN, (EDWARD) GROFF (1904-1968) US editor who began his career as manager of Doubleday Book Stores 1930-34, and who intermittently held various editing positions, in and out of commercial publishing, for the rest of his life; he was, however, primarily a freelance. The first of his many sf ANTHOLOGIES was *The Best of Science Fiction* (anth **1946**), a huge compendium which vied in size and potential influence with Raymond J. HEALY's and J. Francis MCCOMAS's *Adventures in Time and Space* (**1946**), although the latter book was contracted earlier and had first pick of the material. Nevertheless, *The Best of Science Fiction* and its successors from the same publisher – *A Treasury of Science Fiction* (anth **1948**; much cut 1957), *The Big Book of Science Fiction* (anth **1950**; much cut 1957) and *The Omnibus of Science Fiction* (anth **1952**; much cut vt *Science Fiction Omnibus* 1952; much cut vt *Strange Travels in Science Fiction* 1953; much cut vt *Strange Adventures in Science Fiction* 1954 UK; cut 1986 – all cut versions differing in their excisions) – are rewarding compilations. GC wrote a book-review column for GALAXY SCIENCE FICTION from #1 (Oct 1950) until Oct 1955. He also edited for Grosset & Dunlap a series of $1 hardcover sf novels, starting in 1950 with novels by A.E. VAN VOGT, Jack WILLIAMSON and others. The series included the first book publication of Henry KUTTNER's *Fury* (1947 *ASF* as Lawrence O'Donnell; **1950**) with an introduction by GC which has been reprinted in subsequent editions. GC produced anthologies on various themes, including INVASION in *Invaders of Earth* (anth **1952**; much cut 1953 UK; much cut 1955 US; much cut 1962 US; much cut in 2 vols vt *Invaders of Earth* 1962 UK and *Enemies in Space* 1962 UK – all cut versions differing in their excisions), TIME TRAVEL and PARALLEL WORLDS in *Science Fiction Adventures in Dimension* (anth **1953**; cut vt *Adventures in Dimension* 1955 UK; cut

under original title 1965 US), ROBOTS, ANDROIDS and COMPUTERS in *Science Fiction Thinking Machines* (anth **1954**; cut vt *Selections from Science Fiction Thinking Machines* 1955) and MUTANTS in *Science Fiction Adventures in Mutation* (anth **1955**; cut 1955). Later GC became consultant sf editor to Collier Books, for whom he produced the notable anthologies *Great Science Fiction by Scientists* (anth **1962**) and *Fifty Short Science Fiction Tales* (anth **1963**), the latter with Isaac ASIMOV. GC's anthologies were never definitive but were always considered and capable. [MJE/JC]

Other works as editor: *The Science Fiction Galaxy* (anth **1950**); *Possible Worlds of Science Fiction* (anth **1951**); *In the Grip of Terror* (anth **1951**); *Crossroads in Time* (anth **1953**); *The Supernatural Reader* (anth **1953**) with Lucy Conklin; *6 Great Short Novels of Science Fiction* (anth **1954**), not the same collection as *Six Great Short Science Fiction Novels* (anth **1960**), though both are from the same publisher; *Science Fiction Terror Tales* (anth **1955**); *Operation Future* (anth **1955**); *The Graveyard Reader* (anth **1958**); *4 for the Future* (anth **1959**); *Br-r-r-!* (anth **1959**); *13 Great Stories of Science Fiction* (anth **1960**); *Twisted* (anth **1962**); *Worlds of When* (anth **1962**); *12 Great Classics of Science Fiction* (anth **1963**); *17 x Infinity* (anth **1963**); *Dimension 4* (anth **1964**); *Five-Odd* (anth **1964**; vt *Possible Tomorrows* 1972 UK); *5 Unearthly Visions* (anth **1965**); *Giants Unleashed* (anth **1965**; vt *Minds Unleashed* 1970); *13 Above the Night* (anth **1965**); *Another Part of the Galaxy* (anth **1966**); *Seven Come Infinity* (anth **1966**); *Science Fiction Oddities* (anth **1966**; cut vt *Science Fiction Oddities, Second Series* 1969 UK); *Elsewhere and Elsewhen* (anth **1968**; vt in 2 vols *Science Fiction Elsewhen* 1970 UK and *Science Fiction Elsewhere* 1970 UK); *Seven Trips through Time and Space* (anth **1968**).

See also: ALIENS; CYBERNETICS; PUBLISHING.

CONLY, JANE LESLIE [r] ◊ Robert C. O'BRIEN.

CONNER, MIKE Working name of US writer Michael Conner (1951-   ), who used his full name for the first half decade or so of his career, beginning to publish work of genre interest with "Extinction of Confidence, the Exercise of Honesty" in *New Constellations* (anth **1976**) ed Thomas M. DISCH and Charles Naylor. His first novel, *I am Not the Other Houdini* (**1978**; vt *The Houdini Directive* 1989), is a burlesque flirtation with apocalypse set in California in the 21st century. *Groupmind* (**1984**) is less eccentric; but *Eye of the Sun* (**1988**), told with the genre-mixing abundance of many PLANETARY ROMANCES, follows the careening adolescence of three royal children as their FAR-FUTURE world totters into a religious crisis which threatens a long-sustained matriarchy. He won a 1992 NEBULA for "Guide Dog" (1991). [JC]

CONNIE US sf COMIC strip, written and drawn by Frank Godwin (1889-1959) from its beginnings in 1927 until 1944, when it was terminated after several years of dwindling success. The early years of the strip, which featured throughout the madcap adventures of its eponymous flapper heroine, were relatively mundane, but by the mid-1930s Connie had become involved in LOST-WORLDS tales, encounters with mad SCIENTISTS, interplanetary missions and TIME TRAVEL. Godwin was not much admired for his writing, but his complex illustrations, both painterly and draughts-manlike, made the strip memorable. [JC]

CONNINGTON, J.J. Pseudonym for all his fiction of UK writer and chemistry professor Alfred Walter Stewart (1880-1947), best known for his detective novels. His one sf novel was *Nordenholt's Million* (**1923**). A prototype story of world-DISASTER being surmounted, it is realistic, reasoned, sociologically observed and credible. Fireball-mutated denitrifying bacteria destroy the world's vegetation, then die out. A multimillionaire secures the dictatorship of the UK, selects five million people, segregates them in the Clyde valley with supplies, and engineers the collapse of the rest of the country. On the Clyde, nitrogen is synthesized, moral crises take place, there is an atomic-energy breakthrough at the cost of lives, and the exhausted dictator dies. New cities are built. JJC's intellect tackles the scenario seriously and with feeling; though he is occasionally over-"literary", his imagination is firmly anchored in reality. Under his own name he wrote publications on chemistry and, about himself, *Alias J.J. Connington* (**1947**). [DIM]

See also: END OF THE WORLD; HISTORY OF SF; HOLOCAUST AND AFTER.

CONNOLLY, ROY (? -) UK writer of whom nothing is known beyond his collaboration with the equally diffident Frank McIlraith on one sf novel, *Invasion from the Air: A Prophetic Novel* (**1934**), which depicts with some vividness the effects on London of raids using poison gas and incendiaries. The consequences, it is suggested, will include revolution (◊ WAR). [JC]

CONQUEST, JOAN (?1883-1941) UK writer of floridly euphemistic novels of high romance, typical of which are *Leonie of the Jungle* (**1921**), whose eponymous heroine escapes the hypnotic thrall of the goddess Kali in the nick of time, and *Love's Curse* (**1936**), in which the spirit of an Egyptian pharaoh curses two 20th-century lovers. Her two sf novels are *The Reckoning* (**1931**), in which it is presumed that artificial insemination will result in females lacking both morality and reproductive organs, and *With the Lid Off* (**1936**), a future-UTOPIA in which a benevolent Christian dictatorship holds sway. [JC]

CONQUEST, (GEORGE) ROBERT (ACWORTH) (1917-) UK writer, poet and editor, most active as an sf figure in the latter capacity, editing with Kingsley AMIS (*whom see for details*) the **Spectrum** ANTHOLOGIES. RC was educated at Oxford (DLitt), was a member of the Diplomatic Corps 1946-56, and was later literary editor of the *Spectator*. He has an OBE. In addition to much poetry, political history and a non-sf novel, *The Egyptologists* (**1965**) with Amis, he published *A World of Difference* (**1955**), an sf tale whose complicated and discursive plot combines poltical (◊ POLITICS) speculation with a remotely told scientific adventure centred on a new space drive

destined to give humanity a chance to reach beyond the Solar System. [JC]

Other work as editor: *The Robert Sheckley Omnibus* (coll **1973**).

CONQUEST OF SPACE, THE Film (1955). Paramount. Prod George PAL, dir Byron HASKIN, starring Walter Brooke, Eric Fleming, Ross Martin, Mickey Shaughnessy. Screenplay James O'Hanlon, based remotely on *Weltraumfahrt* (**1952**; trans H.J. White as *The Mars Project* **1953** US), by Wernher von Braun (1912-1977). 80 mins. Colour.

The title of this film is taken from the popular-science book *The Conquest of Space* (**1949**) by Chesley BONESTELL and Willy LEY. Though supposedly based on a work of science fact by von Braun, the story, set in the 1980s, of a military research expedition to Mars and back is riddled with implausibilities, both scientific (an asteroid burning in the vacuum of space) and human (the commander, regarded as the only person capable of sustaining the mission, becomes a twitching religious fanatic – at one point uttering the celebrated line: "There are some things that Man is not meant to do"). There is a strange but irrelevant Oedipal conflict, ending with the son killing his father, the commander, when the latter tries to sabotage the ship. The special effects are quite ambitious but clumsily executed, in particular the matte work. A truly awful film, *TCOS* is probably Pal's worst production; it was his last for Paramount. [JB/PN]

See also: SPACE HABITATS.

CONQUEST OF THE EARTH ◊ GALACTICA: 1980.

CONQUEST OF THE PLANET OF THE APES Film (1972). Apjac/20th Century-Fox. Dir J. Lee Thompson, starring Roddy McDowall, Don Murray, Natalie Trundy, Hari Rhodes. Screenplay Paul Dehn, based on characters created by Pierre BOULLE. 86 mins. Colour.

This was the fourth in the ever-weakening series of films beginning in 1968 with PLANET OF THE APES. Caesar (McDowall), the ape born in ESCAPE FROM THE PLANET OF THE APES (1971), is being kept in a circus but comes to resent the human exploitation of apes so much that, with the help of a sympathetic and all too symbolic Black man (Rhodes), he incites his fellow primates to revolt. The film ends with apes victorious over humans after a bloody battle, thus laying the ground for the future situation (there has been a time-warp) of *Planet of the Apes*. All this is crudely simplistic. The novelization is *Conquest of the Planet of the Apes* * (**1974**) by John JAKES. [JB]

CONRAD, EARL (1912-1986) US writer, fairly prolific and sometimes controversial. His sf comprises a NEAR-FUTURE novel, *The Premier* (**1963**), and a collection of short stories, *The Da Vinci Machine: Tales of the Population Explosion* (coll **1969**). [JC]

CONRAD, GREGG [s] ◊ Rog PHILLIPS.

CONRAD, JOSEPH (1857-1924) Naturalized UK writer, born in Poland. His full name was Jósef Teodor Konrad Nalecz Korzeniowski. For most of his life he laboured under the misprision of his early reputation as a teller of sea tales; but posthumously he has received due attention for more complex later works like *Nostromo* (**1904**) and *The Secret Agent* (**1907**). Though it is not sf, "Heart of Darkness" (1902), a dense and potently shaped allegory of guilt, colonialism, alienation and false epiphany in the abyss of Africa, has more than once served as a model for modern sf writers, like Michael BISHOP and Lucius SHEPARD, obsessed by similar concerns: whenever an sf explorer comes across a ravaged cod-godling "white man" in the tropical heart of an alien planet, JC's memory has shaped the tale. Another story, "The Secret Sharer" (1912), has similarly been embraced by Robert SILVERBERG in *The Secret Sharer* (**1988**). With Ford Madox FORD JC wrote *The Inheritors: An Extravagant Story* (**1901**); the people of the title represent a future race, the "Dimensionists", who will come to supersede ordinary mankind. Though the novel is primarily political SATIRE in its projection of the cold, practical, manipulative future humans, it is genuine sf in its use of themes of other DIMENSIONS and EVOLUTION. [JC/PN]

About the author: "Joseph Conrad's Forgotten Role in the Emergence of Science Fiction" by Elaine L. Kleiner, in EXTRAPOLATION, Dec 1973.

See also: CLUB STORY.

CONRAD, M.G. [r] ◊ GERMANY.

CONRAD, PAUL Preferred pseudonym of UK writer and journalist Albert King (1924-   ), an extremely prolific writer in various genres under a series of names: for his ROBERT HALE LIMITED sf he has used PC, his own name, Mark Bannon, Floyd Gibson, Scott Howell, Christopher King and Paul Muller. Born in Northern Ireland, he left school at the age of 14. He is the author of about 120 Westerns, 44 thrillers and 29 romances in addition to his production of 16 sf titles (over 2 years), of which the most notable are perhaps *Ex Minus* (**1974**), as by PC, and *The World of Jonah Klee* (**1976**), as by Christopher King. Most of his work is routine adventure. [JC]

Other works as PC: *Last Man on Kluth V* (**1975**); *The Slave Bug* (**1975**).

As Albert King: *Stage Two* (**1974**).

As Mark Bannon: *The Wayward Robot* (**1974**); *The Assimilator* (**1974**); *The Tomorrow Station* (**1975**).

As Floyd Gibson: *A Slip of Time* (**1974**); *A Shadow of Gastor* (**1975**); *The Manufactured People* (**1975**).

As Scott Howell: *Menace from Magor* (**1974**); *Passage to Oblivion* (**1975**).

As Christopher King: *Operation Mora* (**1974**).

As Paul Muller: *The Man from Ger* (**1974**); *Brother Gib* (**1975**).

CONSTANTINE, MURRAY ◊ Katharine BURDEKIN.

CONSTANTINE, STORM (1956-   ) UK writer whose name, initially a pseudonym, is now her name for all purposes. Her most successful work to date is probably the **Wraeththu** trilogy which began her career: *The Enchantments of Flesh and Spirit* (**1987**), *The Bewitchments of Love and Hate* (**1988**) and *The Fulfilments*

of Fate and Desire (**1989**). The sequence follows the rise of a hermaphroditic race from men (not, at least initially, from women), who take possession of a post-HOLOCAUST Earth devastated by war and pollution. The books focus on the question of whether the Wraeththu, mystically aware and symbolically balanced between male and female yet frequently fascinated by violence and destruction, will prove to be any better than the humans they replace. *The Monstrous Regiment* (dated 1989 but **1990**) is set on a colony world where FEMINISM has gone disastrously wrong and the psychotic ruler – the Dominatrix – plans to confine all men to compounds and milk them for semen to produce children. The sequel, *Aleph* (**1991**), is less inflamed. In *Hermetech* (**1991**) a woman saves an ecologically damaged Earth by means of a sexual coupling, the energies from which are technologically redirected into the planet's "consciousness". SC's novels, which are not really set within an sf framework, give equal weight to the underlying assumptions of science and modern pagan magick. They are all fundamentally concerned with sex and gender (especially androgyny), approached through the realities and potentials of both the male and female experience. The writing itself is vigorous, erotic, highly visual, aesthetically informed by a late punk/Goth sensibility, occasionally somewhat crudely executed, and linguistically shaped by an unusual fusion of intensely contemporary slang and ritualistic "High Style". [NT]

Other works: *Burying the Shadow* (**1992**).

See also: CYBERPUNK; ESP; GAMES WORKSHOP; INTERZONE; NEW WORLDS.

CONTAMINATION ◊ CONTAMINATION: ALIEN ARRIVA SULLA TERRA.

CONTAMINATION: ALIEN ARRIVA SULLA TERRA (vt *Contamination*; vt *Alien Contamination*) Film (1981). Cannon. Dir Luigi Cozzi, starring Ian McCulloch, Louise Marleau, Siegfried Rauch, Martin Mase, Lisa Hahn. Screenplay Cozzi. 85 mins. Colour.

"In Italy," says Cozzi, "when you bring your script to a producer, the first question he asks is . . . What film is your film like?" This is one of several competing Italian attempts to exploit the success of ALIEN (1979). Its opening imitates Lucio Fulci's *Zombi 2* (1979) (mysteriously deserted ship with monstrous cargo docked in New York, and the use of actor McCulloch); and a lot is borrowed from QUATERMASS II (1957). A tolerably lively effort, which repeats too often its image of an alien parasite making characters' stomachs explode in a flurry of guts and blood, this has a Martian MONSTER and a hypnotized astronaut disseminating alien seed-pods around the globe. There's a loud score by Goblin, and some well staged action as resourceful heroes take on zombified alien slaves and an especially ridiculous last-reel monster. [KN]

CONTENTO, WILLIAM G(UY) (1947-   ) US hardware technical support engineer for Cray Research at Lawrence Livermore National Laboratory, and bibliographer. His books, beginning with *Index to Science Fiction Anthologies and Collections* (**1978**) and *Index to Science Fiction Anthologies and Collections: 1977-1983* (**1984**), are essential tools of reference. Researchers wishing to know where to locate short stories in collections and ANTHOLOGIES (and also what books of or about sf were published in a given year) after this period would normally then turn to the annual series compiled by Charles N. BROWN and WGC, and published by LOCUS Press, beginning, in terms of coverage year, with *Science Fiction, Fantasy, & Horror: 1984* (**1990**), and going on through *Science Fiction in Print: 1985* (**1986**), *Science Fiction, Fantasy, & Horror: 1986* (**1987**), *Science Fiction, Fantasy, & Horror: 1987* (**1988**), *Science Fiction, Fantasy, & Horror: 1988* (**1989**), *Science Fiction, Fantasy, & Horror: 1989* (**1990**) and *Science Fiction, Fantasy, & Horror: 1990* (**1991**). Despite very occasional omissions, these are still by far the most comprehensive annual BIBLIOGRAPHIES available, containing useful comment about the nature of each title. They are even more useful from *1988* (**1989**) onwards, as the later volumes contain a Research Index by Hal W. HALL. WGC has also compiled, with Martin H. GREENBERG, *Index to Crime and Mystery Anthologies* (**1990**). [PN]

CONTINENTAL PUBLICATIONS ◊ WONDER STORIES.

CONVENTIONS One of the principal features of sf FANDOM, conventions are usually weekend gatherings of fans and authors, frequently with a programme of sf discussion and events. In FAN LANGUAGE conventions are usually referred to as cons. They are informal, not professionally organized, and with no delegated attendants or, usually, paid speakers. Typical activities include talks, auctions, films, panel discussions, masquerades and banquets.

Although some US sf fans date the first convention to 1936, when a group of fans from New York spent a day with a group from Philadelphia (including Oswald TRAIN), the first formally planned sf convention took place in Leeds, UK, in 1937. Since then regular conventions have been established around the world. In the UK the major annual convention is known as Eastercon (inaugurated 1948), though it was held at Whitsun until 1955 (except 1950, when there was no convention), and has had up to 900 attending; recent venues have included Liverpool, Leeds, Glasgow, Jersey and Blackpool. A second convention, Novacon, was added to the calendar in 1971; it takes place every November in Birmingham and attracts some 300 people. Since the late 1970s there has been an explosion in the number of small conventions held in the UK.

The first US convention was held in New York in 1938 and the first Worldcon, now the premier sf convention, took place there in 1939 (though it was originally so-named because of the World's Fair in New York that year). Worldcon, at which the HUGO Awards are presented, is held annually, usually in the USA, where it has attracted as many as 8000 attending. It has also gone once each to Germany

(1970) and Holland (1990), twice each to Canada (1948 and 1973) and Australia (1975 and 1985), and four times to the UK (1957, 1965, 1979 and 1987). Annual regional conventions have also been long established in North America: major events include Westercon (inaugurated 1948), Midwestcon (inaugurated 1950), Deepsouthcon (inaugurated 1963), Disclave (Washington; inaugurated 1950), Lunacon (New York; inaugurated 1957), Boskone (Boston; inaugurated 1964) and Windycon (Chicago; inaugurated 1974). There are also national conventions in AUSTRALIA, JAPAN and several European countries, including FINLAND, FRANCE, GERMANY, ITALY, the NETHERLANDS and NORWAY. In 1976 one of the international Eurocons (inaugurated 1971) was held in POLAND, the first sf convention in what was then the communist bloc.

Sf conventions are now very numerous, especially in the USA: taking the whole world into account, there are about 150 a year. There are similarities and a degree of overlap between sf cons and those held by fans of COMICS, FANTASY and horror, and also the specialist conventions held by fans of, for example, STAR TREK and DR WHO. [PR/RH]

CONWAY, GERARD F. (1952-   ) US writer who began publishing sf with "Through the Dark Glass" for *AMZ* in 1970. His first sf novel was *The Midnight Dancers* (**1971**). *Mindship* (1971 *Universe*; exp **1974**) is a SPACE OPERA: the mindships of the title are spaceships coordinated by the PSI POWERS of specially trained "corks". Not untypically of sf novels of the time, by the end of the book a gestalt state has been achieved between one cork and his captain. As Wallace Moore, GFC wrote the **Balzan of the Cat People** series: *The Bloodstone* (**1974**), *The Caves of Madness* (**1975**) and *The Lights of Zetar* (**1975**). [JC]

See also: FASTER THAN LIGHT.

CONWAY, TROY ◊ Michael AVALLONE.

COOK, GLEN (CHARLES) (1944-   ) US writer who began his sf career with orthodox stories like his first, "Song from a Forgotten Hill", in *Clarion* (anth **1971**), and with the sf novel *The Heirs of Babylon* (**1972**), in which an authoritarian religious government takes over after the HOLOCAUST. However, he soon became best known for his high FANTASY, especially the **Dread Empire** series, which was notable for its concerted military set-pieces, moderately complex plotting, violence, and a sense of undue haste – he has been exceedingly prolific. The series includes: *A Shadow of All Night Falling* (**1979**); *October's Baby* (**1980**); *All Darkness Met* (**1980**); "Soldier of an Empire Unacquainted with Defeat" (1980); a 2-vol subsequence made up of *The Fire in his Hands* (**1984**) and *With Mercy Toward None* (**1985**); *Reap the East Wind* (**1987**); *An Ill Fate Marshalling*; (**1988**). A further, similar series, the **Chronicles of the Black Company**, perhaps stands out; the first 3 vols – *The Black Company* (**1984**), *Shadows Linger* (**1984**) and *The White Rose* (**1985**) – were assembled as *Annals of the Black Company* (omni **1986**), and were followed by a second sequence, the **Book of the South**, comprising *Shadow Games* (**1989**) and

Dreams of Steel (**1990**); _The Silver Spike_ (**1989**) is set in the same world. A series of humorous fantasies, starring a Chandleresque private eye named Garrett, provides a somewhat relentless light relief, with titles derivative of John D. MacDONALD: _Sweet Silver Blues_ (**1987**), _Bitter Gold Hearts_ (**1988**), _Cold Copper Tears_ (**1988**) – all three assembled as _The Garrett Files_ (omni **1988**) – _Old Tin Sorrows_ (**1989**), _Dread Brass Shadows_ (**1990**) and _Red Iron Nights_ (**1991**). Of his singletons, _A Matter of Time_ (**1985**), a TIME-TRAVEL tale starring detective figures, and _The Tower of Fear_ (**1989**), a strongly plotted fantasy, are the most notable. GC is a writer of considerable energy but little patience. [JC]
Other works: _The Swap Academy_ (**1970**) as by Greg Stevens, GC's first novel, a non-genre erotica title; _The Swordbearer_ (**1982**); the **Starfishers** sequence, comprising _Shadowline_ (**1982**), _Starfishers_ (**1982**) and _Stars' End_ (**1982**), which is related to _Passage at Arms_ (**1985**); the **Darkwar** trilogy: _Doomstalker_ (**1985**), _Warlock_ (**1985**) and _Ceremony_ (**1986**); _The Dragon Never Sleeps_ (**1988**), a SPACE OPERA; _Sung in Blood_ (**1990**), a fantasy.
About the author: _A Glen Cook Bibliography_ (**1983** chap) by Cook and Roger C. SCHLOBIN.

COOK, HUGH (MURRAY WILLIAM) (1957-   ) NEW ZEALAND author, known primarily for his mildly competent and sometimes inventive fantasy series, **Chronicles of an Age of Darkness**, which seems intended for a young-adult readership. His only sf novel, _The Shift_ (**1986** UK), a finalist in the 1985 Young Writers' Competition run by _The Times_ (London) with publishers Jonathan Cape, is a confused tale of deeply undergraduate humour about an alien INVASION and a machine that selectively alters human history. [PN]
Other works: _Plague Summer_ (**1980**), not sf; the **Chronicles of an Age of Darkness** fantasy series, comprising _#1: The Wizards and the Warriors_ (**1986** UK; vt _Wizard War_ 1987 US), _#2: The Wordsmiths and the Warguild, or The Questing Hero_ (**1987** UK; in 2 vols vt _The Questing Hero_ 1987 US and _The Hero's Return_ 1988 US), _#3: The Women and the Warlords_ (**1987** UK; vt _The Oracle_ 1987 US), _#4: The Walrus and the Warwolf_ (**1988** UK), _#5: The Wicked and the Witless_ (**1989** UK), _#6: The Wishstone and the Wonderworkers_ (**1990** UK), _#7: The Wazir and the Witch_ (**1990** UK), _#8: The Werewolf and the Wormlord_ (**1991**) and _#9: The Worshippers and the Way_ (**1992**).

COOK, PAUL H(ARLIN) (1950-   ) US poet and novelist whose infrequent sf stories began with "The Character Assassin" in _Other Worlds #1_ (anth **1979**) ed Roy TORGESON. In his first novel, _Tintagel_ (**1981**), a virus transports its victims, by actualizing their response to MUSIC, into fantasy worlds from which the immune protagonist must rescue them. _Duende Meadow_ (**1985**) depicts the post-HOLOCAUST return of North Americans to the surface of the world, where they find Russian farmers. The lure of transcendence marks PHC's books; if their focus sharpens, they may become substantial. [JC]

Other works: _The Alejandra Variations_ (**1984**); _Halo_ (**1986**); _On the Rim of the Mandala_ (**1987**), a congested SPACE OPERA.
See also: EVOLUTION; MUSIC.

COOK, ROBIN 1. (1931-   ) UK writer, resident for some years in France (in order, he has intimated, to put distance between himself and gangland acquaintances) before his recent return to the UK. He writes thrillers as Derek Raymond, a name he began to use when his career was flagging and his own name was eclipsed by **2.** His last novel as RC, _A State of Denmark, or A Warning to the Incurious_ (**1970**), is a savage and scatological depiction of a NEAR-FUTURE welfare DYSTOPIA in the UK.

2. (1940-   ) US writer of medical horror thrillers whose premises are often extracted from sf. His best-known novel is his first, _Coma_ (**1977**), filmed as COMA (**1978**) by his medical-HORROR confrere Michael CRICHTON. Others include _Brain_ (**1981**), _Fever_ (**1982**), _Godplayer_ (**1983**), _Mindbend_ (**1985**), _Outbreak_ (**1987**), _Mortal Fear_ (**1988**), _Mutation_ (**1989**) and _Harmful Intent_ (**1990**). [JC]
See also: BIOLOGY; GENETIC ENGINEERING; MEDICINE; TECHNOTHRILLER.

COOK, WILLIAM WALLACE (1867-1933) US writer, reportedly pseudonymous, much of whose production appeared after the turn of the century in such magazines as _The_ ARGOSY, and only later in book form, in a stapled format reminiscent of DIME-NOVEL SF. Noteworthy among these books are _A Round Trip to the Year 2000, or A Flight Through Time_ (1903 _The Argosy_; **1925**), in which various contemporary writers travel by SUSPENDED ANIMATION to AD2000, where they observe social conditions, and find themselves popular, and _Adrift in the Unknown, or Adventures in a Queer Realm_ (1904-5 _The Argosy_; **1925**), a satire on US capitalism in which a burglar goes along for the ride with a reformist scientist in his spaceship to MERCURY, where he teaches the kidnapped capitalists he has brought with him some lessons in social justice. WWC was a crude writer, but is of interest in his attempts to combine adventure plots and SATIRE. [JC]
Other works: _Castaway at the Pole_ (1904 _The Argosy_; **1926**); _Marooned in 1492, or Under Fortune's Flag_ (1905 _The Argosy_; **1925**); _The Eighth Wonder, or Working for Miracles_ (1906-7 _The Argosy_; **1925**); _Around the World in Eighty Hours_ (**1925**).
See also: DISCOVERY AND INVENTION; HISTORY OF SF; ROBOTS; TIME TRAVEL.

COOKE, ARTHUR Collaborative pseudonym used on "The Psychological Regulator" (1941) by C.M. KORNBLUTH, Robert LOWNDES, John Michell (1917-1969), Elsie Balter and Donald A. WOLLHEIM. [JC]

COOKE, JOHN ESTES ◊ L. Frank BAUM.

COON, HORACE (1897-1961) US writer in whose _43,000 Years Later_ (**1958**) ALIENS come to a post-HOLOCAUST Earth, become intrigued by the civilization that had gone before, and, through records, explore the 20th-century world to satirical effect. [JC]

COON, SUSAN Pseudonym of US writer Susan

Plunkett (?   -   ), whose **Living Planet** sequence – *Rahne* (**1980**), *Cassilee* (**1980**), *The Virgin* (**1981**) and *Chiy-Une* (**1982**) – skids rather loosely about a GALACTIC-EMPIRE setting, only to terminate in an abrupt and complicated coming-together of humans and ALIENS on the sentient world which gave its name to the final volume.   [JC]

COOPER, C. EVERETT ◊ R. REGINALD.

COOPER, COLIN (SYMONS) (1926-   ) UK writer, active as a scriptwriter for TELEVISION and RADIO. His first sf was a 6-part BBC serial, "Host Planet Earth" (1967). His somewhat downbeat sf novels, *The Thunder and Lightning Man* (**1968**) and *Outcrop* (**1970**), have not had a strong impact on the field. *Dargason* (**1977**) is a story of the NEAR FUTURE in which, for mysterious reasons, listeners to MUSIC become severely affected by a variety of psychologically extreme states; it was perhaps the only sf thriller before Paul H. COOK's *Tintagel* (**1981**) to posit music as a WEAPON.   [JC/PN]
Other works: *The Epping Pyramid* (**1978**).

COOPER, EDMUND (1926-1982) UK writer who served in the British Merchant Navy 1939-45 and who began to publish stories of genre interest with "The Unicorn" (1951), producing a considerable amount of short fiction in the 1950s, much of it assembled (with considerable overlap) in *Tomorrow's Gift* (coll **1958** US), *Voices in the Dark* (coll **1960**) and *Tomorrow Came* (coll **1963**). For one sf adventure series (see listing below) he used the name Richard Avery.

It was as a novelist that EC became most highly regarded, and it was for his earlier novels that he was most appreciated, though later works like *The Overman Culture* (**1971**) showed a continuing (if reluctant) facility in newer modes; in his persistent use of post-nuclear-HOLOCAUST settings he was probably expressing his own conviction about the future course of events. His very first novel, *The Uncertain Midnight* (**1958**; vt *Deadly Image* 1958 US), describes a post-holocaust world in which ANDROIDS are gradually threatening to supplant humankind. *Seed of Light* (**1959**) is a GENERATION-STARSHIP novel in which a small group manages to escape from a devastated Earth. Other novels to incorporate the basic premise that the planet has been rendered to a greater or lesser degree uninhabitable include *The Last Continent* (**1969** US), *The Tenth Planet* (**1973** US) and *The Cloud Walker* (**1973**), which was his best received novel (certainly in the USA) and the last to be much praised. Its message was perhaps conventional, but was competently delivered: even though two nuclear holocausts have afflicted England, the Luddite response of a new church is inappropriate, and the young protagonist properly wins the day with an invention which he uses to defend his village from assailants. As the novel closes, the march of progress is seen to resume.

In general, however, EC's later work lacked much *joie de vivre*, while an anti-FEMINIST point of view – he was quoted as saying of women: "Let them compete against men, they'll see that they can't make it" –

became explicit in his novels *Five to Twelve* (**1968**) and *Who Needs Men?* (**1972**; vt *Gender Genocide* 1973 US), and implicit elsewhere. These attitudes were neither politic, in the heightened atmosphere of the 1970s, nor in fact intrinsically becoming. The stories assembled in *Merry Christmas, Ms Minerva!* (coll **1978**) failed to help. EC died with his reputation at a low ebb; but he was a competent and prolific writer, and a better balance may some day be reached.   [MJE/JC]
Other works: *Wish Goes to Slumberland* (**1960** chap), a fantasy for children; *Transit* (**1964**); *All Fools' Day* (**1966**); *A Far Sunset* (**1967**); *News from Elsewhere* (coll **1968**); *Sea-Horse in the Sky* (**1969**); *Son of Kronk* (**1970**; vt *Kronk* 1971 US); *The Square Root of Tomorrow* (coll **1970**); *Unborn Tomorrow* (coll **1971**); *The Slaves of Heaven* (**1974** US); *Prisoner of Fire* (**1974**); *Jupiter Laughs* (coll **1980**); *A World of Difference* (coll **1980**).

As Richard Avery: The **Expendables** sequence of SPACE OPERAS, comprising *The Deathworms of Kratos* (**1975**), *The Rings of Tantalus* (**1975**), *The War Games of Zelos* (**1975**) and *The Venom of Argus* (**1976**).

About the author: "Hope for the Future: The Science Fiction Novels of Edmund Cooper" and "An Interview with Edmund Cooper" both by James Goddard, in *Science Fiction Monthly* vol 2 #4.

See also: ANTHROPOLOGY; DISASTER; OUTER PLANETS; SCIENCE FICTION BOOK CLUB; SEX; SOCIOLOGY.

COOPER, JAMES FENIMORE (1789-1851) US writer, best known for the **Leather-Stocking Tales** sequence, which includes *The Last of the Mohicans* (**1826**) and many other widely read novels featuring the woodsman Natty Bumppo. In JFC's sf novel, *The Monikins* (**1835**), an English gentleman purchases several captured specimens from an articulate monkey civilization located in a LOST WORLD in the Antarctic, which they describe to him so vividly that he returns there with them, only to find that the monkey civilization parodies 19th-century human politics. As in many PROTO-SCIENCE-FICTION tales of this sort, the protagonist then awakens. *The Crater, or Vulcan's Peak* (**1847**; vt *Man's Reef, or The Crater* 1868 UK) is a UTOPIA set on an ISLAND, which sinks.   [JC]

See also: APES AND CAVEMEN (IN THE HUMAN WORLD).

COOPER, SUSAN (MARY) (1935-   ) UK writer, a graduate in English studies from Oxford, for some time a journalist; now resident in the USA. In her sf novel *Mandrake* (**1964**) the eponymous politician takes over a distressed NEAR-FUTURE England and, in mystical league with the forces of Nature, begins the process of cleansing the Earth of Man, but is stopped just in time. Her juvenile FANTASY series, **The Dark is Rising**, is made up of *Over Sea, Under Stone* (**1965**), *The Dark is Rising* (**1973** US), *Greenwitch* (**1974** US), *The Grey King* (**1975** US) and *Silver on the Tree* (**1977** US). It is thought by many critics to be one of the most distinguished of the mythological fantasy series which, following the success of J.R.R. TOLKIEN's work, were published in a spate during the 1960s and 1970s. The hero of the series, Will Stanton, is at once a small boy and a vessel of ancient powers, and SC shows great skill in blending in him a perfectly natural, unsentimentalized, childish innocence and the sophistication of a mage. The series owed much to Anglo-Saxon and Celtic MYTHOLOGY, but also uses such sf tropes as ALTERNATE WORLDS, TIME PARADOXES and time stasis. *The Grey King* won the 1976 Newbery Award. *Seaward* (**1983** US) once again utilizes Celtic material, this time in a dark hegira into the world of death. [JC/PN]

Other works: *J.B. Priestley: Portrait of an Author* (**1970**) and *Stars in our Hands* (**1977** chap Canada), both nonfiction; *Jethro and the Jumbie* (**1979** chap) and *The Silver Cow* (**1983**), both fantasies for young children.

See also: CHILDREN'S SF.

COOVER, ROBERT (LOWELL) (1932-) US writer who has established a considerable reputation with his novels, in which FABULATION and political scatology mix fruitfully. His work might be seen to represent a POSTMODERNIST intensification of the same milieu excoriated by Richard CONDON. *The Origin of the Brunists* (**1965**) subverts the millennial fantasy tropes at its heart. *The Universal Baseball Association Inc., J. Henry Waugh, Prop.* (**1968**) also denatures its FANTASY premise, the eponymous dreamer's creation of a baseball world to be safe in. *The Public Burning* (**1977**) can be read as an alternate history (◊ ALTERNATE WORLDS) of the early 1950s, taking in the death of the Rosenbergs and examining Richard Nixon – a figure RC also anatomized in *Whatever Happened to Gloomy Gus of the Chicago Bears?* (**1987**). *A Night at the Movies, or You Must Remember This* (**1987**) is a Hollywood fantasia. In *Pinocchio in Venice* (**1991**) the Pinocchio of human flesh, slowly reverting to wood in his old age, returns to his origins. *Pricksongs and Descants* (coll **1969**) contains some stories of sf interest. [JC]

Other works: *Aesop's Forest* (**1986** chap dos).

COPLEY, FRANK BARKLEY (? -?) US writer in whose *The Impeachment of President Israels* (**1912**) a future Jewish US president is impeached for refusing on ethical grounds to make war on Germany, but is vindicated. [JC]

COPPEL, ALFRED Working name used for much of his writing by prolific US author (and wartime fighter pilot) Alfredo José de Marini y Coppel Jr (1921-), along with the pseudonyms Robert Cham Gilman and Sol Galaxan (for 1 story only, 1953). He began publishing sf with "Age of Unreason" for *ASF* in 1947, and published a good deal of magazine fiction in the next decade, though he was in fact producing considerably more in other genres with such action novels as *Hero Driver* (**1954**). His first sf novel was *Dark December* (**1960**), an extremely effective post-HOLOCAUST quest story set in a nuclear-war-devastated USA and featuring the protagonist's search for his lost family. As Gilman, AC published the **Rhada** SPACE-OPERA sequence for tough, older children: *The Rebel of Rhada* (**1968**), *The Navigator of Rhada* (**1969**) and *The Starkahn of Rhada* (**1970**) are not easy reading, and neither is the prequel *The Warlock*

of Rhada (**1985**). *The Burning Mountain: A Novel of the Invasion of Japan* (**1983**) embodies an orthodox alternate-history (◊ ALTERNATE WORLDS) premise in thriller dress, told grippingly: the A-bomb fizzles, necessitating a land invasion of Japan to end WWII; after some delay, a rejuvenated bomb stops the mayhem in 1946. If AC's energies had not been focused elsewhere, he might well have become an important figure in US GENRE SF. [JC]

Other works: Four marginal political thrillers set in the immediate future: *Thirty-Four East* (**1974**) *The Dragon* (**1977**); *The Hastings Conspiracy* (**1980**); *The Apocalypse Brigade* (**1981**).

See also: GALACTIC EMPIRES.

CORBEN, RICHARD (1940-) US illustrator and film animator. He attended the Kansas City Art Institute, and worked for almost a decade with a Kansas City animation company, doing sf illustration (a cover for *FSF* in 1967 was his first sale) and underground COMICS on the side. He became a full-time freelance illustrator in 1972. Better known as a comic-book artist than as an sf illustrator, RC in fact combines the fields in his work: his sf art can look cartoonish, while his comics art has the solid feel of sf illustration. While his men tend to look like "sacks filled with potatoes" and his women are ridiculously huge-breasted, he has a genius for surface texture and for three-dimensional solidity achieved with shading. Much of his best work in sf has been for the SCIENCE FICTION BOOK CLUB and DOUBLEDAY, and, in comics, for MÉTAL HURLANT, especially his two series **Den** and **Rowlff**. He contributed a sequence to the animated film *Heavy Metal* (1981), published the GRAPHIC NOVEL *Bloodstar* (1976) and, with Jan Strnad, produced *New Tales of the Arabian Nights* (**1979**). A somewhat fannish study, with 80 pages of colour illustration and many more in b/w, is *Richard Corben: Flights into Fantasy* (**1982**) by Fershid Bharuch. [PN/JG]

Other works: *Vic and Blood* (graph coll **1989**) with Harlan ELLISON.

CORBETT, CHAN [s] ◊ Nat SCHACHNER.

CORBETT, JAMES (? -?) UK author of popular thrillers specifically written for the lending-library market. His *The Devil Man from Mars* (**1935**) is an interplanetary novel with a poor scientific background (or perhaps it was intended as a parody) in which a Martian, equipped with death rays and hypnotic powers, travels to Earth with, literally, the wind at his back all the way. More sophisticated in content is *The Man who Saw the Devil* (**1934**), a rewrite of Robert Louis STEVENSON's *Strange Case of Dr. Jekyll and Mr. Hyde* (**1886**), in which neither personality is aware of the other's existence. Many of his other works contain some elements of sf and the weird – *Vampire of the Skies* (**1932**), *The Monster of Dagenham Hall* (**1935**), *The Death Pool* (**1936**), *The Man They Could not Kill* (**1936**), *The Man with Nine Lives* (**1938**) *The Moon Killer* (**1938**) and *The Ghost Plane* (**1939**) – but none has any real importance. [JE]

CORELLI, MARIE (1855-1924) UK writer, almost

certainly born Mary (nicknamed "Minnie") Mackay, though she was secretive about her birth, which may have been illegitimate. She wrote extremely popular bestsellers (selling, in her prime, 100,000-copy editions), although her first novel, *A Romance of Two Worlds* (**1886**; rev **1887**) – in which interstellar travel is accomplished at about the turn of the century, through "personal electricity" – and its sequel, *Ardath: The Story of a Dead Self* (**1889**), were only moderately successful. *The Sorrows of Satan* (**1895**), in which a Corelli-like protagonist charismatically cures the Devil of evil, reaches perhaps her peculiar peak. By 1900 her odd brand of sublimated sex, heated religiosity, self-absorbed "female frailty" and unctuous fantasy had begun to lose its appeal; by her death she had been virtually forgotten. Most of her early work can be read as fantasy, though careful explication of the texts may derive a form of religious (◊ RELIGION) explanation for the most extraordinary events. Also of sf interest are *The Young Diana: An Experiment of the Future* (**1915**), about a scientific experiment to make a woman (and hence Woman in general) beautiful, and *The Secret Power* (**1921**), featuring a huge airship and a secret power that triggers a great earthquake in California. [JC]

Other works: *The Soul of Lilith* (**1892**); *Barabbas: A Dream of the World's Tragedy* (**1893**); *Ziska* (**1897**); *Song of Miriam and Other Stories* (coll **1898**); *The Master-Christian* (**1900**); *The Strange Visitation of Josiah McNason: A Christmas Ghost Story* (**1904** chap; vt *The Strange Visitation* 1912 chap); *The Devil's Motor* (**1910** chap); *The Life Everlasting* (**1911**).

About the author: *Now Barabbas was a Rotter* (**1978**) by Brian Masters; "Yesterday's Bestsellers, 1: Marie Corelli" by Brian STABLEFORD in *Million, #1* (1991).

See also: GODS AND DEMONS.

COREY, PAUL (FREDERICK) (1903-   ) US writer in various genres, active from as early as 1934, though his first sf story, "Operation Survival" for *NW*, did not appear until 1962. Most of his early novels are set on farms in the US Middle West; the title of one of them, *Acres of Antaeus* (**1946**), deceptively suggests sf content. His sf novel, *The Planet of the Blind* (**1968**), written for ROBERT HALE LIMITED, is a variation on the theme of the one-eyed man in the country of the blind inaugurated (for sf) by H.G. WELLS in "The Country of the Blind" (1904). [JC]

CORLETT, WILLIAM (1938-   ) UK actor, playwright and novelist, in the latter capacity mostly for older children. He is of sf interest mainly for the **Gate** trilogy – *The Gate of Eden* (**1974**), *The Land Beyond* (**1975**) and *Return to the Gate* (**1975**) – set in a bleak DYSTOPIAN UK of the NEAR FUTURE: social disintegration prefigures the moments of hope and rebuilding in the final volume. *The Dark Side of the Moon* (**1976**) ingeniously parallels the experiences of a kidnapped child with those of an astronaut spiritually adrift in deep space. The **Magician's House** sequence – comprising *The Steps up the Chimney* (**1990**), *The Tunnel behind the Waterfall* (**1991**) and *The Door in the Tree*

(**1992**) – is fantasy. [JC]

CORLEY, EDWIN (1931-1981) US writer whose *Siege* (**1969**) resembles several other US novels of the period in its depiction of a Black revolution centred – as in John WILLIAMS's *Sons of Darkness, Sons of Light* (**1969**) – on Manhattan. His other novels of sf interest include *The Jesus Factor* (**1970**) – which factor prevents the detonation of nuclear weapons, Hiroshima being a hoax intended to prevent future wars – *Acapulco Gold* (**1972**), *Sargasso* (**1977**), and *The Genesis Rock* (**1980**, which foresees a NEAR-FUTURE volcanic eruption under New York. [JC]

CORLEY, JAMES (1947-   ) UK writer and computer programmer whose first novel, *Benedict's Planet* (**1976**), combines SPACE OPERA and some rather technical speculations about the possibility of FASTER-THAN-LIGHT travel in a somewhat overcrowded tale in which the discoverer of a new source of fuel runs into complex trouble. Neither *Orsini Godbase* (**1978**) nor *Sundrinker* (**1980**), written for ROBERT HALE LIMITED, proved significantly more ambitious as novels. [JC]

CORMAN, ROGER (1926-   ) US film-maker, a number of whose films are sf. Born in Los Angeles, he graduated in engineering from Stanford University in 1947, and spent a period in the US Navy and a term at Oxford University before going to Hollywood, where he began to write screenplays; his first sale was *Highway Dragnet* (1954), a picture he coproduced. He soon formed his own company and launched his spectacularly low-budget career. From 1956 he was regularly associated with American International Pictures, a distribution company specializing in cheap exploitation films, often made to fit an already-planned advertising campaign. In 1959 he founded Filmgroup, which distributed its own product, but he returned to AIP in the 1960s for his Edgar Allan POE movies (discussed below). In 1970, with brother Gene and Larry Woolner, Corman founded New World Pictures, which soon overtook AIP as the leading producer and distributor of exploitation films; he sold his share of the company in 1983.

RC's B-movies – mainly Westerns and sf/horror stories at first, later also thrillers, road movies and drugs and rock'n'roll movies, most aimed specifically at teenagers – did much to redefine the various exploitation-movie genres, but only by the 1970s did they begin to attract attention from radical film critics. At first he served only as a producer, but in 1955 he began directing. Sf films he has directed – the dates are those of first release – include *The* DAY THE WORLD ENDED (1956), IT CONQUERED THE WORLD (1956), NOT OF THIS EARTH (1957), ATTACK OF THE CRAB MONSTERS (1957), *War of the Satellites* (1958), *Teenage Caveman* (1958; vt *Prehistoric World*; vt *Out of the Darkness*), *The* WASP WOMAN (1959), LAST WOMAN ON EARTH (1960), *The Little Shop of Horrors* (1960), *Creature From the Haunted Sea* (1961), X – THE MAN WITH THE X-RAY EYES (1963), GAS-S-S-S, OR IT BECAME NECESSARY TO DESTROY THE WORLD IN ORDER TO SAVE IT (1970) and FRANKENSTEIN UNBOUND (1990). The boom for sf films which had begun in the

1950s was dying out by 1963, after which year RC and other quickie-producers made far fewer of them. RC-directed films are rare after 1970; throughout the 1970s and 1980s he concentrated on producing because directing had stopped being fun.

Sf oriented films he has produced, sometimes only as executive producer, include *Monster from the Ocean Floor* (1954; vt *Monster Maker*), *Beast with a Million Eyes* (1955), NIGHT OF THE BLOOD BEAST (1958), *Beast from Haunted Cave* (1959; uncredited), *Attack of the Giant Leeches* (1960; vt *Demons of the Swamp*), DEATH RACE 2000 (1975), PIRANHA (1978), *Deathsport* (1978), *Humanoids from the Deep* (1980; vt *Monster*), BATTLE BEYOND THE STARS (1980), *Galaxy of Terror* (1981; vt *Mindwarp: An Infinity of Terror*; vt *Planet of Horrors*), FORBIDDEN WORLD (1982; vt *Mutant*), *Space Raiders* (1983), NOT OF THIS EARTH (1988 remake), *Crime Zone* (1988), *Lords of the Deep* (1989), *Time Trackers* (1989), BRAIN DEAD (1989) and *Welcome to Oblivion* (1990).

In the 1960s, RC furthered the practice (pioneered by the 1956 US release of GOJIRA) of buying up foreign-language films with spectacular effects and reshooting inserts with well-known US performers to create wholly new films, often farming out the revision jobs to up-and-coming young talent. This explains the presence in the filmographies of Francis Ford Coppola, Peter Bogdanovich and Curtis Harrington of, respectively, *Battle Beyond the Sun* (1963), *Voyage to the Planet of Prehistoric Women* (1966; vt *Gill Woman*) and *Voyage to the Prehistoric Planet* (1965); Harrington also made *Queen of Blood* (1966; vt *Planet of Blood*) in this way. These four films drew on footage from the Soviet films *Niebo Zowiet* (1959; vt *The Sky Calls*; vt *The Heavens Call*) and PLANETA BUR (1962; vt *Planet of Storms*; vt *Storm Planet*; vt *Cosmonauts on Venus*). Throughout his career, indeed, RC has been known for his fostering of young film-makers: as well as Coppola, Bogdanovich and Harrington there have been Martin Scorsese, Monte Hellman, Jonathan Demme, Paul Bartel and Jonathan Kaplan; in the sf-film world specifically he was mentor to James CAMERON, Joe DANTE, Irvin Kershner and John SAYLES.

During his proprietorship of New World, RC became known also as the US distributor of prestigious films by Kurosawa, Bergman, Fellini and Truffaut, but he was up to his old tricks with the US release of NIPPON CHINBOTSU (1973; vt *The Submersion of Japan*) as a truncated travesty, *Tidal Wave* (1974). However, he presided over an inspired re-use of miles of New World footage in *Hollywood Boulevard* (1976), dir Joe Dante and Allan Arkush; this is a skit on low-budget film-making revolving round the production of an sf exploitationer called *Atomic War Brides*.

As a director, RC also worked in the field of supernatural HORROR. *The Undead* (1957) has a TIME-TRAVEL theme in its tale of a prostitute, the REINCARNATION of an executed medieval witch, travelling back into the past but refusing to intervene in her own earlier death because by so doing she would destroy

many futures. Later, RC attracted much critical praise with his series of films based (often insecurely) on the works of Edgar Allan Poe, beginning with *House of Usher* (1960) and mostly starring Vincent Price, of which one of the finest is *The Tomb of Ligeia* (1964), written by Robert Towne, later one of Hollywood's major screenwriters. Only *The Haunted Palace* (1963) – actually based on a story by H.P. LOVECRAFT despite the Poe title – has sf elements: deformed MUTANTS. RC also produced a second Lovecraft adaptation, *The Dunwich Horror* (1969), which was mediocre.

The argument over RC's true worth as a film-maker continues. It is clear that by the 1970s he was mostly pursuing rather than setting trends. His work has attracted a cult following and considerable attention from that school of film critics which holds that there is often a freshness and inventiveness in B-grade films lacking from more "respectable" Hollywood productions. In an interview he said of his sf films: "I was never really satisfied with my work in this field." His autobiography is *How I Made a Hundred Movies in Hollywood and Never Lost a Dime* (**1990**). He played a bit part (as FBI Director Hayden Burke) in the 1991 hit film *The Silence of the Lambs*.   [PN/KN]

Further reading: *The Films of Roger Corman: Brilliance on a Budget* (**1982**) by Ed NAHA; *Roger Corman* (**1985**) by Gary Morris; *Roger Corman: The Best of the Cheap Acts* (**1988**) by Mark McGee.

See also: CINEMA; MONSTER MOVIES.

CORNETT, ROBERT [r] ◊ Kevin D. RANDLE.

CORNWALLIS-WEST, G(EORGE FREDERICK MYDDLETON) (1874-1951) UK writer in whose sf novel, *The Woman who Stopped War* (**1935**), the eponymous heroine sacrifices her virtue in order to gain money to fund the Women's Save the Race League as another WAR approaches. War is halted. But was it worth the cost?   [JC]

CORPSICLE One of the wittiest items of sf TERMINOLOGY. The coinage, credited to Frederik POHL by Larry NIVEN in his essay "The Words in Science Fiction" (in *The Craft of Science Fiction* [anth **1976**] ed Reginald BRETNOR), was first used by Niven in "Rammer" (1971). Formed on the analogy of "popsicle", a US ice-lolly, the word refers to a frozen dead person, preserved in the hope of resuscitation in a medically advanced future (◊ CRYONICS).   [PN]

CORREA, HUGO [r] ◊ LATIN AMERICA.

CORREN, GRACE ◊ Robert HOSKINS.

CORREY, LEE ◊ G. Harry STINE.

CORSTON, (MICHAEL) GEORGE [r] ◊ ROBERT HALE LIMITED.

CORWIN, CECIL [s] ◊ C.M. KORNBLUTH.

CORY, HOWARD L. Collaborative writing name of Jack Owen Jardine (1931-   ) and Julie Ann Jardine (1926-   ), then married; the name was taken from her stage name, Corrie Howard. *The Sword of Lankor* (**1966**), in which natives of a high-GRAVITY planet unknowingly extract valuable crystals for genially manipulative spacefarers, is swashbuckling. In *The Mind Monsters* (**1966** dos) a crash-landed Terran takes over a peculiar alien planet. Jack Owen Jardine's solo sf was written as by Larry MADDOCK. [JC]

CORY & COLLINS ◊ Paul COLLINS.

CORYELL, JOHN RUSSELL [r] ◊ Nick CARTER; Bernarr MacFADDEN.

COSGROVE, RACHEL [r] ◊ E.L. ARCH.

COSMIC MONSTER, THE ◊ *The* STRANGE WORLD OF PLANET X.

COSMIC SCIENCE FICTION ◊ COSMIC STORIES.

COSMIC SCIENCE STORIES UK PULP MAGAZINE. 1 undated issue, cJune 1950, published by Popular Press, London; an abridged reprint of the Sep 1949 issue of SUPER SCIENCE STORIES. The lead novelette was "Minions of Chaos" by John D. MacDONALD. [FHP]

COSMIC STORIES US PULP MAGAZINE. 3 bimonthly issues, Mar-July 1941. Published by Albing Publications; ed Donald A. WOLLHEIM. *CS* was one of 2 companion magazines (the other being STIRRING SCIENCE STORIES) started by Wollheim in 1941. It was cheaply produced (lacking full-colour covers) and had a microscopic editorial budget – most of the stories were not paid for at all, being solicited by Wollheim from his fellow FUTURIANS. The first issue contained a story by Isaac ASIMOV, "The Secret Sense"; C.M. KORNBLUTH contributed a number of stories under various pseudonyms. The title changed with the second issue to *Cosmic Science Fiction*, but the whole venture proved abortive and the magazine was dead within 6 months. [MJE]

COSMIC STRINGS ◊ BLACK HOLES.

COSMOLOGY Cosmology is the study of the Universe as a whole, its nature and its origins. It is a speculative science (there being little opportunity for experiment) and in discussing past writings on the subject it is occasionally difficult to distinguish essays and fictions. Johannes KEPLER's *Somnium* (1634) is basically an essay inspired by the heliocentric theory of the Universe, opposing the Aristotelian system then favoured by the Church (◊ PROTO SCIENCE FICTION). Works of a similar nature include Gabriel DANIEL's *Voyage du monde de Descartes* (1690; trans as *A Voyage to the World of Cartesius* 1692), which popularized the cosmological (and other) theories of René Descartes (1596-1650), and Bernard le Bovyer de FONTENELLE's *Entretiens sur la pluralité des mondes habités* (1686; trans as *The Plurality of Worlds* 1929). An early attempt to describe an infinite Universe with habitable worlds surrounding all the stars was presented as a revelation by Emanuel SWEDENBORG in *De Telluribus* (1758; trans as (short title) *The Earths in Our Solar System and the Earths in the Starry Heavens* 1787). There are several important 19th-century works belonging to this tradition of "semi-fiction". Edgar Allan POE's *Eureka* (1848), elaborating ideas first laid out in "A Mesmeric Revelation" (1844), is a poetic vision embodying intuitive hypotheses about the nature and origins of the Universe; Camille FLAMMARION's *Lumen* (1887; trans 1897) combines religious notions with a powerful scientifically inspired imagination, and J.H. ROSNY aîné's *La légende sceptique* ["The

Sceptical Legend"] (1889) belongs to the same class of works. Edgar FAWCETT's *The Ghost of Guy Thyrle* (1895) includes a cosmic vision, and H.G. WELLS offered a brief – and somewhat ironic – account of a cosmic vision in "Under the Knife" (1896).

In the 20th century this tradition petered out. William Hope HODGSON's *The House on the Borderland* (1908) is better regarded as a late addition to the 19th-century corpus, combining a curious moral allegory with a spectacular vision of the END OF THE WORLD. R.A. KENNEDY's curious philosophical fantasia, *The Triuneverse* (1912), introduced the microcosm and the macrocosm to speculative fiction (◊ GREAT AND SMALL) but is far too absurd to be taken seriously. There is only one cosmic-vision story comparable in scope and ambition to *Eureka* and *La légende sceptique*: Olaf STAPLEDON's classic *Star Maker* (1937; part of discarded first draft published as *Nebula Maker*, 1976).

The early GENRE-SF sf writers were highly ambitious in the scope and scale of their fantasies, but their attitude was conspicuously different from that of the cosmic visionaries. They were interested in adventure, and the viewpoints of their stories remained tied to the experience of their characters. Protagonists sometimes caught brief visionary glimpses of the cosmos, but these were rarely extrapolated at any length. There is a curious narrowness about the tales of the infinite Universe pioneered by E.E. "Doc" SMITH's *Skylark of Space* (1928; 1946), and even such macrocosmic romances as Donald WANDREI's "Colossus" (1934). The bathetic quality of attempts by pulp writers to tune in to the infinite is amply illustrated by the first pulp sf story to develop the idea of the expanding Universe: Edmond HAMILTON's "The Accursed Galaxy" (1935). Hamilton "explained" the expansion by proposing that all the other galaxies might be fleeing in horror from our own, because ours is afflicted with a terrible disease (life). A.E. VAN VOGT's "The Seesaw" (1941; incorporated into *The Weapon Shops of Isher* fixup 1951), in which the formation of the Solar System results from an unfortunate accident whereby a man is caught in a temporal "seesaw", is another example of the tendency of sf writers to minimize the issues of cosmology; ironically, a parodic version of this in *Earthdoom!* (1987) by David LANGFORD and John Grant (◊ Paul BARNETT), in which the Big Bang is "triggered" by an unwitting time traveller, has a far more plausible scientific grounding. The kind of joke embodied in L. Ron HUBBARD's "Beyond the Black Nebula" (1949 as by René Lafayette), in which it is discovered that our Universe is somewhere in the alimentary tract of a macrocosmic worm, is echoed in several other works, including Damon KNIGHT's "God's Nose" (1964) and Robert RANKIN's *Armageddon – The Musical* (1990).

More earnest cosmological visions have been inserted into a number of sf novels, sometimes by means of unusual literary devices. Examples include James BLISH's *The Triumph of Time* (1958; vt *A Clash of

Cymbals), Poul ANDERSON's *Tau Zero* (**1970**) and an episode in Bob SHAW's *Ship of Strangers* (fixup **1978**). Ian WATSON's *The Jonah Kit* (**1975**) casually suggests that the actual cosmos might be a mere shadowy echo of the original creation, while dramatic and symbolic use of the steady-state theory is made in *The Ring of Ritornel* (**1968**) by Charles L. HARNESS. Eccentric cosmological speculations are used to good effect in Philip José FARMER's *The Unreasoning Mask* (**1981**) and in several novels by Barrington J. BAYLEY, including *The Pillars of Eternity* (**1982**) and *The Zen Gun* (**1983**).

Among cosmologists who have dabbled in sf are George GAMOW, who included some cosmological fantasies in his book of didactic fictions *Mr Tomkins in Wonderland* (**1939**), and Fred HOYLE, who incorporated visionary moments into *The Black Cloud* (**1957**) and *The Inferno* (**1973**, with Geoffrey HOYLE).

An *avant-garde* story featuring a juxtaposition between the minutiae of everyday existence and cosmological notions is Pamela ZOLINE's "The Heat-Death of the Universe" (1967). Italo CALVINO produced several eccentric cosmological fantasies, some of which are in *Le Cosmicomiche* (coll of linked stories **1965**; trans as *Cosmicomics* **1968**). Surreal exercises in "alternative cosmology" include Lester DEL REY's *The Sky is Falling* (**1963**), which deals with a pseudo-Aristotelian closed Universe, and two stories in which the Universe is mostly solid, with habitable lacunae: Barrington J. Bayley's "Me and My Antronoscope" (1973) and David LAKE's *The Ring of Truth* (**1982**).

20th-century ASTRONOMY has, of course, gradually revealed the true strangeness of the cosmos; it has popularized such notions as ENTROPY and the Big Bang, and has produced such curious images as that of a hyperspherical Universe which is finite in dimension but infinite in extent. The idea that the Universe may contain vast numbers of BLACK HOLES which themselves may contain universes-in-miniature has lent a new respectability to microcosmic romance, while the notion of PARALLEL WORLDS is thought by some modern physicists to be a likely consequence of quantum theory. The kind of visionary extravagance found in Poe's and Flammarion's cosmological essays pales into insignificance beside such modern popular essays on cosmology as Steven Weinberg's *The First Three Minutes* (**1977**), Paul DAVIES's *Other Worlds* (**1980**) and Stephen Hawking's *A Brief History of Time* (**1988**). The discoveries and speculations reported in such books as these have posed a challenge to contemporary sf writers, several of whom have made interesting attempts to devise fantasies which can contain and do justice to a distinctively modern cosmic perspective Worthy attempts include George ZEBROWSKI's *Macrolife* (**1979**), Charles SHEFFIELD's *Between the Strokes of Night* (**1985**) and Greg BEAR's *Eternity* (**1988**). The inspiration provided by modern cosmology has been adequate to bring about something of a renaissance in the cosmic-vision story; further examples include Michael

BISHOP's "Close Encounter with the Deity" (1986), the visionary sequences in Brian M. STABLEFORD's *The Centre Cannot Hold* (**1990**) and *The Angel of Pain* (**1991**) and David Langford's "Waiting for the Iron Age" (1991). [BS]

See also: ASTRONOMY; BLACK HOLES; ESCHATOLOGY; FASTER THAN LIGHT; METAPHYSICS; PHYSICS.

COSMONAUTS ON VENUS ◊ PLANETA BUR.

COSMOS Fanzine. ◊ FANTASY REVIEW.

COSMOS SCIENCE FICTION AND FANTASY MAGAZINE 1. US DIGEST-size magazine. 4 issues, irregular, Sep 1953-July 1954, published by Star Publications; ed L.B. Cole. This was an unremarkable magazine of moderate standard which published no memorable fiction; the actual editing was done by Laurence M. JANIFER. There was a scoop in #2, "Visitor from Nowhere", an sf story by the mysterious writer of Westerns, B. Traven (?1882-1969).

2. US BEDSHEET-size magazine. 4 issues, bimonthly, May-Nov 1977. Published by Baronet Publishing Co.; ed David G. HARTWELL. *CSFFM* contained a sophisticated mixture of sf and fantasy in an elegant format which included full-colour interior illustration. It serialized a short novel in Fritz LEIBER's **Fafhrd and the Gray Mouser** series, "Rime Isle"; ran Michael BISHOP's The House of Compassionate Sharers"; and featured a number of other major authors; there was a book-review column by Robert SILVERBERG. *CSFAFM* had one of the most promising launches of the decade but, undercapitalized and suffering distribution problems, it folded. [FHP/MJE/PN]

COSTA RICA ◊ LATIN AMERICA.

COSTELLO, P.F. One of the many ZIFF-DAVIS house names, this appeared on over 40 magazine stories 1941-58, but until the late 1940s exclusively for stories by William P. McGivern (1921-1982). It was then sometimes used by Chester S. GEIER, later by Roger P. Graham (Rog PHILLIPS) and probably others still unidentified. "Secret of the Flaming Ring" (1951) and "Space is for Suckers" (1958) have both been attributed to Graham. [PN]

COSY CATASTROPHE A term coined by Brian W. ALDISS in *Billion Year Spree* (**1973**) to describe the comforting ambience shed by the sort of DISASTER tale told by UK writers like John WYNDHAM (*see also* HOLOCAUST AND AFTER). [JC]

CÔTÉ, DENIS (1954-   ) Canadian author whose first two novels, marketed like their successors as juveniles, were *Les Hockeyeurs cybernétiques* (**1983**; trans Jane Brierley as *Shooting for the Stars* **1990**), a tale marked by a high degree of invention, and *Les Parallèles célestes* ["The Celestial Parallels"] (**1983**), which demonstrates considerable literary ambition and talent. The former book begins the **Inactifs** sequence, further volumes including *L'idole des inactifs* ["A Star for the Idle Masses"] (**1989**), *La Révolte des inactifs* ["The Rebellion of the Idle Masses"] (**1990**) and *Le Retour des inactifs* ["The Return of the Idle Masses"] (**1991**). DC won the 1984 Canada Council Award and the Grand prix de la science-fiction et du

Fantastique Québecois. Some of DC's short stories are non-juvenile.   [LP]

Other works: *Les Géants de blizzard* ["The Giants in the Blizzard"] (**1985**); *La Pénombre jaune* ["Yellow Shadow"] (**1986**); *Nocturnes pour Jessie* ["Nocturnes for Jessie"] (**1987**); *Les Prisonniers du zoo* ["Prisoners of the Zoo"] (**1988**); *Terminus cauchemar* ["Terminus Nightmare"] (**1991**); *Les Yeux d'émeraude* ["Eyes of Emerald"] (**1991**).

COTES, MAY ◊ Grant ALLEN.

COTTON, JOHN [s] ◊ John Russell FEARN.

COULSON, JUANITA (RUTH WELLONS) (1933-   ) US writer, briefly a schoolteacher, who began publishing sf with "Another Rib" in *FSF* in 1963 with Marion Zimmer BRADLEY under the shared pseudonym John Jay Wells. With her husband, Robert COULSON, she won the 1965 Best Amateur Publication HUGO for their long-running fanzine YANDRO. JC's first novel, *Crisis on Cheiron* (**1967** dos), like her second, *The Singing Stones* (**1968** dos), is set on a primitive planet in a human-dominated Galaxy; the oppressed species of each planet needs help to survive the inimical influence of large corporations and the like. *Unto the Last Generation* **1975** Canada) deals negatively with population control; *Space Trap* (**1976** Canada) is a First-Contact tale. The romantic coloration of her work is more evident in the **Children of the Stars** family saga of exploration and survival: *Tomorrow's Heritage* (**1981**), *Outward Bound* (**1982**), *Legacy of Earth* (**1989**) and *The Past of Forever* (**1989**). *Star Sister* (**1990**) continues in the same mode. She has also written FANTASY and Gothic novels.   [JC]

Other works: *The Secret of Seven Oaks* (**1972**), *Door into Terror* (**1972**), *Stone of Blood* (**1975**) and *Fear Stalks the Bayou* (**1976**), Gothics; the **Krantin** fantasy series, comprising *The Web of Wizardry* (**1978**) and *The Death-God's Citadel* (**1980**); *Dark Priestess* (**1977**), historical and marginal.

COULSON, ROBERT (STRATTON) (1928-   ) US writer, a long-time fan who edited, with his wife Juanita COULSON, the fanzine YANDRO, winner of a 1965 HUGO. With the exception of *To Renew the Ages* (**1976** Canada), a mildly anti-FEMINISM post-HOLOCAUST adventure, and the less interesting *High Spy* (**1987**), his sf novels have been written with Gene DeWEESE. They include *Gates of the Universe* (**1975** Canada; rev vt *Nightmare Universe* 1985 US), a mildly amusing SPACE OPERA, but more notably the **Joe Karns** sequence of RECURSIVE tales spoofing sf and sf CONVENTIONS, *Now You See It/Him/Them* (**1975**) and *Charles Fort Never Mentioned Wombats* (**1977**). His revision of *But What of Earth?* (**1976** Canada) from the Piers ANTHONY manuscript, published as a collaboration, proved controversial. Anthony (*see his entry*) has argued his sense of the matter at great length; neither author, in fact, approved of the final editing by LASER BOOKS.   [JC]

Other works: Two **Man from U.N.C.L.E.** novelizations with DeWeese, writing together as Thomas Stratton: *The Invisibility Affair* * (**1967**) and *The Mind-Twisters Affair* * (**1967**).

COUNTDOWN Film (1968). William Conrad Productions. Dir Robert Altman, starring Robert Duvall, James Caan. Screenplay Loren Mandel, based on *The Pilgrim Project* (**1964**) by Hank SEARLS. 101 mins cut to 73 mins for UK. Colour.

A year later, *C* would have looked like documentary, for it concerns the first landing on the Moon, which actually took place in 1969. The film's struggle between the USSR and USA to be first to reach the Moon strays from the real-life facts (Searls's original novel was published in 1964), but the behind-the-scenes planning on which the film focuses is gripping. The idiosyncratic, vivid view of personal relationships – here among astronauts and technicians – that typifies Altman's work brings life to the soap-opera elements (astronaut's wife takes to drink, etc.). *C*'s climax is authentically exciting. This is early Altman, and he had no way of preventing a clumsy re-edit or the butchery of the UK print. A number of the later films of Robert Altman (1925-   ) were fantasy or sf: *Brewster McCloud* (1970), *3 Women* (1977), QUINTET (1979) and *Popeye* (1980) most obviously.   [PN]

COUPER, STEPHEN ◊ Stephen GALLAGHER.

COUPLING, J.J. [s] ◊ John R. PIERCE.

COURTENEY, LUKE ◊ Alfred Taylor SCHOFIELD.

COURTIER, S(IDNEY) H(OBSON) [r] ◊ ROBERT HALE LIMITED.

COUTINHO, ALBINO [r] ◊ LATIN AMERICA.

COVER, ARTHUR BYRON (1950-   ) US writer. He was involved in the CLARION SCIENCE FICTION WRITERS' WORKSHOP in 1971-2, and began publishing sf with "Gee, Isn't He the Cutest Little Thing?" in Stephen GOLDIN's *Alien Condition* (anth **1973**). His first novel, *Autumn Angels* (**1975**), with intro by Harlan ELLISON, depicts in hallucinated language a FAR-FUTURE Earth, with LINGUISTIC and cultural jokes proliferating rather exhaustingly. The sequel, *An East Wind Coming* (**1979**), continues to introduce to the end of time cultural icons in pastiche. The stories in *Platypus of Doom and Other Nihilists* (coll of linked stories **1976**) similarly – though with a modest induction of calm – features a sequence of somewhat unhinged parodies of popular figures. Of these early books, only *The Sound of Winter* (**1976**), a love story set in a mutation-riddled post-DISASTER wonderland, attempts to create a more humanly moving outcome. Parody is technically not far removed from novelization, and ABC's next novel, *Flash Gordon* * (**1980**), novelizing the film of that name, was thus perhaps a logical move. Subsequently ABC has written for Byron PREISS some **Time Machine** sharecrops – *The Rings of Saturn* * (**1985**), *American Revolutionary* * (**1985**) and *Blade of the Guillotine* * (**1986**) – as well as two sharecrops – *Planetfall* * (**1988**) and *Stationfall* * (**1989**) – derived from computer games. Other sharecrops include *Isaac Asimov's Robot City, Book 4: Prodigy* * (**1987**) and *Robert Silverberg's Time Tours #5: The Dinosaur Trackers* * (**1992**).   [JC]

COVILLE, BRUCE (1950-   ) US writer of sf and fantasy, almost exclusively juveniles. Of some interest are: *Murder in Orbit* (**1987** UK); *Space Station ICE-3* (**1987**); *My Teacher is an Alien* (**1989**) and its sequels, *My Teacher Fried my Brains* (**1991**) and *My Teacher Glows in the Dark* (**1991**); *Philip José Farmer's The Dungeon #2: The Dark Abyss* * (**1989**), a tie; and the **A.I. Gang** sequence for children – *Operation Sherlock* (**1986**), *Robot Trouble* (**1986**) and *Forever Begins Tomorrow* (**1986**).   [JC]

Other works: *Eyes of the Tarot* (**1983**); *Spirits and Spells* (**1983**); *Waiting Spirits* (**1984**); *Amulet of Doom* (**1985**); *The Monster's Ring* (**1987**); *The Ghost in the Third Row* (**1987**); *The Ghost Wore Gray* (**1988**); *The Unicorn Treasury* (anth **1988**); *How I Survived my Summer Vacation* (**1988**); *Some of my Best Friends are Monsters* (**1988**); *Monster of the Year* (**1989**); *Jeremy Thatcher, Dragon Hatcher* (**1991**); *The Ghost in the Big Brass Bed* (**1991**); *Jennifer Murdley's Toad* (**1992**).

COWAN, FRANK (1844-1905) US writer whose *Revi-Lona: A Romance of Love in a Marvelous Land* (**1879**), is a parody of the lost-race (◊ LOST WORLDS) novels so popular in the late 19th century. It is set, like many of them, in Antarctica, where a council of matriarchs falls under the narrator's sexual sway. The results are syphilis and suicide, death and disaster, and the escape of the hero. Some sharp points are made about UTOPIAS.   [JC]

COWAN, JAMES (1870-1943) US writer whose sf novel, *Daybreak: A Romance of an Old World* (**1896**), features an ambulatory MOON which deposits upon MARS a balloon whose passengers discover there a new defence of Christianity in the form of parallel EVOLUTION and the multiple incarnation of Christ. [JC]

COWIE, DONALD (JOHN) (1911-   ) UK writer (blind since 1984), long resident in Switzerland, author of several crabbed visions of a century in decay. Of sf interest are *The Indiscretions of an Infant, or The Baby's Revenge* (**1945**) and *The Rape of Man, or The Zoo Let Loose* (**1947**), in which the other mammals of the world shake off the human yoke.   [JC]

COWPER, RICHARD Pseudonym of UK writer John Middleton Murry Jr (1926-   ), son of the famous critic; RC also published four non-sf novels under the name Colin Murry, beginning with *The Golden Valley* (**1958**); and, as Colin Middleton Murry – Colin being a nickname – two autobiographical volumes, *One Hand Clapping* (**1975**; vt *I at the Keyhole* 1975 US), which deals mainly with his relationship with his father, and *Shadows on the Grass* (**1977**).

After working for some years as a teacher, and finding his non-sf novels to be only moderately successful, he adopted the Cowper pseudonym for *Breakthrough* (**1967**). Not conventional GENRE SF, being more richly characterized and romantic than is usual, its story of ESP and a kind of reverse REINCARNATION is sensitively told and given unusual reverberations by its use of a leitmotif from Keats. It remains one of RC's finest works, and its romantic theme – of the power of the mind to sense ALTERNATE WORLDS, and

of the flimsiness and limitations of this one's reality, crops up often in his work, sometimes in images of déjà vu; as does its venue, a NEAR-FUTURE Southern England on the cusp of transformation. These characteristics feature in many of the short stories assembled in *The Custodians* (coll **1976**), *The Web of the Magi* (coll **1980**) and *The Tithonian Factor* (coll **1984**), the title story of the first of these collections being much praised in the USA and nominated for several awards. They also inform what is generally considered his best singleton, *The Twilight of Briareus* (**1974**); in this tale England has been transformed, through a disruption in world weather caused by a supernova explosion, into a snowbound Arcadia; from the same apparent source later come psychic influences which lead to complex interaction between humans and ALIENS. The story – like all of RC's best work – is charged with a strange, expectant vibrancy. Its explorations of human PERCEPTION demonstrate an openness not unlike that described in John Keats's remarks about "negative capability" – remarks that RC has quoted in print. Keats's plea was for a kind of waiting expectancy of the mind, which should be kept free of preconceptions. RC does not usually link telepathy with the idea of the SUPERMAN, as is more normally found in US sf uses of the convention; instead, it can be seen in his work as an analogue of "negative capability".

Although the air and style of RC's sf is a long way from traditional HARD SF, its content uses traditional themes. *Kuldesak* (**1972**) deals with an underground society on a post-HOLOCAUST Earth (◊ POCKET UNIVERSE), and one man who finds the surface against the will of an all-powerful COMPUTER. *Clone* (**1972**), which saw RC's first real breakthrough into the US market, is an amusing near-future SATIRE. *Time out of Mind* (**1973**), like the earlier *Domino* (**1971**), rather mechanically applies psi tropes (◊ PSI POWERS) to thriller-like plots involving TIME TRAVEL and the rescue of a future UK from the totalitarian implications of the 20th century. *Worlds Apart* (**1974**) is a not wholly successful comedy, burlesquing several sf CLICHÉS in a story of an alien world on which an sf novel is being written about Urth, while back on Earth an sf writer writes about the alien world. *Profundis* (**1979**) places RC's now-expected mild-mannered telepathic Christ-figure in a huge submarine which has survived nuclear holocaust and is being led around the world by dolphins anxious to keep human violence at bay.

RC remains best known for his **Corlay** trilogy – *The Road to Corlay* (**1978**; with "Piper at the Gates of Dawn" 1976 added, as coll 1979 US), *A Dream of Kinship* (**1981**) and *A Tapestry of Time* (**1982**) – in which what might be called the pathos of expectancy typical of his best work is finally resolved, for the essential parts of the sequence take place in an England 1000 years after changing sea-levels have inundated much low-lying country, creating an archipelago-like venue which hearkens – perhaps consciously – back to Richard JEFFERIES's *After London, or Wild England*

(1885), and which also clearly resembles the West Country featured in Christopher PRIEST's coeval *A Dream of Wessex* (1977). In this land, an oppressive theocracy is threatened by the solace offered through a young lad's redemptive visions of a new faith, whose emblem is the White Bird of Kinship. The sequence proceeds through the establishment of a new church, its stiffening into its own repressive rituals, and its rebirth. Throughout, a sweet serenity of image and storytelling instinct – RC has always been a gripping teller of tales – transfigure conventional plot-patterns into testament. The **Corlay** books so clearly sum up RC's imaginative sense of a redeemed England that it is perhaps unsurprising that he has written relatively little since. [PN/JC]

Other works: *Phoenix* (1968); *Domino* (1971); *Out There Where the Big Ships Go* (coll 1980 US); *The Story of Pepita and Corindo* (1982 chap US); *The Young Student* (1982 chap US); *The Unhappy Princess* (1982 chap US); *The Missing Heart* (1982 chap US); *Shades of Darkness* (1986); *The Magic Spectacles, and Other Tales* (coll 1986 chap).

As Colin Murry: *Recollections of a Ghost* (1960); *A Path to the Sea* (1961); *Private View* (1972), written at the same time as the other non-sf novels.

About the author: "Backwards Across the Frontier" by RC in FOUNDATION 9, 1975.

See also: CHILDREN IN SF; CLONES; DISASTER; ESCHATOLOGY; GOTHIC SF; IMMORTALITY; METAPHYSICS; MILFORD SCIENCE FICTION WRITERS' CONFERENCE; MUSIC; PARALLEL WORLDS; PARANOIA; RELIGION; UNDER THE SEA.

COX, ADRIAN [r] ◊ M.H. ZOOL.

COX, ERLE (1873-1950) Australian novelist and journalist who reviewed for The ARGUS and the *Australasian* 1918-46. His best-known sf novel is *Out of the Silence* (1919 *The Argus*; 1925; rev 1947), about the attempt by a representative of an otherwise extinct super-race to rule first Australia and then the world. The novel exhibits some racist overtones. *Fool's Harvest* (1939) warned against a future INVASION of AUSTRALIA. *The Missing Angel* (1947) is a fantasy about foxing the Devil. [JC]

See also: SUSPENDED ANIMATION.

COX, JOAN (IRENE) (1942-   ) US rancher and author whose first sf novel, *Mindsong* (1979), features a planet terraformed into a Hellenic Eden. Her second, *Star Web* (1980), is somewhat less engaging. [JC]

See also: FASTER THAN LIGHT.

CRACKEN, JAEL [s] ◊ Brian W. ALDISS.

CRACK IN THE WORLD Film (1965). Security Pictures/Paramount. Dir Andrew Marton, starring Dana Andrews, Janette Scott, Kieron Moore, Alexander Knox. Screenplay J.M. White, Julian Halevy. 96 mins. Colour.

An attempt to tap the energy at the Earth's core causes a large and ever increasing crack in the crust. A bid to halt the process with a nuclear explosion sends into space a large chunk of the Earth, which forms a new moon. This ambitious DISASTER movie,

filmed in Spain, is undermined by too small a budget, but is suspensefully directed. [JB/PN]

CRAIG, A.A. [s] ◊ Poul ANDERSON.

CRAIG, ALEXANDER (?   -?   ) Author of the lost-race (◊ LOST WORLDS) novel *Ionia: Land of Wise Men and Fair Women* (1898). Ionia is a singularly pious and anti-Semitic Greek colony in the Himalayas boasting prohibition, eugenics and communism. [JC]

CRAIG, BRIAN ◊ Brian M. STABLEFORD.

CRAIG, DAVID Pseudonym of UK writer and journalist Allan James Tucker (1929-   ), whose **Roy Rickman** series – *The Alias Man* (1968), *Message Ends* (1969) and *Contact Lost* (1970) – a mundane jeremiad about the coming 1970s world crisis, with the UK becoming a Soviet satellite, is sufficiently displaced into sf to be of some interest. [JC]

CRAIG, RANDOLPH [s] ◊ Norvell W. PAGE.

CRAIG, WEBSTER [s] ◊ Eric Frank RUSSELL.

CRAIG, WILLIAM Working name of UK writer Charles William Thurlow-Craig (1901-   ), whose two NEAR-FUTURE sf novels, *Plague Over London* (1939) and *The Tashkent Crisis* (1971), demonstrate a fine consistency of mind through three decades, for in each the Russians are the villains who, with secret weapons and unflagging spite, threaten the world. [JC]

CRAIGIE, DAVID Pseudonym used by illustrator and writer Dorothy M. Craigie (1908-   ) on her books for young adults. As Dorothy Craigie, she has written numerous stories for younger children, from *Summersalts Circus* (1947) to *Nicky and Nigger Join the Circus* (1960); also as Dorothy Craigie she illustrated children's books, including Graham Greene's four in the genre.

As DC, she wrote two sf novels with young protagonists. In *The Voyage of the Luna 1* (1948), which she illustrated under her real name, the two children of famous explorers more or less hijack a Moonbound rocket and encounter various strange species there. *Dark Atlantis* (1951) takes its protagonist three miles down to an ATLANTIS inhabited by intelligent reptiles. [JC]

CRAMER, JOHN G(LEASON) (1934-   ) US scientist and writer; author of the **Alternate View** series of science articles in *ASF* through the 1980s. His HARD-SF novel, *Twistor* (1989), engagingly describes the eponymous invention, which sends folk into other DIMENSIONS, where they find copious supplies of food, while a villainous corporation attempts – in the end unsuccessfully – to corner the device for its own ends. As the novel closes, several new and virgin worlds stand at the brink of being used by humans. [JC]

CRAMER, MILES [s] ◊ Thomas Calvert MCCLARY.

CRANE, ROBERT Pseudonym of Bernard Glemser (1908-1990), UK novelist who worked for his government in the USA after WWII, remaining there after his resignation. Under his own name he wrote several non-genre novels, at least two of which feature a protagonist named Robert Crane. As RC he began to write sf with "The Purple Fields" in 1953, but is best remembered for *Hero's Walk* (**1954**) – the basis for a tv play, "The Voices" (1954) – an intelligent and realistically conceived tale in which superior ALIENS quarantine a militaristic Earth and eventually bomb it to rubble. There is some hope at the novel's close that humanity will be permitted to survive and mature. [JC]

CRAWFORD, NED (? -) UK writer whose *Naming the Animals: A Haunting* (**1980**) congestedly depicts a DYSTOPIAN future, out of which, freighted in symbol, a new Eden implausibly emerges. [JC]

CRAWFORD, WILLIAM L(EVI) (1911-1984) US publisher and editor, one of the first sf fans to become a publisher, editing and producing two SEMIPROZINES: UNUSUAL STORIES – ambitiously announced in 1933 but more or less still-born – and MARVEL TALES, which came out in 1934. At about the same time, after a chapbook anthology assembling "Men of Avalon" by David H. KELLER and "The White Sybil" by Clark Ashton SMITH, he published, in *Mars Mountain* (coll **1935**) by Eugene George KEY, one of the first US GENRE-SF books to be produced by a US SMALL PRESS founded for that purpose, and the first to be released with any expectation that copies would be sold to buyers who did not know the author personally. A second novel, which would have been Andre NORTON's first published sf, was accepted for publication in 1934 but stayed in manuscript – except for a few excerpts – until WLC finally released it 38 years later as *Garan the Eternal* (**1972**). This first press, Fantasy Publications, was followed by Visionary Press, which published *The Shadow over Innsmouth* (**1936**) by H.P. LOVECRAFT; but various projects then foundered, and WLC became successfully active again only in 1945, when as Crawford Publications he released some booklets, including Clifford D. SIMAK's *The Creator* **1946** chap) and an anthology, *The Garden of Fear* (anth **1945** chap); 2 further anthologies, *Griffin Booklet One* (anth 1949) and *The Machine-God Laughs* (anth **1949**), both ed WLC, were under the Griffin Publishing Co. imprint. These enterprises all proved less significant than FANTASY PUBLISHING COMPANY, INC. (or FPCI), which WLC was instrumental in founding in 1947, along with the magazine FANTASY BOOK (editing the latter under the pseudonym Garrett Ford). FPCI was one of the central fan presses of the era, publishing L. Sprague DE CAMP's *The Undesired Princess* (**1951**), L. Ron HUBBARD's *Death's Deputy* (**1948**), A.E. VAN VOGT's and E. Mayne HULL's *Out of the Unknown* (coll **1948**) and other titles of importance; it failed in the end only through incompetent management.

WLC soldiered on through the 1950s and afterwards, hand to mouth, always hopeful and full of projects, some of which were at least partially realized. He edited *Science and Sorcery* (anth **1953**) as Garrett Ford; launched the magazine SPACEWAY in 1953; became publisher of the magazine *Witchcraft & Sorcery* (formerly *Coven 13*) in the 1970s; and became in the mid-1970s a CONVENTIONS entrepreneur. Also, various stray pamphlets appeared. WLC's diverse projects included the publishing of some scarce and interesting material, and it may well have been the unattractive, amateurish production values which characterized all his work that caused his general lack of commercial success; certainly he knew sf, and loved it. [JC/MJE]

CRAWLING EYE, THE ◊ *The* TROLLENBERG TERROR.

CRAZIES, THE (vt *Code Name Trixie*) Film (1973). Cambist Films. Dir George ROMERO, starring Lane Carroll, W.G. McMillan, Harold Wayne Jones. Screenplay Romero, based on a story by Paul McCollough. 104 mins. Colour.

A plane carrying germ-warfare material crashes near a small US town and pollutes the drinking-water, causing an epidemic of homicidal and psychopathic behaviour in the inhabitants. The army moves in and the crazed brutality of the soldiers as they shoot victims of the virus (or trapped innocents) is as bad as the lunacy of their targets. There are strong similarities between this and Romero's best-known film, NIGHT OF THE LIVING DEAD (1968), in that both involve a small group of trapped "normal" people surrounded by nightmare. Romero's exploitation movies are more ambitious than most – wittier, too – and this, as usual, has, half-visible through the blood, a political/cultural subtext about an uncaring society. [JB/PN]

CRAZY RAY, THE ◊ PARIS QUI DORT.

CREASEY, JOHN (1908-1973) UK author, publisher and literary agent who began writing for the BOYS' PAPERS in 1926, turning to adult thrillers in 1932. He wrote 564 books under 13 pseudonyms, but it is doubtful if all were exclusively by him (Michael MOORCOCK was at one time approached to do writing for JC). Like George GRIFFITH with his future-WAR novels, JC exploited contemporary fears of organized crime and of terrorist and revolutionary activities, often including sf elements as an additional horror – for example, his first novel, *Seven Times Seven* (**1932**; rev 1970), depicts a criminal gang equipped with "freezing gas". In later works, beginning with *Dangerous Quest* (**1943**; rev 1965), a futuristic novel about an underground Gestapo group in liberated Yugoslavia, and continuing in his **Dr Palfrey** series (see listing below), sf themes came to the fore. Midget aircraft piloted by zombie-like children attack the world's cities in *The Children of Hate* (**1952**; rev vt *The Children of Despair* 1958 UK; vt *The Killers of Innocence* 1971 US). Human-induced world DISASTER was imminent in *The Flood* (**1955**) and others, while an alien INVASION was defeated in *The Unbegotten* (**1971**). All were sensational in nature, contributing nothing to the genre, and were influential only on the cheap-thriller market. [JE]

Other works include: *The Death Miser* (**1932**; rev 1965); *Men, Maids and Murder* (**1933**; rev 1972); *The Mark of the Crescent* (**1935**; rev 1967); *Death Round the Corner* (**1935**); *The Mystery Plane* (**1936**); *Thunder in Europe* (**1936**; rev 1968); *The Air Marauders* (**1937**); *Carriers of Death* (**1937**; rev 1968), *Days of Danger* (**1937**; rev 1968);

The S.O.S. Flight (**1937**); *Death Stands By* (**1938**; rev 1966); *The Fighting Fliers* (**1938**); *Menace!* (**1938**; rev 1971); *Panic!* (**1939**; rev 1969); *Death by Night* (**1940**); *The Island of Peril* (**1940**; rev 1968); *The Peril Ahead* (**1940**; rev 1964); *Death in Flames* (**1943**; rev 1973 as by Gordon Ashe); *Dark Peril* (**1944**; rev 1958); *The League of Dark Men* (**1947**; rev 1965); *Department of Death* (**1951**); *Four of the Best* (coll **1955**); *The Black Spiders* (**1957**); *A Shadow of Death* (**1968**); *A Blast of Trumpets* (**1975**). **Dr Palfrey** stories: *Traitors' Doom* (**1942**), *The Valley of Fear* (**1943**; vt *The Perilous Country* 1949), *The Legion of the Lost* (**1943**), *The Hounds of Vengeance* (**1945**; rev 1967), *Death in the Rising Sun* (**1945**), *Shadow of Doom* (**1946**), *The House of the Bears* (**1946**; rev 1962), *Dark Harvest* (**1947**; rev 1962), *Sons of Satan* (**1948**; rev 1970), *The Wings of Peace* (**1948**; rev 1964), *The Dawn of Darkness* (**1949**), *The League of Light* (**1949**; rev 1963), *The Man who Shook the World* (**1950**; rev 1958), *The Prophet of Fire* (**1951**), *The Touch of Death* (**1954**), *The Mists of Fear* (**1955**), *The Plague of Silence* (**1958**), *The Drought* (**1959**; vt *Dry Spell* 1967 UK), *The Terror* (**1962**; rev 1970), *The Depths* (**1963**), *The Sleep* (**1964**), *The Inferno* (**1965**), *The Famine* (**1967**), *The Blight* (**1968**), *The Oasis* (**1969**), *The Smog* (**1970**), *The Insulators* (**1972**), *The Voiceless Ones* (**1973**), *The Thunder-Maker* (**1976**) and *The Whirlwind* (**1979**). [JE]

See also: CRIME AND PUNISHMENT.

CREATURE FROM ANOTHER WORLD, THE ◊ *The* TROLLENBERG TERROR.

CREATURE FROM THE BLACK LAGOON, THE Film (1954). Universal. Dir Jack ARNOLD, starring Richard Carlson, Julia Adams, Richard Denning. Screenplay Harry Essex, Arthur Ross, from a story by Maurice Zimm. 3-D. 79 mins. B/w.

A humanoid creature with gills successfully resists attempts by three scientists – attracted to the area by the discovery of a fossilized hand with fins – to take him from his native lagoon in the upper Amazon. One (Denning) is ready to kill it; another (Carlson) hopes to keep it alive. The Gill-Man – lumbering on land but remarkably graceful in the underwater sequences – became one of the icons of Universal's MONSTER MOVIES. Shot in 3-D, the film is richly atmospheric despite its routine script. It became an archetype of the genre through the bizarre eroticism of the Creature's fascination with the third scientist (Adams), especially in the balletic sequence where he swims unseen beneath her in a sensuous mime of intercourse. In some respects Steven SPIELBERG's successful *Jaws* (1975) was a remake of *TCFTBL*. The film had two sequels: REVENGE OF THE CREATURE (1954) and *The* CREATURE WALKS AMONG US (1956).

The novelization is *Creature from the Black Lagoon* * (1954) by Vargo Statten (◊ John Russell FEARN). [PN/JB]

CREATURE FROM THE HAUNTED SEA ◊ Roger CORMAN.

CREATURE WALKS AMONG US, THE Film (1956). Universal. Dir John Sherwood, starring Jeff Morrow, Rex Reason, Leigh Snowden. Screenplay Arthur Ross. 78 mins. B/w.

This is the second, inferior sequel to *The* CREATURE FROM THE BLACK LAGOON (1954) – the first being REVENGE OF THE CREATURE (1954); it was not shot in 3-D, and had a new director. Here the Creature is transformed by fire into a land monster, complete with lungs (and, later, clothes), thereby depriving him of precisely the qualities that made him popular. There is a ludicrous plot about an exploitative scientist (Morrow) making money out of the space programme by building up the Creature's red corpuscles and thus (!) altering his gene structure. [PN/JB]

CREDITS In sf TERMINOLOGY, a credit is a unit of MONEY. Credits are used widely in tales of the future. [PN]

CREEPING UNKNOWN, THE ◊ *The* QUATERMASS XPERIMENT.

CRICHTON, MICHAEL (1942-) US writer and film director; he graduated with an MD from Harvard Medical School. He began publishing sf under the pseudonym John Lange with *Drug of Choice* (1968). Most of the Lange books are thrillers, *A Case of Need* (1968) winning an Edgar Award for Best Mystery Novel of the year; some, such as *Binary* (1972) and *Zero Cool* (1973), make perfunctory use of sf devices in a way typical of the modern post-James-Bond thriller. *Binary* was filmed for tv in MC's directorial début as PURSUIT (1972). Of greater interest are the novels he has written under his own name, many of which are sf or fantasy, beginning with *The Andromeda Strain* (1969), an immediate bestseller soon filmed as *The* ANDROMEDA STRAIN (1971), in which microscopic spores from space attack the US West (◊ DISASTER). MC's medical background is evident in much of his work (◊ MEDICINE). *The Terminal Man* (1972) speculates fascinatingly on the morality and effects of electronic brain implants as a control device, and was the basis of the film *The* TERMINAL MAN (1974), dir Mike Hodges. *Eaters of the Dead* (1976) recounts a savage conflict between Vikings and strange Neolithic people; it is in fact a retelling of the *Beowulf* legend. *Congo* (1980) is a LOST-WORLD story set in Africa, and reads like updated H. Rider HAGGARD. *Sphere* (1987) is an UNDER-THE-SEA thriller about the discovery of a long-sunken spacecraft, anticipating *The* ABYSS (1989). *Jurassic Park* (1990) is a return to the theme of WESTWORLD (discussed below): it effectively argues the risks inherent in uncontrolled GENETIC ENGINEERING, "done in secret, and in haste, and for profit", though the plot itself – dinosaurs reconstituted from genetic scraps cause havoc in the theme park they have been created to stock – is little more than a McGUFFIN; the novel has been optioned for filming by Steven SPIELBERG. All of these novels read a little like film treatments.

After *Pursuit*, MC determined to exercise artistic control over screen adaptations of his work and though he did not do so in the case of *The Terminal Man*, he both scripted and directed WESTWORLD (1973), an intelligent and cleverly commercial film about a ROBOT-manned reconstruction of the Old West (*see also* LEISURE) that falls apart at the seams when a robot gunslinger runs amuck; the book version by MC was *Westworld* (**1974**). He scored his biggest commercial hit as a director with COMA (1978), based on Robin COOK's marginally sf novel, a further exploration of MC's technophobic, PARANOID vision, drawing on his medical background for a conspiracy thriller about a high-tech organ-transplant business that draws its raw material from hospital beds. After a meticulous and underrated period re-creation, *The Great Train Robbery* (1979; vt *The First Great Train Robbery*), adapted from his own novel – not sf – of the same title, MC has rather lost ground as a director, with LOOKER (1981) and RUNAWAY (1984) both failing at the box-office. However, these films, for all their plot failings, are interesting explorations of his fascination with and distrust of an increasingly mechanized society. *Looker* deals with image-generation technology, while *Runaway* casts Tom Selleck as a future policeman whose speciality is tackling dangerously malfunctional household robots. *Physical Evidence* (1989), a non-sf thriller, is his least interesting or personal film to date.

An efficient and intelligent writer and director, MC is capable of producing remarkable work. [JC/PN/KN]
See also: APES AND CAVEMEN (IN THE HUMAN WORLD); CINEMA; HORROR IN SF; MYTHOLOGY; VILLAINS.

CRICHTON, NEIL (?   -   ) Canadian photographer and writer in whose sf novel, *Rerun* (**1976**), a man from 1990 goes back 15 years into his own life of the mid-1970s but does not ultimately profit from his foreknowledge.   [JC]

CRIME AND PUNISHMENT Genre fiction concerned with crime may be roughly divided into detections and thrillers. The former are problem stories; the latter exploit the melodramatic potential of the conflicts inherent in criminal deviation.

Detective stories depend very heavily on ingenuity and generally require very fine distinctions between what is possible and what is not. It is not easy to combine sf and the detective story because in sf the boundary between the possible and the impossible is so flexible, but futuristic detective stories can work, given a sufficiently rigid set of ground rules; thus Isaac ASIMOV was able to create intriguing detections based on the restrictions of his three laws of robotics, most notably *The Naked Sun* (**1957**), and Randall GARRETT was able to write his ingenious **Lord D'Arcy** stories about an ALTERNATE-WORLD detective who must use his powers of ratiocination to solve crimes in which rigorously defined magical laws feature, often being used forensically. There was also a subgenre of early detective stories featuring "scientific detectives" armed not only with the scientific methods of thought made famous by Sherlock Holmes but also with the equipment and arcane knowledge of advanced science; notable works in this vein include *The Achievements of Luther Trant* (coll 1910) by Edwin BALMER and William MacHarg and the many **Craig Kennedy** adventures chronicled by

Arthur B. REEVE, including *The Poisoned Pen* (coll **1911**) and *The Dream Doctor* (fixup **1914**). Hugo GERNSBACK's short-lived SCIENTIFIC DETECTIVE MONTHLY published fiction of this sort, but the speculative aspects of the stories are understandably tentative.

Crime is much more commonly and effectively exploited in sf for its melodramatic potential; the imaginative freedom of sf allows both criminals and crime-fighters to become exotic, and their schemes grandiose, a pattern which underlies Jules VERNE's great creations: Captain Nemo, who features in *Vingt mille lieues sous les mers* (**1870**; trans as *Twenty Thousand Leagues under the Seas* **1872** UK) and its sequel *L'île mystérieuse* (**1874-5**; trans as *The Mysterious Island* **1875** UK); and Robur the Conqueror, who features in *Robur le conquérant* (**1886**; trans as *The Clipper of the Clouds* **1887** UK; vt *Robur the Conqueror* **1887** US) and its sequel *Maître du monde* (**1904**; trans anon as *Master of the World* **1914** UK). PULP-MAGAZINE sf grew up alongside increasingly exotic detective pulps which featured the prototypes of the SUPERHEROES who would ultimately come into their own in COMIC books, most notably DOC SAVAGE. In the early days of scientific romance the scientific supercriminal (often embittered by the world's failure to recognize and reward his genius) was a common character, frequently holding the world (or large parts of it) to ransom. Robert CROMIE's *The Crack of Doom* (**1895**) and Fred T. JANE's *The Violet Flame* (**1899**) feature early examples of world-threatening superscientists. There was a glut of such stories in the 1930s, including *Power* (**1931**) by S. Fowler WRIGHT, *The One Sane Man* (**1934**) by Francis BEEDING and *I'll Blackmail the World* (**1935**) by S. Andrew WOOD. Few apocalyptic threats were fully carried out in such novels, although Neil BELL's *The Lord of Life* (**1933**) is a flamboyant exception. (The tradition is kept alive today by, among others, the plots of the many **James Bond** movies.) Disenchantment with the state of the world allowed many writers of the 1930s to sympathize with world-blackmailers whose demands were humanitarian; C.S. FORESTER's *The Peacemaker* (**1934**) is a notable example, and C.J. Cutcliffe HYNE's *Man's Understanding* (coll **1933**) includes two black comedies suggesting that even the most destructive and unreasonable mad SCIENTIST would be no worse than the actual rulers of the world. Later examples include the atom-bomb story *The Maniac's Dream* (**1946**) by F. Horace ROSE and the **Dr Palfrey** novels by John CREASEY.

Among the early GENRE-SF writers to make use of the stereotyped supercriminal was Murray LEINSTER, whose many versions of it include "A Thousand Degrees Below Zero" (1919), "Darkness on Fifth Avenue" (1929), "The Racketeer Ray" (1932) and "The Earth-Shaker" (1933). John W. CAMPBELL Jr used the formula in "Piracy Preferred" (1930), but he armed his heroes as well as his villain (who reformed and joined the heroes for several sequels). The game of interplanetary super-cops vs super-robbers was pioneered by Edmond HAMILTON in the **Interstellar**

Patrol stories, some of which were reprinted in *Outside the Universe* (1929; **1964**) and *Crashing Suns* (1928-30; coll **1965**), and extravagantly carried forward by E.E. "Doc" SMITH in the **Skylark** series and *Spacehounds of IPC* (1934; **1947**). The conflict in the **Skylark of Space** books, between Richard Seaton and the impressively villainous Blackie DuQuesne, was vigorously sustained; and the later **Lensmen** series (in book form **1948-54**), featured perhaps the most famous genre-sf criminal organization of all: the Eddorian-run interstellar cartel known as Boskone.

Pulp sf writers imagined that future crime would follow much the same pattern as crime today, although they were happy to imagine that romantic crimes like piracy might come back into fashion in outer space – or even in time, as in Ross ROCKLYNNE's "Pirates of the Time Trail" (1943). Retribution, too, tended to follow well established tracks, although one or two writers used sealed time-loops and other gimmicks to design punishments to fit particular crimes; Lester DEL REY's "My Name is Legion" (1942) suggests an appropriate fate for Hitler. One magazine story of the 1940s which attempts to make a significant statement about deviancy and penology is Robert A. HEINLEIN's "Coventry" (1940), which imagines a curious kind of exile, then proceeds to develop one of the most annoying of sf CLICHÉS: the idea that selfish deviants might be harassed as a kind of test to prove their suitability for recruitment into the social élite of a stable society.

When sf writers took to building all kinds of eccentric totalitarian societies for their future scenarios in the 1940s and 1950s, the rectitude of deviancy became a much more open question. As forms of conformity became stranger, so did forms of nonconformity. In Fritz LEIBER's *Gather, Darkness!* (1943; **1950**) the establishment's superscience masquerades as RELIGION, leading the rebels to disguise their own superscience as witchcraft. More sophisticated studies of odd forms of deviancy in warped societies include Wyman GUIN's "Beyond Bedlam" (1951), whose heroine rebels against the obligation to share tenancy of her body with her split personality's *alter ego*, Ray BRADBURY's *Fahrenheit 451* (**1953**), whose meek rebels learn books by heart to save them from would-be burners, and Philip José FARMER's *Dayworld* (**1985**) and its sequels, in which "daybreakers" exceed their allotted active time in an overcrowded world.

In the 1950s, new ideas regarding the treatment of deviants began to appear in some profusion. In "Two-Handed Engine" (1955), by Henry KUTTNER and C.L. MOORE, criminals are attended by robot "furies" to monitor their actions and symbolize their guilt. In Damon KNIGHT's "The Country of the Kind" (1956) criminals are outcast, free to do as they will but utterly lonely – an idea explored with greater intensity in Robert SILVERBERG's "To See the Invisible Man" (1963). Robert SHECKLEY's *The Status Civilization* (**1960**) is a satirical extrapolation of the penal-colony theme, imagining the kind of society which criminals might establish in reaction against the one which exiles them. The notion of the prison colony is taken to a terrible extreme in Cordwainer SMITH's "A Planet Named Shayol" (1961), in which criminals are made to grow extra limbs and organs for harvesting and use in transplants. A much more humane view of the issues involved in crime and punishment is featured in Alfred BESTER's classic sf novel based on Fyodor Dostoyevsky's *Crime and Punishment* (**1866**), *The Demolished Man* (**1953**), in which the obsessed villain ultimately fails to avoid detection by a telepathic policeman, but finds the prospect of punitive "demolition" less terrible than its name implies. Bester's "Fondly Fahrenheit" (1954) is another forceful study in homicidal psychology. New fashions in the real-world treatment of prisoners – especially the notion of "brainwashing" – were extensively featured in borderline-sf thrillers, and taken to surreal lengths in the tv series *The* PRISONER, whose theme was sensitively novelized by Thomas M. DISCH in *The Prisoner* * (**1969**).

Exotic police forces were featured in heroic roles in many sf stories and series in the 1950s. An alien policeman pursues a criminal to Earth in *Needle* (**1950**) by Hal CLEMENT, requiring to inhabit the body of an earthly host in order to do so. Time police – patrolling and protecting history – became commonplace, as in *The End of Eternity* (**1955**) by Isaac Asimov, *Guardians of Time* (1955-60; fixup **1960**) by Poul ANDERSON, and H. Beam PIPER's **Paratime Police** series. Asimov's first sf detective story, *The Caves of Steel* (**1954**), was followed a few years later by the first murder mystery in which Earth is the corpse: Poul Anderson's *After Doomsday* (**1962**). Realistic futuristic police-procedural stories were pioneered by Rick RAPHAEL in an effective series of stories dealing with road-traffic law enforcement in the near future, *Code Three* (fixup **1966**), and were carried forward by such novels as Lee KILLOUGH's *The Doppelganger Gambit* (**1979**), but law enforcers of a rather less conventional kind have understandably remained dominant. Joe Clifford FAUST's *A Death of Honour* (**1987**) imagines that the 21st-century police might be simply too busy to investigate a murder. The vast majority of the novels of Ron GOULART feature crime and detectives in some quirky fashion or other; most notable among them are the **Chameleon Corps** books. (John E. STITH is another writer who mixes HUMOUR, crime and sf, but with less accent on the humour than Goulart.) Although the world of sf crime has remained male-dominated, female detectives have made significant appearances in Rosel George BROWN's *Sibyl Sue Blue* (**1966**; vt *Galactic Sibyl Sue Blue*) and the **St Cyr Interplanetary Detective** series begun by Ian WALLACE in *Deathstar Voyage* (**1969**). SUPERHERO crime-fighters made relatively little impact in written sf until the advent of George R.R. MARTIN's SHARED-WORLD anthology series begun with *Wild Cards* (anth **1986**), but an interesting precursor was featured in Doris PISERCHIA's *Mister Justice* **1973**); *Temps* (anth **1991**), "created by" Neil GAIMAN and Alex Stewart, was the first of a series of shared-world anthologies featuring the crime-fighting escapades of part-time and/or limited-ability superheroes.

A more romantic view of crime is preserved by picaresque sf stories. Although muted for a long time by editorial TABOOS, a considerable body of sf makes heroes of social outsiders and deviants. An early example is Charles L. HARNESS's *Flight into Yesterday* (1949; **1953**; vt *The Paradox Men*), and much of Harness's work features similar heroic outsiders, who tend to be artists when they are not rogues, and are often both. Much of the work of Jack VANCE falls into a similar category. Far less romantic is the eponymous antihero of Harry HARRISON's *The Stainless Steel Rat* (1957-60; fixup **1961**) and its sequels. Philip José Farmer wrote a series featuring **John Carmody**, a criminal who reformed to become a priest, the most notable being *Night of Light* (**1966**). As the taboos eased there appeared criminal heroes who remained both unrepentant and charismatic, including the protagonist of Roger ZELAZNY's *Jack of Shadows* (**1971**) and the narrator of Samuel R. DELANY's "Time Considered as a Helix of Semi-Precious Stones" (1968); Delany is another writer who almost invariably uses miscreant artists as heroes. The most extravagant example of a charismatic criminal in sf is probably the protagonist of Mike RESNICK's *Santiago* (**1986**), who is pursued across the Galaxy by assorted exotic bounty-hunters, most of whom are certainly no better than he turns out to be.

The relativity of crime and the idea of evil in societies which have very different values is widely featured. Earnest variants can be found in such stories as "The Sharing of Flesh" (1968) by Poul Anderson and *Speaker for the Dead* (**1986**) by Orson Scott CARD, in which alien societies license or compel acts which seem to us utterly horrific. Robert Sheckley often addresses the question ironically, as in "Watchbird" (1953), a moral fable about a mechanical law-enforcer's tendency to exceed its brief, and "The Monsters" (1953), which features an alien society in which wife-murder is a moral act. The blackest sf comedy in this vein is probably Piers ANTHONY's "On the Uses of Torture" (1981).

Despite the welter of criminal activity in sf there are very few new crimes, although such DYSTOPIAS as Yegevny ZAMIATIN's *My* (written 1920; trans as *We* **1924**) and George ORWELL's *Nineteen Eighty-four* (**1949**) have taken the rooting-out of political deviance to new extremes in making "thoughtcrimes" detectable and remediable. Crimes of nonconformity often take bizarre forms, as in such J.G. BALLARD stories as "Billenium" (1961), in which the existence of an empty room is wickedly but futilely concealed, and "Chronopolis" (1960), in which the hero illegally winds clocks. Tampering with history is a crime which features only in sf – matched by the singularly appropriate punishment of historical erasure in Robert Silverberg's *Up the Line* (**1969**) – but even this

is no more than an extreme of subversive activity. A more original crime is committed by the protagonist of Piers Anthony's *Chthon* (**1967**), although the extremely nasty prison colony to which he is condemned for it is ordinary in kind. The same situation pertains in the design of punishments, and has done ever since Arthur Conan DOYLE's "The Los Amigos Fiasco" (1892), which anticipated the use of the world's first electric chair but made the consequences of its use exaggeratedly melodramatic. Numerous sf stories have anticipated the use of "electronic tagging", although usually the tags are capable of administering on-the-spot punishment. An early example (although here the "tags" are created by mental conditioning) is featured in "The Analogues" (1952) by Damon Knight; others are in *The Reefs of Space* (**1964**) by Frederik POHL and Jack WILLIAMSON and *The Ring* (**1968**) by Piers Anthony and Robert E. MARGROFF. When the merits of punitive, retributive and rehabilitative theories of penology are compared in sf, the extremism of plausible examples often makes the argument starkly dramatic; examples of Swiftian "modest proposals" abound. An interesting polemical work on penological theory is John J. MCGUIRE's "Take the Reason Prisoner" (1963), and a macabre combination of the punitive and retributive theories is featured in those of Larry NIVEN's stories in which the crime of "organlegging" co-exists with a new penal code whereby criminals are broken up for bodily spare parts. Several of Niven's stories on these lines are among the best examples of the sf detective story; some are collected in *The Long ARM of Gil Hamilton* (coll **1976**).

Since Sherlock Holmes fell into the public domain he has been a popular character in sf stories, appearing in key roles in *Morlock Night* (**1979**) by K.W. JETER, *Sherlock Holmes' War of the Worlds* (**1975**) by Manly Wade and Wade WELLMAN, *Dr Jekyll and Mr Holmes* (**1979**) by Loren D. Estleman and *Time for Sherlock Holmes* (**1983**) by David DVORKIN. Another Victorian figure, from the opposite end of the moral spectrum, who has exerted a similar fascination upon modern writers is the prototypical serial killer Jack the Ripper; several of the stories in the centenary anthology *Ripper!* (anth **1988**; vt *Jack the Ripper* UK) ed Susan CASPER and Gardner DOZOIS are sf.

Theme anthologies concerned with sf crime stories include *Space Police* (anth **1956**) ed Andre NORTON; *Space, Time and Crime* (anth **1964**) ed Miriam Allen DeFORD; and *Computer Crimes and Capers* (anth **1985**) ed Isaac Asimov, Martin H. GREENBERG and Charles G. WAUGH. [BS]

See also: SOCIOLOGY; UTOPIAS.

CRIMES OF THE FUTURE Film (1970). Emergent Films. Prod, dir, written and photographed David CRONENBERG, starring Ronald Mlodzik, Tania Zolty, Jon Lidolt, Jack Messinger. 70 mins. Colour.

This cheaply made, inventive Canadian film, something between an underground and a commercial movie, is chiefly of interest as ushering in – along with *Stereo* (1969) – Cronenberg's distinguished, eccentric and (according to some) disgusting career in sf cinema. With hindsight, we can see many Cronenberg strategies and themes here in embryo: deliberately tasteless SATIRE, the moral corruption of society, human metamorphosis created by irresponsible TECHNOLOGY, sexual metaphor at the heart of the argument, and the contrast of sterile settings with ravages and mutations of the flesh. The film is set in a NEAR FUTURE where humans are devolving (◊ DEVOLUTION) and all women of child-bearing age have been killed by an epidemic spread through a cosmetics additive created by a mad dermatologist (in the House of Skin), thus making procreative pedophilia a likely "crime of the future" and putting a 5-year-old girl (Zolty) at the centre of the barely comprehensible plot.   [PN]

CRIME ZONE ◊ Roger CORMAN.

CRISP, FRANK R(OBSON) (1915-   ) UK writer, at one time in the Merchant Navy. His sf novels, *The Ape of London* (**1959**) and *The Night Callers* (**1960**), are routine adventures deploying thriller and horror elements; their sf displacement is inconsiderable. The latter, involving an alien INVASION, was filmed as *The* NIGHT CALLER (1965).   [JC]

See also: ASTRONOMY; PARASITISM AND SYMBIOSIS.

CRISPIN, A(NN) C(AROL) (1950-   ) US writer who was first known as a competent author of ties, including three for the **Star Trek** enterprise – *Yesterday's Son* ✳ (**1983**) and its direct sequel *Time for Yesterday* ✳ (**1988**), along with *Star Trek, The Next Generation #13: The Eyes of the Beholder* ✳ (**1990**) – and three for the **"V"** sequence – *"V"* ✳ (**1984**), *East Coast Crisis* ✳ (**1984**) with Howard WEINSTEIN and *Death Tide* ✳ (**1985**) with Deborah A. Marshall (◊ "V"). She also collaborated with Andre NORTON on a **Witch World** novel, *Gryphon's Eyrie* (**1984**), before embarking on her first independent work of significance, the **StarBridge** sequence for older children: *StarBridge* (**1989**), *Silent Dances* (**1990**) with Kathleen O'MALLEY and *Shadow World* (**1991**) with Jannean (L.) Elliott. The first volume of the series (projected to contain at least 5 vols) follows the exploits of an extremely bright teenaged girl who becomes involved in problems of galactic scope, and participates in the founding of an Academy for youngsters like herself. The second, rather more interestingly, puts a deaf Academy member of Native American background on an ominous planet where only she can read the signs of ALIEN intelligence. In the third, an alienated male Academy member finds, in a short-lived alien race, challenges that are precisely adapted to his needs. Through these well planned if not strikingly original tales ACC has demonstrated a consistent professionalism about her trade, and considerable generosity about giving good value.   [JC]

CRISPIN, EDMUND Pseudonym for his literary work of UK composer, writer and editor Robert Bruce Montgomery (1921-1978), who remains best known for his nine **Gervase Fen** detective novels. He also reviewed crime fiction for the *Sunday Times* and, as a composer, under his real name wrote the music for many UK films of the 1950s and 1960s, including several of the **Carry On** series. EC did not write sf, but his work as an sf anthologist was of great influence. When *Best SF* (anth **1955**) appeared it was unique in several ways: its editor was a respected literary figure; its publisher (Faber & Faber) was a prestigious one; and it made no apologies or excuses for presenting sf as a legitimate form of writing. Moreover, EC's selection of stories showed him to be thoroughly familiar with sf in both magazine and book form, and his introductions to this and succeeding volumes were informed and illuminating. *Best SF* was followed by *Best SF Two* (anth **1956**), *Three* (anth **1958**), *Four* (anth **1961**), *Five* (anth **1963**), *Six* (anth **1966**) and *Seven* (anth **1970**). It would be difficult to exaggerate the importance of the early volumes in this series in establishing sf in the UK as a respectable branch of literature. EC also edited two sf ANTHOLOGIES for schools, *The Stars and Under* (anth **1968**) and *Outwards from Earth* (anth **1974**), as well as *Best Tales of Terror* (anth **1962**) and *Best Tales of Terror Two* (anth **1965**).   [MJE]

See also: BRITISH SCIENCE FICTION ASSOCIATION; LONGEVITY (IN WRITERS AND PUBLICATIONS); MUSIC.

CRISTABEL Pseudonym of US nurse, professor of nursing, and author Christine Elizabeth Abrahamsen (1916-   ), who wrote at least one Gothic as Kathleen Westcott. She began publishing sf with the florid **Veltakin** sequence of sf adventures: *Manalacor of Veltakin* (**1970**) and *The Cruachan and the Killane* (**1970**). Her singletons were *The Mortal Immortals* (**1971**) and *The Golden Olive* (**1972**). All are written in a style that crosses the romance genre with boys' fiction. [PN/JC]

CRITICAL AND HISTORICAL WORKS ABOUT SF This entry restricts itself to works which generalize about sf, and only in passing mentions books or articles about specific authors or themes (*for which see relevant entries*).

The range and sophistication of sf studies have expanded greatly. Before 1970 very little useful material was available, but since then, and especially during the 1980s, the publication of secondary materials on sf has become an industry. The first work of criticism devoted to US sf is *Hammer and Tongs* (coll **1937** chap) by Clyde F. Beck (?   -1985), which collects still-readable essays from a fanzine, *The Science Fiction Critic*; the first important study, *Pilgrims through Space and Time* (**1947**), by J.O. BAILEY, is historical and thematic, dealing mostly with work published decades previously; value judgments are almost absent, and trivia are discussed alongside works of lasting interest. Despite its limitations, this was a valuable pioneering work. The PILGRIM AWARD for excellence in sf studies was named after it.

Bailey was an academic, but for the next several decades most books about sf were written by fans rather than academic critics. While this meant that their scholarly and critical procedures were often eccentric, and sometimes of indifferent quality, it also introduced considerable vigour into the early days of debate about sf, along with a willingness to plunge into areas of research (ephemeral publications – magazines and FANZINES – as well as books, along with the recording of reminiscences by authors, editors and publishers) avoided by academia; such knowledge of the HISTORY OF SF as is now available to us is very much a product of their initial work. Research is still shallow in many areas of sf's past, and no consensus history yet exists.

The next serious study after Bailey's was *New Maps of Hell* (**1960** US) by Kingsley AMIS, a celebrated novelist with an academic background but, so far as sf was concerned, a fan. Brief and unscholarly, it is nevertheless witty, critical and suggestive; Amis regarded the essential aspects of modern sf as satirical and dystopian (◊ DYSTOPIAS; SATIRE). Unlike Bailey, he took most of his examples from contemporary GENRE SF. Less literary in their approach, and more sober though passionate in their way, were the historical studies of sf by Sam MOSKOWITZ, which, while adopting simplistic critical criteria and not always accurate in detail, were nevertheless important in the huge amount of research they codified for the first time, especially regarding sf in early magazines, but going well beyond that. Three collections of his essays which are often taken to be models of fan scholarship are *Explorers of the Infinite* (coll **1963**), *Seekers of Tomorrow* (coll **1966**) and *Strange Horizons* (coll **1976**) also of note are his *Science Fiction by Gaslight: A History and Anthology of Science Fiction in the Popular Magazines 1891-1911* (anth **1968**) and *Under the Moons of Mars: A History and Anthology of "The Scientific Romance" in the Munsey Magazines, 1912-1920* (anth **1970**), with their long, informative introductions.

Two well known writers of sf, Damon KNIGHT and James BLISH, often took time out to write shrewd, well informed criticism, the latter under the pseudonym William Atheling Jr. Much of Knight's critical work was collected in *In Search of Wonder* (coll **1956**; exp 1967) and of Atheling's in *The Issue at Hand* (coll **1964**) and *More Issues at Hand* (coll **1970**). These books were published by ADVENT: PUBLISHERS, a SMALL PRESS specifically set up to publish books about sf by fan scholars. It was with Knight and Blish that some sort of critical consensus began to emerge about what constituted sf and who were its most influential writers. The first of three critical symposia ed Reginald BRETNOR, also featuring the critical views of sf writers themselves, appeared very early: *Modern Science Fiction: Its Meaning and its Future* (anth **1953**; rev 1979). It was followed by his *Science Fiction, Today and Tomorrow* (anth **1974**) and *The Craft of Science Fiction* (anth **1976**).

The cautious interest being shown in sf by the US academic world bore its first fruits in 1959, in the shape of the critical journal EXTRAPOLATION. For many years this was stencilled, not printed, which suggested that the financial support it was receiving from academia at large was small; nevertheless it lived on. Two further academic magazines about sf followed, both (in different ways) a little livelier: FOUNDATION: THE REVIEW OF SCIENCE FICTION in the UK (1972) and SCIENCE-FICTION STUDIES in the USA (1973). The former – as much fannish as academic – emphasized reviews and critical and sociological studies of contemporary and post-WWII sf; the latter – more strictly academic – concentrated on writers of sf's past plus only the more academically acceptable of the present, with good coverage of European sf and some interesting and, to many, unexpected Marxist criticism. A newcomer has been JOURNAL OF THE FANTASTIC IN THE ARTS (1988).

Some of the best critical writing about sf has appeared in these journals, and also in a great many FANZINES. Unfortunately, fanzines tend to be produced cheaply (and as a result often disintegrate rapidly) and have low circulations; back copies are usually therefore extremely difficult to obtain. Some of the more interesting critical fanzines and SEMIPRO-ZINES from the 1940s through the 1980s were (and in many cases still are) ALGOL, AUSTRALIAN SCIENCE FICTION REVIEW, FANTASY COMMENTATOR, FANTASY NEWS-LETTER, FANTASY REVIEW, JANUS/AURORA, LOCUS, LUNA MONTHLY, NEW YORK REVIEW OF SCIENCE FICTION, QUAR-BER MERKUR, RIVERSIDE QUARTERLY, SCIENCE FICTION & FANTASY BOOK REVIEW, SF COMMENTARY, SCIENCE FICTION EYE, SCIENCE FICTION REVIEW, SCIENCE FICTION TIMES, SFRA NEWSLETTER, SPECULATION, THRUST, VECTOR and WARHOON. The professional sf magazines, too, have regularly published sf criticism, that of *FSF* in particular often being of a high quality, as has been (beginning much later) that of INTERZONE.

By the 1970s a large body of sf criticism had been built up, though much of it was and is difficult to get hold of. The earlier notion that sf should be judged by criteria different from those normally applied to conventional literature began steadily to lose ground in the 1970s to the view that sf is strong enough to be gauged by the same standards that prevail elsewhere in literary criticism. Very naturally, however, the literary analysis of sf tends to this day to be argued thematically and structurally, and to eschew a criticism grounded in concepts of psychological realism on the one hand or metaphorical power on the other. Although this is inevitable, mimetic realism and good characterization being qualities somewhat marginalized by the very nature of sf, it does help explain why even now sf criticism has not generally developed a vocabulary enabling judgmental distinctions to be well made; that is, when explaining why some books and stories are worse than others (an explanation that sf criticism feels called upon to make more seldom than is healthy), it does not usually do the job with much conviction.

The trickle of sf criticism in book form became a small spate around the mid-1970s and something of a torrent later on, but already by 1974 a number of new books had appeared, including studies by Sam

J. LUNDWALL and Donald A. WOLLHEIM in the USA. A major tributary joined the river with *Billion Year Spree* (**1973**) by Brian W. ALDISS; Aldiss later revised and updated this work with David WINGROVE as *Trillion Year Spree* (**1986**), a version that won them both a HUGO. The book is idiosyncratic in some respects, with genuine scholarship of an autodidact kind, although not remotely academic. Many reviewers observed that, in the earlier version of the book, Aldiss's account of the post-WWII period was hurried and not very informative, but this remains an important book, especially in the literary and cultural context it gives for sf ever since the days of Mary SHELLEY, who is Aldiss's candidate for the position of the first *bona fide* sf writer. His cheerful, informal raconteur's tone enlivens without cheapening his many serious points, and comes as a relief after the ponderousness of some previous studies of sf and the defensive fannish enthusiasm of others.

The next important book on sf for the general reader was also by a professional writer from the genre: James E. GUNN's *Alternate Worlds: The Illustrated History of Science Fiction* (**1975**), a balanced and intelligent survey (although coverage of later writers tends to be confined to long lists) which strongly emphasizes the Campbellian tradition of magazine sf in the USA. This book was part of a sudden rush of handsome, illustrated books about sf, some of which are listed under ILLUSTRATION.

A collection of essays by Alexei and Cory PANSHIN, *SF in Dimension* (coll **1976**), argued a coherent if controversial viewpoint. Alexei Panshin had earlier published an interesting study of Robert A. HEINLEIN, and he and his wife would later publish *The World Beyond the Hill: Science Fiction and the Quest for Transcendence* (**1989**), a long book full of incidental insights but whose overall thesis is open to argument. It elicited a devastating review from John CLUTE, always a pungent critic of sf, in *New York Review of Science Fiction* (July 1991), which in turn prompted a correspondence whose overall implication may be that the US-centred, magazine-centred, somewhat inbred and sentimental view of the development of the genre which had dominated sf historians for decades was now being rejected by a new generation of sf critics and scholars. Clute's own book of sf criticism, *Strokes: Essays and Reviews 1966-1986* (coll **1988** US), was an example of the development of a wider perspective on sf, dealing as it does with sf's concerns in terms of their metaphoric resonance – their subtexts – as well as their literal meaning. A sometimes thuddingly literal-minded reading of sf themes, from robots to the colonization of other worlds, had characterized many of the books and articles published on sf prior to the 1980s.

Numerous sf writers apart from those already mentioned have also written well informed and lively sf criticism and essays in sf scholarship; many of these, like Thomas M. DISCH, Gardner DOZOIS, Joanna RUSS, Robert SILVERBERG and Ian WATSON, have not yet had their critical pieces collected in book form. Among those who have are: Algis BUDRYS, with *Benchmarks: Galaxy Bookshelf* (coll **1985**); Samuel R. DELANY, with *The Jewel-Hinged Jaw: Notes on the Language of Science Fiction* (**1977**) and *Starboard Wine: More Notes on the Language of Science Fiction* (coll **1984**), whose structuralist and sometimes POSTMODERNIST criticism is dense and difficult, irritating and interesting; Ursula K. LE GUIN, with *The Language of the Night: Essays on Fantasy and Science Fiction* (coll **1979**; rev 1989 UK); Barry N. MALZBERG, whose *The Engines of the Night: Science Fiction in the Eighties* (**1982**) may not have had the attention it deserves; Norman SPINRAD, with *Science Fiction in the Real World* (coll **1990**), which collects many of his critical columns from ISAAC ASIMOV'S SCIENCE FICTION MAGAZINE; and Brian M. STABLEFORD, whose several well researched books on the subject, including *Scientific Romance in Britain 1890-1950* (**1985**), have done much to dispel the view that sf was primarily a product of PULP MAGAZINES and specialist SF MAGAZINES.

A phenomenon largely of the 1980s was the production of large, multi-author reference works containing critical assessments of sf, of which one of the earliest was the first edition of this encyclopedia (**1979**). The first edition of Neil BARRON's *Anatomy of Wonder: A Critical Guide to Science Fiction* (**1976**; rev 1981; rev 1987) was earlier still, and the book remains one of the best and most accessible critical guides. Others include: the desperately uneven 5-vol *Survey of Science Fiction Literature* (anth **1979**) ed Frank N. Magill, though the actual editing and organization was largely the work of associate editor Keith NEILSON; the largely excellent *Science Fiction Writers: Critical Studies of the Major Authors from the Early Nineteenth Century to the Present Day* (anth **1982**) ed E.F. BLEILER; the 2-vol *Twentieth-Century American Science-Fiction Writers* (anth **1981**) ed David Cowart and Thomas L. Wymer; and *Twentieth-Century Science-Fiction Writers* (anth **1981**; rev 1986; rev 1991) first two edns ed Curtis C. SMITH, with its useful essays badly compromised by poor presentation of bibliographical data. Most of these books are reference works from specialist publishers at prices that may deter lay sf readers, but they are readily located in academic libraries.

None of these books is purely academic in its authorship, but in most of them many of the essays are by academic specialists – for honourable reasons but also, naturally enough, because the publish-or-perish syndrome will always ensure academic contributors willing to work for little or nothing – and it is in the field of academic books on sf that the largest expansion of book publishing on sf has taken place, especially in the 1980s. Long before that there were, aside from Bailey's, two other important early works of academic sf scholarship: *The Imaginary Voyage in Prose Fiction: A History of its Criticism and a Guide for its Study, with an Annotated Check List of 215 Imaginary Voyages from 1700 to 1800* (**1941**) by Philip Babcock

GOVE, and *Voyages to the Moon* (**1948**) by Marjorie Hope NICOLSON. After a long gap, the next academic works of importance (apart from studies of single authors such as of H.G. WELLS and Aldous HUXLEY) were *Voices Prophesying War 1763-1984* (**1966**) by I.F. CLARKE, who followed this work with other studies of sf, and *Yesterday's Tomorrows* (**1968**) by W.H.G. ARMYTAGE. Running concurrently with all these publications, and beginning much earlier, have been the many books on literary UTOPIAS.

Next in the academic line came *Into the Unknown: The Evolution of Science Fiction from Francis Godwin to H.G. Wells* (**1970**) by Robert M. PHILMUS. In the 1970s Darko SUVIN came to the fore as an influential academic critic of sf, his earliest full-scale book being first published in French: *Pour une poétique de la science-fiction* (**1977** Canada; exp in English as *Metamorphoses of Science Fiction: On the Poetics and History of a Literary Genre* **1979** US). Two important later books by Suvin are *Victorian Science Fiction in the U.K.: The Discourses of Knowledge and of Power* (**1983** US) and *Positions and Presuppositions in Science Fiction* (coll **1988** US).

After 1974 the pace of academic publishing increased. The most important studies of the mid-1970s were *New Worlds for Old* (**1974**) by David KETTERER, *Visions of Tomorrow* (coll **1975**) by David SAMUELSON and *Structural Fabulation* (**1975**) by Robert SCHOLES. Scholes went on to collaborate with Eric S. RABKIN on *Science Fiction: History, Science, Vision* (**1977**), one of the best semi-popular accounts of the genre. Rabkin has since published widely in the field.

Scholes's work was much influenced by *Introduction à la littérature fantastique* (**1970** France; trans as *The Fantastic: A Structural Approach to a Literary Genre* **1973**) by Tzvetan TODOROV, a work which has aroused controversy and much interest. Sf criticism, primarily Marxist, structuralist or both, is flourishing in Europe. Other notable European critics are Michel BUTOR, Boris Eizykman (1949-   ), Vladimir GAKOV, Jörg Hienger (1927-   ), Jean-Henri Holmberg (◊ SCANDINAVIA), Julius KAGARLITSKI, Gérard KLEIN, Stanisław LEM, Carlo PAGETTI, Franz ROTTENSTEINER, Martin Schwonke (1923-   ), Jacques van Herp (1923-   ) and Pierre VERSINS. Rottensteiner, who also publishes in English, is one of the most renowned European critics; unfortunately, his best-known book in English, *The Science Fiction Book: An Illustrated History* (**1975**), is not quite up to his own usually high standard. Some exceptionally controversial criticism by Stanisław LEM has been published in English, although his much-discussed *Fantastyka i futurologia* (**1970** Poland), a full-length study of sf, has yet to be translated in full; a small part appeared, with other work, in *Microworlds* (coll trans **1985** US).

Back in the USA, the appearance in the 1970s of many academic courses about sf (◊ SF IN THE CLASSROOM) had repercussions in the publication of anthologies of critical essays. A pioneer editor in this field was Thomas D. CLARESON with *SF: The Other Side of Realism* (anth **1971**), *Voices for the Future: Essays on Major Science Fiction Writers Vol. 1* (anth **1976**) and its two sequels, and *Many Futures, Many Worlds: Theme and Form in Science Fiction* (anth **1977**). Clareson has also published books of his own, his most important work being on the early HISTORY OF SF, as in *Some Kind of Paradise: The Emergence of American Science Fiction* (**1985**), which is more a historical and thematic survey than a critical study. Two critical anthologies about sf aimed at the general reader rather than at the student or teacher are *Science Fiction at Large* (anth **1976**; vt *Explorations of the Marvellous*) ed Peter NICHOLLS and *Turning Points: Essays on the Art of Science Fiction* (anth **1977**) ed Damon Knight. The former book contains several essays which, in their readiness to see shortcomings in sf, may be a particular example of a general lessening of the rather tedious boosterism in many earlier books about the field. Another good, academic critical anthology of the 1970s was *Science Fiction: A Critical Guide* (anth **1979**) ed Patrick PARRINDER.

In the 1980s a great many critical anthologies about sf were published, often choosing their contents from the proceedings of academic conferences or from academic-track programming at sf CONVENTIONS. A number of these are listed in the entries of such individual editors as Martin H. GREENBERG, Donald HASSLER, Eric S. RABKIN and George E. SLUSSER. Many of the academics who have edited such books have also written studies of their own. Among them are perhaps the two most stimulating US academic theoreticians about sf to have risen to prominence in the 1980s: Mark ROSE and Gary K. WOLFE. Rose is the author of *Alien Encounters: Anatomy of Science Fiction* (**1981**), which in its discussion of what he sees as the central paradigms in sf breaks new ground, if controversially. Wolfe is the author of many articles and several books, including *The Known and the Unknown: The Iconography of Science Fiction* (**1979**), perhaps the major study of sf in the recent period, and comes as close as any critic ever has to defining, in useful and quite rigorous theoretical terms, the SENSE OF WONDER that fans so often use to describe what they seek for and find in sf. Unlike many of his academic colleagues, Wolfe writes with clarity, grace and wit, and avoids the jargon that makes so much recent academic analysis of sf so inaccessible to the ordinary reader – and so boring, sometimes, to even the academically trained reader.

The books of two other academic critics of considerable interest have been more narrowly focused than most of the above: H. Bruce FRANKLIN and W. Warren WAGAR. Both write well. Franklin has written, from a Marxist perspective unusual in US criticism, *Robert A. Heinlein: America as Science Fiction* (**1980**) and *War Stars: The Superweapon and the American Imagination* (**1988**). Wagar is the author of a book which is as much a contribution to the history of ideas as it is an analysis of sf specifically: *Terminal Visions: The Literature of Last Things* (**1982**).

In the early 1970s anybody interested in the history

and criticism of sf could have found very little to read on the subject. Now there is too much to cope with, and the difficulty is in locating what might be available and interesting. The "interesting" criterion remains a lottery, but the "availability" criterion can be helped considerably. Here the **Science Fiction and Fantasy Reference Indexes** of Hal W. HALL are very useful, as is **The Year's Scholarship in Science Fiction and Fantasy** series compiled by Marshall B. TYMN and Roger C. SCHLOBIN (*see their entries for details*). An earlier reference is *Science Fiction Criticism: An Annotated Checklist* (**1972**) compiled by Clareson.

Further discussion of secondary materials for the sf researcher will be found in BIBLIOGRAPHIES, CINEMA, DEFINITIONS OF SF and POSTMODERNISM AND SF, and in selected author and theme entries throughout.   [PN]

CRITICAL WAVE UK SEMIPROZINE (1987-current) ed Martin Tudor and Steve Green. *CW* is a bimonthly sf and fantasy newsletter – the schedule often slips by a month – with reviews plus news items covering fantasy, horror and comics as well as sf; it also features interviews and articles. Originally a mimeographed FANZINE, *CW* became professionally printed with #9 and is said to have a circulation above 1000. The editors clearly want it to become the UK equivalent of LOCUS; as of 1992, it still had some way to go.   [RH]

CRITTERS Film (1986). New Line/Smart Egg/Sho films. Dir Stephen Herek, starring Dee Wallace Stone, M. Emmet Walsh, Billy Green Bush, Scott Grimes, Don Opper. Screenplay Herek, Dominic Muir, with additions by Opper. 86 mins, cut to 85 mins. Colour.

Small furry carnivorous aliens with voracious appetites and large teeth (very clearly modelled on the creatures in Joe DANTE's *Gremlins* [1984]) besiege a farmhouse in Kansas and are driven off with the help of alien bounty-hunters. This wholly derivative film has some charm and competence, however, and was a not disastrous début for director Herek, who went on to make BILL & TED'S EXCELLENT ADVENTURE (1989). The sequel, *Critters 2: The Main Course* (1988; vt *Critters 2*), dir Mick Garris, has all the sparkle of a second-generation photocopy, and demonstrates nicely how the 1980s video market had such an insatiable appetite for teenage horror movies that even imitations bred imitations. It was Garris's first film as director, though he was already known as a writer on the tv series AMAZING STORIES.   [PN]

See also: MONSTER MOVIES.

CRITTERS 2: THE MAIN COURSE ◊ CRITTERS.

CROHMĂLNICEANU, OVID S. [r] ◊ ROMANIA.

CROLY, [Reverend] GEORGE (1780-1860) UK clergyman whose novel of IMMORTALITY *Salathiel: A Story of the Past, the Present and the Future* (**1826**; vt *Salathiel the Wandering Jew* 1843 US; vt *Salathiel the Immortal* 1855 UK; vt *Tarry Thou Till I Come* 1901 US) was published anon but soon acknowledged.   [JC]

CROMIE, ROBERT (1856-1907) Irish author of the well known interplanetary sf novel *A Plunge Into Space* (**1890**) in which visitors travel by ANTIGRAVITY to MARS, where they discover humans living under UTOPIAN conditions and a fatal romance ensues; the 1891 edition includes a preface by Jules VERNE. In *The Crack of Doom* (**1895**) something very like atomic energy rather intriguingly threatens the world (the first test of the substance, thousands of years earlier, destroyed the fifth planet to create the ASTEROIDS); though hazily described, RC's use in this novel of a nuclear device to shake civilization marks the first occurrence of a theme which would dominate the next century. Two volumes of a cluttered future HISTORY – *For England's Sake* (**1889**) and *The Next Crusade* (**1897**) – fail, like his remaining works, to retain much interest.   [JC]

Other works: *The King's Oak and Other Stories* (coll **1897**); *A New Messiah* (**1902**); *El Dorado* (**1904**; vt *From the Cliffs of Croaghaun* 1904 US).

See also: CRIME AND PUNISHMENT; END OF THE WORLD; HISTORY OF SF; POWER SOURCES; SPACESHIPS.

CRONENBERG, DAVID (1943-   ) Canadian filmmaker. Crucially a writer as well as a director, DC can be claimed as one of the most important practitioners of sf, in any medium, of the last quarter of the 20th century. From his early student and underground films – *Transfer* (1966), *From the Drain* (1967), *Stereo* (1969) and CRIMES OF THE FUTURE (1970), the tv short *Secret Weapons* (1972) – through his gutsy, increasingly surreal exploitation movies – The PARASITE MURDERS (1974; vt *They Came From Within*; vt *Shivers*), RABID (1976), *The* BROOD (1979), SCANNERS (1980) and VIDEODROME (1982) – to his more mainstream ventures – *The* DEAD ZONE (1983; from Stephen KING's novel), *The* FLY (1986; a remake of the 1958 MONSTER MOVIE), *Dead Ringers* (1989), *The Naked Lunch* (1992; based on William S. BURROUGHS's 1959 novel), and his projected film of J.G. BALLARD's *Crash* (**1973**) – DC has shown a remarkably consistent visual and intellectual style, dealing with the mind-body divide, near-future social, religious and chemical taboos, the MEDIA LANDSCAPE, and the extremes of experience. DC has also worked as an actor, in John Landis's *Into the Night* (1985) and, more notably, Clive Barker's *Nightbreed* (1990). The odd man out in his own filmography is *Fast Company* (1977), an efficient but nondescript movie about drag racing. The highly bizarre violence and mutation, often sexual in nature, of mid-period DC – especially the phallic parasites of *The Parasite Murders* and the sadomasochist visions of *Videodrome* – won him a reputation as the most uncompromising genre *auteur* of his generation, but *The Brood*, an interior-directed family-trauma drama, revealed a vein of icy sensitivity that later yielded *The Fly*, an extraordinarily moving rereading of its hackneyed premise which abjures monster-on-the-loose melodrama for a quietly affecting study of the process of physical change, and *Dead Ringers*, an entirely psychological and non-sf variation on DC's habitual themes that demonstrates how he has created his own category – the Cronenberg Movie – rather than inhabited the sf or HORROR genres in the way that contemporaries like George A. ROMERO and Wes Craven have done. On being hailed as "the King of Venereal Horror", DC commented: "It's a small field, Venereal Horror, but at least I'm king of it." An interesting book of interviews is *Cronenberg on Cronenberg* (coll **1991**) ed Chris Rodley. [KN]

See also: CINEMA; CYBERPUNK; HUMOUR; MONSTERS; PARASITISM AND SYMBIOSIS; PSEUDO-SCIENCE; SEX.

CRONIN, CHARLES BERNARD [r] ◊ Eric NORTH.

CROOK, COMPTON N. [r] ◊ Stephen TALL.

CROSBY, HARRY C. [r] ◊ Christopher ANVIL.

CROSS, JOHN KEIR (1914-1967) UK writer of RADIO scripts before WWII, and later of novels and tv adaptations (one of them being of John WYNDHAM's *The Kraken Wakes*) for the BBC. Some of his books for younger children, written as Stephen MacFarlane, are fantasies; *Lucy Maroon, the Car that Loved a Policeman* (**1944**) and *Mr Bosanko and Other Stories* (coll **1944**) are typical. All his sf novels are for older children; they include *The Angry Planet* (**1945**) and its sequel, *SOS from Mars* (**1954**; vt *The Red Journey Back* 1954 US), both of which represent JKC's transcription of manuscripts "by Stephen MacFarlane" encompassing the first three expeditions to Mars, which discover the vegetable life there to have suffered a Manichaean EVOLUTION into alternative races. *The Owl and the Pussycat* (**1946**; vt *The Other Side of Green Hills* 1947 US) is a fantasy, while *The Flying Fortunes in an Encounter with Rubberface!* (**1952**; vt *The Stolen Sphere* 1953 US) is an early treatment of orbital satellites. Though he wrote several novels as JKC, including *The White Magic* (**1947**) – not a fantasy, although often recorded as such – his best-known work under his own name is *The Other Passenger* (coll **1944**; cut vt *Stories from The Other Passenger* 1961 US), a collection of subtle fantasy tales for adults. He edited *Best Horror Stories* (anth **1956**), *Best Black Magic Stories* (anth **1960**) and *Best Horror Stories 2* (anth **1965**). [JC]

See also: CHILDREN'S SF.

CROSS, POLTON ◊ John Russell FEARN.

CROSS, RONALD ANTHONY (1937-) US writer who began publishing sf with "The Story of Three Cities" in *New Worlds 6* (anth **1973**) ed Michael MOORCOCK and Charles PLATT; the tale's steely moroseness characterizes much of his work in shorter forms. His first novel, *Prisoners of Paradise* (**1988**), similarly renders a GAME-WORLD environment in bleak terms, generating a sense that the **Fantasy-Island**-type trap it depicts is not to be escaped from. [JC]

CROSS, VICTORIA Pseudonym under which UK novelist Annie Sophie ("Vivian") Cory (1868-?1952) published all her work, using the spelling "Crosse" until the death of Queen Victoria; she was briefly notorious for *The Woman who Didn't* (**1895**), written in response to Grant ALLEN's *The Woman who Did* (**1895**). Her only known sf is *Marty Brown, M.P.: A Girl of Tomorrow* (**1935**), which depicts relationships in a 30th-century UK ruled by women: unemployment, war and pollution do not exist, nor is meat eaten, and

there is no prostitution because love is free. [RB]

CROSSEN, KENDELL FOSTER (1910-1981) US writer and editor, active under various names in various PULP-MAGAZINE markets, perhaps most notably as an author of detective stories, his best work being published under his own name and as M.E. Chaber. Though the **Green Lama** series of early 1940s thrillers, published in *Double Detective* as by Richard Foster, and *Murder Out of Mind* (**1945**) as by Ken Crossen, slip close to the fantastic, he began publishing sf proper with two stories in Feb 1951: "The Boy who Cried Wolf 359" in *AMZ* and "Restricted Clientele" in *TWS*. Towards the end of their existences he published a large amount of material with *Startling Stories* and *TWS*; much of this material is intendedly comic, in particular the **Manning Draco** series about an interstellar salesman and his amusing experiences with ALIENS: *Once Upon a Star* (1951-2 *TWS*, fixup **1953**) plus 4 additional stories, "Assignment to Aldebaran" (1953), "Whistle Stop in Space" (1953), "Mission to Mizar" (1953) and "The Agile Algolian" (1954). *Year of Consent* (**1952**), about a COMPUTER that controls the West, expressively conveys the PARANOIA of much US fiction of the period. *The Rest Must Die* (**1959**), as by Foster, follows the story of those who have survived a nuclear attack on New York by happening to be underground in subways or cellars: conflicts ensue. KFC's ANTHOLOGIES – *Adventures in Tomorrow* (anth **1951**; UK edn omits 2 stories) and *Future Tense* (anth **1952**; UK edn omits 7 stories) – include some original stories, are competently selected, and were influential in their time. [JC]

CROW, LEVI [s] ◊ Manly Wade WELLMAN.

CROWCROFT, (WILLIAM) PETER (1925-) UK writer whose *The Fallen Sky* (**1954**) describes a post-HOLOCAUST London reverted to barbarism and a sociologist's attempt to cure himself of violence while simultaneously founding a new civilization. *Monster* (**1980** US) is a horror tale. [JC]

CROWLEY, JOHN (1942-) US writer who has also worked in documentary films and tv since 1966. His sf novels have had a considerable impact on the field, and his fantasies have established him as a figure whose work markedly stretches the boundaries of genre literature.

His first sf novel, *The Deep* (**1975**), is set on a flat discworld resting on a pillar that extends beyond measurement into the circumambient Deep, in which very few stars are visible. On this disc complex feudal conflicts, which seem interminably to repeat a bad year from the War of Roses, are regulated, maintained and when necessary fomented for its own pleasure by the mysterious Being who originally transported to this strange new domain its present inhabitants – humans whose own world was dying. Though the story is told from various points of view, the reader's main perspective is through the eyes of a damaged ANDROID with memory problems sent to record events by the disc's peculiar God. Using sources as widely divergent as James Branch CABELL's **Biography of the Life of Manuel**, Philip José FARMER's **World of Tiers** novels and E.R. EDDISON's *The Worm Ouroboros* (1922), JC constructed a story whose free and supple use of numerous generic conventions marks it as the sort of tale possible only late in the life of any genre.

Beasts (1976) somewhat more conventionally depicts a balkanized USA, but with a complex deployment of sf themes, notable among which are the uses made of biologically transformed animals and of the potential for genuine interspecies empathy. The chilly belatedness of these two books – like all his work they depict worlds caught in the iron claws of a prior authority or Author – warms very considerably in the third, *Engine Summer* (1979), whose title neatly epitomizes JC's abiding central concerns and whose plot – its protagonist finds that his life in a dying post-HOLOCAUST pastoral USA is nothing but a memory interminably replayed, and that he himself is no more than a crystal device replaying those memories on command – exudes a cruel melancholy. But the story which Rush That Speaks represents in his being (and tells) is powerfully moving; and his sleep at the close (though he will soon be turned on again to play himself) is earned.

A similar grave cruelty infuses the TIME TRAVEL cul-de-sacs uncovered in *Great Work of Time* (1991), a tale which depicts the desolate consequences of attempting to control history; it first appeared in *Novelty* (coll 1989), along with some shorter fantasies and "In Blue" a DYSTOPIAN parable.

His major novel, the grave and eloquent *Little, Big* (1981), is primarily a fantasy; partly set in a NEAR-FUTURE USA, this large work puts into definitive form JC's steely nostalgia for the long arm of immortal law. The title itself – which condenses a message repeated throughout the text: "The further in you go, the bigger it gets" – is a restatement in fantasy terms of the process of CONCEPTUAL BREAKTHROUGH central to much sf. The story embeds in the centrifugal world of US fantasy a UK tale of harrowing centripetal inwardness; Smoky Barnable's book-long attempt to enter the world of faerie ends, as it must, in something like death. In the meantime, as the century itself closes, a reborn Barbarossa ravages an unsavable USA. The Renaissance Art of Memory – later utilized by Gene WOLFE, Mary GENTLE and Michael SWANWICK, among others – significantly shapes the geography of the book, with the result that the metamorphoses suffered by its protagonists seem both mathematically foreordained (Lewis CARROLL is a constant presence in the text) and symbolically potent. *Little, Big* has permeated the field. As much cannot be said, perhaps, for *Aegypt* (1987), the first of a projected quartet of novels examining Renaissance neoplatonism with hallucinated concentration; but even the torso of this sequence confirms JC's very considerable shaping power, which is his most significant gift to genre literature. The novelty

of his work is less important than the magnetism of the synthesis it represents. [JC]

Other work: *Beasts/Engine Summer/Little, Big* (omni 1991).

See also: ADAM AND EVE; ALTERNATE WORLDS; FANTASTIC VOYAGES; FANTASY; FAR FUTURE; GODS AND DEMONS; GREAT AND SMALL; MAGIC; METAPHYSICS; MYTHOLOGY; OMNI; OPTIMISM AND PESSIMISM; PASTORAL; PERCEPTION; POCKET UNIVERSE; SCIENCE FANTASY; SWORD AND SORCERY; TIME PARADOXES.

CROWNPOINT PUBLICATIONS ◊ NEBULA SCIENCE FICTION.

CRULS, GASTÃO [r] ◊ LATIN AMERICA.

CRUMP, C(HARLES) G(EORGE) (1862-1935) UK writer whose sf novel, *The Red King Dreams, 1946-1948* (1931), rather demurely satirizes the university life of the NEAR FUTURE. [JC]

CRUMP, IRVING (1887-1979) US writer known almost exclusively for his sequence of prehistoric-sf novels for older children, set in Europe and featuring the resourceful **Og**, who introduces fire to his tribe, fights off giant reptiles and comports himself with commendable dignity throughout: *Og – Son of Fire* (1922), *Og – Boy of Battle* (1925), *Og of the Cave People* (1935) and *Og, Son of Og* (1965). *Mog the Mound Builder* (1931) is set in the Americas. [JC]

CRYOGENICS From a Greek root meaning "cold-producing", this word is used in physics to mean the production of extremely low temperatures and the study of phenomena at those temperatures. The shorter word CRYONICS is more commonly used in sf TERMINOLOGY, especially when, as is usual, it is people or other organic materials that are frozen. [PN]

CRYONICS A term coined in the 1960s by Karl Werner, referring to techniques for preserving the human body by supercooling. R.C.W. Ettinger's *The Prospect of Immortality* (1966) popularized the idea that the corpses of terminally ill people might be "frozen down" in order to preserve them until such a time as medical science would discover cures for all ills and a method of resurrecting the dead. Many sf stories have extrapolated the notion.

The preservative effects of low temperatures have been known for a long time. The notion of reviving human beings accidentally entombed in ice was first developed as a fictional device by W. Clark RUSSELL in *The Frozen Pirate* (1887). In Louis BOUSSENARD's *Dix mille ans dans un bloc de glace* (1889; trans as *10,000 Years in a Block of Ice* 1898) a contemporary man visits the future as a result of a similar accident. Edgar Rice BURROUGHS's "The Resurrection of Jimber Jaw" (1937) is a satirical account of the revival of a prehistoric man and his experiences in the civilized world; Richard Ben SAPIR's *The Far Arena* (1978) is a modern variant involving a Roman gladiator. Freezing is still sf's most popular means of achieving SUSPENDED ANIMATION (*see also* SLEEPER AWAKES), but recent debate about cryonics relates also to the themes of REINCARNATION and IMMORTALITY. The Cryonics Society of California began freezing newly dead people in 1967, and the movement seems to have survived the setback it suffered when a power failure caused a number of frozen bodies to thaw out in 1981, sparking off a chain of lawsuits. The rumour that Walt Disney's body is in a deep-freeze somewhere remains unconfirmed. Interest in the theme is by no means confined to the USA, and two of the major fictional examinations of the prospect are European: Nikolai AMOSOV's *Zapiski iz budushchego* (**1967**; trans as *Notes from the Future* **1970**) and Anders BODELSEN's *Frysepunktet* (**1969**; trans as *Freezing Point* **1971**; vt *Freezing Down* US). Cryonic preservation is still used in stories of TIME TRAVEL into the future, including Frederik POHL's *The Age of the Pussyfoot* (**1969**), Mack REYNOLDS's UTOPIAN *Looking Backward, from the Year 2000* (**1973**) and the Woody Allen film SLEEPER (1973). It is also a common device in stories of slower-than-light SPACE TRAVEL: in E.C. TUBB's **Dumarest** series interstellar travel may by "high" or "low", depending upon whether time is absorbed by the use of drugs or more hazardous cryonic procedures, while James WHITE's *The Dream Millennium* (**1974**) explores hypothetical psychological effects of long-term freezing.

The possible social problems associated with large-scale cryonic projects are explored in various sf stories. Clifford D. SIMAK's *Why Call Them Back from Heaven?* (**1967**) imagines a time when a person can be tried for delaying the freezing of a corpse, permitting "ultimate death", and the financial estates of the frozen have become a political power-bloc, inviting criminal manipulation. A cynical account of the politics of dealing with the dead is offered in Larry NIVEN's "The Defenseless Dead" (1973), which points out that the living have all the votes and that the dead might be an exploitable resource; it was Niven who first used in print Pohl's term CORPSICLES to denote the deep-frozen dead. Ernest TIDYMAN's satirical thriller *Absolute Zero* (**1971**), about a financier who builds up a vast cryonics industry, is similarly cynical. As might be expected, most stories depicting people who try to "cheat" death by having themselves frozen down find suitably ironic ways to thwart them. In "Ozymandias" (1972) by Terry CARR people who take to the cryonic vaults in order to avoid a war fall victim, like the mummified pharaohs of ancient Egypt before them, to professional "tomb-robbers". In Gregory BENFORD's now-anachronistic "Doing Lennon" (1975) an unfrozen John Lennon turns out not to be what he appears or aspires to be. And in ". . . And He not Busy Being Born" (1987) by Brian M. STABLEFORD a bold entrepreneur who succeeds against the odds in delivering himself into a world of immortals find that he still cannot evade his destiny. [BS]

CSERNA, JÓZSEF [r] ◊ HUNGARY.

CSERNAI, ZOLTÁN [r] ◊ HUNGARY.

CUBA ◊ LATIN AMERICA.

CUISCARD, HENRI [s] ◊ Charles DE LINT.

CULBREATH, MYRNA (?   -   ) US writer known

almost exclusively for her collaborations with Sondra MARSHAK as a producer of ties for STAR TREK, including *Star Trek: The New Voyages* ∗ (coll **1976**) and its direct sequel *Star Trek: The New Voyages 2* ∗ (anth **1978**), *The Price of the Phoenix* ∗ (**1977**) and its direct sequel *The Fate of the Phoenix* ∗ (**1979**), *The Prometheus Design* ∗ (**1982**) and *Triangle* ∗ (**1983**), as well as *Shatner: Where No Man . . .: The Authorized Biography of William Shatner* (**1979**) with William SHATNER. [JC]

CULLINGWORTH, N(ICHOLAS) J(OHN) ◊ ROBERT HALE LIMITED.

CULTURAL ENGINEERING A phrase not especially common in sf TERMINOLOGY, although what it refers to is fundamental to the genre. The idea of humans deliberately altering the nature of alien cultures (or of aliens doing it to us), or indeed of doing the same to isolated cultures on Earth, is often evoked in sf, sometimes approvingly, more often disapprovingly. This is especially so in stories in which ANTHROPOLOGY, COLONIZATION OF OTHER WORLDS and SOCIOLOGY are dominant themes. A common form of cultural engineering in sf is the TIME-TRAVEL or PARALLEL-WORLDS story (often both at once) in which some sort of time-police force attempts to engineer past, future or ALTERNATE WORLDS into the most stable and productive conformations. Sf itself can be seen as a form of sublimated cultural engineering in its persistent modelling of societies that differ from our own. [PN]

CULVER, TIMOTHY J. ◊ Donald E. WESTLAKE.

CUMMINGS, M(ONETTE) A. (1914-   ) US writer of short stories in various genres who began publishing sf with "The Bridges of Ool" in *Planet Stories* in 1955. Her collection is *Exile and Other Tales of Fantasy* (coll **1968**). [JC]

CUMMINGS, RAY Working name of US writer Raymond King Cummings (1887-1957), author of over 750 stories under various names in various genres; he was one of the few writers active during the heyday of US PULP-MAGAZINE sf (1930-50) to have begun his career before Hugo GERNSBACK launched *AMZ* in 1926. His first sf of any note is also his best-known story, "The Girl in the Golden Atom" (1919), which appeared, as did much of his early work, in *All-Story Weekly* (◊ *The* ALL-STORY); with its sequel, "People of the Golden Atom", serialized in the same magazine in 1920, this famous story – about a young man who takes a size-diminishing drug and has extraordinary adventures on a microscopic world – became *The Girl in the Golden Atom* (fixup **1922** UK; exp 1923 US) and proved the cornerstone both of RC's reputation and of much of his work from this time on, for he used the idea of the size-diminishing drug and the microscopic world, with many variations, for the rest of his long career (◊ GREAT AND SMALL). *The Girl in the Golden Atom* also constitutes the "Matter" segment of RC's **Matter, Space and Time** trilogy; the "Space" segment contains *The Princess of the Atom* (1929 *The Argosy*; **1950**) and "The Fire People" (1922 *The Argosy*); the "Time" segment takes in *The Man who Mastered Time* (1924 *The Argosy*; **1929**),

The Shadow Girl (1929 *The Argosy*; **1946** UK) and *The Exile of Time* (1931 *ASF*; **1964**).

After the successes of his early years, RC remained prolific, but his mechanical style and the general rigidity of his stories gradually lost him popularity until, in the 1960s, some of his books were nostalgically revived. Typical of his journeyman prose and uneven quality are the **Tama** novels: *Tama of the Light Country* (1930 *The Argosy*; **1965**) and *Tama, Princess of Mercury* (1931 *The Argosy*; **1966**), the heroine of which does very well after being kidnapped from Earth to MERCURY. *Brigands of the Moon* (**1931**), later published in Canada with a mistaken attribution to John W. CAMPBELL Jr, and its sequel *Wandl the Invader* (1932 *ASF*; **1961** dos) are examples of his SPACE-OPERA output, in which space pirates tend to proliferate and humans to defeat terrifying alien monsters.

RC was fundamentally a pulp writer; unlike some of those only a little younger – for example, Murray LEINSTER and Edmond HAMILTON – he was never capable of adapting himself to the changing times, either scientifically or stylistically. His later works could be interchanged with his earliest with very little adjustment. [JC]

Other works: *The Sea Girl* (**1930**); *Tarrano the Conqueror* (1925 *Science and Invention*; **1930**); *Into the Fourth Dimension* (1926 *Science and Invention*; anth **1943** UK), made up of the title novel plus stories by other hands, and not to be confused with *Into the 4th Dimension* (**1981** chap), which reprints only the 1926 tale; *The Man on the Meteor* (1924 *Science and Invention*; **1944** UK); *Beyond the Vanishing Point* (1931 *ASF*; **1958** chap dos); *Beyond the Stars* (1928 *The Argosy*; **1963**); *A Brand New World* (1928 *The Argosy*; **1964**); *Explorers into Infinity* (1927-8 *Weird Tales*; fixup **1965**); *The Insect Invasion* (1932 *The Argosy*; **1967**); "The Snow Girl" (1929 *The Argosy*; in *Famous Fantastic Classics No 1* [anth **1974**]); *Tales of the Scientific Crime Club* (1925 *The Sketch*; coll **1979**).

See also: ASTOUNDING SCIENCE-FICTION; BLACK HOLES; CONCEPTUAL BREAKTHROUGH; FANTASTIC VOYAGES; HISTORY OF SF; PUBLISHING; ROBOTS; SCIENTIFIC ERRORS; TIME TRAVEL.

CUMMINS, HARLE OWEN (? -?) US writer. Of those stories collected in *Welsh Rarebit Tales* (coll **1902**) at least 4, including "The Man who Made a Man" and "The Space Annihilator", have considerable sf interest. In the latter story a MATTER TRANSMITTER is introduced. Other tales are generally FANTASY, some showing the influence of Ambrose BIERCE. [JC]

CUNHA, FAUSTO [r] ◊ LATIN AMERICA.

CUNNINGHAM, E.V. ◊ Howard FAST.

CURREY, L(LOYD) W(ESLEY) (1942-) US specialist bookseller (since 1968) and bibliographer. With David G. HARTWELL he founded (1973) and operated Dragon Press, a SMALL PRESS publishing books about sf, fantasy and horror; the partnership was dissolved in 1979, leaving Hartwell sole owner. Also with Hartwell, he co-edited the GREGG PRESS **Science Fiction Reprint** series 1975-81; alone he edited the Gregg

Press **Masters of Science Fiction and Fantasy** author BIBLIOGRAPHIES 1980-83. LWC's books are: *A Research Guide to Science Fiction Studies: An Annotated Checklist of Primary and Secondary Sources for Fantasy and Science Fiction* (**1977**) with Marshall B. TYMN and Roger SCHLOBIN; *Index to Stories in Thematic Anthologies of Science Fiction* (**1978**) with Tymn, Martin H. GREENBERG and Joseph D. OLANDER; and *Science Fiction and Fantasy Authors: A Bibliography of their Fiction and Selected Nonfiction* (**1979**). This last is his most important work, a standard text which brought new standards of accuracy and scholarship to sf bibliography. Listings for newly covered authors are often published in NEW YORK REVIEW OF SCIENCE FICTION. A second edition of the bibliography is in preparation. [PN]

See also: SF IN THE CLASSROOM.

CURSE OF FRANKENSTEIN ◊ FRANKENSTEIN.

CURSE OF THE FLY Film (1965). Lippert. Dir Don Sharp, starring Brian Donlevy, George Baker, Carole Gray. Screenplay Harry Spalding, based on characters created by George LANGELAAN. 86 mins. Colour.

This UK film is the sequel to the two US films *The FLY* (1958) and RETURN OF THE FLY (1959). The confused script is largely a rehash of them, but Sharp's direction, which concentrates on the mental disintegration of the mad SCIENTIST's wife (Gray), is – occasionally – visually powerful. The results of failed MATTER TRANSMISSION experiments, kept in outhouses in the garden, provide a nice touch. The critical consensus that this is the worst of the three films probably needs revision. [PN]

CURTIES, [Captain] HENRY (1860-?) UK writer whose first sf novel, *Tears of Angels* (**1907**), features its protagonist's conveyance to Alpha Centauri on an angel, who is perhaps weeping; from the star he gains a perspective on Earth, then returns home to find himself in an ALTERNATE-WORLD version of the future. *Out of the Shadows* (**1908**) is a detection with occult elements. *When England Slept* (**1909**) is a future-WAR tale. [JC]

CURTIS, JEAN-LOUIS Pseudonym of French writer Louis Lafitte (1917-). His collection of five satirical sf stories, *Un saint au néon* (coll **1956**; trans Humphrey Hare as *The Neon Halo: The Face of the Future* **1958** UK), very sharply depicts a NEAR-FUTURE world whose centre cannot hold. The tone is vivacious, didactic, circumstantial; its wit is distanced in the *récit* fashion long favoured by French satirists. [JC]

CURTIS, RICHARD A(LAN) (1937-) US editor, literary agent and writer, known mainly in the first capacity for his anthology *Future Tense* (anth **1968**), which is not to be confused with Kendell Foster CROSSEN's *Future Tense* (anth **1952**). He has also published short work, beginning with "Introduction to 'The Saint'" for *Cavalier* in 1968, as well as *Squirm* (**1976**), an sf film novelization (◊ BLUE SUNSHINE). He wrote 1980-92 the **Agent's Corner** column in LOCUS, which has been adapted into book form as *Beyond the Bestseller* (coll **1989**). [JC]

Other works: *How to Prosper in the Coming Apocalypse*

(**1981**); *How to be Your Own Literary Agent* (coll **1983**; exp **1984**); *A Fool for an Agent: Publishing Satires and Verses* (coll **1992** chap).

CURTIS, WADE ◊ Jerry POURNELLE.

CURTIS, WARDON ALLAN (1867-1940) US writer, a contributor to several pre-sf fiction magazines. His most important sf is a short story about a brain transplant, "The Monster of Lake LaMetrie" (1899 *The Windsor Magazine*), in which the brain is human and the recipient body that of a prehistorical survival from a bottomless lake that may lead into a HOLLOW EARTH. WAC also wrote an Arabian-Nights fantasy, "The Seal of Solomon the Great" (1901 *Argosy*) and *The Strange Adventures of Mr Middleton* (coll **1903**), which contains a mixture of Oriental fantasy and bizarre mystery. [JE]

CURTIS WARREN Founded in 1948, one of several UK publishing firms which flourished in the decade after WWII by releasing dozens of purpose-written paperback originals in various popular genres. Before it foundered in 1954, CW had published over 500 novels, 98 of them sf, all of them composed strictly according to length restrictions: in 1948-50, CW books were of 24 or 32pp; in 1950-53, they were of 112 or 128pp; from 1953, 160pp volumes were the rule. CW gained some posthumous fame for having published John BRUNNER's first novel, *Galactic Storm* (**1951**) under the house name Gill HUNT; but their most reliable and prolific author was Dennis HUGHES: as with some of his stablemates, little is known about this author beyond the titles he wrote, mostly under CW house names. Other authors associated with CW (*see their entries for personal pseudonyms*) included William Henry Fleming BIRD, Kenneth BULMER, John Russell FEARN, John S. GLASBY, David GRIFFITHS, Brian HOLLO-WAY, John W. JENNISON and E.C. TUBB. As well as Gill Hunt, house names used for CW sf titles included Berl CAMERON, Neil CHARLES, Lee ELLIOT, Brad KENT, King LANG, Rand LE PAGE, Paul LORRAINE, Kris LUNA, Van REED and Brian SHAW.

It cannot be assumed that *all* books published by CW were written on hire as SHARECROPS; but almost certainly *almost* all of them were. It remains a possibility that some of the 98 titles might have some intrinsic interest, the most likely candidates being those by Fearn, Glasby and Tubb. [JC]
About the publisher: *Curtis Warren and Grant Hughes* (**1985** chap) by Stephen HOLLAND.

CURTONI, VITTORIO [r] ◊ ITALY.

CURVAL, PHILIPPE Pseudonym used by journalist Philippe Tronche (1929-   ), French writer. PC has since the 1950s been associated with the growth of sf in France as bookseller, magazine editor, photographer, chronicler and author. He is a fine stylist whose work is exemplified by a sensual, poetic mood and great affection for his characters. He has written over 20 stories, the first appearing in 1955. *Cette Chère Humanité* (**1976**; trans Steve Cox as *Brave Old World* **1981** UK), which won the 1977 Prix Apollo (◊ AWARDS), conflates the personal extension of lifespans

with the artificial isolation of a future EEC. *Le ressac de l'espace* ["The Breakers of Space"] (**1962**) won the Prix Jules Verne in 1963 and *L'homme à rebours* ["Backwards Man"] (**1974**) was selected as Best French SF Novel of 1974. [MJ/JC]
Other works: *Les fleurs de Vénus* ["Flowers of Venus"] (**1960**); *La fortresse de coton* ["The Cotton Fortress"] (**1967**); *Les sables de Falun* ["The Sands of Falun"] (**1970**); *Attention les yeux* ["Beware, Eyes!"] (**1972**); *Un soupçon de néant* ["A Suspicion of Nothingness"] (**1977**).
See also: FRANCE.

CUSH, GEOFFREY (1956-   ) New Zealand-born writer and journalist, in the UK from the late 1970s. His first novel, *God Help the Queen* (**1987**), was an sf SATIRE about the UK of AD2003, which is in such lamentable condition that only Queen Britannia herself can save it from doublethink and Yankees. [JC]

CUSSLER, CLIVE (ERIC) (1931-   ) US writer, some titles in whose **Dirk Pitt** sequence of TECHNOTHRILLERS are of sf interest. Supremely competent, irresistible to women, slightly sadistic, Pitt is Special Projects Director for the (fictional) American National Under-water and Marine Agency, which engages in specta-cular underwater salvage operations involving exotic technologies. Relevant titles include *Raise the Titanic!* (**1976**), filmed in 1980 as *Raise the Titanic!* dir Jerry Jameson, *Vixen 03* (**1978**), which deals with the hunt for a "Doomsday virus", *Night Probe!* (**1981**), *Pacific Vortex!* (**1983**), which features human divers with artificial gills, *Cyclops* (**1986**), in which a secret MOON colony figures, and *Treasure* (**1988**), a tale of NEAR-FUTURE political manoeuvrings. [NT]
Other works: *Deep Six* (**1984**); *Dragon* (**1990**).

CYBERNETICS In sf TERMINOLOGY this is a word so often misused that its real meaning is in danger of being devalued or forgotten.

The term "cybernetics", derived from a Greek word meaning helmsman or controller, was coined by the distinguished mathematician Norbert WIENER in 1947 to describe a new science on which he and others had been working since 1942. The word first passed into general usage with the publication of his *Cybernetics* (**1948**; rev 1961), subtitled "Control and Communica-tion in the Animal and the Machine". Cybernetics was cross-disciplinary from the beginning; it develo-ped when Wiener and others noticed that certain parallel problems persistently arose in scientific dis-ciplines normally regarded as separate: statistical mechanics, information theory, electrical engineering and neurophysiology were four of the most impor-tant.

Cybernetics has much in common with the parallel study of General Systems Theory, founded by Lud-wig von Bertalanffy in 1940. It is concerned with the way systems work, the way they govern themselves, the way they process information (often through a process known as "feedback") in order to govern themselves, and the way they can best be designed.

The system in question can be a machine or, equally, a human body. The trouble, Wiener found, was that the terminology with which engineers discussed machines led to a very mechanistic approach when applied to human systems, and, conversely, biological terminology led to an over-anthropomorphic approach in discussion of machines (or economic or ecological systems, two other areas where cybernetics is useful). The trick was to construct a new science which would not be biased towards either the mechanical or the biological. In his *An Introduction to Cybernetics* (**1956**), W. Ross Ashby remarked that "cybernetics stands to the real machine – electronic, mechanical, neural or economic – much as geometry stands to a real object in our terrestrial space"; that is, cybernetics is an abstracting, generalizing science. However, science being what it is, always tending towards specialization, the original idea of cybernetics as a cross-disciplinary study is in danger of being forgotten, and now we have specialists in, for example, engineering cybernetics and biological cybernetics. The latter is usually called "bionics", although this word, coined in 1960, is actually a contraction of "biological electronics".

If we use the broad, scientifically accepted definition of "cybernetics", it cannot be delimited as a separate theme in this encyclopedia. Most of the stories discussed under the entries ANDROIDS, AUTOMATION, COMMUNICATION, COMPUTERS, CYBORGS, INTELLIGENCE and ROBOTS will, by definition, be cybernetics stories also. For example, Kurt VONNEGUT Jr's *Player Piano* (**1952**) has at its heart an image of humans incorporated in and subject to an impersonal, machine-like system (◊ AUTOMATION); they effectively become components or "bits" in a cybernetic system.

However, in sf the term "cybernetics" is most often used to mean something narrower – generally the creation of artificial intelligence, or AI. This is indeed a central problem in real-world cybernetics, but by no means the only one. Some cyberneticians hope that analysis of neural systems (i.e., the brain) might lead to the synthesis of simulated intelligences which begin as machines but go on to become self-programming, or even, as in Greg BEAR's *Queen of Angels* (**1990**), self-aware. The first step towards AI in real life is the computer, which is why all computer stories are cybernetics stories also.

Cybernetics also enters sf in the form of the word "cyborg", a contraction of "cybernetic organism". This usage is taken from an area of cybernetics not necessarily related to AI: a person with a wooden leg is a kind of very simple cyborg, because the melding of mechanical and human parts necessitates, whether consciously or not, the use of feedback devices (i.e., it is cybernetic). The study of cybernetics is, at bottom, the study of just such devices, whether they be servo-mechanisms or the messages that travel between eye and hand when we pick up a book from a table.

Surprisingly few sf stories attack the problem of AI

directly; far more commonly, the problem is sidetracked by conjuring up a magic word from the air. Isaac ASIMOV said his robots were POSITRONIC, and left it at that. One of the most comprehensive (if not always comprehensible) cybernetics works in sf is *Destination: Void* (**1966**) by Frank HERBERT, in which the problem is that of building not just a very complex computer but a machine that could be said to be conscious. Herbert actually spells out some of the steps through which this might conceivably be possible, and also goes on to ask those philosophical questions about autonomy and free will which must inevitably hover in the background of any cybernetics story of this kind. Much of the book's terminology is borrowed from Wiener's nonfiction *God & Golem, Inc.* (**1964**). Interestingly, the question "In what respect can a machine be said to have free will?" engenders a parallel question about humans themselves, at least for readers and writers who take the materialist view that the human mind is itself no more than a complex cybernetics system; this "anti-vitalist" view of humanity is common among cybernetics writers. The whole thrust of cybernetics as a study is to point up the resemblances between sciences superficially dissimilar, and the attempt by neurocyberneticians to analyse the mind as a system has led to impassioned attack from people who believe that humanness mystically transcends its own physical constituents.

In real life, attempts to simulate INTELLIGENCE in machines have mainly taken the route of the heuristic programming of computers. This is a way of showing a computer how to solve a problem not by painstakingly going through every possible combination that might lead to a solution – this would take a computer billions of years in an ordinary chess game – but by programming short-cuts into the machine, so that it can gauge the most likely or fruitful directions for analysis. Humans do it automatically; machines have to be taught, but this teaching is the first step towards training a machine how to make choices, a vital step towards consciousness.

The first important sf work to use the terminology of cybernetics was Bernard WOLFE's *Limbo* (**1952**; vt *Limbo '90* UK); he used its basic ideas (sometimes with hostility) in the wide sense, as they relate to computers, war-games, industrial management and the workings of the brain. Cybernetics terminology is used very loosely by Raymond F. JONES in *The Cybernetic Brains* (1950 *Startling Stories*; **1962**), which tells of human brains integrated with computers. Although Jones probably used the term more because it was fine-sounding than for any other reason, this is nonetheless a legitimate cybernetics subject, and is also deployed notably in *Wolfbane* (**1959**) by Frederik POHL and C.M. KORNBLUTH, *Catchworld* (**1975**) by Chris BOYCE and many other stories.

A number of stories about the development of consciousness in computers carry cybernetic implications, though few as far-ranging as those in *Destination: Void*. Some early examples can be found in

Science Fiction Thinking Machines (anth **1954**) ed Groff CONKLIN; also relevant are *The God Machine* (**1968**) by Martin CAIDIN, *Vulcan's Hammer* (**1960**) by Philip K. DICK, *Sagan om den stora datamaskin* (**1966** Sweden; trans as *The Tale of the Big Computer* 1966; vt *The Great Computer, A Vision* 1968 UK; vt *The End of Man?*) by Olof JOHANNESSON, *The Moon is a Harsh Mistress* (**1966**) by Robert A. HEINLEIN, *When Harlie Was One* (**1972**) by David GERROLD and "Synth" (**1966**) by Keith ROBERTS. The reverse progression, of human into machine, occurs in the vignettes of *Moderan* (coll of linked stories **1971**) by David R. BUNCH.

Already-developed machine consciousnesses appear in Roger ZELAZNY's story "For a Breath I Tarry" (**1966**), *Cyberiada* (coll of linked stories **1967** Poland; trans as *The Cyberiad: Fables for the Cybernetic Age* **1974** US) by Stanisław LEM, all the **Berserker** stories by Fred SABERHAGEN, *The Siren Stars* (**1971**) by Richard and Nancy CARRIGAN and *The Cybernetic Samurai* (**1985**) by Victor MILAN. Of these – and they are only a tiny proportion of the total – Lem's fables are the ones that most directly confront the various philosophical paradoxes that machine intelligence involves. A particularly vast, Galaxy-spanning machine consciousness, literally a *deus ex machina*, features in Dan SIMMONS's *Hyperion* (**1989**) and its sequel.

The Steel Crocodile (**1970**; vt *The Electric Crocodile* UK) by D.G. COMPTON is interesting from a cybernetics viewpoint; it is about computer systems, but also analyses the nature of human social systems and examines how the two kinds intermesh. *Gray Matters* (**1971**) by William HJORTSBERG examines disembodied human brain systems linked up in a network. *Spacetime Donuts* (**1981**) by Rudy RUCKER is one of many variants on the theme of a human society controlled repressively by a benevolent computer. *The Black Cloud* (**1957**) by Fred HOYLE dramatizes communication between a human mind and an inorganic intelligence in space; it also raises a number of cybernetic issues. *The Jonah Kit* (**1975**) by Ian WATSON asks cybernetic questions in that part of the story dealing with the imprinting of a human consciousness onto the mind of a whale.

Various compound words have been formed, with dubious etymological exactness, from "cybernetics" – we have already met "cyborg". There are the "Cybermen" and "Cybernauts" – two varieties of dangerous ROBOTS – in the tv series DR WHO and *The* AVENGERS, respectively; here the "cyber" component is merely a buzzword synonym for robot. Two terms where the "cyber" component has considerably more force, CYBERPUNK and CYBERSPACE, warrant their own entries.

The only book that analyses cybernetics issues from an sf perspective is *The Cybernetic Imagination in Science Fiction* (**1980**) by Patricia S. WARRICK, interesting when talking about cybernetic ideas as they are used in sf – often inaccurately in her view – but on less sure ground when discussing the literary quality of the results. "Cyborgs and Cybernetic Intertexts: On Postmodern Phantasms of Body and Mind" by Gabriele Schwab in *Intertextuality and Contemporary American Fiction* (anth **1989**), ed Patrick O'Donnell, is an academic essay on the subject. [PN]

CYBERPUNK Term used to describe a school of sf writing that developed and became popular during the 1980s. The word was almost certainly coined by Bruce BETHKE in his story "Cyberpunk" (**1983** *AMZ*), which had for some time before publication been circulating in manuscript. The term was picked up, either directly or indirectly, by writer and editor Gardner DOZOIS and used by him to characterize a literary movement whose main exponents, at first – in stories from about 1981-2 onwards – were seen as being Bruce STERLING and William GIBSON, along with Rudy RUCKER, Lewis SHINER and perhaps John SHIRLEY. It was not long after the publication of Gibson's first novel, *Neuromancer* (**1984**), that the term began to come into general use, and *Neuromancer* was the book that definitively shaped our sense of the subgenre to which "cyberpunk" refers.

The "cyber" part of the word relates to CYBERNETICS: to a future where industrial and political blocs may be global (or centred in SPACE HABITATS) rather than national, and controlled through information networks; a future in which machine augmentations of the human body are commonplace, as are mind and body changes brought about by DRUGS and biological engineering. Central to cyberpunk fictions is the concept of VIRTUAL REALITY, as in Gibson's **Neuromancer** sequence, where the world's data networks form a kind of machine environment into which a human can enter by jacking into a cyberspace deck and projecting "his disembodied consciousness into the consensual hallucination that was the matrix" (◊ CYBERSPACE). The "punk" part of the word comes from the rock'n'roll terminology of the 1970s, "punk" meaning in this context young, streetwise, aggressive, alienated and offensive to the Establishment. A punk disillusion, often multiple – with progressive layers of illusion being peeled away – is a major component of these works.

Data networks are more than just a part of cyberpunk's subject matter. Density of information, often slipped into stories by near-subliminal means, has from the outset strongly characterized cyberpunk's actual *style*. An important cyberpunk forebear was the film BLADE RUNNER (1982), whose NEAR-FUTURE milieu – mean, drizzling, populous streets lit up by enormous advertisements for Japanese products, alternating street junk with hi-tech – is, in the intensity of its visual infodumps, like a template for a cyberpunk scenario. Even more central to the cyberpunk ethos, however, are the films of David CRONENBERG, whose VIDEODROME (1982) in particular is a central cyberpunk document in its emphasis on bodily metamorphosis, media overload and destructive sex.

Cyberpunk did not spring full-grown from Gibson's

forehead, of course. Indeed, unfriendly critics have rejoiced in locating cyberpunk ancestors, as if this somehow devalued the entire movement; obviously cyberpunk can be read as the apotheosis of various idea-clusters that appeared earlier, but this seems neither surprising nor damaging. Ancestral texts include Bernard WOLFE's *Limbo* (**1952**; vt *Limbo 90* UK), with its prosthetic ironies, Alfred BESTER's *Tiger! Tiger!* (**1956** UK; rev vt *The Stars My Destination* 1957 US), with its protopunk antihero, William S. BURROUGHS's *The Soft Machine* (**1961** France; rev 1966 US) and its various quasi-sequels, with their drug and biological fantasias, Samuel R. DELANY's *Nova* (**1968**), with its streetwise CYBORGS, James TIPTREE Jr's "The Girl who was Plugged In" (1973), with its painful ironies about altered body-image, and Ted MOONEY's *Easy Travel to Other Planets* (**1981**), with its interspecies sex and its information sickness. Other forebears would include J.G. BALLARD, John BRUNNER – notably with *The Shockwave Rider* (**1975**) – Norman SPINRAD, John VARLEY and perhaps even Thomas PYNCHON.

Cyberpunk is often seen as a variety of Postmodernist fiction, a point made by the title of *Storming the Reality Studio: A Casebook of Cyberpunk and Postmodern Science Fiction* (anth **1992**) ed Larry McCaffery. Many of POSTMODERNISM's allegedly principal qualities fit cyberpunk like a glove.

The sense that cyberpunk was almost a political movement, not just a form of fiction, came in part from outside the fictions themselves. There had been nothing like it in the sf world since the NEW-WAVE arguments of the 1960s. In convention panels, in magazines (especially from 1987 in a critical semiprozine, SCIENCE FICTION EYE ed Stephen P. Brown) – in all sorts of media – passionate and sometimes heated arguments took place from about 1985 affirming the cyberpunks as shapers and movers in the sluggish, complacent world of sf publishing. Bruce Sterling's fervour in polemic of this sort was messianic, and it was he who edited the first influential anthology of the movement: *Mirrorshades: The Cyberpunk Anthology* (anth **1986**), whose preface resembles a manifesto. The arguments of Sterling and various of his colleagues have been not merely vigorous but also intelligent about the changing shape of our world (particularly as regards information technology and biological engineering), and many readers must have been attracted by the sense that here was a bunch of writers doing what sf authors are supposed to do best, surf-riding on the big breakers of change and the future. On the other hand, some of the cyberpunk propaganda was so aggressive that it irresistibly reminded older observers of the mid-century politics of the extreme international-socialist left: enjoyable, but tiring to watch.

Some other sf writers, not part of the movement, were a bit taken aback by all the fuss – as well they might have been given the comparatively small amount of published fiction that was receiving such vast hype (the media picked up on cyberpunk in a big way around 1988). On the whole, cyberpunk received a friendly reception, although several of these outside writers seemed to see it as a matter more of tone than of content. Orson Scott CARD wrote a cyberpunk pastiche, "Dogwalker" (1989), that was apparently intended to make a point about this. In his comment on this story when it appeared in his *Maps in a Mirror* (coll **1990**), Card wrote: "But the worst thing about cyberpunk was the shallowness of those who imitated it. Splash some drugs onto brain-and-microchip interface, mix it up with some vague sixties-style counterculture, and then use really self-conscious, affected language, and you've got cyberpunk." This was unfair to much of it, though certainly cyberpunk produced instant CLICHÉS, as in books like *Hardwired* (**1986**) by Walter Jon WILLIAMS (although he rendered them rather well, and is by no means the most cynical-seeming of those who climbed or were hauled onto the bandwagon).

In a magazine piece, "The Neuromantics" (1986; reprinted in *Science Fiction in the Real World* coll **1990**), Norman Spinrad argued cogently that the "romance" component of Gibson's triple-punning title *Neuromancer* ("neuro" as in nervous system; "necromancer"; "new romancer") is basic to the cyberpunk form. Spinrad proposed ingeniously that the cyberpunk authors should in fact be called "neuromantics" (nobody seems to have taken him up on this), for their fiction is "a fusion of the romantic impulse with science and technology". (Spinrad sees romanticism and science as having been damagingly split during the New Wave vs HARD SF debates of the 1960s; only with cyberpunk, he argues, did they fuse together again.) He also argues, correctly, that Greg BEAR is – despite his denials – a cyberpunk writer, and an important one. Certainly the romance element is strong in Bear's work, as is the cyberpunk theme of literally remaking humanity. Gibson is not just mildly romantic: he is deeply so, as affirmed by the continuing homage his earlier work paid to the detective fiction of Raymond Chandler (1888-1959). On the other hand, Sterling's work – notably his **Shaper/ Mechanist** stories – is not very romantic at all. Sterling's cool fictions are perhaps the strangest and most estranging of the cyberpunk stories in that their embracing of the future leaves remarkably few lifelines whereby readers might connect themselves back to the present; his prose, too, is more machine-like than Gibson's (which is notably stylish). All this, while making Sterling's work rather formidable for the reader, goes to show that Spinrad's definition, like most definitions of literary movements, has major exceptions to its rule (◊ DEFINITIONS OF SF).

Cyberpunk has been accused of being a phallocratic movement, and certainly only one woman writer, Pat CADIGAN, is regularly associated with it in the public mind. But surely cyberpunk influence can be seen in the work of, for example, Candas Jane DORSEY, especially in her fine "(Learning About) Machine Sex" (1988), Elizabeth HAND, in *Winterlong* (**1990**), and even perhaps Kathy ACKER, although arguably she influenced cyberpunk more than it influenced her. Other candidates might be Storm CONSTANTINE and MISHA.

Many further writers have been associated with cyberpunk, centrally so in the instances of Tom MADDOX and Richard KADREY, perhaps more marginally so with George Alec EFFINGER, K.W. JETER, Michael SWANWICK and Jack WOMACK; this is far from a fully comprehensive list. These authors, however, along with the others cited above, are by and large sufficiently distinguished to make it clear why cyberpunk made such a splash. To contemplate them all is certainly to evoke a sense of where some of the most exciting US sf action was during the 1980s.

Towards the end of that decade, however, it became clear that the term "cyberpunk" no longer pleased all those whose work it had come to envelop. Perhaps it had begun to represent too many clichés, too many literary constraints, too big a readership wanting more and more of the same. If cyberpunk is dead in the 1990s – as several critics have claimed – it is as a result of euthanasia from within the family. Certainly the effects of cyberpunk, both within sf and in the world at large, have been invigorating; and, since most of its authors still continue to write – if not necessarily under that label – we can safely assume that the spirit of cyberpunk lives on.   [PN]

CYBERSPACE An item of sf TERMINOLOGY introduced by William GIBSON in his novel *Neuromancer* (**1984**). He takes quite an old sf idea, also much discussed by scientists, in imagining a NEAR-FUTURE era in which the human brain and nervous system (biological) can interface directly with the global information network (electrical) by jacking neurally implanted electrodes directly into a networked COMPUTER (or "cyberdeck"). The network then entered by the human mind is perceived by it, Gibson tells us, as if it were an actual territory, almost a landscape, the "consensual hallucination that was the matrix". This is cyberspace. Gibson goes on to imagine that cyberspace might contain not only human minds but also human or godlike simulacra, artefacts of the system created, perhaps accidentally, by AIs. The term "cyberspace" has since been used by other writers. It refers in fact to an imaginary but not wholly impossible special case of VIRTUAL REALITY, which is in our contemporary world a more commonly used term for machine-generated scenarios perceived, in varying degrees, as "real" by those who watch or "enter" them.   [PN]
See also: GODS AND DEMONS.

CYBORGS The term "cyborg" is a contraction of "cybernetic organism" and refers to the product of human/machine hybridization. David Rorvik popularized the idea in *As Man Becomes Machine* (**1971**), writing of the "melding" of human and machine and of a "new era of participant evolution". Elementary medical cyborgs – people with prosthetic limbs or pacemakers – are already familiar, and have been extrapolated in fiction in such works as Bernard

WOLFE's *Limbo* (**1952**; vt *Limbo '90* UK) and Martin CAIDIN's *Cyborg* (**1972**); the tv series *The* SIX-MILLION DOLLAR MAN – which popularized the term "bionic man" – was based on the latter. A more recent example of the cyborg SUPERMAN can be found in Richard LUPOFF's *Sun's End* (**1984**) and *Galaxy's End* (**1988**).

There are two other common classes of cyborg in sf: functional cyborgs are people modified mechanically to perform specific tasks, usually a job of work; adaptive cyborgs are people redesigned to operate in an alien environment, sometimes so completely that their humanity becomes problematic. The subject of the earliest major cyborg novel, *The Clockwork Man* (**1923**) by E.V. ODLE, belongs to the latter category, featuring a man of the future who has a clockwork mechanism built into his head which is supposed to regulate his whole being, and which gives him access to a multidimensional world (◊ DIMENSIONS). The most common form of cyborg portrayed in the early sf PULP MAGAZINES was an extreme version of the medical cyborg (◊ MEDICINE), consisting of a human brain in a mechanical envelope. These are featured in Edmond HAMILTON's "The Comet Doom" (1928) and CAPTAIN FUTURE series, in Neil R. JONES's **Professor Jameson** series, and in Raymond F. JONES's *The Cybernetic Brains* (**1950**; **1962**). Brains immortalized by mechanical preservation often became monstrous, like the ones in Lloyd Arthur ESHBACH's "The Time Conqueror" (1932; vt "Tyrant of Time") and Curt SIODMAK's much-filmed *Donovan's Brain* (**1943**). Some later writers approached the existential situation of humans in mechanized bodies in a much more careful and sophisticated manner; outstanding examples include C.L. MOORE's "No Woman Born" (1944) and Algis BUDRYS's *Who?* (**1958**), both of which focus on the problems of re-establishing identity once the familiar emblems are gone. Existential problems are also to the fore in *The Continuous Katherine Mortenhoe* (**1974**; vt *The Unsleeping Eye*) by D.G. COMPTON, which features a man with tv cameras implanted in his eyes.

An early example of the functional cyborg is strikingly displayed in "Scanners Live in Vain" (1950) by Cordwainer SMITH, which features cyborgs designed for SPACE FLIGHT; this particular theme dominates stories of both functional and adaptive cyborgs. Cyborg spaceships are central to Thomas N. SCORTIA's "Sea Change" (1956), Anne MCCAFFREY's *The Ship who Sang* (coll of linked stories **1969**), Kevin O'DONNELL Jr's *Mayflies* (**1979**) and Gordon R. DICKSON's *The Forever Man* (**1986**), while Vonda MCINTYRE's *Superluminal* (**1983**) features space pilots who require mechanical replacement hearts. Stories dealing with the use of adaptive cyborgs to explore other worlds include Arthur C. CLARKE's "A Meeting with Medusa" (1971), Frederik POHL's *Man Plus* (**1976**) and Paul J. MCAULEY's "Transcendence" (1988). Barrington J. BAYLEY's *The Garments of Caean* (**1976**) has two races of cyborgs adapted to the environment of outer space. Another major theme in stories dealing with functional cyborgs concerns their adaptation to the needs of espionage and war; examples include "I-C-a-BEM" (1961) by Jack VANCE, "Kings who Die" (1962) by Poul ANDERSON and *A Plague of Demons* (1965) by Keith LAUMER. Relatively few stories treat more mundane manipulative functions, although Samuel R. DELANY's *Nova* (1968) makes significant observations *en passant*. Many recent stories feature humans modified in such a way as to be able to plug in directly to COMPUTERS, sometimes working in harness with them to do many kinds of work. Particularly graphic images of this kind can be found in *ORA:CLE* (1984) by Kevin O'Donnell Jr, *Schismatrix* (1985) by Bruce STERLING, *Hardwired* (1986) by Walter Jon WILLIAMS and *Escape Plans* (1986) by Gwyneth JONES; the notion is a staple background element of CYBERPUNK. Not all functional cyborgs involve human flesh: *The Godwhale* (1974) by T.J. BASS features a massive food-collecting cetacean cyborg.

Sf in the cinema and on tv has often used the cyborg as a convenient figure of menace; examples include the DALEKS and Cybermen of DR WHO. Images of cyborg evil in written sf include the Cyclan in E.C. TUBB's **Dumarest** novels and Palmer Eldritch in Philip K. DICK's *The Three Stigmata of Palmer Eldritch* (1964). A more sympathetic cyborg is featured in Dick's *Dr Bloodmoney* (1965), and tv has presented at least one memorable sympathetic image in Harlan ELLISON's *The* OUTER LIMITS script "Demon with a Glass Hand" (1964).

One work which transcends categorization to deal in semi-allegorical fashion with the relationship between human and machine via the symbol of the cyborg is David R. BUNCH's *Moderan* (1959-70; fixup 1971), an assemblage of vignettes about a world where machine-men gradually forsake their "flesh-strips" and retire into mechanized "strongholds" to plot the destruction of their fellows.

A relevant theme anthology is *Human Machines* (anth 1976) ed Thomas N. Scortia and George ZEBROWSKI. [BS]

See also: CYBERNETICS; ROBOTS.

CYBORG 2087 Made-for-tv film (1966). Feature Film Corp. Dir Franklin Adreon, starring Michael Rennie, Karen Steele, Wendell Corey, Warren Stevens, Eduard Franz. Screenplay Arthur C. Pierce. 86 mins. Colour.

This film, which though made for tv achieved theatrical release, has a renegade CYBORG (Rennie) from AD2087 going back to 1966 to prevent a scientist (Franz) from creating a device that will later be used by a totalitarian government for a mind-control programme to which the cyborgs themselves are central. He is followed back in time by two government agents, both cyborgs, but he overcomes them and persuades the scientist to destroy his invention, though he knows that by doing so he will eliminate the possibility of his own existence. When the device is indeed destroyed, he disappears along with everybody's memories of his visit. The narrative has a

better grasp of TIME PARADOXES than usual for tv, but the performances are weak. The plot bears a similarity to that of the much later film TERMINATOR 2: JUDGMENT DAY (1991). [JB]

CYRANO de BERGERAC The form of his name under which French soldier and writer Savinien Cyrano de Bergerac (1619-1655) is best known. He is famous as the hero of a play by Edmond Rostand (1868-1918), *Cyrano de Bergerac* (1898 UK), which made legends of his swordsmanship and the size of his nose. He fought with the Gascon Guard but retired after sustaining bad wounds. Only parts of his major work of PROTO SCIENCE FICTION, *L'autre monde*, were published in posthumous versions, censored (to tone down their heretical elements) by CdB's friend Henri le Bret. *Histoire comique, par Monsieur de Cyrano Bergerac, contenant les états et empires de la lune* (1657 France; trans Tho. St Serf as *Selenarchia: The Government of the World in the Moon* 1659) is complete, but the text of *Fragment d'Histoire comique par Monsieur de Cyrano Bergerac, contenant les états et empires du soleil* (1662 France; trans A. Lovell together with the former item as *The Comical History of the States and Empires of the Moon and Sun*, coll 1687) is partial. Some of the censored text is restored in a French edition of Cyrano's complete works (*Oeuvres* [coll 1957], and both books – *Moon* and *Sun* – are translated from that edition in *Other Worlds: The Comical History of the States and Empires of the Moon and Sun* (trans Geoffrey Strachan omni 1965). It is possible that the remainder of the second part and the third part (*The History of the Stars*) were written but subsequently lost or destroyed.

The hero of the comic histories attempts SPACE FLIGHT by several absurd methods, including ROCKET power. His adventures are SATIRES interrupted by discourses and dialogues regarding contemporary issues in natural philosophy. A classic sequence in the second history has the hero tried for the crimes of humanity by a court of birds. The histories influenced several later satirists, including Jonathan SWIFT and VOLTAIRE. The first part borrows Domingo Gonsales from Francis GODWIN's *The Man in the Moone* (1638), and in the second part Tommaso CAMPANELLA appears as the hero's guide. [BS]

See also: FANTASTIC VOYAGES; FRANCE; HISTORY OF SF; MOON; RELIGION.

CZECH AND SLOVAK SF In Czechoslovakia there are two main groups, the Czechs and the Slovaks, speaking different languages. Sf is written in both.

The history of Czech sf begins in the 19th century, with the first true sf work probably being *Život na Měsíci* ["Life on the Moon"] (1881) by Karel Pleskač. Also of interest are some of the works of the famous mainstream author Svatopluk Čech; for example, *Hanuman* (1884; trans W.W. Strickland 1894 UK), depicting a civil war between two factions of apes (◊ APES AND CAVEMEN), and *Pravý výlet pana Broučka do Měsíce* ["The True Trip of Mr Brouček to the Moon"] (1888). Another important ancestral figure was Jakub

Arbes, who wrote a series of *romanetos* (short novels) on fantastic themes, including *Newtonův mozek* (**1877**; trans Jiří Kral as "Newton's Brain" in *Poet's Lore* [anth **1982** US]), which prefigures the theme of TIME TRAVEL.

The first author to write sf systematically was Karel Hloucha, author of seven novels and story collections, including *Zakletá země* ["Enchanted Country"] (**1910**) and *Sluneční vůz* ["The Solar Waggon"] (**1921**). Aliens that can take the shape of human beings play an important role in Metod Suchdolský's novel *Rusové na Martu* ["Russians on Mars"] (**1907**).

In 1920, the first sf book by Karel ČAPEK was published: the play *R.U.R.* (**1920**; trans **1923**) introduced the word ROBOT into the genre. The 1920s and 1930s were rich in sf novels; each year several titles appeared, with a variety of themes from technological inventions to the political and social aspects of future societies. Among the writers active in this period were Tomáš Hrubý, Jiří Haussmann, Marie Grubhofferová, J.M. Troska (the pseudonym of Jan Matzal) and others. Troska was the most influential, especially with his SPACE OPERA trilogy **Zápas s nebem** ["Struggle With the Skies"] (**1940-41**). At the opposite pole stood Jan Weiss (1890-1972) with his dreamlike mainstream sf novel *Dům o 1000 patrech* ["The Thousand-Storey House"] (**1929**).

After WWII (and especially after the communist coup in 1948) the production of Czech sf decreased, and those few, mainly juvenile works which were published described a more "realistic" NEAR FUTURE. František Běhounek, a well known scientist, wrote seven HARD-SF novels about the apotheosis of science in a communist future, examples being *Akce L* ["Operation L"] (**1956**) and *Robinsoni vesmíru* ["The Space Family Robinson"] (**1958**).

The leading figure of the 1960s, and the symbol of the rebirth of sf, was Josef NESVADBA, whose work is well known also in the English-speaking world. Perhaps the most popular writer of this period, however, was Ludvík Souček (1926-1978), author of nine witty sf-adventure novels and a few story collections, often with elements of the detective story. The first and most popular were the trilogy **Cesta slepých ptáků** ["Voyage of the Blind Birds"] (**1964**) and the collection *Bratři černé planety* ["Brethren of the Black Planet"] (coll **1969**); his last novel, *Blázni z Hepteridy* ["The Madmen from Hepteris"] (**1980**), was published posthumously. Two DYSTOPIAS by mainstream writers are of interest: Jiří Marek's *Blažený věk* ["Cheerful Era"] (**1967**) and Čestmír Vejdělek's *Návrat z Ráje* ["Return from Paradise"] (**1961**). The latter is a complex novel of high literary standard describing the inhabitants of a computer-ruled society who are unaware of their status as slaves. Other interesting writers of the period were Josef Koenigsmark, Václav Kajdoš and Ivan Foustka.

After the heightened activity of the 1960s, the so-called "normalization" of Czech culture following the invasion of Czechoslovakia by the Warsaw Pact countries in 1968 meant that there was another decrease in Czech sf in the first half of the 1970s. At the end of that decade, however, a new wave of writers appeared. The most significant authors of short fiction are Jaroslav Veis (1946-   ), Zdeněk Volný and Ondřej Neff (1945-   ); each has published several books. Veis's *Pandořina skříňka* ["Pandora's Box"] (coll **1979**) is very widely admired. Neff, after the success of his first collection, *Vejce naruby* ["An Inside-Out Egg"] (coll **1985**), turned to novels: his *Měsíc mého života* ["The Moon of My Life"] (**1988**), set in a colony of Moon-miners, is among the best Czech sf. Another fine book from the period, from the usually mainstream writer (although he has also produced four sf novels) Vladimír Páral, is the dystopian *Země žen* ["The Country of Women"] (**1987**). The most important publications for this generation of sf writers were the twin anthologies *Lidé ze souhvězdí Lva* ["People from the Constellation of Leo"] (anth **1983**) and *Železo přichází z hvězd* ["Iron Comes from the Stars"] (anth **1983**), both ed Vojtěch Kantor.

The establishment in 1982 of the Karel Čapek AWARD for the best sf work by new authors encouraged the arrival of a still younger generation of writers – Josef Pecinovský, František Novotný, Eduard Martin and Jan Hlavička are the most significant. Although they have published collections, this group's work primarily attained popularity through anthologies: *Návrat na planetu Zemi* ["Return to Planet Earth"] (anth **1985**) and *Stalo se zítra* ["It Happened Tomorrow"] (anth **1985**), both ed Ivo Železný.

A few sf works have been written by Czech authors in exile, an example being *Maso* ["Meat"] (coll **1981** Canada), a collection of two novellas by Martin Harníček. Another author in exile, Luděk PEŠEK, is published in German and sometimes in English, although he writes in Czech. One novel by Ivo DUKA (pseudonym of Ivo Ducháček and Helena Koldová) was published in English: *Martin and his Friend from Outer Space* (**1955**). Pavel KOHOUT, who left Czechoslovakia in 1968, later published an sf novel (*see his entry for its long title*).

Sf written in Slovak does not have as continuous a tradition, and there are noticeably fewer works. Sf featuring social comment and adventure was published in the 1930s and 1940s by Peter Suchanský, Dežo S. Turčan and Ján Kresánek-Ladčan. After WWII the production of Slovak sf was sporadic and its nature naïve, as in *Luna 2 neodpovedá* ["Luna 2 Doesn't Answer"] (**1958**), one of the three sf novels written by Ján Bajla. Only one author from the 1960s stands out: Jozef Tallo, whose collection is *Vlasy Bereniky* ["The Hair of Berenice"] (coll **1962**). Many more writers emerged in the 1980s: Alta Vášová, Ján Fekete, Jozef Repko and others; they write mainly juvenile fiction. The most successful may be the post-HOLOCAUST novel *Po* ["After"] (**1979**) by Vášová and three juvenile novels by Jozef Žarnay, including *Kolumbovia zo základne Ganymedes* ["Columbuses from

Ganymede Space Station"] (**1983**).

More than 50 sf films have been made in Czechoslovakia, the first of them in the early 1920s. The earliest of real interest are adaptations of stories by Karel Čapek; they are *Bílá nemoc* ["The White Plague"] (1937; vt *Skeleton on Horseback*), dir Hugo Haas, and *Krakatit* (1948), dir Otakar Vávra. From the mid-1950s to 1970, several sf films with animation and live action combined, based loosely on novels by Jules VERNE and using original drawings from French editions of his books, were made by director and animator Karel Zeman: *Cesta do pravěku* (1955; vt *Journey to the Beginning of Time*), VYNÁLEZ ZKÁZY (1958; vt *Weapons of Destruction*), *Baron Prášil* (1961; vt *Baron Münchhausen*), *Ukradená vzducholoď* (1966; vt *The Stolen Airship*) and *Na kometě* (1970; vt *On the Comet*). A completely animated Czech/French coproduction was *La* PLANÈTE SAUVAGE (1973; vt *Fantastic Planet*).

The tradition of Czech sf comedies was launched by Oldřich Lipský with a comedy set in "the 5th century after Sputnik": *Muž z prvního století* ["Man from the First Century"] (1961; vt *Man in Outer Space*). Lipský's other sf films include: a TIME-TRAVEL comedy, *Zabil jsem Einsteina, pánové!* (1969; vt *I Killed Einstein, Gentlemen!*); a parody of pre-WWII pulp detective fiction involving Nick CARTER and a carnivorous plant, perhaps his best film, *Adéla ještě nevečeřela* (1977; vt *Adele Hasn't Eaten Yet*); a Jules VERNE adaptation, *Tajemství hradu v Karpatech* ["Mystery of the Carpathian Castle"] (1981); and *Srdečný pozdrav ze Zeměkoule* ["Cordial Greetings from Earth"] (1982). Miloš Macourek has had a hand in several good sf comedies, notably KDO CHCE ZABÍT JESSII? (1965; vt *Who Would Kill Jessie?*) and *Což takhle dat si špenát* (1976; vt *What Would You Say to Some Spinach?*), and also cowrote the screenplay of ZÍTRA VSTANU A OPAŘÍM SE ČAJEM (1977; vt *Tomorrow I'll Wake up and Scald Myself with Tea*), one of a number of Czech sf films, several of them comedies, based on Josef Nesvadba's stories and novels.

Not many Czech films are "serious" sf, or even straight sf, but those that are include: the space opera IKARIE XB-1 (1963; vt *Voyage to the End of the Universe*); the post-HOLOCAUST story KONEC SRPNA V HOTELU OZÓN (1966; vt *The End of August at the Hotel Ozone*); a film about a visit from deep space, *Akce Bororo* ["Operation Bororo"] (1972?), dir Otakar Fuka; a children's film about First Contact with ALIENS, *Odysseus a hvězdy* ["Odysseus and the Stars"] (1974), dir Ludvík Ráža; a free adaptation of Čapek's *Krakatit* (**1924**), TEMNÉ SLUNCE (1980; vt *The Black Sun*); and, from Slovakia, ecological space sf in *Tretí Šarkan* ["The Third Dragon"] (1985), dir Peter Hledík.

Sf dramas are quite frequent on Czech tv, especially for children. One of the better serials has been *Návštěvníci* ["The Visitors"] (1984), in which an expedition from AD2484, when Earth is endangered by a comet, returns to 1984 to seek help; it was dir Jindřich Polák.

Sf is very popular in Czechoslovakia. It has a wide readership, and print-runs of books by well known authors have been up to 100,000; however, the worsening economic situation in the early 1990s is likely to change that figure dramatically for the worse. On the positive side, a monthly sf magazine, *Ikarie*, was launched in June 1990 under the editorship of Ondřej Neff, who has also edited, with Jaroslav OLŠA jr, «Encyklopedie science fiction» ["Encyclopedia of Science Fiction"] (1992).   [IA/JO]

CZECHOSLOVAKIA ◊ CZECH AND SLOVAK SF.

Da CRUZ, DANIEL (1921-1991) US writer, formerly known for numerous men's action-adventure tales, who began publishing sf with *The Grotto of the Formigans* (**1980**), a novel about African grotto MONSTERS, and who came to more general notice with his **Republic of Texas** or **Forte Family** sequence: *The Ayes of Texas* (**1982**), *Texas on the Rocks* (**1986**) and *Texas Triumphant* (**1987**). The political premises underlying the series – in the late 1990s the USSR, having hoodwinked the supinely liberal US media, has come to dominate the world – have dated, but the exuberance of the tales themselves remains winning. The protagonist, a triple-amputee WWII veteran from the newly free Republic of Texas, arms an old aircraft carrier (itself called *Texas*), and sails off to fight the Russians. Much blood is spilt, and a good time is had by all. *F-Cubed* (**1989**) is a less entrancing TECHNO-THRILLER; but *Mixed Doubles* (**1989**) enjoyably depicts the attempts of a contemporary failed composer who travels back in time to steal MUSIC from those more talented than himself. [JC]

DAGMAR ◊ Lou CAMERON.

DAGMAR, PETER ◊ Frank J. PINCHIN.

DAGNOL, JULES N. [r] ◊ ROBERT HALE LIMITED.

DAHL, ROALD (1916-1990) Welsh-born writer of Norwegian parents who spent periods of his life in the USA, but lived in the UK in his later years; married to the actress Patricia Neal 1953-83. Though his enormous success as an author of children's stories tended to dominate perceptions of his career, he was in fact long best known for his eerie, exquisitely crafted, somewhat poisonous adult tales, many of them fantasies, assembled in *Someone Like You* (coll **1953** US; exp **1961** UK), *Kiss Kiss* (coll **1960** US), *Switch Bitch* (coll **1974** US) and several later collections which often included previous material: *The Best of Roald Dahl* (coll **1978** US); *Tales of the Unexpected* (coll **1979**) and *More Roald Dahl Tales of the Unexpected* (coll **1980**; vt *More Tales of the Unexpected* 1980; vt *Further Tales of the Unexpected* 1981), both

assembled as *Roald Dahl's Completely Unexpected Tales* (omni **1986**); *Two Fables* (coll **1986** chap); *Ah, Sweet Mystery of Life* (coll **1989**); and the posthumous *The Collected Short Stories* (coll **1991**), which includes further work. Not infrequently these stories make use of borderline sf images, such as the unpleasant metamorphosis of human into bee in "Royal Jelly" (1960); but more generally it is the *threat* of sf or supernatural displacement that powers them.

RD's first title was a children's fantasy, *The Gremlins* (**1943** chap US), a short story that became famous because Walt Disney dickered for a time with making an animated film of it (there is no connection with the much later Joe DANTE film *Gremlins*). His only sf novel, *Some Time Never: A Fable for Supermen* (**1948** US), by some margin his worst book, recasts the tale for an adult audience. After attempting to sabotage humanity during WWII, the long-submerged gremlins see that we ourselves are doing the job quite adequately; they take back control of the planet after the nuclear WWIV, but then become extinct in a world bare of humanity. The strained and sour whimsy of this "fable" might be seen – according to RD's critics – as passing directly into his juvenile fantasies, though it would probably be fairer to acknowledge a world of difference between adult spitefulness and the exuberant child's-eye view of grown-ups and the meting of justice unto them presented in *James and the Giant Peach* (**1961** US) and all its successors, the most famous being *Charlie and the Chocolate Factory* (**1964** US), filmed as *Willie Wonka and the Chocolate Factory* (1971); it was assembled with its sequel, *Charlie and the Great Glass Elevator* (**1972** US), as *The Complete Adventures of Charlie and Mr Willy Wonka* (omni **1987**). RD also wrote the screenplay for the **James Bond** film YOU ONLY LIVE TWICE (1967). One late novel for adults followed, the quasi-historical, borderline-STEAMPUNK *My Uncle Oswald* (**1979**), which plays with the notion of "tapping" geniuses such as Freud and Shaw for purposes of artificial insemination

– spermpunk, in short.

But the adult work was, in the end, miserly; the stories for children were, in the end, generously wicked gifts of fable. [JC]

Other works for adults: *Over to You* (coll **1946** US), associational; *Twenty-Nine Kisses from Roald Dahl* (coll **1969**), a compilation; *Boy: Tales of Childhood* (**1984**) and *Going Solo* (**1986**), autobiographical; *Roald Dahl's Book of Ghost Stories* (anth **1983**).

For children: *The Magic Finger* (**1966** chap US); *Fantastic Mr Fox* (**1970** chap); *Danny, the Champion of the World* (**1975**); *The Wonderful Story of Henry Sugar and Six More* (coll **1977**; vt *The Wonderful World of Henry Sugar* 1977 US); *The Enormous Crocodile* (**1978**); *The Twits* (**1980** chap); *George's Marvellous Medicine* (**1981**); *The BFG* (**1982**); *The Witches* (**1983**); *The Giraffe and the Pelly and Me* (**1985**); *Matilda* (**1988**); *Esio Trot* (**1990** chap).

About the author: *Roald Dahl* (**1983**) by Chris Dowling.

See also: HUMOUR; SATIRE.

DAIBER, ALBERT [r] ◊ GERMANY.

DAIKAIJU GAMERA (vt *Gamera*) Film (1966). Daiei. Dir Noriaki Yuasa, starring Eiji Funakoshi, Harumi Kiritachi (and, in the US version, Brian Donlevy, Albert Dekker, Diane Findlay). Screenplay Fumi Takahashi. 88 mins. Colour.

This was Daiei Studios' answer to the enormously successful GOJIRA ["Godzilla"] films from Toho Studios. Gamera is a giant prehistoric turtle, restored to life by nuclear testing. It attacks Tokyo, naturally, but is captured and sent into space. The US version had extra footage showing Americans, not Japanese, discovering how to eliminate Gamera! The **Gamera** films were, apart from the **Gojira** films, Japan's most successful MONSTER MOVIES. The 6 sequels, all dir Yuasa except the first (for which he did the special effects), are: *Gamera Tai Barugon* (1966), dir Shigeo Tanaka, released in English as *Gamera vs. Barugon*, in which Gamera returns from space, now apparently jet-propelled, and fights a giant lizard that has a lethal rainbow field around it; *Gamera Tai Gaos* (1967; vt *Daikaiju Kuchusen*), released in English as *Gamera vs. Gaos* (vt *The Return of the Giant Monsters*), in which Gaos is a bad scaly monster that hates sunlight and Gamera (like Godzilla, he rapidly became a good monster) saves children; *Gamera Tai Viras* (1968; vt *Gamera Tai Uchukaiju Bairasu*), released in English as *Gamera vs. Viras* (vt *Gamera Versus Outer Space Monster Viras*; vt *Destroy All Planets*), in which two boy scouts save Gamera from alien control; *Gamera Tai Guiron* (1969), released in English as *Gamera vs. Guiron* (vt *Attack of the Monsters*), in which Gamera saves children from brain-eating female aliens and their knife-headed monster; *Gamera Tai Daimaju Jaiga* (1970), released in English as *Gamera vs. Jiger* (vt *Gamera vs. Monster X*; vt *Monsters Invade Expo 70*), in which nasty Jiger lays an egg inside Gamera, a parasite hatches and starts sucking his blood, and children in a mini-submarine enter his veins to help out; and *Gamera Tai Shinkai Kaiju Jigura* (1971),

released in English as *Gamera vs. Zigra* (vt *Gamera Versus the Deep Sea Monster Zigra*), in which there is an anti-pollution theme, bad aliens, and a very bad script. [PN]

See also: CINEMA.

DAIKAIJU KUCHUSEN ◊ DAIKAIJU GAMERA.

DAIL, C(HARLES) C(URTIS) (1851-1902) US writer and lawyer whose *Willmoth the Wanderer, or The Man from Saturn* (**1890**; rev c1891) is a real oddity. Though told with no great skill, its narrative, purporting to be that of Willmoth the Saturnian as told towards the end of his several-million-year lifespan, is an eventful affair. Willmoth proceeds from Saturn to Venus (travel via ANTIGRAVITY) and, late in the book, to a prehistoric Earth, whose primitive inhabitants he breeds into *Homo sapiens*. CCD's episodic second novel, *The Stone Giant: A Story of the Mammoth Cave* (**1898**), lies within the overarching context of the first book. It is presented as a translation (by Willmoth) of memoirs by the prehistoric ruler Wymorian, an 8ft (2.4m) giant and founder of ATLANTIS, who is given (by ancient descendants of Willmoth) an elixir of life. There is much talk about the ethics of the IMMORTALITY experiment, which on the whole is a failure – as, notoriously, was Atlantis. [PN/JC]

DAIN, ALEX Pseudonym of Alex Lukeman (? -?), US writer whose sf novel is *The Bane of Kanthos* (**1969** dos), a SPACE OPERA. [JC]

DAKE, CHARLES ROMYN (? -?) US writer whose lost-race (◊ LOST WORLDS) novel, *A Strange Discovery* (**1899**), features a Roman colony in the Antarctic and is notable in that it continues the story of Edgar Allan POE's Gordon Pym. [JC]

DALE, ADAM ◊ Brian HOLLOWAY.

DALE, FLOYD D. (? -) US writer whose first work, *A Hunter's Fire* (**1989**), is a post-HOLOCAUST military-sf adventure. [JC]

DALEKS These sinister ALIENS, bent on universal conquest, mutated and rendered immobile by radioactivity, inhabit metal transporters to become CYBORGS. They were introduced in the tv series DR WHO by writer Terry NATION in *The Hidden Planet* (1963-4), the long-running programme's second story, later filmed as DR WHO AND THE DALEKS (1965); another 1964 tv story was filmed as DALEKS: INVASION EARTH 2150 A.D. (1966). The Daleks returned in many **Dr Who** tv episodes, being the most popular feature of its first decade; only in 1975 did we learn, in *Genesis of the Daleks*, that they had been created by an evil, crippled genius, Davros. [PN]

DALEKS: INVASION EARTH 2150 A.D. (vt *Invasion Earth 2150 A.D.*) Film (1966). AARU. Dir Gordon Flemyng, starring Peter Cushing, Bernard Cribbins, Roberta Tovey, Jill Curzon. Screenplay Milton Subotsky, based on a 6-episode DR WHO tv story by Terry NATION, *The Dalek Invasion of Earth* (1964). 84 mins. Colour.

This was the second movie made by coproducers Milton Subotsky and Max J. Rosenberg to cash in on the popularity of the **Dr Who** tv series, the first being

DR WHO AND THE DALEKS (1965). The DALEKS, almost 200 years on, have invaded Earth (largely unchanged since the 1960s) intending to empty its core and use it as a giant spaceship, but Dr Who and his colleagues, who include a London bobby (Cribbins) from 1966, thwart their plan in a story devoid of dramatic tension or science: Earth's north and south magnetic fields, we are told, meet below Bedfordshire, and can be used to suck the Daleks into oblivion at Earth's centre. The greatest ineptness of the screenplay is its failure to give Dr Who, here played as a doddery old gent by Cushing, anything at all to do. [PN]

DALEY, BRIAN C. (1947-) US writer whose first novels were the SCIENCE-FANTASY **Coramonde** sequence – *The Doomfarers of Coramonde* (**1977**) and *The Starfollowers of Coramonde* (**1979**) – which puts into an ALTERNATE-WORLD setting a tale of MAGIC, court politics and quest, starring a Vietnam veteran who helps his friend, the rightful ruler, fight off an evil sorcerer. Of slightly greater sf interest is the **Alacrity FitzHugh** sequence – *Requiem for a Ruler of Worlds* (**1985**), *Jinx on a Terran Inheritance* (**1985**) and *Fall of the White Ship Avatar* (**1986**) – whose hero, Alacrity, hurtles through sf adventures on a galactic scale. BCD's best single novel has perhaps been *A Tapestry of Magics* (**1983**), a fantasy whose central conceit – a tapestry which is also a magical singularity – recursively recruits into the tale, from various eons and realities, characters both real and fictional, including some of Robert A. HEINLEIN's, perhaps in acknowledgement of Heinlein's own RECURSIVE later fiction.

BCD remains best known, however, for his highly competent and colourful **Star Wars** ties, *Han Solo at Star's End* * (**1979**), *Han Solo's Revenge* * (**1979**) and *Han Solo and the Lost Legacy* * (**1980**), which admirably set out to infill Solo's pre-saga life. Other ties include *Tron* * (**1982**) (◊ TRON) and the two sequences of **Robotech** tv ties with James Luceno, writing together as Jack McKinney: the first comprises *Robotech #1: Genesis* * (**1987**), *#2: Battle Cry* * (**1987**), *#3: Homecoming* * (**1987**), *#4: Battlehymn* * (**1987**), *#5: Force of Arms* * (**1987**), *#6: Doomsday* * (**1987**), *#7: Southern Cross* * (**1987**), *#8: Metal Fire* * (**1987**), *#9: The Final Nightmare* * (**1987**), *#10: Invid Invasion* * (**1987**), *#11: Metamorphosis* * (**1987**) and *#12: Symphony of Light* * (**1987**); the second sequence, the **Sentinels** books, comprises *The Sentinels #1: The Devil's Hand* * (**1988**), *#2: Dark Powers* * (**1988**), *#3: Death Dance* * (**1988**), *#4: World Killers* * (**1988**) and *#5: Rubicon* * (**1988**); both sequences conclude with *Robotech: The End of the Circle* * (**1990**). Luceno and BCD, both still writing as Jack McKinney, continued with some independent titles: *Kaduna Memories* (**1990**), about a detective in 21st-century Manhattan, and the first volumes of the **Black Hole Travel Agency** sequence, *Event Horizon* (**1991**) and *Artifact of the System* (**1991**). It could not be argued that BCD has much built upon the promise of his first books, but nor could it be said that he has ever given bad value. He has become one of the necessary journeymen. [JC]

DALGAARD, NIELS (1956-) Danish academic and sf critic whose PhD research into Danish sf is the first on such a topic to be funded by the Danish Research Council for the Humanities. ND is sf reviewer for the newspaper *Politiken* and editor of the critical journal *Proxima* (since 1981). He wrote the DENMARK entry in this volume. [PN]

DALMAS, JOHN Pseudonym for all his fiction of US writer John R(obert) Jones (1926-), whose first career was as a research ecologist for the US Forest Service. He began publishing with *The Yngling* (**1969** *ASF*; fixup **1971**; rev **1984**), which, with its sequel, *Homecoming* (**1984**) – both assembled as *The Orc Wars* (omni **1992**) – depicts a barbarian future whose history echoes that of the eponymous Norse kings of legend; eventually the hero of the saga leads his neo-Vikings south from the encroaching ice, though their ideal community is soon under threat; «The Yngling and the Circle of Power» (1992) is a prequel. In the **Fanglith** series – *Fanglith* (**1985**) and *Return to Fanglith* (**1987**) – the planet to which criminals are exiled turns out to be Earth; much of JD's work similarly transforms SPACE-OPERA venues into arenas where ironies (or the gods) have free play. In both *The Reality Matrix* (**1986**) and, with Rod Martin (1928-), *The Playmasters* (**1986**) this drift of implication becomes explicit. *The Regiment* (**1987**) and its sequel, *The White Regiment* (**1990**), tell of a group of mercenaries from a military planet sent off to fight until they all die – characters, once again, who are players in others' games. *The General's President* (**1988**) interestingly assumes that a US civilian puppet-leader might convincingly fox his military backers. Though his work is teasingly close to routine, JD is too various and lively to dismiss. [JC]

Other works: *The Varkhaus Conspiracy* (**1983**); *Touch the Stars: Emergence* (**1983**) with Carl Martin (1950-); *The Scroll of Man* (**1985**); *The Walkaway Clause* (**1986**); *The Lantern of God* (**1989**); *The Lizard War* (**1989**); *The Khalif's War* (**1991**).

DALTON, HENRY ROBERT S(AMUEL) (1835-?) UK writer, active to about 1890, whose sf novel *Lesbia Newman* (**1889**) depicts a profound change in UK social attitudes after a disastrous 1890s loss of territory to European powers and the USA, as a consequence of which the eponymous female manages to seduce the Ecumenical Council of 1900 into proclaiming the worship of women. [JC]

DALTON, SEAN ◊ Jay D. BLAKENEY.

DALY, HAMLIN [s] ◊ E. Hoffmann PRICE.

DAMNATION ALLEY Film (1977). Landers-Roberts/Zeitman/20th Century-Fox. Dir Jack Smight, starring Jan-Michael Vincent, George Peppard, Dominique Sanda. Screenplay Alan Sharp, Lukas Heller, based on *Damnation Alley* (1969) by Roger ZELAZNY. 95 mins cut to 91 mins. Colour.

In this travesty the solitary, snarling, Hell's Angel protagonist of Zelazny's novel has become four fairly decent Air Force officers. There are almost no survivors of WWIII. The officers set out from the western USA to cross the country eastwards in "land-mobiles", seeking viable communities. The HOLO-CAUST has tilted Earth's axis, turning the sky into a display of glowing radiation and electrical storms, represented by astonishingly garish and inadequate process work from an obviously low-budget special-effects department. The encounter with mutated, carnivorous cockroaches stands out in an otherwise wholly laughable and random series of stereotyped adventures with murderous hillbillies, floods, a girl, a feral boy and several deaths. [PN]

DAMNED, THE (vt *These Are the Damned*) Film (1961). Hammer/Swallow. Dir Joseph Losey, starring Mac-Donald Carey, Oliver Reed, Shirley Ann Field, Viveca Lindfors, Alexander Knox. Screenplay Evan Jones, based on *The Children of Light* (**1960**) by Henry L. LAWRENCE. 96 mins, cut to 87 mins (UK) and to 77 mins (US). B/w.

Made in the UK by expatriate US director Losey, this film so dismayed the distributors, Columbia, that they kept it on the shelf for two years before releasing it, and then with major cuts. A US visitor to an English seaside town (Carey) becomes involved with the sister (Field) of the leader of some tough, local bikers. The pair accidentally learn of a secret, illegal military project to irradiate children kept in under-ground isolation, thereby rendering them capable of surviving nuclear HOLOCAUST. (The otherwise power-ful film is partly devalued by Losey's casual approach to science; gaffes include the belief that the irradiated children would have abnormally low body tempera-tures but be otherwise healthy!) Ironically, Carey and Field are fatally contaminated by the very children they seek to free. Losey's moral indignation has a paranoid streak, but the film's evocative, allusive imagery is strong, in particular when the children communicate with their obsessed, scientist "father" (Knox) by tv and in the final shots, showing a helicopter hovering like a giant carrion bird over the small boat carrying the dying couple – echoing the grotesque, sometimes bird-like sculptures executed by the scientist's lover (in reality by distinguished sculptress Elisabeth Frink), which stand on the clifftops nearby. *TD* is one of the most memorable sf films of a period when few really good directors would come within miles of the genre. [JB/PN]

See also: CINEMA; PARANOIA.

DAMRON, HILLEL [r] ◊ ISRAEL.

DAN DARE – PILOT OF THE FUTURE UK sf COMIC-strip character, distinguished in appearance by his long chin and by the zigzag on the outer end of each eyebrow. DD was created by Frank HAMPSON for the weekly boys' comic *Eagle*, in which – with the sobriquet "Pilot of the Future" – he appeared with his Lancastrian batman Digby from 1950 until the comic's demise in 1969. Hampson supervised a team of writers, artists, model-makers and photographers to create a totally convincing scenario of the future, as governed by the United Nations Organization. Wri-ters included Eric Eden, David Motton, Alan Stranks

and Chad Varah; artists included Frank Bellamy, Bruce Cornwell, Eric Eden, Donald Harley, Harold Johns, Desmond Walduck and Keith Watson. *DD* stories generally dealt with the exploration of the Solar System, individual stories often centring on conflicts between DD and the Mekon, a green-skinned, dome-headed Venusian despot. Under Hampson's firm control, pictorial authenticity was achieved through the use of scale models, and characters were drawn from photographs of real people; stories were scrutinized for scientific accuracy (Arthur C. CLARKE was adviser for the first six months).

After Hampson's departure in 1959 the writers extended their themes beyond the limitations of the original conception in a series of less convincing adventures across the Galaxy. Continuity became strained and, despite a period of revitalization at the hands of Keith Watson, the strip declined, no new material being published after Jan 1967. A *DD* newspaper strip of 7 frames per week was published in the UK Sunday newspaper *The People* 3 May-26 Nov 1964.

Written by Tom Tulley and drawn at first by Massimo Belardinelli and subsequently by Dave GIBBONS, the character was revived in name only in 2,000 AD (from #1, 26 Feb 1977). The voluble adverse reaction to this from fans of the original strip, along with news of plans for a nostalgic *DD* tv series (to be produced by Paul de Savary), persuaded IPC, *Eagle*'s erstwhile publisher, to relaunch *Eagle* in 1982 as a weekly pulp comic with new *DD* stories featuring the "great grandson" of the original DD. At first top-line artists were used – Gerry Embleton (although he quickly became disillusioned by inconsistent editorial directives and left) and then Ian Kennedy (until 1984) – but the series failed to recreate the credibility of the original, and for a time IPC used less able artists on it until, for a six-week period in 1989, they returned once more to Hampson's original conception (with Keith Watson as artist). The new incarnation of *Eagle* failed to achieve significant sales and became a monthly, reprinting earlier strips alongside new *DD* stories written by Tom Tulley and drawn by David Pugh; it still (early 1992) survives.

In 1982 de Savary's tv series was abandoned unfinished, although a different *DD* tv series is (early 1992) in the process of production by Zenith Films. There have been two RADIO adaptations: the first, starring Noel Johnson, ran continuously on Radio Luxembourg 2 July 1951-25 May 1956; the second, starring Nick Ward, adapted *Eagle*'s original *DD* story and was broadcast by BBC Radio 4 in 1990. Book-length reprints of Hampson's *DD* stories have been published by Dragon's Dream – *The Man from Nowhere* (graph **1979**), *Rogue Planet* (graph **1980**) and *Reign of the Robots* (graph **1981**) – and by Hawk Books – *Pilot of the Future* (graph **1987**), *Red Moon Mystery & Marooned on Mercury* (graph omni **1988**), *Operation Saturn* (graph **1989**), *Prisoners of Space* (graph **1990**) and *The Man from Nowhere* (graph **1991**). DD also starred in a political-SATIRE comic strip written by Grant Morrison and drawn by Rian Hughes, which appeared 1990-91 in *Revolver* and *Crisis* and was published in book form as *Dare* (graph **1991**). A comic-strip parody of *DD*, lampooning contemporary UK politics, ran as *Dan Dire – Pilot of the Future* in 1991 in the satirical magazine *Private Eye*. There have also been two novels: *Dan Dare on Mars* * (**1956**) by Basil Dawson and *Dan Dare – Pilot of the Future* * (**1977**) by Angus Allen, the latter a novelization of the original *Eagle* story.

For more on *DD*'s creator read *The Man who Drew Tomorrow* (**1985**) by Alastair Crompton, and for more on the character read *The Dan Dare Dossier* (**1990**). [RT/ABP/JE]

DANE, CLEMENCE Pseudonym of UK playwright and novelist Winifred Ashton (1888-1965), best remembered for *Broome Stages* (**1931**), a tale of the theatre. She became known to the sf world late in life when she edited the **Novels of Tomorrow** series in 1955-6 for Michael Joseph Ltd, publishing work by John CHRISTOPHER, Harold MEAD and Arthur SELLINGS. Some of her own fiction was of genre interest. *Legend* (**1919**) concerns a supernatural relationship between a dead writer and her biographer. *The Babyons* (**1927**) traces a curse through four generations. *The Arrogant History of White Ben* (**1939**), set in a beleaguered NEAR FUTURE, gives an animate scarecrow the task of leading the UK out of trouble. In *The Saviours* (coll of linked plays **1942**) Merlin attempts to revitalize Britain by giving Arthur's heirs good advice. Some of the stories assembled in *Fate Cries Out* (coll **1935**) are of genre interest. [JC]

DANGER: DIABOLIK ◊ DIABOLIK.

DANGEROUS VISIONS Original ANTHOLOGY ed Harlan ELLISON. *DV* (**1967**) was a massive and influential anthology of 33 stories and copious prefatory material; it became strongly identified with the NEW WAVE in the USA. Among its stories, "Aye, and Gomorrah . . ." by Samuel R. DELANY, "Gonna Roll the Bones" by Fritz LEIBER and "Riders of the Purple Wage" by Philip José FARMER won major awards. *DV* was followed by *Again, Dangerous Visions* (anth **1972**), which was larger still, although it created less stir. It contained two more major-award winners, "When It Changed" by Joanna RUSS and *The Word for World is Forest* (1972; **1976**) by Ursula K. LE GUIN, among its 46 stories. *ADV* used only authors who had not appeared in *DV*. A third and still unpublished instalment, again with wholly new authors – «The Last Dangerous Visions» – has become legendary for its many postponements over 19 years (to 1992), although Ellison is on record (1979) as saying that over 100 stories were bought for it. One sternly adversarial account of its history is the widely discussed *The Last Deadloss Visions* (**1987** chap; rev 1987) compiled/written and published by Christopher PRIEST. [MJE/PN]

See also: TABOOS.

DANIEL, GABRIEL (1649-1728) French writer whose *Voyage du Monde de Descartes* (**1690**; trans T. Taylor as *A Voyage to the World of Cartesius* 1692 UK) is a FANTASTIC VOYAGE whose purpose was to popularize the ideas of the philosopher René Descartes (1596-1650) on COSMOLOGY and other matters. [PN]

See also: PROTO SCIENCE FICTION; SPACE FLIGHT.

DANIEL, YULI (1925-1988) Russian author who wrote as Nikolai Arzhak; he lived in exile after having been imprisoned in 1966 along with his dissident friend, Andrey SINYAVSKY (Abram Tertz), for the writings translated as *This is Moscow Speaking, and Other Stories* (written before 1966; trans Stuart Hood and others **1968** UK). The title story is of sf interest: 10 August 1960 is declared to be Public Murder Day; the point is satirical. The eponymous character in "The Man from MINAP" has the power of predetermining the sex of any child from his loins. [JC]

See also: TABOOS.

DANIELS, LOUIS G. [s] ◊ Daniel F. GALOUYE.

DANIELS, MAX Pseudonym of US writer Roberta Leah Jacobs Gellis (1927-   ), who wrote non-sf as Leah Jacobs. As MD she published two unremarkable sf adventures, *The Space Guardian* (**1978**) and *Offworld* (**1979**). [JC]

DANN, JACK (MAYO) (1945-   ) US writer and anthologist, with a BA in social/political science, who began publishing sf in 1970 with two stories for *Worlds of If* with George ZEBROWSKI, "Dark, Dark the Dead Star" and "Traps". Among his best and most revealing stories of this period was *Junction* (1973 *Fantasy*; exp **1981**), a NEBULA-award finalist in its early form; its young protagonist must leave the eponymous village, the last place on Earth to remain physically stable, to explore the "Hell" of mutability outside. The expansion cogently dramatizes what Gregory FEELEY has suggested is JD's central theme: the rousing of a young man from disaffected solipsism into awareness of the marvels of the noösphere. *Starhiker* (fixup **1977**), set in a heightened SPACE-OPERA venue, similarly puts a young human singer-bard escapee from alien-occupied Earth into an alien spaceship, where he undergoes a series of revelatory experiences (including near self-transcendence on a sentient planet) before returning to his depressed home. The stories assembled in *Timetipping* (coll **1980**) reiterate this basic pattern. Only with *The Man who Melted* (**1984**) did JD expand his canvas by introducing a human subject – his lost wife – for whom the protagonist must search through a baroque world rendered savagely mutable through collective psychoses which have a binding effect on reality.

Despite the clear though strait attainments of his fiction, JD soon became – and has remained – best known as an editor of several strong anthologies: *Wandering Stars* (anth **1974**) and *More Wandering Stars* (anth **1981**) feature sf about Jews; *Faster than Light* (anth **1976**), with George Zebrowski; *Future Power* (anth **1976**), with Gardner DOZOIS, the first of many collaborations with Dozois (see listing below), *Immortals: Short Novels of the Transhuman Future* (anth **1980**);

the impressive *In the Field of Fire* (anth **1987**) with Jeanne Van Buren Dann, about Vietnam. Much of his effort in the 1980s was reportedly devoted to a long non-genre novel whose projected title was «Counting Coup». But for now it seems that, after climaxing his genre career with the creation of a rich and humanized world in *The Man who Melted*, JD has lost his need to write sf.   [JC]

Other works: *Echoes of Thunder* (**1991** chap dos) with Jack C. HALDEMAN II, a TOR BOOKS Double originally designed for DOS publication, but released as a conventional two-item anthology. JD also collaborated with Gardner Dozois on seven of the stories assembled in the latter's *Slow Dancing through Time* (coll **1990**).

Other works as editor: An exclamatory series, all with Dozois: *Aliens!* (anth **1980**), *Unicorns!* (anth **1982**), *Magicats!* (anth **1984**), *Bestiary!* (anth **1985**), *Mermaids!* (anth **1985**), *Sorcerers!* (anth **1986**), *Demons!* (anth **1987**), *Dogtales!* (anth **1988**), *Seaserpents!* (anth **1989**), *Magicats II* (anth **1991**) and *Little People!* (anth **1991**).

About the author: *The Work of Jack Dann: An Annotated Bibliography & Guide* (**1990**) by Jeffrey M. ELLIOT.

See also: ESP; GENERATION STARSHIPS; PSYCHOLOGY; RELIGION; WAR.

DANTE, JOE (1947-   ) US film-maker. Originally a fan writer, JD entered the film industry working for Roger CORMAN's New World in the trailers department, making Filipino movies look more exciting by inserting stock shots of exploding helicopters. His first feature, codirected with Allan Arkush, was *Hollywood Boulevard* (1976), a brisk and breezy SATIRE on low-budget schlock movies featuring many cameo roles, ranging from Dick Miller to Godzilla (◊ GOJIRA), inaugurating JD's tradition of movie-buff in-jokes.

With writer John SAYLES, JD made PIRANHA (1978) and *The Howling* (1981), a pair of effective MONSTER MOVIES with amusing satirical twists (the latter not really sf), and then he gravitated into the orbit of Steven SPIELBERG to direct an episode of *Twilight Zone: The Movie* (adapted from "It's a Good Life" [1953] by Jerome BIXBY) and more famously *Gremlins* (1984), a nasty anecdote in which anarchic monsters chew away at the foundations of a Spielberg-cum-Capra small town.

Following the box-office disappointment of his most personal film, EXPLORERS (1985), a meditation on the SENSE OF WONDER informed by the cultural legacy of Forrest J. ACKERMAN, JD has had less independent control, but has nevertheless delivered a lively, self-aware run of comedies with an edge: INNERSPACE (1987) is a feature-length parody of FANTASTIC VOYAGE (1966), *The 'burbs* (1989) a psychotic neighbourhood comedy, and *Gremlins II: The New Batch* (1990). JD has also contributed episodes to the omnibus film of sf skits, *Amazon Women on the Moon* (1987), and to the tv series AMAZING STORIES (1985-7), *The* TWILIGHT ZONE (2nd series, 1985-7) and *Police Squad* (1982). In 1991 JD became creative consultant for, and directed 4 episodes

of, *Eerie, Indiana* (1991), an NBC tv series about a Tom-Sawyer-type kid and his sidekick who conduct supernatural investigations in a seemingly average but actually weird town.   [KN]

See also: CINEMA; FEMINISM; HORROR IN SF.

DANTE ALIGHIERI (1265-1321) Italian poet. His *La divina commedia* (c1304-21 in manuscript; many translations as *The Divine Comedy*) is an epic poem of 100 cantos in 3 books, each of 33 cantos, with an introduction; the books are *Inferno*, *Purgatorio* and *Paradiso*. It has profoundly affected not only the religious imagination but all subsequent allegorical creation of imaginary worlds in literature generally. For that reason it can (with hindsight) be said to be a work of PROTO SCIENCE FICTION (although it stands at the head of other traditions much older than the sciencefictional); indeed, it *is* sf in the strict sense, albeit the science is medieval. Its subject is cosmological (◊ COSMOLOGY) – it offers us in its worlds of Hell, Purgatory and Heaven (and Earth, Sun and stars) a picture of the way the Universe is structured. The obvious objection to such a view is that the work is theological and philosophical in intent; this is so, but there was no distinction between science and RELIGION when Dante wrote, and he did so with the eye of a scientist, transcending the rational but not deserting it. The tradition that led to sf has *The Divine Comedy* as an ancestor.   [PN]

See also: GODS AND DEMONS; ITALY; MUSIC.

DANVERS, JACK Writing name of Camille Auguste Marie Caseleyr (1909-   ), a Belgian who, after WWII, emigrated to Australia, where he set his sf novel, *The End of it All* (**1962** UK). The tale depicts a nuclear WAR and climaxes in doomed Australian attempts to cope with epidemics unleashed by the opposing forces. In the end extinction is total.   [JC]

DANZELL, GEORGE [s] ◊ Nelson S. BOND.

DARE, ALAN ◊ George GOODCHILD.

D'ARGENTEUIL, PAUL Pseudonym of unidentified US author of *The Trembling of Borealis* (**1899**), set in the USA after a war with Cuba and featuring a revolt of the working classes which brings about a welfare state and the disenfranchisement of Blacks. Given the socialist – albeit racist – bent of the tale, the author's pseudonym can be read as linking wealth to work.   [JC]

d'ARGYRE, GILLES ◊ Gérard KLEIN.

DARIU, AL. N. [r] ◊ ROMANIA.

DARK ANGEL ◊ I COME IN PEACE.

DARKE, JAMES ◊ Laurence JAMES.

DARKMAN Film (1990). Universal. Dir Sam Raimi, starring Liam Neeson, Frances McDormand, Colin Friels, Larry Drake. Screenplay Chuck Pfarrer, Sam Raimi, Ivan Raimi, Daniel Goldin, Joshua Goldin, from a story by Raimi. 91 mins. Colour.

In its violence and simple, over-the-top characterization this is essentially the film equivalent of a comic-book, an "origin of a SUPERHERO" story of sadism and revenge. Darkman, patterned on the Phantom of the Opera (with visual quotes reminding us of other early Universal HORROR films), has had his face and hands horribly mutilated in a gangster attack, and the nerves that transmit pain and pleasure have been severed in hospital. He returns as a half-mad avenger. The sf element – synthetic skin that lasts exactly 99 mins and permits Darkman to duplicate exactly his gangster enemies or appear as briefly normal to his girlfriend – is borrowed from the old sf movie DOCTOR X (1932). There are bravura opening and closing sequences, but *D* is badly constructed (too many writers?) and uninvolving, lacking the insane vigour of Raimi's début film, *The Evil Dead* (1982). [PN]

DARK STAR Film (1974). Jack H. Harris Enterprises. Dir John CARPENTER, starring Brian Narelle, Dan O'Bannon, Joe Saunders, Dre Pahich. Screenplay Carpenter, O'Bannon. 83 mins. Colour.

This cult success, Carpenter's début, was originally a 45min film shot on 16mm by students at the University of Southern California for $6000, but producer Jack H. Harris provided cash for new footage and for transfer to 35mm film stock. *DS* is a SATIRE on space films: the *Dark Star* is a SPACESHIP in which four men are endlessly roaming the Universe on a tedious mission to locate "unstable" worlds and destroy them with thermostellar bombs. Conditions have deteriorated – the COMPUTER is malfunctioning, the life-support systems acting up, the crew in various stages of psychosis, the cryonically maintained captain "dead" but still partly conscious, the ship's mascot (an ALIEN like a beach ball with claws) increasingly belligerent and, worst of all, one of the sentient thermostellar bombs has to be continually coaxed out of exploding prematurely by debates about phenomenology. *DS* ends apocalyptically ("Let there be light!" the bomb decides), with each crew member reaching his desired apotheosis, one boardriding through space and a second undergoing ecstatic union with the stars in an asteroid shower.

Described by one critic as "a *Waiting for Godot* in outer space", *DS* is a sophisticated mixture of black comedy and genuine sf. Technically quite good, its sets and effects are superior to those of sf films costing 10 times its (eventual) $60,000 budget. The novelization is *Dark Star*∗ (1974) by Alan Dean FOSTER. [JB/PN]

See also: CINEMA; SATIRE.

DARLTON, CLARK Pseudonym of German writer, translator and editor Walter Ernsting (1920-   ); he has also written as F. MacPatterson. In the 1950s he edited the German *Utopia-Magazin* (launched 1955), providing it with much original and translated material. In 1957 he began a series of sf publications, **Terra-Sonderband**, and was one of the founding editors and writers, with K.-H. SCHEER, of the PERRY RHODAN series of SPACE OPERAS from 1961. Over 1600 of these booklets had appeared, on a weekly basis, by mid-1992; a slightly expurgated series of English-language translations began with *Enterprise Stardust* (trans **1969** US) and continued through 141 further

instalments to *Phantom Horde* (trans **1979** US). [JC/PN]
See also: GERMANY.

DARNAY, ARSEN (JULIUS) (1936-   ) Hungarian-born writer, in the USA from 1953 and a US citizen from 1961. His first sf story, "Such is Fate", appeared in *If* in 1974; his first novel, *A Hostage for Hinterland* (**1976**), set the pattern for much of his work: in a post-HOLOCAUST USA, where floating CITIES depend upon land-dwelling ecofreak tribesmen for the helium that cools their reactors, crisis erupts into a bleak and somewhat metaphysical confrontation, at the end of which the cities die. A similarly abstract dichotomy, set on a RIMWORLD, is destabilized in *The Siege of Faltara* (**1978**). *The Splendid Freedom* (coll of linked stories **1980**) carries its protagonists, who are linked through REINCARNATION, into a variety of DYSTOPIAS. AD has not published fiction since 1981. [JC]
Other works: *Karma: A Novel of Retribution and Transcendence* (**1978**; vt *The Karma Affair* 1979); *The Purgatory Zone* (**1981**).

DARRINGTON, HUGH (1940-   ) UK writer whose sf novels are *The God Killers* (**1970**) with Tony Halliwell, both authors signing as James Ross, and *Gravitor* (**1971**), which features an oppressed world and a scientific plot to increase GRAVITY, causing chaos . . . to the advantage of the plotters. [JC]

DARWIN, ERASMUS (1731-1802) UK physician, philosopher and poet; grandfather of Charles Darwin (1809-1882). It is for his poetry that ED is of interest to the sf field; in particular, *The Botanic Garden: A Poem, in Two Parts; Part 1: The Economy of Vegetation; Part II: The Loves of the Plants* (as separate poems **1792** and **1789**; **1795**) conveys through its wooden but occasionally powerful couplets a serious speculative message about the chronological depth of EVOLUTION, for which he argued in abominable rhyme – examples of his verse can be found in *The Stuffed Owl* (anth **1930**), ed D.B. Wyndham Lewis (1894-1969) and Charles Lee – clearly presaging the revolutionary thoughts of his grandson.

ED's prose work *Zoonomia: Of the Laws of Organic Life* (**1796**) and the posthumously published poem *The Temple of Nature* (**1802**) both extend the argument, with a wealth of technological and scientific imagery. The extent to which science fired ED's imagination, together with his contemporary popularity, make him an important figure in PROTO SCIENCE FICTION and his work an early outstanding success in terms of sf PREDICTION. He belonged to the period when the imagery of science first entered the consciousness of laymen in general. [JC/PN]
About the author: *Erasmus Darwin* (**1963**) by Desmond King-Hele; Brian W. ALDISS discusses ED at length in *Trillion Year Spree: The History of Science Fiction* (**1986**) with David WINGROVE.

D.A.R.Y.L. Film (1985). World Film Services/ Columbia. Dir Simon Wincer, starring Mary Beth Hurt, Michael McKean, Kathryn Walker, Josef Sommer, Barret Oliver. Screenplay David Ambrose, Allan Scott, Jeffrey Ellis. 100 mins. Colour.

D.A.R.Y.L. is a Data Analysing Robot Youth Life-form but, when "he" (Oliver) wakes up amnesiac in the woods, he thinks he is just a small boy, Daryl. Adopted by a pleasant family, he learns not to show his superintelligence and coordination too obviously and makes local friends, but then is located by the scientists who made him, almost terminated by the military, escapes . . . and so forth. There is a happy ending. This film is fairly obviously aimed at children and is competently and even engagingly made, but it never ignites; even those sf riffs proven successful by Steven SPIELBERG and here borrowed from him (most obviously – ◊ E.T. – the alien being sheltered in suburbia who undergoes death and resurrection) remain comparatively inert. [PN]

DATLOW, ELLEN (SUE) (1949-) US editor, fiction editor of *Omni* from Oct 1981, and editor of seven spin-off anthologies from that magazine 1983-9 (◊ OMNI *for details*). The combination of a decent budget and good critical taste have made ED one of the more influential US sf (and fantasy) editors, and she has by no means restricted her story-buying to work from already established writers. Aside from the **Omni** anthologies she has edited *Blood is Not Enough: 17 Stories of Vampirism* (anth **1989**), its sequel *A Whisper of Blood* (anth **1991**) and *Alien Sex* (anth **1990**), a strong collection of both sf and fantasy (◊ SEX). With Terri WINDLING ED has edited the **Year's Best Fantasy** anthology series: *The Year's Best Fantasy: First Annual Collection* (anth **1988**; vt *Demons and Dreams: The Best Fantasy and Horror 1* UK), *The Year's Best Fantasy: Second Annual Collection* (anth **1989**; vt *Demons and Dreams 2* UK), #3 (anth **1990**), #4 (anth **1991**) and #5 (**1992**). These are certainly the best of their kind – the first two won World Fantasy AWARDS – being very big, very wide-ranging and intelligently selected; ED mainly looks after the horror, Windling the fantasy. [PN]

DAUDET, LÉON [r] ◊ FRANCE.

DAUGHTER OF DESTINY ◊ ALRAUNE.

DAVENPORT, BASIL (1905-1966) US academic and anthologist. His connection with sf began with *An Introduction to Islandia, its History, Custom, Laws, Language, and Geography, as Prepared by Basil Davenport from Islandia* (**1942** chap), a book about *Islandia* (**1942**) by Austin Tappan WRIGHT. Then came a short critical and historical study, *Inquiry into Science Fiction* (**1955**). BD also introduced the anonymously edited critical anthology *The Science Fiction Novel: Imagination and Social Criticism* (anth **1959**; rev 1964), which contains lectures delivered by Alfred BESTER, Robert BLOCH, Robert A. HEINLEIN and C.M. KORNBLUTH at a 1957 symposium at the University of Chicago. His anthologies are in the main fantasy rather than sf. Three were compiled with the aid of Albert Paul Blaustein (Allen DE GRAEFF), uncredited: *Deals with the Devil* (anth **1958**; cut vt *Twelve Stories from Deals with the Devil: An Anthology* 1959), *Invisible Men* (anth **1960**) and *Famous Monster Tales* (anth **1967**). His other anthologies are *Ghostly Tales to be Told* (anth **1950**),

Tales to be Told in the Dark (anth **1953**; cut vt *Horror Stories from Tales to be Told in the Dark* 1960) and *13 Ways to Dispose of a Body* (anth **1966**). [PN]
See also: SF IN THE CLASSROOM.

DAVENPORT, BENJAMIN RUSH (? -?) US writer whose best-known novel is the future-WAR tale *Anglo-Saxons, Onward! A Romance of the Future* (**1898**), in which, led by the US president, Anglo-Saxons dominate the world, including Spain – cf the contemporaneous Spanish-US War. [JC]
Other works: *"Uncle Sam's" Cabins: A Story of American Life, Looking Forward a Century* (**1895**); *Blood Will Tell: The Strange Story of a Son of Ham* (**1902**).

DAVENPORT, GUY (MATTISON) (1927-) US academic, translator and short-story writer, long a teacher at the University of Kentucky, known for his translations from the Greek, his poetry, his literary essays – collected primarily in *The Geography of the Imagination* (coll **1981**) and *Every Force Evolves a Form* (coll **1987**) – and for the FABULATIONS assembled in *Tatlin!* (coll **1974**), *Da Vinci's Bicycle* (coll **1979**), *Trois Caprices* (coll **1981** chap), *Eclogues* (coll **1981**), *The Bowmen of Shu* (**1983** chap), which also appears in *Apples and Pears* (coll **1984**), *The Bicycle Rider* (**1985** chap), which also appears in *The Jules Verne Steam Balloon* (coll **1987**) and *The Drummer of the Eleventh North Devonshire Fusiliers* (coll **1990**). Although J.G. BALLARD and others had insinuated a fascination with French Surrealism into their NEW-WAVE tales, GD's own collaged and hallucinated conflations of data and visuals and *Sehnsucht* – as in "Tatlin!" (1974), the novel-length "The Dawn in Erewhon" (1974), "Au Tombeau de Charles Fourier" (1975), "The Richard Nixon Freischütz Rag" (1976) and "Christ Preaching at the Henley Regatta" (1980) – mediate neatly between the solitary despair of the 1960s work of Ballard and others and the more broadly socialized and nostalgic vision of sf writers like Howard WALDROP. Indeed GD's work can be seen as an important adumbration of the sudden late 1980s growth in alternate-history tales (◊ ALTERNATE WORLDS) which plunder the earlier 20th century for icons and protagonists and for moments of haunting significance. [JC]

DAVENTRY, LEONARD (JOHN) (1915-) UK writer whose first sf novel, *A Man of Double Deed* (**1965**), began the **Claus Coman** series of tales set on an Earth partly recovered from nuclear DISASTER and run by telepaths, one of whom, the protagonist, is assigned the task of solving various problems. The sequel is *Reflections in a Mirage, and The Ticking is in Your Head* (coll **1969** US), two book-length stories, published separately as *Reflections in a Mirage* (**1969**) and *The Ticking is in Your Head* (**1970**). *Terminus* (**1971**) is a grim DYSTOPIA. [JC]
Other works: *Twenty-One Billionth Paradox* (**1971** US); *Degree XII* (**1972**); *You Must Remember Us – ?* (**1980**).

DAVEY, (HENRY) NORMAN (1888-?) UK writer whose *Yesterday: A Tory Fairy-Tale* (**1924**) describes the NEAR-FUTURE secession of the Isle of Wight. Although proof copies of the novel exist entitled «Perhaps» and dated 1914, there is no evidence of the text having actually been published then. ND's other genre works are fantasies; they include the **Matthew Sumner** books: *The Pilgrim of a Smile* (**1921**) and *The Penultimate Adventure* (**1924** chap) – both assembled as *The Pilgrim of a Smile* (omni **1933**) – *Judgment Day* (**1928**) and *Pagan Parable* (**1936**).   [JC]

DAVID, PETER (1954-   ) US writer, many of whose books are signed David Peters. As PD he has concentrated on fantasies like *Knight Life* (**1987**), a tale in which Arthur is put into the modern world, and *Howling Mad: A Tale of Relenting Horror* (**1989**); on film ties like *The Return of Swamp Thing* * (**1989**) and *The Rocketeer* * (**1991**); and on **Star Trek** ties, including one STAR TREK novel, *The Rift* * (**1991**), and several STAR TREK: THE NEXT GENERATION tales: *Strike Zone* * (**1989**), *A Rock and a Hard Place* * (**1990**), *Vendetta* * (**1991**) and *Q-in-Law* * (**1991**).

As David Peters, he is responsible for two sequences: the **Photon** game-tie series – *Photon: For the Glory* * (**1987**), *#2: High Stakes* * (**1987**), *#3: In Search of Mom* * (**1987**), *#4: This is Your Life, Bhodi Li* * (**1987**), *#5: Exile* * (**1987**) and *#6: Skin Deep* * (**1988**) – and the **Psi-Man** series – *Psi-Man* (**1990**), *Psi-Man: Deathscape* (**1991**), *#3: Main Street D.O.A.* (**1991**), *#4: The Chaos Kid* (**1991**) and *#5: Stalker* (**1991**).   [JC]

DAVIDSON, AVRAM (JAMES) (1923-   ) US writer and editor, born in Yonkers, New York; he served in the US Navy 1941-5 and with the Israeli forces in the 1948-9 Arab-Israeli War. An orthodox Jew, though his faith found direct expression very rarely in his stories, he began publishing sf with "My Boy Friend's Name is Jello" (1954) in *FSF*, and early established a reputation for a sometimes obtrusive literacy and considerable wit. "Or All the Seas with Oysters" (1958) won a HUGO. Much of his early fiction appeared in *FSF*, which he edited 1962-4 – it won a Hugo in 1963 – and producing as part of his job *The Best of Fantasy and Science Fiction, 12th Series* (anth **1963**), *13th Series* (anth **1964**) and *14th Series* (anth **1965**). His first novel was *Joyleg* (**1962**) with Ward MOORE (*whom see for details*).

AD's first solo novel, *Mutiny in Space* (**1964**), immediately established his credentials as a writer of superior SPACE OPERA rather in contrast to the manner and style of his short works. Other novels with a similarly straightforward effect include *Rork!* (**1965**), *The Enemy of My Enemy* (**1966**) and, most notably, *Masters of the Maze* (**1965**), an intricate PARALLEL-WORLDS adventure with sharply characterized humans involved in barring interdimensional transit to a remarkably vivid ALIEN race. *The Kar-Chee Reign* (**1966** dos) and *Rogue Dragon* (**1965**) share a relaxedly pan-Galactic FAR-FUTURE perspective on their Earthly venue; *Clash of Star-Kings* (**1966** dos), which along with *Rogue Dragon* was nominated for a NEBULA, is set in a richly realized Mexico which becomes a venue for a game of war amongst returning alien "gods". But even these relatively active tales tend to

subordinate plot to the play of language and a visible affection for the phenomenal world, characteristics increasingly found in his later fiction, where an air of combined flamboyance and meditative calm enriches – but does not always manage to enliven – ornate fantasies like *The Phoenix and the Mirror, or The Enigmatic Speculum* (**1969**), which opens the **Vergil Magus** sequence in a medieval ALTERNATE WORLD whose universal scholastic worldview, encompassing everything from geography to alchemy, turns out to be literally accurate (AD has always been fascinated by PSEUDO-SCIENCE). Vergil goes through a number of adventures in this ornately humanized environment in search of a "virgin mirror" to trade for his stolen virility, but the novel closes without coming to a satisfactory climax, nor does *Vergil in Averno* (**1987**), published as a sequel but in fact set prior to the earlier novel, bring things to a close. This tale, set in a factory town inside a volcano, is a rich and wry parable of the birth of the Renaissance mentality (with the magus himself rather jumping the gun). The **Peregrine** series – *Peregrine: Primus* (**1971**) and *Peregrine: Secundus* (**1981**) – even more relaxedly conveys its protagonist through a wide and intriguing world reminiscent of Classical Rome. *The Island Under the Earth* (**1969**) began a series not yet continued.

AD's notable short fiction has been assembled in several volumes: *Or All the Seas with Oysters* (coll **1962**), *What Strange Stars and Skies* (coll **1965**), *Strange Seas and Shores* (coll **1971**), *The Enquiries of Doctor Eszterhazy* (coll of linked stories **1975**; exp vt *The Adventures of Doctor Eszterhazy* 1990), set in an ALTERNATE-WORLD, RURITANIAN version of late-19th-century Europe, and *The Redward Edward Papers* (coll **1978**), re-sorted in *The Best of Avram Davidson* (coll **1979**) ed Michael KURLAND, and *Avram Davidson: Collected Fantasies* (coll **1982**) ed John SILBERSACK. AD's wit and bookish allusiveness – he is perhaps sf's most explicitly literary author – shine most persuasively in his shorter works, where constraints in length seem to keep him from floundering or self-indulgence and the narrative thread stays in view. Working in short compass seems, too, to excite his extraordinary sense of humour. It is hard to imagine the genre that could encompass him; it is even more difficult to imagine fantasy or sf without him.   [JC]

Other works: *And on the Eighth Day* (**1964**) and *The Fourth Side of the Triangle* (**1965**), both as by Ellery Queen, both detections; *Ursus of Ultima Thule* (fixup **1973**); *Polly Charms the Sleeping Woman* (1975 *FSF*; **1977** chap), an **Eszterhazy** tale; *Magic for Sale* (anth **1983**); *And Don't Forget the One Red Rose* (1975 *Playboy*; **1986** chap); *Marco Polo and the Sleeping Beauty* (**1988**) with Grania (Eve) Davis (1943-   ).

See also: ATLANTIS; COLONIZATION OF OTHER WORLDS; FANTASY; GALAXY SCIENCE FICTION; *The* MAGAZINE OF FANTASY AND SCIENCE FICTION; PASTORAL.

DAVIDSON, HUGH [s] ◊ Edmond HAMILTON.

DAVIDSON, JOHN (1857-1909) UK poet, playwright

and story-writer, best known in the first capacity for *Fleet Street Eclogues* (coll **1893**). *Miss Armstrong's and Other Circumstances* (coll **1896**) contains "An Interregnum in Fairyland", a fantasy tale. "Eagle's Shadow", a future-WAR story, and "The Salvation of Nature", a spoof tale ending in worldwide DISASTER, both feature in the **The Great Men** cycle of CLUB-STORIES collected in *The Great Men, and A Practical Novelist* (omni **1891**), the second title not being of genre interest; both these stories also appear in *The Pilgrimage of Strongsoul and Other Stories* (coll **1896**). *A Full and True Account of the Wonderful Mission of Earl Lavender* (**1895**) is a SATIRE about a self-appointed Nietzschean overman; and the **Testaments** series of poems – especially *The Testament of a Vivisector* (**1901**) – also make use of Nietzsche.

[JC/BS]

See also: END OF THE WORLD.

DAVIDSON, LIONEL (1922-) UK-born writer, resident in Israel, best known for his thrillers, beginning with *The Night of Wenceslas* (**1960**). His second, *The Rose of Tibet* (**1962**), has a lost-race (◊ LOST WORLDS) plot-line. *The Sun Chemist* (**1976**) is borderline sf: the lost formula of Israeli scientist and president Chaim Weizmann (1874-1952) uses the sweet potato as a means of tapping the Sun's power; there is an adventurous quest to find it. *Under Plum Lake* (**1980**) is a fantasy for children with a trip to Paradise under sea and in outer space. [PN]

DAVIDSON, MICHAEL (? -) US author of two sf novels: *The Karma Machine* (**1975**), a dystopian vision of a COMPUTER-dominated world, and *Daughter of Is: A Science Fiction Epic: An "Else-when" Parable* (**1978**), an ALTERNATE-WORLD tale. [JC]

DAVIES, FREDRIC ◊ Ron ELLIK.

DAVIES, HUGH SYKES (1909-1984) UK writer and academic whose surrealist novel *Petron* (**1935**) is, at least retroactively, of some value to sf writers and readers as an early model for contemporary attempts at the rendering of INNER SPACE. *The Papers of Andrew Melmoth* (**1960**) is an interesting story about the EVOLUTION of INTELLIGENCE in rats, quite different, in its quiet literary tone, from the Gothic treatment such subjects normally evoke. [JC/PN]

DAVIES, L(ESLIE) P(URNELL) (1914-) UK writer who has worked also as a pharmacist and as a painter; he now lives in the Canary Isles. His consistently borderline sf often permits a delusional-frame interpretation of the events it depicts, so that frequently it is difficult to distinguish among the genres he utilizes, which include horror, fantasy, suspense thriller and sf. Along with John BLACKBURN and John LYMINGTON, both of whose writing his sometimes resembles, LPD has in a sense founded a new generic amalgam: tales whose slippage among various genres is in itself a characteristic point of narrative interest, with the reader kept constantly in suspense about the generic nature of any climaxes or explanations to be presented.

LPD began publishing sf with "The Wall of Time" for *London Mystery Magazine* in 1960, and published

fiction under a number of pseudonyms, including Leo Barne, Robert Blake, Richard Bridgeman, Morgan Evans, Ian Jefferson, Lawrence Peters, Thomas Phillips, G.K. Thomas, Leslie Vardre and Rowland Welch.

His first novel, *The Paper Dolls* (**1964**), televised in 1968, sets a mystery involving telepathy and murder in the depths of the English countryside, a venue he uses frequently. *Man out of Nowhere* (**1965**; vt *Who is Lewis Pinder?* 1966 US) and *The Artificial Man* (**1965**) can both be read as delusional-frame tales; the latter, about a NEAR-FUTURE secret agent immured in a "fake" English village while his unconscious is probed, was made into the film *Project X* (1968), not to be confused with PROJECT X (1987). LPD's subsequent novels have been, as to genre, variously marketed, but they share an ambivalence in the way they can be read, an occasional glibness of effect, and narrative skill. [JC]

Other works: *Psychogeist* (**1966**); *The Lampton Dreamers* (**1966**); *Tell it to the Dead* (**1966** as by Leslie Vardre in UK; vt *The Reluctant Medium* 1967 US); *Twilight Journey* (**1967**); *The Nameless Ones* (**1967** as by Leslie Vardre in UK; vt *A Grave Matter* 1968 US); *The Alien* (**1968**; vt *The Groundstar Conspiracy* 1972), filmed as *The Groundstar Conspiracy* (1972); *Stranger to Town* (**1969**); *Dimension A* (**1969**); *Genesis Two* (**1969**); *The White Room* (**1969**); *The Shadow Before* (**1970**); *Give Me Back Myself* (**1971**); *What Did I Do Tomorrow?* (**1972**); *Assignment Abacus* (**1975**); *Possession* (**1976**); *The Land of Leys* (**1979** US).

See also: PSYCHOLOGY.

DAVIES, PAUL (CHARLES WILLIAMS) (1946) UK physicist (currently [1992] Professor of Mathematical Physics at the University of Adelaide in Australia), science writer and sf author whose scientific nonfiction is perhaps more distinguished than his sf. His novel *Fireball* (**1987**) has ANTIMATTER pellets impacting Earth and creating chaos; although their actual source is an ALIEN spacecraft, they are interpreted by the USA as a Soviet weapon. The ideas are interesting, the thriller elements routine. However, his academic science books, signed P.C.W. Davies, and his popular science books, signed Paul Davies, are very good. In the former category are *Space and Time in the Modern Universe* (**1977**), *The Forces of Nature* (**1979**), *The Search for Gravity Waves* (**1980**) and *The Accidental Universe* (**1982**), among others. In the latter category are *The Runaway Universe* (**1978**; vt *Stardoom* 1979 UK), *Other Worlds* (**1980**), *The Edge of Infinity* (**1981**), *God and the New Physics* (**1983**), *The Matter Myth* (**1991**) with John GRIBBIN, and *The Mind of God: The Scientific Basis for a Rational World* (**1992**), among others. The speculations tend more towards the theological in the later works. [PN]

See also: COSMOLOGY; METAPHYSICS; PARALLEL WORLDS; SCIENTISTS.

DAVIES, PETE (1959-) UK writer whose first novel, *The Last Election* (**1986**), depicts with singular ferocity a NEAR-FUTURE UK ruled by the Money Party and its senile Nanny; OVERPOPULATION and the total loss of a manufacturing base lead to the government's dissemination of a painkiller which causes premature ageing in the poor. The final election, won by Nanny with the aid of a powerful advertising agency, is soon over. In *Dollarville* (**1989** US), refocusing his Swiftian rage on less local targets, PD constructs an impressively surreal though unspecific venue, a world polluted beyond redemption in which the rich are inconceivably corrupt; in this environment, a decent-hearted advertising man attempts to save a woman ecologist from a porno king; but the world ends. [JC]

DAVIES, WALTER C. [s] ◊ C.M. KORNBLUTH.

DAVIES, W.X. Pseudonym of the unidentified US author of the **Countdown WWIII** sequence of military-sf adventures: *Countdown WWIII: Operation North Africa* (**1984**), #2: *Operation Black Sea* (**1984**), #3: *Operation Choke Point* (**1984**) and #4: *Operation Persian Gulf* (**1984**). [JC]

DAVIS, ELLIS JAMES [r] ◊ ANONYMOUS SF AUTHORS.

DAVIS, FREDERICK C(LYDE) (1902-1977) US writer of pulp fiction, sometimes under pseudonyms. His first book was *The Smiling Killer* (coll *c***1935** chap UK). His most interesting early work was the **Moon Man** sequence, first published from 1933 in *Ten Detective Aces*; after the publication, decades later, of one tale as *The Moon Man* (**1974** chap), the sequence began to be released in book form with *The Night Nemesis: The Complete Adventures of the Moon Man, Volume One* (coll **1985**) ed Gary Hoppenstand and Garyn G. Roberts; however, no further volumes appeared. Under the house name Curtis STEELE, FCD was responsible for the lead novels in the magazine OPERATOR # 5 from Apr 1934 to Nov 1935. 13 of these appeared in book form in 3 separate paperback series: (a) *Legions of the Death Master* (**1966**), *The Army of the Dead* (**1966**), *The Invisible Empire* (**1966**; vt *Operator 5 #2: The Invisible Empire* 1974), *Master of Broken Men* (**1966**), *Hosts of the Flaming Death* (**1966**), *Blood Reign of the Dictator* (**1966**), *March of the Flame Marauders* (**1966**), and *Invasion of the Yellow Warlords* (**1966**); (b) the original first 3 magazine novels republished in chronological order as *The Masked Invasion* (**1974**), *The Invisible Empire* (see above) and *The Yellow Scourge* (**1974**); (c) *Cavern of the Damned* (**1980**), *Legions of Starvation* (**1980**) and *Scourge of the Invisible Death* (**1980**). [JC/PN]

Other work: *The Mole Men Want Your Eyes* (**1976** chap).

DAVIS, GERRY (1930-1991) UK writer, primarily for tv, who collaborated with Kit PEDLER on three sf novels: *Mutant 59: The Plastic Eaters* ∗ (**1972**), derived from their DOOMWATCH tv series, *Brainrack* (**1974**) and *The Dynostar Menace* (**1976**). GD also wrote children's novelizations tied to the DR WHO tv series. [JC]

See also: DISASTER; GENETIC ENGINEERING; POLLUTION.

DAVIS, GRANIA [r] ◊ Avram DAVIDSON.

DAVIS AWARDS ◊ AWARDS.

DAVIS PUBLICATIONS ◊ ASTOUNDING SCIENCE-FICTION; ISAAC ASIMOV'S SCIENCE FICTION MAGAZINE.

DAW BOOKS New York publishing imprint started by Donald A. WOLLHEIM in 1972 (after his departure from ACE BOOKS) with assistance from New American Library. DB (the name derived from Wollheim's initials) publishes only sf and FANTASY, producing 4-5 titles per month. The editorial policy is similar to that followed by Wollheim at Ace: mostly adventure fiction, with a sprinkling of serious works. There has been much series fiction, particularly fantasy and SWORD AND SORCERY, by such authors as Alan Burt Akers (Kenneth BULMER), Marion Zimmer BRADLEY, Lin CARTER, Michael MOORCOCK, John NORMAN and E.C. TUBB, many of whom had followed Wollheim from Ace Books. Major discoveries were C.J. CHERRYH and the fantasy writer Tad Williams (1957-   ), and DB also did much to promote the career of Tanith LEE. An anthology series was **Annual World's Best SF** (◊ WOLLHEIM *for details*). Wollheim's daughter Betsy Wollheim became president in 1985, when her father was seriously ill; by the time of his death in 1990 the number of books published annually by DB was rather lower than it had been early in the 1980s.

[PN/MJE]

Further reading: *Future and Fantastic Worlds: A Bibliographic Retrospective of DAW Books (1972-1987)* (dated 1987 but **1988**) by Sheldon JAFFERY; *An Index to DAW Books* (**1989** chap) by Ian Covell.

DAWN OF THE DEAD (vt *Zombie* Italy; vt *Zombies* UK) Film (1978). Laurel. Dir George ROMERO, starring David Emge, Ken Foree, Scott H. Reininger, Gaylen Ross. Screenplay Romero, with Dario Argento (who also cowrote the music) as script consultant. 127 mins, cut to 125 mins. Colour.

The first of two sequels to NIGHT OF THE LIVING DEAD (1968) – the other was DAY OF THE DEAD (1985) – this was (unusually) premiered in Italy, under the title *Zombie*. DOTD is true sf, not just because of the pseudo-scientific explanation for zombiism but because Romero is interested in zombies not only as occasions for horror – though DOTD remains primarily a HORROR film – but also as phenomena (their sociology, their possible intelligence) in the way that an sf writer might be interested in ALIENS. Where the first film was unremittingly black, this has a comic-strip and satirical humour about it, as four survivors hole up in a shopping mall besieged by zombies and bikers. Jokes about the death of capitalism, even while the capitalist instinct survives, are focused on the many goods displayed in the spotless temple of consumerism. The subtext (we, the working class, are, or could be, the zombies) is spirited though unsubtle, and the film is remembered by most for its violent, brilliantly choreographed action. [PN]

See also: SATIRE.

DAY, BRADFORD M(ARSHALL) (1916-   ) US sf collector and book-dealer whose bibliographical work is one of the foundations on which modern sf scholarship has been built (◊ BIBLIOGRAPHIES). His *The Complete Checklist of Science-Fiction Magazines* (**1961** chap) defines sf widely and lists a number of hero-villain, fantasy and foreign magazines. *The Supplemental Checklist of Fantastic Literature* (**1963**) is a compilation of many titles omitted by or published after the period covered by Everett F. BLEILER's *The Checklist of Fantastic Literature* (**1948**), itself widely revised in 1978. Other works by BMD are *The Checklist of Fantastic Literature in Paperbound Books* (**1965**), *Bibliography of Adventure: Mundy, Burroughs, Rohmer, Haggard* (**1964**) and *An Index on the Weird and Fantastica in Magazines* (**1953**), which indexes most of the Frank A. MUNSEY pulps and many other general-fiction PULP MAGAZINES. All the above were originally published in stencilled format by BMD himself; several have been republished since.   [PN]

See also: ANONYMOUS SF AUTHORS.

DAY, DONALD B(YRNE) (1909-1978) Pioneer sf indexer, resident in Oregon. His *Index to the Science Fiction Magazines 1926-1950* (**1952**), since reissued, has become, along with its successors compiled by other hands (◊ BIBLIOGRAPHIES), an essential tool for sf research.   [PN]

DAY, (GERALD WILLIAM) LANGSTON (1894-?   ) UK writer whose *Magic Casements* (coll **1951**) assembles mythological fantasies, and whose *The Deep Blue Ice* (**1960**) features the experiences of a Victorian mountaineer who is frozen in ice for half a century, and on revival (◊ SLEEPER AWAKES) must face the present day.   [JC]

DAY, LIONEL ◊ Ladbroke BLACK.

DAY AFTER, THE Made-for-tv film (1983). ABC. Dir Nicholas Meyer, starring Jason Robards, Jo-Beth Williams, Steven Guttenberg, John Lithgow, Lori Lethin, William Allen Young and a dozen others. Screenplay Edward Hume. 121 mins. Colour.

Set in Lawrence, Kansas, the film tells of a massive nuclear exchange between the USA and USSR. Many of the missiles hit Kansas and Missouri, targeted because of their numerous Minuteman silos. *TDA* opens a week before nuclear war begins, and ends around six weeks later. The film instantly became a media event, and was hugely publicized and discussed. It was widely – justly but irrelevantly – criticized, especially abroad, for its soap-opera treatment. Meyer's purpose was to bring home a propaganda message to ordinary people, which is precisely what soap-opera characters are perceived to be by most viewers. The film, as the final titles tell us, does give a remarkably mild account of the consequences of atomic war, gruelling though it is. Nevertheless, it was an act of courage for ABC to make this expensive film at all, since nuclear issues at that time were barely touched on by US tv, being unattractive to advertisers, and the nuclear debate was probably quite foreign to many viewers. Also, *TDA* could hardly be seen as apolitical (despite disclaimers by ABC executives): Meyer himself said "the movie tells you that civil defence is useless", and observed that ABC gave him "millions of dollars to go on prime-time tv and call Ronald Reagan a liar". Much of the film is routine in treatment if not subject matter, but it contains several outstanding sequences: the housewife who won't go into the cellar until she finishes

cleaning the house; the lecture to increasingly furious farmers about implausible methods of "decontaminating soil"; a street packed with radiation victims on makeshift mattresses as far as the eye can see.   [PN]

See also: CINEMA.

DAY MARS INVADED EARTH, THE Film (1962). API/20th Century-Fox. Dir Maury Dexter, starring Kent Taylor, Marie Windsor, William Mims, Betty Beall. Screenplay Harry Spalding. 70 mins. B/w.

In this mediocre B-movie, Martians – who consist of pure energy – travel to Earth via radio beam. As in INVASION OF THE BODY SNATCHERS (1956), from which this clearly borrows, they duplicate human beings, killing off the originals, to the horror of a scientist who returns from vacation to find alien minds in the apparent bodies of friends and family and human-shaped ashes in the swimming pool. Unusually, the film ends with the Martians triumphant.   [PN/JB]

DAY OF THE DEAD Film (1985). Laurel. Dir George ROMERO, starring Lori Cardille, Terry Alexander, Joseph Pilato, Richard Liberty, Howard Sherman. Screenplay Romero. 101 mins, cut to 100 mins. Colour.

Romero's plan, after showing the initial zombie attacks (NIGHT OF THE LIVING DEAD [1968]) and the total breakdown of society (DAWN OF THE DEAD [1978]), was to complete the trilogy with a film showing a new coalition between humans and controlled zombies. Partly for budgetary reasons, he settled for something less ambitious. An underground military/storage base is used by a small company of scientists and soldiers in their desperately rushed study of zombie behaviour. Can they be controlled? What causes the infection? The behaviour of both groups becomes increasingly psychotic, with one scientist (Liberty) profaning the military dead by using their bodies to reward zombies in a B.F. SKINNER-style attempt at conditioning, and the senior military officer (Pilato) treating the scientists with insane violence and contempt. One almost likeable zombie, well played by Sherman, shows signs of human memory. Only three people, including the intelligent woman scientist (Cardille) who is the point-of-view character, escape to uncertain sanctuary in this small-scale, beautifully paced, claustrophobic film. *DOTD*, copiously illustrated with scenes of dismemberment and cannibalism, is sickening, but as ever Romero contrives to give metaphoric resonance to his exploitation-movie images.   [PN]

See also: MONSTER MOVIES.

DAY OF THE DOLPHIN, THE Film (1973). Avco-Embassy. Dir Mike Nichols, starring George C. Scott, Trish Van Devere, Paul Sorvino, Fritz Weaver. Screenplay Buck Henry, based on *Un animal doué de raison* (**1967; trans as** *The Day of the Dolphin* **1969**) by Robert MERLE. 105 mins. Colour.

This above-average film, from a director well known for social comedy but new to sf, concerns a marine biologist who succeeds in teaching dolphins to speak English. The first half deals seriously and convincingly with this historic contact between two intelligent species, and conveys the genuine SENSE OF WONDER found in the best sf, but the rest of the story concentrates less interestingly on an attempt by a right-wing group to betray the innocent human-dolphin relationship and use the dolphins to plant mines to assassinate the US President. [JB]

DAY OF THE TRIFFIDS, THE 1. Film (1963). Security Pictures/Allied Artists. Dir Steve Sekely (uncredited), Freddie Francis, starring Howard Keel, Nicole Maurey, Janette Scott, Kieron Moore. Screenplay Philip Yordan, based on *The Day of the Triffids* (**1951**) by John WYNDHAM. 94 mins. Colour.

This unsuccessful version of a good novel had a moderately generous budget, but no sense whatever of how sf works. Thus there is plenty of preaching, lots of florid love interest, but only intermittent attention paid to the basic situation, which, while silly, should have been interesting: most of England's population blinded by light from a meteor shower, and a small group, still sighted, trying to cope with attacks from lethal 7ft (2.1m) mobile vegetables. The triffids are more absurd than frightening.

2. UK tv serial (1981). BBC. Dir Ken Hannam, adapted from Wyndham's novel by Douglas Livingstone, starring John Duttine, Emma Relph. 6 30min episodes (aired outside the UK as a 2-part miniseries). Colour. This was a low-key but successful dramatization of the story, much better than the film. [JB/PN]

DAY THE EARTH CAUGHT FIRE, THE Film (1961). British Lion/Pax/Universal. Prod and dir Val Guest, starring Edward Judd, Janet Munro, Leo McKern. Screenplay Wolf Mankowitz, Guest. 99 mins, cut to 90 mins (US). B/w.

Val Guest, who had made *The* QUATERMASS XPERIMENT (1956) and other sf/horror films for Hammer in the 1950s, excelled himself with this intelligent DISASTER movie about the Earth falling into the Sun after a reckless series of H-bomb tests have knocked it out of orbit. Only more nuclear explosions, properly placed, can save it. The film is made in a crisp, low-key, pseudo-documentary manner, with much of the action set in the offices of the London *Daily Express* newspaper (with former editor Arthur Christiansen playing himself). Les Bowie's low-budget special effects are surprisingly good, including shots of the Thames completely evaporating in the heat. The novelization is *The Day the Earth Caught Fire* * (**1961**) by Barry Wells. [JB/PN]

DAY THE EARTH STOOD STILL, THE Film (1951). 20th Century-Fox. Dir Robert WISE, starring Michael Rennie, Patricia Neal, Hugh Marlowe, Sam Jaffe. Screenplay Edmund H. North, based on "Farewell to the Master" (1940) by Harry BATES. 92 mins. B/w.

Produced at the beginning of the sf boom of the 1950s, this is generally regarded as a classic, though its ethics might be regarded as intemperate; it is, however, directed with pace and impressive economy. An emissary from outer space arrives by flying saucer in Washington, accompanied by an 8ft (2.4m)

ROBOT. The military gets very excited. The soft-spoken, human-seeming ALIEN, Klaatu, has come to warn Earth that his people will not tolerate an extension of human violence into space, but before he can deliver the message he is wounded by a soldier, escapes, and takes a room in a boarding house, where he learns about ordinary people. Later he arranges a demonstration of his powers – the stopping of all electrical equipment, all over the world. Then, his warning still undelivered, he is again shot, this time fatally. But like Christ – the parallel seems deliberate – he rises again and gives his message: unless human violence is curbed the true masters, who are in fact the robots, will "reduce this Earth of yours to a burnt-out cinder". Submission to the rule of implacable, disinterested robots is an authoritarian proposal for a supposedly liberal film. [PN/JB]

DAY THE FISH CAME OUT, THE Film (1967). Michael Cacoyannis Productions/20th Century-Fox. Dir Michael Cacoyannis, starring Tom Courtenay, Sam Wanamaker, Colin Blakely, Candice Bergen, Ian Ogilvy. Screenplay Michael Cacoyannis. 109 mins. Colour.

This NEAR-FUTURE Greek/UK film takes off from a real-life incident in which the US Air Force accidentally lost two H-bombs off the coast of Spain. A NATO bomber crashes into the sea near a small Greek island, losing two H-bombs and a "Doomsday weapon". To keep a low profile, the NATO recovery team arrives disguised as holiday-makers, but this creates the impression that the island is the "in" place to visit, and soon it is swarming with real tourists. Then lethal viruses are released from a metal box found by a fisherman. A strange mixture of slapstick and grim satire, *TDTFCO* is not very coherent, but the final scenes, showing dead fish floating in the black sea while all the tourists, already doomed themselves, dance with frenzied abandon on the beach, are forceful. The novelization is *The Day the Fish Came Out* * (**1967**) by Kay CICELLIS. [JB]

DAY THE WORLD ENDED, THE Film (1956). Golden State/ARC. Prod and dir Roger CORMAN, starring Richard Denning, Adele Jergens, Lori Nelson, Touch (Mike) Connors. Screenplay Lou Rusoff. 81 mins, cut to 79 mins. B/w.

The first sf/horror film to be directed by Corman (although in 1954 he had produced *Monster from the Ocean Floor*), this was, like most of his 1950s films, shot fast (less than a week) on an amazingly small budget (*c*$40,000). *TDTWE* tells of a small group of atomic-war survivors menaced by a MUTANT (created by the radiation) with a bulbous head, three eyes and a taste for human flesh. Corman later improved as a director. [JB/PN]

DC COMICS US COMIC-book publishing company, based in New York, owing much of its commercial success to its ownership of the copyrights in the SUPERHEROES Batman, who is not quite an sf figure, and SUPERMAN, who is.

In Feb 1935 Major Malcolm WHEELER-NICHOLSON published the first US comic book to contain all-new material rather than reprints from newspaper comics sections. His comic book, *New Fun*, ran for 5 issues Feb-Oct 1935, and was reborn in 1936 as *More Fun* (June 1936-Dec 1947). By 1938 Nicholson was publishing *New Adventure Comics* and *Detective Comics*; these were the first comic books to feature regular characters in a series of adventures. However, they didn't pay the bills, and Nicholson eventually settled his debts by handing his company, National Comics, over to his printers, Harry Donenfeld and Jack Leibowitz. Its next publication was *Action Comics*, #1 of which (June 1938) featured the first appearance of the character **Superman**, created by Jerry SIEGEL and Joe Shuster. In May 1939 *Detective Comics* #27 saw the début of **The Batman**, drawn by Bob Kane and written by Bill Finger. The future of the company was assured.

Detective Comics was the first all-new comic book of which each issue was devoted to a single theme. This approach was an instant success, and so the company adopted the initials DC as a trademark, featuring it boldly on (eventually) all of its covers. It bought up Max Gaines's All American Comics in 1945. Donenfeld pioneered the distribution of comic books in the USA, and his efforts were backed up by those of National's stable of editors, writers and artists, who included Alfred BESTER, Otto Binder (◊ Eando BINDER), Gardner FOX, Edmond HAMILTON and Mort WEISINGER. These produced a flood of memorable characters and series including **Aquaman**, **Enemy Ace**, **The Flash**, **Green Lantern**, **Hawkman**, **Sgt Rock**, **Sugar & Spike** and WONDER WOMAN, and *Mystery in Space*, *Rex the Wonder Dog*, *Robin the Boy Wonder* and *Strange Adventures*.

The 1950s saw a change of name to National Periodical Publications and the introduction of romance titles (*Girls Love*), sf (*Strange Adventures*), Westerns (*Hopalong Cassidy*) and licensed character humour (*Bob Hope*, *Jackie Gleason* and *Dean Martin & Jerry Lewis*). In the mid-1950s there was a resurgence in the popularity of superheroes, and many characters abandoned in the previous decade were revived and revamped. This popularity burgeoned in the 1960s and 1970s, and such material constituted a substantial proportion of the company's output, even though there were new titles in the horror, gothic romance and SWORD-AND-SORCERY genres. In 1968 the company was taken over by Warner Bros., and in the early 1980s its official name finally became DC Comics Inc.

The 1980s saw a great expansion of new publishing formats, including limited-series books, softcover and hardcover collections, and GRAPHIC-NOVEL adaptations of the works of leading sf writers such as Larry NIVEN and Robert SILVERBERG. A major contributing factor to the company's recent success has been its exploitations of **The Batman** (now usually known just as **Batman**), allowing artists and writers

– including Frank MILLER, and Alan MOORE and Brian BOLLAND – to evolve a number of highly individual interpretations of his character and milieu. Batman's popularity has, of course, benefited from the films *Batman* (1966), *Batman* (1989) and *Batman Returns* (1992). [RT/SW]

DEAD KIDS (vt *Strange Behavior*) Film (1981). Endeavour/Bannon Glenn/Hemdale. Dir Michael Laughlin, starring Michael Murphy, Louise Fletcher, Dan Shor, Fiona Lewis, Arthur Dignam. Screenplay Laughlin, William Condon. 99 mins, cut to 93 mins. Colour.

This Australian/New Zealand exploitation sf/HORROR movie is set in the US Midwest and has a largely US cast, but was actually shot in New Zealand. It is the first of a projected trilogy (linked by theme only) of which the second is STRANGE INVADERS (1983). At a research centre teenage kids are acting as guinea pigs in experiments in behavioural conditioning (the film is consciously anti-B.F. SKINNER) via a drug injected into the brain – on one occasion, through the eyeball. Some of them become homicidal and murder the children of a now-dead mad SCIENTIST's old enemies. The mad scientist is revealed to be not dead after all. The film – part of the teenage SPLATTER-MOVIE subgenre of the time – has plenty of gore but also wit and intelligence, as well as a rather 1950s style that would be featured again in *Strange Invaders*. [PN]

DEADLY INVENTION, THE ◊ VYNÁLEZ ZKÁZY.

DEADLY RAY FROM MARS, THE ◊ FLASH GORDON.

DEAD ZONE, THE Film (1983). Dino De Laurentiis/Lorimar. Dir David CRONENBERG, starring Christopher Walken, Brooke Adams, Tom Skerritt, Herbert Lom, Anthony Zerbe, Martin Sheen. Screenplay Jeffrey Boam, based on *The Dead Zone* (1979) by Stephen KING. 103 mins. Colour.

Borderline-sf movie about John Smith (Walken), who has an accident, spends five years in a coma, and wakes to learn he has developed a PSI POWER, precognition. The "dead zone" is a blank spot in his visions which may represent the possibility of the future being changed. The more Smith uses his powers, which he is loath to do because of the cargo of pain his visions often carry (and because they age him), the more cut off he becomes from ordinary humanity. He performs several minor miracles, solves an ugly murder mystery, and ultimately prevents WWIII by thwarting the election of a smooth, narcissistic politician (Sheen) who might otherwise, in the future, have plunged the world into holocaust. Cronenberg's least typical and most commercial work, perhaps because King's sprawling novel is a long way removed from the personal material he normally uses, *TDZ* is nevertheless a good and powerful film, notable for its sad, insistent images of winter, correlating with Smith's retreat from life and also with the dead zone of the title. Walken's performance in the main role is admirably lost and icy. [PN]

DEAMER, (MARY ELIZABETH KATHLEEN) DUL-CIE (1890-1972) New Zealand-born writer, in Australia from about 1922, where in association with Norman Lindsay (1879-1969) and others she ruffled some provincial dovecotes. Some of the content of *In the Beginning: Six Studies of the Stone Age and Other Stories* (coll **1909**) reappears in *As It Was in the Beginning* (**1929**), an exercise in prehistoric sf set in Australia, illus Lindsay. *The Devil's Saint* (**1924** UK) is a historical novel with greater elements of FANTASY than normal in her work. *Holiday* (**1940**) is a fantasy of REINCARNATION. [JC]

DEAN, MAL (1941-1974) UK illustrator who died young, of cancer. MD was well known in the jazz world (he illustrated for *Melody Maker*) and in sf for the work he did for NEW WORLDS in the late 1960s and early 1970s; it was especially associated with the **Jerry Cornelius** stories by Michael MOORCOCK and others. His work was mainly in black-and-white with a broad line and much cross-hatching; it was strong, often deliberately unpolished, but the reverse of artless. He favoured surreal juxtapositions, and often worked in the grotesque satirical tradition of Hogarth. [PN]

DEAN, MARTYN [r] ◊ Roger DEAN; Christopher EVANS.

DEAN, ROGER (1944-   ) UK illustrator. Primarily a commercial designer, especially of record-album covers, RD has done some sf and fantasy ILLUSTRATION, and his album and poster art shows a strong fantasy influence. His style is strong, romantic and mannered; he contrasts very finely detailed figures and machines against loosely structured backgrounds. His book *Views* (**1975**) shows his development from a student at the Canterbury School of Art onwards. *Views* was published by Dragon's Dream, a specialist publishing house devoted primarily to UK fantasy illustrators, founded by RD and his brother Martyn Dean; it also publishes under the Paper Tiger imprint. The book *Magnetic Storm* (**1984**), ed Roger and Martyn Dean, details many of the design and publishing projects – often fantastic or sciencefictional – with which they have been associated. RD has been an important influence on UK fantasy illustration, as has his brother, who is more closely associated with book publishing than RD. [JG/PN]

DEARMER, GEOFFREY (1893-?   ) UK writer whose *Saint on Holiday* (**1933**) presents a NEAR-FUTURE UK in which the government is dominated by ministries designed to be of benefit to citizens; it was couched as a topsy-turvydom SATIRE. In *They Chose to be Birds* (**1935**) a preacher of closed mind is unsettlingly duped into "becoming" a bird, and as such learns some Wellsian lessons about the true nature of the world. [JC]
Other works: *Three Short Plays* (coll **1928**), two of which are fantasies.

DEATH LINE (vt *Raw Meat* US) Film (1972). K-L Productions. Dir Gary Sherman, starring Donald Pleasence, Hugh Armstrong, Norman Rossington, David Ladd, Sharon Gurney. Screenplay Ceri Jones, from a story by Sherman. 87 mins. Colour.

In the late 19th century a group of construction workers building an extension to London's underground railway system are buried in a cave-in. In the present, late-night travellers at Russell Square tube station are being murdered (and eaten) by, we slowly learn, troglodytic descendants of the entombed workers who have found their way up, and are now supplementing their diet of rats with human meat. What raises this exploitation movie out of the ordinary is its unexpected shift of perspective – the dawning sympathy we are made to feel for the troglodytes (nearly all of whom have died of a leprosy-like disease): they have almost lost the use of language, but are still able to feel grief and love. [PN]
See also: MONSTER MOVIES.

DEATH OF THE INCREDIBLE HULK ◊ *The* INCREDIBLE HULK.

DEATH RACE 2000 Film (1975). New World. Prod Roger CORMAN. Dir Paul Bartel, starring David Carradine, Simone Griffith, Louisa Moritz, Sylvester Stallone, Mary Woronov. Screenplay Robert Thom, Charles Griffith, based on a story by Ib Melchior. 80 mins. Colour.

In this low-budget black SATIRE about a car race across the USA in the year 2000, the winner is the driver who kills the most pedestrians. "Frankenstein" (Carradine) – who has supposedly been in so many crashes that most of his body has been replaced with artificial parts – is the nation's favourite driver, and surprises everyone at the end by running over the US President as a political gesture. The film's fast pace and lively ironies led many critics to judge it superior to ROLLERBALL (1975), a much more expensive production about the use of brutal sports as an opiate for the masses. A cult classic, *DR2000* has been much imitated. [JB/PN]

DEATH RAYS Rays that could kill, whether by heat or by disintegration, were the staple WEAPONS of pulp sf in the 1920s and 1930s and became a central item of sf TERMINOLOGY. At about the time death rays became old-fashioned in sf, scientists in the real world saw fit to invent the laser, thus retroactively justifying one of sf's fantasies. The death ray always, however, had a basis in historical fact. After the well publicized discoveries of X-rays by Wilhelm Konrad Roentgen (1845-1923) in 1895 and of radioactive emissions by Antoine Henri Becquerel (1852-1908) – he too called them rays – in 1896, the word "ray" entered the popular imagination. One of the earliest literary examples is the "heat ray" used by the Martians in H.G. WELLS's *The War of the Worlds* (**1898**). [PN]

DEATHSPORT ◊ Roger CORMAN.

DEATH WATCH ◊ *Le* MORT EN DIRECT.

de BERGERAC, CYRANO ◊ CYRANO DE BERGERAC.

De CAMP, CATHERINE A. CROOK [r] ◊ L. Sprague DE CAMP.

De CAMP, L(YON) SPRAGUE (1907-   ) US writer, married from 1939 to Catherine A(delaide) Crook (1907-   ), who has collaborated on a number of his books, sometimes without printed credit, although always freely acknowledged by LSDC; the two are increasingly seen to have been a creative team for many years (she is referred to below as CACDC). LSDC was educated at the California Institute of Technology, where he studied aeronautical engineering, and at Stevens Institute of Technology, where he gained a master's degree in 1933. He went to work for a company dealing with patenting, and his first published work was a cowritten textbook on the subject. He then met P. Schuyler MILLER, with whom he collaborated on a novel, *Genus Homo* (1941 *Super Science Stories*; **1950**), which failed to find a publisher for several years. His first published story was "The Isolinguals" (1937) in *ASF*; this was before the arrival of John W. CAMPBELL Jr as editor, but when that happened the two men proved highly compatible, and LSDC soon became a central figure of the GOLDEN AGE OF SF, writing prolifically for *ASF* over the next few years (on one occasion using the pseudonym Lyman R. Lyon), his contributions including the **Johnny Black** series about an intelligent bear: "The Command" (1938), "The Incorrigible" (1939), "The Emancipated" (1940) and "The Exalted" (1940). Some of the better stories from this period were collected in *The Best of L. Sprague de Camp* (coll **1978**).

It was, however, the appearance in 1939 of *ASF*'s fantasy companion UNKNOWN which stimulated his most notable early work, including *Lest Darkness Fall* (1939 *Unknown*; **1941**; rev 1949), in which an involuntary time-traveller to 6th-century Rome attempts to prevent the onset of the Dark Ages; this was the most accomplished early excursion into HISTORY in magazine sf, and is regarded as a classic. Other contributions to *Unknown* included "None but Lucifer" (1939) with H.L. GOLD, *Solomon's Stone* (1942 *Unknown*; **1956**) and the long title stories of *Divide and Rule* (coll **1948**) – the title story alone being republished as *Divide and Rule* (1939 *ASF*; **1990** chap dos) – *The Wheels of If* (coll **1948**), an ALTERNATE-WORLDS story, also cited below in reissued form, and *The Undesired Princess* (coll **1951**), the title story alone being republished in *The Undesired Princess and The Enchanted Bunny* (anth **1990**), the second story being by David A. DRAKE. LSDC was most successful in his collaborations with Fletcher PRATT, whom he met in 1939. Pratt conceived the idea behind their successful **Incomplete Enchanter** series of humorous fantasies in which the protagonist, Harold Shea, is transported into a series of ALTERNATE WORLDS based on various myths and legends. As usual with LSDC, the publication sequence is complex. The main titles are: *The Incomplete Enchanter* (1940 *Unknown*; **1941**), *The Castle of Iron* (1941 *Unknown*; **1950**) and *The Wall of Serpents* (fixup **1960**; vt *The Enchanter Completed* 1980 UK). The first two titles were then assembled as *The Compleat Enchanter: The Magical Misadventures of Harold Shea* (omni **1975**), and all three were eventually put together as *The Intrepid Enchanter* (omni **1988** UK; vt *The Complete Compleat Enchanter* 1989 US); *Sir Harold and the Gnome*

King (**1991** chap) was subsequently added to the **Enchanter** canon. Other collaborations with Pratt were *The Land of Unreason* (**1942**) and *The Carnelian Cube* (**1948**), the latter being published several years after it was written. In 1950, LSDC and Pratt (*whom see for details*) began their **Gavagan's Bar** series of CLUB STORIES, assembled in *Tales From Gavagan's Bar* (coll **1953**; exp 1978).

LSDC joined the US Naval Reserve in 1942, spending the war working in the Philadelphia Naval Yard alongside Isaac ASIMOV and Robert A. HEINLEIN. Afterwards he published a few articles, but hardly any new fiction until "The Animal Cracker Plot" (1949) introduced his **Viagens Interplanetarias** stories, a loosely linked series set in a future where Brazil has become the dominant world power, the stories themselves being sited mainly on three worlds which circle the star Tau Ceti and are named after the Hindu gods Vishnu, Ganesha and Krishna; the planet Krishna was a romantically barbarian world on which LSDC could set, as sf, the kind of PLANETARY ROMANCES he had previously written as fantasy, the market for pure fantasy having disappeared with *Unknown* in 1943. Other planets circling other stars included Osiris, Isis and Thoth. Many of the short stories in the series were included in *The Continent Makers and Other Tales of the Viagens* (coll **1953**); others appeared in *Sprague de Camp's New Anthology of Science Fiction* (coll **1953** UK), and "The Virgin of Zesh" (1953) was assembled together with *The Wheels of If* (1940 *ASF*; **1990** chap dos) in *The Virgin and the Wheels* (coll **1976**). *Rogue Queen* (**1951**), a novel in the series, depicts a matriarchal humanoid society based on a hive structure; it is, with *Lest Darkness Fall*, LSDC's most highly regarded sf work. The remaining novels, an internal series all set on **Krishna**, were *Cosmic Manhunt* (1949 *ASF* as "The Queen of Zamba"; **1954** dos; vt *A Planet Called Krishna* 1966 UK; with restored text and with "Perpetual Motion" added, rev vt as coll *The Queen of Zamba* 1977 US); *The Search for Zei* (1950 *ASF* as the first half of "The Hand of Zei"; **1962**; vt *The Floating Continent* 1966 UK) and *The Hand of Zei* (1950 *ASF* as the second half of "The Hand of Zei"; **1963**; cut 1963), both titles finally being superseded by publication of the full original novel, *The Hand of Zei* (1950 *ASF*; **1982**); *The Tower of Zanid* (1958 *Science Fiction Stories*; cut **1958**; with "The Virgin of Zesh" added, vt as coll *The Virgin of Zesh/The Tower of Zanid* 1983); *The Hostage of Zir* (**1977**); *The Bones of Zora* (**1983**) with CACDC; and *The Swords of Zinjaban* (**1991**) with CACDC. They contain a blend of intelligent, exotic adventure and wry humour characteristic of LSDC's better work, though they do not explore any too deeply either the romantic or the human-condition ironies available to aspiring authors of the planetary romance.

LSDC was in any case not to write much more sf, his later career increasingly being devoted to outright fantasy and to SWORD AND SORCERY. He had gained an interest in the latter category through reading Robert

E. HOWARD's **Conan** stories, and worked extensively on editing and adding to that series. *Tales of Conan* (coll **1955**; vt *The Flame Knife* **1981**) consists of unfinished Howard manuscripts converted into **Conan** stories and completed by LSDC (for remaining titles, see listing below). His nonfiction writings on the sword-and-sorcery genre have been published as *The Conan Reader* (coll **1968**), *Literary Swordsmen and Sorcerers* (**1976**) and *Blond Barbarians and Noble Savages* (**1975** chap). He also edited the anthologies *Swords and Sorcery* (anth **1963**), *The Spell of Seven* (anth **1965**), *The Fantastic Swordsmen* (anth **1967**) and *Warlocks and Warriors* (anth **1970**), and co-edited the critical anthologies *The Conan Swordbook* (anth **1969**) and *The Conan Grimoire* (anth **1972**), both with George H. SCITHERS. LSDC's own first sword-and-sorcery effort was the **Pusadian** sequence of tales assembled as *The Tritonian Ring and Other Pusadian Tales* (coll **1953**); the title novel was later published alone as *The Tritonian Ring* (**1951** *Two Complete Science-Fiction Adventure Books*; **1968**). Later he wrote several stories set in the imaginary world of **Novaria**: *The Goblin Tower* (**1968**), which is his most substantial novel of this type, *The Clocks of Iraz* (**1971**), *The Fallible Fiend* (**1973**), *The Unbeheaded King* (**1983**) and *The Honorable Barbarian* (**1989**) – the first, second and fourth of these five being assembled as *The Reluctant King* (omni **1984**).

LSDC's most notable sf writings after about 1950 were stories like *The Glory that Was* (**1952** *Startling Stories*; **1960**) and the 1956 title story of *A Gun for Dinosaur* (coll **1963**), which also included "Aristotle and the Gun" (**1958**). The first and third of these tales combine TIME-TRAVEL and history themes in a manner similar to *Lest Darkness Fall*; the second is a straightforward time-travel story. LSDC produced one of the earliest books about modern sf, *Science Fiction Handbook* (**1953**; rev 1975) with CACDC; a useful compendium of information and advice for aspiring writers in its original edition, it gained little from its subsequent revision – indeed, the revised version omitted some material of interest. Otherwise he wrote historical novels and nonfiction works, including a book on MAGIC with CACDC: *Spirits, Stars and Spells* (**1966**). His opinions about the nature of FANTASY and the appropriate decorum necessary to write within the genre were expressed in an energetic, if sometimes reactionary, fashion in his many articles. He also wrote definitive lives of H.P. LOVECRAFT – *Lovecraft: A Biography* (**1975**; cut 1976) – and of Robert E. Howard – *Dark Valley Destiny: The Life of Robert E. Howard* (**1983**) with CCDC and Jane Whittington Griffin, the latter book having been preceded by *The Miscast Barbarian* (**1975** chap). In the 1980s, and into his own ninth decade, more and more often in explicit collaboration with CACDC, he maintained a remarkable reputation for consistency of output. He was given the Gandalf (Grand Master) Award for 1976 and the Nebula Grand Master Award for 1978. His recent work seems agelessly smiling. [MJE/JC]

Other works: *Lands Beyond* (**1952**) with Willy LEY, nonfiction, awarded an INTERNATIONAL FANTASY AWARD; *Lost Continents* (**1954**), nonfiction about ATLANTIS and others; *Demons and Dinosaurs* (**1970**), poetry; *The Reluctant Shaman and Other Fantastic Tales* (coll **1970**); *3000 Years of Fantasy and Science Fiction* (anth **1972**) with CACDC; *Scribblings* (coll **1972**); *Tales beyond Time* (anth **1973**) with CACDC; *The Great Fetish* (**1978**); *The Purple Pterodactyls: The Adventures of W. Wilson Newbury, Ensorcelled Financier* (coll of linked stories **1979**); *The Ragged Edge of Science* (**1980**), nonfiction; *Footprints on Sand* (coll **1981**) with CACDC; *Heroes and Hobgoblins* (coll **1981**); *The Incorporated Knight* (fixup **1987**) and its sequel, *The Pixilated Peeress* (**1991**), both with CACDC; *The Stones of Nomuru* (**1988**) with CACDC.

Conan: In terms of internal chronology: *Conan* (coll **1967**) with Lin CARTER and Robert E. Howard; *Conan of Cimmeria* (coll **1969**) with Carter and Howard; *Conan the Freebooter* (coll **1968**) with Howard; *Conan the Wanderer* (coll **1968**) with Carter and Howard, *Conan the Adventurer* (coll **1966**) with Howard, and *Conan the Buccaneer* (**1971**) with Carter, all three being assembled as *The Conan Chronicles* (omni **1990** UK); *Conan the Warrior* (anth **1967**); *Conan the Usurper* (coll **1967**) with Howard; Howard's own *Conan the Conqueror* (**1967** edn) ed LSDP; *The Return of Conan* (**1957**; vt *Conan the Avenger* 1968) with Howard and Bjorn Nyberg; *Conan of Aquilonia* (coll **1977**); *Conan of the Isles* (**1968**) with Carter; *Conan the Swordsman* (coll **1978**) with Carter and Nyberg; *Conan the Liberator* (**1979**) with Carter; *The Blade of Conan* (anth **1979**); *The Spell of Conan* (anth **1980**); *Conan and the Spider God* (**1980**); *Treasure of Tranicos* (**1980**) with Howard; *Conan the Barbarian* * (**1982**) with Carter, a film tie. (For other **Conan** books, ◊ *Robert E.* HOWARD.)

About the author: "Neomythology" by Lin Carter (introduction to LSDC's *Literary Swordsmen and Sorcerers*); *Seekers of Tomorrow* (**1965**) by Sam MOSKOWITZ, Chapter 9; *De Camp: An L. Sprague de Camp Bibliography* (**1983**) by Charlotte Laughlin and Daniel J.H. LEVACK.

See also: APES AND CAVEMEN (IN THE HUMAN WORLD); DISCOVERY AND INVENTION; EDISONADE; END OF THE WORLD; EVOLUTION; FINLAND; HIVE-MINDS; HUMOUR; LINGUISTICS; LONGEVITY (IN WRITERS AND PUBLICATIONS); MATHEMATICS; NEBULA; NUCLEAR POWER; PARALLEL WORLDS; POLITICS; PUBLISHING; SCIENCE FANTASY; SOCIOLOGY; TIME PARADOXES.

De CHAIR, SOMERSET (STRUBEN) (1911-   ) UK writer whose sf novel, *The Teetotalitarian State* (**1947**), is a not particularly bad-tempered SATIRE set in the NEAR FUTURE and directed at the Labour Party, then in power in the UK. [JC]

De CHANCIE, JOHN (1946-   ) US writer who worked in tv in various capacities before beginning to publish sf with his **Skyway Trilogy**: *Starrigger* (**1983**), *Red Limit Freeway* (**1984**) and *Paradox Alley* (**1986**). Based on a truckers-in-space premise with some comic potential, the already crowded tale is complicated by TIME PARADOXES, godlings and much more; the ensuing epic is at points extremely funny. *Crooked House* (**1987**) with Thomas F. MONTELEONE is a horror novel, and the Zelaznyesque **Castle Perilous** sequence – *Castle Perilous* (**1988**), *Castle for Rent* (**1989**), *Castle Kidnapped* (**1989**), *Castle War!* (**1990**), *Castle Murders* (**1991**) and *Castle Dreams* (**1992**) – is fantasy. JDC has also written two biographies: *Peron* (**1987**) and *Nasser* (**1987**). [JC]

DECIMA VITTIMA, LA (vt *The Tenth Victim*) Film (**1965**). Champion/Concordia. Dir Elio Petri, starring Marcello Mastroianni, Ursula Andress, Elsa Martinelli, Massimo Serato. Screenplay Petri, Ennio Flaiano, Tonino Guerra, Giorgio Salvione, based on "The Seventh Victim" (**1953**) by Robert SHECKLEY. 92 mins. Colour.

This French-Italian coproduction is based loosely on Sheckley's story about a future world where, as a safety valve for latent aggression, the government has legalized duels to the death. In the film two participants (Mastroianni and Andress) are highly trained individuals alternating as "hunter" and "victim", each aiming for the 10-kill score that will bring unlimited privileges. The DYSTOPIAN possibilities are neglected in favour of the then-fashionable **James Bond**/thriller approach, with black jokes and posturing in extravagant costumes. The novelization is *The Tenth Victim* ∗ (**1966**) by Robert Sheckley. [JB]

See also: LEISURE.

DEE, ROGER Working name of US writer Roger Dee Aycock (1914-   ) for his fiction, which he began writing with "The Wheel is Death" for *Planet Stories* in 1949; he was a prolific contributor to the sf magazines of the early 1950s. His sf novel, *An Earth Gone Mad* (**1954** dos), is a routine adventure. [JC]

DEEGAN, JON J. House name created by Gordon Landsborough, editor of AUTHENTIC SCIENCE FICTION, and used almost exclusively by UK writer Robert (George) Sharp (?   -?   ) for novels published in that journal, which for some time early in its run filled each issue with one long story. The **Old Growler** series, beginning with "Reconnoitre Krellig II" in 1951, was signed as by JJD, and three of its sequels (all by Sharp) were published in book form as *Amateurs in Alchemy* (**1952**), *Antro, the Life-Giver* (**1953**) and *The Great Ones* (**1953**). Sharp wrote also a TIME-TRAVEL trilogy, *Corridors of Time* (**1953**), *Beyond the Fourth Door* (**1954**) and *Exiles in Time* (**1954**). Of further JJD titles, *Underworld of Zello* (**1952**) is by Sharp; authorship of *The Singing Spheres* (**1952**) is unconfirmed. The much earlier *Horror Castle* (**1936**) was published under Sharp's own name, which he generally used for his crime thrillers. [JC]

DEEPING, (GEORGE) WARWICK (1877-1950) UK popular novelist, the first of whose many books, *Uther & Igraine* (**1903**), was an Arthurian fantasy. *The Man who Went Back* (**1940**), a timeslip epic, takes its protagonist from the 20th-century UK to the time of the Romans, and returns him wiser and better able to cope with the Nazis. *I Live Again* (**1942**) is a REINCARNATION fantasy that likewise terminates heroically in the Blitz. [JC]

DEEPSTAR SIX Film (**1988**). Carolco/Tri-Star. Dir and coprod Sean S. Cunningham, starring Joyce Collins, Greg Evigan, Taurean Blacque, Miguel Ferrer. Screenplay Lewis Abernathy, Geof Miller, based on a story by Abernathy. 99 mins. Colour.

A deep-sea missile base is being installed by underwater station DeepStar Six. Explosives open a vast cavern under the ocean floor, in which dwells a monstrous arthropod; it destroys two submersibles, enters the station, and kills most of the crew one by one. This no-better-than-competent MONSTER MOVIE was the first of the strange-things-in-the-ocean sf films of the period, others being *Lords of the Deep* (**1989**), LEVIATHAN (**1989**) and *The* ABYSS (**1989**). Once revealed, the crayfish-thing is anticlimactic. [PN]

DEER, M.J. ◊ George H. SMITH.

DEFINITIONS OF SF The term "science fiction" came into general use in the 1930s, an early appearance being in Hugo GERNSBACK's editorial to #1 of SCIENCE WONDER STORIES (June 1929). Long before, however, several writers (◊ Edgar FAWCETT; Edgar Allan POE; William WILSON) had made attempts to define species of literary production similar to sf, and other early speculative writers had their own manifestos. Only since the founding of the specialist sf PULP MAGAZINES in the USA has there been any measure of agreement.

The category first referred to by Gernsback as SCIENTIFICTION was described by him thus in the editorial to #1 of AMAZING STORIES (Apr 1926): "By 'scientifiction' I mean the Jules Verne, H.G. Wells and Edgar Allan Poe type of story – a charming romance intermingled with scientific fact and prophetic vision . . . Not only do these amazing tales make tremendously interesting reading – they are always instructive. They supply knowledge . . . in a very palatable form . . . New adventures pictured for us in the scientifiction of today are not at all impossible of realization tomorrow . . . Many great science stories destined to be of historical interest are still to be written . . . Posterity will point to them as having blazed a new trail, not only in literature and fiction, but progress as well."

This notion of sf as a didactic and progressive literature with a solid basis in contemporary knowledge was soon revised as other pulp editors abandoned some of Gernsback's pretensions, but the emphasis on science remained. A new manifesto was drawn up by John W. CAMPBELL Jr for *Astounding Stories*, which, as ASTOUNDING SCIENCE-FICTION, would dominate the field in the 1940s. He proposed that sf should be regarded as a literary medium akin to science itself: "Scientific methodology involves the proposition that a well-constructed theory will not only explain away known phenomena, but will also predict new and still undiscovered phenomena. Science fiction tries to do much the same – and write up, in story form, what the results look like when applied not only to machines, but to human society as well."

Within a few years of the creation of the term "science fiction" a subculture had evolved composed of writers, magazine editors (and, later, book editors), reviewers and fans; stories and novels written within this subculture shared certain assumptions, linguistic and thematic codes which were embedded in the growing literature, and a sense of isolation from the external "mundane" world for which those codes remained cryptic. This whole living matrix, not just the fictional texts that had initially occasioned it, came to be called "science fiction" (◊ GENRE SF).

Once the publishing category had been established, readers and critics began using the term with reference to older works, bringing together all stories which seemed to fit the specifications. However, the first major study of the field's ancestry was undertaken by a person from outside it, the academic J.O. BAILEY in *Pilgrims through Space and Time* (**1947**). He identified his material thus: "A piece of scientific fiction is a narrative of an imaginary invention or discovery in the natural sciences and consequent adventures and experiences . . . It must be a scientific discovery – something that the author at least rationalizes as possible to science."

Many further sf researchers and writers attempted to generate definitions of the form which would demarcate the contemporary genre and assimilate any theoretically eligible earlier work. These definitions included attempts by James BLISH, Reginald BRETNOR, Robert A. HEINLEIN, Damon KNIGHT and Theodore STURGEON, from within the field, and, from scholars and critics more or less closely associated it, by Kingsley AMIS and Sam MOSKOWITZ. Judith MERRIL echoed Campbell's prospectus while borrowing Heinlein's preferred terminology, which replaced the term "science fiction" by "speculative fiction": "Speculative fiction: stories whose objective is to explore, to discover, to *learn*, by means of projection, extrapolation, analogue, hypothesis-and-paper-experimentation, something about the nature of the universe, of man, or 'reality' . . . I use the term 'speculative fiction' here specifically to describe the mode which makes use of the traditional 'scientific method' (observation, hypothesis, experiment) to examine some postulated approximation of reality, by introducing a given set of changes – imaginary or inventive – into the common background of 'known facts', creating an environment in which the responses and perceptions of the characters will reveal something about the inventions, the characters, or both."

The emphasis in all of these earlier definitions falls on the presence of "science", or at least scientific method, as a necessary part of the fiction. The Merril definition, however, clearly (by shifting from science itself to the idea of extrapolation) is rather wider, since it would include stories which depict social change without necessarily making much fuss over scientific development; and indeed such stories were becoming very popular in the magazines during the 1950s and 1960s, the period during which Merril did most of her writing and editing.

Oddly enough, the most obvious element in the magazine sf that is the initial focus of nearly all of these earlier definitions is not much mentioned in them: the overwhelming majority of the sf of this period – especially in the USA – was set in the future. (By contrast, most 19th- and early-20th-century sf was displaced from the normal world through space rather than time.) With an enjoyable lack of responsibility about using the future to teach us about the present, writers like E.E. "Doc" SMITH, in his **Lensman** series, freed the future for "itself", and the effect of this new freedom was, in literary terms, explosive. From this the characteristic (and addictive) flavour of US sf derives: its relaxed embracing of scale and technology, its narrative fluency and, perhaps, its secret impatience with reason. Most descriptive definitions of sf from the period 1940-70 look with hindsight surprisingly unsatisfactory and rather constricting – damagingly indifferent, in fact, to the actual shape of sf texts.

In the 1960s a new line of thought, stemming in large part from the UK, saw sf re-emphasized as a global literature with 19th-century roots rather than as a purely US phenomenon nurtured in the pulp magazines from the 1920s onwards. This wider perspective on sf tends to de-emphasize its science/technology component. The term "science fiction" itself came in for criticism from Brian W. ALDISS, who commented that sf is no more written for scientists than ghost stories are for ghosts. J.G. BALLARD remarked in 1969 that "the idea that a magazine like *Astounding*, or *Analog* as it's now called, has anything to do with the sciences is ludicrous. You have only to pick up a journal like *Nature*, say, or any scientific journal, and you can see that science belongs in a completely different world." In *Billion Year Spree* (**1973**; rev vt *Trillion Year Spree* 1986 by Aldiss and David WINGROVE) Aldiss offered the remark – it seems more an observation describing a philosophical outlook than a definition – that "science fiction is the search for a definition of man and his status in the universe which will stand in our advanced but confused state of knowledge (science), and is characteristically cast in the Gothic or post-Gothic mode" (◊ GOTHIC SF). By placing Mary SHELLEY's *Frankenstein* (**1818**) at the head of this tradition, Aldiss effectively (and influentially) argued that sf was a child begotten upon Gothic Romance by the Industrial and Scientific Revolution of the early 19th century. More recent critics, like Brian M. STABLEFORD in *Scientific Romance in Britain 1890-1950* (**1985**), have likewise somewhat undercut those definitions that appear to fit most closely an idea of sf as a genre first cultured in US magazines (◊ SCIENTIFIC ROMANCE).

The 1970s as a whole witnessed a great upsurge of academic interest in sf (◊ SF IN THE CLASSROOM), especially in the USA, and with it, naturally enough, came more rigorous and formal attempts to define sf.

To teach a subject you need to know what it is; and, especially in the case of sf (which blurs so easily into FANTASY on one side and POSTMODERNIST fictions – FABULATIONS – on another, TECHNOTHRILLERS and political thrillers on a third, mainstream works about scientific discovery on a fourth, not to mention LOST-WORLD stories or UTOPIAS or future-WAR stories or stories set in the prehistoric past), you also need to know what it isn't. Thus in academic definitions there was a new emphasis on drawing the boundaries of sf more precisely, in terms of its literary strategies as well as its ideational content, sometimes using a vocabulary already developed in different spheres of literary criticism by structuralist and other critics.

In 1972 Darko SUVIN defined sf as "a literary genre whose necessary and sufficient conditions are the presence and interaction of estrangement and cognition, and whose main formal device is an imaginative framework alternative to the author's empirical environment". By "cognition" Suvin appears to mean the seeking of rational understanding, and by "estrangement" something akin to Bertolt Brecht's *Verfremdungseffekt*, defined in 1948 thus: "A representation which estranges is one which allows us to recognize its subject, but at the same time make it seem unfamiliar." Perhaps the most important part of Suvin's definition, and the easiest with which to agree, is the emphasis he puts on what he and others have called a "novum", a new thing – some difference between the world of the fiction and what Suvin calls the "empirical environment", the real world outside. The presence of a novum is insufficient in itself, of course, to define sf, since the different and older tradition of fantasy likewise depends on the novum. Peter NICHOLLS, pointing to this particularly blurred demarcation line, argues that sf must by definition follow natural law whereas fantasy may and mostly does suspend it. Fantasy need not be susceptible to "natural" or cognitive explanation; indeed, *super*natural explanation is at fantasy's heart. (Suvin claims that the commercial linking of sf and fantasy is "a rampantly pathological phenomenon". This dividing line is further discussed under MAGIC.) As to estrangement, it arguably has little to do with at least the US tradition of sf (although a great deal to do with European traditions of SATIRE), in which an important component is nostalgia for the familiar – even the familiarly new (◊ CLICHÉS) – and estrangement is significantly absent. John CLUTE has argued that much sf seeks to create the exact opposite of estrangement; that is, it works to make the incredible seem plausible and familiar. Nonetheless, while Suvin's definition would find few who agreed with all of it, it is challenging and has perhaps been the most useful of all in catalysing debate on the issue.

It is to be expected that disagreements of this sort should take place, since sf itself is not homogeneous, and at different times – sometimes both at once – its strategy is either to comment on our own world through the use of metaphor and extrapolation or to create genuine imaginative alternatives to our own world.

The first of these alternatives is the one emphasized in *Structural Fabulation* (**1975**) by Robert SCHOLES, who defines FABULATION as "fiction that offers us a world clearly and radically discontinuous from the one we know, yet returns to confront that known world in some cognitive way". Unqualified, the definition would fit not only GENRE SF but also the fabulations of John BARTH, Richard BRAUTIGAN, Jorge Luis BORGES and Thomas PYNCHON, works which are quite often annexed to sf though having a different characteristic flavour. Scholes recognizes this when he goes on to the specific case of "structural fabulation" (yet another term substituting for "science fiction" and sharing the initials "sf") in which "the tradition of speculative fiction is modified by an awareness of the universe as a system of systems, a structure of structures, and the insights of the past century of science are accepted as fictional points of departure. Yet structural fabulation is neither scientific in its methods nor a substitute for actual science. It is a fictional exploration of human situations made perceptible by the implications of recent science. Its favourite themes involve the impact of developments or revelations derived from the human or physical sciences upon the people who must live with those revelations or developments."

All definitions of sf have a component of prescription (what sf writers *ought* to do, and what their motives, purposes and philosophies *ought* to be) as well as description (what they habitually *do* do, and what kind of things tend to accumulate under the label). It is, however, only in the later academic definitions by authors like Suvin and Scholes, who are noticeably reticent as regards what sf is actually *about*, that we find prescription getting the upper hand. It is possible with almost all definitions, especially of the prescriptive sort, to find examples which do not fit the prescription. No one has yet emerged with a prescription sufficiently inclusive to satisfy all or even most readers. (If the editors of this encyclopedia have erred, it has been on the side of inclusiveness.)

Some other academic definitions have been less inclusive than Suvin's or Scholes's. Leslie FIEDLER, for example, argues (in *Partisan Review* Fall 1965) that the myth of sf is the dream of apocalypse, "the myth of the end of man, of the transcendence or transformation of the human – a vision quite different from that of the extinction of our species by the Bomb, which seems stereotype rather than archetype". In his *New Worlds for Old: The Apocalyptic Imagination, Science Fiction and American Literature* (**1974**) David KETTERER expands on Fiedler's point at length, dividing sf into three categories (according to the type of extrapolation involved) and concentrating on the third: "Philosophically oriented science fiction, extrapolating on what we know in the context of our vaster ignorance, comes up with a startling *donnée*, or rationale, that puts humanity in a radically new perspective." This he sees as a subcategory of "apocalyptic literature" which, by "the creation of other worlds", causes a "metaphorical destruction of [the] 'real' world in the reader's head".

Alvin TOFFLER, author of *Future Shock* (**1970**), a study of the increasing rate of change in the real world, wrote in 1974 that sf, "by dealing with possibilities not ordinarily considered – alternative worlds, alternative visions – widens our repertoire of possible responses to change". Here is the beginning of a definition of sf in terms of its social function rather than of its intrinsic nature, a little more sophisticated than Marshall McLuhan's earlier comment in *The Medium and the Massage* (**1967**): "Science fiction writing today presents situations that enable us to perceive the potential of new technologies."

In 1987 Kim Stanley ROBINSON wrote in FOUNDATION: THE REVIEW OF SCIENCE FICTION that sf was "an historical literature . . . In every sf narrative, there is an explicit or implicit fictional history that connects the period depicted to our present moment, or to some moment of our past." Commenting in 1992 in the NEW YORK REVIEW OF SCIENCE FICTION on this formulation, John Clute suggested that it underlined the sense US sf conveyed of being connected to the linear, time-bound logic of the Western World.

Unfortunately, the clearest (or most aggressive) definitions are often the least definitive, although many sceptics have been attracted to Damon Knight's "Science fiction is what we point to when we say it" or Norman SPINRAD's "Science fiction is anything published as science fiction". Both these "definitions" have a serious point, of course: that, whatever else sf may be, it is certainly a publishing category, and in the real world this is of more pragmatic importance than anything the theorists may have to say about it. On the other hand, the label "sf" on a book is wholly subject to the whims of publishers and editors, and the label has certainly appeared on some very unlikely books. An additional complication arises because some writers fight hard to avoid the label, perhaps feeling that it might deleteriously affect their sales and/or reputations (e.g., Kurt VONNEGUT Jr, John WYNDHAM). Publishers apply similar cautionary measures to potential bestsellers, which are seldom labelled as sf even when that is exactly what they are (although this has been less true in the post-STAR WARS period than in, say, the 1970s), on the grounds that genre sf when so labelled, while normally selling steadily, rarely enters the bestseller class.

There is really no good reason to expect that a workable definition of sf will ever be established. None has been, so far. In practice, there is much consensus about what sf looks like in its centre; it is only at the fringes that most of the fights take place. And it is still not possible to describe sf as a homogeneous form of writing. Sf is arguably not a genre in the strict sense at all – and why should it be? Historically, it grew from the merging of many distinct genres, from utopias to space adventures. Instinctively, however, we may feel that, if sf ever loses its sense of the fluidity of the future and the excitement of our scientific attempts to understand our Universe – in short, as more conservative fans would put it with enthusiasm though conceptual vagueness, its SENSE OF WONDER – then it may no longer be worth fighting over. If things fall apart and the centre cannot hold, mere structural fabulation may be loosed upon the world!

For a listing of many definitions, including some of those referred to but not actually quoted above, a good source is the "Science Fiction" entry in *Critical Terms for Science Fiction and Fantasy* (**1986**) by Gary K. WOLFE. [BS/JC/PN]

DEFOE, DANIEL (1660-1731) UK merchant, professional spy and writer, extremely prolific author of many works of various kinds, though the huge canon of unsigned works attributed to him has in recent years been convincingly diminished. He is best known today for his novel *Robinson Crusoe* (**1719**), which, while not sf, provided a fundamental model for many sf stories (◊ ROBINSONADE). Of interest to students of PROTO SCIENCE FICTION is *The Consolidator, or Memoirs of Sundry Transactions from the World of the Moon* (**1705**; various savagely cut edns under vts 1705-41), in which a mechanical spirit-driven flying machine, the Consolidator, enables various satirical (◊ SATIRE) observations to be made from a lunar viewpoint. *A Journal of the Plague Year* (**1722**), in effect a historical novel set in 1665, a year DD could presumably barely remember, is a prototype of the DISASTER novel. Some associational short work can be found in *Tales of Piracy, Crime, and Ghosts* (coll **1945** US). [JC/PN]

See also: MACHINES; MOON; SPACE FLIGHT.

DEFONTENAY, C(HARLEMAGNE) I(SCHIR) (1814-1856) French writer whose *Star, ou Psi de Cassiopée* (**1854**; trans P.J. Sokolowski as *Star* **1975** US, with intro by Pierre VERSINS) describes the discovery in the Himalayas of a box full of information about life on another planet. The biological and anthropological speculation is interesting; the translation lacks the inventive fluency of the original. [JC/PN]

See also: STARS.

deFORD, MIRIAM ALLEN (1888-1975) US writer, a newspaper reporter for many years; probably known better for her many mystery stories (some award-winning) than for the sf of her later years. Her publications also include such nonfiction as *The Real Bonnie and Clyde* (**1968**) and her work as contributing editor to *The Humanist*. She edited *Space, Time and Crime* (anth **1964**), a collection of sf stories with mystery elements. As an author of sf stories in her own right, she published over 30 items – beginning with "Last Generation" in 1946 for *Harper's Magazine* – in various magazines, though most of the stories in her two collections, *Xenogenesis* (coll **1969**) and *Elsewhere, Elsewhen, Elsehow* (coll **1971**), had first appeared in *FSF*. Her examinations of themes such as nuclear devastation and sexual roles is conducted in a crisp, clearcut style that sometimes lacks grace but never vigour. [JC]

See also: WOMEN SF WRITERS.

DEGAL, ALDION [r] ◊ YUGOSLAVIA.

De GRAEFF, ALLEN Pseudonym of Albert Paul Blaustein (1921-), professor of law at Rutgers from 1955, under which he edited *Human and Other Beings* (anth **1963**). He was uncredited co-compiler of three anthologies with his friend Basil DAVENPORT: *Deals with the Devil* (anth **1958**), *Invisible Men* (anth **1960**) and *Famous Monster Tales* (anth **1967**). [PN]

De HAVEN, TOM (1949-) US writer who began publishing sf with his first novel, *Freaks' Amour* (**1979**), set in 1988 among a group of MUTANTS created by an atomic mishap, and following their lives as itinerant performers. A similar inclination to place a large connected cast in a surreally threatening world impels the otherwise very different *Funny Papers* (**1985**), a kind of urban fantasy/alternate history set at the end of the 19th century in a magic-realist New York (◊ ALTERNATE WORLDS; FABULATION) and concentrating on the newspaper business at the point when COMIC strips were first becoming widely popular. In the long third section of *Sunburn Lake* (coll of linked stories **1988**), TDH applied his easy fabulistic manner to 21st-century New Jersey. Towards the end of the 1980s, however, TDH gave some sense that he was dissipating his energies, producing a sharp but unremarkable tie in *U.S.S.A. Book 1* * (**1987**), a juvenile, *Joe Gosh* (**1988**), which may have been SHARECROPPED, and *Neuromancer: The Graphic Novel: Volume 1* * (graph **1989**) with Bruce Jensen. But the fantasy sequence **Chronicles of the King's Tramp** represented a significant return of energy: *Walker of Worlds* (**1990**) and *The End-of-Everything Man* (**1991**), with further volumes projected, traverse familiar territory – a sequence of PARALLEL WORLDS nested into an ontological hierarchy – with panache and knowing clarity. [JC]

Other works: *Jersey Luck* (**1980**), associational.

See also: CHILDREN'S SF.

DEIGHTON, LEN (1929-) UK writer of spy novels, cookery books and some other nonfiction, still perhaps best known for his early espionage thrillers, such as *The Ipcress File* (**1962**), several of which feature the same undisciplined secret agent. The fourth volume of the series, *Billion-Dollar Brain* (**1966**), is set in an indeterminate NEAR FUTURE and deals with a super-COMPUTER and a private preventive war launched on Russia across the ice from Finland by a mad tycoon; it was filmed as *Billion Dollar Brain* (1967) dir Ken Russell. In *SS-GB* (**1978**) the UK suffers German occupation from 1941 (◊ HITLER WINS). [JC]

DELAIRE, JEAN Pseudonym of Mrs Muirson Blake (? -?), whose date of birth has been listed as an improbably late 1888, editor of *Christian Theosophist*. JD's *Around a Distant Star* (**1904**) has two young fellows travelling on an electrically propelled FASTER-THAN-LIGHT spacecraft to a planet about 1900 light years away, so that, after avoiding carnivorous plants, they can witness through a supertelescope the death and resurrection of Christ. [PN]

Other works: *A Pixie's Adventures in Humanland* (**1926**).

DELANEY, JOSEPH H(ENRY) (1932-) US lawyer and writer, associated through most of his career with *ASF*, for which magazine he began publishing sf with "Brainchild" in 1982 (◊ APES AND CAVEMEN). He made considerable impact with his second story, "In the Face of My Enemy"(1983), which became part of his first solo novel, *In the Face of my Enemy* (fixup **1985**), a SPACE OPERA featuring an immortal shapechanger. His first novel, *Valentina: Soul in Sapphire* (fixup **1984**) with Marc STIEGLER, rather more grippingly depicts the efforts of the eponymous AI to gain memory space in networked mainframes across the world, and to prove her selfhood. *Lords Temporal* (**1987**) is a TIME-TRAVEL tale of some ingenuity. [JC]

See also: COMPUTERS.

DELANY, SAMUEL R(AY) (1942-) US author and critic, one of the most influential and most discussed within the genre; he has taught at several universities from 1975, and from 1988 has been professor of Comparative Literature at the University of Massachusetts. He has a somewhat mixed cultural background: he is Black, born and raised in Harlem, New York, and therefore familiar with the Black ghetto; but his father, a wealthy funeral-parlour proprietor, had the family brought up in privileged, upper-middle-class circumstances – SRD was educated at the prestigious Bronx High School of Science (although he left college after only one term). This double background is evident in all his writing.

He became famous as one of the youthful prodigies of sf. Unusually, his first published sf was a novel, published when he was 20: *The Jewels of Aptor* (**1962** dos; restored 1968; rev 1971 UK); the later versions restore the third of the book which had originally been excised at ACE BOOKS. This was followed by the **The Fall of the Towers** trilogy: *Captives of the Flame* (**1963** dos; rev vt *Out of the Dead City* 1968 UK), *The Towers of Toron* (**1964** dos; rev 1968 UK) and *City of a Thousand Suns* (**1965**; rev 1969 UK), all assembled as *The Fall of the Towers* (omni of rev texts **1970**). Another early novel was *The Ballad of Beta-2* (**1965** dos; text corrected 1977).

The early novels had certain similarities, and some of the themes initiated in them have recurred regularly in SRD's work. The plot structure is almost invariably that of a quest, or some form of FANTASTIC VOYAGE. Physically and psychologically damaged participants are common. An economical use of colourful detail, often initially surprising but logical when considered, is used to flesh out the social background of the stories. There is an interest in MYTHOLOGY, taking the form of metaphorical allusion to existing myths or of an investigation of the way new myths are formed; this is central to *The Ballad of Beta-2*, in which a student anthropologist investigates the facts behind a folk song garnered from a primitive Earth culture which has gone voyaging in a fleet of GENERATION STARSHIPS. This novel also shows an interest in problems of COMMUNICATIONS and LINGUISTICS which was to become central to SRD's work. **The Fall of the Towers**, too, is full of colourful cultural speculation, although its melodramatic story of war, mutations, mad computers and a malign cosmic intelligence is moderately conventional. The original three volumes of **The Fall of the Towers** were set in the same post-HOLOCAUST Earth as *The Jewels of Aptor*; however, the linking references were removed in the revised edition.

SRD published two more novels in 1966: *Empire Star* (**1966** dos; text corrected 1977) and *Babel-17* (**1966**; rev 1969 UK). Both, especially the latter, which won a NEBULA, reveal a notable advance in sophistication. *Babel-17*, whose chapters carry epigraphs from the work of SRD's wife (1961-80), the poet Marilyn Hacker (1942-   ), is about language, and has a poet heroine. In a future galactic society, radio broadcasts in an apparently alien language are received; they are thought to be connected with sabotage and alien invasion. Much of the novel is to do with cracking the language. SRD believes that our PERCEPTION of reality is partly formed by our languages; the invention of different societies in this novel, more intense and imaginative than his previous work, is mostly rendered in terms of thought- and speech-patterns.

In 1967 he began publishing short stories also. Algis BUDRYS (*Gal* Jan 1969) called him "the best science-fiction writer in the world". He was generally seen as being in the forefront of the NEW WAVE, emphasizing cultural speculation, the soft sciences, psychology and mythology over technology and HARD SF. The short story "Aye, and Gomorrah . . ." (1967) won a Nebula, and the novelette "Time Considered as a Helix of Semi-Precious Stones" (1969) won both HUGO and Nebula. These two, with *Babel-17* and *The Einstein Intersection*, his other Nebula-winning novel, can be found in his *The Complete Nebula Award-Winning Fiction* (omni **1986**).

It can be argued that *The Einstein Intersection* (**1967**; 1 chapter restored 1968 UK) is his most satisfying work, along with the next novel, *Nova* (**1968**; text corrected 1969) and the novella *The Star Pit* (1967; **1988** chap dos). The latter can be found in SRD's excellent first collection *Driftglass* (coll **1971**) together with all of his best shorter work of the period. *The Einstein Intersection* is remarkably compressed and densely patterned with allusive imagery. Earth has lost its humans (*how* is never made clear) and their corporeal form has been taken on by a race of aliens who, in an attempt to make coherent sense of the human artefacts among which they live, take on human traditions, too. Avatars of Ringo Starr, Billy the Kid and Christ appear; the hero, a Black musician who plays tunes on his murderous machete, is Orpheus and Theseus. The book is a *tour de force*, though a cryptic one, since the bafflement of the protagonists

trying to make sense of their transformed lives tends to transfer to the reader. SRD's own diaries provide part of the text of the novel. *Nova* is the Prometheus story and the Grail story combined in an ebulliently inventive space opera/quest; the fire from the heavens, the glowing heart of the Grail, is found only at the heart of an exploding nova. Passages of high rhetoric are mingled (as they often are, too, in the work of SRD's contemporary Roger ZELAZNY) with relaxed slang and thieves' argot. The book features a characteristic SRD protagonist, the criminal/outcast/musician/artist whose literary genealogy goes back through Jean Genet (1910-1986) all the way to François Villon (1431-1485). The variety of cultures in these and other novels by SRD has the effect of making morality and ethics seem relative, pluralistic. Divers forms of bizarre human behaviour, many of which would have been seen as antisocial in US society of the time, emerge as natural in the circumstances created. *The Star Pit*, too, is a highly structured work; its central image is that of ant-colony/cage/trap/micro-ecology, and escape is seen to be intimately linked with emotional mutilation, even psychosis.

SRD's next novel – not sf, though with elements of the fantastic – was the pornographic *The Tides of Lust* (**1973**); the title was not his. (A second pornographic novel, *Hogg*, remains unpublished.) It is likely to shock most readers in its evocation of extreme sado-masochism in imagery which is sometimes poetic and often disgusting – and so intended – perhaps as a Baudelairean ritual of passage. It was, indeed, in the mid-1970s that it became generally known that SRD was bisexual. Certainly, all his later work is deeply concerned with the cultural mechanisms – actual, theoretical and sometimes labyrinthine – of eroticism and love. Much light is thrown on the relationship between SRD's own sexuality and the sf he wrote in the 1960s by his much later book, *The Motion of Light in Water: Sex and Science Fiction Writing in the East Village 1957-65* (**1988**; exp vt *The Motion of Light in Water: East Village Sex and Science Fiction Writing: 1960-65; with The Column at the Market's Edge* 1990 UK). This book, frank and priapic to the verge of the scabrous, won a Hugo for Best Non-Fiction.

SRD's next two novels were *Dhalgren* (**1975**; 6th impression has many typographical errors rectified; text further corrected 1977) and *Triton* (**1976**). After a six-year gap in which SRD had published little or no sf, *Dhalgren* was controversial. It is very long, and his critics see it as perilously self-indulgent and flabby, lacking the old economy of effect. It became a bestseller, however, and other critics saw it as his most successfully ambitious work to date. An anonymous youth, the Kid, comes to the violent, nihilist city of Bellona, where order has fled and there are two moons in the sky, though the rest of the NEAR-FUTURE USA is apparently normal. He becomes an artist, couples and fights, and writes a book that might be *Dhalgren* before leaving the city. The opening sentence completes the unfinished final sentence and an enigmatic circle. It is a book primarily about the possibilities and difficulties of a youth culture, and partly about being a writer. *Triton* is more traditionally structured, but in some ways more sophisticated. It presents a series of future societies differentiated mainly along sexual lines; the male protagonist, who begins by displaying a rather insensitive, traditional machismo, ultimately chooses to become a woman, but remains alienated. Triton (a moon of Neptune) is an "ambiguous heterotopia" with a bewildering variety of available lifestyles. The book poses interesting questions about sexuality, and also about freedom of choice.

Since then SRD has published one singleton novel, *Stars in My Pocket Like Grains of Sand* (**1984**), and four books in the **Nevèrÿon** series, which masquerades as SWORD-AND-SORCERY fantasy: *Tales of Nevèrÿon* (coll of linked stories **1979**; rev 1988); *Nevèrÿona* (coll of linked stories **1983**; rev 1989 UK); *Flight from Nevèrÿon* (coll of linked stories **1985**; rev 1989 UK) and *The Bridge of Lost Desire* (coll of linked stories **1987**; rev vt *Return to Nevèrÿon* 1989 UK). *Stars in My Pocket Like Grains of Sand*, the first volume of a projected diptych, is an exotic piece set in a galactic civilization. A complex narrative again asks questions about the arbitrary and parochial nature of our ethical expectations, using various forms of enjoyed degradation to make the point. It is probably SRD's most important work of the 1980s. The **Nevèrÿon** books adopt a similar strategy of culture-building, and play both with and against the readers' expectations. They are, in fact, sf in the sense that they invent alien societies, though technically they are FANTASY, being set in a distant, fantastic, pre-industrial past, and to a degree act as both critique and re-creation of the Mighty-Thewed Barbarian genre. SRD's treatment of the idea of bondage, for example, is infinitely more sophisticated, and somewhat more elusive, than that of, say, John NORMAN in the **Gor** books. Many ideas are explored, from the erotic to the economic, the concept of slavery appearing in both these idea-sets, and the slave-collar itself coming to be the prime erotically charged symbol; the later volumes make clear reference to the AIDS epidemic. Though allusive, ambitious, self-reflexive, seriously intended books, they do return in style to something reminiscent of the wittier, more economic, more playful SRD of the 1960s, and are among the more accessible works of his past two decades.

During the six-year hiatus (from about 1969) in his own fiction, SRD began to pay more attention to other people's. Much of the resulting critical and semiotic writing has been collected in four books: *The Jewel-Hinged Jaw: Notes on the Language of Science Fiction* (coll **1977**), *The American Shore: Meditations on a Tale of Science Fiction by Thomas M. Disch – Angouleme* (**1978**), *Starboard Wine: More Notes on the Language of Science Fiction* (coll **1984**) and *The Straits of Messina* (coll **1989**). Delany's criticism is often structuralist and to a degree POSTMODERNIST, very aware of a contemporary

literary context that goes well beyond sf, sometimes very wordy, but important in its persistent attempt to define sf in terms of the protocols required for reading it. As SRD said in his acceptance speech after receiving the 1985 PILGRIM AWARD for excellence in sf criticism, "We must learn to read science fiction as science fiction." The second of the four books, an analysis of the structure and images of the short story "Angouleme" (1971; later incorporated in *334* [fixup **1972**]) by Thomas M. DISCH, is written with a spectacularly microscopic fastidiousness. *The Straits of Messina* collects mostly pieces by SRD that were originally published as by K. Leslie Steiner, a pseudonym he uses when writing about his own work. The first and third books, essays on the language of sf, are perhaps of the most general interest. A fifth critical book, *Wagner/Artaud: A Play of 19th and 20th Century Critical Fictions* (**1988** chap), does not bear directly on sf.

With Marilyn Hacker SRD edited a series of original anthologies, QUARK, preferring the term "speculative fiction" to "science fiction", and emphasizing experimental writing. There were 4 vols 1970-71.

With hindsight it can be hypothesized that SRD has had different audiences at different points of his career: a very wide, traditional sf readership up to and including *Dhalgren*, which sold nearly a million copies in the USA alone; and a narrower, perhaps more intellectual, campus-based readership thereafter. There is no doubt that by the 1980s his fiction (and criticism) had become less accessible, and the real debate about his career must be whether or not he gained more than he lost with his adoption of a denser style towards the later 1970s. At this point his fiction also began to include more passages of obviously polemical intent, some of whose thrust, especially in their icons of abasement, did not carry conviction for all readers. But, though admirers of SRD's earlier work tend to be heavily polarized in their views of his later work, he by no means disappeared from popular notice. The first two volumes of the **Nevèrÿon** series sold around quarter of a million each. Lower sales on subsequent editions may have been partly due to resistance in the publishing and book-distribution worlds to his increasingly and explicitly controversial texts.   [PN]

Other works: *Empire: A Visual Novel* (graph **1978**), a GRAPHIC NOVEL written by SRD and executed by Howard V. CHAYKIN; *Heavenly Breakfast: An Essay on the Winter of Love* (**1979**), autobiographical, about life in a commune in New York; *Distant Stars* (coll **1981**), which includes *Empire Star* and contains 3 stories not included in *Driftglass*; *We in Some Strange Power's Employ, Move on a Rigorous Line* (1968 FSF; **1990** chap dos).

As editor: *Nebula Award Winners 13* (anth **1980**).

About the author: *The Delany Intersection: Samuel R. Delany Considered as a Writer of Semi-Precious Words* (**1977** chap) by George Edgar SLUSSER; *Worlds out of Words: The SF Novels of Samuel R. Delany* (**1979**) by

Douglas BARBOUR; *Samuel R. Delany: A Primary and Secondary Bibliography, 1962-1979* (**1980**) by Michale W. Peplow and Robert S. Bravard; *Samuel R. Delany* (**1982** chap) by J.B. Weedman; *Samuel R. Delany* (**1985**) by Seth MCEVOY.

See also: ARTS; CHILDREN IN SF; CITIES; CONCEPTUAL BREAKTHROUGH; CRIME AND PUNISHMENT; CRITICAL AND HISTORICAL WORKS ABOUT SF; CYBERPUNK; CYBORGS; DEVOLUTION; FABULATION; FANTASY; FAR FUTURE; GALACTIC EMPIRES; GAMES AND SPORTS; GENETIC ENGINEERING; GOTHIC SF; HEROES; *The* MAGAZINE OF FANTASY AND SCIENCE FICTION; MILFORD SCIENCE FICTION WRITERS' CONFERENCE; MUSIC; MUTANTS; NEW WORLDS; OUTER PLANETS; PARANOIA; PSYCHOLOGY; SCIENCE FANTASY; SEX; SOCIOLOGY; SPACE OPERA; SPECULATIVE FICTION; UTOPIAS; WOMEN AS PORTRAYED IN SCIENCE FICTION.

DELAP, RICHARD (1942-1987) US editor, reviewer and writer who entered the sf world as a fan and soon began to publish book reviews, beginning with pieces in the FANZINE *Granfalloon* and moving on to a column in AMAZING STORIES during the 1960s. In *Delap's Fantasy and Science Fiction Review Magazine* he created a valuable review organ, whose folding was regretted. He co-edited with Terry DOWLING and Gil Lamont *The Essential Ellison* (coll **1987**). His first novel, *Shapes* (**1987**) with Walt LEE, is a horror tale about an extraterrestrial shape-changer.   [JC]

DeLILLO, DON (1936-   ) US writer who very rapidly established a reputation for brilliance and seriousness. His fourth novel, *Ratner's Star* (**1976**), subjects its sf material – it examines the personal and cognitive cruces surrounding the decipherment of a message from the star of the title – to a formidable array of contemporary intellectual procedures, while presenting its numerous characters as in-depth portraits of the fundamental obsessions at the heart of contemporary US intellectual life. The book stands as a model (a rather humbling one for GENRE SF) of the extraordinary complexity of response that any genuine message from the stars would (it is reasonable to assume) elicit. Several DD novels – like *Great Jones Street* (**1973**) and *White Noise* (**1985**) – subject their protagonists to sf-like revelations of the nature of reality through psychotopic drugs and devices; and the game of terror played in *The Names* (**1982**) smacks of OULIPO. Throughout his career, DD has been an author of FABULATIONS, the burden of which has been to expose his characters to unbearable images of the world we live in.   [JC]

About the author: *Introducing Don DeLillo* (anth **1991**) ed Frank Lentricchia.

De LINT, CHARLES (HENRI DIEDERICK HOEFSMIT) (1951-   ) Canadian musician and writer – born as a Canadian citizen in the Netherlands – who established himself during the 1980s as a prolific FANTASY author and as a significant and original contributor to the subgenre of contemporary fantasy, beginning with "The Fane of the Grey Rose" in *Swords Against Darkness IV* (anth **1979**) ed Andrew J. OFFUTT. Some of CDL's short work has appeared as by Tanuki Aki, Henri Cuiscard, Jan Penalurick, Cerin Songweaver and Wendelessen, and one horror novel, *Angel of Darkness* (**1990** US), was as by Samuel M. Key. CDL's output (see list below), which is both various and polished, merits extended consideration; but he is mentioned here primarily for his one sf novel, *Svaha* (**1989** US), a NEAR FUTURE tale set in enclaves established by high-tech Native Americans to fend off the barbarian world outside. A kind of sweetish simplicity sometimes overloads his fantasy tales, especially the earlier ones; it might be surmised that a writer of CDL's energy and ambition may increasingly find that genre-crossing provides him with a necessary stimulus and threat.   [JC]

Other works: *The Oak King's Daughter* (**1979** chap), published, like several other short texts here listed, by CDL's own Triskell Press; *The Moon is a Meadow* (**1980** chap); *A Pattern of Silver Strings* (**1981** chap); *Glass Eyes and Cotton Strings* (**1982** chap); *De Grijze Roose* ["The Grey Rose"] (coll trans Johan Vanhecke et al. **1983** Netherlands); *In Mask and Motley* (**1983** chap); *The Calendar of the Trees* (**1984** chap); *Laughter in the Leaves* (**1984** chap); *Moonheart: A Romance* (**1984** US) and its sequels *Ascian in Rose* (**1987** chap US), *Westlin Wind* (**1989** chap US) and *Ghostwood* (**1990**), all three sequels included in «Spirit Walk» (omni **1992**); *The Riddle of the Wren* (**1984** US); *The Badger in the Bag* (**1985** chap); *The Three Plushketeers and the Garden Slugs* (**1985** chap); *The Harp of the Grey Rose* (**1985** US), the first volume in the projected **Legend of Cerin Songweaver** sequence; *Mulengro: A Romany Tale* (**1985** US); *And the Rafters Were Ringing* (**1986** chap); *Yarrow: An Autumn Tale* (**1986** US); *The Lark in the Morning* (**1987** chap); *Jack, the Giant-Killer: The Jack of Kinrowan: A Novel of Urban Faerie* (**1987** US); *The Drowned Man's Reel* (**1988** chap); *Greenmantle* (**1988** US); *Wolf Moon* (**1988** US); *The Stone Drum* (**1989** chap); a contribution to the SHARED-WORLD **Borderland** enterprise run by Terri WINDLING, *Berlin* * (**1989** chap); two ties – *Philip José Farmer's The Dungeon, #3: The Valley of Thunder* * (**1989** US) and *#5: The Hidden City* * (**1990** US); *Ghosts of Wind and Shadow* (**1990** chap); *The Fair in Emain Macha* (**1985** *Space & Time* #68; exp **1990** dos US); *The Dreaming Place* (**1990** US); *Drink Down the Moon: A Novel of Urban Faerie* (**1990** US); *The Little Country* (**1991** US); *Cafe Purgatorium* (coll **1991** US) with stories, separately, by Dana Anderson; *Hedgework and Guessery* (coll **1991** US); *Uncle Dobbin's Parrot Fair* (**1987** *IASFM*; **1991** chap US); *Our Lady of the Harbour* (**1991** chap US).

See also: CANADA.

de l'ISLE ADAM, VILLIERS [r] ◊ VILLIERS DE L'ISLE ADAM.

DELIUS, ANTHONY (1916-   ) South African poet who eventually moved to the UK. His SATIRE on South African POLITICS and apartheid, *The Last Division* (**1959**), sends a 1980s Union Parliament to a Hell and Devil closely resembling those in Wyndham LEWIS's *The Childermass* (**1928**), where they re-create, under their Premier's inspiration, the social system they left behind. The swingeing satirical power of this book-length poem is remarkable. Its views on South Africa's future contrast markedly with those expressed by Garry ALLIGHAM and are comparable with those of Arthur KEPPEL-JONES, though sharper. Less interestingly, *The Day Natal Took Off* (**1963**) depicts that state's secession from South Africa. [JC]

DELL, DUDLEY [s] ◊ Horace L. GOLD.

DEL MARTIA, ASTRON House name invented by publisher Stephen FRANCES for his own publishing house, and used there by John Russell FEARN on *The Trembling World* (**1949**). The name was then sold on to Gaywood Press, which used it for three more tales: *Dawn of Darkness* (**1951** chap), *Space Pirates* (**1951**) and *Interstellar Espionage* (**1952** chap). The latter story features a security officer called Dog who appears also in *Spawn of Space* (**1951**) by Franz Harkon, an unattributed pseudonym. A fifth ADM story was advertised but never published, although the name was revived by Frances in a reprint of his *One Against Time* (**1954** as by Hank JANSON; **1969** as by ADM). [SH/PN]

DELMONT, JOSEPH Pseudonym of German writer Karl Pick (1873-1935), whose *Die Stadt unter dem Meer* (**1925**; trans anon as *The Submarine City* **1930** UK) features the construction by U-boat crews of an UNDER-THE-SEA city from which it is intended to conquer the world. Some of the stories assembled in English as *The Dead City* (coll trans anon **1932** UK) are sf, as is *Der Ritt auf dem Funken* (**1928**; trans anon as *Mistress of the Skies* **1932** UK). [JC]

del PICCHIA, MENOTTI [r] ◊ LATIN AMERICA.

DELRAY, CHESTER ◊ Francis G. RAYER.

del REY, JUDY-LYNN (1943-1986) US editor. She began her career in 1965 with GALAXY SCIENCE FICTION, becoming associate editor in 1969. Her predecessor was Lester DEL REY; they married in 1971. She moved to BALLANTINE BOOKS in 1973, bringing her husband in on the operation in 1974, and in 1977 was instrumental in forming the Del Rey imprint – named for her – of Ballantine (itself owned by Random House). As editor-in-chief of DEL REY BOOKS, she demonstrated an extraordinary gift for marketing sf and fantasy to an unprecedentedly large audience, and her releases often hit the US bestseller lists. At the time of her death, she had become the dominant figure in US sf and fantasy publishing. Given her physically taxing genetic disability – she was an achondroplastic dwarf, and frequently in pain – the range of her accomplishments in the driven world of New York publishing seemed all the more remarkable.

J-LDR was also responsible for the STELLAR original anthology series: *Stellar 1* (anth **1974**), *Stellar Short Novels* (anth **1976**), *Stellar Science-Fiction Stories #2* (anth **1976**), *#3* (anth **1977**), *#4* (anth **1978**), *#5* (anth **1980**), *#6* (anth **1981**) and *#7* (anth **1981**). [JC]
See also: HUGO; PUBLISHING.

del REY, LESTER Working name of US writer Ramon Felipe San Juan Mario Silvio Enrico Smith Heathcourt-Brace Sierra y Alvarez-del Rey y de los Verdes (1915-). His father was a poor sharecropper of part-Spanish extraction, and LDR's education proceeded in fits and starts before dwindling away after two years in college. After holding a variety of temporary jobs he began to write in the late 1930s, his first published work being "The Faithful" for *ASF* in 1938. This was rapidly followed by his classic ROBOT story, "Helen O'Loy" (1938). Many of his early stories are remarkable for their sentimentality, but the best was the unsentimental suspense story *Nerves* (1942 *ASF*; exp **1956**; rev 1976), about an accident in a NUCLEAR-POWER plant and the struggle to avert a major catastrophe. He stepped up his output after becoming a full-time professional writer in 1950, but this was accompanied by a decline in average quality. He produced several juvenile novels, some as Philip St John (a name he first used in 1939). He wrote also as Erik van Lhin, John Alvarez, Marion Henry, Philip James, Charles SATTERFIELD and Edson MCCANN (the last two pseudonyms being used on collaborations with Frederik POHL, who also used Satterfield on some solo stories). LDR's most notable works of the 1950s and 1960s were: *Preferred Risk* (**1955** with Pohl, writing together as McCann; reprinted 1980 as by Pohl and LDR); the ultra-tough novel of COLONIZATION *Police Your Planet* (1953 *Science Fiction Adventures*; cut **1956** as by Erik van Lhin; rev 1975 as by LDR and Erik van Lhin); and an early novel on the theme of OVERPOPULATION, *The Eleventh Commandment* (**1962**; rev 1970). The second of the short-lived "Galaxy Magabooks" (◊ GALAXY SCIENCE FICTION NOVELS), *The Sky is Falling/Badge of Infamy* (**1963** dos), featured revised versions of two magazine novellas: *The Sky is Falling* (1954 *Beyond* as "No More Stars" with Pohl, writing together as Charles Satterfield; rev 1963 for the Magabook; **1974** dos) and *Badge of Infamy* (1959 *Satellite*; rev 1963 for the Magabook; **1973** dos). Some novels which appeared under his name in 1966-8 were actually written, from LDR's extensive outlines, by Paul W. FAIRMAN; these include *The Runaway Robot* (**1965**), *Rocket from Infinity* (**1966**), *The Infinite Worlds of Maybe* (**1966**), *The Scheme of Things* (**1966**), *Tunnel through Time* (**1966**), *Siege Perilous* (**1966**; vt *The Man without a Planet* 1969) and *Prisoners of Space* (**1968**). His most recent solo novel was *Pstalemate* (**1971**), about the predicament of a man who discovers that he has PSI POWERS, in the knowledge that all psi-powered individuals go insane. *Weeping May Tarry* (**1978**), as by LDR with Raymond F. JONES, is a novel by Jones extrapolating the theme of LDR'S "For I Am a Jealous People" (*Star Short Novels* anth **1954** ed Frederik Pohl).

From the late 1940s, as well as doing a considerable amount of writing, LDR was actively involved with various business and editorial projects. In the early 1950s he was editor of FANTASY MAGAZINE, ROCKET STORIES (under the house name Wade KAEMPFERT), SPACE SCIENCE FICTION and, for a time, SCIENCE FICTION ADVENTURES, leaving all these positions after a dispute in 1953. He edited an anthology of juvenile sf, *The*

Year After Tomorrow (anth **1954**) with Cecile Matschat and Carl Carmer, and one of the many series of **The Best Science Fiction Stories of the Year** – *#1* (anth **1972**), *#2* (anth **1973**), *#3* (anth **1974**), *#4* (anth **1975**) and *#5* (anth **1976**). He selected the GARLAND **Library of Science Fiction** reprint series (45 vols, all 1975) and compiled *Fantastic Science Fiction Art* (**1975**). After the death of P. Schuyler MILLER in 1974 he took over *ASF's* book-review column (he had previously written reviews for *Rocket Stories* under the pseudonym Kenneth Wright, and had done occasional reviews for other magazines under his own name, notably IF in 1968-73). His fourth wife, Judy-Lynn DEL REY (*née* Benjamin), was for some time on the staff of *Gal* and its companions – where he served as features editor 1969-74 – and became sf editor for BALLANTINE BOOKS in the mid-1970s; LDR joined the company in 1977, when it began issuing its sf and fantasy lines under the imprint DEL REY BOOKS – named in honour of her – and he continued to operate these lines alone after his wife's death in 1986 until his retirement at the end of 1991. His history of sf, *The World of Science Fiction: 1926-1976 – The History of a Subculture* (**1979**), focuses narrowly on the US pulp tradition.

LDR was a versatile but rather erratic writer who never fulfilled his early promise. His best work appears in the collections . . . *And Some Were Human* (coll **1948**; with "Nerves" cut, rev vt *Tales of Soaring Science Fiction from . . . And Some Were Human* 1961) and *Gods and Golems* (coll **1973**); much of this is reprinted in *The Best of Lester del Rey* (coll **1978**). There is an interesting autobiographical commentary in *The Early del Rey* (coll **1975**). LDR was given the NEBULA Grand Master award for 1990. [BS]

Other works: *Marooned on Mars* (**1952** juvenile); *Rocket Jockey* (**1952** juvenile, as by Philip St John; vt *Rocket Pilot* UK; reprinted 1978 as by LDR); *Attack from Atlantis* (**1953**), a juvenile; *Battle on Mercury* (**1953**) as by Erik van Lhin, a juvenile; the **Moon** sequence of juvenile tales, comprising *Step to the Stars* (**1954**), *Mission to the Moon* (**1956**) and *Moon of Mutiny* (**1961**); *Rockets to Nowhere* (**1954**) as by Philip St John, a juvenile; *Mission to the Moon* (**1956**), a juvenile; *Robots and Changelings* (coll **1957**); *The Cave of Spears* (**1957**); *Day of the Giants* (1950 *Fantastic Adventures* as "When the World Tottered"; **1959**); *Moon of Mutiny* (**1961**), a juvenile; *Outpost of Jupiter* (**1963**), a juvenile; *Mortals and Monsters* (coll **1965**); *The Best of Hal Clement* (coll **1979**), ed.

About the author: "Lester del Rey" in *Seekers of Tomorrow* (**1967**) by Sam MOSKOWITZ.

See also: ALIENS; ASTOUNDING SCIENCE-FICTION; COSMOLOGY; CRIME AND PUNISHMENT; DISCOVERY AND INVENTION; DYSTOPIAS; ESP; EVOLUTION; GALAXY SCIENCE FICTION; GAMES AND SPORTS; GOLDEN AGE OF SF; HUGO; MARS; MERCURY; MOON; MUTANTS; ORIGIN OF MAN; PREDICTION; PUBLISHING; RELIGION; SATIRE; SOCIAL DARWINISM; SPACESHIPS; VENUS.

DEL REY BOOKS US paperback imprint, founded 1977, a subsidiary of BALLANTINE BOOKS, itself a part of Random House. Some authors developed at Ballantine in the mid-1970s by Judy-Lynn DEL REY and Lester DEL REY had begun to make the bestseller lists, and it was in recognition of this that the new sf/fantasy imprint was named for her. (The original Ballantine imprint is now little used for sf.) Judy-Lynn, who died in 1986, was editor-in-chief and, from 1982, publisher; Lester, the very successful fantasy editor, retired from the company in 1991 at the age of 76. DRB is an sf/fantasy imprint, though it is in fantasy that it has had the majority of its commercial successes, which have been very substantial. Its fantasy authors, some of whom began their career with DRB, have included Piers ANTHONY, James P. BLAYLOCK, Terry Brooks, Stephen DONALDSON, David Eddings, Barbara HAMBLY and Katherine KURTZ. Its sf authors have included Arthur C. CLARKE, Anne McCAFFREY, Larry NIVEN, Frederik POHL and Charles SHEFFIELD. DRB is an important sf/fantasy publisher in terms of big-selling books; it has also published a number of good books. The two categories overlap. [PN]

DELUGE Film (1933). RKO. Dir Felix E. Feist, starring Sidney Blackmer, Peggy Shannon, Lois Wilson. Screenplay John Goodrich, Warren B. Duff, based on *Deluge* (**1928**) by S. Fowler WRIGHT. 70 mins. B/w.

One of the first DISASTER movies, this is an impressive spectacle showing the destruction of New York by a series of earthquakes and tidal waves. There are good special effects by Ned Mann, who later designed and supervised the effects in THINGS TO COME (1936), but the survivors' melodramatic love story is disappointing, and less shocking than the one in the book. The disaster sequence was later used as stock footage, continuing to show up in other films for decades. [JB/PN]

de MADARIAGA (Y ROJO), SALVADOR [r] ◊ Salvador de MADARIAGA.

DeMARINIS, RICK (1934-   ) US writer whose first novel, *A Lovely Monster: The Adventures of Claude Rains and Dr Tellenbeck* (**1975**), applies a sharply fabulistic eye (◊ FABULATION) to Southern California and to the FRANKENSTEIN myth. *Scimitar* (**1977**), set in a similar region, satirically anatomizes the panicky responses of an urban USA to the imploding NEAR FUTURE. *Cinder* (**1978**), contrastingly, celebrates an old man's last days, which he spends (in every sense) in the company of a genie, also ageing and also determined to seize the day. The stories assembled in *Jack & Jill* (coll **1979**) hover at the edge of sf, as do some of the contents of both *Under the Wheat* (coll **1986**) – notably the terrifying title story and "Weeds" – and *The Coming Triumph of the Free World* (coll **1988**). RDM's later novels, *The Burning Women of Far Cry* (**1986**) and *The Year of the Zinc Penny* (**1989**), do not venture into the fantastic. [JC]

DEMIJOHN, THOM Collaborative pseudonym of Thomas M. DISCH and John T. SLADEK on the first edition of their mystery novel (not sf) *Black Alice* (**1968**). The subsequent edition used their real names.

De MILLE, JAMES (1833-1880) Canadian writer and academic, author of much signed fiction and an anonymous, posthumous, Antarctic UTOPIA, *A Strange Manuscript Found in a Copper Cylinder* (**1888**), one of the best 19th-century lost-race (◊ LOST WORLDS) novels. The cylinder's contents describe a shipwreck survivor's discovery of a lost valley at the South Pole, where the climate is temperate, prehistoric animals wander about, and a Semitic people, the Kosekin, has evolved a kindly, cannibalistic society which values darkness, poverty and clement death.   [JC]
See also: CANADA.

DEMON Film. ◊ GOD TOLD ME TO.

DEMONS ◊ GODS AND DEMONS; MAGIC; SUPERNATURAL CREATURES.

DEMON SEED Film (1977). MGM. Dir Donald Cammell, starring Julie Christie, Fritz Weaver, Gerrit Graham, Berry Kroeger. Screenplay Robert Jaffe, Roger O. Hirson, based on *Demon Seed* (**1973**) by Dean R. KOONTZ. 95 mins. Colour.

When the supercomputer Proteus IV is switched on it refuses to obey instructions, in the time-honoured tradition (*for examples* ◊ COLOSSUS, THE FORBIN PROJECT; 2001: A SPACE ODYSSEY). All its terminals are shut down with the inadvertent exception of one, located in its creator's own automated home, which also contains a primitive one-armed robot and the scientist's estranged wife. The COMPUTER takes control of the house, trapping the woman inside and subjecting her to a terrifying (and calculatedly fetishistic) ordeal culminating in its raping her in order to create a new super-race melding human and MACHINE. This up-to-date Luddite variation of the FRANKENSTEIN theme, more HORROR than sf, can perhaps be admired for its bravado in putting its tasteless subtext up there on the surface where everyone can see it. There is indeed a baby.   [JB/PN]
See also: PARANOIA.

DEMONS OF THE SWAMP ◊ Roger CORMAN.

De MORGAN, JOHN (1848-c1920) US writer of fantastic fiction, miscellaneous works and dime novels; said to have been of UK birth. He drew very heavily on the work of H. Rider HAGGARD for models and sources. His adult fantastic fiction included: *He* (**1887**), involving a search for Kallikrates, an immortal who lives on Easter Island; *"It"* (**1887**), with characters from *King Solomon's Mines* (**1886**) like Allan Quatermain, describing further adventures in East Africa seeking the immortal woman, culminating in the discovery of the Missing Link and a clear statement about mutations; and *King Solomon's Treasures* (**1887**), which invokes a surviving pterodactyl and the immortal Macrobi. These works embodied an impressive background of accurate classical and ethnographic data. *King Solomon's Wives* (**1887**) as by Hyder Ragged, sometimes erroneously attributed to JDM, was written by UK legal scholar Sir Henry Chartres Biron (1863-1940).

JDM later became a staff writer for Norman L. Munro (◊ DIME-NOVEL SF) and wrote conventional dime novels. *The Strange Adventures of Two New York Boys in the Realm of the Polar North* (**1890**) describes a lost race (◊ LOST WORLDS) of Old Norse near the North Pole, while *Into the Maelstrom* (**1894**) is concerned with a UTOPIAN society (without crime or evil passions) in a cave world filled with breathable water under the Maelstrom. *In Unknown Worlds* (**1896**), *In Search of the Gold of Ophir* (**1899**) and *Bringing Home the Gold* (**1899**) all deal with Missing Links.   [EFB]

DEMPSEY, HANK [s] ◊ Harry HARRISON.

DENMARK Although one cannot really speak of a Danish sf tradition prior to the 1950s, quite a few Danish authors did write occasional sf works before then. The first such book was Ludvig HOLBERG's *Nicolai Klimii iter Subterraneum* (**1741** in Latin; trans as *A Journey to the World Underground by Nicolas Klimius* **1742**; reprinted 1974), which was among the earliest works in any language to feature a journey inside a HOLLOW EARTH. The 18th century saw a few other satirical and fantastical sf-like works, such as the play *Anno 7603* ["The Year 7603"] (**1785**), a gender-reversal SATIRE, by Johan Hermann Wessel (1742-1785).

The early 19th century saw little Danish sf and fantasy, although Hans Christian Andersen (1805-1875), in addition to his fantasies, wrote a few sf stories, most notably "Om Aartusinder" (1853; trans as "In a Thousand Years" in *The Hans Andersen Library* **1869**). With the arrival of a new rationalism around 1870, the ground was laid for renewed activity in sf, but not much was actually published. A very interesting work from this time is Vilhelm Bergsøe's novella "En reise med Flyvefisken 'Prometheus'" ["A Journey on the Flying Fish 'Prometheus'"] (1869), which tells of a transatlantic journey on a vessel which alternately flies above the water and dives beneath the surface. Authors who worked with UTOPIAN themes included C.F. Sibbern with *Meddelelser af Indholdet af et skrift fra Aaret 2135* ["Report on the Content of Papers from the Year 2135"] (2 vols, **1858** and **1872**) and Otto Møller with *Guld og Ære* ["Gold and Honour"] (**1900**).

The early 20th century saw a number of action-oriented juveniles, chiefly from Niels Meyn (1891-1957), who wrote racist and imperialistic SPACE OPERAS in imitation of Hans Dominik (◊ GERMANY) and various US authors. Satire and social criticism, mostly of a conservative bent, were produced by other contemporary authors, such as Aage Heinberg with *Himmelstormerne* ["Young Titans"] (**1919**).

After WWII and Hiroshima, Danish literature reflected a mixture of fear and enthusiasm towards technology. This, together with the growing US cultural and economic dominance, made for a new trend in Danish sf. Chief among its practitioners was Niels E. Nielsen (1924-   ), whose sf début was in 1952 and who has since written about 40 sf novels. He began as an imitator of Ray BRADBURY, and still harbours a cautious attitude towards TECHNOLOGY, his books usually warning against humankind's usurpation of the powers of the Creator. Among his motifs are nuclear and ecological catastrophe; as early as 1970 he wrote a novel about GENETIC ENGINEERING, *Herskerne* ["The Rulers"] (**1970**).

The 1960s saw increased interest in sf as a result of two principal factors: one was the enthusiasm generated by the US space programme, the other the indefatigable Jannick Storm (1939-   ), who, as editor and translator, introduced a lot of US, UK and Scandinavian sf. Storm was a proponent of the NEW WAVE but also introduced such "classical" writers as Isaac ASIMOV, James BLISH and Frederik POHL.

From the late 1960s onwards this increased interest in the genre led to a number of Danish authors writing occasional sf books. These may be grouped in several ways. Chiefly inspired by the New Wave and COMICS, the "flower children" of the late 1960s saw sf as a new way of telling wondrous tales, as with Knud Holten in *Suma-X* (**1969**). The realists, on the other hand, saw in sf a continuation of realism by other means and created NEAR-FUTURE scenarios; examples are Anders BODELSEN's *Frysepunktet* (**1969**; trans as *Freezing Point* **1971**; vt *Freezing Down*) and Henrik STANGERUP's *Manden der ville være skyldig* (**1973**; trans as *The Man who Wanted to be Guilty* **1982**). Experimental modernists took from the genre part of its inventory and used it for other purposes, as in *Liget og Lysten* ["Corpse and Desire"] (**1968**) by Svend Åge Madsen, which contains sf elements without really being sf. Occultists and ufologists published a number of sf works, best among them being Erwin Neutzsky-Wulff's *Anno Domini* (**1975**) and *Gud* ["God"] (**1976**). Finally, politically conscious writers used near-future scenarios to debate POLLUTION and NUCLEAR POWER. One author who has managed this without his fiction suffering from the politics is Jørgen Lindgreen, whose *Atomer på Næsset* ["Nuclear Plant on the Promontory"] (**1975**) is an effective TECHNOTHRILLER. In the late 1970s and early 1980s a rather disparate group of WOMEN SF WRITERS appeared, ranging from the modernist Dorrit Willumsen, with *Programmeret ti kærlighed* ["Programmed for Love"] (**1981**), to the utopianist Vibeke Grønfeldt, with *Det fantastike barn* ["The Fantastic Child"] (**1982**).

With two exceptions, the authors mentioned above do not consider themselves sf writers, and nor has any of them written more than a single recognizably sf work. Those exceptions – the writers who really know sf – are Bodelsen and Madsen: Bodelsen has published a number of sf short stories, and Madsen has developed his own unique kind of sf with such works as *Tugt og utugt i mellemtiden* ["Virtue and Depravity in the Middle Period"] (**1976**), *Se dagens lys* ["Face the Light of Dawn"] (**1980**) and *Lad tiden gå* ["Let Time Flow"] (**1985**). Later, Inge Eriksen joined them with a very ambitious tetralogy, *Rummet uden tid* ["Space without Time"] (**1983-9**). If a distinctly Danish sf is to develop, it will have to build upon the works of these three. [ND]

DENMARK, HARRISON [s] ◊ Roger ZELAZNY.

DENNIS, BRUCE [s] ◊ David Wright O'BRIEN.

DENNIS, GEOFFREY (POMEROY) (1892-1963) UK writer whose *Harvest in Poland* (**1925**; rev 1931) deals with augurs of a grim future for Europe in supernatural terms. *The End of the World* (**1930**), despite its sf title, is a nonfiction discourse on the ways in which the world might in fact end. It has been suggested by Brian M. STABLEFORD that GD may have also written under the name Guy DENT. [JC]

DENNIS, NIGEL (FORBES) (1912-1989) UK writer whose second novel, *Cards of Identity* (**1955**), is a FABULATION about a post-WWII England whose citizens are so bereft of security that any identity can be imposed on anyone (*see also* PARANOIA); the final section, entitled "The Prince of Antioch, or An Old Way to New Identity", constitutes an entire (and entirely fraudulent) Shakespeare play, hilariously couched. In *A House in Order* (**1966**) identity is again imperilled as the protagonist, under increasingly surreal assault, attempts to act as though WWIII were not happening around him. [JC]

DENT, GUY (?   -   ) Pseudonymous UK writer whose one original contribution to sf, *Emperor of the If* (**1926**), describes two of the possible universes created by a disembodied brain in a laboratory. In the first part the past is superimposed on the present, with vivid descriptions of London being overrun by prehistoric flora and fauna; in the second the locale is a future DYSTOPIA where humans exist under the domination of self-reproducing MACHINES. It has been suggested by Brian M. STABLEFORD that GD was in fact Geoffrey DENNIS. [JE]

See also: ALTERNATE WORLDS; EVOLUTION; FAR FUTURE; SUPERMAN.

DENT, LESTER (1905-1959) US author, best known for his **Doc Savage** novels, which he wrote for DOC SAVAGE MAGAZINE under the house name Kenneth ROBESON (*which see for details*); LD wrote all but 43 of the 181 issues. He also wrote stories under his own name and other crime stories under the pseudonym Tim Ryan. *Lester Dent, the Man Behind Doc Savage* (**1974**) is a study by Robert E. WEINBERG; information about LD and about his work appears also in *Doc Savage: His Apocalyptic Life* (**1973**) by Philip José FARMER. The most complete study is *Bigger than Life: The Creator of Doc Savage* (**1990**) by Marilyn Cannaday. LD was famous in PULP-MAGAZINE circles for his Master Plot: the action-suspense formula he claimed never failed. His prose was described by James STERANKO as "bravura frenzy". [PN/JC]

DENTINGER, STEPHEN [s] ◊ Edward D. HOCH.

DENTON, BRADLEY (CLAYTON) (1958-   ) US writer who began publishing sf with "Music of the Spheres" in *FSF* in 1984, and who caused some impact in the field with his first novel, *Wrack and Roll* (**1986**), a contemporary ALTERNATE-WORLD tale which portrays heavy-metal musicians as the HEROES they might dream of being in a world absolutely divided between the "straight" majority and the anti-authoritarian "wrackers", who are defined by their MUSIC. BD displays an impressive feel for the sustaining myths of heavy metal in his depiction of the wrackers, whose random violence and passion for life are set against the sterility and genocidal tendencies of the straight world as nuclear war approaches. *Buddy Holly is Alive and Well on Ganymede* (**1991**) deploys the same range of knowledge with more feeling, deeper nostalgia, and an improved control of narrative. BD's short stories are generally contemporary fantasies with a moral twist, like "The Calvin Coolidge Home for Dead Comedians" (1988), a fable which attacks the sterile blindness of many Christian conceptions of heaven. [NT]

de PEDROLO, MANUEL [r] ◊ SPAIN.

De POLNAY, PETER (1906-1984) Hungarian-born writer, in the UK from before WWII. Of his very many novels, only *The Stuffed Dog* (**1977**), a TIME-TRAVEL tale, is of genre interest. [JC]

De REYNA, JORGE ◊ Diane DETZER.

DERLETH, AUGUST W(ILLIAM) (1909-1971) US writer and editor, born in Sauk City, Wisconsin, where he spent his life. A correspondent with and devout admirer of H.P. LOVECRAFT, he devoted much of his life to projects aimed at preserving Lovecraft's memory. The most important of these projects was of course the founding, with Donald WANDREI, of the publishing company ARKHAM HOUSE in Sauk City in order to publish Lovecraft's stories; Wandrei later resigned his interest, but AWD carried on until his death, publishing a wide range of weird fiction, including some of his own otherwise very widely published work. He completed a number of unfinished Lovecraft stories and fragments: *The Lurker at the Threshold* (**1945**), *The Survivor and Others* (coll **1957**) and *The Watcher Out of Time and Others* (coll **1974**). In addition, he wrote two volumes of Lovecraft pastiches, *The Mask of Cthulhu* (coll **1958**) and *The Trail of Cthulhu* (coll **1962**), and edited anthologies of such stories by various writers like *The Shuttered Room, and Other Pieces* (anth **1959**) – a title not to be confused with either of the Lovecraft collections likewise entitled (one **1970** UK and one **1971** US, contents differing) – *The Dark Brotherhood, and Other Pieces* (anth **1966**) and *Tales of the Cthulhu Mythos* (anth **1969**; vt in 2 vols as *Tales of the Cthulhu Mythos #1* 1971 and *#2*) 1971). AWD edited Lovecraft's writings for publication, including his letters (in collaboration with Wandrei), and also wrote *H.P.L.: A Memoir* (**1945**) and *Some Notes on H.P. Lovecraft* (**1959** chap).

But AWD's literary activities were by no means dominated by his interest in Lovecraft. He was a prolific and successful writer of regional novels, receiving a Guggenheim Fellowship for this work, and of detective fiction, starting with *Murder Stalks the Wakely Family* (**1934**; vt *Death Stalks the Wakely Family* 1937 UK); he published a series of **Sherlock Holmes** pastiches about the character **Solar Pons**, beginning with *"In Re: Sherlock Holmes"* – *The Adventures of Solar Pons* (coll **1945**; vt *Regarding Sherlock Holmes* 1974; vt *The Adventures of Solar Pons* 1975 UK). His very first story, however – "Bat's Belfry" for *Weird Tales* in 1926

– was of genre interest, and he remained for many years a prolific contributor to WEIRD TALES, mainly under his own name and the pseudonym Stephen Grendon, and to other magazines, including STRANGE STORIES (where he used the name Tally Mason). His best work was assembled in *Someone in the Dark* (coll **1941**), *Something Near* (coll **1945**), *Not Long for This World* (coll **1948**; with 11 stories cut, vt *Tales from Not Long for This World* 1961), *Lonesome Places* (coll **1962**), *Mr George and Other Odd Persons* (coll **1963** as Stephen Grendon; 1964 as AWD; vt *When Graveyards Yawn* 1965 UK as AWD), *Colonel Markesan and Less Pleasant People* (coll **1966**) with the US critic and writer Mark Schorer (1908-1977), and *Dwellers in Darkness* (coll **1976**). He wrote little sf, but his **Tex Harrigan** series was about a newspaperman constantly running across zany sf inventions and the like; it was included in *Harrigan's File* (coll **1975**).

AWD edited a great many anthologies, both sf and weird. His sf anthologies include several large volumes: *Strange Ports of Call* (anth **1948**; much cut 1958), *The Other Side of the Moon* (anth **1949**; cut 1956 UK; much cut 1959 US) and *Beyond Time and Space* (anth **1950**; much cut 1958). His weird anthologies include *Sleep No More* (anth **1944**; cut 1964 UK; much cut vt *Stories From Sleep No More* 1967 US), *Who Knocks?* (anth **1946**; much cut 1964 UK) and *The Sleeping & the Dead* (anth **1947**; vt in 2 vols as *The Sleeping and the Dead* 1964 UK and *The Unquiet Grave* 1964 UK). AWD was one of the pioneering anthologists in the genre.

The history of Arkham House was chronicled in AWD's *Arkham House: The First 20 Years* (**1959** chap) and *Thirty Years of Arkham House, 1939-1969: A History and Bibliography* (**1970** chap). In 1948-9 the company published a magazine, ARKHAM SAMPLER, ed AWD. Competent and literate and highly energetic, AWD was the central figure in bringing lasting popularity to Lovecraft and to other authors such as Clark Ashton SMITH. His own extremely various output awaits comprehensive appraisal. [MJE]

Other works: *100 Books by August Derleth* (**1962**), nonfiction; *The Beast in Holger's Woods* (**1968**).

As editor: *The Night Side* (anth **1947**); *Dark of the Moon: Poems of Fantasy and the Macabre* (anth **1947**); *Far Boundaries* (anth **1951**; cut 1967); *The Outer Reaches* (anth **1951**; cut 1958; vt in 2 vols as *The Outer Reaches* 1963 UK and *The Time of Infinity* 1963 UK); *Night's Yawning Peal* (anth **1952**; much cut 1974); *Beachheads in Space* (anth **1952**; cut 1954 UK; cut 1957 US; with 1 story cut, vt in 2 vols as *Beachheads in Space* 1964 UK and *From Other Worlds* 1964 UK); *Worlds of Tomorrow* (anth **1953**; cut 1954 UK; cut 1958 US; vt in 2 vols as *Worlds of Tomorrow* 1963 UK and *New Worlds for Old* 1963 UK); *Time to Come* (anth **1954**; cut 1959); *Portals of Tomorrow* (anth **1954**); *Fire and Sleet and Candlelight* (anth **1961**), poetry; *Dark Mind, Dark Heart* (anth **1962**); *When Evil Wakes* (anth **1963** UK); *Over the Edge* (anth **1964**); *Travelers by Night* (anth **1967**); *Dark Things* (anth **1971**).

About the author: *August Derleth: A Bibliography*

(1983) by Alison M. Wilson.

See also: PUBLISHING; SMALL PRESSES AND LIMITED EDITIONS.

DERNIER COMBAT, LE (vt *The Last Battle*) Film (1983). Films du Loup. Dir Luc Besson, starring Pierre Jolivet, Jean Bouise, Jean Reno. Screenplay Besson, Jolivet. 92 mins. B/w.

Made by Besson (later one of the best-known French directors of his generation) when only 23, the arty but vigorous *LDC* is low-budget and photographed in black-and-white Cinemascope, and has no dialogue at all. A young man (Jolivet) in an unspeaking post-HOLOCAUST world – holocaust and speechlessness remain unexplained – flies in a restored plane, meets an old doctor, matures, fights a swordsman, conquers a tribal leader and gets a girl. A dwarf lives in a locked car trunk; the tops of high-rise buildings project from the sand; fish fall from the sky; Samurai lurch and scuttle; women are imprisoned. [PN]

De ROUEN, REED R(ANDOLPH) (1917-   ) US writer of half Native American (Oneida) extraction. His sf novel *Split Image* (**1955** UK) mixes SPACE OPERA and speculation on POLITICS and RELIGION in its story of a space flight culminating in a landing on an exact duplicate of Earth. [PN/JC]

DESART, THE EARL OF Working name of UK writer W.U.O'C. Cuffe (1845-1898), whose *The Raid of the "Detrimental"* (**1897**) describes a LOST WORLD in the South Atlantic transformed by its UK inhabitants into an advanced UTOPIA. [JC]

DESMOND, SHAW (1877-1960) Irish novelist, poet, founder of the International Institute for Psychical Research (1934), and author of many works on the afterlife and several sf novels. *Democracy* (**1919**) predicts a revolution in the UK. The DYSTOPIAN *Ragnarok* (**1926**) envisages the destruction of civilization through a world WAR fought by armies equipped with radio-controlled planes and poisonous gases, the narrative concentrating on the derring-do of futuristic fighter pilots. His pessimism continued in *Chaos* (**1938**), which prophesies a future war between the UK and Germany. *World-Birth* (**1938**), possibly stimulated by the works of Olaf STAPLEDON, describes the troubled future history of mankind and the eventual development of an ideal state. This concluding optimism surfaces again in *Black Dawn* (**1944**), where world peace is the dream. His earlier works include two fantasies: *Echo* (**1927**) is a memory of past incarnation (◊ REINCARNATION) and *Gods* (**1921**) centres on industrial exploitation. *Tales of the Little Sisters Of Saint Francis* (coll **1929**) includes some fantasy. [JE]

See also: WEAPONS.

DESTINATION MOON Film (1950). A George Pal Production/Eagle-Lion. Dir Irving Pichel, starring John Archer, Warner Anderson, Dick Wesson, Tom Powers. Screenplay Robert A. HEINLEIN, "Rip" Van Ronkel, James O'Hanlon, based loosely on *Rocket Ship Galileo* (**1947**) by Heinlein. 92 mins. Colour.

DM, the first of George PAL's many sf productions,

has great historical importance: its commercial success initiated the sf film boom of the 1950s after a decade that had contained almost no sf CINEMA at all. It has interest in hindsight, too, in the partial accuracy with which it anticipated the actual Moon landing of 1969. To this day, *DM* stands as a film obviously made by people who knew about science: along with the German rocket expert Hermann Oberth (1894-1989), Heinlein himself acted as technical advisor. The special effects are relatively convincing: astronomical artist Chesley BONESTELL provided the backgrounds for the scenes on the Moon, working with art director Ernst Fegte. The film's biggest predictive error was political, not scientific: it predicted that the first Moon landing, described as "the greatest challenge ever hurled at American industry", would be a truly capitalist affair conducted by private enterprise. *DM* is an austere film, semi-documentary in nature and, aside from a sequence about fuel shortage near the end, rather placid and unexciting. But, despite its colourless script and its low-key performances (except for some ill judged comic relief from the blue-collar radio operator, played by Wesson), *DM* is a film with considerable dignity and, in a quiet way, a genuine SENSE OF WONDER. Its final message – THIS IS THE END OF THE BEGINNING in big block letters – can be seen, in retrospect, as an entirely justified claim. [PN]

See also: MOON; ROCKETS; SPACE FLIGHT.

DESTINATION MOONBASE-ALPHA ◊ SPACE 1999.

DESTINATION SATURN ◊ BUCK ROGERS IN THE 25TH CENTURY.

DESTINIES US "magazine" in paperback-book format published by ACE BOOKS, ed James BAEN, 11 issues, Nov 1978-Aug 1981, last issue undated. The list of contributors to all sections of the magazine – which could equally be thought of as an original-ANTHOLOGY series – was impressive. Book reviews were by Spider ROBINSON, with Orson Scott CARD and Norman SPINRAD taking over from #6. Science-fact articles came from Jerry POURNELLE, among others, and included a five-part series by Poul ANDERSON on the interaction between sf and science. The fiction was mainly short stories and novelettes, many from well known authors like Gregory BENFORD, Card, Larry NIVEN (with Pournelle), Clifford D. SIMAK and Roger ZELAZNY. "Lost Dorsai" by Gordon R. DICKSON won the 1981 HUGO for Best Novella. The emphasis was on HARD SF. The series died when Baen left Ace. However, some time after Baen formed his publishing company Baen Books in 1983, and having published a very similar paperback magazine series, FAR FRONTIERS (1985-6), he resuscitated *Destinies* as *New Destinies*, beginning with *New Destinies, Vol I: Spring 1987* ed Baen, apparently current (1992) though irregular, with 8 issues up to *New Destinies Vol IX* (anth **1990**); there was no *New Destinies Vol V*. The mixture was, as before, of scientific articles and hard-sf stories by authors like Dean ING, Spider Robinson, Charles SHEFFIELD and Harry TURTLEDOVE, as well as pieces from several of the contributors to the original *Destinies*. [RR/PN]

DESTROY ALL MONSTERS ◊ GOJIRA; RADON.

DESTROY ALL PLANETS ◊ DAIKAIJU GAMERA.

De TARDE, JEAN GABRIEL [r] ◊ Gabriel TARDE.

DETECTIVES ◊ CRIME AND PUNISHMENT.

De TIMMS, GRAEME A probable pseudonym. GDT's pulp-style paperback sf novels are *Three Quarters* (**1963**) and *Split* (**1963**). [JC]

DETZER, DIANE Working name used by US writer Diane Detzer de Reyna (1930-   ) for some of her sf, though she has also published much material as Adam Lukens, and some as Jorge de Reyna. She began publishing sf with "The Tomb" for *Science Fiction Stories* in 1958, and soon released a number of novels, from *The Sea People* (**1959**) to *Eevalu* (**1963**), as Adam Lukens. These are varied in subject matter but are generally routine SPACE OPERA. As Jorge de Reyna she published *The Return of the Starships* (**1968**), and under her own name *The Planet of Fear* (**1968**). [JC]
Other works as Adam Lukens: *Conquest of Life* (**1960**); *Sons of the Wolf* (**1961**); *The Glass Cage* (**1962**); *The World Within* (**1962**); *Alien World* (**1963**).

DEVER, JOE [r] ◊ Paul BARNETT; GAMES AND TOYS.

DEVEREUX, EVE ◊ Paul BARNETT.

De VET, CHARLES V(INCENT) (1911-   ) US writer, mostly of short stories, of which he has written over 50 for sf magazines, beginning with "The Unexpected Weapon" for *AMZ* in 1950. In his first sf novel, *Cosmic Checkmate* (1958 *ASF* as "The Second Game"; exp **1962** chap dos; exp vt *Second Game* 1981) with Katherine MACLEAN, an Earthman is sent to investigate a hostile planet whose inhabitants' social advancement depends on proficiency at the national chess-like game (◊ GAMES AND SPORTS). His second novel, *Special Feature* (1958 *ASF*; exp **1975**), rather flatly depicts media involvement in the filming of the depredations of an ALIEN monster in St Louis. After some years of silence, CVDV became active once again in the late 1980s. [JC]

DEVIL-DOLL, THE Film (1936). MGM. Dir Tod Browning, starring Lionel Barrymore, Maureen O'Sullivan, Frank Lawton. Screenplay Browning, Garrett Fort, S. Guy ENDORE, Erich von Stroheim, based on *Burn, Witch, Burn!* (**1933**) by A. MERRITT and "The Witch of Timbuctoo" by Browning. 79 mins. B/w.

In this film by the director of *Dracula* (1931) and *Freaks* (1932) a man (Barrymore) wrongly convicted and sent to Devil's Island returns to Paris, where he uses miniaturized people for revenge. He disguises himself as an old-lady toymaker and sends his 6in (15cm) humans as toys to the homes of his enemies; in the middle of the night the "toys" come to life and carry out his telepathic instructions. The illusion of miniaturization is perfectly created by the use of giant sets and skilfully executed travelling mattes – the work of the MGM special-effects department, then headed by A. Arnold Gillespie. Though the original novel used alchemy for miniaturization, this uses a supposedly scientific electrical device. [JB/PN]

DEVLIN, ROY P. [s] ◊ Thomas P. KELLEY.

DEVOLUTION Sf is usually an optimistic genre, and stories of EVOLUTION on the whole envisage humanity as slowly progressing to higher states. However, a persistent pessimistic note in GENRE SF generally, and to a degree in mainstream sf too, has been to imagine the opposite, the devolution or degeneration of mankind. The note was sounded most famously in H.G. WELLS's *The Time Machine* (**1895**), in which humankind evolves into two races, one physically degenerate, the other with few mental resources. At the end of the book humankind is gone, the Sun is cooling, and a solitary football-shaped creature is seen flopping in the last shallow sea. In George Allan ENGLAND's *Darkness and Dawn* (**1914**) a couple wake after SUSPENDED ANIMATION to find a desolate Earth peopled by subhuman descendants of the survivors of a natural DISASTER. The rhetoric is lurid.

To this day, stories of the HOLOCAUST AND AFTER are often peopled by tribal savages and monstrous MUTANTS, though here the devolution tends to be social rather than biological in emphasis, as in Russell HOBAN's *Riddley Walker* (**1980**), which is unusual in its foregrounding of a devolved (but vivid) language (◊ LINGUISTICS). The possibility of biological devolution was mooted in pseudo-scientific circles a good deal in the early part of the century – it was a favourite notion of the Nazis – and H.P. LOVECRAFT often saw the adherents of his various disgusting cults as devolved into froglike or apelike creatures. The idea that humanity could revert to apedom was almost a CLICHÉ of pulp sf; it is central to, for example, *The Iron Star* (**1930**) by John TAINE, in which rays from a meteor are the mutagenic agent. *La planète des singes* (**1963**; trans as *Planet of the Apes* 1963 US; vt *Monkey Planet* 1964 UK) by Pierre BOULLE, filmed as PLANET OF THE APES (1968), put a later slant on the theme for satirical purposes by having the evolution of apes paralleled by the devolution of humans. The hero of Edmond HAMILTON's "The Man who Evolved" (1931) regresses finally to a blob. Hamilton enjoyed the cosmic pointlessness suggested by ideas of devolution, and often used the theme. On a more serious level, the idea comes up several times in *Last and First Men* (**1930**) by Olaf STAPLEDON, in which the upwards progression of the evolutionary thrust is several times interrupted by devolutionary sequences, rather like someone climbing a slippery hill and occasionally backsliding.

Paddy CHAYEFSKY's *Altered States* (**1978**) gives a new twist to the idea in its interesting if absurd notion that altered states of consciousness (as in a sensory-deprivation tank) may lead to instant alteration of the way our genetic heritage is manifest, our oldest DNA finding bodily expression to produce, in this case, first an apeman and later a blob. This was filmed as ALTERED STATES (1980). Chayefsky admits that his inspiration was Robert Louis STEVENSON's *Strange Case of Dr Jekyll and Mr Hyde* (**1886**), a novel whose protagonist, after experimenting with chemicals, alternates between two states: the highly evolved doctor and the amoral, bestial Hyde. In Stevenson's book what is a subtext in most earlier devolution stories is almost overt: that devolution is a metaphorical equivalent of the Fall of Man.

Social devolution was always a popular theme in genre sf, partly because it gave writers a chance to exploit colourful primitive societies and partly in deference to the cyclic view of HISTORY popularized by Arnold Toynbee (1889-1975). The theme is also common in stories of GALACTIC EMPIRES, where commonly a social breakdown at the centre leads to cultural devolution on the fringes, much as in the Roman Empire. This is the theme of Isaac ASIMOV's **Foundation** trilogy.

The theme of ENTROPY became popular in the 1960s, and with it came a new lease of life for devolution stories. Evolution ever upwards is an example of negentropy, or reverse entropy, and is counter to the general running-down of the cosmos, which in obedience to the laws of thermodynamics moves towards ever decreasing order, ever increasing randomness. (The pessimism of the 1950s and 1960s probably had more to do with the Vietnam War and problems of OVERPOPULATION and starvation than with any revelation from physics, but entropy provided a convenient metaphor for all this.) 1960s writers often envisaged increasing disorder in terms of biological devolution. The theme was touched on by Samuel R. DELANY in *The Ballad of Beta-2* (**1965**), but an earlier and more substantial work was *The Long Afternoon of Earth* (**1962** US; exp vt *Hothouse* 1962 UK) by Brian W. ALDISS, in which a devolved and jungle-like Earth, whose shrunken humans have taken to the trees again, is given a kind of weird charm; life continues fecund even while INTELLIGENCE is lost and the Galaxy subsides towards its heat-death.

Devolution occurs in the work of other writers of FABULATIONS and NEW-WAVE sf, and nowhere are its attractions for the overintellectualized 20th century more clearly shown than in the works of J.G. BALLARD, whose most central and recurring theme this is. Its first clear expression was in his story "The Voices of Time" (1960), in which the countdown to the end of the Universe is accompanied by a series of baroque degenerate mutations and the hero's need for more and more sleep. The tone is as much celebratory as tragic. Ballard's *The Drowned World* (1962) has a hero ever more ready to slough off such human qualities as ambition or even self-preservation as he listens to the insistent call of his bloodstream, whose saltiness recalls a time before life had left the oceans. These inner changes are mirrored in the Earth itself, which has catastrophically reverted to the luxuriance of a new Carboniferous era.

Tales of devolution from the 1970s and 1980s are often curiously close in feeling to their apparent opposite: the stories of evolutionary transcendence that we associate with, for example, Greg BEAR and Ian WATSON. Where we envisage an upwards there

must necessarily be a downwards, too; this is an idea that has haunted many sf writers, notably Michael BISHOP, sometimes metaphorically and sometimes literally. It is close to the latter in his *No Enemy But Time* (**1982**), in which a modern man travels back in time to find marriage and a home with hominids. Which evolutionary direction is upwards, which downwards, and which better, seems to several contemporary writers to be all a matter of perspective, as can be seen in the main 1980s variant on the theme: a devolution that is deliberately biologically (or psychologically) engineered. Several of the CYBERPUNK writers have envisaged such an operation as a means of simplifying the self to a creature who is less prone, perhaps, to the *angst* induced by information overload. A similar idea is found in David ZINDELL's *Neverness* (**1988**), a large part of which deals with the fierce, brave, ice-age Alaloi, a race which "because they wanted to live what they thought of as a natural life . . . back mutated some of their chromosomes, the better to grow strong, primitive children to live on the pristine worlds they hoped to discover". An interesting and even more ferocious devolution, more psychic than physical, is that envisaged in Robert P. HOLDSTOCK's *Mythago Wood* (**1984**) and its sequels, in which the human hind-brain conspires with the power of an ancient woodland to strip the minds of those who walk there down to the blood and bone of their Neolithic forebears and further, back into the days of ice. Most writers of the last few decades who have like Holdstock dealt with this theme have exhibited a strong if ambiguous attraction to the idea, though to an earlier generation devolution appeared straightforwardly repugnant.

The class of stories in which primitive primates confront evolved primates in the present day is discussed under APES AND CAVEMEN; these stories, too, have a bearing on the devolution theme. [PN]

DeWEESE, GENE Working name of US technical writer and author Thomas Eugene DeWeese (1934-   ), who began writing sf with two **Man from U.N.C.L.E.** ties, *The Invisibility Affair* ∗ (**1967**) and *The Mind-Twisters Affair* ∗ (**1967**), both with Robert COULSON and signed, collaboratively, Thomas Stratton. Other novels with Coulson, both authors now signing their own names, include a routine sf adventure for LASER BOOKS, *Gates of the Universe* (**1975** Canada; rev vt *Nightmare Universe* 1985 US) and two spoof RECURSIVE novels about reporter **Joe Karns**, who gets into all kinds of trouble at sf CONVENTIONS; the large number of in-group references made it unlikely that either *Now You See It/Him/Them* (**1975**) and *Charles Fort Never Mentioned Wombats* (**1977**) would gain many readers outside the genre. In the 1980s, GDW concentrated on lively juveniles (see listing below) and on several equally lively **Star Trek** ties: for STAR TREK itself, *Chain of Attack* ∗ (**1987**), its direct sequel *The Final Nexus* ∗ (**1988**), and *Renegade* ∗ (**1991**); and, for STAR TREK: THE NEXT GENERATION, *The Peacekeepers* ∗ (**1988**). [JC/PN]
Other works: *Jeremy Case* (**1976** Canada); *The Wanting*

Factor (**1980**); *Something Answered* (**1983**).

For children: *Major Corby and the Unidentified Flapping Object* (**1979**); *Nightmares from Space* (**1981**); *The Adventures of a Two-Minute Werewolf* (**1983**); the **Calvin Willeford** sequence, comprising *Black Suits from Outer Space* (**1985**; vt *Beepers from Outer Space* 1985), *The Dandelion Caper* (**1986**) and *The Calvin Nullifier* (**1987**); *Whatever Became of Aunt Margaret?* (**1990**).

As Jean DeWeese: Various Gothics, of which *The Reimann Curse* (**1975**; vt *A Different Darkness* 1982 as GDW), *The Moonstone Spirit* (**1975**), *The Carnelian Cat* (**1975**) and *Nightmare in Pewter* (**1978**) have been registered as containing material of genre interest.

DeWEESE, JEAN ◊ Gene DeWEESE.

De WREDER, PAUL ◊ John HEMING.

DEXTER, J.B. ◊ John S. GLASBY.

DEXTER, WILLIAM Pseudonym of UK writer William Thomas Pritchard (1909-   ), whose two sf novels make up a short series. In *World of Eclipse* (**1954**) humans return from internment on the planet of the Vulcanids to repopulate a devastated Earth; *Children of the Void* (**1955**) brings in a runaway world, nuclear conflicts in space, and communication with ethereal descendants of humanity.   [JC]

DEY, FREDERICK VAN RENSSELAER [r] ◊ Nick CARTER; DIME-NOVEL SF; "NONAME".

DIABOLICAL DR MABUSE, THE ◊ *Die* TAUSEND AUGEN DES DR MABUSE.

DIABOLIC INVENTION, THE ◊ VYNÁLEZ ZKÁZY.

DIABOLIK (vt *Danger: Diabolik*) Film (1967). Dino De Laurentiis/Marianne. Dir Mario Bava, starring John Phillip Law, Marisa Mell, Michel Piccoli, Adolfo Celi, Terry-Thomas. Screenplay Bava, Dino Maiuri, Adriano Baracco, Brian Degas, Tudor Gates, based on *fumetti* by Luciana and Angela Giussani. 105 mins, cut to 88 mins. Colour.

This Italian/French coproduction is one of Di Laurentiis's several attempts to film sf COMIC strips, others being BARBARELLA (1967) and FLASH GORDON (1980). Law plays a stylish supercriminal, after the style of Fantômas, the fictional antihero of several thrillers, beginning with *Fantômas* (1913-14); he attempts to steal the entire gold reserves and destroy all the tax records of his country. He is caught at the dénouement in a shower of radiactive molten gold, becoming his own memorial. Directed with visual panache and a sense of fun by Bava, *D* is futuristic but only marginally sf.   [PN]

DIAMOND, JOHN [s] ◊ Barrington J. BAYLEY.

DIANETICS According to its adherents a science, according to its disbelievers a PSEUDO-SCIENCE, founded by L. Ron HUBBARD, at the time a pulp writer whose main market was the sf magazines. Hubbard's sf had always emphasized the powers of the mind and deployed protagonists who maintained to the end a heroic stance against a corrupt Universe. The former interest was translated into real-life terms in the late 1940s, and the latter vision may be what sustained Hubbard against the widespread execration he and his movement received from some quarters, both outside and inside sf.

The editor of *ASF*, John W. CAMPBELL Jr, began experimenting with Hubbard's ideas in 1949 and believed them valid. In May 1950 *ASF* (after much prior publicity) published a long article on Dianetics, seen as a form of psychotherapy that could achieve miraculous results in sweeping away the dross that encumbers ordinary minds, to leave uncovered the SUPERMAN latent in us all. Follow-up publicity went well beyond the sf magazines. Hubbard's *Dianetics: The Modern Science of Mental Health* (**1950**) was published in the same year, and immediately became a bestseller. The attractions of Dianetics were manifold: it could be practised after mere hours of training, with no formal education necessary; it proposed an apparently simple and coherent model of the mind; it offered an explanation of why so many people feel themselves to be unappreciated failures – and, better than that, it offered a cure.

In Dianetics an "auditor" (the therapist) encourages the patient to babble out his/her fantasies. The E-meter, a form of lie-detector, early on came to be an essential item of equipment. In theory, the needle on the meter swings over whenever a traumatic area of memory is uncovered, and the auditor then disposes of the trauma by revealing its meaning. So far, this is rather like an sf version of conventional psychoanalysis. However, Hubbard also taught that traumas could be pre-natal, and eventually that they could have been suffered during previous incarnations (◊ REINCARNATION) right back to the dawn of time. A "clear" – a person who had successfully rid himself/herself of aberrations – would possess radically increased intelligence, powers of telepathy, the ability to move outside the body and to control such somatic processes as growing new teeth, and a photographic memory. Here was the superman figure of so much contemporary pulp sf made flesh – at least if Dianetics worked (◊ EDISONADE).

Film stars took up Dianetics; centres were opened all over the USA; many thousands were converted, including A.E. VAN VOGT, whose own sf had produced many protagonists not unlike Dianetics's "clears". One of Hubbard's assistants was Perry CHAPDELAINE, who later became an sf writer himself. In 1952, after an organizational rift, Hubbard left the Dianetic Foundation and soon advertised his new advance on Dianetics, SCIENTOLOGY, in the entry for which this story is continued.   [PN]

See also: PARANOIA.

DICK, KAY (1915-   ) UK writer and editor whose novel, *They: A Sequence of Unease* (**1977**), resembles thematically and in its experimental structure much of her previous fiction, but is set in a NEAR-FUTURE England where freedom of travel is restricted and cultural activities are actively persecuted. Constructed as a set of linked stories that mirror one another, *They* relates ENTROPY and the youth-culture as enemies of creative values (and middle-class individualism); in relating these levels of meaning,

KD sets up a very moving, though abstract, model of humanistic response to a straitened future.   [JC]

Other works as editor: *The Mandrake Root* (anth **1946**) as Jeremy Scott, *At Close of Eve* (anth **1947**) as Scott and *The Uncertain Element* (anth **1950**), all fantasy anthologies.

DICK, PHILIP K(INDRED) (1928-1982) US writer, one of the two or three most important figures in 20th-century US sf and an author of general significance. He lived most of his life in California, where most of his fiction was set, either literally or by displacing sf protocols into a nightmare of the Pacific Rim. He attended college for one year at Berkeley, operated a record store and ran a classical-music programme for a local radio station; he was married five times, and had three children. From 1950 to 1970 he was intensely and constantly productive – a circumstance only posthumously made clear by the publication of several mainstream novels written during the first years of his career. The order in which he wrote his many novels is of importance in assessing their interrelation, and so the relevant dates are indicated in the discussion below.

He began his career with short magazine fiction – his first published story was "Beyond Lies the Wub" (1952) – and over the next few years came a number of ironic and idiosyncratic short stories, some of which were collected in *A Handful of Darkness* (written 1952-4; coll **1955** UK; with 2 stories cut 1966 UK), *The Variable Man and Other Stories* (written 1952-4; coll **1957**) and *The Book of Philip K. Dick* (written 1952-5; coll **1973**; vt *The Turning Wheel and Other Stories* 1977 UK). The first three and a half volumes of *The Collected Stories of Philip K. Dick* are devoted to these early years. This set, which is definitive, consists of 5 separate titles, all of which suffer from a singularly unhelpful array of vts: *Beyond Lies the Wub* (coll **1987**; vt *The Short Happy Life of the Brown Oxford* 1990); *Second Variety* (coll **1987**; vt *We Can Remember it for You Wholesale*, with "Second Variety" dropped and the new title story added, 1990); *The Father-Thing* (coll **1987**; rev with "Second Variety" added, vt *Second Variety* 1991); *The Days of Perky Pat* (coll **1987**; vt *The Minority Report* 1991) and *The Little Black Box* (coll **1987**; vt *We Can Remember it for you Wholesale* 1991 UK; vt *The Eye of the Sibyl* 1992 US).

PKD's first novels – *The Cosmic Puppets* (written 1953; 1956 *Satellite* as "A Glass of Darkness"; exp **1957** dos) and *Dr Futurity* (written 1953; 1954 *TWS* as "Time Pawn"; exp **1959** dos) – were professional expansions of magazine tales and reveal his fingerprints to hindsight; the former interestingly returns a man to his home-town which, overlaid by manufactured illusion, serves as a battleground for two warring forces who bear the aspects of Ormazd and Ahriman (the opposing principles of Zoroastrian cosmology). PKD's PARANOIA about godlike manipulations of consensual reality marks a theme he would obsessively repeat in less crude form, just as the confusion of humans and mechanical simulacra

adumbrated in the second book might be considered one particular variant of the major theme which runs right through PKD's work: the juxtaposition of two "levels of reality" – one "objectively" determined, the other a world of appearances imposed upon characters by various means and processes.

His first published book, *Solar Lottery* (**1955** dos; rev vt *World of Chance* 1955 UK – each text printing some material the other excludes), has an immediate impact; it is a story belonging to, if not rather dominating, a category prevalent in the early 1950s – the tale in which future society is distorted by some particular set of idiosyncratic priorities: in this case social opportunity is governed by lottery. The plot of the novel is reminiscent of A.E. VAN VOGT, and juxtaposes political intrigues with the utopian quest of the disciples of an eccentric MESSIAH. This interest in messianic figures runs throughout PKD's work as an important subsidiary theme. There are versions of it in *The World Jones Made* (written 1954; **1956** dos), *Vulcan's Hammer* (1956 *Future Science Fiction*; exp **1960**), and in his sf of the 1960s.

But, after writing *The World Jones Made*, a heated authoritarian DYSTOPIA, *Eye in the Sky* (written 1955; **1957**), which sophisticates the reality diseases of his first novel, and the routine *The Man who Japed* (written 1955; **1956** dos), PKD began an exceedingly ambitious – and totally unsuccessful – attempt to break into the mainstream-novel market. From this period came *Mary and the Giant* (written 1953-5; **1987**), *The Broken Bubble* (written 1956; **1988**), *Puttering About in a Small Land* (written 1957; **1985**), *In Milton Lumky Territory* (written 1958-9; **1985**), *Confessions of a Crap Artist* (written 1959; **1975**), *The Man whose Teeth were All Exactly Alike* (written 1960; **1984**) and *Humpty Dumpty in Oakland* (written 1960; **1986** UK). Graceful, wry, vulnerable, pessimistic and wise, they are novels less good only than the best of PKD's intense prime, which began immediately.

Time Out of Joint (written 1958; **1959**) is a bridge novel: its central character, who lives in a peaceful POCKET-UNIVERSE enclave created for him by a war-torn society so that it can exploit his precognitive talents, retains the desire and capacity to defeat illusion and regain objective reality. In later books the author became more and more fascinated by the various unreal worlds he created. In the first of these, the HUGO-winning *The Man in the High Castle* (written 1961; **1962**), his best-known single book, the characters live in an ALTERNATE WORLD in which the Allies lost WWII (◊ HITLER WINS), but one of them eventually learns from the *I-Ching* that the real world – manifest in the alternate through the pages of a novel – is one in which the Allies won (though it is not our world). After this major novel came, in close succession, the writing of three further books which together constitute his finest achievement. *Martian Time-Slip* (written 1962; 1963 *Worlds of Tomorrow* as "All We Marsmen"; exp **1964**) creates a world irradiated by schizophrenic (◊ PARANOIA) perceptions, and moves with frightening intensity – and hilarity – to an elegant transcendental finale. *Dr Bloodmoney, or How We Got Along After the Bomb* (written 1963; **1965**), is built more intricately than any other PKD novel upon a plot-structure whose interconnections and layers themselves work as a portrayal of the world – in this case a post-HOLOCAUST USA. *The Three Stigmata of Palmer Eldritch* (written 1964; **1965**), more extremely than any previous PKD book, inhabits the badlands within which the real and the ersatz interpenetrate: suppliers of a hallucinogenic drug which makes life tolerable for Martian colonists face opposition from the sinister Eldritch, whose own new drug (imaged in language which recalls the Communion wafer) pre-empts reality entirely.

The complexity and stature of these four books were perhaps muffled in the 1960s through their being outnumbered by the less achieved PKD works that were being composed or released at this same time – *We Can Build You* (written 1962; 1969 *AMZ* as "A. Lincoln, Simulacrum", with last chapter added by Ted WHITE; text restored **1972**), *The Game-Players of Titan* (written 1963; **1963**), *The Simulacra* (written 1963; **1964**), *Now Wait for Last Year* (written 1963; **1966**), *Clans of the Alphane Moon* (written 1963-4; **1964**), *The Crack in Space* (written 1963-4; **1966**), *The Zap Gun* (written 1964; **1967**), *The Penultimate Truth* (written 1964; **1964**), *The Unteleported Man* (written 1964-5; first half only **1966** dos; both halves rev 1983, with short inserts by John T. SLADEK rev vt *Lies, Inc* 1984 UK) and *Counter-Clock World* (written 1965; **1967**). None of these stories quite jell in the end – though much happens of considerable interest – and none lack moments of extraordinary cultural and psychological insight, sometimes presented in a language singularly familiar with the large repertory of mind-states accessible through the use of drugs. It was only with a late novel, *A Scanner Darkly* (written 1973; **1977**), that he would explore the more negative human implications of drug-taking, though with an almost hallucinated vehemence.

In his next major novel, *Do Androids Dream of Electric Sheep?* (written 1966; **1968**; vt *Blade Runner* 1982), filmed in 1982 by Ridley SCOTT as BLADE RUNNER, PKD effectively climaxed the series of novels in which mechanical simulacra of human beings – sometimes eminent – figure as agents of illusion. In this tale, which became much more widely known after the film, android animals are marketed to help expiate the guilt people experience because real ones have been virtually exterminated; simultaneously the protagonist must hunt down androids illegally imported from MARS. In so doing, he learns that the society's new MESSIAH may also be a fake; and that the landscapes of decay and imposture may in fact only mirror his own condition. As with so many of PKD's best books – like *Martian-Time Slip*, *Dr Bloodmoney* and *The Three Stigmata of Palmer Eldritch* – the story takes place in a depleted environment, with a small population existing in a derelict world. This sense of

a shrinking world intensifies in PKD's last two "untroubled" works of genius: *Ubik* (written 1966; **1969**), which features the creation of a subjective world by a group of people killed in an accident but restored to a kind of consciousness within a preservative machine, though any final determination of what is real in the book is made superbly problematical; and *A Maze of Death* (written 1968; **1970**), a bleak poisoned exercise in theology which has been described as his single finest work.

From this point in PKD's life, metaphysical questions began to dominate. *Galactic Pot-Healer* (written 1967-8; **1969**) begins almost as a parody, but soon becomes involved in questions of predetermination and the Dualistic conflict between darkness and light. Theological issues are paramount also in the novelette "Faith of Our Fathers" (1967) and in *Our Friends From Frolix 8* (written 1968-9; **1970**), the composition of which is illuminated by *Outline for Our Friends from Frolix 8* (written 1968; **1989** chap).

As the 1970s began, theology gradually segued in PKD's own life into episodes of paranoia and epiphany, climaxing in a religious experience in March 1974 which he spent much of the rest of his life analysing in the form of an "Exegesis", of which a small, integral portion has been published as *Cosmogony and Cosmology* (written 1978; **1987** chap UK); a large selection from this material has been assembled as *In Pursuit of VALIS: Selections from the Exegesis* (**1991**). Both *The Selected Letters of Philip K. Dick: 1974* (coll **1991**) and «The Selected Letters of Philip K. Dick: 1975-76» (coll 1992) focus on the same material; 4 further volumes are projected.

And, after 20 years, the stream of novels became intermittent. *Flow My Tears, the Policeman Said* (written 1970-73; **1974**), which won the JOHN W. CAMPBELL MEMORIAL AWARD, mainly retreads old ground. It was followed by a rather unsatisfactory collaboration with Roger ZELAZNY, *Deus Irae* (written 1964-75; fixup **1976**). *Radio Free Albemuth* (written 1976; **1985**), which began to deal in "healthy" fictional terms with the Exegesis material, was published only after PKD's death.

This latter novel is, in any case, a kind of draft of the finest book of PKD's last years, *VALIS* (written 1978; **1981**), a fragile but deeply valiant self-analysis – he is two characters in the novel, a man who is mad and a man who is not – conducted within the framework of a longing search for the structure of meaning, the Vast Active Living Intelligence System. *The Divine Invasion* (written 1980; **1981**) and *The Transmigration of Timothy Archer* (written 1981; **1982**), which were assembled with their predecessor as *The VALIS Trilogy* (omni **1989**), share obsessional search-patterns but little else. They were the books of a finished writer, in every sense.

The earlier PKD often lost control of his material in ideative mazes and, sidetracked, was unable to find any resolution; but, when he found the tale within his grasp, he was brilliantly inventive, gaining access to imaginative realms which no other writer of sf had reached. His sympathy for the plight of his characters – often far-from-heroic, small, ordinary people trapped in difficult existential circumstances – was unfailing, and his work had a human interest absent from that of writers engaged by complexity and convolution for their own sake. Even the most perilous metaphysical terrors of his finest novels wore a complaining, vulnerable, human face. In all his work he was astonishingly intimate, self-exposed, and very dangerous. He was the funniest sf writer of his time, and perhaps the most terrifying. His dreads were our own, spoken as we could not have spoken them.

[BS/JC]

Other works: *The Ganymede Takeover* (written 1964-6; **1967**) with Ray (R.F.) NELSON; *The Preserving Machine* (written 1953-66; coll **1969**; with 1 story dropped 1971 UK); *The Best of Philip K. Dick* (written 1952-73; coll **1977**) ed John BRUNNER; *A Letter from Philip K. Dick* (written 1960; **1983** chap); *Nazism and the High Castle* (written 1964?; 1964 *Niekas*; **1987** chap dos), published with *Schizophrenia and the Book of Changes* (written 1965?; 1965 *Niekas*; **1987** chap dos); *We Can Remember it for You Wholesale* (written 1965; 1966 *FSF*; **1990** chap), filmed as TOTAL RECALL (1990); *Nick and the Glimmung* (written 1966; **1988** UK), for children; *Warning: We Are Your Police* (written 1967; **1985** chap); *The Golden Man* (written 1952-73; coll **1980**); *The Dark-Haired Girl* (written 1972-5; coll **1988**), mostly nonfiction; *Ubik: The Screenplay* (written 1974; **1985**).

About the author: The literature on PKD is enormous and daily growing. Here are a few representative volumes: *Philip K. Dick: Electric Shepherd* (anth **1975**) ed Bruce GILLESPIE; *Science-Fiction Studies*, Mar 1975 and July 1988, 2 special issues devoted to PKD; *The Novels of Philip K. Dick* (**1984**) by Kim Stanley ROBINSON; *Only Apparently Real: The World of Philip K. Dick* (**1986**) by Paul WILLIAMS; *Mind in Motion: The Science Fiction of Philip K. Dick* (**1987**) by Patricia WARRICK; *To the High Castle: Philip K. Dick: A Life 1928-1962* (**1989**) by Gregg Rickman; *Divine Invasions: A Life of Philip K. Dick* (**1989**) by Lawrence Sutin, perhaps the most clear-sighted of the biographical studies; *Philip Kindred Dick, Metaphysical Conjurer: A Working Bibliography* (latest edn **1990**) by Gordon BENSON Jr and Phil STEPHENSEN-PAYNE.

See also: ACE BOOKS; ALIENS; ANDROIDS; AUTOMATION; BRITISH SCIENCE FICTION AWARD; CITIES; COLLECTIONS; COLONIZATION OF OTHER WORLDS; COMICS; COMPUTERS; CONCEPTUAL BREAKTHROUGH; CYBERNETICS; CYBORGS; ENTROPY; ESP; FANTASTIC VOYAGES; FRANCE; GAMES AND SPORTS; GENETIC ENGINEERING; GODS AND DEMONS; GOTHIC SF; GREAT AND SMALL; HISTORY OF SF; HUMOUR; INVASION; LONGEVITY (IN WRITERS AND PUBLICATIONS); MACHINES; MATTER TRANSMISSION; MEDIA LANDSCAPE; METAPHYSICS; MUSIC; NEW WAVE; NEW WORLDS; OPTIMISM AND PESSIMISM; OUTER PLANETS; PERCEPTION; PHILIP K. DICK AWARD; POLITICS; PSYCHOLOGY; RECURSIVE SF; REINCARNATION; RELIGION; ROBOTS; SATIRE; TIMESCAPE BOOKS; TIME TRAVEL; VIRTUAL REALITY; WEAPONS.

DICKENS, CHARLES (JOHN HUFFHAM) (1812-1870) UK writer, almost certainly the greatest novelist in the English language. CD wrote considerable fantasy – including most famously *A Christmas Carol in Prose, Being a Ghost Story of Christmas* (**1843**) – but no sf proper. However, it has been argued, most explicitly by John CLUTE in *Horror: 100 Best Books* (anth **1988**; rev 1992) ed Stephen Jones and Kim NEWMAN, that the nightmarish, almost futuristic London which figures in several of his later novels, from *Bleak House* (**1853**) through *Our Mutual Friend* (**1865**), was a central influence – *via* G.K. CHESTERTON, Robert Louis STEVENSON and others – in the creation of 19th-century urban England as a stamping-ground for STEAMPUNK. Like William MORRIS, Lord DUNSANY and J.R.R. TOLKIEN after him, CD is central to the geography of sf.

It is also arguable that *Mugby Junction* (anth **1866** chap), a self-contained volume published as an extra Christmas number of CD's magazine *All the Year Round*, may constitute the first SHARED-WORLD anthology of genre interest.

[JC]

Other works: *The Chimes* (dated 1845 but **1844**); *The Cricket on the Hearth* (dated **1846** but 1845); *The Haunted Man, and The Ghost's Bargain* (coll **1848**).

See also: ENTROPY.

DICKINSON, PETER (MALCOLM de BRISSAC) (1927-) UK writer, born in Northern Rhodesia (now Zambia), educated at Eton and King's College, Cambridge; for 17 years assistant editor of the humorous magazine *Punch*. PD is best known for his detective stories, but he has written one adult sf novel, *The Green Gene* (**1973**), an amusing SATIRE on many issues including racial prejudice, set in an ALTERNATE-WORLD UK, where all Celts possess a gene that gives them green skin. It was runner-up for the JOHN W. CAMPBELL MEMORIAL AWARD. An adult detective novel, *King and Joker* (**1976**), is set in an alternate England where George V's elder brother Clarence did not die of pneumonia but lived to become King Victor I; its belated sequel was *Skeleton-in-Waiting* (**1989**). Two other adult thrillers have ambiguously fantastic elements, *Sleep and his Brother* (**1971**) and *Walking Dead* (**1977**).

PD's most important contribution to sf is his **Changes** trilogy for children: in order of internal chronology the novels are *The Devil's Children* (**1971**), *Heartsease* (**1970**) and *The Weathermonger* (**1968**; with chapters 10 and 11 rev, 1969 US), all assembled as *The Changes* (omni **1975**; vt *The Changes Trilogy* 1985; vt *The Changes: A Trilogy* 1991 US). They deal with an inexplicable change in English life when the population suddenly turns against MACHINES and adopts medieval superstitions. *The Devil's Children*, where a 12-year-old girl is adopted by a band of travelling Sikhs, is the most sensitive, and *The Weathermonger*, which features Merlin, the most fantastic and baroque. There are minor inconsistencies in the world picture from book to book.

In 1972 the BBC presented a six-episode sf serial for children, *Man Dog*, written by PD, and novelized as

Mandog * (**1972**) by Lois LAMPLUGH. Escapees from the 26th century transfer their leader's mind into a dog belonging to one of a group of children in the present. They are pursued by future police.

Many of PD's other juveniles have fantastic elements: *Emma Tupper's Diary* (**1971**) is a Loch Ness Monster story; *The Dancing Bear* (**1972**) is a fantasy set in the 5th century; *The Gift* (**1973**) has a telepathic boy in a thriller with mythic overtones; *The Blue Hawk* (**1976**), which won the *Guardian* Award for Best Children's Book of the year, is set in an imaginary ancient kingdom, where the gods are withdrawing their magic from the world; *Chance, Luck and Destiny* (coll **1975**) contains an sf story, "Mr Monnow"; *Annerton Pit* (**1977**) features an ambiguous presence – it may be sciencefictional rather than fantastic – lurking in a mineshaft of ill repute; *Tulku* (**1979**) has fantastic happenings in Tibet; *Healer* (**1983**; vt *The Healer* 1985 US) has a girl with special powers; and *Eva* (**1988**) has a girl's personality transferred to a chimpanzee after a car accident – much social adjustment is necessary.

PD's juveniles are uneven, but at their best they are among the finest in the genre: various, nonconformist and vivid, often giving old themes new life by thinking them through afresh from the beginning, rather than accepting them as givens. [PN]

Other works (all juveniles): *The Iron Lion* (**1973**; rev 1983); *The Flight of Dragons* (**1979**), nonfiction; *The Seventh Raven* (**1983**); *Giant Cold* (**1984** chap); *A Box of Nothing* (**1985**); *Merlin Dreams* (coll of linked stories **1988**); *AK* (**1990**); *A Bone from a Dry Sea* (**1992**).

See also: APES AND CAVEMEN (IN THE HUMAN WORLD); CHILDREN'S SF; MAGIC.

DICK-LAUDER, [Sir] GEORGE (ANDREW) (1917-1981) British Army officer who began a writing career after his retirement from the service. His two sf novels, *Our Man for Ganymede* (**1969**) and *A Skull and Two Crystals* (**1972**), though not innovative, do explore the conventions of SPACE OPERA in a manner both literate and alert. [JC]

DICKSON, CARTER ◊ John Dickson CARR.

DICKSON, GORDON R(UPERT) (1923) Canadian-born writer, resident in the USA since age 13 and long a US citizen. He was educated (along with Poul ANDERSON) at the University of Minnesota, taking his BA in English in 1948, and remains in Minnesota. Through the Minneapolis Fantasy Society, which he re-established after WWII, he became friends with Anderson, with whom he later collaborated on the **Hoka** series – *Earthman's Burden* (coll **1957**), *Star Prince Charlie* (**1975**) and *Hoka!* (coll **1982**) – and with Clifford D. SIMAK. Along with these writers, GRD has shown a liking, often indulged, for hinterland settings peopled by solid farming or small-town stock whose ideologies, when expressed, violate any simple, conservative-liberal polarity, though urban readers and critics tend to respond to them as right-wing. As late as *Wolf and Iron* (1974 *FSF* as "In Iron Years"; much exp **1990**) – which embodies

a SURVIVALIST plot considerably deepened by the author's detailed and compassionate attachment to the kind of hero who understands and loves the physical world – he was still mining this fertile venue.

GRD began publishing sf in 1950 with "Trespass" for *Fantastic Story Quarterly*, written with Anderson, and he has since been a prolific and consistent short-story author; much of this material was assembled in the 1980s in volumes like *The Man from Earth* (coll **1983**), *Dickson!* (coll **1984**; rev vt *Steel Brother* 1985) and *Forward!* (coll 1985), the latter ed Sandra MIESEL, long an advocate of his works.

GRD's first novel, *Alien from Arcturus* (**1956** dos; rev vt *Arcturus Landing* 1979), established from an early date the tone of underlying and rather relentless seriousness which became so marked in later works, while at the same time succumbing to a tendency to displace emotional intensities from human relations between the sexes to those obtaining between human and dependent ALIEN (or, as in *Wolf and Iron*, Terran mammal). The aliens in *Alien from Arcturus* are decidedly cuddly, with shining black noses, and much resemble those who appear in *Space Winners* (**1965**), a juvenile, and *The Alien Way* (**1965**), about an Earthman's telepathic rapport with the representative of a species that may invade. But the strong narrative skills deployed in these comparatively rudimentary SPACE-OPERA tales, along with an idiomatic capacity to write novel-length fiction, has ensured the survival of these relatively unambitious works. Some later singletons – like *Sleepwalker's World* (**1971**), a dystopian vision of OVERPOPULATION, and *The R-Master* (**1973**; rev vt *The Last Master* 1983), in which a society is ambiguously guided by a saviour whose origins lie more in PULP-MAGAZINE ideas than in philosophy – failed to maintain the elation of the earlier books.

While continuing to produce prolifically in the 1950s and 1960s, GRD simultaneously engaged upon a sequence of novels which was to occupy much of his energy for decades. The ongoing **Childe Cycle** – the sf volumes of which are often known as the **Dorsai** series – is intended to present an evolutionary blueprint, in highly dramatized fictional terms, for humanity's ultimate expansion through the Galaxy, as an inherently ethical species. "In order to make this type of story work effectively," GRD has said, "I developed by the late 1950s a new fictional pattern that I have called the 'consciously thematic story'. This was specifically designed to create an unconscious involvement of the reader with the philosophical thematic argument that the story action renders and demonstrates. Because this new type of story has represented a pattern hitherto unknown to readers and writers, my work has historically been criticized in terms that do not apply to it – primarily as if it were drama alone." However, though GRD originally planned to present his thesis through a phased publication of the entire sequence – to include at least three historical titles and three contemporary novels as well as the several books set in the future – only the **Dorsai** books have yet been released, and the full integrity of GRD's argument remains, therefore, undemonstrated.

In rough order of internal chronology, the **Childe Cycle** comprises (1992): *Necromancer* (**1962**; vt *No Room for Man* 1963), *The Tactics of Mistake* (**1971**), *Soldier, Ask Not* (1964 *Gal*; exp **1967**), the short form of which won a HUGO for 1964, and *The Genetic General* (1959 *ASF* as "Dorsai!"; cut **1960** dos; text restored vt *Dorsai!* 1976), all but *Soldier, Ask Not* being assembled as *Three to Dorsai!* (omni **1975**); *The Spirit of Dorsai* (coll of linked stories **1979**) and *Lost Dorsai* (coll of linked stories **1980**; rev 1988 UK), whose title story won a 1981 Hugo, most of both volumes being reassembled with some material preceding *The Genetic General* as *The Dorsai Companion* (coll of linked stories **1986**); and a final grouping of texts, all set about 100 years further into the future: the overlong *Young Bleys* (**1991**), *The Final Encyclopedia* (**1984**) and *The Chantry Guild* (**1988**), the last volume – GRD claimed as early as 1983 – being hived off from a projected final volume to be called *Childe*. As the sequence develops, human space is divided into four spheres plus Old Earth herself, with her vast genetic pool; Dorsai, whose inhabitants are bred as professional soldiers; the Exotic worlds, whose inhabitants are bred to creative (sometimes sybaritic) mind-arts; the worlds (like Newton) which emphasize physical science; and the God-haunted Friendly worlds, where folk are bred for faith. The task of mankind's genetic elite is somehow to merge these variant strains, and the philosophical burden of the sequence tends to be conveyed through plots whose origins lie unabashedly in the SUPERMAN tales of earlier sf. *The Genetic General*, which in its restored form remains the most arousing of these, features Donal Graeme, the central incarnation of a triune evolutionary superman whose earlier life is told in *Necromancer*, and who is reborn as Hal Mayne to climax the series – and the genetic elitism it promulgates – through its final (to date) volumes. The terms GRD uses to describe his superman's capacities – Graeme, for instance, being capable of a potent sort of cognitive intuition – are perhaps best appreciated within the massive, ongoing rhythm of the series; for it is as a novelist, not as a philosopher, that GRD reveals his strength.

Very little of GRD's later fiction, however hastily written some of it may seem, fails to pose questions and arguments about humankind's fundamental nature. From 1960 much of his work has specifically reflected his preoccupation with the concept that humankind is inevitably driven to higher evolutionary states, a notion often expressed, however, in tales – like *None But Man* (**1969**; with 1 story added, as coll 1989) or *Hour of the Horde* (**1970**) – that contrast humankind's indomitable spirit with that of ALIENS whose lack of comparable *élan* makes them into straw horses for *Homo sapiens* to defeat. More serious presentations of material – from the fine *Timestorm* (fixup **1977**) on to ponderous later tales like *Way of the*

Pilgrim (1980 *ASF* as "The Cloak and the Staff"; much exp **1987**) – do generally avoid the graver pitfalls of pulp. Though his sometimes unremitting use of genre conventions to provide solutions to serious arguments has undoubtedly retarded full recognition of his talent and seriousness, the later volumes of the **Childe Cycle** series increasingly enforce a more measured response to his life work.

GRD won the NEBULA for Best Novelette with "Call Him Lord" (1966). He was President of the SCIENCE FICTION WRITERS OF AMERICA 1969-71. In 1981, he won Hugos not only for "Lost Dorsai" but also for a short story, "The Cloak and the Staff". [JC]

Other works: *Mankind on the Run* (**1956** dos; vt *On the Run* 1979); *Time to Teleport* (1955 *Science Fiction Stories* as "No More Barriers"; **1960** chap dos) and *Delusion World* (1955 *Science Fiction Stories* as "Perfectly Adjusted"; exp **1961** dos), both later published in omnibus format (omni **1981**); the **Dilbia** series, comprising *Spacial Delivery* (**1961** dos) and *Spacepaw* (**1969**); *Naked to the Stars* (**1961**); the **Underseas** series, later assembled as *Secrets of the Deep* (omni **1985**) and comprising *Secret Under the Sea* (**1960**), *Secret Under Antarctica* (**1963**) and *Secret Under the Caribbean* (**1964**); *Mission to Universe* (**1965**; rev 1977); *Planet Run* (**1967**; rev as coll with 2 stories added, vt *Planet Run, Plus Two Bonus Stories* 1982) with Keith LAUMER; *The Space Swimmers* (**1967**), which serves as a sequel to *Home from the Shore* (1963 *Gal*; exp **1978**); *Wolfling* (**1969**); *Mutants: A Science Fiction Adventure* (coll **1970**), in which the stories are linked thematically; *Danger – Human* (coll **1970**; vt *The Book of Gordon R. Dickson* 1973); *The Pritcher Mass* (**1972**); *The Outposter* (**1972**); *The Day the Sun Stood Still* (anth **1972**), a common-theme anthology with Poul Anderson and Robert SILVERBERG; *The Star Road* (coll **1973**); *Alien Art* (**1973**), a juvenile, later assembled with *Arcturus Landing* as *Alien Art; Arcturus Landing* (omni **1978**); *Ancient, My Enemy* (coll **1974**); *Gremlins, Go Home!* (**1974**), a juvenile with Ben BOVA; *The Lifeship* (**1976**; vt *Lifeboat* 1978 UK) with Harry HARRISON; the **Dragon and the George** fantasy sequence comprising *The Dragon and the George* (**1976**), *The Dragon Knight* (**1988**) and *The Dragon on the Border* (**1992**); *Gordon R. Dickson's SF Best* (coll **1978**; exp vt *In the Bone* 1987); *The Far Call* (**1978**), a rare NEAR-FUTURE tale of the space programme; *Pro* (**1978**); *Masters of Everon* (**1979**); *In Iron Years* (coll **1980**); *Love Not Human* (coll **1981**); *Survival!* (coll **1984**); *Jamie the Red* (**1984**) with Roland GREEN; *Beyond the Dar al-Harb* (coll **1985**); *Invaders!* (coll **1985**); *The Man the Worlds Rejected* (coll **1986**); *The Last Dream* (coll **1986**); *Mindspan* (coll **1986**) ed Sandra Miesel; *The Forever Man* (**1986**); *Stranger* (coll **1986**); *Guided Tour* (coll **1988**); *Beginnings* (coll **1988**); *Ends* (coll **1988**); *The Earth Lords* (**1989**).

As editor: *Rod Serling's Triple W: Witches, Warlocks and Werewolves* (anth **1963**); *Rod Serling's Devils and Demons* (anth **1967**); *Combat SF* (anth **1975**); *Nebula Winners Twelve* (anth **1978**); the **War and Honor** sequence of SHARED-WORLD anthologies, beginning with *The Harriers* * (anth **1991**) and «Robot Warriors» * (anth **1992**).

About the author: *Gordon R. Dickson: A Primary and Secondary Bibliography* (**1983**) by Raymond H. Thompson; *Gordon Rupert Dickson, First Dorsai: A Working Bibliography* (latest edn **1990** chap) by Gordon BENSON Jr and Phil STEPHENSEN-PAYNE.

See also: ASTOUNDING SCIENCE-FICTION; CANADA; CHILDREN'S SF; COMPUTERS; CYBORGS; ECOLOGY; ECONOMICS; EVOLUTION; GALACTIC EMPIRES; GALAXY SCIENCE FICTION; HUMOUR; INVASION; LINGUISTICS; MATHEMATICS; PARALLEL WORLDS; POLITICS; PSI POWERS; ROBERT HALE LIMITED; SPACESHIPS; TIME TRAVEL; UNDER THE SEA; WAR; WEAPONS.

DIETZ, WILLIAM C(OREY) (1945-) US writer who began to publish sf with *War World* (**1986**), the first volume of his **Sam McCade** sequence of sf adventures about an interstellar bounty hunter, which continued with *Imperial Bounty* (**1988**), *Alien Bounty* (**1990**) and *McCade's Bounty* (**1990**). The galactic venue of the series exhibits some interesting kinks, and McCade himself gradually gains individuality. Singletons include *Freehold* (**1987**), military sf, *Prison Planet* (**1989**), *Cluster Command* (**1989**) with David A. DRAKE – one of the latter's **Crisis of Empire** sequence – and *Matrix Man* (**1990**), a complicated, fast-moving tale set in a NEAR-FUTURE Earth whose seas and population are continuing to rise, and where a nefarious peace foundation (run in fact by a huge corporation) opposes attempts by the Exodus Society to foment emigration. As in his work in general, the right side wins. As an author of entertainments, WCD stands out for his thorough grasp of the devices of sf. [JC]

DIEUDONNE, FLORENCE (LUCINDA) CARPENTER (1850-?) US writer. In her *Rondah, or Thirty-Three Years in a Star* (**1887**) the tale's several protagonists travel through the Solar System in a large ASTEROID (not a star). Transported to this asteroid by a prearranged explosion, the central figure of the tale becomes king of the native bird-people, in fact of vegetable origin, who are replaced by ferocious elves when the worldlet cools down. Much happens. In the end, the protagonist, with his woman, seems destined to rule the Universe. The book is a cacophony of irreconcilable elements, but the author's extremely fertile imagination, when harnessed, manages to create a tale which significantly prefigures 20th-century cosmological SPACE OPERA. *Xartella* (**1891**), self-published, is fantasy. [JC]

Di FATE, VINCENT (1945-) US sf illustrator (name sometimes rendered DiFate). He was born in Yonkers, New York, and like many other sf illustrators attended the Pratt Institute. He began his career doing tv animation for Ralph Bakshi; his first professional sf illustration was for *Analog* (Aug 1969) and most of his magazine work has been for *ASF*. Many of his paintings have been for paperback book covers. His artwork, suprisingly impressionistic for someone who frequently works with technological subjects like spacecraft, is often moody and sombre. He was one of the NASA artists for the Apollo/Soyuz programme in 1975 and has worked for NASA since. He won the HUGO for Best Professional Artist in 1979 and has been nominated many other times. VDF lectures on art and is also well known for his occasional, interesting, long-running column about sf illustration, **Sketches**, from 1976 in the semiprozine ALGOL and in its surviving sister magazine SF CHRONICLE. A book of his work is *Di Fate's Catalog of Science Fiction Hardware* (**1980**) by VDF and Ian Summers. [JG/PN]

See also: ASTOUNDING SCIENCE-FICTION.

DIGEST A term used to describe a magazine format, in contrast to, for example, BEDSHEET and pulp (◊ PULP MAGAZINES), which are both larger. The page size of a digest is approximately 5.5 x 7.5in (about 140 x 190mm), though it can vary slightly; for example, *Gal* was normally a little smaller than *ASF*. *ASF* was the first important sf magazine to turn digest, in 1943, and by the mid-1950s almost all SF MAGAZINES had followed suit, the pulp-magazine format disappearing. By the 1980s, however, many sf magazines had turned to a small-bedsheet, stapled, "slick" format. The digest format is just a little larger than that of the normal paperback book, which averages 4.5 x 7in (about 115 x 180mm); the paperback format has also been used for some magazines, notably *NW* in the mid-1960s. [PN]

DIKTY, T(HADDEUS MAXIM) E(UGENE) (1920-1991) US editor and publisher, married from 1953 to Julian MAY, about whose work he compiled *The Work of Julian May: An Annotated Bibliography & Guide* (**1985**) with R. REGINALD. An early sf fan, TED started an sf checklist on index cards with the collector Frederick Shoyer in 1939, but the cards were lost in WWII. After the war, with Erle Korshak and Mark Reinsberg, he became a bookseller and passed the partially reassembled checklist on to Everett F. BLEILER, who used it to compile *The Checklist of Fantastic Literature* (**1948**) – the first comprehensive BIBLIOGRAPHY in the sf field – which TED and Korshak founded SHASTA PUBLISHERS to put into print. TED was also associated with the setting-up of the publishers Carcosa House. With Bleiler, TED edited an annual ANTHOLOGY series – the first "year's-best" series to appear in the field: *The Best Science Fiction Stories, 1949* (anth **1949**) and *The Best Science Fiction Stories, 1950* (anth **1950**; cut vt *The Best Science Fiction Stories 1951* UK), both assembled as *Science Fiction Omnibus* (omni **1952**); *The Best Science Fiction Stories, 1951* (anth **1951**; cut vt *The Best Science Fiction Stories, Second Series* 1952 UK; further cut vt *The Mindworm* 1967 UK); *The Best Science-Fiction Stories, 1952* (anth **1952**; cut vt *The Best Science Fiction Stories, Third Series* 1953 UK); *The Best Science-Fiction Stories, 1953* (anth **1953**; cut vt *The Best Science Fiction Stories, Fourth Series* 1955 UK); *The Best Science Fiction Stories, 1954* (anth **1954**; cut vt *The Best Science Fiction Stories, Fifth Series* 1956 UK). *Frontiers in Space* (anth **1955**) contains a selection from the second, third and fourth volumes. A second series, **Year's Best Science Fiction Novels**, presented a selection of longer stories: *Year's*

Best Science Fiction Novels, 1952 (anth **1952**; cut vt *Year's Best Science Fiction Novels 1953* UK), *1953* (anth **1953**; cut vt *Category Phoenix* 1955 UK) and *1954* (anth **1954**; cut vt *Year's Best Science Fiction Novels, Second Series* 1955 UK). Together they also edited *Imagination Unlimited* (anth **1952**; cut vt *Men of Space and Time* 1953 UK), which contains stories on each of 15 sciences.

After the collaboration with Bleiler ended, TED went on to produce three further "best" volumes as sole editor: *The Best Science-Fiction Stories and Novels, 1955* (anth **1955**; cut vt *5 Tales from Tomorrow* 1957), *The Best Science-Fiction Stories and Novels, 1956* (anth **1956**; cut vt *6 from Worlds Beyond* 1958) and *The Best Science-Fiction Stories and Novels, Ninth Series* (anth **1958**). He also edited *Every Boy's Book of Outer Space Stories* (anth **1960**) and two theme anthologies about MARS and the MOON: *Great Science Fiction about Mars* (anth **1966**) and *Great Science Fiction Stories about the Moon* (anth **1967**).

In the 1950s, after Shasta had collapsed in ignominy, TED formed Publication Associates with Julian May, and worked closely with her on various projects for the rest of his life, acting as her agent and editor on all her mature work. In 1972, with Darrell C. Richardson, he founded and, with the added help of Robert E. WEINBERG, ran FAX COLLECTOR'S EDITIONS, a publishing enterprise aimed at reprinting material, often in facsimile, from old magazines; at about the same time (though its first title did not appear until 1976), and also with Weinberg (who dropped out after a year), he founded STARMONT HOUSE to produce monographs on individual sf writers, along with some bibliographies and fiction, anonymously editing for the firm one anthology, *Worlds Within Worlds: Four Classic Argosy Tales of Science Fiction* (anth **1991**). Two of his and Julian May's children carried on with the firm after his death. [JC/MJE]

See also: SMALL PRESSES AND LIMITED EDITIONS.

DILLARD, J(EANNE) M. (1954-   ) US writer. Most of her works are STAR TREK ties, including *Mindshadow* * (**1986**), *Demons* * (**1986**), *Bloodthirst* * (**1987**), *Star Trek V: The Final Frontier* * (**1989**), which novelizes the 1989 film, *The Lost Years* * (**1989**) and *The Undiscovered Country* * (**1992**), which novelizes STAR TREK VI: THE UNDISCOVERED COUNTRY (1991). JMD has also written *War of the Worlds: The Resurrection* * (**1988**), tied to the tv series, and *Specters* (**1991**), a horror novel. [JC]

DILLON, LEO (1933-   ) **and DIANE** (1933-   ) US illustrators, the only team (married in 1957) ever to win a HUGO for Best Professional Artist, which they did in 1971. They have been freelancing since 1958, at first working separately. Together their work has covered many fields: record album covers, advertising art, Christmas cards, children's books and movie posters among them; they are among the most respected commercial artists in the USA. Their sf work for ACE BOOKS in the late 1960s (notably for the **Ace Specials**) was particularly good, though perhaps their most celebrated work has been for children's books, winning them Caldecott Medals for *Why*

Mosquitoes Buzz in People's Ears (**1976**) and *Ashanti to Zulu* (**1977**). They have designed especially strong covers for books by Harlan ELLISON. Their sf production has been only occasional since about 1972. Their work is often similar to wood-block prints: rough, sometimes semi-abstract shapes powerfully assembled. They are, however, extremely versatile and work in a variety of styles and media, notably an Art Nouveau-derived look reminiscent of Gustav Klimt (1862-1918), as can be seen in *The Art of Leo and Diane Dillon* (**1981**) ed Byron PREISS. Richard M. POWERS was one of the first to show that semi-abstract images of some sophistication could sell sf; the Dillons went on to prove the point incontrovertibly. [JG/PN]

See also: FANTASY; ILLUSTRATION.

DILOV, LJUBEN [r] ◊ BULGARIA.

DIME-NOVEL SF Dime-novel sf, which was almost wholly boys' fiction, appeared in two media: serially in such BOYS' PAPERS as *Golden Hours*, *Happy Days*, *The Boys of New York* and *Young Men of America*, or as complete stories in series publications like **The Wide Awake Weekly**, **The Boy's Star Library**, **New York Five Cent Library**, the FRANK READE LIBRARY and **The Nugget Library**. The most important publishers were Frank Tousey, Publisher, Norman L. Munro and STREET & SMITH.

Formats varied considerably, from crown-8vo-size books to 9 x 12½in (about 230 x 320mm) saddle-wired (saddle-stitched) pamphlets, but from the turn of the century most dime novels were either saddle-wired single-signature pamphlets of around 8½ x 11in (about 215 x 280mm) or 5 x 7in (about 125 x 180mm) side-stapled paperbound books of several signatures. (All of these formats are rendered here in the US style; i.e., width followed by height.) It is the 8½ x 11in pamphlet – similar in dimension to BEDSHEET-format – that is usually, though not very logically, described as "dime-novel format", but then the term "dime novel" itself is inaccurate, since most commonly they cost a nickel (5¢) or 6¢, rather than a dime (10¢). All dime novels were printed on cheap paper – sometimes very poor indeed – and it is therefore now difficult to locate examples in good condition.

Almost all dime-novel sf falls into three basic categories: the invention story (◊ DISCOVERY AND INVENTION), the lost-race story (◊ LOST WORLDS) and the marvel story. These types occasionally overlap in minor ways.

The invention story originated with Edward S. ELLIS's *The Steam Man of the Prairies* (**1868**), in which Ellis, a prolific and popular writer, adapted the historical Newark Steam Man into a conventional Western story. This first publication seems to have been without influence, but one of the later reprintings (as *The Huge Hunter*, 1876) came to the attention of Frank Tousey, a rival publisher, who commissioned a similar work, *Frank Reade and His Steam Man of the Plains* (*The Boys of New York* 1876 as "The Steam Man of the Plains"; **1892** as by "Noname"), from Harry Enton (pseudonym of Harold Cohen [1854-

1927]). This initiated the important series about the Frank Reade family of inventors (◊ FRANK READE LIBRARY). Enton followed this with two sequels about **Frank Reade**, with steam engines shaped into horses.

These stories, together with Ellis's work, set the pattern for future invention stories. The initial model was the dime-novel Western. Stress was on iron technology, with little or no science; narratives contained random, thrilling incidents, often presented in a disjointed and puerile way. Typical social patterns were: a conscious attempt to capitalize on age conflict, with boy inventors outdoing their elders (◊ EDISONADE); aggressive, exploitative capitalism, particularly at the expense of "primitive" peoples; the frontier mentality, with slaughter of "primitives" (in the first **Frank Reade, Jr.** story Frank kills about 250 Native Americans, to say nothing of destroying an inhabited village); strong elements of sadism; ethnic rancour focused on Native Americans, Blacks, Irish and, later, Mexicans and Jews.

After Enton's three stories and a fourth of unknown authorship, the invention dime novel was taken over by Luis SENARENS, who (with anonymous associates) wrote a long series of **Frank Reade, Jr.** stories 1882-98, culminating in the **Frank Reade Library**. In this series the type of invention shifted to electric air vessels, land rovers and submarines, all showing the strong influence of Jules VERNE. The narrative more typically became one of (frequently inaccurate) geographical exploration and adventure, sometimes incorporating minor lost-race episodes.

The **Frank Reade, Jr.** stories were historically the most important invention stories, but other story chains existed, as did individual stories about other boy inventors with airships or submarines. When the sales of the **Frank Reade Library** languished, Tousey issued a companion series, the **Jack Wright** stories, again by Senarens. Competing boy-inventor series from Street & Smith appeared: the doings of **Tom Edison, Jr.**, written mostly by Philip READE, and **Electric Bob**, written by Robert Toombes. Both series are much superior to the **Frank Reade, Jr.** stories in content and writing, and both are morally less offensive, but neither of them had the cultural impact of Tousey's **Frank Reade Library**.

The dime-novel lost-race story did not necessarily follow the full pattern of its adult counterpart (colonial exploitation, mythic elements, sacred-vs-secular clashes, exotic sex partners, destruction of the land, etc.), but was often a frank chronicle of smugly justified looting. As Senarens said in *Jack Wright and his Prairie Engine* (*The Boys' Star Library* 1892; **1908**), Jack having "liberated" an enormous diamond: "There was no crime in taking it. It was part of an idol, worshipped in lieu of heaven, and wresting such an object from infidels is no crime in the eyes of the Almighty." Typical lost-race dime novels are: *Frank Reade, Jr., and His Electric Coach* (*The Boys of New York* 1890-91; **1893**) by "Noname", with Ancient Hebrews; *The Missing Island* (**1894**) by "Noname",

with Aztecs; *A Trip to the Center of the Earth* (*New York Boys' Weekly* 1878; **1894**) by Howard De Vere (pseudonym of Howard Van Orden), which has acculturated early Americans with interesting speech changes; *The Lost Captain* (1880; **1906**) by Frederick Whittaker, with Old Norse at the North Pole; *Lost at the South Pole* (*The Boys of New York* 1888 as by J.G. Bradley; **1899** as by Capt. Thomas H. Wilson), with strange races; *Among the Fire Worshipers* (*The Boys of New York* 1880 as by Berton Bertrew; **1902** as by Howard Austin), with Aztecs; "Underground" (*Golden Hours* May-July 1890) by Thomas P. Montfort, with Toltecs in Australia; and *Across the Frozen Sea* (**1894**) by "Noname", again with Old Norse at the North Pole. An unusual dime novel for adults is *El Rubio Bravo, King of the Swordsmen* (**1881**) by Col. Thomas Hoyer Monstery, about Aztecs.

Lost-race stories turned up unexpectedly elsewhere. The detective stories about Nick CARTER written by Frederic Rensselaer Dey (1861-1922) under the pseudonym Chickering Carter provide several examples. In *The Index of Seven Stars* (**1907**) and *An Amazonian Queen* (**1907**) Nick has adventures among a lost race of mixed Old Norse and Indian origin, ruled by women, and excels in the gladiatorial arena. A 7-vol series beginning with *Facing an Unseen Terror* (**1907**) and ending with *The Seven-Headed Monster* (**1907**) describes a supercivilization hidden in the foothills of the Himalayas, with flying machines lofted by a new radioactive element: the hidden race has also mastered electricity, vibration and the life force. This time the mighty Nick meets his superior in the wicked scientist Zanabayah.

Lost-race incidents of a more marginal kind frequently occur in invention and geographical-adventure dime novels. In most cases they are concerned with Pre-Columbian American peoples, based loosely on popular American archaeology, and sometimes influenced by the work of H. Rider HAGGARD. In "marvel" dime novels lost-race situations are also common, usually concerning themselves with imaginary peoples possessing high civilizations.

This third group of dime novels, stressing "marvel" elements, emerged in the late 1880s and reached its fullest development in the 1890s and the first decade of the 20th century. The "marvel" tale was no longer a Vernean yarn of geographical adventure or one of Wild West thrills and high jinks, but frankly set its protagonist into extremely fantastic circumstances, often seemingly supernatural, which were almost always rationalized. Instead of savage Indians, Western badmen, malicious "Greasers", pirates, bears, giant snakes, sea serpents, frenzied whales and giant octopuses, it utilized dwarfs, giants, strangely teratological races, outlandish customs, mammoths, magical gems and crystals, bobbing and ducking islands, wonderful cavern worlds and mysterious appearances and disappearances. Inventions, when they appeared, were more likely to be the product of alien races than the brainchildren of boy inventors. Instead of operating steam or electric land rovers, flying ship-hulls and *Nautilus*-like submarines, heroes might encounter bizarre means of transportation: ANTI-GRAVITY airships or vehicles powered by fantastic new energies, sometimes suggested by Bulwer LYTTON's "vril". The purportedly realistic geography of the Vernean dime novel yielded to outlandish ambiences in Antarctica, inside the HOLLOW EARTH or even on other planets.

The central theme of the "marvel" story was no longer mechanical exploitation or destruction of the environment (and weaker peoples), as in the **Frank Reade, Jr.** stories, but encounter with the strange, grotesque, magical and inexplicable. The note of sadism and ethnic rancour that permeated the earlier invention stories was usually lacking, or at least much toned down.

Some marvel elements appeared in the later **Frank Reade, Jr.** stories, but they were found in much finer form in the sometimes very imaginative work of Francis W. DOUGHTY, Fred THORPE and Cornelius SHEA. Other significant marvel stories included *Six Weeks in the Moon* (**1896**) by "Noname" (perhaps Senarens), *Under the World* (*Golden Hours* as "Into the Maelstrom" 1894; **1906**) by John DE MORGAN and "Three Boys from the Moon" (*Happy Days* Aug-Sep 1901) as by Gaston Garne (a Norman L. Munro house name).

Apart from the work of Verne and Haggard, contemporary adult sf had almost no influence on dime-novel sf. Imaginary-WAR stories are rare, the only significant one being "Holland, the Destroyer" (*Golden Hours* 1900-1) by Hal Harkaway (house name used here by Edward T. STRATEMEYER), in which the USA, at war with almost the entire world, is saved by a supersubmarine. Interplanetary elements enter the last **Frank Reade, Jr.** stories and Doughty's pseudonymous *Two Boys on a Trip to an Unknown Planet* (*The Boys of New York* 1989 as by Albert J. Booth; **1901** as by Richard R. Montgomery), but they are fantastic and show no knowledge of contemporary adult work. Weldon J. COBB, a Chicago author, presumably read a US newspaper adaptation of H.G. WELLS's *The War of the Worlds* (*Pearson's Magazine* 1897; **1898**): his *At War with Mars* (*Golden Hours* Sep-Nov 1897; **1907**) reads as near-plagiarism, with Martian cylinders striking in the USA – as an original element, the Martians have fitted out Phobos as an armed space station for the attack on Earth. Cobb's "To Mars with Tesla" (*New Golden Hours* Mar-May 1901) contains an abortive space flight – the landing point proves to be the Southwest desert, not MARS as planned.

The sf dime novel has had a larger influence on later sf than has been generally recognized. The invention story of the **Frank Reade, Jr.** sort led directly, through the Stratemeyer Syndicate, to such boys' fiction as TOM SWIFT (*see also* JUVENILE SERIES). Many early PULP-MAGAZINE sf-adventure stories are simply dime novels translated for an older readership, while individual points of influence are common enough. The situations in Edgar Rice BURROUGHS's Opar and A. MERRITT's Muria ("The Conquest of the Moon Pool" 1919) seem to be indebted to dime novels, while Rex STOUT's *Under the Andes* (*All-Story* 1914; **1984**) is simply a Cornelius Shea sort of story with modifications. A. Conan DOYLE's *The Lost World* (**1912**) was probably influenced by "Noname"'s *The Island in the Air* (**1896**), and David LINDSAY's *A Voyage to Arcturus* (**1920**) possibly by Doughty's *Two Boys on a Trip to an Unknown Planet*. One can also link the episodic structure and strange races in L. Frank BAUM's *The Wonderful Wizard of Oz* (**1900**) with "marvel" dime novels.

There were European equivalents and near-equivalents of Dime Novels, one of the most interesting being the German periodical *Der* LUFTPIRAT UND SEIN LENKBARES LUFTSCHIFF, featuring Captain Mors, which was a pure SPACE-OPERA series, the earliest known. (*For UK equivalents* ◊ BOYS' PAPERS.) [EFB]

DIMENSION 5 (vt *Dimension Four* US) Film (1966). United Pictures and Harold Goldman Associates. Dir Franklin Adreon, starring Jeffrey Hunter, France Nuyen, Harold Sakata, Donald Woods. Screenplay Arthur C. Pierce. 92 mins, cut to 88 mins. Colour.

Adreon and Pierce were the team that made CYBORG 2087 (also 1966). This equally cheap production has Sakata, who played the villain Oddjob in the **James Bond** movie *Goldfinger* (1964), as one of the Chinese communists who plan to blow up Los Angeles by planting an H-bomb. They are foiled by a US secret agent who can go back and forth in time by pressing a button on his belt. [JB]

DIMENSION FOUR ◊ DIMENSION 5.

DIMENSIONS We perceive three spatial dimensions, but theoretical MATHEMATICS is easily capable of dealing with many more. Conventional graphical analysis frequently represents time as a dimension, encouraging consideration of it as the "fourth dimension". The possible existence of PARALLEL WORLDS displaced from ours along a fourth spatial dimension (in the same way that a series of two-dimensional universes might lie next to one another like the pages of a book) is a popular hypothesis in sf, and such worlds are frequently referred to as "other dimensions". The COSMOLOGY of Einstein's General Theory of Relativity (1916), which proposes a four-dimensional model of the Universe in which the notions of space and time are collapsed into a single "spacetime continuum", offered considerable encouragement to sf notions of a multidimensional Universe (or "multiverse"). Many modern occultists and pseudoscientists have followed in the tracks of Johann Zöllner (1834-1882), author of *Transcendental Physics* (**1865**), who borrowed mathematical notions to "justify" the idea of the "astral plane" beloved by spiritualists and Theosophists. J.W. DUNNE used the notion to explain prophetic dreams, eventually constructing a theory of the "Serial Universe", and P.D.

Ouspensky (1878-1947) built a more complex model of the Universe in which time "moves" in a spiral and there are six spatial dimensions.

The possible dimensional limitations of human existence and perception were dramatized by Edwin A. ABBOTT in *Flatland* (**1884**) as by "A Square", which describes a world of two-dimensional beings, one of whom is challenged to imagine our three-dimensional world – encouraging readers, by analogy, to attempt to imagine a four-dimensional world. The challenge was taken up by C.H. HINTON, whose many essays on the subject attempt to "explain" ghosts and to imagine a four-dimensional God from whom nothing in the human world can be hidden. In his story "An Unfinished Communication" (1895) the afterlife involves freedom to move along the time dimension (◊ TIME TRAVEL) to relive and reassess moments of life; he also wrote a Flatland novel, *An Episode of Flatland* (**1907**). H.G. WELLS borrowed Hintonian arguments to "explain" the working of the device in *The Time Machine* (**1895**). The eponymous figure of E.V. ODLE's *The Clockwork Man* (**1923**) could perceive many dimensions when working properly, but while malfunctioning could do no more than flutter back and forth in time, offering the merest hint of the quality of multidimensional life. Algernon BLACKWOOD's "The Pikestaffe Case" (1924) attempts to evoke the non-Euclidean geometry of a dimensional trap lurking within a mirror.

Early GENRE-SF writers who found the notion of dimensions fascinating included Miles J. BREUER, most notably in "The Appendix and the Spectacles" (1928) and "The Captured Cross-Section" (1929), and Donald WANDREI, notably in "The Monster from Nowhere" (1935) and "Infinity Zero" (1936). In E.E. "Doc" SMITH's *Skylark of Valeron* (1934; **1949**) the heroes briefly enter a four-dimensional reality, and in Clifford D. SIMAK's "Hellhounds of the Cosmos" (1932), 99 men enter the fourth dimension in a single grotesque body to fight a four-dimensional monster. Henry KUTTNER's and C.L. MOORE's classic "Mimsy Were the Borogoves" (1943 as by Lewis Padgett) features toys from the future which educate children into four-dimensional habits of thought, but, like most stories of the period, this uses dimensional trickery casually to tie up its plot with a neat knot.

The mathematical discipline of topology inspired several dimensional fantasies: Moebius strips feature in Martin GARDNER's "No-Sided Professor" (1946) and "The Island of Five Colours" (1952), Theodore STURGEON's "What Dead Men Tell" (1949), Arthur C. CLARKE's "Wall of Darkness" (1949) and Homer NEARING Jr's "The Hermeneutical Doughnut" (1954); Klein bottles and tesseracts feature in "The Last Magician" (1951) by Bruce ELLIOTT, "And He Built a Crooked House" (1941) by Robert A. HEINLEIN and "Star, Bright" (1952) by Mark CLIFTON. *Occam's Razor* by David DUNCAN (**1957**) also deploys topological jargon to shore up its dimensional speculations. George GAMOW's popularization of ideas in modern physics, *Mr Tompkins in Wonderland* (coll **1939**), dramatizes certain odd situations very well (although its contents are didactic essays rather than stories).

The notion that spaceships might make use of a fourth-dimensional HYPERSPACE in order to evade the limiting velocity of light is very common in sf, having been initially popularized by Isaac ASIMOV among others, but few stories actually attempt to describe it; it is usually imagined as a chaotic environment which utterly confuses the senses, as in Frederik POHL's "The Mapmakers" (1955) and Clifford D. Simak's "All the Traps of Earth" (1960). The dimensional chaos that might be associated with BLACK HOLES has received closer attention, though these too are most often used as "wormholes" permitting very long journeys to be taken more or less instantaneously. Among the more effective representations of experience in dimensionally distorted environments are Norman KAGAN's "The Mathenauts" (1964), David I. MASSON's "Traveller's Rest" (1965) and Christopher PRIEST's *Inverted World* (**1974**; vt *The Inverted World* US).

In recent years C.H. Hinton's ideas have been revived by Rudy RUCKER, who has used dimensional mathematics very extravagantly in a number of his novels and short stories, including the afterlife fantasy *White Light* (**1980**), the comedy of fourth-dimensional intrusions *The Sex Sphere* (**1983**) and many of the shorter pieces first published in *The 57th Franz Kafka* (coll **1983**) and reprinted, with others, in *Transreal!* (coll **1991**). Rucker is the only modern author to have answered "A Square's" challenge with authentic verve and authority, but A.J. Dewdney's *The Planiverse* (**1984**) is an interesting drama-documentary about a two-dimensional world whose topography recalls Hinton's Flatland more than Abbott's.

Relevant theme anthologies include *Fantasia Mathematica* (anth **1958**) and *The Mathematical Magpie* (anth **1962**), both ed Clifton Fadiman, and *Science Fiction Adventures in Dimension* (anth **1953**) ed Groff CONKLIN. [BS]

See also: INVASION.

DIOMEDE, JOHN K. [s] ◊ George Alec EFFINGER.

DIOSCORIDES, Dr ◊ Pieter HARTING.

DIRAC COMMUNICATOR A device invented by James BLISH for the story "Beep" (1954; exp as *The Quincunx of Time* **1973**), and used by him also in other stories. It is an instantaneous communicator, named after the great theoretical physicist Paul Dirac (1902-1984). Others have since borrowed the device, but more recently Ursula K. LE GUIN's ANSIBLE has been the communicator of preference for sf writers. [PN]

See also: FASTER THAN LIGHT.

DISASTER Cataclysm, natural or manmade, is one of the most popular themes in sf. Tales of future WAR and INVASION belong here, but for convenience are dealt with under those separate headings. Stories which emphasize the nature of the societies which spring up after a great disaster are dealt with under HOLOCAUST AND AFTER.

Central to the disaster tradition are stories of vast biospheric changes which drastically affect human life. Tales of universal floods are at least as old as *The Epic of Gilgamesh* (c2000BC), and other motifs, such as plagues, fires and famines, have an obvious source in the Bible, particularly the Revelation of St John (also known as the Apocalypse, whence the adjective "apocalyptic", frequently applied to this form of sf). Disaster stories appeal because they represent everything we most fear and at the same time, perhaps, secretly desire: a depopulated world, escape from the constraints of a highly organized industrial society, the opportunity to prove one's ability as a survivor. Perhaps because they represent a punishment meted out for the hubris of technological Man, such stories have not been particularly popular in the US sf magazines. The ideology of disaster stories runs counter to the optimistic and expansionist attitudes associated with ASTOUNDING SCIENCE-FICTION and its long-time editor, John W. CAMPBELL Jr. In fact, most examples of the type are from the UK, and it has been suggested that this may be associated with the UK's decline as a world power throughout the 20th century.

However, some of the earliest examples were written at the height of Empire. H.G. WELLS's "The Star" (1897) and M.P. SHIEL's *The Purple Cloud* (1901; rev 1929) are both tales of cataclysm. In the first a runaway star collides with the Earth, and in the second a mysterious gas kills all but two people, a new Adam and Eve. Arthur Conan DOYLE's *The Poison Belt* (1913) also features a gas, but in this case it turns out not to be fatal. After WWI the disaster theme became more common. J.J. CONNINGTON's *Nordenholt's Million* (1923) portrays the social chaos following an agricultural blight caused by a mutation in nitrogen-fixing bacteria. S. Fowler WRIGHT's *Deluge* (1928) and *Dawn* (1929) depict the destruction of civilization by earthquakes and floods, and subsequent attempts to build a new society. John COLLIER's *Tom's A-Cold* (1933; vt *Full Circle* US) and Alun LLEWELLYN's *The Strange Invaders* (1934) both deal effectively with survival in a post-holocaust world. R.C. SHERRIFF's *The Hopkins Manuscript* (1939; rev vt *The Cataclysm*) depicts the Moon's collision with Earth, and is a SATIRE on UK complacency in the face of impending war.

After WWII there was a resurgence, to an even higher level, of the disaster theme. John WYNDHAM's *The Day of the Triffids* (1951) is an enjoyable tale of a world in which all but a few have been blinded and everyone is menaced by huge, poisonous plants. His *The Kraken Wakes* (1953; vt *Out of the Deeps* US) is also a successful blend of invasion and catastrophe themes: sea-dwelling aliens melt Earth's icecaps and cause the inundation of the civilized world. The success of Wyndham's novels inspired many emulators. The most distinguished was John CHRISTOPHER, whose *The Death of Grass* (1956; vt *No Blade of Grass* US) is a fine study of the breakdown of civilized values when a

virus kills all crops. The same author's *The World in Winter* (1962; vt *The Long Winter* US) and *A Wrinkle in the Skin* (1965; vt *The Ragged Edge* US) are also above-average works: one concerns a new Ice Age and the other features earthquakes. Many other UK novelists have dealt in similar catastrophes; e.g., J.T. MCINTOSH in *One in Three Hundred* (1954), John BOLAND in *White August* (1955), Charles Eric MAINE in *The Tide Went Out* (1958; rev vt *Thirst!* 1977), Edmund COOPER in *All Fools' Day* (1966), D.F. JONES in *Don't Pick the Flowers* (1971; vt *Denver is Missing* US) and Kit PEDLER and Gerry DAVIS in *Mutant 59: The Plastic Eaters* * (1972). Keith ROBERTS's *The Furies* (1966), D.G. COMPTON's *The Silent Multitude* (1966) and Richard COWPER's *The Twilight of Briareus* (1974) combine disaster and invasion themes in the Wyndham manner. Fred and Geoffrey HOYLE's *The Inferno* (1973) deals with humanity's attempts to survive devastating cosmic radiation.

There have been several more personal uses of the disaster theme by UK writers – studies in character and psychology rather than adventure stories. An early example was John BOWEN's *After the Rain* (1958). More impressive are J.G. BALLARD's examinations of human "collaborations" with natural disasters: *The Drowned World* (1962 US), *The Burning World* (1964 US; rev vt *The Drought* UK) and *The Crystal World* (1966), which concern the psychological attractions of flooded, arid and crystalline landscapes. Brian W. ALDISS's *Greybeard* (1964) is a well written tale of universal sterility and the impending death of the human race. Several younger UK writers, influenced by Aldiss and Ballard, have produced variations on the cataclysmic theme: Charles PLATT in "The Disaster Story" (1966) and *The City Dwellers* (1970), M. John HARRISON in *The Committed Men* (1971) and Christopher PRIEST in *Fugue for a Darkening Island* (1972). John BRUNNER has made strong admonitory use of the form in his novel of ecological catastrophe, *The Sheep Look Up* (1972). Angela CARTER's *Heroes and Villains* (1969) is a powerful love story set in the aftermath of a disaster, and Doris LESSING's *Memoirs of a Survivor* (1974) is about a passive woman who observes society's collapse from her window.

US disaster novels are fewer in number. Oddly enough, where UK writers reveal an obsession with the weather, US writers show a strong concern for disease. Disastrous epidemics feature in Jack LONDON's *The Scarlet Plague* (1915), George R. STEWART's *Earth Abides* (1949), Richard MATHESON's *I Am Legend* (1954), Algis BUDRYS's *Some Will Not Die* (1961), Michael CRICHTON's *The Andromeda Strain* (1969), Chelsea Quinn YARBRO's *Time of the Fourth Horseman* (1976) and Stephen KING's *The Stand* (cut from manuscript 1978; text largely restored and rev 1990). Of these, Stewart's *Earth Abides* is the outstanding work, containing much sensitive description of landscape and of the moral problems of the survivors. Other notable disaster stories by US writers include *The Second Deluge* (1912) by Garrett P. SERVISS, *Darkness* and Dawn (**1914**) by George Allan ENGLAND, *When Worlds Collide* (**1933**) by Edwin BALMER and Philip WYLIE, *Greener Than You Think* (**1947**) by Ward MOORE, "The XI Effect" (1950) by Philip LATHAM, *Cat's Cradle* (**1963**) by Kurt VONNEGUT Jr, *The Genocides* (**1965**) by Thomas M. DISCH, "And Us, Too, I Guess" (1973) by George Alec EFFINGER, *The Swarm* (**1974**) by Arthur HERZOG and *Lucifer's Hammer* (**1977**) by Larry NIVEN and Jerry POURNELLE.

Japanese sf seems to have a leaning towards disaster themes. Two notable examples are Kobo ABÉ's *Dai-Yon Kampyoki* (**1959**; trans as *Inter Ice Age 4* **1970** US) and Sakyo KOMATSU's *Nippon Chinbotsu* (**1973**; cut trans as *Japan Sinks* **1976**). The latter was filmed in 1973 as NIPPON CHINBOTSU (vt *The Submersion of Japan*; vt *Tidal Wave*).

Disaster is a popular motif in sf in the CINEMA and on TELEVISION. Examples are the US film EARTHQUAKE (1975) and the UK tv series SURVIVORS (1975-7). The disaster-movie boom in the US took place in the 1960s and 1970s, and featured disasters both domestic and sciencefictional; a producer associated with films of both kinds was Irwin ALLEN. Another form is the MONSTER MOVIE (*which see*).

Curiously enough, although the 1980s were generally regarded as a pessimistic decade, the disaster theme in sf seemed largely played out, with only occasional books of any consequence. Among them were *The Birth of the People's Republic of Antarctica* (**1983**) by John Calvin BATCHELOR, which is an ironic account of civilization's collapse, James MORROW's *This is the Way the World Ends* (**1986**), which puts survivors of a global holocaust on trial, Greg BEAR's *The Forge of God* (**1987**), which has Earth destroyed by alien machines, and David BRIN's *Earth* (**1990**), which has Earth in danger of being swallowed up by a small BLACK HOLE at its core. [DP/PN]

See also: COSY CATASTROPHE; DYSTOPIAS; ECOLOGY; END OF THE WORLD; ENTROPY; MUTANTS; NUCLEAR POWER; OPTIMISM AND PESSIMISM.

DISCH, THOMAS M(ICHAEL) (1940-   ) US writer, raised in Minnesota but for many years intermittently resident in New York where, before becoming a full-time writer in the mid-1960s, he worked in an advertising agency and in a bank; he has subsequently lived (and set several tales) in the UK, Turkey, Italy and Mexico. He began publishing sf with "The Double-Timer" for *Fantastic* in 1962; much of his early work appears in *One Hundred and Two H Bombs* (coll **1966** UK; with 2 stories omitted and 2 added 1971 USA; with those 2 new stories omitted along with 2 previous stories, and 7 new stories added vt *White Fang Goes Dingo and Other Funny SF Stories* 1971 UK). "White Fang Goes Dingo", which appears only in the first and third versions of the collection, soon became TMD's second (and rather minor) novel, *Mankind Under the Leash* (1965 *Worlds of If* as "White Fang Goes Dingo"; exp **1966** dos; vt *The Puppies of Terra* 1978 UK); in it ALIENS take over Earth and make pets of mankind for aesthetic reasons. The

hero, White Fang, eventually drives the aliens off, but his feelings towards his period of effortless slavery as a dancing pet remain ambivalent. The first version of *One Hundred and Two H Bombs*, plus one of the stories added to the second edition, plus *Mankind Under the Leash* under its vt *The Puppies of Terra*, all appear in *The Early Science Fiction Stories of Thomas M. Disch* (coll **1977**) ed David G. HARTWELL.

TMD's first novel, *The Genocides* (**1965**), his most formidable early work, also involves alien manipulation of Earth from a perspective indifferent (this time chillingly) to any human values or priorities or conventions of storytelling; this sense of the indifference of society or the Universe pervades his work, helping to distinguish it from US sf in general, which remained fundamentally optimistic about the relevance of human values through the 1960s. In *The Genocides* the aliens seed Earth with enormous plants, in effect transforming the planet into a monoculture agribusiness, an environment in which it gradually becomes impossible for humans to survive. When groups attempt to fight back, the aliens treat them as vermin, worms in the apple of the planet; and, in one of the most chilling conclusions to any sf novel published in the USA, fumigate them.

Echo Round his Bones (**1967**) – later assembled with *The Genocides* and *Mankind Under the Leash* as *Triplicity* (omni **1980**) – is another minor work, but *Camp Concentration* (1967 NW; **1968** UK) is TMD's most sustained sf invention, and represents the highwater mark of his involvement with the UK NEW WAVE (he was one of several Americans, including John T. SLADEK, to be strongly associated with UK rather than US sf in the late 1960s). Told entirely in journal form, *Camp Concentration* recounts its narrator's experiences as an inmate in a NEAR-FUTURE US concentration camp where the military has treated him with Pallidine, a wonder drug which heightens human INTELLIGENCE but causes death within months. Along with his fellow-inmates, the narrator understands he is being used as a kind of self-destructing think tank, experiencing the ecstasy of enhanced intelligence and the agonies of "retribution" – the analogies with Thomas Mann's *Doctor Faustus* (**1947** Sweden; trans **1948** US) are explicit – but his death is averted by a trope-quoting sf climax which has been sharply criticized as a begging of the issues raised.

The next books were less weighty. *Black Alice* (**1968**) with Sladek, writing together as Thom DEMIJOHN, though not sf is reminiscent of both writers. *The Prisoner* ∗ (**1969**) is a tie to the tv series *The* PRISONER. Much of TMD's best work in the years around *Camp Concentration* is in shorter forms, most of the stories being assembled in *Under Compulsion* (coll **1968** UK; vt *Fun with Your New Head* 1971 US) and *Getting into Death* (coll **1973** UK), a title superseded by the superior US edition, *Getting into Death and Other Stories* (coll **1976**), which deletes 5 stories and adds 4. TMD's most famous single story, "The Asian Shore" (1970), which appears in both versions of the collection, renders with gripping verisimilitude the transmutation of a bourgeois Western man into a lower-class urban Turk with family, through a process of possession. Other notable stories from this period include "The Master of the Milford Altarpiece" (1968), "Displaying the Flag" (1973) and "The Jocelyn Shrager Story" (1975). Increasingly, during the 1970s, TMD's best work made use of sf components (if at all) as background to stories of character; in much of this work his protagonists are directly involved, whether or not successfully, in the making of ART, and he increasingly devoted himself to studies of the nature of the artist and of the world s/he attempts to mould but which generally, crushingly, moulds her/him. From this period date his first volumes of poetry (he writes much of his POETRY as "Tom Disch"), the contents of which evince a sharp speculative clarity whose roots are almost certainly generic. After *Highway Sandwiches* (coll **1970** chap), with Marilyn Hacker (1942-   ) and Charles PLATT, and *The Best Way to Figure Plumbing* (coll **1972**), further work appeared in *ABCDEFG HIJKLM NPOQRST UVWXYZ* (coll **1981** chap UK) (the ordering *NPOQRST* being sic), *Burn This* (coll **1982** chap UK), *Here I Am, There You Are, Where Were We?* (coll **1984** chap UK), *Yes, Let's: New and Selected Poems* (coll **1989**), and *Dark Verses and Light* (coll **1991**). Tom Disch is for many readers primarily a poet whose connection with sf, if known, seems secondary.

TMD's most enduring single work of the 1970s is, however, sf. *334* (coll of linked stories **1972** UK), possibly his best book, is set in a near-future Manhattan; the stories, whose linkings are so subtle and elaborate that it is possible – and probably desirable – to read the book as a novel, pivot about the apartment building whose address (334 East 11th Street) is the title of the book (the numbers 3,3,4 also serve as an arithmetical base [◊ OULIPO] for the design and proportions of the text). *334* comprises a social portrait of urban life in about AD2025 in a New York where existence has become even more difficult, intense and straitened than it is now, and where the authorities treat humans no better than TMD's aliens do; but the essence of the book lies in the patterns of survival achieved by its numerous characters, whose aspirations and successes and failures in this darkened urban world do not step over the bounds of what we may expect will become normal experience. *On Wings of Song* (**1979** UK) is likewise set mainly in a near-future New York, and thematically sums up most of the abiding concerns of TMD's career, as well as presenting an exemplary portrait of the pleasures and miseries of art in a world made barbarous by material scarcities and spiritual lassitude; in the final analysis, however, it lacks the complex, energetic denseness of the earlier book.

By this point, he had in any case begun significantly to lessen his production of sf. Neither his massive Gothic novel *Clara Reeve* (**1975**) as by Leonie Hargrave – earlier, with Sladek, he had collaborated on a more

routine Gothic, *The House that Fear Built* (**1966**), the two writing together as Cassandra Knye – nor *Neighboring Lives* (**1981**) with Charles Naylor (1941-   ), an historical analysis in fictional terms of mid-19th-century English literary life, has any genre content. There followed two collections of literate but significantly less engaged genre work – *Fundamental Disch* (coll **1980**; cut 1981 UK) and *The Man who Had No Idea* (coll **1982** UK) – as well as *The Businessman: A Tale of Terror* (**1984**), an intricately metaphysical horror novel. Its thematic partner, *The MD: A Horror Story* (**1991**), a massive and ambitious exercise in the supernatural whose conclusion takes place in a complexly devastated near future, marks only a partial return to the instrumental sf of his early work; however, as a requiem for and an ethical indictment of the US this century, it is as punishing as any of the more conspicuously radical works from the beginning of his career. *Amnesia* (written and programed 1986) is an engaging piece of interactive software. He is the author of two plays, *Ben Hur* (produced 1989) and *The Cardinal Detoxes* (produced 1990), the latter being the subject of a controversy instigated by the Roman Catholic Church. TMD has been theatre critic for *The Nation* for several years, with an intermission in 1991-2.

His virtual departure from sf may be not unconnected to the nature of the field's response to him. Because of his intellectual audacity, the chillingly distanced mannerism of his narrative art, the austerity of the pleasures he affords, and the fine cruelty of his wit, TMD has been perhaps the most respected, least trusted, most envied and least read of all modern first-rank sf writers. He received the JOHN W. CAMPBELL MEMORIAL AWARD for *On Wings of Song* in 1980, but has otherwise gone relatively unhonoured by a field normally over-generous with its kudos. [JC]

Other works: *Alfred the Great* ∗ (**1969**) as by Victor Hastings, an associational film tie; *Orders of the Retina* (coll **1982** chap), poetry; *Ringtime: A Story* (**1983** chap); *Torturing Mr Amberwell* (**1985** chap); *The Tale of Dan de Lion* (**1986** chap), a tale in verse; *The Brave Little Toaster* (1981 *Fantasy Annual IV*; **1986** chap) and *The Brave Little Toaster Goes to Mars* (**1988** chap), juveniles; *The Silver Pillow: A Tale of Witchcraft* (dated 1987 but **1988**).

As editor: A series of incisive theme anthologies of unusually high calibre, comprising *The Ruins of Earth* (anth **1973**), *Bad Moon Rising* (original anth **1973**) and *The New Improved Sun: An Anthology of Utopian Science Fiction* (anth **1975**); two additional anthologies with Charles Naylor, *New Constellations* (anth **1976**) and *Strangeness* (anth **1977**).

About the author: *The American Shore: Meditations on a Tale of Science Fiction by Thomas M. Disch – Angouleme* (**1978**) by Samuel R. DELANY; *A Tom Disch Checklist: Notes Toward a Bibliography* (**1983** chap) by Chris DRUMM.

See also: BRITISH SCIENCE FICTION AWARD; CHILDREN IN SF; CITIES; CONCEPTUAL BREAKTHROUGH; CRIME AND PUNISHMENT; CRITICAL AND HISTORICAL WORKS ABOUT SF; DISASTER;

DYSTOPIAS; END OF THE WORLD; ENTROPY; ESCHATOLOGY; FANTASY; GOTHIC SF; HORROR IN SF; HUMOUR; INVASION; MATTER TRANSMISSION; MESSIAHS; MUSIC; MYTHOLOGY; NEW WORLDS; OMNI; OPTIMISM AND PESSIMISM; OVERPOPULATION; PHILIP K. DICK AWARD; POLLUTION; PSYCHOLOGY; SEX; SUPERMAN; UTOPIAS; VENUS.

DISCOVERY AND INVENTION These two topics are dealt with together because it is difficult to separate them, the discovery of a new principle usually being followed by the invention of a means of exploiting it. The discovery of new places is dealt with in COLONI-ZATION OF OTHER WORLDS and LOST WORLDS. Invention, too, is discussed in other entries, including IMAGINARY SCIENCE, MACHINES, POWER SOURCES, PREDICTION, TECH-NOLOGY and TRANSPORTATION.

The invention story was prominent in 19th-century sf, notably in the works of Jules VERNE, who could almost be said to have invented it. Vernean inven-tions, particularly of new kinds of transport, were a feature of DIME-NOVEL SF. Yankee knowhow and inventiveness were carried into the past with Mark TWAIN's *A Connecticut Yankee in King Arthur's Court* (**1889**). (A modern version of Twain's story, with a more sophisticated view of HISTORY, is *Lest Darkness Fall* [**1941**] by L. Sprague DE CAMP.) Edward Everett HALE invented orbital satellites in "The Brick Moon" (1869). Later in the century the US inventor Thomas Alva Edison (1847-1931) became a hero figure; his exploits were much imitated in sf, and his name often borrowed (◊ EDISONADE); some of these stories are also described under SCIENTISTS. Rudyard KIPLING invented the transatlantic airmail postal service in "With the Night Mail" (1905). H.G. WELLS invented a huge number of devices – some fantastic, as in *The Time Machine* (**1895**), and some realistic, as with the tanks in "The Land Ironclads" (1903) and atomic war in *The World Set Free* (**1914**). Samuel CHAPMAN's *Doctor Jones' Picnic* (**1898**) features a busy inventor who creates a huge aluminium BALLOON and a homoeopathic cure for cancer. The index of Everett F. BLEILER's *Science-Fiction: The Early Years* (**1990**) lists 134 stories and novels according to their particular inventions, those for "g" being "gasoline substitute, ghost condensor, gravity storage apparatus, gun-powder engine"; other letters of the alphabet produce examples just as eccentric.

The invention story had an especially strong vogue in the early PULP MAGAZINES, where it was equalled in popularity as an sf subject only by the future-WAR story and the lost-race story. Examples are: George Allan ENGLAND's *The Golden Blight* (1912 *Cavalier*; **1916**), in which a gold-disintegrator effects economic revolution; William Wallace COOK's *The Eighth Wonder* (1906-7 *Argosy*; **1925**), in which an eccentric inventor threatens to steal the world's electricity supply with a huge electromagnet; and Garrett P. SERVISS's *The Moon Metal* (**1900**), in which a MATTER TRANSMITTER is invented to obtain artemisium, a rare valuable metal, from the Moon.

The years 1900-30 were largely those of scientific OPTIMISM, and in the pulps Hugo GERNSBACK was one of its prophets. Before founding AMAZING STORIES he did well with his magazine SCIENCE AND INVENTION, which featured much technological fiction. His own *Ralph 124C 41+* (1911-12 *Modern Electrics*; fixup **1925**) is one of the most celebrated of those novels whose *raison d'être* is to catalogue the inventions of the future; they include tv.

The discovery/invention story continued to pop up every now and then outside GENRE SF, as in C.S. FORESTER's *The Peacemaker* (**1934**), in which a pacifist invents a magnetic disrupter which stops machinery; E.C. LARGE's *Sugar in the Air* (**1937**), in which a process for artificial photosynthesis is discovered; and Wil-liam GOLDING's play *The Brass Butterfly* (1956 as "Envoy Extraordinary"; **1958**), in which a brilliant inventor in ancient Greece is given short shrift by his ruler, who sees the new inventions as an unpleasing threat to the *status quo*. But it was inside genre sf that the invention story found its true home, though tending to become more sombre when the central metaphor of Mary SHELLEY's *Frankenstein* (**1818**) – the inventor being destroyed by his creation – was given contemporary relevance by the dropping of the atom bomb over Hiroshima. Even before that, stories featuring NUCLEAR POWER, such as Lester DEL REY's "Nerves" (1942), had been very much aware of the dangers of such inventions. John W. CAMPBELL Jr, both as a writer and as editor of *ASF*, was taking a gloomier view of technological advance by the late 1930s, although his own *The Mightiest Machine* (1934 *ASF*; **1947**) had been a jolly romp, featuring the invention of a SPACESHIP which can take its energy direct from the stars. Campbell's *ASF* continued through the 1940s to publish a number of invention stories, in which scientific plausibility was empha-sized as never before in genre sf. The results included Robert A. HEINLEIN's "Waldo" (1942 *ASF* as by Anson MacDonald; vt *Waldo: Genius in Orbit* **1958**). This is a gripping, optimistic invention story; the term WALDO is still used today for remote-control devices. George O. SMITH's **Venus Equilateral** stories (*ASF* 1942-5; coll as *Venus Equilateral* **1947**) feature much inventive work in radio COMMUNICATIONS across the Solar System. *ASF*'s invention syndrome was given a boost by James BLISH's **Okie** stories, which feature the SPINDIZZY, one of the most attractive of all sf inven-tions; they appeared 1950-54, and in book form as the first 2 vols of the **Cities in Flight** tetralogy: *Earthman, Come Home* (**1955**) and *They Shall Have Stars* (**1956** UK; vt *Year 2018!* US). *ASF* sometimes struck a lighter note *vis-à-vis* inventions, notably in the **Galloway Gal-legher** stories (1943-8) by Lewis Padgett (Henry KUTTNER). These feature an inventor whose creative faculties are released by the intake of large quantities of alcohol, and his irritating robot sidekick; they were collected as *Robots Have No Tails* (coll of linked stories **1952**) as by Kuttner. Meanwhile *ASF*'s competitors were also featuring lighthearted invention stories alongside the more doom-laden variety. A notable example of the former was the **Lancelot Biggs** series of SPACE OPERAS by Nelson S. BOND, which appeared mostly in *Fantastic Adventures* (1939-40) and were collected in revised form as *Lancelot Biggs: Spaceman* (coll of linked stories **1950**). Biggs, the thin genius who bumbles around but gets there in the end, is typical of sf's more stereotyped inventors. Many other relevant genre-sf stories are collected in *Science Fiction Inventions* (anth **1967**) ed Damon KNIGHT.

Many famous sf discoveries have been made through a process of CONCEPTUAL BREAKTHROUGH, and about 40 of them are discussed under that rubric. One in particular is worthy of attention here: "Noise Level" (1952) by Raymond F. JONES. In this tale, which in its emphasis on the potential power of the human mind sums up the whole ethos of Campbell's *ASF*, a counterfeit invention is the occasion of conceptual breakthrough. A group of scientists are shown an apparently *bona fide* film of an ANTIGRAVITY device, the inventor of which has been killed. In their attempt to duplicate it they break through to a new understanding of physics, only to discover that the original was a fraud, the stratagem having been devised to exert psychological pressure on them to rethink their worldviews.

Discovery/invention themes still proliferate in sf, as by the nature of the genre they always will. Important examples from the 1950s onward have been: Fred HOYLE's *Ossian's Ride* (**1959**), in which a sinister-seeming cartel has cordoned off southwest Ireland as an invention-producing area; Kurt VONNEGUT Jr's *Cat's Cradle* (**1963**), in which havoc is wreaked by a newly discovered form of ice which freezes everything it touches; Isaac ASIMOV's *The Gods Themselves* (**1972**), in which a new energy source, the positron pump, is invented with a great show of plausibility; and Bob SHAW's *Other Days, Other Eyes* (fixup **1972**), based on his short story "Light of Other Days" (1966), which features "slow glass", one of the most convincing and original inventions of sf (it slows down light, thus effectively allowing events to be viewed after a time-lapse; the privacy-invading social consequences are intriguingly explored). Arthur C. CLARKE's *Fountains of Paradise* (**1979**), a classically optimistic work of technological invention, envisages the building in a NEAR-FUTURE Earth of a 36,000km (22,400 mile) tower to be used as a space elevator.

One of the most interesting subthemes, which has persisted strongly into the 1990s, is found in stories relating the discoveries of ALIEN artefacts, very often with a subsequent desire to exploit them. Some, such as A.E. VAN VOGT's "A Can of Paint" (1944) and Robert SHECKLEY's "One Man's Poison" (1953; vt "Untouched by Human Hands") and "Hands Off" (1954), are basically comedies about the dangers of the incomprehensible ("One Man's Poison" contains the line "I don't eat anything that giggles"). But the theme has serious ramifications, too. Such stories often create a tension between the longing and wonder aroused by the thought that we are not

alone, together with a sense of despair at the ambiguity of such objects and the doubt whether they will ever be understood. Such is Arthur C. Clarke's "Sentinel of Eternity" (1951; vt "The Sentinel"), the basis for the film 2001: A SPACE ODYSSEY (1968); the story tells of the discovery of a strange monolith on the Moon. Clarke's *Rendezvous with Rama* (**1973**) is entirely devoted to the exploration of, and failure to fully comprehend, a vast, apparently unmanned spaceship which enters the Solar System (◊ BIG DUMB OBJECTS). The psychological repercussions of Man's inability to comprehend the alien are well explored in Frederik POHL's *Gateway* (**1977**), where abandoned alien spaceships are discovered and used, but not understood; the reaching out so symbolized is obsessive, seductive and murderous.

Gateway and the subsequent novels in Pohl's **Heechee** series are sociologically almost the reverse of the *ASF* stories referred to above, perhaps reflecting the lowering of self-esteem and morale in the West from the late 1960s onward. Whereas *ASF* published tales of human ingenuity conquering the unknown, Pohl's stories envisage humanity as bewildered by the discovery of superior technology in much the same way as Bushmen in our own world might be baffled by the products of the industrial West. The metaphor for this in Arkady and Boris STRUGATSKI's novella "Piknik na obochine" (1972; trans as "Roadside Picnic" in *Roadside Picnic/Tale of the Troika*, coll **1977**) is of humans discovering enigma as they scrabble like rats through trash left by alien picnickers. The theme, not always so pessimistically expressed, is common in the sophisticated new wave of 1980s space opera as represented by authors like Greg BEAR and Paul J. MCAULEY, and also by Charles SHEFFIELD's *Divergence* (**1991**). A GOTHIC-SF variant of the theme appears in the malign consequences of the discovery of a long-buried alien spacecraft on Earth in Stephen KING's *The Tommyknockers* (**1987**). [PN]

DiSILVESTRO, ROGER L. (1949-   ) US writer whose first novel of genre interest was *Ursula's Gift* (**1988**), a humorous fantasy. His second, *Living with the Reptiles* (**1990**), spoofs the ethical tomfooleries of that form of the TIME-TRAVEL tale in which the protagonist changes history to save/destroy/play with the future. In this case the protagonists, after acquiring the necessary equipment in what remains of the Amazon jungle, pass into the 9th century, where shenanigans are soon afoot. [JC]

DISINTEGRATOR In sf TERMINOLOGY, one of the commonest items of the sf armoury (◊ WEAPONS), especially in SPACE OPERA of the 1930s and 1940s. The device may have been a product of squeamishness – or perhaps just neatness – since it creates a maximum of destruction with a minimum of bleeding pieces left to sweep up afterwards. The disintegrator first reached a wide audience with the COMIC strip BUCK ROGERS IN THE 25TH CENTURY in 1935, as a result of which toy disintegrators were very popular with kids in the late 1930s. [PN]

DISRAELI, BENJAMIN (1804-1881) UK novelist and statesman, MP from 1837 and, in 1868 and again 1874-80, Prime Minister. He became Lord Beaconsfield. His almost-forgotten youthful novel *The Voyage of Captain Popanilla* (**1828**; published anon) has an innocent savage from a South Seas UTOPIA voyaging to an imaginary country closely resembling a satirized England. Modern sf normally uses actual ALIENS rather than savages as their innocent observers in books of this kind, but the principle is the same. BD features RECURSIVELY in *The Difference Engine* (**1990** UK) by Bruce STERLING and William GIBSON. [PN]

DITMAR AWARDS ◊ AWARDS.

DIXIE, [Lady] FLORENCE (CAROLINE) (1855-1905) UK traveller and writer whose nonfiction *Across Patagonia* (**1880**) captures something of her FEMINIST urgency. In *Gloriana, or The Revolution of 1900* (**1890**) a woman disguised as a man is elected Prime Minister of the UK and, though unmasked, establishes full equality between the sexes; by 1999, a woman-ruled UK beneficently dominates its Federated Empire. *Isola, or The Disinherited: A Revolt for Women and All the Disinherited* (**1903**), a play, depicts the coming to UTOPIAN plenitude of the society of Saxcoberland on the planet Erth, which is similar but not identical to Earth. [JC]
About the author: *Victorian Women Travel Writers* (**1982**) by Catherine Barnes Stevenson.

DIXON, CHARLES UK writer, problematically identified as Charles Dixon (1858-1926), an ornithologist of some renown. The sf novel written by him or some other CD is *Fifteen Hundred Miles an Hour* (**1895**), a boys' tale featuring the interplanetary exploits of some young protagonists who travel to MARS via an electric SPACESHIP. [JC]

DIXON, DOUGAL (1947-) UK writer whose *After Man: A Zoology of the Future* (**1981**) and *Man After Man: An Anthropology of the Future* (**1990**) provide quasi-factual views of a FAR-FUTURE Earth in which *Homo sapiens*, having exhausted the planet, soon becomes extinct, giving way (in a fashion reminiscent of the work of Olaf STAPLEDON) to succeeding forms of life. Similarly couched in a TIME-TRAVEL framework, but less taxing in its assumptions, is a Byron PREISS tie, *Time Machine #7: Ice Age Explorer* * (**1985**). [JC]
See also: EVOLUTION.

DIXON, FRANKLIN W. ◊ Harriet S. ADAMS.

DIXON, ROGER (1930-) UK accountant and writer whose epic adventure about humankind's future fate, *Noah II* (**1970** US; rev 1975 UK), is based on a story idea by RD and his agent, Basil Bova, and began the aborted **Quest** series. A second novel, *The Cain Factor* (**1975**) as by Charles Lewis, mixes SEX and apocalypse as a man and a woman escape a post-HOLOCAUST Earth to become the ADAM AND EVE of a new planet. [JC]
See also: GENERATION STARSHIPS; SPACESHIPS.

DIXON, THOMAS (1864-1946) US writer whose *The Fall of the Nation* (1915-16 *National Sunday Magazine*; **1916**) graphically depicts the conquest of the USA by the Imperial Confederation of Europe, dominated by Germany. After years of occupation, a singularly ferocious US womanhood helps the men of the USA expel the enemy. [JC]
See also: INVASION.

DÖBLIN, ALFRED [r] ◊ GERMANY.

DOCKWEILER, JOSEPH H. [r] ◊ Dirk WYLIE.

DOC SAVAGE MAGAZINE US PULP MAGAZINE, pulp-size Mar 1933-Dec 1943, DIGEST-size Jan 1944-Sep/Oct 1948, pulp-size Winter 1948-Summer 1949. 181 issues Mar 1933-Summer 1949. Monthly until Feb 1947, then 4 bimonthly issues, then quarterly from Winter 1948. Published by STREET & SMITH; ed John Nanovic 1933-43.
DS was perhaps the best of the sf-oriented pulp-hero magazines. Each issue had a novel published under the pseudonym Kenneth Robeson, and many contained short adventure stories as well; a considerable majority of the novels were the work of Lester DENT (*whom see, and* ◊ *especially* ROBESON *for further* **Doc Savage** *details*). The most usual sf elements were superscientific WEAPONS and visits to LOST WORLDS; TELEPORTATION featured once. A master SCIENTIST, almost superhuman in intelligence and strength, Doc Savage was actually Clark Savage, the "Man of Bronze". The success of the series led to imitations, most notably SUPERMAN, whose debt to *DS* is evident in his name – Clark Kent, the "Man of Steel". [FHP/MJE]

DOC SAVAGE: THE MAN OF BRONZE Film (1975). Warner Bros. Dir Michael Anderson, starring Ron Ely, Paul Wexler. Screenplay George PAL, Joseph Morheim based on "The Man of Bronze" (1933) by Kenneth ROBESON. 100 mins. Colour.
There were 181 novels in DOC SAVAGE MAGAZINE, and at one point producer George Pal announced that he hoped to film them all, but this, based on the first of them, was a flop. Muscular superscientist hero Doc fights with a villain over a fountain of liquid gold owned by a remote tribe in South America. The sf elements are very marginal. The film is treated in a joky manner reminiscent of the 1966-8 **Batman** tv series, but Anderson, who later made the disappointing LOGAN'S RUN (1976), is too ponderous a director to carry off this sort of camp nostalgia with flair. It was not until Steven SPIELBERG's *Raiders of the Lost Ark* (1981) that the ambience of the sf/adventure pulps was recreated with the right mixture of respect and amusement. [PN/JB]

DR CYCLOPS Film (1940). Paramount. Dir Ernest B. Schoedsack, starring Albert Dekker, Janice Logan, Thomas Coley, Charles Halton. Screenplay Tom Kilpatrick. 75 mins. Colour.
A mad scientist in the Peruvian jungle is using radioactivity to miniaturize living things, and shrinks some US explorers who find his laboratory to an average height of 12in (30cm). Made by the director of KING KONG (1933), *DC* is a fast-paced, visually inventive film (though the dialogue is leaden), largely taken up by desperate efforts to survive a series of perils. Dekker's portrayal of the ruthless Dr Thorkel – shaven head, bulky body, thick-lensed glasses – as

the "god" toying sadistically with his little creations before casually destroying them is truly menacing; whether by design or accident, he resembles what was to become the caricature of the "beastly Jap" during WWII. The illusion of miniaturization – supervised by Farciot Edouart, one of the innovators in that area of trick photography – is very convincing. The novelization, *Dr Cyclops* * (**1940**), was published under the house name Will GARTH, and was probably the work of Alexander SAMALMAN. [JB/PN]

See also: GREAT AND SMALL.

DR JEKYLL AND MR HYDE 1. Film (1932). Paramount. Prod and dir Rouben Mamoulian, starring Fredric March, Miriam Hopkins, Rose Hobart. Screenplay Samuel Hoffenstein, Percy Heath, based on *Strange Case of Dr. Jekyll and Mr. Hyde* (**1886**) by Robert Louis STEVENSON. 98 mins, cut to 90 mins, cut to 81 mins. B/w.

While Stevenson's suggestion is that civilization may be only skin-deep, his tale of a decent, prim society doctor, Dr Jekyll, who transforms himself with a new drug into the brutal libertine, Mr Hyde, does not exactly abandon the religious concept of original sin; it does, however, reconcile it with 19th-century scientific thought, calling on Darwin (humanity's animal heritage) and prefiguring Freud (the id sometimes overwhelming the ego). Silent film versions (made in 1908, 1910, 1912, 1913 and three in 1920) were usually taken from one of the several melodramatic stage productions rather than directly from the original novel, and tended to present Hyde (as in the 1920 version played by John Barrymore) as a caricature of evil – that is, as a victim of his own Original Sin.

In Mamoulian's 1932 version, which remains the most interesting, Hyde's appearance is almost that of Neanderthal Man (◊ APES AND CAVEMEN), and his joyfully ferocious behaviour results not from inherent evil but from uncontrollable primitive drives. The most compelling of these is sexual – this is one of the classic *loci* of the theme of SEX in sf – though as the film progresses it is accompanied by an increasing capacity for cruelty. All this comments, apparently deliberately, on the repressed society in which Jekyll has been reared. The film, atmospheric and convincing, is an acknowledged classic, especially famous for the heartbeats on the soundtrack and the convincing transformation scenes. When re-released after the Hollywood Production Code was established in 1934, it had 10 minutes cut (sexual censorship), seldom restored since.

2. Film (1941). MGM. Dir Victor Fleming, starring Spencer Tracy, Ingrid Bergman. Screenplay John Lee Mahin. 127 mins. B/w.

Growing pressures of censorship took some of the sexual edge from this glossy remake and, although the film is still gripping – largely because of Bergman's appealing vulnerability as the tart – it seems bland after the raw energy of Mamoulian's version.

3. Subsequent film versions – including *The Two*

Faces of Dr Jekyll (1960; vt *House of Fright* US), which had a plain Jekyll turning into a handsome Hyde, *The Strange Case of Dr Jekyll and Mr Hyde* (1967), a made-for-tv film, *I, Monster* (1970), *Dr Jekyll and Sister Hyde* (1971), where Martine Beswick plays Hyde as a woman in a film seemingly designed for fetishists, *The Man with Two Heads* (1972; vt *Dr Jekyll und Mr Blood*), *Dr Black and Mr Hyde* (1975) and *Docteur Jekyll et les femmes* (1981; vt *The Blood of Dr Jekyll*), a particularly perverse version dir Walerian Borowczyk – have simply been variations of the formula, some more ingenious than others, but none with the impact of the 1932 production. [PN/JB]

DR. M Film (1989). NEF Filmproduktion/Ellepi Film/Cléa Productions. Dir Claude Chabrol, starring Alan Bates, Jennifer Beals, Jan Niklas, Hanns Zischler. Screenplay Sollace Mitchell from a story by Thomas Bauermeister, inspired by *Dr Mabuse, der Spieler* (trans Lilian A. Clare **1923** UK) by Norbert Jacques (1880-1954). 116 mins. Colour.

Although in clear homage to Fritz LANG's three **Dr Mabuse** films (◊ DR MABUSE, DER SPIELER), this German, Italian and French coproduction is not Langian in style. An epidemic of suicides in a NEAR-FUTURE Berlin, investigated by detectives from both East (Zischler) and West (Niklas), is connected to the Theratos holiday camps whose mysterious owner (the "Mabuse" figure, Marsfeldt, played by Bates) has been conditioning holiday-makers by hypnosis to kill themselves, his thesis being that death is fundamentally what we all crave. Marsfeldt, a perversely charming philosopher surviving thanks to a life-support system, has wide media holdings and intends to brainwash the whole of Berlin into oblivion via a tv broadcast. This sophisticated film focuses on the dream-like quality of a world dominated by media images and on the difficulty of locating any firm reality within it. [PN]

DR MABUSE, DER SPIELER (vt *Dr Mabuse, the Gambler*) Film (1922). Ullstein/UCO Film/Decla Bioscop/UFA. Dir Fritz LANG, starring Rudolf Klein-Rogge, Alfred Abel, Aud Egede Nissen, Gertrud Welcker, Bernhard Goetzke. Screenplay Thea VON HARBOU, loosely based on *Dr Mabuse, der Spieler* (trans Lilian A. Clare **1923** UK) by Norbert Jacques (1880-1954). In 2 parts, 95 mins and 100 mins. B/w.

Although on the face of it just a sensational melodrama about a ruthless businessman/scientist intent on world gangsterism, this film anticipates several 20th-century sf themes, both written and filmed. It pictures a Germany sinking into anarchy and corruption, ready to be exploited by a man – more of an evil genius – to whom chaos is almost an end in itself. Mabuse (Klein-Rogge) has strong hypnotic powers and can summon visions to control the weak. The DYSTOPIA depicted looks forward to any number of sf books and films. The chaos-lover whose weapons are as much psychological as technological seems to anticipate, for example, the novels of Alfred BESTER. The idea of a decaying society controlled and exploited by a secret group – the essence of cultural PARANOIA – appears throughout sf, often in the early novels of C.M. KORNBLUTH and Frederik POHL, for example. The film shows how artistically potent the themes of pulp fiction can be when distilled and concentrated, and imaged with such ferocity. In Part One, *Ein Bild der Zeit* ["An Image of our Time"], Mabuse and his web of henchmen penetrate and corrupt society at all levels. In Part Two, *Inferno – Menschen der Zeit* ["Inferno – Men of our Time"], Mabuse becomes wholly mad and is incarcerated in an asylum. Lang, who went on to make the sf films METROPOLIS (1926) and *Die* FRAU IM MOND (1929; vt *The Woman in the Moon*), also made two Mabuse sequels, *Das Testament des Dr Mabuse* (1933; vt *The Testament of Dr Mabuse*) and *Die* TAUSEND AUGEN DES DR MABUSE (1960; vt *The Thousand Eyes of Dr Mabuse*; vt *The Diabolical Dr Mabuse*). In the early 1960s five further Mabuse films were made in Germany, not by Lang.   [PN]

See also: DR. M.

DR MABUSE THE GAMBLER ◊ DR MABUSE, DER SPIELER.

DR NO Film (1962). Eon/United Artists. Dir Terence Young, starring Sean Connery, Ursula Andress, Joseph Wiseman, Jack Lord. Screenplay Richard Maibaum, Johanna Harwood, Berkely Mather, based on *Dr No* (**1958**) by Ian FLEMING. 105 mins. Colour.

This UK film was the first in the hugely successful **James Bond** series, at first loosely based on Fleming's novels and later featuring original stories. The villain, whose cinematic forebears include Fu Manchu, Captain Nemo and METROPOLIS's Rotwang – like Rotwang, Dr No possesses mechanical hands – attempts to blackmail the USA, working from a remote Caribbean island, by deflecting its Cape Canaveral rockets off course. UK secret agent Bond brings his plans to an end by boiling him in a pool containing an atomic reactor. *DN*'s mordant humour, its sexism, its visual flashiness and the foiled attempt by a supervillain to rule the world with a superscientific device set the pattern for the entire series, most of which are marginally sf in the pulp-adventure manner of **Doc Savage** (◊ DOC SAVAGE MAGAZINE). The two most obviously sciencefictional sequels are YOU ONLY LIVE TWICE (1967) and MOONRAKER (1979).   [JB]

See also: CINEMA.

DOCTOROW, E(DGAR) L(AURENCE) (1931-   ) US writer who remains best known for *Ragtime* (**1975**), a novel that evokes the past with an hallucinatory power which edges its real-life and fictional characters into a fable-like milieu (◊ FABULATION). His sf novel, *Big as Life* (**1966**), depicts satirically what happens in New York when enormous beings suddenly appear in the city streets.   [JC]

DR STRANGELOVE OR: HOW I LEARNED TO STOP WORRYING AND LOVE THE BOMB Film (1963). Hawk/Columbia. Prod and dir Stanley KUBRICK, starring Peter Sellers, George C. Scott, Sterling Hayden, Keenan Wynn, Slim Pickens. Screenplay Kubrick, Terry Southern (1924-   ), Peter GEORGE, based on *Two Hours to Doom* (**1958**; vt *Red Alert* US) by Peter Bryant (pseudonym of Peter George). 94 mins. B/w.

This, the first of Kubrick's three sf films, has worn well, with its curious blend of black comedy, documentary realism and almost poetic homage to the very machines (B-52s and their nuclear cargo) that he shows as destroying the world. The original novel was a serious story about an insane US general who launches a pre-emptive attack on Russia without presidential authority, but Kubrick opted for a grotesquely satirical and very funny treatment, helped by a strong cast including Peter Sellers, who plays three roles: one is Dr Strangelove, a sinister ex-Nazi, generally seen as burlesquing a distinguished real-life SCIENTIST. The appalling point of the film is the way the vision of Armageddon attracts the very protagonists whose job it is to prevent it: Strangelove is sexually aroused by the idea of cleansing HOLOCAUST, and it excites the lunatic general and even the bomber pilot (Pickens), who rides his own bomb down with Texan whoops of triumph as Vera Lynn's voice rises plangently into "We'll Meet Again". The novelization is *Dr Strangelove or: How I Learned to Stop Worrying and Love the Bomb* ∗ (**1963**) by Peter George.

The film received the 1965 HUGO for Best Dramatic Presentation.   [PN/JB]

See also: CINEMA; PARANOIA.

DR WHO UK tv series (1963-   ). BBC TV. Created by Sydney Newman, Donald Wilson. 1st-season prod Verity Lambert, story editor David Whitaker; Dr Who played by William Hartnell Nov 1963-Oct 1966. 26 seasons to date, 695 episodes to Dec 1989, mostly 25 mins per episode. Seasons 1-6 b/w; subsequent seasons colour.

In this longest-running UK sf tv series for children, Dr Who, eventually revealed as a Time Lord, travels back and forth in time and space, accompanied by various people (sometimes children, sometimes men, usually young women), in his TIME MACHINE, the *Tardis*. Stories have varied in length from 1 to 14 episodes, the most common length through 1974 being 6 episodes, and subsequently 4.

The first episode (Nov 1963) concerned a young girl who puzzles two of her schoolteachers with her unusual knowledge of history. They follow her into what appears to be a police telephone box but is in fact a time machine (whose interior is many times larger than its exterior) owned by her irritable and eccentric grandfather, Dr Who. As the machine cannot be properly controlled they are all whisked off to the Stone Age, where they remain for the following 3 episodes.

The series had a modest following at first; it was not until the second story, *The Dead Planet*, written by Terry NATION, that it achieved mass popularity, mainly because of the introduction of the DALEKS. Until 1990 the series returned to UK tv every year; it was not introduced to US tv until 1982, when it quickly developed a cult following.

Because the Doctor has the ability periodically to regenerate his entire body, the series has been able to outlast its original star, the crusty William Hartnell, and to introduce a succession of new leading men. Patrick Troughton (Nov 1966-June 1969), Jon Pertwee (Jan 1970-June 1974), Tom Baker (Dec 1974-Mar 1981) and Peter Davison (Jan 1982-Mar 1984) represented a gradual change away from eccentricity, reversed by the casting of Colin Baker (Mar 1984-Dec 1986) and Sylvester McCoy (Sep 1987 onwards). Peter Cushing took the role in two films, DR WHO AND THE DALEKS (1965) and DALEKS: INVASION EARTH 2150 A.D. (1966); Richard Hurndall took the place of the late Hartnell in *The Five Doctors* (1983); and Michael Jayston played the Doctor's evil incarnation from the future in the 14-episode *The Trial of a Time Lord* (1986).

While the b/w episodes featuring Hartnell and Troughton are spikier and stranger, the show probably hit its peak between the Pertwee and Davison versions, with Tom Baker's long-lived, Harpo-Marxish Time Lord the most popular of all and the writers of the 1970s gradually revealing more of the secrets of the Time Lords that had been hinted at since the first. In the late 1980s the show lost direction (some say thanks to the tiredness of John Nathan-Turner's regime as producer, begun Aug 1980) and the BBC experimented with it – lengthening it, moving it from its long-established Saturday teatime slot to a weekday, and, finally, putting it on an indefinite suspension where, neither cancelled nor renewed, it remains as of mid-1992. While early seasons were 10 months long, in the 1970s most seasons were 6-7 months, and from 1982 they were 3 months.

Although the programme has long since settled into a pattern, with stories usually featuring at least one monster, there has been plenty of room for experiment. The authors have unblushingly pirated hundreds of ideas from PULP-MAGAZINE sf, but often make intelligent and sometimes quite complex use of them. It seems probable that, certainly in the 1970s, the programme attracted as many adult viewers as children. With the increasing sophistication of the scripts and the expertise of the special effects and make-up – from which many other programmes could learn a great deal about what can be done on a low budget – *DW* became a notably self-confident series, juggling expertly with many of the great tropes and images of the genre. It is the most successful SPACE OPERA in the history of tv, not excluding STAR TREK. Storylines often feature political SATIRE. At its worst merely silly, at its best it has been spellbinding.

Other notable cast members over the years have included Carole Ann Ford (Dr Who's granddaughter), Frazer Hines (Jamie), Anneke Wills (Polly), Michael Craze (Ben), Deborah Watling (Victoria), Wendy Padbury (Zoe), Nicholas Courtney (the Brigadier), Katy Manning (Jo), Roger Delgado (Dr Who's great enemy, the Master), Elizabeth Sladen (Sarah Jane), Louise Jameson (Leela), John Leeson (the voice of K-9, the Doctor's robot dog, one of the most successful of the media's cute ROBOTS), Mary Tamm (Romana), Lalla Ward (the regenerated Romana), Sarah Sutton (Nyssa), Janet Fielding (Tegan), Nicola Bryant (Peri), Anthony Ainley (the Master again), Bonnie Langford (Mel) and Sophie Aldred (Ace). Producers of the series after Verity Lambert (who lasted into the 3rd season) have included Innes Lloyd, Peter Bryant, Barry Letts, Philip Hinchcliffe, Graham Williams and John Nathan-Turner. Story editors, all of whom have written episodes, have included Dennis Spooner, Gerry DAVIS, Derrick Sherwin, Terrance Dicks (1968-74), Robert Holmes, Anthony Read, Douglas ADAMS, Christopher H. Bidmead, Eric Saward (1982-6) and Andrew Cartmell. Other writers have included Terry Nation, David Whitaker, John Lucarotti, Brian Hayles, Kit PEDLER, Malcolm Hulke, Don Houghton, Robert Sloman, Bob Baker and Dave Martin, Robert Banks Stewart, David Fisher, Stephen GALLAGHER, Johnny Byrne, Terence Dudley, Peter Grimwade, Pip and Jane Baker, and Ben Aaronovitch.

There are now very many spin-off books from the series, ranging from episode guides through annuals, encyclopedias, scholarly studies and published scripts to a *Tardis* cookbook. There is a magazine, *Dr Who Monthly*, with more than 160 issues. Every story has now been novelized, with 151 titles published from the 1970s through late 1990. In 1991, all existing scripts having been novelized, a post-tv sequence of releases, **The New Doctor Who Adventures**, was instituted, the first sequence being the **Timewyrm** series: *Timewyrm: Genesis* ∗ **(1991)** by John Peel, *Exodus* ∗ **(1991)** by Terrance Dicks, *Apocalypse* ∗ **(1991)** by Nigel Robinson and *Revelation* ∗ **(1991)** by Paul Cornell. A comprehensive **Dr Who** bibliography would itself be book-size. [JB/PN/KN]

See also: SHARED WORLDS; STEAMPUNK.

DR WHO AND THE DALEKS Film (1965). AARU. Dir Gordon Flemyng, starring Peter Cushing, Roy Castle, Jenny Linden, Roberta Tovey. Screenplay Milton Subotsky, based on the second DR WHO tv story, 1963-4, the 7-episode *The Dead Planet* by Terry NATION. 85 mins. Colour.

Dr Who – played colourlessly by Cushing as a polite old man – is inadvertently taken to a dying planet with his granddaughters and an accident-prone young man (Castle) as a result of the latter falling onto the controls of the Doctor's time-and-space machine, the *Tardis*. They find a city occupied by DALEKS about to wipe out their ancient human enemies, the Thals, with a neutron bomb; despite their fierceness the Daleks prove ridiculously easy to immobilize. *DWATD* shows something about the 1960s in having Dr Who, famous in later incarnations as a crafty expert in nonviolent resolution of conflict, hawkishly urging the pacifist Thals to war. This crudely made children's-film remake of the early tv story in which the Daleks made their début is of interest mainly to **Dr Who** completists wishing to see Cushing in the role, which he never played on tv; though inferior to its original, it is at least superior to the even more tepid film sequel, DALEKS: INVASION EARTH 2150 A.D. (1966). [PN]

DOCTOR X Film (1932). First National/Warner Bros. Dir Michael Curtiz (1888-1962), starring Lionel Atwill, Fay Wray, Lee Tracy, Preston Foster. Screenplay Robert Tasker, Earl Baldwin, based on a play by Howard W. Comstock and Allen C. Miller. 77 mins. Original prints two-strip Technicolor, later b/w.

A series of cannibalistic murders committed when the Moon is full prove, in this blend of sf, HORROR and the whodunnit, to have been committed by a SCIENTIST maddened by the effect of his newly invented synthetic flesh, from which he can grow a temporary artificial arm. Curtiz's customary hard-edged direction enlivens this early, low-budget pot-boiler. A more sophisticated version of the central idea is found in DARKMAN (1990). [JB/PN]

DR. YEN SIN US PULP MAGAZINE. 3 bimonthly issues, May/June-Sep/Oct 1936. Published by Popular Publications; ed Rogers Terrill. *DYS* was a follow-up to an earlier Popular title, The MYSTERIOUS WU FANG, itself intended to capitalize on the popularity of Sax ROHMER's **Fu Manchu**; in fact the cover of #1 had originally been painted for the previous title. All issues featured lead novels by Donald E. Keyhoe (1897-1988), whose several books on flying saucers later helped foment the UFO craze of the early 1950s. Yen Sin was a conventional yellow-peril supervillain, intent on world conquest with the aid of superscience. His opponent, Michael Traile, had been accidentally deprived of the ability to sleep, so read a lot. The lead novel of #1 was reprinted by Robert E. WEINBERG as *Pulp Classics No. 9* (**1976**). [MJE/PN]

DODD, ANNA BOWMAN (1855-1929) US writer whose anti-socialist sf novel, *The Republic of the Future, or Socialism a Reality* (**1887**), set in AD2050, offers a scathing and comical portrait of egalitarianism brought to the uttermost, resulting in a technologically advanced antlike society. The tale actively deprecates FEMINISM. [JC]

DODDERIDGE, ESMÉ (1916-) US writer whose *The New Gulliver, or The Adventures of Lemuel Gulliver, Jr. in Capovolta* (**1979**) brings its protagonist into a well run feminist (◊ FEMINISM) UTOPIA, which he rather likes. [JC]

DOENIM, SUSAN [s] ◊ George Alec EFFINGER.

DOLAN, BILL ◊ Tom WILLARD.

DOLD, DOUGLAS (MERIWETHER) (c1890-1932/6) US editor and writer, elder brother of Elliott DOLD, with whom in 1915 he joined the Serbian army. As a result of injuries sustained in combat, he gradually became blind, but this affliction did not prevent him from editing *The Danger Trail* magazine, presiding over Clues, Incorporated (which published *Clues: A Magazine of Detective Stories*), or publishing several borderline sf/adventure tales. The last of these

appears to have been "Valley of Sin" in *Miracle Science and Fantasy Stories* (which he also helped edit) in 1931. According to Murray LEINSTER, DD died of pneumonia after his house caught fire and the firemen sprayed him with water. [RB]
See also: ASTOUNDING SCIENCE-FICTION.

DOLD, (WILLIAM) ELLIOTT (Jr) (1892-1957) US illustrator, son of noted psychiatrist William Elliott Dold (1856-1942) and younger brother of Douglas DOLD. ED studied art at the College of William and Mary in Virginia to 1912, and with his brother joined the Serbian army in 1915. Although his 44 Art Deco drawings for Harold HERSEY's *Night* (**1923**) are perhaps his finest work, ED is now best remembered for his interior ILLUSTRATIONS for the early sf PULP MAGAZINES, also in an Art Deco idiom. Using only black and white (with virtually no greys), he was a master at depicting looming, massive, superbly detailed and intricate MACHINES that dwarfed their human operators, whom he depicted with relative indifference. ED contributed to ASTOUNDING SCIENCE-FICTION 1934-8, and was one of that magazine's finest interior illustrators; his illustrations for its serialization of E.E. "Doc" SMITH's *Skylark of Valeron* (1934 *ASF*; **1949**) are considered classics. He edited, did colour covers and wrote a lead story for Hersey's short-lived MIRACLE SCIENCE AND FANTASY STORIES (1931). His last sf appearances were in 1941, when he painted covers for COSMIC STORIES and STIRRING SCIENCE STORIES. [RB/JG]
See also: ASTOUNDING SCIENCE-FICTION.

DOLEZAL, ERICH [r] ◊ AUSTRIA.

DOLINSKY, MIKE Working name used by US screenwriter Meyer Dolinsky (1923-) for his sf novel, *Mind One* (**1972**), in which two psychiatrists discover that a drug meant to treat psychosis actually engenders TELEPATHY (*see also* ESP), and find themselves relating warmly to each other (they are of opposite sexes); as one of them is a Jesuit priest, an element of RELIGION soon enriches the tale. As Meyer Dolinsky, MD wrote 3 episodes for the tv series *The OUTER LIMITS*. [JC]

DOLPIN, REX [r] ◊ Peter SAXON.

DOMECQ, H. BUSTOS ◊ Adolfo BIOY CASARES; Jorge Luis BORGES.

DOMINIK, HANS [r] ◊ GERMANY.

DONALDSON, STEPHEN R(EEDER) (1947-) US writer who remains best known for the two formidably ambitious **Chronicles of Thomas Covenant the Unbeliever** high-fantasy sequences. Although he was a FANTASY writer of central importance in the 1970s and 1980s, and winner of the JOHN W. CAMPBELL AWARD for most promising writer in 1979, and although characters in **Mordant's Need** (see listing below) shift worlds via gates which arguably work according to sf conventions governing MATTER TRANSMISSION, SRD did not become of strong sf interest until the publication of the first volumes of his ongoing **Gap** sequence of Galaxy-spanning SPACE OPERAS: *The Gap into Conflict: The Real Story* (**1990** UK), *The Gap into Vision: Forbidden Knowledge* (**1991**) and *The*

Gap into Power: A Dark and Hungry God Arises (**1992**), with several further volumes projected. The volumes to date are characterized by a pounding bluntness of prose, a plot-pattern which makes some superficial homage to traditional space opera, and an underlying extremism in the creation of character (both the villain and the seeming hero are almost supernaturally monstrous) and in the expression of sexual violence. It is hard to predict what dark climax is being mounted. [JC]

Other works: The **Chronicles of Thomas Covenant the Unbeliever**, comprising *Lord Foul's Bane* (**1977**), *The Illearth War* (**1977**) and *The Power that Preserves* (**1977**); its sequel, the **Second Chronicles of Thomas Covenant the Unbeliever**, comprising *The Wounded Land* (**1980**), *The One Tree* (**1982**) and *White Gold Wielder* (**1983**); a slim pendant to the sequences, *Gilden-Fire* (**1981**); *Daughter of Regals and Other Tales* (coll **1984**), not to be confused with *Daughter of Regals* (**1984**), which prints only the title story of the previous volume; *Epic Fantasy in the Modern World: A Few Observations* (**1986** chap), nonfiction; the **Mordant's Need** books, in effect one novel published in 2 vols as *The Mirror of Her Dreams* (**1986** UK) and *A Man Rides Through* (**1987**).

As Reed Stephens: An associational detective-novel sequence comprising *The Man who Killed his Brother* (**1980**), *The Man who Risked his Partner* (**1984**) and *The Man who Tried to Get Away* (**1990**).

See also: DEL REY BOOKS; SWORD AND SORCERY.

DONNE, MAXIM ◊ Madelaine DUKE.

DONNELLY, IGNATIUS (1831-1901) US writer and politician, famous for his study *Atlantis: The Antediluvian World* (**1882**), which was responsible for a considerable resurgence of interest in the legend of ATLANTIS, and for *The Great Cryptogram* (**1888**), in which he attempted to prove by cryptographic analysis that Francis BACON wrote Shakespeare's early plays. His most important sf novel was *Caesar's Column* (**1890**; early editions under the pseudonym Edmund Boisgilbert), which countered the UTOPIAN optimism of Edward BELLAMY with the argument that society was evolving towards greater inequality and catastrophic WAR rather than towards peace and plenty. ID wrote two other fantasies of social criticism: *Doctor Huguet* (**1891**), in which the racist protagonist exchanges bodies with a Black man, and *The Golden Bottle* (**1892**), in which a gold-making device is instrumental in the overthrow of capitalism. [BS]

See also: CITIES; LOST WORLDS; POLITICS; SOCIAL DARWINISM.

DONOVAN, DICK ◊ J.E. Preston MUDDOCK.

DONOVAN'S BRAIN Film (1953). Dowling Productions/United Artists. Dir Felix Feist, starring Lew Ayres, Gene Evans, Nancy Davis. Screenplay Feist, based on *Donovan's Brain* (**1943**) by Curt SIODMAK. 83 mins. B/w.

One of three films based on Siodmak's novel of the same name, the others being *The* LADY AND THE MONSTER (1944) and VENGEANCE (vt *The Bruin*) (1963).

A scientist keeps a dead businessman's brain artificially alive, but it has an evil, telepathic influence over him. Feist, whose previous sf film was DELUGE (1933), directs unspectacularly, but gets a good performance from Ayres, who accomplishes the transitions from his natural to his possessed state very well. The female lead later married Ronald Reagan. Despite its sf elements, the film is more GOTHIC than scientific – the brain itself is ludicrous. *DB* was parodied in *The* MAN WITH TWO BRAINS (1983). [JB]

DONSON, CYRIL [r] ◊ ROBERT HALE LIMITED.

DOOMWATCH 1. UK tv series (1970-72). BBC TV. Prod Terence Dudley. Series devised by Kit PEDLER, Gerry DAVIS. Starring John Paul, Simon Oates, Robert Powell, Wendy Hall, Joby Blanchard. Writers included Dudley, Pedler, Davis, Dennis Spooner, Don Shaw, Martin Worth, Brian Hayles, John Gould. Dirs included Dudley, Jonathan Alwyn, David Proudfoot, Lennie Mayne, Eric Hills, Darrol Blake. 3 seasons, 57 50min episodes. Colour.

In this drama series, the first about dangers to Earth's ECOLOGY, a group of scientists – aggressively ready to take on the Establishment and headed by caustic Dr Quist (John Paul) – is set up as a watchdog over the rest of the scientific community. Stronger safeguards in the use of everything from chemical weapons and pesticides to new drugs and *in vitro* fertilization are urged, while some lines of research should be abandoned altogether; the not too deeply hidden subtext appeared to be that scientific research is dangerous *per se*. Pedler and Davis departed before the 3rd season, repudiating what they claimed was *D*'s increasing lack of seriousness, but in fact from the beginning the hoariest sf CLICHÉS had appeared beneath the display of social conscience; apart from its overbearingly moralizing tone there was little difference between *D* and the mad-SCIENTIST movies of the 1930s and 1940s.

2. Film (1972). Tigon. Dir Peter Sasdy, starring Ian Bannen, Judy Geeson, John Paul, Simon Oates, George Sanders. Screenplay Clive Exton, based on the BBC TV series. 92 mins. Colour.

A familiar horror-film plot is given a fashionable rationale, in what is effectively a feature-film episode of the tv series. Visitors to a fishing village on a remote offshore island are met with hostility; grossly malformed people are being hidden away. The distortions – in fact, acromegaly – have resulted not from the workings of Hell but from the dumping of pituitary growth hormone (intended as an additive to animal feed) in the sea nearby, although the horror stereotypes suggest the two possible causes are topologically identical. Sasdy directed with style but was handicapped by a banal script. [JB/PN]

DOONER, PIERTON W. (1844-?1907) US writer whose *Last Days of the Republic* (**1880**) was the first US Yellow Peril novel, and demonstrates the terribly common dynamic by which a guilty party, or nation, feels compelled to transfer its guilt to the victim or victim-nation: in 1880, the year of the book's publication, the USA had been using Chinese coolies for some time as forced labour, and in terms of this dynamic it was high time to accuse them of being a menace. In the novel, the coolies nefariously gain civil rights from cowardly Whites, and use their ill gotten power to gain control of the Pacific coastal states, from which point the collapse of Washington is only a matter of time. [JC/PN]

DOPPELGANGER (vt *Journey to the Far Side of the Sun*) Film (1969). Century 21 Productions/Universal. Prods Gerry and Sylvia ANDERSON. Dir Robert Parrish, starring Ian Hendry, Roy Thinnes, Patrick Wymark, Lyn Loring, Herbert Lom. Screenplay by the Andersons, Donald James. 101 mins, cut to 94 mins (US). Colour.

The first live-action feature from the Anderson production team responsible for a number of tv series featuring puppets in sf adventure scenarios, *D*, though panned by most critics, displays its illogical plot with some style. Scientists discover a counter-Earth, an exact duplicate of Earth that is always hidden on the opposite side of the Sun – a centuries-old idea that popped up occasionally in pulp sf, as in *Split Image* (**1955**) by Reed DE ROUEN. An expedition is mounted to reach the counter-Earth, and the confusions of the subsequent story, involving sabotage, characters meeting themselves and apparent conspiracy between the two planets, are compounded by the fact that the story is told in flashbacks by a scientist in a mental asylum, giving a *Dr Caligari*-like ambiguity to the whole film. [JB/PN]

DORER, FRANCES (CATHERINE) (? -) US writer, always with Nancy Dorer, who began to publish work of genre interest with *When Next I Wake* (dated 1978 but **1979**) as by Frank Dorn, and whose most ambitious effort was the **Eagle** sequence of sf adventures, all dated 1979 but published 1980: *By Daybreak the Eagle* (**1980**), *Wings of the Eagle* (**1980**) and *Return of the Eagle* (**1980**). Singletons include *Appointment with Yesterday* (dated 1978 but **1979**), *Sunwatch* (**1979**), *Where No Man has Trod* (dated 1979 but **1980**) and *Two Came Calling* (dated 1979 but **1980**). [JC]

DORER, NANCY (JANE) [r] ◊ Frances DORER.

DORMAN, SONYA (HESS) (1924-) US writer who began publishing sf in 1963 with "The Putnam Tradition" for *AMZ*, and who established a reputation in the field for intensely written, sometimes highly metaphorical stories. They are surprisingly unlike her rather straightforward POETRY, for which she is generally best known; the first of her verse collections was *Poems* (coll **1970**). *Planet Patrol* (fixup **1978**), a juvenile, is sf. [JC]

DORN, FRANK ◊ Frances DORER.

DORRINGTON, ALBERT (1871-?) UK writer whose death-date is undetermined: he may have been the AD who died in Australia in 1953. He was best known for *The Radium Terrors* (**1912**), which combines Yellow Peril fears with the then widespread fascination for the powers of radium. The plot unmemorably details a conspiracy on the part of the former to use the latter. *The Half-God* (**1933**) features super-radium. [JC]

Other works: *Our Lady of the Leopards* (**1911**), a fantasy.

DORSEY, CANDAS JANE (1952-) Canadian writer, arts journalist and social worker, author of three early volumes of poetry and co-editor of *Tesseracts*[3] (anth **1991**) with Gerry Truscott. CJD began publishing work of genre interest with "Columbus Hits the Shoreline Rag" in *Getting Here* (anth **1977**) ed Rudy Weibe; her terse, complex stories, assembled in *Machine Sex* (coll **1988**), polemically re-use and rework sf and fantasy tropes from a FEMINIST perspective, engaging most memorably, and fascinatedly, in the title story, "(Learning About) Machine Sex", with the phallocentrisms of much CYBERPUNK. The protagonist of the tale, a computer-design prodigy and occasional hooker, débuted in CJD's first novel, the undistinguished *Hardwired Angel* (**1985**), written with Nora Abercrombie. [RK]

See also: CANADA.

DOS(-à-DOS) When two books are bound together so that they share one spine, but with their texts printed upside-down in respect to each other, the composite volume is described in the publishing trade as being bound dos-à-dos (literally "back-to-back"). Such a volume has two front covers and two title pages, which the reader can confirm by turning any example upside-down, when a second front cover will appear, right way up, and a second text, likewise. Almost always – though not invariably – the format has been used in sf for paperback originals, the two best known mass-market publishers to have done this being ACE BOOKS in their **Ace Doubles** series and TOR BOOKS in their **Tor Doubles** series; some SMALL PRESSES have also engaged in the practice. For the convenience of readers and collectors we use the word "dos" in our book ascriptions in this encyclopedia to designate any edition of a title making up one half of a dos-à-dos twin.

A problem arises. Towards the end of their existence as a line, **Tor Doubles** began to appear with the 2 titles presented sequentially; in strict bibliographical terms these late issues were, in fact, anthologies, just as two earlier series – the **Belmont Doubles** and the **Dell Binary Stars** – were, strictly speaking, anthologies. If – as was almost never the case – any of the individual titles reprinted in these series had been originally published as books, the resulting volume would have then been technically describable as an omnibus. But readers do not tend to think of the volumes in these series as being either anthologies or omnibuses; readers (and we) tend to think of them as two titles bound together. We have therefore – in deliberate violation of bibliographical protocol – extended the use of the word "dos" in our book ascriptions to include all titles of publishers' series which "feel" "dos"-like.

In this encyclopedia we designate as "dos" all

genuine dos-à-dos bindings; we also designate as "dos" all other series-linked bindings that contain two but no more than two titles, each title being named on the cover.

DOUBLEDAY US general publisher which in the 1950s was one of the first US hardcover houses to institute an sf line, an early title being *Waldo & Magic, Inc.* (coll **1950**) by Robert A. HEINLEIN. (The Doubleday imprint, Doubleday & Company, Inc., should not be confused with that of their associated company, Nelson Doubleday, Inc., publishers of the US SCIENCE FICTION BOOK CLUB.) Once the Doubleday line was established it published about 30 titles a year, its authors in due course including many who at the time were comparatively unknown, such as George Alec EFFINGER, Octavia BUTLER, John CROWLEY, M. John HARRISON, Stephen KING, Josephine SAXTON and Kate WILHELM. D also published many established authors, some of whom had previously published mainly in paperback: they included Isaac ASIMOV, Avram DAVIDSON, Philip K. DICK, Harry HARRISON, Heinlein, C.M. KORNBLUTH, Barry MALZBERG, Bob SHAW and Roger ZELAZNY. D's anthology series have included CHRYSALIS, UNIVERSE and **Nebula Award Stories** (◊ NEBULA). D was both loved and loathed by sf authors: loved because it was a reliable market not afraid to take risks with innovative material that was not obviously commercial, loathed because its advances were small, its book production often cheap, and its book promotion negligible. In 1981 D (whose sf editor for the difficult years 1977-89 was Pat LoBrutto) halved the size of the list. In 1986 it and associated companies, including Dell/Delacorte and the Science Fiction Book Club (but not the New York Mets) were sold for $475 million to the German company Bertelsmann, which already owned BANTAM BOOKS and which thereby became one of the largest sf/fantasy publishers in the USA, with around 170 titles a year.

In 1987 the old Doubleday line was revamped, the imprint now being called **Doubleday Foundation** after Isaac Asimov's **Foundation** books (they had not initially been published by Doubleday, but Asimov came to the firm in the early 1950s and remained faithful to it until his death). The new list was very much more consciously innovative than its predecessors, and ambitious novels by authors like Dan SIMMONS and Sheri S. TEPPER soon began to appear; books under this imprint often went on to be paperbacked by **Bantam Spectra**. During 1991, however, **Doubleday Foundation** was merged into **Bantam Spectra**, and the Doubleday name ceased to be relevant to sf publishing. [PN]

DOUGHTY, CHARLES M(ONTAGU) (1843-1926) UK explorer and writer whose *Travels in Arabia Deserta* (**1888**) profoundly influenced T.E. Lawrence (1888-1935), among others. The difficult, archaic language of CMD's later work, a series of book-length poems, has kept them from wide circulation. Two are of some sf interest: *The Cliffs* (**1909**) features an airborne "Persanian" invasion of England, which is success-

fully repelled; in *The Clouds* (**1912**) a similar invasion is successful, and England occupied. Both poems are designed as warnings to complacent Britons, and share many of the characteristics of the INVASION stories popular before WWI. [JC]

DOUGHTY, FRANCIS W(ORCESTER) (1850-1917) US numismatist, scholar and miscellaneous writer whose well written, ingenious and original dime novels (◊ DIME-NOVEL SF) have often been considered the finest examples of the category. His better stories present a succession of highly imaginative strokes, often with good historical backgrounds. *"I"* (**1887**) describes a double quest, for a beautiful She Who Is Never Seen and for a remarkable manuscript hidden by Saint Cyprian. *The Cavern of Fire* (**1888**) uses as its departure points (a) the theory that the Mound Builders were ancient Greeks and (b) a HOLLOW EARTH filled with teratological peoples. *Two Boys' Trip to an Unknown Planet* (**1889**) is an astronomical fantasy, often on a mythic level, set on a planet circling Sirius; it may have been a source of motifs for David LINDSAY's *A Voyage to Arcturus* (**1920**). *"Where?"* (**1889-90**) takes place in a strange Antarctica filled with grotesque peoples and superscientific devices reminiscent of Bulwer LYTTON's *vril*. *3,000 Miles through the Clouds* (**1892**), which takes elements from Jules VERNE's *The Mysterious Island* (trans **1875**), puts three comrades into wildly imaginative situations in an Arctic crater. Perhaps also by Doughty is *Al and his Air-Ship* (**1903**) as by Gaston Garne, which describes scientifically advanced giants in Antarctica, remarkable flying machines powered by a *vril*-like source, and other marvels. An adult sf novel, *Mirrikh* (**1892**), although highly imaginative, was not especially successful. [EFB]

DOUGLAS, CAROLE NELSON (1944-   ) US writer who began her career as a feature writer 1967-84 for the St Paul *Pioneer Press*. Her first novels, like *Amberleigh* (**1980**), were historical romances. She has become best known for energetic, layered high-fantasy tales like *The Six of Swords* (**1982**), the first volume in her **Kendri and Irissa** sequence, which continues with *Exiles of the Rynth* (**1984**), *Keepers of Edanvant* (**1987**), *Heir of Rengarth* (**1988**) and *Seven of Swords* (**1989**). Though she has been an infrequent author of sf, the **Probe** sequence – *Probe* (**1985**) and *Counterprobe* (**1988**) – is of some interest for its slow unfolding of the mystery behind the amnesia afflicting a young woman who has PSI POWERS and who turns out to be what the title says she is: a probe inserted by ALIENS into the human world to gather data. But love intervenes. It may be the case that CND will never wish to shake herself completely free of romance idioms and plotlines; but, if she does so, she might become one of the significant genre writers of the 1990s. [JC]

Other works: The **Crystal** books, *Crystal Days* (**1990**) and *Crystal Nights* (coll **1990**), associational, with some of the same cast appearing in a fantasy, *Catnap: A Midnight Louie Mystery* (**1992**); *Good Night, Mr*

Holmes ∗ (**1990**) and *Good Morning, Irene* ∗ (**1991**), associational pastiches of **Sherlock Holmes**; the projected **Taliswoman Trilogy**, beginning with *Cup of Clay* (**1991**).

See also: SUPERMAN.

DOUGLAS, GARRY ◊ Garry KILWORTH.

DOUGLAS, IAIN [r] ◊ ROBERT HALE LIMITED.

DOUGLAS, JEFF ◊ Andrew J. OFFUTT.

DOUGLAS, (GEORGE) NORMAN (1868-1952) UK writer of superb meditative travel books and some fiction, his best known novel being *South Wind* (**1917**). *Unprofessional Tales* (coll **1901**), as by Normyx, consists mainly of fantasies; but in two novels of his late maturity he dramatized his strongly misogynist and persuasively "pagan" views in venues familiar to the reader of sf. *They Went* (**1920**; rev **1921**) subversively promulgates a UTOPIAN aestheticism in a land much like doomed Lyonesse. Through the tale of half-divine Linus and his imposition of a rigid civilization upon the world, *In the Beginning* (**1927** Italy), an example of prehistoric sf, expresses – with a more vigorous loathing than Thomas Burnett SWANN could muster 40 years later – the sense that humanity's rise entailed the destruction of Eden, and of the sentient, pagan, amoral creatures who dwelt there. [JC]

Other works: *Nerinda* (**1929** Italy).

DOUGLASS, ELLSWORTH Probably the pseudonym of Elmer Dwiggins (? -?), about whom little is known. ED wrote "The Wheels of Dr Ginochio Gyves" (1899 *Cassell's Magazine*), about a gyroscopically controlled space vessel, with Edwin PALLANDER. His sf novel, *Pharoah's Broker: Being the Very Remarkable Experiences in Another World of Isidor Werner (Written by Himself)* (**1899** UK), is an interplanetary romance set on MARS, where parallel EVOLUTION has resulted in a society almost identical to that of Egypt in the time of Joseph. In the end the hero, having been a grain-broker in Chicago, is able to take on Joseph's role. [PN/JC]

DOWDING, HENRY WALLACE (?1888-?1967) US writer who was most active in the 1920s. His sf novel, *The Man from Mars, or Service, for Service's Sake* (**1910**), is occupied for much of its length with its protagonist's search for a McGUFFIN document, but shifts in its later moments to be a long description, on the part of the protagonist's employer, of his time on MARS, which planet is small, quite close to Earth, and UTOPIAN. [JC]

DOWLING, TERRY (1947-) Australian lecturer in English, tv performer, songwriter and writer. One of the most interesting new voices in local sf, TD is beginning to glean international praise as well. His master's thesis was, unusually for AUSTRALIA, about sf – its topic was J.G. BALLARD and the Surrealists. "The Man who Walks Away behind the Eyes" (1982 OMEGA SCIENCE DIGEST) inaugurated an sf career that has so far been devoted exclusively to short fiction (approaching 30 stories to date); his work was at first too obviously indebted to Cordwainer SMITH and Jack VANCE, but later developed an individual voice. TD's

idiosyncratic but vivid between-the-lines style is perhaps best displayed in his **Tyson** stories, some of which are collected in *Rynosseros* (coll of linked stories **1990**) and *Blue Tyson* (coll **1992**): they tell of Tom Tyson, captain of the sandship *Rynosseros*, in which he roams the strange, high-tech Ab'o societies of a future Australia's outback, occasionally undergoing mystical epiphanies. TD's oblique surrealism is again well shown in a second series, collected as *Wormwood* (coll of linked stories **1991**). With Richard DELAP and Gil Lamont he edited *The Essential Ellison* (coll **1987**) by Harlan ELLISON. [PN]

DOWNING, PAULA E. Working name of US attorney, municipal judge and writer Paula Elaine Downing King (1951-), who writes also as Paula King; she is married to T. Jackson KING. PED began publishing work of genre interest with "Loni's Promise" for *Discoveries* in 1989. Her first novel, *Mad Roy's Light* (**1990**) as Paula King, is an sf adventure featuring a human woman who must come to terms with her life within an interstellar trade guild while at the same time striving to comprehend the ALIEN Li Fawn, who mercilessly use biological engineering (◊ GENETIC ENGINEERING) to modify other species for their own purposes. Her second, *Rinn's Star* (**1990**), plays something of a game of words with its title, as the telepathic protagonist Rinn, who lives on an interesting planet and travels between the stars, also sees her own personal star wax and wane erratically as she shoots from one culture to another, each having a different attitude towards her background and her gift. In *Flare Star* (**1992**) a colony planet is devastated when its sun flares. [JC]

DOWNMAN, FRANCIS ◊ Ernest OLDMEADOW.

DOYLE, [Sir] ARTHUR CONAN (1859-1930) UK writer known primarily for his work outside the sf field and in particular for his **Sherlock Holmes** stories. Born in Edinburgh and educated by Jesuits, he studied medicine at Edinburgh University and initiated his own practice in Portsmouth in 1882, supplementing his income by writing. The first **Holmes** novel was *A Study in Scarlet* (**1887**). His historical novels, *Micah Clarke* (**1889**) and *The White Company* (**1891**), were relatively unsuccessful, but the first series of **Holmes** short stories in *The* STRAND MAGAZINE (1891-2) secured his popularity. His interest in subjects on the borderline between science and mysticism is evident in a potboiler about supernatural vengeance from the mysterious East, *The Mystery of Cloomber* (**1889**), and in a short novel of telepathic vampirism, *The Parasite* (**1895**). Although the **Holmes** stories suggest an incisively analytical and determinedly rationalistic mind, ACD was fascinated by all manner of occult disciplines, including hypnotism, Theosophy and oriental mysticism; following the death of his son he became an ardent convert to Spiritualism.

ACD's first SCIENTIFIC ROMANCE, *The Doings of Raffles Haw* (**1891**), is a hurriedly written account of a gold-maker who becomes disenchanted with the fruits of his philanthropy. His early sf short stories include "The Los Amigos Fiasco" (1892), in which an experimental electric chair "supercharges" a criminal instead of killing him, and the personality-exchange story "The Great Keinplatz Experiment" (1894). ACD abandoned sf during the early decades of his literary success but returned before WWI to make his most important contribution to the genre: following "The Terror of Blue John Gap" (1910) – about a monstrous visitor from an underground world – and a satirical account of "The Great Brown-Pericord Motor" (1911) came *The Lost World* (**1912**), a classic LOST-WORLD novel in which the redoubtable Professor Challenger leads an expedition to a plateau in South America where dinosaurs still survive. In a sequel, *The Poison Belt* (**1913**), the Earth faces disaster as a result of atmospheric poisoning. "The Horror of the Heights" (1913) is an account of strange forms of life inhabiting the upper atmosphere. The novelette "Danger!" (1914; reprinted in *Danger!, and Other Stories*, coll **1918**) is Doyle's contribution to the imminent-WAR genre, anticipating submarine attacks on shipping – a prophecy received sceptically by the Admiralty but validated within months.

ACD's post-WWI passion for the paranormal, which led him to such excesses as the endorsement of Elsie Wright's and Frances Griffiths's clumsily faked photographs of the "Cottingley fairies" in *The Coming of the Fairies* (**1922**), strongly infects his later sf. In *The Land of Mist* (**1926**) Challenger is converted to spiritualism; the remaining stories in the series – which can be found alongside the titular occult romance in *The Maracot Deep and Other Stories* (coll **1929**) as well as in *The Professor Challenger Stories* (omni **1952**; vt *The Complete Professor Challenger*) – are weak, though "When the World Screamed" (1929) is a striking early LIVING-WORLD tale.

ACD's earlier short stories, including numerous fantasies and a few trivial sf stories not mentioned above, exist in many collections, including *The Captain of the Polestar and Other Tales* (coll **1890**), *The Great Keinplatz Experiment, and Other Stories* (coll **1894** US; rev vt *The Great Keinplatz Experiment, and Other Tales of Twilight and the Unseen* 1919 US), and *Round the Red Lamp: Being Facts and Fancies of Medical Life* (coll **1894**), most of whose contents are reprinted in *The Conan Doyle Stories* (coll **1929**). *The Best Science Fiction of Arthur Conan Doyle* (coll **1981**), ed Charles G. WAUGH and Martin H. GREENBERG, collects almost all of his shorter sf; one notable exception is an interesting essay in alternative history ($\lozenge$ ALTERNATE WORLDS), "The Death Voyage" (*The Strand* 1929).

Since **Sherlock Holmes** fell into the public domain the character has been popular in sf stories, appearing in key roles in, among others, *Morlock Night* * (**1979**) by K.W. JETER, *Sherlock Holmes' War of the Worlds* * (**1975**) by Manly Wade and Wade WELLMAN, *Exit Sherlock Holmes* * (**1977**) by Robert Lee HALL, *Dr Jekyll and Mr Holmes* * (**1979**) by Loren D. Estleman and *Time for Sherlock Holmes* * (**1983**) by David DVORKIN.

Druid's Blood (**1988**) by Esther M. Friesner features Holmes (here called Brihtric Donne) in an alternate world where MAGIC works; ACD himself appears as Arthur Elric Boyle. The first novel of this "revival", *The Seven-Per-Cent Solution* (**1974**) by Nicholas Meyer is of sf interest in that it involves early psychoanalysis ($\lozenge$ PSYCHOLOGY) and the father of psychoanalysis himself, Sigmund Freud (1856-1939). A relevant anthology is *Sherlock Holmes through Time and Space* (anth **1984**) ed Isaac ASIMOV, Martin H. GREENBERG and Charles G. WAUGH. [BS]

Other works: *The Best Supernatural Tales of Arthur Conan Doyle* (coll **1979** US) ed E.F. BLEILER; *The Supernatural Tales of Sir Arthur Conan Doyle* (anth **1987**) ed Peter HAINING.

See also: ATLANTIS; BIOLOGY; CRIME AND PUNISHMENT; DIME-NOVEL SF; DISASTER; ESCHATOLOGY; HISTORY OF SF; HORROR IN SF; MACHINES; MEDICINE; MONEY; PARASITISM AND SYMBIOSIS; POWER SOURCES; PSI POWERS; RADIO; SCIENTISTS; SERIES; UNDER THE SEA.

DOZOIS, GARDNER (1947-   ) US writer, anthologist and, from 1985 (with the Jan 1986 issue), editor of ISAAC ASIMOV'S SCIENCE FICTION MAGAZINE, winning 5 HUGOS between 1988 and 1992; he is married to Susan CASPER. He began publishing sf in 1966 with "The Empty Man" for *If*, but it was not until after military service (in which he worked as a military journalist) that he began producing such stories as "A Special Kind of Morning" (1971) and "Chains of the Sea" (1972), which made him a figure of some note in the latter-day US NEW WAVE, causing some misapplied criticism of his "pessimism" and general lack of interest in storytelling; both stories are included in *The Visible Man* (coll **1977**), which assembles his best early work, and reappear in «Geodesic Dreams: The Best Short Fiction of Gardner Dozois» (coll 1992).

His first novel, *Nightmare Blue* (**1975**) with George Alec EFFINGER, a fast-paced adventure, demonstrates a dangerous facility on both authors' parts. Much more important – and less "professional" – is his first solo novel, *Strangers* (1974 *New Dimensions*; exp 1978), an intense and well told love story between a human male and an ALIEN female, set on her home planet, in a Galaxy humans signally do not dominate; her death from bearing his child is biologically inevitable (the plot's derivation from Philip José FARMER's *The Lovers* [1961] can be seen as homage) and stems from a mutual incomprehension rooted in culture and the intrinsic solitude of beings (*see also* SEX). Never a prolific author, though fluently capable as an editor, GD has collaborated frequently with associates in the writing of stories, many of which are assembled in *Slow Dancing through Time* (coll **1990**) with Susan CASPER, Jack DANN, Jack C. HALDEMAN II and Michael SWANWICK. *The Peacemaker* (1983 *IASFM*; **1991** chap) won a NEBULA for 1983 and "Morning Child" a Nebula for 1984.

GD has written considerable sf criticism, and in *The Fiction of James Tiptree, Jr* (**1977** chap) he constructed an analysis which was not to be disqualified by Alice Sheldon's revelation that she was TIPTREE. An anthology, *Writing Science Fiction and Fantasy: Twenty Dynamic Essays by Today's Top Professionals* (anth **1991**), extols dynamic professionalism. His first fiction anthologies, intelligently edited and of continuing interest, are *A Day in the Life* (anth **1972**), *Future Power* (anth **1976**) with Dann, and *Another World* (anth **1977**). Subsequent anthologies, all ed with Dann (except as noted), are *Aliens!* (anth **1980**), *Unicorns!* (anth **1982**), *Magicats!* (anth **1984**), *Bestiary!* (anth **1985**), *Mermaids!* (anth **1985**), *Sorcerers!* (anth **1986**), *Demons!* (anth **1987**), *Dogtales!* (anth **1988**), *Ripper!* (anth **1988**; vt *Jack the Ripper* 1988 UK) with Casper, *Seaserpents!* (anth **1989**), *Dinosaurs!* (anth **1990**), *Magicats II* (anth **1991**) and *Little People!* (anth **1991**). Later singleton anthologies were *The Best of Isaac Asimov's Science Fiction Magazine* (anth **1988**), *Time Travelers* (anth **1989**), *Transcendental Tales from Isaac Asimov's Science Fiction Magazine* (anth **1989**), *Isaac Asimov's Aliens* (anth **1991**), *Isaac Asimov's Robots* (anth **1991**) with Sheila Williams, *The Legend Book of Science Fiction* (anth **1991** UK) and *Modern Classics of Science Fiction* (anth **1992**).

In 1977 GD took over an ongoing year's-best anthology from Lester DEL REY and edited several **Best Science Fiction Stories of the Year** ANTHOLOGIES: *Sixth Annual Collection* (anth **1977**), *Seventh Annual Collection* (anth **1978**), *Ninth Annual Collection* (anth **1979**) and *Best Science Fiction Stories of the Year* (anth **1981**). After the termination of this series, he launched a further ongoing sequence, **The Year's Best Science Fiction**: *First Annual Collection* (anth **1984**), *Second Annual Collection* (anth **1985**), *Third Annual Collection* (anth **1986**), *Fourth Annual Collection* (anth **1987**; vt *The Mammoth Book of Best New Science Fiction* 1987 UK), *Fifth Annual Collection* (anth **1988**; vt *Best New SF 2* 1988 UK), *Sixth Annual Collection* (anth **1989**; vt *Best New SF 3* 1989 UK) *Seventh Annual Collection* (anth **1990**; vt *Best New SF 4* 1990 UK), *Eighth Annual Collection* (anth **1991**; vt *Best New SF 5* 1991 UK) and *Ninth Annual Collection* (anth **1992**). [JC]

See also: CONCEPTUAL BREAKTHROUGH; CRITICAL AND HISTORICAL WORKS ABOUT SF; CYBERPUNK; HISTORY OF SF; INVISIBILITY; OMNI; PARASITISM AND SYMBIOSIS; POLLUTION; SHARECROP.

DR In this encyclopedia's alphabetical listing, "Dr" is, as is conventional, treated as if spelled out in full – i.e., as "Doctor".

DRAGON ◊ GAMES AND TOYS.

DRAGON PUBLICATIONS ◊ VARGO STATTEN SCIENCE FICTION MAGAZINE.

DRAGONS ◊ SUPERNATURAL CREATURES.

DRAKE, DAVID A(LLEN) (1945-   ) US lawyer and writer who served as the Assistant Town Attorney in Chapel Hill, North Carolina, 1972-80. He became a full-time writer in 1981, although his first story, the H.P. LOVECRAFT pastiche "Denkirch", had appeared much earlier, in *Travellers by Night* (anth **1967**) ed August W. DERLETH. Though the wide success of his

various military-sf novels and series and SHARED-WORLD enterprises has perhaps had a simplifying effect on his reputation, DAD has, in fact, from the beginning of his career written a wide variety of work, both stories and novels, a range perhaps best encapsulated in his first collection of unconnected stories, *From the Heart of Darkness* (coll **1983**), which assembles sf, fantasy and horror tales written from 1974 onwards and set in the past, present and future. From early in his career, his prose has been spare and telling though occasionally, in some of the more routine sf adventures, seemingly no more than cost-efficient.

DAD first came to wide notice with his **Hammer's Slammers** sequence of military-sf tales set in a SPACE-OPERA Galaxy: *Hammer's Slammers* (coll **1979**; exp 1987), *#2: Cross the Stars* (**1984**), *#3: At Any Price* (**1985**), *#4: Counting the Cost* (**1987**), *#5: Rolling Hot* (**1989**) and *#6: The Warrior* (**1991**). It is very noticeable that the mercenaries involved in this sequence, and in most of DAD's other military sf, are (as it were) soldiers on the ground, and that representatives of the officer class generally merit the suspicion with which they are greeted. Though its general political vision could not be described as anarchist, DAD's work lacks – possibly as a consequence of his indifference to the loquacious cod stoicism ascribed by other writers to officer classes in general – a sense of philosophizing import, gaining much thereby, so that he can concentrate on the moment-to-moment exigencies of honorable mercenary soldiering. The **Fleet** sequence of SHARED-WORLD anthologies, created and ed by DAD and Bill FAWCETT – *The Fleet* * (anth **1988**), *#2: Counter Attack* * (anth **1988**), *#3: Breakthrough* * (anth **1989**), *#4: Sworn Allies* * (anth **1990**), *#5: Total War* * (anth **1990**) and *#6: Crisis* * (anth **1991**) – does not depart markedly from this mature restraint. The **Crisis of Empire** sequence, essentially written as TIES by his collaborators – *Crisis of Empire #1: An Honorable Defense* * (**1988**) with Thomas T. THOMAS, *#2: Cluster Command* * (**1989**) with William C. DIETZ and *#3: The War Machine* * (**1989**) with Roger MacBride ALLEN – rather more flamboyantly follows the plummeting career of a captain who reaches bottom in the third volume but whom we expect, in projected continuations, to save the Empire. The **Northworld** sequence – *Northworld* (**1990**), *#2: Vengeance* (**1991**) and *#3: Justice* (**1992**) – sets its military operations on a world which operates as a gateway to several ALTERNATE-WORLD settings. The **General** sequence with S.M. STIRLING – expected to run several volumes beyond *The Forge* (**1991**) and «The Hammer» (**1992**) – features yet another military officer, befriended on his far-off planetary home by a battle COMPUTER planning to re-establish a Galactic Federation.

With *The Dragon Lord* (**1979**), an exercise in Arthurian SWORD AND SORCERY, DAD began to publish singletons set in various venues and times, and of varying quality. *Time Safari* (coll of linked stories **1982**) makes one of the hoary CLICHÉS of TIME-TRAVEL tales –

the dinosaur hunt – vividly present to the mind's eye through the well researched verisimilitude of the telling. *Birds of Prey* (**1984**) brings Ancient Rome, again through time travel, vividly to life, as does *Killer* (1974 *Midnight Sun #1*; **1985**) with Karl Edward Wagner (1945-   ). *Bridgehead* (**1986**) combines time travel with interstellar military action and intrigue. *Dagger* * (**1988**) is a tied contribution to the **Thieves' World** enterprise, and *Explorers in Hell* * (**1989**) with Janet E. MORRIS is part of the **Heroes in Hell** enterprise. *Old Nathan* (coll of linked stories **1991**), set in a traditional USA, nostalgically tells tales of a crabby but lovable ghost-hunter. Today there seems very little to stop DAD from writing exactly what he wishes to write. [JC]

Other works: *Skyripper* (**1983**); *The Forlorn Hope* (**1984**); *Active Measures* (**1985**), *Kill Ratio* (**1987**) and *Target* (**1989**), all three with Janet E. Morris; *Fortress* (**1986**); *Lacey and his Friends* (coll of linked stories **1986**); the **World of Crystal Walls** fantasy sequence, beginning with *The Sea Hag* (**1988**), further volumes projected; *Ranks of Bronze* (**1986**); *Vettius and his Friends* (coll of linked stories **1989**); *Surface Action* (**1990**); *The Hunter Returns* (**1991**), adapted from *Fire-Hunter* (**1951**) by Jim Kjelgaard (1910-1959); *The Military Dimension* (coll **1991**); *The Jungle* * (**1991**), based on (and printed with) "Clash by Night" (1943) as by Lawrence O'Donnell, a joint pseudonym of Henry KUTTNER and C.L. MOORE, and here ascribed, some think erroneously, to Kuttner alone; «*Starliner*» (1992).

As editor: The **Starhunters** sequence of reprint stories, comprising *Men Hunting Things* (anth **1988**), *Things Hunting Men* (anth **1988**) and *Bluebloods* (anth **1990**); the **Space** sequence, all with Martin H. GREENBERG and Charles G. WAUGH, comprising *Space Gladiators* (anth **1989**), *Space Infantry* (anth **1989**) and *Space Dreadnoughts* (anth **1990**); *A Separate Star* (anth **1989**) and *Heads to the Storm* (anth **1989**), both with Sandra MIESEL and both constituting a tribute to Rudyard KIPLING; *The Eternal City* (anth **1990**) with Greenberg and Waugh.

See also: ALIENS; GAMES AND SPORTS; VENUS; WAR; WEAPONS.

DRAYTON, HENRY S(HIPMAN) (1840-1923) US writer whose lost-race (◊ LOST WORLDS) novel, *In Oudemon: Reminiscences of an Unknown People* (**1900**), features a 100-year-old English colony in South America which is technologically advanced, telepathic, socialist and Christian. [JC]

DREAMSCAPE Film (1984). Bella Productions/Zupnik-Curtis Enterprises. Dir Joseph Ruben, starring Dennis Quaid, Max Von Sydow, Christopher Plummer, Eddie Albert, Kate Capshaw, David Patrick Kelly. Screenplay David Loughery, Chuck Russell, Ruben, based on a story by Loughery. 99 mins. Colour.

A gambler with psychic powers (Quaid) is persuaded to take part in experiments in "dreamlinking" at a research centre. He learns how to enter other people's dreams and interact with them. There is a plot to murder the President, who has been having dreams of nuclear holocaust, by using an evil psychic to assassinate him during a nightmare, but the Quaid character intervenes in the dream. The theme can be traced back at least to "Dreams are Sacred" (1948 *ASF*) by Peter Phillips, and a similar notion would later be the focus of the **Nightmare on Elm Street** movies. In *D* the penny-dreadful thriller plot is so ludicrous that it is only the dreams themselves that have much entertainment value. The effects are lively, especially in the climactic vision of Washington in flames after the Bomb. [PN]

See also: VIRTUAL REALITY.

DREAM WORLD US DIGEST-size magazine. 3 quarterly issues, Feb-Aug 1957; published by ZIFF-DAVIS; ed Paul W. FAIRMAN. Subtitled "Stories of Incredible Powers", *DW* was initiated as a response to the success of similar issues of FANTASTIC, with stories of wish-fulfilment sometimes featuring PSI POWERS. #1 reprinted stories by Thorne Smith and P.G. WODEHOUSE, but the magazine included little fiction of note, although Harlan ELLISON and Robert SILVERBERG contributed amusing stories. [FHP/MJE]

DREW, WAYLAND (1932-   ) Canadian teacher and writer who began publishing sf with *The Wabeno Feast* (**1973**), a complex tale about HOLOCAUST and its roots, in which three narrative strands all tangibly cohere – the 18th-century journal of an early entrepreneur who confronts the heart of darkness in the pale wabeno (an Indian shaman), the canoe trip of a Canadian couple through the wilderness upon which the earlier visitor has already stamped the seal of the civilized world, and a NEAR-FUTURE flight into the same but now savaged wilderness on the part of escapees from a DISASTER directly tied to the spoliation of the planet. After *Dragonslayer* * (**1981** US), a film tie, WD composed in **The Erthring Cycle** another post-holocaust narrative – *The Memoirs of Alcheringia* (**1984** US), *The Gaian Experiment* (**1985** US) and *The Master of Norriya* (**1986** US) – which describes the founding of a secret underground society, the Yggdrasil Project, via which it is hoped to surmount inevitable planetary catastrophe. But, as the final volume moves to a quiet, sombre close, the reader will perhaps be reminded of the dying fall which concludes George R. STEWART's *Earth Abides* (**1949**). [JC]

Other works: **batteries not included** * (**1987** US), novelizing * BATTERIES NOT INCLUDED (1987); *Willow* * (**1988** US), another film tie; *Halfway Man* * (**1989**).

DREXEL, JAY B. [s] ◊ Jerome BIXBY.

DRUERY, CHARLES THOMAS (1843-1917) UK writer, often on UK flora, whose didactic novel, *The New Gulliver, or Travels in Athomia* (**1897**), presents its shrunken narrator with strange new perspectives on the natural world. [JC]

DRUGS The use of drugs, both real and imaginary, is a common theme in sf, notably in CYBERPUNK. The topic is discussed in detail under PERCEPTION, and a little under NEW WAVE and PSYCHOLOGY. Film and tv treatments of the theme include ALTERED STATES, DOOMWATCH, LIQUID SKY and THX 1138. A small selection of the many sf authors who have used drug themes is: Brian W. ALDISS, Ralph BLUM, Karin BOYE, William S. BURROUGHS, Don DeLILLO, Philip K. DICK, Charles DUFF, Mick FARREN, William GIBSON, Evan HUNTER, Aldous HUXLEY, K.W. JETER, Richard KADREY, Irwin LEWIS, Talbot MUNDY, Geoff RYMAN, Lucius SHEPARD, Norman SPINRAD, Bruce STERLING, Robert Louis STEVENSON and Ian WATSON. [PN]

DRUILLET, PHILIPPE (1944-) Innovative French artist with an epic imagination and an astringent pen-line style who cofounded with Moebius (Jean GIRAUD) and others the publishing company Les Humanoïdes Associés and the imaginative graphic-fiction magazine MÉTAL HURLANT in 1975; much of the content of the latter has been published in English in the US magazine HEAVY METAL. Brought up in Spain, PD was a photographer until the publication of his first strip *Lone Sloane* (graph coll **1967**; intro by Maxim JAKUBOWSKI), a bawdy SPACE OPERA influenced by US CINEMA and HEROIC FANTASY. A unique illustrator, often clumsy in his portrayal of the human face, PD has enlarged the graphic structures of the sf COMIC strip and created a wild, flamboyant, morally ambiguous universe of crazed architectures and monstrous ALIENS. The increasingly obsessive **Lone Sloane** adventures were continued in *Les 6 voyages de Lone Sloane* ["The Six Journeys of Lone Sloane"] (graph coll **1972**) and, with script by Jacques Lob, *Delirius* (graph coll **1973**) – together collected in English as *Lone Sloane – Delirius* (graph omni trans **1975** UK) – followed by *Yragael* (graph coll **1974** with script by Michel Demuth) and *Urm le fou* (graph coll **1975**) – together collected in English as *Yragael – Urm* (graph omni trans Pauline Tennant **1976** UK). PD tackled SWORD AND SORCERY in his adaptation of Michael MOORCOCK's **Elric of Melniboné** with script by Jakubowski and Demuth as *Elrick* (graph **1973**; with script by Moorcock as *Elric* **1973** UK). *La nuit* ["The Night"] (graph **1977**), a sombre panorama of urban warfare, was completed after the traumatic experience of his wife's dying from cancer in 1975. His other works include *Vuzz* (graph **1974**), *Retour à Bakaam* ["Return to Bakaam"] (graph **1975**) with script by François Truchaud, *Mirages* (graph **1976**), *Salammbo* (graph **1983**) and *Nosferatu* (graph coll **1982**; trans **1991** US), the last being a collection of black-and-white strips first published in the magazine *Pilote*. During the mid-1980s PD was commissioned to create the internal decor for the Paris Metro station at Porte de la Villette; he has also produced sculpture and created a children's sf animated tv series, *Bleu* (52 26min episodes, 1989-current). [MJ/RT]

See also: FANTASY; ILLUSTRATION.

DRUMM, CHRIS (1949-) US bookseller, publisher and bibliographer who has published under the imprint Chris Drumm Booklets a large number of chapbooks containing stories and other work by R.A. LAFFERTY and others. Beginning in 1983, his BIBLIO-

GRAPHIES, all arranged with an economic practicality sometimes missing from this field, include works on Algis BUDRYS, Hal CLEMENT, Thomas M. DISCH, James E. GUNN, Lafferty, Larry NIVEN, Mack REYNOLDS, John T. SLADEK and Richard WILSON; in this encyclopedia they are listed under the authors treated (*whom see*). [JC]

DRUMM, D.B. House pseudonym used on Dell Books' post-HOLOCAUST **Traveler** series of SURVIVALIST FICTION, initiated by Ed Naha, with most of the novels thought to be the work of John SHIRLEY. (◊ Ed NAHA for details.) [PN]

DRURY, ALLEN (STUART) (1918-) US writer of a sequence of novels depicting US political (◊ POLITICS) life from a point roughly similar to real-life 1960 and growing into a full-fledged history of the NEAR FUTURE. The bent is conservatively anti-communist, and the satirical effects are often telling, though sometimes tendentious. The series comprises *Advise and Consent* (**1959**), which won a Pulitzer, *A Shade of Difference* (**1962**), *Capable of Honor* (**1966**), *Preserve and Protect* (**1968**), *Come Nineveh, Come Tyre: The Presidency of Edward M. Jason* (**1973**), in which world communism topples an unready USA into chaos, and *The Promise of Joy (The Presidency of Orrin Knox)* (**1975**), in which a war between the USSR and China further challenges the pacifist- and liberal-ridden republic. *The Throne of Saturn* (**1971**), in which the Russians attempt to sabotage the USA's first manned expedition to MARS, is similar in tone but otherwise unconnected to the series. Two later books, *The Hill of Summer: A Novel of the Soviet Conquest* (**1981**) and its sequel, *The Roads of Earth* (**1984**), break no new ground. [JC]

DRYASDUST ◊ M.Y. HALIDOM.

DUANE, DIANE E(LIZABETH) (1952-) US writer, most respected for her work in fantasy. She is married to fantasy author Peter Morwood (1956-), with whom she has collaborated on three books. She began writing fantasies with the **Epic Tale of the Five** sequence – *The Door into Fire* (**1979**) and *The Door into Shadow* (**1984**), later extended with *The Door into Sunset* (**1992**) – and continued with the **Wizard** sequence: *So You Want to Be a Wizard?* (**1983**), *Deep Wizardry* (**1985**) and *High Wizardry* (**1990**), all three being assembled as *Support Your Local Wizard* (omni **1990**). Of more direct sf interest are several successful STAR TREK ties: *The Wounded Sky* * (**1983**), *My Enemy, My Ally* * (**1984**), *The Romulan Way* * (**1987**) with Morwood, *Spock's World* * (**1988**) and *Doctor's Orders* * (**1990**). Though the smooth power of her best fantasies does not transmit perfectly to her sf ties, the **Star Trek** examples are by no means negligible. Other ties include *Guardians of the Three #2: Keeper of the City* * (anth **1989**) and *Space Cops: Mindblast* * (**1991**), both with Morwood, and *Space Cops: Kill Station* * (**1992**). [JC]

Du BOIS, THEODORA (McCORMICK) (1890-1986) US writer best known for her many detective novels, though *The Devil's Spoon* (**1930**), featuring visitors from other worlds, and *Sarah Hall's Sea God* (**1952**) are fantasies. In her sf novel, *Solution T-25* (**1951**), the

USSR wages successful nuclear war against the USA. An underground resistance, faking collaboration with the occupation forces, develops Solution T-25, which dissolves the Soviet leadership's authoritarian personality structures, turning them into benign humorists incapable of commanding their forces. [JC] **Other works:** *Armed with a New Terror* (**1936**) and *Murder Strikes an Atomic Unit* (**1946**), both associational.

Du BOIS, WILLIAM PÈNE (1916-   ) US writer, illustrator and art editor and designer for *Paris Review*. His own novels, which he illustrates himself (he also illustrates other writers' books), are usually juveniles, though the illustrations are of general interest. He began publishing with stories like *Elizabeth, the Cow Ghost* (**1936**), *Giant Otto* (**1936**), and *The Flying Locomotive* (**1941**), and much of his work employs fantasy elements. The ANTIGRAVITY device featured in *Peter Graves* (**1950**) verges on sf, and *The Twenty-One Balloons* (**1946**) is a full-fledged sf novel: a retired professor, travelling across the Pacific by BALLOON in 1883, is forced down on Krakatoa, where he finds a UTOPIA in full swing, financed by its inhabitants' secret trips to civilization to sell diamonds, which they have in plenty. The famous eruption of that year finishes the experiment, but everyone escapes by balloon. [JC]

See also: CHILDREN'S SF.

DUDGEON, ROBERT ELLIS (1820-1904) UK homeopathic doctor, author of the UTOPIAN novel *Colymbia* (**1873**, published anon). Written in a spirit of competition with *Erewhon* (**1872**; rev 1903) by Samuel BUTLER, who was RED's patient, it is set on an equatorial archipelago in the Pacific and tells of a lost race (◊ LOST WORLDS) of Englishmen interbred with Oceanic natives; their submarine city is powered by tidal energy. Their remarkably free sexual practices allow RED to satirize those of Victorian England. *Colymbia* is livelier and more original than most of its kind. [PN]

See also: ANONYMOUS SF AUTHORS.

DUDINTSEV, VLADIMIR (1918-   ) Russian writer whose novel *Not by Bread Alone* (1956 *Novy Mir*; trans **1957** US) seemed at first to proclaim the Soviet thaw, but he was publicly reprimanded for it soon after its publication. *Novogodniaia skazka* (1956 *Novy Mir*; trans Gabriella Azrael as *A New Year's Tale* **1960** chap US; vt *A New Year's Fable* 1960 chap US; first book publication in USSR 1965) is a kind of sf morality tale in which the protagonist, by composing himself for his expected death, discovers a new source of cheap light and heat. [JC]

DUDLEY-SMITH, TREVOR [r] Elleston TREVOR.

DUFF ◊ AWARDS.

DUFF, CHARLES (St LAWRENCE) (1894-1966) Irish translator and writer whose sf play, *Mind Products Limited: A Melodrama of the Future in Three Acts and an Epilogue* (**1932** Netherlands), though breezily deprecatory of the 1960 world it depicts, introduces an inventive range of extrapolatory material, including mind control (and X-ray vision) through drugs, carplanes and tv phones, all contributing to a ČAPEK-like vision of totalitarianism in a world gone mad. [JC]

DUFFY, MAUREEN (PATRICIA) (1933-   ) UK writer whose novels tend to explore marginalized figures, many of them women viewed from a FEMINIST angle; typical is the protagonist of *Gor Saga* (**1981**) televised as *First Born* in 1988 – who is the child of a gorilla mother fertilized by human semen (◊ APES AND CAVEMEN), and who grows into articulate adulthood in an alienating NEAR-FUTURE UK. MD's nonfictional *The Erotic World of Faery* (**1972**) takes a determinedly Freudian view of that subject. [JC]

See also: ANTHROPOLOGY; GENETIC ENGINEERING; WOMEN SF WRITERS.

DUKA, IVO Joint pseudonym of émigré Czech writers Ivo Ducháček (1913-c1988) and his wife Helena Koldová (? -   ), based in the USA from 1948. Ducháček was in charge of the Czech broadcasting department of the Voice of America, where he worked under his mother's name, Čermák. Their sf novel for children, in English, is *Martin and his Friend from Outer Space* (chap **1955** US). [PN]

See also: CZECH AND SLOVAK SF.

DUKE, MADELAINE (ELIZABETH) (1925-   ) UK writer and physician, born in Switzerland of Dutch parents, active under her own name and at least two pseudonyms in a variety of genres including sf novels (which she describes as "cartoons"). *Claret, Sandwiches and Sin: A Cartoon* (**1964** as by Maxim Donne; 1966 as by MED) depicts a world insecurely amalgamated, after a nuclear conflict, into two political divisions: Africa and the Rest of the World. Any politician who risks war is eliminated by an underground organization. The protagonist of the sequel, *This Business of Bomfog: A Cartoon* (**1967**), is "Maxim Donne" – author of *Claret, Sandwiches and Sin*, a successful novel that has inspired the assassination of a number of world leaders. In 1989, Bomfog (Brotherhood-of-Man-Fatherhood-of-God), the organization responsible, now runs the UK in a fashion MED depicts in somewhat hectic language as DYSTOPIAN. *Flashpoint* (**1982**) features a scientist who plans to use a new nuclear power system to enforce global sanity. [JC]

Du MAURIER, DAPHNE (1907-1989) UK writer, granddaughter of George DU MAURIER, famous for dark-hued romances (like *Rebecca* [**1938**]), usually set in Cornwall and often – like her first, *The Loving Spirit* (**1931**), a ghost story – tinged with the supernatural; drugs send the protagonist of *The House on the Strand* (**1969**) into medieval Cornwall. Her one sf novel, *Rule Britannia* (**1972**), subjects a NEAR-FUTURE Cornwall to US INVASION, during which the natives rebel against the tasteless Yankees. Among DDM's short stories are "The Birds", from *The Apple Tree: A Short Novel and Some Stories* (coll **1952**; vt *Kiss Me Again, Stranger* 1953 US; vt *The Birds and Other Stories* 1963 UK), which was made by Alfred Hitchcock into *The* BIRDS (1963), and "Don't Look Now", from *Not After Midnight* (coll

1971; vt *Don't Look Now* 1971 US), which Nicholas Roeg filmed as *Don't Look Now* (1973). [JC]

Other works include: *The Breaking Point: Eight Stories* (coll 1959; vt *The Blue Lenses, and Other Stories* 1970); *Echoes from the Macabre: Selected Stories* (coll 1976); *Classics of the Macabre* (coll 1987; vt *Daphne Du Maurier's Classics of the Macabre* 1987 US).

Du MAURIER, GEORGE (LOUIS PALMELLA BUS-SON) (1834-1896) UK illustrator, cartoonist and writer, known almost exclusively today as the author of *Trilby* (1894), whose famous villain, Svengali, is a preternaturally competent mesmerist. The progatonists of GDM's first novel, *Peter Ibbetson* (1891), share each other's dreams, in which they return to their idyllic childhood. His last novel, *The Martian* (1897 US), lackadaisically tells through hindsight the life story of a sensitive but mysterious Spiritualist who turns out to have been a Martian all her life. [JC]

Other works: *A Legend of Camelot* (coll 1898), whose title poem is mildly fantasticated.

See also: PSI POWERS.

DUNCAN, BRUCE ◊ Irving A. GREENFIELD.

DUNCAN, DAVE Working name of Scottish-born petroleum geologist and writer David John Duncan (1933-   ), in Canada from 1955. His singleton novels have divided fairly evenly between fantasy and sf. The first, *Shadow* (1987 US), is a SCIENCE-FANTASY tale of dynasties in trouble on a strange planet "light-years hence". *A Rose-Red City* (1987 US) complicatedly puts its 20th-century protagonist into a walled UTOPIA, where demons (and the Minotaur) oppose his attempts to extract Ariadne from the world. *West of January* (1989 US) is a crowded PLANETARY ROMANCE set on a world whose day and orbit are of approximately the same duration and in which a not particularly attractive hero – his name is Knobil and, as the book is at times comical in intent, the K can be assumed silent – has adventures all day long, some of which carry subtle stings in their tails. *Strings* (1990 US), also sf, features a significantly naïve protagonist caught up in events the book's readers understand better than he, as a desperately terminal Earth must be escaped, via superstring transport, and a princess must be succoured. DD's work has all the flamboyance of tales written strictly for escape, but (as has been noted by critics) never for long allows his readers to forget what kind of problems he is inviting them to dodge. His most virtuoso passages seem almost brazenly to dance with despair. [JC]

Other works: The **Seventh Sword** fantasy sequence, comprising *The Reluctant Swordsman* (1988 US), *The Coming of Wisdom* (1988 US) and *The Destiny of the Sword* (1988 US); the **Man of his Word** fantasy sequence, comprising *Magic Casement* (1990 US), *Faery Lands Forlorn* (1991 US), *Perilous Seas* (1991 US) and *Emperor and Clown* (1992); *Hero!* (1991 US), an sf juvenile; *The Reaver Road* (1992), a fantasy.

DUNCAN, DAVID (1913-   ) US writer of popular fiction in several genres, perhaps as well known for his few sf novels as for any other work, though his first novel with an sf content, *The Shade of Time* (1946), which deals with "atomic displacement", was (as he records) accepted for publication only after Hiroshima. His books of the 1950s, more widely distributed within the sf markets, have been better remembered, though he also scripted several films, including *The* TIME MACHINE (1960), and wrote a screenplay for *The* OUTER LIMITS. *Dark Dominion* (1954) is a well told melodrama concerning a new element, magellanium, which varies in weight according to the position of the star Sirius, and which is finally used to power a spaceship. *Beyond Eden* (1955; vt *Another Tree in Eden* 1956 UK) contrasts different routes towards fulfilment – materially, through a vast water-making project, and spiritually, via crystals that expand humankind's nature in the direction of gestalt empathy. *Occam's Razor* (1957) explores, within the context of a threatening nuclear war, the impact of the arrival of two humans – though one is horned – from a PARALLEL WORLD. DD has since fallen silent. [JC]

Other work: *The Madrone Tree* (1949), a fantasy.

See also: DIMENSIONS; MATHEMATICS.

DUNCAN, RONALD (FREDERICK HENRY) (1914-1982) UK novelist, poet and playwright; Benjamin Britten's librettist for the opera *The Rape of Lucretia* (1946). He was generally best known for works outside the sf field. *The Dull Ass's Hoof* (coll 1941) contains some fantasy plays. Some of the stories in *The Perfect Mistress and Other Stories* (coll 1969), *A Kettle of Fish* (coll 1971), *The Tale of Tails* (coll 1975) and *The Uninvited Guest* (coll 1981) are fables with sf components. RD's sf novella, *The Last Adam* (1952 chap), features a last man who, being something of a misogynist, comes across the last woman and leaves her. [JC]

Other works: *This Way to the Tomb* (1946) and *The Death of Satan* (1955), fantasy plays; *Mr and Mrs Mouse* (1977), a fairy tale.

DUNE Film (1984). Dino De Laurentiis/Universal. Dir David Lynch, starring Kyle MacLachlan, Francesca Annis, Kenneth McMillan, Sting, Sean Young, many others. Screenplay Lynch, based on *Dune* (fixup 1965) by Frank HERBERT. 137 mins. Colour.

Seldom has a big-budget genre film been so execrated by fans and film critics alike. Certainly its narrative is confused to the point of incoherence, showing signs of last-minute, lunatic cutting. Certainly the many-layered story of Herbert's original, with its complex intellectual structure (occasionally also vague), is here largely reduced to melodrama. Certainly the distilled grotesquerie with which Baron Harkonnen and his nephew Feyd Rautha (McMillan and Sting) are envisaged belongs to a world more disgusting than anything invented by Herbert. Certainly the final three-quarters of a long novel is reduced to a ludicrously fast-moving half-hour or so. Yet the film was, after all, made by David Lynch, master of weirdness, whose previous films had been

Eraserhead (1976) and *The Elephant Man* (1980), and whose subsequent works would include *Blue Velvet* (1986) and the pilot of *Twin Peaks* (1989) – remarkable movies all. It may be time to reappraise *D*, which Lynch clearly conceived in terms of emblematic tableaux, like scenes from some stately, hieratic pageant. Much of the production design – but not the sandworms – was wonderfully original and exotic; the camerawork (by Freddie Francis) made confident, artistic use of light and shade, glowing golds and deep shadows. However bad the film may have been in some respects, the neo-Baroque of the whole thing, not least in the Harkonnen sequences, is one of the most interesting attempts yet to capture a look and a feeling for sf that does not simply depend (as Herbert's original did not) on technological gimmickry. Bits of this bad film are close to masterful. [PN]

See also: STEAMPUNK.

DUNN, KATHERINE (KAREN) (1945-   ) US writer, teacher and radio personality whose third novel, *Geek Love* (**1989**), is a densely told tale of a family which breeds its own freaks through a kind of GENETIC ENGINEERING; in the end the book reads, however, not as sf, but as an extremely expert FABULATION on the primordial theme of the family romance. KD's novel is not to be confused with *The Geek* (**1969**) by Alice Louise Ramirez, which is narrated by a chicken. [JC]

DUNN, PHILIP M. [r] ◊ Saul DUNN.

DUNN, SAUL Pseudonym used by UK writer and publisher Philip M. Dunn (1946-   ) for the original publication of his books in the UK, though he used his own name for their US release; he was also the director of Pierrot Publishing, a packaging-cum-publishing firm which became insolvent in 1981, owing large sums. SD was reported to have moved to India for religious reasons. Releases generated by the company included Brian W. ALDISS's *Brothers of the Head* (**1977**), Peter DICKINSON's *The Flight of Dragons* (**1979**) and Harry HARRISON's *Great Balls of Fire! A History of Sex in Science Fiction Illustration* (**1977**); all were heavily illustrated. SD wrote two SPACE-OPERA sequences, the **Steeleye** books – *The Coming of Steeleye* (**1976**), *Steeleye – The Wideways* (**1976**) and *Steeleye – Waterspace* (**1976**) – and the **Cabal** tales – *The Cabal* (**1978**; 1981 US under his own name), *The Black Moon* (**1978**; 1982 US under his own name) and *The Evangelist* (**1979**; 1982 US under his own name). [JC]

DUNNE, J(OHN) W(ILLIAM) (1875-1949) UK writer and engineer, responsible for designing the first UK military aeroplane *c*1907. Though his two fantasies – *The Jumping Lions of Borneo* (**1937** chap) and the more ambitious *An Experiment with St George* (**1939**) – are of some mild interest, JWD is now remembered almost exclusively for his theories about the nature of time, which he developed in order to explain his sense that dreams are often precognitive. In *An Experiment with Time* (**1927**; rev 1929; rev 1934) he began to articulate his appealing thesis that time was not a linear flow but a sort of geography, accessible to the dreaming

mind. In later books, such as *The Serial Universe* (**1934**), *The New Immortality* (**1938**), *Nothing Dies* (**1940**) and the posthumous *Intrusions?* (**1955**), he ludicrously sophisticated the theory, postulating various numbered levels of Time leading by an infinite regress to God; but his early work resonated perfectly with the time-hauntedness of interbellum UK writers from E.F. BENSON to the children's author Alison Uttley (1884-1976) to – most famously – J.B. PRIESTLEY, whose **Time Plays** are indebted to JWD, and whose nonfictional *Over the Long High Wall: Some Reflections and Speculations on Life, Death and Time* (**1972**) guardedly advocates JWD's more fruitful intuitions. [JC]

See also: DIMENSIONS; TIME TRAVEL.

DUNSANY, LORD Working name of Edward John Moreton Drax Plunkett (1878-1957), 18th Baron Dunsany, prolific Irish author of stories, novels, essays and plays. Though primarily a writer of FANTASY, he is of sf interest through the widespread influence of his language and imagery. Late in life he wrote one sf novel, *The Last Revolution* (**1951**), about MACHINES in revolt. His influence, especially on writers of HEROIC FANTASY, was strong from almost the beginning of his long career, when he published a series of FANTASY collections whose contents are linked by imagery and reference: *The Gods of Pegana* (coll of linked stories **1905**), *Time and the Gods* (coll **1906**), *The Sword of Welleran* (coll **1908**), *A Dreamer's Tales* (coll **1910**), *The Book of Wonder: A Chronicle of Little Adventures at the Edge of the World* (coll **1912**), *Fifty-One Tales* (coll **1915**; vt *The Food of Death: Fifty-One Tales* 1974 US), and *Tales of Wonder* (coll **1916**: vt *The Last Book of Wonder* 1916 US). The stories in these intermittently brilliant volumes made creative use of influences from Wilde and Yeats through William MORRIS – along with the very specific effect of the play *The Darling of the Gods* (**1902**) by David Belasco (1859-1931) and John L. Long (1861-1927), with its misty fake-oriental setting. Through their sustained otherworldliness and their muscular delicacy, these stories in turn exerted a potent influence on later writers.

In his second phase as a fantasist – after a rather ostentatious spurning of the genre during WWI – LD turned to novels like *The Chronicles of Don Rodriguez* (**1922**; vt *Don Rodriguez: Chronicles of Shadow Valley* 1922 US), *The King of Elfland's Daughter* (**1924**) and *The Charwoman's Shadow* (**1926**); the second of these did much to give geographical reality to the secondary universe (◊ J.R.R. TOLKIEN) of high fantasy. His third phase consists of the **Jorkens** CLUB STORIES: *The Travel Tales of Mr Joseph Jorkens* (coll **1931**), *Jorkens Remembers Africa* (coll **1934** US; vt *Mr Jorkens Remembers Africa* 1934 UK), *Jorkens Has a Large Whiskey* (coll **1940**), *The Fourth Book of Jorkens* (coll **1947**) and *Jorkens Borrows Another Whiskey* (coll **1954**). Along with works by Robert Louis STEVENSON and G.K. CHESTERTON, these tales focused the attention of sf and fantasy writers upon the late Victorian and Edwardian club story as a suggestive mode for storytelling; Arthur C. CLARKE,

Sterling LANIER and Spider ROBINSON are among the many who have written in it. LD's work as a fantasist is of high intrinsic merit, and his influence is pervasive. [JC]

Other works: *Tales of War* (coll **1918**); *Unhappy Far-Off Things* (coll **1919**); *Tales of Three Hemispheres* (coll **1919** US); two macabre novels, *The Blessing of Pan* (**1927**) and *The Curse of the Wise Woman* (**1933**); two novels in which men's minds are transferred into animals' bodies, *My Talks with Dean Spanley* (**1936**) and *The Strange Journeys of Colonel Polders* (**1950**); *The Man who Ate the Phoenix* (coll **1949**); *The Little Tales of Smethers* (coll **1952**); *The Sword of Welleran and Other Tales of Enchantment* (coll **1954**; contents differ from the 1908 vol); 3 compilations ed Lin CARTER, *At the Edge of the World* (coll **1970**), *Beyond the Fields We Know* (coll **1972**) and *Over the Hills and Far Away* (coll **1974**); *Gods, Men and Ghosts* (coll **1972**) ed E.F. BLEILER; *The Ghosts of the Heaviside Layer and Other Fantasms* (coll **1980** US); also numerous pamphlets and plays.

About the author: *Biography of Lord Dunsany* (**1972**) by Mark Amory; *Lord Dunsany: King of Dreams* (**1959**) by Hazel Littlefield; *Literary Swordsmen and Sorcerers* (**1976**) by L. Sprague DE CAMP.

See also: SWORD AND SORCERY.

DUNSTAN, ANDREW [s] ◊ A. Bertram CHANDLER.

DURRELL, LAWRENCE (GEORGE) (1912-1990) UK poet and novelist best known for the **Alexandria Quartet** (1957-60). His sf novel sequence, *Tunc* (**1968**) and *Nunquam* (**1970**), assembled as *The Revolt of Aphrodite* (omni **1974**), subjects sf material to intensely literary scrutiny. In the first volume, Merlin, a burgeoning multinational corporation, co-opts the protagonist, Felix Charlock, into constructing a super-COMPUTER, which can predict the future and which drives him to madness; in the second volume, Felix is cured in order to create an ANDROID lady – echoing an LD obsession – perfectly duplicating a destroyed lover of the boss of Merlin; but the android is also destroyed in a NEAR-FUTURE world choked with evil and images of corruption. [JC]

See also: MYTHOLOGY.

DUSTY AYRES AND HIS BATTLE BIRDS US PULP MAGAZINE. 12 issues, July 1934-July 1935; published by Popular Publications; ed Rogers Terrill. Each issue contained a novel by Robert Sidney BOWEN Jr in which Dusty and his sidekicks fought off the menace of the Black Invaders, led by an Asian warlord bent on world domination. The magazine, genuine NEAR-FUTURE sf, was a revival of a more conventional aviation pulp, *Battle Birds*, in an attempt to pull in the readership of the previous title for what was in fact a brand new magazine with a new hero and a new, futuristic storyline. It continued the numeration of *Battle Birds*, beginning with vol 5 #4 and ending with vol 8 #3. Five of the stories were reprinted as paperbacks in 1966 (*for details* ◊ BOWEN). [FHP/MJE]

DVORKIN, DANIEL [r] ◊ David DVORKIN.

DVORKIN, DAVID (1943-) UK-born author, long in the USA, whose first novel of strong interest, after

the unremarkable *The Children of Shiny Mountain* (**1977**; vt *Shiny Mountain* 1978 UK) and *The Green God* (**1979**), was *Time for Sherlock Holmes* * (**1983**). This RECURSIVE tale takes the detective, who has found the secret of eternal youth, through a tortuous plot (much TIME TRAVEL is involved) from the time of H.G. WELLS (concerned at Professor Moriarty's theft of the Time Machine to seesaw through the eons, doing evil) to a Martian future where, after a DYSTOPIAN interlude, he prepares to lead humanity to the stars. Unfortunately, the telling is somewhat flat, an ailment of style which afflicted DD through the next several books. *Budspy* (**1987**), set in an ALTERNATE WORLD featuring a victorious Germany (◊ HITLER WINS), is greyly half-convincing; and *The Seekers* (**1988**) and *Central Heat* (**1988**), both set in the same universe, again lack a sense of full conviction, though much of the detail-work is, as usual, applied with considerable intelligence. *Central Heat* is plotted with all DD's love of intricacy: ALIENS have decided that Earth has failed to breed decent citizens and so abduct the Sun, although ensuring that our planet ricochets into an orbit around Jupiter and Saturn, which have been thrown together; properly instructed as to how to go about igniting the joined gas giants into a tiny new sun, the remnants of humanity begin to learn how to cope. With *Ursus* (**1989**), DD shifted into horror. [JC]

Other works: Three STAR TREK ties: *The Trellisane Confrontation* * (**1984**), *Timetrap* * (**1988**) and *Star Trek: The Next Generation #8: The Captain's Honor* * (**1989**) with Daniel Dvorkin (1969-), his son.

See also: CRIME AND PUNISHMENT.

DWIGGINS, W(ILLIAM) A(DDISON) (1880-1956) US writer on typography and, through his association with the Mergenthaler Linotype Company, designer of several well known typefaces, including Electra and Caledonia. He is known within the sf field for designing and illustrating the luxurious 1931 edition of H.G. WELLS's *The Time Machine*. His sf play, *Millennium 1* (**1945**) – published in an edition he designed and illustrated – depicts an ambiguous UTOPIA in which machines have revolted and humans must fight to recover their hegemony. [JC]

DWYER, DEANNE ◊ Dean R. KOONTZ.

DWYER, JAMES FRANCIS (1874-1952) US writer, most of whose books – like *The White Waterfall* (**1912**), *The Spotted Panther* (**1913**) and the stories assembled in *"Breath of the Jungle"* (coll **1915**) – are Oriental fantasies of little interest, though *Evelyn: Something More than a Story* (**1929**) translates the prurient primitivism of the earlier books into the future, and *Hespamora* (**1935** UK) combines elements of DYSTOPIAN satire with an incursion of pagan deities. The **Spillane** series, *The Lady with Feet of Gold* (**1937** UK) and *The City of Cobras* (**1938** UK), returned to JFD's old haunts. [JC]

Other works: *Cold-Eyes* (**1934**).

DWYER, K.R. ◊ Dean R. KOONTZ.

DYE, CHARLES (1927-1955) US writer who began publishing sf with "The Last Orbit" for *AMZ* in 1950.

He was active for the next half-decade, soon publishing his only sf novel, *Prisoner in the Skull* (**1952**), in which ordinary *Homo sapiens* and a form of SUPERMAN engage in thriller-like confrontations. He was married briefly (1951-3) to Katherine MacLEAN, who wrote "The Man who Staked the Stars" (1952) and "Syndrome Johnny" (1951) under his name. The latter story contains an amazingly early account of a genetic-recombination technique (gene splicing), in which a "piggyback" virus transports genetic material (a silicon-using gene) into human cells. [JC/PN]

DYER, ALFRED [r] ◊ ROBERT HALE LIMITED.

DYING EARTH A not uncommon category of sf story which has now developed its own melancholy mythology. ◊ FAR FUTURE. [JC]

DYNAMIC SCIENCE FICTION US PULP MAGAZINE published by Columbia Publications; ed R.A.W. LOWNDES. 6 issues, Dec 1952-Jan 1954. Much of the fiction *DSF* printed was mediocre, but it published 2 2-part critical articles of some note by James E. GUNN: "The Philosophy of SF" (Mar-June 1953) and "The Plot-Forms of SF" (Oct 1953-Jan 1954). 3 numbered issues were reprinted in the UK in 1953. [BS]

DYNAMIC SCIENCE STORIES US PULP MAGAZINE, a short-lived companion to MARVEL SCIENCE STORIES. 2 issues, Feb 1939 and Apr/May 1939, published by Western Fiction Publishing Corp.; ed Robert O. Erisman. #1 featured the novel *Lord of Tranerica* (**1966**) by Stanton A. COBLENTZ; #2 included stories by L. Sprague DE CAMP and Manly Wade WELLMAN. *DSS* was an average pulp magazine with no distinctive qualities. #1 appeared as a UK reprint in 1939. [MJE]

DYSON, FREEMAN J(OHN) (1923-   ) UK-born theoretical physicist and FRS; professor at the Institute for Advanced Study, Princeton, since 1953, and now a US citizen. FJD's main work has been in quantum field theory, but he is well known in sf for the concept of the DYSON SPHERE, which he introduced in a short paper for *Science* in 1960 (vol 131 p1667). In this paper, which was concerned with locating and communicating with extraterrestrial civilizations, Dyson argued that any such civilization would probably be millions of years old and that Malthusian pressure would have led to its energy requirements being equal to the total output of radiation from its star. It would therefore reconstruct its solar system so as to form an artificial biosphere completely enclosing its sun. This and related schemes, like the basic notion behind his *Ringworld* (**1970**), are discussed by Larry NIVEN in his article "Bigger than Worlds" (1974; reprinted in *A Hole in Space* coll **1974**). An sf novel which makes use of an actual Dyson Sphere is Bob SHAW's *Orbitsville* (**1975**). The "Cuckoo" in *Farthest Star* (**1975**) by Frederik POHL and Jack WILLIAMSON is revealed in the sequel, *Wall Around a Star* (**1983**), to be a Dyson Sphere.

FJD's theorizing has many times gone beyond his own speciality to cover topics as diverse as the Greenhouse Effect, galactic COLONIZATION, GENETIC ENGINEERING and the use of the SOLAR WIND for space-

sailing. His many essays are a treasure trove for sf writers, some being collected in *Infinite in All Directions* (coll **1988** US). His set of autobiographical sketches, *Disturbing the Universe* (**1979** US), tells entertaining tales of intellectual adventure. It was a student of Dyson's who made headlines in 1976 by designing a workable nuclear weapon using only published sources. [TSu/PN]

See also: ENTROPY; XENOBIOLOGY.

DYSON SPHERE Item of sf TERMINOLOGY; named for a concept put forward by the physicist Freeman J. DYSON.

DYSTOPIAS The word "dystopia" is the commonly used antonym of "eutopia" (◊ UTOPIAS) and denotes that class of hypothetical societies containing images of worlds worse than our own. An early user of the term was John Stuart Mill (1806-1873), in a parliamentary speech in 1868, but its recent fashionableness probably stems from its use in *Quest for Utopia* (**1952**) by Glenn Negley (1907-1988) and J. Max Patrick (1908-   ). Anthony BURGESS argued in *1985* (**1978**) that "cacotopia" would be a more apt term.

Dystopian images are almost invariably images of future society, pointing fearfully at the way the world is supposedly going in order to provide urgent propaganda for a change in direction. As hope for a better future grows, the fear of disappointment inevitably grows with it, and when any vision of a future utopia incorporates a manifesto for political action or belief, opponents of that action or belief will inevitably attempt to show that its consequences are not utopian but horrible. The very first work listed in I.F. CLARKE's bibliography of *The Tale of the Future* (3rd edn **1978**) is a tract of 1644 warning of the terrible disaster which would follow were the monarchy to be restored.

Dystopian images began to proliferate in the last decades of the 19th century. Utopian and dystopian images are contrasted in the rival cities of Frankville and Stahlstadt in *The Begum's Fortune* (**1879**; trans **1880**) by Jules VERNE. The greedy materialism which has created Stahlstadt is also the underlying ideology of H.C. MARRIOTT-WATSON's *Erchomenon* (**1879**). Walter BESANT produced two significant early dystopias in *The Revolt of Man* (**1882**), in which women (◊ WOMEN AS PORTRAYED IN SCIENCE FICTION) rule with disastrous consequences, and *The Inner House* (**1888**), in which IMMORTALITY has led to social stagnation. The great utopian H.G. WELLS produced his images of dystopia, too – forecasts of what the world must be like if the forces of socialism did not triumph – in "A Story of the Days to Come" (1897) and *When the Sleeper Wakes* (**1899**; rev vt *The Sleeper Awakes*, **1910**). He also produced the first ALIEN dystopia in his description of Selenite society in *The First Men in the Moon* (**1901**). Robert Hugh BENSON's *Lord of the World* (**1907**) is a hysterical protest against secularism, humanism and socialism which ends with the apocalypse.

The single most prolific stimulus to the production of dystopian visions has been the political polarization of capitalism and socialism. Anti-capitalist dystopias include *The Iron Heel* (**1907**) by Jack LONDON, *The Air Trust* (**1915**) by George Allan ENGLAND, and *Useless Hands* (**1920**; trans **1926**) by Claude FARRÈRE. Anti-socialist dystopias, which are more numerous, include *The Unknown Tomorrow* (**1910**) by William LE QUEUX, *Crucible Island* (**1919**) by Condé B. PALLEN, *Unborn Tomorrow* (**1933**) by John KENDALL, *Anthem* (**1938**) by Ayn RAND and *The Great Idea* (**1951**; vt *Time Will Run Back*) by Henry HAZLITT. Anti-fascist dystopias include *Land under England* (**1935**) by Joseph O'NEILL, *The Wild Goose Chase* (**1937**) by Rex WARNER and *The Lost Traveller* (**1943**) by Ruthven TODD. Anti-German dystopias from before and after the rise of the Nazi Party include Owen GREGORY's *Meccania* (**1918**), Milo HASTINGS's *City of Endless Night* (**1920**) and *Swastika Night* (**1937**) by Murray Constantine (◊ Katharine BURDEKIN) (*see also* HITLER WINS).

Although these works are emotional reactions against ideas which seem various, the basic fears which they express are very similar. The emphasis may differ, but the central features of dystopia are ever present: the oppression of the majority by a ruling élite (which varies only in the manner of its characterization, not in its actions), and the regimentation of society as a whole (which varies only in its declared ends, not in its actual processes). In his attempt to imagine the "rationalized" state of the Selenites, Wells took as his dystopian model the ant-nest (◊ HIVE-MINDS) and this has seemed the epitome of dystopian organization to many other writers. J.D. BERESFORD's and Esmé Wynne-Tyson's *The Riddle of the Tower* (**1944**) suggests that the fundamental danger facing society is "Automatism" – the trend toward the victory of organic society over the individual – whatever political philosophy is invoked to justify it. The most detailed analysis of this anxiety, and perhaps the most impressively ruthless of all dystopias, is *My* (trans as *We* **1924**) by Yevgeny ZAMIATIN, and the most luridly horrible development of it is to be found in George ORWELL's *Nineteen Eighty-four* (**1949**), which in part expressed Orwell's despair of the UK working class and its capacity to revolt (or even be revolted).

Because animosity against specific political programmes was the most important force provoking early dystopian visions, the tradition did not immediately engage in contradictory argument the main basis for utopian optimism, which is a more generalized faith in the idea of progress, both social and technological. It was not long, though, before there appeared dystopian images reflecting an emotional reaction against technological advance. The world of E.M. FORSTER's "The Machine Stops" (**1909**) is perhaps the first dystopia created by technological sophistication; the story's argument is halfhearted, concentrating on the question of what would happen when the MACHINES broke down rather than on the horrors of living with them while they were still functioning. A confident assertion that scientific progress would make the world a worse place to live in because it would allow society's power groups more effectively to oppress others was made by Bertrand RUSSELL in *Icarus, or The Future of Science* (**1924**), his reply to J.B.S. HALDANE's optimistic *Daedalus* (**1924**). Aldous HUXLEY's satirical dystopia *Brave New World* (**1932**) is also an ideological reply to *Daedalus*, raising awkward questions about the quality of life in a LEISURE society. S. Fowler WRIGHT's *The New Gods Lead* (coll **1932**) is a scathing indictment of the values of technocracy and "the utopia of comforts". The general pessimism of the UK SCIENTIFIC ROMANCE in this period was countered mainly by hopes of transcendence (*via* the evolution of a new and better species of mankind) rather than by faith in political reform.

This suspicion of technology, though running directly counter to Hugo GERNSBACK's optimism for an "Age of Power Freedom", is surprisingly widespread in early GENRE SF. In "Paradise and Iron" (**1930**) by Miles J. BREUER a mechanical brain established to coordinate a mechanistic utopia becomes a tyrant. In "City of the Living Dead" (**1930**) by Laurence MANNING and Fletcher PRATT, machines that simulate real experience allow people to live in dream worlds, sustained by mechanical "wombs", and thereby bring about the total stagnation of society. Scepticism in regard to technological miracles is a hallmark of the work of David H. KELLER, whose dystopian fantasies include "The Revolt of the Pedestrians" (**1928**), in which automobilists who have lost the power of self-locomotion rule oppressively over mere pedestrians. Most stories of this kind feature some kind of rebellion against the adverse circumstances described. The reversion to a simpler way of life is celebrated by Keller in "The Metal Doom" (**1932**) as enthusiastically as it is in the hysterically technophobic *Gay Hunter* (**1934**) by J. Leslie MITCHELL.

Revolution against a dystopian regime was to become a staple plot of GENRE SF, partly because such a formula offered far more melodramatic potential than utopian planning. The standard scenario involves an oppressive totalitarian state which maintains its dominance and stability by means of futuristic technology, but which is in the end toppled by newer technologies exploited by revolutionaries. The standard genre-sf answer to the problem posed by Russell in *Icarus* is, therefore, that élites empowered by technology will lose their interest in further technological progress, and will probably try to suppress it – with the result that its clandestinely developed fruits will become the instruments of their overthrow. Examples from the 1940s of this formula are "If This Goes On ..." (**1940**) and *Sixth Column* (**1941**; **1949**) by Robert A. HEINLEIN, *Gather, Darkness!* (**1943**; **1950**) by Fritz LEIBER, *Tarnished Utopia* (**1943**; **1956**) by Malcolm JAMESON and *Renaissance* (**1944**; **1951**; vt *Man of Two Worlds*) by Raymond F. JONES. In the SF MAGAZINES of the 1950s this formula became more refined and increasingly stylized. There appeared a whole generation of sf novels in which individual power groups come to dominate society, shaping it to their special interests. Advertising executives run the world in the archetype of this subspecies, *The Space Merchants* (**1953**) by Frederik POHL and C.M. KORNBLUTH; insurance companies are in charge in *Preferred Risk* (**1955**) by Edson McCann (Pohl and Lester DEL REY); supermarkets in *Hell's Pavement* (**1955**; vt *Analogue Men*) by Damon KNIGHT; racketeers in *The Syndic* (**1953**) by Kornbluth; doctors in *Caduceus Wild* (**1959**; rev **1978**) by Ward MOORE and Robert Bradford; and a cult of hedonists in *The Joy Makers* (fixup **1961**) by James E. GUNN. All these novels are, in a sense, gaudy fakes that use dystopian images for melodramatic convenience; they select their villains with a vigorous disregard for plausibility and a cheerful animus against some personal *bête noire*. They tend to be ABSURDIST exaggerations rather than serious political statements. In this period genre sf produced only one genuine dystopian novel, the classic *Fahrenheit 451* (**1953**) by Ray BRADBURY, which leaves its ruling élite anonymous in order to concentrate on the means by which oppression and regimentation are facilitated, with the powerful key image of the firemen whose job is to burn books. In many of the lesser genre-sf novels of the 1950s, revolution against an oppressive and stagnant society is seen as a difficult irrelevance, escape by SPACESHIP becoming a key image.

Outside the sf magazines the post-WWII period produced a remarkable series of very varied dystopian novels – remarkable not only for their diversity and characteristic intensity but also for a tendency to black comedy. Aldous Huxley's *Ape and Essence* (**1948**) is an anti-scientific polemic; Evelyn WAUGH's *Love among the Ruins* (**1953**) is a vitriolic political satire; Bernard WOLFE's *Limbo* (**1952**) plays in macabre fashion with the idea of (literal) "disarmament". Even the more earnest works, like Gerald HEARD's enigmatic *Doppelgangers* (**1947**), SARBAN's *The Sound of His Horn* (**1952**), David KARP's *One* (**1953**), L.P. HARTLEY's *Facial Justice* (**1960**) and Anthony Burgess's *A Clockwork Orange* (**1962**), possess a curious surreal quality. Many of these novels are neither accusations directed at particular social forces nor attempts to analyse the nature of the dystopian state, but seem to be products of a new kind of incipient despair; only a few – notably *Doppelgangers* – offer a significant note of hope in their account of rebellion against evil circumstance. This, it appears, was a period of history in which US-UK society lost its faith in the probability of a better future, and the dystopian image was established as an actual pattern of expectation rather than as a literary warning device.

Genre sf soon followed this lead – and so prominent was the dystopian image in magazine sf that the transition from fakery to "realism" was very easily achieved. During the 1960s a whole series of reasons for believing in a dystopian future were discovered – to justify rather than to cause the pessimistic outlook typical of the time. OVERPOPULATION – a theme ignored since the days of Malthus – began to inspire dystopian horror stories, most impressively in *Make Room! Make Room!* (**1966**) by Harry HARRISON, *Stand on Zanzibar* (**1968**) by John BRUNNER and *The World Inside* (**1971**) by Robert SILVERBERG. The awful prospects of POLLUTION and the destruction of the environment were extravagantly detailed in Brunner's *The Sheep Look Up* (**1972**) and Philip WYLIE's *The End of the Dream* (**1972**). When Alvin TOFFLER proposed in *Future Shock* (**1970**) that the sheer pace of change threatened to make everyday life unendurable, Brunner was able to complete a kind of "dystopian tetralogy", following the two books cited above and *The Jagged Orbit* (**1969**) with *The Shockwave Rider* (**1975**). Thomas M. DISCH's *334* (fixup **1972**) is a dark vision of the NEAR FUTURE in which human resilience is tested to the limit by the stresses and strains of everyday life.

Perhaps strangely, MAINSTREAM dystopias of the late 1960s and 1970s seem rather weak-kneed compared to those of the preceding decades. Michael FRAYN's *A Very Private Life* (**1968**), Adrian MITCHELL's *The Bodyguard* (**1970**), Ira LEVIN's *This Perfect Day* (**1970**) and Lawrence SANDERS's *The Tomorrow File* (**1975**) all seem stereotyped. Perhaps there was little scope left for originality once the most all-inclusive and ruthless image of a horrible and degenerate future had been provided by William S. BURROUGHS in *Nova Express* (**1964**), or perhaps it was simply that dystopian imagery came to be taken for granted to such an extent that it could be deployed only in an almost flippant manner – as by the CYBERPUNK writers of the 1980s. It is arguable that the only new ground broken by literary dystopias of the 1970s and 1980s, whether in the mainstream or in genre sf, related to FEMINIST images of oppressive masculinity; notable examples include *Walk to the End of the World* (**1974**) by Suzy McKee CHARNAS, *Woman at the Edge of Time* (**1976**) by Marge PIERCY, *The Handmaid's Tale* (**1985**) by Margaret ATWOOD, and *Bulldozer Rising* (**1988**) by ANNA LIVIA.

The significance of the firm establishment of a dystopian image of the future in literature should not be underestimated. Literary images of the future are among the most significant expressions of the beliefs and expectations we apply in real life to the organization of our attitudes and actions. Notable studies of dystopian fiction include *From Utopia to Nightmare* (**1962**) by Chad Walsh, *The Future as Nightmare* (**1967**) by Mark R. HILLEGAS, and *Science Fiction and the New Dark Age* by Harold L. Berger (**1976**). In *New Maps of Hell* (**1960**) Kingsley AMIS argues that the dystopian tradition is the most important strand in the tapestry of modern sf. A relevant theme anthology is *Bad Moon Rising* (anth **1973**) ed Thomas M. Disch.   [BS]
See also: DISASTER; MEDIA LANDSCAPE; OPTIMISM AND PESSIMISM; SOCIOLOGY.

EARNSHAW, BRIAN (1929-   ) UK author of the fine chase thriller *And Mistress Pursuing* (**1966**) and a complex sf thriller, *Planet in the Eye of Time* (**1968**), which encompasses, via TIME TRAVEL, the period of the crucifixion (◊ MESSIAHS; RELIGION) and addresses the problems of a dying Galaxy. His later work within the genre has all been for children. The **Dragonfall** series includes *Dragonfall Five and the Space Cowboys* (**1972**), *Dragonfall Five and the Royal Beast* (**1972**), *Dragonfall Five and the Empty Planet* (**1973**), *Dragonfall Five and the Hijackers* (**1974**), *Dragonfall Five and the Master Mind* (**1975**), *Dragonfall Five and the Super Horse* (**1977**) and *Dragonfall Five and the Haunted World* (**1979**). The **Star Jam Pack** series, featuring an interstellar rock group, includes *Starclipper and the Song Wars* (**1985**), *Starclipper and the Snowstone* (**1986**) and *Starclipper and the Galactic Final* (**1987**). [JC]

Other works: *The Rock Dog Gang* (**1987**); *Planet of the Jumping Beans* (**1990** chap).

EARTH DEFENSE FORCE ◊ CHIKYU BOEIGUN.

EARTH DIES SCREAMING, THE Film (1964). Lippert/Planet. Dir Terence Fisher, starring Willard Parker, Virginia Field, Dennis Price. Screenplay Henry Cross, from a story by Harry Spalding. 62 mins. B/w.

This is the first of three sf films that Terence Fisher (best known for his Hammer Horror films) made during the 1960s; the others were ISLAND OF TERROR (1966) and NIGHT OF THE BIG HEAT (1967). The UK has been invaded by alien-controlled robots. Survivors are besieged by corpses animated by the robots, so that the film is an inferior forerunner to NIGHT OF THE LIVING DEAD (1968). Like the other films in the series, all similar in theme, *TEDS* is handicapped by a clumsy script, a tiny budget and a director uninterested in sf. [JB]

EARTH GIRLS ARE EASY Film (1988). De Laurentiis/Kestrel. Dir Julien Temple, starring Geena Davis, Jeff Goldblum, Jim Carrey, Damon Wayans, Julie Brown. Screenplay Brown, Charlie Coffey, Terrence E. McNally. 100 mins. Colour.

Three fur-covered humanoid aliens crash their spaceship in a swimming pool in the San Fernando Valley, Los Angeles. They meet a Valley girl (Davis), who arranges for them to be shaved and trendily dressed. They learn about local customs. This very light comedy with songs (good words, so-so tunes) was made by a UK director who downplayed the alienness of the aliens (they are good at dancing, piano playing and sex) in favour of the alienness of the San Fernando Valley, photographed in lurid primary colours and observed with all the astonished voyeurism of some tyro anthropologist confronted by pygmy headhunters. *EGAE* is slight, but much funnier than MY STEPMOTHER IS AN ALIEN (1988), on a very similar theme. [PN]

See also: CINEMA.

EARTHQUAKE Film (1974). Universal. Dir Mark Robson, starring Charlton Heston, Ava Gardner, George Kennedy, Lorne Greene, Genevieve Bujold. Screenplay George Fox, Mario Puzo. 123 mins. Colour.

We include this as a representative member of a class of marginally sf films, DISASTER movies, which normally deal with events that, while they have not yet happened, plausibly might in the NEAR FUTURE. In practice the feeling of most disaster films is not sciencefictional, their point being to generate an emotional thrill through the disaster itself rather than to investigate causes and effects. This example, commercially very successful, shows the destruction of Los Angeles by a major earthquake, and as usual focuses on a small group who struggle to survive. Technically the film is adroit, though the human relationships are stilted and stereotyped. It is a showcase for some of Hollywood's best special-effects men, many of whom were persuaded to come out of retirement to work on it; one of them, Clifford Stine, had created the effects in Universal's series of sf/horror films in the 1950s, including *The* INCREDIBLE SHRINKING MAN (1957). The film's gimmick was the introduction of "Sensurround", a system intended to disturb audiences with low-frequency vibrations generated by powerful electro-acoustic horns placed at the front and rear of the theatre. [JB]

EARTH VS. THE FLYING SAUCERS (vt *Invasion of the Flying Saucers*) Film (1956). Clover/Columbia. Prod Charles H. Schneer. Dir Fred F. Sears, starring Hugh Marlowe, Joan Taylor. Screenplay George Worthing Yates, Raymond T. Marcus, based on a story by Curt SIODMAK. 83 mins. B/w.

This film was suggested by *Flying Saucers from Outer Space* (**1953**) by Donald E. Keyhoe (1897-1988), and was made to cash in on the UFO mania of the period. After a simple misunderstanding, there are spectacular scenes of destruction as aliens in saucers attempt to defeat Earth using ray-guns. The militaristic story is ill written and badly paced. Though done on a small budget, Ray HARRYHAUSEN's elegant special effects – the only reason for watching the film – are impressive, particularly in the climactic battle sequence, when flying saucers drop out of the sky and crash into famous Washington landmarks. [JB]

EASTERLEY, ROBERT ◊ Robert POTTER.

EAST GERMANY ◊ GERMANY.

EASTON, EDWARD Pseudonym of US writer Edward P. Malerich (1940-), author of *The Miscast Gentleman* (**1978**), a mildly intriguing TIME-TRAVEL tale, and *The Pirate of Hitchfield* (**1978**). [JC]

EASTON, M(ALCOLM) COLEMAN (1942-) US writer who is also employed in computer science and engineering research. He began publishing sf with "Superflare" as Coleman Brax for *FSF* in 1980, using that pseudonym for some further magazine stories; in collaboration with Clare BELL, with whom he lives, some titles are projected under a joint pseudonym, Clare Coleman. His early novels – like the sequence comprising *Masters of Glass* (**1985**) and *The Fisherman's Curse* (**1987**) – are fantasy. *Swimmers Beneath the Night* (**1987**), set on a water-covered planet and critical of the science which has populated it with bioengineered settlers, is sf. With *Spirits of Cavern and Hearth* (**1988**) he reverted to fantasy and to his favourite venue, a world vibrant with spirits. [JC]

EASTON, THOMAS A(TWOOD) (1944-) US critic, writer and biology teacher (he holds a PhD in theoretical biology) who is best known for the **Reference Library** book-review column he has written for *ASF* since 1979, where he covers a wide range of titles with strict fairness, though not often granted the room to delve deep. His first story was "Next" for *Adam* in 1974, and he has since published at least 50 tales in magazines, sometimes as Sam Atwood. His sf novels *Sparrowhawk* (**1990**), *Greenhouse* (**1991**) and *Woodsman* (**1992**) are all set in a world rather mechanically dominated by a biological revolution, with genimals – genetically engineered animals – replacing cars and indeed almost anything imaginable. Reversals of this sort are generally effected for purposes of SATIRE, but it is clear that for TAE the perils and pleasures of the invention have been

sufficient. [JC]

EATON COLLECTION ◊ J. LLOYD EATON COLLECTION.

EBIRAH, HORROR OF THE DEEP ◊ GOJIRA.

EC COMICS Company founded in 1945 by M.C. Gaines (1896-1947), creator of the format of the modern COMIC book and original partner in DC COMICS. The initials stood for both Educational and Entertaining Comics. After Gaines's death the company passed to his son, William M. Gaines (1922-1992), who revamped the line to his own taste. Educational Comics was wound down and Entertaining Comics was transformed into a line of anthology titles that included two sf comic books – *Weird Science* and *Weird Fantasy* – which were the poorest sellers, but which survived because of his personal support. Various artists drew the sf stories, which ranged from the clichéd and absurd to the surprisingly good; most were written by editor Albert B. Feldstein, though some were by Otto Binder (◊ Eando BINDER). Feldstein also "borrowed" stories from authors such as Anthony BOUCHER, Ray BRADBURY, Fredric BROWN, John COLLIER and Richard MATHESON. In 1952 Bradbury noted the unauthorized adaptations but, enjoying them, simply wrote and requested payment, which Gaines forwarded. This led to official adaptations of Bradbury stories.

In 1954 increasing concern about juvenile delinquency and the "harmful influence" of comic books led to the two sf titles combining as *Weird Science-Fantasy*. Such minor measures failed to stem the flow of criticism, and EC abandoned its entire comic-book line in 1955 to concentrate on *MAD Magazine*.

EC influenced various creators, including the underground comics artists of the 1960s and several writers, notably Stephen KING, but the main influence was from EC's horror titles, not their sf titles. A number of collections of EC material have appeared, including two collections of Bradbury adaptations by Albert B. Feldstein: *The Autumn People* (coll **1965**), horror, and *Tomorrow Midnight* (coll **1966**), sf.

Russ Cochran's **The Complete EC Library** reprints the entire run in large hardcovers, and Gladstone Comics are reissuing most of the titles as monthly reprints. [ZB/BF]

ECKERT, ALLAN W(ESLEY) (1931-) US writer, mainly of works of natural history, for which he has five times been nominated for the Pulitzer Prize. His sf novel, *The HAB Theory* (**1976**), is based on the neo-Velikovskian idea of poleshift (◊ PSEUDO-SCIENCE; Immanuel VELIKOVSKY): lay theoreticians realize that the Earth is about to flip over on its axis with the obvious catastrophic consequences, but of course the ivory-tower bastions of Orthodox Science refuse to listen. The HOLOCAUST duly afflicts an underprepared humanity. The **Mesmerian Annals** – *The Dark Green Tunnel* (**1984**) and *The Wand* (**1986**) – are juvenile fantasies. [JC/JGr]

ECO, UMBERTO (1932-) Italian academic and writer, famed for his work in history, philosophy, literary criticism and semiotics. While his novels are not explicitly sf, he shares with much of the best of the genre a central concern with both the nature of ideas and the moral significance of the methods by which we determine what is true. *Il Nome della Rosa* (**1980**; trans William Weaver as *The Name of the Rose* **1983** US/UK) is a medieval detective story (and a story about detection), an exploration of the detective's empirical approach to the world and the importance of humour, set against the fanatical certainties of medieval Christianity. *Il Pendolo di Foucault* (**1988**; trans William Weaver as *Foucault's Pendulum* **1989** US) tells the story of a group of Italian intellectuals who, appalled by the stupidity of the books on mysticism and occult history that they publish for a living, decide to construct their own conspiracy theory of history, and discover that the human PERCEPTION of reality is more subtle than they had anticipated (◊ FABULATION). UE's fiction is remarkably inventive, sophisticated and humorous, expressive of a profound love for life over sterile abstraction. [NT/PhR]

Other works: *Travels in Hyperreality* (coll trans William Weaver *et al* **1987** US), journalism and essays.

See also: ITALY.

ECOLOGY Ecology is the study of organisms in relation to their environment. It is a relatively new discipline, the first notable work on the subject being *Animal Ecology* (**1927**) by Charles Elton (1900-1990). The complexity of the environmental relationships which determine the success, or even the survival, of populations has been realized only within the last half-century. The same period has seen a dramatic increase in the world's population and the virtual destruction of the natural environment in many populous areas, and such issues as the protection of food chains and increasing the efficiency of ecological systems have become extremely important.

As is to be expected with respect to a scientific discipline no older than GENRE SF, there are very few early stories with ecological themes. W.H. HUDSON's fantasies of a mode of human life harmonized with Nature – particularly *A Crystal Age* (**1887**) – can be seen, with hindsight, as related to the theme, but their inspiration was mystical rather than scientific. An early story on an ecological theme is J.D. BERESFORD's "The Man who Hated Flies" (1929), a parable about a perfect insecticide which precipitates an ecocatastrophe by obliterating the pollinators of many plant species. Early sf writers were often oblivious to the simplest matters of ecology in their pictures of LIFE ON OTHER WORLDS, providing abundant carnivorous species without the herbivore populations required to sustain them; Edgar Rice BURROUGHS's image of Mars is a cardinal example. The only early PULP-MAGAZINE writer whose work showed anything more than a rudimentary consciousness of the subject was Stanley G. WEINBAUM. After WWII, however, writers began to use a good deal more ingenuity in their representations of ALIEN ecology, and produced numerous puzzle stories in which explorers on other worlds have to figure out peculiar

relationships in the local fauna and flora. Examples are William TENN's "The Ionian Cycle" (1948), several stories by Clifford D. SIMAK – notably "You'll Never Go Home Again" (1951; vt "Beachhead") and "Drop Dead" (1956) – James H. SCHMITZ's "Grandpa" (1955), Brian W. ALDISS's **PEST** (Planetary Ecological Survey Team) series (1958-62) and a series by Jack SHARKEY begun with "Arcturus Times Three" (1961). More sophisticated examples are Richard MCKENNA's "Hunter Come Home" (1963), Neal BARRETT's *Highwood* (**1972**) and John BOYD's *The Pollinators of Eden* (**1969**). Jack VANCE's "Winner Loses All" (1951) is an interesting oddity with no human characters. Michael G. CONEY has deployed ecological puzzles in a number of novels, including *Syzygy* (**1973**) and *Hello Summer, Goodbye* (**1975**; vt *Rex*).

Inevitably, the COLONIZATION OF OTHER WORLDS has come to be seen more and more in ecological terms. Ecological planning is necessarily of central concern in stories dealing with TERRAFORMING. Thus an elementary strategy of ecological control is the key to the invasion of the land areas of VENUS in *Fury* (**1950**; vt *Destination Infinity*) by Henry KUTTNER, and in many novels about the colonization of MARS – e.g., Kim Stanley ROBINSON's *Red Mars* (**1992** UK). The great majority of ecological-problem stories involving colonization derive their problems through slight distortion of ecological systems on Earth, or through simple analogy. Relatively few authors have been willing to take on the job of attempting to construct an alien ecology in some detail, although Johannes KEPLER made some interesting observations about the ways in which life might adapt to a lunar habitat in his *Somnium* (**1634**). Notable modern examples include numerous stories by Hal CLEMENT, including *Cycle of Fire* (**1957**) and *Close to Critical* (1958; **1964**), Brian W. Aldiss's *The Long Afternoon of Earth* (fixup **1962** US; exp vt *Hothouse* UK), Poul ANDERSON's *Fire Time* (**1974**), Alan Dean FOSTER's *Midworld* (**1975**), Gordon R. DICKSON's *Masters of Everon* (**1979**), Aldiss's **Heliconia** trilogy (**1982-5**), Donald KINGSBURY's *Courtship Rite* (**1982**), Larry NIVEN's *The Integral Trees* (**1983**) and its sequel *The Smoke Ring* (**1987**), Paul J. MCAULEY's *Four Hundred Billion Stars* (**1988**) and Sheri S. TEPPER's *Grass* (**1989**).

The precariousness of the human ecological situation has gradually but inevitably become one of the major themes of sf. The possibility of a worldwide DISASTER caused by soil-exhaustion is explored in A.G. Street's *Already Walks Tomorrow* (**1938**) and Edward S. HYAMS's *The Astrologer* (**1950**), both of which point out that ecological planning will be made difficult by the tendency of politicians to think about only the short term. Significant cautionary tales about ecological catastrophes include Ward MOORE's *Greener than You Think* (**1947**), in which a species of grass outcompetes all other plant life, and John CHRISTOPHER's *The Death of Grass* (**1956**; vt *No Blade of Grass*), in which a blight affecting grass species destroys most of the world's crops. Early magazine sf stories which focus on mankind's future ecological problems include Damon KNIGHT's "Natural State" (1954; vt *Masters of Evolution* **1959**) and C.M. KORNBLUTH's "Shark Ship" (1958).

Ecocatastrophe stories picked up considerable impetus in the 1960s from a number of nonfictional warnings that things could only get worse as a result of OVERPOPULATION and POLLUTION. The alarmist Paul Ehrlich (1932-   ), author of *The Population Bomb* (**1968**), used a quasidocumentary fictional framework for a brief summary of his predictions in "Ecocatastrophe" (1969). The greenhouse effect was later added to the list, followed by the decay of the ozone layer, leading to such extreme ecocatastrophe stories as *Ecodeath* (**1972**) by William Jon WATKINS and E.V. (Gene) SNYDER, *The Nitrogen Fix* (**1980**) by Hal Clement and *Nature's End* (**1986**) by Whitley STRIEBER and James Kunetka, and such all-inclusive ones as David BRIN's *Earth* (**1990**). Many ecocatastrophe stories are notable for their bitter irony – most sf writers who use the theme seem to feel that we will get no more than we deserve if we destroy our environment and poison ourselves – but even writers who are neither angry nor despairing tend to accept that an ongoing ecological crisis will be one of the most obvious features of the NEAR FUTURE.

Intensification of ecological awareness helped to lend a new subtlety and sophistication to the disaster story, which spawned a new subspecies dealing with the delicate aesthetics of corrosive changes in mankind's physiological and psychological relationship with the environment. Gerald HEARD's "The Great Fog" (1944) is an early example; others are *The Year of the Cloud* (**1970**) by Theodore L. THOMAS and Kate WILHELM, George Alec EFFINGER's "And Us, Too, I Guess" (1973) and George TURNER's *The Sea and Summer* (**1987**; vt *Drowning Towers*). The most detailed exploration of such possibilities has been carried out by J.G. BALLARD in such novels as *The Wind from Nowhere* (**1962**), *The Drowned World* (**1962**), *The Burning World* (**1964**; vt *The Drought*) and *The Crystal World* (**1966**).

Stories concerned with the ecology of alien worlds have recently tended to take on a strong element of mysticism. In the real world the word "ecology" has acquired quasicharismatic status, encouraged by vulgarizations of the "Gaia hypothesis" enunciated by James Lovelock (1919-   ); this points out that the ecosphere has certain built-in homeostatic mechanisms and that evolving earthly life created the atmospheric environment in which it now exists. For many people "ecology" has come to symbolize a lost sense of harmony with the world at large, and various commune movements have tried to make ecological awareness an antidote to alienation. The word "symbiosis" (◊ PARASITISM AND SYMBIOSIS) is often invoked in this context. In sf, ecological mysticism is very obvious in such parables as Robert F. YOUNG's *The Last Yggdrasil* (1959 as "To Fell a Tree"; exp **1982**), such evocations of the Eden myth as Mark

CLIFTON's *Eight Keys to Eden* (**1960**) and such curious biological allegories as Jacqueline LICHTENBERG's *Dushau* (**1985**) and its sequels. It is central to the mystical ritualization of water relations featured in Robert A. HEINLEIN's *Stranger in a Strange Land* (**1961**) and Frank HERBERT's *Dune* (**1965**). In Piers ANTHONY's *Omnivore* (**1968**) ecological relationships themselves are transformed into a mystical pattern. This mysticism is evident also in many stories set on Earth, including Frank Herbert's *The Green Brain* (**1966**), Hilbert SCHENCK's *At the Eye of the Ocean* (**1980**), Norman SPINRAD's *Songs from the Stars* (**1980**), Somtow Sucharitkul's (◊ S.P. SOMTOW) *Starship and Haiku* (**1984**) and Scott Russell SANDERS's *Terrarium* (**1985**).

Two anthologies featuring ecocatastrophe stories are *Saving Worlds* (anth **1973**; vt *The Wounded Planet*) ed Roger ELWOOD and Virginia KIDD, and *The Ruins of Earth* (anth **1971**) ed Thomas M. DISCH.   [BS]

ECONOMICS The word "economics" derives from a Greek word signifying the art of household management. Its modern usage has been extended by analogy to pertain to the management of the industry and finances of nations. Medieval economic "theory" was dominated by ethical considerations, and evaluative judgments still remain entangled with the science; economics thus has the capacity to arouse powerful passions in spite of its frequent designation as "the dismal science". This is very evident in fiction dealing with economic systems. Thomas MORE's *Utopia* (**1516**; trans **1551**) is largely a treatise on economic matters, and much subsequent UTOPIAN literature has been concerned with economic theory's relationships with political power and social justice.

The idea that economics should attempt to shed its ethical entanglements and be reformulated in terms of "natural laws" was popularized by "The Grumbling Hive", the poem which formed the headpiece of *The Fable of the Bees, or Private Vices, Publick Benefits* (**1714**) by Bernard de Mandeville (1670-1733). The poem and the tract advanced the thesis that, if the market were allowed to find its own equilibrium while individuals attempted to maximize their profits in open competition (no matter how greedily), the community as a whole would benefit. This notion was later taken up by Adam Smith (1723-1790) in *The Wealth of Nations* (**1776**). In the 19th century the rise of various socialist movements, latterly armed with their own Marxist theory of economics, brought a good deal of ideological conflict into economic thought at both academic and popular levels. This conflict is very evident in a great deal of 19th-century utopian fiction. *Voyage en Icarie* (**1840**) by Étienne Cabet (1788-1856) and *The Happy Colony* (**1856**) by Robert Pemberton were among the earliest socialist utopias, although their arguments are moral rather than scientific. Theodore HERTZKA's *Freiland* (**1890**; trans **1891**) and its sequel were among several novels exploring the pros and cons of a mixed economy, but there are relatively few 19th-century *laissez-faire* utopias. By the end of the century the argument was becoming confused by the interest which utopian novelists were taking in AUTOMATION and TECHNO-LOGY, but economic egalitarianism remained a central issue in such technological utopias as Edward BEL-LAMY's *Looking Backward, 2000-1887* (**1888**) and the many ideological replies produced in its wake. Like many other US socialists, Bellamy took more inspiration from Henry George (1839-1897) – author of *Progress and Poverty* (**1879**) – than from Marx. (George's influence is also very strong in the works of M.P. SHIEL, and his ideas can still be found echoing in the writings of Barrington J. BAYLEY.) Despite Marx's 20th-century status as a figurehead there are surprisingly few outrightly Marxian utopias; the best example is *Sur la pierre blanche* (**1905**; trans as *The White Stone* **1910**) by Anatole FRANCE.

Relatively few 20th-century utopias give more priority to economic considerations than to political or technological issues; notable exceptions are Robert ARDREY's *World's Beginning* (**1944**) and Henry HAZLITT's *The Great Idea* (**1951**; vt *Time Will Run Back*). The longest and most extravagant economic tract cast as fiction this century is Ayn RAND's *Atlas Shrugged* (**1957**), a pioneering work of Libertarian apologetics in which the world's capitalists go on strike in protest against the forces of creeping socialism (◊ LIBERTA-RIANISM). Marxist economic theory is more prominen-tly featured in DYSTOPIAS like Jack LONDON's *The Iron Heel* (**1907**) and in SATIRES like Upton SINCLAIR's *The Millennium* (**1924**). Sharper and more flamboyant economic satire can be found in Archibald MARSHALL's *Upsidonia* (**1915**), about a world where the profit motive operates in reverse, and in Leon STOVER's *The Shaving of Karl Marx* (**1982**), which slyly suggests that the policies which Lenin instituted after the Russian Revolution have far more in common with the ideas of H.G. WELLS than with those of Marx.

The early PULP-MAGAZINE sf writers were not much concerned with economics, tending to take the historical continuity of the American Dream for granted, although Fred MacISAAC's "World Brigands" (1928) is an interesting story from the nonspecialist pulps in which the burden of WAR debt leads to a war between the USA and its former allies. When John W. CAMPBELL Jr took over ASTOUNDING SCIENCE-FICTION, economic issues were returned to the sf agenda. They were taken up by Robert A. HEINLEIN, whose "The Roads Must Roll" (1940) is about a strike called by "Functionalists" – proponents of the theory that the greatest economic rewards should go to the people with the most vital jobs. Heinlein's "Let There be Light . . ." (1940 as by Lyle Monroe) includes cynical asides about the suppression of innovations by power groups who have a heavy investment in existing technologies – a notion whose variants include items of modern folklore as well as the themes of stories; "Logic of Empire" (1941) has some similarly cynical comments on the economics of slavery; and "The Man who Sold the Moon" (1950) concerns the struggle to finance the first Moon

voyage. Heinlein's economic theorizing was compre-hensively updated in *The Moon is a Harsh Mistress* (**1966**), which helped to popularize the acronym tanstaafl ("there ain't no such thing as a free lunch"); his uncompromising Libertarianism – which has echoes of SOCIAL DARWINISM – set an important example within the genre, instituting a tradition vigorously carried forward by Poul ANDERSON, Jerry POURNELLE, G.C. EDMONDSON and L. Neil SMITH, among others, and led to the founding of the Prometheus AWARD.

Other pulp stories in which the emphasis on economic considerations is central include "The Iron Standard" (1943) by Lewis Padgett (Henry KUTTNER and C.L. MOORE), in which Earthmen force reluctant aliens to help them by disrupting their economy and threatening the power structure of a static society, and "The Helping Hand" (1950) by Poul Anderson, a neat parable about the economics of "foreign aid". Economic issues are also to the fore in Anderson's series about interstellar trader Nicholas van Rijn and his associates, notably "Margin of Profit" (1956) and the novelettes collected as *Trader to the Stars* (coll **1964**). Oddly enough, the other writer of the 1950s strongly associated with Campbell who showed a very strong interest in economics was Mack REYNOLDS, whose parents were devout socialists and whose ideas were strongly influenced by the three-times socialist candidate for the US Presidency Eugene Debs (1855-1926). Reynolds's efforts range from the wry "Subversive" (1962), the satirical *Tomor-row Might Be Different* (1960 as "Russkies, Go Home!"; exp **1975**) and the melodramatic "Ultima Thule" (1961; in fixup *Planetary Agent X* **1965**) to the fascinat-ing thought-experiment described in *The Rival Rige-lians* (1961 as "Adaptation"; exp **1967**), in which visiting Earthmen divide an alien world's nations in order to compare the power of free enterprise and Marxist planning as forces of social evolution. Reynolds went on to write a series of utopian novels cast in a Bellamyesque mould, beginning with *Looking Backward, from the Year 2000* (**1973**) and *Equality in the Year 2000* (**1977**).

A rather different approach to economic issues was manifest in the magazine GALAXY SCIENCE FICTION, where the emphasis was on satirical irony. The author who best embodied the outlook of the magazine – and who eventually became its editor – was Frederik POHL, whose economic fantasies stand in sharp contrast to those of Heinlein, Anderson and Reynolds. In his collaboration with C.M. KORNBLUTH, *The Space Merchants* (**1953**), the economy of the USA has been driven to extremes of conspicuous con-sumption in order to maintain economic growth, and the advertising industry has become the linchpin of government. In "The Midas Plague" (1954) the situation is further exaggerated, every citizen having a burdensome consumption quota as the nation strives to cope with the abundance of machine-produced goods. In "The Tunnel under the World"

(1955) an artificial world exists only to test advertising pitches. In another collaboration with Kornbluth, *Gladiator-at-Law* (**1955**), the stock market is supreme, manipulated by corporations run by reclusive super-geriatrics. A further notable *Gal* satire is "Cost of Living" (1952) by Robert SHECKLEY, in which the middle class can maintain its standard of living only by mortgaging the future income of its children. Satirical economic fantasies are seen also in the work of Damon KNIGHT, whose *Hell's Pavement* (fixup **1955**; vt *Analogue Men*) features consumption quotas in a future USA ruled by commercial interests, and whose *The People Maker* (1957 as "A for Anything"; exp **1959**; rev vt *A for Anything* 1961 UK) explores the socio-economic consequences of the invention of a matter-duplicator. The latter makes an interesting contrast with two other stories on the same theme: George O. SMITH's "Pandora's Millions" (1945), in which civilization collapses as a result, and Ralph Williams' "Business As Usual, During Alterations" (1958), in which it doesn't. The manipulation of consumers in pursuit of economic stability is investigated also in more impressionistic stories, including Rosel George BROWN's "Signs of the Times" (1959) and J.G. BALLARD's "The Subliminal Man" (1963).

Although the satirical tradition has been carried forward by such novels as Pohl's solo sequel to *The Space Merchants*, *The Merchants' War* (**1984**), the dominant species of economic speculation in contemporary US sf is Libertarian polemic, as seen in such novels as G.C. Edmondson's *The Man who Corrupted Earth* (**1980**) and Ben BOVA's *Privateers* (**1985**), both of which imagine entrepreneurs boldly taking charge of the conquest of space after pusillanimous US governments have given up on it. The vulnerability of the modern world to economic catastrophe is a minor theme in several sf novels, including *The Visitors* (**1980**) by Clifford D. SIMAK, in which generous aliens do the damage, and *Wolf and Iron* (**1990**) by Gordon R. DICKSON, in which we have done it to ourselves. Stories of ecocatastrophe (◊ ECOLOGY) often include commentaries on the economic problems associated with OVERPOPULATION and "underdevelopment"; *The Sea and Summer* (**1987** vt *Drowning Towers*) by George TURNER is a notable example. The evolving economic problems of the Third World have also been brought into sharp focus by Bruce STERLING in "Green Days in Brunei" (1985) and *Islands in the Net* (**1988**). Now that communism seems on the wane, Libertarian polemics will presumably become less strident and alarmist, and the problems involved in the economic rescue of formerly communist nations may begin to attract as much attention from those writers seriously interested in the NEAR FUTURE as the problems of Third World poverty.

A relevant anthology is *Tomorrow, Inc.: SF Stories about Big Business* (anth **1976**) ed Martin Harry GREENBERG and Joseph D. OLANDER.   [BS]

See also: MONEY; POLITICS; SOCIOLOGY.

ECUADOR ◊ LATIN AMERICA.

EDDISON, E(RIC) R(UCKER) (1882-1945) UK civil servant, writer and scholar of Old Norse. His first work of fiction and most considerable single work, *The Worm Ouroboros* (**1922**), is an erudite HEROIC FANTASY written in archaic English; the initial protagonist, Lessingham, is transported from Earth to a fantasy MERCURY, where it will be his function to observe mighty conflicts, heraldic battles and quests, and magical turns of plot, all destined to recur forever, as the title implies. The **Zimiamvian** trilogy, whose internal chronology reverses that of publication, is made up of *The Mezentian Gate* (**1958**), posthumously assembled, *A Fish Dinner in Memison* (**1941** US) and *Mistress of Mistresses: A Vision of Zimiamvia* (**1935**). Beyond the presence of Lessingham, who has become (like all the cast) an avatar of the divine, the sequence's main connection with *The Worm Ouroboros* is that it is set in the (Platonic) heaven of the earlier novel. The tales are discursive, metaphysical, learned, linguistically adventurous and engrossing. ERE's influence on the sf genre, as with writers like Lord DUNSANY and J.R.R. TOLKIEN, lies mainly in the powerful example of his language and the sustained "otherness" of his creation.   [JC]

Other works: *Styrbiorn the Strong* (**1926**); *Egil's Saga: Done into English Out of the Icelandic with an Introduction, Notes, and an Essay on Some Principles of Translation* (trans 1930).

About the author: "Superman in a Bowler: E.R. Eddison" in *Literary Swordsmen and Sorcerers: The Makers of Heroic Fantasy* (**1976**) by L. Sprague DE CAMP; "The *Zimiamvian* Trilogy" by Brian Attebery in *Survey of Modern Fantasy Literature* (anth **1983**) ed Frank Magill.

See also: FANTASY; PLANETARY ROMANCE; SWORD AND SORCERY.

EDISONADE Daedalus was the first inventor hero. But he was also a bureaucrat, building his labyrinth as a king's wage-slave or sharecropper, and for that reason this entry, which is about a US dream of freelance heroism, cannot be spent defining the "daedalusade". As used here the term "edisonade" – derived from Thomas Alva Edison (1847-1931) in the same way that "ROBINSONADE" is derived from Robinson Crusoe – can be understood to describe any story which features a young US male inventor hero who uses his ingenuity to extricate himself from tight spots and who, by so doing, saves himself from defeat and corruption and his friends and nation from foreign oppressors. The invention by which he typically accomplishes this feat is not, however, simply a WEAPON, though it will almost certainly prove to be invincible against the foe and may also make the hero's fortune; it is also a means of TRANSPORTATION – for the edisonade is not only about saving the country (or planet) through personal spunk and native wit, it is also about lighting out for the Territory. Once the hero reaches that virgin Territory, he will find yet a further use for his invention: it will serve as a certificate of ownership.

Magically, the barefoot boy with cheek of tan will discover that he has been made CEO of a compliant world; for a single, revelatory maxim can be discerned fueling the motor heart of the edisonade: the conviction that to tinker with is to own.

Daedalus could never, therefore, have starred in an edisonade. Could Thomas Alva Edison himself have done so? Why should we head this entry with his name, rather than that of Nikola Tesla (1856-1943), who inspired Weldon COBB's *To Mars with Tesla* (**1901**), or Hiram Maxim (1840-1916), who inspired George GRIFFITH's *The Outlaws of the Air* (**1895**)? It certainly might be claimed that Edison was no more inventive than either of these figures; and he certainly worked for hire. Edison's life and career, when examined, hardly add up to an appropriate model for E.E. "Doc" SMITH's Richard Seaton, the inventor-hero of the **Skylark** series, who seems almost definitively to embody the dream we are attempting to describe. In his early years, true enough, Edison was a practical professional, a tinkerer of genius, and the inventor (or inspired improver) of a wide range of implements, most of them electrical, from the phonograph to the lightbulb. But, beginning in the 1880s, he transformed himself into an advertiser of genius whose main subject was himself, and from this point the mythopoeic power of the Edison name outstripped that of his rivals, no mean publicists themselves. For nearly half a century, the senatorial Sage of Menlo Park waxed ever greater in the public imagination, writing articles, making speeches, chairing commissions, granting oracular interviews whose subject was, very frequently, weapons he claimed to be about to unveil which would make the USA utterly invincible and war impossible. From 1890 he claimed more than once – or those whom he may have hired to ghost some of his articles claimed – that he had invented devices of war which did not, in fact, exist outside his imagination, or which had been created by others (perhaps his employees). It may be of interest to note that the language in which these claims were made bore a strong resemblance to the urgent telegraphese Mark TWAIN fell into whenever he was expounding a technical notion; much of *A Connecticut Yankee at King Arthur's Court* (**1889**) is so couched, and the resemblance between the Boss protagonist of that novel and the self-image of Edison expressed in his writings is most striking. In his later years Edison was, in short, something of a fraud; he may have served as a model when L. Frank BAUM was creating the Wizard of Oz. But this, one might argue, could be precisely the point. It might be relevant to note that not only are edisonades dreams which come true for the protagonist but they also embody the shaping fantasies of that protagonist, who is not in the end as innocent as he seems. Like Edison himself, the hero of the edisonade is at some level, conscious or unconscious, an impostor or confidence-man.

The first proto-edisonade was probably the first dime novel (◊ DIME-NOVEL SF) to feature a boy inventor, Edward S. ELLIS's *The Steam Man of the Prairies* (**1868**), and the first edisonade proper was the **Tom Edison, Jr.** sequence of dime novels (**1891-2**) by Philip READE. Young orphan Tom (ostensibly unrelated to Thomas Alva) responds to the challenge of his enemies by inventing a succession of ever more impressive devices, most of which double as weapons and forms of self-propelling transport. In these and other similar tales, the presence of the US frontier as a barrier to be penetrated is nearly always evident, though sometimes only subliminally; and the topological similarity between penetrating a frontier and penetrating knowledge through CONCEPTUAL BREAKTHROUGH is nowhere more clearly expressed than in the boys' edisonades written at a time when the USA's literal frontiers were only just snapping shut.

Oddly enough, however, the first adult novel to make use of Edison was not by a US author at all. VILLIERS DE L'ISLE-ADAM's *L'Ève future* (**1886**; trans as *The Eve of the Future* **1981** US; new trans as *Tomorrow's Eve* **1982** US) introduces a character, Thomas Alva Edison, who rescues a handsome young lord from despair at his fiancée's crassness by providing an impeccable ANDROID duplicate. It may be that Edison the "electrician" was given so significant a role in this tale because electricity itself had an almost occult significance for late 19th-century romantics like Villiers, who in a sense created a decadent version of the edisonade before any adult edisonades had in fact been written. The first adult US example did not, in fact, appear for over a decade. It was not until the newspaper publication of Garrett P. SERVISS's *Edison's Conquest of Mars* (1898 *The New York Journal*; **1947**), a tale of quite extraordinary thematic clarity, that the native edisonade took on its mature shape – in complete ignorance of Villiers' oblique use of the fabulous inventor. Written as a direct – and consciously US – response to the defeatist implications of H.G. WELLS's *The War of the Worlds* (**1898**), the tale depicts Edison himself inventing weapons of great power in an unfettered and spunky response to the continuing threat from the external enemies. Armed with a disintegrating weapon and ANTIGRAVITY, and accompanied by most of the world's best SCIENTISTS, Thomas Alva heads to Mars, where he commits triumphant genocide before granting the survivors colonial status. It should be noted that Edison's inventions and his conquest of Mars are both consequences of the actions of others: he and the USA he represents are innocents; they are *forced* to respond to a wicked world with the Trickster effrontery of their native genius; and afterwards they are *forced* to become owners of what their genius has conquered.

Between Serviss and E.E. Smith, many edisonades repeated the basic story in plots which often represented a US version of the European future-WAR novel. Three can stand as examples. In J.S. BARNEY's *L.P.M.: The End of the Great War* (**1915**) a US scientist called Edestone invents enough weapons to defeat the corrupt and aggressive nations of Europe, and to establish a world government; in J.U. GIESY's *All for His Country* (**1915**) a young US inventor's gravity-defying airplane is sufficient to defeat Japanese aggressors; and in Cleveland Langston MOFFETT's *The Conquest of America* (**1916**) Edison himself reappears as a repository of anti-socialist US virtue and the creator of an invention sufficient to see off the aggressive Germans. In all cases, the aggression is from without; the weapons are invented by a free spirit who is not on hire to a corrupt government; and in the end the world is passed into the ownership of innocent Americans who had wished only to be left alone to enjoy their virgin paradise.

This basic story has been an essential shaper of US realpolitik for more than a century, and its manifestations are far broader than those encompassed by the relatively simple edisonade, whose precarious concentration on a tangibly implausible model hero seemed to guarantee its early death as a literary form. The 43 **Doctor Hackensaw** stories (1921-5) by Clement FEZANDIE, though amusingly varied in their presentation of the Doctor's scientific feats, seemed more an epilogue than a way forward. But the edisonade was saved by SPACE OPERA. E.E. Smith's **Skylark** sequence gave Edison the Galaxy as playground and estate, provided an infinity of frontiers to penetrate, territories to stumble into and to claim, and entrepreneurial empires to build in all innocence. The Smithian edisonade remains central to entertainment space opera to this day.

It might seem, however, that GENRE SF as a whole outgrew the edisonade by about 1940, when John W. CAMPBELL Jr's GOLDEN AGE OF SF was at its height, and for a few years at least it looked as though hillbilly Tricksters with the Touch had become comic turns whose proper place was in the less serious pages of *Unknown* and in the light-fingered grasp of such writers as L. Sprague DE CAMP. But a glance at the central male role model promulgated by the core authors of the Golden Age might disabuse readers of this assumption, for the Competent Man is Thomas Alva Edison in sheep's clothing, disguised mainly by his genuine proficiency (because writers like Robert A. HEINLEIN were the first sf authors able actually to convey the feel and describe the *process* of Higher Tinkering) and by his ability to explain himself. But, in being able to explain himself, the Competent Man of the 1940s, as created by Heinlein and his followers, soon began to *advocate* his line of thought; as soon as this happened, innocence fled.

For, the moment the frank lad of the primitive edisonade begins to have to justify himself, Huck Finn the Trickster becomes a flim-flam man or, even worse, a prophet. L. Ron HUBBARD's Church of Scientology is in truth the Church of Edison. The overbearing protagonist of Heinlein's later novels is in truth the Sage of Menlo Park after one too many interviews. Only the unexamined edisonade is worth

reading. Once looked at with an eye to the main chance, it turns sour, self-serving and entrepreneurial, and we find ourselves in the land of some HARD-SF writers of the 1980s, whose protagonists are never poor, and never lose, and never give; nor would it perhaps be stretching the term too far to find in the ruthless protagonists of much SURVIVALIST FICTION ghostly and solipsistic echoes of the edisonades of a more innocent time – when the hero did not have to understand the consequences of his triumphs. Much worse than a Thomas Alva Edison who doesn't know the score is a Thomas Alva Edison who does. [JC]

Further reading: *War Stars: The Superweapon and the American Imagination* (**1988**) by H. Bruce FRANKLIN.

EDMONDS, HARRY (MORETON SOUTHEY) (1891-1989) UK writer of several adventure novels and of some NEAR-FUTURE sf novels, beginning with *The North Sea Mystery* (**1930**), which features land-launched torpedoes which threaten to sink the entire Royal Navy. In *The Riddle of the Straits* (**1931**), a WAR story set in 1935, the UK and Japan find themselves pitted against the USSR and the USA; a Channel Tunnel saves the UK from embargo. In *Red Invader* (**1933**), Russia and Germany are once again involved, this time in intrigues against the UK. In *The Professor's Last Experiment* (**1935**; rev vt *The Secret Voyage* 1946) a vast war is halted when the protagonist broadcasts a "radiation" wave which stops all the engines of conflict. After WWII, HE continued in the same vein with *The Clockmaker of Heidelberg* (**1949**), featuring a new form of submarine propulsion, as well as a neo-Nazi germ-warfare plot centred in Brazil. A sequel, *The Rockets (Operation Manhattan)* (**1951**), hints at the violent end of all civilization. [JC]

Other works: *Wind in the East* (**1933**); *The Death Ship, or The Tragedy of the "Valmiera" as Related by Chief Officer James Stanley* (**1933**).

EDMONDS, PAUL [s] ◊ Henry KUTTNER.

EDMONDSON, G.C. Working name of Mexican-born US writer and translator José Mario Garry Ordoñez Edmondson y Cotton (1922-   ) for all his writing except his Westerns, which are as by Kelly P. Gast, J.B. Masterson and Jake Logan. He published his first sf, "Blessed are the Meek", in *ASF* in 1955, and was active in the magazines for the next decade, particularly in *FSF*, where his **Mad Friend** stories appeared. Assembled as *Stranger than You Think* (coll of linked stories **1965** chap dos), they describe the effects their narrator's mad friend manages to elicit from the world about him, and his explanations thereof. GCE's first novel, *The Ship that Sailed the Time Stream* (**1965** dos; rev 1978) and its sequel, *To Sail the Century Sea* (**1981**), are amusingly and graphically told FANTASTIC-VOYAGE tales involving a US ship and its inadvertent TIME TRAVELS. They remain his most successful books.

Chapayeca (**1971**; vt *Blue Face* 1972), set in Mexico, and *T.H.E.M.* (**1974**), are both fluently written but less exhilarating to read. More impressively, *The Aluminum Man* (**1975**) confronts some Native Americans – depicted with great sympathy, as always in GCE's work – with a crash-landed ALIEN looking for fuel. *The Man who Corrupted Earth* (**1980**) fails to carry over the complex cynicism of Mark TWAIN's "The Man that Corrupted Hadleyburg" but is in its own right an amusing presentation of the notion that free enterprise can conquer space when governments falter at the task (◊ ECONOMICS; LIBERTARIANISM). After writing a paranoid singleton, *The Takeover* (**1984**) with C.M. Kotlan, in which Russians briefly conquer the USA through nuclear blackmail, GCE produced, also with Kotlan, a complex sf sequence – *The Cunningham Equations* (**1986**), *The Black Magician* (**1986**) and *Maximum Effort* (**1987**). The entangled thriller conventions dominant in this trilogy feverishly pit genetic transformations of the human species against the dubious intercession of AIs in the long process of growth, amid constant references to Yaqui Indian culture. The mix is perhaps too rich for coherence. In the end, it is his constant engagement with the region and the people of his early years that lifts GCE's work above routine entertainment. [JC]

Other works: #12 in the **Spaceways** sequence: *Star Slaver* (**1982**) as John CLEVE (with Andrew J. OFFUTT).

See also: POLITICS; SPACE FLIGHT.

EDMONDSON, WALLACE [s] ◊ Harlan ELLISON.

EDUCATION ◊ SF IN THE CLASSROOM.

EDWARDS, DAVID (?   -   ) US writer whose *Next Stop Mars!* (**1960**) sends another first space flight to that planet. [JC]

EDWARDS, F.E. [s] ◊ William F. NOLAN.

EDWARDS, GAWAIN ◊ Edward PENDRAY.

EDWARDS, MALCOLM (JOHN) (1949-   ) UK editor and critic, educated at Cambridge, where he graduated in anthropology. Long active in UK sf FANDOM, he edited the BRITISH SCIENCE FICTION ASSOCIATION journal VECTOR 1972-4, worked as sf editor for GOLLANCZ 1976-7, and was administrator of the SCIENCE FICTION FOUNDATION 1978-80 and editor of its journal FOUNDATION: THE REVIEW OF SCIENCE FICTION #13-#19; he was a contributing editor to the first (1979) edition of this encyclopedia. In the early 1980s he returned to Gollancz, whose sf list he improved and where he rose rapidly in influence, becoming Publishing Director. He left Gollancz in 1989 to join Grafton Books, a division of HarperCollins, of which he is now (1992) Publishing Director, Trade Fiction, responsible among other things for the sf/fantasy list. MJE became President of WORLD SF in 1990.

In the late 1970s MJE began work, always in collaboration, on the text of a series of books – mostly picture-books – about sf and fantasy. With Robert P. HOLDSTOCK he produced a series of sf and fantasy coffee-table books with fairly brief texts: *Alien Landscapes* (**1979**), *Tour of the Universe: The Journey of a Lifetime – The Recorded Diaries of Leio Scott and Caroline Luranski* (**1980**), *Magician: The Lost Journals of the Magus Geoffrey Carlyle* (**1982**), *Realms of Fantasy* (**1983**) and *Lost Realms* (**1985**). None of these could be taken very seriously, though the first has interesting artwork.

Another collaborative illustrated book was *Spacecraft in Fact and Fiction* (**1979**) with Harry HARRISON. MJE's most interesting book, a collaboration with Maxim JAKUBOWSKI and this time not a picture-book, is *The Complete Book of Science Fiction and Fantasy Lists* (**1983**; rev vt *The SF Book of Lists* 1983 US), compiled for the trivia buff and often very funny, but also containing – if the reader can cope with the absence of an index – a great deal of solid information about sf not easily found elsewhere. [PN]

See also: BRITISH SCIENCE FICTION AWARD; INTERZONE.

EDWARDS, NORMAN Collaborative pseudonym of Terry CARR and Ted WHITE, used on one minor novel, *Invasion from 2500* (**1964**). [JC]

EDWARDS, PETER (1946-   ) UK writer and civil servant whose sf novel, *Terminus* (**1976**), rather ponderously sets in motion a political conflict in a 22nd-century, post-HOLOCAUST Eurafrica which a sado-masochist secret society is attempting to dominate. The hero's discovery of an ancient city on MARS confuses all issues. [JC]

EFFINGER, GEORGE ALEC (1947-   ) US writer long resident in New Orleans. He entered sf writing via the 1970 CLARION SCIENCE FICTION WRITER'S WORKSHOP, having 3 stories in the workshop's first anthology, *Clarion* (anth **1971**), ed Robin Scott WILSON. His first published story was "The Eight-Thirty to Nine Slot" for *Fantastic* in 1971. Some early work was written as by John K. Diomede or Susan Doenim. Within a very short time GAE established himself as a writer of stylish, surrealistic sf stories, becoming a regular contributor to such series anthologies as ORBIT, NEW DIMENSIONS and UNIVERSE as well as the major magazines; and, despite a steady production of novels, he was for at least a decade most admired for this work, much of which was assembled in *Mixed Feelings* (coll **1974**), *Irrational Numbers* (coll **1976**), *Dirty Tricks* (coll **1978**), *Idle Pleasures* (coll **1983**) and *The Old Funny Stuff* (coll **1989**); "Schrödinger's Kitten" (**1988**), not yet collected, won both HUGO and NEBULA for Best Novelette.

At the same time, *What Entropy Means to Me* (**1972**), GAE's first novel, did gain praise from Theodore STURGEON and Robert SILVERBERG among others, and was nominated for a Nebula. It is an elaborate, multi-layered work, combining elements of SPACE OPERA, family romance and quest fable within a self-referential discourse about the impulses and restraints of creation. *Relatives* (fixup **1973**), less well received, fails to unify its disparate parts, which tell of one man in three PARALLEL WORLDS. *Nightmare Blue* (**1975**) with Gardner DOZOIS and *Those Gentle Voices: A Promethean Romance of the Spaceways* (**1976**) were dithering attempts to disguise a lack of creative impetus through demonstrations of professional skill. For some time, it seemed that he would always remain a better short-story writer than novelist, the knowledgeable, witty master of a sly tone and unlikely subject matter, with a particular interest in various kinds of games (◊ GAMES AND SPORTS), but failing to fulfil his promise. His very considerable capacity to dazzle – and an adroit use of parallel-world conventions, with characters dodging into changed identities with frivolous inevitability – led undoubtedly to a body of work unduly packed with exercises.

"Many of my stories interlock," he once said, "and some day I will figure out a kind of chronology and key to the business." Perhaps fortunately, he has never published anything of the sort, and the wise absurdities (◊ FABULATION) of his best work have never been tampered with. After two moderately successful novels – *Death in Florence* (**1978**; vt *Utopia 3* 1980) and *Heroics* (**1979**) – he began the 1980s with the darkly DYSTOPIAN *The Wolves of Memory* (**1981**), whose surreal *mise-en-scène* effortlessly draws the book's brooding hero into the depths. In the self-referential dance of motif and character of *The Nick of Time* (**1985**) and its sequel, *The Bird of Time* (**1986**), he at last successfully manifested at novel length his long-felt need to present TIME TRAVEL as a form of play. Appalling ill health and other disasters severely afflicted him during these years, but *When Gravity Fails* (**1987**), *A Fire in the Sun* (**1989**) and *The Exile Kiss* (**1991**), the first three books of the **Marîd Audran** sequence, are perhaps his most successful books to date. In these novels, the technological and electronic complexities of the 21st-century Middle East are fully as dazzling as the dervish of alternating realities so dominant in GAE's previous work. In attempting to flourish in this CYBERPUNK hive, the protagonist of the series becomes an Everyman-survivor, an example for those of GAE's readers who expect someday to live there. A career that seemed underachieving has become one of major interest. [JC/DP]

Other works: Novelizations of scripts from the tv series PLANET OF THE APES: *Man the Fugitive* * (**1974**), *Escape to Tomorrow* * (**1975**), *Journey into Terror* * (**1975**) and *Lord of the Apes* * (**1976**); *Felicia* (**1976**) and *Shadow Money* (**1988**), both non-genre; *Look Away* (**1990** chap); *The Zork Chronicles* * (**1990**), humorous novelization of a fantasy game; *The Red Tape War: A Round-Robin Science Fiction Novel* (**1991**) with Jack L. CHALKER and Michael D. RESNICK.

See also: DISASTER; ECOLOGY; ENTROPY; GAME-WORLDS; OMNI; PHYSICS; THEODORE STURGEON MEMORIAL AWARD.

EFREMOV, IVAN ANTONOVICH [r] ◊ Ivan Antonovich YEFREMOV.

EGAN, GREG (1961-   ) Australian writer who began publishing work of genre interest with his first novel, *An Unusual Angle* (**1983**), a fantasy, and whose first short stories were also fantasy. From the mid-1980s, however, he has increasingly concentrated on sharply written sf with an emphasis on BIOLOGY, the best of them – tales like "The Caress" (1990) and "Learning to Be Me" (1990) – raising considerable expectations for his first sf novel, «*Quarantine*» (1992 UK). [JC]

See also: INTERZONE.

EGAN, KEVIN (?   -   ) US writer whose sf novel,

The Perseus Breed (**1988**), features the mysterious disappearance of certain women over a number of years. [JC]

EGBERT, H.M. ◊ Victor ROUSSEAU.

EGLETON, CLIVE (FREDERICK) (1927-   ) UK soldier and writer who began to publish novels with the **Garnett** sequence – *A Piece of Resistance* (**1970**), *Last Post for a Partisan* (**1971**) and *The Judas Mandate* (**1972**) – about UK post-nuclear-HOLOCAUST resistance to the Russians who occupy the islands; in the end, a government-in-exile is formed and the invaders, drained by a China war, retreat. *State Visit* (**1976**) is about the assassination of the Queen in order to prevent German reunification. CE specializes in spy thrillers. [JC]

EGREMONT, MICHAEL ◊ Michael HARRISON.

EHRLICH, MAX (SIMON) (1909-1983) US writer initially active as an author of RADIO plays for various series, including *The Shadow*. His first novel, *The Big Eye* (**1949**), concerns an attempt by astronomers to terrify humanity into world peace by announcing that a visiting planet is due to hit Earth; the planet misses narrowly. *The Edict* (**1971**) is based on ME's own screenplay for the film Z.P.G. and deals with an embargo on births. *The Reincarnation of Peter Proud* (**1974**), filmed in 1974 to his own screenplay, is a quest novel whose protagonist attempts to track down information about his former self, the murder of whom recurs in his dreams; his adventures continue in *Reincarnation in Venice* (**1979**; vt *The Bond* 1980 UK). ME was a proficient writer who tended to use sf protocols as much to alarm as to illuminate. [JC]

Other works: *Dead is the Blue* (**1964**), a borderline-sf nuclear-submarine story; *The Savage is Loose* * (**1974**), for which film (1974; dir George C. Scott) he also wrote the screenplay; *Shaitan* (**1981**), fantasy.

EIDLITZ, WALTHER ◊ TRANSPORTATION.

EIDOLON Australian SEMIPROZINE, published from North Perth, Western Australia, by Eidolon Publications, quarterly from #1, Autumn 1990 (published in May 1990), current, 8 issues to 1992, ed Jeremy G. Byrne, Keira McKenzie, Robin Pen, Richard Scriven, Jonathan Strahan, Chris Stronach.

This elegant, A5 desk-top published perfect-bound magazine has the appearance of an academic critical journal, but in fact publishes mainly sf/fantasy fiction, with some articles and reviews. It is available through subscription rather than from newsstands. *E* has had surprising success, with fiction on the whole superior to that of its east-coast rival, AUREALIS, and won a 1991 Ditmar (◊ AWARDS) for Best Fanzine/Semiprozine. It has published stories by Terry DOWLING, Greg EGAN, Leanne Frahm, Rosaleen LOVE, Philippa Maddern and Sean MCMULLEN, among others. [PN]

EINSTEIN, CHARLES (1926-   ) US writer who published his first sf story, "Tunnel 1971", in *Saturn* in 1957. His NEAR-FUTURE novel *The Day New York Went Dry* (**1964**) depicts a water shortage in that city which comes to a crisis in the drought of 1967. A hurricane then saves the city and its politicians. [JC]

EISENBERG, LARRY (1919-   ) US writer and for many years Co-Director of the Electronics Laboratory at Rockefeller University. He began publishing sf with "The Mynah Matter" as Lawrence Eisenberg for *Fantastic Stories* in 1962, and became known for his comic sequence of stories about **Emmett Duckworth**; many of these were assembled in his only collection, *The Best Laid Schemes* (coll **1971**). As an inventor whose devices crucially misfire, Duckworth might seem a cheap target, but LE presents his recurring disasters with winning sympathy. The stories describing the relationship of humans to the ALIEN **Sentients** were very much darker in import, though never unrelentingly so. After the beginning of the 1980s, LE became relatively inactive. [JC]

EISENSTEIN, ALEX (1945-   ) US writer whose work has been exclusively in collaboration with his wife, Phyllis EISENSTEIN, beginning with "The Trouble with the Past" for *New Dimensions 1* (anth **1971**) ed Robert SILVERBERG; although only about 5 stories are bylined with both names, their collaborative efforts extend throughout her work. [JC]

EISENSTEIN, PHYLLIS (1946-   ) US writer, whose first sf was "The Trouble with the Past" (1971), written in collaboration with her husband, Alex EISENSTEIN, in *New Dimensions 1* (anth **1971**) ed Robert SILVERBERG. She and her husband have written other stories together, and he is influential also on work signed only by PE. Her first novel, *Born to Exile* (1971-4 *FSF*; fixup **1978**), is a deft, romantic, episodic fantasy about a witch minstrel who can teleport. There followed perhaps her best work, *Sorcerer's Son* (**1979**), also fantasy, an oedipal quest involving magical apprenticeship. Her next two books were sf romances, *Shadow of Earth* (**1979**) and *In the Hands of Glory* (**1981**). The former is a racy ALTERNATE-WORLD story in which the heroine has to cope with the male chauvinism of a US Midwest belonging to a world in which the Spanish Armada won. PE's praiseworthy narrative facility in this productive period may have left her other capacities as a writer somewhat unstretched. She slowed down, for a time publishing only short fiction and in no great quantity, then returned seven years later with two fantasy sequels: *The Crystal Palace* (**1988**), sequel to *Sorcerer's Son*, and *In the Red Lord's Reach* (**1989**), sequel to *Born to Exile*. Both were marked by a change of pace to something almost languid, more reflective and metaphoric than before, with some gain and some loss. [PN]

See also: MAGIC.

EISFA ◊ YANDRO.

EISLER, STEVEN ◊ Robert P. HOLDSTOCK.

EKLUND, GORDON (1945-   ) US writer, born in Seattle, where he now lives. He published his first sf, "Dear Aunt Annie", a NEBULA nominee, with *Fantastic* in 1970. In the early and productive years of his career he published dozens of stories in sf magazines (none have been collected), writing as Wendell Stewart

once; until his work as E.E. SMITH (see below), he published all his books under his own name. His work was initially various though uneven. Both his first novel, *The Eclipse of Dawn* (**1971**), and his fourth and best solo effort, *All Times Possible* (**1974**), anatomize with pessimistic force the US political landscape and share an interest in the psychology and tactics of leadership. The sf elements in the first – mainly some intrusive ALIENS – tend to jar, but the PARALLEL-WORLDS structure of *All Times Possible* intensifies and darkens the picture of political realities at work through the second quarter of the 20th century. Although a sometimes careless writing style and a tendency to prolixity mar these books, they are still significant contributions to the theme of POLITICS in sf. *A Trace of Dreams* (**1972**) is also a novel of some weight, but some other modestly exploratory works are comparatively commonplace: *Inheritors of Earth* (1951 *Future Combined with Science Fiction Stories* as "Incomplete Superman"; exp **1974**), with Poul ANDERSON, stumblingly expands the latter's original story; *Beyond the Resurrection* (**1973**) and *The Grayspace Beast* (**1976**) lack the eloquence necessary to give full life to the concepts they present.

GE collaborated with Gregory BENFORD (*whom see for details*) on the series of stories which eventually became *If the Stars Are Gods* (fixup **1977**), the title story of which, in its original form, won a 1974 Nebula for Best Novelette; it is GE's most sustained work (and one of Benford's finest as well). *Find the Changeling* (**1980**), also with Benford, less impressively recounts the hunt on a colony-world for a shape-changing alien. Subsequent novels show a lessening of energy. The **Lord Tedric** series of SPACE OPERAS is not remarkably successful. The first volume, *Lord Tedric* (1954 *Universe Science Fiction*; exp **1978**) – was expanded from an original story by E.E. "Doc" Smith and was published as a collaboration, though GE was not credited in the UK edition; *Space Pirates* (**1979**) and *Black Knight of the Iron Sphere* (**1979**; vt *The Black Knight of the Iron Sphere* 1979 UK), both entirely by GE, were published as collaborations in the USA and as by Smith alone in the UK; the final volume, *Alien Realms* (**1980**), appeared under the Smith name in both countries. After *The Garden of Winter* (**1980**) GE fell silent for some years, returning to the scene with a juvenile, *A Thunder on Neptune* (**1989**). [JC]

Other works: *Serving in Time* (**1975** Canada); *Falling toward Forever* (**1975** Canada); *Dance of the Apocalypse* (**1976** Canada); two **Star Trek** ties, *The Starless World* * (**1978**) and *Devil World* * (**1979**); *The Twilight River* (**1979** dos).

See also: ALTERNATE WORLDS; GODS AND DEMONS; HITLER WINS; JUPITER; LIVING WORLDS; OUTER PLANETS; RELIGION; ROBOTS; STARS; SUN.

ELDER, MICHAEL (AIKEN) (1931-   ) Scottish actor and writer in various genres, some of whose earlier novels, written in the 1950s, deal with theatrical themes. He began writing sf with *Paradise is Not Enough* (**1970**) for ROBERT HALE LIMITED, and thereafter produced a number of fairly routine adventures for that firm. Most notable are the **Barclay** SPACE-OPERA adventures involving COLONIZATION and its perils: *Nowhere On Earth* (**1972**), which also deals with problems of OVERPOPULATION, and its sequels *The Perfumed Planet* (**1973**; vt *Flight to Terror* 1973 US), *Down to Earth* (**1973**), *The Seeds of Frenzy* (**1974**) and *The Island of the Dead* (**1975**). His other connected books are *Mindslip* (**1976**) and its sequel *Mindquest* (**1978**) and *Oil-Seeker* (**1977**) and its sequel *Oil-Planet* (**1978**). ME's ambitions do not generally extend beyond entertainment, though a dour DYSTOPIAN bent of thought is sometimes allowed to surface. [JC]

Other works: *The Alien Earth* (**1971**); *The Everlasting Man* (**1972**); *A Different World* (**1974**); *Centaurian Quest* (**1975**); *Double Time* (**1976**).

ELDERSHAW, M. BARNARD Collaborative pseudonym used by Australian writers and critics Marjorie Faith Barnard (1897-1987) and Flora Sydney Patricia Eldershaw (1897-1956) for four well regarded mainstream novels 1929-37; nearly all the writing was done by Barnard, with Eldershaw being the critical editorial eye. A fifth novel, also published as by MBE and the most distinguished work under this pseudonym, was by Barnard alone: *Tomorrow and Tomorrow* (cut **1947**; text restored vt *Tomorrow and Tomorrow and Tomorrow* 1983 UK) is a political novel whose framing story is set in the 24th century, where a historical novelist living in the Tenth Commune (once the Riverina) has written a book about Australia from 1924 to *c*1950, the years of Depression and WWII. The novel within a novel, entitled *Little World Left Behind*, is a striking picture of an Australia well known to Barnard, seen as if from a future perspective. As she had finished writing the book by 1944, the later events of WWII and its supposed aftermath – including the burning of Sydney by its anguished inhabitants – are pure sf, as is the future in which the novelist lives, a blighted, indifferent UTOPIA. Indeed the whole novel is very sophisticated, very unusual sf, part of whose subject is the elusiveness of HISTORY and its relation to fiction.

The book's publisher, unknown to Barnard, submitted it before publication to the censor, who saw it as politically subversive and therefore mutilated the latter part, thus bearing witness to the same repressive forces that give the novel its theme; later editions have the text restored. [PN]

See also: AUSTRALIA.

ELDRIDGE, PAUL (1888-1982) US languages teacher and writer, best known for the sf-fantasy trilogy he wrote with George S. VIERECK (*whom see for details*): *My First Two Thousand Years: The Autobiography of the Wandering Jew* (**1928**), *Salome. The Wandering Jewess* (**1930**; cut vt *Salome: 2000 Years of Love* 1954) and *The Invincible Adam* (**1932**). *Prince Pax* (**1933** UK), also with Viereck, provides an idealistic RURITANIAN king with a high-tech WEAPON: world peace, on his terms, ensues. [JC]

See also: ADAM AND EVE; IMMORTALITY; ORIGIN OF MAN;

POCKET UNIVERSE.

ELDRIDGE, ROGER (?   -   ) UK writer whose first sf book was a juvenile, *The Shadow of the Gloom-World* (**1977**). His second, *The Fishers of Darksea* (**1982**), is an ambitious adult tale set in an Eskimo culture with a tradition of shamanism; the visions endured by the protagonist are ironically revealed to be merely circumstantial, for the tribe has been genetically adapted to handle radioactive ore, and the MONSTERS seen in shamanic trance are merely human overseers, suitably shielded. [JC]

ELECTRICAL EXPERIMENTER ◊ SCIENCE AND INVENTION.

ELEK, ISTVÁN [r] ◊ HUNGARY.

ELGIN, SUZETTE HADEN Working name of US poet, author and teacher Patricia Anne Suzette Wilkins Elgin (1936-   ) for her sf. She combines writing with a professional specialization in LINGUISTICS, having a PhD in linguistics from the University of California, San Diego; she was a professor of linguistics at San Diego State University 1972-80, now emeritus, and has published widely in her specialist field. Her sf began in 1969 with "For the Sake of Grace" in *FSF*, which was incorporated into *At the Seventh Level* (**1972**), part of an ongoing series featuring the interstellar adventures of Trigalactic Intelligence Service agent **Coyote Jones**; with *The Communipaths* (**1970** dos) and *Furthest* (**1971**), it was assembled as *Communipath Worlds* (omni **1980**). Further titles, *Star-Anchored, Star-Angered* (**1979**) and *Yonder Comes the Other End of Time* (**1986**), did little to lessen the somewhat distressing discrepancy between the ramshackleness of the **Coyote Jones** plots and the terse eloquence of their descriptions of the meaning-systems of and COMMUNICATION with alien cultures, in which the condition of women (particularly in *Furthest*) is described with sufficient point that the books are used as FEMINIST texts.

A second series, the **Ozark trilogy** – *Twelve Fair Kingdoms* (**1981**), *The Grand Jubilee* (**1981**) and *And then There'll be Fireworks* (**1981**), assembled as *The Ozark Trilogy* (omni **1982**) – cannot be said to solve her inability to find plots of a sufficient knottiness to hold her attention (the young heroine of the series, whose magic secretly rules the planet Ozark, is in a coma for much of the final volume); but SHE's linguistic inventiveness, and her light-hearted detailing of the magic-based Ozark culture, give the books a charm they do not convey in synopsis. (*Yonder Comes the Other End of Time* is also set in this milieu.) Far more interesting, though still fumblingly plotted, is SHE's third series, *Native Tongue* (**1984**) and *The Judas Rose* (**1987**), in which a lame initial premise – a 1991 Amendment to the US Constitution declares women inferior to men on the basis of "scientific" evidence – fails much to hamper tightly narrated tales of the creation of a "womanlanguage" for self-protection (though the tongue itself is only fleetingly presented). The caricatured unpleasantness of almost all men, which both heightens and trivializes the first volume, becomes less significant in the second; superior ALIENS have arrived, and the fragile carapace of male superiority gets short shrift. But the pleasures and lessons of SHE's texts continue to lie more in texture than in premise.

In 1978, SHE founded the SCIENCE FICTION POETRY ASSOCIATION. [JC]

See also: POETRY.

ELIADE, MIRCEA [r] ◊ ROMANIA.

ELIMINATORS Film (1986). Altar/Empire. Prod Charles BAND. Dir Peter Manoogian, starring Andrew Prine, Denise Crosby, Patrick Reynolds, Conan Lee, Roy Dotrice. Screenplay Paul DeMeo, Danny Bilson. 96 mins, cut to 91 mins. Colour.

Enjoyable exploitation frolic whose plot defies précis, but involves a mad SCIENTIST (he wants to be a Roman emperor) in the jungle with a TIME MACHINE, the weary CYBORG Mandroid (his unhappy creation), the tough heroine Colonel Nora, the ROBOT SPOT (a dead ringer for R2D2), the martial artist Kuji, riverboats, prehistoric humans and a FORCE FIELD. Screenwriters Bilson and DeMeo also wrote producer Band's two best films, TRANCERS (1984) and ZONE TROOPERS (1985). [PN]

ELIOTT, E.C. Pseudonym of UK writer Reginald Alec Martin (1900-   ), whose **Kemlo** sequence of CHILDREN'S SF novels had a powerful emotional impact on many of their youthful UK readers, shaping the thoughts towards sf of an entire generation of them. The sequence is: *Kemlo and the Crazy Planet* (**1954**), *Kemlo and the Zones of Silence* (**1954**), *Kemlo and the Sky Horse* (**1954**), *Kemlo and the Martian Ghosts* (**1954**), *Kemlo and the Craters of the Moon* (**1955**), *Kemlo and the Space Lanes* (**1955**), *Kemlo and the Star Men* (**1955**), *Kemlo and the Gravity Rays* (**1956**), *Kemlo and the Purple Dawn* (**1957**), *Kemlo and the End of Time* (**1957**), *Kemlo and the Zombie Men* (**1958**), *Kemlo and the Space Men* (**1959**), *Kemlo and the Satellite Builders* (**1960**), *Kemlo and the Space Invaders* (**1961**) and *Kemlo and the Masters of Space* (**1963**). Kemlo and his friends, living with their parents in SPACE HABITATS, are young adolescents of the first generation to be born in space, and can therefore breathe vacuum. Despite this implausibility, the tales of the children's adventures are surprisingly enjoyable for their type and vintage – the spacestation settings, with families and above all children *routinely* Up There, were innovative (at least in children's sf); the characters seemed real, rather than being grim-jawed adult male heroes or indestructible precocious superbrats; and the books as a whole compare favourably with those being produced at about the same time by, for example, Captain W.E. JOHNS. A second, much shorter series, the **Tas** books, stopped after *Tas and the Space Machine* (**1955**) and *Tas and the Postal Rocket* (**1955**). [JC/DRL]

See also: JUVENILE SERIES.

ELITE ◊ GAMES AND TOYS.

ELIVAS, KNARF ◊ Frank SAVILE.

ELLERMAN, GENE [s] ◊ Basil WELLS.

ELLERN, WILLIAM B. [r] ◊ E.E. SMITH.

ELLIK, RON(ALD) (1938-1968) US computer programmer, author and well known sf fan, co-editor with Terry CARR of a HUGO-winning FANZINE, FANAC (1958-61). RE was co-author of *The Universes of E.E. Smith* (**1966**) with Bill EVANS (*whom see for details*). Under the joint pseudonym Fredric Davies he wrote with Steve Tolliver *The Man From U.N.C.L.E. #14: The Cross of Gold Affair* * (**1968**). RE died in a car accident the day before he was to have been married. [PN]

ELLIOT, JEFFREY M. (1947-   ) US academic – professor of political science at North Carolina Central University – and writer who has published prolifically in several areas. Much of his work in sf has been in collaboration with Robert REGINALD, including the second version of Reginald's *The Attempted Assassination of John F. Kennedy* (**1977** chap) as by Lucas Webb, which JME helped to revise into a format designed to be used in teaching, retitling it *If J.F.K. Had Lived: A Political Scenario* (exp **1978** chap). Also with Reginald (the latter as Michael Burgess) JME compiled *The Work of R. Reginald: An Annotated Bibliography & Guide* (**1985** chap). Other BIBLIOGRAPHIES include *The Work of George Zebrowski: An Annotated Bibliography & Guide* (**1986** chap; exp 1990) with Reginald, *The Work of Jack Dann: An Annotated Bibliography & Guide* (**1990**) and *The Work of Pamela Sargent: An Annotated Bibliography & Guide* (**1990** chap). JME also ed *Starclimber: The Literary Adventures and Autobiography of Raymond Z. Gallun* (**1991**). [JC]

Other works: A sequence of interview books comprising *Science Fiction Voices #2: Interviews with Science Fiction Writers* (coll **1979** chap), *#3* (coll **1980** chap) and *#4* (coll **1982** chap); *Literary Voices #1* (coll **1980** chap); *The Future of the Space Program: Large Corporations & Society: Discussions with 22 Science-Fiction Writers* (coll **1981** chap) and *Fantasy Voices: Interviews with American Fantasy Writers* (coll **1982** chap); also *Kindred Spirits: An Anthology of Gay and Lesbian Science Fiction Stories* (anth **1984**).

About the author: *The Work of Jeffrey M. Elliot: An Annotated Bibliography & Guide* (**1984** chap) by Boden Clarke (Robert REGINALD).

ELLIOT, JOHN (1918-   ) UK writer, primarily for tv, who collaborated with Fred HOYLE on two serials, A FOR ANDROMEDA and *The* ANDROMEDA BREAKTHROUGH, and the subsequent novelizations under the same titles (**1962** and **1964** respectively). He is not to be confused with the John Elliott (note spelling) who wrote the anti-Chinese/Soviet political thriller *Dragon's Feast* (**1970**), itself a work of borderline sf. [JC]

ELLIOT, LEE House name used for three sf novels published by CURTIS WARREN, one each by William Henry Fleming BIRD and Dennis HUGHES and one – *Overlord New York* (**1953**) – by an as yet unidentified author. [JC]

ELLIOTT, BRUCE (WALTER GARDNER LIVELY STACY) (1914-1973) US writer and editor, active mainly in the sf field in the early 1950s, beginning with "Fearsome Fable" for FSF in 1951. His sf novels – *Asylum Earth* (1952 *Startling Stories*; **1968**) and *The*

Rivet in Grandfather's Neck (**1970**) – are routine adventures. [JC]

See also: DIMENSIONS.

ELLIOTT, ELTON P. [r] ◊ Richard E. GEIS.

ELLIOTT, GEORGE P(AUL) (1918-1980) US writer and academic, many of whose short stories were sf or fantasy. He is best remembered for the title story in *Among the Dangs* (coll **1960**), which deals with an imaginary South American tribe and has been widely reprinted within and outside the genre; his essay "Discovering the Dangs", in *Conversions: Literature and the Modernist Deviation* (coll **1971**), discusses, biographically and theoretically, the creation of an sf text. Two other stories from that collection, including the anti-racist parable "The NRACP", and five of those assembled in *An Hour of Last Things* (coll **1968**), most notably "Into the Cone of Cold", are also sf. Although it has been listed in sf bibliographies, *David Knudson* (**1962**) is in fact an associational novel dealing with nuclear guilt and the aftereffects of radiation poisoning. [JC/GF]

ELLIOTT, H(ARRY) CHANDLER (1907-) Canadian-born US physician, university teacher of medicine and writer, in whose sf novel, *Reprieve from Paradise* (**1955**), Polynesians have established a worldwide culture after an atomic HOLOCAUST. Their civilization is described in sometimes amusing detail, though an enforced breeding plan soon sours the picture. The introduction of an Antarctic UTOPIA then complicates matters further. [JC]

See also: GAMES AND SPORTS; TRANSPORTATION.

ELLIOTT, JANICE (1931-) UK writer since 1962 of sophisticated novels of domestic passion. Her sf novel, *The Summer People* (**1980**), places in a NEAR-FUTURE world one of her typical casts, who decide it would be a good idea, while society collapses offstage, to remain ensconced in their holiday resort for the time being. An Arthurian sequence for older children – *The King Awakes* (**1987**) and *The Empty Throne* (**1988**) – arouses the once and future king into a post-HOLOCAUST UK. *The Sadness of Witches* (**1987**) is a tale of the occult. [JC]

ELLIOTT, NATHAN ◊ Christopher EVANS.

ELLIOTT, RICHARD ◊ Richard E. GEIS.

ELLIOTT, SUMNER LOCKE (1917-1991) Australian-born playwright, tv scriptwriter and novelist, resident in the USA from 1948, becoming a US citizen. Several of his novels, many of which have Australian settings, have been televised. His novel *Fairyland* (**1988**) is about growing up gay in Australia. His only sf is *Going* (**1975**), about life and love in a slightly DYSTOPIAN future in which euthanasia at age 65 is compulsory. The heroine, close to this age, reflects on her life. [PN]

ELLIS, ALBERT C(HARLES) (1947-) US writer who began publishing sf with "Fire in the Sky" in *Vertex* in 1974, and who subsequently wrote two modest but readable sf adventures, *Death Jag* (dated 1979 but **1980**) with Jeff Slaten, and *Worldmaker* (**1985**). [JC]

ELLIS, CRAIG House name used 1940-43 in *AMZ* by David Vern (◊ David V. REED) and Lee Rogow. [JC]

ELLIS, D.E. (? -) UK writer briefly active in the early 1960s with "Stress" for *NW* in 1961 and the routine *A Thousand Ages* (**1961**). [JC]

ELLIS, EDWARD S(YLVESTER) (1840-1916) US teacher, editor and author of boys' books, popular history, miscellaneous work and a very large number of US dime novels, mainly Westerns, under his own name and many pseudonyms. His enormous bibliography, though studied exhaustively by Denis Rogers (in various issues of *Dime Novel Round-Up*), remains unsettled. ESE established the dime novel as a commercial field with *Seth Jones* (**1860**), and instigated DIME-NOVEL SF through his adaptation of the historical Newark Steam Man into a Western: *The Steam Man of the Prairies* (**1868**; vt *The Huge Hunter, or The Steam Man of the Prairies* 1876; vt *Baldy's Boy Partner, or Young Brainerd's Steam Man* 1888); sf soon became one of the popular dime-novel genres. ESE's use of the Steam Man (not a ROBOT, simply a man-shaped mobile steam engine which cannot go into reverse) was uninspired, with little recognition of the potential of the device. *The Steam Man* has been conveniently reprinted in E.F. BLEILER's *Eight Dime Novels* (anth **1974**) with a full introduction to the field. Of ESE's huge body of work, a few others are of some interest: *Land of Mystery* (**1889**), a lost-race (◊ LOST WORLDS) tale, *The Monarch of the Air* (**1907**), a fantastic aeronautics story as by Seward D. Lisle (an anagram pseudonym), and *The Dragon of the Skies* (**1915** UK). [EFB/JC]

See also: EDISONADE; HISTORY OF SF.

ELLIS, T(HOMAS) MULLETT (1850-1919) UK poet and writer whose sf novel, *Zalma* (**1895**), features the protracted NEAR-FUTURE attempts of the eponymous wrong-side-of-the-bed Russian-Spanish princess to revenge herself on the heir to the throne of England, who has for unclear reasons swiftly annulled their morganatic marriage. Anthrax-bearing balloons are brought into play, and the tale closes on a possible Europe-wide socialist upheaval. [JC]

See also: WEAPONS.

ELLISON, HARLAN (JAY) (1934-) US writer, the most controversial and among the finest of those writers associated with sf whose careers began in the 1950s. He was born and raised in Ohio, attending Ohio State University for 18 months before being asked to leave, one of the reasons for his dismissal being rudeness to a creative-writing professor who told him he had no talent. HE had already become deeply involved in Cleveland fandom, producing material for and later taking over the Cleveland SF Society's magazine, *Science-Fantasy Bulletin* (later *Dimensions*). In a profile contributed to the *FSF* Special Harlan Ellison Issue (July 1977), Robert SILVERBERG, his near contemporary, vividly portrayed the young HE as insecure, physically fearless, extraordinarily ambitious and hyperkinetic, dominating any room he entered. Much the same could be said about the short stories which made him famous (initially in sf circles, later outside them) and won him a remarkable number of awards – 7 HUGOS and 3 NEBULAS – for these tales have almost unfailingly reflected and magnified their author's character and concerns.

By 1955 HE was in New York, rooming with Silverberg and producing numerous stories. His first professional sf appearance came early in 1956 with "Glowworm" for *Infinity Science Fiction*, and he soon began to publish very prolifically indeed, with well over 150 stories and pieces in a variety of genres by the end of 1958. Much of this initial production is coarse and derivative, mixing strong early influences like Nelson Algren (1909-1981) with models derived from successful magazine writers of the time. In these years, HE used a number of pseudonyms: in fanzines, Nalrah Nosille; for short stories in crime, sex and other genre magazines, Sley Harson (in collaboration with Henry SLESAR), Landon Ellis, Derry Tiger, Price Curtis and Paul Merchant; in sf magazines the house names Lee ARCHER (one story), E.K. JARVIS (one story) and Clyde MITCHELL (one story) and the personal pseudonyms Jay Charby, Wallace Edmondson, Ellis Hart, Jay Solo and, from 1957, Cordwainer Bird, a name which after 1964 he used to designate material that (generally through conflict with tv producers) he partially disclaimed.

Not long after reaching New York, HE assumed a false identity and ran as a member of a gang from Red Hook, Brooklyn, called the Barons. This 10-week stint gained him material which he used directly in the first of his infrequent novels, *Rumble* (**1958**; vt *Web of the City* 1975), which early demonstrated, in the vigour and violence of its urban imagery, the ambivalent hold of the CITY on his imagination. HE is one of the relatively few writers of his generation to deal constantly and impassionedly with the turbulent complexities of the modern US city (an engagement furthered in sf, decades later, by the CYBERPUNK movement). More material drawn from contemporary urban life may be found in *The Deadly Streets* (coll **1958**; exp 1975), *The Juvies* (coll **1961**), *Gentleman Junkie and Other Stories of the Hung-up Generation* (coll **1961**; rev 1975) and *Rockabilly* (**1961**; rev vt *Spider Kiss* 1975), as well as in the autobiographical street-gang study *Memos from Purgatory: Two Journeys of Our Times* (**1961**). None of this material is technically sf, but HE has consistently deprecated the making of distinctions between generic and non-generic writing in his own works.

After serving in the US Army, HE moved to Chicago in 1959 as editor of *Rogue Magazine*, where later he was also involved in the creation of Regency Books. By 1962 he was in Los Angeles, where he has remained. During this time, while continuing to write for many markets, he was beginning to establish a maverick reputation within sf, though his first sf books – *The Man with Nine Lives* (fixup **1960** dos) and *A Touch of Infinity* (coll **1960** dos) – display an uneasy

conformity to the constraints of late-1950s magazine sf. *Ellison Wonderland* (coll **1962**; vt *Earthman, Go Home* 1964; with new introduction and with "The Forces that Crush" deleted and "Back to the Drawing Boards" added, rev 1974; rev 1984) is likewise uneasy, containing stories whose conventional premises are shaken apart by the violent rhetoric of their telling. HE was still very much feeling his way; of major sf writers, he was among the earliest to find his voice – raw thrusts of emotion rattle even the most "commercial" of his early stories – but among the slowest to find forms and markets through which to project it.

After much struggle, by 1963 HE had established himself as a successful tv writer, contributing scripts to such series as *Route 66*, *The Alfred Hitchcock Hour* and *The Untouchables*, with considerable work for *Burke's Law* as well as two scripts for *The* OUTER LIMITS in 1964 – one of these, "Demon with a Glass Hand" (1964), won the Writers' Guild of America Award for Outstanding Script – two scripts for *The* MAN FROM U.N.C.L.E. in 1966-7, and a STAR TREK episode, "The City on the Edge of Forever" (1967), which won a Hugo for Best Dramatic Presentation in 1968 and a Writers' Guild of America Award for Most Outstanding Script, Dramatic Episode, of 1967-8. A later foray into tv – his attempt to create a series based on the concept of a GENERATION STARSHIP – was something of a fiasco. The series, *The* STARLOST, was Canadian-made and lasted only one season, 1973; and so many changes were made to HE's original concept that he disowned the programme, signing the pilot episode Cordwainer Bird. The original script (not the one filmed) received a Writers' Guild of America Award for Best Dramatic Episode Script (HE is the only scenarist to have won the award three times), and was later novelized as *Phoenix without Ashes* * (**1975**) with Edward BRYANT. A thinly disguised account of the whole affair formed the plot of a *roman à clef* by Ben BOVA, *The Starcrossed* (**1975**). More recently, HE served as creative consultant for the first season of the revived *The* TWILIGHT ZONE.

At around the same time that he began his tv career, HE began publishing the short stories that have made his name. Many of them appear in his books of the late 1960s: *Paingod and Other Delusions* (coll **1965**; with "Sleeping Dogs" added exp 1975) and *I Have No Mouth & I Must Scream* (coll **1967**; rev 1983), both assembled as *The Fantasies of Harlan Ellison* (omni **1979**); *From the Land of Fear* (coll **1967**); *Love Ain't Nothing but Sex Misspelled* (coll **1968**; with 9 stories removed and an intro, 1 story and 2 articles added 1976), which mixes sf and non-sf, though the 2nd edn retains mainly non-genre material; *The Beast that Shouted Love at the Heart of the World* (coll **1969**; with "Along the Scenic Route", "The Place with no Name" and "Shattered Like a Glass Goblin" cut 1976 UK), the US edition being a corrupt text; and *Over the Edge: Stories from Somewhere Else* (coll **1970**). *Alone Against Tomorrow: Stories of Alienation in Speculative Fiction* (coll **1971**; UK edn in 2 vols as *All the Sounds of Fear* 1973 and *The Time of the Eye* 1974, the latter containing new intro) represents HE's first attempt (of several) to re-sort his material, and provides a good summary of his best 1960s work. Further attempts at sorting include *Approaching Oblivion: Road Signs on the Tread-mill toward Tomorrow* (coll **1974**), which contains a moving autobiographical analysis of the roots of his writing; and the superb *Deathbird Stories: A Pantheon of Modern Gods* (coll **1975**; rev **1984**), which reassem-bles many of his best stories into a kind of cycle about Man's relation to the GODS and horrors within and without him. ("Pretty Maggie Moneyeyes", maybe his most moving tale, is again reprinted here, finding at last a fit context. This story of the quasidelusional rapport between a gambler and a female spirit trapped within a slot machine definitively expresses what might be called an Ellisonian pathos about the sadness and rage of men and women, lovers, victims, users: solitaries all, in a gashed world.) But *Deathbird Stories* was not a true retrospective, and the confusion caused by the release of many and frequently revised titles, often with overlapping contents, was cleared up only with the publication of *The Essential Ellison: A 35-Year Retrospective* (coll **1987**), a huge and grip-ping overview of his entire career.

From the mid-1960s on, HE began to amass a large number of Hugos and Nebulas: both were awarded in 1966 for "'Repent, Harlequin!' Said the Ticktock-man" (1965), later published with James STERANKO as *"Repent, Harlequin!" Said the Ticktockman* (graph **1978** chap); a 1968 Hugo (Short Story) for "I Have No Mouth and I Must Scream" (1967), a most scarifying expression of the true dehumanizing consequences of nuclear war; a 1969 Hugo (Short Story) for "The Beast that Shouted Love at the Heart of the World" (1968); a 1974 Hugo (Best Novelette) for "The Deathbird" (1973); and a 1969 Nebula (Best Novella) for "A Boy and his Dog" (1969). This last was made into a successful film (◊ A BOY AND HIS DOG), itself awarded a 1976 Hugo, not shared by HE, for Best Dramatic Presentation. He also won a 1975 Hugo for Best Novelette for "Adrift Just off the Islets of Langerhans, Latitude 38° 54' N, Longitude 77° 00' 13" W", an Edgar from the Mystery Writers of America for "The Whimper of Whipped Dogs" (1973), a 1978 Nebula and Hugo for Best Short Story for "Jeffty is Five" and a 1986 Hugo for Best Novelette for "Paladin of the Lost Hour" (1985).

It was during these prime years that HE also began editing his famous series of NEW-WAVE sf ANTHOLOGIES with DANGEROUS VISIONS (anth **1967**; vt in 3 vols *Dangerous Visions #1* 1969, *#2* 1969 and *#3* 1969) and *Again, Dangerous Visions* (anth **1972**; vt in 2 vols *Again, Dangerous Visions I* 1973 and *II* 1973); these books were striking for the general excellence of their contents and for the extensive, deeply personal annotations supplied by HE. For this success – and self-exposure – he was to pay. A third volume, «The Last Dangerous Visions», was announced at the start of the 1970s but still (1992) awaits publication. A

series of illnesses impaired HE's fitness for the huge task of annotating what had soon become an enor-mous project; and an inherent stubbornness seemed to prevent him from closing the enterprise down after its time – the high tide of the 1960s New Wave movement, created in part by the first volume of the series – had inevitably passed.

For several years, HE had in addition to his fiction and his screenwriting activities begun to produce a considerable body of nonfiction – essays, reviews, polemics, culture cartoons, memoirs. Much of this material has now been published in book form. *The Glass Teat: Essays of Opinion on the Subject of Television* (coll **1970**) and *The Other Glass Teat* (coll **1975**) engage trenchantly with their subject; *Sleepless Nights in the Procrustean Bed* (coll **1984**) collects general essays, as does *An Edge in My Voice* (coll **1985**), both containing severe assaults on hypocrisies of government (and individuals); *Harlan Ellison's Watching* (coll **1989**) contains film criticism; and *The Harlan Ellison Horn-book* (coll **1990**) is a sequence of sometimes fairly ratty confessional essays.

From about 1970, though the quality of his work was by no means inferior, HE began to publish markedly fewer stories; and from about 1980 an understandable inclination to cultural melancholia began to be noticed. New titles, some as disting-uished as anything from earlier decades, were assem-bled in *Strange Wine* (coll **1978**), *Shatterday* (coll **1980**), *Stalking the Nightmare* (coll **1982**) and *Angry Candy* (coll **1988**), generating a sense of the painful maturity of an author passionately engaged not only with himself – an engagement whose dangerous allure he has never denied – but with the essential gestures of rage and love and self-betrayal that mark our species. He has increasingly engaged his large energies as a writer in creating parable after parable – only some of them couched in anything like a conventional sf idiom – that illuminate the late years of the century, sometimes luridly, always with a genuine and redeeming pain. For all the scattershot rawness of his wilder work, at the end of the day – as *All the Lies that Are My Life* (**1980**) tormentedly exposes – HE is a representative speaker of the things that count.   [JC]

Other works: *Sex Gang* (**1959**) as by Paul Merchant; *Doomsman* (1958 *Imagination Science Fiction* as "The Assassin"; **1967** chap dos); *Partners in Wonder: Harlan Ellison in Collaboration with . . .* (coll **1971**), collabora-tions with various writers; *No Doors, No Windows* (coll **1975**); *The City at the Edge of Forever* * (**1977**), a **Star Trek** spin-off; *The Illustrated Harlan Ellison* (graph coll **1978**); *The Book of Ellison* (anth **1978**) with Andrew PORTER; *Medea: Harlan's World* (anth **1985**), one of the earlier SHARED-WORLD anthologies, and perhaps the best; *Night and the Enemy* (graph **1987**) with Ken Steacy; *Eidolons* (**1988** chap); *Footsteps* (**1989** chap); *Vic and Blood: The Chronicles of a Boy and His Dog* (graph coll of linked stories **1989**) with Richard CORBEN; *Run for the Stars* (1957 *Science Fiction Adventures*; rev **1991** chap dos), in a TOR BOOKS Double published in anthology format; *Dreams with Sharp Teeth* (omni **1991**) containing *I Have No Mouth and I Must Scream*, *Deathbird Stories* and *Shatterday*, all texts corrected.

About the author: *FSF* Special Harlan Ellison Issue (July 1977); *Harlan Ellison: Unrepentant Harlequin* by George Edgar SLUSSER (**1977**); *Harlan Ellison: A Bibliographical Checklist* (**1973**; 2nd edn in *Fantasy Research & Bibliography* #1-#2 1980-81) compiled by Leslie Kay Swigart – the latter title is unusually thorough and comprehensive and, given its coverage of HE's intensely productive early years, remains useful.

See also: AMAZING STORIES; AUTOMATION; BRITISH SCIENCE FICTION AWARD; CHILDREN IN SF; CINEMA; COMICS; COMPUTERS; CYBORGS; ESCHATOLOGY; FANTASY; GALAXY SCIENCE FICTION; GAMES AND SPORTS; HITLER WINS; HOLOCAUST AND AFTER; INVISIBILITY; MACHINES; *The* MAGAZINE OF FANTASY AND SCIENCE FICTION; MESSIAHS; MILFORD SCIENCE FICTION WRITERS' CONFERENCE; MUSIC; MYTHOLOGY; NEW WORLDS; OPTIMISM AND PESSIMISM; RELIGION; SEX; TABOOS; *The* TERMINATOR; TRANSPORTATION; WOMEN SF WRITERS.

ELMORE, ERNEST (CARPENTER) (1901-1957) UK actor and writer, author of about 30 detective novels as John Bude. In *The Steel Grubs* (**1928**) a Dartmoor convict finds some ALIEN eggs, which hatch into ferrophage grubs that eat first the iron bars of his cell and then much of First Industrial Revolution England. *This Siren Song* (**1930**) features some McGUFFIN inventions. *The Lumpton Gobbelings* (**1954**), his most famous title, describes an invasion by Little People of the village of Lumpton, scandalizing the villagers. [JC]

ELOUS, MARV ◊ Robert E. VARDEMAN.

ELPHINSTONE, MARGARET (1948-   ) Scottish writer of at least two gardening books who began publishing sf with "Spinning the Green" in *Despatches from the Frontiers of the Female Mind* (anth **1985**) ed Jen Green and Sarah LEFANU. Her sf sequence, the **Incomer** series – *The Incomer* (**1987**) and *A Sparrow's Flight* (**1989**) – applies a FEMINIST perspective to the post-HOLOCAUST story of the arrival of a wandering musician in a far-northern village and his winter-long residence there, and to further examinations of the post-patriarchal, post-technological world that is slowly revealed. [JC]

EL SALVADOR ◊ LATIN AMERICA.

ELSTAR, DOW [s] ◊ Raymond Z. GALLUN.

ELTON, BEN Working name of UK tv comedian, playwright and novelist Benjamin Charles Elton (1959-   ), well known for the contumely of his stand-up verbal SATIRE. His first sf novel, *Stark* (**1989**), is set in a NEAR-FUTURE Australia threatened by a typical late-20th-century entrepreneur, and by the END OF THE WORLD through POLLUTION, which the industrialists responsible hope to evade by leaving the planet to its victims – us. *Gridlock* (**1991**) less successfully dramatizes a sudden UK-wide traffic jam. [JC]

See also: TRANSPORTATION.

ELWOOD, ROGER (1933-   ) US editor who produced a number of reprint ANTHOLOGIES in the 1960s, mostly in collaboration with Vic Ghidalia (1926-   ) or Sam MOSKOWITZ, and who burst into prominence in the early 1970s when, with indefatigable salesmanship, he sold a huge number of ORIGINAL ANTHOLOGIES –about 80 in all (including a number of short books for young children), according to his claim – to a variety of publishers. At one time it was estimated that RE alone constituted about a quarter of the total market for sf short stories, and such dominance led to criticism of his restrictions on the free use of SEX and RELIGION as themes. Notable among his many anthologies were: *Future City* (anth **1973**); *Saving Worlds* (anth **1973**; vt *The Wounded Planet* 1974) with Virginia KIDD; the **Continuum** sequence, whose 4 vols –*Continuum #1* (anth **1974**), *#2* (anth **1974**), *#3* (anth **1974**) and *#4* (anth **1975**) – featured 8 different 4-part series; and *Epoch* (anth **1975**) with Robert SILVERBERG. Collections ed RE included *The Many Worlds of Poul Anderson* (coll **1974**) and *The Many Worlds of Andre Norton* (coll **1974**). RE was also responsible for the short-lived magazine ODYSSEY, the LASER BOOKS series of sf adventures from Canada, and *Starstream Comics* (1976). Later, as the oversaturated anthology market contracted, he diversified into editing the sf lines of various publishers – Bobbs-Merrill, Pinnacle and Pyramid, in addition to Laser. As a devout Christian, RE also wrote evangelical and inspirational works, and in the late 1980s several novels that were similarly inspirational, including the **Angelwalk** sequence – *Angelwalk: A Modern Fable* (**1988**) and *Fallen Angel* (**1990**) – and some singletons: *The Christening* (**1989**), *The Frankenstein Project* (**1991**) and *Wise One* (**1991**). [MJE/JC]

Other works (as editor): *Alien Worlds* (anth **1964**) and *Invasion of the Robots* (anth **1964**), both ghost-edited by Sam Moskowitz; *Strange Signposts* (anth **1966**); *The Human Zero* (anth **1967**) with Moskowitz; *The Time Curve* (anth **1968**); *Alien Earth* (anth **1969**) with Moskowitz; *Other Worlds, Other Times* (anth **1969**) with Moskowitz; *The Little Monsters* (anth **1969**) and *More Little Monsters* (anth **1973**), both with Vic Ghidalia; *Beware the Beasts* (anth **1970**) with Ghidalia; *The Horror Hunters* (anth **1971**) with Ghidalia; *Young Demons* (anth **1971**) with Ghidalia; *Signs and Wonders* (anth **1972**); *And Walk Now Gently through the Fire* (anth **1972**); *The Venus Factor* (anth **1972**) with Ghidalia; *Androids, Time Machines and Blue Giraffes* (anth **1973**) with Ghidalia; *Demon Kind* (anth **1973**); *Frontiers I: Tomorrow's Alternatives* (anth **1973**) and *Frontiers II: The New Mind* (anth **1973**); *Monster Tales: Vampires, Werewolves and Things* (anth **1973**); *Omega* (anth **1973**); *The Other Side of Tomorrow* (anth **1973**); *Science Fiction Adventures from Way Out* (anth **1973**); *Science Fiction Tales: Invaders, Creatures and Alien Worlds* (anth **1973**); *Showcase* (anth **1973**); *Strange Things Happening* (anth **1973**); *Children of Infinity* (anth **1973**); *Future Quest* (anth **1973**); *Flame Tree Planet: An Anthology of Religious Science-Fantasy* (anth **1973**); *Ten Tomorrows* (anth **1973**); *The Berserkers* (anth **1974**); *Chronicles of a Comer* (anth **1974**); *Crisis* (anth **1974**); *The Extraterrestrials* (anth

1974); *Future Kin* (anth **1974**); *Horror Tales: Spirits, Spells and the Unknown* (anth **1974**); *The Graduated Robot and Other Stories* (anth **1974**); *The Learning Maze* (anth **1974**); *More Science Fiction Tales: Crystal Creatures, Bird-Things and other Weirdies* (anth **1974**); *Survival from Infinity* (anth **1974**); *The Far Side of Time* (anth **1974**); *The Long Night of Waiting* (anth **1974**); *Strange Gods* (anth **1974**); *Vampires, Werewolves, and Other Monsters* (anth **1974**); *Beware More Beasts* (anth **1975**) with Ghidalia; *Dystopian Visions* (anth **1975**); *Future Corruption* (anth **1975**); *The Gifts of Asti* (anth **1975**); *In the Wake of Man* (anth **1975**); *Tomorrow: New Worlds of Science Fiction* (anth **1975**); *The 50-Meter Monsters and Other Horrors* (anth **1976**); *Visions of Tomorrow* (anth **1976**); *Futurelove* (anth **1977**) ed anon, perhaps because it dealt in part with sexual matters; *A World Named Cleopatra* (anth **1977**); *Spine-Chillers: Unforgettable Tales of Terror* (anth **1978**) with Howard GOLDSMITH.

For younger children (ed anon): *The Graduated Robot* (anth **1973** chap); *Adrift in Space* (anth **1974** chap); *Journey to Another Star* (anth **1974** chap); *The Killer Plants* (anth **1974** chap); *The Mind Angel* (anth **1974** chap); *The Missing World* (anth **1974** chap); *Night of the Sphinx and Other Stories* (anth **1974** chap); *The Tunnel* (anth **1974** chap).

See also: CHILDREN IN SF; COMICS; SHARED WORLDS; TABOOS; THEATRE.

ELY, DAVID Working name of US journalist and writer David Eli Lilienthal (1927-   ), perhaps best known for such psychological thrillers as *The Tour* (**1967**). Some of the stories in *Time Out* (coll **1968**) contain fantasy elements. His first sf novel, *Seconds* (**1963**), had some initial success and was made into the John FRANKENHEIMER film SECONDS (1966), financed by and starring Rock Hudson. Both book and film revolve around an organization which transforms middle-aged men into young, Rock-Hudson-like he-men. At first the change is exciting, but soon the nightmares start. The protagonist of DE's second sf novel, *A Journal of the Flood Year* (**1992**), discovers that a huge wall designed to reclaim part of the American continental shelf from the Atlantic has begun to leak, but the rigidly stratified world, of which the wall is a potently rendered symbol, attempts to block any awareness of the oncoming and inevitable DISASTER. [JC]

See also: PSYCHOLOGY.

EMBRYO Film (1976). Cine Artists. Dir Ralph Nelson, starring Rock Hudson, Diane Ladd, Barbara Carrera, Roddy McDowall. Screenplay Anita Doohan, Jack W. Thomas, based on a story by Thomas. 105 mins. Colour.

In this variation on the FRANKENSTEIN theme, a scientist (Hudson), while experimenting on a premature foetus with a growth hormone, creates in weeks a fully developed 25-year-old woman (Carrera). She has a virtually blank mind, and the scientist, like Pygmalion, moulds her personality and introduces her into society. The result is an intelligent but morally crippled creature whom he ultimately destroys. Despite its modern hardware, the film is really a reworking of the old GOTHIC theme – as in the German silent films HOMUNCULUS (1916) and ALRAUNE (1928) – about the basic evil of beings who are created by unnatural means and are therefore without souls. It is not a good film. The novelization is *Embryo* * (**1976**) by Louis CHARBONNEAU. [JB/PN]

EMECHETA, (FLORENCE ONYE) BUCHI (1944-   ) Nigerian-born writer, in the UK from 1962, author of a number of semi-autobiographical novels which vividly describe the lives of African women in the industrial UK during the years of its decline. *The Rape of Shavi* (**1983**), set in the NEAR FUTURE, describes the effect upon the African country of Shavi when a horde of refugees from a European nuclear HOLOCAUST descends like locusts. [JC]

EMERSON, WILLIS GEORGE (1856-1918) US writer, mostly of Westerns, whose lost-race (◊ LOST WORLDS) novel *The Smoky God, or A Voyage to the Inner World* (**1908**) is set in a HOLLOW-EARTH Eden, on the John Cleves SYMMES model, where a race of long-lived giants worships the interior sun. [JC]

EMPIRE STRIKES BACK, THE Film (1980). Lucasfilm/20th Century-Fox. Executive prod George LUCAS. Dir Irvin Kershner, starring Mark Hamill, Harrison Ford, Carrie Fisher, Billy Dee Williams, Frank Oz. Screenplay Leigh BRACKETT, Lawrence Kasdan, based on a story by Lucas. 124 mins. Colour.

A first viewing of this blockbuster sequel to STAR WARS (1977) sweeps the viewer along with the colour and spectacle of its various space-opera venues: frozen and swampy planets, hide-and-seek among asteroids, and a climax in the sky station of Cloud City. A repeated screening reveals its weakly episodic nature, where heroic freedom fighters struggle repetitively against the Galactic Empire. Luke Skywalker (Hamill) is coached in spiritual control by a green puppet, Yoda, operated by Frank Oz of tv's *Muppets*, in a sequence more banal than metaphysical. After too much pointless action and not enough character exploration, a genuine mythic (and Freudian) charge is belatedly evoked when evil Darth Vader reveals himself during a duel with good Luke to be his father, and in one or two scenes we are allowed to recognize in Luke a potential for harm, lending the film a much needed moral complexity. Brackett was dying of cancer as she drafted the script (she received a posthumous HUGO for it), which was heavily revised by Kasdan, but nevertheless and despite its faults *TESB* retains distant echoes of the florid and witty grandeur of her own SPACE OPERAS. The *Star Wars* trilogy was completed with *The* RETURN OF THE JEDI (1983). A book about the film is *Once Upon a Galaxy: A Journal of the Making of The Empire Strikes Back* (**1980**) by Alan Arnold (1922-   ). The novelization is *The Empire Strikes Back* * (**1980**) by Donald F. GLUT. [PN]

EMSH, ED ◊ Ed EMSHWILLER.

EMSHWILLER, CAROL (FRIES) (1921   ) US writer

who began to publish sf with "This Thing Called Love" for *Future* in 1955. She was married from 1949 to Ed EMSHWILLER, with whom she occasionally collaborated; but from the beginning of her career the razor-sharp exactness of her language and the subversive power of the themes she expressed with such dangerous precision have marked her as a unique voice. Though she published much of her early work in *FSF*, and later in Damon KNIGHT's ORBIT and similar anthologies, she has never been identified as a GENRE-SF writer. Her language is too much in the foreground for that; and the unrelenting clarity with which she deconstructs the narrative and thematic conventions central to the genre (◊ FABULATION) has disqualified almost all of her stories from being read simply as tales. In her hands, sf conventions become models of our deep estrangement from ourselves (especially women; ◊ WOMEN AS PORTRAYED IN SCIENCE FICTION) and from the world. Early stories can be found in *Joy in Our Cause* (coll **1974**). *Verging on the Pertinent* (coll **1989**) assembles corrosively elegant non-genre work. *The Start of the End of it All* (coll **1990** UK; rev **1991** US) collects stories as close to sf or fantasy as she is likely to compose. CE's first novel, *Carmen Dog* (**1988** UK), is a FEMINIST fable which draws obvious but very deftly pointed lessons from the transformation of women into dogs and dogs into women. [JC]

Other works: *Venus Rising* (**1992** chap).

EMSHWILLER, ED Working name of US illustrator and film-maker Edmund Alexander Emshwiller (1925-1990); he often signed his sf artwork "Emsh". He studied art at the University of Michigan, the École des Beaux Arts in Paris, and the Art Students League in New York. Astonishingly prolific, Emsh did cover and interior art, beginning with *Gal* in 1951, for more than two dozen magazines including *AMZ*, *FSF* (which he dominated through the 1950s) and *Startling Stories*, along with hundreds of book covers, both hardback and paperback; his work for ACE BOOKS alone would have made his reputation. He and Frank Kelly FREAS were the undisputed rulers of the sf-art realm during the 1950s and early 1960s, and among the few sf artists of the time able to make a decent living from their work. EE shared the first HUGO for Best Cover Artist with Hannes BOK in 1953; he won further Hugos in 1960, 1961, 1962 and 1964; the only other cover artists to win Hugos in that period were Freas and Roy G. KRENKEL.

EE also painted abstract expressionist canvases for gallery exhibition and worked in experimental 16mm movie-making. *Dance Chromatic* (1959), his first film, and *Thanatopsis* (1962) are still remembered. He turned to full time moviemaking in 1964, thereafter doing only occasional sf artwork as a favour to friends. His 38min *Relativity* (1966) is regarded by many critics as one of the greatest short films ever made. This second career was notably distinguished, the Museum of Modern Art being one of many bodies to recognize its importance. In 1971 he began working with videotape, then a very new medium; and he

was artist-in-residence at the Television Laboratory, WNET/13 in New York, winning yet more awards. He later (1981-6) became provost of the School of Film and Video at the California Institute of the Arts. EE was married to Carol EMSHWILLER.

As an sf artist, EE worked fast and skilfully, seeming equally at home in every sf illustrative mode, whether dramatic, symbolic or humorous. His style was vigorous but polished-seeming, though his actual lines (especially in interior artwork) tended to be rough, assured and full of character. While there is no denying his talent, he may have worked too speedily: from the perspective of the 1990s, little of his sf artwork seems especially memorable, and nobody then or now seems to have bothered to produce a book of his work. But in the 1950s he represented a definite step up from the colourful crudeness of most ILLUSTRATION for the PULP MAGAZINES. [JG/PN]

See also: ASTOUNDING SCIENCE-FICTION; GALAXY SCIENCE FICTION.

EMTSEV, MIKHAIL (TIKHONOVICH) (1930-   ) Russian scientist and writer whose most significant work has been accomplished in collaboration with Eremei PARNOV, also a trained scientist. They began their career with HARD-SF stories in 1961, publishing titles like *Uravneniie s Blednogo Neptuna* (coll **1964**; title story trans Helen Saltz Jacobson as "The Pale Neptune Equation" in *New Soviet Sf*, anth **1979** US), *Padeniie Sverkhnovoi* ["The Fall of the Supernova"] (**1964**), *Zelenaia Krevetka* ["The Green Shrimp"] (**1965**), *Tri Kvarka* ["Three Quarks"] (**1969**) and others. "'Vozvratite Liubov'!" (**1966**; trans Arthur Shkarovsky as "Bring Back Love" in *Everything but Love* anth **1973** Russia) was a remarkable first (and accurate) prediction of the neutron bomb. In *More Diraka* ["The Dirac Sea"] (**1967**) the scientist's moral responsibility is discussed, while *Dusha Mira* (**1964**; trans Antonina W. Bouis as *World Soul* **1978** US) combines Frankensteinian horrors with detailed speculation on the collective consciousness. Their most sophisticated novel, *Klotchia T'my Na Igle Vremeni* ["Turfs of Darkness on the Needle of Time"] (**1970**), is a TIME-TRAVEL fantasy with, as protagonist, a historian engaged in the study of all "reincarnations" of fascism through the ages. EP and Parnov discontinued their partnership in 1970. [VG]

See also: HIVE-MINDS.

ENCOUNTER AT RAVEN'S GATE ◊ INCIDENT AT RAVEN'S GATE.

ENDANGERED SPECIES Film (1982) Alive Enterprises/MGM-UA. Dir Alan Rudolph, starring Robert Urich, JoBeth Williams, Paul Dooley, Hoyt Axton, Peter Coyote. Screenplay Rudolph, John Binder, from a story by Judson Klinger, Richard Woods. 92 mins. Colour.

This exploitation movie, made in the wake of sensationalist reports emerging from rural areas of the US Midwest about mutilated cattle, features a vacationing New York detective (Urich) uneasily teaming with a local woman sheriff in Colorado

(Williams), first to investigate dead cattle falling from the sky and later to probe the roles of local conservative extremists and a paramilitary group. The explanation is nerve-gas testing, part of a rightwing conspiracy with implied official backing. This is a post-Watergate PARANOIA movie made by a well regarded director who did rather better in other films. [PN]

END OF AUGUST AT THE HOTEL OZONE, THE ◊ KONEC SRPNA V HOTELU OZÓN.

END OF THE WORLD Together with UTOPIAS and cautionary tales, apocalyptic visions form one of the three principal traditions of pre-20th-century futuristic fantasy. Visions inspired by the religious imagination go back into antiquity (◊ MYTHOLOGY; RELIGION), but the influence of the scientific imagination did not make itself felt in literature until the late 19th century, and the end-of-the-world theme maintained many of its religious overtones until very recently. The phrase itself has become looser in meaning; once the Comte du Buffon (1707-1788) had in *Epochs of Nature* (**1780**) popularized the notion that a whole series of "worlds" had occupied the Earth's surface, the finality of any particular end of the world became dubious. A wide spectrum, within which no firm dividing line can be drawn, extends from authentically apocalyptic visions to accounts of large-scale DISASTER; it would therefore be over-pedantic in this discussion to construe "world" as "planet".

The earliest SCIENTIFIC ROMANCES of world's end were the products of Romanticism: the anti-progressive *The Last Man, or Omegarus and Syderia* (**1806**) by Jean-Baptiste Cousin de Grainville (1746-1805) and Mary SHELLEY's gloomy Great Plague story *The Last Man* (**1826**). Thomas Campbell (1777-1844) also wrote a poem on the "Last Man" theme, and Thomas Hood (1799-1845) parodied it. Plagues were to remain one of the standard literary means of depopulating the world and destroying society, but the cosmic-disaster story rapidly became a particular favourite of scientific romance. Edgar Allan POE's "The Conversation of Eiros and Charmion" (1839) is an early comet-strike story, but many more followed Camille FLAMMARION's popularization of the idea in various magazine articles of the 1890s. Notable examples include George GRIFFITH's *Olga Romanoff* (**1894**) and H.G. WELLS's "The Star" (**1897**). These are NEAR-FUTURE stories, but FAR-FUTURE stories of the ultimate end of life on Earth began to appear in the same period. Flammarion's own apocalyptic fantasy *La fin du monde* (**1893-4**; trans as *Omega: The Last Days of the World* **1897** US) allows the Earth to survive its brush with a comet, but leaps ahead to describe the freezing of the world when the Sun cools. Wells did likewise in *The Time Machine* (**1895**), and Gabriel TARDE's *Underground Man* (**1896**; trans **1905**) imagines a much more rapid cooling. A similarly long-range view is taken in George C. WALLIS's "The Last Days of Earth" (1901). The visionary sequence in William Hope HODGSON's *The House on the Borderland* (**1908**) makes the death of the Earth a minor incident in a

grander scheme – an implication of irrelevance which is also used with telling effect in J.D. BERESFORD's "A Negligible Experiment" (1921) and Olaf STAPLEDON's *Star Maker* (**1937**).

End-of-the-world stories are frequently ambivalent, their writers often taking delight in contemplation of the destruction of everything that they hate. Robert CROMIE's *The Crack of Doom* (**1895**) – one of many tales of threatened apocalypses which are aborted in the nick of time – gives the scientist who wants to put an end to the human story abundant space to present his case. Wells thought that large-scale destruction was a necessary prelude to utopian regeneration, and M.P. SHIEL's *The Purple Cloud* (**1901**), in which Earth is depopulated by a cloud of cyanogen gas, contrives nevertheless to end with a triumphant affirmation of the progressiveness of EVOLUTION. John DAVIDSON's "The Salvation of Nature" (1887) is far more cynical, as is James Elroy FLECKER's "The Last Generation" (1908), in which mankind accepts extinction voluntarily. 20th-century religious apocalyptic fantasies – notable among them R.H. BENSON's *Lord of the World* (**1907**) – tend to revel in the expectation that an imminent end of the world will put a well deserved end to apostasy and decadence. There was a dramatic resurgence of apocalyptic scientific romance after WWI, among them many bitter parables arguing that modern men and women thoroughly deserved to lose all the gifts of civilization because of their stupid inability to refrain from warfare. Notable examples include Edward SHANKS's *The People of the Ruins* (**1920**), Cicely HAMILTON's *Theodore Savage* (**1922**; rev vt *Lest Ye Die* 1928), Neil BELL's *The Seventh Bowl* (**1930** as by Miles), John GLOAG's *Tomorrow's Yesterday* (**1932**) and J. Leslie MITCHELL's *Gay Hunter* (**1934**).

In fictions of this subgenre the impending end of the world is often foreseen (sometimes mistakenly) by the characters involved, and there are many stories in which those armed with foresight set out to make what preparations they can (usually derided by their neighbours – but they laughed at Noah, too). Examples include *The Second Deluge* (**1912**) by Garrett P. SERVISS, *Nordenholt's Million* (**1923**) by J.J. CONNINGTON, *When Worlds Collide* (**1933**) by Philip WYLIE and Edwin BALMER and "Ark of Fire" (1937-8) by John Hawkins. There are many stories in which only a few people are able to escape atomic war, in shelters, or to escape into space when the Sun goes nova; examples include *Death of a World* (**1948**) by J. Jefferson FARJEON and *One in Three Hundred* (**1954**) by J.T. MCINTOSH. A more subtle version explores the effect on various characters of the knowledge (again sometimes mistaken) that the world will end. Early examples are William MINTO's *The Crack of Doom* (**1886**) and Hugh KINGSMILL's "The End of the World" (1924); more recent ones are "The Last Night of the World" (1951) by Ray BRADBURY, "The Last Day" (1953) by Richard MATHESON and *On the Beach* (**1957**) by Nevil SHUTE.

The early sf PULP MAGAZINES featured numerous

luridly bleak visions of the end of the human race, and of the Earth itself, including Donald WANDREI's "The Red Brain" (1927), Amelia Long's "Omega" (1932) and L.H. Morrow's "Omega – The Man" (1933), but such stories appeared alongside others which were confident that mankind could outlast the Earth, if necessary, and need not be unduly troubled by the prospect of its end – a notion rarely met outside the magazines, although a notable exception is J.B.S. HALDANE's "The Last Judgment" (1927). Humanity lives on beyond the death of Earth in John W. CAMPBELL Jr's "Voice of the Void" (1930) and Arthur C. CLARKE's supremely smug "Rescue Party" (1946) – but Campbell also wrote stories in which mankind became extinct and Clarke's "The Nine Billion Names of God" (1953) makes an apocalyptic joke out of the smugness of Western Man. The theme continued to evoke mixed emotions no matter what new twists were given to it. Edmond HAMILTON's "Requiem" (1962) is a poignant story which regrets the commercial exploitation of the Earth's death as a spectacular tv show for a Galaxy-wide audience.

The idea that we might easily destroy ourselves and our world as our WEAPONS of war become ever more powerful gained ground steadily throughout the 1920s and 1930s. The atomic bomb in H.G. Wells's *The World Set Free* (1914) is fairly feeble, but the one in Harold NICOLSON's *Public Faces* (1932) is more like the real thing. The "ultimate deterrent" or "Dooms-day weapon" was introduced (and used) in *The Last Man* (1940; vt *No Other Man*) by Alfred NOYES. Such anxiety became extreme in Alfred BESTER's "Adam and No Eve" (1941), in which atomic destruction requires evolution to begin all over again in the sea. After Hiroshima the possibility of imminent atomic holocaust was clear to everyone, and lent new pertinence to apocalyptic thinking. It seemed entirely likely that the world would end with a bang and not a whimper after all, despite the broad sexual pun in the title of Damon KNIGHT's last-man-meets-last-woman story, "Not with a Bang" (1950). Notable examples of atomic-HOLOCAUST stories include *Shadow on the Hearth* (1950) by Judith MERRIL, *The Long Loud Silence* (1952) by Wilson TUCKER and *Level 7* (1959) by Mordecai ROSHWALD. The depth of the anxiety is perhaps better reflected by SATIRES and black comedies than by earnest speculation; notable examples of bitterly ironic apocalypses include Ward MOORE's *Greener than You Think* (1947), L. Sprague DE CAMP's "Judgment Day" (1955), Kurt VONNEGUT Jr's *Cat's Cradle* (1963) and Peter GEORGE's *Dr Strangelove* (1963). Fritz LEIBER's ironically despairing vignettes, including "A Pail of Air" (1951), "The Moon is Green" (1952) and "A Bad Day for Sales" (1953), are particularly effective in combining poignancy with irony. The urgency of the anxiety is reflected also in bleakly downbeat stories whose nihilistic temper is most unusual for a pulp-descended genre; examples include Robert A. HEINLEIN's "Year of the Jackpot" (1952), E.C. TUBB's "Tomorrow" (1954) and Robert

SILVERBERG's "Road to Nightfall" (1958). The post-WWII decade also produced sf's boldest novel about the end of the Universe: James BLISH's *The Triumph of Time* (1958; vt *A Clash of Cymbals*).

This pattern of ironic despair, bitter satire and grimly pessimistic "realism" extended into the 1960s and 1970s, when many more causes for the sense of imminent doom were popularized, including OVER-POPULATION and POLLUTION. Notable apocalyptic black comedies from this period include *The Genocides* (1965) by Thomas M. DISCH and "The Big Flash" (1969) by Norman SPINRAD. "When We Went to See the End of the World" (1972) by Robert Silverberg is more slickly ironic. A savage sense of despair is evident in "We All Die Naked" (1969) by James Blish and in *The End of the Dream* (1972) by Philip Wylie. A note of ironic innovation was struck by Poul ANDER-SON's *After Doomsday* (1962), the first ever whodunnit in which the Earth itself is the murder victim; equally ironic in its own way is the ingenious "Inconstant Moon" (1971) by Larry NIVEN, in which a sudden increase in the Moon's brightness reveals to those who can deduce its meaning that the Sun has gone nova and that dawn will bring destruction.

The increasing familiarity and plausibility of the idea of an imminent apocalypse has promoted the production of surreal apocalyptic visions both inside and outside the genre. Examples include the title story of *Up and Out* (coll 1957) by John Cowper POWYS, *Ice* (1967) by Anna KAVAN, both stories in *Apocalypses* (coll 1977) by R.A. LAFFERTY, *God's Grace* (1982) by Bernard MALAMUD and *Galapagos* (1985) by Kurt Vonnegut Jr. A similar spirit is detectable in those CYBERPUNK stories which use the obliteration or radical metamorphosis of Earthly civilization almost as a throwaway idea; examples include Bruce STER-LING's *Schismatrix* (1985) and Michael SWANWICK's *Vacuum Flowers* (1987). The end of the Universe is similarly relegated to throwaway status in Charles SHEFFIELD's *Between the Strokes of Night* (1985). An authentic emotional depth is, however, conserved by such poignantly bitter accounts as Hilbert SCHENCK's *A Rose for Armageddon* (1982), Frederik POHL's "Fermi and Frost" (1985) and James K. MORROW's heart-rending *This is the Way the World Ends* (1986).

The end of the Cold War may soothe anxieties about nuclear war, and the anticipated hysteria which forms the basis of such sardonic millenarian fantasies as Russell M. GRIFFIN's *Century's End* (1981) and John KESSEL's *Good News from Outer Space* (1989) is not to be taken seriously, but there has recently been a boom in cosmic-disaster stories occasioned by the fashionability of the celebrated question: "If we're not alone in the Universe, where *are* they?" Apocalyptic "explanations" of this presumed enigma include *Across the Sea of Suns* (1984) by Gregory BENFORD and *The Forge of God* (1987) by Greg BEAR.

A theme anthology is *The End of the World* (anth 1956) ed Donald A. WOLLHEIM. A notable collection of essays on apocalyptic literature is *The End of the World* (anth **1983**) ed Eric S. RABKIN, Martin H. GREENBERG and Joseph D. OLANDER. [BS]

See also: ENTROPY; FAR FUTURE.

END OF THE WORLD Film. ◊ PANIC IN YEAR ZERO!

END OF THE WORLD, THE Film. ◊ *La* FIN DU MONDE.

ENDORE, S(AMUEL) GUY (1901-1970) US writer and translator, some of whose realistic FANTASY novels can in a marginal sense be considered as sf (◊ PSYCHOLOGY). The best known is *The Werewolf of Paris* (**1933**), set in the shambles of 1871 Paris, where a French soldier is succumbing to lycanthropy; this represents on a human scale the civic trauma of the body politic as the Commune falls. *Methinks the Lady* (**1945**), a courtroom drama, explains its central female Jekyll-and-Hyde character in Freudian terms. Though having relatively little influence on the sf field, SGE was a highly effective purveyor of sexual fantasies; he did not mince words. He collaborated on the scripts of the films *The* DEVIL-DOLL and *Mad Love* (a version of ORLACS HÄNDE). [JC]

Other works: *The Man from Limbo* (**1930**).

See also: GOTHIC SF; SUPERNATURAL CREATURES.

ENEMY FROM SPACE ◊ QUATERMASS II.

ENEMY MINE Film (1985). Kings Road Entertainment/20th Century-Fox. Dir Wolfgang Petersen, starring Dennis Quaid, Louis Gossett Jr. Screenplay Edward Khmara, based on *Enemy Mine* (1979 *IASFM*; **1989** chap dos) by Barry B. LONGYEAR. 108 mins, cut to 93 mins. Colour.

During a space battle between humans and the reptilian (and hermaphroditic) Dracs, two pilots, one from each species, crashland on an inimical planet. The human (Quaid) and the Drac (Gossett) first try to kill one another, but soon reach an uneasy *rapprochement*, which warms into mutual respect and affection. When the Drac dies giving birth, the man raises the infant. It is later captured by illegal slaver/miners, its adoptive father being left for dead. However, he returns with assistance, the miners are defeated, and the child is saved. This uneven film works quite well on the intimate level, with excellent small moments of culture clash and mutual education; Gosset's performance is memorably good. On the larger scale, the effects creating the planetary surface and, at the end, the Drac planet are striking. But the film's earnest liberalism is both preachy and slickly sentimental, with too many scenes designed to evoke tearful, kneejerk responses; and overall it seems more selfconscious than the much earlier ROBINSON CRUSOE ON MARS (1964), the Crusoe-Friday parts of which its plot somewhat resembles. The novelization is *Enemy Mine* * (**1985**) by Barry B. Longyear and David GERROLD. [PN]

See also: CINEMA.

ENERGY ◊ COSMOLOGY; ENTROPY; NUCLEAR POWER; POWER SOURCES; PHYSICS; SUN.

ENGDAHL, SYLVIA LOUISE (1933-   ) US writer, employed in the field of computer programming 1957-67. Her novels, though marketed as juveniles, appeal as well to adults for their intelligence and humanity. *Enchantress from the Stars* (**1970**) and its sequel *The Far Side of Evil* (**1971**) are perhaps her best-known works. The first describes, with suggestive analogues between traditional and technological versions of crucial events (to a savage, all technology is MAGIC), the early career of Elena, who is in the Anthropological Service and must protect the "primitive" culture of one planet from a technologically more advanced culture from a neighbouring world. The second continues her career on another planet, which SLE describes as a totalitarian DYSTOPIA. A second series consists of *This Star Shall Abide* (**1972**; vt *Heritage of the Star* 1973 UK), *Beyond the Tomorrow Mountains* (**1973**) and *The Doors of the Universe* (**1981**). The societal design in these books, set on a planet with an imposed RELIGION, takes, not unusually, the shape of a pyramid, with benign but hidden representatives of an alien race ruling the world; more surprising is SLE's refusal to dismantle – after the time-honoured pattern – this hierarchy. [JC/PN]

Other works: *Journey Between Worlds* (**1970**).

As editor: *The Universe Ahead: Stories of the Future* (anth **1975**) with Rick Roberson; *Anywhere, Anywhere: Stories of Tomorrow* (anth **1976**).

Nonfiction: *The Planet-Girded Suns: Man's View of the Other Solar Systems* (**1974**); *The Subnuclear Zoo: New Discoveries in High Energy Physics* (**1977**) with Rick Roberson.

See also: CHILDREN'S SF.

ENGEL, LEONARD (1916-1964) US author, with Emanuel S. PILLER, of one of the very first Cold War dreadful-warning nuclear-WAR novels, *The World Aflame: The Russian-American War of 1950* (**1947**), in which the USA's monopoly of the A-bomb – and use of it in a first strike – proves insufficient to crush the Red hordes; a despairing humaneness invests the final pages. LE also edited a nonfiction anthology, *New Worlds of Modern Science* (anth **1956**). [JC]

ENGEL, LYLE KENYON (1915-1986) Canadian editor, book packager and writer; he edited UNCANNY TALES 1940-43 in Canada, and SPACE SCIENCE FICTION MAGAZINE and *Tales of the Frightened* in 1957. He also produced the **Richard Blade** SWORD-AND-SORCERY sequence, writing an unknown number of the titles under the house name Jeffrey Lord (most were by Roland J. GREEN). Through his packaging firm, Book Creations Inc., LKE created the **Kent Family Chronicles**, which made their author, John JAKES, famous. [JC]

ENGELHARDT, FREDERICK [s] ◊ L. Ron HUBBARD.

ENGH, M(ARY) J(ANE) (1933-   ) US librarian and writer whose first sf novel, *Arslan* (**1976**; vt *A Wind from Bukhara* 1979 UK), established a strong underground reputation in its first incarnation as a paperback original; a hardbound edition has since been released. *Arslan*, a young warlord from NEAR-FUTURE Turkestan, has enigmatically conquered both the USA and the USSR. He personally occupies the small Illinois town of Kraftsville, mentally and physically seducing a teenage boy while at the same time driving the book's protagonist into a state of powerful ambivalence about the cunning rape of his land. The book is subtle, seductive and very frightening. *The House in the Snow* (**1987**) is a juvenile of marginal interest. *Wheel of the Winds* (**1988**), a complex tale set on an alien planet and told from an alien perspective, perhaps inevitably lacks the hypnotic grip of *Arslan*, but the deadpan narrative "face" of this superficially cold novel conceals layers of passion. The main CONCEPTUAL BREAKTHROUGHS offered by the novel will be those experienced by the reader.   [JC]

ENGINEERING ◊ DISCOVERY AND INVENTION; MACHINES; TECHNOLOGY; TRANSPORTATION.

ENGLAND, GEORGE ALLAN (1877-1936) US explorer and author of, *inter alia*, 5 sf novels and over a dozen magazine serials and short stories from 1905 on; these appeared predominantly in Frank A. MUNSEY's magazines, where he was one of the more popular writers of the pre-1926 period, ranking as the closest rival in sf to Edgar Rice BURROUGHS. His stories were occasionally derivative: his serial "The House of Transformation" (1909) and his short story "The Thing from – Outside" (1923) are reminiscent of, respectively, H.G. WELLS's *The Island of Dr Moreau* (**1896**) and Algernon BLACKWOOD's "The Willows" (1907).

Several themes recur in his writings. IMMORTALITY and the elixir of youth appear in his LOST-WORLD serial "Beyond White Seas" (1909-10) and in another serial, "The Elixir of Hate" (1911), which presents more sophisticated characterization and ethical analysis than appears elsewhere in his PULP-MAGAZINE work. Socialist thought, in the mode of Jack LONDON, shapes the anticapitalist stances of *The Air Trust* (**1915**) and *The Golden Blight* (1912 *Cavalier*; **1916**); the first centres on a monopoly on air, the second on a ray that temporarily changes gold to ash. The latter has strong racist overtones, as does his most popular work, a long post-HOLOCAUST novel set in a devastated USA about 1000 years hence, *Darkness and Dawn* (1912-13 *Cavalier* as 3 separate serials, "Darkness and Dawn", "Beyond the Great Oblivion" and "The Afterglow"; fixup **1914**; rev in 5 vols as *Darkness and Dawn* 1964, *Beyond the Great Oblivion* 1965, *The People of the Abyss* 1966, *Out of the Abyss* 1967, and *The Afterglow* 1967).

Other works of interest include "The Empire of the Air" (1914), a serialized novel of INVASION by immaterial beings from the fourth DIMENSION, and "June 6, 2016" (1916), a short story with elaborate future gadgetry and a feminist twist. *The Flying Legion* (**1920**) is a heist story of the NEAR FUTURE involving advanced weaponry and the theft from Mecca of Islam's most sacred relic. "The Fatal Gift" (1915), a serial, deals with the production of a superwoman by plastic surgery. Lesser works are: "The Time Reflector" (1905), about an invention for viewing the past; "A Message from the Moon" (1907), in which advertising matter is projected onto the Moon; "My Time Annihilator" (1909), ostensibly about TIME TRAVEL to the past but really about madness; "He of the Glass Heart"

(1911), featuring an artificial heart; and "Drops of Death" (1922), a scientific detective story. "The Tenth Question" (1916), a mathematical puzzle story (◊ MATHEMATICS), was later rewritten by Stanley G. WEINBAUM as "Brink of Infinity" (1936).   [JE/EFB]

Other works: *Keep Off the Grass* (**1919**).

See also: CITIES; DEVOLUTION; DISASTER; DISCOVERY AND INVENTION; DYSTOPIAS; EVOLUTION; HISTORY OF SF; INVISIBILITY; MONEY; MONSTERS; POLITICS; VILLAINS.

ENGLAND, JAMES [r] ◊ ROBERT HALE LIMITED.

ENGLING, RICHARD (DAVID GEORGE PATRICK) (1952-   ) US writer whose NEAR-FUTURE sf novel, *Body Mortgage* (**1989**), tells in a CYBERPUNK idiom the tale of a Chicago private eye on the track of a body-parts scam in the immediate run-up to the millennium. RE's obvious competence would show more clearly, perhaps, in a more fully original setting.   [JC]

See also: MEDICINE.

ENGLISH, CHARLES [s] ◊ Charles NUETZEL.

ENSTROM, ROBERT (WILLIAM) (1946-   ) US industrial chemist and writer whose first novel, *Encounter Program* (**1977**), attempts to deal with a late-century sf problem – how to cope with ALIENS when we encounter them – in the language of SPACE OPERAS published 50 years earlier, when the problem was easier to solve. *Beta Colony* (**1980**) commits similar errors of register.   [JC]

ENTON, HARRY [r] ◊ DIME-NOVEL SF; FRANK READE LIBRARY; "NONAME".

ENTROPY In its strict meaning, "entropy" is a thermodynamics term, first used by the German physicist Rudolf Clausius (1822-1888) in 1850 to describe the amount of heat that must be put into a closed system to bring it to a given state. The Second Law of Thermodynamics – often stated in terms of work as "it is impossible to produce work by transferring heat from a cold body to a hot body in any self-sustaining process" – can alternatively be rendered: "Entropy always increases in any closed system not in equilibrium, and remains constant for a system that is in equilibrium."

To put it less technically: whenever there is a flow of energy some is always lost as low-level heat. For example, in a steam engine, the friction of the piston is manifested in non-useful heat, and hence some of the energy put into it is not turned into work. There is no such thing as a friction-free system, and for that reason no such thing as a perfect machine. Entropy is a measure of this loss. In a broader sense we can refer to entropy as a measure of the order of a system: the higher the entropy, the lower the order. There is more energy, for example, tied up in complex molecules than in simple ones (they are more "ordered"); the Second Law can therefore be loosely rephrased as "systems tend to become less complex". Heat flows, so ultimately everything will tend to stabilize at the same temperature. When this happens to literally everything – in what is often called the heat-death of the Universe – entropy will have reached its maximum, with no order left, total randomness, no life, the end. (There is, however, an argument about whether the concept of entropy can properly be related to the Universe as a whole.) Of course, the amount of usable energy in the Universe, primarily supplied by the stars, is unimaginably huge, and the heat-death of the Universe is billions of years away. Isaac ASIMOV's amusing "The Last Question" (1956) has a supercomputer, which for aeons has been worrying about the heat-death, reversing entropy at the last possible moment. The scientist Freeman DYSON, in "Time Without End: Physics and Biology in an Open Universe" (*Review of Modern Physics* July 1979), confronts the same question with a similar optimism and, one must assume, rather better mathematics. Local images of entropy, like the huge red Sun at the end of H.G. WELLS's *The Time Machine* (**1985**), long antedate the general use of the word; indeed, dying-Earth stories generally (◊ END OF THE WORLD) can be seen as entropy stories, both literally and metaphorically.

Although "entropy" has been a technical term for a long time, it is only since the early 1960s that it has, in its extended meaning, become a fashionable concept (although the word sometimes popped up in sf earlier, as in *House of Entropy* [**1953**] by H.J. CAMPBELL as Roy SHELDON). Since the 1960s, to the annoyance of some scientifically minded people, the extended concept of increasing entropy includes holes wearing in socks, refrigerators breaking down, coalminers going on strike, and death. These are indeed all examples of increasing disorder in a technical though not necessarily a moral sense. Life itself is a highly ordered state, and in its very existence is an example of negative entropy (negentropy). It is as if, though the Universe is running down, there are whirlpools of local activity where things are winding up. All forms of information, whether in the form of the DNA code or the contents of this encyclopedia, can be seen as examples of negentropy. It is natural, then, that a popular variant on the entropy story is the DEVOLUTION story.

Entropy has become a potent metaphor. It is uncertain who first introduced the term into sf, but it is likely that Philip K. DICK, who makes much of the concept in nearly all his work, was the first to popularize it. He spells it out in *Do Androids Dream of Electric Sheep?* (**1968**), where entropy, or increasing disorder, is imaged as "kipple": "Kipple is useless objects, like junk mail or match folders after you use the last match or gum wrappers or yesterday's homeopape. When nobody's around, kipple reproduces itself . . . the entire universe is moving towards a final state of total, absolute kippleization."

It was, however, in NEW-WAVE writing, especially that associated with the magazine NEW WORLDS, that the concept of entropy made its greatest inroads into sf. J.G. BALLARD has used it a great deal, and did so as early as "The Voices of Time" (1960), in which a count-down to the end of the Universe is accompanied by more localized entropic happenings, includ-

ing the increasing sleepiness of the protagonist. Pamela ZOLINE's "The Heat Death of the Universe" (1967), about the life of a housewife, is often quoted as an example of the metaphoric use of entropy. Another example is "Running Down" (1975) by M. John HARRISON, whose protagonist, a shabby man who perishes in earthquake and storm, "carried his own entropy around with him". The concept appears in the work of Thomas M. DISCH, Barry N. MALZBERG, Robert SILVERBERG, Norman SPINRAD and James TIPTREE Jr as a *leitmotiv*, and also in nearly all the work of Brian W. ALDISS, which typically displays a tension between entropy and negentropy, between fecundity and life on the one hand, stasis, decay and death on the other. Outside GENRE SF, Thomas PYNCHON has used images of entropy many times, especially in *Gravity's Rainbow* (**1973**). George Alec EFFINGER's *What Entropy Means to Me* (**1972**) is not in fact a hardcore entropy story at all (apart from a tendency for things to go wrong), but Robert Silverberg's "In Entropy's Jaws" (1971) is a real entropy story and a fine one, exploring the metaphysics of the subject with care. Although it was in the 1960s and 1970s that the entropy-story peaked, the image is still used, as in Dan SIMMONS's *Entropy's Bed at Midnight* (**1990** chap).

Colin GREENLAND once wrote a critical book called *The Entropy Exhibition: Michael Moorcock and the UK "New Wave"* (**1983**), and it is indeed Moorcock who has perhaps made more complex use of entropy and negentropy than any other sf writer, and not just in *The Entropy Tango* (fixup **1981**); the two concepts run right through his **Dancers at the End of Time** and **Jerry Cornelius** sequences. Jerry Cornelius seems for a long time proof against entropy, and keeps slipping into alternate realities as if in hope of finding one whose vitality outlives its decay, but like a Typhoid Mary he carries the plague of entropy with him, and ultimately, especially after the death of his formidably vital and vulgar mother, succumbs to it himself, becoming touchingly more human, though diminished.

In all of these works, entropy is a symbol or metaphor through which the fate of the macrocosm, the Universe, can be linked to the fate of societies and of the individual – a very proper subject for sf. Negentropy versus entropy is usually seen as an unequal battle, David against Goliath, but sickness, sorrow, rusting, cooling and death contrive to be held at bay, locally and occasionally, by passion and movement and love. Looked at from this perspective, entropy is one of the oldest themes in literature, the central concern, for example, of Shakespeare, Donne, Milton and – especially – Charles DICKENS.   [PN]

ERDMAN, PAUL E(MIL) (1932-   ) Canadian writer, formerly consulting economist to the European Coal and Steel Community and a senior banker in Switzerland. Some of his thrillers are genuine NEAR-FUTURE sf of an interesting kind. Sf writers usually imagine future changes that are technological or political, seldom ECONOMIC. Like the CYBERPUNK authors, though more "bestseller" than cyberpunk in style, PEE recognizes the supra-national importance of giant cartels in the world of tomorrow (and today). His thrillers involve the manipulation of financial institutions; they portray a financial world of frightening instability in which economic collapse followed by global disorder and war could be catalysed by the actions of only a few unscrupulous persons. After the success of *The Billion Dollar Killing* (**1973**) and *The Silver Bears* (**1974**), both set more or less in the present, PEE wrote three NEAR-FUTURE novels: *The Crash of '79* (**1976**), *The Last Days of America* (**1981**) and *The Panic of '89* (**1986**), in each of which world catastrophe is only a year or two ahead. In the first, oil money destabilizes the US banking system and then the world's, and there are prophetic observations about Iran. [PN]

Other works: *The Palace* (**1987**).

See also: HISTORY OF SF.

ERICKSON, STEVE Working name of US writer Stephen Michael Erickson (1950-   ), active as a journalist for some years before his first novel, *Days Between Stations* (**1985**), quickly established his reputation as an author of dark, journey-haunted, surreal FABULATIONS about the USA and the 20th century. Labyrinthine figurations of apocalypse dominate his grey and hyperbolic landscapes; but a powerful sense of geography, notable also in the first Surrealists, gives each of his novels a local habitation. *Days Between Stations*, set mainly on an allegorically split river, features the attempts of two sensually linked people to make sense of their pasts; *Rubicon Beach* (**1986**) is a more specific allegory of the USA, as are *Tours of the Black Clock* (**1989**) and the semidocumentary *Leap Year* (**1989**). Although sf instruments sometime protrude through the texture of these tales, they are in no telling sense works of genre. [JC]

ERIKSEN, INGE [r] ◊ DENMARK.

ERMAN, JACQUES DeFOREST [s] ◊ Forrest J. ACKERMAN.

ERNSBERGER, GEORGE [r] ◊ AVON FANTASY READER.

ERNST, PAUL (FREDERICK) (1899-1985) US writer, mostly of short fiction for pulp markets, sometimes under his own name and sometimes (once in *Weird Tales*) under the pseudonym Paul Frederick Stern; he should not be confused with the Paul Ernst (1886-?   ) who wrote 1930s detective novels. His first published story may have been "The Temple of Serpents" for *Weird Tales* in 1928, and he remained extremely active throughout the 1930s, writing for sf, fantasy and hero magazines. In the last capacity, under the house name Kenneth ROBESON, he was responsible for much of the contents of *The Avenger*, writing all 23 novel-length stories for that magazine in 1939, each featuring **The Avenger**, a SUPERHERO who fought a wide range of villains; the Robeson house name had already been made popular by Lester DENT in DOC SAVAGE MAGAZINE, and it was in an attempt to cash in on the success of the name that it was offered for PE's use.

These tales all appeared in book form in the 1970s as *Justice, Inc* * (**1972**), *The Yellow Hoard* * (**1972**), *The Sky Walker* * (**1972**), *The Devil's Horns* * (**1972**), *The Frosted Death* * (**1972**), *The Blood Ring* * (**1972**), *Stockholders in Death* * (**1972**), *The Glass Mountain* * (**1973**), *Tuned for Murder* * (**1973**), *The Smiling Dogs* * (**1973**), *River of Ice* * (**1973**), *The Flame Breathers* * (**1973**), *Murder on Wheels* * (**1973**), *Three Gold Crowns* * (**1973**), *House of Death* * (**1973**), *The Hate Master* * (**1973**), *Nevlo* * (**1973**), *Death in Slow Motion* * (**1973**), *Pictures of Death* * (**1973**), *The Green Killer* * (**1974**), *The Happy Killers* * (**1974**), *The Black Death* * (**1974**), *The Wilder Curse* * (**1974**) and *Midnight Murder* * (**1974**), the last being from 1940. (Subsequent **The Avenger** novels in the 1970s series were originals written by Ron GOULART, also as Robeson.) PE's **Doctor Satan** series in *Weird Tales* is fantasy along conventional hero-villain lines; five of these stories were reprinted as *Dr Satan* (coll **1974** chap) ed Robert E. WEINBERG. His sf stories – the first of which were "The Black Monarch" (**1930** *Weird Tales*) and "Marooned under the Sea" (**1930** *ASF*) – include "The Microscopic Giants" (**1936**) and "Nothing Happens on the Moon" (**1939**). PE was less prolific after the 1930s. [PN/JC]

See also: ASTOUNDING SCIENCE-FICTION.

ERNSTING, WALTER [r] ◊ Clark DARLTON; GERMANY.

ERSKINE, GEORGE [r] ◊ Ian CAMERON.

ERSKINE, THOMAS (1788-1870) UK writer, mostly of religious texts, whose anonymously published SATIRES, *Armata: A Fragment* (**1816**) and *The Second Part of Armata* (**1817**), both assembled as *Armata: A Fragment* (omni **1817**), describe a society on another planet rather similar to Earth and reachable via our South Pole, to which it is attached. [JC]

ERTZ, SUSAN (1894-1985) UK popular novelist, active for much of the century, whose one sf novel, *Woman Alive* (**1935**), flips the more usual last-man-alive theme in a story of the last woman alive, after all other females have died of a post-war plague in 1985. [JC]

ESCAPE FROM NEW YORK Film (1981). Avco Embassy/International Film Investors/Goldcrest. Dir John CARPENTER, prod Larry Franco and Debra Hill, starring Kurt Russell, Lee Van Cleef, Donald Pleasence, Ernest Borgnine, Harry Dean Stanton, Adrienne Barbeau, Isaac Hayes. Screenplay Carpenter, Nick Castle. 99 mins. Colour.

The idea is wonderful. In 1997 the whole of Manhattan Island is a penal colony, surrounded by minefields and unscalable walls and inhabited by criminal scum and crazies. In this inferno lands the US President (a creepy performance from Pleasence) after a plane crash. War-hero and criminal Snake Plissken (Russell), implanted with 24-hour-fused explosives to ensure his voluntary return, is sent in to get the President out. Looking like an attempt to recapture some of the brilliance of Carpenter's first major thriller, *Assault on Precinct 13* (1976), the film instead loses itself in routine though colourful macho confrontations; it is a little reminiscent of the exploitation formula of the MAD MAX sequence, and is not helped by Russell's inexpressive performance.   [PN]

ESCAPE FROM THE PLANET OF THE APES Film (1971). Apjac/20th Century-Fox. Dir Don Taylor, starring Roddy McDowall, Kim Hunter, Bradford Dillman, Natalie Trundy, William Windom. Screenplay Paul Dehn, based on characters created by Pierre BOULLE. 97 mins. Colour.

This is the third of the five PLANET OF THE APES films. When the late UK screenwriter Paul Dehn – author of *Quake, Quake, Quake* (coll **1961**), a series of parody verses, illustrated by Edward Gorey, on the aftermaths of the nuclear age – had been working on the second (BENEATH THE PLANET OF THE APES [1970]) he had been told it would be the last, so he decided to end the film by destroying the whole world with an atomic explosion. Four months later he received a telegram from Fox saying: "Apes exist, sequel required." His ingenious answer was to send three of the apes by TIME TRAVEL back to before the world exploded. They arrive in the contemporary USA and immediately become the centre of a violent controversy which results in their deaths, but not before the female who featured in the first two films has given birth to a baby ape. This mixture of SATIRE and action/adventure is much more sentimental than its hard-edged predecessors, but more entertaining than those that followed. The novelization is *Escape from the Planet of the Apes* ∗ (**1974**) by Jerry POURNELLE. [JB/PN]

ESCAPE OF MEGAGODZILLA, THE ◊ GOJIRA.

ESCAPE TO WITCH MOUNTAIN ◊ Alexander KEY.

ESCHATOLOGY Eschatology is the class of theological doctrine pertaining to death and the subsequent fate of the soul, and to the ultimate fate of the world. Stories of the FAR FUTURE and the END OF THE WORLD can be categorized as eschatological, but are considered separately; this section deals mainly with the idea of personal survival after death.

Ancient Egyptian RELIGION included an inordinately complex set of eschatological beliefs (explored in sf in Roger ZELAZNY's *Creatures of Light and Darkness* [**1969**]) which influenced most subsequent eschatologies. Christian eschatology is, of course, basically dualistic, contrasting Heaven and Hell, but it has variants which are more complex, incorporating Purgatory and Limbo, and including an involved demonology. A common strategy employed by sf writers writing pure FANTASY (as for instance in the magazine UNKNOWN) is to import a judicious measure of common sense into settings derived from classical MYTHOLOGY or the Christian demonological schema, usually with comic results – although unorthodox horror stories sometimes result.

The growth of the SCIENTIFIC ROMANCE in the late 19th century coincided with the growth of the Spiritualist movement. The Spiritualists popularized an eroded version of Christian eschatology with some added jargon involving the "astral plane" and like concepts. Spiritualist beliefs influenced several early

sf writers, including Camille FLAMMARION and Arthur Conan DOYLE; Doyle's later works – particularly *The Land of Mist* (**1926**) and "The Maracot Deep" (in *The Maracot Deep and Other Stories* coll **1929**) – are markedly affected. There is an abundance of Spiritualist fiction, but whether any of this can be considered sf is dubious, despite the pseudo-scientific endeavours of Johann Zöllner (1834-1882), author of *Transcendental Physics* (**1865**), and other psychic theorists. The most heavily sciencefictionalized of these Spiritualist fantasies is Allen UPWARD's *The Discovery of the Dead* (**1910**), which recounts the revelations of a "necroscope". An early pulp-sf writer who dabbled in Spiritualist fiction was Ralph Milne FARLEY, as in *Dangerous Love* (**1931**; **1946**). More interesting is David LINDSAY's interstellar fantasy *A Voyage to Arcturus* (**1920**), which inverts conventional Spiritualist ideas and routine eschatological aspirations, imagining an intrinsically painful destiny.

The idea that scientists might one day prove the existence of the elusive soul and build traps for it is featured in Charles B. STILSON's curious "Liberty or Death!" (1917; vt "The Soul Trap"), and is developed more ambitiously in *The Weigher of Souls* (**1931**) by André MAUROIS. Maurois may have borrowed his inspiration from the fantasy *Spirite* (**1865**; trans **1877**) by Théophile Gautier (1811-1872), and his example inspired in its turn Romain GARY's satirical soul-trapping story *The Gasp* (**1973**), in which the inexhaustible energy of the soul is quickly exploited as an industrial resource. In all these examples, as in most stories in which people supposedly trespass on divine prerogatives, no good comes of it all. Nor does it in Maurice RENARD's *Le docteur Lerne, sous-dieu* (**1908**; trans as *New Bodies for Old* **1923** US), when an experiment in metempsychosis ends with the imprisonment of a person's soul in the engine of a motor car. An experiment in communication with the dead ends tragically in *The Edge of Running Water* (**1939**; vt *The Unquiet Corpse*) by William M. SLOANE. A curious corollary of the conviction that "there are things Man is not meant to know" is the profusion of afterlife fantasies in which characters realize only at the story's end that they have been dead since its beginning; two which transcend the banality of the plot are Ray BRADBURY's "Pillar of Fire" (1948) and Flann O'BRIEN's *The Third Policeman* (**1967**).

C.S. LEWIS's theological fantasy *The Great Divorce* (**1945**) acknowledges that some of the ideas used in formulating its image of Heaven are borrowed from sf, but sf writers were slow to develop the hypothesis that future TECHNOLOGY might succeed in securing the life after death that God and Nature had failed to provide. Robert SHECKLEY's melodrama of technological REINCARNATION, *Immortality Delivered* (**1958**; exp vt *Immortality, Inc.* 1959), is an early example which skates lightly over the experience of disembodied existence and the question of ultimate destiny. Thomas M. DISCH's *On Wings of Song* (**1979**) features a technology which grants out-of-body experiences to almost everyone, but Disch is likewise coy about the possibility of universal life after death. A similar hesitancy is seen in the many stories which Philip José FARMER has devoted to eschatological matters, including *Inside Outside* (**1964**), *Traitor to the Living* (**1973**) and the **Riverworld** series. More ambitious and more convincing stories of technological afterlife include Robert SILVERBERG's "Born with the Dead" (1974), Lisa TUTTLE's "The Hollow Man" (1979) and Lucius SHEPARD's account of biotechnological zombies, *Green Eyes* (**1984**). Silverberg had earlier written *To Live Again* (**1969**) on a less interesting eschatological theme; here the personas of living persons are regularly "recorded" so that, after the death of the body, the most recent recording can be introduced into the mind of a host. Similar recording processes are featured – without the consequent overcrowding of skulls on which Silverberg focuses – in other stories of reincarnation, including John VARLEY's *The Ophiuchi Hotline* (**1977**) and Michael BERLYN's nasty-minded *Crystal Phoenix* (**1980**).

Some writers have sciencefictionalized the Christian notion of the soul, imagining it as an alien symbiont (◊ PARASITISM AND SYMBIOSIS) which invests living beings and survives their deaths. Clifford D. SIMAK, in *Time and Again* (**1951**; vt *First He Died* 1953), makes no attempt to describe the life led by such symbionts when apart from their hosts, but Bob SHAW, in *The Palace of Eternity* (**1969**), is more ambitious, equating the pseudoastral plane with the extradimensional HYPERSPACE employed by the starships to transcend Einsteinian limitations. In Deane ROMANO's *Flight from Time One* (**1972**) the astral plane is no sooner discovered by science than exploited, but the novel follows the exploits of "astralnauts" without saying anything about the spirits of the departed. Rudy RUCKER's *White Light* (**1980**) is much more courageous and ingenious in following the venerable example of C.H. HINTON by recruiting mathematical speculations about infinity (and Cantor's extrapolated hierarchy of infinities on infinities) to construct a metaphysics which includes an afterlife. Harlan ELLISON's "The Region Between" (1970) is a bold surreal melodrama featuring soul-predation. A particularly poignant story in which science ultimately reveals that human personalities do live on after death is Richard COWPER's "The Tithonian Factor" (1983), which considers the plight of those who have already accepted an inferior technology of IMMORTALITY. Special eschatologies are sometimes devised for individual characters: death as metamorphosis is often featured in the work of Charles L. HARNESS and the later work of Robert A. HEINLEIN, and is notable in Thomas M. DISCH's *Camp Concentration* (**1968**). ALIENS often fare better than humans in this breed of sf, having some kind of afterlife built into their BIOLOGY; examples can be found in Poul ANDERSON's "The Martyr" (1960), George R.R. MARTIN's "A Song for Lya" (1974) and Nicholas YERMAKOV's *The Last Communion* (**1981**) and its sequels. Some writers have

developed this line of thought on a grander scale, moving eschatological speculation to a level which takes in entire species, or even the entire Universe. Arthur C. CLARKE's *Childhood's End* (**1953**) features the transcendent "apotheosis" of mankind's superior descendants, producing an image very similar to that evoked by the heretical Jesuit and evolutionist Pierre Teilhard de Chardin (1881-1955); Teilhard's ideas are overtly invoked in George ZEBROWSKI's *The Omega Point Trilogy* (omni **1983**).

Although they are not sf, mention must be made of a recent group of quasi-Dantean fantasies by sf writers. *Inferno* (**1975**) by Larry NIVEN and Jerry POURNELLE was the apparent inspiration for a series of SHARED-WORLD anthologies and novels "created" by Janet E. MORRIS, begun with *Heroes in Hell* (anth **1986**) and *The Gates of Hell* (**1986**); Robert Silverberg's contributions featuring Gilgamesh were subsequently reassembled in *To the Land of the Living* (fixup **1989**). A much more earnest and varied theme anthology – one of the best of its kind – is *Afterlives* (anth **1986**) ed Pamela SARGENT and Ian WATSON, whose contributions, mostly original to the volume, range over the entire spectrum of eschatological fantasy and sf. Outstanding among the sf stories are Gregory BENFORD's "Of Space-Time and the River", Rudy Rucker's "In Frozen Time" and Watson's own "The Rooms of Paradise"; Watson is also the author of the very eschatological novel *Deathhunter* (**1981**).   [BS]
See also: COSMOLOGY; ENTROPY; GODS AND DEMONS; METAPHYSICS.

ESENWEIN, J(OSEPH) BERG ◊ ANTHOLOGIES.

ESHBACH, LLOYD ARTHUR (1910-   ) US writer and publisher, and an sf enthusiast from an early age. Though his work as a publisher has always – and probably rightly – been deemed his main contribution to the field, a splurge of novels in the 1980s, after he had been inactive as a writer for many years, has focused some attention on his auctorial work. He began publishing sf with "The Man with the Silver Disc" for *Scientific Detective* in 1930, and for some years wrote fairly prolifically for the PULP MAGAZINES; the best of this early work was assembled in *The Tyrant of Time* (coll **1955**), a volume published by his own FANTASY PRESS, which he had formed in 1946; it was probably the best of the SMALL PRESSES founded after the war to put into book form the novels and stories that had been accumulating in magazines since the founding of AMAZING STORIES in 1926. In 1952 he began a short-lived companion imprint, Polaris Press. For Fantasy Press LAE edited the first published book about modern sf: *Of Worlds Beyond: The Science of Science Fiction Writing* (anth **1947**), a symposium of essays by such authors as John W. CAMPBELL Jr, Robert A. HEINLEIN and A.E. VAN VOGT. *Over My Shoulder: Reflections on a Science Fiction Era* (**1983**), told in memoir form, is a history of the sf specialist presses from the 1930s to the 1950s.

In the 1980s LAE turned again to fiction. He edited P. Schuyler MILLER's **Alice in Wonderland** parody,

Alicia in Blunderland (1933 *Science Fiction Digest* as by Nihil; **1983**), and he sorted out and completed a manuscript left by his old friend E.E. "Doc" SMITH, publishing it as *Subspace Encounter* (**1983**) by Smith, ed LAE. His major work of the decade, the **Gates of Lucifer** sequence – *The Land Beyond the Gate* (**1984**), *The Armlet of the Gods* (**1986**), *The Sorceress of Scath* (**1988**) and *The Scroll of Lucifer* (**1990**) – does not forge its way into new territory, though the facility which LAE displays in putting his protagonist through various paces in various mythic venues is notable in an author so long inactive. Like Jack WILLIAMSON's, his career has extended throughout almost the entire history of the modern GENRE SF, which he continues to grace in his supporting role. [JC/MJE]
See also: CYBORGS; LONGEVITY (IN WRITERS AND PUBLICATIONS); SPECULATIVE FICTION.

ESP An acronym (for extra-sensory perception) popularized by the pioneering exercise in parapsychology *Extra-Sensory Perception* (1934) by J.B. Rhine (1895-1980), which attempted to repackage folkloristic notions of "second sight" or a "sixth sense" in scientific jargon. Definitions of the term "ESP" vary, but it may be taken to include clairvoyance, telepathy and precognition; many modern sf stories deal also with a restricted kind of telepathy, empathy, in which only feelings and not thoughts may be perceived. Stories about new senses and eccentric augmentations of existing ones are covered in the article on PERCEPTION. Rhine's investigations of ESP eventually broadened out to take in a fuller spectrum of wild talents; for stories about psychokinesis, teleportation and mental fire-raising ◊ PSI POWERS.

The late 19th century saw a boom in occult romances featuring various kinds of extra-sensory perceptions; attempts by the Society for Psychical Research and other bodies to account for such phenomena in scientific terms helped bring many such romances close to the sf borderline, and encouraged more thoughtful consideration of the implications of possessing these powers. *A Seventh Child* (**1894**) by "John Strange Winter" (Henrietta Stannard [1856-1911]), *Kark Grier: The Strange Story of a Man with a Sixth Sense* (1906) by Louis TRACY and *The Sixth Sense* (**1915**) by Stephen McKenna (1885-1967) are trivial, but they helped pave the way for Muriel JAEGER's *The Man with Six Senses* (**1927**), the first attempt to extrapolate such a hypothesis carefully and painstakingly – and to conclude that it might better be reckoned a curse than a blessing. Some early pulp-sf stories were also cautionary tales, including Edmond HAMILTON's "The Man who Saw the Future" (1930) and "The Man with X-Ray Eyes" (1933).

The notion that new powers of ESP might be developed in the course of humankind's future EVOLUTION, although treated sceptically by H.G. WELLS, was developed by several of the UK writers he influenced, including J.D. BERESFORD in *The Hampdenshire Wonder* (**1911**) and Olaf STAPLEDON in *Last and First Men* (**1930**). It also became a standard theme in

GENRE SF, where in the late 1930s Rhine's work began to attract interest along with that of Charles FORT, whose *Wild Talents* (1932) had dealt extensively with ESP. ESP quickly became part of the standard repertoire of the pulp SUPERMAN, much encouraged by A.E. VAN VOGT's *Slan* (1940 *ASF*; **1946**), in which a new race of telepaths struggles against the prejudices of ordinary mortals – a theme further explored in such later novels as Henry KUTTNER's *Mutant* (1945-52 *ASF*; fixup **1953**) and George O. SMITH's *Highways in Hiding* (**1956**). John W. CAMPBELL Jr, the editor of ASTOUNDING SCIENCE-FICTION, was eventually to become a fervent admirer of Rhine, and ESP stories featured very prominently in the post-war "psi-boom" which he engineered. Important products of this boom included James BLISH's *Jack of Eagles* (**1952**; vt *ESP-er* 1958), Wilson TUCKER's *Wild Talent* (**1954**) and Frank M. ROBINSON's *The Power* (**1956**). The variant title of the first-named is a significant use of the term ESPER (found also in Lloyd BIGGLE Jr's *The Angry Espers* [**1961** dos]), which had first been popularized in *The Demolished Man* (**1953**) by Alfred BESTER, a bold pioneering attempt to depict a society into which espers are fully integrated. Because the psi-boom years coincided with the early years of the Cold War, Campbell's writers paid a good deal of attention to the utility of telepathy in espionage – a frequent theme in the solo and collaborative works of Randall GARRETT. Telepaths still occasionally find such employment in such works as Stephen GOLDIN's *Mindflight* (**1978**), Daniel Keys MORAN's *Emerald Eyes* (**1988**) and especially the **Sensitives** series by Herbert Burkholz (1932-   ) – *The Sensitives* (**1987**) and *Strange Bedfellows* (**1988**) – but probably do more socially useful work as psychotherapists, like those in John BRUNNER's *The Whole Man* (1958-9 *Science Fantasy*; fixup **1964**; vt *Telepathist* UK) and Roger ZELAZNY's *The Dream Master* (**1966**). ESP is sometimes invoked as a solution to the problem of COMMUNICATION with ALIENS, although the logic of this is somewhat suspect (thought is largely couched in language); one of the more intelligent exercises in this vein is Edward LLEWELLYN's *Word-Bringer* (**1986**).

Sf writers, ever on the side of progress, usually side with ESP-powered supermen against those who hate and fear them. Theodore STURGEON's work includes many stories in which an ESP-based psychological community is seen as a possible and highly desirable solution to ordinary human alienation; examples include *The Dreaming Jewels* (**1950**; vt *The Synthetic Man*), *More than Human* (fixup **1953**) and ". . . And My Fear is Great" (1953). Other genre-sf writers who showed a consistently thoughtful and positive interest in ESP-talented characters while the psi-boom gradually lost its impetus included Zenna HENDERSON, in the long-running **People** series collected in *Pilgrimage* (coll of linked stories 1961) and *The People: No Different Flesh* (coll of linked stories 1966), James H. SCHMITZ, in the **Telzey Amberdon** series and *Agent of Vega* (coll 1960), Arthur SELLINGS, most notably in *Telepath* (1962) and *The Uncensored Man* (1964), Frank HERBERT, especially in the series begun with *Dune* (1965), Marion Zimmer BRADLEY in the **Darkover** series, and Dan MORGAN in the trilogy begun with *The New Minds* (1967).

In Sturgeon's stories ESP often compensates for other inadequacies – a common theme strikingly displayed in such stories as Gene WOLFE's "The Eyeflash Miracles" (1976) and John VARLEY's "The Persistence of Vision" (1978). In more extreme Sturgeon stories, particularly *More than Human* and *The Cosmic Rape* (1958), the acquisition of telepathic powers becomes a kind of transcendental breakthrough. Similarly transcendental ideas of psionic "cosmic community" cropped up occasionally in the work of Clifford D. SIMAK, notably in *Time is the Simplest Thing* (1961). Not all sf stories, however, place ESP in a positive light. The kind of telepathic "gestalt-mind" featured in *More than Human* is given more sceptical treatment in *The Inner Wheel* (1970) by Keith ROBERTS. The possible embarrassments of telepathy are pointed out in Walter M. MILLER's "Command Performance" (1952; vt "Anybody Else Like Me?"). Such novels as André MAUROIS's *La machine à lire les pensées* (1937; trans as *The Thought-Reading Machine* 1938 UK) suggest that ESP abilities might be utterly insignificant (though the Emotional Registers in the latter book are purely mechanical devices), but other stories tend to an opposite extreme; even Sturgeon, in his empath story "Need" (1961), recognized that an ability to sense other people's pain might constitute an appalling burden. Numerous tales, notably Lester DEL REY's *Pstalemate* (1971) and Jack DANN's *The Man who Melted* (1984), propose that people endowed with ESP might very readily become insane, and the well adjusted esper generally has to be credited with an ability to screen out unwanted images, thoughts and feelings lest he or she should lose his or her true self, as the hero of Roger ZELAZNY's *Bridge of Ashes* (1976) routinely does. Unfortunate consequences of ESP endowment are elaborately described in such novels as Joanna RUSS's *And Chaos Died* (1970), Mike DOLINSKY's *Mind One* (1972), Robert SILVERBERG's *Dying Inside* (1972) and Leigh KENNEDY's *The Journal of Nicholas the American* (1986). Partly as a result of these sceptical analyses, the idea that ESP might play a crucial role in future human evolution has lost much of its fashionableness, although it is a subsidiary element in Storm CONSTANTINE's not-altogether-earnest **Wraeththu** trilogy (1987-9).

Sf stories which isolate some aspect of ESP for specific consideration usually deal (as do most of the above examples) with telepathy, but there is also a notable tradition of stories dealing specifically with precognition, and with the apparent paradoxes which arise from having knowledge of the future. Characters whose foresight of the future is perversely impotent extend from the hero of J.D. Beresford's "Young Strickland's Career" (1921) to the heroine of C.J. CHERRYH's aptly titled "Cassandra" (1978); and

Philip K. DICK's "precogs", including the one in *The World Jones Made* (1956), rarely get much joy out of their abilities. Brian M. STABLEFORD's "The Oedipus Effect" (1991) borrows Karl Popper's term for the effects which predictions have on the outcome of situations in order to examine the paradoxicality of precognitive talents. Robert Silverberg's *The Stochastic Man* (1975) considers precognition in much the same sceptical way that his *Dying Inside* had examined telepathy. Precognition of a patchy and teasingly perverse kind is a common element in thrillers on the sf borderline; a notable example is Stephen KING's *The Dead Zone* (1979).

Despite the inconsistency displayed by supposedly talented subjects and the fact that several of his best performers were ultimately exposed as frauds, Rhine's intellectual descendants have managed to cling to sufficient credibility to support the production of numerous thrillers which deploy ESP without admitting to being sf; examples include *Mind out of Time* (1958) by Angela TONKS and *The Mind Readers* (1965) by Margery Allingham (1904-1966), though the latter uses a mechanical device for mind-reading rather than ESP proper. Parapsychological research labs are a common setting for stories on this borderline. Lifestyle fantasists who pass themselves off as clairvoyants or "psychics" are sometimes avid to help the police solve crimes; their negligible success rate is, of course, much improved by their fictional counterparts. Barry N. MALZBERG's and Bill PRONZINI's *Night Screams* (1979) is an ironic reflection of the phenomenon, which remains a popular theme in the CINEMA and TELEVISION.

Two theme anthologies are *14 Great Tales of ESP* (anth 1969) ed Idella Purnell Stone and *Frontiers II: The New Mind* (anth 1973) ed Roger ELWOOD.   [PN/BS]

ESPER In sf TERMINOLOGY, a person who is able to use one or other of the powers of ESP; ESP is usually regarded as including such "passive" powers as telepathy (mind-reading) and perhaps precognition and clairvoyance; and occasionally also the "active" psychic abilities – those that interact with the world of matter, such as TELEKINESIS. However, most sf writers reserve the terms PSIONICS or PSI POWERS for the full spectrum of such abilities, reserving "ESP" for telepathy. James BLISH's novel *Jack of Eagles* (1952) was given the variant title *ESP-er* in a 1958 reprint.   [PN]

ESSEX HOUSE A short-lived (1968-9) Los Angeles publishing imprint, a subsidiary of Milton Luros's Parliament News, Inc., specializing in highbrow erotica. Many Essex House novelists were young serious writers (several of them poets), and some used scenarios drawn from sf and fantasy, including future DYSTOPIAS, as settings for their pornography. About half the 42 titles published by EH were sf/fantasy; they included novels by Philip José FARMER, Richard E. GEIS, David MELTZER (perhaps the most distinguished), Michael Perkins (1942-) and Hank STINE, of which a number were ambitious, some literary, and most somewhat joyless – even emetic –

and redolent of 1960s radicalism. The unusual aspirations of this imprint are generally attributed to its young editor, Brian Kirby, who also edited the pornographic books of the sister imprint, Brandon House. [PN]

Further reading: "Essex House: The Rise and Fall of Speculative Erotica" by Maxim JAKUBOWSKI in *Foundation* #14 (1978); *The Secret Record: Modern Erotic Literature* (**1976** US) by Michael Perkins.

See also: SEX.

ET ◊ EXTRATERRESTRIAL.

ETCHEMENDY, NANCY H. (1952-   ) US writer whose three sf novels – *The Watchers of Space* (**1980**), *Stranger from the Stars* (**1983**) and *The Crystal City* (**1985**) – are juveniles, but whose stories, beginning with "Clotaire's Balloon" (1984), tend to be richly coloured, wry fantasies. She has also written some sf and fantasy POETRY. [JC]

ETERNITY SCIENCE FICTION US BEDSHEET-size SEMI-PROZINE. 4 issues July 1972-1975, 2 issues 1979-80; published and ed Stephen Gregg from South Carolina. *ESF* was well produced (two covers by Stephen FABIAN) and contributors included David R. BUNCH, Barry N. MALZBERG and Roger ZELAZNY, as well as early work by Ed BRYANT and Glen COOK, with some emphasis on experimental fiction and poetry. Like most such magazines it seems to have been undercapitalized and to have had inadequate distribution. [FHP/PN]

ÉTRANGE AVENTURE DE LEMMY CAUTION, UNE ◊ ALPHAVILLE.

E.T.: THE EXTRATERRESTRIAL Film (1982). Universal. Dir and coprod Steven SPIELBERG, starring Dee Wallace, Henry Thomas, Peter Coyote, Robert McNaughton, Drew Barrymore. Screenplay Melissa Mathison. 115 mins. Colour.

10-year-old Elliott (Thomas) meets an alien, "E.T.", who has been accidentally left outside Los Angeles when his spacecraft and its crew – which we infer includes his parents – is forced to depart rapidly to avoid a search party sent out by a human task force. Elliott and E.T., who demonstrates various PSI POWERS, become friends. E.T. wants to "phone home", and builds a communications device out of household objects. But he soon begins to sicken in our fallen world, as does Elliott, now emotionally linked to E.T. As the task force finally targets the alien traces they are searching, and invades Elliott's home (where he lives with his two siblings and his mother: the father has left home for good), E.T. becomes terminally ill. After the apparent death of the alien child, Elliott recovers and discovers that, like Jesus, E.T. is not in fact dead (or is resurrected). With the help of Elliott and his friends, and proving in the nick of time that he can still levitate bicycles, E.T. escapes the adults, returns to the rendezvous, is reunited with his kind; and leaves.

Almost certainly the most commercially successful film ever made, *E.T.* confidently alternates finely controlled sentiment and humour, the choreography of all this being almost flawless. But for some it is not a film that grows in the memory; for them the loneliness of the lizard-like but soft-eyed E.T., whose parents have left him, and of Elliott (another E...T), remains merely sad in a curiously unreverberant way. Countering this response, however, is the luminosity of the film, and a sense that its presentation of the epiphanies of childhood is truly joyful. The careful structuring of emotional release can be seen in the handling of adult males. They are first seen (only from the waist down) as hulking and affectless, but turn out to be concerned and sympathetic as E.T. sickens drastically; and the most empathetic of them is clearly destined to marry the deserted mother. Elliott's elder brother undergoes a similar transformation earlier in the film. There are echoes throughout of J.M. Barrie's *Peter Pan* (**1904**), as envisioned in the Walt Disney film *Peter Pan* (1953); this was also to be the source of Spielberg's later *Hook* (1991). [JC]

See also: CINEMA; HISTORY OF SF.

EUGENICS ◊ GENETIC ENGINEERING.

EUROPEAN SCIENCE FICTION AWARDS ◊ AWARDS.

EVANS, BILL Working name of US chemist and writer William Harrington Evans (1921-1985) for his sf studies, which began with bibliographical and other work in the 1940s and 1950s, mostly in *The Fanzine Index*, a journal he published with Bob Pavlat through 1952, and which was later assembled into a single volume, *Fanzine Index: Listing Most Fanzines from the Beginning through 1952, including Titles, Editors' Names, and Data on Each Issue* (**1965**). With Francis T. Laney he published the early *Howard Philips Lovecraft (1890-1937): A Tentative Bibliography* (**1943** chap). BE's work in the sf field culminated in an extensive introduction to E.E. "Doc" SMITH, *The Universes of E.E. Smith* (**1966**), on which he collaborated with Ron ELLIK. Most of the book is a concordance of themes and characters, though there is some critical content. BE did the **Skylark** series, Ellik the **Lensman** books. [JC]

EVANS, CHRISTOPHER (D.) (1951-   ) Welsh-born UK chemist who became a full-time writer in 1979 after some years in the pharmaceutical industry, and who has published sf and fantasy novels under his own name and as Christopher Carpenter, Nathan Elliott, Robert Knight and John Lyon, and some non-genre fiction as by Evan Christie and Alwyn Davies. His first publications, released more or less simultaneously, were the rather bad *Plasmid* * (**1980**) as by Robert Knight, a film tie to an untraceable (and perhaps unmade) movie, and the impressive *Capella's Golden Eyes* (**1980**), an extremely English version of a CONCEPTUAL-BREAKTHROUGH tale, set on a colony planet inhabited also by reclusive ALIENS – English because of the mundane detailing of life on Gaia, because the protagonist has no real access to the roots of power or change, and because any chances for conceptual breakthrough are in any case co-opted by a plot in which Gaia's first masters are simply replaced by a Chinese management team from Earth. *The Insider* (**1981**), set in a NEAR-FUTURE UK, depicts the plight of an alien symbiont forced to transform its new human host into an "alienated" outcast from society. *In Limbo* (**1985**) further intensifies CE's characteristic insistence on the isolation of human beings in a world they can neither comprehend nor control, an insistence not significantly modified by the more intensive use of local colour and expansive plotting in *Chimeras* (coll of linked stories **1992**), about an artist's complex and ambiguous relationship to the eponymous new art form (◊ ARTS). It remains to be seen whether CE will be able to accommodate his desolate visions within GENRE SF, which is characteristically outward-thrusting, or whether – as seems may be the case – he will find it increasingly uncongenial.

With Robert P. HOLDSTOCK, CE has edited OTHER EDENS, a strong anthology series comprising *Other Edens* (anth **1987**), *#II* (anth **1988**) and *#III* (anth **1989**). He responded to the controversy surrounding the extensive presence of organizations linked to SCIENTOLOGY at the 1987 World Science Fiction Convention (held in Brighton, UK) by editing *Conspiracy Theories* (anth **1987** chap), in which a variety of views were expressed, most of them critical of that presence. [JC]

Other works:
As Christopher Carpenter: *The Twilight Realm* (**1985**).
As Nathan Elliott: The **Hood Army Trilogy**, comprising *Earth Invaded* (**1986**), *Slaveworld* (**1986**) and *The Liberators* (**1986**), juvenile sf; the **Star Pirates** sequence, also juveniles, comprising *Kidnap in Space* (**1987**), *Plague Moon* (**1987**) and *Treasure Planet* (**1987**).
As John Lyon: *The Summoning* (**1985**).
Nonfiction: *Science Fiction as Religion* (**1981** chap) with Stan Gooch (1932-   ); *The Guide to Fantasy Art Techniques* (**1984**) with Martyn Dean, a picture book; *Lightship* (**1985**), text to visuals by Jim BURNS; *Writing Science Fiction* (**1988** chap US); *Dream Makers: Six Fantasy Artists at Work* (**1988**) with Martyn Dean, a picture book; *Airshow* (graph coll **1989**), text to visuals by Philip Castle.
See also: PARASITISM AND SYMBIOSIS.

EVANS, E(DWARD) EVERETT (1893-1958) US sf fan and writer. He began in the latter capacity late in life and had mixed success, though there is no doubt of the affection in which other Californian sf writers and fans held him, as evinced in the many tributes to him from writers such as E.E. "Doc" SMITH and A.E. VAN VOGT included in a compilation of his macabre fantasy stories, *Food for Demons* (coll **1971**). This was originally conceived as a homage to the man, and set up and printed, though not bound, as early as 1959; it contains his best work. EEE's novels were digestible but routine. The adventures of ESPER spy **George Hanlan** in *Man of Many Minds* (**1953**) and its sequel, *Alien Minds* (**1955**), are without much bite; and EEE's juvenile, *The Planet Mappers* (**1955**), is also very mild. He collaborated with E.E. Smith, whom he admired greatly, on one story, which Smith expanded into the novel *Masters of Space* (1961-2 *If*; **1976**). [JC]

EVANS, GERALD (1910-   ) UK writer, born in Wales, who began publishing sf with "Pebbles of Dread" for *TWS* in 1940, and who wrote one sf adventure, *The Black Sphere* (**1952**) as by Victor LA SALLE. A later collection, *Shadows in Landore* (coll **1979**), was self-published. [SH]

EVANS, IAN ◊ Angus WELLS.

EVANS, I(DRISYN) O(LIVER) (1894-1977) South-African-born UK civil servant and, especially after his retirement in 1956, editor and writer. His first book of sf relevance was the nonfiction *The World of Tomorrow* (**1933**), about possible future inventions, partly illustrated with reproductions of artwork from sf magazines, and thus – almost accidentally – the first anthology of sf ILLUSTRATION. He later specialized in the works of Jules VERNE, many of which he translated and edited for the **Fitzroy** edition of Verne's work in translation, beginning in 1958; some of these were reprinted by ACE BOOKS. Unfortunately, in editing Verne IOE occasionally abridged him cruelly, rendering him more of a simple boys'-action writer than was in fact the case. IOE wrote *Jules Verne and his Work* (**1965**) and edited *Science Fiction through the Ages 1* (anth **1966**) and *Science Fiction through the Ages 2* (anth **1966**), the first volume of which is restricted to pre-20th-century sf. He also edited *Jules Verne – Master of Science Fiction* (coll **1956**), which assembles extracts from Verne's novels. [PN]

EVANS, MORGAN ◊ L.P. DAVIES.

EVE OF DESTRUCTION Film (1991). Orion. Dir Duncan Gibbons, starring Gregory Hines, Renée Soutendijk. Screenplay Gibbons, Yale Udoff. 98 mins. Colour.

Soutendijk is good, both as Eve, a Defense Department scientist, and as Eve VIII, the military ROBOT that she creates in her own image. Armed with endless firepower and a nuclear bomb, the robot destroys the men Eve secretly hates, several male chauvinists and the police who try to stop her. Some critics see Eve VIII as a female "terminator" (◊ *The* TERMINATOR [**1984**]), but she also recalls the Id Monster of FORBIDDEN PLANET (1956). *EOD*'s supposed FEMINISM is unsubtle and suspect: a scene in which Eve first teases and then castrates a loutish man is so extreme that it may in fact be intentionally misogynist. Nevertheless, Eve VIII – beautiful, elegant, stony-faced, murderous and bulletproof – is one of the most effective villains of recent years. Hines's performance as a military troubleshooter is mediocre. [MK]

EVERYTHING YOU ALWAYS WANTED TO KNOW ABOUT SEX (BUT WERE AFRAID TO ASK) Film (1972). Jack Rollins and Charles H. Joffe Productions/ United Artists. Dir Woody Allen, starring Allen, Gene Wilder, Louise Lasser, John Carradine, Burt Reynolds, Tony Randall. Screenplay Allen, suggested by the nonfiction *Everything You Always Wanted to Know about Sex, but Were Afraid to Ask* by David Reuben. 88 mins. Colour.

This engaging collection of filmed anecdotes satirizes various sexual obsessions and movie genres;

two episodes can charitably be defined as sf. One involves a giant, mobile female breast that breaks out of a mad SCIENTIST's laboratory and ravages the countryside, in the manner of a 1950s MONSTER MOVIE. The other dramatizes a seduction attempt by comparing the interior processes of the human body to those of a mechanized production line, with white-suited technocrats running things from the "Brain Room" while brawny, hard-hatted workers cope with the heavy equipment of the penis. Allen plays one of a group of sperm cells nervously waiting to go into action in the manner of paratroopers about to be dropped into enemy territory. Allen soon returned to sf satire with SLEEPER (1973).   [JB]

EVIL FORCE, THE ◊ 4D MAN.

EVOLUTION There is, inevitably, an intimate connection between the development of evolutionary philosophy and the history of sf. In a culture without an evolutionary philosophy most of the kinds of fiction we categorize as sf could not develop. Like the idea of progress, evolutionary philosophy flourished in late-18th-century France, and it was first significantly represented in literature by RESTIF DE LA BRETONNE's evolutionary fantasy *La découverte Australe par un homme volant* ["The Southern-Hemisphere Discovery by a Flying Man"] (**1781**), an allegorical treatment of ideas partly derived from the Comte du Buffon (1707-1788). In the early-19th-century *Philosophie zoologique* (**1809**), the Chevalier de Lamarck (1744-1829) developed a more elaborate evolutionary philosophy, introducing the key notion of adaptation, and paved the way for Charles Darwin (1809-1882) and his theory of natural selection, promulgated in *The Origin of Species* (**1859**). Because we have fallen into the habit of labelling various theoretical heresies "Lamarckian", it is easy to forget that for most of the 19th century Lamarck was the more influential writer, especially in France. In the UK, Darwin was ardently championed by T.H. Huxley (1825-1895) and the sociologist Herbert Spencer (1820-1903), and his ideas took much firmer hold in the UK than elsewhere. Thus there was a sharp divergence of emphasis between French and UK evolutionary sf, and this lasted well into the 20th century. The writers who pioneered the tradition of French evolutionary fantasy were Camille FLAMMARION, most notably in *Lumen* (**1887**; trans **1897**) and *Omega* (trans **1894**), and J.H. ROSNY aîné in his many prehistoric fantasies, in "Les xipéhuz" (**1887**; trans as "The Shapes" 1968) and in "La mort de la terre" (**1910**; trans as "The Death of the Earth" 1978). Jules VERNE's only evolutionary fantasy, *La grande forêt, le village aérien* (**1901**; trans I.O. Evans as *The Village in the Treetops* 1964 UK), is also Lamarckian.

Lamarck's successor, Henri Bergson (1859-1941), whose theory of "creative evolution" made much of the notion of the *élan vital* – which Lamarck had rejected – seems to have provided the seed of one of the most important UK evolutionary fantasies, J.D. BERESFORD's *The Hampdenshire Wonder* (**1911**), but for the most part UK writing was dominated by the implications of Darwinian theory and the catchphrases by which it was vulgarized: "the survival of the fittest" and "the struggle for existence". H.G. WELLS was taught by T.H. Huxley in the early 1890s, and remained ever-anxious that the qualities which had shaped human nature for survival in the struggle for existence might prevent our ever achieving a just society – a fear powerfully reflected, in different ways, in *The Time Machine* (**1895**), *The Island of Dr Moreau* (**1896**), *The War of the Worlds* (**1898**) and *The Croquet Player* (**1936** chap). (An interesting antidote to Wellsian pessimism is administered in one of the several sequels to *The Time Machine*: David LAKE's *The Man who Loved Morlocks* * [**1981**].) The ominous spectres arising from the harsher versions of Darwinian philosophy also feature strongly in *Erewhon* (**1872**) by Samuel BUTLER (who also wrote several anti-Darwinian tracts) and intrude upon most of the speculative fiction of Grant ALLEN (who wrote several pro-Darwinian tracts). The political implications of the careless transplantation of Darwinian ideas into theories of social evolution (◊ SOCIAL DARWINISM) were such that Wells's one-time fellow-Fabian George Bernard SHAW renounced Darwinism in favour of neo-Lamarckism on political grounds, and his play *Back to Methuselah* (**1921**) was published with a long introductory essay explaining this renunciation. Similar steps were taken by T.D. Lysenko (1898-1976), in the name of Soviet communism, and Luther Burbank (1849-1926), in the name of US fundamentalism. It was not widely realized that the implications of Darwinism were not necessarily as harsh as vulgar Darwinians tended to assume. An interesting allegorical popularization of a more humane Darwinism is Gerald HEARD's *Gabriel and the Creatures* (**1952**; vt *Wishing Well* 1953). The influence of Darwinian ideas can be seen in such US works as Edgar FAWCETT's *The Ghost of Guy Thyrle* (**1895**) and Austin BIERBOWER's *From Monkey to Man* (**1894**); the latter is an early attempt to present *Genesis* as an allegory of evolution.

Human evolution was explored by writers in terms of its probable past (◊ ANTHROPOLOGY; ORIGIN OF MAN) and possible future. Wells's classic essay, "The Man of the Year Million" (1893), imagined mankind as evolution might remake us, with an enormous head and reduced body, eyes enlarged but ears and nose vestigial – an image which became a stereotype adopted by many other writers. It became a cliché in early PULP-MAGAZINE sf, although most writers took a dim view of the "fitness" of such individuals, and usually represented them as effete entities doomed to extinction; "Alas, All Thinking!" (1935) by Harry BATES is a graphic example. Few pulp writers, though, had much idea of the actual implications of Darwinism, and they produced very few extrapolations which could stand up to rigorous examination – a state of affairs which still persists. Most sf writers contemplating the evolutionary future of mankind have been inordinately taken with the idea of sudden, large-scale mutations of a kind in which modern

Darwinians do not believe ($\lozenge$ MUTANTS). Many stories appeared in which mutagenic radiation accelerated evolution to a perceptible pace, including John TAINE's *The Iron Star* (**1930**) and *Seeds of Life* (1931; **1951**) and Edmond HAMILTON's "Evolution Island" (1927). Hamilton's fiction also showed a persistent interest in the pseudo-scientific notion of retrograde evolution ($\lozenge$ DEVOLUTION), which had earlier been luridly featured in George Allan ENGLAND's *Darkness and Dawn* (**1914**) and which crops up also in Olaf STAPLEDON's curiously un-Darwinian *Last and First Men* (**1930**). In Hamilton's "The Man who Evolved" (1931) a man who bathes himself in mutagenic radiation first turns into the man-of-the-year-million stereotype and then regresses, ending up as a blob of undifferentiated protoplasm. Equally pseudo-scientific, though more interesting, is Edgar Rice BURROUGHS's "extrapolation" of Haeckel's law ("ontogeny recapitulates phylogeny") in *The Land that Time Forgot* (1918; **1924**); in this romance the recapitulation takes place during active life rather than embryonically. Similar schemes are credited to alien life-systems in Theodore STURGEON's "The Golden Helix" (1954) and James BLISH's *A Case of Conscience* (**1958**).

Sf of the 1920s and 1930s was frequently pessimistic about the long-term evolutionary prospects of mankind, but bold success stories are featured in J.B.S. HALDANE's "The Last Judgment" (1927) and Laurence MANNING's *The Man who Awoke* (1933; fixup **1975**). The former influenced and the latter was influenced by the most detailed and most extravagant of all evolutionary fantasies, Stapledon's *Last and First Men*. This extraordinary study of mankind's many descendant species, extending over a timespan of billions of years, exhibits an odd combination of optimism and pessimism further extrapolated on the grander stage of *Star Maker* (**1937**), whose experimentally inclined God-figure is working His way through an evolving series of Creations. Those sf stories in which the human evolutionary story does not end with eventual extinction or with the acquisition of a stabilizing IMMORTALITY usually propose, like Shaw in *Back to Methuselah*, that there will eventually be a transcendence that frees human intelligence from its association with frail flesh, and that our ultimate descendants will be more-or-less godlike entities of "pure thought" – an idea which echoes continually through E.E. "Doc" SMITH's work and crops up briefly but rather disturbingly in Robert A. HEINLEIN's *Methuselah's Children* (1941; rev **1958**). A particularly memorable pulp sf evocation of this sort of motif is Eric Frank RUSSELL's "Metamorphosite" (1946). Even when mankind fails to stay the distance – as in John W. CAMPBELL Jr's "The Last Evolution" (1932), where it is our machines, not their creators, which ultimately achieve the state of "pure consciousness" – this is conventionally seen as the logical end-point of evolution, as it still is in such novels as *The Singers of Time* (**1990**) by Frederik POHL and Jack WILLIAMSON and *Eternal Light* (**1991**) by Paul J. MCAULEY. Given that

images of the next stage in human evolution ($\lozenge$ SUPERMAN) usually invoke pseudo-scientific notions about mental powers ($\lozenge$ ESP) based on Cartesian illusions about mental ghosts in bodily machines, the idea that evolution tends towards disembodiment is a natural and psychologically plausible extrapolation, though arguably rather silly. The post-WWII boom in stories of human mental evolution produced a number of stories which invoked the notion of a universal evolutionary schema. The most notable were Arthur C. CLARKE's *Childhood's End* (**1953**), which shows a whole generation of Earthly children undergoing a kind of metamorphic apotheosis to fuse with the "cosmic mind", and two stories by Theodore Sturgeon: *More than Human* (fixup **1953**) and *The Cosmic Rape* (**1958**), which deploy similar imagery on a smaller scale, using the idea of collective mental gestalts. Another interesting example of such a schema is to be found in the material linking the short stories in *Galaxies like Grains of Sand* (**1959**; full text restored **1979**) by Brian W. ALDISS, which proposes that the next step in human evolution might be complete somatic awareness and control. A more modest schema of human evolution, past and future, underlies Gordon R. DICKSON's **Childe Cycle** novels, and is elaborated in some detail in his *The Final Encyclopedia* (**1984**). A remarkable philosophical allegory surreally re-examining many ideas about mankind's possible future evolution is Robert SILVERBERG's *Son of Man* (**1971**). The most widely seen (but by no means most widely understood) symbolic representation of evolutionary apotheosis is that contained in the final frames of the film 2001: A SPACE ODYSSEY (1968).

Last and First Men also includes in its multifaceted discussion of future human evolution the possibility – first raised in Haldane's essay *Daedalus, or Science and the Future* (**1923**) – that humans might take charge of their own physical evolution by means of what is nowadays termed GENETIC ENGINEERING, but this line of inquiry was not widely explored until much later. Damon KNIGHT's *Masters of Evolution* (1954 as "Natural State"; exp **1959**) features the anti-technological "muckfeet", who have allegedly progressed beyond the need for machines and cities in acquiring biological control of their environment, but stories of this kind, inspired by a growing interest in ECOLOGY and a corollary antipathy towards CITIES (*see also* DYSTOPIAS; MACHINES), have been heavily outnumbered by those which – following Aldous HUXLEY's example in *Brave New World* (**1932**) – consider the idea of tampering with human nature implicitly horrific. Examples include Frank HERBERT's *The Eyes of Heisenberg* (**1966**) and T.J. BASS's *Half Past Human* (**1971**), the latter featuring a "human hive" – an image invoked in many stories as a highly unfortunate but nevertheless probable destiny for evolving human society ($\lozenge$ HIVE-MINDS), most notably in J.D. BERESFORD's and Esmé Wynne-Tyson's *The Riddle of the Tower* (**1944**). The idea that our future evolution might involve turning ourselves into CYBORGS – memorably pioneered by

E.V. ODLE's remarkable *The Clockwork Man* (**1923**) – has usually been treated with similar unenthusiasm. The idea of any future metamorphosis of the human species, however modest, is repugnant to many whose aesthetic standards are not unnaturally defined by our present ideals: even to those who abhor anything that might smack of Nazism, the desirable notion of "men like gods" inevitably conjures up an image of serried ranks of Aryan matinée idols. One sf writer who has tried particularly hard to escape this imaginative straitjacket is Ian WATSON, whose exuberant adventures in evolutionary possibility extend to bizarre extremes in *The Gardens of Delight* (**1980**) and *Converts* (**1984**).

A surprising number of sf stories look forward – often with a curious inverted nostalgia – to the time when mankind's day is done and we must pass on our legacy to the inheritors of Earth (or of the Universe). Usually the inheritors are machines, as in Lester DEL REY's "Though Dreamers Die" (**1944**) and Edmond Hamilton's "After a Judgment Day" (**1963**), but sometimes they are animals, as in Del Rey's "The Faithful" (**1938**), Clifford D. SIMAK's *City* (**1944-51**; fixup **1952**) and Terry BISSON's "Bears Discover Fire" (**1990**). Olof JOHANESSON, in *The Tale of the Big Computer* (**1966**; trans **1968**; vt *The Great Computer*), plots an evolutionary schema in which the function of mankind is simply to be the means of facilitating machine evolution; while L. Sprague DE CAMP's and P. Schuyler MILLER's ironic *Genus Homo* (**1941**; **1950**), Neal BARRETT Jr's puzzle-story *Aldair in Albion* (**1976**), Dougal DIXON's fascinating picture-book *After Man: A Zoology of the Future* (**1981**) and Kurt VONNEGUT Jr's jeremiad *Galapagos* (**1985**) all describe new species which take up the torch of evolutionary progress after mankind's demise. Such stories have strong ideative links with extravagant ALTERNATE-WORLD stories which contemplate alternative patterns of earthly evolution, notably Guy DENT's *Emperor of the If* (**1926**), Harry HARRISON's *West of Eden* (**1984**) and its sequels – in which primitive men must compete with intelligent descendants of the dinosaurs – and Stephen R. BOYETT's *The Architect of Sleep* (**1986**), in which it is raccoons rather than apes that have given rise to sentient descendants.

Accounts of ALIEN evolution are separately considered in the section on LIFE ON OTHER WORLDS, but mention must be made here of the frequent recruitment of the ideas of convergent evolution and parallel evolution to excuse the dramatically convenient deployment of humanoid aliens. Writers conscientious enough to construct a jargon of apology for such a situation often argue that the logic of natural selection permits intelligence to arise only in upright bipeds with binocular vision and clever hands, and that, had such bipeds not evolved from lemurs, they might instead have evolved from catlike or even lizardlike ancestors. There are, however, relatively few stories which actually turn on hypotheses of this kind; examples include Philip LATHAM's "Simpson"

(**1954**), one of several stories about humanlike aliens who are not as similar to us as they seem, and Lloyd BIGGLE's *The Light that Never Was* (**1972**), which addresses the question of whether "animaloid" species are necessarily inferior to "humanoid" ones.

Alternative life-systems capable of Lamarckian evolution are featured in a few stories, including Barrington J. BAYLEY's "Mutation Planet" (**1973**) and Brian M. STABLEFORD's "The Engineer and the Executioner" (**1975**; rev **1991**).

The Butlerian idea that machines may eventually begin to evolve independently of their makers has become increasingly popular as real-world COMPUTERS have become more sophisticated; images of such evolutionary sequences have become more complex, as in James P. HOGAN's *Code of the Lifemaker* (**1983**). Several recent images of universal evolutionary schemas – notably the one featured in Gregory BENFORD's *Across the Sea of Suns* (**1984**) and the trilogy begun with *Great Sky River* (**1988**) – imagine a fundamental ongoing struggle for existence between organic and inorganic life-systems. The beginnings of such a division are evident in Bruce STERLING's series of stories featuring the Shapers and the Mechanists, which culminates in *Schismatrix* (**1985**). A related but somewhat different Universe-wide struggle for existence is revealed in the concluding volume of Stableford's **Asgard** trilogy, *The Centre Cannot Hold* (**1990**), and an even stranger one is first glimpsed in *The Angel of Pain* (**1991**), the second volume of another Stableford trilogy.

Mutational miracles still abound in modern sf, in such apocalyptic stories of future evolution as Greg BEAR's *Blood Music* (**1985**), and there is a strong tendency to mystify evolution-related concepts such as "ECOLOGY" and "symbiosis" (◊ PARASITISM AND SYMBIOSIS) in a fashion which is at best interestingly metaphorical and at worst hazily metaphysical. Patterns of evolution on alien worlds (◊ LIFE ON OTHER WORLDS) are often placed in the service of some kind of Edenic mythology, and this is true even in the work of writers well versed in the biological sciences. Perhaps this is not unduly surprising in an era when religious fundamentalists are still trying to fight the teaching of Darwinism in US schools, and to have equal time given to "Creation Science". Some evolutionary philosophers have not yet given up hope of producing a crucial modification of the Darwinian account of evolution which is more aesthetically appealing; the latest to attempt it has been Rupert Sheldrake in *The Science of Life: The Hypothesis of Formative Causation* (**1981**), an idea adapted to sf use by Paul H. COOK in *Duende Meadow* (**1985**). Given the continued success of Darwinism as a source of explanations, however, it is lamentably unfortunate that so few sf stories have deployed the theory in any reasonably rigorous fashion.   [BS]

See also: BIOLOGY.

EWALD, CARL (1856-1908) Danish writer whose *Two-Legs* (trans Alexander Teixeira de Mattos **1906** US) narrates the rise of Man from the significantly jaundiced viewpoint of the animals over which he would soon have dominion. Two other books of genre interest have not been translated into English. [JC]

EWERS, HANNS HEINZ (1871-1943) German writer, spy in Mexico and the USA in WWI, and early member of the Nazi Party. SUPERMEN predominate in his fiction, much of which remains untranslated. He is noted mainly for a series of novels about **Frank Braun** – anthropologist and *Übermensch* – some of which are sf. The young hero of *Der Zauberlehrling* (**1907**; trans Ludwig Lewisohn as *The Sorcerer's Apprentice* **1927** US) hypnotizes his "inferior" Italian mistress into a spurious sainthood – complete with stigmata – which in the end he makes real by helping crucify her. In *Alraune* (**1911**; trans S. Guy ENDORE **1929** US), which was filmed 5 times 1918-52 (◊ ALRAUNE), Braun uses artificial insemination to breed from the dregs of society – a sex criminal and a prostitute – the soulless eponymous female whose name reflects in German her likeness to a mandrake root, and whose vampirical powers prove almost fatal to him. In *Vampir* (**1921**; trans Fritz Sallagher as *Vampire* **1934** US; vt *Vampire's Prey* 1937 UK) Braun appears as a macabre alter ego of the author, spying in Mexico during WWI while at the same time becoming a vampire. [JC]

Other works: *Blood* (coll trans Erich Posselt and Sinclair Dombrow **1930** US), *contes cruels*.

EWING, FREDERICK R. ◊ Theodore STURGEON.

EWING, JENNY ◊ F. Yorick BLUMENFELD.

EWOK ADVENTURE, THE (vt *Caravan of Courage*) Made-for-tv film (1984). Lucasfilm/Korty Films for ABC TV. Executive prod George LUCAS. Dir John Korty, starring Eric Walker, Aubree Miller. Screenplay Lucas. 120 mins, cut to 97 mins. Colour.

When the family spaceship crashes on an alien moon, the parents are captured by a monster and their two children cared for by Ewoks, the teddy-bear aliens first seen in RETURN OF THE JEDI (1983). After a long trek, the children and Ewoks save the parents. *TEA* is disappointing by adult standards, but children like it – and it *is* a children's film. The special effects are surprisingly poor considering Lucasfilm's STAR WARS experience. Lucas's story is vestigial and the Ewoks, though clearly intended to be cute, are charmless; Philip STRICK described their faces as "a fixed, unblinking mask set in a rictus of amiability". *TEA* was released theatrically overseas as *Caravan of Courage*. A second tv movie, *Ewoks: The Battle for Endor* (1985), though slightly better, had no theatrical release. [PN]

EWOKS AND DROIDS ◊ George LUCAS.

EWOKS: THE BATTLE FOR ENDOR ◊ *The* EWOK ADVENTURE.

EXOBIOLOGY ◊ XENOBIOLOGY.

EXPEDITION MOON ◊ ROCKETSHIP X-M.

EXPERIMENTER PUBLISHING CO. ◊ AMAZING STORIES; Hugo GERNSBACK.

"EXPLORABILIS" ◊ Eliza HAYWOOD.

EXPLORERS Film (1985). Edward S. Feldman/Paramount. Dir Joe DANTE, starring Ethan Hawke, River Phoenix, Jason Presson. Screenplay Eric Luke. 109 mins. Colour.

Three schoolboys, tipped off by a dream, employ a computer to help create a sphere that can move very quickly and is impervious to gravity; they use it to power a spacecraft they build out of junk. Far above Earth they find a spaceship with, inside it, two aliens – their view of humanity entirely gleaned from old tv programmes – who turn out likewise to be kids on a joyride. This strange film was apparently aimed at pre-teens, but the grotesque aliens (more like cartoons than extraterrestrials) and their tv/radio obsession seem directed far more at adults. Perhaps because of this uncertainty about the audience, *E*, the most personal of Dante's films, was a box-office failure. Despite its self-indulgence it has wonderful moments, captures well that sense of dream and yearning in children known to sf fans of whatever age as the SENSE OF WONDER, and deftly pinpoints many points of collision between the child's world and the adult's. [PN]

See also: CINEMA.

EXTRAPOLATION ◊ PREDICTION.

EXTRAPOLATION Critical magazine, ed Thomas D. CLARESON from its inception in Dec 1959; Clareson was joined by Donald M. HASSLER from the Winter 1987 issue, and Hassler became sole editor from the Spring 1990 issue; 2 numbers a year at first, quarterly since Spring 1979; current. It began as *The Newsletter of the Conference on Science-Fiction of the MLA* (the MLA being the Modern Languages Association). *E* was first published from the English Department of the College of Wooster, Ohio, and since Spring 1979 has been published by the Kent State University Press, Ohio.

E was very much the product of one person, Clareson (although it had a large editorial board), without whose enthusiasm it might not have survived. He continues as Emeritus Editor today. It was the first of the academic journals about sf; its successors have included FOUNDATION: THE REVIEW OF SCIENCE FICTION, then SCIENCE-FICTION STUDIES and, much more recently, JOURNAL OF THE FANTASTIC IN THE ARTS. *E* is a journal more notable for feature articles than for reviews, polemics or ongoing debate. While its standard has been variable – there have certainly been flat spots – the same can be said of the other critical magazines. In its long career it has published articles of all kinds, though generally concentrating more on scholarship than on criticism. A long-running feature (until 1981) was the annual survey, "The Year's Scholarship in Science Fiction and Fantasy", compiled first by Clareson and later by Marshall B. TYMN and Roger C. SCHLOBIN; it continued as a separate publication from Kent State from 1982. *E*'s existence as the earliest public platform for sf studies significantly advanced them; historically important, *E* continues to be relevant and sometimes stimulating, although too few of its articles are of interest outside a rather narrow academic community. *E*'s rare first 10 years' issues were reprinted in book form by GREGG PRESS as *Extrapolation, a Science Fiction Newsletter, Vols 1-10* (anth **1978**) ed Clareson. [PN]

EXTRA-SENSORY PERCEPTION In sf TERMINOLOGY, usually known by its acronym, ESP (*which see for details*). [PN]

EXTRATERRESTRIAL In sf TERMINOLOGY, a creature (usually intelligent) from beyond TERRA. When used as a noun, and occasionally in its adjectival mode, the word may be shortened to "et" or "ET" (pronounced "eetee"). ◊ ALIENS; LIFE ON OTHER WORLDS. [PN]

EXTRO Northern Irish magazine, A4 format, Feb-July 1982, 3 issues, published bimonthly by Specifi Publications, ed Paul Campbell. During its brief existence – terminated when its bank manager dishonoured an overdraft arrangement – *E* published fiction by Brian W. ALDISS, Garry KILWORTH, Christopher PRIEST, Bob SHAW, John T. SLADEK, Ian WATSON, James WHITE and others (notably Ian MCDONALD's first story), along with interviews, essays and book reviews. [RH]

EYES WITHOUT A FACE ◊ *Les* YEUX SANS VISAGE.

EYRAUD, ACHILLE ◊ VENUS.

FABIAN, STEPHEN E. (1930-   ) US illustrator who worked in electronics until 1973. Self-trained as a freelance sf illustrator, he worked as a fan artist in the late 1960s. At the age of 43 he graduated to the professional SF MAGAZINES, mostly *AMZ* and *Fantastic*, with both cover art and interiors; he was less active in the 1980s than the 1970s. His art is distinctive, with a strong sense of formal design; it is for his dramatic interior black-and-white work, reminiscent of Virgil FINLAY's and prepared on textured coquille board, that he is best known. Book covers and interior illustrations include work for SMALL PRESSES such as Donald M. Grant, Byron PREISS and UNDERWOOD-MILLER. Books devoted to SEF's work include *Letters Lovecraftian: An Alphabet of Illuminated Letters Inspired by the Works of the Late Master of the Weird Tale, Howard Phillips Lovecraft* (**1974**), *Fantastic Nudes* (**1976**) and *Fantastic Nudes: 2nd Series* (**1976**), which are collected with other material in *Fantasy by Fabian* (**1978**), *The Best of Stephen Fabian* (**1976**), *More Fantasy by Fabian* (**1979**) and *Fabian in Color* (**1980**). Many of these are ed and published Gerry de la Ree (?   -1993), who also published much of Virgil Finlay's work. SEF has seven times been nominated for a HUGO.   [PN/JG]

See also: FANTASY.

FABULATION We do not intend to make here – or to quote – any sustained theoretical argument about the nature of fabulation as the term was conceived by Robert SCHOLES in *The Fabulators* (**1967**) and amplified in his *Structural Fabulation* (**1975**). Our starting point must be GENRE SF, our central concern throughout this encyclopedia. In the entry on MAINSTREAM WRITERS OF SF we contrast the writers of genre sf, and the circumstances under which they write, with writers and their circumstances in what has come to be known as the mainstream. Here, we contrast the inherent nature of genre sf with the inherent nature of the central literature of the postmodern world (◊ POSTMODERNISM AND SF for a more sharply focused view of Postmodernism as a movement and a condition of mind). In using the single term "fabulation" instead of several – over and beyond Postmodernism, a critical roster might include ABSURDIST SF, Fictionality, MAGIC REALISM, SLIPSTREAM SF and Surfiction – we know we are offering a grossly oversimplified snapshot of the modern literary environment (or nests of environments). But the alternative would be to make a thousand individual choices, often inevitably controversial, as we attempted to label each non-"realistic" non-genre sf novel according to its precise place in an ever-shifting mosaic of prescriptive definitions. One term will have to do.

Over the course of the 20th century, sf readers have grown used to thinking of genre sf as substantially different (in manner, in substance and in intention) from the great stream of realistic novels which increasingly dominated the English-speaking literary since the middle of the 18th century, a dominance which was challenged only in the first decades of our own era. Helped along by critics from within the genre, like Alexei and Cory PANSHIN in their contentious *The World Beyond the Hill* (**1989**), sf readers have further grown accustomed to thinking that it was genre sf itself that dethroned the mimetic novel from its position of dominance in 1926, and that the continued popularity of "realistic" fiction has been a kind of confidence game. We feel that something like the reverse is true: that genre sf – which we repeat is our central concern throughout this encyclopedia – is essentially a *continuation* of the mimetic novel, which it may have streamlined but certainly did not supplant; and that the onslaught of Modernism (and its successors) on the mimetic novel was also an onslaught upon the two essential assumptions governing genre sf.

The first assumption is that both the "world" and the human beings who inhabit it can be seen whole, and described accurately, in words. The writers who created the great novels of the 19th century wrote in that assumption, and their novels were written as though they opened omniscient windows into reality. What the novel said and what was true were the same thing. Writers of genre sf have never abandoned this assumption. The explorations of Henry James (1843-1916) in the inherent *unreliability* of words – and the consequent unreliability of narrators – awoke no appreciative response in the mind of Hugo GERNSBACK, and it was not until the 1970s and 1980s that sf or fantasy was published (by writers like Jonathan Carroll, Samuel R. DELANY and Gene WOLFE) which accepted, 70 years late, the Jamesian intuition. In the world outside, however, after WWI, serious literary critics and readers almost universally granted the case of Modernist writers – nearly all of them the spiritual children of Henry James – that the "real" world could never be grasped whole, but that it was the high and difficult task of writers to forge fallen words into a semblance of the world, and to take an artificer's joy in the task of construction.

The second assumption is that the "world" – whether or not it can be seen whole through the distorting glass of words – does in the end have a story which can be told. That story might be the knotty and problematical revelation of the truth of the Christian faith as unfolded in the later work of T.S. Eliot (1888-1965); or the March of Progress that Alexei and Cory Panshin claim to have traced, beginning with the planet-bound storytellers of the 19th century whose descendants bounded ever upwards toward the GOLDEN AGE OF SF, exploring the Galaxy *en passant*. What underlying story is being told is less important than the fact that, for writers of genre sf, some form of "meta-narrative" lies beneath the tale, ensuring the connectivity of things. The huge proliferation of future HISTORIES and novel sequences in genre sf does not simply reflect market strategies; it also represents a belief that the world is tellable. It is that belief, whether held by Modernists like T.S. Eliot (and Gene Wolfe) or pure genre writers like E.E. "Doc" SMITH, that has been called into question by the various Postmodernist movements, and which lies at the heart of most fabulations.

We can now say what we mean in this encyclopedia by a "fabulation": *a fabulation is any story which challenges the two main assumptions of genre sf: that the world can be seen; and that it can be told.* We have chosen to use the term "fabulation" because it seems to us the best blanket description of the techniques employed by those writers who use sf devices to underline that double challenge, and whose work is thus at heart profoundly antipathetic to genre sf. A typical fabulation, then, is a tale whose telling is *foregrounded* in a way which emphasizes the inherent arbitrariness of the words we use, the stories we tell (Magic Realism, for instance, can be seen as a subversion of the "official" stories which are told by "rational" means and authorities), the characters whose true nature we can never plumb, the worlds we can never step into. (An unfriendly critic might say that fabulations are all means and no substance; but that is perhaps to miss the Postmodernist point that all previous stories were likewise, albeit secretly, all means and no "substance".) By foregrounding the means of telling a tale, fabulations articulate what might be called the *fableness* of things: the fableness of the world itself in some Magic Realism; the fableness of the political and social world in some Absurdist sf; the fableness of the aesthetic object in Postmodernism as a whole; and – finally – the fableness of fables in Fabulation itself.

Authors whose works (or some of whose works) are, in our terms, fabulations include Paul ABLEMAN, Paul AUSTER, John BARTH, Donald BARTHELME, Adolfo BIOY CASARES, Michael BLUMLEIN, Jorge Luis BORGES, Bruce BOSTON, Scott BRADFIELD, Richard BRAUTIGAN, Christine BROOKE-ROSE, Ed BRYANT, David R. BUNCH, Anthony BURGESS, William BURROUGHS, Dino BUZZATI, Italo CALVINO, Angela CARTER, Jerome CHARYN, Barbara COMYNS, Robert COOVER, Arthur Byron COVER, Tom DE HAVEN, Don DeLILLO, Rick DeMARINIS, Thomas M. DISCH, E.L. DOCTOROW, Katherine DUNN, Umberto ECO, George Alec EFFINGER, Carol EMSHWILLER, Steve ERICKSON, Karen Joy FOWLER, Carlos FUENTES, Felix GOTSCHALK, Alasdair GRAY, MacDonald HARRIS, M. John HARRISON, Carol HILL, William HJORTSBERG, Russell HOBAN, Trevor HOYLE, Harvey JACOBS, Langdon JONES, Franz KAFKA, Robert KELLY, Jerzy KOSINSKI, William KOTZWINKLE, Joseph McELROY, Sheila MacLEOD, Michael MOORCOCK, Haruki MURAKAMI, Vladimir NABOKOV, Flann O'BRIEN, John Cowper POWYS, Christopher PRIEST, Thomas PYNCHON, Peter REDGROVE, Philip ROTH, Salman RUSHDIE, James SALLIS, Josephine SAXTON, Arno SCHMIDT, Lucius SHEPARD, John T. SLADEK, Norman SPINRAD, Stefan THEMERSON, David THOMSON, Boris VIAN, Gore VIDAL, William T. VOLLMANN, Alice WALKER, Rex WARNER, William WHARTON, Gene WOLFE, Stephen WRIGHT, Rudolf WURLITZER and Pamela ZOLINE. [JC]

See also: OULIPO.

FABULOUS WORLD OF JULES VERNE, THE ◊ VYNÁLEZ ZKÁZY.

FACE OF FU MANCHU, THE Film (1965). Anglo-Amalgamated. Dir Don Sharp, starring Christopher Lee, Nigel Green, Tsai Chin, Howard Marion-Crawford, James Robertson Justice. Screenplay Harry Alan Towers, based on the characters created by Sax ROHMER. 96 mins. Colour.

The first of a series of films produced by Harry Alan Towers in which Christopher Lee portrayed the oriental master-fiend, Tsai Chin played Fu's insidious daughter (renamed Lin Tang from Rohmer's Fah Lo Suee) and a succession of square-jawed heroes – Nigel Green, Douglas Wilmer, Richard Greene – played Sir Denis Nayland Smith of Scotland Yard. This first entry is by far the best of the batch, shot imaginatively on Irish locations which stand in for England and Tibet in the 1920s, and with devices reminiscent of the old movie serials, such as a gas which kills an entire village and a superexplosive, both deployed in Fu's scheme to control the world.

Sharp's direction is fast-paced, with full rein given to the mild sadomasochism of the originals as victims are whipped or confined to cabinets which slowly fill with Thames water. This is a richly entertaining pastiche of the old style, although less delirious than *The* MASK OF FU MANCHU (1932), in which Fu was played by Boris Karloff. Sharp stayed with the series for *Brides of Fu Manchu* (1966), which was almost up to standard, but after the inferior *Vengeance of Fu Manchu* (1967), dir Jeremy Summers, the series was turned over to international hack Jesus Franco for the disastrous *Castle of Fu Manchu* (1968) and *Blood of Fu Manchu* (1968; vt *Kiss and Kill*). [KN]

FAGAN, H(ENRY) A(LLAN) (1889-1963) South African judge and writer, Chief Justice of the Supreme Court of South Africa 1956-9. In his sf novel *Ninya* (**1956** UK) survivors of a crash landing on the Moon encounter many strange adventures. [JC]

FAHRENHEIT 451 Film (1966). Anglo-Enterprise and Vineyard/Universal. Dir François Truffaut, starring Julie Christie, Oscar Werner, Cyril Cusack, Anton Diffring. Screenplay Truffaut, Jean-Louis Richard, based on *Fahrenheit 451* (**1953**) by Ray BRADBURY. 112 mins. Colour.

Bradbury's angry parable is about a future in which all books are banned. The hero (Werner) is a member of the Fire Brigade, whose function is not to put out fires but to burn books. He first questions the regime and then rebels totally, incinerating the fire chief instead of the books, escaping from the city and joining a rural community whose members are each memorizing a book, word for word, in order to preserve it. The film is more ambiguous than the book and, so to speak, lacks its fire; Truffaut seems not altogether to accept Bradbury's moral simplicity. This is particularly evident at the end, with the book people murmuring aloud the words they are committing to memory, while plodding about the snow-covered landscape like zombies. The words may be saved but literature itself seems dead. The film is well photographed by Nicolas Roeg, later the celebrated director of, among others, *The* MAN WHO FELL TO EARTH (1976). [JB/PN]

See also: CINEMA; COMMUNICATIONS.

FAIL SAFE Film (1964). Max E. Youngstein-Sidney Lumet. Dir Sidney Lumet, starring Henry Fonda, Dan O'Herlihy, Walter Matthau, Frank Overton, Fritz Weaver. Screenplay Walter Bernstein, based on *Fail-Safe* (**1962**) by Eugene L. BURDICK and Harvey WHEELER. 111 mins. Colour.

A mistaken US nuclear attack on Moscow nearly initiates WWIII, a quandary resolved only by the US President's decision to bomb New York as an apologetic gesture. *FS* had the misfortune to be released soon after DR STRANGELOVE OR: HOW I LEARNED TO STOP WORRYING AND LOVE THE BOMB (1963), and the public preferred the vigorous black farce of Stanley KUBRICK's film to the wordy, low-key documentary style of Lumet's. The unlikely premise is lent conviction by some good performances, but this "message"

film is at once too diagrammatic and too like soap opera in such simplistic portrayals as Hawkish Professor, Liberal President and Conscience-Stricken Air-Force General. [PN]

FAIRBAIRNS, ZÖE (ANN) (1948-) UK writer and FEMINIST whose one sf novel, *Benefits* (**1979**), presents a DYSTOPIAN vision of the fate of women in the 21st century, as advances in reproductive technologies permit greater male control, in fear and loathing, over the female half of the race. [JC]

See also: WOMEN SF WRITERS.

FAIRMAN, PAUL W. (1916-1977) US editor and writer in several genres, including crime stories and erotica. His first published sf story was "No Teeth for the Tiger" for *AMZ* in 1950, and for some years thereafter he was a regular contributor to the ZIFF-DAVIS magazines under his own name, the pseudonyms Robert Lee and Mallory Storm, and various house pseudonyms, including E.K. JARVIS, Clee GARSON and Paul LOHRMAN. He was the first editor of IF, Mar-Nov 1952, but departed after 4 issues to join the Ziff-Davis staff. He left Ziff-Davis in 1954 but returned in Dec 1955 and became editor of AMAZING STORIES and FANTASTIC from May 1956, a position he held until Sep 1958. He launched the short-lived DREAM WORLD in 1957. He was the principal user of the Ivar JORGENSEN pseudonym, publishing under that name *Ten from Infinity* (**1963**; vt *The Deadly Sky* 1970; vt *Ten Deadly Men* 1975), *Rest in Agony* (**1963**; vt *The Diabolist* 1973) and *Whom the Gods Would Slay* (1951 *Fantastic Adventures*; **1968**). Two of his magazine stories were filmed: "Deadly City" (1953 *If* as Jorgensen) as TARGET EARTH! (1954) and "The Cosmic Frame" (1953 *AMZ*) as *Invasion of the Saucer Men* (1955; vt *Invasion of the Hell Creatures*). Several of his books were novelizations of tv scripts, including *The World Grabbers* * (**1964**), based on an episode from *One Step Beyond*, and *City under the Sea* * (**1965**), based on the film *City under the Sea* (1965; vt *War Gods of the Deep*). Other books issued under his own name were the sf novel *I, the Machine* (**1968**) and the horror-story collection *The Doomsday Exhibit* (coll **1971**). He wrote one pseudonymous novel in collaboration with Milton LESSER, *The Golden Ape* (1957 *AMZ* as "Quest of the Golden Ape" as by Adam CHASE and Ivar Jorgensen; **1959** as by Chase).

PWF wrote several juvenile novels based on outlines by Lester DEL REY and published under del Rey's byline, including *The Runaway Robot* (**1965**), *Tunnel through Time* (**1966**), *Siege Perilous* (**1966**; vt *The Man without a Planet* 1969) and *Prisoners of Space* (**1968**). *Rocket from Infinity* (**1966**), *The Infinite Worlds of Maybe* (**1966**) and *The Scheme of Things* (**1966**) may also have been by PWF but have not been acknowledged as such. He wrote one juvenile, *The Forgetful Robot* (**1968**), under his own name. [BS]

Other works: *A Study in Terror* * (**1966**; vt *Sherlock Holmes Versus Jack the Ripper* 1967 UK) as by Ellery Queen; *The Frankenstein Wheel* (**1972**).

See also: UNDER THE SEA.

FALCONER, KENNETH [s] ◊ C.M. KORNBLUTH.

FALCONER, LEE N. ◊ Julian MAY.
FALCONER, SOVEREIGN ◊ Craig STRETE.
FALDBAKKEN, KNUT [r] ◊ SCANDINAVIA.
FAMOUS FANTASTIC MYSTERIES US PULP MAGA-
ZINE which published 81 issues, Sep/Oct 1939 (vol 1
#1) June 1953 (vol 14 #4). It was originally part of the
Frank A. MUNSEY chain but was sold to Popular
Publications, which published it from Mar 1943. Mary
GNAEDINGER was editor throughout.

Although it published a few original stories, *FFM*
was basically a reprint magazine – perhaps the most
distinguished; it was originally founded to reprint
science fantasy from the Munsey pulps. After the sale
to Popular it switched to the reprinting of novels and
stories not previously published in magazines. The
first few monthly issues used much short material,
with novels serialized, but, after going bimonthly in
Aug 1940, *FFM* presented a complete novel in every
issue. The early issues featured novels by such
Munsey regulars as Ray CUMMINGS, George Allan
ENGLAND, A. MERRITT and Francis STEVENS. Novels
reprinted from original hardback editions included
several by H. Rider HAGGARD, William Hope HODG-
SON, John TAINE, E. Charles VIVIAN, H.G. WELLS and
S. Fowler WRIGHT. Through offering access to such
material *FFM* allowed many pulp-sf fans to broaden
their acquaintance with non-pulp material – extending even to such authors as G.K. CHESTERTON and
Franz KAFKA. The quality of illustration was also
exceptionally high – Virgil FINLAY did much of his best
work for the magazine, including 27 covers; 26 covers
were by Lawrence Sterne STEVENS. During the WWII
years publication was sometimes irregular.

A Canadian reprint edition ran Feb 1948-Aug 1952;
this was the second Canadian reprinting of *FFM*, the
first being the Canadian SUPER SCIENCE STORIES.　　[BS]
FAMOUS SCIENCE FICTION US DIGEST-size magazine. 9 issues, Winter 1966 (vol 1 #1) to Spring 1969
(vol 2 #3). One of the reprint magazines ed R.A.W.
LOWNDES for Health Knowledge Inc., it used material
from the PULP MAGAZINES of the 1930s plus 16 original
short stories by Greg BEAR, Miriam Allen DeFORD,
Philip K. DICK and others. The most notable of its
reprints was Lawrence MANNING's **The Man who
Awoke** series (1933 *Wonder Stories*; Summer 1967-
Summer 1968). To issues 2-6 Lowndes contributed a
series of editorials, **Standards in Science Fiction**, later
reprinted as *Three Faces of Science Fiction* (**1973**).　　[BS]
FANAC US FANZINE, ed from Berkeley by Terry CARR
and Ron ELLIK (1958-61) and subsequently (1961-3) by
Walter Breen. *Fanac* was a small but frequent publication carrying information on sf writers and events
and news of sf fans and their activities. Its informal
and humorous style was popular and became a
model for later fanzines. Contributors included well
known fans and professional writers. *Fanac* won the
HUGO for Best Fanzine in 1959.　　[PR]
FANCHER, JANE S(UZANNE) (1952-　　) US writer
who began publishing genre material with two
GRAPHIC NOVELS based on the work of C.J. CHERRYH:

Gate of Ivrel: Claiming Rites * (graph **1987**) and *Gate of
Ivrel: Fever Dreams* * (graph **1988**). In her own right JSF
wrote the **Cantrell** sequence of SPACE OPERAS set in a
Cherryhesque habitat-dominated Galaxy – *Groundties*
(**1991**) and *Uplink* (**1992**) – and featuring the protagonist's attempts to deal with a COMPUTER-generated
crisis on a colony planet inhabited by the descendants
of Native Americans. Both tales are high-pitched in
tone, complex and promising.　　[JC]
FANCIFUL TALES OF TIME AND SPACE US DIGEST-
size magazine. 1 issue, Fall 1936, published by
Shepard & Wollheim; ed Donald A. WOLLHEIM.
FTOTAS contained a mixture of weird, sf and fantasy
stories, including work by August DERLETH, David
KELLER and H.P. LOVECRAFT, as well as the first
publication of Robert E. HOWARD's poem "Solomon
Kane's Homecoming". *FTOTAS* was, strictly speaking, a SEMIPROZINE, rather like the earlier MARVEL TALES
– which is to say that, despite the print run being only
200, the magazine was for sale – although it seems to
have found no adequate distribution.　　[FHP/MJE]
FANDOM The active readership of sf and fantasy,
maintaining contacts through FANZINES and CONVEN-
TIONS. Fandom originated in the late 1920s, shortly
after the appearance of the first SF MAGAZINES. Readers
contacted each other, formed local groups (some of
which, notably the SCIENCE FICTION LEAGUE, were
professionally sponsored), and soon began publication of APAS and other amateur magazines, which
came to be known collectively as fanzines. The first
organized convention was held in Leeds, UK, in 1937
and the first World SF Convention in New York in
1939 (although it gained its name from the holding in
that year of the World's Fair in New York). From the
1920s to the 1950s, when sf was a minority interest,
the number of people in fandom was small, probably
no more than 500 at any one time. Since the 1960s,
however, the number has steadily increased to over
10,000 – though this figure, of course, represents no
more than a tiny fraction of the wider sf readership.
Fandom is, like GENRE SF, primarily a US phenomenon, though other English-speaking countries
quickly adopted the concept. Continental Europe,
Japan and elsewhere followed much later; but
increasing translation of and interest in sf has now
spread fandom to some 30 countries, from Mexico to
Norway. It is made up of both readers and writers of
sf; many authors started as fans and many fans have
written sf, so there is no absolute distinction between
the two groups. Fans themselves are mainly young
and male with higher education and a scientific or
technical background, but exceptions are numerous
and the stereotype is becoming less pronounced.
Many more women entered fandom in the 1970s and
1980s.

Fandom is not a normal hobbyist group. It has been
suggested that, if sf ceased to exist, fandom would
continue to function quite happily without it. That is
an exaggeration; but it indicates the difference
between sf fans and ostensibly similar groups

devoted to Westerns, romances, detective fiction, etc. The reason may lie in the fact that sf is a speculative literature and consequently attractive to readers actively interested in new ideas and concepts, in addition to those idly seeking entertainment. Early fans took part in rocketry, radical politics and quasi-utopian experiments; later fans seem to find fanzines, conventions and the interaction of fandom itself a sufficient outlet for their energies and ideas. Though fandom has a tradition and history, even a FAN LANGUAGE, fans are notably independent; relatively few belong to national organizations such as N3F or the BRITISH SCIENCE FICTION ASSOCIATION, and many publish individual and independent fanzines, a fact that at least one outside sociologist – Fredric Wertham (1895-1981) in *The World of Fanzines* (**1973**) – has found remarkable and even "unique".

There is a fannish word "fiawol", an acronym for "fandom is a way of life": the joke is not altogether untrue. Just as sf is unrestricted in the scope of its interests, so too are fans and fandom. Fandom is thus a collection of people with a common background in sf and a common interest in communication, whether through discussion, chatter, correspondence or fanzine publishing. The result is more nearly a group of friends, or even a subculture, than a simple fan club or a literary society.

There have always been divergent interest groups within fandom, and during the 1980s these tended to split more obviously. The most basic division, perhaps, is between those fans whose main love is written sf and the so-called media fans, who prefer sf in the form of CINEMA, TELEVISION or COMICS. Even among fans of written sf, fanzine fans and convention fans have become separate groups, though there is substantial overlap; comics fans have their own conventions, and there are other special-interest groups in media fandom who may be primarily interested in, for example, STAR TREK (the "Trekkies") or DR WHO; there is even a games fandom, with a particular interest in role-playing games (◊ GAMES AND TOYS).

Various aspects of US fan history are covered in, among others, *The Immortal Storm* (**1954**) by Sam MOSKOWITZ, *All our Yesterdays* (**1969**) and *A Wealth of Fable* (**1976** in mimeo form) by Harry WARNER Jr, *The Futurians* (**1977**) by Damon KNIGHT and *The Way the Future Was: A Memoir* (**1978**) by Frederik POHL. The fullest history of UK fandom takes the form of a fanzine, *Then*, written and published by Rob Hansen: the 180pp of #1, #2 and #3 (1988-91) cover the story to the end of the 1960s; more are projected.   [PR/PN]

See also: FAPA; FUTURIANS; OMPA; RATFANDOM.

FANE, BRON ◊ R.L. FANTHORPE.

FANE, JULIAN (CHARLES) (1927-   ) UK writer of literary bent whose DYSTOPIA, *Revolution Island* (**1979**), was one of the last UK visions of a union-dominated left-wing future. It was published just before the incoming administration of Margaret Thatcher (1979-90) put an end, for this century, to the relevance of

this sort of warning.   [JC]

FAN LANGUAGE Sf enthusiasts, in common with other groups, have evolved their own terminology and usage. This language comprises words and phrases used in the writing of sf itself and also the more arcane and whimsical jargon of FANDOM and FANZINES.

Most sf readers are familiar with the shorthand of their literature, and words like "spaceship", "robot", "time-machine" and even "ftl drive", "spacewarp" and "ray-gun" need little or no glossing. These words, however, originated in sf and required explanation when first coined (◊ TERMINOLOGY). Only the growth in popularity of sf has led to the acceptance of such terms as part of everyday English. The language of fandom, however, has a more restricted use and thus is less familiar. Much of it was initially associated with fanzines, including the specialized art of duplicating them, and much of it resulted from simple contraction: "corflu", for example, was nothing stranger than correcting fluid (for stencils). It is a sign of the march of time – and of the very widespread use of COMPUTER networks in fandom – that terms like "corflu" have gained an air of ancient quaintness; another sign of the times is that contemporary fans tend to accept neologisms from the world of computing rather than to generate their own. Of more general interest are words which describe fan attitudes and behaviour. Examples are: "egoboo" (from "ego-boost"), the satisfaction gained from praise or recognition, such as seeing one's name in print; "mundane", a non-fan; "slash fiction", fan-generated stories about sexual intimacy between famed fictional characters, always male, the best known examples being the Kirk/Spock slash tales; and acronyms like "to gafiate" (get away from it all – to leave fandom). Some of these contractions, acronyms and neologisms fill a linguistic need ("slash fiction" describes a phenomenon not otherwhere comprehended); others simply enrich the sense of affinity that fandom – like any other grouping of this sort – was partly created to foster. In general, fan argot is anything but freemasonical, and never amounts to anything like a secret code to baffle outsiders. For fans, outsiders are identifiable not so much by their failure to use certain terms as by their tendency to misuse others. The best example of this is perhaps "sf", the usual contraction used by sf fans; journalists and other nonsympathetic outsiders can readily be identified by their use of the repugnant "SCI-FI"; older fans sometimes use the contracted adjective stfnal, short for "scientifictional" (◊ SCIENTIFICTION).

Various guides to fan language have been published (by fans) in the USA and UK. Wilson TUCKER's *Neofan's Guide* (**1955**; rev 1973; rev 1984) is a useful introduction, and Roberta Rogow's *Futurespeak: A Fan's Guide to the Language of Science Fiction* (**1991**), though erratic, covers much new ground.   [PR/JC]

FANTAST ◊ *The* FUTURIAN.

FANTASTIC US DIGEST-size magazine, companion to

AMAZING STORIES; published by ZIFF-DAVIS (Summer 1952-June 1965), Ultimate Publishing Co. (Sep 1965-Oct 1980); ed Howard BROWNE (Summer 1952-Aug 1956), Paul W. FAIRMAN (Oct 1956-Nov 1958), Cele GOLDSMITH (Dec 1958-June 1965; as Cele G. Lalli from July 1964), Joseph ROSS (Sep 1965-Nov 1967), Harry HARRISON (Jan-Oct 1968), Barry N. MALZBERG (Dec 1968-Apr 1969), Ted WHITE (June 1969-Jan 1979), Elinor Mavor (Apr 1979-Oct 1980; initially under the pseudonym Omar Gohagen). From Nov 1980 *Fantastic* was merged with *AMZ*. After the title was bought by Sol Cohen's Ultimate Publishing Co. in 1965 it mainly published reprints until mid-1968; the reprint policy was finally phased out completely under White soon after he took over from Malzberg. For much of its early life *F* was bimonthly, but at its height – in the Goldsmith period – it went monthly, beginning with Feb 1957. The Ultimate Publishing version began in Sep 1965 as a bimonthly, but the magazine went onto a quarterly schedule in 1976. The title underwent numerous minor changes, appearing as *Fantastic Science Fiction* (Apr 1955-Feb 1958), *Fantastic Science Fiction Stories* (Sep 1959-Sep 1960), *Fantastic Stories of Imagination* (Oct 1960-June 1965) and *Fantastic Stories* at various periods.

Browne originally intended *F* to attract a wider audience than *AMZ*, and published tales under bylines famous outside the sf field, including Raymond Chandler, Truman Capote, Mickey Spillane and Evelyn WAUGH (the Spillane byline was probably not authentic). After 1953, when it absorbed the much older FANTASTIC ADVENTURES, *F* deteriorated to become a downmarket sf magazine indistinguishable from *AMZ*. But from 1958, under the more adventurous editorship of Goldsmith, it improved dramatically, becoming arguably the best fantasy magazine existing. Fritz LEIBER revived his **Fafhrd and Gray Mouser** for an issue containing only his stories (Nov 1959), and the series remained an irregular feature. Authors whose first published stories appeared in *F* include Thomas M. DISCH, Ursula K. LE GUIN and Roger ZELAZNY. David BUNCH was a regular (and controversial) contributor. Following a bad period in the mid-1960s after the magazine was sold, *F* improved again under White, featuring a notable series of articles by Alexei and Cory PANSHIN, **Science Fiction in Dimension** (1970-73), publishing much early work by Gordon EKLUND and some excellent covers by Stephen FABIAN. New **Conan** stories by L. Sprague DE CAMP and Lin CARTER helped to boost circulation a little, but the magazine's situation remained financially precarious despite the fact that "adult fantasy" had been spectacularly revived as a paperback genre. Its deterioration after White quit was rapid and deservedly terminal.

Although the words "science fiction" appeared on the cover at different times for four or five years, *F* was always mainly known for fantasy, being particularly strong in SWORD AND SORCERY.

An undated bimonthly UK reprint ran for 8 issues, published by Strato Publications Dec 1953-Feb 1955. An anthology of stories from *F* is *The Best from Fantastic* (anth **1973**) ed Ted White.   [BS]

FANTASTIC ADVENTURES US PULP MAGAZINE published by ZIFF-DAVIS as a companion to AMAZING STORIES. 128 issues May 1939-Mar 1953. *FA* began as a bimonthly, BEDSHEET-size, but maintained a monthly schedule from vol 2 #1 (Jan 1940) for most of its existence, shrinking to PULP-MAGAZINE size in June 1940. To Dec 1949 it was ed Raymond A. PALMER, and from then until May/June 1953 (when it merged with the one-year-old Ziff-Davis DIGEST magazine FANTASTIC) by Howard V. BROWNE. William L. HAMLING was managing editor Nov 1947-Feb 1951.

The bulk of *FA*'s contents were provided by a small stable of Chicago writers using a variety of house pseudonyms, although Palmer did publish several stories by Edgar Rice BURROUGHS 1939-42 and some material by established sf and fantasy writers – Robert BLOCH was a frequent contributor. The magazine was at its best under Browne's editorship in 1950-51, when it published Theodore STURGEON's first novel, *The Dreaming Jewels* (Feb 1950; **1950**), and notable long stories by Lester DEL REY, Walter M. MILLER and William TENN. *FA* hardly bears comparison with its rival *ASF*'s short-lived but excellent companion UNKNOWN, but sf writers given *carte blanche* to write pure fantasy for *FA* did often produce readable fiction with a distinctive whimsical and ironic flavour. The mass-produced material it published was of quite negligible interest.

In 1941-3 and 1948-51 unsold issues were bound up in threes and sold as *Fantastic Adventures Quarterly*, there being 8 such in the first series, Winter 1941-Fall 1943, and 11 in the second, Summer 1948-Spring 1951. There were 2 UK editions: the first released 2 short (32pp) numbered issues in 1946, the second reprinted 24 numbered issues 1950-54, abridged from US issues dated Mar 1950-Jan 1953.   [BS]

FANTASTIC ADVENTURES QUARTERLY ◊ FANTASTIC ADVENTURES.

FANTASTIC ADVENTURES YEARBOOK One of the many reprint DIGEST-size magazines issued by Sol Cohen's Ultimate Publishing Co., which in 1965 had bought rights to the ZIFF-DAVIS sf magazines. Its only issue, containing stories reprinted from FANTASTIC ADVENTURES 1949-52, was released in 1970.   [BS/PN]

FANTASTIC JOURNEY, THE US tv series (1977). Bruce Lansbury Productions/Columbia Pictures TV/NBC. Prod Leonard Katzman. Writers included Michael Michaelian, Kathryn Michaelian Powers and the story editor, D.C. FONTANA. Dirs included Andrew V. McLaglen (pilot episode), Vincent McEveety. Starring Carl Franklin, Roddy McDowall, Jared Martin. One season, pilot episode of 75 mins plus 9 50min episodes. Colour.

The pilot episode has explorers entering the Bermuda Triangle, an ocean area in which planes and ships are reputed to disappear; but, after an effectively eerie opening in which their boat is consumed by a pulsating green cloud, it becomes evident that they are still within the borders of tv-formula-land. Reaching an island that "isn't on the map", they meet a 23rd-century human, Varian (Martin), and discover that the landscape consists of segments of past and future time and space, an idea perhaps inspired by Fred HOYLE's *October the First is Too Late* (**1966**). This concept allows the protagonists to encounter a new (stereotyped) culture every week, each within walking distance. Silly and somewhat repetitive adventures take place. The series was quickly dropped.

[JB/PN]

FANTASTIC NOVELS US bimonthly reprint PULP MAGAZINE, companion to FAMOUS FANTASTIC MYSTERIES, which it somewhat resembled. 5 issues July 1940-Apr 1941, published by the Frank A. MUNSEY Corp.; it was revived by Popular Publications to publish 20 more issues Mar 1948-June 1951, with the numeration of the second series following directly on from that of the first. It was ed in both incarnations by Mary GNAEDINGER.

FN used a great deal of material by A. MERRITT. #1 featured *The Blind Spot* (1921; **1951**) by Austin HALL and Homer Eon FLINT, serialization of which had begun in *Famous Fantastic Mysteries*, and all subsequent issues except the last featured a complete novel. Other authors whose work was reprinted included Ray CUMMINGS and George Allan ENGLAND.

2 issues of a UK edition appeared in 1950 and 1951, the second (undated) issue confusingly appearing as #1. There were 17 issues of a Canadian reprint, Sep 1948-June 1951, identical to the US issues. [BS/PN]

FANTASTIC PLANET ◊ *La* PLANÈTE SAUVAGE.

FANTASTIC SCIENCE FICTION US BEDSHEET-size magazine, ed Walter B. GIBSON, the prolific pulp writer and creator of **The Shadow**. Only 2 issues appeared, #1 (Aug 1952) published by Super Science Fiction Publications, #2 (Dec 1952) by Capitol Stories, both of Connecticut.

This inferior magazine, whose stories featured simplistic and chauvinistic adventure, should not be confused with FANTASTIC, also begun in 1952, which for Apr 1955-Feb 1958 was likewise titled *Fantastic Science Fiction*. [BS/PN]

FANTASTIC SCIENCE FICTION STORIES ◊ FANTASTIC.

FANTASTIC SCIENCE THRILLER UK juvenile pocketbook series published by Stanley Baker Ltd. There were 6 issues, all in 1954. [BS]

FANTASTIC STORIES ◊ FANTASTIC.

FANTASTIC STORIES OF IMAGINATION ◊ FANTASTIC.

FANTASTIC STORY MAGAZINE ◊ FANTASTIC STORY QUARTERLY.

FANTASTIC STORY QUARTERLY US reprint PULP MAGAZINE, 23 issues Spring 1950-Spring 1955, the title changing after #4 to *Fantastic Story Magazine*; published by Best Books, a subsidiary of Standard Magazines. Sam MERWIN Jr was editor until Fall 1951, being succeeded by Samuel MINES and then by

Alexander SAMALMAN for the last 2 issues.

Most of the reprints were from STARTLING STORIES and THRILLING WONDER STORIES; early issues carried a good deal of material from Hugo GERNSBACK's WONDER STORIES. *FSQ* used a few original stories, including Gordon R. DICKSON's first, "Trespass!" (1950), written with Poul ANDERSON, and occasionally went outside the chain for reprints – e.g., publishing A.E. VAN VOGT's *Slan* (1940 *ASF*; **1946**; rev 1951) in the Summer 1952 issue. Most issues carried a complete novel. There was a Canadian edition of the first 4 numbers. [BS]

FANTASTIC UNIVERSE US DIGEST-size magazine, last 6 issues PULP-MAGAZINE size. 69 issues June/July 1953-Mar 1960, published by Leo MARGULIES's King-Size Publications to July 1959, then by Great American Publications. *FU* began as a bimonthly, but went monthly in Sep 1954 and held to that schedule for most of its life except Nov 1958-Sep 1959, when it was again bimonthly. Ed Sam MERWIN Jr June-Nov 1953; Beatrice Jones Jan-Mar 1954; Leo Margulies May 1954-Aug 1956; Hans Stefan SANTESSON Sep 1956-Mar 1960.

FU's material spanned the entire fantasy spectrum; in effect it became the poor man's MAGAZINE OF FANTASY AND SCIENCE FICTION. There was no interior artwork until July 1959. Two important stories were "Who?" (1955) by Algis BUDRYS, which formed the basis of his *Who?* (**1958**), and "Curative Telepath" (1959) by John BRUNNER, which formed the basis of his *The Whole Man* (**1964**; vt *Telepathist* UK). 16 of the best stories from its pages were published in *The Fantastic Universe Omnibus* (anth **1960**) ed Santesson. [BS/PN]

FANTASTIC VOYAGE Film (1966). 20th Century-Fox. Dir Richard Fleischer, starring Stephen Boyd, Raquel Welch, Edmund O'Brien, Donald Pleasence. Screenplay Harry Kleiner, based on a story by Otto Clement and J. Lewis (i.e., Jerome) BIXBY. 100 mins. Colour.

A submarine and its crew of medical experts – plus a double-agent saboteur (Pleasence) – are miniaturized and injected into the bloodstream of an important scientist in order to remove by laser a blood-clot from his brain. In the finale – a race to escape before they revert to full size while still inside the body – they exit via a tear duct with only seconds to spare. The special effects by L.B. Abbott, Art Cruickshank and Emil Kosa Jr are impressive, as are the sets – duplicating in giant size various organs of the body, such as the heart, lungs and brain – designed by art director Dale Hennesy with spectacular histological surrealism. This vivid spectacle, however, does not compensate for the ham acting, the irrelevance of Ms Welch's lingered-on breasts, and the puerile melodrama. The novelization was *Fantastic Voyage* ∗ (**1966**) by Isaac ASIMOV. A film using a very similar theme is Joe DANTE's INNERSPACE (1987). [PN/JB]

See also: GREAT AND SMALL.

FANTASTIC VOYAGES The fantastic voyage is one of the oldest literary forms, and remains one of the basic frameworks for the casting of literary fantasies. Of the prose forms extant before the development of the novel in the 18th century, the fantastic voyage is the most important in the ancestry of sf ($\lozenge$ PROTO SCIENCE FICTION). Among others, Johannes KEPLER's *Somnium* (**1634**), Francis BACON's *New Atlantis* (**1627**), Tommaso CAMPANELLA's *City of the Sun* (**1623**) and CYRANO DE BERGERAC's *Other Worlds* (**1657-62**) all take this form, as do the oldest of all works which can be claimed as ancestors of sf: the Sumerian *Epic of Gilgamesh*, from the third millennium BC, and HOMER's *Odyssey*, from the first.

The fantastic voyage continued to dominate speculative fiction and the SCIENTIFIC ROMANCE long after the rise of the novel, whose basic pretence was the painstaking imitation of experience (what the critic Ian Watt calls "formal realism"). It is partly because of this formal separation of speculative literature from the development of 19th-century social literature that there remains something of a gulf between speculative fiction and the literary MAINSTREAM today. The first sf story cast in the form of a novel was Mary SHELLEY's *Frankenstein* (**1818**), but there were very few comparable works written in the succeeding century. The bulk of Jules VERNE's imaginative work falls in the category of *voyages imaginaires*, and many of H.G. WELLS's scientific romances adopt a similar form. Among the important fantastic voyages which today may be classified as sf are: *The Man in the Moone* (**1638**) by Francis GODWIN, *Gulliver's Travels* (**1726**) by Jonathan SWIFT, *Nicolai Klimii iter subterraneum* (**1741** in Latin; exp 1745; trans as *A Journey to the World Under-Ground* **1742** UK) by Ludwig HOLBERG, *A Short Account of a Remarkable Aerial Voyage and Discovery of a New Planet* (**1813**) by Willem BILDERDIJK, *Symzonia* (**1820**) by Adam SEABORN, *A Voyage to the Moon* (**1827**) by Joseph ATTERLEY, *Voyage au centre de la terre* (**1863**; exp 1867; trans as *Journey to the Centre of the Earth* **1872** UK) and *Vingt mille lieues sous les mers* (**1870**; trans as *Twenty Thousand Leagues under the Sea* **1872** UK) by Jules Verne, and *Across the Zodiac* (**1880**) by Percy GREG. These voyages took their heroes over the Earth's surface, into worlds underground and beneath the sea, to the Moon and to other planets. Important new scope for the fantastic voyage was revealed in the last few years of the 19th century by H.G. Wells in *The Time Machine* (**1895**), which opened up the limitless vistas of the future to planned tourism, and by Robert W. COLE in *The Struggle for Empire* (**1900**), the first major interstellar adventure story. These new imaginative territories were to prove immensely significant for 20th-century imaginative literature. The fantastic voyage has, of course, also remained central within the literature of the supernatural imagination, much of which was also ill adapted to the form of the novel. As supernatural fantasy has been influenced and infiltrated by the scientific imagination it has been the fantastic voyage, far more than any other narrative form, that has provided a suitable medium for "hybrid" works; thus a considerable number of 20th-century fantastic voyages are difficult to classify by means of the standard genre borderlines. In this no-

man's-land within the territories of imaginative literature exist virtually all the works of writers such as William Hope HODGSON, Edgar Rice BURROUGHS and A. MERRITT, and various individual novels of note: Frigyes KARINTHY's Gulliverian *Voyage to Faremido and Capillaria* (**1916** and **1922**; trans omni **1966**), David LINDSAY's *A Voyage to Arcturus* (**1920**), Ruthven TODD's *The Lost Traveller* (**1943**), the title story of John Cowper POWYS's *Up and Out* (coll **1957**), *The Phantom Tollbooth* (**1961**) by Norton Juster (1929-   ) and Michel Bernanos's *The Other Side of the Mountain* (**1967**; trans **1968**).

When Hugo GERNSBACK first demarcated sf as a genre in the 1920s he co-opted Verne, Wells and Merritt, and also Ray CUMMINGS, author of fantastic voyages into the atomic microcosm ($\lozenge$ GREAT AND SMALL). It was not long before E.E. "Doc" SMITH's *The Skylark of Space* (**1928**; **1946**) took PULP-MAGAZINE sf, at FASTER-THAN-LIGHT speeds, into the greater Universe beyond the limits of the Solar System. Other milieux were quickly introduced. Edmond HAMILTON's "Locked Worlds" (**1929**) adapted the notion of PARALLEL WORLDS from supernatural fantasy, and the first pulp sf voyages into a future replete with ALTERNATE WORLDS were undertaken in Jack WILLIAMSON's *The Legion of Time* (**1938**; **1952**). A significant refinement in the interstellar fantastic voyage, the GENERATION STARSHIP, was introduced a few years later, most significantly in Robert A. HEINLEIN's "Universe" (**1941**).

Voyages into the "inner spaces" of the human mind had also long been commonplace in supernatural fantasy, but a sciencefictional jargon of support for such adventures was slow in arriving. Notable early examples are "Dreams are Sacred" (**1948**) by Peter Phillips and "The Mental Assassins" (**1950**) by Gregg Conrad (Rog PHILLIPS).

Most of these milieux were reachable only by means of literary devices whose practicability was highly dubious if not flatly impossible. Space travel was the one hypothetical variant of the fantastic voyage into which it was possible to introduce rigorous attempts at realism ($\lozenge$ SPACESHIPS), although the technologies involved have inevitably became dated with the passage of time. Notable attempts from various periods include Verne's *De la terre à la lune* (**1865**) and *Autour de la lune* (**1870**), Konstantin TSIOLKOVSKY's *Beyond the Planet Earth* (**1920** Russia; trans **1960**), Laurence MANNING's "Voyage of the Asteroid" (**1932**) and Arthur C. CLARKE's *Prelude to Space* (**1951**). The purely facilitative character of devices like TIME MACHINES and interdimensional portals should not, however, be deemed to disqualify them as means to be deployed in serious speculative fictions; indeed, they are vitally necessary

The opening up of these vast imaginary territories gave sf writers limitless scope for invention. There is no speculation – whether physical, biological, social or metaphysical – that cannot somehow be made incarnate and given a space of its own within the conventions of sf. Voyages into fluid worlds where anything and everything may happen – where the characters become helpless victims of chaos or god-like creators – may be envisaged, as in M.K. JOSEPH's *The Hole in the Zero* (**1967**), as may voyages into mathematical abstraction like "The Mathenauts" (1964) by Norman KAGAN. Sf has drawn up a framework of conventions and a vocabulary of literary devices which not only makes such adventures conceivable but renders them relatively comfortable. It is a potential that sf writers have, for various reasons, been greatly inhibited from exploiting to the full, but they have – whatever their failings – established significant signposts within all these hypothetical realms.

At its simplest the fantastic voyage is a set of episodes whose function is simply to present a series of dramatic encounters, but it is rare to find the form used with no higher ambition than to offer a pleasant distraction. Many voyages which pretend to be doing that – like Lewis CARROLL's **Alice** books – actually present worlds whose bizarre aspects reflect the real world ironically and subversively. The same is true even of many relatively crude pulp sf stories like Francis STEVENS's *The Heads of Cerberus* (1919; **1952**), Garret SMITH's *Between Worlds* (1919; **1929**), John TAINE's *The Time Stream* (1931; **1946**) and Stanton A. COBLENTZ's *Hidden World* (1935 as "In Caverns Below"; **1957**), and in such unconvincing films as VOYAGE TO THE BOTTOM OF THE SEA (1961) and FANTASTIC VOYAGE (1966). In very many cases the fantastic voyage has allegorical implications, which are most obvious when the voyage is also a quest, as it very often is in modern genre fantasy, which tends to follow the paradigm of J.R.R. TOLKIEN's *The Lord of the Rings* (3 vols **1954-5**). The quest may be for a person, an object or a place, but the movement through a hypothetical landscape is usually paralleled by a growth towards some kind of maturity or acceptance in the protagonist's mind. The growth is towards self-knowledge or CONCEPTUAL BREAKTHROUGH in the psychologically oriented variants which lie within or close to the borders of sf; examples include *Rasselas* (**1759**) by Samuel JOHNSON, *Non-Stop* (**1958**; vt *Starship* US) by Brian W. ALDISS, *The Drowned World* (**1962**) by J.G. BALLARD and *Inverted World* (**1974**) by Christopher PRIEST. In stories of this kind the relationship between the environment of the story and the inner space of the protagonists's psyche is often complex and subtle; in the work of Philip K. DICK, from *Eye in the Sky* (**1957**) to *A Scanner Darkly* (**1977**), characters are continually forced to undertake nightmarish journeys into milieux where the distinction between real and unreal is hopelessly blurred and their personal inadequacies are painfully exposed.

Any list of notable fantastic voyages in modern sf is necessarily highly selective, but some of the most important and interesting which have appeared since 1926 are as follows: *The World Below* (**1929**) by S. Fowler WRIGHT, *Out of the Silent Planet* (**1938**) by C.S. LEWIS, *The Voyage of the Space Beagle* (1939-50; fixup **1950**) by A.E. VAN VOGT, *Big Planet* (1952; **1957**) by Jack VANCE, "Surface Tension" (1952) by James BLISH, *Mission of Gravity* (**1954**) by Hal CLEMENT, *The City and the Stars* (**1956**) by Arthur C. CLARKE, *The Einstein Intersection* (**1967**) and *Nova* (**1968**) by Samuel R. DELANY, *Picnic on Paradise* (**1968**) by Joanna RUSS, *Space Chantey* (**1968**) by R.A. LAFFERTY, *Tau Zero* (**1970**) by Poul ANDERSON, *Downward to the Earth* (**1970**) and *Son of Man* (**1971**) by Robert SILVERBERG, *Ringworld* (**1970**) by Larry NIVEN, *The Infernal Desire Machines of Dr Hoffman* (**1972**; vt *War of Dreams*) by Angela CARTER, *Hiero's Journey* (**1973**) by Sterling E. LANIER, *Orbitsville* (**1975**) by Bob SHAW, *Galaxies* (**1975**) by Barry N. MALZBERG, *Engine Summer* (**1979**) by John CROWLEY, *The Hitch Hiker's Guide to the Galaxy* (**1979**) and *The Restaurant at the End of the Universe* (**1980**) by Douglas ADAMS, **The Book of the New Sun** (**1980-83**) by Gene WOLFE, *The Void Captain's Tale* (**1983**) and *Child of Fortune* (**1985**) by Norman SPINRAD, *The Travails of Jane Saint* (**1986**) by Josephine SAXTON and *Hyperion* (**1989**) by Dan SIMMONS. [BS]

FANTASY There is no DEFINITION OF SF that excludes fantasy, other than prescriptive definitions so narrow that, were they applied, this encyclopedia would be reduced to 10 per cent of its present length. We are talking about problems of definition raised by not a minority but a majority of all genre writings. Among the GENRE-SF writers whose work would be excluded are Terry BISSON, Ray BRADBURY, Orson Scott CARD, John CROWLEY, Avram DAVIDSON, Samuel R. DELANY, Thomas M. DISCH, Harlan ELLISON, Philip José FARMER, Ursula K. LE GUIN, Fritz LEIBER, Michael MOORCOCK, Andre NORTON, Tim POWERS, Keith ROBERTS, Geoff RYMAN, Lucius SHEPARD, Dan SIMMONS, Jack VANCE, John VARLEY, Gene WOLFE and Roger ZELAZNY – many of the ablest and most popular writers in the sf field. Most or all of these writers (and several hundred more names could easily be added) have written occasional works that would be accepted by almost all readers as fantasy, but that is not the point; rather it is that any definition of sf that insists upon limiting true sf to scientific or "cognitive" modes of thought, and extrapolation from known realities, would exclude *the whole body of their work*. It is not that Delany or Le Guin are unscientific; indeed, they are not. But the science is not the whole story; their work is deeply imbued with fantasy motifs, fantastic modes of thought, narrative connections deriving from the logic of myth, metaphors from magical or religious belief, narrative resonances evoking a backward corridor of time long preceding the ages of science and technology. Certainly most of us can and do accept nearly all the above as true sf writers, but that is because most of us are not wedded to prescriptive definitions of sf. In the real world, we recognize that both sf and fantasy, if genres at all, are impure genres. They are not homogeneous. Their fruit may be sf but the roots are fantasy, and the flowers and leaves, perhaps, something else again.

It is, of course, quite simple to erect a theoretical system that distinguishes the genres, though in practice it is not especially helpful, for the reasons given above. The usual way is to regard fantasy as a subset of fiction, a circle within a circle. (The bit between inner and outer circles is mimetic fiction, which cleaves to known reality. Mimetic or "realistic" fiction is itself fairly recent; the distinctions being made here could not have been made before the 18th century.) Within the inner circle of fantasy – the fiction of the presently unreal – is a smaller circle still, a subset of a subset, and this is sf. It shares with fantasy the idea of a novum: some new element, something that distinguishes the fiction from reality as presently constituted. A novum could be a vampire or a colonized planet. The sub-subset that is sf insists that the novum be explicable in terms that adhere to conventionally formulated natural law; the remainder, fantasy, has no such requirement.

To cut the definition to an irreducible minimum: mimetic fiction is real, fantasy is unreal (but ◊ FABULATION); sf is unreal but natural, as opposed to the remainder of fantasy, which is unreal and supernatural. (Or, simpler still, sf could happen, fantasy couldn't.)

Several things follow from this sort of argument. The first is that all sf is fantasy, but not all fantasy is sf. The second is that, because natural law is something we come to understand only gradually, over centuries, and which we continue to rewrite, the sf of one period regularly becomes the fantasy of the next. What we regard as natural or possible depends upon the consensus reality of a given culture; but the idea of consensus reality itself is an ideal, not an absolute: in practice there are as many realities as there are human consciousnesses. A reader who believes in astrology will allow certain fictions to be sf that an astronomer would exclude. Although the point is seldom made, it could be said that the particular consensus reality to which sf aspires is that of the scientific community.

In this encyclopedia we do not use the word "fantasy" in the sense suggested in the previous three paragraphs: that is, as a supergenre which includes sf. This is because we have practical problems to contend with: the hardest part in determining which authors should and should not be given entries in this encyclopedia was deciding which fantasy authors were sufficiently sf-like to be included (see Introduction for further discussion). To make any sort of distinction at all, we had to regard "fantasy" as the contents of the middle circle excluding the sf circle, in which the novum is supernatural; in other words, "fantasy", as we use the word throughout this book, is fiction about the impossible. Even then, the distinction is quite extraordinarily difficult; again and again the sf fruit has roots of fantasy; even HARD SF regularly uses fantastic or IMAGINARY SCIENCE.

Although academics, especially those specializing in genre studies, have written many volumes attempting to make the sort of distinction we speak of, the sf community has been decidedly pragmatic and has generally ducked the issue. To take two major AWARDS, the HUGO and the NEBULA, and one less known, the PHILIP K. DICK AWARD, it is sometimes not realized that there is nothing in their constitutions to prevent them being given to works of fantasy rather than sf; indeed, they often are. Hugo-winners include Fritz Leiber's "Ill Met in Lankhmar" (1970) and Robert BLOCH's "That Hell-Bound Train" (1958); Nebula-winners include Pat MURPHY's *The Falling Woman* (1986) and Ursula K. Le Guin's *Tehanu: The Last Book of Earthsea* (1990); Philip K. Dick award-winners include Tim Powers' *The Anubis Gates* (1983) and Patricia Geary's *Strange Toys* (1987). There are many more such.

Or take the genre magazines, and consider how many have titles deliberately including both genres: FANTASTIC SCIENCE FICTION STORIES, *The* MAGAZINE OF FANTASY AND SCIENCE FICTION, SCIENCE FANTASY, and a number of others. Or consider that the genre newspaper LOCUS, along with the annual bibliographies it publishes, gives full coverage to sf, fantasy and horror and makes no clear distinction between them. Consider that the most recent academic journal about sf deliberately titles itself to include fantasy also: JOURNAL OF THE FANTASTIC IN THE ARTS. (We do not wish to start any hares about whatever differences may be discernible between Fantasy and the Fantastic.) Or consider the Italian word for sf, "fantascienza", which combines the two genres in the word itself; the Russian word is "fantastika". Indeed, consider that the general thrust of the European (though not UK) literary tradition is to regard fantasy and sf as two aspects of the same phenomenon; it is notable that several European authors of such entries in this encyclopedia as ROMANIA are more inclusive about what constitutes sf than this encyclopedia is as a whole. (European theoretical critics, however, can be very *ex*clusive in their definitions; Tzvetan TODOROV muddied the waters in *Introduction à la littérature fantastique* [**1970**; trans as *The Fantastic: A Structural Approach to a Literary Genre* **1973**], which sees the fantastic, not very helpfully, as occupying the area where the reader hesitates between imputing a rational or a supernatural explanation to the events described, which would exclude most fantasy from "the fantastic"; and another celebrated European critic, Darko SUVIN, has claimed that the commercial linking of sf and fantasy, whether in marketing or in critical terms, is "a rampantly pathological phenomenon". Suvin is the best known of those critics who have offered the kind of prescriptive definition of sf noted above.)

In the face of this widespread conspiracy to ignore generic boundaries wherever possible (a conspiracy to which most bookshops belong) it may seem quixotic to attempt distinctions at all. Yet we feel that a book calling itself *The Encyclopedia of Science Fiction* must make at least some attempt to prevent "sf proper" from being wholly swamped by the necessarily much larger number of entries (especially author entries) that a wholly inclusive policy about fantasy would entail.

The task is not impossible, though necessarily subjective. The most important thing perhaps – difficult to pin down because it involves style as well as content – is to regard fantasy as sf-like when it adopts a cognitive approach to its subject matter, even if that subject matter is MAGIC. Although both are given entries in this book, most people would agree that Ursula Le Guin's **Earthsea** books are more sciencefictional in tone – even though set in worlds where magic works and where dragons exist – than, say, H.P. LOVECRAFT's stories of the **Cthulhu Mythos**, though the latter are in fact explicable in sf terms where the former are not; that is, Lovecraft's Elder Gods, spawned in space or in other worlds, can be seen as enormously powerful ALIEN invaders. In practice, though, Lovecraft's readers seldom give his work an sf reading of this sort, because his tone is fundamentally and unmistakably GOTHIC and antirational: Le Guin is an explainer, Lovecraft prefers the weird, the sinister and the inexplicable. In other words, supernatural fantasy approaches the condition of science fiction when its narrative voice implies a post-scientific consciousness. Conversely, sf (like, for example, much of that by Andre Norton or, in a different way, by Ray Bradbury) approaches the condition of fantasy when its narrative voice implies a mystical or even anti-scientific consciousness.

Authors who use fantasy elements in sf regularly rationalize their fundamentally GOTHIC motifs, Anne MCCAFFREY's dragons being an excellent example: many further examples are given in the entries on GODS AND DEMONS, GOLEM, MAGIC, MONSTERS, MYTHOLOGY and SUPERNATURAL CREATURES, these all being areas where sf and fantasy commonly collide. Conversely, when writers of HARD SF like Robert A. HEINLEIN, Poul ANDERSON and Larry NIVEN write fantasy, as they often have done, it is amusing to note how the old habits persist; they regard the marvellous and the magical with a rationalist scrutiny, treating MAGIC (which see) rather as Le Guin does, as if it were a science. The distinction between magic and science is not wholly clear at the best of times; Arthur C. CLARKE has commented that "any sufficiently advanced technology is indistinguishable from magic". Larry Niven and David GERROLD's *The Flying Sorcerers* (**1971**) is constructed around this precept.

A story parodying the transmutation of fantasy into sf by use of scientific jargon is Isaac ASIMOV's "Pâté de Foie Gras" (**1956**), an sf version of "The Goose that Laid the Golden Eggs". When the rationalization of fantasy elements is merely cursory (substituting, say, an ALTERNATE WORLD reached through a Dimensional Gate for something resembling what Alice found down the rabbit burrow) we would be inclined to call the result fantasy still, though others would call it sf. This kind of fiction perhaps began with Edgar Rice BURROUGHS's **Barsoom** books in the early decades of this century, in which an unexplained superscience tends to stand in for magic. A convenient term for these stories is SCIENCE FANTASY, and they are discussed under that rubric; many "science fantasy" stories are also PLANETARY ROMANCES (*which see*).

One reason why so much fantasy rather resembles sf is its use of many sciencefictional motifs (though it has to be said that the *range* of motifs is much narrower than that found in sf proper, since not much fantasy contains anything other than occult technology; there are few ROBOTS and CYBORGS and SPACESHIPS). Theme entries in this book representing the most notable sf and borderline-sf motifs of this sort are ALTERNATE WORLDS, ATLANTIS, DIMENSIONS, ESP, FANTASTIC VOYAGES, IMMORTALITY, PSI POWERS, REINCARNATION, SUSPENDED ANIMATION and TIME TRAVEL. All of these are commonplace in fantasy, most of them commonplace in sf also. Indeed, sf set in worlds where psi powers work can often be read as it if were fantasy; such, towards the sf end of the spectrum, are Marion Zimmer BRADLEY's **Darkover** novels and, towards the fantasy end, Christopher STASHEFF's *The Warlock in Spite of Himself* (**1969**) and its sequels. A sophisticated variant is *The Deep* (**1975**) by John CROWLEY, which adroitly plays upon the generic expectations of the reader in such a way that what appears to be HEROIC FANTASY comes to seem, retrospectively, pure sf.

Fantasy itself is not homogeneous; various terms are used, often not very precisely, to characterize its various kinds. An interesting distinction, made by Marshall B. TYMN, Kenneth J. Zahorski and Robert H. Boyer in the introduction to *Fantasy Literature: A Core Collection and Reference Guide* (**1979**), is between high fantasy, set in a fully realized secondary world, and low fantasy, which features supernatural intrusions into our own world. Most HORROR fiction takes the latter form; most SWORD AND SORCERY (or HEROIC FANTASY) takes the former. Although this encyclopedia contains many examples of both high and low fantasy, it is probably high fantasy (in this definition) that is the closest to sf: high fantasy and sf typically create imaginary worlds (alternate to our own). Thus Frank HERBERT's *Dune* (**1965**) and J.R.R. TOLKIEN's *The Lord of the Rings* (**1954-5**), though the one is sf and the other high fantasy, have in the imaginative intensity of their detailed world-creation a great deal in common (but ◊ PLANETARY ROMANCE for an argument that the two styles of fiction differ essentially in that one is set on a planet, the other in a landscape). The kind of fantasy which creates such detailed, self-consistent alternate worlds, whatever we call it, is certainly the kind most written by sf writers "on vacation". Such is Poul Anderson's *Three Hearts and Three Lions* (**1953**; exp **1961**) and Jack Vance's *The Dying Earth* (coll **1950**). Such worlds were never peculiar to sf writers, however. Further back, many of the works of Lord DUNSANY are effectively set in a coherent, alternate universe, as are those of E.R. EDDISON and James Branch CABELL, all three being quite unconnected to genre sf when they wrote, though all three have since had repercussions in sf that go beyond the merely stylistic. An even more notable work of fantasy is the **Gormenghast** sequence **(1946-59)** by Mervyn PEAKE; this may not be set in a fully fledged alternate world, but it does contain all the conceptual creativity that another writer might have lavished on an entire planet focused upon one emblematic building and its occupants.

In its marketing, sword-and-sorcery fiction was for some time sold very much as if it were a form of sf – perhaps in part because many of the same writers have been involved in both genres, like L. Sprague DE CAMP, C.L. MOORE, Henry KUTTNER, Leigh BRACKETT, Jack Vance and Fritz Leiber; the term "sword and sorcery" is said to have been coined by Leiber. The archetypal sword-and-sorcery writer at the pulp end of the spectrum was Robert E. HOWARD in his **Conan** series of the 1930s, mostly in *Weird Tales* (1932-6); while not sf, these stories were set in a coherent and quite carefully imagined world (presented as an enormously archaic version of our own). Sword and sorcery (the term is often used in a derogatory manner, which partly explains its gradual displacement by the term HEROIC FANTASY) is generally a form of high fantasy.

The overlap of supernatural-horror fiction with sf is rather smaller than the overlap of high fantasy with sf, though still very substantial indeed; this area of overlap is discussed under the rubrics GOTHIC SF and HORROR IN SF.

In children's fiction (◊ CHILDREN'S SF) the interweaving of sf with fantasy motifs is intrinsic and can seldom be untwined, as is especially obvious in UK and Australian work, such as that of Alan GARNER, Diana Wynne JONES, Victor KELLEHER, William MAYNE and Robert WESTALL.

So far we have stressed the ways in which sf and fantasy get mixed up together. In fact the position of the genre analyst is by no means hopeless, for distinctions between high fantasy (or even fantasy generally) and sf are quite real, however elusive, and they extend very much further than fantasy-equals-impossible versus sf-equals-possible. Such distinctions always work better, of course, at the ends of the spectrum rather than at its centre, where apparent opposites become merged (or balanced) together. At the extreme fantasy end of the spectrum the imaginary worlds tend, strongly, to be conceptually static; history is cyclical; the narrative form is almost always the quest for an emblematic object or person; the characters are emblematic too, most commonly of a dualistic (even Manichean) system where good confronts evil; most fundamentally of all, the protagonists are trapped in pattern. They live in a determinist world, they fulfil destiny, they move through the steps of an ancient dance. At the extreme sf end of

the spectrum the stories are set in kinetic venues that register the existence of change, history is evolutionary and free will operates in a possibly arbitrary universe whose patterns, if they exist at all, may be only those imposed upon it (or, according to some quantum theorists, created in it) by its human observers. If there is truth in this argument, then it follows that the important distinction between fantasy and sf is more philosophical than technological, a matter of METAPHYSICS.

There is one final group of fantasists, the fabulators (◊ FABULATION), who create fantastic changes (often quite minor) in everyday reality, often ironically or for purposes of SATIRE, rather than for the creation of frissons of horror or romantic adventure. Such a work is Franz KAFKA's *Die Verwandlung* (1916; trans as *The Metamorphosis* 1937), in which a man is turned into a beetle. Many such works stem from traditions of fable and ABSURDIST literature, sometimes taking the form of MAGIC REALISM. John BARTH, Angela CARTER, Richard CONDON and Thomas PYNCHON are only four of the several hundred such writers who receive entries in this encyclopedia, including some whose associations with genre sf have been rather closer, like Barry N. MALZBERG, Kurt VONNEGUT Jr, and Robert SHEA and Robert Anton WILSON, whose **Illuminatus** trilogy **(1975)** puts a range of fantasy and sf devices to absurdist ends in a black comedy proposing PARANOIA as the most fully appropriate response to modern life.

In the 1970s fantasy (and its variant labels like Epic Fantasy, Heroic Fantasy and so forth) became an important area of book marketing. Some alarmist observers believed that the density of fantasy publication was such that sf as a viable, separate marketing category was doomed. In fact, sf has proved able to weather the storm, but fantasy publishing continues strongly into the 1990s, only slightly abated, especially in the area of trilogies and series whose points of reference (sometimes approaching plagiarism) continue in the main to be Robert E. Howard and, especially, J.R.R. Tolkien. One effect of fantasy's publishing success (and to a lesser degree that of horror) may have been to make genre-crossing, which was always common, even more popular. K.W. JETER and George R.R. MARTIN move from sf to horror; Terry PRATCHETT, Michael Scott ROHAN, Robert HOLDSTOCK and others from sf to fantasy; Stephen KING, contrariwise, moves sometimes from horror to sf; James P. BLAYLOCK contrives, dizzyingly, to occupy all such worlds simultaneously, as do John Crowley and arguably Gene Wolfe; fantasy writers like John M. FORD or Barbara HAMBLY or David GEMMELL invent sf-like worlds; supposedly hard-sf writer Orson Scott Card is repeatedly drawn to PASTORAL fantasy; William GIBSON, Elizabeth HAND, even Greg BEAR, put GODS AND DEMONS into CYBERPUNK worlds; R.A. MACAVOY, Patricia MCKILLIP and Sheri S. TEPPER turn from high fantasy to sf; Brian M. STABLEFORD turns to SCIENTIFIC ROMANCES about vampires and werewolves. In the face of this insouciance on the part of the makers of sf and fantasy, the wise critic will eschew rigid prescription. Beyond the very various distinctions already suggested, no consistent demarcation-line between sf and fantasy should be extractable from a reading of this encyclopedia. Certainly none was intended. [PN]

FANTASY Title used on two early UK sf magazines. The first was a PULP magazine published by George Newnes Ltd., ed T. Stanhope Sprigg. It produced 3 issues 1938-9. The second, subtitled "The Magazine of Science Fiction", was a saddle-stapled DIGEST issued by the Temple Bar Publishing Co., ed Walter GILLINGS. It too lasted 3 issues, Dec 1946 and Apr and Aug 1947. Eric Frank RUSSELL and John Russell FEARN were featured in both series, and the second magazine featured 3 early stories by Arthur C. CLARKE (2 pseudonymous, as by E.G. O'Brien and Charles Willis). The second magazine was killed by paper restrictions, but Gillings was able to use some of his backlog of stories when he became the first editor of SCIENCE FANTASY in 1950. [BS/PN]

FANTASY AMATEUR PRESS ASSOCIATION ◊ FAPA.

FANTASY AND SCIENCE FICTION The often-used short form of the title of *The* MAGAZINE OF FANTASY AND SCIENCE FICTION, often referred to, in this encyclopedia and elsewhere, as *FSF*. [PN]

FANTASY BOOK 1. Magazine, BEDSHEET-format for 2 issues, then various DIGEST-size formats. 8 issues July 1947-Jan 1951; irregular. Published by FANTASY PUBLISHING COMPANY INC.; ed Garrett Ford (pseudonym of William L. CRAWFORD). *FB* was generally an undistinguished and erratic magazine. Some issues appeared in three different editions with different covers. *FB* is best remembered for publishing in #1 "The People of the Crater", the first sf story by Andre NORTON (as Andrew North) and, in #6 (Jan 1950), Paul Linebarger's first story as Cordwainer SMITH, "Scanners Live in Vain". When it ceased publication it left incomplete a Murray LEINSTER serial, "Journey to Barkut"; this later appeared in full in STARTLING STORIES (Jan 1952), and in book form as *Gateway to Elsewhere* (**1954**).

2. US SEMIPROZINE, BEDSHEET-format. 23 issues Oct 1981-Mar 1987, ed Dennis Mallonee and Nick Smith from California, bimonthly, then quarterly from #4. Unlike the first *FB*, to which it was unconnected, this published almost no sf, concentrating on fantasy and horror. Its authors included R.A. LAFFERTY, Alan Dean FOSTER and Ian WATSON. Circulation seldom rose above 3000. [MJE/PN]

FANTASY COMMENTATOR US FANZINE (1943-current), ed from New York by A. Langley SEARLES, 43 issues to 1992. The original run of 26 issues, 1943-53 – quarterly before 1950 and then irregular – featured well written, scholarly articles about contemporary fantasy writers and an impressive series of bibliographies. *FC* was notable at this time for publishing the series of articles about FANDOM by Sam MOSKOWITZ that later became *The Immortal Storm* (**1954**) and for the original material it carried by A.

MERRITT, Henry KUTTNER, David H. KELLER, H.P. LOVECRAFT and William Hope HODGSON. *FC* was suspended in 1953 but revived in 1978 with #29 (facsimiles of #27-#28, which had been set up in 1953 but not published, were released in 1986). Up to 1950 *FC* appeared quarterly, thereafter irregularly. Its current incarnation was annual to 1990, semiannual thereafter. Regular contributors to the current version include Moskowitz and Mike ASHLEY. *FC* remains strong in scholarship about early sf and fantasy. [RH]

FANTASY FICTION/FANTASY STORIES US DIGEST-size magazine. 2 issues, May and Nov 1950, published by Magabook, ed Curtis Mitchell. "Old and New Fantasy Stories but Always the Best" was the slogan of this shortlived magazine, whose stories were largely reprinted from general PULP MAGAZINES of the 1930s and early 1940s. It also offered prizes for reports of true fantastic experiences and of haunted houses. #2 was retitled *Fantasy Stories*, carried a lengthy UFO feature ("Flying Saucer Secrets Blabbed by Mad Pilot", as the cover put it), and was three months late. #3 never materialized.

The final 3 issues of the 1950s FANTASY MAGAZINE, an unconnected publication, were also titled *Fantasy Fiction*. [MJE]

FANTASY HOUSE ◊ VENTURE SCIENCE FICTION.

FANTASY MAGAZINE/FANTASY FICTION 1. US DIGEST-size magazine. 4 issues, Feb, June, Aug, Nov 1953, all but #1 under the latter title, published by Future Publications, New York, ed Lester DEL REY, under his own name for #1–#3 and under the house name Cameron Hall for #4. All issues had covers by Hannes BOK. #1 featured a **Conan** novelette revised by L. Sprague DE CAMP from Robert E. HOWARD's unpublished "The Black Stranger". The contents, of quite good quality, were almost exclusively fantasy, much of it rather in the style of UNKNOWN.

2. *Fantasy Magazine* was a vt 1934-7 of a celebrated FANZINE, *Science Fiction Digest*, founded 1932, of which Julius SCHWARTZ was one of the editors. This in turn had incorporated *The Time Traveller*, often regarded as the first true fanzine (#1, Jan 1932), which Schwartz had published with Mort WEISINGER. *FM* published original fiction, factual articles, reviews, gossip and biographical pieces. [BS/PN]

FANTASY NEWSLETTER ◊ FANTASY REVIEW.

FANTASY PRESS An early US SMALL PRESS specializing in sf/fantasy, historically important in the growth of genre-sf PUBLISHING before sf was discovered by mass-market book houses. It was founded by Lloyd Arthur ESHBACH in 1946, based in Reading, Pennsylvania. It published a number of works in hardcover by such authors as John W. CAMPBELL Jr, L. Sprague DE CAMP, E.E. "Doc" SMITH, Stanley G. WEINBAUM and Jack WILLIAMSON. It folded in 1955 at a time when small-press publishing was in crisis. In 1958 Eshbach sold the company and its stock to GNOME PRESS. [MJE/PN]

FANTASY PUBLISHING COMPANY INC. US SMALL PRESS based in Los Angeles and specializing in sf/fantasy, generally known by its initials FPCI. One of the many semiprofessional publishing enterprises of William L. CRAWFORD, FPCI was one of the less notable companies to start issuing magazine sf in book form in the late 1940s and the 1950s. Its authors included L. Sprague DE CAMP, L. Ron HUBBARD, Olaf STAPLEDON, John TAINE and A.E. VAN VOGT, but only lesser works of theirs. Crawford also published the magazines FANTASY BOOK and later SPACEWAY and *Witchcraft and Sorcery* (formerly *Coven 13*) under the FPCI imprint, in addition to various occult titles and books by Emil PETAJA and others.

The pre-WWII incarnation of the company, then known just as Fantasy Publishers, had brought out the magazines MARVEL TALES and UNUSUAL STORIES; and an associated company, Visionary Publishing Co., had published *The Shadow over Innsmouth* (**1936**) by H.P. LOVECRAFT. [MJE/PN]

FANTASY REVIEW 1. UK FANZINE, ed Walter GILLINGS. 18 issues 1947-50. Gillings, previously editor of several UK SF MAGAZINES – TALES OF WONDER (1937-42), STRANGE TALES (1946) and FANTASY (1946-7) – found himself needing an outlet for his energies after the demise of the latter title and began *FR*, which was almost identical in format and content to his earlier fanzine *Scientifiction* (7 issues 1937-8) and later fanzine *Cosmos* (3 issues 1969). It carried reviews and sf news items, and was professional in appearance. For its last 3 numbers the title changed to *Science-Fantasy Review*. When in 1950 Gillings was given the editorship of SCIENCE FANTASY, the new sister magazine to Nova Publications' NEW WORLDS, he incorporated *Science-Fantasy Review* into its first 2 issues as a news-chat section; this disappeared when John CARNELL assumed the editorship of *Science Fantasy* with #3.

2. US monthly critical SEMIPROZINE, founded as *Fantasy Newsletter* by Paul C. Allen in Rochester, NY, as, literally, an 8pp newsletter in June 1978, but becoming a magazine in Jan 1980, ceasing publication in Oct 1981. It was revived at once, however, by Robert Collins, director of the International Conference on the Fantastic in the Arts at Florida Atlantic University. The magazine, which had always published interesting features, gained much strength when amalgamated at the beginning of 1984 with SCIENCE FICTION AND FANTASY BOOK REVIEW (Neil BARRON, editor of the latter, becoming review editor) with a new title, *Fantasy Review*, but a continuation of the previous numeration. (The logo showed *SF & Fantasy Review* for several months, with the "SF" very small; it was soon dropped.) *FR* had the widest (though not necessarily deepest) sf-book-review coverage in the US and probably the world, covering fantasy and horror as well as sf. Later review editors were Carol McGuirk and Rob Latham. Quite handsomely produced, *FR* had the usual difficulty in finding a commercially viable market for a magazine of the standard desired by the editor, and folded with #103, July/Aug 1987. The review section lives on less usefully in annual form, beginning 1988, as SCIENCE FICTION AND FANTASY BOOK REVIEW ANNUAL, with

Collins and Latham co-editors. [PN]

FANTASY STORIES ◊ FANTASY FICTION.

FANTASY TIMES US FANZINE (1941-69) ed James V. Taurasi Sr (1917-1991), briefly by Sam MOSKOWITZ during WWII, Taurasi again, and Frank Prieto Jr from 1966. Published erratically until 1946, *FT* thereafter established itself as a straightforward sf and fantasy newsletter containing news, notes and reviews. In 1957 its title changed to *Science Fiction Times*, and publication continued under this title until #465, in 1969. Though its contents were mostly routine records of events, the magazine did attract some attention from publishers and authors; James BLISH was its book reviewer for a time (c1956). *FT* won the HUGO for Best Fanzine in 1955 and 1957. Its news-reporting function was effectively taken over by LOCUS. A short-lived Spanish edition, *Tiempo de Fantasia*, was published in 1949, and a successful German version, *SF Times*, began publication in 1958, at first as a straight translation, later – especially under the editorship of Hans Joachim ALPERS – as a serious German fanzine in its own right (◊ GERMANY). [PR/PN]

FANTAZIA 2000 ◊ ISRAEL.

FANTHORPE, R(OBERT) L(IONEL) (1935-) UK writer who became a schoolteacher and preacher. From 1954 to 1965 RLF was an sf writer of remarkable productivity, towards the end of that period producing novels on a weekly schedule for BADGER BOOKS and associated imprints, for which he was paid £25 a volume, dictating his tales into a battery of tape-recorders for transcription by members of his family or by friends. The rushed endings of many of his novels were a result of this practice, as he often did not know how close he was to his allotted word-length until batches of typing had been completed; if a tale had reached its length while still in mid-plot, it would be truncated forthwith. It has been claimed of RLF that he was the world's most prolific writer in the genre. His first story, written at the age of 16, was "Worlds without End" as by Lionel Roberts for FUTURISTIC SCIENCE STORIES in 1952. His first novel, *Menace from Mercury* (**1954**), was published under the house name Victor LA SALLE; other house names under which he would work were John E. MULLER and Karl ZEIGFREID. Within a few years he was responsible for the vast majority of Badger's sf and supernatural output, both novels and collections of stories, some of the former and all of the latter being included in the numbered series **Supernatural Stories**. (RLF's practice with stories was generally to provide all the contents of a particular issue, using several pseudonyms in addition to his own name, creating in effect a series of collections. It is as collections that these titles are listed in this entry, under the title and name story listed on the cover, though in fact this title might not actually appear within, and pseudonymous work by other authors occasionally appears in collections otherwise by RLF; we have here violated our normal practice of designating such books as anthologies.) After Badger Books folded, RLF fell silent, though he made a brief comeback as a fiction writer with *The Black Lion* (**1979**), written in collaboration with his wife, Patricia Fanthorpe (1938-   ); it is a not-unsuccessful fantasy, the first of a projected (but still incomplete) trilogy.

One series of some interest, published under the Bron Fane pseudonym, chronicles the adventures of the Bulldog Drummond-like **Val Stearman** and the immortal La Noire: "The Seance" (1958), "The Secret Room" (1958), "Valley of the Vampire" (1958), "The Silent Stranger" (1959), "The Other Line" (1959), "The Green Cloud" (1959), "Pursuit" (1959), "Jungle of Death" (1959), "The Crawling Fiend" (1960), "Curtain Up" (1960), "The Secret of the Lake" (1960), "The Loch Ness Terror" (1961), "The Deathless Wings" (1961), "The Green Sarcophagus" (1961), "Black Abyss" (1961), "Forbidden City" (1961), "The Secret of the Pyramid" (1961), "Something at the Door" (1961), "Forbidden Island" (1962), "Storm God's Fury" (1962), "Vengeance of the Poltergeist" (1962), "The Persian Cavern" (1962), "The Chasm of Time" (1962), "The Voice in the Wall" (1962), "Cry in the Night" (1962), "The Nine Green Men" (1963), "The Man who Never Smiled" (1963), "Return Ticket" (1963), "The Room that Never Was" (1963), "The Walker" (1963), *Softly By Moonlight* (**1963**), "The Thing from Sheol" (1963), "The Man who Knew" (1963), *Unknown Destiny* (**1964**), "The Warlock" (1964), *The Macabre Ones* (**1964**), "The Troll" (1964), "The Walking Shadow" (1964), "The Lake Thing" (as Pel Torro, 1964), "The Accursed" (1965), "The Prodigy" (1965), *U.F.O. 517* (**1965**), "Girdle of Fear" (1965), "Repeat Programme" (1966) and "The Resurrected Enemy" (1966).

Apart from those listed below in connection with book titles, RLF's pseudonyms included Neil Balfort, Othello Baron, Noel Bertram, Oben Lerteth, Elton T. Neef, Peter O'Flinn, René Rolant, Robin Tate and Deutero Spartacus. All but the last are partial anagrams of his name.   [MJE]

Other works:

As R.L. Fanthorpe: *Resurgum* (coll **1957**); *Secret of the Snows* (coll **1957**); *The Flight of the Valkyries* (coll **1958**); *The Waiting World* (**1958**); *Watchers of the Forest* (coll **1958**); *Call of the Werewolf* (coll **1958**); *The Death Note* (coll **1958**); *Mermaid Reef* (coll **1959**); *Alien from the Stars* (**1959**); *Fiends* (**1959**); *Space-Borne* (**1959**); *The Ghost Rider* (coll **1959**); *Hyperspace* (**1959**); *Doomed World* (**1960**); *The Man who Couldn't Die* (coll **1960**); *Out of the Darkness* (**1960**); *Satellite* (**1960**); *Asteroid Man* (**1960**); *Werewolf at Large* (coll **1960**); *Hand of Doom* (**1960**); *Whirlwind of Death* (coll **1960**); *Flame Mass* (**1961**); *Fingers of Darkness* (coll **1961**); *Face in the Dark* (coll **1961**); *Devil from the Depths* (coll **1961**); *Centurion's Vengeance* (coll **1961**); *The Golden Chalice* (**1961**); *The Grip of Fear* (coll **1961**); *Chariot of Apollo* (coll **1962**); *Hell has Wings* (coll **1962**); *Graveyard of the Damned* (coll **1962**); *The Darker Drink* (coll **1962**); *Curse of the Totem* (coll **1962**); *Space Fury* (**1962**); *Goddess of the Night* (coll

1963); *Moon Wolf* (coll **1963**); *Avenging Goddess* (coll **1964**); *Death has Two Faces* (coll **1964**); *The Shrouded Abbot* (coll **1964**); *Bitter Reflection* (coll **1965**); *Neuron World* (**1965**); *The Triple Man* (**1965**); *Call of the Wild* (coll **1965**); *Vision of the Damned* (coll **1965**); *The Sealed Sarcophagus* (coll **1965**); *The Unconfined* (**1966**); *Stranger in the Shadow* (coll **1966**); *Curse of the Khan* (coll **1966**); *Watching World* (**1966**); *The Story of St Francis of Assisi* (**1989**), nonfiction; *Three of the Earliest SF Stories by Lionel Fanthorpe* (coll **1991** chap); *Collection of Documents Referring to Lionel Fanthorpe's Early Writings* (coll **1991** chap).

As Erle Barton: *The Planet Seekers* (**1964**).

As Lee Barton: *The Unseen* (**1963**); *The Shadow Man* (**1966**).

As Thornton Bell: *Space Trap* (**1964**); *Chaos* (**1964**).

As Leo Brett: *The Drud* (coll **1959**); *The Return* (coll **1959**); *Exit Humanity* (**1960**); *The Microscopic Ones* (**1960**); *The Faceless Planet* (**1960**); *March of the Robots* (**1961**); *Black Infinity* (**1961**); *Mind Force* (**1961**); *Nightmare* (**1962**); *Face in the Night* (**1962**); *The Immortals* (**1962**); *The Frozen Tomb* (coll **1962**); *They Never Come Back* (**1963**); *The Forbidden* (**1963**); *From Realms Beyond* (**1963**); *Phantom Crusader* (coll **1963**); *The Alien Ones* (**1963**); *Power Sphere* (**1963**).

As Bron Fane: *The Crawling Fiend* (coll **1960**); *Juggernaut* (**1960**; vt *Blue Juggernaut* 1965 US); *Last Man on Earth* (**1960**); *Rodent Mutation* (**1961**); *Storm God's Fury* (coll **1962**); *The Intruders* (**1963**); *Somewhere Out There* (**1963**); *The Thing from Sheol* (coll **1963**); *Nemesis* (**1964**); *Suspension* (**1964**); *The Walking Shadow* (coll **1964**).

As L.P. Kenton: *Destination Moon* (**1959**).

As Victor La Salle (house name): ◊ Victor LA SALLE.

As John E. Muller (house name): *A 1000 Years On* (**1961**); *The Mind Makers* (**1961**); *The Ultimate Man* (**1961**); *Forbidden Planet* (**1961**); *The Uninvited* (**1961**); *Crimson Planet* (**1961**); *The Venus Venture* (**1961**; 1965 US as by Marston Johns); *The Return of Zeus* (**1962**); *Perilous Galaxy* (**1962**); *The Eye of Karnak* (**1962**); *Infinity Machine* (**1962**); *Uranium 235* (**1962**); *The Man who Conquered Time* (**1962**); *Orbit One* (**1962**; 1966 US as by Mel Jay); *Micro Infinity* (**1962**); *Beyond Time* (**1962**; 1966 US as by Marston Johns); *Vengeance of Siva* (**1962**); *The Day the World Died* (**1962**); *The X-Machine* (**1962**); *Reactor XK9* (**1963**); *Special Mission* (**1963**); *Dark Continuum* (**1964**); *Mark of the Beast* (**1964**); *The Exorcists* (**1965**); *The Negative Ones* (**1965**); *The Man from Beyond* (**1965**); *Spectre of Darkness* (**1965**); *Beyond the Void* (**1965**); *Out of the Night* (**1965**); *Phenomena X* (**1966**) and *Survival Project* (**1966**).

As Phil Nobel: *The Hand from Gehenna* (coll **1964**).

As Lionel Roberts: *The Incredulist* (coll **1954**); *Guardians of the Tomb* (coll **1958**); *The Golden Warrior* (coll **1958**); *Dawn of the Mutants* (**1959**); *Time Echo* (**1959**; 1964 US as by Robert Lionel); *Cyclops in the Sky* (**1960**); *The In-World* (**1960**); *The Face of X* (**1960**; 1965 US as by Robert Lionel); *The Last Valkyrie* (**1961**); *The Synthetic Ones* (**1961**); *Flame Goddess* (**1961**).

As Neil Thanet: *Beyond the Veil* (**1964**); *The Man who Came Back* (**1964**).

As Trebor Thorpe: *The Haunted Pool* (coll **1958**); *Five Faces of Fear* (**1960**); *Lightning World* (**1960**); *Voodoo Hell Drums* (coll **1961**).

As Pel Torro: *Frozen Planet* (**1960**); *World of the Gods* (**1960**); *The Phantom Ones* (**1961**); *Legion of the Lost* (**1962**); *The Strange Ones* (**1963**); *Galaxy 666* (**1963**); *Formula 29X* (**1963**; vt *Beyond the Barrier of Space* 1969 US); *The Timeless Ones* (**1963**); *Through the Barrier* (**1963**); *The Last Astronaut* (**1963**); *The Face of Fear* (**1963**); *The Return* (**1964**; vt *Exiled in Space* 1969 US); *Space No Barrier* (**1964**; vt *Man of Metal* 1969 US); *Force 97X* (**1965**).

As Olaf Trent: *Roman Twilight* (coll **1963**).

As Karl Zeigfreid (house name): *Gods of Darkness* (**1962**); *Walk through Tomorrow* (**1963**); *Android* (**1962**); *Atomic Nemesis* (**1962**); *Zero Minus X* (**1962**); *Escape to Infinity* (**1963**); *Radar Alert* (**1963**); *World of Tomorrow* (**1963**; vt *World of the Future* 1964 US); *The World that Never Was* (**1963**); *Projection Infinity* (**1964**); *No Way Back* (**1964**); *Barrier 346* (**1965**); *The Girl from Tomorrow* (**1965**).

FANZINE A fanzine is an amateur magazine produced by sf fans. The term "fanzine", coined by Russ Chauvenet in 1941, has been borrowed and used by comics collectors, wargamers, "underground" publishers and other non-sf enthusiasts. The fastest-growing category in the mid-1980s was the soccer fanzine.

The first known fanzine was *The Comet* (May 1930) ed Raymond A. PALMER for the Science Correspondence Club, followed by *The Planet* (July 1930) ed Allen Glasser for the New York Scienceers. However, both of these were mainly about science, although the second did include reviews of the professional sf magazines. Some regard the first true fanzine – certainly the first major one – as *The Time Traveller* (#1, Jan 1932) ed Julius SCHWARTZ and Mort WEISINGER. Schwartz, with others, went on to publish *Science Fiction Digest* (◊ FANTASY MAGAZINE). These and other early fanzines were straightforward publications dealing exclusively with sf or amateur science, and were produced by local fan groups founded in the USA by the more active readers of contemporary professional SF MAGAZINES. However, as interest grew and sf fans formed closer contacts and friendships, individual fans began publishing for their own amusement, so that fanzines became more diverse and their contents more capricious; fan editors also began to exchange fanzines and to send out free copies to contributors and letter-writers. Thus fanzines abandoned any professional aspirations in exchange for informality and an active readership – characteristics that persist to the present and distinguish fanzines from conventional hobbyist publications. From the USA the idea spread to the UK, where Maurice Hanson and Dennis Jacques started NOVAE TERRAE (later ed E.J. CARNELL as the forerunner of NEW WORLDS) in 1936. Since then fanzine publishing has proliferated and many thousands of titles have appeared. Probably 500-600 fanzines are currently in production, the majority in North America but with substantial numbers from the UK, Australia and Western Europe, and occasional items from Japan, South America, South Africa, New Zealand, Turkey and Eastern Europe.

Many modern sf writers started their careers in FANDOM and published their own fanzines; Ray BRADBURY, for example, produced 4 issues of *Futuria Fantasia* (1939-41), which contained *inter alia* his first published stories. Other former fanzine editors include James BLISH, Kenneth BULMER, John CHRISTOPHER, Harlan ELLISON, Damon KNIGHT, C.M. KORNBLUTH, Charles Eric MAINE, Michael MOORCOCK, Frederik POHL, Robert SILVERBERG and Ted WHITE. Some still find time to publish: Wilson TUCKER, for example, has continued to produce *Le Zombie* since 1938.

Fan editors are of course free to produce whatever they like, and so fanzines vary dramatically in production, style and content. Normally they are duplicated, photocopied or printed, consisting of anything from a single sheet to 100+ pages, and with a circulation of from 5 to 5000 copies, though the tendency in the 1980s has been to call fanzines with a circulation of over 1000 SEMIPROZINES. The smaller fanzines are often written entirely by the editor and serve simply as letter substitutes sent out to friends; others have limited distribution within amateur press associations such as FAPA and OMPA. The larger fanzines, with an average circulation of 200-500, fall into three main categories, with considerable overlap: those dealing with sf (containing reviews, interviews, articles and discussions); those dealing with sf fans and fandom (containing esoteric humour); and those dealing with general material (containing anything from sf to Biblical engineering). (A further category consists of fanzines exclusively publishing amateur fiction; these are not listed in this volume unless widely enough circulated to be regarded as semiprozines.) On the fringe there are specialist fanzines catering for FANTASY and SWORD-AND-SORCERY fans, others devoted to cult authors such as J.R.R. TOLKIEN, H.P. LOVECRAFT and Robert E. HOWARD, and yet others which deal with sf films or tv series such as STAR TREK. Since 1955 there has been a Best Fanzine category in the HUGO Awards, and since 1984 a Best Semiprozine category also.

A selection of 36 important fanzines – some now regarded as semiprozines – from different periods of fandom receive full entries in this volume: ALGOL, *The* ALIEN CRITIC, ANSIBLE, AUSTRALIAN SF REVIEW, AUSTRALIAN SF REVIEW: SECOND SERIES, BIZARRE, CRITICAL WAVE, FANAC, FANTASY COMMENTATOR, FANTASY MAGAZINE, FANTASY REVIEW, FANTASY TIMES, FILE 770, *The* FUTURIAN, HYPHEN, JANUS/AURORA, LOCUS, LUNA MONTHLY, NIEKAS, NOVAE TERRAE, PSYCHOTIC, QUANDRY, QUARBER MERKUR, RIVERSIDE QUARTERLY, SCIENCE FICTION: A REVIEW OF SPECULATIVE FICTION, SF CHRONICLE, SF COMMENTARY, SCIENCE FICTION EYE, SLANT, SPECULATION, THRUST, VECTOR, *The* VORTEX, WARHOON, XERO and YANDRO. Data on another dozen or so fanzine titles are available by following up cross-references. The majority of the above are critical magazines, and many are listed again under CRITICAL AND HISTORICAL WORKS ABOUT SF. [PR/PN]

FAPA The commonly used acronym for the Fantasy Amateur Press Association, formed in 1937 in the USA by Donald A. WOLLHEIM to facilitate distribution on an APA basis of FANZINES published by and for members; it was the first of many such groups. Early contributors included E.J. CARNELL, Robert A.W. LOWNDES, Sam MOSKOWITZ, Frederik POHL, Wilson TUCKER and Richard WILSON. Current members include Moskowitz, F.M. BUSBY and Robert SILVERBERG. [PR]

FARCA, MARIE C. (1935-) US writer whose first sf novel, *Earth* (**1972**), is a competent adventure. Her second, *Complex Man* (**1973**), is a sequel set on another planet. [JC]

FAR FRONTIERS US "magazine" in paperback-book format; it could also be regarded as an original anthology series. Quarterly, published by Baen Books, ed Jerry POURNELLE and Jim BAEN and (uncredited) John F. CARR; 7 issues, from *Far Frontiers* (anth **1985**) at the very beginning of that year to *Far Frontiers Vol VII* (anth Winter **1986**). At this point Baen revived (as solo editor) his very similar **Destinies** series of magazines/anthologies as *New Destinies* with #1 in Spring 1987 (◊ DESTINIES), and *Far Frontiers* came to an end. Something of a shop-window for upcoming Baen Book publications, *FF* featured several book excerpts. Its emphasis was on HARD SF, sometimes militaristic, and on good science-fact articles; authors of the latter included Robert L. FORWARD, John GRIBBIN, Pournelle and G. Harry STINE. Authors of stories included Greg BEAR, David BRIN, John DALMAS, Dean ING, Vernor VINGE and Timothy ZAHN. [PN]

FAR FUTURE Fred Polak's *The Image of the Future* (**1973**) identifies two distinct categories of images of the distant future, which he called the "future of prophecy" and the "future of destiny". Prophets, although they refer to the future, are primarily concerned with the present: they issue warnings about the consequences of present actions and demand that other courses of action be adopted. Their images are images of the historical future which will grow out of human action in the present day (◊ NEAR FUTURE). To the second category of images, however, present concerns are usually irrelevant; these are images of the ultimate future, taking the imagination as far as it can reach. Such visions are related to ESCHATOLOGY and often feature the END OF THE WORLD; others depict a world where everything has so changed as to have become virtually incomprehensible, or a world which has attained some ultimate UTOPIAN state of perfection.

Scientifically inspired images of the far future could not come into being until the true age of the Earth and therefore the scope of possible change were understood – an understanding first popularized by Sir Charles Lyell (1797-1875) in *Principles of Geology* (**1830**). Even then it was not until the establishment of the theory of EVOLUTION that writers found a conceptual tool which made it possible for them to imagine the kinds of changes which might plausibly take place. W.H. HUDSON's *A Crystal Age* (**1887**), which belongs to the utopian school, embraces an evolutionary philosophy of a curiously mystical kind, and such traces of mysticism are retained by very many representations of the far future. Most early images of the far future accepted estimates of the likely age of the Sun based on the tacit, natural but false assumption that its heat was produced by combustion; the far-future Earth is thus represented as a cold, dark and desolate place from which life is slowly disappearing. We find such imagery in H.G. WELLS's *The Time Machine* (**1895**), George C. WALLIS's "The Last Days of Earth" (1901) and William Hope HODGSON's *The House on the Borderland* (**1908**). Hodgson's *The Night Land* (**1912**) is bizarre as well as bleak, offering a phantasmagorical vision of a decaying world inherited by frightful monsters. The optimistic far-future vision which concludes George Bernard SHAW's *Back to Methuselah* (**1921**) is predicated on the assumption that mind can and will cast off the confining shackles of matter. More elaborate but no less striking imagery is featured in the concluding section of Guy DENT's *Emperor of the If* (**1926**), in which our insane descendants are no longer human in form or ability but remain all too human in psychological terms. S. Fowler WRIGHT's *The World Below* (incorporating *The Amphibians* [**1924**]; **1929**) is equally ambitious, and contrives to transcend the images of decay and desolation associated with so many other visions. These works were quickly followed by Olaf STAPLEDON's monumental attempt to track the entire evolutionary future of mankind, *Last and First Men* (**1930**), partly based on a blueprint provided by J.B.S. HALDANE in "The Last Judgment" (1927). Other than millenarian fantasies, which claim that the future of destiny is imminent, very few novels link the two images of the future defined by Polak within a coherent historical narrative; *Last and First Men* is by far the most outstanding example, although Camille FLAMMARION's *Omega* (trans **1894**) had earlier brought the two into rather awkward juxtaposition.

The early sf PULP MAGAZINES featured several far-future visions of the end of the world, but had little to compare with the imagery of the UK SCIENTIFIC ROMANCES. One notable story that presents the extinction of mankind's remote descendants as one more stage in a continuing process of change is "Seeds of the Dusk" (1938) by Raymond Z. GALLUN, in which a much-changed Earth is "invaded" and "conquered" by spores from another world. Gallun's "When Earth is Old" (1951) has time travellers negotiating with sentient plants to assure the rebirth of the species. The quest for some such rebirth is a common motif in far-future stories, and time travellers from the present frequently contrive to turn the evolutionary tide that is sweeping humanity towards extinction, as in such stories as John W. CAMPBELL Jr's "Twilight" (1934 as by Don A. Stuart). The idea of reigniting a senescent Sun in order to give Earth and mankind a new lease of life is poignantly deployed in Clark Ashton SMITH's "Phoenix" (1954) and extravagantly developed in Gene WOLFE's **Book of the New Sun** tetralogy (**1980-83**). Such notions arise from false analogies drawn between the life of an individual and that of a species, alleging that species may "age" and become "senescent". The popularity of such ideas in sf is not surprising, given the influence of similar analogies between individuals and cultures in the work of philosophers of history like Oswald Spengler (1880-1936). Spengler's ideas were a strong influence on James BLISH, whose most memorable accounts of the far future are "Watershed" (1957) and *Midsummer Century* (**1972**). Images of an aged world that has returned to its "second childhood" are sometimes as affectionate as rose-tinted images of human retirement; the classic example is John CROWLEY's *Engine Summer* (**1979**).

Clark Ashton Smith set the most lushly exotic of all his series in Zothique, the "last continent" – a bizarre and decadent world in which magic flourishes. The stories, all written in the 1930s, were eventually collected in *Zothique* (coll **1970**). Zothique offered Smith more imaginative freedom than his distant-past scenario Hyperborea precisely because it was irredeemably decadent. A similar but less fervent series of fantasies is Jack VANCE's *The Dying Earth* (coll **1950**), whose later sequels include *The Eyes of the Overworld* (fixup **1966**), which contains a stronger strain of picaresque comedy. A. MERRITT never used the far future as a setting, but his lavish descriptions of exotic landscapes influenced a number of far-future fantasies; Henry KUTTNER and C.L. MOORE, who wrote a series of Merritt-influenced novels in the 1940s, offered a Merrittesque far future in *Earth's Last Citadel* (1943; **1964**).

The classic pulp sf story of the far future is Arthur C. CLARKE's Stapledon-influenced *Against the Fall of Night* (1948; **1953**; rev vt *The City and the Stars* **1956**). Its imagery is stereotyped – a bleak, derelict Earth with cities whose handsome, incurious inhabitants are parasitic upon their machines – but its perspectives widen dramatically to take in the whole cosmos, where mankind may yet seek a further and more glorious destiny. This was to become a central myth of sf, and many images of GALACTIC EMPIRE include nostalgic portraits of stagnant backwater Earth. These are not, of course, images of the future of destiny but rather attempts to perpetuate and magnify the historical image – as is obvious in the many epics which construct galactic history by analogy with Earthly history.

Images of far-future Earth became more varied in the sf of the 1950s; notable examples include a number of highly stylized and semi-allegorical vignettes by Fritz LEIBER, including "When the Last Gods Die" (1951) and "The Big Trek" (1957), as well as many fine stories by Brian W. ALDISS, including the later items in *The Canopy of Time* (coll **1959**; rev vt

Galaxies Like Grains of Sand), "Old Hundredth" (1960), the stories making up *The Long Afternoon of Earth* (fixup **1962** US; exp vt *Hothouse* UK), "A Kind of Artistry" (1962) and "The Worm that Flies" (1968). As with all the stories in this category, these tend towards FANTASY, and some controversy was stirred up by a particularly memorable image in *The Long Afternoon of Earth*, in which gigantic cobwebs stretch between the Earth and the Moon, whose faces are now perpetually turned to one another. Other innovative uses of far-future settings can be seen in John BRUNNER's elegiac adventure story *The 100th Millennium* (**1959**; rev vt *Catch a Falling Star* 1968), Samuel R. DELANY's exotic romance *The Jewels of Aptor* (**1962**), Jack Vance's elegant political allegory *The Last Castle* (**1966**), Michael MOORCOCK's *angst*-ridden *The Twilight Man* (**1966**; vt *The Shores of Death*) and Crawford KILIAN's exotic romance of maturation *Eyas* (**1982**).

Michael Moorcock's fondness for far-future settings encouraged him to break new ground in his **Dancers at the End of Time** trilogy (**1972-6**) and various other works associated with it. In this series, whose tone ranges from extravagant SATIRE to perverse sentimentality, the ultimate future is inhabited by humans with godlike powers who must perpetually seek diversion from the tedium of their limitless existence. Other writers who have made frequent and significant use of far-future imagery in recent times include Robert SILVERBERG, in such works as the surreal *Son of Man* (**1971**) and "This is the Road" (1973), Doris PISERCHIA, in such works as *A Billion Days of Earth* (**1976**) and *Earth in Twilight* (**1981**), and Michael G. CONEY in *The Celestial Steam Locomotive* (**1983**), *Gods of the Greataway* (**1984**) and other associated works.

There are no anthologies dealing specifically with this theme, and it is worth noting that Harry HARRISON's attempt to compile a companion volume to his near-future anthology *The Year 2000* (anth **1970**), to be entitled «The Year 2,000,000», failed to attract sufficient suitable submissions. The theme does not lend itself readily to conventional plot and character development. [BS]

See also: DEVOLUTION; ENTROPY; MYTHOLOGY.

FARJEON, J(OSEPH) JEFFERSON (1883-1955) UK writer, prolific (often as Anthony Swift) in the detective genre and as a playwright. The RURITANIAN *Mountain Mystery* (**1935**) depicts the small country of Weldheim, which loses itself to history after WWI, becoming a kind of LOST WORLD. *Death of a World* (**1948**) depicts the arrival of aliens on a dead Earth and their reading of the diary (which makes up the bulk of the text) kept by a last survivor of the nuclear DISASTER that ended all life (◊ END OF THE WORLD). [JC]

Other works: *The Invisible Companion and Other Stories* (coll **1946** chap), fantasies.

FARLEY, RALPH MILNE Pseudonym of US writer and teacher Roger Sherman Hoar (1887-1963) for all his sf work except two 1938 stories published in *AMZ* as by Lt John Pease. He was educated at Harvard and had a remarkably varied career, which included teaching such subjects as mathematics and engineering, inventing a system of aiming large guns by the stars, and serving as a Massachusetts state senator. His early work in the pulp-sf field was written in obvious imitation of Edgar Rice BURROUGHS and was contributed to *The* ARGOSY – notably his most famous series, the **Radio Man** series, featuring **Miles Cabot**, which began with *The Radio Man* (1924 *Argosy*; **1948**; vt *An Earthman on Venus* 1950) and continued with *The Radio Beasts* (1925 *Argosy*; **1964**), *The Radio Planet* (1926 *Argosy*; **1964**), "The Radio Man Returns" (1939 *AMZ*) and "The Radio Minds of Mars" (1955 *Spaceway*, part 1 only; part 2 in *Spaceway* 1969). Other "radio" stories – including novels which did not reach book form, such as "The Radio Flyers" (1929 *Argosy*) and "The Radio Gun-Runners" (1930 *Argosy*) – are out of series. The tales, at first absurdly boosted by *The Argosy* as scientifically accurate, are devoted to the adventures of Cabot, mostly on VENUS, the Radio Planet, and still have admirers. Along with another novel, *The Hidden Universe* (1939 *AMZ*; with "We, the Mist" as coll **1950**), *The Radio Man* was later assembled as *Strange Worlds* (omni **1953**). RMF was a rough-hewn, traditional SENSE OF WONDER writer, and as a consequence became relatively inactive with the greater sophistication of the genre after WWII. [JC/PN]

Other works: *Dangerous Love* (fixup **1946** chap UK); *The Immortals* (1934 *Argosy*; **1947** chap UK); *The Omnibus of Time* (coll **1950**).

See also: ALIENS; COMICS; ESCHATOLOGY; HISTORY OF SF; HIVE MINDS; MATTER TRANSMISSION; PLANETARY ROMANCE; PULP MAGAZINES; TIME PARADOXES; TIME TRAVEL.

FARMER, PHILIP JOSÉ (1918-   ) US writer. Although a voracious reader of sf in his youth, PJF was a comparatively late starter as an author, and his first story, "O'Brien and Obrenov" for *Adventure* in 1946, promised little. A part-time student at Bradley University, he gained a BA in English in 1950, and two years later burst onto the sf scene with his novella *The Lovers* (1952 *Startling Stories*; exp **1961**; rev 1979). Although originally rejected by John W. CAMPBELL Jr of ASTOUNDING SCIENCE-FICTION and H.L. GOLD of GALAXY SCIENCE FICTION, it gained instant acclaim and won PJF a 1953 HUGO for Most Promising New Author. It concerned XENOBIOLOGY, PARASITISM and SEX, an explosive mixture which was to feature repeatedly in PJF's best work. After writing such excellent short stories as "Sail On! Sail On!" (1952) and "Mother" (1953), PJF became a full-time writer. His second short novel, *A Woman a Day* (1953 *Startling Stories*; rev **1960**; vt *The Day of Timestop* 1968; vt *Timestop!* 1970), was billed as a sequel to *The Lovers* but bore little relation to the earlier story. "Rastignac the Devil" (1954) was a further sequel. PJF then produced two novels, both of which were accepted for publication but neither of which actually saw print at the time, the first due to the folding of STARTLING STORIES (it eventually appeared as *Dare* [**1965**]). The second, «I Owe for the Flesh», won a contest held by

SHASTA PRESS and Pocket Books, but the Pocket Books prize money was used by Shasta founder Melvin Korshak to pay bills, Shasta foundered, and the manuscript was lost (the idea eventually formed the basis of the **Riverworld** series; see below). This double disaster forced PJF to abandon full-time authorship, a status to which he did not return until 1969.

Nevertheless, he produced many interesting stories over the next few years, such as the **Father Carmody** series in *The* MAGAZINE OF FANTASY AND SCIENCE FICTION, published in book form as *Night of Light* (1957 *FSF*; exp **1966**) and *Father to the Stars* (coll of linked stories **1981**), featuring a murderous priest who becomes ambiguously involved in various theological puzzles on several planets. The best of the sequence is *Night of Light*, a nightmarish story of a world where the figments of the unconscious become tangible. Other notable stories of this period include "The God Business" (1954), "The Alley Man" (1959) and "Open to Me, My Sister" (1960; vt "My Sister's Brother"). The last named is the best of PJF's biological fantasies (◊ BIOLOGY); like *The Lovers*, it was repeatedly rejected as "disgusting" before its acceptance by *FSF*.

PJF's first novel in book form was *The Green Odyssey* (**1957**), a picaresque tale of an Earthman escaping from captivity on an alien planet; the intricately colourful medieval culture of this planet, the high libido of its women, the mysteries buried within the sands of the desert over which the hero must flee, and the admixture of rapture and disgust with which the hero treats the venue – all go to make this novel, along with Jack VANCE's *Big Planet* (1952 *Startling Stories*; cut **1957**; full text 1978), a model for the flowering of the PLANETARY ROMANCE from the 1960s on. It was the first of many entertainments PJF has written over the years. Later novels in a not dissimilar vein include *The Gate of Time* (**1966**; exp vt *Two Hawks from Earth* 1979), *The Stone God Awakens* (**1970**) and *The Wind Whales of Ishmael* (**1971**), the last-named being an sf sequel to Herman MELVILLE's *Moby-Dick* (**1851**). *Flesh* (**1960**; rev 1968) is more ambitious: a dramatization of the ideas which Robert GRAVES put forward in *The White Goddess* (**1947** US), it presents a matriarchal, orgiastic society of the future. Rather heavy-handed in its humour, it was considered a "shocking" novel on first publication. *Inside Outside* (**1964**), a novel about a scientifically sustained afterlife, also contains some extraordinary images and grotesque ideas which resonate in the mind, though the book suffers from a lack of resolution. The novella "Riders of the Purple Wage" (1967) – later collected in *The Purple Book* (coll **1982**) and *Riders of the Purple Wage* (coll **1992**) – won PJF a 1968 Hugo; written in a wild and punning style, it is one of his most original works. It concerns the tribulations of a young artist in a UTOPIAN society, and has a more explicit sexual and scatological content than anything PJF had written before. "The Oogenesis of Bird City" (1970) is a related story.

The novels assembled as *The World of Tiers* (omni in 2 vols **1981**; vt *World of Tiers #1* 1986 UK and *#2* 1986 UK) show PJF in a lighter vein, though the architectural elaborateness of the universe in which they are set prefigures **Riverworld**. The original volumes are *The Maker of Universes* (**1965**; rev 1980), *The Gates of Creation* (**1966**; rev 1981), *A Private Cosmos* (**1968**; rev 1981), *Behind the Walls of Terra* (**1970**; rev 1982) and *The Lavalite World* (**1977**; rev 1983). The sequence unfolds within a series of POCKET UNIVERSES, playgrounds built by the masters – who are perhaps gods, originally humanoid – whose technology is unimaginable. The most notable character is the present-day Earthman Paul Janus Finnegan (his initials, PJF, show that this ironic observer serves as a stand-in for the author: it is a signal repeated often in later work); he is also called Kickaha, under which significantly Native American name he acts out the role of a trickster hero indulging in merry, if bloodthirsty, exploits. The books sag in places, but have moments of high invention; and the Jungian models upon which the main characters are constructed supply one key to the understanding of *Red Orc's Rage* (**1991**), a novel which RECURSIVELY dramatizes the use of the previous titles in the series as tools in role-playing therapy for disturbed adolescents.

At about the same time, ESSEX HOUSE, publishers of pornography, commissioned PJF to write three erotic fantasy novels, taking full advantage of the new freedoms of the late 1960s. *The Image of the Beast* (**1968**), the first of the **Exorcism** trilogy, is an effective parody of the private eye and Gothic horror genres. It was followed by a perfunctory sequel, *Blown, or Sketches Among the Ruins of my Mind* (**1969**), both being run together into one novel as *The Image of the Beast* (omni **1979**); the third **Exorcism** volume, *Traitor to the Living* (**1973**), was not published by Essex House. The Essex House contract was completed with *A Feast Unknown: Volume IX of the Memoirs of Lord Grandrith* (**1969**), the first volume of the **Lord Grandrith/Doc Caliban** series, followed by *Lord of the Trees* (**1970** dos) and *The Mad Goblin* (**1970**; vt *Keepers of the Secrets* 1985 UK), the latter two being assembled as *The Empire of the Nine* (omni **1988** UK). *A Feast Unknown* is a brilliant exploration of the sado-masochistic fantasies latent in much heroic fiction, and succeeds as SATIRE, as sf and as a tribute to the creations of Edgar Rice BURROUGHS and Lester DENT. It concerns the struggle of Lord Grandrith (Tarzan) and Doc Caliban (Doc Savage) against the Nine, a secret society of immortals. It is a narrative *tour de force*.

All three books point to an abiding concern (or game) that would occupy much of PJF's later career: the tying of his own fiction (and that of many other authors) into one vast, playful mythology. Much of this is worked out in the loose conglomeration of works which has been termed the **Wold Newton Family** series, all united under the premise that a meteorite which landed near Wold Newton in 18th-century Yorkshire irradiated a number of pregnant women and thus gave rise to a family of mutant SUPERMEN. This family includes the characters involved in the **Lord Grandrith/Doc Caliban** books, as well as several other texts devoted to Tarzan, though excluding *Lord Tyger* (**1970**), which is about a millionaire's attempt to create his own ape-man and is possibly the best written of PJF's novels (◊ APES AND CAVEMEN). Central to **Wold Newton** is *Tarzan Alive: A Definitive Biography of Lord Greystoke* (**1972**), a spoof biography in which PJF uses Joseph Campbell's ideas (from *The Hero With a Thousand Faces* [**1949**]) to explore the nature of the HERO's appeal. The appendices and genealogy, which link Tarzan with many other heroes of popular fiction, are at once a satire on scholarship and a serious exercise in "creative mythography". Tarzan appears again in *Time's Last Gift* (**1972**; rev 1977), a preliminary novel for a subseries about **Ancient Africa**, set in a colony of ATLANTIS and employing settings from Burroughs and H. Rider HAGGARD. *Hadon of Ancient Opar* (**1974**) and *Flight to Opar* (**1976**) continue the series. Other works which contain **Wold Newton** material include "Tarzan Lives: An Exclusive Interview with Lord Greystoke" (1972), "The Obscure Life and Hard Times of Kilgore Trout" (1973), *Doc Savage: His Apocalyptic Life* (**1973**; rev 1975), *The Other Log of Phileas Fogg* (**1973**), "Extracts from the Memoirs of 'Lord Greystoke'" (1974), "After King Kong Fell" (1974), *The Adventure of the Peerless Peer* (**1974**), *Ironcastle* (**1976**), a liberally rewritten version of J.H. ROSNY aîné's *L'étonnant voyage de Hareton Ironcastle* (**1922**), and *Doc Savage: Escape from Loki: Doc Savage's First Adventure* (**1991**). Other characters incorporated into the sequence include Sherlock Holmes, Jack the Ripper, James Bond and Kilgore Trout, a Kurt VONNEGUT character under whose name PJF also published *Venus on the Half-Shell* (**1975**). As a whole, the series parlays its conventions of "explanation" into something close to chaos.

Though these various books perhaps best express his playfully serious manipulations of popular material to express a sense of the Universe as chaotically fable-like, PJF gained greatest popular acclaim with his **Riverworld** series, set on a planet where a godlike race has resurrected the whole of humanity along the banks of a multi-million-mile river. The series is made up of *To Your Scattered Bodies Go* (**1965-6** *Worlds of Tomorrow*; fixup **1971**), *The Fabulous Riverboat* (**1967-71** *If*; fixup **1971**), *The Dark Design* (**1977**), *Riverworld and Other Stories* (coll **1979**), *The Magic Labyrinth* (**1980**), *Riverworld War: The Suppressed Fiction of Philip José Farmer* (coll **1980**), *The Gods of Riverworld* (**1983**) and *River of Eternity* (**1983**), the last being a rediscovered rewrite of the lost «I Owe for the Flesh». The first of these won a 1972 Hugo. Such historical personages as Sir Richard Burton (1821-1890), Samuel Clemens (Mark TWAIN) and Jack LONDON explore the terrain and relate to one another in their search to understand, in terms mundane and metaphysical, the new universe which has tied them together. As surviving characters begin to overdose on the freedoms (or powers) they have discovered in themselves, the plots of the later volumes become increasingly chaotic, perhaps deliberately.

After *The Unreasoning Mask* (**1981**), an extremely well constructed SPACE OPERA about a search for God, who comprises the Universe but is still a vulnerable child, PJF embarked on the **Dayworld** series, whose premise derives from "The Sliced-Crossways Only-on-Tuesday World" (1971): in a vastly overcrowded world, the population is divided into seven, each cohort spending one day of the week awake and the rest of the time in "stoned" immobility. In *Dayworld* (**1985**), *Dayworld Rebel* (**1987**) and *Dayworld Breakup* (**1990**), this premise becomes increasingly peripheral in a tale whose complications invoke A.E. VAN VOGT. Here, as in all his work, PJF is governed by an instinct for extremity. Of all sf writers of the first or second rank, he is perhaps the most threateningly impish, and the most anarchic. [DP/JC]

Other works: *Strange Relations* (coll **1960**); *The Alley God* (coll **1962**); *Fire and the Night* (**1962**), associational; *Cache from Outer Space* (**1962** dos; rev as coll with "Rastignac the Devil" and "They Twinkled like Angels" vt *The Cache* 1981); *The Celestial Blueprint and Other Stories* (coll **1962** dos); *Tongues of the Moon* (1961 *AMZ*; exp **1964**); *Reap: The Baycon Guest-of-Honor Speech* (**1968** chap); *Love Song* (**1970**), associational; *Down in the Black Gang, and Others* (coll **1971**); *The Book of Philip José Farmer, or The Wares of Simple Simon's Custard Pie and Space Man* (coll **1973**; rev 1982); *Dark is the Sun* (**1979**); *Jesus on Mars* (**1979**); *Flesh, and Lord Tyger* (omni **1981**); *Greatheart Silver* (coll of linked stories **1982**); *A Barnstormer in Oz* (**1982**); *Stations of the Nightmare* (1974-5 in *Continuum* #1-#4 ed Roger ELWOOD; coll of linked stories **1982**); *The Classic Philip José Farmer* (coll **1984** in 2 vols); *The Grand Adventure* (coll **1984**); *Fantastic Voyage II* (**1985**).

As editor: *Mother Was a Lovely Beast: A Feral Man Anthology of Fiction and Fact about Humans Raised by Animals* (anth **1974**).

About the author: "Philip José Farmer" by Sam MOSKOWITZ, in *Seekers of Tomorrow* (1966); "Thanks for the Feast" by Leslie A. Fiedler, in *The Book of Philip José Farmer* (1973); *Philip José Farmer* (1980) by Mary T. Brizzi; *Magic Labyrinth of Philip José Farmer* (1984 chap) by E.L. Chapman; *Philip José Farmer: Good-Natured Ground Breaker: A Working Bibliography* (2nd edn 1990 chap) by Gordon BENSON Jr and Phil STEPHENSEN-PAYNE.

See also: ALIENS; COMICS; CONCEPTUAL BREAKTHROUGH; COSMOLOGY; CRIME AND PUNISHMENT; ESCHATOLOGY; FANTASY; GAMES AND TOYS; GAME-WORLDS; GODS AND DEMONS; GOTHIC SF; MARS; MESSIAHS; MYTHOLOGY; OVERPOPULATION; PARANOIA; PSYCHOLOGY; REINCARNATION; RELIGION; SOCIOLOGY; TABOOS; THRILLING WONDER STORIES; VILLAINS.

FARNSWORTH, DUNCAN [s]. ◊ David Wright O'BRIEN.

FAR OUT! Australian sf magazine (1985), DIGEST-format, 3 issues, published from Western Australia by Far Out Enterprises, ed anon Pamela Klacar. Subtitled "Australia's own sf/fantasy magazine", *FO!* published fiction of an amateurish nature by unknown writers. Though (astonishingly) given national distribution, it soon silently disappeared. [PN]

FARRELL, JOHN WADE [s] ◊ John D. MACDONALD.

FARREN, MICK (1943-   ) UK writer and ex-rock musician, first active in a band, the Deviants, 1967-70; he then edited the underground paper *IT* 1970-73 and founded the underground comic *Nasty Tales* – prosecuted for obscenity in a well known trial – in which, with Chris Rowley and Chris Welch, he produced a comic strip with sf content, **Ogoth the Wasted**. His first sf novel was *The Texts of Festival* (**1973**), set in a surrealistic post-HOLOCAUST England; this novel and his subsequent **Jeb Stuart Ho** trilogy – *The Quest of the DNA Cowboys* (**1976**), *Synaptic Manhunt* (**1976**) and *The Neural Atrocity* (**1977**) – radiate a late-1960s aura of apocalyptic, hip hyperbole, sometimes effectively. *The Last Stand of the DNA Cowboys* (**1989**) is a loose sequel. The world of the trilogy especially is almost deliriously polymorphic, full of images out of Westerns and other genres and references to dope, rock and the hippy subculture generally, and can be seen as a clear precursor of CYBERPUNK, though without COMPUTERS, and laced throughout with the kind of drug use which later writers like William GIBSON were able to avoid through the various delights of CYBERSPACE.

MF's next novels were similar in texture. Both *The Feelies* (**1978**; rev 1990 US), a left-oriented SATIRE whose premise resembles that of John D. MACDONALD's "Spectator Sport" (1950), and the dithery *The Song of Phaid the Gambler* (**1981**; rev vt in 2 vols as *Phaid the Gambler* 1986 US and *Citizen Phaid* 1987 US) seemed paralysed by their 1960s provenance. After *Protectorate* (**1984**) his work began to seem derivative of the cyberpunk writers who had followed him. *Corpse* (**1986**; vt *Vickers* 1988 US), *The Long Orbit* (**1988** US; vt *Exit Funtopia* 1989 UK) and *Armageddon Crazy* (**1989** US) have in common violent action, desolate NEAR-FUTURE venues and spiritual malaise. *Their Master's War* (**1988** US) concerns the ruthless use of helpless species in an unending interstellar conflict. [JC]

Other works: *Mars – The Red Planet* (**1990** US).

FARRÈRE, CLAUDE Pseudonym of French writer Frédéric Charles Pierre Édouard Bargone (1876-1957), author mainly of "colonial" novels after the model of Pierre Loti (1850-1923). His sf books are *La maison des hommes vivants* (**1911**; trans Arthur Livingston as *The House of the Secret* 1923 US) and, more notably, *Les condamnés à mort* (**1920**; trans Elisabeth Abbott as *Useless Hands* 1926 US; 1973 US as by Charles Bargone), whose harsh social-Darwinist terms render a 1990s workers' revolt as bleakly pathetic: when the "useless hands" go on strike, they are disintegrated by a new weapon and machines take over their jobs. [JC]

Other works: *Black Opium* (coll trans Samuel Putnam **1929** US), tales linked by reference to opium.

See also: AUTOMATION; DYSTOPIAS; SOCIAL DARWINISM.

FAST, HOWARD (MELVIN) (1914-   ) US writer best known for his work outside the sf field: historical novels under his own name and detective novels and thrillers as E.V. Cunningham. *The Unvanquished* (1942) and *Spartacus* (1951), both as HF, are perhaps his most familiar titles. He began publishing sf with "Wrath of the Purple" for *AMZ* in 1932, but did not actively produce sf until the later 1950s, when he started a long association with *FSF*. His sf and fantasy stories have been collected in *The Edge of Tomorrow* (coll 1961), *The General Zapped an Angel* (coll 1970) and *A Touch of Infinity* (coll 1973); all the stories in the latter two volumes were reassembled as *Time and the Riddle: Thirty-One Zen Stories* (coll 1975). His work is sharply political in implication – he was a member of the Communist Party 1943-56, being imprisoned for contempt of Congress in 1947 – and eschews most of the cruder satisfactions of genre fiction. Harlan ELLISON, among others, has expressed high praise for HF's stories, but admiration, though widespread, is not universal. Some critics have seen their occasionally religiose moralizing as cloying and their ideative content as trite. *Phyllis* (1962), as by E.V. Cunningham, is a borderline novel in which a US and a Soviet scientist come together to try to force their governments to ban the bomb by threatening to explode two themselves. In "The Trap", a novel-length tale which occupies most of *The Hunter and The Trap* (coll 1967), the US Government secretly attempts to raise exceptional children in a monitored environment; when the Department of Defense attempts to view the results the children, now telepathic, close themselves off from the world to breed *Homo superior*.   [JC]

Other works: *Tony and the Wonderful Door* (1968; vt *The Magic Door* 1980), a juvenile.

See also: SATIRE.

FAST, JONATHAN (DAVID) (1948-   ) US composer and writer, son of Howard FAST, who wrote music before coming to sf with "Decay" for *FSF* in 1975. His first novel, *The Secrets of Synchronicity* (1977; vt *Prisoner of the Planets* 1980 UK), is a complex SPACE OPERA which, unusually for the form, treats an expanding capitalism as inherently repressive of true freedom. In *Mortal Gods* (1978) a similar enemy maintains control over a culture shaped by the possibilities of GENETIC ENGINEERING. The tone of his writing, which is generally light, and his plotting, which is contrived, tend to obscure the political arguments underlying his work.   [JC]

Other works: *The Inner Circle* (1979); *The Beast* (1981), a fantasy.

FASTER THAN LIGHT According to Relativity the velocity of light is limiting: no matter how objects alter their velocity relative to one another, the sum of their velocities can never exceed the ultimate constant *c* (the velocity of light in a vacuum); moreover, the measurement of *c* is unaffected by the velocity of the measurer. The apparently paradoxical implications of this statement are avoided because objects travelling at high velocities relative to one another are subject to different frames of measurement, by which each appears to the other to be subject to a distortion of time. As a consequence, SPACESHIPS which make interstellar journeys at velocities close to light-speed relative to their points of origin are subject to a time-dilatation whereby the travellers age more slowly than the people they left at home. A good popularization of such ideas can be found in George GAMOW's book of scientific fables *Mr Tompkins in Wonderland* (coll 1939 chap).

Some "relativistic" effects of FTL travel are described in Camille FLAMMARION's pre-Einsteinian cosmic fantasy *Lumen* (1887; trans 1897), but other early sf writers, including the pioneers of pulp SPACE-OPERA, ignored such matters, even after Relativity theory had come into being. As the intellectual respectability of such ignorance declined, however, the limiting velocity of light increasingly became an awkward inconvenience to writers of interstellar adventure stories, necessitating the development of a series of facilitating devices – often involving "space-warps", interdimensional dodges into HYPERSPACE or "subspace", or, more recently, TACHYON drives or BLACK-HOLE-related "wormholes" – to enable the science-fictional imagination to retain GALACTIC EMPIRES and their effectively infinite supply of earthlike ALIEN worlds ripe for COLONIZATION. Faster-than-light communication systems like James BLISH's DIRAC transmitter and Ursula K. LE GUIN's ANSIBLE require similar justificatory fudges. Such literary devices cannot, in fact, succeed in setting aside the logical difficulties which arise if Einstein's theory is true, but FTL drives of various kinds are so very useful in avoiding the inconveniences of GENERATION STARSHIPS that many writers of HARD SF insist on clinging to the hope that the theory may be imperfect in such a way as to permit an exploitable loophole. *Faster than Light* (anth 1976), a theme anthology ed Jack DANN and George ZEBROWSKI, includes, as well as the stories, several essays combatively arguing the case. Other writers, however, have found the time-dilatation effects associated with relativistic star-travel a rich source of plot ideas.

John W. CAMPBELL Jr was the writer who laid the groundwork for such facilitating devices as the space-warp (in *Islands of Space*, 1931; 1957) and hyperspace (in *The Mightiest Machine*, 1934; 1947), where the term made its début; where he led legions followed. Stories which work harder than most to make such notions plausible include Robert A. HEINLEIN's *Starman Jones* (1953), Murray LEINSTER's *The Other Side of Nowhere* (1964), A. Bertram CHANDLER's *Catch the Star Winds* (1969) and David ZINDELL's *Neverness* (1988). Memorable imagery relating to hypothetical means of FTL travel can be found in James Blish's tales of cities-become-starships by courtesy of the SPINDIZZY, *Cities in Flight* (omni 1970), and in Kenneth BULMER's "Strange Highway" (1960) and Bob SHAW's *The Palace of Eternity* (1969). Some memorable imagery attempting (mistakenly, as it later turned out) to envisage real relativistic visual effects can be found in Frederik POHL's "The Gold at the Starbow's End" (1972; exp as *Starburst* **1982**). Many sf stories suggest that the pilots of FTL spaceships may have to be specially adapted to the task, sometimes by cyborgization (◊ CYBORGS), becoming more-or-less alienated from their own kind; notable examples include Cordwainer SMITH's "Scanners Live in Vain" (1950), Gerard F. CONWAY's *Mindship* (**1974**), Joan COX's *Star Web* (**1980**), Vonda MCINTYRE's *Superluminal* (**1984**), Melissa SCOTT's trilogy begun with *Five Twelfths of Heaven* (**1985**), and Emma BULL's *Falcon* (**1989**). Norman SPINRAD's *The Void-Captain's Tale* (**1983**) deals ironically with sf symbolism of this general kind, featuring a phallic spaceship powered by a libidinous "psychological drive".

Sf stories which play with time-dilatation effects include Fredric BROWN's flippant "Placet is a Crazy Place" (1946), L. Ron HUBBARD's earnest *Return to Tomorrow* (1950; **1954**), Blish's "Common Time" (1953), Heinlein's *Time for the Stars* (**1956**), which deploys, literally, the celebrated "twins paradox", Vladislav Krapivin's "Meeting my Brother" (trans 1966), Joe HALDEMAN's *The Forever War* (fixup **1975**), Larry NIVEN's *A World Out of Time* (fixup **1976**), Tom Allen's "Not Absolute" (**1978**) and George TURNER's *Beloved Son* (**1978**). Such effects are taken to spectacular extremes in Poul ANDERSON's *Tau Zero* (**1970**), whose protagonists are permitted to outlive the Universe, and in Pohl's and Jack WILLIAMSON's even more expansive *The Singers of Time* (**1991**).

The elementary changes have now been rung, but there is probably further scope for intriguing time-dilatation plots. One such is *Redshift Rendezvous* (**1990**) by John E. STITH, set on a starship in a version of hyperspace in which the velocity of light is so low (22mph/35kph) that its passage is visible, and relativistic phenomena are obvious at walking speed. In the mean time, FTL facilitating devices will undoubtedly continue to do sterling work for the extravagantly inclined sf writer. [BS]

FAUCETTE, JOHN M(ATTHEW) Jr (1943-) US writer whose sf novels, including *Crown of Infinity* (**1968**) and *The Age of Ruin* (**1968**), are routine works, the first a SPACE OPERA, the second a post-DISASTER odyssey. The **Peacemakers** series, in which alien invaders are fought to a negotiated truce, comprises *The Warriors of Terra* (**1970**) and *Siege of Earth* (**1971**). [JC]

FAULCON, ROBERT ◊ Robert P. HOLDSTOCK.

FAUST, JOE CLIFFORD (1957-) US copywriter and author who began publishing sf with "The Jackalope's Tale" for *Wyoming Rural Electric News* in 1983. His first novel, *A Death of Honor* (**1987**), is an sf mystery set in a 21st century moderately displaced in the direction of CYBERPUNK, where a Constitutional Amendment has entitled victims of crime to pursue the perpetrators; the mystery itself is worked out with extremely satisfying care. His second novel, *The Company Man* (**1988**), enters even more familiar

cyberpunk territory by featuring a protagonist who steals data for a large corporation which partially runs the decaying world, and who soon faces a moral crisis. In the **Angel's Luck** trilogy – *Desperate Measures* (**1989**), *Precious Cargo* (**1990**) and *The Essence of Evil* (**1990**) – JCF created a romping SPACE OPERA whose spiralling intricacies of plot, as the freelance protagonists who run the starship *Angel's Luck* get into deeper and deeper waters, are recounted with the rigorous plot-control for which he has become known and with a sly sustaining humour. As a professing Christian, JCF has an avowed allegiance to what he has called "old-fashioned virtues"; so far, however, his tales show no signs of doctrinal purpose. [JC]

See also: CRIME AND PUNISHMENT.

FAWCETT, BILL Working name of US anthologist, packager and writer William Brian Fawcett (1947-). His fiction has generally been collaborative: examples include *Cold Cash Warrior* (**1989**) with Robert ASPRIN and *Lord of Cragslaw* * (**1989**) with Neil Randall, a novel tied to the **Guardians of the Three** sequence, *Lord of Cragslaw* * (**1989**) (*for details of books with David A. DRAKE and Christopher* STASHEFF, *see their entries*). Solo, BF has been responsible for the **SwordQuest** fantasy sequence: *Quest for the Unicorn's Horn* (**1985**), *Quest for the Dragon's Eye* (**1985**), *Quest for the Demon Gate* (**1986**) and *Quest for the Elf King* (**1987**). As anthologist, he created the **War Years** sequence of ties, including *War Years #1: The Far Stars War* * (anth **1990**), *#2: The Siege of Arista* * (anth **1991**) with Stasheff, and *#3: The Jupiter War* * (anth **1991**). Also with Stasheff, he ed *The Crafters* (anth **1991**). [JC]

See also: SHARED WORLDS.

FAWCETT, EDGAR (1847-1904) US writer, known primarily for his work outside the sf field. Most of his 40 or so novels belong to the realist school associated with his contemporary William Dean HOWELLS, but (like Howells) BF also wrote imaginative works. He provided a manifesto for a species of fiction which he called "realistic romance", which is very similar to some DEFINITIONS OF SF: "Stories where the astonishing and peculiar are blent with the possible and accountable. They may be as wonderful as you will, but they must not touch on the mere flimsiness of miracle. They can be excessively improbable, but their improbability must be based upon scientific fact, and not upon fantastic, emotional and purely imaginative groundwork." This statement is from the introduction to *The Ghost of Guy Thyrle* (**1895**), a novel whose hero discovers a drug which separates his soul from his body and must undertake a voyage into the further reaches of the cosmos when his uninhabited body is cremated. Earlier and more modest works in the same vein are *Douglas Duane* (**1887**), a personality-exchange story, *Solarion* (**1889**), a novel about a dog with artificially augmented intelligence, and *The Romance of Two Brothers* (**1891**), which features a problematic elixir of life. *The New Nero* (**1893**), a study in abnormal psychology concerning a man who believes himself to be a mass murderer, is of borderline interest. Some of EF's POETRY is also relevant, most notably "In the Year Ten Thousand" in *Songs of Doubt and Dream* (coll **1891**). An early supernatural story of some note is "He, She and It" (1871). He copyrighted several unpublished manuscripts, some of which appear to have been sf.   [BS]

About the author: "The Realistic Romances of Edgar Fawcett" by Brian M. STABLEFORD, *Foundation* #24 (Feb 1982).

See also: COSMOLOGY; EVOLUTION; MOON; RELIGION.

FAWCETT, E(DWARD) DOUGLAS (1866-1960) UK writer and mystical thinker, long resident in Switzerland. His first (and best-known) sf novel, *Hartmann the Anarchist, or The Doom of the Great City* (**1893**), illustrated by Fred T. JANE, features a 1920s anarchist revolution against a wicked, capitalist UK, with London being destroyed by airships; but, in the face of opposition and gripped by guilt, the rebel Hartmann eventually destroys himself and the *Attila*, his fearsome airship, and all is well. The HOLLOW EARTH featured in *Swallowed by an Earthquake* (**1894**), a juvenile, is non-Symmesian (◊ John Cleves SYMMES) and uncompellingly cluttered with prehistoric reptiles. *The Secret of the Desert, or How We Crossed Arabia in the "Antelope"* (**1895**) is about a secret amphibious tank which crosses Arabia, finding there a lost race (◊ LOST WORLDS) of Phoenicians.   [JC]

FAWCETT, FAUSTO [r] ◊ LATIN AMERICA.

FAWCETT, F(RANK) DUBREZ (1891-1968) UK writer active in various genres under his own name and several others from 1923; non-sf pseudonyms included Cass Borelli, Henri Dupres, Madame E. Farra, "GRIFF", Eugene Glen, Duke Linton, Coolidge McCann, Elmer Eliot Saks, Ben Sarto and Hank Spencer. Much of his output consisted of such thrillers as *Miss Otis Comes to Piccadilly* (**1946**), as by Ben Sarto, and its many quite popular successors. *The Wonderful Isle of Ulla-Gapoo* (**1946**) is a mild fantasy. FDF's only known sf novel proper is *Hole in Heaven* (**1954**), about a human body possessed by an otherdimensional ALIEN. *Air-Gods' Parade* (**1935**), as by Simpson Stokes, and *The Dubious Adventures of Baron Munchhausen* (**1948**) may be of some interest.   [JC]

FAX COLLECTOR'S EDITIONS US SMALL PRESS established by T.E. DIKTY with Darrell C. Richardson in 1972, and devoted to publishing material from and about PULP MAGAZINES. Its publications include several collections of obscure Robert E. HOWARD stories, two anthology series in facsimile under the titles **Famous Fantastic Classics** and **Famous Pulp Classics**, and *The Weird Tales Story* (**1977**), a large volume written and ed Robert E. WEINBERG. An associated and more prolific company, also founded by Dikty, is STARMONT HOUSE.   [MJE]

FAYETTE, J.B. ◊ JUPITER; OUTER PLANETS.

FEARING, KENNETH (1902-1961) US poet and novelist, known mainly for mysteries like *The Big Clock* (**1946**), a tale whose atmosphere adumbrates the *film-noir* tonality of later US fantasy. Within a mystery frame, *The Loneliest Girl in the World* (**1951**) is border-

line sf. KG's only sf novel proper is *Clark Gifford's Body* (**1942**), which gravely and literately portrays a future US civil war.   [JC]

FEARN, JOHN (FRANCIS) RUSSELL (1908-1960) UK writer; extremely prolific, he used many pseudonyms. During the 1930s he wrote for magazines, including the US PULP MAGAZINES, but during WWII he switched to books. He became a central figure in the post-WWII paperback boom, writing numerous Westerns, crime stories and probably some romances as well as his sf, most of which appeared under the names Vargo Statten and Volsted GRIDBAN (the latter pseudonym being taken over from E.C. TUBB). In the pulps he wrote many stories as Thornton Ayre and Polton Cross, and also used the names Geoffrey Armstrong, Dennis Clive, John Cotton and Ephriam Winiki; his sf books and crime stories with sf elements include items signed with the personal pseudonyms Spike Gordon, Conrad G. Holt, Laurence F. Rose, John Russell and Earl Titan, and the house names Astron DEL MARTIA, "GRIFF", Paul LORRAINE and Brian SHAW.

JRF's first GENRE-SF work was the early SUPERMAN story *The Intelligence Gigantic* (1933 *AMZ*; **1943**). It was followed by the extravagant *Liners of Time* (1935 *AMZ*; **1947**) and its sequel "Zagribud" (1937 *AMZ*; cut vt *Science Metropolis* by Vargo Statten **1952**); he subsequently wrote a good deal for ASTOUNDING SCIENCE-FICTION while it was edited by F. Orlin TREMAINE, contributing numerous "thought-variant" stories, some of which he later expanded into Vargo Statten novels, including *Nebula X* (1946 as "The Multillionth Chance" by JRF; rev **1950**), *The Sun Makers* (1937 as "Metamorphosis" by JRF; rev **1950**), *The Avenging Martian* (1938 as "Red Heritage" by JRF; rev **1951**), *The Renegade Star* (1935 as "The Blue Infinity" by JRF; rev **1951**), *The Inner Cosmos* (1937 as "Worlds Within" by JRF; rev **1952**), *To the Ultimate* (1936 as "Mathematica" and "Mathematica Plus" by JRF; rev **1952**) and *The Dust Destroyer* (1934 as "The Man who Stopped the Dust" by JRF; rev **1953**).

Four Thornton Ayre novelettes in FANTASTIC ADVENTURES featuring the superwoman – or **Golden Amazon** – Violet Ray were extensively revised into the novel *The Golden Amazon* (1939-43; **1944**), which was reprinted in the *Toronto Star Weekly* to such acclaim that 23 sequels followed, the last appearing posthumously there in 1961. Those which have subsequently appeared in book form are: *The Golden Amazon Returns* (1945; **1949**; vt *The Deathless Amazon* 1953 Canada), *The Golden Amazon's Triumph* (1946; **1953**), *The Amazon's Diamond Quest* (1947 as "Diamond Quest"; **1953**), *The Amazon Strikes Again* (1948; **1954**), *Twin of the Amazon* (1948; **1954**), *Conquest of the Amazon* (1949; **1973** chap) and *Lord of Atlantis* (1949; **1991** chap). Two other series are Edgar Rice BURROUGHS imitations: the **Clayton Drew** interplanetary romances *Emperor of Mars* (**1950**), *Warrior of Mars* (**1950**), *Red Men of Mars* (**1950**) and *Goddess of Mars* (**1950**); and the **Anjani** sequence of **Tarzan** imitations signed Earl Titan: *The Gold of Akada* (**1951**) and *Anjani, the Mighty* (**1951**). JFR also wrote the book of the notable 1954 schlock-horror film *The* CREATURE FROM THE BLACK LAGOON, *The Creature from the Black Lagoon* * (**1954**) as Vargo Statten.

Scion, publishers of Vargo Statten, created the VARGO STATTEN SCIENCE FICTION MAGAZINE, although JRF did not become its editor immediately; it underwent several title changes in the course of its short life.

JRF's writing was unpolished and his use of ideas imaginatively reckless, but his best work is vigorous and occasionally vivid. His works have sometimes proved popular in translation; he enjoyed something of a boom in Italy in the 1970s.   [BS]

Other works as JRF: *Slaves of Ijax* (**1947** chap); *From Afar* (**1982** chap); *No Grave Need I* (**1984** chap); *The Slitherers* (**1984** chap).

As Hugo Blayn: *What Happened to Hammond?* (**1951**).

As Dennis Clive: *Valley of Pretenders* (*c***1942** chap US); *The Voice Commands* (*c***1942** chap US).

As Polton Cross: *Other Eyes Watching* (**1946**).

As Astron del Martia (house name): *The Trembling World* (**1949**).

As Spike Gordon: *Don't Touch Me* (**1953**).

As Volsted Gridban: *The Dyno-Depressant* (**1953**); *Magnetic Brain* (**1953**); *Moons for Sale* (**1953**); *Scourge of the Atom* (1948 as "After the Atom" by JRF; rev **1953**); the **Herbert** sequence, comprising *A Thing of the Past* (**1953**) and *The Genial Dinosaur* **1954**); *Exit Life* (1941 as "The World in Wilderness" by Thornton Ayre; rev **1953**); the **Adam Quirke** sequence, comprising *The Master Must Die* (**1953**) and *The Lonely Astronomer* (partly based on "Death at the Observatory" 1938 by JRF; **1954**); *The Purple Wizard* (**1953**); *The Frozen Limit* (**1954**); *I Came – I Saw – I Wondered* (**1954**).

As "Griff" (house name): *Liquid Death* (**1953**).

As Conrad G. Holt: *Cosmic Exodus* (**1953** chap).

As Paul Lorraine (house name): *Dark Boundaries* (**1953**).

As Laurence F. Rose: *The Hell-Fruit* (**1953** chap).

As John Russell: *Account Settled* (**1949**).

As Brian Shaw (house name): *Z-Formations* (**1953**).

As Vargo Statten: *Operation Venus* (**1950**); *Annihilation* (**1950**); *The Micro-Men* (**1950**); *Wanderer of Space* (**1950**); *2000 Years On* (**1950**); *Inferno!* (**1950**); *The Cosmic Flame* (**1950**); *Cataclysm* (1944 as "The Devouring Tide" by Polton Cross; rev **1951**); *The Red Insects* (**1951**); *The New Satellite* (**1951**); *Deadline to Pluto* (**1951**); *The Petrified Planet* (**1951**); *Born of Luna* (**1951**); *The Devouring Fire* (**1951**); *The Catalyst* (**1951**); *The Space Warp* (**1952**); *The Eclipse Express* (**1952**); *The Time Bridge* (1942 as "Prisoner of Time" by Polton Cross; rev **1952**); *The Man from Tomorrow* (1950 as "Stranger in our Midst" by JRF; rev **1952**); *The G-Bomb* (1941 as "The Last Secret Weapon" by Polton Cross; rev **1952**); *Laughter in Space* (1939 as "Laughter out of Space" by Dennis Clive; rev **1952**); *Across the Ages* (1952 as "Glimpse" by JRF; **1952** chap); *The Last Martian* (**1952** chap); *Worlds to Conquer* (**1952** chap); *De-Creation* (**1952** chap); *The Time Trap* (**1952** chap); *Ultra Spectrum* (**1953**); *Black-Wing of Mars* (1953 as "Winged Pestilence" by JRF; **1953**); *Man in Duplicate* (**1953**); *Zero Hour* (1952 as "Deadline" by JRF; **1953**); *The Black Avengers* (**1953**); *Odyssey of Nine* (**1953**); *Pioneer 1990* (1940 as "He Conquered Venus" by JRF; rev **1953**); *The Interloper* (**1953**); *Man of Two Worlds* (**1953**); *The Lie Destroyer* (**1953**); *Black Bargain* (**1953**); *The Grand Illusion* (**1953**); *Wealth of the Void* (**1954**); *A Time Appointed* (**1954**); *I Spy* (**1954**); *The Multi-Man* (**1954**); *1,000 Year Voyage* (**1954**); *Earth 2* (**1955**).

About the author: *The Multi-Man* (**1968** chap) by Philip HARBOTTLE.

See also: BOYS' PAPERS; CLONES; TIME TRAVEL.

FEELEY, GREGORY (**1955-**   ) US critic and writer whose essays and book reviews have appeared throughout the 1980s in various journals from the *Washington Post* to FOUNDATION. Sometimes adversarial, unfailingly intelligent, they represent a cold-eyed view of a genre he loves by a critic immersed in its material. Although he began publishing sf with "The Light at the End of the Penumbra" in *Ascents of Wonder* (anth **1977**) ed David GERROLD, GF did not become active as an author of fiction for about a decade. His first novel, *The Oxygen Barons* (**1990**), served therefore as a sort of début, surprising some by turning out to be a HARD-SF tale of a terraformed Moon (◊ TERRAFORMING). In what seems a perfectly standard fashion, colonists and a giant corporation are at loggerheads; it is only the labyrinth of the plot that exposes the novel as other than orthodox.   [JC]

FEGHOOTS ◊ Reginald BRETNOR; *The* MAGAZINE OF FANTASY AND SCIENCE FICTION.

FEKETE, GYULA [r] ◊ HUNGARY.

FELDSTEIN, ALBERT B. [r] ◊ EC COMICS.

FELICE, CYNTHIA (LINDGREN) (**1942-**   ) US writer who began publishing sf with "Longshanks" for *Galileo 2* in 1976. Her first novel, *Godsfire* (**1978**), depicts an ALIEN planet inhabited by felines who dominate the local humans but who have never seen their sun because of the unending rain. Almost too well constructed – almost facile in its zestful plotting – the book demonstrated CF's technical skill, her romantic inclinations and a tendency to slough off hard solutions. Her next book, *The Sunbound* (**1981**), for instance, failed to produce a protagonist capable of hewing to CF's intricate plot demands without seeming an arbitrary creation, yet the family romance at the tale's heart required characters who could be intrinsically believed in. Of her later solo singletons, *Downtime* (**1985**) interestingly combined a longevity intrigue in a distant solar system, aliens, and romance, but *The Khan's Persuasion* (**1991**) once again demonstrated a gap between the quality of her sf perceptions and the easy flow of the plotty romance idiom through which she presents characters. CF's two collaborations with Connie WILLIS, *Water Witch* (**1982**) and *Light Raid* (**1989**), benefit from Willis's significantly harsher mind but are still somewhat heavily plotted.   [JC]

Other works: *Eclipses* (**1983**); *Double Nocturne* (**1986**); *Iceman* (**1991**).

See also: WEAPONS.

FEMINISM Although a genre defined and long dominated by men, sf has a particular affinity with feminism. This became clear in the 1970s with the publication of such challenging books as *The Female Man* (**1975**) by Joanna RUSS, *Walk to the End of the World* (**1974**) and *Motherlines* (**1978**) by Suzy McKee CHARNAS and *Woman on the Edge of Time* (**1976**) by Marge PIERCY.

One of the most obvious attractions of sf to women writers – feminist or not – is the possibilities it offers for the creation of a female HERO. The demands of realism in the contemporary or historical novel set limits which do not bind the universes available to sf. Although the history of sf reveals few heroic, realistic, or even original images of women (◊ WOMEN AS PORTRAYED IN SCIENCE FICTION), the genre had a potential recognized by the women writers drawn to it in the 1960s and 1970s. The desire to write (or read) about women who wield swords, pilot spaceships or simply lead lives from which the threat of male violence is absent might be seen as escapist, but such imaginings can also be read as part of a political agenda. As Pamela SARGENT wrote in a letter to *Frontiers: A Journal of Women Studies*, Fall 1977, "Science-fiction writers are limited only by human potential, not human actualities. Sf can serve to show women, and men, how large that potential can be." And Suzy McKee Charnas remarked in the same journal: "Women's realities are still highly circumscribed by various forms of oppression . . . One place for us to imagine new strengths, goals, and ways of being human is in the world of fantasy, where we can work around our present limitations in ways that may help to point us . . . out of and beyond those limitations."

Despite the reputation sf has as a mind-expanding, possibly subversive, always questioning form, these strengths were seldom brought to bear on the subject of male/female relationships, sexual roles or the idea of "woman's place" prior to the rise of the Women's Liberation Movement. As Kingsley AMIS pointed out in *New Maps of Hell* (**1960** US), "Though it may go against the grain to admit it, science-fiction writers are evidently satisfied with the sexual status quo." He was referring, of course, to male sf writers. With a very few exceptions (e.g., Philip WYLIE's *The Disappearance* [**1951**], Theodore STURGEON's *Venus Plus X* [**1960**] and John WYNDHAM's "Consider Her Ways" [**1956**]), the men who tried to imagine alternatives to patriarchy did so only to "prove" how nasty and impossible life would be without the "natural" dominance of woman by man. (For more novels featuring women-ruled societies ◊ SOCIOLOGY.)

One of the major challenges of modern feminism has been to the idea that gender roles and relations are in some way permanent, arising from a natural and immutable law. In *The Dialectic of Sex: The Case for Feminist Revolution* (**1970**) Shulamith Firestone located the site of women's oppression in their role as child-bearers and -rearers, and argued that feminist revolution would not be possible until women were freed not only from the sole responsibility for child-rearing (which should be taken by society as a whole) but also, by technology, from the tyranny of reproduction. Although the idea that women might have to give up the physical act of child-bearing in order to achieve a truly egalitarian society has never achieved wide popularity, the force of Firestone's argument is powerfully illustrated in Marge Piercy's *Woman on the Edge of Time*, and its influence can be traced also in the writings of Charnas, Russ and Sally Miller GEARHART.

Not all work by women writers is feminist – not even when it concentrates on the "woman question" – and there are different interpretations of what comprises feminist sf. The only specifically labelled feminist sf list from any publisher is the one established by The Women's Press in the UK under the direction of Sarah LEFANU in 1985. Anything published by The Women's Press, sf included, is considered, by definition, feminist, and is often ghettoized in bookshops. Yet many of the books on this list were first published in the USA and even in the UK by nonfeminist houses either as straightforward sf, as for example *A Door into Ocean* (**1986**) by Joan SLONCZEWSKI, or as mainstream literature, like *The Book of the Night* (**1984**) by Rhoda Lerman (1936-   ). The Women's Press list also includes books by writers who had not previously been seen as, and would not define themselves as, feminist writers, such as Josephine SAXTON and Tanith LEE.

Diane Martin, an editor of the fanzine *Aurora* (where sf stands for "speculative feminism" – ◊ JANUS/AURORA), in 1990 proposed, with tongue slightly in cheek, "The Martin Scale" as a tool for measuring the feminist content of a work of sf or fantasy:

Level One: Doubts about patriarchy/women escaping victimization (e.g., most Andre NORTON novels)

Level Two: Men and women as equals (e.g., *Dreamsnake* [**1978**] by Vonda MCINTYRE)

Level Three: Women are better than men on some levels (e.g., *FrostFlower and Thorn* [**1980**] by Phyllis Ann Karr)

Level Four: Women are uniformly better than men (e.g., Jessica Amanda Salmonson's **Tomoe Gozen** saga)

Level Five: Can't live with 'em/can't live without 'em (e.g., "The Women Men Don't See" [1973] by James TIPTREE Jr)

Level Six: Men are tragically flawed and pitiable (e.g., *Native Tongue* [**1984**] by Suzette Haden ELGIN)

Level Seven: Men as slaves (e.g., B-movies like *Amazon Women on the Moon* [1987]; ◊ Joe DANTE)

Level Eight: Separatism is necessary for survival (e.g., *The Gate to Women's Country* [**1988**] by Sheri S. TEPPER)

Level Nine: Positive depiction of lesbian/feminist utopias (e.g., *The Shore of Women* [**1986**] by Pamela Sargent)

Level Ten: Parthenogenesis and/or scenes of actual castration (e.g., *Motherlines* [1978] by Suzy McKee Charnas)

In what is probably the most thoughtful and accessible survey of the topic, *In the Chinks of the World Machine: Feminism and Science Fiction* (1988; vt *Feminism and Science Fiction* 1989 US) by Sarah Lefanu, the author makes a distinction between feminist sf and "feminized sf". The latter, she argues, while it challenges established sexism by valuing women and feminine values over men and masculinity, and has been an important influence on the development of sf as a whole, does not dispute the man/woman paradigm or question the construction of gender as more radical feminist writings do. Feminist ideas are able to flourish within sf despite reader resistance because, she claims, sf at its best "deploys a sceptical rationalism as its subtext" and "feminism is based upon a profound scepticism: of the 'naturalness' of the patriarchal world and the belief in male superiority on which it is founded".

A forerunner to modern feminist sf can be seen in the spate of utopian stories written by women as part of the movement for women's rights which began in the 19th century. Unlike the utopias of male writers, these fictions always question the sexual status quo and foreground the position of women, sometimes – as in Mary E. Bradley LANE's *Mizora* (1890) and Charlotte Perkins GILMAN's *Herland* (1914; 1979) – by depicting an all-women society and showing its superiority to societies in which men rule.

The utopian tradition in women's writing was forgotten in subsequent decades until its rediscovery by feminist scholars in the 1970s, and there is some worry that, however well established women writers may seem now, the same fate may befall feminist sf. Russ has described many of the ways in which women's work is discounted in *How to Suppress Women's Writing* (1983); and, in "An Open Letter to Joanna Russ" in *Aurora 25* (1987), Jeanne Gomoll expressed her feeling that her own experiences of FANDOM and sf in the 1970s were being rewritten by men choosing to ignore the impact of feminism and characterize a whole decade as "boring" because their personal interests were not always given priority. To many, women as well as men, the revolution is over, equality has been won, and we are living in a post-feminist age. In addition, the label "feminist" has never been either safe or comfortable; while it had in the 1970s – particularly in the USA – a certain novelty value, by the mid-1980s to be called a feminist writer was to be announced as writing for a limited audience of like-minded readers.

On the positive side, the impact of feminism can be seen even in much nonfeminist sf. Men as well as women writers are more interested in creating believable female characters; and, as a ground for "thought experiments" relating to gender, social relations and new ways of being human – topics central to feminism – sf is extremely fertile. [LT]

Further reading: *Future Females: A Critical Anthology* (anth 1981) ed Marlene S. Barr; *Feminist Futures: Contemporary Women's Speculative Fiction* (1984) by Natalie M. Rosinski; *Women Worldwalkers: New Dimensions of Science Fiction and Fantasy* (anth 1985) ed Jane B. Weedman; *Writing Beyond the Ending: Narrative Strategies of Twentieth-Century Women Writers* (1985) by Rachel Blau DuPlessis; *Feminist Utopias* (1989) by Francis Bartkowski.

FENDALL, PERCY (?   -?   ) UK author known solely for his sf novel *Lady Ermyntrude and the Plumber: A Love Tale of MCMXX* (1912). After the passage of the Great Compulsory Work Act and the suppression of the House of Lords, everybody must work to live. [JC]

FENN, LIONEL ◊ Charles L. GRANT.

FERGUSON, BRAD Working name of US writer Bradley Michael Ferguson (1953-   ). His two **Star Trek** ties are *Crisis on Centaurus* * (1986) and *A Flag Full of Stars* * (1991). He has also written one independent title, *The World Next Door* (1990), in which a post-HOLOCAUST Earth is set as an ALTERNATE WORLD to our own. [JC]

FERGUSON, HELEN ◊ Anna KAVAN.

FERGUSON, NEIL (1947-   ) UK writer who began publishing sf with "The Monroe Doctrine" for *Interzone* in 1983, and through the 1980s released several sharply conceived tales, revealing more than once a deep interest in US life.

His first book, *Bars of America* (coll 1986), not sf, is a collection of tales and musings set in the heart of that country. His first sf novel, *Putting Out* (1988), presents a NEAR-FUTURE US political race in terms of the semiotics of dressing, with all the sensitivity to signs so often found in exiles, voluntary or forced. *Double Helix Fall* (1990), also linguistically inventive and darkly obsessed with the USA's visions of its own demise, presents – in the guise of a homage to the world and style of Philip K. DICK – an original rendering of that sense of demise, for in the USA of this novel it has become a matter of political and religious orthodoxy that to be born is to die, and that the world into which one dies is a stratified Hell. A ROBOT detective helps, in the nick of time, to loosen the death-grip. [JC]

FERMAN, EDWARD L(EWIS) (1937-   ) US editor, son of Joseph W. FERMAN; ELF formally took over the editorship of *The* MAGAZINE OF FANTASY AND SCIENCE FICTION in Jan 1966, a post in which he remained until June 1991, having previously been managing editor since Apr 1962 under Avram DAVIDSON and then his father. Under ELF's editorship *FSF* generally prospered: for many years it was one of only two sf magazines – *ASF* being the other, with both now being joined by ISAAC ASIMOV'S SCIENCE FICTION MAGAZINE – to have maintained a regular schedule, and its circulation has remained fairly stable. *FSF* won the HUGO for Best Magazine four years in succession (1969-72) under ELF and, after that category was dropped, ELF won the replacement Hugo for Best

Editor in 1981, 1982 and 1983. It would be fair to say that, although the magazine has lost much of its distinctive flavour of the 1950s, larger market forces and changes in the nature of the genre have had much to do with that diminution of specialness. In 1991 ELF appointed Kristine Kathryn RUSCH as editor, retaining the post of publisher.

During his long stay at the helm, ELF edited various anthologies drawn from the magazine, including several volumes of the **Best from Fantasy and Science Fiction** series (see listing below). There were also four anniversary volumes: *Twenty Years of the Magazine of Fantasy and Science Fiction* (anth **1970**) with Robert P. MILLS, *The Best from Fantasy and Science Fiction: A Special 25th Anniversary Anthology* (anth **1974**), *The Magazine of Fantasy and Science Fiction: A 30-Year Retrospective* (anth **1980**) and *The Best from Fantasy & Science Fiction: A 40th Anniversary Anthology* (anth **1989**). With Barry N. MALZBERG ELF collaborated on a notable original anthology, *Final Stage* (anth **1974**; rev 1975), a reprint collection, *Arena: Sports SF* (anth **1976**) and *Graven Images: Three Original Novellas of Science Fiction* (anth **1977**).   [MJE/JC]

Other works: *Once and Future Tales from the Magazine of Fantasy and Science Fiction* (anth **1968**); *The Magazine of Fantasy and Science Fiction, April 1965* (anth **1981**) with Martin H. GREENBERG; *The Best Fantasy Stories from the Magazine of Fantasy & Science Fiction* (anth **1986**); *The Best Horror Stories from the Magazine of Fantasy and Science Fiction* (anth **1988**; in 2 vols US 1989; vt *The Best of Modern Horror: Twenty-Four Tales from the Magazine of Fantasy and Science Fiction* 1989 UK) ed with Anne Devereaux Jordan.

The Best from Fantasy and Science Fiction: *The Best from Fantasy and Science Fiction: 15th Series* (anth **1966**); *16th Series* (anth **1967**); *17th Series* (anth **1968**); *18th Series* (anth **1969**); *19th Series* (anth **1971**); *20th Series* (anth **1973**); *22nd Series* (anth **1977**); *23th Series* (anth **1980**); *24th Series* (anth **1982**).

FERMAN, JOSEPH W(OLFE) (1906-1974) US publisher and editor, born in Lithuania. After a long career with the magazine *American Mercury*, JWF became involved with *The* MAGAZINE OF FANTASY AND SCIENCE FICTION from its inception, was listed Aug 1954-Oct 1970 as Publisher and Dec 1964-Dec 1965 as Editor, a position to which his son, Edward L. FERMAN, succeeded him. He also founded VENTURE SCIENCE FICTION as a companion to *FSF*; it ran 1957-8 under the editorship of Robert P. MILLS, with a second series being published 1969-70 under the editorship of Edward L. Ferman. JWF edited an anthology of stories from *Venture: No Limits* (anth **1964**).   [MJE/PN]

FERRING, DAVID ◊ David S. GARNETT.

FEZANDIE, (ERNEST) CLEMENT (1865-1959) US writer and playwright based initially in New York, though he lived and travelled in the Middle East in later life, and died in Belgium. His sf novel, *Through the Earth* (**1898**), is about a transportation-tube through the planet from New York to Australia, which gives its first passenger an experience in free

fall but suffers from melting at the Earth's core and must be abandoned. The sequel, «A Trip to Venus», still awaits publication. It is likely that CF's early work, with its didactic bias, was appreciated by Hugo GERNSBACK, and his **Dr Hackensaw** series (◊ EDISONADE) appeared first in Gernsback's SCIENCE AND INVENTION in 43 instalments, from "The Secret of Artificial Respiration" (1921) to the novel "A Journey to the Center of the Earth" (1925), with two concluding stories published the next year in *AMZ*.   [JC]

See also: APES AND CAVEMEN (IN THE HUMAN WORLD); HOLLOW EARTH; MATTER TRANSMISSION; SERIES.

FIALKO, NATHAN (1881-?   ) Soviet writer, resident in the USA, who translated his own uneven sf novel into English as *The New City: A Story of the Future* (**1925**; trans and rev **1937**). It depicts first Soviet then US society with strongly DYSTOPIAN views of both.   [JC]

FICHMAN, FRED (?   -   ) US writer whose *SETI* (**1990**) pits its teenaged hero against both US and Soviet governments in the race to make First Contact. He does surprisingly well.   [JC]

See also: ALIENS.

FICKS, R. SNOWDEN [r] ◊ ROBERT HALE LIMITED.

FICTIONEERS, INC. ◊ ASTONISHING STORIES; SUPER SCIENCE STORIES.

FIEDLER, LESLIE A(ARON) (1917-   ) US critic whose piercing and mythopoeic views on the relationship between US culture and literature were first expressed in *Love and Death in the American Novel* (**1960**), where he describes sf as a "typically Anglo-Saxon" form, although later, in *Waiting for the End* (coll **1964**), he states that "Even in its particulars, the universe of science fiction is Jewish". He has long espoused the work of such sf writers as Samuel R. DELANY. *In Dreams Awake* (anth **1975**) assembles material of interest, and *Olaf Stapledon: A Man Divided* (**1983**) is an invigorating if sometimes eccentric examination of STAPLEDON. His fiction, like *The Messengers will Come no More* (**1974**), tends to FABULATION.   [JC]

See also: DEFINITIONS OF SF.

FIELD, GANS T. ◊ Manly Wade WELLMAN.

FIEND WITHOUT A FACE Film (1957). Amalgamated/MGM. Dir Arthur Crabtree, starring Marshall Thompson, Terence Kilburn, Kim Parker, Peter Madden, Kynaston Reeves. Screenplay Herbert J. Leder, based on "The Thought-Monster" (*Weird Tales* 1930) by Amelia Reynolds Long. 74 mins. B/w.

This is one of the two sf/HORROR films made by Amalgamated in the UK (the other was FIRST MAN INTO SPACE [1958], also starring Marshall Thompson) but set in North America. *FWAF* is much more interesting than the other, despite the absurdity of its basic premise. An elderly SCIENTIST (Reeves) accidentally creates, with his new thought-wave amplifier, a number of creatures consisting of pure energy. Invisible at first, they commit a series of murders by sucking out their victim's brains through holes made at the base of the neck; but in the final sequences, when the creatures have trapped the protagonists in a remote house, they gradually materialize as disembodied brains with trailing spinal cords and twitching tendrils. The lunatic climax has a quality of genuine nightmare, with the brains – animated in imaginative stop-motion photography by Florenz von Nordhoff and K.L. Ruppel – leaping and plopping about like demonic frogs. This is the ultimate in anti-intellectual movies. [JB/PN]

See also: MONSTER MOVIES.

FIGGIS, N.P. (1939-   ) Irish archaeologist and writer whose fourth novel, *The Fourth Mode* (**1989**), sensitively depicts a small town and the natural life surrounding it as a nuclear holocaust first threatens, then arrives. [JC]

FILE 770 US FANZINE of the 1980s, ed from Los Angeles by Mike Glyer, bimonthly for most of its life. A newsletter covering FANDOM, with emphasis on North America, it was begun when the previous US "newszine" (fanzine devoted to items of news), *Karass*, ed Linda Bushyager, folded. The focus of *F770*, much of whose contents are written in Glyer's no-nonsense style, is convention news and reports. It won HUGOS for Best Fanzine in 1984, 1985 and 1989, and Glyer won the Hugo for Best Fan Writer in 1984, 1986 and 1988. [RH]

FILM ◊ CINEMA.

FINAL COUNTDOWN, THE Film (1980). Bryna Company/United Artists. Dir Don Taylor, starring Kirk Douglas, Martin Sheen, Katharine Ross, James Farentino. Screenplay David Ambrose, Gerry DAVIS, Thomas Hunter, Peter Powell, based on a story by Hunter, Powell, Ambrose. 105 mins. Colour.

An aircraft carrier on manoeuvres off Hawaii in 1980 is caught in a strange storm which turns out to be a time-warp. The vessel is deposited in the same spot in 1941, just before the attack on Pearl Harbor. Action is eschewed for interminable ethical debate about altering history, as the captain (Douglas) agonizes whether or not to shoot down the Japanese planes which will shortly bomb the US naval base; a second time-warp renders decision unnecessary. The film is wholly pointless, ill acted, and a complete waste of a perfectly good ship, the *Nimitz*, which the US Navy had allowed the production company (Kirk Douglas and family) to use. [PN]

FINAL PROGRAMME, THE (vt *The Last Days of Man on Earth*) Film (1973). Goodtimes Enterprises/Gladiole Films/MGM-EMI. Dir Robert Fuest, starring Jon Finch, Jenny Runacre, Sterling Hayden, Harry Andrews, Hugh Griffith, Julie Ege, Patrick Magee, Derrick O'Connor. Screenplay Fuest, based on *The Final Programme* (**1968**) by Michael MOORCOCK. 89 mins. Colour.

In this first film to feature Moorcock's polymorph protagonist, Jerry Cornelius, style triumphs over content. Originally a set-designer, Fuest is best known for *The Abominable Dr Phibes* (1971), an extravagantly theatrical horror-film spoof, and for the many episodes that he directed of *The* AVENGERS. *TFP* looks impressive, but not much of Moorcock's creation remains. Cornelius's father has died, leaving a

hidden microfilm on which is the final (computer) programme of the title. Those involved in the hunt for the film include Jerry (Finch), his evil brother (O'Connor), and the awesome Miss Brunner (Runacre), who has a tendency to consume her lovers, bones and all. The Moorcock original was not as strong as the other three books of his **Jerry Cornelius** tetralogy, but none the less was sophisticated in its ironies, which Fuest here reduces (literally in one case) to a series of knowing winks. When Moorcock defines his characters in terms of their personal style, this is often a form of criticism; for Fuest, by contrast, strong style is apparently to be admired. The apotheosis of the book is rendered farcical in the film, which substitutes a grinning Neanderthal for Moorcock's original hermaphroditic MESSIAH. [PN/JB]

FINCH, SHEILA (ROSEMARY) (1935-   ) UK-born writer, in the USA from 1962 or earlier, who began publishing sf with "The Confession of Melakos" for *Sou-wester* in 1977. Her first novel, *Infinity's Web* (**1985**), rather confusedly describes the lives of five versions of one protagonist who live in various ALTERNATE WORLDS, and who gradually gain a sense of the mutual web they inhabit. Though far more devoted to generic pleasures than Joanna RUSS in *The Female Man* (**1975**), whose structure is superficially similar, the novel still generates a clear and telling FEMINIST perspective. Her professional training in linguistics permeates her second novel, *Triad* (**1986**), another very full story, involving a woman run Earth government, a female mission to a planet where several ALIEN races seem to congregate, and pirates. She is now, perhaps unfairly, best known for the **Shaper Exile** sequence – *The Garden of the Shaped* (**1987**), *Shaper's Legacy* (**1989**) and *Shaping the Dawn* (**1989**) – as the first volume at least of this PLANETARY ROMANCE is awkwardly written, dumping three separate genetic versions of human stock upon a new planet, and sorting them out in terms of an unconvincing biological determinism. The second volume is more toughly argued, but the third moves too easily into the plot arabesques common to this subgenre. SF is still (1992) in the wings, but gives the impression she is capable of stepping into full view at any time. [JC]

See also: GENETIC ENGINEERING.

FIN DU MONDE, LA (vt *The End of the World*) Film (1931). L'Écran d'Art. Dir Abel Gance, starring Gance, Victor Francen, Colette Darfeuil, Sylvie Grenade, Jeanne Brindeau, Samson Fainsilber. Screenplay Gance, suggested by a story by Camille FLAMMARION. 105 mins, cut to 91 mins, cut to 54 mins. B/w.

This tells of a comet's approach to Earth and of the upheavals (natural and cultural) that ensue. There are orgies, and the rise of a totalitarian leader (Francen), obviously approved by the director, who would soon prove sympathetic to fascism. As with most of Gance's films, which were usually independently produced, it took many years to complete. *LFDM* was made as a silent film, but sound effects were later added by the producers, who sacked Gance and cut the film's length. (Gance was still working on one version in 1949.) A shortened 54min English version, repudiated by Gance, was released in 1934; it was supervised by V. Ivanoff and the script was adapted by H.S. Kraft. The film is extravagant, and fits one description of Gance's work as hovering "between the ludicrous and the majestic"; a more unkind critic might see it as somewhere between the grandiose and the banal. [PN/JB]

FINE, STEPHEN (? -) US screenwriter and author whose first novel, *Molly Dear: The Autobiography of an Android, or How I Came to my Senses, Was Repaired, Escaped my Master, and Was Educated in the Ways of the World* (**1988**), rewrites Daniel DEFOE's *Moll Flanders* (**1722**) as the memoirs of a 21st-century ANDROID to satirical effect. Her innocence – assisted by memory wipes – resembles that of VOLTAIRE's Candide, or almost any of John T. SLADEK's child ROBOTS in a cruel world. Some of the points about Molly's legal enslavement are sharply made. [JC]

FINE PRESSES ◊ SMALL PRESSES AND LIMITED EDITIONS.

FINLAND Sf in Finland, now over a century old, has been diverse, with few clear-cut lines of development. The earliest story was the serial "Muistelmia matkaltani Ruskealan pappilaan uuden vuoden aikoina vuonna 1983" ["Memoirs of My Trip to the Vicarage of Ruskeala around New Year 1983"] (1883, in the newspaper *Aura*) by Evald Ferdinand Jahnsson. Apart from a few children's stories, early Finnish sf took the form of future, sometimes socialist, UTOPIAS. The Moon was reached by an icy ball in "Matka kuuhun" ["Voyage to the Moon"] (1887) by Tyko Hagman, but the first true sf was the novella "Tähtien tarhoissa" ["Among the Stars"] (1912) by Arvid Lydecken, which was about Helsinki in AD2140, a Martian attack, a voyage to Mars and the beginning of peaceful coexistence on Earth after Mars has been destroyed by impacting asteroids.

Fear of Bolshevism during WWI produced several imaginary-WAR novels, the first being the excellent *Ylös helvetistä* ["Up from Hell"] (**1917**) by Konrad Lehtimäki. In *Suur-Isänmaa* ["The Great Fatherland"] (**1918**) by Kapteeni Teräs, Finland defeats Russia, forces the UK's surrender and becomes a superpower. *Kohtalon kolmas hetki* ["Fate's Third Moment"] (**1926**) by Aarno Karimo tells about a war in 1967-8 between Finland and the Soviet Union, which nation (in a defence union with the Mongols) is totally devastated by strange Finnish inventions. A typical hero of the period would be a scientist-inventor. The most curious of these "engineer novels" is *Neljännen ulottuvuuden mies* ["Man of the Fourth Dimension"] (**1919**) by H.R. Halli, in which a new chemical substance enables its users to see and walk through solid objects. The best book of this period, *Viimeisellä hetkellä* ["At the Last Moment"] (**1922**), also by Halli, creates a daring time perspective into Earth's distant future.

There were fewer sf books in the 1930s. Among the more notable are *The Diamondking of Sahara* (**1935**), written in English by Sigurd Wettenhovi-Aspa, and *Undred från kraterön* ["The Wonder of Crater Island"] (**1939**), written in Swedish by Ole Eklund. There were 30 sf books published in the 1940s. The most popular were the **Atorox** series by Outsider (pseudonym of Aarne Haapakoski) whose eponymous character was a ROBOT: *Atorox, ihmisten valtias* ["Atorox, Lord of Humans"] (**1947**), *Atorox kuussa* ["Atorox on the Moon"] (**1947**), *Atorox Marsissa* ["Atorox on Mars"] (**1947**), *Atorox Venuksessa* ["Atorox on Venus"] (**1947**), *Atorox Merkuriuksessa* ["Atorox on Mercury"] (**1948**) and *Atoroxin paluu v. 2948* ["The Return of Atorox in AD2948"] (**1948**). The most remarkable book of the period, however, was Volter Kilpi's *Gulliverin matka Fantomimian mantereelle* ["Gulliver's Travel to the Continent of Fantomimia"] (**1944**), where Gulliver leaves the 18th century for the 20th.

The term "science fiction" itself came to Finland in 1953 with translations of US books, and the 1950s saw growing enthusiasm for sf; the publisher Otava held a competition, "Adventures in the World of Technology", whose winner was Armas J. Pulla with *Lentävä lautanen sieppasi pojat* ["The Boys Were Snatched by a Flying Saucer"] (**1954**), in which antlike Martians intend to invade Earth. Other books of the decade were juvenile adventures. Sf writers of the 1950s, each with several books, include Osmo Ilmari and Antero Harju, and Ralf Parland (who wrote in Swedish).

The 1960s were poor years for Finnish sf. The only notable novel of the period was *Paikka nimeltä Plaston* ["A Place Called Plaston"] (**1968**) by Erkki Ahonen, set on a planet whose devolved inhabitants live in herds, controlled by COMPUTERS. Ahonen's subsequent books, *Tietokonelapsi* ["The Computer Child"] (**1972**), about a human embryo's excised brain interfaced with a computer, and *Syvä matka* ["Deep Voyage"] (**1976**), about the evolution of consciousness on another planet, are Finland's most important sf novels. Further books worth mentioning from the 1970s are: *Viimeinen uutinen* ["The Last News"] (**1970**) by Risto Kavanne, about NEAR-FUTURE power politics; *Rösterna i den sena timmen* ["Voices in the Late Hours"] (**1971**) by Bo Carpelan, about the feelings of people under the threat of nuclear war; and *Aurinkotuuli* ["Wind from the Sun"] (**1975**) by Kullervo Kukkasjärvi (1938-).

The first Finnish sf magazine, *Spin*, began as a FANZINE in 1977. It was followed by *Aikakone* ["Time Machine"] (1981), *Portti* ["The Gate"] (1982), *Tähtivaeltaja* ["Star Wanderer"] (1982) and *Ikaros* (1986). Besides translations, these magazines publish short fiction by Finnish writers, who before had had to be content with occasional publication in mainstream periodicals. *Aikakone* has grown to the point that it singlehandedly supports its own fandom and sf *milieu*, with new young authors appearing.

Recent Finnish sf is represented by *Auruksen tapaus*

["The Case of Aurus"] (**1980**) by Jukka Pakkanen, a vision of the future; *Amos ja saarelaiset* ["Amos and the Island People"] (**1987**) by the well known MAIN-STREAM writer Hannu Salama, telling in a stylistically compact way of the world after a nuclear WAR; *Katajanukke* ["The Juniper Doll"] (**1988**), a first novel by Pekka Virtanen; and *Messias* ["Messiah"] (**1989**) by Kari Nenonen, the story of Christ's cloning from the Shroud of Turin and of the consequences. The anthologies *Jäinen vaeltaja* ["The Ice Wanderer"] (anth **1986**), *Atoroxin perilliset* ["The Heirs of Atorox"] (anth **1988**) and *Tähtipuu* ["Startree"] (anth **1990**) contain mainly short stories by new Finnish writers – among the best of whom are Johanna Sinisalo, Ari Tervonen and Eeva-Liisa Tenhunen – selected from magazines and writing competitions. The annual Finnish award for best short story is the Atorox AWARD.

Tales from Finnish mythology, as collected from legends and ballads to form the epic poem *Kalevala* from 1828 to 1849, have not only nourished Finnish writers – as in Pekka Virtanen's "Kanavat" ["Canals"] (1985), Veikko Rekunen's "Viimeinen laulaja" ["The Last Singer"] (1985) and Ernst Lampén's *Taivaallisia tarinoita* ["Heavenly Stories"] (coll **1918**) – but have also influenced the works of writers abroad, as for example Emil PETAJA's four-novel **Kalevala** sequence – *Saga of Lost Earths* (**1966**), *The Star Mill* (**1966**), *The Stolen Sun* (**1967**) and *Tramontane* (**1967**) – as well as his *The Time Twister* (**1968**) and, by L. Sprague DE CAMP and Fletcher PRATT, *Wall of Serpents* (1953-4; **1960**). [JI]
See also: SCANDINAVIA.

FINLAY, VIRGIL (WARDEN) (1914-1971) US illustrator. VF worked in both colour and black-and-white, but is best known for the latter, where his unique, painstaking stippling gained him fame although, because of the slow process involved, not fortune. Nonetheless he was prolific. His earliest work was an interior illustration for *Weird Tales* in 1935. Though it was in black-and-white interior work that he excelled – several thousand pieces – he also painted many covers, including 16 for *Weird Tales* and 24 for *Famous Fantastic Mysteries*. His work appeared also in *A. Merritt's Fantasy Magazine, Fantastic Novels, Fantastic Story Quarterly* and about 27 other sf/fantasy magazines. He often added sparkling bubbles to his illustrations, partly as a decorative device and partly to modestly conceal parts of naked women. He was stronger in fantasy than sf, excelling (it was a common paradox) in the two extremes of the glamorous and the macabre, both meticulously executed. His early work was more abstractly stylized than the later, and suggested a toughness which later became smoothed under an expert commercial veneer. Possibly the greatest craftsman in the history of sf ILLUSTRATION, VF revolutionized its quality. The HUGO system arrived a little late for VF; though he was nominated 7 times, he won only once, in the very first year, 1953 – the only award ever given for Best Interior Illustration. He had only small success doing book covers, mostly 1949-58, which his style did not

really suit. Sadly, the collapse in SF-MAGAZINE publishing in the mid-1950s – with the surviving magazines being DIGESTS rather than PULP MAGAZINES and so having fewer illustrations – forced VF away from sf as his main market, and through the late 1950s and the 1960s he worked largely on astrological illustrations. Many portfolios and books of his work have been published, the first being *A Portfolio of Illustrations by Virgil Finlay* (coll **1941**) published by *Famous Fantastic Mysteries*. Books include *Virgil Finlay* (**1971**) ed Donald M. GRANT, and *The Book of Virgil Finlay* (**1975**) and *Virgil Finlay Remembered* (**1981**) ed Gerry de la Ree (? -1993), these latter being 2 out of 12 books of and about Finlay's art ed de la Ree. [JG/PN]
See also: COMICS; FANTASY; SEX; SPACESHIPS.

FINN, RALPH L(ESLIE) (1912-) UK novelist and journalist who published widely. Of some sf interest are three novels based on the time theories of J.W. DUNNE: *The Lunatic, the Lover, and the Poet* (**1948**), *Twenty-Seven Stairs* (**1949**) and *Time Marches Sideways* (**1950**), the latter a love story set in London. *Captive on the Flying Saucers* (c**1950**) and *Freaks against Supermen* (c**1951**), both conventional sf stories, gain some interest from their mild erotic content. [JC]
See also: TIME TRAVEL.

FINNEY, CHARLES G(RANDISON) (1905-1984) US newspaperman and writer, based in Arizona, who spent the years 1927-9 with the US infantry in Tientsin, China; an oriental influence pervades most of his work. His novels and stories, though FANTASY rather than sf, have been influential throughout the field, especially his famous *The Circus of Dr Lao* (**1935**), filmed insensitively as *The Seven Faces of Dr Lao* (1963). CGF's work was a strong influence on Ray BRADBURY in particular, as the latter's anthology, *The Circus of Dr Lao and Other Improbable Stories* (anth **1956**), demonstrates. The novel depicts the effect upon a small Arizona town of Dr Lao's circus, which is full of mythical beasts and demigods, all of whom actually live within his tents: they are simultaneously pathetic and awe-inspiring, and the townspeople soon find themselves acquiring unwanted self-knowledge as they confront the caged GODS. The erotic intensity of these confrontations is remarkable. *The Magician out of Manchuria* (**1976** UK), which first appeared as an omnibus under that title (omni **1968**) with *The Unholy City* (**1937**), is set in China, and agreeably lightens the message of Lao. *The Unholy City* itself is a somewhat unwieldy allegory. *The Ghosts of Manacle* (coll **1964**) assembles much of CGF's short fiction. [JC]
Other works: *Past the End of the Pavement* (**1939**), associational.
See also: MYTHOLOGY.

FINNEY, JACK Working name of US author Walter Braden Finney (1911-), whose career began when he was 35; he published his first work in the genre, "Such Interesting Neighbors" for COLLIER'S WEEKLY, in 1951. Although he is as well known for sf as for anything else, he did not specialize in the field, adapting his highly professional skills to mysteries and general fiction as well. Stories from his first years as a writer of sf can be found in *The Third Level* (coll **1957**; vt *The Clock of Time* 1958 UK) and later ones in *I Love Galesburg in the Springtime: Fantasy and Time Stories* (coll **1963**) – both asembled as *About Time: Twelve Stories* (omni **1986**) – and *Forgotten News: The Crime of the Century and Other Lost Stories* (coll **1983**). Many are evocative tales of escape from an ugly present into a tranquil past, or into a PARALLEL WORLD, or wistful variants of the theme when the escape fails. His best-known work is *The Body Snatchers* (**1955**; vt *Invasion of the Body Snatchers* 1973; rev 1978), twice filmed as INVASION OF THE BODY SNATCHERS: in 1956 by Don Siegel and in 1978 by Philip Kaufman. The book – perhaps less plausibly than the film versions – horrifyingly depicts the INVASION of a small town by interstellar spores that duplicate human beings, reducing them to dust in the process. The menacing spore-people who remain symbolize, it has been argued, the loss of freedom in a 1950s USA obsessed by the problems of "conformism". JF's further books were smoothly told, more involving, perhaps less pertinent. *The Woodrow Wilson Dime* (1960 *Saturday Evening Post*; exp **1968**) is a PARALLEL-WORLDS novel. *Time and Again* (**1970**) sets a time traveller in the New York of 1882, which is meticulously evoked. *Marion's Wall* (**1973**) movingly displaces the ghost of a 1926 film star into the present day. Generally, in a JF story, sf or fantasy devices open the door into new worlds and are then forgotten. The worlds thus made available are, all the same, engrossing. [JC]

Other works: Both *The Woodrow Wilson Dime* and *Marion's Wall* appear with *The Night People* (**1977**) in *3 by Finney* (omni **1987**).

See also: TIME TRAVEL; UTOPIAS.

FIREBALL XL5 UK tv series (1962-3). AP Films for ATV/ITC. Created by Gerry and Sylvia ANDERSON; prod Gerry Anderson. Dirs included Alan Pattillo, John Kelly, Bill Harris. Writers included the Andersons, Alan Fennell, Anthony Marriott, Dennis Spooner. 1 full season and 1 part season. 39 25min episodes. B/w.

This was the second of the Andersons' "Super-Marionation" animated-puppet sf series for children, the first being SUPERCAR and the third being STINGRAY; it was the last made in black-and-white and the first to be networked in full in the USA (on NBC). Steve Zodiac is a space pilot, part of World Space Fleet (based in the Pacific Ocean); his spacecraft XL5 patrols other star systems. This is a true SPACE OPERA, in its way a predecessor of STAR TREK. Sidekicks include Venus, a glamorous blonde space doctor, Professor Mat Matic, a Genius, and Robert the Robot. Stories involved, *inter alia*, space pirates, a glass-surfaced planet and Ice Men. Planetary transport was by jetmobile. Derek Meddings's special effects, mostly achieved through use of clever models, are good. [PN]

FIREFOX Film (1982). Warner Bros. Dir Clint Eastwood, starring Eastwood, Freddie Jones, Nigel Hawthorne, Warren Clarke. Screenplay Alex Lasker, Wendell Wellman, based on *Firefox* (**1977**) by Craig THOMAS. 136 mins. Colour.

The sf aspect of the film is a new Russian fighter, the MIG 31 or "Firefox", which can fly at Mach-5 and operates through electronic translation of the pilot's brain patterns (thought control). Eastwood is the US pilot smuggled into the USSR to steal it and fly it out. The movie is split in two, the difficult voyage in disguise to the Soviet air base being tense and well accomplished, the flight back out (with a STAR WARS-style dogfight) merely silly, especially since the much-discussed thought control turns out to have no real plot function at all. The film never even considers that such a raid might precipitate WWIII. [PN]

FIRESTARTER Film (1984). Universal. Dir Mark L. Lester, starring David Keith, Drew Barrymore, Freddie Jones, Heather Locklear, Martin Sheen, George C. Scott. Screenplay Stanley Mann, based on *Firestarter* (**1980**) by Stephen KING. 114 mins. Colour.

The novel is not one of King's best, but it hardly deserved this messy adaptation. A young girl, Charlie (Barrymore), has pyrotic powers and can start fires by mental concentration alone. Naturally, a CIA-like organization ("the Shop") wishes to exploit her powers as a new WEAPON, and just as naturally she incinerates them in a final (rather small) holocaust. Scott plays the evil Native-American assassin who wishes to absorb Charlie's powers. The film is pure CLICHÉ from beginning to end, and not very competent at that level. Far superior in the teenage PSI POWERS line is the very similar *The* FURY (1978) and, of course, CARRIE (1976), both dir Brian De Palma, and the latter also based on a King novel. [PN]

FIRST COMICS ◊ COMICS.

FIRST CONTACT ◊ COMMUNICATIONS.

FIRST FANDOM AWARDS ◊ AWARDS.

FIRST MAN INTO SPACE Film (1958). Amalgamated/MGM. Dir Robert Day, starring Marshall Thompson, Marla Landi, Robert Ayres, Bill Edwards. Screenplay John C. Cooper, Lance Z. Hargreaves, from "Satellite of Blood" by Wyott Ordung. 77 mins. B/w.

This is the second of two sf films made by Amalgamated in the UK that pretend to be set in the USA (the other was FIEND WITHOUT A FACE [1957]). *FMIS* seems to imitate *The* QUATERMASS XPERIMENT (1955; vt *The Creeping Unknown*): a test pilot ejects from his high-flying aeroplane and returns to Earth enveloped in a repulsive, crusty substance that turns him into an inhuman, blood-drinking monster (the blood giving him the oxygen he needs!). As in the **Quatermass** film, there are moments of pathos, but *FMIS* is generally derivative and routine. Released around the time of the first orbital satellites, *FMIS*, with its deceptive title, must have lured audiences expecting something scientific and quasidocumentary; indeed, despite its lurid content, it is soberly and stiffly directed. [JB/PN]

FIRST MEN IN THE MOON Film (1964). Columbia.

Prod Charles H. Schneer. Dir Nathan Juran, starring Edward Judd, Martha Hyer, Lionel Jeffries. Screenplay Nigel KNEALE, Jan Read, from *The First Men in the Moon* (1901) by H.G. WELLS. 107 mins, cut to 103 mins. Colour.

This watered-down version of Wells's classic novel is for the most part low farce, with too much random slaughtering of Selenite aliens, but still contrives to be entertaining. An eccentric Victorian inventor who has developed an ANTIGRAVITY material flies to the Moon in a spherical "spaceship". He and his companions are captured by insect-like Moon people but eventually escape, inadvertently leaving behind cold-germs which destroy the Moon's population. Ray HARRYHAUSEN's Moon creatures are rather good, as are the sets.

A previous version of *FMITM* was made in 1919 by British Gaumont, dir J.V. Leigh. [JB/PN]

FIRTH, N. WESLEY Working name of UK writer Norman Firth (1920-1949), who began his career during WWII writing pulp Westerns and thrillers. He wrote stories variously as Rice Ackman, Earl Ellison, Leslie Halward and perhaps other names; his first sf publication remains untraced. His first novel, *Terror Strikes* (1946 chap), is of some interest through its extremely close resemblance to H.G. WELLS's *The Invisible Man* (1897). *Spawn of the Vampire* (1946 chap) is a hastily concocted horror tale. NF was a writer of potential worth, but died (of TB) at the age of 29 before proving it. [SH]

FISCHER, LEONARD (? -) Canadian writer whose *Let Out the Beast* (1950) is a post-HOLOCAUST-reversion-to-savagery book in which it is the protagonist who – unusually – becomes the feared enemy of those engaged in trying to rebuild civilization. [JC]

FISH, LEONARD G. (? -) UK author of some short fiction under his own name and as by David Campbell, and of several minor sf adventures: *Planet War* (1952) as by Fysh, *After the Atom* (1953) as by Victor LA SALLE, and *Beyond the Solar System* (1954) as by Claude Haley. [SH]

FISHER, JAMES P. (? -) US writer whose sf novel *The Great Brain Robbery* (1970) is a rather lightweight adventure in which an ALIEN tries to steal a student's unusual brain. [JC]

FISHER, LOU (1940-) US writer. After spending 20 years writing IBM computer manuals, he began publishing sf with "Triggerman" for *Gal* in 1973. His first novel, *Sunstop 8* (1978), is a SPACE OPERA; his second, *The Blue Ice Pilot* (1986), features a space war made possible by developments in CRYONICS. [JC]

FISHER, VARDIS (ALVERO) (1895-1968) US writer, raised in a Mormon family; his best-known single novel, *Children of God* (1939), is about the Mormons. His **Testament of Man** sequence covers the whole of human history, extending into many volumes the basic strategy which shapes several novels by F. Britten AUSTIN, the 6 vols of Johannes V. JENSEN's *The Long Journey* (1922-4) and other early-20th-century celebrations of the drama of EVOLUTION. Of sf interest in the **Testament** are the first 5 titles, which deal with prehistory: *Darkness and the Deep* (1943), *The Golden Rooms* (1944), *Intimations of Eve* (1946), *Adam and the Serpent* (1947) and *The Divine Passion* (1948), which comprise a formidable attempt at sustained anthropological sf. [JC]

See also: ADAM AND EVE; ORIGIN OF MAN.

FISK, NICHOLAS Pseudonym of UK author David Higginbottom (1923-), who writes exclusively for children. His first sf tale was *Space Hostages* (1967), in which his tastes for HARD-SF backgrounds and realistically flawed protagonists were competently expressed. The former reaches full expression in tales like *Trillions* (1971) and *Antigrav* (1978). *A Rag, a Bone, and a Hank of Hair* (1980), on the other hand, gravely and movingly concentrates on its emotionally torn protagonist, a young genius in an arid far-future DYSTOPIA commanded to observe a small family of reconstructed "primitives", who have been drugged into repeating the same fake 1940 day over and over again, so that he may garner experimental data about raw humans. In the end, both family and protagonist are killed by the masters of the terrible world. NF is a smooth writer, but the world he envisages – as demonstrated in *A Hole in the Head* (1991), a harrowing tale of the Earth at the brink of ecological catastrophe – is fraught. [JC]

Other works: *Grinny* (1973); *High Way Home* (1973); *Little Green Spacemen* (1974 chap); *The Witches of Wimmering* (1976); *Wheelie in the Stars* (1976 chap); *Time Trap* (1976); *Escape from Splatterbang* (1978 chap; vt *Flamers* 1979 chap); *Monster Maker* (1979); the **Starstormers** sequence, comprising *Starstormers* (1980), *Sunburst* (1980), *Catfang* (1981), *Evil Eye* (1982) and *Volcano* (1983); *Robot Revolt* (1981); *Sweets from a Stranger* (coll 1982); *On the Flip Side* (1983); *You Remember Me!* (1984); *Dark Sun, Bright Sun* (1986); *Living Fire* (coll 1987); *Mindbenders* (1987); *Backlash* (1988); *The Talking Car* (1988 chap); *The Telly is Watching You* (1989); *The Worm Charmers* (1989); *The Back-Yard War* (1990 chap); *The Model Village* (1990); *Extraterrestrial Tales* (omni 1991) assembling *Space Hostages*, *Trillions* and *On the Flip Side*; *Pig Ignorant* (1991).

See also: CHILDREN'S SF; RADIO.

FISKE, TARLETON [s] ◊ Robert BLOCH.

FITZGERALD, HUGH ◊ L. Frank BAUM.

FITZGERALD, WILLIAM [s] ◊ Murray LEINSTER.

FITZGIBBON, (ROBERT LOUIS) CONSTANTINE (LEE-DILLON) (1919-1983) US writer of politically oriented fiction and other works who became a naturalized Irish citizen. His first sf novel, *The Iron Hoop* (1949), describes an occupied city in WWIII. *When the Kissing Had to Stop* (1960) depicts in Anglophobe terms the self-destruction of a UK dominated by a Communist-inspired government. Less known but more remarkable, *The Golden Age* (1975) treats the post-HOLOCAUST recuperation of the UK in terms of the myth of Orpheus. [JC]

Other works: *The Rat Report* (1980).

FITZ-GIBBON, RALPH EDGERTON (c1904-) US writer, long active as a journalist. His sf novel, *The Man with Two Bodies* (**1952**), offers parapsychological explanations for the mysteries suggested by the title. [JC]

FIVE Film (1951). Columbia. Prod, written, dir Arch Oboler, starring Susan Douglas, William Phipps, James Anderson, Charles Lampkin, Earl Lee. 93 mins, cut to 89 mins (UK). B/w.

The first "after the bomb" film, *F* concerns five US survivors – a mountaineer, a pregnant girl, a token Black, a cashier and an adventurer. This is a gloomy art film with low-budget, grainy photography, a scientifically bogus explanation for the five's survival, much talking, a racial murder and two deaths from radiation, but the theme itself retains some power. Oboler had worked extensively in radio before entering the film industry in 1945 with *Strange Holiday* and *Bewitched*, both based on his own radio plays. *F* is basically a sermon against the prejudices and insanities that may lead to atomic war. [JB/PN]

FIVE MILLION YEARS TO EARTH ◊ QUATERMASS AND THE PIT.

FIXUP A term first used by A.E. VAN VOGT to describe a book made up of previously published stories fitted together – usually with the addition of newly written or published cementing material – so that they read as a novel. Aware that fixups are immensely more common in GENRE SF than in any other literature in the world, we borrowed the term for the 1979 edition of this encyclopedia, and continue to use it now; an example is van Vogt's own *The War Against the Rull* (fixup **1959**). We do, however, recognize that it is not always an easy description to apply with accuracy. It is, for instance, sometimes impossible to know whether or not a series of connected stories may have been extracted from an already-written book, which for some would make it impossible to describe that book as a fixup; some readers and authors, in other words, feel that the term can be applied only to novels assembled from previously existing work.

We disagree. A book which is written *so as* to be broken up for prior magazine publication may well, in our view, constitute a perfectly legitimate example of the form, though we do recognize that when we call such a text a fixup we are making a critical judgment as to the internal nature – the *feel* – of that text. We should perhaps emphasize, therefore, that the term is not, for us, derogatory. In fact, the fixup form may arguably be ideal for tales of epic sweep through time and space. It is perhaps no accident that Robert A HEINLEIN's seminal GENERATION-STARSHIP tale, "Universe" (1941), ultimately became part of *Orphans of the Sky* (fixup **1963** UK). [JC]

FLAGG, FRANCIS Pseudonym of US writer George Henry Weiss (?1898-1946), who appeared in *Weird Tales* and then began publishing sf with "The Machine Man of Ardathia" for *AMZ* in 1927. He published 20 or so typical pulp-sf stories over the next decade, some of his later work being in collaboration

with Forrest J. ACKERMAN. He was a comparatively careful writer. In his posthumously published sf tale, *The Night People* (**1947** chap), an escaped convict takes a drug-induced trip to another planet. [JC]

See also: ASTOUNDING SCIENCE-FICTION; CANADA.

FLAMMARION, (NICHOLAS) CAMILLE (1842-1925) French astronomer and writer. One of the first major popularizers of ASTRONOMY, he took great delight in the flights of imagination to which his studies in COSMOLOGY inspired him. In 1858, the year he entered the Paris Observatory as a student, he wrote an unpublished scientific romance, «Voyage extatique aux régions lunaires, correspondence d'un philosophe adolescent». His two major fascinations were the possibilities of LIFE ON OTHER WORLDS and of life after death, and these interests are reflected by his earliest major works: *La pluralité des mondes habités* ["The Plurality of Inhabited Worlds"] (**1862**) and *Les habitants de l'autre monde* ["The Inhabitants of the Other World"] (**1862**), the latter being "revelations" transmitted by the medium Mlle Huet. His most important work in the popularization of science was *Astronomie populaire* (**1880**; trans as *Popular Astronomy* **1894**). He dramatized ideas from his earlier nonfiction book *Les mondes imaginaires et les mondes réels* (**1864**; trans as *Real and Imaginary Worlds* **1865** US) in three of his *Récits de l'infini* (coll **1872**; trans S.R. Crocker as *Stories of Infinity* **1874** US): "The History of a Comet", "Lumen" and "In Infinity". The second, consisting of a series of dialogues between a man and a disembodied spirit which is free to roam the Universe at will, includes observations about the implications of the finite velocity of light and many images of otherworldly life adapted to ALIEN circumstances. These stories were revised and expanded for separate publication as *Lumen* (**1887**; trans A.M. and R.M., with some new material, **1897** US). Notions taken from these dialogues were embodied in the REINCARNATION romances *Stella* (**1877** France) and *Uranie* (**1889**; trans Mary Serrano as *Uranie* **1890** US; new trans Augusta Rice Stetson as *Urania* **1891** US). CF's boldest SCIENTIFIC ROMANCE, however, is *La fin du monde* (**1893-4**; trans anon as *Omega: The Last Days of the World* **1897** US), an epic of the future. Although it is as much essay as story, this is a notable work, akin to H.G. WELLS's *The Time Machine* (**1895**) and William Hope HODGSON's *The House on the Borderland* (**1908**) in presenting a striking vision of the END OF THE WORLD. CF's scientific reputation was injured by his passionate interest in Spiritualism (in later life he was an intimate of Arthur Conan DOYLE), but his was a major contribution to the popularization of science and to the literature of the scientific imagination. [BS]

See also: ESCHATOLOGY; EVOLUTION; FAR FUTURE; FASTER THAN LIGHT; FRANCE; HISTORY OF SF; MARS; RELIGION; STARS; SUN.

FLASH GORDON 1. US COMIC strip created by artist Alex RAYMOND for King Features Syndicate. *FG* appeared in 1934, at first in Sunday, later in daily newspapers. Its elaborately shaded style and exotic storyline made it one of the most influential sf strips. It was taken over in 1944 by Austin Briggs, then in 1948 by Mac Raboy, and since then has been drawn by Dan Barry (with contributions from artists Harvey Kurtzman and Wally WOOD and writer Harry HARRISON) and Al Williamson, and more recently written by Bruce Jones and illustrated by Gray MORROW. Various episodes have been released in comic-book form – including a 9-part series from DC COMICS written and drawn by Dan Jurgens (1988) – and also in book form. It continues today.

The scenario of FG is archetypal SPACE OPERA. Most episodes feature Flash locked in combat with the villain, Ming the Merciless of the planet Mongo. Flash's perpetual fiancée, Dale Arden, and the mad SCIENTIST Hans Zarkov play prominent roles. (In later episodes Zarkov's craziness was played down and he became a straightforward sidekick to Flash.) The décor shifts between the futuristic (DEATH RAYS, rocketships) and the archaic (dinosaurs, jungles, swordplay) with a fine contempt for plausibility, rather in the manner of Edgar Rice BURROUGHS's romances. Although begun quite cynically in conscious opposition to the earlier BUCK ROGERS IN THE 25TH CENTURY, FG quickly developed its own individuality, emphasizing a romantic baroque against the cool technological classicism of its predecessor, to which it is artistically very much superior.

The strip was widely syndicated in Europe. When, during WWII, the arrival of various episodes was delayed, the strip was often written and drawn by Europeans. One such writer was Federico Fellini (1920-   ).

The FG comic strip has had many repercussions in other media. It led to a popular radio serial, to a short-lived pulp magazine (FLASH GORDON STRANGE ADVENTURE MAGAZINE), and in the late 1930s to several film serials starring Buster Crabbe; later came a tv series and a film (see below). A full-length film parody, FLESH GORDON, appeared in 1974.

An early FG novel was *Flash Gordon in the Caverns of Mongo* (**1937**) by Raymond. A paperback series of five FG short novels, based on the original strips, with Alex Raymond credited, consisted of *Flash Gordon 1: The Lion Men of Mongo* * (**1974**), *Flash Gordon 2: The Plague of Sound* * (**1974**), *Flash Gordon 3: The Space Circus* * (**1974**), *Flash Gordon 4: The Time Trap of Ming XIII* * (**1974**) and *Flash Gordon 5: The Witch Queen of Mongo* * (**1974**). The first four were "adapted by Con Steffanson", a house name; #1-#3 were the work of Ron GOULART; #4 was by Carter BINGHAM and #5, also by Bingham, was published under his name.

2. Serial film. 13 2-reel episodes (1936). Universal. Dir Frederick Stephani, starring Buster Crabbe, Jean Rogers, Charles Middleton, Frank Shannon, Priscilla Lawson. Screenplay Stephani, George Plympton, Basil Dickey, Ella O'Neill, based on the comic strip. B/w.

The film FG was the nearest thing to PULP-MAGAZINE space opera to appear on the screen during the 1930s.

Flash, Dale and Zarkov go to the planet Mongo in Zarkov's backyard-built spaceship to find the cause of an outbreak of volcanic activity on Earth. Ming the Merciless (a wonderfully hammy performance from Middleton) is behind it all and plans to invade Earth. Our heroes spend the next 12 episodes surviving various exotic hazards before outwitting Ming in the final reel. Though more lavish than the average serial (the budget was a record $350,000), FG has the cheap appearance of most: unconvincing special effects, sets and costumes borrowed from a variety of other films, and plenty of stock footage. However, it remains great fun, romantic and fantastical. Ill edited versions of the first and second halves were released theatrically as *Spaceship to the Unknown* (1936) (97 mins) and *Perils from the Planet Mongo* (1936) (91 mins).

The follow-up was *Flash Gordon's Trip to Mars* (1938), dirs Ford Beebe, Robert F. Hill, with the same leading actors – Ming is back again – and Beatrice Roberts as the evil queen who turns humans to "clay people". The setting was changed from Mongo to Mars after the success of Orson Welles's 1938 RADIO adaptation of *The* WAR OF THE WORLDS. 15 two-reel episodes. Screenplay Ray Trampe, Norman S. Hall, Wyndham Gittens, Herbert Dolmas. The 99min edited-down version was *The Deadly Ray from Mars* (1938).

The final FG movie serial was *Flash Gordon Conquers the Universe* (1940), dir Ford Beebe, Ray Taylor, with the same leading actors except that Carol Hughes replaced Jean Rogers as Dale Arden. 12 two-reel episodes. Screenplay George H. Plympton, Basil Dickey, Barry Shipman. This, the weakest of the three, kills off Ming (again) at the end. The 87min edited-down version was *Purple Death From Outer Space* (1940).

The three FG film serials continue to have a cult following and are regularly revived on tv and in the cinema.

3. US tv series (1951) from DuMont, starring Steve Holland. It was low-budget and universally execrated, lasting only one season.

4. Film (1980). Columbia/EMI/Warner. Prod Dino De Laurentiis. Dir Michael Hodges, starring Sam J. Jones, Melody Anderson, Topol, Max Von Sydow, Brian Blessed, Timothy Dalton. Screenplay Lorenzo Semple Jr, based on the early episodes of the comic strip by Raymond. 115 mins. Colour.

As a producer, De Laurentiis has always had a weakness for over-the-top, fantastic parodies (sometimes successful, as in DIABOLIK [1967] and BARBARELLA [1967]) but here his instincts let him down badly. Apart from the fetishistic costumes (leather, spikes, etc.) there is little of interest in this tongue-in-cheek, lurid fantasy, which tries to make a comic-strip virtue of wooden acting. The plot is largely derived from the 1936 film serial, and the rushed special effects similarly recall the ludicrousness of that film. The romantic elements are subjugated to a rather listless kinkiness. [PN/JB]

See also: CINEMA.

FLASH GORDON CONQUERS THE UNIVERSE ◊ FLASH GORDON.

FLASH GORDON STRANGE ADVENTURE MAGA-ZINE US BEDSHEET-size PULP MAGAZINE. 1 issue, Dec 1936, published by C.J.H. Publications; ed Harold HERSEY. The featured novel was "The Master of Mars" by James E. Northfield. *FGSAM*, intended to be a monthly juvenile magazine, was notable for its coloured interior illustrations in a comic-strip format. A failed attempt to cash in on the popularity of the comic strip FLASH GORDON, its sole issue is now a rare collector's item. [FHP/MJE]

FLASH GORDON'S TRIP TO MARS ◊ FLASH GORDON.

FLECKER, (HERMAN) JAMES ELROY (1884-1915) UK poet, playwright and novelist best known for *Hassan* (**1922**), a fantasy play with an Arabian Nights flavour. His only novel, *The King of Alsander* (**1914**), was also a fantasy. He is of sf interest for *The Last Generation: A Story of the Future* (**1908** chap), whose narrator is spirited into times moderately close to the present where he witnesses the self-willed extinction of the human race through a refusal to breed more children into this vale of tears. He is then taken much further forward, where he discovers that apes (see APES AND CAVEMEN) are destined to become the masters of the planet and "try again". This tale was later collected along with some fantasies in *Collected Prose* (coll **1920**). [JC]

See also: END OF THE WORLD.

FLEHR, PAUL [s] ◊ Frederik POHL.

FLEMING, HARRY ◊ William Henry Fleming BIRD.

FLEMING, IAN (LANCASTER) (1908-1964) UK writer, brother of Peter FLEMING. Neither the use of advanced technological gadgetry nor the fantastic plots of his enormously successful **James Bond** sequence of thrillers makes them genuine sf. The closest any of them comes to an sf plot is *Moonraker* (**1955**), whose eponymous rocket is rather ahead of its time. Many of IF's novels have been filmed, usually with additional sf-like gadgetry and completely reworked plots. The first of these films were DR NO (1962); YOU ONLY LIVE TWICE (1967) featured Bond crushing an attempt at world domination which involved the kidnapping of orbital satellites. MOON-RAKER (1979) involves an orbital satellite and the Space Shuttle. [JC/PN]

See also: ISLANDS; TECHNOTHRILLER; VILLAINS.

FLEMING, (ROBERT) PETER (1907-1971) UK travel writer and novelist, brother of Ian FLEMING. He is known mainly for such travel books as *Brazilian Adventure* (**1933**). In his spoof sf novel, *The Flying Visit* (**1940**), Adolf Hitler parachutes into the UK with amusing results. The tale was reprinted, along with a fantasy, "The Man with Two Hands", in *With the Guards to Mexico! and Other Excursions* (coll **1957**). *The Sixth Column: A Singular Tale of our Time* (**1951**), a satirical political thriller set in an implied NEAR FUTURE, verges on sf. [JC]

Other works: Some of the tales in *A Story to Tell* (coll **1942**) are fantasies; *Invasion 1940* (**1957**; vt *Operation Sea Lion* 1957 US), a nonfiction study of German preparations to invade the UK, speculatively presents a successful assault (◊ HITLER WINS).

FLEMING, STUART [s] ◊ Damon KNIGHT.

FLESCH, HANS [r] ◊ GERMANY.

FLESH FOR FRANKENSTEIN ◊ FRANKENSTEIN.

FLESH GORDON Film (1974). Mammoth/Graffiti. Dir Michael Benveniste, Howard Ziehm, starring Jason Williams, Suzanne Fields, John Hoyt. Screenplay Benveniste, William Hunt. 90 mins, cut to 84 mins, cut to 78 mins. Colour.

This burlesque of FLASH GORDON began as a cheap soft-porn film, but became relatively expensive as the special effects became more elaborate. Work on it continued for nearly two years and many special-effects technicians were involved, some uncredited; they included Jim Danforth, Dave Allen, Rick Baker, Greg Jein, George Barr and Dennis Muren. Several of the effects sequences include model animation of a high standard, in particular the climax, when a monster, the Great God Porno, clutching the heroine, scales a building in the manner of KING KONG while muttering a series of surly asides. A duel with an animated insect-creature rivals the best of Ray HARRY-HAUSEN's work. The makers were so pleased with the effects that they cleaned it up a bit, and it was released without the feared X-rating. Most of the jokes are variants on the undergraduate ploy of inserting sexual references – e.g., there is a penis-aurus – into a context that was originally downright puritanical. [JB]

FLETCHER, GEORGE U. ◊ Fletcher PRATT.

FLETCHER, JOSEPH SMITH (1863-1935) UK writer of popular fiction, much of it for boys. *The Wonderful City* (**1894**), for instance, carries its youthful protagonist to a doomed lost race (◊ LOST WORLDS) in Central America. *Morrison's Machine* (**1900**), an adult tale, analyses the relationship of scientific Man to the MACHINES he was creating at the turn of the century (◊ SCIENTISTS). *The Three Days' Terror* (**1901**), like *The Ransom for London* (**1914**), deals with NEAR-FUTURE threats to the stability of the UK. [JC]

Other works: *The Air-Ship, and Other Stories* (coll **1903**); *The Wheatstack, and Other Stories* (coll **1909**); *Many Engagements* (coll **1923**); *The Matheson Formula* (**1929** US); *The House in Tuesday Market* (**1930**); *The Man in No. 3, and Other Stories of Crime, Love and Mystery* (coll **1931**).

FLIGHT OF THE NAVIGATOR Film (1986). Producers Sales/New Star Entertainment/Walt Disney. Dir Randal Kleiser, starring Joey Cramer, Veronica Cartwright, Cliff De Young, Howard Hesseman, Paul Mall. Screenplay Michael Burton, Matt MacManus, based on a story by Mark H. Baker. 89 mins. Colour.

Made for children, this might – one would think – be rather disturbing for them. A 12-year-old (Cramer) returns home after a fall and finds the wrong people living there. The police take him to where his family now live, where he learns that it is eight years later, that he has been missing, presumed dead, and that his kid brother has become his post-pubertal big brother. Tests reveal that our hero has strange brainwaves, some of which are read by a computer as a picture of a flying saucer, just like one that has recently been found but has proved unopenable. The boy locates the saucer and meets inside it the robotic alien Max (Mall), who clearly recognizes him, addressing him as The Navigator, an aspect of his recent past which is news to him, since he lost his memory after the saucer's crashlanding. Because he has been travelling at FASTER-THAN-LIGHT speeds to the alien's planet and back, the boy has not grown noticeably older. Unhappy at his role in this unnerving future, he persuades Max to return him (normality comfortingly restored) back through time to 1978. This film presents what is actually rather a nightmare scenario, and carries it off with considerable aplomb for the first half; but it sinks quickly into routine post-E.T.: THE EXTRATERRESTRIAL scenes once the flying saucer and alien have been introduced. [PN]

FLIGHT UNLIMITED ◊ SHAYOL.

FLINT, HOMER EON (1892-1924) US writer (born Flindt) whose work appeared mainly in the Frank A. MUNSEY magazines from the teens of the century. His first sf story was "The Planeteer" for *All-Story Weekly* in 1918; it deals with sexual rivalry and personal ambition in a Bellamistic (◊ Edward BELLAMY) society. Its sequel, "The King of Conserve Island" (1918), describes the corruption and collapse of the socialist world under the propaganda attacks of a reactionary, capitalist society. The **Dr Kinney** stories examine the implications of various political ideas: "The Lord of Death" (1919) describes the ultimate Spencerian survival of the fittest on MERCURY; "The Queen of Life" (1919) is based on the opposite point of view, preservation of life for its own sake and Malthusianism on a VENUS characterized by superscience; "The Devolutionist" (1921) covers the ambivalences of an efficient, more or less benevolent dictatorship and a bumblingly anarchistic or democratic underground; and the final story, "The Emancipatrix" (1921), contrasts a hive world and primitive humans on a ring-shaped planet. In the last two stories, the alien contact takes place by means of an apparatus acquired from Venus. HEF's writing style and PULP-MAGAZINE habits did not always adequately express his deep interest in the emergence of behavioural and historical patterns from various political and social philosophies. The series was much later assembled as *The Devolutionist and The Emancipatrix* (1921 *Argosy*; coll of linked stories **1965**) and *The Lord of Death and The Queen of Life* (1919 *All-Story Weekly*; coll of linked stories **1965**).

HEF is remembered in part for the mystery of his death (having picked up a hitchhiker – who turned out to have had a criminal record – he was found dead in his crashed car) and rather more for his sf novel with Austin HALL (*whom see for details*), *The Blind*

Spot (1921 *Argosy*; **1951**). However, the **Dr Kinney** stories are his real legacy. [EFB/JC]

See also: HISTORY OF SF; PARALLEL WORLDS; PLANETARY ROMANCE.

FLIPSIDE OF DOMINICK HIDE, THE Made-for-tv film (1980). BBC TV. Dir Alan Gibson, starring Peter Firth, Caroline Langrishe, Pippa Guard, Patrick Magee. Teleplay Gibson, Jeremy Paul. 95 mins. Colour.

This was an unexpected success, winning several awards. Hide (Firth) travels back in a flying saucer (◊ UFOS) from the somewhat austere AD2130 to contemporary London to do historical research. A Candide-figure, he is confused but cheerful about what he finds, falls in love, and (of course) becomes his own great-great-great-grandfather. This film is unusual in not being pessimistic about modern life, and uses its future perspective cleverly to provide a sort of instant nostalgia for the present day. The sequel, *Another Flip for Dominick* (1982), 85 mins, made by and starring the same people, has Hide revisiting the past in search of a missing colleague; it is less memorable. [PN]

FLUTE, MOLLY ◊ Eileen LOTTMAN.

FLY, THE 1. Film (1958). 20th Century-Fox. Dir Kurt Neumann, starring Al (David) Hedison, Patricia Owens, Vincent Price. Screenplay James Clavell, based on "The Fly" (1957) by George LANGELAAN. 94 mins. Colour.

A scientist experimenting with MATTER TRANSMISSION accidentally gets mixed with a fly and ends up with its head and arm (or leg). He has retained his own brain, however, and with the help of his wife tries to reverse the procedure. But the complementarily deformed fly refuses to be caught, and the scientist is driven to commit suicide by putting his head in a steam press. The final sequence shows the fly, with tiny scientist's head and arm, trapped in a spider's web and screaming "Help me!" (which makes one wonder where the fly's brain ended up). An absurd film whose ludicrous excesses are amusing, and lavishly produced for a horror/MONSTER movie, it was a financial success and spawned two low-budget sequels, RETURN OF THE FLY (1959) and CURSE OF THE FLY (1965). [JB]

2. Film (1986). Brooksfilms/20th Century-Fox. Dir David CRONENBERG, starring Jeff Goldblum, Geena Davis, John Getz. Screenplay Charles Edward Pogue, Cronenberg, based on the Langelaan story. 100 mins, cut to 96 mins. Colour.

This blackly comic remake is radically more sophisticated and more horrific than its original. In this version the (this time unmarried) scientist's accident leads to a melding of genetic material, and his transformation into fly is gradual and protracted. With it comes a sexual and creative potency and a capacity for destruction hitherto only latent in the idealistic, repressed Seth Brundle, movingly acted by Goldblum. As usual Cronenberg confronts the vulnerable and ephemeral nature of the human body by imagining it metamorphosed; where other people use words to create metaphor, Cronenberg uses the flesh, ambiguously evoking exultation and disgust, the grotesque and the beautiful. [PN]

See also: CINEMA; SEX.

FLY II, THE Film (1989). Brooksfilms/20th Century-Fox. Dir Chris Walas, starring Eric Stoltz, Daphne Zuniga, Lee Richardson. Screenplay Mick Garris, Jim Wheat, Ken Wheat, Frank Darabont, based on a story by Garris. 104 mins. Colour.

This is a genuine sequel to the 1986 remake of *The* FLY, not just a lame excuse for more horrific "fly" effects. Chris Walas, the skilled technician who created those effects for the earlier film, here made his directorial début, and surprised many by doing so assured a job of it. Seth Brundle's girlfriend, made pregnant by him in the previous film, dies after giving birth to a "monster"; beneath the larva-like casing is an apparently normal baby. At age 5, however, the child has a near-adult appearance and superintelligence. His adoptive father, head of Bartok Industries, is secretly determined to exploit both Brundle's son and his MATTER-TRANSMISSION device, realizing that the genetic melding the device allows gives him a handle for controlling "the form and function of all life". The subtext is more reassuring than in CRONENBERG's earlier film, and *TFII* becomes a retelling of *Beauty and the Beast*, with a crude but satisfying comeuppance for Bartok at the end. Though Cronenberg is the one popularly supposed to show disgust for the flesh, it is Walas whose more conventional affection for normality has the effect of reducing the son's metamorphosis to a mere occasion for horror. This deeply conservative film is less subtle than its predecessor, though it has interesting Freudian reverberations, and many people will prefer Walas's emphasis on the corruption of an external agency (Industry) to Cronenberg's emphasis on the tragic divisions of the Self. [PN]

See also: CINEMA; MONSTER MOVIES.

FLYING SAUCERS ◊ UFOS.

FLYING SAUCERS FROM OTHER WORLDS ◊ OTHER WORLDS.

FLYNN, MICHAEL F(RANCIS) (1947-   ) US writer who began publishing sf with "Slan Libh" in *ASF* in 1984, and who soon became identified as one of the most sophisticated and stylistically acute 1980s *Analog* regulars, some of his work appearing as by Rowland Shew. His first novel, *In the Country of the Blind* (1990), is an alternate-history thriller based on the premise that Charles BABBAGE's early-19th-century COMPUTER did in fact work, and is being used by a secret society to predict (and therefore to control) events. A 20th-century woman hacker discovers the conspiracy and exposes its databases by use of a computer worm. Babbage's computer, by coincidence, features similarly in *The Difference Engine* (1990 UK) by William GIBSON and Bruce STERLING. MFF's second novel was *Fallen Angels* (1991) with Larry NIVEN (*whom see for details*) and Jerry POURNELLE. His third, *The Nanotech Chronicles* (1991), presents, with all MFF's engagingly

lurid competence, a tale which exploits current speculations about the future of molecular engineering. MFF is on the verge of becoming a central creator of HARD SF. [JC]

See also: ASTOUNDING SCIENCE-FICTION; MACHINES; STEAMPUNK.

FÖLDES, PÉTER [r] ◊ HUNGARY.

FOLINGSBY, KENNETH A possible pseudonym of a probable Scotsman whose *Meda: A Tale of the Future* (1891), though the events it recounts turn out to be a dream, remains of interest for the imaginative scope of the AD5575 depicted, in which large-headed brainy "Scotonians" are fed by ambient electricity, possess ANTIGRAVITY, and represent the end of a long (and detailed) world-history, including a comet HOLOCAUST. The protagonist begins to have erotic longings, and awakens. [JC]

FOLLETT, JAMES (1939-   ) UK writer of fiction and technical material; most of his sf work has been for BBC TV or BBC RADIO. His sf work, which is not remarkable, includes: *The Doomsday Ultimatum* (1976); *Ice* (1978); *Earth Search* (1981), based on his BBC radio serial; *Torus* (1990); *Trojan* (1991), about a computer virus from Mars. [JC]

FOLLETT, KEN Working name of UK writer Kenneth Martin Follett (1949-   ), most famous for thrillers like *Storm Island* (1978; vt *The Eye of the Needle* 1978 US), but who, under pseudonyms, has also written some sf. *The Power Twins and the Worm Puzzle: A Science Fantasy for Young People* (1976) as by Martin Martinsen was a juvenile; *Amok: King of Legend* (1976) as by Bernard L. Ross was marginal fantasy; *Capricorn One* * (1978) as by Ross was one of two novelizations – the other being by Ron GOULART – of the film CAPRICORN ONE (1978). [JC]

FONTANA, D(OROTHY) C(ATHERINE) (1939-   ) US writer, primarily for tv; she was associated with STAR TREK as its story editor, eventually writing *Vulcan's Glory* * (1989) for the series of novelizations. She was later involved with the two tv series *The* FANTASTIC JOURNEY and LOGAN'S RUN. *The Questor Tapes* * (1974) is based on a series pilot written by Gene RODDENBERRY and Gene L. Coon, who created *Star Trek*, and released as *The* QUESTOR TAPES. It tells of the creation of an ANDROID who eventually plans to combat evil in secret. The pilot did not lead to a series. DCF has written a number of tv episodes in addition to her work as a story editor. [JC]

See also: WAR OF THE WORLDS.

FONTENAY, CHARLES L(OUIS) (1917-   ) US newspaperman and writer, born in Brazil and raised in Tennessee, spending his life there. He was a member of the *If* stable from the publication of his first story, "Disqualified", in 1954, and wrote three somewhat routine sf novels: *Twice Upon a Time* (1958 dos), *Rebels of the Red Planet* (1961 dos), an intrigue set on Mars, and *The Day the Oceans Overflowed* (1964), in which the manner of their doing so is scientifically ill motivated. CLF is no longer active in the field. *Epistle to the Babylonians* (1969), nonfiction, deals in part with the philosophy of science.   [JC]

FONTENELLE, BERNARD LE BOVYER DE (1657-1757) French man of letters whose work pointed forward to the Age of Reason; nephew of the dramatist Corneille. He wrote much, and one of his most important books became a seminal influence on PROTO SCIENCE FICTION: *Entretiens sur la pluralité des mondes habités* (**1686**; trans J. Glanvill as *The Plurality of Worlds* **1929**). This is one of the earliest works ever written popularizing science, notably ASTRONOMY, for the layman, which it does by wittily presenting its speculations – many about the possibility of LIFE ON OTHER WORLDS – in the form of conversations after dinner between the author and a marquise. In 1697 he became permanent secretary of the the Académie des Sciences, a post he held for 44 years.   [PN]

See also: COSMOLOGY; FRANCE; STARS; VENUS.

FOOD OF THE GODS Film (1976). AIP. Prod and dir Bert I. Gordon, starring Marjoe Gortner, Pamela Franklin, Ralph Meeker, Ida Lupino. Screenplay Gordon, based on a "portion" of *The Food of the Gods and How it Came to Earth* (**1904**) by H.G. WELLS. 88 mins. Colour.

Set on an island off the coast of British Columbia, *FOTG* tells of a miraculous foodstuff which oozes from the ground and causes gigantism in all infant creatures that eat it (◊ GREAT AND SMALL). Animated wasps, plastic caterpillars and out-of-focus chickens (all huge) are wholly unconvincing, but the giant rats (ordinary rats shot in miniature sets) are marginally plausible – which is more than can be said for most of the actors and all of the script, though Meeker is effectively creepy as the wicked industrialist out to exploit the Food. Nothing of the Wells novel survives in this rat-drowning epic, which purports to be a revenge-of-Nature film – like so many from its ECOLOGY-conscious period.   [PN]

FORBES, ALEXANDER (1882-?   ) US writer whose sf novel, *The Radio Gunner* (**1924**), depicts a future WAR set in 1937 between Northern Europe, in alliance with the USA, and the Constantinople Coalition. AF's predictive powers were poor and his eponymous hero, who knows how to locate radios, fails to enthrall.   [JC]

FORBIDDEN PLANET Film (1956). MGM. Dir Fred McLeod Wilcox, starring Walter Pidgeon, Anne Francis, Leslie Nielsen, Warren Stevens. Screenplay Cyril Hume, based on a story by Irving Block and Allen ADLER. 98 mins. Colour.

Although Wilcox was new to sf cinema (his best-known film was *Lassie Come Home*, [1943]), *FP* is one of the most attractive movies in the genre. Some of the more interesting resonances of *FP* stem from its being an updated version of Shakespeare's *The Tempest* (c1611). Prospero is Morbius, an obsessive scientist living alone with his daughter Altaira (the virginal Miranda figure) on the planet Altair IV. Ariel is a charming metal creature, Robby the Robot (who became so popular – the first ROBOT star since METROPOLIS – that another film, *The* INVISIBLE BOY

[1957], was made as a special vehicle for him). The film opens with a spaceship landing to investigate the fate of a colony whose sole survivors are Morbius and Altaira. The crew is menaced by an invisible Caliban, which proves to be a "Monster from the Id" and eventually destroys its unwitting creator, Morbius; holocaust follows. Altaira is saved.

The plot, mixing the tawdry and the potent, is very sophisticated for the time – astonishingly so for a film originally designed for a juvenile audience, especially in the intimations of incestuous feelings of the father for the daughter. The dialogue is slick and unmemorable. The best sequences involve a tour of the still-functioning artefacts, spectacular and mysterious, dwarfing the humans passing among them, of an awesomely powerful vanished race, the Krel. The visual treatment of *FP* was unsurpassed until 2001: A SPACE ODYSSEY, made 12 years later. Despite its flaws, it remains one of the few masterpieces of sf cinema.

Forbidden Planet ∗ (**1956**), based on the film, was by W. J. Stuart (Philip MacDONALD).   [PN]

See also: INTELLIGENCE; MONSTER MOVIES; MUSIC; PARANOIA; VILLAINS.

FORBIDDEN WORLD (vt *Mutant*) Film (1982). New World. Dir Allan Holzman, starring Jesse Vint, June Chadwick, Dawn Dunlap, Linden Chiles, Fox Harris, Raymond Oliver. Screenplay Tim Curnen. 86 mins. Colour.

This cheap imitation of ALIEN (1979), from Roger CORMAN's New World exploitation factory, is distinguished by its gleefully sleazy nature and amusing cynicism. An outer-space troubleshooter (Vint) is awakened from cryo-sleep (◊ CRYONICS), casually informed that he is now younger than his son, and despatched to a remote planet where a genetically engineered organism has run amok. Although generally predictable, this is fast-paced and does produce one astonishing coup by having its MONSTER, which replicates the cell structure of anything it devours, defeated when a terminally ill scientist feeds it his own cancerous liver, an organ he has removed during anaesthetic-free self-surgery. Vint's grimy hero imports a bit of welcome humour, and the film makes good use of the generically required exploitation elements, intercutting a formulaic sex scene with oddly poignant vignettes of the space-station staff whiling away the time at the end of the Universe. Some of *FW*'s sets and effects crop up again in ANDROID (1982).   [KN]

FORBIN PROJECT, THE ◊ COLOSSUS, THE FORBIN PROJECT.

FORCE FIELD In sf TERMINOLOGY – unlike physics, where it has a different meaning – a force field (sometimes a force shield) is usually an invisible protective sphere or wall of force. Throughout the 1930s and 1940s the force field performed sterling service, notably in E.E. "Doc" SMITH's **Skylark** and **Lensmen** series, where force fields under attack glow red and orange and then all the way up through the spectrum until they reach violet and black and break down. Force fields are also a sovereign remedy against DEATH RAYS and usually bullets, too, though not against swords in Charles L. HARNESS's *Flight into Yesterday* (1953; vt *The Paradox Men* dos), in which the efficacy of the shield is directly proportional to the momentum of the object it resists; this property of force fields gives Harness a good excuse to introduce swordplay (where the momentums are relatively small) into a technologically advanced society – an example that other writers were not slow to follow. Robert SHECKLEY's "Early Model" (1956) tells of a force field so efficient that it renders its wearer almost incapable of carrying out any action at all that might conceivably endanger him. The eponymous device in Poul ANDERSON's *Shield* (1963) can recharge its batteries by soaking up the kinetic energy of the bullets it stops. But these are comparatively late examples, when the concept was sufficiently familiar in sf to allow parody and sophisticated variations.

It is the essence of an sf force field that by a kind of judo it converts the energy of an attacking force and repels it back on itself. Few writers, however, were able to give – or concerned to try to give – a convincing rationale for forces being conveniently able to curve themselves around an object and to take on some of the properties of hard, resistant matter. A well ground mirror might more plausibly carry out the same function, at least against death rays. The true rationale for the force field and for its close relations, the tractor beam (which pulls objects towards the beamer) and the pressor beam (which pushes them away), is that – like FASTER THAN LIGHT travel – they help tell stories. [PN]

FORD, ASHTON ◊ Don PENDLETON.

FORD, DOUGLAS MORET (?   -?   ) UK writer whose *A Time of Terror: The Story of a Great Revenge (A.D. 1910)* (1906; vt *A Time of Terror: The Story of a Great Revenge (A.D. 1912)* 1908) pits the UK, aided by a valiant underground organization, against the Kaiser's invading forces. *The Raid of Dover: A Romance of the Reign of Woman, A.D. 1940* (1910) was fairly mild-mannered. [JC]

FORD, FORD MADOX (1873-1939) UK writer and editor, born (Joseph Leonard) Ford (Hermann) Madox Hueffer into a literary family of German descent. In protest at German behaviour in WWI he changed his name to FMF, though typically he refrained from doing so until hostilities had ended; original books and reprints after 1919 are signed FMF. A versatile man of letters, founder/editor of the *English Review* and the *Transatlantic Review*, he is best known for *The Good Soldier* (1915) and the four **Tietjens** novels assembled as *Parade's End* (omni 1950 US). His first book, *The Brown Owl* (1892), was a children's fantasy. *The Inheritors: An Extravagant Story* (1901) with Joseph CONRAD (*whom see for details*) is sf. Fantasies include *Mr Apollo* (1908), *The "Half Moon": A Romance of the Old World and the New* (1909), a complex story of 17th-century witchcraft, and *Ladies whose Bright Eyes* (1911), a TIME-TRAVEL tale. *The Simple*

Life Limited (1911), as by Daniel Chaucer, attacks utopianism. FMF inserted into the murkily RURITANIAN *The New Humpty-Dumpty* (1912), also as by Daniel Chaucer, a rather savage caricature of H.G. WELLS, who appears as Herbert Pett, a "cockney" Great Thinker and philanderer, with a high-pitched voice, who fatally intermixes sex and revolution. *Vive le Roy* (1936 US) delineates a struggle for power in a future monarchical France. [JC]

FORD, GARRETT ◊ William L. CRAWFORD.

FORD, JOHN M. (1957-   ) US writer. He is author of some children's fiction under an unrevealed pseudonym. He began publishing sf under his own name with "This, Too, Reconcile" for *ASF* in 1975. His **Alternities Corporation** sequence appeared in magazines 1979-81. His first novel, *Web of Angels* (1980), can be seen in retrospect as a quite remarkable rendering of the basic venues exploited by CYBERPUNK some years later, though its traditional rite-of-passage plot bears little resemblance to the quest-for-Nirvana structure given definitive form by William GIBSON in *Neuromancer* (1984). Beyond that basic distinction in dynamic thrust, however, and beyond JMF's failure (or disinclination) to make use of *film-noir* icons and the hegemony of corporate Japan, the eponymous commmunication/data web much resembles CYBERSPACE, though intergalactic in scope; the cowboy hacker protagonist hired out to a merchant prince is also familiar, as are the Web's automatic defence systems – Geisthounds – which hunt him remorselessly. JMF's second novel, *The Princes of the Air* (1982), is a florid SPACE OPERA whose detail is more enthralling than its span. *The Dragon Waiting* (1983) is an ALTERNATE-WORLD fantasy set in an unChristianized (and dragonless) medieval Europe; it won the 1984 World Fantasy AWARD. *The Final Reflection* * (1984) and *How Much for Just the Planet?* * (1987) are STAR TREK ties; *The Scholars of Night* (1988) is an associational thriller; *Casting Fortune* * (coll 1989), set in the **Liavek** SHARED-WORLD enterprise, contains in "The Illusionist" a book-length tale of theatrical MAGIC; and *Fugue State* (1987 in *Under the Wheel* ed Elizabeth Mitchell; 1990 dos) is a complex sf exploration of an imprisoned psyche. There is (1992) perhaps some sense that JMF may be damaging his commercial career through his inability to create a definitive style or mode; but his originality is evident, a shifting feisty energy informs almost everything he writes, and that career is still young. [JC]

Other works: *On Writing Science Fiction (The Editors Strike Back!)* (anth 1981) with Darrell SCHWEITZER and George H. SCITHERS.

See also: FANTASY; GAMES AND TOYS; POETRY; TIMESCAPE BOOKS.

FOREST, JEAN-CLAUDE [r] ◊ BARBARELLA.

FORESTER, C(ECIL) S(COTT) (1899-1966) UK writer best known for his work outside the sf field, especially the **Horatio Hornblower** novels (from 1937). In addition to several sf stories – including the substantial HITLER-WINS novella, "If Hitler had Invaded

England" (1960), which was posthumously collected in *Gold from Crete* (coll **1971**) – he published a novel, *The Peacemaker* (**1934** US), about a pacifist mathematician and schoolteacher who tries to force peace on the world through his invention of a magnetic disruptor that stops machinery. He fails. [JC]

Other works: *Poo-Poo and the Dragons* (**1942** US), a juvenile fantasy.

See also: CRIME AND PUNISHMENT; DISCOVERY AND INVENTION.

FORGOTTEN FANTASY US DIGEST-size magazine. 5 issues Oct 1970-June 1971, published by Nectar Press, Hollywood, ed Douglas MENVILLE. *FF* reprinted some ancient fantasy stories, but the long novel serialized in #1-#4, *The Goddess of Atvatabar* (**1892**) by William R. BRADSHAW, was probably too dated to be successful even in the nostalgia market. A second serial, *Hartmann, the Anarchist* (**1893**), by E. Douglas FAWCETT, began in #5. With his associate editor, R. REGINALD, Menville went on to publish in book form the **Forgotten Fantasy Library** (1973-80), 24 vols of reprint material. [FHP/PN]

FORMAN, JAMES D(OUGLAS) (1932-   ) US writer whose sf novels are for a young-adult audience. They began with *Call Back Yesterday* (**1981**) and its sequel, *Doomsday Plus Twelve* (**1984**), a studiedly and effectively admonitory presentation of nuclear HOLOCAUST as an event having little to do – contra much wish-fulfilment SURVIVALIST FICTION – with post-Bomb opportunities for self-fulfilment. In the first volume, a teenaged US girl's flirtation in the Middle East sets off, through a chain of stupidities, the final war; in the second, 12 years later, a young girl persuades the remnants of the US Army not to try to attack a benevolent Japan, which has had nothing to do with the war. *Cry Havoc* (**1988**), somewhat less interestingly, features the creation of killer dogs through GENETIC ENGINEERING gone awry. [JC]

FORREST, HENRY J. (?   -?   ) UK writer known only for the early sf UTOPIA, *A Dream of Reform* (**1848**), which tamely introduces the usual visitor to a mildly socialist planet designed on anti-industrial lines. The book is thus a vague precursor to the work of William MORRIS. [JC]

FORREST, MARYANN Pseudonym of an unidentified Australian writer in whose *Here (Away from it All)* (**1969** UK; vt *Here* 1970 US) the residents of a Mediterranean island must deal with the consequences of the HOLOCAUST. [JC]

FORSTCHEN, WILLIAM R. (1950-   ) US writer whose work has been restricted almost exclusively to series, beginning with the **Ice Prophet** sequence – *Ice Prophet* (**1983**), *The Flame upon the Ice* (**1984**) and *A Darkness upon the Ice* (**1985**) – set on Earth at some point in the future after an ecological disaster has caused the planet to become icebound. In this world technology has, according to the orthodox sf assumptions, been foolishly banned, and the eponymous prophet heralds a revival of science; but the intricacies of the realpolitik which doom him personally,

and the beauties of the ice world itself, go some way to keep the sequence from being unduly familiar. The **Gamester War** novels – *The Alexandrian Ring* (**1987**) and *The Assassin Gambit* (**1988**) – show a similar competence and a whole-hearted involvement in the most far-reaching dictates that SPACE OPERA can demand on those who treat its premises seriously, featuring a race of intergalactic overlords who permit the citizens of Earth and many other planets to engage in vast GAME-WORLD-like conflicts and to import, through TIME TRAVEL, figures like Alexander the Great to fight wagered wars on the enormous ringworld that serves as arena. The **Crystal** series, written with Greg Morrison – *The Crystal Warriors* (**1988**) and *The Crystal Sorcerers* (**1991**) – is fantasy. The **Lost Regiment** sequence – *Rally Cry!* (**1990**), *Union Forever* (**1991**) and *Terrible Swift Sword* (**1992**) – reworks the basic structure of the **Gamester War** books, this time from the perspective of a Civil War Union troop transported through time to a medieval planet secretly dominated by remote aliens. *Into the Sea of Stars* (**1986**) is a singleton. WRF is a genre writer of shining efficiency, and is technically capable of the most ambitious work. [JC]

See also: GAMES AND SPORTS.

FORSTER, E(DWARD) M(ORGAN) (1879-1970) UK writer of essays and novels, the best known being *A Passage to India* (**1924**). *The Celestial Omnibus, and Other Stories* (coll **1911**) assembles several fantasies of interest, but EMF's importance to sf lies wholly in his short story "The Machine Stops" (1909), collected in *The Eternal Moment* (coll **1928**), which includes further fantasies. Both books were assembled as *Collected Short Stories* (coll **1947**; vt *Collected Tales* 1974 US). Cast in the form of a warning look at the distant future, rather in the mode of H.G. WELLS's *The Time Machine* (**1895**), "The Machine Stops" directly attacks, as many critics noted and as EMF himself acknowledged, the rational World State that Wells promulgated in *A Modern Utopia* (**1905**). In the hivelike underground society EMF envisions, freedom and (paramountly) the value of the individual human's personal relations with others of his kind have been eliminated. When the state collapses – when the machine stops – the depersonalized ciphers underground perish, while above, on the surface, a few genuine humans survive. In any study of the relation of DYSTOPIA to UTOPIA, the story is of vital interest. [JC]

See also: AUTOMATION; CITIES; HISTORY OF SF; LEISURE; TECHNOLOGY; VIRTUAL REALITY.

FORSYTH, FREDERICK (1938-   ) UK writer who gained fame with his first novel, *The Day of the Jackal* (**1971**), and whose books are generally political thrillers. *The Shepherd* (**1975** chap), however, is a sentimental timeslip fantasy about a WWII pilot, and both *The Devil's Alternative* (**1979**) and *The Negotiator* (**1989**) are NEAR-FUTURE thrillers, the first predicting the failure of the Russian harvest, the second predicting (wrongly) a Soviet-generated crisis. [JC]

FORT, CHARLES (HOY) (1874-1932) US journalist and

author. Working from extensive notes collected mainly from newspapers, magazines and scientific journals, CF compiled a series of books containing information on "inexplicable" incidents and phenomena. Though characterized as an anti-scientist, CF reserved his attacks for the "scientific priestcraft" and their dogmatic "damning" of unconventional or unwanted observations. CF's own belief was simply a monistic faith in the unity of all things, and this forms the principal connection between his apparently unrelated groups of data. His books are written in an eccentric style and are interspersed with wilfully absurd theories and ideas. The first two, both still (1992) unpublished, were called simply «X» and «Y»; «X» proposes that Earth is controlled from MARS and «Y» supports the HOLLOW-EARTH hypothesis. *The Book of the Damned* (1919) and *New Lands* (1923) are largely concerned with astronomical and meteorological events, while *Lo!* (1931) and *Wild Talents* (1932) are more interested in human and animal phenomena. The four published books are crammed with data, and the sheer bulk of information is impressive; however, there is no attempt to evaluate the numerous reports cited, so that silly-season urban legends and hoax stories are jumbled in with a too-sparse leavening of more reliable accounts. Reading CF therefore feels much like eating a stew of dubious provenance: the taste is good but one worries about what went into it. CF himself was perfectly aware that much of his data was, to say the least, doubtful; of *The Book of the Damned* he wrote: "This book is fiction, like *Gulliver's Travels*, *The Origin of Species*, Newton's *Principia*, and every history of the United States." Moreover, he was reluctant to invent theories (other than whimsical ones) to account for his data – a humility that distances his books from the sketchy fantasies of later writers such as Erich VON DÄNIKEN.

After CF's death, compilation of data was continued by the Fortean Society, founded in 1931 by a group that included Ben HECHT, John Cowper POWYS, Alexander Woollcott (1887-1943) and Theodore Dreiser (1871-1945), and in the journals *Doubt* (US) and *Lo!* (UK). Information is currently collected by the International Fortean Organization, who publish *INFO Journal*, and by the UK publication *Fortean Times*. Prominent modern Forteans include William F. Corliss, John Michell and Robert J.M. Rickard.

CF's list of bizarre observations and events (from astronomical heresies to teleportation cases), together with his demand for original and undogmatic interpretation, influenced and stimulated many sf writers. CF's most enthusiastic sf follower was Eric Frank RUSSELL, who considered him "the only real genius sf ever had"; Russell's *Sinister Barrier* (1943) and *Dreadful Sanctuary* (1951) are based on Fortean ideas. Damon KNIGHT, another author influenced by CF, published a standard biography, *Charles Fort, Prophet of the Unexplained* (1970). The influence of CF's ideas on sf was particularly strong in the magazines ed John W.

CAMPBELL Jr, *Unknown* and *ASF*. Fortean elements rarely appear in more recent written sf, though Patrick TILLEY's *Fade-Out* (1975) is one exception, and films such as CLOSE ENCOUNTERS OF THE THIRD KIND (1977), with its discovery of the famous "lost" Flight 19, maintain the tradition. [PR/JGr]

See also: ASTOUNDING SCIENCE-FICTION; ESP; Vol MOLES-WORTH; PARANOIA; PSEUDO-SCIENCE; PSI POWERS; TELEKINESIS; TELEPORTATION.

FORWARD, ROBERT L(ULL) (1932-   ) US physicist and writer, senior scientist at Hughes Research Laboratories and one of the most devoted HARD-SF authors of the 1980s. He began publishing sf with "I Demand the Stars for my Children!" as Susan Lull for *Galileo* in 1979, and made a very considerable impact with his first novel, *Dragon's Egg* (1980), which, along with its sequel *Starquake!* (1985), is set in a most intriguing venue – a NEUTRON STAR whose surface GRAVITY is 67,000,000,000 gees – and concentrates on the immensely enjoyable ALIEN cheela who inhabit this venue, living and evolving at an enormous rate (a generation passes in 37 minutes). The human scientists who visit the cheela of Dragon's Egg inadvertently civilize them over a 24-hour period. In the sequel the cheela, now evolved far beyond their glacial human teachers, very quickly explore the entire Galaxy, though the catastrophe of the title soon complicates the plot, leading to further rapid-fire EVOLUTION, invention and mind-play.

RLF's second successful novel, *The Flight of the Dragonfly* (1982-3 *ASF* as "Rocheworld"; exp **1984**; exp 1985; orig full version restored, vt *Rocheworld* 1990), posited a second world of almost equal fascination. On the eponymous dumb-bell-shaped double-planet is placed an alien race whose individuals are characterized more strongly than are the humans involved in an exploratory mission there. (Despite the striking resemblance in storylines and the titles, this novel is unrelated to the earlier series.) Once again the self-confident articulacy of RLF's scientific mind dominates proceedings, and the novel concludes (as did his first) with a symposium which analyses the ideas underlying the book. However, the unfortunate corollary to this style of novel-writing is that, when no scientific conceit governs the structure of the tale, character and plot can prove, as in RLF's case, a poor substitute. *Martian Rainbow* (1991), which has no such central world-building conceit to govern it, consequently fails to convince in its simplistic rendering of a Russian-US conflict on Mars, or in the cardboard triumphalism of its human cast. More than almost any other hard-sf writer, RLF dazzles within his bailiwick and embarrasses outside it. [JC]

Other works: *Timemaster* (1992), a LIBERTARIAN tale.

Nonfiction: *Future Magic* (1988); *Mirror Matter: Pioneering Antimatter Physics* (1988) with Joel Davis.

See also: ASTRONOMY; PLANETARY ROMANCE; SCIENTISTS; STARS.

FOSS, CHRIS(TOPHER) (1946-   ) UK illustrator. CF studied architecture at Cambridge University, and has worked in sf ILLUSTRATION since 1970, primarily as a cover artist; he uses brush and airbrush to excellent effect. He is best known in sf circles for his hardware, particularly his SPACESHIPS: intricate, asymmetrical, almost Gothic, these have been deeply influential not only on other UK illustrators but also on film designers. Ever since STAR WARS (1977), most movie spacecraft look as if they have been designed by CF, even though they have not – although he did work as a concept artist on ALIEN (1979). (Paradoxically, outside sf, CF is better known in commercial illustration for his detailed figure studies; he did the many romantically erotic drawings for Alex COMFORT's *The Joy of Sex* [1972] and *More Joy of Sex* [1973].) CF's smooth, airbrushed, representational style, demonstrated on hundreds of covers, spearheaded a revolution in UK sf paperback design in the 1970s, and had many imitators. It was what the market wanted, and after a decade had become almost tedious in its predictability – though that was the publishers' fault, not CF's. His sf work is often a celebration of technology – monstrous spaceships or vast robots, beautiful and deadly, rear up over landscapes and skyscapes where humans are absent or tiny – yet the effect is bracing. *Science Fiction Art* (1976), with an introduction by Brian W. ALDISS, is a portfolio of his work; others are *21st Century Foss* (1978) and *The Chris Foss Portfolio* (1990). *Diary of a Spaceperson* (1990) is unusual and not wholly successful in combining the erotic with the scientific in what purports to be the illustrated diary (written by CF) of a spacewoman who has sexual congress with an alien plant. [PN]

See also: TECHNOLOGY.

FOSTER, ALAN DEAN (1946-   ) US writer, raised in Los Angeles; interestingly, he has listed Carl Barks (1901-   ), the long-unacknowledged creator of the best COMIC strips and books in the Disney stable, as one of his formative influences (on his depiction of older characters). ADF began publishing sf with "Some Notes Concerning a Green Box" for *The Arkham Collector* in 1971, and has collected short stories in *With Friends Like These . . .* (coll 1977), its companion, *. . . Who Needs Enemies?* (coll 1984), and *The Metrognome and Other Stories* (coll 1990). ADF is best known, however, for a prolific and generally competent output of novels and novelizations.

Several of his best books fit into a loose double sequence of novels set in a multifarious Galaxy dominated by the **Humanx Commonwealth**, a venue well suited as an arena for SPACE OPERAS and encounters with ALIEN races. The central sequence follows the life of young Flinx, an orphan with PSI POWERS and the friendship of a highly potent pet alien named Pip, and comprises (in order of internal chronology): *For Love of Mother-Not* (1983); a connected trilogy made up of ADF's first novel, *The Tar-Aiym Krang* (1972), *Orphan Star* (1977) and *The End of the Matter* (1977); *Bloodhype* (1973); and *Flinx in Flux* (1988). A second, looser sequence consists of *Nor Crystal Tears* (1982);

Midworld (1975); a connected trilogy made up of *Icerigger* (1974), *Mission to Moulokin* (1979) and *The Deluge Drivers* (1987), the three comprising his best work to date; *Voyage to the City of the Dead* (1984); and *Sentenced to Prism* (1985). Sometimes reminiscent of the earlier work of Poul ANDERSON, the sequence is expansive and colourful, though tending to melodrama and prone to the fable-like use of such sf and fantasy elements as ESP and dragons.

Individual novels have tended more to a clearheaded commercial exploitation of various genre categories, though *Cachalot* (1980), whose whale-like aliens are of interest, *The Man who Used the Universe* (1983) and *Cyber Way* (1990) perhaps stand out.

Of ADF's numerous novelizations, the most notable are possibly *Dark Star* * (1974), based on DARK STAR (1974), *Star Wars* * (1976), as by George LUCAS, the director of STAR WARS (1977), *Alien* * (1979), based on ALIEN (1979), *Aliens: A Novelization* * (1986), based on ALIENS (1986), and *Alien³* * (1992), based on ALIEN³ (1992). [JC]

Other works: *Luana* (1974); *The Horror on the Beach* (1978 chap); the **Spellsinger** sequence of high-fantasy romps, comprising *Spellsinger at the Gate* (1983; vt in 2 vols as *Spellsinger* 1983 and *The Hour of the Gate* 1984) and *The Day of the Dissonance* (1984), both assembled as *Season of the Spellsong* (omni 1985), and *The Moment of the Magician* (1984), *The Path of the Perambulator* (1985) and *The Time of the Transference* (1986), all assembled as *Spellsinger's Scherzo* (omni 1987); *Slipt* (1984); *The I Inside* (1984); *Into the Out Of* (1986); *Glory Lane* (1987); *To the Vanishing Point* (1988); *Maori* (1988); *Quozl* (1989); the **The Damned** series beginning with *A Call to Arms* (1991) and *The False Mirror* (1992); *Cat-A-Lyst* (1991).

Novelizations: The **Star Trek Logs**, comprising *Star Trek Log One* * (coll 1974), *Star Trek Log Two* * (coll 1974), *Star Trek Log Three* * (coll 1975), *Star Trek Log Four* * (coll 1975), *Star Trek Log Five* * (coll 1975), *Star Trek Log Six* * (coll 1976), *Star Trek Log Seven* * (coll 1976), *Star Trek Log Eight* * (coll 1976), *Star Trek Log Nine* * (coll 1977), *Star Trek Log Ten* * (1978); *Splinter of the Mind's Eye* * (1978), a **Star Wars** novel; *The Black Hole* * (1979); *Outland* * (1981); *Clash of the Titans* * (1981); *The Thing* * (1982); *Krull* * (1983); *The Last Starfighter* * (1984); *Shadowkeep* * (1984), based on a computer game; *Starman* * (1984); *Pale Rider* * (1987); *Alien Nation* * (1988).

As editor: *The Best of Eric Frank Russell* (coll 1978); *Animated Features and Silly Symphonies* (anth 1980); *Smart Dragons, Foolish Elves* (anth 1991) with Martin H. GREENBERG.

See also: ECOLOGY; GAMES AND TOYS; HUMOUR; TRANSPORTATION; UFOS.

FOSTER, GEORGE C(ECIL) (1893-?   ) UK writer whose first novel of genre interest, *The Lost Garden* (1930), is a fantasy in which survivors of ATLANTIS experience world history up to the present. In *Full Fathom Five* (1930) prehistoric episodes are linked by REINCARNATION to scenes set in the present. *Awakening*

(1932) subjects the contemporary (and the future) world to the perspective of a soldier awakening from suspended animation. *Cats in the Coffee* (1938), under the *nom de plume* Seaforth, presents through reincarnation a retrospective vision of prehistory, and *We Band of Brothers* (1939), also as by Seaforth, combines future-WAR events and elucidatory conversations between a man of the deep future and a man of the deep past. *The Change* (1963) is routine. In almost all his work, conventional plots are twisted to make room for perspectives on the nature of human history; in this sense, GCF illuminates a central strategy of the UK SCIENTIFIC ROMANCE.   [JC/PN]

See also: IMMORTALITY.

FOSTER, M(ICHAEL) A(NTHONY) (1939-   ) US writer, former data-systems analyst and sequentially a Russian linguist and ICBM launch-crew commander to the US Air Force; he is also a semiprofessional photographer. After some poetry, published privately as *Shards from Byzantium* (coll 1969 chap) and *The Vaseline Dreams of Hundifer Jones* (coll 1970 chap), he began to publish sf with the ambitious **Ler** trilogy about a race of genetically created SUPERMEN. *The Gameplayers of Zan* (1977), a very long novel formally constructed on the model of an Elizabethan tragedy, describes a period of climactic tension between the ler and the rest of humanity, and is set on Earth. *The Warriors of Dawn* (1975), published first but set later, is a more conventional SPACE OPERA in which a human male and a ler female are forced to team up to try to solve a complexly ramifying problem of interstellar piracy. *The Day of the Klesh* (1979) brings the ler and the eponymous race of humans together on a planet where they must solve their differences. The books are slow in the telling, but impressively detailed in their construction of ler culture and language. The **Morphodite** sequence which followed comprises *The Morphodite* (1981), *Transformer* (1983) and *Preserver* (1985), and similarly uses devices of genetic manipulation to buttress complex plots, though in this case the shape-changing, revolution-fomenting protagonist dominates the tale as trickster and superman. *Waves* (1980) rather sluggishly recalls Stanisław LEM's *Solaris* (1961) in a tale of political intrigue on a planet whose ocean is intelligent. The four novellas collected in *Owl Time* (coll 1985) are told in challengingly various modes, and derive strength from their mutual contrast. MAF's career to date could be seen as a prelude to the major book which should bring him the acclaim he merits.   [JC]

See also: GENETIC ENGINEERING; LIVING WORLDS; PLANETARY ROMANCE.

FOSTER, RICHARD ◊ Kendell Foster CROSSEN.

FOSTER, W(ALTER) BERT(RAM) (1869-1929) US author of two borderline sf novels, *The Eve of War* (1904) and *The Lost Expedition* (1905).   [JC]

FOUNDATION: THE REVIEW OF SCIENCE FICTION UK semi-academic journal, published by the SCIENCE FICTION FOUNDATION of North East London Polytechnic (now known as the University of East London) from Mar 1972, current, 54 numbers to Summer 1992, 3 numbers a year. #1-#4 ed Charles BARREN, #5-#13 ed Peter NICHOLLS, #14-#19 ed Malcolm EDWARDS, #20-#36 ed David PRINGLE, #37 onwards ed Edward JAMES. Much of the journal's flavour has resulted from the work of long-running features editor Ian WATSON, who held that position from #10 (1976) to #51 (1991). The most influential reviews editors have perhaps been John CLUTE (#20-#47) followed by Colin GREENLAND (from #47). Other members of the editorial board have included Kenneth BULMER, George HAY and Christopher PRIEST.

F:TROSF has a distinctive flavour regarded by US readers as typically UK, though in fact some of its editors have been foreigners. After a shaky beginning, it soon became perhaps the liveliest and indeed the most critical of the big three critical journals – the others being EXTRAPOLATION in the USA and SCIENCE FICTION STUDIES in Canada – though lacking the academic authority of at least the latter. Since there is very little formal use of sf in UK universities, there is no academic base to provide a rigidly scholarly features section. The real strengths of *F:TROSF* have always been its book reviews and its willingness to publish articles about current sf; it has been weaker in theoretical and historical studies. Nevertheless, it has provided a platform for serious sf criticism in the UK. Its contributors – often professional writers of fiction rather than academics – have tended to be more aggressively judgmental, and more intent upon defining a critical canon for sf, than their politer US colleagues. All of this may explain why its readership appears to be less academic than that of the other scholarly journals, consisting more of fans and sf writers. The US scholar Gary K. WOLFE sees *F:TROSF*, not wholly unadmiringly (and only in part incorrectly), as partaking of "certain traditions of fan scholarship". From the beginning a feature of *F:TROSF* has been the **Profession of Science Fiction** series (43 to date) of autobiographical pieces by sf writers; a selection of **Profession** essays appeared later as *The Profession of Science Fiction* (anth 1992) ed Edward James and Maxim JAKUBOWSKI. The first 8 issues of *F:TROSF* were republished in book form as *Foundation, Numbers 1 to 8: March 1972-March 1975* (1978) with intro by Peter Nicholls.   [PN]

4D MAN (vt *The Evil Force* UK; vt *Master of Terror* US) Film (1959). Fairview/Universal. Coproduced and dir Irwin Shortess Yeaworth Jr, starring Robert Lansing, Lee Meriwether, James Congdon. Screenplay Theodore Simonson, Cy Chermak, from an idea by Jack H. Harris. 85 mins. Colour.

A small, interesting film made by the same producer/director team, Jack H. Harris and Yeaworth, that had already made *The* BLOB (1958). Lansing plays a scientist who uses his brother's research on the amplification of brainwaves and finds that as a result he can interpenetrate with solid matter – walk through walls, etc. The unfortunate side-effect is that he draws on the lifeforce of others (an idea used again in LIFEFORCE [1985]), which renders them instantly dead of old age. There is a love triangle, and some brooding *angst* from Lansing, who oscillates between delight in his new power and guilt.   [PN]

FOUR-SIDED TRIANGLE Film (1952). Hammer. Dir Terence Fisher, starring Barbara Payton, Stephen Murray, John Van Eyssen. Screenplay Paul TABORI, Fisher, based on *The Four-Sided Triangle* (1939 *AMZ*; exp **1949**) by William F. TEMPLE. 81 mins, cut to 71 mins. B/w.

A scientist builds a machine capable of duplicating human beings. He duplicates the woman he loves but who is in love with another man, only to have the duplicate, too, fall in love with that other man. This is a low-budget film and suffers from it; there appear to be no prints now in circulation.   [JB]

FOURTH DIMENSION ◊ DIMENSIONS.

FOWLER, KAREN JOY (1950-   ) US writer with degrees in political science and north Asian studies. She began publishing sf with "Recalling Cinderella" in *L. Ron Hubbard Presents Writers of the Future, Vol II* (anth **1986**) ed Algis BUDRYS, and caused considerable stir in the sf field with the quality of the work assembled in her first collection, *Artificial Things* (coll **1986**), which helped gain her the 1987 JOHN W. CAMPBELL AWARD for Best New Writer. Her short stories – later collections are *Peripheral Vision* (coll **1990** chap) and *Letters from Home* (anth **1991** UK), which contains separate tales by her, Pat CADIGAN and Pat MURPHY – gave a first and entirely deceptive appearance of reticence, but soon revealed steely ironies, an insistence on the essential solitude of her protagonists (which evoked FEMINIST arguments about alienation but did not dwell upon the specifics of oppression or male-female discord) and an urgent hilarity. Some stories, like "Face Values", are pure sf; others shift into fantasy or FABULATION, giving ambiguous cues as to any "proper" reading.

This sure-footed refusal to give her readers much epistemological security – much sense that her worlds could be firmly apprehended – also governed the telling of KJF's first novel, the remarkable *Sarah Canary* (**1991**), which – along with John FOWLES's *A Maggot* (**1985**) – may be the finest First Contact novel (◊ COMMUNICATIONS) yet written. A strange female figure – woman or alien, no one knows, or can even formulate the question – arrives in the state of Washington in 1873 and is dubbed Sarah Canary, because of the birdlike sounds she makes. In attempting to deal with her, the Chinese worker to whom she has attached herself is exposed to a long array of those living beings that the sciences of the 19th century have attempted to control through "knowledge": Indians, Blacks, the insane, immigrants, women, animals, artists, confidence men. Sarah Canary, who stands for them all in the indescribable melody of her Being, finally disappears, never having said a word. As an emblem of the enigma behind the idea of First Contact she is perhaps definitive. As a dramatization of the self-deluding imperialisms of knowledge, *Sarah Canary* is equally convincing.   [JC]

Other work: *The War of the Roses* (1985 *IASFM*; **1991** chap).

See also: INTERZONE; SOCIOLOGY; WRITERS OF THE FUTURE CONTEST.

FOWLER, SYDNEY ◊ S. Fowler WRIGHT.

FOWLES, JOHN (ROBERT) (1926-   ) UK writer who remains perhaps most famous for his first novel, *The Collector* (**1963**), but whose second novel, *The Magus* (**1965** US; rev 1977 UK), especially in the conciser revised version, more powerfully explores the labyrinths of obsession and manipulation underlying, in all of JF's work, the rigmaroles of daylight reality. In this novel a series of seemingly supernatural contrivances separates the unpleasant protagonist from his love and from any security, causing him to learn something about himself before happiness is allowed to reign; rational explanations in the end from the Daedalus-like magus do little to attenuate a sense of magic-realist entrapment. Of JF's other novels, *A Maggot* (**1985**) is sf. Set in the 18th century, it superlatively explores the epistemology of First Contact – the study of the possible nature of human PERCEPTIONS of something genuinely ALIEN, genuinely Other – by telling a version of the life-story of the mother of Ann Lee (1736-1784), historical founder of the Shaker religion; the woman's response to the insoluble knot of PERCEPTIONS visited upon her when she inadvertently stumbles upon some time travellers, possibly from Earth's future, is a literal seedbed (she is pregnant at the time) for Enthusiasm.   [JC]

FOX, GARDNER F(RANCIS) (1911-1986) US lawyer and author, who began writing in 1937 for DC COMICS, including SUPERMAN. Arguably his most important work was for COMICS: he wrote over 4000 comic-book stories, and created **The Flash** as well as the first SUPERHERO team, the **Justice League of America**, in 1940. In the 1960s he was one of those responsible for reviving many of the superheroes from the 1940s and also created new characters, like **The Atom** and **Adam Strange**. He began publishing sf/fantasy in non-graphic form with "The Weirds of the Woodcarver" for *Weird Tales* in 1944. He used several pseudonyms at this time, including Jefferson Cooper, Jeffrey Gardner and James Kendricks, though not for sf. He was an active contributor to *Planet Stories* from 1945, and soon established a reputation for historical romances like *The Borgia Blade* (**1953**), not beginning to publish sf novels, either under his own name or under his later pseudonyms Rod Gray, Simon Majors and Bart Somers, until *Five Weeks in a Balloon* ✻ (**1962**), which novelizes the film of the Jules VERNE novel. GFF's first sf novel proper is *Escape Across the Cosmos* (**1964**), in which a man fights a menace from another DIMENSION; it was plagiarized as *Titans of the Universe* in various 1978 editions, variously as by Brian James Royal, James Harvey and Moonchild. His best is probably *The Arsenal of Miracles* (**1964** dos), which combines SPACE OPERA, GALACTIC EMPIRES and a romantically conceived hero who prefigures the interest in

HEROIC FANTASY which dominated GFF's later output. His sf series are the two fantasy-like **Alan Morgan** adventures – *Warrior of Llarn* (**1964**) and *Thief of Llarn* (**1966**) – and, as by Bart Somers, the **Commander Craig** space operas: *Beyond the Black Enigma* (**1965**) and *Abandon Galaxy!* (**1967**). GFF was an efficient story-teller with no visible pretensions to significance or thematic originality.   [JC/PN]

Other works: *The Hunter out of Time* (**1965**); *The Druid Stone* (**1967**), as by Simon Majors; the **Kothar** series of heroic-fantasy novels, comprising *Kothar – Barbarian Swordsman* (coll of linked stories **1969**), *Kothar of the Magic Sword!* (**1969**), *Kothar and the Demon Queen* (**1969**), *Kothar and the Conjuror's Curse* (**1970**) and *Kothar and the Wizard Slayer* (**1970**); *Conehead* (**1973**); the **Kyrik** heroic-fantasy series, comprising *Kyrik: Warlock Warrior* (**1975**), *Kyrik Fights the Demon World* (**1975**), *Kyrik and the Wizard's Sword* (**1976**) and *Kyrik and the Lost Queen* (**1976**); *Carty* (**1977**).

As Rod Gray (house name): Of the soft-porn **Lady from L.U.S.T.** sequence, those by GFF and of some sf interest are *The Poisoned Pussy* (**1969**), *Laid in the Future* (**1969**), *Blow my Mind* (**1970**) and *The Copulation Explosion* (**1970**).

FOX, SAMUEL MIDDLETON (1856-1941) UK writer whose sf novel, *Our Own Pompeii: A Romance of Tomorrow* (**1887**), a fairly mild-mannered SATIRE of high society, features a pleasure city on the Riviera which proves too expensive to run.   [JC]

FPCI ◊ FANTASY PUBLISHING COMPANY INC.

F.P.1 ANTWORTET NICHT Film (1932). UFA. Dir Karl Hartl, starring Hans Albers, Sybille Schmitz, Paul Hartmann, Peter Lorre. Screenplay Walter Reisch, Kurt SIODMAK, based on *F.P.1 Antwortet Nicht* (**1932**) by Siodmak. 111 mins. B/w.

F.P.1 has been described as being in the tradition of METROPOLIS (1926) and *Die FRAU IM MOND* (1929), but Karl Hartl was no Fritz LANG. It is a slow-moving film about the construction of a giant floating runway (*Flugzeug Platform 1*) to be moored in mid-Atlantic for refuelling transatlantic flights, but is actually more concerned with a tedious love triangle. The story is about an intrepid aviator who sees flight as a near-mystical experience, and about sabotage and noble renunciations – all pulp materials, but with none of the slickness or verve of similar Hollywood films of the period. At great expense a flying platform was actually built for the film, on the island of Oie. The same production team made GOLD (1934).

An English version (◊ FP1 DOESN'T ANSWER) and a French one, starring Charles Boyer, were made of *F.P.1* at the same time as the German version. [JB/PN]

F.P.1 DOESN'T ANSWER Film (1932). UFA. Technical credits as for FP1 ANTWORTET NICHT, but starring Conrad Veidt, Jill Esmond and Leslie Fenton. 90 mins. B/w.

This is the shorter English-language version of the German film, and was shot at the same time. The acting is better than in the German version.   [PN]

FRAME, JANET (PATTERSON) (1924-   ) New Zealand writer of several novels, the most intense of which explore the world through the telling perceptions of protagonists categorized as psychiatrically disturbed. *Intensive Care* (**1970** US) is told in part through the eyes of a young woman defined as mentally deficient in a post-HOLOCAUST world where those so described are killed after being experimented upon. *The Carpathians* (**1988** UK) is a fantasy set in an imaginary country.   [JC]

FRANCE The history of France's relationship with sf is one of long flirtation, marked through the centuries by episodic outbursts of passion and, in recent times, by an increasing shift from authorship to readership, from the active to the passive role, as more and more people become avid consumers of the US/UK sf tradition. A few remarkable French writers of sf have emerged, but, although the 1970s were an active period for French sf, no truly indigenous school of writing has yet taken shape.

A quest for "great ancestors" in the corpus of French literature would be endless. Many texts – some vintage classics, some long-forgotten oddities – show that FANTASTIC VOYAGES, the search for UTOPIA, and speculation about other worlds and alien forms of society were constant preoccupations. People tend to overlook the fact that the last parts of François RABELAIS's *Gargantua and Pantagruel* (**1532-64**; trans **1653-94**), especially *L'isle sonante* ["The Ringing Island"] (**1562**), are clearly set in the future and almost constitute an early style of SPACE OPERA with their processing of foreign languages, customs and landscapes.

One century later, interest in the otherworldly asserted itself in works such as CYRANO DE BERGERAC's *Histoire comique contenant les états et empires de la lune* (**1657**; trans as *A Voyage to the Moon* **1659**) and Bernard le Bovyer de FONTENELLE's *Entretiens sur la pluralité des mondes habités* (**1686**; trans J. Glanvill as *The Plurality of Worlds* **1929**), but it is in the 18th century that we encounter the most direct forerunner of sf in its modern sense, in the form of the *conte philosophique*, or philosophical tale. Conditions were then ideal for the emergence of something akin to sf: the *Siècle des Lumières* was one of universal curiosity, of philosophical audacity and political revolution; it gave birth to all-encompassing spirits such as that of Denis Diderot (1713-1784) and saw the writing of the *Encyclopédie* (**1751-2**), which merged the two aspects of culture, literary and scientific, the divorce of which would be one of the main sources of the decline of French sf in our time.

The conventions of the *conte philosophique* – which generally takes the shape of a fantastic voyage – are predecessors to those of sf: the voyage to the far island symbolizes what we now imagine in interplanetary travel, and the islanders themselves stand for what are now aliens, while the study of their civilizations serves as a mirror/criticism of our institutions. Conversely, the satire of French (= European) society as seen through foreign eyes was a device that had already been used by Charles Montesquieu (1689-1755) in his *Lettres persanes* ["Persian Letters"] (**1721**).

The genre could be illustrated by numerous stories (Pierre VERSINS states that "at the beginning of the 18th century, at least one speculative work was published each year"), but among its landmarks were VOLTAIRE's *Micromégas* (Berlin **1750**; France **1752**), Louis-Sébastien MERCIER's *L'an deux mille quatre cent quarante* (**1771**; trans as *Memoirs of the Year Two Thousand Five Hundred* **1772**), RESTIF DE LA BRETONNE's *La découverte australe* ["The Southern-Hemisphere Discovery"] (**1781**) and Giacomo CASANOVA di Seingalt's *Isocameron* (**1788**), an early story of travel to the centre of the Earth. Such was the vogue of speculation that in 1787 a publisher started a list of **Voyages imaginaires** which ran to 36 volumes and may be considered the first sf series ever.

Perhaps the most significant sf figure of the early 19th century was Félix Bodin, whose *Le Roman de l'avenir* ["The Romance of the Future"] (**1834**) consists of a long theoretical discussion of the nature of futuristic fiction, this being a preface to a fragmentary or unfinished novel about a future, in which mechanized warfare appears. As Paul K. ALKON demonstrates in *Origins of Futuristic Fiction* (**1987**), Bodin's book presents an aesthetic which – significantly for sf – refers not only to a genre which takes the future as its subject but to one that itself will exist only in the future. The remainder of the 19th century would seem to be entirely dominated by the formidable silhouette of Jules VERNE, but it was a very active period in other respects too, carrying on the *élan* of the preceding era. Scientific achievements and the Industrial Revolution gave birth to popular novels in the same way that philosophical turmoil had produced its share of *contes*. Verne himself stands apart because he was the first writer to be systematic about it and build his whole work according to a vast design, as described by his publisher Hetzel in 1867: "His aim is to sum up all knowledge gathered by modern science in the fields of *geography, geology, physics, astronomy*, and to remake, in his own attractive and picturesque way, the history of our Universe." From then to his death in 1905, Verne gave Hetzel the 64 books which make up his **Voyages extraordinaires**, subtitled "Voyages dans les mondes connus et inconnus" ["Voyages into the Known and Unknown Worlds"]. Jacques Van Herp (1923-   ), who himself wrote a large number of works of CHILDREN'S SF as Michel Jansen, has argued that the huge success Verne enjoyed, basically among adolescents, drove serious critics and historians away from him, so that – in France anyway – one may trace back to Verne the lame academic quarrel about whether sf, or "anticipation", is high literature or not. Indeed, that question had never been raised before; it took a bourgeois system of education (see below) to institute class-struggle among books. Verne's work went the way of *Robinson Crusoe* or *Treasure Island*: that of a sort

of universal reputation which does not preclude underestimation or misunderstanding. Until recently, Verne was ignored by the universities, but fascinated such diverse minds as those of Raymond Roussel (who called him "le plus grand génie littéraire de tous les siècles" ["the greatest literary genius of all time"]), Michel BUTOR and Michel Foucault (1926-1984).

Among Verne's contemporaries in the field, one should at least mention the astronomer Camille FLAMMARION and his *Récits de l'infini* (**1872**; trans as *Stories of Infinity: Lumen – History of a Comet in Infinity* **1874**) and the novelist cum draftsman Albert ROBIDA, who was no less prolific than Verne, whom he parodied in his *Voyages très extraordinaires de Saturnin Farandoul* (1879; for book publication ◊ ROBIDA) which purportedly took their hero "into all the countries known and even unknown to Mr Jules Verne". Robida proved himself a visionary as well as a humorist in his *Le vingtième siècle* ["The Twentieth Century"] (**1882**), *La vie électrique* ["The Electric Life"] (**1883**) and "La guerre au vingtième siècle" ["War in the 20th Century"] (*La caricature* 1883).

By the turn of the century, however, the one name Verne had to contend with was that of J.H. ROSNY aîné, a writer who possibly deserves as much consideration. The Rosnys, two brothers of Belgian extraction, started together a writing career that was eventually to win them seats in the Académie Goncourt, but we are concerned only with the numerous stories and the 17 novels of Rosny aîné (the elder brother), which run from the prehistoric, such as *La guerre du feu* ["The War of Fire"] (**1909**), through the cataclysmic *La mort de la terre* ["Death of the Earth"] (**1910**) to the futuristic *Les navigateurs de l'infini* ["Navigators of the Infinite"] (**1925**). Rosny aîné consistently brought to the field, besides a solid scientific culture, a breadth of vision at times worthy of Olaf STAPLEDON.

The period ranging from the 1880s to the 1930s, largely predating the US boom of the 1920s, was the true golden age of French sf: we might call it France's pulp era. Not that there ever existed any specific sf magazines, but wide-circulation periodicals such as *Journal des voyages* and *La science illustrée* – and, later, *Je sais tout*, *L'Intrépide* and the very important *Sciences et voyages* – regularly ran stories and serialized novels of "anticipation". Sf was thus lent a degree of respectability by being introduced as an extension of travel and adventure stories. In the general title given to his work, Jules Verne had proceeded similarly from "known" to "unknown" worlds.

Apart from isolated works by nonspecialists such as *L'Ève future* (**1886**; trans as *The Eve of the Future* **1981** US; new trans as *Tomorrow's Eve* **1982** US) by VILLIERS DE L'ISLE-ADAM, *L'île des pingouins* (**1908**; trans as *Penguin Island* **1909**) by Anatole FRANCE and *Le Napus, fléau de l'an 2227* ["The 'Disappearance': Scourge of the Year 2227"] (**1927**) by Léon Daudet (1868-1942), this period gave birth to a host of popular writers:

Paul d'Ivoi, Louis BOUSSENARD, then Gustave Le Rouge, Jean de La Hire, André Couvreur, José Moselli, René Thévenin, etc. All were not of equal worth, but three names are outstanding: Maurice RENARD, author of the amazing *Le docteur Lerne* (**1908**; trans as *New Bodies for Old* **1923**), which he dedicated to H.G. WELLS; Jacques SPITZ, whose best novel was *L'oeil du purgatoire* ["The Eye of Purgatory"] (**1945**) and whose earlier *L'agonie du globe* (**1935**; trans as *Save the Earth* **1936**) was given a UK edition; and Régis Messac (1893-1943), whose *Quinzinzinzili* (**1935**) and *La cité des asphyxiés* ["City of the Suffocated"] (**1934**) exhibit a sinister mood and grim humour that deserve to gain him a new audience today.

WWII put an end to this thriving period, and during the 1940s only one writer of note appeared: René BARJAVEL, with *Ravage* (**1943**; trans as *Ashes, Ashes* **1967**) and *Le voyageur imprudent* (**1944**; trans as *Future Times Three* **1971**). At the end of WWII two factors were to bear heavily on the future of sf in France. The first was the growing separation, at school, in the universities and in all thinking circles, between *les littéraires* and *les scientifiques*. This made for a lack of curiosity on the part of aspiring novelists about science and its possible effects on the shapes of our lives, and drove many talents away from the genre, which was definitely viewed as teenager-fodder. France had, as it were, ceased to dream about its own future – and about the future generally. Second, whatever interest in these matters existed was satisfied from another source, the USA. In the years following WWII the French public discovered all at once jazz, US films, thrillers and the US GOLDEN AGE OF SF. One key personality of the period was Boris VIAN, novelist, songwriter, film buff and jazz musician, who translated both Raymond Chandler and A.E. VAN VOGT. This was the time of the creation of *Le club des savanturiers* by Michel Pilotin, Vian, Raymond Queneau and Audiberti. In 1951, Queneau wrote an introductory essay in *Critique*: "Un nouveau genre littéraire: les sciences-fictions" ["A New Literary Genre: SF"], followed two years later by Michel Butor, with "La crise de croissance de la science-fiction" (1953 *Cahiers du Sud*; trans as "SF: The Crisis of its Growth", *Partisan Review* 1967; reprinted in *SF: The Other Side of Realism* [anth **1971**] ed T. CLARESON).

Sf was again fashionable but mainly in translated form. Between 1951 and 1964, the **Rayon fantastique** series published 119 titles, mostly US; it was followed in 1954 by **Présence du Futur**, which still exists today. By the end of the decade some French names were appearing on the list of the former (Francis Carsac [pseudonym of François Bordes (1919-1977)], Philippe CURVAL and Albert Higon, pseudonym of Michel Jeury [1934-]) and the latter (Jacques STERN-BERG, Jean Hougron), but for the most part French authors were published, often under pseudonyms, in the less prestigious **Fleuve noir** series, created in 1951. The best of these were Stefan WUL, B.R. Bruss (Roger Blondel), Kurt Steiner (André Ruellan) and

Gilles d'Argyre (Gérard KLEIN).

In 1953 Éditions Opta launched the French editions of *Gal* and *FSF*, *Galaxie* and *Fiction*, whose contents differ notably from those of their US models. These two would remain for many years the principal outlet for US stories and a springboard for new French talents, including critics. But such were few and far between. The initial impetus given by the discovery of US sf in the 1950s slowed down during the following decade. One magazine which devoted more space to indigenous authors, *Satellite*, had a brief life. Among the new writers, Michel Demuth, Alain Dorémieux and Gérard Klein were soon absorbed by editorial responsibilities and their output consequently became irregular.

The most personal voice during this period and the succeeding years has been that of Philippe Curval who, from *Le ressac de l'espace* ["The Breakers of Space"] (**1962**) through *Cette chère humanité* ["This Dear Humanity"] (**1976**), has consistently maintained a high standard while never imitating the US model. Beside him we should again mention Michel Jeury, who resumed writing (under his own name) with *Le temps incertain* ["Uncertain Time"] (**1973**), and Daniel Drode (1932-), whose only novel was *Surface de la planète* ["Surface of the Planet"] (**1959**). Mainstream writers occasionally tackled sf: Pierre BOULLE with *La planète des singes* (**1963**; trans as *Planet of the Apes* **1963**; vt *Monkey Planet* UK); Robert MERLE with *Un animal doué de raison* (**1967**; trans as *The Day of the Dolphin* **1969**) and *Malevil* (**1972**; trans **1974**); and Claude Ollier, an adept of the *nouveau roman*, with *La vie sur Epsilon* ["Life on Epsilon"] (**1972**).

In the 1970s the situation underwent new changes, once more due to a definite influence: that of the UK NEW WAVE and in particular post-NEW-WORLDS sf. J.G. BALLARD's later work, along with that of such US writers as Thomas M. DISCH, Harlan ELLISON, Norman SPINRAD and, above all, Philip K. DICK, had a tremendous impact on the new generation of readers who lived through the 1968 student uprising and saw the possibilities of making powerful political statements in speculative form. Several young authors who began writing in the mid-1960s (Daniel WALTHER, Jean-Pierre Andrevon, Jean-Pierre Hubert) readily took that route, and were followed by a batch of newcomers, with Dominique Douay, Pierre Pelot and Philippe Goy the best among them.

Nevertheless, the effervescence of the late 1970s did not survive into the 1980s. Lack of enthusiasm on the part of the public? Overabundance of books? Difficulties linked to general publishing problems? It was the beginning of a critical period in which the number of sf imprints, about 40 during the late 1970s, diminished to a half-dozen. The so-called "New French SF", sometimes inordinately politicized, was the first victim of this crisis. Partly because of its excesses, readers and editors grew weary of French sf authors, who then tried to explore different paths and attract recognition through other means. Some, mostly newcomers, reacted by turning to a form-oriented sf – that is, to a greater preoccupation with style, poetry and experimental writing (Emmanuel Jouanne, Antoine Volodine) – to the point where they sometimes forgot the true nature of the genre. Others were tempted into expressing their personal universes, often powerfully fantastic in kind. Among these were Jean-Marc Ligny, Jacques Barbéri, Francis Berthelot and particularly Serge Brussolo who, in less than 10 years, made his mark with some 40 novels – including such definite masterpieces as *Aussi lourd que le vent* ["As Heavy as the Wind"] (**1981**), *Carnaval de fer* ["Iron Carnival"] (**1983**) and *La nuit du bombardier* ["Night of the Bomber"] (**1989**) – and became the most original and most popular sf writer of his generation. Finally, a third category of authors put their craft into the service of a "neo-classical" sf which invited the reader to reflect upon contemporary issues (ECOLOGY, the media, COMPUTERS, genetics, cultural intermingling) though without giving up the traditional lures of exoticism and adventure. They include G.-J. Arnaud and his long series **La compagnie des glaces** ["The Ice Company"], which has run since 1981, Bernard Simonay with *Phénix* (**1986**) and Joël Houssin with *Les Vautours* ["The Vultures"] (**1986**) and *Argentine* (**1989**), all books which have found a large audience and won awards.

Today French sf shows a paradoxical face: it includes many talented writers, usually well detached from the UK-US influence, whether long-established authors or newcomers to the genre such as Richard Canal, Pierre Stolze, Raymond Milési and Colette Fayard. But, on the other hand, the dwindling of publishing imprints, magazines and columns – or their outright disappearance (*Fiction* ceased in 1989) – gives the unfortunate impression that the domain is definitely in peril. Thus, the best French authors – notably those with a long career behind them – are now inclined to abandon sf and turn to horror (◊ HORROR IN SF) which, courtesy of Stephen KING, has become increasingly popular (Andrevon, Brussolo), or to mainstream literature (Sternberg, Jeury, Pelot, Andrevon, Curval, Volodine), or to screenplays (Ruellan, Pelot, Houssin), a far more lucrative field.

One would think that the existence of an active, passionate FANDOM – thanks to which the French sf milieu has been holding its own CONVENTIONS since 1974 – would have given a boost to the national production, but such is not the case. French fandom remains self-centred, and is more devoted to its own byzantine arguments than to the task of working efficiently to enlarge sf's public recognition. In other words, fans complain about their preferred literature being locked up in a ghetto, but never do anything really helpful to change that. Only a handful of critics – sometimes translators, editors or writers themselves (Curval, Jeury, Klein) – have tried and are still trying to publish in mainstream magazines or newspapers regular columns or interviews meant to

defend and exemplify sf (French or not) to the general public, who are often ill informed about the genre.   [RL/JCh]

Further reading: *Encyclopédie de l'utopie, des voyages extraordinaires et de la science-fiction* (**1972** Switzerland) by Pierre Versins; *Histoire de la science-fiction moderne* (**1973**) by Jacques SADOUL; *Panorama de la science-fiction* (**1973** Belgium) by Jacques Van Herp; the preface by Gérard KLEIN to *Sur l'autre face du monde & autres romans scientifiques de "Science et voyages"* (anth **1973**) ed A. Valerie; *Malaise dans la science-fiction* (**1977**) by Klein; also useful are 4 anthologies of French sf short stories, *Les Mondes francs*, *L'Hexagone halluciné*, *La Frontière éclatée* and *Les Mosaïques du temps* (**1988–90**) ed Klein, Ellen Herzfeld and Dominique Martel.

FRANCE, ANATOLE Working name of Anatole-François Thibault (1844-1924), French writer active from the early 1860s until his death. His essayistic "pagan" SATIRES seem perhaps less relevant now than formerly, their amused rationality failing to bite with sufficient savagery into targets like official religion and sexual prudery. Of sf interest are *Sur la pierre blanche* (**1905**; trans Charles E. Roche as *The White Stone* **1910**), in which a group of intellectuals prognosticates a White Peril (the Yellow races being at risk) and the rise of Socialism; and *L'île des pingouins* (**1908**; trans A.W. Evans as *Penguin Island* **1909** UK), in which humanity's evolutionary course is allegorized satirically through the transformation into humans – after they have been baptised in error – of a race of penguins, who repeat human history. In *La révolte des anges* (**1914**; trans Mrs Wilfrid Jackson as *The Revolt of the Angels* **1914** UK), a fantasy and AF's finest novel, an angel – corrupted by the world of books – realizes that his fallen brethren were in the right. AF won the Nobel Prize for Literature in 1921.   [JC]

Other works: *Thaïs* (**1890**; trans, almost certainly by Charles Carrington, **1901** France); *L'Etui de Nacre* (coll **1892**; trans Henry Pene du Bois as *Tales from a Mother-of-Pearl Casket* **1896** US; vt *Mother of Pearl* **1908** UK); *Le Puits de Sainte Clare* (coll **1895**; trans, almost certainly by Charles Carrington, as *The Well of St Clare* **1903** France); *Honey-Bee* (trans Mrs John Lane **1911** UK), a tale first published with other fantasies in *Balthazar* (coll **1889**; trans Mrs John Lane **1909** UK); *Les Sept Femmes de la Barbe-Bleu, et autres contes merveilleux* (coll **1909**; trans Mrs D.B. Stewart as *The Seven Wives of Bluebeard, and Other Marvellous Tales* **1920** UK).

See also: ECONOMICS; FRANCE; UTOPIAS.

FRANCES, STEPHEN (DANIEL) (1917-1989) UK publisher and pulp writer who lived in Spain from the early 1950s. In the mid-1940s he founded his own publishing company, Pendulum Publications, which released a variety of genre fiction, including sf. The editor of his sf line, Frank ARNOLD, introduced SDF to John CARNELL, a meeting that led to the birth of NEW WORLDS in 1946; but after only 3 issues the company was sold (and liquidated).

SDF then founded his own self-named company. For it he penned a series of fast-moving US-style thrillers as by Hank JANSON; they achieved remarkable success at the time. Also for it he created the house name Astron DEL MARTIA (*which see*), but soon sold the name to Gaywood Press to help finance his move to Spain. Later he wrote three sf novels as by Hank Janson: *The Unseen Assassin* (**1953**), a routine tale in which an alien disease threatens to wipe out humanity, *Tomorrow and a Day* (**1955**), a stronger post-HOLOCAUST tale, and *One Against Time* (**1956** as by Janson; 1969 as by Del Martia), a TIME-TRAVEL tale pitting a mathematician against the World Council from a future threatened by his genius. SDF's later novel, *The Disorientated Man* (**1966**; vt *Scream and Scream Again* 1967 US) as by Peter SAXON, a mad-SCIENTIST tale filmed in 1969 as SCREAM AND SCREAM AGAIN, was heavily revised by W. Howard BAKER. [SH]

About the author: *The Trials of Hank Janson* (**1991**) by Stephen HOLLAND.

FRANCHISE ◊ SHARECROP.

FRANCIS, RICHARD H. Working name of UK author and academic Richard Francis (1945-   ), who added a fictitious "H" to distinguish himself from Dick Francis, the thriller writer. RHF's first novel, *Blackpool Vanishes* (**1979**), tells the quirky, extremely English story of what happens when microscopic ALIENS kidnap the town of Blackpool. *Swansong* (**1986**) is a mildly fantastic SATIRE on Margaret Thatcher's UK, the Falklands War and the brutally unexpected disasters of both personal and political history. [NT]

See also: UFOS.

FRANK, PAT (HARRY HART) (1907-1964) US journalist and author; a government official during WWII, he later served with the UN. Though his three sf novels are well known within the field, PF was not generally identified as an sf author. His first novel, *Mr Adam* (**1946**), exploits the fears of contamination felt in the USA after Hiroshima. All men but one are sterilized by a nuclear DISASTER; the experiences of the sole fertile male are rather feebly rendered as comical, providing grounds for a SATIRE on government procedures. *Forbidden Area* (**1956**; vt *Seven Days to Never* 1957 UK) also deals – more grimly – with the atomic question, in a thriller plot involving sabotage and near-HOLOCAUST. In his most famous novel, *Alas, Babylon* (**1959**), the disaster is again nuclear, but this time it is not averted. In a part of Florida that has survived the holocaust, the inhabitants of a small town manage, perhaps rather implausibly, to cope (◊ PASTORAL; ROBINSONADE) and modestly to flourish; domestic verisimilitude and apocalypse mingle here attractively, and the book was both made into a play and televised. PF's work draws its clear emotional force from the deep fears of nuclear devastation many Americans suffered, with some cause, during the 1950s. [JC]

FRANKAU, GILBERT (1884-1952) UK writer known mainly for his work outside the sf field, most notably his Byronesque verse novel *One of Us* (**1912**) and dozens of popular romances. *The Seeds of Enchantment*

(**1921**) is a lost-race (◊ LOST WORLDS) fantasy which features contrasting UTOPIAS in the wilds of Indochina. His posthumous sf novel, *Unborn Tomorrow: A Last Story* (**1953**), depicts a 50th-century Roman Catholic world where a beam which destroys all explosives has enforced a happy return to a pre-industrial lifestyle. [JC]

Other work: *Son of the Morning* (**1949**).

FRANKE, HERBERT W(ERNER) (1927-   ) Austrian-born writer and scientist who, after receiving a doctorate in Vienna in 1950, moved to Munich, where he taught cybernetic aesthetics at the University of Munich. After publishing considerable nonfiction in the 1950s, mostly on either speleology or computer graphics, he also began publishing sf, at first speculative short stories like those assembled in *Der grüne Komet* ["The Green Comet"] (coll **1960**), *Einsteins Erben* ["Einstein's Heirs"] (coll **1972**) and *Zarathustra kehrt zurück* ["Zarathustra Returns"] (coll **1977**). He has also published several novels beginning with *Das Gedankennetz* (**1961**; trans Christine Priest as *The Mind Net* 1974 US). *Der Orchideenkäfig* (**1961**; trans Christine Priest as *The Orchid Cage* 1973 US) complexly depicts, in HWF's typically speculative, somewhat dry manner, the profound transformative effects of a mysterious planet on its human explorers. *Zone Null* (**1970**; trans **1974** US) sets up between a future Free World and an apparently defeated and deserted Zone Null a metaphysical questioning of the true aims of society and of the intermingled values of both opposed sides. In *Transpluto* (**1982**), which is typical of his later work, a mysterious planet hornswoggles a team of Earthmen, keeping them from leaving the Solar System. HWF is one of the first contemporary German sf writers whose work ranks with that in English and other European languages. [JC]

Other works: *Die Glasfalle* ["The Glass Trap"] (**1961**); *Die Stahlwüste* ["The Steel Desert"] (**1962**); *Fahrt zum Licht* ["Expedition to Light"] (**1962**); *Planet der Verlorenen* ["Planet of the Lost"] (**1963**) as by Sergius Both; *Der Elfenbeinturm* ["The Ivory Tower"] (**1965**); *Ypsilon Minus* (**1976**); *Ein Kyborg namens Joe* ["A Cyborg Named Joe"] (**1978**); *Sirius Transit* (**1979**); *Schule für Übermenschen* ["School for Supermen"] (**1980**); *Paradies 3000* ["Paradise 3000"] (**1981**); *Keine Spur vom Leben* ["No Trace of Life"] (**1982**); *Die Kälte des Weltraums* ["The Coldness of Space"] (**1982**); *Tod eines Unsterblichen* ["Death of an Immortal"] (**1982**); *Endzeit* ["End of Time"] (**1985**); *Der Atem der Sonne* ["The Breath of the Sun"] (**1986**); *Zentrum der Milchstrasse* ["The Centre of the Milky Way"] (**1990**); *Spiegel der Gedanken* ["Mirror of Thought"] (coll **1990**).

See also: AUSTRIA; GERMANY.

FRANKENHEIMER, JOHN (1930-   ) US film director. A graduate of the 1950s school of live tv drama, JF first attracted attention as a film-maker with melodramas centred on youth and social issues: *The Young Stranger* (1956), *The Young Savages* (1961), *All Fall Down* (1961) and *The Birdman of Alcatraz* (1962).

However, in his direction of *The* MANCHURIAN CANDI-DATE (1962), *Seven Days in May* (1964) and SECONDS (1966), all based on successful novels, JF revealed a distinctive fantastic vision, rooted in the realities of the USA of the 1950s and 1960s, which would be a great influence on the 1970s run of post-Watergate conspiracy movies, like Alan J. Pakula's *The Parallax View* (1974) and William Richert's *Winter Kills* (1979). *Seven Days in May*, in which the USA is threatened by a military coup, and *The Manchurian Candidate* are political fantasies focusing on the precariousness of the presidency, while *Seconds*, one of the scariest films of the 1960s, is a nightmare about rejuvenation. These exercises in unease are confidently shot in black-and-white with the Expressionist imagination of a top-drawer TWILIGHT ZONE episode, and feature a brilliant oddball casting of his stars. JF's films at this stage are a vision of a grey-suited corporate USA gone wrong, with recurrent themes of brainwashing, surveillance, assassination and Kafkaesque bureau-cracies, many of which returned in his still-underrated comic-book gangster fantasy *99 & 44/100% Dead* (1974; vt *Call Harry Crown*) and the large-scale terrorist thriller *Black Sunday* (1977). He had a commercial success with *The French Connection II* (1975), but his return to sf with PROPHECY (1979), a hokey, expensive MONSTER MOVIE, was a major disappointment, and his more recent films have tended to be bland adaptations of best-selling thrillers.   [KN]

See also: CINEMA; PARANOIA.

FRANKENSTEIN Film (1931). Universal. Dir James Whale, starring Boris Karloff, Colin Clive, Mae Clarke, Edward van Sloan, Dwight Frye. Screenplay Garrett Fort, Robert Florey, Francis Edward Faragoh, based on an adaptation by Florey and John L. Balderston of the play by Peggy Webling, based in turn on *Frankenstein, or The Modern Prometheus* (**1818**) by Mary SHELLEY. 71 mins. B/w.

This remains the most famous of the Frankenstein films, although it was not the first. (The Edison Company made a 16min version in 1910; it was dir J. Searle Dawley and starred Charles Ogle as the Monster. A second version, also US, was the 70min *Life without Soul* in 1915, dir Joseph W. Smiley.) Dr Frankenstein is a SCIENTIST who builds an artificial man using parts from stolen bodies. He succeeds, with the aid of an electrical storm, in bringing the creature to life but, because his assistant has provided the brain of a criminal rather than that of a "normal" man (a clumsy plot device which has nothing to do with Shelley's novel), the creation proves difficult to control. Eventually the FRANKENSTEIN MONSTER es-capes, accidentally kills a small girl, and is pursued and apparently slain by angry villagers (originally the Monster killed Frankenstein, too, but the studio substituted a happy ending).

The film remains a semi-classic today. With his atmospheric lighting, smooth tracking shots and numerous low-angle shots that were never obtrusive but made effective use of the high-ceilinged sets – particularly Frankenstein's laboratory – Whale suc-ceeded in making a HORROR film of some grandeur, with an undertone of ironic humour. Much of the credit must go to Karloff for his fine (unspeaking) performance as the pathetic Monster, considerably helped by Jack Pierce's famous make-up; Karloff's success here doomed him to horror roles for the rest of his life.

There have been numerous sequels and remakes. The sequel BRIDE OF FRANKENSTEIN (1935), also dir Whale, is the best film he ever made. Other, increasingly awful, sequels from Universal were *Son of Frankenstein* (1939), *Ghost of Frankenstein* (1942), *Frankenstein Meets the Wolfman* (1943), *House of Frank-enstein* (1945) and *Abbott and Costello Meet Frankenstein* (1948). In 1957 the UK company Hammer Films remade the original, calling it *Curse of Frankenstein* (vt *Birth of Frankenstein*), and then made *The Revenge of Frankenstein* (1958), *The Evil of Frankenstein* (1964), *Frankenstein Created Woman* (1966), *Frankenstein Must Be Destroyed* (1969) and *The Horror of Frankenstein* (1970), ending with *Frankenstein and the Monster from Hell* (1973). Five of these were dir Terence Fisher, and nearly all featured Peter Cushing's interestingly tense and upright performance as Baron von Frankenstein. Andy Warhol produced in Italy a 3-D SPLATTER-MOVIE pornographic version (remarkably tasteless on all counts) dir Paul Morrissey (or possibly an uncredited Antonio Margheriti): *Carne per Frankenstein* (1973; vt *Flesh for Frankenstein*; vt *Andy Warhol's Frankenstein*). A successful parody/homage movie was *Young Frank-enstein* (1974), dir Mel Brooks. Other versions of the story, mostly exploitation films, were made in Italy and Spain. Two more US titles are *Frankenstein 1970* (1958), dir Howard W. Koch and starring an ageing Boris Karloff, and *Frankenstein Meets the Space Monster* (1965; vt *Mars Invades Puerto Rico*), which is not about Frankenstein at all. There are many more.

An interesting attempt to recreate Mary Shelley's original novel, including its finale in the Arctic (all previous films had changed the story), is the 3-hour made-for-tv film *Frankenstein: The True Story* (1973), Universal/NBC, dir Jack Smight, from a script by Christopher Isherwood and Don Bachardy, starring James Mason, David McCallum and Michael Sarra-zin. It was theatrically released, cut to 123 mins. The teleplay was published as *Frankenstein: The True Story*∗ (**1973**), by Isherwood and Bachardy.

A book about versions of the story is *Hideous Progenies: Dramatizations of Frankenstein from Mary Shelley to the Present* (**1990**) by Steven Earl Forry. [JB/PN]

See also: FRANKENSTEIN UNBOUND; GOTHIC SF; MONSTER MOVIES; SEX.

FRANKENSTEIN MONSTER The term is in general use, not only in sf TERMINOLOGY but in common parlance, to mean a MONSTER that ultimately turns and rends its irresponsible creator. Note that in the original novel Frankenstein was the name of the creator and not of the monster, though in popular

usage it is often assumed that the monster itself is Frankenstein. In critical talk, Frankenstein is often equated with Prometheus and Dr Faustus, two other legendary figures who were guilty of *hubris* in their quest for knowledge, and struck down.   [PN]
See also: FRANKENSTEIN; HORROR IN SF; MONSTER MOVIES; Mary SHELLEY.

FRANKENSTEIN: THE TRUE STORY ◊ FRANKEN-STEIN.

FRANKENSTEIN UNBOUND (vt *Roger Corman's Frankenstein Unbound*) Film (1990). Warner Brothers. Dir Roger CORMAN, starring John Hurt, Raul Julia, Bridget Fonda, Nick Brimble, Katherine Rabbett, Jason Patric, Michael Hutchence. Screenplay Corman, F.X. Feeney, based on *Frankenstein Unbound* (1973) by Brian W. ALDISS. 85 mins. Colour.

This philosophical (about the dangers of the Promethean impulse) TIME-TRAVEL horror/fantasy was the first film directed by Corman for 20 years. A 21st-century scientist (Hurt) is time-warped into 19th-century Switzerland. On one side of Lake Geneva the Byron/Shelley ménage is living; on the other the plot of Mary SHELLEY's *Frankenstein, or The Modern Prometheus* (1818) is being played out. Hurt gets involved with both sets of characters and winds up whisking MONSTER and maker off to an ice-age future for a splattery plot resolution, laced with conservative lectures about the evils of science. Some of the plentiful laughs may be intended, given that Aldiss's playful novel is in part a comedy, though Fonda is ridiculous as the dainty but promiscuous Mary. There are some cheapskate effects, but Raul Julia is good as the mad visionary; the angry-at-the-world FRANKEN-STEIN MONSTER (Brimble) comes with impressive details like scarred eyeballs; and the GOTHIC horror set-pieces are directed with unselfconscious panache.   [KN]

FRANKLIN, EDGAR Working name used for his publications by US writer Edgar Franklin Stearns (1879-?   ), whose *Mr Hawkins' Humorous Inventions* (coll of linked stories **1904**), all reprinted from *The ARGOSY*, features the eponymous inventor/scientist comically failing to make a series of devices, such as the pumpless pump, work properly; the series continued to 1915 in various of the Frank A. MUNSEY magazines.   [JC]
See also: HUMOUR.

FRANKLIN, H. BRUCE (1934-   ) US critic, John Cotton Dana Professor of English and American Studies at Rutgers. In 1961 HBF gave at Stanford one of the earliest university courses in sf in the USA. In 1972 he was dismissed by Stanford for giving speeches protesting the university's involvement in the Vietnam War – a case well known to those interested in questions of academic freedom. His *Future Perfect: American Science Fiction of the Nineteenth Century* (anth **1966**; rev 1968; exp and rev 1978) has been one of the most influential of sf ANTHOLOGIES, in drawing attention to the sheer volume of 19th-century sf. A later HBF anthology, containing sf

about nuclear weapons, is *Countdown to Midnight* (anth **1984**). HBF's two other books about sf are *Robert A. Heinlein: America as Science Fiction* (**1980**) and *War Stars: The Superweapon and the American Imagination* (**1988**). The former relates HEINLEIN's career to contemporary US history from a Marxist perspective; the latter is a pungent and important study about the US preoccupation with super-WEAPONS in fact and fiction, and the way in which the fact has been influenced by the fiction. HBF has published many other critical articles on sf and is among the genre's most respected commentators. He received the PILGRIM AWARD in 1983. He has been a consulting editor of SCIENCE-FICTION STUDIES since its inception.   [PN]
See also: CRITICAL AND HISTORICAL WORKS ABOUT SF; SF IN THE CLASSROOM; WAR.

FRANKOWSKI, LEO A. (1943-   ) US writer known principally for his ALTERNATE-WORLD series, the **Adventures of Conrad Stargard**: *The Cross-Time Engineer* (**1986**), *The High-Tech Knight* (**1989**), *The Radiant Warrior* (**1989**), *The Flying Warlord* (**1989**) and *Lord Conrad's Lady* (**1990**), with further volumes projected. The series features a Polish-US engineer, Stargard, who in the first volume is transported to medieval Poland via TIME TRAVEL. He settles down quite happily to the task of reshaping his native land into a country capable of surviving the next perilous decades, being overseen all the while by the time-travellers who have mistakenly conveyed him there. By changing the technology of medieval Poland, Stargard is of course changing timelines – in perfectly orthodox sf-adventure fashion – but the author's clear indifference to the plotting rigours expected in tales of this sort increasingly detracts from the flow of the story. *Copernick's Rebellion* (**1987**) deals with GENETIC ENGINEERING in a NEAR-FUTURE Polish setting, where LAF's inability to create women (though he is strong on breasts) is seriously irritating.   [JC]

FRANK READE LIBRARY US DIME-NOVEL SF series, BEDSHEET size. 191 issues (#188-#191 are reprints of #1-#4) 24 Sep 1892-8 Aug 1898, weekly to 8 June 1894 (#82), biweekly from then on. Cost 5¢. Published by Frank Tousey, Publisher, New York. (Partial reissue 1902-4, partial UK reprint.) All issues were printed on very poor paper and seldom survive in good condition; the 1902-4 reissue, with coloured covers, is sometimes considered more desirable than the first printing.

This was the earliest serial publication devoted solely to sf, with more issues than all of Hugo GERNSBACK's sf magazines put together, each containing a single or a half story about **Frank Reade** (4 stories) or **Frank Reade, Jr.** (179 stories). All but the last were attributed to "NONAME" on their appearance in the *FRL*. About one-quarter of the stories were reprints from other Tousey BOYS' PAPERS (*The Boys of New York*, *The Five Cent Wide Awake Library*, *Happy Days*); the remainder were originals. As a whole, they comprise the most significant US dime-novel series, and in their exuberance (and stereotyped action), their humour (and their racism), their inventiveness (and the merciless repetition of similar inventions and WEAPONS), they represent the best and worst of the tradition.

It is impossible to attain final bibliographical certainty about a series of this sort, but E.F. BLEILER's *The Frank Reade Library* (omni 10 vols **1979-86**), which reprints the entire sequence, casts as much light as can ever be hoped for. It is not known, for instance, how many authors wrote as "Noname", a house pseudonym used for mysteries and Westerns as well as sf, though it is certain that the first **Frank Reade** story – *Frank Reade and his Steam Man of the Plains* (1876 *The Boys of New York* as by Harry Enton; **1892** as *Frank Reade Library #12* as by "Noname") – was by Harold Cohen (1854-1927), who normally wrote as Enton. The tale was almost certainly commissioned by Frank Tousey in emulation of Edward S. ELLIS's *The Steam Man of the Prairies* (**1868**). Three more **Frank Reade** episodes followed (the first two written by Cohen), all involving steam-driven TRANSPORTATION devices whose main use (it is one of the less attractive features of the sequence, many of whose episodes were set in the US West) seemed to be that of slaughtering large numbers of Native Americans.

In 1882, **Frank Reade, Jr.**, son of **Frank Reade**, took over the action, beginning with *Frank Reade, Jr., and his Steam Wonder* (1882 *The Boys of New York*; **1893** as *Frank Reade Library #20*). The popularity of these stories presumably inspired Tousey to institute **The Frank Reade Library** itself in 1892. The first 50 issues or so generally reprinted tales from 1880s Tousey magazines; the remaining issues, beginning 1893, were mostly original titles. It is probable that most of the **Frank Reade, Jr.** stories were written by Luis SENARENS, and *en masse* they suffered visibly from this hugely prolific author's carelessness, cheap jingoism, racist stereotyping and lackadaisical plotting. But, tedious or not, the sequence managed to make use of most of the sf venues and devices available at the close of the 19th century; in particular, airships and submarines and various other means of TRANSPORTA-TION – which served simultaneously as devastating weapons and means of near-magical travel (◊ EDISO-NADE) – almost always featured prominently in the adventures of the indefatigable boy inventor. Significant issues include #48, *Frank Reade, Jr., Exploring a River of Mystery* (1890 *Five Cent Wide Awake Library*; **1893**), not by Senarens, which has fantastic geography and travels in Africa and is based on Henry Stanley's books or newspaper dispatches, and #133: *The Island in the Air* (**1896**), probably by Senarens, perhaps the first consideration of Roraima (in British Guiana) as a LOST WORLD, almost certainly a source for *The Lost World* (**1912**) by A. Conan DOYLE. More typical, however, is the long episodic novel *Frank Reade, Jr., and his Queen Clipper of the Clouds* (1889 *The Boys of New York*; **1893**) by Senarens.

The **Frank Reade Library**, however, does not contain all the adventures of the inventive Reade family. There are at least two uncollected stories about **Frank Reade, Jr.** and one about **Frank Reade** (Sr.). The last, *Franke Reade, the Inventor, Chasing the James Boys with his Steam Team* (**1890**), stands apart from the series and is the only **Frank Reade** story not attributed to "Noname". The third member of the Reade family, **Frank Reade, III**, stars in *Young Frank Reade and his Electric Air Ship* (**1899**) and perhaps in other unlocated stories. [EFB/JC]

FRASER, Sir RONALD (ARTHUR) (1888-1974) UK writer and civil servant. Most of his work, like his first novel, *The Flying Draper* (**1924**; rev **1931**), utilizes fantasy or sf devices – in the initial case self-levitation – to create allegorical or philosophical arguments; the unmistakably Wellsian draper, for instance, finds that the ability to fly enforces "higher" thoughts. In *Flower Phantoms* (**1926**) an orchid responds to the protagonist's nubility by showing her the secrets of sex. In *Beetle's Career* (**1951**), which is sf, a super-weapon is shown to have beneficial side-effects. In the **Venus** quartet – *A Visit from Venus* (**1958**), *Jupiter in the Chair* (**1958**), *Trout's Testament* (**1960**) and *City of the Sun* (**1961**) – various inhabitants of the Solar System confer about a number of mildly pressing topics. In an elegant, generally painless manner, RS concentrated throughout his career on novels of controlled wit, mild SATIRE and admissible sentiment; only occasionally would these entertainments move into the darker regions. [JC]

Other works: *Landscape with Figures* (**1925**), an oriental fantasy; *Miss Lucifer* (**1939**); *The Fiery Gate* (**1943**); *Sun in Scorpio* (**1949**); *A Work of Imagination: (The Pen – the Brush – the Well)* (**1974**), a novel of occultism.

See also: PSYCHOLOGY.

FRATZ, D(ONALD) DOUGLAS (1952-   ) US editor who founded the energetic sf news and reviews journal THRUST in 1973, renaming it *Quantum* with #36 (**1990**). He remains (1992) its editor and (from #5) its publisher. [JC]

FRAU IM MOND, DIE (vt *By Rocket to the Moon*; vt *The Girl in the Moon*; vt *The Woman in the Moon*) Film (1929). UFA. Dir Fritz LANG, starring Gerda Maurus, Willy Fritsch, Gustav von Wangenheim, Fritz Rasp, Klaus Pohl. Screenplay Lang, Thea VON HARBOU, based on *Frau im Mond* (**1928**) by von Harbou. 156 mins, cut to 107 mins, cut to 97 mins. B/w.

After the success of METROPOLIS, Fritz Lang's next sf film was a disappointment. Overlong (in its original form) and melodramatic, it concerns an ill matched group of people travelling to a MOON which seems little different from the Swiss Alps, airlessness and low gravity being ignored: the explorers are able to amble about picking up chunks of precious metal and jewels (the trip having been arranged by industrial-ists who believe, correctly, that the Moon is rich in gold). The build-up to the take-off, however, is much more convincing; Lang used rocket experts Hermann Oberth (1894-1989) and Willy LEY as technical advis-ers, and the model rocket they produced was prophetic in its design – it was even constructed in two stages. The blast-off itself was also impressive, with good camera-work by Oskar Fischinger and effects by Konstantin Tschetwerikoff. Later the Nazis withdrew the film from distribution and destroyed the rocket model, afraid that its accuracy would give away secrets about their own development of military ROCKETS. [JB/PN]

See also: CINEMA; GERMANY.

FRAYN, MICHAEL (1933-   ) UK novelist, journalist and playwright, best known for such work outside the sf field as the novel *Towards the End of the Morning* (**1967**; vt *Against Entropy* 1967 US), which despite its vt is not sf. *The Tin Men* (**1965**) is a SATIRE on the computerization of human consciousness. *A Very Private Life* (**1968**) describes a sanitized Earth with mankind divided into those who live inside germ-free enclaves and those who live outdoors; some ambivalence is expressed throughout as to whether what is being described is a DYSTOPIA or simply a *mise en scène*: MF lacks, in other words, the ready animus so often found in MAINSTREAM WRITERS when they appropriate sf tropes – almost always imprudently – for satirical purposes. [JC]

Other works: *Sweet Dreams* (**1973**), an afterlife fantasy.

See also: AUTOMATION; LINGUISTICS.

FRAZER, SHAMUS Pseudonym of UK writer James Ian Arbuthnot Frazer (1912-   ), whose sf novel, *A Shroud as Well as a Shirt* (**1935**), describes a succession of NEAR-FUTURE political conflicts which lead finally to a world war. *Blow, Blow Your Trumpets* (**1945**) is a comic satirical fantasy set in the time of Noah, and explains the necessity of the Flood. [JC]

FRAZETTA, FRANK (1928-   ) US illustrator, born Frank Frazzetta. A New Yorker, he studied at the Brooklyn Academy of Fine Arts and was then active almost exclusively in COMICS 1944-63, working on both BUCK ROGERS IN THE 25TH CENTURY and FLASH GORDON and spending 9 years on *Li'l Abner*. By the time he came to prominence as a comics illustrator, working on *Creepy* for Warren Publications (from 1965) and later *Vampirella*, he had already been introduced (in 1964) to paperback-book-cover ILLUSTRATION by his friend Roy G. KRENKEL, first for ACE BOOKS and then for Lancer Books. He quickly became known (like Krenkel) for HEROIC-FANTASY illustrations, especially (from 1966) for his covers for Lancer's reissue of Robert E. HOWARD's **Conan** books. Some of his work was sf. He won his only HUGO for Best Professional Artist in 1966, but the lack of further Hugos did not imply a diminution in popularity – on the contrary, although his following was largely, presumably, among FANTASY rather than sf fans. Around this time FF set up, with his wife, a company to sell posters he had designed; later he also painted for a number of calendars. Portfolios produced at this time included the two volumes entitled *Burroughs Artist Frank Frazetta* (portfolio **1968** and **1973**). A further breakthrough was the publication of *The Fantastic Art of Frank Frazetta* (**1975**), which was

followed by *Frank Frazetta Book Two* (**1977**) and then *Three* (**1978**), *Four* (**1980**) and *Five* (**1985**). By the 1980s, however, FF's fame extended well beyond narrow genres: his work was spread over many commercial areas, and his output of specifically fantasy/sf illustration became very small – although it did include the **Death Dealer** novels by James R. Silke with FF, from 1988, based on an idea (and covers) by FF, as well as covers for the L. RON HUBBARD PRESENTS WRITERS OF THE FUTURE series of original anthologies. Film work by FF includes *Fire and Ice* (1982), an animated SWORD-AND-SORCERY feature film, produced by Ralph Bakshi and FF, partly designed by FF.

FF's vigorous paintings of heavily muscled heroes, often fighting, are notable for their dynamic sense of movement (in contrast, perhaps, to work by Boris VALLEJO and other later, smoother illustrators who are often referred to as having inherited FF's mantle); he is famous, too, for his lush wide-hipped women, often chained or menaced but equally often shown as threatening Amazon Queens. His work has been accused of sexism and criticized as cheaply melodramatic, but at its best it is undeniably spirited and powerful. In the heroic-fantasy mode, FF has been one of the most influential illustrators of the century. [PN]

See also: SEX.

FRAZIER, ROBERT (ALEXANDER) (1951-   ) US editor and writer, most active as a poet, whose several published volumes include *Peregrine* (coll **1978**), *Perception Barriers* (coll **1987**) and *Co-Orbital Moons* (coll **1988**). He has edited 2 vols of sf POETRY, *The Rhysling Anthology: Best Science Fiction Poetry of 1982* (anth **1983** chap) and *Burning with a Vision: Poetry of Science and the Fantastic* (anth **1984**), and is editor of *StarLine*, the newsletter of the SCIENCE FICTION POETRY ASSOCIATION. As an author of fiction, he began relatively late, his first sf story, "Across Those Endless Skies", appearing in *In the Field of Fire* (anth **1987**) ed Jack DANN and Jeanne Dann. He is perhaps most noted for the extended "Summer People", his contribution to *Nantucket Slayrides* (coll **1989**), the other stories in which are by Lucius SHEPARD. RF wrote the POETRY entry in this encyclopedia. [JC]

See also: ISAAC ASIMOV'S SCIENCE FICTION MAGAZINE; SF IN THE CLASSROOM.

FREAS, (FRANK) KELLY (1922-   ) US illustrator, the most popular sf artist in the history of the field; the list of his accomplishments is staggering. Since he entered the field in 1950 he has painted hundreds of covers for 28 magazines, most famously for *ASF* from 1953 (interior work also) but including also *FSF*, *Planet Stories* and *If*, as well as for many book publishers, including ACE BOOKS, GNOME PRESS, DAW BOOKS and all the covers for LASER BOOKS. The gritty realism of his and Ed EMSHWILLER's work in the 1950s redefined sf art during that period. He also painted many covers for *Mad Magazine* and designed the astronauts' shoulder patch for the Skylab 1 mission. His art has been collected in a portfolio from ADVENT:

PUBLISHERS, *Frank Kelly Freas* (portfolio **1957**), and in 2 books, *Frank Kelly Freas: The Art of Science Fiction* (**1977**) and *Frank Kelly Freas: A Separate Star* (**1984**). Much of his work, sometimes reminiscent of that of Edd CARTIER, is relaxedly humorous, featuring vigorous vagabonds, amiable aliens and a selection of jaunty scoundrels. He has won numerous awards, including 10 HUGOS for Best Professional Artist. [JG/PN]
See also: ASTOUNDING SCIENCE-FICTION; ILLUSTRATION.

FREEDMAN, NANCY (1920-   ) US actress and writer whose sf novel, *Joshua Son of None* (**1973**), one of the earliest novels to deal with cloning (◊ CLONES), depicts the intrigue surrounding the childhood and adolescence of Joshua Francis Kellogg, cloned in 1963 from the body of John F. Kennedy. [JC]
Other works: *The Immortals* (**1976**), borderline sf.

FREEDOM: THE VOICE FROM EIN HAROD ◊ ISRAEL.

FREEJACK Film (1992). Morgan Creek/Ronald Shusett/ Warner Bros. Dir Geoff Murphy, starring Emilio Estevez, Mick Jagger, Rene Russo, Anthony Hopkins, Jonathan Banks. Screenplay Steven Pressfield, Ronald Shusett, Dan Gilroy, based on *Immortality, Inc.* (**1958**; exp 1959) by Robert SHECKLEY. 108 mins. Colour.

From the producers of TOTAL RECALL (1990) and the New Zealand director of *The* QUIET EARTH (1985), this disappointing adaptation jettisons much that was interesting in the original book, including the metaphysical speculation about the relation of mind to body and the "scientific" explanations of ghosts, zombies and a technological IMMORTALITY. This is a thriller set 20 years in the future, when rich people with ailing bodies transfer their personalities into healthy bodies hijacked from the past (including our present). Jagger is rather good as the sinister and ubiquitous bodysnatcher who grabs a racing-car driver (Estevez) just as he is about to die violently. Joe Alves's mildly CYBERPUNK production design owes a lot to BLADE RUNNER (1982). [PN]

FREKSA, FRIEDRICH [r] ◊ GERMANY.

FRENCH, PAUL ◊ Isaac ASIMOV.

FRENKEL, JAMES R. (1948-   ) US editor, married to Joan D. VINGE since 1980. In the late 1970s and early 1980s he was with Dell Books, where he ed anon the **Binary Star** books, each comprising two titles bound sequentially (◊ DOS): *Binary Star #1* containing *Destiny Times Three* (**1978** dos) by Fritz LEIBER and *Riding the Torch* (**1978** dos) by Norman SPINRAD, #2 containing *The Twilight River* (**1979** dos) by Gordon EKLUND and *The Tery* (**1979** dos) by F. Paul WILSON, #3 containing *Dr Scofflaw* (**1979** dos) by Ron GOULART and *Outerworld* (**1979** dos) by Isidore HAIBLUM, #4 containing *Legacy* (**1980** dos) by Joan D. VINGE and *The Janus Equation* (**1980** dos) by Steven G. SPRUILL, and #5 containing *Nightflyers* (**1981** dos) by George R.R. MARTIN and *True Names* (**1981** dos) by Vernor VINGE. In 1983 he founded BLUEJAY BOOKS, whose strong but underfunded list was forced to cease trading in 1986. [JC]

FREWIN, ANTHONY (1947-   ) UK publisher and writer, who also worked for five years as an assistant to the film director Stanley KUBRICK. His *One Hundred Years of Science Fiction Illustration: 1840-1940* (**1974**) has a well chosen selection of sf ILLUSTRATIONS, many – unusually – from the 19th century, with a full chapter on Albert ROBIDA. [PN]

FREY, JAMES N. (?   -   ) US writer whose *The Elixir* (**1986**) was a GOTHIC-SF/fantasy story of Nazi Germany, where Hitler's secret weapon is the eponymous aid to IMMORTALITY. [JC]

FREZZA, ROBERT (1956-   ) US writer who began publishing sf with "Max Weber's War" for *AMZ* in 1987. His sf novel, *A Small Colonial War* (**1990**), replays the Boer War on a colony planet, although without Kaffirs. The Imperial military forces, predictably, find the transplanted post-HOLOCAUST Afrikaners tough meat. [JC]

FRIEDBERG, GERTRUDE (TONKONOGY) (1908-1989) US writer who also taught. Her career as a playwright began early, with *Three Cornered Moon* (**1933**), which was later filmed, but she began publishing sf only in 1963, with "The Short and Happy Death of George Frumkin" for *FSF*. Her fine sf novel *The Revolving Boy* (**1966**) strikingly tells the story of a child sensitive from his unique birth in free fall to signals, possibly intelligent in origin, from beyond the Solar System. He reveals his sensitivity by being forced to adjust himself – revolving balletically – so that his body is aligned in the direction from which the signals come. [JC]

FRIEDELL, EGON (1878-1938) Austrian writer best known for his seminal *Cultural History of Modern Times* (**1927-32**), a text which effectively inaugurated the discipline of cultural history. As a Jew, his position became intolerable when the Nazis invaded Austria, and he committed suicide. His wry homage to H.G. WELLS, *Die Rückkehr mit der Zeitmaschine* (apparently written *c*1935; **1946** Germany; trans Eddy C. Bertin as *The Return of the Time Machine* 1972 US), complete with a spoof correspondence between himself as narrator and Wells's secretary, purports to reprint the Time Traveller's narrative of his later journeys. The story, told with a literate wit reminiscent of some of Karel ČAPEK's lighter work, depends on complex mathematical doubletalk for its demonstration of the ultimate futility of TIME TRAVEL. [JC]

FRIEDMAN, MICHAEL JAN (1955-   ) US writer, mostly notably of STAR TREK and STAR TREK: THE NEXT GENERATION ties, though he has also written a singleton, *The Glove of Maiden's Hair* (**1987**), a fantasy set in contemporary New York, and the **Vidar** fantasy sequence about a son of Odin: *The Hammer and the Horn* (**1985**), *The Seekers and the Sword* (**1985**) and *The Fortress and the Fire* (**1988**). MJF's **Star Trek** novels are *Double, Double* ∗ (**1989**), *Legacy* ∗ (**1991**) and *Faces of Fire* ∗ (**1992**). His **Star Trek: The Next Generation** novels are *A Call to Darkness* ∗ (**1989**), *Doomsday World* ∗ (**1990**) with Carmen CARTER, Peter DAVID and Robert Greenberger, *Fortune's Light* ∗ (**1991**) and *Reunion* ∗ (**1991**). [JC]

FRIEL, ARTHUR O(LNEY) (1885-1959) US writer and

explorer, most of whose work appeared in PULP MAGAZINES, including the **McKay, Knoulton and Ryan** sequence of lost-race (*see* LOST WORLD) tales set in South America and featuring the exploits of Americans, who eventually establish a kingdom somewhere close to Peru. Those published as books – *The Pathless Trail* (**1922**), *Tiger River* (**1923**), in which men are transformed into beasts by a strange Circean wine, *The King of No Man's Land* (**1924**) and *Mountains of Mystery* (**1925**) – were marginal as sf; but "In the Year 2000" (**1928** *Adventure*), which never reached book form, is set after a world war in which White men have triumphed. [JC]

FRIEND, ED ◊ Richard WORMSER.

FRIEND, OSCAR J(EROME) (1897-1963) US writer and editor who worked for the Standard Magazine chain on CAPTAIN FUTURE, STARTLING STORIES and THRILLING WONDER STORIES during 1941-4, a period when these magazines were most specifically aimed at adolescents. The editorial director at the time was Leo MARGULIES, with whom OJF later edited 3 anthologies (see below). After the death of Otis Adelbert KLINE in 1946, OJF became head of Kline's literary agency. He was intermittently active as a writer from before 1920, concentrating on horror, Western and detective tales, sometimes as Owen Fox Jerome, his first sf story proper being "Of Jovian Build" for *Thrilling Wonder Stories* in 1938. His first novel, *The Hand of Horror* (**1927**) as by Jerome, was a horror tale involving hynotism. His sf books – *The Kid from Mars* (**1940** *Startling Stories*; **1949**), *Roar of the Rocket* (**1940** *TWS*; **1950** chap Australia) and *The Star Men* (**1963**) – are unremarkable but entertaining. [MJE/JC]
Other works: *From Off this World* (anth **1949**), *My Best Science Fiction Story* (anth **1949**) and *The Giant Anthology of Science Fiction* (anth **1954**; cut vt *Race to the Stars* 1958), all with Leo Margulies.
See also: ALIENS.

FRIGGENS, A. [r] ◊ Eric BURGESS.

FRITCH, CHARLES E. (*c*1920-) US writer and editor who began publishing sf with "The Wallpaper" for *Other Worlds* in 1951. He edited the magazine GAMMA 1963-5. His stories, written for a variety of markets but sharing a certain glibness and snappiness of effect, are collected in *Crazy Mixed-Up Planet* (coll **1969**) and *Horses' Asteroid* (coll **1970**). Many are spoofs. [JC]

FROESE, ROBERT (1945-) US academic and writer whose sf novel, *The Hour of Blue* (**1990**), presents the strangely consoling notion that Gaia herself is beginning to respond defensively to humanity's rape of the planet, and that the forests in Maine (the state where RF himself teaches) are transforming themselves. [JC]

FROGS Film (1972). American International. Dir George McCowan, starring Ray Milland, Sam Elliott, Joan van Ark, Lynn Borden. Screenplay Robert Hutchison, Robert Blees. 90 mins. Colour.
A cheerful exploitation movie, its director's début and part of the 1970s Revenge-of-Nature boom (◊ MONSTER MOVIES), *F* is a rather well made ecological

fable in which upper-crust layabouts living on a bayou are disposed of by frogs, spiders, leeches, snakes and snapping turtles (all normal size, but in large numbers), apparently as a payback for Mankind's ill treatment of Nature: a sort of amphibian *The BIRDS* (1963). [PN]

FROM BEYOND Film (1986). Taryn/Empire. Executive prod Charles BAND. Dir Stuart Gordon, starring Jeffrey Combs, Barbara Crampton, Ken Foree, Ted Sorel, Carolyn Purdy-Gordon. Screenplay Dennis Paoli, based on "From Beyond" (1934) by H.P. LOVECRAFT. 85 mins. Colour.
With three of the same leading players, the same production team, and one of Lovecraft's fringe sf stories as its original, this is effectively a sequel to RE-ANIMATOR (1985), and was made as a direct result of that film's success. Lovecraft's idea was that stimulating the pineal gland might open a window to another DIMENSION peopled by MONSTERS. The film adds an element of sexual stimulation to that (psychiatrists in bondage gear, etc.), a not unreasonable reading of Lovecraft's lurid but repressed imaginings, but the main variation is the glee and (occasional) wit with which the disgusting monsters from beyond are set into action. Though an undergraduate-style exercise in SPLATTER-MOVIE bad taste, *FB* is less gory than *Re-Animator*. [PN]

FROM THE EARTH TO THE MOON Film (1958). Waverly/RKO. Dir Byron HASKIN, starring Joseph Cotton, George Sanders, Deborah Paget. Screenplay Robert Blees, James Leicester, adapted from Jules VERNE's *De la terre à la lune* (**1865**) and *Autour de la lune* (**1870**), the two published together in English translation as *From the Earth to the Moon* (**1873**). 100 mins. Colour.
Using a new explosive, a projectile carrying human passengers is fired at the Moon from a huge cannon. Paget plays a pretty stowaway. The film, shot in Mexico, is slow-moving and has painful dialogue; it is perhaps the dullest sf movie ever made. There are no scenes on the Moon. A comic version, bearing no relation to Verne's novel, was the UK *Jules Verne's Rocket to the Moon* (1967; vt *Those Fantastic Flying Fools*) dir Don Sharp, in which a series of farcical misadventures – the rocket lands in Russia, not on the Moon – keeps the story effectively Earthbound. [PN/JB]

FROST, JASON Zebra Books house name, used almost exclusively by US writer Raymond Obstfeld (1952-) for the **Warlord** sequence of post-HOLOCAUST sf adventures with a survivalist message: *The Warlord* (**1983**), *The Warlord #2: The Cutthroat* (**1984**), *#3: Badland* (**1984**), *#4: Prisonland* (**1985**) and *#5: Terminal Island* (**1985**). *#6: Killer's Keep* (**1987**) was written as JF by Rich Rainey. A singleton film tie, *Invasion U.S.A.* * (**1985**), was by Obstfeld. [JC]

FTL Acronym, often used in sf TERMINOLOGY, for FASTER THAN LIGHT.

FUENTES, CARLOS (1929-) Mexican diplomat and writer whose acerbic MAGIC REALISM – a more worldly version of that idiom than found in the works of his coeval, Gabriel García Márquez (1928-   ) – has featured in stories and novels from the 1950s on. They include: *Aura* (**1962**; trans **1965** chap US), a ghost story which incorporates elements of vampirism; *La Cabeza de la Hidra* (**1978**; trans Honi Werner as *The Hydra Head* **1978** US), set just before the outbreak of WWIII in Mexico; *Terra Nostra* (**1975**; trans Margaret Sayers Peden **1976** US), a vast FABULATION about the entire Earth (though centred in an ALTERNATE-WORLD Paris); and *Cristobál nonato* (**1987**; trans Alfred MacAdam and CF as *Christopher Unborn* **1989** US), a NEAR-FUTURE lament for Mexico and the world narrated by a child still in the womb.   [JC]

See also: LATIN AMERICA.

FUENTES, ROBERTO [r] ◊ Piers ANTHONY.

FUGA DAL BRONX ◊ 1990: I GUERRIERI DAL BRONX.

FUKKATSO NO HI (vt *Virus*) Film (1981). Haruki Kadokawa Films. Dir Kinji Fukasaku, starring Masao Kusakari, Chuck Connors, Glenn Ford, Olivia Hussey, George Kennedy, Henry Silva, Robert Vaughn. Screenplay Koji Takada, Gregory Knapp, Fukasaku, from *Fukkatsu No Hi* (**1964**) by Sakyo KOMATSU. 155 mins, cut to 108 mins. Colour.

It is difficult to judge this reputedly expensive Japanese DISASTER film, which was very successful in Japan, because the export version was severely cut – but one cannot believe it was ever very good. A germ-warfare virus is stolen and accidentally released; only those in very cold areas survive. Then the crazed US Chief of Staff (Silva) sets off a nuclear strike. In the Antarctic, 864 shivering male survivors share 8 women. The story is told as flashback, with a Japanese (Kusakari) looking like a bearded scarecrow about to walk, implausibly, from Washington DC to the Antarctic. (In the Japanese version he makes it.) The characters are appallingly stereotyped. This is a simplistic melodrama with nothing serious to say.   [PN]

FULLER, ALVARADO M(ORTIMER) (1851-?   ) US writer whose sf novel, *A.D. 2000* (**1890**; vt *Back to Life A.D. 2000* **1911**), wakes its protagonist (◊ SLEEPER AWAKES) in the UTOPIAN culture of AD2000. A single party rules North America, and electrical inventions (after a great disaster with "aluminum bronze", electricity has become the chief source of power) dominate the exiguous storyline.   [JC]

FULL SPECTRUM US ORIGINAL-ANTHOLOGY series published by BANTAM BOOKS since 1988, created by Lou ARONICA, 3 issues to date (Spring 1992): *Full Spectrum* (anth **1988**), ed Aronica with Shawna MCCARTHY, *#2* (anth **1989**), ed Aronica with Pat Lobrutto, McCarthy and Amy Stout, and *#3* (anth **1991**), ed Aronica with Betsy Mitchell and Stout. These are fat, prestigious volumes – an unusual publishing ploy at a time when conventional wisdom says sf ANTHOLOGIES sell badly – presumably designed to publicize the **Bantam Spectra** sf line and to announce that Bantam remains a leader in the sf market. To date their only major award-winner has been "Bible Stories for Adults, No. 17: The Deluge" (**1988**) by James MORROW, which won

a NEBULA, but a high count of *FS* stories have been shortlisted for awards, and *FS* itself won a Locus Award for Best Anthology in its first year. *FS* publishes a fairly high proportion of "literary" stories and a low proportion of HARD SF, and mixes well known authors with promising unknowns.   [PN]

FU MANCHU For a listing of some of the films in which Sax ROHMER's oriental supervillain, armed with the weapons of superscience, appeared, ◊ *The* FACE OF FU MANCHU.   [PN]

FUNNELL, AUGUSTINE (1952-   ) Canadian writer whose two sf novels, *Brandyjack* (**1976**) and its sequel, *Rebels of Merka* (**1976**) – the only titles published by LASER BOOKS actually to have been written by a Canadian – were unremarkable SPACE OPERAS. In the 1980s AF began to publish short fiction in US magazines.   [JC]

FUQUA, ROBERT Pseudonym of Chicago-based US illustrator Joseph Wirt Tillotson (?   -   ), used by him on sf cover paintings (although some of his black-and-white work appeared under his own name). For some time a staff artist for ZIFF-DAVIS magazines, RF painted 25 covers for *AMZ* 1938-44 and 7 for *Fantastic Adventures*. In the 1950s, away from Ziff-Davis, he contributed to the Chicago magazines *Imagination* and *Other Worlds*. He might have been better known had he worked also for New York-based publishers, but he always restricted himself to Chicago. One of the more prominent sf illustrators of the 1930s and 1940s, RF used very bright colours to compensate for poor reproduction processes. His melodramatic style – the very essence of PULP-MAGAZINE sf – perfectly complemented the lurid Ziff-Davis fiction.   [JG/PN]

FUREY, MICHAEL ◊ Sax ROHMER.

FURTINGER, ZVONIMIR [r] ◊ YUGOSLAVIA.

FURY, THE Film (1978). Frank Yablans Presentations/ 20th Century-Fox. Dir Brian De Palma, starring Kirk Douglas, John Cassavetes, Charles Durning, Amy Irving, Fiona Lewis, Andrew Stevens. Screenplay John Farris, based on his *The Fury* (**1976**). 118 mins. Colour.

After his success with CARRIE (1976), it seems cynical of director De Palma to have made another film about destructive teenage PSI POWERS so quickly. This one has an intricate plot with standard ingredients: the secret government agency experimenting with WEAPONS (in this case, human weapons), the paranoid (◊ PARANOIA) sense that everything is manipulated by this agency, the FRANKENSTEIN theme of the monster that turns on its creator, and (a Frankenstein subtheme) Freudian hostility between children and parents. The two teenagers who can telekinetically cause blood to spurt from every available orifice of those they attack (or even to explode them) are both corrupted by their power, one deeply, one mildly. The film is a vivid string of fireworks, with De Palma as usual manipulating audience response with bravura, but not creating anything that is more than the sum of its exploitative parts.   [PN]

FUTRELLE, JACQUES (1875-1912) US writer and theatrical manager, on the editorial staff of the *Boston American*; he drowned when the *Titanic* sank. The stories assembled in his **Thinking Machine** books about the scientific detective August S.F.X. Van Dusen – *The Thinking Machine* (coll **1907**; vt *The Problem of Cell 13* 1917) and *The Thinking Machine on the Case* (coll **1908**) – are properly detections, though Van Dusen's methods verge on sf. *The Thinking Machine* (coll **1959**) ed Tony Simon contains "The Problem of Cell 13" and 2 other stories. Larger selections have been ed E.F. BLEILER as *Best "Thinking Machine" Stories* (coll **1973**) and *Great Cases of the Thinking Machine* (coll **1976**). *The Diamond Master* (**1909**; exp with "The Haunted Bell" as coll *c***1912**), which is sf, revolves melodramatically around the artificial manufacture of diamonds; the added novella is a supernatural tale involving Van Dusen. [JC]

FUTURE, THE There are relevant entries throughout, but ◊ especially CYBERPUNK; END OF THE WORLD; FAR FUTURE; FUTUROLOGY; HOLOCAUST AND AFTER; NEAR FUTURE; PREDICTION.

FUTURE COMBINED WITH SCIENCE FICTION ◊ FUTURE FICTION.

FUTURE COMBINED WITH SCIENCE FICTION STORIES ◊ FUTURE FICTION.

FUTURE COP ◊ TRANCERS.

FUTURE COP 2 ◊ TRANCERS.

FUTURE FANTASY AND SCIENCE FICTION ◊ FUTURE FICTION; SWAN AMERICAN MAGAZINE.

FUTURE FICTION US magazine. 17 issues Nov 1939-July 1943, 48 further issues May/June 1950-Apr 1960. Published by Blue Ribbon Magazines, later Double Action Magazines and (from Apr 1941) Columbia Publications; ed Charles D. HORNIG (Nov 1939-Apr 1941) and Robert A.W. LOWNDES (Aug 1941-Apr 1960). *FF* began as a companion magazine to SCIENCE FICTION, with similar editorial policies. It absorbed its parent magazine in Oct 1941, changing its title to *Future Combined with Science Fiction*. Under Lowndes's editorship it began to feature stories by such fellow FUTURIANS as James BLISH, C.M. KORNBLUTH and Donald A. WOLLHEIM, often under pseudonyms. It also carried some of the earliest magazine covers done by Hannes BOK. The title changed again to *Future Fantasy and Science Fiction* in Oct 1942, and finally to *Science Fiction Stories* in Apr 1943. The 2 issues of this final wartime incarnation are virtually identical in appearance to *Science Fiction*, but as they continue the numbering of *FF* they are considered part of its run.

FF was one of the many magazines to fall victim to wartime paper shortages, but it was revived under the same editor in 1950 as *Future Combined with Science Fiction Stories*, which became *Future Science Fiction Stories* in Jan 1952 and, finally, *Future Science Fiction* in May 1952. It changed from PULP to DIGEST size in June 1954. It was one of several respectable but mediocre magazines edited on shoestring budgets by Lowndes during the 1950s. The volume numbering

was taken over by *The* ORIGINAL SCIENCE FICTION STORIES with its Jan 1955 issue (vol 5 #4), suggesting the death of *Future Science Fiction*; however, the latter reappeared a little later in 1955, apparently unhurt, with #28. (The numeration of Columbia's magazines has baffled generations of collectors.) There were 2 UK reprint runs of *FF*, 14 issues 1951-4 in pulp format, and 11 digest issues 1957-60. [MJE/PN]

FUTURE HISTORIES ◊ especially GALACTIC EMPIRES; HISTORY IN SF; NEAR FUTURE; PREDICTION; WAR.

FUTURE PUBLICATIONS ◊ FANTASY MAGAZINE/FANTASY FICTION; SCIENCE FICTION ADVENTURES.

FUTURE SCIENCE FICTION 1. Variant title of FUTURE FICTION in its 1950s incarnation.

2. Australian DIGEST-size magazine. 6 numbered, undated issues (2 in 1953, 3 in 1954, 1 in 1955) published by Frew Publications, Sydney, plus 2 (1967) published by Page Publications, NSW; ed anon. The Frew series used a mixture of US reprints, 13 new US stories and 4 new Australasian stories; the Page series reprinted #4 and #6 from the Frew publications, renumbering them #1 and #2. A companion magazine to both versions was POPULAR SCIENCE FICTION. [FHP/PN]

FUTURE SCIENCE FICTION STORIES ◊ FUTURE FICTION.

FUTURE WAR ◊ HISTORY OF SF; INVASION; WAR.

FUTUREWORLD Film (1976). AIP. Dir Richard T. Heffron, starring Peter Fonda, Blythe Danner, Arthur Hill. Screenplay Mayo Simon, George Schenck. 104 mins. Colour.

An inferior sequel to WESTWORLD (1973), set in the same theme park, Delos, *F* lacks the unity and impact of Michael CRICHTON's original film. In a newly built area of Delos, devoted to dramatizing the future, there are several diverting scenes irrelevant to the main plot, which is one of PULP-MAGAZINE sf's oldest: a mad SCIENTIST (revealed at the end to be himself a ROBOT) creates robot duplicates of influential people to enable him to rule the world. His plan is uncovered by two journalists reporting the grand opening. *F* is rather ill organized and crude. The novel *Futureworld* * (**1976**) was adapted by John Ryder Hall (William ROTSLER) from the screenplay. [JB]

FUTURIAN, THE UK FANZINE (1938-40), ed from Leeds by J. Michael Rosenblum. A continuation of the Leeds SCIENCE FICTION LEAGUE's *Bulletin* (1937), *The Futurian* was a small printed publication featuring fiction, poems and articles by leading sf fans of the day, including Arthur C. CLARKE, Ralph Milne FARLEY, John Russell FEARN, David H. KELLER, Frederik POHL and William F. TEMPLE. Other important pre-WWII UK fanzines were John CHRISTOPHER's *The Fantast*, Jonathan BURKE's and Charles Eric MAINE's *Satellite*, Donald Mayer's *Tomorrow* (incorporating Walter GILLINGS's *SCIENTIFICTION*) and Maurice K. Hanson's NOVAE TERRAE (later NEW WORLDS). Under the title *Futurian War Digest* (1940-45), Rosenblum's fanzine became a focal point for UK fandom during the WWII years when sf and amateur publishing faced considerable difficulties. It was revived as *The New Futurian* 1954-8. [PR]

FUTURIANS A New York sf group active 1938-45, notable for radical politics and the conviction that sf fans should be forward-looking and constructive; the name came from J. Michael Rosenblum's UK fanzine, *The* FUTURIAN. Though deeply involved in FANZINE publishing and internal fan politics, The Futurians also brought together many young fans who hoped to become sf writers. Members included Isaac ASIMOV, James BLISH, C.M. KORNBLUTH, David KYLE, Robert A.W. LOWNDES, Frederik POHL – who describes this period in *The Way the Future Was: A Memoir* (**1978**) – Richard WILSON and Donald A. WOLLHEIM; also associated with the group were Hannes BOK, Damon KNIGHT – who in *The Futurians* (**1977**) published an informal history of the group – Judith MERRIL and Larry T. SHAW. [PR/PN]

FUTURIAN WAR DIGEST ◊ *The* FUTURIAN.

FUTURISTIC SCIENCE STORIES UK pocketbook-size magazine. 16 issues, numbered, undated, 1950-58, published by John Spencer, London; ed John S. Manning (pseudonym of publishers Sol Assael and Michael Nahum). *FSS* was one of 4 almost identical low-quality juvenile sf magazines – all of minimal interest – published by Spencer; the others were TALES OF TOMORROW, WONDERS OF THE SPACEWAYS and WORLDS OF FANTASY. #1-#15 appeared 1950-54; #16 did not appear until 1958. (*For more information on Spencer's publications* ◊ BADGER BOOKS.) [FHP]

FUTURISTIC STORIES UK pulp-size magazine. 2 undated issues, 1946, published by Hamilton & Co., Stafford; ed anon. *FS* was poor-quality, juvenile, and of little interest. A companion magazine was STRANGE ADVENTURES. [FHP]

FUTUROLOGY The word "futurology" is a neologism coined in 1943 by a refugee German professor of sociology, Ossip K. Flechtheim, then teaching in a US college. He argued for a concerted effort by sociologists, historians, psychologists, economists and political scientists to examine social and technological trends as a means of learning the true shape of coming things. He sent his proposals to Aldous HUXLEY, who took them up with enthusiasm, and thereby conveyed the word into the language. Now futurologists are everywhere except perhaps in the very poorest countries.

History shows that human beings are *ab origine* future-directed animals. Ever since *Homo erectus* began the long trek out of Africa and into Eurasia, the horizon-watchers have known that their survival might well depend on what they found over the hill, in the no-man's time of the day after. But the literature of proposals and projections about future things appears as a mere blip at the end of civilization's 10,000-year record. It is strange, too, that UTOPIAS, DYSTOPIAS, forecasts, projections and sf are in origin, and still largely, a Western intellectual activity. All these future-oriented activities may have begun with the first modern utopias to present the

other-history of the better society. Thomas MORE's *Utopia* (Part Two **1516** in Latin; trans Ralphe Robynson with the later Part One **1551**) and Francis BACON's *New Atlantis* (1627; **1629**) contained ideologies which had already worked their benign effects in the could-be of imagined lands, and might serve as guides for achieving a more perfect way of life in the real world of a reformed England. In the beginning, then, the future was another place, and the VIRTUAL REALITY of word-generated social systems and behaviour patterns in the utopias made for a most effective connection between today and tomorrow.

There was still a long way to go before considered forecasts. The world had to wait for the new ideas about the progress of mankind that, in the mid-18th century, were to mark out the base for a calculus of probabilities. In his very influential *Philosophical Review of the Successive Advances of the Human Mind* (**1750**) Anne Robert Jacques Turgot (1727-1781), then a student at the Sorbonne, provided the historical evidence that allowed him to indicate the main lines of human progress. Since, he argued, mankind had advanced from primitive beginnings to the glorious days of Louis XV, it followed that the human race would "go on advancing, although at a slow pace, towards greater perfection". The details of this march forward awaited the work of men like Adam Smith (1723-1790), who in his *Wealth of Nations* (**1776**) reduced the entirety of ECONOMICS, industry and commerce to a Newtonian universe of actions and reactions.

At around this time the great divide between fiction and prediction began to narrow, as the first tales of the future spread their message of the centuries ahead. The most important was Louis-Sébastien MERCIER's *L'an 2440* (1771; trans as *Memoirs of the Year Two Thousand Five Hundred* **1772**), which described a better future world in which the social ideals of the Enlightenment had prevailed: constitutional monarchs, deism the universal religion, education for all. The most telling register of expected change was in the technology of the future: a Suez Canal, rapid BALLOON transportation between continents, and "all sorts of machines for the relief of Man in laborious works".

Still the would-be predictors awaited the theories and techniques that would help them provide for the whole of society what Adam Smith had provided for a part. New means of assessment and measurement swiftly arrived. In 1798 Thomas Malthus (1766-1834) published his notorious *Essay on the Principle of Population*, in which he pessimistically linked the future of humanity to the potentially geometrical growth of population and the merely arithmetical growth of the rations that sustained it, a situation that could be balanced only if vast numbers died. A tremendous debate about humankind's future followed, partly because this early example of Future Shock had coincided with the publication by Edward Jenner (1749-1823) of his paper on the *Causes and*

Effects of the Variolae Vaccinae, which provided the first marvellous promise that the future would be different. By that time James Watt's steam engine was providing power on an unprecedented scale, and the Industrial Revolution was on the point of transforming the world.

It seems strange, with change so rapidly manifesting itself, that it was almost a century before straightforward forecasts like *Dans cent ans* ["In 100 Years"] (**1892**) by Charles Richet (1850-1935) came to be published. But in the 19th century the "certainty factor" persuaded everyone that change and technological development could be accommodated within the known social system. The same, but better, was the slogan – or, in the Tennysonian phrase, the great world would "spin for ever down the ringing grooves of change". So people invented new methods to measure the changes they considered most important. The first decennial census of 1801 began the continuing measure of population; the Belgian mathematician Lambert Quételet (1796-1874) adopted the Laplace probability theory to produce the crucial concept of the Average Man. Also significant was the first attempt to analyse the new literature of the future in *Le roman de l'avenir* ["The Novel of the Future"] (**1834**) by Félix Bodin (◊ FRANCE). Another sign was the inauguration of the British Association for the Advancement of Science in 1831.

The flood of forecasting literature did not take place until around 1890, beginning with sustained discussion about the next great WAR (a discussion catalysed by the War of 1870). Its first major prediction was the work of Polish banker and statistician Ivan Gottlieb de Bloch (1836-1902), who produced the classic analysis in *The War of the Future in its Technical, Economic and Political Relations* (**1897**). His findings, ignored by the generals, led him to forecast a great war of entrenchment. Soon forecasts became part of popular writing: weekly magazines occasionally featured articles with illustrations of flying machines, motor cars and television. Some two dozen books were published at this time about the future, including George Ermann on the imperial German future in *Deutschland im Jahre 2000* ["Germany in the Year 2000"] (**1891**), the influential *Esquisse de l'organisation politique et économique de la societé future* (**1899**; trans P.H. Lee Warner as *The Society of To-Morrow* **1904**) by Gustave de Molinari (1819-1911), and the collection by Edward Carpenter (1844-1929) of the expectations of 10 eminent socialists in *Forecasts of the Coming Century* (coll **1897**). The most widely read of them all in the Anglo-Saxon world was the series of articles by H.G. WELLS in *Fortnightly Review* in 1900, published as *Anticipations* (**1901**).

The next advances in the investigation of the future followed two major innovations between the two world wars. In the 1920s the publishing house Kegan Paul, Trench & Trubner brought out a series of 86 monographs in their **Today and Tomorrow** series, in which scientists, sociologists, philosophers, theologians and others set down their expectations of the future. One was J.B.S. HALDANE's *Daedalus, or Science and the Future* (**1924**), which accurately forecast advances in biology that gave Aldous Huxley important ideas for *Brave New World* (**1932**). The series was widely reported and did much to publicize thinking about the future. More important, however, was the first major state initative in this regard. The US President, Herbert Hoover, in 1930 appointed a National Resources Committee "to examine and report upon recent social trends in the United States with a view to providing such a review as might supply a basis for the formulation of large national policies looking to the next phase in the nation's development". The committee, drawing on the resources of field-survey techniques formulated at the University of Chicago, presented their conclusions in their report *Recent Social Trends* (**1932**), which provided a model for the USA and an example to the rest of the world.

The development of techniques for investigating the future accelerated during WWII, especially the Operational Research procedures borrowed from the UK by the US Army Air Force. These proved so successful in the air war that General Henry Arnold established a research centre to investigate possible developments in warfare. This had the codename RAND (Research and Development), and in 1948 the project team set up an independent non-profit organization known as the RAND Corporation. It had immense influence on military planning and on presidential decisions about the manufacture of nuclear weapons; it was the first "think tank", and from it came the System Development Institute and the Hudson Institute. The latter gained world notoriety when Herman Kahn (1922-1983) published books such as *On Escalation* (**1968**) that took the hardest of looks into the future. Indeed, this was a period of rapid growth in futurology, with a great many books and journals published on the subject. Kahn's books were among the best-known, but futurology's limitations as a science can be seen very clearly in his *Things to Come* (**1972**), a book about what to expect in the 1970s and 1980s. The index has no entries for oil, gasoline, energy, resources or power; Kahn's only remark about the Arabs is to say that, because the West is their only market, we need expect no problems of supply. Sf writers, too, were unsuccessful in predicting the energy crisis, but few as blandly and so close to the time when it happened as this.

A very influential, albeit flawed, work of futurology was the report of the Club of Rome on OVERPOPULATION and diminishing resources, excerpts from which were published as *The Limits to Growth* (**1972**). Alvin TOFFLER's book *Future Shock* (**1970**) was a bestselling work of SOCIOLOGY rather than futurology; it documented the increasing rate of change in the 20th century, but was comparatively cautious in making specific predictions about the future. At the other extreme were books of popularization like *The Next Ten Thousand Years* (**1974**) by Adrian BERRY, a work of technological optimism packed with "what-ifs" and predictions rather than futurology *per se*. There are many of these.

The modern "science" of futurology is the forecasting of the future (usually the NEAR FUTURE) by projection and extrapolation from current trends, statistics, population figures, political groupings, availability of resources, economic data, etc. It cannot be called a science proper, since too many of the factors involved are imponderable (and often unknown), but its tools are statistical analysis and the computer simulation of various models.

It may seem that the futurologist and the sf writer are involved in the same trade, but they share a certain unease about one another. Futurologists work primarily on what can be quantified, and to a large degree their projections depend on the future being the same as the past. Population projections for the UK, for example, were for a long time too high because demographers were unable to quantify the factors that persuade people to have fewer children. Sf writers are not actually in the prediction business, but when they deal with the near future they normally write a "what-if?" scenario, which may involve discontinuities with the past. In practice, this is only to say that the factors sf writers deal with include a good deal of guesswork and invention. What makes sf writers unreliable as predictors is the nature of that "what if?". It may appeal to the writer because of its intrinsic interest or its function as a warning symbol, rather than for its likelihood. Writers often do not believe in it themselves; they are writing stories, not prophecies. Also, the sf writer is often ignorant of the mechanisms, such as those of ECONOMICS, which must play an important role in any realistic story of future cause and effect.

Where sf writers have an advantage is in the ability to adopt a multidisciplinary approach; they are often good at what is sometimes known as lateral thinking. In a sense the advantage sf writers have is their very irresponsibility: they cannot be held accountable for the nature of their scenarios; the details do not have to be justified. This allows sf writers to survey a far

greater range of possibility than the comparatively restricted futurologist. The writer can take the unexpected into account, and history tells us that the unexpected does indeed often happen. Sf itself may give direction to change, through a process of self-fulfilling prophecy, by presenting images of the future which grip people's minds; e.g., the US space programme, which could not have been funded without popular support, or the multistorey apartment blocks that were built by local authorities in such disastrously great numbers in the UK after WWII, designed by a generation of architects reared on the utopian-sf visual imagery of the 1920s.

Neither futurologists nor sf writers have done very well at PREDICTION, though perhaps the writers' emphasis on the lives of individuals seems more humane than the futurologists' statistical projections about the masses. Many examples of sf about the general area also covered by futurology can be found under TECHNOLOGY, ECOLOGY, NEAR FUTURE, OVERPOPULATION and WAR. John BRUNNER is one notable writer who has written novels of this kind. Often, of course, Brunner and others are not so much predicting as trying to avert; they hope their ghastly scenarios will be influential as a kind of early-warning system. Arthur C. CLARKE, on the other hand, has used much optimistic futurological speculation in both his factual books and his fiction.

Sf itself has also produced futurologists as characters, the best known being the exponents of PSYCHOHISTORY in Isaac ASIMOV's **Foundation** series. [IFC/PN]

FYFE, H(ORACE) B(OWNE) (1918-   ) US writer whose first sf story, "Locked Out", appeared in *ASF* in 1940 but who became active, mainly with stories in *ASF*, only after WWII army service. By 1967, when he became inactive, he had published nearly 60 stories. His **Bureau of Slick Tricks** tales (*ASF* 1948-52) are typical of John W. CAMPBELL's need for stories in which humans inevitably outwit thick-skulled (often bureaucratic) ALIENS. In his novel, *D-99* (fixup **1962**), which continues the series, Department 99 of the Terran government has the job of finagling citizens out of jams on other planets and flummoxing thicker species. The tone is fortunately light. [JC]

FYSH ◊ Leonard G. FISH.

GADALLAH, LESLIE (1939-   ) Canadian writer best known for her **Cat's Pawn** sequence – *Cat's Pawn* (**1987** US) and *Cat's Gambit* (**1990** US) – in which a human protagonist becomes involved with the eponymous catlike alien Orioni, themselves involved in a desperate war against the invading Kazi, who dominate much of the Galaxy by the end of the second volume, which ends on an unusual downbeat, suggesting that further volumes may be projected. *The Loremasters* (**1988** US), a singleton, less impressively pits a civilized enclave against a horde of barbarians on an energy-starved future Earth.   [JC]

GADE, HENRY [s] ◊ Raymond A. PALMER.

GAIL, OTTO WILLI (1896-1956) German writer of popular fiction, two of whose astronautical novels were published in Hugo GERNSBACK's *Science Wonder Quarterly*: *Der Schuss ins All* (**1925**; trans Francis Currier 1929 as *The Shot into Infinity*; **1975** US) and its sequel, *Der Stein vom Mond* (**1926** trans Francis Currier 1930 as "The Stone from the Moon"). *Hans Hardts Mondfahrt: Eines abenteuerliche Erzählung* (**1928**; trans anon as *By Rocket to the Moon: The Story of Hans Hardt's Miraculous Flight* **1931** US) is a juvenile. All three aim at a technical realism unusual for the time.   [JC]

See also: GERMANY; SPACESHIPS.

GAIMAN, NEIL (RICHARD) (1960-   ) UK writer, in the USA from 1992, who has specialized in the scripting of fantasy and sf comics and GRAPHIC NOVELS, but who began publishing work of genre interest with a story, "Featherquest", for *Imagine* in 1984. His first book, *Ghastly Beyond Belief* (anth **1985**) with Kim NEWMAN, presents various kinds of bad writing to be found in sf and fantasy. His first visual book was *Violent Cases* (graph **1987**) with Dave MCKEAN, a dark urban fantasy in graphic-novel form. He then began to write comics in earnest, with extended stints as scripter for *The Sandman* (1988-current) and *Miracle Man* (1990-current), the latter being a genuine sf comic with a UTOPIAN turn (◊ CAPTAIN MARVEL). The **Sandman** stories – one of

which, "A Midsummer Night's Dream" (1990), won a 1991 World Fantasy Award for Best Short Story – have been published in book form as *The Sandman: The Doll's House* (graph coll **1990**) with Mike Dringenberg and Malcolm Jones III, *The Sandman: Preludes and Nocturnes* (graph coll **1991**) with Dringenberg, Jones and Sam Kieth, and *The Sandman: Dream Country* (graph coll **1991**) with various artists; a long tale, which transmutes dark-fantasy material evocative of the work of Jonathan Carroll (1949-   ), was contained in 6 further issues (1991-2) of the comic and is projected for book release as «A Game of You» (graph **1992**) with Shawn McManus and Colleen Doran. His further graphic novels are *Black Orchid* (graph **1991**) and *Signal to Noise* (1989-90 *The Face*; rev as graph **1992**), both with Dave McKean, and «The Books of Magic» (graph coll 1993 US) with various artists. *Good Omens: The Nice and Accurate Prophecies of Agnes Nutter, Witch* (**1990**; rev 1991 US) with Terry PRATCHETT is a comic fantasy novel about the Four Horsemen, who do not quite end the world. Unlike graphic novelists such as Alan MOORE, NG has tended to combine draconian verbal economy with an ample romanticism, so that his tales carry, sometimes effortlessly, a burden of half-uttered resonances. He cowrote the entry on the GRAPHIC NOVEL for this encyclopedia.   [JC]

Other works: *Don't Panic: The Official Hitch Hiker's Guide to the Galaxy Companion* (**1988**; rev 1992); *Now We Are Sick: A Sampler* (anth **1986** chap) ed with Stephen Jones (1953-   ), booklet produced to publicize and sell rights in the next book; *Now We Are Sick* (anth **1991** chap) ed with Stephen Jones, assembling original poems; *Temps Volume l* (anth **1991**) ed with Alex STEWART.

See also: CRIME AND PUNISHMENT; SHARED WORLDS; SUPERMAN.

GAKOV, VLADIMIR Pseudonym of Russian critic and editor Mikhail (Andreevich) Kovalchuk (1951-   ), a trained physicist who began publishing sf criticism in 1976, soon giving up his science career for professional journalism. His three critical works on sf are *Vitok Spirali* ["The Curve of a Spiral"] (**1980**), *Tchetyre Puteshestviiaa Na Mashine Vremeni* ["Four Trips in the Time Machine"] (**1983**) and *Ultimatum* ["The Ultimatum"] (**1989**), the last being an historical study of the relationship between fact and fiction in the nuclear arms race. Among his various anthologies, of interest to English-speaking readers is *World's Spring* (anth **1979** Sweden). A contributor to various English-language reference editions, he has revised or written many of the entries on Russian sf in this encyclopedia.   [VG/JC]

See also: CRITICAL AND HISTORICAL WORKS ABOUT SF; RUSSIA.

GALACTICA: 1980 US tv series (1980). Universal MCA/ABC-TV. Creator, executive prod Glen A. LARSON. Most episodes written by Larson. Regular cast included Lorne Greene, Kent McCord, Barry Van Dyke, Robyn Douglass. 3 pilot 50min episodes followed by 7 50min episodes.

The pilot, *Galactica Discovers Earth*, a three-part made-for-tv film sequel to the tv series BATTLESTAR GALACTICA, was successful enough to convince ABC-TV to commission a new series. Rushed into production, aimed at an early-evening time slot where special rules applied about what children can watch, and underrehearsed, it flopped badly and was soon jettisoned. In the pilot, *Galactica* finds Earth too undeveloped to fight off the Cylons and attempts are made via TIME TRAVEL to improve the situation. The remaining episodes are all set on Earth and feature Cylon attacks. The pilot, dir Sidney Hayers, with sections of 2 further episodes, was theatrically released as *Conquest of the Earth* (1980). Generally the series was shown on tv abroad as if part of *Battlestar Galactica*.   [PN]

GALACTIC EMPIRES In *The Universe Makers* (**1971**) Donald A. WOLLHEIM attempts to distil from the range of futuristic visions presented by magazine sf a basic pattern – a "cosmogony of the future" – in which stages 3-5 (there are 8 in all) describe "the rise and fall of the Galactic Empire", which is thus enshrined as the central myth of GENRE SF. ("Empire" is here used with a general, almost metaphorical meaning, rather than in its politically definitive sense.) The galactic empire was a necessary invention: an imaginative framework which could accommodate any number of "Earth-clone" worlds on which writers might deploy ordinary human characters in confrontation with any imaginable social and biological system. Very many modern sf stories are designed to fit into such a framework, taking advantage of the fact that it has become established as a convention which needs no explanation.

Much of the credit for the establishment of the convention must go to Isaac ASIMOV, whose **Foundation** series (1942-50; fixups **1951-3**) set the most influential example, although it is possible to trace the idea back to earlier roots. As long ago as 1900

Robert W. COLE had imagined Victoria's glorious British Empire extending its dominion to the stars, so that ours should not be the only sun never to set upon it. Confederations of worlds within the Solar System were common in pulp sf from its inception, and these were extended into the Galaxy in such novels as *Galactic Patrol* (1937-8; **1950**) by E.E. "Doc" SMITH. Asimov, however, was the writer who provided the essential historical framework for such a concept. He did so by relatively straightforward analogy with past empires, reversing the analytical historical perspective of such works as *The History of the Decline and Fall of the Roman Empire* (**1776-88**) by Edward Gibbon (1737-1794) to produce the predictive science of PSYCHOHISTORY. With a single flourish, a whole prospectus for the future of the human race – allowing virtually limitless possibilities so far as events on a finer scale were concerned – was established. Asimov used the convenient historical pattern himself as a background for other works, including *The Stars Like Dust* (**1951**) and *The Currents of Space* (**1952**). Robert A. HEINLEIN's painstaking attempt to develop a future HISTORY step by step became an empty endeavour after the **Foundation** series, and later efforts seem distinctly half-hearted. James BLISH's **Cities in Flight** (**1955-62**) succeeds more through its key image of the star-travelling CITIES than through its framework, derived from the philosophy of cyclic history developed by Oswald Spengler (1880-1936). Poul ANDERSON, who developed his own scheme for use in his **Technic History** series and many other stories and novels, was able to take a great deal for granted because Asimov had prepared the way.

Writers of the 1940s who employed the galactic-empire framework include C.L. MOORE, in *Judgment Night* (1943; **1952**), Edmond HAMILTON, in *The Star Kings* (1947; **1949** vt *Beyond the Moon*) and – most extravagantly – A.E. VAN VOGT in such stories as "Recruiting Station" (1942; in *Masters of Time* coll **1950**). Van Vogt was not at all hesitant about borrowing the entire apparatus of historical empires, and replayed the most melodramatic phase of Roman history – presumably borrowed via Robert GRAVES's *I, Claudius* (**1934**) – in his **Linn** series, *Empire of the Atom* (1946-7; fixup **1957**) and *The Wizard of Linn* (1950; **1962**). The background proved particularly useful in the colourful brand of adventure sf featured by PLANET STORIES, and it was very extensively used therein, notably by Leigh BRACKETT, Alfred COPPEL and Poul Anderson (in his early SPACE OPERAS). During the 1950s SCIENCE FICTION ADVENTURES, the magazine closest in editorial philosophy to *Planet Stories*, likewise made extensive use of it, particularly in stories written for the US version by Robert SILVERBERG and for the UK version by Kenneth BULMER.

In addition to Anderson, several other post-WWII writers have made consistent and elaborate use of a galactic civilization as a reservoir for unusual worlds.

These include Jack VANCE, notably in *The Languages of Pao* (**1958**), *The Dragon Masters* (**1963**) and in virtually all of his work during the 1960s and 1970s, John BRUNNER, notably in *Endless Shadow* (**1964**) and *The World Swappers* (**1959**), Cordwainer SMITH, in his **Instrumentality** series, and E.C. TUBB, in his **Dumarest** series. Few writers have, however, concerned themselves in any but the most superficial way with the sociopolitical structure of the galactic community. Anderson has done significant work in this vein, and so has Gordon R. DICKSON, notably in the **Dorsai** series, but most are prepared to leave the community in a state of disorganization or nebulous harmony. Only rarely do works appear in which there actually is a powerful, autocratic, imperial system of government – the most conspicuous modern example is the film STAR WARS (**1977**) and its sequels – and the word "empire" is often substituted by "league", "federation" or some other such variant. Most works of this kind are either US or (like the German PERRY RHODAN series) products of cultural coca-colonization, and the political model employed for galactic civilization is very often the US system writ large – an ideal summed up by the final line of Asimov's *The Stars Like Dust* and conscientiously supported by innumerable episodes of STAR TREK. It is interesting to note the relative unwillingness of genre-sf writers, even when they take the entire Galaxy for their setting, to create new political or economic modes, although Iain M. BANKS's galactic culture in *Consider Phlebas* (**1987**), *The Player of Games* (**1988**) and *Use of Weapons* (**1990**) is refreshingly alien to the US model. Galactic empires are almost always ruled by humans, and human empires are often at war with ALIEN empires. An amusing antidote to this conventional human chauvinism is *The Zen Gun* (**1983**) by Barrington J. BAYLEY, in which men become so effetely decadent that their erstwhile underlings, the pigs, take over.

It is more or less taken for granted in post-WWII works that any galactic federation will have a relatively untamed frontier, almost always called "the rim" (◊ GALACTIC LENS). First popularized by A. Bertram CHANDLER's long-running **Rim Worlds** series, the galactic empire's equivalent of the Wild West features fairly prominently in modern SPACE OPERA, notably in C.J. CHERRYH's relatively sophisticated stories of that type, which include *Merchanter's Luck* (**1982**) and *Rimrunners* (**1989**). In such stories freelance starship pilots take the place of cowboy gunfighters; in recent years such roles have very frequently been filled by female characters, partly as a result of the influence of *Star Trek* in recruiting female readers and writers into the sf community.

Any list of post-WWII sf novels using the galactic-empire framework is bound to be highly selective, but some of the more notable stories which actually deal with issues relating to the community rather than to specific worlds within it are: *Star Bridge* (**1955**) by Jack WILLIAMSON and James E. GUNN, *Citizen of the Galaxy* (**1957**) by Heinlein, *Starmaster's Gambit* (**1957**

France; trans **1973**) by Gérard KLEIN, *Way Station* (**1963**) by Clifford D. SIMAK, *Empire Star* (**1966**) by Samuel R. DELANY, *The Ring of Ritornel* (**1968**) by Charles L. HARNESS, *Rite of Passage* (**1968**) by Alexei PANSHIN, *Voyage to Dari* (**1974**) by Ian WALLACE, *Beyond Heaven's River* (**1980**) by Greg BEAR, *Light on the Sound* (**1982**) by S.P. SOMTOW, *Star of Gypsies* (**1986**) by Silverberg, and the **Hyperion** books (**1989-90**) by Dan SIMMONS.

The definitive theme anthology is *Galactic Empires* (anth 2 vols **1976**) ed Brian W. ALDISS. [BS]

See also: COLONIZATION OF OTHER WORLDS; COMMUNICATIONS; SOCIOLOGY.

GALACTIC LENS This term, from ASTRONOMY, makes frequent appearance in sf. It refers to the fact that our Galaxy is (like many others) approximately lens-shaped – it is a disc containing spiral arms, but like a lens it has a central bulge. Our own position in the Galaxy is quite a long way from the core; when we look towards the centre of the "lens", the direction in which the stars are clustered most thickly, we see the so-called Milky Way. Towards the outer rim of the "lens", stars are comparatively sparse, not only in terms of the numbers lying in our line of sight but also in fact. Many sf writers have set stories on planets circling such stars. Such worlds were dubbed Rim Worlds by A. Bertram CHANDLER, and the term (often as "Rimworld") has since become commonplace in sf. [PN]

GALAXAN, SOL [s] ◊ Alfred COPPEL.

GALAXY ◊ GALAXY SCIENCE FICTION.

GALAXY MAGABOOKS ◊ GALAXY SCIENCE FICTION NOVELS.

GALAXY MAGAZINE ◊ GALAXY SCIENCE FICTION.

GALAXY OF TERROR ◊ Roger CORMAN.

GALAXY PUBLISHING CORPORATION ◊ BEYOND FANTASY FICTION; GALAXY SCIENCE FICTION.

GALAXY SCIENCE FICTION US DIGEST-size magazine, Oct 1950 to a single undated issue in 1980. Published by World Editions (Oct 1950-Sep 1951), Galaxy Publishing Corp. (Oct 1951-May 1969), Universal Publishing and Distributing Corp. (July 1969-Sep/Oct 1979), Avenue Victor Hugo (1980); ed H.L. GOLD (Oct 1950-Oct 1961), Frederik POHL (Dec 1961-May 1969), Ejler JAKOBSSON (July 1969-May 1974), James BAEN (June 1974-Oct 1977), John J. PIERCE (Nov 1977-Mar/Apr 1979), Hank STINE (June/July-Sep/Oct 1979), Floyd Kemske (1980). The monthly schedule from the beginning to Dec 1958 was broken only by the omission of Dec 1955. It was bimonthly Feb 1959-Apr 1968. June 1968-Apr 1971 the schedule was monthly, except that June 1969 and Jan 1970 were omitted, and Aug/Sep 1970 and Oct/Nov 1970 were single issues. May/June 1971-July/Aug 1973 the schedule was bimonthly, returning to a shaky monthly schedule Sep 1973-June 1978, the issues for May, Nov and Dec 1975 being omitted, as were those for Apr, June, Aug 1976; Dec 1977-Jan 1978 was a single issue. After June 1978, the final issues were Sep 1978, Nov/Dec 1978, Mar/Apr 1979, June/July 1979, Sep/Oct 1979 and one 1980 issue released in summer.

The first publisher of *Gal* was an Italian company which, having incurred heavy losses trying to launch another magazine in the USA, approached H.L. Gold for alternative suggestions. He proposed an sf magazine, and *Gal* came into existence. From the outset, *Gal*'s payment rates equalled the best in the field – a minimum of three cents a word – and it adopted the digest format already taken by its most successful contemporaries, ASTOUNDING SCIENCE-FICTION and *The* MAGAZINE OF FANTASY AND SCIENCE FICTION. These two with *Gal* were the most important sf magazines of the 1950s through to the mid-1970s.

The new magazine was an immediate success. *ASF* was at this time following John W. CAMPBELL Jr's newfound obsession with DIANETICS and was otherwise more oriented towards TECHNOLOGY. Gold's editorial policy was comparatively free-ranging: he was interested in PSYCHOLOGY, SOCIOLOGY and SATIRE and other HUMOUR, and the magazine reflected this. Like Campbell, he worked closely with his writers (mostly by telephone, as he was confined to his apartment by acute agoraphobia) and is said to have had a hand in the conception of many of the famous stories he published, notably Alfred BESTER's *The Demolished Man* (Jan-Mar 1952; **1953**). In its first year *Gal* included such stories as: Clifford D. SIMAK's "Time Quarry" (Oct-Dec 1950), in book form *Time and Again* (**1951**); Fritz LEIBER's "Coming Attraction" (Nov 1950); Damon KNIGHT's "To Serve Man" (Nov 1950); Isaac ASIMOV's "Tyrann" (Jan-Mar 1951), in book form *The Stars Like Dust* (**1951**); Ray BRADBURY's "The Fireman" (Feb 1951), in book form *Fahrenheit 451* (exp **1953**); C.M. KORNBLUTH's "The Marching Morons" (Apr 1951); Edgar PANGBORN's "Angel's Egg" (June 1951); Wyman GUIN's "Beyond Bedlam" (Aug 1951); and Robert A. HEINLEIN's *The Puppet Masters* (Sep-Nov 1951; **1951**).

The magazine maintained a comparable quality through its early years, and in 1953 shared the first HUGO for Best Magazine with *ASF*, while Bester's *The Demolished Man*, in its *Gal* version, won the first Hugo for Best Novel. Although the magazine's fiction encompassed a considerable variety of styles and preoccupations, the approach most identified with Gold's magazine is the irony and social satire of such authors as Knight, Leiber, Pohl and Robert SHECKLEY. With the Mar 1952 issue, Willy LEY began his science column, **For Your Information**, which he continued until his death in 1969. Groff CONKLIN was book reviewer from the beginning to Oct 1955.

A weakness of the early *Gal* was that the cover art was mainly crude and undistinguished. The June 1951 issue, however, featured the first cover by Emsh (Ed EMSHWILLER), whose humorous approach was well suited to the magazine's contents and became identified with it.

Further stories which appeared in Gold's *Gal* included: Pohl and Kornbluth's "Gravy Planet" (June-Aug 1952), in book form *The Space Merchants* (**1953**);

Theodore STURGEON's "Baby is Three" (Oct 1952), part of *More than Human* (fixup **1953**); Asimov's *The Caves of Steel* (Oct-Dec 1953; **1954**); Pohl and Kornbluth's *Gladiator-at-Law* (June-Aug 1954; **1955**); Bester's *The Stars My Destination* (Oct 1956-Jan 1957; **1956**; vt *Tiger! Tiger!* UK); Pohl and Kornbluth's *Wolfbane* (Oct-Nov 1957; **1959**); Leiber's Hugo-winning *The Big Time* (Mar-Apr 1958; **1961**); Avram DAVIDSON's Hugo-winning "Or All the Sea with Oysters" (May 1958); and Sheckley's "Time-Killer" (Oct 1958-Feb 1959), in book form *Immortality Delivered* (**1958**; exp vt *Immortality, Inc.* 1959). A prize contest sponsored by *Gal* drew no worthwhile entries, so Frederik Pohl and Lester DEL REY were prevailed upon to collaborate on a "prize-winning" novel, which appeared as *Preferred Risk* (June-Sep 1955; **1955:**) by Edson MCCANN. *Gal* had a short-lived fantasy companion, BEYOND FANTASY FICTION, in 1953-5, and in 1959 its publishers acquired IF, which Gold also edited. In Sep 1958 the title changed to *Galaxy Magazine*, after which it varied between the two (with a period when it was called simply *Galaxy*). Beginning with the Feb 1959 issue it changed to bimonthly publication, with more pages per issue.

In 1961 Gold was forced to retire following a car accident. He was succeeded as editor of *Gal* and *If* by Frederik Pohl. Pohl widened the magazine's policy still further, to include more fantasy-oriented material. Jack VANCE and Cordwainer SMITH became regular contributors, Vance with such stories as *The Dragon Masters* (Aug 1962; **1963**), which won a Hugo, *The Star King* (Dec 1963-Feb 1964; **1964**) and *The Last Castle* (Apr 1966; **1966**), which also won a Hugo, and Smith with "The Boy who Bought Old Earth" (Apr 1964; exp vt *The Planet Buyer* **1964**), "The Dead Lady of Clown Town" (Aug 1964) and many others. Larry NIVEN was one of Pohl's discoveries, and Frank HERBERT and Robert SILVERBERG became further regular contributors. Other notable stories from his editorship include: Simak's "Here Gather the Stars" (June-Aug 1963), in book form *Way Station* (**1963**); Gordon R. DICKSON's "Soldier, Ask Not" (Oct 1964), which won a Hugo; Harlan ELLISON's "'Repent, Harlequin,' Said the Ticktockman" (Dec 1965) and "The Beast that Shouted Love at the Heart of the World" (June 1968), both of which won Hugos and the former also a NEBULA; Poul ANDERSON's "To Outlive Eternity" (June-Aug 1967), in book form *Tau Zero* (**1970**); and Silverberg's "Hawksbill Station" (Aug 1967) and "Nightwings" (Sep 1968), which won a Hugo. As Gold was notorious for unnecessary editorial tampering with the stories he published, so was Pohl famed for indiscriminately altering their titles. Algis BUDRYS began a notable book-review column in 1965.

Pohl's *Gal* was consistently an interesting magazine, but it was less successful, with sf fans at least, than his *If*, which under Pohl won three consecutive Hugos. Pohl also commenced three companion magazines: WORLDS OF FANTASY and INTERNATIONAL SCIENCE FICTION came and went swiftly; WORLDS OF

TOMORROW was more durable.

In June 1968 *Gal* resumed monthly publication. The following year it changed ownership and editorship again. Ejler Jakobsson gave *Gal* the subtitle "The Best in Pertinent Science Fiction", and the appearance was revamped in a seeming attempt to give the magazine more contemporary appeal; for a time it included a comic strip, **Sunpot**, by Vaughn BODÉ. One notable occurrence during Jakobsson's editorship was the featuring of two consecutive serials by Robert Silverberg: *Downward to the Earth* (Nov 1969-Mar 1970; **1970**) and *Tower of Glass* (Apr-June 1970; **1970**). Theodore Sturgeon took over as book reviewer (Jan 1972-July 1975), his column proving less lively than might have been expected. On the whole, the magazine failed to develop under Jakobsson's editorship, and it reverted to a bimonthly schedule with the May/June 1971 issue, though a patchy monthly schedule began again Sep 1973. In June 1974 he was succeeded by James Baen.

In Jan 1975, *Gal* absorbed *If*. After a period in the doldrums, 1976 saw a revival in the magazine's fortunes. Contributors included Niven, John VARLEY and Roger ZELAZNY. Pohl's *Gateway* (Nov 1976-Mar 1977; **1977**) was a notable serial which won both Hugo and Nebula. The magazine featured book reviews by Spider ROBINSON (from Aug 1975) and a science column by Jerry POURNELLE. However, despite the strength of the fiction, distribution faltered, and the monthly schedule was adhered to only patchily in 1975, 1976 and 1977.

Baen left in 1977 to become sf editor of ACE BOOKS, and was succeeded by John J. Pierce, who sadly presided over *Gal*'s slow collapse – payment rate dropping, good authors hard to find except for the ever-loyal Pohl – to be followed briefly by Hank Stine (2 issues). Then *Gal* was sold to the publishers of CALILEO; ed Floyd Kemske, it lasted for only 1 more issue (in large format). The mess is witnessed by the fact that Pohl's serialized novel *Jem* (Nov-Dec 1978-1980; **1979**) took two years to serialize, under three editors, finishing long after the book had been published.

There have been numerous anthologies of stories from *Gal*, for details of which see the entries for its first four editors. *Galaxy Magazine: The Dark and the Light Years* (**1986**) by David L. Rosheim is good on hard facts about the magazine but very restricted on interpretation and context.

A UK edition, from Strato Publications, began in Jan 1953 (reprinting the Oct 1952 US edition). It was labelled vol 3 #1. #2 reprinted the preceding US issue (Sep 1952). The UK edition continued to follow the original, erratically at first, and from #7 began to shorten the US edition. It continued to be numbered continuously (dropping the "vol 3" after #12) until #94 (Feb 1961). From #72 (Feb 1959) it was an exact reprint of the US edition with a different title page. From Dec 1961 only the cover was different, and from Dec 1962 the US edition was imported. A second UK edition,

published by Gold Star Publications, ran for 5 issues in 1967, reprinting six months after the US original (Jan/Feb 1967 UK was June 1966 US), printing US editions complete apart from the changed date. Then, again, the US edition was distributed. In 1972 a third UK edition began, from Universal-Tandem Publishing Co., who overprinted the US edition with price and issue number: the May/Jun 1972 issue was #1, and a total of 25 numbered issues were published, ending with #25, Jan 1975. However, the numbering was not continuous; it ran #1-#10, #11, #11, #12, #12, #12, #14, #17-#25. Thereafter the US edition was distributed. [MJE/PN]

See also: GOLDEN AGE OF SF.

GALAXY SCIENCE FICTION NOVELS A companion series to GALAXY SCIENCE FICTION. The first 31 issues of these numbered books, which resembled magazines, were published irregularly, 1950-57, in DIGEST format, and a further 4, 1957-9, were issued in standard paperback format. #1-#7 (1950-51) were published by World Editions, #9-#35 (1952-9) by Galaxy Publishing Corp. The series was then taken over by Beacon Books, a publisher specializing in mild pornography, which brought out 11 further issues, #36-#46 (1959-61), still in paperback format, usually with lurid covers and suggestive titles.

The original series featured several classics of magazine sf, including *Sinister Barrier* (1939 *Unknown*; **1943**) by Eric Frank RUSSELL (#1), *Legion of Space* (1934 *ASF*; **1947**) by Jack WILLIAMSON (#2) and *Lest Darkness Fall* (1939 *Unknown*; **1941**) by L. Sprague DE CAMP (#24). Notable novels from outside the genre, often abridged, included *The Amphibians* (**1924**) and *The World Below* (**1929**) by S. Fowler WRIGHT (#4 and #5) and *Odd John* (**1935**) by Olaf STAPLEDON (#8). There were also some original novels, including *Prelude to Space* (**1951**) by Arthur C. CLARKE (#3) and *Empire* (**1951**) by Clifford D. SIMAK (#7). Original novels with a sexy slant published in the Beacon Books series include *Flesh* (**1960**) by Philip José FARMER (#41) and *The Male Response* (**1961**) by Brian W. ALDISS (#45), while such innocuous works as A.E. VAN VOGT's *The House that Stood Still* (**1950**) and Cyril JUDD's *Outpost Mars* (**1952**) were retitled, respectively, *The Mating Cry* (rev vt 1960) (#44) and *Sin in Space* (rev vt 1961) (#46).

In 1963 there appeared a second companion series to *Gal*, *Galaxy Magabooks*, each volume consisting of two short novels by a single author. There were only 3 issues: #1 and #2 came in 1963; the later #3 was *And My Fear is Great/Baby is Three* (**1965** dos) by Theodore STURGEON. Award Books issued a number of paperbacks as "Galaxy Science Fiction Novels" in the early 1970s, but these did not constitute a series. [BS]

GALILEO US BEDSHEET-size magazine. 16 issues Sep 1976-Jan 1980, with #11/12, May 1979, being a double issue. Planned as quarterly, but bimonthly to Sep 1978, then irregular, with the last 4 issues bimonthly. Published by Avenue Victor Hugo, Boston, Massachusetts; ed Charles C. RYAN.

Published on a small budget, *G* hoped to survive

through subscription sales rather than newsstand distribution. 8000 copies of #1 were printed and sold. In magazine terms this is small, but the circulation steadily increased, at least initially. Printed on cheap newsprint, and using a number of stories by little-known writers, *G* began quietly but showed signs of improvement by #3. The great Renaissance scientist was evoked in the title because *G* was planned to emulate his "indomitable spirit ... [and] undying quest for knowledge". Almost half of *G*, like most 1970s sf magazines, was devoted to science-fact articles, reviews, interviews etc. Contributors included Brian W. ALDISS, Ray BRADBURY (poetry), Robert CHILSON, Hal CLEMENT (science fact), John KESSEL, Connie WILLIS and Larry NIVEN, the latter with a serialization of *The Ringworld Engineers* (1979; **1980**). *G* became quite a good magazine, but perished because of distribution problems. [PN]

GALLAGHER, STEPHEN (1954-) UK scriptwriter and author who first came to prominence with sf scripts, notably the RADIO series "The Last Rose of Summer", which he adapted as his first novel, *The Last Rose of Summer* (**1978**) – from which derived *Dying of Paradise* (**1982**) and its sequel, *The Ice Belt* (**1983**), both as by Stephen Couper – and episodes for DR WHO, two of which he novelized: *Doctor Who and Warrior's Gate* * (**1982**) and *Doctor Who – Terminus* * (**1983**), both as by John Lydecker. In the 1980s SG began to establish a reputation as one of the UK's most successful HORROR writers, though some of his books have strong sf overtones. *Chimera* (**1982**) is a variation on the Frankenstein myth in which the monster is a hybrid apeman (◊ APES AND CAVEMEN) created by a government research project in DNA manipulation (◊ GENETIC ENGINEERING); it was serialized on UK tv in 1991. *Oktober* (**1988**) is about an experimental drug that allows the protagonist to control other people's nightmares. While often lacking originality of ideas, SG's work is marked by strong characterization, good plotting and extensive background detail, particularly when police-procedural material is being presented. [AC/PR]
Other works: *Saturn 3* * (**1980**), novelizing the movie SATURN 3 (1980), and based on its screenplay by Martin AMIS; *Follower* (**1984**); *Valley of Lights* (**1987**); *Down River* (**1989**); *Rain* (**1990**); *The Boat House* (**1991**).

GALLICO, PAUL (WILLIAM) (1897-1976) US journalist, screenwriter and novelist, sports editor of the New York *Daily News* for 12 years, known mainly for such works outside the sf field as *The Snow Goose* (**1941** chap), a sentimental novella extremely popular in the wartime UK. *The Foolish Immortals* (**1953**) is an eternal-youth novel. [JC]
Other works: *The Abandoned* (**1950**); *Love of Seven Dolls* (**1954**); *Ludmila: A Story of Liechtenstein* (**1954** chap Liechtenstein); *Thomasina: The Cat who Thought She was God* (**1957**); *The Silent Miau* (**1964**); *The Man who was Magic: A Tale of Innocence* (**1967**); *The House that Wouldn't Go Away* (**1979** UK); *The Best of Paul Gallico* (coll **1988**).

GALLUN, RAYMOND Z(INKE) (1911-) US author and technical writer, now retired. He was born and educated in Wisconsin, and has been a considerable traveller since. He began publishing sf stories at the age of 19 in 1929 with "The Space Dwellers" in *Science Wonder Stories* and "The Crystal Ray" in *Air Wonder Stories*. In the 1930s he published frequently in F. Orlin TREMAINE's *ASF*, his most famous contributions being the **Old Faithful** series: "Old Faithful" (1934), "The Son of Old Faithful" (1935) and "Child of the Stars" (1936), the first of these novelettes featuring a sympathetically conceived Martian – much in contrast to the then dominant sf convention that ALIENS were to be depicted as monstrous – and the other two featuring that Martian's descendants. Along with other stories, the three were collected in *The Best of Raymond Z. Gallun* (coll **1978**). During his prolific years – he published most of his 120 plus stories during 1929-42 – RZG also used the pseudonyms Arthur Allport, Dow Elstar, E.V. Raymond and William Callahan in his magazine fiction, publishing his first book, *The Machine that Thought* (**1939** *Science Fiction Stories*; c**1940-42** chap) as Callahan. His style was rough-hewn, but he plotted his work with vigour and packed it with ideas, often decidedly original: from a very early date, many of his stories show an interest in BIOLOGY and GENETIC ENGINEERING not widely shared by his contemporaries. He became inactive in the 1940s and, though he has published again since about 1950, he has never regained the popularity of his early years, although one of his finest stories, reprinted in the *Best* volume, was "The Restless Tide" (1951 *Marvel Science Fiction*). He published nothing 1961-74, but remained intermittently active through the 1980s.

RZG's first novel, "Passport to Jupiter" (1950 *Startling Stories*), never appeared as a book. The style of the first to do so, *People Minus X* (roughly based on "Avalanche", 1935 *ASF* as by Dow Elstar; **1957**), continued to reflect his many years of writing in a four-square idea-oriented style for the PULP MAGAZINES, and unsurprisingly derives its energy from the concepts which flood it, including body-miniaturization, body-recording, the transfiguration of human volunteers into space-resistant ANDROIDS, and much more. *The Planet Strappers* (**1961**) is more routine, but *The Eden Cycle* (**1974**) is a carefully written, slow-moving study of humans who, having received from aliens the gift of IMMORTALITY and a capacity to reinhabit imaginatively – through a kind of VIRTUAL REALITY – various epochs of world history (◊ HISTORY IN SF), find themselves less and less capable of responding to their experiences.

RZG is a writer – along with Edmond HAMILTON and Stanley G. WEINBAUM – whose writing reflected the expectations of magazine readers of the early 1930s; and like Hamilton (Weinbaum died early) his development after 1945 was tied, for good and for ill, to those early days. Late novels, like *Skyclimber* (**1981**), set on MARS, and *Bioblast* (**1985**), about the early years of a mutant SUPERMAN, may therefore lack some essential degree of appeal to today's audiences because they are crude, because they avoid sex, because their protagonists are unsubtle. But the sense of purpose persists, as does a humane vigour – as a late memoir, *Starclimber: The Literary Adventures and Autobiography of Raymond Z. Gallun* (**1991**) ed Jeffrey M. ELLIOT, amply conveys. RZG is the best of those pre-1939 sf writers who failed to remain well known into the current nostalgic period. [JC]

About the author: «The Work of Raymond Z. Gallun: An Annotated Bibliography & Guide» (1993) by Jeffrey M. Elliot.

See also: ASTOUNDING SCIENCE-FICTION; FAR FUTURE; JUPITER; LONGEVITY (IN WRITERS AND PUBLICATIONS); OUTER PLANETS; SOCIAL DARWINISM.

GALOUYE, DANIEL F(RANCIS) (1920-1976) US writer who was born and died in New Orleans, Louisiana; a naval test pilot during WWII, he subsequently worked as a journalist, though the delayed effect of war injuries forced him to retire in 1965. He began to publish sf with "Rebirth" for *Imagination* in 1952, and appeared frequently in the magazines for about a decade with such tales as "Tonight the Sky Will Fall" (1952) and "The City of Force" (1959), characterized by a combination of a strong HARD-SF structure and a treatment of psychological concerns that was sometimes a touch uneasy. Twice he wrote (1953-4) as Louis G. Daniels. Stories from this period are collected in *The Last Leap and Other Stories of the Super-Mind* (coll **1964** UK) and *Project Barrier* (coll **1968** UK); neither volume appeared in the USA.

DFG's first novel, *Dark Universe* (**1961**), a POCKET-UNIVERSE tale (*see also* CONCEPTUAL BREAKTHROUGH), remains his most popular and is probably his best (it was nominated for a HUGO). Long after a nuclear HOLOCAUST, the survivors' descendants live sightless far underground. Their culture – from daily routine through cosmological concerns – is grippingly and originally conceived, though the book closes with a somewhat anticlimactic escape from darkness into a new age of "enlightenment". His next novels, *Lords of the Psychon* (**1963**), based roughly on "City of Force" (1959), *Counterfeit World* (**1964** UK; vt *Simulacron-3* 1964 US) and *The Lost Perception* (**1966** UK; vt *A Scourge of Screamers* 1968 US), share the same technical ingenuity and a continuing interest in worlds where the PERCEPTION of reality is controlled and restricted, where indeed the worlds themselves are arbitrary constructs, *Counterfeit World* being particularly interesting in this respect. In a sense it is a novel-length reworking of Frederik POHL's "The Tunnel Under the World" (1954), both being about construct-worlds designed for market research; it was filmed for tv in Germany in 1973 by Rainer Werner Fassbinder as WELT AM DRAHT (1973; vt *World on a Wire*). DFG's last novel, *The Infinite Man* (**1973**), was less successful.

DPG was never really able to capitalize on the promising beginning he had made as an sf writer. It may be that his war injuries kept him from a longer and more fruitful career. [JC]

See also: GREAT AND SMALL; MEDIA LANDSCAPE; PSYCHOLOGY; VIRTUAL REALITY.

GAMBI PUBLICATIONS ◊ ODYSSEY.

GAMERA A giant prehistoric turtle who starred in a number of MONSTER MOVIES from the Daiei Studios. The first of these was DAIKAIJU GAMERA (1966), in the entry for which are detailed also the other **Gamera** films. [JGr]

GAMES AND SPORTS This entry deals with games as a theme within sf. Games based on sf are treated under GAMES AND TOYS.

Just as sf's concern with the ARTS has been dominated by stories about the decline of artistry in a mechanized mass society, so its concern with sports has been much involved with representing the decline of sportsmanship. There is a marked tendency in contemporary sf to assume that the audience-appeal of futuristic sports will be measured by their rendering of violence in terms of spectacle: the film ROLLERBALL (1975) is perhaps the clearest expression of this notion.

There are two forms of stereotyped competitive violence which are common in sf: the gladiatorial circus and the hunt. The arena is part of the standard apparatus of romances in the Edgar Rice BURROUGHS tradition, and extends throughout the history of sf to such modern variants as that found in the **Dumarest** series by E.C. TUBB (**1967** onwards). Combat between human and ALIEN is the basis of Fredric BROWN's popular "Arena" (1944) and a host of similar stories, while many visions of a corrupt future society foresee the return of bloody games in the Roman tradition – Frederik POHL's and C.M. KORNBLUTH's *Gladiator-at-Law* (**1955**) is a notable example. The **BattleTech** SHARED-WORLD series (*see also* Robert THURSTON) moves the formula on to a galactic stage. Ordinary hunting is extrapolated to take in alien prey in such stories as the **Gerry Carlyle** series by Arthur K. BARNES (1937-46; coll **1956** as *Interplanetary Hunter*), and a familiar variant has mankind as the victim rather than the hunter; examples include *The Sound of his Horn* (**1952**) by SARBAN, *Come, Hunt an Earthman* (**1973**) by Philip E. HIGH and many works by Robert SHECKLEY, ranging from "Seventh Victim" (1953) and "The Prize of Peril" (1958) to such recent novels as *Victim Prime* (**1986** UK) and *Hunter/Victim* (**1987** UK). A notable series of relevant theme anthologies is the 3-vol **Starhunters** series (1988-90) ed David A. DRAKE. The oft-presumed equivalence between the spectator-appeal of sport and that of dramatized violence reached its peak in Norman SPINRAD's "The National Pastime" (1973) and the film DEATH RACE 2000 (1975).

An opposing trend is one which suggests that the people of the future might substitute rule-bound war games for actual wars, thus avoiding large-scale slaughter of civilians. The idea was first mooted by George T. CHESNEY in *The New Ordeal* (**1879**); sf versions of it include "Mercenary" (1962; exp vt *Mercenary from Tomorrow* **1968**) and its sequel *The*

Earth War (**1963**) by Mack REYNOLDS and the **Gamester War** series begun with *The Alexandrian Ring* (**1987**) by William R. FORSTCHEN, and also a number of films, including GLADIATORERNA (1968) and ROBOT JOX (1990).

The sf sports story is almost entirely a post-WWII phenomenon, although the pre-WWII pulps did feature Clifford D. SIMAK's "Rule 18" (1938) – in which one of the ever-popular "all-time great" teams is actually assembled – and one or two rocket-racing stories, such as Lester DEL REY's "Habit" (1939); and much earlier van Tassel SUTPHEN had included a couple of golfing-sf stories in his *The Nineteenth Hole: Second Series* (coll **1901**). Many early post-WWII stories are accounts of man/machine confrontation (◊ MACHINES; ROBOTS). Examples include the golf story "Open Warfare" (1954) by James E. GUNN, the boxing stories "Title Fight" (1956) by William Campbell Gault and "Steel" (1956) by Richard MATHESON, the chess story "The 64-Square Madhouse" (1962) by Fritz LEIBER, and the motor-racing story "The Ultimate Racer" (1964) by Gary Wright, who also wrote a fine bobsled-racing sf story in "Mirror of Ice" (1967). The changing role of the automobile in post-WWII society provoked a number of bizarre extrapolations, including H. Chandler ELLIOTT's violent "A Day on Death Highway" (1963), Roger ZELAZNY's story about a car-fighting matador, "Auto-da-Fé" (1967), and Harlan ELLISON's "Along the Scenic Route" (1969). Other popular sf themes are often combined with sf sports stories. Gambling of various kinds appears in many ESP stories, for obvious reasons, and superhuman powers are occasionally employed on the sports field, as in Irwin Shaw's "Whispers in Bedlam" (1973) and George Alec EFFINGER's "Naked to the Invisible Eye" (1975). Stories which examine the possible impact of biotechnology on future sports include Howard V. Hendrix's "The Farm System" (**1988**) and Ian MC-DONALD's "Winning" (**1990**). Full-length novels about future sport are relatively rare; examples include *The Mind-Riders* (**1976**) by Brian M. STABLEFORD, about boxing, and *The New Atoms Bombshell* (**1980**) by Robert Browne (Marvin Karlins [1941-   ]), about baseball.

Games are used as a key to social advancement and control in a number of stories, including *The Heads of Cerberus* (1919; **1952**) by Francis STEVENS, *World out of Mind* (**1953**) by J.T. MCINTOSH, *Solar Lottery* (**1955**; vt *World of Chance*) by Philip K. DICK and *Cosmic Checkmate* (**1962**) by Katherine MACLEAN and Charles V. DE VET. Some sf stories produce future or alternate worlds where games are fundamental to the social fabric, as in Hermann HESSE's *Das Glasperlenspiel* (**1943**; trans M. Savill as *Magister Ludi* **1949** US; preferred trans Richard and Clara Winston as *The Glass Bead Game* 1969 US) and Gerald MURNANE's *The Plains* (**1982**); a vicious games-based culture is successfully attacked by the protagonist of Iain M. BANKS's space opera *The Player of Games* (**1988**). In other novels by Philip K. Dick, including *The Game-Players of Titan* (**1963**) and *The Three Stigmata of Palmer Eldritch* (**1965**), games function as levels of pseudo-

reality. Sf writers who have shown a particular and continuing interest in games or sports include Barry N. MALZBERG, who often uses surreal games to symbolize frustrating and ultimately unbeatable alienating forces – as in the apocalyptic *Overlay* (**1972**) and *Tactics of Conquest* (**1974**), and in the quasi-allegorical *The Gamesman* (**1975**) – George Alec EFFINGER, who also uses game situations as symbols of the limitations of rationality and freedom, notably in "Lydectes: On the Nature of Sport" (1975) and "25 Crunch Split Right on Two" (1975), and Piers ANTHONY, who often uses games to reflect the structures of his plots, notably in *Macroscope* (**1969**), *Ox* (**1976**), *Steppe* (**1976**) and *Ghost* (**1988**). The game which has most frequently fascinated sf writers is chess, featured in Charles L. HARNESS's "The Chess-players" (1953) and Poul ANDERSON's "The Immortal Game" (1954) as well as Malzberg's *Tactics of Conquest*. John BRUNNER's *The Squares of the City* (**1965**) has a plot based on a real chess game, and Ian WATSON's *Queenmagic, Kingmagic* (**1986**) includes a world structured as one (as well as worlds structured according to other games, including Snakes and Ladders!). Gérard KLEIN built the mystique of the game into *Starmaster's Gambit* (**1958**; trans **1973**). A version of chess crops up in the work of Edgar Rice Burroughs – in *The Chessmen of Mars* (**1922**) – and a rather more exotic variant plays an important role in *The Fairy Chessmen* (**1951**; vt *Chessboard Planet*; vt *The Far Reality*) by Lewis Padgett (Henry KUTTNER and C.L. MOORE). An anthology of chess stories is *Pawn to Infinity* (anth **1982**) ed Fred SABERHAGEN.

In recent years the rapid real-world evolution of electronic arcade games and home-computer games has sparked off a boom in stories where such games become too real for comfort. Notable examples include "Dogfight" (1985) by Michael SWANWICK and William GIBSON, *Octagon* (**1981**) by Saberhagen, *True Names* (1981; **1984**) by Vernor VINGE, *Ender's Game* (1978; exp **1985**) by Orson Scott CARD, *God Game* (**1986**) by Andrew M. GREELEY and *Only You Can Save Mankind* (**1992**) by Terry PRATCHETT (*see also* VIRTUAL REALITY). Stories of space battles whose protagonists are revealed in the last line to be icons in a computer-game "shoot 'em up" may have succeeded Shaggy God stories (◊ ADAM AND EVE) as the archetypal folly perpetrated by novice writers (although Fredric Brown's similarly plotted "Recessional" [1960], where the protagonists are chessmen, has been much anthologized). Many computer-game scenarios are, of course, sciencefictional, as are many of the scenarios used in fantasy role-playing games (◊ GAMES AND TOYS; GAME-WORLDS).

When it comes to inventing new games, sf writers have had very limited success. There have been one or two interesting descriptions of sports played in gravity-free conditions, but these are usually incidental to the real concerns of the stories in which they occur; stories set in SPACE HABITATS frequently include descriptions of "flying" games played in the vicinity of the rotational axis. Sling-gliding, in which glides are accelerated by massive steel whips, is a plausible and dangerous sport featured in *The Jaws that Bite, the Claws that Catch* (**1975**; vt *The Girl with a Symphony in her Fingers*) by Michael G. CONEY. The sport of hussade, which plays a major part in Jack VANCE's *Trullion: Alastor 2262* (**1973**), is unconvincing. The board-game vlet in Samuel R. DELANY's *Triton* (**1976**) is cleverly presented, but the details of play are necessarily vague. This game was first written about by Joanna RUSS in "A Game of Vlet" (**1974**).

Games and sports are also very common in FANTASY and SCIENCE FANTASY, especially that set in post-HOLOCAUST or primitive worlds, as in Piers Anthony's early trilogy (1968-75) collected as *Battle Circle* (omni **1977**), or *Eclipse of the Kai* ✳ (**1989**) by Joe Dever and John Grant (◊ Paul BARNETT), which features vtovlry, a rugby analogue played triangularly and with throwing-axes. Indeed, the metaphoric nuances of games enliven fantasy of all sorts, from the croquet and card games in Lewis CARROLL's **Alice** books to Sheri S. TEPPER's **True Game** series; in both cases the arbitrary and obsessive nature of games-playing becomes an image of life itself.

A relevant theme anthology is *Arena: Sports SF* (anth **1976**) ed Barry N. Malzberg and Ed FERMAN. [BS/PN]
See also: LEISURE.

GAMES AND TOYS For games as a theme within sf ◊ GAMES AND SPORTS. This entry deals with games and toys based on sf.

Sf games have quite a long history. The first, fairly quiet, phase comprised board games or card games based on a successful film, tv series or comic strip. The second phase, the commercial explosion in sf and fantasy games (and toys), dates back only to the 1970s, and came about as a consequence of three factors: the introduction in 1974 of *Dungeons and Dragons* (*D&D*), a very successful role-playing game (RPG); the introduction of the home computer, which only at the very end of the 1970s developed any real market penetration (though an early sf computer strategy game, *Star Trek*, was on display at the Worldcon in Australia in 1975) and the increasing realization by business people of the fortunes to be made by marketing products associated with successful films and tv shows, everything from bars of soap through books and comics to games and toys. The first massive campaign of this sort in the sf field was associated with the film STAR WARS (1977).

The first phase. Sf scenarios lend themselves readily to strategy games or war games (the latter being a specialized case of the former), often played on boards marked out in various grid patterns. Board games of this sort can be traced back to chess and Wei-ch'i, but miniature wargaming effectively began with H.G. WELLS, as described in his books *Floor Games* (**1911**) and *Little Wars: A Game for Boys* (**1913**); he was probably, despite his denials, influenced by *Kriegspiel*, a military training tool then used in Germany. The immediate ancestor of sf games is

Gettysburg (1958), designed by Charles Roberts, the first board game dedicated to simulating a single military event. It led to a plethora of such games, including simulations of imaginary events.

Once speculative warfare was admitted by gamers to be legitimate, the field was open to games like *Lensman* (1971), based on E.E. "Doc" SMITH's series of novels. Featuring space combat, it was largely a variant on existing naval simulations, with the addition of such sf tropes as FORCE FIELDS and tractor beams. Later games include: *Robert Heinlein's Starship Troopers* (1976), a clever and complex development from Robert A. HEINLEIN's original scenario, *John Carter of Mars* (1979), based on Edgar Rice BURROUGHS's **Barsoom** books, and *Dune* (1979), based on Frank HERBERT's novel. The first sf game with an original scenario (that is, not based on a book or film) was *Cosmic Encounter* (1977), a strategy card game in which players, as alien species with differing powers, competed to extend their "sphere of influence". The first fantasy board game may have been *War of the Ring* (1978), based on J.R.R. TOLKIEN's *The Lord of the Rings* (**1954-5**).

The second phase. Until the mid-1970s most games inspired by sf and fantasy were essentially glosses on existing forms, substituting Mars for Mayfair or Nazgul for Nazis. Then new game-forms appeared, notably role-playing games, which took their inspiration from fantasy and sf at a much more fundamental level. *Dungeons and Dragons* (1974), the first published RPG, inspired by Tolkien's books and other fantasy sources, was created by Gary Gygax (1938-   ) and Dave Arneson. *D&D* was soon popular with students and sf fans, and by 1981 their company, TSR Inc., was earning $20 million a year. In RPGs a referee (or "dungeon master") acts as story-teller, prepares – or describes according to parameters set out by the games company – an environment through which the players move, and presents the players with a series of problems such as monsters, booby traps and complicated puzzles. The players control "characters", defined in terms of various ratings, and roll dice to see whether they have succeeded or failed. Players tend to feel intense identification with their characters.

Other companies saw the potential of the market and launched their own fantasy RPGs, but the earliest were little more than variations on the *D&D* theme. *Runequest* (1978), published by Chaosium, was the first really innovative successor, providing a detailed and consistent fantasy GAME-WORLD, complete with history, human and nonhuman races, religions and politics. Meanwhile *Traveller* (1977), published by GDW Inc., was the first sf RPG to be launched, and it too later added its own detailed background. Set in a SPACE-OPERA universe, *Traveller* would feel familiar to readers of such writers of HARD SF as Poul ANDERSON and Jerry POURNELLE.

By now it was clear that game referees were prepared to buy accessory materials, such as rules supplements, prepared adventures, pads for recording details of characters, etc., and would buy more material for an existing game in preference to a new game. Games not supported by such accessories soon stopped selling. An early RPG trend was increasing complexity of rules. *Chivalry and Sorcery* (1977), published by Fantasy Games Unlimited, tried to simulate every detail of medieval life, and play slowed to a crawl under the burden of dice rolling and rules consultation needed for every action. *Advanced Dungeons and Dragons* (1978-9), published by TSR, much more successfully added several hundred thousand words to the *D&D* rules.

Most 1970s RPGs used invented game-worlds, or left their backgrounds vague, but in the 1980s many RPGs were licensed from popular sf and fantasy works. Among these were *Call of Cthulhu* (1981), published by Chaosium, based on H.P. LOVECRAFT's horror stories, *Stormbringer* (1981), published by Chaosium, based on Michael MOORCOCK's novels, *Star Trek* (1983), published by FASA, based on the tv series, *Marvel Super Heroes* (1984), published by TSR, based on MARVEL COMICS, *Ringworld* (1984), published by Chaosium, based on Larry NIVEN's novel, *Star Wars* (1987), published by West End Games, based on STAR WARS, *Buck Rogers XXVc: The 25th Century* (1988), published by TSR, based on the comic strip BUCK ROGERS IN THE 25TH CENTURY, *Humanx Commonwealth* (1989), published by Steve Jackson Games, based on the series of books by Alan Dean FOSTER, *Uplift* (1990), published by Steve Jackson Games, based on the novel by David BRIN, and *Aliens* (1991), published by Leading Edge Games, based on the film ALIENS.

Sf games in original settings range from the Wellsian STEAMPUNK *Space 1889* (1989), published by GDW, through the humorously DYSTOPIAN *Paranoia* (1984), published by West End Games, through space opera such as *Spacemaster* (1986), published by Iron Crown Enterprises, to the increasingly popular CYBERPUNK setting: *Shadowrun* (1989), published by FASA, *Dark Conspiracy* (1991), published by GDW, and *Cyberpunk* (1991), published by Steve Jackson Games (see below).

The first mass-market UK RPGs also appeared in the 1980s, all from GAMES WORKSHOP. *Golden Heroes* (1984) was an unsuccessful SUPERHERO RPG. *Judge Dredd* (1985), based on JUDGE DREDD, did better, as did *Warhammer Fantasy* (1986). No other UK RPG manufacturer has achieved much success. All the most important RPG companies are US, notably TSR, Chaosium, FASA, Steve Jackson Games, GDW and West End Games. TSR probably sells more RPG material than all the others combined.

Some RPGs are PBM (play by mail); these may be administered and refereed by commercial organizations, which charge a fee and often use a computer database.

Many RPG manufacturers use a core game system for several genres, so that players need learn only one set of rules. By far the most prolific is **GURPS** (1988; Generic Universal Role Playing System), from Steve Jackson Games, which has supplements in every genre from fantasy, sf and horror to Wild West, pirates and modern warfare, and leases rights from a range of sources, including *Witch World* (1988), based on the novels by Andre NORTON, *Riverworld* (1989), based on the novels by Philip José FARMER, *Wild Cards* (1989), based on the WILD CARDS original anthologies, themselves inspired by an RPG played by several of the authors, and *The Prisoner* (1991), based on *The PRISONER*. (This company gained considerable notoriety when computers, manuscripts and materials for *Cyberpunk* were seized by the FBI, who believed that the company was preparing "a handbook for computer crime".) Similarly Chaosium's **Runequest** system was modified for *Call of Cthulhu, Stormbringer, Ringworld* and other RPGs. GDW's near-future war RPG *Twilight 2000* (1987) was the basis for their hard-sf *2300 AD* (1989) and other games. West End Games also have a generic system, **TORG** (1990).

It seems likely that the early 1990s will see a major shake-out of RPG manufacturers, since there are too many games chasing too few customers; there are currently at least 10 horror RPGs and six cyberpunk variants. At any given time there are likely to be several RPG magazines in production, but they tend to be short-lived. The oldest and most regular are *Dragon* from TSR, *White Dwarf* from Games Workshop and *Challenge* from GDW. *Dragon* and *Challenge* often publish fiction.

An important RPG variant is the Live Role-Playing Game, in which players dress as their characters, fight with blunt or padded weapons, and explore real caves or fake ruins. Numerous groups are involved in these activities.

A growing branch of publishing, especially for children, is the role-playing gamebook, the book itself being the game. Such books, often part of series like the **Fighting Fantasy Gamebook** series, offer branching narratives where at various points the reader is invited to make a choice, as between, say, "Go left" and "Go right", with a different scenario following according to the choice made. Usually the reader has first defined, by rolling dice or otherwise, the various attributes (skill, stamina, good fortune, etc.) that s/he carries to the game. Successful authors in the field include Steve Jackson (1951-   ), Ian Livingstone and Joe Dever (1956-   ). Although most such books are fantasy, some are sf, as for example Dever's **Freeway Warrior** series.

In the 1970s, at the same time as the rise of RPGs, the COMPUTER game *Adventure* (vt *Colossal Cave*), designed by Crowther and Wood, was the prototype for computer games that used simple typed commands to explore the secrets and eliminate the obstacles of a "world" described in lively detail by the computer. At first the only players were computer professionals and students who had access to the mainframe computers then required for play, but the games became much more widely popular in the early 1980s as the first mass-market personal computers appeared. The original *Adventure* was easily converted to most machines, and soon new games added larger vocabularies, better parsing (conversion of typed input into game instructions) and more complicated worlds. *Zork* (1982), published by Infocom, typified these adventures early on, but more recent "adventure games" of this sort are very much more sophisticated. In the USA, Infocom produced a number of good adventure games with sf scenarios, including *Planetfall* (1984), *Starcross* (1984), the dystopian *A Mind Forever Voyaging* (1985) and – based on Douglas ADAMS's best-selling novel – *The Hitchhiker's Guide to the Galaxy* (1984). Also notable was the sf **Silicon Dream** trilogy from Level 9 in the UK, beginning with *Snowball* (1983). Several multiple-player games appeared, the most successful being MUD (Multi-User Dungeon) (1982), played over computer networks or via modem.

By the late 1980s many of the concepts used in RPGs had found their way into computer adventures, which were beginning to use animated graphics, sound and more flexible control methods. Several RPGs were converted to computer form, notably *Advanced Dungeons and Dragons*, in *Pool of Radiance* (1989) published by SST, and later games. Computer adventures of the late 1980s and the 1990s often involve as many as 4-6 characters, much like those in RPGs, and these sometimes act independently of the player's instructions.

While most RPGs stay in production for several years, the shelf life of most computer games is measured in months, and they become obsolete as systems evolve. Despite complaints from the minority of players who had enjoyed the language-oriented input and output of earlier computer adventure games, almost all computer adventures now rely on highly detailed graphics, and often include music and electronically generated speech. Unfortunately, these embellishments mean that a game which runs on one type of computer must be completely rewritten to run on another. Conversion is usually expensive and difficult, and a game which is famous on one or two systems may be unknown elsewhere. A new trend is rapid growth in the sheer size of programs: some adventures are supplied on seven or more floppy disks. The huge *King's Quest 5* (1990), published by Sierra, is most conveniently purchased as a CD-ROM disk.

While sf scenarios are at their most interesting (and their closest to written sf) in these so-called "adventure" games, they are even more common in "arcade" games. Where adventure games require skill at problem-solving (and sometimes language skills), arcade games put a premium on the dexterity of the player or players with joystick or pushbutton controls, and often involve manoeuvring small screen figures on moving platforms or around various moving threats, and shooting down moving obstacles (which in early arcade classics were space invaders or asteroids). Such scenarios – though visually much more elaborate – are still common in the arcade games produced, for example, by the Japanese computer-games company Nintendo. A classic game mixing strategy (trading between planetary systems) and arcade skills (space combat) is *Elite* (1984 UK), originally published by Acornsoft and now available in diverse versions, including Nintendo. The modern computer adventure game commonly contains elements of play (requiring timing and dexterity) taken from arcade games; sometimes these games are known as "arcade adventures".

Games presently under development will present their players with a VIRTUAL-REALITY scenario; their players will wear helmets, gloves, etc., in which visual display units and WALDO sensors will be incorporated. The subjective experience approximates the feeling of being placed in and able to interact with a real alternate world. Such developments are still at comparatively early stages (although of course they have been commonplace in sf since the 1940s).

There has naturally been considerable cross-fertilization between RPGs and computer adventures on the one hand, and sf and fantasy in other media on the other. While many RPGs are based either on literary sources or on tv or film, it is now not unusual for the fiction to be based on the game. Several sf games have appeared with novels set in the worlds they present as part of the games package. TSR's games have spawned numerous novels, comics and a tv cartoon series. Novel TIES have been based on RPGs, especially D&D and computer adventures, such as *Zork*. Several well known authors have emerged from hobby writing, including John M. FORD. For more on this aspect of publishing ◊ GAMEWORLDS, themselves a specialized aspect of SHARED WORLDS.

Games playing itself has become a common activity in sf scenarios in films and books (it is used to conscript a space pilot in *The* LAST STARFIGHTER [1984], for example), especially those directed at adolescents. *Space Demons* (**1986**) by Gillian RUBINSTEIN is not untypical in sucking its protagonists into a ruthless computer-games world, much as in the film TRON (1982). (*See also* CYBERSPACE.)

There are many active RPG fans, and this group has a considerable overlap with sf and fantasy FANDOM generally. Annual CONVENTIONS include Origins and Gencon, in the USA, and the UK's Gamesfair, and are usually commercially organized (unlike most sf conventions). FANZINES tend to be short-lived and irregular. There is not nearly so much fan activity among computer-games enthusiasts.

RPGs have frequently come under fire from religious fundamentalists and other pressure groups, who appear to believe that their depictions of MAGIC and SUPERNATURAL CREATURES are likely to deprave and corrupt. Any suicide by an RPG player may be blamed on the genre, despite evidence suggesting that suicide rates among RPG players are lower than average. It can be argued that such games are psychologically disruptive, sometimes distracting their players from education and other matters which should take a higher priority, but this is true of most hobbies. It can equally be argued, especially with some of the sf games (which may require, for example, a good working knowledge of physics and chemistry), that games-playing can be educational.

From a commercial point of view, sf toys are more important than sf games, and they have at least as long a history. Wind-up toy robots had become popular by the mid-1950s, but they can be regarded as simply the latest incarnation of the "automata" that were being built as toys as early as the 18th century and celebrated in PROTO-SCIENCE-FICTION stories such as "Der Sandmann" (1816; trans as "The Sandman") by E.T.A. HOFFMANN and "The Artist of the Beautiful" (1844) by Nathaniel HAWTHORNE.

Marketing campaigns for toys connected to hit movies like *Star Wars* made many millions of dollars and became the target of angry opposition from parents and educators when, in the 1980s, they became connected to the sort of tv shows often viewed by children on a Saturday morning – usually animated cartoons or animated puppet programmes. Three notable offenders were the sf tv programmes *Transformers*, *He-Man* and *Teenage Mutant Ninja Turtles*, all of which, whatever their virtues as entertainment, could be seen as 25-minute advertisements designed to encourage children to put pressure on their parents to buy toys which would enable them, in play, to reproduce the on-screen adventures (*see also The* TRANSFORMERS – THE MOVIE, MASTERS OF THE UNIVERSE and TEENAGE MUTANT NINJA TURTLES). An additional criticism, perhaps less securely based, is that many such programmes, including these three, encourage childen to indulge in fantasies of violence. The commercial clout of these product-advertising programmes – not all of them sf (*Care Bears* is a non-sf example) – can be enormous, spawning major industries. The USA and Australia are among the worst offenders; the UK has some regulations designed to minimize this sort of advertising-masquerading-as-entertainment to a captive audience of children, and some European countries have banned such programmes altogether. [MR/BF/ZB/PN]
Further reading: On games, *Heroic Worlds: A History and Guide to Role-Playing Games* (1991) by Lawrence Schick, and *Adventure Games for Microcomputers: An Annotated Directory of Interactive Fiction* (1991) by Patrick R. Dewey; on toys, *Zap! Ray Gun Classics* (1991) by Leslie Singer.

GAMES WORKSHOP UK company specializing in fantasy-adventure role-playing games and models (◊ GAMES AND TOYS) whose subsidiary, GW Books, under the editorship of David PRINGLE (with Neil Jones 1990-91), between 1989 and 1991 produced a range of novels and story collections in three series relating to three of the company's games: **Warhammer** (HEROIC FANTASY), **Warhammer 40,000** (heroic fantasy/SPACE OPERA) and **Dark Future** (ALTERNATE-WORLD/ CYBERPUNK/car action). Writers who contributed novels included Brian Craig (Brian M. STABLEFORD), David Ferring (David S. GARNETT), Ian WATSON and Jack Yeovil (Kim NEWMAN), while the collections, ed Pringle (one with Neil Jones), featured work by these authors and, among others, S.M. Baxter, Myles Burnham (Eugene Byrne), Ralph T. Castle (Charles PLATT), Storm CONSTANTINE, Charles Davidson (Charles Stross), Sean Flynn (Paul J. MCAULEY), Nicola Griffith, Neil Jones and William King. Ranging from the conventional to the very offbeat, GW Books' output was superior to the highly successful stream of games-related fictions from the TSR stable (◊ GAME-WORLDS), perhaps because Pringle, editor of INTER-ZONE, drew on the contributors to that magazine. In 1992 it was announced that rights in these works had been bought by Box Tree Books. GW has also published many games manuals and two art books, one featuring Les Edwards, the other John Blanche and Ian MILLER. [KN]

GAME-WORLDS These are worlds designed by the manufacturers of games, almost always role-playing games (or gamebooks) or computer adventure games (◊ GAMES AND TOYS). In the case of RPGs the parameters of the "world" (the fictional setting in which the game takes place) will be set out in the handbooks which form the central part of the game package; in the latter, much of the world's setting is described on screen by the computer program itself, and additional information may be given in the associated printed material. Since the mid-1980s it has been common for the more successful games of either sort to generate associational material, which may include stories, novels and COMIC books set in the world of the game. Thus George Alec EFFINGER's *The Zork Chronicles* ∗ (1990) is set in a world first described in the computer adventure game *Zork* (1982 US), published by Infocom, and subsequently the setting for several other Infocom games.

The US games company TSR Inc. has been especially prolific in commissioning books associated with their role-playing games, though these are usually fantasy rather than sf – as books set in game-worlds tend generally to be. An example is TSR's *Forgotten Realms Fantasy Adventure: Pool of Radiance* ∗ (1989) by James M. Ward and Jane Cooper Hong. The role-playing game *Shadowrun* (1989 US), published by FASA, has generated a game-worlds series, set in a world where fantasy and CYBERPUNK elements are uneasily married, of which one is *Secrets of Power: Volume 2: Shadowrun: Choose Your Enemies Carefully* ∗ (1991) by Robert N. Charrette. The **BattleTech** novels by Robert THURSTON are more straightforwardly sf, specifically SPACE OPERA. These are merely arbitrary examples of what is now a widespread phenomenon: it constitutes, for example, a sizeable proportion of the Roc sf/fantasy list of Penguin Books. Since game-worlds series books are often written by a variety of authors who are seldom the same people who invented the world in the first place, the game-world can be seen as a special case of the SHARED WORLD.

Authors whose book publications are solely set in game-worlds do not necessarily receive entries in this volume; many are absent. Nonetheless, though much fiction set in game-worlds is hack work, some is not. For example, the novels in the **Demon Download** subseries by Jack Yeovil (Kim NEWMAN), set in GAMES WORKSHOP's **Dark Future** world, are good, original works in the CYBERPUNK mode.

Many games are set in worlds previously established in book form, as with *Riverworld* (1989), published by Steve Jackson Games, based on the novels by Philip José FARMER. This volume does not accept such settings as true game-worlds, which must have originated in a games format. [PN]

GAMMA US DIGEST-size magazine. 5 issues 1963-5, published by Star Press, N. Hollywood; ed William F. NOLAN for 3 issues, then Jack Matcha and Charles E. FRITCH. The fiction in this magazine – a blend of sf and fantasy – was of good quality, many stories being by Californian writers with film connections, like Charles BEAUMONT and Richard MATHESON, and there were some fine covers by Morris Scott Dollens and John Healey. Its irregularity of publication sped its demise. [FHP/PN]

GAMOW, GEORGE (1904-1968) Russian-born physicist involved in the development of quantum theory at Göttingen and later a colleague of Niels Bohr (1885-1962) and Ernest Rutherford (1871-1937). After 1935 he lived in the USA, holding the chair of theoretical physics at George Washington University. After important work on stellar evolution, he turned to investigating the Big Bang, becoming the most ardent proselytizer for that theory of the Universe's origins, in contradiction to the then important Steady State theory advocated by, notably, Fred HOYLE. Beyond his technical work, GG is known for his 10 or more scientific popularizations, beginning with *The Birth and Death of the Sun* (**1940**) and including *One Two Three . . . Infinity* (**1947**; rev 1960). His three books about **Mr Tompkins** are particularly attractive: *Mr Tompkins in Wonderland* (coll **1939** chap UK) and *Mr Tompkins Explores the Atom* (coll **1944** chap UK), both being assembled as *Mr Tompkins in Paperback* (omni **1965** UK), and *Mr Tompkins Learns the Facts of Life* (coll **1953** chap UK; exp with Martynas Ycas vt *Mr Tompkins inside Himself* 1967). Couched in narrative form, these books gracefully and intelligently explore the wonders of science, with Tompkins magically visiting embodied demonstrations of the scientific world, and even exploring his own body. Though technically juvenile, the books have a wide appeal. GG also wrote at least one sf story for adults, "The Heart on the Other Side" (1931), written to celebrate Bohr's 70th birthday and later published in *The Expert Dreamers* (anth **1963**) ed Frederik POHL. [JC]

See also: ALTERNATE WORLDS; COSMOLOGY; DIMENSIONS; FASTER THAN LIGHT; GREAT AND SMALL.

GANDON, YVES (1899-?   ) French novelist. His *Le dernier Blanc* (**1945**; trans A.M. as *The Last White Man*

1948 UK) depicts, on familiar lines, the chemical warfare of the future featuring a toxin deadly only to whites. Other borderline sf works include *Après les hommes* ["After Men"] (**1963**), involving an ethical ferromagnetic race, and *La ville invisible* ["The Invisible Town"] (**1953**). *En pays singulier* ["In a Remarkable Country"] (coll **1949**) contains some sf. [JC/PN]

GANICK, NICHOLAS [r] ◊ ROBERT HALE LIMITED.

GANN, ERNEST K(ELLOGG) (1910-1991) US writer, usually of thrillers, whose *Brain 2000* (**1980**) is an sf spoof in which the extraction of oil from parts of the world causes gravitational and orbital disturbances. A smart child solves all our problems. [JC]

GANN, WILLIAM D. (1878-1955) US businessman and writer whose sf novel, *The Tunnel Thru the Air, or Looking Back from 1940* (**1927**), features a protagonist whose Fundamentalist belief in the Bible gives him sufficient predictive prowess to dodge a great depression (which WDG dates 1928-32), while at the same time impelling him to invent various superweapons, which are used to defend the USA against her external enemies. New York is then renamed the City of the Lord. All ends happily. [JC]

GANSOVSKY, SEVER (FELIKSOVICH) (1918-1990) Russian writer, a dominant figure of the 1960s and 1970s, well known for his radio plays, some of them sf, and also well regarded for his HARD-SF short stories and novellas, which were assembled in *Shagi V Neizvestnoie* ["Steps into the Unknown"] (coll **1963**), *Shest' Geniev* ["Six Geniuses"] (coll **1965**), *Tri Shaga K Opasnosti* ["Three Steps towards Danger"] (coll **1969**), *Idyot Tchelovek* ["Man is Coming"] (coll **1971**) and *Tchelovek, Kotoryi Sdelal Baltiiskoie More* ["The Man who Made the Baltic Sea"] (coll **1981**). Some of his better stories appear in *World's Spring* (anth **1979** Sweden) ed Vladimir GAKOV, and further stories were assembled as *The Day of Wrath* (coll trans Alexander Repyev **1989** Russia). A novel, *Vinsent Van-Gog* ["Vincent Van Gogh"] (**1971**) is a TIME-TRAVEL tale raising general philosophical questions about the artist's destiny. [VG]

GANTZ, KENNETH F(RANKLIN) (1905-   ) US writer, mostly of nonfiction, and USAF editor. His sf novel, *Not in Solitude* (**1959**; rev 1961), fictionalizes a first voyage to MARS and describes the probable environment faced by the travellers. [JC]

GARBO, NORMAN (1919-   ) US writer in whose borderline sf novel, *The Movement* (**1969**), exaggerated late-1960s-style confrontations between US students and police lead to a full-scale uprising with retaliatory bombing by the government. [JC]

GARBY, Mrs LEE HAWKINS (1890-?   ) The wife of a school-friend of E.E. "Doc" SMITH, with whom she collaborated on *The Skylark of Space: The Tale of the First Inter-Stellar Cruise* (written 1915 20; 1928 *AMZ*; **1946**; cut rev 1958), for which she was credited. The 1958 abridgement of this famous SPACE OPERA may have eliminated most and perhaps all of her contribution, as she was no longer listed as co-author. [JC]

GARDEN, DONALD J. [r] ◊ ROBERT HALE LIMITED.

GARDNER, ERLE STANLEY (1889-1970) US lawyer and writer, most famous for the **Perry Mason** detective novels, beginning with *The Case of the Velvet Claws* (**1933**). He was extremely prolific and, although he spent almost no time at all on sf, managed to produce enough fiction to fill *The Human Zero: The Science Fiction Stories of Erle Stanley Gardner* (coll **1981**) ed Martin H. GREENBERG and Charles G. WAUGH. The tales, which first appeared in *The Argosy* around 1930, are efficient but unmemorable pulp sf, and now seem both dim and mechanical. [JC]

See also: APES AND CAVEMEN (IN THE HUMAN WORLD).

GARDNER, JEROME ◊ ROBERT HALE LIMITED.

GARDNER, JOHN 1. (1926-   ) UK writer who was a minister for several years before becoming an agnostic, a drama critic, and the creator of the **Boysie Oakes** sequence of spy thrillers spoofing Ian FLEMING's **James Bond** books, most famously in *The Liquidator* (**1964**); one Boysie Oakes tale, *Founder Member* (**1969**), involves its hero in a SEX experiment in space. More recently, JG has written a number of novels continuing the **James Bond** saga itself. Among his many other novels, mostly thrillers, *Golgotha* (**1980**; vt *The Last Trump* 1980 US), is a NEAR-FUTURE thriller whose apocalyptic imagery may owe something to JG's early theological training. [JC]

2. Full name John Champlin Gardner (1933-1982), US writer and academic who achieved popularity with his large contemporary novel, *The Sunlight Dialogues* (**1972**). His third work of fiction, *Grendel* (**1971**), is a mordant retelling of the Beowulf legend from the MONSTER's point of view, and renders – more pointedly than Thomas Burnett SWANN's similar elegies – Anglo-Saxon Man's triumphs as allegorical of the rise of the cruel, modern, industrial world. Further works that contain fantastic elements include *Jason and Medeia* (**1973**), a fantasy novel in verse, several tales assembled in *The King's Indian: Stories and Tales* (coll **1974**), *In the Suicide Mountains* (**1977**), a juvenile based on Russian folk themes, and *Freddy's Book* (**1980**). *Mickelsson's Ghosts* (**1982**) attempts to subsume the ghost story and other narrative conventions into a mundane frame. Though clearly attracted to various supernatural and classical traditions, JG had little apparent interest in the sf or fantasy genres, which are scantly treated in *On Moral Fiction* (**1978**), in which he argued for a traditional viewpoint, abjuring what he saw as POSTMODERNIST nihilism. He died in a motorcycle accident. [GF/JC]

About 2: *World of Order and Light: The Fiction of John Gardner* (**1984**) by G.L. Morris.

See also: MYTHOLOGY.

GARDNER, MARTIN (1914-   ) US mathematician, conjurer, journalist and author; his BA is in philosophy from the University of Chicago. His *In the Name of Science* (**1952**; rev vt *Fads and Fallacies in the Name of Science* 1957) is an iconoclastic and amusing nonfiction book about PSEUDO-SCIENCE: cults, fads and hoaxes existing on the fringes of science, with chapters on HOLLOW-EARTH and flat-Earth theories, pyramidology, UFOS and other subjects. Of particular interest to sf readers may be its references to Sir Arthur Conan DOYLE, Charles FORT, L. Ron HUBBARD, Richard SHAVER. More recent works in the same debunking line are *Science: Good, Bad and Bogus* (coll **1981**) and *Notes of a Fringe-Watcher* (**1988**). MG's *The Ambidextrous Universe* (**1964**; exp 1979; rev 1982), on the other hand, concerns serious science; moving from simple questions of symmetry to profound problems of physical philosophy, it is one of the finest works of scientific popularization.

From 1956 until 1981 MG wrote the **Mathematical Games** column in *Scientific American*, and a number of collections of these pieces have been published in book form, including *The Unexpected Hanging and Other Mathematical Diversions* (**1969**) and *Mathematical Carnival* (**1975**). His *The Incredible Dr Matrix* (fixup **1977**) brings together a number of spoof stories from that column about the eponymous numerologist and rogue, a practitioner of several of the shady cults described in MG's earlier book. Also of note are his *The Annotated Alice* (**1960**), a densely glossed edition of Lewis CARROLL's two **Alice** books – it is supplemented by *More Annotated Alice* (**1990**) – and *The Annotated Snark* (**1962**), a similar treatment of Carroll's *The Hunting of the Snark* (**1876** chap).

From the launching of ISAAC ASIMOV'S SCIENCE FICTION MAGAZINE (1977) MG had a MATHEMATICS column there, with puzzles often posed in the form of sf stories; many of these have been collected as *Science Fiction Puzzle Tales* (coll **1981**) and *Puzzles from Other Worlds* (coll **1984**). A further volume, collecting actual sf stories (not simply puzzle stories) in a similar vein is *The No-Sided Professor* (coll **1987**). Collections of essays, some with an sf connection, are *Order and Surprise* (coll **1983**) and *Gardner's Whys and Wherefores* (coll **1989**). *Logic Machines and Diagrams* (**1958**; rev 1982) also refers to sf. [PN/JE]

See also: DIMENSIONS; PARANOIA.

GARDNER, NOEL [s] ◊ Henry KUTTNER.

GARIS, HOWARD R(OGER) (1873-1962) US writer known mainly for such work outside the sf field as his **Uncle Wiggily** series, whose 15,000 episodes were widely syndicated. For the Edward STRATEMEYER Syndicate he wrote, under the house pseudonym Roy ROCKWOOD and according to plot outlines from Stratemeyer, the first 6 vols of the **Great Marvel** series: *Through the Air to the North Pole* (**1906**), *Under the Ocean to the South Pole* (**1907**), *Five Thousand Miles Underground* (**1908**), *Through Space to Mars* (**1910**), *Lost on the Moon* (**1911**) and *On a Torn-Away World* (**1913**); 3 later volumes are of unknown authorship. These tales were of considerable imaginative power, not emulated by his contributions to the TOM SWIFT series, for which he wrote – again to Stratemeyer synopses – the first 35 (of 38) episodes under the house name Victor APPLETON, from *Tom Swift and his Motor-Cycle, or Fun and Adventure on the Road* (**1910**) to HRG's last, *Tom Swift and his Giant Magnet, or Bringing up the Lost Submarine* (**1932**). (R. REGINALD's *Science Fiction and*

Fantasy Literature: A Checklist, 1700-1974 [**1979**] gives all 35 titles.) [JC/EFB]

Other works: Many juveniles, including *Tom of the Fire Cave* (**1927**); the **Rocket Riders** books, *Rocket Riders Across the Ice, or Racing against Time* (**1933**), *Rocket Riders over the Desert, or Seeking the Lost City* (**1933**), *Rocket Riders in Stormy Seas, or Trailing the Treasure Divers* (**1933**) and *Rocket Riders in the Air, or A Chase in the Clouds* (**1934**).

GARLAND Garland Publishing, Inc., New York, is a US specialist publisher of a wide range of reference works and facsimile reprints, only some of which are related to sf. In 1975 G published the **Garland Library of Science Fiction**: 45 titles, selected by Lester DEL REY, issued in durable editions. The series was criticized, partly for some idiosyncratic choices – unexceptional novels by Stanton A. COBLENTZ, H. Beam PIPER and George O. SMITH – but chiefly for choosing inferior versions of the books to reproduce. Intended as an accompanying critical history by Del Rey was *The World of Science Fiction: 1926-1976: The History of a Subculture* (**1979**), which in the event appeared from DEL REY BOOKS first and then from G in 1980. Among G's very occasional books of genre interest since that time have been *The Literature of Fantasy: A Comprehensive, Annotated Bibliography of Modern Fantasy Fiction* (**1979**) by Roger C. SCHLOBIN, *Science Fiction and Fantasy Series and Sequels: A Bibliography, Volume 1: Books* (**1986**) by Tim Cottrill, Martin H. GREENBERG and Charles D. WAUGH, and *Horror Literature: A Reader's Guide* (**1990**) and *Fantasy Literature: A Reader's Guide* (**1990**), both ed Neil BARRON. [MJE/PN]

GARNE, GASTON ◊ Francis W. DOUGHTY.

GARNER, ALAN (1934-   ) UK writer, primarily for children; he has lived all his life near Alderley Edge, Cheshire, the setting for nearly all his fiction. AG is widely thought one of the finest, though most difficult, children's writers of his generation. Most of his work is FANTASY, rooted in his knowledge of local archaeology and MYTHOLOGY. His first two books form a short series for younger children: *The Weirdstone of Brisingamen* (**1960**; vt *The Weirdstone* 1961 US) and *The Moon of Gomrath* (**1963**); his third, *Elidor* (**1965**), can be read as borderline sf. The mood here darkens in a story of teenagers faced with a threat (and a quest) from an ALTERNATE WORLD, which impinges menacingly on their own. AG's first fully mature work is *The Owl Service* (**1967**), in which a bitter Welsh legend re-enacts itself among modern children, faced with fully adult problems of love, jealousy and death. AG's theme has always been a kind of TIME TRAVEL, but the time is inner and psychic; his stories rework archetypal patterns, usually involving pain, loss, desire, rage and the need for an almost unattainable courage.

AG's next book, *Red Shift* (**1973**), is in no conventional sense a children's book (*see also* CHILDREN'S SF). In compressed, elliptical prose, primarily dialogue, he reverts to the theme of the past working out its problems in the present, as a time shift, focused on a Neolithic axe-head, moves the protagonist backwards and forwards in a choppy and wrenching way between *alter egos* in the twilight of the Roman Empire in Britain, the Civil War of the 17th century and now.

AG's last fiction of note is a sparely written, quasi-autobiographical tetralogy for rather younger children: *The Stone Book* (**1976**), *Tom Fobble's Day* (**1977**), *Granny Reardun* (**1977**) and *The Aimer Gate* (**1978**), later published together as *The Stone Book Quartet* (omni **1983**; vt *The Stone Quartet* US). Though these books are neither sf nor fantasy, the old themes recur. [PN]

Other works: *The Lad of the Gad* (**1981**).

Retold folktales: *The Hamish Hamilton Book of Goblins* (coll **1969**); *Alan Garner's Fairy Tales of Gold* (coll **1980**; rev vt *Fairytales of Gold* **1989** illus Michael Foreman); *Alan Garner's Book of British Fairy Tales* (coll **1984**); *A Bag of Moonshine* (coll **1986**).

As editor: *The Guizer: A Book of Fools* (anth **1975**), which in addition to tales by others contains many folktales retold by AG.

About the author: *A Fine Anger: A Critical Introduction to the Work of Alan Garner* (**1981**) by Neil Philip; "Inner Time" by Alan Garner in *Science Fiction at Large* (anth **1976**; vt *Explorations of the Marvellous*) ed Peter NICHOLLS.

See also: FANTASY; RADIO.

GARNER, GRAHAM ◊ Donald Sydney ROWLAND.

GARNER, ROLF ◊ Bryan BERRY.

GARNETT, DAVID (1892-1981) UK writer, member of the famous Garnett family which includes his grandfather, Richard GARNETT, his father, Edward GARNETT, and his mother, the translator Constance Garnett (1862-1946); DG was also an intimate member of the Bloomsbury Group. His first novel under his own name is also his most famous, the fantasy *Lady into Fox* (**1922** chap); like its inferior successor, VERCORS' *Sylva* (**1961**; trans **1962**), this is an allegory of metamorphosis, in this instance from demure wife into vixen, with tragic results. A FEMINIST reading of the book is both elucidating and inescapable; it was famously parodied by Christopher Ward (1868-1943) in *Gentleman into Goose* (**1924** chap). *A Man in the Zoo* (**1924**) is also fantasy. *The Grasshoppers Come* (**1931**) fascinatingly combines aviation and allegory in a borderline-sf tale. *Two by Two: A Story of Survival* (**1963**) retells the story of Noah (quite possibly a portrait of DG's friend T.H. WHITE) and the Flood. DG translated André MAUROIS's *A Voyage to the Island of the Articoles* (**1927**; trans **1928** UK). *The White/Garnett Letters* (coll **1968**), which he edited, are of great value to students of both his work and White's. [JC]

Other works: *A Terrible Day* (**1932**); *Purl and Plain, and Other Stories* (coll **1973**); *The Master Cat: The True and Unexpurgated Story of Puss in Boots* (**1974**).

GARNETT, DAVID S. (1947-   ) UK writer with a BSc in economics, author of about 50 books, many of them novels, in various genres and under various names. To differentiate himself from the elder David

GARNETT he created a middle initial, and in the USA signed his early books Dav Garnett; he has published novels also as David Lee and David Ferring. Though his sf has always been action-oriented and dominated by SPACE-OPERA conventions, his first book, *Mirror in the Sky* (**1969** US), guys those traditions with disillusioned but moderate spite. His third novel, *Time in Eclipse* (**1974**) – written like its 1970s successors for ROBERT HALE LIMITED – is a comparatively ambitious effort set on a war-torn Earth whose guardian is an amnesiac obscurely bound to a vast COMPUTER. Much of his work is marred by haste, so that the anarchic subtexts pervading his most routine tales can seem unintended. Their subversiveness, however, is certainly deliberate. As editor, DSG was responsible for an original story anthology series, *Zenith: The Best in New British Science Fiction* (anth **1989**) and *Zenith 2: The Best in New British Science Fiction* (anth **1990**); when the sequence was terminated, he initiated – with the approval of Michael MOORCOCK – a new incarnation of NEW WORLDS, this time in anthology form, beginning with *New Worlds* (anth **1991**) and *New Worlds 2* (anth **1992**). DSG also ed *The Orbit Science Fiction Yearbook 1* (anth **1988**), #2 (anth **1989**) and #3 (anth **1990**), distinguished from other year's-best anthologies by its smaller size and greater concentration on critical material, each volume including essays on the sf scene by Brian W. ALDISS, John CLUTE and DSG himself. [JC]

Other works: *The Starseekers* (**1971** US); *The Forgotten Dimension* (**1975**); *Phantom Universe* (**1975**); *Cosmic Carousel* (coll **1976**).

As **David Lee:** *Destiny Past* (**1974**).

As **David Ferring:** *The Hills Have Eyes Part 2* ✻ (**1984**), novelizing a horror film; the **Konrad** trilogy set in the **Warhammer** fantasy gaming world (◊ GAMES WORKSHOP), comprising *Konrad* ✻ (**1990**), *Shadowbreed* ✻ (**1991**) and «Warblade», the third vol being caught in limbo when the line shut down.

See also: ANTHOLOGIES; GAME-WORLDS.

GARNETT, EDWARD (1868-1936) UK writer and man of letters, son of Richard GARNETT, husband of Constance Garnett, father of David GARNETT. His greatest fame was as an enormously influential publishers' reader for several UK firms; among the writers whose careers he significantly helped were Joseph CONRAD, E.M. FORSTER and W.H. HUDSON. The sf SATIRES assembled in *Papa's War* (coll dated 1918 but probably **1919**) reveal a freethinking, controversial, clear-headed teller of tales and allegories. [JC]

GARNETT, RICHARD (1835-1906) UK librarian and writer, Chief Keeper at the British Museum, father of Edward GARNETT, grandfather of David GARNETT. His *The Twilight of the Gods and Other Tales* (coll **1888**; exp 1903) is a well known collection of fables and other fantasies, some of which touch on sf themes. [JC]

GARON, MARCO ◊ Marco GARRON; Dennis HUGHES.

GARRETT, (GORDON) RANDALL (PHILLIP DAVID) (1927-1987) US writer whose first publication was a **Probability Zero** vignette in ASTOUNDING

SCIENCE-FICTION in 1944. He went on to become a prolific writer for that magazine in the 1950s and early 1960s. He was at one time part of the ZIFF-DAVIS stable writing for AMAZING STORIES and FANTASTIC, when he and his sometime collaborator Robert SILVERBERG ran a "fiction factory" together. He used the pseudonyms David Gordon and Darrel T. Langart as well as numerous house names; he has frequently been listed as having written the *ASF* stories signed Walter Bupp, although these are now known to have been by John BERRYMAN. His most notable collaborations with Silverberg were the **Nidor** series, *The Shrouded Planet* (fixup **1957**) and *The Dawning Light* (**1958**), which appeared as by Robert Randall; other collaborations were signed Gordon Aghill and Ralph BURKE, and some stories signed under house names Alexander BLADE, Richard GREER, Ivar JORGENSEN, Clyde MITCHELL, Leonard G. SPENCER, S.M. TENNESHAW and Gerald VANCE may be further RG/Silverberg collaborations. He also collaborated with Laurence M. JANIFER, usually as Mark PHILLIPS, under which name they produced a trilogy of PSI-POWER stories: *Brain Twister* (1959 *ASF* as "That Sweet Little Old Lady"; **1962**), *The Impossibles* (1960 *ASF* as "Out Like a Light"; **1963**), and *Supermind* (1960-61 *ASF* as "Occasion for Disaster"; **1963**).

RG's most impressive solo work is the series of stories first published in *ASF* between 1964 and 1976 – reprinted in *Too Many Magicians* (**1967**), *Murder and Magic* (coll **1979**) and *Lord Darcy Investigates* (coll **1981**), and finally assembled in *Lord Darcy* (omni **1983**) – featuring the exploits of the detective Darcy in an ALTERNATE WORLD where MAGIC works according to Frazerian laws whose implications are being gradually unravelled by the scientific method. RG's earlier sf books were *Unwise Child* (**1962**; vt *Starship Death* 1982), about a sentient machine, and *Anything You Can Do . . .* (**1963**) as by Darrel T. Langart, about a battle between a superhuman and an ALIEN. RG was fond of producing parodies in verse and prose: he wrote comic verse for The MAGAZINE OF FANTASY AND SCIENCE FICTION and "Parodies Tossed" (1956) for SCIENCE FICTION QUARTERLY, and he guyed the **Feghoot** shaggy-dog stories (written for *FSF* by Reginald BRETNOR as Grendel Briarton) in the adventures of **Benedict Breadfruit**, written for *AMZ* as Grandall Barretton. With Janifer he wrote a bawdy comic fantasy in which the deities of Classical MYTHOLOGY return to preside over a high-tech future, *Pagan Passions* (**1959**). His best humorous work was collected in *Takeoff!* (coll **1980**) and *Takeoff Too* (coll **1987**); a more eclectic selection was assembled in *The Best of Randall Garrett* (coll **1982**) ed Silverberg. Always a devout man – despite the occasional wildness of his lifestyle – RG virtually dropped out of sf writing for a long period in the 1970s, and took Holy Orders for a while. He eventually abandoned the priesthood and married his third wife, Vicki Ann Heydron, with whom he plotted the **Gandalara** series of heroic fantasies; these appeared as collaborations, although in fact Heydron wrote them while RG was hospitalized in the wake of a serious attack of viral meningitis. The series comprises *The Steel of Raithskar* (**1981**), *The Glass of Dyskornis* (**1982**), *The Bronze of Eddarta* (**1983**), *The Well of Darkness* (**1983**), *The Search for Ka* (**1984**), *Return to Eddarta* (**1985**) and *The River Wall* (**1986**). The first 3 were assembled as *The Gandalara Cycle, Volume 1* (omni **1986**) and the second 3 as *The Gandalara Cycle, Volume 2* (omni **1986**). [BS]

See also: CRIME AND PUNISHMENT; ESP.

GARRON, MARCO A CURTIS WARREN house name used exclusively for jungle novels derived from Edgar Rice BURROUGHS's **Tarzan of the Apes** sequence; most were sf or fantasy. Under the spelling Marco Garron appeared the **Azan the Apeman** series – *The Lost City* (**1950**), *The Missing Safari* (**1950**), *Tribal War* (**1951**), *White Fangs* (**1951**), *King Hunters* (**1951**) and *Jungle Fever* (**1951**) – which so closely mimicked **Tarzan** that after the first 6 releases the Burroughs estate was able to gain an injunction banning any further publications; it is possible they were written by D.A. GRIFFITHS. Writing as Marco Garon (note spelling), Dennis HUGHES (*whom see for details*) published a second series, the **Rex Brandon** novels, sufficiently remote from **Tarzan** to avoid further legal action. [JC]

GARSON, CLEE House name used on the ZIFF-DAVIS magazines by Paul W. FAIRMAN (1 story, "Nine Worlds West", *Fantastic Adventures* Apr 1951), David Wright O'BRIEN and perhaps others. In all, there were 13 CG stories 1942-55. [PN]

GARSON, PAUL (1946-   ) US teacher and writer whose *The Great Quill* (**1973**) is set in a baroquely degenerate post-HOLOCAUST England; there are satirical effects. [JC]

GARTH Blond, square-jawed, musclebound, time-travelling COMIC-strip character created for the London *Daily Mirror* by artist Steve Dowling and BBC producer Gordon Boshell as the UK's answer to FLASH GORDON. Scripted by Don Freeman, G first appeared, floating ashore on a raft, on 24 July 1943, and soon became a kind of fantasy troubleshooter. In *The Seven Ages of Garth* (Sep 1944-Jan 1946) Freeman introduced G's Doctor-Zarkov equivalent, Professor Lumière, whose magic word "karma" put G in touch with his previous lives.

The finest scripts were written 1953-66 by Peter O'Donnell (1920-   ), who introduced G's eternal lover Astra in *The Last Goddess* (1965). Jim Edgar provided moderately imaginative scripts throughout the next two decades on three basic themes: TIME TRAVEL, journeys to distant planets, and earthbound adventures that usually had sf elements. Angus Allan provided a few scripts in the late 1980s.

Steve Dowling retired in 1968 and his assistant, John Allard, took over as artist. In 1971 the *Daily Mirror* secured the services of Frank Bellamy (1919-1976), one of the finest strip illustrators of his day, whose beautifully rendered drawings made G the most attractive-looking UK newspaper strip then published. On Bellamy's sudden death the art chores were taken on by Martin Asbury; for some years Asbury's art was polished, enthusiastic and inventive, but it suddenly deteriorated in the mid-1980s and today seems hurried and shoddy. Tim Quinn has recently started to do the scripting.

The *Daily Mirror* published 3 collections: *The Last Goddess* (graph coll **1966**), *The "Daily Mirror" Book of Garth 1975* (graph coll **1975**) and *1976* (graph coll **1976**). Single-story collections were published by John Dakin/The Newspaper Strip Society: *Sapphire* (graph **1980**), *Night of the Knives* (graph **1980**), *The Doomsmen* (graph **1981**), *Mr Rubio Calls* (graph **1981**) and *Bride of Jenghiz Khan* (graph **1981**). 2 collections of Bellamy stories were published by Titan: *The Cloud of Balthus* (graph coll **1985**) and *The Women of Galba* (graph coll **1985**). [RT/SW]

GARTH, WILL House name used on *Thrilling Wonder Stories, Startling Stories* and CAPTAIN FUTURE 1937-41 by Otto BINDER, Edmond HAMILTON, Henry KUTTNER, Mort WEISINGER and possibly others. The film novelization of DR CYCLOPS, *Dr Cyclops* * (**1940**) as by WG, has been attributed to Kuttner, who confusingly wrote a TWS short story of that title in the same year, and to Manly Wade WELLMAN, who did not write it. It was almost certainly by Alexander SAMALMAN. [PN/JC]

GARVIN, RICHARD M(cCLELLAN) (1934-1980) US writer whose career had been in advertising. His two sf novels with Edmond G. Addeo are *The FORTEC Conspiracy* (**1968**) and *The Talbot Agreement* (**1968**). In the former, a crashlanded alien ship infects Earth with a deadly disease; the latter novel is borderline sf with espionage elements. A solo novel was *The Crystal Skull* (**1974**). [JC]

GARY, ROMAIN Pseudonym of French writer and diplomat Romain Kacewgari (later changed to Kassevgari) (1914-1980) born in Tiflis, Georgia, of Polish parents. In WWII he was active in the French Resistance. RG was much praised for such novels outside the sf field as *Les racines du ciel* (**1956**; trans Jonathan Griffin as *The Roots of Heaven* **1958** US), for which he was awarded the Prix Goncourt. An early and untranslated sf novel, *Tulipe* (**1946**), is about the Blacks taking over Earth. In his later work he utilizes generic material usually to point up ethical issues, and *La danse de Gengis Cohn* (**1967**; trans by RG as *The Dance of Genghis Cohn* **1968** US), with its sequel, *La tête coupable* (**1968** trans by RG as *The Guilty Head* **1969** US), are certainly FABULATIONS. Rather similar to the inferior *On A Dark Night* (**1949**) by Anthony WEST, they depict a supernatural transference of a victim's personality into the body of a Nazi. In *Genghis Cohn* it is Cohn himself, a Yiddish comedian, who, as a dybbuk, enters the mind of the SS officer who ordered the massacre in which Cohn was shot. The novel takes place in the late 1960s, with the former officer, now a police superintendent, obsessed by his dybbuk, who torments him, and with Germany itself tormented by an incursion of allegorical figures representative of her spiritual plight. *Gloire à nos illustres pionniers* (coll **1962**; trans Richard Howard as

Hissing Tales **1964** US) contains some sf, notably the title story. In *The Gasp* (**1973** US; in French as *Charge d'âme* **1978** France) it turns out that the *élan vital* which escapes from the body at the moment of death can be used in warfare. RG was a sharp, clear-headed and passionate novelist of considerable stature. [JC]

Other work: *The Talent Scout* (ms? trans John Markham Beach **1961** US).

See also: ESCHATOLOGY; HISTORY OF SF; POWER SOURCES; RELIGION.

GAS GIANT Item of sf TERMINOLOGY invented by James BLISH; it proved so useful that it is now often used by astronomers. It refers to the fact that four of the planets of our Solar System are not comparatively small and dense, like Earth and MARS, but extremely large, and consist mainly of substances like hydrogen, helium, methane and ammonia. Even in the cold at the outer edge of our Solar System, these planets are of low density, being essentially globes of gas and liquid. The four gas giants – often called the Jovian Planets – in our Solar System are JUPITER, Saturn, Uranus and Neptune (◊ OUTER PLANETS). The fact that there are two kinds of planet in the Solar System is of great interest to scientists constructing theories of its evolution; it is believed that gas-giant planets have been detected orbiting a few nearby stars. [PN]

GASKELL, JANE Working name of UK writer Jane Gaskell Lynch (1941-), whose dozen books include *Strange Evil* (**1957**), her first, written when she was 14; it features fairies from another world, claustrophobic conflicts in that world, and an aura of Gothic pubescence throughout. *King's Daughter* (**1958**) is set in ancient ATLANTIS, where a cache of even more ancient nerve gas is discovered; the book is remotely connected, through a shared character, with the **Cija** sequence of Atlantean tales – *The Serpent* (**1963**; vt in 2 vols *The Serpent* 1975 and *The Dragon* 1975), *Atlan* (**1965**), *The City* (**1966**) and *Some Summer Lands* (**1977**). The non-Atlantean Princess Cija is involved, via forced marriage, in complex conflicts between northern forces and the quasihuman dwellers of the island state. As things fall apart, sex and sorcery abound, but the princess eventually reaches home again. In genre terms the series uneasily marries sf and the popular romance; it is full of vigorous and exuberant invention and occasionally overheated prose. *The Shiny Narrow Grin* (**1964**) is a comedy about vampires. *A Sweet Sweet Summer* (**1969**) scathingly exposes an anarchic NEAR-FUTURE England to the gaze of invading extraterrestrials. *Sun Bubble* (**1990**) is a fantasy. [JC]

GÁSPÁR, LÁSZLÓ [r] ◊ HITLER WINS; HUNGARY.

GAS-S-S-S, OR IT BECAME NECESSARY TO DESTROY THE WORLD IN ORDER TO SAVE IT (vt *Gas! or It Became Necessary to Destroy the World in Order to Save It*) Film (1970). San Jacinto/AIP. Prod and dir Roger CORMAN, starring Robert Corff, Elaine Giftos, Bud Cort, Talia Coppola. Screenplay George Armitage. 79 mins cut to 77 mins. Colour.

In Corman's belated attempt to cash in on the hippy/counterculture movements of the 1960s, a poison gas makes everyone over 25 die of old age and the young inherit the USA. There is topsy-turvy chaos in this black comedy, with conservative Middle Americans going on a rampage of destruction while Hell's Angels attempt to protect the old way of life (golf links, etc.), but a cheerfully workable society begins to emerge. Edgar Allan POE occasionally appears on a motorcycle, with the Raven perched on his shoulder and Lenore on pillion. The film was made with Corman's legendary speed and cheapness, and with a general sense of expansive euphoria. AIP disliked it, re-editing it drastically without Corman's knowledge, so he went on to set up his own production/distribution company, New World. [JB]

See also: CINEMA.

GATE, THE UK SEMIPROZINE, irregular, 3 issues to date, published by Richard Newcombe, #1 1989 in paperback book format ed Maureen Porter, subsequent issues (1990 and 1991) A4 format ed Paul Cox, no publication dates given. *TG* is primarily a fiction magazine (stories by son and father Sean and Barrington J. BAYLEY, Storm CONSTANTINE, Kim NEWMAN, Andy Sawyer, Brian M. STABLEFORD, Ian WATSON, James WHITE and others), but carries a regular film column by Newman. [RH]

GAUGER, RICK Working name of US writer Richard C. Gauger (? -), who began publishing sf with "The Vacuum-Packed Picnic" for *Omni* in 1979. His sf novel, *Charon's Ark* (**1987**), pleasingly depicts the hijacking of a 747 full of students, who are taken to the moon of Pluto. Charon turns out to be an Ark, its function being to carry life across the Galaxy: it needs new crew members. [JC]

GAUGHAN, JACK Working name of US illustrator John Brian Francis Gaughan (1930-1985). JG made his first professional sale while still in school at the Dayton Art Institute; he went full-time in the mid-1950s. Prolific in both covers and interior art, he was most closely associated with GALAXY SCIENCE FICTION, for which he was Art Editor 1969-72 and painted 38 covers over the years; he also did 29 covers for *If*, 11 covers for *FSF*, 7 for *IASFM* and others for many other magazines. But, although his cover work was more than competent, it was his spare, often nearly abstract black-and-white interior ILLUSTRATIONS that dominated the field in the 1960s. He worked for paperback and hardcover book publishers, too, most notably ACE BOOKS. Famous for his generosity in donating artwork to FANZINES, he is the only illustrator to have won HUGOS for both Best Fan Artist and Best Professional Artist in the same year (1967); he won the Professional Artist award again in 1968 and 1969. Throughout the 1970s and 1980s his work became less in demand and he was in increasingly poor health, as a result producing very little sf work. [JG]

See also: ASTOUNDING SCIENCE-FICTION.

GAWRON, JEAN MARK (1953-) French-born US writer whose first sf novel, *An Apology for Rain* (**1974**), traces the travels of a woman in search of her brother through a surreal USA. It was followed by *Algorithm* (**1978**), a further linguistic allegorizing of quest motifs. [JC]

GAWSWORTH, JOHN Pseudonym of UK editor and writer (Terence Ian) Fytton Armstrong (1912-1970) for most of his work of genre interest, though he signed some work with his real name. He was a close colleague of M.P. SHIEL, creating a Shiel checklist in the bibliographical *Ten Contemporaries* (**1932**) and editing *The Best Short Stories of M.P. Shiel* (coll **1948**). His poetry was traditional, and his occasional stories are of relatively little interest; his importance to sf and fantasy lies primarily in the large anthologies he assembled in the 1930s, including *Strange Assembly* (anth **1932**), *Full Score* (anth **1933**) as Fytton Armstrong, *New Tales of Horror by Eminent Authors* (anth **1934**), *Thrills, Crimes and Mysteries* (anth **1935**), *Thrills* (anth **1936**), *Crimes, Creeps and Thrills* (anth **1936**) and *Masterpiece of Thrills* (anth **1936**). [JC]

GAY, ANNE (1952-) UK teacher and writer who began publishing sf with "Wishbone" in *Gollancz-Sunday Times Best SF Stories* (anth **1987**) ed anon. Her first novel, *Mindsail* (**1990**), very promisingly describes an alien planet to which the passengers of a crashed human starship have had to adjust, gradually evolving into fragmented and warring societies in the process. Romance elements – the female protagonist's rather prolonged search for a husband – interfere to some extent with the revelations, but the book leaves a vivid memory trace.

The Brooch of Azure Midnight (**1991**), an sf tale with some of the tone of the "gate romance" common to FANTASY from the time of H.P. LOVECRAFT, confronts an expanding Terran culture with the challenge and opportunity of wormhole access to the stars. [JC]

GAY, J. DREW ◊ L. Edgar WELCH.

GAYLE, HENRY K. (1910-) Canadian writer and civil servant whose horror/sf novel, *Spawn of the Vortex* (**1957**), plays on the nuclear-testing PARANOIA of the 1950s. Underwater tests activate a horde of MONSTERS who advance upon the USA. [JC]

GAYTON, BERTRAM (? -?) UK writer whose sf novel, *The Gland Stealers* (**1922**), deals lightly with physical rejuvenation achieved – apparently – by transplanting glands from apes into the bodies of elderly humans. [JC]

See also: MEDICINE.

GEAR, KATHLEEN O'NEAL (1954-) US writer with extensive training in American prehistory; married to W. Michael GEAR. Her first sf, the **Powers of Light** trilogy – *An Abyss of Light* (**1990**), *Treasure of Light* (**1991**) and *Redemption of Light* (**1991**) – was published as by Kathleen M. O'Neal. With an occasionally oppressive relentlessness about the moral and theological issues involved, it presents an intergalactic conflict between humans and the ALIEN Magistrates who have established a coercive "peace" in terms inescapably evocative of the Jewish experi-

ence during the 20th century; moments of awkwardness failed to muffle the impressive intensity of the long tale. With W. Michael Gear (*whom see for details*), and writing now as KO'NG, she has begun the **Ancient Americans** sequence, projected to cover the entire prehistory of North America. *Sand in the Wind* (**1990**), solo, is an historical novel. [JC]

GEAR, W. MICHAEL (1955-) US writer with extensive training in American archaeology; married to Kathleen O'Neal GEAR. He began publishing sf with the competent **Spider** sequence – *The Warriors of Spider* (**1988**), *The Way of Spider* (**1989**) and *The Web of Spider* (**1989**) – about the conflict between a newly discovered lost-colony offshoot of humanity and the reactionary Directorate which attempts to control human space. The former, who are of Native American stock and worship a god called Spider, are sexually and culturally irresistible to the women who first discover them, but WMG fortunately has too many complex interstellar doings to present for sentimental romancing to dominate the proceedings. The **Ancient Americans** sequence, all written with Kathleen O'Neal Gear – *People of the Wolf* (**1990**), *People of the Fire* (**1991**) and *People of the Earth* (**1992**), with 7 further volumes planned – has, because of its carefully plausible venue, little fantasy or sf content beyond occasional reference to true visions derived from proper shamanistic practice; but of course the prehistoric-sf subgenre was always likely, as our knowledge of the past gained definition, to be transformed into fictionalized history. Other sf novels include *The Artifact* (**1990**), *Starstrike* (**1990**) and the **Forbidden Borders** sequence – *Forbidden Borders: Requiem for the Conqueror* (**1991**) and #2: *Relic of Empire* (**1992**), with at least 1 further volume projected – about an Earth prevented by a GRAVITY barrier from reaching more than a few nearby star systems. [JC]

GEARHART, SALLY MILLER (1931-) US author of lesbian-FEMINIST works – including *A Feminist Tarot* (**1976**) with Susan Rennie – and Professor of Speech and Communication Studies at San Francisco State University. Her sf book, one of the most extreme of those that envisage men and women as effectively different races, is *The Wanderground: Stories of the Hill Women* (coll of linked stories **1980**). It is set in the outlaw, all-women, UTOPIAN hill communities of a future when men are restricted to the CITIES and dependent on TECHNOLOGY, while women (in a somewhat New Age manner) have developed PSI POWERS through harmony with Nature. Even the Gentles, men no longer driven by violence, know that "maleness touched women only with the accumulated hatred of centuries". [PN]

See also: PASTORAL.

GEE, MAGGIE (1948-) UK writer whose first published novel, *Dying in Other Words* (**1981**), is a morbid experimental work which could be interpreted as having ghostly elements. In *The Burning Book* (**1983**) an ordinary contemporary family's problems are overshadowed by auctorial asides reminding the reader of the fragility of human life, as demonstrated by Hiroshima, Nagasaki and the HOLOCAUST that will occur at the end of the novel. *Where are the Snows?* (**1991**) takes her protagonists from the early 1980s through to a pessimistically drawn 21st century. [PH] **Other works:** *Light Years* (**1985**); *Grace* (**1989**).

GEE, MAURICE (GOUGH) (1931-) NEW ZEALAND writer best known for a trilogy of non-genre novels: *Plumb* (**1978** UK), *Meg* (**1981** UK) and *Sole Survivor* (**1983** UK). His juvenile fantasies – *Under the Mountain* (**1979**), later a tv series, and *The World Around the Corner* (**1980**) – are routine quests. More complex is the **World of O** trilogy – *The Halfmen of O* (**1982**), *The Priests of Ferris* (**1984**) and *Motherstone* (**1985**) – which moves from unquestioning use of sf/fantasy conventions to a less certain view of morality: the human saviours of the ALTERNATE WORLD of O realize that its inhabitants must discover their own solution to the problem of good and evil, even at the price of their sentience. MG's virtues include a strong sense of character and place. [MMacL]

GEIER, CHESTER S. (1921-1991) US writer and editor, very active in the ZIFF-DAVIS stable (for *AMZ* and *Fantastic Adventures*) in the 1940s, where he published a large amount of routine material under his own name and pseudonyms including Guy Archette and the house names Alexander BLADE, P.F. COSTELLO, Warren KASTEL, S.M. TENNESHAW, Gerald VANCE and Peter WORTH. "Forever is too Long" (1947 *Fantastic Adventures*) is book-length, as is "Outlaw in the Sky" (1953 *AMZ*) as by Archette, which is essentially a Western with a few sf transpositions. CSG was an advocate of the Richard SHAVER "mystery" and founded a club in his honour, editing the *Shaver Mystery Magazine* on its behalf. Although he was one of the most prolific of PULP-MAGAZINE writers, his stories have never been collected in book form, and only one, "Environment" (1944), has been anthologized. [JC]
See also: COLONIZATION OF OTHER WORLDS.

G-8 AND HIS BATTLE ACES US PULP MAGAZINE. 110 issues Oct 1933-June 1944. Monthly to Apr 1941, bimonthly thereafter. Published by Popular Publications; ed Rogers Terrill and, later, Alden H. Norton (1903-1987). All the novels were the work of one of the most prolific of all pulp authors, Robert J. Hogan (1897-1963), who also wrote under pseudonyms the short stories which filled out each issue. Hogan, who wrote *The* MYSTERIOUS WU FANG and other magazines as well, was under editorial instruction to send in his material as he wrote it, without any revision; the amount of editing subsequently necessary is described by Damon KNIGHT in *Hell's Cartographers* (anth **1975**), ed Brian W. ALDISS and Harry HARRISON. G-8 is the leader of a US fighter squadron in WWI, which combats a wide variety of fantastic enemy menaces. Only some of the novels were sf, and the magazine was not as futuristic as its companion, DUSTY AYRES AND HIS BATTLE BIRDS. [MJE/PN]

GEIS, RICHARD E(RWIN) (1927-) US writer,

editor and sf fan, best known since 1953 for producing and contributing significantly to a fanzine, PSYCHOTIC, and later a semiprozine, *The* ALIEN CRITIC, both of which were, confusingly, at different times known as *Science Fiction Review*. He has published other FANZINES. His vigorously anti-highbrow judgements were for a long time influential in the sf field; between 1969 and 1983 he 6 times won a HUGO for Best Fanzine and a further 7 times for Best Fan Writer.

His first published story was "Flight Game" for *Adam* in 1959. He concentrated thereafter on pornographic fiction, with well over 100 titles, both soft and hardcore. Not many had sf or fantastic themes. Exceptions are the **Roi Kunzer** books – *The Sex Machine* (**1967**) and *The Endless Orgy* (**1968**) – and the singletons *Raw Meat* (**1969**), *The Arena Women* (**1972**) and, as by Peggy Swenson, *A Girl Possessed* (**1973**). Three further erotic sf novels by REG were self-published, mimeographed limited editions: *Canned Meat* (**1978**), *Star Whores* (**1980**) and *The Corporation Strikes Back* (**1981**). More recently, writing with Elton P. Elliott as Richard Elliott, he wrote the **John Norris** thrillers set on a NEAR-FUTURE Earth suffering from sun-flares caused by a star-wars snafu – *Sword of Allah* (**1984**) and *The Burnt Lands* (**1985**) – as well as the singletons *The Master File* (**1986**) and *The Einstein Legacy* (**1987**). [JC/PN]
See also: SEX.

GEMINI MAN ◊ *The* INVISIBLE MAN.

GEMMELL, DAVID A. (1948-) UK journalist and then full-time author, primarily of HEROIC FANTASY. His first FANTASY series, **The Drenai Saga**, consists of *Legend* (**1984**; vt *Against the Horde* 1988 US), *The King Beyond the Gate* (**1985**), *Waylander* (**1986**) and *Quest for Lost Heroes* (**1990**), the first 3 being collected, along with an additional story, as *The Drenai Tales* (omni **1991**). DAG's inclusion in this volume is largely due to his second series, the **Sipstrassi** novels, which are SCIENCE FANTASY: *Wolf in Shadow* (**1987**; vt *The Jerusalem Man* 1988 US), *Ghost King* (**1988**), *Last Sword of Power* (**1988**) and *The Last Guardian* (**1989**). The components of the series are linked by the Sipstrassi stones of healing and/or destruction, whose source is ATLANTIS. The middle two volumes, which have Arthurian resonances, are set in Britain during and after the Roman occupation, but the framing works are set in a post-HOLOCAUST venue 300 years after Earth's axis has been tilted by an Immanuel VELIKOVSKY-style DISASTER; echoes of Erich VON DÄNIKEN's PSEUDO-SCIENCE books also abound. The Dying Earth setting (◊ FAR FUTURE) is well achieved; there is TIME TRAVEL between Atlantis and its future; ESP, GENETIC ENGINEERING and IMMORTALITY are other themes.

DAG's subsequent works have been: *Knights of Dark Renown* (**1989**), featuring PARALLEL WORLDS; the **Macedon** sequence of historical fantasies set in an ALTERNATE-WORLD Greece at the time of Alexander, to date comprising *Lion of Macedon* (**1990**) and *Dark Prince* (**1991**), in the second of which Aristotle (who else?) knows the secret of portals through time and space that lead to parallel worlds; and *Morningstar* (**1992**), which introduces a bard and an ambiguous hero faced with necromancy and Vampyre Kings. DAG is accomplished and tough-minded, and interestingly varies (but not too much) stereotypical generic situations. [PN]

See also: HISTORY OF SF; MAGIC.

GENERAL SEMANTICS A quasiphilosophical movement founded in Chicago in 1938 by Count Alfred KORZYBSKI, whose *Science and Sanity* (**1933**) was the basic handbook of the movement. GS had a surprising success, peaking in the 1940s and 1950s. It teaches that first unsanity and later insanity are caused by adherence to an Aristotelian worldview, by which is meant the use of the two-valued either-or logic which Korzybski saw as being built into Indo-European language structures. From this simple beginning – with much of which linguistic philosophers, including Ludwig Wittgenstein (1889-1951), would be unlikely to differ very profoundly – was developed a confused and confusing psychotherapeutic system which, like L. Ron HUBBARD's DIANETICS, promised to focus the latent abilities of the mind. It may have seemed to its more naïve adherents that GS held out the promise of turning Man into SUPERMAN by teaching non-Aristotelian (null-A or Ā) habits of thought. The movement, whose critics saw it as a PSEUDO-SCIENCE, probably had some influence on the development of Dianetics, but its best-known repercussion in sf was the composition of two novels by A.E. VAN VOGT featuring a non-Aristotelian superman hero, Gilbert Gosseyn (often read as a pun on "go sane"): *The World of Ā* (1945 *ASF*; rev **1948**; rev with intro 1970; vt *The World of Null-A*) and *The Pawns of Null-A* (1948-9 *ASF* as "The Players of Ā"; **1956**; vt *The Players of Null-A* UK). [PN]

GENERATION STARSHIPS For writers unwilling to power their starships with FASTER-THAN-LIGHT drives or to make use of a relativistic time contraction, there is a real problem in sending ships between the stars: the length of the voyage, which would normally span many human lifetimes. The usual answers are to put the crew into SUSPENDED ANIMATION, as in James WHITE's *The Dream Millennium* (**1974**), to send germ cells only, as in Kurt VONNEGUT Jr's "The Big Space Fuck" (1972), or to use a generation starship, whereby the human beings who reached the destination would be the remote descendants of the original, long-dead crew, intervening generations having lived and died aboard the journeying vessel.

It was probably Konstantin TSIOLKOVSKY who first saw the necessity for using generation starships in the COLONIZATION OF OTHER WORLDS; he presented the idea in "The Future of Earth and Mankind", which was published in a Russian anthology of scientific essays in 1928 but may have been conceived even earlier. Tsiolkovsky here argued for the construction in the future of space-going "Noah's Arks": he envisaged such journeys as taking many thousands

of years.

The first GENRE-SF use of the notion was probably Don WILCOX's "The Voyage that Lasted 600 Years" (1940) in *AMZ*. Here the captain of the ship is in hibernation, but wakes every 100 years to check on progress. Each time he wakes he finds great social changes among the successive descendants of the crew, and a sinking into brutality accompanied by plague. His successive appearances render him an object of superstitious awe to the tribesmen on board. The theme of social change and degeneration inaugurated by Wilcox was to become the dominant motif of such stories. (In *Seekers of Tomorrow* [**1966**] Sam MOSKOWITZ claims the first generation-starship story to be Laurence MANNING's "The Living Galaxy" [1934], which is set in a small, self-powered world and so does not fully embody the concept.)

The other dominant theme was presented in the following year in an altogether more famous story, "Universe" (1941) by Robert A. HEINLEIN, and in its sequel in *ASF* the following month, "Common Sense" (1941); the two were published in book form as *Orphans of the Sky* (fixup **1963** UK). In this classic generation-starship story the crew have forgotten that they are on a ship and have descended to a state of rigidly stratified and superstitious social organization; the unusually intelligent hero discovers the truth in a traumatic CONCEPTUAL BREAKTHROUGH. Indeed generation-starship stories remained paradigmatic for the conceptual-breakthrough theme, and are important, too, in rite-of-passage stories showing the growth from puberty to adulthood (◊ POCKET UNIVERSES). Brian W. ALDISS, who loved the idea but thought it crudely developed by Heinlein, devoted his first novel, *Non-Stop* (**1958**; vt *Starship* US), to a very successful reworking of the same theme. Other stories in which surviving generations think of the ship as a world and not a mode of transport are "Spacebred Generations" (1953; vt "Target Generation") by Clifford D. SIMAK, "Ship of Shadows" (1969) by Fritz LEIBER, in which the ship is not strictly a starship, though the degenerated society is similar, and Harry HARRISON's amazing *Captive Universe* (**1969**), in which the crew and colonists have been transformed, in an act of insane CULTURAL ENGINEERING, into medieval monks and Aztec peasants.

Some stories begin at the outset of or after the end of a generation-starship voyage. Arthur C. CLARKE's early story "Rescue Party" (1946) has Earth evacuated in the face of a coming nova, the evacuees heading confidently towards the stars in a giant fleet of primitive generation rocketships. Brian M. STABLEFORD's *Promised Land* (**1974**) tells of a society of colonists whose social structure is based on that developed over generations in the starship on which they arrived.

An interesting variant which appears in several stories, most notably John BRUNNER's "Lungfish" (1957; vt "Rendezvous with Destiny" USA), has the ship itself taking on the role in its occupants' minds of surrogate mother; even on reaching their destination they will not leave the womb. This theme is also prominent in the Simak story mentioned above.

The generation-starship idea has been used little outside genre sf, though a spectacular exception is the epic poem *Aniara* (**1956**; trans **1963**) by the Nobel Prize-winning Swedish poet Harry MARTINSON. An opera by Karl-Birger Blomdahl (1916-1968), *Aniara*, based on the poem, was performed in 1959. The story pits human values against inhuman technology on a generation starship.

Among the more interesting stories about social changes on generation starships are the Aldiss, Harrison, Heinlein, Leiber and Simak tales already cited, along with: *The Space-Born* (**1956**) by E.C. TUBB; *Rite of Passage* (**1968**) by Alexei PANSHIN (though, since the starship in question can travel also through HYPERSPACE, this is not a pure example of the subgenre); *The Ballad of Beta-2* (**1965**) by Samuel R. DELANY; *Rogue Ship* (1947-63; fixup **1965**) by A.E. VAN VOGT; *Seed of Light* (**1959**) by Edmund COOPER; *The Star Seekers* (**1953**) by Milton LESSER, which features a four-way division of society in a hollowed-out asteroid; *Alpha Centauri – or Die!* (1953 *Planet Stories* as "Ark of Mars"; fixup **1963** dos) by Leigh BRACKETT; *200 Years to Christmas* (**1961**) by J.T. MCINTOSH, which features a competently thought-out but conventional cyclic history within the ship; "Bliss" (1962) by David ROME; and *Noah II* (**1970** US; rev 1975 UK) by Roger DIXON.

Some enterprising variants on the theme are found. In Arthur SELLINGS's "A Start in Life" (1951) a plague decimates the ship, leaving two 5-year-old survivors to be raised by ROBOTS. Judith MERRIL's "Wish Upon a Star" (1958) features a ship originally crewed by 20 women and four men, with a resultant matriarchal society. Chad OLIVER's "The Wind Blows Free" (1957) takes the birth-trauma theme to its logical conclusion with a story about a man who, goaded to near-madness by the claustrophobic society of the ship, opens an airlock only to find that the ship landed on a planet some centuries back.

Harlan ELLISON wrote the script for a generation-starship tv series, *The* STARLOST, made in Canada, disastrously, in 1973. Ellison repudiated the series as it stood, and used his derisive pseudonym Cordwainer Bird in the credits; his original script for the pilot episode appears as "Phoenix without Ashes" in *Faster than Light* (anth **1976**) ed Jack DANN and George ZEBROWSKI, and was also novelized as *Phoenix without Ashes* * (**1975**) with Edward BRYANT.

From the mid-1970s the theme has been used only sparsely. An interesting variation is found in Damien BRODERICK's idea-packed *The Dreaming Dragons* (**1980**), in which a generation TIME MACHINE is uncovered beneath Ayers Rock in the Australian desert. In Pamela SARGENT's juvenile novel *Earthseed* (**1983**) the generation starship is a hollowed-out asteroid occupied by teenagers. In Kevin O'DONNELL Jr's *Mayflies* (**1979**) the lives of humans seem ephemeral (hence the title) by contrast with the near-immortal human

brain, embedded in the ship's computer, which (only partially) controls those lives; and the voyage accomplished in Frank M. ROBINSON's *The Dark Beyond the Stars* (**1991**) is ultimately circular. [PN]

GENESIS II Made-for-tv film (1973). CBS-TV. Dir John Llewellyn Moxey, starring Alex Cord, Mariette Hartley, Percy Rodriguez, Ted Cassidy. Screenplay Gene RODDENBERRY. 90 mins. Colour.

Produced by Roddenberry, the creator of STAR TREK, this was a pilot for a tv series that was never made. After a SUSPENDED-ANIMATION experiment goes wrong, a scientist wakes in a future world which is suffering from the aftermath of a nuclear HOLOCAUST. Ordinary humans are ruled tyrannously by MUTANTS. Aided by his primitive vitality, the hero helps overcome the rulers. A similar format was used by Roddenberry in two further attempts to launch series; these were released as PLANET EARTH and STRANGE NEW WORLD. [JB]

GENETIC ENGINEERING In his remarkable prophetic essay *Daedalus, or Science and the Future* (**1924**) J.B.S. HALDANE looked forward optimistically to a day when biologists have "invented" a new species of alga to solve the world's food problem, and in which "ectogenetic" children born from artificial wombs can be strategically modified by eugenic selection. Nothing was known in 1924 about the biochemistry of genetics, so Haldane spoke mainly in terms of "selective breeding", but he nevertheless anticipated not merely some of the possible practical applications of direct genetic manipulation but also the likely response of the popular imagination. He observed that there is always extreme resistance against "biological inventions" because they are initially perceived as blasphemous perversions. Following the decipherment, in the late 1950s, of the genetic code carried by DNA molecules, the genetic engineering of bacteria has become commonplace, and contemporary sf reflects the strength of this resistance in no uncertain terms. Despite the strong tradition of technophilia which exists in HARD SF, there is still relatively little sf championing the cause of genetic engineering.

The careful "engineering" of living creatures by surgery is featured in a few early sf stories, most notably H.G. WELLS's *The Island of Dr Moreau* (**1896**), but it was not until Haldane wrote his essay that more ambitious projects of human engineering were featured – in Olaf STAPLEDON's *Last and First Men* (**1930**), and in Aldous HUXLEY's satirical development of ideas from *Daedalus* in *Brave New World* (**1932**), in which ectogenetic embryos are nutritionally and environmentally controlled to fit them for life as "alphas", "betas" or "gammas". Julian Huxley (1887-1975), brother of Aldous and friend of Haldane and Wells, wrote a notable horror-sf story along the same lines: "The Tissue-Culture King" (1927). Haldane's sister, Naomi MITCHISON, later extrapolated ideas from *Daedalus* in a sceptical way in *Not by Bread Alone* (**1983**). In the early sf PULP MAGAZINES David H. KELLER wrote several stories about quasiblasphemous tampering with human form and nature, most notably

"Stenographer's Hands" (1928), about a eugenic experiment to breed the perfect typist, with reduced initiative and a wasted body but jolly capable hands. An early pulp-sf story involving true genetic engineering was "Proteus Island" (1936) by Stanley G. WEINBAUM, which echoes its model, *The Island of Dr Moreau*, in presuming that "the nature of the beast" cannot be changed as easily as its physical form. Artificial organisms designed for particular purposes appear in minor roles in several stories, a notable example being the "familiars" employed by the fake witches in Fritz LEIBER's *Gather, Darkness!* (1943 *ASF*; **1950**), and, once A.E. VAN VOGT had used "gene transformation" to create superhumans in *Slan* (1940 *ASF*; **1946**), vague and unspecified forms of genetic engineering became standard methods of creating the pulp-sf SUPERMAN. The most adventurous use of genetic engineering in 1940s sf was in Robert A. HEINLEIN's *Beyond this Horizon* (1942 *ASF* as by Anson MacDonald; **1948**), the first story to describe (not altogether convincingly) a society which routinely uses eugenics and genetic engineering to ensure the physical and mental fitness of the population, and to address the moral questions thus raised.

The first sf writer to cultivate a more accurate understanding of possible genetic engineering techniques, and the first to confront these possibilities with a far-reaching but disciplined imagination, was James BLISH. *Titan's Daughter* (1952 in *Future Tense* as "Beanstalk"; exp **1961**) features a race of giant humans created by stimulated polyploidy (spontaneous polyploidy – doubling of the chromosome complement – is not uncommon in plants, and usually results in giantism) and echoes Wells's *The Food of the Gods* (**1904**). Blish moved on to consider the possible utility of genetic engineering in adapting humans for the COLONIZATION OF OTHER WORLDS in his PANTROPY series, written around the novelette "Surface Tension" (1952) – about microscopic humans engineered for life in small pools of water – and collected in *The Seedling Stars* (fixup **1956**). The final section of the book looks forward to the day when Earth, much changed by time, will itself become an alien environment to be re-seeded with "adapted men". This idea, of specially engineering individuals to "conquer" alien worlds, was taken up by other writers of the period, including Philip K. DICK in *The World Jones Made* (**1956**) and Poul ANDERSON in "Call me Joe" (1957). The idea that an engineered race might be necessary to undertake SPACE FLIGHT itself was later developed by Samuel R. DELANY in "Aye, and Gomorrah . . ." (1967). Other stories from the 1950s dealing with experiments in genetic engineering are *Masters of Evolution* (1954 as "Natural State"; exp **1959**) by Damon KNIGHT and "They Shall Inherit" (1958) by Brian W. ALDISS. The notion of modifying animals into human form was developed extensively by Cordwainer SMITH in his stories of the Underpeople, who cannot breed true, having been modified by somatic engineering – a modification of the genes in

the specialized cells of a differentiated embryo or an adult organism which does not affect the germ plasm. (The different implications of somatic engineering and the engineering of egg cells are not always appreciated by users of the theme.)

Interest in genetic engineering was inevitably renewed in the 1960s, although many early stories concentrated on the very modest notion of producing CLONES. Alarmism was rife: the UK tv series DOOMWATCH, whose purpose was overtly propagandistic, helped to awaken many people to some of the implications of biological engineering. Its first episode became the basis for the novel *Mutant-59* ∗ (**1972**) by Kit PEDLER and Gerry DAVIS, about the "escape" of a bacterium engineered to metabolize plastic, and many other episodes also featured biological engineering of various kinds. The idiosyncratic note of horror struck by many of the scripts recurs in many subsequent tv plays, including two about the possibility of creating "transgenic" hybrids of human and ape (◊ APES AND CAVEMEN): *First Born* (1989), notionally based on Maureen DUFFY's satire *Gor Saga* **1981**), and *Chimera* (1991), adapted by Stephen GALLAGHER from his own novel *Chimera* (**1982**).

The first attempts to use genetic-engineering techniques to cure genetic deficiency diseases have already been made, and the possibility of eliminating such diseases has become a commonplace background element in sf. The notion that a radiation-affected world might desperately require such processes of repair is ironically developed in David J. SKAL's *When We were Good* (**1981**) and Christopher HODDER-WILLIAMS's post-HOLOCAUST *The Chromosome Game* (**1984**). The use of somatic engineering for cosmetic purposes is the focus of such stories as "Cinderella's Sisters" (1989) and "Skin Deep" (1991) by Brian M. STABLEFORD. The possibility of further altering the human condition by genetic engineering remains much more controversial. The plight of ordinary humans growing old in a world already inherited by their engineered superchildren is explored in *Anvil of the Heart* (**1983**) by Bruce T. HOLMES. Other alarmist tales in a similar vein include Robin COOK's *Mutation* (**1989**) and Geoff RYMAN's *The Child Garden* (**1989**), which feature very different developments of the assumption that programmes of improvement involving genetic-engineering techniques might have unforeseen and unfortunate side-effects. Relatively modest functional modifications of humans include adaptation for aquatic life and for life in low gravity: *Inter Ice Age 4* (**1959**; trans **1970**) by Kobo ABÉ is the most notable novel dealing with the former theme, Lois McMaster BUJOLD's *Falling Free* (**1988**) the most notable dealing with the latter (and also raises interesting questions about the obsolescence of functional modifications). Frank HERBERT was consistently interested in the more bizarre variations of the theme, as displayed in *The Eyes of Heisenberg* (**1966**) and *Hellstrom's Hive* (**1973**), although the superman-breeding programme in *Dune* (**1965**) is a pedestrian affair of long-range eugenics. Genetic-engineering techniques are fundamental to the Protean futures of many stories by John VARLEY, including *The Ophiuchi Hotline* (**1977**) and "Options" (1979), a story of promiscuous sex-changes. The widespread use of such techniques is also a premise of Bruce STERLING's **Shaper & Mechanist** stories, culminating in the novel *Schismatrix* (**1985**), and of C.J. CHERRYH's monumental *Cyteen* (**1988**). Charles SHEFFIELD's series begun with *Sight of Proteus* (**1978**) is more extravagant, and the technology involved is highly fanciful.

Exotically engineered human societies established on other worlds are featured in several sf novels, the most notable being the hermaphrodite society in Ursula K. LE GUIN's *The Left Hand of Darkness* (**1969**). More recent COLONIZATION stories involving genetic engineering include *The Warriors of Dawn* (**1975**) and *The Gameplayers of Zan* (**1977**) by M.A. FOSTER, *Manseed* (**1982**) by Jack WILLIAMSON, and *The Garden of the Shaped* (**1987**) by Sheila FINCH.

As real-world genetic engineering makes rapid progress, sf writers have acquired a better sense of what actually goes on in the laboratory, reflected in such stories as Richard S. Weinstein's "Oceans Away" (1976), which deals with the creation of intelligent cephalopods, and John GRIBBIN's *Father to the Man* (**1989**), one of the most intelligent stories about an artificial half-human being. There is still, however, a marked tendency for the strategic endeavours of scientists to be unceremoniously set aside in favour of the miracles of MUTATION, as they are in Greg BEAR's *Blood Music* (**1985**). It cannot be said that sf writers have as yet explored the real potential which genetic-engineering technologies hold for the radical remaking of the human world, but a beginning of sorts is made by the speculative future history *The Third Millennium* (**1985**) by Brian Stableford and David LANGFORD, and by Stableford's various spinoff short stories, some of which are collected in *Sexual Chemistry: Sardonic Tales of the Genetic Revolution* (coll **1991**). [BS]

See also: BIOLOGY; MEDICINE.

GENONE, HUDOR Pseudonym of US writer William James Roe (1843-1915) for his sf and fantasy; he also produced some non-genre work under his own name and as G.I. Cervus. He was a freethinker – a disposition of mind found with surprising infrequency among 19th-century sf writers – and in *Inquirendo Island* (**1886**) he dramatized in unmistakable terms his negative feelings about Christianity. The protagonist, shipwrecked on the eponymous mid-Atlantic ISLAND, discovers that its inhabitants have constructed a topsy-turvy RELIGION, which they follow with pious zeal, out of their ancestors' bad memories of their own shipwreck and out of idolatry directed towards the arithmetic text which is the only printed book to have survived. *Bellona's Husband* (**1887**) takes its protagonists via spaceship to MARS, where they find a humanlike society distinguished from ours mainly by the fact that Martians live backwards in time; this may be the earliest example of the notion of time reversal being given full-fledged narrative form. Both novels stand out by virtue of the pungency of their thought and their story-telling clarity. [JC]

Other works: *The Last Tenet Imposed upon the Khan of Thomathoz* (**1892**), a fantasy.

GENRE SF By this term, used widely in this encyclopedia, we mean sf that is either *labelled* science fiction or is instantly recognized by its readership as belonging to that category – or (usually) both. The implication is that any author of genre sf is conscious of working within a genre with certain habits of thought, certain "conventions" – some might even say "rules" – of storytelling. These conventions are embedded primarily in a set of texts which are generally agreed to contain them. This might seem to be a circular definition, as though one were saying that genre sf is a set of conventions located in genre-sf stories; but it is in fact a spiral. A text published in 1930 may describe something – say a form of MATTER TRANSMISSION – so well that in 1935 the description has become recognized as a model or convention; and in 1940 a second text may be published which shows its agreement with the convention by repeating it, with variations which themselves enrich it. Partly this spiral is created by sf readers, and partly it governs the expectations of those who so define themselves, and who establish their sense of the true nature of genre sf from many sources: from the spiral of books and stories certainly, but also from film, tv and personal interactions (◊ FANDOM; CONVENTIONS), and finally from an abiding sense shared by most members of the sf "community" that genre sf is an intrinsic part of US history and literature. In its narrowest sense, then, a genre-sf tale will be a story written after 1926, published (or theoretically publishable) in a US SF MAGAZINE or specialist sf press (◊ PUBLISHING; SMALL PRESSES AND LIMITED EDITIONS), and conspicuous for its signals that it is honouring the compact between writers and readers to respect the protocols embedded in the texts which make up the canon. (The term "protocols" has been used in this way by several scholars of sf, notably Samuel R. DELANY and Mark ROSE.)

To work variations on these protocols is clever (and indeed required); but to abandon them is to leave home. For many years, leaving home in this fashion (as, for instance, Kurt VONNEGUT Jr was deemed to have done) was considered a form of treason; for some writers and readers, this attitude remains. Similarly, works of fiction which use sf themes in seeming ignorance or contempt of the protocols – often works from so-called MAINSTREAM WRITERS OF SF – frequently go unread by those immersed in genre sf; and, if they *are* read, tend to be treated as invasive and alien . . . and incompetent. This snobbery (which reverses that very frequently expressed about genre sf by the mainstream) is perhaps unfortunate as a general rule, though in many particular instances it is fully justified.

Though this encyclopedia focuses primarily on genre sf, and though genre sf is central to our sense of the nature of sf as a whole, we also conceive non-genre sf as an essential part of the picture. This encyclopedia therefore includes much of it; other works, such as *The New Encyclopedia of Science Fiction* (**1988**) ed James E. GUNN, have been unwilling to trespass far in this direction, and have proved in practice (and occasionally by precept) unwilling to accord genuine sf status to work written outside the protocols and outside North America. The question as to whether or not international non-genre-based sf is *true* sf has, moreover, become inflamed and politicized; and to discuss non-genre sf in an encyclopedia of sf has at times been regarded by some critics, especially in the USA, as a radical ideological decision. The editors of this volume are content to pay as much attention to these views as they warrant, and agree that if it is ideological to regard, say, Murray Constantine (◊ Katharine BURDEKIN) and George R. STEWART (non-genre sf) as being just as important to the HISTORY OF SF as, for example, Arthur Leo ZAGAT and Miles J. BREUER (genre sf), then this is indeed an ideological encyclopedia.

In the 1960s, 1970s and 1980s literary academics have very often talked about genre. By "genre" they almost invariably refer, as Gary K. WOLFE puts it in *Critical Terms for Science Fiction and Fantasy* (**1986**), to "a group of literary works with common defining characteristics" and "major formal, technical or even thematic elements that unite groups of works". This academic approach, which rightly tends to draw very heavily upon genre sf for examples, is likely to generate formal DEFINITIONS OF SF which fairly closely resemble the sets of protocols for writing genre sf. It is almost certainly right that this is so. But it seems no partially satisfactory definition of sf (there is no *fully* satisfactory definition of sf) has yet been written so as to include only genre sf. Some critics – like, famously, Darko SUVIN – have attempted to define the genre of sf in terms which would in fact logically *exclude* most genre sf from serious consideration. The point we would make here is this: when we use the term "genre sf" in this encyclopedia, we are not making a short-cut definition of the genre of sf; we are referring to those sf works which honour the contract.

This topic is raised, directly and by implication, at many points in this volume, including the entries mentioned above, and in the article on PULP MAGAZINES. [PN/JC]

GENTLE, MARY (1956-) UK writer who began publishing with a fantasy for young adults, *A Hawk in Silver* (**1977**; rev 1985 US), and who came to general notice with her **Orthe** sequence – *Golden Witchbreed* (**1983**) and *Ancient Light* (**1987**) – which, despite the fantasy ring of the first title, is sf. The protagonist of both volumes, a woman diplomat/entrepreneur in the complexly defined employ of an Earth dominated

by vast corporations, comes to Orthe in an attempt to open the planet to exploitation, but discovers the densely described humanoid Orthean culture a seeming match for the desires of her masters. Her trek across Orthe, which takes much of *Golden Witchbreed* and which is replicated in feel in *Ancient Light*, gives the sequence the typical plot-structure and landscape of PLANETARY ROMANCE, though MG is, in fact, far less entranced by scene-setting than are the creators of the modern form (e.g., Jack VANCE). The final import of the sequence – despite the sf pleasures entailed in the discovery of an ancient race whose technological hubris once seared the world, and of a huge ancient artifact (◊ BIG DUMB OBJECTS) – is anything but conducive to any sense that Orthe is a planetary Secret Garden. The protagonist is older in the second volume, Orthean culture has been fatally touched by the allure of human TECHNOLOGY, disturbances transform the old comity, which is now torn by ethnic conflicts, and the revanchist descendants of the ancient Golden Witchbreed do finally use the secret weapon which gives that second volume its title. The Secret Garden – which lies at the heart of the true planetary romance – becomes, in MG's hands, the Third World.

Some of the stories assembled in *Scholars and Soldiers* (coll **1989**) are sf, but in the late 1980s MG turned to FANTASY, and in the **White Crow** sequence – *Rats and Gargoyles* (**1990**) and *The Architecture of Desire* (**1991**) – created an ALTERNATE WORLD or multiverse whose scenery and idiom were superficially reminiscent of Michael MOORCOCK's metaphysical romances; but MG was far more interested than Moorcock in the arguments that might sustain such a universe, deriving a rationale to sustain them – like John CROWLEY before her – from Renaissance Neoplatonism. In the first novel, it is seen that the world is sustained in the memory of a cabal of gods. In the second, set in an alternate England which mirrors Cromwellian times, the female protagonist begins, at great cost to herself and others, to outgrow the toys of MAGIC; MG has always been an author of FEMINIST inclinations, and she presents the sins committed by the White Crow in this novel as non-gender hubris and complacency. It may be hoped that the harsh, flexible urgency of MG's fantasies will shape an equally complex new sf vision. [JC]

Other works: *The Weerde #1* * (anth **1992**) ed with Roz KAVENEY; *Villains!* * (anth **1992**) ed with Kaveney; *Grunts!* (**1992**), a parodic sf/fantasy.

See also: GODS AND DEMONS; MILFORD SCIENCE FICTION WRITERS' CONFERENCE; PSEUDO-SCIENCE; SHARED WORLDS.

GENTRY, CURT (1931-) US writer whose NEAR-FUTURE sf novel, *The Last Days of the Late, Great State of California* (**1968**), vividly depicts a San Andreas Fault DISASTER, though its ecological arguments, blaming Man for the destruction of the state, are somewhat laboured. [JC]

GEORGE, EDWARD E. ◊ Robert E. VARDEMAN.

GEORGE, PETER (BRYAN) (1924-1966) UK writer and

ex-RAF officer whose life and career seem to have been obsessed by nuclear WAR and its consequences. His best-known sf novel, *Two Hours to Doom* (**1958**; vt *Red Alert* 1958 US) as by Peter Bryant, was a straightforward story in which a preventive war, inaugurated by a general, almost leads to worldwide HOLOCAUST, and he may have had some mixed feelings about its satirical transmogrification into Stanley KUBRICK's brilliant DR STRANGELOVE: OR, HOW I LEARNED TO STOP WORRYING AND LOVE THE BOMB (1963), in which doomsday is neither averted at the last moment nor entirely unwelcomed. *Dr Strangelove: or, How I Learned to Stop Worrying and Love the Bomb* * (**1963**) was credited solely to PG, though the influence of Terry Southern (1924-   ), who co-wrote the film-script, is everywhere evident. A further sf novel, *Commander-1* (**1965**), follows the desperate struggles of survivors after a nuclear war. PG's suicide followed soon after, during the composition of yet another novel on the same theme, to have been entitled «Nuclear Survivors».   [JC]

See also: END OF THE WORLD; SCIENTISTS.

GERGELY, MIHÁLY [r] ◊ HUNGARY.

GERHARDI, WILLIAM Legal name during his pub-lishing career of UK writer William Gaerhardie (1895-1977); he partially reverted to Gaerhardie in his later, inactive years. He is best known for works outside the sf field like *Futility* (**1922**). His END-OF-THE-WORLD novel *Jazz and Jasper: The Story of Adam and Eva* (**1928**; vt *Eva's Apple: A Story of Jazz and Jasper* 1928 US; vt *My Sinful Earth* 1947 UK; vt *Doom* 1974) depicts a Lord Beaverbrook figure and his entourage in their com-plex lives and later, after a huge cataclysm, hurtling through space on a chip of rock which is all that remains of Earth. *The Memoirs of Satan* (**1932**) with Brian Lunn (Hugh KINGSMILL's brother) is fantasy.   [JC]

GERMANO, PETER B. [r] ◊ Jack BERTIN.

GERMANY This entry covers the whole of Germany, including the former GDR (East Germany). There is a separate entry for AUSTRIA, with which there is a small and inevitable overlap: many books by Austrian writers were in fact published in Germany, and many Austrians have lived in Germany – some, indeed, working in the German publishing industry.

The roots of German sf can be traced back to the 17th century, when the astronomer Johannes KEPLER's *Somnium* (**1634** in Latin; trans into German as *Traum von Mond* 1898; trans E. Rosen as *Kepler's "Somnium"* 1967) reflected, in semifictional form, on life on the Moon. Considered a masterpiece of its time is the picaresque novel *Der abenteuerliche Simplizissimus* (**1669**; trans A.T.S. Goodricke as *The Adventurous Simplicissimus* 1912 UK; retrans H. Weissenborn and L. Macdonald 1963 UK) by Johann Jakob Christoffel von Grimmelshausen (1622-1676), which contains, *inter alia*, episodes about utopian societies and plans as well as a journey to the Moon.

The 18th century saw publication of *Wunderliche Fata einiger Seefahrer* (4 parts **1741-43**), usually known as *Insel Felsenburg* ["Felsenburg Island"], by Johann Gottfried Schnabel (1692-1752). This book, very popular at the time, combined elements of the UTOPIA, the ROBINSONADE and the episodic adventure novel, and could be regarded as the earliest German forerunner of adventure sf. Further utopian novels of the 18th and early 19th century are *Dreyerley Wir-kungen: Eine Geschichte aus der Planetenwelt* ["Triple Effects: A Story from the World of Planets"] (**1789**) and *Urani: Königin von Sardanopalien im Planneten Sirius* ["Urania: Queen of Sardanopolis in the Planet Sirius"] (**1790**) – both by Johann Friedrich Ernst Albrecht (1752-1814), who normally wrote "knight-and-robber" novels – and **Die schwarzen Brüder** ["The Black Brotherhood"] (**1791-5**) by Heinrich Zschokke (1771-1848), a sensationalist trilogy about a secret society; its third novel is set in the 24th century, when humanity is used as a kind of livestock for ALIENS. Another early work is *Ini: Ein Roman aus dem 21. Jahrhundert* ["Ini: A Novel from the 21st Century"] (**1810**) by Julius von Voss (1768-1832). Important to the development of German sf is the story "Der Sandmann" (1816; trans as "The Sandman") by E.T.A. HOFFMANN, the most important author of the Schwarze Romantik ["Black Romantic"] movement in Germany. The story, which has been reprinted innumerable times, tells of Dr Coppelius, who constructs an automaton in the shape of a human being; it is one of the first ROBOT stories.

But the real pioneer of German sf was Kurd LASSWITZ, a teacher at the Gymnasium Ernestinum in Gotha, who wrote the most important classical German sf novel, *Auf zwei Planeten* (**1897**; cut 1948; cut again 1969; trans Hans J. Rudnick, much cut, as *Two Planets* 1971 US). It is the story of a confrontation of human and Martian cultures, the latter being techni-cally and ethically superior. Lasswitz, who regarded ethical development as dependent on scientific and technological development, included impressive technical predictions: a spokewheel-shaped space station, rolling roadways, synthetic materials, solar cells and much more. Influenced by the German idealist philosopher Immanuel Kant (1724-1804), his work was didactic and focused on philosophical conceptions for the future. He published a number of short stories and novellas, several of which have been translated into English, and two further sf novels, less popular, which remain untranslated. These are *Aspira* (**1906**) and *Sternentau* ["Star Dew"] (**1909**).

Wholly different, but no less remarkable, are the many works of sf by the scurrilous visionary Paul Scheerbart (1863-1915), who in *Lesabèndio* (**1913**) and the story collection *Astrale Novelletten* ["Astral Novel-ettes"] (coll **1912**), for example, populated the cos-mos with grotesque and tremendously imaginative beings reminiscent of the creations of the later writer Olaf STAPLEDON. Much of Scheerbart's work has been reissued in Germany. This is not the case with the interesting *In Purpurner Finsternis* ["In Purple Dark-ness"] (**1895**) by M(ichael) G(eorg) Conrad (1846-

1927), an sf utopia mainly set in a labyrinth of caves, and critical of Germany under Kaiser Wilhelm.

German FANTASTIC VOYAGES and adventures of the Jules VERNE type arrived with the novels of Robert Kraft (1869-1916) and F.W. MADER. Kraft, touted by his publishers as "the German Jules Verne", wrote in addition to countless adventure novels and sea novels the 10-issue dime-novel series **Aus dem Reiche der Phantasie** ["From the Realms of Imagination"] (**1901**), whose protagonist's adventures include trips to the Stone Age and the Moon. (It was probably the first DIME-NOVEL SF series in Germany. This form of publication, *Groschenhefte*, saddle-stapled booklets very similar to one of the several popular dime-novel formats in the USA, continued very much longer in Germany than it did in the USA – see below.) Typical of Kraft's book publications are *Im Panzermobil um die Erde* ["Round the World in a Tank"] (**1906**), *Im Aeroplan um die Erde* ["Round the World in a Plane"] (**1908**), *Der Herr der Lüfte* ["Lord of the Air"] (**1909**), *Die Nihilit-Expedition* ["The Nihilit Expedition"] (**1909**) – a lost-race (◊ LOST WORLDS) novel – and *Die neue Erde* ["The New Earth"] (**1910**), a post-HOLOCAUST novel. F.W. Mader wrote juvenile adventure novels, often set in Africa and reminiscent of H. Rider HAGGARD, and sometimes, as in *Die Messingstadt* ["City of Brass"] (**1924**), with utopian as well as fantastic elements. His space adventure *Wunderwelten* (**1911**; trans Max Shachtman as *Distant Worlds: The Story of a Voyage to the Planets* **1932** US) is one of the most important sf novels of the Kaiser's period.

Other German sf writers popular in the first two decades of the 20th century include: Carl Grunert (1865-1918), author of *Der Marsspion und andere Novellen* ["The Martian Spy and Other Novelettes"] (coll **1908**); Albert Daiber, author of *Vom Mars zur Erde* ["From Mars to Earth"] (**1910**); Oskar Hoffmann (1866-?   ), whose many works included the dime-novel series **MacMilfords Reisen im Universum** ["MacMilford's Voyages into the Universe"] (1902-3); and Robert Heymann (1879-?   ), author of *Der unsichtbare Mensch vom Jahr 2111* ["The Invisible Man of the Year 2111"] (**1909**). Finally, there was the classic novel *Der Tunnel* (**1913**; trans anon as *The Tunnel* **1915**) by Bernhard KELLERMANN (rendered Bernard Kellerman in the English translation), about the building of a tunnel between England and the Continent; it was filmed as *Der* TUNNEL (1933).

One of the most successful sf series of the time in the field of dime novels/pulp adventures, and one of the earliest purely sf periodicals anywhere, was *Der* LUFTPIRAT UND SEIN LENKBARES LUFTSCHIFF (1908-11), totalling 165 adventures.

Between the two World Wars an especially German type of sf came into being, namely the scientific-technical *Zukunftsroman* (future novel), a term which gave its name to the genre, being only gradually replaced, from the early 1950s onward, by the foreign designation "science fiction", which was eventually naturalized. By far the most popular author of the

Zukunftsroman – the spectrum of whose themes was fixed much more strictly than that of US-UK "science fiction" – was unquestionably Hans Dominik (1872-1945), whose nearly 20 books – his first novel was *Die Macht der Drei* ["The Power of the Three"] (**1922**) – sold several million copies in total. Dominik's books are clumsy and badly written, but they survive on the frisson given by their technically oriented adventure, and were probably also successful because their distinctly nationalistic overtones – the German engineer being seen as superior to all others in the world – suited the spirit of a Germany in which National Socialism was on the rise. Other representatives of the *Zukunftsroman* were Rudolf H(einrich) Daumann (1896-1957), St(anislaw) Bialkowski (1897-?   ), Karl August von Laffert (1872-1938), Hans Richter (1889-1941) and Walther Kegel (1907-1945). A further popular author in this line was Freder van Holk, a pseudonym of Paul Alfred Müller (1901-1970), who also published as Lok Myler; under these pseudonyms he wrote the successful dime-novel series **Sun Koh, der Erbe von Atlantis** ["Sun Koh: Heir of Atlantis"] (1933-6), with 150 issues, and **Jan Mayen** (1935-9), with 120 issues. The former deals with an Atlantean in modern London, planning, with supertechnology, to control ATLANTIS when it reappears. Sf of this type had great influence on the first postwar generation of German sf authors.

Among the more interesting novels of prewar German sf are those of Otto Willi GAIL, whose works include *Hans Hardts Mondfahrt* (**1928**; trans anon as *By Rocket to the Moon: The Story of Hans Hardt's Miraculous Flight* **1931**). Before writing, he consulted the German rocket pioneer Max Valier and was able to give a technically exact (according to the knowledge of the time) description of a flight to the Moon and of other space plans since realized. Another writer who like Gail had some of his work translated into English and published in Hugo GERNSBACK's sf magazines was Otfried von Hanstein (1869-1959). The five novels concerned included *Mond-Rak 1: Eine Fahrt inns Weltall* (**1929**; trans Francis Currier as "Between Earth and Moon" 1930 *Wonder Stories Quarterly*).

But perhaps the sf writer of the period best known abroad was Thea VON HARBOU, who had collaborated with her husband, film director Fritz LANG, on the screenplays of several sf films including the great classic METROPOLIS (1926) and also *Die* FRAU IM MOND (1929). Von Harbou's turgid novelizations were *Metropolis* * (**1926**; trans anon **1927** UK) and *Frau im Mond* * (**1928**; trans Baroness von Hutten as *The Girl in the Moon* **1930** UK; cut vt *The Rocket to the Moon, from the Novel, The Girl in the Moon* 1930 US), the latter being published in Germany before the film was released. An unusual theme is dealt with in *Druso: Oder die gestohlene Menschheit* ["Druso, or The Stolen Mankind"] (**1931**; trans Fletcher PRATT as "Druso" 1934 *Wonder Stories*) by Friedrich Freksa (1882-1955), a novel about superhumans that reaches far into the future, but which is sadly marred by racist and fascist undertones. This is almost opposite, politically, to *Utopolis* (**1930**) by Werner Illing (1895-1979), which is a socialist utopia in which workers defeat rebellious capitalists.

Utopolis, however, is at the more literary end of the spectrum. It was one of several impressive sf novels published by non-genre authors between the wars. Among the others were *Tuzub 37* (**1935**) by Paul Gurk (1880-1953), a strange "green" dystopia in which a flayed and totally concreted Nature rises up against the mankind who did this, and *Balthasar Tipho* (**1919**) by Hans Flesch (1895-1981), a strong apocalyptic novel. The most celebrated of the writers who occasionally experimented with sf themes was Alfred Döblin (1878-1957), who went into exile in France in 1933 and then the USA in 1941. Two of his books are surreal, metamorphic sf of very considerable power: *Wadzek's Kampf mit der Dampfturbine* ["Wadzek's Struggle with the Steam-Machine"] (**1918**) and *Berge, Meere und Giganten* ["Mountains, Seas and Giants"] (**1924**; rev vt *Giganten* ["Giants"] 1931). In the latter, somewhat earlier than Olaf Stapledon, with whom he has been compared, Döblin deals with GENETIC ENGINEERING as a means of evolving the capacities of a future race of humans. His work was a potent influence on Cordwainer SMITH's sf. All of these works, however, stand somewhat outside what most readers would regard as sf proper.

There were further stories of the future from more "literary" German writers after WWII, though the one best known in the English-speaking world was in fact by an Austrian, Franz WERFEL: *Stern der Ungeborenen* (**1946** Austria; trans Gustave O. Arlt as *Star of the Unborn* **1946**). Others were *Die Stadt hinter dem Strom* (**1947**; trans P. de Mendelssohn as *The City Beyond the River* **1953**) by Hermann Kasack (1896-1966), a political satire with futuristic sequences, which was made into an opera; *Heliopolis* (**1949**) by Ernst JÜNGER; and *Nein: Die Welt der Angeklagten* ["No: The World of the Accused"] (**1950**) by Walter Jens (1923-), set in a totalitarian DYSTOPIA reminiscent of George ORWELL's *Nineteen Eighty-four* (**1939**). In a much less solemn vein is *Die Gelehrtenrepublik* (**1957**; trans Michael Horovitz as *The Egghead Republic: A Short Novel from the Horse Latitudes* **1979** UK) by Arno SCHMIDT, with its MUTANTS and its language games. Several German writers, much affected by the horrors of WWII and especially the shock of the atomic bombing of Hiroshima, wrote post-HOLOCAUST novels; these included *Wir fanden Menschen* ["We Found Men"] (**1948**) by Hans Wörner (1903-), *Blumen wachsen im Himmel* ["Flowers Grow in the Heavens"] (**1948**) by Hellmuth Lange (1903-), *Helium* (**1949**) by Ernst von Khuon (1915-) and *Die Kinder des Saturn* ["The Children of Saturn"] (**1959**) by Jens Rehn, whose real name was Otto Jens Luther (1918-1983).

The world of GENRE SF began changing after WWII. The first US sf in translation was issued from 1951 onwards by the publishers Gebrüder Weiss in their hardcover line, **Die Welt von Morgen**, whose first publications, from 1949 on, had been reprints of Hans Dominik; later on, and importantly, they published the juveniles of Robert A. HEINLEIN and Arthur C. CLARKE. The first adult HARD SF bound in hard covers was in the short-lived **Rauchs Weltraum-Bücher** series, all 1953, from Karl Rauch publishers, ed Gotthard Günther (1900-1985), one being an anthology ed Günther, *Überwindung von Raum und Zeit* ["Conquest of Space and Time"] (anth **1953**), and the other three being books by John W. CAMPBELL Jr, Jack WILLIAMSON and Isaac ASIMOV. Each had a long, critical afterword by Günther. This line made the term "science fiction" known to German readers for the first time, and is now legendary to fans and collectors. In terms of copies sold at the time, it was a flop.

The division of Germany into East and West after WWII also influenced the development of genre sf. While in the GDR literature generally, and therefore sf, had to serve socialism, in the FRG sf publishing at first saw itself in terms of the traditional *Zukunftsroman*. Thus reprints were issued of Dominik's work and of dime-novel series by Freder van Holk/Lok Myler.

A specialized form of publishing turned out to be significant for sf: cheaply produced hardbacks with millboard covers, issued in small print runs for commercial circulating libraries. Before the circulating libraries fell victim in the late 1950s and early 1960s to the altered leisure-time behaviour of the readership, more than 500 sf novels were published in this format. Even though most of them were trash, they nevertheless prepared the way for a growing generation of native German authors, as well as publishing translations into German for the first time of books by E.E. "Doc" SMITH, A.E. VAN VOGT, Philip K. DICK, Clifford D. SIMAK and others.

The second and more important pathway into postwar German sf writing was provided by the publishers of pulp adventures. The long and continuous German tradition of publishing dime-novel booklets is only now, in the 1990s, fading away. Some reprints of prewar sf of this kind have already been mentioned, but it was above all the three publishers Pabel, Lehning and Moewig who dominated in this field. In 1953 Pabel started the pulp line **Utopia-Zukunftsromane**, later supplemented by **Utopia-Grossband**, **Utopia-Kriminal** and the first German sf magazine, *Utopia-Magazin*. In 1956 Lehning followed up with reprints of circulating-library titles in its pulp line **Luna-Utopia-Roman**, and in 1957 Moewig joined the scene with **Terra**, followed by **Terra-Sonderband** and *Galaxis*, a German edition of GALAXY SCIENCE FICTION. It was Pabel which succeeded in popularizing the term "science fiction" in Germany. At the beginning of the **Utopia-Zukunftsromane** line the stories consisted of serial adventures in the **Jim Parker** series, but later they shifted to novels independent of series, and from 1955 on also translations (mostly short novels) of

Murray LEINSTER, Eric Frank RUSSELL and many others. Quite a number of the best and most popular US sf novels and novellas appeared amid all this material published by Pabel and the other companies, but most were translated rather badly and, as the format was limited to a fixed number of pages, often drastically cut, a practice that continued in German sf translations for a long time, since early paperbacks, too, had a rigidly restricted page count.

It was Walter Ernsting (1920-), first at Pabel and later at Moewig, who could be regarded as the engine that propelled the growing sf industry. He wrote sf adventures under the pseudonym Clark DARLTON; along with K.H. SCHEER he soon became the most popular author of German adventure sf, and as an editor he was responsible for altering publishers' policies (in part towards the publication of more of the UK-US type of sf), editing both *Utopia-Magazin* and the pulp publishing lines (the immediate predecessors of paperback publishing as understood in the English-speaking world) **Utopia-Grossband** and **Terra-Sonderband**, the latter continuing as the paperback line **Terra-Taschenbuch**. Ernsting is, of course, most famous for founding **Perry Rhodan** with Scheer in 1961. It is the most popular pulp-adventure sf series in the HISTORY OF SF; to 1991 more than 1600 short novels had been published in it, not to mention numerous reprints, paperbacks, hardcovers and the spin-off **Atlan** series, which itself has published a massive number of titles. The Perry Rhodan print-run – it is published weekly – is around 200,000 copies for the first edition. The series was and still is written by a team (◊ PERRY RHODAN *for further details*).

Another important editor was Günther M. Schelwokat (1929-1992), who edited much of the sf production of Moewig and (after they had both come under the same ownership) Pabel. Because of the power he had in selecting new authors for the various lines and series, he has been called the John W. Campbell of the German pulps.

Further pulp series include **Mark Powers**, **Ad Astra**, **Ren Dhark**, **Rex Corda**, **Raumschiff Promet**, **Die Terranauten** and **Zeitkugel**, all coming and going in the past few decades, most of them trying (and failing) to repeat the success of **Perry Rhodan** with similar concepts. However, on a smaller scale, the **Orion** series is still thriving, originally in the pulp format but now in paperback reprints; its novelizations and ongoing novels, about 145 of them, many by Hans Kneifel (1936-), are based on the successful German tv SPACE OPERA series *Raumpatrouille – Die phantastichen Abenteuer des Raumschiffes Orion* ["Space Patrol – The Fantastic Adventures of the Space Ship Orion"], which began, like STAR TREK, in 1966, and which, also like *Star Trek*, slowly built up a considerable fan following.

Until the 1960s, paperbacks were the exception rather than the rule in German publishing, being brought out only by smaller publishers. Genre sf mainly remained a feature of the pulp scene and seemed to be unsaleable outside that milieu. This changed when, in 1960, the publishing house Goldmann began a hardcover sf line (with the Austrianborn Herbert W. FRANKE as consulting editor) and then, from 1962, a paperback line that continues today. In 1960, too, the publisher Heyne began, at first sporadically but then vigorously, to publish sf. Heyne developed into one of the bestselling publishers of paperbacks generally, not just in sf; but sf remained a central part of its publishing programme and today, with Wolfgang JESCHKE as editor, it is undisputed leader of the sf market, publishing over 100 paperbacks a year, mostly translations. Just as Ernsting and Schelwokat forced the pace of sf pulpadventure publishing in Germany, so Jeschke was the person most responsible for sf's development as a paperback literature in Germany. With his line of sf paperbacks, including sub-lines like **Classics** and **Bibliothek der Science Fiction**, and his ability to select the best work, Jeschke fulfilled his intention of presenting the whole spectrum of sf from all over the world. Another notable paperback line was **Fischer Orbit** (1972-4), based on Damon KNIGHT's ORBIT anthologies and extended to include novels and collections, mainly of US origin, but including the first collection of new and classic German sf stories, *Science Fiction aus Deutschland* ["Science Fiction from Germany"] (anth **1974**), ed H.J. ALPERS and Ronald M. Hahn (1948-).

In the late 1960s and the 1970s, publishers like Marion von Schröder, Lichtenberg, Insel and Hohenheim began hardcover or quality paperback sf lines, but all were finally cancelled, including Hohenheim's project to publish a 15-vol hardcover series, ed H.J. Alpers and Werner Fuchs (1949-), to chronicle sf history with the best stories of the best authors; only 6 vols appeared. Indeed, after the boom that lasted from the late 1970s to the early 1980s, during which Bastei-Lübbe, Knaur, Moewig, Pabel and Ullstein all began new paperback lines or extended existing ones, there was a severe contraction. Today only Heyne, Goldmann and BasteiLübbe remain competitive.

Unlike the English-language countries, Germany has no magazine-based tradition of short-story publication. There had been a magazine of the fantastic, *Der Orchideengarten* ["The Garden of Orchids"] (1919-21), but it was only in the 1950s, with *Utopia-Magazin* (1955-9; 26 issues) and *Galaxis* (1958-59; 15 issues), that the first sf magazines were published. Later attempts to establish magazines, mostly from smaller publishers, failed. **Perry Rhodan** did not successfully make the transition from pulp weekly booklet to magazine in *Perry Rhodan Magazin*. Other publications in magazine format were *Comet*, *2001*, *Star SF* and a German edition of OMNI, but all finally failed. However, forums for short stories do remain, mainly occasional anthologies from Heyne, ed Wolfgang Jeschke. Earlier there had been the **Kopernikus** series, a kind of magazine in paperback (1980-88; 15

vols) ed H.J. Alpers from Moewig; the **Polaris** series from Insel/Suhrkamp (1973-85; 8 vols) ed Franz ROTTENSTEINER; and a series of paperbacks (1980-84) from Goldmann, ed Thomas LeBlanc (1951-   ).

Let us turn from publishing to writing, and look at the major German sf authors since WWII. We can start in the 1950s in the field of pulp adventure with the work of Walter Ernsting (writing as Clark Darlton) and K.H. Scheer. The former reached Erich VON DÄNIKEN territory before von Däniken did with his tales of past extraterrestrial visits to Earth, and was best known for his TIME-TRAVEL stories. Scheer specialized in military-technological space opera. In the 1960s Herbert FRANKE came to prominence as the first German-language sf writer to tackle really ambitious themes. Later, in the 1960s and 1970s, he was joined (at first just in the field of short stories) by Jeschke. Also of interest is Otto BASIL, who like Franke was an Austrian, with his ALTERNATE-WORLD novel *Wenn das der Führer wüste* (**1966**; cut trans Thomas Weyr as *The Twilight Man* **1968** US). This story of Nazi Germany's victory in WWII, followed by a postwar decay of the Third Reich after Hitler's death as his heirs struggle for power, can be compared to *The Man in the High Castle* (**1962**) by Philip K. DICK.

In the 1970s Carl Amery (1922-   ), a leading German MAINSTREAM WRITER, turned his attention to sf themes, inspired by Walter M. MILLER's *A Canticle for Leibowitz* (**1960**). With 3 excellent books, original in both their idiom (Bavarian) and their concepts, he played variations on the themes of time travel, the fall of Western culture, and alternate worlds; these were *Das Königsprojekt* ["The King Project"] (**1974**), the short novel *Der Untergang der Stadt Passau* ["The Fall of the City of Passau"] (**1975**), and *An den Feuern der Leyermark* ["At the Fires of the Leyermark"] (**1979**), Leyermark being an old name for Bavaria. Franke wrote further remarkable novels, notably *Zone Null* (**1970**; trans **1974** US) and *Ypsilon Minus* (**1976**).

In the 1980s Wolfgang Jeschke raised his profile, proving himself an excellent novelist with *Der letzte Tag der Schöpfung* (**1981**; trans Gertrud Mander as *The Last Day of Creation* 1981 US) and *Midas* (**1989**; trans 1990 US). Thomas R.P. Mielke (1940-   ), up to then an almost unnoticed pulp writer, surprised everybody with the thematically bizarre novel *Das Sakriversum* ["The Vestryverse"] (**1983**), in which he described how two mutated tribes, who for centuries have kept themselves hidden in the roof-vault of a cathedral, survive a war waged with neutron bombs. With *Die Parzelle* ["The Piece of Land"] (**1984**) Werner Zillig (1949-   ) wrote a remarkable novel about countercultures which realize their utopian and radical ideas in protected areas. *Die Enkel der Raketenbauer* ["Grandchildren of the Rocket-Builders"] (**1980**) by Georg Zauner (1920-   ) is a cutting, ironic novel about a postnuclear Bavaria. A notable dystopian novel is *Erwins Badezimmer oder Die Gefährlichkeit der Sprache* ["Erwin's Bathroom, or The Perilousness of Language"] (**1984**) by Hans Bemmann (1922-   );

and Richard Hey (1926-   ) published in *Im Jahr 95 nach Hiroshima* ["In the Year 95 after Hiroshima"] (**1982**) an outstanding post-holocaust novel dealing with a new ice age and the vanishing of European culture. Other authors worth notice include Rainer Erler (1933-   ), mainly a tv screenwriter and director, Reinmar Cunis (1933-1989) and Michael Weisser (1948-   ). Known primarily for short stories are Thomas Ziegler (the pen-name of Rainer Zubeil [1956-   ]), Karl Michael Armer (1950-   ), Horst Pukallus (1949-   ), Gerd Maximović (1944-   ), Peter Schattschneider (1950-   ) (◊ AUSTRIA) and Ronald M. Hahn, the latter mostly with SATIRES.

In the postwar GDR, sf was expected to serve socialism and to be subordinate to the concepts of party functionaries, and was anyway for a long time regarded with suspicion. The first East German sf novel was *Die goldene Kugel* ["The Golden Ball"] (**1949**) by Ludwig Turek (1898-1975). During the whole of the 1950s in the GDR only 11 sf books, plus 50 or so short stories scattered here and there, were published. In the 1950s and 1960s authors like Eberhard Del'Antonio (1926-   ), the Brazilian-born Carlos Rasch (1932-   ), Günther Krupkat (1905-   ) and Karl-Heinz Tuschel (1928-   ), and in the 1970s and 1980s Klaus Frühauf (1933-   ), Rainer Fuhrmann (1940-   ), Peter Lorenz (1944-   ), Michael Szameit (1950-   ) and others wrote an upright, arid, often didactic sf that was miles away, thematically and in literary quality, from all international standards. But from the 1970s onward the GDR also began to produce weightier voices, with Heiner Rank (1931-   ), Gerhard Branstner (1927-   ), Gert Prokop (1932-   ), Erik Simon (1950-   ) and several collaborative teams: Alfred Leman (1925-   ) and Hans Taubert (1928-   ); Johanna (1929-   ) and Günter (1928-   ) Braun; and Karlheinz (1950-   ) and Angela (1941-   ) Steinmüller. *Die Ohnmacht der Allmächtigen* ["The Impotence of the Omnipotent Ones"] (**1973**) by Heiner Rank, *Der Irrtum des Grossen Zauberers* ["The Error of the Great Sorcerer"] (**1972**) and *Unheimliche Erscheinungsformen auf Omega XI* ["Strangely Shaped Apparitions on Omega XI"] (**1974**), both by Johanna and Günter Braun, and *Andymon* (**1982**) and *Pulaster* (**1986**), both by Karlheinz and Angela Steinmüller, are examples of sf books that are full of ideas and well written, and need not fear international comparison.

In the GDR, translated sf was very largely from RUSSIA and other socialist countries; Western sf was seldom published and Western adult fantasy never. There were few East German sf paperbacks; most books were hardcovers from Das Neue Berlin and Neues Leben, as well as pulp booklets from the **Das neue Abenteuer** and **kap** lines. Only in recent years has the term "science fiction" been used, and it appeared on only one line of books, a short-running paperback series. Ekkehard Redlin (1919-   ), as editor of *Das Neue Berlin*, was an important influence on East German sf, and later both Olaf R. Spittel

(1953-   ) and especially Erik Simon had a huge influence on the scene. With *Die Science-fiction der DDR: Autoren und Werke: Ein Lexicon* ["Sf in the GDR: Authors and Works: A Dictionary"] (**1988**), these two wrote what is effectively a small encyclopedia of East German sf (a shorter version had appeared earlier, in 1982). Simon, who also edits for *Das Neue Berlin*, has edited an annual, with stories and critical essays, entitled **Lichtjahr** ["Lightyear"] (5 vols 1980-86).

Sf publishing in the united Germany of today has few book lines, is dominated by Heyne, and is in general the domain of US-UK authors. Outside the **Perry Rhodan** pulps, no German sf author is able to earn his or her living from sf alone; the one marginal exception is Wolfgang E. Hohlbein (1953-   ), a bestselling author of, primarily, fantasy. In recent years some SMALL PRESSES have published sf, either in limited editions or in attempts to break into the upmarket area of hardcovers and quality paperbacks. Among them are Corian, Fantasy Productions, Fabylon, Laurin and Edition Phantasia. Besides the book market, sf writers can look to a small market for high-quality radio plays, which has been supported over the years by radio editors and directors like Horst Krautkrämer, Andreas Weber-Schäfer and, above all, Dieter Hasselblatt (1926-   ).

There has been quite a lot of critical and scholarly literature about sf in Germany. The SEMIPROZINE *Science Fiction Times*, which began in 1958 as a straight translation of the US *Science Fiction Times*, itself a variant title of FANTASY TIMES, began to publish original German material in the early 1960s. It is now the longest-lasting critical journal in Germany; also important in this respect is Franz Rottensteiner's QUARBER MERKUR. There have been several academic studies of sf, sometimes written from a sociological or political viewpoint. Begun in 1985, *Phantastichen Literatur*, ed Joachim Körber, is a continuously updated bibliographical resource for both sf and fantasy from Corian. Standard references include *Lexicon der Science Fiction Literatur* (**1980**; rev 1988; new edn projected for 1992) and *Reclams Science Fiction Führer* (**1982**), the former from Heyne, the latter from Reclam, both ed Hans Joachim Alpers, Werner Fuchs and Ronald M. Hahn, with Wolfgang Jeschke as a further editor of the Heyne books.

Sf cinema had a good start in Germany in the silent period with the serial HOMUNCULUS (1916), Fritz LANG's DR MABUSE, DER SPIELER (1922) and METROPOLIS (1926), and Robert Wiene's ORLACS HÄNDE (1925). Indeed, the German film industry continued strongly into the early 1930s, with sf and fantastic themes quite popular. Other sf films of this period are ALRAUNE (1928), *Die* FRAU IM MOND (1929), F.P.1 ANTWORTET NICHT (1932), *Die* HERRIN VON ATLANTIS (1932; vt *Lost Atlantis*), *Der* TUNNEL (1933), and GOLD (1934). German sf cinema in the postwar period has been, on the whole, disappointing, and the films deserving of entries are comparatively few: *Die* TAUSEND AUGEN DES DR MABUSE (1960), *Der* GROSSE VERHAU (1970; vt *The Big Mess*), Rainer Erler's OPERATION GANYMED (1977), and KAMIKAZE 1989 (1982). Fassbinder's made-for-tv movie WELT AM DRAHT (1973; vt *World on a Wire*) is also of substantial interest.   [HJA]

GERNSBACK, HUGO (1884-1967) Luxembourg-born writer and editor who emigrated to the USA in 1904. Intensely interested in electricity and radio, he designed batteries and by 1906 was marketing a home radio set. In 1908 he launched his first magazine, *Modern Electrics*, where he later published his novel *Ralph 124C 41+* (1911-12 *Modern Electrics*; fixup **1925**). While deficient as fiction, the tale clearly shows his overriding interest in sf as a vehicle of PREDICTION, being a catalogue of the marvellous TECHNOLOGY of the 27th century. *Modern Electrics* later became *Electrical Experimenter*, for which he wrote a series of apocryphal scientific adventures of **Baron Munchausen** (*sic*): "How to Make a Wireless Acquaintance" (1915), "How Munchausen and the Allies Took Berlin" (1915), "Munchausen on the Moon" (1915), "The Earth as Viewed from the Moon" (1915), "Munchausen Departs for the Planet Mars" (1915), "Munchausen Lands on Mars (1915), "Munchausen is Taught Martian" (1915), "Thought Transmission on Mars" (1916), "Cities of Mars" (1916), "The Planets at Close Range" (1916), "Martian Amusements" (1916), "How the Martian Canals are Built" (1916) and "Martian Atmosphere Plants" (1917). The series was reprinted in *AMZ* in 1928. In 1920 another title-change brought into being SCIENCE AND INVENTION, in which HG regularly printed sf. The Aug 1923 issue was devoted to what he then termed "scientific fiction". The following year HG solicited subscriptions for an sf magazine to be called *Scientifiction*; but it was not until April 1926 that there appeared the first issue of AMAZING STORIES, the first true sf magazine in English. HG was publisher and editor, although much of the actual editorial work was done by T. O'Conor SLOANE, his elderly associate editor. *AMZ* was an immediate commercial success, and in 1927 HG published AMAZING STORIES ANNUAL, which in turn spawned AMAZING STORIES QUARTERLY. In 1929, however, his Experimenter Publishing Company was forced into bankruptcy, almost certainly by Bernarr MACFADDEN, and HG lost control of the journals he had founded, though he immediately bounced back by founding another company and starting 4 more magazines: AIR WONDER STORIES, SCIENCE WONDER STORIES, *Science Wonder Quarterly* and SCIENTIFIC DETECTIVE MONTHLY, the first 2 being amalgamated the following year as WONDER STORIES. His empire declined through the 1930s (though other projects prospered), with *Scientific Detective Monthly* (which changed its name to *Amazing Detective Tales*) lasting less than a year, WONDER STORIES QUARTERLY (as *Science Wonder Quarterly* had become) ceasing publication in 1933, and *Wonder Stories* being sold in 1936 to become THRILLING WONDER STORIES. In 1939 he published 3 issues of an early sf COMIC, *Superworld Comics*, and in 1953 he published his last sf magazine, SCIENCE

FICTION PLUS, with HG named as editor but with Sam MOSKOWITZ as managing editor; it ran for 7 issues. A rather different HG publication, *Sexology*, enjoyed more lasting success.

Opinions vary on the beneficence of HG's influence on GENRE SF. Moskowitz has termed him the "Father of Science Fiction" (in "Hugo Gernsback: 'Father of Science Fiction'" in *Explorers of the Infinite* [**1963**]), while Brian W. ALDISS said of his emphasis on supposed scientific accuracy that it had "the effect of introducing a deadening literalism" into the field (in *Trillion Year Spree* by Aldiss and David WINGROVE [**1986**]). HG gave the genre a local habitation and a name; but he bestowed upon his creation a provincial dogmatism and an illiteracy that bedevilled US sf for years. The Science Fiction Achievement Awards are named the HUGOS in his honour; and he himself was given a special Hugo in 1960.   [MJE]

Other works: *The Ultimate World* (**1971**).

See also: ASTOUNDING SCIENCE-FICTION; AUTOMATION; BENELUX; CITIES; CRIME AND PUNISHMENT; DEFINITIONS OF SF; DYSTOPIAS; FABULATION; FANTASTIC VOYAGES; GOLDEN AGE OF SF; HEROES; HISTORY OF SF; ILLUSTRATION; MACHINES; MEDIA LANDSCAPE; NEAR FUTURE; NUCLEAR POWER; OPTIMISM AND PESSIMISM; ORIGIN OF MAN; POLITICS; POWER SOURCES; PROTO SCIENCE FICTION; PSYCHOLOGY; PULP MAGAZINES; ROCKETS; SCIENTISTS; SPACE FLIGHT; SPACE OPERA; TRANSPORTATION; UTOPIAS; WEAPONS.

GERNSBACK PUBLICATIONS Publishing company. ◊ SCIENCE FICTION PLUS.

GERRARE, WIRT Pseudonym of UK writer William Oliver Greener (1862-?   ) for most of his work, both fiction and nonfiction, though at least one thriller appeared under his real name. His first novel of any interest, *Rufin's Legacy: A Theosophical Romance* (**1892**), features a Russian female spy who uses her astral body nefariously. *Phantasms: Original Stories Illustrating Posthumous Personality and Character* (coll **1895**) assembles fantasies about a psychic investigator. *The Warstock: A Tale of To-Morrow* (**1898**) is a genuine sf novel in which a group of brilliant inventors establishes in Morocco an advanced city-state called Cristalia, seemingly armoured against invasion. But Germany, using fifth-columnists, takes over, though without reckoning on the eponymous weapon, a device which randomly triggers ammunition dumps worldwide. The scientists then reoccupy the city and prepare to rule the world from their technological meritocracy.   [JC]

GERROLD, DAVID Pseudonym of US author and scriptwriter Jerrold David Friedman (1944-   ), who was raised in Southern California, gaining a BA in theatre arts there. His earliest commercial sales were tv scripts, the first of them a well known STAR TREK episode, "The Trouble with Tribbles" (1967), which became the subject of one of his two books about the series, *The Trouble with Tribbles* (**1973**), which includes the script plus a nonfiction narrative. The other, *The World of Star Trek* (**1973**; rev **1984**), perceptively analyses the strengths and weaknesses of the show,

and recounts its travails in the world of network tv; he also wrote one **Star Trek** tie, *The Galactic Whirlpool* ∗ (**1980**). A contribution to the **Star Trek: The Next Generation** book sequence, *Encounter at Farpoint* ∗ (**1987**), followed after several years; he briefly worked on the tv series STAR TREK: THE NEXT GENERATION.

DG's first novel, *The Flying Sorcerers* (**1971**) with Larry NIVEN, is a lively attempt to give a scientific rationale to a variety of incidents – which to the observers seem like MAGIC – when an explorer is stranded on a primitive planet. His first solo novel, *Space Skimmer* (**1972**), deals with a man's search for a vanished GALACTIC EMPIRE and its spaceships, described in the title. Perhaps his best-known work is *When Harlie was One* (fixup **1972**; rev vt *When H.A.R.L.I.E. was One (Release 2.0)* **1988**), which deals with the evolution of artificial INTELLIGENCE in a COMPUTER, discussing many of the problems of life with an air of profundity not wholly justified by the content (the revised version improves the telling, but does not significantly sophisticate DG's rendering of AI). *With a Finger in my I* (coll **1972**) assembles some of his occasionally precious short stories; the title story (**1972**) is a fantasy about solipsism and PERCEPTION showing a strong if slightly undergraduate sense of verbal play. *Yesterday's Children* (**1972**; exp **1980**; vt *Starhunt* **1987**) is a SPACE OPERA, with conflict between a captain and first officer on a starship. *The Man who Folded Himself* (**1973**) deals in jerky, short-sentenced prose with a hero who meets other versions of himself, doubled through TIME PARADOX, and makes love to several of them in an orgy of reciprocal narcissism. *Moonstar Odyssey* (**1977**) deals with an extraterrestrial hermaphroditic society whose members do not have to settle into one sex until after adolescence. In both books, a superficial obedience to "Californian" concepts of the free lifestyle revert to more traditional readings of human morality.

In the 1980s – a decade during which he did extensive work for tv – DG's writings lost some of their freshness, and his dependency on earlier sf models for inspiration became more burdensome. The **War Against the Chtorr** sequence – *A Matter for Men* (**1983**; rev **1989**), *A Day for Damnation* (**1984**; exp **1989**) and *A Day for Revenge* (**1989**), with the first versions of the first 2 titles assembled as *The War Against the Chtorr: Invasion* (omni **1984**) – mixes countercultural personal empowerment riffs *à la* HEINLEIN with violent action scenes as the worm-like Chtorr continue to assault Earth, with no end in sight. Other novels, like *The Galactic Whirlpool* (**1980**) and *Enemy Mine* ∗ (**1985**) with Barry B. LONGYEAR – the novelization of ENEMY MINE, a film based on a Longyear story – show a rapid-fire competence but are not innovative. *Chess with a Dragon* (**1987**) is an amusing but conceptually flimsy juvenile. There is a growing sense that DG might never write the major novel he once seemed capable of – not because he has lost the knack, but because he refuses to.   [JC]

Other works: *Battle for the Planet of the Apes* ∗ (**1973**);

Deathbeast (**1978**); *Voyage of the Star Wolf* (**1990**).

As editor: Several 1970s anthologies with Stephen GOLDIN (uncredited): *Protostars* (anth **1971**), *Generation: An Anthology of Speculative Fiction* (anth **1972**), *Science Fiction Emphasis 1* (anth **1974**), *Alternities* (anth **1974**) and *Ascents of Wonder* (anth **1977**); *Norman Jacobs & Kerry O'Quinn Present Starlog's Science Fiction Yearbook, Vol 1* (anth **1979**) with Dave Truesdale.

See also: CLONES; CYBERNETICS; FANTASY; GRAVITY; TERRAFORMING.

GESTON, MARK S(YMINGTON) (1946-   ) US writer and attorney whose remarkable first novel *Lords of the Starship* (**1967**) was published while he was still a student at Kenyon College. This work, which establishes the dark mood of all his fiction and is like its immediate successors set in a weary, war-torn FAR-FUTURE Earth, describes a dilapidated, decadent, centuries-long attempt to construct an enormous SPACESHIP whose completion would transform the fortunes of everyone involved and mark a phase of rebirth. The project is, however, a shambles and a sham, and the novel closes in ENTROPY and despair. *Out of the Mouth of the Dragon* (**1969**) conveys the same mood, introducing prosthetic weaponry that turns many of his characters virtually into CYBORGS without making them any more capable of transforming ancient ways, ancient obsessions. Cultures, weapons, ideas and their embodiments in doom-ridden characters and decaying cities also permeate his third novel, *The Day Star* (**1972**), and his fourth, *The Siege of Wonder* (**1976**), in which all the themes of his previous books are wrapped up in the perversion and death of a magical unicorn. MSG then fell silent for nearly 20 years: «Mirror to the Sky» (**1992**) may mark, however, his welcome return to active work.   [JC]

See also: MAGIC; MYTHOLOGY.

GHIDORAH SANDAI KAIJU CHIKYU SAIDAI NO KESSAN ◊ GOJIRA; RADON.

GHIDRAH, THE THREE-HEADED MONSTER ◊ GOJIRA; RADON.

GHOSTS ◊ ESCHATOLOGY; SUPERNATURAL CREATURES.

GIANT BEHEMOTH, THE ◊ BEHEMOTH, THE SEA MONSTER.

GIANT CLAW, THE Film (1957). Clover/Columbia. Dir Fred F. Sears, starring Jeff Morrow, Mara Corday, Morris Ankrum. Screenplay Samuel Newman, Paul Gangelin. 76 mins. B/w.

A giant bird from outer space decides to build a nest on Earth. It is conveniently protected by an ANTI-MATTER shield, so that attempts to kill it at first prove futile, but eventually the field is nullified by scientists shooting mu-mesons and all ends happily – though not for the bird. This is a much-loved terrible film, mainly because of the bird: quite appallingly designed, it is possibly the most laughter-provoking creature in the history of MONSTER MOVIES.   [JB/PN]

GIANTS ◊ GREAT AND SMALL.

GIANT SPIDER INVASION, THE Film (1975). Group 75/Transcentury. Dir Bill Rebane, starring Steve Brodie, Barbara Hale, Alan Hale, Leslie Parrish.

Screenplay Robert Easton, Richard L. Huff. 76 mins. Colour.

Noted by one critic, Michael Weldon, as the MONSTER MOVIE with the worst special effects since *The GIANT CLAW* (1957), this is fondly remembered as the one where the giant spider was built out of a modified Volkswagen. The spiders, whose eggs are mistaken for diamonds by a greedy farmer, emerge from a BLACK HOLE (yes) near a small Midwest town, which they terrorize. The script has wonderfully highbrow moments. "It all fits – Einstein's general theory of relativity – everything!" cries Steve Brodie, the tough guy who laconically copes with the situation. The best spider movie of the period was KINGDOM OF THE SPIDERS (1977), and the best since then has been ARACHNOPHOBIA (1990).   [PN]

GIBBARD, T.S.J. ◊ ROBERT HALE LIMITED.

GIBBON, LEWIS GRASSIC ◊ J. Leslie MITCHELL.

GIBBONS, DAVE Working name of prolific, award-winning UK COMIC-strip artist David Chester Gibbons (1949-   ); using a bold, firm line style, he specializes in the SUPERHERO genre. Born in St Albans, Hertfordshire, he trained as a surveyor and began his artistic career providing ILLUSTRATIONS and strips for fanzines. He turned professional in 1973, drawing **The Wriggling Wrecker** for the D.C. Thompson comic *Wizard*. Further strips with an sf flavour followed until, in 1975, he began work on the Nigerian superhero **Powerman**, his monthly 16pp episodes alternating with those by Brian BOLLAND to produce a fortnightly publication schedule. DG was one of the initial team of artists on 2,000 AD, drawing **Harlem Heroes** and **Robusters** and co-creating **Rogue Trooper** with writer Gerry Finley-Day. DG drew a number of DR WHO episodes for the UK division of MARVEL COMICS, and in 1981 began a long association with the US publisher DC COMICS, drawing **The Creeper**, 12 issues of **Green Lantern** and a SUPERMAN tale called "For the Man who Has Everything", written by Alan MOORE. His greatest achievement to date, also written by Moore, has been the phenomenally successful WATCHMEN (12-vol series 1986-7; graph **1987** US; with additional material 1988 US); this ALTERNATE-WORLD superhero story, rich in semiotics, won a special category for Best Other Forms in the 1988 Hugo Awards (◊ HUGO for discussion of this category). DG's next major project was *Give Me Liberty* (graph **1990**), written by Frank MILLER. DG has recently begun to establish himself as a writer with a **Superman/Batman** team-up (1991) and a **Batman vs Predator** comic book (1992), both for DC.   [RT]

See also: DAN DARE – PILOT OF THE FUTURE; GRAPHIC NOVEL.

GIBBONS, (RAPHAEL) FLOYD (PHILLIPS) (1886-1939) US writer, mostly of war stories; well known as a war correspondent. *The Red Napoleon* (**1929**) is a future-WAR tale featuring a modern-day Mongol dictator, Karakhan, who conquers much of the world, miscegenating as he goes in a deliberate onslaught upon the racist White nations. He is eventually defeated by the USA. In 1941, in Bermudan exile with the dying Karakhan, Gibbons – who appears as his journalist self throughout – recounts these events with some sympathy. [JC]

See also: INVASION; VILLAINS.

GIBBS, LEWIS Pseudonym of Joseph Walter Cove (1891-?), a UK writer whose sf novel, *Late Final* (**1951**), deals with a post-WWIII England. [JC]

Other works: *Parable for Lovers* (**1934**).

GIBSON, COLIN (? -) NEW ZEALAND writer whose second novel, *The Pepper Leaf* (**1971**), is a NEAR-FUTURE sf tale set in New Zealand. Fearful of nuclear catastrophe, a small group of vegetarian nudists expose themselves to survival conditions, and their cruel interactions, described in a tense, allusive style, provide a model for, or allegory of, the human condition *in extremis*. [JC]

GIBSON, EDWARD (1936-) US Skylab astronaut whose sf novel, *Reach* (**1989**), set in the more remote NEAR FUTURE, argues for a continuation of the space programme via the story of an expedition sent to discover the nature of an ALIEN lifeform. This proves unfriendly; but the case for human exploration of our potential domain is presented with commendable clarity. [JC]

GIBSON, FLOYD ◊ Paul CONRAD.

GIBSON, WALTER B(ROWN) (1897-1985) US newspaper journalist, editor and writer who founded and ran *Tales of Magic and Mystery* (1927-8) – where he published his first piece of genre interest, "The Miracle Man of Benares", in 1927 – as well as *True Strange Stories* (1929) for Bernarr MACFADDEN, and FANTASTIC SCIENCE FICTION (1952); this latter lasted only 2 issues, and is not to be confused with FANTASTIC, also founded 1952. Variously prolific, he remains best known under the house name Maxwell Grant – though "pseudonym" would perhaps be a more accurate term, as WBG wrote almost 300 novels as Grant, most for the celebrated pulp magazine *The Shadow* (325 issues 1931-49), whose hero – originating in a 1930 radio series – is a mysterious vigilante who often walks by night. WBG wrote most (not all) of these, but only 25 or so contain sf themes, those later republished as books being *Charge, Monster* (1934; **1977**), *The Silent Death* (**1978**) and *The Death Giver* (**1978**). Other **Shadow** episodes republished in book form include *The Living Shadow* (**1933**), *The Shadow and the Voice of Murder* (**1940**), *Return of the Shadow* (**1963**) as WBG, *The Weird Adventures of the Shadow* (coll **1966**) as WBG, and (all first published in *The Shadow*) *The Weird Adventures of the Shadow: Grove of Doom* (1933; **1969**), *The Eyes of the Shadow* (1931; **1969**), *The Shadow Laughs!* (1931; **1969**), *The Death Tower* (1932; **1969**), *The Ghost Makers* (1932; **1970**), *Hidden Death* (1932; **1970**), *Gangdom's Doom* (1931; **1970**), *The Black Master* (1932; **1974**), *The Mobsmen on the Spot* (1932; **1974**), *Red Menace* (1931; **1975**), *Silent Seven* (1932; **1975**), *Hands in the Dark* (1932; **1975**), *Double "Z"* (1932; **1975**), *The Crime Cult* (1932; **1975**), *The Romanoff Jewels* (1932; **1975**), *The Crime Oracle* (1936; **1975**), *Teeth of the Dragon*

(1937; **1975**), *Kings of Crime* (1932; **1976**), *Shadowed Millions* (1933; **1976**), *Green Eyes* (1932; **1977**), *The Creeping Death* (1933; **1977**), *The Shadow's Shadow* (1933; **1977**), *Fingers of Death* (1933; **1977**), *Murder Trail* (1933; **1977**), *Grey Fist* (1934; **1977**), *Charg, Monster* (1934; **1977**) and *Zemba* (1935; **1977**). **The Shadow** titles published as by WBG include *The Mask of Mephisto and Murder by Magic* (coll **1975**), *A Quarter of Eight and The Freak Show Murders* (coll **1978**), *Crime Over Casco and The Mother Goose Murders* (coll **1979**), *The Shadow Scrapbook* (coll **1979**), *Jade Dragon and House of Ghosts* (coll **1981**) and *The Shadow and the Golden Master* (coll of linked stories **1984**). WBG also wrote *Rod Serling's The Twilight Zone* * (coll **1963**; cut vt *Chilling Stories from Rod Serling's The Twilight Zone* 1965) and *Twilight Zone Revisited* * (coll **1964**). [JC]

GIBSON, WILLIAM (FORD) (1948-) US-born writer, in Canada since 1968, when he moved north after being rejected by his draft-board. After some time in Toronto – where a significant proportion of his fellow expatriates had come to Canada in protest against the Vietnam War – he moved in 1972 to Vancouver, a Pacific Rim city where attention was uneasily focused upon increasingly dominant Japan across the waters. (It could be argued that the Vancouver attitude toward imperial Japan, and to its Hong Kong "sidekick", provides a model for the numb, colonized acquiescence to a new world order so characteristic of occidentals in the **Neuromancer** trilogy which made WG famous.) WG began publishing sf with "Fragments of a Hologram Rose" for *Unearth* in 1977, and by 1983 had produced most of the fiction later assembled in *Burning Chrome* (coll **1986** US); some of these tales, like "Johnny Mnemonic" (1981) and the 1982 title story, were set in the **Neuromancer** universe, and were, therefore, early examples of what would soon become known as CYBERPUNK (*which see for detailed examination of the movement*).

WG did not invent cyberpunk, nor has he ever claimed to have done so. Bruce BETHKE's "Cyberpunk" (1983) supplied the name, and Gardner DOZOIS, in a 1983 article, defined the movement by applying the term to works set in COMPUTER-driven, high-tech NEAR-FUTURE venues inhabited by a slumbound streetwise citizenry for whom the new world is an environment, not a project. In terms of traditional US sf, this was heresy, and WG's enormous success as an sf writer must have seemed an ominous harbinger of the death of traditional sf. His novels treat traditional sf instruments and themes as unforegrounded figures in the complex mosaic of urban life; they shift the grounds of sf displacement inwards from cyber (as it were) to punk; the world they describe is old, and whether or not it can be understood – in WG's work it generally cannot – its inhabitants are consumers, not makers. The essential displacement from which they suffer – like so many protagonists of Modernist and POSTMODERNIST literature – is the loss of an integrated self. For the inhabitants of WG's world, selfhood has emptied itself into the instruments of the world, and in book after book – like cases of flesh – his characters are found hacking the wilderness for Cargo.

Canadian sf – from A.E. VAN VOGT down through Gordon R. DICKSON and beyond – has always tended to lock its protagonists into grey wilderness environments impenetrable to CONCEPTUAL BREAKTHROUGH, where they survive as displaced souls, longing for transcendence. As a Canadian writer, therefore – through his own displacing act of emigration – WG was well placed to write the definitive cyberpunk book. All he needed to add to the new territory he had embraced was – in his remarkably fluent and attentive prose – gear, brand-names, Japanese corporations and mean streets. But in the end the void of the wilderness interpenetrates the things of the world, and generates a sense that they are ultimately vain. The **Neuromancer** trilogy – *Neuromancer* (**1984** US), *Count Zero* (**1986** UK) and *Mona Lisa Overdrive* (**1988** UK) – is all about escaping the flesh.

The protagonist of *Neuromancer* – which won the HUGO, NEBULA, and PHILIP K. DICK AWARDS – is a matrix cowboy or outlaw hired to link a digital version of his mind into CYBERSPACE itself (cyberspace being a worldwide computer matrix of information experienced by any plugged-in sentience as an infinitely complex and chambered VIRTUAL-REALITY labyrinth) and, once "inside", to steal data. The "outside" world of the book is a near-future USA (although never named as such) dominated by Japanese corporations, one of which may be his employer. The plot itself harks back, as does much of the imagery, to the classic mean-streets California thrillers of Raymond Chandler (1888-1959) and Ross Macdonald (pseudonym of Kenneth Millar [1915-1983]); and, true to those models – and to what might be called WG's Canadian pessimism about changing the world – none of the characters of *Neuromancer* have anything but an eavesdropping relationship to the true roots of power. The story eventually moves from Earth into near space, where complex orbiting arcologies house the AIS which, perhaps, secretly run the world; but the protagonist does not covertly long to run the world in their stead. His longing is to transcend the flesh which pulls him back from the bliss of cyberspace. The second and third volumes of the sequence, though more sophisticated as novels, inevitably fail to advance much further – in traditional sf terms – towards working out the implications of the **Neuromancer** world, which remains a wilderness. The AIs of the first volume have suffered a traumatized, cataclysmic coming to self-awareness, and now haunt cyberspace in the guise of voodoo godlings. A wide range of characters appears throughout *Count Zero* and *Mona Lisa Overdrive*, but they share an underlying paralysis; and, as a novelist burdened with the task of creating new tales, WG inevitably pays a price for his refusal to countenance any normal sf sorting-out of the world. Hints given at the end of the last volume of a sudden interstellar growth of perspective

singularly fail to convince.

Cyberpunk in WG's hands, then, was an assault on future HISTORY. *Neuromancer* in particular was treated by much of its huge readership as a manual for surviving in style. That WG is uncannily sensitive to manners and idioms may have, for many of his readers, obscured the underlying bleakness of his vision. After spending some time writing filmscripts in Hollywood, however, he allowed that bleakness to come unmistakably to the fore in *The Difference Engine* (**1990** UK) with Bruce STERLING. The book is a sustained work of RECURSIVE SF – Benjamin DISRAELI and characters from his work appear throughout – a STEAMPUNK evocation of an ALTERNATE WORLD 19th-century UK dominated by the supposition that in about 1820 Charles BABBAGE succeeded in his attempt to construct the title's COMPUTER. The world that explodes into reality as a consequence of Babbage's triumph is, in *The Difference Engine*, a cruel and polluted DYSTOPIA, a land dominated by calculation, measurement and severely "practical" reason. Vast arterial roads ransack a choking London; huge masonical edifices house the new totalitarian bureaucracy which operates the Engines; and a conscious AI is a-borning. Though the book is at points unduly narrow in conception, and congested as a tale, its ultimate effect is very considerable.

Today WG seems on the verge of becoming sf's moralist. [JC]

See also: ACE BOOKS; CANADA; CHILDREN IN SF; CLICHÉES; FANTASY; GAMES AND SPORTS; GODS AND DEMONS; GOTHIC SF; HISTORY OF SF; MEDIA LANDSCAPE; MUSIC; OMNI; OPTIMISM AND PESSIMISM; PARANOIA; SPACE HABITATS; TECHNOLOGY; VILLAINS.

GIESY, J(OHN) U(LRICH) (1877-1948) US physiotherapist and PULP-MAGAZINE writer, author of many stories, most not sf, in *Argosy* and *All-Story Weekly* 1914-34. *All for His Country* (1914 *Cavalier*; **1915**), which combines plot-material from the future-WAR genre and from the EDISONADE, pits a young inventor's radium-powered gravity-defying plane against the treacherous Japanese; ominously, JUG also accuses Japanese-Americans from California of betrayal. The **Jason Croft** or **Palos** trilogy – *Palos of the Dog Star Pack* (1918 *All-Story Weekly*; cut **1965**), *The Mouthpiece of Zitu* (1919 *All-Story Weekly*; cut **1965**) and *Jason, Son of Jason* (1921 *Argosy*; cut **1966**) – features Croft's adventures on Palos, a planet of Sirius. Derivative of Edgar Rice BURROUGHS's Martian stories, these novels are also highly practical, for Croft triumphs not through his own strength but because of an encyclopedic knowledge of Earth's technologies of destruction. JUG's further sf includes a UTOPIA, "In 2112" (1912 *Cavalier*), written with his frequent collaborator, the Utah lawyer Junius Smith (1883-1945), and a number of humorous stories about the eccentric **Dr Xenophon Xerxes Zapt**. JUG's sf – tempered as it is by a devout belief in astrology – has dated and is now of merely historical interest, but for years he was considered second only to Burroughs as an author of interplanetary romances. [RB/JC]

GIGAMESH AWARD ◊ AWARDS.

GIGANTIS ◊ GOJIRA.

GIGANTIS THE FIRE MONSTER ◊ GOJIRA.

GIGER, H.R. Working name of Swiss artist and theatre and film designer – but not illustrator – Hansruedi Giger (1940-   ). He began developing his distinctive style in the early 1970s. Strikingly grotesque, morbid, necrophile, it draws heavily on the Surreal and the decadent traditions, his acknowledged influences including Arnold Böcklin (1827-1901), Hieronymus Bosch (1460-1516), Salvador Dali (1904-1989) and Antonio Gaudí (1852-1926), and there are clear resemblances also to the paintings of Max Ernst (1891-1976). It is perhaps from Ernst and Gaudí that he first took his main trademark, the combination of organic with machine-like forms, which has been termed "biomechanoid". The first two books of his work were *A Rh+* (**1971**) and *H.R. Giger* (**1976**), but it was the third, *H.R. Giger's Necronomicon* (**1977**) – the title pays appropriate homage to H.P. LOVECRAFT – which drew the attention of the US and UK public to his work.

Among these readers were the producers of the film ALIEN (1979), who invited HRG to help in the alien designs. (They had also heard of his weird 1975 designs for the unmade Jodorowsky version of DUNE.) The spectacular results, done from working drawings subsequently published in *H.R. Giger's Alien* (**1979**; rev vt *Giger's Alien Film Design* 1989), revolutionized the look of sf cinema to a degree it would be difficult to overstate; it has since been much imitated in many films, including SATURN 3 (1980), LIFEFORCE (1985) and even VIDEODROME (1982), though it is doubtful if HRG has profited from this. The idea that alien MACHINES might not look like ours – along with the very idea of the organic machine – was inventive, and in sf-cinema terms an important step away from anthropomorphism. (Some, though, would argue that the incorporation into HRG's aliens and their artefacts of penis and vagina shapes is as anthropomorphic as you can get.) HRG was unhappy with the execution of his designs for the film *Poltergeist II* (1986). Considering the fame of his film work, it is surprising he has done so little.

He continued through the 1980s with very much the same kind of airbrushed painting in ink and acrylics: death/sex/machine imagery of staggering banality according to some, shocking Surrealism according to others; and his seminal influence in the sf field now seems to have been almost accidental, though it is not the first time Surrealism has influenced sf. His 1980s work can be seen in *H.R. Giger: N.Y. City* (**1981** chap), *H.R. Giger: Retrospektive, 1964-1984* (**1984**), *Giger's Necronomicon Two* (**1986**) and *H.R. Giger's Biomechanics* (**1988**; trans Clara Häricht Frame 1990 US). [PN]

See also: FANTASY; ILLUSTRATION.

GIJSEN, WIM [r] ◊ BENELUX.

GILBERT, JOHN (1926-   ) US writer whose sf novel, *Aiki* (**1986**), sets a gladiatorial martial-arts tale in 21st-century New York. [JC]

GILBERT, (WILLIAM) STEPHEN (1912-   ) UK writer whose first novel, *The Landslide* (**1943**), is a PARALLEL-WORLDS fantasy of some complexity in which primeval eggs, exposed by the titular slide, begin to hatch. His second, *Monkeyface* (**1948**), movingly explores the familiar territory of the self-aware ape (◊ APES AND CAVEMEN). His best-known sf novel, *Ratman's Notebooks* (**1968**; vt *Willard* 1971 US), is fundamentally a horror tale. Ratman conceives a special relationship with rats, comes precariously to dominate and commune with them, and leads their vengeful incursions on the world at large; but there is a comeuppance. The book was filmed as *Willard* (1971). [JC]

GILCHRIST, JOHN ◊ ROBERT HALE LIMITED.

GILES, GEOFFREY [s] ◊ Walter GILLINGS.

GILES, GORDON A. [s] ◊ Eando BINDER.

GILFORD, C(HARLES) B(ERNARD) (1920-   ) US teacher and writer whose sf novel, *The Liquid Man* (**1969**), features a scientist and a problem in undesired metamorphosis, the nature of which is clear from the title. [JC]

GILLESPIE, BRUCE (1947-   ) Australian educational-books editor, critic and from 1969 publisher of a FANZINE (current), SF COMMENTARY, where much of his writing on sf has appeared. Some of this was reprinted in *Philip K. Dick: Electric Shepherd* (critical anth **1975**) ed BG, published by Norstrilia Press, a SMALL PRESS named in honour of Cordwainer SMITH and founded by BG with Carey Handfield and Rob Gerrand; Norstrilia, now long silent, published more than 20 books, many of sf relevance. A later fanzine (from 1984) is *The Metaphysical Review*, which also carries occasional critical pieces. BG has received 9 Ditmar AWARDS for fan writing and publishing and 2 William Atheling Jr Awards for criticism. [PN]

See also: AUSTRALIA.

GILLIATT, PENELOPE (ANN DOUGLAS) (1932-   ) UK writer best known for her work outside the sf field, including the esteemed screenplay for *Sunday, Bloody Sunday* (1971). Her sf novel, *One by One* (**1965**), depicts a NEAR-FUTURE London hit by a devastating plague. [JC]

GILLILAND, ALEXIS A(RNALDUS) (1931-   ) US cartoonist and writer who won HUGOS as Best Fan Artist in 1980, 1983, 1984 and 1985; he also won the JOHN W. CAMPBELL AWARD for Best New Writer of 1982. As an official in the US Federal Government 1956-82, serving mainly as a chemist and specification writer, AAG was well situated to spoof bureaucracy, though his first sf books, the **Rosinante** trilogy – *The Revolution from Rosinante* (**1981**), *Long Shot for Rosinante* (**1981**) and *The Pirates of Rosinante* (**1982**) – significantly stop short of depicting all forms of government as intrusion. Set on a colony planet chafing at bureaucratic interference from faraway Earth, the sequence amusingly depicts first the successful revolt, then the dawning realization of the colonists that their COMPU-

TERS have taken control. *The End of the Empire* (**1983**) features, contrastingly, a protagonist who works to defend a GALACTIC EMPIRE against a comically conceived LIBERTARIANISM, on the grounds that too *little* government is no less damaging than too much. AAG's second series, the **Wizenbeak** sequence – *Wizenbeak* (**1986**) and *The Shadow Shaia* (**1990**) – is fantasy, featuring a comical wizard who had appeared in cartoon form in previous years. AAG's books of cartoons, where Wizenbeak can also be found, include *The Iron Law of Bureaucracy* (graph coll **1979**), *Who Says Paranoia Isn't "In" Anymore* (graph coll **1985**) and *The Waltzing Wizard* (graph coll **1990**).   [JC]

GILLINGS, WALTER (1912-1979) UK journalist and editor, active in FANDOM from the early 1930s; he published (1937-8) 7 issues of an historic FANZINE, *Scientifiction*. This activity led to his editing the first true UK sf magazine, TALES OF WONDER (1937-42). Immediately after WWII he joined the author Benson HERBERT to create the Utopian Publications imprint, which issued sf, fantasy and some soft-core pornography in cheap paperback format; this included the AMERICAN FICTION and STRANGE TALES series. WG then edited the 3 issues of FANTASY (1946-7). After its demise he produced the professional-looking fanzine FANTASY REVIEW (1947-50); when, in 1950, he was given the editorship of the new professional magazine SCIENCE FANTASY, the fanzine was incorporated as a section of the first 2 issues. John CARNELL took over editorship of *Science Fantasy* with #3 (Winter 1951/2), and WG dropped out of sf activities for some years. He then produced another fanzine, *Cosmos*, for 3 issues in 1969, and also appeared regularly in VISION OF TOMORROW (1969-70) with a series about the HISTORY OF SF in the UK, and again as a columnist in SCIENCE FICTION MONTHLY (1974-6), where he also had a column as Thomas Sheridan – the pseudonym under which he had years earlier published the first of his 3 sf stories, "The Midget from Mars" for *Tales of Wonder* in 1938. Another story, "Lost Planet" (*Fantasy* 1946), was published as by Geoffrey Giles.   [PN]

See also: BRITISH SCIENCE FICTION ASSOCIATION; SF MAGAZINES.

GILLMORE, INEZ HAYNES Pseudonym of US writer Inez Haynes Irwin (1873-1970), whose sf novel, *Angel Island* (**1914**), conveys an almost surreal FEMINIST message with considerable competence. After five men are shipwrecked on the eponymous island (in the ROBINSONADE tradition) and tame the beautiful winged women who inhabit it by clipping their wings and breeding with them, the tale gradually makes explicit a kind of consciousness of outrage on the part of the caged beings.   [JC]

GILLMORE, PARKER (?   -?   ) UK writer, mostly of travel books published 1869-93. His sf novel, *The Amphibion's [sic] Voyage* (**1885**), is a tale shaped suspiciously like a travelogue, but manages to evoke some interest for the eponymous land-and-sea vehicle, which carries its passengers into encoun-

ters with a sea monster or two.   [JC]

GILL WOMAN ◊ Roger CORMAN; PLANETA BUR.

GILMAN, CHARLOTTE PERKINS (1860-1935) US editor, writer and lecturer, and an important figure in the history of US FEMINISM. Although by no means negligible, her later fiction was clearly dedicated to the promulgation of a copious flow of radical thought. However, her first story, *The Yellow Wall Paper* (1892 *New England Magazine*; **1899** chap) as by Charlotte Perkins Stetson, was long read as a relatively straightforward tale of horror; it took no substantial task of decoding for later readers to understand that the powerful delusional imagery of the tale reflects the intolerable stress felt by its autobiographical protagonist at being forced to act out the role of a compliant and sequestrated female. CPG divorced her husband in 1894, after having moved to California; she then spent half a decade lecturing before remarrying. The rest of her life was productive. She founded, edited, and wrote almost the entire contents of *The Forerunner*, an issues-oriented journal which ran 1909-16; here first appeared many of the stories assembled decades later as *The Yellow Wallpaper and Other Writings* (coll **1989**). This volume does not include the book-length feminist UTOPIA "Moving the Mountain" (1911 *The Forerunner*), set in 1940 after women have decided that enough is enough and have taken over running the USA on a basis of humane, socialist equality. More famously, *Herland* (1914 *The Forerunner*; **1979**), along with its sequel "With Her in Ourland" (1916 *The Forerunner*), depicts an isolated parthenogenetic society 2000 years hence. Three men stumble into this gentle, humorous, wise utopian venue; one idolatrously reveres women, one is a male chauvinist, and the third narrates. In the sequel, a woman from Herland visits the USA, which she finds worthy of very considerable comment. An autobiography, *The Living of Charlotte Perkins Gilman* (**1935**), was published after CPG, aged 75, had discovered she had cancer and committed suicide.   [JC]

About the author: *To Herland and Beyond: The Life and Work of Charlotte Perkins Gilman* (**1990**) by Ann J. Lane.

See also: POLITICS.

GILMAN, ROBERT CHAM ◊ Alfred COPPEL.

GILMORE, ANTHONY Collaborative pseudonym used in *Astounding Stories of Super-Science* by Harry BATES and Desmond W. HALL, respectively editor and assistant editor of that magazine, for the enthusiastically received **Hawk Carse** series, put into book form as *Space Hawk* (1931-2 *ASF*; fixup **1952**). Carse and his Black assistant, Friday, are intrepid space adventurers dedicated to driving the Yellow Peril, in the form of the evil Dr Ku Sui, from the spaceways. Bates later revived the character, without Hall, in "The Return of Hawk Carse" (1942).   [MJE]

See also: ASTOUNDING SCIENCE-FICTION.

GILSON, BARBARA ◊ Charles GILSON.

GILSON, CHARLES (JAMES LOUIS) (1878-1943) UK writer, best known for fantasies like *The Cat and the*

Curate (**1934** US), in which a cat is transformed into a seductive Middle Eastern lady, and for LOST-WORLD tales like *The Lost Island* (**1910**) and, as by Barbara Gilson, *Queen of the Andes* (**1935**). Other novels with sf elements, generally for a juvenile market, include *The Pirate Aeroplane* (**1913**), *The Realm of the Wizard King* (**1922**) and *The City of the Sorcerer* (**1934**).   [JC]

GINSBURG, MIRRA (1919-   ) Russian-born US editor, writer and translator. She began her translating career with a version of Mikhail BULGAKOV's "The Fatal Eggs" for *FSF* in 1964, and later translated an abridged version of his *Master i Margarita* as *The Master and Margarita* (**1967**). Other translations include a collection of stories by Yevgeny ZAMIATIN, *The Dragon: Fifteen Stories by Yevgeny Zamyatin* (coll trans from various sources **1967**), a new version of his *We* (**1920**; **1972**), and a juvenile sf novel by Lydia OBUKHOVA, *Lilit* (trans as *Daughter of Night* **1974**). She has edited and translated the stories for 3 collections of Soviet sf (◊ RUSSIA; SOVIET UNION): *Last Door to Aiya* (anth **1968**), *The Ultimate Threshold* (anth **1970**) and *The Air of Mars and Other Stories of Time and Space* (juvenile anth **1976**). MG also edited *The Fatal Eggs and Other Soviet Satire* (anth **1965**), which contains several fantasies. She has written books for very young children.   [JC/PN]

GIPE, GEORGE (1933-1986) US writer known within the sf field for several competent film ties: *Resurrection* * (**1980**), *Gremlins* * (**1984**) (◊ Joe DANTE), *Explorers* * (**1985**) (◊ EXPLORERS) and *Back to the Future* * (**1985**) (◊ BACK TO THE FUTURE).   [JC]

GIR ◊ Jean GIRAUD.

GIRAUD, JEAN (1938-   ) French artist (now resident in the USA); staggeringly prolific, remarkably inventive and influential, he is better known in the sf field as Moebius. With his loose, eloquent line style, JG is considered one of Europe's major talents, and his work has influenced an entire generation of fantasy and sf artists. Born in Fontenoy-sous-Bois, near Paris, he displayed from childhood a love of illustration. His early influences were classic US COMIC strips and the engravings of Gustave Doré (1833-1883). He attended the École des Arts Appliqués 1954-6, and then wrote and drew a Western comic strip before being drafted into the French army. On discharge in 1960 he worked as an assistant to the Belgian comics artist Joseph Gillain (1914-1980) and later illustrated a series of encyclopedia-like books. It was at this time that he created the sobriquet Moebius, which he first attached to a series of dark-humoured comic strips. In 1963 he met writer Jean-Michel Charlier (1924-1989), and together they created the Western series **Lieutenant Blueberry** for the magazine *Pilote*; this work was collected in 29 vols (**1965-90**; **1977-9** UK), of which 26 were drawn by JG as "Gir".

In the late 1960s he began illustrating, as Moebius, a line of French sf books and magazines and created a number of groundbreaking sf strips. In 1975 he cofounded the magazine MÉTAL HURLANT ["Screaming Metal"] with fellow-artist Philippe DRUILLET and writer Jean-Pierre Dionnet (1947-   ). For this magazine he created *Le bandard fou* ["The Horny Goof"] (1975), *Le garage hermétique de Jerry Cornelius* ["The Airtight Garage of Jerry Cornelius"] (from 1975), *Arzach* (1976), *The Long Tomorrow* (1976), scripted by Dan O'Bannon, and **Les aventures de John Difool** ["The Adventures of John Difool"] (1982-9), a multi-part epic written by film-maker Alejandro Jodorowski: *L'Incal noir* ["The Dark Incal"] (graph **1982**), *L'Incal lumière* ["The Bright Incal"] (coll **1983**), *Ce qui est en bas* ["What's Below"] (graph **1984**), *Ce qui est en haut* ["What's Above"] (graph **1985**), *Le cinquième essence I* ["The Fifth Essence: I"] (graph **1987**), *Le cinquième essence II* (graph **1988**) and *Les mystères de l'Incal* ["The Mysteries of the Incal"] (graph **1989**). The **Incal** stories have been translated into English as *Incal #1* (**1988** UK/US), *#2* (**1988** UK/US) and *#3* (**1988** UK/US).

Keeping track of JG's Moebius material is a bibliographer's nightmare. Books in French include *Gir 30 x 40* (graph **1974**), *Le bandard fou* ["The Horny Goof"] (graph **1975**), *Arzach* (graph **1976**), *John Watercolor et sa redingote qui tue* ["John Watercolor and his Killer Overcoat"] (graph **1976**), *L'homme, est il bon?* ["Is Man Good?"] (graph **1977**), *Cauchemar blanc* ["White Nightmare"] (graph **1978**), *Le garage hermétique* ["The Airtight Garage"] (graph **1979**), *Tueur des mondes* ["World Killer"] (graph **1979**), *Moebius 30 x 30* (graph **1979**), *Double evasion* (graph **1981**), *L'Homme programmé* ["The Programmed Man"] (graph **1981**), *Le disintegré reintegré* ["The Disintegrated Reintegrated"] (graph **1982**), *Mémoire du futur* ["Memory of the Future"] (graph **1983**), *Sur l'étoile* ["Upon a Star"] (graph **1983**), *Venise céleste* ["Heavenly Venice"] (graph **1984**), *L'Univers de Gir* ["Gir's Universe"] (graph **1985**), *Starwatcher* (graph **1986**), *Le saga du crystal* ["Crystal Saga"] (graph **1987**), *Les jardins d'Aedena* ["The Gardens of Aedena"] (graph **1987**), *Made in LA* (graph **1988**), *La citadel aveugle* ["The Blind Citadel"] (graph **1989**), *Nineteen Eighty eight* (graph **1990**), *Les vacances du Major* ["Major's Holiday"] (graph **1990**) and *La déesse* ["The Goddess"] (graph **1990**). Collected works in English include *Moebius 1: Upon a Star* (graph coll **1986** US), *#2: Arzach and Other Fantasy Stories* (graph coll **1986** US), *#3: The Airtight Garage* (graph coll **1987** US), *#4: The Long Tomorrow and Other Science Fiction Stories* (graph coll **1988** US), *#5: The Gardens of Aedena* (graph coll **1988** US), *6: Pharagonesia and Other Strange Stories* (graph coll **1988** US), *#7: The Goddess* (graph coll **1989** US) and a collection of graphics, illustrations and sketches under the title *The Art of Moebius* (graph coll **1989** US).

In 1985 JG relocated to Santa Monica, California, and set up Starwatcher Graphics to publish his posters, graphics and other fine-art pieces, and to promote himself as a conceptual designer. He illustrated one two-episode **Silver Surfer** story, in a surprise team-up with Stan LEE: *Parable* (1988-9 US). He also illustrated an ecological story for a special "Earth Day" issue of *Concrete* (1991 US). Meanwhile spin-off series in comic-strip form from his creations such as **The Airtight Garage** and **Incal** have been published as collaborative ventures with other artists and writers; these contribute, from a fabric of interlocking themes, to the creation of a Moebius universe. They include **The Elsewhere Prince** (1990 US), **The Man from Ciguri** (1990-91 US), **The Onyx Overlord** (4-issue comic-book series beginning 1992 US) and **Legends of Arzach** (6-issue series of short stories accompanied by colour artwork commissioned from leading artists in the comics medium, beginning 1992 US).

JG has also been influential in designing for and storyboarding films. Alejandro Jodorowski hired him in 1976 to storyboard his projected film adaptation of Frank HERBERT's novel *Dune* (fixup **1965**), a venture eventually abandoned through lack of funding. JG designed spacesuits and uniforms for Ridley SCOTT's ALIEN (1979). He designed the animated feature *Les maîtres du temps* ["The Time Masters"] (1982) dir René Laloux, based on *L'orphelin de Perdide* ["The Orphan from Perdide"] (**1958**), the novel by Stefan WUL, and worked on Disney's TRON (1982) and on *Nemo*, a Japanese animated film (based on Winsor MCCAY's **Little Nemo in Slumberland**), in production in 1992. He designed the creature for James CAMERON's 1989 film *The* ABYSS.

A French postage stamp designed by and in honour of JG was issued in 1988. [RT/MJ]

See also: HEAVY METAL.

GIRL FROM U.N.C.L.E., THE ◊ *The* MAN FROM U.N.C.L.E.

GIRL IN THE MOON, THE ◊ *Die* FRAU IM MOND.

GIVINS, ROBERT C(ARTWRIGHT) (1845-1915) US writer whose sf novel, *A Thousand Miles an Hour* (**1913**), might stand as a compendium of misunderstood science; examples are the concept of an airplane whose vertical screw allows it to remain still while the world turns, and the notion that gravity stops 40 miles up. [JC]

GLADIATORERNA (vt *The Peace Game*; vt *The Gladiators*) Film (1968). Sandrews/New Line. Dir Peter WATKINS, starring Arthur Pentelow, Frederick Danner, Kenneth Lo, Björn Franzen. Screenplay Nicholas Gosling, Watkins. 105 mins, cut to 91 mins. Colour.

Watkins uses his customary cinema-verité approach in this Swedish film about NEAR FUTURE in which, as a surrogate for full-scale war, small teams of soldiers fight it out under the guidance of a COMPUTER. He generates considerable righteous indignation over this, rather pointlessly in that such a system does not exist in reality and is unlikely ever to do so. The battle games are not well staged and the film lacks the impact of Watkins's other sf films, which include *The* WAR GAME (1965), PRIVILEGE (1966) and PUNISHMENT PARK (1971). A very similar theme was much later used in ROBOT JOX (1990). [JB/PN]

GLADIATORS, THE ◊ GLADIATORERNA.

GLAMIS, WALTER [s] ◊ Nat SCHACHNER.

GLASBY, JOHN S(TEPHEN) (1928-) UK writer,

chemist and astronomer, Fellow of the Royal Society of Astronomy, author of popularizing texts in that field and of a large number of stories and novels in various genres for pulp publishers of the 1950s and 1960s. Like R.L. FANTHORPE – alongside whom he supplied BADGER BOOKS with most of their sf and fantasy titles – and Dennis HUGHES, he severely curtailed his production when market conditions changed, publishing only one sf novel, *Project Jove* (**1971** US), after 1970, although in about 1990 he began to publish short stories once again. Like his colleagues, JSG wrote mainly under a range of pseudonyms and house names, beginning with *Satellite B.C.* (**1952**), *Time and Space* (**1952**) and *Zero Point* (**1952**), all these titles being collaborations with Arthur ROBERTS, sharing the house name Rand LE PAGE; JSG's most frequently used personal pseudonym was A.J. Merak. Though much of his work, either solo or in collaboration, was hasty and unremarkable, JSB was entirely capable of more memorable work, especially perhaps in some early stories which showed the influence of A.E. VAN VOGT. [JC]

Other works:

As John Adams: *When the Gods Came* (**1960**).

As R.L. Bowers: *This Second Earth* (**1967**).

As Berl CAMERON (house name): *Cosmic Echelon* (**1952**) with Arthur Roberts; *Sphero Nova* (**1952**) with Roberts.

As J.B. Dexter: *The Time Kings* **1958**).

As Victor LA SALLE (house name): *Dawn of the Half-Gods* (**1953**); *Twilight Zone* (**1954**).

As Rand Le Page: See above.

As Paul LORRAINE (house name): *Zenith-D* (**1952**) with Arthur Roberts.

As John C. Maxwell: *The Time Kings* (**1958**).

As A.J. Merak: *Dark Andromeda* (**1954**); *Dark Conflict* (**1959**); *The Dark Millennium* (**1959**); *No Dawn and No Horizon* (**1959**; vt *The Frozen Planet* 1969 US); *Barrier Unknown* (**1960**); *Hydrosphere* (**1960**).

As John E. MULLER (house name): *Alien* (**1961**); *Day of the Beasts* (**1961**); *The Unpossessed* (**1961**).

As J.L. Powers: *Black Abyss* (**1960**).

As Karl ZEIGFREID (house name): *The Uranium Seekers* (**1953**); *Dark Centauri* (**1954**).

GLASKIN, G(ERALD) M(ARCUS) (1923-) Australian writer whose sf novel *A Change of Mind* (**1959** UK) concerns a hypnotic mind-transference between two men, with much emotional activity – and melodrama – consequent upon the changeover. GM has also written a series of nonfiction books, beginning with *Windows of the Mind: The Christos Experiment* (**1974**), describing experiments purporting to involve a form of psychic TIME TRAVEL *à la* J.W. DUNNE. [JC]

See also: PSEUDO-SCIENCE.

GLASSFORD, WILFRED ◊ Wilfred Glassford MCNEILLY.

GLEN AND RANDA Film (1971). UMC. Dir Jim McBride, starring Steven Curry, Shelley Plimpton, Woodrow Chambliss, Garry Goodrow. Screenplay

Lorenzo Mans, Rudolf WURLITZER, McBride. 94 mins. Colour.

The film opens with a shot of a naked man and woman walking hand-in-hand through a dreamlike setting, but it soon becomes clear that this is not the Garden of Eden but a post-HOLOCAUST USA. The young couple drift through the shattered debris of civilization in a search for the mythical city of Metropolis, encountering other survivors along the way; Randa (Plimpton) dies in childbirth, but Glen (Curry) continues his quest. Though made independently for very little money (shot on 16mm and later blown up to 35mm), *GAR* is more interesting than most of its kind due to McBride's ingenuity in creating an evocatively desolate and sometimes beautiful setting out of existing landscapes; the film is austere but hopeful. McBride has not done much commercial work, but he did go on to make the excellent thriller *The Big Easy* (1986). [JB/PN]

GLOAG, JOHN (1896-1981) UK writer, primarily in the fields of social history, architecture and design. His first sf novel, *Tomorrow's Yesterday* (1932), strongly influenced by H.G. WELLS's *The Time Machine* (1895) and Olaf STAPLEDON's *Last and First Men* (1930), is a satirical criticism of contemporary society as viewed by our successors, a race of cat people who have mastered TIME TRAVEL. Time manipulation featured prominently in several of JG's short stories and, through a drug capable of unlocking ancestral memories, in the novel *99%* (1944). His other novels, again with strong satirical overtones, are chiefly concerned with the effect of new discoveries on society. In *The New Pleasure* (1933) a chemical is used to heighten the sense of smell; in *Winter's Youth* (1934) a rejuvenation process adds 30 years to one's life; and in *Manna* (1940) a fungus that appeases hunger creates a lethargic population. *Tomorrow's Yesterday* was reprinted, with slight revisions, in *First One and Twenty* (coll 1946), which also incorporates 10 stories from *It Makes a Nice Change* (coll 1938). Other fantasy stories appear in *Take One a Week* (coll 1950).

After a long period away from the field, JG published a series of historical fantasy novels, *Caesar of the Narrow Seas* (1969), *The Eagles Depart* (1973) and *Artorius Rex* (1977), which attracted comparison with the works of Susan COOPER. [JE]

Other works: *Artifex, or The Future of Craftsmanship* (1926 chap), nonfiction; *Sacred Edifice* (1937); *Slow* (1954).

About the author: "The Future Between the Wars: The Speculative Fiction of John Gloag" by Brian M. STABLEFORD in *Foundation* (1980).

See also: BIOLOGY; END OF THE WORLD; HISTORY IN SF; HISTORY OF SF; POLITICS; REINCARNATION; WAR; WEAPONS.

GLOSSOP, [Captain] REGINALD (1880-?   ) UK writer, long resident in France, remembered almost exclusively for *The Orphan of Space* (1926), which lamely prefigures C.S. LEWIS's **Ransom** trilogy in the conceit that Earth is a diseased planet barred from the higher spheres. The plot concerns the collaboration

of a kind of spirit of Gaia with the ghost of a long-dead Chinese scientist to pass the secret of atomic energy on to the protagonists in 1935, so that they can cleanse the planet of its ailment. Some of RG's other novels were vanity-published. [JC]

Other works: *The Coming Invasion* (1903 chap); *The Crystal Globe* (1922); *The Magic Mirror* (1923); *Burning Sands* (1928 France); *The Ghastly Dew* (1932), a future-WAR tale in which the Channel Tunnel is a threat; *The Egyptian Venus* (1946).

GLUT, DONALD F(RANK) (1944-   ) US writer whose first publications of interest were nonfiction studies like *The Frankenstein Legend* (1973) and *The Dracula Book* (1975), and who also wrote filmscripts. His first novel, *Bugged* (1974), is fantasy; his second, *Spawn* (1976 Canada), is an sf tale featuring intelligent dinosaurs. What seems to have been an extensive interest in the subject led to the **New Adventures of Frankenstein** sequence – *Frankenstein Lives Again* (1977; exp 1981), *Terror of Frankenstein* (1977), *Bones of Frankenstein* (1977 UK) and *Frankenstein Meets Dracula* (1978 UK) – as well as to a further nonfiction title, *The Frankenstein Catalog* (1984), a useful bibliographical companion to the subject. DFG has also written a tie, *The Empire Strikes Back* * (1980), novelizing *The* EMPIRE STRIKES BACK; this text was also published as *The Empire Strikes Back: The Illustrated Edition* * (1980) and assembled in *The Star Wars Trilogy* * (omni 1987) along with the two other relevant novelizations, by Alan Dean FOSTER (writing as George LUCAS) and James KAHN. [JC]

GLYN JONES, RICHARD (1946-   ) UK illustrator and publisher. He graduated from Sheffield University and went on to postgraduate work in experimental psychology. With no formal art training, he began illustrating with underground COMIC strips and became, along with Mal DEAN, the most important illustrator for NEW WORLDS under the editorship of Michael MOORCOCK. He was designer for the last few issues, and also for the succeeding paperback book series. His work shows surprising and inventive contrasts between dark and light spaces, and a striking sense of design. He has also done book covers. In the 1980s he set up a SMALL PRESS in London, Xanadu Publishing, which has produced *Science Fiction: The 100 Best Novels* (1985) by David PRINGLE and other genre-related titles. ` [PN]

GLYNN, A(NTHONY) A(RTHUR) (1929-   ) UK journalist and writer whose sf novels – both routine pulp productions typical of UK publishing at the time – are *Search the Dark Stars* (1961), under the BADGER BOOKS house name John E. MULLER, and *Plan for Conquest* (1963). Though he preferred sf, AAG wrote mostly Westerns. [JC]

GNAEDINGER, MARY (1898-1976) US editor who, as an employee of the Frank A. MUNSEY chain of PULP MAGAZINES, was made editor in 1939 of the new magazine FAMOUS FANTASTIC MYSTERIES. She edited all 81 issues of the magazine, which eventually ceased publication in 1953, as well as two companion magazines: FANTASTIC NOVELS, published 1940-41 and again 1948-51, and A. MERRITT'S FANTASY MAGAZINE, published 1949-50. All three were devoted to reprinting old stories. [MJE]

GNOME PRESS US specialist SMALL PRESS founded in 1948 by Martin GREENBERG and David A. KYLE. It was the most eminent of the fan publishers of sf, and produced more than 50 books, surviving into the early 1960s. It published many of the major sf authors, and in some cases, as with Robert E. HOWARD's **Conan** series (published in 6 books 1950-55) and Isaac ASIMOV's **Foundation** series (published in 3 books 1951-3), was responsible for the manner in which their stories were collected into book form. Other authors included Arthur C. CLARKE, Robert A. HEINLEIN and C.L. MOORE. An associated imprint was Greenberg: Publisher, and in 1958 GP bought out the stock of FANTASY PRESS. Most of GP's books were hardcover, but some saw simultaneous softcover editions. GP was important in the transitional period between GENRE SF as a magazine phenomenon and its arrival in mass-market book PUBLISHING. [MJE/PN]

GOBLE, NEIL (1933-) US Air Force officer, technical writer, and author of a borderline-sf novel, *Condition Green: Tokyo* (**1967**). His first published sf was "Master of None" (*ASF* 1962). *Asimov Analyzed* (**1972**), published by MIRAGE PRESS, is perhaps too respectful toward its subject, and is now out of date. [PN]

GODBER, NOËL (LAMBERT) (1881-?) UK writer of several light novels, the first of which, *Amazing Spectacles* (**1931**), boasts some sf content: a pair of spectacles allows its wearer to see through clothing. [JC]
Other works: *Keep it Dark!* (**1932**).

GODFREY, HOLLIS (1874-1936) US writer in whose sf novel, *The Man who Ended War* (**1908**), the inventor of a radioactive metal-disintegrating beam (a nuclear weapon of sorts, probably the first in world literature) threatens to destroy the world's warships, one by one, if the great powers refuse to disarm. They resist and he carries out his threat, finally killing himself with his own beam, thereby protecting the secret of its manufacture. [JC]
Other works: *Dave Morrell's Battery* (**1912**).

GODFREY, MARTYN N. (1949-) Canadian writer whose sf, mostly aimed at the young-adult market, includes *The Vandarian Incident* (**1981**), *Alien War Games* (**1984**), *The Last War* (**1986**) – a post-HOLOCAUST tale – *More than Weird* (**1987**) and *I Spent my Summer Vacation Kidnapped into Space* (**1990** US). To date none has markedly striven to stand out from the routine. [JC]

GODS AND DEMONS The word "God" (or "Gods") is one of the commonest of all nouns in sf story and novel titles. Although this frequency is partly fuelled by the interest in RELIGION that has characterized sf from its earliest days, we must seek further to explain the sheer scale of the phenomenon.

The sf writer is a creator of imaginary worlds; in that sense his activity is godlike. It is, then, natural that he or she should especially enjoy fantasies (some might say delusions of grandeur) about superbeings with the ability to create and manipulate whole worlds. But it is not only power fantasies that feed into sf stories about gods; just as important are fantasies of impotence (sf's fascination with the uses of power extending as often to the manipulated as to the manipulators) in which we ourselves are the puppets of (or have even been created by) godlike beings. The idea that we are property – a favourite notion of Charles FORT's – feeds strongly into sf tales of PARANOIA, which are often stories of gods to whom we are subject; one of the commonest forms of METAPHYSICS in sf is to ask whether the universe is wholly arbitrary, or whether its patterns of meaning are somehow planned (though not by us), which brings us full circle back to religion again.

A particularly common form of the "we are property" story tale is the retelling of the story of ADAM AND EVE (*which see for examples*) in terms of what Brian W. ALDISS has termed "Shaggy God" stories: recastings of biblical myth into an sf framework. A common variant is that in which some sort of alien power or god seeds Earth with mankind (Adam and Eve in the first instance), or transmutes the existing ape-people, as in the film 2001: A SPACE ODYSSEY, where the alien/god takes the form of a black monolith. Such stories were given a new lease of life during the 1970s and early 1980s by the enormous popularity of PSEUDO-SCIENCE books by Erich VON DÄNIKEN, who saw ancient alien astronauts as having visited Earth eons ago, bearing technological gifts, and now remembered in race memory as gods. The modern sf version of this motif has strange, enormous alien artefacts (◊ BIG DUMB OBJECTS) made – often in space – by a now forgotten race of alien Builders for their own godlike purposes, but seeming to us like incomprehensible sacred relics.

Although sf analogues to the One God are comparatively rare in GENRE SF, even in its early days, quite a few works of earlier borderline sf consider the nature of the Christian God. Marie CORELLI apparently considered religious experience to be electric in nature, and in *A Romance of Two Worlds* (**1886**; rev 1887) postulated a God who manifests himself electrically. In *A Voyage to Arcturus* (**1920**), David LINDSAY created analogues of the more conventional Christian and Jewish images of God, only to dismiss them in every case as false and cheap in a universe where only pain and personal striving are meaningful. (Analogues of Christ are very much more common in sf than those of God the Father, and are discussed under MESSIAHS.)

God-stories in sf are nearly always rationalized, seldom mystical. Many stories are based on the notion that a highly advanced society might seem godlike to a more primitive one, and in many tales of COLONIZATION OF OTHER WORLDS the narrative turns on the difficulties and responsibilities of being seen in this light; an example is *Trudno byt' bogom* (**1964**; trans as *Hard to be a God* **1973**) by the brothers STRUGATSKI. Conversely, other stories present humans as confronted by some form of galactic intelligence which is so high in the order of life as to seem godlike. A very early work by Clifford D. SIMAK, *The Creator* (1935; **1946**), features a world-creating alien; the same author's *A Choice of Gods* (**1972**) proposes a godlike galactic principle. Eric Frank RUSSELL's "Hobbyist" (1947) envisages a god who created life in the Galaxy for mere aesthetic pleasure. A benevolent being does the same thing in Olaf STAPLEDON's *Star Maker* (**1937**) in an altogether more serious treatment of the theme; like several sf writers Stapledon wished to dispense with the anthropomorphic aspects of Christianity while preserving a sense of cosmic meaning and pattern. Not all galactic intelligences are benevolent; James TIPTREE Jr has a godlike galaxy-destroyer in *Up the Walls of the World* (**1978**). Arthur C. CLARKE proposes a ravening "mad mind" in *The City and the Stars* (1948; exp **1956**), but that was created by Man.

The Clarke novel raises an interesting notion that recurs quite often, in many forms, from the technological to the quasi-mystical: that a lower form of life might be able to create a higher. A number of stories concern computers that attain godlike powers (*see* COMPUTERS *for a list*), sometimes alone and sometimes through a transcendental fusion with their operators, as in *Catchworld* (**1975**) by Chris BOYCE. A recent example of the computer-god story on an epic scale is Dan SIMMONS's 2-vol **Hyperion Cantos** sequence – *Hyperion* (**1989**) and *The Fall of Hyperion* (**1990**) – in which human-created AI networks become the secret manipulators of all things, among their tools being other god-avatars (including the paingod Shrike); the books' titles (and structures) reflect Keats's famous poems about the fall of the old gods and the rise of the new. Indeed the **Hyperion** sequence became overnight the definitive "gods in sf" story, playing almost every imaginable variant on the theme.

More metaphysical methods of god-creation are just as common. A.E. VAN VOGT, whose career has largely been devoted to creating SUPERMAN figures, devised the ultimate (though not the most interesting) variant in *The Book of Ptath* (1943; **1947**; vt *Two Hundred Million A.D.* 1964; vt *Ptath* 1976), in which a god is created through the force of his followers' prayers, his power being proportional to their number – a vision which governs the most serious of Terry PRATCHETT's **Discworld** novels, *Small Gods* (**1992**). Gods are created in the flesh in Philip José FARMER's *Night of Light* (1957; exp **1966**) through the transcendental union of very good (or very bad) men once every seven years, when the local sun emits a mysterious radiation. In Frank HERBERT's *The God Makers* (**1972**) humans deliberately create a god using a blend of mystical, psychological and technological means. In this case Herbert's writing was not equal to his theme; and, indeed, god-stories generally meet severe literary problems in attempting to render transcendental

experience through GENRE-SF stereotypes. One of the most interesting variants on the theme of the artificially created god is found in Philip K. DICK's *A Maze of Death* (**1970**), in which a series of mystifying false realities are created, ultimately involving salvation through a godlike Intercessor; only late in the novel is it revealed that the realities and their god are all part of a construct imposed by the computer of a crippled starship.

The focus of interest in most sf god-stories is, paradoxically, not religious, though, in the case of Dick and some others, metaphysical questions about reality are certainly raised. More common are god-stories about the exercise of power or the burden of responsibility, or both. The theme is an old one, for the work of the SCIENTIST has been seen by many as a usurpation of powers that are properly God's; such is the case in Mary SHELLEY's *Frankenstein* (1818; rev 1831), where a scientist creates life but cannot create a soul to go with it. A number of variants have been sardonic. James Branch CABELL features several demiurges (world-makers) in his **Poictesme** fantasies – notably *The Silver Stallion* (**1926**), where Creation occurs through the boredom of a god whose cosmic perspective leads readily to a detachment seen by its victims as sadistic. This image of less-than-perfect god-creators became almost a CLICHÉ in genre sf. Robert SHECKLEY, for example, has often proposed rather harassed and incompetent gods, overworked and put upon, as in *Dimension of Miracles* (**1968**), and Douglas ADAMS echoed this in his **Hitch Hikers' Guide to the Galaxy** books. More seriously, in "Microcosmic God" (**1941**) Theodore STURGEON has an irresponsible scientist playing god to a miniature world, whose inhabitants he cruelly goads into accelerated technological development. Ursula K. LE GUIN examines the metaphysical aspects of the fallible-god theme, in a manner reminiscent of Dick's work, in *The Lathe of Heaven* (**1971**). All these works emphasize questions of responsibility.

The "delusions of grandeur" aspect of god stories became, starting in the 1960s, the speciality of two very notable sf writers: Philip José Farmer and Roger ZELAZNY. Zelazny's "gods" are often, in fact, technologically advanced superhumans, who for not always explained reasons are able to take on "aspects" of godhood, often analogous to those of the gods of legend; the Greek myths in *This Immortal* (**1966**), the Hindu pantheon in *Lord of Light* (**1967**) and the Egyptian pantheon in *Creatures of Light and Darkness* (**1969**). His *Isle of the Dead* (**1969**) features a feud between gods, and his **Amber** series features reality changes brought about by quasi-gods in worlds which are constantly changing copies of some Platonic original, beyond which some more ultimate god-figure might be hidden. Many (if not most) of Farmer's books deal with gods, notably the two series set on artificial worlds: the **Tierworld** series and the **Riverworld** series. The latter series is the archetype of the "we are property" theme, in which resuscitated humans are the playthings of the gods, and the former emphasizes the all-too-human qualities of the gods that do the manipulating. Artificial worlds of this type can usefully be called POCKET UNIVERSES (*which see for further examples*), and have become an sf staple. Farmer and Zelazny regularly and ironically undercut their god-themes with the use of a colloquial and streetwise tone, juxtaposing the sublime with the ridiculous, and this habit has permeated many subsequent examples of the pocket-universe novel. Two writers who have adopted this sort of tone in pocket-universe stories, in which protagonists are manipulated by god figures like pieces on a games board (or perhaps *are* gods without knowing it), are Piers ANTHONY (sometimes) and Jack L. CHALKER, the latter so devoted to the theme that it embraces almost the whole of his massive output.

One pocket-universe variant is the novel set in a VIRTUAL REALITY (*which see for examples*) generated by human or artificial intelligences. In the last two books of his **Neuromancer** trilogy (1986-88) William GIBSON has the virtual reality of CYBERSPACE actually occupied by gods within the machine itself, these taking the form of voodoo deities. (The sf voodoo theme, in which archetypal aspects of human behaviour are incarnate – somewhere in the hindbrain? – as gods, may well become a new cliché, one of its more interesting manifestations being in Greg BEAR's *Queen of Angels* [1990].)

Philip K. Dick's obsession with godhood runs through much of his work, and indeed entered his life. *Our Friends from Frolix 8* (1970) and *Galactic Pot-Healer* (1969) both feature alien quasi-gods and their effect on humans. *The Three Stigmata of Palmer Eldritch* (1965), as the title suggests, is about a god-being, once a businessman but now inhuman and metallic, who is able to bring about menacing reality-changes that seem almost to be beyond good and evil. Dick's nightmares of ordinary people being cosmically manipulated carry an emotional charge much more intense than genre sf is normally able to produce. Towards the end of his career, theology became his over-riding theme to an extravagant degree, as in *The Divine Invasion* (1982).

Much more straightforward gods appear in that small group of books whose genesis goes back to the idea in medieval astrology that each of the planets has a tutelary spirit. Such is the case in C.S. LEWIS's trilogy about **Ransom**, whose inspiration is directly Christian. The aliens in the novella "If the Stars are Gods" (1974), the title story of the fixup novel of the same name (1977) by Gordon EKLUND and Gregory BENFORD, believe that the universe is controlled by gods located in suns (an idea to be found in William Blake's poetry); the amusing *Dogsbody* (1975) by Diana Wynne JONES is another to make use of the notion. A more sciencefictional version of the same theme is in the living stars of Frank Herbert's *Whipping Star* (1970) and its sequel *The Dosadi Experiment* (1977). Indeed Herbert is, like Dick, a writer for

whom godlike figures are the central theme in a majority of his work, most celebratedly in the transformed Paul Atreides (something of a maimed god) in the 6 novels of the **Dune** sequence (1965-85), notably *God Emperor of Dune* (1981).

Further sf god-novels of note include (some at the fantasy end of the spectrum): *The Man who was Thursday: A Nightmare* (1908) by G.K. CHESTERTON, in which a recruiter of secret agents turns out to be God; *The Circus of Dr Lao* (1935) by Charles FINNEY, in which demigods are caged in a circus; most novels by Thomas Burnett SWANN and (though sometimes obscurely) most novels by Gene WOLFE, including *There are Doors* (1988); Harlan ELLISON's *Deathbird Stories: A Pantheon of Modern Gods* (coll 1975; rev 1984); *Strata* (1981) by Terry Pratchett, as well as his **Discworld** sequence; *Courtship Rite* (1982) by Donald KINGSBURY; *Winterking* (1984) by Paul HAZEL; *Planet of Whispers* (1984) by James Patrick KELLY, in which whispers from the right side of the brain are interpreted as the voice of God; *Waiting for the Galactic Bus* (1988) by Parke GODWIN, in which aliens take the roles of God and the Devil; *The Ring* (1988) by Daniel Keys MORAN, a Wagner-pastiche in which the gods are genetically engineered superbeings; *Neverness* (1988) by David ZINDELL, which has a godlike entity whose being is made up of many star systems and who can be reached only by solving mathematical theorems; *Rats and Gargoyles* (1990) by Mary GENTLE; *The Werewolves of London* (1990) by Brian M. STABLE-FORD; and *The Face of the Waters* (1991) by Robert SILVERBERG (who has written earlier god-novels, too), in which God is a planetary consciousness.

Gods are comparatively rare in sf CINEMA, two exceptions being the appalling RED PLANET MARS (1952), where God turns out to be real and in charge of Mars, and GOD TOLD ME TO (1976; vt *Demon*), where God the son is reincarnated as a hermaphrodite who tells his subjects to commit mass murder.

The concept of demons and devils is equally common in sf, but usually at a quite trivial level: they tend, as in non-horror FANTASY generally, to be seen simply as frightening and malicious entities derived from medieval Christian ideas of Hell, and are quite often played for laughs. There are many demonology stories with sf elements, such as the time-warping demon in Anthony BOUCHER's "Snulbug" (1941) and the other-dimensional alien blood-drinker in Henry KUTTNER's "Call Him Demon" (1946). Norvell W. PAGE's "But without Horns" (1940) uses demonic imagery in a story of a telepathic MUTANT. Demons proper often appear in SWORD AND SORCERY; demonic creatures of darkness were all in a day's work to Robert E. HOWARD's Conan. Particularly unpleasant aliens are often given demonic form (sometimes with talk about racial memory) in genre-sf stories, as in van Vogt's second published story, "Discord in Scarlet" (1939; in *The Voyage of the Space Beagle* fixup 1950) – which may have been the (unacknowledged) source of the film ALIEN – and Keith LAUMER's *A Plague of Demons* (**1965**), both truly nasty creations. A famous twist on the theme is found in Arthur C. Clarke's *Childhood's End* (**1950**; exp **1953**), in which mankind is confronted by aliens shaped exactly like the Devil (racial precognition of their arrival explains his bat-winged image in Christian mythology) but turn out to have mournfully paternalistic natures. Several sf-oriented fantasies by HARD-SF writers have imagined that Hell and its demons are real, and created a kind of quasi-scientific rationale for them. An early example is Robert A. HEINLEIN's "The Devil Makes the Law" (**1940**; with vt as 2nd title story of *Waldo and Magic, Inc.* coll **1950**); more recent examples are *Operation Chaos* (**1956-9** *FSF*; fixup **1971**) by Poul ANDERSON and the DANTE ALIGHIERI pastiche *Inferno* (**1975**) by Larry NIVEN and Jerry POURNELLE. Demons are, of course, by no means peculiar to Christianity, though in some other mythologies they are hardly to be distinguished from malign or death-dealing gods, as in the demonic green-eyed boy god who haunts the degenerate CYBERPUNK future of Elizabeth HAND's *Winterlong* (**1990**).

The strong prevalence of god (and devil) themes in sf strongly suggests that, as a genre, sf is not quite the hard-headed, extrapolative literature its proponents sometimes claim. On the other hand, at a time when many actual physicists publish books attempting to reconcile COSMOLOGY or quantum mechanics with the idea of God, it is hardly surprising if sf writers do the same. [PN]

See also: GOTHIC SF; MAGIC; MONSTERS; SUPERNATURAL CREATURES.

GOD TOLD ME TO (vt *Demon*) Film (**1976**). Larco. Prod and dir Larry Cohen, starring Tony Lo Bianco, Deborah Raffin, Sandy Dennis, Richard Lynch. Screenplay Cohen. 89 mins. Colour.

It is as well that Larry COHEN has his own production company, Larco, since it is impossible to imagine any other company taking on so eccentric a project. This is perhaps the most baroque sf movie ever made. A devout Catholic detective (Lo Bianco) investigates separate instances of mass murder linked by the assassins' confessions that God had told them to do it. Another link is the enigmatic Bernard (Lynch), revealed only at the end to be the hermaphroditic product of a virgin birth – he has a vagina – fathered by a sort of cross between an alien from a flying saucer (◊ UFOS) and a pentecostal fire. Now a MESSIAH, he is responsible for the various murders, having used PSI POWERS to programme the murderers. He offers to bear a child to the (childless) detective, who has only recently learned, to his dismay, that he himself is also the product of an alien-fathered virgin birth. Other directors faced with this bizarre material would have concentrated on the monstrous Bernard; Cohen typically turns it around into a study of the detective's feelings of religious guilt. For all its sophisticated religious symbolism, the film is structured as if it were a conventional *policier*. [PN]

See also: CINEMA; GODS AND DEMONS.

GODWIN, FRANCIS (**1562-1633**) English bishop and writer, most noted for his striking description of a lunar UTOPIA in the posthumously and anonymously published *The Man in the Moone, or A Discourse of a Voyage Thither by Domingo Gonsales, the Speedy Messenger* (**1638**). The flight to the low-gravity MOON, accomplished in a flying machine drawn by "gansas" (wild geese) who winter there, is described with some realism; FG cautiously allows that Nicolaus Copernicus (1473-1543) may have been right in some of his theories. (Domingo Gonsales reappears as a character in sf in work by CYRANO DE BERGERAC.) FG's book was reprinted many times in the following centuries – apparently often cut – and was perhaps the most influential work of PROTO SCIENCE FICTION. It is available in *The Man in the Moone: An Anthology of Antique Science Fiction* (anth **1971**) ed Faith K. Pizor and T. Allan Comp. [PN]

See also: FANTASTIC VOYAGES.

GODWIN, FRANK [r] ◊ CONNIE.

GODWIN, PARKE (**1929-**) US writer who began publishing work of genre interest with "Unsigned Original" for *Brother Theodore's Chamber of Horrors* (anth **1977**) ed Marvin KAYE "and Brother Theodore" (a Kaye pseudonym). PG has since been more or less equally associated with fantasy and sf, though most of the stories assembled in *The Fire when it Comes* (coll **1984**) are the former, the title novella winning a 1982 World Fantasy Award. As an sf writer, PG remains best known for the first two volumes of the **Masters of Solitude** sequence, both with Marvin Kaye: *Masters of Solitude* (**1978**) and *Wintermind* (**1982**); a projected third volume has yet to appear. Set in a post-HOLOCAUST USA, the first volume depicts a conflict between rural followers of a diseased mutant form of Christianity and a CITY in which a science-based worldview is encapsulated; in the second, a personal drama and an interesting half-breed protagonist intensify the grain of narrative, but peculiarly diminish the sense, given off by the earlier book, of a large sf occasion. *A Cold Blue Light* (**1983**), also with Kaye (*whom see for the sequel*), is a ghost story which confusingly mixes sf and supernatural rationales. PG's second sf sequence, written solo, the **Snake Oil** series – *Waiting for the Galactic Bus* (**1988**), *The Snake Oil Wars, or Scheherazade Ginzberg Strikes Again* (**1989**) – is an erratically amusing but ultimately very dark-complected SATIRE on RELIGION and US society at large, refracted through the behaviour of the two ALIENS who were responsible for breeding *Homo sapiens* in the first place, and have now taken on the roles of God and Devil; the assault on Christian fundamentalism is explicit. Though a writer whose flamboyance sometimes unhinges his plots, PG remains a figure whose relative obscurity is fully undeserved. [JC]

Other works: The **Firelord** Arthurian fantasy sequence, comprising *Firelord* (**1980**), *Beloved Exile* (**1984**) and *The Last Rainbow* (**1985**); *A Memory of Lions* (**1983**), associational; *A Truce with Time* (**1988**), contemporary fantasy; *Invitation to Camelot* (anth **1988**); *Sherwood* (**1991**), a Robin Hood fantasy, with a sequel projected.

See also: GODS AND DEMONS.

GODWIN, TOM (1915-1980) US writer whose life and career were afflicted by disease and misfortune: kyphosis had misshapen his spine, family tragedies caused him to leave school after third grade, and he was an alcoholic. He published the first of approximately 30 sf stories, "The Gulf Between", in *ASF* in 1953, and soon after wrote his most famous tale, "The Cold Equations" (1954), in which a girl stowaway on a precisely payloaded spaceship must be jettisoned by the one-man crew because to transport her extra mass would require more fuel than the starship carries, so making disaster inevitable and dooming also the colony to which the ship is heading. TG's first two novels, *The Survivors* (**1958**; vt *Space Prison* 1960) and its sequel *The Space Barbarians* (**1964**), tell of the abandoned human survivors of an alien prison planet who wait 200 years for revenge, then undergo SPACE-OPERA adventures involving a demoralized Earth and telepathic allies but ultimately demonstrating – in the approved *ASF* fashion – humanity's inextinguishable spirit. A similar bias governs *Beyond Another Sun* (**1971**), an anthropological sf novel in which aliens observe Man on another planet. TG wrote relatively little, and almost always within the expansionist tradition fostered by John W. CAMPBELL. What he did write, however, exhibited a fine clarity of conception and considerable narrative verve, though his characterizations were sometimes sentimental. [JC]

About the author: "Tom Godwin: A Personal Memory" (1990) by Diane Godwin Sullivan, in *Quantum #37*.

See also: ANTHROPOLOGY; ANTIGRAVITY; COLONIZATION OF OTHER WORLDS; MOON; PHYSICS; PROTO SCIENCE FICTION; RELIGION; SPACE FLIGHT.

GODZILLA The anglicized version of GOJIRA.

GOG Film (1954). Ivan Tors/United Artists. Dir and ed Herbert L. Strock, starring Richard Egan, Constance Dowling, Herbert Marshall. Screenplay Tom Taggart, from a story by Tors. 85 mins. 3-D. Colour.

In this slow-moving film, originally in 3-D, experiments are being carried out on human subjects in a secret underground laboratory to determine whether manned space flight is possible. Various pieces of equipment start to behave in a lethal fashion: a man loses his life in a centrifuge, another is frozen to death in a high-altitude chamber, a third is killed by high-frequency sound. Finally two experimental ROBOTS, Gog and Magog, go berserk. These accidents turn out to be the work of a foreign power which has taken over the lab's COMPUTER by means of instructions transmitted from a high-flying aircraft. The film's style is similar to that of the tv series SCIENCE FICTION THEATRE (1955-7), also produced by Tors. [JB/PN]

GOGOL, NIKOLAI ◊ RUSSIA.

GOHAGEN, OMAR ◊ AMAZING STORIES; FANTASTIC.

GOJIRA (vt *Godzilla, King of the Monsters*; vt *Godzilla*) Film (1954 Japan; exp with new footage 1956 US). Toho/Embassy. Dir Inoshiro Honda, starring Takashi Shimura, Akira Takarada, Akihiko Hirata (and Raymond Burr in US version). Screenplay Takeo Murata, Honda, based on a story by Shigeru Kayama. 98 mins cut to 81 mins for US release. B/w.

This was the first of a long series of Japanese (◊ JAPAN) films featuring Gojira (anglicized as Godzilla), a 400ft (120m) amphibious dinosaur that breathes fire; the name is a portmanteau word from "gorilla" and "kujira" ["whale"]. The film was bought by a US company which released it internationally in 1956 as *Godzilla, King of the Monsters* (vt *Godzilla*), replacing segments featuring a Japanese reporter by footage starring Raymond Burr. This first Gojira film was basically a conventional MONSTER MOVIE (nuclear radiation revives a prehistoric monster in the Pacific Ocean and it proceeds to devastate Tokyo), but over the years the sequels have become increasingly esoteric, not to say silly. Originally Toho Studio's special effects (supervised until his death in 1970 by Eiji Tsuburaya) for the **Gojira** series were fairly impressive, but they became more perfunctory. Unlike Willis H. O'BRIEN's and Ray HARRYHAUSEN's monsters – achieved with stop-motion animation of puppets – Gojira was created using either a man in a suit or small mechanized models.

Between *Gojira* and GOJIRA 1985 (1985) there were 14 other **Gojira** films: *Gigantis* (1955; vt *Gojira No Gyakushu*) released in English as *Gigantis the Fire Monster* (1959; vt *Godzilla Raids Again*; vt *The Return of Godzilla*), with the monster's name changed; *King Kong Tai Gojira* (1962), released in English as *King Kong vs. Godzilla*, very successful financially; *Mosura Tai Gojira* (1964; vt *Gojira Tai Mothra*), released in English as *Godzilla vs. The Thing* (vt *Godzilla vs. Mothra*), featuring the likeable giant moth from MOSURA (1961) and thought by some to be the best of the series; *Kaiju Daisenso* (1965), released in English as *Invasion of Astro-Monster* (vt *Battle of the Astros*; vt *Monster Zero*; vt *Invasion of Planet X*), in which Gojira and RADON for the first time are weapons of rather than threateners of Earth; *Ghidorah Sandai Kaiju Chikyu Saidai No Kessan* (1965; vt *Chikyu Saidai No Kessan*), released in English as *Ghidrah, the Three-Headed Monster*, in which Gojira, Radon and Mosura defend Earth from the nastiest of Toho's monsters, previously introduced in *Kaiju Daisenso*; *Nankai No Daiketto* (1966), dir Jun Fukuda, released in English as *Ebirah, Horror of the Deep* (vt *Godzilla vs. the Sea-Monster*), in which giant crab Ebirah is defeated, the first of the series not to be directed by Honda; *Gojira No Musuko* (1967), dir Fukuda, released in English as *Son of Godzilla*, a comical children's film; *Kaiju Soshingeki* (1968), dir Honda, released in English as *Destroy All Monsters* (vt *Operation Monsterland*; vt *The March of the Monsters*), in which all 11 Toho monsters to date are feebly on display; *Oru Kaiju Daishingeki* (1969), dir Honda, released in English as *Godzilla's Revenge*, too much a rerun of old footage; *Gojira Tai Hedora* (1971), dir Yoshimitsu Banno, released in English as *Godzilla vs. The Smog Monster* (vt *Godzilla Versus Hedora*), in which the emphasis changes from anti-nuclear-weaponry-and-radiation to anti-pollution, and Gojira has become an undignified, friendly buffoon; *Gojira Tai Gaigan* (1972), dir Fukuda, released in English as *War of the Monsters* (vt *Godzilla on Monster Island*), in which pollution-ridden aliens try to take over Earth; *Gojira Tai Megaron* (1973), dir Fukuda, released in English as *Godzilla vs. Megalon*, in which Megalon is a giant cockroach; *Gojira Tai Mekagojira* (1974), dir Fukuda, released in English as *Godzilla vs. the Bionic Monster* (vt *Godzilla vs. the Cosmic Monster*), in which Gojira battles his alien-controlled cyborg double; *Mekagojira No Gyakushu* (1975), dir Honda to celebrate Gojira's 20th birthday, released in English as *Terror of Mechagodzilla* (vt *The Escape of Megagodzilla*; vt *Monsters from the Unknown Planet*), a partial return to form, in which aliens again use bad monsters in an invasion of Earth fought off by good monsters.   [PN]

See also: CINEMA; COMICS; GREAT AND SMALL.

GOJIRA 1985 (vt *Godzilla 1985*) Film (1985). Toho/New World. Dir Kohji Hashimoto, R.J. Kizer, starring Raymond Burr (in US version), Keiju Kobayashi, Ken Tanaka. Screenplay Shuichi Nagahara, Lisa Tomei, from a story by Tomoyuki Tanaka. 120 mins, cut to 91 mins USA and 87 mins UK. Colour.

The original screenplay from GOJIRA (1954) is not credited, but this is effectively a remake of the first film; although it purports to be a sequel, it ignores the other 14 sequels as if they had never happened. Again the radioactive giant dinosaur attacks ships, then destroys Tokyo. Again footage starring Burr as a reporter is spliced in for the US market (the US/UK versions are half an hour shorter than the Japanese). The plotting is dire; its main genuflection to modernity is the Japanese opposition to US and Russian insistence that Gojira should be nuked. The dialogue and characterization of this MONSTER MOVIE are laughable; but the special effects are better than the first time around.   [PN]

GOLD (vt *L'Or*) Film (1934). UFA. Dir Karl Hartl, starring Hans Albers, Friedrich Kayssler, Lien Deyers, Michael Bohnen, Brigitte Helm. Screenplay Rolf E. Vanloo. 120 mins. B/w.

This German film was made by much the same team that had made F.P.1 ANTWORTET NICHT two years earlier, but is more spectacular and also more nationalistic. German scientists are hired by a megalomaniac Scottish tycoon who wishes to build a nuclear reactor to transmute base metal into gold. The ethics of the heroes eventually prevail, and the successful prototype is destroyed. The laboratory sequences, with dazzling electrical effects, are impressive, but the film as a whole is somewhat leaden.

A French-language version, *L'or*, dir Serge de Poligny, was made at the same time with a different cast, though Brigitte Helm, the love interest,

appeared in both.   [JB/PN]

GOLD, H(ORACE) L(EONARD) (1914-) Canadian-born writer and editor, in the USA from an early age, though retaining dual nationality. HLG began his sf career with several sales to *Astounding Stories* in the mid-1930s, the first being "Inflexure" (1934). At that time he wrote under the pseudonyms Clyde Crane Campbell and Leigh Keith, a gambit necessitated, he has said, by antisemitism on the part of the publishers. After a hiatus, he returned to the magazine under his own name with "A Matter of Form" (1938), becoming a regular contributor to UNKNOWN with such stories as "Trouble with Water" (1939), an enjoyable humorous MAGIC story, and "None but Lucifer" (1939), a collaboration with L. Sprague DE CAMP. He was later assistant to Mort WEISINGER on the magazines CAPTAIN FUTURE, START-LING STORIES and THRILLING WONDER STORIES (1939-41), from which he moved on to true-detective magazines, COMICS and radio scripts. During these years he occasionally used two further pseudonyms, Richard Storey in 1943 and Dudley Dell in 1951.

In 1950 he started GALAXY SCIENCE FICTION, which from the outset he made one of the leading sf magazines, and for the editing of which he remains best known – indeed, notorious. Afflicted with acute agoraphobia as a result of his wartime experiences, HLG worked from his apartment, doing much of his work by telephone. The emphasis of *Gal* reflected his interests in PSYCHOLOGY and SOCIOLOGY, as well as HUMOUR, and like John W. CAMPBELL Jr – with whom in 1953 he shared the first HUGO to be given for editing a professional magazine – he was credited with suggesting many ideas which his contributors turned into famous stories; he also earned a reputation for overediting. An interesting companion magazine, BEYOND FANTASY FICTION, which he also edited, lasted 10 issues 1953-5. He edited GALAXY SCIENCE FICTION NOVELS, an sf and fantasy reprint series of variable quality, in the same format as *Gal*. Later still he became editor of IF when it was taken over by *Gal*'s owner. He retired from editing both *Gal* and *If* in 1961.

Over the period of his editorship, HLG compiled a number of anthologies from the pages of *Gal*: *Galaxy Reader of Science Fiction* (anth **1952**; cut to 13 out of 33 stories 1953 UK), *Second Galaxy Reader of Science Fiction* (anth **1954**; with 11 stories removed, cut vt *The Galaxy Science Fiction Omnibus* 1955 UK), *The Third Galaxy Reader* (anth **1958**), *Five Galaxy Short Novels* (anth **1958**), *The Fourth Galaxy Reader* (anth **1959**), *The World that Couldn't Be and 8 Other Novelets from Galaxy* (anth **1959**), *Bodyguard, and Four Other Short Novels from Galaxy* (anth **1960**), *The Fifth Galaxy Reader* (anth **1961**), *Mind Partner and 8 Other Novelets from Galaxy* (anth **1961**) and *The Sixth Galaxy Reader* (anth **1962**). He also edited one independent anthology, *The Weird Ones* (anth **1962**).

Some of HLG's stories were collected in *The Old Die Rich* (coll **1955**). *What Will They Think of Last?* (**1976**) is a selection of his editorials from *Gal* with an autobiographical postscript. [MJE]

See also: QUESTAR.

GOLDEN AGE OF SF It has been said, cynically, that the Golden Age of sf is 14.

Certainly there is no objective measure by which we can say that the sf of any one period was notably superior to that of any other. Nonetheless, in conventional usage (at least within FANDOM) older readers regularly refer quite precisely to the years 1938-46 as sf's Golden Age, and younger readers, though not necessarily convinced, had not yet jettisoned the term when the first edition of this encyclopedia was published in 1979. In 1992 it is not a term so often used, though books like *The World Beyond the Hill: Science Fiction and the Quest for Transcendence* (**1989**) by Alexei and Cory PANSHIN still argue for the primacy of this period as a peak in sf's development.

There is little argument about when the Golden Age began. The term is nearly always used of genre magazine sf (◊ GENRE SF), and it is almost always seen as referring to the period ushered in by John W. CAMPBELL Jr's assumption of the editorship of ASTOUNDING STORIES in Oct 1937. (By 1938 he had altered the title to *Astounding Science-Fiction*.) Within a few years Campbell had managed to take over not only many of the best (and youngest) working writers of the period, such as L. Ron HUBBARD, Clifford D. SIMAK, Jack WILLIAMSON, L. Sprague DE CAMP, Henry KUTTNER and C.L. MOORE (the last three often in his companion magazine UNKNOWN), but to develop such new writers as Lester DEL REY, Eric Frank RUSSELL (who had a couple of stories in *ASF* before Campbell arrived), Theodore STURGEON and especially the big three, Robert A. HEINLEIN, Isaac ASIMOV and A.E. VAN VOGT. These writers dominated genre sf until their younger contemporaries Alfred BESTER, James BLISH, Ray BRADBURY, Arthur C. CLARKE, C.M. KORNBLUTH and Frederik POHL, after sometimes protracted apprenticeships, emerged as new forces in the late 1940s and early 1950s. But, as soon as these new names are evoked, it becomes clear that it is difficult to say in what sense the Golden Age could be said to have stopped in 1946, or anywhere in the 1940s. Certainly Campbell's *ASF* was in the latter 1940s receiving quite high-class competition from STARTLING STORIES, and a few years later from GALAXY SCIENCE FICTION and the MAGAZINE OF FANTASY AND SCIENCE FICTION, and by the 1950s it was coming to be seen as a force for conservatism in magazine sf rather than its spearhead. The "end" of the Golden Age may have had more reality, then, for devotees of *ASF* than for sf readers in general.

Certainly 1938-46 was a period of astonishing activity (among comparatively few writers), the time when most of the themes and motifs of sf were taking their modern shape, which in some cases proved almost definitive and in others continued to be reworked and modified, as is the way of genres. It was also the great age of the PULP MAGAZINES (most of which were dead or transfigured into DIGESTS by early in the 1950s), the period in which genre sf belonged primarily to magazines rather than books, which gave the magazine readers something of a sense of belonging to a kind of secret brotherhood (not a sisterhood: the Golden Age stories were by and large written by men for young male readers.)

A balanced reading of genre sf since Campbell would probably see it as becoming progressively more mature; it would also see (as sf became more popular) much mechanical reworking of the Golden Age themes by hack writers, whose increasing numbers may have partly obscured the steady improvement in the upper echelons of the genre. Certainly there were slack periods, the late 1950s being one such and the late 1970s another, but only with tunnel vision and nostalgia could the claim seriously be made that the period of WWII marked a high point in sf that has never been reached again. Indeed, by the 1980s the Golden Age "classics" of sf, which until then had been reprinted constantly, began to drift quietly from the marketplace as they proved less and less accessible to succeeding generations of readers.

It is interesting to turn to one of the anthologies of the Golden Age period – perhaps *Adventures in Time and Space* (anth **1946**) ed Raymond J. HEALY and Francis MCCOMAS, or the relevant sections of *The Astounding-Analog Reader* (anth in 2 vols **1973**) ed Harry HARRISON and Brian W. ALDISS, or *The Science Fiction Hall of Fame* (anth **1970**) ed Robert SILVERBERG – and see how banal the writing and retrospectively creaky the plot devices even of the supposed classics often seem. Isaac Asimov's "Nightfall" (1941) retains the potency of its original idea, but the working out is laboured; Lester del Rey's "Helen O'Loy" (1938) is sentimental and patronizingly sexist. The soaring ideas of Golden Age sf were all too often clad in an impoverished pulp vocabulary aimed at the lowest common denominator of a mass market. It would not hurt to remember, also, that the Golden Age was an almost purely US phenomenon, restricted to the not very large readership of a tiny handful of ephemeral magazines. This is not to devalue it; but to keep things in proportion we should remember that elsewhere (in the UK, and in the USA outside the magazines) non-genre sf books of real literary quality were being published and had already been published which had nothing to do at all with what Campbell was offering.

But, when all the caveats have been stated – including the almost undeniable counterclaim that sf now is by and large better written than it was then – there is a residue of truth in the Golden Age myth. For older readers, certainly, there has been nothing since then to give quite the same adrenalin charge (not too far removed from the SENSE OF WONDER). It may be a matter of context. Today we *expect* sf to present us with amazing concepts (as it still, sometimes, does), but in the 1940s this stuff seemed (except for unusually sophisticated readers, which the pulps were not aimed at anyway) to spring miraculously from nowhere at all. In the years 1938-46 the wild and yearning imaginations of a handful of genre writers – who were mostly very young, and conceptually very energetic indeed – laid down entire strata of sf motifs which enriched the field greatly. In those years the science component of sf became spectacularly more scientific and the fiction component more assured. It was a quantum jump in quality, perhaps the greatest in the history of the genre, and, in gratitude to that, perhaps the term Golden Age *should* be enshrined.

As, indeed, it has been by the authors of many histories and commentaries on the genre, from James E. GUNN to Donald A. WOLLHEIM: the Golden Age does not lack defenders. [PN]

GOLDEN ARGOSY, THE ◊ *The* ARGOSY.

GOLDIN, STEPHEN (1947-) US writer, married to Kathleen SKY 1962-82. He began publishing sf with "The Girls on USSF 193" for *If* in 1965 and was runner-up for a NEBULA for Best Short Story with "The Last Ghost" (1971). His early novels – his first, *Herds* (1975 Canada), was like its immediate successors written for LASER BOOKS – were stereotyped adventures, and he was better known for an ongoing series of E.E. "Doc" SMITH spin-offs, the **Family D'Alembert** sequence. The first volume, *The Imperial Stars* * (1964 *If*; exp **1976**) was directly based on a Smith story about the members of a large family who spend their lives saving the Galaxy from a variety of threats; subsequent volumes – *Stranglers' Moon* * (**1976**), *The Clockwork Traitor* (**1977**), *Getaway World* * (**1977**), *Appointment at Bloodstar* * (**1978**; vt *The Bloodstar Conspiracy* 1978 UK), *The Purity Plot* * (**1978**), *Planet of Treachery* * (**1982**), *Eclipsing Binaries* * (**1983**), *The Omicron Invasion* * (**1984**) and *Revolt of the Galaxy* * (**1985**) – were derived from the initial premise. Aside from these, his later work is more varied. *The Eternity Brigade* (**1980**) is an interestingly nightmarish vision of warfare among various mercenary soldiers whose personalities have been reincarnated (◊ REINCARNATION). *A World Called Solitude* (**1981**) is a somewhat overburdened drama of identity. The light **Rehumanization of Jad Darcy** sequence, with Mary Mason, begins in *Jade Darcy and the Affair of Honor* (**1988**) at a café called Rix's on an entrepôt planet much like, one supposes, Morocco in 1942; the series continues with *Jade Darcy and the Zen Pirates* (**1990**). SG cannot be called an original force in sf, but he seldom violates his brief of providing well crafted entertainments. He has been editor of SFWA BULLETIN. [JC]

Other works: *Caravan* (**1975** Canada); *Scavenger Hunt* (**1976** Canada) and its sequel, *Finish Line* (**1976** Canada); *Assault on the Gods* (**1977**); *Mindflight* (**1978**); a **Star Trek** novel: *Trek to Madworld* * (**1978**); *And Not Make Dreams Your Master* (**1981**); *The Business of Being a Writer* (**1982**) with Kathleen SKY, nonfiction; the **Parsina Saga**, comprising *Shrine of the Desert Mage* (**1988**), *The Storyteller and the Jann* (**1988**) and *Crystals*

of Air and Water (**1989**), fantasy.

As editor: SG anonymously collaborated with David GERROLD on several 1970s anthologies – *Protostars* (anth **1971**), *Generation: An Anthology of Speculative Fiction* (anth **1972**), *Science Fiction Emphasis 1* (anth **1974**), *Alternities* (anth **1974**) and *Ascents of Wonder* (anth **1977**).

See also: ALIENS; ESP; SPACE OPERA.

GOLDING, LOUIS (1895-1958) UK writer, several of whose popular novels are on Jewish themes. *The Doomington Wanderer* (coll **1934**; vt *This Wanderer* 1935 US; cut in 2 vols vt *The Call of the Hand and Other Stories* 1944 chap UK and *The Vicar of Dunkerly Briggs* 1944 chap UK) contains several romantically couched fantasy tales. *The Pursuer* (**1936**) sets a psychological parable of a man obsessed by his Conradian "shadow" in an ALTERNATE WORLD very similar to our own, while *Honey for the Ghost* (**1949**) tells a similar tale of possession as a ghost story. [JC]

Other works: *The Miracle Boy* (**1927**), a religious fantasy; *Pale Blue Nightgown: A Book of Tales* (coll **1944**), fantasies; *The Frightening Talent* (**1973**).

GOLDING, WILLIAM (GERALD) (1911-) UK writer, awarded the 1983 Nobel Prize for Literature. He wrote a pre-WWII book of *Poems* (coll **1934**), but remained a provincial schoolmaster until the publication of his first and best-known novel, *Lord of the Flies* (**1954**), later filmed twice as LORD OF THE FLIES (1963, 1990), a superficially simple story about a group of schoolchildren trapped on an ISLAND when their plane is shot down while evacuating them from a nuclear HOLOCAUST. Left alone, the boys – who bear the same names as the schoolboy heroes in R.M. Ballantyne's *The Coral Island* (1858) – soon revert (◊ DEVOLUTION) to tribal savagery. Beyond its obvious allegorizing repudiation of its model, the novel constitutes a complex utterance about the darkness of the human condition and the shapes human nature takes when "free" to do so.

WG's second novel, *The Inheritors* (1955), written in part as a reaction to H.G. WELLS's "The Grisly Folk" (1921), could be seen as anthropological sf (◊ ANTHROPOLOGY; ORIGIN OF MAN); it views through the eyes of a Neanderthal the morally ambiguous triumph of Cro-Magnon Man. *Pincher Martin* (1956; vt *The Two Deaths of Pincher Martin* 1957 US) is as much sf as Ambrose BIERCE's "An Occurrence at Owl Creek Bridge", with which it has frequently been compared. A castaway on a tiny rock in the ocean, Pincher seems to be surviving with desperate defiance; but, as the ending makes clear, the rock he clings to is the same shape as a diseased tooth he touches constantly with his tongue, and his "survival" may well be no more than a last flicker of pre-purgatorial consciousness. WG's contribution to *Sometime, Never* (anth 1956) ed anon, a book including also stories by John WYNDHAM and Mervyn PEAKE, is "Envoy Extraordinary", a long tale subsequently made into a play, *The Brass Butterfly* (1957 US; rev 1958 UK), about Alexandrian Greek inventor Phanocles' attempts to get his steam engine, gun, pressure-cooker and printing-press accepted by the Roman emperor, who in refusing these gifts proves philosophically wiser than the inventor. The story also appears in *The Scorpion God* (coll **1971**) along with two fantasies.

WG's relation to sf is as tangential as his relation to the conventional mainstream novel; especially in his early works, he treads the line between allegory and novel with astonishingly fruitful results.   [JC]

About the author: Critical literature on WG is extensive and widely available.

See also: CONCEPTUAL BREAKTHROUGH; DISCOVERY AND INVENTION; HISTORY IN SF; HISTORY OF SF; SOCIOLOGY.

GOLDMAN, STEPHEN H. ◊ James E. GUNN.

GOLDSMITH, CELE (1933-   ) US editor of SF MAGAZINES who in 1956-8 was assistant editor and then managing editor of AMAZING STORIES and FANTASTIC under Paul W. FAIRMAN, becoming editor of both in Dec 1958; she held this position until June 1965, when the magazines were sold and ceased for a time to publish original stories. Under her editorship the quality of both improved markedly; she was prepared to encourage experiment and was particularly sensitive to new writers. Among the authors whose first published stories appeared in her magazines were Thomas M. DISCH, Roger ZELAZNY and Ursula K. LE GUIN; the latter said of CG, in *The Wind's Twelve Quarters* (coll **1975**), that she was "as enterprising and perceptive an editor as the science fiction magazines ever had". CG married in 1964, becoming Cele G. Lalli.   [MJE]

See also: WOMEN SF WRITERS; ZIFF-DAVIS.

GOLDSMITH, HOWARD (1943-   ) US research psychologist and writer whose fiction – including *The Whispering Sea* (**1976**), *The Shadow, and Other Strange Tales* (coll **1977** chap), *Terror by Night, and Other Strange Tales* (coll **1977**) and *Invasion: 2200 A.D.* (**1979**) – was designed for "reluctant readers". With Roger ELWOOD he produced the anthology *Spine-Chillers: Unforgettable Tales of Terror* (anth **1978**).   [JC]

GOLDSTEIN, LISA (1953-   ) US writer who began writing work of genre interest with *The Red Magician* (**1982**), a fantasy based on Hungarian motifs and venues and set during the Holocaust; it won the American Book Award for that year. With considerable intensity, and in a style which treats sf and fantasy material through a MAGIC-REALIST looking-glass, LG has since then consistently submitted her protagonists – who are in any case generally alienated from mainstream life – to deeply alienating venues which are themselves threatened with radical transformation. *The Dream Years* (**1985**) – alternating sequences of which are set in a 1920s Paris succumbing to the tenets of Surrealism, and at the crisis point of the Events of 1968 – is a timeslip romance which conflates the artistic movement for a transformed reality with the later moment in history when it seemed, for an instant, that the world might shift. *A Mask for the General* (**1987**), set in a DYSTOPIAN 21st-century USA, depicts an opposition between the General who rules the land and the mask-makers who tap tribal depths, who create totem visages for their friends and enemies, and who wish to transform the General into one of them, human again, no longer alienated. The alienation suffered by the protagonists of *Tourists* (1984 *IASFM*; much exp **1989**) is superficially more conventional, for the land of Amaz in which they find themselves caught – as emissaries of a USA which represents a version of reality no longer valid in this new world – seems at first glance no more than a typical Middle Eastern backdrop. But the US family's search for a 1000-year-old document of seeming archaeological interest swerves dizzyingly into an attempt to trace a course between two converging topologies of reality, and to survive the clash. Though readable in sf terms, *Tourists* displays much of the same feel for the labyrinth of the Orient that found more fantastic expression in *The Arabian Nightmare* (**1983**) by Robert Irwin (1946-   ). Some of LG's relatively few short stories were assembled in *Daily Voices* (coll **1989**).   [JC]

See also: ARTS; TIME TRAVEL.

GOLEM The medieval Jewish legend of the Golem comprises a set of PROTO-SCIENCE-FICTION stories about the maker and the made. Several well known rabbis and Judaic scholars of the Middle Ages and early Renaissance had Golem stories ascribed to them, the most elaborate cycle being that connected with Rabbi Judah Loew ben Bezalel (1512-1609), the Maharal of Prague, a controversial and admired sage and community leader. "His" version of the Golem, Joseph, is an automaton made from the sand and mud lining the Vltava River. To animate him, the rabbi orders one of his assistants to make a circuit of the figure 7 times, entrusting him with combinations of letters to utter as he does so; subsequently the rabbi and his assistants recite *Genesis* ii.7, which refers to the creation of Man as a single entity, and the Golem comes to "life". This Prague version of the legend contains explicit discussions of the Golem as artificial human being and as human instrument: a being without past or future. Three uniquely human faculties are denied it: inclination, either to good or evil; the soul associated with language; and the power to engender. It is used to inspect the streets of the Prague ghetto.

The tale of the Golem is important to sf not because of any primacy it might claim regarding the concept of an artificial creature but because it is a narrative, and because it centrally concerns the making of the most complex tool imaginable: something (or someone) who looks, and superficially acts, like us. It is a study in how we shape the environment to meet our needs, and how we relate to that changed environment while dead labour assists in the structuring of live labour. It augments Joanna RUSS's curiously neglected suggestion that work is one of the central concerns of sf.

Several earlier tales and fragments of tales, including some Talmudic references, have survived. One significant version of the legend is associated with a rabbi of Chelm near Lublin in Poland; in this variant there is a fear that the creature may grow, and it is destroyed. The Chelm version gave rise to Christian developments of the material into what might be called the Promethean GOTHIC: tales in which a nameless rabbi manages to deactivate the creature, but is himself smothered in its fall.

Of 20th-century responses to the fable, the most famous is probably Gustav MEYRINK's *Der Golem* (**1914**; cut trans Madge Pemberton as *The Golem* **1928** US; full version of trans 1976 US). In *He, She and It* (**1991**; vt *Body of Glass* 1992 UK) Marge PIERCY retells the tale to enforce an analogy between the Golem and CYBORGS. [EMP]

GOLIGORSKI, EDUARDO ◊ LATIN AMERICA.

GOLLANCZ UK publishing house, properly styled Victor Gollancz Ltd, famous (until its sale to the US company Houghton Mifflin in 1990) as one of the last family companies in UK publishing; in 1992 it was taken over by the Cassell group of companies. Its early strength was in political polemic; its main postwar strengths were detective fiction and sf: from the early 1960s to the late 1980s it was the premier UK publisher of sf books in hardcover, both native and US. In the past half decade it has faced greater competition, but it is still (1992) one of the market leaders. Its earlier history as a publisher, with some gripping stuff from the files, is told in *Gollancz: The Story of a Publishing House: 1929-1978* (**1978**) by Sheila Hodges.

Victor Gollancz (1893-1967), the firm's founder in 1928, had always been interested in the fantastic; though he was never to publish any sf by H.G. WELLS, one of his inaugural books was Wells's *The Open Conspiracy* (**1928**), and within a year he was publishing reissues of several works by M.P. SHIEL and a new novel by E.H. VISIAK. In the 1930s came Charles FORT's *Lo!* (**1931**), which flopped badly, the first translation of Franz KAFKA's *Der Prozess* (written 1914-15; **1925**; trans Willa and Edwin Muir as *The Trial* **1937**), sf novels by Murray Constantine (Katharine BURDEKIN), Andrew MARVELL, Joseph O'NEILL, R.C. SHERRIFF, Francis STUART and others, and five novels by Charles WILLIAMS. One of G's most valued authors was George ORWELL, but Victor Gollancz turned down *Animal Farm* (**1945**) when it was submitted to him in 1944, seeing its anti-Stalinism as inappropriate at a time when Russia, the UK's ally, was suffering during the war. Later he also rejected Orwell's *Nineteen Eighty-four* (**1949**).

Though this was an unpromising beginning to the postwar period, G did publish a number of good sf titles in the 1950s, both non-genre and GENRE SF, the latter including a 1954 edition of Theodore STURGEON's *More than Human* (**1953**); none, however, was labelled as "science fiction". This term and the sf list proper (20 or so books a year) were introduced by Hilary Rubinstein, Victor Gollancz's nephew, after Gollancz had in 1961 published Kingsley AMIS's study

of sf, *New Maps of Hell* (**1960** US). Most of the early big names were US: Hal CLEMENT, Harry HARRISON, Robert A. HEINLEIN, Frederik POHL, Robert SHECKLEY, Clifford D. SIMAK and others. The first important UK writer to be added was J.G. BALLARD, with *The Drowned World* (**1962**). For the next two decades Gollancz's plain yellow jackets with black typography came to seem almost synonymous with UK-published hardcover sf. (Since the mid-1980s pictorial jackets have been phased in for most of the major sf and fantasy authors.) Other important UK writers joining Gollancz were Arthur C. CLARKE, Richard COWPER, Keith ROBERTS, Bob SHAW and Ian WATSON, with later additions including Robert P. HOLDSTOCK, Paul J. MCAULEY, Phillip MANN and Terry PRATCHETT, several of whom made their débuts with Gollancz. Subsequent US authors included Philip K. DICK, William GIBSON, Ursula K. LE GUIN and Robert SILVERBERG. The children's list included Peter DICKINSON. After Rubinstein left in 1963, John Bush took over the list until the early 1980s, when Malcolm EDWARDS took over (spending larger sums on books than Gollancz had previously allowed), being followed by Richard Evans in 1989. Gollancz sf editors have normally held very senior positions in the company, sf providing a major contribution to the company's profit. [PN]

GOOCH, STAN [r] ◊ Christopher EVANS.

GOODCHILD, GEORGE (1885-1969) UK thriller and adventure writer and playwright. His first sf novel, *The Eye of Abu* (**1927**) as by Alan Dare, was an Atlantean (◊ ATLANTIS) LOST-WORLD novel relating the discovery of the Fountain of Youth. As GG he followed this with *The Monster of Grammont* (**1927**), marginally sf, *The Emperor of Hallelujah Island* (**1930**), about a kingdom of criminals, *A Message from Space* (**1931**) and *Doctor Zil's Experiment* (**1953**), in which survivors of a world-destroying DISASTER undergo various tribulations. [JE/BS]

GORDON, BERT I. ◊ *The* AMAZING COLOSSAL MAN; FOOD OF THE GODS.

GORDON, DAVID [s] ◊ Randall GARRETT.

GORDON, DONALD ◊ Ian CAMERON.

GORDON, MILLARD VERNE [s] ◊ Donald A. WOLLHEIM.

GORDON, NEIL ◊ A.G. MacDONELL.

GORDON, REX Most frequently used pseudonym of UK writer S(tanley) B(ennett) Hough (1917-) for his sf work, although under his own name he has published *Mission in Guemo* (**1953**), the borderline-sf thriller *Extinction Bomber* (**1956**) and *Beyond the Eleventh Hour* (**1961**), a story of nuclear HOLOCAUST in which all the major nations of the world except the UK and India destroy themselves. As RG, he began publishing sf with *Utopia 239* (**1955**), whose protagonists escape a nuclear holocaust by TIME TRAVEL into the future, where a sexually liberated UTOPIA uses its high technology to survive the consequences of the final war. *No Man Friday* (**1956**; vt *First on Mars* 1957 US), a ROBINSONADE which is perhaps RG's strongest book, retells Crusoe's adventures on MARS, in quietly convincing terms, though the science is sometimes shaky; the film ROBINSON CRUSOE ON MARS (**1964**) does not credit RG, though the storyline bears notable resemblances. *First to the Stars* (**1959** US; vt *The Worlds of Eclos* 1961 UK) is thematically similar: a crash-landed man and woman try to survive and breed without any cultural aids at all. *First Through Time* (**1962** US; vt *The Time Factor* 1964 UK) is a time-travel thriller that asks most of the standard questions about predestination. Throughout his career RG showed a strong grasp of human motivation that jarred against a rather superficial use of sf themes and scientific knowledge in general; his underlying pessimism about humanity has seemed as a consequence rather underargued. [JC]

Other works: *Utopia Minus X* (**1966** US; vt *The Paw of God* 1967 UK); *The Yellow Fraction* (**1969** US); *Creative Writing* (nd but *c*1983 chap) as by S.B. Hough, nonfiction.

GORDON, RICHARD A. [s] ◊ Stuart GORDON.

GORDON, SPIKE [s] ◊ John Russell FEARN.

GORDON, STUART Pseudonym of Scottish writer Richard Gordon (1947-   ), who also writes as Alex R. Stuart and published his first sf story – "A Light in the Sky" for *NW* in 1965 – as Richard A. Gordon. His first sf novel, *Time Story* (**1972**), describes a criminal's attempt to flee retribution via TIME TRAVEL. In his **Eyes** books – *One-Eye* (**1973** US), *Two-Eyes* (**1974** US) and *Three-Eyes* (**1975** US), assembled as *The Eyes Trilogy* (omni **1978**) – the MUTANT One-Eye triggers the forces of chaos in an apocalyptic post-HOLOCAUST land where humanity fights a losing battle against genetic decay; in increasingly elaborated prose (SG's main fault as a writer is an inadequate control over imagery) the trilogy proceeds to a complex self-confrontation of mankind. *Smile on the Void: The Mythhistory of Ralph M'Botu Kitaj* (**1981** US) ponderously guys late-20th-century susceptibilities in the "biography" of an almost certainly fake MESSIAH. *Fire in the Abyss* (**1983** US), though terribly overcrowded, impressively plants the Elizabethan sailor Sir Humphrey Gilbert (1537-1583) via time travel into an apocalyptically dissolving present-day. The **Watchers** trilogy – *Archon* (**1987**), *The Hidden World* (**1988**) and *The Mask* (**1988**) – is another extremely complex time-travel fantasy, in the opposite direction, as 20th-century personal traumas intersect, in medieval and Reformation France, with the cultural ills of the present and the NEAR FUTURE. SG's language has baroque vigour and his plots are increasingly inventive; he lacks mainly a capacity to moderate and therefore give verisimilitude to the rush of notions. [JC]

Other works: *Suaine & The Crow God* (**1975**).

As Alex R. Stuart: Several novels, of which *The Outlaws* (**1972**), *The Devil's Rider* (**1973**) and *The Bike from Hell* (**1973**) have fantasy/sf components.

GORER, GEOFFREY (EDGAR) (1905-1985) UK anthropologist and writer whose *Nobody Talks Politics* (**1936**) is a SATIRE on UK POLITICS of the 1930s as seen through the eyes of a young man woken from a 10-year trance. Its Epilogue is set in the NEAR FUTURE. [JC]

GORGO Film (1960). King Bros/MGM. Dir Eugène Lourié, starring Bill Travers, William Sylvester, Vincent Winter. Screenplay John Loring, Daniel Hyatt, based on a story by Lourié and Hyatt. 78 mins. Colour.

A prehistoric reptile is captured off a small island in the Irish Sea, taken to London and put on show. But the 65ft (20m) creature turns out to be a mere infant, as everyone discovers when its 150ft (45m) mother comes to collect it, demolishing bits of London in the process. We are allowed to sympathize with the monsters and cheer their escape. Good use is made of locations, and there are interesting special effects by Tom Howard. The monsters are achieved by the cheap man-in-a-suit technique, but are effective nonetheless. Lourié had once worked as an art director for Jean Renoir, and his latter-day reputation as director of sea-going MONSTER MOVIES was a sad come-down (◊ *The* BEAST FROM 20,000 FATHOMS; BEHEMOTH, THE SEA MONSTER), but *G* is atmospheric and crisply made. The novelization, with wholly irrelevant soft-core pornographic additions, is *Gorgo* * (**1960**) by Carter BINGHAM. [JB/PN]

GORODISCHER, ANGÉLICA [r] ◊ LATIN AMERICA.

GOTHIC SF In current usage a "Gothic" is a romantic novel which has a strong element of the mysterious or the supernatural and which usually features the persecution of a woman in an isolated locale; but this restricted and specialized use of the word has nothing to do with sf. The term "Gothic" entered critical terminology with the publication of *The Castle of Otranto* (**1765**), subtitled "A Gothic Story", by Horace Walpole (1717-1797). As in architecture, the word originally referred to a medieval style. Although the Middle Ages had for much of the 18th century been thought of as barbaric, a nostalgia had now developed for the romantic splendours of an idealized Middle Ages that never existed. Gothic novels in imitation of Walpole's ghostly tale became quite common as the century drew to a close; indeed their popularity was closely allied to the growth of Romantic literature generally.

The Gothic may be seen as a reaction to the emphasis on reason which prevailed in the Enlightenment, the intellectual world of the 18th century. In a world ruled by Order, where Isaac Newton (1642-1727) had explained the mechanics of the Solar System, Carolus Linnaeus (1707-1778) had shown how plants and animals could be logically classified, Adam Smith (1723-1790) had written of the apparently immutable laws of ECONOMICS, and sermons in church regularly pictured God as a kind of master watchmaker who had wound the Universe up and left it to tick like a perfectly regulated mechanism, some room needed to be left for mystery, the marvellous, the evil, the inexplicable. The movement was probably given impetus at the beginning of the 19th century by science itself becoming remystified

511 _____ GOTHIC SF

through all the work being done on the strange forces of electromagnetism, and also by a crumbling social stability, as signalled by many political revolutions across the Western World.

Such is the background against which Mary SHELLEY's *Frankenstein* (**1818**; rev 1831) should be read. With this book, along with the contemporary works of E.T.A. HOFFMANN and a little later Edgar Allan POE, the use of science in fiction was becoming assimilated into a literary movement which emphasized mystery over knowledge, and the dangers of Man trespassing in a territory rightfully God's. The linking of science with the Gothic may have been partly a historical accident, and the balance was soon to be partly rectified by the sometimes laboured common sense of Jules VERNE (even he produced a Gothic hero, in Captain Nemo), but it certainly had repercussions in sf which have by no means died away. Brian W. ALDISS, in his critical work *Billion Year Spree* (**1973**; rev with David WINGROVE as *Trillion Year Spree* 1986), argues that sf "is characteristically cast in the Gothic or post-Gothic mould". That may be putting it too strongly, but Aldiss's view is certainly a useful antidote to the commoner views that sf is a literature either of technology or of UTOPIAS and anti-utopias.

Certainly from Mary Shelley's day to now, much sf has been devoted to secrets, to inexplicable violence and wildness lurking beneath the veneer of civilization and to the ALIEN and the monstrous bursting in on us from the outside; Gothic sf emphasizes danger, and attacks the complacency of those of us who imagine the world to be well lit and comfortable while ignoring that outside all is darkness. Gothic sf characteristically clothes these fears in quasiscientific talk, but in spirit it is quite opposed to the outlook of the SCIENTIST. The prototype is perhaps Robert Louis STEVENSON's *Strange Case of Dr Jekyll and Mr Hyde* (**1886**) – which, in its story of a respectable doctor whose *alter ego* is a brutish sensualist and a living monument to the reality of Original Sin, can be read as an allegory of the violent subconscious struggling with the conscious mind – for the archetypal Gothic story is the tale of the Thing in the Cellar, in which an everyday world of surface conceals the menacing depths (and subtexts). Other sf writers of the 19th century who worked in the Gothic mode were Bulwer LYTTON, Ambrose BIERCE and Arthur MACHEN.

In the 20th century, the Gothic mode was largely hived off into the genre of occult/horror, but it never lost its kinship with sf. WEIRD TALES was the archetypally Gothic PULP MAGAZINE, and several of its authors wrote sf too. H.P. LOVECRAFT, of course, is as pure an instance of the Gothic writer as can be found in this century, but some of the same qualities can be found in writers who were much more closely associated with sf than Lovecraft ever was. About two-thirds of all sf films (◊ CINEMA), especially MONSTER MOVIES, are pure Gothic. PARANOIA in sf nearly always falls into the Gothic mode.

The Gothic idea of the Promethean or Faustian mad scientist (◊ CONCEPTUAL BREAKTHROUGH; SCIENTISTS) punished for assuming the creative powers belonging to the gods or God (sometimes for creating artificial life without a soul) was central to sf early in this century, as in the films ALRAUNE (1928) and FRANKENSTEIN (1931). Other sf variants of Gothic images are the renegade ROBOT (along with all ghost-in-the-machine stories), most Luddite stories, most stories of manipulation by beings who may be GODS AND DEMONS, nearly all stories rationalizing SUPERNATURAL CREATURES, most stories about ambiguous ALIEN artefacts; indeed, to put it more widely still, most stories in which the Universe proves unamenable to rational (or "cognitive") understanding.

It is so easy to find Gothic elements in even the most celebrated writers of sf that there is little point in listing actual books containing them. Sf writers whose work is consistently Gothic are, among many others: John BLACKBURN, James P. BLAYLOCK, Ray BRADBURY, S. Guy ENDORE, Robert P. HOLDSTOCK, K.W. JETER, Stephen KING, Nigel KNEALE, Dean R. KOONTZ, Richard MATHESON, Kim NEWMAN, Tim POWERS, Maurice RENARD, Sax ROHMER, Dan SIMMONS, Curt SIODMAK, Lisa TUTTLE and Chelsea Quinn YARBRO; it is no coincidence that nearly all of these have written HORROR fiction as well. But there are strong Gothic elements in other sf writers whose work is considered less borderline. These include – again, among a hundred others – Brian W. Aldiss, Alfred BESTER, James BLISH, Algis BUDRYS, Richard COWPER, Samuel R. DELANY, Philip K. DICK, Thomas M. DISCH, Philip José FARMER, William GIBSON, George R.R. MARTIN, Michael MOORCOCK, Geoff RYMAN, Fred SABERHAGEN, Hilbert SCHENCK, Lucius SHEPARD, Lew SHINER, Michael SWANWICK, Sheri S. TEPPER, Jack VANCE, Howard WALDROP, Gene WOLFE, John WYNDHAM and Roger ZELAZNY. If the case for the prevalence of Gothic sf is correct, then we must see it as so deeply engrained that it cannot be considered a mere sport or mutant form of the genre.

There has always been a tension in sf between the Classical desire for order and understanding – for the Universe that can be *known* – and the Romantic desire (which fits the observable facts to date) that the Universe should continue to surprise us, hold secrets and malignities. This latter desire (or fear, or both) is the Gothic, and its coexistence with the Classical or cognitive, in most major sf writers of our century, is not a paradox; the place where the two forces meet (Classical and Romantic, cognitive and Gothic) might almost be described as the central place where sf happens, the seeding-ground for its fertility. If this is the case, then Brian Aldiss's above-noted comment (◊ DEFINITIONS OF SF) is not as eccentric as some have found it; moreover, those definitions that see sf as exclusively cognitive (like Darko SUVIN's) are missing the point; they are prescriptive, not descriptive. Sf remains a Romance literature. Its vaunted SENSE OF WONDER arises as much from its Gothic as from its scientific elements, and will continue to do so as long as the Thing in the Cellar keeps lashing its tail.   [PN]

See also: FANTASY; HISTORY OF SF.

GOTLIEB, PHYLLIS (FAY) (1926-   ) Canadian writer probably best known for her POETRY. She took an MA with the University of Toronto in English language and literature, and married a professor of computer science, whom she credits for assistance on her second sf novel. She began publishing sf with "A Grain of Manhood" for *Fantastic* in 1959 and gained considerable praise for her first novel, *Sunburst* (**1964** US), which treats feelingly of the growth of a connected group of MUTANT children, of their harrowing difficulties, of the gestalt concord they arrive at, and of their coming to (a somewhat overplotted) accord with the surrounding world. Complexities of kinship and identity also pervade her **Sven Dahlgren** books – *O Master Caliban!* (**1976** US) and *Heart of Red Iron* (**1989** US) – which take place on a planet set aside for environmental experiments. In the first the young four-armed Dahlgren must confront and defeat the sentient ROBOTS which have seized power from his scientist father; in the second he must calibrate the needs of various ALIEN races and come to terms with his own humanity. PG's stories – some of the best are assembled in *Son of the Morning and Other Stories* (coll **1983** US) – also tend to investigate questions of human nature through sf tropes, like PSI POWERS, that are congenial to that sort of exploration. A second series, the **Starcats** books – *A Judgement of Dragons* (**1980** US), *Emperor, Swords, Pentacles* (**1982** US) and *The Kingdom of the Cats* (**1985** US) – features interstellar travel and other sf trappings attuned to SCIENCE FANTASY needs. With Douglas BARBOUR she edited *Tesseracts²* (anth **1987**), a series – #1 ed Judith MERRIL – designed to showcase Canadian sf.   [JC]

See also: CANADA.

GOTSCHALK, FELIX C. (1929-   ) US writer and psychologist who began publishing sf with "Outer Concentric" and "The Examination" for *New Dimensions 4* (anth **1974**) ed Robert SILVERBERG. In a relatively short time he established a reputation as an author of high linguistic energy whose stories emoted a ruthless savvy about the future. Many of his tales are narrated through stunning linguistic displays of the emotional and physiological ways of being that humans display in isolation and in their relations to the social world; these ways of being are constantly articulated by the protagonists in a flow of brilliant jargon, with the result that existence and the LINGUISTIC perception of existence become identical. The effect is exhilarating and also rather terrifying. FCG's first novel, *Growing Up in Tier 3000* (**1975**), is set in a world very similar to that of many of the tales, and deploys a similarly searching sense of the surface of events and of identities, though its plot moves with some difficulty: in an energy-quarantined, savagely competitive, complexly automated DYSTOPIAN future society, young children show their readiness to take over from their elders (in a *reductio ad absurdum* of the Whorfian hypothesis that language structure deter-

mines our conceptualization of the world) by understanding the languages necessary for survival in the hyperkinetic new. At least two further novels have been written and await publication; but the aggressive ingenuity of his style, and the oddly high-strung gallantry of his attitude to the futures in store for the human race – that they are to be endured with grace, but never "won" – make his work unlikely to reach a wide market.   [JC]

See also: CITIES; FABULATION; TABOOS.

GOTTESMAN, S.D. Pseudonym used on magazine stories by C.M. KORNBLUTH 1940-42, once solo, 5 times with Frederik POHL, and twice with both Pohl and Robert A.W. LOWNDES.   [PN]

GOTTLIEB, HINKO (1886-1948) Yugoslav writer, editor and lawyer whose sf novel, *The Key to the Great Gate* (trans Fred Bolman and Ruth Morris from the Serbo-Croat **1947** US), was first composed in an Italian concentration camp (the manuscript was destroyed and had to be reconstructed later). An imprisoned SCIENTIST, having learned how to expand and contract the Einsteinian spacetime continuum, dazzles and befuddles his Nazi guards, gradually becoming an effective symbol of human dignity and the freedom of the spirit. The book is also funny.   [JC]

GOULART, RON(ALD JOSEPH) (1933-   ) US writer, born in California, where he lived until the late 1960s and which he has made the setting (whether or not literally so) for much of his sf. After graduation he worked in an advertising agency; he has put on record the influence of this experience on the forming of his concise, polished style. He published his first sf, "Letters to the Editor", in *FSF* in 1952, and wrote many stories before the appearance of his first sf novel, *The Sword Swallower* (**1968**), which features the **Chameleon Corps** of shapeshifting agents; the book – like much of his ensuing work – is set in a SPACE-OPERA venue called the **Barnum System** which much resembles Southern California: urbanized, helter-skelter, crazed and balkanized, the planets of this system, where the Corps originates, are populated in large part by traditional comic stereotypes or humours, deftly drawn. Again like many of its successors, the novel features a gangly detective on the trail of a complex crime (◊ CRIME AND PUNISHMENT); his need to search out clues and suspects takes him (conveniently) through a wide spectrum of scenes and characters. Similarities of plot and setting (and numerous cross-references) dog any anatomizer of series in the RG universe, but other books specifically connected to the Barnum System include *The Fire-Eater* (**1970**), *Death Cell* (**1971**), *The Chamelon Corps and Other Shape Changers* (coll **1972**), *Plunder* (**1972**), *Shaggy Planet* (**1973**), *Flux* (**1974**), *Spacehawk, Inc.* (**1974**), *A Whiff of Madness* (**1976**), *The Wicked Cyborg* (**1978**), *Daredevils, Ltd* (**1987**), *Starpirate's Brain* (**1987**) and *Everybody Comes to Cosmo's* (**1988**); the **Star Hawk** sequence of novels – *Empire 99* (**1980**) and *The Cyborg King* (**1981**), based on the COMIC strip illustrated by Gil Kane – are also set in Barnum. Along with the remarkable *After Things Fell Apart* (1970), these books share a swiftness of telling, a constant hilariousness and a cogency; elsewhere, jokes sometimes seem to guide the storylines, which can be flimsy.

Much of RG's work is, in fact, journeyman, though even in the most desultory tale his smooth dialogue-driven style is always recognizable. In the mid-1970s and 1980s he wrote under various pseudonyms (including the house names Kenneth ROBESON and Con Steffanson, as well as personal pseudonyms like Chad Calhoun, R.T. Edwards, Ian R. Jamieson, Josephine Kains, Jillian Kearny, Howard Lee, Zeke Masters, Frank S. Shawn and Joseph Silva) a large number of novelizations and other routine work (see listing below for titles of genre interest). As RG, his **Vampirella** series – *Bloodstalk* * (1975), *On Alien Wings* * (1975), *Deadwalk* * (1976), *Blood Wedding* * (1976), *Deathgame* * (1976) and *Snakegod* * (1976) – put a character derived from comic books into thin prose. The **Wild Talents** sequence, which includes *A Talent for the Invisible* (1973) and *Hello, Lemuria, Hello* (1979), and the **Gypsy** sequence about an identity-quest, which includes *Quest of the Gypsy* (1976) and *Eye of the Vulture* (1977), similarly lacked their author's full attention.

A darker, sharper, more attentive aspect of the RG vision of California-as-Barnum can be seen in those of his novels – *Wildsmith* (1972), among others – which feature the highly humanized, eccentric, wilful ROBOTS which are perhaps his most enduring creation. Quite remarkably comic in their deadpan obsessiveness and pernickety sang-froid, they serve also as genuinely effective icons of a time – the NEAR FUTURE – and a place – either Southern California itself or the world which it portends – caught in the throes of convulsive change.

The slightness of RG's plotting does at times make his satirical intent difficult to perceive; an underlying saliency can be detected more clearly, perhaps, in collections like *What's Become of Screwloose? and Other Inquiries* (coll 1971), *Broke Down Engine and Other Troubles with Machines* (coll 1971), *Nutzenbolts and More Troubles with Machines* (coll 1975) and *Skyrocket Steele Conquers the Universe and Other Media Tales* (coll 1990) – the last being connected with the novel *Skyrocket Steele* (1980). *Odd Job No. 101 and Other Future Crimes and Intrigues* (coll 1975), *Calling Dr Patchwork* (1978), *Big Bang* (1982) and *Brainz, Inc.* (1985) make up the **Odd Jobs** sequence, whose interest diminishes with extension.

Though he is prolific and acute, it can still be said of RG that his dark wit and adroit handling of plot and theme have not yet been directed to a project of a scope sufficient to give those talents full play. [JC]
Other works: *Gadget Man* (1971); *Clockwork's Pirates* (1971 dos); *Ghost Breaker* (coll 1971 dos); *Hawkshaw* (1972); *The Tin Angel* (1973), later assembled with *Flux* as *Flux and The Tin Angel* (omni 1978 UK); *Shaggy Planet* (1973); *When the Waker Sleeps* (1975); *The Hellhound Project* (1975); *The Enormous Hourglass*

(1976); *Challengers of the Unknown* * (1977); *Crackpot* (1977); *The Emperor of the Last Days* (1977); *The Panchronicon Plot* (1977); *Nemo* (1977); *Capricorn One* * (1978) (◊ CAPRICORN ONE); *Dr Scofflaw* (1979 dos); *Hail Hibbler* (1980); *The Robot in the Closet* (1981); *Brinkman* (1981); *Upside Downside* (1982); 3 **Battlestar Galactica** novels, all with Glen A. LARSON, *Greetings from Earth* * (1983), *Experiment in Terra* * (1984) and *The Long Patrol* * (1984); *Hellquad* (1984); *The Prisoner of Blackwood Castle* (1984); *Suicide, Inc.* (1985); *Galaxy Jane* (1986); *The Curse of the Obelisk* (1987); *The Tijuana Bible* (1989). The introduction to William SHATNER's extremely Goulart-like *TekWar* (1989) thanks RG for his help; this book and its two sequels, *TekLords* (1991) and *TekLab* (1991), have been attributed to RG.

As Josephine Kains: *The Devil Mask Mystery* (1978); *The Curse of the Golden Skull* (1978); *The Green Lama Mystery* (1979); *The Whispering Cat Mystery* (1979); *The Witch's Tower Mystery* (1979); *The Laughing Dragon Mystery* (1980).

As Howard Lee: Two **Kung Fu** novels: *Chains* (1973) and *Superstition* (1973).

As Frank S. Shawn: Books in the **Phantom** series: *The Veiled Lady* * (1973); *The Golden Circle* * (1973); *The Mystery of the Sea Horse* * (1973); *The Hydra Monster* * (1973); *The Goggle-Eyed Pirates* * (1974); *The Swamp Rats* * (1974).

As Kenneth Robeson (house name): Books in the **The Avenger** series: *The Man from Atlantis* * (1974); *Red Moon* * (1974); *The Purple Zombie* * (1974); *Dr Time* * (1974); *The Nightwitch Devil* * (1974); *Black Chariots* * (1974); *The Cartoon Crimes* * (1974); *The Death Machine* * (1974); *The Blood Countess* * (1975); *The Glass Man* * (1975); *The Iron Skull* * (1975); *Demon Island* * (1975).

As Con Steffanson (house name): Books in the **Flash Gordon** series: *The Lion Men of Mongo* * (1974); *The Plague of Sound* * (1974); *The Space Circus* * (1974).

As Joseph Silva: *The Island of Dr Moreau* * (1977) (◊ *The* ISLAND OF DR MOREAU); *Stalker from the Stars* * (1977) with Lein Wein and Mary Wolfman; *Holocaust for Hire* * (1979), a **Captain America** novel. The pseudonym plays on the name of one of RG's many private eyes, Jose Silvera.

As editor: *The Hardboiled Dicks* (anth 1965); *Lineup Tough Guys* (anth 1966); *The Great British Detective* (1982); *The Encyclopedia of American Comics* (1990), for which he also wrote about half the entries.

Nonfiction: *The Assault on Childhood* (1972); *Cheap Thrills: An Informal History of the Pulp Magazines* (1972); *An American Family* (1973); *The Adventurous Decade: Comic Strips in the Thirties* (1976); *Focus on Jack Cole* (1986 chap); *The Great Comic Book Artists* (1986) and *The Great Comic Book Artists Volume 2* (1988); *Ron Goulart's Great History of Comic Books* (1986); *The Dime Detectives* (1988).

See also: HUMOUR; MEDIA LANDSCAPE; ROBERT HALE LIMITED; SATIRE; TIME TRAVEL.

GOULD, ALAN [s] ◊ Michael A. BANKS.

GOULD, F(RANCIS) CARRUTHERS (1844-1925) UK illustrator and writer, creator of a large number of sharply satirical political cartoons in the decades before WWI. *"Who Killed Cock Robin?", and Other Stories for Children Young and Old* (coll **1896**) assembled various parodic animal fables, among which "The Great Beetle War" comes closest to sf. *Explorations in the Sit-tee Desert, Being a Comic Account of the Supposed Discovery of the Ruins of the London Stock Exchange some 2000 Years Hence* (**1899** chap) is a surprisingly effective and pointed SATIRE written from a post-HOLOCAUST viewpoint. [JC]

GOULD, F(REDERICK) J(AMES) (1855-1938) UK writer of numerous works in which he espoused an agnostic philosophy. His sf novel, *The Agnostic Island* (**1891**), exposes some Christian missionaries to a society which threatens their beliefs. [JC]

GOVE, PHILIP BABCOCK (1902-?   ) US academic, author of *The Imaginary Voyage in Prose Fiction: A History of its Criticism and a Guide for its Study, with an Annotated Check List of 215 Imaginary Voyages from 1700 to 1800* (**1941**; reissued by ARNO PRESS 1975). Though in no sense a book about sf *per se*, it is one of the most important and reliable tools for the researcher into 18th-century FANTASTIC VOYAGES, about which few books have been written. [PN]

See also: CRITICAL AND HISTORICAL WORKS ABOUT SF.

GOWLAND, JOHN STAFFORD (1898-?   ) UK writer whose sf novel, *Beyond Mars* (**1956**), treats, perhaps rather primitively, space travel to the Moon and beyond by use of ANTIGRAVITY. [JC]

GRABIEN, DEBORAH (?   -   ) UK writer. Her first novel, *Woman of Fire* (**1988**; vt *Eyes in the Fire* 1989 US), is fantasy. Her second, the post-HOLOCAUST *Plainsong* (**1990** US), is an unsentimental PASTORAL tale about the arrival of a new Messiah in a plague-devastated land. [JC]

GRAEME, BRUCE [r] ◊ Anthony ARMSTRONG.

GRAHAM, DAVID [r] ◊ ROBERT HALE LIMITED.

GRAHAM, J(OHN) M(ICHAEL) [r] ◊ ROBERT HALE LIMITED.

GRAHAM, P(ETER) ANDERSON (?   -1925) UK writer on rural themes whose post-HOLOCAUST novel, *The Collapse of Homo Sapiens* (**1923**), written in the apocalypse-obsessed aftermath of WWI, identifies the fall of mankind with the defeat of the UK by an alliance of coloured powers, which themselves soon disintegrate, leaving the world to shrink and degenerate. The traveller who is moved through time to witness this disaster puts much of the blame for the UK's unreadiness upon trade-union nihilists. [JC]

GRAHAM, ROBERT ◊ Joe HALDEMAN.

GRAHAM, ROGER PHILLIPS [r] ◊ Rog PHILLIPS.

GRAHAM, TOM ◊ Sinclair LEWIS.

GRAHAME-WHITE, CLAUDE (1879-1959) UK author of two sf juveniles with Harry HARPER (*whom see for details*): *The Air-King's Treasure* (**1913**) and *The Invisible War-Plane: A Tale of Air Adventure in the Great Campaign* (**1915**). [JC]

GRANT, ANTHONY ◊ ROBERT HALE LIMITED.

GRANT, CHARLES L. (1942-   ) US writer who has restricted himself since the late 1970s almost exclu-

sively to horror and fantasy fiction (see listing below), mainly under his own name (sometimes in the form C.L. Grant), though he has written books as by Felicia Andrews, Steven Charles, Lionel Fenn and Geoffrey Marsh. He began publishing work of genre interest with "The House of Evil" for *FSF* in 1968, but really became active only after the mid-1970s with the release of his first novels, the **Parric** family series of post-HOLOCAUST tales: *The Shadow of Alpha* (**1976**), *Ascension* (**1977**) and *Legion* (**1979**). Set in a balkanized USA ravaged by a Plague Wind and beset with petty dictators and crazed ANDROIDS, all three novels – they form part of a much longer, uncompleted sequence – are told in a somewhat heated style possibly derived from the example of Samuel R. DELANY, and perhaps more suitably applied, as CLG has seemingly decided, to other genres. Further novels containing sf elements include *The Ravens of the Moon* (**1979**), but the precepts of horror fiction are generally dominant. Of his horror, the best known titles fit into the **Oxrun Station** sequence. He has edited two notable series – **Shadows** and two of the **Night Visions** anthologies – and a useful manual, *Writing and Selling Science Fiction* (anth **1976**). His "A Glow of Candles, a Unicorn's Eye" won the 1978 Best Novelette NEBULA. [JC]

Fantasy and horror titles:

Oxrun Station: *The Hour of the Oxrun Dead* (**1977**); *The Sound of Midnight* (**1978**); *The Last Call of Mourning* (**1979**); *The Grave* (**1981**); *The Bloodwind* (**1982**); a 19th-century trilogy internal to the Oxrun sequence and comprising *The Soft Whisper of the Dead* (**1982**), *The Dark Cry of the Moon* (**1986**) and *The Long Night of the Grave* (**1986**); *Nightmare Seasons* (fixup **1982**); *The Orchard* (**1986**); *Dialing the Wind* (**1989**).

Singletons: *A Quiet Night of Fear* (**1981**); *Tales from the Nightside* (coll **1981**); *A Glow of Candles and Other Stories* (coll **1981**); *The Nestling* (**1982**); *Night Songs* (**1984**); *The Teaparty* (**1985**); *The Pet* (**1986**); *For Fear of the Night* (**1988**); *In a Dark Dream* (**1989**); *Stunts* (**1990**); *Fire Mask* (**1991**); *Something Stirs* (**1991**).

As Felicia Andrews: *Mountainwitch* (**1980**).

As Steven Charles: The **Private Academy** sequence of sf/horror novels for a young-adult audience, comprising *Nightmare Session* (**1986**), *Academy of Terror* (**1986**), *Witch's Eye* (**1986**), *Skeleton Key* (**1986**), *The Enemy Within* (**1987**) and *The Last Alien* (**1987**).

As Lionel Fenn: The **Quest for the White Duck** sequence of comic fantasies, comprising *Blood River Down* (**1986**), *Web of Defeat* (**1987**), *Agnes Day* (**1987**) and *The Seven Spears of the W'dch'ck* (**1988**); the **Kent Montana** series of comic sf tales, which invoke Hollywood icons through the adventures of a failed actor, comprising *Kent Montana and the Really Ugly Thing from Mars* (**1990**), *Kent Montana and the Reasonably Invisible Man* (**1991**) and *Kent Montana and the Once and Future Thing* (**1991**).

As Geoffrey Marsh: The **Lincoln Blackthorne** thrillers, *The King of Satan's Eyes* (**1984**), *The Tale of the Arabian Knight* (**1986**), *The Patch of the Odin Soldier* (**1987**) and *The Fangs of the Hooded Demon* (**1988**).

As editor (series): The **Shadows** anthologies, comprising *Shadows* (anth **1978**; vt *Shadows II* 1987 UK), #2 (anth **1979**), #3 (anth **1980**), #4 (anth **1981**; vt *Shadows* 1987 UK), #5 (anth **1982**), #6 (anth **1983**), #7 (anth **1984**), #8 (anth **1985**), #9 (anth **1986**) and #10 (anth **1987**), the entire series being showcased in *The Best of Shadows* (anth **1988**) and *Final Shadows* (anth **1991**); of the **Night Visions** anthologies, *Night Visions 2* (anth **1985**; vt *Night Visions: Dead Image* 1987; vt *Night Terrors* 1989 UK) and *Night Visions 4* (anth **1987**; vt *Night Fears* 1989 UK) uncredited for the UK versions; the **Greystone Bay** anthologies, comprising *The First Chronicles of Greystone Bay* * (anth **1985**), *Doom City* * (anth **1987**) and *The SeaHarp Hotel* * (anth **1990**).

As editor (singletons): *Nightmares* (anth **1979**); *Horrors* (anth **1981**); *Terrors* (anth **1983**); *The Dodd, Mead Gallery of Horror* (anth **1983**); *Midnight* (anth **1985**); *After Midnight* (anth **1986**).

GRANT, DAVID ◊ Craig THOMAS.

GRANT, JOHN ◊ Paul BARNETT.

GRANT, MARK ◊ David F. BISCHOFF.

GRANT, MAXWELL STREET & SMITH house name under which Walter B. GIBSON (*whom see for details*) wrote some 300 novels, usually about **The Shadow**. He was followed by Dennis LYNDS (*whom also see*). [JC]

GRANT, RICHARD (1952-   ) US writer; he lives with Elizabeth HAND. RG began writing work of genre interest with "Drode's Equations" for *New Dimensions 12* (anth **1981**) ed Marta RANDALL, and came to rapid prominence with three novels of mixed sf/fantasy provenance, set in the same post-HOLOCAUST land, almost certainly the USA, but transfigured by time and events. The first, *Saraband of Lost Time* (**1985**), is set much the deepest into this venue, so far into the future that the rather shambling plot mainly serves the PLANETARY-ROMANCE function of guiding the reader through the world, whose contours have reminded some critics of M. John HARRISON's **Viriconium**. The rich array of protagonists featured in *Rumours of Spring* (**1987**) is reminiscent of the same source, though RG seems quite visibly to have taken more pleasure in creating characters than Harrison ever has; the plot involves a quest, hampered by spiritual ENTROPY, for the Gaian spirit of the forest which is beginning to assault the desultory evening cultures of humankind. Beyond Harrison, authors freely used as models by RG include James P. BLAYLOCK and John CROWLEY; but the amalgam has a recognizable flavour of its own. *View from the Oldest House* (**1989**) casts its net even more widely, bringing in allusions to figures from Milton to James Joyce to Archibald MacLeish to Thomas PYNCHON, in addition to all the above; the story itself, set in a NEAR-FUTURE, HOLOCAUST-haunted version of the same domain, tends to founder in these labyrinths of reference, just as its protagonist founders in his search for a self. A fourth novel, «Through the Heart» (1992), sharpens in sf terms RG's abiding venue: North America after the Fall. [JC]

See also: ANTI-INTELLECTUALISM IN SF; PHILIP K. DICK AWARD.

GRANT, ROBERT (1852-1940) US novelist chiefly remembered for *Unleavened Bread* (**1900**). With John Boyle O'REILLY (1844-1890), an Irish writer who escaped Australian exile to live in the USA, J.S. of Dale (a pseudonym of US lawyer Frederick Jessup Stimson [1855-1943]) and J.T. Wheelwright (1856-1925), also a New England lawyer, RG wrote *The King's Men: A Tale of To-morrow* (**1884**), set in a republican UK around the 1940s, during a period of Royalist rebellion (like that of Bonnie Prince Charlie 200 years earlier). There is a great deal of tangled action, and some sf artillery. Republicanism triumphs. [JC]

GRANVILLE, AUSTYN (?   -?   ) 19th-century US author, resident for some years in Australia. His racy, bigoted lost-race (◊ LOST WORLDS) novel *The Fallen Race* (**1892**), one of the earliest sf books set in Australia, shares the belief in a great inland sea which in real life led to the disappointment or death of many explorers. Stranded in the desert, a doctor finds a lost race developed, absurdly, from the primeval union of aboriginals and kangaroos; its people, almost spherical in shape, are ruled by a White (human) queen. The protagonist outwits a palace revolution, survives the amorous attentions of a female spheroid, establishes – through technological knowhow and CULTURAL ENGINEERING – a middle-class UTOPIA, and marries the queen. [PN]

Other works: *If the Devil Came to Chicago* (**1894**) with W. Wilson Knott, a reformist fantasy about vice.

See also: SEX.

GRAPHIC NOVEL To speak of the graphic novel is to speak of a particular kind of COMIC book, but to do so after about 1985 is to risk applying what has become a marketing term to questions of definition, transforming a practical distinction into what looks superficially like a separate genre.

The graphic novel proper is a self-contained narrative in comic-book form. It is almost never, in other words, part of an ongoing series like **Fantastic Four** (from 1961), though there are exceptions, like Dave SIM's **Cerebus the Aardvark** (from 1977), a connected series of stories projected to extend to 300 issues. It should be noted, too, that many graphic novels are initially published episodically in comic-book format, whether or not originally conceived as a single narrative, only subsequently reaching the state which readers tend to recognize as that of a graphic novel; that is, a large (often quarto-sized), usually perfect-bound volume of anywhere from 50 to 300 pages.

Through the 20th century, many books have been published which present a fictional tale primarily or solely through a sequence of pictures; the first important artist to become involved in graphic storytelling was probably Frans Masereel (1889-1972), whose nonverbal narratives in woodcut – culminating in *Die Stadt* (**1925**; as *The City* 1988 UK) – vividly encapsulated a 1920s sense of the new century in imagery reminiscent of the medieval Dance of Death. Books like Szegeti Szuts's *My War* (**1931**), might also seem to constitute part of a tradition which led directly to the graphic novels of the 1970s, but this is almost certainly misleading. Though many graphic-novel writers and illustrators are clearly aware of various forms of visual narrative – including recent painterly experiments in visual narration like *A Humument: A Treated Victorian Novel* (**1980**) by Tom Phillips (1937-   ) – the graphic novel itself derives from the very specific conventions of the comic, in particular from the extraordinarily sophisticated, cinema-derived narrative techniques which have been developed over the decades by comic-book artists, and which distinguish the comic from all other forms of visual storytelling. Masereel may have collaborated on film work (with directors like Abel Gance [1889-1981]), but only after having created his novels in terms which were cognate with but which did not borrow directly from the early CINEMA. No more is a recent figure like Glen Baxter a graphic novelist, as we are using the term. His *The Billiard Table Murders: A Gladys Babbington Morton Mystery* (**1990**) is certainly a visual novel; but Baxter is a cartoonist rather than a comic-book artist, and his visual pages are frozen images which highlight and comment upon the narrative action, whereas in a true graphic novel the images *carry* the action. The difference is as between night and day.

Though comic-derived tales – like *He Done Her Wrong: The Great American Novel: And Not a Word in it – No Music, Too* (**1930**) by Milt Gross (1895-1953) – were not uncommon from an early date, the term "graphic novel" was coined, possibly by the author himself, to describe what was itself in fact a collection of linked stories, *A Contract with God* (graph **1978**) by Will Eisner (1917-   ), but it did not become a widely used label until the release of a strangely ill matched trio – *Maus* (1980-85 *Raw*; graph **1987**) by Art Spiegelman (1948-   ), WATCHMEN (1986-7; graph **1987**) by Alan MOORE and Dave GIBBONS, and *Batman: The Dark Knight Returns* (1986; graph **1986**) by Frank MILLER – raised the profile of the serious narrative comic book and, in large part because of the low prestige of the comic-book medium, instigated a commercial need for a distinguishing term ("Adult Comic" had already been taken by comics with explicit sexual content).

Today, however, many so-called graphic novels are no more than costly collections of entirely routine SUPERHERO tales and the like. Among titles that, by contrast, deserve to be noticed are *Ed the Happy Clown* (1986; graph **1989**) by Chester BROWN, *The Magician's Wife* (1986 France; graph **1987** US) by Jerome CHARYN and François Boucq, *Violent Cases* (graph **1987**) by Neil GAIMAN and Dave MCKEAN, the various graphic novels serialized in LOVE AND ROCKETS – including *Human Diastrophism* (graph **1989**) by Gilbert Hernandez (1957-   ) and *Ape Sex* (graph **1989**) by Jaime Hernandez – *Elektra: Assassin* (1986-7; graph **1987**) by Frank Miller and Bill SIENKIEWICZ, *V for Vendetta* (1982-5; graph **1990**) by Alan Moore and David Lloyd, *A*

Small Killing (graph **1991**) by Moore and Oscar Zarate and *The Complete New Statesmen* (graph **1990**) by John Smith (1967- .   ) with Jim Baikie, Duncan Fegredo and Sean Phillips.

The term may have become a commercial tag, but its very existence represented an opportunity for ambitious comic-book artists and writers to begin to test the boundaries of their medium, to demonstrate the organized complexity possible in the interplay between the conventions of written narrative and visual storytelling. The best graphic novels are more than the sum of their parts; they are visions of the world which cannot be paraphrased into any other medium.   [NG/JC]

GRATACAP, LOUIS POPE (1851-1917) US naturalist and writer whose first sf novel, *The Certainty of a Future Life on Mars: Being the Posthumous Papers of Bradford Torrey Dodd* (**1903**), remains his best known. Dying in the conviction that dead humans transcendentally ascend to a Martian REINCARNATION as embodied spirits, the narrator's father is soon communicating from there by radio with his son. Martian society, he reports, is UTOPIAN – with natives of the planet as servants – and Mars itself has canals; an essay on MARS by the Italian astronomer Giovanni Schiaparelli (1835-1910) closes the volume. *A Woman of the Ice Age* (**1906**) is a turgid prehistoric romance. *The Evacuation of England: The Twist in the Gulf Stream* (**1908**) pins its expectations of catastrophe on the completion of the Panama Canal; the ensuing mini Ice Age persuades the UK monarchy to transplant itself to Australia. *The Mayor of New York: A Romance of the Days to Come* (**1910**) is set in AD2000, when "suicidariums" gently gas the willing and anarchism threatens the independent state of New York. In *The New Northland* (**1915**) a lost race (◊ LOST WORLDS) of Hebrew-speaking dwarfs inhabits a clement hollow in the Arctic, where their possession of vast amounts of radium seals their fate, for the protagonist decides that these riches must be exploited. LPG's range was wide, incorporating much material which has become central to sf, but his books are overlong, choked by his compulsive didacticism, and consequently unreadable today.   [JC]

Other works: *The End: How the Great War was Stopped* (**1917**), a fantasy in which the risen dead terrify the living into stopping the war.

GRAUSTARK ◊ RURITANIA.

GRAUTOFF, FERDINAND HEINRICH (1871-1935) German historian and writer, known in English for two pseudonymous works of fiction. In *"1906" – Der Zusammenbruch der alten Welt* (**1905**; trans G. Herring as *Armageddon 190-* **1907** UK) as by Seestern, the USA instigates a future WAR with Germany which is catastrophic for Europe but beneficial for Russia and the USA. *Bansai!* (**1908**; trans anon as *Banzai!* **1908** Canada) as by Parabellum pits the USA against the Japanese, with results initially disastrous for the USA, though the invading armies of the East are eventually driven all the way back past the Rocky

Mountains to the sea. [JC]

See also: INVASION.

GRAVEL, GEARY (1951-   ) US writer and (since 1978) a Certified Sign Language Interpreter. He began publishing sf with *The Alchemists* (**1984**); it and its sequel, *The Pathfinders* (**1986**), make up the first 2 volumes of the **Autumnworld Mosaic** sequence, set in a Galaxy abandoned by superior ALIENS after they have passed their technologies on to the human race, which proceeds to conquer the neighbouring planetary systems, sometimes to the detriment of existing inhabitants. The first novel describes an attempt on the part of a human group to thwart the "expansionists" on a planet occupied by nonsentient humanoids; the second involves a damaging plunge into the "dark beyond space" where as-yet-unrevealed mysteries of cosmogony reside. Further volumes are projected. The **Fading Worlds** series – *A Key for the Nonesuch* (**1990**) and *Return of the Breakneck Boys* (**1991**) – is a SCIENCE-FANTASY adventure set in a mysterious GAME-WORLD-like arena, into which the protagonist initially stumbles when he uses a borrowed key to gain access to, as he thinks, a toilet. Further volumes of this series, too, are projected. GG continues to seem a polished writer who has not quite yet unleashed what seems a considerable talent. [JC]

GRAVES, C(HARLES) L(ARCOM) [r] ◊ E.V. LUCAS.

GRAVES, ROBERT (VON RANKE) (1895-1985) UK poet, novelist and critic, best known for an active poetic career, extending from the beginning of WWI into the 1970s, and for such novels as *I, Claudius* (**1934**). His tendentious claim that he wrote fiction solely for commercial reasons does little to explain the high quality of all but his first novel, the RURITANIAN extravaganza *No Decency Left* (**1932**) with Laura Riding (1901-1991), together writing as Barbara Rich. *The Golden Fleece* (**1944**; vt *Hercules, My Shipmate* 1945 US) is an erudite fantasy of considerable power. His UTOPIAN sf novel *Watch the North Wind Rise* (**1949** US; vt *Seven Days in New Crete* 1949 UK) complexly dramatizes some ideas concerning the nature of POETRY and its ideal relation to the world that he had earlier expounded in *The White Goddess* (**1947** US), a nonfiction study. *Seven Days* is framed as a possible dream of its protagonist, a poet called into the future by the Poet-Magicians who rule utopian New Crete, and whose worship of the White Goddess benefits from her literal existence; but the book provides no clear-cut advocacy of the utopia it describes, and indeed it becomes clear that the Goddess has arranged for the poet's intrusion precisely so that he may – like so many visitors to utopias – unbalance what has become a sterile society. The escapist, timeless nature of New Crete, and the mediocre poetry it produces, are depicted with considerable ambivalence by RG, who allows no "winners" in his quest for a view of the world that will appropriately balance the opposing forces of whole-witted timefulness and half-witted utopia. [JC]

Other works: *The Shout* (**1929** chap).

About the author: There is much critical literature about RG in general. On *Seven Days in New Crete* the following are useful: Fritz LEIBER's "Utopia for Poets and Witches" in RIVERSIDE QUARTERLY 4 (1970), Robert H. Canary's "Utopian and Fantastic Dualities in Robert Graves's *Watch the North Wind Rise*" in SCIENCE-FICTION STUDIES 4 (1974) and Peter Briggs's "Watch the North Wind Rise" in *Survey of Modern Fantasy Literature* (anth 1983) ed Frank N. Magill.

See also: ANTHROPOLOGY; GALACTIC EMPIRES; *The* MAGAZINE OF FANTASY AND SCIENCE FICTION; MYTHOLOGY.

GRAVES, VALERIE ◊ Marion Zimmer BRADLEY.

GRAVITY The force of gravity is the most inescapable and unvarying fact of terrestrial life, and when writers first sent characters into SPACESHIPS and on to other planets the phenomenon of low gravity, or of no gravity at all, figured prominently among the wonders of space. Many early authors did not realize that complete weightlessness is a consequence of free fall, but this soon became a fact to be taken for granted in describing SPACE FLIGHT, and now few writers bother to emphasize it. A delightful account of the attractions of weightlessness was given by Fritz LEIBER in "The Beat Cluster" (1961); a more straightforward introduction is contained in Arthur C. CLARKE's *Islands in the Sky* (**1952**). In Bob SHAW's *The Ragged Astronauts* (**1986**) the most difficult part of interplanetary travel by BALLOON (no free fall here) between two mutually orbiting planets only 5000 miles (8000km) or so apart, and with a common atmosphere, is the transition of the weightless zone where the two gravitic pulls cancel out.

Weightlessness in practice is more likely to be a nuisance than anything else. The favoured method of providing "artificial gravity" in a spaceship or SPACE HABITAT is to spin the ship about an axis to generate a centrifugal force acting outward from the axis, so that the vessel's wall becomes the "floor". The visual paradoxes associated with a "gravity" that acts outwards on the inside of a hollow object were exploited in the film 2001: A SPACE ODYSSEY (1968), in Arthur C. CLARKE's *Rendezvous with Rama* (**1973**), and in Harry HARRISON's *Captive Universe* (**1969**). Few writers apart from Clarke mention the Coriolis force, a sideways force on a moving object which also results from a spinning system, and makes things tend to move in circles; it might be a severe disadvantage in a very large spinning spaceship. The Coriolis force is not encountered if the gravity is provided by a constant linear acceleration, nor if the problem is solved outside known science by having recourse to gravity generators such as SPINDIZZIES.

Centrifugal force also comes into play on rapidly rotating planets, where it combines with the force of gravity to define the direction of the vertical. Since the surface of a planet tends to be generally at right angles to the combined centrifugal and gravitational forces, the centrifugal force can be treated for most practical purposes as a part of the gravity, having the effect of decreasing the gravity at the equator (where it is already likely to be lower because of the shape of the planet), as in Hal CLEMENT's *Mission of Gravity* (**1954**). This novel tells of the very high gravity on the massive, rapidly rotating, discus-shaped planet of Mesklin, and of the effect of these conditions on the psychology of the planet's intelligent lifeforms. In our Solar System high gravity, nowhere near as extreme as Mesklin's, can be found on JUPITER; this is described in Poul ANDERSON's "Call Me Joe" (1957), James BLISH's "Bridge" (1952) – the story which describes the development of spindizzies – and Arthur C. Clarke's "A Meeting with Medusa" (1971), from which was developed *The Medusa Encounter* (**1990**) by Clarke and Paul PREUSS.

Much stronger gravitational forces than these can be expected near the very massive but small objects composed of collapsed matter (◊ NEUTRON STARS; PHYSICS). Not just the gravitational field's overall strength is important: the *variations* in its strength between different locations can exert forces even on an object in free fall. These are called "tidal forces" (the tides on Earth, caused by the difference between the Moon's gravitational pull on opposite sides of Earth, provide the most familiar example). Tidal forces feature in Larry NIVEN's "Neutron Star" (1966) and "There is a Tide" (1968). A collapsing star of sufficient mass (about three times that of the Sun) would pass through the neutron-star stage to become a BLACK HOLE – some high-gravity stories of the 1970s and 1980s are discussed under that heading – and there has been a large amount of sf set around (or even within) such venues.

The wish for a method of manipulating gravity has been a rich source of IMAGINARY SCIENCE, indeed ANTIGRAVITY has been something of a philosopher's stone to sf writers, and is discussed in some detail in that entry. The attraction of antigravitational themes grows from a kind of resentment at the inescapable restraints gravity imposes on us in the real world. Cecelia HOLLAND deals in rather cavalier manner with gravity in *Floating Worlds* (**1976**), the worlds of the title being cities floating above Saturn and Uranus. David GERROLD's *Space Skimmers* (**1972**) exploits an imaginary gravitic effect (using gravity as a kind of point applied to a surface) which yields an attractive spaceship designed as if by M.C. Escher. *Walkers on the Sky* (**1976**) by David J. LAKE owes more to wish fulfilment than to science, but does offer a technological explanation for the behaviour summarized in the title.

Gravity as a theme has naturally been in the main the province of HARD-SF writers like Hal Clement and Larry Niven. Working very much in their tradition are the physicist Robert L. FORWARD, who has written two interesting novels about a lifeform living in intensely high-gravity conditions on the surface of a neutron star – *Dragon's Egg* (**1980**) and its sequel *Starquake!* (**1985**) – and Stephen BAXTER, whose *Raft* (**1991**) is set in an ALTERNATE UNIVERSE where gravity, instead of being (to simplify) the weakest of the fundamental forces, as it is in our Universe, is one of

the strongest; the results are described with élan. [TSu/PN]

GRAY, ALASDAIR (JAMES) (1934-) Scottish painter, playwright and author who began publishing work of genre interest with "The Star" for *Collins Magazine for Girls and Boys* in 1951; this tale was gathered, along with a wide variety of sf fables and FABULATIONS, in *Unlikely Stories, Mostly* (coll **1983**). His first and most substantial novel was *Lanark: A Life in Four Books* (**1981**), a vast tale whose burly narrative voice shoulders aside questions of genre as impertinences; the protagonist is born, lives and dies in Glasgow, whence, transformed into an alter ego named Lanark, he is transported to the regimented subterranean DYSTOPIA of Unthank, which is of course Hell but which also – as he enters the "Epilogue" – becomes the text of *Lanark*, through which he wages his way. *1982 Janine* (**1984**) is a metaphysical fantasy, with some of the same embedded entwinings of life and book. *The Fall of Kelvin Walker: A Fable of the Sixties* (**1985**) and *Something Leather* (**1990**) are associational, as are the tales assembled in *Lean Tales* (coll **1985**), which also includes work by James Kelman and Agnes Owens. *McGrotty and Ludmilla, or The Harbinger Report* (1975 as BBC radio play; **1990**) is a mildly poisonous SATIRE of UK life and politics set in a moderately displaced ALTERNATE WORLD, and *Poor Things: Episodes from the Early Life of Archibald McCandless M.D. Scottish Public Health Offices* (**1992**) fabulates the Frankenstein story (◊ FRANKENSTEIN MONSTER) and FEMINISM. Though published by mainstream houses, most of AG's books have been designed by him in his own unmistakable style, so that his oeuvre is unique inside and out. [JC]

See also: CITIES.

GRAY, CURME (1910-1980) US writer in whose complex sf novel *Murder in Millennium VI* (**1951**) a homicide case shakes a matriarchal DYSTOPIA thousands of years hence – murder being inexplicable to the inhabitants of this world. The focus of interest in the novel is the gradual unveiling of the fact that a gradual transition – not back to patriarchy but to some synthesis – is under way. There is a detailed analysis in *In Search of Wonder* (**1956**) by Damon KNIGHT, the admiring tone of which has not been universally shared. [JC]

GRAY, ROD ◊ Gardner F. FOX.

GRAZIER, JAMES (? -) US writer in whose awkwardly written *Runts of 61 Cygni C* (**1970**) humans encounter approximately humanoid aliens and lots of kinky sex on the planet 61 Cygni C. [JC]

Other works: *Hydra* (**1969**) as by James A. Grazier, a juvenile.

GREAT AMERICAN PUBLICATIONS ◊ FANTASTIC UNIVERSE.

GREAT AND SMALL One of the commonest fantastic devices in literature and legend is the alteration of scale. MYTHOLOGY and folklore abound with giants and miniature humans, and different perspectives dependent upon changes of scale are central to many of the SATIRES recognized today as works of PROTO SCIENCE FICTION, most notably Jonathan SWIFT's *Gulliver's Travels* (**1726**) and VOLTAIRE's *Micromégas* (**1750** Berlin; 1752 France; trans **1753**). Mark TWAIN's uncompleted works include "Three Thousand Years among the Microbes" (written 1905; 1967), in which a germ called Huck inhabits the body of a tramp, recalling Morgan ROBERTSON's earnest medical fantasy "The Battle of the Monsters" (1899). Modern satires using distortion of scale in other ways include Joe Orton's *Head to Toe* (**1971**), J.G. BALLARD's "The Drowned Giant" (1964; vt "Souvenir") and Jessamyn WEST's *The Chilekings* (**1967**). The first SCIENTIFIC ROMANCE of the microcosm was "The Diamond Lens" (1858) by Fitz-James O'BRIEN, in which a scientist discovers a tiny humanoid woman in a water-drop. The tactic of shrinking human beings to insect-size in order that they may observe the small-scale wonders of the natural world is common in didactic sf, ranging from Alfred Taylor SCHOFIELDEN's *Travels in the Interior* (**1887**; as by Luke Courteney) through Edwin PALLANDER's *The Adventures of a Micro-Man* (**1902**) and Bob OLSEN's "The Ant with the Human Soul" (1932) to Donald SUDDABY's *Lost Men in the Grass* (**1940**) as by Alan Griff. More ambitious didactic microcosmic fantasies can be found in George GAMOW's *Mr Tompkins Explores the Atom* (**1944**). Adventure stories in which humans are pitted against giant insects and monstrous spiders are commonplace, ranging from Sara Coleridge's curious fantasy *Phantasmion* (1837) through the stories assembled in Murray LEINSTER's *The Forgotten Planet* (1920-53; fixup **1954**) to the series begun with *Spider World: The Tower* (**1987**) by Colin WILSON; a duel with a spider is the high-point of the film *The* INCREDIBLE SHRINKING MAN (1957) based on Richard MATHESON's *The Shrinking Man* (**1956**).

The idea that there might be worlds within worlds was popularized by the Rutherford-Bohr model of the atom as a tiny "solar system" with electrons orbiting the nucleus. The notion that all the atoms of our Universe might be solar systems in their own right, and all of our Universe's solar systems themselves atoms in a macrocosm, was developed by several writers, appearing first in *The Triuneverse* (**1912**) by R.A. KENNEDY. The PULP-MAGAZINE writer who made the theme his own was Ray CUMMINGS, whose works in this vein include the microcosmic romances *The Girl in the Golden Atom* (1919-20; fixup **1921**), *The Princess of the Atom* (1929; **1950**) and *Beyond the Vanishing Point* (1931; **1958**) and the macrocosmic romance *Explorers into Infinity* (1927-8; **1965**). Other pulp writers who borrowed the theme from Cummings include Harl VINCENT, for "The Microcosmic Buccaneers" (1929), S.P. MEEK for "Submicroscopic" (1931), Donald WANDREI for "Colossus" (1934), Jack WILLIAMSON for "The Galactic Circle" (1935) and Festus PRAGNELL for *The Green Man of Kilsona* (1935 as "The Green Man of Graypec"; **1936**; vt *The Green Man of Graypec* 1950 US). Numerous other pulp-sf stories featured miniaturized men, including "A Matter of

Size" (1934) by Harry BATES, "He who Shrank" (1936) by Henry L. HASSE, whose protagonist is both giant and miniature man while shrinking through a whole series of worlds-within-worlds, "Fury from Lilliput" (1949) by Murray LEINSTER, "Chaos in Miniature" (1952) by H.J. CAMPBELL, and the classic "Surface Tension" (1952) by James BLISH. Despite the inherent logical flaws in the notion (to do with the relationships between mass, strength and organic complexity) the idea of human miniaturization has retained sufficient fascination to encourage writers to continue to fudge the issue; it crops up in such novels as *Atta* (**1953**) by Francis Rufus BELLAMY, *Cold War in a Country Garden* (**1971**) by Lindsay GUTTERIDGE and *The Men Inside* (**1973**) by Barry N. MALZBERG, and in such films as DR CYCLOPS (1940), *The Incredible Shrinking Man*, FANTASTIC VOYAGE (1966) and INNERSPACE (1987). The process of fudging can be ingenious, sometimes recruiting the notion of the expanding Universe, as in the playful "Prominent Author" (1954) by Philip K. DICK and *Land of Dreams* (**1987**) by James P. BLAYLOCK. An interesting attempt to accommodate the microcosmic romance to more modern atomic theory is "Nor Iron Bars" (1957) by James Blish. An intriguing recomplication of the theme involves the depiction of miniature worlds whose time-flow is more rapid than ours, as in "Pygmy Planet" (1932) by Jack Williamson, "Microcosmic God" (1941) by Theodore STURGEON, *Edge of Time* (**1958**) by David Grinnell (Donald A. WOLLHEIM) and *Dragon's Egg* (**1980**) by Robert L. FORWARD, which is set on a NEUTRON STAR, the rapid time-flow being a relativistic consequence of the huge surface GRAVITY. Miniature worlds constructed for specific purposes are featured in "The Tunnel under the World" (1954) by Frederik POHL and *Counterfeit World* (**1964** UK; vt *Simulacron-3* 1964 US) by Daniel F. GALOUYE.

Giants are usually treated less sympathetically than very tiny characters, for obvious reasons; the oversized heroes of *The Food of the Gods* (**1904**) by H.G. WELLS and *Titan's Daughter* (**1961**) by James Blish are notable exceptions. The giant ALIENS in Raymond F. JONES's *The Alien* (**1951**) and Blish's *The Warriors of Day* (**1953**) are menacing, although the one in Joseph L. GREEN's *Gold the Man* (**1971**; vt *The Mind Behind the Eye*) isn't. In films which invert the theme of *The Incredible Shrinking Man*, including *The* AMAZING COLOSSAL MAN (1957) and *Attack of the 50-Foot Woman* (1958), the central characters become figures of menace, although the charismatically gargantuan star of KING KONG (1933) has always generated sympathy, as has his one-time saurian rival GOJIRA. When human beings must live as scavengers in worlds populated by alien giants, as in Kenneth BULMER's *Demon's World* (**!964**; vt *The Demons*), William TENN's *Of Men and Monsters* (1963 *Gal* as "The Men in the Walls"; exp **1968**) and the tv series LAND OF THE GIANTS, they are the obvious heroes, but when humans are the giants sympathy usually attaches to the tiny aliens, even when – as in A. Bertram CHANDLER's "Giant Killer"

(1945) – they are not humanoid. The notion of social stratification based on more moderate differences of size is cleverly developed in the fantasies of Sharon Baker (1938-1991) set on the planet Naphar, including *Quarrelling, They Met the Dragon* (**1984**).

John CHRISTOPHER's *The Little People* (**1967**) is the most sciencefictional of the many notable juvenile fantasies which feature tiny races living fugitive lives in the human world; others include T.H. WHITE's *Mistress Masham's Repose* (**1946**) and the two series begun with *The Borrowers* (**1952**) by Mary Norton (1903-1992) and *Truckers* (**1989**) by Terry PRATCHETT. By far the best modern fantasy to include aspects of microcosmic romance is John CROWLEY's *Little, Big* (**1981**), and it is to the realms of FANTASY that most of the themes dealing with microcosms and macrocosms really belong. [BS]

See also: COSMOLOGY; FANTASTIC VOYAGES.

GREATOREX, WILFRED ◊ 1990.

GREAT SCIENCE FICTION / SCIENCE FICTION GREATS One of the many reprint DIGEST-size magazines published by Sol Cohen's Ultimate Publishing Co. employing the reprint rights acquired when Cohen bought AMAZING STORIES and FANTASTIC. 21 issues were released, quarterly Oct 1965-Spring 1971, the first 12 under the title *Great Science Fiction*, #13-#16 as *Science Fiction Greats* and #17-#21 as *SF Greats*.

The contents were mostly short stories by well known authors, reprinted from the period when Cele GOLDSMITH edited *AMZ* and *Fantastic*. #13 was devoted entirely to Robert SILVERBERG and #14 entirely to Harlan ELLISON. This was one of Cohen's better publications, for he was selecting from an interesting period in the history of his source magazines. [BS]

GREAT SCIENCE FICTION STORIES ◊ TREASURY OF GREAT SCIENCE FICTION STORIES.

GREELEY, ANDREW M(ORAN) (1928-) US Roman Catholic priest and writer, several of whose books have been nonfiction texts on matters of faith; among the rest are detective novels (sometimes with paranormal elements) and some fantasy and sf, beginning with *Nora Maeve and Sebi* (**1976** chap), a short fantasy tale, and *The Magic Cup* (**1979**), a fantasy set in medieval Ireland. *God Game* (**1986**) depicts a priest introduced by COMPUTER to a fantasy GAME-WORLD. *The Final Planet* (**1987**) features the Irish Catholic captain of a desperately wandering starship called *Iona* from the planet Tara, who must descend to a very secular planet to see if colonists are admissible, almost (but never quite) bedding a female scientist *en passant. Angel Fire* (**1988**) is a SCIENCE-FANTASY novel about an Irish-descended Nobel Prize-winning scientist – he has been honoured for the already discredited "punctuated equilibrium" theory of EVOLUTION – blessed with a literal guardian angel, who protects him very well. *Sacred Visions* (anth **1991**) ed with Michael CASSUTT (and Martin H. GREENBERG anon) assembles a wide range of stories about RELIGION. [JC]

See also: GAMES AND SPORTS; VIRTUAL REALITY.

GREEN, HENRY Pseudonym of UK industrialist and writer Henry Vincent Yorke (1905-1973), author of several laconic but richly thought-through novels from *Blindness* (**1926**) to *Doting* (**1952**). His one sf tale, *Concluding* (**1948**), set 50 years hence in a DYSTOPIAN socialist UK, presents through imagery and dialogue a complex vision of a world in which humanity and Nature are irretrievably dissevered. [JC]

GREEN, HILARY [r] ◊ ROBERT HALE LIMITED.

GREEN, I.G. Pseudonym of US writer Ira Greenblatt (? -), in whose *Time Beyond Time* (**1971**) the hero is either killed by lightning or caught in a "time-nexus" and cast into a disease-free ATLANTIS, where he finds himself immortal and becomes embroiled in many exciting adventures. [JC]

GREEN, JEN [r] ◊ Sarah LEFANU.

GREEN, JOSEPH (LEE) (1931-) US writer of sf and technical journalism who began publishing sf in 1962 with "The Engineer" in *NW*. *An Affair with Genius* (coll **1969** UK) assembles some of his better early work. Although many of his 60 stories to date (not all sf) have appeared in the USA – along with popular-science articles in *ASF* that demonstrate the lucid gift of exposition visible also in his fiction – it was in the UK that he first established his name, and there that most of his books were first published. *The Loafers of Refuge* (1962-3 *NW*; fixup **1965** UK), his first novel, chronicles the gradual coming together, to their mutual benefit, of colonizing humans and humanlike natives on the planet Refuge, mainly through the mediation of the protagonist (◊ COLONIZATION OF OTHER WORLDS). JG's best novel to date is probably his second, *Gold the Man* (**1971** UK; vt *The Mind Behind the Eye* 1972 US), which deals very competently (though not in depth) with a variety of themes from SUPERMAN to ALIENS and INTELLIGENCE. Gold is *Homo sapiens* born with about 4oz (120g) of extra association neocortex. As an adult he is asked to "operate" a brain-damaged giant invader from inside its head (◊ GREAT AND SMALL). Returning, thus incorporated, to the alien's blandly UTOPIAN home planet, he works out the reason for the imminent destruction of its sun: sentient sunspots. All ends well. Further novels include *Conscience Interplanetary* (1965-71 var mags, fixup **1972** UK), the uneven story of a Conscience whose job it is – in an unhappy replay of the protagonist's role in *The Loafers of Refuge* – to adjudicate as to the INTELLIGENCE of alien species before allowing human beings to exploit their planets. JG has become inactive in the field. [JC]

Other works: *Star Probe* (**1976** UK); *The Horde* (**1976** Canada).

See also: COMMUNICATIONS; MATTER TRANSMISSION.

GREEN, MARTIN (BURGESS) (1927-) UK academic and writer, long resident in the USA. Some of his studies of the linkages between culture and literature, like "Science and Sensibility" (in *Science and the Shabby Curate of Poetry* coll **1964**) and *Children of the Sun* (**1976**), express a remote interest in GENRE SF. His one attempt at fiction, *The Earth Again Redeemed: May 26* to July 1, 1984, on *This Earth of Ours and its Alter Ego: A Science Fiction Novel* (**1977**), uneasily posits an ALTERNATE WORLD where the Roman Catholic Church has blocked the development of science, and where a visiting CYBORG from our own ruined timeline detects clear signs of coming disaster. [JC]

See also: ANTIMATTER.

GREEN, NUNSOWE Pseudonym of unidentified UK writer of the sf discussion novel, *A Thousand Years Hence; Being Personal Experiences as Narrated by . . .* (**1882**). Though the featured tour of the future turns out to have been a dream, the novel invokes a wide range of sf notions, from ESP to TERRAFORMING. [JC]

GREEN, ROBERT (? -) Canadian writer and musician whose *The Great Leap Backwards* (**1968**) depicts a future where COMPUTERS have taken over the cities, leaving the countryside in a natural state. [JC]

GREEN, ROGER (GILBERT) LANCELYN (1918-1987) UK author, scholar, critic and translator (from classical Greek), with a special interest in FANTASY. Among his many works those most relevant to sf studies are *C.S. Lewis* (**1963**), *C.S. Lewis: A Biography* (**1974**) with Walter Hooper, and *Into Other Worlds: Space-Flight in Fiction, from Lucian to Lewis* (**1957**). The latter is one of the earlier books on sf, but is primarily pitched at a rather anecdotal and trivial level. His *Andrew Lang* (**1946**) throws light on an author whose relationship to sf has been almost forgotten (◊ Andrew LANG); a later study, *Andrew Lang* (**1962** chap), is less thorough. RLG's allegorical and old-fashioned fantasy, *From the World's End* (**1948**), is about visionary dreams in an old house. *The Land Beyond the North* (**1958**) carries Jason and the Argonauts ultimately to a sacrifice at Stonehenge. [PN]

Other works (nonfiction): *Tellers of Tales* (**1946**); *The Story of Lewis Carroll* (**1949**); *Fifty Years of Peter Pan* (**1954**); *J.M. Barrie* (**1960** chap).

As editor: *The Diaries of Lewis Carroll* (2 vols **1953**); *Modern Fairy Stories* (anth **1955**); *Fairy Stories* (coll **1958**) by Mary Molesworth; *Thirteen Uncanny Tales* (anth **1970**); *A Book of Magicians* (anth **1973**; vt *A Cavalcade of Magicians* US); *Strange Adventures in Time* (anth **1974**); *The Complete Fairy Tales of George MacDonald* (coll **1977**); *The Unknown Conan Doyle* (coll **1984**) with John Michael Gibson. This list is selective; RLG as editor and reteller produced almost 100 books for children.

See also: PROTO SCIENCE FICTION.

GREEN, ROLAND J(AMES) (1944-) US writer whose first sale was the first volume in the **Wandor** SWORD-AND-SORCERY sequence (see listing below), though his first published work was a volume in the similar **Richard Blade** sequence (see listing below) under the house name Jeffrey Lord. His sf has generally been written in collaboration, notably 2 vols in the **Janissaries** sequence of military novels with Jerry POURNELLE, *Janissaries: Clan and Crown* (**1982**) and *Janissaries III: Storms of Victory* (**1988**). Others include: *Jamie the Red* (**1984**) with Gordon R. DICKSON; a continuation of H. Beam PIPER's **Paratime Police/Lord**

Kalvan books with John F. CARR, *Great King's War* ∗ (**1985**); and *The Book of Kantela* (**1985**) with Frieda Murray (RJG's wife). The **Peace Company** series of military sf novels – *Peace Company* (**1985**), *These Green Foreign Hills* (**1987**) and *The Mountain Walks* (**1989**) – are by RJG alone, as is the **Starcruiser Shenandoah** sequence, comprising *Squadron Alert* (**1989**), *Division of the Spoils* (**1990**) and *The Sum of Things* (**1991**). In these works it is difficult to pin down any strongly individual tone. [JC]

Other works: The **Wandor** books, comprising *Wandor's Ride* (**1973**), *Wandor's Journey* (**1975**), *Wandor's Voyage* (**1979**) and *Wandor's Flight* (**1981**); *Throne of Sherran: The Book of Kanetal* (**1985**); novels tied to Robert E. HOWARD's **Conan**, *Conan the Valiant* ∗ (**1988**), *Conan the Guardian* ∗ (**1991**) and *Conan the Relentless* ∗ (**1992**).

As Richard Blade: #9 through #37 (except #30) of the **Richard Blade** series, *Kingdom of Royth* (**1974**), *Ice Dragon* (**1974**), *Dimension of Dreams* (**1974**), *King of Zunga* (**1975**), *The Golden Steed* (**1975**), *The Temples of Ayocan* (**1975**), *The Towers of Melnon* (**1975**), *The Crystal Seas* (**1975**), *The Mountains of Brega* (**1976**), *Warlords of Gaikon* (**1976**), *Looters of Tharn* (**1976**), *Guardians of the Coral Throne* (**1976**), *The Forests of Gleor* (**1977**), *Empire of Blood* (**1977**), *The Dragons of Englor* (**1977**), *The Torian Pearls* (**1977**), *City of the Living Dead* (**1978**), *Master of the Hashomi* (**1978**), *Wizard of Rentoro* (**1978**), *Treasure of the Stars* (**1978**), *Gladiators of Hapanu* (**1979**), *Pirates of Gohar* (**1979**), *Killer Plants of Binaark* (**1980**), *The Ruins of Kaldac* (**1981**), *The Lords of the Crimson River* (**1981**), *Return to Kaldac* (**1983**) and *Warriors of Luittan* (**1984**).

As John CLEVE: *Spaceways #15: Starship Sapphire* (**1984**) with Andrew J. OFFUTT, writing together as Cleve.

As editor: 2 vols in the **War World** SHARED-WORLD anthologies created by Jerry Pournelle: *The Burning Eye* ∗ (anth **1988**) and *Death's Head Rebellion* ∗ (anth **1990**), both with John F. Carr.

GREEN, SHARON (1942-) US writer who came to notice for her **Terrilian Sequence** of sadomasochistic novels in the manner of John NORMAN, with which the advertising copy explicitly linked them. The sequence is *The Warrior Within* (**1982**), *The Warrior Enchained* (**1983**), *The Warrior Rearmed* (**1984**), *The Warrior Challenged* (**1986**) and *The Warrior Victorious* (**1988**); they differ from Norman's in being set on a more plausible planet. Other series directed to the same market include the **Jalav/Amazon Warrior** sequence – *The Crystals of Mida* (**1982**), *An Oath to Mida* (**1983**), *Chosen of Mida* (**1984**), *The Will of the Gods* (**1985**) and *To Battle the Gods* (**1986**) – and the **Diana Santee, Spaceways Agent** sequence: *Mind Guest* (**1984**) and *Gateway to Xanadu* (**1985**). The **Far Side of Forever** sequence – *The Far Side of Forever* (**1987**) and *Hellhound Magic* (**1989**) – is more traditional fantasy. Other titles include *Lady Blade, Lord Fighter* (**1987**), projected to initiate a series, *The Revel Prince* (**1987**), *Mists of the Ages* (**1988**), also projected to start a series, and *Dawn Song* (**1990**). [JC]

GREEN, STEPHEN ◊ Neil BELL.

GREEN, TERENCE M(ICHAEL) (1947-   ) Canadian teacher and writer who began publishing work of genre interest with "Of Children in the Foliage" in *Aurora: New Canadian Writing 1979* (anth **1979**) ed Morris Wolfe; the story was gathered with further lean and subtle tales in *The Woman who is the Midnight Wind* (coll **1987**). In his short fiction TMG, like many Canadian writers, tenders a vision which might be called melancholy humanism. His first novel, *Barking Dogs* (**1988** US), on the other hand, opens that vision out but, to do so, forcibly transforms Toronto into a mean-streets venue suitable for displays of high-tech weaponry displays by a vengeful cop. In *Children of the Rainbow* (**1992**) a descendant of the *Bounty* mutineers undergoes TIME-TRAVEL stress and imprisonment. [JC]

See also: CANADA.

GREENBERG, MARTIN (1918-   ) US publisher and anthologist, not to be confused with Martin H. GREENBERG. In 1948 he cofounded with David A. KYLE and others GNOME PRESS, one of the small but important early publishers of GENRE SF in hardcover format. MG edited 7 anthologies for Gnome, of which *Coming Attractions* (anth **1957**) consisted of sf-related nonfiction articles. The others were *Men Against the Stars* (anth **1950**; cut vt *9 Stories from Men Against the Stars* 1963), *Travelers of Space* (anth **1951**), with 16 illustrations by Edd CARTIER, *Journey to Infinity* (anth **1951**), *Five Science Fiction Novels* (anth **1952**; with novels by Fritz LEIBER and A.E. VAN VOGT omitted, cut vt *The Crucible of Power* 1953 UK), *The Robot and the Man* (anth **1953**) and *All About the Future* (anth **1955**). Most are loosely thematic. [PN]

See also: SMALL PRESSES AND LIMITED EDITIONS.

GREENBERG, MARTIN H(ARRY) (1941-   ) US anthologist and academic, not to be confused with Martin GREENBERG. He has a doctorate in Political Science (1969) and has taught at the University of Wisconsin – Green Bay since 1975, currently holding the position of Professor of Regional Analysis, Political Science, and Literature and Language. Most of his own writing, like *Bureaucracy and Development: A Mexican Case Study* (**1970**), has been in the field of political science; his sf writing has been restricted to two reference tools, *Index to Stories in the Thematic Anthologies of Science Fiction* (**1978**) with Joseph D. OLANDER and Marshall B. TYMN, and *Science Fiction and Fantasy Series and Sequels: A Bibliography – Volume 1: Books* (**1986**) with Tim Cottrill (1958-   ) and Charles G. WAUGH.

It is as an anthologist – primarily of sf and fantasy, although he has also edited many anthologies in other genres – that MHG has become a dominant figure, working both solo and with colleagues, usually Olander and Waugh, either separately or together, and with the occasional collaboration of MHG's wife, Rosalind M. Greenberg. Team anthologies – anthologies put together by two or more professional anthologists who divide up the various tasks involved, which include everything from story research and selection through copyright searches down to selling the actual book – were not unknown before MHG began to work, but he very quickly established himself in a commanding position, and by 1992 had published at least 450 anthologies, primarily assembling reprint and original material of interest to sf and fantasy readers. His efficiency as an anthologist is self-evident, and the quality of the product is rarely negligible, though some titles show a lack of daring in their selection of contents: this flatness stands in odd contrast to the imaginativeness of most of the concepts presented, for it is clear that MHG has a high talent for conceiving hook themes and titles.

Most of the huge array is made up of fiction anthologies, but several nonfiction titles have appeared, including the **Writers of the Twenty-First Century** series of anthologies reprinting critical articles on major writers, all ed with Olander: *Isaac Asimov* (anth **1977**), *Ray Bradbury* (anth **1980**), *Arthur C. Clarke* (anth **1977**), *Philip K. Dick* (anth **1983**), *Robert A. Heinlein* (anth **1978**) and *Ursula K. Le Guin* (anth **1979**). Other nonfiction anthologies include *Fantastic Lives: Autobiographical Essays by Notable Science Fiction Writers* (anth **1981**), *The End of the World* (anth **1983**) with Olander and Eric S. RABKIN, *The Legacy of Olaf Stapledon* (anth **1989**) with Charles Elkins and Patrick A. McCarthy, and *No Place Else: Explorations in Utopian and Dystopian Fiction* (anth **1983**) with Olander and Rabkin.

Of the fiction anthologies, many have been edited by MHG either alone or with his team (by which term we refer not to contractual relationships – about which we claim no knowledge – but to the text partnerships so clearly in evidence), but in addition a large number also credit as co-editor a "name" writer – often a fiction author associated with the subject of the book in question. Although it is probable that some of these "name" editors did little more than approve contents assembled by the team, most of the MHG/"name" anthologies are genuine collaborative efforts. For this reason, and because there is little profit in duplicating long ranks of titles, we list all MHG/"name" anthologies (of which there are nearly 200) in the entries for the "name" writers involved rather than below. Of MHG's collaborators (some are academics who are not part of the MHG team) we treat the following as "name" writers: Robert ADAMS (6 titles), Poul ANDERSON (5, MHG anon in 1), Piers ANTHONY (1), Isaac ASIMOV (127), Gregory BENFORD (6), Robert BLOCH (1; MHG anon), Orson Scott CARD (1; MHG anon), Terry CARR (1), Arthur C. CLARKE (1; MHG anon), David A. DRAKE (4), Alan Dean FOSTER (1), Andrew M. GREELEY (1, with Michael CASSUTT, MHG anon), Damon KNIGHT (1), Barry N. MALZBERG (2), Richard MATHESON (1), Walter M. MILLER (1), William F. NOLAN (3), Andre NORTON (2), Frederik POHL (4), Bill PRONZINI (1), Fred SABERHAGEN (1), Robert SILVERBERG (10), S.M. STIRLING (2), Robert E. WEINBERG (1) and Jane YOLEN (5), of which only the

Yolen titles are listed below.

The first MHG anthologies, beginning with *Political Science Fiction* (anth **1974**) with Patricia WARRICK, were clearly designed to appeal to teachers; opinions were strongly divided about the usefulness of some of their accompanying critical apparatus. The **Through Science Fiction** educational sequence includes: *Introductory Psychology Through Science Fiction* (anth **1974**; exp 1977) with Harvey Katz and Warrick; *Anthropology Through Science Fiction* (anth **1974**) with Carol Mason and Warrick; *Sociology Through Science Fiction* (anth **1974**) with Joseph D. Olander and Warrick; *School and Society Through Science Fiction* (anth **1974**) with Olander and Warrick; *American Government Through Science Fiction* (anth **1974**) with Olander and Warrick; *The New Awareness: Religion Through Science Fiction* (anth **1975**) with Warrick; *Run to Starlight: Sports Through Science Fiction* (anth **1975**) with Olander and Warrick; *Social Problems Through Science Fiction* (anth **1975**) with John Milstead, Olander and Warrick; *The City: 2000 A.D.: Urban Life Through Science Fiction* (anth **1976**) with Ralph S. Clem and Olander; *Marriage and the Family Through Science Fiction* (anth **1976**) with Val Clear, Olander and Warrick; *Criminal Justice Through Science Fiction* (anth **1977**) with Olander; *No Room For Man: Population and the Future Through Science Fiction* (anth **1979**) with Ralph S. Clem and Olander; *Dawn of Time: Prehistory Through Science Fiction* (anth **1979**) with Silverberg and Olander. They were not addressed to a wide audience.

Later titles, which tended to appeal to more general markets, lacked pedagogical aids and began to feature the name collaborators listed above. The topical range of these anthologies is enormous, and many of them are cited in relevant theme entries throughout this encyclopedia. We list them below in the following order: first, MHG alone; next, MHG with non-team collaborators; finally, MHG with team collaborators (sometimes plus non-team collaborators). Each subdivision of the listing is in chronological order. [JC]

Other works:

MHG alone: *The Classic Philip José Farmer 1952-1964* (coll **1984**) and *The Classic Philip José Farmer 1964-1973* (coll **1984**); *The Best of Margaret St Clair* (coll **1985**); *The Best of Marion Zimmer Bradley* (coll **1985**; cut 1990 UK); *Ursula K. Le Guin: Five Complete Novels* (omni **1985**) ed anon; *Amazing Stories: Visions of Other Worlds* (anth **1986**); *The Best Science Fiction of Isaac Asimov* (coll **1986**) ed anon; *Amazing Science Fiction Anthology: The Wonderful Years, 1926-1935* (anth **1987**), *The War Years, 1936-1945* (anth **1987**) and *The Wild Years, 1946-1955* (anth **1987**); *The Best of Pamela Sargent* (coll **1987**); *Bart Science Fiction Triplet #1* (anth **1988**), only vol published; *Foundation's Friends: Stories in Honor of Isaac Asimov* (anth **1989**); *The Asimov Chronicles: Fifty Years of Isaac Asimov* (coll **1989**; vt in 6 vols as *The Asimov Chronicles #1* 1990, *#2* 1990, *#3* 1990, *#4* 1991, *#5* 1991 and *#6* 1991); *The Further Adventures of Batman* * (anth **1989**) and *The Further Adventures of the Joker* * (anth

1990); *Mummy Stories* (anth **1990**); *The Diplomacy Guild* (anth **1990**); *Christmas on Ganymede, and Other Stories* (anth **1990**); *The Leiber Chronicles* (coll **1990**); *The Fantastic Adventures of Robin Hood* (anth **1991**); *Fantastic Chicago* (anth **1991**); *Isaac's Universe #1: The Diplomacy Guild* * (anth **1991**) and *#2: Phases in Chaos* * (anth **1991**); *New Stories from The Twilight Zone* * (anth **1991**); *Nightmares on Elm Street: Freddy Krueger's Seven Sweetest Dreams* * (anth **1991**); *After the King: Stories in Honor of J.R.R. Tolkien* (anth **1992**).

MHG with non-team collaborators:

MHG with John L. Apostolou: *The Best Japanese Science Fiction Stories* (anth **1989**).

MHG (anon) with Barbara Brenner, Seymour Reit and Howard Zimmerman: *The Bank Street Book of Science Fiction* (anth **1989**); *The Bank Street Book of Fantasy* (anth **1989**).

MHG with Alan BRENNERT (anon): *Stories from the New Twilight Zone* * (anth **1991**).

MHG with John W. CAMPBELL Jr: *Astounding Science Fiction, July 1939* (anth **1981**) – the July 1939 issue of *ASF* in facsimile.

MHG with Edward L. FERMAN: *The Magazine of Fantasy and Science Fiction, April 1965* (anth **1981**) – the Apr 1965 issue of *FSF* in facsimile.

MHG with Ed Gorman: *Stalkers: All New Tales of Terror and Suspense* (anth **1989**); *Solved* (anth **1991**).

MHG (anon) with Robert McCammon: *Under the Fang* (anth **1991**).

MHG with Francis M. Nevins: *Hitchcock in Prime Time* (anth **1985**).

MHG (anon) with Byron PREISS: *The Ultimate Werewolf* (anth **1991**); *The Ultimate Dracula* (anth **1991**); *The Ultimate Frankenstein* (anth **1991**).

MHG with Patrick L. Price: *Fantastic Stories: Tales of the Weird & Wondrous* (anth **1987**).

MHG with Stanley SCHMIDT: *Unknown Worlds: Tales from Beyond* (anth **1988**).

MHG and Robert E. WEINBERG with Stefan R. Dziemianowicz: *Weird Tales: 32 Unearthed Terrors* (anth **1988**); *Rivals of Weird Tales: 30 Great Fantasy & Horror Stories from the Weird Fiction Pulps* (anth **1990**); *Famous Fantastic Mysteries: 30 Great Tales of Fantasy and Horror from the Classic Pulp Magazines Famous Fantastic Mysteries and Fantastic Novels* (anth **1991**).

MHG with Jane Yolen: *Werewolves* (anth **1988**); *Things that Go Bump in the Night* (anth **1989**); *Vampires* (anth **1991**).

MHG with team collaborators:

MHG with Rosalind M. Greenberg: *Phantoms* (anth **1989**); *Horse Fantastic* (anth **1991**).

MHG and R.M. Greenberg with Charles G. Waugh: *14 Vicious Valentines* (anth **1988**).

MHG with Joseph D. Olander: *Tomorrow, Inc.: SF Stories about Business* (anth **1976**); *The Best of John Jakes* (coll **1977**); *Time of Passage* (anth **1978**); *Science Fiction of the Fifties* (anth **1979**).

MHG and Olander with Patricia Warrick: *Science Fiction: Contemporary Mythology: The SFWA-SFRA Anthology* (anth **1978**).

MHG and Olander with Charles G. Waugh: *Mysterious Visions: Great Science Fiction by Masters of the Mystery* (anth **1979**).

MHG with Charles G. Waugh: *Love, 3000* (anth **1980**); *The Human Zero: The Science Fiction Stories of Erle Stanley Gardner* (coll **1981**); *The Fantastic Stories of Cornell Woolrich* (coll **1981**); *The Best Science Fiction of Arthur Conan Doyle* (coll **1981**); *Hollywood Unreel: Fantasies about Hollywood and the Movies* (anth **1982**); *The Fantastic Saint* (coll **1982**); *The Arbor House Celebrity Book of Horror Stories* (anth **1982**); *Cults! An Anthology of Secret Societies, Sects, and the Supernatural* (anth **1983**); *Alternative Histories: Eleven Stories of the World as it Might Have Been* (anth **1986**); *The Alternate Asimovs* (coll **1986**) ed anon; *Baker's Dozen: 13 Short Horror Novels* (anth **1987**); *Battlefields beyond Tomorrow: Science Fiction War Stories* (anth **1987**); *House Shudders: An Anthology of Haunted House Stories* (anth **1987**); *Vamps: An Anthology of Female Vampire Stories* (anth **1987**); *East Coast Ghosts* (anth **1989**); *Cults of Horror* (anth **1990**); *Devil Worshippers* (anth **1990**); *Back from the Dead* (anth **1991**); *Robot Warriors* (anth **1991**); *A Newbery Christmas* (anth **1991**).

MHG and Waugh with Frank D(avid) McSherry Jr (1927-   ): *Baseball 3000* (anth **1981**); *Treasury of American Horror Stories* (anth **1985**); *Strange Maine* (anth **1986**); *Cinemonsters* (anth **1987**); *Nightmare in Dixie* (anth **1987**); *Pirate Ghosts of the American Coast* (anth **1988**); *Red Jack* (anth **1988**); *Yankee Witches* (anth **1988**); the **Haunting, Spine-Chilling Stories** sequence, comprising *Dixie Ghosts* (anth **1988**), *Eastern Ghosts* (anth **1990**), *New England Ghosts* (anth **1990**), *Western Ghosts* (anth **1990**) and *Ghosts of the Heartland* (anth **1990**); *Haunted New England* (anth **1988**); *Fantastic World War II* (anth **1990**) with MHG and Waugh anon; *Civil War Ghosts* (anth **1991**); *Hollywood Ghosts* (anth **1991**); *Great American Ghost Stories* (anth **1991**); *The Fantastic Civil War* (anth **1991**) with MHG and Waugh anon.

MHG and Waugh with Carol Serling: *Rod Serling's Night Gallery Reader* * (anth **1987**).

MHG and Waugh with Jenny-Lynn Waugh: *101 Science Fiction Stories* (anth **1986**).

MHG and Waugh with Jane Yolen: *Dragons and Dreams* (anth **1986**); *Spaceships and Spells* (anth **1987**).

See also: ALTERNATE WORLDS; AMAZING STORIES; ANTHOLOGIES; ANTHROPOLOGY; CHILDREN IN SF; COMPUTERS; CRITICAL AND HISTORICAL WORKS ABOUT SF; LONGEVITY (IN WRITERS AND PUBLICATIONS); *The* MAGAZINE OF FANTASY AND SCIENCE FICTION; SHARED WORLDS; SOCIOLOGY.

GREENBERGER, ROBERT [r] ◊ Michael Jan FRIEDMAN.

GREENBERG: PUBLISHER ◊ GNOME PRESS; Martin GREENBERG.

GREENFIELD, IRVING A. (1928-   ) US writer in various genres, noted for expansive historical fantasies. *Waters of Death* (**1967**), *Succubus* (**1970**; as by Campo Verde 1977) and *The Stars Will Judge* (**1974**; vt *Star Trial* 1977) apply a lush though highly readable psychologizing style to routine sf matters. As Bruce Duncan he wrote *Mirror Image* (**1968** chap dos), a

minor work. [JC]

Other works: *The UFO Report* (**1967**), nonfiction; *The Others* (**1969**); *The Ancient of Days* (**1973**); *A Play of Darkness* (**1974**); *To Savor the Past* (**1975**); *Aton* (**1975**); *The Face of Him* (**1976**); *Julius Caesar is Alive and Well* (**1977**); *The Gods' Temptress* (**1978**), a fantasy; *The Fate of an Eagle* (**1990**); the **Depth Force** series of military-sf novels, comprising *Depth Force* (**1984**), *Depth Force #2: Death Dive* (**1984**), *#3: Bloody Seas* (**1985**), *#4: Battle Stations* (**1985**), *#5: Torpedo Tomb* (**1986**), *#6: Sea of Flames* (**1986**), *#7: Deep Kill* (**1986**), *#8: Suicide Run* (**1987**), *#9: Project Discovery* (**1988**), *#10: Death Cruise* (**1988**), *#11: Ice Island* (**1988**), *#12: Harbor of Doom* (**1989**), *#13: Warmonger* (**1989**), *#14: Deep Rescue* (**1990**) and *#15: Torpedo Treasure* (**1991**).

GREENHOUGH, TERRY Working name of UK writer Terence Greenhough (1944-   ) for most of his fiction, though he used the pseudonym Andrew Lester for the routine novel *The Thrice-Born* (**1976**), about persecuted hermaphrodites on a distant planet. TG began publishing sf with "The Tree in the Forest" for *Science Fiction Monthly* in 1974. His first novel, *Time and Timothy Grenville* (**1975**), typically of this writer somewhat discursively exploits an uneasy, oppressive relation between the world at large and its protagonist in a story of complex TIME TRAVEL and ALIENS, in which Earth itself proves to be at stake. [JC]
Other works: *The Wandering Worlds* (**1976**); *Thought-world* (**1977**); *The Alien Contract* (**1980**).

GREENLAND, COLIN (1954-   ) UK writer and academic who took a PhD in sf at Oxford, publishing his thesis in revised form as *The Entropy Exhibition: Michael Moorcock and the UK "New Wave"* (**1983**). This text also includes extensive examinations of the works of Brian W. ALDISS and J.G. BALLARD and gives competent readings of these and other authors, though it (understandably) fails to provide anything like a definitive modelling of the notoriously portable field and slippery topic of the NEW WAVE and its prime organ, NEW WORLDS. CG later edited, with Eric S. RABKIN and George E. SLUSSER, *Storm Warnings: Science Fiction Confronts the Future* (anth **1987** US). Beyond some further critical pieces – and *Death is no Obstacle* (**1992**), a book-length interview with Michael MOORCOCK, mostly about the latter's work – his interest had by this point shifted towards fiction, though he was to take on the position of Reviews Editor for FOUNDATION: THE REVIEW OF SCIENCE FICTION in 1990.

CG began publishing works of genre interest with "Miss Otis Regrets" for *Fiction Magazine* in 1982. His first novel, *Daybreak on a Different Mountain* (**1984**), a fantasy, wrestles mildly with an ENTROPY-laden plot and venue, and with a range of New Wave influences forgivable in a book coming from a scholar's loaded mind. Two further fantasies set in different parts of the same world, *The Hour of the Thin Ox* (**1987**) and *Other Voices* (**1988**), gradually demonstrated a sharpening, meticulously intelligent, cold, quiet narrative voice, and plots which carefully picked at some of the unthinking assumptions, general to FANTASY, about war and peace, prejudice and love. Of much greater sf interest was his fourth novel, *Take Back Plenty* (**1990**), a devotedly exuberant SPACE OPERA which won the ARTHUR C. CLARKE AWARD and the BRITISH SCIENCE FICTION AWARD. The story involves much tried-and-true material – from the MARS where the tale begins to the tough female space-tramp who runs her own ship and is in all sorts of trouble, and on to the ALIENS who dominate human space – and indeed there are moments when CG seems all too knowing. But the neatly calipered parodies are accomplished with love, lacking any trace of the disdain that has tended to disfigure much UK space opera; and the high jinks are genuinely earned. *In the Garden: The Secret Origin of the Zodiac Twins* (**1991** chap) is a short prequel. CG has become, quite suddenly, one of the dominant figures of his generation of sf writers. He contributed the entry on Bruce STERLING to this encyclopedia. [JC]

Other works: *Magnetic Storm* (graph **1984**) with Martyn Dean and Roger DEAN; *Interzone: The First Anthology* (anth **1985**) ed with John CLUTE and David PRINGLE.

See also: INTERZONE; MILFORD SCIENCE FICTION WRITERS' CONFERENCE; OUTER PLANETS; SCIENCE FICTION FOUNDATION; SPACE FLIGHT; WOMEN AS PORTRAYED IN SCIENCE FICTION.

GREENLEAF, WILLIAM (? -) US writer whose year of birth has been given as 1917. He began publishing sf with his first novel, *Timejumper* (**1980**), an adventure incorporating an unusually subtle presentation of the rite of passage central to the sf genre. His further novels share a common galactic background, though it is clear he is interested in that background not to challenge it with cosmogonies and alarums but in order to add verisimilitude to tales of humans caught off-balance in the vast Universe, and attempting to cope. *The Tartarus Incident* (**1983**) lovingly describes an accident which dumps an untrained group of humans on the planet of the title. *The Pandora Stone* (**1984**) is a tale of detection involving an AI and a return to an almost deserted Earth, where wisdom still resides. *Starjacked!* (**1987**) and *Clarion* (**1988**) cover similar ground, perhaps rather hurriedly. [JC]

GREENLEAF PUBLISHING ◊ IMAGINATION; IMAGINATIVE TALES.

GREENLEE, SAM (1930-) US writer whose NEAR-FUTURE sf novel, *The Spook who Sat by the Door* (**1969**), features a Black uprising in a near-contemporary USA. [JC]

See also: POLITICS.

GREENWALD, HARRY J. ◊ ROBERT HALE LIMITED.

GREENWOOD PRESS US specialist publishing house, based in Westport, Connecticut, whose books are largely academic and sometimes bibliographical; it has a special interest in sf, and is one of the major academic publishers in this area. GP has published commentaries on sf by Martha A. Bartter (1989), Thomas D. CLARESON (1984), Bud Foote (1990), Donald M. HASSLER (1982), John J. PIERCE (1987 and

1989), Gary K. WOLFE (1986) and others, and anthologies of critical essays on sf ed Michael R. COLLINGS, Thomas P. Dunn and Richard D. Erlich, Martin H. GREENBERG, Robert E. Myers, Donald Palumbo, Robert Reilly, Carl B. YOKE and others, many in GP's **Contributions to the Study of Science Fiction and Fantasy** series, which began in 1982 and has (by 1992) published over 40 volumes. Some of the anthologies have been selected from conference proceedings of the annual International Conference on the Fantastic in the Arts. Other GP books are the splendid *Science Fiction, Fantasy, and Weird Fiction Magazines* (**1985**) ed Marshall B. TYMN and Mike ASHLEY, and *A Biographical Dictionary of Science Fiction and Fantasy Artists* (**1988**) by Robert E. WEINBERG, both standard references. GP has also published complete runs of many famous sf magazines (mostly PULP MAGAZINES) in microfiche, including *AMZ*, *Planet Stories* and *Startling Stories*. [PN]

See also: SF IN THE CLASSROOM.

GREER, RICHARD ZIFF-DAVIS house name used once by Robert SILVERBERG and Randall GARRETT, on the story "The Great Klandar Race" (*AMZ* 1956), and twice during 1956-7 by others (unidentified). [PN]

GREER, TOM Working name of Irish surgeon Thomas Greer (1846/7-1904) for his writing; he lived in the UK from about 1880. In his *A Modern Daedalus* (**1885**) an Irish lad invents a one-man flying device which straps to the shoulders. The UK Government attempts to persuade him to use it against Ireland. Though he longs simply for peace, UK military action forces him onto the side of the revolutionaries, and a squadron of Irish fliers gains independence for their oppressed island home. [JC]

GREG, PERCY (1836-1889) UK poet, novelist and historian, son of the prolific essayist William Rathbone Greg (1809-1881); PG also wrote as Lionel G. Holdreth. His first work of genre interest was "Guy Neville's Ghost" for *Blackwood's* in 1865; the nonfiction *The Devil's Advocate* (**1878**) contains some speculative material. He was author of an important early sf novel, *Across the Zodiac: The Story of a Wrecked Record* (**1880**) (◊ FANTASTIC VOYAGES), which is perhaps most significant for its detailed depiction of the protagonist's journey to MARS through the use of apergy, an ANTIGRAVITY force (the concept provided a model for many later novels) which he uses to propel his SPACESHIP, whose construction is carefully described. Once on Mars, a more orthodox detailing of UTOPIA ensues: the Martians' version, though technologically advanced and benignly monarchical, suffers from scientific literalism (wrong thoughts are criminal) and dubious sexual morality (women are bought and sold). Finding himself allied to an opposing group of telepaths who believe in family life, the protagonist is embroiled in a final conflict and loses friends and wife, though the telepaths win the war. He escapes to his spaceship and the novel ends abruptly. *Across the Zodiac* remains readable. [JC/BS]

See also: HISTORY OF SF; POWER SOURCES.

GREGG PRESS US publisher of reprints in hardcover, a subsidiary of G.K. Hall & Co. The **Gregg Press Science Fiction Reprint Series**, ed David G. HART-WELL with Lloyd W. CURREY as associate editor, included a variety of novels and collections dating from the 18th century until recent times. Among them were several new volumes, including *Alyx* (coll **1976**; vt *The Adventures of Alyx* 1985 UK) by Joanna RUSS. GP also published books of critical material about sf drawn from such academic journals as SCIENCE-FICTION STUDIES and FOUNDATION. The GP reprints – many of which represented the first hardcover editions of out-of-print paperback originals – were regarded by critics as the best of the several sf reprint hardcover series, all aimed primarily at libraries; new and often lengthy introductions to the fiction reprints, by leading critics and authors, were a useful feature. 1978 was a peak year for the series, with 61 titles published. In 1980 it became clear that the backlist inventory was too large, and the roster of new publications was radically cut down. During 1980-84 Currey alone edited the GP **Masters of Science Fiction and Fantasy** author bibliographies, which covered 18 writers in 14 volumes. GP stopped publishing sf in 1984, and disappeared on being absorbed into Macmillan in Spring 1991. [PN/MJE]

GREGOR, LEE [s] ◊ Tony ROTHMAN.

GREGORY, JOHN ◊ Robert HOSKINS.

GREGORY, OWEN (? -) Pseudonym of the UK author of *Meccania, the Super State* (**1918**), a futuristic DYSTOPIA describing a German mechanical and totalitarian society taken to its logical extreme. It contrasts interestingly with the portrait of a dystopian Germany in Milo HASTINGS' *City of Endless Night* (**1920**). [JE]

See also: HISTORY OF SF; POLITICS.

GREMLINS Film. ◊ Joe DANTE.

GRENDON, STEPHEN ◊ August W. DERLETH.

GREY, CAROL [s] ◊ Robert A.W. LOWNDES.

GREY, CHARLES ◊ E.C. TUBB.

GRIBBIN, JOHN (1946-) UK writer known mostly for his very numerous science popularizations. Most of his novels have been in collaboration and have tended to a certain narrative predictability, though the science content has always been impressively presented. *Sixth Winter* (**1979**) with Douglas (William) Orgill (1922-1984) is a HARD-SF tale dealing with the coming of a new ice age. *Brother Esau* (**1982**), again with Orgill, charts the events following the discovery of the Yeti. *Double Planet* (**1988**) and its remote sequel *Reunion* (**1991**), both with Marcus CHOWN, are set in the same universe, though 1000 years apart. In the first, astronauts must intercept a comet thought to be on collision course with Earth; in the second the lunar population comes under the influence of a cult claiming to hold the secret to the replenishment of the MOON's atmosphere. JG's only solo novel, *Father to the Man* (**1989**), arguably his best book, is a readable and witty tale of a geneticist hero pitted against a world of spreading religious fundamentalism. The

Ragnarok Alternative (**1991**) with D.G. COMPTON is a NEAR-FUTURE cautionary tale in a traditional vein: a SCIENTIST threatens to end human civilization unless peace is declared; almost inadvertantly, Ragnarok does indeed occur. [MB]

Other works: Very many science books, including: *The Jupiter Effect* (**1974**) and *Beyond the Jupiter Effect* (**1983**), both with Stephen Plagemann (◊ Immanuel VELIKOVSKY); *White Holes: Cosmic Gushers in the Universe* (**1977**); *In Search of Schrödinger's Cat* (**1984**); *Blinded by the Light* (**1991**).

See also: ANTHROPOLOGY; APES AND CAVEMEN (IN THE HUMAN WORLD); BLACK HOLES; GENETIC ENGINEERING; PARALLEL WORLDS.

GRIDBAN, VOLSTED Pseudonym initially used by E.C. TUBB for 3 novels written for Scion Publications: *Alien Universe* (**1952**), *Reverse Universe* (**1952**) and *Debracy's Drug* (**1953**). Tubb then used the name on 2 novels for the Milestone Press – *Planetoid Disposals, Ltd* (**1953**) and *Fugitive of Time* (**1953**) – but Scion objected and reclaimed the name, which was used thereafter by John Russell FEARN (*whom see for titles*). [BS]

"GRIFF" House name of Modern Publications, used by John Russell FEARN on the sf novel *Liquid Death* (**1953**) and on non-sf works by F. Dubrez FAWCETT. [JC]

GRIFF, ALAN ◊ Donald SUDDABY.

GRIFFIN, BRIAN (1941-) UK writer who published two unremarkable sf novels for ROBERT HALE LIMITED, *The Nucleation* (**1977**) and *The OMEGA Project* (**1978**). He is better remembered for the competent *Apertures: A Study of the Writings of Brian Aldiss* (**1984**) with David WINGROVE. [JC]

GRIFFIN, P(AULINE) M. (1947-) US writer known initially as the author of the untaxing **Star Commandos** military-sf sequence set in an interstellar venue: *Star Commandos* (**1986**), *Star Commandos #2: Colony in Peril* (**1987**), *#3: Mission Underground* (**1988**), *#4: Death Planet* (**1989**), *#5: Mind Slaver* (**1990**), *#6: Return to War* (**1990**), *#7: Fire Planet* (**1990**), *#8: Jungle Assault* (**1991**) and *#9: Call to Arms* (**1991**). PMG has also published several fantasy stories, including material contributed to Andre NORTON's **Witch World** sequence, such as "Oath-Bound" in *Tales of the Witch World* * (anth **1987**) ed Norton and *Witch World: The Turning: Storms of Victory* * (**1991**) with Norton. [JC]

GRIFFIN, RUSSELL M(ORGAN) (1943-1986) US academic and writer who began publishing sf with his first novel, *The Makeshift God* (**1979**), an overwritten and overlong but notably intelligent romance of origins, set initially in a drab Arab-dominated marginally pre-CYBERPUNK USA, and then on a planet which houses mysteriously significant data about the deep human past. *Century's End* (**1981**) takes another blackly satirical look at the NEAR FUTURE of Earth, generating comparisons between RMG and writers like Kurt VONNEGUT Jr and – more relevantly – John T. SLADEK. In *The Blind Man and the Elephant* (**1982**) RMG tackled a theme dear to Sladek, the consequences of thrusting a tabula-rasa personality into a meat-grinder world – in Sladek's case it is usually a young ROBOT that loses its innocence; in RMG's it is a fast-maturing and monstrous experiment in cloning. The novel closes, after some very funny passages, in a state of utter despair. RMG's final novel, *The Timeservers* (**1985**), returns to the relative extroversion of his first in the story of a young soldier's confrontation with CLONES, far stars and telepathic ALIENS. RMG's premature death halted a career which could have soared. [JC]

See also: END OF THE WORLD; MONSTERS.

GRIFFITH, GEORGE Working name of UK traveller, journalist and writer George Chetwynd Griffith-Jones (1857-1906), the son of a clergyman and one of the most influential sf writers of his time. He appeared frequently in the pre-sf MAGAZINES and PULP MAGAZINES, particularly PEARSON'S WEEKLY and PEARSON'S MAGAZINE, writing as GG or, for some short stories, as Levin Carnac. He was instrumental in the transformation of the future-WAR novel to a more sensational form, capitalizing on contemporary political anxiety; and he helped make up a literary coterie, including William LE QUEUX, M.P. SHIEL and Louis TRACY, which specialized in the genre.

GG first established himself with *The Angel of the Revolution* (1893 *Pearson's Weekly*; rev **1893**) and its sequel *Olga Romanoff* (1893-4 *Pearson's Weekly* as "The Syren of the Skies"; rev **1894**). In the first a revolutionary organization equipped with aerial battleships creates a reformed society under the government of a world federation; the second, set 125 years later, describes the upheaval which transforms this UTOPIAN state to one of total anarchy. Both are remarkable for their foresight of battle tactics in air warfare and for their anticipation of radar, sonar and nuclear weapons. They include elements which would only later become commonplace, notably the struggle by international cartels for world domination and the apocalyptic visions of Armageddon on Earth and of DISASTER from the heavens by comet. These elements can be found also in *The Outlaws of the Air* (1894-5 *Short Stories*; rev **1895**), *Gambles with Destiny* (coll **1898**), *The Great Pirate Syndicate* (1898 *Pick-Me-Up*; rev **1899**), *The Lake of Gold* (**1903**), *A Woman Against the World* (**1903**), *The World Masters* (**1903**), *The Stolen Submarine* (**1904**), *The Great Weather Syndicate* (**1906**), *The World Peril of 1910* (**1907**) and *The Lord of Labour* (**1911**).

From early in his career GG was overshadowed by H.G. WELLS, a fact which caused him to diversify his work, in search of critical acclaim. Such praise never came, although he produced notable examples of several themes: IMMORTALITY featured in *Valdar the Oft-Born* (1895 *Pearson's Weekly*; rev **1895**) and *Captain Ishmael* (**1901**), the latter also being an early example of the PARALLEL-WORLDS theme; the LOST-WORLD theme in *The Romance of Golden Star* (1895 *Short Stories* as "Golden Star"; rev **1897**), *The Virgin of the Sun* (**1898**) and *A Criminal Croesus* (**1904**); SPACE FLIGHT in *A Honeymoon in Space* (1900 *Pearson's Magazine* as "Stories

of Other Worlds"; exp **1901**); the fourth DIMENSION in *The Mummy and Miss Nitrocris* (fixup **1906**; vt *The Mummy and the Girl* UK); telepathy in *A Mayfair Magician* (**1905**; vt *The Man with Three Eyes* UK); RELIGION in *The Missionary* (**1902**); and the supernatural in *Denver's Double* (**1901**), *The White Witch of Mayfair* (**1902**) and *The Destined Maid* (**1908**).

GG's influence on contemporary UK sf was extensive, from E. Douglas FAWCETT's *Hartmann the Anarchist* (**1893**) through to Cyril Seymour's *Comet Chaos* (**1906**) and John MASTIN's *The Stolen Planet* (**1906**), and can still be seen today, as in Michael MOORCOCK's 19th-century pastiches. (Since GG's anti-US stance precluded US publication of many of his works, his influence there has been negligible.) Several of his novels have been reprinted in recent times, as well as a collection of unreprinted stories, *The Raid of "Le Vengeur"* (coll **1974**) ed George LOCKE. [JE]

Other works: *Briton or Boer?* (**1897**); *The Gold Finder* (**1898**); *The Justice of Revenge* (**1901**); *The Sacred Skull* (**1908**).

About the author: "War: Warriors of If" in *Strange Horizons: The Spectrum of Science Fiction* (**1976**) by Sam MOSKOWITZ.

See also: EDISONADE; END OF THE WORLD; HISTORY OF SF; MARS; MERCURY; MOON; NEAR FUTURE; NUCLEAR POWER; POLITICS; PROTO SCIENCE FICTION; REINCARNATION; TECHNOLOGY; TRANSPORTATION; VENUS; WEAPONS.

GRIFFITH, MARY (?1800-1877) US horticultural writer and novelist whose early futuristic UTOPIA, *Three Hundred Years Hence* (**1950**), originally appeared as one of the stories in *Camperdown, or News from our Neighbourhood* (coll **1836**), published as by An Author of our Neighbourhood. In an extremely early use of the SLEEPER-AWAKES convention, the tale takes its protagonist 200 years forward into an automated, urban world where women are emancipated, slavery is abolished, drunkards are pilloried, good hygiene is enforced, dogs are extinct and Shakespeare is expurgated. It is a bluestocking world, but one created with a substantial force of imagination. [JC/PN]

See also: SUSPENDED ANIMATION.

GRIFFITHS, DAVID ARTHUR (? -) UK writer whose obscurity is only marginally lessened by the knowledge that, while working for CURTIS WARREN, he invited E.C. TUBB to write his first novels. Under the house name Gill HUNT DAG wrote *Vega* (**1951**) and *Fission* (**1952**); under the house name King LANG he wrote *Gyrator Control* (**1951**), *Astro-Race* (**1951**), *Task Flight* (**1951**), *Rocket Invasion* (**1951**) and *Projectile War* (**1951**); and under the house name David Shaw he wrote *Laboratory "X"* (**1950**), *Planet Federation* (**1950**) and *Space Men* (**1951**). Though unconfirmed, there is a strong possibility that DAG was the author of 6 **Tarzan**-derived novels under the house name Marco GARRON. [JC]

GRIFFITHS, JOHN (C.) (1934-) UK writer in whose sf novel, *The Survivors* (**1965**), an assorted group of folk hang on in a Cornish cave after China starts WWIII. A nonfiction (and significantly unliterary) study, *Three Tomorrows: American, British and Soviet Science Fiction* (**1980**), treats the genre as a forum, defined according to the sociological principles of Karl Mannheim (1893-1947), for predictive utterances that illustrate national characters. [JC]

GRILE, DOD ◊ Ambrose BIERCE.

GRIN, ALEXANDER [r] ◊ RUSSIA.

GRINNELL, DAVID ◊ Donald A. WOLLHEIM.

GRIP ◊ L. Edgar WELCH.

GROGAN, GERALD (1884-1918) UK writer, killed in WWI. His sf novel, *A Drop in Infinity* (**1915**), carries its unwilling protagonists via a mad SCIENTIST's device into an empty but congenial PARALLEL WORLD. A lengthy ROBINSONADE evolves during which the protagonists become reconciled to their lot, have children, survive a crisis and find themselves finally isolated from Earth. [JC]

GRØNFELDT, VIBEKE ◊ DENMARK.

GROOM, (ARTHUR JOHN) PELHAM (?   -   ) UK writer whose long series of **Peter Mohune** novels were mostly crime stories; the last two, however, concern themselves with the implications of nuclear power. In *The Fourth Seal* (c**1947**) Mohune comes across a secret society which has privately developed atomic fission. In *The Purple Twilight* (**1948**) he travels to MARS in search of the descendents of ATLANTIS, finding instead telepathic members of a dying Martian race, who tell him they themselves destroyed Atlantis in self-defence, but later fell into an arms race leading to the nuclear civil war that sterilized them all. When Mohune returns to Earth he finds a similar arms race developing, with similar sterilizing weapons. He tells of his experiences – in vain. [JC]

GROSSE VERHAU, DER (vt *The Big Mess*) Film (1970). Kairos Film. Prod and dir Alexander Kluge, starring Siegfried Graue, Vincenz Starr, Maria Sterr, Silvia Forsthofer. Screenplay Kluge, Wolfgang Mai. 86 mins. B/w and colour.

This West German comedy is by a director – a leading light of the German New Wave – whose apprenticeship was with Fritz LANG. It is an amusing DYSTOPIA set in AD2034, when the Galaxy has been opened up to entrepreneurs, and monopoly capitalism – in this case the Suez Canal Company – is rampant. *DGV* focuses on two not especially bright astronauts caught in the muddle of the system, who smuggle, wreck spaceships for scrap or do deals with insurance companies. The imagery of working stiffs in ramshackle spacecraft points forward to ALIEN (1979). [PN]

GROUSSET, PASCHAL ◊ André LAURIE.

GROVE, FREDERICK PHILIP (1897-1948) German-born Canadian writer, born Felix Paul Greve. His output included realistic novels, rural studies and the sf SATIRE *Consider Her Ways* (written 1913-23; **1947**), which presents the notes of an amateur scientist in telepathic contact with three ants, members of an exploratory team from South America. Their comments on the nature of Man and human society are pointed, and the picture of ant society is remarkably detailed. The novel has never received due

attention. [JC]

See also: CANADA.

GROVE, PETER J. [r] ◊ ROBERT HALE LIMITED.

GROVE, W. (?   -?   ) UK writer of whom nothing is known except that he was the author of *A Mexican Mystery* (**1888**) and its sequel, *The Wreck of a World* (**1889**), which trace the coming to a kind of consciousness of the MACHINES of Earth; they then breed other machines and revolt, driving humanity from the continental USA by about 1950. [JC]

GROVES, J(OHN) W(ILLIAM) (1910-   ) UK writer, variously employed, who began publishing sf with "The Sphere of Death" for *AMZ* in 1931, but whose career consisted mainly of desultory magazine publications until his first novel for ROBERT HALE LIMITED, *Shellbreak* (**1968**), in which a man awakens in AD2505 armed with knowledge that helps him to topple a corrupt dictatorship. *The Heels of Achilles* (**1969**) presents a world in which the dead have come mysteriously to life. [JC]

GRUBER, MARIANNE [r] ◊ AUSTRIA.

GRUNERT, CARL [r] ◊ GERMANY.

GUERARD, ALBERT JOSEPH (1914-   ) Influential US critic and novelist, who has taught at Amherst College, Harvard University and Stanford University. He has long been an advocate of US experimentalist fiction. His sf novel *Night Journey* (**1950**) depicts an idealistic soldier against the background of a useless NEAR-FUTURE European WAR. The loss of his illusions is rendered with psychological acuity. [JC]

GUERNSEY, H.W. [s] ◊ Donald WANDREI.

GUERRE PLANETARI ◊ *Il* PIANETA DEGLI UOMINI SPENTI.

GUIN, WYMAN (WOODS) (1915-1989) US pharmacologist, advertising executive and writer who began publishing sf with "Trigger Tide" as Norman Menasco for *ASF* in 1950, though his career can be said really to have begun with "Beyond Bedlam" (1951) which, like most of his best work of the 1950s and early 1960s, appeared first in *Gal* and was subsequently included in *Living Way Out* (coll **1967**; exp vt *Beyond Bedlam* 1973 UK). "Beyond Bedlam" is a brilliant novelette describing an Earth about 1000 years hence where drugs enforce a strictly regulated schizophrenia (◊ PARANOIA) in every human being in a five-days-on, five-days-off routine, each body being inhabited alternately by two personalities, the balance between whom nullifies Man's subconscious aggressions, thus eliminating the "paranoid wars" of the "ancient Moderns". But passion and art likewise disappear. The good and evil of this system are explored with a literacy and verisimilitude that make it a genuinely interesting variation on Aldous HUXLEY's vision of drug-enforced stability in *Brave New World* (**1932**). Similar hyperbolic distortions of the "normal" world govern stories like "My Darling Hecate" (1953) and "The Delegate from Guapanga" (1964). *The Standing Joy* (**1969**), a PARALLEL-WORLDS story set in a nostalgically rendered other Earth, features a SUPERMAN, a good deal of harmless SEX and a general sense of missed focus. WG will be remembered for the power of his early stories.   [JC]

See also: CRIME AND PUNISHMENT; GALAXY SCIENCE FICTION; PSYCHOLOGY; SOCIOLOGY.

GU JUNZHENG ◊ CHINESE SF.

GULL, RANGER ◊ Guy THORNE.

GUNN, JAMES E(DWIN) (1923-   ) US writer, critic and teacher, born in Kansas City and educated at the University of Kansas, where he is now a professor of English and journalism and Director of the Center for the Study of Science Fiction. He began publishing sf with "Communications" for *Startling Stories* in 1949 as Edwin James, a disguise he dropped for good in 1952 after 10 stories. Throughout his career, JEG's favoured form has been the short story or novelette; his best book-length fictions have been either collaborations or assemblages of shorter material. He has also published considerable sf criticism, beginning with excerpts from his MA thesis in *Dynamic Science Fiction* (1953-4) and continuing with the brief *The Discovery of the Future: The Ways Science Fiction Developed* (**1975**). More notable is a competent illustrated survey of sf, *Alternate Worlds: The Illustrated History of Science Fiction* (**1975**), although it inevitably suffers from superficiality in its attempt at comprehensive coverage of later years, with many writers appearing only as names in paragraph-long lists. For this critical work JEG won the 1976 PILGRIM AWARD. More recently, he edited *The New Encyclopedia of Science Fiction* (**1988**), a shortish and film-dominated text which is in no way a sequel to or otherwise connected with the first edition of *The Encyclopedia of Science Fiction* (**1979**) ed Peter NICHOLLS.

JEG's first two books were SPACE OPERAS. *This Fortress World* (**1955**) pits its protagonist against a repressive future religion. *Star Bridge* (**1955**), with Jack WILLIAMSON, shows through a sometimes pixilated intricacy of plotting the mark of its senior collaborator's grasp of the nature of good space opera. Everyone, it turns out, is being manipulated, for the salvation of mankind, by an immortal Chinese with a parrot. *Station in Space* (coll of linked stories **1958**) assembles several uninteresting early tales about how Man is tricked into space exploration for his own good. *The Joy Makers* (fixup **1961**) describes, in JEG's dark, ponderous, cumulatively impressive manner, a society whose members are controlled by synthetic forms of release that corrode their sense of reality. In *The Immortals* (fixup **1962**), JEG's best known work, a mutation confers IMMORTALITY upon a group of people who become collectively known as Cartwrights; as their condition is transmissible to others by blood transfusion, they are forced underground by the understandable desire of mortal men to attain immortality. The hospital setting of the book adds verisimilitude. As The IMMORTAL (1969), it became a made-for-tv series, which JEG novelized as *The Immortal* ∗ (**1970**).

JEG's second novel to gain general esteem, *The Listeners* (fixup **1972**), makes productive use of its episodic structure in depicting the installation of an electronic listening post to scan for radio messages from the stars, and the 100-year wait that ensues. JEG's somewhat morose style (in his better moments he evokes a kind of sense of the melancholy of wonder) nicely underlines the complex institutional frustrations and rewards of this long search. Indeed, his forte seems to lie in the narrative analysis of stress-ridden administrations and their administrators; and his best work is usually set in organizations or among groups of people forced to cooperate. Women (◊ WOMEN AS PORTRAYED IN SCIENCE FICTION), however, tend to be excluded from the higher purposes of such organizations, and are sometimes depicted balking at the sacrifices men must make to reach the stars. Nevertheless, JEG has made a considerable success of his chosen length and venue, and his later works – particularly *Crisis!* (fixup **1986**) – can ruminate absorbingly on the administration of humanity's problems to come.   [JC]

Other works: *Future Imperfect* (coll **1964**); *The Witching Hour* (coll **1970**); *The Burning* (fixup **1972**); *Breaking Point* (coll **1972**); *Some Dreams are Nightmares* (coll **1974**), containing short stories from *Station in Space*, *The Joy Makers* and *The Immortals*; *The End of the Dreams: Three Short Novels About Space, Happiness and Immortality* (coll **1975**), containing long stories from *Station in Space*, *The Joy Makers* and *The Immortals*; *The Magicians* (1954 *Beyond* as "Sine of the Magus"; exp **1976**); *Kampus* (**1977**); *The Dreamers* (1977 in *Triax* ed Robert SILVERBERG as "If I Forget Thee"; exp **1980**; vt *The Mind Master* 1982); *Tiger! Tiger!* (written 1952; **1984** chap); *The Unpublished Gunn* (coll **1992** chap).

Nonfiction: *Teacher's Manual: The Road to Science Fiction* (**1980** chap) with Stephen H. Goldman (? -1991), who also served as Associate Editor for JEG's *New Encyclopedia* and was its major contributor; *Isaac Asimov: The Foundations of Science Fiction* (**1982**), for which he received a 1983 HUGO; *Inside Science Fiction: Essays on Fantastic Literature* (coll **1992**).

As editor: The 4 vols of **The Road to Science Fiction** sequence, comprising *From Gilgamesh to Wells* (anth **1977**), *From Wells to Heinlein* (anth **1979**), *From Heinlein to Here* (anth **1979**) and *From Here to Forever* (anth **1982**).

About the author: *A James Gunn Checklist* (**1984** chap) by Chris DRUMM.

See also: ALIENS; ANTI-INTELLECTUALISM IN SF; ASTRONOMY; BIBLIOGRAPHIES; COMMUNICATIONS; CRITICAL AND HISTORICAL WORKS ABOUT SF; DYSTOPIAS; GALACTIC EMPIRES; GAMES AND SPORTS; GENRE SF; GOLDEN AGE OF SF; HUGO; ISAAC ASIMOV'S SCIENCE FICTION MAGAZINE; JOHN W. CAMPBELL MEMORIAL AWARD; LEISURE; MAGIC; MEDICINE; NEBULA; PSYCHOLOGY; RELIGION; SCIENCE FICTION WRITERS OF AMERICA; SOCIOLOGY; UTOPIAS.

GUNN, NEIL M(ILLER) (1891-1973) Scottish writer and civil servant, author of many novels, the first being *Grey Coast* (**1926**). It and some others – like *Morning Tide* (**1931**), *The Last Glen* (**1932**), *Second Sight* (**1940**) and *The Silver Bough* (**1948**) – contain fantasy elements of interest. *The Green Isle of the Great Deep* (**1944**), a sequel to *Young Art and Old Hector* (**1942**), describes the experiences of an old man and a young boy in an underground realm which turns out to be a sterile and totalitarian land of the dead: their protests to God are successful. *The Serpent* (**1948**) is a TIME-TRAVEL story. *The Well at World's End* (**1951**), whose title acknowledges a debt to William MORRIS, sums up NMG's style, which is rich and sometimes sentimental, and his abiding concern, which is the evocation of an idealized Scotland. [JC]

GUNNARSSON, THORARINN (1957-) US writer who has been strongly identified with FANTASY because of *Song of the Dwarves* (**1988**), its sequel *Revenge of the Valkyrie* (**1989**), plus *Make Way for Dragons!* (**1990**), sequelled by *Human, Beware!* (**1990**), both sequences humorous. The **Starwolves** sequence – *The Starwolves* (**1988**), *Starwolves: Battle of the Ring* (**1989**) and *Starwolves: Tactical Error* (**1991**) – is rousing SPACE OPERA, opposing human warriors to a sentient space fortress. [JC]

GÜNTHER, GOTTHARD [r] ◊ GERMANY.

GURK, PAUL [r] ◊ GERMANY.

GURNEY, DAVID ◊ Patrick BAIR.

GURNEY, JAMES (1958-) US illustrator, raised in California, studied at the Art Center College of Design in Pasadena. JG made his sf début with a cover for *FSF* in 1982, but his real baptism of fire that year was working as one of only two background painters on the animated SWORD-AND-SORCERY film *Fire and Ice* (**1982**). JG, who works in oils, primarily paints book covers; he has also done historic and prehistoric paintings for *National Geographic*. His style is one of the most painterly in sf since the retirement of John SCHOENHERR; in a field that emphasizes surface slickness, JG is refreshing. His influences are eclectic, but include Norman Rockwell (1894-1978). His popular *Dinotopia: A Land Apart from Time* (**1992**) is an art book, with text also by JG, telling of a 19th-century LOST WORLD in which humans coexist with intelligent dinosaurs. [JG/PN]

See also: ILLUSTRATION.

GUTTERIDGE, LINDSAY (1923-) UK writer. His sf series featuring **Matthew Dilke** – *Cold War in a Country Garden* (**1971**), *Killer Pine* (**1973**) and *Fratricide is a Gas* (**1975**) – calls upon themes from espionage to ECOLOGY to buttress far-fetched tales of a government agent miniaturized with some companions (◊ GREAT AND SMALL) to test the chances of counteracting OVERPOPULATION by resettling the world with a miniaturized mankind. [JC]

GYERTYÁN, ERVIN [r] ◊ HUNGARY.

HABER, KAREN Working name of Karen Lee Haber Silverberg (1955-   ), US writer and anthologist, married to Robert SILVERBERG since 1987. She began publishing work of genre interest with "Madre de Dios" for *FSF* in 1988, and came to general notice with the **Fire in Winter** sequence, which traces the fortunes of a family of PSI-POWERED mutants and their threatened subculture in a 21st-century USA: *The Mutant Season* (**1989**) with Silverberg, *The Mutant Prime* (**1990**) and *Mutant Star* (**1992**), with a further volume projected. Silverberg's influence was initially evident – the first volume was derived from his "The Mutant Season" (1973) – but KH soon established her own identity as a sharp, warm teller of tales. A singleton, *Thieves Carnival* (**1990** chap dos), prequels Leigh BRACKETT's *The Jewel of Bas* (1944 *Planet Stories*; **1990** dos), with which it was paired as a TOR BOOKS Double. With Silverberg, KH co-edited the new sequence of UNIVERSE anthologies, carrying on from Terry CARR's original series: *Universe 1* (anth **1990**) and *Universe 2* (anth **1992**), with further volumes projected. [JC]

HABĪBĪ, AMIL ◊ ARABIC SF.

HACKETT, [General Sir] JOHN (WINTHROP) (1910-   ) British Army officer (retired) and writer, whose *The Third World War: August 1985* (**1978**; rev 1982) and *The Third World War: The Untold Story* (coll **1982**), both written with the help of a think-tank of soldiers, journalists and diplomats, together describe the course of a (largely) conventional war betweeen (mostly) NATO and the Warsaw Pact in a mock historical style. The books represent an attempt to alert the public to the dangers posed by war against the Soviet bloc, and remain interesting largely because of the authenticity and detail of their descriptions of what such a conflict might actually have been like. [NT]

HADLEY, ARTHUR T(WINING) (1924-   ) US journalist and writer whose successful novel, *The Joy Wagon* (**1958**), uses a borderline-sf treatment of COMPUTERS in a sharply comic send-up of the US electoral system. The computer runs for President and almost wins. [JC]

See also: POLITICS.

HADLEY, FRANKLIN ◊ Russ R. WINTERBOTHAM.

HADLEY PUBLISHING COMPANY US specialist SMALL PRESS, 1947-8, based in Providence, Rhode Island, owned by Thomas P. Hadley. It grew out of (or was a renaming of) Buffalo Book Co., under which name it published *The Time Stream* (1931 *Wonder Stories*; **1946**) by John TAINE and *The Skylark of Space* (1928 *AMZ*; **1946**) by E.E. "Doc" SMITH. A very short-lived company, HPC was notable for publishing John W. CAMPBELL Jr's first book, *The Mightiest Machine* (1934-5 *ASF*; **1947**), A.E. VAN VOGT's *The Weapon Makers* (1943 *ASF*; **1947**; rev vt *One Against Eternity* 1952) and L. Ron HUBBARD's *Final Blackout* (1940 *ASF*; **1948**). The company was bought out by Donald M. Grant (1927-   ) and became the Grandon Company; later, under his own name, Grant became an important small-press publisher of fantasy. [MJE/PN]

HAGGARD, [Sir] H(ENRY) RIDER (1856-1925) UK civil servant, lawyer, agricultural expert and writer. HRH spent the years 1875-81 in the Colonial Service in South Africa, where he gained much of the material for his fiction. On his return to the UK he read for the bar while at the same time beginning to produce novels and other work. With his third and fourth novels, *King Solomon's Mines* (**1885**) and the even more successful *She: A History of Adventure* (1886-7 *The Graphic*; cut **1886** US; text restored 1887 UK; *The Annotated She* [**1991** US] ed Norman Etherington is a variorum text with erratic additional notes) HRH was catapulted into fame, and soon left the bar; he was knighted in 1912. These novels of anthropological sf remain his most famous; they established a pattern he would follow for the rest of his career. That pattern might be described as a central model for Edgar Rice BURROUGHS and the SCIENCE-FANTASY subgenre whose popularity attended the latter's revival in the 1960s: it is a pattern in which realistic portraits of the contemporary world (in HRH's case South Africa) are combined with backward-looking displacements (in his case invoking LOST WORLDS, IMMORTALITY and REINCARNATION) to give a general effect of deep nostalgia. HRH was fascinated by ruins, ancient civilizations and primitive customs. His allied interest in the PSEUDO-SCIENCE of Spiritualism link him to such contemporaries as Bulwer LYTTON and Marie CORELLI, though in fact his central literary friendships were with Andrew LANG and Rudyard KIPLING; he shared with the latter a *fin de siècle* sense – which proved entirely accurate – that the British Empire was on the wane. His prose was sometimes overblown, but he was a gifted storyteller with a powerful imagination and the ability to create memorable heroic figures, like the Zulu Umslopogaas, whose early life is the subject of the remarkable *Nada the Lily* (**1892** US).

Umslopogaas appears also in HRH's principal sequence, the novels about white hunter **Allan Quatermain** which gave Africa to the world as a haven in the mind's eye. Here the **Quatermain** books are given in order of internal chronology, the dates of their settings preceding the titles: 1835-8 *Marie* (**1912**); 1842-69 *Allan's Wife* (**1887**), which was incorporated into *Allan's Wife and Other Tales* (coll **1889**); 1854-6 *Child of Storm* (**1913**); 1859 *Maiwa's Revenge* (**1888**); 1870 *The Holy Flower* (**1915**); vt *Allan and the Holy Flower* 1915 US); 1871 *Heu-Heu, or The Monster* (**1924**); 1872 *She and Allan* (**1921** US); 1873 *The Treasure of the Lake* (**1926** US); 1874 *The Ivory Child* (**1916**); 1879 *Finished* (**1916** US); 1879 "Magepa the Buck" in *Smith and the Pharaohs and Other Tales* (coll **1920**); 1880 *King Solomon's Mines*; 1882 *The Ancient Allan* (**1920**); 1883 *Allan and the Ice Gods: A Tale of Beginnings* (**1927**); 1884-5 *Allan Quatermain: Being an Account of his Further Adventures and Discoveries in Company with Sir Henry Curtis, Bart., Commander John Good, and one Umslopogaas* (**1887**; cut vt *Allan Quatermain and the Lost City of Gold* * 1986, the text being shaped into a film novelization). Not all these books could be described as science fantasy, but all project that sense of desiderium – the longing for that which is lost – that lies at the heart of true science fantasy; and those titles written late in HRH's career – like *The Ancient Allan*, a tale of love-death set in Egypt, and *Allan and the Ice Gods*, in which Quatermain is thrown back in time by means of a drug and inhabits the body of a paleolithic man – tend to express their author's potent (but submerged) sexuality in venues so remote that a suppressed libidinousness can become, occasionally, almost explicit.

It is, however, in the **Ayesha** sequence that HRH's Victorian libido found easiest release from the chains of the present. In *She: A History of Adventure* (rewritten for the movies by Don Ward as *She: The Story Retold* * **1949** US), *Ayesha: The Return of She* (**1905**; vt *The Return of She: Ayesha* 1967 US), *She and Allan*, which provides a link with the **Quatermain** series,

and *Wisdom's Daughter: The Life and Love Story of She-Who-Must-Be-Obeyed* (**1923**), HRH created, in the immortal and subversive Ayesha, what has come to seem an abiding emblem of that longing for "primitive" transcendence that typically marks the end of eras. The sudden ageing of Ayesha in the first volume of the sequence (later volumes dally inconsequentially with her earlier life) has an effect both tragic and petty. *The World's Desire* (**1890**), with Andrew Lang, a pendant to the main series, carries Odysseus into new adventures, during which he discovers that Helen of Troy and Ayesha are one. A knotted eroticism also infuses *When the World Shook: Being an Account of the Great Adventure of Bastin, Bickley, and Arbuthnot* (**1919**), a novel plotted in part by Kipling (who later helped HRH with *Allan and the Ice Gods*): the three eponymous Victorians find the high priest of ATLANTIS in SUSPENDED ANIMATION; having caused the first Flood, he is about to start another; his daughter, likewise discovered, causes ructions in the hearts of the three.

HRH can seem both heated and evasive to modern readers, but read in context he is a figure of very considerable power, a stirrer in deep waters. [DP/JC]
Other works: *Cleopatra: Being an Account of the Fall and Vengeance of Harmachis, the Royal Egyptian, as Set Forth by his Own Hand* (**1889** US); *Beatrice* (**1890**); *Eric Brighteyes* (**1891**); *Montezuma's Daughter* (**1893**); *The People of the Mist* (**1894**); *Heart of the World* (**1895**); *The Wizard* (**1896**); *Swallow: A Tale of the Great Trek* (**1899** US); *Elissa, the Doom of Zimbabwe: Black Heart & White Heart* (coll **1900** US; rev vt *Black Heart and White Heart and Other Stories*; title story of US edition only, vt *Elissa, or The Doom of Zimbabwe* 1917 UK); *Lysbeth: A Tale of the Dutch* (**1901** US); *Stella Fregelius: A Tale of Three Destinies* (**1903** US); *Pearl-Maiden: A Tale of the Fall of Jerusalem* (**1903**); *The Brethren* (**1903**); *Benita* (**1906**; vt *The Spirit of Bambatse* 1906 US); *The Yellow God: An Idol of Africa* (**1908** US); *The Ghost Kings* (**1908**; vt *The Lady of the Heavens* 1908 US); *The Lady of Blossholme* (**1909**); *Morning Star* (**1910**); *Queen Sheba's Ring* (**1910**); *Red Eve* (**1911**); *The Mahatma and the Hare: A Dream Story* (**1911**); *The Wanderer's Necklace* (**1914**); *Moon of Israel: A Tale of the Exodus* (**1918**); *The Missionary and the Witch-Doctor* (**1920** chap US); *The Virgin of the Sun* (**1922**); *Queen of the Dawn: A Love Tale of Old Egypt* (**1925**); *Mary of Marion Isle* (**1929**; vt *Marion Isle* 1929 US); *Belshazzar* (**1930**). There are various omnibuses.

About the author: *Bibliography of the Works of H. Rider Haggard* (**1947**) by J.E. Scott; *The Cloak that I Left* (**1951**) by Lilias Rider Haggard; *Rider Haggard: His Life and Work* (**1960**) by Morton Cohen; *The Wheel of Empire* (**1967**) by Alan Sandison; *Rider Haggard* (**1984**) by Norman Etherington.

See also: ANTHROPOLOGY; DIME-NOVEL SF; HISTORY OF SF; ORIGIN OF MAN; PULP MAGAZINES; RADIO (USA); SERIES; SEX.

HAGGARD, WILLIAM Pseudonym of Richard Clayton (1907-   ), UK civil servant whose political thrillers, usually featuring Colonel Russell (retired in later volumes) of the Secret Service, sometimes extrapolate on current political trends, after the fashion of their genre. *Slow Burner* (**1958**) has some sf content relating to the atomic-power process described by the title. The skulduggery in *Venetian Blind* (**1959**) concerns Negative Gravity, "a prize beyond price. The conquest of space, the ultimate weapon"; it proves chimerical. *The Bitter Harvest* (**1971**) deals with germ warfare. [JC]

HAHN, RONALD M. [r] ◊ GERMANY.

HAHN, STEVE ◊ Stephen ROBINETT.

HAIBLUM, ISIDORE (1935-) US writer, born, educated and based in New York, where he has set much of his fiction. The humour expressed in his novels is Yiddish in style (IH is himself a Jew), especially in his first sf novel, *The Tsaddik of the Seven Wonders* (**1971**). IH writes a fluent though sometimes rather disarranged kind of comic sf, of which *The Wilk are Among Us* (**1975**; rev 1979) is a representative example, with its amusingly overcomplicated plot, its frenetic spoofing of the ALIENS-in-our-midst theme, and its general failure to take hold of its materials. *Nightmare Express* (**1979**), a comparatively ambitious ALTERNATE-WORLD detective novel, and a later mystery series set in the 21st century – *The Mutants are Coming* (**1984**) and *Out of Sync* (**1990**) – maintain a similar tone. His attempts to amalgamate Yiddish humour and sf themes are of technical interest. [JC]
Other works: *The Return* (**1973**); *Transfer to Yesterday* (**1973**); three novels featuring a detective named **Dunjer**, being *Interworld* (**1977**), *Outerworld* (**1979** dos) and *Specterworld* (**1991**); two novels featuring the **Siscoe and Block** detective team, being *The Identity Plunderers* (**1984**) and *The Hand of Ganz* (**1985**).

HAIGH, RICHARD (? -) UK author of one routine SPACE OPERA for ROBERT HALE LIMITED, *The Golden Astronauts* (**1980**), and of a series of horror novels, *The Farm* (**1984**) and *The City* (**1986**), both featuring man-eating pigs. [JC]

HAILE, TERENCE J. (? -?1980) UK author of two sf novels remarkable for their clumsiness and their apparent ignorance of basic physical laws. In *Space Train* (**1962**) a farmer builds a rocket-powered train which, as a consequence of sabotage, takes off into space. There he encounters interplanetary crabs before returning to Earth. *Galaxies Ahead* (**1963**) is similarly implausible. [NT]

HAILEY, JOHANNA ◊ Sharon JARVIS.

al-HAKĪM, TAWFĪQ (1898-1986) Regarded along with Nobel-prize winning author Najīb Mahfūz as the most important modern Egyptian writer, author of over 50 books of short stories, novels, dramas and essays, some of sf interest. In 1947 he published his first sf short story, "Fī sana malyūn" ["In the Year Million"]. His most interesting sf works are plays. In *Rihla ilā al-ghad* (**1950**; trans as "Voyage to Tomorrow" 1981) he uses relativistic TIME TRAVEL during interstellar flight, in something of a homage to H.G. WELLS. Two one-act plays have sf themes: *Shāir alā al-qamar* (**1972**; trans as "Poet on the Moon" 1981) and Taqrīr

qamarī ["Moon Account"] (**1972**). The first uses sf metaphor in a story about the struggle of Art to assert its place in society; the second tells of two extraterrestrials writing a report about life on Earth. English translations of "Voyage to Tomorrow" and "Poet on the Moon" can be found in *Plays, Prefaces and Postscripts* (2 vols, coll **1981**). His essays about the future in *Hadīth maa al-kawkab* ["Conversation with the Planet"] (coll **1974**) have sf relevance, as do some other works. [JO]
See also: ARABIC SF; THEATRE.

HALAM, ANN ◊ Gwyneth JONES.

HALBERSTAM, MICHAEL J(OSEPH) (1932-1980) US medical doctor and writer whose *The Wanting of Levine* (**1978**) depicts a 1988 US presidential campaign which ends in the election of the Jewish politician Levine, whose wry wisdom may bring the nation back from the violent civil strife that has already begun to balkanize the land. [JC]

HALDANE, CHARLOTTE (FRANKEN) (1894-1969) UK writer, married to J.B.S. HALDANE and sister-in-law of Naomi MITCHISON. Her sf novel, *Man's World* (**1926**), set in a 21st-century society which divides women into whores and sainted breeders (◊ WOMEN AS PORTRAYED IN SCIENCE FICTION), takes an ambivalent attitude towards the eugenic thinking (◊ GENETIC ENGINEERING) responsible for such a state, but eventually seems to suggest that the social cost of improving the human stock by fiat has been too high. The racism delineated – Whites have risen to new biological heights while Blacks are systematically poisoned – is also ambivalent in the telling. Two fantasies are *Melusine, or Devil Take Her!* (**1936**), about the survival of witches in Christian Europe, and *The Shadow of a Dream* (**1952**). [JC]

HALDANE, J(OHN) B(URDON) S(ANDERSON) (1892-1964) UK biologist, brother of Naomi MITCHISON. He dabbled in sf in an incomplete and posthumously published novel, *The Man with Two Memories* (**1976**), about a man's mental link with an inhabitant of another world. JBSH's bold speculative essays heavily influenced significant works by other writers. *Daedalus, or Science and the Future* (**1924**), the first of the long-running series of **Today & Tomorrow** pamphlets, is a classic anticipation of GENETIC ENGINEERING, and provided the image of the future sarcastically extrapolated by Aldous HUXLEY in *Brave New World* (**1932**). The semifictional "The Last Judgment" in *Possible Worlds* (coll **1927**) provides an evolutionary prospectus for the human race which was extensively elaborated by Olaf STAPLEDON in *Last and First Men* (**1930**). JBSH's wife Charlotte HALDANE drew heavily on his ideas for *Man's World* (**1926**). "On Being the Right Size", also from *Possible Worlds*, discusses problems of scale in sf (e.g., giants 10 times human size but with – unworkably – the same proportions). *My Friend Mr Leakey* (coll of linked stories **1937**) is a book of fantasies for children. [BS]
About the author: *J.B.S.: The Life and Work of J.B.S. Haldane* (**1968**) by Ronald W. CLARK.

HALDEMAN, JACK C(ARROLL) II (1941-   ) US
writer who began publishing sf with "Garden of
Eden" for *Fantastic* in 1971. His 50 or so stories have
tended to avoid the more serious SPACE-OPERA themes,
sticking generally to GAMES-AND-SPORTS tales about
ROBOT football players, precognitive STARS, and the
like. His first novel, *Vector Analysis* (**1978**), sets
problems in space and sees them solved. His second,
Perry's Planet * (**1980**), is a **Star Trek** tie, and his third,
with his wife Vol Haldeman and Andrew J. OFFUTT,
all signing as John CLEVE, is *Spaceways #11: The Iceworld
Connection* (**1983**). *There is No Darkness* (fixup **1983**)
with his brother Joe HALDEMAN, amusedly pits a hick
from the hinterlands of a colony planet against some
interstellar difficulties, leading picaresquely to the
saving of the Universe. *Bill, the Galactic Hero on the
Planet of the Zombie Vampires* * (**1991**) with Harry
HARRISON is slapstick. But not all JCH's work has been
determinedly light; some of his earlier stories – like
"Songs of Dying Swans" (1976), about the death of
some genetically altered humans – show genuine
aesthetic skills, a sense of bluff cunning which came
more and more to the fore in the 1980s. He remains
perhaps most at ease in collaborations; his contributions to *Slow Dancing Through Time* (coll **1990**), an
assembly of stories written by various authors in
collaboration with Gardner DOZOIS, are among his
best work. *Echoes of Thunder* (**1991** chap dos) with Jack
DANN is also of interest.   [JC]

See also: MATHEMATICS.

HALDEMAN, JOE Working name of US writer Joseph
William Haldeman (1943-   ). JH took a BS in
physics and astronomy before serving as a combat
engineer in Vietnam (1967-9), where he was severely
wounded, earning a Purple Heart; later, in 1975, he
took an MFA. The range of degrees was an early
demonstration of the complexity of his interest in the
HARD SF with which he has sometimes been identified;
and his experiences in Vietnam have marked everything he has since written, including his first book,
War Year (**1972**), a non-sf novel set there. He began
publishing sf with "Out of Phase" for *Gal* in 1969, and
came to sudden prominence with the critical and
popular success of his first sf novel, *The Forever War*
(1972-4 *ASF*; fixup **1974**), which, with "You Can
Never Go Back" (1975), makes up a series whose
description of the life of soldiers in a future WAR
counterpoints and in some ways rebuts Robert A.
HEINLEIN's vision in *Starship Troopers* (**1959**). In *The
Forever War* interstellar travel is effected by "collapsar
jumps", which are subjectively instantaneous but
which in fact take many years to accomplish, so that
they work as a kind of one-way TIME TRAVEL; sent by
this means to fight in engagement after engagement
on different planets, soldiers are doomed to total
alienation from the civilization for which they are

fighting, and if they make too large a jump face the
risk of coming into battle with antiquated weaponry.
Their deracination is savage, their camaraderie cynically manipulated. As a portrait of the *experience* of
Vietnam the book is remarkable. It won a Ditmar (◊
AWARDS), a NEBULA and a HUGO; the first volumes of a
GRAPHIC-NOVEL version are *The Forever War 1* (graph
1991) and *The Forever War 2* (graph **1991**), both
illustrated by Marvano.

Mindbridge (**1976**), a novel whose narrative techniques are suggested by its dedication to John Dos
Passos (1896-1970) and John BRUNNER, is composed in
alternating sequences of straight narration, reportage, excerpts from books (some written long after
the events depicted), graphs and other devices. The
story itself is a not unconventional space epic, with
MATTER TRANSMISSION, telepathy-inducing "toys" –
actually small aquatic animals – abandoned by an
extinct race of godlike aliens, and so forth. *All My Sins
Remembered* (fixup **1977**) returns to the existential
chaos of Earth, and introduces an enduring model of
the JH protagonist: a competent hero whose identity
is threatened from without, by the manipulations of
worldly powers, and from within, by the need to
make sense of an existence without ultimate meaning. In JH's novels, making sense of things is itself an
act of heroism. As his most typical books revolve
around this task – and are resolved in its often
ambiguous accomplishment – it is not surprising that
he has rarely written sequels. Once the goal has been
reached, the story ends.

The only exception to this pattern is the **Worlds**
sequence comprising *Worlds* (**1981**), *Worlds Apart*
(**1983**) and *Worlds Enough and Time* (**1992**). These
books, which also differ from his typical work in
featuring a female protagonist, are distinguished by
the broad compass of their portrayal of a NEAR-FUTURE
Earth under the threat of nuclear HOLOCAUST, which
is soon realized. In the surviving SPACE HABITATS –
each a small world representative of a different kind
of civilization – some sense must be made of the
human enterprise: the relict planet must be preserved
and, in the third volume, humanity must attempt to
reach the stars. JH's other novels of the 1980s are only
intermittently successful. *Tool of the Trade* (**1987**), a
TECHNOTHRILLER, repeats in a damagingly affectless
manner the themes of earlier books; and *Buying Time*
(**1989**; vt *The Long Habit of Living* 1989 UK) weakens a
central tale about the purchasing of IMMORTALITY by a
displeasing failure to address the kind of society in
which this might be acceptable, or the kind of human
who might pursue the goal. But *The Hemingway Hoax*
(**1990**), the magazine version of which won a Nebula
as Best Novella, movingly entangles its typical JH
protagonist in a complex set of dilemmas (and
ALTERNATE WORLDS) which test to the utmost his
capacity to retain moral choice, to remain even
approximately whole.

JH's stories, assembled in *Infinite Dreams* (coll **1979**)
and *Dealing in Futures* (coll **1985**), are of subsidiary

interest to his novels – though "Tricentennial" (1976) won a Hugo – but sometimes illustrate with clarity the themes which drive them. Throughout his career there has been a sense – not usual in US sf – that JH thinks of his novels as necessary acts in a lifelong enterprise, a moral theatre whose meaning will be defined only when he finishes. It is perhaps for this reason that he is not good at repeating himself, that those books in which he attempts to do so are surprisingly bad, and that after two decades his readers continue to await each new title – each new act in the existential drama – with very substantial interest. [JC]

Other works: Two borderline sf **Attar** spy novels, *Attar's Revenge* (**1975**) and *War of Nerves* (**1975**), under a Pocket Books house name, Robert Graham; two **Star Trek** novels, *Planet of Judgment* * (**1977**) and *World without End* * (**1979**); *There is No Darkness* (**1983**) with his brother Jack C. HALDEMAN II (*whom see for details*); *More than the Sum of his Parts* (1985 *Playboy*; **1991** chap).

As editor: *Cosmic Laughter* (anth **1974**); *Study War No More* (anth **1977**); *Nebula Award Stories Seventeen* (anth **1983**); three anthologies with Martin Harry GREENBERG and Charles G. WAUGH, being *Body Armor: 2000* (anth **1986**), *Supertanks* (anth **1987**) and *Space-Fighters* (anth **1988**).

About the author: *Joe Haldeman* (**1980**) by Joan Gordon.

See also: ALIENS; ASTOUNDING SCIENCE-FICTION; BLACK HOLES; COLONIZATION OF OTHER WORLDS; FASTER THAN LIGHT; HIVE-MINDS; ISAAC ASIMOV'S SCIENCE FICTION MAGAZINE; MEDICINE; POETRY.

HALE, EDWARD EVERETT (1822-1909) Prolific US writer, contributing editor to *The Atlantic Monthly*, Unitarian preacher and abolitionist; he is best known today for the title story (1863) of *The Man without a Country and Other Tales* (coll **1868**). *Sybaris and Other Homes* (coll **1869**), describing a UTOPIAN colony of Sybarites uncovered on an ISLAND off the coast of Italy, is of sf interest. A second utopian fiction, *Ten Times One is Ten: The Possible Reformation* (**1871**), as by Frederick Ingham, is constructed as a fantasy of socially beneficial haunting; it first appeared (1870) in EEH's own journal *Old and New*, which he founded to espouse the ideals embodied in the tale. *Hands Off* (1881 *Harper's New Monthly Magazine*; **1895** chap) interestingly places two time-travelling spirits in Biblical Egypt, where as an experiment they construct an ALTERNATE WORLD in which the patriarch Joseph excapes captivity, with disastrous results. Of primary interest to sf readers are "The Brick Moon" (1869) and its short sequel, "Life in the Brick Moon" (1870) – both revised into one story in *His Level Best and Other Stories* (coll **1872**), later reprinted in *The Brick Moon and Other Stories* (coll **1899**), and published independently as *The Brick Moon* (**1971** chap) – which comprise probably the first attempt to describe an artificial Earth satellite, along with its accidental launching into orbit and the attempts of those stranded upon it

to survive. [JC]

Other works: *Back to Back: A Story of Today* (**1878**; exp vt *How They Lived in Hampton: A Study of Practical Christianity Applied in the Manufacture of Woollens* 1888), a utopian speculation in story form.

About the author: "The Real Earth Satellite Story" in *Explorers of the Infinite* (**1963**) by Sam MOSKOWITZ.

See also: DISCOVERY AND INVENTION; HISTORY OF SF; SPACE HABITATS.

HALE, ROBERT, LIMITED ◊ ROBERT HALE LIMITED.

HALEY, CLAUDE ◊ Leonard G. FISH.

HALIBUT, EDWARD [s] ◊ Richard WILSON.

HALIDOM, M.Y. Pseudonym of an unidentified UK writer who wrote also as Dryasdust, under which name he is perhaps best known for the 3-vol *Tales of the Wonder Club* (coll **1899-90**; each vol subsequently published as by MYH vt *Tales of the Wonder Club: First Series* 1903; *Second Series* 1904; *Third Series* 1905). Most of the stories assembled are supernatural. *The Wizard's Mantle* (**1890**; rev 1903 as by MYH) also appeared initially as by Dryasdust. Further titles, all as by MYH, and some including suggestions of sf, were *The Spirit Lovers* (coll **1903**), *A Weird Transformation* (**1904**), about a reanimated corpse, *The Woman in Black* (**1906**), *Zoë's Revenge* (**1908**), *The Poet's Curse* (**1911**) and *The Poison Ring* (**1912**). [JC]

HALL, AUSTIN (*c*1885-1933) US writer who claimed to have written over 600 stories in various pulp genres, mainly Westerns. He began publishing sf and fantasy with "Almost Immortal" for *All-Story Weekly* in 1916. "The Rebel Soul" (1917 *All-Story Weekly*) and its sequel, the book-length "Into the Infinite" (1919 *All-Story Weekly*), typically infuse immortality-through-vampirism and TIME TRAVEL with pulp clichés, not always ineffectively; in their concern with the nature of human personality all three are derivative of Robert Louis STEVENSON's *Strange Case of Dr Jekyll and Mr Hyde* (**1886** chap). Possibly confused by the collaborative process, *The Blind Spot* (1921 *Argosy*; **1951**) with Homer Eon FLINT cloaks a central plot – involving an interdimensional gateway into a PARALLEL WORLD – in layers of unresolved melodrama. Cruelly, Damon KNIGHT quoted extensively from it in a critical piece (reprinted as part of Chapter 3 of *In Search of Wonder* [coll **1956**; exp 1967]) to demonstrate its infelicities. A sequel, *The Spot of Life* (1932 *Argosy*; **1964**), was by AH alone; it offers scientific explanations for the gateway (or blind spot) plus doses of dynastic politicking in the parallel world. *People of the Comet* (1923 *Weird Tales*; **1948**), a weaker tale, is a variant on the theme of solar-system-as-atom in a greater macrocosm (◊ GREAT AND SMALL). [JC]

See also: HISTORY OF SF; MARS.

HALL, DESMOND W(INTER) (1909-1992) US writer and editor who served as assistant editor of *Astounding Stories of Super Science* (◊ ASTOUNDING SCIENCE-FICTION) under Harry BATES 1930-33, also collaborating with Bates as a writer under the pseudonyms H.G. WINTER and, more famously, Anthony GILMORE; as Gilmore they produced the popular **Hawk Carse**

series, which reached book form as *Space Hawk* (coll of linked stories **1952**). DWH also wrote some stories under his own name as well as one under an unidentified pseudonym for *Weird Tales*. After F. Orlin TREMAINE took over from Bates, DWH continued as assistant editor for a time before being promoted to the editorship of the magazine *Mademoiselle*. In "Gold on Gold", in *What Will They Think of Last?* (**1976**), H.L. GOLD claimed that it was DWH rather than Tremaine who actually ran *ASF*. [MJE]

HALL, FRANCES (? -) US writer, author of *Pretender* (**1979**) with Piers ANTHONY. [JC]

HALL, HAL(BERT) W(ELDON) (1941-) US bibliographer, Special Formats Librarian at Texas A & M University Library. His useful series of BIBLIOGRAPHIES began with *SFBRI: Science Fiction Book Review Index, 1970* (**1971** chap), and volumes relating to each year have been published in each succeeding year up to *Vol 15, 1984* (**1985** chap); since then, each volume now titled **Science Fiction and Fantasy Book Review Index**, there have been *Vol 16, 1985* (**1988** chap), *Vol 17, 1986* (**1988** chap) and *Vol 18, 1987* **1990** chap). Three retrospective books collecting and revising these are *Science Fiction Book Review Index 1923-1973* (**1975**), *Science Fiction Book Review Index 1974-1979* (**1981**) and *Science Fiction and Fantasy Book Review Index 1980-1984* (**1985**), the last with Geraldine L. Hutchins. All are most useful to the researcher: comprehensive and accurate, they contain also a great deal of data about sf magazine publication. On this latter subject HWH has published *A Checklist of Science Fiction Magazines* (**1972** chap) and *The Science Fiction Magazines: A Bibliographical Checklist of Titles and Issues through 1982* (**1983** chap).

A second series of reference works began with *Science Fiction Research Index, Vol 1* (**1979** chap) and *Vol 2* (**1982** chap), running to date to *Vol 7* (**1987**) and *Vol 8* (**1990** chap). A collection of the first 6 vols plus additions is the monumental *Science Fiction and Fantasy Reference Index, 1878-1985: An International Author and Subject Index to History and Criticism* (2 vols **1987**), to which vols 7 and 8, which bring the story up to 1987, are the initial supplements. Subsequent supplements are included in the annual bibliographies ed Charles N. BROWN and William G. CONTENTO: *Science Fiction, Fantasy, & Horror: 1988* (**1989**), *1989* (**1990**), *1990* (**1991**) and *1991* (**1992**). There are, of course, omissions – it is not possible to examine the review pages of every newspaper in the world – but these works are the best available for determining the location of reviews and articles on anything from CYBERPUNK through NIGHT OF THE LIVING DEAD to TOLKIEN.

The continually expanding computer database in which HWH has stored all this material also contains information on the location of important sf/fantasy book and magazine COLLECTIONS, and HWH has published various articles on this subject – one written with Neil BARRON in *Anatomy of Wonder: A Critical Guide to Science Fiction, Third Edition* (**1987**) ed

Barron – and one book, *Science/Fiction Collections: Fantasy, Supernatural & Weird Tales* (**1983**).

HWH is on the editorial board of EXTRAPOLATION. [PN]

Other works: *Chad Oliver: A Preliminary Bibliography* (**1985** chap; rev vt *The Work of Chad Oliver* 1990); *The Work of Louis L'Amour: An Annotated Bibliography and Guide* (**1991**).

See also: CRITICAL AND HISTORICAL WORKS ABOUT SF.

HALL, JAMES [s] ◊ Henry KUTTNER.

HALL, JOHN RYDER ◊ William ROTSLER.

HALL, NORMAN [r] ◊ ROBERT HALE LIMITED.

HALL, ROBERT LEE (1941-) US writer and high-school teacher whose first novel, *Exit Sherlock Holmes* (**1977**; rev 1977 UK), purports to be a lost Watson manuscript telling more about the relationship of Holmes and Moriarty. As in David DVORKIN's later *Time for Sherlock Holmes* (**1983**), TIME TRAVEL fuels the plot. [JC]

HALL, RODNEY (1935-) Australian poet and writer, Chairperson since 1991 of the Australia Council, a body responsible for government arts policy and funding. His long, vivid, humorous, baroque fourth novel, *Kisses of the Enemy* (**1987**), is set in the NEAR FUTURE in an Australia now a republic. A campaign of cultural subversion unsettles a nation that has hitherto offered little resistance to its rape by foreign opportunists. [PN]

HALL, RONALD (1929-) UK writer in whose sf novel, *The Open Cage* (**1970**), an escaped con returns to a violently altered and apocalyptic world. [JC]

HALL, SANDI (1942-) UK-born writer, journalist and feminist activist, resident variously in Canada, Zambia, NEW ZEALAND, Australia, the USA and Mexico. In New Zealand she belonged to the "Broadsheet" collective, founded the NZ Women's Party, and publicly announced her lesbianism. In the NEAR-FUTURE *The Godmothers* (**1982** UK), her first novel, two groups of women in a well realized feminist AD2095 oppose patriarchal oppression. *Wingwomen of Hera* (**1987** US), the first volume of the projected **Cosmic Botanists** sequence, is less didactic: the collision of patriarchal and feminist values is background for a strong plot with convincing societies and characters. SH writes well; and refreshingly believes that a feminist future does not necessarily imply UTOPIA. [MMacL]

HALLE, LOUIS J(OSEPH) (1910-) US academic and writer whose UTOPIA, *Sedge* (**1963**), contrasts a community which isolates itself from civilization for hundreds of years with the increasingly frenetic world beyond the gates. [JC]

HALLEN, A.L. (? -?) UK writer whose *Angilin: A Venite King* (**1907**) is among several novels by early writers that prefigure the PLANETARY ROMANCES of Edgar Rice BURROUGHS, though without the flair. The planet in question is VENUS; the protagonist is an Earthman who transports his psyche there in an attempt to find his dead love; the plot is ornate and dynastic, and features airships. [JC]

HALLI, H.R. [r] ◊ FINLAND.

HALLIWELL, TONY ◊ Hugh DARRINGTON.

HALLOWEEN III: SEASON OF THE WITCH Film (1983). Dino De Laurentiis. Prod Debra Hill, John CARPENTER. Dir Tommy Lee Wallace, starring Tom Atkins, Stacey Nelkin, Dan O'Herlihy. Screenplay Wallace (but primarily by Nigel KNEALE, uncredited). 98 mins. Colour.

Not at all a true sequel to the "stalk and slash" **Halloween** films, this is a horror film with an sf rationale. Crazed Irish entrepreneur Cochran (O'Herlihy), infuriated by Halloween's commercial degradation, plans to restore to it its proper mystical significance. Using microchips manufactured from a stolen Stonehenge monolith, he manufactures and sells huge numbers of Halloween masks that will hideously destroy their child wearers when triggered by an electronic pulse relayed through tv advertisements. Kneale had his name taken off the credits, disgusted at this becoming more and more like a SPLATTER MOVIE, but a true eeriness remains to balance the physical horrors (not all of which are merely arbitrary), especially in the dark-suited, polite ANDROID killers and in the menacing sleepy streets of the company town. Directed by a Carpenter protégé, this film has the enjoyably grisly flavour of Carpenter's own. [PN]

HALLUS, TAK ◊ Stephen ROBINETT.

HALSBURY, EARL OF Working name of UK writer Hardinge Goulburn Giffard, Second Earl of Halsbury (1880-1943). His future-WAR novel, *1944* (**1926**), depicts a cataclysmic conflict in which the USSR attacks the UK from the air, leaving only a few survivors. The protagonist, a modern Noah, prepares to leave the shattered island by ark, but is told that the USSR has been itself obliterated, and returns to build a new UK. [JC]

HAM, BOB (? -) US author of the **Overload** sequence of post-HOLOCAUST series of military-sf adventures comprising *Overload #1: Personal War* (**1989**), *#2: The Wrath* (**1989**), *#3: Highway Warriors* (**1989**), *#4: Tennessee Terror* (**1989**), *#5: Atlanta Burn* (**1990**), *#6: Nebraska Nightmare* (**1990**), *#7: Rolling Vengeance* (**1990**), *#8: Ozark Payback* (**1991**), *#9: Huntsville Horror* (**1991**), *#10: Michigan Madness* (**1991**), *#11: Alabama Bloodbath* (**1991**) and *#12: Vegas Gamble* (**1991**). [JC]

HAMBLY, BARBARA (1951-) US author, primarily of FANTASY, based in Southern California. She entered genre publishing with the **Darwath Trilogy** fantasy sequence, published by DEL REY BOOKS: *The Time of the Dark* (**1982**), *The Walls of Air* (**1983**) and *The Armies of Daylight* (**1983**). In these a historian and a biker from Los Angeles find themselves in a struggle between Good and Evil in a PARALLEL WORLD where MAGIC works; the conventional fantasy situation is invigorated to a degree by the lively treatment. Her **Sun Wolf** fantasy sequence, to date open-ended, is more original in both style and matter: *The Ladies of Mandrigyn* (**1984**), *The Witches of Wenshar* (**1987**) –

reissued together as *The Unschooled Wizard* (omni **1987**) – and *The Dark Hand of Magic* (**1990**). These novels have, without preaching, an attractive element of FEMINISM in their depiction of the women in their medieval fantasy world, some of whom are mercenaries, others at least potentially self-reliant.

In the **Windrose** series – *The Silent Tower* (**1986**) and *The Silicon Mage* (**1988**), reissued together as *Darkmage* (omni **1988**) – BH, who had previously used occasional sf ideas in her fantasy, produced a true genre-bending sequence in its apposition of science and magic by placing two parallel worlds (one ours) in phase in a story involving an evil sorcerer's consciousness embedded in a COMPUTER as "a series of subroutines". BH's sole pure sf novel to date is *Those who Hunt the Night* (**1988**; vt *Immortal Blood* UK 1988), which was marketed as HORROR. It is a good whodunnit in the STEAMPUNK manner, set in Victorian England, about a skilled investigator hired to protect vampires – rationalized as a race parallel to humanity but with somewhat different ethics – from whoever is murdering them. Magicians (persecuted) behave once again rather as displaced SCIENTISTS in the initial world of the projected **Sun-Cross** sequence: *The Rainbow Abyss* (**1991** UK) and *The Magicians of Night* (**1992**). The latter book, with savage irony, transports one of these true magicians into our own world among the occultists and pseudo-scientists clustered around Hitler in Nazi Germany.

BH has created her own corner of the FANTASY market, characteristically pressing occasional sf ideas into the service of her fundamentally fantastic themes, but without pushing too hard against fantasy/sf genre constraints. Her books – by no means potboilers, and sometimes painful – are normally vigorous, interesting and alert within her self-imposed format. [PN]

Other works: *The Quirinal Hill Affair* (**1983**; vt *Search the Seven Hills* 1987), an historical whodunnit; *Ishmael* * (**1985**) and *Ghost Walker* * (**1991**), both STAR TREK ties; *Dragonsbane* (**1986**), fantasy; *Beauty and the Beast* * (**1989**) and *Beauty and the Beast: Song of Orpheus* * (**1990**), novelizing tv episodes from BEAUTY AND THE BEAST.

See also: HISTORY OF SF.

HAMILTON, CICELY Pseudonym under which UK novelist, playwright, actress and feminist Cicely Mary Hamill (1872-1952) published all her adult work, though her children's fiction, including some stories for the **Sexton Blake** series, was written as by Scott Rae and by Max Hamilton. Her best-known plays are eloquently suffragist; they include *How the Vote was Won* (**1910**) with Christopher St John, in which the outcome predicted by the title is achieved when those women without means go on strike. Her sf novel, *Theodore Savage: A Story of the Past or the Future* (**1922**; rev vt *Lest Ye Die* 1928), bitterly depicts a future WAR in whose aftermath the people of the UK, driven out of the cities, revert to superstitious barbarism. The ironically named protagonist lives to a great age in a small village full of savages who think of pre-collapse artifacts as obscene. CH is one of the first – and among the darkest – of those UK sf novelists whose vision of things was shaped by WWI, which they saw as foretelling the end of civilization. [JC]

See also: END OF THE WORLD; HISTORY IN SF.

HAMILTON, CLIVE ◊ C.S. LEWIS.

HAMILTON, EDMOND (MOORE) (1904-1977) US writer, married to Leigh BRACKETT from 1946. With E.E. "Doc" SMITH and Jack WILLIAMSON, he was one of the prime movers in the development of US sf, sharing with those writers in the creation and popularization of classic SPACE OPERA as it first appeared in PULP MAGAZINES from about 1928. His first story, "The Monster-God of Mamurth" for *Weird Tales* in 1926, which vulgarized the florid weird-science world of Abraham MERRITT, only hinted at the exploits to come, though EH found SCIENCE FANTASY a fertile vein, collecting this story and others in his first book, *The Horror on the Asteroid & Other Tales of Planetary Horror* (coll **1936** UK). Only two years later, with the publication of "Crashing Suns" (1928 *Weird Tales*), he was writing genuine space opera of the sort with which he soon became identified: the Universe-spanning tale in which an Earthman and his comrades (not necessarily human) discover a cosmic threat to the home Galaxy and successfully – either alone, or with the aid of a space armada, or both – combat the ALIENS responsible for the threat. Science or pseudo-science served as a magically enabling doubletalk for the easier presentation of interstellar action, and the scope, colour and dynamic clarity of this liberated action did much to define the SENSE OF WONDER for a generation of readers, who rewarded EH with several nicknames in recognition of his gift, variously "World-Destroyer", "The World Wrecker", or "World-Saver Hamilton".

Though not technically part of the series, "Crashing Suns" is structurally identical to the six **Interstellar Patrol** stories, which followed immediately; when they were (with the exception of "The Sun People" [1930]) finally reprinted in the 1960s, this story was properly included, giving its title to the second volume. *Outside the Universe* (1929 *Weird Tales*; **1964**) and *Crashing Suns* (coll **1965**) represent, with faults and virtues grandly magnified, the heart of EH's early work – and the heart, therefore, of space opera. Others of his works contributing to the creation of the form include *The Metal Giants* (1926 *Weird Tales*; **1932** chap), "The Comet Doom" (1928) and "The Universe Wreckers" (1930). The main failure of EH's work is a lack of cohesion, through the lack of any sense of strategic plotting; that lack would of course be remedied in the work of E.E. Smith. EH persisted with the format through the 1930s, with gradually diminishing success, occasionally under pseudonyms including Robert Castle, Hugh Davidson, Robert Wentworth and the house name Will GARTH; and – dangerously for his career – occupied much of his time in the early 1940s with the smoother but

significantly less lively **Captain Future** series, published 1940-50 by Standard Magazines in CAPTAIN FUTURE (1940-44) and afterwards in *Startling Stories* (1945-6 and 1950-51).

Not all the **Captain Future** stories were by EH. Five were signed with the house name Brett STERLING, of which two were by EH and three – "Worlds to Come" (1943), "Days of Creation" (1944) and *The Tenth Planet* (1944 *CF*; **1969**) – were by Joseph SAMACHSON, with one further title – *The Solar Invasion* (1946 *Startling Stories*; **1969**) – being by Manly Wade WELLMAN. Each tale was written to a rigorous formula in which the super-scientist protagonist, backed by three aides (one ROBOT, one ANDROID and one brain in a box), brings an interstellar villain to justice. EH's **Captain Future** titles eventually released in book form are *Danger Planet* (1945 *Startling Stories* as "Red Sun of Danger"; **1968**, as by Sterling), *Outlaw World* (1946 *Startling Stories*; **1969**), *Quest Beyond the Stars* (1942 *Captain Future*; **1969**), *Outlaws of the Moon* (1942 *Captain Future*; **1969**), *The Comet Kings* (1942 *Captain Future*; **1969**) – which was probably the outstanding tale among them – *Planets in Peril* (1942 *Captain Future*; **1969**), *Calling Captain Future* (1940 *Captain Future*; **1969**), *Captain Future's Challenge* (1940 *Captain Future*; **1969**), *Galaxy Mission* (1940 *Captain Future* as "The Triumph of Captain Future"; **1969**), *The Tenth Planet* (1944 *Captain Future* as "Magic Moon"; **1969**, as by Sterling), *The Magician of Mars* (1941 *Captain Future*; **1969**) and *Captain Future and the Space Emperor* (1940 *Captain Future*; **1969**). 11 further novels remain in magazine form: "Captain Future and the Seven Space Stones" (1941), "Star Trail to Glory" (1941), "The Lost World of Time" (1941), "The Face of the Deep" (1943), "The Return of Captain Future" (1950), "Children of the Sun" (1950), "The Harpers of Titan" (1950), "Pardon My Iron Nerves" (1950), "Moon of the Unforgotten" (1951), "Earthmen no More" (1951) and "Birthplace of Creation" (1951). The original idea for *Captain Future* had come from Mort WEISINGER, a senior editor with the Standard Magazines group. Later, in 1941, Weisinger shifted over to DC COMICS, and took many of his top writers with him, including EH, who worked for some time in the mid-1940s as a staff writer on SUPERMAN, along with Henry KUTTNER and others.

Unfortunately for EH, his work in comics and his involvement with *Captain Future* (which was aimed primarily at teenaged boys) made it initially somewhat difficult for him to be accepted after WWII as the competent and versatile professional he had in fact been for years, a writer with a much wider range than was generally realized, one who had already produced several stories whose comparatively sober verisimilitude prefigured post-WWII requirements. After his marriage to Brackett in 1946 his output diminished, but its quality increased, a fact obscured by the publication in book form over the next years of material from his early career – like *Tharkol, Lord of the Unknown* (1939 *Startling Stories*; **1950** UK), in which

Martians invade Earth for its water – and by his habitual rehashing of space-opera conventions in old-fashioned epics like *The Sun Smasher* (1954 *Universe*; **1959** dos), *Battle for the Stars* (1956 *Imagination* as by Alexander BLADE; exp **1961**) and *Fugitive of the Stars* (1957 *Imagination*; rev **1965** dos). His final series, the **Starwolf** tales about tough interstellar adventurer Morgan Chane, is similarly antiquated in premise, but told in a clean-cut trimmed-down language which has won it supporters. The sequence comprises *The Weapon from Beyond* (**1967**), *The Closed Worlds* (**1968**) and *World of the Starwolves* (**1968**), all three being assembled as *Starwolf* (omni **1982**).

At the same time, however, EH was writing novels which, though in the space-opera tradition, were more carefully composed and darker in texture. It is for these novels, plus *The Monsters of Juntonheim* (1941 *Startling Stories* as "A Yank at Valhalla"; **1950** UK; vt *A Yank at Valhalla* 1973 dos US), that he is now mainly remembered. The best is probably *The Haunted Stars* (**1960**), in which well characterized humans face a shattering mystery on the MOON: the secret of star travel left by long-dead ALIENS, along with dark warnings. *The Star Kings* (**1949**; vt *Beyond the Moon* 1950), whose plot reflects *The Prisoner of Zenda* (**1894**) by Anthony Hope (1863-1933) (◊ RURITANIA), is grander in scope but less impressively written: its sequels are collected in *Return to the Stars* (coll of linked stories **1970**), and both volumes are assembled as *Chronicles of the Star Kings* (omni **1986** UK). Other titles of interest from this flourishing period are *City at World's End* (**1951**), *The Star of Life* (1947 *Startling Stories*; rev **1959**) and *The Valley of Creation* (1948 *Startling Stories*; rev **1964**), a strongly written SWORD-AND-SORCERY tale with an sf dénouement.

EH shared with his long-time colleague Jack Williamson a capable and flexible attitude towards the post-WWII genre and its markets (in contrast to the third great originator of US space opera, E.E. Smith, who was a generation older). Through his ability to evolve a cleaner and more literate style to meet these new demands, and to apply this style to his old generic loves, EH wrote novels at the end of his career that read perfectly idiomatically as novels of the 1960s, as evidenced also in two compendiums of his shorter work: *What's It Like Out There? and Other Stories* (coll **1974**) and the posthumous *The Best of Edmond Hamilton* (coll **1977**) ed Leigh Brackett. In the end, it can be said of EH that he took space opera seriously enough to make it good. [JC]

Other works: *Tiger Girl* (**1945** chap UK); *Murder in the Clinic* (coll **1946** chap UK); *Doomstar* (**1966**); *The Lake of Life* (1937 *Weird Tales*; **1978** chap).

As editor: *The Best of Leigh Brackett* (anth **1977**).

About the author: *Leigh Douglass Brackett and Edmond Hamilton: A Working Bibliography* (**1988** chap) by Gordon BENSON Jr.

See also: AIR WONDER STORIES; AMAZING STORIES; ASTER-OIDS; COLONIZATION OF OTHER WORLDS; COMICS; COMPU-TERS; COSMOLOGY; CRIME AND PUNISHMENT; CYBORGS; DEVOLUTION; END OF THE WORLD; ESP; EVOLUTION; FANTASTIC VOYAGES; GALACTIC EMPIRES; HEROES; HISTORY OF SF; INVASION; INVISIBILITY; ISLANDS; JUPITER; LIVING WORLDS; MARS; MATTER TRANSMISSION; MUTANTS; MYTHOLOGY; PARALLEL WORLDS; PARANOIA; PUBLISHING; RELIGION; SPACE FLIGHT; STARS; SUN; WAR; WEAPONS.

HAMILTON, (ANTHONY WALTER) PATRICK (1904-1962) UK writer best known for plays like *Rope* (**1929**) and for several acute and supple novels of hopelessness in the UK of the 1930s. His sf novel *Impromptu in Moribundia* (**1939**) further explores this milieu through its dreamlike exploration of another planet where Earth's customs are seen inverted, as in a distorting mirror. *Hangover Square* (**1941**) is a split-personality murder mystery. [JC]

HAMILTON, TODD CAMERON [r] ◊ P.J. BEESE.

HAMILTON, VIRGINIA (ESTHER) (1936-) US writer, mostly of juveniles, and of very considerable interest in that field for the exploratory intensity of her work, from *Zeely* (**1967**) on, and for the depth of her presentation of the complex experience of being Black in the USA. Several of her early tales, like *M.C. Higgins, the Great* (**1974**) and *Sweet Whispers, Brother Rush* (**1982**), are fantasies. Of particular sf interest is the **Justice Cycle** – *Justice and her Brothers* (**1978**), *Dustland* (**1980**) and *The Gathering* (**1981**) – describing the slow growth of a sibling gestalt into an entity which may well prefigure a higher form of humanity. The relationship between the siblings, as Justice begins to realize that she must take control over her identical-twin elder brothers, is developed with great skill. [JC]

Other works: *The Magical Adventures of Pretty Pearl* (**1983**); *The People Could Fly: American Black Folk-Tales* (coll **1985**); *The Dark Way: Stories from the Spirit World* (coll **1990**).

See also: SUPERMAN.

HAMILTON & CO. ◊ AUTHENTIC SCIENCE FICTION.

HAMLET, OVA [s] ◊ Richard A. LUPOFF.

HAMLING, WILLIAM L(AWRENCE) (1921-) US writer and editor. Active as an sf fan in the late 1930s and early 1940s, he published a number of stories, the first of which, "War with Jupiter" with Mark Reinsberg, appeared in AMAZING STORIES in 1939. WLH later went to work for ZIFF-DAVIS under Raymond A. PALMER, and was managing editor of *AMZ* and FANTASTIC ADVENTURES 1948-50. In 1951 he became editor and publisher of IMAGINATION, having bought the title from Palmer. He added a companion, IMAGINATIVE TALES, and continued both until late 1958. In 1955 he started an early men's magazine, *Rogue*. In the late 1960s his publishing company Greenleaf Classics, which specialized in erotic novels, ran badly foul of US pornography laws for publishing an illustrated edition of a Congressional investigation of pornography, an offence for which he was imprisoned along with his co-publisher Earl Kemp (1929-), compiler of the pamphlets *Who Killed Science Fiction?: An Affectionate Autopsy* (anth **1960** chap) and *Why is a Fan?* (anth **1961** chap). Greenleaf Classics and its associated imprints (Adult Books, Candid Reader, Companion Books, Ember Library, Idle Hour Books, Late House Library, Leisure Books, Nightstand Books, Pleasure Readers and Regency Books) published over 50 titles of sf pornography; they are listed in *The Science Fiction Collector 4* (**1977**) ed J. Grant Thiessen and in Donald H. TUCK's *The Encyclopedia of Science Fiction and Fantasy through 1968, Volume 3: Miscellaneous* (**1982**). Greenleaf published several of the early works of Harlan ELLISON. [MJE/PN]

HAMMOND, KEITH ◊ Henry KUTTNER.

HAMMURA, RYO [r] ◊ JAPAN.

HAMPSON, FRANK (1917-1985) UK artist who almost singlehandedly brought the UK COMIC strip into the scientific age. When the Rev. Marcus Morris and FH originated the *Eagle* comic in 1949-50, FH created the sf strip DAN DARE – PILOT OF THE FUTURE for its full-colour front pages. What made the strip so revolutionary was FH's genius for colour, draughtsmanship and characterization, and his ability to create authentic future technology. He brought the comic strip closer to the CINEMA than any other UK artist before him, with panoramas, close-ups and a great feeling for movement and sequence. Until 1959, together with a team of artists, scriptwriters and scientific advisers, FH controlled the cult spaceman on his adventures across the Solar System. He abandoned **Dan Dare** to draw an impressive life of Christ in comic-strip form, *The Road of Courage* (1959-60; graph **1981**); apart from a short stint on **Lady Penelope** for *TV21* in 1964, this was his last comic strip. Indeed, dogged by ill health and bitter about his shabby treatment by *Eagle*'s publishers, he produced very little published work at all after this, although he illustrated seven books for very young children for the publisher Ladybird Books and produced two sf spreads for MARVEL COMICS's UK **Spider-Man** title in 1976. He received the Italian Yellow Kid award in 1975. [ABP/RT]

See also: RADIO.

HANCOCK, H(ARRIE) IRVING (1868-1922) US martial arts specialist and writer, mostly for boys, who remains of sf interest for the **Conquest of the United States** sequence – *The Invasion of the United States, or Uncle Sam's Boys at the Capture of Boston* (**1916**), *In the Battle for New York, or Uncle Sam's Boys in the Desperate Struggle for the Metropolis* (**1916**), *At the Defense of Pittsburgh, or The Struggle to Save America's "Fighting Steel" Supply* (**1916**) and *Making the Stand for Old Glory, or Uncle Sam's Boys in the Last Frantic Drive* (**1916**) – set around 1920 and depicting the invasion of the USA by a Germany already victorious in Europe. Slightly advanced airplanes are in evidence, as is much action. Germany loses. [JC]

HAND, ELIZABETH (1957-) US writer and critic who began publishing fiction with "Prince of Flowers" for *Twilight Zone Magazine* in 1988. Her first novel, *Winterlong* (**1990**), set on Earth some hundreds or thousands of years hence, combines sf and fantasy materials in a way made familiar by writers of

PLANETARY ROMANCES from Jack VANCE through Gene WOLFE to Richard GRANT (with whom she lives). The tale features baroque bioengineering, mythical resonances and ornate psychopathologies intensely glimpsed; the prose is occasionally very powerful, but the book is rather too long. A second volume set in the same universe, *Aestival Tide* (**1992**), showed a formidable improvement in its pacing and confirmed EH as a significant presence in the field. [JC]

See also: CYBERPUNK; FANTASY; GODS AND DEMONS; HOLOCAUST AND AFTER.

HANDLEY, MAX (ADRIAN ROBERT) (1945-) US writer known in the sf world only for *Meanwhile* (**1977**), an intricately comic FABULATION crammed to bursting point with devices from the whole spectrum of sf and fantasy, all introduced by a sharply knowledgeable hand. [JC]

HANDMAID'S TALE, THE Film (1990). Cinecom/Bioskop. Dir Volker Schlöndorff, starring Natasha Richardson, Faye Dunaway, Aidan Quinn, Elizabeth McGovern, Victoria Tennant, Robert Duvall. Screenplay Harold Pinter (1930-), based on *The Handmaid's Tale* (**1985**) by Margaret ATWOOD. 108 mins. Colour.

A near-future USA, some time after a right-wing coup, is now a patriarchal, fundamentalist, totalitarian state, suppressive of all liberal thought and especially of women, who have no rights at all. The heroine is a "handmaid", one of the few women whose reproductive systems have survived the (very vaguely specified) ravages of chemical pollution and radiation from power-plants. A handmaid's duty is to bear children to important men, conception taking place at ceremonies where she is sandwiched between piously thrusting husband and demure wife; the baby is taken by the wife. This US/German adaptation was perhaps doomed to failure. The believability of Atwood's original novel depends largely on texture, on irony, on the watchful but partially submissive consciousness through which its events are filtered: novels of this kind are notoriously difficult to film. Stripped of this fineness of observation, *THT*'s lurid future is so diagrammatic – despite excellent performances – that suspension of disbelief becomes impossible. The most terrifying aspect of the novel, the wounded complicity with which many of its women consent to their own dehumanization, is weakened by making the film's heroine (Richardson) an active revolutionary who finally cuts the throat of her owner, played by Duvall, whose portrayal of nearly unconscious hypocrisy – he sees himself as a kind man – is the best thing in the film. [PN]

HANDS OF A STRANGER ◊ ORLACS HÄNDE.

HANDS OF A STRANGLER ◊ ORLACS HÄNDE.

HANDS OF ORLAC, THE ◊ ORLACS HÄNDE.

HANLEY, JAMES (1901-1985) Irish writer, in the UK from around the time he began – with *Drift* (**1930**) – to publish his many novels and collections. His only sf, *What Farrar Saw* (**1946**; rev as coll, vt *What Farrar Saw and Other Stories* 1984), set in a NEAR FUTURE land much like war-depleted England, presents a country choked by both an invidious class system and huge traffic jams, which serve as a metaphor for social sclerosis. The jams are cleared with bombs, but the system seems intact. [JC]

HANNA, W.C. (?1910-   ) US writer in whose *The Tandar Saga* (**1964**) the natives of Tandar cruise space looking for habitable planets. [JC]

HANNAN, ROBERT CHARLES (?   -?   ) UK writer whose first sf novel, *The Betrothal of James* (**1898**), attempts to extract some humour from the fact that female cats must be sacrificed in the production of a rejuvenation pill. *Thuka of the Moon* (**1906**), a fantasy in which lunar deities amuse themselves by creating various humanlike beings, awkwardly prefigures Philip José FARMER's **World of Tiers** POCKET-UNIVERSE sequence. In *The Electric Man* (performed 1906; **1910** chap), a play, a primitive ROBOT is mistaken for the hero, with farcical consequences. [JC]

HANSEN, KARL (1950-   ) US writer who began publishing sf with "A Red, White and Blue Fourth of July" in *2076: The American Tricentennial* (anth **1976**) ed Edward BRYANT, and who published stories fairly frequently in the late 1970s. His first novel, *War Games* (**1980** as "Sergeant Pepper" in *The Berkley Showcase #5* ed Victoria Schochet; exp **1981**), is a surprisingly searing military-sf vision; it is set in the loose **Hybrid** universe, as is his second, *Dream Games* (**1985** *Omni* as "Dreams Unwind"; exp **1985**), which less interestingly describes a rebellion against a COMPUTER-controlled DYSTOPIA. Further volumes of the **Hybrid** series are anticipated. [JC]

HANSEN, L(OUISE) TAYLOR (?   -   ) US writer who published numerous sf stories and popular science articles in the PULP MAGAZINES from 1929 to at least 1948, beginning with "The Undersea Tube" for *AMZ* in 1928; this details the failure of a subway under the Atlantic. She probably attended the University of California Los Angeles for graduate work in science. Her stories, which revolve around hard-science explanations or technological problems, tend to include many diagrams. *The Ancient Atlantic* (**1969**), nonfiction, deals with the geological and mythic history of the Atlantic Ocean. [JD]

HANSON, VERN Working name of UK writer Victor Joseph Hanson (1920-   ), author of a number of some routine sf published over a brief span: *The Twisters* (coll **1963**), *Creatures of the Mist* (**1963**), *Claws of the Night* (**1964**) and *The Grip of Fear* (coll **1964**). [JC]

HÄPNA! ◊ SCANDINAVIA.

HARBEN, WILL(IAM) N(ATHANIEL) (1858-1919) US writer, most of whose novels variously depict life in the South. "In the Year Ten Thousand" (1892 *Arena*) is a UTOPIAN sketch espousing vegetarianism. His sf novel, *The Land of the Changing Sun* (**1894**), is a LOST-WORLD tale featuring an underground utopia/dystopia, Alpha, founded 200 years earlier under the Arctic by a group of inventive Englishmen, who espouse a rigid eugenic regime, and who heat and light their habitat with an artificial sun, which moves

on tracks and changes colour pleasingly. Intruding magma threatens their world, and they decide to evacuate Alpha in advanced submarines. [JC]
See also: HISTORY OF SF.

HARBINSON, W(ILLIAM) ALLEN (1941-   ) UK writer who has concentrated on the sf of PARANOIA, generally rooted in the notion that ALIENS are either investigating our planet or governing us, or both. The **Projekt Saucer** sequence – in order of internal chronology, *Projekt Saucer #1: Inception* (**1991** US) and *Genesis* (**1980**; vt *Projekt Saucer #2: Genesis* 1991 US) – connects UFOS and superscience in a global conspiracy. *Otherworld* (**1984**) collapses under the burden of attempting to make stylistic bricks out of material of this sort, but *The Light of Eden* (**1987**; vt *Eden* 1987 US) more successfully follows the psychiatric examination of some humans who gradually make it clear that they are not in fact hallucinating an alien presence in the land. *Dream Maker* (**1991**) suggests that UFOs in need of energy from human minds are sucking holes in the ozone layer. [JC]

HARBOTTLE, PHILIP (JAMES) (1941-   ) UK local government officer and sf researcher. PH is the world authority on the works of John Russell FEARN, whose literary estate he represents and with whom he has posthumously collaborated, completing several stories. His bibliographical study of Fearn is *The Multi-Man* (**1968** chap). PH is an expert in publishing data relating to UK GENRE SF, especially in magazine form, and has contributed research to several UK books about sf. He edited the magazine VISION OF TOMORROW for its 12 issues, Aug 1969-Sep 1970, as well as, anon, 3 anthologies: *Eternal Rediffusion* (anth **1973** chap), *Flight on Titan* (anth **1973** chap) and *Passage to Saturn* (anth **1973** chap). His work as a whole has been summarized in 2 linked volumes, «Vultures of the Void: A History of British Science Fiction, 1946-1956» (1992 US) and «British Science Fiction Paperbacks, 1949-1956» (1992 US), both with Steve HOLLAND. [PN/JC]

HARCOURT, GLENN [r] ◊ Carter SCHOLZ.

HARDING, LEE (JOHN) (1937-   ) Australian freelance photographer and writer who began publishing sf with "Displaced Person" for *Science Fantasy* in 1961; he eventually expanded this story as *Displaced Person* (**1979**; rev vt *Misplaced Persons* 1979 US). Aimed – like *The Weeping Sky* (**1977**) and *Waiting for the End of the World* (**1983**), which are equally impressive – at a teenage audience, it memorably imprisons its protagonist in a world turning to grey just as the grim solitude of his own life becomes painfully manifest. This use of sf plots to explore character became a kind of trademark of the LH novel. During the 1960s, sometimes writing as Harold G. Nye, he concentrated on magazine work, twice winning a Ditmar AWARD, in 1970 for "Dancing Gerontius" (1969) and in 1972 for the magazine version of his first novel, *Fallen Spaceman* (**1971** *If*; rev **1973**; rev 1980 US), a juvenile. His adult novels – *A World of Shadows* (**1975** UK) and *Future Sanctuary* (**1976** Canada) – have been perhaps less notable than his juveniles, though the last impressively anatomizes a desolate NEAR-FUTURE Australia. His other juveniles include *The Children of Atlantis* (**1976**), *The Frozen Sky* (**1976**), *Return to Tomorrow* (**1977**) and *The Web of Time* (**1980** UK); they are sombre and clear. LH has edited *Beyond Tomorrow: An Anthology of Modern Science Fiction* (anth **1976**; cut 1977 UK), *The Altered I: An Encounter with Science Fiction* (anth **1976**), which presents some of the productions of an sf workshop in Australia presided over by Ursula K. LE GUIN, and *Rooms of Paradise* (anth **1978**). [JC]

See also: CHILDREN'S SF; PSYCHOLOGY.

HARDING, RICHARD Pseudonym of US writer Robert Tine (? -), author of the **Outrider SURVIVALIST** sequence: *The Outrider* (**1984**), *#2: Fire and Steel* (**1984**), *#3: Blood Highway* (**1984**), *#4: Bay City Burnout* (**1985**) and *#5: Built to Kill* (**1985**). As usual, the HOLOCAUST is vengefully enjoyed. [JC]

HARD SF Item of sf terminology used by sf FANDOM and readers; it has sometimes overlapped in meaning with "hardcore sf", often used in the 1960s and 1970s to mean the kind of sf that repeats the themes and (to a degree) the style of the GENRE SF written during the so-called GOLDEN AGE OF SF. Though still sometimes used in a way that implies the element of nostalgia associated with "hardcore sf", the term "hard sf" now seems to refer to something rather simpler, as summarized by Allen STEELE (in "Hard Again" in NEW YORK REVIEW OF SCIENCE FICTION, June 1992): "Hard sf is the form of imaginative literature that uses either established or carefully extrapolated science as its backbone." Steele goes on to regret the association in many readers' minds of hard sf with "a particular political territory – usually located somewhere on the far right", an association which, while certainly sometimes justifiable, has cultural origins that cannot easily be elucidated.

The commonly used distinction between hard and SOFT SCIENCES runs parallel to that between hard and SOFT SF. Theme entries in this volume which deal with the so-called hard sciences include, but are not restricted to, ASTRONOMY, BLACK HOLES, COMPUTERS; COSMOLOGY, CYBERNETICS, FASTER THAN LIGHT, GRAVITY, MATHEMATICS, NUCLEAR POWER, PHYSICS, POWER SOURCES, ROCKETS, SPACE FLIGHT, SPACE SHIPS, TECHNOLOGY and WEAPONS. All but the most puristic reader would probably accept also BIOLOGY, GENETIC ENGINEERING and TERRAFORMING as appropriate material for hard sf. But it is possible to write a kind of hard sf about almost anything, as can be exemplified by Brian M. STABLEFORD's rationalizing treatment of vampires in *The Empire of Fear* (**1988**). Hard sf should not, however, wilfully ignore or break known scientific principles, yet stories classified as "hard sf" often contain, for example, ESP, SUPERMAN, FASTER-THAN-LIGHT and TIME-TRAVEL themes (*see also* IMAGINARY SCIENCE). While a rigorous definition of "hard sf" may be impossible, perhaps the most important thing about it is, not that it should include real science in any great detail, but that it should respect the scientific spirit; it should seek to provide natural rather than supernatural or transcendental explanations for the events and phenomena it describes. [PN]

HARD TO BE A GOD ◊ TRUDNO BYT' BOGOM.

HARDWARE Film (1990). Palace/Millimeter/A Wicked Films Production. Dir Richard Stanley, starring Stacey Travis, Dylan McDermott, John Lynch, William Hootkins. Screenplay Stanley, based (it was admitted after a threatened lawsuit) on a 1980 JUDGE DREDD story. 94 mins, but many prints shortened to avoid adults-only rating. Colour.

In a radioactive city in an apparently post-HOLOCAUST near future, a dope-smoking sculptress is given a military robot's head to incorporate into a steel sculpture. It reincorporates itself using pieces of the sculpture, thereby taking the film from the technopunk-DYSTOPIA genre into the Luddite killer-ROBOT genre. The 24-year-old director, Stanley, had a track record in so-called Industrial Music rock videos, and the eclectic, pack-rat junk sensibility which this suggests (a bit of Andrei TARKOVSKY here, a bit of Dario Argento there, a bit of CYBERPUNK everywhere) surprisingly transcends cliché in the images if not the script. Though *H* is basically a simple low-budget SPLATTER MOVIE, it is unusually inventive in its design and in several of the characters, notably Hootkins as a rotund sadistic voyeur. The crazed robot is a Mark 13, and the film's epigraph is adapted from (where else?) the Gospel According to St Mark, Chapter 13: "No flesh shall be spared." [PN]

See also: CINEMA.

HARDY, DAVID A(NDREWS) (1936-) UK illustrator, known as much for his astronomical paintings in the accurate tradition of Chesley BONESTELL as for his sf work. DH learned his craft at the Margaret Street College of Art in Birmingham, and was soon painting for the British Interplanetary Society. Some of his best early work was to illustrate a nonfiction book by Patrick MOORE, *Sun, Myth, and Men* (**1954**); DAH later illustrated and cowrote with Moore *Challenge of the Stars* (**1972**). His work has appeared on magazine and book covers, most notably (beginning 1971) many covers for *FSF*, the magazine for which he developed his famous "Space Gumby", a green alien which lent humour to his vivid astronomical scenes. He was an important artist for VISION OF TOMORROW, and worked also for *Science Fiction Monthly*, *If* and *Gal*. Other book credits include *Galactic Tours* (**1981**) with Bob SHAW and artwork for *Atlas of the Solar System* (**1982**) and *Visions of Space* (**1989**). [JG/PN]

HARDY, PHIL(IPPE) (1945-) UK expert on rock music and film, on both of which subjects he has published widely, having been founding editor of Studio Vista's **Rockbooks** series and of the magazine *Music Business*. Among his notable books on film those most relevant to sf are *The Aurum Film Encyclopedia: Science Fiction* (**1984**; vt *Science Fiction: The Complete Film Sourcebook* 1985 US; rev 1991) and *The Aurum Film Encyclopedia: Horror* (**1985**; vt *The Encyclo-*

pedia of Horror Movies 1987 US; rev projected 1993), both of which he edited and partly wrote. Well edited, containing detailed credits and critical annotations on well over 1000 films each, these books are – despite inevitable small errors and on rare occasion weird judgments – about the most readable and useful reference works in book form on their subjects (◊ CINEMA). There are more comprehensive filmographies available, but PH's are much the most comprehensive to contain critical comment. The *Science Fiction* volume – whose 1991 updating was largely the work of Kim NEWMAN – is the only current (1992) book to be more comprehensive in the field than this encyclopedia. [PN]

HARGRAVE, JOHN (GORDON) (1894-1982) UK writer and illustrator. At age 17 he became the chief cartoonist for the London *Evening News*; he also illustrated several books of interest, including a 1909 edition of Jonathan SWIFT's *Gulliver's Travels* (**1726**) and *Black Tales for White Children* (coll **1914**) by C.H. Stigland. His work was all in black-and-white, with effects that ran from the forceful to the jagged. He became involved in the Boy Scout movement during WWI, then left it to found a rival organization, the Kibbo Kift, whose principles he advocated in a quasi-UTOPIAN novel, *Young Winkle* (**1925**); he invented an automatic aircraft navigator; and he was involved in Social Credit, a theory that advocated the redistribution of resources to increase purchasing power. Of his nonfiction, *The Life and Death of Paracelsus* (**1951**) is of note. His sf novel, *The Imitation Man* (**1931**), depicts the life of an artificially created homunculus with the power of ESP who causes a good deal of furore but soon dies. [JC]

See also: SUPERMAN.

HARGRAVE, LEONIE ◊ Thomas M. DISCH.

HARKER, KENNETH (1927-) UK author with a training in physics. His sf novels – *The Symmetrians* (**1966**), which concerns a DYSTOPIAN response to nuclear HOLOCAUST, and *The Flowers of February* (**1970**) – are straightforward but uninspired. [JC]

HARMON, H.H. [s] ◊ Robert Moore WILLIAMS.

HARMON, JIM Working name of US writer and RADIO producer James Judson Harmon (1933-), who began publishing sf with "The Smuggler" for *Spaceway* in 1954, and who became active in the magazine field. A nonfiction book, *The Great Radio Heroes* (**1967**), discusses SUPERMAN and other programmes and characters of sf interest. A similarly well documented nostalgic study is *The Great Movie Serials: Their Sound and Fury* (**1972**) by JH and Donald F. GLUT. JH also contributed a number of articles to RIVERSIDE QUARTERLY. [JC/PN]

HARNESS, CHARLES (LEONARD) (1915-) US patent attorney and writer, born in Texas. His first published story was "Time Trap" for *ASF* in 1948, a convoluted time-loop story involving the working of tremendous time-forces off-stage and a quasitranscendental experience as the hero goes back in time to remake the world. His subsequent output shows a

remarkable consistency in echoing and developing these themes. His first two novels, *Flight into Yesterday* (1949 *Startling Stories*; exp **1953**; vt *The Paradox Men*) and *The Ring of Ritornel* (**1968**), feature cycles in time and HEROES who undergo transcendental metamorphoses in order to manipulate their own destinies and that of the human race; both novels are shamelessly melodramatic, and have an obvious kinship with the work of A.E. VAN VOGT. Shorter works in the same vein include "The New Reality" (1950) – sf's best ADAM AND EVE story – and "Stalemate in Space" (1949; vt "Stalemate in Time"). The first phase of his career (1948-53) may well have ended because of his failure to sell the remarkable novella "The Rose" (1953 AUTHENTIC SCIENCE FICTION; title story of *The Rose* [coll **1966** UK], which also includes "The New Reality" and "The Chessplayers") to a US market. This striking allegory of the opposed worldviews of science and the ARTS is a memorable exemplar of the particular kind of SUPERMAN story which represents future human EVOLUTION in metamorphic terms. Its reprinting in the 1960s was the result of the interest in CLH's work of Michael MOORCOCK, who reprinted several CLH stories in NEW WORLDS, and this may have been responsible for Harness's second burst of creativity, which produced *The Ring of Ritornel* and several shorter works drawing on his experience as a lawyer, including "An Ornament to his Profession" (1966) and "The Alchemist" (1966). (CLH had earlier drawn on this experience in writing whimsical articles and stories for *ASF* as Leonard Lockhard, sometimes working in collaboration with Theodore L. THOMAS.)

CLH returned to sf writing for a third time with the futuristic infernal romance *Wolfhead* (1977-8 *FSF*; **1978**), one of several sf novels to borrow heavily from DANTE ALIGHIERI and to recast the myth of Orpheus and Eurydice. He has been moderately prolific since then, aided by his retirement from legal work in 1981. *The Catalyst* (**1980**) is one of several CLH stories featuring quasimiraculous scientific discoveries made in frank defiance of supposedly rational procedures. The transcendental time-looping of his earlier novels is reiterated in *Firebird* (**1981**), *Krono* (**1988**), and – in an un-space-operatic fashion – in *Lurid Dreams* (**1990**), whose out-of-body time traveller meets up with Edgar Allan POE. *Redworld* (**1986**) is an eccentric *Bildungsroman* set on a peculiar alien world, which may be in part a transfiguration of the author's early life. His fondness for outrageously melodramatic courtroom dramas in which absolutely everything is rigged against the defendant, first displayed in "Probable Cause" (1968), is echoed in *The Venetian Court* (**1982**) and *Lunar Justice* (**1991**).

CLH is an original, stylish and imaginatively audacious writer whose relative neglect is difficult to understand. His most recent books may not have quite the scope and exuberant panache of his earlier efforts, but it is nevertheless unfortunate that the works of such a colourful and highly readable writer should still be condemned, with one recent exception, to appear only as ephemeral paperback originals. Despite his one-time fashionability in the UK, none of his recent works has been published there. [BS]

About the author: *Charles L. Harness: Attorney in Space: A Working Bibliography* (**1992** chap) by Phil STEPHENSEN-PAYNE.

See also: COMPUTERS; COSMOLOGY; CRIME AND PUNISHMENT; ESCHATOLOGY; FORCE FIELD; GALACTIC EMPIRES; GAMES AND SPORTS; HISTORY IN SF; JUPITER; MEDICINE; METAPHYSICS; MOON; MUSIC; MYTHOLOGY; RECURSIVE SF; SCIENTISTS; SUN; TIME PARADOXES; WEAPONS.

HARNÍČEK, MARTIN [r] ◊ CZECH AND SLOVAK SF.

HARPER, GEORGE W(ILLIAM) (1927-   ) US volcanologist and writer, often of nonfiction pieces for journals like *ASF*. His only sf novel, *Gypsy Earth* (**1982**), is a full-flung SPACE OPERA in the manner of the pre-WWII masters of that form, pitting valiant Terrans against vast invading spacefleets, which they initially destroy. The modernity of the tale was perhaps revealed by the destruction of Earth partway through; but survivors in the eponymous hollow ASTEROIDS wreak revenge, and humanity survives. [JC]

HARPER, HARRY (1880-1960) UK author with Claude GRAHAME-WHITE of two sf juveniles, *The Air-King's Treasure* (**1913**) and *The Invisible War-Plane: A Tale of Air Adventure in the Great Campaign* (**1915**). In the latter an airship is concealed by paint which (it is claimed) neither absorbs nor reflects light. Much later HH wrote two solo works of semifictional FUTUROLOGY, *Winged World* (**1946**) and *Dawn of the Space Age* (**1946**). [PN]

HARPER, RORY (?   -   ) US writer who began publishing sf with *Petrogypsies* (1985 in *Far Frontiers* ed John F. CARR and Jerry POURNELLE; exp **1989**), an essentially comic novel set in what seems to be an ALTERNATE WORLD where oil exploration is done by bio-constructs piloted by "gypsies", whose skills dominate the venue. [JC]

See also: POWER SOURCES.

HARPER, VINCENT (?   -?   ) US writer whose sf novel, *The Mortgage on the Brain, Being the Confessions of the late Ethelbert Craft, MD* (**1905**), describes an electric-shock treatment which alters personality beneficially and undermines many then-conventional views of the nature of the mind. The story is a melodramatic hotchpotch, but is of interest in its reference to the ego, which is described (as in the title) as holding no more than a mortgage on its habitat: this idea has found sophisticated support in late-20th-century studies of the workings of the mind. [JC]

See also: PSYCHOLOGY.

HARRINGTON, ALAN (1919-   ) US writer, author of *The Immortalist* (**1969**), a work of speculative nonfiction. His sf novel, *Paradise 1* (**1977**), set in the 21st century, tells of potential IMMORTALITY and of a continuing struggle to wrest humanity free of its

contract with death. [JC]

HARRIS, CLARE WINGER (1891-1968) US writer (known also as Mrs F.C. Harris), the first woman to publish sf in the specialized 1920s PULP MAGAZINES, beginning with "A Runaway World" for *Weird Tales* in 1926. "The Fate of the Poseidonia" (1927) won third prize in an *AMZ* contest. She experimented with a female point of view in "The Fifth Dimension" (1928), and her stories generally feature strong women, most notably Sylvia, airplane pilot and mechanic in "The Ape Cycle" (1930). Her work often dealt with beings on the borders of humanity – CYBORGS and ape-people (◊ APES AND CAVEMEN) in particular. She assembled her work in *Away from Here and Now* (coll **1947**). [JD]

HARRIS, FRANK Working name of UK writer and editor James Thomas Harris (1856-1931), who spent some years as a lawyer in the USA and who is now best known for his erotic autobiography, *My Life and Loves* (**1922-7**), which first appeared in 5 privately published volumes. In *Pantopia* (in *Undream'd of Shores* [coll 1924] as "The Temple of the Forgotten Dead"; much exp **1930** US) a young man is shipwrecked somewhere in the South Atlantic, finding himself on a utopian ISLAND whose Spanish-speaking socialist inhabitants make use of radar, lasers and atomic power, and who as a matter of course do what is good for their race in a natural fashion. Unfortunately, also as a matter of course, they execute strangers. Luckily the hero is saved by a privileged maiden, and both eventually escape. [JC]

HARRIS, J. HENRY (?   -?   ) UK writer whose uneasily fin-de-siècle sf novel, *A Romance in Radium* (**1906**), follows the investigative journey to Earth of a feathered female ALIEN, a member of an angel-like species from 100,000,000 miles away; her people are confused as to why earlier visitors stayed on our planet and became mortal. The answer is SEX – or, as JHH puts it, marriage. Angels, it seems, cannot get enough of marriage. [JC]

HARRIS, JOHN BEYNON [r] ◊ John WYNDHAM.

HARRIS, JOHNSON ◊ John WYNDHAM.

HARRIS, LARRY M(ARK) [r] ◊ Laurence M. JANIFER.

HARRIS, MACDONALD Pseudonym used by US writer and academic Donald William Heiney (1921-   ) for all his fiction which, though composed in a smooth and accessible style, tends significantly to foreground any elements of fantasy (◊ FABULATION) with which it may deal. *Bull Fever* (**1973**) treats a modern family romance in terms of the myth of the Minotaur. *The Balloonist* (**1976**) recounts a failed 1897 BALLOON expedition to the North Pole in terms reminiscent of Jules VERNE's **Voyages extraordinaires**; indeed, the book is dedicated to Verne. *The Little People* (**1986**) takes its title from the myth of faerie, though in a delusional frame. *Glowstone* (**1987**) posits a kind of ALTERNATE WORLD in which a woman strongly reminiscent of Marie Curie (1867-1934) makes identical scientific discoveries. *Screenplay* (**1982**), a TIME-TRAVEL tale, deposits its hero in a *film-noir* dream of 1920s Hollywood. Several of the stories assembled in *The Cathay Stories and Other Fictions* (coll **1988**) carry a contemporary Marco Polo backwards in time to the increasingly fabulous world of the original (1254-1324). [JC/GF]

HARRIS, RAYMOND (1953-   ) US writer who began publishing sf with his first novel, *The Broken Worlds* (**1986**), an attractive picaresque adventure. *Shadows of the White Sun* (**1988**) seems at first assessment almost too complex – it is set in a FAR-FUTURE Solar System dominated by revenant star-sailors whose descendents occupy seven SPACE HABITATS called the Hypaethra, orbiting the Sun, while a computer-created ANDROID race occupies the planet Veii in exchange for ritual tribute paid to the Despot who dominates the habitats. But embedded within this surround are a convincing murder mystery, a trek and an examination of character. Echoes of both Frank HERBERT and Gene WOLFE are detectable, not to RH's discredit. Complications of venue and plot affect *The Schizogenic Man* (**1990**) more seriously, with a 21st-century balkanized, computer-run, city-state USA where lives change according to periodic lotteries, and a TIME-TRAVEL plot that further shuffles the reality cards; the novel was the 1991 runner-up for the PHILIP K. DICK AWARD. RH's work has yet to come fully into focus, but there is a sense that this may happen very soon. [JC]

HARRIS, ROGER [r] ◊ Michael MOORCOCK

HARRIS-BURLAND, J(OHN) B(URLAND) (1870-1926) UK writer whose first novels of sf interest, *Dacobra, or The White Priests of Ahriman* (**1903**) and *The Princess of Thora* (**1904** US; vt *Dr Silex* 1905 UK as JBH-B), were signed Harris Burland. The first tale sets in an occult frame a wide range of supernatural subjects including IMMORTALITY; the second, a LOST-WORLD novel, features a race of lost Normans who have developed into SUPERMEN in an enclave at the North Pole. *The Gold Worshipers* (**1906** US), as JBH-B, returns to one of the subjects of the first novel – the transubstantiation of metals – in a congested tale of greed, gold-making and amply reimbursed remorse. [JC]

Other works: *Workers in Darkness* (**1908**), borderline.

HARRISON, CRAIG (1942-   ) UK-born NEW ZEALAND playwright and writer whose work embodies consistently anti-racist themes. *Broken October: New Zealand 1985* (**1976**) posits political terrorism and racial conflict resulting in a US-backed military takeover. In *The Quiet Earth* (**1981**), filmed as *The* QUIET EARTH (1985), a GENETIC-ENGINEERING disaster depopulates the planet. The insane protagonist realizes, in a moment of CONCEPTUAL BREAKTHROUGH that vindicates his PARANOIA, that he has caused the DISASTER. *Days of Starlight* (**1988**) pits scientists against the US military after a holographic recorder of Earth's history is discovered. Technically excellent, CH's work is sometimes uninvolving. [MMacL]

HARRISON, HARRY (1925-   ) US writer, born Henry Maxwell Dempsey (though his father changed his name to Harrison soon after HH's birth), now usually resident, after many years of travelling, in Ireland. HH began his career as a commercial artist in the later 1940s, working chiefly in comics as an illustrator and writer, often in collaboration with Wallace A. WOOD, supplying illustrations as well to magazines like GALAXY SCIENCE FICTION and eventually having a stint as art director of *Picture Week*. At the same time – being from an early age an sf enthusiast and friendly with many writers through his membership of the Hydra Club, a New York group of sf professionals – he began to think about writing. Damon KNIGHT, then editor of WORLDS BEYOND and one of the Hydra Club members, commissioned some illustrations from HH for that magazine; he then – far more importantly – bought HH's first story, "Rock Diver", which appeared in *Worlds Beyond* in 1951. HH's short fiction appeared regularly from then, sometimes as by Felix Boyd or Hank Dempsey. In 1953 HH served as editor of ROCKET STORIES for 1 issue (#3) under the house name Wade KAEMPFERT. In later years, HH was also for short periods in charge of the magazines *Impulse* (◊ SCIENCE FANTASY), AMAZING STORIES and FANTASTIC.

In 1957, from Mexico, HH sold his first story to John W. CAMPBELL Jr for ASTOUNDING SCIENCE-FICTION, thereby initiating a long and close relationship with both editor and magazine. This was his first tale featuring the interstellar-criminal-turned-law-enforcer Slippery Jim DiGriz, the **Stainless Steel Rat**, HERO of a set of fast-moving adventures with a broad leavening of HUMOUR: *The Stainless Steel Rat* (fixup **1961** US), *The Stainless Steel Rat's Revenge* (**1970** US) and *The Stainless Steel Rat Saves the World* (**1972** US) – all assembled as *The Adventures of the Stainless Steel Rat* (omni **1977**) – plus *The Stainless Steel Rat Wants You!* (**1979** US), *The Stainless Steel Rat for President* (**1982** US), *A Stainless Steel Rat is Born* (**1985** US) and *The Stainless Steel Rat Gets Drafted* (**1987** UK). (HH did the jacket illustrations for the UK hardcover editions of the second and third books.) HH always remained a stout defender of Campbell, even though as editor and critic his attitude often seemed diametrically opposed to Campbell's increasingly stiff-necked social and political views. He edited Campbell's *Collected Editorials from Analog* (coll **1966**), was filmed at a working lunch with Campbell and Gordon R. DICKSON, a session which resulted in the Harrison-Dickson collaborative novel *The Lifeship* (**1976** US; vt *Lifeboat* 1978 UK), and after Campbell's death edited a memorial anthology, *Astounding* (anth **1973**; vt *The John W. Campbell Memorial Anthology* 1974 UK).

HH's first published novel appeared a year before *The Stainless Steel Rat*: *Deathworld* (**1960** US; vt *Deathworld 1* 1973 UK). Its highly kinetic description of the COLONIZATION of a planet crammed with hostile life established him as a vigorous writer of intelligent action adventures. Further volumes in the **Deathworld** series are *Deathworld 2* (**1964** US; vt *The Ethical Engineer* 1964 UK) and *Deathworld 3* (**1968** US), all three being assembled as *The Deathworld Trilogy* (omni

1974 US); "The Mothballed Spaceship" (1973) was an associated short story. The third series begun by HH in his early years (though the second volume was not to appear for three decades) was the **Bill, the Galactic Hero** sequence, starting with *Bill, the Galactic Hero* (**1965** US), a sharp extended lampoon of aspects of stories by Robert A. HEINLEIN, Isaac ASIMOV and even HH himself. The later volumes of the series declined, unfortunately, into undirected slapstick: *Bill, the Galactic Hero: The Planet of the Robot Slaves* (**1989** US; vt *Bill, the Galactic Hero on the Planet of Robot Slaves* 1989 UK), *Bill, the Galactic Hero on the Planet of Bottled Brains* (**1990** US) with Robert SHECKLEY, *Bill, the Galactic Hero on the Planet of Tasteless Pleasure* (**1991**) with David F. BISCHOFF, *Bill, the Galactic Hero on the Planet of the Zombie Vampires* (**1991**) with Jack C. HALDEMAN II, and *Bill, the Galactic Hero on the Planet of Ten Thousand Bars* (**1991**; vt *Bill, the Galactic Hero on the Planet of the Hippies from Hell* 1992 UK) with Bischoff.

Most of HH's singletons are also of interest. They include: a group of stories exploring the ROBOT theme, *War with the Robots* (coll **1962** US); the examination of MATTER TRANSMISSION in *One Step From Earth* (coll **1970** US); a parody of E.E. SMITH in *Star Smashers of the Galaxy Rangers* (**1973** US); *Captive Universe* (**1969** US), an unusual GENERATION-STARSHIP story using a background of Aztec culture (◊ CONCEPTUAL BREAKTHROUGH; POCKET UNIVERSE); *Tunnel through the Deeps* (**1972** US; vt *A Transatlantic Tunnel, Hurrah!* 1972 UK), a PARALLEL-WORLD novel in which the American Revolution failed and the British Empire still flourishes; and *Skyfall* (**1976** UK), a fairly conventional DISASTER novel. Some, however, like *Invasion: Earth* (**1982** US), seem to parody nothing but their author's own attempts to parody bad SPACE OPERA. In contrast, *Make Room! Make Room!* (**1966** US) is a serious – indeed, impassioned – novel of OVERPOPULATION, gravely told and well formed. It formed the basis of the film SOYLENT GREEN (1973), though much of its substance was lost in transition; the film nevertheless won the 1973 NEBULA for Best Dramatic Presentation.

Later series of interest include the **To the Stars** sequence – *Homeworld* (**1980** US), *Wheelworld* (**1981** US) and *Starworld* (**1981** US), all three being assembled as *To the Stars* (omni **1981**) – which combine muscular sf-adventure plotting with sharp narrative analyses of UK and US life. Far more important, however, is the **Eden** series – *West of Eden* (**1984** US), *Winter in Eden* (**1986** US) and *Return to Eden* (**1988** US) – an ambitiously conceived ALTERNATE-WORLD sequence based on the assumption that the dinosaurs did not suffer extinction and, in the due course of time, have evolved into saurians skilled at biotechnology. Their encounter with a savage humanity, and the irreconcilable differences between two intelligent species warring for Lebensraum, is intrinsically interesting, tightly and informatively told, and dramatically gripping as the slowly approaching Ice Age adds intensity to the strife and the sense of peril. Along with his earliest sf adventures and *Make Room!*

Make Room!, the **Eden** books are by a considerable margin HH's best work.

For many years HH's close professional association with Campbell was balanced by his even closer personal and professional association with Brian W. ALDISS, a figure dauntingly averse to the Campbellian vision. Together they founded the critical magazine *SF Horizons*, whose two issues served as a litmus test for sf criticism; they edited an annual **Best SF** anthology (see listing below); they collaborated on other anthologies, such as *Nebula Award Stories Two* (anth **1967** US), *Farewell, Fantastic Venus! A History of the Planet Venus in Fact and Fiction* (anth **1968** UK; cut vt *All about Venus* 1968 US), *The Astounding-Analog Reader, Volume One* (anth **1972** US; vt in 2 vols as *The Astounding-Analog Reader, Volume One* 1973 UK and *The Astounding-Analog Reader, Volume Two* 1973 UK) and *The Astounding-Analog Reader, Volume Two* (anth **1973** US); and they assembled the **Decade** series – *Decade: The 1940s* (anth **1975**), *Decade: The 1950s* (anth **1976**) and *Decade: The 1960s* (anth **1977**).

HH has been hard to pin down. He has lived everywhere. He was an author of the hardest of hard-sf adventure novels while at the same time mercilessly spoofing the conventions – and politics – of that literature. He is deeply American, and deeply expatriate. He might spend the rest of his career writing bad-joke spin-offs from his own earlier work, or he might compose his masterpiece. After 40 years, there is still no knowing.   [MJE/JC]

Other works: *Planet of the Damned* (**1962** US; vt *Sense of Obligation* 1967 UK) and its sequel, *Planet of No Return* (**1981** US); *Vendetta for the Saint* * (**1964** US) as Leslie CHARTERIS; *Plague from Space* (**1965** US; vt *The Jupiter Legacy* 1970 US); *Two Tales and 8 Tomorrows* (coll **1965** UK); *The Technicolor Time Machine* (**1967**); *The Man from P.I.G.* (**1968** US; with additional story as coll vt *The Men from P.I.G. and R.O.B.O.T.* 1974 UK), a juvenile; *The Daleth Effect* (**1970** US; vt *In Our Hands, the Stars* 1970 UK); *Prime Number* (coll **1970** US); *Spaceship Medic* (**1970** UK); *Stonehenge* (**1972** US; exp vt *Stonehenge: Where Atlantis Died* 1983 US) with Leon E. STOVER; *Montezuma's Revenge* (**1972** US) and *Queen Victoria's Revenge* (**1974** US), linked associational novels; *The California Iceberg* (**1975** UK); *The Best of Harry Harrison* (coll **1976** US; rev 1976 UK); *Great Balls of Fire: A History of Sex in Science Fiction Illustration* (**1977** UK), nonfiction; *Spacecraft in Fact and Fiction* (**1979**) with Malcolm EDWARDS, nonfiction; *Mechanismo* (**1978**), nonfiction; *Planet Story* (**1979** UK); *The QE II is Missing* (**1980** UK), associational; *A Rebel in Time* (**1983** US).

As editor: *Apeman, Spaceman: Anthropological Science Fiction* (anth **1968** US) with Leon E. Stover; the **Author's Choice** anthologies, in which authors chose their own favourites and said why, comprising *Backdrop of Stars* (anth **1968** UK; vt *SF: Authors' Choice* 1968 US), *SF: Author's Choice 2* (anth **1970** US), *#3* (anth **1971** US) and *#4* (anth **1974** US); the **Best SF** annual series, all with Brian W. Aldiss, comprising

Best SF: 1967 (**1968** US; vt *The Year's Best Science Fiction No 1* 1968 UK), *The Year's Best Science Fiction No 2* (anth **1969** UK; exp vt *Best SF: 1968* 1969 US), *The Year's Best Science Fiction No 3* (anth **1970** UK; vt *Best SF: 1969* 1970 US), *The Year's Best Science Fiction No 4* (anth **1971** UK; vt *Best SF: 1970* 1971 US), *The Year's Best Science Fiction No 5* (anth **1972** UK; vt *Best SF: 1971* 1972 US), *Best SF: 1972* (anth **1973** US; vt *The Year's Best Science Fiction No 6* 1973 UK), *Best SF: 1973* (anth **1974** US; cut vt *The Year's Best Science Fiction No 7* 1974 UK), *Best SF 1974* (anth **1975** US; cut vt *The Year's Best Science Fiction No 8* 1975 UK) and *The Year's Best Science Fiction No 9* (anth **1976** US; vt *Best SF: 1975* 1976 US); *Blast Off: S.F. for Boys* (anth **1969** UK; rev vt *Worlds of Wonder* 1969 US); *Four for the Future: An Anthology on the Themes of Sacrifice and Redemption* (anth **1969** UK); the **Nova** series of original sf stories, comprising *Nova 1* (anth **1970**), *#2* (anth **1972** US), *#3* (anth **1973** US; vt *The Outdated Man* 1975 US) and *#4* (anth dated 1974 but **1975** US); *The Year 2000* (anth **1970** US); *The Light Fantastic* (anth **1971** US) and *Ahead of Time* (anth **1972** US), the latter with Theodore J. Gordon; *A Science Fiction Reader* (anth **1973** US) with Carol Pugner; *Science Fiction Novellas* (anth **1975** US) with Willis E. MCNELLY; *Hell's Cartographers* (anth **1975** UK) with Brian W. Aldiss; *There Won't Be War* (anth **1991**) with Bruce MCALLISTER.

About the author: *Harry Harrison* (last rev 1985 chap) by Gordon BENSON Jr; *Harry Harrison* (**1990**) by Leon STOVER.

See also: ANTHOLOGIES; ANTHROPOLOGY; ARTS; ATLANTIS; AUTOMATION; CHILDREN'S SF; COMICS; CRIME AND PUNISHMENT; DYSTOPIAS; EVOLUTION; FAR FUTURE; GOLDEN AGE OF SF; GRAVITY; JOHN W. CAMPBELL MEMORIAL AWARD; MAINSTREAM WRITERS OF SF; MEDIA LANDSCAPE; MEDICINE; MESSIAHS; MYTHOLOGY; POLLUTION; RADIO; RELIGION; ROBERT HALE LIMITED; SATIRE; SEX; TABOOS; TRANSPORTATION; UNDER THE SEA.

HARRISON, HELGA (SUSAN BARBARA) (1923-) UK writer whose sf novel, *The Catacombs* (**1962**), depicts with some irony a post-HOLOCAUST world in which "Crishuns", having persuaded themselves that they warrant special attention, await salvation. [JC]

HARRISON, MICHAEL (1907-1991) UK writer in various genres, mostly not sf. He wrote an early film novelization, *The Bride of Frankenstein* * (**1936**) as Michael Egremont, and some of the stories assembled in *Transit of Venus* (coll **1936**) are of fantasy interest. His first and most interesting sf novel, *Higher Things* (**1945**), is clearly influenced by H.G. WELLS. An impoverished young man, caught in the trammels of a clerical position but with dreams of higher things, finds in himself the power to levitate, which he does at crucial moments in his rather melancholy life to escape his and the world's muddles. He then makes a long (probably delusional) flight to confront the Dictator (Hitler) and to discuss with him the world's fate, a middle-period Wellsian excursion which is succeeded by a Wellsian quietus: the protagonist, haunted by PARANOIA, decides to escape the world entirely in a levitated, airtight gondola. *The Darkened Room: An Arabesque* (**1951**) is like *Higher Things* set in the mythical town of Rowcester; it features a cat kept artificially alive to further a blackmail scheme. *The Brain* (**1953**) devotes itself to a mushroom cloud which becomes sentient. [JC]

Other works: *The Exploits of the Chevalier Dupin* (coll **1968** US) and *Murder in the Rue Royale* (coll **1972**) are collections of mystery stories extending the canon of Edgar Allan POE's seminal detective.

See also: PSI POWERS.

HARRISON, M(ICHAEL) JOHN (1945-) UK writer and rock-climber, closely identified in the 1960s with NEW WORLDS, where he published his first sf story, "Baa Baa Blocksheep", in 1968, and for which he later wrote some of the best tales using the **Jerry Cornelius** template, or icon, from the series created by Michael MOORCOCK. He also wrote considerable criticism for *NW*, usually as Joyce Churchill, and served for some time as its literary editor. Typical work from this period was assembled in *The Machine in Shaft Ten and Other Stories* (coll **1975**), which reveals its NEW-WAVE provenance in narrative discontinuities and subheads after the fashion of J.G. BALLARD. His first novel, *The Committed Men* (**1971**; rev 1971 US), is an impressive post-HOLOCAUST story set in a fractured England, centring physically on the ruins of the motorways, and generating a powerful sense of entropic dismantlement. His third, *The Centauri Device* (**1974** US), is a significantly disgruntled SPACE OPERA, perhaps his least successful book, and one which demonstrates MJH's persistent discomfort with the escapist conventions of this sort of sf. Unsurprisingly, the doomsday device of the title duly blows up the Galaxy.

As the first volume of his **Viriconium** sequence, though much simpler than later instalments, his second novel, *The Pastel City* (**1971**), is of greater interest. It is a FAR-FUTURE science fantasy set on a bleak Dying Earth, whose description plays on SWORD-AND-SORCERY imagery, though nothing happens of a magical nature. Viriconium itself is both the land – conveyed with a growing capacity to portray in words the physical world – and the city at the end of time which dominates it. The second volume of the sequence, *A Storm of Wings* (**1980** US), rewrites its predecessor in language whose intensity is both surreal and topographically exact, so that an orthodox tale of alien INVASION becomes a series of bleak *tableaux vivants* as witnessed through the insectoid perceptions of the invaders. *In Viriconium* (**1982**; vt *The Floating Gods* 1983 US), the final novel of the sequence, is far more abstract, rendering the *fin de siècle* transports of its plot in language of a fixating painterly density. The UK versions of the stories assembled as *Viriconium Nights* (coll **1984** US; much rev 1985 UK) – and later brought together with *In Viriconium* as *Viriconium* (omni **1988**) – focus even more intensely upon the task of seeing their dying landscapes with utter exactitude, so that the inhabitants of the city present their failed artistries in terms less and less reassuring to any sense that they are able to inhabit a fantasy world; this sense of the closing of the world was intensified in *The Luck in the Head* (1983 *Interzone* text alone, as MJH; text rev as graph **1991**) with Ian MILLER, which darkly re-viewed a tale from the UK collection. The reality of things seen comes, in the end, to be the only reality to which MJH will give allegiance in the sequence; all else is unearned.

The central lesson to be extracted from his work – that any personal escape from the world must be earned by attending to that very world, for only when self and city and rockface are seen with true sight do we know what it is we wish to leave – is reiterated in most of the stories assembled in *The Ice Monkey and Other Stories* (coll **1983**), some of which are sf tales of a striking and obdurate coldness, and in *The Course of the Heart* (**1992**), where a partial fulfilment of the longing enacts a stringent penalty. In *Climbers* (**1989**), an associational novel about rock-climbing, the lesson is driven home with something like ferocity. The protagonists of this book are losers and obsessives, and the land they climb is dreadful with the weight of being; in a sense, therefore, the book truly defines the end of the **Viriconium** sequence and the preceding sf tales, because for MJH the only difference between the lords and ladies in science fantasy and climbers clinging to a rock in the real world is that the latter know where they are. [JC] **Other works:** *Fawcett on Rock* (**1987**) as by Ron Fawcett, nonfiction.

See also: CITIES; ENTROPY; DISASTER; NEW WRITINGS IN SF; PERCEPTION.

HARRISON AWARD ◊ WORLD SF.

HARRY AND THE HENDERSONS (vt *Bigfoot and the Hendersons* UK) Film (1987). Amblin/Universal. Dir William Dear, starring John Lithgow, Melinda Dillon, Joshua Rudoy, David Suchet, Don Ameche, Kevin Peter Hall. Screenplay Dear, William E. Martin, Ezra D. Rappaport. 111 mins. Colour.

This amiable, well made film is sf only in that it deals with a lost race (◊ LOST WORLDS). Harry is a Bigfoot, an 8ft (2.4m) intelligent hairy anthropoid, a shy native of the US Northwest. He is knocked down by the car of and then temporarily adopted by the Henderson family of Seattle. Made by Steven SPIELBERG's production company, Amblin Entertainment, *HATH* is effectively a variation on the theme of his E.T.: THE EXTRATERRESTRIAL (1982), in which the innocent ALIEN, healer of human hurt, pursued by the unthinking mob, is this time a father- rather than a child-figure. The occasional tartness of the film's wit compensates for the its almost excessive sweetness; this proved to be a commercial miscalculation.

The novelization is *Harry and the Hendersons* ∗ (**1987**; vt *Bigfoot and the Hendersons* 1987 UK) by Joyce THOMPSON. There has also been a tv sitcom based on the film. [PN]

See also: APES AND CAVEMEN (IN THE MODERN WORLD).

HARRYHAUSEN, RAY (1920-) US special-effects supervisor, long based in the UK, associated with many sf and fantasy films. As a boy his main interests were sculpture and palaeontology. The desire to see his own clay figures move on the screen, aroused by KING KONG (1933), stimulated his interest in photography and special effects. While Willis H. O'BRIEN, who had animated King Kong, was preparing to make MIGHTY JOE YOUNG (1949), RH approached him, showed sample footage of his work on 16mm, and was hired as his assistant on this film and on the subsequent abortive project *El Toro Estrella*, about a boy, a bull and a dinosaur. RH and O'Brien then went their separate ways, though they later teamed up briefly to work on the dinosaur sequences in the pseudo-documentary *Animal World* (1956).

RH supervised the effects in The BEAST FROM 20,000 FATHOMS (1953), which was a success. He then formed a partnership with producer Charles H. Schneer that continued through his active career. Their first film together was IT CAME FROM BENEATH THE SEA (1955); it was followed by EARTH VS. THE FLYING SAUCERS (1956) and 20 MILLION MILES TO EARTH (1957). By then the sf film boom was in decline and they decided that their next project would be a mythic fantasy. In 1958 they made *The Seventh Voyage of Sinbad*, the first animation film of its type in colour. It proved a huge financial success and similar fantasies followed: *The Three Worlds of Gulliver* (1960), MYSTERIOUS ISLAND (1961) and *Jason and the Argonauts* (1963). Then there was a shift back to sf with FIRST MEN IN THE MOON (1964), ONE MILLION YEARS BC (1966) and *The* VALLEY OF GWANGI (1969).

In the 1970s and 1980s their output fell and they returned to the format of their best-loved films, *The Seventh Voyage of Sinbad* and *Jason and the Argonauts*. Their three further films in the same vein were *The Golden Voyage of Sinbad* (1973), *Sinbad and the Eye of the Tiger* (1977) and *Clash of the Titans* (1981). In the latter (an adaptation of the Perseus legend) they attempted, by using distinguished actors in supporting roles, to counter criticisms that their films had become 5min dollops of monster-fighting stitched together with 15min stretches of pointless running about and bad acting. It remained a relative disappointment, not helped by the inclusion of an insufferable mechanical owl patterned on LucasFilm's R2D2 in STAR WARS (1977) – a film which, ironically, was deeply influenced by RH's earlier fantasies. The alien craft of *Earth vs. the Flying Saucers* and the Ymir of *20 Million Miles to Earth* probably stand as RH's best animation, and *Jason and the Argonauts* as his best film. While his effects were very influential state-of-the-art stuff in the 1950s and 1960s, he proved reluctant to adapt to the 1980s and 1990s boom in computer-assisted animation. He has gracefully retired, now sculpting figures from his films and acting as spiritual godfather to his pupils-cum-successors, Jim Danforth, David Allen and Phil Tippett. He appears, thinly disguised, as "Roy Holdstrom" in Ray BRADBURY's *A Graveyard for Lunatics* (**1990**). [JB/KN]

HART, ELLIS [s] ◊ Harlan ELLISON.

HARTING, PIETER (1812-1885) Dutch polymath, immensely prolific in scientific fields such as biology, medicine and geology. His one sf novel, *Anno 2065* (**1865** as by Dr Dioscorides; trans anon as *Anno Domini 2071* 1871 UK), posits a liberal world 200 years hence which is at peace, has new sources of power, and is highly industrious. [JC]

HARTLEY, L(ESLIE) P(OLES) (1895-1972) UK novelist and short-story writer known mainly for his works outside the sf field, especially for *The Go-Between* (**1953**) and for the trilogy comprising *The Shrimp and the Anemone* (**1944**), *The Sixth Heaven* (**1946**), which has some slight fantasy content, and *Eustace and Hilda* (**1947**). His ghost stories – some of the finest from this century – were variously collected in *Night Fears and Other Stories* (coll **1924**), *The Killing Bottle* (coll **1932**), *The Travelling Grave and Other Stories* (coll **1948** US), *The White Wand* (coll **1954**), *Two for the River* (coll **1961**) and *Miss Carteret Receives and Other Stories* (coll **1971**); these and more were assembled in *The Complete Short Stories of L.P. Hartley* (coll **1973** in 2 vols). His sf novel, *Facial Justice* (**1960**), deals sourly but sensitively with personal dilemmas after humanity has re-emerged from underground after a nuclear DISASTER. Many of the precepts of the subsequent DYSTOPIA satirize the welfare state and English socialism. For women, true equality involves a literal equality of physical appearance, with poignant effects. It has been argued that, when the female protagonist unmasks the dictator responsible, showing her to be an ancient and envious hag, the author reveals a fundamental misogyny; the point is moot. [JC]

See also: HISTORY OF SF; POLITICS.

HARTLIB, SAMUEL (*c*1600-1660) Polish-born scientist, chemist and writer, in the UK from about 1625. SH was the author of a Royalist UTOPIA, *A Description of the Famous Kingdome of Macaria* (**1641**). A facsimile edition was published in 1961 in the USA. [JC]

HARTMAN, EMERSON B. (1890-?) US writer whose *Lunarchia: That Strange World Beneath the Moon's Crust* (**1937**) began a projected interplanetary sequence in the Edgar Rice BURROUGHS vein with the discovery of a colourful civilization within the Moon. No further volumes appeared. [JC]

Other work: *The Giant of the Sierras* (**1945**).

HARTRIDGE, JON (1934-) UK writer associated, like Brian W. ALDISS, with the *Oxford Mail*, of which he was features editor. His sf novels, *Binary Divine* (**1969**) and *Earthjacket* (**1970**), take a dark view of Earth's crowded, DYSTOPIAN, urbanized future. [JC]

HARTWELL, DAVID G(EDDES) (1941-) US editor, publisher and critic, with a PhD from Columbia in Comparative Medieval Literature. He published and edited *The Little Magazine* (1965-88), a literary magazine, and since 1988 has been reviews editor of *The* NEW YORK REVIEW OF SCIENCE FICTION, published by Dragon Press, the SMALL PRESS of which he was

partner 1973-8 and is now proprietor. He edited the short-lived COSMOS SCIENCE FICTION AND FANTASY MAGAZINE 1977-8.

His substantial influence in the sf world has been mainly, however, as an editor and/or advisor for various commercial sf publishers, including Signet (1971-3), Berkley/Putnam (1973-8), GREGG PRESS (1975-86) – an academic publisher of important sf reprints – Pocket Books/Simon & Schuster (1978-83), where he was responsible for their important TIMESCAPE BOOKS sf imprint, TOR BOOKS (1984-current), where he is consulting sf editor, Arbor House (1984-8) and William Morrow (1988-91). His career – a tightrope walk – testifies to the difficulties DGH has partly conquered in reconciling the conflicting demands of art and commerce, especially during his tenure with Pocket Books' **Timescape** programme, where he published many distinguished titles, including Gene WOLFE's **Book of the New Sun** tetralogy (**1980-3**).

The anthologies DGH has edited include: *The Battle of the Monsters and Other Stories* (anth **1977**) with L.W. CURREY, 19th-century sf; *Christmas Ghosts* (anth **1987**) with Kathryn Cramer (1962-), ghost stories; *The Spirits of Christmas* (anth **1989**) with Cramer, ghost stories; *The Dark Descent* (anth **1987**; reprinted in 3 vols 1990), horror stories; *Masterpieces of Fantasy and Enchantment* (anth **1988**); *Masterpieces of Fantasy and Wonder* (anth **1989**); and *The World Treasury of Science Fiction* (anth **1988**). DGH won a World Fantasy AWARD in the Special Award/Professional category in 1988, and has 7 times been nominated for a HUGO as Best Editor. He has written a number of critical essays on sf; and his *Age of Wonders: Exploring the World of Science Fiction* (**1984**) is wide-ranging, informal and anecdotal, treating sf and FANDOM as both a literary and a sociological phenomenon. [PN]

See also: PHILIP K. DICK AWARD.

HARVEY, FRANK (LAIRD) (1913-1981) US writer whose collection of stories, *Air Force!* (coll **1959**), concentrates on that branch of the armed services, but with a NEAR-FUTURE setting which includes manned satellites and the like. [JC]

HARVEY, JAMES ◊ Gardner F. FOX.

HARVEY, M(ARY) ELAYN (1945-) US writer whose sf novel, *Warhaven* (**1987**), the first volume of a projected trilogy, puts its young protagonist through a series of trials, at the end of which he has clearly prepared himself to become one of the Guardians who covertly supervise a variety of spacefaring races. Throughout, his solutions to problems tend, unusually, to dodge the use of force. [JC]

HASKIN, BYRON (1899-1984) US film director. His film career began in 1919 when he became an assistant cameraman for Louis J. Selznick. He directed 4 films in 1927, but later worked mostly as a cinematographer; he supervised the special-effects department for Warner Bros. 1936-47. In 1947 he began directing again with *I Walk Alone*, a Hal Wallis production. In 1952 he formed a creative partnership with producer George PAL, directing several films for him. The first of these was WAR OF THE WORLDS (1953); it was followed by *The Naked Jungle* (1954), CONQUEST OF SPACE (1955) and *The* POWER (1968), the latter codirected with Pal. Other sf movies directed by BH were FROM THE EARTH TO THE MOON (1958) and ROBINSON CRUSOE ON MARS (1964). He also directed many tv episodes, including several in *The* OUTER LIMITS. BH's background in special effects meant that he never neglected them in his films, unlike many other sf film-makers of the 1950s. His work as a director was likable – as in Disney's *Treasure Island* (1950) – but uninspired: *War of the Worlds* derives impact from its spectacle, but most of his other sf films are merely competent. Probably his most interesting and personal film, on which he had a fair degree of control, was *Robinson Crusoe on Mars*. He retired in 1967. [JB]

HASSE, HENRY L. (1913-1977) US fan and sf writer who frequently worked in collaboration with others, notably A. Fedor (with whom he published his first story, "The End of Tyme" for *Wonder Stories* in 1933), Emil PETAJA, whose pseudonym E. Theodore Pine he once shared, and Ray BRADBURY, with whom he collaborated on Bradbury's first professional story, "Pendulum" (1941). His best-known story is the novelette "He who Shrank" (1936) (◊ GREAT AND SMALL). An sf novel, *The Stars Will Wait* (**1968**), is unremarkable. [JC]

HASSLER, DONALD M(ACKEY II) (1937-   ) US academic and scholar of sf, based at Kent State University, Ohio. DMH was President of the SCIENCE FICTION RESEARCH ASSOCIATION 1985-6, and became managing editor of the journal EXTRAPOLATION with the Summer 1986 issue, co-editor with the Winter 1987 issue, and editor with the Spring 1990 issue. He was a pioneer in the early 1980s of "academic tracks" in world sf-CONVENTION programming. Books by DMH relating to sf are *Erasmus Darwin* (**1973** chap), *The Comedian as the Letter D: Erasmus Darwin's Comic Materialism* (**1973** Netherlands), *Comic Tones in Science Fiction: The Art of Compromise with Nature* (**1982**), *Hal Clement, Reader's Guide 11* (**1982** chap) and *Isaac Asimov, Reader's Guide 40* (**1991** chap). Collections of critical essays ed DMH are *Patterns of the Fantastic: Academic Programming at Chicon IV* (anth **1983**), *Patterns of the Fantastic II* (anth **1984**) and, with Carl B. YOKE, *Death and the Serpent: Immortality in Science Fiction and Fantasy* (anth **1985**). [PN]

See also: CRITICAL AND HISTORICAL WORKS ABOUT SF; IMMORTALITY.

HASSLER, KENNETH W(AYNE) (1932-   ) US personnel specialist and writer whose routine sf novels are *The Glass Cage* (**1969**), *Destination: Terra* (**1970**), *The Dream Squad* (**1970**), *A Message from Earth* (**1970**), *Intergalac Agent* (**1971**) and *The Multiple Man* (**1972**). [JC]

HASTINGS, GEORGE GORDON (?   -?   ) US writer whose sf novel, *The First American King* (**1904**), carries two protagonists – the more important being a brilliant inventor – by SUSPENDED ANIMATION to the USA of AD1975. They find it to be a RURITANIAN

empire assaulted from within by Federated Nihilists, who eventually take power and establish – in singularly unstrict accordance with their name – a benevolent welfare state. Rather unusually, GGH approves, and the novel ends peacefully. [JC]

HASTINGS, HUDSON [s] ◊ Henry KUTTNER.

HASTINGS, MILO (MILTON) (1884-1957) US nutritionist, editor and writer, sometimes on agricultural subjects – *The Dollar Hen* (**1909**) is a nonfiction text about hens. With striking accuracy, his future-WAR sf centres on conflict between either Japan or Germany and the rest of the world. Set around 1950, "In the Clutch of the War-God: The Tale of the Orient's Invasion of the Occident" (1911 *Physical Culture*) effectively espouses the cause of eugenical Japan against a bigoted USA, which loses the war but becomes healthy. Set around AD2150, and far more impressive, *City of Endless Night* (1919 *True Story* as "Children of 'Kultur'"; rev **1920**) describes a Germany partly defeated after centuries of warfare, but remaining impregnable underground within a great dome which shelters Berlin. Here a proto-Nazi DYSTOPIA has taken shape, with under-races genetically distinguished from one another (and from the sybaritic ruling class) by a ruthless breeding programme; thought-control is universal. The imagery of this striking novel links it with the German Expressionist cinema and films like Fritz LANG's METROPOLIS (1926), as well as to dystopian fictions like HUXLEY's *Brave New World* (**1932**). [JC]

See also: HISTORY OF SF; POLITICS.

HATCH, GERALD Pseudonym of US writer Dave Foley (?   -   ), whose sf novel, *The Day the Earth Froze* (**1963**), was one of a series published by Monarch Books on similar themes, including Charles FONTENAY's *The Day the Oceans Overflowed* (**1964**) and Christopher ANVIL's *The Day the Machines Stopped* (**1964**). [JC]

HAUNTED PALACE, THE ◊ Roger CORMAN.

HAUPTMANN, GERHART (JOHANN ROBERT) (1862-1946) German playwright and novelist, winner of the 1912 Nobel Prize for Literature, whose greatest plays were performed before the turn of the century and whose novels were written later. Of sf interest is *Die Insel der grossen Mutter, oder Das Wunder von Ile des Dames: Eine Geschichte aus dem Utopischen Archipelagus* (**1924**; trans Willa and Edwin Muir as *The Island of the Great Mother* **1925** US). The subtitle – "The Miracle of the Île des Dames: A Tale from the Utopian Archipelago" – fairly describes the complex mood of GH's ROBINSONADE, which portrays a matriarchal ISLAND society founded after a shipwreck, and follows the young men who, upon being exiled to another part of the Isle of Women, soon revolt, ending an ideal world. [JC]

Other works: *Hanneles Himmelfahrt* (**1893**; trans **1894** UK) and *Die versunkene Glocke* (**1896**; trans C.H. Meltzer as *The Sunken Bell* **1898** UK) and *Till Eulenspiegel* (**1928**), fantasy plays.

HAUSER'S MEMORY Made-for-tv film (1970).

Universal/NBC TV. Dir Boris Sagal, starring David McCallum, Susan Strasberg, Lilli Palmer, Robert Webber, Leslie Nielsen. Screenplay Adrian Spies, based on *Hauser's Memory* (**1968**) by Curt SIODMAK. 100 mins. Colour.

Siodmak's 1968 novel is an updated but equally absurd variation on the theme of his novel *Donovan's Brain* (**1943**), which was filmed three times (◊ DONOVAN'S BRAIN; *The* LADY AND THE MONSTER; VENGEANCE): a dead man's mind somehow exerts influence on the living. This time DNA material taken from the brain of a dead German Nazi scientist in order to preserve his scientific knowledge is injected into a young US Jewish scientist (McCallum). The conflicts created within the hero's mind by this experiment in memory-transfer have dramatic potential, mostly wasted as the film degenerates into a conventional thriller about the CIA versus the Russians. At the end, Hauser's memory now dominating the hero, a melodramatic revenge takes place. [JB]

HAWEL, RUDOLF [r] ◊ AUSTRIA.

HAWKE, SIMON ◊ Nicholas YERMAKOV.

HAWKES, JACQUETTA (1910-   ) UK archaeologist and writer, known mainly for such works outside the sf field as *The Land* (**1951**). She was married to J.B. PRIESTLEY. *Fables* (coll **1953**; vt *A Woman as Great as the World and Other Fables* 1953 US) includes "The Unites", a long exemplary tale which combines fantasy and DYSTOPIAN sf: God sends down an investigative angel to find out why humans have grown silent. The angel reports that, although *Homo sapiens* has degenerated into a breed of hive-dwelling automata through too sedulous a striving after equality, dissidents have begun to recreate human conflict and difference. God seems pleased. *Providence Island: An Archaeological Tale* (**1959**) is a fairly late example of anthropological sf (◊ ANTHROPOLOGY), in which an expedition comes across survivors from the Magdalenian culture of the late Paleolithic living within an extinct volcano on a Pacific ISLAND. They have highly developed empathic and PSI POWERS, developed as a kind of cultural alternative to technological prowess; they use these powers to fend off US nuclear tests. *A Quest for Love* (**1980**) is a REINCARNATION fantasy. [JC]
See also: LOST WORLDS.

HAWKIN, MARTIN Working name of UK writer Martin Hawkins (?   -   ) for his INVASION novel, *When Adolph Came* (**1943**), featuring an ALTERNATE WORLD in which the Germans conquer the UK (◊ HITLER WINS). An underground movement soon begins to turn the tables. [JC]

HAWKINS, WARD (1912-1990) US writer who spent most of his career producing Westerns, usually in collaboration with his elder brother, John Hawkins. In the 1980s WH wrote tv scripts and the **Borg and Guss** sequence of humorous sf adventures – *Red Flame Burning* (**1985**), *Sword of Fire* (**1985**), *Blaze of Wrath* (**1986**) and *Torch of Fear* (**1987**) – starring Harry Borg and his sidekick Guss the lizard-man in an alternate-universe (◊ ALTERNATE WORLDS) Galaxy. [JC]

HAWKWOOD, ALLAN ◊ H. BEDFORD-JONES.

HAWTHORNE, NATHANIEL (1804-1864) US writer known primarily for his work outside the sf field. One of the formative figures in US literature, NH was intrigued throughout his writing career by themes we would now call sf. His extensive notebooks outline dozens of projected sf works, some of which he was able to complete, while others he worked on unsuccessfully until his death. A long line of doctors, chemists, botanists, mesmerists, physicists and inventors parade their marvellously creative and destructive skills through his fiction, even the most apparently fantastic events being given naturalistic explanations. Thus much of his writing at least borders on sf.

In three of his four major romances, sf elements run as a main undercurrent. A secret medical experiment controls the plot of *The Scarlet Letter* (**1850**); the main action of *The House of the Seven Gables* (**1851**) derives from hypnotism (◊ PSYCHOLOGY) and a strange inherited disease; all the major events in *The Blithedale Romance* (**1852**) flow from a major topic of 19th-century sf, mesmeric control. A SCIENTIST's quest for the elixir of life is the subject of *Dr Heidegger's Experiment* (1837 *Salem Gazette*; **1883** chap) and two unfinished, posthumously published romances, all possibly differing draft attempts at the same basic story: the title story of *The Dolliver Romance and Other Pieces* (1864 *The Atlantic Monthly* as "The Dolliver Romance"; coll **1876**), and *Septimius: A Romance* (**1872** UK; vt *Septimius Felton, or The Elixir of Life* 1872 US). Some stories, such as "The Man from Adamant" (1837), come directly from pseudo-scientific curiosities NH encountered as editor of *The American Magazine of Useful and Entertaining Knowledge*.

NH's short work of interest appeared in *Twice-Told Tales* (coll **1837**; exp in 2 vols 1842), *Mosses from an Old Manse* (coll **1846**) and *The Snow-Image and Other Twice-Told Tales* (coll **1852**). Three of his early stories had profound influences on subsequent 19th-century sf, and all three still stand as masterpieces of the genre. In "The Birthmark" (1843) a lone genius who has invented numerous scientific marvels commits the fatal error of attempting to remove the one blemish which keeps his wife from being perfect, a tiny birthmark which makes this lovely woman disgusting to him. "The Artist of the Beautiful" (1844) describes the creation of an automaton butterfly which, for another lone inventive genius, substitutes for love, sex and biological procreation. In "Rappaccini's Daughter" (1844) a scientist attempts to make his only child impervious to the evils of the world by filling her with secret poisons, but is foiled by his arch-rival. Part of the enduring power of these three tales comes from their deep penetration into the psychology of a group of men emerging in NH's society, the technical-scientific élite. NH's sf extends the achievements of Mary SHELLEY's *Frankenstein* (**1818**) into the dawn of the age of modern science and the literature that is part of that age's culture, modern sf. [HBF]

Other works: *Doctor Grimshawe's Secret* (**1883**); *The Ancestral Footstep* (**1883**); *The Ghost of Doctor Harris* (**1900** chap); *The Dolliver Romance, and Kindred Tales* (coll **1900**); *The Complete Short Stories of Nathaniel Hawthorne* (coll **1959**), assembling 72 tales; *The Snow Image and Uncollected Tales* (coll **1974**) ed E.F. BLEILER; *Young Goodman Brown and Other Short Stories* (coll **1992**).

See also: ARTS; BIOLOGY; CLICHÉS; GAMES AND TOYS; HISTORY OF SF; HORROR IN SF; MACHINES; MEDICINE.

HAWTON, HECTOR (1901-   ) UK writer and Humanist, at one time managing director of the Rationalist Press Association. The **Col. Max Masterson** sequence – *Tower of Darkness* (**1950**), *Blue-Eyed Buddha* (**1951**), *Black Emperor* (**1952**) and *The Lost Valley* (**1953**) – verges on sf, the final volume being a lost-race (◊ LOST WORLDS) tale. *Operation Superman* (**1951**) is an old-fashioned yarn about a man whose INTELLIGENCE has been much heightened by shock-treatment experiments in a Nazi concentration camp.   [JC/PN]

HAY, GEORGE Working name of UK writer, editor and sf enthusiast Oswyn Robert Tregonwell Hay (**1922-**   ), who began publishing sf in the early 1950s with *Flight of the "Hesper"* (**1951**), *Man, Woman and Android* (**1951**), *This Planet For Sale* (**1952**) and, as by King LANG, *Terra!* (**1953**). Turning to editing, he produced *Hell Hath Fury* (anth **1963**), a collection of stories from UNKNOWN; *The Disappearing Future* (anth **1970**); *Stopwatch* (anth **1974**), an original anthology with stories by John BRUNNER, Ursula K. LE GUIN, Christopher PRIEST, A.E. VAN VOGT and others; *The Edward De Bono Science Fiction Collection* (anth **1976**), a selection of stories chosen to illustrate De Bono's theories of "lateral thinking"; *The Necronomicon* (anth **1978**), a hoax assemblage of texts, dominated by Colin WILSON, arguing that a certain manuscript was passed obscurely from the Renaissance alchemist John Dee on down to H.P. LOVECRAFT, with «The R'lyeh Text» (anth **1993**) projected to continue in the same vein; and the **Pulsar** sequence of original anthologies, *Pulsar 1* (anth **1978**) and *Pulsar 2* (anth **1979**), with stories from Robert HOLDSTOCK and Ian WATSON as well as older figures like van Vogt. The first volume of a long-meditated collection, *The John W. Campbell Letters, Volume One* (coll **1986** US) ed Perry A. CHAPDELAINE, Tony Chapdelaine and GH, was welcomed for the light it shed on numerous moments of sf history; a second volume is projected (◊ John W. CAMPBELL Jr). From the end of the 1960s, GH worked to establish some formal organization to promote sf in the UK, and was instrumental in the establishment of the SCIENCE FICTION FOUNDATION, of which he remains a council member, espousing in that role his continuing sense that sf provides an armamentarium of tools for coping with the future.   [MJE/JC]

HAY, JACOB (1920-   ) US writer whose sf novel, *Autopsy for a Cosmonaut* (**1969**; vt *Death of a Cosmonaut* 1970 UK), with John M. KESHISHIAN, describes a NEAR-FUTURE space crisis in which NASA attempts a space rendezvous with a Soviet satellite suspected of harbouring a nuclear warhead.   [JC]

HAY, JOHN Working name of Australian writer and farmer John Warwick Dalrymple-Hay (1928-   ). In his sf novel, *The Invasion* (**1968** UK), a NEAR-FUTURE war begins after a US test missile devastates China, whose retaliation includes the waging of atomic WAR on the coastal cities of Australia. Inland survivors band together to resist the invaders.   [JC]

HAY, W(ILLIAM) DELISLE (?   -?   ) UK writer and Fellow of the Royal Geographical Society, known for his writings on New Zealand matters. His first sf novel, *The Doom of the Great City, Being the Narrative of a Survivor, written A.D. 1942* (**1880**), retains interest for the vividness with which it depicts the collapse of London through the onslaught of a poisonous fog (◊ POLLUTION), though the piety of the reportage is vicious. *Three Hundred Years Hence, or A Voice from Posterity* (**1881**), which is more substantial (but even less pleasant), is a future HISTORY told as a series of smug lectures delivered in AD2180, long after the White races have committed genocide on all Blacks and Orientals, and created a technological and political paradise on Earth.   [JC]

HAYES, FREDERICK WILLIAM (1848-1918) UK painter, playwright and writer whose sf novel, *The Great Revolution of 1905, or The Story of the Phalanx* (**1893**), describes from a 1930s perspective the successful efforts of the socialist middle-class "Phalanx" to take over the UK.   [JC]

HAYNES, JOHN ROBERT ◊ Philip WILDING.

HAYWARD, WILLIAM STEPHENS (?   -?   ) UK writer, prolific author of adventure novels for three decades after about 1860, whose sf novel, *The Cloud King, or Up in the Air and Down in the Sea* (**1865**), features a balloon trip to an African LOST WORLD in which low gravity seems to help keep the natives from ageing.   [JC]

See also: BOYS' PAPERS.

HAYWOOD, ELIZA (FOWLER) (?1693-1756) UK actress, publisher and most prolific female writer of her time. Much of her work was scandalous, containing thinly veiled characterizations of notable contemporaries. *The Adventures of Eovaai, Princess of Ijavea: A Pre-Adamitical History* (**1736**; vt *The Unfortunate Princess* 1741) is an allegorical political SATIRE set before the destruction of Earth's second moon and featuring, among many accounts of sorcery, the visitation by mechanical means of an extraterrestrial (this was several years before the appearance of VOLTAIRE's *Micromégas* [**1751**]). EH also wrote *Memoirs of a Certain Island Adjacent to the Kingdom of Utopia* (2 vols **1725-6**), an anonymously published allegorical UTOPIA built around a series of sexual scandals, and *The Invisible Spy* (**1755**) as by "Explorabilis", in which an INVISIBILITY belt is used to eavesdrop on society gossip. The anonymous satirical LOST-WORLD novel *Memoirs of the Court of Lilliput* (**1727**) was (perhaps wrongly) attributed to her by Alexander Pope in 1729.   [JE]

About the author: *The Life and Romances of Mrs Eliza*

Haywood (**1915**) by G.F. Whicker.

HAZEL, PAUL (1944-   ) US writer whose **Finn-branch Trilogy** makes use of some sf devices, though primarily a Celtic fantasy about a hero – and underworld god – named Finn, told in a dense, difficult style which nevertheless has very considerable power. The first 2 vols, *Yearwood* (**1980**) and *Undersea* (**1982**), are moderately orthodox, though recounted with unconventional intensity, but the third, *Winterking* (**1984**), is set in an ALTERNATE-WORLD version of a contemporary USA riven by the numinous presence of gods and threatened by terminal transformation; in this respect the book resembles John CROWLEY's *Little, Big* (**1981**). All 3 vols have been assembled as *The Finnbranch* (omni **1986** UK). [JC]

See also: GODS AND DEMONS.

HAZLITT, HENRY (1894-   ) US journalist and author in whose sf novel, *The Great Idea* (**1951**; vt *Time Will Run Back* 1952 UK), the communist Wonworld society of the future is transformed back into a free-market capitalist society, the agent of change being the dictator's son. The communism of this society is more Soviet than Marxist. [JC]

See also: DYSTOPIAS; ECONOMICS.

HAZZARD, WILTON [s] ◊ Margaret ST CLAIR.

HEADLINE PUBLICATIONS ◊ SUPER-SCIENCE FICTION.

HEAL, PENELOPE [r] ◊ M.H. ZOOL.

HEALY, RAYMOND J(OHN) (1907-   ) US editor who, in collaboration with J. Francis MCCOMAS, compiled the 35-story, 1000pp *Adventures in Time and Space* (anth **1946**; cut vt *Selections from Adventures in Time and Space* 1954; recut vt *More Adventures in Time and Space* 1955; text restored, vt *Famous Science-Fiction Stories* 1957), which remains a definitive anthology of magazine sf up to 1945 and is credited with considerable influence in helping to give GENRE SF literary respectability. RJH later pioneered the original sf ANTHOLOGY with *New Tales of Space and Time* (anth **1951**) and *9 Tales of Space and Time* (anth **1954**), which included notable stories by such writers as Isaac ASIMOV, Anthony BOUCHER and Ray BRADBURY. [MJE/JC]

See also: ASTOUNDING SCIENCE-FICTION; GOLDEN AGE OF SF.

HEARD, GERALD Working name of UK author and speculative journalist H(enry) F(itzgerald) Heard (1889-1971), which he used for both fiction and nonfiction in the UK; in the USA, where he lived after 1937, he wrote his fiction as H.F. Heard. He is perhaps best remembered for his association with Aldous HUXLEY in investigations of the Vedanta cult and for such speculative studies as *The Ascent of Humanity* (**1929**) and *The Third Morality* (**1937**). His UFO popularization *The Riddle of the Flying Saucers: Is Another World Watching?* (**1950**; rev 1953), was well received, although time has passed it by. Some of his detective and horror fictions featuring **Mr Mycroft** – *A Taste for Honey* (**1941**; vt *A Taste for Murder* 1955), *Reply Paid* (**1942**) and *The Notched Hairpin* (**1949**) – are borderline-sf pastiches of Arthur Conan DOYLE's **Sherlock Holmes** stories; *Murder by Reflection* (**1942**)

features a killing done by radiation poisoning. The title story of *The Great Fog and Other Weird Tales* (coll **1944**; vt *The Great Fog: Weird Tales of Terror and Detection* 1946; with 2 stories added and 1 dropped, rev under first title 1947 UK) is a DISASTER tale, the mould-derived Great Fog destroying all civilization. In the title story of *The Lost Cavern* (coll **1948**) a man is held captive by intelligent bats. Set in the 19th century, *The Black Fox: A Novel of the 'Seventies* (**1950** UK) is a supernatural tale, the fox being Anubis. *Doppelgangers: An Episode of the Fourth, the Psychological, Revolution, 1997* (**1947**), which is sf, rather laboriously sets up a conflict among three factions, each of whose philosophies is in didactic opposition to the others'. *Gabriel and the Creatures* (**1952**; vt *Wishing Well* 1953 UK) recasts some of GH's evolutionary speculation in sf form for children. [JC]

See also: DYSTOPIAS; ECOLOGY; EVOLUTION; *The* MAGAZINE OF FANTASY AND SCIENCE FICTION.

HEARD, H.F. [r] ◊ Gerald HEARD.

HEARTBEEPS Film (1981). Universal. Dir Allan Arkush, starring Bernadette Peters, Andy Kaufman, Randy Quaid. Screenplay John Hill. 79 mins. Colour.

Obviously disliked by its distributors, who trimmed it by 10 minutes before release (not enough action) and then allowed it to sink almost without trace, this film is a mildly amusing, perhaps over-cute, extremely silly comedy about two domestic ROBOTS (male and female) who escape from the repair shop and fall in love. It oscillates between gentle SATIRE and over-the-top sentimentality. The robots (Peters and Kaufman in all-over plastic) are well realized. [PN]

HEATH, PETER Pseudonym of US writer Peter Fine (1938-   ), whose novels *The Mind Brothers* (**1967**), *Assassins from Tomorrow* (**1967**) and *Men who Die Twice* (**1968**) comprise the routine thriller-like **Mind Brothers** sf series. [JC]

HEATH, ROYSTON ◊ George C. WALLIS.

HEAVY METAL Glossy BEDSHEET-size US colour COMIC-strip magazine inspired by the French magazine MÉTAL HURLANT and reprinting English-language versions of mainly sf and fantasy material from this and other French, Italian and Spanish sources alongside similar matter by select US contributors. Published monthly Apr 1977-Dec 1985, quarterly from the Winter (i.e., January) 1986 issue and then bimonthly from Mar 1989, *HM* has built a reputation for high quality in both presentation and content; in an editorial during 1985 it claimed a readership of over 2 million. Monthly issues carried serialized material in episodes of varying length, causing an often uncomfortable segmentation of some stories; the change to quarterly publication introduced a policy of presenting only complete stories and full-length GRAPHIC NOVELS. *HM*'s list of contributors reads like a roster of the world's best artists and writers of comic-strip sf, and the following is only a selection: Enki BILAL, Vaughn BODÉ, Caza, Howard V. CHAYKIN, Richard CORBEN, Guido Crepax, Philippe DRUILLET, Fernando Fernandez, Juan Giminez, Jean GIRAUD

(Moebius), Jeff Jones, Rod Kierkegaard, Tanino Liberatore, Milo Manara, Georges Pichard, José Ribera, Aleuteri Serpieri, Jacques Tardi, Daniel Torres and Berni Wrightson. In addition to the regular issues there have been several "Specials", including *Son of Heavy Metal* (1983), *Heavy Metal's Even Heavier Metal* (1984), *Bride of Heavy Metal* (1986) and *Best of Heavy Metal* (1986). *HM* has also published a line of graphic novels, most of which previously appeared as serials in the magazine.

The animated film *Heavy Metal* (1981) dir Gerald Potterton displayed animated improvisations on themes and characters featured in *HM*. A live-action sequel, *Heavy Metal's Burning Chrome*, was planned but never realized. [RT]

HECHT, BEN (1894-1964) US journalist, novelist, playwright, film scriptwriter and publisher, associated with Bohemian literary circles before becoming prominent in Hollywood night-life in the early 1930s. His writings are particularly notable for their cynicism, iconoclasm and irony. Many of his short stories border on SCIENCE FANTASY, most vividly "The Adventures of Professor Emmett" (in *A Book of Miracles* coll **1939**) (◊ HIVE-MINDS); some were influenced by the works of Charles FORT. BH is best known in the sf field for *Fantazius Mallare* (**1922**) and its sequel *The Kingdom of Evil* (**1924**), an erotic and supposedly decadent account of a descent into madness; the first volume was successfully prosecuted for obscenity on the grounds of its illustrations (by Wallace Smith). [JE]

Other works: *Eleven Selected Great Stories* (coll **1943**); *Miracle in the Rain* (**1943**); *The Collected Stories of Ben Hecht* (coll **1945**).

HECHT, FRIEDRICH [r] ◊ AUSTRIA.

HEINBERG, AAGE [r] ◊ DENMARK.

HEINE, IRVING ◊ Dennis HUGHES.

HEINE, WILLIAM C(OLBOURNE) (1919-) Canadian writer in whose NEAR-FUTURE *The Last Canadian* (**1974**; vt *Death Wind* 1976 US; vt *The Last American* 1986 Canada) a plague survivor flees northwards into ice and snow. [JC]

HEINLEIN, ROBERT A(NSON) (1907-1988) US writer, educated at the University of Missouri and the US Naval Academy, Annapolis. After serving as a naval officer for five years, he retired due to ill-health in 1934, studied physics at UCLA for a time, then took a variety of jobs before beginning to publish sf in 1939 with "Lifeline" for *ASF*, a magazine whose GOLDEN AGE he would profoundly shape, just as he rewrote US sf as a whole in his own image. RAH may have been the all-time most important writer of GENRE SF, though not its finest sf writer in strictly literary terms; his pre-eminence from 1940 to 1960 was both earned and unassailable. For half a century he was the father – loved, resisted, emulated – of the dominant US form of the genre.

He came to the role naturally. Unlike most of John W. CAMPBELL Jr's pre-WWII recruits to *ASF*, he entered the field as a mature man, already in his 30s,

with one genuine career (the military) honourably behind him. He was smart, aggressive, collegial, competent and highly inventive. And he worked fast. By 1942 – when he stopped writing to do his WWII service as an engineer at the Naval Air Experimental Station, Philadelphia – he had already published almost 30 stories, including three novels which would only later be released in book form. Moreover, it had soon been made clear that those stories published under his own name – like "Requiem" (1940), "The Roads Must Roll" (1940), "Blowups Happen" (1940) and the short novel "If This Goes On . . ." (1940; rev 1953) – fitted into a loose **Future History**, the schema for which Campbell published in *ASF* in 1941. As a device for tying together otherwise disparate stories, and for establishing a privileged (and loyal) group of readers familiar with the overall structure into which individual units were magically inserted, RAH's outline of the future was an extraordinarily acute idea. It was imitated by many other writers (with considerable success by Poul ANDERSON and Larry NIVEN, to name but two), but for many years only RAH's and perhaps Isaac ASIMOV's similar scheme – by priority, and by claiming imaginative copyright on the imagined future – were able to generate a sense of genuine CONCEPTUAL BREAKTHROUGH. RAH himself largely abandoned his **Future History** after 1950 (if the RECURSIVE novels of his last years are discounted for the moment); all the short stories in the sequence were soon assembled in book form as *The Man who Sold the Moon* (coll **1950**; with 2 stories cut 1951), *The Green Hills of Earth* (coll **1951**) and *Revolt in 2100* (coll **1953**). Two early novels also belonged to the series: *Methuselah's Children* (1941 *ASF*; rev **1958**), which concerns an extended family of near-immortals, and *Orphans of the Sky* (fixup **1963** UK) – assembling *Universe* (1941 *ASF*; **1951** chap) and "Common Sense" (1941 *ASF*) – which contains an innovative presentation of the GENERATION STARSHIP concept. With *Methuselah's Children*, the three collections were republished – "Let There Be Light" (1950) being omitted and "Searchlight" (1962) and "The Menace from Earth" (1957) added – in *The Past through Tomorrow* (omni **1967**; with *Methuselah's Children* omitted, cut 1977 UK).

Not all of RAH's early writing consisted of **Future History** stories, although most of his non-series work was initially published under the pseudonyms Anson MacDonald, Lyle Monroe, John Riverside and Caleb Saunders, including the novels *Sixth Column* (1941 *ASF* as MacDonald; **1949** as RAH; vt *The Day After Tomorrow* 1951) and *Beyond this Horizon* (1942 *ASF* as MacDonald; **1948** as RAH). In *Sixth Column* an Asiatic INVASION of the USA is defeated by a resistance – disguised as a RELIGION – which uses superscientific gadgets to accomplish "miracles". The original idea came from Campbell, who had incorporated it in the then unpublished novella "All" (in Campbell's *The Space Beyond* [coll **1976**]). *Beyond this Horizon* describes a future society of material plenty where people spend their time seeking the meaning of life ($\Diamond$ GENETIC ENGINEERING). Some of RAH's best stories belong to this period: "And He Built a Crooked House" (1941), about an architect who inadvertently builds into another dimension; "By His Bootstraps" (1941 as by MacDonald), a superb TIME-PARADOX fantasia; and "They" (1941), a fantasy about solipsism. "Waldo" (1942 as by MacDonald), about a crippled inventor who lives in a satellite, gave rise to a significant item of TERMINOLOGY, the real-life equivalents of the protagonist's remote-control lifting devices subsequently being known as WALDOES. These stories, and the later non-series stories, are collected in various volumes: *Waldo and Magic, Inc.* (coll **1950**; vt *Waldo: Genius in Orbit* 1958), *Assignment in Eternity* (coll **1953**; in 2 vols, vt *Assignment in Eternity* 1960 UK and *Lost Legacy* 1960 UK), *The Menace from Earth* (coll **1959**), *The Unpleasant Profession of Jonathan Hoag* (coll **1959**; vt *6 X H* 1961), *The Worlds of Robert A. Heinlein* (coll **1966**) and *Requiem: New Collected Works* (coll **1992**) ed Eric KOTANI.

In a style which exuded assurance and savvy, RAH's early writing blended slang, folk aphorism, technical jargon, clever understatement, apparent casualness, a concentration on people rather than gadgets, and a sense that the world described was real; it was a kind of writing able to incorporate the great mass of necessary sf data necessary without recourse to the long descriptive passages and deadening explanations common to earlier sf, so that his stories spoke with a smoothness and authority which came to seem the very tone of things to come. His characters were competent men of action, equally at home with their fists and a slide-rule ($\Diamond$ EDISONADE) and actively involved in the processes and procedures (political, legal, military, industrial, etc.) which make the world turn. Described in tales whose apparent openness concealed very considerable narrative craft, these characters seemed genuinely to inhabit the worlds of tomorrow. By the end of his first three years of writing, RAH had domesticated the future.

In the years 1943-6 RAH published no fiction, but in 1947 he expanded his career – and the potential reach of genre sf as a marketable literature – in two new directions: he sold a number of short stories to the *Saturday Evening Post* and other "slick" magazines; and he published – with Scribner's, a highly respectable mainstream firm – the first US juvenile sf novel to reflect the new levels of characterization, style and scientific plausibility now expected in the field. *Rocket Ship Galileo* (**1947**) is not an outstanding work (its young heroes confront and defeat a gaggle of conspiring Nazis on the Moon) but it was the first in a series that represents the most important contribution any single writer has made to CHILDRENS' SF. (It also formed the basis of a film, DESTINATION MOON [1950], scripted by RAH.) *Space Cadet* (**1948**), the second in the series, renders RAH's own experiences at Annapolis in sf terms. With the third, *Red Planet:*

A Colonial Boy on Mars (**1949**; text restored 1989), which recounts the adventures of two young colonists and their Martian "pet", RAH came fully into his own as a writer of sf for teenagers. A strong narrative line, carefully worked-out technical detail, realistic characters and brisk dialogue are the leading virtues of this and most of his later juveniles, which include *Farmer in the Sky* (**1950**), *Between Planets* (**1951**), *The Rolling Stones* (**1952**; vt *Space Family Stone* 1969 UK), *Starman Jones* (**1953**), *The Star Beast* (**1954**), *Tunnel in the Sky* (**1955**), *Time for the Stars* (**1956**), *Citizen of the Galaxy* (**1957**) and *Have Space Suit – Will Travel* (**1958**). The last three of these, along with *Starman Jones* and *The Star Beast*, rank among the very best juvenile sf ever written; their compulsive narrative drive, their shapeliness and their relative freedom from the didactic rancour RAH was beginning to show when addressing adults in the later 1950s all make these books arguably his finest works.

After 1950 RAH wrote very little short fiction – the most notable piece is the time-paradox tale "All You Zombies" (1959) – concentrating for some years on the highly successful stream of juveniles, although never abandoning the adult novel. *The Puppet Masters* (**1951**; text restored 1989) is an effective if rather hysterical INVASION story, and a prime example of PARANOIA in 1950s sf. *Double Star* (**1956**), about a failed actor who impersonates a galactic politician ($\Diamond$ RURITANIA), won a HUGO, and is probably his best adult novel of the 1950s, although the mellow and charming *The Door into Summer* (**1957**), a TIME TRAVEL story, is also much admired; all three books were assembled as *A Heinlein Trio* (omni **1980**).

His next novel, however, was something else entirely. *Starship Troopers* (**1959**), originally written as a juvenile but rejected by Scribner's because of its violence, is the first title in which RAH expressed his opinions with unfettered vigour. A tale of interstellar WAR, it won a 1960 Hugo but also gained RAH the reputation of being a militarist, even a "fascist". The plot as usual confers an earned adulthood upon its young protagonist, but in this case by transforming him from a pacifist into a professional soldier. This transformation, in itself dubious, is rendered exceedingly unpleasant (for those who might demur from its implications) by the hectoring didacticism of RAH's presentation of his case. Father-figures, always important in his fiction, tended from this point on to utter unstoppable monologues in their author's voice, and dialogue and action become traps in which any opposing versions of reality were hamstrung by the author's aggrieved partiality.

But this, for good and for ill, was the fully unleashed Heinlein. His next novel, *Stranger in a Strange Land* (**1961**; text restored 1990), a stronger work which won him another Hugo, is even more radical. Valentine Michael Smith, of human stock but raised on Mars, returns to Earth armed with his innocence and the PSI POWERS bequeathed to him by the Martians. After meeting Jubal Harshaw and being tutored by this ultimate surrogate-father and know-all voicebox for RAH himself, Valentine begins his transformation into a MESSIAH-figure, demonstrates the nature of grokking – a term which RAH created for this book – and eventually "discorporates", a form of dying which is painless and which can be freely imposed upon others. This costless discorporation of human beings marks the book as a FANTASY, and not, perhaps, as one very markedly adult; and it was unfortunate for Sharon Tate that its dreamlike smoothness (a smoothness even more winningly evident in the much longer restored version) could, if his claims are to be credited, be translated into this-worldly action by the sociopathic murderer Charles Manson. However, among those capable of understanding the nature of a fiction, it has proved to be RAH's most popular novel, in the later 1960s becoming a cult-book among students (who were drawn to it, presumably, by its iconoclasm and by RAH's apparent espousal of free love and mysticism), and remains by far the best of the books he wrote in his late manner.

There followed 2 minor works, *Podkayne of Mars: Her Life and Times* (**1963**), an inferior juvenile which proved to be his last, and *Glory Road* (**1963**), a largely unsuccessful attempt at SWORD AND SORCERY. *Farnham's Freehold* (**1964**), another long and opinionated novel of ideas, invokes rather unpleasantly a Black despotism in the USA of the FAR FUTURE (*see also* POLITICS; SURVIVALIST FICTION), and begins to fully articulate a theme that obsessed the late RAH: the notion of the family as utterly central. From this time onward, hugely extended father-dominated families, sustained by incest and enlarged by mating patterns whose complex ramifications required an increasing use of time travel and ALTERNATE WORLDS, would tend to generate the plots of his novels. Before he plunged fully into this final phase, however, RAH published *The Moon is a Harsh Mistress* (**1966**), which won a 1967 Hugo and marked a partial return to his best form. About a revolution among Moon-colonists – many historical parallels being made evident with the War of Independence – it is of value partly because it shows the nature of RAH's political views very clearly. Rather than being a fascist, he was a right-wing anarchist, or "libertarian" (◊ LIBERTARIANISM), much influenced by SOCIAL DARWINISM.

But the fact that RAH's politics are a prime concern in discussions of his later novels points to the sad decline in the quality of dramatization in his sf. As Alexei PANSHIN, his most astute earlier critic, pointed out, RAH once dealt in "facts" but latterly he dealt only in "opinions-as-facts". And as these opinions-as-facts were uttered in RAH's voice by domineering monologuists, his last novels increasingly conveyed a sense of flouncing solitude, and were frequently described – with justice – as exercises in solipsism; for, no matter how many characters filled the foreground of the tale, his casts ultimately proved either cruelly disposable or members of the one enormous intertwined family whose begetter bore the countenance, and spieled the tracts, of the author. *I Will Fear No Evil* (**1970**) is an interminable novel about a rich centenarian who has his mind transferred to the body of his young secretary; it brought into the open the espousal of free sex (and inevitable babies begat upon wisecracking women who long to become gravid) first evident in *Stranger in a Strange Land*. *Time Enough for Love, or The Lives of Lazarus Long* (**1973**), a late coda to the **Future History** series, was perhaps the most important of the late books in that it established the immortal Long, a central character in *Methuselah's Children*, as RAH's final – and most enduring – *alter ego*. Other novels which revolve around Lazarus Long include *"The Number of the Beast"* (**1980** UK), *The Cat who Walks through Walls* (**1985**) and *To Sail Beyond the Sunset* (**1987**). *Friday* (**1982**) and *Job: A Comedy of Justice* (**1984**) similarly gathered other works from RAH's prime into the late fold. The final effect of these novels – in direct contrast to their joke-saturated telling – was one of embitterment. By devaluing everything in the Universe except for the one polymorphic family, RAH effectively repudiated the genre whose mature tone he had himself almost singlehandedly established, and the USA whose complex populism he had so vividly expressed. In the end, the father of sf abandoned his children.

RAH was guest of honour at three World SF Conventions, in 1941, 1961 and 1976. His works remained constantly in print. He has repeatedly been voted "best all-time author" in readers' polls such as those held by LOCUS in 1973 and 1977, and in 1975 he was recipient of the First Grand Master NEBULA. His death in 1988 was deeply felt. [DP/JC]

Other works: *The Discovery of the Future . . . Speech Delivered by Guest of Honor at 3d World Science Fiction Convention* (**1941** chap); *Tomorrow, the Stars* (anth **1951**); *The Robert Heinlein Omnibus* (omni **1958** UK), containing *The Man who Sold the Moon* and *The Green Hills of Earth*, which is not to be confused with *A Robert Heinlein Omnibus* (omni **1966** UK), containing *Beyond this Horizon*, *The Man who Sold the Moon* and *The Green Hills of Earth*; *Three by Heinlein* (omni **1965**; vt *A Heinlein Triad* 1966 UK), containing *The Puppet Masters* and *Waldo and Magic, Inc.*; *The Best of Robert Heinlein* (coll **1973** UK; vt in 2 vols as *The Best of Robert Heinlein 1939-1942* 1977 UK and *The Best of Robert Heinlein 1947-1959* 1977 UK); *The Notebooks of Lazarus Long* (**1978** chap), being extracts from *Time Enough for Love*; *Expanded Universe* (coll **1980**), including much nonfiction; *Grumbles from the Grave* (coll **1989**) ed Virginia Heinlein, a first selection of letters with other material; *Starship Troopers/The Moon is a Harsh Mistress/Time Enough for Love* (omni **1991**); *Tramp Royale* (written 1953-4; **1992**), travel memoir.

About the author: "One Sane Man: Robert A. Heinlein" by Damon KNIGHT, in *In Search of Wonder* (**1956**; rev 1967); "Robert A. Heinlein" by Sam MOSKOWITZ, in *Seekers of Tomorrow* (**1966**); *Heinlein in*

Dimension (**1968**) by Alexei Panshin; "First Person Singular: Heinlein, Son of Heinlein" by James BLISH, in *More Issues at Hand* (**1970**); *Robert A. Heinlein: A Bibliography* (**1973** chap) by Mark OWINGS; *Robert A. Heinlein: Stranger in his Own Land* (**1976**; much rev 1977) by George Edgar SLUSSER; *The Classic Years of Robert A. Heinlein* (**1977**) by Slusser; *Robert A. Heinlein* (anth **1978**) ed J.D. OLANDER and Martin H. GREENBERG; *Robert A. Heinlein: America as Science Fiction* (**1980**) by H. Bruce FRANKLIN; "Robert Λ. Heinlein" by Peter NICHOLLS, in *Science Fiction Writers* (**1982**) ed E.F. BLEILER; «A Robert A. Heinlein Cyclopedia: A Guide to the Persons, Places, and Things in the Fiction of America's Most Popular Science Fiction Author» (**1992**) by Nancy Bailey Downing, a 500pp guide which we list in the expectation that it will fill a need.

See also: ALIENS; ANTI-INTELLECTUALISM IN SF; ARTS; ASTOUNDING SCIENCE-FICTION; AUTOMATION; CHILDREN IN SF; CLONES; COLONIZATION OF OTHER WORLDS; COMPUTERS; CRIME AND PUNISHMENT; CRITICAL AND HISTORICAL WORKS ABOUT SF; CYBERNETICS; DEFINITIONS OF SF; DIMENSIONS; DISCOVERY AND INVENTION; DYSTOPIAS; ECOLOGY; ECONOMICS; END OF THE WORLD; ESCHATOLOGY; EVOLUTION; FANTASTIC VOYAGES; FASTER THAN LIGHT; GALACTIC EMPIRES; GALAXY SCIENCE FICTION; GAMES AND TOYS; GODS AND DEMONS; HISTORY IN SF; HISTORY OF SF; HIVE-MINDS; IMMORTALITY; JUPITER; JUVENILE SERIES; LINGUISTICS; LONGEVITY (IN WRITERS AND PUBLICATIONS); MACHINES; *The* MAGAZINE OF FANTASY AND SCIENCE FICTION; MAGIC; MARS; MATHEMATICS; MONSTERS; MOON; MUSIC; MUTANTS; NEAR FUTURE; NUCLEAR POWER; OPTIMISM AND PESSIMISM; PARALLEL WORLDS; PARASITISM AND SYMBIOSIS; PASTORAL; PHYSICS; POCKET UNIVERSE; PREDICTION; PSYCHOLOGY; PUBLISHING; RADIO; ROCKETS; SF IN THE CLASSROOM; SEX; SOCIOLOGY; SPACE FLIGHT; SPACESHIPS; SPECULATIVE FICTION; SUPERMAN; TECHNOLOGY; TERRAFORMING; TRANSPORTATION; UFOS; VENUS; VILLAINS; WEAPONS; WOMEN AS PORTRAYED IN SCIENCE FICTION.

HELLFIRE Film (1986). Manley. Written and dir William Murray, starring Kenneth McGregor, Sharon Mason, Julie Miller, Jon Maurice, Joseph White. 89 mins. Colour.

In 1997 a revolutionary power source, Hellfire, is a controversial issue. Terrorists destroy a space station in an attempt to stop the project which, while it could produce pollution-free energy, also – as in *Fire Pattern* (**1984**) by Bob SHAW and *Torched* (**1986**) by James Blackstone (John BROSNAN) – tends to produce spontaneous human combustion. A private eye (McGregor) is hired by a cool blonde (Miller) to investigate her murderous tycoon brother, who controls Hellfire. Stereotyped hardboiled underworld events are foregrounded, while an understated but quite effective future vision serves as background. Director Murray is clumsy with actors and action scenes alike, and, while the sparkly combustion trick is quite impressive, the futuristic vehicles are unconvincing. [KN]

See also: SPACE HABITATS.

HELPRIN, MARK (1947-) US writer who served in the British Merchant Navy and the Israeli armed

forces, experiences transmuted in *A Dove of the East and Other Stories* (coll **1975**). He is best known for his only genre work, *Winter's Tale* (**1983**), an epic fable set in an imaginary New York. The novel attempts to be a fantastic history of the city in the 20th century, celebrating the forces which gave birth to it, and catapulting it towards an ambiguously redemptive apocalypse at the end of the century. MH employs sf images and ideas (such as extraordinary MACHINES and TIME TRAVEL), but at heart the book remains a fairytale, concerned more with MAGIC than with science. [PR]

Other works: *Swan Lake* (**1989** chap), fantasy based on the ballet.

HEMING, JOHN W(INTON) (1900-1953) Extremely prolific Australian writer who began publishing sf novels with *The Living Dead* (**1942**) and was associated during WWII with the Australian firm Currawong Publishers in the release of native sf, US imports being banned at the time. He wrote one novel, *Time Marches Off* (**1942** chap), as Paul de Wreder. [JC]

Other works: *Subterranean City* (**1942** chap); *King of the Underseas* (**1942** chap); *Other Worlds* (**1942** chap); *From Earth to Mars* (**1943** chap); *In Aztec Hands* (**1944** chap); *The Weird House* (**1951**).

HEMINGWAY, AMANDA (1955-) UK writer who began publishing work of genre interest with "The Alchemist" in 1981 for that year's issue of the Faber & Faber **Introduction** series of anthologies. Her first novel, *Pzyche* (**1982**), places an uncomfortable and virginal female protagonist on a mineral-rich, art-obsessed planet, where she unappreciatively undergoes a series of adventures. [JC]

HEMYNG, (SAMUEL) BRACEBRIDGE (1841-1901) UK writer best known in the USA for the **Jack Harkaway** boys' stories from 1871, but responsible for many other tales. His sf novel, *The Commune in London, or Thirty Years Hence* (**1871** chap), is an anti-Communard version of the 1871 uprising in Paris as translated into a shocked UK. [JC]

HENDERSON, ZENNA (1917-1983) US writer and schoolteacher who frequently used her teaching experience in Arizona and elsewhere as a base for her stories; perhaps significantly, given her treatment of ALIENS as emblems of our better selves, during WWII she taught interned Japanese-Americans in a relocation camp. Her first story was "Come on, Wagon!" for *FSF* – the magazine with which she is mostly strongly associated – in 1951; soon after, with "Ararat" (1952), she began publishing in *FSF* the series of stories about **The People** which comprises her central achievement. Put together with framing devices as *Pilgrimage: The Book of the People* (fixup **1961**) and *The People: No Different Flesh* (coll of linked stories **1966**) – and assembled as *The People Collection* (omni **1991** UK) – the sequence recounts over a long timespan the arduous experiences of a group of aliens with PSI POWERS who have been shipwrecked on Earth and must try to survive as well and fully as possible; although outwardly indistinguishable from humans, they are morally superior. A further story, "The Indelible Kind" (1968), appears with unconnected stories in *Holding Wonder* (coll **1971**); this collection, along with *The Anything Box* (coll **1965**), assembles most of ZH's stories independent of **The People**. The same decorous warmth infuses all her work, sometimes overly reducing tensions and contrasts, but usually demonstrating her humane talent to advantage, though her wholesomeness can be vitiating. [JC]

See also: CHILDREN IN SF; ESP; *The* MAGAZINE OF FANTASY AND SCIENCE FICTION; PASTORAL; SUPERMAN; WOMEN SF WRITERS.

HENHAM, ERNEST G(EORGE) (1870-?   ) UK writer whose first novel of genre interest, *Tenebrae* (**1898**), features the depredations of a monstrous spider. *Bonanza: A Story of the Outside* (**1901**) is a tale of the Arctic Gold Rush in which prospectors stumble across a valley protected by a magnetic FORCE FIELD. *The Feast of Bacchus* (**1907**) is a horror fantasy. As John Trevena, EGH wrote two novels of interest: *Furze the Cruel* (**1907**), a fantasy, and *The Reign of the Saints* (**1911**), an sf tale set 200-300 years in the future at a point when an internally divided UK is threatened by revolutionary strife. [JC]

HENRY, MARION [s] ◊ Lester DEL REY.

HENSLEY, JOE L(OUIS) (1926-   ) US writer and Indiana Judicial Circuit Court judge 1975-88, active as an author of suspense novels, one of which, *The Poison Summer* (**1974**), was named in the *New York Times* Best of the Year List in 1974. He began publishing sf with "Treasure City" for *Planet Stories* in 1952, and appeared with some frequency in the field, sometimes as J.L. Hensley and once, in collaboration with Alexei PANSHIN, as Louis J.A. Adams. Much of his best work appears in *Final Doors* (coll **1981**), including two collaborations with Harlan ELLISON. His work is vigorous and action-oriented, possibly to a fault in his only sf novel, *The Black Roads* (**1976** Canada), a chase story set in a post-HOLOCAUST USA whose integral web of roads is dominated by a tyrannous organization; a rebellion is in the works. [JC]

HERBERT, [Sir] A(LAN) P(ATRICK) (1890-1971) UK humorist, writer and politician, prolific for 60 years after he began publishing light verse in *Punch*, some of it fantastic, around 1910. *The Red Pen* (**1927** chap), the libretto for a radio opera with music (not included) by Geoffrey Toye (1889-1942), is a NEAR-FUTURE story in which artists arrange for the nationalization of the arts. *Number Nine, or The Mind-Sweepers* (**1951**) and its loose sequel, *Made for Man* (**1958**), also set in the near future, are political SATIRES, good-tempered except on the matter of divorce, in which area APH's liberal instincts caused him to disagree profoundly with Church of England doctrines. A late example of his long-extended **Misleading Cases** sequence, "Reign of Error?" in *Bardot M.P.?* (coll **1964**), addresses the legal question of the criminal responsibility of a COMPUTER. [JC]

HERBERT, BENSON (1912-1991) UK writer with a master's degree in science who began publishing sf in US magazines with "The World Without" for *Wonder Stories* in 1931 and was fairly active in the 1930s. *Crisis! – 1992* (1935 *Wonder Stories* as "The Perfect World"; **1936**) deals with the ominous passage of another planet close to Earth's orbit, and with what humans discover when they land on it: the planet is actually a giant SPACESHIP. The book was prefaced by M.P. SHIEL. During WWII BH wrote several very short, moderately exuberant SPACE OPERAS: *Hand of Glory: Strange Adventures in the Pennines* (**?1943** chap); *Thieves of the Air* (**?1943** chap) with Festus PRAGNELL; *Strange Romance* (**1943** chap) and *The Red-Haired Girl* (**1944** chap). With Walter GILLINGS as director, BH financed and founded Utopia Publications, which published some sf, including the AMERICAN FICTION series and STRANGE TALES. [JC/PN]

HERBERT, BRIAN (PATRICK) (1947-   ) US writer, son of Frank HERBERT, who began publishing sf with his third book and first novel, *Sidney's Comet* (**1983**), a comic SATIRE – the eponymous comet being composed of human garbage – set in the 27th century; the sequel, *The Garbage Chronicles* (**1985**), is also perhaps somewhat desultory. Both feature, *inter alia*, amusing parodies of his father's stylistic quirks. *Sudanna, Sudanna* (**1985**), set on a surreally conceived planetoid, describes the lives of its resident bureaucracy-ridden ALIENS in a tone that determinedly shifts from HUMOUR to gravity and back. *Man of Two Worlds* (**1986**), with Frank Herbert, frolics rather cumbrously with reality games, and its presentation of ALIENS who dream us up is not always coherent, though the final pages, when humans dream back, are more exhilarating. *Prisoners of Arionn* (**1987**) again juxtaposes aliens (conceived with an elaborate though somewhat skittish lightness of touch) and human society (in this case San Francisco) in a plot which uneasily details the former's kidnapping of the latter, while at the same time examining with genuine insight some family relationships. If BH was in fact wrestling with genres in an attempt to intermingle them fruitfully, an inadequate control over narrative structure was proving detrimental to the attempt. This sense of virtuous effort and only partial success persists through *The Race for God* (**1990**) and *Memory-makers* (**1991**) with Marie Landis. It is, all the same, of continuing interest to follow his career; he is an author who, at any point it seemed, might get the note right. [JC]

Other work: *The Notebooks of Frank Herbert's Dune* (**1988**), ed.

See also: TRANSPORTATION.

HERBERT, FRANK [s] ◊ Bill RANSOM.

HERBERT, FRANK (PATRICK) (1920-1986) US writer born in Tacoma, Washington, and educated at the University of Washington, Seattle. FH worked as a reporter and editor on a number of West Coast newspapers before becoming a full-time writer. He lived in Washington State.

He began publishing sf with "Looking for Something?" for *Startling Stories* in 1952. During the next decade he was an infrequent contributor to the sf magazines, producing fewer than 20 short stories (which nevertheless constituted a majority of his short fiction; he never made a significant impact with work below novel length). At this time he also wrote one novel, *The Dragon in the Sea* (1955 *ASF* as "Under Pressure"; **1956**; vt *21st Century Sub* 1956; vt *Under Pressure* 1974), a much praised sf thriller containing complex psychological investigations aboard a submarine of the future. His emergence as a writer of major stature commenced with the publication in *ASF* in 1963-4 of "Dune World", the first part of his **Dune** series. It was followed in 1965 by "The Prophet of Dune"; the two were amalgamated into *Dune* (fixup **1965**), which won the first NEBULA for Best Novel, shared the HUGO, and became one of the most famous of all sf novels.

Dune is a novel of extraordinary complexity. It encompasses intergalactic POLITICS of a decidedly feudal nature, the development of PSI POWERS, RELIGION – specifically the reluctant but inevitable evolution of its protagonist into a MESSIAH – and WAR. Its primary impact, however, lay in its treatment of ECOLOGY, a theme which it brought into the forefront of modern sf readers' and writers' awareness. The desert planet Arrakis, with its giant sandworms and its Bedouin-like human inhabitants, the Fremen, clinging to the most precarious of ecological niches through fanatical scrupulousness in water conservation, is possibly the most convincing PLANETARY-ROMANCE environment created by any sf writer. With its blend (or sometimes clash) of complex intellectual discourse and Byzantine intrigue, *Dune* provided a template for FH's more significant later work. Sequels soon began to appear which carried on the arguments of the original in testingly various manners and with an intensity of discourse seldom encountered in the sf field. *Dune Messiah* (**1969**) elaborates the intrigue at the cost of other elements, but *Children of Dune* (**1976**) recaptures much of the strength of the original work and addresses another recurrent theme in FH's work – the EVOLUTION of Man, in this case into SUPERMAN; both these novels, along with the original, were assembled as *The Great Dune Trilogy* (omni **1979** UK). *God Emperor of Dune* (**1981**) followed, then *Heretics of Dune* (**1984** UK) and *Chapter House Dune* (**1985** UK; vt *Chapterhouse: Dune* 1985 US), these three being assembled as *The Second Great Dune Trilogy* (omni **1987** UK). The last volume of the sequence is comparatively desultory, but *God Emperor of Dune* and *Heretics of Dune*, like the enormously extended development section in the first movement of a great symphony, work and rework the initial material into more and more elaborate presentations of the initial themes. As a whole, the sequence almost fully justified FH's decision – certainly astute in marketing terms – to so comprehensively draw out his original inspiration.

Although **Dune** dominated his career from 1965 –

much later a film based on it, DUNE (1984), was released – FH began in the mid-1960s to publish other novels and series with admirable regularity. *The Green Brain* (**1966**) features mutated insects which achieve corporate intelligence (◊ HIVE-MINDS). *Destination: Void* (**1966**; rev 1978), a clotted novel on a CYBERNETICS theme, concentrates on the construction of an AI aboard a starship, where it comes to the conclusion that it is God (◊ GODS AND DEMONS). The **Pandora** sequence, all written with Bill RANSOM – *The Jesus Incident* (**1979**), *The Lazarus Effect* (**1983**) and *The Ascension Factor* (**1988**) – follows on from *Destination: Void*, exploring in exhaustive detail the implications of the earlier book while placing in a PLANETARY-ROMANCE frame the complex and developing relationship between God-"protected" human stock and the natives of Pandora. *The Eyes of Heisenberg* (**1966**) is about GENETIC ENGINEERING and IMMORTALITY, and *The Heaven Makers* (**1968**; rev 1977) again copes with immortality. *The Santaroga Barrier* (**1968**), describing a higher order of INTELLIGENCE evolved within an isolated, near-UTOPIAN community, served to emphasize the thematic centrality of intelligence throughout FH's work, in which consistent attempts are made not only to suggest different, or evolved, types of intelligence but to describe them in detail. Among contemporary sf writers only Ian WATSON has addressed this theme as frequently and as convincingly. ALIEN intelligence (*see also* LIVING WORLDS) is examined in *Whipping Star* (**1970**; rev 1977) and, more searchingly, in its sequel *The Dosadi Experiment* (**1977**) which, while orchestrating a plot of multi-levelled intrigue, describes several different alien species in detail, examines the effect of an experiment in extreme OVERPOPULATION, and gifts its hero and heroine with advanced PSI POWERS, including total mind transference.

FH's other sf novels include: *The God Makers* (1960 *Fantastic* as "The Priests of Psi"; exp **1972**), in which a god is reified through human endeavours; the rather surly *The White Plague* (**1982**), in which a man driven into mad misogyny destroys the women of the world; and the minor *Man of Two Worlds* (**1986**) with his son Brian HERBERT. More important than any of these, however, is *Hellstrom's Hive* (**1973**), which derives its title from the film *The Hellstrom Chronicle* (1971) but otherwise has little connection with it. Arguably FH's most successful novel after *Dune*, this presents in persuasive detail an underground colony of humans selectively bred, on insect-hive principles, into various specializations. In this society the individual's existence is of minor importance; the continuation of the hive as a functioning entity is paramount. The novel points up the contradictions of a society which in its own terms is a successful utopia, but which from an outside human viewpoint is horrific.

Much of FH's work makes difficult reading. His ideas were genuinely developed concepts, not merely decorative notions, but they were sometimes embodied in excessively complicated plots and articulated in prose which did not always match the level of thinking, so that much of his writing seemed dense and opaque. His best novels, however, were the work of a speculative intellect with few rivals in modern sf. [MJE/JC]

Other works: *The Worlds of Frank Herbert* (coll **1970** UK; with 1 story added 1971 US); *Soul Catcher* (**1972**), a non-sf novel; *The Book of Frank Herbert* (coll **1973**); *The Best of Frank Herbert* (coll **1975** UK; cut vt *The Best of Frank Herbert: 1952-1970* 1976 UK; text restored vt in 2 vols as *The Best of Frank Herbert 1952-1964* 1977 UK and *The Best of Frank Herbert 1965-1970* 1977 UK); *Direct Descent* (fixup **1980**); *The Priests of Psi* (coll **1980** UK); *Eye* (coll **1985**).

Nonfiction: *Survival and the Atom* (coll **1952**); *New World or No World* (anth **1970**), an environmental anthology; *Threshold: The Blue Angels Experience* (**1973**); *Without Me, You're Nothing: The Essential Guide to Home Computers* (**1980**) with Max Barnard; *The Maker of Dune: Insights of a Master of Science Fiction: Frank Herbert* (coll **1987**) ed Tim O'Reilly; *The Notebooks of Frank Herbert's Dune* (**1988**) ed Brian Herbert.

About the author: *Frank Herbert* (**1980**) by David M. Miller; *Frank Herbert* (**1981**) by Timothy O'Reilly; *The Dune Encyclopedia* (anth **1984**) ed Willis E. McNELLY; *Dune Master: A Frank Herbert Bibliography* (**1988**) by Daniel J.H. Levack.

See also: ASTOUNDING SCIENCE-FICTION; COMMUNICATIONS; COMPUTERS; ESP; FANTASY; FORCE FIELD; GALAXY SCIENCE FICTION; GAMES AND TOYS; HISTORY IN SF; LINGUISTICS; LONGEVITY (IN WRITERS AND PUBLICATIONS); MUSIC; PARANOIA; SPACESHIPS; UNDER THE SEA.

HERBERT, WILLIAM Pseudonym of the unidentified UK author of *The World Grown Young* (**1891**), a placidly tendentious record of NEAR-FUTURE reforms imposed benevolently from above upon a grateful UK by its richest citizen. Attacks by Russia and the USA are routinely defeated. [JC]

HERCK, PAUL van [r] ◊ Paul VAN HERCK.

HERNÁDI, GYULA [r] ◊ HUNGARY.

HERNAMAN-JOHNSON, FRANCIS (1879-1949) UK medical researcher and author of *The Polyphemes: A Story of Strange Adventures Among Strange Beings* (**1906**). The beings, giant intelligent Moon-worshipping ants from a Pacific island, just fail to conquer the world, despite their use of "X Magnetism" to power flying machines which bomb Europe. [JC]

HEROES Sf began to produce a distinctive kind of hero well before the beginning of the 20th century. As might be expected, sf writers – most of whom expressed interest (sometimes monitory) in the advancement of science – soon found models for heroic action in SCIENTISTS (or, perhaps more accurately, inventors). From early in its history, the US dime novel (◊ DIME-NOVEL SF) featured young protagonists who invented their way out of dire straits in a thousand tales, and who soon took on many of the advertised characteristics of the most charismatic US

inventor/scientist of the 19th century, Thomas Alva Edison (◊ EDISONADE *for details*); well into the 20th century, heroes on the edisonade model figured large in GENRE SF, generally in SPACE OPERA between the World Wars, although the influence of the Edison myth can be detected also in Robert A. HEINLEIN's Competent Man.

At the same time, it cannot be denied that in much sf the figure of the scientist remained far too remote and enigmatic to stand as a hero, and it was only rarely – as in H.G. WELLS's *The Time Machine* (**1895**) – that adult sf featured scientists in roles that gave them the opportunity to assume protagonist burdens of heroism. Over against the heroes of the edisonade, sf very frequently featured young heroes who had become entangled with matters of superscience entirely by accident: a certain bewildered astonishment was a constant feature of the role. FLASH GORDON and BUCK ROGERS are heroes of this type, as is John Star, hero of Jack WILLIAMSON's *The Legion of Space* (**1934**; **1947**). And whether or not their creators deemed them to be inventor/scientist heroes – as C.M. KORNBLUTH argued in "The Failure of the Science Fiction Novel as Social Criticism" (1959) – the worldview of E.E. SMITH's heroes and all their kind is that of small children, and their adventures are daydreams which proceed according to the pattern of make-believe games. This pattern, common to almost all action-adventure fiction, stands out particularly clearly in PULP-MAGAZINE sf simply because the scope of the make-believe is so great. Edgar Rice BURROUGHS's **Barsoom** novels are perhaps the ultimate in literary daydreams, and the enduring attraction of such fantasies is shown by the constant proliferation of their imitators. Edmond HAMILTON's CAPTAIN FUTURE stories and the PERRY RHODAN adventures are examples of more strictly sciencefictional variants.

In the 1940s John W. CAMPBELL Jr used his influence as editor of ASTOUNDING SCIENCE-FICTION to urge sf writers to modify the standard pulp hero by putting much greater emphasis on problem-solving aptitude and engineering skill. Archetypes of this new image included the staff of George O. SMITH's *Venus Equilateral* (1942-5 *ASF*; fixup **1947**), who were forever scribbling equations and designs on the tablecloths in Joe's Bar. It might be argued that this was very limited progress, and that the new image appealed to the worldview of the adolescent in the process of learning, upgrading mental competence at the expense of physical prowess, but really coming no nearer to genuine characterization. Certainly there is a great deal of sf which is attractive to the adolescent – and particularly to the alienated adolescent, bound more closely to a private mental world – and, just as E.E. Smith's Lensmen relate to their Arisian mentors in the same way that children relate to adults, a similar relationship, but at a later stage, is reflected in Poul ANDERSON's **Flandry** series, in which the hero's flamboyant behaviour and contempt for imperial decadence relates very well to the mood of adolescent rebellion. The conscientiously unorthodox Campbell had a particular fondness for scientist-heroes who were determined paradigm-breakers, and this was shared by many of his writers. Even nonscientist heroes are frequently portrayed in magazine sf as diehard rebels against stultifying orthodoxy, and the iconoclast who demonstrates by his delinquency that he is fit for membership in the social élite is an annoying sf CLICHÉ. Although there were few true antiheroes in sf before, say, the emergence of Michael MOORCOCK's Jerry Cornelius in *The Final Programme* (1965-7 *NW*; **1968**) – Harry HARRISON's Stainless Steel Rat (in *The Stainless Steel Rat* [**1961**] and its sequels) being too lovable a rogue to qualify – there was a long pre-existent tradition of heroic bloody-mindedness in magazine sf.

As a more mature approach to characterization began to appear in sf during the 1940s, the heroic stature of its protagonists inevitably began to be compromised. True heroes are implicitly unrealistic characters of more-than-human dimensions, and the pulp SUPERHEROES who had existed on the fringe of sf, like DOC SAVAGE, were largely diverted into the world of the COMICS, where SUPERMAN became the archetype of a vast legion of caped crusaders. In the sf pulps, too, superhumans became heroes, following a prototype established by A.E. VAN VOGT in *Slan* (1940 *ASF*; **1946**). The vanVogtian hero is always adrift in a hostile world whose circumstances are beyond his understanding, but he is possessed of awesome, temporarily dormant powers whose ultimate flowering will enable him spectacularly to prevail. This slightly schizoid stereotype became increasingly common, and also more elaborate and extravagant. Later works in this vein frequently feature heroes who exhibit an odd combination of vulnerability and godlikeness; several examples can be found in the work of Roger ZELAZNY (*see also* PARANOIA). It is, of course, the function of heroes to appease the psychological forces within us that must necessarily be repressed in the day-to-day routine of adult intercourse with the world, and there is really no need to worry – as the psychoanalyst Fredric Wertham (1895-1981) did in *The Seduction of the Innocent* (**1954**) – that the fascination of children and sf fans with superheroes might be perverted or fascistic. The utility of social outsiders in heroic roles is also, inevitably, reflected in the increasingly common use of ALIENS as heroes, and sometimes MACHINES (although ROBOTS and sentient COMPUTERS pose problems when employed as foci for reader-identification). These trends too began in the 1940s but became more pronounced in subsequent decades. The most extreme cases of "outsider" heroes are perhaps to be found in CYBORG stories which use brains-in-boxes as viewpoint characters.

Despite the processes of sophistication which have reduced many of its protagonists to a more human scale, modern sf has carried forward the trends which were set in the 1940s, albeit in more selfconscious –

and often frankly humorous – ways. The noble rebel against oppressive authority remains commonplace, his activities celebrated with awesome sentimentality in such novels as Michael D. RESNICK's *Santiago* (**1986**). The oppressed child-become-superhero has also been provided with a striking new archetype in Orson Scott CARD's *Ender's Game* (1977 *ASF*; exp **1985**), although Card's anxiety about the propriety of this genocidal power-fantasy led him to pad out the expanded version with much philosophical debate and to produce sequels in which Ender becomes a kind of saintly redeemer. Comic-book superhero fantasy has moved back into a closer alliance with written fiction, reflected in such projects as George R.R. MARTIN's WILD CARDS series of multi-authored "mosaic novels" or BRAIDS. It is noticeable that modern comic-book superheroes are very often social outsiders, the TEENAGE MUTANT NINJA TURTLES providing a striking example. The market-encouraged overlap between sf and HEROIC FANTASY has helped to maintain much older kinds of hero despite acute problems of plausibility. Sciencefictional transfigurations of Greek and other hero-myths are surprisingly numerous, most notable among them R.A. LAFFERTY's *Space Chantey* (**1968**) and Tim POWERS's *Dinner at Deviant's Palace* (**1985**), and Grail Quests are also featured in such novels as Samuel R. DELANY's *Nova* (**1968**). Antiheroes have been very much in fashion in recent times thanks to the CYBERPUNK movement, but the parallel fashionability of militaristic sf (◊ WAR) has resulted in a wide spectrum of heroic types which ranges from steadfastly honourable soldiers through mercenaries to determined followers of a SURVIVALIST ethos. Female heroes were almost unknown in sf before 1960, although sweet-natured "heroines" were to be found in abundance, but as more and more female writers have moved into sf this imbalance has been spectacularly redressed; a great deal of contemporary sf has now taken on the burden of appeasing the frustrations of women in much the same way that 1940s sf appeased the frustrations of adolescent boys. Although the path of progress was first mapped by feminist writers like Joanna RUSS, creator of the troubled-but-competent **Alyx**, female heroes are now so numerous in certain roles – notably that of starship pilot – that such assignments no longer seem propagandistic.

SCIENTISTS, for the most part, are still out in the cold, rarely afforded even moderate heroic status: an accurate but sad reflection of contemporary social attitudes. [BS/JC]

See also: ANTI-INTELLECTUALISM IN SF; VILLAINS.

HEROIC FANTASY In the TERMINOLOGY of sf/fantasy readers, this term began in the late 1970s to overtake SWORD AND SORCERY as the name of the subgenre which we choose – perhaps arbitrarily – to discuss under the latter head. The two terms (which both continue in common but diminished usage into the 1990s) are close but not identical in meaning. However, the nuances that distinguish them differ according to the writer (or blurb-writer) who uses them, though perhaps "Heroic Fantasy" comprehends a greater range of possible fictions. There is probably no argument about the twin poles of Heroic Fantasy (or Sword and Sorcery) being the gentlemanly works of J.R.R. TOLKIEN and the far-from-gentlemanly works of Robert E. HOWARD, especially his **Conan** series. Other terms applied both critically and commercially to fantasy have proliferated; they include Adult Fantasy, High Fantasy, Epic Fantasy, Quest Fantasy and SCIENCE FANTASY, but none are susceptible to any rigorous definition that would correspond to the variations in actual usage. By the 1990s the compulsion felt by publishers to label their books generically had slackened – it may have proved counterproductive – and many works of Heroic Fantasy now have merely the word FANTASY on the cover, or no descriptive word at all. [PN]

See also: MAGIC; PLANETARY ROMANCE.

HERON-ALLEN, EDWARD [r] ◊ Christopher BLAYRE.

HERRICK, ROBERT (1868-1938) US academic and writer best known for *The Master of the Inn* (**1908**), whose eponymous hero cures the mentally ill by making them work hard and contemplate, too. His one sf novel, *Sometime* (**1933**), set 1000 years hence, describes the visit of some Africans to a post-ice-age North America, where the races have finally bred together, sexual prudishness has been cast off at last, and the CITIES have been abandoned. RH clearly approves all these changes. [JC]

HERRIN VON ATLANTIS, DIE (vt *L'Atlantide*; vt *Lost Atlantis*; vt *The Mistress of Atlantis*) Film (1932). Nero Film. Dir G.W. Pabst (1885-1967), starring Brigitte Helm and (German version) Gustav Diessl, (French version) Jean Angelo, (English version) John Stuart. Screenplay Ladislaus Vajda, Hermann Oberländer, based on *L'Atlantide* (**1919**) by Pierre BENOIT. 87 mins. B/w.

This German film is based on Benoit's lurid popular novel about Antinea, the Queen of ATLANTIS (in this case a city beneath the North African desert), who lures a succession of men to their doom and displays their mummified bodies in a bizarre trophy room. The similarities between this and H. Rider HAGGARD's *She* (**1887**) are obvious.

L'Atlantide has been filmed several other times: the first was a tedious 1921 French version dir Jacques Feyder; in 1948 a kitsch US version, *Siren of Atlantis* (vt *Atlantis*; vt *Queen of Atlantis*), was dir Arthur Ripley, Greg R. Tallas, Douglas Sirk and John Brahm, starring Maria Montez; and in 1961 a French/Italian coproduction, *Antinea, L'Amante della Città Sepolta* (vt *Atlantis, the Lost Kingdom*) – not to be confused with ATLANTIS, THE LOST CONTINENT prod George PAL in 1960 – was dir Edgar G. Ulmer and Giuseppe Masini. The Pabst film is superior to these others, not only for its visual flair but also for Brigitte Helm's striking performance as the queen (she is also remembered for her dual role as heroine and evil robot in METROPOLIS [1926]). It is, however, slow-moving, and

no one could take this pulp romance seriously.

Three versions, in German, French and English, were made simultaneously with Helm starring in all, although otherwise the casts were different. [JB/PN]

HERSEY, HAROLD (BRAINERD) (1893-1956) US editor, publisher, story writer and poet. A man of great energy and relatively little talent, HH edited such sf PULP MAGAZINES as THRILL BOOK, MIRACLE SCIENCE AND FANTASY STORIES and *Mystery Adventures*, though most of his editorial work was not sf-related. His early writing, all negligible, appeared under various pseudonyms; but *Night* (coll **1923**), a POETRY collection, has superb artwork by Elliott DOLD, and *Pulpwood Editor* (**1937**) is an informative (albeit anecdotal) look at the pulp-magazine world. [RB]

See also: ALTERNATE WORLDS; INTELLIGENCE; OVERPOPULATION; THEATRE.

HERSEY, JOHN (1914-) US novelist and journalist, perhaps best known for his early report, *Hiroshima* (**1946**). His *White Lotus* (**1965**) is an ALTERNATE-WORLDS story in which China conquers the USA and makes slaves of White Americans, including the teenager renamed White Lotus. *The Child Buyer* (**1960**) is a NEAR-FUTURE story – told in the form of a courtroom drama – in which corporations bid for effective ownership of child prodigies. *My Petition for More Space* (**1974**) is a radically DYSTOPIAN rendering of an enormously regimented Earth bedevilled by OVERPOPULATION problems – the protagonist lives in a tiny cubicle and petitions, vainly, for an extra foot in each direction. [JC]

HERSHMAN, MORRIS (1920-) US writer whose sf novel, *Shareworld* (**1972**; vt *The Crash of 2086* 1976), takes a DYSTOPIAN view of the stock market dominating the entire world and anticipates a final and definitive Crash. [JC]

HERTZKA, THEODOR (1845-1924) Austrian economist and author of the influential socialist UTOPIA, *Freiland: Ein Sociales Zukunftsbild* (**1890**; trans Arthur Ransom – *not* Arthur Ransome [1884-1967] – as *Freeland: A Social Anticipation* 1891 UK) and its sequel, *Eine Reise nach Freiland* (**1893**; trans anon as *A Visit to Freeland, or The New Paradise Regained* 1894 UK; vt *A Trip to Freeland* 1905 US). These offer little in the way of fictional pleasures in the bland portrayal of their African setting, but most unusually manage to depict an ideal society in terms that sound genuinely livable. It may be the case that they fail satisfactorily to suggest a convincing relationship between private and public control of production (◊ ECONOMICS), but all the same the books inspired a Freeland Society in the USA, and some local colonies were actually established. [JC]

See also: AUSTRIA.

HERVEY, MAURICE H. (? ?) UK writer active at the end of the 19th century. The protagonist of his sf novel, *David Dimsdale, M.D.: A Story of Past and Future* (**1897**), awakens in 1920 (◊ SLEEPER AWAKES) to find ubiquitous electrical advances plus the daughter of the woman he'd loved in 1895. He ends up marrying the daughter.   [JC]

HERVEY, MICHAEL (1914-   ) UK writer who moved to Australia in 1951; he is author of an estimated 3500 short stories in various genres. His sf work is minor; it includes a future-UTOPIA tale, *Strange Hunger* (**1946**), and some of the stories assembled in *The Queer-Looking Box* (coll **1944** chap), *Murder Medley* (coll **1945** chap), *Horror Medley* (coll **1946** chap) and *Creeps Medley* (coll **1946** chap).   [SH]

HERZL, THEODOR [r] ◊ AUSTRIA; ISRAEL.

HERZOG, ARTHUR (III) (1927-   ) US writer and editor who has also worked with the Peace Corps and as a political manager. His first sf novel, *The Swarm* (**1974**), convincingly posits an ecological catastrophe when the African honey-bee mutates and invades North America (◊ ECOLOGY; HIVE-MINDS). Partly based on fact (African bees have indeed bred with South American bees to form a large and belligerent hybrid), the novel is well researched and written, as are *Earthsound* (**1975**), in which a seismologist attempts to warn sceptical New Englanders of an approaching earthquake and is thought to be merely hysterical, and *Heat* (**1977**; rev 1989), which is an early attempt to deal with the greenhouse effect. In later novels, AH moved less convincingly towards SATIRE. In *IQ 83* (**1978**) an attempt to retune DNA predictably backfires, and the **America** series – *Make Us Happy* (**1978**) and *Glad to Be Here* (**1979**) – takes him shakily into the realms of DYSTOPIA.   [PN/JC]

Other works: *Aries Rising* (**1980**); *The Craving* (**1982**).

See also: DISASTER.

HERZOG, ÉMILE [r] ◊ André MAUROIS.

HESKY, OLGA (LYNFORD) (1912-1974) UK editor and writer in whose wry and somewhat Surrealist sf novel, *The Purple Armchair* (**1961**), the ALIEN who resembles an armchair and is purple must decide whether or not the human race – caught in a near-future DYSTOPIA dominated by COMPUTERS – should survive. Eventually the "chair" says no.   [JC]

HESSE, HERMANN (1877-1962) German-born writer, a Swiss citizen from 1923. His long career culminated with the publication of his largest novel, *Das Glasperlenspiel* (**1943**; trans M. Savill as *Magister Ludi* **1949** US; preferred trans Richard and Clara Winston as *The Glass Bead Game* 1969 US); it was largely as a result of this novel that HH was awarded the 1946 Nobel Prize for Literature. Set in a future land closely resembling Europe, it is a complex UTOPIA whose structure revolves around the eponymous game. For the inhabitants of the community of Castilia, under the guidance of Joseph Knecht, their Magister Ludi (or Master of Games), the undescribed aesthetic and intellectual disciplines of the game culminate in experiences that – by analogy with the music of J.S. Bach – serenely resolve the dissonances of the outside world. Knecht's biography constitutes the bulk of the novel, and his poems and essays are published in an appendix. Through these texts, which are suffused with allusions to and renderings of the world-transcending subtleties and graces of the Castilian

mind-plays, Knecht's life has a sometimes exalting effect on the reader, though Knecht himself must eventually repudiate the game for a more humane vision of utopia.

HH's great popularity in translation in the 1960s and 1970s derives more directly, however, from earlier and more accessible works, like *Siddharta* (**1922**; trans Hilda Rosner **1954** UK) and *Der Steppenwolf* (**1927**; trans Basil Creighton as *Steppenwolf* **1929** UK; trans rev 1963), in which Jungian depth psychology, Indian mysticism and *Weltschmerz* are perhaps overpalatably combined; these and others of his novels can be read – unwisely – to emphasize any fantasy elements, for at their core they are meditations on transcendence.   [JC]

Other works: *Demian* (**1919**; trans W.J. Strachan **1958** UK); *Die Morgenlandfahrt* (**1932**; trans Hilda Rosner as *The Journey to the East* **1956** chap UK); *Strange News from Another Star* (coll trans **1972** US) and *Pictor's Metamorphoses and Other Fantasies* (coll trans Rika Lesser **1982** US), collecting his fantasies, some of which are sf.

See also: ARTS.

HETZEL, JULES [r] ◊ Jules VERNE.

HEVESI, LUDWIG [r] ◊ AUSTRIA.

HEXT, HARRINGTON ◊ Eden PHILLPOTTS.

HEY, RICHARD [r] ◊ GERMANY.

HEYDON, J(OSEPH) K(ENTIGERN) (?   -?   ) UK writer whose *World D* (**1935**), as told to him by "Hal P. Trevarthen, Official Historian of the Superficies", describes the creation of an UNDER-THE-SEA culture, Helioxenon; the detail is considerable, sometimes Catholic. On the jacket the novel was credited to Trevarthen.   [JC]

HEYDRON, VICKI ANN [r] ◊ Randall GARRETT.

HEYMANN, ROBERT [r] ◊ GERMANY.

HICKS, GRANVILLE (1901-1982) US writer, editor and broadcaster, most of whose significant work lay in the field of cultural studies, initially from a Marxist standpoint, though from 1939 he became disillusioned with any form of communism. His first novel, *The First to Awaken* (**1940**) with Richard M. Bennett, was a SLEEPER-AWAKES tale whose protagonist reaches the year AD2040 via SUSPENDED ANIMATION and finds there a literately described and mutedly sane socialist UTOPIA.   [JC]

HIDDEN, THE Film (1988). New Line-Heron Joint Venture/Third Elm Street Venture. Dir Jack Sholder, starring Kyle MacLachlan, Michael Nouri, William Boyett. Screenplay Bob Hunt. 97 mins. Colour.

A quiet stockbroker goes on a homicidal spree. We learn his body is temporarily occupied by a homicidal slug-like ALIEN, which moves from body to body but is soon recognizable from its behaviour. Police detective Beck (Nouri) works with an FBI man (MacLachlan) who turns out to be an alien cop in a human body. Finally, after six body changes, the Ferrari-driving alien killer is defeated. *TH* is a fast-moving, violent, well made formula film with no intellectual ambitions but an interesting, ambiguous ending. The story is sufficiently close to that of Hal CLEMENT's *Needle* (**1950**; vt *From Outer Space* 1957) as to make one wonder why he received no screen credit. The oddly coupled human/alien cop team was to become an instant film cliché: ◊ ALIEN NATION and I COME IN PEACE. [PN]

See also: MONSTER MOVIES.

HIDDEN WORLD, THE US magazine PULP MAGAZINE-size, 16 issues, Spring 1961-Winter 1964, published and ed Raymond A. PALMER. This was a quarterly publication, handling SHAVER-Mystery and flying-saucer (◊ UFOS) material, and purporting to be science fact rather than science fiction. #1 elaborated on the Shaverian "Mantongue" language. Circulation had by the end dropped from 10,000 to 2000; the issue marked Winter 1964 was in fact released in 1966. [FHP/PN]

HIGH, PHILIP E(MPSON) (1914-   ) UK writer, variously employed for a number of years before beginning to publish sf in 1955 with "The Statics" for *Authentic Science Fiction*; he contributed to UK magazines, especially NEBULA SCIENCE FICTION, for several years before publishing his first sf novel *The Prodigal Sun* (**1964** US), which set the model for most of those to follow. His sense of the world is pessimistic, but he overlays that sense with plots of an epic cast. In this first novel, characteristically, an Earthman possessing powers enhanced through his upbringing by an ALIEN race returns to his grim home planet, rousing it. Other novels combining social comment and adventure include *No Truce with Terra* (**1964** dos US), *The Mad Metropolis* (**1966** dos US; vt *Double Illusion* 1970 UK) and *These Savage Futurians* (**1967** dos US). *The Time Mercenaries* (**1968** dos US) interestingly places a 20th-century submarine into a time when mankind has lost its genetic capacity to fight; the resurrected crew (having been artificially preserved) dutifully saves mankind from aliens. Though constrained by his dystopian sense of the possibilities of Man's future, PEH has been capable of writing enjoyable adventures, though without fully stretching his dark imagination. His later work, written largely for ROBERT HALE LIMITED, was less engaging. [JC]

Other works: *Reality Forbidden* (**1967** dos US); *Twin Planets* (**1967** US); *Invader on my Back* (**1968**); *Butterfly Planet* (**1971**); *Come, Hunt an Earthman* (**1973**); *Sold – For a Spaceship* (**1973**); *Speaking of Dinosaurs* (**1974**); *Fugitive from Time* (**1978**); *Blindfold from the Stars* (**1979**).

See also: SUN.

HIGHLANDER II: THE QUICKENING Film (1990). Davis-Panzer/Lamb Bear Entertainment. Dir Russell Mulcahy, starring Christopher Lambert, Sean Connery, Virginia Madsen, Michael Ironside, Allan Rich. Screenplay Peter Bellwood, from a story by Brian Clemens and William Panzer, based on characters created by Gregory Widen. 100 mins. Colour.

This is a sequel to *Highlander* (1986), which was a pure fantasy about two immortals, one good (with amnesia) and one bad, who battle through the centuries. The sequel begins in 1999 with the sword-wielding immortal Scotsman (Lambert again) saving humanity by building a shield to replace the destroyed ozone layer. Moving forward to AD2034 we find a corporate DYSTOPIA in the subtropical twilight (shot in Argentina) beneath the shield, which is now maintained only for corporate profit, the ozone layer being in much better condition, though this is kept secret. The protagonist – who turns out to be an ALIEN – oscillates unnervingly between youth and age, mortality and IMMORTALITY, before disposing of the shield and the alien warlord (Ironside) who has temporarily become a partner of the corporate villains. Rumoured production problems and budget cuts may explain the incoherence of what could have been much more fun. [PN]

HIGH TREASON Film (1929). Gaumont. Dir Maurice Elvey, starring Benita Hume, Jameson Thomas, Basil Gill, James Carew. Screenplay L'Estrange Fawcett, based on a play by Noel Pemberton-Billing. 95 mins, cut to 69 mins. B/w.

This forgotten curiosity, one of the earliest UK sound movies, was quite a big film in its day, when it was seen as a kind of English METROPOLIS (1926) – a comparison that does not for an instant hold water. Set in the world of 1940 (a Channel tunnel, tv, aeroplanes landing on London skyscrapers), it envisages a tense political situation between United Europe, to which England belongs, and a United America. The Peace League saves the world from war by assassinating the leader of United Europe. The production design is singularly unstriking and the story absurd. [PN]

HIGHWAYMAN, THE ◊ Glen A. LARSON.

HILL, CAROL (DeCHELLIS) (1942-   ) US writer whose first novel, *Jeremiah 8:20* (**1970**), is a raucous FABULATION about the Apocalypse. Her second, *Let's Fall in Love* (**1975**), spoofs sex, pornography and politics in a vaguely fantastic 1970s milieu. *The Eleven Million Mile High Dancer* (**1985**; vt *Amanda and the Eleven Million Mile High Dancer* 1988 UK), equally flamboyant in diction, carries its female astronaut protagonist into metaphysical (and Theory-of-Indeterminacy-and-Zen-evoking) contact with the eponymous representation of the nature of the Universe. [JC]

HILL, DOUGLAS (ARTHUR) (1935-   ) Canadian-born writer and editor, in the UK from 1959. Most of his early books were nonfiction, *The Supernatural* (**1965**) with Pat Williams, and *Magic and Superstition* (**1968**) being of interest to a genre audience. His involvement in sf and fantasy began through his editing of anthologies like *Window on the Future* (anth **1966**) and *Way of the Werewolf* (anth **1966**); he served as Associate Editor of *NW* in 1967-8. He began a long sequence of novels for younger and older children (◊ CHILDREN'S SF) with *Coyote the Trickster* (**1975**) with Gail Robinson. Several series ensued: the **Last Legionary** sequence of SPACE OPERAS – *Galactic Warlord* (**1979**), *Deathwing over Veynaa* (**1980**), *Day of the Starwind*

(1980), *Planet of the Warlord* (1982) and *Young Legionary: The Earlier Adventures of Keill Randor* (1982), all but the last (a prequel) being assembled as *The Last Legionary Quartet* (omni 1985) – which builds effectively on an interplanetary revenge quest; the **Huntsman** sequence – *The Huntsman* (1982), *Warriors of the Wasteland* (1983) and *Alien Citadel* (1984) – set on an Earth enslaved by alien invaders; and the **ColSec** sequence – *Exiles of ColSec* (1984), *The Caves of Klydor* (1984) and *ColSec Rebellion* (1985) – whose young protagonists strive for freedom after being shipwrecked on an unknown planet. His only adult sf novels, *The Fraxilly Fracas* (1989) and its sequel, *The Colloghi Conspiracy* (1990), are also space opera, and share with his juveniles an engaging briskness, though psychological depths tend to remain unplumbed. [JC]

Other works: *The Exploits of Hercules* (1978); *Have Your Own Extra-Terrestrial Adventure* (1983 chap); the **Talents** series of fantasies, comprising *Blade of the Poisoner* (1987) and *Master of Fiends* (1987); *Penelope's Pendant* (1990).

For younger children: *Moon Monsters* (1984 chap); *How Jennifer (and Speckle) Saved the Earth* (1986 chap); *Goblin Party* (1988 chap); *Penelope's Pendant* (1990); *The Tale of Trellie the Troog* (1991 chap).

As editor: *The Devil his Due* (anth 1967); *Warlocks and Warriors* (anth 1971); *Tribune 40* (anth 1977), not sf or fantasy; *The Shape of Sex to Come* (anth 1978), of stories about SEX; *Alien Worlds* (anth 1981); *Planetfall* (anth 1986).

HILL, ERNEST (1915-   ) UK writer who began publishing sf with "The Last Generation" for *NW* in 1954, and who published some stories of interest, most notably the DYSTOPIAN "Atrophy" (1965 in *New Writings in SF #6*, ed John CARNELL). His novels – the rather desultory SPACE OPERA *Pity about Earth* (1968 dos US), *The GC Radiation* (1971) and *The Quark Invasion* (1978), the latter two being written for ROBERT HALE LIMITED – are of less interest. [JC]

HILL, H. HAVERSTOCK ◊ J.M. WALSH.

HILL, JOHN ◊ Dean R. KOONTZ.

HILL, ROGER [r] ◊ Glen A. LARSON.

HILL, RUSSELL (?   -   ) US writer whose sf novel, *Cold Creek Cash Store* (1986), presents an unremarkable vision of a post-HOLOCAUST refuge in California. [JC]

HILL, WILLIAM BOYLE (?   -   ) Writer, probably UK, whose novel *A New Earth and a New Heaven* (1936) is of exceedingly moderate sf interest for its advocacy of a garden-city subtopian future, but which comes somewhat to life on its protagonists' visit to a LOST WORLD – in the heart of Australia – whose inhabitants are in touch with MARS. [JC]

HILLEGAS, MARK R. (1926-   ) US sf critic and professor of English who has been based at Southern Illinois University. In 1961 he gave, at Colgate, one of the first university-level classes in sf in the USA (◊ SF IN THE CLASSROOM). His academic study *The Future as Nightmare: H.G. Wells and the Anti-Utopians* (1967)

deals primarily with such MAINSTREAM WRITERS of DYSTOPIAS as Karel ČAPEK, Aldous HUXLEY, C.S. LEWIS, George ORWELL and Yevgeny ZAMIATIN; it has become a standard reference. A later work ed MRH is *Shadows of Imagination: The Fantasies of C.S. Lewis, J.R.R. Tolkien and Charles Williams* (anth 1969). His sf criticism, which includes a number of essays, was all published in the 1960s and 1970s. He won the PILGRIM AWARD in 1992. [PN]

HILLMAN PERIODICALS ◊ WORLDS BEYOND.

HILTON, JAMES (1900-1954) UK writer, in the USA from 1935, known mainly for slightly sentimental mainstream novels like *Good-bye Mr Chips* (1934). His romantic LOST-WORLD novel, *Lost Horizon* (1933), is set in the hidden Tibetan valley of Shangri-La (his coinage), and deals with IMMORTALITY. The book is emotionally moving, and was extremely popular; it has been filmed twice (◊ LOST HORIZON). [JC]

Other works: *Nothing So Strange* (1947 US), associational, about an experimental scientist and the Manhattan Project.

See also: ANTHROPOLOGY; UTOPIAS.

HINE, MURIEL (?   -   ) UK writer whose *The Island Forbidden to Man* (1946) seemed to espouse the feminist UTOPIA hinted at in the title (◊ FEMINISM), but did not give it long for this world. [JC]

HINGLEY, RONALD (FRANCIS) (1920-   ) UK lecturer in Russian studies and writer whose sf novel *Up Jenkins!* (1956) satirically presents a UK split in two, the northern half remaining more or less free, the southern half, People's Britain, being ruled in totalitarian fashion. The SATIRE of People's Britain is deft. [JC]

HINTON, C(HARLES) H(OWARD) (1853-1907) UK author whose many essays about the fourth and other DIMENSIONS in space and time are collected along with some works of fiction in *Scientific Romances* (coll 1886) and *Scientific Romances: Second Series* (coll 1902). His interest was partly inspired by Edwin ABBOTT's *Flatland* (1885), and he wrote a novel of his own set on a circular two-dimensional world, *An Episode of Flatland* (1907). His other sf story is "Stella", in *Stella and An Unfinished Communication* (coll 1895; reprinted as part of *Scientific Romances: Second Series*), a short novel about an invisible girl which antedated H.G. WELLS's *The Invisible Man* (1896). "An Unfinished Communication" is a metaphysical fantasy which represents life after death as freedom to move in the fourth dimension (time) through the moments of life, "unlearning" and re-evaluating. "The Persian King", in *Scientific Romances*, is a curious allegory applying mathematical logic to Christian ideas of atonement. Interest in CHH's work has recently been revived by virtue of the attention paid to it in stories and essays by Rudy RUCKER. [BS]

See also: ESCHATOLOGY; INVISIBILITY; MATHEMATICS; RELIGION.

HINZ, CHRISTOPHER (1951-   ) US writer who made a considerable impact with the **Paratwa** sequence: *Liege-Killer* (1988) – which won the Compton

Crook/Stephen Tall AWARD for Best First Novel – *Ash Ock* (**1989**) and *The Paratwa* (**1991**). From the first, the sequence has given off a sense of professional polish and hurry, densely packing a wide variety of 1980s adventure-sf conventions into an intensely realized post-HOLOCAUST setting dominated by SPACE HABITATS which contain those who escaped before the end of life on Earth. Technology is controlled, but pressure is building; and when the Paratwa – pre-holocaust, genetically primed assassins – begin to reappear, CH soon engages a large cast in violent action, as the villains are hunted down and their masters (the Ash Ock) are exposed. It could not be claimed that the second and third volumes of the sequence show any deep originality, but the impersonal vigour of the narrative strikes a responsive note. A singleton, *Anachronisms* (**1988**), also demonstrates CH's canny adherence to demanding genre models in the tale of a corporation-owned survey ship – packed with CYBORGS, ESPERS, obsessed SCIENTISTS, a paramilitary cadre, and Realpolitik-driven AIS – which must face the threat of a seemingly undefeatable ALIEN which assaults them from an about-to-be-exploited planet. The parallels with the movies ALIEN (1979) and ALIENS (1986) are too explicit not to have been meant as a homage, and demonstrate that the sophisticated models of action in space deployed by those films had become necessary to high-quality, cutting-edge written adventure sf. CH is an alert follower. [JC]

HIRD, JAMES DENNIS (1850-?1920) UK writer involved in 19th-century temperance movements and Christian socialism. His *Toddle Island; Being the Diary of Lord Bottsford* (**1894**), an Erewhonian UTOPIA set on an ISLAND in the Pacific, rather effectively satirizes much of UK intellectual life. [JC]

HIRSCHMAN, EDWARD [r] ◊ Edgar Rice BURROUGHS.

HISTORY IN SF The real history of the world and the many alternative histories which might have replaced it (◊ ALTERNATE WORLDS) are extensively featured in sf stories of TIME TRAVEL and PARALLEL WORLDS, but sf writers have also drawn much inspiration from history in designing hypothetical futures. Sometimes, like Charles L. HARNESS in *Flight into Yesterday* (1949 *Startling Stories*; exp **1953**; vt *The Paradox Men*) and James BLISH in *Cities in Flight* (1950-62 var mags; omni **1970**), they have made use of actual theories – from Arnold Toynbee (1889-1975) in the former case, Oswald Spengler (1880-1936) in the latter – which have claimed to detect authentic cyclic patterns in history; more commonly, though, they have simply borrowed the past as a convenient template. Thus Miles J. BREUER and Jack WILLIAMSON replayed the story of the American Revolution as the story of the revolt of the MOON's colony against its Earthly masters in *The Birth of a New Republic* (1930 *AMZ*; **1981**); Robert A. HEINLEIN later did this more convincingly in *The Moon is a Harsh Mistress* (**1966**). Isaac ASIMOV gave to this process of borrowing a new gloss of sophistication in the first phase of his **Foundation** series (1942-50 *ASF*; in 3 vols **1951-3**; as *The Foundation*

Trilogy omni **1963**) by inventing his own futuristic science of PSYCHOHISTORY, by which Edward Gibbon's retrospective analysis of the decline and fall of the Roman Empire is transmuted into Hari Seldon's prophetic analysis of the decline and fall of the GALACTIC EMPIRE. Seldon's Plan, however, can change these deterministic prophecies by social engineering. Interestingly, a later novel by Asimov, *The End of Eternity* (**1955**), argues as strongly against social engineering as the **Foundation** series argued for it.

Toynbee eventually recanted the cyclic theory outlined in *A Study of History* (12 vols **1934-61**), and the earlier quasideterministic theories of Giambattista Vico (1668-1744) and Spengler's *Decline of the West* (**1918-22**) never quite attained academic respectability, but the attractions of such theories to sf writers are obvious. Blish's fascination with Spengler became deep, respectful and altogether serious, and A.E. VAN VOGT drew inspiration from Spengler in *The Voyage of the Space Beagle* (fixup **1950**). Toynbeean ideas continued to echo various writers' works, including Frederik POHL's and C.M. KORNBLUTH's "Critical Mass" (1961), in which they are quoted directly, Frank HERBERT's *Dune* (fixup **1965**), which seems to draw on Toynbee's picture of the Janissary-supported Turkish courts of the later Middle Ages, and Larry NIVEN's *A World out of Time* (**1967**), which uses the Toynbee-derived notion of "water-monopoly empires" – i.e., empires founded on irrigation control. Philosophers of history who dealt in NEAR-FUTURE climaxes rather than recurrent cycles – G.W.F. Hegel (1770-1831) and Karl Marx (1818-1883) are the most obvious examples – have naturally been of less interest to sf writers.

The PULP MAGAZINES inherited from the dime novels (◊ DIME-NOVEL SF) a striking "mythologized" version of the USA's recent past in the Western genre, which glorified the "frontier spirit". This myth (*see also* SOCIAL DARWINISM) was transferred to sf, where it became the animating force of countless stories about the exploration of the Solar System and the COLONIZATION OF OTHER WORLDS. The reflection of this mythical version of US history has maintained a tenacious hold over the images of the future contained in GENRE SF, and has been elaborated in various ways, sometimes painfully naïve and sometimes quite extraordinary. (The phenomenon is not, of course, restricted to fiction; the idea of space as a "high frontier" requiring conquest by bold pioneers informs much actual political rhetoric, and may be regarded as NASA's guiding myth.) It is not only US history *per se* which is reflected in stories of space pioneering; US writers have been perfectly willing to adapt "relevant" bits of more distant history, producing such images as those in Poul ANDERSON's *The High Crusade* (**1960**), H. Beam PIPER's *Space Viking* (**1963**) and Ben BOVA's *Privateers* (**1985**). Anderson has been a particularly prolific and artful borrower of entrepreneurial models from the past, taking in explorers, privateers, merchant princes and all manner of military empire-builders.

Unlike US genre sf, UK SCIENTIFIC ROMANCE was heavily influenced by more pessimistic metaphysical notions of eternal recurrence. As citizens of an empire in decline rather than descendants of mythical pioneers, UK writers inherited a rather different attitude to the past, reflected in such elegiac and defeatist fantasies of cyclic history as Edward SHANKS's *The People of the Ruins* (1920), Cicely HAMILTON's *Theodore Savage* (1922) and John GLOAG's "Pendulum" (*c*1930) and *Tomorrow's Yesterday* (1932). J.B. PRIEST-LEY's **Time** plays dealt more delicately and not quite so darkly with similar philosophical ideas. Olaf STAPLEDON adopted a more robust view of future history in his classic *Last and First Men* (1930), toying with cyclicity but eventually discarding it in favour of a more open-ended philosophy of progress, but even he could not shake off a pessimistic conviction that whatever civilizations rise up must ultimately decline and fall. The pulp-sf writers were sometimes suspicious of the idea of progress, but in general they had much more faith in the notion that contemporary civilization was destined to thrive and expand for some considerable time; such future histories as Laurence MANNING's in *The Man who Awoke* (1933 *Wonder Stories*; fixup 1975) and the far more elaborate patterns drawn in the future-history series of Heinlein and Anderson are conspicuously open-ended. Relatively few pulp visionaries imagined that any significant and irreversible rot was likely to set in before the Galactic Empire had attained a glorious zenith. (◊ GALACTIC EMPIRES for the argument that the open framework supplied by Asimov's **Foundation** series proved so comprehensive as to render unnecessary the sort of future history worked out with such pains by Heinlein and in rather less detail by later writers.)

In somewhat similar fashion, UK writers of scientific romance have often tended to see the past as something inelastically resistant to change. William GOLDING's inventor in "Envoy Extraordinary" (1956; play version *The Brass Butterfly* 1958) fails ignominiously to interest the Roman Empire in gunpowder, the steam engine and the printing press, just as the scientist in Ronald W. CLARK's *Queen Victoria's Bomb* (1967) finds that his invention arouses little excitement in Victorian England. (It was, of course, the UK that produced Herbert Butterfield [1900-1979], the historian who wrote the clever satire *The Whig Interpretation of History* [1931] in an attempt to expose the absurdity of belief in progress, and also the folly of that kind of history written, perhaps unwittingly, to flatter a society's image of itself; many works of sf, even though set in the future, are open to the criticism of "whiggery".) In sharp contrast, the hero of L. Sprague DE CAMP's classic pulp timeslip story *Lest Darkness Fall* (1939 *Unknown Worlds*; 1941; rev 1949) averts the Dark Ages by means of a series of small and subtle technological fixes, and many genre writers felt it necessary to set up corps of "time police" to protect history from casual spoliation by careless or evil-minded time-travellers. Examples include Anderson's *The Guardians of Time* (fixup 1960) and *The Corridors of Time* (1965), Barrington J. BAYLEY's *The Fall of Chronopolis* (1974) and Diana Wynne JONES's *A Tale of Time City* (1987); however, Fritz LEIBER's **Change War** series includes one story, "Try and Change the Past" (1958), whose basic point is the impossibility of changing history at all.

It was not until the spectre of the Bomb caught up with US sf writers that tragic images of historical recurrence – like that in Walter M. MILLER's classic *A Canticle for Leibowitz* (1955-7 *FSF*; fixup 1960), which portrays a future Dark Age in which learning has once more retreated to the monasteries – began to appear in some quantity. More pessimistic philosophies of history, like the one deployed in Kornbluth's "The Only Thing We Learn" (1949) and the one detected by John F. CARR in the stories he collected for H. Beam PIPER's posthumous *Empire* (coll 1981), also began to infect genre sf in this period. More recently, the aftermath of world-scale HOLOCAUST has been much more widely exploited as a setting for historical "replays" in such novels as Paul O. WILLIAMS's **Pelbar Cycle**, begun with *The Breaking of Northwall* (1981), and Kim Stanley ROBINSON's *The Wild Shore* (1984). However, the progressive optimism of US sf has generally been maintained, being unrepentantly and exuberantly displayed in such fantasies of history as D.R. BENSEN's ironic *And Having Writ . . .* (1978) and Poul Anderson's *The Boat of a Million Years* (1989). Anderson and other US writers in the same vein have always taken it for granted that liberal democracy is the evolutionary ideal of all political systems.

Although UK sf has absorbed much of the imaginative drive of US sf since the importation of the genre label, its more thoughtful exponents have always maintained a relatively modest and sceptical attitude to the dynamics of history, as displayed in such novels as Brian W. ALDISS's *An Age* (1967; vt *Cryptozoic!* US and later UK edns), Andrew STEPHENSON's *The Wall of Years* (1979) and Ian WATSON's *Chekhov's Journey* (1983). [TS/BS]

HISTORY OF SF Sf is an impure genre (◊ DEFINITIONS OF SF) which did not finally take shape until the late 19th century, although all its separate elements existed earlier. If the labelling of any earlier story as sf depended only on the presence of sf elements there would be many such. The Babylonian *Epic of Gilgamesh*, for example, has a FANTASTIC VOYAGE and a great world-flood, and in those respects it qualifies; but such retrospective labelling is not very useful, since there is no sense at all in which we can regard sf as a genre conscious of *being* a genre before the 19th century. Sf proper requires a consciousness of the scientific outlook, and it probably also requires a sense of the possibilities of change, whether social or technological. A cognitive, scientific way of viewing the world did not emerge until the 17th century, and did not percolate into society at large (◊ FUTUROLOGY) until the 18th (partly) and the 19th (to a large extent); a sense of the fragility of social structures and their potential for change did not really become widespread until the political revolutions of the late 18th century. These questions are discussed further under PROTO SCIENCE FICTION, in which entry a number of early scientific fictions, from Johannes KEPLER through CYRANO DE BERGERAC and Jonathan SWIFT, along with even earlier writers, are treated.

The main elements which eventually, in varying proportions, became melded into sf are as follows: (1) the FANTASTIC VOYAGE; (2) the UTOPIA (along with the Anti-Utopia and the DYSTOPIA); (3) the *conte philosophique*, or Philosophical Tale (◊ SATIRE); (4) the GOTHIC; (5) the TECHNOLOGICAL and SOCIOLOGICAL Anticipation, especially as it developed into the US tradition of the tale of DISCOVERY AND INVENTION in the dime novels (◊ DIME-NOVEL SF; EDISONADE). As with sf, these constituent genres are not generically pure: for instance, the Fantastic Voyage is combined with the Dystopia in Jonathan Swift's *Gulliver's Travels* (1726; rev 1735); the Gothic is combined with the Anticipation in *The Mummy!* (1827) by Jane LOUDON.

The two figures most important to sf in the early 19th century were Mary SHELLEY and Edgar Allan POE, both of whom wrote Gothic romances informed with a degree of scientific speculation, standing out in this respect from isolated, freakish speculations such as Captain Adam SEABORN's *Symzonia* (1820), one of the earliest of the many novels based on the idea of a HOLLOW EARTH, and *A Voyage to the Moon* (1827) by Joseph ATTERLEY. By the middle of the century a number of US writers, in particular, were making use of sf elements in their work, notably Nathaniel HAWTHORNE, Herman MELVILLE and Fitz-James O'BRIEN, as was Lord LYTTON in the UK. In the 1860s Jules VERNE began to publish something more strongly resembling modern sf than anything written by his predecessors. His books were described as "Extraordinary Voyages" by his publisher; many of them deal directly with the impact of NEAR-FUTURE technology. After Verne, and to some extent because of his success, the sf trickle became a torrent.

The next figure whose work had a truly transformative impact on early sf was H.G. WELLS, in many of whose stories – which began to be published in the 1890s – the Gothic, the Utopia and the Anticipation are closely bound together and reworked into a form which all readers today recognize as inarguably sf. Most sf since Wells's has adhered more or less closely to the Wellsian balances between abstract speculation and characterization and between scientific and sociological speculation.

Though Wells's achievement was great, it is too simple by far to imagine – as earlier accounts of the genre did to a greater or lesser extent – that sf jumped straight from Verne to Wells and then exploded into the form we know today. Wells had many contemporaries who wrote sf, and many predecessors; between the publication of Verne's first sf novel, *Cinq*

semaines en ballon (1863; trans as *Five Weeks in a Balloon, or Journeys and Discoveries in Africa, by Three Englishmen* 1869 US), and Wells's first, *The Time Machine* (1895 US; rev 1895 UK), the genre had been consolidating and expanding. Notable titles from the period are, in chronological order: *The Steam Man of the Prairies* (1868) by Edward S. ELLIS, "The Brick Moon" (1869) by Edward Everett HALE, *The Battle of Dorking* (1871 chap) by George T. CHESNEY, *The Coming Race* (1871) by Lytton, *Erewhon* (1872) by Samuel BUTLER, *Récits de l'infini* (1872 France; trans as *Stories of Infinity: Lumen* 1873) by Camille FLAMMARION, *Frank Reade and his Steam Man of the Plains* (as "The Steam Man of the Plains" 1876; 1892) by Harry Enton (◊ FRANK READE LIBRARY), *She* (1887) by H. Rider HAGGARD, *Across the Zodiac* (1880) by Percy GREG, *Flatland* (1884) by Edwin A. ABBOTT, *After London* (1885) by Richard JEFFERIES, *L'Ève future* (1886; trans as *The Eve of the Future* 1981 US) by VILLIERS DE L'ISLE-ADAM, *Strange Case of Dr Jekyll and Mr Hyde* (1886) by Robert Louis STEVENSON, "Les xipéhuz" (1887; trans as "The Shapes") by J.H. ROSNY aîné, *A Crystal Age* (1887) by W.H. HUDSON, *Looking Backward, 2000-1887* (1888) by Edward BELLAMY, *A Connecticut Yankee in King Arthur's Court* (1889) by Mark TWAIN, *A Plunge into Space* (1890) by Robert CROMIE, *News from Nowhere* (1890) by William MORRIS, *Olga Romanoff* (1894) by George GRIFFITH, *A Journey to Mars* (1894) by Gustavus POPE, and *The Call of the Cosmos* (1895 Russia; trans 1963) by Konstantin TSIOLKOVSKY. The above list is highly selective; it is only as a result of recent bibliographical research – carried out by many scholars including Tom CLARESON, I.F. CLARKE, Lyman Tower SARGENT, Darko SUVIN and pre-eminently Everett F. BLEILER in *Science-Fiction: The Early Years* (dated 1990 but 1991) – that we have become able to see how radically incomplete it is. Bleiler lists 618 sf works (stories and novels) for this same period 1863-95. Despite the comparative lack of well remembered names among the authors of sf in that period, it is now clear that the last three decades of the 19th century were the seed-bed for the modern genre. Wells did not spring from nowhere; he refined an existing tradition.

In the 1880s and after, many new and inexpensive MAGAZINES appeared, and quite a few of them published sf stories, as did the dime novels (◊ DIME-NOVEL SF) in the USA and the BOYS' PAPERS in the UK a little later, and with the advent of the PULP MAGAZINES (as opposed to the "slicks") in the late 1890s the market for magazine sf expanded still more. These changes meant that sf was for the first time finding a truly popular audience, but one whose expectations of literature were often crude; the prime demand was for an action-packed story. By Wells's time a rift between the SCIENTIFIC ROMANCE and pulp sf was beginning to open.

Several of the pre-Wells titles listed above initiated subgenres which were to prove popular. *The Steam Man of the Prairies* inaugurated sf in dime-novel format, usually featuring boys involved in the creation and use of marvellous inventions (these were the years when Thomas Alva Edison [1847-1931] was becoming a national hero in the USA; ◊ EDISONADE). Sf dime novels continued until the 1900s, at which time they were gradually replaced by such JUVENILE SERIES as TOM SWIFT and by the stories in the new PULP MAGAZINES. H. Rider Haggard's *She*, a great success, led to the massive popularity of the LOST-WORLD romance; this continued with some vitality into the 1930s, and is not quite extinct even today. George T. Chesney's *The Battle of Dorking* ushered in the era of the future-WAR story, which often featured INVASION, perhaps the most popular of all the fringe sf genres in the late 19th century. Wells's *The War of the Worlds* (**1898**) popularized the extraterrestrial invasion. Future-war stories remain popular today, especially in interstellar venues, but their great era ended with the start of WWI, which so devastatingly failed to fulfil future-war writers' expectations of a vivid and rapidly concluded conflict.

The earlier potted histories of sf that jumped from Verne (1863) to Wells (1895) tended to do the same for the years between Wells and *AMZ* (1926), as if the intervening years were comparatively empty. Yet the period 1895-1926 is considerably more packed than even 1863-95. There is not space here to give titles; authors whose sf largely appeared in the first instance in magazines include Frank AUBREY, Edgar Rice BURROUGHS, William Wallace COOK, Ray CUMMINGS, George Allan ENGLAND, Ralph Milne FARLEY, Homer Eon FLINT, Austin HALL, Murray LEINSTER, A. MERRITT, Victor ROUSSEAU and Garrett P. SERVISS; those primarily remembered for book publication include Edwin Lester ARNOLD, J.D. BERESFORD, Karel ČAPEK, J.J. CONNINGTON, Arthur Conan DOYLE, E.M. FORSTER, Owen GREGORY, Will N. HARBEN, Milo HASTINGS, William Hope HODGSON, Fred T. JANE, Rudyard KIPLING, Kurd LASSWITZ, David LINDSAY, Jack LONDON, John MASTIN, E.V. ODLE, Max PEMBERTON, Maurice RENARD, M.P. SHIEL, Guy THORNE, E. Charles VIVIAN, Edgar WALLACE, S. Fowler WRIGHT and Yevgeny ZAMIATIN.

From an sf point of view, the most important magazines before the arrival of the specialist sf magazines were those published by Frank A. MUNSEY in the USA and, in the UK, PEARSON'S MAGAZINE and PEARSON'S WEEKLY. Many reputations were made in the magazines, the most influential being that of Edgar Rice Burroughs; his first work was "Under the Moons of Mars", which appeared in 1912 in Munsey's ALL-STORY MAGAZINE as by Norman Bean and later in book form, expanded as *A Princess of Mars* (**1917**), under his own name. Burroughs's great popularity did much to skew magazine sf away from scientific and social speculation towards the PLANETARY ROMANCE – adventures in colourful and usually primitive other-worldly landscapes – in effect creating the genre which would later become known as SCIENCE FANTASY.

By 1926 the split between mainstream and genre sf was becoming pronounced; mainstream sf is explained in detail in MAINSTREAM WRITERS OF SF, but here we can briefly say that it is sf by writers (often already established as authors of non-sf novels and stories) working outside the traditions of magazine sf, and who often (though not always) appear to be ignorant of the very existence of those traditions. At worst, this leads to an inordinate amount of reinventing the wheel; at best, writers like Olaf STAPLEDON or John GLOAG or Aldous HUXLEY or André MAUROIS have been free to write serious books for adults without the constrictions imposed by PULP-MAGAZINE editors aiming at a predominantly juvenile and not especially literate readership. But it is only with hindsight that we can refer to these authors as mainstream: because "science fiction" as a marketing label was not a term widely used in the USA in the 1930s and was hardly used at all in the UK before the 1950s, we can hardly be surprised if writers in the UK failed to adhere to sf's generic protocols. Is there any point in calling a river the main stream before the tributary exists?

However, Olaf Stapledon did not write in a vacuum, any more than had his predecessor H.G. Wells. Brian M. STABLEFORD, in *Scientific Romance in Britain 1890-1950* (**1985**), makes a powerful case for the Scientific Romance, tales characterized by a moderate gloom (◊ OPTIMISM AND PESSIMISM), long temporal perspectives (◊ EVOLUTION) and a paucity of HEROES. Arguably many Scientific-Romance authors – who tend to be regarded by modern critics (especially in the USA) as mainstream – were in fact conscious of writing in an sf tradition, but one rather different from that developing in the US magazines: it was UK-based, and it was nurtured in hardcover books rather than magazines, but for all practical purposes it was indeed an sf tradition. In the UK it is only since the 1940s that the magazine GENRE-SF tradition and the Scientific Romance tradition have really merged, in the work of Arthur C. CLARKE, John WYNDHAM and others.

GENRE SF was usually published in the first instance in magazine format (at least until the paperback book revolution of the 1950s). The first English-language magazine devoted wholly to sf was AMAZING STORIES, founded in 1926 by Hugo GERNSBACK; it was subtitled "The Magazine of Scientifiction" (◊ SCIENTIFICTION). Many SF MAGAZINES followed, although not in large numbers before the 1940s. The usual modern term "science fiction" was hardly used before the early 1930s, and did not pass into general parlance before John W. CAMPBELL Jr took over the editorship of *ASF*. But genre sf was becoming readily distinguishable as a separate entity. Until the 1960s the perception of middle-class readers was that sf by authors like Aldous HUXLEY, George ORWELL and George R. STEWART was "respectable" (they would probably not have described it as sf) while genre sf was not. Perhaps to rectify this sort of prejudice, most of the earlier books about sf heavily emphasized genre sf, and in so doing distorted the history of sf as a whole. A high proportion (although less than half) of the authors represented in this volume are not genre-sf writers, and those who published before, say, 1955, might not even have understood the "sf" label had it been applied to their work, which it almost invariably was not (and in many cases is not today). The standard histories usually give a passing nod to Huxley and Orwell, but the sheer scale of sf publication outside the magazine tradition is still not generally realized – works by writers as diverse as John COLLIER and L.P. HARTLEY, William GOLDING, C.S. LEWIS, Oscar LEWIS, Sinclair LEWIS and Wyndham LEWIS, Vladimir NABOKOV and Rex WARNER and Herman WOUK.

In the 1930s, indeed, magazine sf was at rather a low ebb, though at this time the new subgenre of SPACE OPERA was being developed almost entirely within the magazines. The extraordinary growth in sf publishing since WWII has caused us to forget its relative unimportance up to the end of the 1930s. Out of many hundreds of specialized pulp magazines, only a few were devoted to sf; it is unlikely that, in those days, sf had more than 2-3 per cent of the pulp market. Many magazine-sf writers turned their hand to any of half a dozen pulp genres. It was not until a generation of sf specialists began publishing in the magazines at the end of the decade that the so-called Golden Age of (magazine) sf began. There were specialist forerunners of course, notable among them being John W. CAMPBELL Jr (often writing as Don A. Stuart), Edmond HAMILTON, E.E. "Doc" SMITH, John TAINE, Stanley G. WEINBAUM and Jack WILLIAMSON; but little of it is as enjoyable to read now as once it was. Magazine sf of the 1930s is important mainly for what it led to, especially when Campbell took over the editorship of *ASF* in Oct 1937 (*for the detailed story* ◊ ASTOUNDING SCIENCE-FICTION *and* GOLDEN AGE OF SF), and magazine sf began to become mature; during 1938-46 many of its most celebrated writers – Isaac ASIMOV, Alfred BESTER, James BLISH, Arthur C. CLARKE, Robert A. HEINLEIN, Frederik POHL, A.E. VAN VOGT and many others – made their débuts.

The sf that was published in the magazines during the Golden Age was to be the basis of the sf book-publishing boom which – in both hardcovers and paperback, first by specialist SMALL PRESSES and then by mass-market publishers – was a phenomenon of the 1950s and has continued unabated ever since. At first the majority of these sf books reprinted their material directly from the magazines. The gradual shift of emphasis from magazine to book publication (until the late 1960s, unlike the case in any other branch of literature, prior publication in a magazine was still the rule rather than the exception) won genre sf a much larger readership than ever before; by the 1970s sf constituted around 10 per cent of all English-language fiction published, and with the growing readership came a greater public acceptance of sf as "respectable". Sf book publishing is discussed under the rubrics SF PUBLISHING and ANTHOLOGIES.

The increase in maturity of genre sf during the 1940s was only relative. Most sf publishers from 1926 seem to have assumed that their main readership was made up of teenage boys, as is obvious in both editorial and advertising material right through the era of the sf PULP MAGAZINES at least to 1950 – and after. The publisher Donald A. WOLLHEIM is on record as believing this, and we can see confirmation in the remarkable but adventure-story-oriented sf lists he edited from the 1950s, first at ACE BOOKS and later at DAW BOOKS. A similar targeting of the young readership has been adopted successfully by DEL REY BOOKS. On the other hand, Jim BAEN, editor of GALAXY SCIENCE FICTION in the mid-1970s, believes surveys support him in showing that the readership reaches its median age in the mid-20s. No market surveys yet carried out have been extensive or reliable enough to prove the point one way or the other, though it has long been obvious that there is actually more than one sf market. Whatever the truth of the matter, the belief that the readership was young and primarily male was sufficient to discourage genre sf from including complex or experimental writing; the vocabulary of the pulp magazines, while vigorous, was mostly undemanding. Before the cultural shifts of the 1960s, which affected all fiction publishing, genre sf normally observed TABOOS about SEX, bad language and RELIGION. Even in the 1970s these taboos were ingrained deeply enough to cause some able writers to abandon sf altogether, or to talk publishers into printing their books without the ghetto-izing "sf" label on the cover.

The domination of Campbellian sf within the genre began to falter with the inauguration of two important new magazines, *The* MAGAZINE OF FANTASY AND SCIENCE FICTION in 1949 and GALAXY SCIENCE FICTION in 1950. The former emphasized literacy and style to an extent unprecedented in sf-magazine publishing, and the latter specialized in witty SATIRE, often sociological rather than technological, written by such important writers as Alfred BESTER, C.M. KORNBLUTH and Frederik POHL, Robert SHECKLEY, William TENN and, occasionally, Philip K. DICK. During the 1950s and 1960s, the emphasis of genre sf shifted from the hard sciences (engineering, astronomy, physics, etc.) to the SOFT SCIENCES (sociology, psychology, etc.). Stories of PSI POWERS and ESP had been popular ever since the first appearance of A.E. van Vogt's *Slan* (1940 *ASF*; **1946**; rev 1951), but they absolutely boomed in the 1950s; the market eventually became saturated (as it did at about the same time with flying-saucer stories; ◊ UFOS), and the psi story subsided to a lower though constant level in the 1960s. The 1950s were also notable for the first real sf boom in the movies (◊ CINEMA; MONSTER MOVIES), though the films were rather different from most written sf of the period. The most obvious change in 1950s sf is surprisingly seldom discussed: the shift in protagonists from highly trained, self-reliant and in control of events to baffled, ordinary and subject to manipulation by the powerful in society.

As worries about POLITICS, ECOLOGY and OVERPOPU-LATION grew in the 1960s, an already perceptible shift away from simple optimism began to accelerate (◊ OPTIMISM AND PESSIMISM). This move is much con-nected in readers' minds with the advent of the NEW WAVE, though this was never an easily definable movement – indeed, it was not an organized move-ment at all – and its outward signs lay as much in a greater willingness to adopt more complex narrative strategies as in any generally downbeat attitude. But pessimism in sf certainly did increase in the late 1960s, reflecting massive cultural changes taking place in Europe and the USA, as did left-wing political attitudes; most previous genre sf had either been dead to POLITICS or had adopted a stance interpreted by many as right-wing (◊ LIBERTARIANISM; SOCIAL DARWINISM). The late 1960s were also notable for seizing on the idea of ENTROPY as a useful all-purpose metaphor.

Isaac Asimov, looking back from 1981, described magazine sf of 1926-38 as "adventure dominant", that of 1939-50 as "technology dominant", and that of 1950 on as "sociology dominant". James E. Gunn preferred to describe the Campbell years as "science-dominant", and added a fourth category, "style dominant", for the period beginning in the mid-1960s. John CLUTE's shorthand account, given in 1992, is rather different: "In 1942 . . . the inner tale of sf was a tale of empire . . . in 1952, it was hubris . . . in 1962, solipsism . . . in 1972, retribution . . . in 1982, memory . . . in 1992, the inner tale of sf is a tale of exogamy." This, though an initially cryptic-seeming formulation, is one for which most readers would find it surprisingly simple to provide supporting examples.

By the 1960s sf was being read so much more widely than before that its ideas, and its iconography generally, had begun dramatically to feed back into mainstream fiction – previously the intellectual traffic had been mostly the other way. While some writers, such as Kurt VONNEGUT Jr, J.G. BALLARD and Michael MOORCOCK, succeeded (to varying degrees) in shrug-ging off the sf taint, other writers were embracing sf, so that, although it might be controversial to claim some of the works of Angela CARTER, Romain GARY, Russell HOBAN, Thomas PYNCHON and Angus WILSON (and many others) as pure sf, there is little question that their thrillers, romances or fabulations drew on sf among their more obvious sources.

Since 1960 there has been a complex cross-fertilization of genres. While, at the intellectual end of the spectrum, FABULATIONS have been making more and more use of sf images and themes, at the popular end fantasy, horror and DISASTER novels have borrowed heavily from sf, as has the bestseller (itself now a definable genre). As an example of the latter, *The Crash of '79* (**1976**) by Paul E. ERDMAN is pure sf extrapolation, though it uses the conventional narra-tive strategies of the bestseller in its tale of NEAR-FUTURE disaster in POLITICS and ECONOMICS. Barbara HAMBLY and David GEMMELL are only two of the writers who import sf elements into their fantasies. At the beginning of the 1990s, generic labelling is less insistent than it was a decade earlier, and bookshops regularly place sf on the same shelves as fantasy and horror (as, indeed, they have for a long time); in some cases the books are by the same authors.

With hindsight, it might seem that sf as a separate, definable genre was a phenomenon of, say, 1926-65. By the 1990s hard sf, arguably the heart of the genre in an earlier era, had shrunk to a comparatively small section of the overall sf market. A significant cultural change took place in 1992 when the SCIENCE FICTION WRITERS OF AMERICA officially agreed to admit fantasy and horror writers to their ranks (in practice, many had been there for years), the organization changing its name to the Science Fiction and Fantasy Writers of America. Many of the stories in Gardner DOZOIS's **Year's Best Science Fiction** anthologies are so far removed from their generic roots that they would not appear out of place in, say, *The New Yorker*. At the same time, a Postmodernist (◊ POSTMODERNISM AND SF) nostalgia for sf of an earlier, simpler period became apparent from the number of pastiche works pub-lished by sf writers in the 1980s and 1990s that referred selfconsciously and often to the genre's own history. (Three early examples are Michael MOOR-COCK's **Dancers at the End of Time** sequence, Brian W. ALDISS's *Frankenstein Unbound* [**1973**] and Christ-opher PRIEST's *The Space Machine* [**1976**].) The ages of development and consolidation have passed, it some-times seems, to be replaced by an age of rococo decoration.

While these developments have been more obvious since the late 1980s, they are no more than a culmination of a genre-mixing process that has been continuing since the New Wave of the 1960s. An important strand in this has been the commercial success of sf, largely catalysed by films, notably 2001: A SPACE ODYSSEY (1968), STAR WARS (1977), and Steven SPIELBERG's CLOSE ENCOUNTERS OF THE THIRD KIND (1977) and E.T.: THE EXTRATERRESTRIAL (1982). The result of this success was a much greater awareness in the 1980s of sf as a commercial "product" to be packaged like any other, and aimed at the juvenile end of the market. The 1980s rapidly became a bibliographer's nightmare, with the proliferation of various BRAIDS and TIES, many of them SHARECROPS: tv and film novelizations and spin-offs, SERIES, SHARED WORLDS, GAME-WORLDS and so on. Most of these categories had existed earlier, but never on the massive scale of the 1980s and the present. Though patient readers could find good work within them, the commercial impera-tives generating them led all too obviously to an absolute deluge of hack work, far greater than had been visible in sf book publishing previously. Many sf authors have argued that this mass of "product" is drowning out the individuality of what publishers call the midlist: that portion of their booklist that sells reliably if not in huge numbers, and without much in the way of promotion – the portion to which books by most of the better sf authors belong. Fortunately, apocalyptic premonitions of sf's imminent death by drowning seem (as usual) premature; if anything, greater numbers of exciting sf writers emerged in the 1980s than in the 1970s. Sf, by marrying outside the genre (one of the meanings of "exogamy" in Clute's terms), is more likely to disappear by a generalized cultural absorption than through neglect. At the beginning of the 1980s LOCUS was listing about 180 new English-language genre-sf novels each year; by the end of the decade the figure was about 280 (the *Locus* figures are likely to be on the low side). This is not necessarily a proof of the genre's health, but it certainly does not look like a symptom of terminal illness.

By the end of the 1980s the sf-film boom was wavering and, as ever, sf on tv was still not having the good fortune that eager producers – intending to ride on the film boom of the early 1980s – kept (and still keep) hoping for, generally destroying all hope of real success by playing it safe and producing programmes of staggering banality. The few surviving professional sf magazines had dwindling circulations, even ISAAC ASIMOV'S SCIENCE FICTION MAGAZINE (founded 1977), which could be regarded as the only new US sf magazine to approach the high quality of what had been the big three: *ASF*, *FSF* and *Galaxy*. In another part of the sf landscape the news was more cheerful: as desktop publishing, using comparatively cheap home computers, became possible, there was in the mid-1980s a proliferation of SEMIPROZINES, some containing fiction, some containing criticism, and some both. These magazines, even though usually of quite small circulation, soon proved something of a nursery and a debating ground for many young writers; this compensated, to a degree, for the shrinking of the professional-magazine market.

The most exciting sf event of the 1980s was the advent of CYBERPUNK (with William GIBSON and Bruce STERLING cast as its prophets); despite the obvious hyperbole with which it was greeted by the media publicity machines, cyberpunk certainly represented a real invigoration of the genre – and came closer than anything else in the period to revitalizing hard sf as well. [PN]

Further reading: A very much fuller account of sf's history can be gained by following up the various cross-references in the above entry. Many ANTHOLOGIES of sf from specific periods are available, and book reprint series have brought older works back into the light. Numerous books on the history of sf are discussed under CRITICAL AND HISTORICAL WORKS ABOUT SF.

HITCHCOCK, RAYMOND (JOHN) (1922-) Indian-born UK writer and cartoonist whose **Percy** books – *Percy* (**1969**) (filmed in 1971 as *Percy*) and *Percy's Progress* * (**1972**), the latter written as a film novelization – find mirth in penis transplantation. *Venus 13: A Cautionary Space Tale* (**1972**) also deals

lightly with sex, depicting the complications that surround a eugenic mating in a space satellite. [JC]

HITCH HIKER'S GUIDE TO THE GALAXY, THE Tv series (1981). BBC TV. Written and created by Douglas ADAMS, prod Alan J.W. Bell, associate prod John Lloyd, starring Simon Jones as Arthur Dent, David Dixon as Ford Prefect, Mark Wing-Davey as Zaphod Beeblebrox and Sandra Dickinson as Trillian. 6 35min episodes, re-edited to 7 episodes for first US release. Colour.

This tv serial began life as 2 6-part BBC radio programmes, #1 in 1978, #2 in 1980 (2 episodes cowritten with its producer John Lloyd, who also received a production credit on the tv series), which had built up a massive (for radio) cult following; commercially released recordings of the radio broadcasts sold widely. Adams then turned his scripts into the bestselling novels *The Hitch Hiker's Guide to the Galaxy* (**1979**) and *The Restaurant at the End of the Universe* (**1980**). Two further volumes followed, but it was the 12 radio programmes (and perhaps the first two books) that formed the basis for the tv script. Adams had substantial tv experience, having been a script editor on DR WHO. The tv series was very funny indeed (although less liked by many aficionados than the original radio version) and was notable for the sophisticated graphics with which the eponymous talking Guidebook itself was animated. The series belongs to a very English school of comparatively deadpan (and somewhat cruel) absurd humour, based on the implicit premise that the Universe is arbitrary and unkind, especially to the English, and suffers from galloping ENTROPY. Although US tv seldom produces work of this sort, the programme was successful there also, although not to the same extent as in the UK. It is often replayed. [PN]

HITLER WINS For nearly half a century it has been an enjoyable creative exercise to imagine what kind of ALTERNATE WORLD might have evolved had Germany won WWII, and many novels and stories have been written to explore that assumption. But the first Hitler-wins tales were not exercises in reconstructing history; *Swastika Night* (**1937**) by Murray Constantine (◊ Katharine BURDEKIN), was not set in an alternate world, and nor were the several others published 1939-45. Any Hitler-wins story published before the end of WWII falls under the general category of the future-WAR or INVASION tale, and was almost certainly designed as a dreadful warning of the consequences of defeat. Examples include *Loss of Eden* (**1940**; vt *If Hitler Comes* 1941) by Douglas Brown (1907-) and Christopher Serpell, *Then We Shall Hear Singing* (**1942**) by Storm JAMESON, *Grand Canyon* (**1942**) by Vita SACKVILLE-WEST, *When the Bells Rang* (**1943**) by Anthony ARMSTRONG and Bruce Graeme (1900-), and *When Adolf Came* (**1943**) by Martin HAWKIN. A subcategory – novels in which Hitler seems about to win, but loses an important battle or secret at the last moment – includes many borderline tales of warfare and espionage; among the serious examples are detailed fictional prognoses like Fred ALLHOFF's *Lightning in the Night* (1939 *Liberty*; **1979**), which predicts a US readiness to use nuclear weapons against Germany as a final resort.

The death of Hitler in 1945 marked the end of the real WWII in Europe, but for any number of reasons – the astonishing intensity of the evil he represented; the dreadful clarity of the consequences had the Allies failed; the melodramatic intensity of the conflict itself, with the whole war seeming (then and later) to turn on linchpin decisions and events; and (shamingly) the cheap aesthetic appeal of Nazism, with its Art Deco gear, its brutal élites, its Blitzes and Panzer strikes, its secrecy and paranoia – WWII very soon became a focus for speculative thought, and it was only a few months before the first alternate-world Hitler-wins tale was published (in HUNGARY): László Gáspár's *Mi, I. Adolf* ["We, Adolf 1"] (**1945**). The first significant example in English was SARBAN's *The Sound of his Horn* (**1952**), which sinuously intertwines sadism and aesthetics into a vision of decadence with roots in Germany's mythic past. This book may have influenced – and certainly served as a tonal precedent for – several works both within the field, like Keith ROBERTS's "Weihnachtsabend" (1972), and outside it, as in non-alternate-history novels of Germany like Gabriel Fielding's *The Birthday King* (**1962**) and Michel Tournier's *Le Roi des Aulnes* (**1970**; trans Barbara Bray as *The Erl-King* **1972** UK).

The most famous single Hitler-wins sf tale is probably Philip K. DICK's *The Man in the High Castle* (**1962**), in which Hitler's victory becomes a kind of poisonous backdrop for a complex tale; and the most telling commentary on the moral underside of the subgenre is Norman SPINRAD's *The Iron Dream* (**1972**), in which the young Hitler, a failure at politics, becomes a pulp novelist whose tale *Lord of the Swastika* exploits, to savagely ironic effect, some of the responses of many readers to tales of "genuine" Nazi triumph.

Half a century after the end of WWII, new Hitler-wins stories are less common, but the number written during this intervening period has been remarkable. They include Hilary BAILEY's "The Revolt of Frenchy Steiner" (1964), Otto BASIL's *Wenn das der Führer wüsste* (**1966**; cut trans Thomas Weyr as *The Twilight Men* **1968** US), Greg BEAR's "Though Road No Whither" (1985), David BRIN's "Thor Meets Captain America" (1986), Len DEIGHTON's *SS-GB* (**1978**), David DVORKIN's *Budspy* (**1987**), Gordon EKLUND's "Red Skins" (1981), Harlan ELLISON's STAR TREK teleplay "The City on the Edge of Forever" (shown 1967), Gary Gygax's and Terry Stafford's *Victorious German Arms: An Alternate Military History of World War II* (**1973** chap), Robert Harris's *Fatherland* (**1992**), James P. HOGAN's *The Proteus Operation* (**1985**), Trevor HOYLE's *Q: Through the Eye of Time* (**1977**), the film IT HAPPENED HERE (1966), C.M. KORNBLUTH's "Two Dooms" (1958), Fritz LEIBER's *The Big Time* (**1961**), Brad LINAWEAVER's *Moon of Ice* (**1988**), Norman Longmate's (1931–   ) *If Britain had*

Fallen * (**1974**), based on a 1972 BBC programme, Kenneth Macksey's *Invasion: The German Invasion of England, July 1940* (**1980**), Richard MEREDITH's *Run, Come See Jerusalem* (**1976**), in which the Nazis do eventually lose, though only after nuking Chicago, Frederic MULLALLY's *Hitler has Won* (**1975**), Eric NORDEN's *The Ultimate Solution* (**1973**) and Andre NORTON's *The Crossroads of Time* (**1956**).

An interesting theme anthology is *Hitler Victorious* (anth **1986**) ed Gregory BENFORD and Martin Harry GREENBERG, which contains several of the stories listed above. Peter FLEMING's *Invasion 1940* (**1957**; vt *Operation Sea Lion* 1957 US) describes in great detail the preparations Germany made to invade the UK in 1940, speculating in the last chapter on what might have happened had a successful invasion occurred. WWII, Fleming suggests, might in that event have been won by Hitler. [JC]

HIVE-MINDS A hive-mind is the organizing principle of the community in those insect species of which the basic reproductive unit is the hive, organized around a single fertile female, the queen. The term is used more loosely in some sf stories, often referring to any situation in which minds are linked in such a way that the whole becomes dominant over the parts.

Because the organization of social-insect communities is so very different from that of mammal communities, while showing a degree of structural complexity comparable only to human societies, ants and their kindred have always held a particular fascination for sf writers, and the ant-nest is the most obvious model for an ALIEN society. Early expressions of this fascination include "The Empire of the Ants" (1905) by H.G. WELLS, "The Adventures of Professor Emmett" (1939) by Ben HECHT, "The Ant with the Human Soul" (1932) by Bob OLSEN, "Doomsday Deferred" (1949) by Will F. Jenkins (Murray LEINSTER) and "Come and Go Mad" (1949) by Fredric BROWN. Wells's *The First Men in the Moon* (**1901**) was the first of many to depict an alien hive-society. Giant ants and wasps are among the standard figures of menace employed by sf writers; notable examples are found in Ralph Milne FARLEY's *The Radio Man* (1924 *Argosy*; **1948**), Frank A. RIDLEY's *The Green Machine* (**1926**), Alfred Gordon BENNETT's *The Demigods* (**1939**), the film THEM! (1954) and Keith ROBERTS's *The Furies* (1966). Real-world scares concerning "killer bees" have been reflected in such novels as Arthur HERZOG's *The Swarm* (**1974**) and the associated Irwin ALLEN film. "The Empire of the Ants" and other stories portray hive-insects as serious contenders to end human domination of Earth, but Frank HERBERT's *The Green Brain* (**1966**) imagines a multispecies insect hive evolving in order to protect the world's ecological balance against the short-sighted policies of humankind.

Most sf novels which imagine hivelike human societies find the idea repugnant, and it is often cited as the ultimate totalitarian DYSTOPIA; examples include *The Human Termites* (1929 *AMZ*: **1979**) by David H. KELLER, *The Riddle of the Tower* (**1944**) by

J.D. BERESFORD and Esmé Wynne-Tyson and *Morrow's Ants* (**1975**) by Edward HYAMS. L. Sprague DE CAMP's wry *Rogue Queen* (**1951**) features the revolutionary overthrow of a hivelike state. Some recent sf writers have been more conscientiously ambivalent – examples include T.J. BASS's *Half Past Human* (**1971**), Frank Herbert's *Hellstrom's Hive* (**1973**) and Robert SILVERBERG's *The Queen of Springtime* (**1989**) – but their eventual verdict remains negative. Less hivelike group-minds are not uncommon in sf stories dealing with ESP, and the idea that some kind of group-mind represents the evolutionary destiny of the species crops up frequently; it figures extensively as an image of transcendental social harmony in Olaf STAPLEDON's *Last and First Men* (**1930**) and *Star Maker* (**1937**), and is memorably developed in Theodore STURGEON's *More than Human* (**1953**) and "To Marry Medusa" (**1958**; exp vt *The Cosmic Rape* **1958**) and in Arthur C. CLARKE's *Childhood's End* (**1953**). The loss of individuality is, however, still seen as a horrific prospect in such novels as *Enemies of the System* (**1978**) by Brian W. ALDISS and *Dusha Mira* (**1964**; trans Antonina W. Bouis as *World Soul* **1978** US) by Mikhail EMTSEV and Eremei PARNOV.

The ambivalence with which many recent sf stories regard hive-minds derives mainly from the association of group-minds with the notion of transcendent EVOLUTION, but there has also been a tendency for recent sf writers calculatedly to question the assumptions made by their forerunners. Thus, whereas in *Starship Troopers* (**1959**) Robert A. HEINLEIN was content to assume that human individualism and alien hive-organization must fight a fundamental Darwinian struggle for existence, Joe HALDEMAN was prepared to suggest in *The Forever War* (**1974**) that mankind might be greatly enriched by making peace with the aliens. The alien hive-minds in Barrington J. BAYLEY's "The Bees of Knowledge" (**1975**) and Keith LAUMER's *Star Colony* (**1981**) are treated with some respect, and Orson Scott CARD followed up the genocidal *Ender's Game* (**1977** *ASF*; exp **1985**) with *Speaker for the Dead* (**1986**), in which the guilt-stricken hero searches for a suitable home for the last surviving alien queen. The most detailed and sympathetic sf image of an alien hive-society is that in *Serpent's Reach* (**1982**) by C.J. CHERRYH; another clever deployment is in Linda STEELE's *Ibis* (**1985**), an ironic account of a love affair between an alien female and a human male. The actual genetic politics of hive-organization – revelation of which has been the greatest triumph of the sociobiology of Edmund O. Wilson (1929-   ) – whereby the misnamed "queen" stands revealed as a helpless sex-slave forced to work to the genetic advantage of her sisters, has not yet found significant reflection in sf.   [BS]

See also: COMMUNICATION; LIVING WORLDS; POLITICS; SUPERMAN.

HJORTSBERG, WILLIAM (REINHOLD) (1941-   )
US writer, much of whose work – like his first novel, *Alp* (**1969**), or his third, *Toro! Toro! Toro!* (**1974**) – is

FABULATION. *Gray Matters* (**1971**), which is sf, grounds its fantastic episodes in a future UTOPIA where people are reborn (◊ REINCARNATION) from entombment as "Cerebromorphs" within an enormous CYBERNETIC complex only when they have achieved some transcendence of their personal identities. *Falling Angel* (**1978**), filmed as *Angel Heart* (**1987**), grippingly marries detection and horror in a secret-sharer tale of striking grimness.   [JC]
Other works: *Symbiography* (**1973**); *Tales and Fables* (coll **1985** chap).

H-K PUBLICATIONS ◊ COMET.

HLOUCHA, KAREL [r] ◊ CZECH AND SLOVAK SF.

H-MAN, THE ◊ BIJO TO EKITAI NINGEN.

HOBAN, RUSSELL (CONWELL) (1925-   ) US-born writer and illustrator, in the UK from 1969. After serving in WWII, he worked in advertising and tv until the mid-1960s, becoming a full-time writer in 1967. Most of his many titles are children's books, about 50 of them being illustrated texts for younger children, like the first, *What Does It Do and How Does It Work?* (**1959**), and (to mention only one of many stunning fables) *La Corona and the Tin Frog* (**1974** *Puffin Annual*; **1979** chap). Although not sf, his early masterpiece for children cannot go unnoticed: the potent allegorical burden of *The Mouse and his Child* (**1967**) may in fact have hampered its acceptance by the younger readers for whom it was ostensibly written, for the epic quest of a clockwork mouse and his son for a secure haven – where they will no longer need to undergo the existential trauma of needing to be rewound – is metaphorically dense and abidingly melancholy, and the Dolls' House they eventually reach does not absolve them from their own form of mortality. In other words, *The Mouse and his Child*, like all the greatest children's books, is best read twice: as a child, and again later.

It was not until the 1970s that RH began to write the adult novels for which he has become best known, beginning with *The Lion of Boaz-Jachin and Jachin-Boaz* (**1973**), a FABULATION in which the raw Being of the long-dead lion of the world is embraced by the eponymous father and son in a moment of unity. Both *Kleinzeit* (**1974**) and *Turtle Diary* (**1976**) offer worlds displaced by language, though not on analysis literally fantastic. But RH's next novel, *Riddley Walker* (**1980**), for which he received the JOHN W. CAMPBELL MEMORIAL AWARD in 1982, is a genuine – and quite extraordinary – sf novel, set 2000 or so years after the HOLOCAUST in southern England, just as the barbarian societies of the land have rediscovered the use of gunpowder. It is a situation much explored in the sf of the latter half of the 20th century, and RH's penetration of the moral and cultural complexities involved is acute; but what distinguishes the book from other attempts to represent something like a full sense of how it might actually seem to inhabit such a world is its language (◊ LINGUISTICS), a remarkably inventive and internally consistent presentation of an evolved and living tongue. The often-quoted first sentence of the novel gives something of the flavour: "On my naming day when I come 12 I to gone front spear and kilt a wyld boar he parbly ben the las wyld pig on the Bundel Downs any how there hadnt ben none for a long befor him nor I aint looking to see none agen." In this tongue, legends – like the tale of the "Littl Shynin Man the Addom" – seem told in a timeless present tense, and Riddley Walker's own groping progress towards an understanding of the dangers of a return to the old ways also seems told for the first time.

Subsequent novels have been fabulations of intriguing complexity, while some of the tales assembled in *The Moment under the Moment* (coll **1992**) are of moderate genre interest. *Pilgermann* (**1983**) allows its 11th-century protagonist to inhabit various eras in a kind of ghost form. *The Medusa Frequency* (**1987**) heavily foregrounds the myths of Orpheus and Medusa in the tale of a 20th-century novelist who, like the twinned parent and son of RH's first adult novel, strives to find the moment, or the tongue, or the tale, that will join together in Being all that is asunder. But the later novel stops short of finding that Story. Only in *Riddley Walker* do the levels seem, at moments, to inhabit one another – do story and the world trick the eye into seeming one.   [JC]

See also: ANTHROPOLOGY; DEVOLUTION; HISTORY OF SF.

HOBANA, ION [r] ◊ ROMANIA.

HOCH, EDWARD D(ENTINGER) (1930-   ) US writer best known for his crime novels and stories. With the short story "Co-Incidence" (1956), as by Irwin Booth, he began publishing detection-oriented sf, later using as well the pseudonyms Stephen Dentinger, Pat McMahon and R.L. Stevens. The numerous stories featuring detective **Simon Ark**, who claims to be 2000 years old – some collected in *The Judges of Hades and Other Simon Ark Stories* (coll **1971**), *City of Brass and Other Simon Ark Stories* (coll **1971**) and *The Quests of Simon Ark* (**1984**) – are marginal sf or fantasy. EDH's sf series featuring Earl Jazine of the **Computer Cops** mixes sf and detection in action tales of 21st-century crises involving computer crimes. The series includes "Computer Cops" (1969), *The Transvection Machine* (**1971**), *The Fellowship of the HAND* (**1973**) and *The Frankenstein Factory* (**1975**). Within his range, EDH is a briskly competent storyteller.   [JC]

HODDER-WILLIAMS, (JOHN) CHRISTOPHER (GLAZEBROOK) (1926-   ) UK writer, pilot, composer and sound engineer. His first novel, *The Cummings Report* (**1957**) as by James Brogan, was not sf. He began publishing sf with *Chain Reaction* (**1959**), which concerns itself, as does almost all of his fiction, with the relationship between Man and the machine technology he has created, in this case through a mystery plot about radiation sickness spread by food. His next three novels were aviation stories, sharing the same general theme, but since *The Main Experiment* (**1964**) he has written only sf, almost always in the form of novels with NEAR-FUTURE scenarios. These include *Fistful of Digits* (**1968**), which introduces self-

programming computers to an obsessive tale about loss of individuality, and *The Silent Voice* (**1977**), about the human brain's capacity to receive radio waves directly – to potentially ominous effect. *The Chromosome Game* (**1984**), set 200 years after a nuclear HOLOCAUST, grimly argues that human nature will soon, once again, disastrously express itself in the old way. CH-W's novels combine social and cultural concerns typical of UK post-WWII writers with somewhat melodramatic plotting and stiff characterization of a rather male-chauvinist variety; the effect is sometimes sharp, but more often uneasy.   [JC]

Other works: *The Egg-Shaped Thing* (**1967**; the UK hardcover edition is definitive); *98.4* (**1969**); *Panic O'Clock* (**1973**); *Cowards' Paradise* (**1974**; UK paperback slightly rev); *The Prayer Machine* (**1976**); *The Thinktank that Leaked* (**1979**).

See also: GENETIC ENGINEERING; PARANOIA.

HODGART, MATTHEW (JOHN CALDWELL) (1916-   ) UK academic, Professor of English at Sussex University from 1964. His continuation of Jonathan SWIFT's *Gulliver's Travels* (1727), *A New Voyage to the Country of the Houyhnhnms* (**1969** chap), is a SATIRE on the 1960s upheavals in higher education in the UK.   [JC]

HODGE, T. SHIRBY Pseudonym of US writer Roger Sherman Tracy (1841-1926). His sf novel, *The White Man's Burden: A Satirical Forecast* (**1915**), is set in AD5000, by which period the warlike and primitive White races have been restricted to North America while, in Black-dominated Africa, anarchism and scientific genius have generated a UTOPIAN world. A White invasion suffers ignominious defeat, and the narrator – a (White) interloper from the 20th century – returns to his own time. Considering its period, the book is remarkable for declining to treat Blacks as inherently inferior to Whites.   [JC]

See also: POLITICS.

HODGKINS, DAVID C. [s] ◊ Algis BUDRYS.

HODGSON, WILLIAM HOPE (1877-1918) UK writer who ran away to sea in his youth and was deeply affected by his experiences aboard ship: he never lost a profound fascination, reflected in all his poetry and most of his stories and essays, for the mysteries of the sea. His fantastic sea stories – the first was "From the Tideless Sea" (1906 *The London Magazine*) – owe an obvious debt to the traditions of supernatural fiction, but he derived his horrific imagery mainly from the scientific imagination; notable examples are "The Voice in the Night" (1907), in which castaways are transformed by a fungus they have been obliged to eat, and "The Stone Ship" (1914), in which an ancient wreck is raised to the surface by a volcanic eruption, bringing many weird creatures with it. In his first novel, *The Boats of the "Glen Carrig"* (**1907**), a ship's crew is marooned on an island near a land of floating seaweed inhabited by bizarre and terrible lifeforms. His second, *The House on the Borderland* (**1908**; recent paperback edns cut), is a remarkable visionary fantasy in which a man living in a house which apparently co-exists in two worlds undertakes an allegorical spiritual odyssey through time and space, witnessing the destruction of the Solar System. *The Ghost Pirates* (**1909**) also juxtaposes the known world with an alien counterpart as a ship "slips" into intermediacy and its crew witness strange and frightening manifestations. His last-published novel, *The Night Land* (**1912**), describes in a peculiar mock-archaic style an epic FAR-FUTURE journey across the face of a much altered and monstrously populated Earth. The allegorical aspect of WHH's novels embodies a conviction that horrid evil forces move beneath the surface of reality, sometimes becoming vilely manifest in creatures such as the spirit which possesses the SCIENTIST in the blasphemous fantasy "Eloi, Eloi, Lama Sabachthani" (written 1912; 1919 as "The Baumoff Explosion") and the entity manifested in "The Hog", the last of his **Carnacki** series of stories featuring an occult detective, gathered as *Carnacki the Ghost-Finder* (coll **1913**; exp **1947**).

Some of his short stories were collected in *Men of the Deep Waters* (coll **1914**), *The Luck of the Strong* (coll **1916**) and *Captain Gault* (coll **1917**), though the last has no fantastic material. The best were reprinted in the ARKHAM HOUSE collection *Deep Waters* (coll **1967** US); Arkham had earlier reprinted all four of his novels in *The House on the Borderland and Other Novels* (omni **1946** US). Some of his stories were further reprinted in *Masters of Terror, Volume One: William Hope Hodgson* (coll **1977**), and some unreprinted stories were assembled in *Out of the Storm* (coll **1975**), which features also a biography of WHH by Sam MOSKOWITZ that draws heavily on research conducted by R. Alain Everts, whose Strange Company issued in 1988 a set of 15 booklets containing stories by WHH in their magazine versions (some had been revised for book publication). Other booklets containing previously unreprinted stories are the British Fantasy Society's *William Hope Hodgson: A Centenary Tribute 1877-1977* (coll **1977** chap) and *Demons of the Sea* (coll **1992** chap) ed Sam Gafford; the latter also contains 3 of WHH's essays, including the futuristic SATIRE "Date 1965: Modern Warfare" (1908).

For some reason, possibly involving US copyright protection, WHH arranged for privately printed editions of drastically condensed versions of several of his books. The short version of *The Night Land*, initially issued in *Poems and The Dream of X* (coll **1912** chap), has been separately reprinted as *The Dream of X* (**1977** chap), while the abridgement of two **Carnacki** stories in *Carnacki, the Ghost Finder, and a Poem* (coll **1910** chap) is reprinted alongside the condensed novel from *The Ghost Pirates, a Chaunty and Another Story* (coll **1909** chap) in *Spectral Manifestations* (coll **1984** chap). Ian Bell, the compiler of *Spectral Manifestations*, has also edited a collection of essays about WHH, *Visions and Venturers* (anth **1987** chap). [BS]
See also: BIOLOGY; COSMOLOGY; END OF THE WORLD; FANTASTIC VOYAGES; HISTORY OF SF; HORROR IN SF; ISLANDS; MESSIAHS; MONSTERS; PARALLEL WORLDS; PULP MAGAZINES; RELIGION; STARS; SUN.

HOFFMAN, LEE Working name of US sf fan and writer Shirley Bell Hoffman (1932-   ); she was married for a time to Larry T. SHAW. LH is probably better known for her Westerns than for her sf, which she began publishing with a short novel, *Telepower* (**1967** chap), following it with *The Caves of Karst* (**1969**), *Always the Black Knight* (**1970**) and *Change Song* (**1972**). The last-named is, typically of her work, a polished, unpretentious adventure in which a juvenile protagonist on an unspecified planet, similar to but probably not Earth, succeeds in acquiring self-knowledge along with adult power. *In and Out of Quandry* (coll **1982** chap dos) is a short collection of essays and tales, mostly humorous (◊ QUANDRY). [JC]
See also: UNDER THE SEA.

HOFFMANN, E(RNST) T(HEODOR) A(MADEUS) (1776-1822) German composer, painter, lawyer, judge and writer. About 1808 he changed his third given name from Wilhelm to Amadeus in homage to Mozart, and for many years he thought of himself primarily as a musician, being intensely involved in all aspects of MUSIC from composition to criticism. His first story, "Gluck", was not written until 1809, so that it was only in the last 15 years of his life that he turned to the artform in which he did his most significant work: his tales. These expressed a grotesque Romanticism more effectively than those of any other writer of his time and, variously translated and assembled, have strongly influenced European literature. His only completed novel, *Die Elixiere des Teufels* (**1813-16**; trans R.P. Gillies as *The Devil's Elixir* **1824** UK; vt *The Devil's Elixirs* **1963**), typically concerns itself with a monk seduced by the Devil. Collections of his shorter works are *Fantasiestücke* ["Fantasy Pieces"] (coll **1814-15**), *Nachtstücke* ["Night Pieces"] (coll **1816-17**) and *Die Serapionsbruder* (coll **1818-21**; trans Alexander Ewing in 2 vols as *The Serapion Brethren* **1886** and **1892**, both UK); early English translations from various sources include *Hoffman's Strange Stories* (coll trans anon **1855** US), *Hoffmann's Fairy Tales* (coll trans L. Burnham **1857** US) and *Weird Tales of E.T.W.* [sic] *Hoffmann* (coll trans T.J. Bealby in 2 vols **1885** UK); convenient recent assemblies include E.F. BLEILER's *The Best Tales of Hoffmann* (coll of old trans **1967** US), *Selected Writings of E.T.A. Hoffmann* (coll trans Leonard J. Kent and Elizabeth C. Knight in 2 vols **1969** US) and *Three Märchen of E.T.A. Hoffmann* (coll trans Charles E. Passage **1971** US). Three of ETAH's stories formed the basis of the opera *Tales of Hoffmann* (1881) by Jacques Offenbach (1819-1880), which was filmed in 1951.

ETAH, like his celebrated successor in the GOTHIC, Edgar Allan POE, was interested in contemporary science, and especially in the psychological theories of Emanuel SWEDENBORG and the animal magnetism espoused by Franz Mesmer (1734-1815); his stories in this vein have influenced later sf. His best-known story, "Der Sandmann" ["The Sandman"] (1816), features the sinister spectacle-maker Dr Coppelius and the beautiful automaton he builds, with which the hero falls in love. Predating Mary SHELLEY's *Frankenstein* (**1818**), this story is an important forerunner of ROBOT and ANDROID stories. It formed the basis of the ballet *Coppelia* (1870) by Léo Delibes (1836-1891). [JC/PN]

See also: GAMES AND TOYS; GERMANY; HORROR IN SF; MACHINES; SCIENTISTS; THEATRE.

HOFFMANN, OSKAR [r] ◊ GERMANY; *Der* LUFTPIRAT UND SEIN LENKBARES LUFTSCHIFF.

HOGAN, ERNEST (? -) US writer who began publishing sf with "The Yenagloshi Express" for *AMZ* in 1986. His first novel, *Cortez on Jupiter* (**1990**), uses the subversive tone of CYBERPUNK to tell the tale of a countercultural street artist looking for fulfilment, travelling from the usual hyperbolic NEAR-FUTURE Southern California by jagged stages to JUPITER, where he confronts without blinking an ALIEN species with whom it has been death for more mundane souls to speak. *High Aztech* (**1992**) is set in the Tenochtitlán (aka Mexico City) of AD2045. There is an explosiveness about the tale, and about EH's short fiction, which marks him as a figure of interest for the 1990s. [JC]

HOGAN, JAMES P(ATRICK) (1941-) UK-born systems-design engineer and writer, in the USA from 1977 and a full-time author from 1979. His first novel (and first publication), *Inherit the Stars* (**1977**), aroused interest for the exhilarating sense it conveys of scientific minds at work on real problems and for the genuinely exciting scope of the sf imagination it deploys. The book turned out to be the first volume in the **Minervan Experiment** sequence, being followed by *The Gentle Giants of Ganymede* (**1978**) and *Giants' Star* (**1981**), all three being assembled as *The Minervan Experiment* (omni **1981**; vt *The Giants Omnibus* 1991). Much later, the sequence continued with *Entoverse* (**1991**), a tale that laboriously expands the initial premise through the use of a parallel universe in which, rather oddly for a writer pugnaciously associated with the HARD-SF wing of the genre, only MAGIC can cope with the strangeness of the physical world – in the earlier volumes of the sequence the reader was safely in the hands of an author who brooked no such nonsense. The sequence is in fact a hard-sf fable of humanity's origins – we are the direct descendants of the highly aggressive inhabitants of the destroyed fifth planet, who would have conquered the Galaxy had they not blown themselves up – and espouses a vision of the Universe in which other species must learn to cope with the knowledge that we will, some day, come into our inheritance. Although JPH could not maintain the flow of speculative thought that drove the first volumes, the sequence stands as his best work.

Other novels variously succeed in presenting HEROES – generally clumped into male-bonded affinity groups – and scientific problems of a similar nature. In *The Genesis Machine* (**1978**) one of these heroes averts the END OF THE WORLD. In *Voyage from Yesteryear*

(**1982**) a colony world, governed according to the kind of Trickster Libertarianism of old and honoured *ASF* writers like Eric Frank RUSSELL, effortlessly faces down and flummoxes an attempt by Earth to re-establish control. In *Code of the Lifemaker* (**1983**) a ROBOT civilization on Titan is saved from similarly corrupt Earth corporations. But in *Endgame Enigma* (**1987**) a NEAR-FUTURE Russian threat to dominate the world via armed satellite is recounted with leaden flippancy, and this brought to the fore a problem JPH has presented to his readers from the first. Though most of them either share or accept his right-wing POLITICS, and tolerate his editorial intrusions about personal *bêtes-noires* like the ECOLOGY movement, JPH's extreme awkwardness as a stylist and creator of character has made his books difficult, at times, actually to read. When he abandons his strengths – his hard-edged sense of how SCIENTISTS think, and his joyful capacity to stretch the terms of SPACE OPERA – this gaucheness is difficult to ignore. It is to be hoped that he will return to the game of thought. [JC]

Other works: *The Two Faces of Tomorrow* (**1979**); *Thrice Upon a Time* (**1980**); *The Proteus Operation* (**1985**), a HITLER-WINS story; *Minds, Machines & Evolution* (coll **1988**); *The Mirror Maze* (**1989**); *The Infinity Gambit* (**1991**).

See also: ALTERNATE WORLDS; AUTOMATION; EVOLUTION; LIBERTARIAN SF; MOON; NUCLEAR POWER; UTOPIAS.

HOGAN, ROBERT J. [r] ◊ G 8 AND HIS BATTLE ACES; *The* MYSTERIOUS WU FANG.

HOLBERG, LUDVIG, [Baron] (1684-1754) Danish playwright, essayist and historian. Born in Bergen, Norway, LH studied at Copenhagen and settled permanently in Denmark, where he was appointed professor at Copenhagen University, first of philosophy, later of metaphysics and of Latin rhetoric, and finally of history (1730). A prolific author, he published several voluminous poems, 32 comedies and the satirical novel *Nicolai Klimii iter subterraneum* (**1741** in Latin; exp 1745; trans anon as *A Journey to the World Under-Ground. By Nicolas Klimius* **1742** UK; vt *The Journey of Niels Klim to the World Underground* 1960 US; vt *A Journey to the World Underground* 1974 US). This is a satirical UTOPIAN novel, deriding LH's contemporary world and inspired primarily by Jonathan SWIFT's *Gulliver's Travels* (**1726**; rev 1735), Thomas MORE's *Utopia* (Part 2 **1516** in Latin; both parts 1551 in English) and Montesquieu's *Lettres persanes* (**1721**). One of the most influential 18th-century SATIRES, it describes the FANTASTIC VOYAGE of Niels Klim through a hole in a mountain (the name Holberg can be translated as "hollow mountain") into a HOLLOW EARTH, where he finds a minute sun circled by the planet Nazar, whose inhabitants show a societal pattern diametrically opposed to that of the contemporary stereotype: WOMEN are the dominant sex and males perform only menial tasks. It is notable that Holberg's novel was considered dangerously radical in Denmark; the English translation preceded publication in Danish by 47 years. [J-HH]

See also: BIG DUMB OBJECTS; DENMARK.

HOLBROOK, JOHN [s] ◊ Jack VANCE.

HOLDSTOCK, ROBERT P(AUL) (1948-   ) UK writer with an MSc in medical zoology from the London School of Hygiene and Tropical Medicine. He spent 1971-4 in medical research before becoming a full-time writer, though he had published his first story, "Pauper's Plot", for *NW* as early as 1968. He wrote much of his short fiction in the following years. Among the more notable stories are the novelettes "Travellers" (1976), a TIME-TRAVEL tale, and "The Time Beyond Age" (1976); others are collected in *In the Valley of the Statues* (coll **1982**). After the mid-1970s his writing broke into two superficially incompatible categories. Under the house names Ken BLAKE and Richard KIRK, and as Robert Black, Chris Carlsen, Steven Eisler and notably Robert Faulcon, he published (see listing below) at least 20 novels, novelizations and works of popular sf "nonfiction", almost all of them hasty commercial efforts but infused, nevertheless, with a black intensity of action that gave even clichéd SWORD-AND-SORCERY plots something of a mythic intonation. At the same time, under his own name, he began to publish sf novels like *Eye Among the Blind* (**1976**) and *Earthwind* (**1977**), in both of which he uneasily attempted to accommodate the compulsive mythologizing of his dark fantasies to "normal" sf worlds. The result was a series of books whose narrative energies seem hampered by decorum: the interplay between ALIENS and alienation in *Eye Among the Blind* is effective but ponderously expressed; *Earthwind* utters slow-moving hints at the powers of a "chthonic" atavism; and *Where Time Winds Blow* (**1981**), the best of these early books, ornately but without much movement posits an environment suffering arbitrary transfigurations through time-shifts.

With the publication of *Mythago Wood* (**1984**), however, RH's two careers suddenly and thankfully converged in a tale whose elaborate proprieties of rationale are driven by narrative energies and an exuberance of language previously restricted in crude form to his **Berserker** novels, written as Chris Carlsen. Much expanded from his short 1981 fantasy of the same title, *Mythago Wood* is FANTASY rather than sf only if it is wrong to consider the creation of a rational model for conceiving racial archetypes a proper subject for sf. The frame of the tale is indeed obdurately rational, and the "mythagoes" discovered – and transmuted – by the contemporary protagonist are appropriate expressions of what might be called the unconscious tale of the race: they are that tale made animate, and each mythago bears a name or names – and enacts the nature – of those archetypes that embody, for Britons, the permutations of that tale. The wood from which they come – like the interior lands for which the protagonists of much UK fantasy long – is huger inside than out, and in describing it RH engages in language of a metaphoric density rarely encountered in marketable fiction. The book won the 1986 World Fantasy AWARD. Its sequel,

Lavondyss: Journey to an Unknown Region (**1988**), only increases the intensity of the cooperation between rational discourse and *Sehnsucht* (a term C.S. LEWIS employed to describe the melancholy longing for "something that has never actually appeared in our experience", and by which he meant to designate the impulse behind certain kinds of fantasy). The longing of the protagonists of *Lavondyss* to enter the "unknown region" where archetypes shape themselves into the human story is absolute, and it gives the book much of its potency as an explication of mythopoeisis. Several of the stories assembled in *The Bone Forest* (coll **1991**) serve as pendants to the central novels; and *The Fetch* (**1991**), a fantasy, traverses similar terrain. In transforming the Matter of Britain into archetypal sf, RH has re-assembled old material, and old generic devices, into a new territory for fiction.   [JC]

Other works: *Encyclopedia of Science Fiction* (**1978**), Consultant Editor; *Necromancer* (**1978**), paranormal horror; *Elite: The Dark Wheel* * (**1984** chap), novella based on a computer game; *Bulman* * (**1984**) and *One of Our Pigeons is Missing* * (**1984**), associational tv novelizations; *The Emerald Forest* * (**1985**), novelizing the John BOORMAN film.

As Ken Blake (house name): *Cry Wolf* * (**1981**), *The Untouchables* * (**1982**), *Operation Susie* * (**1982**) and *You'll be All Right* * (**1982**), associational titles in the **The Professionals** series.

As Robert Black: *Legend of the Werewolf* * (**1976**) and *The Satanists* * (**1977**), both novelizing films.

As Chris Carlsen: The **Berserker** series, comprising *Shadow of the Wolf* (**1977**), *The Bull Chief* (**1977**) and *The Horned Warrior* (**1979**).

As Steven Eisler: The linking texts for 2 vols of reprinted illustrations, being *Space Wars Worlds and Weapons* (**1979**) and *The Alien World* (**1980**).

As Robert Faulcon: The **Night Hunter** sequence, comprising *The Stalking* (**1983**) and *The Talisman* (**1983**), both assembled as *The Stalking* (omni **1987**), *The Ghost Dance* (**1984**) and *The Shrine* (**1984**), both assembled as *The Ghost Dance* (omni **1987**), and *The Hexing* (**1984**) and *The Labyrinth* (**1987**), both assembled as *The Hexing* (omni **1988**).

As Richard Kirk (house name): *Swordsmistress of Chaos* * (**1978**) with Angus WELLS, writing together as Kirk, *A Time of Ghosts* * (**1978**) and *Lords of the Shadows* * (**1979**), being titles in the **Raven** series.

Nonfiction: *Alien Landscapes* (**1979**), *Tour of the Universe: The Journey of a Lifetime – The Recorded Diaries of Leio Scott and Caroline Luranski* (**1980**), *Magician: The Lost Journals of the Magus Geoffrey Carlyle* (**1982**), *Realms of Fantasy* (**1983**) and *Lost Realms* (**1985**), all written with Malcolm EDWARDS, all primarily picture books.

As editor: *Stars of Albion* (anth **1979**) with Christopher PRIEST; the **Other Edens** series of original anthologies, all with Christopher EVANS, comprising *Other Edens* (anth **1987**), *Other Edens II* (anth **1988**) and *Other Edens III* (anth **1989**).

See also: BRITISH SCIENCE FICTION AWARD; DEVOLUTION; GOTHIC SF; MYTHOLOGY; NEW WRITINGS IN SF.

HOLKAR, MO [r] ◊ M.H. ZOOL.

HOLLAND ◊ BENELUX.

HOLLAND, CECELIA (1943-   ) US writer whose numerous historical novels, beginning with *The Firedrake* (1966), have explored with striking vividness many of the genuine "alternate worlds" on Earth. One of these, still-born as a tale set in Mongol China, became the sf novel *Floating Worlds* (1976), a formidably long and complex SPACE OPERA involving conflict in the Solar System between Inner and Outer Planets. A wide range of contrasting societies, on an anarchist Earth and on the OUTER PLANETS themselves, provide a convincing background for the presentation of characters of unusual complexity. The protagonist is a woman, subtly drawn, ambivalent in her motivations, highly believable; on the Outer Planets, the description of the floating cities (◊ GRAVITY) is likewise believable, and involving.

Though not sf, *Home Ground* (1981), which puts an sf writer into a UTOPIAN commune, makes its points in the RECURSIVE mode which has become familiar within the genre. *Pillar of the Sky* (1985) combines historical research and fantasy in a story centred on Stonehenge.   [JC]

See also: WOMEN SF WRITERS.

HOLLAND, STEPHEN (1962-   ) UK bibliographer and critic who has also scripted some COMICS, including a 1989 story for *The Cursed Land* and a 1990 story for *Computer Killer*. His main work has been in the almost infinitely perplexing field of post-WWII UK paperback publishers and authors, and he has done much to clarify the two decades after 1945, a period rife with pseudonymous titles, ephemeral publications, fly-by-night publishers and reticent authors. His bibliographical studies, most of them short but illuminating, include *Scion and Dragon Books* (1984 chap), *Modern Fiction* (1984 chap), *Curtis Warren and Grant Hughes* (1985 chap), *John Spencer and Badger Books* (1985 chap), *Gaywood Press, Compact Books and Hank Janson Publishers* (1986 chap), *Piccadilly Novels* (1986 chap), *Digit Books* (1986 chap), *Brown Watson* (1986 chap), *R. & L.W. Locker/Harborough/Archer* (1987 chap), *Viking/WDL/Consul* (1987 chap), *Hamilton & Panther* (1987 chap), *The Sexton Blake Library* (1988 chap), *Paul Renin: A Bibliographical Checklist* (1990 chap), *The Gramol Group* (1990 chap) and *The Mike Western Story* (1990 chap). *The Trials of Hank Janson* (1991) and *The Fleetway Companion* (anth in 2 vols 1992) were more commodious presentations of this material. His work as a whole has been summarized in two linked volumes, «Vultures of the Void: A History of British Science Fiction, 1946-1956» (1992 US) and «British Science Fiction Paperbacks, 1949-1956» (1992 US), both with Philip HARBOTTLE. He has contributed several entries to this encyclopedia. [JC]

HOLLOWAY, BRIAN (?   -   ) UK writer of whom nothing is known beyond the fact that he wrote sf novels under a number of CURTIS WARREN house

names: *Destination Alpha* (1952) as Berl CAMERON, *Titan's Moon* (1952) as Neil CHARLES, *Southern Exploration* (1953) as Adam Dale, *Trans-Mercurian* (1952) as King LANG, *"A" Men* (1952) as Rand LE PAGE, *Beyond Geo* (1953) as Arn ROMILUS, and *Lost World* (1953) as Brian SHAW. He also wrote two sf novels for the firm under personal pseudonyms: *The Mortals of Reni* (1953) as Von Gruen and *Red Storm* (1952) as Brian Storm.   [JC]

HOLLOW EARTH The concept of the Earth as a hollow, spherical shell with a habitable, internal concave surface accessible through polar openings or caves, or by mechanical bores, has long been a significant motif in sf. The idea's dual origins, from RELIGION and PSEUDO-SCIENCE, are still potent. Traditionally Hell was sited inside the Earth, a notion that persisted at least until the 18th century, when a theologian proposed that Earth's rotation was caused by the damned scrambling to escape from Hell. In pseudo-science the astronomer Edmond Halley (1656-1742), to account for magnetic phenomena, suggested in a paper published by the Royal Society in 1692 that Earth (and the other planets) consisted of concentric, nested spheres surrounding a small central sun, with, possibly, openings at the poles.

The first important use of Halley's concept came in Ludvig HOLBERG's *Nicolaii Klimii iter subterraneum* (1741 in Latin; exp 1745; trans anon as *A Journey to the World Under-Ground. By Nicolas Klimius* 1742 UK; vt *The Journey of Niels Klim to the World Underground* 1960 US; vt *A Journey to the World Underground* 1974 US), in which a young Norwegian falls through the Earth's crust to the hollow interior, where he has adventures on an inner planet and on the concave shell among nonhuman intelligent beings. Derivative from Holberg's work is Giacomo CASANOVA's *Icosameron* (1788; cut trans Rachel Zurer as *Casanova's 'Icosameron'* 1986 US), which is concerned, *inter alia*, with ALIEN lifeforms inside the Earth.

The largest impetus to modern hollow-Earth fiction came from a persuasive US soldier, John Cleves SYMMES, who revitalized and publicized Halley's theory of concentric spheres and polar openings. *Symzonia* (1820) by Adam SEABORN (an unidentified pseudonym), a pleasant early IMAGINARY VOYAGE, satirizes Symmes's ideas; it also comments, *à clef*, on the political structures of Europe and the USA. It has been suggested that Edgar Allan POE's "MS Found in a Bottle" (1833) and *The Narrative of Arthur Gordon Pym* (1838) are indebted to Symmes and *Symzonia*, but it is more probable that Poe had in mind the caves and water engine involved in the traditional Abyss of Waters.

Much the best known hollow-Earth stories are Edgar Rice BURROUGHS's **Pellucidar** novels: *At the Earth's Core* (1914 *All-Story*; **1922**), *Pellucidar* (1915 *All-Story-Cavalier*; **1923**) and several sequels. Based loosely on Symmes, these stories develop Burroughs's usual themes: Gibson-girl romance, frustrated sexual assaults and dominance (here empire-building among naïve natives) against a background of palaeontological survivals. While the earlier stories are rational in their assumptions, later ones slip into supernaturalism involving REINCARNATION and Hell. For Burroughs the Moon, too, is hollow, as in *The Moon Maid* (1923-25 *Argosy-All-Story*; **1925**).

The concept of the hollow Earth has otherwise been used for the most varied fictional purposes. In a dystopian attack on FEMINISM, *Pantaletta* (**1882** US) by "Mrs J. Wood" (probably a man), the world within is run by arrogant dominant woman who have changed even personal pronouns to avoid sexism. "Vera Zarovitch"'s (◊ Mary E. Bradley LANE) *Mizora* (1880-81 *Cincinatti Commercial*; **1890** US), on the other hand, posits a feminist, socialist UTOPIA, where males are no longer biologically necessary. In *Nequa* (**1900**) by Jack ADAMS the themes are sexual equality, altruism and socialism. The "single tax" proposed by the US economist Henry George (1839-1897) offers the leit-motif for Byron Welcome's *From Earth's Centre* (**1894** US), and an odd mixture of occultism, anarchism and Fourierist socialism supports the story thread of M. Louise Moore's *Al Modad* (**1892** US). John Uri LLOYD's *Etidorhpa* (**1895**) describes occult advancement as the narrator progresses to the centre; George W. Bell's *Mr Oseba's Last Discovery* (**1904** New Zealand) promotes New Zealand real estate by comparing that country to the edenic interior; and "My Bride from Another World" (1904 *Physical Culture*) by "Rev. E.C. Atkins" plugs for Bernarr MacFADDEN's hygienics – nudism, vegetarianism and back-to-Nature. *Plutoniia* (1915; **1924**; trans as *Plutonia* **1957**) by the great Russian geologist Vladimir Afanasevich OBRUCHEV is frankly written as a simple introduction to palaeontology. Obruchev adds a new supposition: the Earth solidified hollow, and a comet knocked a hole in the shell, permitting access.

Fantastic adventure with less message characterizes Charles Willing BEALE's *The Secret of the Earth* (**1899**), William R. BRADSHAW's occult *The Goddess of Atvatabar* (**1892**), Frank Powell's lurid boys' thriller *The Wolf-Men* (**1905** UK), Roy ROCKWOOD's boys' book *Five Thousand Miles Underground* (**1908**), William J. Shaw's *Under the Auroras* (**1888** US), Fred THORPE's serialized DIME NOVEL "In The World Below" (1897 *Golden Hours*) and Park Winthrop's "The Land of the Central Sun" (1903 *Argosy*).

A religious note is not uncommon. In the later stories of the paranoid Shaver mystery (◊ Richard S. SHAVER) the inner world is a Hell; however, edenic stories, in which creation took place inside the Earth, like Casanova's *Icosameron*, are more frequent. There is an internal CITY called Eden in Willis George EMERSON's *The Smoky God or, A Voyage to the Inner World* (**1908**). In William A. Miller's *The Sovereign Guide* (**1989** US) Eden still exists, though overgrown, as does the tomb of ADAM AND EVE. Seaborn's *Symzonia* and Beale's *The Secret of the Earth* both consider surface humans as descendants of exiles from the interior.

The gravitational peculiarities of a hollow Earth are seldom utilized. Exceptions are Clement FEZANDIE's "A Journey to the Center of the Earth" (1925 *Science and Invention*) and Konstantin TSIOLKOVSKY's "Dreams of Earth and Sky" (1895; trans in *The Call of the Cosmos* coll **1963**).

In most cases the writers cited do not take the hollow-Earth concept seriously. On the whole, the hollow Earth is simply a convenient alien place for odd adventures or panaceas, but it would be easy enough to work out a psychoanalytic or other metaphoric interpretation of the motif.

True hollow-Earth stories should not be confused with stories set in deep cave-systems, another very common theme. Two of the most famous underground stories of this type are LYTTON's *The Coming Race* (**1871**; vt *Vril: The Power of the Coming Race* 1972 US) and Jules VERNE's *Voyage au centre de la terre* (**1863**; exp 1867; trans anon as *Journey to the Centre of the Earth* 1872 UK). A third example, not often thought of as being such, and especially prone to the psychoanalytic interpretation, is Lewis CARROLL's *Alice's Adventures in Wonderland* (**1865**).

Hollow-Earth stories still show up occasionally in the modern period. Among the more interesting are "Black as the Pit, from Pole to Pole" (1977 *New Dimensions 7*) by Howard WALDROP and Steven UTLEY, Richard A. LUPOFF's *Circumpolar!* (**1984**) and Rudy RUCKER's *The Hollow Earth* (**1990**). Nothing is ever crystal clear in a novel by James P. BLAYLOCK, but *The Digging Leviathan* (**1984**) appears also to be marginally a hollow-Earth story. It is interesting that all these tales are couched as nostalgic pastiche (and often close to MAGIC REALISM), as if merely to mention a hollow Earth today were to evoke a wondrous past time. [EFB]

HOLLY, JOAN HUNTER A late working name of US writer Joan Carol Holly (1932-1982), who before 1970 signed herself J. Hunter Holly. JHH had a degree in psychology and conducted creative-writing work-shops as well as doing her own work; a benign brain tumour, removed in 1970, interrupted her career 1966-70, and she later suffered further ill health. She began publishing sf with a novel, *Encounter* (**1959**), in which Man and inimical ALIEN confront one another. Much of her work – including *The Flying Eyes* (**1962**), *The Dark Planet* (**1962**) and *The Time Twisters* (**1964**) – involves melodramatic alien INVASIONS and other traumatic encounters. Among her better stories, written after her illness, are "The Gift of Nothing" (1973) and "Psi Clone" (1977). *Keeper* (**1976** Canada) and *Shepherd* (**1977** Canada) make up a short DYSTO-PIAN series in which one man opposes an oppressive regime JHH wrote straightforward adventure novels whose dark undertones were of interest. [JC]

Other works: *The Green Planet* (**1960**); *The Gray Aliens* (**1963**; vt *The Grey Aliens* 1964 UK); *The Running Man* (**1963**); *The Dark Enemy* (**1965**); *The Mind Traders* (**1966**); *The Assassination Affair* * (**1967**), #10 in the MAN FROM U.N.C.L.E. series; *Death Dolls of Lyra* (**1977**).

See also: WOMEN SF WRITERS.

HOLLYWOOD BOULEVARD ◊ Roger CORMAN; Joe DANTE.

HOLM, SVEN (1940-) Danish novelist who works in various modes, from realism to KAFKA-inspired modernism. His one sf work, *Termush, Atlanterhavs-kysten* (1967; trans Sylvia Clayton as *Termush* 1969 UK), tells of the psychological problems encountered by a group of rich survivors dwelling in their luxury shelter after a nuclear HOLOCAUST. While bona fide sf, *Termush* is also a parable of the alienation of modern, materialistic Man. [DN/JC]

HOLMBERG, JOHN-HENRI [r] ◊ SCANDINAVIA.

HOLMES, A.R. [s] ◊ Harry BATES.

HOLMES, BRUCE T. (? -) US writer whose sf novel, *Anvil of the Heart* (1983), presents with some poignance one of the potential nightmares attendant upon the successful GENETIC ENGINEERING of the human species: the slow death of the last pre-altered humans as their children confront a new world. [JC]

HOLMES, H.H. [s] ◊ Anthony BOUCHER.

HOLOCAUST AND AFTER This is part of a giant cluster of themes which has always played a central role in sf, both GENRE SF and MAINSTREAM. It is impossible to dissect out the different aspects of this cluster so that they are mutually exclusive; hence there is some overlap between this entry and ADAM AND EVE (many sf tales deal with a second genesis after catastrophe), ANTHROPOLOGY (the emphasis is often on tribal patterns forming in a brutalized and diminished population), EVOLUTION and DEVOLUTION (evolutionary change has since the 18th century been linked with natural catastrophe), ENTROPY (holocaust is one of the more dramatic aspects of everything running down), HISTORY IN SF (human-inspired disasters are often seen as part of a Toynbeean or Spenglerian process of historical cycles), the END OF THE WORLD (holocaust on a major scale), ECOLOGY (interference with nature is often seen as the bringer of disaster), MEDICINE (the agent of holocaust is often plague), MUTANTS (the use of nuclear weapons is often seen as leading to massive mutation in plants, animals and humans), NUCLEAR POWER (the most popular agent of holocaust in fiction since WWII), OPTIMISM AND PESSIMISM and SURVIVALIST FICTION (which is all too often written by men for men, featuring men shooting other men after civilization's convenient collapse). The catastrophe variants are summarized under DISASTER; particular aspects of catastrophe are discussed in most of the above entries. Here we concentrate on the many stories whose focus is not so much the disaster itself but the kind of world in which the survivors live, and which they make for themselves.

The aftermath of holocaust may be the most popular theme in sf; this encyclopedia mentions at least 400 examples at novel length. The genre is as old as sf itself: a convenient starting point is Mary SHELLEY's second sf novel, *The Last Man* (1826), in which plague crosses Europe from the Middle East,

leaving one survivor in Rome who is possibly the last man. Natural catastrophe, too, strikes in Herrmann LANG's *The Air Battle: A Vision of the Future* (1859), in which European civilization is destroyed by flood and earthquake, but a benevolent North-African federation brings peace to the world, Black leading White back to social order.

The novel in which the post-holocaust story takes on its distinctive modern form is Richard JEFFERIES's *After London* (1885), in which the author's strategy is to set the novel thousands of years after the catastrophe has taken place; in this way an interesting, alienating perspective is gained. The hero takes his own society (as in most later stories in this vein it is quasimedieval) for granted; he endeavours to reconstruct the nature of the fallen civilization that preceded it, and also the intervening years of barbarism. Ever since Jefferies's time the post-holocaust story has tended to follow this pattern; for every book whose hero lived through the holocaust itself – John CHRISTOPHER's *The Death of Grass* (1956; vt *No Blade of Grass* US), filmed as NO BLADE OF GRASS (1970), and Robert MERLE's *Malevil* (1972 France; trans 1974), filmed as MALEVIL (1981), being examples – there are several whose story begins long after the disaster is over but while its effects are still making themselves felt.

Though such stories continue to fascinate, there has been surprisingly little variation in the basic plot: disaster is, in the average scenario, seen as being followed by savage barbarism and a bitter struggle for survival, with rape and murder commonplace; such an era is often succeeded by a rigidly hierarchical feudalism based very much on medieval models. When the emphasis falls on struggle and brutality, as it very often does, we have in effect an awful-warning story. But often the new world is seen as more peaceful and ordered, more in harmony with Nature, than the bustle and strife of civilization. Such stories are often quasi-UTOPIAS in feeling and PASTORAL in their values. There is no denying the attraction of such scenarios: they tempt us with a kind of life in which the individual controls his or her own destiny and in which moral issues are clear-cut.

In mature versions of the post-holocaust story there is usually an emotional resonance developed from a tension between loss and gain, with the simplicities of the new order not wholly compensating for the half-remembered glories and comforts of the past. This is the case with George R. STEWART's *Earth Abides* (1949), and may explain why, despite its occasionally fulsome prose, that novel has attained classic status.

The first two decades of the 20th century saw no particular boom in the genre, but at least two works are still well remembered: Jack LONDON's *The Scarlet Plague* (1914) and S. Fowler WRIGHT's *Deluge* (1928) (sequelled by *Dawn* [1929]); in both cases the catastrophe is natural. This was so of most holocaust stories in those days of comparative innocence. Even after WWI, mankind's capacity for self-destruction was seldom seen as efficient enough to operate on a global scale. Other relevant stories of the period are Garrett P. SERVISS's *The Second Deluge* (**1912**), George Allan ENGLAND's *Darkness and Dawn* (**1914**), an unusually optimistic story of reconstruction, J.J. CONNINGTON's *Nordenholt's Million* (**1923**) and P. Anderson GRAHAM's cranky racist *The Collapse of Homo Sapiens* (**1923**).

Connington's book made much of the reconstruction of TECHNOLOGY; from this point on the relationship of technology to the post-holocaust world, and the often ambiguous feelings of the latter towards it, became prominent. Thomas Calvert MCCLARY's *Rebirth* (1934 *ASF*; **1944**) is a casually callous account of a SCIENTIST so disgusted by what he self-righteously regards as the decadence of modern civilization that he invents a ray which causes everyone to forget all acquired knowledge, including how to talk: starting from instinct, the smartest and toughest re-educate themselves in technology in about 10 years; most die. Edwin BALMER's and Philip WYLIE's *When Worlds Collide* (**1933**), with its reconstruction sequel *After Worlds Collide* (**1934**), has a scientific elite escaping a doomed Earth in a giant rocket and rebuilding on a new planet, at the same time fighting off communists; it was filmed as WHEN WORLDS COLLIDE (1951). Stephen Vincent BENÉT's "The Place of the Gods" (1937; vt "By the Waters of Babylon") blends superstitious fear and plangent nostalgia in telling of a barbarian boy's response to the technological wonders of a ruined CITY; its sentimentality was to become a recurrent note in many such tales after WWII: it ends, "We must build again."

Many of the authors cited have not been closely connected with GENRE SF. The post-holocaust theme, particularly in the UK, has had a strong attraction for MAINSTREAM writers, perhaps because it offers such a powerful metaphor for exploring Man's relation with his social structures: it pits art against Nature. Two strong UK examples from the 1930s are Alun LLEWELLYN's *The Strange Invaders* (**1934**) and John COLLIER's *Tom's A-Cold* (**1933**; vt *Full Circle* USA); both evoke the atmosphere of a fallen society with considerable intensity of feeling. An interesting French novel published during WWII was *Ravage* (**1943**; trans Damon KNIGHT as *Ashes, Ashes* **1967** US) by René BARJAVEL, in which the disappearance of electricity turns France rural.

After the Hiroshima bombing a new period began in which, unsurprisingly, the post-holocaust story came to seem less fantastic; it also became more popular, and developed a distinctively apocalyptic atmosphere, a heavy emphasis on a supposed antitechnological bias among the survivors, and a concentration on the results of nuclear power in general and radiation in particular. The mood was darker in that imagined catastrophes were now primarily man-made. Man became pictured as a kind of lemming bent on racial suicide – through nuclear, biological and chemical warfare in stories of the 1940s and 1950s, and through POLLUTION, OVERPOPULATION and

destruction of Earth's ecosphere in many stories since the 1960s.

Among the darker scenarios set after nuclear war are: Judith MERRIL's *Shadow on the Hearth* (**1950**); Wilson TUCKER's *The Long Loud Silence* (**1952**); Ward MOORE's "Lot" (1953) with its sardonic sequel "Lot's Daughter" (1954), the uncredited bases for PANIC IN YEAR ZERO (1962); Mordecai ROSHWALD's *Level 7* (**1959**); Pat FRANK's *Alas, Babylon* (**1959**), more optimistic than the others about the possibility of re-ordering society; Alfred COPPEL's *Dark December* (**1960**); and Fritz LEIBER's extremely savage "Night of the Long Knives" (1960; vt "The Wolf Pair"), which can be found in *The Night of the Wolf* (coll **1966**). Novels which place a greater emphasis on the kinds of society developed after the holocaust are: Algis BUDRYS's *False Night* (**1954**; text reinstated and exp, vt *Some Will not Die* 1961; rev 1978), a very grim book; Margot BENNETT's *The Long Way Back* (**1954**), in which civilized Africans send a colonizing expedition to legendary Great Britain, where they find Whites still living in caves; *Dark Universe* (**1961**) by Daniel F. GALOUYE, set in an underground POCKET UNIVERSE; Edgar PANGBORN's *Davy* (**1964**), *The Judgment of Eve* (**1966**) and *The Company of Glory* (**1975**); Brian W. ALDISS's *Non-Stop* (**1958**; vt *Starship* USA) and *Greybeard* (**1964**), the latter dealing with life after mass sterility has struck humanity; Philip K. DICK's *Do Androids Dream of Electric Sheep?* (**1968**), where pollution has destroyed the animal kingdom, and which, much changed, was the basis of the film BLADE RUNNER (1982); and John BOWEN's *After the Rain* (**1958**), dealing with the psychology of the survivors of a great flood.

Paramount among such books is Walter M. MILLER's *A Canticle for Leibowitz* (fixup **1960**), an ironic black comedy about the ways in which a post-holocaust civilization's history recapitulates the errors of its predecessor. The story is set largely in an abbey, where fragments of half-understood technological knowledge have been kept alive by the Church. The book is vivid, morose and ebulliently inventive; it has been very influential.

Miller's vision of technology as being (though morally neutral) at once saviour and destroyer is echoed in several books, including some already cited, in which an antitechnological majority, usually medieval in social structure and rigidly conservative in outlook, is unable to suppress the scientific curiosity of young malcontents; two good examples are Leigh BRACKETT's *The Long Tomorrow* (**1955**) and John WYNDHAM's *Re-Birth* (**1955** US; rev vt *The Chrysalids* UK). (The English disaster novel at this time was dominated by Wyndham and by John CHRISTOPHER, both writing several post-holocaust novels.) At a more popular, adventure-story level, several writers have picked up the idea (found also in the Brackett and Wyndham novels) of a secret enclave of scientifically advanced technocrats in an otherwise primitive world. Such is the situation in Piers ANTHONY's trilogy collected as *Battle Circle* (omni **1977**), which began with *Sos the Rope* (**1968**). A film pitting barbarians against an island of technology is ZARDOZ (1973), where the sympathy, as often happens, is with the barbarian. In stories of this type technology is generally feared, since it was through technology that mankind almost destroyed itself; a furtive technology is pitted against MAGIC in a FAR-FUTURE post-holocaust venue in Fred SABERHAGEN's trilogy consisting of *The Broken Lands* (**1968**), *The Black Mountains* (**1971**) and *Changeling Earth* (**1973**), but here, despite a tenuous rationale, the tone of the story is more that of SWORD AND SORCERY than of sf proper. Indeed, many sword-and-sorcery stories are set in a post-holocaust period when mankind has taken the route of magic rather than science; the rather silly idea is presumably that if we give up depending on technology we may be able to work miracles instead. In one of the commonest variants the magic is rationalized: the post-holocaust society develops PSI POWERS.

With the increased publicity given to the so-called counterculture in the late 1960s (reflected in sf by the NEW WAVE), post-holocaust stories of rather a different kind became popular. Hell's-Angels-style motorcycle gangs roam a ruined world in two colourful romances, Roger ZELAZNY's *Damnation Alley* (**1969**), badly filmed with many changes as DAMNATION ALLEY (1977), and Steve WILSON's *The Lost Traveller* (**1976**); the same idea is used more subtly in a grimmer work, Brian W. Aldiss's *Barefoot in the Head* (fixup **1969**), as motorcyclists roll through the debris of a Europe half-destroyed by the use of psychedelic drugs as weapons. J.G. BALLARD's *oeuvre* is made up largely of post-holocaust stories; he has evoked catastrophes of all sorts, manmade and natural, sudden and protracted, and often his protagonists act in psychic collaboration with the forces that threaten humanity's security. Scarred motorways continue to link up the decaying communities of M. John HARRISON's forceful first novel, *The Committed Men* (**1971**), which has something of a Ballardian bleakness but a rather tougher survival mentality in the protagonists. Other notable post-holocaust stories of the late 1960s and the 1970s are *Heroes and Villains* (**1969**) by Angela CARTER, "The Snows are Melted, the Snows are Gone" (1969) by James TIPTREE Jr, "The Lost Continent" (1970) by Norman SPINRAD, *The End of the Dream* (**1972**) by Philip Wylie, returning to a theme he first worked with 40 years earlier, *Hiero's Journey* (**1973**) by Sterling LANIER, *Winter's Children* (**1974** UK) by Michael CONEY, *Earthwreck!* (**1974**) by Thomas N. SCORTIA, *Walk to the End of the World* (**1974**) by Suzy McKee CHARNAS, *Where Late the Sweet Birds Sang* (fixup **1976**) by Kate WILHELM, *The Stand* (cut **1978**, text largely restored and rev **1990** UK) by Stephen KING, and *Dreamsnake* (fixup **1978**) by Vonda N. MCINTYRE.

A fine story from this period was "A Boy and his Dog" (1969) by Harlan ELLISON, interestingly filmed as A BOY AND HIS DOG (1975). Indeed, the 1960s, and more prolifically the 1970s, saw many variations on the post-holocaust theme in the CINEMA aside from those already mentioned, including ON THE BEACH (1959), *The* WORLD, THE FLESH AND THE DEVIL (1959), *The* DAY OF THE TRIFFIDS (1963), *L' ultimo uomo della terra* (1964; vt *The Last Man on Earth*); KONEC SRPNA V HOTELU OZON (1966; vt *The End of August at the Hotel Ozone*), NIGHT OF THE LIVING DEAD (1968), *The* BED-SITTING ROOM (1969), GAS-S-S-S (1970), GLEN AND RANDA (1970), *The* OMEGA MAN (1971), NIPPON CHINBOTSU (1973; vt *The Submersion of Japan*; vt *Tidal Wave*), *The* ULTIMATE WARRIOR (1975), JUBILEE (1978), QUINTET (1979) and MAD MAX (1979); UK tv took up the idea with SURVIVORS (1975-7). The success of *Mad Max* not only produced two sequels but began a whole cycle of post-holocaust colourful-barbarian action thriller films that continued right through the 1980s, including 1990: I GUERRIERI DEL BRONX (1982; vt *Bronx Warriors*) and CITY LIMITS (1984). In fact the 1980s was a period in which the post-holocaust venue became primarily used as a conveniently barbaric backdrop for feats of romantic adventure and, perhaps more worryingly, for the macho acts of rapine and savagery that characterize SURVIVALIST FICTION, which became very popular at this time. Although the post-holocaust genre remained popular in the 1980s film industry, and produced a strange variety of films, it produced no great ones, perhaps the most telling being George A. ROMERO's DAY OF THE DEAD (1985). Others were FUKKATSU NO HI (1980; vt *Virus*), MEMOIRS OF A SURVIVOR (1981), *Le* DERNIER COMBAT (1983; vt *The Last Battle*), RED DAWN (1984), NIGHT OF THE COMET (1984), *The* QUIET EARTH (1985), SLIPSTREAM (1989) and HARDWARE (1990).

Earlier, post-holocaust venues had by the 1970s become popular in CHILDREN'S SF, a particularly good book being *Z for Zachariah* (**1975**) by Robert C. O'BRIEN. Too often, however, such books were designed to teach moral lessons of the currently approved kind, often simplistically; the typical holocaust of 1980s children's books features ecological spoliation brought about by evil capitalists, one of the livelier examples being *Scatterlings* (**1991**) by Isobelle CARMODY.

While post-holocaust scenarios in films (and in COMICS, where they became extremely popular) were tending to trivialize the genre, it remained an important and still very popular element in serious sf in book form. Interesting and rather admirable are the 7 **Pelbar** books of Paul O. WILLIAMS, beginning with *The Breaking of Northwall* (**1981**), in which fragmented societies in a rural post-holocaust USA begin slowly to knit themselves together. Another good series was Richard COWPER's **Corlay** trilogy (1976-82), a contemplative PASTORAL work set in England centuries after low-lying areas have been covered by the rising sea. William BARNWELL's **Blessing** trilogy (1980-81) features a fantastic quest in a world recovering after a holocaust deliberately brought about for metaphysical reasons. Storm CONSTANTINE's **Wraeththu** trilogy (1987-9) presents luridly but with some flair a hermaphroditic race arising in a devastated world. Notable single novels from the 1980s and since include *Voices in Time* (**1980**) by Hugh MacLENNAN, *In the Drift* (fixup **1984**) by Michael SWANWICK, *The Postman* (**1985**) by David BRIN, *Wolf in Shadow* (**1987**; vt *The Jerusalem Man* 1988 US) by David GEMMELL, *The Sea and Summer* (**1987**; vt *Drowning Towers* 1988 US) by George TURNER, *The Wall around Eden* (**1989**) by Joan SLONCZEWSKI, *Winterlong* (**1990**) by Elizabeth HAND and *Bone Dance: A Fantasy for Technophiles* (**1991**) by Emma BULL. But the outstanding post-holocaust novel of the decade was probably *Riddley Walker* (**1980**) by Russell HOBAN, in which the nature of the future civilization is vividly evoked through its devolved language (◊ LINGUISTICS).

Life after the holocaust is a theme that continues to grip the imagination. The idea of destroying our crowded, bureaucratic world and then rebuilding afresh offers an exciting psychic freedom. The rusting symbols of a technological past protruding into a more primitive, natural, future landscape are among the most potent of sf's icons. [PN]

HOLT, CONRAD G. ◊ John Russell FEARN.

HOLTBY, WINIFRED (1898-1935) UK writer who espoused, in *South Riding* (**1936**) and other novels and essays, the informed, complex FEMINISM which was also reflected in her near-future SATIRE, *The Astonishing Island* (**1933**): the island satirized is not Tristan da Cunha, from which the bewildered protagonist hails, but the UK. [JC]

HOLTEN, KNUD [r] ◊ DENMARK.

HOLT-WHITE, W(ILLIAM EDWARD BRADDEN) (1878-?) UK writer in various genres, author of 7 novels of sf interest. In *The Earthquake: A Romance of London in 1907* (**1906**) the ruined capital is taken in hand by an aristocratic Prime Minister. In *The Man who Stole the Earth* (**1909**), which begins as a RURITANIAN pot pourri of politics and romance, a love-lorn inventor bombs most of Europe into submission in his drive to wed the daughter of the King of Balkania, forcing the world, *en passant*, into a state of peace. *The Prime Minister's Secret* (**1910**) is marginal sf. *Helen of All Time* (**1910**) rather remarkably compresses into one volume an advanced airship (◊ TRANSPORTATION) and the REINCARNATION of Helen of Troy. *The Man who Dreamed Right* (**1910**), though suffering from WH-W's general tendency to overpack his tales to the point of parody, rather movingly depicts an innocent man whose dreams predict the future, and who is destroyed at the hands of the world's rulers (including Teddy Roosevelt), all desperate to corner his power. *The World Stood Still* (**1912**) not entirely plausibly describes the catastrophic effect on the world when its financiers go on strike; and *The Woman who Saved the World* (**1914**) concerns NEAR-FUTURE terrorism. [JC]

HOLZHAUSEN, CARL JOHAN [r] ◊ SCANDINAVIA.

HOME-GALL, EDWARD REGINALD [r] ◊ William Benjamin HOME-GALL.

HOME-GALL, WILLIAM BENJAMIN (1861-1936) UK writer, much of whose work was boys' fiction, including *Beyond the Northern Lights* (**1903**) as by Reginald Wray, a LOST-WORLD tale set near the North Pole. *The Dweller in the Half-Light* (**1923**), also as by Wray, is fantasy for adults. WBH-G's son, Edward Reginald Home-Gall (1899-   ), was the most prolific of all authors of boys' stories next to Frank Richards (usual pseudonym of Charles Hamilton [1876-1961]), and was responsible for two **Human Bat** tales: "Caught in the Spider's Web" (**1950**) and *The Human Bat v. the Robot Gangster* (**1950**). [JC]

HOMER (*c*800BC) The most famous of early Greek poets, generally supposed to be the author of the *Iliad* and the *Odyssey*; these were probably not written down until the 6th century BC, and come to us in much later versions. The *Odyssey* is not, of course, sf, but stands paradigmatically at the head of the PROTO-SCIENCE-FICTION genre of the FANTASTIC VOYAGE. In Homer's day the Mediterranean was a *tabula rasa*, just as the worlds of outer space are today; to say that the *Odyssey* is a kind of first-millennium-BC template for PLANETARY ROMANCE may be to confuse the sublime with the ridiculous, but its aspiring spirit, always seeking to learn what is over the next horizon, testifies to the longevity of those human feelings which today are fed into the reading and writing of sf. [PN]

See also: MUSIC; MYTHOLOGY.

HOMUNCULUS (vt *Homunculus der Führer*) Serial film (1916). Deutsche Bioscop. Dir Otto Rippert, starring Olaf Fønss, Friedrich Kühne. Script Otto and Robert Neuss, based on a story by Robert Reinert. 6 episodes; total length 401 mins. B/w.

This 6-part silent German serial, the most popular of the WWI period, tells of an artificial man created by a scientist (Kühne) who wants to make a perfect creature of pure reason. But the result, Homunculus (the Danish actor Fønss), resents the fact that he is not a real human being (and has no soul); after being driven from country to country he becomes the dictator of a large, unnamed nation and plans to conquer the world, being finally destroyed by a convenient bolt of lightning. *H* contains seminal themes of the GOTHIC variety, foreshadowing many sf/HORROR films: the archetypal mad SCIENTIST, the inherent evil of TECHNOLOGY and scientific progress, superhuman ANDROIDS, conquest of the world and a fiery, apocalyptic climax. [JB]

HOMUNCULUS DER FÜHRER ◊ HOMUNCULUS.

HONEY, I SHRUNK THE KIDS Film (1989). Walt Disney. Dir Joe Johnston, starring Rick Moranis, Matt Frewer, Thomas Brown, Amy O'Neill, Robert Oliveri. Screenplay Ed NAHA, Tom Schulman, from a story by Stuart Gordon, Brian Yuzna and Ed Naha. 93 mins. Colour.

Eccentric inventor Szalinski (Moranis) builds a miniaturizing machine which is accidentally activated, shrinking his own two children and those of his macho next-door neighbour. Swept up in the trash they emerge in the garden, have adventures, fall tentatively in love (the two eldest), return, almost get eaten in a bowl of breakfast cereal, and are ultimately regrown. The special effects sequences are well done and the film is fun. [PN]

HONG KONG ◊ CHINESE SF.

HOOBLER, THOMAS (?1944-   ) US writer of an sf adventure, *The Hunters* (**1978**) with Burt WETANSON, and of *Dr Chill's Project* (**1987**; vt *Dr Chill* 1989 UK), an sf juvenile involving PSI POWERS.   [JC]

HOOVER, H(ELEN) M(ARY) (1935-   ) US writer, all of whose novels of sf interest have been juveniles for older children. First were *Children of Morrow* (**1973**) and its sequel, *Treasures of Morrow* (**1976**), a post-HOLOCAUST sequence which, in describing a reactionary state and its pro-TECHNOLOGY successor, plumps cautiously for the latter; the books demonstrate a smoothly searching style and a grasp of character. HMH soon showed her competence with a wide range of venues and themes. *The Delikon* (**1977**), again set on Earth, investigates a political revolution. The protagonist of *The Rains of Eridan* (**1978**), set on an ALIEN world where scientific stations are assaulted by waves of seemingly unnatural fear, uncovers the mystery without betraying the methods and goals of science. *Return to Earth* (**1980**), set a millennium hence on Earth, humanizes a thriller plot through its close portrayal of a growing friendship between an old man and a young girl – friendship between generations being unusually evident in HMH's work. The two young protagonists of *This Time of Darkness* (**1980**) transcend the bleak POCKET-UNIVERSE society in which they have been raised. *Another Heaven, Another Earth* (**1981**) intriguingly presents a complex vision of human limitations on a colony planet which is demonstrably inimical to life. Throughout, HMH shows a deft attentiveness to the problem of engaging her readership in tales of worlds whose solidity precludes easy triumphs for young protagonists, but which gives them a chance to achieve an enlightened freedom; always there is a sense that in the end the lessons awaiting readers in her texts are unequivocally meant to be learned. Her novels are, in the best sense, didactic.   [JC]
Other works: *The Lost Star* (**1979**); *This Time of Darkness* (**1980**); *The Bell Tree* (**1982**); *The Shepherd Moon: A Novel of the Future* (**1984**); *Orvis* (**1987**; vt *Journey through the Empty* 1990 UK); *The Dawn Palace: The Story of Medea* (**1988**); *Away is a Strange Place to Be* (**1990**).
See also: CHILDREN'S SF.

HOPE, LAURA LEE ◊ Harriet S. ADAMS.

HOPKINS, JAMES [r] ◊ William F. NOLAN; Robert REGINALD.

HORLAK, E.E. ◊ Sheri S. TEPPER.

HORLER, SYDNEY (1888-1954) UK writer, most of whose 150 novels are thrillers, some importing sf devices in the form of fantastic inventions and/or MCGUFFINS. Some of the **Paul Vivanti** sequence – specifically *The Mystery of No. 1* (**1925**; vt *The Order of the Octopus* 1926 US), *The Screaming Skull, and Other Stories* (coll **1930**; cut c1945), *The Worst Man in the World* (**1930**), *Lord of Terror* (**1935**) and *Virus X* (**1945**) – are of interest in their admixture of occult and fragmentary superscience elements, with DEATH RAYS making an appearance or two. The title story in *The*

Man who Shook the Earth (coll **1933**) features an attempt to blackmail the world by a SCIENTIST who has discovered the secret of atomic energy.   [JC]
Other works: *The Formula: A Novel of Harley Street* (**1933**; vt *The Charlatan* 1934 US); *The Vampire* (**1935**); *The Evil Messenger* (**1938**); *The House with the Light* (**1948**); *The House of the Uneasy Dead* (**1950**); *The Face of Stone* (**1952**).

HORN, PETER House name used in ZIFF-DAVIS magazines by Henry KUTTNER once, for "50 Miles Down" (*Fantastic Adventures* 1940), and by David Vern (◊ David V. REED) twice, also in 1940.   [JC/PN]

HORNE, R. HENGIST [s] ◊ Richard Henry HORNE.

HORNE, RICHARD HENRY (1803-1884) UK writer credited by William WILSON as the author of what is, according to Wilson's DEFINITION OF SF, an exemplary work of "Science-Fiction": *The Poor Artist, or Seven Eye-sights and One Object* (**1871**), a didactic novella in which a struggling artist achieves success by reproducing seven different images of a coin as perceived by various woodland creatures. RHH signed some of his other work R. Hengist Horne.   [BS]
See also: PERCEPTION.

HORNER, DONALD W(ILLIAM) (1874-?   ) UK astronomer, meteorologist and writer who specialized in popular-science texts. Though published as boys' fiction, *By Aeroplane to the Sun: Being the Adventures of a Daring Aviator and his Friends* (**1910**) offers a numerate and complex vision of a high-tech NEAR FUTURE, featuring picturephones, tv and electric cars, and describing the protagonists' usual tour of the Solar System with prescient realism. The ship operates by a kind of ION DRIVE; its inhabitants, some of whom are women, use pressure suits when necessary; and the planets themselves, as well as the cool SUN, offer a wide range of challenges. *Their Winged Destiny: Being a Tale of Two Planets* (**1912**; vt *The World's Double: Being a Tale of Two Planets* 1913) expands the scope of the earlier book, sending its astronauts from a possibly doomed Earth to its double in orbit around Alpha Centauri. Both novels demonstrate the speed with which the advance of science – DWH was of course no amateur – was engendering radical changes in the venues and plotting conventions that went to make up GENRE SF long before the founding of AMAZING STORIES in 1926.   [JC]

HORNIG, CHARLES D. (1916-   ) US editor whose career began in 1933 when, as a young sf fan, he started a FANZINE called *The Fantasy Fan* and happened to send a copy of it to Hugo GERNSBACK. By coincidence, Gernsback was at that time looking for a new managing editor for WONDER STORIES, and was so impressed by CDH's editorial that he decided to offer him the post. At 17, CDH became the youngest-ever sf magazine editor, attending evening classes at the same time until he finished high school. He edited *Wonder Stories* Nov 1933-Apr 1936, when the magazine was sold to another publisher and became THRILLING WONDER STORIES. CDH did not give up his fan activities, continuing *The Fantasy Fan* on a monthly basis until early 1935. At Gernsback's instigation he began the SCIENCE FICTION LEAGUE, a club centred on *Wonder Stories*. CDH initiated a "new-story" policy in an attempt to emulate the "thought-variant" stories published by F. Orlin TREMAINE in *ASF*; but this did not achieve many notable results – although he did publish Stanley G. WEINBAUM's first story, "A Martian Odyssey" (1934), to great acclaim. He published one story of his own under the pseudonym Derwin Lesser, used again in articles he contributed to the magazine SCIENCE FICTION, which he edited from its inception in Mar 1939. He also edited two companion magazines: FUTURE FICTION and SCIENCE FICTION QUARTERLY. None of these magazines achieved any distinction; they were taken over (and the first 2 titles amalgamated) by Robert A.W. LOWNDES in 1941. A convinced pacifist, CDH was a conscientious objector to WWII, and in 1942 was assigned to a public-service forestry camp. He left in 1943 and was imprisoned later the same year as an absolute objector to all forms of wartime service. [MJE]

HORROR! ◊ CHILDREN OF THE DAMNED.

HORROR CHAMBER OF DR FAUSTUS, THE ◊ *Les* YEUX SANS VISAGE.

HORROR EXPRESS ◊ PANICO EN EL TRANSIBERIANO.

HORROR IN SF The often propounded notion that sf is a literature of rational, scientifically based extrapolation is in most instances false. Much sf is anti-science, for reasons partly historic and perhaps partly intrinsic. The famous remark of the Spanish painter Goya (1746-1828) that the Sleep of Reason breeds Monsters is inarguable in its most obvious meaning: when rationality is in abeyance, terrible things happen. But the phrase seems to allow a rather different interpretation, one of great significance to sf: that it is science itself which, when it dreams, dreams monsters; in other words, the link between the bright light of science and the darkness of monstrousness is a link of blood and kinship. Certainly much sf might lead us to suppose that this apparent paradox is true.

Brian W. ALDISS argued in *Billion Year Spree* (**1973**) that sf "was born from the Gothic mode" in the 19th century (◊ GOTHIC SF), and that was also one of the birthplaces of horror fiction; certainly many of sf's early manifestations were horrible indeed, with E.T.A. HOFFMANN's malign ROBOT-maker Coppelius, Mary SHELLEY's FRANKENSTEIN MONSTER, Robert Louis STEVENSON's Jekyll and Hyde, Nathaniel HAWTHORNE's poison-saturated daughter of the scientist Rappaccini, and Edgar Allan POE's rotting M. Valdemar being celebrated but not untypical examples.

In the flurry of fantastic fiction published in magazines and PULP MAGAZINES between, say, 1880 and 1930, occult and supernatural fiction and sf were so closely related as to be disentangled only with the greatest difficulty, and sometimes not very convincingly. Ambrose BIERCE, Algernon BLACKWOOD, Arthur Conan DOYLE, William Hope HODGSON, Arthur MACHEN and A. MERRITT are only a few of the very many writers of that half-century whose work hovered between sf's light and horror's darkness. Even during and after the 1930s, when pulp fiction was being more and more categorized into separate groups, we find that it was not just the sf magazines like *AMZ* and *ASF* that published sf: much sf, of an often horrific kind, continued to appear in WEIRD TALES, a magazine largely devoted to supernatural fiction. Even H.P. LOVECRAFT wrote some borderline sf. In the ordinary world, science, then as now, came in two guises: on the one hand it offered a gleaming, safe future; on the other it carried us to the brink of apocalypse. Its medical research might unleash new diseases, its robots run amok, its intellectualism generate a race with huge brains and withered bodies, its physics create death rays or atomic bombs. Science was ungodly; it might even awaken the dead.

Sf is, even now, by and large written by ordinary people rather than scientists. This was almost exclusively so in the 1930s, and it is no wonder that much of the sf of those early years gave science a bad press. Many people agree that sf should be about science, but that has never meant that sf should *like* science. The anti-scientism of much 1930s sf (also visible at the more reputable end of the spectrum in the work of writers like C.S. LEWIS) did no more than reflect the fears of the 1930s, fears that are in no wise abated in the 1990s. Public anxieties aroused by science and technology are bound to manifest themselves in fiction, especially horror fiction; this is natural and unsurprising. The only surprising thing about it is that so many commentators on the genre are surprised by it. These commentators have, of course, endeavoured to banish sf/horror from the sf genre, and some have actually contrived DEFINITIONS OF SF intended to do just this. Wishing, however, does not make it so; and the fact is that the supposed splitting in the 1920s and 1930s of the fantastic-fiction tradition into separate genres of sf, horror and FANTASY never really took place – or, at least, that the process was never completed.

This failure to exorcise the demons from sf is most visible in sf CINEMA. To this day maybe half of *all* sf movies are horror movies. Of the 250 or so films given entries in this encyclopedia that could be cited to demonstrate the case, a few dozen or so of the most prominent should be sufficient. In the 1920s we had DR JEKYLL AND MR HYDE, METROPOLIS, ALRAUNE (vt *Unholy Love*; vt *Daughter of Destiny*) and ORLACS HÄNDE (vt *The Hands of Orlac*); in the 1930s we had FRANKENSTEIN, MAD LOVE, *The* INVISIBLE MAN, KING KONG and ISLAND OF LOST SOULS; in the 1940s (when there was almost no sf cinema at all) we had DR CYCLOPS and *The* LADY AND THE MONSTER; the 1950s offered rich pickings with *The* THING, *The* BEAST FROM 20,000 FATHOMS, INVADERS FROM MARS, THEM!, *The* QUATERMASS XPERIMENT, TARANTULA, INVASION OF THE BODY SNATCHERS, *The* BLOB and I MARRIED A MONSTER FROM OUTER SPACE, among very many others; things slowed down a little in the 1960s with VILLAGE OF THE DAMNED, *The* DAMNED, *The* BIRDS, X – THE MAN WITH THE X-RAY EYES, DR STRANGELOVE: OR HOW I LEARNED TO STOP WORRYING AND LOVE THE BOMB, TERRORE NELLO SPAZIO (vt *Planet of the Vampires*), SECONDS, WEEKEND, QUATERMASS AND THE PIT, NIGHT OF THE LIVING DEAD and SCREAM AND SCREAM AGAIN; in the 1970s we saw *A* CLOCKWORK ORANGE, FROGS, *The* CRAZIES, IT'S ALIVE!, WESTWORLD, *The* PARASITE MURDERS, *The* STEPFORD WIVES, BUG, DEMON SEED, COMA, PIRANHA, *The* BROOD and, most notably of all, ALIEN; in the 1980s there were ALTERED STATES, SATURN 3, SCANNERS, *The* THING, VIDEODROME, *Der* LIFT, *The* TERMINATOR, RE-ANIMATOR, *The* FLY, PREDATOR, MONKEY SHINES, THEY LIVE, SOCIETY, TREMORS, HARDWARE, DARKMAN and ALIENS; already in the 1990s we have had TERMINATOR 2: JUDGMENT DAY and ALIEN3. All of these are sf. All of these can be described as horror.

There is something going on here beyond anxieties about science. It is the theme (discussed in detail under GOTHIC SF and again under MONSTER MOVIES) of the incursion of the irrational into an apparently calm and ordered venue – an intrusion that in the real world we all fear with good reason; for this fear (which is for some an active desire) we may need a catharsis in harmless fictional form. It is a theme for which the metaphoric flexibility of sf is peculiarly well adapted to cater. The worldview of PARANOIA is one that sf has often adopted.

Horror itself, as a separate genre, has roots older than those of sf, and had begun to develop its distinctive patterns by the time of the Romantic movement in the very early 19th century – a little earlier than sf. Like sf it was by the 1930s widely if incorrectly considered as distinct from other literary genres. Horror did not, however, become a major genre in the mass market until the late 1970s and early 1980s – a boom that partly resulted from Stephen KING's popularity – and later in the 1980s it began to seem as if the horror wave had already crested. It is a genre defined not by its content but by its presumptive effect – this is why it so readily overlaps with other genres which *are* identified by their content; we know that horror-sf is common, and lately there has been a mini-boom in horror Westerns. Various critical attempts have been made, seldom very convincingly, to distinguish between horror and weird fiction, or horror and terror, or even horror and the New Gothic. (The term "horror" is regarded by some as an unpleasant lowest-common-denominator word for the genre, hence the occasional search for something that sounds more respectable, such as "dark fantasy"; but some contrary writers glory in even less attractive terms, like the current "splatterpunk" [*see also* SPLATTER MOVIES]. Regardless of what terms critics use, the predominant marketing term remains "horror".) Horror fiction can be either psychological horror – often psychopaths cutting up women with sharp instruments, sometimes the inner landscapes of maimed minds – or supernatural horror, or very often both, stories in the second category being (perhaps) no more than an externalization of the demons conjured up within the first.

When sf collides with horror it is, curiously enough, usually via the supernatural category, though very often in a rationalized format (◊ GODS AND DEMONS; GOLEM; SUPERNATURAL CREATURES) where some kind of quasiscientific explanation is given – as in Richard MATHESON's *I Am Legend* (**1954**) and Brian M. STABLE-FORD's *The Empire of Fear* (**1988**), both vampire novels – for apparently unnatural, and often horrible, manifestations. (The term MONSTER is sometimes reserved for more overtly sciencefictional horrors, like the carnivorous killer in *Alien*.) Just as sf often uses horror motifs, so too does horror sometimes use sf motifs, as in Joe R. Lansdale's *The Drive-In 2: Not Just One of Them Sequels* (**1989**), in which a "big red comet" causes carnivorous dinosaurs to manifest in a metamorphosed Texas. Lansdale is one of the many interesting writers lacking entries in this encyclopedia because their use (if any) of sf tropes is so inexplicable; but his borderline case does serve to show up the insecurity any scholar must feel in attempting to dissect horror, fantasy and sf out from each other.

There seems little point in listing here sf authors whose work contains major horror components; such a list would be not only unmanageably long but also rather arbitrary, for such genre-crossing occurs in work of very varied literary ambition and for a variety of purposes, some horror-sf stories being admonitory fables, others exercises in the provision of rollercoaster thrills, still others tales of mental breakdown and the hallucinatory worlds such illness can produce. As argued above, horror cannot easily be defined by content, only by its desired effect, which may be a matter of auctorial tone, or of lethal subtext. Coagulations of horror with sf have come from authors as various as Ray BRADBURY and Thomas M. DISCH, Charles BEAUMONT and Dan SIMMONS, Clark Ashton SMITH and L. Ron HUBBARD, Frank Belknap LONG and Dean R. KOONTZ, Gerald KERSH and K.W. JETER. The theme of CHILDREN IN SF, in particular, is a hothouse for such crossovers.

With sf cinema it is possible to be very much more specific: the *auteur* directors who have specialized in blending sf with horror are first and foremost David CRONENBERG and then, still importantly, Larry COHEN, Roger CORMAN, George A. ROMERO and Ridley SCOTT, in turn followed perhaps by Charles BAND, James CAMERON, John CARPENTER, Michael CRICHTON and Joe DANTE, along with the important film-writer Nigel KNEALE.

There are many books and magazines about horror. A particularly useful quarterly magazine that sometimes considers horror-sf crossover books – and a better informed and more intelligent review than many magazines in the field – is *Necrofile: The Review of Horror Fiction* ed Stefan Dziemianowicz, S.T. Joshi and Michael Morrison, published by Necronomicon Press, Rhode Island, USA, since Summer 1991. [PN]

HORSNELL, HORACE (1882-1949) UK drama critic and novelist whose *Man Alone* (1940) describes the experiences of the last man on Earth as he wanders through London after the final DISASTER. *Castle Cottage* (1940) is a ghost story and *The Cool of the Evening* (1942) a rather gentle ADAM-AND-EVE fable set at the close of Adam's life. [JC]

HORTON, GORDON T. [r] ◊ ROBERT HALE LIMITED.

HOSHI, SHIN'ICHI (1926-   ) One of the pioneers of Japanese sf. SH, who has specialized in the short-short story, became the first full-time sf writer in JAPAN. His stories were influential on the younger generation, and he was largely responsible for the popularization of sf and its way of thinking. He has developed a writing style that gives an sf flavour even to his non-sf works, and which is appropriate to his attacks on everyday values. Although he is sometimes called the Japanese Ray BRADBURY, his writings are more satirical than poetic: comparison with Fredric BROWN might be closer to the mark. A graduate of Tokyo University, he helped Takumi SHIBANO found *Uchujin*, the first Japanese FANZINE, in 1957; his first professional sale, "Sekisutora" ["Sextra"] (1957), had originally been published in *Uchujin* #2. His best known story is "Bokkochan" (1958; trans under same title *FSF* 1963); it also appeared in *Jinzo Bijin* ["A Man-Made Beauty"] (coll 1961). By 1983 he had published over 1000 stories, including two sf/fantasy novels: *Muma No Hyoteki* ["Target of Nightmare"] (1964), in which a ventriloquist is controlled by his doll, and *Koe No Ami* ["Net of the Voice"] (1970), in which a telephone network becomes conscious and takes control of human society. Other works have included historical novellas, collections of unconventional short essays, and fictionalized documentaries including biographies of his father and grandfather. An important multivolume retrospective is *Hoshi Shin'ichi No Sakuhinshu* ["The Complete Works of Shin'ichi Hoshi"] (coll 1974). Two books of English translations are *The Spiteful Planet and Other Stories* (coll trans 1978 Tokyo) and *There was a Knock* (coll trans 1984 Tokyo), the latter collecting short-short stories. [TSh]

HOSKINS, ROBERT (1933-) US writer and editor. RH began publishing sf with "Feet of Clay" for *If* in 1958 as by Phillip Hoskins. He worked as a literary agent 1967-8, and served as senior editor with Lancer Books from 1969 until the firm closed in 1972. His first published novel, *Evil in the Family* (1972) as by Grace Corren, is a TIME-TRAVEL fantasy. *The Shattered People* (1975) is FAR-FUTURE sf, pitting a primitive culture against a technological civilization which has been exploiting it. The **Stars** sequence – *Master of the Stars* (1976 Canada), *To Control the Stars* (1977) and *To Escape the Stars* (1978) – is based loosely on RH's "The Problem Makers" (1963), and describes a cluster of galactic civilizations, connected by a system of ancient stargates, over a period of eons. *Legacy of the*

Stars (1979) as by John Gregory is an sf adventure unconnected to the sequence. RH's books make no claims to be anything more than entertaining action adventures.

As an anthologist, RH is of primary importance as editor of the INFINITY series of original anthologies: *Infinity #1* (anth 1970), *#2* (anth 1971), *#3* (anth 1972), *#4* (anth 1972) and *#5* (anth 1973). [PN/JC]

Other works: *Tomorrow's Son* (1977); *Jack-in-the-Box Planet* (1978), juvenile sf; *The Attic Child* (1979) as by Grace Corren; *The Night Runner: The Gemini Run* ∗ (1979) as by Michael Kerr.

Other works as editor: *First Step Forward* (anth 1969); *The Stars Around Us* (anth 1970); *Swords against Tomorrow* (anth 1970); *The Far-Out People* (anth 1971); *Tomorrow One* (anth 1971); *Wondermakers* (anth 1972); *Strange Tomorrows* (anth 1972); *The Edge of Never* (anth 1973), fantasy; *Wondermakers 2* (anth 1974); *The Liberated Future* (anth 1974); *The Future Now: Saving Tomorrow* (anth 1977); *Against Tomorrow* (anth 1979).

HOUGH, S(TAN) B. [r] ◊ Rex GORDON.

HOUGHTON, CLAUDE Pseudonym of Claude Houghton Oldfield (1889-1961), a UK writer known primarily outside the sf field. He declared that all his work was based on the thesis that modern civilization must collapse "because it no longer believes it has a destiny"; thus his novels of ideas occasionally stray into the surreal, the supernatural or the sciencefictional. His one borderline-sf novel is *This was Ivor Trent* (1935), which examines the effect upon a writer of a vision which reveals to him a man of the future. His first novel, *Neighbours* (1927), is an intriguing study in abnormal PSYCHOLOGY whose narrator makes an obsessive study of his "next-door neighbour", unaware of the fact that he is merely an alienated facet of his subject's mind. Some of CH's later works also feature eccentric psychologies, but their fantastic elements are minimal. *Julian Grant Loses his Way* (1933) is a bitterly misanthropic character-study cast in the form of a posthumous fantasy. *Three Fantastic Tales* (coll 1934 chap) contains 3 brief philosophical fantasies. [BS]

See also: SUPERMAN.

HOUSE, [Colonel] EDWARD MANDELL (1858-1938) US political figure – in his refusal of official duties rather like an earlier Bernard Baruch (1870-1965) – involved with President Woodrow Wilson in setting up the League of Nations. *Philip Dru, Administrator: A Story of Tomorrow, 1920-1935* (1912) is a surprisingly wide-ranging exercise in political sf. After a cartel of corrupt business tycoons attempts to suborn the US Government, Dru instigates a new Civil War, wins, and in place of the old US Government establishes a radical UTOPIA that features universal suffrage and other "socialist" innovations. He then saves the rest of the world. [JC]

HOUSEHOLD, GEOFFREY (1900-1988) UK writer who remains best known for *Rogue Male* (1938), the first of a run of thrillers whose intensely stoic lone protagonists condemn the political world, seeking authenticity in the soil and in autonomous acts, like the attempted assassination of Hitler which forms the premise of this book. GH's first novel, *The Terror of Villadonga* (**1936**; rev vt *The Spanish Cave* 1936 US), for older children, describes the discovery of a prehistoric sea-beast. *The Third Hour* (**1937**) sends its protagonist to South America in search of UTOPIA. *The Dance of the Dwarfs* (**1968**) is set in the Amazon basin, where feral prehistoric survivals cause some horrific damage. *The Cats to Come* (**1975**) is a fantasy about a future Earth ruled by cats. *Hostage: London; The Diary of Julian Despard* (**1977**) is a NEAR-FUTURE thriller. *The Sending* (**1980**) is a dark fantasy. *Summon the Bright Water* (**1981**) is a SCIENCE-FANTASY tale invoking ATLANTIS. *Arrows of Desire* (**1985**), set in a crumbling post-HOLOCAUST UK, expresses once again, and for the final time, GH's profound doubt that humanity could ever govern itself with dignity. [JC]

HOUSE NAMES ◊ PSEUDONYMS.

HOUSMAN, LAURENCE (1865-1959) UK writer, brother of the poet A.E. Housman (1859-1936) and best known for his plays and for several volumes of fantasy stories, including *Gods and their Makers* (coll **1897**; with stories added, vt *Gods and Their Makers and Other Stories* coll 1920), *What Next? Provocative Tales of Faith and Morals* (coll **1938**) and *Strange Ends and Discoveries* (coll **1948**). Some of his work for children, such as his first book, *A Farm in Fairyland* (coll **1894**), and some of his plays, such as *Possession* (**1921**), are also of fantasy interest, as is his novel *Trimblerigg* (**1924**). Closer to an sf interest are his two RURITANIAN tales, *John of Jingalo: The Story of a Monarch in Difficulties* (**1912**; vt *King John of Jingalo* 1912 US) and its sequel *The Royal Runaway, and Jingalo in Revolution* (**1914**); in both novels there is a running commentary on UTOPIAN social solutions, particularly with regard to WOMEN's rights. [JC]

Other works: *All-Fellows: Seven Legends of Lower Redemption* (coll **1896**) and *The Cloak of Friendship* (coll **1905**), both assembled with 1 additional story as *All-Fellows and the Cloak of Friendship* (omni **1924**); *The House of Joy* (coll **1895**) and *The Field of Clover* (coll **1898**), both recast, with *A Farm in Fairyland*, as *Moonshine and Clover* (coll **1922**) and *A Doorway to Fairyland* (coll **1923**); *The Blue Moon* (coll **1904**); *Ironical Tales* (coll **1926**).

HOUSTON, DAVID Pseudonym of US writer Houston Force Lumpkin III (1938-   ), who produced sf books with some intensity for a few years. Generally unremarkable, though competent, his works began with *Alien Perspective* (**1978**) and an sf-adventure sequence comprising *Gods in a Vortex* (**1979**) and *Wingmaster* (**1981**). He then wrote a series of novels tied to the TALES OF TOMORROW tv series: *Tales of Tomorrow #1: Invaders at Ground Zero* * (**1981**), *#2: Red Dust* * (**1981**), *#3: Substance X* * (**1981**) and *#4: Ice from Space* * (**1982**). He was also responsible for *Swamp Thing* * (**1982**) with Len Wein, a SWAMP THING film tie. [JC]

HOVORKA, ROBERT L(EO) Jr (1955-   ) US writer

whose first sf novel, the SPACE OPERA *Derelict* (**1988**), is reminiscent of ALIEN (1979). [JC]

HOWARD, (JOHN) HAYDEN (?   -   ) US writer who began publishing sf with "It" for *Planet Stories* in 1952. His sf novel, *The Eskimo Invasion* (fixup **1967**), set (rather unusually) in Canada, comprises a speculative view of OVERPOPULATION problems through a story about a group of Eskimos transformed into an apparently benign, fast-breeding new species. [JC]

HOWARD, IVAN (?   -   ) US editor who produced 7 anthologies 1962-4 for Belmont books, and nothing since: *The Weird Ones* (anth **1962**; IH uncredited), *Escape to Earth* (anth **1963**), *Novelets of Science Fiction* (anth **1963**), *Rare Science Fiction* (anth **1963**), *6 and the Silent Scream* (anth **1963**), *Way Out* (anth **1963**) and *Things* (anth **1964**). [PN]

HOWARD, ROBERT E(RVIN) (1906-1936) US writer. REH wrote no sf – although *Almuric* (1939 *Weird Tales*; **1964**) is a PLANETARY ROMANCE in the manner of Edgar Rice BURROUGHS – but his association with H.P. LOVECRAFT and WEIRD TALES helped to maintain the sf community's interest in his extravagant SWORD-AND-SORCERY stories. His few contributions to Lovecraft's **Cthulhu Mythos** do not bring out the sf elements. He was the real parent and inspiration of the sword-and-sorcery (or HEROIC FANTASY) genre (although earlier writers have been retrospectively recruited to it by historians), which existed as an enclave of the sf marketplace until FANTASY became a marketing category in the late 1960s, after which REH's work enjoyed a spectacular posthumous boom. His first professionally published story was "Spear and Fang" for *Weird Tales* in 1925; he quickly became an amazingly prolific writer of vigorous adventure fiction in several pulp genres.

REH's most celebrated works are those which comprise the **Conan the Barbarian** series; 17 of these appeared in *Weird Tales* 1932-6, and 4 more were published posthumously. The series has been extended vastly, first by the fan Bjorn Nyberg (1929-   ), whose pastiche novel was edited by L. Sprague DE CAMP; then De Camp turned several other unpublished REH stories into **Conan** stories, and he and Lin CARTER wrote many more around fragments and outlines as well as creating pastiches of their own. Further adventures have been produced by Andrew J. OFFUTT, Robert Jordan (1948-   ) and Steve PERRY, among others. The popularity of the series was further enhanced by the film *Conan the Barbarian* (1981) starring Arnold Schwarzenegger, although it de-emphasized the fantasy element. The bibliography of the series is inordinately complicated, but the whole of the authentic canon can be found in 5 GNOME PRESS vols: in order of internal chronology, *The Coming of Conan* (coll **1953**; includes 2 non-series stories, 2 revisions and some supplementary material), *Conan the Barbarian* (coll **1955**), *The Sword of Conan* (coll **1952**), *King Conan* (coll **1953**) and *Conan the Conqueror* (1935 *Weird Tales* as "The Hour of the Dragon"; **1950**; rev vt *The Hour of the Dragon* 1977).

Gnome also issued the De Camp/Nyberg *The Return of Conan* (**1957**; vt *Conan the Avenger*) and the De Camp revisions in *Tales of Conan* (coll **1955**). Lancer published 11 vols of a 12-vol set, later completed and reissued by ACE BOOKS: again in order of internal chronology, these are *Conan* (coll **1967**), *Conan of Cimmeria* (coll **1969**), *Conan the Freebooter* (coll **1968**), *Conan the Wanderer* (coll **1968**), *Conan the Adventurer* (coll **1966**), *Conan the Buccaneer* (**1971**; by De Camp and Carter), *Conan the Warrior* (coll **1967**), *Conan the Usurper* (coll **1967**), *Conan the Conqueror* (**1967**), *Conan the Avenger* (**1968**), *Conan of Aquilonia* (coll **1977**; by De Camp and Carter) and *Conan of the Isles* (**1968** by De Camp and Carter). Using the original magazine texts, Donald M. Grant issued handsome illustrated editions of many of the REH stories including *The People of the Black Circle* (**1974**), *A Witch Shall Be Born* (**1975**), *The Tower of the Elephant* (coll **1975**), *Red Nails* (**1975**), *Rogues in the House* (coll **1976**), *The Devil in Iron* (coll **1976**), *Queen of the Black Coast* (coll **1978**), *Pool of the Black One* (coll **1986**) and *The Hour of the Dragon* (**1989**). A Berkley paperback series advertised as "the authorized edition" and ed Karl Edward Wagner includes *The Hour of the Dragon* (**1977**), *The People of the Black Circle* (coll **1977**) and *Red Nails* (coll **1977**). There is also an omnibus, *The Conan Chronicles* (omni **1989**). Two MARVEL COMICS based on the character are *Conan the Barbarian* and *The Savage Sword of Conan*.

Other REH sword-and-sorcery series include one set in Conan's imaginary prehistoric world, collected in *King Kull* (coll **1967**, ed and with additional material by Lin Carter; rev excluding Carter items, vt *Kull, the Fabulous Warrior King* 1978). Others are collected in *Bran Mak Morn* (coll **1969**; cut vt *Worms of the Earth* 1987) and *Red Shadows* (coll **1968**; vt in 3 vols as *The Moon of Skulls* 1969, *The Hand of Kane* 1970 and *Solomon Kane* 1971).

REH wrote at high speed and his work is unsophisticated, but it is vigorous, fast-paced and easy to read. His suicide – after learning of his mother's imminent death – brought to a premature end what might have been an extraordinarily productive career.   [MJE/BS]
Other works: *Skull-Face and Others* (coll **1946**; vt in 3 vols as *Skull-Face and Others* 1976 UK, *The Valley of the Worms, and Others* 1976 UK and *The Shadow Kingdom* 1976 UK); *Always Comes Evening* (coll **1957**), poetry; *The Dark Man and Others* (coll **1963**; cut vt *Pigeons from Hell* 1976); *Wolfshead* (coll **1968**); *Tigers of the Sea* (coll **1976**); *The Book of Robert E. Howard* (coll **1976**); *The Second Book of Robert E. Howard* (coll **1976**); *The Robert E. Howard Omnibus* (coll **1977**); *Sword Woman* (coll **1977**); *Black Canaan* (coll **1978**); *The Gods of Bal-Sagoth* (coll **1979**); *Lord of the Dead* (coll **1981**); *Cthulhu: The Mythos and Kindred Horrors* (coll **1987**) ed David A. DRAKE; *Shadows of Dreams* (coll **1989**), poetry.
About the author: *The Miscast Barbarian* (**1975** chap) by L. Sprague De Camp, reprinted in *Literary Swordsmen and Sorcerers* (coll **1976**); *The Last Celt* (**1976**) by Glenn Lord, bio-bibliography by the agent of REH's estate; *The Annotated Guide to Robert E. Howard's Sword & Sorcery* (**1976** chap) by Robert E. WEINBERG; *The Ultimate Guide to Howardia 1925-1975* (**1976**) ed Wayne Warfield; *The Dark Barbarian: The Writings of Robert E. Howard: A Critical Anthology* (**1984**) ed Don Herron.
See also: ARKHAM HOUSE; ATLANTIS; FANZINE; GODS AND DEMONS; MAGIC; PUBLISHING; SEX; SMALL PRESSES AND LIMITED EDITIONS.

HOWARD, TROY ◊ Lauran Bosworth PAINE.
HOWARD, WARREN F. [s] ◊ Frederik POHL.
HOWELL, SCOTT ◊ Paul CONRAD.
HOWELLS, WILLIAM DEAN (1837-1920) US writer, best known for his many realist novels from 1870 onwards. His UTOPIAN sequence, *A Traveller from Altruria* (1892-3 *Cosmopolitan*; **1894**) and *Through the Eye of the Needle* (Part One 1894 *Cosmopolitan*; exp **1907**), is a deceptively mild-mannered assault on the pretensions of late-19th-century US democracy and culture, seen from the perspective of a dreamlike visitor from Altruria, a land where the principles of Christianity and of the US Constitution, taken literally, result in an ethical form of socialism. In the second volume the visitor returns to Altruria with his US bride, and both send letters back describing that land, whose nature is somewhat influenced by the work of Edward BELLAMY, more so by that of William MORRIS. Capitalism has been replaced by a genuine altruistic "neighbourliness", and the two books attack hypocrisy and the more ruthless forms of capitalism in a manner both unmistakable and highly telling, even though gently put. *Letters of an Altrurian Traveller* (1893-4 *Cosmopolitan*; **1961**) assembles bridging material WDH published only in magazine form; *The Altrurian Romances* (omni **1968**) reprints everything. Much the same narrative technique reappears movingly in *The Seen and Unseen at Stratford-on-Avon* (**1914**), whose revived but ghostly Shakespeare, addressing the 20th-century narrator, sweetly defends his right to be considered the author of his own plays; the book is an answer to Mark TWAIN's *Is Shakespeare Dead?* (**1909**) which, after the fashion of the time, argues Francis BACON's authorship. *Questionable Shapes* (coll **1903**) and *Between the Dark and the Daylight* (coll **1907**), neither sf, assemble (along with other work) CLUB STORIES in which the psychologist Wanhope scientifically debunks the ghost stories of his fellow members.   [JC]
Other works: *The Undiscovered Country* **1880**; *The Leatherwood God* (**1916**).
As editor: *Shapes that Haunt the Dusk* (anth **1907**) with Henry Mills Alden.

HOWES, JANE ◊ Wilmar H. SHIRAS.
HOWL, MARCIA YVONNE [r] ◊ Sharon JARVIS.
HOWLING, THE ◊ Joe DANTE.
HOYLE, [Sir] FRED (1915-   ) UK astronomer and writer, famed in the former capacity for his maverick views on many subjects, including a long-held advocacy of the Steady State theory of the creation of the Universe, a concept replaced after much acrimony by the currently orthodox Big Bang theory. A possible consequence of his combative attitude towards

theory and his colleagues was the apparent weariness which afflicted him in 1973, the year of his knighthood, when he resigned his posts at Cambridge University as Plumian professor of ASTRONOMY and experimental philosophy, and as director of the Cambridge Institute of Theoretical Astronomy, which he had founded. He subsequently much increased the rate of his writing, both fiction and nonfiction. The first in the latter category, and his first book, *The Nature of the Universe* (**1950**), had eloquently popularized his COSMOLOGY in 1950s terms, as had what is possibly his most important popularization, *Frontiers of Astronomy* (**1955**); later works, like *Astronomy and Cosmology* (**1975** US), *Astronomy Today* (**1975**; vt *Highlights in Astronomy* 1975 US) and *The Universe According to Hoyle* (**1982** US), aggressively updated those arguments. More unusual postulates about the nature of the Universe were presented – with Chandra Wickramasinghe – in books such as *Lifecloud: The Origin of Life in the Universe* (**1979**), *Diseases from Space* (**1979**), *Evolution from Space* (**1981**) and *Cosmic Life-Force* (**1988**), which argue that complex organic molecules, including viruses, form in the nuclei of comets and are deposited on Earth during close encounters or impacts; they join the gene pool, making EVOLUTION possible. *Ice: The Ultimate Human Catastrophe* (**1981**) argues that a new Ice Age is imminent.

It could be argued that FH's formidable reputation and powers as a scientific intellect have obscured the true nature of his sf, none of which is told with anything like a strict adherence to scientific principles, plausible or speculative. His first novel, *The Black Cloud* (**1957**) postulates the arrival of a sentient cloud of gas from space which – in a manner reminiscent of the work of Edmond HAMILTON – proceeds to blot off the Sun's rays from Earth, killing the scientists who attempt full-scale COMMUNICATION with it, because such an intense exposure to the cloud's mentality overwhelmingly displaces their human conception of reality. In later novels offers of transcendence would affect FH's SCIENTISTS like catnip, giving them the chance both to escape "orthodox" science and to demonstrate an impatient contempt for civilian dealings: his books, which typically read as mystical romps into the transcendental, are of absorbing interest for their aggressive presentation of the argument that science-educated people are more fit to govern than arts-educated people, partly because numeracy is a necessary qualification for rulers but also because civilians face life through a tangle of disenabling emotions. FH's work, therefore, when it is not expressive of a holiday escapism, is consistently political (◊ POLITICS) in orientation.

Ossian's Ride (**1959**), his second novel, is told initially in a manner reminiscent of John Buchan (1875-1940) or Geoffrey HOUSEHOLD: a protagonist, on the run in rough-and-tumble Ireland from a posse of incompetent agents, gradually uncovers an underlying sf plot – at which point the book changes course utterly. Stranded ALIENS plan to transform Earth into

a rationalized, high-tech, skyscraper-packed UTOPIA, by force if necessary: they offer to recruit the protagonist, who joins them gladly. With John ELLIOT, FH next published *A for Andromeda* * (**1962**) and *Andromeda Breakthrough* * (**1964**), adapted from their tv serials with those titles (*which see*). With the exception of one further solo novel, *October the First is Too Late* (**1966**), an emotionally disjointing excursion through time-slipped areas of Earth, and a collection of stories, *Element 79* (coll **1967**), FH for some 20 years concentrated exclusively on collaborative work; *Comet Halley* (**1985**) noticeably lacked the drive of his collaborations. The obvious power of his personality is reflected in the fact that the novels written with Elliot, and the more important ones with his son Geoffrey HOYLE, differ in no significant way from the early solo efforts.

In the first novel with Geoffrey, *Fifth Planet* (**1963**), an alien intelligence offers, as usual, a challenge – and an ultimate marriage of minds – to a scientist who must attempt to make sense of events on Achilles, a grassy, wandering planet. *Rockets in Ursa Major* (**1962** as unpublished children's play by FH; rev **1969**) and its sequel, *Into Deepest Space* (**1974** US), are spasmodic SPACE OPERAS involving an ALIEN-guided trip through a BLACK HOLE. The protagonist of *The Incandescent Ones* (**1977** US), trapped on a DYSTOPIAN Earth, finds to his relief that he is an ANDROID, and thus entitled to discorporate into the higher consciousnesses who inhabit Jupiter. *The Westminster Disaster* (**1978**) welcomes a terrorist-inspired nuclear destruction of London, with the buildings of Whitehall coming "down like so many rotten fruit". But most interesting perhaps is *The Inferno* (**1973**), in which an explosion at the galactic core wipes out all human life except for small groups, mainly in Scotland, which an impatient scientist comes to rule: as wish-fulfilment, the tale is perhaps more self-revealing than many "civilian" authors would dare to pen; the power of the book, nevertheless, is very considerable. By this point, FH and his son had become adept at a style whose apparent disjointedness concealed an intensity which scathed the mundane world. In his best work, FH demonstrates not the power of scientific method but the personal allure of transcendental intoxication. His appeal is straightforward. In his hands, sf does not explain. It releases.   [JC/PN]

Other works: *The Small World of Fred Hoyle: An Autobiography* (**1986**).

With Geoffrey Hoyle: *Seven Steps to the Sun* (**1970**); *The Molecule Men and The Monster of Loch Ness: Two Short Novels* (coll **1971**); the **Professor Gamma** series of juvenile novels, comprising *The Energy Pirate* (**1982** chap), *The Frozen Planet of Azuron* (**1982** chap), *The Giants of Universal Park* (**1982** chap) and *The Planet of Death* (**1982** chap).

See also: ANTI-INTELLECTUALISM IN SF; CONCEPTUAL BREAKTHROUGH; CYBERNETICS; DISASTER; DISCOVERY AND INVENTION; INTELLIGENCE; LIVING WORLDS; MATHEMATICS; PARALLEL WORLDS; PHYSICS.

HOYLE, GEOFFREY (1941-   ) UK writer, author of several sf novels with his father, Fred HOYLE (*whom see for details*). *2010: Living in the Future* (**1972**) is a nonfiction exercise in FUTUROLOGY for children.   [JC]

HOYLE, TREVOR (1940-   ) UK writer who has, most unusually, been able to apply an erudite surrealism to works directed towards a mass market. He had not, however, yet mastered this technique for his first novel, *The Relatively Constant Copywriter* (**1972**), a dourly joky FABULATION which he self-published. He remains best known for his **Q** series – *Q: Seeking the Mythical Future* (**1977**), *Q: Through the Eye of Time* (**1977**) and *Q: The Gods Look Down* (**1977**) – set in a variety of ALTERNATE WORLDS and detailing the work and crises of its overall protagonist, a Myth Technologist who, in the second volume, must cope with the re-creation, on an alternate world, of an experimental Adolf Hitler whose existence threatens to leak into our own familiar Earth (◊ HITLER WINS). TH's mature range was demonstrated by the publication in the same year, 1979, of *This Sentient Earth* (**1979** US; vt *Earth Cult* 1979 UK), an unremarkable sf adventure, and *The Man who Travelled on Motorways* (**1979**), an intensely crafted hegira through the apocalyptic inscapes of a UK approaching the end. *The Last Gasp* (**1983** US; rev 1990) is a salutary dreadful-warning tale about terminal POLLUTION, implying very clearly that humanity's behaviour could be described as lemming-like. *Vail* (**1984**), once again focusing on motorways, presents a NEAR-FUTURE UK in DYSTOPIAN terms. *K.I.D.S.* (**1987**; vt *Kids* 1990 US) is a horror tale which climaxes in nuclear HOLOCAUST. It may be that, in finding several audiences, TH has failed to find any one audience that properly recognizes him; but he still has readers, and they continue to look for his work.   [JC]
Other works: Three BLAKE'S SEVEN tv ties, being *Blake's Seven* * (**1977**; vt *Terry Nation's Blake's 7: Their First Adventure* 1988 US), *#2: Project Avalon* * (**1979**; vt *Terry Nation's Blake's 7: Project Avalon* 1988 US) and *#3: Scorpio Attack* * (**1971**; vt *Terry Nation's Blake's 7: Scorpio Attack* 1988 US); *The Rock Fix* (**1977**); *The Stigma* (**1980**).

HOYNE, THOMAS TEMPLE (1875-1946) US writer, a popularizer of ECONOMICS topics and author of *Intrigue on the Upper Level: A Story of Crime, Love, Adventure and Revolt in 2050 A.D.* (**1934**), in which a primitive, hierarchical, gangster-run capitalist society is riven by discontent among the lower orders, and is eventually overthrown.   [JC]

HRUSKA, ALAN (?   -   ) US writer whose sf novel, *Borrowed Time* (**1984**), attempts with some success to suggest analogies and crossings between various ALTERNATE WORLDS and the bicameral human brain.   [JC]

HUANG HAI [r] ◊ CHINESE SF.

HUBBARD, L(AFAYETTE) RON(ALD) (1911-1986) US writer in many genres, including sf and fantasy, and subsequent quasireligious figure whose founding of DIANETICS and in 1952 the Church of SCIENTOLOGY led

to much controversy, which continues. He began publishing sf with "The Dangerous Dimension" for *ASF* in 1938, and remained active until, more than a decade later, he transferred his creative gifts to the RELIGION he founded. He wrote under his own name and as Kurt von Rachen, Rene Lafayette and Frederick Engelhardt; other names remain unrevealed. Though there is no hard and fast line, his fantasy, much of it published in *Unknown*, was frequently as by LRH, and his sf, mostly in *ASF*, was frequently pseudonymous (although at least 12 items, some of them full-length though yet-unreprinted novels, appeared in *ASF* as by LRH). Certainly LRH was for John W. CAMPBELL Jr, in the throes of creating his GOLDEN AGE OF SF, a worthwhile and prolific contributor to the two journals, though he was not a member of that small group – L. Sprague DE CAMP, Robert A. HEINLEIN and Isaac ASIMOV being the prime movers – who were rewriting the rules of generic plausibility in terms which survived for many years. Retrospective attempts to elect LRH to that central role are best seen as gestures of loyalty from those sympathethic to his later career.

His best-known early sf novel, *Final Blackout* (**1940** *ASF*; **1948**), grimly describes a world devastated by many wars in which a young army officer becomes dictator of the UK, which he organizes to fend off a decadent USA. It cannot be denied that the book veers extremely close to the fascism its text explicitly disavows. But sf was clearly not LRH's forte, and most of his work in the genre reads as tendentious or laboured or both. As a writer of fantasy, however, he wrote with an occasionally pixilated fervour that is still pleasing, and sometimes reminiscent of the screwball comedies popular in the 1930s cinema. *Slaves of Sleep* (**1939** *Unknown*; **1948**), with its sequel "The Masters of Sleep" (1950), his best-known fantasy, is laid in the Arabian Nights environment set aside for him by Campbell as his exclusive bailiwick in *Unknown*. The darkly PARANOID *Fear* (**1940** *Unknown*; **1957**) was perhaps rather stronger and more original, and demonstrated a powerful capacity to hook the reader into worlds where normal logic is distressingly maladaptive; it appeared also as one of the 2 novellas in *Typewriter in the Sky/Fear* (**1940** *Unknown* for "Typewriter in the Sky"; coll **1951**) and as one of the 2 novellas in *Fear & The Ultimate Adventure* (**1939** *Unknown* for "The Ultimate Adventure"; coll **1970**). "Typewriter in the Sky", a slyly effective self-referential FABULATION, may be his most permanently memorable work. *Return to Tomorrow* (1950 *ASF* as "To the Stars"; **1954**) is a remarkably ruthless SPACE OPERA (◊ SOCIAL DARWINISM). The **Ole Doc Methuselah** stories, as by Rene Lafayette, have been assembled as *Ole Doc Methuselah* (1947-50 *ASF*; coll **1970**). He wrote other series, too, notably the **Conquest of Space** series (as Lafayette) in *Startling Stories*, all but the last story in 1949: "Forbidden Voyage", "The Magnificent Failure", "The Incredible Destination", "The Unwilling Hero", "Beyond the

Black Nebula", "The Emperor of the Universe" and "The Last Admiral" (1950). As Kurt von Rachen he wrote the **Kilkenny Cats** series, all in *ASF*: "The Idealists" (1940), "The Kilkenny Cats" (1940), "The Traitor" (1941), "The Mutineers" (1941) and "The Rebels" (1942). In general his early work, though composed with delirious speed, often came to haunt his readership, and its canny utilization of SUPERMAN protagonists came to tantalize them with visions of transcendental power.

The vulnerability of the sf community – from Campbell and A.E. VAN VOGT down to the naïvest teenage fans – to this lure of transcendence may help account for the otherwise puzzling success first of Dianetics, then of Scientology itself, which gained many early recruits from sf; for, both as technique and as religion, these very US bodies of doctrine centrally posited a technology of self-improvement, a set of instructions to follow in order to liberate the transcendent power within one (◊ EDISONADE). LRH became very wealthy on the proceeds of his intuition concerning "spiritual technology", and departed the sf field for many years, not to return until the publication of *Battlefield Earth: A Saga of the Year 3000* (**1982**), an enormously long space opera composed in an idiom that seemed embarrassingly archaic. This was followed by the **Mission Earth** "dekalogy", a 10-vol sequence whose farcical overemphases fail to disguise an overblown tale that would have been more at home in the dawn of the PULP MAGAZINES; it comprises *The Invaders Plan* (**1985**), *Black Genesis* (**1986**), *The Enemy Within* (**1986**), *An Alien Affair* (**1986**), *Fortune of Fear* (**1986**), *Death Quest* (**1987**), *Voyage of Vengeance* (**1987**), *Disaster* (**1987**), *Villainy Victorious* (**1987**) and *The Doomed Planet* (**1987**). The posthumous publication of some of these books has led to speculation as to their true authorship. The sequence was released by LRH's own firm, Bridge Publications, and was heavily promoted, reflecting LRH's – and his intellectual heirs' – apparent desire to re-establish his reputation in the sf world. At the same time, he inaugurated the WRITERS OF THE FUTURE CONTEST and the Writers of the Future workshops for new authors, some of whom have reported benefits (◊ Algis BUDRYS *for further discussion*); the associated anthology series is L. RON HUBBARD PRESENTS WRITERS OF THE FUTURE. In the early 1990s, much of LRH's early work was scheduled for reissue from Bridge Publications; and in 1992 it was announced that an underground crypt had been constructed near Petrolia, California, by an arm of the Church of Scientology known as the Church of Spiritual Technology, to house "the religious works of L. Ron Hubbard and other key religious works of mankind". [JC/PN]

Other works: *Buckskin Brigades* (**1937**; rev 1987; further rev 1987), associational; *Death's Deputy* (**1940** *Unknown*; **1948**) and *The Kingslayer* (coll **1949**; vt *Seven Steps to the Arbiter* 1975), also bound together as *From Death to the Stars* (omni **1953**); *Triton and Battle of Wizards* ("Triton" 1940 *Unknown*; "Battle of Wizards"

1949 *Fantasy Book*; coll **1949**), also bound with Ed Earl REPP's *The Radium Pool* (coll **1949**) as *Science Fantasy Quintet* (anth **1953**); *The Case of the Friendly Corpse* (1941 *Unknown*; **1991**).

Nonfiction: *Dianetics: The Modern Science of Mental Health* (**1950**) and very many others of this type, including *This is Scientology: The Science of Certainty* (**1955** UK), *Scientology: The Fundamentals of Thought* (**1956** UK) and *The Phoenix Lectures* (**1968** UK).

See also: ALIENS; ASTOUNDING SCIENCE-FICTION; COSMOLOGY; FASTER THAN LIGHT; HORROR IN SF; MEDICINE; MESSIAHS; MUSIC; POLITICS; PSI POWERS; PSYCHOLOGY; SPACESHIPS; VIRTUAL REALITY; WAR.

HUBSCHMAN, THOMAS (?   -   ) US author of two unremarkable sf adventures, *Alpha-II* (dated 1979 but **1980**) and *Space Ark* (**1981**). [JC]

HUDSON, JAN ◊ George H. SMITH.

HUDSON, MICHAEL ◊ Michael KUBE-McDOWELL.

HUDSON, W(ILLIAM) H(ENRY) (1841-1922) UK naturalist and writer, born in Argentina. His fine quasi-UTOPIAN novel of the FAR FUTURE, *A Crystal Age* (**1887** anon; signed, with a new preface, 1906) depicts small, self-sufficient, matriarchally organized households living in harmony with Nature. The protagonist, tragically, cannot adapt to their PASTORAL way of life. A similar quasisupernatural harmony with the Amazonian forest is enjoyed by the wild girl Rima – the last of her race – in the affectingly powerful novel *Green Mansions* (**1904**); she is ultimately destroyed by the local Indians, who are no more in tune with Nature than is the unhappy civilized protagonist. Both stories are remarkable anticipations of modern ecological mysticism (◊ ECOLOGY). "Marta Riquelme", in *El Ombú* (coll **1902**), is an equally feverish fantasy in which the eponymous woman undergoes sorrow-induced metamorphosis into a bird. *A Little Boy Lost* (**1905**) is a children's fantasy which further develops Hudson's peculiar fascination with maternal figures. [BS]

See also: ANONYMOUS SF AUTHORS; HISTORY OF SF; SLEEPER AWAKES.

HUEFFER, FORD MADOX [r] ◊ Ford Madox FORD.

HUGHES, DENNIS (TALBOT) (?   -   ) UK writer, one of several authors of paperback originals for obscure houses in the late 1940s and 1950s who have remained reticent – or indifferent – about revealing much about themselves as individuals. DH was among the most prolific, producing some 60 known sf novels in less than half a decade. Like John S. GLASBY and the even more prolific R.L. FANTHORPE, DH made use of a wide range of sf themes with considerable invention, especially on some of his later fantasy stories, which often feature allegorical and/or dream sequences; but the books themselves were slackly written, albeit with some improvement over the years. This carelessness was entirely understandable given the sweat-shop conditions of his employment. [JC]

Works include:

As Dennis (or Denis) Hughes: *The Earth Invasion*

Battalion (**1950**); *Murder by Telecopter* (**1950**); *Formula 695* (**1950**); *War Lords of Space* (**1950**); *Moon War* (**1951**). **As Marvin Ashton:** *People of Asa* (**1953**).

As Ray Barry: *Death Dimension* (**1952**); *Blue Peril* (**1952**); *Gamma Product* (**1952**); *Humanoid Puppets* (**1952**); *Ominous Folly* (**1952**).

As George Sheldon Browne (or Brown): *Destination Mars* (**1951**); *The Planetoid Peril* (**1952**); *The Yellow Planet* (**1954**).

As Berl CAMERON **(house name):** *Maid of Thuro* (**1952**); *Lost Aeons* (**1953**).

As Dee Carter: *Blue Cordon* (**1952**); *Chloroplasm* (**1952**); *Purple Islands* (**1953**).

As Neil CHARLES **(house name):** *Twenty-Four Hours* (**1952**); *The Land of Esa* (**1953**); *Beyond Zoaster* (**1953**); *Pre-Gargantua* (**1953**); *World of Gol* (**1953**); *Research Opta* (**1953**).

As Lee ELLIOT **(house name):** *Bio-Muton* (**1952**).

As Marco Garon (house name): The **Rex Brandon** jungle fantasies, loosely derived from **Tarzan**, comprising *Jungle Allies* (**1951**), *Death Warriors* (**1951**), *Black Fury* (**1951**), *White Gold* (**1951**), *Black Sport* (**1951**), *Bush Claws* (**1951**), *Silent River* (**1951**), *Veldt Warriors* (**1951**), *Leopard God* (**1952**), *Snake Valley* (**1952**), *Fire Tribes* (**1952**) and *Mountain Gold* (**1952**) (◊ Marco GARRON).

As Irving Heine: *Dimension of Illion* (**1955** chap).

As Gill HUNT **(house name):** *Elektron Union* (**1951**); *Hostile Worlds* (**1951**); *Planet X* (**1951**); *Space Flight* (**1951**); *Spacial Ray* (**1951**).

As Von KELLAR **(house name):** *Ionic Barrier* (**1953**).

As Brad KENT **(house name):** *Biology "A"* (**1952**); *The Fatal Law* (**1952**); *Catalyst* (**1952**).

As John Lane: *Maid of Thuro* (**1952**); *Mammalia* (**1953**).

As Rand LE PAGE **(house name):** *Asteroid Forma* (**1953**).

As Grant Malcolm: *The Green Mandarin Mystery* (**1950**).

As G.R. Melde: *Pacific Advance* (**1954**).

As Van REED **(house name):** *House of Many Changes* (**1952**).

As Russell Rey: *The Queen People* (**1952**); *Valley of Terror* (**1953**).

As William Rogersohn: *North Dimension* (**1954**); *Amiro* (**1954**).

As Arn ROMILUS **(house name):** *Brain Paleo* (**1953**); *Organic Destiny* (**1954**).

As E.R. Royce: *Experiment in Telepathy* (**1954**).

HUGHES, EDWARD P. (? -) US writer who began publishing sf with "In the Name of the Father" for *FSF* in 1980. His first novel, *The Long Mynd* (**1985**), depicts a post-HOLOCAUST world which has been brought into being by PSI POWERS. *Master of the Fist* (coll of linked stories **1989**) repeats significant elements of the first venue. [JC]

HUGHES, MONICA (1925-) UK-born writer, from 1952 in CANADA, where she has won several awards in recognition of her novels for older children, including the Canada Council Children's Literature Prize in 1982 and 1983. Her first sf novels, *Crisis on Conshelf Ten* (**1975**) and its sequel, *Earthdark* (**1977** UK), utilize an UNDER-THE-SEA and a Lunar setting to explore in a humane fashion the crises of adolescents in venues which, typically of her work in general, encompassingly keep them alive, but at a cost. This irony of survival – it is an irony likely to evoke an acute response from young readers – is very much sharpened in the **Isis** sequence, for which MH remains best known: *The Keeper of the Isis Light* (**1980** UK), *The Guardian of Isis* (**1981** UK) and *The Isis Pedlar* (**1982** UK). The protagonist of the sequence, a deeply isolated orphan teenager, is initially alone on the planet Isis except for a guardian ROBOT. It is only when human settlers arrive that she discovers that she has been bio-engineered into a kind of reptile for survival purposes, and must from this point adjust to her job as warden and to her solitude. Other series include the DYSTOPIAN **Arc One** sequence – *Devil on My Back* (**1984** UK) and *The Dream Catcher* (**1986** UK) – and *Sandwriter* (**1985** UK) and its sequel, *The Promise* (**1989**).

Singletons of interest include: *The Tomorrow City* (**1978** UK), which again demonstrates the costs of survival through the story of a young girl who is blinded by the great COMPUTER designed by her father to protect her environment; *Beyond the Dark River* (**1979** UK), a post-HOLOCAUST tale set in the prairies of northern Canada; *Ring-Rise, Ring-Set* (**1982** UK), again set in a threatened Canada; and *Invitation to the Game* (**1990**), in which the implicit PARANOIA of some of MH's earlier work becomes frighteningly articulate, as a seemingly benevolent 21st-century government transports unemployable adolescents to an unknown destination, where they will be very happy. [JC]

Other works: *The Beckoning Lights* (**1982**); *Space Trap* (**1983**).

See also: CHILDREN'S SF.

HUGHES, TED (1930-) Working name of UK poet Edward James Hughes for all his writing. Best known for volumes of dark, violent verse such as *Crow* (coll **1970**; rev 1971), which like all his work features representations of other species in terms hinting at mythic metamorphoses, he has been Poet Laureate since 1984. Of sf interest is his children's story, *The Iron Man: A Story in Five Nights* (**1968**; vt *The Iron Giant* 1968 US), in which a frightening but friendly iron man defends the world against a dragon from space, ultimately persuading it to sing the music of the spheres, a sound which soothes humanity's terrible lust for war and causes peace; it was made into a musical (◊ MUSIC), *The Iron Man* (1989) by Pete Townshend (1945-). Also for children, *What is the Truth? A Farmyard Fable for the Young* (**1984** chap) and *Ffangs the Vampire Bat and the Kiss of Truth* (**1986** chap), both written in a style that intermingles verse and prose, are complex tales mixing didactic concerns with flights of sf hyperbole. Much of his verse for children, variously collected in volumes like *Moon-Whales* (coll 1976 US; rev 1988 UK), is fantasy. [JC]

HUGHES, ZACH Working name of US writer Hugh Zachary (1928-) for almost all his sf; he uses his real name for other work, and has written as well under various pseudonyms, including Evan Innes, Peter Kanto and Pablo Kane. His novels in the sf field are expertly devised and readable and frequently surprisingly dark in their implications. *The Book of Rack the Healer* (**1973**) and its sequel *Thunderworld* (**1982**) explore with some complexity first a post-HOLOCAUST USA, then a planet whose ALIEN population renders humanity's survival problematic. *The Legend of Miaree* (**1974**) again subjects alien races to a reading which is pessimistic about the chances of species survival. *Tide* (**1974**) and *The St Francis Effect* (**1976**) are more routine but *Seed of the Gods* (**1974**) sharply parodies the Erich VON DÄNIKEN books. Other novels, like *The Stork Factor* (**1975**), *For Texas and Zed* (**1976**) and *Tiger in the Stars* (**1976** Canada), variously exploit SPACE-OPERA themes, sharing with his first books an inventive knack for aliens. Without undue emphasis, elements of a shared background link several of these titles – *Killbird* (**1980**), for instance, is clearly set in the same universe as *The Legend of Miaree* – and ZH's work gives a general sense of only casually developed potential, along with very considerable unevenness: *Sundrinker* (**1987**), another tale of aliens, features as protagonist a mobile plant, arguing the plausibility of the premise with some force; while *The Dark Side* (**1987**) is a conventional space opera. In the end, ZH gives the air of being a professional writer less than fully attentive to the genre. [JC]

Other works: *Pressure Man* (**1980**); *Gold Star* (**1983**); *Closed System* (**1986**); *Life Force* (**1988**); *Mother Lode* (**1991**).

As Evan Innes: The **America 2040** sequence of SPACE-OPERA adventure SHARECROPS comprising *America 2040* (**1986**), #2: *The Golden World* (**1986**), #3: *The City in the Mist* (**1987**), #4: *The Return* (**1988**) and #5: *The Star Explorer* (**1988**).

As Pablo Kane: *A Dick for All Seasons* (**1970**).

As Peter Kanto: Of his numerous sex novels under this name, *The World where Sex was Born* (**1968**) and *Rosy Cheeks* (**1969**) are of some interest.

As Hugh Zachary: *Gwen, in Green* (**1974**); *The Revenant* (**1988**).

HUGI, MAURICE G. [r] ◊ INVASION; Brad KENT.

HUGIN ◊ SCANDINAVIA.

HUGO The almost invariably used term, in honour of Hugo GERNSBACK, for the Science Fiction Achievement Award; it has been an official variant of the formal title since 1958. Hugos were first awarded at the 1953 World SF CONVENTION; the idea was then dropped for a year (1954), but since 1955 the awards have been annual. They have always been the amateur or fan awards as opposed to, say, the NEBULA or PHILIP K. DICK AWARD, which are voted on by different categories of professional reader. The original idea, from fan Hal Lynch, was based on the National Film Academy Awards (Oscars). The award takes the form of a rocketship mounted upright on fins. The first model was designed and produced by Jack McKnight; from 1955 a similar design by Ben Jason has normally been used. The rockets have been

cast since 1984 (except 1991) in Birmingham, UK, at the foundry of prominent fan Peter WESTON; in 1992 they were gold-plated to celebrate the 50th Worldcon.

Awards are made in several classes, which have varied in definition and number from year to year. They are given primarily for fiction, but classes for editing, artwork, film and tv, fan writing and illustration have also been included; moreover, occasional unclassified special awards have been given. The rules governing awards are made, and often remade, at Worldcon business meetings, held annually. Winners in each class are chosen by ballot; since 1960 the voters have been limited annually to members of the forthcoming Worldcon (anyone can buy membership without actually attending the convention). The occasional special awards, however, are made by Worldcon committees. Voting on Hugos is always carried out postally before the convention begins; counting is done using the single transferable ballot, often known as the Australian ballot (after the system used in Australian lower-house elections), the least successful contender's votes being redistributed, using second or subsequent preferences, after each count, until one candidate has a clear majority. There was no nominating procedure up to 1958. Since 1959 there have been ballots for nominations, distributed to fans generally until 1963, when they were limited to the membership of the current and previous year's Worldcon, except in 1965 and 1967.

World conventions are held over Labor Day Weekend in September, and Hugos are given for publication or activity in the preceding calendar year. Hence, for example, a novel which wins a 1998 Hugo will have been published in 1997 (though, if it also wins a Nebula, the latter will be known confusingly as the 1997 Nebula). "No award" votes have for many years been permitted, and have resulted occasionally in void classes. Since 1963, story series and tv series have been excluded from the short-fiction and drama classes; thus in 1968 five individual STAR TREK episodes were nominated for the drama award, while in 1962 Brian W. ALDISS was able to win the short-fiction award with a series, the **Hothouse** stories.

The definitions of the various categories of short fiction have varied. There was no short-fiction award in 1953. In the years 1955-9 there were only two classes of short fiction: novelette and short story. These were amalgamated 1960-66 as "short fiction"; few short stories were nominated during this period. In 1967 the novelette class was reintroduced, and a new class, novella, was included from 1968. In 1970-72 the only two classes were short story and novella. Since 1973 there have again been three classes of short fiction. Since the early 1970s a novella has been defined as being 17,500-40,000 words, a novelette as 7500-17,500 words, a short story as any fiction shorter than a novelette and a novel as any fiction longer than a novella.

Since 1971, the drama category has included

recordings. In 1973 the professional-magazine class changed to a professional-editor class, to acknowledge the increasing importance of original ANTHOLOGIES. In 1980 the new category of nonfiction book was added, the first award being given to the first edition of this encyclopedia, and subsequent awards have gone to books of criticism, scholarship, artwork, reminiscence and science fact: a category in which GRAPHIC NOVELS compete with encyclopedias is perhaps too much of a grab-bag; the 1989 Worldcon committee did choose specifically to exclude *A Brief History of Time* (**1988** US) by Stephen Hawking (1942-), causing some slight controversy. Since 1984 the new category of SEMIPROZINE has been included, for publications midway between FANZINES and professional magazines.

The Hugos have for many years been subject to criticism on the grounds that awards made by a small, self-selected group of hardcore fans do not necessarily reflect either literary merit or the preferences of the sf reading public generally; hardcore FANDOM probably makes up less than 1 per cent of the general sf readership. Certainly Hugos have tended to be given to traditional HARD SF, and have seldom been awarded to experimental work, but they have been, on the whole, surprisingly eclectic. While many awards have gone to (good but) conservative writers like Poul ANDERSON, Robert A. HEINLEIN, Clifford D. SIMAK and Larry NIVEN, they have also been given to such doyens of the NEW WAVE as Harlan ELLISON, Roger ZELAZNY and James TIPTREE Jr, and to a number of works of literary excellence which quite fail to conform to the standard patterns of genre expectation, such as Walter M. MILLER Jr's *A Canticle for Leibowitz* (**1959**) and Ursula K. LE GUIN's *The Dispossessed* (**1974**). Neither was Fritz LEIBER's eccentric *The Big Time* (1958; **1961**), which won the award before going into book format, a traditionalist selection. The rival award, the NEBULA, is chosen by professional writers, but there is no evidence that they have consistently selected works of superior literary merit; indeed, some critics would argue the contrary case, that the Hugo voters have proved themselves marginally the more reliable judges. Though good books are often ignored, and in some years individual awards have seemed strange, the track record of the Hugos has been, on the whole, quite honourable. Another cavil is that both Hugo and Nebula, being US-centred, are notably chauvinistic, and awards to non-US writers have been rare. Nevertheless, despite all the criticisms to which both awards are readily subject, they are of real value to their recipients in increasing book sales.

Up-to-date listings of the rules under which Hugo awards are made can be found in the programme booklets for each Worldcon, as Article II of the Constitution of the World Science Fiction Society. Much of the Hugo-winning short fiction is available in a series of anthologies edited by Isaac ASIMOV (*whom see for details*).   [PN]

Novels:
1953: Alfred BESTER, *The Demolished Man*
1955: Mark CLIFTON and Frank RILEY, *They'd Rather be Right*
1956: Robert A. HEINLEIN, *Double Star*
1957: no award
1958: Fritz LEIBER, *The Big Time*
1959: James BLISH, *A Case of Conscience*
1960: Robert A. Heinlein, *Starship Troopers*
1961: Walter M. MILLER Jr, *A Canticle for Leibowitz*
1962: Robert A. Heinlein, *Stranger in a Strange Land*
1963: Philip K. DICK, *The Man in the High Castle*
1964: Clifford D. SIMAK, *Way Station*
1965: Fritz Leiber, *The Wanderer*
1966: Roger ZELAZNY, ". . . And Call Me Conrad" and Frank HERBERT, *Dune* (tie)
1967: Robert A. Heinlein, *The Moon is a Harsh Mistress*
1968: Roger Zelazny, *Lord of Light*
1969: John BRUNNER, *Stand on Zanzibar*
1970: Ursula K. LE GUIN, *The Left Hand of Darkness*
1971: Larry NIVEN, *Ringworld*
1972: Philip José FARMER, *To Your Scattered Bodies Go*
1973: Isaac ASIMOV, *The Gods Themselves*
1974: Arthur C. CLARKE, *Rendezvous with Rama*
1975: Ursula K. Le Guin, *The Dispossessed*
1976: Joe HALDEMAN, *The Forever War*
1977: Kate WILHELM, *Where Late the Sweet Birds Sang*
1978: Frederik POHL, *Gateway*
1979: Vonda N. McINTYRE, *Dreamsnake*
1980: Arthur C. CLARKE, *The Fountains of Paradise*
1981: Joan D. VINGE, *The Snow Queen*
1982: C.J. CHERRYH, *Downbelow Station*
1983: Isaac Asimov, *Foundation's Edge*
1984: David BRIN, *Startide Rising*
1985: William GIBSON, *Neuromancer*
1986: Orson Scott CARD, *Ender's Game*
1987: Orson Scott Card, *Speaker for the Dead*
1988: David Brin, *The Uplift War*
1989: C.J. Cherryh, *Cyteen*
1990: Dan SIMMONS, *Hyperion*
1991: Lois McMaster BUJOLD, *The Vor Game*
1992: Lois McMaster Bujold, *Barrayar*
Short fiction to 1972:
1955
Novelette: Walter M. Miller Jr, "The Darfstellar"
Short Story: Eric Frank RUSSELL, "Allamagoosa"
1956
Novelette: Murray LEINSTER, "Exploration Team"
Short Story: Arthur C. Clarke, "The Star"
1957
No award
1958
Short Story: Avram DAVIDSON, "Or All the Seas with Oysters"
1959
Novelette: Clifford D. Simak, "The Big Front Yard"
Short Story: Robert BLOCH, "That Hell-Bound Train"
1960
Short Fiction: Daniel KEYES, "Flowers for Algernon"

1961
Short Story: Poul ANDERSON, "The Longest Voyage"
1962
Short Fiction: Brian W. ALDISS, the **Hothouse** series
1963
Short Fiction: Jack VANCE, "The Dragon Masters"
1964
Short Story: Poul Anderson, "No Truce with Kings"
1965
Short Fiction: Gordon R. DICKSON, "Soldier, Ask Not"
1966
Short Fiction: Harlan ELLISON, "'Repent, Harlequin!' said the Ticktockman"
1967
Novelette: Jack Vance, "The Last Castle"
Short Story: Larry Niven, "Neutron Star"
1968
Novella: Anne MCCAFFREY, "Weyr Search" and Philip José Farmer, "Riders of the Purple Wage" (tie)
Novelette: Fritz Leiber, "Gonna Roll Those Bones"
Short Story: Harlan Ellison, "I Have no Mouth and I Must Scream"
1969
Novella: Robert SILVERBERG, "Nightwings"
Novelette: Poul Anderson, "The Sharing of Flesh"
Short Story: Harlan Ellison, "The Beast that Shouted Love at the Heart of the World"
1970
Novella: Fritz Leiber, "Ship of Shadows"
Short Story: Samuel R. DELANY, "Time Considered as a Helix of Semi-Precious Stones"
1971
Novella: Fritz Leiber, "Ill Met in Lankhmar"
Short Story: Theodore STURGEON, "Slow Sculpture"
1972
Novella: Poul Anderson, "The Queen of Air and Darkness"
Short Story: Larry Niven, "Inconstant Moon"
Novellas from 1973:
1973: Ursula K. Le Guin, "The Word for World is Forest"
1974: James TIPTREE Jr, "The Girl who Was Plugged In"
1975: George R.R. MARTIN, "A Song for Lya"
1976: Roger Zelazny, "Home is the Hangman"
1977: Spider ROBINSON, "By Any Other Name" and James Tiptree Jr, "Houston, Houston, Do You Read?" (tie)
1978: Spider and Jeanne ROBINSON, "Stardance"
1979: John VARLEY, "The Persistence of Vision"
1980: Barry B. LONGYEAR, "Enemy Mine"
1981: Gordon R. Dickson, "Lost Dorsai"
1982: Poul Anderson, "The Saturn Game"
1983: Joanna RUSS, "Souls"
1984: Timothy ZAHN, "Cascade Point"
1985: John Varley, "PRESS ENTER ■"
1986: Roger Zelazny, "Twenty-four Views of Mount Fuji, by Hokusai"
1987: Robert Silverberg, "Gilgamesh in the Outback"
1988: Orson Scott Card, "Eye for Eye"
1989: Connie WILLIS, "The Last of the Winnebagos"

1990: Lois McMaster Bujold, "The Mountains of Mourning"
1991: Joe Haldeman, "The Hemingway Hoax"
1992: Nancy KRESS, "Beggars in Spain"
Novelettes from 1973:
1973: Poul Anderson, "Goat Song"
1974: Harlan Ellison, "The Deathbird"
1975: Harlan Ellison, "Adrift Just Off the Islets of Langerhans: Latitude 38° 54' N, Longitude 77° 00' 13" W"
1976: Larry Niven, "The Borderland of Sol"
1977: Isaac Asimov, "The Bicentennial Man"
1978: Joan D. Vinge, "Eyes of Amber"
1979: Poul Anderson, "Hunter's Moon"
1980: George R.R. Martin, "Sandkings"
1981: Gordon R. Dickson, "The Cloak and the Staff"
1982: Roger Zelazny, "Unicorn Variation"
1983: Connie Willis, "Fire Watch"
1984: Greg BEAR, "Blood Music"
1985: Octavia E. BUTLER, "Bloodchild"
1986: Harlan Ellison, "Paladin of the Lost Hour"
1987: Roger Zelazny, "Permafrost"
1988: Ursula K. Le Guin, "Buffalo Gals, Won't You Come Out Tonight"
1989: George Alec EFFINGER, "Schrödinger's Kitten"
1990: Robert Silverberg, "Enter a Soldier. Later, Enter Another"
1991: Michael D. RESNICK, "The Manamouki"
1992: Isaac Asimov, "Gold"
Short Stories from 1973:
1973: R.A. LAFFERTY, "Eurema's Dam", and Frederik Pohl and C.M. KORNBLUTH, "The Meeting" (tie)
1974: Ursula K. Le Guin, "The Ones who Walk Away from Omelas"
1975: Larry Niven, "The Hole Man"
1976: Fritz Leiber, "Catch that Zeppelin"
1977: Joe Haldeman, "Tricentennial"
1978: Harlan Ellison, "Jeffty is Five"
1979: C.J. Cherryh, "Cassandra"
1980: George R.R. Martin, "The Way of Cross and Dragon"
1981: Clifford D. Simak, "Grotto of the Dancing Deer"
1982: John Varley, "The Pusher"
1983: Spider Robinson, "Melancholy Elephants"
1984: Octavia E. Butler, "Speech Sounds"
1985: David Brin, "The Crystal Spheres"
1986: Frederik Pohl, "Fermi and Frost"
1987: Greg Bear, "Tangents"
1988: Lawrence WATT-EVANS, "Why I Left Harry's All-Night Hamburgers"
1989: Michael D. Resnick, "Kirinyaga"
1990: Suzy McKee CHARNAS, "Boobs"
1991: Terry BISSON, "Bears Discover Fire"
1992: Geoffrey Landis, "A Walk in the Sun"
Nonfiction book:
1980: Peter NICHOLLS, editor, *The Science Fiction Encyclopedia*
1981: Carl SAGAN, *Cosmos*
1982: Stephen KING, *Danse Macabre*
1983: James E. GUNN, *Isaac Asimov: The Foundations of*

Science Fiction

1984: Donald H. TUCK, *The Encyclopedia of Science Fiction and Fantasy: Volume 3: Miscellaneous*

1985: Jack WILLIAMSON, "Wonder's Child: My Life in Science Fiction

1986: Tom Weller, *Science Made Stupid*

1987: Brian W. Aldiss with David WINGROVE, *Trillion Year Spree*

1988: Michael WHELAN, *Michael Whelan's Works of Wonder*

1989: Samuel R. Delany, *The Motion of Light in Water*

1990: Alexei and Cory PANSHIN, *The World Beyond the Hill*

1991: Orson Scott Card, *How to Write Science Fiction and Fantasy*

1992: *The World of Charles Addams*

Dramatic presentation:

1958: Outstanding movie, *The* INCREDIBLE SHRINKING MAN

1960: *The* TWILIGHT ZONE

1961: *The Twilight Zone*

1962: *The Twilight Zone*

1963: no award

1965: Special drama, DR STRANGELOVE OR: HOW I LEARNED TO STOP WORRYING AND LOVE THE BOMB

1967: "The Menagerie" (STAR TREK)

1968: "City on the Edge of Forever" (*Star Trek*)

1969: Drama, 2001: A SPACE ODYSSEY

1970: Dramatic, news coverage of Apollo XI

1971: no award

1972: *A* CLOCKWORK ORANGE

1973: SLAUGHTERHOUSE FIVE

1974: SLEEPER

1975: *Young Frankenstein*

1976: *A* BOY AND HIS DOG

1977: no award

1978: STAR WARS

1979: SUPERMAN

1980: ALIEN

1981: *The* EMPIRE STRIKES BACK

1982: *Raiders of the Lost Ark*

1983: BLADE RUNNER

1984: RETURN OF THE JEDI

1985: 2010

1986: BACK TO THE FUTURE

1987: ALIENS

1988: *The Princess Bride*

1989: *Who Framed Roger Rabbit*

1990: *Indiana Jones and the Last Crusade*

1991: *Edward Scissorhands*

1992: TERMINATOR 2: JUDGMENT DAY

Professional magazine:

1953: GALAXY SCIENCE FICTION and ASTOUNDING SCIENCE-FICTION (tie)

1955: *ASF*

1956: *ASF*

1957: US, *ASF*; UK, NEW WORLDS

1958: *FSF*

1959: *FSF*

1960: *FSF*

1961: *ASF*

1962: *ASF*

1963: *FSF*

1964: *ASF*

1965: *ASF*

1966: IF

1967: *If*

1968: *If*

1969: *FSF*

1970: *FSF*

1971: *FSF*

1972: *FSF*

Professional editor:

1973: Ben BOVA

1974: Ben Bova

1975: Ben Bova

1976: Ben Bova

1977: Ben Bova

1978: George H. SCITHERS

1979: Ben Bova

1980: George H. Scithers

1981: Edward L. FERMAN

1982: Edward L. Ferman

1983: Edward L. Ferman

1984: Shawna MCCARTHY

1985: Terry CARR

1986: Judy-Lynn DEL REY (declined by Lester DEL REY)

1987: Terry Carr

1988: Gardner DOZOIS

1989: Gardner Dozois

1990: Gardner Dozois

1991: Gardner Dozois

1992: Gardner Dozois

Publisher:

1964: ACE BOOKS

1965: BALLANTINE BOOKS

Professional artist (early awards differently named):

1953

Interior Illustrator: Virgil FINLAY

Cover Artist: Ed EMSHWILLER and Hannes BOK (tie)

1955

Illustrator: Frank Kelly FREAS

1956

Illustrator: Frank Kelly Freas

1957

No award

1958

Illustrator: Frank Kelly Freas

1959

Illustrator: Frank Kelly Freas

1960

Illustrator: Ed Emshwiller

1961

Illustrator: Ed Emshwiller

1962: Ed Emshwiller

1963: Roy G. KRENKEL

1964: Ed Emshwiller

1965: John SCHOENHERR

1966: Frank FRAZETTA

1967: Jack GAUGHAN

1968: Jack Gaughan
1969: Jack Gaughan
1970: Frank Kelly Freas
1971: Leo and Diane DILLON
1972: Frank Kelly Freas
1973: Frank Kelly Freas
1974: Frank Kelly Freas
1975: Frank Kelly Freas
1976: Frank Kelly Freas
1977: Rick STERNBACH
1978: Rick Sternbach
1979: Vincent DI FATE
1980: Michael WHELAN
1981: Michael Whelan
1982: Michael Whelan
1983: Michael Whelan
1984: Michael Whelan
1985: Michael Whelan
1986: Michael Whelan
1987: Jim BURNS
1988: Michael Whelan
1989: Michael Whelan
1990: Don MAITZ
1991: Michael Whelan
1992: Michael Whelan

Semiprozine:
1984: Charles N. BROWN, ed LOCUS
1985: Charles N. Brown, ed *Locus*
1986: Charles N. Brown, ed *Locus*
1987: Charles N. Brown, ed *Locus*
1988: Charles N. Brown, ed *Locus*
1989: Charles N. Brown, ed *Locus*
1990: Charles N. Brown, ed *Locus*
1991: Charles N. Brown, ed *Locus*
1992: Charles N. Brown, ed *Locus*

Fan magazine/amateur publication/fanzine:
1955: James V. Taurasi and Ray Van Houten, eds FANTASY TIMES
1956: Ron Smith, ed *Inside* and *Science Fiction Advertiser*
1957: James V. Taurasi, Ray Van Houten and Frank Prieto, eds *Science Fiction Times* (◊ FANTASY TIMES)
1959: Terry Carr and Ron ELLIK, eds FANAC
1960: F.M. and Elinor BUSBY, Burnett Toskey and Wally Weber, eds *Cry of the Nameless*
1961: Earl KEMP, "Who Killed Science Fiction?"
1962: Richard Bergeron, ed WARHOON
1963: Richard and Pat LUPOFF, eds XERO
1964: George SCITHERS, ed *Amra*
1965: Robert and Juanita COULSON, eds YANDRO
1966: Camille Cazedessus Jr, ed *ERB-dom*
1967: Ed Meskys and Felice Rolfe, eds NIEKAS
1968: George Scithers, ed *Amra*
1969: Richard E. GEIS, ed SCIENCE FICTION REVIEW
1970: Richard E. Geis, ed *Science Fiction Review*
1971: Charlie and Dena Brown, eds *Locus*
1972: Charlie and Dena Brown, eds *Locus*
1973: Michael Glicksohn and Susan WOOD Glicksohn, eds *Energumen*
1974: Andy Porter, ed ALGOL, and Richard E. Geis, ed

The ALIEN CRITIC (tie)
1975: Richard E. Geis, ed *The Alien Critic*
1976: Charlie and Dena Brown, eds *Locus*
1977: Richard E. Geis, ed *Science Fiction Review*
1978: Charlie and Dena Brown, eds *Locus*
1979: Richard E. Geis, ed *Science Fiction Review*
1980: Charlie and Dena Brown, eds *Locus*
1981: Charlie and Dena Brown, eds *Locus*
1982: Charlie and Dena Brown, eds *Locus*
1983: Charlie and Dena Brown, eds *Locus*
1984: Mike Glyer, ed FILE 770
1985: Mike Glyer, ed *File 770*
1986: George "Lan" Laskowski, ed *Lan's Lantern*
1987: David LANGFORD, ed ANSIBLE
1988: Pat Mueller, ed *Texas SF Enquirer*
1989: Mike Glyer, ed *File 770*
1990: Leslie Turek, ed *The Mad 3 Party*
1991: George "Lan" Laskowski, ed *Lan's Lantern*
1992: Dick and Nicki Lynch, ed *Mimosa*

Fan writer:
1967: Alexei PANSHIN
1968: Ted WHITE
1969: Harry WARNER, Jr
1970: Bob (Wilson) TUCKER
1971: Richard E. Geis
1972: Harry Warner, Jr
1973: Terry Carr
1974: Susan WOOD
1975: Richard E. Geis
1976: Richard E. Geis
1977: Richard E. Geis and Susan Wood (tie)
1978: Richard E. Geis
1979: Bob SHAW
1980: Bob Shaw
1981: Susan Wood
1982: Richard E. Geis
1983: Richard E. Geis
1984: Mike Glyer
1985: David Langford
1986: Mike Glyer
1987: David Langford
1988: Mike Glyer
1989: David Langford
1990: David Langford
1991: David Langford
1992: David Langford

Fan artist:
1967: Jack GAUGHAN
1968: George BARR
1969: Vaughn BODÉ
1970: Tim Kirk
1971: Alicia Austin
1972: Tim Kirk
1973: Tim Kirk
1974: Tim Kirk
1975: William ROTSLER
1976: Tim Kirk
1977: Phil Foglio
1978: Phil Foglio
1979: William Rotsler

1980: Alexis GILLILAND
1981: Victoria Poyser
1982: Victoria Poyser
1983: Alexis Gilliland
1984: Alexis Gilliland
1985: Alexis Gilliland
1986: joan hanke-woods
1987: Brad Foster
1988: Brad Foster
1989: Brad Foster and Diana Gallagher Wu (tie)
1990: Stu Shiffman
1991: Teddy Harvia
1992: Brad Foster

Other Hugo awards:
1953
#1 Fan personality: Forrest J. ACKERMAN
Excellence in fact articles: Willy LEY
New sf author or artist: Philip José Farmer
1956
Feature writer: Willy Ley
Most promising new author: Robert Silverberg
Book reviewer: Damon KNIGHT
1958
Most outstanding actifan (active fan): Walter A. Willis
1966
Best all-time series: Isaac Asimov, **Foundation** series
Best Other Forms:
A category added by the Committee in 1988 and voted on, so it was not a Special Committee Award (see below). It was won by Alan MOORE and Dave GIBBONS for a GRAPHIC NOVEL, WATCHMEN. However, this particular award has mysteriously disappeared from subsequent official lists of past Hugo Winners, so its status is not clear.

Special Committee Awards:
Not strictly Hugo awards, these have been given from time to time to people as various as Hugo Gernsback for being "The Father of Science Fiction" in 1960, Pierre VERSINS for his *L'Encyclopédie de l'Utopie et de la science fiction* in 1973 and Chesley BONESTELL for his illustrations in 1974. We do not list them in full.

See also: JOHN W. CAMPBELL MEMORIAL AWARD; SF MAGAZINES; WOMEN SF WRITERS.

HULL, E(DNA) MAYNE (1905-1975) Canadian-born US writer, married from 1939 to A.E. VAN VOGT, who collaborated with her on most of her work, either in its original magazine form or by expanding it for book publication. She began publishing sf with "The Flight that Failed" for *ASF* in 1942, and made her greatest impact with the **Arthur Blord** series, later assembled by van Vogt as *Planets for Sale* (1943-6 *ASF*; fixup **1954** with both authors credited); and with the magazine version of *The Winged Man* (1944 *ASF*; exp van Vogt **1966** with both authors credited). The collection *Out of the Unknown* (coll **1948**) was credited to both writers, and consisted of 6 stories, 3 each, according to their original bylines. EMH ceased writing sf and fantasy when she became involved in DIANETICS. [JC]

HUMANOIDS FROM THE DEEP ◊ Roger CORMAN;

L'ISOLA DEGLI UOMINI PESCE.

HUME, FERGUS(ON WRIGHT) (1859-1932) UK writer raised in New Zealand, and who may have been born there; he lived in the UK at least from 1886, when *The Mystery of a Hansom Cab* (**1886**) made his name. It was followed by about 140 further books, most of them novels, some being fantasy and a few sf, including *The Year of Miracle: A Tale of the Year One Thousand Nine Hundred* (**1891**), a DISASTER novel in which the UK is depopulated by a plague. *The Island of Fantasy* (**1892**) is a marginal UTOPIA set on a Mediterranean island. *The Nameless City: A Romany Romance* (**1893**), *The Expedition of Captain Flick* (**1896**) and *The Mother of Emeralds* (**1901**) are LOST-WORLD novels, the first featuring a secret Gypsy land, the second set in the Indian Ocean and featuring ancient Greeks, and the third set in Peru, where Incans have developed an underground civilization based on electricity. [JC]
Other works: *The Gentleman who Vanished: A Psychological Phantasy* (**1890**; vt *The Man who Vanished* 1892 US); *Aladdin in London* (**1892**); *Chronicles of Faeryland* (coll **1892**); *The Harlequin Opal* (**1893**); *The Dwarf's Chamber, and Other Stories* (coll **1896**); *For the Defense* (**1898** US); *The Sacred Herb* (**1908**); *The Blue Talisman* (**1912**); *A Son of Perdition: An Occult Romance* (**1912**).

HUMOUR There is a false belief that sf and humour do not mix. Certainly sf has produced many bad jokes – Arthur C. CLARKE's *Tales From the White Hart* (coll of linked stories **1957**) is entirely devoted to them – but from the beginning it has also produced many good ones. Much sf humour takes the form of social SATIRE, and stories of this kind are discussed mainly in that entry. While the discussion below naturally includes satires also, it focuses on sf that elicits laughter rather than a wry smile.

The wittiest sf writers of the late 19th century were probably Mark TWAIN, Samuel BUTLER, Ambrose BIERCE and H.G. WELLS. The humour of Twain's *A Connecticut Yankee in King Arthur's Court* (**1889**), like so much humour generally, is rooted in self-confident prejudice: Twain clearly found the bumbling incompetence of the Middle Ages irresistibly funny. Butler's satire in *Erewhon* (**1872**) often consists of topsy-turvy analogies, as in the comparison between UK churches and Erewhonian banks, pointing up the self-interest Butler supposed to be the motive for religious devotion. Bierce's short stories often have a grim and macabre humour. Wells's, on the other hand, are often jolly, as in "The Truth about Pyecraft" (1903). Other early works of sf humour are *Mr Hawkins' Humorous Inventions* (coll of linked stories **1904**) by Edgar FRANKLIN and *Button Brains* (**1933**) by J. Storer CLOUSTON, a novel that introduced several ROBOT jokes which have since been overused.

Also working in the 1930s was John COLLIER, whose short stories amuse through the sometimes poisonous sharpness of their language and a cruel sense of the ironies of life. Roald DAHL and – to a degree – Gerald KERSH were to write rather similar stories later on, but these writers, working in the tradition of VILLIERS DE L'ISLE-ADAM's *Contes cruels* ["Cruel Stories"] (coll **1883**), were primarily fantasists who used sf themes only occasionally.

Occasional humorists have consistently popped up in GENRE SF, and with the advent of the magazine UNKNOWN in 1939 they had a platform. *Unknown* specialized in whimsical fantasy, sometimes dealing with SUPERNATURAL CREATURES, very often set in ALTERNATE WORLDS. Anthony BOUCHER was an important contributor, and many of his stories of this type are collected in *The Compleat Werewolf* (coll **1969**). Even better remembered are the **Harold Shea** stories by L. Sprague DE CAMP and Fletcher PRATT, later collected as *The Complete Enchanter* (coll **1975**): propelled back into versions of a mythic or literary past, Shea has a terrible time coming to terms with the local customs in worlds where MAGIC works. The early 1940s also saw a whole series of broad but accomplished jokes by Eric Frank RUSSELL, usually featuring cunning protagonists who deflate the pretensions of the brutal, the stupid and the pompous in various interplanetary venues. Examples from a slightly later period, when Russell had perfected his wisecracking style, are ". . . And Then There Were None" (1951), *Wasp* (**1957**) and *The Space Willies* (1956 *ASF*; exp **1958**; vt *Next of Kin* UK). From the same period come many of Fredric BROWN's amusing stories, like "Placet is a Crazy Place" (1946), in which the eponymous planet meets itself during its orbit, creates hallucinations, is undermined by heavy-matter widgie birds and becomes the locale for horrendous puns. Brown's outrageous inventions have appeared in many collections, including *Angels and Spaceships* (coll **1954**; vt *Star Shine*) and *Nightmares and Geezenstacks* (coll **1961**). A less well known funny sf book of that period is *The Sinister Researches of C.P. Ransom* (coll of linked stories **1954**) by Homer NEARING Jr.

Humorous genre sf is more common in short stories than at novel length. Three of sf's premier humorists worked commonly and perhaps at their best in this form, with the result that, perhaps, their full stature has not been generally recognized: Henry KUTTNER, William TENN and Robert SHECKLEY. Kuttner's humour may have dated the most quickly, but "The Twonky" (1942 as by Lewis Padgett) is a classic (filmed in 1952 as *The* TWONKY), as are his **Hogben** stories (1947-9) and the **Galloway Gallegher** series, collected as *Robots Have No Tails* (1943-8 *ASF*; coll **1952**). Tenn's style is more polished; but it is Sheckley who for many years remained the most consistent humorist of them all. Nothing is ever quite what it seems in Sheckley's urbane stories, and, with an inventiveness that lasted through the 1950s and 1960s, he depicted the naïve but sometimes successful struggles of little men against an unimaginably absurd and rather menacing cosmos. Philip K. DICK, although a fundamentally more serious writer, had something of the same quality, and most of his novels have a rich sense of the various comic ways in which the life of the future might thwart us; he is especially well known for robots that talk back.

Both Dick and Sheckley often published in GALAXY SCIENCE FICTION, a magazine that, notably under Horace GOLD, encouraged wit, satire and a moderately demanding literacy in its writers, who also included Frederik POHL and Alfred BESTER, both of whom were as much at home with the humorous story as with the serious sf for which they are best remembered. Bester's "The Men who Murdered Mohammed" (1958), a wry and funny TIME-PARADOX story, appeared in *FSF*, the home of Reginald BRETNOR's appalling **Ferdinand Feghoot** series of vignettes with punning punch-lines.

Most well known sf authors have tried their hand at humour at one time or another, sometimes rather heavy-handedly, as in Keith LAUMER's **Retief** series or Gordon R. DICKSON's and Poul ANDERSON's **Hoka** series. More successful in this line has been Harry HARRISON, who has often amusingly parodied the excesses of genre sf, as in the **Stainless Steel Rat** stories and in *Bill, the Galactic Hero* (**1965**). A wry, Irish humour of sharp observation comes often from Bob SHAW, who also has a good line in pastiche; his comic novel *Who Goes Here?* (**1977**) straight-facedly produces a spaceship which has a matter transmitter at each end, and thus can be driven by being repeatedly transmitted through its own length.

Comic sf of the 1960s and 1970s tended strongly towards satire, and its comedy – especially that of the NEW WAVE – was often black. Nearly all of John T. SLADEK's work is of this sort; it tends more towards irony than farce (although he has also written raucously funny farce, notably in parody), blending comedy with nightmare in tales that often deal with technology running amok and mankind being manipulated. His one-time collaborator Thomas M. DISCH is one of the most formidable of sf's wits and stylists, though again it is the wry smile rather than the outright laugh that is evoked. Michael MOORCOCK often deals in a comedy of unexpected juxtapositions, as in his **Dancers at the End of Time** series, where time-travellers constantly misunderstand one another's customs. In the same period, however, Ron GOULART became known for knockabout, satiric farce. Gaining notoriety late in the 1960s, R.A. LAFFERTY is offbeat in quite another way. His bizarre, quasi-surrealist humour depends strongly on the exuberant idiosyncracy of his language; his flamboyantly tall stories are seen by some as morally stringent, dismissed by others as empty games. His work has never fitted the conventions of genre sf, floating somewhere between sf and fantasy. The same could be said of the **Illuminatus** trilogy (1975) by Robert SHEA and Robert Anton WILSON, a rambling story of conflicting conspiracies and secret cults which persuasively argues for the accuracy of a paranoid (◊ PARANOIA) view of POLITICS; a sometimes bloodshot view of the vagaries of human behaviour is expressed through farce, wisecracks and general lunacy.

One of the least plausible of all comic sf novels is Piers ANTHONY's *Prostho Plus* (**1971**), featuring a kidnapped Earth dentist forced to practise on a hideous variety of alien teeth; it is carried off, against all the odds, with verve. Anthony subsequently became known for comic fantasy rather than comic sf, his tone being in the tradition set by De Camp and Pratt in their *Unknown* stories. Along with Christopher STASHEFF's **Warlock** series, Anthony's novels set a trend, in the 1970s and 1980s, for novels sited in alternate fantasy worlds featuring slapstick, agonizing puns, and a Twain-like juxtaposition of modernisms with archaisms. Alan Dean FOSTER, Craig Shaw Gardner, Robert ASPRIN and many others have worked in this subgenre, which has proved commercially very successful, though it includes more dire undergraduate humour than is digestible for grown-up readers. The first great success story of written sf humour in the 1980s – a decade not generally notable for funny sf – was Douglas ADAMS. Other producers, on a much smaller scale, were Rudy RUCKER and Howard WALDROP in the USA and (more recently) Robert RANKIN in the UK.

Humour notoriously translates badly, and the wit of Stanisław LEM in such works as *Cyberiada* (coll **1965**; trans as *The Cyberiad* **1974**) and "Kongres Futurologiczny" (**1971**; trans as *The Futurological Congress* **1974**), while attested by his Polish readership as being full of subtle ironies and linguistic fireworks, appears rather crude in the English-language versions.

Sf humour has been a mainstay of both the small and large screens. In the USA, humorous tv series have included MY FAVORITE MARTIAN, MY LIVING DOLL, MORK AND MINDY and ALF, most of these being sitcoms in which human foibles become all too clear when seen from an alien perspective. A very selective list of humorous sf movies from the USA would include *The* ABSENT-MINDED PROFESSOR, ANDROID, BILL AND TED'S EXCELLENT ADVENTURE, DARK STAR, DR STRANGELOVE OR: HOW I LEARNED TO STOP WORRYING AND LOVE THE BOMB; EARTH GIRLS ARE EASY, FLESH GORDON, *The* ICE PIRATES, *The* MAN WITH TWO BRAINS, MEET THE APPLEGATES, MONKEY BUSINESS, *The* NUTTY PROFESSOR, *The* PRESIDENT'S ANALYST, REAL GENIUS, *The* ROCKY HORROR PICTURE SHOW, SCHLOCK, SHORT CIRCUIT, SLEEPER, SPACED INVADERS, TERRORVISION and WEIRD SCIENCE, a list which should, perhaps, include as well the films of Larry COHEN and David CRONENBERG which, though mostly sf/horror, are also shot through with dark humour, as are some SPLATTER MOVIES, like RE-ANIMATOR. No clear conclusion can be drawn from the list, which contains few really good films and few really bad. It does contain a notable amount of pastiche and parody, something that normally occurs fairly late in the history of any genre, and it is interesting to note that the majority of the films listed are quite recent; many are aimed at a younger audience.

The story is a little different in the UK, where sf humour for the big screen is rare and, when it does appear, usually poor, as in MORONS FROM OUTER SPACE.

But there is a long tradition of light-hearted humour in UK tv, which bubbled up strongly in much of the long-running DR WHO series. It did not, however, reach cult proportions until the tv version of the radio success *The* HITCH HIKER'S GUIDE TO THE GALAXY appeared in 1981. This was written by Douglas Adams, whose **Hitch Hiker** books, developed from the radio series, became bestsellers. Behind the extremely funny absurdity of the series there seems to be a mournfully nihilist view of life on Earth (and in the cosmos), where nothing means very much at all, and we are all shuttlecocks racketed around by fate or, if it comes to that, ENTROPY. A similar view of the soft white underbelly of human existence reappeared in 1988 in the (also very successful) tv series RED DWARF, a SPACE OPERA with an unbelievably small cast, only one of them indubitably both human and alive.

There is one line of development visible among the variety of authors named in this entry: sf humour has by and large been pessimistic. The ordinary guy battered by circumstance, trying to find meaning or justice in a Universe where these commodities may be nonexistent, is a character running through from Collier via Sheckley, Dick and Sladek to reach perhaps its apotheosis in Adams. Indeed Kurt VONNEGUT Jr, probably the most famous of all sf humorists, fits squarely into this tradition. In, for example, *The Sirens of Titan* (**1959**) and *Cat's Cradle* (**1963**) – and with a somewhat more brittle and fatalistic air in *Slaughterhouse-5* (**1969**) – Vonnegut contrives scenarios at once witty, sardonic and nihilistic, though in the earlier books the nihilism is softened by the affection he shows for the absurd and doomed ambitions of his protagonists. Some see Vonnegut as a fierce wit in the tradition of Jonathan SWIFT; others find his black comedies increasingly facile, repetitive, and disfigured by the literary equivalent of nervous tics. So it goes.

David LANGFORD's parodic bent infiltrates much of his fiction, though it is most clearly expressed in *The Dragonhiker's Guide to Battlefield Covenant at Dune's Edge: Odyssey Two* (coll **1988**), which assembles parodies of various writers and tendencies. But the great UK comic success of the 1980s is Terry PRATCHETT, whose **Discworld** books climb to the top of bestseller lists with satisfying regularity, and who writes work both joyful and delightful, allowing the little man his triumphs as well as his agonies. Most readers would call these books fantasies, but they are, after all, set on a planet other than Earth. It is, one must confess, a very *flat* planet, and perched on the back of a giant turtle ... [PN]

HUNGARY Sf in the modern sense evolved tentatively in Hungary in the 1870s, although it had had forerunners. The end of the 18th century was characterized by the popularity of FANTASTIC VOYAGES and UTOPIAS. French and other sources inspired *Tariménes utazása* ["The Voyage of Tariménes"] (**1804**) by György Bessenyei (1747-1811). The hero, who gets to an unknown country, not only describes the perfect order of the state but also presents a copy of its constitution. Another important fantastic utopia was *Utazás a Holdba* ["Voyage to the Moon"] (**1836**) by Ferenc Ney (1814-1899), a novel in which travellers find that the Moon has everything they miss on Earth: the possibility of happiness and the happiness of equality. János Munkácsy (1802-1841), in his *Hogy áll a világ a jövö században?* ["How Stands the World in the Next Century?"] (**1838**), describes the wonderful future development of TRANSPORTATION and many social changes: deadly WEAPONS are put aside and conflicts between states are settled by competitive poetry recitals. The first Hungarian SPACE OPERA was *Végnapok* ["The Final Days"] (**1847**) by Miklós Jósika (1794-1865). This apocalyptic novel had an immense success. The story takes place on Earth in a FAR-FUTURE ice age.

Mór JÓKAI is justly regarded as the greatest author produced by Hungary. He was very prolific – his collected works run to several hundred volumes. His most important works of fantasy and sf are *Óceánia* about a romantic ATLANTIS, *Fekete gyémántok* (**1870**; trans A. Gerard as *Black Diamonds* 1896), set in a North Polar sea, *Egész az északi pólusig* ["All the Way to the North Pole"] (**1876**), in which ancient patriarchs and fairy-like ladies are revived from frozen hibernation to facilitate the author's criticism of contemporary society, and *Ahol a pénz nem Isten* ["Where Money is not a God"] (**1904**), describing the life of a happy island community, and hinting at the possibility of the fall of the Austro-Hungarian empire. Along with these sometimes Edgar Allan POE-like fantasies comes Jókai's most significant sf novel, *A jövö század regénye* ["The Novel of the Next Century"] (**1872**), whose story is founded in the invention of a marvellous new material, "ichor". Airplanes made of ichor serve the heroes, who dominate global communications and trade; declaring war on anarchistic Russia, they fight the last war of mankind and create eternal peace. The novel then moves onto the cosmic scale: a comet menaces Earth but is fought off by mankind, the Moon is colonized and the Solar System is conquered.

Jókai's disciple Titusz Tóvölgyi (1838-1918) wrote a surprisingly interesting novel about the future socialist state: *Az új világ* ["The New World"] (**1888**). Elsewhere, besides sociopolitical novels there were fantasies of markedly scientific foundation, like *Repülögépen a Holdba* ["On an Airplane to the Moon"] (**1899**) by István Makay (1870-1935), another Jókai disciple, which, antedating H.G. WELLS, describes a society of cave-dwelling Selenites. *Barna Arthur* ["Arthur Barna"] (**1880**) by Gusztáv Beksics (1847-1906) has an African volcano spreading flowing gold over the country, with the consequent bankruptcy of trusts, banks and states.

In the first half of the 20th century the authors gathering around the journal *Nyugat* ["West"] were attracted almost without exception to the fantastic,

and with them sf reached artistic heights once more; they include Dezsö Kosztolányi (1885-1935), Géza Csáth (1888-1919), Géza Laczkó (1884-1953), Gyula Szini (1876-1932), László Cholnoky (1879-1929), Béla Balázs (1884-1949) and Margit Kaffka (1880-1918). Unfortunately, only two names are known in the English-speaking world: Frigyes KARINTHY and Mihály BABITS.

Karinthy wrote a good many stories about TIME TRAVEL, DISASTER, PSI POWERS and so on, but these are surpassed by his philosophical novels. *Utazás Faremidóba* (**1916**) and *Capillária* (**1921**), which have been assembled as *Voyage to Faremido/Capillaria* (omni trans Paul TABORI 1965 Hungary; 1966 US), are sardonic sequels to Jonathan SWIFT's stories of Gulliver and his travels. The former deals with problems of AI and the latter describes the conflict between men and women in an UNDER-THE-SEA empire. *Mennyei riport* ["A Report from the Heavens"] (**1937**), the surprising story of a journey to the next world, is an important precursor of modern sf.

The novels of the poet Mihály Babits stand out for their literary merit and for the interest of their ideas. In *Gólyakalifa* ["Storks' Caliph"] (**1916**; trans as *King's Stork* 1948 Hungary; retrans anon as *The Nightmare* 1966), his first novel, he created a world of pure fantasy; the protagonist is a young man living a surreal double life. Another novel, *Elza pilóta, avagy a tökéletes társadalom* ["The Pilot Elza, or The Perfect Society"] (**1933**), is a description of an episode in an age of eternal war, its protest against fascism being pointed at a time when fascism was spreading rapidly.

Utazás Kazohiniában ["A Voyage in Kazohinia"] (**1941** censored; text restored 1946) by Sándor Szathmáry (1897-1974) is a bitter, Swiftian (and Karinthyan) SATIRE describing a new journey of Gulliver. Kazohinia is divided into two parts, one where exaggerated rationalism prevails, the other ruled by the uncontrolled power of the instincts.

In the Fall of 1945 László Gáspár (? -) produced his short novel *Mi, I. Adolf* ["We, Adolf 1"] (**1945**), subtitled "If the Germans had Won". In this postwar nightmare, fascism rules by terror and weaponry, and all peoples are slaves of the Germans (◊ HITLER WINS).

The two decades after WWII did not favour Hungarian sf – Soviet sf, along with the theoretical views it espoused, dominated the sf published in Hungary – and only one item from this period is memorable: *Az ibolyaszínü fény* ["The Violet Light"] (**1956**) by Péter Földes (1916-), a juvenile adventure that presents interesting ideas. In 1968, however, the publishing house Móra began a paperback sf series under the imprint **Kozmosz Fantasztikus Könyvek**. In 1972 Móra followed this with the magazine *Galaktika*, ed Péter KUCZKA, which started as a quarterly and is now a monthly, with a circulation of 50,000. Its younger stablemate (since 1985) is *Robur*, a bimonthly sf magazine for juvenile readers, with a circulation of

80,000-100,000. Other publishers now publish sf, though the Móra book series, also long under the editorship of Kuczka, remains the most significant.

Today 25-30 authors in Hungary are engaged in sf, although many of them work also in other genres. Among the older authors is Mária Szepes (1908-   ), who in *Tükörajtó a tengerben* ["Mirror Door in the Sea"] (1976), *Surayana élö szobrai* ["Living Statues of Surayana"] (1971) and *Napszél* ["Sunwind"] (1983) draws her figures of fantasy with great psychological force. She introduced ESP motifs to Hungarian sf, mainly through her first and most influential novel, *A vörös oroszlán* ["The Red Lion"] (1946), the story of an alchemist living through the centuries and from sin to redemption. Iván Boldizsár (1912-1988) belonged to the same generation; his *Születésnap* ["Birthday"] (1959) is a TIME-TRAVEL novel. The most famous book of István Elek (1915-   ) is a juvenile adventure, *Merénylet a világürben* ["An Attempt in Space"] (1967). József Cserna (1899-1975) wrote a number of admonitory stories about nuclear WAR, the destruction of the ECOLOGY and other dangers menacing mankind.

Next comes the generation of writers now in their 50s and 60s, like Gyula Fekete (1922-   ), an excellent novelist in the realistic tradition. His sf works are all utopian and educational, whether set on unknown islands or on distant planets. In *A szerelmesek bolygója* ["Planet of Lovers"] (1964) he deals satirically with juvenile morals and life-values; in *Triszex* ["Trisex"] (1974) he predicts changes in family life and in human relationships. His most famous work is *A kék sziget* ["The Blue Island"] (1976), a harmonious UTOPIA. Gyula Hernádi (1926-   ) is a restless, experimenting author; he blends surrealism with real and fictitious documents. His significant novels are *Az eröd* ["The Fortress"] (1971), *Az elnökasszony* ["Madame President"] (1978) and *Hasfelmetszö Jack* ["Jack the Ripper"] (1982). Zoltán Csernai (1925-   ) is one of the most popular sf writers. His main focus is on encounters between ALIENS and humans in the past and present; this provides the background to his trilogy *Titok a világ tetején* ["Secret on the Top of the World"] (1961), *Az özönvíz balladája* ["The Ballad of the Flood"] (1964) and *Atlantisz* ["Atlantis"] (1968). His *Boldogságcsinálók* ["Producers of Happiness"] (1974) is an interesting psychological novel. Among his several short stories, "Kövek" ["Stones"] (1974) is perhaps the best of all Hungarian sf short stories; it has been much translated. Péter Zsoldos (1930-   ) is an sf author in the US-UK tradition, his recurrent subjects being SPACE FLIGHT and ROBOTS. His best novels are *Feladat* ["The Task"] (1971), *Ellenpont* ["Counterpoint"] (1973), *Távoli tüz* ["A Distant Fire"] (1969), *A Viking visszatér* ["Return of the Viking"] (1967) and *A holtak nem vetnek árnyékot* ["The Dead Cast No Shadows"] (1983). Ervin Gyertyán (1925-   ) prefers a humorous, satirical attitude *Kibernerosz* ["Cyberneros"] (1963) and *Isten óvd az elnököt!* ["God Save the President!"] (1971), paying special

attention to the differences between Man and MACHINE, and also to the nature of identity. Two sf works by Miklós Rónaszegi (1930-   ), *A rovarok lázadása* ["Revolt of the Insects"] (1969) and *Ördögi liquor* ["Liquor of the Devil"] (1972), were published as juveniles, although there is nothing juvenile about their themes: the first analyses the mechanisms of fascism and the second unveils ways in which modern society dehumanizes and manipulates.

Novels of adventure and scientific inspiration have been written also by Klára Fehér (1922-   ), László Nemes (1920-   ) and Tibor Dáné (1923-   ). Dezsö Kemény (1925-   ) melds sf with the crime story. *Az utolsó ember* ["The Last Man"] (1982) by Péter Bogáti (1924-   ), a ROBINSONADE about the last survivor of world HOLOCAUST, bears comparison with better-known treatments of the subject. László András (1919-1988), György Nemes (1910-   ), András Kürti (1922-   ) and Rudolf Weinbrenner (1923-1987) are all writers who have enriched Hungarian sf with one or two books. A rather different coloration can be found in *A Kozmosz tizenötödik törvénye* ["The Fifteenth Law of the Cosmos"] (1984) by Mihály Gergely (1921-   ), a novel in which alien visitors try to force humanity into peace and intelligent cooperation.

Perhaps the most important member of the younger generation is Péter Szentmihályi Szabó (1945-   ). His collection of short stories *A sebezhetetlen* ["The Invulnerable"] (coll 1978) tries out every voice and technique of sf; *A tökéletes változat* ["The Perfect Variety"] (1983) is a DYSTOPIA about contradictory social systems in the distant future. Two very prolific younger authors are László L. Lörincz (1939-   ) and István Nemere (1944-   ). Lörincz's collection of short stories *A nagy kupola szégyene* ["The Shame of the Great Dome"] (coll 1982) deals with CRIME AND PUNISHMENT and with problems of social isolation. His novels, such as *A hosszú szafari* ["The Long Safari"] (1984) and *A földalatti piramis* ["The Underground Pyramid"] (1986), are much appreciated for their exciting plots, richness of ideas and beautiful style. Nemere's most successful novels (out of about 60) are *A kozmosz korbácsa* ["The Whip of the Cosmos"] (1982), *Az acélcápa* ["The Steel Shark"] (1982) and *A neutron akció* ["The Neutron Project"] (1982).

One MAINSTREAM WRITER who has occasionally turned to sf is Péter Lengyel, who wrote the prizewinning *Ogg második bolygója* ["Ogg's Second Planet"] (1969). [PK]

HUNGER, ANNA ◊ R. DeWitt MILLER.

HUNT, GILL House name used 1950-52 by the UK paperback publisher Curtis Warren. The authors who have used the name (*for titles see their entries*) are John BRUNNER, David GRIFFITHS, Dennis HUGHES, John JENNISON and E.C. TUBB. Because it was Brunner's first book, *Galactic Storm* (1951) has become the best-known of the GH titles; it is not, however, significantly less routine than its stablemates. [JC]

HUNTER, EVAN Once the main pseudonym and now

the adopted legal name of the US writer born S.A. Lombino (1926-), who remains best known as Ed McBain, under which byline he has written at least 50 laconic police procedurals as well as some action-detections in the John D. MacDONALD mould. As EH he is most famous for novels like *The Blackboard Jungle* (**1954**), and his later career has had little to do with sf, most of his work in the genre appearing – under his own name and as Richard Marsten and Hunt Collins – in the 1950s. This early output included a number of magazine sf stories, published 1953-6 – some of which were assembled in *The Last Spin* (coll **1960** UK) and *Happy New Year, Herbie* (coll **1963**) – and the screenplay for Alfred Hitchcock's *The* BIRDS (1963). His first three sf novels were juveniles: the protagonist in *Find the Feathered Serpent* (**1952**) utilizes his father's TIME-TRAVEL device to return to – and to participate in – the founding of the Mayan empire; *Rocket to Luna* (**1953**), as by Richard Marsten, puts students on the first trip to the Moon; and *Danger! Dinosaurs!* (**1953**), as by Marsten, again takes its heroes by time-travel into an exciting era. His first adult sf novel, *Tomorrow's World* (1954 *If* as "Malice in Wonderland" as by EH; exp **1956**; vt *Tomorrow and Tomorrow* 1956), as by Hunt Collins, takes a somewhat satirical look at a future dominated by organized DRUG addicts. In a marketing decision somewhat at odds with EH's normal practice, the book was later published unchanged (1979 UK) as by Ed McBain: it is certainly not in the McBain style. *Nobody Knew They Were There* (**1971**) is set in 1974, but is a tale of campus violence only marginally displaced into sf. The plot of *Ghosts* (**1980**), one of his extensive series of 87th Precinct police-procedural novels as by Ed McBain, surprisingly hinges on parapsychological manifestations (◊ ESP), to the detriment of its merit as a detection. EH's long inactivity as an sf writer has been the genre's loss.   [JC]

See also: LEISURE; PULP MAGAZINES.

HUNTER, E. WALDO [s] ◊ Theodore STURGEON.

HUNTER, NORMAN (GEORGE LORIMER) (1899-) UK writer first active before WWII. He lived in South Africa 1949-70, a period during which he published nothing. He was also a professional conjurer, and wrote on this subject. His classic CHILDREN'S SF series about **Professor Branestawm** and his inventions – *The Incredible Adventures of Professor Branestawm* (coll **1933**), *Professor Branestawm's Treasure Hunt* (coll **1937**), *Stories of Professor Branestawm* (coll **1939**), *The Peculiar Triumph of Professor Branestawm* (coll **1970**), *Professor Branestawm up the Pole* (coll **1972**), *Professor Branestawm's Great Revolution* (coll **1974**), *Professor Branestawm 'round the Bend* (coll **1977**) and *Professor Branestawm's Perilous Pudding* (coll **1979**) – delightfully involves the professor and his extraordinary devices in various exploits and entanglements. There followed a compilation, *The Best of Branestawm* (coll **1980**), and a series of booklets: *Professor Branestawm and the Wild Letters* (**1981** chap), *Professor Branestawm's Pocket Motor Car* (**1982** chap), *Professor Branestawm's Mouse*

War (**1982** chap), *Professor Branestawm's Crunchy Crockery* (**1983** chap) and *Professor Branestawm's Hair-Raising Idea* (**1983** chap). The initial titles inspired a 1969 UK tv series. NH also wrote a number of tales for younger children, many of them revolving around the King and Queen of Incrediblania.   [JC]

HUNTER, S.L. ◊ Nicholas YERMAKOV.

HUNTING, (HENRY) GARDNER (1872-1958) US writer whose sf novel *The Vicarion* (**1926**; exp 1927) features a device which gives sight of the past. As a consequence, murders can be solved, politics cleaned up and the true events of history understood at last.   [JC]

See also: MACHINES.

HURD, DOUGLAS (RICHARD) (1930-) UK Conservative politician and writer, in the former capacity serving his government for an extended period at Cabinet level. His sf novels are, perhaps understandably, NEAR-FUTURE thrillers in which the UK must survive threats from within and without (◊ POLITICS). *Send Him Victorious* (**1968**) with Andrew Osmond (1938-) features threats of political upheaval from within. *The Smile on the Face of the Tiger* (**1969**) sees China demanding Hong Kong back from her imperial masters (a plot which has, of course, become part of history). *Scotch on the Rocks* (**1971**) describes a Scottish liberation movement (and may be prophetic).   [JC]

Other works: *Truth Game* (**1972**).

HURD, GALE ANNE (1955-) US film producer who cut her teeth on Roger CORMAN's New World Pictures' exploitation movies; she was production manager on BATTLE BEYOND THE STARS (1980) and coproduced the car-chase movie *Smokey Bites the Dust* (1981) with Corman. She came to prominence with the excellent low-budget independent film *The* TERMINATOR (1984), whose screenplay was cowritten by her and her then husband James CAMERON (also a graduate of the Corman school of low-budget film-making skills): both were in their 20s; he directed and she produced. This was sufficient to get them the high-status job of producing and directing ALIENS (1986), which they did with panache. They next worked together on *The* ABYSS (1989), whose screenplay (by Cameron) contained *roman à clef* elements in its story of the break-up of a marriage between two highflying professionals; they had separated personally by then, and to a degree professionally, although GAH worked as executive producer on TERMINATOR 2: JUDGMENT DAY (1991), perhaps the most expensive film ever made. (The actual producer was B.J. Rack.) GAH's expertise with genre movies was underwritten by the two sf films she produced apart from Cameron, ALIEN NATION (1988) and TREMORS (1990), the latter being an especially craftsmanlike work. Although it is difficult to gauge the creative influence of producers as opposed to directors, GAH's track record is impressive; her films (even the low-budget ones) are polished and look good, and she seems to have an affinity with sf subjects.   [PN]

HURWOOD, BERNHARDT J(ACKSON) (1926-1987)

US writer who wrote occult books for younger readers – like *Strange Curses* (coll **1975**) and *By Blood Alone* (**1979**) – the **Man from T.O.M.C.A.T.** soft-porn quasithriller sequence as by Mallory T. Knight, comprising *The Man from T.O.M.C.A.T. #1: The Dozen Deadly Dragons of Joy* (**1967**), *#2: The Million Missing Maidens* (**1978**), *#3: The Terrible Ten* (**1967**), *#4: The Dirty Rotten Depriving Boy* (**1967**), *#5: Tsimmis in Tangier* (**1968**), *#6: The Malignant Metaphysical Menace* (**1968**), *#7: The Ominous Orgy* (**1969**), *#10: The Peking Pornographer* * (**1969**) and *The Bra-Burner's Brigade* (**1971**). The **Invisibles** sequence, comprising *The Invisibles* (**1971**) and *The Mind Master* (**1973**), were sf stories about a mad SCIENTIST who conducts experiments on human subjects. *Kingdom of the Spiders* * (**1977**) was a film tie (◊ KINGDOM OF THE SPIDERS). [JC]

HUTCHINSON, DAVID (CHRISTOPHER) (1960-) UK writer who published 4 volumes of stories at a very early age – *Thumbprints* (coll **1978**), *Fools' Gold* (coll **1979**), *Torn Air* (coll **1980**) and *The Paradise Equation* (coll **1981**) – and then moved into journalism. The deftness and quiet humaneness of his work seemed better than precocious, and it came as welcome news in the late 1980s that he was turning his attention again to sf. [JC]

HUXLEY, ALDOUS (1894-1963) UK novelist and man of letters whose fame was freshest in the 1920s, a decade which his work, conveying as it did an overwhelming sense of psychic aftermath, captured precisely; his best fiction, like *Point Counter Point* (**1928**), was written then. From 1937 he lived in the USA. He is today almost certainly remembered most widely for his seminal DYSTOPIA, *Brave New World* (**1932**), a book which established such words as "soma" (originally from Sir Thomas MORE's *Utopia* [**1517**]) and "feelie" in the English language, and which contributed to social and literary thought a definite model of pharmacological totalitarianism. (Soma is a kind of psychedelic drug used as a social control; the feelies are multisense – or "VIRTUAL REALITY" – movies, developed for the same reason.) *Brave New World* depicts a future Earth in which the expression of dissonant emotions and acts is rigorously controlled from above, ostensibly for the betterment of all, though in fact the motives of those in power are, as always, self-serving. Babies, once decanted, are chemically adjusted to grow to assume the body-type and intelligence required at that moment by society, and as a result enter into the appropriate castes, from Alpha to Epsilon (◊ GENETIC ENGINEERING). Sex and all other relationships are casual, without dissonance or affect. As in any dystopia, the story both illustrates and exposes this plastic paradise, and presents opportunities for discussion about it. One protagonist goes to a Savage Reservation (where, as a kind of control, a few old-style humans are permitted their exemplary culture) and there rescues a young woman in trouble; he returns with her and her Savage son to the central society. To this she proves unable to adjust: after

causing general disgust through her display of visible diseases and her horrifying descent into age, she overdoses despairingly on soma. Her son does little better, though the fracas he causes gains him and two discontented citizens an interview with Mustapha Mond, one of the 10 World Controllers, who argumentatively justifies the price paid for stability. When the unconvinced Savage attempts to live alone and so to replicate the conditions necessary for the creation of high art, he is soon driven by the mass MEDIA into committing suicide.

As argument and as SATIRE, *Brave New World* is a compendium of usable points and quotable jibes – the substitution of Ford for God being merely the best known – and has provided material for much subsequent fiction. Its pessimistic accounting of the sterility and human emptiness of utopian communities shaped by a reductive scientism has caused the book to be read as a decisive refutation of those UTOPIAS of H.G. WELLS – e.g., *Men Like Gods* (**1923**) – whose strident OPTIMISM about scientific utopianism even Wells himself could not manage to support with much imaginative conviction. *Brave New World Revisited* (coll **1958**), later assembled with its predecessor (omni **1960**), is a nonfiction series of essays on the themes of the novel from the perspective of 25 years later.

After moving to the USA, AH wrote two novels in which utopia/dystopia debates are continued. *Ape and Essence* (**1948**), powerfully dystopian, is set in AD2108 after an atomic and bacteriological final WAR. From New Zealand, which has been left untouched, a researcher visits the USA, where he discovers a literally devilish society: human nature and science have gone savagely wrong, and females – now contemptuously known as "vessels" – come into oestrus for only two weeks in the year, after Belial Day. The pessimism of the book is unalleviated, and its presentation, as a kind of ideal filmscript, horrific and disgusted. *Island* (**1962**) presents a utopian alternative to the previous books, though without much energy. Pala – the ISLAND in question – is set safely in the Indian Ocean, and has long enjoyed a mildly euphoric existence, sustained spiritually by religious practices derived from Tantric Buddhism, and physically by moksha, a sort of benign soma, whose psychedelic effects smooth the rough edges of the world. But the book itself is powerless to convince.

Of AH's other work, *After Many a Summer Dies the Swan* (**1939**; vt *After Many a Summer* 1939 UK), in which a Californian oil magnate rediscovers an 18th-century longevity compound and its macabre consequences (◊ APES AND CAVEMEN *for other tales that evoke images of* DEVOLUTION), and *Time Must Have a Stop* (**1944**), one of whose protagonists undergoes posthumous experiences, are both of genre interest.

AH was at his most striking in those of his novels, some technically sf, which treated their fictional content as subservient to the matters being discussed and illuminated. The literacy of his style, and the apparent sophistication of his transcendental thought, have perhaps impressed traditional sf readers and critics more than he deserved. There is no denying, however, the extreme importance of the example of his thought in the intellectual development of the genre. [JC]

About the author: There are many critical studies. Lilly Zahner's *Demon and Saint in the Novels of Aldous Huxley* (**1975**) provides clear analysis and an adequate bibliography. Other studies include *Aldous Huxley: A Study of the Major Novels* (**1968**) by Peter Bowering, and *Aldous Huxley, Satire and Structure* (**1969**) by Jerome Meckier.

See also: ANTHROPOLOGY; AUTOMATION; BIOLOGY; CRITICAL AND HISTORICAL WORKS ABOUT SF; EVOLUTION; FUTUROLOGY; HISTORY OF SF; IMMORTALITY; LEISURE; MACHINES; MAINSTREAM WRITERS OF SF; MUSIC; PERCEPTION; SOCIOLOGY; TECHNOLOGY; THEATRE.

HYAMS, EDWARD S(OLOMON) (1910-1975) UK writer, prolific in various genres, fiction and nonfiction, from before WWII; he was also active as a translator. Although not widely known as a writer of sf or fantasy, he published several novels of sf interest. *Not in Our Stars* (**1949**) depicts the discovery of a fungus of use in biological warfare. *The Astrologer* (**1950**) is an early novel on the ecological theme of soil exhaustion, and the DISASTER its protagonist tries to avert by denying men sex, like Lysistrata. *The Final Agenda* (**1973**) places a worldwide organization of anarchists in power in a NEAR-FUTURE venue, and traces with considerable sympathy their attempts to found an ecological UTOPIA. *Morrow's Ants* (**1975**) is about the creation of a HIVE-MIND. Typically of writers not identified with the genre, ESH tends to use sf components in a didactic fashion, although in his case to considerable effect. [JC]

Other works: *The Wings of the Morning* (**1939**), a Wellsian discursive novel set just before a future WAR; *Sylvester* (**1951**; vt *998* 1952 US); *The Last Poor Man* (**1966**); *The Death Lottery* (**1971**); *Prince Habib's Iceberg* (**1974**).

See also: ASTRONOMY; ECOLOGY; SCIENTISTS.

HYDE, CHRISTOPHER (1949-   ) Canadian writer, generally of TECHNOTHRILLERS, beginning with *The Wave* (**1979** US) and continuing with titles like *Styx* (**1982** US), *Jericho Falls* (**1988** UK), *Crestwood Hills* (**1988** US), *Egypt Green* (**1989** US) and *White Lies* (**1990** US). The last features a mentally suspect NEAR-FUTURE US President who puts out a contract on himself. [JC]

HYDE, SHELLEY ◊ Kit REED.

HYDER, ALAN (?   -?   ) UK writer known only for the remarkable *Vampires Overhead* (**1935**), in which comet-hopping vampires invade Earth, causing general devastation; the tale is told with very considerable vigour. It was included in a list prepared in 1983 by Karl Edward Wagner for *Twilight Zone* of the 13 best sf HORROR novels. [JC]

HYMAN, MIRANDA ◊ Miranda MILLER.

HYNE, C(HARLES) J(OHN) CUTCLIFFE (WRIGHT)

(1866-1944) UK writer. He utilized his ample travelling experience in creating the popular **Captain Kettle** series which appeared in PEARSON'S MAGAZINE and later in the cinema; *Captain Kettle on the Warpath* (coll **1916**), *The Rev. Captain Kettle* (coll **1925**), *Mr Kettle, Third Mate* (**1931**) and *Ivory Valley* (**1938**) are the only volumes to contain sf elements. He is best known for *The Lost Continent* (**1900**), set in ATLANTIS at the time of its destruction. CJCH began writing sf with *Beneath Your Very Boots* (**1889**), a LOST-WORLD tale set in caves under England, following it up with a ROBINSONADE, *The New Eden* (**1892**), later turning to future WAR with *Empire of the World* (**1910**; vt *Emperor of the World* 1915) and to the Wandering-Jew theme with *Abbs, His Story through Many Ages* (**1929**). This diversity of ideas was even more prevalent in his short stories, particularly *The Adventures of a Solicitor* (coll of linked stories **1898**) as by Weatherby Chesney, which contains stories about INVISIBILITY, ROBOTS, SPACE FLIGHT and rejuvenation, together with several GOTHIC and weird fantasies. CJCH, one of the most prolific writers of early magazine sf, is now almost forgotten. [JE]

Other works: *The Recipe for Diamonds* (**1893**); *The Stronger Hand* (coll **1896**), *The Foundered Galleon* (1898-9 *Scraps* as by Weatherby Chesney and Alick Jones; 1902) as by Weatherby Chesney; *The Adventures of an Engineer* (coll of linked stories **1903**) as by Weatherby Chesney; *Atoms of Empire* (coll **1904**); *Red Herrings* (coll **1918**); *West Highland Spirits* (coll **1932**); *Man's Understanding* (coll **1933**), some sf; *Wishing Smith* (**1939**).

See also: CRIME AND PUNISHMENT; WEAPONS.

HYPERION PRESS US publisher based in Westport, Connecticut. HP's relevance to sf is through its photographically reproduced reprint series, **Classics of Science Fiction**; HP was the first publisher to undertake such a series, preceding ARNO PRESS, GARLAND and GREGG PRESS. The series editor was Sam MOSKOWITZ, who also provided introductions to many of the volumes; the books selected were primarily drawn from the late 19th and early 20th centuries. The first series, published 1974, had 23 vols; the second, published 1976, had 19 vols. HP also brought back into print 6 anthologies and collections of criticism by Moskowitz. [MJE/PN]

HYPERSPACE In sf TERMINOLOGY, a kind of specialized space through which SPACESHIPS can take a short cut in order to get rapidly from one point in "normal" space to another far distant. The term was probably invented by John W. CAMPBELL Jr in *Islands of Space* (1931 *Amazing Stories Quarterly*; **1957**). It is now so thoroughly incorporated into the conventions of GENRE SF that few sf writers feel called upon to explain its meaning, although Robert A. HEINLEIN gave a particularly clear account in *Starman Jones* (**1953**). Hyperspace is often seen as a space of higher DIMENSION through which our three-dimensional space can be folded or crumpled, so that two apparently distant points may almost come into contact. Sometimes, as in Frederik POHL's "The Mapmakers" (1955), hyperspace is seen as a POCKET

UNIVERSE, a kind of visitable map with a one-to-one correspondence to our own Universe (with all points hopefully arranged in the same order). In "FTA" (1974) by George R.R. MARTIN, although hyperspace exists, travel by it takes longer. In *Redshift Rendezvous* (**1990**) by John E. STITH a starship has to cope with the fact that the velocity of light in hyperspace is 22mph (35kph); relativistic effects thus occur at very modest velocities.

The prohibitions in Relativity theory against travelling FASTER THAN LIGHT are not really circumvented with devices like SPACE WARPS or hyperspace, since it is actually FTL *journeys* and not FTL *velocities* that are prohibited, a point often not appreciated by sf writers; if an FTL journey takes place via hyperspace, the fact remains that the arrival might be witnessed by observers elsewhere in the Universe as preceding the take-off, and Relativity prohibits the principle of causality being broken by the reversal of cause and effect.

A relevant article is "Hyperspace" by David LANGFORD in *The Science in Science Fiction* (**1982**) by Peter NICHOLLS, Brian M. STABLEFORD and Langford. [PN/TSu]

HYPHEN Northern Irish FANZINE (1952-65) ed from Belfast by Walt Willis, with Chuck Harris and later Ian McAuley; probably the most famous of humorous fanzines. The quality and style of *H*'s writing made it not only one of the most admired fanzines of its time but also gave it considerable prestige and influence in FANDOM. Contributors included Robert BLOCH, Damon KNIGHT, Bob SHAW, William F. TEMPLE and James WHITE. There was a single-issue revival in 1987. [PR/RH]

HYPNOSIS ◊ PSYCHOLOGY.

ICARUS XB-1 ◊ IKARIE XB-1.

ICEMAN Film (1984). Universal. Prod Norman Jewison. Dir Fred Schepisi, starring Timothy Hutton, John Lone, Lindsay Crouse. Screenplay Chip Proser, John Drimmer, from a story by Drimmer. 99 mins. Colour.

Set in the Arctic (shot in Canada), *I* tells of a Neanderthal dug out of the ice, thawed, resuscitated and studied. Eschewing the caveman clichés (◊ APES AND CAVEMEN) of films like TROG (1970), it adopts a sensitive and supposedly realistic manner, much being made of Neanderthal LINGUISTICS. But the story is so thin as to be almost invisible, and the film sags tediously as eco-clichés of the period lead to predictable clashes between the anthropologist, on the side of life, and the female scientist, on the side of cold-blooded research. The scientific methods on display are laughably inept and unlikely. [PN]

ICE PIRATES, THE Film (1984). MGM/United Artists. Dir Stewart Raffill, starring Robert Urich, Mary Crosby, Michael D. Roberts, Anjelica Huston, John Matuszak, Ron Perlman. Screenplay Raffill, Stanford Sherman. 94 mins. Colour.

Sf parodies have seldom worked well in the cinema, but this is an exception. Jason (Urich) is a pirate captain of a spaceship (he and his crew carry cutlasses and wear high boots) who raids merchant ships for ice (the planets in this area being arid), meets a princess and has adventures. The film's success depends on the script's real knowledge (unusual in the movies) of written sf's dafter conventions as well as the CLICHÉS of sf cinema; both are neatly caricatured. Particularly lunatic is the final battle in a time warp, with the heroic contenders visibly ageing, the day being saved by the hero's baby who grows rapidly into a man and repels the elderly boarders. There is a small, irritating, chest-bursting ALIEN scuttling around, and Anjelica Huston buckles an expert swash. The farce is played straight enough to work, and the whole thing, though sometimes too broad, is agreeably genial. Raffill went on to direct *The* PHILADELPHIA EXPERIMENT (1984). [PN]

I COME IN PEACE (vt *Dark Angel* US) Film (1989). Vision. Dir Craig R. Baxley, starring Dolph Lundgren, Brian Benben, Matthias Hues. Screenplay Jonathan Tydor and Leonard Maas Jr. 91 mins. Colour.

Good cop (Lundgren) and silly FBI man (Benben) go up against ALIEN drug dealer in Houston, with brief assistance from alien cop. *ICIP* is rather like a downmarket ALIEN NATION and also borrows from *The* HIDDEN. The alien, who is collecting human endorphins, is big and uses a razor-edged self-propelled compact disc as a weapon. This formula action movie is only partially redeemed by Mark Helfrich's brisk editing. It ends thus: *Alien:* "I come in peace." *Lundgren:* "And you go in pieces, asshole!" [PN]

IDLER, THE UK magazine published monthly by Chatto & Windus (later by Dawburn & Ward and others), ed Jerome K. Jerome and Robert BARR – both jointly and separately – and by Arthur Lawrence, Sidney H. Sime, and others, Feb 1892-Mar 1911.

Although comparatively short-lived, *TI* published much sf, mainly through the leanings of its founding editors, both (at times) fantasy authors and both of whom contributed sf stories to its pages. Other notable contributors in its early days were Edwin Lester ARNOLD, Arthur Conan DOYLE, Mark TWAIN and H.G. WELLS. *TI* continued to publish fantasy and sf from writers such as Patrick Vaux, William Hope HODGSON and Paul Bo'ld until its demise. Many stories from *TI* were reprinted in MCCLURE'S MAGAZINE. [JE]

IDRĪS, YŪSUF ◊ ARABIC SF.

IF US DIGEST-size magazine. 175 issues Mar 1952-Nov/Dec 1974. It was founded by the Quinn Publishing Co. with Paul W. FAIRMAN as editor, but James L. QUINN quickly assumed the editorial chair himself, in Nov 1952, holding it until Damon KNIGHT took over Oct 1958-Feb 1959. There were no issues Feb-July

1959 because the title was sold during that year to Digest Productions and became a companion to GALAXY SCIENCE FICTION under the editorship of *Gal's* editor H.L. GOLD, who stayed in the post July 1959-Sep 1961. Frederik POHL assumed the editorship Nov 1961. From July 1963 the publisher operated as Galaxy Publishing Corp. *Gal* and *If* were both sold in 1969 to the Universal Publishing and Distributing Co., and Ejler JAKOBSSON took over as editor of both in July 1969. James BAEN became editor with the Mar/Apr issue in 1974, shortly before the magazine folded. For most of its life it was bimonthly, but Mar 1954-June 1955, and again July 1964-May 1970, it was monthly. The latter period was its heyday; it won HUGOS for Best Magazine in 1966, 1967 and 1968. *If* was at first merely subtitled *Worlds of Science Fiction*, but in Nov 1961 the cover logo – though not the spine – was altered to *Worlds of If Science Fiction*. *If* absorbed its bimonthly companion, WORLDS OF TOMORROW, in 1967.

The most notable story appearing in *If* during the Quinn period – during one year of which, 1953-4, Larry SHAW did most of the actual editing – was James BLISH's classic *A Case of Conscience* (Sep 1953; exp **1958**). At its height, under Pohl, the magazine featured several Hugo-winning stories, including Robert A. HEINLEIN's *The Moon is a Harsh Mistress* (Dec 1965-Apr 1966; **1966**), Larry NIVEN's "Neutron Star" (Oct 1966) and Harlan ELLISON's "I Have No Mouth and I Must Scream" (Mar 1967); other stories included Samuel R. DELANY's "Driftglass" (June 1967). In this period the magazine also featured A.E. VAN VOGT's return to sf-writing after a long absence, and the fourth volume of E.E. "Doc" SMITH's **Skylark** series, nearly 30 years after the third – *Skylark Du Quesne* (June-Oct 1965; **1966**). Under Jakobsson's editorship the magazine resumed playing second fiddle to *Gal* and gradually declined until it was merged with its companion as of Jan 1975. It had been, overall, one of the more distinguished sf magazines. Writers who made their débuts in *If* include David R. BUNCH, Larry Niven, William F. NOLAN, Andrew OFFUTT and Alexei PANSHIN.

Artwork was quite good from early on. Ed VALI-GURSKY was the first art editor – replaced by Mel Hunter in 1955 – and introduced Kelly FREAS's and Kenneth Fagg's work to the magazine. Later artists included Jack GAUGHAN, Gray MORROW and Wally WOOD.

The history of *If*'s UK editions is inordinately complex. Strato Publications reprinted 15 numbered issues from the 1953-4 period, and a further 18 (beginning again at #1) in 1959-62. Gold Star Publications marketed a UK edition Jan-Nov 1967 whose issues were dated 10 months later than the otherwise identical US editions. Copies of the UPD version were imported 1972-4 and numbered for UK release, the numbers running #1-#9 and then, astonishingly, #11, #1, #13, #3, #4 and #5! The last issue of *If* was never distributed in the UK.

Two anthologies of stories from *If*, in magazine format, were released as *The First World of If* (anth **1957**) and *The Second World of If* (anth **1958**), both ed Quinn. There followed *The If Reader of Science Fiction* (anth **1966**) and *The Second If Reader of Science Fiction* (anth **1968**), both ed Pohl. More recent collections have been *The Best from If* (anth **1973**) ed anon, *The Best from If Vol II* (anth **1974**) ed The Editors of If Magazine, and *The Best from If Vol III* (anth **1976**) ed James Baen. [BS/PN]

IGGULDEN, JOHN (1917-) Australian author whose sf work is restricted to an unremarkable DYSTOPIAN novel, *Breakthrough* (**1960** UK), in which a dictator uses implanted radio-controlled devices for purposes of repression. [JC]

IGNOTUS, CORONEL [r] ◊ SPAIN.

IJÄS, JYRKI (NIILO JUHANI) (1943-) Finnish film editor, translator and journalist, the first of whose (few) sf stories was "Koekaniini" ["Guinea Pig"] in 1968. One of the founders of *Aikakone* magazine (◊ FINLAND), he is also publisher and editor of *Ikaros* magazine, winner of the Finnish Kosmoskynä award in 1988, editor of *Ensimmäinen yhteys* ["First Contact"] (anth **1988**) and an sf critic. He wrote the entry on FINLAND for this encyclopedia. [PN]

IKARIE ◊ CZECH AND SLOVAK SF; Jaroslav OLŠA.

IKARIE XB-1 (vt *Voyage to the End of the Universe*; vt *Icarus XB-1*) Film (1963). Filmové studio Barrandov. Dir Jindřich Polák, starring Zdeněk Štěpánek, Radovan Lukavský, Dana Medřická. Screenplay Pavel Juráček, Polák. 81 mins, cut to 65 mins. Colour.

This interesting Czech film is set in a giant spaceship (with elaborate interiors designed by Jan Zázvorka) on a long exploratory mission. The shipboard routines, coolly observed, create the impression of a culture alien to ours. The stock situations of comparable US-UK films and tv series (STAR TREK and SPACE 1999, for example) are mostly avoided by the Czech writers, although the build-up of suspense when the spaceship encounters a wreck floating in space adds a touch of SPACE OPERA. The ending – the spaceship reaches a planet that we realize is contemporary Earth – is a US addition to the otherwise savagely cut print used for US and UK release. [JB/PN]

See also: CINEMA.

ILIĆ, DRAGUTIN [r] ◊ YUGOSLAVIA.

ILIEV, GEORGI [r] ◊ BULGARIA.

ILLING, WERNER [r] ◊ GERMANY.

ILLUSTRATED MAN, THE Film (1968). SKM Productions/Warner-Seven Arts. Dir Jack Smight, starring Rod Steiger, Claire Bloom, Robert Drivas, Don Dubbins, Jason Evers. Screenplay Howard B. Kreitsek, based on *The Illustrated Man* (coll **1951**) by Ray BRADBURY. 103 mins. Colour.

Bradbury's idea of a man whose various tattoos each represent a different tale did not completely work as an afterthought framework to link the stories of his collection, and it is even less successful in the film, which Bradbury hated. The stories are "The Long Rains" (astronauts lost on Venus), "The Veldt" and "The Last Night of the World"; only "The Veldt" (VIRTUAL-REALITY nursery animals come to life and are used by future children to dispose of parents) is anything other than limp and literal-minded. The same actors appear in each episode; apparently Smight, the director, was aiming at an atmosphere of downbeat enigma and malign destiny, with Steiger, the tattooed man, as a constantly reincarnated loser. Another Bradbury anthology film is VEL'D (1987).   [PN/JB]

ILLUSTRATION 1. From the Beginnings to 1978 The historical function of art in sf has been to illustrate rather than interpret; this reflects the hard-edged nature of early GENRE SF itself, which portrayed technics-dominated society rather than interpreting its *raisons d'être*; just as this kind of sf was popular science plus human- or wonder-interest, so the illustrations were there to provide page-interest. When these functional attitudes weakened, sf illustrations became freer, aspiring to illumination rather than diagram. Today their relationship to text is often generic rather than specific.

Before the SF MAGAZINES, there is little that can be regarded as pure generic sf illustration, though the art history of that early period of sf publication awaits research. Inspiration was derived on the one hand from black-and-white masters of graphic pun, such as Jean Ignace Grandville (1803-1847), Richard ("Dicky") Doyle (1824-1883) and the astonishing Albert ROBIDA, or specialists in futuristic WAR like Fred T. JANE, and on the other hand from more "serious" artists, such as Gustave Doré (1832-1883) and John Martin (1789-1854). The latter in particular, the first artist of the immense, has had great influence; his mighty visions were natural material for Hollywood, and echoes of them abound in, for instance, the original KING KONG (1933).

The other matter upon which the first generation of sf illustrators could rely was the spate of pictures of scientific and engineering marvels appearing in the press; a later generation turned to NASA handouts. Many drawings in Hugo GERNSBACK's early magazines in particular can be traced directly to sawn-down or blown-up versions of the Eiffel Tower and the thermionic valve or tube. Such illustrations accompanied stories which were often cautionary in nature: scientific experiments could result in DISASTER; interstellar gas and renegade planets were hazards in Earth's path; ROBOTS were prone to rape inventors' daughters – but still TECHNOLOGY had to go on. The illustrations were diagrams to enforce the thesis, and often set over a line or two of actual text.

Yet the subservient role of the sf artist is by no means the whole story. Even in the most commercial period it was recognized that the impact of the cover sold the magazine or paperback; in consequence, care and money went into the cover art. Some artists worked at their best on covers not just because the pay was better. Dedication was a more noteworthy characteristic than artistic excellence among this low-salaried breed of men.

Because of printing deadlines some publishers, particularly those with a "stable" of magazines, commissioned covers before stories. As a result, a writer might be asked to write a tale to fit a picture; this doubtful privilege gave the writer his name on the cover but could also entail a cut in the already mean rates of payment.

In this way, magazine art developed and became, even if in small compass, a tradition, with names of prolific illustrators like Frank R. PAUL, Virgil FINLAY and Emsh (Ed EMSHWILLER) dominating the field. Interior art became increasingly less tied to text, just as text became less tied to technics. It was free to indulge in the pleasantly hazy symbolism of a Paul ORBAN, the immaculacy of an Alex SCHOMBURG, or even the whimsicality of an Edd CARTIER. It was also at liberty to fudge on the detail in which members of the previous generation of illustrators, such as Frank R. Paul and Elliott DOLD, had gloried. Increasingly, the magazine covers symbolized the spirit of the magazine rather than depicting an incident in an actual story; the series of covers Emsh executed for GALAXY SCIENCE FICTION in the early 1960s provides a noteworthy example of this.

Increased paper and production costs in the 1940s hit the PULP MAGAZINES hard; as they dwindled, the COMIC book – which grew out of comic strips – rose in popularity. Hal Foster (1892-1982) had started the ever-popular Tarzan strip in 1929, in the same year that BUCK ROGERS IN THE 25TH CENTURY, drawn by Dick CALKINS and written by Philip NOWLAN, appeared on the scene. What Tarzan did for Africa, Buck did for space. Success bred imitators: the 1930s brought the caveman ALLEY OOP, a sort of anti-Tarzan (by Vincent Hamlin), **The Phantom** (Lee Falk and Ray Moore), BRICK BRADFORD (Clarence Gray and William Ritt), and the much admired FLASH GORDON, elegantly drawn by Alex RAYMOND. From such SUPERHEROES it was only a step to the king of them all, SUPERMAN. Created by Jerry SIEGEL and Joe Shuster, two sf fans, this character began life in a comic book, *Action Comics*, in 1938, and was a success from the start. Like Flash and Buck before him, Superman went into RADIO and then into films. By 1941, the fortnightly comic-book version had reached a circulation of 1,400,000. The day of the superhero had dawned.

MARVEL COMICS introduced **The Fantastic Four** in 1961; since then Marvel's fabulous but fallible beings – **The Spider-Man, The Incredible Hulk, The Silver Surfer** and the rest of the grotesques – have changed the nature of comics and, on the whole, improved the standard of draughtsmanship in the field. But the most astonishing developments came from France, in particular from the group of artists (of whom Philippe DRUILLET was one) working for the magazine MÉTAL HURLANT. Here the mood was of brooding unease rather than action; sophisticated surreal effects were achieved without recourse to balloons or commentary.

As the written word affected artwork, so artwork

ILLUSTRATION _____ 612

influenced the written word. There was a period in sf when interiors of SPACESHIPS were vast, shadowy, and echoing; they came complete with cast-iron doors opening directly onto space and equipped with doorknobs for handles. That was the influence of Calkins's **Buck Rogers**. Raymond's **Flash Gordon** had similar effects, and his line of galactic romance, with proud queens dressed in fur-tipped boots and haughty expressions, and usurping villains lurking behind the arras with axe and ray-gun, is with us yet. The enormous vacuum-vehicles of Christopher FOSS spring from A.E. VAN VOGT's epics – and will surely inspire future van Vogts.

Imitation is promoted by systems of tight deadlines and tighter payrolls; whatever comes to hand must be used. Artists, like writers, still borrow heavily from each other. In the jungle world of the pulps, artists moved easily from one genre to another, depending on the corporation employing them. We should be surprised not that there is so little individuality but that there is so much. Hubert ROGERS, *ASF*'s chief artist throughout much of the 1940s, produced many covers for other STREET & SMITH magazines; Frank Kelly FREAS, an *ASF* illustrator of infinite jest, created *Mad Magazine*'s lunatic optimist Alfred E. Neuman ("What, me worry?").

In the magazines of the early post-Gernsback period the mode depended heavily on horror and GOTHIC, perhaps because here was a convention readily to hand, waiting to be adapted. Finlay, Lawrence (Lawrence Sterne STEVENS), Hannes BOK, Alexander LEYDENFROST and Cartier are names that spring to mind. These artists of the macabre secured and kept a great following: Finlay and Bok in particular have become revered since their deaths. Leydenfrost, son of a Dutch illustrator, produced some of the most imaginative MONSTERS in the business; they are frequently based on insect morphology.

Later sf artists were able to forge an idiom more in tune with the technophile nature of sf. The precept of Frank R. PAUL was decisive here. An artist with training as an architect, Paul was possibly Gernsback's most remarkable discovery. This prodigious talent created his own brand of future CITY, with its sensuously curving lines an exotic amalgam of Byzantium and the local movie palace, owing something to the Art Deco movement. The same patterns were exaggerated in paranoid style by Elliot DOLD, who developed an intense poetry of machinery. During this period, H.W. WESSO also produced spirited interpretations of mighty cities and machineries, as did Leo MOREY and Orban, but it was the purity of line of Charles SCHNEEMAN and Rogers that best conveyed the aspirations of technocratic culture, where the merely human dwindles in the light of its aseptic artefacts.

Few sf illustrations are memorable in their own right; they come and they go. An exception must be made for Schneeman's idealistic picture of E.E. "Doc" SMITH's hero, Kimball Kinnison, the Grey Lensman,

striding along with two formidable alien allies (*ASF* Oct 1939). Together with Rogers's cover for Robert A. HEINLEIN's "The Roads Must Roll" (*ASF* Nov 1939), it represents a synthesis of that immaculate metal-clad future towards which many thought the world was rolling. Of course it was an illusion: WWII was already raging in Europe. In place of Rogers, Freas became *ASF*'s most popular artist; he specialized in roughnecks with guns.

ASF was iconoclastic, aware of its brand-image as the intellectual's sf magazine. The emphasis was on the word, which got things done, not the drawing, which was merely decorative; in consequence, much interior artwork was dull. For vigour, one turned to lesser magazines, to the crowded Herman Vestals in *Startling Stories* and *Planet Stories*, or to Rod RUTH in *Fantastic Adventures*, whose spirited sketches for "Queen of the Panther World" by Berkeley LIVINGSTON (July 1948) still retain their power.

Of the new 1950s magazines, *Gal* has already been mentioned. Its misty interior illustrations appeared refreshingly contemporary; best-remembered exponents of this style are William Ashman, Don Sibley, Dick Francis and the alarming Kossin. Among the names rising to prominence in the 1960s were John SCHOENHERR, Mel Hunter (1929-   ) and Jack GAUGHAN. By this time, the magazines had tidied up their typography, imitating their powerful rivals in the paperback industry; it is in paperback books that most of the traditional art is aired nowadays.

With sf motifs pervading certain strata of popular MUSIC, sf and fantasy art made formidable appearances on record album sleeves. Notably, Roger DEAN's striking composites of machine, insect, animal and bone have convincing power. Dean and the remarkably fecund Patrick Woodroffe (1940-   ) published collections of their own work, as did Karel THOLE, King Surrealist of sf art.

The new professional magazines of the later 1970s relied heavily on old modes of illustration. GALILEO did best, with Tom Barber striving towards something fresh. But it seemed undeniable that innovations would be more likely to occur elsewhere. Innovation follows cash flow: movies, tv and record-album covers adopted, on a wide front, an idiom that virtually began in the magazines. That early work, for many reasons, can never be repeated; for aesthetic reasons, it cannot be ignored. A number of books of the 1970s deal, in whole or in part, with sf illustration: *Hier, L'an 2000* (**1973** France; trans as *2000 A.D.: Illustrations from the Golden Age of Science Fiction Pulps* **1975**) by Jacques SADOUL; *One Hundred Years of Science Fiction Illustration* (**1974**) by Anthony FREWIN; *Science Fiction Art* (**1975**) by Brian W. ALDISS and *A Pictorial History of Science Fiction* (**1976**) by David A. KYLE.   [BWA]

2. From 1978 to 1992 This has been a period of few sf magazines: *Gal* died and the circulations of those that survived slipped inexorably downhill. The new UK magazine INTERZONE (begun 1982) unevenly experimented with cover art in many styles, Ian MILLER's bizarre, STEAMPUNK machines being among the more memorable results. The balance, so far as sf illustration was concerned, became permanently tilted in this period away from magazines and towards the covers of paperback books and the dust-jackets of hardcovers, and even here (remuneration in the book business not being highly competitive) some of the more successful artists, like Frank FRAZETTA, worked only briefly in the field before moving on to other forms of commercial art. A big success on book covers of the late 1970s were the erotic fantasies of Boris VALLEJO, whose busty bimbos in bondage harked back with a kind of frozen tastelessness to the era of the pin-up girl, but after a while his work could most easily be bought in the form of calendars.

Through much of the 1970s and 1980s UK sf paperback book covers were dominated by space pictures in a smooth, airbrushed style, with vast spacecraft looming – a style which most critics associated with Chris FOSS. Tim WHITE and Jim BURNS, Foss's heirs as the most successful UK sf illustrators, worked easily in this mode, though much of the best work of both is in other styles. Anthony ROBERTS and Angus MCKIE were also among the guilty parties. Burns was the first UK artist to win a HUGO for his work. While the style lasted, it looked to the casual bookshop browser as if all UK-published sf was effectively the same book.

In the USA, sf cover art was dominated through the 1980s by the paintings of Michael WHELAN, meticulous and vivid but perhaps with a rather-too-commercial predictability. He has created what will surely be an all-time record by failing to win the Hugo for Best Professional Artist only twice in the years 1980-1991 inclusive, winning 10 Hugos in all in that category, and an 11th for Best Non-Fiction Book. Some find that the covers of one of his closer competitors, Don MAITZ (who also won a Hugo), have more movement and vigour. Many of Maitz's covers are fantastic rather than technological, and the move away from icons of technology as a means of selling sf in book form was if anything even more pronounced in the USA during the 1980s than in the UK. Sf books sometimes featured the work of almost purely fantastic artists like ROWENA or the well achieved Art Nouveau pastiche of Thomas CANTY (although decorative styles based on woodcuts, stained glass and late-19th-century illustration had previously been used, to very great effect, by Leo and Diane DILLON). Other notable US cover artists of the 1980s include James GURNEY, Barclay SHAW and Darrell SWEET.

It is surprising that Surrealist book covers have been used comparatively seldom for sf, despite the memorable work of Richard POWERS in the USA (BALLANTINE BOOKS during the 1950s) in this supposedly more up-market and respectable style. Others to adopt a semi-Surrealist style were Brian LEWIS in the UK, Paul LEHR in the USA and Karel THOLE in Europe, but none of these are artists whose work is at all typical of the 1980s. The best known sf-Surrealist of our time is, like Thole, a European, and deeply influenced by the traditions of decadent graphic art that were always so much stronger in Europe than in the USA. This is H.R. GIGER, the Swiss painter whose work became justly celebrated in the USA with the film ALIEN (1979), for which he designed both monsters and spacecraft. His biomorphic creations are both phallic and vulval in a manner that, had it appeared in comic strips in the 1950s, would have justified the hysteria of Dr Fredric Wertham (1895-1981), whose book *The Seduction of the Innocent* (**1954**) charged that coded vaginas appeared in the shading of some comics drawing. (These and similar charges led directly to the introduction of the Comics Code in 1955.) Giger is not a cover artist, and has had only a small influence in that field.

It may be that sf illustration as a separate genre is slowly dying away, with the advent of the paperback book not really compensating for the death of the magazines in providing a niche for it. Certainly, there is not much in the sf art of the late 1980s/90s to get excited about; most of the development has been in fantasy art (and much of that, too, deals in visual stereotypes). While general standards are much higher than they were in, say, the PULP MAGAZINES, the sense of lurid freedom seems to have disappeared now that publishers carefully commission book covers which, normally, are designed to attract without giving offence.

In one area there have been great advances: the COMICS, once again. Most comics art is poor, but some is very good indeed. A new development in comics, the GRAPHIC NOVEL, has showcased artists, either working in close collaboration with writers or writing their own scenarios, some of whom are exceptional; they include Enki BILAL, Brian BOLLAND, Dave GIBBONS, Dave MCKEAN and Frank MILLER. But this is a wholly different art from sf illustration proper, comics being themselves a storytelling medium whereas magazine illustrations and book covers have the more static function of rendering icons designed to label the publication as being sf (or fantasy) and then to sell it, not to further the story.

See the Introduction for lists of comics artists and sf illustrators who receive entries in this encyclopedia. [PN]

See also: SEX.

ILLUSTRATORS OF THE FUTURE CONTEST ◊ WRITERS OF THE FUTURE CONTEST.

IMAGINARY SCIENCE Imaginary science is extremely common in sf; it is not at all the same thing as PSEUDO-SCIENCE. The difference is that the adherents of the pseudo-sciences believe them to be true, whereas the sf writer who uses imaginary science knows perfectly well that it is untrue.

Sf has often been criticized for scientific illiteracy, sometimes unfairly, for, while it does produce many simple SCIENTIFIC ERRORS, it commonly uses presently impossible science for two good reasons, neither of them ignorant: (a) what is impossible now may one day become possible; (b) imaginary science may be essential for plot purposes. An example of the first category is the common sf device of MATTER TRANSMISSION. All matter can be described in terms of information and, since all information can be transmitted, then one may legitimately theorize that matter transmission (or at least matter reconstruction) does not transgress the laws of Nature as we know them, even though the practical problems are so vast as to seem, at present, insuperable. (Instantaneous matter transmission, the most common form portrayed in sf, is another kettle of fish: it violates Relativity in the same way as any other mode of FASTER-THAN-LIGHT travel, such as via HYPERSPACE.) Similarly, SUSPENDED ANIMATION is not possible now but, with advances in CRYONICS, one day it may be.

We are primarily concerned here with the second category: the imaginary scientific device which does indeed contradict what we know of the sciences, usually PHYSICS, but which allows the writer a kind of imaginative freedom extremely difficult to obtain otherwise. The five best-known examples are ALTERNATE WORLDS; ANTIGRAVITY; FASTER-THAN-LIGHT (or FTL) travel and COMMUNICATION; INVISIBILITY; and TIME TRAVEL. A separate entry is devoted to each of these.

The game – it is indeed a game – is to produce as plausible a rationalization for the impossible as the author's artistry will allow, and it is precisely this skill that worries the scientific purist. Thus James BLISH, in his **Cities in Flight** series (1955-62; omni **1970**), explains his SPINDIZZY by referring to work by real theoretical physicists with an air of such bland conviction that a generation of sf readers may have grown up believing that antigravity is possible. Similarly, H.G. WELLS in *The Invisible Man* (**1897**) rattles on about refraction with a perfectly straight face. Blish did not believe in antigravity, nor Wells in invisibility: their aim was simply to rationalize the surrealistic central images of their story – US cities flying through space in Blish's book, and a suit and a mask being removed to reveal nothing behind them in Wells's. The imaginary science was there to clear the way, and, of course, to lend conviction to the tale.

Time travel is perhaps the clearest example. The ingenuity of sf writers is constantly aimed at subverting the prohibitions physics appears to place on time travel – some to do with causality – because, critically, time travel gives narrative access to the past and the future, and opens up exactly that perspective that is central to sf's finest achievements. Through its (almost certainly impossible) use, sf writers have achieved the freedom to consider things both possible and real, as in the fields of HISTORY, EVOLUTION and even METAPHYSICS – all three in the case of the great original, H.G. Wells's *The Time Machine* (**1895**). A puritanical demand for universal scientific responsibility (the genre is called science *fiction* after all) would instantly destroy this and many others of sf's

most intellectually rigorous works.

The publication of many books of scientific popularization in the 1970s and 1980s, particularly those about the relationship of quantum physics to COSMOLOGY, gave new credence to some of the imaginary sciences. If some real scientists were prepared to contemplate quantum-mechanical explanations for ALTERNATE WORLDS, or time-travelling particles like TACHYONS, or the possibility that BLACK HOLES may provide portals to other, distant areas of time or space (or even to "different universes"), then why should not sf authors be allowed the same imaginative warrant? The imaginary sciences took on a new lease of life, and Schrödinger's cat became, belatedly, an overnight success. The cynic, of course, might argue that this is simply a case of sf feeding back into science.

A controversial example of imaginary science is the employment of ESP or PSI POWERS – which might more properly be seen as within the province of the pseudo-sciences – as central to the story. Some sf writers, such as Alfred BESTER and Blish, have used psi powers exactly as they might use other imaginary sciences, as an evocative and useful plot device; other sf writers appear to be propagandizing on behalf of parapsychology, or at least succumbing to the lure of wish fulfilment. In SUPERMAN tales especially, the science involved tends to be pseudo rather than imaginary, and perhaps open to criticism on that account.

Writers of HARD SF often like to develop a realistic extrapolation from one imaginary change in scientific laws, or even in the fundamental constants of the Universe. Thus Bob SHAW, in *The Ragged Astronauts* (**1986**), invents a universe where pi equals exactly 3 (and where – perhaps as a remote consequence? – interplanetary travel between two planets closely orbiting one another is possible by balloon); Stephen BAXTER's *Raft* (**1991**) takes place in a universe where the force of GRAVITY is very much stronger than in ours; John E. STITH's *Redshift Rendezvous* (**1990**) proposes that in HYPERSPACE the velocity of light is 22 mph (35kph).

Sf writers have been inventive in creating imaginary scientific devices – such as the "slow glass" of Shaw's poignant "Light of Other Days" (1966) and others, which allows us to view the past because light takes so long to penetrate a sheet of the material – and occasionally even new sciences. An early example of the latter, and still one of the best, is Alfred JARRY's 'pataphysics, the science of imaginary solutions. Isaac ASIMOV was especially prolific in creating new sciences, such as POSITRONICS and PSYCHOHISTORY, though in these cases he was somewhat evasive about the details of how they worked; he has also used such old imaginary-science favourites as miniaturization (◊ GREAT AND SMALL), in *Fantastic Voyage* (**1966**), and in *The Gods Themselves* (**1972**) he came up with an "electron pump" that provides us with a limitless supply of electricity (electrons) in return for positrons supplied to an alternate universe. His most absurd coup in the imaginary-science line was "thiotimoline", described in "The Endochronic Properties of Resublimated Thiotimoline" (1948), which parodies the dusty style of a scientific report, and in its several sequels. Thiotimoline is, in effect, a time-travelling chemical which effortlessly reverses cause and effect. Ursula K. LE GUIN likewise came up with a new science in a spoof-scientific paper, "The Author of the Acacia Seeds and Other Extracts from the *Journal of the Association of Therolinguistics*" (1974); therolinguistics is the study of animal language and literature.

One real science is thus far imaginary, in the sense that it has no available subject matter: XENO-BIOLOGY. [PN]

IMAGINARY VOYAGES A term much used in the TERMINOLOGY of sf/fantasy critics, probably derived from the French, whose name for the genre is *"voyages imaginaires"*. From this term was also derived **Voyages extraordinaires**, the overall series title used by publisher Hetzel on the novels of Jules VERNE. In this encyclopedia the theme is treated under FANTAS-TIC VOYAGES and PROTO SCIENCE FICTION. A book on the subject is *The Imaginary Voyage in Prose Fiction* (1941) by Philip Babcock GOVE. [PN]

IMAGINATION US DIGEST-size magazine. 63 issues. First released Oct 1950 by the Clark Publishing Co., ed Raymond A. PALMER. Early in 1951, with #3, it was acquired by William L. HAMLING's Greenleaf Publishing Co., and continued with Hamling as editor until Oct 1958. Beginning as a bimonthly, it operated a six-weekly and then briefly a monthly schedule Sep 1952-July 1955. Until July 1955 its full title was *Imagination: Stories of Science and Fantasy*; from Oct 1955 it became *Imagination Science Fiction*. Hamling followed a policy of including a short novel in each issue. Among his most frequent contributors were Kris NEVILLE and Daniel F. GALOUYE, both of whom published much of their early work in *I*; others were Milton LESSER, Dwight V. SWAIN and, towards the end of *I*'s career, Edmond HAMILTON. *I* dealt primarily in routine SPACE OPERA, and featured an unusually high number of titles ending in exclamation marks. [BS]

IMAGINATIVE TALES US DIGEST-size magazine. 26 issues. A bimonthly companion to IMAGINATION, *IT* was published by William HAMLING's Greenleaf Publishing Co., ed Hamling, Sep 1954-Nov 1958. The last 3 issues, July-Nov 1958, were published under the title *Space Travel* (but continued the previous numeration) in a doomed effort to capture the post-Sputnik space-enthusiast market.

IT began as a humorous FANTASY magazine, the first 6 issues featuring complete novels in the style of Thorne Smith (1892-1934) by Charles F. Myers and Robert BLOCH, but from Sep 1955 it reverted to a policy identical to that of its companion, featuring only sf, with a short novel heading every issue. Regular writers included Edmond HAMILTON, Geoff St Reynard (Robert W. Krepps) and Dwight V. SWAIN,

while the supporting short fiction was principally supplied by authors from the regular stable writing for the ZIFF-DAVIS magazines *AMZ* and *Fantastic*. [BS]

IMAGINE . . . ◊ CANADA.

I MARRIED A MONSTER FROM OUTER SPACE Film (1958). Paramount. Dir Gene Fowler Jr, starring Tom Tryon, Gloria Talbot, Ken Lynch. Screenplay Louis Vittes, from a story by Fowler and Vittes. 78 mins. B/w.

Another manifestation of the rampant PARANOIA of the 1950s, *IMAMFOS* might be called an sf version of *I Married a Communist*. In this enjoyably tasteless MONSTER MOVIE, a young woman's fiancé, on the way to his wedding, is captured and replaced by a shape-shifting ALIEN, one of a group whose mission on Earth is to breed with human women in an attempt to replenish their own declining population. The sexual subtext of some other sf B-movies is here brought out into the open, notably in the famous wedding-night scene where a flash of lightning reveals to the audience (but not the wife) the alien lineaments beneath the nervous cigarette-smoking husband's face. But the woman, who grows suspicious of her "spouse" over the next year, convinces a "real" man of what is happening and he organizes a rescue party. The aliens, impervious to bullets, are destroyed when dogs are set on them, and dissolve into writhing, bubbling alien knots. At various points, surprisingly, some sympathy for the aliens is deliberately roused, and in this respect *IMAMFOS* is more interesting than the otherwise deservedly more celebrated INVASION OF THE BODY SNATCHERS (1956), whose story, in part, it imitates. Gene Fowler, a former editor for Fritz LANG, directed well. [PN/JB]

See also: INVASION; SEX.

IMMORTAL, THE US tv series (1969-71). Paramount/ABC TV. Concept based on the novel *The Immortals* (fixup 1962) by James E. GUNN. Executive prod Tony Wilson. Prod Lou Morheim. Dirs included Joseph Sargent (pilot), Mike Caffey. Writers included Robert Specht, Stephen Kandel, Dan Ullman. Starring Christopher George, Carol Lynley, Don Knight, David Brian, Barry Sullivan. 75min pilot, followed by 15 50min episodes. Colour.

In the 1969 pilot Ben Richards (George) is discovered to have a rare blood-type which renders him immune to disease and to the ageing process. An elderly millionaire wants to keep him locked up as a human fountain of youth, but he escapes to search for his long-lost brother, who may have the same type of blood. The 1970 series reverts to the formula of the hunted man – others are after him, too – having adventures on his travels. The novelization is *The Immortal* ✶ (1970), also by Gunn. [JB]

IMMORTALITY Immortality is one of the basic motifs of speculative thought; the elixir of life and the fountain of youth are hypothetical goals of classic intellectual and exploratory quests. What is usually involved is, strictly speaking, extreme longevity and freedom from ageing – the uselessness of the former without the latter is reflected in the myth of Tithonus and in Jonathan SWIFT's account of the Struldbruggs.

One thing immediately noticeable about this rich literary tradition is that immortality is often treated as a false goal, sometimes as a curse recalling the infinitely tedious punishments meted out to Ixion, Tantalus, Sisyphus and the Wandering Jew. It is understandable that GOTHIC fantasies such as *St Leon* (**1799**) by William Godwin (1756-1836), *Melmoth the Wanderer* (**1820**) by Charles MATURIN, *The Wandering Jew* (**1844-5**) by Eugène Sue (1804-1857), *Auriol* (**1850**) by W. Harrison Ainsworth (1805-1882) and *The Death Ship* (**1888**) by W. Clark RUSSELL should be suspicious; these are cautionary tales, warning against the emptiness of dreams (though a cynic might equally suggest sour grapes). It is perhaps surprising, though, that early sf writers mostly followed suit. Walter BESANT's *The Inner House* (**1888**) proposes that immortality would lead to social sterility – an opinion echoed by many later writers, including Martin SWAYNE in *The Blue Germ* (**1918**), Harold Scarborough (1897-1935) in *The Immortals* (**1924**) and Aldous HUXLEY in *After Many a Summer Dies the Swan* (**1939**; vt *After Many a Summer* UK). Stories which take a brighter view – like George C. FOSTER's *The Lost Garden* and the trilogy by George S. VIERECK and Paul ELDRIDGE begun with *My First Two Thousand Years* (**1928**) – usually have only a few privileged immortals living in a world of mortals. When George Bernard SHAW expressed enthusiasm for universal longevity in *Back to Methuselah* (**1921**), Karel ČAPEK added a rebutting preface to his own play *The Makropoulos Secret* (**1925**) to explain his own opinion that it would be an unmitigated curse even for a single individual.

This difference of opinion remains very evident in sf. In some stories immortality is the beginning of limitless opportunity; in others it represents the ultimate stagnation and the end of innovation and change. We find the former view in such early pulp stories as "The Jameson Satellite" (1931) by Neil R. JONES and *The Man who Awoke* (1933; fixup **1975**) by Laurence MANNING, and its converse in David H. KELLER's "Life Everlasting" (1934; title story of *Life Everlasting and Other Tales* [**1947**]) and John R. PIERCE's "Invariant" (1944). In later magazine sf, the former attitude is implicit in J.T. MCINTOSH's "Live For Ever" (1954) and James BLISH's "At Death's End" (1954), while the latter is seen in Damon KNIGHT's "World without Children" (1951). Frederik POHL's *Drunkard's Walk* (**1960**), Brian W. ALDISS's "The Worm that Flies" (1968) and Bruce MCALLISTER's "Their Immortal Hearts" (1980). There is, however, a general acceptance of the fact that the *desire* for immortality is immensely powerful, and that it constitutes the ultimate bribe; lurid dramatizations of this supposition include Jack VANCE's *To Live Forever* (**1956**), James E. GUNN's *The Immortals* (1955-60; fixup **1962**), John WYNDHAM's *Trouble with Lichen* (**1960**), Norman SPINRAD's *Bug Jack Barron* (**1969**), Bob SHAW's *One Million Tomorrows* (**1970**), Robert SILVERBERG's *The Book of*

Skulls (**1972**), Thomas N. SCORTIA's "The Weariest River" (1973) and Mack REYNOLDS's and Dean ING's *Eternity* (**1984**). There have been numerous notable sf novels featuring immortal heroes, including A.E. VAN VOGT's *The Weapon Makers* (1943; **1952**), Wilson TUCKER's *The Time Masters* (**1953**; rev 1971), Clifford D. SIMAK's *Way Station* (**1963**), Roger ZELAZNY's *This Immortal* (**1966**) and Robert A. HEINLEIN's *Time Enough for Love* (**1973**). But the dominant opinion seems to be that boredom and sterility must eventually set in. Raymond Z. GALLUN's *The Eden Cycle* (**1974**) is an extended study of this presumed phenomenon, and the protagonists of Michael MOORCOCK's **Dancers at the End of Time** sequence (1972-6) must go to extreme and absurd lengths to keep *ennui* at bay.

Some of the modern stories dealing with the theme are scrupulously analytical, and are among the finest exercises in speculative thought that the genre has produced. Most are respectful of the problematic aspects of longevity, but almost all eventually favour the prospect; notable examples of extended *contes philosophiques* in this vein include Robert Silverberg's "Born with the Dead" (1974) and *Sailing to Byzantium* (**1985**), Octavia E. BUTLER's *Wild Seed* (**1980**), Pamela SARGENT's *The Golden Space* (**1982**), Kate WILHELM's *Welcome, Chaos* (**1983**) and Poul ANDERSON's epic *The Boat of a Million Years* (**1989**). A particularly notable negative story is "The Tithonian Factor" (1983) by Richard COWPER, in which hasty users of a technology which gives them a Struldbrugg-like longevity are discomfited by the subsequent discovery that humans do indeed have a joyous spiritual afterlife. Damon Knight's "Dio" (1957), Marta RANDALL's *Islands* (**1976**; rev 1980) and Frederik POHL's *Outnumbering the Living* (**1990** UK) are interesting stories about lone mortals in societies of immortals.

Research in biotechnology following the cracking of the genetic code has encouraged speculation that technologies of longevity are a real prospect, and a new immediacy was introduced into the theme when R.C.W. Ettinger's *The Prospect of Immortality* (**1964**) popularized the idea that CRYONIC preservation might allow people now living to be preserved until the day when they might benefit. Though satirized in such novels as Anders BODELSEN's *Freezing Down* (**1971**; vt *Freezing Point*), this notion inspired a curious political "manifesto" in Alan HARRINGTON's *The Immortalist* (**1969**), followed by his extravagant novel *Paradise 1* (**1977**); Harrington prefers the term "emortality", which signifies an immunity to ageing but not to injury. Technologies of longevity and genetically engineered emortality play a central role in Brian M. STABLEFORD's and David LANGFORD's future history *The Third Millennium* (**1985**), and the theme is a constant preoccupation in Stableford's recent solo work, notably *The Empire of Fear* (**1988**). A collection of essays on immortality in sf is *Death and the Serpent* (anth **1985**) ed Carl B. YOKE and Donald M. HASSLER. A theme anthology is *Immortal* (anth **1978**) ed Jack DANN. [BS]

See also: ESCHATOLOGY; GODS AND DEMONS; HIVE-MINDS; LOST-WORLDS; MEDICINE; RELIGION; SUPERMAN.

IMPOSSIBLE VOYAGE, AN ◊ VOYAGE À TRAVERS L'IMPOSSIBLE.

IMPULSE ◊ SCIENCE FANTASY.

INCIDENT AT RAVEN'S GATE (vt *Encounter at Raven's Gate*) Film (1988). Hemdale. Dir Rolf de Heer, starring Steven Vidler, Celin Griffen, Ritchie Singer, Vince Gil, Saturday Rosenberg. Screenplay Marc Rosenberg, de Heer. 89 mins. Colour.

Australian cinema has produced a number of under-appreciated genre items, such as *The Last Wave* (1978) and *Razorback* (1984). This is another, a conspiracy-cum-UFO movie which locates its bizarre storyline in a dried-up, mean-spirited outback. It starts awkwardly with an unnecessary flashback structure, and risks alienating audiences accustomed to complete explanations for all manifestations, but is otherwise an outstanding atmospheric nail-biter. As in the best 1950s cheapies – IT CAME FROM OUTER SPACE (1953) is the particular touchstone evoked – the fantastic elements are used to bring out the tensions of the human characters. The pressures on an already uptight policeman turn him into a menace who competes with the influence of the offscreen ALIENS as the source of the film's HORROR, so that *IARG* wavers between the psycho-movie and alien-encounter genres. Though the film does not produce tentacled monstrosities, it does have a few impressively unsettling moments in the invaded-transformed Raven's Gate farmhouse. [KN]

INCREDIBLE HULK, THE US tv series (1977-82). Universal/CBS-TV. Created by Kenneth Johnson (executive prod), starring Bill Bixby, Lou Ferrigno, Jack Colvin. Prods included Nicholas Corea, James D. Parriott, Charles Bowman, Bob Sherman. Dirs included Johnson, Bowman, Kenneth Gilbert, Jeffrey Hayden, Reza Badiyi, Jack Colvin. Writers included Johnson, Parriott, Corea, Karen Harris and Jill Sherman, Richard Christian MATHESON. 5 seasons, 2 100min pilots plus 79 50min episodes. Colour.

The series is based on the MARVEL COMICS character of the same name. Mild-mannered scientist Dr David Banner (Bixby) subjects himself to gamma radiation and turns temporarily into a violent, green, 7ft (2.15m) hulk (Ferrigno), a condition that repeats itself whenever he is under stress. The Hulk persona never speaks. Banner has many adventures while on the run, trailed by abrasive investigative reporter McGee (Colvin), who suspects the truth. Only a handful of episodes – notably the 2-part "Prometheus", which involves a meteor freezing Banner/Hulk into an intermediate state – have any sf components aside from the initial SUPERHERO premise. In this formulaic but popular series the Hulk is much more polite (and lacklustre) than his frenzied comic-book counterpart.

The 2 pilots and a further 2-episode story were syndicated in the USA and released as movies elsewhere: *The Incredible Hulk* (1977), *Return of the Incredible Hulk* (1977; a retitling of "Death in the Family") and *Bride of the Incredible Hulk* (1978; a retitling of "Married"). 2 made-for-tv movies, both dir Bill Bixby, are *Trial of the Incredible Hulk* (1979) and *Death of the Incredible Hulk* (1990). [PN/JB]

INCREDIBLE MELTING MAN, THE Film (1977). Quartet Productions/AIP. Written and dir William Sachs, starring Alex Rebar, Burr DeBenning, Ann Sweeny, Michael Aldredge. Additional dialogue Rebecca Ross. 84 mins. Colour.

By 1977 the idea of an astronaut returning to Earth after being contaminated by some space infection was well and truly a CLICHÉ subgenre of the MONSTER MOVIE, an early example being The QUATERMASS XPERIMENT (1955). This time the infection causes great strength, the desire to eat human flesh, and an unfortunate skin disease that gives the astronaut a strong resemblance to man-shaped porridge. Some sequences are rather good, but the special effects are laughable. [PN]

INCREDIBLE SHRINKING MAN, THE Film (1957). Universal. Dir Jack ARNOLD, starring Grant Williams, Randy Stuart, April Kent. Screenplay Richard MATHESON, based on his own *The Shrinking Man* (**1956**). 81 mins. B/w.

This is one of the few truly classic sf films of the 1950s. The basic premise is unscientific, but that does not detract from the power of this story about a man (Williams) who becomes contaminated by a radioactive cloud and starts to shrink. What were once safe and comforting to him become increasingly threatening as he continues to diminish. There is severe sexual anxiety as his wife (Stuart) looms ever larger above him (and patronizes him). In due course his cat becomes a monster and the prosaic confines of his own basement, into which he escapes, become a surrealist jungle. Eventually he disappears completely as the wind blows through autumn leaves and the stars glitter above in a curiously joyful epiphany. Matheson's mature script is intelligently handled by Arnold. Clifford Stine's special effects are a paradigm for how these things should be done.

A supposedly comic partial remake starring Lily Tomlin, *The Incredible Shrinking Woman* (1981), dir Joel Schumacher, purports to be a SATIRE on the consumer society. [PN/JB]

See also: GREAT AND SMALL; HONEY, I SHRUNK THE KIDS; HUGO; MUTANTS; PARANOIA.

INCREDIBLE SHRINKING WOMAN, THE ◊ The INCREDIBLE SHRINKING MAN.

INFINITY Original paperback anthology series ed Robert HOSKINS, published by Lancer Books, and presented as a lineal descendant of the magazine INFINITY SCIENCE FICTION (1955-8), whose editor, Larry T. SHAW, was also connected with Lancer; the covers bore the slogan "New Writings in Speculative Fiction". *I* was a competent but not outstanding series. Regular contributors included Poul ANDERSON, Barry N. MALZBERG and Robert SILVERBERG; Alan BRENNERT and George ZEBROWSKI made their débuts in its pages. *Infinity One* (anth **1970**) reprinted Arthur C. CLARKE's

"The Star" (1955) from the first issue of its spiritual ancestor; all other stories were originals. Later volumes were *Infinity Two* (anth **1971**), *Three* (anth **1972**), *Four* (anth **1972**) and *Five* (anth **1973**). The series was terminated when its publisher went bankrupt.

[MJE/PN]

INFINITY SCIENCE FICTION US DIGEST-size magazine. 20 issues Nov 1955-Nov 1958, published by Royal Publications, ed Larry T. SHAW; irregular, with 4 months between some issues, 1 month between others. *ISF* was one of the most interesting of the flood of new sf magazines in the early and mid-1950s. Its first issue featured Arthur C. CLARKE's HUGO-winning story "The Star", and the magazine went on to publish other good stories by such authors as Isaac ASIMOV, James BLISH, Algis BUDRYS, Damon KNIGHT and C.M. KORNBLUTH; Harlan ELLISON made his début here with "Glow Worm" (1956). Robert SILVERBERG was another regular – and sometimes prolific – contributor; #20 contained book reviews by him and also 3 of his stories (including "Ozymandias", published as by Ivar Jorgenson). Damon Knight had earlier been *ISF*'s regular critic; much of the material in *In Search of Wonder* (**1956**; rev 1967) originated in *ISF*. After the first issue, all the covers were painted by Ed EMSHWILLER. The original anthology series INFINITY described itself as the "lineal descendant" of *ISF*.

[MJE]

ING, DEAN (1931-   ) US writer whose work makes effective use of his years in the Air Force (1951-5) and in the engineering profession (1957-70), and reflects in its pragmatic tone – though not in its plotting, which can be pixilated – his training in behavioural psychology (PhD in speech, 1974). Much of his fiction can be described as SURVIVALIST, insofar as military tales set in a post-HOLOCAUST USA necessarily inhabit survivalist terrain; but the violence of his better work is relatively restrained, and the libertarianism (◊ LIBERTARIAN SF) which underpins his conception of proper behaviour cannot be described as unthinking. Collections like *High Tension* (coll **1982**) and *Firefight 2000* (coll **1987**), the latter including both fiction and nonfiction, amply demonstrate the cogency of his concerns.

DI began writing sf with "Tight Squeeze" for *ASF* in 1955, though he became active only in the late 1970s. His first novel, *Soft Targets* (**1979**), interestingly copes with terrorism in a NEAR-FUTURE setting, though a besetting weakness for melodrama diverts attention from the serious points he makes about the fatal precariousness of societies in the advanced Western World. DI is, in fact, much less interested in that precariousness than in its consequences, and his most significant work, the **Ted Quantrill** sequence – *Systemic Shock* (**1981**), *Single Combat* (**1983**) and *Wild Country* (**1985**) – is set in a desolated and paranoid post-Bomb USA under the thumb of a theocracy. (The similarity of this setting to Robert A. HEINLEIN's **Future History** is sufficiently obvious to count as a homage.) Quantrill's life, as he matures, presents a

model of and argument for the individual who admits no restraints upon his behaviour but his own recognizance. That Quantrill does not behave poorly derives, perhaps, more from the author's decency than from any notion that near-absolute autonomy makes one fully human. Other titles of interest include several novels written as with Mack REYNOLDS, who died in 1983, though some of them at least were probably crafted entirely by DI from Reynolds's outlines; they are *Eternity* (**1984**), *Home Sweet Home: 2010 A.D.* (**1984**), *The Other Time* (**1984**), in which an archaeologist uses TIME TRAVEL to help the Aztecs defeat the Spanish, *The Lagrangists* (**1983**), *Chaos in Lagrangia* (**1984**), *Trojan Orbit* (**1985**) and *Deathwish World* (**1986**). His solo books include *Anasazi* (coll of linked stories **1980**), *Pulling Through* (coll **1983**), which comprises a short ROBINSONADE and a series of survivalist articles designed to add versimilitude to the course of the main story, and *The Big Lifters* (**1988**), a HARD-SF tale in which entrepreneurship wins the day. In general, DI presents what might be called the acceptable face of survivalism.

[JC]

Other works: *Blood of Eagles* (**1986**), associational; *The Ransom of Black Stealth One* (**1989**); *Cathouse* * (fixup **1990**), tales set in Larry NIVEN's Man-Kzin universe; *The Nemesis Mission* (**1991**); *Silent Thunder* (**1991** chap dos).

About the author: *The Work of Dean Ing: An Annotated Bibliography and Guide* (**1990** chap) by Scott A. Burgess.

See also: COLONIZATION OF OTHER WORLDS; IMMORTALITY; SOCIAL DARWINISM.

INGHAM, FREDERICK ◊ Edward Everett HALE.

INGREY, DEREK (?   -   ) UK writer whose post-HOLOCAUST sf novel, *Pig on a Lead* (**1963**), describes the dead-end life of the last surviving humans in the UK – two men, who soon kill each other, and a boy, who survives in the company of a young Eve-figure and the eponymous pig. Told in a marvellous pot pourri of styles, the book makes effective use of many black-humour routines.

[JC]

INGRID, CHARLES ◊ Rhondi VILOTT.

INNER SPACE In sf TERMINOLOGY, an antonym to "outer space". The term was probably first used in the sf field by Robert BLOCH in a speech at the 1948 Worldcon, but was not widely disseminated at that time. However, in "They Come from Inner Space" (1954 *The New Statesman*) – an essay he later included in *Thoughts in the Wilderness* (coll **1957**) – J.B. PRIESTLEY more conspicuously suggested that sf mistakenly attempted to explore "the other side of the Sun rather than . . . the hidden life of the psyche". "Beyond all these topical tales, fables and legends" lay "deep feelings of anxiety, fear, and guilt" which themselves required exploration. "Having ruined this planet," he continued, "we take destruction to other planets. This very extension in space of our activities is desolating, at least to minds that are not entirely childish, because it is a move, undertaken in secret despair, in the wrong direction." Whether J.G.

BALLARD's first use of the term in 1962 was a separate coining or reflected a memory of this essay, it is clear that he intended to designate something not dissimilar. (It is also possible that he had read "Invasion from Inner Space" [1959 *Star Science Fiction #6*] by Howard Koch, a story about sceptical COMPUTERS revolutionizing society, but this is obviously a rather different usage.) The term soon became a commonplace, especially with reference to NEW-WAVE writers (like Ballard) who came into prominence in the mid-1960s. [JC/PN]

See also: GREAT AND SMALL; MUSIC.

INNERSPACE Film (1987). Amblin/Warner Bros. Steven SPIELBERG as an executive prod. Dir Joe DANTE, starring Dennis Quaid, Martin Short, Kevin McCarthy, Fiona Lewis, Meg Ryan. Screenplay Jeffrey Boam, Chip Proser, based on a story by Proser. 120 mins. Colour.

In this parody of FANTASTIC VOYAGE (1966), tough test pilot Tuck (Quaid) is accidentally injected into feeble Jack (Short) while in a miniaturized state. Tuck, though tiny, can to a degree control Jack. In a confused and sometimes unfunny plot, villainous industrial spies pursue a microchip McGUFFIN and a miniaturized killer is also injected into Jack. Adventures happen. All Dante's films have delightful moments, but this, an attempt to make good commercially after the débacle of EXPLORERS (1985), seems oddly impersonal while at the same time trying too hard. The inside-the-body effects are good. The technical adviser on the movie was Gentry LEE. [PN]

See also: CINEMA.

INNES, EVAN ◊ Zach HUGHES.

INSIDE US FANZINE. ◊ HUGO; RIVERSIDE QUARTERLY.

INTELLIGENCE Intelligence is necessarily one of the issues discussed in the entries on ANTI-INTELLECTUALISM IN SF, CYBERNETICS, MUTANTS and SUPERMAN. MACHINE intelligence is discussed under COMPUTERS and ROBOTS. This entry is restricted to stories in which the emphasis is on the actual workings of intelligence in living beings.

Much sf refers to intelligence, but a surprisingly small amount gives a good idea of what the workings of a superior or different intelligence would feel like or even look like. In many stories of abnormally intelligent supermen or mutants we have to take the intelligence on trust. Such intelligences were favourites with A.E. VAN VOGT, but their workings are often less than transparent to the reader, as is the case with the hero of his *The World of Ā* (1945 *ASF*; rev **1948**; rev vt *The World of Null-A* 1970), whose blinding leaps of non-Aristotelian logic are frequently incomprehensible and on the face of it rather silly.

The first sf story of any significance about intelligence was probably *The Curse of Intellect* (**1895**) by Frank Challice Constable, in which an ape is given human intelligence (◊ APES AND CAVEMEN); the first of real importance was *The Hampdenshire Wonder* (**1911**; vt *The Wonder* US) by J.D. BERESFORD, in which the focus of interest is on the feelings of a superintelligent child growing up in a world of what seem to him

subnormals. A colder and harsher reworking of the same theme was twice undertaken by Olaf STAPLEDON, in *Odd John* (**1935**), about an abnormally intelligent human whose spiritual powers are also highly developed, and in *Sirius* (**1944**), about an intelligent dog. In some ways the latter work is the more successful, perhaps because of the problem in stories of this kind of finding a form of language appropriate to describing an experience which by its very nature cannot be fully comprehended by either the reader – or indeed the writer.

One way around the problem of increasing intelligence is to begin with an animal or a moron, so that the higher intelligence is not hopelessly out of reach of our own. This strategy has been adopted in several GENRE-SF stories, of which the two best known are *Brain Wave* (**1954**) by Poul ANDERSON and "Flowers for Algernon" (1959) by Daniel KEYES, later much exp as *Flowers for Algernon* (**1966**). The latter, filmed as CHARLY (1968), is a moving story, told largely through his own diaries, of intelligence artificially induced in a moron. Sadly, the process is only temporary; while hero and reader are given a glimpse, surprisingly convincing, of what genius must feel like, the gates of the golden city are soon barred, and the story ends with an itching discomfort in the subnormal mind of the hero and an almost intolerable feeling of loss in the reader's.

Superintelligence is often pictured as going along with what seems to ordinary humans a cold indifference and a casual amorality. Perhaps this demonstrates a sour-grapes syndrome. We do not like the thought of being relegated to a minor place in the evolutionary scheme; and, as EVOLUTION is traditionally carried out by a "Nature red in tooth and claw", we half expect that a race of geniuses would treat us cruelly. A prototype of this kind of story is John TAINE's *Seeds of Life* (1931 *AMZ*; **1951**), in which an accident with radiation transforms a surly laboratory technician into a cruel, glowing supermind in the body of an Adonis; the sense we are given of the workings of his mind is vivid enough to transcend the pulp crankiness of the story's ideas of evolution. Here, too, the growth of intelligence is reversible.

Many adults are ready enough to see even normal children as essentially ALIEN creatures, and a flourishing subgenre has been the story of the superchild (◊ CHILDREN IN SF), often turning on his or her relationship with parents or guardians. Henry KUTTNER reverted to this theme several times, as in "Mimsy Were the Borogoves" (1943, as Lewis Padgett), in which a teaching machine from the future has frightening effects on children, and "When the Bough Breaks" (1944, again as Padgett), in which a peculiarly nauseating superbaby gives his parents a hard time. "Star Bright" (1952) by Mark CLIFTON is a typically pulp version of the intelligence theme in which the manifestations of high intelligence in children – where the real interest of the story might have lain – rapidly develop into what are in effect magical powers. The two most thoughtful and mature novels in this subgenre are probably *Children of the Atom* (1948-50 *ASF*; fixup **1953**) by Wilmar H. SHIRAS, which incorporates the classic story "In Hiding" (1948), in which an extremely intelligent boy attempts, in self-protection, to behave just like any other child, but is discovered, and *The Fourth "R"* (**1959**; vt *The Brain Machine*) by George O. SMITH, in which the intelligence of a 5-year-old has been trained artificially by a machine which reinforces learning mechanisms in the brain. Both books deal sensitively with the contrast between intellectual maturity and emotional immaturity, and are surprisingly plausible in their scenarios of ways in which superintelligence might show itself in action.

Two other relevant stories from the 1950s are C.M. KORNBLUTH's "The Marching Morons" (1951), a vividly unpleasant story of a future which has become polarized between morons and geniuses, the former in much greater numbers because the middle classes know more about contraception (an interesting not-very-hidden assumption here), and *The Black Cloud* (**1957**) by Fred HOYLE, in which a cloud-intelligence in space accidentally injures and even kills those who attempt to communicate with it, their human intellects being too fully programmed and inflexible to cope with the new data. Something similar happens to the people in the film FORBIDDEN PLANET (1956) who subject themselves to the intelligence-raising machinery of the Krel.

A number of stories have hinged on the COLONIZATION OF OTHER WORLDS under an imagined future law which states that the worlds of intelligent beings must be either left alone or at least treated with great care. Thus the measurement of alien intelligence becomes a question of politics. H. Beam PIPER's *Little Fuzzy* (**1962**) is of this kind, as is Joseph GREEN's *Conscience Interplanetary* (1965-71 var mags; fixup **1972**), though Green does not really develop the potential of the theme. Perhaps the most interesting novel about surveying the nature of alien life and intelligence is Naomi MITCHISON's *Memoirs of a Spacewoman* (**1962**).

Other variations on the intelligence theme include: Olof JOHANNESSON's *Sagan om den stora datamaskinin* (**1966**; trans as *The Big Computer: A Vision* **1968** UK; vt *The Tale of the Great Computer: A Vision* 1968 US; vt *The End of Man?* 1969 US), which is actually a history of intelligence, written in the future, seeing human intelligence as an evolutionary step towards machine intelligence; "The Planners" (1968) by Kate WILHELM, about the acceleration of the genetic transmission of intelligence in apes; and "Eurema's Dam" (1972) by R.A. LAFFERTY, about a genius whom the author disingenuously describes as stupid. This last story is one of a long line of genre-sf yarns about *idiots savants* who construct various marvellous machines and theories without having the least idea about what they are doing. A major work on the evolution of intelligence is Thomas M. DISCH's *Camp Concentration*

(**1968**), a highly structured novel which describes, through a series of recurrent images and thematic leitmotifs, an experiment in drug-induced raising of intelligence among deserters and conscientious objectors in a prose whose increasing richness and difficulty reflect the ever-increasing intelligence of the narrator. Oscar ROSSITER's *Tetrasomy 2* (**1974**) is a black comedy about a young doctor in whom a sudden acceleration of intelligence is catalysed by a vegetable-like superbeing; the doctor's inability to use his improved mind with any social *sang froid* poses a problem not generally considered in this type of story.

The question of intelligence testing comes up in many UTOPIAS and DYSTOPIAS, and is analysed interestingly in "Intelligence Testing in Utopia" by Carolyn H. Rhodes in EXTRAPOLATION, Dec 1971. Among the works she discusses in which this theme is central are *The Messiah of the Cylinder* (**1917**; vt *The Apostle of the Cylinder*) by Victor ROUSSEAU, *Player Piano* (**1952**; vt *Utopia 14*) by Kurt VONNEGUT Jr, *The Rise of the Meritocracy* (**1958**) by Michael YOUNG, *The Child Buyer* (**1960**) by John HERSEY and *World out of Mind* (**1953**) by J.T. MCINTOSH.

Two sf novelists whose work consistently speculates on the nature of intelligence and the various directions in which it may evolve are Frank HERBERT and Ian WATSON, both heavily committed to the possibility of some form of transcendent intelligence. In Herbert's work the theme is seen most clearly in the **Dune** series and in *The Dosadi Experiment* (**1977**), though it appears in all his novels. As with van Vogt, however, it is not always clear exactly how his "other" intelligences operate. With Herbert, much depends on enigmatic hints and clues, as if he knew more than he's telling; this is reflected in his plots, which combine abstruse metaphysical speculation with conspiratorial, cloak-and-dagger manipulations in a sometimes confusing way. Nonetheless, Herbert has at times evoked the *difference* of evolved intelligences with great feeling. Where Herbert hints, Watson analyses and chips patiently away at his recurrent theme, approaching it from a slightly different angle in each of his novels of the 1970s and in some later ones. Unlike those sf writers who seem to fear the thought of a transcendent intelligence, Watson desires it, while recognizing how such an evolution may be quite alien to our present selves. Bringing to bear an impressive arsenal of analytic tools taken from ANTHROPOLOGY, CYBERNETICS, LINGUISTICS, PSYCHOLOGY, semiotics and neurology, he is ready to tackle ambitious projects; in particular he has attempted, with partial success but sometimes drily, to evoke the feeling of a supermind whose processes are more lateral, analogizing and synthesizing than sequential in the traditional mode of human logic. Examples can be found in *The Embedding* (**1973**), *The Martian Inca* (**1977**) and *Alien Embassy* (**1977**). Similarly, Damien BRODERICK's *The Judas Mandala* (**1982**; rev 1990) is notable for the intellectual arabesques produced by its evolved intelligences, hovering just this side of comprehensibility.

In the 1980s the intelligence theme became less important in genre sf, though Stephen KING's *The Tommyknockers* (**1987**) has a lively if pulp-style treatment of a popular notion in sf – that contact with aliens or their artefacts may cause a rapid evolution of our intelligence – most famously evoked in the film 2001: A SPACE ODYSSEY (1968). In King's novel the artefact is an ancient spacecraft dug up in Maine. Robert SILVERBERG's *At Winter's End* (**1988**) features a FAR-FUTURE primitive tribe whose apparently human intelligence is the result of an experiment in primate evolution. In *The Divide* (**1990**) by Robert Charles WILSON a man whose superintelligence was created by a hormonal experiment during his childhood attempts to cope with his alienation by splitting his mind; this creates two wholly different personalities, one apparently average. But generally the emphasis of 1980s sf has shifted away from intelligence examined in isolation towards the nature of consciousness and the workings of the mind in general. This is one of the recurrent themes in Greg BEAR's work. His *Blood Music* (**1985**) has a transformation of humanity brought about by intelligent microorganisms, and *Queen of Angels* (**1990**) envisages a society in which most people are "therapied" by molecule-scale machines made possible by developments in NANO-TECHNOLOGY; the same book features direct exploration/mapping of the mind and its subroutines, consciousness alteration through vodoun ("voodoo"), and the growth to self-consciousness of an AI.

The idea of biological engineering of the mind appears also in Geoff RYMAN's *The Child Garden* (**1989**), in which almost the whole of humanity is educated by the direct importation of tailored DNA into the brain through viral infection. Ironically the heroine, who is immune to viruses, is very intelligent, and the book makes an important distinction between knowledge and intelligence, emphasizing how the conventional "grammars" of thought create a conformism antipathetic to true creativity. In this case (and often, no doubt, in the real world) education can muffle intelligence. [PN]

INTERNATIONAL FANTASY AWARDS UK awards, made annually 1951-7 (not 1956). The idea came from four UK enthusiasts, including John Beynon Harris (John WYNDHAM). The IFAs were presented to the authors of the best fantasy or sf book of the year, with a second category for the best nonfiction book likely to be of interest to sf readers; the nonfiction class was dropped after 1953. Winners were selected by a panel of prominent sf personalities; from 1952 the panel was international. The award took the form of a trophy. Once the HUGOS had been successfully launched, some of the *raison d'être* for the IFAs was gone, but in their time they were given to some excellent and imaginatively chosen works, most of which would have had almost no chance of winning any of the major US AWARDS. The first IFA was presented at the 1951 UK sf CONVENTION, the last at the London Worldcon in 1957. [PN]

1951
Fiction: George R. STEWART, *Earth Abides*
Nonfiction: Willy LEY and Chesley BONESTELL, *The Conquest of Space*
1952
Fiction: John COLLIER, *Fancies and Goodnights*
Nonfiction: Arthur C. CLARKE, *The Exploration of Space*
1953
Fiction: Clifford D. SIMAK, *City*
Nonfiction: Willy Ley and L. Sprague DE CAMP, *Lands Beyond*
1954
Theodore STURGEON, *More than Human*
1955
Edgar PANGBORN, *A Mirror for Observers*
1957
J.R.R. TOLKIEN, *Lord of the Rings*

INTERNATIONAL SCIENCE FICTION US DIGEST-size magazine. 2 issues, Nov 1967 and June 1968, published by Galaxy Publishing Corp., ed Frederik POHL. The interesting idea of reprinting stories from all over the world – authors ranging from Arkady STRUGATSKI (RUSSIA) through Hugo Correa (Chile [◊ SOUTH AMERICA]) to Damien BRODERICK (AUSTRALIA) – sadly but unsurprisingly met with no success.

[FHP/PN]

INTERNATIONAL STORYTELLER ◊ STORYTELLER.
INTERPLANETARY ROMANCE ◊ PLANETARY ROMANCE.

INTERZONE UK magazine, current, #1 Spring 1982, small-BEDSHEET (A4) format, saddle-stapled, continuously numbered, on slick paper from #41, Nov 1990, quarterly to #24, Summer 1988; bimonthly to #34, Mar/Apr 1990; monthly thereafter. *IZ* was first published and edited by a collective made up of John CLUTE, Alan Dorey, Malcolm EDWARDS, Colin GREENLAND, Graham James, Roz KAVENEY, Simon Ounsley and David PRINGLE. This group shrank: James left after #2, Edwards after #4, Kaveney after #7, Clute and Dorey after #10, and Greenland after #12. From #13, Autumn 1985, the only editors were Ounsley and Pringle, although some previous editors continued to act as advisory editors. Since #25, Sep/Oct 1988, when the magazine went bimonthly, the sole editor (and publisher) has been David Pringle, who was from the outset one of the major forces behind its publication. *IZ* had reached #62 by Aug 1992. Begun as an idealistic exercise by a group of fans and writers at a time when the UK had almost no market for sf short stories, it has grown into by far the most distinguished UK sf magazine since NEW WORLDS and SCIENCE FANTASY. In appearance and content it is a fully professional magazine, although its subscription base is only around 2000; its comparatively low circulation (by US standards) requires it to be classed as a SEMIPROZINE in HUGO voting.

IZ published perhaps too many downbeat stories in its early issues, hoping rather too obviously to revive something of the feeling of Michael MOORCOCK's *NW* and its NEW-WAVE glories. However, it slowly developed – certainly by 1985-6 – a real personality of its own. From #13 (Autumn 1985) Nick Lowe has contributed a sophisticated film-review column; from #16 (Summer 1986) John Clute has been the featured and inimitable senior book reviewer. Since then the nonfiction component has continually improved: a second book-review column by Paul J. MCAULEY was added from #23 (Spring 1988), and Mary GENTLE has reviewed with increasing frequency. Good interviews have appeared regularly, as well as literary and market analysis in the interesting **Big Sellers** series; Wendy Bradley began to review, amusingly, both tv shows and fantasy fiction; and Charles PLATT and Bruce STERLING (separately) contributed occasional columns of (deliberately) controversial polemics.

All of this gave the magazine a good bone structure on which the skin and musculature of the fiction could be adequately supported. It has slowly become clear that this one magazine, despite its slender resources and comparatively small readership, has been largely (if not solely) responsible for catalysing a second new wave of UK sf. Its younger UK authors have included Paul J. McAuley, Steve BAXTER, Keith BROOKE, Eric BROWN, Richard Calder (1955-   ), Neil FERGUSON, Nicola Griffith, Simon D. Ings (1965-   ), Ian Lee (1951-   ), Ian MCDONALD, Ian R. MacLeod, Kim NEWMAN and Charles Stross, among many others, coming in to join already established writers like Brian W. ALDISS, J.G. BALLARD, Barrington J. BAYLEY, M. John HARRISON, Gwyneth JONES, Garry KILWORTH, Keith ROBERTS, Brian M. STABLEFORD and Ian WATSON. Australian Greg EGAN has been an especially notable contributor, as has, though more seldom, the Canadian Geoff RYMAN. Good US contributors have included Greg BEAR, Michael BLUMLEIN, Scott BRADFIELD, Paul Di Filippo, Thomas M. DISCH, Karen Joy FOWLER, Richard KADREY, Geoffrey A. Landis, Pat MURPHY, Rachel POLLACK and Michael SWANWICK.

This represents, so far as UK sf writing is concerned, a spectacular upturn in both the quality and the quantity of sf by new writers, after long years of near-stagnation in the 1970s and early 1980s. It is not so much the UK writers' uniform brilliance – they are by no means always brilliant – as the sense of vigour and community they arouse by their regular appearance together in this magazine; this is what has revitalized UK sf, and incidentally encouraged the starting up of many other small UK semiprozines in IZ's wake. Pringle as editor has occasionally, and somewhat unfairly, been accused of playing it too safe and commercial in recent years, after publishing much experimental fiction early on. More commonly he is regarded as having got the balance between SOFT SF and HARD SF, the experimental and the old-style fast-paced narrative, about right. In the late 1980s and the 1990s, IZ has been intelligently eclectic.

Both cover art and interior art have been of uneven quality. The most notable artist consistently associated with *Interzone* – he was Art Editor for a time – is Ian MILLER. [PN]
See also: INTERZONE: THE ANTHOLOGY.

INTERZONE: THE ANTHOLOGY UK anthology series, mainly reprint (from the magazine INTERZONE), part original, 5 vols to date. These are *Interzone: The 1st Anthology* (anth **1985**) ed David PRINGLE with John CLUTE and Colin GREENLAND, *The 2nd Anthology* (anth **1987**) ed Pringle with Clute and Simon Ounsley, *The 3rd Anthology* (anth **1988**) ed Pringle with Clute and Ounsley, *The 4th Anthology* (anth **1989**) ed Pringle with Clute and Ounsley, and *The 5th Anthology* (anth **1991**) ed Pringle with Clute and Lee Montgomerie. Original stories have appeared in #1 (1 story), #4 (3 stories) and #5 (2 stories), their authors including Geoff RYMAN and Cherry WILDER. [PN]

INVADERS, THE US tv series (1967-8). A Quinn Martin Production for ABC TV, created by Larry COHEN. Prod Alan Armer. Writers included Don Brinkley, Dan Ullman, Jerry SOHL, Robert Collins. Dirs included Joseph Sargent, Paul Wendkos, Sutton Roley. 43 50min episodes. Colour.

Roy Thinnes stars as a man who has witnessed a landing by ALIENS in a UFO but is unable to get anyone to believe him. The aliens, from a doomed planet, are trying to take over Earth by infiltration: able to take on human form, they can be distinguished only by the odd angle of their little fingers; when dead their bodies evaporate leaving only a pile of ashes, so lasting proof of their existence is almost impossible to establish. The rigid formula – in each episode the hero discovers and foils a new alien plot, but remains unable to convince the authorities – meant that there was little variation, and the series was cancelled after the second season. Larry Cohen, whose idea the series was, later became celebrated for his low-budget independent films, usually, as here, featuring an ordinary man facing horrible incursions on the one hand and an uncaring, unimaginative or conspiratorial establishment on the other. Perhaps *TI* came too late: it belonged, in spirit, to the PARANOID sf version of the Communist-spy scares of the 1950s, as in Robert A. HEINLEIN's *The Puppet Masters* (**1951**), the tv serial QUATERMASS II (**1955**) and the film INVASION OF THE BODY SNATCHERS (**1956**).

Two short series of books based on *TI* were published in the USA (3 books) and the UK (4 books). The 2 to appear in both series are *The Invaders* * (**1967**; vt *The Meteor Men* UK as by Anthony LeBaron) by Keith LAUMER, #1 in the USA and #2 in the UK; and *The Halo Highway* * (**1967**; vt *Army of the Undead* US) by Rafe BERNARD, #1 in the UK and #3 in the USA. Invaders #2 in the USA was *Enemies from Beyond* * (**1967**) by Laumer; #3 and #4 in the UK were *The Night of the Trilobites* * (**1968**) and *The Autumn Accelerator* * (**1969**), both by Peter LESLIE. [JB/PN]
See also: MONSTER MOVIES.

INVADERS FROM MARS 1. Film (1953). National Pictures/20th Century-Fox. Dir William Cameron

Menzies, starring Jimmy Hunt, Helena Carter, Arthur Franz, Leif Erickson. Screenplay Richard Blake (and John Tucker Battle, uncredited). 78 mins (82 mins in Europe). Colour.

A small, disturbing, curiously memorable film by the director of THINGS TO COME (1936), made for children but capable of terrifying them. Through a little boy's eyes we see ALIENS from a UFO take over the minds of everyone in a town, beginning with the boy's own parents. The army moves in, there is an underground battle and the aliens are defeated. The boy wakes up and realizes that it was all a dream . . . but then he once again sees the UFO land behind his house. (Extra footage was shot for the European print to substitute for the all-a-dream ending, which it was felt would be unpopular; more recent prints have combined both versions.)

Although *IFM* was cheaply made, Menzies produced – through the use of mildly expressionistic sets (reinforcing the dream idea) and a camera placed to give us a child's-eye view – a powerful sf metaphor for the loneliness and alienation of a child whose world seems subtly wrong. The image of human bodies concealing incomprehensible and menacing alien motives was, in its PARANOIA, an important one in US sf cinema, especially during the 1950s Communist-spy phobias.

2. Film (1986). Cannon. Prods Menahem Golan, Yoram Globus. Dir Tobe Hooper, starring Hunter Carson, Karen Black, Timothy Bottoms, Louise Fletcher. Screenplay Dan O'Bannon, Don Jakoby, based on original. 99 mins. Colour.

Disappointing (although astonishingly faithful) remake by a director more at home with exploitation horror movies. The more sophisticated special effects (Martians created by Stan Winston) and the updating of the setting serve only to throw the original's flaws into high relief. What carried eerie conviction on the small screen becomes merely silly on the big one, especially as Hooper's direction sinks into near-incoherence in the pacing of the finale. The best bits, unsurprisingly, are straight from the HORROR genre: possessed parents chewing horribly burnt bacon, a malicious schoolteacher eating a live frog, etc. [PN/JB]
See also: INVASION; MONSTER MOVIES.

INVADERS FROM THE DEEP ◊ STINGRAY.

INVASION Futuristic fiction in the UK was given a tremendous boost by the success of George T. CHESNEY's clever piece of propaganda, *The Battle of Dorking* (1871), which put the case for army reform and rearmament by offering a dramatic illustration of the ease with which the UK might fall to an invading German army. This became the foundation-stone of a subgenre of future-WAR stories whose history is described in I.F. CLARKE's excellent *Voices Prophesying War 1763-1984* (**1966**). Significant exercises in similar alarmism published in the run-up to WWI included *The Great War in England in 1897* (**1894**) by William LE QUEUX, *The Riddle of the Sands* (**1903**) by Erskine CHILDERS, *The Invasion of 1910* (**1906**) by Le Queux and

When William Came (**1913**) by SAKI. P.G. WODEHOUSE's early novel, *The Swoop!* (**1909**), was a parody of the subgenre. The invaders were usually German, but stories of French invasion were frequently used as cautionary tales against the folly of building a Channel Tunnel, such as Max PEMBERTON's *Pro Patria* (**1901**). UK SCIENTIFIC ROMANCE was to a large extent an outgrowth and elaboration of this kind of fiction; and a crucial CONCEPTUAL BREAKTHROUGH was made by H.G. WELLS in *The War of the Worlds* (**1898**), which imagined that an invasion of the Earth by technologically superior ALIENS might appear to Britons in much the same light as the eventually genocidal invasion of Tasmania by Europeans had appeared to the luckless Tasmanians (*see also The* WAR OF THE WORLDS). Although it was (very narrowly) anticipated in some respects by Kurd LASSWITZ's *Auf zwei Planeten* (**1897**; cut trans as *Two Planets* **1971**), Wells's novel was far more influential in making the role of invader central to the fictional image of the alien for the next half-century.

Mundane invasions remained fairly commonplace in UK fiction between the wars, although the fear of occupation *per se* was outweighed and largely superseded by the fear of the aerial bombardment which might be its prelude; in the UK such stories far outnumbered stories of alien invasion, although there were some notable examples of the latter: G. McLeod WINSOR's *Station X* (**1919**) and Bohun LYNCH's *Menace from the Moon* (**1925**), as well as the Martian invasion included in Olaf STAPLEDON's future history *Last and First Men* (**1930**). This general dearth of alien-invasion stories is understandable. Separated from continental Europe by a mere 22 miles, the UK was especially vulnerable to the threat of invasion – and Britons understood how narrowly such a fate had been averted in 1588 and again in Napoleonic times.

The USA was far less vulnerable to such anxieties – although they found expression in such novels as Thomas DIXON's *The Fall of a Nation* (**1916**) and Floyd GIBBONS's *The Red Napoleon* (**1929**), as well as in various lurid accounts of the "Yellow Peril", including Parabellum's (Ferdinand GRAUTOFF's) *Banzai!* (**1909**), Philip Francis NOWLAN's **Buck Rogers** stories (1928-9) and the series begun by Arthur Leo ZAGAT with "Tomorrow" (1939) – but in general the possibility of alien invasion probably seemed to US citizens not too much more remote than the probability of invasion by another nation.

Early pulp melodramas of alien invasion include J. Schlossel's "Invaders from Outside" (1925), Nictzin Dyalhis's "When the Green Star Waned" (1925), Edgar Rice BURROUGHS's *The Moon Maid* (**1926**), Edmond HAMILTON's "The Other Side of the Moon" (1929) and John W. CAMPBELL Jr's *Invaders from the Infinite* (1932 *AMZ Quarterly*; **1961**). An interesting story by P. Schuyler MILLER in which the "invasion" is by spores rather than sentient beings is "The Arrhenius Horror" (1931), a theme which he recapitulated in "Spawn" (1939); a later development of it was Jack

FINNEY's *The Body Snatchers* (**1955**; vt *Invasion of the Body Snatchers*), filmed twice as INVASION OF THE BODY SNATCHERS. Alien-invasion stories quickly became a staple of the specialist sf pulps, and Campbell went on to conduct a sober and rather peculiar analysis of the idea of alien conquest and the subjugation of humankind in four of his "Don A. Stuart" stories: "The Invaders" (**1935**), "Rebellion" (**1935**), "Out of Night" (**1937**) and "The Cloak of Aesir" (**1939**) – stories somewhat at odds with his later conviction that humanity was destined to get the better of any and all alien species. One of the side-effects of this later human chauvinism was Campbell's de-emphasizing of alien-invasion stories in ASTOUNDING SCIENCE-FICTION – it is surprising how few such stories appeared in *ASF* in the decade separating *The Dark Destroyers* (1938 as "Nuisance Value"; **1959**) by Manly Wade WELLMAN from "Late Night Final" (1948) by Eric Frank RUSSELL, even though such stories could certainly (as did both the examples cited) champion the human against the nonhuman. Joseph J. MILLARD's *The Gods Hate Kansas* (**1941**; rev **1964**) is a notable example from elsewhere.

A sparse but interesting line of stories featuring invasions launched from UNDER THE SEA runs from Owen Oliver's antique "Out of the Deep" (1904) and Eden PHILLPOTTS's *The Owl of Athene* (**1936**) to John WYNDHAM's *The Kraken Wakes* (**1953**; vt *Out of the Deeps* US) and Murray LEINSTER's *Creatures of the Abyss* (**1961**). These often bring the typical features of mundane and alien invasion stories into uneasy combination.

Hypothetical Asian invasion continued to crop up occasionally in GENRE SF – as in Robert A. HEINLEIN's *Sixth Column* (1941 *ASF* as by Anson MacDonald; **1949**; vt *The Day after Tomorrow*) and C.M. KORN-BLUTH's *Not this August* (**1955**; vt *Christmas Eve* UK) – although they were easily outnumbered by attempted and successful conquests of a more exotic kind, even if most of these were featured in the less prestigious magazines. Invasions came not only from outer space but from other DIMENSIONS, as in Murray LEINSTER's "The Incredible Invasion" (1936 *ASF*; **1955** dos as *The Other Side of Here*), from the microcosm, as in "Invaders from the Atom" (1937) by Maurice G. Hugi (1904-1947), and eventually from the future, as in *Invasion from 2500* (**1964**) by Norman Edwards (Terry CARR and Ted WHITE). Among the more bizarre alien invasions is Fredric BROWN's "The Waveries" (1945), in which electrical energy-beings hijack our airwaves. Despite the sobering conclusion of *The War of the Worlds*, in which lowly bacteria must compensate for human impotence, confidence in human ability to repel alien invaders sooner or later always ran high in pulp sf, one lone man occasionally being adequate to the task, as in A.E. VAN VOGT's "The Monster" (1948). In some stories, of course, humans are themselves the alien invaders of other worlds, and works of this kind (which rarely appeared in *ASF*) were often fiercely critical of such human follies

as racism and imperialism; examples range from Edmond Hamilton's "A Conquest of Two Worlds" (1932) through Robert Silverberg's *Invaders from Earth* (**1958** dos) and *Downward to the Earth* (**1970**) to Ursula K. LE GUIN's *The Word for World is Forest* (1972 in *Again, Dangerous Visions* ed Harlan ELLISON; **1976**).

From their earliest inception, stories of invasion featured a paranoid anxiety that the invaders might already be lurking undetected in our midst. William Le Queux was an indefatigable propagator of the notion that a Fifth Column of German agents was already in the UK, preparing to play its part in open conflict, and many US Yellow-Peril novels likewise featured Fifth Columnists. This kind of PARANOIA could be taken to extremes in sf, where aliens could easily be credited with the power to masquerade as humans. The notion was understandably attractive to low-budget film-makers, and it was extravagantly deployed in the magazines and in the CINEMA during the McCarthy witch-hunts of the early Cold War period. The new wave of paranoid alien-invasion stories was launched by Murray Leinster's *The Brain-Stealers* (1947 *Startling Stories* as "The Man in the Iron Cap"; **1954**) and Ray BRADBURY's "Zero Hour" (1947), but it really hit its stride with Heinlein's *The Puppet Masters* (**1951**), quickly followed by INVADERS FROM MARS (1953), Eric Frank RUSSELL's *Three to Conquer* (**1955**), *Invasion of the Body Snatchers* (1956) and I MARRIED A MONSTER FROM OUTER SPACE (1958). By this time, however, the comic potential of alien invasion was being more widely exploited, too, in such works as Fredric Brown's *Martians Go Home!* (**1955**) and Richard WILSON's *The Girls from Planet 5* (**1955**). The possibility of benign invasions was considered, notably by Arthur C. CLARKE in *Childhood's End* (**1953**), by Algis BUDRYS in "Silent Brother" (1956) and (somewhat perversely) by Theodore STURGEON in *The Cosmic Rape* (**1958**).

By the 1960s the alien-invasion story appeared to be old hat, fit for cynical display in such stories as Thomas M. DISCH's *The Genocides* (**1965**), in which humans are relegated to the status of irrelevant vermin, and his *Mankind under the Leash* (**1966**; vt *The Puppies of Terra* UK), in which they become pets; or surreal parody, in such works as Keith LAUMER's *The Monitors* (**1966**) and Philip K. DICK's and Ray NELSON's *The Ganymede Takeover* (**1967**); or romantic nostalgia in such works as Robert SILVERBERG's *Nightwings* (fixup **1969**). Serious treatments of the theme were rare: William BURKETT's *Sleeping Planet* (**1965**) and Piers ANTHONY's *Triple Détente* (1968 *ASF* as "The Alien Rulers"; exp **1974**) do not quite qualify, although Gordon R. DICKSON's *The Alien Way* (**1965**) and John BRUNNER's *The Day of the Star Cities* (**1965**; rev vt *Age of Miracles* 1973) might. More recent attempts to revitalize the theme have been relatively few in number; by far the most determined and most successful is *Footfall* (**1985**) by Larry NIVEN and Jerry POURNELLE, a conscientiously controlled melodrama. Other notable examples include Jack CHALKER's *Dan-*

cers in the Afterglow (**1978**) and the "invasion" subplot of Gregory BENFORD's *Across the Sea of Suns* (**1984**).

A notable theme anthology of early genre stories is Groff CONKLIN's *Invaders of Earth* (anth **1952**). [BS/DP]

INVASION Film (1966). Merton Park/AIP. Dir Alan Bridges, starring Edward Judd, Valerie Gearon, Yoko Tani, Lyndon Brook. Screenplay Roger Marshall, based on a story by Robert Holmes. 82 mins. B/w.

This interesting UK film tells of two humanoid aliens who crash-land on Earth outside a country hospital. It turns out that one is a prisoner of the other. Further aliens, members of an extraterrestrial police force, arrive and demand that the hospital doctor hand over the prisoner; when their request is refused they place an impenetrable FORCE FIELD around the hospital, but are finally outwitted by the protective doctor. Bridges creates a powerfully strange atmosphere despite a very small budget.   [JB/PN]

INVASION EARTH 2150 AD ◊ DALEKS – INVASION EARTH 2150 AD.

INVASION OF ASTRO-MONSTER ◊ GOJIRA; RADON.

INVASION OF PLANET X ◊ GOJIRA; RADON.

INVASION OF THE BEE GIRLS Film (1973). Centaur/Sequoia. Dir Denis Sanders, starring William Smith, Anitra Ford, Victoria Vetri, René Bond. Screenplay Nicholas Meyer. 85 mins. Colour.

This softcore erotic movie – perhaps inspired by *The* WASP WOMAN (1959) – has deservedly developed a minor cult reputation for the outrageousness of its tacky if typical exploitation premise, that SEX is death. A woman becomes a nymphomaniacal but sterile "queen bee", and conscripts housewives and other women to join the group; they are covered with jelly and irradiated, and emerge as beautiful human-seeming ALIENS, wearing dark glasses to conceal their insect eyes. They kill their male victims through repeated induction of orgasm. The story hinges on the murder investigation. Part parody, the film is intermittently amusing and arguably perversely proto-FEMINIST. Meyer went on to cowrite *The* NIGHT THAT PANICKED AMERICA (1975), to write and direct TIME AFTER TIME (1979), to direct STAR TREK II: THE WRATH OF KHAN (1982), to direct *The* DAY AFTER (1983), to cowrite STAR TREK IV: THE VOYAGE HOME (1986), and to cowrite and direct STAR TREK VI: THE UNDISCOVERED COUNTRY (1992). He has also written excellent **Sherlock Holmes** pastiches (◊ Sir Arthur Conan DOYLE.)   [PN]

INVASION OF THE BODY SNATCHERS 1. Film (1956). Allied Artists. Prod Walter Wanger. Dir Don Siegel, starring Kevin McCarthy, Dana Wynter, Carolyn Jones, King Donovan. Screenplay Daniel Mainwaring, Sam Peckinpah (uncredited), based on *The Body Snatchers* (**1955**) by Jack FINNEY. 80 mins. B/w.

PARANOIA was the dominant theme running through much sf cinema of the 1950s. Nowhere was it better realized than in this subtle and sophisticated movie, directed by B-film veteran Siegel, about vegetable pods from outer space that turn into emotionless replicas of human beings, in the process replacing the usually sleeping originals. Whether the film reflects right-wing paranoia about a secret takeover by communists or left-wing paranoia about the increasing power of the McCarthyists has been much argued; either way, the theme is loss of individual identity and of human feeling. The original downbeat ending, in which the pods are victorious, was diluted by the addition of a prologue and epilogue set in hospital, the latter showing the authorities finally believing in the existence of the pods. These scenes are often cut in modern prints. The film has been very highly praised: it is possibly the most discussed B-movie in the history of US film, and was the first of many 1950s sf films to be remade.

2. Film (1978). Solofilm/United Artists. Dir Philip Kaufman, starring Donald Sutherland, Brooke Adams, Leonard Nimoy, Veronica Cartwright, Jeff Goldblum. Screenplay W.D. Richter, based on the Finney novel. 115 mins. Colour.

This unusually interesting remake shifts the emphasis from political to sociological, from cohesive small town to alienating big city (San Francisco), where it is more difficult at the best of times to tell who is a pod and who isn't, a point made by the psychiatrist (Nimoy). The script is witty, making satirical points about Californian society in the late 1970s, so intent upon development and change that becoming a pod is almost a logical next step. Kaufman's direction is confident, but sometimes too ominous.   [PN]

See also: CINEMA; INVASION; MONSTER MOVIES.

INVASION OF THE FLYING SAUCERS ◊ EARTH VS. THE FLYING SAUCERS.

INVENTION ◊ DIME-NOVEL SF; DISCOVERY AND INVENTION; EDISONADE; MACHINES; SCIENTISTS; TECHNOLOGY.

INVENTION OF DESTRUCTION ◊ VYNÁLEZ ZKÁZY.

INVISIBILITY The fantasy of being able to make oneself invisible is a common childhood daydream. As with all such daydreams, literary treatments of the theme tend to be cautionary tales; the three-decker novel *The Invisible Gentleman* (**1833**) by James Dalton is the most extravagant example. No good comes of it in such early sf stories as Edward Page MITCHELL's "The Crystal Man" (1881), H.G. WELLS's classic *The Invisible Man* (**1897**) and Jack LONDON's "The Shadow and the Flash" (1903), though C.H. HINTON was unconcerned with moralizing in "Stella" (1895). Almost as common as stories of *being* invisible are stories of confrontation with invisible adversaries, in which feelings of fear and insecurity with no immediate and obvious cause are dramatically symbolized. Many stories in this vein inhabit the borderland between supernatural fantasy and sf; notable examples include Fitz-James O'BRIEN's "What Was It?" (1859), Guy de Maupassant's "The Horla" (1887), Ambrose BIERCE's "The Damned Thing" (1893), George Allan ENGLAND's "The Thing from Outside" (1923), H.M. Egbert's *The Sea Demons* (**1925**; ◊ Victor ROUSSEAU), Edmond HAMILTON's "The Monster-God of Mamurth" (1926), H.P. LOVECRAFT's "The Dunwich Horror" (1929), Eric Frank RUSSELL's *Sinister Barrier*

(1939; **1943**; rev 1948) and Murray LEINSTER's *War with the Gizmos* (**1958**). Invisibility is a staple of cinematic special effects, displayed to good effect in the classic *The* INVISIBLE MAN (1933) – based on Wells's novel and borrowing some inspiration from Philip WYLIE's *The Murderer Invisible* (**1931**) – but not so well in its inferior sequels, and with varying success in 3 tv series, all likewise called *The* INVISIBLE MAN, featuring invisible crime-fighters and secret agents.

In more recent sf, invisibility – sometimes more metaphorical than literal – is usually deployed symbolically. An invisible manned bomb-carrier is featured in "For Love" (1962; vt "All for Love") by Algis BUDRYS. In Damon KNIGHT's "The Country of the Kind" (1956) and Robert SILVERBERG's "To See the Invisible Man" (1963) criminals are "exiled" from society in that people simply refuse to see them, so that they suffer agonies of loneliness; the notion is inverted in Gardner R. DOZOIS's "The Visible Man" (1975), in which other people become invisible to the outcast. The idea of unnoticed communities existing in the interstices of everyday society is developed by Fritz LEIBER in *The Sinful Ones* (1950 *Fantastic Adventures* as "You're All Alone"; exp **1953**; rev 1980) and Christopher PRIEST's *The Glamour* (**1984**). Stories in which people fade from original inconsequentiality into literal or metaphorical invisibility include Charles BEAUMONT's "The Vanishing American" (1955), Harlan ELLISON's "Are You Listening?" (1958) and Sylvia Jacobs's "The End of Evan Essant" (1962). More extensive and elaborate accounts of the existential politics of individual invisibility can be found in H.F. SAINT's *Memoirs of an Invisible Man* (**1987**), filmed as MEMOIRS OF AN INVISIBLE MAN (1992), and Thomas BERGER's *Being Invisible* (**1988**). A pseudo-technological essay at achieving invisibility is depicted in *The* PHILADELPHIA EXPERIMENT (1984). A theme anthology is *Invisible Men* (anth **1960**) ed Basil DAVENPORT. [BS]

INVISIBLE AGENT, THE ◊ *The* INVISIBLE MAN.

INVISIBLE BOY, THE Film (1957). Pan/MGM. Dir Herman Hoffman, starring Richard Eyer, Philip Abbott, Diane Brewster, Harold J. Stone. Screenplay Cyril Hume, based on "The Invisible Boy" (1956; vt "The Brain Child") by Edmund COOPER. 90 mins. B/w.

In this well written and made film for children, a 10-year-old boy (Eyer) assembles a ROBOT from pieces brought back from the future by a time-traveller, and ends up with Robby the Robot, who had won the hearts of audiences in FORBIDDEN PLANET (1956). Robby comes under the influence of a malign, fully aware supercomputer – probably the first such in movies – and somewhat irresponsibly makes the boy an INVISIBILITY potion. More importantly, he helps the COMPUTER – which is planning to conquer the world – by implanting electronic receivers in the brains of prominent men, but redeems himself at the end when he ignores the computer's command to kill the boy and instead destroys the computer, with the implicit moral that machines shaped like men are more trustworthy than machines shaped like MACHINES. [JB/PN]

INVISIBLE MAN, THE 1. Film (1933). Universal. Dir James Whale, starring Claude Rains, Gloria Stuart, Henry Travers, William Harrigan, Una O'Connor. Screenplay R.C. SHERRIFF, Philip WYLIE, based on *The Invisible Man* (**1897**) by H.G. WELLS. 71 mins, cut to 56 mins. B/w.

This excellent black comedy tells of a scientist who discovers a drug that causes INVISIBILITY but whose side-effect is megalomania. Wearing black goggles over a face wrapped in bandages, he is memorably menacing. After a series of crimes he is trapped by police (his footprints in the snow betray his presence) and shot, slowly regaining visibility as his life ebbs away. Whale's direction is full of his usual idiosyncratic touches, with much humour derived from baffled minor characters. John Fulton's special effects are very sophisticated for the period, and were widely imitated. One of the most successful Wells adaptations, this made Claude Rains a star almost purely on the basis of his mellifluous voice. *TIM* is archetypal in its not-unsympathetic portrait of the SCIENTIST as over-reacher – it contains the much-copied line: "I meddled in things that Man must leave alone."

2. Universal's progressively inferior and silly variations on the theme – not true sequels – were *The Invisible Man Returns* (1940), *The Invisible Woman* (1940), *The Invisible Agent* (1942), *The Invisible Man's Revenge* (1944) and *Abbott and Costello Meet the Invisible Man* (1951). Over 30 other films use the invisibility theme, some crediting Wells's novel as a source.

3. UK tv series (1958-9). ATV. Created and prod Ralph Smart, starring the voice of Tim Turner. 2 seasons, 26 25min episodes. B/w. In this un-Wellslike version, the unfortunate hero divides his time between seeking an antidote for his condition and fighting crime. Lisa Daniely and Deborah Watling played the hero's sister and niece.

4. US tv series (1975-6). Universal TV for NBC. Created and prod Harve Bennett, Steve Bochco. Dirs included Robert Michael Lewis, Alan Levi, Sigmund Neufeld Jr. Writers included Bochco, James D. Parriott. 1 season, 75min pilot plus 12 50min episodes. Colour.

David McCallum stars as a scientist who discovers a way of turning himself invisible but cannot regain visibility. A plastic-surgeon friend makes him a skin-coloured mask identical with his pre-invisibility face. The pilot episode concerns his attempts to keep the formula from the military; in later episodes the plots revolve, tepidly, around his work as a secret agent.

5. The above series had mediocre ratings, so in 1976 Universal replaced McCallum with Ben Murphy, changed the title to *Gemini Man*, and started the story again from the beginning. 1 season, 75min pilot plus 11 50min episodes (only 5 broadcast by NBC). Colour. Murphy plays a secret agent who can control his invisibility with a wristwatch-like device, but can remain safely invisible for only 15 minutes a day. This version flopped, too, and was cancelled before all completed episodes were shown. The producer, Harve Bennett, was having greater success elsewhere with *The* SIX MILLION DOLLAR MAN. [PN/JB]

INVISIBLE MAN RETURNS, THE ◊ *The* INVISIBLE MAN.

INVISIBLE MAN'S REVENGE, THE ◊ *The* INVISIBLE MAN.

INVISIBLE WOMAN, THE ◊ *The* INVISIBLE MAN.

ION DRIVE A common item of sf TERMINOLOGY derived from a theoretical means of ROCKET propulsion. Chemically fuelled rockets are hampered by the necessity of carrying large burdens of fuel. Other systems, including the ion drive, propose using much lighter fuels, compensating for the decrease in the mass available for propulsion by ejecting it at correspondingly higher velocities. Ions (charged particles) can be accelerated to enormous velocities using a magnetic field, and so would seem an ideal fuel. Also, since all elements can be ionized (albeit with varying degrees of difficulty), ion-drive rockets could theoretically make use of pretty well any substance to hand. Although an ion drive would produce only a small acceleration because of the relatively tiny masses involved, this could be maintained for months or years, so that very high terminal velocities could be achieved. The first tests in space of such a system began in 1971 with the SERT (Space Electric Rocket Test) satellites; the propellant was ionized mercury and the electric power was derived from solar cells. [PN]

IONNESCU, DEMETRIU G. [r] ◊ ROMANIA.

IRELAND, DAVID (1927-   ) Australian writer whose *A Woman of the Future* (**1979** US), his best known work, depicts a bizarre but positively conceived future which his protagonist finds congenial. *City of Women* (**1981** UK), on the other hand, presents a FEMINIST vision of separatism whose ending befits its *Alice in Wonderland* style, as the vision turns out to be the hallucination of a lonely woman. *Archimedes and the Seagle* (**1984**), a fantasy, presents the memoirs of a dog. [JC]

ISAAC ASIMOV'S SCIENCE FICTION MAGAZINE US DIGEST-size magazine. Quarterly from Spring 1977, bimonthly from Jan/Feb 1978, monthly from Jan 1979, 4-weekly from Jan 1981. Published by Davis Publications; ed George H. SCITHERS Spring 1977-Feb 1982, Kathleen Moloney Mar 1982-Dec 1982, Shawna MCCARTHY Jan 1983-Feb 1986, Gardner DOZOIS Mar 1986 to date. IASFM was sold to Dell Magazines, part of the BANTAM/DOUBLEDAY/Dell publishing group, early in 1992; the first redesigned version under the new management is projected to be Nov 1992, and the title is projected to become at that time *Asimov's Science Fiction*.

Asimov was named as "Editorial Director" of this sf magazine, which was titled to take advantage of his popularity; the first 3 issues featured his photograph on the cover, and he contributed a great many chatty editorial articles. IASFM was commercially successful – at least relative to other sf magazines – from the outset, though its contents under Scithers's editorship were on the whole light and undemanding. However, it continued to mature, especially under McCarthy and then Dozois, until by the mid- and late 1980s it was clearly the most accomplished and vigorous magazine on the US market, with an extraordinarily high number of its stories nominated for, and winning, various awards. Through the 1980s its circulation was similar to, although in most years somewhat lower than, that of the market leader, its sister publication *Analog* (◊ ASTOUNDING SCIENCE-FICTION), which Davis Publications had bought in 1980. The circulations of sf magazines generally dropped steadily during the 1980s, so even IASFM, by a long way the best of them, limped along with about 74,000 in 1991 (79,000 for *Analog*), down from almost 109,000 in 1978.

IASFM is popular with fans. Scithers was awarded the HUGO for Best Professional Editor in 1978 and 1980, McCarthy in 1984, and Dozois in 1988, 1989, 1990 and 1991; all of these are effectively awards for the magazine. New writers who have made their débuts in its pages, or at least had much of their early work published there, included, under Scithers alone, Barry B. LONGYEAR and S.P. SOMTOW, both of whom, in successive years, won the JOHN W. CAMPBELL AWARD for best new sf writer of the year. Hugo- and NEBULA-winning stories have been Longyear's *Enemy Mine* (1979; **1989** chap dos), "Fire Watch" (1982) by Connie WILLIS, "Hardfought" (1983) by Greg BEAR, "The Peacemaker" (1983) by Dozois, "Speech Sounds" (1983) by Octavia E. BUTLER, "PRESS ENTER ■" (1984) by John VARLEY, "Bloodchild" (1984) by Butler, "Twenty-four Views of Mount Fuji, by Hokusai" (1985) by Roger ZELAZNY, "Fermi and Frost" (1985) by Frederik POHL, "Sailing to Byzantium" (1985) by Robert SILVERBERG, "Portraits of His Children" (1985) by George R.R. MARTIN, "Gilgamesh in the Outback" (1986) by Silverberg, "R&R" (1986) by Lucius SHEPARD, "The Girl who Fell into the Sky" (1986) by Kate WILHELM, "Eye for Eye" (1987) by Orson Scott CARD, "Why I Left Harry's All-Night Hambúrgers" (1987) by Lawrence WATT-EVANS, "The Blind Geometer" (1987) by Kim Stanley ROBINSON, "Rachel in Love" (1987) by Pat MURPHY, "The Last of the Winnebagos" (1988) by Willis, "Ripples in the Dirac Sea (1988) by Geoffrey A. Landis, "Enter a Soldier. Later: Enter Another" (1989) by Silverberg, "Boobs" (1989) by Suzy McKee CHARNAS, *The Hemingway Hoax* (**1990**) by Joe HALDEMAN, "The Manamouki" (1990) by Michael D. RESNICK, "Bears Discover Fire" (1990) by Terry BISSON, *Stations of the Tide* (**1991**) by Michael SWANWICK and "Beggars in Spain" (1991) by Nancy KRESS. This density of award-winning is without precedent in sf-magazine publishing, and says much for Dozois's editorial discernment and skill. Indeed, if Dozois can be criticized at all, it is perhaps on the grounds that he chooses stories first for their literary quality and only second for their generic positioning: IAFSM may in the 1970s have been a HARD-SF magazine, but under

Dozois it has on the whole been quite the reverse, with many of the stories being only marginally sf or fantasy (so that sometimes *IASFM* can look like *The New Yorker*), being as little bound by rigid generic expectations as was, say, NEW WORLDS under Michael MOORCOCK. In the case of Dozois, this does not seem to have brought about any substantial backlash from conservative readers.

The nonfiction features of *IASFM* have ranged through, *inter alia*, editorial musings by Isaac Asimov, an excellent mathematical column by Martin GARDNER, book reviews by Baird SEARLES – later joined by a separate and very energetic books column from Norman SPINRAD – literary articles by James E. GUNN in earlier issues, poems by various hands, notably Robert FRAZIER, and a games column (◊ GAMES AND TOYS) by Matthew J. Costello. [PN]

See also: JAPAN.

ISLAND AT THE TOP OF THE WORLD, THE ◊ Ian CAMERON; LOST WORLDS.

ISLAND OF DR MOREAU, THE Film (1977). Cinema 77/AIP. Dir Don Taylor, starring Burt Lancaster, Michael York, Nigel Davenport, Barbara Carrera. Screenplay John Herman Shaner, Al Ramrus, based on *The Island of Dr Moreau* (**1896**) by H.G. WELLS. 98 mins. Colour.

In this slow-moving and trite remake of ISLAND OF LOST SOULS (1932), a young castaway (York) on a remote ISLAND learns that Dr Moreau (Lancaster), resident SCIENTIST, is carrying out experiments to give animals human characteristics; some of the resulting hybrids live in the jungle and worship Moreau as a god. Unlike the novel and the first film, where the hybrids were cruelly created by vivisection, these are formed by GENETIC ENGINEERING; thus this version's Wellsian references to the House of Pain become puzzlingly irrelevant. The novelization (so much for Wells!) is *The Island of Dr Moreau* * (**1977**) by Joseph Silva (Ron GOULART). [JB/PN]

ISLAND OF LOST SOULS Film (1932). Paramount. Dir Erle C. Kenton, starring Charles Laughton, Richard Arlen, Leila Hyams, Kathleen Burke, Bela Lugosi, Alan Ladd, Randolph Scott. Screenplay Waldemar Young, Philip WYLIE, based on *The Island of Dr Moreau* (**1896**) by H.G. WELLS. 72 mins. B/w.

Though somewhat altered from the Wells original, and adding such Hollywood touches as a seductive Panther Girl, this memorable film incorporates much of the novel's moody atmosphere. A young couple is shipwrecked on an ISLAND where the leering, whip-cracking Moreau (Laughton), by means of vivisection and other cruel medical techniques, is trying to turn animals into men. (Wells disliked the depiction of his twisted idealist, Moreau, as a sadist.) The pathetic beast-men – rendered with first-rate and often horrific make-up – are kept in check by their belief that Moreau is a god. But, when they see him murdering his human assistant and thereby breaking one of his own commandments, their fear of him dissolves and they carry him off to the House of Pain – the laboratory where they were all created – and wreak bloody, surgical vengeance. A remake was *The* ISLAND OF DR MOREAU (1977). [JB]

See also: MONSTER MOVIES.

ISLAND OF MUTATIONS ◊ L'ISOLA DEGLI UOMINI PESCE.

ISLAND OF TERROR (vt *Night of the Silicates*) Film (1966). Planet/Universal. Dir Terence Fisher, starring Peter Cushing, Edward Judd, Carole Gray, Eddie Byrne. Screenplay Alan Ramsen, Edward Andrew Mann. 89 mins. Colour.

This is one of the 3 films with an sf theme made for Planet by Terence Fisher, best known for his HORROR movies, of which this, despite its sf trappings, is one. (The others are *The* EARTH DIES SCREAMING [1964] and NIGHT OF THE BIG HEAT [1967].) Giant mutated viruses, the product of cancer research gone wrong, get loose on a small island and kill their victims by sucking their bones out of their bodies. There are some well choreographed shocks. As the monsters, which look like animated piles of porridge, can move only slowly, it is unclear how they overtake their prey. [JB/PN]

ISLAND OF THE BURNING DAMNED ◊ NIGHT OF THE BIG HEAT.

ISLANDS Islands play a crucial role in imaginative fiction, providing geographical microcosms in which the consequences of various types of scientific or political hypotheses may be incarnated and made available for inspection by visitors from the world at large. An archetypal island venue is ATLANTIS, mentioned as early as the time of ancient Greece by the philosopher PLATO. Many an island has played host to a UTOPIA, including Thomas MORE's *Utopia* itself (**1516** in Latin; trans **1551**), Austin Tappan WRIGHT's *Islandia* (**1942**) and Jacquetta HAWKES's *Providence Island* (**1959**); not very many have harboured DYSTOPIAS. Islands also feature extensively in SATIRE, notably those displayed in Jonathan SWIFT's *Gulliver's Travels* (**1726**). Although rarely fantastic, the islands featured in ROBINSONADES are also of some significance in the history of PROTO SCIENCE FICTION. Islands are the natural refuge of weird lifeforms in many early fantasies of EVOLUTION, including William Hope HODGSON's "The Voice in the Night" (1907). An island was the natural "laboratory" for the daring scientific experiment carried out in H.G. WELLS's *The Island of Dr Moreau* (**1896**), the prototypic island-sf story and the significant inspiration of such later works as S. Fowler WRIGHT's *The Island of Captain Sparrow* (**1928**), the 1940 title story of Adolfo BIOY CASARES's *The Invention of Morel and Other Stories* (trans **1964**), and – of course – Brian W. ALDISS's *Moreau's Other Island* (**1980**; vt *An Island Called Moreau* US). A very different experiment – an attempt to produce super-INTELLIGENCE (by somewhat fraudulent means) in a child cut off from the world – is carried out on M.P. SHIEL's *The Isle of Lies* (**1909**). An artificial island is featured in Jules VERNE's *L'île à hélice* (**1895**; trans as *The Floating Island* **1896**; vt *Propeller Island*).

Early pulp sf made considerable use of islands in its

thought-experiments. Notable weird lifeforms are featured in "Fungus Isle" (1923) by Philip M. Fisher and in "Nightmare Island" (1941) by Theodore STURGEON. Even more exotic fauna appear in Edgar Rice BURROUGHS's *The Land that Time Forgot* (1924), Stanley G. WEINBAUM's "Proteus Island" (1936) and Edmond HAMILTON's "The Isle of Changing Life" (1940). However, the scope for the deployment of undiscovered islands in fiction shrank dramatically during the early part of the century, and although such defiant-minded authors as Lance SIEVEKING, in *The Ultimate Island* (1925), would not be put off, most writers transferred their more extravagant thought-experiments to remoter locations. Apparently innocuous islands continued to be used, however, as bases for the hatching of nefarious schemes in many NEAR-FUTURE thrillers, ranging from Edmund SNELL's *Kontrol* (1928) to Ian FLEMING's *Dr No* (1962), and for such social experiments as those carried out in Aldous HUXLEY's *Island* (1962) and Scott Michel's *Journey to Limbo* (1963). Extraterrestrial islands play a significant role in many sf stories about watery worlds, notably the floating islands of VENUS in C.S. LEWIS's *Perelandra* (1943) and the "islands" thrown up by the sentient ocean in Stanisław LEM's *Solaris* (1961; trans 1970).

The symbolic significance of the word "island" has maintained its prominence in stories which treat artificial satellites, SPACE HABITATS, asteroids, planets or even galaxies as islands in the void, and it continues to supply neat titular metaphors to such novels as Raymond F. JONES's *This Island Earth* (1952), filmed as THIS ISLAND EARTH (1954), Marta RANDALL's *Islands* (1976) and Bruce STERLING's *Islands in the Net* (1988). A series of particularly ingenious metaphorical changes have been rung by Gene WOLFE in "The Island of Dr Death and Other Stories" (1970), which has been assembled with "The Death of Dr Island" (1973), "The Doctor of Death Island" (1978) and "Death of the Island Doctor" in *The Wolfe Archipelago* (coll 1983). Exotic robinsonades continue to be written, often ironically; examples include "The Terminal Beach" (1964) and *Concrete Island* (1974), both by J.G. BALLARD.

Because islands supply a strictly delimited space, rather like a stage set, in which a plot may develop, they are ideal for certain kinds of narrative exercise. Even if it were not for their specific "laboratory function", therefore, they would have a significant continuing role to play in sf. Recent works illustrative of this role include Hilbert SCHENCK's *A Rose for Armageddon* (1982) and *Chronosequence* (1988) and Garry KILWORTH's *Cloudrock* (1988), in which an atoll is left high and dry after the surrounding ocean has vanished. The Galápagos islands, which played a crucial role in guiding Darwin to the theory of evolution by natural selection, are afforded a key symbolic role in Kurt VONNEGUT Jr's bitter futuristic fantasy *Galapagos* (1985). [BS/DP]

ISOLA DEGLI UOMINI PESCE, L' (vt *Island of Mutations*; vt *Screamers*) Film (1978). Dania-Medusa/New World. Dir Sergio Martino (and Joe DANTE, US version only), starring Barbara Bach, Claudio Cassinelli, Richard Johnson, Beryl Cunningham, Joseph Cotten (and Cameron Mitchell, Mel Ferrer, US version only). Screenplay Martino, Sergio Donati, Cesare Frugoni. 99 mins, cut to 91 mins. Colour.

This is a wild Italian schlock picture, seemingly inspired by the flop *The* ISLAND OF DR MOREAU (1977). In 1891 a shipwrecked doctor (Cassinelli) encounters a tribe of man/fish hybrids, created for sound ethical reasons by a mad SCIENTIST (Cotten) but being exploited by a vintage Victorian villain (Johnson) to recover the sunken treasures of ATLANTIS. A heroine strutting in riding boots (Bach) and the villain's voodoo priestess mistress (Cunningham) play roles in a demented story which contains an immensely enjoyable collection of *Boy's Own* CLICHÉS. For US release (as *Screamers*) the film was slightly recut by Roger CORMAN's New World and given a much gorier prologue dir Joe Dante, with guest stars Ferrer and Mitchell – neither a stranger to Italian exploitation – being chomped by MUTANT leftovers from *Humanoids from the Deep* (1980). [KN]

ISRAEL Israel's traditional orientation towards the West, the initially UTOPIAN character of Zionism – partly inspired by founding Zionist ideologue Binyamin Zev (Theodor) Herzl's polemic *Der Judenstaat* (1896; trans as *The Jewish State* 1946) and short novel *Altneuland* (1902; trans as *Old-New Land* 1947) – and the country's adherence to its own form of democracy ought to have made it a promised land for speculative literature. But, despite the seminal influence within the genre of Jewish writers and editors, sf has never attained more than marginal stature within Israel.

Survival in this pressure-cooker region has stunted the capacity of many Israelis to contemplate alternate realities. Indeed Hebrew, the new *lingua franca* of Israel, seems ill suited to sf. Unlike Yiddish, whose rich cadences nourished the dreamlike imageries of an Isaac Bashevis Singer (1904-1991), modern Hebrew is leaner and less fanciful. Redeemed from a language hitherto used for liturgical purposes, it was also more limited, early on, in its ability to describe TECHNOLOGY. Indeed, merely agreeing a Hebrew term for sf (initially *mada dimioni* ["imaginary science"] and ultimately, in the late 1970s, *mada bidioni* ["science fabrication"]) severely challenged the semantic abilities of Israel's small sf community.

In the 1950s, brief forays by publishers tantalized would-be fans with a few Hebrew translations of novels by Robert A. HEINLEIN and Fredric BROWN before ending in bankruptcy. So too ended three plunges into sf magazine publishing with *Mada Dimioni* (1958, 13 issues), *Cosmos: Sipurei Mada Dimioni* ["Cosmos: Stories of Science Fiction"] (1958, 4 issues) and *Flash Gordon* (1963, 7 issues); none published work by local authors. The only Israeli sf writer of note in this period, Mordecai ROSHWALD, had his apocalyptic novels *Level Seven* (**1959** UK) and *A Small Armageddon* (**1962** UK) published abroad; neither was translated into Hebrew, and Roshwald, whose work is unrecognized in Israel, eventually settled in the UK.

The election to power of the Likud bloc in 1977 heralded a period of consumerism in Israel that permitted a brief boom in sf. Encouraged by young Israelis' new spending power and by the success of such films as STAR WARS (1977), publishers embarked upon ambitious schedules of mostly translated sf. By the onset of the long recession following the 1982 invasion of Lebanon, nearly 200 of the classic books of modern sf had been translated.

Of several new sf magazines, few survived long, but *Fantazia 2000* merits special notice. Launched in 1978, it nourished a group of local writers and a small, vigorous fan community during its 44-issue, six-year life. Among its writers was Hillel Damron, author of the critically well received *Milchemet Ha'minim* ["The War of the Sexes"] (**1982**), set in a post-HOLOCAUST underground colony where a society of sexual equals devolves into full-scale subjugation of males.

Before the Lebanon War, Israeli sf tended to be reticent on POLITICS, but the 1982 watershed altered this. Another *Fantazia* graduate, David Melamed, whose first collection, *Tsavua B'Corundy* ["A Hyena in Corundy"] (coll **1980**), contains stories with little immediate relevance to Israel, powerfully recounted in his third novel, *Ha'Halom Ha'Rivi'i* ["The Fourth Dream"] (**1986**) – unequalled for its nightmare tones if not for its narrative drive – the travails of an Israeli refugee in Germany after a NEAR-FUTURE fall of the Jewish state.

Melamed's dystopian excursion followed two other landmark works. In 1983 the prominent left-wing columnist Amos Kenan published *Ha-Derech L'Ein Harod* (**1983**; trans as *The Road to Ein Harod* **1986**), which postulated a NEAR-FUTURE military takeover of Israel. It was not his first speculative novel – that being the more surreal *Shoah II* ["Holocaust II"] (**1973**) – but it was the only Israeli sf novel ever awarded a peace prize by the Palestine Liberation Organization. Although the book embraces well known sf and TECHNOTHRILLER tropes, Kenan vehemently denied its genre roots, no doubt because of the Israeli literary establishment's low esteem of sf. A second significant DYSTOPIA was written by the established novelist Binyamin Tammuz (d1990): *Pundako Shel Yermiyahu* ["Jeremiah's Inn"] (**1984**) is a broad comic SATIRE about an Israel taken over by religious zealots. A grimmer version of the future is Yitzhak Ben-Ner's *Ha'malachim Ba'im* ["Angels are Coming"] (**1987**), in which world atomic apocalypse has spared Israel, but by the 21st century life within the theocratic state is characterized by street violence, persecution of the secular minority and widespread alienation.

Zirmat Ha'hachamim ["Genes for Genius, Inc."] (**1982**) and *Luna: Gan Eden Geneti* ["Luna: The Genetic

Paradise"] (**1985**) by geneticist Ram Moav, about GENETIC ENGINEERING of humans, inspired accusations of fascism on the part of the author, who had written the two books while terminally ill. Ruth Blumert's *Ha'Tzariach* ["The Turret"] (**1983**) is a fantasy reminiscent of Mervyn PEAKE's **Gormenghast** trilogy.

Israel is not an important centre for sf film-making. The most notable foreign production has been Menachem Golan's low-budget, post-HOLOCAUST feature *America 3000* (1985; video release only), dir David Engelbach with a cast of comely Israeli and US Amazons. Poet and *avant-garde* film-maker David Avidan directed *Sheder Min Ha'atid* (1981; vt *Message from the Future*) in English about future humans visiting present-day Israel; it is execrable. Ricki Shelach's James BLISH-influenced short film *Ishur Nehita* ["Permission to Land"] (1978) tells of a visiting alien. Both films may have reflected that SENSE OF WONDER inspired among Israelis by the visit of Egypt's President Anwar Sadat. The 1989 adaptation, shot in English, of Amos Kenan's 1983 novel as *Freedom: The Voice from Ein Harod* failed to achieve Western distribution. Directed by prolific producer/director Doron Eran and shot for $2 million, *Freedom* was one of the most expensive films ever produced domestically, but suffered from the Israeli army's refusal to donate the use of military matériel; the peculiar lead casting of US actor Anthony Peck and Italian model Allesandra Mussolini (grandaughter of Il Duce) also detracted from its believability. In 1990 the Israeli film-maker Avi Nesher wrote and directed a Los-Angeles-shot $7 million technothriller, «Nameless» (vt «Timebomb»), as yet unreleased.

A small body of sf criticism emerged in the 1980s, the first regular column outside the sf magazines being Sheldon TEITELBAUM's in the *Jerusalem Post* (1981-5). Orzion Bartana, a professor of literature at Tel Aviv University, published Israel's first critical book on sf: *Ha'fantazia b'siporet Dor Hamdina: Fantasy in Israeli Literature in the Last Thirty Years* (**1989**). The vagaries of the sf scene are discussed in "Sociological Reflections on the History of Science Fiction in Israel" (SCIENCE-FICTION STUDIES Mar 1986) by Nachman Ben Yehuda, a Hebrew University sociologist and early contributor to *Fantazia 2000*.   [ST]

ITALY To trace an Italian sf tradition is not easy, because of the well established split in Italy between scientific language and "literary culture". It is of doubtful relevance to read DANTE ALIGHIERI's great poem *La divina commedia* (c1304-1320 in manuscript; trans as *The Divine Comedy*) as a sort of sf journey; Dante used his theological allegory to create a world that in terms of medieval consciousness was perfectly real. It may be more fruitful to consider as PROTO SCIENCE FICTION the chronicle of Marco Polo's marvellous voyage to India, China and Japan, *Milione* ["One Million Stories"] (**1298**): the meeting of the Venetian merchant with the alien Eastern world does have the flavour of a First Contact. In his *Le città invisibili* (**1972**; trans as *Invisible Cities* **1974**), Italo CALVINO rewrites

Marco Polo's work as a Borgesian catalogue of mysterious and fascinating towns, conceived by an endless imaginative process.

FANTASTIC VOYAGES and UTOPIAN landscapes are the most effective contributions of Italian literature to the development of a genre that would eventually merge into sf, as in the Renaissance poem *Orlando Furioso* (**1506**) by Ludovico Ariosto (1474-1533), based on the mythical history of Charlemagne and his Paladins. In this the palace of the wizard Atlante is a bewitched place of unrequited desires and bitter delusions, and the knight Astolfo, in his search for the brain of mad Orlando, rides on the wings of the Hippogriff to the Moon, where he visits a large valley, the land of forgotten dreams and wasted passions.

A century later the philosopher Tommaso CAMPA-NELLA evoked the City of the Sun, whose utopia is after the political ideas of PLATO. The male inhabitants have abolished private property, own all in common (women included) and believe in natural RELIGION, not in historical Christianity. This tale, first written though not first published in Italian, was *Città del sole* (written 1602-12; **1623** in Latin as *Civitas Solis*; trans in *Ideal Commonwealths* **1885** as "The City of the Sun").

In the 18th century – the Age of Reason, but also of a keen interest in exotic worlds – Italian culture enthusiastically hailed the satirical-fantastical mood of Jonathan SWIFT's *Gulliver's Travels* (**1726**; rev 1735) and VOLTAIRE's *Candide* (**1759**). Among the manifold imitators of Swift (and of his French disciple, the Abbé Desfontaines [1685-1745]) was the Venetian-Armenian Zaccaria Seriman, whose lively account of the fantastic voyage of a British hero is *Viaggi di Enrico Wanton alle terre incognite australi ed ai regni delle scimmie e dei cinocefali* ["Enrico Wanton's Travels to the Unknown Lands of the Southern Hemisphere and to the Kingdoms of the Monkeys and of the Dog-Headed People"] (**1764**). Although issued in French, Giacomo CASANOVA's huge novel *Icosameron* (**1788**) was partly drafted in Italian. Beyond its encyclopedic farrago of scientific and philosophical meditations, *Icosameron* establishes a well known imaginative pattern: two young protagonists (brother and sister) discover an underground world where total harmony rules the lives of the Megamicri ("Big-Littles").

Italian Romanticism was not deeply involved in the industrial and scientific upheavals of the 19th century. There was no Italian equivalent of Mary SHEL-LEY's *Frankenstein* (**1818**; rev 1831) or of the Faustian short stories of Edgar Allan POE and Nathaniel HAWTHORNE. (The main literary problems of Italy were connected with the struggle for national independence, achieved in 1861, and the need for a common language.) All the same, the major Italian Romantic poet Giacomo Leopardi (1798-1837), inspired by the example of Galileo Galilei (1564-1642), did deal with the relationship between the scientific and the literary imagination, as shown in the fabulous scenery of some of his *Operette morali* (coll **1827**; preferred trans Patrick Creagh as *Moral Tales* **1988**

UK). One of the most fascinating *operette* is the dialogue between the anatomist Federico Ruysch and his mummies, reborn at the beginning of a new cosmic cycle.

Although Italy had neither a Jules VERNE nor an H.G. WELLS, the end of the 19th century did offer a minor literature of extraordinary journeys into the future, such as the utopian world explored in *L'Anno 3000: Sogno* ["The Year 3000: A Dream"] (**1897**) by Paolo Mantegazza. The enormously popular Emilio Salgari (1862-1911), creator of the Malayan pirate **Sandokan**, also published futuristic tales such as *La meraviglie del duemila* ["The Marvels of the Year 2000"] (**1907**).

Fantasy, both in the GOTHIC form and in the sphere of the wonderful and the whimsical, appeals to the modern Italian reader much more than the cognitive rhetoric of GENRE SF; this is certainly why Giacinto Spagnoletti, a well known scholar of Italian literature, has labelled native sf "neo-fantastico". The tradition is a long one. Outstanding examples of fantasy appear in the *fin de siècle* works of the so-called "Scapigliati" ["The Dishevelled Ones"], a Milanese cultural movement fighting against tradition and provincialism; in the "metaphysical" fiction of Massimo Bontempelli (1884-1960), whose *Eva ultima* ["The Ultimate Eve"] (**1923**) was inspired by De Chirico's painting; and, more recently, in the hallucinatory world of Dino BUZZATI's short stories and his novel of military life in a forgotten fortress, *Il deserto dei Tartari* (**1940**; trans as *The Tartar Steppe* **1952**).

Critics detect a "true" sf production in Italian only from the period after WWII. Much of this specialized sf was arguably not culturally Italian, in that it was heavily influenced by the US-UK canon as enthusiastically presented by publishers, notably the **Romanzi di Urania** series published since 1953 by Arnoldo Mondadori under the editorship of Giorgio Monicelli (inventor of the neologism "fantascienza" for "science fiction"). Even today some of the younger Italian authors, especially those groomed by the main Italian sf-publishing house, Editrice Nord, employ traditional US-UK sf formulae, sometimes with the addition of fashionable brushstrokes taken from J.R.R. TOLKIEN or Jorge Luis BORGES: Luigi Menghini and Vittorio Catani are examples.

But a more Italian trend has been advocated since the 1960s by a group of writers who, while basically accepting the formulaic conventions of sf, emphasize the need for psychological insight, a "human" perception of the alien and a (somewhat sceptical) moral probing into the triumphs of technology. Among them Lino Aldani – an accomplished and witty storyteller, as in *Quarta dimensione* ["Fourth Dimension"] (coll **1963**) – Sandro Sandrelli, Inisero Cremaschi and Gilda Musa are certainly worth mentioning. All four cooperated in the clever monthly review *Il Futuro* ["Future"] (1963-4); this and other Italian sf magazines (notably *Gamma* in the mid-1960s and *Robot* in the mid-1970s) were short-lived and, except for *Il Futuro*, had to rely heavily on US-UK material. Other novelists from the 1960s and 1970s, employing mainly formulaic devices, are Roberta Rambelli, Ugo Malaguti, Gianni Montanari, Roberto Vacca – one of the very few with a scientific background, author of *Il robot e il minotauro* ["The Robot and the Minotaur"] (**1959**) – and Vittorio Curtoni, who is also the author of an informative history of modern Italian sf, *Le frontiere dell'ignoto* ["Frontiers of the Unknown"] (**1977**).

Unquestionably, the proper tool for Italian writers to use in combining the scientific imagination, on the one hand, with the subjective universe(s) of fantasy, on the other, is the short story, as is evidenced by such representative anthologies as *I labirinti del terzo pianeta* ["The Labyrinths of the Third Planet"] (anth **1964**), ed I. Cremaschi and G. Musa, and *Universo e dintorni* ["Universe and Surroundings"] (anth **1978**), ed I Cremaschi.

In the 1980s the emergence of a group of young women sf writers in Italy confirmed an international development. Daniela Piegai, perhaps the best of them, creates in *Il mondo non è nostro* ["The World is Not Ours"] (**1989**) a technological version of KAFKA's castle, whose inhabitants are entrapped in a sort of temporal vortex, unable to return to the external world.

Contemporary non-genre Italian sf exists: some of the best of those postwar novelists usually thought of as MAINSTREAM WRITERS have shown a highly original imagination in handling sf themes and symbols. A mad astronaut is imprisoned in a living starship in Tommaso LANDOLFI's *Cancroregina* (**1950**; in *Cancerqueen and Other Stories* coll trans **1971** US); the achievements of scientific progress are ironically explored by Primo LEVI in *Storie naturali* ["Tales of the Natural World"] (coll **1966**), whose contents make up part of *The Sixth Day* (coll trans **1990** US); wandering on an untouched Earth from which mankind has suddenly disappeared, a solitary survivor lives his grotesque and suicidal loneliness in Guido Morselli's posthumously published *Dissipatio H.G.* ["Disappearance of the Human Race"] (**1977**); the impact of the scientific imagination, and the history of science, help shape the fantastic narrative of *Il pendolo di Foucault* (**1988**; trans William Weaver as *Foucault's Pendulum* **1989** US) by Umberto ECO. One outstanding sf writer – although he did not like to be referred to as such – was Italo CALVINO, as when he shaped his complicated web of scientific fables and myths in *Le Cosmicomiche* (coll of linked stories **1965**; trans William Weaver as *Cosmicomics* **1968** US). Contemporary non-genre sf seems obsessed by theological and religious themes. In *1994: La nudità e la spada* ["Year 1994: The Nakedness and the Sword"] (**1990**), Ferruccio Parazzoli builds up an anti-Catholic *coup-d'état* in a grim, NEAR-FUTURE Italy, while in *Ascolta, Israele* ["Hearken, Israel!"] (**1991**) Ugo Bonanate creates an ALTERNATE WORLD where Judaism is the only Western religion, early Christian communities have been wiped out, and the Gospels are buried in a hidden place until

their sensational discovery by a team of astonished international scholars . . .

Italian cinema inclines more towards HORROR than sf but, hovering between the two, a few quite good Italian films play on the theme of cosmic catastrophe, as in *La morte viene dallo spazio* (**1958**; vt *Death from Outer Space*; vt *The Day the Sky Exploded*), dir Paolo Heusch, and *Il* PIANETA DEGLI UOMINI SPENTI ["Planet of the Soulless People"] (**1961**; vt *Battle of the Worlds*; vt *Planet of the Lifeless Men*), dir Anthony Dawson (Antonio Margheriti). Another sf/horror blend, TERRORE NELLO SPAZIO (**1965**; vt *Planet of the Vampires*), dir Mario Bava, was in some ways a predecessor of ALIEN (**1979**). More commonly, Italian sf films exploit already successful foreign films: CONTAMINATION: ALIEN ARRIVA SULLA TERRA (**1981**; vt *Contamination*) mimics *Alien*; **1990**: I GUERRIERI DEL BRONX (**1982**; vt *1990: Bronx Warriors*) owes a lot to ESCAPE FROM NEW YORK (**1981**); and L'ISOLA DEGLI UOMINI PESCE (**1978**; vt *Island of Mutations*; vt *Screamers*) seems inspired by The ISLAND OF DR MOREAU (**1977**). Possibly the one real contribution of Italian cinema to sf lies in the field of satire and parody, exemplified by Tinto Brass's *Il disco volante* (**1964**; vt *The Flying Saucer*), Elio Petri's *La* DECIMA VITTIMA (**1965**; vt *The Tenth Victim*), based on a story by Robert SHECKLEY, and Mario Bava's DIABOLIK (**1967**; vt *Danger: Diabolik*).

Italian sf criticism is stronger on the utopian tradition and modern DYSTOPIA than it is on GENRE SF, owing perhaps to the activities of Vito Fortunati, founder of the Centre for Utopian Studies in Bologna, and to the publications of A. Monti and C. PAGETTI on H.G. Wells and of D. Guardamagna and S. Manferlotti on Aldous HUXLEY, George ORWELL and Anthony BURGESS. A handful of critics deal with contemporary sf: C. Pagetti with *Il senso del futuro* ["The Sense of the Future"] (**1970**; rev edn projected), F. Ferrini with *Che cosa è la fantascienza* ["What is SF?"] (**1970**), S. Solmi with *Saggi sul fantastico* ["Essays on Fantastic Literature"] (coll **1978**), which includes his seminal essay on sf published in 1953, R. Giovannoli with *La scienza della fantascienza* ["Science and Science Fiction"] (**1982**), S. Salvestroni with *Semiotica dell'imaginazione* ["Semiotics of the Imaginary"] (**1984**), on Russian sf, A. Caronia with *Il Cyborg* ["Cyborgs"] (**1985**), on the artificial human in sf, O. Palusci with *Terra di Lei* ["Herland"] (**1990**), on the female imagination in sf, and F. La Polla on sf cinema and tv.   [CP]

IT CAME FROM BENEATH THE SEA Film (**1955**). Clover/Columbia. Prod Charles H. Schneer. Dir Robert Gordon, starring Kenneth Tobey, Faith Domergue, Donald Curtis. Screenplay George Worthing Yates, Hal Smith, based on a story by Yates. 77 mins. B/w.

In this MONSTER MOVIE a giant octopus is affected by atomic radiation – as so often in the genre – and goes on a destructive rampage, attacking San Francisco and demolishing various landmarks, including the Golden Gate Bridge, before being destroyed by an atomic torpedo. The film, unimportant in itself, marks the beginning of the long partnership between producer Schneer and special-effects supervisor Ray HARRYHAUSEN, who was limited here by the small budget: his animated octopus, for instance, has only six tentacles. [JB/PN]

IT CAME FROM OUTER SPACE Film (1953). Universal. Dir Jack ARNOLD, starring Richard Carlson, Barbara Rush, Charles Drake. Screenplay Harry Essex, based on a screen treatment by Ray BRADBURY. 80 mins. 3-D. B/w.

This was Arnold's, and Universal's, first venture into the sf/HORROR genre; it was also the first sf film to exploit a desert location (here the Mojave Desert), and the first 3-D film released in widescreen format. Research by Bill WARREN, in *Keep Watching the Skies! Volume 1* (**1982**), shows conclusively that much more of Bradbury's original treatment was used than for many years had been thought the case, and that Bradbury's creative input was greater than screenwriter Essex's. This is a genuinely alarming film about an ALIEN spaceship that crashlands in the desert. The shapeshifting aliens, more frightened – it turns out – than inimical, and needing assistance to repair their ship, begin duplicating local inhabitants. Not quite a classic, but historically important, *ICFOS* is a well made, moody film. The human-duplication theme was to become a cinematic CLICHÉ (◊ MONSTER MOVIES; PARANOIA). [PN/JB]

IT CONQUERED THE WORLD Film (1956). Sunset/American International. Prod and dir Roger CORMAN, starring Peter Graves, Lee Van Cleef, Beverly Garland. Screenplay credited to Lou Rusoff, actually by Charles B. Griffith. 71 mins. B/w.

This film only just survives its ridiculous monster (cone-shaped with fangs) and the usual hurried air of a Corman production, but there's plenty of interest in the tale of an idealistic but weak scientist (Van Cleef) who brings a Venusian to Earth, where it proceeds to let him down badly by embarking on conquest. The scheme (Earth people reduced to subservient zombies by the bites of small batlike things generated by the monster) is foiled by another scientist (Graves), and there is a subtext about loss of individuality and emotion similar to that in the better-known INVASION OF THE BODY SNATCHERS (also 1956). [PN]

IT HAPPENED HERE Film (1966). Rath/Lopert. Dir Kevin Brownlow, Andrew Mollo, starring Pauline Murray, Sebastian Shaw, Fiona Leland, Honor Fehrson. Screenplay Brownlow, Mollo. 99 mins, cut to 93 mins. B/w.

ALTERNATE-WORLD stories are rare in sf cinema. This UK film is an exception; it shows what might have happened had Nazi Germany successfully invaded the UK (◊ HITLER WINS). Shot in a realistic, documentary-like style, it is a remarkable achievement when one takes into account that it is virtually an amateur film, made over a period of years by Brownlow and Mollo working mainly at weekends

and using nonprofessional talent. Its release date, 1966, is three years later than the copyright date. Sadly, it was never widely shown. [JB]

IT LIVES AGAIN (vt *It's Alive II*) Film (1978). Larco/Warner Bros. Prod and dir Larry COHEN, starring Frederic Forrest, Kathleen Lloyd, John P. Ryan, John Marley. Screenplay Cohen. 91 mins. Colour.

This sequel to IT'S ALIVE (1974) has the MUTANT child's father from the previous film warning another young couple that the pregnant wife may also produce a mutant baby and that the government is systematically terminating all such pregnancies, even though he has learned that the monsters will respond to parental affection. There follows a continuing clash between, on the one hand, the group determined to save the babies and, on the other, a government group – including another father of a mutant baby – equally determined to kill them. Apart from being a devastating study in marital stress, the film also asks (but does not answer) questions of an sf kind about the possible purpose of this apparently horrible mutation. Primarily, however, the mutants symbolize the way in which families and society as a whole can be torn apart by diversions from the norm. Like most of Cohen's films, *ILA* is deeply subversive of the conventional social pieties. The exploration of these ideas is continued in the further sequel, *It's Alive III: Island of the Alive* (1986), which blends schlock horror with extraordinary sensitivity in Cohen's typical but unsettling manner. Here the mutants have been isolated on an island contaminated by radioactivity, two of them producing a child of their own, while once again a father (Michael Moriarty) has to come to terms with his abhorrent role as star in a media freak show. [PN]

See also: MONSTER MOVIES.

IT'S A BIRD! IT'S A PLANE! IT'S SUPERMAN! ◊ SUPERMAN.

IT'S ALIVE Film (1974). Larco/Warner Bros. Prod and dir Larry COHEN, starring John Ryan, Sharon Farrell, Andrew Duggan, Guy Stockwell. Screenplay Cohen. 91 mins. Colour.

A MUTANT baby (the mother has taken a new drug) kills all the medical staff in the delivery room and leaps through a skylight to go on a rampage, killing a woman, a milkman and several policemen. Although the plot is evidently ludicrous, as a witty, low-budget MONSTER MOVIE *IA* is more than satisfactory. The baby, wisely presented in a series of fast, almost subliminal shots, is disturbing because it does what all babies do – crawl around on the floor. Far more disturbing is the transition from seeing the baby as monstrous menace to seeing it as somebody's child. The father (Ryan), who joins the hunt, tries unsuccessfully to protect his offspring in a curiously moving though absurd climax set in Los Angeles' storm drains, deliberately evoking the finale of THEM! (1954). The two sequels are IT LIVES AGAIN (1978; vt *It's Alive II*) and *It's Alive III: Island of the Alive* (1986). [JB/PN]

See also: CINEMA.

IT'S ALIVE II ◊ IT LIVES AGAIN.

IT'S ALIVE III: ISLAND OF THE ALIVE ◊ IT LIVES AGAIN.

IT! THE TERROR FROM BEYOND SPACE Film (1958). Vogue/United Artists. Dir Edward L. Cahn, starring Marshall Thompson, Shawn Smith, Kim Spalding. Screenplay Jerome BIXBY. 69 mins. B/w.

In this largely mediocre film there are good, tense moments. The crew of a spaceship returning from Mars discover that "something" has stowed away: a monster which attacks crew members (for their blood and soft parts) and stores their bodies in the ship's ventilation system as future snacks. The survivors are slowly forced to retreat, section by section, as the seemingly invulnerable creature takes over the ship. An effective build-up of suspense takes place so long as the monster is kept vague and shadowy. The ending (the crew don spacesuits then asphyxiate the monster by draining the craft of oxygen) is one of several plot similarities to the later ALIEN (1979), but *I!TTFBS* itself cannot claim great originality, being reminiscent of A.E. VAN VOGT's (uncredited) "The Black Destroyer" (1939). [JB]

IVERSON, ERIC G. ◊ Harry TURTLEDOVE.

IZBAVITELJ ◊ YUGOSLAVIA.

JABLOKOV, ALEXANDER (1956-   ) US writer who began publishing sf with "Beneath the Shadow of her Smile" for *IASFM* in 1985, and who has since been fairly prolific in short forms, several stories being set in a future Boston. In its darkly suave competence, his first novel, *Carve the Sky* (**1991**), demonstrates the benefits of this work. The story, which opens on a clement, richly complex, low-tech Earth, soon begins to argue that a viable human culture might consciously wish to inhabit a PLANETARY-ROMANCE venue, and indeed so legislate. Later portions of the tale, set on an outward-bound spaceship and introducing an elaborate set of metaphors linking art (◊ ARTS) to the structure of the Universe, are marginally less impressive. His second novel is «A Deeper Sea» (1989 *IASFM*; exp 1992). [JC]

See also: SPACE FLIGHT.

JACKSON, BASIL (1920?-   ) Canadian author of several unremarkable NEAR-FUTURE sf novels, mostly for ROBERT HALE LIMITED: *Epicenter* (**1976** UK), *Supersonic* (**1976** UK), *Rage Under the Arctic* (**1977** UK), *The Night Manhattan Burned* (**1979** US) and *Spill!* (**1979** UK). [JC]

JACKSON, SHIRLEY (1919-1965) US short-story writer and novelist, married from 1940 to the literary critic Stanley Edgar Hyman (1919-1970), with whom she wrote (but was solely credited for) *Life Among the Savages* (**1953**) and *Raising Demons* (**1957**), two light memoirs of family life whose effect was radically dissimilar to that of her fiction, none of which is sf in any orthodox sense. Much of her work – like her first story, "Janice" (1937) – comprises psychological studies of women at the end of their tether. She became famous for one story, "The Lottery" (1948), which established her reputation as an author of GOTHIC fiction; the ritual stoning which climaxes the tale is perhaps more easily explicable in terms of HORROR than of sf, but the New England in which the event occurs betrays the profile of a land suffering the aftermath of the some vast CATASTROPHE. Most of the remaining stories assembled in *The Lottery, or The Adventures of James Hardis* (coll **1949**) are fantasies of alienation. Unnamed but tangible catastrophe is the explicit subject of *The Sundial* (**1958**), in which 12 of her New England characters await the END OF THE WORLD. *The Haunting of Hill House* (**1959**), filmed as *The Haunting* (1963) by Robert WISE, is a superb ghost story. [JC]

Other works: *Hangsaman* (**1951**); *We Have Always Lived in the Castle* (**1962**); *Come Along with Me* (coll **1968**); *The Lottery; The Haunting of Hill House; We Have Always Lived in the Castle* (omni **1991**).

JACOBI, CARL (RICHARD) (1908-   ) US writer; also editor of several journals, including the *Minnesota Quarterly*. His insinuatingly evocative short fiction is mainly of horror and fantasy interest, much of it appearing in *Weird Tales*, though he also produced some sf, mostly SPACE OPERA. He began publishing with "The Haunted Ring" for *Ghost Stories* in 1931, and collected some of his large output in *Revelations in Black* (coll **1947**; vt *The Tomb from Beyond* 1977 UK), *Portraits in Moonlight* (coll **1964**), *Disclosures in Scarlet* (coll **1972**) and *East of Samurinda* (coll **1989**). [JC]

JACOBS, HARVEY (1930-   ) US writer whose work, much of it taking on a MAGIC-REALIST glow, generally depicts the nature and fate of the urban Jew, especially in New York. His more fable-like tales, many of which appear in *The Egg of the Glak and Other Stories* (coll **1969**), are not dissimilar to some of Bernard MALAMUD's. The title story (1968) and "In Seclusion" (1968), with which he began publishing stories in the sf magazines, typically demonstrate HJ's sharply sardonic use of sf elements to make moral points about man's inhumanity to man in a cold world. [JC]

JACOBSON, DAN (1929-   ) South African novelist, in the UK from the early 1950s. Moral fervour and a harsh eloquence about his tortured homeland characterize novels like *The Trap* (**1955**). *The Confessions of Joseph Baisz* (**1977**) is set in a tyrannical DYSTOPIA, and *Her Story*

(1987) is an examination in sf and feminist terms of a desolate post-HOLOCAUST environment. [JC]

JACOMB, CHARLES ERNEST (1888-?   ) UK journalist and editor, author of one sf novel, *And A New Earth* (1926), which combines the UTOPIAN and future-WAR genres: an élitist, eugenic society is forced to defend itself with advanced weaponry against the major powers. Civilization is destroyed by a comet, and post-HOLOCAUST culture develops again very slowly. [JE]

JADE, SYMON Pseudonym of US writer Michael Eckstrom (?   -   ), responsible for the **Starship Orpheus** sequence of sf adventures: *Return from the Dead* (1982), *Cosmic Carnage* (1983) and *Alter Evil* (1983). [JC]

JAEGER, MURIEL (c1893-?   ) UK writer who took an English degree at Oxford and was a minor member of a group of women writers including Winifred HOLTBY and Dorothy L. Sayers (1893-1957). Her first sf work, *The Question Mark* (1926), depicts a UTOPIAN UK of 200 years hence (as witnessed by a waker from a cataleptic trance; ◊ SLEEPER AWAKES) and shows strongly the influences of H.G. WELLS and William MORRIS. In *The Man with Six Senses* (1927) a weakly youth, endowed with unrefined ESP talents, is helped towards maturity by a sympathetic girlfriend; the promise of originality shown in this novel was never realized, perhaps because of discouraging sales. *Hermes Speaks* (1933) follows the consequences, in the worlds of POLITICS and ECONOMICS, of adherence to the prophecies of a fake medium. *Retreat From Armageddon* (1936), a peripheral future-WAR novel in which a group of people withdraw from the ensuing conflagration to a remote country house where they philosophize on Man's shortcomings, is notable for its advocacy of GENETIC ENGINEERING. It, too, met with little success, and MJ stopped writing fiction. [JE]

About the author: *Dangerous by Degrees: Women at Oxford and the Somerville College Novelists* (1989) by Susan J. Leonardi.

See also: LEISURE; SUPERMAN.

JAFFERY, SHELDON (R.) (?   -   ) US attorney, editor and bibliographer. In the latter capacity he has concentrated on fantasy and horror, beginning with *Horror and Unpleasantries* (1982), an ARKHAM HOUSE bibliography, later incorporated into his *The Arkham House Companion* (1989). His guides to WEIRD TALES – *The Collector's Index to Weird Tales* (1985) with Fred Cook – and to DAW BOOKS – *Future and Fantastic Worlds* (dated 1987 but 1988) – are also useful tools. He has edited *Sensuous Science Fiction from the Weird and Spicy Pulps* (anth 1982), *Selected Tales of Grim and Grue from the Horror Pulps* (anth 1987) and *The Weirds: A Facsimile Selection of Fiction from the Era of the Shudder Pulps* (anth 1987). [JC]

JAHN, MIKE Working name of US writer Joseph Michael Jahn (1943-   ), most of whose work of sf interest has been in ties for the tv series *The* SIX MILLION DOLLAR MAN: *Wine, Women, and War* ∗ (1975), *The Rescue of Athena One* ∗ (1975), *The Secret of Bigfoot Pass* ∗ (1976) and *International Incidents* ∗ (1977). *The Invisible Man* ∗ (1975) is another tv tie. MJ has also contributed *Omega Sub* ∗ (1991) and *City of Fear* ∗ (1991) to the **Omega Sub** sf adventure series under the house name J.D. CAMERON. *The Olympian Strain* (1980) and *Armada* (1981) are singletons. [JC]

JAHNSSON, EVALD FERDINAND [r] ◊ FINLAND.

JAKES, JOHN (WILLIAM) (1932-   ) US writer best known for sf and fantasy before his **Bicentennial** series of novels, which traces the fictional history of a US family over the past 200 years; it achieved extraordinary bestsellerdom, undoubtedly justifying, at least financially, his decision to retire from the genre. Most of his shorter work, beginning with "The Dreaming Trees" for *Fantastic Adventures* in 1950, was written by the 1960s – a good selection appearing as *The Best of John Jakes* (coll 1977) ed Martin H. GREENBERG and Joseph D. OLANDER – and he published his last sf novel in 1973. He generally displayed competence, but his early work lacked bite and his later novels, though sharper, were published in some obscurity. He was in any case from the first actively involved in other genres, and published at least 20 books, including several historicals as by Jay Scotland, before *When the Star Kings Die* (1967), the first volume in the **Dragonard** series of SPACE OPERAS, marked his full-scale entry into the field. The 3 novels in the sequence – the others are *The Planet Wizard* (1969) and *Tonight We Steal the Stars* (1969 dos) – follow the adventures of the Dragonard clan as they guard II Galaxy and its corporate "star kings" against various perils. His second series, the **Brak the Barbarian** SWORD-AND-SORCERY epic, includes *Brak the Barbarian* (coll of linked stories 1968), *Brak the Barbarian versus the Sorceress* (1963 *Fantastic* as "Witch of the Four Winds"; exp 1969; vt *Brak the Barbarian – The Sorceress* 1970 UK; vt *The Sorceress* 1976 UK), *Brak the Barbarian versus the Mark of the Demon* (1969; vt *Brak the Barbarian – The Mark of the Demons* 1970 UK; vt *The Mark of the Demons* 1976 UK), *Brak: When the Idols Walked* (1964 *Fantastic Stories*; exp 1978) and *The Fortunes of Brak* (coll 1980). The deep debt of these stories to Robert E. HOWARD's **Conan** tales was acknowledged in the publication of *Mention my Name in Atlantis* (1972), an amusing pastiche of the subgenre.

Out of the several sf novels JJ published 1969-73, three stand out. *Six-Gun Planet* (1970) depicts a deliberately archaic colony planet called Missouri complete with ROBOT gunfighters, just as in the later film WESTWORLD (1973). *Black in Time* (1970) presents vignettes from Black history dramatized through a TIME-TRAVEL plot device. *On Wheels* (1973), set about a century hence, tautly depicts a mobile US subculture whose members live, breed and die on wheels, whether in large trailers or on their own vehicles, never leaving the Interstate highway system, never dropping below 40mph (65kph). Their god is the Texaco Firebird, which they see only at the moment of death. As SATIRE the story is simple but gripping, like most of JJ's best work. [JC]

Other works: *The Asylum World* (**1969**); *The Hybrid* (**1969**); *Secrets of Stardeep* (**1969**) and *Time Gate* (**1972**), both juveniles, later brought together as *Secrets of Stardeep, and Time Gate* (omni **1982**); *The Last Magicians* (**1969**); *Mask of Chaos* (**1970**); the **Gavin Black** novels, being *Master of the Dark Gate* (**1970**) and *Witch of the Dark Gate* (**1972**); *Monte Cristo #99* (**1970**); *Conquest of the Planet of the Apes* * (**1974**); *Excalibur!* (**1980**) with Gil Kane.

See also: COLONIZATION OF OTHER WORLDS; SOCIOLOGY; TRANSPORTATION.

JAKOBER, MARIE (1941-) Canadian writer whose only sf novel, *The Mind Gods* (**1976** UK), confronts on another planet a materialist, tolerant society with a repellent spiritual creed. With some subtlety the outcome is shown to be not altogether, morally, on the side of the liberals. [PN]

JAKOBSSON, EJLER (1911-1986) Finnish-born editor, in the USA from 1926. He became a PULP-MAGAZINE writer in the 1930s and joined the staff of one of the pulp chains, Popular Publications, in 1943. He briefly had responsibility for ASTONISHING STORIES and SUPER SCIENCE STORIES, but both magazines were already in the process of closing down due to paper shortages and Frederik POHL's departure. EJ remained with the company and became editor on its revival in 1949 of *Super Science Stories*, a position he retained until the magazine again (and finally) ceased publication in 1951; Damon KNIGHT was his assistant for part of this period. EJ returned to SF-MAGAZINE editing in 1969, when he took over the editorship of GALAXY SCIENCE FICTION and IF – again in succession to Pohl. With the assistance of Judy-Lynn DEL REY and Lester DEL REY, he attempted to make the magazine more contemporary and trendy, with mixed results, though Robert SILVERBERG praised his work. He was succeeded as editor by Jim BAEN in mid-1974. During EJ's editorship the following anthologies were published (his name did not appear on their title pages): *The Best from Galaxy Vol I* (anth **1972**) ed The Editors of Galaxy Magazine; *The Best from If* (anth **1973**) ed anon; *The Best from Galaxy Vol II* (anth **1974**) ed The Editors of Galaxy Magazine; *The Best from If Vol II* (anth **1974**) ed The Editors of If Magazine. [MJE]

JAKUBOWSKI, MAXIM (1944-) UK writer, critic, publisher, bookseller, translator and anthologist. He was educated in France and writes in both French and English. After some time as a company director in the flavour industry, he turned to publishing, becoming Managing Director of Virgin Books (1980-83) and then taking up directorships of Zomba and Rainbird. Since 1988 he has run the Murder One bookshop, London, specializing in mysteries; since 1991 this has incorporated the New Worlds sf outlet. As a writer he has published about 25 books, those in English mostly concerning rock music and the mystery field. Generally more at ease in short-story length, in both French and English, he began publishing fiction of genre interest in English with

"Lines of White on a Sullen Sea" for *NW* in 1969, which took place in the **Jerry Cornelius** SHARED WORLD opened by Michael MOORCOCK for contributors to the magazine. MJ's sf has tended to be marginal, and his preoccupation with doomed love, music, sex and death has more often been expressed in mainstream fiction. A prolific anthologist in France (9 vols), he has also edited several English-language anthologies: *Travelling towards Epsilon: An Anthology of French Science Fiction* (anth trans Beth Blish and MJ **1977**), *Twenty Houses of the Zodiac: An Anthology of International Science Fiction* (anth **1979**), *Lands of Never* (anth **1983**) and *Beyond Lands of Never* (anth **1984**), the latter two being original fantasy. With Malcolm EDWARDS he wrote *The Complete Book of Science Fiction and Fantasy Lists* (**1983**; rev vt *The SF Book of Lists* 1983 US), and with Edward JAMES he edited *The Profession of Science Fiction* (anth **1992**), a selection of pieces taken from the journal FOUNDATION: THE REVIEW OF SCIENCE FICTION. [MJ/PN/JC]

JALES, MARK [r] ◊ ROBERT HALE LIMITED.

JAMES, DAKOTA Pseudonym used for his fiction by US academic Bernard (Joseph) James (1922-), whose sf novels *Greenhouse* (**1984**) and its sequel, *Milwaukee the Beautiful* (**1987**), are set in a Wisconsin gradually isolated from the rest of a balkanized USA by the greenhouse effect. In the first DJ riskily assumes that the effect will be gravely consequential by 1997; but the second, set further in the future, agilely explores the implications of a Latin American invasion of independent Milwaukee. [JC]

JAMES, EDWARD (FREDERICK) (1947-) UK academic and editor who began teaching at University College, Dublin, in 1970, and moved to York University in 1978, where he became Director of the Centre for Medieval Studies in 1992. He has been the editor of FOUNDATION: THE REVIEW OF SCIENCE FICTION since 1986; in that capacity he has compiled an *Index to Foundation, 1-40* (**1988**) and edited with Maxim JAKUBOWSKI *The Profession of Science Fiction* (anth **1992**), which assembles autobiographical pieces first published in the journal. [JC]

JAMES, EDWIN [s] ◊ James E. GUNN.

JAMES, LAURENCE (1942-) UK paperbacks editor and then writer active under his own name and under at least 9 pseudonyms and house names, including Jonathan May, in various genres including Westerns, thrillers, historical romances and soft-core pornography. Over one four-year period he averaged about a book a month. As LJ he began publishing sf with "And Dug the Dog a Tomb" for *New Worlds Quarterly 3* (anth **1972**), an sf development of Samuel Beckett's *Waiting for Godot* (trans **1954**), though under his own name he is best known for a series of paperback SPACE OPERAS featuring **Simon Rack** and his Galactic Security Service Comrades: *Earth Lies Sleeping* (**1974**), *Starcross* (**1974**; vt *War on Aleph* 1974 US), *Backflash* (**1975**), *Planet of the Blind* (**1975**) and *New Life for Old* (**1975**). These are swiftly told but otherwise unremarkable. The **Dark Future** series of post-HOLOCAUST adventures for a young-adult audience includes *The Revengers* (**1992**) and *Beyond the Grave* (**1992**). For adults and as James Axler he wrote the SURVIVALIST-FICTION **Death Lands** post-holocaust military-sf series: *Death Lands #1: Red Holocaust* (**1986** Canada), *#2: Pilgrimage to Hell* (**1987** Canada), *#3: Neutron Solstice* (**1987** Canada), *#4: Crater Lake* (**1987** Canada), *#5: Northstar Rising* (**1988** Canada), *#6: Pony Soldiers* (**1988** Canada), *#7: Dectra Chain* (**1988** Canada), *#8: Ice and Fire* (**1988** Canada), *#9: Red Equinox* (**1989** Canada), *#10: Time Nomads* (**1989** Canada), *#11: Latitude Zero* (**1991** Canada), *#12: Seedling* (**1991** Canada) and *#13: Dark Carnival* (**1992** Canada). As James McPhee he wrote the similar **Survival 2000** sequence, dealing with events after an ASTEROID strikes Earth: *Survival 2000 #1: Blood Quest* (**1991**), *#2: Renegade War* (**1991**) and *#3: Frozen Fire* (**1991**). [JC]

Other works: *Electric Underground – A City Lights Reader* (anth **1973**); the **Witches** sequence, all as by James Darke, comprising *The Prisoner* (**1983**), *The Trial* (**1983**), *The Torture* (**1983**), *The Escape* (**1984**), *The Feud* (**1986**) and *The Plague* (**1986**).

JAMES, PHILIP [s] ◊ (1) Lester DEL REY; (2) James CAWTHORN.

JAMES, R. ALAN [r] ◊ ROBERT HALE LIMITED.

JAMES BLISH AWARD ◊ AWARDS.

JAMESON, FREDRIC [r] ◊ POSTMODERNISM AND SF.

JAMESON, MALCOLM (1891-1945) US writer who began producing fiction only after cancer forced him to retire from a nonwriting life which had included a career in the US Navy. He began publishing sf with "Eviction by Isotherm" for *ASF* in 1938, and wrote prolifically until his death. His books were all posthumously published. *Atomic Bomb* (**1944** *Startling Stories* as "The Giant Atom"; rev **1945**) is a NEAR-FUTURE story of an atomic explosion. *Bullard of the Space Patrol* (1940-45 *ASF*; coll of linked stories **1951**; omitting "The Bureaucrat" cut 1955) is a set of SPACE-OPERA tales for juveniles ed Andre NORTON. In *Tarnished Utopia* (1943 *Startling Stories*; **1956**) two people awaken from SUSPENDED ANIMATION to find themselves in conflict with a dictatorship. [JC]

See also: ASTEROIDS; DYSTOPIAS; NUCLEAR POWER.

JAMESON, (MARGARET) STORM (1891-1986) UK novelist, the first woman to gain a BA from Leeds University (1912), known mainly for family-chronicle novels such as those assembled as *The Triumph of Time* (omni **1932**). Her sf novels derive from her interest in the POLITICS of change, and extrapolate extremist political "solutions" into the NEAR FUTURE. *In the Second Year* (**1936**) projects a fascist UK. In *Then We Shall Hear Singing* (**1942**) a victorious German Reich dominates an unnamed country, but is unable to eliminate the resistance of the individual consciousness (◊ HITLER WINS). Set after an off-stage atomic HOLOCAUST, *The Moment of Truth* (**1949**) describes a UK ruled by communists. Only in *The World Ends* (**1937**) as by William Lamb does SJ permit herself some elegiac tranquillity: in this novel the world ends quietly (but thoroughly) flooded, and a patriarchy

comes into being. [JC]

JAMES TIPTREE, JR. AWARD ◊ AWARDS.

JANE, FRED T. Working name of UK writer and illustrator Frederick Thomas Jane (1865-1916), best known for founding the **Jane's Fighting Ships** series (from **1898**). *Blake of the "Rattlesnake", or The Man who Saved England* (**1895**) is a NEAR-FUTURE story in which, through a series of engagements, modern torpedoes save the UK from the Russians and the French. Artificially created according to an ancient Egyptian formula, the protagonist of *The Incubated Girl* (**1896**) upsets the contemporary UK with her soulless purity, her vegetarianism and her goddesslike charisma. *To Venus in Five Seconds: An Account of the Strange Disappearance of Thomas Plummer, Pillmaker* (**1897**) takes its kidnapped narrator to VENUS, where he sets off a conflict between the natives – intelligent giant insects – and the ancient Egyptians who have been resident there for some time, including his lady kidnapper; the humorous effects in this tale are clearly intentional. *The Violent Flame: A Story of Armageddon and After* (**1899**) features a mad SCIENTIST who brings about the END OF THE WORLD – which, Gaia-like, is a living entity – with a disintegrator ray. The narrator and his wife survive to be a new ADAM AND EVE. FTJ's fiction, though crude, conveys a genuine speculative impact; his ILLUSTRATIONS, not only of his own work but also of future-war novels by George GRIFFITH and E. Douglas FAWCETT, focus on WAR and WEAPONS, though some more interesting sequences, like "Guesses at Futurity" (1894-5 *Pall Mall Magazine*), show a wide-ranging visual sense of things to come. He was also of note as an illustrator of some of Arthur Conan DOYLE's **Sherlock Holmes** stories. [JC/PN]

See also: CRIME AND PUNISHMENT; HISTORY OF SF; MATTER TRANSMISSION; TRANSPORTATION.

JANIFER, LAURENCE M(ARK) (1933-) US writer – in several genres – and performing musician. Born Larry Mark Harris – a name used on his fiction until 1963 – he reverted to the old family name, which had been discarded by an immigration officer when LMJ's grandfather had gained entry to the USA from Poland. Some of his non-sf books – mostly erotica – appeared under the pseudonyms Alfred Blake and Barbara Wilson. His first sf publication was "Expatriate" for *Cosmos* in 1953. Much of his sf has been written in collaboration, including early works with Randall GARRETT and some later ones with S.J. TREIBICH. With Garrett he wrote a bawdy mythological fantasy, *Pagan Passions* (**1959**), as by Randall Garrett and Larry M. Harris, for the Beacon Books series of GALAXY SCIENCE FICTION NOVELS and 3 novels as Mark PHILLIPS featuring confrontations between a secret-service agent and various PSI-POWERED individuals: *Brain Twister* (1959 *ASF* as "That Sweet Little Old Lady"; **1962**), *The Impossibles* (1960 *ASF* as "Out Like a Light"; **1963**) and *Supermind* (1960-61 *ASF* as "Occasion for Disaster"; **1963**).

LMJ's first solo novel was *Slave Planet* (**1963**). The

Wonder War (**1964**), though credited to Janifer alone, appears from the dedication to have been written in collaboration with Michael KURLAND. *You Sane Men* (**1965**; vt *Bloodworld* 1968) describes a world where sadism is the aristocratic way of life. *A Piece of Martin Cann* (**1968**) features psi-assisted psychotherapy. LMJ's most ambitious novel is *Power* (**1974**), a study of the POLITICS of rebellion; similar themes are tackled in *Reel* (**1983**). The lively **Knave** series – *Survivor* (**1977**) and its sequels *Knave in Hand* (**1979**) and *Knave and the Game* (coll of linked stories **1987**) – feature an interplanetary troubleshooter, Knave, who is somewhat in the mould of Keith LAUMER's Retief. LMJ's 3 novels with Treibich, the **Angelo di Stefano** series, are comedies: *Target: Terra* (**1968**), *The High Hex* (**1969**) and *The Wagered World* (**1969**). A collection of his short fiction is *Impossible?* (coll **1968**). LMJ edited the anthology *Masters' Choice* (anth **1966**; vt in 2 vols *SF: Master's Choice* 1968 UK; vt *18 Greatest Science Fiction Stories* 1971 US). [BS]

See also: MUSIC.

JANSON, HANK Initially a personal pseudonym of Stephen FRANCES but eventually a house name used by other UK writers for various publishers. Authors writing as HJ included Harry Hobson (1908-   ), Harold Ernest Kelly (1900-1969), James MOFFATT, Victor NORWOOD and Colin Simpson. Most HJ titles were thrillers. [JC]

See also: ADAM AND EVE.

JANUS/AURORA US feminist sf FANZINE (1975-90) ed from Madison, Wisconsin, by Jan Bogstad, Jeanne Gomoll and Diane Martin (#1-#3 by Bogstad, #4-#17 by Bogstad and Gomoll, #18-#26 by Martin). *Janus* (which became *Aurora* with #19) was born as FEMINISM began making itself felt in sf in the mid-1970s. It carried articles by Samuel R. DELANY, Suzette Haden ELGIN, Joanna RUSS and Jessica Amanda Salmonson (1950-   ), and interviews with Octavia E. BUTLER, Suzy McKee CHARNAS, Jo CLAYTON, Elizabeth A. LYNN, Clifford D. SIMAK, John VARLEY, Joan D. VINGE and Chelsea Quinn YARBRO. Through reviews and articles, *J/A* examined critically the depiction of sexuality in sf, WOMEN AS PORTRAYED IN SCIENCE FICTION, sf by women, women in fandom and the feminist SMALL PRESSES. Right up to its demise it worked to prevent the contribution of WOMEN SF WRITERS being ignored. In the penultimate issue Gomoll wrote an "Open Letter to Joanna Russ" pointing out that the dismissal of 1970s sf by CYBERPUNK writers was the sort of attempt to erase the contribution of women that Russ had highlighted in *How to Suppress Women's Writing* (**1983**). Many, such as Delany and Sarah LEFANU, who used *J/A* extensively in her own researches into sf and feminism, agreed. *J/A* is likely to remain one of the best sources for research into the discourse between sf and feminism that took place in the 1970s and 1980s. [RH]

JANVIER, IVAN or PAUL [s] ◊ Algis BUDRYS.

JANVIER, THOMAS A(LLIBONE) (1849-1913) US novelist who was also active as a journalist. His lost-race (◊ LOST WORLDS) novel, *The Aztec Treasure House* (**1890**), didactically describes a surviving remnant of the Aztec empire. In *The Women's Conquest of New York* (**1894**), published anon, Tammany Hall misguidedly enfranchises females, who run amok until threatened with physical violence by their aroused spouses. *In the Sargasso Sea* (**1898**) is a ROBINSONADE in which a shipwrecked sailor survives aboard his disabled vessel in a maze of seaweed, finds a treasure trove, and escapes. *In Great Waters* (coll **1901**) contains fantasies. [JC]

See also: ANTHROPOLOGY.

JAPAN It seems that the continuing attention the Japanese people give to their ancient legends and fantastic stories has made them receptive to modern fantasies and sf, and the rationalization of a chaotic Universe which such stories offer. Appropriately, the history of Japanese sf begins during the 1870s, a period of violently rapid modernization in Japan, with translations of the works of Jules VERNE. The native Japanese sf writers of this era, such as Shunro Oshikawa (1877-1914), show his strong influence. One of Oshikawa's most popular books is *Kaitei Gunkan* ["Undersea Warship"] (**1900**), a future-WAR novel about a conflict between Japan and Russia, which effectively predicted the actual war of 1904-5. Between the two World Wars, new writers of straight sf and fantasy began to appear, the most popular and capable among them being Juza Unno (1897-1949), who wrote stories influenced by the newly developing US sf; stories of his such as *Chikyu Tonan* ["The Stolen Earth"] (**1936**) and *Yojigen Hyoryu* ["Marooned in the 4-D World"] (**1946**) were, although not highly regarded as literature, loved by young readers.

It was only after WWII, however, that sf became widely popular. A few ambitious publishers attempted series of translated sf stories, though most of these experiments failed due to limited sales. Notable among them were a series of 7 anthologies from *Amazing Stories* (all 1950) and 20 volumes of the **Gengensha SF Series** (1956-7); these began the process of establishing an sf audience in Japan. This audience was soon catered for by the first successful venture, the **Hayakawa SF Series** (1957-74), published by Hayakawa Publishing Co., which issued 318 volumes, mostly of translations but also including about 50 Japanese originals; another paperback series, **Hayakawa SF Bunko** (1970-current), reached its 940th volume in 1991 (all translations), including reprints from the earlier series. The same company's **Hayakawa JA Series** of original works (1973-current) has reached about 340 volumes. Hayakawa has also published hardback sf series. In competition with Hayakawa, the Tokyo Sogensha Co. began its own translation series (1963-current), which has reached some 300 volumes; early on it featured Edgar Rice BURROUGHS's **Barsoom** books and E.E. "Doc" SMITH's works. Asahi Sonorama's series of Japanese originals (1975-current) numbers over 500, most of them sf. Sanrio Co. published almost 200 titles in **Sanrio SF**

Bunko (1978-84). Other publishers, such as Kadokawa Shoten, Kodansha, Shinchosa, Shueisha and Seishinsha, publish both translated and original sf or fantasy on a smaller scale. The NEW WAVE in the 1960s and CYBERPUNK in the 1980s affected Japanese sf and stimulated several writers to work in these styles.

In 1957 the FANZINE *Uchujin* ["Cosmic Dust"] was founded, and began publishing original Japanese work; nearly half of the sf writers in Japan today started there. With 190 issues and a circulation of about 1000, *Uchujin* remains Japan's leading fanzine. In 1960 the first successful professional sf magazine in Japan was launched by Hayakawa: *SF Magazine* began as a reprint vehicle for *FSF*, but shortly began to publish original material, which soon predominated. *SF Magazine* proved a success, celebrating its 400th issue in Oct 1990 with a lavish special issue. The second professional sf magazine, *Kiso-Tengai* ["Fantastic"], began in 1975 and has folded twice, each time being revived by a fresh publisher; by 1990 it had reached almost 100 issues. *SF Adventure* (1979-current), published by Tokuma Shoten, has reached its 145th issue, and *Shishioh* ["Lion King"] (1985-current), published by Asahi Sonorama, has reached its 69th. Three Japanese versions of US magazines, ISAAC ASIMOV'S SCIENCE FICTION MAGAZINE, titled *SF Hoseki* ["SF Jewels"] (1979-81), STARLOG (1979-87) and OMNI (1982-9), and two quarterly SEMIPROZINES, *SF-ISM* (1981-5) and *SF No Hon* ["SF Books"] (1982-6), also attracted readers, but not enough to survive. Though magazine circulation figures are classified in Japan, the best estimate is that the top magazine sells about 50,000 copies.

Today, in the early 1990s, about 400 Japanese original and 150 translated sf books are published each year (excluding reprints, game books and juveniles), a figure that varies according to criteria for distinguishing between sf and non-sf. (The term "sf" is in Japanese rather inclusive, embracing much that an occidental sf purist would reject. The numbers cited therefore include light fantasies, which have recently been popular.) Though the borderline between hardback and paperback publication is difficult to determine in the Japanese system, probably about a quarter of these are hardbacks. Paperbacks generally sell about 20-30,000 copies in the first print run, though there are many exceptions. As in other countries, most Japanese sf readers are of secondary-school/university age.

Japanese FANDOM began to reveal itself in 1962 with the first Japanese sf CONVENTION in Tokyo, attended by about 200 fans; the 30th convention, i-con, was held in Kanazawa, Ishikawa-Prefecture, in 1991 with about 1700 attendees; the 1983 convention, Daicon-4, held in Osaka, was the biggest to date, with about 4000. The site selection for conventions is presided over by the Federation of Science Fiction Groups of Japan, founded 1965, which also regulates the voting for the Sei'un AWARDS, the Japanese equivalent of the HUGOS, established in 1970. The categories are: Novel (Japanese and translation), Short Story (Japanese and translation), Media Presentation, Comics, Nonfiction, and Artist. The Nippon SF Taisho ("Taisho" means "Big Award"), the Japanese equivalent of the NEBULA, begun in 1980, is given to the single most prominent product of Japanese sf in the preceding year.

The first Japanese sf film was GOJIRA (1954; vt *Godzilla*). It was followed by many other MONSTER MOVIES such as RADON (1956; vt *Rodan*), MOSURA (1961; vt *Mothra*), DAIKAIJU GAMERA (1966; vt *Gamera*) and GOJIRA 1985 (1985; vt *Godzilla 1985*), and also by straight sf offerings like CHIKYU BOEIGUN (1957; vt *The Mysterians*), BIJO TO EKITAI NINGEN (1958; vt *The H-Man*), NIPPON CHINBOTSU (1973; vt *The Submersion of Japan*; cut vt *Tidal Wave*), FUKKATSU NO HI (1981; vt *Virus*) and SENGOKU JIEITAI (1981; vt *Time Slip*). Most of these were from Toho-Eiga or Kadokawa-Eiga Co. (Eiji Tsuburaya [1901-1970], who worked with Toho-Eiga, was famous for his special effects.) Monster and sf-adventure series flooded TELEVISION, too, but were less successful than animated tv series like *Tetsuwan Atom* (1963-5; vt *Astroboy*), the first of them, and *Gatchaman* (1972-4) and *Uchusenkan Yamato* ["Space Battlecruiser Yamato"] (1974-5). Many of these series have also been shown abroad. Recently, full-length animated feature films, such as Hayao Miyazaki's *Kaze no Tano no Nausika* (1984; vt *Nausica*) and *Tonari no Totoro* (1988; vt *My Neighbour Totoro*) and Katsuhiro OTOMO's *AKIRA* (1987), have been highly regarded by the general public as well as sf fans. Most such animations are derived from COMICS (by the same authors), comics being an important form of publication not only for children but also for young adults in Japan.

Among Japanese sf authors, the best known abroad is Kobo ABÉ, author of *Dai-Yon Kampyoki* (**1959**; trans as *Inter Ice Age 4* **1970**); he is, however, fundamentally a writer of mainstream literature. Other stories by popular MAINSTREAM WRITERS have been highly regarded in sf circles. Two such, by Hisashi Inoue in 1981 and Makoto Shiina in 1990, won the Nippon SF Taisho in their respective years. The reputation of Haruki MURAKAMI – whose work includes *Hitsuji o meguru boken* (**1982**; trans Alfred Birnbaum as *A Wild Sheep Chase* **1989** US) and *Sekai no owar to hard-boiled wonderland* (**1984**; trans Alfred Birnbaum as *Hard-Boiled Wonderland and the End of the World* **1991** US) – is also spreading widely.

Osamu TEZUKA, the writer/artist for *Astroboy*, is regarded as a kind of Japanese Walt Disney: he produced the first animated film series for tv in Japan and is a top name in sf and other comics. Other important writer/artists in comics are Fujio Fujiko (1933-), Shotaro Ishinomori (1938-), Reiji Matsumoto (1938-), Go Nagai (1945-) and Katsuhiro Otomo.

Shin'ichi HOSHI has written more than 1000 short stories, with many translated into other languages. His "Bokkochan" (1958; trans *FSF* June 1963) was the first

Japanese sf story to be translated into English. Hoshi's work was critical in the popularization of sf in the early days in Japan. Sakyo KOMATSU is a sort of symbol of Japanese sf. Many of his novels are panoramic in scope, dealing in broad strokes with the destiny of the Universe and with *Homo sapiens*'s place in it. He is best known abroad as the author of *Nippon Chinbotsu* (**1973**; cut trans **1976** as *Japan Sinks*), which sold about 4 million copies in Japan alone and, as mentioned above, was filmed. Yasutaka Tsutsui (1934-   ) is noted for his sharply satirical comic situation fantasies – sometimes called slapstick sf – such as *Vietnam Kanko Kosha* ["The Vietnam Sightseeing Co."] (**1967**), but his recent bestselling stories are considered mainstream rather than sf. Ryo Hammura (1933-   ) won the Naoki Award – the most prestigious Japanese literary prize – in 1974. He is best known for his earlier fantasy books, which created a fictitious history of ancient Japan, but a more recent bestseller, *Misaki Ichiro no Teiko* ["The Resistance of Ichiro Misaki"] (**1988**), is centrally sf, describing the tragedy of a SUPERMAN. Hammura also wrote the novel on which was based the film SENGOKU JIETAI. Ryu Mitsuse (1928-   ) combines a HARD-SF surface with poetic form in such perceptive novels as *Hyakuoku no Hiru to Sen'oku no Yoru* ["Ten Billion Days, a Hundred Billion Nights"] (**1967**), an sf variation on the Buddhist theme of transience. Taku Mayumura (1934-   ) is noted for his serious attempts to create a future history (◊ HISTORY IN SF), a representative work being *Shiseikan* ["Governors of the Worlds"] (**1974**), a book in a series describing the rise and fall of a galactic government.

Among the younger authors, Masaki Yamada (1950-   ) is a born sf writer, one of the second generation of Japanese sf authors. His first story, the novella "Kami-Gari" ["God Hunters"] (1974), deals with the fight against the unseen and ruthless government of Almighty God. Baku Yumemakura (1951-   ) became a bestselling sf writer through violent adventure novels, but his recent *Jogen no Tsuki o Taberu Shishi* ["The Lion that Ate the Crescent Moon"] (**1989**) is highly poetic and symbolic; he won both the Sei'un Award and the Nippon Sf Taisho with this novel. Chohei Kambayashi (1953   ) could be called a typical VIRTUAL-REALITY writer. His novel *Sento-Yosei Yukikaze* ["Fairy Fighter Yukikaze"] (**1984**) deals with the man-machine interface when a ROBOT fighter plane fights an alien machine race. Yoshiki Tanaka (1952-   ) writes a variety of historical fantasies. The most popular among them is *Ginga Eiyu Densetu* ["The Legend of Galactic Heroes"] (**1982**), which tells of a space war and is based on the ancient Chinese story "Three Kingdoms".

Among women sf writers, perhaps Motoko Arai (1960-   ) is the most typical, with her rather easy-to-read style of fantasy. Quite different is Mariko Ohara (1959-   ), who writes CYBERPUNK stories. Kaoru Kurimoto (1953-   ) is prolific in the field of HEROIC FANTASY. Many other women writers of light fantasy have enjoyed popularity in recent years.

A study in English is *Japanese Science Fiction: A View of a Changing Society* (**1989**) by Robert Matthew. Several of the writers mentioned above are represented in translation in *The Best Japanese Science Fiction Stories* (anth **1989** US) ed John L. Apostolou with Martin H. GREENBERG. [TSh]

JARRY, ALFRED (1873-1907) French writer who carried the fruits of his scientific education into his surreal avant-garde writing, particularly the influence of the French evolutionary philosopher Henri Bergson (1859-1941). AJ's famous play *Ubu roi* (**1896**; trans **1951** UK) and its several sequels – including *Ubu enchaîné* (**1900**; trans B. Keith and G. Legman as *King Turd* **1953** UK) – helped found the THEATRE of the absurd, and he created the mock-science of 'pataphysics (◊ IMAGINARY SCIENCE), which studies exceptions rather than laws and aspires to provide imaginary solutions to practical problems. H.G. WELLS's *The Time Machine* (**1895**) inspired him to write the speculative essay "How to Construct a Time Machine" (1899) (◊ TIME TRAVEL). His most sciencefictional work is *Le surmâle* (**1901**; trans Barbara Wright as *The Supermale* **1964** UK; rev 1968), a comic fantasy featuring a SUPERMAN who, nourished on superfood, wins an extraordinary bicycle race against a six-man team and performs astonishing feats of erotic endurance before perishing in the passionate embrace of an amorous MACHINE. Also of interest is the disorganized and extravagant "neoscientific romance" *Gestes et opinions du docteur Faustroll, 'Pataphysician* (**1911**; trans as "Exploits and Opinions of Dr Faustroll, 'Pataphysician" in *Selected Works of Alfred Jarry* ed Roger Shattuck and Simon Watson-Taylor, coll **1965** UK). There are minor fantastic elements in his hallucinatory first novel, *Les jours et les nuits* (**1897**; trans Alexis Lykiard as *Days and Nights* **1989** in an edition which also includes the mythological extravaganza *L'autre Alceste* [**1947** chap] trans Simon Watson-Taylor as "The Other Alcestis") and in his bawdy historical romance *Messaline* (**1901**; trans John Harman as *Messalina* **1985** UK). AJ's influence on modern sf writers (◊ ABSURDIST SF; FABULATION) is best exemplified by J.G. BALLARD's "The Assassination of John Fitzgerald Kennedy Considered as a Downhill Motor Race" (1967), which echoes AJ's "Commentaire pour servir à la construction pratique de la machine à explorer le temps" (1900), most familiar in trans as "The Crucifixion of Christ Considered as an Uphill Bicycle Race" (1965). [BS]
Other works: *Caesar-Antichrist* (**1895**; trans Antony Melville as *Caesar Antichrist* **1992** UK).

JARVIS, E.K. ZIFF-DAVIS house name used 1942-58 on *AMZ*, *Fantastic Adventures* and *Fantastic* for over 45 stories, primarily by Robert Moore WILLIAMS, who used the name as a personal pseudonym until the 1950s, when Paul W. FAIRMAN, Harlan ELLISON and Robert SILVERBERG – 1 identified story each – also wrote as EKJ. [JC]

JARVIS, SHARON (1943-   ) US writer whose fiction has all been written with collaborators under joint pseudonyms. As Jarrod Comstock she published with Ellen M. Kozak the **These Lawless Worlds** sequence of mildly erotic sf: *The Love Machine* (**1984**) and *Scales of Justice* (**1984**). As Johanna Hailey she published with Marcia Yvonne Howl (1947-) two elf fantasies: *Enchanted Paradise* (**1985**) and *Crystal Paradise* (**1986**). As H.M. Major she published with Kathleen Buckley the **Alien Trace** sf sequence, equally mild in its eroticism: *The Alien Trace* (**1984**) and *Time Twister* (**1984**). As SJ, she edited *Inside Outer Space: Science Fiction Professionals Look at their Craft* (anth **1985**). [JC]

JASON, JERRY ◊ George H. SMITH.

JAVOR, FRANK A. Working name of US writer Francis Anthony Jaworski (1916-), who has written an estimated 10,000 "how to" articles for service magazines. He has appeared infrequently in sf magazines from 1963, his first story being "Patriot" for *ASF*; three tales were included in the Judith MERRIL **Year's Best S-F** series of anthologies. The **Eli Pike** series of sf novels – *The Rim-World Legacy* (**1967**; exp as coll vt *The Rim-World Legacy and Beyond* 1991), *Scor-Sting* (**1990**) and *The Ice Beast* (**1990**) – comprises 3 capably framed intrigues on RIMWORLDS, where Pike must maintain some sort of order. The series manages, despite the quarter-century gap between episodes, to remain fresh. [JC]

JAY, MEL ◊ John E. MULLER.

JAY, PETER (1937-) UK writer, economist and former diplomat who served as the UK Ambassador to the USA 1977-9. His future HISTORY, *Apocalypse 2000: Economic Breakdown and the Suicide of Democracy* (**1987**) with Michael STEWART, was inefficient as fiction but acute about the pleasures and miseries of late capitalism. [JC]

JEAN, ALBERT ◊ Maurice RENARD.

JEEVES, (BYRON) TERRY [r] ◊ Mike ASHLEY.

JEFFERIES, (JOHN) RICHARD (1848-1887) UK naturalist and novelist. The son of a farmer, he showed remarkable powers of observation when writing about Nature, describing it in a poetic style from an animist viewpoint that was devoid of sentimentality. This was particularly noticeable in his first fantasy novel, *Wood Magic: A Fable* (**1881**; cut vt *Sir Bevis: A Tale of the Fields* 1889); semi-autobiographical, it features a young boy who has the ability to communicate with animals, birds and plants, and was primarily concerned with the social and political structure of the local animal kingdom and the struggles of a contender for the throne. A sequel, the famous *Bevis: The Story of a Boy* (**1882**), appeared a year later, but with the emphasis on the pleasures and intrigues of childhood rather than the hero's supernatural abilities.

For the last six years of his life RJ's health was severely in decline, and his thoughts turned to the future and to speculation. The result was *After London, or Wild England* (**1885**), a post-HOLOCAUST novel which describes, from the viewpoint of a future historian, an England reverted to rural wilderness: the novel's first part describes the lapse into barbarism, the specific reasons for the disaster being deliberately kept vague, and the second details the medieval-style society that has come into being and tells of a voyage of discovery on a great inland lake that now covers the centre of England. *After London* is a first-class example of Victorian sf and proved very popular at the time; its influence can be traced through W.H. HUDSON's *A Crystal Age* (**1887**) to John COLLIER's *Tom's A-Cold* (**1933**; vt *Full Circle: A Tale* US). RJ's earlier political SATIRE, *Jack Brass: Emperor of England* (**1873**), can loosely be construed as fantasy. [JE]

See also: CITIES; HISTORY OF SF; PASTORAL; POLLUTION; UTOPIAS.

JEFFERSON, IAN ◊ L.P. DAVIES.

JEFF HAWKE UK COMIC strip created by writer Eric Souster and artist Sidney Jordan (1930-). Some scripts were written by William Patterson and many of the later ones by Jordan. *JH* first appeared in 1954 in the London *Daily Express*, and ceased in 1974. During its lifetime it was the UK's leading sf comic strip. The overall scenario depicted Earth as a primitive planet on the periphery of a highly advanced galactic civilization, whose deposed emperor, Chalcedon, was a frequent adversary. Individual stories, of which there were over 60, contained standard sf concepts interspersed with plots based on theories similar to those of Erich von DÄNIKEN (Vishnu and Shiva as interplanetary visitors, Aladdin's lamp as a dead space-pilot's communicator, etc.). The storylines were original for a comic strip, and kept abreast of contemporary technological progress. Softcover reprints have been published as *Jeff Hawke Book 1* (graph coll **1985**) and *Jeff Hawke Book 2: Counsel for the Defence* (graph coll **1986**), with covers by Brian BOLLAND, who also worked briefly on the strip; hardcover collections have appeared in Italy. *JH* also appeared briefly in 1955-6, drawn by Ferdinando Tacconi, in the children's colour comic *Express Weekly*. [JE/RT]

JENKINS, WILL F. [r] ◊ Murray LEINSTER.

JENNINGS, PHILLIP C. (1946-) US writer who began publishing work of genre interest with "Tadcaster's Doom" for *FSF* in 1986, and who during the next few years published over 30 often pyrotechnical stories, several of which described a world dominated by "bugs" – personalities in electronic storage. Some of the best of these stories are assembled as *The Bug Life Chronicles* (coll **1989**). PCJ's first novel, *Tower to the Sky* (**1988**), set in the same universe, explosively depicts a human campaign in 3700CE to escape the crowded Solar System and the Gatekeepers who bar us from the stars, via the eponymous skyscraper; this contains much of humankind within it, is tall enough to reach into space, and is convertible into a starship. PCJ's exuberance is intermittently chaotic, but he now seems to be exercising greater control over his material; the next years may see work of very considerable worth. [JC]

JENNISON, JOHN W(ILLIAM) (? -?1969) UK

writer, one of several who became active as mass-producers of genre fiction for UK paperback houses and who remained reticent about personal details during their careers. From about 1945 to the year in which it is thought he may have died, JWJ seems to have written over 100 novels under at least 40 pseudonyms, mostly thrillers and Westerns. He began to publish his routine but occasionally engaging sf with two novels as Edgar Rees Kennedy, *Conquerors of Venus* (**1951**) and *The Mystery Planet* (**1952**). Working for CURTIS WARREN, he then published: under the house name Neil CHARLES, *Para-Robot* (**1952**); under the Gill HUNT name, *Station 7* (**1952**) and *Zero Field* (**1952**); and under the King LANG name, *Spaceline* (**1952**). After *Invasion from Space* (**1954**) as Matthew C. Bradford, however, he ceased producing sf for some time, returning in the mid-1960s with the marginal *Supercar in the Black Diamond Trail* (**1965**) as JWJ. Generally as John Theydon, a name he had used since 1946 for non-sf tales, he then published a sequence of STINGRAY tv ties – *Stingray* * (**1965**), *Stingray: Danger in the Deep* * (**1965**) as JWJ, and *Stingray and the Monster* * (**1966**) – a sequence of THUNDERBIRDS tv ties – *Thunderbirds* * (**1966**), *Calling Thunderbirds* * (**1966**), *Thunderbirds: Ring of Fire* * (**1966**), *Thunderbirds: Lost World* * (**1966**) as JWJ, and *Lady Penelope: The Albanian Affair* * (**1967**) – and a sequence of **Captain Scarlet** tv ties (◊ CAPTAIN SCARLET AND THE MYSTERONS) – *Captain Scarlet and the Mysterons* * (**1967**; vt *Captain Scarlet* 1989) and *Captain Scarlet and the Silent Saboteur* * (**1967**). JWJ's last known sf book, again as Theydon, was another tv tie, *The Angels and the Creeping Enemy* * (**1968**). [JC]

JENS, WALTER [r] ◊ GERMANY.

JENSEN, AXEL (1932-) Norwegian writer, active since 1955. His DYSTOPIAN sf novel, *Epp* (**1965**; trans anon **1967** UK), describes in chillingly grey, fragmented prose a world where people live isolated from one another in cells and file reports on their similarly treacherous, alienated "neighbours". [JC]

JENSEN, JOHANNES V(ILHELM) (1873-1950) Danish poet, novelist and essayist, awarded the Nobel Prize for Literature in 1944. He is best known for *Den Lange Rejse* (6 vols **1908-22** Denmark; all but vol 5 trans Arthur G. Chater, vols 1-2 as *The Long Journey: Fire and Ice* **1922** UK, vols 3-4 as *The Cimbrians: The Long Journey II* **1923** UK, and vol 6 as *Christopher Columbus: The Long Journey III* **1924** UK; vol 5, *Skibet* ["The Ship"] [**1912**], remains untranslated), an epic myth spanning humanity's development from its origins in a temperate Scandinavian Eden before the Ice Age through to the threshold of modern times with the explorations of Christopher Columbus. The translated portions were later released in 1 vol as *The Long Journey* (omni **1933** US). JVJ also published several collections of "myths" that remain untranslated. [JE]

See also: ANTHROPOLOGY; ORIGIN OF MAN.

JENSEN, KRIS (1953-) US writer who began publishing sf with her first novel, *FreeMaster* (**1990**); it and its sequel, *Mentor* (**1991**), made up the **Ardel**

series, in which an unscrupulous interstellar corporation is baulked from exploiting a mineral-rich planet inhabited by ALIENS with PSI POWERS. Of greatest interest are the detailed descriptions of the strange BIOLOGY of the Ardellans, which help give the sequence its PLANETARY-ROMANCE flavour. [JC]

JENSEN, NORMAN [r] ◊ ROBERT HALE LIMITED.

JEPPSON, J.O. [r] ◊ Janet ASIMOV.

JEPSON, EDGAR (ALFRED) (1863-1938) UK schoolteacher and writer, prolific in various popular genres from 1895; some of his books are of sf interest. Half-RURITANIA, half-DYSTOPIA, the imaginary land-locked Asian country in *The Keepers of the People* (**1898**) has been ruled for generations by Englishmen; the novel encroaches on sf from several angles. *The Horned Shepherd* (**1904**) and *No. 19* (**1910**; vt *The Garden at 19* 1910 US) are both fantasies, the first about a new incarnation of a god which has also been Pan, the second about the attempts of a magus (who resembles Aleister Crowley [1875-1947]) to summon Pan. In *The Moon Gods* (**1930**), a lost-race (◊ LOST WORLDS) tale, 20th-century aviators discover a Carthaginian city in the African desert. [JC/BS]

JEROME, OWEN FOX ◊ Oscar J. FRIEND.

JERSILD, P(ERS) C(HRISTIAN) (1935-) Swedish writer whose translated sf novels – *En Levande Själ* (**1980**; trans Rika Lesser as *A Living Soul* **1988** UK) and *Efter Floden* (**1982**; trans Lone Tygesen Blecher and George Blecher as *After the Flood* **1986** US) – are both DYSTOPIAS, the latter a post-HOLOCAUST tale of some ferocity. [JC]

JESCHKE, WOLFGANG (1936-) German editor and writer, winner of the 1987 Harrison AWARD for achievements in international sf. He began to publish sf with "Die Anderen" ["The Others"] in 1959, but first became strongly involved with the genre in 1969 as editor of Kindlers Literaturlexikon's series of sf paperbacks. In 1973 he took over Heyne Verlag's sf publishing line, a job he retains (1992) and in which he has been responsible for introducing many important works to the German market. He has also edited more than 100 anthologies, from 1970 on, many containing material translated from the English. WJ's first novel was *Der Letzte Tag der Schöpfung* (**1981**; trans Gertrud Mander as *The Last Day of Creation* **1984** US), in which a US group uses TIME TRAVEL to acquire Middle Eastern oil, evading the problems posed by modern-day local governments; TIME PARADOXES ensue. In *Midas* (**1987**; author's trans **1990** UK), set on a NEAR-FUTURE Earth which has suffered severe ecological damage, a primitive matter-replication technique has been discovered, but the copies of humans thus produced are crude and cannot live longer than a few months. WJ's writing is humanist in orientation and strongly (on occasion overbearingly) ironic in tone, but is sometimes betrayed by a certain lack of subtlety and originality. [NT]

See also: CLONES; GERMANY; POWER SOURCES.

JESSEL, JOHN [s] ◊ Stanley G. WEINBAUM.

JE T'AIME, JE T'AIME Film (1967). Parc/Fox Europa.

Dir Alain Resnais, starring Claude Rich, Olga Georges-Picot, Anouk Ferjac. Screenplay Resnais, Jacques STERNBERG. 94 mins, cut to 82 mins. Colour.

A failed suicide is co-opted into a dangerous scientific experiment; he is to be sent back into the past for one minute. The experiment has proved safe for mice, but humans are conscious of time and memory in a way that animals are not, and the protagonist is trapped in a series of not-quite-random time oscillations around the point of an unhappy love affair. Where Resnais's previous study of time and memory, *Last Year at Marienbad* (1961), was a triumph for the cameraman, this film is a triumph for the editor. Some of the oscillations last only seconds, some minutes, sometimes replaying the same scene (with subtle variations) several times over, sometimes visiting fantasy events as if this second time around they were real – memory, with its distortions, carrying the same metaphysical weight as fact. The TIME MACHINE itself is organic and womb-like, and from it the hero emerges into the amniotic fluid of the sea. This is a very striking sf film, though only almost incidentally sf; it uses the idea of TIME TRAVEL to explore the extent to which we can, or cannot, withdraw ourselves from our own pasts, and hence from the processes of time. The screenwriter, Sternberg, is an sf writer of distinction and sophistication. [PN]

See also: CINEMA.

JETÉE, LA (vt *The Jetty*; vt *The Pier*) Short film (1963). Argos/Arcturus Films. Produced, written and dir Chris Marker, starring Hélène Chatelain, Jacques Ledoux, Davos Hanich. 29 mins. B/w.

This celebrated French short film is often seen as a breakthrough in sf narration that has yet to be equalled. With voice-over narration and composed entirely of still photographs (though there is one brief sequence – a close-up of a girl winking – that gives the impression of movement) the film is nearer in theme and approach to the NEW-WAVE sf of the 1960s than to traditional TIME-TRAVEL stories in the CINEMA or in literature. Set in a post-HOLOCAUST Paris where the concept of passing time is disappearing and the principle of cause-and-effect is therefore being lost, this subtle and complex film shows an attempt being made to send back in time a man obsessed by his memory of a woman's face, since the existence of memory suggests that time still exists for him. He is also sent into the future where he finds the remembered face is a witness to his own death. [JB/PN]

JETER, K.W. (1950-) US writer of importance as an author of horror novels, the highly charged claustrophobia of his style fitting the essential affect of that genre rather better than it does sf. His early work, generally conceived in sf terms, gives off an air of hectic congestion which sometimes interferes with the presentation of ideas, the articulation of a barrier through which to penetrate; for him, as for most HORROR writers, CONCEPTUAL BREAKTHROUGHS tend to end in tears. Nevertheless, his first published novel,

Seeklight (**1975** Canada), fascinatingly combines tried-and-true narrative conventions (its protagonist is the scion of an ex-leader, whose rivals need to kill the lad) with exorbitant reality-twists (a sociologist intermittently uses advanced technology to intervene and to make queries about the action). *The Dreamfields* (**1976** Canada) similarly juxtaposes contrasting realities, in this case a land of dreams occupied by ALIENS but dominated by sick human teenagers. *Morlock Night* (**1979**) is a sequel to H.G. WELLS's *The Time Machine* (**1895**) which both extends the original story and, by conveying a Morlock invasion backwards in time to the sewers of late 19th-century-London, may well constitute the first significant STEAMPUNK novel, long before the flush period of that subgenre in the late 1980s. But *Soul Eater* (**1983**), KWJ's first outright horror novel, is more accomplished than any of these.

KWJ's most significant sf may lie in the thematic trilogy comprising *Dr Adder* (**1984**) – his first novel (written 1972), long left unpublished because of its sometimes turgid violence – *The Glass Hammer* (**1985**) and *Death Arms* (**1987** UK). Philip K. DICK read *Dr Adder* in manuscript and for years advocated it; and it is clear why. Though the novel clearly prefigures the under-soil airlessness of the best urban CYBERPUNK, it even more clearly serves as a bridge between the defiant reality-testing PARANOIA of Dick's characters and the doomed realpolitiking of the surrendered souls who dwell in post-1984 urban sprawls. In each of these convoluted tales, set in a devastated Somme-like NEAR-FUTURE USA, KWJ's characters seem to vacillate between the sf traditions of resistance and cyberpunk quietism. In worlds like these, the intermittent flashes of sf imagery or content are unlasting consolations.

Although sometimes technically sf, KWJ's later novels have altogether abandoned the consolations of sf. *Dark Seeker* (**1987**) is a horror novel about DRUGS which invokes Charles Manson. *Infernal Devices: A Mad Victorian Fantasy* (**1987**) is another steampunk tale, quite hilarious at points, but not reassuring in its use of sf devices that its protagonist signally misunderstands. *Mantis* (**1987**) is again horror, as are *In the Land of the Dead* (**1989** UK), *The Night Man* (**1990**) and *Wolf Flow* (**1992**). Only *Madlands* (**1991**), set in a parodic, ENTROPY-choked Disneyland-like Los Angeles, and *Farewell Horizontal* (**1989**), set in the FAR FUTURE, are sf, and their technical adventurousness does not dispel the sense that KWJ is making a slow farewell to the genre. [JC]

About the author: *A Checklist of K.W. Jeter* (**1991** chap) by Tom Joyce and Christopher P. STEPHENS.

See also: CRIME AND PUNISHMENT; FANTASY; GOTHIC SF; MEDICINE; PSYCHOLOGY.

JET JACKSON, FLYING COMMANDO ◊ CAPTAIN MIDNIGHT.

JETTY, THE ◊ La JETÉE.

J. LLOYD EATON AWARD ◊ AWARDS.

J. LLOYD EATON COLLECTION In 1969 the late Donald Wilson, University Librarian at the University of California, Riverside Library (now the Tomás Rivera Library), purchased a COLLECTION of 7500 volumes of sf and fantasy from the estate of J. Lloyd Eaton MD. Eaton had for several decades collected many rare and unusual monographs of sf, including such items as *Varney the Vampire* (**1847**) and Frank AUBREY's *King of the Dead* (**1903**), ceasing his active interest in the field about 1956. For the first decade after its purchase, the collection remained in storage, uncatalogued and inaccessible to researchers. In 1978 Robert REGINALD and George Edgar SLUSSER successfully proposed an annual conference centred on the Eaton Collection, and in 1979 Slusser was appointed Curator. Simultaneously the Rivera Library began actively cataloguing the newer parts of the collection, while making retrospective purchases of missing items and adding current materials. Cataloguing of the old books was completed with a federal grant in the late 1980s; unfortunately, the *Dictionary Catalog of the J. Lloyd Eaton Collection of Science Fiction and Fantasy Literature, University of California, Riverside* (3 vols **1982**) was compiled long before the task had been completed.

The collection now includes 100,000+ items, having been supplemented with the acquisition of the Douglas MENVILLE collection (10,000 paperbacks and esoterica), the Terry CARR collection (20,000 FANZINES), the Rick Sneary (1927-1990) collection (40,000 fanzines) and the manuscripts of several contemporary sf writers, plus 10,000 superhero COMICS, 10,000 boys' books, 500 shooting scripts of sf and fantasy films, the Michael CASSUTT collection of screenplays and teleplays, and some foreign-language material. Access to this, the largest academic library collection of fantastic literature, is available to legitimate scholars and to members of the university community.		[RR]

JOE 90 UK tv series (1968-9). A Century 21 Production for ITC/ATV. Devised by Gerry and Sylvia ANDERSON, prod David Lane (with Reg Hill as executive prod). Script editor Tony Barwick. Dirs included Peter Anderson, Leo Eaton, Alan Perry, Desmond Saunders. Writers included Barwick, Shane Rimmer, Gerry and Sylvia Anderson. 30 25min episodes. Colour.

This was the last and one of the least popular of the sf animated-puppet series made for children in "SuperMarionation" by the Andersons – though TERRAHAWKS (1983-6), in which the puppets were electronically operated in a process Anderson called "Supermacromation", was still to come. The hero, Joe, is a 9-year-old boy whose scientist father has devised a method of transferring specialist brain patterns into his mind, armed with which (looking innocent) he becomes a test pilot, a brain surgeon and so on, working as a special agent for the World Intelligence Network. *J90* collapsed after 1 season, perhaps because it appeared more childish than most of its immediate predecessors in the **SuperMarionation** tv shows.		[PN]

JOHANNESSON, OLOF Pseudonym of Swedish scientist and writer Hannes Olof Goesta Alfvén

(1908-), winner of the 1970 Nobel Prize for Physics. His sf novel, *Sagan om den stora datamaskinin* (**1966**; trans as *The Big Computer: A Vision* **1968** UK; vt *The Tale of the Great Computer: A Vision* 1968 US; vt *The End of Man?* 1969 US) purports to be a history of Earth written in the future by a COMPUTER (or perhaps by a human). Its drily witty fundamental premise is that mankind is merely an intermediate step in the EVOLUTION of MACHINES.		[JC/PN]

Other works: *Världen-spegelvärlden: Kosmologi och antimateria* (**1966** trans as *Worlds-Antiworlds: Antimatter in Cosmology* **1966** US), as by H. Alfvén, nonfiction.

See also: AUTOMATION; CYBERNETICS; INTELLIGENCE.

JOHANSSON, GEORGE [r] ◊ SCANDINAVIA.

JOHNS, AYRESOME ◊ George LOCKE.

JOHNS, KENNETH Pseudonym used for collaborations between Kenneth BULMER and John NEWMAN on a long series of science-fact articles for *NW* and *Nebula* 1955-61.		[JC]

JOHNS, MARSTON ◊ R.L. FANTHORPE; John E. MULLER.

JOHNS, [Captain] W(ILLIAM) E(ARLE) (1893-1968) UK writer who began producing boys' action adventures in 1930; his total output exceeded 200 volumes. He became famous in particular for the 80 or more **Biggles** novels, of which two – *Biggles Hits the Trail* (**1935**) and *Biggles – Charter Pilot: The Adventures of Biggles & Co on a World-Wide Cruise of Scientific Investigation* (**1943**) – have some sf content. Of WEJ's other works, of particular sf interest is the **"Tiger" Clinton** sequence: *Kings of Space* (**1954**), *Return to Mars* (**1955**), *Now to the Stars* (**1956**), *To Outer Space* (**1957**), *The Edge of Beyond* (**1958**), *The Death Rays of Ardilla* (**1959**), *To Worlds Unknown* (**1960**), *The Quest for the Perfect Planet* (**1961**), *Worlds of Wonder* (coll **1962**) and *The Man who Vanished into Space* (**1963**). These novels feature "Tiger" Clinton, his son Rex and Professor Brane, the first humans in space, who meet strange new races and become caught up in interplanetary war.		[AC/JC]

JOHNSON, DENIS (1949-) US writer whose second novel, *Fiskadoro* (**1985**), is set in post-HOLOCAUST Key West, where an aged inhabitant confuses the desolate USA with Vietnam, where she lived during the US action. For sf readers, that is likely to be the only innovation apparent in this intensely conceived tale, but it is striking.		[JC]

JOHNSON, GEORGE CLAYTON (1929-) US writer who wrote 3 sf stories for GAMMA 1963-5 and was co-author with William F. NOLAN of *Logan's Run* (**1967**), which was filmed as LOGAN'S RUN (1976) and inspired a tv series. *Scripts and Stories Written for The Twilight Zone* (coll **1977**) and *Writing for The Twilight Zone* (coll **1981**) assemble scripts created for that programme. He also wrote at least one script for STAR TREK.		[JC]

See also: OVERPOPULATION.

JOHNSON, JAMES B(LAIR) (1944-) US writer who began publishing sf with his first novel, *Daystar and Shadow* (**1981**), in which a post-HOLOCAUST USA is depicted. More interesting, though the voltage of innovation remains low, is *Trekmaster* (**1987**), set on a rediscovered colony planet whose inhabitants are divided over the issue of reunion with the Galactic Federation; included are some dynastic romance, a rite of passage and a cohabiting ALIEN species. Further novels in the same general vein, though showing an increasing competence, are *Mindhopper* (**1988**), *Habu* (**1989**) and *A World Lost* (**1991**).   [JC]

JOHNSON, KEN Working name of US bibliographer Kenneth R. Johnson (?   -   ), whose main work, undertaken with Jerry BOYAJIAN, has been a series of indexes to the SF MAGAZINES: *Index to the Science Fiction Magazines 1977* (**1982** chap), *1978* (**1982** chap), *1979* (**1981** chap), *1980* (**1981** chap), *1981* (**1982** chap), *1982* (**1983** chap) and *1984* (**1985** chap). Both authors also began an associated enterprise comprising *Index to the Semi-Professional Fantasy Magazines, 1982* (**1983** chap) and *Index to the Semi-Professional Magazines, 1983* (**1984** chap). With Hal W. HALL and George Michaels he compiled *The Science Fiction Magazines: A Bibliographical Checklist of Titles and Issues through 1983* (**1983** chap).

KJ is not to be confused with the UK horror writer Kenneth R(ayner) Johnson (?   -   ), author of *Zoltan, Hound of Dracula* * (**1977**; vt *Hounds of Dracula* 1977 US; vt *Dracula's Dog* 1977 US), *The Succubus* (**1979**) and *The Cheshire Cat* (**1983** US).   [JC]

JOHNSON, L(EROY) P(ETER) V(ERNON) (1905-   ) UK writer whose *In the Time of the Thetans* (**1961**) features unpleasant Thetans, who resemble starfish.   [JC]

JOHNSON, OWEN M(cMAHON) (1878-1952) US writer in various genres. The protagonist of *The Coming of the Amazons: A Satirical Speculation on the Scientific Future of Civilization* (**1931**) finds on awakening in AD2181 from SUSPENDED ANIMATION that women rule and that a simple sex-role reversal accounts for humiliating changes in masculine behaviour. He resists vigorously, but without success. Unlike most stories on this theme, the book treats women with some sympathy.   [JC]

JOHNSON, SAMUEL (1709-1784) UK poet, critic, lexicographer and author of one novel, *The History of Rasselas: Prince of Abissinia* (**1759**; rev 1759), written to pay for his mother's funeral (he got £100 for the first printing). It is of interest to the student of PROTO SCIENCE FICTION for its sustained meditation on the nature of and chances of obtaining human happiness (*see also* UTOPIAS; DYSTOPIAS). The initial setting of the tale is a secret valley, from which Rasselas hopes to escape in a flying machine (in the event it fails – SJ's spirit was inimical to unsustained flights of fancy); also featured is an astronomer who believes himself responsible for weather control. The book is an archetypal example of the important sf theme of CONCEPTUAL BREAKTHROUGH. The most attractive 20th-century critical edition was ed 1927 by R.W. Chapman; a useful recent critical edition was ed 1977 by Geoffrey Tillotson and Brian Jenkins.   [JC/PN]

See also: ASTRONOMY; FANTASTIC VOYAGES.

JOHNSTONE, D(AVID) LAWSON (?   -?   ) UK

writer, mostly of novels for older children, including *The Mountain Kingdom* (**1888**), a Jules VERNE-style LOST-WORLD tale whose young protagonists travel into the Kingdom of the Smoking Mountains (in Tibet), which is inhabited by descendents of ancient Greeks; our heroes thwart a rebellion against the monarch. *The Paradise of the North* (**1890**; cut 1894) similarly uncovers a lost world, but this time at the North Pole and inhabited by Norsemen. *The White Princess of the Hidden City* (**1898**) uncovers yet another, now in Central America and inhabited by Whites whose claim to the Americas – in accordance with 19th-century fantasies of racial justice – is found to antedate that of the Amerindians.   [JC]

JOHNSTONE, WILLIAM W. (1938-   ) US writer who has written at least 85 novels since his first in 1980, being best known for Westerns; he has also written some horror. His **Ashes** sequence of SURVIVALIST-FICTION military post-HOLOCAUST sf novels comprises *Out of the Ashes* (**1983**), *Fire in the Ashes* (**1984**), *Anarchy in the Ashes* (**1984**), *Blood in the Ashes* (**1985**), *Alone in the Ashes* (**1985**), *Wind in the Ashes* (**1986**), *Smoke from the Ashes* (**1987**), *Danger in the Ashes* (**1988**), *Valor in the Ashes* (**1988**), *Trapped in the Ashes* (**1989**), *Death in the Ashes* (**1990**), *Survival in the Ashes* (**1990**) and *Fury in the Ashes* (**1991**). The premise of the first volume is, perhaps, surprisingly frank: shocked by the imposition of gun control, a group of patriotric US citizens bring about the nuclear holocaust in the expectation that a better world will, phoenix-style, be born. The remaining volumes of the sequence attempt to demonstrate how right they were.   [JC]

Other works: The **Devil** series, comprising *The Devil's Kiss* (**1980**), *The Devil's Heart* (**1983**), *The Devil's Touch* (**1984**) and *The Devil's Cat* (**1987**); *Wolfsbane* (**1982**); *The Uninvited* (**1982**); *Crying Shame* (**1983**); *Nursery* (**1983**); *Sweet Dreams* (**1985**); *Cat's Cradle* (**1986**); *Jack-in-the-Box* (**1986**); *Rockinghorse* (**1986**); *Baby Grand* (**1987**) with Joseph E. Keene; *Sandman* (**1988**); *Carnival* (**1989**); *Cat's Eye* (**1989**); *Darkly the Thunder* (**1990**); *Watchers in the Woods* (**1991**).

JOHN W. CAMPBELL AWARD Award for the best new sf writer of the year, selected by votes of sf fans and presented at the World Sf CONVENTION during the HUGO ceremony. Sponsored by Condé-Nast, publishers of *Analog*, the JWCA was instituted in 1972 in tribute to John W. CAMPBELL Jr, its celebrated editor, who died in 1971. Davis Publications continued the sponsorship when *Analog* passed into their hands. The anthology series NEW VOICES, ed George R.R. MARTIN, was devoted to printing original novellas (written a few years later) by, in each volume, a given year's finalists; it ceased after 5 vols. Several of the winners were at the time of receiving the JWCA primarily fantasy writers.   [PR/PN]

Winners:

1973: Jerry POURNELLE
1974: Lisa TUTTLE and Spider ROBINSON
1975: P.J. Plauger
1976: Tom REAMY

1977: C.J. CHERRYH
1978: Orson Scott CARD
1979: Stephen R. DONALDSON
1980: Barry B. LONGYEAR
1981: Somtow Sucharitkul (S.P. SOMTOW)
1982: Alexis GILLILAND
1983: Paul O. WILLIAMS
1984: R.A. MACAVOY
1985: Lucius SHEPARD
1986: Melissa SCOTT
1987: Karen Joy FOWLER
1988: Judith MOFFETT
1989: Michaela Roessner
1990: Kristine Kathryn RUSCH
1991: Julia Ecklar
See also: WOMEN SF WRITERS.

JOHN W. CAMPBELL MEMORIAL AWARD Created by Harry HARRISON and Brian W. ALDISS, this is given annually in July for the best sf novel of the previous year published in English, selected by a committee of academic critics and sf writers. The membership of the jury has undergone a number of changes, and the award has been variously administered from first the USA, then the UK, Ireland, Sweden and then back to the USA at the University of Kansas at Lawrence in 1979, since when the committee has been chaired by James E. GUNN. The selections have at times been criticized as overintellectual; the first was judged by some to be untrue to the memory of Campbell. (In response, one judge commented that it was no good trying to guess what Campbell would have chosen; the only honest thing to do was to choose for oneself: "You can't second-guess the dead.") The award, which has not been well publicized, got off to a shaky start, but there is certainly room for an award voted on by a small panel of experts, as opposed to fans (the HUGO) or writers (the NEBULA). The winning books have generally been in interesting contrast to the Hugo and Nebula winners, and include distinguished work that might otherwise have largely escaped notice. [PN]

Winners:
1973: Barry N. MALZBERG, *Beyond Apollo*; special trophy for excellence in writing to Robert SILVERBERG
1974: Arthur C. CLARKE, *Rendezvous with Rama*, and Robert MERLE, *Malevil* (tie)
1975: Philip K. DICK, *Flow My Tears, the Policeman Said*
1976: Wilson TUCKER, *The Year of the Quiet Sun* (special retrospective award)
1977: Kingsley AMIS, *The Alteration*
1978: Frederik POHL, *Gateway*
1979: Michael MOORCOCK, *Gloriana*
1980: Thomas M. DISCH, *On Wings of Song*
1981: Gregory BENFORD, *Timescape*
1982: Russell HOBAN, *Riddley Walker*
1983: Brian W. ALDISS, *Helliconia Spring*
1984: Gene WOLFE, *The Citadel of the Autarch*
1985: Frederik Pohl, *The Years of the City*
1986: David BRIN, *The Postman*
1987: Joan SLONCZEWSKI, *A Door Into Ocean*

1988: Connie WILLIS, *Lincoln's Dreams*
1989: Bruce STERLING, *Islands in the Net*
1990: Geoff RYMAN, *The Child Garden*
1991: Kim Stanley ROBINSON, *Pacific Edge*
1992: Bradley DENTON, *Buddy Holly is Alive and Well on Ganymede*

JÓKAI, MÓR or MAURUS (1825-1904) Very prolific Hungarian novelist, the dominant literary figure of 19th-century HUNGARY, frequently translated and still very highly regarded. Many of his 100 or more novels are violent historical tales, full of catastrophic incident. *Az aranyember* (1872; trans Mrs H. Kennard as *Timar's Two Worlds* 1888 UK), which contrasts a hectic and hysterical urban life with an idyllic UTOPIA established on an "ownerless island" in the Danube, is not really sf, despite the title of its first English translation. MJ did, however, write a number of anticipations in novels and in short fiction, few of which have been translated into English but many into German. *Tales from Jokai* (coll trans R. Nisbet Bain 1904 UK) contains "The City and the Beast" (1858), which deals with ATLANTIS and its destruction, plus three *contes cruels*. An untranslated novel, *Oceánia* (1846), is also about Atlantis. The most important sf by MJ, likewise untranslated into English, is *A jövö század regénye* ["The Novel of the Next Century"] (1872), a dazzlingly inventive 3-vol novel of the future. *Egész az északi pólusig* ["All the Way to the North Pole"] (1876) is also sf, featuring SUSPENDED ANIMATION; *Ahol a pénz nem Isten* ["Where Money is not a God"] (1904) is a utopian ROBINSONADE; *Fekete gyémántok* (1870; trans A. Gerard as *Black Diamonds* 1896) has a scientist seeking to create a utopia; it is partly set in an Arctic sea. [PN/JC]
Other work: *Told by the Death's Head* (trans 1902 of *Egy hirhedett kalandor a tizenhetedil századból* 1904).

JONES, D(ENNIS) F(ELTHAM) (1917-1981) UK writer who served as an officer in the Royal Navy in WWII and was variously employed afterwards. He began publishing sf with the first – and best – volume of his **Colossus** trilogy, *Colossus* (1966), effectively filmed as COLOSSUS, THE FORBIN PROJECT (1969). In both book and film, Charles Forbin has helped to create a master COMPUTER designed to coordinate all the defences of the Western World; however, the Soviets have been building a similar computer, Guardian. In an impressive scene, the two computers exchange information. Soon Colossus gains consciousness and takes over the world. The sequels, *The Fall of Colossus* (1974 US) and *Colossus and the Crab* (1977 US), expand from the first volume (in the process diluting its admonitory impact) by introducing complicated plots, religious sects that worship Colossus, and irritated Martians; ultimately everything comes to a transcendental stop. Some of DFJ's other novels are of interest. In *Implosion* (1967) most women have become sterile, those who remain fertile being tied to a grimly DYSTOPIAN regime. *Denver is Missing* (1971 US; vt *Don't Pick the Flowers* 1971 UK) subjects the city to geological devastation. *Earth Has Been Found* (1979

US; vt *Xeno* 1979 UK) burdens an unsuspecting Earth with an alien INVASION. All these later novels succumb with excessive ease to a slick gloominess, caught in which his characters show little scope for action or development, and by the end of his career his work had lost most of its initial glum panache. [JC]

Other works: *The Floating Zombie* (**1975**); *Bound in Time* (**1981**).

See also: DISASTER.

JONES, DIANA WYNNE (1934-   ) UK writer whose name is sometimes incorrectly rendered as Diana Wynne-Jones, although not on her books; probably the premier UK writer of children's FANTASY today. She began her writing career as a playwright, with three plays produced in London 1967-70, then published her first novel (for adults and not sf), *Changeover* (**1970**). Her second, *Wilkin's Tooth* (**1973**; vt *Witch's Business* 1974 US), was for children (as opposed to teenagers), as were her next half-dozen or so. She hit her stride with her third novel, *The Ogre Downstairs* (**1974**), which is very funny indeed about the results of children playing with a magic alchemy set while at the same time dealing honestly and movingly with some quite difficult human problems. DWJ went on to write stories which, no matter how indirect or devious their plots, always maintain an extraordinarily clearsighted directness about sometimes painful human relationships.

All her work for children is fantastic, and most is shot through with HUMOUR; some is fantasy with sf elements (precognition, ALTERNATE WORLDS); some is borderline sf; some is sf proper. *Dogsbody* (**1975**), borderline sf, features the incarnation of the star Sirius, exiled for an alleged murder, into the body of a terrestrial dog. *The Homeward Bounders* (**1981**) features a child trapped in a seemingly endless series of PARALLEL WORLDS. Perhaps DWJ's best sf novel is *Archer's Goon* (**1984**), a splendidly convoluted mystery involving TIME PARADOXES, alternate worlds, PARANOIA, writer's block and a cheerful thug; it was dramatized by the BBC as a six-part tv serial in 1992. *A Tale of Time City* (**1987**), her most overtly sciencefictional story, concerns a city outside time having trouble with the fabric of reality as it sends patrollers up and down the time-stream.

Fine fantasies from the 1970s include: *Eight Days of Luke* (**1975**), which has Norse gods amusingly manifest on Earth; the **Dalemark** sequence, comprising *Cart and Cwidder* (**1975**), *Drowned Ammet* (**1977**) and *The Spellcoats* (**1979**), the latter, one of her best books, being set in the mythic prehistory of the other two; and *Power of Three* (**1976**), which regards humans from an alien (or fairy) perspective. The **Dalemark** series is projected to be completed with «The Crown of Dalemark» (1993).

Through the 1980s DWJ's target audience seemed, mostly, to become older. This is the case with *The Time of the Ghost* (**1981**), perhaps her darkest work, and especially of her moving reworking of the old ballad "Tam Lin" in *Fire and Hemlock* (**1985**). Other good books of the period include the intricate *Howl's Moving Castle* (**1986**) and its sequel *Castle in the Air* (**1990**). Her best-known series is the **Chrestomanci** sequence: *Charmed Life* (**1977**), *The Magicians of Caprona* (**1980**), *Witch Week* (**1982**) and *The Lives of Christopher Chant* (**1988** US); Chrestomanci is an enchanter who polices MAGIC across the parallel worlds. *Black Maria* (**1991**; vt *Aunt Maria* 1991 US) has children trapped in a seaside town held under the magical sway of their appalling aunt.

Hidden Turnings (anth **1989**) is an ORIGINAL ANTHOLOGY of fantasy stories for teenagers. A new departure is DWJ's fantasy for adults «A Sudden Wild Magic» (**1992** US). [PN]

Other works: *Who Got Rid of Angus Flint?* (**1978** chap); *The Four Grannies* (**1980** chap); *Warlock at the Wheel, and Other Stories* (coll **1984**), containing a **Chrestomanci** story; *The Skivers' Guide* (**1984**); *Wild Robert* (**1989** chap); *Chair Person* (**1989** chap).

See also: CHILDREN'S SF; GODS AND DEMONS; MILFORD SCIENCE FICTION WRITERS' CONFERENCE; MYTHOLOGY.

JONES, EDDIE (1935-   ) UK illustrator. One of the most prolific UK sf artists, EJ is also one of the few in the field to be self-taught. His first professional work was published in 1958 in *Nebula* and *NW*. He illustrated part-time until 1969, when he became art director for VISION OF TOMORROW. He has done sf covers for many publishers in the UK and Germany – notably Sphere Books in the UK and Bastei Verlag, Fischer and Pabel in Germany – as well as elsewhere, including the USA. His style is representational and uses rich, glowing colours; he is best known for SPACESHIPS and other forms of space hardware. [JG]

JONES, (THOMAS FREDERICK) GONNER (?   -   ) UK writer of *The Dome* (**1968**), in which the eponymous brain is in charge of a future CITY. [PN]

JONES, GWYNETH (ANN) (1952-   ) UK writer who became best known in the 1980s for three complex adult sf novels, though most of her books have been juveniles, beginning with *Water in the Air* (**1977**), a fantasy. From her fourth novel, *Dear Hill* (**1980**), she has written sf and fantasy exclusively. *Ally Ally Aster* (**1981**) and *The Alder Tree* (**1982**), both as by Ann Halam, exploit Norse and Gothic material. *King Death's Garden* (**1986**), as by Halam, is a darkly subtle, smoothly stark ghost story set in Brighton, where GJ lived. Set in post-HOLOCAUST Inland, which is governed on deep-ecology lines by women, the **Zanne** series – *The Daymaker* (**1987**), *Transformations* (**1988**) and *The Skybreaker* (**1990**), all as by Halam – is bracingly sf. Young rebellious Zanne slowly learns to control her innate rapport with the forbidden high-tech artifacts of the old patriarchal world-destroying hegemony, and becomes, willy-nilly and by protracted stages, an active agent in the sane preservation of Inland. GJ's only 1980s juvenile under her own name, *The Hidden Ones* (**1988**), is a contemporary urban fantasy. In *Dinosaur Junction* (**1992**), as by Halam, the young protagonist is confronted with dilemmas relating to TIME TRAVEL and meets a dinosaur.

GJ's first novel for adults, *Divine Endurance* (**1984**), remains her most widely admired. Like the **Zanne** books, it is set in a post-holocaust land governed by a matriarchy, but neither setting nor premise are presented with the clarity appropriate in a juvenile text. No dates are given, but GJ's enormously complex Southeast Asia venue has a dying-Earth (◊ FAR FUTURE) feel; and the matriarchical society she depicts is riven by profound ambivalences. The protagonist, a female android named Chosen Among the Beautiful, and the eponymous cat which accompanies her, dangerously agitate the scene by arriving in it, and a civil conflict begins to devastate the long polity of the land. The hard melancholy and sustained density of the book are unique in recent sf. *Escape Plans* (**1986**) attempts some of the same density of effect through an acronym-heavy style and a bruising presentation of the COMPUTER-run DYSTOPIAN world in which the action takes place, but the sacrificial descent from other-world luxury of the female protagonist and her implication in an inevitable revolt have little of the resonance of her predecessor's structurally identical gift of self. *Kairos* (**1988**) – which with the previous two books makes up a kind of thematic trilogy featuring profoundly divided women who descend into the world and redeem it – is set in a NEAR-FUTURE UK degenerating into fascism or anarchy. The title of the book is a theological term designating the moment of fullness in time when Christ appears, and clearly glosses the dramatic centre of each volume of the implied trilogy. In this case the female protagonist descends into the disintegrating UK's netherworld through ingesting a drug, Kairos, which literally recasts reality around her. The world she creates is cleansed of the grosser forms of evil. *White Queen* (**1991**) moves beyond the pattern of the previous books, confronting its protagonists (and the planet) with an INVASION of ALIENS who themselves rewrite human perceptions of, and therefore the rules that bind, reality. In 1992 the book shared the first James Tiptree, Jr. Award with Eleanor ARNASON's *A Woman of the Iron People* (**1991**).

In her adult books GJ is a writer of nearly unforgiving intensity, and on occasion an incompetent storyteller. But the rewards for understanding her are so considerable that the task of learning how to do so seems light enough. [JC]

Other works: *The Influence of Ironwood* (**1978**) and *The Exchange* (**1979**), associational juveniles.

See also: AUTOMATION; CYBORGS; INTERZONE; WOMEN AS PORTRAYED IN SCIENCE FICTION.

JONES, LANGDON (1942-) UK short-story writer, editor and musician, strongly associated with NEW WORLDS during its NEW-WAVE period both as contributor – he published all his sf stories there, beginning with "Storm Water Tunnel" in 1964 – and in various editorial capacities. His most memorable work, most of it experimental in form and characterized by a strongly angular narrative style, appears in *The Eye of the Lens* (coll **1972**). LJ's wide taste as an editor was demonstrated in *The New SF* (anth **1969**); he also collaborated with Michael MOORCOCK in assembling *The Nature of the Catastrophe* (anth **1971**), which contained a number of **Jerry Cornelius** stories from *NW* written by Moorcock and others. The first published version of Mervyn PEAKE's *Titus Alone* (**1959**) had been heavily edited because of Peake's degenerative illness, and LJ was responsible for the reconstruction work resulting in the posthumous 1970 publication of the definitive version of the book. [JC]

See also: ARTS; MUSIC.

JONES, MARGARET (? -) UK writer and lecturer in human communication studies. In *The Day They Put Humpty Together Again* (**1968**; vt *Transplant* 1968 US) prosthetic-surgery techniques are used to wire an artist's head to a criminal's libidinous torso. *Through the Budgerigar* (**1970**) is a fantasy. [JC]

JONES, MERVYN (1922-) UK writer best known for his many novels outside the sf field and for journalism with the political magazine *New Statesman*. *On the Last Day* (**1958**) is a NEAR-FUTURE story about attempts during WWIII to build a new intercontinental missile. [JC]

JONES, NEIL R(ONALD) (1909-1988) US writer who until his retirement in 1973 worked as a New York State unemployment insurance claims investigator. His first story, "The Death's Head Meteor" (the first sf story to use the word "astronaut") for *Air Wonder Stories* in 1930, shares with almost all his fiction a very generalized common background, a future HISTORY – one of the earliest seen in US genre sf – which is given some explanation in "Time's Mausoleum" (1933), a story from the **Professor Jameson** series. Against a background of epic advances and conflicts in the 24th and 26th centuries, Professor Jameson arranges for his corpse to be preserved indefinitely in orbit. After millions of years, long after all other humans have died, he is woken by the ROBOT Zoromes, which encase his brain in metal and give him the chance to travel the Universe in search of knowledge and adventure. He embraces the opportunity. The first **Jameson** story, "The Jameson Satellite", dates from 1931. Most of the pre-WWII stories in the series appeared in *AMZ*, and most of the somewhat inferior later instalments in *Super Science Stories* and *Astonishing Stories*. The first 16 stories of the sequence were collected much later as *The Planet of the Double Sun* (coll **1967**), *The Sunless World* (coll **1967**), *Space War* (coll **1967**), *Twin Worlds* (coll **1967**) and *Doomsday on Ajiat* (coll **1968** including 2 previously unpublished stories). The stories that did not reach book form are "The Cat-Men of Aemt" (1940), "Cosmic Derelict" (1941), "Slaves of the Unknown" (1942), "Parasite Planet" (1949), "World without Darkness" (1950), "The Mind Masters" (1950) and "The Star Killers" (1951); of the 7 further hitherto-unpublished stories "Exiles from Below" appeared in the SEMIPROZINE *Astro-Adventures* in 1987.

NRJ was a vigorous, straightforward writer whose style and concerns were typical of the first blossoming of sf at the end of the 1920s. [JC]

See also: CYBORGS; IMMORTALITY; UNDER THE SEA.

JONES, RAYMOND F. (1915-   ) US writer, very active for about 15 years after he first appeared in *ASF* in 1941 with "Test of the Gods". He was virtually silent in the 1960s; some novels appeared in the 1970s. His best-known short story is the witty "Noise Level" (1952), an archetypal *ASF* tale of CONCEPTUAL BREAKTHROUGH, scientific advance taking place through destruction of a previous paradigm: SCIENTISTS are told that ANTIGRAVITY exists, and so proceed to invent it. The story had two sequels, "Trade Secret" (1953) and "The School" (1954). During his most prolific – and most exciting – period he wrote 1 story, "Utility" (1944), under the pseudonym David Anderson. Two collections, *The Toymaker* (coll **1951**) and *The Non-Statistical Man* (coll **1964**), gather much of this work.

RFJ's first novel, also from that time, is probably his best. *Renaissance* (1944 *ASF*; **1951**; vt *Man of Two Worlds* 1963) is a long, complicated PARALLEL-WORLDS adventure with an exciting narrative – WAR, superscience and echoes of nuclear HOLOCAUST – and a number of lively variations on favourite sf themes. *The Alien* (**1951**), the story of the discovery of an ancient ALIEN artifact in the ASTEROID belt, likewise displays strong narrative drive. *This Island Earth* (1949-50 *TWS*; fixup **1952**) begins with beleaguered ALIENS secretly using human scientists in order to resist an enemy in an intergalactic war which threatens to engulf Earth. The protagonist finally persuades them that, by allowing their tactics to be dictated by vast COMPUTERS, they have become predictable to the enemy. But he may be too late. The film version, THIS ISLAND EARTH (1954), begins well but loses interest when it diverges – perhaps inevitably – from the book.

RFJ's 1950s juveniles are also good. They are *Son of the Stars* (**1952**), *Planet of Light* (**1953**) and *The Year when Stardust Fell* (**1958**).

After *The Secret People* (**1956**; vt *The Deviates* 1959) and *The Cybernetic Brains* (1950 *Startling Stories*; **1962**) RFJ became comparatively inactive, and more recent novels, like *Syn* (**1969**) and *Weeping May Tarry* (**1978**), the latter with Lester DEL REY, show a much diminished energy. Though not generally an innovator in the field, RFJ, during his first period of activity, produced solid, well crafted HARD-SF adventures. [JC/PN]

Other works: *Voyage to the Bottom of the Sea* * (**1965**), a tie to the tv series VOYAGE TO THE BOTTOM OF THE SEA; *Moonbase One* (**1971**); *Renegades of Time* (**1975** Canada); *The King of Eolim* (**1975** Canada); *The River and the Dream* (**1977** Canada).

See also: ASTOUNDING SCIENCE-FICTION; CYBERNETICS; CYBORGS; DISCOVERY AND INVENTION; DYSTOPIAS; GREAT AND SMALL; ISLANDS; PHYSICS; POWER SOURCES; SUSPENDED ANIMATION.

JONES, RICHARD GLYN [r] ◊ Richard GLYN JONES.

JONES, ROBERT F(RANCIS) (1934-   ) US journalist (with *Time-Life*) and writer whose sf novel, *Blood Sport: A Journey up the Hassayampa* (**1974**; vt *Ratnose* 1975 UK), follows a man and his son up the Hassayampa River, along whose banks the future, the present and the past exist simultaneously, together with every imaginable culture as well as the villain Ratnose, against whom the protagonists must prove themselves. [JC]

JONG, ERICA (MANN) (1942-   ) US poet and novelist, best known for the FEMINIST energy of her first novel, *Fear of Flying* (**1971**). Her only tale of genre interest, *Serenissima* (**1987**), is a timeslip fantasy with some sf language inattentively buttressing the premise. The protagonist, haunted amid the playfully sketched glitterati of the Venice film festival, slips back to the 16th century (◊ TIME TRAVEL), where she meets a vacationing Shakespeare and has sex with him. Dying, she is – anticlimactically – reborn in the here and now. [JC/JG]

JORDAN, SIDNEY [r] ◊ JEFF HAWKE.

JORGENSEN, IVAR Floating PSEUDONYM first used in the ZIFF-DAVIS magazines AMAZING STORIES and FANTASTIC, subsequently used in IF, IMAGINATION and IMAGINATIVE TALES. Its main user was Paul W. FAIRMAN (*whom see for details*), who employed it for 3 books: *Ten from Infinity* (**1963**; vt *The Deadly Sky* 1971; vt *Ten Deadly Men* 1976), *Rest in Agony* (**1963**; vt *The Diabolist* 1972) and *Whom the Gods Would Slay* (1951 *Fantastic Adventures*; **1968**). One of Fairman's stories as by IJ, "Deadly City" (1953 *If*), was filmed as TARGET EARTH! (1954). Other writers who may have used the name IJ include Harlan ELLISON, Randall GARRETT and Robert SILVERBERG, although IJ should not be confused with Ivar Jorgenson, a later pseudonym of Silverberg's. [BS]

JORGENSON, IVAR [s] ◊ Robert SILVERBERG.

JOSEPH, M(ICHAEL) K(ENNEDY) (1914-1981) UK-born and Oxford-educated New Zealand writer and professor of English; his first novels were not sf. *The Hole in the Zero* (**1967** UK) begins as an apparently typical SPACE-OPERA adventure into further dimensions at the edge of the Universe, but quickly reveals itself as a linguistically brilliant, complex exploration of the nature of the four personalities involved as they begin out of their own resources to shape the low-probability regions into which they have tumbled. Ultimately the novel takes on allegorical overtones. As an examination of the metaphorical potentials of sf language and subject matter, it is a significant contribution to the field. In 1969 MKJ also produced a scholarly edition of Mary SHELLEY's *Frankenstein* (1818). [JC]

Other works: *The Time of Achamoth* (**1977**).

See also: FANTASTIC VOYAGES; NEW ZEALAND.

JÓSIKA, MIKLÓS [r] ◊ HUNGARY.

JOURNAL OF THE FANTASTIC IN THE ARTS US academic critical journal sponsored by the International Association for the Fantastic in the Arts, current, theoretically quarterly but irregular after the first 4 issues (1988), with a further 6 issues during

1989–April 1992. Vol 1 #1-#4 published M.E. Sharpe, Inc., New York, subsequent issues by Orion Publishing, New York. Executive ed Carl B. YOKE; other eds Marshall B. TYMN, Roger SCHLOBIN and Robert A. Collins.

This comparatively recent addition to the specialist academic journals dealing with sf (◊ EXTRAPOLATION; FOUNDATION; SCIENCE-FICTION STUDIES) has, on the whole, been vigorous and (mostly) eschews excessive critical jargon. Because its remit includes the whole range of the fantastic, including not only sf but also FANTASY, HORROR and FABULATION, it has a certain amplitude the others lack – usefully so in a period of literary history when generic boundaries are rapidly dissolving – but by the same token it sometimes appears unfocused. However, some of the issues have been thematic, vol 1 #4 being about POSTMODERN-ISM, vol 2 #2 about CINEMA, vol 2 #3 about Doris LESSING and vol 3 #1 about art, for example. The portfolios of fantastic art have been largely disastrous, but otherwise *JOTFITA* seems a promising addition to the field. [PN]

JOURNAL WIRED Semi-annual SEMIPROZINE from a SMALL PRESS in paperback-book form ("bookazine"), Winter 1989-Summer/Fall 1990, 3 issues only, published and ed from California and Colorado by Andy Watson and MARK V. ZIESING. This hip, elegant and short-lived periodical ran fiction by a mixture of interesting new writers and better known names (like Paul Di Filippo, Colin GREENLAND, Rudy RUCKER and Lewis SHINER), interviews (William BURROUGHS and others) and commentary by Lucius SHEPARD and others on politics, rock'n'roll, movies and even sf. At 363pp, the last issue was very big. Some stories are sf. If the term NEW WAVE were still used, this would have been a new-wave magazine. [PN]

JOURNEY INTO SPACE ◊ Charles CHILTON; RADIO.

JOURNEY THROUGH THE BLACK SUN ◊ SPACE 1999.

JOURNEY TO THE CENTER OF THE EARTH Film (1959). 20th Century-Fox. Prod Charles Brackett. Dir Henry Levin, starring Pat Boone, James Mason, Arlene Dahl, Thayer David, Peter Ronson, Diane Baker. Screenplay Walter Reisch, Brackett, based on *Voyage au centre de la terre* (**1864**) by Jules VERNE. 132 mins. Colour.

A lively and literate screenplay (cowritten by producer Brackett, one of the Hollywood giants), vigorous if stereotyped characterization, good performances and a charming duck called Gertrud make this superior among the numerous Verne adaptations of the 1950s. There is a real SENSE OF WONDER in some of the underground sequences – which involve labyrinthine caverns, a great ocean at the centre of the HOLLOW EARTH, the remains of ATLANTIS and statutory dinosaurs (iguanas with fins attached) – though the special effects are uneven. The escape from the centre riding a lava jet on an Atlantean altar of serpentine up a presumably 3,900-mile (6,250km) volcanic shaft is merely absurd; but, despite plot changes – including a rival expedition led by a satisfyingly villainous

Icelander played by David – *JTTCOTE*, set in the 1880s, is true in spirit to its stirring original. [PN]

JOURNEY TO THE CENTER OF TIME Film (1967). Borealis/Dorad. Dir David L. Hewitt, starring Scott Brady, Gigi Perreau, Anthony Eisley, Abraham Sofaer. Screenplay David Prentiss. 82 mins. Colour.

Hewitt had been co-screenwriter and special-effects director of *The* TIME TRAVELERS (1964), dir Ib Melchior, and *JTTCOT* is a remake of the earlier film. A pointless, low-budget exercise, certainly no better than the original, it does contain an additional sequence – a battle against a dinosaur – set in the past. [PN]

JOURNEY TO THE FAR SIDE OF THE SUN ◊ DOPPELGANGER.

J.S. OF DALE Pseudonym of F.J. Stimson. ◊ Robert GRANT.

JUBILEE Film (1978). Waley-Malin Production/Megalovision. Written and dir Derek Jarman, starring Jenny Runacre, Little Nell, Toyah Willcox, Jordan, Orlando, Richard O'Brien, Ian Charleson, Adam Ant. 104 mins. Colour.

This was the first solo film by Jarman, one of the doyens of gay, experimental and gender-bending cinema in the UK. The film, which displays a strong sense of irony about the glories of England, was made to be released just in time for Queen Elizabeth II's Jubilee celebrations. Queen Elizabeth I (Runacre) is given the power to glimpse the future. This is (for us) a NEAR-FUTURE London which is decayed, punk and anarchic, though retaining a certain youthful energy (most characters being in their early 20s). The forced decadence of the action is more middle-class Chelsea than streetwise, and the film – with all its orgies, its castrations, its shootings and its music arranged by Brian Eno – is theatrical high camp. [PN]

JUDD, CYRIL Pseudonym used for their 2 collaborative novels by C.M. KORNBLUTH and Judith MERRIL (*both of whom see for further details*): *Outpost Mars* (**1952**; rev vt *Sin in Space* 1961) and *Gunner Cade* (**1952**). [BS]

JUDGE DREDD Judge (Joe) Dredd is an ultra-tough, mean, ruthless, granite-jawed lawman of the future Mega-City One. The strip of which he is the HERO (or maybe antihero) was created by Pat Mills, John Wagner and Carlos Esquerra (artist). It first appeared in 2,000 AD #2 (5 Mar 1977), drawn by Mike McMahon, and more than 800 issues later continued to dominate that COMIC. In a world after the atomic HOLOCAUST, the millions of survivors are crowded into vastly overpopulated Mega-CITIES whose soaring crime rate is dealt with by the Judges, a breed of genetically selected men and (rarely) women. Dressed in black leather with massively chunky insignia and exaggerated elbow-, knee- and shoulder-pads, riding heftily armoured motorcycles with ultra-wide wheels, these law officers have the power to dole out on-the-spot sentences ranging from multi-credit fines to life sentences in far-flung penal colonies. Early stories featured an occasional sidekick, Walter the Wobot, a ROBOT valet with a speech defect. The story-lines, mostly by John Wagner and Alan Grant (variously credited to them under their own names and a number of their pseudonyms), quickly established a high standard of plotting and characterization, with a significant thread of grittily humorous social SATIRE. From this fertile source flowed a rich succession of original ideas that served to establish JD as one of the most popular comic-strip characters ever created. Throughout, both storytelling and characterization have been enriched by a strong element of continuity introduced by Pat Mills, who has also written a number of the stories, including "The Cursed Earth" (25 episodes, 1978) and "The Apocalypse War" (25 episodes, 1982) sequences. Artists on *JD* have included Brian BOLLAND, Esquerra, Ian Gibson, John Higgins, Can Kennedy, Brendan McCarthy, McMahon, Colin MacNeil, Ron Smith and a host of others.

A few of *JD*'s colleagues have become prominent enough to feature in spin-off strips of their own: Judge Anderson of PSI Division, a female Judge with PSI POWERS; Judge Death, a Judge from another DIMENSION where all lifeforms have been sentenced to death, a verdict he has been empowered to enforce throughout the universes; and Judge Armour, JD's equivalent in the city called Brit Cit.

The phenomenal popularity of *JD* has led to a proliferation of spin-off publications, including among others 2 monthly black-and-white reprint titles (*Best of 2,000 AD Monthly*, which does not focus on JD, and *The Complete Judge Dredd*, which does) and more recently a monthly *Judge Dredd, The Megazine*, with mostly full-colour painted artwork, published in different formats for the UK and US editions and featuring serial stories, some starring JD, which cross over with the parent comic. Reprint books have been published by Titan Books in the **The Chronicles of Judge Dredd** series and the **Judge Dredd Graphic Paperbacks** series, both from 1988, with further material constantly being added; there are also annuals, yearbooks and other titles.

A separate company, Eagle Comics, was set up to exploit *JD* in the USA, reprinting his early *2,000 AD* adventures but in colour and adapted for the US comic-book format; the practice was taken over by Quality Comics. Both enterprises overcame the problem of incompatible page proportions by stretching the image on a laser copier; this had the effect of making all the characters appear tall and skinny. JD took a further ponderous step across the international stage with the publication of a DC COMICS/Fleetway collaboration, *Judgement on Gotham* (graph **1991**), featuring a **Judge Dredd/Batman** team-up; this was written by the Wagner-Grant team and painted by the talented high-flier Simon Bisley. In late 1992 a projected series of novels featuring JD was being actively commissioned, and it was reported that a film was in production. [RT]

See also: GAMES AND TOYS.

JUENGER, ERNST ◊ Ernst JÜNGER.

JUGOSLAVIA ◊ YUGOSLAVIA.

JULES VERNE-MAGASINET ◊ Sam J. LUNDWALL; SCANDINAVIA.

JULES VERNE'S ROCKET TO THE MOON ◊ FROM THE EARTH TO THE MOON.

JÜNGER, ERNST (1895-   ) German writer whose early works reflected his experiences in WWI. *Auf den Marmorklippen* (**1939**; trans Stuart Hood as *On the Marble Cliffs* **1947** UK as by Ernst Juenger) – though its status as a classic of resistance to Nazism has been somewhat shaken by analysis of its broodingly passive austerity regarding political action – is a peculiarly resonant allegory of the destruction of a civilized country by an incursion of vandal-like conquerors. *Gläserne Bienen* (**1957**; trans Louise Bogan and Elizabeth Mayer as *The Glass Bees* **1960** US as by Ernst Juenger) also applies an allegorical mode to the story of the creation and use of ROBOT bees for industrial work. *Heliopolis* (**1949**), an ironical UTOPIA, remains untranslated. [JC]

See also: GERMANY.

JUPITER Jupiter's importance in sf is derived from its status as the largest planet in the Solar System and also the most accessible – because nearest to Earth – of the GAS GIANTS. Its four major moons – Ganymede, Callisto, Io and Europa – were discovered by Galileo, but it was not until 1892 that the US astronomer Edward Barnard (1857-1923) discovered the fifth. About a dozen others have been discovered in the 20th century. The visible "surface" of Jupiter is an outer layer of a very dense, deep atmosphere and is thus fluid, though it does have one enigmatic feature that has endured at least since 1831: the Great Red Spot.

Jupiter was included in various interplanetary tours inspired by the religious imagination, and is prominent in several 19th-century interplanetary novels, including *A World of Wonders* (**1838**) by Joel R. Peabody, the anonymously published *The Experiences of Eon and Eona* (**1886**; by J.B. Fayette) and John Jacob ASTOR's *A Journey in Other Worlds* (**1894**), in which it is a "prehistoric" version of Earth, replete with dinosaurs, etc. It is a parallel of Earth in *A Fortnight in Heaven* (**1886**) by Harold Brydges (1858-1939) and in the anonymous *To Jupiter via Hell* (**1908**). As astronomical discoveries were popularized, however, the credibility of an Earthlike Jupiter waned rapidly. The last significant novel to use a Jovian scenario for straightforward UTOPIAN modelling was Ella SCRYMSOUR's *The Perfect World* (**1922**), though pulp-sf writers squeezed a little more melodramatic life out of the notion. Edmond HAMILTON's "A Conquest of Two Worlds" (1932) tells the harrowing tale of the human invasion of Jupiter, and Edgar Rice BURROUGHS sent John Carter there to fight the eponymous "The Skeleton Men of Jupiter" (1943).

Many exotic romances set beyond the orbit of Mars employ the satellites of Jupiter. Ganymede is featured in E.E. "Doc" SMITH's *Spacehounds of IPC* (1931 *AMZ*; **1947**) and in Leigh BRACKETT's "The Dancing Girl of Ganymede" (1950), and Io features in two notable early pulp-sf stories: Stanley G. WEINBAUM's "The Mad Moon" (1935) and Raymond Z. GALLUN's "The Lotus Engine" (1940).

John W. CAMPBELL Jr required contributors to ASTOUNDING SCIENCE-FICTION to pay more attention to what was actually known about the planets. Early applications of this new realism to Jupiter are "Heavy Planet" (1939) by Lee Gregor (Milton A. Rothman; ◊ Tony ROTHMAN) and "Clerical Error" (1940) by Clifford D. SIMAK. Simak revisited Jupiter in his curious "Desertion" (1944), in which humans undergo biological metamorphosis in order to enjoy a paradisal existence there. Isaac ASIMOV set one of his earliest stories, "The Callistan Menace" (1940), in the neighbourhood, then turned his attention to Jupiter itself in "Not Final!" (1941), in which hostile aliens are discovered there, and in "Victory Unintentional" (1942), in which Jovians fail to realize that their visitors are ROBOTS rather than men. Two classic magazine sf stories dealing with conditions on Jupiter are James BLISH's "Bridge" (1952 *ASF*; incorporated into *They Shall Have Stars* fixup **1956**; vt *Year 2018!*), in which a colossal experiment to test hypotheses tests also the psychological resilience of the experimenters, and Poul ANDERSON's "Call Me Joe" (1957), about the everyday life of an artificial centaur-like creature designed for the Jovian environment. Anderson later made use of a similar background in *Three Worlds to Conquer* (**1964**) – the worlds being Jupiter, Ganymede and Earth – in which Ganymede comes into focus as a possible site for a colony, a notion developed also by Robert A. HEINLEIN in *Farmer in the Sky* (**1950**), Anderson again in *The Snows of Ganymede* (1955 *Startling Stories*; **1958**) and Robert SILVERBERG in *Invaders from Earth* (**1958**). Blish, however, recognized that such COLONIZATION would require considerable GENETIC ENGINEERING (which he called PANTROPY), as displayed in "A Time to Survive" (1956 *FSF*; incorporated into *The Seedling Stars*, fixup **1957**).

Although it has become obvious that humans could never live on Jupiter, the idea of a descent into its atmosphere continues to attract attention. Such descents are featured in Isaac Asimov's *Lucky Starr and the Moons of Jupiter* (**1957** as by Paul French; vt *The Moons of Jupiter*), the brothers STRUGATSKI's "Destination: Amaltheia" (1960; trans 1962), Arthur C. CLARKE's "A Meeting With Medusa" (1971) and its elaboration as *The Medusa Encounter* (**1990**) by Paul PREUSS, Ben BOVA's *As on a Darkling Plain* (**1972**) and Gregory BENFORD's and Gordon EKLUND's "The Anvil of Jove" (1976; incorporated into *If the Stars are Gods*, fixup **1977**). Several of these stories cling to the hope that Jupiter might harbour alien life of some kind, albeit nothing remotely humanoid, as does Benford's juvenile novel *Jupiter Project* (**1975**; rev 1980). By far the most spectacular use to which Jupiter has recently been put, however, is in Arthur Clarke's *2010: Odyssey Two* (**1982**), in which it is elevated to the status of a second sun by monolithic *di ex machina* in

order to give a crucial boost to evolution on Europa – an idea echoed in Charles L. HARNESS's *Lunar Justice* (**1991**). Europa (as revealed by the Voyager probes) is also the centre of attention in Charles SHEFFIELD's *Cold as Ice* (**1992**). A relevant theme anthology is *Jupiter* (anth **1973**) ed Frederik and Carol POHL.   [BS]

JUPITER AWARD ◊ AWARDS.

JUST IMAGINE Film (1930). Fox. Dir David Butler, starring El Brendel, Frank Albertson, Maureen O'Sullivan, John Garrick. Screenplay David Butler, Ray Henderson, G.G. DeSylva, Lew Brown. 113 mins. B/w.

The failure of this expensive sf blockbuster – one of a flood of musicals that appeared after the advent of sound in movies – may help explain why Hollywood kept clear of sf subjects (except in the context of horror) for so long afterwards, but it was the whimsicality of the silly story, rather than its sf content, that led to *JI*'s failure. A man is struck by lightning while playing golf in 1930 and wakes to find himself in New York in 1980. There follows a stowing-away on a spaceship and a romantic-triangle plot between man, girl and beautiful Martian, interspersed with banal musical numbers. The special effects are good for their period, and the sets by art directors Stephen Goosson and Ralph Hammeras are spectacular, in particular the huge, futuristic model, which cost $250,000 to build, of New York City. This CITY of the future is imaginatively designed and just as memorable as its obvious progenitor, the one in METROPOLIS (1926).   [JB]

See also: MUSIC.

JUVENILE SF ◊ CHILDREN'S SF.

JUVENILE SERIES When dime novels (◊ DIME-NOVEL SF) declined and disappeared in the 1900s – partly because of public outcry against their supposed evil effect on boys, and partly because of increasing competition from the PULP MAGAZINES, which had become comparable in price – the torch of juvenile sf was taken up by a new format, illustrated hardcover juvenile book series, and the ideas in these began to range more widely. The **Great Marvel** series (9 books 1906-35) by Roy ROCKWOOD – the first hardcover sf series on record – began featuring interplanetary explorations and discoveries with *Through Space to Mars, or The Longest Journey on Record* (**1910**), and was surpassed in quality as juvenile-series sf only by Carl H. CLAUDY's later **Adventures in the Unknown** series (1933-4), the 4 vols of which told of TIME TRAVEL, journeys into the fourth DIMENSION and discoveries of ALIEN intelligences on MARS and in the Earth's crust. Although their plots were at least as strong as those of the contemporary GERNSBACK magazine stories, they proved less popular than the tales of the Earthbound TOM SWIFT (1910-41). In the years 1910-40 there were dozens of other book series aimed at teenage boys and many had themes of scientific invention – natural enough at a time when Edison and Ford were two of the greatest US heroes (◊ EDISONADE) – but those named above are the most fondly remembered.

In the 1930s juvenile series began to appear in a new format, the **Big Little Books**, squat, card-bound 3in x 4in (7.5cm x 10cm upright) volumes which alternated full-page illustrations with text pages. Derived from the COMICS, they included novelizations of BUCK ROGERS IN THE 25TH CENTURY, FLASH GORDON and SUPERMAN. Their demise came in the late 1940s, at which time Robert A. HEINLEIN's juveniles were becoming successful, heralding a new wave of hardcover CHILDREN'S SF series, some of which were novelized adventures derived from popular TELEVISION series.

Tom Swift (or, more accurately, his son) reappeared in the 1950s together with TOM CORBETT: SPACE CADET, **Rip Foster** and others, all united by their interplanetary settings, a feature shared by Isaac ASIMOV's **Lucky Starr** series (1952-8; originally as by Paul French) and by E.C. ELIOTT's **Kemlo** series (1954-63).   [JE/PN]

KADREY, RICHARD (1957-   ) US writer, rock musician and illustrator; he did the cover for INTER-ZONE #9 and the vigorous though somewhat derivative collage illustrations for *Dream Protocols* (coll **1992** chap) by sf poet Lee Ballentine (1954-   ); he has also contributed articles to SCIENCE FICTION EYE and *Whole Earth Review*. His first published sf was "The Fire Catcher" (*Interzone* 1985; *Omni* 1986). Not wholly assimilated influences like CYBERPUNK and J.G. BALLARD give an element of pastiche to his early work, including his novel *Metrophage* (**1988**), but the latter transcends it in a vigorous and inventive tale of a mean-streetwise drug pusher's problems in a NEAR-FUTURE Los Angeles that is being eaten alive by urban decay, police corruption and corporate cynicism. It reads like a supercharged arcade game that appals even its creator.   [PN]

KAEMPFERT, WADE House pseudonym (pronounced Kemfer) used by the editors of ROCKET STORIES: Lester DEL REY on the first 2 issues and Harry HARRISON on the #3.   [PN]

KAFKA, FRANZ (1883-1924) Czech novelist, not usually or profitably considered a writer of fantasy or sf, though some of his stories – such as *In der Strafkolonie* (**1919** chap; trans 1933; trans Willa and Edwin Muir as title story in *The Penal Colony* coll **1948** US; vt *In the Penal Settlement* 1949 UK) and *Die Verwandlung* (**1915**; trans A.L. Lloyd as *The Metamorphosis* 1937 chap UK) – present through a prose of hallucinated transparency a world radically displaced from normal reality (◊ FABULATION). The former tells of an execution machine which incises moral slogans on the victim's body; the latter is a horrifying allegory of alienation in which a young man is transformed overnight into a huge beetle. Other fables are included in *The Great Wall of China* (coll trans Willa and Edwin Muir **1933** UK) and *The Transformation and Other Stories: Works Published during Kafka's Lifetime* (coll trans Malcolm Pasley **1992** UK), which presents a new version of *Die Verwandlung* plus other material

whose release FK sanctioned. His most famous works – none finished and all published posthumously (and despite his apparent wishes that they be destroyed on his death) – are his three novels: *Amerika* (written 1911-14; **1927**; trans Willa and Edwin Muir **1938** UK), *Der Prozess* (written 1914-15; **1925**; trans Willa and Edwin Muir as *The Trial* **1937** UK) and *Das Schloss* (written 1921-22; **1926**; trans Willa and Edwin Muir as *The Castle* **1930** UK). Though all share a vision of the menacing absurdity of the world (◊ ABSURDIST SF), when read in chronological order of writing they present an illuminating sequence from the persecuted innocence of *Amerika*'s protagonist (literally displaced into a surrealistic New World) to the confidence-man ingenuities of K., the protagonist of *The Castle*, who seems almost capable of forcing the 20th-century world to give him meaning and a room. FK's work is Modernist, its fable-like quality indefinably dreamlike; his influence, which has been enormous, permeates much of modern sf's attempts to get at the quality of life in dislocated, totalitarian, surrealistic or merely inscrutable venues.   [JC]

About the author: The literature on FK is enormous. A recent study of interest is *Franz Kafka* (**1990**) by Pietro Citati.

See also: AUSTRIA; FANTASY; MONSTERS; PARANOIA.

KAGAN, JANET (1945-   ) US writer who began publishing sf with a STAR TREK tie, *Uhura's Song* * (**1985**), reckoned to be one of the better novels attached to that enterprise. Her second novel, *Hellspark* (**1988**), carries some of the same digestible competence into an sf adventure whose heroine (attended by a sentient AI) must defend the inhabitants of a valuable planet from a predatory corporation, helped in her task by her very considerable competence in kinesics and LINGUISTICS. More interesting is *Mirabile* (coll of linked stories **1991**), a loosely linked portrait of the eponymous planet, which is inhabited by natives and colonized by humans. The latter import flora and fauna whose

DNA has been genetically engineered to provide the new colony with all sorts of lifeforms. However, the records (of what will sprout from what) have been lost, and the heroine must cope with a variety of comic crises. [JC]

KAGAN, NORMAN (? -) US writer whose occasional sf stories, from "The Mathenauts" for *If* in 1964, have sometimes dealt vigorously and amusingly with MATHEMATICS as a subject, and tend to feature extroverted mathematicians as protagonists. NK also wrote *The Cinema of Stanley Kubrick* (**1972**; exp **1989**). [JC]

See also: DIMENSIONS; FANTASTIC VOYAGES.

KAGARLITSKI, JULIUS (IOSIFOVICH) (1926-) Russian critic and professor of European drama at the State Theatrical Institute in Moscow. JK, one of the leading Russian critics to have a strong interest in sf, published the first and most comprehensive study in the then USSR of an individual sf author: *Herbert Wells* (**1963**; trans as *The Life and Thought of H.G. Wells* 1966 UK; considerably rev and exp vt *Vggiadyvaias v Griadusheie* ["Staring into the Future"] 1989). He later edited a 15-vol set of Wells's collected works (**1965**). *Tchto Takoie Fantastika?* ["What is the Fantastic?"] (**1974**) is a popular history of the genre, and has been translated into several languages (not English). JK won, unusually, the Chief Award of the Polish Ministry of Culture, and, again unusually, in 1972 the PILGRIM AWARD for services to sf studies. [PN/VG]

See also: CRITICAL AND HISTORICAL WORKS ABOUT SF; RUSSIA.

KAHN, JAMES (1947-) US physician and writer who began publishing sf with "Mobius Trip" in 1971, but who has been most active as a novelist, usually of film adaptations. His **New World** trilogy – *World Enough and Time* (**1980**), *Time's Dark Laughter* (**1982**) and *Timefall* (**1987**) – initially depicts a fantasy-like FAR-FUTURE Earth in which GENETIC ENGINEERING on the part of the self-destructing human race has generated vampires, centaurs, semi-sentient cats, ANDROIDS and other creatures, all of which roam through something like Southern California. The first volume floridly introduces the cast, with some *Grand Guignol* episodes. The second, perhaps the most interestingly baroque, carries its human protagonist through a love affair, the begetting of a goddesslike child who wantonly transfigures the world in her death-throes, and his return (with the child's mother) through time to Eden. The third volume, set in Colombia, fails to bring the complex structure of the sequence into clear focus, though the power of the JK's imagery remains vivid in the reader's mind. *The Echo Vector* (**1988**) is a medical thriller that verges on sf. JK's novelizations are competent. [JC]

Film novelizations: *Poltergeist* * (**1982**) and its sequel, *Poltergeist II: The Other Side* * (**1986**); *Star Wars: Return of the Jedi* * (**1983**), novelizing RETURN OF THE JEDI (1983); *Indiana Jones and the Temple of Doom* * (**1984**); *The Goonies* * (**1985**).

See also: MESSIAHS.

KAIJU DAISENSO ◊ GOJIRA; RADON.
KAIJU SOSHINGEKI ◊ GOJIRA; RADON.
KAINS, JOSEPHINE ◊ Ron GOULART.
KAMBAYASHI, CHOHEI [r] ◊ JAPAN.
KAMIKAZE 1. Variant title of the film KAMIKAZE 1989 (1982).

2. Film (1986). Les Films du Loup/ARP/Gaumont. Dir Didier Grousset, starring Richard Bohringer, Michel Galabru, Dominique Lavanant, Riton Liebman, Kim Massee, Harry Cleven. Screenplay Luc Besson, Grousset. 89 mins. Colour.

An amusingly black film with a serious point, *K* tells of a brilliant unemployed scientist, obsessed with tv, who invents a ray-gun which, when pointed at the screen, can kill anyone appearing live on it. When slimy presenters on French afternoon tv start getting blasted mid-announcement, a rumpled *flic* (Bohringer), with the help of a roomful of boffins, sets out to hunt the killer. This French film is something of a throwback to the international 1970s cycle of sf-tinged PARANOIA movies. Like *The Parallax View* (1974) and *Winter Kills* (1979), or the home-grown *Écoute Voir* (1979), *K* mixes bizarre assassination hardware and computerized complications with the traditional down-at-heel strengths of the *policier* as it follows its two central characters down their own labyrinths. Galabru is outstanding as the murderer, starting out as a sympathetic loser but becoming a psychopath who whites his face and dresses up as a Mishima-style samurai. [KN]

KAMIKAZE 1989 (vt *Kamikaze*; vt *Kamikaze '89*) Film (1982). Regina Ziegler/Trio/Oase/ZDF. Dir Wolf Gremm, starring Rainer Werner Fassbinder, Boy Gobert, Günther Kaufmann, Nicole Heesters, Franco Nero. Screenplay Robert Katz, Gremm, based on *Mord pa 31* (**1965**; trans as *Murder on the 31st Floor* **1966**) by Per WAHLÖÖ. 106 mins. Colour.

In the Germany of 1989 people have no problems. They are entertained around the clock by a gigantic multimedia corporation, operating from a 30-floor building. Police Lieutenant Jansen (Fassbinder), investigating a bomb threat against the corporation, discovers the existence of a 31st floor where idealistic journalists are developing plans to make people more intellectual. Their plans are never realized: the corporation keeps an eye on all free-thinkers. Fassbinder's very physical performance, his last (he died in 1982), is all that makes this worth seeing more than once. The rest of this playful West German adaptation of Wahlöö's DYSTOPIAN novel mixes sf and mystery elements with no great individuality. Fassbinder had earlier directed an sf film, the made-for-tv WELT AM DRAHT (1973). [JK]

KAMIN, NICK Pseudonym of US writer Robert J. Antonick (1939-), whose sf novels *Earthrim* (**1969** dos), a heavily plotted melodrama set on a tyrannized Earth, and *The HEROD Men* (**1971**), both feature adventure plots somewhat awkwardly presented. [JC]

KANDEL, MICHAEL (1941-) US writer, translator

and book editor, best known until the late 1980s for his brilliant translations from the Polish of works by Stanisław LEM, among them a pyrotechnic rendering of the novella "Kongres Futurologiczny" (1971 Poland) as *The Futurological Congress* (**1974** US), many of whose wordplays are of necessity MK's. *The Cosmic Carnival of Stanisław Lem* (coll **1981**), which MK assembled, contains excerpts from previously translated novels plus some stories. MK's own novels reflect, perhaps, his immersion in the Eastern European tradition. *Strange Invasion* (**1989**) describes, with dissecting humour, an alien tourist invasion of Earth. *In Between Dragons* (**1990**) subjects a fantasy-game-like universe to an equally wry analysis. *Captain Jack Zodiac* (**1991**), in a fashion reminiscent of the way post-HOLOCAUST traumas were surreally ignored in *The* BED-SITTING ROOM, exposes its zany cast to a USA gone terminally insane after the Bomb has been dropped.   [JC]

KANE, PABLO ◊ Zack HUGHES.

KANE, WILSON House name used by ZIFF-DAVIS on 4 stories 1958-9 in *AMZ* and *Fantastic*; at least 1, unidentified, was by Robert BLOCH.   [PN]

KANER, H(YMAN) (1896-1973) Romanian-born UK writer and civil servant who published his own books from Llandudno in Wales. Of them, two full-length novels stand out: *People of the Twilight* (**1946**), a PARALLEL-WORLDS tale, and *The Sun Queen* (**1946**), which features instantaneous TRANSPORTATION and a race of beings dwelling within the SUN.   [JC]
Other works: *Squaring the Triangle* (coll **1944** chap); *Fire-Watcher's Night* (coll **1944** chap); *Hot Swag* (coll **1945** chap); *The Cynic's Desperate Mission* (coll **1946** chap); *Ape-Man's Offering* (coll **1946** chap); *The Naked Foot* (coll **1946** chap); *The Terror Catches Up* (coll **1946** chap); *Ordeal by Moonlight* (coll **1947** chap).

KANTO, PETER ◊ Zack HUGHES.

KANTOR, MacKINLAY (1904-1977) US writer best known for such works outside the sf field as *Andersonville* (**1955**), a long novel set during the US Civil War, the area of his deepest concern. That war is also the setting for *If the South had Won the Civil War* (**1961**), the ALTERNATE-WORLDS thesis of the title being a favourite crux for US writers in the genre.   [JC]

KAPITÄN MORS DER LUFTPIRAT See *Der* LUFTPIRAT UND SEIN LENKBARES LUFTSCHIFF.

KAPLAN, ALINE BOUCHER (1947-   ) US marketing executive and writer who began publishing sf with *Khyren* (**1988**), in which the protagonist finds herself transported from her conventional existence into a world where female worth is measured by fertility; the FEMINIST implications of the tale are not heavily underlined. ABK's second novel, set in the same universe, is *World Spirits* (**1992**).   [JC]

KAPP, COLIN (1928-   ) UK writer and worker in electronics. He began publishing sf with "Life Plan" for *NW* in 1958, where his best work soon appeared, including "Lambda 1" (**1962**), which gave its title to the John CARNELL collection, *Lambda 1* (anth **1964**), and *Transfinite Man* (**1964** US; vt under the 1963 mag

title *The Dark Mind* **1965** UK), in which a fierce unkillable SUPERMAN protagonist pits himself against the corrupt Failway [*sic*] Terminal in duels extending through various DIMENSIONS – access to which the Terminal attempts to control. Despite CK's otherwise unextraordinary plotting, the combination of invulnerability and rage in the tale generates a sense of nearly uncontrollable energy, imparting to this one book something of the exhilaration of Keith LAUMER and a touch of the complexity of Alfred BESTER, whose Gully Foyle – from *Tiger! Tiger!* (**1956** UK) – is clearly evoked. CK's later publications include a sequence of problem-solver tales assembled as *The Unorthodox Engineers* (coll of linked stories **1979**), a short series comprising *The Patterns of Chaos* (**1972**) and *The Chaos Weapon* (**1977** US), the former featuring a SUPERHERO implausibly capable of manipulating chaos, and the **Cageworld** sequence of SPACE OPERAS centred on a DYSON SPHERE: *Cageworld* (**1982**; vt *Search for the Sun!* 1983 US), *The Lost Worlds of Cronus* (**1982**) and *The Tyrant of Hades* (**1982**).   [JC]
Other works: *The Wizard of Anharitte* (**1973**); *The Survival Game* (**1976** US); *Manalone* (**1977**); *The Ion War* (**1978** US); *The Timewinders* (**1980**).
See also: NEW WORLDS; NEW WRITINGS IN SF; TRANSPORTATION.

KARAGEORGE, MICHAEL [s] ◊ Poul ANDERSON.

KAREL AWARD ◊ WORLD SF.

KARIG, WALTER (1898-1956) US journalist and novelist, a pseudonymous author for many years of the **Nancy Drew** detective series and others. *War in the Atomic Age?* (**1946** chap) compresses into very few pages a sequence of 21st-century superscience duels between the USA and Galaxia – they include atomic warfare, FORCE FIELDS, biological WEAPONS and underwater ROBOT tanks. The USA wins hands down. In his sf fantasy, *Zotz!* (**1947**), a man – given the ancient power to kill by pointing his hand and saying "Zotz!" – is frustrated by bureaucracy in his attempts to help the USA win WWII; the effect is mildly satirical.   [JC]

KARIMO, AARNO [r] ◊ FINLAND.

KARINTHY, FRIGYES (1887-1938) Hungarian writer and translator, best known for his work outside the sf field, mostly humorous SATIRES first published in newspapers; he also translated works by Jonathan SWIFT and Mark TWAIN, among others, into Hungarian. His two continuations of Swift's *Gulliver's Travels* (1726) – *Utazás Faremidóba* (**1916**) and *Capillária* (**1921**) – were assembled as *Voyage to Faremido/Capillaria* (omni trans Paul TABORI **1965** Hungary). The first carries FK's version of Gulliver to a ROBOT society, the second to one ruled by women. Sharp-tongued and convincingly Swiftian, they are impressive introductions to his melancholy, sometimes savage view of the 20th century. His career, and his prescient use of robots as symbols of the dawning new age, were similar to Karel ČAPEK's, but he pulled fewer punches. FK was a dangerous writer.   [JC]
See also: FANTASTIC VOYAGES; HUNGARY.

KARP, DAVID (1922-   ) US writer whose sf novel

One (**1953**; vt *Escape to Nowhere* 1955) is a notable MAINSTREAM use of sf modes as a way of expressing DYSTOPIAN views about the future. Though distinctly less convincing than such predecessors as Arthur KOESTLER's *Darkness at Noon* (**1940**) and George ORWELL's *Nineteen Eighty-four* (**1949**), it does present a salutarily grim and sharply described vision of a totalitarian future USA and the brutal mind-control that must be imposed if the state is to survive. Part of the novel's interest lies in its sometimes sympathetic insight into the mind of inquisitor as well as victim. *The Day of the Monkey* (**1955**) is a fantasy. [JC]

See also: POLITICS.

KASACK, HERMANN [r] ◊ GERMANY.

KASTEL, WARREN ZIFF-DAVIS house name used on magazine stories by Chester S. GEIER and possibly others 1948-50, and by Robert SILVERBERG in 1957. [JC]

KASTLE, HERBERT D(AVID) (1924-1987) US writer best known outside the genre. He began publishing sf with "The York Problem" for *If* in 1955. His one sf novel, *The Reassembled Man* (**1964**; exp vt *Edward Berner is Alive Again!* 1975; vt *The Three Lives of Edward Berner* 1976 UK) depicts without excessive originality the transformation by aliens of a human into a sexually supercharged SUPERMAN. [JC]

KAUL, FEDOR (? -?) German writer. His sf novel, *Die Welt ohne Gedächtnis* (trans Winifred Ray as *Contagion to this World* **1933** UK), begins conventionally enough with a deformed SCIENTIST, thwarted in love, determining to revenge himself on the world by releasing dangerous bacteria he has developed; these turn out to have a memory-erasing effect on humans. The scientist's love-affair forgotten, the novel becomes a post-HOLOCAUST vision in which the remnants of mankind mutate into a roving race of giants in harmony with Nature. The scientist grows old and – remarkably – dies forgiven. [JC]

KAVAN, ANNA Name under which French-born, much travelled UK writer born Helen Woods Edmonds (1901-1968) wrote her fiction from 1940, having previously signed herself under her married name, Helen Ferguson; the orphaned protagonist of *Let Me Alone* (**1930**) and *A Stranger Still* (**1935**) is named Anna Kavan, and Edmonds eventually became AK by deed poll. Her life, which ended in suicide, was tragically complicated by heroin addiction, and in most of her work fantasy and mental illness surreally intermingle. She was well known for work outside the sf field, though her last work, the sf novel *Ice* (**1967**), is as familiar to readers as anything she wrote. It depicts, through compulsively intense imagery which links her with Franz KAFKA and the Surrealists generally, a post-HOLOCAUST search for a woman through a world increasingly shadowed by an approaching ice age. An earlier novel, *Eagles' Nest* (**1958**), traverses the same quest landscape, though in fantasy terms. Later editions of *Ice* carry an introduction by Brian W. ALDISS, in which he claims AK as one of the great sf writers; he also edited the posthumous *My Madness: The Selected Writings of Anna Kavan* (coll

1990). [JC]

Other works: *Asylum Piece and Other Stories* (coll **1940**); *House of Sleep* (**1947** US; vt *Sleep has his House* 1948 UK); *A Bright Green Field* (coll **1958**); *Julia and the Bazooka* (coll **1970**); *My Soul is in China* (coll **1975**).

See also: END OF THE WORLD; WOMEN SF WRITERS.

KAVANNE, RISTO [r] ◊ FINLAND.

KAVENEY, ROZ (1949-) UK critic, editor and writer. Her sf criticism, beginning in the late 1970s (before 1980 as by Andrew Kaveney), has appeared in specialist journals like FOUNDATION and in non-genre outlets like the Washington *Post* and *Books and Bookmen*; it is marked by a seemingly off-hand general erudition and a knowing sharpness about the field. Much of her non-sf writing has concentrated on issues like FEMINISM, gay rights and censorship. She began publishing sf with "A Lonely Impulse" in *Temps: Volume One* * (anth **1991**), "devised by" Neil GAIMAN and Alex Stewart. She edited *Tales from the Forbidden Planet* (anth **1987**) and *More Tales from the Forbidden Planet* (anth **1990**) as well as two SHARED-WORLD anthologies: *The Weerde* * (anth **1992**) and *Villains* * (anth **1992**), both with Mary GENTLE. [JC]

See also: INTERZONE.

KAY, SAMUEL M. ◊ Charles DE LINT.

KAYE, MARVIN (NATHAN) (1938-) US writer, usually of fantasy and horror, noted here primarily for the **Masters of Solitude** sf sequence: *Masters of Solitude* (**1978**) and *Wintermind* (**1984**), both written with Parke GODWIN (*whom see for details*). The supernatural novel *A Cold Blue Light* (**1983**), also with Godwin, is less successful; and its sequel, *Ghosts of Night and Morning* (**1987**), by MK alone, is neither sf nor supernatural. Early in his career, MK wrote some stories as Brother Theodore. [JC]

Other works: The **Umbrella/Fillmore** fantasy sequence, comprising *The Incredible Umbrella* (fixup **1979**) and *The Amorous Umbrella* (**1981**); *The Possession of Immanual Wolf and Other Improbable Tales* (coll **1981**).

As editor: *Brother Theodore's Chamber of Horrors* (anth **1975**) "with Brother Theodore" (i.e., MK under that pseudonym); *Fields and Creatures* (anth **1975**); *Ghosts* (anth **1981**) with Saralee Kaye; *Masterpieces of Terror and the Supernatural* (anth **1985**) with S. Kaye; *Devils and Demons* (anth **1987**) with S. Kaye; *Weird Tales: The Magazine that Never Dies* (anth **1988**) with S. Kaye; *Witches and Warlocks* (anth **1990**); *Haunted America: Star-Spangled Supernatural Stories* (anth **1991**); *Lovers and Other Monsters* (anth **1992**); *Fantastique* (**1992**).

KDO CHCE ZABÍT JESSII (vt *Who Would Kill Jessie?*) Film (1965). Filmové studio Barrandov. Dir Miloš Macourek, Václav Vorlíček, starring Jiří Sovák, Dana Medřická, Olga Schoberová, Karel Effa, Juraj Višný. Screenplay Macourek, Vorlíček. 80 mins. B/w.

This very funny Czechoslovak film was conceived for children, but the makers realized that the idea had satirical potential. An overworked professor (Sovák) becomes obsessed with a newspaper comic strip featuring a voluptuous heroine, Jessie (Schoberová), who is constantly being pursued by two villains – a malicious cowboy (Effa) and a displeasing analogue of SUPERMAN (Višný). He dreams a lot about Jessie. The straitlaced wife of the professor (Medřická), also a scientist, has invented a dream-manipulator with which she hopes to eradicate her husband's lascivious dreams, but it malfunctions and the three comic-book characters materialize in their apartment, causing upheaval. This exhilarating, well made film deserves wider distribution. [JB/PN]

KEA, NEVILLE [r] ◊ ROBERT HALE LIMITED.

KEARNEY, (ELFRIC WELLS) CHALMERS (1881-1966) Australian-born writer, in the UK most of his life, author of the nonfiction *Rapid Transit in the Future* (only 2nd edn recorded, **1911**). His UTOPIA, *Erone* (**1943**; rev 1945), an old-fashioned love-story set in a rather sentimentalized communist society on Uranus, had some popular success, though now forgotten. A short pamphlet, *The Great Calamity* (**1948** chap), itemizes the destruction of most of the world. [JC]

KEATING, H(ENRY) R(EYMOND) F(ITZWALKER) (1926-) UK writer, almost exclusively of detective novels, notably those featuring **Inspector Ghote** of the Bombay CID. His two sf novels are *The Strong Man* (**1971**), a DYSTOPIAN tale of a dictator and the ambiguous consequences of his removal, and *A Long Walk to Wimbledon* (**1978**), in which a man treks laboriously across London to visit his wife just after a DISASTER has devastated the capital. [JC]

KEAVENEY, JAMES R. ◊ Arthur H. LANDIS.

KEE, ROBERT (1919-) UK broadcaster and writer. *A Sign of the Times* (**1955**) is set in the NEAR FUTURE, where regimentation rules along lines familiar in post-WWII UK fiction. [JC]

KEENE, CAROLYN ◊ Harriet S. ADAMS.

KEENE, DAY (1904-1969) US writer, mostly of detective novels and film and tv scripts. In his sf novel, *World without Women* (**1960**) with Leonard PRUYN, the few remaining women find themselves in DYSTOPIAN circumstances. [JC]

KEITH, LEIGH [s] ◊ Horace L. GOLD.

KELLAR, VON House name used for 2 routine sf adventures published by CURTIS WARREN: *Ionic Barrier* (**1953**) by Dennis HUGHES and *Tri-Planet* (**1953**), whose authorship has not been ascertained. [JC]

KELLEAM, JOSEPH E(VERIDGE) (1913-1975) US writer and civil servant, an occasional contributor to the sf field since publishing his first story, "Rust", in *ASF* in 1939. His first novel, *Overlords from Space* (**1956** dos), is a routine tale in which ALIEN conquerors of Earth are defeated at last. *The Little Men* (**1960**) and its sequel, *Hunters of Space* (**1960**), whose characters are derived from European MYTHOLOGY, traces the fight between **Jack Odin** and the villainous Grim Hagen, first under the Earth, then in space; various princesses and dwarfs attend. In *When the Red King Woke* (**1966**), which may be sf, a mysterious monarch sleeps off-planet in a bubble; as readers of Lewis CARROLL might expect, when the king awakes the planet dies. [JC]

See also: ROBOTS.

KELLEHER, VICTOR (MICHAEL KITCHENER) (1939-) Australian lecturer in English and now full-time writer. Born in London, VK spent 20 years in Africa before emigrating to New Zealand (1973) and then Australia (1976). VK's major theme in the sf and FANTASY (he makes no sharp distinction between the two genres) for adolescents for which he is best known is the tension between cyclic/seasonal time and linear time. His sf includes *The Green Piper* (**1984**), *Taronga* (**1986**) and *The Makers* (**1987**); his fantasy includes *Master of the Grove* (**1982**) – Australian Children's Book of the Year – *Baily's Bones* (**1988**), *The Red King* (**1989**), *Brother Night* (**1990**) and *Del-Del* (**1991**), and also his early novels *Forbidden Paths of Thual* (**1979**) and *The Hunting of Shadroth* (**1981**). *Papio* (**1984**) is an adventure story. His post-HOLOCAUST novel for adults, *The Beast of Heaven* (**1985**), won a Ditmar AWARD for best Australian sf. He has written four non-sf books for adults. [JW]

See also: AUSTRALIA; CHILDREN'S SF.

KELLER, DAVID H(ENRY) (1880-1966) US writer, physician and psychiatrist, deeply involved in the last capacity in WWI work on shell shock; he published a great deal of technical work in his professional role. As a writer of fantasy and sf he was active but unpublished for many years before the period 1928-35, his first sf sale being "The Revolt of the Pedestrians" (◊ DYSTOPIA) to *AMZ* in 1928. For the next decade he appeared widely in *Weird Tales* and other PULP MAGAZINES, including AMAZING STORIES, where he published "The Metal Doom" (1932), in which advanced civilization ends when all metal begins to rust. He fell out of wide public notice with the onset of the GOLDEN AGE OF SF, whose optimism about the workability of the Universe he clearly did not share. He remained active in FANDOM, however, and – it is rumoured – wrote a large number of stories, some of which appeared in the 1940s; others were published in the 1970s in response to the continuing appeal of his apparently primitive fiction.

DHK's sf is probably inferior to his horror and fantasy work. *The Thing in the Cellar* (1932 *Weird Tales*; **1940** chap), for instance, works almost as a hydraulic metaphor (in the Freudian manner) of the relationship between the upstairs daylight of consciousness and the blind tide of unconsciousness beneath our floors. It is much superior to the sf story published as his first book, *The Thought Projector* (**1930** chap).

His sf was conservative – against the spirit of the age – in its presentation of the risks inherent in all science; the eponymous detective of the **Taine of San Francisco** sequence of sf stories (1928-47) generally operates so as to conceal, rather than expose, the truth behind things. Much of DHK's sf concerns dilemmas created by GENETIC ENGINEERING – the stories in Brian M. STABLEFORD's *Sexual Chemistry* (coll **1991**) are readable as a direct rebuttal to DHK's unvarying pessimism – and tends to end in arbitrary apocalypse. His novels are similar. In his first, *The Human Termites* (1929 *Science Wonder Stories*; **1979** chap), the human race is almost seen off by invading social insects. Other early novels have not reached book form. In "Life Everlasting" (1934 *AMZ*), which appears in *Life Everlasting and Other Tales of Science, Fantasy and Horror* (coll **1947**), the human race must choose between IMMORTALITY and fertility. The second (and considerably longer) title in *The Solitary Hunters; and The Abyss* (coll **1948**) again demonstrates, by detailing the terrible consequences of any removal of human repressions, DHK's sense of the fragility of the psychic order.

Several of his full-length books were story collections, with some sf included in a preponderantly fantasy mix. They include *At the Sign of the Burning Hart* (coll of linked stories **1938** France; with appendix added, vt *At the Sign of the Burning Hart: A Tale of Arcadia* 1948 US), which is UTOPIAN, *Tales from Underwood* (coll **1952**), *The Folsom Flint and Other Curious Tales* (coll **1969**), *The Street of Queer Houses and Other Tales* (coll **1976**) and *The Last Magician: Nine Stories from "Weird Tales"* (coll **1978** chap). [JC]

Other works: *Wolf Hollow Bubbles* (?**1934** chap); *Men of Avalon* (**1935** chap dos); *The Waters of Lethe* (**1937** chap); *The Television Detective* (**1938** chap); *The Devil and the Doctor* (fixup **1940**), in which Satan is a HERO-figure; *The Eternal Conflict* (1939 *Les Primaires*, part only; **1949**); *The Homunculus* (**1949**); *The Final War* (**1949** chap); *The Lady Decides* (**1950**); *A Figment of a Dream: A New Allegorical Fantasy* (**1962** chap).

See also: AIR WONDER STORIES; AUTOMATION; BIOLOGY; HIVE-MINDS; MACHINES; MEDICINE; PSYCHOLOGY; ROBOTS; SMALL PRESSES AND LIMITED EDITIONS; TECHNOLOGY; TRANSPORTATION.

KELLERMANN, BERNHARD (1879-1951) German writer whose sf novel, *Der Tunnel* (**1913**; trans anon as *The Tunnel* **1915** UK), tells the epic story, sometimes in heartfelt terms, of the construction of a transatlantic tunnel. It was the basis of the German film *Der* TUNNEL (1933) and its UK remake, *The* TUNNEL (1935). [JC]

See also: GERMANY; TRANSPORTATION.

KELLEY, LEO P(ATRICK) (1928-) US novelist, for some time also an advertising copywriter. He began publishing sf with "Dreamtown, U.S.A." for *If* in 1955. Several of his sf novels likewise concentrate on societies which invidiously dominate their inhabitants by psychological means, as in his second, *Odyssey to Earthdeath* (**1968**). His first, *The Counterfeits* (**1967**), as by Leo F. Kelley, similarly puts sociological sf into a routine adventure frame. An oddly affectless baroque style sometimes jars against the stories he tells, pretending an urgency it fails to convey through plots of a fashionable grimness; but he has been a readable contributor to the genre. [JC]

Other works: *Time Rogue* (**1970**); *The Accidental Earth* (**1970**); *The Coins of Murph* (**1971**); *Brother John* * (**1971**); *Time: 110100* (**1972**; vt *The Man from Maybe* 1974 UK); *Mindmix* (**1972**); *Mythmaster* (**1973**); *The Earth Tripper* (**1973**); a series of short juveniles, comprising *Time Trap* (**1977** chap), *Star Gold* (**1978** chap; vt *Alien Gold*

1983), *Backward in Time* (**1979** chap), *Death Sentence* (**1979** chap), *Earth Two* (**1979** chap), *Prison Satellite* (**1979** chap), *Sunworld* (**1979** chap), *Worlds Apart* (**1979** chap), *Night of Fire and Blood* (**1979** chap), *Dead Moon* (**1979** chap), *King of the Stars* (**1979** chap), *On the Red World* (**1979** chap), *Where No Sun Shines* (**1979** chap), *Vacation in Space* (**1979** chap) and *Good-bye to Earth* (**1979** chap).

As editor: *Themes in Science Fiction* (anth **1972**); *Fantasy, the Literature of the Marvelous* (anth **1973**); *The Supernatural in Fiction* (anth **1973**).

KELLEY, THOMAS P. (1905-1982) Ex-prizefighter and, in his own description, "King of the Canadian pulp writers", author mostly of adventure fiction and "true crime", as well as of the sf novel "A Million Years in the Future" (1940 *Weird Tales*), which never reached book form. Four fantasy novels are *I Found Cleopatra* (1938 *Weird Tales*; cut **1946**), *The Face that Launched a Thousand Ships* (fixup **1941**), *Tapestry Triangle* (**1946** UK), featuring an immortal Chinese and a race of Amazons, and *The Gorilla's Daughter* (**1950**). He contributed under pseudonyms, including Gene Bannerman, Roy P. Devlin and Valentine North, to the Canadian UNCANNY TALES and wrote 40 scripts for *Out of the Night*, a radio programme specializing in supernatural tales. [PN/JC]

See also: CANADA; WEAPONS.

KELLEY, WILLIAM MELVIN (1937-) US writer whose celebrated short novel *A Different Drummer* (**1959**) is a borderline-sf fable telling of Black history in an imaginary southern state of the USA, and ending with a mass emigration of all Blacks from the state in 1957. [PN]

Other works: *Dem* (**1967**); *Dunsford Travels Everywhere* (**1970**).

See also: POLITICS.

KELLOGG, MARJORIE BRADLEY (1946-) US scenery designer and writer who published her first three novels as by M. Bradley Kellogg to avoid confusion with another Marjorie Kellogg, but from 1991 used her full name. Her first novel, *A Rumor of Angels* (**1983**), is unexceptional, but the **Lear's Daughters** sequence – *The Wave and the Flame* (**1986**) and *Reign of Fire* (**1986**), both written with NASA climatologist William B(rigance) Rossow (1947-) and assembled as *Lear's Daughters* (omni **1987**) – somewhat more interestingly devotes much attention to the ECOLOGY and violent climatic extremes of a potential colony planet, though the conflict between the advocates of exploitation and those of alliance with the pacific cave-dwelling weather-predicting natives lacks originality. MBK's fourth novel, *Harmony* (**1991**), is a large and ambitious tale set on an Earth dominated by centuries of POLLUTION, with almost all humans now living in large, strictly controlled domes. But some artists – here MBK again shows an untoward softness of mind – have somehow managed to live in the open, and the book moves slowly towards a wholesome resolution of the conflict between ensuring safety and embracing the world. [JC]

KELLY, FRANK K(ING) (1914-) US writer who began to publish sf with "The Light Bender" for *Wonder Stories* in 1931, and who rapidly became known for SPACE-OPERA tales of some bleakness, though later titles were infused with an idealistic glow. He stopped writing sf in 1935, turning to non-genre fiction and political histories, and it was not until 45 years later that his sf work became available again, with the release of *Starship Invincible* (coll **1979**). FKK cofounded the Center for the Study of Democratic Institutions in 1959, and the Nuclear Age Peace Foundation in 1982. [JC]

KELLY, JAMES PATRICK (1951-) US writer who began to publish after attending his first CLARION SCIENCE FICTION WRITERS' WORKSHOP in 1974. With "Dea Ex Machina" for *Gal* in 1975, the first of about 40 tales to 1992, he began very quickly to establish himself as an author whose work contained, within a sometimes sober demeanour, considerable pyrotechnic charge. In the selfconscious 1980s controversy between CYBERPUNK and "Humanist" modes of sf discourse, he was located with the latter, but like most "Humanists" he has disavowed the distinction – and indeed published a story, "Solstice" (1985), in Bruce STERLING's *Mirrorshades* (anth **1986**). Some of his short work is collected in *Heroines* (coll **1990**). He is perhaps best known for *Freedom Beach* (fixup **1985**) with John KESSEL – an author with whom he has also collaborated on separate stories. In the book several characters find themselves in an interzone in which "reality" and dreamwork wed surreally, and must make sense of their surroundings. The control they exercise can be seen as allegorical of the creative act.

Of greater interest are JPK's solo novels, *Planet of Whispers* (**1984**) and *Look into the Sun* (**1989**), which start the open-ended **Messengers Chronicles**. Whatever message is carried by the various species who link the Galaxy into a communications network has not been revealed so far. The first tale, set on the planet Aseneshesh, explores in voluminous detail the native race of near-immortal bearlike beings whose mental workings are derived from the attractive hypotheses developed by Julian Jaynes in *The Origin of Consciousness in the Breakdown of the Bicameral Mind* (**1976**). In Jaynes's book, and in JPK's novel, preconscious sentients – i.e., preliterate humans, including Homer – "hear" right-brain "whispers" which they understand to be the voices of the gods, and in this fashion hallucinate normative diktats which shape their culture. No humans appear in the novel. In the second volume, set partly on a depleted Earth, a young architect is recruited by Messengers to travel to Aseneshesh, being engineered en route into the semblance of an Asenesheshian, with a computer-implant substituting for the right-brain voice of God. Aseneshesh is vividly depicted in the two books, in a PLANETARY-ROMANCE style reminiscent at times of Jack VANCE; but the plotting has a slow rigour typical of all JPK's work. He stands at the verge of recogni-

tion as a major writer. [JC]

See also: CHILDREN IN SF; GODS AND DEMONS.

KELLY, ROBERT (1935-) Extremely prolific US poet; a professor of English. His novel *The Scorpions* (**1967**) has been read as sf because of its baroque rendering of a psychiatrist's conviction that a rich patient does in fact have contact with the Scorpions, a race of ultraviolet people. However, like *Cities* (**1971** chap), the book is more plausibly viewed as a FABULATION, depicting US life after the fashion of Harry Mathews (1930-) and Thomas PYNCHON. In the 1980s RK began to publish short fiction in the same vein, collected in *A Transparent Tree: Fictions* (coll **1985**). [JC]

KELLY, WILLIAM PATRICK (1848-1916) UK writer in whose *Doctor Baxter's Invention* (**1912**) it proves possible to transfer insanity and homicidal behaviour from one person to another via blood transfusions. [JC]

KEMLO ◊ E.C. ELIOTT.

KEMP, EARL An associate of William L. HAMLING (*whom see for details*) and recipient of a 1961 fan-writing HUGO. [JC]

KENAN, AMOS [r] ◊ ISRAEL.

KENDALL, GORDON ◊ S.N. LEWITT; Susan SHWARTZ.

KENDALL, JOHN Pseudonym of UK writer Margaret Maud Brash (1880-?), author of *Unborn Tomorrow* (**1933**), a futuristic DYSTOPIA describing dehumanization, regimentation and subsequent revolution in the UK under communism. [JE]

See also: POLITICS.

KENDALL, MAY [r] ◊ Andrew LANG.

KENEALLY, THOMAS (MICHAEL) (1935-) Australian writer best known for *Bring Larks and Heroes* (**1967** UK) and for *Schindler's Ark* (**1983** UK), which won the Booker Prize, but who has several times edged into generic displacements to contain a remarkably intense and occasionally visionary imagination. His first novel, *The Place at Whitton* (**1964** UK), is horror. *Blood Red, Sister Rose* (**1974** UK) is an historical fantasy. *Victim of the Aurora* (**1977**), which can be read as a detection, *feels* like sf in that it depicts Antarctica exactly as an sf writer might depict an alien planet. *Ned Kelly and the City of the Bees* (**1978** UK) is juvenile sf. The eponymous human foetus in *Passenger* (**1979** UK) has been transformed by laser-scan into a conscious and articulate being. [JC]

KENNAWAY, JAMES Pseudonym of Scottish writer James Ewing Peebles (1928-1968), best known for such works outside the sf field as *Tunes of Glory* (**1956**). His borderline sf novel is *The Mind Benders* * (**1963**), which applies MAINSTREAM tactics to a story about brainwashing and the psychological consequences of overexposure to experimental conditions of sensory deprivation. The book was written from his script for the 1963 film of the same name. [JC]

See also: PSYCHOLOGY.

KENNEALY, PATRICIA Working name of US writer Patricia Kennealy Morrison (1946-), "married" to rock singer Jim Morrison (1943-1971); she appeared in a cameo role in Oliver Stone's film *The Doors* (1991). Her sf oscillates – in a manner common to much 1980s work – between fantasy and sf, in the end seeming more the former than the latter. However, her **Keltiad** sequence – *The Copper Crown* (**1985**), *The Throne of Scone* (**1986**) and *The Silver Branch* (**1988**) – is set in space, being an expansive SPACE-OPERA reworking of the Arthurian Cycle. A second sequence, the **Tales of Arthur**, beginning with *The Hawk's Gray Feather* (**1990**) – further volumes are projected – is set 1000 or so years before the first; the tale is set on a single world and a PLANETARY-ROMANCE idiom dominates, so it is hard to read the book as sf. The marriage of modes, however, remains of genuine potential interest. [JC]

KENNEDY, EDGAR REES ◊ John W. JENNISON.

KENNEDY, LEIGH (1951-) US writer, in the UK since 1985; married to Christopher PRIEST from 1988. Her sf stories, beginning with "Salamander" for *ASF* in 1977, combine generic sharpness of address and a "literary" density. "Her Furry Face" (1983), perhaps her best-known single work, exemplifies this duality of effect in a striking presentation of love between species, human and primate (◊ APES AND CAVEMEN); it was assembled, with very various companions, in *Faces* (coll **1986**). *The Journal of Nicholas the American* (**1986**) depicts with alarming exactitude the anguish of paranormal empathy (◊ ESP), which drives the young man who inherits the gift almost to insanity. [JC]

Other work: *Saint Hiroshima* (**1987**), associational.

KENNEDY, R.A. (? -?) UK metaphysical writer whose curious sf work, written as by "The Author of Space and Spirit" is *The Triuneverse: A Scientific Romance* (**1912**). Set in the future, after the destruction of Mars and other events, it has only a thin narrative, being mainly taken up with cosmological speculations about the fabric of the Universe. [JC]

See also: COSMOLOGY; GREAT AND SMALL; LIVING WORLDS.

KENT, BRAD House name used on 4 routine sf adventures published by CURTIS WARREN, 3 by Dennis HUGHES and *Out of the Silent Places* (**1952**) by Maurice G(aspard) Hugi (1904-1947). [JC]

KENT, KELVIN Pseudonym used on the **Pete Manx** series in *Thrilling Wonder Stories* (1939-44), individually by Arthur K. BARNES (4 stories) and Henry KUTTNER (6 stories), and on the 2 they wrote in collaboration: "Roman Holiday" (1939) and "Science is Golden" (1940). [PN]

KENT, MALLORY [s] ◊ Robert A.W. LOWNDES.

KENT, PHILIP ◊ Kenneth BULMER.

KENTON, L.P. ◊ R. Lionel FANTHORPE.

KENWARD, JAMES (MACARA) (1908-) UK author, mostly of nonfiction studies and memoirs. *Summervale* (**1935**) is a tale in which a man is transformed into a dog. The framing narrative of *The Story of the Poor Author* (coll of linked stories **1959**) is sf; it involves SPACESHIPS. [JC]

KENYON, ROBERT O. [s] ◊ Henry KUTTNER.

KEPLER, JOHANNES (1571-1630) German astronomer, one-time assistant to Tycho Brahe (1546-1601) and later imperial mathematician and astrologer to the Holy Roman Emperor Rudolph II. JK's contribution to ASTRONOMY – most notably his 3 laws of planetary motion – provided vital groundwork for Newton's cosmological synthesis. In 1593 JK prepared a dissertation on the heliocentric theory, which explained how events in the heavens would be seen by an observer stationed on the MOON; a new draft, in which the observer is conveniently placed on the Moon by a demon conjured up by his mother, was prepared in 1609 (the manuscript was stolen in 1611 and JK later had to defend his own mother against an accusation of witchcraft, a charge which may have been encouraged by the literary device). Between 1620 and 1630 he annotated the essay extensively, but he died while it was being prepared for publication; it finally appeared as *Somnium* (**1634** in Latin; definitive trans in *Kepler's "Somnium"* by Edward Rosen **1967**; a cut trans had earlier appeared in *Beyond Time and Space*, anth **1950** ed August W. DERLETH). The last section constructs a hypothetical ECOLOGY for the Moon, a significant pioneering exercise in the imagination of LIFE ON OTHER WORLDS. [BS]

See also: BIOLOGY; COSMOLOGY; FANTASTIC VOYAGES; GERMANY; HISTORY OF SF; PROTO SCIENCE FICTION; SPACE FLIGHT.

KEPPEL-JONES, ARTHUR (MERVYN) (1909-) South African-born writer, in Canada from 1959, whose *When Smuts Goes: A History of South Africa from 1952 to 2010* (**1947**) takes a gloomy view of the apartheid-ridden future of that country. It is a respectable – though minor – contribution to the future-HISTORY genre. [JC]

See also: POLITICS.

KERN, GREGORY ◊ E.C. TUBB.

KERR, MICHAEL ◊ Robert HOSKINS.

KERSH, GERALD (1911-1968) Russian-born UK writer, active from the mid-1930s, very prolific in shorter forms; known mainly for such work outside the sf field as *Night and the City* (**1938**) and *They Die with their Boots Clean* (**1941**). Many of his numerous short stories are sf or fantasy, and had their original book appearance in collections such as *The Horrible Dummy and Other Stories* (coll **1944**), *Neither Man nor Dog* (coll **1946**), *Sad Road to the Sea* (coll **1947**), *The Brighton Monster* (coll **1953**), *Men without Bones* (coll **1955** UK; with differing contents, rev 1962 US), *The Ugly Face of Love* (coll **1960**), *The Terribly Wild Flowers* (coll **1962**) and *The Hospitality of Miss Tolliver* (coll **1965**). Two US compilations, *On an Odd Note* (coll **1958** US) and *Nightshade and Damnations* (coll **1968** US), the latter ed Harlan ELLISON, conveniently abstract some of GK's fantasies and sf from his other short stories, which often take the shape of anecdotes told to a narrator (sometimes identified as GK himself), so that much of his work tends to verge upon the tall-tale or CLUB-STORY genre; *The Best of Gerald Kersh* (coll **1960**) is more general. In "Whatever Happened to Corporal

Cuckoo?" (1953) the corporal tells GK of his 500 years of soldier life following a mysterious cure given to him about 1537 (◊ IMMORTALITY). "Voices in the Dust of Annan" (1947) is a post-HOLOCAUST tale starring fairies. In "Men without Bones" a tropical explorer tells us of a species of loathsome invertebrates, adding the hypothesis that we are really Martians.

GK's novels are perhaps less impressive. *The Weak and the Strong* (**1945**) grotesquely carries its cast – trapped underground – into claustrophobic fantasy realms, and *An Ape, a Dog, and a Serpent: A Fantastic Novel* (**1945**) fabulates a history of film-making with borderline sf elements. *The Great Wash* (**1953**; vt *The Secret Masters* 1953 US) is an sf novel in which the usual narrator – GK – becomes gradually involved in a plot to inundate most of the world and to rule the remains on authoritarian lines. The subplot of *Brock* (**1969**) revolves around a new form of nuclear explosive. But GK's strengths as an author are everywhere evident: a strong and vivid sense of character, a colourful style and a capacity to infuse his stories with a deep emotional charge (sometimes sentimentalized). He has strong admirers. [JC]

See also: HORROR IN SF; HUMOUR.

KESHISHIAN, JOHN M. (1923-   ) US doctor of medicine and writer whose sf novel, with Jacob HAY (*whom see for details*), is *Autopsy for a Cosmonaut* (**1969**; vt *Death of a Cosmonaut* 1970 UK). [JC]

KESSEL, JOHN (JOSEPH VINCENT) (1950-   ) US academic and writer who began publishing sf with "The Silver Man" for *Galileo* in 1978, and whose short fiction rapidly established him as an author of cunningly pastiche-heavy, erudite stories. His two best known early tales – both assembled with other work in *Meetings in Infinity: Allegories & Extrapolations* (coll **1992**) – are probably "Not Responsible! Park and Lock It!" (1981) and *Another Orphan* (1982 *FSF*; **1989** chap dos), which won a NEBULA in 1983; in both, an urgent extremism of metaphor tends to enforce allegorical readings. This extremism with the materials of genre sf also dominates much of JK's first novel, *Freedom Beach* (**1985**) with James Patrick KELLY, a tale whose characters find themselves occupying allegorical venues construed according to the styles of various authors, from Aristophanes to Groucho Marx. Of greater interest, perhaps, is his first solo novel, *Good News from Outer Space* (fixup **1989**), a sustained but dizzying look at the human animal as the millennium approaches, identity crises eat into men and women, the dead are medically reawoken, and dreams of redeeming ALIENS raddle the large cast. There are echoes of Philip K. DICK, but a gonzo Dick, and of Barry N. MALZBERG's allegorized urban desolation (and black wit) – but JK's desolation, very frighteningly and very movingly, is populous with human faces, however fractured. JK seems to be one of the writers capable of bending the tools of sf inward upon the human psyche. [JC]

See also: END OF THE WORLD; *The* MAGAZINE OF FANTASY AND SCIENCE FICTION.

KESTEVEN, G.R. Pseudonym of UK teacher and writer Geoffrey Robins Corsher (1911-   ), some of whose stories for children have been published under his own name. Of sf interest is *The Pale Invaders* (**1974**), a post-HOLOCAUST tale set in the FAR FUTURE and describing the impact upon an isolated valley culture of the discovery of technologies which reveal much hitherto hidden history. *The Awakening Water* (**1977**) has less impact. [JC]

KETTERER, DAVID (ANTHONY THEODOR) (1942-   ) UK-born Canadian academic (with a DPhil from the University of Sussex) based at Concordia University, Montreal. His *New Worlds for Old: The Apocalyptic Imagination, Science Fiction, and American Literature* (**1974**) interestingly, though in rather academic terminology, links apocalyptic themes in US MAINSTREAM literature with similar obsessions in genre sf. *The Rationale of Deception in Poe* (**1979**) covers the whole of Edgar Allan POE's writing, including the PROTO SCIENCE FICTION; a briefer work on Poe is *Edgar Allan Poe: Life, Work, and Criticism* (chap **1989**). *Frankenstein's Creation: The Book, the Monster, and Human Reality* (**1979**) is another of DK's later works which, to a degree, enlarge on the thesis of his first. DK's critical work is widely respected and by no means "one-note", but it does often return to the idea of "metaphorical transcendence". *The Science Fiction of Mark Twain* (coll **1984**) ed DK contains 120pp of Introduction and critical apparatus. DK attracted much attention with *Imprisoned in a Tesseract: The Life and Work of James Blish* (**1987**). An important new work is *Canadian Science Fiction and Fantasy* (**1992**), a critical and historical survey with bibliography. [PN]

See also: CANADA; CRITICAL AND HISTORICAL WORKS ABOUT SF; DEFINITIONS OF SF; SENSE OF WONDER; WOMEN AS PORTRAYED IN SCIENCE FICTION.

KETTLE, LEROY [r] ◊ John BROSNAN.

KETTLE, (JOCELYN) PAMELA (1934-   ) UK writer, author of a historical novel, *Memorial to the Duchess* (**1968**) as by Jocelyn Kettle, and of the sf novel *The Day of the Women* (**1969**), in which sex-role reversal is instituted – and deplored. [JC]

KEY, ALEXANDER (HILL) (1904-1979) US writer who began publishing novels for children with *The Red Eagle* (**1930**), and who moved into CHILDREN'S SF with the **Sprockets** sequence: *Sprockets: A Little Robot* (**1963**), *Rivets and Sprockets* (**1964**) and *Bolts – A Robot Dog* (**1966**). These books were not likely, however, to seize a wide audience, and it was only with the **Witch Mountain** sequence – *Escape to Witch Mountain* (**1968**) and *Return from Witch Mountain* * (**1978**) – that AK's easy sentimentality was attached to a narrative strong enough to bear it, as two orphan children on the run gradually come to realize that they are in fact ALIENS with powers (and memories) foreign to their ignorant hosts. Both stories were filmed by Walt Disney, in 1975 and 1978 respectively, both dir John Hough. An earlier alien orphaned on Earth had featured in *The Forgotten Door* (**1965**). Other singletons of interest include *The Golden Enemy* (**1969**), set thousands of

years hence when the descendants of the survivors of nuclear HOLOCAUST must face their human nature, and *Flight to the Lonesome Place* (**1971**), where a young mathematical genius flees his oppressors into a space to which only he can understand the route.   [JC]
Other works: *The Incredible Tide* (**1970**); *The Preposterous Adventures of Swimmer* (**1973**); *The Magic Meadow* (**1975**); *Jagger, the Dog from Elsewhere* (**1976**); *The Sword of Aradel* (**1977**); *The Case of the Vanishing Boy* (**1979**).
See also: SMALL PRESSES AND LIMITED EDITIONS; SUPERMAN.

KEY, EUGENE G(EORGE) (1907-   ) US author whose sf collection, *Mars Mountain* (coll **1936**), published by William L. CRAWFORD's semi-professional company Fantasy Publications, was the first full-length book to appear from any US publishing house specializing in sf, and so the precursor of great things to come. Otherwise the 3 stories assembled are unremarkable.   [JC]

KEYES, DANIEL (1927-   ) US writer and university lecturer in English. He began his sf career as associate editor of MARVEL SCIENCE FICTION, Feb-Nov 1951, and it was in that magazine that his first published story, "Precedent" appeared (1952). He is known mainly for one excellent novel, *Flowers for Algernon* (1959 *FSF*; exp **1966**), winner of a 1960 HUGO in its magazine form and of a 1966 NEBULA for the full-length book version, on which was based the film CHARLY (1968). It is the story, largely in the first person, of Charlie Gordon, whose INTELLIGENCE, starting at IQ 68, is artificially increased to genius level (◊ MEDICINE; SUPERMAN). The mouse Algernon has preceded him in this course, but Algernon soon dies, and Gordon's main contribution to science is his working out of the "Algernon-Gordon Effect", by which "artificially induced intelligence deteriorates at a rate of time directly proportional to the quantity of the increase". The last pages of the novel, detailing the loss of Charlie's faculties, are extremely moving. His treatment as an object of scientific curiosity throughout his ordeal underlines the book's points about deficiencies in the scientific method as applied to human beings. *The Touch* (**1968**; vt *The Contaminated Man* 1977 UK), a borderline-sf tale about the psychological consequences of an industrial accident involving radioactive contamination, has received less attention. After long silence, a new novel from DK was projected for the early 1990s.   [JC]
See also: ALIENS; CINEMA; CONCEPTUAL BREAKTHROUGH; *The* MAGAZINE OF FANTASY AND SCIENCE FICTION; NUCLEAR POWER; PSYCHOLOGY; RADIO.

KEYES, THOM (1943-   ) UK writer whose sf novels, *The Battle of Disneyland* (**1974**) and *The Second Coming* (**1979**), apply the tools of sf SATIRE, without excessive energy, to NEAR FUTURE USA.   [JC]

KEYHOE, DONALD E. [r] ◊ DR. YEN SIN; EARTH VS. THE FLYING SAUCERS; UFOS.

KEYNE, GORDON [s] ◊ H. BEDFORD-JONES.

KHAN, OBIE ◊ Robert E. VARDEMAN.

KIDD, (MILDRED) VIRGINIA (1921-   ) US literary agent and writer, married to James BLISH 1947-63,

who began to publish professionally in the early 1950s, writing at least 1 story with Blish; her first solo sf story, "Kangaroo Court", did not appear until much later, in *Orbit 1* (anth **1966**) ed Damon KNIGHT. She edited 3 strong ORIGINAL ANTHOLOGIES: *Millennial Women* (anth **1978**; vt *The Eye of the Heron, and Other Stories* 1980 UK), *Interfaces* (anth **1980**) with Ursula K. LE GUIN, and *Edges* (anth **1980**), also with Le Guin. As a literary agent from 1965, she became known for her FEMINIST views and – although she did not handle only WOMEN WRITERS – for representing a highly capable range of feminist authors, including Carol EMSHWILLER, Le Guin, Josephine SAXTON and James TIPTREE Jr.   [JC]

KILIAN, CRAWFORD (1941-   ) US-born writer, in Canada from 1967, who began publishing sf with *The Empire of Time* (**1978** US), the first volume of the **Chronoplane Wars** sequence. This sequence – which continued with *The Fall of the Republic* (**1987** US) and *Rogue Emperor: A Novel of the Chronoplane Wars* (**1988** US) – is dominated by the discovery in a savagely declining NEAR-FUTURE USA of the I-Screens, through which travel to a series of ALTERNATE WORLDS is possible. Each Earth is located uptime or downtime of our base reality but, ominously, uptime is uninhabitable, seemingly because of the effects of an alien INVASION; the protagonist gradually uncovers a seamy truth. Perhaps more interestingly, *Icequake* (**1979**) and its sequel *Tsunami* (**1983**) – the latter set in Vancouver – depict an Earth very much closer to home, with the ozone layer gone and the Antarctic icecap beginning to melt disastrously. *Eyas* (**1982**) moves into the very FAR FUTURE, where the eponymous primitive gingers his tribe into readiness for the dawn of a new age. *Brother Jonathan* (**1985** US) describes the effect of experiments which permit human-animal interfaces, these soon being invaded by AIS in typical CYBERPUNK fashion. *Lifter* (**1986** US) is a fairly unserious tale about ANTIGRAVITY and *Gryphon* (**1989** US) somewhat unadventurously deals with an alien invasion. CK's work can be analysed in terms of its Canadianness, its emphasis on themes of survival (◊ CANADA); but he slips too often into generic dogpaddling for this kind of analysis to be entirely fruitful.   [JC]
Other works: *Wonders, Inc.* (**1968**), a juvenile; *Greenmagic* (**1992**), a fantasy.

KILLDOZER Made-for-tv film (1974). Universal TV/ABC. Dir Jerry London, starring Clint Walker, Carl Betz, Neville Brand. Teleplay Richard Mackillop, Theodore STURGEON, based on Sturgeon's "Killdozer" (1944). 74 mins. Colour.

Though derived from Sturgeon's own well known story about a huge futuristic bulldozer that becomes possessed by an ALIEN force from outer space, this tv movie does not live up to its potential. The story is a tightly constructed description of the battle between the machine and a group of men on a Pacific island; the film pads this material out with clichéd emotional conflicts between the human characters.   [JB]

KILLOUGH, (KAREN) LEE (1942-   ) US writer and

Chief Technologist at the Department of Radiology, Kansas State University Veterinary Medical Teaching Hospital. She began publishing sf with "Caveat Emptor" for *ASF* in 1970, and since then has published about 30 stories, perhaps most notably the tales assembled as *Aventine* (coll of linked stories **1982**), set in an artist's colony in a decadent future whose resemblance to that depicted in J.G. BALLARD's *Vermilion Sands* (**1971** US) led some critics to brand it as merely derivative, though others accepted it as a homage. Her first novel, *A Voice out of Ramah* (**1979**) – set on a planet where 90 per cent of males are ritually slaughtered at puberty – is typical of much of her work in its plumping for unexceptionable presentations of various issues (FEMINISM in this case) while at the same time tending to stumble over the generic working-out of those presentations. *The Doppelgänger Gambit* (**1979**) and its sequels, *Spider Play* (**1986**) and *Dragon's Teeth* (**1990**), are police procedurals starring **Janna Brill and Mama Maxwell** and set in a USA that must be wary of COMPUTERS; and *Blood Hunt* (**1987**) and its sequel *Bloodlinks* (**1988**) are police-procedural fantasies dealing with a cop's confrontation of the fact that he has become a vampire. In both series there is a recurring sense that unexamined plots have tended to dominate proceedings. LK's singletons are various. *The Monitor, the Miners, and the Shree* (**1980**) amiably deals with the issue of human exploitation of alien planets. *Deadly Silents* (**1981**) again involves the police, though this time on another world. *The Leopard's Daughter* (**1987**) is a vibrant fantasy set in Africa. [JC]

Other work: *Liberty's World* (**1985**).

See also: ARTS; CRIME AND PUNISHMENT.

KILPI, VOLTER [r] ◊ FINLAND.

KILWORTH, GARRY (DOUGLAS) (1941-   ) UK writer who began to publish sf and fantasy stories and novels in the mid-1970s on retiring after 18 years' service as a cryptographer in the RAF; raised partly in Aden, he has travelled and worked in the Far East and the Pacific. He published his first sf story, "Let's Go to Golgotha", in *The Gollancz/Sunday Times Best Sf Stories* (anth **1975**), having won the associated competition, and some of his many stories have been assembled as *The Songbirds of Pain* (coll **1984**) and «In the Country of Tattooed Men» (coll **1993**); he has written novels as Garry Douglas. His first sf novel, *In Solitary* (**1977**), is set on an Earth whose few remaining humans have for over 400 years been dominated by birdlike ALIENS, and deals with a human rebellion whose moral impact is ambiguous; the novel is the first of several combining generic adventurousness – indeed opportunism, for GK seldom accords his full attention to the raw sf elements in his tales – and an identifiably English dubiety about the roots of human action. Consequences of such action in a GK novel are seldom simple, rarely flattering. *The Night of Kadar* (**1978**) places humans hatched from frozen embryos on an alien planet whose culture has an Islamic coloration, where they must attempt to understand

their own nature. *Split Second* (**1979**) similarly isolates a contemporary human in the mind of a Cro-Magnon. *Gemini God* (**1981**) again uses aliens to reflect the human condition. *A Theatre of Timesmiths* (**1984**) isolates a human society in an ice-enclosed city (◊ POCKET UNIVERSE) as computers fail and questions about the meaning of human life must be asked. *Cloudrock* (**1988**) pits brothers – GK often evokes kinship intimacies – against themselves and each other in a further pocket-universe setting. *Abandonati* (**1988**), set in a desolate NEAR-FUTURE London, reflects grittily upon the implications for the UK of the last decades of this century. GK's non-genre novels (see listing below) follow the same pattern; of them, *Witchwater Country* (**1986**), among his finest works, has autobiographical elements. At the end of the 1980s, in an apparent break with his sf career, he began to publish animal fantasies: *Hunter's Moon: A Story of Foxes* (**1989**; vt *The Foxes of First Dark* 1990 US), *Midnight's Sun: A Story of Wolves* (**1990**) and *Frost Dancers: A Story of Hares* (**1992**), in all of which he scrutinized nonhuman terrestrial life with an unblinking eye. Much of his short fiction is uneven; but in his novels GK has developed into an observer whose reports are both subtle and frank. [JC]

Other works: *Spiral Winds* (**1987**), *In the Hollow of the Deep-Sea Wave: A Novel and Seven Stories* (coll **1989**) and *Standing on Shamsan* (**1992**), all containing some fantasy elements; a juvenile series comprising *The Wizard of Woodworld* (**1987**) and *The Voyage of the Vigilance* (**1988**); *Trivial Tales* (coll **1988** chap); *The Rain Ghost* (**1989**), *Dark Hills, Hollow Clocks: Stories from the Otherworld* (coll **1990**), *The Drowners* (**1991**), a ghost story, and *The Third Dragon* (**1991**), associational, all juveniles.

As Garry Douglas: *Highlander* * (**1986**), a film novelization; *The Street* (**1988**), horror.

See also: INTERZONE; ISLANDS; MESSIAHS; RELIGION; TIME TRAVEL.

KIMBERLY, GAIL (1937-   ) US writer who began publishing work of genre interest with "The Prince and the Physician" for *Medical Opinion & Review* in 1969, and who has been moderately productive in short forms ever since. She has written young-adult adventure novels under the house name Dayle Courtney and a Gothic, *Secret of the Abbey* (**1980**) as by Alix Andre. Her sf novel is *Flyer* (**1975**), a meditative tale of an Earth occupied by MUTANTS who fly and swim. *Dracula Began* (**1976**) is horror. [JC]

KIMBRIEL, KATHARINE ELISKA (1956-   ) US writer whose work of sf interest – though she has published some fantasy stories – is restricted to the **Nuala** sequence: *Fire Sanctuary* (**1986**), *Fires of Nuala* (**1988**) and *Hidden Fires* (**1991**). Threatened by mutations (caused by high radioactivity in the planetary crust) and by intergalactic war, the inhabitants of the eponymous long-lost colony planet must cope with intrigues, spies, dynastic disputes and an extremely harsh climate. The plots are sometimes congested, but KEK's sense of local colour and her capacity to create genuinely engaging characters have made the sequence into something more than routine.   [JC]

KING, ALBERT [r] **or CHRISTOPHER** ◊ Paul CONRAD.

KING, JOHN ◊ Ernest L. MCKEAG.

KING, JOHN ROBERT (1948-   ) UK writer whose *Bruno Lipshitz and the Disciples of Dogma* (**1976**) rather uneasily juggles a number of ingredients in a complex plot: an ALIEN invasion, a strange RELIGION, interpersonal conflicts and dollops of adventure.   [JC]

KING, PAULA ◊ Paula E. DOWNING.

KING, STEPHEN (1947-   ) US writer of HORROR fiction. With over 80 million books in print already – his first book was published less than 20 years ago – he is probably the most successful bestseller novelist in history; the example of his success has revolutionized the horror-fiction business, which is considerably more flourishing in 1990 than it was in 1975.

At first he was attracted to sf, beginning with the unpublished novel «The Aftermath» (written when he was 16) and, commercially, with "The Glass Floor" for *Startling Mystery Stories* in 1967. *Night Shift* (coll **1978**) collects much of his early short fiction, his main market then being *Cavalier*; it includes some grisly sf in the pulp style. He was perhaps diverted from a conventional sf career by the response of Donald A. WOLLHEIM to his first novel submission: "We here at Ace Books are not interested in negative Utopias."

SK has since concentrated on horror/fantasy with occasional sf grounding, as exemplified by the focus on PSI POWERS, notably TELEKINESIS, in his first published novel, *Carrie* (**1974**), successfully filmed as CARRIE (1976). Other paranormal talents feature in *The Dead Zone* (**1979**) (precognition) and *Firestarter* (**1980**) (pyrokinesis), both also filmed (◊ *The* DEAD ZONE and FIRESTARTER). While SK does not have the analytical approach of the HARD-SF writer, and is not especially interested in "explanations" of his GOTHIC creations, he has a down-to-earth quality which gives even his purely supernatural fiction a true sf "feel"; he eschews the nebulous; he describes and specifies with some exactness.

Under his own name SK has written two further novels which are sf by any measure (though both incorporate elements from other genres). The earlier and better is *The Stand* (abridged from manuscript **1978**; with text largely restored, rev **1990** UK), a long and intelligent story of the HOLOCAUST AND AFTER in the USA, beginning with the accidental release of a germ-warfare virus by the US military; in the second half of the book a supernatural struggle between powers of light and darkness weakens the impact from an sf point of view, but the novel remains a very superior example of its genre, clearly owing something to George R. STEWART's *Earth Abides* (**1949**), but not imitative of it. *The Tommyknockers* (**1987**) is gothic horror dressed in sf clothes, a lurid, eminently readable tale of an alien SPACESHIP buried for millions of years and now dug up, and of the effects it has on people nearby: sudden technological brilliance, physiological changes and a melding into a group mind.

The Talisman (**1984**), with Peter Straub, is an uneasy collaboration in which two very strong individual voices seem to muffle one another; primarily a fantasy quest, it uses the sf device of PARALLEL WORLDS, as does the ongoing **Dark Tower** fantasy series by SK alone: to date *The Dark Tower: The Gunslinger* (**198?**), *#2: The Drawing of the Three* (**1987**) and *#3: The Waste Lands* (**1991**); different in tone from most of SK's work – and perhaps more demandingly inventive than usual – these have an undeniable mythic charge, partly because of the alienated-adolescent theme that runs through them. As the series continues, and especially in the third volume, it has looked more like sf and less like pure FANTASY, both in its post-holocaust imagery and in its use of a self-aware AI as a major threat to the protagonists.

SK wrote four early novels (the first three before *Carrie* came out) subsequently published as paperback originals as by Richard Bachman: *Rage* (**1977**), *The Long Walk* (**1979**), *Roadwork* (**1981**), and *The Running Man* (**1982**). Shortly after the publication of a fifth, *Thinner* (**1984**), Bachman's cover was blown, and an omnibus edition of the first four out-of-print Bachman titles was published as *The Bachman Books: Four Early Novels by Stephen King* (omni **1985**; vt *The Bachman Books: Four Novels by Stephen King* UK). *The Long Walk* and *The Running Man* are both fringe sf about futuristic sadistic sports events, the first a marathon walk where those who fall behind are shot, the second duelling to the death as a tv game show; the latter was filmed as *The* RUNNING MAN (1987).

It is generally held that most films based on SK's novels, stories and original screenplays are poor. In fact *Carrie*, *The Shining* (1980), *The Dead Zone* (1983), *Cujo* (1983), *Stand By Me* (1986) and *Misery* (1990) are all strong films, although SK dislikes the second. Fantasy/horror films aside from those already mentioned are *Salem's Lot* (tv miniseries 1979), *Creepshow* (1982), *Christine* (1983), *Cat's Eye* (1984), *Children of the Corn* (1984), *Silver Bullet* (1985), *Creepshow II* (1987), *Pet Sematary* (1989), *Graveyard Shift* (1990) and *It* (tv miniseries 1990). *Return to Salem's Lot* (1987) dir Larry COHEN is "based on characters created by Stephen King". *Tales from the Darkside: The Movie* (1990), an anthology film based on the tv series of the same name, contains an adaptation of SK's "The Cat from Hell" (1977). SK rightly repudiated the sf film *The* LAWNMOWER MAN (1992), allegedly based on a short story by him, as having nothing to do with his work, and won a lawsuit demanding that his name be removed from the credits. He wrote an original screenplay for the horror film *Sleepwalkers* (1992; vt *Stephen King's Sleepwalkers*).

One film adaptation of a story by SK – "Trucks" (1973) – was directed by King himself from his own screenplay: *Maximum Overdrive* (1986). Though not as bad as some critics stated, it flopped commercially. Technically sf, it has Earth passing through the tail of a comet that mysteriously gives self-awareness to MACHINES (trucks, lawnmowers, hairdryers, electric carving knives, etc.), which then revolt against humans. This paranoid fantasy is crudely made with very broad stereotypes, but at least one sequence, of a boy cycling through a quiet township littered with bodies, suggests latent cinematic talent.

SK's occasional critical commentaries, the reverse of academic in style, are usually observant and interesting. *Danse Macabre* (**1981**), a study of horror in books, films and comics, won a HUGO for Best Nonfiction Book in 1982.

SK's pungent prose, his sharp ear for dialogue, his disarmingly laid-back, frank style, along with his passionately fierce denunciations of human stupidity and cruelty (especially to CHILDREN), put him among the more distinguished of "popular" writers. [PN]
Other works: *'Salem's Lot* (**1975**); *The Shining* (**1977**); *The Monkey* (**1980** chap); *Cujo* (**1981**); *The Raft* (**1982** chap); *The Plant* (**1982** chap); *Creepshow* (coll **1982**); *Different Seasons* (coll **1982**); *Pet Sematary* (**1983**), one of SK's finest works; *Christine* (**1983**; text differs slightly in UK edition); *Cycle of the Werewolf* (**1983**; exp as coll with film screenplay "Silver Bullet" **1985**); *The Eyes of the Dragon* (**1984**; rev 1987); *Skeleton Crew* (coll **1985**; exp by 1 story 1985); *It* (**1986**; the 1st edn was the German translation as *Es* [**1986**]); *Misery* (**1987**); *My Pretty Pony* (**1988** chap); *Dolan's Cadillac* (**1989** chap); *The Dark Half* (**1989** UK); *Four Past Midnight* (coll **1990**); *Needful Things* (**1991**); *Gerald's Game* (**1992**).
Nonfiction includes: *Nightmares in the Sky* (**1988**), a book of photographs by "F-Stop Fitzgerald" with minimal contribution by SK; *Bare Bones: Conversations on Terror with Stephen King* (coll **1988**); *Feast of Fear: Conversations with Stephen King* (coll **1989**).
About the author: *Fear Itself: The Horror Fiction of Stephen King* (coll **1982**) ed Tim UNDERWOOD and Chuck MILLER; *Stephen King: The Art of Darkness* (**1984**; rev 1986) by Douglas E. Winter; *The Stephen King Companion* (coll **1989**) ed George Beahm; many others, including at least 10 from STARMONT HOUSE.
See also: CINEMA; CLICHÉS; DISASTER; DISCOVERY AND INVENTION; EC COMICS; ESP; FRANCE; INTELLIGENCE; MEDIA LANDSCAPE; MUSIC.

KING, T(HOMAS) JACKSON (Jr) (1948-) US archaeologist and writer, married to Paula E. DOWNING. He began publishing sf with his first novel, *Retread Shop* (**1988**), a somewhat congested but pleasingly vivid tale of the upbringing of a young human in the SPACE HABITAT of the title, and of his complicated dealings with alien merchants and crises of various sorts. The energy of the telling constitutes a forecast of much further work. [JC]
KING, VINCENT Pseudonym of UK writer, artist and teacher Rex Thomas Vinson (1935-), who worked in Cornwall and began publishing sf with "Defence Mechanism" for *New Writings in SF No 9* (anth **1966**) ed E.J. CARNELL. His more successful novels, like *Light a Last Candle* (**1969** US) and *Candy Man* (**1971** US), tend to combine elements of epic and grotesque sf adventure with a characteristically English darkness of emotional colouring and a tendency towards down-

beat conclusions. [JC]
Other works: *Another End* (**1971** US); *Time Snake and Superclown* (**1976**).

KINGDOM OF THE SPIDERS Film (1977). Arachnid Productions/Dimension. Dir John "Bud" Cardos, starring William SHATNER, Tiffany Bolling, Woody Strode. Screenplay Richard Robinson, Alan Caillou, from a story by Jeffrey M. Sneller, Stephen Lodge. 95 mins, cut to 90 mins. Colour.

In its modest way, this is one of the better films in the revenge-of-Nature cycle (◊ MONSTER MOVIES). Near a small town in Arizona, tarantulas whose ECOLOGY has undergone changes because of crop-dusting sprays are migrating north in large numbers and apparently acting with communal intelligence (◊ HIVE-MINDS). Starting small and building to local apocalypse, the film is crisply made, the masses of spiders (normal size) are believable, and the end, though clearly echoing Hitchcock's *The* BIRDS (1963), offers a genuine minatory thrill with its vision of a whole town cocooned in spider-silk, its occupants now preserved as food. Shatner plays the vet trying to puzzle out why the normally solitary spiders are acting in concert. [PN]
KING-HALL, LOU Working name of UK writer Louise (variously Luise) Olga Elisabeth King-Hall (1897-), whose *Fly Envious Time* (**1944**) posits a NEAR-FUTURE world in which eugenics dominates and women have achieved full equality; WWIII follows rather rapidly, in 1999. Her brother was Stephen KING-HALL. [JC]
KING-HALL, (WILLIAM) STEPHEN (RICHARD) (1893-1966) UK naval officer, writer and politician; brother of Lou KING-HALL. His military experiences (1914-29) influenced his work as a writer, especially the long series of admonitory newsletters he published from 1936 for 30 years, first as the *K-H News Service* and later under other names. *Posterity* (**1927** chap), a play, is fantasy; it appears also in *Three Plays and a Plaything* (coll **1933**) along with "The Republican Princess", a RURITANIAN spoof. In *Post-War Pirate* (**1931**) a submarine uses a newly invented gas to disable shipping. *Bunga-Bunga* (**1932**) is a SATIRE set on an ISLAND where anything is permitted. *Number 10 Downing Street* (**1948**), a play which depicts an occupied UK, takes place in the mid-1950s. His last novel, *Men of Destiny* (**1960**; vt *Moment of No Return* 1961 US), is again set in the NEAR FUTURE. [JC]
KING KONG 1. Film (1933). RKO. Dir Merian C. Cooper, Ernest B. Schoedsack, starring Fay Wray, Robert Armstrong, Bruce Cabot. Screenplay James A. Creelman, Ruth Rose, from a story by Cooper, with credit also given to Edgar WALLACE. Special effects designed and supervised by Willis H. O'BRIEN. 100 mins. B/w.

The classic MONSTER MOVIE. On a remote island inhabited by unfriendly natives and prehistoric MONSTERS, of which the most powerful is a giant APE called Kong, a young actress (Wray) from a visiting film unit is kidnapped by tribesmen and offered to Kong, a gift which he eagerly accepts. She is rescued and Kong is captured and taken to New York, where he is exhibited, escapes, rampages, recaptures the girl (for whom he appears to cherish strong feelings), and makes a last defiant stand on top of the Empire State Building before being machine-gunned down by a squadron of biplanes.

Although *KK* is an early film, its special effects are still very convincing today, many being the product of the technique of stop-motion photography that had been pioneered by O'Brien in *The* LOST WORLD (1925). The classic status of *KK*, which has become one of the great mythopoeic works of the 20th century, has probably to do with the ambiguous feelings – much as with its fairy-tale model, "Beauty and the Beast" – created by the film towards Kong himself: terror at his savagery; admiration for his strength, naturalness and effortless regality in his primeval surroundings; and pity for his squalid end – the most memorable of all cinematic images of Nature destroyed in the CITY. This ending is also an image of the great destroyed by the small: the humans are dwarfed by the ape and indeed by the city they have created, a feeling emphasized by the ambience of the Great Depression, with a bored, impoverished populace ready to grasp at any ersatz marvel but panicking when it finds itself faced with the real thing. Yet another polarity is that of innocence destroyed by sophistication, a feeling enhanced by the crucial story-element of Kong's capture being to do with the shooting of a movie. The narrative moves with élan, and the film has been almost as popular with critics as with the general public.

The disappointing sequel was SON OF KONG (1933). Another Willis O'Brien giant ape, not quite so big, starred in MIGHTY JOE YOUNG (1949; vt *Mr Joseph Young of Africa*).

2. Film (1976). Dino De Laurentiis/Paramount. Dir John Guillermin, starring Jessica Lange, Jeff Bridges, Charles Grodin, Ed Lauter. Screenplay Lorenzo Semple Jr, based on the 1933 screenplay. 134 mins. Colour.

In this lavish and heavily publicized remake, it is an oil-company executive who leads the expedition to Kong's island. Kong is taken back to the USA in an oil supertanker. His last stand is on top of the World Trade Center, and he is shot dead by a group of helicopter gunships.

This version did not use model animation and was therefore more restricted – and indeed more primitive – in its effects: most shots of Kong show a man in an ape suit. The original set-piece battles between Kong and prehistoric monsters are gone. The vigorous narrative of the original is here slowed down by didactic, moralizing scenes in a manner which suggests that the new Hollywood has a much lower opinion of the intelligence of the public than the old one did. The delicate balance of the original between pity and terror is here shifted towards pity, and Kong is softened. Tragedy becomes at best pathos, yet

many scenes remain moving, and the startlingly vulgar heroine (now feminist and tough, no longer a limp screamer) has a more interesting role than her original. In a flurry of self-contradiction, *KK* seems designed to be spoof, tragedy, nostalgia-epic, spectacle and allegory about "the rape of the environment by big business" – all rolled into one.   [JB/PN]

See also: CINEMA; GREAT AND SMALL; LOST WORLDS.

KING KONG TAI GOJIRA ◊ GOJIRA.

KING KONG VS. GODZILLA ◊ GOJIRA.

KINGSBURY, DONALD (MacDONALD) (1929-   ) US-born academic and writer, in Canada from 1948, a teacher of mathematics at McGill University from 1956 until his retirement in 1986. He began publishing sf with "Ghost Town" for *ASF* in 1952; although he produced relatively little for nearly 30 years, his intermittent appearances in *ASF*, with both fiction and nonfiction, were generally noticed. What could not have been noted – because of the sparseness of his production and the wide-ranging nature of his underlying construct – was that almost everything he wrote shared a common future HISTORY, somewhere into the middle of which his first novel, *Courtship Rite* (**1982** US; vt *Geta* 1984 UK), fitted smoothly; indeed, the polished sweep and exuberance of this large epic PLANETARY ROMANCE must have owed something to DK's long familiarity with its sustaining Universe. The planet Geta is a venue which amply contains: several warring cultures for whom all aspects of life are agonistic; complicated group marriages; an elaborate ethical and ecological justification of cannibalism in a world of terrible scarcity (◊ ECOLOGY); and the highly productive worship of a God in the sky (in fact, in a standby orbit, the starship that seeded the world) who rewards worship by raining down computer chips full of precious data. The plot, involving the forced courtship of a woman from another culture by members of a group marriage, is perhaps less convincing than the background; but the pace is sufficient to intrigue and to engage even those readers who might be dubious about the Libertarian assumptions underlying certain elements of the unrelenting agons of Geta.

DK's second novel, *The Moon Goddess and the Son* (1979 *ASF*; exp **1986**), is set so early in his Future History that the NEAR-FUTURE setting of certain parts of the tale seems directly extrapolative of current thinking about space technologies. The HARD-SF arguments, about the design and construction of space stations capable of grappling space freighters into dock, are as gripping as this sort of narrative can sometimes be; and later sections, featuring the eponymous Diana a generation or so further on, adequately point a way forward into romance. A third novel, "The Survivor", forms the bulk of *Man-Kzin Wars IV* ∗ (anth **1991**) in the Larry NIVEN **Man-Kzin Wars** SHARED-WORLD enterprise; it is bleak and exorbitant, and constitutes a self-sufficient tale.

DK is a writer whose energy is conspicuous, and

whose imagined Universe does not lack ambition. At the time of writing, further connective tissue is still wanting, but can be hoped for. [JC]

See also: ANTHROPOLOGY; CANADA; GODS AND DEMONS.

KING-SIZE PUBLICATIONS ◊ FANTASTIC UNIVERSE.

KINGSMILL, HUGH Working name of UK writer and anthologist Hugh Kingsmill Lunn (1899-1949), who remains best known for *An Anthology of Invective and Abuse* (anth **1929**). *The Dawn's Delay* (coll **1924**) contains "The End of the World", of interest for its vision of a Solar System populated by various species, and "W.J.", about a future WAR in 1966-72. *The Return of William Shakespeare* (**1929**) presents within a sketchy sf frame the thoughts and activities of a Shakespeare reconstituted in the 20th century (◊ ARTS; REINCARNATION). In revised form both of these volumes were assembled as *The Dawn's Delay* (omni **1948**). With Malcolm Muggeridge (1903-1990), HK wrote two SATIRES rendering NEAR-FUTURE doings in the form of newspaper stories: *Brave Old World: A Mirror for The Times* (**1936**) and *Next Year's News* (**1938**). A much-loved figure, HK appears in novels and reminiscences of writers like William GERHARDI and Lance SIEVEKING. [JC]

See also: END OF THE WORLD; SUN.

KINGSTON, JEREMY 1. Full name Jeremy Hervey Spencer Kingston (1931-   ), UK writer, mostly of plays. His novel, *Love Among the Unicorns* (**1968**), a surreal fantasy set in South America, features a LOST WORLD.

2. Pseudonym under which John Gregory BETAN-COURT wrote *Robert Silverberg's Time Tours #6: Caesar's Time Legion* * (**1991**). [JC]

KINROSS, ALBERT (1870-1929) UK writer in various genres whose *The Fearsome Island* (**1896**), most of which takes the form of a recently discovered 16th-century manuscript, describes its protagonist's experiences after being shipwrecked on an unknown ISLAND full of alarms and delights – including a huge mechanical man, an ominous castle which has many perilous marvels, and a Caliban-like native. The maker of all this, it turns out, is a cruel Spanish inventor who left his homeland long ago on a pre-Columbian expedition to the Americas. Some of the stories in *Within the Radius* (coll **1901**) are sf. [JC]

KINVIG UK tv series (1981). London Weekend Television. Created and written by Nigel KNEALE. Prod and dir Les Chatfield; starring Tony Haygarth, Patsy Rowlands, Colin Jeavons, Prunella Gee. 7 25min episodes. Colour.

This most recent of Kneale's many sf plays and series for tv was a sitcom, fuelled apparently by a certain animus against sf FANDOM, about two lunatic fans living seedy urban lives, one of whom (Haygarth) has a fat wife (Rowlands) and a fat dog, and is entranced by an ALIEN from Mercury (Gee) in the guise of a beautiful customer at his electrical repair shop. He has adventures with her (she wearing a variety of sexy catsuits) and helps ward off an INVASION of Earth by the alien Xux. The scripts lacked the precision required for decent farce, and the invasive canned laughter did not help. Kneale's belief that sf fans are typologically identical with UFO cultists, and that both have an obsessive need for alien glamour to lighten their ghastly lives, was offensive to some viewers. [PN]

KIPLING, ARTHUR WELLESLEY (?   -   ) UK author, possibly pseudonymous, of 2 future-WAR novels. *The New Dominion* (**1908**) pits the USA triumphantly against Japan and *The Shadow of Glory* (**1910**) visualizes a worldwide conflict, mainly naval. [JC]

KIPLING, (JOSEPH) RUDYARD (1865-1936) UK poet, short-story writer and novelist, known mainly for such works outside the sf field as *Plain Tales from the Hills* (coll **1888** India) and *Kim* (**1901**). He won the Nobel Prize for Literature in 1907. Before the age of 27, RK wrote a considerable number of stories containing elements of fantasy and horror. Some, like "The Strange Ride of Morrowbie Jukes" (1885), are to be found in *The Phantom 'Rickshaw, and Other Tales* (coll **1888** India; rev 1890 UK), the title story of which is also fantasy; others appear in *Life's Handicap, Being Stories of Mine Own People* (coll **1891**) and *Many Inventions* (coll **1893**), which includes "The Lost Legion" (1892). *The Brushwood Boy* (1895; **1899** chap) is fantasy, as are the various linked and unlinked stories assembled in *The Jungle Book* (coll **1894**) and *The Second Jungle Book* (coll **1895**), while *Just So Stories for Little Children* (coll **1902**) contains classic children's fables. *"They"* (**1905** chap) is a ghost story. *Puck of Pook's Hill* (coll **1906**) and its sequel, *Rewards and Fairies* (coll **1910**), contain a series of stories about the formation and growth of Britain as told by Puck to two children. In several of his late stories, all of which are complex, elliptic, highly crafted and deeply pessimistic, RK made some ambiguous use of supernatural principles of explanation; of these, "A Madonna of the Trenches" and "The Wish House", both from 1924, are assembled along with "The Gardener" in *Debits and Credits* (coll **1926**), which has a claim to being his finest collection. These tales are not comfortably amenable to either sf or fantasy reading, but they demonstrate the power of hinted supernatural themes in writing of high virtuosity. *The Complete Supernatural Stories of Rudyard Kipling* (coll **1987**) conveniently assembles this category of his output, as does «John Brunner Presents Kipling's Fantasy» (coll 1992) ed John BRUNNER. *Thy Servant a Dog: Told by Boots* (**1930** chap), not included in either collection, is an animal fantasy of almost perverse fervour.

Sf proper appears infrequently in RK's work, though "The Finest Story in the World" (1891), whose protagonist reflects on previous incarnations, and "A Matter of Fact" (1892), about a modern sea-serpent sighting – both assembled in *Many Inventions* – are arguably sf, as are "The Ship that Found Herself" (1895) and "007" (1897) from *The Day's Work* (coll **1898**). Other early tales include "Wireless" (1902; in

Traffics and Discoveries [coll **1904**]), in which amateur-radio experiments make communication possible between a shop assistant and John Keats; "The House Surgeon", in *Actions and Reactions* (coll **1909**), explains a ghost in terms of PSI POWERS; "In the Same Boat" (1911), in *A Diversity of Creatures* (coll **1917**), suggests a prenatal cause for bouts of irrational dread; "The Eye of Allah", in *Debits and Credits*, describes the ALTERNATE HISTORY that is almost generated when a microscope falls into the hands of medieval English churchmen; and "Unprofessional" (1930), assembled in *Limits and Renewals* (coll **1932**), suggests that planetary "tides" may affect human tissue.

RK's most notable and unmistakably sf stories are perhaps *With the Night Mail: A Story of 2000 A.D.* (1905 *McClure's Magazine*; **1909** chap US) and its sequel, "As Easy as A.B.C." (1912), which was collected in *A Diversity of Creatures*. Both tales revolve about the Aerial Board of Control, or A.B.C., which dominates the world. The first is a dramatized travelogue, depicting some incidents on a dirigible journey from London to Québec, and is accompanied by an appendix of futuristic advertisements; in the second – a somewhat DYSTOPIAN vision of centralized government probably based on Wellsian models – agents of the A.B.C. fly to Chicago to deal with a revolt of the local underclass, whose demands for a return of democracy have generated attacks by the rest of the population. The A.B.C. – though not necessarily the political views it stands for – has influenced writers as far apart as Michael ARLEN and Rex WARNER. Although its reprint of *With the Night Mail* is incomplete, «John Brunner Presents Kipling's Science Fiction» (coll 1992) ed John Brunner is otherwise thorough in its coverage of this part of RK's work.

Although RK was not an sf writer by inclination, his intense, somewhat feverish talent makes even the least characteristic of his works of more than peripheral interest to the sf reader. [JC]

About the author: Literature on RK is extensive. Charles Carrington's *Rudyard Kipling* (**1955**) is the definitive biography, while J.M.S. Tompkins's *The Art of Rudyard Kipling* (**1959**) very competently surveys both prose and poetry. RK's own posthumous, sanitized autobiographical fragment, *Something of Myself* (**1937**), is of some interest. Angus WILSON's *The Strange Ride of Rudyard Kipling* (**1977**) combines biography and criticism in a sustained, intense study. Also interesting is *Rudyard Kipling and his World* (**1977**) by Kingsley AMIS.

See also: APES AND CAVEMEN (IN THE HUMAN WORLD); DISCOVERY AND INVENTION; HISTORY OF SF; PREDICTION; TRANSPORTATION.

KIPPAX, JOHN Pseudonym of UK writer John Charles Hynam (1915-1974). He was a regular contributor to the UK sf magazines during 1955-61, publishing over 30 stories in that time. His first two stories appeared in Dec 1954: "Dimple" in *Science Fantasy* and "Trojan Hearse" in *NW*. The latter was a collaboration with Dan MORGAN, with whom he also published a SPACE-OPERA series – *A Thunder of Stars* (**1968**), *Seed of Stars* (**1972** US), *The Neutral Stars* (**1973** US) and, by JK alone, *Where No Stars Guide* (**1975**) – about the Space Corps team of the *Venturer Twelve*. [JC]

KIRBY, JACK (1917-   ) US comic-book illustrator, born Jacob Kurtzberg. One of the giants in the COMICS industry, he began his 50+-year career in 1935 working on newspaper comic strips (with a break in 1936, animating **Popeye** cartoons for Max Fleischer). He later broke into the comic-book field, creating **Captain America** with Joe Simon in 1941 for Timely Comics (later MARVEL COMICS); he also worked on CAPTAIN MARVEL. His main claim to fame, however, was his work in the 1960s for Marvel Comics, by then under the direction of Stan LEE. In 1961 JK created **The Fantastic Four** (a group of SUPERHEROES), one of the most popular series in the history of the genre. He also created, or helped create, dozens of other superheroes, including **The Incredible Hulk**, which helped launch Marvel to the top of the business. He left the Lee organization in 1970 and for a while worked for DC COMICS, where he produced an interesting group of four interconnected superhero comics, including *New Gods* (referred to as "Kirby's Fourth World"), before returning to Marvel. JK's style is blocky, almost primitive, but with a power and sense of drama that many other comics artists lack. His use of motion-picture techniques (such as still-frame storytelling) and dramatic perspectives has influenced most of today's comics artists. His work is reproduced in *Origins of Marvel Comics* (**1974**), *Son of Origins of Marvel Comics* (**1975**) and *Bring on the Bad Guys* (**1976**), all ed Stan Lee, and in many more recent and accessible collections, including #2-#4, #6-#8, #13 and #14 of the **Marvel Masterworks** series (1986 onwards). [JG/RH/PN]

KIRBY, JOSH (1928-   ) UK illustrator, trained at Liverpool School of Art. JK's work in sf began with covers for the 1956 paperback of Ian FLEMING's *Moonraker* (**1955**) and for *Authentic Science Fiction*. Most of his art has been for paperback covers, for publishers including Corgi, Panther and New English Library and, in the USA, ACE BOOKS, BALLANTINE BOOKS, DAW BOOKS and Lancer Books. His style is colourful and intricate, and often designed on a small scale: the painting is frequently no larger than the book cover itself. His trademark is the grotesquerie of his creations. He belongs to a tradition derived more obviously from grotesque fantasists like Arthur Rackham than from sf illustrators. JK's work has been strongly identified, in the 1980s and since, with both hardcover and paperback editions of the novels of Terry PRATCHETT, with whom he shares a cover credit for the richly illustrated *Eric* (**1990**) – even Pratchett imitators often get JK covers. A book of his work is *Voyage of the Ayeguy* (**1981**). *The Josh Kirby Poster Book* (**1989**), in large format and introduced by Pratchett, contains 13 posters. [JG/PN]

See also: FANTASY.

KIRCHER, ATHANASIUS (1602-1680) German priest

and scientist who predicted the germ theory of disease. For his relevance to sf, ◊ MARS, MERCURY, OUTER PLANETS, RELIGION and VENUS, in each of which entries there is reference to AK's speculative, visionary round-trip to the planets, *Itinerarium Exstaticum* ["A Journey in Rapture"] (**1656** Rome).   [PN]

KIRK, RICHARD ◊ Robert P. HOLDSTOCK; Angus WELLS.

KIRKHAM, NELLIE (? -) UK writer whose sf novel, *Unrest of Their Time* (**1938**), used contrasting colours of type to represent the simultaneity of lives lived in different periods by the one protagonist. [JC]

KIRST, HANS HELLMUT (1914-1989) German writer best known for his novels about WWII. His NEAR-FUTURE sf novel, *Keiner Kommt Davon* (**1957**; trans Richard Graves as *The Seventh Day* **1959** US; vt *No One Will Escape* **1960** UK), deals with the period directly preceding WWIII and with the atomic HOLOCAUST that then kills off the cast.   [JC]

KISS ME DEADLY Film (1955). Parklane. Prod and dir Robert Aldrich, starring Ralph Meeker, Albert Dekker, Paul Stewart, Maxine Cooper, Gaby Rogers, Chloris Leachman. Screenplay A.I. Bezzerides, based remotely on *Kiss Me Deadly* (**1952**) by Mickey Spillane. 105 mins. B/w.

This extraordinary *film noir*, now recognized as one of the greatest of its period, substitutes a boxful of radioactivity – a kind of surrogate atom bomb – for the packet of narcotics everyone seeks control of in Spillane's original. In a sadly tarnished world, the lethal Pandora's Box takes on a glamour which literally shines out – destroying the world – at the apocalyptic climax. Painful and furious, *KMD* gives an extraordinarily abrasive quality to the stereotypes of the private-eye genre, but it is the box itself that dominates the movie, growing from an apparent MCGUFFIN into an icon of a menacing future, the object of worship in an impoverished present which, by implication, yearns for the hard white light that abolishes all shadows.   [PN]

See also: CINEMA.

KJELGAARD, JIM [r] ◊ David A. DRAKE.

KLASS, PHILIP [r] ◊ William TENN.

KLEIN, GÉRARD (1937-) French writer, anthologist, critic and editor. An economist by profession, GK is one of the few European sf writers known in the USA. He has used the pseudonyms Gilles d'Argyre, François Pagery and Mark Starr. His first stories, heavily influenced by Ray BRADBURY, appeared in 1955 when he was only 18 years old, and he soon made a major impact on the field in France, publishing over 40 delicately crafted stories 1956-62 (60 by 1977), while also establishing himself as a forceful and literate critic of the genre with a series of 30 penetrating essays in various publications. His first novel, *Le gambit des étoiles* (**1958**; trans C.J. Richards as *Starmaster's Gambit* **1973** US), a clever and wide-ranging adventure yarn, shows the increasing influence that US GENRE SF was having on GK, a trend which comes strongly to the fore in novels like *Le*

temps n'a pas d'odeur (**1963**; trans P.J. Skolowski as *The Day before Tomorrow* **1972** US) and *Les seigneurs de la guerre* (**1971**; trans John BRUNNER as *The Overlords of War* **1973** US); these, though well conducted and interesting, lack the poetic invention of his early work. From 1969, GK edited the **Ailleurs et Demain** imprint for publisher Robert Laffont, where he was instrumental in introducing some of the major modern US-UK sf writers to the French public while also encouraging the better local authors – Philippe CURVAL, Michel Jeury, Christian LÉOURIER, André Ruellan and Stefan WUL. Many of GK's works feature an imagery and even a structure influenced by chess.   [MJ]

Other works: *Agent galactique* ["Galactic Agent"] (**1958**) as by Mark Starr; *Embûches dans l'espace* ["Ambushes in Space"] (**1958** as by François Pagery); *Les perles du temps* ["Pearls of Time"] (coll **1958**); *Chirurgiens d'une planète* ["Planet-Surgeons"] (**1960**) as by Gilles d'Argyre; *Les voiliers du soleil* ["Sailors of the Sun"] (**1961**) as by d'Argyre; *Le long voyage* ["The Long Journey"] (**1964**) as by d'Argyre; *Les tueurs du temps* (**1965**; trans C.J. Richards as *The Mote in Time's Eye* **1975** US), as by d'Argyre in France, GK in USA; *Le sceptre du hasard* ["The Sceptre of Chance"] (**1966**) as by d'Argyre; *Un chant de pierre* ["Stone Song"] (coll **1966**); *La loi du talion* ["The Law of Retaliation"] (coll **1973**); *Histoires comme si* ["Stories as If"] (coll **1975**); *Anthologie de la science-fiction française* (anth in 3 vols **1975**, **1976**, **1977**) with others; *Le Livre d'or du Gérard Klein* ["The Book of Gold of Gérard Klein"] (coll **1979**).

See also: CRITICAL AND HISTORICAL WORKS ABOUT SF; FRANCE; GALACTIC EMPIRES; GAMES AND SPORTS; LIVING WORLDS.

KLINE, OTIS ADELBERT (1891-1946) US songwriter, author and literary agent, active in music before beginning to write popular fiction in several genres, predominantly fantasy, in the early 1920s, most notably for *Weird Tales* and *The Argosy*. With the exception of marginal sf tales like "The Bride of Osiris" (1927) and space adventures such as "Race Around the Moon" (1939), most of his genre work is HEROIC FANTASY, and is generally thought to have been written in competition with (and slavishly derived from) Edgar Rice BURROUGHS's PLANETARY ROMANCES. The **Robert Grandon** sequence is typical: comprising *The Planet of Peril* (**1929**), *The Prince of Peril* (**1930**) and *The Port of Peril* (**1932** *Weird Tales* as "Buccaneers of Venus"; **1949**), it carries the swashbuckling Grandon to VENUS, where he rises from slavery to marry a princess; the later adventures expand upon this. Linked to this series through the character of Dr Morgan – a scientist who makes interplanetary transfers easy – are *The Swordsman of Mars* (**1933** *Argosy*; **1960**) and its sequel, *The Outlaws of Mars* (**1933** *Argosy*; **1960**). In *Maza of the Moon* (**1930**) the P'an-ku who rule the MOON bomb Earth after Earth bombs them. *Call of the Savage* (**1931** *Argosy* as "Jan of the Jungle"; **1937**; vt *Jan of the Jungle* **1966**) and its sequel *Jan in India* (**1935** *Argosy*; **1974**) again ape

Burroughs, the target this time being Tarzan. In his later years, OAK's time was almost entirely taken up by his literary agency. Violently coloured, crudely racist and sniggeringly sexist, his tales represent pulp fiction at its worst, but they retain a raw compulsiveness. [JC]

Other works: *The Man who Limped and Other Stories* (coll of linked stories **1946**); *Tam, Son of the Tiger* (1931 *Weird Tales*; **1962**); *Bride of Osiris and Other Weird Tales* (coll **1975** chap).

See also: COMICS; MARS; PUBLISHING.

KNEALE, (THOMAS) NIGEL (1922-) UK author and screenwriter, married to Judith Kerr (1923-), a well known children's author. After attending the Royal Academy of Dramatic Art and working as an actor, NK began writing short stories, 26 of which – some horror or fantasy – appear in *Tomato Cain and Other Stories* (coll **1949**). Since then most of his writing work has been for TELEVISION and film, often using sf themes, most commonly consisting of scientific rationalizations of ancient motifs from HORROR fiction and MYTHOLOGY. His first major tv success was in 1953 with a serial, *The* QUATERMASS EXPERIMENT. In 1954 he successfully adapted George ORWELL's *Nineteen Eighty-four* (**1949**) for BBC TV; it caused much controversy. Two more **Quatermass** serials for BBC TV were QUATERMASS II (1955) and QUATERMASS AND THE PIT (1958-9). All three were adapted into feature films by Hammer Films, as *The* QUATERMASS XPERIMENT (1955; vt *The Creeping Unknown*), QUATERMASS II (1957; vt *Enemy from Space*) and QUATERMASS AND THE PIT (1968; vt *Five Million Years to Earth*). NK coscripted the second of these films, and scripted the third. The tv scripts were published as *The Quatermass Experiment: A Play for Television in Six Parts* * (1953 BBC TV; rev **1959**), *Quatermass II: A Play for Television in Six Parts* * (1955 BBC TV; rev **1960**) and *Quatermass and the Pit: A Play for Television in Six Parts* * (1958-9 BBC TV; rev **1960**). NK also scripted FIRST MEN IN THE MOON (1964) and the horror film *The Witches* (1966), adapted from novels by H.G. WELLS and Peter Curtis respectively.

Three further tv plays, "The Road" (1963), "The Year of the Sex Olympics" (1969) and "The Stone Tape" (1972) have been collected in *The Year of the Sex Olympics and Other TV Plays* (coll **1976**). The first is an 18th-century ghost story in which the ghosts are apparitions of 20th-century TECHNOLOGY; the second deals satirically with a future tv-watching population and improved methods of apathy control; the third again combines Gothic horror with messages across time. In 1971 "The Chopper", about a biker's ghost, was televised as part of the OUT OF THE UNKNOWN series. The 1975 ATV tv series *Beasts* was scripted by NK, the beasts in question ranging from psychological to supernatural.

In 1979 Quatermass returned, this time to ITV, in a new tv serial (4 parts) entitled QUATERMASS. An edited-down version, retitled *The Quatermass Conclusion*, was intended for cinema release, but in the UK was released only on videotape. It had in fact been written a decade earlier for BBC TV, and its plot (featuring mystically inclined flower children about to be harvested by ALIENS *via* messages beamed through stone circles) seemed curiously old-fashioned. The book version by NK, *Quatermass* (**1979**), which appeared concurrently, is not a novelization, and diverges in detail from the tv series. A more sinister version of the same theme appears in NK's script for the film HALLOWEEN III: SEASON OF THE WITCH (1983), in which microchips made out of a Stonhenge monolith are used to booby-trap children's Halloween masks with a hideous destruction device, this being the plot of a madman who wishes (as perhaps NK does) that the true meaning of Halloween had not been vulgarized.

It had now become clear from NK's sf/horror work that he had little interest in, or even knowledge of, sf proper, a genre about which he has consistently expressed contempt (sf being "very disappointing and horribly overwritten" and sf fans, he said in a 1979 interview, being either fat with wispy wives or wispy with fat ones); it is interesting, for example, that the two films he repudiated as having vulgarized his scripts, *Quatermass II* – which he has kept from circulation for years – and *Halloween III*, are among the better ones. With hindsight, there is a clear pattern in NK's work of ordinary people being seen as stupid and ignorant, and ready prey for the supernatural or sciencefictional forces that will almost inevitably attempt to control them. There is a seigneurial, Edwardian element in this, a recoiling from the vulgar. It is worth labouring the point, because he is certainly a much better than average scriptwriter – the **Quatermass** series especially is exemplary – and his scripts have been, paradoxically, very influential on sf, at least at the GOTHIC and irrational margin of the genre where sf meets fantasy and horror (and particularly among film and tv producers, who never expect sf to make sense anyway).

NK's revulsion against what he saw sf as standing for came into gloomy focus with the 1981 tv series KINVIG, which attempts to call forth derisory laughter at the granting (through the introduction of a very beautiful ALIEN) of two sf fans' romantic longings for mysteries in a mundane world; it is a sitcom notable for its contemptuous treatment of the leading characters. [PN]

See also: MUSIC; PSEUDO-SCIENCE; SUPERNATURAL CREATURES.

KNEBEL, FLETCHER (1911-?1992) US journalist and novelist, most of whose books are political thrillers, not excepting his borderline-sf books. *Seven Days in May* (**1962**), with Charles W. BAILEY, later filmed (◊ John FRANKENHEIMER), describes an attempted military coup in the USA. *Night of Camp David* (**1965**) tells of a NEAR-FUTURE President of the USA who goes mad and almost destroys the country. In *Trespass* (**1969**), set in 1973, a Black activist group takes over White properties and upsets the FBI. [JC/PN]

KNEIFEL, HANS [r] ◊ GERMANY; PERRY RHODAN.

KNIGHT, DAMON (FRANCIS) (1922-) US writer

and editor; his third marriage was to Kate WILHELM. Like many sf writers, DK became involved in sf FANDOM at an early age, and by 1941 was a member of the FUTURIANS in New York, where he shared an apartment with Robert A.W. LOWNDES and met James BLISH, C.M. KORNBLUTH, Frederik POHL and others. (In *The Futurians: The Story of the Science Fiction "Family" of the 30's that Produced Today's Top SF Writers and Editors* [1977] he published a candid history of the group and its era.) His first professional sale was a cartoon to *AMZ*. His first story was "Resilience" (1941) in STIRRING SCIENCE STORIES, edited by another Futurian, Donald A. WOLLHEIM; but DK's career as a short-story writer lay fallow for several years. In 1943 he became an assistant editor with Popular Publications, a PULP-MAGAZINE chain. Later he worked for a literary agency, then returned to Popular Publications as assistant editor of SUPER SCIENCE STORIES. In 1950-51 he was editor of WORLDS BEYOND, but the magazine ran for only 3 issues; later he edited IF for 3 issues 1958-9.

DK made his initial strong impact on the field as a book reviewer, and is generally acknowledged to have been the first outstanding GENRE-SF critic. His very first piece – a fanzine review (in Larry SHAW's *Destiny's Child*) of the 1945 *ASF* serial version of A.E. VAN VOGT's *The World of Ā* (**1948**) – remains perhaps his best known; it is in any case one of the most famous works of critical demolition ever published in the field, inspiring considerable revisions in the published book, and being credited (perhaps a touch implausibly) for van Vogt's eventual slide from preeminence. DK later reviewed books for a number of amateur and professional magazines, notably INFINITY and *The* MAGAZINE OF FANTASY AND SCIENCE FICTION, expressing throughout a sane and consistent insistence on the relevance of literary standards to sf. His early reviews were collected in *In Search of Wonder* (coll **1956**; rev 1967), and won him a HUGO in 1956. He stopped reviewing entirely when *FSF* declined to print a negative response to Judith MERRIL – probably the review of *The Tomorrow People* (**1960**) which appears in *In Search of Wonder*. In 1975 he received a retrospective PILGRIM AWARD from the SCIENCE FICTION RESEARCH ASSOCIATION.

DK's 1940s stories – including occasional collaborations with Blish, once using the collaborative pseudonym Donald Laverty, and 3 times as Stuart Fleming – were of only mild interest until the release in 1949 of his ironic END OF THE WORLD story "Not With a Bang" in one of the first issues of *FSF*. This magazine, and GALAXY SCIENCE FICTION even more so, now provided markets in which DK could develop his urbane and darkly humorous short stories – including the famous "To Serve Man" (1950), "Four in One" (1953), "Babel II" (1953), "The Country of the Kind" (1955) and "Stranger Station" (1956) – though as the decade advanced, and as his perspectives on the human enterprise darkened, even these markets proved too narrow, and he was forced to publish

some of his finest work in lesser journals, where his scouring, revisionary, anatomical rewrites of the genre's already sclerotic conventions could appear in safe obscurity. DK's reputation as a writer has primarily rested on the short stories published during the 1950s and, to a lesser extent, the 1960s; they are adult and sane and have not dated. His best work has been assembled in various collections, including *Far Out* (coll **1961**), *In Deep* (coll **1963**; cut 1964 UK), *Off Center* (coll **1965** dos; exp vt *Off Centre* 1969 UK), *Turning On* (coll **1966**; exp 1967 UK) and *Rule Golden* (coll **1979**); later collections like *Late Knight Edition* (coll **1985**), *One Side Laughing: Stories Unlike Other Stories* (coll **1991**) and *God's Nose* (coll **1991**) tend to mix early and later work.

From the first, novels presented something of a difficulty for DK. Most of them – like his first, *Hell's Pavement* (fixup **1955**; vt *Analogue Men* 1962), a DYSTOPIAN story of a future society with humanity under psychological control, *Masters of Evolution* (1954 *Gal* as "Natural State"; exp **1959** chap dos) and *The Sun Saboteurs* (1955 *If* as "The Earth Quarter"; **1961** dos) – were expanded from stories, losing in the process the compressed drivenness of his short work. Of them all, only *The People Maker* (**1959**; rev vt *A for Anything* 1961 UK) and the late *The World and Thorinn* (fixup **1981**), a scintillating picaresque derived from some 1960s tales, seem comfortably to fill the longer format; and by the mid-1960s he appeared to have turned his attention permanently elsewhere.

Like Frederik Pohl, DK became adept at all aspects of the writing business, having worked as magazine editor, short-story writer, novelist and critic. He now involved himself in formalizing the professional collegiality so important to the sf field, first by cofounding, with Blish and Merril, the MILFORD SCIENCE FICTION WRITERS' CONFERENCE in 1956, which he ran (soon with Wilhelm) for over 20 years, later participating in its spiritual offspring, the CLARION SCIENCE FICTION WRITERS' WORKSHOP writing seminar, for which he edited *The Clarion Writers' Handbook* (anth **1978**); and second by being largely responsible for founding the SCIENCE FICTION WRITERS OF AMERICA, serving as its first president 1965-7. At about the same time he began to issue well conceived reprint ANTHOLOGIES like *A Century of Science Fiction* (anth **1962**), *First Flight* (anth **1963**; vt *Now Begins Tomorrow* 1969; exp vt *First Voyages* 1981 with Martin H. GREENBERG and Joseph D. OLANDER), *Tomorrow x 4* (anth **1964**), *A Century of Great Short Science Fiction Novels* (anth **1964**) and many others. He also translated a number of French sf stories, some for publication in *FSF*, and collected them as *13 French Science-Fiction Stories* (anth **1965**). But his greatest editorial achievement during these years was the ORBIT series of ORIGINAL ANTHOLOGIES that he began in 1966, and which would become the longest-running and most influential series of that sort yet seen in the field; among writers strongly identified with **Orbit** were Gardner DOZOIS, R.A. LAFFERTY, Kate WILHELM and Gene WOLFE.

In the 1980s, after the end of **Orbit**, DK became more active as a writer again, though without making a huge impression on a new generation of readers. But if *The Man in the Tree* (**1984**) seems unduly slack and irony-poor in its presentation of a contemporary MESSIAH figure, DK returned to something like form, though without quite the energy of earlier efforts, in the wickedly UTOPIAN sequence comprising *CV* (**1985**), *The Observers* (**1988**) and *A Reasonable World* (**1991**), about ALIEN parasites who turn out not to be the PARANOIA-justifiying plague of 1950s sf but moralistic symbionts who enforce something like rational behaviour upon humanity's leaders; in the third volume, a plethora of sf devices and utopian appeals somewhat weakens the pleasurable sting, but the series as a whole seems young at heart, and DK's cognitive energy remains clearly evident – as also demonstrated by the autumnal ironies of *Why Do Birds* (**1992**), in which the world is brought to an end. There is still a sense that he may have a mind to continue to shock the sf world. [MJE/JC]

Other works: *Beyond the Barrier* (**1964**); *The Rithian Terror* (1953 *Startling Stories* as "Double Meaning"; exp **1965** dos); *Mind Switch* (**1965**; vt *The Other Foot* 1966 UK); *Three Novels* (omni **1967**; vt *Natural State and Other Stories* 1975 UK); *World without Children, and The Earth Quarter* (coll **1970**) including *The Sun Saboteurs* as "The Earth Quarter", its magazine title; *Two Novels* (omni **1974**) presenting *The Rithian Terror* and *The Sun Saboteurs*, both under their magazine titles; *The Best of Damon Knight* (coll **1976**); *Better than One* (coll **1980**) with Kate Wilhelm; *Rule Golden/Double Meaning* (omni **1991**) presenting the collection *Rule Golden* plus *The Rithian Terror* as *Double Meaning*.

Nonfiction: *Turning Points: Essays on the Art of Science Fiction* (anth **1977**), critical essays; *Creating Short Fiction* (**1981**; rev 1985).

As editor: *Beyond Tomorrow* (anth **1965**); *The Dark Side* (anth **1965**); *The Shape of Things* (anth **1965**); *Cities of Wonder* (anth **1966**); *Nebula Award Stories 1965* (anth **1966**); *Science Fiction Inventions* (anth **1967**); *Worlds to Come* (anth **1967**); *The Metal Smile* (anth **1968**); *One Hundred Years of Science Fiction* (anth **1968**); *Toward Infinity* (anth **1968**); *Dimension X* (anth **1970**; in 2 vols, the 2nd vol vt *Elsewhere x 3* 1974 UK); *A Pocketful of Stars* (anth **1971**); *First Contact* (anth **1971**); *Perchance to Dream* (anth **1972**); *Science Fiction Argosy* (anth **1972**); *Tomorrow and Tomorrow* (anth **1973**); *The Golden Road* (anth **1973**); *A Shocking Thing* (anth **1974**); *Happy Endings* (anth **1974**); *Science Fiction of the Thirties* (anth **1975**); *Monad 1* (anth **1990**) and *Monad 2* (anth **1992**).

The Orbit anthologies: *Orbit 1* (anth **1966**); *Orbit 2* (anth **1967**); *Orbit 3* (anth **1968**); *Orbit 4* (anth **1968**); *Orbit 5* (anth **1969**); *Orbit 6* (anth **1970**); *Orbit 7* (anth **1970**); *Orbit 8* (anth **1970**); *Orbit 9* (anth **1971**); *Orbit 10* (anth **1972**); *Orbit 11* (anth **1972**); *Orbit 12* (anth **1973**); *Orbit 13* (anth **1974**); *Orbit 14* (anth **1974**); *Orbit 15* (anth **1974**); *Orbit 16* (anth **1975**); *Orbit 17* (anth **1975**); *Best Stories from Orbit: Volumes 1-10* (anth **1975**); *Orbit 18* (anth **1976**); *Orbit 19* (anth **1977**); *Orbit 20* (anth

1978); *Orbit 21* (anth **1980**).

About the author: "All in a Knight's Work" by James Blish, *Speculation* 29, 1971; "Ragged Claws" by DK in *Hell's Cartographers* (anth **1975**) ed Brian W. ALDISS and Harry HARRISON.

See also: ANTI-INTELLECTUALISM IN SF; ARTS; COMMUNICATIONS; COSMOLOGY; CRIME AND PUNISHMENT; CRITICAL AND HISTORICAL WORKS ABOUT SF; DEFINITIONS OF SF; DISCOVERY AND INVENTION; ECOLOGY; ECONOMICS; EVOLUTION; GENETIC ENGINEERING; IMMORTALITY; INVISIBILITY; MONSTERS; NEBULA; PARASITISM AND SYMBIOSIS; SF MAGAZINES; SCI FI; SPACE HABITATS; TABOOS; TRANSPORTATION.

KNIGHT, HARRY ADAM ◊ John BROSNAN.

KNIGHT, NORMAN L(OUIS) (1895-1972) US writer and pesticide chemist for the Department of Agriculture until his retirement in 1963. He was not a prolific writer, publishing only 11 stories altogether, the first of which was the novella "Frontier of the Unknown" for *ASF* in 1937. He made his main contribution by collaborating with James BLISH on *A Torrent of Faces* (**1967**). This novel – whose UNDER-THE-SEA sequences and amphibious Tritons (genetically engineered humans; ◊ GENETIC ENGINEERING) are taken from NLK's first story and from "Crisis in Utopia" (1940 *ASF*) – depicts an ambiguously UTOPIAN Earth whose trillion people (◊ OVERPOPULATION) must face up to the challenge of an approaching meteor. [JC]

See also: ASTEROIDS.

KNIGHT, ROBERT ◊ Christopher EVANS.

KNIGHT RIDER ◊ Glen A. LARSON.

KNOWLES, W(ILLIAM) P(LENDERLEITH) (1891-   ) UK writer whose *Jim McWhirter* (**1933**), set in 1953, advances towards a not unusual socialist UTOPIA via a sequence of very violent catastrophes, including an emission of poison gases from within the crust of the Earth. [JC]

KNOX, CALVIN M. ◊ Robert SILVERBERG.

KNOX, G.D. [r] ◊ T.C. WIGNALL.

KNOX, [Monsignor] RONALD A(RBUTHNOTT) (1888-1957) UK Roman Catholic priest (converted 1917, ordained 1919) and extremely prolific writer. Among his many books are several then-popular detective novels, volumes of parodies, a new translation of the Testaments, and some genre work. *A Still More Sporting Adventure!* (**1911**) with Charles R.L. Fletcher (1857-1934), published anon, takes two women back in time to spy on Queen Dido in Carthage, thus parodying *An Adventure* (**1911**) by Charlotte Moberly and Eleanor Jourdain, a bestselling nonfiction tale of the authors' experiences via supposed timeslip in Versailles. *Absolute and Abitofhell* (**1915** chap), as by R.A.K., is a fantasy poem about Noah's Ark; with further material, some of genre interest, it was republished in *Essays in Satire* (coll **1928**). *Memories of the Future: Being Memoirs of the Years 1915-1972 Written in the Year of Grace 1988 by Opal, Lady Porstock* (**1923**) satirizes the type of evolutionary UTOPIA most closely identified with H.G. WELLS. The story is perhaps too cleverly told, and its imitation of the genteel memoir too exact in places. *Other Eyes* *than Ours* (**1926**), which features an apparatus for communicating with the dead, is in fact hoax sf, the device having been concocted to bring an obsessive to his senses. [JC]

KNYE, CASSANDRA ◊ Thomas M. DISCH; John T. SLADEK.

KOCH, ERIC (1919-) German-born writer and tv producer, in Canada from 1935, three of whose novels are of some sf interest. In *The French Kiss: A Tongue in Cheek Political Fantasy* (**1969**), set in a NEAR-FUTURE Canada threatened – as usual – by separatism, a reincarnated colleague of Napoleon muses on De Gaulle's similarity to the long-dead Emperor. *The Leisure Riots: A Comic Novel* (**1973**) suggests that, in 1980, the enforced leisure of the executive class will trigger riots. In *The Last Thing You'd Want to Know* (**1976**) a "witch" becomes US President, sweeping all before her except one tortured ex-Nazi. EK was sometimes amusing, but fatally inattentive to questions of verisimilitude. [JC]

KOESTLER, ARTHUR (1905-1983) Hungarian-born author and journalist who narrowly avoided execution in the Spanish Civil War and spent the rest of his life in the UK and France, becoming a naturalized UK citizen in 1940. All his books after the famous DYSTOPIA *Darkness at Noon* (trans Daphne Hardy **1940**) were written in English. Several of the speculative, philosophical works of his later career have a direct interest for sf readers and have probably been influential on sf writers. They include *The Sleepwalkers: A History of Man's Changing Vision of the Universe* (**1959**), *The Act of Creation* (**1964**), *The Case of the Midwife Toad* (**1971**) – about the "Lamarckian" inheritance of acquired characteristics (◊ EVOLUTION; PSEUDO-SCIENCE) – and *The Roots of Coincidence* (**1972**). His play, *Twilight Bar: An Escapade in Four Acts* (written 1933; English version **1945**), is a UTOPIAN fantasia set on a world-ISLAND visited by ALIENS who threaten to destroy human life unless we better ourselves immediately. *The Age of Longing* (**1951**), is NEAR-FUTURE sf, a discussion novel set in France; it distils his intimate experience with European thought and POLITICS into a prediction of the nature of our response to a threatened INVASION from the East. *The Call Girls: A Tragi-Comedy* (**1972**) is a discussion novel on sf-related themes. AK was an important speculative thinker, many of whose ideas challenged (sometimes with some success) "orthodox" scientific and social thought. He several times expressed contempt for sf. [JC]

See also: THEATRE.

KOHOUT, PAVEL (1928-) Czech poet, playwright, novelist and, since his emigration in 1968, émigré activist. Though his early poetry had been pro-communist, his politics changed and his work remained unpublished in Czechoslovakia in the period 1968-89; some was published there in 1990. His sf novel, which deals with the political persecution of a man who can control ANTIGRAVITY, is *Bílá kniha o kauze Adam Juráček, profesor tělocviku a kreslení*

na Pedagogické škole v K., kontra Sir Isaac Newton, profesor fyziky na univerzitě v Cambridge (written 1970 and circulated in samizdat form; **1978** Canada; trans Alec Page as *White Book: Adam Juracek, Professor of Drawing and Physical Education at the Pedagogical Institute in K., vs. Sir Isaac Newton, Professor of Physics at the University of Cambridge* **1977** US). [JO]

See also: CZECH AND SLOVAK SF; THEATRE.

KOLCHAK: THE NIGHT STALKER US tv series (1974-5). Francy Productions for Universal TV/ABC. Created Jeff Rice. Executive prod Darren McGavin. Prod Paul Playton, Cy Chermak. Story consultant David Chase. 20 50min episodes. Colour.

This fondly remembered series was a spin-off from a successful made-for-tv movie, *The Night Stalker* (1972), prod Dan Curtis and written Richard MATHESON, about a vampire in contemporary Las Vegas. This led to a feature-length sequel, *The Night Strangler* (1973), also written by Matheson, about a youth serum produced from murdered women. The tv series was partly sparked off by the enthusiasm of McGavin, star of the two movies, who became *K:TNS*'s executive producer. He again played the reporter, Kolchak, who each week uncovered some fantastic threat. Unable to persuade anyone in authority of its existence, he was usually obliged to combat the menace alone. Most episodes featured supernatural creatures; sf-related episodes were "They Have Been, They Will Be, They Are" (ALIEN intervention), "The Energy Eater" (invisible creature feeds on radioactivity), "Mr. R.I.N.G." (government-created killer ROBOT), "The Primal Scream" (cells from the Arctic grow into a prehistoric ape-creature) and "The Sentry" (lizardlike monster). The series was entertaining and atmospheric, but too unvarying in its rigidly formulaic stories. [JB]

KOLUPAYEV, VIKTOR (DMITRIEVICH) (1936-) Russian writer who made a striking début in 1966, soon becoming a leading author of SOFT SF; his work has been likened to that of Ray BRADBURY. His lyrical short stories are assembled in *Slutchitsia Zhe S Tchelovekom Takoie!* ["What Can Happen to a Man?"] (coll **1972**), *Katcheli Otshel'nika* (coll **1974**; trans Helen Saltz Jacobson with somewhat differing contents as *Hermit's Swing* **1980** US) and *Poiushii Les* ["The Singing Forest"] (coll **1984**). VK's only novel is the controversial and somewhat unsuccessful *Firmenny Poezd "Fomitch"* ["The 'Fomitch' Special Train"] (**1979**). [VG]

KOMAN, VICTOR (1944-) US writer who began publishing sf with "When it Worked" for *New Libertarian Notes* in 1976. Much of his subsequent output has emphasized material and points of view that could be characterized under the LIBERTARIANISM rubric. After publishing *Saucer Sluts* (**1980**), and collaborating with Andrew J. OFFUTT under the joint pseudonym John CLEVE for two **Spaceways** sf adventures, *#13: Jonuta Rising!* (**1983**) and *#17: The Carnadyne Horde* (**1984**), VK released his first novel of substance, *The Jehovah Contract* (**1985** Germany, trans as *Der*

Jehova-Vertrag; **1987** US), in which a Los Angeles private eye is commissioned, in 1999, to kill God; the ensuing events might be considered blasphemous by some readers. In *Solomon's Knife* (**1989**) abortions are averted through a medical technique which allows the transfer of foetuses into the wombs of infertile women who want a child. *The Prometheus Meltdown* (**1990**) is a round-robin libertarian tale whose other contributors were Brad LINAWEAVER, J. Neil SCHULMAN, Robert SHEA, L. Neil SMITH and Robert Anton WILSON. [JC]

KOMARČIĆ, LAZAR [r] ◊ YUGOSLAVIA.

KOMATSU, SAKYO (1931-   ) Japanese novelist and essayist regarded as the premier sf writer of his country. His main novels consistently deal with large subjects: the destiny of the Universe and *Homo sapiens*'s place within it. They are highly regarded for their panoramic vision and the encyclopedic knowledge they display. A graduate of Kyoto University, SK worked at many jobs from factory manager to comedy writer. His first sf was the novelette "Chi Niwa Heiwa Wo" ["Peace on Earth"] (1961); nominated later for the Naoki Award, Japan's most prestigious literary prize, it was reprinted in *Chi Niwa Heiwa Wo* (coll **1963**) along with other early short fiction. His most popular work is the DISASTER novel *Nippon Chinbotsu* (**1973**; trans Michael Gallagher, cut by one-third, as *Japan Sinks* **1976** US; vt *Death of the Dragon* 1978). It sold about four million copies in JAPAN and was filmed by Toho Eiga as NIPPON CHINBOTSU (1973) with a very limited release in the West as *The Submersion of Japan*; the film was later rereleased in the West as *Tidal Wave* (1974), cut to two-thirds and with new scenes added by producer Roger CORMAN. In the novel the Japanese archipelago begins to slide inexorably into the Japan Trench. Beyond its well worked-out geological basis, *Japan Sinks* is effective as an obviously deeply felt elegy for Japan herself in all her physical and cultural fragility: the story has no heroes or villains, the main focus of our attention being the dying of the country.

SK's novel *Sayonara Jupiter* ["Goodbye Jupiter"] (**1982**) was also filmed by Toho Eiga, in 1984 (vt, tastelessly, *Bye-Bye Jupiter*), prod and dir SK himself, who also wrote the screenplay. It features a scheme to turn Jupiter into a small Sun to render the outer Solar System habitable; the book predated Arthur C. CLARKE's *2010: Odyssey Two* (**1982**), which uses the same central image. SK's most recent novel, *Kyomu Kairo* ["Gallery of Nothingness"] (**1987**), has an immortal "Artificial Existence" (developed in an AI laboratory) riding a spaceship to research a mysterious "SS" (super-structure), a cylinder 1.2 light years in diameter and 2 light years in length, which suddenly appears 5.8 light years from Earth (◊ BIG DUMB OBJECTS). SK's other main works include *Nippon Apache-Zoku* ["Japanese Apache"] (**1964**), *Fukkatso No Hi* ["The Day of Resurrection"] (**1964**), filmed as FUKKATSO NO HI (1981; vt *Virus*), *Hateshi Naki Nagare No Hateni* ["At the End of Endless Flow"] (**1966**), an

extraordinary tale of PARALLEL WORLDS and human EVOLUTION, *Tsugu Nowa Dareka?* ["Who Succeeds Humanity?"] (**1972**), which won the Sei'un AWARD, and *Shuto Shoshitsu* ["The Disappearance of Tokyo"] (**1985**), which won the Nippon SF Taisho.

SK is active also as a journalist and publicist – for example, as a consultant for and organizer of Expos. In 1970 he conducted the "International SF Symposium", recognized as the first truly worldwide gathering of sf authors, including 5 delegates from the USSR as well as Brian W. ALDISS, Arthur C. CLARKE and Frederik POHL. [TSh/JC]

KONEC SRPNA V HOTELU OZÓN (vt *The End of August at the Hotel Ozone*) Film (1966). Československý armádní film. Dir Jan Schmidt, starring Ondrej Jariabek, Beta Poničanová, Magda Seidlerová, Hana Vítková. Screenplay Pavel Juráček. 87 mins. B/w.

This Czech film is set in a desolate landscape 15 years after a nuclear HOLOCAUST. A band of brutalized women survivors live primitively (in what looks to Western eyes like an art-film version of an exploitation movie), not really understanding the occasional remnants they come across of the old world. One such survival is a deserted hotel; another is its proprietor, who alas for him is too old to be of any use to them. The film's bleakness is monotonous. [PN]

KOONTZ, DEAN R(AY) (1945-   ) US writer of much fiction under various names. He began his career with a number of sf novels; since 1975 he has concentrated on HORROR, becoming one of the best-selling authors in that genre, and a figure of genuine significance for his well crafted and very various work, though he lacks Peter Straub's panache and Stephen KING's compelling sense of locality. Much of his horror output first appeared (see listing below) as by Brian Coffey, Deanne Dwyer, K.R. Dwyer, Leigh Nichols, Anthony North, Richard Paige and Owen West; from the 1980s, these titles when reprinted are acknowledged as by DRK or Dean Koontz (on many of his more recent books the middle initial is omitted). Sf titles have appeared also as by David Axton, John Hill and Aaron Wolfe.

DRK began publishing sf in 1967 with "Soft Come the Dragons" for *FSF*, which with other stories was collected in *Soft Come the Dragons* (coll **1970** dos). His first novel, *Star Quest* (**1968** dos), was followed by at least 20 more sf novels within half a decade. The sensibility that would find horror congenial quickly revealed itself in a tendency to write stories in which, cruelly and effectively, the boundaries of human identity were stretched. Monstrous children – who classically embody a horror at the potential aliens beneath the human skin – appear in *Beastchild* (**1970**) and *Demon Seed* (**1973**), filmed as DEMON SEED (1977); and MUTANTS and CYBORGS and ROBOTS appear throughout, notably in books like *Anti-Man* (**1970**) and *A Werewolf Among Us* (**1973**). As an sf writer, DRK managed frequently to transcend the plotting conventions he seemed to obey and the forced "darkness" of imagery and style to which he was prone, and to create worlds of invasive mutability. Of those novels written within a more normal sf frame, *Nightmare Journey* (1975) stands out; though over-complicated, it impressively depicts a world 100,000 years hence when humanity, thrust back from the stars by an incomprehensible ALIEN intelligence, goes sour in the prison of Earth, where radioactivity has speeded mutation, causing a religious backlash.

DRK's large body of work contains some surprises; there are comic novels like *The Haunted Earth* (1973), drolleries like *Oddkins* (1988), and several fantasies. Some of his horror novels – like *Night Chills* (1976) and *Lightning* (1988) – are plotted around sf premises, but the use of these is clearly subordinate to the mode within which they fit as arbitrary enabling devices; they are best discussed as HORROR. In the end, the effect of his work is oddly diffuse. After 50 books, the portrait of the artist remains blurred.   [JC]

Other works: *The Fall of the Dream Machine* (**1969** dos); *Fear that Man* (**1969** dos); *Dark Symphony* (**1970**); *Dark of the Woods* (**1970** dos); *Hell's Gate* (**1970**); *The Crimson Witch* (**1971**); *A Darkness in My Soul* (**1972**); *Warlock!* (**1972**); *Time Thieves* (**1972** dos); *The Flesh in the Furnace* (**1972**), *Starblood* (**1972**); *Hanging On* (**1973**); *After the Last Race* (**1974**); *The Vision* (**1977**); *Whispers* (**1980**); *Phantoms* (**1983**); *Darkness Comes* (**1984** UK; vt *Darkfall* 1984 US); *Twilight Eyes* (**1985**; exp 1987 UK); *Strangers* (**1986**); *Watchers* (**1987**); *The House of Thunder* (**1988** UK); *The Shadow Sea* (**1988**); *Midnight* (**1989**); *The Bad Place* (**1990**); *Cold Fire* (**1991**); *Three Complete Novels* (omni **1991**), assembling *The Servants of Twilight* (under its vt *Twilight*), *Darkfall* and *Phantoms*; *Hideaway* (**1992**).

As David Axton: *Prison of Ice* (**1976**), sf.

As Brian Coffey: *Blood Risk* (**1973**); *Surrounded* (**1974**); *Wall of Masks* (**1975**); *The Face of Fear* (**1977**; 1978 UK as K.R. Dwyer; 1989 UK as DRK); *The Voice of the Night* (**1980**; 1989 UK as DRK).

As Deanne Dwyer: *Demon Child* (**1971**); *Legacy of Terror* (**1971**); *Children of the Storm* (**1972**); *The Dark of Summer* (**1972**); *Dance with the Devil* (**1973**).

As K.R. Dwyer: *Chase* (**1972**; 1988 UK as DRK); *Shattered* (**1973**; 1989 UK as DRK); *Dragonfly* (**1975**).

As John Hill: *The Long Sleep* (**1975**), sf.

As Leigh Nichols: *The Key to Midnight* (**1979**; 1990 UK as DRK); *The Eyes of Darkness* (**1981**; 1989 as DRK); *The House of Thunder* (**1982**; 1988 as DRK); *Twilight* (**1984**; vt *The Servants of Twilight* 1985 UK; under original title, 1988 US as DRK); *Shadowfires* (**1987**; 1990 as DRK).

As Anthony North: *Strike Deep* (**1974**), not sf/fantasy.

As Richard Paige: *The Door to December* (**1985**; 1987 UK as Leigh Nichols; 1991 UK as DRK).

As Owen West: *The Funhouse* * (**1980**; with new afterword 1992 as DK), film novelization; *The Mask* (**1981**; 1988 as DRK).

As Aaron Wolfe: *Invasion* (**1975** Canada), sf.

Nonfiction: *Writing Popular Fiction* (**1972**); *How to Write Best Selling Fiction* (**1981**), which incorporates parts of the earlier book.

About the author: *A Checklist of Dean R. Koontz* (last rev **1990** chap) by Christopher P. STEPHENS.

See also: BIOLOGY; GOTHIC SF; MEDIA LANDSCAPE; MONSTERS.

KORNBLUTH, C(YRIL) M. (1923-1958) US writer. A member of the FUTURIANS fan group, he published prolifically during the years 1940-42 in magazines edited by fellow Futurians Donald A. WOLLHEIM and Frederik POHL. His first sf publication was "Stepsons of Mars" with Richard WILSON, writing together as Ivar TOWERS, for *Astonishing Stories* in 1940; his first solo sf story was "King Cole of Pluto" for *Super Science Stories* as S.D. GOTTESMAN, also in 1940. He used many other pseudonyms, both for solo work and for work written in collaboration with Pohl (and sometimes others, including Robert A.W. LOWNDES); these included Arthur COOKE, Cecil Corwin, Walter C. Davies, Kenneth Falconer, Paul Dennis Lavond and Scott MARINER. (He also wrote 1 non-sf novel in the early 1950s as Simon Eisner and 4 as Jordan Park.) After WWII, in which he served as an infantryman and was decorated, CMK went into journalism. He resumed writing sf in 1947, using his own name, and quickly established himself as a brilliant short-story writer. His classic works include "The Little Black Bag" (1950), about the misuse of a medical bag timeslipped from the future (◊ MEDICINE), and the controversial SATIRE "The Marching Morons" (1951), about a future where the practice of birth control by the intelligentsia has had a spectacularly dysgenic effect (◊ INTELLIGENCE). Such stories as "With These Hands" (1951) and "The Goodly Creatures" (1952) are delicate and sensitive, but much of his work is deeply ingrained with bitter irony. "The Cosmic Charge Account" (1956) is a black comedy about a little old lady who finds the power to remake her environs. "Shark Ship" (1958) is an early alarmist fantasy about OVERPOPULATION and POLLUTION. The ALTERNATE-WORLD story "Two Dooms" (1958) is one of the better studies of a world in which the Nazis won WWII (◊ HITLER WINS).

CMK wrote two routine novels in collaboration with Judith MERRIL as Cyril JUDD: *Outpost Mars* (**1952**: rev vt *Sin in Space* 1961), about the colonization of MARS, and *Gunner Cade* (**1952**), about a future in which WAR is a spectator sport (◊ GAMES AND SPORTS). His first solo sf novel, *Takeoff* (**1952**), is a weak NEAR-FUTURE story about the building of the first Moon ROCKET; but when CMK began working again in collaboration with Frederik Pohl they produced a classic, *The Space Merchants* (**1952** *Gal* as "Gravy Planet"; **1953**), about a world run by advertising agencies in the service of capitalist consumerism. This became the archetype of a whole generation of sf novels which showed the world of the future dominated by one particular institution or power group. Two other collaborations with Pohl – the episodic satirical comedy *Search the Sky* (**1954**; rev by Pohl 1985) and *Gladiator-at-Law* (**1955**) – belong to the same subspecies. The last novel CMK wrote with

Pohl was *Wolfbane* (**1957**; rev by Pohl 1986), in which the Earth is moved out of its orbit by ALIENS who capture humans in order to use their bodies in a vast COMPUTER complex. CMK and Pohl also wrote two non-sf novels, *A Town is Drowning* (**1955**) and *Presidential Year* (**1956**). Collaborative stories continued to appear for four years after CMK's premature death, and Pohl wrote some more stories from CMK's ideas in the early 1970s, one of which – "The Meeting" (1972) – won a HUGO. Some of the collaborative short stories are reprinted in the overlapping collections *The Wonder Effect* (coll **1962**), *Critical Mass* (coll **1977**) *Before the Universe* (coll **1980**) and *Our Best* (coll **1986**). CMK's other solo novels are undistinguished: *The Syndic* (**1953**) ironically depicts a future USA run by organized gangsterism in a semi-benevolent fashion; *Not this August* (**1955**; vt *Christmas Eve* 1956 UK; exp by Pohl under first title 1981) describes a revolution in a future USA which has been conquered by communists.

The best of CMK's short work is collected in *The Explorers* (coll **1954**; with 1 story cut and 4 added, vt *The Mindworm and Other Stories* 1955 UK), *A Mile Beyond the Moon* (coll **1958**; paperback omits 3 stories) and *The Marching Morons* (coll **1959**). Eclectic selections from these volumes are *Best SF Stories of Cyril M. Kornbluth* (coll **1968**) and *The Best of C.M. Kornbluth* (coll **1976**), the latter ed Pohl. A selection of early stories originally signed Cecil Corwin is *Thirteen O'Clock and Other Zero Hours* (coll **1970**) ed James BLISH. CMK's essay "The Failure of the Science Fiction novel as Social Criticism" (in *The Science Fiction Novel* coll **1959** intro by Basil DAVENPORT) is an important early piece of sf criticism, sharply pointing out the genre's shortcomings. His widow, Mary Kornbluth, compiled *Science Fiction Showcase* (anth **1959**) as a memorial.　　　　　　　　　　　　　　　　　　[BS]

Other work: *Gunner Cade, Plus Takeoff* (omni **1983**).

See also: ANTI-INTELLECTUALISM IN SF; ARTS; COLONIZATION OF OTHER WORLDS; CYBERNETICS; DYSTOPIAS; ECOLOGY; ECONOMICS; GALAXY SCIENCE FICTION; GOLDEN AGE OF SF; HEROES; HISTORY IN SF; HISTORY OF SF; INVASION; LEISURE; LIBERTARIAN SF; *The* MAGAZINE OF FANTASY AND SCIENCE FICTION; MEDIA LANDSCAPE; OPTIMISM AND PESSIMISM; PARANOIA; PSYCHOLOGY; SF IN THE CLASSROOM; SCIENTISTS; SOCIOLOGY; SPACE HABITATS; SUPERNATURAL CREATURES; TIME TRAVEL; UFOS; VENUS.

KORNWISE, ROBERT [r] ◊ Piers ANTHONY.

KORZYBSKI, ALFRED (HABDANK SKARBEK) (1879-1950) Polish-born aristocrat (a count) sent after WWI to the USA as an artillery expert. He remained, and wrote a quasiphilosophical text, *Science and Sanity* (**1933**), which became the basic handbook of the GENERAL SEMANTICS movement, later to prove so influential on the writer A.E. VAN VOGT. With the support of a Chicago millionaire, AK set up the Institute of General Semantics in 1938.　　　　　　[PN]

About the author: *Fads and Fallacies in the Name of Science* (1957; rev exp vt of *In the Name of Science* 1952) by Martin GARDNER.

See also: PSEUDO-SCIENCE.

KOSINSKI, JERZY (NIKODEM) (1933-1991) Polish writer whose harrowing experiences as a child in WWII are reflected in his first novel, *The Painted Bird* (**1965**; rev 1976), a hallucinated picaresque set in the surrealistic landscape of war-devastated Poland; its child protagonist – like JK himself – is driven mute by his experiences. JK regained the power of speech at the age of 15, moved to the USA in 1958, and wrote all his fiction in English. Most of his novels are shaped as mosaics of deracination (◊ FABULATION), and tales like *Cockpit* (**1975**) displace these chips of reality in an sf direction. His nearest approach to sf proper, *Being There* (**1970**), treats the US political system as one from which any meaning has been evacuated; its vacant-minded protagonist, named Chance, reflects through his media-shaped emptiness the desires and delusions of the world, while at the same time being selected to run for high office; it was filmed as *Being There* (1979). JK's later years were not happy. Illness, false accusations of plagiarism, insinuations that he had fabricated elements of his childhood experiences, a failing career, and the fatalism that has often afflicted survivors of the Holocaust attended him. He committed suicide.　　[JC]

About the author: *Jerzy Kosinski: The Literature of Violation* (**1991**) by Welch D. Everman.

See also: ABSURDIST SF.

KOTANI, ERIC Pseudonym used by US astrophysicist and writer Yoji Kondo (1933-　　) for all his fiction. He has been professor of astrophysics at the University of Oklahoma (1972-7), the University of Houston (1974-7), the University of Pennsylvania (from 1978) and concurrently the George Mason University (from 1989), with over 100 scientific papers to his credit. He has edited the journal *Comments on Astrophysics* since 1979, was President of the International Astronautical Union Commission on Astronomy from Space 1985-8, and received a NASA Medal for Exceptional Scientific Achievement in 1990. Compared with the evident achievements of his academic career, his fiction has been quite deliberately lightweight, though vigorously speculative within those limits, consisting in general of adventures substrated by HARD-SF concerns. He is perhaps best known for a NEAR-FUTURE sequence written in collaboration with John Maddox ROBERTS: *Act of God* (**1985**), *The Island Worlds* (**1987**) and *Between the Stars* (**1988**). The action is at times congested, and is somewhat unrelentingly military in orientation, but the vision that unfolds of a bustling and expanding Solar System frequently exhilarates. *Delta Pavonis* (**1990**), also with Roberts, is again an sf adventure; and *Supernova* (**1991**) with Roger MacBride ALLEN, probably his most interesting novel to date, recounts with gripping verisimilitude the scientific process involved in discovering that a nearby star is due to go nova and flood Earth with hard radiation – which happens.　　　　　[JC]

Other works: *Requiem: New Collected Works by Robert A. Heinlein* (coll **1992**) ed EK.

KOTLAN, C.M. [r] ◊ G.C. EDMONDSON.

KOTZWINKLE, WILLIAM (1938-   ) US writer who began his career with several novels for children (see listing below); his genre-crossing FABULATIONS – some of them making use of sf material – created something of a literary stir in the 1970s. These early tales for adults – like *Hermes 3000* (**1972**), *Fata Morgana* (**1977**), set in the Paris of 1871 and plausibly describable as proto-STEAMPUNK, and *Herr Nightingale and the Satin Woman* (**1978**) – tend to treat genre boundaries as thresholds through which characters pass from more or less everyday realities into fantastic or sf-like worlds which rewrite those realities in allegorical terms, sometimes feyly. *Doctor Rat* (**1976**), on the other hand, never shifts from one plane, and seems all the more extraordinary for that consistency. The tale is mostly narrated by an elderly laboratory rat, his mind jumbled by too much maze-running, who sees himself as an active collaborator with the human experimenters; the destiny of the animal world, he feels, is that it be subjected to such experiments for the ultimate good. Crises in the ECOLOGY, however, drive the brutalized animals to form a global consciousness, and war ensues between Man and animals; Doctor Rat heroically quells revolt in the lab, until eventually he is the only animal left alive.

WK is best known in the sf world for some excellent film ties. They include *E.T., The Extra-Terrestrial, in his Adventure on Earth* * (**1982**) – which appeared at the same time as a text for younger readers, *E.T., The Extra-Terrestrial Storybook* * (**1982** chap) – and *E.T., The Book of the Green Planet* * (**1985**; cut for younger readers 1985 chap), based on a story by Stephen SPIELBERG (◊ E.T.: THE EXTRA-TERRESTRIAL) and designed to work as a bridge between the first **E.T.** film and its yet-unmade successor. It too was accompanied by a text for younger readers, *E.T., The Storybook of the Green Planet: A New Storybook* * (**1985** chap), probably derived from the cut version of the main title. A further tie, *Superman III* * (**1983**), is perhaps less memorable.

At the same time WK continued to produce fabulations, including *Christmas at Fontaine's* (**1982**), *Great World Circus* (**1983**), *Queen of Swords* (**1984**), *The Exile* (**1987**), in which a contemporary US actor is transported back to Nazi Germany, where he gets involved in black-market activities, and *The Midnight Examiner* (**1989**), a perhaps overbroad comedy in which a journalist – an ideal kind of protagonist for the typical WK novel – becomes tangled in a world of Mafia revenges, voodoo and other sorceries. Short work has been assembled in *Elephant Bangs Train* (coll **1971**), *Trouble in Bugland: A Collection of Inspector Mantis Mysteries* (coll **1983**) – **Sherlock Holmes** pastiches for younger readers – *Jewel of the Moon* (coll **1985**), *Hearts of Wood and Other Timeless Tales* (coll **1986** chap) – mostly fairytales – and *The Hot Jazz Trio* (coll **1989**), which contains 3 long stories, each involving a transgressive journey from "normal" reality into other worlds, including the Land of the Dead. Because he crosses genres with such ease, WK could fairly be accused of frivolity; but the charge itself seems frivolous when his harsher texts are looked at square.   [JC/PN]

Other works for children: *The Fireman* (**1969**); *The Ship that Came Down the Gutter* (**1970**); *Elephant Boy: A Story of the Stone Age* (**1970**); *The Oldest Man and Other Timeless Stories* (coll **1971**); *The Supreme, Superb, Exalted, and Delightful, One and Only Magic Building* (**1973**); *The Leopard's Tooth* (**1976** chap); *The Ants who Took away Time* (**1978** chap), in which the Solar System must be searched for the ant-dismembered Watch which keeps Time together; *Dream of Dark Harbor* (**1979**); *The Nap Master* (**1979**); *The Empty Notebook* (**1990**).

KOZAK, ELLEN [r] ◊ Sharon JARVIS.

KOZUMI, REI [r] ◊ Takumi SHIBANO.

KRAFT, ROBERT [r] ◊ GERMANY.

KRAJEWSKI, MICHAL DYMITR [r] ◊ POLAND.

KRAKATIT ◊ Karel ČAPEK; CZECH AND SLOVAK SF; TEMNÉ SLUNCE.

KRENKEL, ROY G(ERALD Jr) (1918-1983) US illustrator. A lifelong resident of New York, he studied at Burne Hogarth's School of Visual Arts after WWII and started his career at EC COMICS, where he became friends with Frank FRAZETTA. A great deal of his art, heavily influenced by the work of J. Allen ST JOHN and also by the Australian artist Norman Lindsay (1879-1969), was published in the SWORD-AND-SORCERY fanzine *Amra* (◊ George H. SCITHERS), where it came to the attention of Donald A. WOLLHEIM of ACE BOOKS. Ace were planning to reprint many of the works of Edgar Rice BURROUGHS, and Krenkel's style fitted perfectly. RGF did about 20 of these Burroughs covers, and because of their popularity won a 1963 HUGO as Best Professional Artist; when he could not meet all the deadlines, he got Wollheim to ask Frazetta onto the project, thus launching Frazetta's sf career. Krenkel also did covers for DAW BOOKS, some interior work for sf magazines and, most celebratedly, cover and interior illustrations for several Robert E. HOWARD collections published by Donald M. Grant. Though his covers were good, it was with his pen-and-ink work, his first love, that he was most at home; it is both delicate and spirited. All his best work was in the field of HEROIC FANTASY. A book of his work is *Cities & Scenes from the Ancient World* (**1974**).   [JG/PN]

See also: COMICS.

KRESS, NANCY (ANNE) (1948-   ) US writer who began publishing sf with "The Earth Dwellers" for *Gal* in 1976, and whose first novels were fantasies like *The Prince of Morning Bells* (**1981**), a quest tale during which, surprisingly, the young princess involved ages into an old woman before the close, and *The Golden Grove* (**1984**), which, again surprisingly, treats Greek myth with something of the iron darkness it merits. After a further fantasy novel, *The White Pipes* (**1985**), and an intermittently rewarding collection, *Trinity and Other Stories* (coll **1985**), which includes the

NEBULA-winning "Out of All Them Bright Stars" (1985), NK moved forthrightly into sf with her fourth novel, the slow-moving but cumulatively impressive *An Alien Light* (**1988**), set on a planet inhabited by two sets of irreconcilably opposed humans, the descendants of the people from a starship that crashed there centuries earlier after a battle with the ALIEN Ged. All knowledge of this history has been lost, and the Ged set up a huge technological honey-trap to entice humans inside for study, as they have found the territoriality and attendant aggressiveness of *Homo sapiens* baffling. What they learn from the two sets of stranded humans does not lead them to feel that they will win the war against a species whose savagery seems ultimately unopposable. *Brain Rose* (**1990**), just as impressively, presents an extremely grim NEAR-FUTURE Earth whose inhabitants are harassed by an AIDS-like disease which eats memory; the protagonists of the tale sign up for medically dubious Previous Life Access Surgery (◊ MEDICINE), which is intended somehow to counter the dimming out of the world itself through a "genuine" return to the past. *Beggars in Spain* (**1991**), a novella, is set within a framework familiar to most sf readers: a group of specially bred children who need no sleep must band together to defend themselves against the jealousy and oppressive behaviour of normal humans. But within this frame NK embeds speculations about not only GENETIC ENGINEERING but also the ethical consequences of "superiority" (◊ SUPERMAN) in a world which demands an "ecology of help" to survive; the novella version won a NEBULA, and the full-length version, «Beggars in Spain» (**1992**), which expands the novella into an ironic saga set partly in space, is almost certainly her best work yet. There seem few subjects that NK, in an already fascinating career, will be unable to assimilate. [JC]

See also: ANTHROPOLOGY; ISAAC ASIMOV'S SCIENCE FICTION MAGAZINE; *The* MAGAZINE OF FANTASY AND SCIENCE FICTION.

KRING, MICHAEL K. (1952-) US writer whose **Space Mavericks** series of SPACE OPERAS – *The Space Mavericks* (**1980**) and *Children of the Night* (**1981**) – carries its protagonists through various adventures but not to their destination planet: the conclusion to the series was never published, due to difficulties experienced by MKK's publisher, Leisure Books. [JC]

KROL, GERRIT [r] ◊ BENELUX.

KRONOS Film (1957). Regal/20th Century-Fox. Prod and dir Kurt Neumann, starring Jeff Morrow, Barbara Lawrence, John Emery. Screenplay Laurence Louis Goldman, from a story by Irving Block. 78 mins. B/w.

A scientist is possessed by an alien lifeform of pure energy. Shortly afterwards (the incidents are connected) an "asteroid" (actually a flying saucer) deposits a huge mechanical creature on a Mexico beach. When activated, it moves across the countryside, crushing anything and anyone in its path: its aim is to destroy power stations and absorb their energy, too much of which ultimately causes it to explode after it has been deliberately short-circuited. The script of this low-budget MONSTER MOVIE is mediocre, but Kronos itself is such an unusual monster that it stands out among all the giant reptiles, giant insects, etc., of the 1950s sf boom. Prod/dir Kurt Neumann's other sf films include ROCKETSHIP X-M (1950) and the very successful *The* FLY (1958). [JB/PN]

KUBE-McDOWELL, MICHAEL P. Pseudonym of US writer Michael Paul McDowell (1954-), who attached his wife's name, Kube, to his own in order to avoid confusion with Michael M. McDowell at a time when both authors were writing scripts for the tv series *Tales from the Darkside*. His first published sf story, "The Inevitable Conclusion" for *AMZ* in 1979, also marked the inception of his **Trigon Disunity** sequence, comprising his first three novels – *Emprise* (**1985**), *Enigma* (**1986**) and *Empery* (**1987**) – along with other tales like "Antithesis" (1980). Though failing to rise above some of the less attractive assumptions held by popular writers in the sf field about the comical incompetence of politicians compared to the world-changing nerve of scientific entrepreneurs (◊ EDISONADE), the series triumphs through the expansive exuberance of its premise: that an earlier wave of humanity had long ago colonized the Galaxy, and that the apparent ALIENS whose probing has reawakened contemporary humanity's interest in the stars – and revitalized a decaying planet – are in fact our own cousins; the final volume moves, less convincingly, into a vision of the human species melding its differences through a form of communion. *Alternities* (**1988**) similarly combines efficient action, in this case among a number of ALTERNATE WORLDS, and marginally vapourish speculations about the human species; but *The Quiet Pools* (**1990**), MPK-M's best novel to date, successfully coordinates action and thought in a story about the ambiguous nature of humanity's drive outwards to the stars, carried through the troubled consciousness of a man who is genetically incapable – just as most of humanity has always been – of denying the planet, of leaping into space. The book's genetic determinism, which is much too explicit to have been inadvertent, is both bleak and bracing. Rather more baldly, *Exile* (**1992**) takes the sclerotic China of 1988's Tiananmen Square massacre as a model for the construction of a rigid, terraformed colony world in the throes of a tragic confrontation with its own youth. MPK-M has become, quite suddenly, one of the authors to watch. [JC]

Other works: *Photon: Thieves of Light* * (**1987**) as Michael Hudson, a tv adventure tie; *Isaac Asimov's Robot City #1: Odyssey* * (**1987**), the first of the tied ROBOT sequence.

See also: COMMUNICATIONS.

KUBIN, ALFRED [r] ◊ AUSTRIA.

KUBRICK, STANLEY (1928-) US film-maker, resident in the UK. Born in New York, the son of a doctor, he early became obsessed with photography; *Look* magazine hired him as soon as he left school.

Motion pictures became his dominant interest, and he left *Look* after four years to make two short films with his own money and then two feature films, *Fear and Desire* (1953) and *Killer's Kiss* (1955), borrowing the production money from relatives. By then he had also become a fully qualified cameraman. In 1956 he made *The Killing*, which attracted the attention of critics, and his reputation was further enhanced by *Paths of Glory* (1957); he directed most of *Spartacus* (1960). In 1961 he moved to the UK and, with *Lolita* (1962), began the cycle of films that have made him internationally famous. In 1963 he made his first sf film, DR STRANGELOVE OR: HOW I LEARNED TO STOP WORRYING AND LOVE THE BOMB, and at the end of 1965 he started work on 2001: A SPACE ODYSSEY, which he completed in 1968. His next film was also sf – the controversial A CLOCKWORK ORANGE (1971). Breaking away from sf but remaining true to his concerns, SK's continued his slim output with *Barry Lyndon* (1975), from W.M. Thackeray's novel *The Luck of Barry Lyndon* (1844; **1852**), *The Shining* (1980), from Stephen KING's bestselling *The Shining* (**1977**), and *Full Metal Jacket* (1987), from *The Short Timers* (**1979**), a Vietnam novel by Gustav Hasford (1947-   ). Having avoided direct involvement in Peter Hyam's 2010, the sequel to *2001*, SK is currently (1992) planning a return to sf with an adaption of Brian W. ALDISS's "Super-Toys Last All Summer Long" (1969).

SK is one of the few film-makers who has succeeded in maintaining control over all aspects of his films (*Spartacus* was the exception), and his personal style is stamped on all his work, its most obvious characteristic being a cool and ironic wit. His films manifest a formidable intelligence, unusual in a maker of high-budget spectaculars. SK is reported to have an almost obsessive desire for perfection, which shows itself in a fastidious attention to detail. Critics have emphasized the intellectual authority of SK's work – though some see him as merely cold-bloodedly stylish – but he is also, and perhaps primarily, a consummate showman. His sf work is notable for distasteful, ultimately impotent protagonists dwarfed or cowed by enigmatic, dehumanizing TECHNOLOGY; but his main theme, older than sf, appears to be Original Sin.   [JB/KN/PN]

See also: CINEMA; COMMUNICATIONS; MUSIC; ORIGIN OF MAN; PARANOIA.

KUCZKA, PÉTER (1923-   ) Hungarian publisher and critic who, beginning in the 1960s, was a powerful force in the renaissance of Hungarian sf, even during a period of Hungarian history not conducive to literary experiment (though the situation was liberalized in the 1970s). In 1968 PK took over as controller and editor of the publisher Móra's brand-new sf imprint **Kozmosz Fantasztikus Könyvek**, which was and remains the most important sf publisher in HUNGARY in terms of both original Hungarian sf and translations. In 1972 Móra followed this paperback series with the magazine *Galaktika*, ed PK, first as a quarterly and now as a monthly with a circulation of

about 50,000; it has several times won awards as the best sf magazine in Europe. He also introduced sf into the Hungarian Writers' Association (no easy task in a country whose *literati* and academics have often regarded sf with revulsion), has been from the outset (1972) connected with the Eurocons (trans-European sf CONVENTIONS), and is a director of WORLD SF. Like all impresarios he has been criticized, but he has done more for Hungarian sf than any other individual. He has published a variety of essays on sf, many in Hungarian, some in English, and is the author of the entry on HUNGARY in this encyclopedia.   [PN]

KUNETKA, JAMES [r] ◊ Whitley STRIEBER.

KUPPORD, SKELTON Pseudonym of UK writer J. Adams (?   -?   ), whose sf novel, *A Fortune from the Sky* (**1903**), features several inventions that are all linked to "panergon", which is capable of generating a profitable sky-writing ray but which its inventor soon uses, more conventionally, as a DEATH RAY. Soon the UK is ringed with victims, mostly innocent ones. In the end, world peace is enforced.   [JC]

KUPRIN, ALEXANDER (IVANOVICH) [r] ◊ RUSSIA.

KURD LASSWITZ AWARD ◊ AWARDS.

KURLAND, MICHAEL (JOSEPH) (1938-   ) US writer who began publishing sf in 1964 with "Elementary" with Laurence M. JANIFER for *FSF* and *Ten Years to Doomsday* (**1964**) with Chester ANDERSON. The latter is a lightly written alien-INVASION novel, full of harmless violence in space and on other planets. MK then participated in the writing of an unusual trilogy comprising *The Butterfly Kid* (**1967**) by Anderson, *The Unicorn Girl* (**1969**) by MK and *The Probability Pad* (**1970**) by T.A. WATERS. The books all feature the various authors as characters. *The Unicorn Girl* deals with a number of sf themes in a spoof idiom which is sometimes successful; MATTER TRANSMISSION and invasions abound. Although MK has perhaps gained most recognition for his suspense novel *A Plague of Spies* (**1969**), which won an Edgar Allan Poe Scroll from the Mystery Writers of America, his later sf has admirers for its briskness and its bright touristic promenades through various venues.

Transmission Error (**1970**) is an adventure set on a colourful planet. *Pluribus* (**1975**), a post-HOLOCAUST novel, though breaking no new ground makes effective use of its US locations. *The Whenabouts of Burr* (**1975**) is an ALTERNATE-WORLDS tale featuring Aaron Burr (1756-1836). *The Princes of Earth* (**1978**), a crowded juvenile, takes its young backwater-planet protagonist to school on Mars. *The Last President* (**1980**) with S.W. Barton (pseudonym of Barton Stewart Whaley [1928-   ]) posits the survival of a Nixon-like President in office and his subsequent destruction of democracy. *Star Griffin* (**1987**), another tale whose main flaw is crowdedness, sets its protagonist a series of detective puzzles on an overpopulated Earth choked with sects, some of which may be opposing the development of a FASTER-THAN-LIGHT vehicle. *Perchance* (**1989**) initiates a projected sequence of humorous TIME-TRAVEL tales, to be

called **The Chronicles of Elsewhen**. Unlike many lesser (and some more significant) writers, MK puts the themes and venues of sf to work in a professional manner, with no radical innovations but always imparting a sense of secure competence. [JC]
Other works: The War, Inc series, sf, comprising *Mission: Third Force* (**1967**), *Mission: Tank War* (**1968**) and *A Plague of Spies*; *Tomorrow Knight* (**1976**); two **Sherlock Holmes** pastiches, being *The Infernal Device* ∗ (**1979**) and *Death by Gaslight* ∗ (**1982**); *Psi Hunt* (**1980**); *First Cycle* (coll **1984**) with H. Beam PIPER; a fantasy series set in the **Lord Darcy** universe created by Randall GARRETT, comprising *Ten Little Wizards* ∗ (**1988**) and *A Study in Sorcery* ∗ (**1989**), the latter again invoking Sherlock Holmes; *Button Bright* (**1990**), borderline sf.

KURTÉN, BJÖRN (OLAF) (1924-1988) Finnish palaeontologist and writer; his fiction appeared in Swedish. His sf novels – *Den svarta tigern* (**1978** Sweden; trans BK as *Dance of the Tiger* **1980** US with foreword by Stephen Jay Gould) and *Mammutens Radare* (**1984** Sweden; trans BK as *Singletusk* **1986** US) – fascinatingly apply late-20th-century speculations about EVOLUTION to the old subgenre of prehistoric sf (◊ ANTHROPOLOGY; ORIGIN OF MAN), offering the suggestion that blond and burly Neanderthals fell fatally in love with their Black, beautiful, neotenous Cro-Magnon neighbours, bringing them home to engage in sterile matches. Neoteny can be defined as an indefinite prolongation of childlike behaviour and physical proportions; the notion that our ancestors rose to preeminence through cuteness is intriguing. [JC]

KURTZ, KATHERINE (IRENE) (1944-   ) US writer employed in various fields including oceanography and cancer research, as well as a stint as instructional designer for the Los Angeles Police Department. Her fiction, basically FANTASY, has been dominated from the beginning by the unfolding **Chronicles of the Deryni** sequences, all set in a highly detailed, coherent ALTERNATE WORLD whose society is hierarchical and in many of its aspects medieval Welsh. By internal chronology they are: **The Legends of Camber of Culdi**, comprising *Camber of Culdi* (**1976**), *Saint Camber* (**1978**) and *Camber the Heretic* (**1980**); **The Heirs of Saint Camber**, comprising *The Harrowing of Gwynedd* (**1989**) and *The Chronicles of the Deryni* (omni **1985**), which assembles her first novel, *Deryni Rising* (**1970**), *Deryni Checkmate* (**1972**) and *High Deryni* (**1973**); and **The Histories of King Kelson**, comprising *The Bishop's Heir* (**1984**), *The King's Justice* (**1985**) and *The Quest for Saint Camber* (**1986**). These chronicles tell the history of a group of humans whose witchlike PSI POWERS, the explanation for which hovers between sf and mysticism, cause them to be persecuted by a medieval Church. The first novel is perhaps the best, but the whole is generally much above average for HEROIC FANTASY and is well characterized, although sometimes archaic and modern language clash. Appended to the series are 2 supplementary volumes:

The Deryni Archives (**1986**) and *Deryni Magic: A Grimoire* (**1991**). Her other work of interest includes *The Legacy of Lehr* (**1986**), juvenile sf. [JC/PN]
Other works: *Lammas Night* (**1983**); *The Adept* (**1991**) with Deborah Turner Harris (1951-   ), the first of a projected series.
See also: DEL REY BOOKS; MAGIC.

KUTTNER, HENRY (1914-1958) US writer. His interest in WEIRD TALES early led him to correspond with H.P. LOVECRAFT and others; his first sale to the magazine was a poem, followed by "The Graveyard Rats" (1936). His stories for it included a Robert E. HOWARD-like SWORD-AND-SORCERY series collected as *Elak of Atlantis* (1938-41; coll of linked stories **1985**). He began to publish sf stories in 1937 with "When the Earth Lived" for *TWS*. His early sf work included a series about the movie business of the future: "Hollywood on the Moon" (1938), "Doom World" (1938), "The Star Parade" (1938), "The Energy Eaters" (1939) and "The Seven Sleepers" (1940), the last two in collaboration with Arthur K. BARNES. (He and Barnes also wrote together as Kelvin KENT.) HK achieved a certain notoriety with the slightly risqué stories he wrote for MARVEL SCIENCE STORIES, notably "The Time Trap" (1938). He used many pseudonyms in this part of his career, and even more after marrying C.L. MOORE in 1940, when the two wrote very many stories in collaboration; these names included Paul Edmonds, Noel Gardner, James Hall, Keith Hammond, Hudson Hastings, Robert O. Kenyon, C.H. Liddell, K.H. Maepen, Scott Morgan and Woodrow Wilson Smith. HK also published stories under various house names, including Will Garth, as whom he wrote "Dr Cyclops" (1940), a novelette confusingly unconnected with the novelization of that same year's film DR CYCLOPS, a state of affairs not clarified by the release of the HK tale as the title story of *Dr Cyclops* (anth **1967**) ed anon (◊ Will GARTH for more details).

After their marriage in 1940, most of HK's and Moore's works were to some extent joint efforts – it is said that each could pick up and smoothly continue any story from wherever the other had left off. Moore seems to have been the more fluent and perhaps the more assiduous (indeed, talented) writer, but HK's wit, deftly audacious deployment of ideas and neat exposition complemented her talents very well. During WWII they became part of John W. CAMPBELL Jr's stable of writers working for ASTOUNDING SCIENCE-FICTION. It was then that they devised their best known pseudonyms, Lewis Padgett and Lawrence O'Donnell, much of their best work appearing initially under these names. The Padgett stories are ingenious and slickly written, often deploying offbeat HUMOUR. HK was the sole author of the Padgett **Galloway Gallegher** series collected as *Robots Have No Tails* (1943-8; coll of linked stories **1952** as by Padgett; 1973 as HK; paperback as by HK; vt *The Proud Robot: The Complete Galloway Gallegher Stories* 1983 UK). Other notable Padgett stories include "The Twonky" (1942), filmed as *The* TWONKY (1952), and the classic "Mimsy Were the Borogoves" (1943), about educative toys timeslipped from the future. Two Padgett short novels, *Tomorrow and Tomorrow & The Fairy Chessmen* (1946-7; coll **1951**; 1st story published separately as *Tomorrow and Tomorrow* 1963 UK; 2nd story published separately vt *Chessboard Planet* 1956 US and vt *The Far Reality* 1963 UK), are intensely recomplicated tales in the tradition of A.E. VAN VOGT, whose influence is also evident in the **Baldy** series about persecuted SUPERMEN, assembled as *Mutant* (1945-53; fixup **1953** as by Padgett; 1954 UK as HK). Most of the O'Donnell stories were Moore's work, including the remarkable "Clash By Night" (1943), whose sequel *Fury* (1947 as by O'Donnell; **1950**; vt *Destination Infinity* 1958 US) was a collaboration.

HK and Moore wrote many colourful novels for STARTLING STORIES during the 1940s. "When New York Vanished" (1940) and *The Creature from beyond Infinity* (1940 as "A Million Years To Conquer"; **1968**) are slapdash sf probably by HK alone, but subsequent works – which became archetypes of the hybrid genre SCIENCE FANTASY – neatly fused HK's vigorous plotting with Moore's romanticism. These included *The Dark World* (1946 as by HK; **1965** as by HK), *Valley of the Flame* (1946 as by Keith Hammond; **1964** as by HK), "Lands of the Earthquake" (1947 as by HK), *The Mask of Circe* (1948 as by HK; **1971**), *The Time Axis* (1949 as by HK; **1965**), *Beyond Earth's Gates* (1949 as "The Portal in the Picture" by HK; **1954** dos as by Padgett and Moore) and *Well of the Worlds* (1952 as by HK; as a GALAXY SCIENCE FICTION NOVEL by Padgett **1953**; vt *The Well of the Worlds* as by HK 1965 US). The first, second and fifth were combined in *The Startling Worlds of Henry Kuttner* (omni **1987**). *Earth's Last Citadel* (1943 *Argosy* as by HK and Moore; **1964** as by Moore and HK) also belongs to this sequence, although one other *Startling Stories* novel, "Lord of the Storm" (1947 as by Hammond), does not. For *Startling*'s companion THRILLING WONDER STORIES HK wrote the humorous **Hogben** series about an ill assorted family of MUTANT hillbillies: "Exit the Professor" (1947), "Pile of Trouble" (1948), "See You Later" (1949) and "Cold War" (1949). In 1950 HK and Moore went to study at the University of Southern California; they wrote a number of mystery novels thereafter but very few sf stories. HK graduated in 1954 and went on to work for his MA, but died of a heart attack before it was completed.

During his career HK rarely received the credit his work merited, and was to an extent overshadowed by his own pseudonyms. His reputation as one of the most able and versatile of modern sf writers has risen steadily since. His influence on the young Ray BRADBURY was considerable, and many later writers have acknowledged their debt to him. His short stories are distributed over numerous overlapping collections: *A Gnome There Was* (coll **1950** as by Padgett), *Ahead of Time* (coll **1953**), *Line to Tomorrow*

(coll **1954** as by Padgett), *No Boundaries* (coll **1955** as by HK and Moore), *Bypass to Otherness* (coll **1961**), *Return to Otherness* (coll **1962**), *The Best of Kuttner, Volume 1* (coll **1965** UK) and *Volume 2* (coll **1966** UK), *The Best of Henry Kuttner* (coll **1975**) with intro by Ray Bradbury, *Clash by Night and Other Stories* (coll **1980** UK as by HK and Moore), *Chessboard Planet and Other Stories* (coll **1983** UK as by HK and Moore) and *Secret of the Earth Star and Others* (coll **1991**). Another early sword-and-sorcery series was collected in *Prince Raynor* (1939 *Strange Stories*; coll **1987** chap), while 3 early non-sf stories are in *Kuttner Times Three* (coll **1988** chap). [MJE/BS]

See also: ANTI-INTELLECTUALISM IN SF; ATLANTIS; AUTOMATION; CHILDREN IN SF; COLONIZATION OF OTHER WORLDS; COMICS; CRIME AND PUNISHMENT; DIMENSIONS; DISCOVERY AND INVENTION; ECOLOGY; ECONOMICS; ESP; FANTASY; FAR FUTURE; GAMES AND SPORTS; GODS AND DEMONS; GOLDEN AGE OF SF; INTELLIGENCE; MESSIAHS; OUTER PLANETS; PARALLEL WORLDS; PSI POWERS; RECURSIVE SF; RELIGION; ROBOTS; SCIENTISTS; SUPERMAN [character]; TIME TRAVEL; UFOS; UNDER THE SEA; VENUS.

al-KUWAYRĪ, YŪSUF [r] ◊ ARABIC SF.

KYLE, DAVID A. (*c*1912-   ) US sf fan, writer, illustrator, owner of several radio stations, and publisher. DK is a member of "first fandom", having been active in the field since 1933. Until the 1970s his writing activities were only occasional. His first published sf was "Golden Nemesis" for *Stirring Science Stories* in 1941. In 1948, with Martin GREENBERG, he founded the fan publishing company GNOME PRESS, which maintained what were probably the highest standards of any of the SMALL PRESSES of the period; DK designed several of the book jackets. For much of the 1970s DK was resident in the UK, where he wrote two well and lavishly illustrated coffee-table-style books on sf, the first dealing primarily with the HISTORY OF SF and the second with sf's dominant themes: *A Pictorial History of Science Fiction* (**1976**) and *The Illustrated Book of Science Fiction Ideas and Dreams* (**1977**). Both are descriptive rather than analytic, and the main interest of their texts, which are conservatively skewed towards HARD SF of the so-called GOLDEN AGE OF SF, is in their well informed data about sf PUBLISHING.

When E.E. "Doc" SMITH's **Lensman** books were reissued in the early 1980s, new novels were published by other hands, continuing and infilling the series. DK, who had been a friend of Smith, wrote 3 of these: *The Dragon Lensman* (**1980**), *Lensman from Rigel* (**1982**) and *Z-Lensman* (**1983**). The second, perhaps the most interesting, is about an ALIEN who has progressed to the level of Second Stage Lensman. DK succeeded to a degree in capturing the flavour of Smith, but not his compulsiveness. [PN]

See also: BRITISH SCIENCE FICTION AWARD; FUTURIANS; ILLUSTRATION; NEW WAVE.

LACH-SZYRMA, W(LADISLAW) S(OMERVILLE)
(1841-1915) UK Anglican clergyman and author who
began writing his series of interplanetary romances
featuring the travels around the Solar System of the
winged Venusian Aleriel in a magazine story in 1865;
this was incorporated into *A Voice from Another World*
(**1874** as by WSL-S; exp vt *Aleriel, or A Voyage to Other
Worlds* as by the Rev. W.S. Lach-Szyrma 1883).
Aleriel's further travels were chronicled in his anonymous **Letters from the Planets** series in *Cassell's
Family Magazine*, 9 stories (1887-93) which were
reprinted in *Worlds Apart* (anth **1972**) ed George
LOCKE. *Under Other Conditions* (**1892**), which belongs
to the series, tells of another Venusian's adventures
on Earth. These rather preachy stories concentrate on
sightseeing and ethics, but fair-mindedly stress that
other planetary conditions may lead to other customs. Lach-Szyrma could be considered a minor
forerunner to C.S. LEWIS. [PN]

See also: MARS; MOON; VENUS.

LACKEY, MERCEDES [r] ◊ C.J. CHERRYH; Anne
McCAFFREY; Andre NORTON.

LADY AND THE MONSTER, THE Film (1944).
Republic. Prod and dir George Sherman, starring
Vera Ralston, Richard Arlen, Erich von Stroheim,
Sidney Blackmer. Screenplay Dane Lussier, Frederick
Kohner, based on *Donovan's Brain* (**1943**) by Curt
SIODMAK. 86 min. B/w.

This is the first of the 3 film versions of Siodmak's
novel; the others are DONOVAN'S BRAIN (1953) and
VENGEANCE (1963; vt *The Brain*). Financial wizard
W.H. Donovan is killed when his plane crashes in the
desert. An obsessive SCIENTIST (von Stroheim), whose
laboratory is nearby, removes the undamaged brain
and keeps it alive in a glass tank, but it gradually
takes over the minds of those around it, forcing them
to commit a series of evil deeds. The photography is
atmospheric, but the film overall is routine GOTHIC
melodrama. [JB/PN]

See also: CINEMA.

LAFARGUE, PHILIP Pseudonym of UK writer and
physician Joseph Henry Philpot (1850-1939), whose
The Forsaken Way: A Romance (**1900**) depicts the UK at
the close of the 20th century as a romantic ruin. After
falling in love, the protagonist leaves his monastery
and starts a new life. [JC]

LAFAYETTE, RENE [s] ◊ L. Ron HUBBARD.

LAFFERTY, R(APHAEL) A(LOYSIUS) (1914-   ) US
writer who worked in the electrical business until
retiring in 1971; he came to writing only in his 40s,
publishing his first sf, "Day of the Glacier", with *The
Original Science Fiction Stories* in 1960. Over the next
25 years (he reportedly retired from writing at the age
of about 70) he produced many stories – about 200
have been published – and a number of novels. The
extremely active SMALL-PRESS interest in his work gave
birth to a large number of titles in the late 1980s, most
of them short collections, but much RAL material
remains apparently in manuscript, including several
of the titles mentioned in *The Complete Book of Science
Fiction and Fantasy Lists* (**1983**) by Malcolm EDWARDS
and Maxim JAKUBOWSKI.

There are reasons for this apparent neglect of a
writer whose originality and whose value to the sf/
fantasy world have never been questioned. From the
first, RAL demonstrated only the slenderest interest
in making his stories conform to any critical or
marketing definition of either sf or fantasy. He has
fairly been described as a writer of tall tales, as a
cartoonist, as an author whose tone is fundamentally
oral; his conservative Catholicism has been seen as
permeating every word he writes (or has been
ignored); he has been seen as a ransacker of old
MYTHOLOGIES, and as a flippant generator of new
ones; he delights in a vision of the world as being
irradiated by conspiracies both godly and devilish,
but at times pays scant attention to the niceties of
plotting; he has been understood by some as essentially light-hearted and by others as a solitary,
stringent moralist; he is technically inventive, but

lunges constantly into a slapdash sublime; his skill in the deploying of various rhetorical narrative voices is manifest, but these voices are sometimes choked in baroque flamboyance. He was awarded a 1973 HUGO for Best Short Story for "Eurema's Dam" (1972); and in the 1960s and 1970s, partly through his (in retrospect tenuous) association with the NEW WAVE, he was seen as a figure of looming eccentricity and central import. For his career's sake, it was certainly unfortunate that his response to renown seems to have been an intensification of the oddness of his product; final judgement on the effect of this failure to observe normal canons of writing still awaits a coherent presentation of his work as a whole. However, though many stories remain uncollected, RAL did assemble several volumes which grant some view of the entirety, including *Nine Hundred Grandmothers* (coll **1970**), *Strange Doings* (coll **1972**), *Does Anyone Else Have Something Further to Add?* (coll **1974**), *Ringing Changes* (coll **1984**; 1st published in Dutch trans as *Dagan van Gras, Dagan van Stro* ["Days of Grass, Days of Straw"] 1979), *Golden Gate and Other Stories* (coll **1982**), *Through Elegant Eyes: Stories of Austro and the Men who Know Everything* (coll **1983**), and *Lafferty in Orbit* (coll **1991**), which puts together all the work originally published in Damon KNIGHT's ORBIT series of original anthologies (1967-80). Many other stories have been printed as chapbooks (see listing below).

RAL's first three novels, *Past Master* (**1968**), *The Reefs of Earth* (**1968**) and *Space Chantey* (**1968** dos), all appeared within a few months of one another, causing some stir. Pre-publication praise for *Past Master* (accolades from New-Wave writers Samuel R. DELANY, Roger ZELAZNY and Harlan ELLISON) demonstrated the impact his work was beginning to have, and, though it can be said that the US New Wave amounted more to an iconoclastic tone of voice than a programme, its generally sardonic air proved bracing to such mature writers as RAL, whose entry at age 45 into the field seemed to betoken its growing maturity. *Past Master* places Sir Thomas More on the planet Astrobe, where he is tricked into becoming World President and suffers once again a martyr's death: the contrasts between UTOPIA and life are laid down without the normal derision. *Space Chantey* retells HOMER's *Odyssey* as SPACE OPERA, very rollickingly, and is the most representative of RAL's attempts to liberate sagas by transposing them into a rambunctious, myth-saturated, never-never-land future. In *The Reefs of Earth* (RAL's first-completed novel) a passel of ALIEN children bumptiously attempt to rid Earth of humans, and fail. More complexly, *Fourth Mansions* (**1969**), possibly RAL's most sustained single novel, articulates with some clarity the basic underlying bent of his best work: a protagonist (or several) finds a pattern of flamboyant, arcane, dreamlike clues to a conspiracy (or conspiracies) between Good and Evil whose outcome will determine the moral nature of reality to come; and enters

the fray joyously (though confusingly) upon the side of the angels.

Though much of RAL's work shares characters, and plot segments shuttle back and forth from book to book, he has written only one explicit genre series, the **Argos Mythos**: *Archipelago: The First Book of The Devil is Dead Trilogy* (**1979**), *The Devil is Dead* (**1971**), *Promontory Goats* (**1988** chap Canada), *How Many Miles to Babylon?* (**1989** chap Canada) and *Episodes of the Argo* (coll **1990** chap Canada), the latter including the conclusion of the long-written third part of the series, the **More than Melchisedech** sequence, whose full publication has now begun with *Tales of Chicago* (**1992**). The **Argos Mythos** treats a group of WWII buddies as reincarnations of Jason's Argonauts, and engages them in a long, myth-saturated battle against Evil. Later novels, like *Arrive at Easterwine: The Autobiography of a Ktistec Machine* (**1971**), the life story of a COMPUTER which also features in some stories as well, begins to evince a tangledness that comes, at times, close to incoherence. "The Three Armageddons of Enniscorthy Sweeny", the second novel-length tale assembled in *Apocalypses* (coll **1977**), suggests that the comprehensive power of opera (◊ MUSIC) might, in an alternate world, stop war. *Dotty* (**1990** chap Canada), though not directly part of the **Argos Mythos** and ostensibly not sf or fantasy at all, embraces the "mundane" world, sf, fantasy, Jason, the Argonauts and much else in 96 packed pages. Even now the full explication of the extremities of RAL's large universe remains impossible; for it seems there is more to come.   [JC]

Other works: *The Fall of Rome* (**1971**); the **Coscuin Chronicles**, historical novels transfigured into fable, of which have been published *The Flame is Green* (**1971**) and *Half a Sky* (**1984**); *Okla Hannali* (**1972**), historical; *Not to Mention Camels: A Science Fiction Fantasy* (**1976**); *Funnyfingers & Cabrito* (coll **1976** chap); *Horns on their Heads* (**1976** chap); *Aurelia* (**1982**); *Annals of Klepsis* (**1983**); *Snake in his Bosom and Other Stories* (coll **1983** chap); *Four Stories* (coll **1983** chap); *Heart of Stone, Dear and Other Stories* (coll **1983** chap); *Laughing Kelly and Other Verses* (coll **1983** chap); *The Man who Made Models and Other Stories* (coll **1984** chap); *Slippery and Other Stories* (coll **1985** chap); the first two chapters of *My Heart Leaps Up (1920-28)* (**1986** chap), followed by chapters 3 and 4 (**1987** chap), 5 and 6 (**1987** chap), 7 and 8 (**1988** chap) and 9 and 10 (**1990** chap), making up the first volume of the projected **In a Green Tree** sequence, the second volume of which, *Grasshoppers & Wild Honey (1928-1942)*, was continued on the same basis, starting with chapters 1 and 2 (**1992** chap); *Serpent's Egg* (**1987** UK; 1 story added to the limited issue to make coll 1987); *The Early Lafferty* (coll **1988** chap Canada) and *The Early Lafferty II* (coll **1990** chap Canada); *East of Laughter* (**1988** UK; with 1 story added to the limited issue to make coll); *Strange Skies* (coll **1988** chap Canada), verse; *The Back Door of History* (coll **1988** chap Canada); *The Elliptical Grave* (**1989**; with 1 story added to the limited issue to make coll 1989); *Sindbad: The 13th Voyage* (**1989**); *Mischief Malicious (and Murder Most Strange)* (coll **1991** chap Canada), which contains work from as early as 1961; «Iron Tears» (coll 1992).

Nonfiction: *It's Down the Slippery Cellar Stairs* (coll **1984** chap), *True Believers* (coll **1989** chap); *Cranky Old Man from Tulsa: Interviews with R.A. Lafferty* (coll **1990** chap Canada).

About the author: *An R.A. Lafferty Checklist* (**1991** chap) by Dan Knight.

See also: CITIES; END OF THE WORLD; FANTASTIC VOYAGES; HEROES; HUMOUR; INTELLIGENCE; LINGUISTICS; MESSIAHS; PERCEPTION; REINCARNATION.

LAGRANGE POINT In 1772 the French mathematician Joseph Louis Lagrange (1736-1813) calculated that in the orbit of Jupiter around the Sun there would be two stable positions, one 60° ahead of the planet, the other 60° behind, where a comparatively tiny mass would remain in stable orbit around the Sun rather than being swept up Jupiter's gravitational field. (More than a century later two groups of ASTEROIDS, the Trojans, were found at these positions in Jupiter's orbit.) This is a general principle, part of what is sometimes called the three-body problem, although usually more than 3 bodies must be considered; for example, if planning to site a SPACE HABITAT at one of the Lagrange Points (or Lagrangian Points) of the Earth-Moon system, one must take into account also the gravitational presence of the Sun (the mass of the habitat itself can be discounted as trivially small). There are 5 Lagrange Points in the Earth-Moon system; they are not absolutely fixed in relation to the Earth and Moon but, because of the Sun's influence, slowly circle "Lagrange Regions". They are numbered L1 to L5.

The Princeton physicist Gerard K. O'Neill (1927-1992), an important propagandist for space colonies, argued in *The High Frontier* (**1977**) that good sites for such colonies would be L4 and L5, 60° ahead of and behind the Moon in its orbit. He particularly liked L5, and this region soon became something of an sf CLICHÉ as the site for fictional space cities consisting of clusters of habitats. [PN]

LAIDLAW, MARC (1960-   ) US writer who began publishing work of genre interest with "A Hiss of Dragon" with Gregory BENFORD for *Omni* in 1978. Though he published solo stories with some frequency in the 1980s, his best known short work is perhaps the group of mathematically oriented tales written with Rudy RUCKER, such as "Chaos Surfari" (1989). ML's first novel, *Dad's Nuke* (**1985**), is a SATIRE of suburban life and Christian fundamentalism set in a NEAR-FUTURE community effectively sealed off from the rest of the disintegrating USA; ritual technological fixes for anxiety include having a personal nuclear power plant and a baby adapted (◊ GENETIC ENGINEERING) to recycle the wastes into her lead-lined diapers. ML's second novel, the amusing *Neon Lotus* (**1988**), follows the consequences of the REINCARNATION of a Tibetan Buddhist sage as a young girl in a highly

technologized USA. «Kalifornia» (1993) is a further satire. [NT]

See also: TECHNOLOGY; WEAPONS.

LAING, ALEXANDER (KINNAN) (1903-1976) US writer, editor and academic, noted for his books on the sea, for editing *The Haunted Omnibus* (anth **1937**; vt *Great Ghost Stories of the World* 1939), and for his murder novel, *The Cadaver of Gideon Wyck, by a Medical Student* (**1934**), which hinges on horrific changes to the human body. Two further books with fantastic elements are *Dr Scarlett: A Narrative of his Mysterious Behavior in the East* (**1936**) and its sequel, *The Methods of Dr Scarlett* (**1937**). In collaboration with Thomas PAINTER, AL wrote an sf thriller, *The Motives of Nicholas Holtz, Being the Weird Tale of the Ironville Virus* (**1936**; vt *The Glass Centipede, Retold from the Original Sources* 1936 UK). Persuasively authentic in its use of biological data, it is a well told story of the creation of artificial life in the form of a deadly virus, and of the dangers that beset the man who investigates the ensuing deaths. [PN]

See also: MONSTERS.

LAKE, DAVID J(OHN) (1929-   ) Indian-born Australian writer (he emigrated in 1967), originally a UK citizen; his education (a Jesuit school in India, a BA in English at Cambridge, a diploma in linguistics and a PhD in English) is reflected in the texture of his sf work, as is his teaching in Vietnam, Thailand and India (1959-67). After publishing several works of criticism, including the strongly argued, somewhat controversial *The Canon of Thomas Middleton's Plays* (**1975**) and a volume of poetry, *Hornpipes and Funerals* (coll **1973**), which deals with some of the themes of his fiction, he began publishing sf with the first of his **Breakout Novels** sequence, *Walkers on the Sky* (**1976** US). It was followed by *The Right Hand of Dextra* (**1977** US) and *The Wildings of Westron* (**1977** US), both set on Dextra; by *The Gods of Xuma, or Barsoom Revisited* (**1978** US) and *Warlords of Xuma* (**1983** US), which constitute a riposte to the sexism and crudity of E.R. BURROUGHS's **Barsoom** novels; and by *The Fourth Hemisphere* (**1980**), set on yet another planet. All the books in the sequence share certain fundamental premises: in WWIV (AD2068) Earth destroys itself, and by AD2122 the colonies of the Moon are also in the throes of terminal conflict; but, before the final collapse, interstellar ships break out of the Solar System in search of suitable planets for COLONIZATION. The novels to date are set on various of these planets and share comparatively simple, action-packed surface narratives matched with considerable complexity of implication, some of it Jungian. *Walkers on the Sky*, set AD12117, entertainingly carries a young man across a terraformed world irradiated by planes of force whose operation explains the dreamlike behaviour indicated by the title. *The Right Hand of Dextra*, set earlier, in AD2687, intermingles biological, religious and colonization themes in the story of the reconciliation between incompatible forms of biological organization on a planet whose human colonists are religious fundamentalists insensitive to the vital questions surrounding Dextra's weird ECOLOGY.

Of books lying outside this central sequence, the most interesting is perhaps *The Man who Loved Morlocks* (1981). Ostensibly a sequel to H.G. WELLS's *The Time Machine* (1895), it also works as a sustained and loving critique of that book, of its author and of the late-19th-century mind-sets which shaped both. *Ring of Truth* (1982; vt *The Ring of Truth* 1984 US) is a POCKET-UNIVERSE tale of surreal intensity whose climax – unusually for this sort of book – provides no soothing explanation for the shape of the world. *The Changelings of Chaan* (1985) and *West of the Moon* (1988) are juveniles. Despite an occasional truculent stiffness of diction, DJL is a writer of fully realized fictions whose work, almost always, flows with thought. [JC]
See also: ALIENS; AUSTRALIA; COSMOLOGY; EVOLUTION; GRAVITY; SOCIOLOGY; TIME TRAVEL; TRANSPORTATION.

LALLI, CELE G. [r] ◊ Cele GOLDSMITH.

LA MASTER, SLATER (1890-?   ) US writer whose *Cupid Napoleon* (1928 *Argosy-All-Story* as "Luckett of the Moon"; **1934**) is a delusional interplanetary romance whose satirical effects are seriously jumbled. *The Phantom in the Rainbow* (1929) is marginal sf. [JE/JC]

LAMB, WILLIAM ◊ Storm JAMESON.

LAMBE, DEAN R. [r] ◊ Michael A. BANKS.

LAMBERT, S.H. ◊ Neil BELL.

LAMBOURNE, JOHN Form of his name used on books by UK writer John Battersby Crompton Lamburn (1893-?   ), brother of Richmal Crompton (1890-1969), authoress of the **Just William** children's books. JL's *The Kingdom that Was* (1931) and its sequel *The Second Leopard* (1932) are mildly allegorical, subduedly humorous works describing how, 50,000 years ago, the apathetic rulers of the animal kingdom were led to abdicate in favour of mankind. JL also wrote *The Unmeasured Place* (1933), about a female vampire-cum-were-leopard. [JE]

LAMPLUGH, LOIS (1921-   ) UK editor and writer whose *Mandog* * (**1972**) novelizes Peter DICKINSON's script for a tv tale for children. [JC]

LAMPTON, CHRIS Working name of US writer Christopher Lampton (1950-   ), who began writing sf with *The Seeker* (**1976** Canada) with David F. BISCHOFF. He continued with two further competent sf adventures, *Cross of Empire* (**1976** Canada) and *Gateway to Limbo* (**1979**). [JC]

LANCE, KATHRYN (1943-   ) US writer. Much of her work has consisted of non-sf tales for children, often as by Lynn Beach (see listing below). Her sf has been restricted to the **Pandora** sequence – *Pandora's Genes* (1985) and *Pandora's Children* (1986) – set in a post-HOLOCAUST world where pluck and luck seem set to ensure a viable future. [JC]
Other works, as Lynn Beach: contributions to the **Find your Fate: G.I. Joe** sequence, including *G.I. Joe: Operation Jungle Doom* * (**1986**), *G.I. Joe: Operation Time Machine* * (**1987**) and *Invisibility Island* * (**1988**); the **Phantom Valley** sequence of fantasy adventures

starring a warlock boy, comprising *Phantom Valley #1: H.O.W.L. High* (**1991**), *#2: The Evil One* (**1991**), *#3: The Dark* (**1991**) and *#4: Scream of the Cat* (**1992**); other titles, variously attached to juvenile fantasy series, include *Secrets of the Lost Island* * (**1984** chap), *The Attack of the Insecticons* * (**1985** chap), *Conquest of the Time Master* * (**1985**), *The Haunted Castle of Ravencurse* * (**1985**) and *Invaders from Darkland* * (**1986**).

LANCOUR, GENE Working name of Gene Lancour Fisher (1947-   ), US author of the SWORD-AND-SORCERY **Dirshan** series about Dirshan the God-Killer, a barbarian warrior: *The Lerios Mecca* (**1973**), *The War Machines of Kalinth* (**1977**), *Sword for the Empire* (**1978**) and *The Maneaters of Cascalon* (**1979**). GL's next book was sf: *The Globes of Llarum* (**1980**) puts a mercenary on the side of rebel independents against a giant corporation on a frontier planet; complications routinely ensue. [PN]

LANDIS, ARTHUR H(AROLD) (1917-1986) US author and editor. While editing for *Dealer's Voice*, a motorcycle magazine, AHL convinced his publisher to begin a new fantasy magazine, *Coven 13*, which AHL edited for 4 issues Sep 1969-Mar 1970 before the title passed to William L. CRAWFORD. The 4-part serial "Let There Be Magick" in *Coven 13*, by AHL as James R. Keaveney, became *A World Called Camelot* (1969-70; rev **1976**) as by AHL, and was followed in the same series by *Camelot in Orbit* (**1978**), *The Magick of Camelot* (**1981**) and *Home – To Avalon* (**1982**). In the first novel a cultural engineer, or "Adjuster", is sent from Earth to the second planet of Fomalhaut, known as Camelot, a world where MAGIC works, rather as in Christopher STASHEFF's **Warlock** series. Sf meets SWORD AND SORCERY in a whimsical manner throughout the series, whose quality deteriorates. The final volume is set on a different world. [PN]

LANDIS, MARIE [r] ◊ Brian HERBERT.

LAND OF THE GIANTS US tv series (1968-70). An Irwin Allen Production for 20th Century-Fox TV/ABC. Created Irwin ALLEN, also executive prod. Writers included Bob and Esther Mitchell, Bob and Wanda Duncan, Richard Shapiro, Dan Ullman, William Welch. Dirs included Harry Harris, Nathan Juran, Sobey Martin, Irwin Allen (1st episode only). Regular cast Gary Conway, Kurt Kasznar, Don Marshall, Heather Young, Don Matheson, Deanna Lund, Stefan Arngrim. Special effects L.B. Abbott, Art Cruickshank, Emil Kosa Jr. 2 seasons, 51 50min episodes. Colour.

Carrying on in the tradition of such films as DR CYCLOPS and *The* INCREDIBLE SHRINKING MAN (◊ GREAT AND SMALL) as well as an earlier tv series, WORLD OF GIANTS, the first episode showed 7 people aboard a future "stratocruiser" passing through a space/time-warp into a world similar to 20th-century Earth, but where all things, including people, are 12 times larger. The series concerned their predictable encounters with giant people and giant props. Three novelizations by Murray LEINSTER are *Land of the Giants* * (**1968**), *Land of the Giants #2: The Hot Spot* * (**1969**) and

#3: *Unknown Danger* * **(1969)**. Others were *Land of the Giants: Flight of Fear* * **(1969)** by Carl Henry RATHJEN and *Land of the Giants: The Mean City* * **(1969)** by James Bradwell. [JB/PN]

LANDOLFI, TOMMASO (1908-1979) Italian writer, active as an author of short fictions from 1929. Three selections have appeared in English: *Gogol's Wife and Other Stories* (coll trans Raymond Rosenthal, John Longrigg and Wayland Young **1963** US), *Cancerqueen and Other Stories* (coll trans Raymond Rosenthal **1971** US) – which includes the short title novel, *Cancroregina* (**1950**; first trans Jack Murphy as "Cancroregina" 1950 *Botteghe Oscure*), about a mad astronaut imprisoned in a living starship – and *Words in Commotion and Other Stories* (coll trans Kathrine Jason **1986** US), a volume taken mostly from *La più belle pagine di Tommaso Landolfi* ["The Best Pages of Tommaso Landolfi"] (coll **1982**), a compilation introduced by Italo CALVINO, who compares TL to writers like VILLIERS DE L'ISLE-ADAM. TL's laconic, surreal, testing FABULATIONS, which also resemble those of Jorge Luis BORGES and Franz KAFKA, clearly influenced Calvino in turn. [JC]

LAND THAT TIME FORGOT, THE Film (1975). Amicus. Dir Kevin Connor, starring Doug McClure, John McEnery, Susan Penhaligon. Screenplay Michael MOORCOCK, James CAWTHORN, adapted from *The Land that Time Forgot* (**1924**) by Edgar Rice BURROUGHS. 95 mins. Colour.

This UK film was the first of 3 LOST-WORLD Burroughs adaptations produced by Amicus, the others being AT THE EARTH'S CORE (1976) and The PEOPLE THAT TIME FORGOT (1977). A German U-boat – with a contingent of male Germans, Britons and one American, plus a young woman – discovers Caprona, a long-lost landmass near the South Pole. It is crawling with prehistoric monsters and cavemen who do their best to destroy the invaders, with little success. The film ends with a volcanic eruption and the marooning of the hero and heroine. The various monsters are unconvincing. The script by Moorcock and Cawthorn was altered extensively by the producers. [JB]

LANE, JANE Pseudonym of UK writer Elaine Dakers (1905-1978), author of many esteemed historical novels. Her post-HOLOCAUST sf novel, *A State of Mind* (**1964**), is set in an ORWELL-like DYSTOPIA. [JC]

LANE, JOHN ◊ Dennis HUGHES.

LANE, MARY E. BRADLEY (? -?) US writer of whom nothing is known other than that she may have been the author of *Mizora: A Prophecy: A Mss. Found Among the Private Papers of Princess Vera Zarovitch: Being a True and Faithful Account of her Journey to the Interior of the Earth, with a Careful Description of the Country and its Inhabitants, their Customs, Manners and Government* (*Cincinatti Commercial* 1880-81; **1890** anon; 1975, with 2 prefaces, as by Mary E. Bradley Lane). This obscure, part-radical, part-conservative UTOPIA is set mainly within a HOLLOW EARTH, where an all-woman society (◊ FEMINISM) whose children are produced by parthenogenesis has an advanced technology and stringent laws: they have eliminated brunettes and all men, and by eugenics have produced a race of blonde superwomen. With men gone, crime is gone. The book is notable for the ruthlessness of its social speculations, quite extreme for 19th-century utopian writing. [PN]

LANG, ALLEN KIM (1928-) US writer who began publishing sf with "Machine of Klamugra" for *Planet Stories* in 1950 and wrote a good number of action stories in the following decade. *Wild and Outside* (**1966**) sends a US baseball shortstop to subdue a planet of alien musclemen. [JC]

LANG, ANDREW (1844-1912) Scottish man of letters well known for a wide range of literary activity, including novels, poetry, belles-lettres, anthropology, children's books and (perhaps most familiar to current readers) anthologies of traditional fables and tales retold for children, with some added hagiographical and historical material, much of the work being done by his wife; numerous volumes followed the first of these, *The Blue Fairy Book* (anth **1889**). The rather delicate fantasy content of many of his children's tales gives them a nostalgic interest for some adults today; representative are: *The Gold of Fairnilee* (**1888**); *Prince Prigio* (**1889**) and *Prince Ricardo of Pantouflia: Being the Adventures of Prince Prigio's Son* (**1893**), which has a trip to the Moon on a flying horse, both titles being assembled as *My Own Fairy Book* (omni **1895**); and *Tales of a Fairy Court* (coll **1906**), which contains more **Prince Prigio** stories.

Some of AL's adult fiction contains more bracing material, however, though *Much Darker Days* (**1884**; rev 1885) as by A. Hugh Longway, which parodies *Dark Days* (**1884**) by Hugh Conway (1847-1885), does so without venturing into the sensational fantasies of its target, and *That Very Mab* (**1885**), written with May Kendall – the pseudonym of Emma Goldworth (1861-?1931) – and published anon, is a rather feeble SATIRE involving the return of the fairy queen to a 19th-century England where (we discover incidentally) interplanetary travel exists. The title story of *In the Wrong Paradise and Other Stories* (coll **1886**) is less ineffectual in its dramatization of the dictum that one man's paradise is another man's hell. In the same volume, "The Romance of the First Radical" is an early example of anthropological sf (◊ ANTHROPOLOGY; ORIGIN OF MAN), predating H.G. WELLS's "A Story of the Stone Age" (1897) by more than a decade. Why-Why, a revolutionary Ice Age citizen, falls in love with Verva, asks intolerable questions of his tribe, and comes to a sad end. "The End of Phaeacia" (same volume) is a lost-race (◊ LOST WORLDS) tale in which a missionary is shipwrecked on a South Sea ISLAND that turns out to be the Homeric Phaeacia. *The Mark of Cain* (**1886**) introduces, late in the action, a flying machine as *deus ex machina* to solve a court case. Some of the pieces collected in *Old Friends: Essays in Epistolary Parody* (coll **1890**) represent a forerunner format for the writing of RECURSIVE SF.

Considerably more durable is AL's collaboration

with his friend H. Rider HAGGARD, whose *She* (**1887**) he parodied in *He* (**1887**), written with Walter Herries Pollock (1850-1926) and published anon. After this, AL joined with Haggard to write *The World's Desire* (**1890**), a novel which combines Haggard's crude, sometimes haunting vigour and AL's chastely pastel classicism; despite occasional longueurs, the resulting tale of Odysseus's last journey to find Helen in Egypt is a moving, frequently eloquent romance, coming to a climax with Odysseus's discovery that Helen is the avatar of Ayesha (of Haggard's *She*) and his death at the hands of his son. *The Disentanglers* (coll of linked stories **1901** chap US; much exp 1902 UK), AL's last book of adult fiction, is fundamentally uncategorizable, though its sections have some resemblance to the CLUB STORY; some of its episodes deal with submarines, occult sects, spectres and so forth, all used – as Roger Lancelyn GREEN noted in the best work on AL, *Andrew Lang* (**1946**) – to replace the traditional "magical devices of the fairy tale" with the latest scientific developments, though retaining the magical function. Copious, but flawed by a disheartening dilettantism, AL's work lies just the wrong side of major ranking in the sf/fantasy field, just as in his other areas of concentration. [JC]

Other works: *Pictures at Play, or Dialogues of the Galleries* (coll **1888**) with W.E. Henley (1849-1903), as by Two Art-Critics; *A Monk of Fife: A Romance of the Days of Jeanne d'Arc* (**1895**); *When it was Light: A Reply to "When it was Dark"* (**1906**), an anon response to Guy THORNE's 1903 novel; *Tales of Troy and Greece* (coll **1907**).

LANG, FRITZ (1890-1976) Austrian film-maker who, after trouble with the Nazis, left Germany for France in 1933 and emigrated to the USA in 1934. He was originally trained as an architect but preferred the graphic arts; during the years before WWI he supported himself as a cartoonist and caricaturist. He turned to writing after being wounded during WWI, producing several popular thrillers and fantasy romances. After WWI ended he entered the German film industry and began directing a series of lavish melodramas, such as *Die Spinnen* (1919; vt *The Spiders*), many of which were sf-related, involving lost races (◊ LOST WORLDS), technology-driven plots to take over the world, etc. In this vein was the first **Dr Mabuse** film, DR MABUSE, DER SPIELER (1922; vt *Dr Mabuse, the Gambler*). In 1923-4 he made a majestic 6hr fantasy, based directly on the myth rather than on Wagner: *Die Nibelungen* (released as 2 separate films, *Siegfrieds Tod* [vt *Siegfried*] and *Kriemhilds Rache* [vt *Krimhild's Revenge*]). Like all FL's German films, this was cowritten with his wife, Thea VON HARBOU. In 1925 he started work on another epic, his first real sf film, METROPOLIS (1926); it is deservedly the most celebrated of all sf films of the silent period. Von Harbau novelized the script as *Metropolis* * (**1926**; trans anon **1927** UK). FL's other major sf film was *Die FRAU IM MOND* (1929; vt *The Girl in the Moon*); von Harbou's novelization, *Frau im Mond* * (**1928**; trans

Baroness von Hutten as *The Girl in the Moon* 1930 UK; cut vt *The Rocket to the Moon; From the Novel, The Girl in the Moon* 1930 US) was published in Germany before the film was released.

FL's German films of the 1930s included the famous murder movie *M* (1931), which introduced Peter Lorre, and *Das Testament des Dr Mabuse* (1933; vt *The Testament of Dr Mabuse*). The latter, parts of which were interpreted as anti-Nazi, involved the master criminal operating through hypnotic powers and even undergoing a form of REINCARNATION, transferring his mind into the body of the director of the lunatic asylum in which he had been locked up at the end of the previous film.

FL directed 22 films during his first 25 years in the USA, mostly low-budget though often impressive thrillers, such as *Fury* (1936), *You Only Live Once* (1937) and *The Big Heat* (1953). The nearest thing to another sf film he ever directed was his last film, made back in Germany, *Die TAUSEND AUGEN DES DR MABUSE* (1960; vt *The Thousand Eyes of Dr Mabuse*; vt *The Diabolical Dr Mabuse*). The influence of FL's harsh, expressive style on genre cinema, especially on thrillers, psychological thrillers and sf films, has been incalculable. He was a master at depicting the compulsiveness and the politics of power, and most film critics regard him as a great director. [PN/JB]

Further reading: *The Cinema of Fritz Lang* (**1969** US) by Paul M. Jensen; *Fritz Lang* (**1976** UK) by Lotte Eisner; *Fritz Lang: The Image & The Look* (**1981** US) by Stephen Jenkins.

See also: CINEMA; CITIES; COMICS; GERMANY; ROCKETS.

LANG, HERRMANN (? -?) Ostensibly a German writer and professor in the Polytechnic School at Karlsruhe, with publications in chemistry. However, there seems to have been no German edition of his sf novel, *The Air Battle: A Vision of the Future* (ostensibly trans **1859**), and HL is most likely the pseudonym of a UK writer. The novel presents in short compass a remarkable portrait of a world several millennia hence, long after European civilization has been destroyed by floods and earthquakes; the peace-loving Black rulers of the country of Sahara dominate Africa, and in a final battle with other powers utilize their great heavier-than-air machines to establish a beneficial hegemony over the world. Remarkably for a novel of this period, miscegenation is strongly approved of, and the White woman whose adventures the plot traces is destined to marry a Black man. [JC]

See also: HOLOCAUST AND AFTER; POLITICS; WAR.

LANG, KING House name used by CURTIS WARREN on several sf novels: five by David GRIFFITHS and 1 each by George HAY, Brian HOLLOWAY, John William JENNISON and E.C. TUBB. [JC]

LANG, SIMON Pseudonym of US screenwriter and author Darlene Hartman (1934-). SL's SPACE OPERAS – *All the Gods of Eisernon* (**1973**) and continuing with *The Elluvon Gift* (**1975**) – constitute a loose series, both featuring the Terran starship **Skipjack** and both set in the same galactic venue. The first novel is the more ambitious, presenting in the planet Eisernon an idyllic picture of an ALIEN race ecologically integrated with Nature. Both books feature more ominous aliens, too, and suffer from their all too clear resemblance to STAR TREK, for which SL had written. [JC]

LANGART, DARREL T. ◊ Randall GARRETT.

LANGE, HELLMUTH [r] ◊ GERMANY.

LANGE, JOHN ◊ Michael CRICHTON.

LANGE, OLIVER (1927-   ) A pseudonym. In OL's *Vandenberg* (1971; vt *Defiance: An American Novel* 1984) the eponymous hero fights to the death against Soviet takeover of the USA, retreating to the Rocky Mountains to die undefeated. [JC]

LANGELAAN, GEORGE (1908-   ) French-born UK writer and journalist, active for many years in the USA before returning to France. His collection of sf/horror stories, *Out of Time* (coll 1964 UK), includes "The Fly" (1957), a macabre story of an unsuccessful experiment in MATTER TRANSMISSION, in which the scientist ends up with the head of a fly. It was filmed as *The* FLY (1958), with various sequels. He has published several works in French, including *Nouvelles de l'anti-monde* ["Tales of the Anti-World"] (coll 1962) and *Le vol de l'anti-g* ["The Flight of Anti-G"] (1967). [JC/PN]

LANGFORD, DAVID (ROWLAND) (1953-   ) UK writer, critic and sf fan, in the latter capacity recipient of 6 HUGO awards for fan writing – some of the best of his over 450 pieces are assembled as *Platen Stories* (coll 1987 chap) – plus 1 Best FANZINE Hugo for his self-produced news magazine, ANSIBLE. DL began to publish sf with "Heatwave" for *New Writings in SF 27* (anth 1975) ed Kenneth BULMER. His first book-length fiction, *An Account of a Meeting with Denizens of Another World, 1871* (1979) as by William Robert Loosley and ed DL, centres on a spoof 19th-century report of a Close Encounter; its main narrative was summarized as if factual, without permission or payment, by Whitley STRIEBER in his "fiction based on fact", *Majestic* (1989). In DL's one serious novel, *The Space Eater* (1982), emissaries from a devastated Earth are sent by an unpleasant form of MATTER TRANSMISSION to a distant colony planet, where they must stop the local military from ripping the fabric of the Universe. *The Leaky Establishment* (1984), borderline sf, hilariously examines a crisis involving lost nuclear warheads at what many readers have assumed is Aldermaston Atomic Weapons Research Establishment (where DL, who has an MA in physics, worked 1975-80). In *Earthdoom!* (1987) with John Grant (Paul BARNETT), a parody of the DISASTER novel, a multitude of catastrophes afflicts the world, more or less simultaneously. *The Dragonhiker's Guide to Battlefield Covenant at Dune's Edge: Odyssey Two* (coll 1988) assembles parodies of sf and fantasy writers. Though some of his short fiction is entirely serious, DL remains best known for the witty and ironic humour of his fan writing – perhaps best distilled in the

fanzine *Twll Ddu* (1976-83) – and most of his full-length fiction, although it is sometimes over-broad. It is surprising that a writer so obviously gifted has as yet produced so little sf of real substance.

DL has also written, often in collaboration, a variety of nonfiction texts of sf interest, all imaginatively conceived and soundly based: *War in 2080: The Future of Military Technology* (1979), *Fact and Fallacies: A Book of Definitive Mistakes and Misguided Predictions* (1981) with Chris MORGAN, *The Science in Science Fiction* (1982) with Peter NICHOLLS and Brian STABLEFORD, *Micromania: The Whole Truth about Home Computers* (1984), which is a reworking for the UK market of Charles PLATT's *Micromania: The Whole-Truth Home Computer Handbook* (1984), and *The Third Millennium (A History of the World: AD 2000-3000)* (1985) with Stableford. [JC/NT]

Other works: *The Necronomicon* (anth 1978) ed George HAY, DL's contribution being to construct a hoax history of the "lost occult text" invented by H.P. LOVECRAFT; *The Transatlantic Hearing Aid* (1985 chap), nonfiction; *A Novacon Garland* (coll 1985 chap dos), fiction and nonfiction; *Critical Assembly* (coll 1987), book reviews; *Let's Hear it for the Deaf Man* (coll 1992 chap US) ed Ben Yalow, nonfiction.

See also: ANTHROPOLOGY; BLACK HOLES; BRITISH SCIENCE FICTION AWARD; COSMOLOGY; GENETIC ENGINEERING; HUMOUR; HYPERSPACE; IMMORTALITY; NEW WRITINGS IN SF; PREDICTION; PSEUDO-SCIENCE; UFOS; UTOPIAS; WEAPONS.

LANGUAGES ◊ LINGUISTICS.

LANIER, STERLING E(DMUND) (1927-   ) US editor and writer. SEL did 6 years' graduate work at the School of Anthropology and Archeology at the University of Pennsylvania before working as an editor, mainly for Chilton Books for periods during 1961-7; he persuaded the firm to publish Frank HERBERT's *Dune* (fixup 1965). He subsequently turned freelance, working as as a sculptor and jeweller and as a writer.

His first published story was "Join our Gang?" for *ASF* in 1961, but the majority of his short work belongs to the **Brigadier Ffellowes** series published in *FSF*. Like Lord DUNSANY's **Jorkens** stories or Arthur C. CLARKE's *Tales from the White Hart* (coll 1957), the Ffellowes tales are examples of the CLUB STORY, as narrated by the eponymous brigadier; they mostly involve the irruption of mythical creatures into the real world. They are assembled in *The Peculiar Exploits of Brigadier Ffellowes* (coll 1972) and *The Curious Quest of Brigadier Ffellowes* (coll 1986). SEL's first novel was a good children's fantasy, *The War for the Lot* (1969), about a young boy telepathically selected to defend a tract of wilderness from city rats. His second remains his most important: *Hiero's Journey* (1973) – and its sequel, *The Unforsaken Hiero* (1983), both being assembled as *Hiero Desteen* (omni 1984) – is a long and inventive quest tale set in a teeming post-HOLOCAUST world 5000 years after an atomic war. Radiation dangers and recidivist mutant SCIENTISTS still haunt this venue, threatening Hiero, who treks down from

Canada searching for a mythical COMPUTER which might help reconstruct things. In the second volume, which returns to the plot of *The War for the Lot*, Hiero telepathically marshals some animal allies and fights off an invasion of the Unclean Masters. Not precisely innovative, the sequence succeeds through its author's fluent and ingeniously varied cast of characters. A later singleton, *Menace under Marswood* (**1983**), tamely repeats some of the same material on a terraformed MARS.   [JC/MJE]

See also: FANTASTIC VOYAGES; MUTANTS; MYTHOLOGY.

LAO SHE [r] ◊ CHINESE SF.

LARGE, E(RNEST) C(HARLES) (? -1976) UK plant pathologist and occasional fiction writer. *Sugar in the Air* (**1937**) is a notable and original sf novel bitterly describing the conflicts which arise between scientific and commercial interests during the development of an industrial process of artificial photosynthesis. Its sequel, *Asleep in the Afternoon* (**1939**), is a SATIRE whose frame narrative about the tribulations of an author is interwoven with a frivolous sf story about a device for inducing sleep. In the more adventurous sarcastic fantasy *Dawn in Andromeda* (**1956**) God translocates a representative sample of humanity by way of experiment; the political evolution of the community and the spontaneous regeneration of RELIGION confound the UTOPIAN schemes of the original group but cannot suppress mechanical progress.   [BS]

See also: DISCOVERY AND INVENTION; SCIENTISTS; SOCIOLOGY.

LARSON, GLEN A. (1937-) US TELEVISION producer, perhaps best known as producer of BATTLESTAR GALACTICA (from 1978). However, GL had been long involved with tv previously, being responsible for *Quincy*, *McCloud*, *BJ and the Bear* and other non-sf programmes before he turned to sf. All the sf tv series that GAL has produced have been simplistic, grossly formulaic, and generally contemptuous of science; in interviews he has adopted a cavalier attitude about the various SCIENTIFIC ERRORS pointed out to him. However, he remained loyal to sf/fantasy programming on tv for a number of years. Subsequent series of this kind for which he received the "Created by" credit include: the **Battlestar Galactica** sequel-series GALACTICA 1980 (1980); BUCK ROGERS IN THE 25TH CENTURY (1979-81); his most successful series, *Knight Rider*, 4 seasons, 83 episodes 1982-6, starring David Hasselhoff as Michael Knight, the former police officer almost killed in an accident who is given a new identity and groovy futuristic car controlled by a COMPUTER called KITT (Knight Industries Two Thousand), to help him catch bad people as a kind of licensed vigilante; *Manimal*, 8 episodes 1983, about a shapeshifting crimefighter, Jonathan Case (Simon MacCorkindale), who catches bad people by adopting the guise of panther, eagle, etc.; *Automan*, 11 episodes 1983-4, starring Desi Arnaz Jr as the computer expert who creates Automan (Chuck Wagner), the world's first living holographic image, to catch bad people; and *The Highwayman*, 10 episodes 1987-8,

another road-movie series in which future law enforcers, Highwaymen, use futuristic vehicles to catch bad people, starring Sam Jones.

GL was given cover credit for writing, always in collaboration, the **Battlestar Galactica** series of tied novels, including *Battlestar Galactica* * (**1978**) with Robert THURSTON, *Battlestar Galactica #2: The Cylon Death Machine* * (**1979**) with Thurston, *#3: The Tombs of Kobol* * (**1979**) with Thurston, *#4: The Young Warriors* * (**1980**) with Thurston, *#5: Galactica Discovers Earth* * (**1980**) with Michael RESNICK, *#6: The Living Legend* * (**1982**) with Nicholas YERMAKOV, *#7: War of the Gods* * (**1982**) with Yermakov, *#8: Greetings from Earth* * (**1983**) with Ron GOULART, *#9: Experiment in Terra* * (**1984**) with Goulart, *#10: The Long Patrol* * (**1984**) with Goulart, *#11: The Nightmare Machine* * (**1985**) with Thurston, *#12: "Die, Chameleon!"* * (**1986**) with Thurston, *#13: Apollo's War* * (**1987**) with Thurston and *#14: Surrender the Galactica!* * (**1987**) with Thurston. With Roger Hill, GL wrote a series of **Knight Rider** ties: *Knight Rider* * (**1983**), *#2: Trust Doesn't Rust* * (**1984**), *#3: Hearts of Stone* * (**1984**) and *#4: The 24-Carat Assassin* * (**1984** UK).   [PN/JC]

Other works: *The Hardy Boys and Nancy Drew Meet Dracula* * (**1978**) with Michael Sloan.

LA SALLE, VICTOR House name used on early paperback sf novels published by John Spencer & Co. (later BADGER BOOKS). *Menace from Mercury* (**1954**) was the first-published novel of the prolific R.L. FANTHORPE (his only VLS title). *Dawn of the Half-Gods* (**1953**) and *Twilight Zone* (**1954**) were by John S. GLASBY. The remainder were: *The Black Sphere* (**1951**) by Gerald EVANS, *After the Atom* (**1953**) by Leonard G. FISH, and *Assault from Infinity* (**1953**), *The Seventh Dimension* (**1953**) and *Suns in Duo* (**1953**), all by Tom W. WADE.   [SH/MJE]

LASERBLAST Film (1978). Irwin Yablans. Prod Charles BAND. Dir Michael Rae, starring Kim Milford, Cheryl Smith, Gianni Russo. Screenplay Franne Schacht, Frank Ray Perilli. 80 mins. Colour.

In this ill made, low-budget exploitation movie a miserable teenager finds in the desert an amulet and a laser left by ALIENS. The amulet makes his eyes glow red; taken over by the alien persona, he revenges himself with the laser on people who pick on him, also exploding many cars and a *Star Wars* poster before the returning aliens get him.   [PN]

LASER BOOKS Canadian sf imprint initiated in 1975 by Harlequin Books, the US publisher of Mills & Boon romances, under the editorship of Roger ELWOOD. The books were restricted to a formula which specified a male protagonist, an upbeat ending, no sex or atheism, and a minimum of long words. All Laser Book covers were the work of Frank Kelly FREAS. The series was suspended early in 1977 after 57 books had appeared. The Laser formula made it unlikely that books of any literary quality would be published, but some were interesting, including K.W. JETER's début, *Seeklight* (**1975**), and Ray NELSON's *Blake's Progress* (**1975**; rev vt *Timequest* 1985 US).   [MJE]

LASKI, MARGHANITA (1915-1988) UK writer, one of the most prolific contributors of material (over 250,000 wordslips) to the Oxford English Dictionary. Though she was not an avowed author of sf, her work often edged snappishly into the fantastic, and she early demonstrated an uncircumscribed sense of good writing in *The Patchwork Book: A Pilot Omnibus for Children* (anth **1946**), whose sf contents included several stories by H. Rider HAGGARD, Edgar Allan POE, Jules VERNE and others. *Love on the Super-Tax* (**1944**) borders on sf in its depiction of a wartime transformation of the UK. *Tory Heaven* (**1948**) is a class-ridden spoof UTOPIA set in an ALTERNATE-WORLD UK in which the Conservative Party has won the 1945 election. *The Victorian Chaise Longue* (**1953**) is a fantasy in which two invalids, 100 years apart, switch identities. *The Offshore Island* (written 1954; **1959** chap) is a strongly pacifist sf play set in a UK continuing to suffer the effects of nuclear HOLOCAUST after 10 years of war. It stingingly condemns (while linking) the sexual prudery and political ruthlessness of the great powers. Two volumes of nonfiction – *Ecstasy* (**1961**) and *Everyday Ecstasy* (**1980**) – deal sympathetically with categories of experience often used within the genre as agents or symbols of transition to a better world.   [JC]

Other works: *The Tower* (**1974** chap US).

LASSWITZ, KURD (1848-1910) German Kantean philosopher, historian of science, novelist and short-story writer. As the first major sf writer in German, he holds the same place in GERMANY as do H.G. WELLS in the UK and Jules VERNE in France. He taught philosophy for many years at the Gymnasium Ernestinum in Gotha, and it is symptomatic of 19th-century German intellectual culture that he irradiated his fiction with theoretical speculation; there is no KL fiction without a lesson. In "German Theories of Science Fiction" (1976 *Science-Fiction Studies*) William B. Fischer claims on KL's behalf that many of his ideas directly prefigure later critics' use of terms like "extrapolation" and "analogue", and translates as follows from KL's introduction to the short-story collection *Bilder aus der Zukunft* ["Images of the Future"] (coll **1878**): "Many inferences about the future can be drawn from the historical course of civilization and the present state of science; and analogy offers itself to fantasy as an ally." The seriousness of KL's didactic impulse can be seen in the strong emphasis he places in his fiction on establishing a plausible imaginary world whose hypothetical nature will be governed, and given verisimilitude, by the resemblance to scientific method evident in its realization.

Unsurprisingly, the stories that embody these overriding concerns tend to be more effective as broad technological and scientific canvases than as studies in character. The tales collected in *Bilder aus der Zukunft* read consequently almost like illustrated tours of various "superior terrestrial cultures located in the future". (A short story from this volume was published in *Overland Monthly* in 1890 as "Pictures of the Future".) Further short stories are collected in *Seifenblasen* ["Soap Bubbles"] (coll **1890**), 2 stories from this volume appearing (trans Willy LEY 1953 and 1955) in *FSF*, and *Nie und Nimmer* ["Never, Ever"] (coll **1902**); 2 sf novels, *Aspira* (**1906**) and *Sternentau* ["Star Dew"] (**1909**), have not been translated into English.

KL's major work is his long sf novel, *Auf zwei Planeten* (**1897**; cut 1948; cut again 1969; trans Hans J. Rudnick, much cut, as *Two Planets* **1971** US), in which mankind confronts a superior Martian culture when a Martian SPACE HABITAT is discovered above the North Pole along with an enclave at the pole itself. After useless defiance of the Martians, Earth is put under a benign protectorate, and humans gradually begin a process of self-improvement at the same time that the Martians on Earth become decadent. Ultimately mankind rebels, equality between the two planets is established, and Earth seems destined to a UTOPIAN future. The book incorporates much technological speculation, including details about life on MARS – based on the theories of Percival Lowell (1855-1916) – possible alien forms of biology (◊ XENOBIOLOGY), and the nature of mankind, actual and potential. It was deeply influential upon at least two generations of German youth, as the epigraph to the 1971 translation by Wernher von Braun (1912-1977) attests; and E.F. BLEILER has speculated that it was important in shaping Hugo GERNSBACK's "technologically based liberalism".

In 1981, the Kurd Lasswitz AWARDS were established to honour, in a fashion meant to reflect the HUGO, the best German sf published during the previous year.   [JC]

See also: HISTORY OF SF; INVASION.

LAST BATTLE, THE ◊ *Le* DERNIER COMBAT.

LAST DAYS OF MAN ON EARTH, THE ◊ *The* FINAL PROGRAMME.

LAST MAN ON EARTH, THE ◊ *L'*ULTIMO UOMO DELLA TERRA.

LAST STARFIGHTER, THE Film (1984). Lorimar/Universal. Dir Nick Castle, starring Lance Guest, Dan O'Herlihy, Catherine Mary Stewart, Norman Snow, Robert Preston. Screenplay Jonathan Betuel. 101 mins. Colour.

In this cheerful, derivative wish-fulfilment story, Alex (Guest), who lives in a trailer park, is a teenage whiz at computer arcade games. Attaining the highest-ever score on the *Starfighter* game, he is conscripted (though at first refusing) by its inventor, an alien (Preston), to play a real-life version of the game in a real starfighter and so save the Galaxy from the invasion of the Ko-Dan Empire. While he is offworld, his place on Earth is taken by a robot simulacrum; this leads to amusing problems. Made for a juvenile audience, *TLS* is achieved with such good humour (and interesting computer animation for the space battles) that it survives its silliness to become quite a good film. The novelization is *The Last*

Starfighter * (**1984**) by Alan Dean FOSTER. (*For further discussion of computer-game/real-life confusions* ◊ CYBER-SPACE; VIRTUAL REALITY.) [PN]

LAST WOMAN ON EARTH Film (1960). Filmgroup. Prod and dir Roger CORMAN, starring Antony Carbone, Betsy Jones-Moreland, Edward Wain (pseudonym of Robert Towne). Screenplay Towne. 71 mins. Colour.

For unexplained reasons (war?) the world is drained of oxygen for several hours; the lone survivors (as far as we know) are three scuba divers: two men (one wealthy and aggressive, one effete and intellectual) and the first man's wife. Scientifically silly and poorly acted, with scriptwriter Towne – later celebrated for *Chinatown* (1974) and other films – called in to play the intellectual part at the last minute, *LWOE* still has compelling moments. For a quickie-movie the script is remarkably mannered; yet it may be a sharper, less sentimental film than the more famous *The* WORLD, THE FLESH AND THE DEVIL (1959), on which it was presumably modelled. [PN]

LATHAM, PHILIP Pseudonym used for his sf by US astronomer Robert Shirley Richardson (1902-1981). He began publishing sf in the magazines in 1946 with "N-Day" for *ASF*, and continued to 1977, with 20 or so stories in all; many had astronomical themes (◊ ASTRONOMY). The most anthologized is "The Xi Effect" (1950), in which Earth is found to be in a segment of the Universe that is contracting. Many of the later stories, oddly, are as much about MAGIC as they are HARD SF. PL wrote two CHILDREN'S SF stories: *Five against Venus* (**1952**) and *Missing Men of Saturn* (**1953**), and around the same time also wrote scripts for the juvenile tv series CAPTAIN VIDEO. As Robert S. Richardson he wrote astronomical articles for sf magazines, the story "Kid Anderson" (1962), the semifictional *Second Satellite* (**1956**), and over 10 books on astronomy, including the juvenile *Exploring Mars* (**1954**; vt *Man and the Planets* UK). [PN]

See also: DISASTER; OUTER PLANETS; PHYSICS; SCIENTISTS; SUN; VENUS.

LATHE OF HEAVEN, THE Made-for-tv film (1980). TV Laboratory WNET/13, New York, for PBS. Prod and dir David R. Loxton and Fred Barzyk, starring Bruce Davison, Kevin Conway, Margaret Avery. Teleplay Roger E. Swaybill, Diane English, based on *The Lathe of Heaven* (**1971**) by Ursula K. LE GUIN. 120 mins. Colour.

Made outside the commercial system for Public Television, this may be the best sf tv-movie ever made, with innovative use of existing reality (futuristic high-rises in Dallas, for example) substituting for expensive sets. The visual consultant was Ed EMSHWILLER. The story of George Orr (Davison), who can dream permanent changes to reality, is both here and in Le Guin's chilling original a moral fable rather like the fairy-tales about three wishes. Orr's talent is exploited by an ambitious psychiatrist (Conway), but every time he tries to dream a better world something frightful goes wrong, OVERPOPULATION being cured by

plague or, later, racism cured by everybody turning grey. The deliquescence of reality, whose binding glue is ultimately in danger of dissolving (the ending is ambiguous), is subtly caught, and the viewer has to be observant to register every change. [PN]

See also: VIRTUAL REALITY.

LATIN AMERICA Although deeply influenced by US-UK sf, modern sf in Latin America is also affected by the fantastic traditions of Indian and colonial times, and in some instances by a conscious decision to depart from English-speaking traditions. "Anglo-Saxon sf explores in one way: the way in which Anglo-Saxons think and feel," writes Argentinian critic and author Claudio Omar Noguerol. "Latin-American sf explores as only a person immersed in the turbulence of Latin America can do it."

Since the continent produces very little technology and scientific research but is a consumer (and sometimes victim) of technological advance, its sf has stressed the social, economic and political costs of progress. In that respect, Latin-American sf has paralleled the NEW-WAVE movement of the 1960s in the US and UK, with the added advantage (albeit dubious) of not being restricted by the market pressures of pulp publishing: in most Latin-American countries publishers have yet to exploit the commercial potential of sf. Sf as a *literary* pursuit is more notable than in countries where mass-marketability is a requisite. Sf novels are relatively scarce; sf is more often than not in the form of short fiction and, frequently, POETRY. Its authors are commonly social scientists or professional writers, only a very few coming from the ranks of the hard sciences.

Latin-American sf is also very close to the political turmoil that surrounds it, and has frequently been the only available channel for social criticism when and where military dictatorships have been in control. Therefore, although there is a certain overall Latin-American identity, it is not always easy to generalize. Argentina, Cuba and Mexico, for instance, have such widely different histories, geographies, political systems and inhabitants that sometimes the Spanish language (and some universal aspirations) are the only common ground shared by their literature; in the case of Portuguese-speaking Brazil there is also the language barrier. Unfortunately, US and UK market conditions have made it almost impossible for Spanish- or Portuguese-language sf writers to publish in those countries.

Argentina

Under the influence of such writers of the fantastic as Macedonio Fernández (1874-1952), the Uruguayan-born Horacio Quiroga (1878-1937), Roberto Arlt (1900-1942) and Leopoldo Lugones (1874-1938) – as well as the undefinable work of Jorge Luis BORGES, which often borders on unconventional sf – and of sf precursors such as E.L. Holmberg (1852-1937), author of *Viaje maravilloso del señor Nic Nac* ["The Wonderful Voyage of Mr Nic Nac"] (**1875**), the magazine *Más allá* ["Beyond"] (1953-7) published 48 issues featuring the work of the first modern generation of sf writers in the country. The second generation – heralded by the short-lived magazine *Revista de ciencia ficción y fantasía* ["Magazine of Science Fiction and Fantasy"] (1977) – arrived in the 1970s and 1980s and has been especially interested in social issues as well as language; sf's rebirth was in part due to the downfall of the military regime. This allowed the creation of the Círculo Argentino de Ciencia Ficción y Fantasia ["Argentinian Circle of Science Fiction and Fantasy"] and the publishing of several FANZINES (*Unicornia azul, Nuevo-mundo, Clepsidra* and *Sinergia,* among others, plus *Axxón,* published in diskette form) as well as professional magazines, like *Parsec* and *Minotauro,* and scores of books. Argentina hosts the annual South-American sf and fantasy convention, Consur.

Among the best known Argentinian authors are Borges, Adolfo BIOY CASARES and Angélica Gorodischer (1929-   ), whose 2-vol *Kalpa Imperial* ["Imperial Kalpa"] (coll vol 1 1983, vol 2 1984) is one of the best stylistic examples of modern Latin-American sf, though she sometimes veers towards pure fantasy. Other books by her are *Opus dos* ["Opus Two"] (coll 1967), *Bajo las jubeas en flor* ["Under the Flowering Jubeas"] (coll 1973) and *Casta luna electrónica* ["Chaste Electric Moon"] (coll 1977). The work of Eduardo Goligorski (1931-   ), author of *A la sombra de los bárbaros* ["Under the Shadow of the Barbarians"] (coll 1977), is closer to conventional sf. He became one of the few Latin-American writers to publish in *FSF* – with "When the Birds Die" (1967) – and edited the most representative 1960s Argentinian sf anthology, *Los argentinos en la Luna* ["Argentinians on the Moon"] (anth 1968). Other writers include: Carlos Gardini, author of *Mi cerebro animal* ["My Animal Brain"] (1983) and *Sinfonía cero* ["Zero Symphony"] (1984); Magdalena Mouján Otaño; Emilio Rodrigué, author of *Plenipotencia* ["Full Powers"] (coll 1967); Alberto Vanasco (1925-   ), who collaborated with Goligorski in *Memorias del futuro* ["Memories of the Future"] (anth 1966) and *Adiós al mañana* ["Goodbye to Tomorrow"] (anth 1966); Daniel Barbieri (1951-   ), author of *Domún* (1991); Spanish-born Marcial Souto (1947-   ), author of *Para bajar a un pozo de estrellas* ["To Go Down a Well of Stars"] (coll 1985); and Sergio Gaut vel Hartman (1947-   ), author of *Cuerpos descartables* ["Disposable Bodies"] (coll 1985).

Cuba

Sf in Cuba originated in the poetry of Oscar Hurtado (1919-1977), as in *La ciudad muerta de Korad* ["The Dead City of Korad"] (1964), and the stories and novels of Angel Arango (1926-   ), which include (*¿A dónde van los cefalomos?* ["Where do the Cephalhoms Go?"] (coll 1964), *El planeta negro* ["The Black Planet"] (coll 1966), *Robotomaquia* ["Robotomachy"] (coll 1967), *El arco iris del mono* ["The Monkey's Rainbow"] (coll 1980), *Transparencia* ["Transparency"] (coll 1982) and *Coyuntura* ["Juncture"] (coll 1984). Cuban sf has been influenced both by Caribbean magical traditions and by Soviet sf – there were no real precedents for Cuban sf before the 1959 revolution. Although no specialized Cuban sf magazines exist, sf stories were well received in most periodical publications and dozens of titles were published every year until, in 1990, Cuban publishing began to suffer severe problems owing to lack of paper.

Cuban sf began to find its own identity through the work of Arango and of Miguel Collazo (1936-   ), author of *El libro fantástico de Oaj* ["The Fantastic Book of Oaj"] (1966), *El viaje* ["The Journey"] (1968), *Onoloria* and *El arco de Belén* ["The Arch of Bethlehem"]. It has a strongly political trend but also, less expectedly, purely fantastic and clearly erotic traits, best exemplified by the work of Daína Chaviano (1957-   ), first winner in the sf category (established 1979) of the national literary award, the David, with her short-story collection *Los mundos que amo* ["The Worlds I Love"] (coll 1980). Her other books to date are *Amoroso planeta* ["Loving Planet"] (coll 1983), *Historias de hadas para adultos* ["Fairytales for Adults"] (coll 1986), *Cuentos de una abuela extraterrestre* ["Stories from an Extraterrestrial Grandmother"] (1988) and *El abrevadero de los dinosaurios* ["The Waterhole of the Dinosaurs"] (coll 1990). Other Cuban sf writers to be noted are: Gregorio Ortega (1926-   ), author of *Kappa*[15] (1982); Chely Lima (1957-   ) and Alberto Serret (1947-   ), a vanguardist couple who collaborated on *Espacio abierto* ["Open Space"] (coll 1983); F. Mond, author of *Con perdón de los terrícolas* ["You'll Excuse Us, Earthmen"] (1983); Agustín de Rojas (1949-   ), author of *Espiral* ["Spiral"] (1982); Gabriel Céspedes (1946-   ), author of *La nevada* ["The Snowstorm"] (1985); and Félix Lizárraga (1958-   ), author of *Beatrice* (1982). Most of these have won the David.

Mexico

The history of sf in Mexico perhaps begins with a FANTASTIC-VOYAGE story whose title has been lost. It was written by the Franciscan monk Manuel Antonio de Rivas and was cited among the charges (later dismissed) brought against him in 1773 by the Inquisition. In this story he defended the experimental method and the philosophy of the Age of Reason, and like many others of his time used a tale of the Moon and of ALIENS as a pretext for social criticism. In the early decades of this century the Modernist poet Amado Nervo (1870-1919), with his story "La última guerra" ["The Last War"] (1920), and the soldier-novelist Francisco L. Urquizo (1891-1969), with *Mi tío Juan* ["My Uncle Juan"] (1934), wrote the first works that are clearly sf. It was not until the 1960s, when hundreds of sf books translated from English and published in SPAIN reached the country, that Mexicans began to write sf consistently. A short-lived magazine, *Crononauta,* and several books – notably *Mexicanos en el espacio* ["Mexicans in Space"] by Carlos Olvera and *La nueva prehistoria* ["The New Prehistory"] (coll 1968) by Colombian-born René

Rebetez – fuelled interest in the genre. Also influential were the 1960s COMIC-book series **Los supersabios** ["The Super-Scientists"] by Germán Butze and the short stories of Costa Rican-born Alfredo Cardona Peña, the dean of Mexican sf, notably "La niña de Cambridge" ["The Cambridge Girl"]. Peña's books include *Fábula contada* ["Fable Told"] (coll **1972**) and *Los mejores cuentos de magia y misterio* ["The Best Magic and Mystery Stories"] (coll **1990**). Among those considered to be the first generation of Mexican sf writers are: Manú Dornbierer, author of *Después de Samarkanda* ["After Samarkand"] (**1977**); María Elvira Bermúdez (1912-1989) (short stories); Tomás Mojarro (1932-), author of *Trasterra* (**1973**); Marcela del Río, author of *Proceso a Faubritten* ["Trial Against Faubritten"] (**1976**); Agustín Cortés Gaviño (1946-), author of *Hacia el infinito* ["Towards the Infinite"] (**1968**) and (*¿De donde . . . ?* ["Whence . . . ?"] (**1969**). All of these have published books as well as short stories in mainstream magazines, though none has made sf the centre of his or her work. Some MAINSTREAM WRITERS have also approached sf themes; e.g., José Agustín, author of *Cerca del fuego* ["Near the Fire"], José Emilio Pacheco, author of *La sangre de Medusa* ["Medusa's Blood"], and, most notably, the internationally celebrated Carlos FUENTES, author of *Cristóbal nonato* (**1987**; trans Alfred MacAdam and the author as *Christopher Unborn* **1989** US).

Between these efforts around the 1960s and the rebirth of Mexican sf in 1984 the main interest was again Anglo-Saxon sf, although there was a small, continuing publication of sf stories in scientific, mainstream and literary magazines. 1984 saw the establishment, through the efforts of Celine Armenta, biologist and fan, of the Puebla SF Short Story National Award. This sparked off open interest in the genre among literally hundreds of (mostly young) Mexican writers. Many of these now devote themselves exclusively or primarily to sf and fantasy (although several also write crime fiction, as do many of their colleagues among Cuban and Argentinian sf writers). This second generation has attempted to create a peculiarly Mexican sf, with characters, scenery and circumstances corresponding to the Mexican urban and rural reality, while at the same time sufficiently accessible to foreign readers. This has been evident in the 7 stories to date that have won the Puebla Award, all of which, along with some "honourable mentions", have been published in the bimonthly science magazine *Ciencia y desarrollo* ["Science and Development"]. The first anthology of second-generation Mexican sf was *Más allá de lo imaginado* ["Beyond the Imagined"] (anth 2 vols **1991**) ed Federico Schaffler, with 26 authors represented.

Other recent sf books include: *Vértigos y barbaries* ["Vertigos and Barbarisms"] (coll **1988**) by Irving Roffe; *Absurdo concursante* ["The Absurd Contestant"] (coll **1988**) and *Breve eternidad* ["Brief Eternity"] (coll **1991**) by Federico Schaffler; *Los ojos de Ciro* ["Ciro's Eyes"] (coll **1984**) by Juan Cervera; *Dime con quién andas y te diré quién herpes* (coll **1985**) and *Apenas seda azul* ["Only Blue Silk"] (coll **1987**) by Gonzalo Martré; *Miríada* ["Thousand"] (coll **1991**) and the critical essay *La ciencia ficción: literatura y conocimiento* ["Science Fiction: Literature and Knowledge"] (**1991**) by Gabriel Trujillo; and *Escenas de la realidad virtual* ["Scenes From Virtual Reality"] (coll **1991**) by Mauricio-José SCHWARZ. A new annual award, the Kalpa, has been announced; the first national convention, ConPuebla, was held in 1991; and a new SEMIPROZINE, *Estacosa* ["Thisthing"], was launched in Nov 1991. There is room for some optimism in the predominantly bleak scene of sf publishing. [M-JS]

Brazil
The most important PROTO SCIENCE FICTION from Brazil is "Páginas da História do Brasil, escritas no Ano 2000" ["Pages of a History of Brazil, Written in the Year 2000"] (1868-72 in the newspaper *O Jequitinhonha*) by Joaquim Felicio dos Santos (1828-1895), a satirical work set in the future. Works with clear sf elements by mainstream writers from the earlier part of the 20th century include: *A liga dos Planetas* ["The League of the Planets"] (**1923**) by Albino Coutinho (1860-1940), which features space travel to utopian VENUS and MARS; *A Amazonia Misteriosa* ["The Mysterious Amazon"] (**1925**) by Gastão Cruls (1888-1959), an adventure novel featuring a tribe of warrior women (descended from the Incas) and a German SCIENTIST who performs Moreau-like experiments on Indians; *O Presidente Negro* ["The Black President"] (**1926**; vt *O Choque das Raças* ["Clash of the Races"]) by Monteiro Lobato (1882-1948), a SATIRE with racist overtones set in a future USA; and *República 3000* ["The Republic of 3000"] (**1930**; vt *A Filha do Inca* ["The Inca's Daughter"]) by Menotti del Picchia (1892-1988), an adventure novel featuring a futuristic lost city.

Brazil's first writer of GENRE SF was Jeronimo Monteiro (1908-1970), a rarity in the literary scene of that time in that he was an enthusiast for US sf, and for mysteries and popular fiction in general. In the 1930s he wrote and directed a radio series about the adventures of a detective, **Dick Peter**, who faced dangers of a sciencefictional kind; these stories were later published by him under the pseudonym Ronnie Wells. In 1964 he founded the Brazilian Society of SF, and shortly before his death he edited issues dated 1970-71 of the Brazilian version of *FSF*, *Magazine de Ficção Científica*, which lasted only 20 issues. He wrote many sf books, often for children. His best adult novel is *Fuga para Parte Alguma* ["Escape to Nowhere"] (**1961**).

There was something of a boom in Brazilian sf in the 1960s, due primarily to Gumercindo Rocha Dorea, founder of the GRD publishing house and affectionately known as "the Brazilian Campbell". In 1960 he began publishing collections of sf and fantasy, alternating translations of US authors with Brazilian writers, including some from the mainstream. Two important anthologies edited by him were *Antologia Brasileira de Ficção Científica* ["Brazilian Anthology of SF"] (anth **1961**) and *Histórias do Acontecerá* ["Tales from the Will-Happen"] (anth **1961**). Another publishing house, Edart, run by Alvaro Malheiros, did a similar job on a smaller scale. Together, these SMALL PRESSES created the first wave of true sf in Brazil.

New authors of the time included: Dinah Silveira de Queiroz (1910-1982), with *Eles herdarão a Terra* ["They Shall Inherit Earth"] (coll **1960**) and others; André Carneiro (1922-   ), perhaps the senior living Brazilian sf writer, with *Diário da Nave Perdida* ["Diary of the Lost Spaceship"] (coll **1963**), *O Homem que Adivinhava* ["The Man who Guessed Right"] (coll **1966**) and others; Rubens T. Scavone (1925-   ), with *O Diálogo dos Mundos* ["Dialogue of the Worlds"] (coll **1961**) and others; and Fausto Cunha (1923-   ), with *As Noites Marcianas* ["Martian Nights"] (coll **1960**) and others.

In 1969 a major sf symposium was held in conjunction with the Festival Internacional de Cinema in Rio de Janeiro. This event brought to Brazil some of the great names of sf, including Brian W. ALDISS, J.G. BALLARD, Alfred BESTER, Arthur C. CLARKE, Harlan ELLISON, Robert A. HEINLEIN and A.E. VAN VOGT. It was organized by José Sanz, an active editor and prolific translator of sf who afterwards presented, in *SF Symposium/FC Simpósio* (anth **1969**), English and Portuguese versions (the latter trans A. Arruda) of talks given at the meeting, which aroused temporary enthusiasm; generally, however, even though the 1960s writers mentioned above mostly continued into the 1970s, Brazilian sf was in decline.

A minor renaissance has been taking place since the mid-1980s, beginning with the appearance of some lively sf FANZINES and fan organizations like the "Club de Leitores de Ficção Científica" ["Sf Readers' Club"], created by Roberto C. Nascimento in 1985. The first stories of several new writers appeared in fanzines like *Somnium*, *Hiperespaço* and *Antares* or in fan anthologies like *Verde . . . Verde . . .* ["Green . . . Green . . ."] (anth **1988**) ed Sergio Fonseca. Writers closely associated with the fan movement include: Jorge Luiz Calife, whose projected HARD-SF trilogy begins with *Padrões de Contato* ["Patterns of Contact"] (**1985**); Henrique V. Flory with *Só Sei que não Vou por Aí* ["All I Know is that I Won't Go that Way"] (coll **1989**); Roberto Schima with *Pequenas Portas do Eu* ["Little Doors of the I"] (coll **1987**); José dos Santos Fernandes with *Do Outro Lado do Tempo* ["At the Other Side of Time"] (coll **1990**); Ivanir Calado with *A Mãe do Sonho* ["The Mother of Dream"] (**1990**); and Braulio TAVARES, who won a Portuguese sf award with *A Espinha Dorsal da Memória* ["The Backbone of Memory"] (coll **1989**).

Some mainstream writers have written borderline sf works during the 1980s; e.g., Marcio Souza with *A Ordem do Dia* ["Order of the Day"] (**1983**), Ignacio de Loyola Brandão with *Não Verás País Nenhum* ["You Will See No Country"] (**1982**), Herberto Salles with *A Porta de Chifre* ["The Horn Door"] (**1982**), and Floro

Freitas de Andrade, whose *Jogo Terminal* ["Terminal Game"] (**1988**) won the Nova Award for Best Book by a Brazilian Author. A recent first novel by songwriter and performance artist Fausto Fawcett, *Santa Clara Poltergeist* (**1991**), mixes CYBERPUNK elements and PSI POWERS in a NEAR-FUTURE Rio de Janeiro.   [BT]

Beneath is an incomplete listing of important sf authors and titles from the other Latin American countries. In some instances we can give no more than an author's name; further research into this field is eagerly awaited.

Chile

Eduardo Barredo (1942-   ): *Encuentros paralelos* ["Parallel Encounters"] (**1987**), *Los muros del silencio* ["The Walls of Silence"] (**1987**).

Hugo Correa (1926-   ): *El que merodea en la lluvia* ["The Prowler in the Rain"] (**1968**), *Los titeres* ["The Puppets"] (**1969**), *Cuando Pilato se opuso* ["When Pilate Said No"] (**1971**), *Los altisimos* ["The Highest Ones"] (**1973**).

Antoine Montagne: *Los superhomos* ["The Superhumans"] (**1963**), *Acá del tiempo* ["This Side of Time"] (**1968**), *No morir* ["Not to Die"] (**1971**).

Barredo is in exile in Cuba, where he has written most of his books, which are mainly for a juvenile readership. Correa was called by Bernard Goorden "the first Latin-American classic", and has published some stories in magazines and anthologies in the USA.

Colombia

Antonio Mora Vélez (1942-   ): *Glitza* (**1979**), *Lorna es una mujer* ["Lorna is a Woman"] (**1986**), *El juicio de los dioses* ["The Judgment of the Gods"] (coll **1982**).

Alberto Gaviria Coronado: *Brujos cósmicos* ["Cosmic Sorcerers"] (**1974**; rev 1984).

Mario Loperra.

Costa Rica

Alberto Cañas.

Ecuador

Abdón Ubidia (1944-   ): *Divert Inventos* ["Diversions/Inventions"] (coll **1989**).

El Salvador

Alvaro Menén Desleal.

Peru

José B. Adolph: *El retorno de Aladino* ["Aladdin's Return"] (coll **1968**), *Hasta que la muerte* ["Till Death Do Us"] (coll **1971**), *Invisible para las fieras* ["Invisible to Beasts"] (coll **1972**), *Cuentos del relojero abominable* ["Tales of the Abominable Watchmaker"] (coll **1974**), *Mañana fuimos felices* ["Tomorrow We Were Happy"] (coll **1975**), *Mañana de las ratas* ["Morning of the Rats"] (**1978**).

Santo Domingo

Juan Bosch.

Uruguay

Saúl Ibargoyen, a poet.

Carlos María Federici.

Elvio E. Gandolfo.

Mario Levrero (1940-   ): *La máquina de pensar en Gladys* ["The Machine to Think about Gladys"] (coll

1967), *El lugar* ["The Place"] (**1982**).

Venezuela

Luis Britto García (1940-   ): *Abrapalabra* [the title is a pun on abracadabra] (**1979**) and *Rajatabla* (coll **1987**).

Pedro Berroeta: *La salamandra* ["The Salamander"] (**1973**).

David Alizo.

Ileana Gómez.

Armando José Sequera.   [M-JS/BT]

LA TOURETTE, AILEEN (1946-   ) US-born writer, in the UK from 1968, whose advocacy of a radical FEMINISM informs most of her work, all of which is sophisticatedly told. Her sf novel, *Cry Wolf* (**1986**), however, assays a somewhat jumbled moral scan of the events leading up to a nuclear HOLOCAUST in language both too ornately self-referential and too abstract to convey much of the subsequent shattered world as it attempts to sort truth from myth and to build anew.   [JC]

LAUMER, (JOHN) KEITH (1925-1993) US writer who used his experiences in the US armed forces and Diplomatic Corps to considerable advantage in his sf work. He served in the army 1943-5, studied architecture and graduated with a BScArch from the University of Illinois in 1952, served in the USAF 1953-6, and then joined the US Foreign Service. He rejoined the USAF as a captain in 1960. He began publishing sf in 1959 with "Greylorn" for *AMZ*, and for more than a decade remained extremely prolific, producing three major series and two minor ones along with a number of independent novels; after 1973, affected by illness, he published more sparingly.

The most interesting of KL's series is the **Imperium** sequence, comprising his first novel, *Worlds of the Imperium* (**1962** dos; with 2 stories added to make coll, rev 1982), *The Other Side of Time* (**1965**) and *Assignment in Nowhere* (**1968**) – both assembled as *Beyond the Imperium* (omni **1981**) – and *Zone Yellow* (**1990**). The Imperium dominates a complex nest of PARALLEL-WORLDS universes, and strives to maintain the stability of its chosen time-stream. As opposed to the grimmer and perhaps more plausible versions of the same task expressed in novels like Barrington BAYLEY's *The Fall of Chronopolis* (**1974** US), KL takes an essentially optimistic view of this kind of situation, treating it in a no-nonsense, problem-solving manner. Also related, if only thematically, to the **Imperium** series is *Dinosaur Beach* (**1971**), a tale of TIME PARADOXES in which a role similar to that of the Imperium is played by Nexx Central. A second series, the parallel-worlds comic novels featuring **Lafayette O'Leary** – *The Time Bender* (**1966**), *The World Shuffler* (**1970**), *The Shape Changer* (**1972**) and *The Galaxy Builder* (**1984**) – attempts to replay a similar scenario in terms of slapstick, with only moderate success.

KL's other major series depicts the adventures of interstellar diplomatic troubleshooter Jaime **Retief** on a variety of alien worlds: *Envoy to New Worlds* (coll **1963**; exp vt *Retief: Envoy to New Worlds* 1987), *Galactic Diplomat* (coll **1965**), *Retief's War* (**1966**), *Retief and the Warlords* (**1968**), *Retief: Ambassador to Space* (coll **1969**), *Retief of the CDT* (coll **1971**), *Retief's Ransom* (**1971**; with new title story added to make coll, rev vt *Retief and the Pangalactic Pageant of Pulchritude* 1986), *Retief: Emissary to the Stars* (**1975**; exp 1979), *Retief: Diplomat at Arms* (coll **1982**), *Retief to the Rescue* (**1983**), *The Return of Retief* (**1984**), *Retief in the Ruins* (coll **1986**) and *Reward for Retief* (**1989**). Retief's unchanging role is to mediate between the residents of alien worlds, some of them nefarious, and his bumbling superiors in the Terran Diplomatic Corps, and to solve various sticky problems, almost all couched in comic terms, sometimes amusingly. Here as elsewhere, the KL bibliography is tangled; putting aside titles which partially replicate earlier titles, **Retief** collections assembled entirely from earlier volumes include *Retief at Large* (coll **1978**) and *Retief Unbound* (omni **1979**), containing *Retief's Ransom* plus 5 stories from *Envoy to New Worlds*.

KL's singletons are varied, ranging from broad HUMOUR like *The Monitors* (**1966**), filmed as *The MONITORS* in 1969, to taut, efficient sf thrillers whose structures amalgamate SPACE OPERA and the favourite sf theme of the coming to awareness of the SUPERMAN. Best of them is *A Plague of Demons* (**1965**), in which a tough human is biologically engineered into a sort of superman so that he can deal with a threat to Earth, and finds – after a long, remarkably sustained chase sequence ending in his capture by some singularly efficient aliens – that for centuries Earth has been being despoiled of its best fighting men, who, like himself, are taken off-planet and surgically transformed into command centres for gigantic, armed fighting machines embroiled in an eons-long interstellar war. In this CYBORG form, he regains autonomy, organizes a revolt of his fellow cyborg-supertanks and prepares to carry – fabulously armed – his message of freedom to the stars. Thematically associated with this novel are the **Bolo** books – *Bolo: The Annals of the Dinochrome Brigade* (coll of linked stories with new linking material **1976**) and *Rogue Bolo* (coll of linked stories **1986**), both assembled, with 1 piece missing, as *The Compleat Bolo* (omni **1990**), plus the weak *The Stars Must Wait* (**1990**) – which recount the long history of a military unit of constantly upgraded quasisentient tanks.

In *A Plague of Demons*, and in other novels such as *A Trace of Memory* (**1963**), *The Long Twilight* (**1969**), *The House in November* (**1970**; with 1 story added to make coll, rev 1981), *Dinosaur Beach* and *The Infinite Cage* (**1972**), the essential KL superman takes shape: often an orphan, usually a loner, he discovers the world to be a persecuting snare and delusion, and gradually comes to realize that his PARANOIA is justified, for his frustrated human competence is no more than a cloak disguising his true – at times godlike – superiority. Once he has become a superman he is able to transcend the world of normals, and often takes that world over, though behind the scenes. It is for novels in which this wish-fulfilment version of the superman is expressed that KL will be best remembered, though his tendency to repeat earlier inspirations in slackened form seems to have damaged his later efforts even in this favourite mode; books such as *The Ultimax Man* (**1978**) or *End as a Hero* (**1985**) are significantly weak by comparison with his early work. But at his best KL wrote polished and succinct daydreams of sf transcendence that served as models of their kind. [JC]

Other works: *The Great Time Machine Hoax* (**1964**); *Embassy* (**1965**), an associational novel whose protagonist, Brion Bayard, shares his name but no other circumstances with the hero of the **Imperium** sequence; *Catastrophe Planet* (**1966**; with added pieces to make coll, rev vt *The Breaking Earth* 1981); *Earthblood* (**1966**) with Rosel George BROWN (*whom see for details*); *Nine by Laumer* (coll **1967**); *Galactic Odyssey* (**1967**); *Planet Run* (**1967**; with 1 story by each added to make coll, rev 1982) with Gordon R. DICKSON; *The Day Before Forever and Thunderhead* (coll **1968**); *The Invaders* * (coll **1967**; vt *The Meteor Men* UK) as by Anthony LeBaron and *Enemies from Beyond* * (coll **1967**), adapting stories from *The* INVADERS; *The Afrit Affair* * (**1968**), *The Drowned Queen* * (**1968**) and *The Gold Bomb* * (**1968**), adapting stories from *The* AVENGERS; *Greylorn* (coll **1968**; vt *The Other Sky* 1968 UK); *It's a Mad, Mad, Mad Galaxy* (coll **1968**); *Time Trap* (**1970**); *The Star Treasure* (**1971**; with stories added to make coll, rev 1986); *Once There was a Giant* (coll **1971**), a different book from *Once There was a Giant* (coll **1984**), the first title containing 8 stories, the second 2 novellas; *Timetracks* (coll **1972**); *The Big Show* (coll **1972**); *Night of Delusions* (**1972**; with 2 stories added to make coll, rev vt *Knight of Delusions* 1982); *The Glory Game* (**1973**); *The Undefeated* (coll **1974**); *The Best of Keith Laumer* (coll **1976**); *Star Colony* (fixup **1982**); *Chrestomathy* (coll **1984**); *Judson's Eden* (**1991**); *Alien Minds* (coll **1991**); «Back to the Time Trap» (**1992**).

As editor: *Five Fates* (anth **1972**).

About the author: *Keith Laumer, Ambassador to Space: A Working Bibliography* (last rev **1990** chap) by Gordon BENSON Jr and Phil STEPHENSEN-PAYNE.

See also: ALTERNATE WORLDS; GODS AND DEMONS; HIVE-MINDS; INVASION; PSI POWERS; PSYCHOLOGY; ROBERT HALE LIMITED; WEAPONS.

LAURIE, ANDRÉ Pseudonym of Paschal Grousset (1845-1909), French politician and author. His first political novel, *Le rêve d'un irreconciliable* ["Dream of a Diehard"] (**1869**) and several political works were published under his real name, but thereafter he used the AL pseudonym. While living as a *communard* exile in London, AL wrote the original version of the book which was later published as *The Begum's Fortune* (**1879**) as by Jules VERNE. Laurie legally renounced title to the story, as he did with *The Southern Star Mystery* (**1884**), rewritten and published as by Verne. Both authors put their name to *L'épave du Cynthia* (**1885**; trans as *Salvage from the Cynthia* **1958** UK). It was a strange collaboration, AL being politically a long way

to the left of Verne. Of AL's several sf novels, 5 have been translated into English. The best known is *Les exiles de la Terre, Séléne Company Limited* (**1887**; trans anon as *The Conquest of the Moon: A Story of the Bayouda* **1889** UK), in which the MOON is drawn from its orbit to land in the Sahara desert. AL wrote of the discoveries of scientifically advanced societies in *The Secret of the Magian, or The Mystery of Ecbatana* (**1890** France; trans **1891** UK) and *Atlantis* (**1895**; trans L.A. Smith as *The Crystal City Under the Sea* 1896 UK; vt *The Crystal City* 1896 US), and of a transatlantic tunnel in *De New York à Brest en sept heures* (**1888**; trans anon as *New York to Brest in Seven Hours* 1890 UK). His most critically acclaimed work, *Spiridon le muet* ["Spiridon the Mute"] (**1909** France), remains untranslated. [JE/PN]

Other works: *Axel Eberson, the Graduate of Upsala* (**1891** France; trans **1892** UK).

See also: BOYS' PAPERS; NEAR FUTURE; UNDER THE SEA.

LAVERS, NORMAN (1935-) US writer whose sf novel, *The Northwest Passage* (**1984**), engages in an experiment (◊ POSTMODERNISM) familiar to readers of the modern novel: the book comprises a "text", complete with a scholarly apparatus which is itself, of course, part of the "text". In this case, a far-future editorial apparatus surrounds the late-20th-century scholarly edition of an 18th-century manuscript. The title proves to have a more than geographical context. [JC]

LAVERTY, DONALD Pseudonym used by James BLISH and Damon KNIGHT in collaboration. [JC]

LAVOND, PAUL DENNIS [s] ◊ C.M. KORNBLUTH; Robert A.W. LOWNDES; Frederik POHL.

LAWHEAD, STEPHEN R. (1950-) US writer of Christian sf and fantasy, beginning with the **Dragon King** fantasy trilogy: *In the Hall of the Dragon King* (**1982**), *The Warlords of Nin* (**1983**) and *The Sword and the Flame* (**1984**). Of sf interest are *Dream Thief* (**1983**) and the **Emphyrion** sequence: *The Search for Fierra* (**1985**) and *The Siege of Dome* (**1986**), both titles being assembled as *Emphyrion* (omni **1990** UK). A further fantasy sequence, the **Pendragon Cycle** – *Taliesin* (**1987**), *Merlin* (**1988**) and *Arthur* (**1989**) – Christianizes (or re-Christianizes) Arthurian legends. The catechizing impulse evident in earlier titles seems to have been moderated in later productions. [JC]

Other works: *Howard Had a Spaceship* (**1986**), juvenile; *The Paradise War* (**1991**).

LAWNMOWER MAN, THE Film (1992). Allied Vision Lane Pringle/Fuji Eight Co. Dir Brett Leonard, starring Jeff Fahey, Pierce Brosnan, Jenny Wright, Geoffrey Lewis. Screenplay Leonard, Gimel Everett. 108 mins. Colour.

The full title is *Stephen King's The Lawnmower Man*, but the film has been repudiated by KING, angry at the cynicism whereby his old (1975) short story was purchased to exploit the marketing power of his name and then effectively discarded through being altered out of recognition. In this dumb rewrite of both FRANKENSTEIN (1931) and CHARLY (1968), an obsessive SCIENTIST (Brosnan) uses a VIRTUAL-REALITY hook-up, along with intelligence-raising drugs, to change the local handyman (Fahey), an affable simpleton, into a homicidal SUPERMAN with telekinetic powers who ultimately downloads himself into the USA's information networks in order to "cleanse this diseased planet". The film's concepts and dialogue are uniformly contemptible – noting in awe that his creation has learned Latin in two hours, the brilliant scientist says: "It took me a year just to learn the Latin alphabet!" The virtual-reality effects on which the film relies (the suggestion being that computer-generated scenery makes you clever) are not remotely like reality, and are routine in execution. [PN]

LAWRENCE ◊ Lawrence Sterne STEVENS.

LAWRENCE, HENRY L(IONEL) (1908-　) UK writer whose *The Children of Light* (**1960**) deals with the effects of radiation. It was used as the basis for a 1961 film, *The* DAMNED. [JC/PN]

LAWRENCE, J(UDITH) A(NN) (?　-　) US writer and artist, long resident in Greece, married to James BLISH from 1964 until his death in 1975, collaborating with him (sometimes without credit) on some of the later ties he wrote for the STAR TREK enterprise. She was credited as co-author of *Star Trek 12* * (coll **1977** US) and was solely responsible for *Mudd's Angels* * (**1978** US). [JC]
See also: MILFORD SCIENCE FICTION WRITERS' CONFERENCE; NEBULA.

LAWRENCE, JIM Working name of US writer James Duncan Lawrence (1918-　), whose sf consists of the unremarkable **Man from Planet X** sequence – *The Man from Planet X #1: She-Beast* (**1975**) and *#2: Tiger by the Tale* (**1975**), both as by Hunter Adams – and 2 novels tied to SHARED-WORLD franchises: *ESP McGee and the Haunted Mansion* * (**1983** chap) for the **ESP McGee** series, and *The Cutlass Clue* * (**1986**) for the **A.I. Gang** series. [JC]

LAWRENCE, LOUISE Pseudonym of Elizabeth Rhoda Wintle (1943-　), UK writer who began publishing sf for young adults with *Andra* (**1971**), and who early became noted for the marked and sensitive intelligence of her settings and characters. *The Power of Stars* (**1972**), in which an extraterrestrial force transfixes human teenagers, and *Star Lord* (**1978**; rev 1987), in which a boy protects the eponymous alien from the government, are characteristic; as are *The Wyndcliffe* (**1974**) and its sequel, *Sing and Scatter Daisies* (**1977**), an intricate romance fantasy. Her shorter work is assembled in *Extinction is Forever and Other Stories* (coll **1990**). [JC]
Other works: *The Earth Witch* (**1981**); *Calling B for Butterfly* (**1982**); *Children of the Dust* (**1985**); *Moonwind* (**1986**); *The Warriors of Taan* (**1986**).
See also: STARS.

LAWRENCE, STEPHEN ◊ Lawrence Sterne STEVENS.

LAZARUS, HENRY (?　-?　) UK writer, active in the 1890s, whose *The English Revolution of the Twentieth Century: A Prospective History* (**1894**), caused some stir through its advocacy of a welfare state following a revolution led by the forces of Labour. [JC]

LAZENBY, NORMAN A(USTIN) (1914-　) UK pulp writer, prolific as an author of Westerns and detective novels, and a minor contributor to GENRE SF. He began publishing sf with "A Matter of Size" for *Fantasy* in 1946, and continued to publish stories under various names for several years, and then again for a few years after 1970. *The Coming of the Beetle Men* (coll **1949** chap; the cover title was *Terror Trap*) contains 1 sf story. His only sf novel is *The Brains of Helle* (fixup **1953**) as by Bengo Mistral. [SH]

LEA, HOMER (1876-1912) US writer in whose "Yellow Peril" tale, *The Valor of Ignorance* (**1909**), a racially contaminated USA – riddled also with FEMINISTS – must attempt to gird its loins against a Japanese INVASION. But Japan wins, gaining California and other Pacific regions. In 1942, the book enjoyed the unusual privilege of being reprinted in both Japan and the USA. [JC]

LEACOCK, STEPHEN (BUTLER) (1869-1944) Canadian economist and writer of many books of humorous sketches, the most famous being perhaps *Sunshine Sketches of a Little Town* (coll **1912**). Sf often featured as the target of the more fantastical of these sketches, beginning with spoofs like "The Man in Asbestos", which parodies H.G. WELLS's *The Time Machine*, and other stories in *Nonsense Novels* (coll **1911** UK). *The Iron Man and the Tin Woman, with Other Such Futurities: A Book of Little Sketches of To-day and Tomorrow* (coll **1929** US) and *Afternoons in Utopia: Tales of the New Time* (coll **1932** US) contain the highest proportion of this sort of material – UTOPIAS being a favourite target – but examples can be found in many of his collections. [JC]
Other works: *Moonbeams from the Larger Lunacy* (coll **1917** UK); *Frenzied Fiction* (coll **1918** UK); *The Hohenzollerns in America, With the Bolsheviks in Berlin, and Other Impossibilities* (coll **1919** UK); *Winsome Winnie and Other New Nonsense Novels* (coll **1920** UK).
See also: CANADA.

LEAHY, JOHN MARTIN (1886-1967) US PULP-MAGAZINE author and illustrator who contributed sf to *Science and Invention* and *Weird Tales*, in which latter appeared *Drome* (1927; **1952**), a LOST-WORLD tale set in caves under California. [JE/EFB]

LEBAR, JOHN ◊ Harold Bell WRIGHT.

LeBARON, ANTHONY ◊ Keith LAUMER.

LeCALE, ERROL ◊ Wilfred Glassford MCNEILLY.

Le CLÉZIO, J(EAN)-M(ARIE) G(USTAVE) (1940-　) Mauritius-born French writer, known primarily for his work outside the sf field; he took his degree in literature at Nice University. He is a major contemporary author in the ABSURDIST tradition, his work often bordering on sf and the surreal through a minute examination of physical phenomena and aspects of reality. His hallucinatory scrutiny of manifestations of madness in the world at large is best demonstrated in *Les géants* (1973; trans Simon Watson-Taylor as *The Giants* 1975 US), set in Hyperbolis, a nightmare shopping complex in a futuristic CITY. [MJ]

Other works include: *Le procès-verbal* (**1963**; trans Daphne Woodward as *The Interrogation* **1964** US); *La fièvre* (coll **1964**; trans Daphne Woodward as *Fever* **1966** US); *Le déluge* (**1965**; trans Peter Green as *The Flood* **1967** US); *Terra Amata* (**1967**; trans Barbara Bray **1969** US); *Le livre des fuites* (**1969**; trans Simon Watson-Taylor as *The Book of Flights* **1972** US); *La guerre* (**1970**; trans Simon Watson-Taylor as *War* **1973** US); *Voyages de l'autre côté* ["Journeys on the Other Side"] (**1975**).

See also: MEDIA LANDSCAPE.

LEE, DAVID ◊ David S. GARNETT.

LEE, GENTRY (B.) (? -   ) US writer who held several important posts in NASA's deep-space exploration programme and was a screenwriter for Carl SAGAN's *Cosmos* tv series. His sf has been written exclusively in collaboration with Arthur C. CLARKE (*whom see for details*); at least initially, the senior partner provided outlines based on ideas generated by both writers, and then the books themselves were written by GL. *Cradle* (**1988**), the first and weakest, is a First-Contact drama exhibiting little of Clarke's economy or intensity. Following on from Clarke's solo *Rendezvous with Rama* (**1973**), the **Rama** sequence – *Rama II* (**1989** UK) and *The Garden of Rama* (**1991**), with at least 1 further vol projected – shows a continual improvement. GL has proved competent at conveying technical information, though tending to lapse into an "airport novel" approach when it comes to dealing with human beings.   [NT]

LEE, MATT [s] ◊ Sam MERWIN.

LEE, ROBERT [s] ◊ Paul W. FAIRMAN.

LEE, SHARON [r] ◊ Steve MILLER.

LEE, STAN (1922-   ) US COMIC-book writer and executive, born Stanley Leiber; his name has been legally changed to Lee. Before WWII he began to establish himself in the New York comics publishing world, in 1939 joining Timely Comics, Inc., the firm for which Jack KIRBY invented **Captain America**. SL remained with Timely – which soon became Atlas Comics, then MARVEL COMICS in 1963, without changing its corporate identity – for the whole of his career, serving as its editor 1942-72, and as its publisher and editorial director from 1972, concentrating on film productions after 1978. His career was not of particular importance for the student of sf until 1961, when – with Kirby, who had spent many years away from Marvel – he began to create a new type of comic-book SUPERHERO, with titles like **The Fantastic Four** (from 1961) and **The Incredible Hulk** (from 1962); other comics created at this time included **Spiderman** (initiated in *Amazing Fantasy* in 1962) as drawn by Steve Ditko, whose angular, repressed style greyly evoked the pedestrian urban life which the hero tried to transcend. Over the next half decade SL (usually with Kirby) initiated a number of similar comic books including **The Avengers** (from 1963), into which Kirby reintroduced his **Captain America**, X-MEN (from 1963) and **Thor** (separate comic from 1966, character introduced in *Journey into Mystery* in 1962). These comics, most of them scripted by SL –

according to the "Marvel Method", which involved much initial collaboration between artist and writer – were remarkable for eschewing the template structures of previous work in the field (characters neither ageing nor suffering significant change). SL's protagonists grew up, aged, suffered, exhibited human frailties and changed their minds about things; their superpowers were often explicitly seen as compensatory wish-fulfilments, allowing them – though never permanently – to transcend their personal problems. In hindsight, SL's 1960s work was a major influence on the creation of the GRAPHIC NOVEL in the 1980s, especially perhaps the work from about 1965 on, when his continuing storylines began to develop space-operatic complexities; most memorable were those episodes of **The Fantastic Four** in which the heroes became involved in intergalactic disputes with the planet-devouring (but rather sympathetic) Galactus and his moody sidekick, the Silver Surfer, a nonhuman rider of space imprisoned by Galactus within Earth's atmosphere where, misunderstood and reviled, he time and again (as featured in **The Silver Surfer** 1968-70) saved humanity from itself.

The above account should be read in the context of Jack Kirby's repeated claims during the 1980s that SL was an administrator rather than a writer – indeed, that he actually wrote *none* of the comics for which he received writing credit. The editors of this encyclopedia are not in a position to evaluate those claims.

In 1970 Kirby left Marvel; though he would return later, it is arguable that SL's domination of the comic-book world, as both editor and writer, began to slip from about this time. For instance, it was Roy Thomas who fruitfully introduced into Marvel's generic mix a number of themes and characters from HEROIC FANTASY (including Robert E. HOWARD's **Conan** in *Conan the Barbarian* from 1970), and though Marvel Comics featured ever more spectacular and sf-like situations, there was a sense of decreasing ebullience; routine situations began to predominate.

SL is not to be confused with the Stan Lee who has written novels such as *The God Project* (**1990**), a NEAR-FUTURE thriller with metaphysical import.   [JC]

See also: SUPERMAN.

LEE, TANITH (1947-   ) UK writer, first of fantasies for children, beginning with *The Dragon Hoard* (**1971**), and then, after *The Birthgrave* (**1975** US), primarily of fantasies for adults. Both these areas of concentration lie outside our proper remit, but it can be said that she is an inventive and fertile writer, that she has encompassed her primary theme – the ethical and sexual initiation of an adolescent character into a volatile world s/he herself will shape, often through renunciation – in a wide variety of modes, and that, although her work differs vastly in tone and subject matter from that of C.J. CHERRYH, both writers share a daunting comprehensiveness. TL, however, has not (yet) assembled her various singletons and series into one shared universe.

The Birthgrave and its sequels, *Vazkor, Son of Vazkor*

(**1978** US; vt *Shadowfire* 1979 UK) and *Quest for the White Witch* (**1978** US), are sf by virtue of the ending of the first volume, in which Earthmen arrive in a spaceship to tell the albino heroine the true, non-supernatural explanation for the compulsions she feels and the voices she hears inside her head – and, having awoken with amnesia in the heart of a volcano and wreaked considerable damage upon the world with her untutored powers, she is by this time sorely in need of some reassurance. The second and third volumes deal primarily with her son, who must deal with his own powers and learn that his mother is not evil. At trilogy's end, immortal and forgiving, they commit incest. *Don't Bite the Sun* (**1976** US) and *Drinking Sapphire Wine* (**1977** US), both assembled as *Drinking Sapphire Wine* (omni **1979**), form a genuine sf sequence set in a FAR-FUTURE world somewhat resembling that in Michael MOORCOCK's **Dancers at the End of Time** series, treated in this case as a DYSTOPIA whose citizens, superficially free to shape-change and cavort, are in fact prisoners of the protectiveness of their artificial environment. *Electric Forest* (**1979** US) depicts the rite of passage of an ugly child on a planet where her appearance is shocking. *Day by Night* (**1980** US) is set on non-rotating mirror-worlds unconscious of each other's existence. *Sabella, or The Blood Stone* (**1980** US) and its sequel, *Kill the Dead* (**1980** US) – both assembled as *Sometimes, After Sunset* (omni **1980** US) – associate vampirism with Mars. *The Silver Metal Lover* (**1981** US) concerns a love affair between a woman and a ROBOT or ANDROID. *Days of Grass* (**1985** US) is set a century or so after an ALIEN invasion. TL's sf, though she is clearly conversant with its instruments, makes such individual use of the normal displacements of the genre that nothing – from robots to cosmogony – fails to serve her primary impulses as a storyteller. For TL, sf is a kind of metaphysical pathos: it illustrates her children.

Of her several volumes of stories, some of which are exceptional, the most far-ranging are probably *Dreams of Dark and Light: The Great Short Fiction* (coll **1986** US), *Forests of the Night* (coll **1989**) and *Women as Demons: The Male Perception of Women through Space and Time* (coll **1989**). [JC]

Other works:
Juvenile fantasies: *Princess Hynchatti and Some Other Surprises* (coll **1972**); *Animal Castle* (**1972**); *Companions on the Road* (**1975**) and *The Winter Players* (**1976**), both assembled as *Companions on the Road and The Winter Players: Two Novellas* (omni **1977** US); *East of Midnight* (**1977**); *The Castle of Dark* (**1978**); *Shon the Taken* (**1979**); *Prince on a White Horse* (**1982**), assembled with *The Castle of Dark* as *Dark Castle, White Horse* (omni **1986** US).

Adult fantasies: *The Betrothed* (**1968** chap); *Volkhavaar* (**1977** US); the **Tales from the Flat Earth** sequence, comprising *Night's Master* (**1978** US), *Death's Master* (**1979** US) and *Delusion's Master* (**1981** US), all assembled as *Tales from the Flat Earth: The Lords of Darkness* (omni **1987** US), plus *Delirium's Mistress: A Novel of the Flat Earth* (**1986** US) and *Night's Sorceries* (coll **1987** US), both assembled as *Tales from the Flat Earth: Night's Daughter* (omni **1987** US); the **Wars of Vis** sequence, comprising *The Storm Lord* (**1978** US) and *Anackire* (**1983** US), both assembled as *The Wars of Vis* (omni **1984** US), plus *The White Serpent* (**1988** US); *Lycanthia, or The Children of Wolves* **1981** US); *Unsilent Night* (coll **1981** chap US); *Cyrion* (coll of linked stories **1982** US); *Sung in Shadow* (**1983** US); *Red as Blood, or Tales from the Sisters Grimmer* (coll **1983** US); *The Beautiful Biting Machine* (**1984** chap); *Tamastara, or The Indian Nights* (coll **1984** US); *The Gorgon and Other Beastly Tales* (coll **1985** US); *Madame Two Swords* (**1988** US); *A Heroine of the World* (**1989** US); the **Secret Book of Paradys** sequence, comprising *The Book of the Damned* (coll of linked stories **1988**) and *The Book of the Beast* (**1988**), both assembled as *The Secret Book of Paradys* (omni **1991** US); *The Blood of Roses* (**1990** US); *The Black Unicorn* (**1991** US); *Into Gold* (**1986** IASFM; **1991** chap); the **Blood Opera** sequence, beginning with *Dark Dance* (**1992**), further volumes projected; *Heart-Beast* (**1992**), a werewolf novel.

See also: CHILDREN'S SF; DAW BOOKS; FEMINISM; RADIO; SUPERNATURAL CREATURES.

LEE, THOMAS (?   -?) UK writer, active in the late 19th century, identified by Darko SUVIN in *Victorian Science Fiction in the UK* (**1983**) as a North London plasterer and publican. TL's sf novel, *Falsivir's Travels: The Remarkable Adventures of John Falsivir, Seaman, at the North Pole and in the Interior of the Earth* (**1886**), is a HOLLOW-EARTH tale. The narrator discovers a race of giants oppressed by a race of normal-sized humans, along with other features that E.F. BLEILER has suggested mark the author's attempts to satirize the UK of the 19th century. [JC]

LEE, WALT(ER WILLIAM) (1931-   ) US film-writer and consultant with a 1954 BS in physics. His monumental self-published *Reference Guide to Fantastic Films: Volume 1 A-F* (**1972**), *Volume 2 G-O* (**1973**) and *Volume 3 P-Z* (**1974**) contains upwards of 20,000 entries. Fantasy, occult and horror films feature more largely than pure sf, but the latter is dealt with thoroughly. The work remains a useful research tool for anyone dealing with sf CINEMA, although commentary on the actual content of the films it covers is very minimal. He later collaborated with Richard DELAP on an sf horror novel about a shape-changing ALIEN, *Shapes* (**1987**). [PN]

LEE, WILLIAM ◊ William S. BURROUGHS.

LEESON, ROBERT (ARTHUR) (1928-   ) UK editor and writer, active from the mid-1940s. He began publishing his books for children, in which he has since specialized, with *Beyond the Dragon Prow* (**1973**), an historical romance. Of sf interest is the **Time Rope** sequence – *Time Rope* (**1986**), *Three Against the World* (**1986**), *The Metro Gangs Attack* (**1986**) and *At War with Tomorrow* (**1986**) – in which a sharp social awareness of the contemporary world is focused through a TIME-TRAVEL plot with ample conflicts. [JC]

Other works: *The Third Class Genie* (**1975**); *Slambash*

Wangs of a Compo Gormer (**1987**); *Landing in Cloud Valley* (**1991**), which begins the projected **Cloud Valley** sequence.

LEE TUNG (?   -   ) Indian writer whose interesting sf novel, *The Wind Obeys Lama Toru* (**1967**), is a complex story about OVERPOPULATION in which fertility and sterility drugs act and counteract, driving the population up and down disastrously. [JC]

LEFANU, SARAH (1953-   ) UK academic whose *Despatches from the Frontiers of the Female Mind* (anth **1985**), ed with Jen Green (1954-   ), provided a forum for WOMEN SF WRITERS. The FEMINISM illustrated in that book could serve readers as a backdrop for *In the Chinks of the World Machine* (**1988**; vt *Feminism and Science Fiction* 1989 US), a solid nonfiction analysis of the work of several contemporary sf writers, most notably Suzy McKee CHARNAS, Ursula K. LE GUIN, Joanna RUSS and James TIPTREE Jr. Through readings of some acuteness, SL argues that GENRE SF has provided a conceptual opportunity for women writers to speak in their own autonomous voices, unimprisoned by the patriarchal modes dominant in more "normal" literatures. [JC]

LEGER, RAYMOND [r] ◊ Raymond MacDONALD.

LEGION OF SUPER-HEROES COMIC-book series about a group of superpowered youths in the 30th century, published by DC COMICS. The LOS-H first appeared in *Adventure Comics* #247 (April 1958) in a **Superboy** story written by Otto Binder (◊ Eando BINDER) and then featured in various SUPERMAN titles (ed Mort WEISINGER) before gaining their own series in *Adventure Comics* #300. Writers have included Jerry SIEGEL, Edmond HAMILTON, Paul Levitz and Jim Shooter, whose first story appeared when he was only 13, a logical extension of Weisinger's policy of incorporating reader suggestions. Many LOS-H characters were designed by fans, and its leadership was regularly decided by readers' votes. LOS-H appeared in *Adventure Comics* #300-#380 (Sep 1962-May 1969), then in *Action Comics* #378-#392 (July 1969-Sep 1970); it then became a regular back-up feature in *Superboy*, appearing Mar 1971-Aug 1977 in #172-#173, #176, #183-#184, #188, #190-#191, #193, #195 and #197-#230. At this point there was a title change. *Superboy* became *Superboy and the Legion of Super-Heroes* from #231 (Sep 1977), and this became just *Legion of Super-Heroes* for #259-#313 (Jan 1980-July 1984). Then there began a new "deluxe" series, produced on higher-quality stock; also called *Legion of Super-Heroes*, it ran from #1 to #63 (July 1984-Aug 1989). The older title of the same name was from #314 renamed *Tales of the Legion of Super-Heroes*, featuring new material to #325 (July 1985) and thereafter reprinting the "deluxe" title on a one-year-behind schedule. A new series, again called *Legion of Super-Heroes*, began with #1 (Nov 1989) 3 months after the last issue of the old, and (1991) is current. The present writers are Tom and Mary Bierbaum.

Much of LOS-H's sf content was quaint even when it first appeared, but sf continues as an important and evolving part of the series, even if in uneasy balance with its SUPERHERO basis. [ZB/BF]

LE GUIN, URSULA K(ROEBER) (1929-   ) US writer, based in Portland, Oregon. Her first novel was published in 1966; by 1970 she was spoken of as one of the most important writers within the field. Her reputation has extended far beyond the readership of GENRE SF, while within the genre she has been honoured with 5 HUGOS and 4 NEBULAS; more attention has been paid to her by the academic community than to any other modern sf writer.

UKLG is the daughter of Dr Alfred and Theodora Kroeber, the former a celebrated anthropologist who has published much work on Native Americans, the latter a writer best known for *Ishi in Two Worlds* (**1961**). UKLG was thus brought up in academic surroundings; her own education, with an undergraduate degree from Radcliffe and a master's degree from Columbia, was in Romance Literatures of the Middle Ages and Renaissance, particularly French. She wrote POETRY (some of it collected in *Wild Angels* [coll **1975** chap]) and a number of unpublished realistic novels, mostly set in an imaginary Central European country, before turning to sf. (It is generally assumed that her two **Orsinia** books, both set in 19th-century "Orsinia", *Orsinian Tales* [coll of linked stories **1976**] and *Malafrena* [**1979**] – neither sf or fantasy – are reworkings of this 1950s Central European material.) Typically, UKLG's tales set a man in an alien (and perhaps alienated) world, and follow him on a quest, until he makes a CONCEPTUAL BREAKTHROUGH and proves an agent for the reconciliation of the sundered parts; the quest often takes the form of a winter journey.

All her early published stories were bought by Cele GOLDSMITH for *AMZ* and *Fantastic*, her first published genre piece being "April in Paris" for *Fantastic* in 1962; like much of her early work this is more FANTASY than sf, though she makes no rigorous distinction between the two, as she notes in "A Citizen of Mondath" (1973) and other essays in *The Language of the Night: Essays on Fantasy and Science Fiction* (coll **1979**; rev with biblio omitted 1989 UK) ed Susan WOOD.

Much of UKLG's earlier work, generally known as the **Hainish** series, is set in a common universe. The people from the planet Hain once seeded the habitable worlds of our part of the Galaxy with human life; this has resulted in great cultural variety, useful for a writer who grew up with ANTHROPOLOGY as an everyday discipline. Five novels, two novellas and several short stories belong to the sequence, which covers about 2500 years of future HISTORY, beginning 300-400 years from now.

UKLG's first three novels come late in the sequence's internal chronology. They are *Rocannon's World* (**1966** dos; text corrected 1977), *Planet of Exile* (**1966** dos) and *City of Illusions* (**1967**), and were collected as *Three Hainish Novels* (omni **1978**). In *Rocannon's World* an ethnographer is marooned on a primitive planet with which he comes to terms only with difficulty; finally, in giving himself to the planet, he receives in return the gift of "mindspeech" or telepathy (◊ ESP). *Planet of Exile*, set over 1000 years later, has mindspeech in normal use; a Terran colony is struggling to survive on a planet whose natives they despise; under pressure the two communities are finally able to merge. *City of Illusions* is set on a cowed Earth ruled by the human-seeming but alien Shing invaders who have the hitherto unknown art of "mindlying". The amnesiac hero turns out, when his memory is restored, to be a messenger from the planet of the previous book; able to detect mindlying, he will be the agent of destruction for the malign Shing.

Perhaps the generic structures of these books are too conventional to sustain fully the weight of meaning they are required to bear. But, though apprentice work, all show, well developed, the typical UKLG strategy of shaping a story around recurrent motifs, which gain in richness and density as the action juxtaposes them in new patterns, until it might almost be said that the motifs *are* the story. Many of these are the simple archetypal symbols that have always dominated myth and poetry: darkness and light, root and branch, winter and spring, submission and arrogance, language and silence. These are not seen by UKLG as polarities or opposed forces; rather, they are twin parts of a balanced whole, each deriving meaning from the other. UKLG's dualism, insofar as it exists, is not so much in the Western philosophical tradition (where progress is often seen to derive from the tension of antitheses, as in Marxist dialectics) as in the Eastern Taoist tradition, where the emphasis is on balance, mutuality (as in *yin* and *yang*) and an ordered wholeness. However, while Jungian archetype and the tenets of Taoism play a central role in all UKLG's work, critical commentaries on UKLG have emphasized them almost too much; they are by no means the whole story.

The first work of UKLG's maturity as a writer is *The Left Hand of Darkness* (**1969**), which won both Hugo and Nebula awards for best novel. The story is told in a prose notable for its clarity and evocative precision. Once again an ethnologist visits a planet, this time Gethen, whose people are androgynous; normally neuter, they have the capability of becoming either male or female at the peak of their sexual cycle; the world itself is snow-bound. The professional observer cannot hold aloof from events; in the novel's most moving sequence, a long, lonely journey across the ice, he reaches a painful understanding with, and a reciprocated love for, the Gethenian protagonist. Because the Gethenians appear initially to be like us, the reading experience – a gradual understanding of the *differences* between Gethenians and us – invites thoughtfulness about the nature of SEX and sexism in our world, and of cultural chauvinism generally. These four **Hainish** novels were reprinted along with "The Word for World is Forest"

(see below) as *Five Complete Novels* (omni **1985**).

The next two important items in the **Hainish** sequence are novellas: "Vaster than Empires and More Slow" (**1971**) and *The Word for World is Forest* (1972 in *Again, Dangerous Visions* ed Harlan ELLISON; **1976**). The former story, its title taken from Andrew Marvell's "To his Coy Mistress", is set just after the action of *Rocannon's World*, and the latter, which won a 1973 Hugo as Best Novella, rather earlier. Both set humans on alien planets; the first (◊ LIVING WORLDS) is inhabited by only a sentient plant network (the previous line of the Marvell poem is "My vegetable love should grow"); the second planet is occupied by a much-exploited native race, in a situation clearly made to articulate parallels with the Vietnam War. In both cases a kind of union is gained through human surrender to otherness, and alienation is imaged as violence, madness and ravening egoism. UKLG's stories are remarkably persuasive and consistent in their outlook, although the answers tend to come less easily in the work of her middle period, whose major work was the fifth and last novel in the **Hainish** sequence.

This was *The Dispossessed: An Ambiguous Utopia* (**1974**), which won a Hugo and a Nebula, and is widely regarded as UKLG's most richly textured sf work. This is not a book in which difficulties are readily surmounted; a central image is the wall. The novel stands at the head of the **Hainish** sequence, for it tells the life of a physicist whose new MATHEMATICS (by another conceptual breakthrough) will result in the ANSIBLE, the instantaneous-communication device (◊ FASTER THAN LIGHT) necessary if the League of All Worlds – the galactic network about which the sequence is constructed – is to come into being. Two inhabited worlds, one a moon of the other, have different systems of POLITICS: one is an anarchy (reminiscent of that proposed in real life by Kropotkin), the other is primarily capitalist. The hero, Shevek, is not completely at home in either society. The book has been read as pitting a UTOPIA against a DYSTOPIA, but, as the book's subtitle implies, there are seldom absolutes in UKLG's work; the attractive anarchist society is in some ways blinkered and emotionally regimented (with the willing collaboration of its people). Ideationally the novel is very strong, but a slight didactic dryness in the telling – which, perhaps deliberately, hinders any simple emotional identification with the hero – alienated some readers. Nonetheless, it is a deeply imagined work of art. The short story "The Day before the Revolution" (1974) is an introduction to the anarchist society of *The Dispossessed*, being the tired, unromantic last memories of that society's founder; it, too, won a Nebula.

One interesting non-**Hainish** novel was published before *The Dispossessed*. Set in the imaginative territory generally associated with Philip K. DICK, *The Lathe of Heaven* (**1971**) tells of a man who through his dreams can bring alternate reality structures into being. In its interest in METAPHYSICS, it is of a piece with her other work, including her fantasy (see below). It was intelligently dramatized for US tv as *The* LATHE OF HEAVEN.

Through all this period (1962-74), UKLG also wrote non-**Hainish** fiction, including the Hugo-winning "The Ones who Walk Away from Omelas" (1973), a bitter, deft parable about the cost of the good life, and "Nine Lives" (1969), a moving story of CLONES mining an alien planet. With the exception of *The Word for World is Forest*, all UKLG's early short fiction can be found in *The Wind's Twelve Quarters* (coll **1975**; UK paperback in 2 vols), her first and best collection. UKLG has published fewer sf short stories since then. One of them, *The New Atlantis* (1975 as title story of *The New Atlantis* ed Robert SILVERBERG; **1989** chap dos), is a dark NEAR-FUTURE story, in which a ruined ECOLOGY is causing the USA (along with its frightened and frightening state apparatus) to sink into darkness just as ATLANTIS's white towers re-emerge above the sea; it ends ambiguously – as much of UKLG's later fiction does – with the cry of the Atlanteans: "We are here. Where have you gone?" This is one of the stories in UKLG's second collection, *The Compass Rose* (coll **1982**), an occasionally whimsical book which had a mixed critical reception, as did the novella *The Eye of the Heron* (1978 in *Millennial Women* ed Virginia KIDD; **1982** UK), an over-diagrammatic political fable whose translucent simplicity approaches self-parody. UKLG's most recent collection is *Buffalo Gals and Other Animal Presences* (1971-87 var mags; coll **1987**), stories and poems about animals, many being previously collected, but featuring the first book appearance of "Buffalo Gals, Won't You Come Out Tonight?"; this Hugo-winning story recounts a human girl's meeting with incarnations of Native American spirit animals (including Coyote).

It became clear in UKLG's fiction after *The Dispossessed* (including the **Orsinia** sequence) that her strongly utopian impulse was taking over. This is unusual in postwar sf, whether genre sf or mainstream. Because utopian fiction tends not to be plot-driven, much of her fiction since 1974 has seemed a little static: it consciously demands a more contemplative kind of attention than that dictated by most sf. It is a difficult, quixotic demand, since it requires that the reader will accept a cultural re-education. The clearest example is the most recent and biggest of her sf novels, *Always Coming Home* (**1985**). This is an experiment: a collage of verse, reports, tales, drawings by Margaret Chodos, an associated cassette of music by Todd Barton, and even recipes, all relating to the matriarchal society of the Kesh, who live in California's Napa Valley in a future long after some catastrophic event has sunk the coastal cities. An intermittent narrative tells of a woman who marries into, then flees from, a masculine, aggressive society. Utopia is here approached by way of a fictional anthropology, which focuses on its society not by asking the sf question, "How did it get that way?", but

simply asking: "What is it?"

UKLG's FANTASY stories may be her most personal work, and have given some of her readers more pleasure than anything she has written. The **Earthsea** trilogy, austere but vivid, is a major work whose appeal goes far beyond the teenagers at whom in the first instance it was aimed: *A Wizard of Earthsea* (**1968**), *The Tombs of Atuan* (**1971**) and *The Farthest Shore* (**1972**; slightly cut 1973 UK), collected as *Earthsea* (omni **1977**; vt *The Earthsea Trilogy* 1979). Set on ISLANDS in an ocean world, the trilogy tells of training in a MAGIC so rigorous in its principles as to be easily understood as a form of alternate science. The books recount episodes in the apprenticeship, the full-powered maturity and the final death-quest of a magician, Ged. A grave joyfulness pervades the trilogy, which is perhaps more maturely thoughtful (while remaining exciting) than the comparable **Narnia** series of C.S. LEWIS. However, over the next decade a certain backlash against UKLG became evident from the women's movement. It was alleged that, especially in this trilogy, Le Guin saw men as the actors and doers in the world (magicians are male) while women remain the still centre, the well from which they drink. UKLG's FEMINISM certainly altered in nature over the next two decades (as evident in *Always Coming Home*), and she also made a kind of restitution by writing a fourth novel in the **Earthsea** series: *Tehanu: The Last Book of Earthsea* (**1990**). It is a sad, powerful, quiet book about the strength of women (and the ultimate impotence of Ged); it won a Nebula.

UKLG has edited 3 anthologies: *Nebula Award Stories 11* (anth **1976**), *Interfaces* (anth **1980**) and *Edges* (anth **1980**), the last 2 with Virginia Kidd. She also published a second collection of nonfiction pieces, mostly literary essays and reviews, *Dancing at the End of the World: Thoughts on Words, Women, Places* (coll **1989**). In 1989 she received the PILGRIM AWARD for services to sf criticism.

The limpid, serene clarity of her fables, whether in fantasy, sf or even the quasihistorical fiction of her **Orsinia** stories, is powerful, and has won her many loyal friends, even in the genre readership which some see her as having abandoned. Why else would this group continue to award her Hugos and Nebulas through to the end of the 1980s? It is possible that UKLG has been overpraised, but she has given much to the genre, not least by showing (through example) how the traditional novelist's interest in questions of character and moral growth need not be alien to sf. John CLUTE once wrote of her as "eminently sane, humanitarian, concerned" but went on to lament her "fatal lack of *risk*". This may be overstatement, but it points to a quality in her work that has been observed by other critics. It is true that UKLG's demure certainties could, perhaps, be more open to the random and the unpredictable. But can self-confidence justly be evidenced as a flaw?   [PN]

Other works: *From Elfland to Poughkeepsie* (**1973** chap), a critical pamphlet; *Dreams Must Explain Themselves* (coll **1975** chap), a pamphlet which has a story, an essay, a speech and an interview; *The Water is Wide* (**1976** chap); *Very Far Away from Anywhere Else* (**1976**; vt *A Very Long Way from Anywhere Else* 1976 UK), a contemporary love story, not sf, directed at teenagers; *Walking in Cornwall: A Poem for the Solstice* (1976 chap); *Leese Webster* (**1979** chap), for children; *The Beginning Place* (**1980**; vt *Threshold* 1980 UK), a poignant fantasy novel for young adults about an ambiguously desirable alternate world; *Gwilan's Harp* (1977 *Redbook*; **1981** chap); *Hard Words and Other Poems* (coll **1981** chap); the **Adventures in Kroy** sequence for children, comprising *The Adventures of Cobbler's Rune* (**1982** chap) and *Solomon Leviathan's Nine Hundred and Thirty-First Trip around the World* (**1983** chap); *In the Red Zone* (**1983** chap); *The Visionary: The Life Story of Flicker of the Serpentine* (**1984** chap dos), a prepublished excerpt from *Always Coming Home* (**1985**); *King Dog: A Screenplay* (**1985** dos), based on Hindu myth; *Wild Oats and Fireweed . . . New Poems* (coll **1988** chap); *A Visit from Dr Katz* (**1988** chap), for children; *Catwings* (**1988** chap) and *Catwings Return* (**1989** chap), both for children; *Fire and Stone* (**1989** chap) with illustrator Laura Marshall, for children; *Way of the Water's Going: Images of the Northern California Coastal Range* (**1989**) with Ernest Waugh and Allan Nicholson, nature photographs printed with excerpts from *Always Coming Home*; *The Lathe of Heaven/The Dispossessed/The Wind's Twelve Quarters* (omni **1991**); *The Eye of the Heron & The Word for World is Forest* (omni **1991** UK); *Searoad: The Chronicles of Klatsand* (coll **1991**), not sf/fantasy, 10 short stories set on the Oregon coast.

About the author: SCIENCE-FICTION STUDIES, Nov 1975, is a Le Guin issue, concentrating on the sf; *The Farthest Shores of Ursula K. Le Guin* (chap **1976**) by George Edgar SLUSSER; *Ursula K. Le Guin* (anth **1979**) ed M.H. GREENBERG and J.D. OLANDER; *Ursula K. Le Guin: Voyager to Inner Lands and to Outer Space* (anth **1979**) ed Joe De Bolt; *Ursula K. Le Guin* (**1984**) by Charlotte Spivack; *Ursula K. Le Guin* (anth **1986**) ed Harold Bloom, in which most notes and documentation from the original essays have been unaccountably dropped; *Ursula K. Le Guin's The Left Hand of Darkness* (anth **1987**) ed Bloom.

See also: ACE BOOKS; AMAZING STORIES; ANTI-INTELLECTUALISM IN SF; CHILDREN'S SF; CITIES; COLONIZATION OF OTHER WORLDS; CRITICAL AND HISTORICAL WORKS ABOUT SF; GENETIC ENGINEERING; GODS AND DEMONS; IMAGINARY SCIENCE; INVASION; LEISURE; LIBERTARIAN SF; LIFE ON OTHER WORLDS; LINGUISTICS; *The* MAGAZINE OF FANTASY AND SCIENCE FICTION; MAINSTREAM WRITERS OF SF; MUSIC; MYTHOLOGY; OPTIMISM AND PESSIMISM; PASTORAL; PERCEPTION; PHYSICS; POETRY; SCIENCE FICTION FOUNDATION; SCIENTISTS; SOCIOLOGY; VIRTUAL REALITY; WOMEN SF WRITERS.

LEHMANN, RUDOLF CHAMBERS (1856-1929) UK politician, lawyer and writer, involved in the journal *Punch* 1890-1919 and composing for initial publication there *"Mr Punch's" Prize Novels* (coll **1892**), which includes parodies of H. Rider HAGGARD, Jules VERNE and the future-WAR subgenre. A later volume, *The Adventures of Picklock Holes* (coll **1901**), contains at least 1 sf story in addition to its parodies of Arthur Conan DOYLE. [JC]

LEHR, PAUL (1930-) US illustrator. After graduation, PL studied illustration at the prestigious Pratt Institute, and sold his first sf painting to *Satellite* in 1958. Since then he has done hundreds of book-cover paintings as well as covers for *ASF*, *Omni* and non-sf magazines such as *Saturday Evening Post*, *Life* and *Time*. Over the 30-plus years PL has been involved with sf his art has become less realistic, and the greys that dominated his early work have been replaced by more vivid colours. His paintings often contain strange, egg-shaped objects, and sometimes his people seem insignificant and symbolic. With the increasing reliance on realism in sf ILLUSTRATION during the 1980s, PL's sf artwork became less in demand from publishers. [JG]

LEHTIMÄKI, KONRAD [r] ◊ FINLAND.

LEIBER, FRITZ (REUTER Jr) (1910-1992) US writer, father of Justin LEIBER. FL majored in psychology and physiology at the University of Chicago, then spent a year at a theological seminary. His subsequent career included periods as an editor (chiefly with *Science Digest*) and as a drama teacher. He became interested in writing through voluminous correspondence with a college friend, Harry Fischer; it was Fischer who in 1934 suggested the characters of **Fafhrd and the Gray Mouser**, whose HEROIC-FANTASY adventures were central to FL's career. Both men worked intermittently on embellishments to the saga, as described in detail by FL in his essay "Fafhrd and Me" (included in *The Second Book of Fritz Leiber* coll **1975**) and further discussed in *Fafhrd & Me* (coll **1991** chap); Fischer was important to FL as both a friend and an inspiration, and was the model for the Gray Mouser, FL viewing himself as Fafhrd. In 1939 "Two Sought Adventure", the first published story of the sequence and FL's first story, appeared in *Unknown*; he was still adding to the series half a century later. It comprises *Swords and Deviltry* (coll **1970**), *Two Sought Adventure* (coll **1957**; exp and rev vt *Swords Against Death* 1970) and *Swords in the Mist* (coll **1968**) – all assembled as *The Three Swords* (omni **1989**) – plus *Swords Against Wizardry* (coll **1968**), *The Swords of Lankhmar* (1961 *Fantastic* as "Scylla's Daughter"; exp **1968**) and *Swords and Ice Magic* (coll **1977**; with 6 of the 8 stories cut vt *Rime Isle* 1977) – all assembled as *Swords' Masters* (omni **1990**) – plus *The Knight and Knave of Swords* (coll **1988**). From fairly prosaic beginnings the series developed into a complex and enjoyable cycle owing little to the standard clichés of its subgenre (for which FL is credited with coining the widely used description SWORD AND SORCERY). The mood varies from sombre introspection to broad comedy, and there is a very wide range of invention. On its original publication, the long story *Ill Met in*

Lankhmar (1970 in *Swords and Deviltry*; **1990** dos) won both HUGO and NEBULA awards. *The Swords of Lankhmar*, which adds a strong element of sophisticated fetishistic sex to its other virtues – as does the book-length title story in *The Knight and Knave of Swords* – has strong claims to be considered the best modern HEROIC-FANTASY novel, as well as FL's own best novel.

FL was noted also for his fantasies in modern settings, and was almost certainly the most influential model for the sudden creation in the 1980s of the subgenre of Contemporary (or Urban) Fantasy. FL's examples include: "Smoke Ghost" (1941); *Conjure Wife* (1943 *Unknown*; assembled in *Witches Three*, omni **1952**, ed Fletcher PRATT; as a solo book **1953**), a novel of 20th-century witchcraft which has twice been filmed – as *Weird Woman* (1944) and *Burn, Witch, Burn* (1961; vt *Night of the Eagle*) – as well as being adapted for tv; "The Man who Made Friends with Electricity" (1962); and *Our Lady of Darkness* (**1977**), a subtle and touching Gothic with strong autobiographical elements. Other fantasy tales include "Gonna Roll the Bones" (1967), published in DANGEROUS VISIONS, which won a Hugo and a Nebula and later appeared, with other tales of interest, in *The Ghost Light* (coll **1984**); in it a compulsive gambler finds himself playing dice with the Devil, the stake being his soul. "Belsen Express" (1975) won both the Lovecraft Award and the August Derleth Award. FL's further awards for fantasy included the 1975 Grand Master of Fantasy (Gandalf) Award and the 1976 Life Achievement Lovecraft Award; the 1981 Grand Master Nebula Award was presented for his work as a whole. He won altogether 6 Hugos (2 for novels), 4 Nebulas and about 20 other awards.

FL's first important work of sf was *Gather, Darkness!* (1943 *ASF*; **1950**), in which a religious dictatorship ($\diamond$ RELIGION) is overthrown by rebels who disguise their superscience (colourfully, if by far-fetched logic) as witchcraft. *Destiny Times Three* (1945 *ASF*; **1957**) is a neglected ALTERNATE-WORLDS variant. In the early 1950s he became a regular contributor to GALAXY SCIENCE FICTION, for which he wrote a number of notable stories, chiefly social SATIRE. Paramount among these is "Coming Attraction" (1951), depicting an unpleasantly decadent future USA. *The Green Millennium* (**1953**) shows some similar thematic concerns, particularly regarding sexual mores. He then fell silent for four years, through alcoholism (about which he was candid).

His return to sf in 1958 was vigorous, his first stories introducing the **Change War** series, built around a TIME-PARADOX war being fought through time and space and ALTERNATE WORLDS by two factions, the "Spiders" and the "Snakes". The sequence comprises *The Big Time* (1958 *Gal*; **1961** dos) along with most of *The Mind Spider and Other Stories* (coll **1961** dos; rev 1976), this material being variously reassembled as *The Change War* (coll of linked stories **1978**; cut vt *Changewar* 1983). *The Big Time*, which takes place entirely in one room (an R & R location

called the Place, sited beyond normal realities) is suggestive of a play in prose form, and thus reflects FL's background in theatre; both his parents were Shakespearean actors and his father appeared in many films, and FL himself acted on both stage and screen, including a small part in the Greta Garbo film *Camille* (1936). *The Big Time* won a Hugo as Best Novel, as did his most ambitious sf work, *The Wanderer* (**1964**), a long DISASTER novel telling of the havoc caused by the arrival of a strange planet in the Solar System. Its mosaic narrative technique, through which events are observed through a multiplicity of viewpoints, foreshadowed the profusion of such novels and films in the 1970s. FL won a further Hugo for "Ship of Shadows" (1969), a novella first published in a special FL issue of *FSF*, and completed the double of Hugo and Nebula awards for the third time with "Catch that Zeppelin!" (1975), a vivid if inconclusive PARALLEL-WORLDS story. Selections of his best short fiction include *The Best of Fritz Leiber* (coll **1974** UK), *The Worlds of Fritz Leiber* (coll **1976**), *The Ghost Light* (noted above) and *The Leiber Chronicles: Fifty Years of Fritz Leiber* (coll **1990**) ed Martin H. GREENBERG.

Despite his many awards FL never quite established an identity as an sf writer in the way he had for his fantasy; for this reason his work has sometimes been undervalued. His work reflected his various enthusiasms – cats, chess and the theatre are all recurrent motifs – and beliefs, notably a distaste for sexual repression and hypocrisy; but the variety of his approaches was considerable. His prose is ebullient; its idiosyncrasies occasionally appear mannered, but its baroque and colourful qualities are usually prevented from becoming slapdash by the precision with which he used words, and by the appositeness of his imagery, at least in his fantasies. FL was never quite as comfortable in sf, where a straining for effect is more often noticeable. Many of his sf works, he revealed, were fantasies rewritten when the fantasy market began to contract. By refusing to create an easily recognizable template for his sf and then adhering to it, he may have sacrificed some popularity; in compensation, he was the only sf and fantasy writer of his generation to be still developing and producing his best work in the late 1970s. [MJE/JC]

Other works: *Night's Black Agents* (coll **1947**; cut vt *Tales from Night's Black Agents* 1961; original text with 2 stories added, exp 1978); *The Sinful Ones* (1950 *Fantastic Adventures* as "You're All Alone"; exp by other hands as title story of the Universal Giant Edition #5 anth **1953**; cut vt as title story of *You're All Alone* coll **1972**; text restored **1980**); *The Silver Eggheads* (1958 *FSF*; exp **1962**), an example of RECURSIVE SF; *Shadows with Eyes* (coll **1962**); *Ships to the Stars* (coll **1964** dos); *A Pail of Air* (coll **1964**); *Tarzan and the Valley of Gold* * (**1966**), one of only 2 **Tarzan** spin-offs ever authorized by the Edgar Rice BURROUGHS estate (the other being by Joan D. VINGE); *The Night of the Wolf* (coll **1966**); *The Secret Songs* (coll **1968** UK); *Night Monsters* (coll **1969** chap dos; exp 1974 UK); *A Specter* *is Haunting Texas* (**1969**), discussed more fully under SPACE HABITATS; *The Demons of the Upper Air* (coll 1969 chap), poetry; *The Book of Fritz Leiber* (coll **1974**); *Heroes and Horrors* (coll **1978**); *Sonnets to Jonquil and All* (coll **1978** chap), poetry; *Bazaar of the Bizarre* (coll **1978**); *Ship of Shadows* (coll **1979** UK), not to be confused with *Ship of Shadows* (1969 *FSF*; **1989** chap dos), which reprints only the title story; *Ervool* (**1980** chap); *The World Fantasy Awards 2* (anth **1980**) with Stuart David Schiff; *Riches & Power* (**1982** chap); *The Mystery of the Japanese Clock* (**1982** chap), nonfiction; *In the Beginning* (**1983** chap); *Quicks around the Zodiac: A Farce* (**1983** chap); *Conjure Wife/Our Lady of Darkness* (omni **1991**); 2 **Fafhrd and the Gray Mouser** GRAPHIC-NOVEL versions by Howard V. CHAYKIN, *Fafhrd and the Gray Mouser Book 1* (graph **1991**) and *Book 2* (graph coll **1991**). **About the author:** The special FL edition of *FSF*, July 1969; "The Profession of Science Fiction: XII: Mysterious Islands" by FL in FOUNDATION 11/12 (**1977**); *Fritz Leiber* (**1980** chap) by Jeff Frane; *Fritz Leiber* (**1983**) by Tom Staicar; *Fritz Leiber, Sardonic Swordsman: A Working Bibliography* (last rev **1990**) by Gordon BENSON Jr and Phil STEPHENSEN-PAYNE; *Witches of the Mind: A Critical Study of Fritz Leiber* (**1991**) by Bruce Byfield.

See also: ANTHOLOGIES; ANTI-INTELLECTUALISM IN SF; ARKHAM HOUSE; ARTS; ASTOUNDING SCIENCE-FICTION; CITIES; CRIME AND PUNISHMENT; DYSTOPIAS; END OF THE WORLD; FANTASY; FAR FUTURE; GAMES AND SPORTS; GENERATION STARSHIPS; GENETIC ENGINEERING; GRAVITY; HITLER WINS; HOLOCAUST AND AFTER; INVISIBILITY; LONGEVITY (IN WRITERS AND PUBLICATIONS); H.P. LOVECRAFT; The MAGAZINE OF FANTASY AND SCIENCE FICTION; MAGIC; MEDIA LANDSCAPE, MUTANTS; ROBOTS; SUPERNATURAL CREATURES; TRANSPORTATION; UFOS; WAR.

LEIBER, JUSTIN (FRITZ) (1938-   ) US academic and writer, son of Fritz LEIBER. A Professor of Philosophy at the University of Houston, JL has used sf as a medium for speculation in his field of interest, the philosophy of the mind. His first novel, *Beyond Rejection* (**1980**), which begins the **Beyond** sequence, deals in considerable detail with the problems associated with transplanting the recorded mind of a man into the body of a woman (who has a prehensile tail). In *Beyond Humanity* (**1987**) JL contrasts human INTELLIGENCE with those of COMPUTERS and enhanced-intelligence chimpanzees (◊ APES AND CAVEMEN) as humans, computer and chimpanzee cooperate to contact extraterrestrial intelligence. The sequence concludes with *Beyond Gravity* (**1988**), set in 22nd-century Houston and Oxford. JL has also written a number of academic books on similar themes, including *Can Animals and Machines Be Persons?* (**1985**), which uses an sf scenario – a legal case between a space-exploration company and a Civil Liberties Union over whether a chimpanzee and a computer used on a space station should be treated as tools or as employees. [TA]
Other works: The **Saga of the House of Eigin** sequence, comprising *The Sword and the Eye* (**1984**) and *The Sword and the Tower* (**1985**).

LEIGH, STEPHEN (W.) (1951-   ) US writer and musician who began publishing sf with "A Rain of Pebbles" for *ASF* in 1977, and who sometimes releases short stories as Lee Stevens. The first novel of his **Neweden** sequence – *Slow Fall to Dawn* (**1981**), *Dance of the Hag* (**1983**) and *A Quiet of Stone* (**1984**) – brought him into some prominence through its depiction of the attractive feudal culture obtaining upon the eponymous planet, whose name seemed, initially, only moderately ironic. Later episodes, however, demonstrate the fragility of Neweden mores in a SPACE-OPERA context that dissipates the network of mutual obligations that makes the thieves' guild at the sequence's heart so attractive a vehicle for sf adventures. Further sf novels of interest include: *The Bones of God* (**1986**), an interplanetary tale pitting a solitary prophet against the oppressive Judeo-Christian RELIGION that dominates Old Earth; *Crystal Memory* (**1987**), a complex novel in which problems typical of sf adventures – a female space-freighter pilot attempts to recover her erased memories and to avenge the death of her young son – are placed in a context featuring interestingly depicted MARS colonies, ALIEN incursions, zombies, intrigue and loss; and *The Abraxis Marvel Circus* (**1990**), a humorous fantasy, choked with variously comic characters and rock musicians, about reviving the dead. SL has written several ties in recent years, and his career has consequently lost some focus. [JC]
Other works: *Dr Bones #1: The Secret of the Lona* * (**1988**); *Isaac Asimov's Robot City: Robots and Aliens #1: The Changeling* * (**1989**); *The Next Wave #2: Alien Tongue* (**1991**), including an essay by Rudy RUCKER.

LEIGHTON, EDWARD ◊ G.J. BARRETT.

LEINSTER, MURRAY Pseudonym under which US writer William Fitzgerald Jenkins (1896-1975) was best known in the sf field, and under which he wrote almost all his work in the genre; exceptions were a few stories in magazines, mainly those in the **Bud Gregory** series as by William Fitzgerald, and a small number as by Will F. Jenkins. He remained active as an sf writer from 1919, when his first story, "The Runaway Skyscraper", about a building falling backwards through time, was published in *Argosy*, until about 1970. Like most contributors to the pre-WWII US sf PULP MAGAZINES, he published a great deal of material that did not reach book form until after 1945. His first book publication, *Murder Madness* (**1931**), as its title indicates did not aim directly at the sf market (then still nascent in the USA), though the book is in fact sf. *The Murder of the U.S.A.* (**1946**; vt *Destroy the U.S.A.* 1950 Canada) as by Will F. Jenkins was again directed as much to the mystery as to the sf market, though its plot (the hero solves the mystery of who dropped 300 A-bombs on US cities) is more sf than locked-room. Because of the pile-up of magazine material, many of ML's post-WWII book publications contained or reworked early stories, and were often rather dated in plotline and character development; ironically, it was at this time that he was publishing his best work in the magazines, stories that competed on equal terms with those by writers 20 years newer to the field.

ML's first series was the set of 4 off-beat **Masters of Darkness** or **Preston-Hines** superscience-blackmail stories contributed to *The Argosy*, 1929-30, and never collected in book form. The more widely known **Bud Gregory** series comprises the 3 stories in *Out of this World* (coll **1958**) and "The Seven Temporary Moons" (1948); all 4 were originally published in *TWS*. Bud is a hillbilly whose intuitive knack with high technology allows him to solve various superscience problems. Of more interest is the **Med Service** sequence, *S.O.S. from Three Worlds* (coll **1967**), *The Mutant Weapon* (**1959** dos), *Doctor to the Stars: Three Novelettes of the Interstellar Medical Service* (coll **1964**) and *This World is Taboo* (**1961**); all but *Doctor to the Stars* were assembled as *The Med Series* (omni **1983**). In these stories and novels, Calhoun and the "being" Murgatroyd act as troubleshooters in various far-flung crises; the tales are robust and adventurous, but rudimentary compared to the inventiveness of James WHITE's **Sector General** tales (*see also* MEDICINE). The **Joe Kenmore** novels – *Space Platform* (**1953**), *Space Tug* (**1953**), and *City on the Moon* (**1957**) – make up a juvenile series about the crisis-ridden first years of the near-future US space effort, told in melodramatic terms that have not worn well.

ML's best years as an sf writer were undoubtedly the decade following WWII, a period during which his finest short stories were published, among them "First Contact" (1945), "Doomsday Deferred" (1949) as by Jenkins, "The Lonely Planet" (1949), "If You Was a Moklin" (1951) and "Exploration Team" (1956), which won the 1956 HUGO for Best Novelette and became part of *Colonial Survey* (1955-6 ASF; fixup **1956**; vt *Planet Explorer* 1957), perhaps his most enjoyable single volume, though his individual short stories are generally superior to his book-length work. When ML did contrive FIXUPS of short material, the result was often disappointing. His first classic story, for instance, "The Mad Planet" (1920), on being incorporated into *The Forgotten Planet* (1920-53 var mags; fixup **1954**), exposed to view implausibilities that may have been tolerable in a 1920 short story but which, 30 years later in book form, failed to convince. His novels, which were frequently unambitious and repetitive, generally stretched beyond their proper span, and seemed written for a less demanding market than his best stories (which appeared in many journals, including *ASF* and *Gal*). A good selection of these tales can be found in *Monsters and Such* (coll **1959**); *The Best of Murray Leinster* (coll **1976** UK) ed Brian Davis is much inferior to *The Best of Murray Leinster* (coll **1978**) ed J.J. PIERCE.

The last decade of ML's career boasted numerous publications, but no substantial works were conceived after the mid-1950s – though *The Pirates of Zan* (**1959** dos), a competent but unremarkable space opera, won some praise. In this book, and in almost every full-length title ML published after WWII, the *Galaxy* serves as a template which scamps and engineers tinker with to their own advantage, and to the advantage of small communities on Earth or elsewhere. "According to the fiction tapes," as ML puts it in *The Pirates of Zan*, "the colonized worlds of the galaxy vary wildly from one another. In cold and unromantic fact, it isn't so. Space travel is too cheap and sol-type solar systems too numerous to justify the settlement of hostile worlds." It is perhaps revealing that variations, in this quote, are seen as innately hostile. In any case, the ML universe had little room for CONCEPTUAL BREAKTHROUGH, and the similarities in background from one novel to another were sufficiently numerous that his later books made up one loose series. Allied to this template view of the Universe was a deepening political simplicity of view, rather right-wing in orientation (a viewpoint common to many sf writers of his generation), which led to the frequent depiction of cartoon-like confrontations between the USA and underhanded enemies, in the resolving of which means tended to dominate ends. In *Timeslip!* ∗ (**1967**) and *The Time Tunnel* ∗ (**1967**), based on episodes from the tv series TIME TUNNEL – another ML novel, *Time Tunnel* (**1964**), is confusingly unrelated to this series – the past is paradoxically restructured by executive fiat to make life safe for democracy. But the paradox seems unconscious.

The high and only superficially simple competence of the stories remains as ML's memorial. In this work he speaks with a directness to the heart of magazine sf and its readership with a craftsmanship and consistency that warrant the nickname he was given: the Dean of SF. [JC]

Other works: *Fight for Life* (1947 *Startling Stories*; **1949**); *The Last Space Ship* (1946-7 *TWS*; fixup **1949**); *Sidewise in Time* (coll **1950**); *Conquest of the Stars* **1952** (chap Australia); *The Unknown* (**1952** chap Australia); *The Black Galaxy* (1949 *Startling Stories*; **1954**); *The Brain-Stealers* (1947 *Startling Stories* as "The Man in the Iron Cap"; **1954** dos); *Gateway to Elsewhere* (1950 *Fantasy Book*; 1952 *Startling Stories* as "Journey to Barkut"; **1954** dos); *Operation: Outer Space* (**1954**); *The Other Side of Here* (1936 *ASF* as "The Incredible Invasion"; rev **1955** dos); *War with the Gizmos* (**1958**); *Four from Planet 5* (**1959**); *The Monster from Earth's End* (**1959**); *The Aliens* (coll **1960**); *Men into Space* ∗ (**1960**), based on the tv series; *Twists in Time* (coll **1960**); *Creatures of the Abyss* (**1961**; vt *The Listeners* 1969 UK); *The Wailing Asteroid* (**1960**); *Operation Terror* (**1962**); *Talents, Incorporated* (**1962**); *The Duplicators* (**1964** dos); *The Greks Bring Gifts* (**1964**); *Invaders of Space* (**1964**); *The Other Side of Nowhere* (**1964**); *Get Off my World!* (coll **1966**); *Space Captain* (**1966** dos); *Checkpoint Lambda* (**1966**); *Miners in the Sky* (**1967**); *Space Gypsies* (**1967**); ties based on the tv series LAND OF THE GIANTS, comprising *Land of the Giants* ∗ (**1968**), *#2: The Hot Spot* ∗ (**1969**) and *#3: Unknown Danger* ∗ (**1969**); *A Murray Leinster Omnibus* (omni **1968**), assembling *Operation Terror, Checkpoint*

Lambda and *Invaders of Space*; *Last Murray Leinster Interview* (**1983** chap) with Ronald Payne.

As editor: *Great Stories of Science Fiction* (anth **1951**).

About the author: *Murray Leinster (Will F. Jenkins): A Bibliography* (**1970** chap) by Mark OWINGS.

See also: ALIENS; ALTERNATE WORLDS; AMAZING STORIES; ASTEROIDS; ASTOUNDING SCIENCE-FICTION; COLONIZATION OF OTHER WORLDS; COMMUNICATIONS; CRIME AND PUNISHMENT; FASTER THAN LIGHT; GREAT AND SMALL; HIVE-MINDS; INVASION; INVISIBILITY; LIVING WORLDS; LONGEVITY (IN WRITERS AND PUBLICATIONS); MACHINES; MOON; OUTER PLANETS; PARALLEL WORLDS; PARASITISM AND SYMBIOSIS; SPACE FLIGHT; SPACESHIPS; TIME PARADOXES; TIME TRAVEL.

LEISURE The gradual AUTOMATION of industry and the progressive reduction of working hours has already extended the amount of leisure time which citizens of the developed nations have, and most contemporary images of the future assume that everyone will have even more of it in times to come. The majority of people, for whom work is a necessary but unpleasant burden, regard this as a highly desirable outcome; but sociologists and sf writers tend to be more sceptical. UTOPIAN satires like Muriel JAEGER's *The Question Mark* (**1926**) and Aldous HUXLEY's *Brave New World* (**1932**) offer horrified and disapproving visions of the people of the future giving themselves over to frivolous and intellectually vacuous pursuits, all in the worst possible taste. Had Huxley lived to see contemporary tv, Torremolinos and Euro-Disney he would undoubtedly have said "I told you so", as he did with regard to far less garish spectacles in *Brave New World Revisited* (coll **1958**).

GENRE-SF writers, who are themselves part of the entertainment industry, might be expected to look upon leisure with a kinder eye, but for the most part they have not. E.M. FORSTER's censorious question about what happens when "The Machine Stops" (1909) is echoed even in such pulp melodramas as Miles J. BREUER's "Paradise and Iron" (1930) and Laurence MANNING's and Fletcher PRATT's strikingly vivid "The City of the Living Dead" (1930). Frederik POHL's and C.M. KORNBLUTH's biting SATIRE on consumerism, *The Space Merchants* (**1953**), kicked off a whole series of similar sarcastic fantasies, notably Shepherd MEAD's *The Big Ball of Wax* (**1954**), Pohl and Kornbluth's *Gladiator-at-Law* (**1955**) and Harold LIVINGSTON's *The Climacticon* (**1960**). The most thoughtful and carefully focused of these was probably James E. GUNN's *The Joy Makers* (1954-5; fixup **1961**), in which a cult of hedonism gradually takes over the world; it concludes with a vision more refined but every bit as striking as that in Manning's and Pratt's story, in which the vast majority of people live cocooned in life-support systems experiencing nothing but engineered dreams. *Tomorrow's World* (**1956**; vt *Tomorrow and Tomorrow*) by Hunt Collins (Evan HUNTER) is exceptional in defending the supporters of Vicarious Experience against their puritanically inclined opponents, and is one of the few sf stories to assume that the people of the future will

sensibly accept the Epicurean dictum that pleasure, despite being the only true end of human experience, ought to be taken in moderation. Other images of technologically supported total escapism are featured in Arthur C. CLARKE's "The Lion of Comarre" (1949), John D. MacDONALD's "Spectator Sport" (1950), John T. SLADEK's "The Happy Breed" (1967) and Mack REYNOLDS's *Perchance to Dream* (**1977**) and *After Utopia* (**1977**). The majority opinion seems to be that such escapists need to be brought back to reality whether they like it or not, and that those appointed to achieve that end need not be overly scrupulous in so doing.

The leisure pursuits traditionally associated with cultural élites inevitably get a better press in sf's images of the future than do those associated with the lower orders; comparison of the works considered in the entries on the ARTS and GAMES AND SPORTS will readily confirm this, but even stories about the finer arts often deal in images of enervated decadence, like those featured in J.G. BALLARD's stories of *Vermilion Sands* (coll **1971**). A great many sf stories propose that sadistic spectator "sports" of the kind which went on in the Roman arena are likely to make a comeback in the future, their lapse into apparent obsolescence being a temporary imposition of censorship rather than a permanent refinement of feeling. Indeed, the current popularity of sf war games (◊ GAMES AND TOYS; GAME-WORLDS; VIRTUAL REALITY) has led to the production of TIES in which entire GALACTIC EMPIRES become writ-large arenas for carefully staged and extraordinarily bloody conflicts. Robert SHECK-LEY's neatly satirical stories about sadistic futuristic games, including "Seventh Victim" (1953; filmed as *La* DECIMA VITTIMA [1965]) and "The Prize of Peril" (1958), were inflated by popular demand into the film-associated melodrama *The Tenth Victim* * (**1966**) and ultimately into the series of novels including *Victim Prime* (**1987**) and *Hunter/Victim* (**1988**), whose narrative dispiritedness might be seen as an ironic comment on the awful absurdity of their saleability. When they are not revisiting the past, sf images of future leisure tend to be firmly anchored in the trends of the present – as witness the recent rash of stories about the Theme Parks of the future, including the series begun by Larry NIVEN and Steven BARNES with *Dream Park* (**1981**) as well as Michael CRICHTON's *Jurassic Park* (**1991**). The extension of the MEDIA LANDSCAPE to take in mass-produced dreams, as featured in many stories – including Chelsea Quinn YARBRO's *Hyacinths* (**1983**) and James MORROW's *The Continent of Lies* (**1984**) – is seen by most writers as a natural extrapolation of the trend towards privacy and subjection to personal whim which led from cinema to tv to the VCR; and stories involving such technologies frequently echo – often calculatedly – contemporary disputes about the uses and alleged abuses of these media.

The unfortunate correlates of leisure are, of course, boredom and purposelessness. The threat of boredom is seen by very many sf stories as something so likely to spoil the experience of IMMORTALITY as to make it almost worthless – a contention which is surely breathtaking in its closed-mindedness. Many sf stories similarly argue that, because the use of TECHNOLOGY to supply all our basic needs would rob our lives of a sense of purpose, we would be far better off engaged in a constant struggle for existence. HARD SF has characteristically adopted and adapted the frontier mythology of US history in order to extrapolate the struggle for existence onto a galactic stage, thus ducking the question of excessive leisure altogether, although on occasion hard-sf writers are inclined to take it for granted that time liberated from more vulgar forms of work will naturally be devoted, by all those capable of such intellectual effort, to scientific inquiry. (Indeed, many hard-sf writers seem unable to devise suitably sciencefictional leisure-time activities for their characters. In many books the protagonists seem to entertain themselves either by dabbling in quantum physics or by engaging in sex, with very little – such as reading thrillers or going to the movies – in between.) Aside from four-dimensional chess or a hobby of dabbling in xeno-archaeology, Sf novels which depict in some detail and without disapproval the leisure pursuits of imaginary cultures generally do so in connection with low-tech cultures whose leisure is both limited and evidently purposive; the works of Jack VANCE offer many examples, although the single most elaborate exercise in this vein is Ursula K. LE GUIN's *Always Coming Home* (1985).

It is arguable that one of the great failures of the sciencefictional imagination has been the inability to envision laudable ways in which the leisured classes of the future might make use of that leisure. Even stories which depict all-powerful immortals successfully keeping boredom at bay generally assume that their projects and methods will be essentially silly, like those of the central characters of Michael MOORCOCK's **Dancers at the End of Time** series (1972-7). Godlike beings in sf usually behave like spoiled children – although perhaps this is not entirely surprising, given that the gods people have actually believed in have mostly behaved in much the same fashion. Perhaps, on the other hand, the concept of "leisure" is implicitly ambiguous; if so, sciencefictional accounts of future leisure can do little else but unpack that ambiguity, exposing its paradoxicality for purposes of lamentation or mockery, according to taste. [BS/DP]

LEITHAUSER, BRAD (1953-   ) US poet and novelist whose sf novel, *Hence* (1989), is a near-future FABULATION – itself told as from a point considerably further into the future – in which a boy plays against a COMPUTER for the world chess championship. Style and matter are at times reminiscent of the work of Vladimir NABOKOV. [JC]

LEM, STANISŁAW (1921-   ) Polish writer, critic and polymath, winner of numerous awards including the 1973 Polish State Literary Award. Born in Lwów, he has described his childhood and adolescence charmingly in the autobiographical *Wysoki zamek* ["High Castle"] (1966 Poland). SL's study of medicine was interrupted in WWII by the Nazi occupation, when he worked as a car mechanic and welder; these experiences closely inform his first-written novel (not sf), *Szpital Przemienienia* (1982 Poland; trans William Brand as *Hospital of the Transfiguration* 1988 US). In 1946 he moved to Cracow (he now lives in Italy), received his MD and wrote lyrical verse and essays on scientific methodology until he ran foul of the Soviet state's adulation of the Lamarckian biological theories of T.D. Lysenko (1898-1976) (◊ EVOLUTION; PSEUDO-SCIENCE), and was research assistant in a scientific institute. Another "naturalistic" novel, *Czas nieutracony* ["Time Saved"] (1955), depicts an intellectual finding his way from solitude to sociopolitical meaning; it likewise was written in the 1940s. In the meantime SL had switched to sf; he has published over two dozen books so far, with translations into at least 30 languages and several million copies sold. His early sf novels, *Astronauci* ["The Astronauts"] (1951 Poland) and *Oblok Magellana* ["The Magellan Nebula"] (1955 Poland), are works of a beginner and limited by some of the conventions of "socialist realism", but are still interesting and contain a number of SL's constant themes (the threat of global destruction and militarism; human identity); their UTOPIAN naïvety is shaped by the committed humanism characteristic of one axis of his work. His other axis, a black grotesque, appears in *Dzienniki Gwiazdowe* (coll 1957 Poland; gradually exp until by 1971 there were 14 "voyages" and 8 other **Ijon Tichy** stories; trans in 2 vols, vol 1 trans Michael KANDEL as *The Star Diaries* 1976 US, vol 2 trans Joel Stern and Maria Swiecicka-Ziemianek as *Memoirs of a Space Traveler: Further Reminiscences of Ijon Tichy* 1982 US), which develops into a parable-like expression.

The dozen years after the "Polish October" of 1956 were the golden noon of SL. He published 17 books: 5 sf novels; 10 partly overlapping books of sf short stories including the **Pirx the Pilot** cycle (see below), the "robotic fairy tales" of *Bajki robotów* (coll 1964 Poland) and the **Trurl-Klapaucius** or **Cyberiad** cycle (see below); *Noc ksiezycowa* (coll 1963 Poland), 1 sf play and 3 tv plays; nonfiction including the "cybernetic sociology" of *Dialogi* (1957 Poland); and the crown of SL's speculation and key to his fiction, *Summa technologiae* (1964 Poland), a breathtakingly brilliant and risky survey of possible social, informational, cybernetic, cosmogonic and biological engineering in Man's game with Nature.

Eden (1959 Poland; trans Marc E. Heine as *Eden* 1989 US), *Solaris* (1961 Poland; trans Joanna Kilmartin and Steve Cox [from French trans] 1970 US), *Niezwyciezony* (1964 Poland; trans Wendayne Ackerman [from German trans] as *The Invincible* 1973 US) and *Opowieści o pilocie Pirxie* (coll 1968 Poland; trans in 2 vols as *Tales of Pirx the Pilot* 1979 US and *More Tales of Pirx the Pilot* **1982** US) use the mystery of strange beings, events and localities to educate their protagonists into understanding the limitations and strengths of humanity; *Solaris* was filmed as SOLARIS (1971). These parables for our age are fittingly open-ended: their tenor is that no closed reference system is viable in the age of CYBERNETICS and rival political absolutisms; the protagonists are redeemed by ethical and aesthetic insight rather than by hardware, abstract cognition or power – thence SL's strong, at times oversimplifying but salutary critique of English-language sf in his *Fantastyka i futurologia* (**1970** Poland; excerpts trans with other material as coll *Microworlds: Writings on Science Fiction and Fantasy* **1985** US) for abusing the potentials of the new in gimmicks and disguised fairytales. His critique of equally anthropomorphic banalities in Soviet sf was effected by means of his immense popularity and liberating influence there. In between the two leviathans, SL used the experience of Central European intellectuals (◊ ALBANIA, BULGARIA, CZECHOSLOVAKIA, HUNGARY, POLAND, ROMANIA, RUSSIA, SOVIET UNION) to fuse a bright, humanistic hope with a bitter, historical warning. This double vision subverts both the "comic inferno" approach and a deterministic utopianism by juxtaposing the black flickerings of the former with the bright horizons of the latter. Such a style of wit places SL in the *contes philosophiques* tradition of Jonathan SWIFT and VOLTAIRE. Even his grotesque stories, where no "cruel miracles" redeem the often disgusting limits of Man – such as *Cyberiada* (coll **1965** Poland; trans Kandel as *The Cyberiad* **1974** US), collecting many of the **Trurl-Klapaucius** stories – are informed by such humanizing fun, black SATIRE or allegorical iconoclasm.

Signs of an ideological dead-end, if not exhaustion, showed in about 1968, prompting further formal experimentation and a furious brilliance in SL's writing. In *Glos pana* (**1968** Poland; trans Kandel as *His Master's Voice* **1983** US), SL's radical doubts about human self-determination and sovereignty, and therefore about possibilities of COMMUNICATION with other people (not to mention other civilizations), began threatening to distort the fictional form of the novel into solipsist musings, lectures and ideational adventure. *His Master's Voice* may have avoided that by a *tour de force* of narrative tone, but SL learned some lessons from this near-escape: he turned to a brilliantly innovative series of briefer second-order glosses at the borderland of fiction and treatise. *Doskonala próżnia* (coll **1971** Poland; trans Kandel as *A Perfect Vacuum* **1978** US) – mainly composed of reviews of nonexistent books, which simultaneously characterize and persiflage their targets – and *Wielkość urojona* (coll **1973** Poland; trans Marc E. Heine with 2 pieces from *Golem XIV* [coll **1973**] as *Imaginary Magnitude* **1984** US) range from thumbnail sketches of grisly futuristic follies to developments of *Summa technologiae* ideas on "intellectronics" (artificially heightened intelligence) and "phantomatics" (illus-

ory existence). We find the latter in the most grimly hilarious and longest work of this period, a further **Ijon Tichy** story, "Kongres Futurologiczny" (in coll *Bezsenność* **1971** Poland; trans Kandel as *The Futurological Congress* **1974** US), as well as SL's deeply rooted though atheistic theologico-cosmogonic obsessions. Only in the 1980s, with the awkward but ferocious assault upon human cognitive pretensions contained in *Fiasko* (**1986** Poland; trans Kandel as *Fiasco* **1987** US), did he return to novel-length structures.

SL's overflowing linguistic inventiveness, matching his controversial ideational plenty, is partly lost in translation, though the short stories assembled as *Mortal Engines* (coll trans **1977** US), *The Cosmic Carnival of Stanisław Lem* (coll trans Kandel **1981**) and *One Human Minute* (coll trans Catherine S. Leach **1986** US) reveal some of the exuberance of the writing. Nonetheless, SL's peculiar geopolitical vantage-point – enabling him effectively to transcend both cynical pragmatism and abstract utopianism – his stubborn warnings against static "final solutions", his position at the crossroads of major European cultures and ethics, joined to an intense internalization of problems from cybernetics and information theory, his fusion of dilemmas from ultramodern science and the oldest cosmogonic heresies, his dazzling formal virtuosity – all mark him as one of the most significant sf writers of our century, and a distinctive voice in world literature.   [DS]

Other works: *Czlowiek z Marsa* (1946 Poland, apparently only as episodes in a weekly); *Sezam* ["Sesame"] (coll **1955** Poland); *Sledztwo* (**1959** Poland; trans Adele Milch as *The Investigation* **1974** US), ontological mystery rather than sf; *Inwazja z Aldebarana* ["Invasion from Aldebaran"] (coll **1959** Poland); *Powrót s gwiazd* (**1961** Poland; trans as *Return from the Stars* **1980** US); *Pamietnik znaleziony w wannie* (**1961** Poland; trans Michael Kandel and Christine Rose as *Memoirs Found in a Bathtub* **1973** US); *Ksiega robotów* ["The Book of Robots"] (coll **1961** Poland); *Wejście na orbite* ["Getting into Orbit"] (coll **1962** Poland), essays on technology and fiction; *Polowanie* ["The Hunt"] (coll **1965** Poland); *Ratujmy kosmos* (coll **1966** Poland); *Opowiadania* (coll **1969** Poland); *Rozprawy i szkice* (coll **1974** Poland), essays on literature, sf and science; *Katar* (**1977** Poland; trans anon as *The Chain of Chance* **1978** UK); *Wisja Lokalna* ["The Scene of the Crime"] (**1982**), an **Ijon Tichy** novel.

About the author: "To My Readers" by Stanisław Lem, *Poland* 5, 1973; "Language and Ethics in Solaris" by Edward Balcerzan, *Science-Fiction Studies: Selected Essays on Science Fiction 1973-1975* (**1976**) ed R.D. MULLEN and Darko SUVIN; "Stanisław Lem, Rationalist and Sensualist" by Jerzy Jarzębski, SCIENCE-FICTION STUDIES July 1977; "Lem in Review (June 2238)" by Michael KANDEL, *Science-Fiction Studies* Mar 1977; "Stanisław Lem on Men and Robots" by Kandel, EXTRAPOLATION Dec 1972; *New Worlds for Old* (**1974**) by David KETTERER; "European SF" by Ursula K. LE GUIN,

Science-Fiction Studies Spring 1974; "The Open-Ended Parables of Stanisław Lem and *Solaris*" by Darko Suvin, afterword to *Solaris* (trans **1970**) and rev for 1976 edn; *Stanisław Lem* (**1985**) by Richard E. Ziegfeld; special SL issue of *Science Fiction Studies* (vol 13, part 3, whole #4, 1986).

See also: ALIENS; ASTRONOMY; AUTOMATION; CONCEPTUAL BREAKTHROUGH; CRITICAL AND HISTORICAL WORKS ABOUT SF; DISCOVERY AND INVENTION; HUMOUR; ISLANDS; LIVING WORLDS; MACHINES; METAPHYSICS; PERCEPTION; PHYSICS; ROBOTS; SCIENCE FICTION WRITERS OF AMERICA; SPACE HABITATS; SPACESHIPS; SUPERNATURAL CREATURES.

L'ENGLE, MADELEINE Working name of US actress and writer Madeleine L'Engle Camp (1918-   ), whose first play, *18 Washington Square, South* (**1944**), was produced in 1940, and who performed on the stage during the early 1940s. Her first novel, *The Small Rain* (**1945**), and some of its successors are non-genre fictions for adult audiences, but from *And Both Were Young* (**1949**) most of her work has been for children. She gained immediate and lasting acclaim for *A Wrinkle in Time* (**1962**), which was both her first sf novel and the first volume of the **Meg Murray** sequence, which includes also *A Wind in the Door* (**1973**), *A Swiftly Tilting Planet* (**1978**), *Many Waters* (**1986**) and *An Acceptable Time* (**1989**). *A Wrinkle in Time*, which won the 1963 Newbery Medal and various later awards, follows the adventures of the children of Dr Murray, a scientist abducted to a distant planet where he is held in thrall to a central COMPUTER intelligence. The tight plot and ample moral scope of the tale make Meg Murray's rescue of her father into one of the more memorable moments in CHILDREN'S SF. Later novels similarly expose the Murray family to adventures and stresses, and develop a telling portrait of complex young people. The **Canon Tallis** sequence – *The Arm of the Starfish* (**1965**) and *The Young Unicorns* (**1968**) – is also of interest. ML'E's singletons include *Dance in the Desert* (**1969**) and *The Sphinx at Dawn* (coll of linked stories **1982**). [JC]

LENGYEL, PÉTER [r] ◊ HUNGARY.

LÉONARD, FRANÇOIS [r] ◊ BENELUX.

LEONARD, GEORGE H. (1921-   ) US writer whose two sf novels, *Beyond Control* (**1975**) and *Alien* (**1977**; vt *Alien Quest* 1981 UK), explore competently – but without much energy – the conventions of the sf-adventure tale; the latter is unconnected with the 1979 film of the same name. GHL is also the author of a classic work of PSEUDO-SCIENCE (or possibly spoof), *Someone Else is on Our Moon* (**1976**), which explains many features of the lunar landscape in terms of the mighty engineering feats of ALIEN colonists – and, *inter alia*, characterizes Galileo as a "feisty pioneer". [JC/JGr]

See also: UFOS.

LEOPARDI, GIACOMO [r] ◊ ITALY.

LÉOURIER, CHRISTIAN (1948-   ) French writer, author of *Les montagnes du soleil* (**1971**; trans anon as *The Mountains of the Sun* 1973 US), an interesting

socio-anthropological novel mapping the rediscovery of Earth after a cataclysmic deluge. CL has since written principally for children. [MJ]

LE PAGE, RAND House name used by CURTIS WARREN for some routine SPACE OPERAS. Authors included William Henry Fleming BIRD, John S. GLASBY, Brian HOLLOWAY, Dennis HUGHES and David O'BRIEN. *Beyond These Suns* (**1952**) was by Cyril Protheroe. On the wrappers, RLP was described as "the French master of modern science fiction". [SH/JC]

L'EPY, HELIOGENES de Pseudonym of an unidentified 17th-century UK writer whose *A Voyage into Tartary, Containing a Curious Description of that Country* (**1689**) depicts, perhaps for the first time, the discovery of a LOST WORLD. The circular city of Heliopolis in central Asia, inhabited by descendants of ancient Greeks, is a republican UTOPIA which maintains remarkable control over its own advanced technologies; a museum contains relics of flying machines and other devices. [JC]

About the author: "L'Epy's *A Voyage into Tartary*. An Enlightenment Ideal Society" by E.F. BLEILER in *Extrapolation* (summer 1988) records Bleiler's pioneering investigation of this author and his text.

LE QUEUX, WILLIAM (TUFNELL) (1864-1927) French-born UK journalist and author of over 100 books in a variety of genres, though most of his most popular works were espionage thrillers in the vein of E. Phillips OPPENHEIM – he claimed, unconvincingly, to be a spy himself – and detective novels, often with oriental colouring. He wrote a number of fantasies in the vein of H. Rider HAGGARD, with some immediate but no lasting success, and a number of romances, like *Stolen Souls* (**1895**), whose generic definition shifts between suspense and the occult. He is best remembered today for his two future-WAR/INVASION novels: *The Great War in England in 1897* (**1894**) and *The Invasion of 1910: With a Full Account of the Siege of London* (**1906**; cut vt *The Invasion* 1910), the latter written with the anon collaboration of H(erbert) W(rigley) Wilson (1866-1940). Both books were serialized in English newspapers before being separately published, and both aroused considerable stir, particularly the latter, with its letter of commendation from the distinguished soldier and statesman Lord Roberts (1832-1914), who shared WLQ's anti-German views (and collaborated with him on two nonfiction dreadful-warning books, *The Great War* [**1908**] and *Spies of the Kaiser* [**1909**]). Though both novels were told with every trick WLQ had acquired in his years of journalism, and though the latter is replete with diagrams of the threatened invasion from Germany, the ultimate effect of each book is of a laboured turgidity of effect. A further tale whose title hints at similar contents, *England's Peril* (**1899**), is fundamentally an espionage thriller. WLQ persistently utilized Germany as the opponent in his work; even after WWI, stories like *The Terror of the Air* (**1920**) attempt to present a world in constant danger of Teutonic aggression. The sf of WLQ's last years is consistently routine. He is fundamentally a figure of pre-WWI interest. [JC]

Other works: *Zoraida: A Romance of the Harem and the Great Sahara* (**1895**); *The Great White Queen: A Tale of Treasure and Treason* (**1896**); *The Eye of Istar: A Romance of the Land of No Return* (**1897**), one of several lost-race novels (◊ LOST WORLDS); *A Madonna of the Music Halls* (**1897**; vt *A Secret Sin* 1913); *The Veiled Man* (coll **1899**); *The Sign of the Seven Sins* (**1901**); *The Closed Book* (**1904**); *The Unknown Tomorrow: How the Rich Fared at the Hands of the Poor* (**1910**); *The House of Whispers* (**1910**); *The Great God Gold* (**1910**); *No 70 Berlin* (**1915**); *The Mystery of the Green Ray* (**1915**); *"Cinders" of Harley Street* (coll **1916**), featuring a doctor with PSI POWERS; *The Zeppelin Destroyer: Being some Chapters of Secret History* (**1916**); *The Unbound Book* (**1916**); *The Bomb-Makers* (**1917**); *The Rainbow Mystery: Chronicles of a Colour-Criminologist* (coll **1917**); *The Little Blue Goddess* (**1918**); *The Voice from the Void* (**1922**); *The Gay Triangle* (**1922**), featuring a car with collapsible wings; *Tracked by Wireless* (**1922**); *The Broadcast Mystery* (**1925**); *Double Nought* (**1927**); *The Chameleon* (**1927**; vt *Poison Shadows* 1927 US); *The Secret Formula* (**1928**).

See also: DYSTOPIAS; WEAPONS.

LERANGIS, PETER (? -) US writer of a variety of ties, including 3 titles in the Byron PREISS **Time Machine** sequence – *The Amazing Ben Franklin* * (**1987** chap), *The Last of the Dinosaurs* * (**1988**) and *Time Machine, Special Edition: World War II Code Breaker* * (**1989**) – a STAR TREK novel, *Star Trek IV, the Voyage Home* * (**1986** chap) (◊ STAR TREK IV: THE VOYAGE HOME), and a **Find Your Fate – G.I. Joe** tale, *The Sultan's Secret* * (**1988**). [JC]

LEROUX, GASTON (1868-1927) French writer of mystery novels who remains best known for *Le Fantôme de l'Opéra* (**1910**; trans Alexander Teixeira de Mattos as *The Phantom of the Opera* **1911** UK), a tale of horror filmed in 1925 (rereleased with sound 1930), 1943, 1962, 1983 (for tv), 1989 and 1990 (for tv) and used as the basis for a highly successful 1986 musical. His first novel of direct genre interest, *La Double Vie de Theophraste Longuet* (**1904**; trans anon as *The Double Life* **1909** US; new trans Edgar JEPSON as *The Man with the Black Feather* 1912 UK), is a horror fantasy. *Balaoo* (**1912**; trans Alexander Teixeira de Mattos **1913** UK) is an sf tale featuring a Missing Link in a detective role (◊ APES AND CAVEMEN). *The Bride of the Sun* (trans anon **1915** US) ventures into LOST-WORLD territory. *The Amazing Adventures of Carolus Herbert* (trans Hannaford Bennett **1922** UK) and its sequel *The Veiled Prisoner* (trans Hannaford Bennett **1923** UK), recount the exploits of a mysterious captain and his super-submarine in WWI. *La Machine à assassiner* (**1924**; trans anon as *The Machine to Kill* **1935** US) features a ROBOT murderer. GL's use of sf material was opportunistic; a fair estimate of his skill as a novelist almost certainly awaits better translations. [JC]

Other works: *The Burgled Heart* (coll trans Hannaford Bennett **1925** UK; vt *The New Terror* 1926 US), which includes some *contes cruels*; *The Haunted Chair* (trans

anon **1931** US); *The Kiss that Killed* (trans anon **1934** US).

LERTETH, OBEN [s] ◊ R.L. FANTHORPE.

LESLIE, DESMOND (PETER ARTHUR) (1921-) UK writer, son of Shane Leslie and best known for co-authoring with George Adamski (1891-1965) the famous UFO book *Flying Saucers have Landed* (**1954**; exp by Leslie 1970). Of sf interest is *Angels Weep* (**1948**), a right-wing DYSTOPIA, and *The Amazing Mr Lutterworth* (**1958**), in which ALIENS avert the destruction of the planet through a device which provides unlimited energy: a Time of Splendour ensues. [JC]

Other work: *How Britain Won the Space Race* (**1982**) with Patrick MOORE, illustrated spoof account of a 19th-century UK space programme.

See also: MUSIC.

LESLIE, O.H. [s] ◊ Henry SLESAR.

LESLIE, PETER (1922-) UK author, journalist and actor, most of whose books have been borderline-sf ties contributed to tv spin-off series, beginning with 2 titles for the INVADERS sequence: *#3: The Night of the Trilobites* * (**1968**) and *#4: The Autumn Accelerator* * (**1969**). His tales for the MAN FROM U.N.C.L.E. series included: *The Finger in the Sky Affair* * (**1966**), which is #5 in the UK and #23 in the US numbering; *The Radioactive Camel Affair* * (**1966**), #7 UK and #7 US; *The Diving Dames Affair* * (**1967**), #10 UK and #9 US; *The Splintered Sunglasses Affair* * (**1968**), #14 UK and #16 US; and *The Unfair Fare Affair* * (**1968**), #17 UK and #18 US. For the GIRL FROM U.N.C.L.E. series he wrote #4: *The Cornish Pixie Affair* * (**1967**). [JC/PN]

Other work: *Hell for Tomorrow* (**1966**).

LESSER, DERWIN [s] ◊ Charles D. HORNIG.

LESSER, MILTON (1928-) US writer, more recently author of many crime novels and a few sf stories under what is now his real name, Stephen Marlowe. His sf mostly appeared in the ZIFF-DAVIS magazines, including his first story, "All Heroes are Hated" (1950), but he was an active fan for some years before that. His other pseudonyms for sf included Adam CHASE, C.H. Thames and the house name S.M. TENNESHAW; he has also written thrillers as Thames, Andrew Frazer and Jason Ridgway, as well as an **Ellery Queen** novel, *Dead Man's Tale* (**1961**). He wrote the juvenile sf novels *Earthbound* (**1952**), *The Star Seekers* (**1953**), *Stadium Beyond the Stars* (**1960**) and *Spacemen Go Home* (**1961**). Novels reprinted from magazines are *Recruit for Andromeda* (1953 *Imagination* as "Voyage to Eternity"; exp **1959**), *Secret of the Black Planet* (1952 *AMZ* as "Secret of the Black Planet" and "Son of the Black Chalice"; fixup **1965**), and *The Golden Ape* (1957 *AMZ* as "The Quest of the Golden Ape" by Adam Chase and Ivar JORGENSEN; **1959** as by Chase), which latter he wrote in collaboration with Paul W. FAIRMAN. ML also edited the anthology *Looking Forward* (anth **1953**). He abandoned sf in the early 1960s, but some of his recent thrillers, notably the supernatural horror story *Translation* (**1976**) and *The Valkyrie Encounter* (**1978**), both as Marlowe, have fantastic elements; these are much more effective

than his routine action-adventure sf.   [BS]
See also: GENERATION STARSHIPS.

LESSING, DORIS (1919-   ) Persian (Iranian)-born Southern Rhodesian (Zimbabwean) writer, in UK from 1949. She is best known for her searching examinations of the position of women in the world in such novels as *The Golden Notebook* (**1962**) The 5 vols of her **Children of Violence** sequence deal more expansively with the same problems, and *The Four-Gated City* (**1969**), which ends the series, moves in its final pages rapidly into the NEAR FUTURE, providing in this fashion a somewhat apocalyptic perspective on the preceding volumes from a viewpoint tinged with Sufi mysticism. This Persian form of Islam, influenced by Indian religions, is centrally concerned with the union of the soul with a Higher Being, in terms which are at times surprisingly literal, invoking a kind of drama of the steps one may take in order to achieve transcendence and the permanence of the soul. Much of DL's later work, especially the **Canopus in Argos: Archives** sequence, can be seen as exegetical of Sufist precepts.

Before and after the latter series, however, DL wrote four singletons of some sf interest. *Briefing for a Descent into Hell* (**1971**) puts a schizophreniac through a mythic journey. *The Summer Before the Dark* (**1973**) submits to a similar voyage of external/internal discovery a woman at a point of crisis in her life. In *The Memoirs of a Survivor* (**1974**) a woman watches the end of urban civilization from her window, never leaving her room, while a young girl grows up beside her, giving some muted hope for human continuity; it was filmed as MEMOIRS OF A SURVIVOR (1981). *The Fifth Child* (**1988** US) explores with considerable intensity the consequences of giving birth to an infant so destructive of the humans around him that he seems to be a genuine changeling. Far more expansively than these "domestic" novels, the **Canopus in Argos: Archives** books place the crises of human self-striving into a metaphysically conceived interstellar frame. Each individual novel in the sequence – *Re: Colonised Planet 5, Shikasta* (**1979** US), *The Marriage Between Zones Three, Four, and Five* (**1980** US), *The Sirian Experiments* (**1981** US), *The Making of the Representative for Planet 8* (**1982** US) and *The Sentimental Agents in the Volyen Empire* (**1983** US) – depicts an exemplary drama of the soul, as inhabitants of various planets, under the distant aegis of the Canopan Empire, attempt to come to terms with sexuality, politics, mortality and transcendence. Shikasta is Earth; the other novels make use of other venues. Everywhere the drive – sometimes thwarted – is towards literal union with universal principles (or God). The series exudes, at times, a piety not normally associated with sf; but at others the perspectives it opens are illuminating. In DL's hands, the instruments of sf become parables.   [JC]
Other work: *No Witchcraft for Sale: Stories and Short Novels* (coll **1956** Russia).
About the author: *Doris Lessing* (**1983** chap) by Lorna

Sage; *Doris Lessing* (**1985**) by Mona Knapp; *Unexpected Universe of Doris Lessing* (**1985**) by Katherine Fishburn.
See also: ADAM AND EVE; DISASTER; MAINSTREAM WRITERS OF SF; MUSIC; WOMEN SF WRITERS.

LESSNER, ERWIN (CHRISTIAN) (1898-1959) US writer in whose *Phantom Victory: The Fourth Reich 1945-1960* (**1944**) an underground cadre of Nazi officers successfully conspires to conquer the world in the name of a resurgent Germany (◊ HITLER WINS).   [JC]

LESTER, ANDREW ◊ Terry GREENHOUGH.

LESTER, EDWARD (1831-1905) UK clergyman and writer in whose *The Siege of Bodike: A Prophecy of Ireland's Future* (**1886**) the separation of Ireland from the ruling UK is prevented in large part by the narrator, in a BALLOON; and the landlords return. [JC]

LESTER, IRVIN [s] ◊ Fletcher PRATT.

L'ESTRANGE, MILES Pseudonym of an unidentified late-19th-century UK writer whose *What We are Coming To* (**1892**) describes in satirical terms its narrator's response to a rationalized England where women have been emancipated. *Platonia: A Tale of Other Worlds* (**1893**) rather more interestingly presents its narrator with an ancient design for a spacecraft which takes him to the eponymous planet, located this side of Mars, where an oddity of the atmosphere permits telescopic perusal of our world as it was 100 years before.   [JC]

LEVACK, DANIEL J.H. (?   -   ) US bibliographer and critic, author of several author BIBLIOGRAPHIES including *Fantasms: A Bibliography of the Literature of Jack Vance* (**1978** chap with Tim UNDERWOOD; rev vt *Fantasms II* 1979 with Underwood and Kurt Cockrum; rev 1979), *PKD: A Philip K. Dick Bibliography* (**1981**; rev 1988), *Amber Dreams: A Roger Zelazny Bibliography* (**1983**) and *Dune Master: A Frank Herbert Bibliography* (**1988**). The leisurely production schedules of some academic firms in the sf field may account for the failure of the Frank HERBERT bibliography or of the Philip K. DICK text in its 1988 "revision" to incorporate posthumous data.   [JC]

LEVEN, JEREMY (1941-   ) US writer whose two sf novels, *Creator* (**1980**) and *Satan: His Psychotherapy and Cure by the Unfortunate Dr Seymour Kassler, J.S.P.S.* (**1982**), both apply a sometimes portentous mainstream sensibility to generic conceits. In the first, the attempted creation of a CLONE to replace a dead wife activates considerable brooding about a variety of issues. In the second a COMPUTER turns out to house the eponymous Principle, invoking thoughts about the mind and the brain.   [JC]
See also: PSYCHOLOGY; RELIGION.

LEVENE, MALCOLM (1937-   ) UK writer whose *Carder's Paradise* (**1968**) describes the mixed blessings of a completely automated society whose inhabitants are kept busy by complex entertainments.   [JC]

LEVENE, PHILIP [r] ◊ J.L. MORRISSEY.

LEVETT, OSWALD [r] ◊ AUSTRIA.

LEVI, PRIMO (1919-1987) Italian survivor of Auschwitz, industrial chemist, autobiographer, essayist and writer of fiction: one of the most

distinguished men of letters of his generation, winning international fame late in life. In much of his work – e.g., *Il sistema periodica* (**1975**; trans Raymond Rosenthal as *The Periodic Table* **1984** US) – metaphors drawn from science illuminate subjects normally thought of as literary or historical, in a manner unusual in Europe generally and especially unusual for a writer in ITALY, a country where the gap between the two cultures is especially wide. This is true also of his sf stories, mostly sharp, ironical fables, almost reductionist, that nevertheless often metamorphose into direct affirmations of the values of life in a way unusual in sf anywhere. Many feature a discomforting exploitation of strange inventions, or a distancing alien perspective on human life. PL's sf stories appear in 2 Italian collections, *Storie naturali* (coll **1966**) as by Damiano Malabaila, and *Vizio di forma* (coll **1977**), collected together in English as *The Sixth Day and Other Tales* (trans Raymond Rosenthal omni **1990** US). A typical story is "Excellent is the Water", where a gradual increase in the viscosity of water in an Italian river spreads to become a worldwide phenomenon, thereby serving as an image of the torpor and lethargy of the heart's flow in our 20th-century world.   [PN]
Other works: *La Chiave a Stella* (**1978**; trans William Weaver as *The Monkey's Wrench* **1986** US; vt *The Wrench* 1987 UK) contains embedded fabular tales.
See also: CLONES.

LEVIATHAN Film (1989). Gordon Co./Filmauro. Dir George P. Cosmatos, starring Peter Weller, Richard Crenna, Amanda Pays. Screenplay David Peoples and Jeb Stuart, based on a story by Peoples. 98 mins. Colour.
      One of several undersea-ALIEN movies of the period, *L* most resembles (and improves on) DEEPSTAR SIX (1988), especially in the near-identical finale. In this efficiently scary but routine horror-adventure film, miners at an undersea base discover a sunken Russian submarine which turns out to have been the jettisoned arena for dangerous experiments in genetic manipulation. Two of the miners, infected, mutate into a shapeshifting MONSTER of familiar format, like a downmarket cross between the menaces in ALIEN and the 1982 remake of *The* THING. Few survive.   [PN]
See also: MONSTER MOVIES.

LEVIE, REX DEAN (1937?-   ) US businessman and writer whose *The Insect Warriors* (**1965**) deals with problems humans face on a world where they are the size of insects.   [JC]

LEVIN, IRA (1929-   ) US playwright and novelist whose first book, *A Kiss Before Dying* (**1953**), is an extremely impressive chiller. He is best known for the fantasy *Rosemary's Baby* (**1967**), in which the Devil impregnates a young woman; the book was filmed by Roman Polanski in 1968. IL moved into sf proper with *This Perfect Day* (**1970**), a DYSTOPIAN view of a cybernetically regimented future (◊ COMPUTERS), and *The Stepford Wives* (**1972**), which was soon filmed (◊ *The* STEPFORD WIVES), a horrific morality tale about a US suburb whose men have turned their womenfolk into compliant ROBOTS. The last 3 titles were assembled as *Three by Ira Levin* (omni **1985**). His most impressive book is perhaps *The Boys from Brazil* (**1976**), filmed as *The* BOYS FROM BRAZIL, a complex story involving the cloning (◊ CLONES) of cells from Adolf Hitler's body in order to later impregnate a number of women with young Hitlers, whom a Brazilian neo-Nazi group headed by Dr Josef Mengele tries to raise in environments as close as possible to that in which the Führer himself was raised. IL applies to sf themes meticulous style and plotting, along with a certain fascination with the multitude of ways in which women can be violated.   [JC]
Other works: *Nightmares: Three Great Suspense Novels* (omni **1981**), assembling *A Kiss Before Dying*, *Rosemary's Baby* and *The Stepford Wives*; *Sliver* (**1991**), associational.
See also: HISTORY OF SF; SATIRE.

LEVY, DAVID (1913-   ) US film executive and writer in whose *The Gods of Foxcroft* (**1970**) the protagonist awakes from SUSPENDED ANIMATION to find the world of 500 years hence suffering under ecologically disastrous circumstances which have forced humans into cramped habitats; meanwhile, ALIENS are observing us from space.   [JC]

LEWIN, LEONARD C. (1916-   ) US writer whose spoof paper, *Report from Iron Mountain: On the Possibility and Desirability of Peace* (**1967**), presents the conclusions of a US Government commission formed to consider the economic and political threat of world peace. In a tone of cunningly egregious Realpolitik, the commission urges that the world be kept on a continual WAR-footing. *Triage* (**1972**) is a NEAR-FUTURE novel about growing political oppression in the USA; the government secretly applies the wartime medical practice of triage to social "problems" with the aim of eliminating them – literally (◊ OVERPOPULATION).   [JC]

LEWIS, ANTHONY R(ICHARD) (1941-   ) US bibliographer who compiled, solo and with others, various indexes for the New England Science Fiction Association, including *The N.E.S.F.A. Index to the Science Fiction Magazines and Original Anthologies, 1966* (**1969** chap), *1967* (**1968** chap), *1968* (**1969** chap), *1969* (**1970** chap), *1966-1970* (**1971** chap), *1971-1972* (**1973** chap) with Andrew Adams WHYTE, *1973* (**1974** chap) with Whyte, *1974* (**1975** chap) with Whyte and George Flynn, *1975* (**1976** chap) with Whyte, *1976* (**1977** chap) with Whyte and Jerry BOYAJIAN, *1977-78* (**1983** chap) with Whyte, *1979-1980* (**1982** chap) with Whyte, *1981* (**1982** chap) with Whyte, *1982* (**1983** chap) with Whyte, *1983* (**1984** chap) with Whyte, *1984* (**1985** chap), *1985* (**1986** chap), *1986* (**1988** chap) and *The N.E.S.F.A. Index to Short SF, 1987* (**1989** chap). Other works have included *The Best of Astounding* (anth **1978**) as by Tony Lewis, *Concordance to Cordwainer Smith* (**1984** chap) and, most interestingly, *An Annotated Bibliography of Recursive Science Fiction* (**1990** chap).   [JC]
See also: BIBLIOGRAPHIES; RECURSIVE SF.

LEWIS, BRIAN (1929-1978) UK illustrator. A skilled

painter whose work dominated UK sf magazine covers in the mid- and late 1950s, BL often showed a strong influence from Surrealists such as Paul Klee (1879-1940) and Max Ernst (1891-1976), perhaps partly mediated through the book-cover illustration of Richard POWERS. This style was encouraged for a time by the editor John CARNELL in *Science Fiction Adventures* (19 covers), *NW* (41 covers) and *Science Fantasy* (21 covers), although some of these were representational, a manner BL adopted when it was required of him. His colours were strong and plain and seemed laid on thickly, an impression few other illustrators give. Besides his work in sf magazines, BL drew COMIC strips in newspapers (for a time he worked on DAN DARE – PILOT OF THE FUTURE) and then went into stop-motion film animation and children's puppet films. [JG/PN]

See also: ILLUSTRATION.

LEWIS, CAROLINE ◊ Harold BEGBIE.

LEWIS, CHARLES ◊ Roger DIXON.

LEWIS, C(LIVE) S(TAPLES) (1898-1963) UK author and critic, born in Belfast; Fellow of Magdalen College, Oxford, 1925-54, and finally Professor of Medieval and Renaissance English at Cambridge. Most of his writing, whether directly or indirectly, was Christian apologetics; this was as true of his autobiography *Surprised by Joy* (**1955**) as of the fantasy *The Screwtape Letters* (**1942**; exp vt *The Screwtape Letters and Screwtape Proposes a Toast* 1961), in which an older devil writes letters of advice to a younger, devising various means of winning human souls. In Oxford CSL was friendly with Charles WILLIAMS (another Anglican) and J.R.R. TOLKIEN (a Roman Catholic). All three were Christian moralists with a strong interest in allegory or fantasy, and (with others) they formed a casual society, the Inklings, during whose meetings they read to each other from works in progress.

CSL's most popular fiction is for children, and is allegorical FANTASY, although it uses many sf devices, including TIME TRAVEL, other DIMENSIONS and PARALLEL WORLDS. The kingdom of **Narnia**, to which various human children travel, is ruled by a lion, Aslan, who is "crucified" by a wicked witch. There are many excitingly described perils, most with a direct Christian allegorical application. Widely loved by children as straightforward fantasy, the series is: *The Lion, the Witch and the Wardrobe* (**1950**), *Prince Caspian* (**1951**), *The Voyage of the "Dawn Treader"* (**1952**), *The Silver Chair* (**1953**), *The Horse and his Boy* (**1954**), *The Magician's Nephew* (**1955**), which comes first in terms of the internal chronology, and *The Last Battle* (**1956**); omnibuses include *Prince Caspian & The Voyage of the Dawn Treader* (omni **1990**) and *Tales of Narnia: The Silver Chair & The Last Battle* (omni **1990**). Two fantasies for adults are *The Great Divorce* (**1945** chap), a minor allegory about Heaven and Hell, and *Till We Have Faces* (**1956**), a dark retelling of the myth of Cupid and Psyche which some of his admirers consider his best work.

CSL's primary contribution to sf proper is the **Cosmic Trilogy** (or **Ransom Trilogy**) about the linguist Dr Ransom, who like Christ is at one point offered as a ransom for mankind: *Out of the Silent Planet* (**1938**), *Perelandra* (**1943**; vt *Voyage to Venus* 1953), and *That Hideous Strength* (**1945**; cut 1955; cut version vt *The Tortured Planet* 1958 US). The first two novels are PLANETARY ROMANCES with elements of medieval mythology. Each planet is seen as having a tutelary spirit; those of the other planets are both good and accessible, while that of Earth is fallen, twisted and not known directly by most humans. These two books are powerfully imagined, although their scientific content is intermittently absurd. The effect of lesser GRAVITY on Martian plant and animal life is rendered with great economy and vividness, as is Ransom's first sight of the water world of Venus, a rich exercise in PERCEPTION; in a passage as purely evocative of a sense of alien wonder as anything in sf, Ransom's human eyes cannot at first make sense of the strangeness about him. The religious allegory of *Perelandra*, however, in which an evil SCIENTIST plays Satanic tempter to the female ruler of Venus, a new Eve, is deeply conservative and also – in its courtly, romantic (and some may think dehumanizing) view of womanhood – sexist. Lewis's ideology of gender is spelled out in detail in a number of essays and in the critical book *A Preface to Paradise Lost* (**1942**), which can be seen as a template for *Perelandra*.

The third volume, *That Hideous Strength*, is set on contemporary Earth, and is more directly occult in its genre machinery than either of its predecessors. The fury of CSL's attack on scientific "humanism" or "scientism" (science directed towards purely worldly ends) is very nearly unbalanced, and leads to grossly melodramatic caricature of scientists and government-supported research units in general, and of H.G. WELLS in particular, here grotesquely envisaged as a vulgar cockney journalist, Jules. The book's attack on government indifference to ECOLOGY won it a new audience in the late 1960s. CSL's attitude towards any form of modernism was neatly encapsulated by a remark he made during a lecture on medieval poetry in 1938: "And then the Renaissance came and spoiled everything." The three books are collected in *The Cosmic Trilogy* (omni **1990**).

Some of CSL's minor essays in and about sf, including a transcript of a talk with Brian W. ALDISS and Kingsley AMIS, can be found in the posthumous *Of Other Worlds* (coll **1966**) ed Walter Hooper, which includes 2 stories originally published in *FSF*. A later posthumous work is *The Dark Tower and Other Stories* (coll **1977**) ed Hooper. It has been strongly suggested by Kathryn Lindskoog (1934-) in *The C.S. Lewis Hoax* (**1988**) that the Reverend Hooper – CSL's secretary for only one month – forged various items of posthumously published CSL material included in *The Dark Tower*, a charge which has been rebutted. Lindskoog has offered a vigorous counter-rebuttal in "The Dark Scandal: Science Fiction Forgery" (1992 *Quantum* #42), but in that year it was revealed that she herself had been forging evidence (letters) – indeed, she admitted as much. What there can be no doubt about is that the works assembled by Hooper have affected readers as being both sexually poisonous and egregiously amateur. [PN]

Other works: *Dymer* (chap **1926**), a narrative fantastic poem as by Clive Hamilton; *The Pilgrim's Regress: An Allegorical Apology for Christianity, Reason and Romanticism* (**1933**; rev 1943); *On Stories, and Other Essays in Literature* (coll **1982**; vt *Of This and Other Worlds* 1984); *Boxen: The Imaginary World of the Young C.S. Lewis* (**1985**).

As editor: *Essays Presented to Charles Williams* (anth **1947**), including the influential "On Fairy-Stories" by Tolkien.

About the author: About 50 book-length studies of CSL's life and work exist, perhaps the most distinguished biography being *C.S. Lewis: A Biography* (**1990**) by A.N. Wilson. Further biographical material appear in *Shadowlands: The Story of C.S. Lewis and Joy Davidman* (**1985**) by Brian Sibley, based on Bill Nicholson's tv drama *Shadowlands*, which was also a successful stage play. Other studies include: *Shadows of Imagination: The Fantasies of C.S. Lewis, J.R.R. Tolkien and Charles Williams* (anth **1969**; exp 1979) ed Mark R. HILLEGAS, which contains an entertaining and passionate attack on CSL by the Marxist biologist and author J.B.S. HALDANE; *The Longing for a Form: Essays on the Fiction of C.S. Lewis* (coll **1977**) ed Peter J Schakel; *The Literary Legacy of C.S. Lewis* (**1979**) by Chad Walsh; *C.S. Lewis: His Literary Achievement* (**1987**) by C.N. MANLOVE.

See also: ALIENS; ANTI-INTELLECTUALISM IN SF; CHILDREN'S SF; CONCEPTUAL BREAKTHROUGH; ESCHATOLOGY; FANTASTIC VOYAGES; GODS AND DEMONS; HORROR IN SF; ISLANDS; LIFE ON OTHER WORLDS; LINGUISTICS; LIVING WORLDS; *The* MAGAZINE OF FANTASY AND SCIENCE FICTION; MAGIC; MAINSTREAM WRITERS OF SF; MARS; MESSIAHS; MYTHOLOGY; RELIGION; SOCIAL DARWINISM; VENUS.

LEWIS, IRWIN (1916-   ) US writer who began publishing sf with "To Invade New York" for *ASF* in 1963. This story's basic idea was incorporated into his first novel, *The Day They Invaded New York* (**1964**), in which invading ALIENS confuse New Yorkers by fouling the transportation systems of the great city. A second novel, *The Day New York Trembled* (**1967**), creates its chaos through a pain-relieving drug and its unexpected consequences. [JC]

LEWIS, OSCAR (1893-1992) US editor and writer whose ALTERNATE-WORLD novel, *The Lost Years* (**1951**), depicts the last years of Abraham Lincoln in a world where he was never assassinated. [JC]

LEWIS, (ERNEST MICHAEL) ROY (1913-   ) UK novelist and journalist, editor of *New Commonwealth* 1953-4, later with the *Economist* and *The Times*, and the author of several political/sociological studies. His sf novel, *What We Did to Father* (**1960**; vt *The Evolution Man* 1963), amusingly concentrates human cultural EVOLUTION during the Pleistocene into the hands of one man, the narrator's father, all of whose discoveries

are seen in terms of their extrapolated effects. Not surprisingly, the parricide which ends the book is nothing if not proto-neo-Freudian. [JC]

See also: ORIGIN OF MAN.

LEWIS, (HARRY) SINCLAIR (1885-1951) US writer, highly esteemed in the 1920s and 1930s for such novels as *Main Street* (**1920**) and *Babbitt* (**1922**) and first US winner of the Nobel Prize for Literature (1930), but with much diminished reputation today. His first novel, *Hike and the Aeroplane* (**1912**) as by Tom Graham, is a juvenile centred on a futuristic 200mph (320kph) aircraft; *Arrowsmith* (**1925**) is not so much sf as fiction about science, contrasting the idealism of the research SCIENTIST with the avarice and greed of the medical profession in general. SL's sf novel, *It Can't Happen Here* (**1935**), warns of how a Nazi-like regime could come to power in the USA. SL pays little attention to the nature of political institutions in this book, but that is not to say that he is guilty of political naïvety (◊ POLITICS): his analysis of how fascist regimes can come to power largely through the "little man's" apathy and perceived powerlessness is a potent example of the dreadful-warning tale. His NEAR-FUTURE scenario contrasts interestingly with Gordon EKLUND's very similar portrait of 1930s authoritarianism in *All Times Possible* (**1974**), though in the latter case there is an ALTERNATE-WORLDS framework. [JC]

LEWIS, (PERCY) WYNDHAM (1884-1957) UK writer and painter, known in the latter capacity as the instigator of Vorticism. His illustrations for Naomi MITCHISON's *Beyond This Limit* (**1935** chap) constitute a co-creation of the book, which she acknowledged. As an author, he was responsible for determinedly Modernist manifestos such as *The Caliph's Design: Architects! Where is Your Vortex?* (**1919** chap) and novels such as *The Apes of God* (**1930**). Of particular sf interest is **The Human Age**, a trilogy comprising *The Childermass* (**1928**; rev 1956), *Monstre Gai* and *Malign Fiesta*, the two latter novels being first published together as *The Human Age: Book Two Monstre Gai, Book Three Malign Fiesta* (**1955**). Like Philip José FARMER's **Riverworld** series, though with greater impact, **The Human Age** depicts the posthumous existence of various characters. Pulley and Satters, the two freshly deceased protagonists of *The Childermass*, observe and join in the jousting, linguistic and intellectual, that surrounds the Bailiff, a sort of doorkeeper who decides the eligibility of applicants to the Magnetic City, and who, in *Monstre Gai*, takes them into the Third City, a DYSTOPIA based on the post-WWII UK and its Welfare State. Finding life difficult there, they all go on to Matapolis in *Malign Fiesta*, but Matapolis is Hell, and punishments abound; there is a sense of suffocating evil. A fourth volume, «The Trial of Man», in which the two protagonists were to be transported to Heaven, remained unwritten. The arduousness of *The Childermass*, a major 20th-century novel, has kept many readers from its much more clear-cut sequels. WL is much less read than read about, a situation to be deplored. [JC]

See also: ROBERT HALE LIMITED.

LEWITT, S.N. Working name of US writer Shariann Lewitt (1954-   ); the N. stands for "Nothing". She began publishing sf with "St Joey the Action" in *Perpetual Light* (anth **1982**) ed Alan Ryan. After *First and Final Rites* (**1984**), a fantasy novel published as by Shariann Lewitt, she released the first of the military SPACE OPERAS with which she soon became identified: *White Wing* (**1985**) with Susan M. SHWARTZ, writing together as Gordon Kendall. *Angel at Apogee* (**1987**), her first book as SNL and perhaps her best, features a complicated (at times congested) PLANETARY-ROMANCE plot in which much fighting co-exists with the author's punk sensibility; it tells the story of a female pilot who must come to terms with the two submerged races which revolt against her father's hegemony over the planet in question. Other novels which similarly stretch the conventions of military sf include *Cyberstealth* (**1989**) – and its sequel *Dancing Vac* (**1991**) – and *Blind Justice* (**1991**). Her ties in the **U.S.S.A.** SHARED-WORLD enterprise, *U.S.S.A. Book 2* ＊ (**1987**) and *Book 4* ＊ (**1987**), are of less interest, but *Cybernetic Jungle* (**1992**), set in a near-future CYBERPUNK Brazil, is a complex (although perhaps not entirely original) tale. [JC]

LEY, WILLY (1906-1969) German-born scientist and scientific writer who emigrated to the USA in 1935. In Germany he had been part of a small group which, early on, had believed in the potential of rocket propulsion (some went on to become famous for the construction of the V2). His first book was *Die Fahrt ins Weltall* ["Journey into Space"] (**1926**); his second, *Die Möglichkeit der Weltraumfahrt* ["The Possibility of Interplanetary Travel"] (**1928**), was to be one of the inspirations behind the film (and book) *Die* FRAU IM MOND (1929; vt *The Girl in the Moon*). In the USA his well researched, precise science articles became a notable feature of the SF MAGAZINES, especially ASTOUNDING SCIENCE-FICTION (from 1937) and AMAZING STORIES (from 1940). He became Science Editor of GALAXY SCIENCE FICTION in Sep 1952, having in March of that year begun there a science column which would last until his death. During the brief period when science-fact articles were a HUGO category, he received 2. He wrote 3 sf stories as Robert Willey.

WL was also a prolific author of books on science, especially on ROCKETS and SPACE FLIGHT. Perhaps his best-known (and certainly most beautiful) book was *The Conquest of Space* (**1949**), with splendid illustrations, many in colour, by Chesley BONESTELL; it won the nonfiction category of the INTERNATIONAL FANTASY AWARD in 1951. *Lands Beyond* (**1952**) with L. Sprague DE CAMP, a historical account of strange explorations and discoveries, won the same award in 1953. Of the science-fact writers intimately connected with GENRE SF, only De Camp, Arthur C. CLARKE and Isaac ASIMOV could rival WL. One of the Moon's craters is named in his honour. [PN]

Other works (all nonfiction): *The Lungfish and the Unicorn* (**1941**; rev vt *The Lungfish, the Dodo and the Unicorn* 1948); *The Days of Creation* (**1941**; rev 1952); *Shells and Shooting* (**1942**); *Rockets* (**1944**; rev vt *Rockets and Space Travel* 1947; rev vt *Rockets, Missiles and Space Travel* 1951; rev 1957; rev vt *Rockets, Missiles and Men in Space* 1968); *Dragons in Amber* (**1951**); *Engineer's Dreams* (**1954**); *Salamanders and Other Wonders* (**1955**); *The Exploration of Mars* (**1956**; vt *Project Mars* 1962 UK) with Wernher von Braun (1912-1977), illus Bonestell; *Satellites, Rockets and Outer Space* (**1958**; rev 1962); *Space Stations* (**1958**); *Space Travel* (**1958**); *Exotic Zoology* (**1959**) featuring rearranged selections from his previous books on natural history; *Watchers of the Skies* (**1963**); *Beyond the Solar System* (**1964**) illus Bonestell; *Missiles, Moonprobes and Megaparsecs* (**1964**); *Ranger to the Moon* (**1965**); *On Earth and in the Sky* (coll **1967**); *Another Look at Atlantis* (coll **1969**); *The Drifting Continents* (**1969**); *Events in Space* (**1969**); *Gas Giants: The Largest Planets* (**1969**); *Visitors from Afar: The Comets* (**1969**).

See also: SPACE HABITATS; SUN.

LEYDENFROST, A(LEXANDER) (1889-1961) US illustrator born in Hungary, where he lived until he was 34; his father was a Dutch illustrator. Although forgotten by most fans today, AL was one of the best sf artists of the 1940s, particularly when elements of fantasy or horror were required. His often grotesque, heavily shadowed and hideous forms sprawled across the pages of such magazines as *Planet Stories*, *Super Science Stories*, *Astonishing Stories* and *Famous Fantastic Mysteries*. While AL's black-and-white ILLUSTRATIONS were strong and dynamic with expressive lines and stark contrasts, his colour work, which included 2 covers for *Planet Stories*, was strained and awkward. In the 1920s and 1930s he had worked as an interior designer and commercial artist, and many of his later illustrations were for the "slicks", notably *Esquire* and *Life*. His sons Bob and Harry both briefly illustrated for *Planet Stories* in the mid-1940s. [JG/PN]

L5 ◊ LAGRANGE POINT.

LIBERTARIAN SF A political movement (◊ POLITICS) originating in and largely confined to the USA, libertarianism is a form of anarchism – or "minarchism", the desire for an extremely limited state – which emphasizes (nonviolent) competition rather than the voluntary cooperation proposed by the older strand of anarchist thinking, as exemplified by the writings of such theorists as Peter Kropotkin (1842-1921) or, in the sf field, by Ursula K. LE GUIN's *The Dispossessed* (**1974**). The libertarian branch is generally characterized as a "right-wing" type of anarchism (in the sense that the [traditional] anarcho-syndicalists are "left-wing") through the premise that voluntarily entered contracts are the only form of social interaction that can be literally enforced (as opposed to, for example, state taxation as a way of funding a democratically elected government). A common libertarian assumption is that, in the absence of government intervention, the free market will bring about almost unlimited growth in available technology and personal wealth, thus solving any problems of human poverty. These views are frequently associated with a belief in "positive thinking" and a fundamental OPTIMISM about human potential.

Uniquely among political movements, many of libertarianism's most influential texts have been by sf writers. Books from both inside and outside the genre which strongly affected the early development of the movement include Ayn RAND's *Atlas Shrugged* (**1957**), most of the early works of Robert A. HEINLEIN (up to, and culminating in, *The Moon is a Harsh Mistress* [**1966**]) and, to a lesser extent, C.M. KORNBLUTH's *The Syndic* (**1953**). These works could be said to be "proto-libertarian" in nature – a description which applies particularly to Rand, founder of the allied Objectivist philosophy. Explicitly libertarian fictions, with their characteristically detailed alternative societies and economic systems, did not begin to appear until the 1970s, with the publication of J. Neil SCHULMAN's *Alongside Night* (**1979**) and the **Illuminatus!** trilogy (**1975**) by Robert SHEA and Robert Anton WILSON. This trilogy – along with associated texts such as the **Schrödinger's Cat** books from 1981 – probably represents the best of libertarian sf. Other recent novels of significance have been F. Paul WILSON's *An Enemy of the State* (**1980**) and the long series of mildly comic adventures by L. Neil SMITH beginning with *The Probability Broach* (**1980**). Authors currently writing from a libertarian perspective include Melinda SNODGRASS (the **Circuit** trilogy), James P. HOGAN (notably in *Voyage from Yesteryear* [**1982**]), Victor KOMAN, Brad LINAWEAVER, Victor MILAN, Jerry POURNELLE and Vernor VINGE.

The Prometheus and Prometheus Hall of Fame trophies (◊ AWARDS) are given annually by the Libertarian Futurist Society for, respectively, the best libertarian novel of the year and the past novel most worth retrospective attention. While nonsympathizers may be repelled by libertarian sf's frequent concentration on adventure rather than character, its sometimes casual attitude towards violence, and its loose association with the principles of SOCIAL DARWINISM, the libertarian writers themselves might argue that they have made a genuine and deep-felt commitment to their vision of human freedom. It seems likely that the influence of the movement within sf will grow. [NT]

LIBRARIES OF SF ◊ COLLECTIONS.

LICHTENBERG, JACQUELINE (1942-   ) US writer who began publishing sf with "Operation High Time" for *Worlds of If* in 1969, but soon concentrated on fan fiction set in the OPEN UNIVERSE permitted by the owners of STAR TREK; *Star Trek Lives!* (**1975**) with Sondra MARSHAK and Joan Winston is a famous nonfiction description of the early days of **Star Trek** fandom. Her first book was *House of Zeor* (**1974**), the initial volume of the **Sime/Gen** sequence, also an open-universe series, which continued with *Unto Zeor, Forever* (**1978**), *First Channel* (**1980**) with Jean

LORRAH, *Mahogany Trinrose* (**1981**), *Channel's Destiny* (**1982**) with Lorrah, *RenSime* (**1984**) and *Zelerod's Doom* (**1986**) with Lorrah. The series is set 1000 years after a mutation has split the human race into Gens and Simes; the latter survive by sucking life force ("selyn") from the former, a process that is fatal unless effected through a specially mutated Sime called a Channel. *First Channel* and *Channel's Destiny* describe the first appearance of Channels in a society which has been reduced to near-barbarism by undeclared war between the two subspecies. *House of Zeor* and later volumes (in terms of internal chronology) follow the gradual evolution of a compromise, and move toward a sense that the two subspecies together may form a whole greater than the sum of the parts. The considerable success of the series may be partially due to the sexual connotations of the Sime/Gen relationship, particularly the Simes' use of remarkably phallic tentacles to (sometimes forcibly) acquire selyn.

A second sequence, the **Molt Brothers** series – *Molt Brother* (**1982**) and *City of a Million Legends* (**1985**) – deals with relationships between humans and members of a reptilian species (the Kren) who must choose special companions to guard them when they moult. The **Dushau** trilogy – *Dushau* (**1985**), *Farfetch* (**1985**) and *Outreach* (**1986**) – tells the story of a rebellion against a repressive galactic empire by the human heroine and a group of alien empaths who establish rapport with planetary ecologies.

Although JL's prose is sometimes undistinguished and her backgrounds are routine, she has acquired many dedicated readers through writing about intensely emotional cross-species relationships based on mutual affection and need. [NT]

Other works: *Those of My Blood* (**1988**) and its sequel, *Dreamspy* (**1989**).

See also: ECOLOGY.

LIDDELL, C.H. [s] ◊ Henry KUTTNER.

LIEBERMAN, ROBERT (HOWARD) (1941-   ) US writer who worked initially as a teacher of mathematics and physics at university level until becoming a full-time writer in 1979. His third novel, *Baby* (**1981**), tells of the consequences when an elderly spinster gives virgin birth to a child with a beautiful singing voice. *Perfect People* (**1986**) sets its post-holocaust DYSTOPIA in an underground CITY. [JC]

LIFE AFTER DEATH ◊ ESCHATOLOGY; REINCARNATION.

LIFEFORCE Film (1985). Cannon. Dir Tobe Hooper, starring Steve Railsback, Peter Firth, Frank Finlay, Mathilda May, Patrick Stewart. Screenplay Dan O'Bannon, Don Jakoby, based on *The Space Vampires* (**1976**) by Colin WILSON. 101 mins. Colour.

Astronauts exploring Halley's Comet discover three humanoid ALIEN bodies in suspended animation in crystal containers in a derelict alien spacecraft, and recover them. All but one of the astronauts die; the strange bodies awaken back in London, and prove to be shapeshifting vampiric lifeforms which, by sucking the lifeforce from people, turn them into withered zombies who themselves can pass on the zombie infection. Soon London becomes a zombie city. The narrative borders on incoherence, non sequiturs abound, and the film is a melodramatic travesty, especially the performance of Finlay as a "thanatologist" (student of death). And yet it has its virtues. John Dykstra, famous for his work in STAR WARS (1977), produces arresting special effects, and Hooper, best known for *The Texas Chainsaw Massacre* (1974), directs with an intensity verging on the hysterical. The film, though a mess (partly through being based on Wilson's heavily philosophical but muddled novel), is original and, despite all the zombies, avoids cliché. May's nude performance as the female alien is striking.   [PN]

LIFE ON OTHER WORLDS Early interplanetary travellers invariably discovered worlds which were markedly akin to Earth. Without a theory of EVOLUTION for a guide, let alone any but the most primitive awareness of ECOLOGY, the imaginative creation of other-worldly life was inevitably a haphazard and arbitrary process. One notable exception is Johannes KEPLER's attempt to imagine lunar life in the last pages of *Somnium* (**1634**). There is little in most other pre-20th-century accounts to distinguish other worlds from the strange Earthly lands featured in many travellers' tales and romances ($\lozenge$ ANTHROPOLOGY; FANTASTIC VOYAGES; LOST WORLDS). Camille FLAMMARION was the first writer to apply Lamarckian and Darwinian ideas to the construction of hypothetical ALIEN worlds, in *Les mondes imaginaires et les mondes réels* (**1864**; trans as *Real and Imaginary Worlds* **1865** US) and *Lumen* (1872; exp **1887**); and his later romance of other-worldly reincarnation, *Urania* (**1890**), offers a description, albeit relatively undetailed, of the Martian biosphere. Flammarion's contemporary, C.I. DEFONTENAY, gave a comprehensive description of life on another world in *Star, ou Psi de Cassiopée* (**1854**; trans as *Star* **1975** US), but biological speculation was muted. Most late-19th-century interplanetary romances similarly feature pseudo-human races and are vehicles for political and sociological rather than biological hypothesis. Exotic milieux are used merely to provide local colour for interplanetary tourists, as in George GRIFFITH's *A Honeymoon in Space* (**1901**). Edgar FAWCETT's *The Ghost of Guy Thyrle* (**1895**) takes some trouble to convey an impression of the multifariousness of life on other worlds, but does not pause for detailed description. Even H.G. WELLS, a writer whose biological training qualified him to take on the job of designing an alien life-system, shirked the task; the Selenite society in *The First Men in the Moon* (**1901**) is given only the most cursory supportive ECOLOGY. Wells's French contemporary J.H. ROSNY aîné was similarly shy until 1922, when he included a fairly elaborate description of an alien life-system in his LOST-WORLD story *L'étonnant voyage de Hareton Ironcastle* (**1922**; rewritten rather than trans by Philip José FARMER as *Ironcastle*, **1976**).

The favourite abode of other-worldly life in early sf was MARS, and an approximate consensus image of the Martian biosphere slowly grew up, much encouraged by *Mars as the Abode of Life* (**1908**) by the eccentric US astronomer Percival Lowell (1855-1916). The red deserts and the canals became CLICHÉS but, whether Mars was seen as a decadent world or as a primitive one, its biosphere tended to be somewhat stripped-down. A lush Mars is featured in Edwin Lester ARNOLD's daydream fantasy *Lieut. Gullivar Jones: His Vacation* (**1905**; vt *Gulliver of Mars*), the first of many novels to use the red planet as a backcloth for a swashbuckling adventure story, but Arnold and his successor in this vein, Edgar Rice BURROUGHS, were understandably uninterested in serious biosphere-design. A similar blithe disregard for matters of rational plausibility is exhibited not only by the great legion of Burroughs imitators – Otis Adelbert KLINE, Ralph Milne FARLEY, J.U. GIESY, Lin CARTER, Gardner F. FOX, Alan Burt Akers (Kenneth BULMER) *et al.* – but also by less derivative sf writers who adapted the underlying philosophy to their own purposes. Leigh BRACKETT, Ray BRADBURY and C.L. MOORE have helped to maintain a calculatedly nonrealistic image of Mars long beyond its natural lifespan, and Bradbury's curious amalgam of impossible romanticism and heavy nostalgia, exhibited in *The Martian Chronicles* (coll **1950**; vt *The Silver Locusts*), remains so powerful that it still affects contemporary works like Ian McDONALD's *Desolation Road* (**1988**). Indeed, the influence of this romantic image has been so great that it has had quite a marked influence upon supposedly realistic treatments of the planet like Arthur C. CLARKE's *The Sands of Mars* (**1951**) and James BLISH's *Welcome to Mars* (**1967**).

Some early GENRE-SF writers did make an effort to introduce more variety and a greater degree of plausibility into their accounts of extraterrestrial life. Laurence MANNING's "The Wreck of the Asteroid" (1932), Jack WILLIAMSON's "The Moon Era" (1932) and Leslie F. STONE's "The Hell Planet" (1932) all show enterprise in this regard, but the story most remembered today as a crucial turning-point in the sophistication of other-worldly melodrama is "A Martian Odyssey" (1934) by Stanley G. WEINBAUM. Weinbaum went on to write a whole series of adventure stories set against the backgrounds of various weird alien ecologies, but no one seemed able to take up where he left off. John W. CAMPBELL Jr's **Penton and Blake** series (1936-8; fixup as *The Planeteers* **1966**) is imitative of Weinbaum but much weaker. In 1939 Clifford D. SIMAK began a series intended to deal in a realistic manner with conditions on each of the planets in turn; of the 4 stories he completed the last, "Tools" (1942), is the most notable. Eric Frank RUSSELL, in the course of his own series of exploration stories – collected in *Men, Martians, and Machines* (coll of linked stories **1956**) – produced the memorable "Symbiotica" (1944), but did little more in this line. Outside genre sf, very few writers tackled the problem of describing life on worlds unlike Earth. Olaf STAPLEDON's *Star*

Maker (**1937**) is admirably wide-ranging but short on detail, save for one long description of a very Earthlike world. The fullest descriptions of other-worldly life offered by non-genre writers are to be found, oddly enough, in allegories inspired by the religious imagination: David LINDSAY's *A Voyage to Arcturus* (**1920**) and C.S. LEWIS's *Out of the Silent Planet* (**1938**) and *Perelandra* (**1943**; vt *Voyage to Venus*).

The sophistication of post-WWII sf encouraged attempts to tackle the problem of constructing strange alien life-systems more realistically. "Grandpa" (**1955**) by James H. SCHMITZ is a notable study of a complex marine lifecycle on an Earth-type planet. Conscientious attempts to design ecologies for unearthly physical circumstances were regularly made by Hal CLEMENT, most notably in *Mission of Gravity* (1953 *ASF*; **1954**), *Cycle of Fire* (**1957**) and *Close to Critical* (1958 *ASF*; **1964**), and by Poul ANDERSON, especially in "Call me Joe" (**1957**), *War of the Wing-Men* (**1958**; vt *The Man who Counts*) and *Three Worlds to Conquer* (**1964**). Anderson also produced a non-fiction work, *Is There Life on Other Worlds?* (**1963**), an early popularization of the speculative science of XENOBIOLOGY – the study of extraterrestrial life. Isaac ASIMOV wrote essays on this subject, and one of its leading exponents, Carl SAGAN, has also written sf. One of the most intriguing nonfictions in the field is *Extraterrestrial Encounter* (**1979**) by Chris BOYCE, another sf writer. One writer of the post-WWII period whose name is particularly associated with the detailed presentation of alien worlds is Jack VANCE, whose interest in alien ecology is linked to a strong concern for cultural ANTHROPOLOGY. His alien worlds usually have human populations cleverly adapted to and integrated into the native ecology, and his works carefully combine romanticism and earnest specula-tion (*see also* PLANETARY ROMANCE); outstanding among his many novels in this vein are *Son of the Tree* (1951 *TWS*; **1964**), *Big Planet* (1952 *Startling Stories*; **1957**), *The Houses of Iszm* (1954 *Startling Stories*; **1964**), *The Languages of Pao* (**1958**), *The Dragon Masters* (**1963**), *The Blue World* (**1966**) and *Emphyrio* (**1969**). There also grew up in this post-WWII period, in calculated opposition to the romantic school of other-worldly adventures, a school of fiction which represented human life on other worlds as a grim and terrible battle against implacably hostile circumstances (◊ COLONIZATION OF OTHER WORLDS).

Popularization in the 1960s of the notion of impend-ing ecological crisis in the real world brought about a significant change in emphasis in sf. The notion of "conquering" other worlds and mastering harsh environments by hard work and sheer determination – which reached its peak in such novels as Tom GODWIN's *The Survivors* (**1958**; vt *Space Prison*) and Harry HARRISON's *Deathworld* (**1960**) – found new ideological opposition in many stories emphasizing the notion of harmonious order (◊ ECOLOGY). Alien ecospheres possessing such perfection are often depicted, with mankind featuring either as an

unthinking destroyer or as a candidate for member-ship whose case has yet to be judged. Such stories often embody a strong element of mysticism (◊ RELIGION; MYTHOLOGY). The representation of alien ecospheres as problematic Gardens of Eden has since become so commonplace as to be almost ritual; notable examples of the careful extension of this metaphor include Mark CLIFTON's *Eight Keys to Eden* (**1960**), Richard M. MCKENNA's "Hunter Come Home" (1963), John BOYD's ironic *The Pollinutors of Eden* (**1969**), Ursula K. LE GUIN's *The Word for World is Forest* (1972; **1976**), Neal BARRETT's *Highwood* (**1972**), Brian STABLEFORD's *The Paradise Game* (**1974**) and *The Gates of Eden* (**1983**), Stanisław LEM's *Edem* (**1959**; trans as *Eden* **1989** US) and Michael D. RESNICK's *Paradise* (**1989**). Many of these works echo the forest fantasies of the great pioneer of ecological mysticism, W.H. HUDSON. The 1960s also produced two thorough and detailed accounts of human populations in alien environ-ments which are particularly impressive: Frank HER-BERT's *Dune* (fixup **1965**), with its description of life on the desert world Arrakis, and Ursula K. Le Guin's *The Left Hand of Darkness* (**1969**), which describes the life of hermaphroditic humans on the world of Winter. The scope which sf offered for much more detailed and considered modelling of alien environments was increased considerably during this period by virtue of the popularity of series novels, and, although interest remained focused almost exclusively on life-systems native to planets habitable by humankind, the found-ations of various notable exercises in long-term "worldbuilding" were laid down. Marion Zimmer BRADLEY's **Darkover** series and Anne MCCAFFREY's **Pern** series provided models for various subsequent endeavours on a smaller scale. Much of this work is so heavily romanticized that it exists on the border-line between sf and FANTASY, being little more realistic in its speculative components than the Burroughsian romances which it has largely replaced, but the most competent writers in this vein of planetary romance bring considerable intelligence to bear on their work; one who has been consistently ambitious is C.J. CHERRYH, whose descriptions of other-worldly life in such novels as *The Faded Sun* (3 vols **1979-80**) and *Serpent's Reach* (**1980**) are outstanding.

The depiction of authentically alien life-systems has always been handicapped by the problems involved in using such systems as backgrounds to entertaining stories. An enormous amount of work goes into the design of an entire alien world, and it is not easy to blend that kind of artistry with the less esoteric creation of sensitive characterization and well-made plots. The most conscientious efforts of writers like Hal Clement and those who have followed in his footsteps – including Robert L. FORWARD in *The Flight of the Dragonfly* (**1984**; exp vt *Rocheworld* 1990) and Larry NIVEN in *The Integral Trees* (**1984**) and *The Smoke Ring* (**1987**) – run into acute problems in trying to integrate the enormous amounts of information they must get across with some kind of suspenseful narrative; Forward's novel was drastically cut for its first publication in the interests of finding a reasonable balance; its later reissue, restoring the additional information for the benefit of purists, required appendices full of graphs and diagrams. Novels which attempt to present an image of everyday life on alien worlds, without the benefit of human observers – notable examples include John BRUNNER's *The Crucible of Time* (**1984**), Brian HERBERT's *Sudanna, Sudanna* (**1985**) and Charles L. HARNESS's *Redworld* (**1986**) – suffer inevitable problems of reader-identification, and tend to take on an ironic, if not outrightly satirical, edge even if that was not the author's primary intention. Given these difficulties, it is not entirely surprising that the most memorable images of other-worldly life are often highly artificial, contained in stylized narratives whose main purpose is allegorical. [BS]

See also: BIOLOGY; COLONIZATION OF OTHER WORLDS; HIVE-MINDS; LIVING WORLDS.

LIFT, DE (vt *The Lift*) Film (1983). Sigma Films. Dir Dick Maas, starring Huub Stapel, Willeke Van Ammelrooy. Screenplay and music Maas. 99 mins. Colour.

This neat Dutch horror film with an sf rationale, dubbed atrociously into English, tells of a homicidal lift (elevator) in a high-rise office building. The lift is controlled by an organic, living computer (biochip), manufactured in Japan, which has run amuck and reprogrammed itself. The film belongs to the anti-technology tradition of killer MACHINES, common in sf cinema, to which also belong DEMON SEED (1977) and RUNAWAY (1984). [PN]

LIGHT, JOHN [r] ◊ ROBERT HALE LIMITED.

LIGHTNER, A(LICE) M(ARTHA) (1904-1988) US writer and entomologist who began publishing her sf, all of which is for children, with "A New Game" for *Boy's Life* in 1959. Her first published novel, *The Rock of Three Planets* (**1963**) – its sequels were *The Planet Poachers* (**1965**) and *The Space Ark* (**1968**) – was followed by several other effective juveniles, though she came to general sf notice only with *The Day of the Drones* (**1969**), a post-HOLOCAUST story set half a millennium after a nuclear WAR. (This was actually her first-written novel; originally written for adults, it had been revised for publication as a juvenile.) As in Margot BENNETT's *The Long Way Back* (**1954**), Black Africa has survived. The two young protagonists, sent north on an exploratory mission, discover that the White remnants of UK civilization have evolved into a hive society (◊ HIVE-MINDS), and at a high cost save one (male) drone, who may (or may not) prove acceptable to the Black society back home. AML also wrote a number of nonfiction books of dramatized natural science as Alice L. Hopf, her married name. [JC]

Other works: *Doctor to the Galaxy* (**1965**); *The Galactic Troubadours* (**1965**); *The Space Plague* (**1966**); *The Space Olympics* (**1967**); *The Thursday Toads* (**1971**); *Star Dog* (**1973**); *Gods or Demons?* (**1973**); *The Space Gypsies*

(**1974**); *Star Circus* (**1977**).

See also: CHILDREN'S SF.

LIMITED EDITIONS ◊ SMALL PRESSES AND LIMITED EDITIONS.

LINAWEAVER, BRAD (1952-) US writer who came to general notice with his first novel, *Moon of Ice* (1982 *AMZ*; exp **1988**), set in an ALTERNATE WORLD where a Nazi-controlled Europe and a freedom-loving USA confront each other in a nuclear standoff (◊ HITLER WINS). The original novella (itself revised in 1986) conveys considerable impact in its description of the confrontation between the supremely pragmatic and practical Joseph Goebbels and a mystical inner circle of the SS which plans to replace humanity by Übermenschen. The novel, which also contains the story of Goebbels's daughter's life as an anarchist revolutionary and the portrait of an explicitly LIBERTARIAN US citizen, adds little to the original. [NT]

LINCOLN, MAURICE Pseudonym of a UK writer, apparently born in 1887, whose two sf novels display an uneasy bantering tone and slyly cluttered plots which make his or her identification of some potential interest. In *Nothing Ever Happens* (**1927**) two young UK men are transported to an unlocatable island run by an impossibly old Master – it is possible T.H. WHITE's similar *The Master* (**1957**) owes some debt to this book – where they are induced to breed with his daughters and discover that he himself breeds ANDROIDS. In *The Man from Up There* (**1929**) a similar duo discovers – and attempts to profit from – a Cyclopean giant from the Moon, whose arrival on Earth has stopped all radio transmissions for days. Eventually the giant goes home. [JC]

LINDBOHM, DÉNIS [r] ◊ SCANDINAVIA.

LINDGREEN, JØRGEN [r] ◊ DENMARK.

LINDNER, ROBERT (MITCHELL) (1914-1956) US psychoanalyst and prison psychologist who reported on his work in the latter capacity in *Rebel Without a Cause* (**1944**). "The Jet-Propelled Couch", a long narrative essay which appears in *The Fifty-Minute Hour: A Collection of True Psychoanalytic Tales* (coll **1955**; vt *The Jet-Propelled Couch* UK), absorbingly examines and analyses the sf-based fantasies of one of his patients, who retreated from an intolerable childhood, adolescence and adulthood through progressive immersion in an elaborate SPACE-OPERA universe, to which he believed he was regularly transported and in which he was the ruler of a planet. His rationalization of his role in this universe was impeccably couched in sf terms, with alternate time-streams playing a considerable role, and provides an explanation *in extremis* for sf's imaginative power over adolescents. Also of interest is one effect of RL's curative strategy: he pretended to enter into his patient's universe with him, and eventually was himself fascinated and almost ensnared by it. Roger ZELAZNY's *The Dream Master* (**1966**) develops the implications of RL's experience in bravura fashion. [JC]

See also: PARANOIA; PSYCHOLOGY.

LINDSAY, DAVID (1878-1945) UK writer remembered today almost entirely for his first novel, *A Voyage to Arcturus* (**1920**), in which he rather high-handedly makes use of a range of sf and fantasy devices to transport a man to the planet Tormance, where he is destined to undergo a series of baroque adventures. In fact the journey to this planet is a mystical inner passage into a state where ethical precepts, and all the other slings and arrows to which the protagonist's soul is vulnerable, are embodied in the extraordinary Tormance lifeforms. The metaphysic thus unfolded is of a compelling ornateness, and may – it has been suggested – have inspired C.S. LEWIS'S **Cosmic Trilogy**. *The Haunted Woman* (**1922**) is a more conventional FANTASY in which a similarly allegorical reading of the Ocean of Story is constantly underlined. *The Adventures of M. de Mailly* (**1926**; vt *A Blade for Sale* 1927 US) is a historical novel, while *Sphinx* (**1923**), *Devil's Tor* (**1932**) and *The Violet Apple & The Witch* (coll **1975** US) are all fantasies. *The Violet Apple* (**1978**) contains only the first tale. [JC]

About the author: *The Strange Genius of David Lindsay* (anth **1970**) by J.B. Pick, E.H. VISIAK and Colin WILSON; *David Lindsay* (**1982** chap) by Gary K. WOLFE.

See also: CONCEPTUAL BREAKTHROUGH; DIME-NOVEL SF; ESCHATOLOGY; FANTASTIC VOYAGES; GODS AND DEMONS; HISTORY OF SF; LIFE ON OTHER WORLDS; MYTHOLOGY; PERCEPTION.

LINDSAY, RICHARD [r] ◊ ROBERT HALE LIMITED.

LINDSAY, (NICHOLAS) VACHEL (1879-1931) US poet, the clanging primitivism of whose best known work, the poems assembled in *The Congo and Other Poems* (coll **1914**), may have been ingenuous. Of sf interest is *The Golden Book of Springfield, being the Review of a Book that will Appear in the Autumn of the year 2018, and an Extended Description of Springfield, Illinois, in that Year* (**1920**), a prose work in which a world government is envisioned. [JC]

LINGUISTICS Linguistics is the study of language, how languages work, what their function is, how they are constructed and whence they are derived. As a discipline it has leapt to academic prominence since the 1960s. Languages play a surprisingly important role in sf, and many stories turn on linguistic issues. The theme overlaps, naturally, with that of COMMUNICATIONS, and also to some extent with those of ANTHROPOLOGY and PERCEPTION, inasmuch as a language tells us a great deal about the culture that uses it and the way that culture perceives the world. This entry concentrates primarily on verbal languages in sf. Other ways of giving information are dealt with under COMMUNICATIONS, and two examples will suffice here. Terry CARR's "The Dance of the Changer and the Three" (1968) is set on an alien planet whose natives are energy forms; their language is dancing; for no clear reason they destroy many humans for whom they seem to feel no enmity, and survival depends on the correct reading of the dance. John VARLEY invents a nonverbal linguistic UTOPIA in the 1978 title story of *The Persistence of Vision* (coll **1978**),

in which a sighted man enters a community of people who are blind and deaf; they communicate through touch (and sex) in a language more subtle and immediate than he can at first grasp.

Much earlier C.S. LEWIS and J.R.R. TOLKIEN both used their considerable philological expertise in their fictions. The former's *Out of the Silent Planet* (**1938**) speaks interestingly of the different grammars and vocabularies of the three Martian languages, and plays some rather facile linguistic tricks to show up what Lewis regarded as the arrogance of humanistic SCIENTISTS. Tolkien's *The Lord of the Rings* (3 vols **1954-5**; omni **1968**) is unusual in that its very genesis was largely linguistic: Tolkien invented his imaginary languages (carefully glossed and explained in the many appendices) before he wrote the books. If we accept linguistics as a science – it is arguably the "hardest" (or "most scientific") of the SOFT SCIENCES – then we might argue that the fiction of Tolkien, usually regarded as FANTASY, at least approaches sf in its linguistic aspects.

Sf stories in which linguistics plays a subsidiary role are very much more common than sf stories actually *about* linguistics. Most writers who set stories in the future (or in the past, if it comes to that) ignore the problem of language-change, but some have confronted the problem, with various degrees of success; many of these attempts are discussed by Walter E. MEYERS in what is by far the best study of the topic, *Aliens and Linguists: Language Study and Science Fiction* (**1980**). Although sf writers normally realize that their craft requires a good understanding of the hard sciences (physics, etc.), many have no training in nor understanding of linguistics; and nor, very often, do they seem to feel this as a lack. Thus stories turning on points of ALIEN or future language are often patchy; the ways in which grammar, vocabulary and speech-sounds evolve do not seem to be widely understood.

Examples of sf stories demonstrating linguistic change, whether fanciful or plausible, are: Alfred BESTER's "Of Time and Third Avenue" (1951), Bester being generally very much alive to the forms of language; Robert A. HEINLEIN's "Gulf" (1949), with its future speedtalk; Anthony BURGESS's *A Clockwork Orange* (**1962**), with its NEAR-FUTURE Russian-derived Nadsat slang; George ORWELL's *Nineteen Eighty-four* (**1949**), with its Newspeak, designed to reinforce "proper" social attitudes; Poul ANDERSON's "Time Heals" (1949), with a futurified pronunciation; Felix C. GOTSCHALK's *Growing Up in Tier 3000* (**1975**), where a great variety of future colloquialisms are evoked; and Michael FRAYN's *A Very Private Life* (**1968**), whose future languages are more lively than plausible. A more generalized linguistic gusto is displayed in, for example, Benjamin APPEL's *The Funhouse* (**1959**), Arthur Byron COVER's *Autumn Angels* (**1975**) and much of the output of R.A. LAFFERTY.

A GENRE-SF writer who is always aware of linguistic problems is L. Sprague DE CAMP; his article "Language for Time Travelers" (1938) – similar material is incorporated into his *Science-Fiction Handbook* (**1953**; rev 1975) – was probably the first account of linguistic problems in sf. His stories, sometimes rather ploddingly, reflect this interest, as in "The Wheels of If" (1940), set in an ALTERNATE WORLD where the Norman Conquest did not take place and so English has never been Frenchified (although here De Camp gets Grimm's Law of sound-changes quite wrong, in terms of both its effect and the historical period to which it refers), and in the **Viagens Interplanetarias** series, in which the space pidgin Intermundos is heavily influenced by Brazilian space crews.

Orwell's Newspeak, although the most celebrated example of language-control being used by the state to impose social conformity and an unthinking acceptance of the way things are, was by no means the first. Yevgeny ZAMIATIN's *We* (trans **1924**) has a heavily conformist, mechanical language that reflects the regimentation of society. Anthony BOUCHER's interesting TIME-TRAVEL story "Barrier" (1942) likewise features such a language, along with a daffy collocation of future linguists all researching via TIME MACHINES. A tour de force of conformist-language creation is the story told by the Ascian prisoner-of-war in Gene WOLFE's *The Citadel of the Autarch* (**1983**), expressing entirely in patriotic slogans a tale of the individual spirit. The whole of Wolfe's **Book of the New Sun**, indeed, is alive with linguistic invention, not least in its use of words from the classical Greek to express concepts at once futuristic and archaic.

Language is an important aspect of the above stories, but is not their *raison d'être*. Three kinds of story in which linguistics becomes central are those where humans communicate with animals (1) or with aliens (2), or endeavour to translate dead alien languages (3).

Two good examples in the first group are *Un animal doué de raison* (**1967**; trans as *The Day of the Dolphin* **1969**) by Robert MERLE and *Slave Ship* by Frederik POHL, in both of which animals who must be spoken to are used as military weapons. Ursula K. LE GUIN's amusing spoof scientific paper, based on the idea that animals and insects have not only languages but also artforms, "The Author of the Acacia Seeds and Other Extracts from *The Journal of the Association of Therolinguistics*" (1974), is probably not intended entirely as a joke. Many stories other than Merle's have looked at cetacean-human communication, a subject popularized from 1961 in a series of nonfiction books by the experimental psychologist John C. Lilly. Among such stories are those in David BRIN's **Uplift War** sequence, particularly *Startide Rising* (**1983**; rev 1985), whose advanced dolphins have undergone GENETIC ENGINEERING, and Ted MOONEY's *Easy Travel to Other Planets* (**1981**), in which a love story between woman and dolphin, to which linguistic questions are central, takes place against a backdrop of global Information Sickness.

First Contact stories (◊ ALIENS; ANTHROPOLOGY)

necessarily involve linguistics unless, as once was frequent, the issue is dodged by the use of some kind of magical translation box. However, there are many such stories that do involve linguistic questions, notably including the series about galactic intelligence agent **Coyote Jones** by Suzette Haden ELGIN, who spent a decade as a professor of linguistics. John BERRYMAN's "Berom" (1951) has an amusing variant on the theme, in which incomprehensible visiting aliens turn out to be speaking in a UK commercial cable code of the 1920s that they have picked up by radio. The **Hoka** series by Poul Anderson and Gordon R. DICKSON features aliens who understand language quite literally, with sometimes comic results. Frank HERBERT's *Whipping Star* (**1970**) conjures up, in a story of humans making contact with aliens who turn out to be STARS, so intense a miasma of semantic confusions (as recurs regularly in his work) that the narrative structure and human interest of the story are very nearly overwhelmed. Roger ZELAZNY's "A Rose for Ecclesiastes" (1963), a verbally brilliant story with a depth of feeling seldom found in sf, has a poet-linguist chosen to attempt contact with the few remaining Martians, and to translate their high language and their holy texts; his complacency is punctured. Chad OLIVER's *The Winds of Time* (**1957**) has some expertly worked-out descriptive field linguistics in operation in a story of interstellar aliens waking from SUSPENDED ANIMATION on Earth. Edward LLEWELLYN's *Word-Bringer* (**1986**) is another First Contact story (about an alien ROBOT emissary to Earth) with linguistic ramifications. The film CLOSE ENCOUNTERS OF THE THIRD KIND (1977) ends with a prolonged epiphany when the occupants of a flying saucer (◊ UFOS) finally consent to make contact, communication being initiated through a linguistic code of flickering lights and a sequence of crashing chords. Another film, ICEMAN (1984), has a prolongedly earnest linguistic sequence about attempted contact with a resuscitated Neanderthal (◊ APES AND CAVEMEN). David I. MASSON, a devoted student of linguistics, may have written the First Contact story with the best-informed linguistic detail in "Not So Certain" (1967), which shows one kind of problem that may bedevil the most well intentioned exo-culture specialists. This was republished in his *The Caltraps of Time* (coll **1968**), which also contains the amusing "A Two-Timer" (1966), in which an inadvertent time traveller from the 17th century describes in his own English what he finds in the 20th – not least, semantic bafflement.

Stories of archaeological linguistics are less common. H. Beam PIPER's "Omnilingual" (1957), probably his best story, has a woman seeking a Rosetta Stone with which to interpret the writings of a dead Martian civilization; she ultimately finds it in the periodic table of the elements.

Other sf works focusing strongly on linguistics include *Hunter of Worlds* (**1977**) by C.J. CHERRYH, herself a linguist; and the **Cuckoo** series – *The Farthest Star* (fixup **1975**) and *Wall Around a Star* (**1983**) – by

Frederik Pohl and Jack WILLIAMSON. These are recent and quite sophisticated, but one of the best sf books about linguistic problems was much earlier: Jack VANCE's *The Languages of Pao* (1958) is one of the most intelligent uses in genre sf of the idea that the perception of reality by different races is reflected in, and to a degree actually determined by, the languages they speak; hence CULTURAL ENGINEERING can be carried out by the teaching of new languages. In real-life linguistics this view is strongly identified with the writings of Dr Benjamin Whorf (1897-1941) in his studies of Native American languages. Whorf's theories of linguistic relativity are most obviously reflected in sf terms in Samuel R. DELANY's *Babel-17* (1966), a complexly structured novel about communication which takes language itself as the central image; a web of different languages is threaded through the spy-story plot, in which an alien code turns out to be only paradoxically alien. It is Babel-17, a perfect analytical language which has no word for "I"; this absence Delany sees as its strength and also its weakness. (Meyers, in his book cited above, admonishes Delany for not then knowing as much about linguistics as the confident tone of *Babel-17* might suggest.) Delany's interest in language and linguistic philosophy has continued, and is reflected in much of his work, including the curious dialects he created in *Nova* (1968) and also his critical book, *The Jewel-Hinged Jaw: Notes on the Language of Science Fiction* (coll 1977).

The use of linguistic devices in the actual telling of a story, to reflect along Whorfian lines the nature of the human or alien cultures described, is a difficult narrative skill. Suzette Haden Elgin attempts it only occasionally in her series *Native Tongue* (1984) and *The Judas Rose* (1987), but there is considerable interest in her account of the creation of the secret language Womanspeak (or "La'Adan") used by a disempowered female underclass as one weapon in their struggle to subvert the self-satisfied world of men. The film MAD MAX BEYOND THUNDERDOME (1985), a post-HOLOCAUST exploitation thriller, is the last place one might have expected to find a linguistic thesis, but the devolved language of an isolated community of children is presented with considerable imagination (and a not inconsiderable beauty). The linguistic tour de force of the 1980s, however, was *Riddley Walker* (1980) by Russell HOBAN, a story of a post-holocaust England actually told in the devolved but vivid language of its inhabitants; the astonishing thing is not so much the attempt – many sf writers have done the same thing on a smaller scale – but its success at novel length. Other sf writers may have had much to say about linguistic concepts, but none has ever so sustainedly shown such a language in action, nor so successfully – and movingly – revealed the culture of its speakers in so doing.

If Whorf has been the one powerful influence on sf linguistic scenarios, another may come to be Noam Chomsky (1928-   ), whose view that all human languages share a deep structure which is perhaps genetically determined is to some extent at odds with Whorf's view that our conceptual categorization of the world is determined by our native language; where Whorf stressed diversity, Chomsky stresses unity. Sf had added little to this debate, nor seemed very conscious of it, until 1973, when the ideationally exuberant Ian WATSON first attracted the attention of the sf readership. Most of his novels feature linguistic thought somewhere in their usually complex structure, and his first, *The Embedding* (1973), is certainly *the* sf linguistics novel *par excellence*, with all three of its subplots linking language and PERCEPTION in interweaving stories of alien, South American Indian and computer-imposed languages, and the differing subjective realities they may or may not succeed in generating. An important essay by Watson is "Towards an Alien Linguistics" (1975 *Vector*), reprinted in *The Book of Ian Watson* (coll 1985 US), in which he considers questions of epistemology and hazards the thought that there may be "a topological grammar of the universe, which reflects itself in the grammars of actual languages" – Chomsky writ very large indeed. Watson is one of those theorists who have used arguments from quantum mechanics to support the solipsistic view that the Universe exists as an external structure only through the consciousnesses of its participants and observers; language, in Watson's scheme, is reflexive, Nature sending a message to itself – an intellectual position that, if correct, would place linguistics as the scientific discipline right at the heart of sf. [PN]

Further reading: Aside from those cited above, two useful texts about linguistics in sf are *Linguistics and Language in Science Fiction-Fantasy* (1975) by Myra Edwards BARNES and an interesting essay on the popular subject of word-coinage by sf writers, "The Words in Science Fiction" by Larry NIVEN in *The Craft of Science Fiction* (anth 1976) ed Reginald BRETNOR.

LINKLATER, ERIC (ROBERT RUSSELL) (1899-1974) Scottish writer proficient in various genres though best remembered for his novels, beginning with *White Maa's Saga* (1929). Much of his work is fantasy, like *The Devil's in the News* (1934) and many of the stories collected in *God Likes them Plain* (coll 1935), *Sealskin Trousers* (coll 1947) and *A Sociable Plover* (coll 1957). *The Impregnable Women* (1938) is a NEAR-FUTURE rewrite of Lysistrata in which the women of Europe band together, go on sexual strike, and end a futile war (◊ WOMEN AS PORTRAYED IN SCIENCE FICTION). Similar in attitude were EL's WWII conversation plays, notably *The Raft and Socrates Asks Why* (1942 chap), *The Great Ship and Rabelais Replies* (1944 chap) and *Crisis in Heaven: An Elysian Comedy* (1944 chap), which employed fantasy elements as didactic pointers. His two children's novels, *The Wind on the Moon* (1944) and *The Pirates in the Deep Green Sea* (1949), are both attractive fantasies, in the latter of which Davy Jones and all the drowned pirates under the sea are discovered guarding the great knots that tie latitudes and longitudes together to keep the world from splitting. *A Spell for Old Bones* (**1949**) is a fantasy set in a mythical 1st-century Scotland. In *A Terrible Freedom* (**1966**) a man finds the characters of his dream world taking over the real one. [JC]

See also: *The* MAGAZINE OF FANTASY AND SCIENCE FICTION.

LINUS ◊ Pierre CHRISTIN.

LIN YUTANG Working name of Chinese-US novelist, essayist and academic Lin Yü-t'ang (1895-1976). In *The Unexpected Island* (**1955** UK; vt *Looking Beyond* 1955 US) refugees from several world HOLOCAUSTS establish a conservative UTOPIA on an isolated ISLAND. [JC]

LIONEL, ROBERT ◊ R.L. FANTHORPE.

LIPPINCOTT, DAVID (McCORD) (1925-   ) US writer and advertising executive whose NEAR-FUTURE political thriller *E Pluribus Bang!* (**1970**) finds the US President involved in the murder of a Secret Service agent he finds in bed with his wife. *Tremor Violet* (**1975**) is a DISASTER novel about earthquakes in Los Angeles. [JC]

Other works: *Voice of Armageddon* (**1974**); *The Blood of October* (**1977**); *Black Prism* (**1980** UK; vt *Dark Prism* 1981 US).

LIQUID SKY Film (1982). Z Films. Dir Slava Tsukerman, starring Anne Carlisle, Paula E. Sheppard, Susan Doukas, Otto von Wernherr. Screenplay Tsukerman, Carlisle, Nina V. Kerova. 112 mins. Colour.

ALIENS who have landed their tiny flying saucer on the roof of a Manhattan penthouse observe the lives of strange young people: fashionable, drug-using, white-faced Punk/New Wavers. The aliens are attracted to chemicals released when humans use heroin ("liquid sky") and/or achieve orgasm, killing the humans or causing them to disappear at the moment of endorphin saturation. When looking through alien eyes we see this in psychedelic patterns. This elegant, sometimes funny, sometimes obscene art film, something of an anthropological documentary about an alienated, self-brutalized human subculture, was made by a group of Russian *émigrés* in New York – effectively aliens themselves – and features a German (that is, alien) alien-hunter. [PN]

See also: SEX.

LISLE, SEWARD D. ◊ Edward S. ELLIS.

LITTELL, JONATHAN (?1969-   ) US writer whose *Bad Voltage: A Fantasy in 4/4* (**1989**) depicts a CYBERPUNK Paris with confused verve. The young protagonist (he is Black; the first edition's cover shows him White) moves from underground criminal activities to the upper world of the rich, which mirrors the lower. The energies of the book are expended scattershot, but attractively. [JC]

LITTLE SHOP OF HORRORS, THE ◊ Roger CORMAN.

LI TUNG [r] ◊ LEE TUNG.

LIVIA, ANNA [r] ◊ ANNA LIVIA.

LIVINGSTON, BERKELEY (1908-   ) US writer whose sf appeared only in the ZIFF-DAVIS magazines *AMZ* and *Fantastic Adventures*. Some 50 stories appeared 1943-50, under either his own name or the house names Alexander BLADE and Morris J. Steele. His only book was *Meteor of Death* (**1954** chap Australia). He is noted for the quantity rather than the quality of his work. [JE/PN]

See also: ILLUSTRATION; LEISURE.

LIVINGSTON, HAROLD (1924-   ) US writer, often of tv scripts, whose fourth book, *The Climacticon* (**1960**), spoofs SEX obsessions in a borderline-sf tale. [JC]

LIVING WORLDS The notion that a planet might be a living creature is a rather startling one; indeed, it was initially used purely for its shock value. In R.A. KENNEDY's remarkable philosophical extravaganza *The Triuneverse* (**1912**), MARS begins to reproduce by binary fission and its daughter cells devour much of the Solar System. In "When the World Screamed" (1929) by Arthur Conan DOYLE a hole is drilled through the Earth's "skin" and the living flesh within reacts against the violation. Other attempts to exploit this shock value include Edmond HAMILTON's "The Earth-Brain" (1932), Jack WILLIAMSON's "Born of the Sun" (1934) – in which the Sun is living, the planets are its eggs, and Earth hatches – and Nelson BOND's "And Lo! The Bird" (1950). The perishability of easy shock value inevitably gives rise to an escalation of scale; Laurence MANNING soon took the idea to its extreme in "The Living Galaxy" (1934).

The notion of living STARS seems to fascinate sf writers more than that of living planets. Austere stellar intelligences are featured in *Star Maker* (**1937**) by Olaf STAPLEDON, though Stapledon discarded a first draft which featured the exploits of intelligent nebulae; it was later published as *Nebula Maker* (**1976**). (An intelligent nebula, albeit a very small one, figures also in Fred HOYLE's *The Black Cloud*, **1957**.) There are vestiges here of the occasional medieval equation of stars and angels, seen also in William Blake's poem "The Tiger" (1794). More recent examples of living stars are found in Gérard KLEIN's *Starmaster's Gambit* (**1958**; trans **1973**), Frederik POHL's and Jack Williamson's *Starchild* (**1965**) and *Rogue Star* (**1969**), Frank HERBERT's *Whipping Star* (**1970**) and *If The Stars are Gods* (fixup **1977**) by Gregory BENFORD and Gordon EKLUND. Living planets have become rare, although visiting spacemen offend one in Ray BRADBURY's "Here There Be Tygers" (1951), but planets whose whole ecospheres are single individuals, often imbued with consciousness, are not uncommon. The planetary spirits in the **Cosmic Trilogy** (**1938-45**) by C.S. LEWIS are somewhat rarefied, as are the curious world-consciousnesses featured in Theodore STURGEON's "Case and the Dreamer" (1972) and Neal BARRETT's *Stress Pattern* (**1974**), but more mundane life-systems which comprise single vast organisms are featured in such stories as Murray LEINSTER's "The Lonely Planet" (1949), Doris PISERCHIA's *Earthchild* (**1977**), M.A. FOSTER's *Waves* (**1980**), Brian M. STABLEFORD's "Wildland" (1989) and Isaac ASIMOV's *Nemesis* (**1989**). The most popular model for such integrated ecospheres is the forest, displayed in "Process" (1950) by A.E. VAN VOGT, "The Forest of Zil" (1967) by Kris NEVILLE, and "Vaster than Empires and More Slow" (1971) by Ursula K. LE GUIN. The most impressive presentation of a truly ALIEN world-intelligence is Stanisław LEM's *Solaris* (**1961**; trans **1970**), many features of which are prefigured in his *Edem* (**1959**; trans as *Eden* **1989**). The recent popularization of James Lovelock's "Gaia hypothesis" has encouraged writers to pay more attention to highly integrated ecospheres, but the most radical repersonalization of the Earth is that in David BRIN's *Earth* (**1990**), in which the planet undergoes metamorphosis into a gargantuan AI – perhaps the most extravagant *deus ex machina* ever deployed. [BS]

See also: BIOLOGY; HIVE-MINDS.

LLEWELLYN, (DAVID WILLIAM) ALUN (1903-   ) UK writer active in several genres, including political SATIRE. His sf novel *The Strange Invaders* (**1934**), like John COLLIER's *Tom's A-Cold* (**1933**), builds upon the deeply felt elegiac mood of Richard JEFFERIES's post-HOLOCAUST novel *After London* (**1885**). Set in a new ice age and told in an intensely worked, harsh style, it depicts a tribal society in a future USSR where Marx, Lenin and Stalin are revered as saints in a barbarian religion; the world has, long ago, been nearly destroyed by war. The novel's focus is INVASION by great lizard-like successors to humanity, which the inhabitants of a small settlement finally defeat at great cost. [JC]

Other works: *Confound their Politics* (**1934**), a political satire set in imaginary countries; *Jubilee John* (**1939**).

See also: DISASTER.

LLEWELLYN, EDWARD Working name of Welsh-born Canadian writer and doctor Edward Llewellyn-Thomas (1917-1984), who held professorships variously in pharmacology, medicine, electrical engineering and psychology. Most of his work is set loosely in the same universe, with his first 3 novels – *The Douglas Convolution* (**1979** US), *The Bright Companion* (**1980** US) and *Prelude to Chaos* (**1983** US) – constituting a trilogy about a 22nd-century Earth suffering from widespread female infertility. The muscularly told first volume follows the arrival in this world, via TIME TRAVEL, of an ingenious mathematician, who proves invaluable to the Order of fertile women; the second presents a tour of the world dominated by this Order; the third is a weak prequel. In *Salvage and Destroy* (**1984** US) EL moved into SPACE OPERA, though genetics continues to play a role in a complex plot involving two immortal species of aliens, one of which becomes involved with Earth. *Fugitive in Transit* (**1985** US) similarly confronts humans with representatives of galactic civilization, in this case the Galactic Transit Authority, which is chasing the woman who has discovered a stargate. *Word-Bringer* (**1986**) presents its protagonist with the discovery – familiar to readers of Clifford D. SIMAK – that aliens have left on Earth a device which spreads knowledge for free, engendering all sorts of scientific

advances. Though he did not seem destined to become a major writer in the field, EL's tales are literate, numerate and attractively marked by their frequent use of active and personable WOMEN as protagonists. [JC]

See also: CANADA; ESP; LINGUISTICS.

LLOYD, JOHN URI (1849-1936) US chemist, author of *Etidorhpa, or The End of Earth* (**1895**; rev 1901), a metaphysical FANTASTIC VOYAGE in which the narrator is led by a blind humanoid to a LOST WORLD in the interior of the Earth, where he gains occult enlightenment into the higher forms of love (the title is *Aphrodite* reversed). *Etidorhpa*, which went through at least 11 editions, is noteworthy for its bitter attack on the rational sciences. Like other notable HOLLOW-EARTH works of the period, it derives from the theories of John Cleves SYMMES. [JE/JC]

LOBATO, MONTEIRO [r] ◊ LATIN AMERICA.

LOCKE, GEORGE (WALTER) (1936-   ) UK writer, one-time pharmacist, antiquarian bookseller and bibliographer. He began publishing sf with "The Human Seed" for *Authentic* in 1957, and under the name Gordon Walters published a number of sf stories in the 1960s, but no sf books; his novels, *Pattern of Terror* (**1987**) and *A Spectre-Room of Fancy* (**1989** chap) as by Ayresome Johns, are detective tales of "impossible crimes" and the supernatural. His most important publications have been in the BIBLIOGRAPHY of sf and fantasy; though his researches have been far-ranging, the emphasis has been on 19th-century interplanetary romances, which he annotated in *Voyages in Space: A Bibliography of Interplanetary Fiction, 1801-1914* (**1975** chap). *Ferret Fantasy's Christmas Annual for 1972* (**1972** chap), *Ferret Fantasy's Christmas Annual for 1973* (**1974** chap) and *Ferret Fantasy's Christmas Annual for 1974* (**1975** chap), which contains *inter alia* short bibliographies of this material, led to the excellent *Science Fiction First Editions: A Select Bibliography and Notes for the Collector* (**1978** chap). *A Spectrum of Fantasy: The Bibliography and Biography of a Collection of Fantastic Literature* (**1980**) applied the same combination of bibliographic exactitude and anecdotal commentary to a description of his own extremely large library. Many books not previously understood to merit admission to the canon of sf and fantasy were first cited in these volumes; a second **Spectrum** volume is projected. His SMALL PRESS, Ferret Fantasy, has so far issued 15 books of sf, fantasy and mystery interest. [JC]

Other works: *Worlds Apart* (anth **1972**), ed, early interplanetary fiction in facsimile; *At the Mountains of Murkiness and Other Parodies* (anth **1973**), ed anon; *From an Ultimate Dim Thule* (**1973**), a study of fantasy illustrator Sidney H. Sime, and *The Land of Dreams* (**1975**), an illustrated survey of Sime; *The Affair of the Lost Compression and Other Stories* (anth **1975** chap); *Guardians of the Lilac Moon, or The Downfall of Dakeevle the Dire* (**1980** chap), a tale for children; *Thirty Years of Dustwrappers: 1884-1914* (**1988** chap); *Pearson's Weekly: A Checklist of Fiction 1890-1939* (**1990**).

LOCKE, RICHARD ADAMS (1800-1871) US journalist and editor, usually regarded as author of the famous "Moon Hoax". In 1835 several issues of the New York *Sun* carried articles purporting to describe the inhabitants of the MOON and their environs as observed by the distinguished astronomer Sir John Herschel (1792-1871) through a new, high-magnification telescope. It remains unclear which of several variously titled chapbook versions of the original hoax is in fact the original edition. Title variations include *Great Astronomical Discoveries Lately Made by Sir John Herschel at the Cape of Good Hope* and *A Complete Account of the Late Discoveries in the Moon* (both **1835** chap; under first title rev 1841; rev vt *The Moon Hoax, or A Discovery that the Moon has a Vast Population of Human Beings* 1859 US; vt *The Great Moon Hoax of Richard Adams Locke* 1886). The book has also been dubiously ascribed to Joseph Nicolas Nicollet, but the consensus is that the work was indeed RAL's. The effectiveness of the hoax was comparable to the reactions to Edgar Allan POE's "Balloon Hoax" (1844 New York *Sun*), which was purchased for the paper by RAL, then one of its editors, and the Orson Welles broadcast of *The* WAR OF THE WORLDS (1938). *The Moon Hoax, or A Discovery that the Moon has a Vast Population of Human Beings* (anth **1859**; exp with new intro by Ormond Seavey **1975**) presents the original text plus later material. [JE]

See also: ASTRONOMY.

LOCKHARD, LEONARD [s] ◊ Charles L. HARNESS; Theodore L. THOMAS.

LOCUS US SEMIPROZINE, 1968-current, ed Charles N. BROWN (calling himself Charlie Brown in earlier days), published by Locus Publications (in Oakland, California, since the 1970s), 378 issues to July 1992. *Locus* was founded in New York by Brown with Ed Meskys and Dave Vanderwerf as a one-sheet news FANZINE; when Brown's partners dropped out, his then wife Marsha Brown joined him as co-editor. At that time the magazine appeared between fortnightly and monthly. Brown divorced, became sole editor, remarried in 1970, and his new wife Dena Brown became the new co-editor. *Locus* (and the Browns) moved to the San Francisco area in 1972, a year after winning its first of many Best Fanzine HUGOS.

In 1976 Charles Brown gave up his job as an electrical engineer and began to edit *Locus* full-time (Dena Brown had worked full-time on it 1972-5). He divorced again in 1977, and since then has been sole editor; the magazine effectively became a semiprozine at this point, since Brown was attempting to earn a living from it alone; the first paid employee was hired in 1977. During the 1970s the newsletter became a monthly, increased in size, and began (from 1974) listing all sf books published in the USA. By 1980 the circulation had topped 5000, reaching 7000 in 1984. In 1983 it increased to 48pp an issue and switched to computer setting; it became fully desktop published with laser typesetting from 1986.

By the 1990s *Locus* (now 74pp as of June 1992) had long been established as *the* trade newspaper of sf; its paid circulation was stable at c8500. Its clear superiority over all other news magazines in the field has been confirmed by the astonishing number of Hugos (16) it has now received: 8 for Best Fanzine to 1983, and a further 8 since 1984 for Best Semiprozine; i.e., a Hugo for every year the latter category has been in existence. The predictability of *Locus*'s annual Hugo has proved irritating to some in the sf world. Wholly professional in appearance, *Locus* excels in its news coverage (with regular columns from overseas, including the UK and much of Europe, Australia, Russia, China and occasionally various Latin American countries). Its book-review coverage is very ample, taking up a large proportion of the magazine. Brown's policy of not printing strongly adverse reviews, while understandable in view of the magazine's reliance on the book trade for advertising, is unfortunate. The policy matters less in practice than in theory, since most reviews are intelligent and well informed, although some readers find them somewhat bland overall. Nonetheless, *Locus* is indispensable for professionals in the sf field, and was one of the most important references used in the compilation of this encyclopedia. *Locus* polls its readers annually about their favourites in different categories of sf publishing (◊ AWARDS), and there is a case for arguing that the Locus Awards are more securely based across the sf readership than are the more celebrated Hugos. *Locus* also surveys annually its subscribers' ages, occupations, reading habits, etc. Locus Publications also publishes books (*for further details of which* ◊ Charles N. BROWN *and* William CONTENTO). [PN]

LOCUS AWARDS ◊ AWARDS.

LOFTING, HUGH [r] ◊ CHILDREN'S SF.

LOGAN, CHARLES (1930-   ) UK writer, and nurse for the mentally handicapped. *Shipwreck* (**1975**) won the 1975 Gollancz/*Sunday Times* sf contest jointly with Chris BOYCE's *Catchworld* (**1975**). Calmly and inexorably, it tells the story of the inevitable death of a man whose spaceship lands disabled on a planet whose ECOLOGY is unfriendly to human survival. That this grim anti-ROBINSONADE presents the most likely outcome of such an occurrence has not made it any more popular with sf fans. [JC]

LOGAN'S RUN 1. Film (1976). MGM/United Artists. Dir Michael Anderson, starring Michael York, Jenny Agutter, Richard Jordan, Peter Ustinov, Farrah Fawcett-Majors. Screenplay David Zelag Goodman, based on *Logan's Run* (**1967**) by William F. NOLAN and George Clayton JOHNSON. 118 Mins. Colour.

One of the largest, most "prestigious" sf films of the decade, this was also one of the most sluggish, reducing its lively source, Nolan's and Johnson's novel, to a bland affair whose lavishness is all decoration, no substance. Set in a domed city where no one is allowed to pass their 30th birthday – official killers, "Sandmen", disposing of those who refuse their ritual suicide – the film concerns a renegade

Sandman and his girlfriend, who attempt to reach the legendary "Sanctuary" outside. But Sanctuary does not exist; instead they find a mildewed Washington DC, inhabited by the only living old man. They decide that old age is a good thing and return to the dome to spread the news. During interrogation, the reformed Sandman confuses the city COMPUTER to the point where it blows itself up, along with the city.

LR's youth autocracy exists in a conceptual vacuum and is riddled with contradiction, and the film's attack on its sterile UTOPIA is – typically of much patronizing sf cinema of the period – simplistic to the point of banality. There are livelier film versions of the theme, one being GAS-S-S-S (1970).

2. US tv series (1977-8), based on the film. An MGM TV Production for CBS. Prod Ben Roberts, Ivan Goff. Executive prod Leonard Katzman. Story editor D.C. FONTANA. Writers included Fontana, Saul David, Harlan ELLISON. Dirs included Paul Krasny, Curtis Harrington. 1 season, 75min pilot plus 13 50min episodes. Colour.

The two men who created and produced the popular crime-busting programme *Charlie's Angels* – both admitted they knew nothing about sf – made this short-lived tv series designed to exploit the film. For budgetary reasons the series was set outside the film's domed city. It concerns the adventures of Logan (Gregory Harrison), Jessica (Heather Menzies) and Rem (Donald Moffat), the latter – a comic ANDROID with nonbiological components – having been hastily introduced to exploit the popularity of the two ROBOTS in STAR WARS (1977). These three characters search for Sanctuary while pursued by deadly Sandmen from the city, moving from one DYSTOPIAN situation to another, all this portrayed at the level of comic-book stereotype. [JB/PN]

LOGGEM, MANUEL van [r] ◊ BENELUX.

LOGSDON, SYD (?1950-   ) US writer whose first sf novel, *Jandrax* (**1979**), is a PLANETARY ROMANCE about a sexually active scout who is also tough on planets. SL's second, *A Fond Farewell to Dying* (1978 *Gal* as "To Not Go Gently"; exp **1981**), is a far more interesting post-HOLOCAUST tale set in 23rd-century India. A long-standing conflict with a Muslim nation to the north frames the humanly complex story of a Westerner's research into cloning (◊ CLONES) to compensate for the post-nuclear sterilization suffered by most of the world. The sense that cloning barbarously parodies Hindu beliefs in REINCARNATION permeates the text, whose very considerable competence makes SL's subsequent silence all the more regrettable. [JC]

LOHRMAN, PAUL House name used on the ZIFF-DAVIS magazines by Richard SHAVER, Paul W. FAIRMAN and perhaps others on 7 stories 1950-53. "The World of the Lost" (*Fantastic Adventures* 1950) has been definitely attributed to Shaver. [PN]

LONDON, JACK Working name of US writer John Griffith London (1876-1916), known primarily for his work outside the sf field. After leaving school at the age of 14, JL spent 7 years of adventure and hardship as an oyster pirate, sailor, hobo, prisoner and Klondike gold-seeker. During this period, he gave himself an education steeped in the most influential scientific and philosophic theories of the late 19th century – Darwinism (◊ EVOLUTION; SOCIAL DARWINISM), Nietzscheism and Marxism (◊ ECONOMICS; POLITICS) – which he was to amalgamate in his voluminous writings. These writings consist of adventure tales, socialist essays and fiction, autobiographical narratives, and about 20 works of sf, including 4 novels.

His first sf story, "A Thousand Deaths" (1899), combines some key themes of 19th-century sf: a cold-hearted lone SCIENTIST uses his own son in revivification experiments and is then dematerialized by a super-weapon invented by the son. "The Rejuvenation of Major Rathbone" (1899) displays a "rejuvenator" extracted from a "lymph compound". "The Shadow and the Flash" (1903) has two competing scientific geniuses attaining INVISIBILITY, one by perfecting a pigment that absorbs all light, the other by achieving pure transparency. In "The Enemy of All the World" (1908) a lone genius invents a superweapon and terrorizes the world. Racism runs through much of JL's sf, most shockingly in "The Unparalleled Invasion" (1910): after the White nations have wiped out the Chinese with an aerial germ-warfare assault, a joyous epoch can begin of "splendid mechanical, intellectual, and art output". One major area of JL's sf is the prehistoric world (◊ ANTHROPOLOGY; ORIGIN OF MAN), which is explored in *Before Adam* (**1906**), his first sf novel – which uses a favourite theme, atavism, as a device to project a consciousness into the past – as well as in "The Strength of the Strong" (1911). Atavism appears also in "When the World was Young" (1910), in which a "magnificent" and "yellow-haired" savage shares the body of a successful California businessman, and in *The Star Rover* (**1915**; vt *The Jacket* 1915 UK), a novel based partly on the reported revelations of one Ed Morrell, who had experienced a dissociation of mind from body under torture in San Quentin. In *The Scarlet Plague* (1912 *London Magazine*; **1914**) human history is viewed as cyclical; the post-HOLOCAUST world of the NEAR FUTURE has reverted to primitive tribal existence. The novella "The Red One" (1918) describes a contemporary stone-age society that has turned a mysterious sphere from outer space into the centrepiece of a death cult.

Several of JL's sf works deal with the struggle between the capitalist class, trying to establish a fascist oligarchy, and the proletariat, striving for socialism. "A Curious Fragment" (1908), set in the 28th century, shows one of the ruling oligarchs encountering a severed arm bearing a petition from his industrial slaves, though a more optimistic view appears in "Goliah" (1908), in which a "scientific superman" masters the ultimate energy source, Energon, becomes master of the world's fate, and inaugurates a millennium of international socialism;

both stories are assembled in *Curious Fragments: Jack London's Tales of Fantasy Fiction* ed Dale L. Walker (coll **1975**). In "The Dream of Debs" (**1909**) a near-future general strike brings the capitalist class to its knees. JL's finest achievement in sf, and perhaps his masterpiece, is the DYSTOPIAN *The Iron Heel* (**1907**), which predicts a 20th-century fascist oligarchy in the USA and recounts, through documents discovered by scholars in the socialist 27th century, the epic revolutionary struggle of the enslaved proletariat.

Many of JL's shorter works can be found reprinted in *The Science Fiction of Jack London* ed Richard Gid Powers (coll **1975**), which also has a good introduction. [HBF]

About the author: *Jack London: A Bibliography* (last rev **1973**) by H.C. Woodbridge; *Jack London* (**1984** chap) by Gorman Beauchamp.

See also: DISASTER; HISTORY OF SF; MEDICINE; PULP MAGAZINES; REINCARNATION; TABOOS.

LONG, CHARLES R(USSELL) (1904-1978) US writer whose 2 routine sf novels are *Infinite Brain* (**1957**) and *The Eternal Man* (**1964**). Both are filled with action, the first on a distant planet, the second on an Earth replete with human and alien immortals. [JC]

LONG, DUNCAN (1949-) US writer and editor of a SURVIVALIST newsletter. His first novel, *Anti-Grav Unlimited* (**1988**), features a super-competent tinker/inventor hero (◊ EDISONADE) who – in a post-HOLOCAUST atmosphere almost perfectly designed to serve as an arena for his exploits – uses his ingenious ANTIGRAVITY device to defeat a corporate cabal. The book is well crafted. [JC]

LONG, FRANK BELKNAP (1903-) US writer of sf and fantasy whose working life extended from 1924 to the 1980s. He produced poetry very early, the best of it appearing in *A Man from Genoa and Other Poems* (coll **1926**) and *The Goblin Tower* (**1935**), but is most noted for the weird fantasy he wrote from the beginning of his fiction career, publishing his first stories, "The Desert Lich" and "Death Waters" in WEIRD TALES in 1924. Influenced by H.P. LOVECRAFT, who had promoted the acceptance of his first work and who remained a close colleague until his death in 1937, FBL tended to create worlds in his mentor's style with a slender sf base. He frequently told of his friendship, personal and professional, with Lovecraft, and gave additional details in the valuable introduction and running notes to *The Early Long* (coll **1976**), which assembles stories from 1924-44, the period of his prime as a writer of sf and fantasy. The contents of his first ARKHAM HOUSE volume, *The Hounds of Tindalos* (coll **1946**; cut 1963), were variously excerpted as *The Dark Beasts* (coll **1963**) and *The Black Druid and Other Stories* (coll **1975** UK); these stories represent the cream of his work. A more recent Arkham collection, *The Rim of the Unknown* (coll **1972**), draws from the same prime material.

The post-WWII years saw a change of emphasis in FBL's long career, with much more sf being written and published, beginning with *John Carstairs: Space Detective* (coll of linked stories **1949**) which, with "The Ether Robots" (**1942**) and "The Heavy Man" (**1943**), formed a series about **John Carstairs**, detective and biological expert. Most of FBL's sf deals with future-Earth situations, space travel occurring relatively infrequently (*Space Station No 1* [**1957** dos] occurs off Earth, but the setting is not too distant), though much of his earlier sf featured TIME TRAVEL. Several of his sf books concentrate on INVASION plots in which aliens menace our world, as in *Lest Earth be Conquered* (**1966**; vt *The Androids* 1969 US) and *Journey into Darkness* (**1967**); others, like *It was the Day of the Robot* (**1963**) and *This Strange Tomorrow* (**1966**), depict intrigue-filled future-Earth societies. Some of his later books, like *Survival World* (**1971**) and *The Night of the Wolf* (**1972**), a HORROR fantasy, are among his better works. FBL has published hundreds of short stories over his career, in addition to those collected in his own books; a proper estimate of his stature will have to take them into account, as well as the more routine sf novels of his later years, which for some time obscured the shorter work for which he will finally be remembered. His full-length study, *Howard Phillips Lovecraft: Dreamer on the Nightside* (**1975**), is also of interest. [JC]

Other works: *Woman from Another Planet* (**1960**); *The Mating Center* (**1961**); *Mars is my Destination* (**1962**); *Three Steps Spaceward* (1953 *Fantastic Universe* as "Little Men of Space"; **1963**); *The Horror from the Hills* (1931 *Weird Tales*; **1963**); *Odd Science Fiction* (coll **1964**; vt *The Horror from the Hills* 1965 UK, not to be confused with the 1963 US title, which prints the novel only); *The Martian Visitors* (**1964**); *Mission to a Star* (1958 *Satellite*; **1964**); *So Dark a Heritage* (**1966**); *. . . And Others Shall be Born* (**1968** dos); *The Three Faces of Time* (**1969**); *Monster from Out of Time* (**1970**); *In Mayan Splendor* (coll **1977**), poetry; *When Chaugnar Wakes* (**1978** chap), poem; *Night Fear* (coll **1979**) ed Roy TORGESON; *Rehearsal Night* (**1981** chap); *Autobiographical Memoir* (**1985** chap).

As Lyda Belknap Long: *To the Dark Tower* (**1969**); *Fire of the Witches* (**1971**); *The Shape of Fear* (**1971**); *The Witch Tree* (**1971**); *Hour of the Deadly Nightshade* (**1972**); *Legacy of Evil* (**1973**); *The Crucible of Evil* (**1974**).

See also: LONGEVITY (IN WRITERS AND PUBLICATIONS); PARALLEL WORLDS; ROBERT HALE LIMITED; SMALL PRESSES AND LIMITED EDITIONS.

LONG, LYDA BELKNAP ◊ Frank Belknap LONG.

LONG, WESLEY [s] ◊ George O. SMITH.

LONGBEARD, FREDERICK [s] ◊ Barry B. LONGYEAR.

LONGEVITY ◊ IMMORTALITY.

LONGEVITY (IN WRITERS AND PUBLICATIONS) A curious phenomenon in GENRE SF is the extreme longevity of some of its writers and many of its publications. In referring to the longevity of writers, we mean their professional lives rather than the span between their births and deaths. Although sf careers spanning more than 50 years are not usual, neither are they especially uncommon. The present records may be those held by Jack WILLIAMSON (1908-), whose first published story was "The Metal Man" (1928) in *AMZ* and who was still writing at the time of *Beachhead* (**1992**), a span of 64 years; and by Frank Belknap LONG (1903-   ), whose first published story was "The Desert Lich" (1924) in *Weird Tales*, and who was active at least until 1986, making a span of 62 years. Others to break the 50-year mark have included Lloyd Arthur ESHBACH (1910-   ), who has published comparatively little fiction but has played an important role in sf publishing, and whose writing career nevertheless runs 60 years from "The Man with the Silver Disc" (1930) to *The Scroll of Lucifer* (**1990**); Andre NORTON (1912-   ), whose first novel, not sf, was *The Prince Commands* (**1934**) – her first sf being "The People of the Crater" (1947) as by Andrew North – and whose most recent book is *Songsmith* (**1992**) with A.C. CRISPIN, a span of 58 years; Raymond Z. GALLUN (1910-   ), who began with "The Space Dwellers" (1929) and whose most recent novel was *Bioblast* (**1985**), a span of 56 years (increased to 62 years if we take into account his sf memoir *Starclimber* [**1991**]); Clifford D. SIMAK (1904-1988), whose first published sf was "The World of the Red Sun" (1931) and whose last was *Highway of Eternity* (**1986**), a span of 55 years; L. Sprague DE CAMP (1907-   ), who began with "The Isolinguals" (1937) and who recently published *The Swords of Zinjaban* (**1991**) with his wife Catherine A. Crook de Camp, a span of 54 years; Frederik POHL (1919-   ), who published a slew of short stories under pseudonyms in 1940-41 and whose most recent book is *Mining the Oort* (**1992**), a span of 52 years; Fritz LEIBER (1910-1992), who began with "Two Sought Adventure" (1939) in *Unknown* and whose late collection *The Leiber Chronicles: Fifty Years of Fritz Leiber* (coll **1990**) ed Martin H. GREENBERG announces his writing lifespan on the cover; and Murray LEINSTER (1896-1975), whose first published sf was "The Runaway Skyscraper" (1919) and whose last was *Land of the Giants No 3: Unknown Danger* (**1969**), a span of 50 years. Among non-genre writers who nevertheless published several books of sf, the prolific Eden PHILLPOTTS (1862-1960) had altogether a 70-year career (1889-1959), and his fantasy writing career ran 54 years from *A Deal With the Devil* (**1895**) to *Address Unknown* (**1949**). Even a comparative youngster, in terms of natural lifespan, like Isaac ASIMOV (1920-1992), whose career began when he was very young with "Marooned Off Vesta" (1939), managed a 50-year span up to the solo novel *Nemesis* (**1989**), and indeed continued to write stories, collaborative novels and articles until only months before his death early in 1992. Robert A. HEINLEIN (1907-1988), even though he began writing quite late, managed 48 years between "Lifeline" (1939) and *To Sail Beyond the Sunset* (**1987**).

The lengths of these professional lives and of others like them are not merely trivial material for the record books. They came about partly because the sf community, made up of writers, editors, publishers, agents, critics and fans, exists *as a community* – a community which, sometimes sentimentally, and in the face of a clear decline in their writing power, cares for its elders (although surprisingly many have continued to write well, Fritz Leiber being a particularly clear example). It is ironic that the literature of the future is, to a degree, in the hands of men and women of the past; and there is no doubt that many young writers, trying to get published, have cursed the names of Asimov or Heinlein, who not only took up valuable space in the bookstores but also, it must have seemed, would *never* stop writing.

The longevity of these careers is matched by the longevity of the texts. There is no other genre which keeps its classic texts in print or focuses on its past with anything like the same selfconscious zeal as sf does. In sf, work dating as far back as the mid-1930s, like the **Lensman** books of E.E. "Doc" SMITH, was still finding new readers in the 1980s. The writers of the GOLDEN AGE OF SF – Asimov, Heinlein, Simak, James BLISH, A.E. VAN VOGT, Ray BRADBURY, Arthur C. CLARKE and many others – are recycled for each generation (though some, like Simak and van Vogt, seem at last to be fading from sight). The same is true of more recent classics (some of them almost 40 years old now) by Jack VANCE, Frank HERBERT, Philip K. DICK and a host of others.

The oddity of this is that contemporary visions of the future exist side-by-side with rivals that, in the context of our century of rapid change, are ancient history. What confuses the issue further is the tendency of sf, like the Worm Ouroboros, to eat its own tail (or its own parents). There is a strangely conservative self-cannibalism in the sf culture, always redigesting "new" ideas which might easily be 60 years old, and this practice is not restricted to its lower echelons. Of all genres, one might expect sf – with its focus on change and the future – to be the one whose cutting edge would be continually resharpened. But, faced with the actual situation, we might cynically propose that sf is more like a wave, whose constituent molecules – the writers working at any one time – are always changing, but which seems as it approaches us to be *exactly the same wave* it was while still distant.

There are good aspects, however, to the longevity of successful sf texts. Sf's generic stability is a function of its past co-existing with its present, and it is for this reason, too, that sf's icons take on such density and richness, so that it has become the most resonant of all popular literatures. Its words and its metaphors and its narrative structures carry not just the burden of yesterday but also that of some of yesterday's excitement (and these images are not static; they slowly grow and change with the years, like a tree).

An sf that was always genuinely new would be intolerable; it would concuss us with future shock. The reward for sf's longevity is that it remains workable; the cost, too often, is that it is also kept familiar and safe.   [PN]

LONGWAY, A. HUGH ◊ Andrew LANG.

LONGYEAR, BARRY B(ROOKES) (1942-   ) US

writer and editor who ran a printing company with his wife before beginning to write in 1977. He soon published his first sf story, "The Tryouts" for *IASFM* in 1978. Before his 1981 hospitalization for alcoholism and addiction to prescription drugs – an experience which forms the basis of the non-sf novel *Saint Mary Blue* (**1988**) – he had already published prolifically, sometimes as by Frederick Longbeard. Most of the short fiction for which he remains best known was soon released, most notably the stories assembled in *Manifest Destiny* (coll **1980**), which explore their shared universe – dominated by a ruthlessly expanding Earth – with considerable intensity. *Enemy Mine* (1979 *IASFM*; **1989** chap dos), which appeared in that volume, won both HUGO and NEBULA and was filmed as ENEMY MINE (**1985**), with the collaboration of David GERROLD, BBL novelized the film version as *Enemy Mine* * (**1985**). In both versions, a human and an ALIEN, caught in the bitter conflict occasioned by human expansion, are isolated together on a primitive planet and must cooperate or die. *The Tomorrow Testament* (**1983**) is a loose sequel to the tale, reiterating in competently extended form its lessons.

At the same time, BBL began to publish his **Circus** sequence – comprising, in order of internal chronology, *City of Baraboo* (coll of linked stories **1980**), *Elephant Song* (**1982**) and *Circus World* (coll of linked stories **1981**) – about the escape of a circus troop from Earth, its misadventures, its colonizing of the planet Momus, and the final triumph of its representatives as an interstellar act. Most of the contents of *It Came from Schenectady* (coll **1984**) had first appeared by 1981. In 1980 BBL won the JOHN W. CAMPBELL AWARD for Best New Writer.

After the gap caused by his hospital experience, BBL returned to active work with a sharp DYSTOPIA about OVERPOPULATION, *Sea of Glass* (**1987**), told from the viewpoint of a child whose birth was illegal but promulgated by the COMPUTER which struggles coldly to deal with the huge excess of humans on the planet. Later novels like *Naked Came the Robot* (**1988**), *The God Box* (**1989**), *Infinity Hold* (**1989**) and *The Homecoming* (**1989**) are variously of interest, but exhibit some intermittent sense of fatigue. At the same time, the alert clarity and genre cunning of BBL's best work seem potentially available to him, and may surface at any point in the 1990s. [JC]

Other works: *Science Fiction Writer's Workshop – I: An Introduction to Fiction Mechanics* (**1980**).

See also: ISAAC ASIMOV'S SCIENCE FICTION MAGAZINE.

LÖNNERSTRAND, STURE [r] ◊ SCANDINAVIA.

LOOKER Film (1981). Ladd Co./Warner Bros. Dir Michael CRICHTON, starring Albert Finney, James Coburn, Susan Dey, Leigh Taylor Young. Screenplay Crichton. 94 mins cut to 90 mins. Colour.

L was intended by Crichton as a comedy, but the studio wanted a suspense thriller, and the result falls confusingly between the two. Three models, after having undergone surgery to make them even more beautiful, are murdered, and the plastic surgeon (Finney) wonders why. Villainous company Digital Matrix, whose employees have guns which create time-lapses in the victims, plans to use computer-generated human images (the murder of their human originals is never explained) in a tv advertising campaign designed to exploit the LOOKER (Light Ocular-Oriented Kinetic Emotive Responses) system for mind-control by hypnosis. *L* seems to be badly cut, since it is full of loose ends and non sequiturs. The sequences of computer imaging are striking, the SATIRE against the advertising business heavy-handed. [PN]

LOOMIS, NOEL (MILLER) (1905-1969) US writer and editor, active in the magazine field for some time, publishing work under his own name and as Benjamin Miller, and a book as by Silas Water. Though his first novel, *Murder Goes to Press* (**1937**), was a thriller, he was most successful as an author of Westerns. In his first sf novel, *City of Glass* (1942 *Startling Stories*; exp **1955**), based on his first sf story, three men are time-warped into a desolate distant future on Earth; "Iron Men" (1945) is a sequel. A second novel, *The Man with Absolute Motion* (**1955**) as by Silas Water, is likewise set in a desolate venue; in this case the Universe is running out of energy. After saving the Universe, the eponymous hero takes an Eve figure back to a depopulated Earth, and plans to breed. [JC]

LOOSLEY, WILLIAM ROBERT [r] ◊ David LANGFORD.

LORAN, MARTIN ◊ John BAXTER.

LORD, GABRIELLE (1946-   ) Australian author, mostly of thrillers, who has been publishing novels since 1980. Her fourth, *Salt* (**1990**), is a routine post-HOLOCAUST novel set in Australia in AD2075, the holocaust having been the product of OVERPOPULATION, POLLUTION and dreadful damage to the ECOLOGY. [PN]

LORD, JEFFREY ◊ Lyle Kenyon ENGEL; Roland GREEN; Ray NELSON.

LORD OF THE FLIES 1. Film (1963). Allen-Hodgdon Productions/Two Arts. Dir Peter Brook, starring James Aubrey, Tom Chapin, Hugh Edwards, Roger Elwin. Screenplay Brook, based on *The Lord of the Flies* (**1954**) by William GOLDING. 91 mins. B/w.

Set in the NEAR FUTURE, the film concerns a group of English schoolboys whose plane crash-lands on a remote island. With two exceptions the boys quickly revert to savagery, resulting in the murder of one of them. *LOTF* can be interpreted in several ways: as a demonstration of the validity of the belief in Original Sin; as a variation on H.G. WELLS's theme that civilization is only skin-deep (also demonstrated by the implication that WWIII is taking place elsewhere); or as an indictment of the English public-school system. It is an honest but "literary" (and not very cinematic) rendition of a story that works better as a novel.

2. Film (1990). Castle Rock Entertainment/Nelson Entertainment/A Jack's Camp/Signal Hill production. Dir Harry Hook, starring Balthazar Getty, Chris Furrh, Daniel Pipoly. Screenplay Sarah Schiff, based on the Golding novel. 90 mins. Colour.

This updated remake (the boys are US rather than UK) is well made, and its less than reverent adherence to its distinguished source does not hurt it. The main adaptation is to modify the hanged pilot of the original into a badly injured pilot who arrives on the island with the boys, crawls into a cave and comes to be regarded as a MONSTER. [JB/PN]

LORDS OF THE DEEP ◊ Roger CORMAN.

LÖRINCZ, LÁSZLÓ L. [r] ◊ HUNGARY.

LORRAH, JEAN (*c*1942-   ) US writer and academic, professor of English at Murray State University in Kentucky. For the sf reader her writing career has perhaps seemed to lack focus, being broken into three areas of concentration. After fan involvement in the **Star Trek** OPEN UNIVERSE, she began publishing sf with the first of her collaborations with Jacqueline LICHTENBERG, *First Channel* (**1980**), a volume in the latter's **Sime/Gen** sequence; though this and *Channel's Destiny* (**1982**) and *Zelerod's Doom* (**1986**) are worthy companions to Lichtenberg's solo efforts, JL was perceived as the junior partner in the enterprise, a perception modified by the publication of her solo venture in the sequence, *Ambrov Keon* (**1986**). Her second area of concentration was the **Savage Empire** series of fantasies concerning MAGIC: *Savage Empire* (**1981**), *Dragon Lord of the Savage Empire* (**1982**), *Captives of the Savage Empire* (**1984**), *Flight to the Savage Empire* (**1986**) with Winston A. Howlett, *Sorcerers of the Frozen Isles* (**1986**), *Wulfston's Odyssey: A Tale of the Savage Empire* (**1987**) with Howlett, and *Empress Unborn* (**1988**). It is with her third focus, novels written for STAR TREK and STAR TREK: THE NEXT GENERATION, that she has become perhaps most identified: *Full Moon Rising* * (**1976** chap), *The Night of the Twin Moons* * (**1976**), *Epilogue, Part 1* * (**1979** chap) and *Epilogue, Part 2* * (**1979** chap), *Jean Lorrah's Sarek Collection* * (coll **1980**), *The Vulcan Academy Murders* * (**1984**) and *The IDIC Epidemic* * (**1988**) are contributions to **Star Trek** proper, and *Survivors* * (**1989**) and *Metamorphosis* * (**1990**) contributions to **Star Trek: The Next Generation.** [JC]

LORRAINE, ALDEN [s] ◊ Forrest J. ACKERMAN.

LORRAINE, LILITH One of at least 5 pseudonyms of Mary Maude Wright (née Dunn) (1894-1967), US writer, poet, editor and radio lecturer, who regularly published sf in the 1930s PULP MAGAZINES. *The Brain of the Planet* (**1929** chap), from Hugo GERNSBACK's **Science Fiction** series, is a FEMINIST socialist UTOPIA, as is her "Into the 28th Century" (1930 *Science Wonder Quarterly*). Her favourite themes included classless societies, revised gender roles and ESP. Between 1937 and 1967 she also edited poetry magazines and wrote much verse, including *Banners of Victory* (coll **1937** chap), *Beyond Bewilderment* (coll **1942** chap), *They* (**1943** chap), *The Day before Judgement* (coll **1944** chap) and *Trailing Clouds of Glory* (coll **1947** chap), *Call on the Rocks 1944-47* (coll **1947** chap); *Let the Patterns Break* (omni **1947**) assembles the previous volumes. The later *Wine of Wonder* (coll **1951** chap) was advertised as being the first volume of POETRY devoted to sf. It

is hard to say that LL had an individual voice, though she did at times effectively translate common poetic idioms into sf terms. In 1940 she founded Avalon, a poetry association. [JD/JC]
About the author: "Empress of the Stars" by Steve Sneyd in *Fantasy Commentator* #43, 1992.

LORRAINE, PAUL House name for CURTIS WARREN used by William Henry BIRD for *Two Worlds* (**1952**), John Russell FEARN for *Dark Boundaries* (**1953**) and John S. GLASBY for *Zenith-D* (**1952**). [PN/JC]

LORY, ROBERT (EDWARD) (1936-   ) US public relations adviser and writer who began publishing sf with "Rundown" for *Worlds of If* in 1963; his stories have been assembled as *A Harvest of Hoodwinks* (coll **1970** dos). His sf novels, mostly light, fantasy-laced adventures, are unambitious but competent; they include *Identity Seven* (**1974**) and *The Thirteen Bracelets* (**1974**). The **Trovo** series – *The Eyes of Bolsk* (**1969** dos) and *Master of the Etrax* (**1970**) – and the **Shamryke Odell** sequence – *Masters of the Lamp* (**1970** dos) and *The Veiled World* (**1972** dos) – are SCIENCE FANTASY of an undemanding sort. [JC]
Other works: 2 horror/fantasy series: the **Dracula** sequence, comprising *Dracula Returns!* (**1973**), *The Hand of Dracula* (**1973**), *Dracula's Brother* (**1973**), *Dracula's Gold* (**1973**), *Drums of Dracula* (**1974**), *The Witching of Dracula* (**1974**), *Dracula's Lost World* (**1974**), *Dracula's Disciple* (**1975**) and *Challenge to Dracula* (**1975**), featuring an immortal Dracula who has survived ATLANTIS; the **Horrorscope** sequence, comprising *The Green Flames of Aries* (**1974**), *The Revenge of Taurus* (**1974**), *The Curse of Leo* (**1974**) and *Gemini Smile, Gemini Kill* (**1975**).

LOST ATLANTIS ◊ *Die* HERRIN VON ATLANTIS.

LOST CONTINENT, THE Film (1968). Hammer/20th Century-Fox. Dir Michael Carreras, starring Eric Porter, Hildegard Knef, Suzanna Leigh, Darryl Read. Screenplay Michael Nash, based on *Uncharted Seas* (**1938**) by Dennis WHEATLEY. 98 mins. Colour.

A ramshackle freighter wanders into the Sargasso Sea and becomes trapped in a "lost continent" of seaweed. Passengers and crew then face the onslaught of various menaces, including a giant octopus, a giant crab, carnivorous seaweed and, finally, a lost race (◊ LOST WORLDS) whose people, descended from Spanish conquistadores, travel in BALLOONS. Bad but enjoyable, wholly absurd; good art direction. [JB/PN]

LOST HORIZON 1. Film (1937). Columbia. Dir Frank Capra, starring Ronald Colman, Jane Wyatt, Sam Jaffe, Edward Everett Horton, H.B. Warner. Screenplay Robert Riskin, based on *Lost Horizon* (**1933**) by James HILTON. 133 mins, cut to 118 mins, then to 109 mins; but full print now available. B/w.

In this memorably sentimental, deft, trite, enormously popular UTOPIAN/LOST-WORLD film set in the Himalayas, survivors of a plane crash find themselves in the mysterious, tranquil city of Shangri-La. It is ruled by the High Lama, a kindly old buffer, who tells them that war and disease do not exist here and that if they remain in the city they will live for ever.

After some time the hero (Colman) leaves with his brother and a Shangri-La woman, who ages with appalling speed away from her home. After a brief return to civilization, Colman realizes that he has abandoned true happiness, and is last seen, hauntingly, struggling through the snow and in long shot, reaching the gate of the forbidden city as the bells ring out and the audience weeps.

2. Film (1973). Columbia. Prod Ross Hunter. Dir Charles Jarrott, starring Peter Finch, Liv Ullman, Sally Kellerman, George Kennedy, Charles Boyer, Michael York. Screenplay Larry Kramer. 150 mins, cut to 143 mins. Colour.

Long, lush, sluggish remake with banal songs (by Hal David and Burt Bacharach) and much stilted dialogue in Hollywood's philosophical vein. The original piece of hokum was orchestrated by Capra with skill and conviction; this unmagical version was a box-office failure. [JB/PN]

LOST IN SPACE US tv series (1965-68). An Irwin Allen Production in association with Van Bernard Productions for 20th Century-Fox Television/CBS. Created Irwin ALLEN, also executive prod. Story consultant Anthony Wilson. Writers included Peter Packer, William Welch, Bob and Wanda Duncan, Carey Wilbur, Barney Slater. Dirs included Harry Harris, Sutton Roley, Nathan Juran, Don Richardson, Sobey Martin. 3 seasons, 83 50min episodes. 1st season b/w; colour from 2nd.

LIS was aimed primarily at children. The Robinsons' spacecraft is sabotaged by an enemy agent, causing them to crash-land on a remote planet. The group consists of the family of 5 – the series was originally to be called *Space Family Robinson* – along with a young male co-pilot (Mark Goddard) and the whining saboteur, Dr Smith, played with comic but sinister effect by Jonathan Harris; the Robinsons were played by June Lockhart, Guy Williams, Angela Cartwright, Marta Kristen and Billy Mumy. There was also a ROBOT, whose catch-phrase was "That does not compute". Though remote, the planet soon became a stopping-off point for practically every space-travelling alien or monster in the Galaxy, each episode seeing the arrival of some new visitor. After the first season the Robinsons got back into space themselves. As the series progressed the young boy (Mumy) and the ambiguous Dr Smith became the central characters, together with the robot, while the others receded more and more into the background. The stories, at first straight sf, became more and more fantastic. *LIS* was probably the most enjoyable of Irwin Allen's many excursions into televised sf. *Lost in Space* ∗ (**1967**) by Dave VAN ARNAM and Ron Archer (Ted WHITE) is a novelization. [JB/PN]

LOST PLANET, THE 1. Film serial (1953). Columbia. Dir Spencer G. Bennet, starring Judd Holdren, Vivian Mason, Ted Thorpe, Forrest Taylor, Michael Fox. Script George H. Plympton, Arthur Hoerl. This 15-part children's series – Hollywood's last sf serial – featured an investigative reporter, a mad SCIENTIST, a

ROBOT and an attempted alien INVASION of Earth. Individual "chapters" had titles like "Blasted by the Thermic Disintegrator" and "Snared by the Prysmic Catapult".

2. UK tv serial (1954). BBC TV. Prod Kevin Sheldon, starring Peter Kerr, Jack Stewart, Mary Law. Script by Angus MacVicar, based on his *The Lost Planet* (**1953**). 6 25min episodes. B/w. This was one of the first sf-related BBC TV serials for children; previously it had been a very popular RADIO serial. An atomic-powered spacecraft takes a group, including one child, to the lost planet of Hesikos. A sequel, *Return to the Lost Planet*, based on MacVicar's *Return to the Lost Planet* (**1954**), was produced the following year. We can find no evidence for the assertion in *The Encyclopedia of TV Science Fiction* (**1990**) by Roger Fulton that MacVicar is a pseudonym of Andre NORTON. [PN/JB]

LOST RACES ◊ ANTHROPOLOGY; LOST WORLDS.

LOST WORLD, THE 1. Film (1925). First National. Dir Harry O. Hoyt, starring Wallace Beery, Lewis Stone, Bessie Love, Lloyd Hughes. Script Marion Fairfax, based on *The Lost World* (**1912**) by Arthur Conan DOYLE. 9700ft (approx 105 mins, cut to 60 mins). B/w, with some tinted sequences.

Wallace Beery makes an unlikely Professor Challenger in this slow-moving, wordy (a large number of dialogue frames) silent version of the famous novel about the discovery of an almost inaccessible South American plateau, a LOST WORLD in which prehistoric creatures, including dinosaurs and apemen, still live. The film is relatively faithful to the book, certainly more so than the 1960 remake (see below), though one departure occurs at the climax when the brontosaurus taken back to London by Challenger to confound the snooty doubters of the Royal Society breaks free and goes on a rampage that ends with the destruction of Tower Bridge (in the book it was a small pterodactyl that escaped), a forerunner of many sequences in later MONSTER MOVIES. The film is interesting chiefly because of its special effects, the work of stop-motion photography pioneer Willis H. O'BRIEN. It was the first feature film to make large-scale use of model animation combined with live action.

2. Film (1960). 20th Century-Fox. Dir Irwin ALLEN, starring Claude Rains, Michael Rennie, Jill St John, David Hedison, Fernando Lamas. Screenplay Allen, Charles Bennett. 97 mins. Colour.

This rather lifeless remake contains all the usual Irwin Allen banalities, with the customary reliance on spectacle to carry the film. The special effects, supervised by L.B. Abbott, are certainly spectacular; this time the various dinosaurs were portrayed using live lizards photographically enlarged, and their death throes, when the plateau is engulfed by volcanic fire, are alarmingly realistic. [JB]

LOST WORLDS This rubric covers lost races, lost cities, lost lands: all the enclaves of mystery in a rapidly shrinking world that featured so largely in the sf of the late 19th and early 20th centuries. This subgenre was obviously a successor to the FANTASTIC VOYAGES of the 18th century and earlier, but there are important distinctions to be drawn. The earlier tales had belonged to a world which was still geographically "open"; at the time Jonathan SWIFT wrote *Gulliver's Travels* (**1726**), Australia had yet to be discovered by Europeans and Africa had yet to be explored. The lost-world story, however, belonged to a cartographically "closed" world: in Jules VERNE's and H. Rider HAGGARD's day unknown territories were fast disappearing. The options were running out, and hence the 19th-century lost lands tended to be situated in the most inaccessible regions of the globe: the Amazon basin, Himalayan valleys, central-Asian and Australian deserts, at the poles, or within the HOLLOW EARTH. These works are also distinguishable from earlier travellers' tales by their much greater "scientific" content. The new sciences of geology, ANTHROPOLOGY and, above all, archaeology had a considerable influence on Verne, Haggard and their successors. For a while, the fiction was concurrent with the reality (at least in the popular mind). From the discoveries of Troy and Nineveh to those of Machu Picchu and Tutankhamun's tomb, there flourished a "heroic age" of archaeology and scientific exploration, of which the fiction was a natural concomitant.

The fiction was often based on PSEUDO-SCIENCE rather than real science, for example the many ATLANTIS stories which followed the success of Ignatius DONNELLY's nonfiction *Atlantis, the Antediluvian World* (**1882**). Tales of undiscovered worlds within the Earth tended to be based on the crackpot geology of John Cleves SYMMES. Perhaps the best of all inner-world fantasies (though not set in a full-scale Symmesian Hollow Earth) is *Voyage au centre de la terre* (**1863**; exp 1867; trans anon as *Journey to the Centre of the Earth* **1872** UK) by Jules Verne, in which explorers reach a subterranean sea by way of an extinct volcano. Other underground lost worlds include LYTTON's *The Coming Race* (**1871**; vt *Vril: The Power of the Coming Race* 1972 US), William N. HARBEN's *The Land of the Changing Sun* (**1894**), John M. LEAHY's *Drome* (1927 *Weird Tales*; **1952**), Stanton A. COBLENTZ's *Hidden World* (1935 *Wonder Stories* as "In Caverns Below"; **1957**) and Joseph O'NEILL's *Land Under England* (**1935**). The Hollow-Earth story "Black as the Pit, from Pole to Pole" (**1977**) by Steven UTLEY and Howard WALDROP is a pastiche of this whole tradition.

The archetypes of the lost-race story are, in the main, unrepentantly romantic. Edgar Rice BURROUGHS was an extensive contributor to the subgenre (with, for example, *The Land that Time Forgot* [1918 *Blue Book*; **1924**] and most of his **Tarzan** novels) but its most famous exponent was a generation earlier: H. Rider Haggard, whose lost-race fantasies include *King Solomon's Mines* (**1885**), *Allan Quatermain* (**1887**), *She* (**1887**) – these two introducing the hugely popular erotic motif of the beautiful queen, or high priestess,

who attempts to seduce the hero – *The People of the Mist* (**1894**), *The Yellow God* (**1908**) and *Queen Sheba's Ring* (**1910**); the publication dates of these novels span the period when the species was in its heyday. Other notable examples are William WESTALL's *The Phantom City* (**1886**), James DE MILLE's *A Strange Manuscript Found in a Copper Cylinder* (**1888**) and Thomas JANVIER's *The Aztec Treasure House* (**1890**). The best-known individual work in the genre may be *The Lost World* (**1912**) by Arthur Conan DOYLE, a perennially popular adventure story about the discovery of surviving prehistoric creatures on a South American plateau (◊ *The* LOST WORLD). The species was popular in the general-fiction pulps but was in decline by the time the first SF MAGAZINES appeared, though lost-world stories by A. MERRITT – *The Face in the Abyss* (1923-30 *Argosy*; fixup **1931**) – and by A. Hyatt VERRILL – *The Bridge of Light* (1929; **1950**) – proved influential on some later sf writers. John TAINE's *The Purple Sapphire* (**1924**) and *The Greatest Adventure* (**1929**) have stronger sf elements than usual, though somewhat vaguely described superscientific technology was common enough in the subgenre. Other authors of lost-race stories include Grant ALLEN, Austyn GRANVILLE, Andrew LANG, William LE QUEUX, John MASTIN, S.P. MEEK, Talbot MUNDY, Hume NISBET, Gordon STABLES, Rex STOUT, E. Charles VIVIAN and S. Fowler WRIGHT.

Even from the 1930s, when fewer lost-world stories were being published, there were occasional popular successes. The film KING KONG (1933) opens in a lost world. James HILTON's mystical Tibetan romance of IMMORTALITY, *Lost Horizon* (**1933**), was a bestseller (◊ LOST HORIZON). Later examples can be found in the work of Dennis WHEATLEY, including *The Fabulous Valley* (**1934**), *Uncharted Seas* (**1938**), which was filmed as *The* LOST CONTINENT, and *The Man who Missed the War* (**1945**).

Only very occasional lost-race novels have appeared since WWII. Ian CAMERON's *The Lost Ones* (**1961**; vt *Island at the Top of the World*) is set in the Arctic and was filmed by Disney as *The Island at the Top of the World* (1974) dir Robert Stevenson. *Stones of Enchantment* (**1948**) by Wyndham MARTYN, *The City of Frozen Fire* (**1950**) by Vaughan WILKINS, *Lost Island* (**1954**) by Graham McINNES and *The Rose of Tibet* (**1962**) by Lionel DAVIDSON seem rather old-fashioned. Gilbert PHELPS's *The Winter People* (**1963**), though, is an intelligent novel about an eccentric South American explorer and his discovery of a remarkable tribe. Stephen TALL's *The People beyond the Walls* (**1980**) is a remarkably late example. Generally, though, postwar lost-race stories edge close to pastiche; several examples are given in the HOLLOW EARTH entry.

The fact that this species of fantasy was so little influenced by scientific thought may be a result of its being largely anachronistic (and therefore implausible) from its beginnings. Once TRANSPORTATION technology had allowed Phileas Fogg to achieve his object, the lost-race fantasy owed more to the desire that enclaves of mystery should exist than to the likelihood that they did. Even from the point of view of sociological or political thought-experiments, the genre had surprisingly little to offer. The lost-race story is obviously an opportunity for the setting up of imaginary UTOPIAS and DYSTOPIAS, but these elements are not as common as might be expected, and most of the stories listed above – which include the best-remembered classics of the genre – are quite straightforward romantic adventure. It has been suggested, too, that such stories allow exercises in imaginary cultural ANTHROPOLOGY, but few of these stories are of any real interest in this respect – an exception being the late example *Providence Island: An Archaeological Tale* (**1959**) by Jacquetta HAWKES – and they have more to offer the student of popular mythology – in which context they are discussed by Brian Street in *The Savage in Literature* (**1975**). Oddly enough there is more and better cultural anthropology in offworld stories of planetary exploration and COLONIZATION OF OTHER WORLDS (mostly postwar), subgenres that largely superseded the lost-race story, than there are in lost-race stories set on Earth.

Science-Fiction: The Early Years (**1990**) by Everett F. BLEILER lists and describes some hundreds of lost-race stories up to 1930, its index allowing a sort by scientific advancement (from barbaric to superscientific), or by location (Antarctic to Siberia), or by racial derivation (from Atlantean via Hebrew and Old Norse to Phoenician). A relevant essay is "Lost Lands, Lost Races: A Pagan Princess of Their Very Own" by Thomas D. CLARESON in *Many Futures, Many Worlds* (anth **1977**) ed Clareson.   [DP/BS/PN]

See also: APES AND CAVEMEN (IN THE HUMAN WORLD); ISLANDS; PASTORAL.

LOTT, S. MAKEPEACE Working name of UK author Stanley Makepeace-Lott (?   -   ), whose *Escape to Venus* (**1956**) is an ORWELL-influenced DYSTOPIAN view of a VENUS colony established 60 years after a 1980 world war.   [JE]

LOTTMAN, EILEEN (1927-   ) US writer of ties, mainly for the *The* BIONIC WOMAN tv series: *The Bionic Woman #1: Welcome Home Jaime* * (**1976**; vt *Double Identity* 1976 UK as by Maud Willis) and *#2: Extracurricular Activities* * (**1977**; vt *A Question of Life* 1977 UK as by Maud Willis). Singleton ties include *The Devil's Rain* * (**1975**) as by Willis and *Through the Looking Glass* * (**1976**) as by Molly Flute.   [JC]

LOUDON, JANE (WEBB) (1807-1858) UK author of many books on popular natural history and gardening, and of *The Mummy! A Tale of the Twenty-Second Century* (**1827**; much rev 1828), published anon. Around a somewhat melodramatic plot – the Mummy of Cheops conspires with a Roman Catholic priest in AD2126 to control the choice of the next Queen of England – JL assembles a number of elaborate speculations about inventions of the future, including mechanical farming, movable housing and weather control, among the more plausible.   [JC]

See also: HISTORY OF SF; NEAR FUTURE; UTOPIAS.

LOVE, ROSALEEN (1940-   ) Australian author, science journalist and lecturer in the history and philosophy of science. RL has been publishing short fiction – not all sf – since 1985, and has won a number of Australian MAINSTREAM awards for her stories. The astringent sf FABULATIONS collected in *The Total Devotion Machine and Other Stories* (coll **1989** UK) are wry, intelligent and often funny; RL's style is straight-faced irony. Her subject matter is often FEMINIST or ecological.   [PN]

See also: AUSTRALIA.

LOVE AND ROCKETS US COMIC book created in 1981 by the brothers Gilbert (1957-   ), Jaime and Mario Hernandez. #1, self-published, featured a 40pp future-apocalyptic chase-thriller, "BEM", by Gilbert; it introduced tail-chasing supersleuth Castle Radium as well as Luba, a continuing star of much of Gilbert's output. Also in #1 were some short pieces by Jaime; one of these, "Mechan-X", introduced the characters Maggie, Hopey and Rand Race, who featured in #2's 40pp story "Mechanics", which told of a group of prosolar mechanics (essentially, super-repairmen) who are trying to fix a crashed rocket-ship in a primordial jungle. Except for later references to Maggie's prosolar job and a brief strip about a little Black girl in outer space ("Rocky"), the sf elements have since disappeared from *LAR* – a fact often regarded by the magazine's enthusiasts as being all to the good. Fantagraphics has published *LAR* since reprinting #1 in 1982, and also brought out Jaime's "Mechanics" as a 3-issue colour comic in 1985.   [SW]

LOVECRAFT, H(OWARD) P(HILLIPS) (1890-1937) US writer who spent almost all his life in Providence, RI, maintaining social contacts mainly by mail. He joined the United Amateur Press Association (◊ APA) in 1914 and produced much of his early fiction in connection with this enterprise, which also allowed him to come in touch with Clark Ashton SMITH, Frank Belknap LONG and others. He began to publish professionally with the serial release of *Herbert West Reanimator* (1922 *Home Brew*; **1977** chap), but only began to establish himself when he started, with "Dagon" (1923), publishing in WEIRD TALES; his prolific correspondence with many other of its writers made him a key influence on that magazine: without his background presence its highly significant contribution to the development of US weird fiction would have been considerably weakened. His disciples included Robert BLOCH, August W. DERLETH, Henry KUTTNER and E. Hoffman PRICE. Derleth, with assistance from Donald WANDREI, founded ARKHAM HOUSE to reprint HPL's work, and the imprint was later to provide a haven for other writers influenced by HPL, including Ramsey Campbell and Brian Lumley. Colin WILSON is another modern writer who has written Lovecraftian novels, notably *The Philosopher's Stone* (**1969**).

Although HPL's primary reputation is as a HORROR writer, his later works – those of his stories belonging to the **Cthulhu Mythos** – attempted to develop a distinctive species of "cosmic horror", employing premises drawn from sf: other DIMENSIONS, INVASION by ALIENS, and interference with human cultural and physiological EVOLUTION. He tried to convey a sense that the Universe is essentially horrible and hostile to humankind by means of a distinctive prose style which extends by gradual degrees from a quasiclinical mode into passages of dense, highly adjectival description. A notable essay by HPL on the historical roots of his fiction is *Supernatural Horror in Literature* (1939; **1945**). HPL encouraged other writers to use the background of the **Cthulhu Mythos**; *The Reader's Guide to the Cthulhu Mythos* (**1969**; rev 1973) by Robert E. WEINBERG and Edward P. Berglund lists many such writers including (in addition to those already cited) Lin CARTER, Robert E. HOWARD, Fritz LEIBER, Robert A.W. LOWNDES and Manly Wade WELLMAN. HPL's principal **Cthulhu Mythos** stories – which include his best works – are "The Nameless City" (1921), "The Festival" (1925), *The Colour out of Space* (1927; **1982** chap), "The Call of Cthulhu" (1928), "The Dunwich Horror" (1929), "The Whisperer in Darkness" (1931), "The Dreams in the Witch-House" (1933), "The Haunter of the Dark" (1936), *The Shadow over Innsmouth* (**1936**), "The Shadow out of Time" (cut 1936; 1939), *At the Mountains of Madness* (cut 1936; 1939; **1990** chap), *The Case of Charles Dexter Ward* (cut 1941; 1943; dated 1951 but **1952** UK) and "The Thing on the Doorstep" (1937).

The first Arkham House HPL collection was *The Outsider and Others* (coll **1939**), which contained all his major works except *The Case of Charles Dexter Ward*, which first appeared in book form in the subsequent Arkham volume *Beyond the Wall of Sleep* (coll **1943**). *Marginalia* (coll **1944**) included some stories HPL had revised for other writers as well as essays, fragments and appreciations; a complete collection of such revisions is *The Horror in the Museum and Other Revisions* (coll **1970**; cut vt *Nine Stories from The Horror in the Museum* 1971; vt in 2 vols as *The Horror in the Museum* 1975 UK and *The Horror in the Burying Ground* 1975 UK; rev and corrected **1989**). HPL's complete works can be obtained in 3 vols: *The Dunwich Horror and Others* (coll **1963**; cut vt *The Colour out of Space, and Others* 1964; full text vt *The Best of H.P. Lovecraft* 1982; corrected text under original title 1985), a title not to be confused with *The Dunwich Horror, and Other Weird Tales* (coll **1945**); *At the Mountains of Madness and Other Novels* (coll **1964**; cut 1968 UK; again cut 1971 US; corrected text under original title 1985); and *Dagon and Other Macabre Tales* (coll **1965**; much cut vt *Dagon* 1967 UK; UK edn again cut, vt *The Tomb* 1969 UK; corrected text of original version 1986). The bibliography of the many other collections drawn from the corpus is inordinately complicated, and is supplemented by many chapbooks recovering all manner of trivia; the most frequently reprinted eclectic selections are *The Haunter of the Dark* (coll **1951** UK), which was a cut version of *Best Supernatural Stories of H.P. Lovecraft* (coll **1945**), both ed Derleth, *The Doom that Came to Sarnath* (coll **1971**) ed Lin Carter

and *Bloodcurdling Tales of Horror and the Macabre: The Best of H.P. Lovecraft* (coll **1982**). Several SMALL PRESSES have been and are dedicated to the celebration of his works, most notably the Necronomicon Press, which publishes the journal *Lovecraft Studies* ed S.T. Joshi, and, since 1990, when it took the title over from Cryptic Publications, the long-running *Crypt of Cthulhu* ed Robert M. Price. Several bibliographies of primary and secondary sources have been published, including Joshi's *H.P. Lovecraft: An Annotated Bibliography* (**1981**). These small presses have given a home to early work by several modern writers of note, including Thomas Ligotti (1953-   ).

Derleth wrote many stories based on fragmentary texts by HPL or on notes for unwritten stories, including the novel *The Lurker at the Threshold* (**1945**), the stories in *The Survivor and Others* (coll **1957**) and 2 stories in *The Shuttered Room and Other Pieces* (coll **1959**; cut 1970 UK), which also contains some HPL juvenilia and essays about him; it is not to be confused with *The Shuttered Room* (coll **1971**). All the Derleth "collaborations" are assembled in *The Watchers Out of Time and Others* (coll **1974**); all but *The Lurker at the Threshold* had been in *The Shadow out of Time and Other Tales of Horror* (coll **1968** UK), along with the 6 which *The Haunter of the Dark* omitted from its parent collection. The Derleth stories are weak exercises in pastiche, and Derleth's editing of HPL's own stories came in for some criticism in the 1980s on the grounds of alleged insensitivity and distortion, necessitating the corrected editions of the 3 Arkham House collections.   [BS]

Other works: This list is selective, not including all small-press publications, nor items of Lovecraftiana containing little or no actual fiction by him: *Fungi from Yuggoth* (coll **1941**), poetry, not to be confused with vt of 1963 collection (see below); *The Lurking Fear* (coll **1947**; vt *Cry Horror!* 1958), not to be confused with either *The Lurking Fear* (coll **1964** UK) or *The Lurking Fear* (coll **1971**), all 3 with differing contents, or with *The Lurking Fear* (1928 *Weird Tales*; **1977** chap), which reprints the story alone; *The Curse of Yig* (coll **1953**); *Dreams and Fantasies* (coll **1962**); *The Dream-Quest of Unknown Kadath* (1943; **1955**), not to be confused with *The Dream-Quest of Unknown Kadath* (coll **1970**) ed Lin Carter; *Something about Cats, and Other Pieces* (coll **1949**), revisions, essays, notes, etc.; *Collected Poems* (coll **1963**; cut vt *Fungi from Yuggoth and Other Poems* 1971); *Selected Letters 1911-1937* (5 vols **1965-76**); *Uncollected Prose and Poetry* (coll **1978**) ed S.T. Joshi and Marc Michaud.

About the author: *Lovecraft: A Look Behind the Cthulhu Mythos* (**1972**) by Lin CARTER; *Lovecraft: A Biography* (**1975**) by L. Sprague DE CAMP; *Howard Phillips Lovecraft: Dreamer on the Nightside* (**1975**) by Frank Belknap LONG; *The Dream Quest of H.P. Lovecraft* (**1978**) by Darrell SCHWEITZER; *The H.P. Lovecraft Companion* (**1977**) by Philip A. Schrefler; *The Major Works of H.P. Lovecraft* (**1977**) by John Taylor Gatto; *H.P. Lovecraft* (**1982**) by S.T. Joshi; *H.P. Lovecraft: A Critical Study*

(1983) by Donald R. Burleson.

See also: ASTOUNDING SCIENCE-FICTION; DEVOLUTION; FANTASY; FANZINE; GAMES AND TOYS; GOTHIC SF; INVISIBILITY; MÉTAL HURLANT; MONSTERS; OPEN UNIVERSE; PARALLEL WORLDS; PARANOIA; PSEUDO-SCIENCE; PSYCHOLOGY; PUBLISHING; SUSPENDED ANIMATION.

LOVEJOY, JACK (1937-   ) US writer with an advanced degree in Roman history who began publishing work of genre interest with *The Rebel Witch* **(1978)**, a fantasy for children. His first sf novels, *Star Gods* (dated 1978 but **1979**) and *The Hunters* **(1982)**, combine sf-adventure routines with some cultural extrapolation. The **Vision of Beasts** sequence – *Creation Descending* **(1984)**, *The Second Kingdom* **(1984)** and *The Brotherhood of Diablo* **(1985)** – is set in a fairly remote post-HOLOCAUST USA, where California has become an archipelago and the mainland is overrun by MUTANTS known as "gunks".   [JC]

Other works: *Magus Rex* **(1983)**, a fantasy; *Black Sky* **(1990)**, a TECHNOTHRILLER; *Guardians of the Three #4: Defenders of Ar* * **(1990)**, a SHARED-WORLD fantasy tie.

LOVELOCK, JAMES (EPHRAIM) [r] ◊ Michael ALLABY; BIOLOGY; ECOLOGY; LIVING WORLDS.

LOVE ROMANCES PUBLISHING CO. ◊ PLANET STORIES; TOPS IN SCIENCE FICTION.

LOVE WAR, THE Made-for-tv film (1970). Paramount/ABC-TV. Dir George McCowan, starring Lloyd Bridges, Angie Dickinson, Harry Basch, Dan Travanti. Screenplay Guerdon Trueblood, David Kidd. 74 mins. Colour.

Six aliens from two warring planets arrive on Earth for a duel to the death to decide which of those planets is the victor. Four are eliminated; one survivor (Bridges) opts to try to stop the fight, remain on Earth, merge with the natives, and have a relationship with a woman (Dickinson). He promises that they will marry as soon as he can overcome the other survivor, whom he knows to be closing in for the kill. The surprise revelation of his fiancée's true identity will not surprise B-movie and sf fans. This is an unpretentious and entertaining sf thriller.   [JB]

LOVIN, ROGER [r] ◊ ROBERT HALE LIMITED.

LOW, A(RCHIBALD) M(ONTGOMERY) (1888-1956) UK academic, inventor and writer, president of the British Interplanetary Society for a period; in 1917 he invented a flying bomb. In his first sf novel, *Adrift in the Stratosphere* (1934 *Scoops* as "Space"; **1937**), a juvenile, the young protagonists accidentally take off in a professor's rocket-ship. In *Mars Breaks Through* **(1937)** a scientist possessed by a Martian can bring about world peace, but seems unwilling to. *Satellite in Space* **(1956)** is a SPACE OPERA in which humans, including an old-time Nazi, meet aliens from the asteroid belt. AML also wrote two nonfiction prognoses, *The Future* **(1925)** and *It's Bound to Happen* **(1950**; vt *What's the World Coming To?* 1951 US).   [JC]

Other works: *Peter Down the Well* **(1933)**, a juvenile.

See also: BOYS' PAPERS.

LOWNDES, ROBERT A(UGUSTINE) W(ARD) (1916-   ) US writer and editor, often referred to as "Doc" Lowndes, a member of the FUTURIANS fan group and collaborator on several stories with other members of the group under the names Arthur COOKE, S.D. GOTTESMAN, Paul Dennis Lavond and Lawrence WOODS. His first story, "The Outpost at Altark" for *Super Science* in 1940, was written in collaboration with fellow-Futurian Donald A. WOLLHEIM, uncredited. For his solo work in the early 1940s RAWL used the names Carol Grey, Mallory Kent, and Richard Morrison; later he added Carl Groener, Wilfred Owen Morley, Robert Morrison, Michael Sherman and Peter Michael Sherman, and once collaborated with James BLISH as John MacDOUGAL.

RAWL edited FUTURE FICTION and SCIENCE FICTION QUARTERLY for Columbia Publications from early 1941 until their demise in 1943, and again throughout their shoestring revival in the early 1950s under various titles. He also edited DYNAMIC SCIENCE FICTION (1952-4) and *Science Fiction Stories* (1954-5) for Columbia Publications, continuing to edit the latter under its new name, ORIGINAL SCIENCE FICTION STORIES, from 1955 until the chain folded in 1960, when he began editing for Health Knowledge Inc. He gradually added a number of fantasy magazines to the latter publisher's line, including *The* MAGAZINE OF HORROR in 1963, *Startling Mystery Stories* in 1966, FAMOUS SCIENCE FICTION in 1966, *Weird Terror Tales* in 1969 and *Bizarre Fantasy Tales* in 1970, but all became defunct in 1970. He was also the editor of the Avalon Books sf line 1955-67.

RAWL wrote a hectic action-adventure novel in collaboration with Blish, *The Duplicated Man* (1953 *Dynamic Science Fiction* as by Blish and Michael Sherman; **1959**), and later edited the posthumous *The Best of James Blish* (coll **1979**). He also produced three solo novels: *The Mystery of the Third Mine* **(1953)**, which is a juvenile, *The Puzzle Planet* **(1961)** and *Believers' World* (1952 *Space* as "A Matter of Faith" as by Michael Sherman; exp **1959**); in the third and most interesting of these, inhabitants of three lost colonies have developed an eccentric RELIGION. His best short stories are H.P. LOVECRAFT-like items such as "The Abyss" (1941) and "The Leapers" (1942 as Carol Grey; rev vt "Leapers" 1968). His literary columns from *Famous Science Fiction* were assembled as *Three Faces of Science Fiction* (coll **1973** chap).   [BS/PN/JC]

LOXMITH, JOHN [s] ◊ John BRUNNER.

L. RON HUBBARD PRESENTS WRITERS OF THE FUTURE Original anthology series, ed Algis BUDRYS, made up of stories by entrants to the WRITERS OF THE FUTURE CONTEST and published by Bridge Publications in the USA and New Era in the UK; both publishing houses were originally set up to publish DIANETICS and SCIENTOLOGY textbooks, but had already begun publishing fiction with the novels of L. Ron HUBBARD's unexpected second career in fiction. The contest is quarterly (though an annual award is given also), and most of the anthology stories are first, second or third place-getters. Some fine writers have made their début in this series (which has survived the controversy surrounding it) – not surprisingly, considering the fairly lavish nature of the awards involved. They include Robert Touzalin (Robert REED), Karen Joy FOWLER, David ZINDELL and Dave WOLVERTON. Anthologies to date, all ed Budrys, are *L. Ron Hubbard Presents Writers of the Future* (anth **1985**), *Vol. II* (anth **1986**), *Vol. III* (anth **1987**), *Vol. IV* (anth **1988**), *Vol. V* (anth **1989**), *Vol. VI* (anth **1990**) and *Vol. VII* (anth **1991**). [PN]

LUCAS, E(DWARD) V(ERRALL) (1868-1938) UK editor and writer, the author of innumerable "weekend" essays and tamely belletristic travel books. Of his several novels, *The War of the Wenuses* (**1898**), with C(harles) L(arcom) Graves (1856-1944), is of interest as a mildly sexist parody of H.G. WELLS's *The War of the Worlds* (**1898**). *Wisdom while You Wait* (**1903**), also with Graves, mocks the future Americanization of the world in the form of a parody encyclopedia. *Mr Pulteney* (**1910** chap) as by E.D. Ward – a pseudonym which is simply EVL's first name – is fantasy, featuring a hotel with an ANTIGRAVITY garden for the use of suicides. Wells and Winston Churchill make appearances. [JC]

LUCAS, F(RANK) L(AURENCE) (1894-1967) UK writer and critic, better known in the latter capacity. Of his fiction, *The Woman Clothed with the Sun and Other Stories* (coll of linked stories **1937**), like much of the work of F. Britten AUSTIN, presents a didactic rendering of mankind's destiny through a story-sequence, in this case extending from AD53 to 1995, ending in an exemplary cleansing of the human species from the world. [JC]

LUCAS, GEORGE (1944-   ) US film-maker. He attended the University of Southern California Film School and as a graduate student made an sf short there entitled *THX 1138:4EB* (1967), which won film festival awards. Working in 1968 as an assistant to Francis Ford Coppola he made a highly praised documentary about the filming of Coppola's *The Rain People* (1969); then in 1969, with Coppola as executive prod, Lucas began a feature-film version, THX 1138 (1971), of his sf short; it was well received by critics but not a popular success. His second feature, *American Graffiti* (1973) – about small-town Californian teenagers in the 1950s – established him as a commercial film-maker. Nonetheless, GL had difficulty setting up his next film – a project he had been planning for several years. His hardships were amply recompensed when it was released as STAR WARS (1977) and had the highest box-office takings of any film to that date.

Star Wars was singly responsible for the sf film boom (and to a lesser extent the literary boom) of the late 1970s and early 1980s, but GL swiftly announced his intention to retire from directing and stick to producing. He has kept that vow, although the films produced under his aegis bear his obvious personal stamp and his directors' personalities are invariably obscured. *The* EMPIRE STRIKES BACK (1980), dir Irvin Kershner, and RETURN OF THE JEDI (1983), dir Richard

Marquand, conclude the trilogy, persistently rumoured to be only the middle section of a 9-film triptych GL has long had on the back burner. There have been frequent suggestions that the next trilogy, tentatively entitled *The Clone Wars*, a prequel to the 3 extant films, is due to go into production, but as of 1992 this seems very unlikely. Lucasfilm (GL's company) has made several spinoffs from the **Star Wars** universe, including the tv movies *The* EWOK ADVENTURE (1984; theatrically released overseas as *Caravan of Courage*) and *Ewoks: The Battle for Endor* (1985). GL sanctioned a new series of **Star Wars** spin-off books in the 1990s, beginning with Timothy ZAHN's *Star Wars: Heir to the Empire* * (**1991**).

Although his partnership with his contemporary and rival Steven SPIELBERG has yielded the three commercially successful borderline-fantasy **Indiana Jones** films, GL has otherwise often had trouble away from the **Star Wars** universe, failing to make much impact with his productions of the banal fairytales *Labyrinth* (1986) dir Jim Henson and *Willow* (1988) dir Ron Howard, and scoring a disastrous miss with *Howard the Duck* (1986; vt *Howard . . . A New Breed of Hero*), an adaptation from the comic books. With Francis Ford Coppola and Michael Jackson, GL made *Captain EO*, a short (viewable only in Disneyland, Disneyworld and the EPCOT Center) employing various sophisticated new techniques and rumoured to have cost over $20 million, despite being only 17 mins long. He has also produced a tv series, *The Young Indiana Jones Chronicles* (begun 1992).

With his pack-rat borrowings from sf, fantasy and Hollywood's past – not to mention his conspicuous espousal of the mythical ideas of Joseph Campbell's *The Hero with a Thousand Faces* (**1949**) – GL undoubtedly opened up the cinema for a wave of big-budget sf movies in the 1980s, even while he ensured that its level remained juvenile. The novelization *THX 1138* * (**1971**) was by Ben BOVA, and the novelization *Star Wars* * (**1976**), attributed to GL, may have been by Alan Dean FOSTER. Many other books have been spun-off from the **Star Wars** trilogy. [KN/PN]

About the film-maker: *Skywalking: The Life and Films of George Lucas* (**1983**) by Dale Pollock.

See also: CINEMA; SWORD AND SORCERY.

LUCENO, JAMES (?   -   ) US writer whose main work has been in collaboration with Brian C. DALEY (*whom see for details*) under the joint pseudonym Jack McKinney, but who has also written two solo sf adventures: *A Fearful Symmetry* (**1989**), a NEAR-FUTURE thriller about the coming of the Millennium and the arrival of ALIENS, and *Illegal Alien* (**1990**), an interplanetary SEX spoof. [JC]

LUCIAN (*c*120-180) Syrian-Greek writer, known also as Lucian of Samosata; born in Samosata, capital of Commagene, in Syria. He early became an advocate and practised at Antioch, but soon set out on the travels which were to help provide the verisimilitude underlying the fantastic surface of some of his works. He visited Greece, Italy and Gaul, studied philosophy in Athens, and eventually became procurator of part of Egypt, where he died. The number of works attributed to him varies with criteria of authenticity, but at least 80 titles have been suggested, some certainly spurious. His works can be subdivided into various categories, some of little interest to the student of PROTO SCIENCE FICTION: works of formal rhetoric, numerous essays, biographies and the prose fictions – which include *The True History* and the possibly spurious *Lucius, or The Ass* – and the series of Dialogues which comprise L's most important work, and to the form of which he gave his name.

The Lucianic Dialogue mixes PLATO's Dialogues, Old and New Comedy, and Menippean Satire into a racy, witty, pungent form ideally suited to the debunking activities with which L is most associated, and which are his most important bequest; his influence on these lines extends from Sir Thomas MORE and Erasmus (?1466-1536) to the dialogue-based SATIRES of Thomas Love Peacock (1785-1866) and others. The Lucianic Dialogue of greatest sf interest is the *Icaro-Menippus*, in which Menippus, disgusted with the fruitless animadversions of Earthly philosophers, acquires a pair of wings and flies first to the MOON, whence he is able to get a literal (i.e., visual) perspective on the nature of mankind's follies, and second to Olympus, where he meets Jupiter and watches that god deal with men's prayers (which arrive fartlike through huge vents). Jupiter proves moderately venal, but does in the end threaten to destroy the acrimonious philosophers who drove Menippus to flight. Other Dialogues of interest include the *Charon*, *Timon*, the 26 *Dialogues of the Gods* and the *Dialogues of the Dead*.

Though less important, the prose fictions are vital proto sf. *The True History* – taking off from the numerous unlikely travellers' tales that proliferated at the time – is an extremely enjoyable and frequently scatological debunking exercise. L travels with 50 companions to the Moon, where they become embroiled in a space war; they then fly past the Sun and back to Earth, where they land in the sea and are soon swallowed by an enormous whale, from which they escape and visit various ISLANDS, where L's fertile imagination piles marvel upon lunatic marvel. With regard to fantasy and the spirit of romance, *The True History* is detumescent. Its influence extends to François RABELAIS and Jonathan SWIFT. *Lucius, or The Ass* is important as a cognate of or original for Apuleius's *The Golden Ass* (cAD200; vt *Metamorphoses*), about a magician's helper who is turned into an ass, suffers much, and is finally retransformed by a goddess. Lucius's picaresque adventures, and the earthy manner of their telling, provided models for picaresque counterattacks on idealistic fiction from Miguel de Cervantes (1547-1616) onwards.

L is vital to that somewhat problematic line of descent of prose fictions which leads eventually to what we might legitimately think of as sf proper. Though he has often been misunderstood as being himself a romancer, he was in fact a consistent (and often savage) debunker of the idiom and ideals of romance. His attitude to the FANTASTIC VOYAGES of his supposed descendants would not have been that of the typical proud father.

There are various translations, the earliest in English being *A Dialog of the Poet Lucyan* (trans **1530** UK); *The Complete Works of Lucian* (trans in 4 vols **1905** UK) is useful. [JC]

About the author: "Lucian's True History as SF" by S.C. Fredericks in SCIENCE-FICTION STUDIES, vol 3, part 1, Mar 1976.

LUCIAN Pseudonym of a UK writer whose *1920: Dips into the Near Future* (1917 *The Nation*; coll of linked stories **1918** chap) sharply examines a UK inherently deformed by years of unending war. [JC]

LUCIE-SMITH, EDWARD [r] ◊ POETRY.

LUDWIG, EDWARD W(ILLIAM) (1920-   ) US writer and publisher whose *The Mask of John Culon* (1970) awakens its protagonist from SUSPENDED ANIMATION into a DYSTOPIA dominated by a repressive RELIGION. *The 7 Shapes of Solomon Bean and 14 Other Marvelous Stories of Science Fiction and Fantasy* (coll **1983**) contains some similar material. [JC]

LUFTPIRAT UND SEIN LENKBARES LUFTSCHIFF, DER ["The Pirate of the Air and his Navigable Airship"] German DIME-NOVEL series, popularly known as **Kapitän Mors der Luftpirat**; it has no connection with a 1948 series of the same name. One of the most popular series of its day, its author or authors are unknown, but well known writers like Oskar Hoffmann (1866-?   ) may have been involved; and, since its adventures take place alternately on Earth and in space, it may have been written by two people. 165 32pp issues were published 1908-11, at first by the Druck- und Verlagsgesellschaft m.b.h. in Berlin and, retitled simply **Der Luftpirat**, from #94 by Verlag Moderner Lektüre, also in Berlin. In 1914 #65-#86 were republished as #1-#22 of the series **Der Fliegerteufel**, published by Verlag P. Lehmann G.m.b.h. in Berlin. During WWI the series was proscribed by the military as "trash". DLUSLL anticipates many SPACE OPERAS, having an interplanetary background – there are numerous adventures with Venusians, Martians, crystal ROBOTS and MONSTERS of all kinds on the planets of the Solar System. Many issues have blueprints of Mors's spaceship on the back cover. Captain Mors, the Man with the Mask, is a Nemo-like fugitive from mankind who, with his crew of Indians, fights against evil. There is a case for calling this the first sf magazine. [FR]

LUKENS, ADAM ◊ Diane DETZER.

LUKODIANOV, ISAI (BORISOVICH) [r] ◊ Evgeny VOISKUNSKY.

LULL, SUSAN [s] ◊ Robert L. FORWARD.

LUNA, KRIS A house name used twice for CURTIS WARREN publications: *Stella Radium Exchange* (**1952**) by David O'BRIEN and *Operation Orbit* (**1953**) by William Henry Fleming BIRD. [JC]

LUNA MONTHLY US FANZINE (1969-77), published by

Frank and Ann F. Dietz from New Jersey, ed Ann F. Dietz, 67 issues, schedule varying from monthly to quarterly, stapled DIGEST-size, litho. *LM* was notable for its professionalism and its exceptionally thorough review coverage, for which it is a useful research tool. Reviews – some by Greg BEAR – were often good; Mark Purcell's column **The International Scene** was consistently well informed. Paul WALKER conducted interesting interviews with sf writers.   [PN]

LUNAN, DUNCAN (ALASDAIR) (1945-   ) Scottish writer, generally of nonfiction books and articles in popular science, with a concentration on space exploration and related topics; titles include *Man and the Stars* (**1974**), *New Worlds for Old* (**1979**) and *Man and the Planets* (**1983**). The first of these presented and supported the hypothesis that historical radio anomalies might best be accounted for in terms of a ROBOT probe from an ALIEN culture parked at one of the Earth-Moon system's LAGRANGE POINTS; the anomalies have now been otherwise explained, but DL's exposition of his case, based on sound science rather than PSEUDO-SCIENCE, does not lack integrity. As an sf writer, DL began publishing stories with "Renaissance" for the *Glasgow University Magazine* in 1964, although his first fully professional sale, "The Moon of Thin Reality", did not appear until 1970 (in *Gal*). In *Starfield: Science Fiction by Scottish Writers* (anth **1989**) DL demonstrated some of the range of sf currently being written in his home country.   [JC/JGr]

LUNDBERG, KNUD (1920-   ) Danish writer whose *Det olympiske håb* (**1955**; trans Eiler Hansen and William Luscombe as *The Olympic Hope* **1958** UK) suggests that the 1996 Olympics might be plagued by the use of DRUGS to improve the performance of athletes.   [JC]

LUNDIN, CLAËS [r] ◊ SCANDINAVIA.

LUNDWALL, SAM J(ERRIE) (1941-   ) Swedish author, editor, critic, translator (of about 400 books, many sf), professional photographer, tv producer, film director, composer, singer (several records) and publisher. His first published work was an sf play for Swedish radio, broadcast in 1952 when he was 11 years old. Enormously active in sf FANDOM since 1956, SJL began selling stories in 1963. His first book was a collection, *Visor i vår tid* (coll **1965**). His next book was sold in SJL's own translation to ACE BOOKS: *Science Fiction: från begynnelsen till våra dagar* (**1969**; exp trans SJL as *Science Fiction: What It's All About* **1971**); it was one of the earlier studies of sf in English.

Beginning 1970, SJL has written a number of novels, 4 of which have been translated into English. In *Alice's World* (**1970** dos US; trans SJL as *Alice, Alice!* **1974** Sweden) a spaceship returning to an abandoned Earth finds it occupied by mythic and literary beings. SJL's SATIRE can be vicious, as in *King Kong Blues* (**1974**; trans SJL as *AD 2018, or The King Kong Blues* **1975** US), about advertising; at other times it is despondent – as in *Bernhards magiska sommar* ["Bernhard's Magical Summer"] (**1974**), the third in a trilogy beginning with *No Time for Heroes* (**1970** dos

US; trans SJL as *Inga Hjältar här* Sweden **1972**) and *Bernhard the Conqueror* (**1973**; trans SJL as *Uppdrag i universum* Sweden **1973**) – or hilarious, as in *Mörkrets furste* ["The Prince of Darkness"] (**1975**), probably his best novel, a burlesque of turn-of-the-century DIME NOVEL SF.

From 1970 he edited the Askild & Kärnekull sf line, thereby reviving Swedish publishing interest in sf. In 1973 he left to form his own house, Delta, which lasted until 1991, specializing in new and reprinted sf, averaging some 20 sf books a year. Under the Delta imprint SJL also edited the revived *Jules Verne-Magasinet*, Sweden's only professional sf magazine (◊ SCANDINAVIA), which in its first incarnation had run 1940-48; it is still published, now under his personal imprint, Sam J. Lundwall Fakta & Fantasi. SJL's careful BIBLIOGRAPHY of sf published in Sweden, both original and translated, is *Bibliografi över science fiction & fantasy, 1741-1973* (**1974**), the 2nd revision of a work which originally appeared in 1962; the sequel is *Bibliografi över science fiction & fantasy, 1974-83* (**1984**). His anthology series **Den fantastika romanen**, 4 vols (1973-4), collects documents of sf history with critical comment. A later 18-vol anthology series ed SJL was **Det hände i morgon** ["It Happened Tomorrow"].

Another work in English is *Science Fiction: An Illustrated History* (**1979** US), which argues the primacy and greater sophistication of European over US sf. SJL's most recent book in English is *The Penguin World Omnibus of Science Fiction* (anth **1986**) ed with Brian W. ALDISS, which in its eclectic, mostly non-US content could be seen as a footnote to his earlier argument.

Among the dozen or so novels SJL has written since 1975, *CRASH* (**1980**) is about the adventures of a Swedish sf author in the US publishing world. His most ambitious project is a series (novels, stories, poems) set in a probabilistic ALTERNATE WORLD, a flat Earth facing dissolution into other probability formats; the scientific underpinning is rooted in quantum physics. Only 3 short stories from the series have been translated into English, "Nobody Here But Us Shadows" (1975 *Gal*), "Take Me Down the River" (1979) and "Time Everlasting" (1986). The central novels of the series are *Fängelsestaden* ["Prison City"] (**1978**), *Flicka i fönster vid världens kant* ["Girl in the Window at the Edge of the World"] (**1980**), *Tiden och Amélie* ["Time and Amélie"] (**1986**), *Gestalter i sten* ["Figures in Stone"] (**1988**), *Frukost bland ruinerna* ["Breakfast in the Ruins"] (**1988**) and *Vasja Ambartsurian* ["Vasja Ambartsurian"] (**1990**).

SJL has been a pivotal figure in Swedish sf as author, editor, publisher, entrepreneur and translator. He updated the SCANDINAVIA entry in this encyclopedia.   [J-HH/PN]
See also: CRITICAL AND HISTORICAL WORKS ABOUT SF; MYTHOLOGY.

LUPOFF, RICHARD A(LLEN) (1935-   ) US writer who worked in computers until he became a full-time writer in 1970. He was first active in sf fandom; the fanzine XERO, which he co-edited with his wife Pat, won a HUGO in 1963. A series of articles therein about COMICS later formed the core of *All in Color for a Dime* (1970), which RAL co-edited with Don Thompson. He contributed a long-running book-review column to the fanzine ALGOL. RAL is also an expert on Edgar Rice BURROUGHS, and as fiction editor of Canaveral Press in the early 1960s he supervised the republication of many of Burroughs's works. His *Edgar Rice Burroughs: Master of Adventure* (1965; rev 1968; rev 1975) is probably the best short introduction; *Barsoom: Edgar Rice Burroughs and the Martian Vision* (1976) is also useful.

After *The Case of the Doctor who Had No Business, or The Adventure of the Second Anonymous Narrator* (1966 chap), a RECURSIVE tale involving Burroughs and Arthur Conan DOYLE's Dr Watson, RAL's first published fiction was the novel *One Million Centuries* (1967; rev 1981), a colourful adventure of the FAR FUTURE in a pastiche style (the object being in this case Burroughs) which would mark most of his career. Pastiche and recursiveness feed naturally into one another, and it is at times difficult, despite his clear and abundant intelligence, to identify a unique RAL voice. His short stories include a series of parodies of other sf writers published in FANTASTIC under the pseudonym Ova Hamlet and assembled as *The Ova Hamlet Papers* (coll 1979 chap); several were earlier incorporated into *Sacred Locomotive Flies* (fixup 1971). He has also used the pseudonym Addison Steele. One of RAL's most notable stories is the satirical "With the Bentfin Boomer Boys on Little Old New Alabama" (in *Again, Dangerous Visions* 1972 ed Harlan ELLISON), which eventually became the fine *Space War Blues* (fixup 1978), a nearly surrealist tale of race wars fought in space between human colonies; it and *Sword of the Demon* (1977), a novel based and styled on Japanese mythology, came very close to giving him a recognizable profile in the field, but his chameleon facility won out, and each new story bore a new facet usually borrowed with a grin. His other 1970s novels are various but insufficiently memorable. *The Triune Man* (1976) deals with the split personality of a comic-strip artist. OVERPOPULATION, ecocatastrophe and sf in-jokes are coped with in *The Crack in the Sky* (1976; vt *Fool's Hill* 1978 UK), shipwreck on a dehydrated planet in *Sandworld* (1976), and a female werewolf in *Lisa Kane* (1976).

Two series dominated the 1980s. The **Twin Planet** books – *Circumpolar!* (1984) and *Countersolar!* (1986) – carry pastiche to the point of MAGIC REALISM. The first, in its depiction of an ALTERNATE-WORLD Earth – with a Symmesian hole ingeniously implanted in the centre of its doughnut shape (◊ HOLLOW EARTH) – has evoked comparisons with the work of James P. BLAYLOCK; historical figures star in a race across the gap. The second less interestingly moves into the 20th century and features a large cast of undifferentiated real people. The **Sun's End** sequence – *Sun's End* (1984) and *Galaxy's End* (1988) with a 3rd vol projected – is

of greater interest, exploiting the fascination with Japanese culture that RAL first showed in *Sword of the Demon* in a complex SPACE-OPERA venue – although this does not prevent a certain amount of nostalgic pastiche of early-20th-century cultural modes and icons. But there still remains in RAL's work a sense of focus frustrated, of ambition deferred.   [MJE/JC]

Other works: *Into the Aether* (1974; rev as graph vt *The Adventures of Professor Thintwhistle and His Incredible Aether Flyer* 1991 with Steve Stiles); *The Return of Skull-Face* (1977), "collaboration" with Robert E. HOWARD; *Nebogipfel at the End of Time* (1979 chap); *Stroka Prospekt* (1982 chap); *The Digital Wristwatch of Philip K. Dick* (dated 1985 but 1986 chap); *Lovecraft's Book* (1985); *The Forever City* (1988); *The Comic Book Killer* (1988), associational; *Philip José Farmer's The Dungeon #1: The Black Tower* * (1988) and *#6: The Final Battle* * (1990).

As Addison E. Steele: Two **Buck Rogers** tv ties, *Buck Rogers in the 25th Century* * (1978) and *That Man on Beta* * (1979).

As editor: *The Reader's Guide to Barsoom and Amtor* (anth 1963 chap); *The Comic-Book Book* (anth 1973) with Don Thompson; *What If? #1: Stories that Should Have Won the Hugo* (anth 1980) and its sequel, *What If? #2* (anth 1981).

See also: CITIES; CYBORGS; SUSPENDED ANIMATION.

LURGAN, LESTER Pseudonym of UK writer Mabel Winfred Knowles (1875-1949), author of various popular novels including *The League of the Triangle* (1911). LL's sf novel, *A Message from Mars* * (1912), based on an 1899 play by Richard Ganthony, may have been used as well as the play in creating the film version, *A MESSAGE FROM MARS* (1913). The story deals with the effects on humans of the arrival of a messenger from MARS with words of good sense about our earthly dilemmas.   [JC]

See also: SATIRE.

LUSTBADER, ERIC [r] ◊ Eric VAN LUSTBADER.

LUTHER, RAY ◊ Arthur SELLINGS.

LUXEMBOURG ◊ BENELUX.

LYDECKEN, ARVID [r] ◊ FINLAND.

LYDECKER, JOHN ◊ Stephen GALLAGHER.

LYMINGTON, JOHN Pseudonym of UK writer John Newton Chance (1911-1983), prolific author of novels and stories, mostly detections, under his real name. His first novels of genre interest were two juvenile fantasies, *The Black Ghost* (1947) and *The Dangerous Road* (1948), both as by David C. Newton; a later sf novel, *The Light Benders* (1968), as by Jonathan Chance, is unremarkable. Under his own name he published the **Bunst** series of children's stories – *Bunst and the Brown Voice* (1950), *Bunst the Bold* (1950), *Bunst and the Secret Six* (1951) and *Bunst and the Flying Eye* (1953) – which deploy sf elements, though casually. His first novel as JL, later made into a film (◊ *The* NIGHT OF THE BIG HEAT), was *The Night of the Big Heat* (1959), about an alien INVASION, and much of his subsequent work constituted a set of variations on the theme of alien or natural menace to Earth, though not at the imaginative level of his predecessors (and likely models), John WYNDHAM and John CHRISTOPHER. JL's use of genuine science is minimal and most of his books (many of which feature MONSTERS) operate at the level of B-grade sf/horror films, where menace strikes unexpectedly in a lazy, rural setting. Some of the better titles of this sort are *The Giant Stumbles* (**1960**), *Froomb!* (**1964**) – probably his best single novel of societal collapse (the title is an acronym for fluid's running out of my brakes) – *The Green Drift* (**1965**), *Ten Million Years to Friday* (**1967**), and *Give Daddy the Knife, Darling* (**1969**). He wrote with some verve but little style, and there are many clichés of character. His short stories, collected in *The Night Spiders* (coll **1964**), are routine. It might be said that JL's main deficiency as a writer of sf was a lack of interest in the forward thrust of the genre; he was, at heart, a HORROR writer. [JC/PN]

Other works: *The Grey Ones* (**1960**); *The Coming of the Strangers* (**1961**); *A Sword Above the Night* (**1962**), assembled with *The Grey Ones* as (omni **1978** US); *The Sleep Eaters* (**1963**); *The Screaming Face* (**1963**); *The Night Spiders* (**1964**); *The Star Witches* (**1965**); *The Nowhere Place* (**1969**); *The Year Dot* (**1972**); *The Sleep Eaters* (**1973**); *The Hole in the World* (**1974**); *A Spider in the Bath* (**1975**); *The Laxham Haunting* (**1976**); *Starseed on Gye Moor* (**1977**); *The Waking of the Stone* (**1967**); *A Caller from Overspace* (**1979**); *Voyage of the Eighth Mind* (**1980**); *The Power Ball* (**1981**); *The Terror Version* (**1982**); *The Vale of Sad Banana* (**1984**).

LYNCH, (JOHN GILBERT) BOHUN (1884-1928) UK writer and caricaturist in whose *Menace from the Moon* (**1925**) – which blends interplanetary, LOST-WORLD and future-WAR themes – descendants of a MOON colony established by 17th-century Europeans attack the Earth with heat-rays. It contains many references to the works of Bishop John WILKINS. [JE]

Other work: *A Muster of Ghosts* (anth **1924**; vt *The Best Ghost Stories 1924* US), ed.

See also: INVASION.

LYNCH, FRANCES ◊ D.G. COMPTON.

LYNDS, DENNIS (1924-   ) US editor and writer whose sf consists of 2 sf adventures as by Michael Collins – *Lukan War* (**1969**) and *The Planets of Death* (**1970**) – and several late contributions under the house name Maxwell Grant to the **The Shadow** book sequence, earlier titles in which had been mainly reprints of lead novels from the pulp magazine *The Shadow* (1931-49), mostly by Walter B. Gibson (also as Grant). DL's additions followed on from Gibson's last contribution to the series (*Return of the Shadow* * [**1963**]): *The Shadow Strikes* * (**1964**), *Shadow Beware* * (**1965**), *Cry Shadow!* * (**1965**), *The Shadow's Revenge* * (**1965**), *Mark of the Shadow* * (**1966**), *Shadow Go Mad* * (**1966**), *The Night of the Shadow* * (**1966**) and *Destination Moon* * (**1967**). [JC]

LYNN, ELIZABETH A. (1946-   ) US writer who began publishing work of genre interest with "We All Have to Go" for *The Berkley Showcase* (anth **1976**) ed Victoria Schochet and John SILBERSACK. This was assembled with other early work in *The Woman who Loved the Moon and Other Stories* (coll **1981**). Her early sf stories and her first novel, *A Different Light* (**1978**), share certain assumptions about the nature of the Universe, including the existence of HYPERSPACE, used here both to facilitate storytelling and as an existential cusp for her protagonists – like the cancer-stricken artist in the novel, who must decide whether or not to seize the day by travelling where he needs to go by hyperspace, even though such travel will mortally intensify his illness. In her second and best-received novel, *The Sardonyx Net* (**1981**), EAL applies a similar ironic torsion to a tale whose moral premises seem initially unproblematic – slavery is bad for a planet, drugs are bad for society, sadism is bad for the soul – but which become significantly less clearcut in the telling. Although the slavery which obtains in one mercenary planet in the Galaxy is never justified, its operations are seen as complexly interactive; and the sadism of the captain and slavetrader turns out to express so vividly his violated inner state that he almost becomes the protagonist of the book. Most of her remaining work – including the effective **Chronicles of Tornor** sequence, comprising *Watchtower* (**1979**), *The Dancers of Arun* (**1979**) and *The Northern Girl* (**1980**) – has been fantasy, and as the 1980s progressed she wrote less and less sf. Given the sophisticated use to which she has put conventional sf-adventure plots and venues, this slow departure seems most regrettable. [JC]

Other works: *The Red Hawk* (**1984** chap); *The Silver Horse* (**1984**), a fantasy for children; *Tales from a Vanished Country* (coll **1990**), stories all previously published in earlier volumes.

LYNN, GREY (?   -   ) UK writer (possibly pseudonymous) whose *The Return of Karl Marx* (**1941**) features the rising of the philosopher from his grave by unexplained means. After exposure to the degenerate UK of 1940 he returns, sadly, to his place of rest. [JC]

LYON, JOHN ◊ Christopher EVANS.

LYON, LYMAN R. [s] ◊ L. Sprague DE CAMP.

LYON, RICHARD K. ◊ Andrew J. OFFUTT.

LYONS, DELPHINE C. ◊ Evelyn E. SMITH.

LYTTON (EDWARD GEORGE EARLE LYTTON BULWER), FIRST BARON (1803-1873) UK writer, known as Edward Bulwer until 1838, when he became Sir Edward Bulwer. He became Sir Edward Bulwer-Lytton in 1843 when he succeeded to the Knebworth estate on his mother's death. His name is often rendered as Sir Edward Bulwer-Lytton, or simply as Bulwer Lytton; the standard editions of his collected works give his name as Lord Lytton. He became Colonial Secretary in 1858-9 (he signed the documents creating British Columbia and Queensland), and was raised to the peerage as First Baron Lytton in 1866.

As a writer, he was most significant for such fashionable and trendsetting novels as *Pelham* (**1828**), though he is best remembered for *The Last Days of Pompeii* (**1834**). He was versatile and prolific in several genres, and his collected works fill over 110 volumes. His powerful interest in the occult, or more specifically in doctrines associated with the Rosicrucians, surfaces throughout his work, becoming explicit in *Zanoni* (**1842**) and *A Strange Story* (**1862**; rev 1863), which feature ruminations on the proper route to the attainment of the elixir of life and on other occult themes. *The Haunted and the Haunters, or The House and the Brain* (1859 *Blackwood's Magazine*; **1905** chap) is a more convincing haunted-house tale which qualifies as marginal sf through its quasiscientific explanations in terms of mesmerism (animal magnetism). His sf novel is *The Coming Race* (**1871**; vt *Vril: The Power of the Coming Race* 1972 US), a UTOPIA set in an underground LOST WORLD inhabited by an evolved form of *Homo sapiens*, larger and wiser than surface dwellers. This race derives its moral and physical virtue from vril, an electromagnetic form of energy of universal utility which fuels flying machines and automata, and even makes telepathy possible. (The UK beef-tea Bovril took its name from vril.) Females of the Vril-ya are superior to men, a circumstance which shapes the book's thin plot. A human visitor from the surface is condemned to death for eugenic reasons but two women fancy him, taking the initiative as is normal for Vril-ya; with the aid of one of them he escapes to tell his tale. He understands little of his superiors' lives, however, and masters nothing of their arts and sciences. Soon, it is clear, the world above will be visited in turn and *Homo sapiens* will be exterminated. Lytton's lack of horror at science, and the professionalism of his text, help explain the extremely wide influence of *The Coming Race*, which is one of the seminal sf texts before the age of H.G. WELLS.   [JC]

Other works: *Asmodeus at Large* (**1833**); *Godolphin* (**1833**); *The Pilgrims of the Rhine* (coll **1834**), which contains "The Fallen Star", perhaps the first story to consider primitive Man from an ethnographic point of view; *The Student* (coll **1835**).

About the author: *Strange Stories, and Other Explorations in Victorian Fiction* (**1971**) by Robert Lee Wolff; *Gothic Immortals: The Fiction of the Brotherhood of the Rosy Cross* (**1990**) by Marie Roberts.

See also: ANONYMOUS SF AUTHORS; DIME-NOVEL SF; GOTHIC SF; HISTORY OF SF; HOLLOW EARTH; POWER SOURCES; PROTO SCIENCE FICTION; PSEUDO-SCIENCE.

McALLISTER, ANGUS (?   -   ) Scottish writer whose first novel, *The Krugg Syndrome* (**1988**), briefly conceals the mild-mannered and amusing tale of a country boy in the big city by suggesting for a few pages that his personality has been replaced by that of a telepathic alien. AM's second novel, *The Canongate Strangler* (**1990**), plays more darkly with Doppelgänger themes in a tale of possession, murder and (once again) ESP. [JC]

McALLISTER, BRUCE (HUGH) (1946-   ) US writer, editor and academic, director since 1974 of the creative-writing programme at the University of Redlands, California, and Professor of English from 1983. He has written at least 40 stories since starting to publish sf in 1963 with "The Faces Outside" (for *If*), which is also the title story of a long-projected collection of his best work. "The Boy" (1976) – a peculiarly revolting, skilful tale of the entropic life of a reconstructed Peter Pan and Wendy on a less than utopian ISLAND – is an exercise about, and to some extent in, literary sadism, which at the same time gives exemplary form to his ongoing obsessions with psychic and physical entrapment and with the alienation of human beings in worlds they have not made. His first novel, *Humanity Prime* (**1971**), which takes some material from "The Faces Outside" and was used as his thesis for an MFA degree in creative writing, ingeniously depicts the complex underwater environment of the planet Prime, where humans have, after 3000 years, become deeply adapted to their aquatic life; they cope with both the demented CYBORG starship which brought them there and an incursion of reptile-like aliens. His second novel, the elegant and incandescent *Dream Baby* (**1989**), is set in Vietnam during the darkest years of US involvement there, and recounts the long excruciation of a nurse whose paranormal power (she has precognitive dreams about the deaths of soldiers: the title is an imperative) leads her, under the control of a secret military unit, into the heart of the darkness.

BM edited *SF Directions* (anth **1972**), the special sf issue of the New Zealand journal *Edge* (Autumn/Winter **1973**), which comprised a sizeable anthology of original stories, and the fine *Their Immortal Hearts* (anth **1980**), to which he contributed the title novella. Because his first novel was published in a dying series (it was a late **Ace Special**), because his second novel speaks unrelentingly of painful matters, and because his shorter work remains scattered, BM continues to be relatively obscure long past the point at which he should have attained considerable prominence. [JC]

About the author: *The Work of Bruce McAllister: An Annotated Bibliography & Guide* (**1985** chap; rev **1986**) by David Ray Bourquin.

See also: IMMORTALITY; WAR.

MAC AND ME ◊ *The* PHILADELPHIA EXPERIMENT.

MacAPP, C.C. Pseudonym used by US colour printer Carroll M. Capps (?1917-1971) in his writing career, which began – after illness forced his retirement – with "A Pride of Islands" in 1960 for *If*, with which magazine (and its stablemates) he was associated for the balance of his short career. Much of his fiction concerns itself with alien-INVASION themes, notably the **Gree** stories (in *If* and *Worlds of Tomorrow* 1965-6) and his first novel, *Omha Abides* (1964-6 *Worlds of Tomorrow*; fixup **1968**), in which a long-lasting alien occupation is opposed by Terrans whose Native-American nature finds expression also in CCM's most ambitious novel, *Worlds of the Wall* (1964 *Fantastic*; exp **1969**), an intriguing adventure of initiation and self-fulfilment set in a strange other-dimensional world. Though most of his work skimps character development in favour of action-oriented plots, CCM's last novel, *Bumsider* (**1972**), pays more attention to the development of his cast's personalities. In general he wrote clearly and excitingly, and his range was still growing at the time of his death; the early truncation of his career was much regretted. [JC]

Other works: *Prisoners of the Sky* (1966 *If*; exp **1969**);

Secret of the Sunless World (**1969**) as Carroll M. Capps; *Recall Not Earth* (**1970**); *Subb* (**1968** *If*; fixup **1971**).

McARTHUR, JOHN ◊ Arthur WISE.

MacAULAY, DAVID (ALEXANDER) (1946-   ) US writer, much of whose work, beginning with *Cathedral: The Story of its Construction* (**1973**), has concentrated on architectural subjects, a focus reflected in *Unbuilding* (**1980** chap), which depicts in pictures and text the hypothetical demolition of the Empire State Building. Of more specific sf interest are *Motel of the Mysteries* (graph **1979** UK), a comic FABULATION whose surreal twists cleverly evoke displaced worlds, and *Baaa* (**1985** chap), a fantasy SATIRE in which sheep take over the world. [JC]

MACAULAY, (EMILIE) ROSE (1881-1958) UK author of 23 novels from 1906, the most famous being her last, *The Towers of Trebizond* (**1956**). Some of these books – like *And No Man's Wit* (**1940**), in which a mermaid appears – venture edgily into fantasy. *What Not: A Prophetic Comedy* (**1918**; libellous passages cut 1919), set several years after the conclusion of WWI, depicts the coming to power in the UK of an autocratic government designed to counter postwar crises. (Although copies exist of the 1918 version, which portrays a newspaper proprietor attempting political blackmail, it may never have been officially released.) *Mystery at Geneva: An Improbable Tale of Singular Happenings* (**1922**) is set in an undefined NEAR FUTURE where a monarchist counter-revolution has replaced the Bolsheviks in Russia and a reporter (a woman in drag) helps save the League of Nations from a conspiracy designed to restore communism. *Orphan Island* (**1924**) is a borderline UTOPIA (*see also* ISLANDS) set in the 19th and 20th centuries and satirizing conventional Victorian social and sexual mores. [JC]

About the author: *Rose Macaulay: A Writer's Life* (**1991**) by Jane Emery.

See also: POLITICS.

McAULEY, PAUL J. (1955-   ) UK biologist and writer. He began publishing sf with "Wagon, Passing" for *IASFM* in 1984; his best shorter work is collected in *The King of the Hill and Other Stories* (coll **1991**). With his first novel, *Four Hundred Billion Stars* (**1988** US), he launched conspicuously into a far-reaching series which, combining SPACE-OPERA plots and cosmological speculations, fruitfully amalgamated influences from both US and UK traditions: H.G. WELLS and Larry NIVEN consort, sometimes uncomfortably, in these tales of interstellar warfare, world-building and universe-creation. Further volumes are *Of the Fall* (**1989** US; vt *Secret Harmonies* 1989 UK) and the very substantial *Eternal Light* (**1991**), which best exemplifies to date PJM's control over the instruments of 1990s HARD SF: wormholes, agathics to forestall death, GENETIC ENGINEERING and cosmogony on the hugest scale. The series itself ostensibly concerns the attempts of an almost fatally wearied corporation-run Earth – reminiscent of Cordwainer SMITH – to fend off the panicked aggressions of an ancient starfaring species, itself hiding from enemies of its own ilk; but the pleasures of this ongoing sequence seem more and more to lie in the increasingly comprehensive physical history of the entire Universe adumbrated in *Eternal Light*. PJM is potentially a major writer of his form of sf. [JC]

Other work: *In Dreams* (anth **1992**) with Kim NEWMAN.

See also: ALIENS; AMAZING STORIES; BLACK HOLES; COLONIZATION OF OTHER WORLDS; CYBORGS; DISCOVERY AND INVENTION; ECOLOGY; EVOLUTION; GAMES WORKSHOP; INTERZONE; METAPHYSICS; OPTIMISM AND PESSIMISM; PARANOIA; PHILIP K. DICK AWARD; WOMEN AS PORTRAYED IN SCIENCE FICTION.

MacAULEY, ROBIE (MAYHEW) (1919-   ) US writer, active as a non-genre story writer from 1947 but almost certainly best known for his first novel, *The Disguises of Love* (**1952**). His second, *A Secret History of Time to Come* (**1979**), sf, displays some literary finesse in traversing a post-DISASTER terrain, but is unoriginal. [JC]

MacAVOY, R(OBERTA) A(NN) (1949-   ) US writer, primarily of FANTASY – which tends to be quirky, well written and scholarly about historical detail – and of one sf novel. Her first book, *Tea with the Black Dragon* (**1983**), is a witty contemporary fantasy about the friendship that grows between a middle-aged woman musician and an ageless Oriental who is probably the human incarnation of a dragon. The sequel was *Twisting the Rope: Casadh an t'Súgáin* (**1986**). The **Trio for Lute** trilogy – *Damiano* (**1983**), *Damiano's Lute* (**1984**) and *Raphael* (**1984**), collected as *A Trio for Lute* (omni **1985**) – is set in an ALTERNATE-WORLD Renaissance Italy, France and Moorish Spain where MAGIC works. *The Book of Kells* (**1985**) features time-travel from the present day to a god-frequented 10th-century Ireland. *The Grey Horse* (**1987**), also set in Ireland (Connemara in the late 19th century), is a finely told, complex romance about local resistance to the Land League, featuring a *púca*, or fairy-horse.

RAM's sf novel is *The Third Eagle* (**1989**), an entertaining romance about a naïve Native-American warrior's learning experiences on a variety of planetary and spacecraft venues; though promising, it is less focused than most of her fantasy. RAM returned to fantasy with the ongoing **Lens of the World** trilogy, to date comprising *Lens of the World* (**1990**) and *King of the Dead* (**1991**): more coming-of-age material set in an imaginary medieval world. RAM has become an important fantasist, especially in the unfamiliarity of her material, which has enlivened a genre specializing all too often in retreads. [PN]

See also: JOHN W. CAMPBELL AWARD; PHILIP K. DICK AWARD.

McBAIN, ED ◊ Evan HUNTER.

McBAIN, GORDON (DUNCAN III) (1946-1992) US teacher and writer who, in his brief sf career, wrote the moderately appealing but unremarkable **Exoterra** young-adult sf series: *The Path of Exoterra* (**1981**) and *Quest of the Dawnstar* (**1984**). [JC]

McCAFFREY, ANNE (INEZ) (1926-   ) US writer,

now living in Ireland. Most of her work is sf, though tinged with the tone and instruments of FANTASY. She began publishing with "Freedom of the Race" for Hugo GERNSBACK's *Science Fiction Plus* in 1953, but became active only a decade or so later with her first novel, *Restoree* (**1967**), which rather conventionally, though with tongue in cheek, tells the story of a young woman who is flayed alive by alien flesh-eaters, is saved, and with her skin restored has some adventures. Soon AM began publishing the linked novels and stories that have made her reputation as a writer of romantic, heightened tales of adventure explicitly designed to appeal – and to make good sense to – a predominantly female adolescent audience.

Her major series is set in a long-lost Earth colony, **Pern**, a world whose humans, symbiotically pair-bonded with tame, time-travelling, telepathic and telekinetic dragons, engage in high adventures and defend the planet from the poisonous Threads. It comprises several shorter units: *Dragonflight* (fixup **1968**) (containing the 1968 HUGO-winner "Weyr Search" and the 1968 NEBULA-winner "Dragon Rider"), *Dragonquest* (**1971**) and *The White Dragon* (**1978**) are assembled as *The Dragonriders of Pern* (omni **1978**); *Dragonsong* (**1976**), *Dragonsinger* (**1977**) and *Dragondrums* (**1979**), which are juveniles, are assembled as *The Harper Hall of Pern* (omni **1979**); *Moreta, Dragonlady of Pern* (**1983** UK; exp **1983** US) and *Nerilka's Story* (**1986**) are closely connected. Further titles include *Dragonsdawn* (**1988**), a prequel to the overall sequence, which is directly followed by *The Renegades of Pern* (**1989**) and *All the Weyrs of Pern* (**1991**). *A Time When: Being a Tale of Young Lord Jaxom, his White Dragon Ruth, and Various Fire-Lizards* (**1975** chap) is connected to the series; *Dragonflight* (graph **1991**) is the first of a projected series of graphic-novel versions of the material. Though the tone is that of fantasy, the premises underlying **Pern** are orthodox sf; even the dragons turn out to have been bio-engineered eons previously by humans as a defence against a vacuum-traversing spore. *The Dragonlover's Guide to Pern* (**1989**) with Jody Lynn Nye (1957-   ) may be of assistance to readers.

Other series include: the **Pegasus** or **Talents** books – *To Ride Pegasus* (fixup **1973**), which deals with a corps of parapsychological investigators in the near future and is notable for its political conservatism, *Pegasus in Flight* (**1990**), these two being assembled as *Wings of Pegasus* (omni **1991**) – the **Ireta** books – *Dinosaur Planet* (**1978** UK) and *Dinosaur Planet Survivors* (**1984**), both being assembled as *The Ireta Adventure* (omni **1985**) – the **Killashandra** tales – *The Crystal Singer* (**1974-5** *Continuum* ed Roger ELWOOD; fixup **1982** UK), *Killashandra* (**1985**), and *Crystal Line* (**1992**) and the **Planet Pirates** books – *Sassinak* (**1990**) with Elizabeth MOON, *The Death of Sleep* (**1990**) with Jody Lynn Nye, and *Generation Warriors* (**1991**) with Moon; the **Rowan** sequence, comprising *The Rowan* (**1990**) and *Damia* (**1992**), features a powerful female telepath

who engages in adventures and much sex with an even more powerful male telepath named Jeff Raven.

AM's early singletons include *Decision at Doona* (**1969**) – disappointingly sequeled much later by *Crisis on Doona* (**1992**) with Jody Lynn Nye – and *The Ship who Sang* (fixup **1969**) – unexcitingly sequeled by *PartnerShip* (**1992**) with Margaret Ball (1947-   ) and *The Ship who Searched* (**1992**) with Mercedes Lackey (1950-   ) – the two 1969 books being assembled with *Restoree* as *The Worlds of Anne McCaffrey* (omni **1981** UK). Though less popular than the **Pern** books, these (the sequels excepted) are perhaps more clearly inventive. *The Ship who Sang*, for instance, intriguingly presents a deformed girl who is grafted into a SPACESHIP (◊ CYBORGS) and in effect becomes the ship; the emotional difficulties facing a musical lady spaceship are many (◊ MUSIC). Later singletons, like *The Coelura* (**1983** chap) – strangely assembled with *Nerilka's Story* from the **Pern** sequence as *Nerilka's Story & The Coelura* (omni **1987**) – tend to downgrade their sf premises in favour of romance. AM's stories, including some connected work, have been collected in *Get Off the Unicorn* (coll **1977**). Though her work has been criticized as oversentimental, AM is among the most popular writers in her particular subgenre. [JC]

Other works: *The Mark of Merlin* (**1971**), *Ring of Fear* (**1971**) and *The Kilternan Legacy* (**1975**), none sf or fantasy, and all assembled as *Three Women* (omni **1990**); *The Smallest Dragonboy* (**1982** chap Ireland); *Stitch in Snow* (**1984** Ireland) and *The Year of the Lucy* (**1986** Ireland), neither being sf or fantasy; *The Girl who Heard Dragons* (**1985** chap); *Habit is an Old Horse* (coll **1986** chap); *The Lady* (**1987**; vt *The Carradyne Touch* **1988** UK), a romance; *Rescue Run* (**1991** chap), an sf novella.

As editor: *Alchemy & Academe* (anth **1970**); *Cooking Out of This World* (anth **1973**), a collection of recipes supplied by various sf writers.

About the author: *Anne McCaffrey, Dragonlady and More: A Working Bibliography* (latest rev **1989** chap) by Gordon BENSON Jr and Phil STEPHENSEN-PAYNE.

See also: ARTS; COLONIZATION OF OTHER WORLDS; DEL REY BOOKS; PLANETARY ROMANCE; PSI POWERS; SCIENCE FANTASY; WOMEN AS PORTRAYED IN SCIENCE FICTION; WRITERS OF THE FUTURE CONTEST.

McCANN, ARTHUR [s] ◊ John W. CAMPBELL Jr.

McCANN, EDSON Pseudonym used by Frederik POHL and Lester DEL REY on the novel *Preferred Risk* (**1955**), hurriedly written for a GALAXY SCIENCE FICTION novel competition because no acceptable submission had been received. Cast in the same mould as Pohl's and C.M. KORNBLUTH's *The Space Merchants* (**1953**), it features a world dominated by insurance companies. [BS]

See also: SATIRE.

McCARTHY, SHAWNA (?   -   ) US editor who served 1983-5 as editor of ISAAC ASIMOV'S SCIENCE FICTION MAGAZINE and 1985-8 as sf editor of BANTAM BOOKS. For *IASFM* she produced 4 anthologies: *Isaac*

Asimov's Wonders of the World (anth **1982**), *Isaac Asimov's Aliens & Outworlders* (anth **1983**), *Isaac Asimov's Space of Her Own* (anth **1984**; vt *Isaac Asimov's Space of Your Own* 1984 UK; cut under original title 1989) and *Isaac Asimov's Fantasy!* (anth **1985**; cut 1990). With Lou ARONICA of Bantam she was involved in the FULL SPECTRUM original-anthology series, editing *Full Spectrum* (anth **1988**) with Aronica and *Full Spectrum 2* (anth **1989**) with Aronica, Patrick LoBrutto and Amy Stout. [JC]

McCAY, (ZENAS) WINSOR (1867-1934) US COMIC-strip artist and creator of animated cartoons, of seminal importance in both fields. His earliest years were obscure (it is not known where he was born; his name is sometimes given as Winsor Zenic McCay, and his year of birth as 1869 or 1871), but by 1889 he was employed in Chicago as an engraver in a printing firm, and during the 1890s he worked as a freelance poster painter and as an in-house artist at Cincinnati's Vine Street Dime Museum before, in 1898, starting his newspaper career by doing editorial cartoons for the *Cincinnati Commercial Tribune*. By 1900 WM had switched papers and was drawing his first comic strip, **Tales of the Jungle Imps**, signed Felix Fiddle.

His new interest in strips and success as a cartoonist for *Life* led to his moving in 1902 to New York, where he began to work for the two New York papers owned by James Gordon Bennett (1841-1918): the *New York Herald* as WM and the *New York Telegram* as "Silas". A cascade of humorous allegories followed, including **A Pilgrim's Progress by Mr Bunion**, **Hungry Henrietta**, **Poor Jake** and **Little Sammy Sneeze**. 1904 saw the début of WM's nightmarish **Dreams of the Rarebit Fiend**, which carried its characters into a variety of very frightening dyspepsia-generated dream experiences; it appeared in book form as *Dreams of a Rarebit Fiend* (graph coll **1905**; rev 1973). The success of this strip inspired his masterpiece, **Little Nemo in Slumberland**, which appeared in the *New York Herald* (1905-11), then for William Randolph Hearst papers under the title *In the Land of Wonderful Dreams* (1911-14), then for the *Herald-Tribune* (1924-7) under the original title. The first sequence was the most innovative and inspired, and soon selections were reprinted as *Little Nemo in Slumberland* (graph coll **1909**). Later titles included an adaptation by Edna Sarah Levine, *Little Nemo in Slumberland* ∗ (**1941**) illus WM, and *The Complete Little Nemo in Slumberland* (graph coll **1989-90**) ed Richard Marschall, a definitive version in 4 vols of the 1905-11 strip, reproducing the original colours; a 5th vol, *The Complete Little Nemo in Slumberland: In the Land of Wonderful Dreams* (graph coll **1991**), also ed Marschall, reprinted the 1911-12 strips from the second sequence. Many of the first-sequence episodes – all drawn in WM's florid, hallucinatory, meticulously crafted, architectonic, poster-like Art Nouveau style – were straightforward dream fantasies; but later sustained sequences – like those dealing with Shantytown, with Befuddle Hall,

and with a voyage by airship into outer space during 1909 – intermittently displayed an sf-like verisimilitude; as pioneering explorations into the techniques of narrating complex visions through sequential drawings, the strip as a whole was of vital importance.

While busy with *Little Nemo*, WM was also able to continue with other graphic work, including many individual drawings, those making up the *Spectrophone* series of visions of the future being of particular sf interest. After he moved to Hearst, he began concentrating on political cartoons from a conservative point of view; but continued to issue enormously detailed prophetic drawings involving vast airships, cityscapes and catastrophes. Some of these have been assembled as *Daydreams & Nightmares: The Fantastic Visions of Winsor McCay* (graph coll **1988**) ed Richard Marschall.

WM also took a central role in the development of the animated cartoon – indeed, some claim that he invented the art of animation. In whatever medium he worked, he drew with incredible speed; this gave rise to the vaudeville act he presented from 1906, during which he executed a series of 40 chalk drawings, one every 30 seconds, showing a man and a woman ageing while the orchestra played a suitable melody. From here it was a logical step to animation. With astonishing industry, he hand-painted each frame of his cartoons; beginning in 1909 he produced 10 short films: *Little Nemo* (1911), which required c4000 drawings; *The Story of a Mosquito* (1912; vt *How a Mosquito Operates*); *Gertie, the Dinosaur* (1914), which required c10,000 drawings; *The Sinking of the Lusitania* (1918), the most ambitious, requiring c25,000 drawings done in much more detail than in the earlier films; *The Centaurs*, a fantasy film, *Flip's Circus* and *Gertie on Tour*, these 3 being done c1918-21 and surviving only as fragments; and 3 **Dreams of the Rarebit Fiend** shorts, all released in 1921: *The Pet, Bug Vaudeville* and *The Flying House*. In *The Pet* household animals drink an elixir and swell to huge proportions; a 10-storey cat ravages a city and, KING-KONG-style, is assailed by airships. *Bug Vaudeville* is a **Silly Symphonies**-style (but pre-Disney) fantasy. In *The Flying House* a couple, escaping their creditors, fit out their house with wings and a propeller and fly off into outer space where, *inter alia*, they meet a giant on the Moon. It is not certain why WM gave up animation after these successes, but it was possibly because he thought – wrongly, as was soon proven by **Felix the Cat** and Walt Disney's **Alice** and **Oswald the Lucky Rabbit** – that animation, as an artform, was a deadend street to whose end he had come. He continued to produce newspaper strips and illustrations, however, until the end of his life. [JC/JGr/SW]
Further reading: "Winsor McCay" by John Canemaker in *The American Animated Cartoon: A Critical Anthology* (anth **1980**) ed Danny Peary and Gerald Peary; *Winsor McCay: His Life and Art* (**1987**) by John Canemaker; *Comic Artists* (**1989**) by Richard Marschall.
McCLARY, THOMAS CALVERT (?1909-1972) US

speechwriter and ghostwriter whose sf appeared in *ASF* in the 1930s under his own name and under the pseudonyms Thomas Calvert, Miles Cramer and Calvin Peregoy – the latter for the **Doctor Conklin** series in *ASF* in 1934-5. For *Unknown* he wrote "The Tommyknocker" (1940). Basic to his two sf novels, *Rebirth: When Everyone Forgot* (1934 *ASF*; **1944**) and *Three Thousand Years* (1938 *ASF*; **1954**), is the theory, reminiscent of Buckminster Fuller (1895-1983), that a small scientific elite unhindered by the opportunism of businessmen and politicians could keep the world running in decency and comfort. Both are worked out in post-HOLOCAUST settings, intentionally and instantaneously precipitated in the former by means of a ray which obliterates all memory and in the latter by the transition of all lifeforms to a state of SUSPENDED ANIMATION. In both books the idealistic theory is set up only to be exploded. [JE/RB/PN]

MacCLOUD, MALCOLM (? -) US writer of two sf juveniles for older children, *The Tera Beyond* (**1981**) and *A Gift of Mirrorvax* (**1981**), the latter attempting with only moderate success to make plausible a mirror Earth on the other side of the Sun. [JC]

MacCLURE, VICTOR (THOM MacWALTER) (1887-1963) UK writer of popular fiction. His *Ultimatum: A Romance of the Air* (**1924**; vt *The Ark of the Covenant: A Romance of the Air and of Science* 1924 US) tells of world disarmament brought about by pacifists armed with dirigibles carrying a sleep gas and a ray that transmutes elements. They also possess atomic energy and other weapons invented by their dying South American "Master". After the US President is converted to their cause, peace ensues. [JC/PN]

See also: AIR WONDER STORIES; WEAPONS.

McCLURE'S MAGAZINE US "slick" magazine published by S.S. McClure, ed Ida Tarbell and others. Monthly June 1893-Jan 1926 (irregularly towards the end). Recommended June 1926 as a romance magazine. Merged with *Smart Set* in Apr 1929.

Initially conceived as the US edition of *The* IDLER, *MM* appeared as a new magazine with original stories and features, although some sf was reprinted from *The Idler*. *MM*'s best remembered sf publication is Rudyard KIPLING's *With the Night Mail: A Story of 2000 AD* (1905; **1909** chap US). Two interesting disaster stories were "Within an Ace of the End of the World" (1900) by Robert BARR and "The End of the World" (1903) by Jules Guerin. Jack LONDON's "The Unparalleled Invasion" (1910) is a future-WAR Yellow-Peril story in which the author, famous as a believer in the Brotherhood of Man, recommends genocide of the Chinese. A serialized novel was Cleveland MOFFETT's *The Conquest of America: A Romance of Disaster and Victory: U.S.A. 1921 A.D.* (May-Aug 1915 as "The Conquest of America in 1921"; **1916**). [JE/PN]

MacCOLL, HUGH (? -?) UK author of *Mr Stranger's Sealed Packet* (**1889**), an interplanetary novel describing a spaceship journey to MARS and the discovery there of two races of Earth origin, one of which has attained a UTOPIAN ideal (◊ EVOLUTION). Although lacking the depths of Percy GREG's influential *Across the Zodiac* (**1880**), the book proved popular and may in turn have influenced H.G. WELLS, especially in its account of the death of a Martian through exposure to bacteria in Earth's atmosphere. [JE]

McCOLLUM, MICHAEL A. (1946-) US writer and control-systems engineer specializing in aerospace propulsion. MAM began publishing sf with "Duty, Honor, Planet" for *ASF* in 1979. His first novel, *A Greater Infinity* (fixup **1982**), established the pattern he would follow through the 1980s: a complex SPACE-OPERA adventure plot involves humans (in this case Terrans) with one or more alien races as wars, quests and challenges galore generate a sense of movement. The **Makers** series – *Life PROBE* (**1983**) and *Procyon's Promise* (**1985**) – and the **Antares** series – *Antares Dawn* (**1986**) and *Antares Passage* (**1987**) – are in this mould, but *Thunderstrike!* (**1989**) deals more mundanely with what happens when a comet strikes Earth, and *The Clouds of Saturn* (**1991**) concerns human and internecine strife in the cloud-cities colonizing Saturn. MAM's touch is usually light, and accusations of racism – occasioned by the sorry fate Africa suffers in the **Makers** books – seem almost certainly misdirected. [JC]

McCOMAS, J(ESSE) FRANCIS (1911-1978) US editor and writer who published a number of sf stories under his own name – including "Shock Treatment" (1954) and "Parallel" (1955) – and as Webb Marlowe. He was co-editor with Raymond J. HEALY of the 35-story ANTHOLOGY *Adventures in Time and Space* (anth **1946**; cut vt *Selections from Adventures in Time and Space* 1954; recut vt *More Adventures in Time and Space* 1955; text restored vt *Famous Science-Fiction Stories* 1957), which was initially published by Random House, one of the two or three most prestigious literary publishers of the time, and whose contents – a very wide selection from the new US sf of the previous decade – were made available for the first time to a wide non-genre audience. It was in this anthology that he published his first story, "Flight into Darkness" (1946) as by Webb Marlowe. JFM was also joint editor with Anthony BOUCHER of *The* MAGAZINE OF FANTASY AND SCIENCE FICTION from #1 (1949) until Aug 1954, though he has not generally received his due share of credit for establishing the direction of that magazine. He also co-edited with Boucher the first 3 vols of the **Best from FSF** sequence: *The Best from Fantasy and Science Fiction* (anth **1952**), #2 (anth **1953**) and #3 (anth **1954**). He remained advisory editor of *FSF* until March 1962. JFM was a member of the Mystery Writers of America. [MJE/JC]

Other works as editor: *The Graveside Companion* (anth **1962**); *Crimes and Misfortunes* (anth **1970**); *Special Wonder: The Anthony Boucher Memorial Anthology of Fantasy and Science Fiction* (anth **1970**; in 2 vols vt *Special Wonder #1* 1971 and #2 1971).

See also: ASTOUNDING SCIENCE-FICTION; GOLDEN AGE OF SF.

McCORD, GUY [s] ◊ Mack REYNOLDS.

McCOY, ANDREW Pseudonym of South African-born Australian writer André Jute (1945-   ), who has concentrated as AM on violent tales of conflict in the continent of his birth, most of them verging into the NEAR FUTURE. Novels as AM include *Atrocity Week* (**1978** UK), *The Insurrectionist* (**1979** UK), *African Revenge* (**1980** UK), *Blood Song* (**1983** UK), *Cain's Courage* (**1985** UK), *Survivors and Winners* (**1986** UK) and *The Meyeresco Helix* (**1988** UK). Under his own name he has published tales of a similar nature though less aggressively told: *Reverse Negative* (**1982** UK), *Festival* (**1982** UK), *Sinkhole* (**1982** UK) and *Iditarod* (**1990** UK). [JC]

MacCREIGH, JAMES ◊ Frederik POHL.

McCRUMB, SHARYN [r] ◊ RECURSIVE SF.

McCULLOUGH, COLLEEN (1937-   ) Working name of Australian writer Colleen McCullough-Robinson, who remains most famous for *The Thorn Birds* (**1977**). *A Creed for the Third Millennium* (**1985** US), set in the 21st century, has a familiar plot in which a charismatic figure ambiguously revitalizes a disillusioned world. *The Ladies of Missolonghi* (**1987** UK) is a ghost story. [JC]

McCUTCHAN, PHILIP (1920-   ) UK writer, a Sandhurst graduate, author of several routine sf thrillers, most of them in his **Commander Shaw** series, which began with *Gibraltar Road* (**1960**) and closed with *Corpse* (**1980**). Of these, *Skyprobe* (**1966**), *The Screaming Dead Balloons* (**1968**), *The All-Purpose Bodies* (**1969**) and *The Bright Red Business Men* (**1969**) make the clearest use of sf instruments, though never centrally. The Commander's function, which is to involve himself with espionage and to save the world from mad SCIENTISTS who grow extraterrestrial fungi, construct malign CYBORGS, etc., generally necessitates the destruction of any sf device before the story's end. [JC/PN] **Other works:** *Bowering's Breakwater* (**1964**), a UK liner faces trouble after the start of a nuclear world war; *A Time for Survival* (**1966**), a post-HOLOCAUST story of unremitting bleakness; *The Day of the Coastwatch* (**1968**), a DYSTOPIA; *This Drakotny . . .* (**1971**); *Flood* (**1991**), the northern polar icecap melts.

McDANIEL, DAVID (1939-1977) US writer who also wrote as Ted Johnstone. He published a SPACE OPERA, *The Arsenal Out of Time* (**1967**), and a number of tv spin-offs, most of them in the MAN FROM U.N.C.L.E. series. They are *The Dagger Affair* * (**1966**), *The Vampire Affair* * (**1966**), *The Monster Wheel Affair* * (**1967**), *The Rainbow Affair* * (**1967**), *The Utopia Affair* * (**1968**) and *The Hollow Crown Affair* * (**1969**). He also wrote a spin-off from the tv series The PRISONER, *The Prisoner #2: Number Two* * (**1969**; vt *Who is Number Two?* 1982 UK). [JC]

McDERMOT, MURTAGH Pseudonym of a UK or Irish author whose satirical MOON-voyage novel, *A Trip to the Moon* (**1728**), describes various remarkable sights and beings after the fashion of CYRANO DE BERGERAC. The necessary propulsion is provided by gunpowder. [JC]

McDERMOTT, DENNIS[s] ◊ P. Schuyler MILLER.

McDEVITT, JACK Working name of US writer John Charles McDevitt (1935-   ), who began publishing sf with "The Emerson Effect" for *Twilight Zone* in 1981, coming to prominence with "Cryptic" (1984), a tale whose theme – First Contact between humans and the ALIEN races who are sending communications across space – was elaborated in his first novel, *The Hercules Text* (**1986**). Despite the occasional descent into CLICHÉS in his plotting and his politics (even as early as 1986 the vision of the USA coming close to war with the USSR over ownership of the information in the signals lacked extrapolative vigour), JMcD managed in this tale to concentrate very effectively on the human dimensions of the conundrum posed by the existence of a COMMUNICATION whose contents, when deciphered, might well devastate human civilization; and the Roman Catholic viewpoint of one of the SCIENTISTS involved in decoding the message is presented with an obvious sympathy which does not hamper the storytelling, which involves threats of violent skulduggery. JMcD's second novel, *A Talent for War* (**1988**), set in a galactic venue eons hence, similarly sets a religious frame around the central quest plot, in which a young man must thread his way through the unsettled hinterlands dividing human and alien space in his search for the secret that may retroactively destroy the reputation of a human who has been a hero in the recent wars. In both novels, JMcD wrestles valiantly with the task he has set himself: that of imposing an essentially contemplative structure upon conventions designed for violent action. He comes, at times, close to success. [JC]

See also: PHILIP K. DICK AWARD.

MacDONALD, ANSON ◊ Robert A. HEINLEIN.

MacDONALD, GEORGE (1824-1905) Scottish author and editor, noted for his fairy tales. His former occupation as a clergyman was reflected in his allegorical fantasies, *Phantastes: A Faerie Romance for Men and Women* (**1858**) and *Lilith* (**1895**; rev 1924), the latter work being his closest to sf. Based on the premise that an infinite number of three-dimensional universes can exist in a four-dimensional frame (◊ PARALLEL WORLDS), *Lilith* draws heavily from the Talmud in its enigmatic description of a search, set in both this Universe and another, for the self. It compares interestingly with David LINDSAY's *A Voyage to Arcturus* (**1920**).

After GM's death, his son Greville wrote three fantasy novels as well as the biographical *George MacDonald and his Wife* (**1924**). [JE/JC] **Other works:** *Adela Cathcart* (coll **1864**; rev 1882 to exclude fantasy stories); *The Portent: A Story of the Inner Vision of the Highlanders, Commonly Called the Second Sight* (**1864**; rev as coll vt *The Portent and Other Stories* 1909; original novel vt *Lady of the Mansion* 1983 US); *Dealings with the Fairies* (**1867**); *At the Back of the North Wind* (**1870**), *The Princess and the Goblin* (**1871** US) and *The Princess and Curdie* (**1882** US), a series for children; *Works of Fancy and Imagination* (10 vols **1871**); *The Wise Woman: A Parable* (**1875**; vt *A Double Story* 1876 US; vt *Princess Rosamund* US; vt *The Lost Princess* 1895 UK); *The Flight of the Shadow* (**1891**); *The Fairy Tales of George MacDonald* (coll in 5 vols **1904**); *Fairy Tales* (**1920**); *The Light Princess* (coll **1961**) ed Roger Lancelyn GREEN; *Evenor* (coll **1972**) ed Lin CARTER; *Visionary Novels: Lilith; Phantastes* (omni **1954** US; vt *Phantastes; and Lilith* 1962 UK); *The Gifts of the Child Christ: Fairy Tales and Stories for the Childlike* (coll in 2 vols; **1973** US) ed Glenn Edward Sadler; *The Gold Key and The Green Life* (anth **1986**), the second story being by Fiona Macleod (pseudonym of William Sharp [1824-1905]); *The Day Boy and the Night Girl* (**1988** chap); *Little Daylight* (**1988** chap).

About the author: There is a mass of critical work on GM. Of particular genre interest is *The Renaissance of Wonder in Children's Literature* (**1977**; vt *Renaissance of Wonder: The Fantasy Worlds of C.S. Lewis, J.R.R. Tolkien, George MacDonald, E. Nesbit and Others* 1980 US) by Marion Lochhead (1902-1985).

See also: ADAM AND EVE; MUSIC.

McDONALD, IAN (1960-   ) UK writer, a resident of Northern Ireland, who began publishing sf with "The Islands of the Dead" for *Extro* in 1982; this, with other short work, was assembled as *Empire Dreams* (coll **1988** US). He very quickly demonstrated a fascination with garish sf impedimenta and a habit of rococo elaboration which made him both a highly promising writer and potentially a wilfully eccentric one. His first novel, *Desolation Road* (**1988** US), has been described as *The Martian Chronicles* (coll **1950**) crossed with *One Hundred Years of Solitude* (**1967**; trans **1970**), a joke limited in accuracy only by its failure to add Cordwainer SMITH to Ray BRADBURY and Gabriel García Márquez (1928-   ). IM is not so much being influenced or writing pastiche as appropriating deftly from other writers the precise gestures needed to make ideological or emotional points about the human implications of TERRAFORMING or cyborgization (◊ CYBORGS). *Out on Blue Six* (**1989** US) describes a failed UTOPIA, a standard theme in the UK during the Thatcher years, working both to rehabilitate socialist ideals and to acknowledge legitimate criticism; it combines standard Robert A. HEINLEIN motifs – the Man, or in this case Woman, who Learns Better – some A.E. VAN VOGT mystification about amnesiac Hidden Masters, and a catalogue of DYSTOPIAN and heterotopian fragments, plus chunks of Grail quest and a lot of shooting and running around. *King of Morning, Queen of Day* (1985 in *Empire Dreams*; exp **1991** US), which won the PHILIP K. DICK AWARD in 1992, is a fantasy about Irish identity across the generations which manages in its third (contemporary) section to assimilate much of the feel of CYBERPUNK. *Hearts, Hands and Voices* (**1992**; vt *The Broken Land* 1992 US), set in a tropical venue much resembling Asia (though the religious conflicts have an Irish ring), replicates the technique of his first novel; in this case his models are Geoff RYMAN's novels *The Unconquered Country*

(**1986**) and *The Child Garden* (**1988**).   [RK]

Other work: *Speaking in Tongues* (coll **1992**).

See also: CITIES; COLONIZATION OF OTHER WORLDS; GAMES AND SPORTS; INTERZONE; MARS; NEW WORLDS; WOMEN AS PORTRAYED IN SCIENCE FICTION.

MacDONALD, JOHN D(ANN) (1916-1986) US writer and ex-lieutenant colonel in the US Army, known mainly for such well written thrillers as *The Brass Cupcake* (**1950**) and the 21 **Travis McGee** novels (1964-85), which evolved from escapist tales of derring-do into impassioned laments for the human race and the planet. None of his sf, which began early in his career with "Cosmetics" for *ASF* in 1948, significantly anticipates JDM's late mood; the best of his 50 or so short stories, nearly all written 1948-53, were assembled in *Other Times, Other Worlds* (coll **1978**). His two early sf novels, *Wine of the Dreamers* (**1951**; vt *Planet of the Dreamers* 1953 UK) and *Ballroom of the Skies* (**1952**), were both polished and proficient adventures in PARANOID sf involving extraterrestrial manipulations of humanity, inadvertent in the first book and, in the second, as part of a winnowing process to select good leadership material. A later novel, *The Girl, the Gold Watch, & Everything* (**1962**), is a complicated spoof adventure in which a man inherits a watch which, when correctly used, speeds up time for the owner, rendering him invisible to the people in real, apparently frozen, time, and thereby giving him great power. All 3 novels were assembled as *Time and Tomorrow* (omni **1980**).

JDM occasionally wrote sf stories under the pseudonyms John Wade Farrell and Peter Reed.   [JC/PN]

About the author: *Bibliography of the Published Works of John D. MacDonald* (**1980**) by Walter and Jean Shine.

See also: LEISURE; PULP MAGAZINES.

MacDONALD, PHILIP (1899-1980) Scottish-born author of detective novels and screenplays, in California from 1931; he was best known for thrillers like *The Rasp* (**1924**) and *X v. Rex* (**1933** as by Martin Porlock), of which at least four, including *The List of Adrian Messenger* (**1959**), were filmed. His 23 screenplay credits included *Rebecca* (1940), *The Body Snatcher* (1945) and the sf film *Tobor the Great* (1954). PM published occasional sf stories in *FSF* and elsewhere in the 1940s and 1950s, and as W.J. Stuart wrote *Forbidden Planet* * (**1956**), based on FORBIDDEN PLANET (1956), a film novelization of higher quality than usual.   [PN/JC]

McDONALD, RAYMOND Joint pseudonym of US writers Raymond Leger (1883-?   ) and Edward McDonald (1873-?   ), whose sf novel, *The Mad Scientist: A Tale of the Future* (**1908**), features the increasingly dangerous – or effective – interventions of the said SCIENTIST in the dealings of US businessmen and of the US Government itself. The scientist's inclinations are socialist but, surprisingly for 1908, the authors are ambiguous about whether or not he is a menace pure and simple; and the protagonists of the tale find themselves again and again having to cope with uncomfortable revelations – from fraud to conspiracies with German strikebreakers – brought into the open by the scientist's numerous inventions. [JC]

McDONALD, STEVEN E(DWARD) (1956-   ) Jamaican writer who began publishing sf with "Empty Barrels" for *ASF* in 1978, was most noted for "Ideologies" (1980), and whose first novel, *The Janus Syndrome* (1981 US), put into SPACE-OPERA guise a tale involving racial oppression, romantic exaggerations of material, and masquerades. Unfortunately, he then fell silent. [JC]

MacDONELL, A(RCHIBALD) G(ORDON) (1895-1941) Scottish writer who began his career as author with a series of thrillers as Neil Gordon; one of these, *The Professor's Poison* (1928), was sf. From 1933, AGM wrote under his own name. In *Lords and Masters* (1936) an industrial struggle between traditional steel manufacturers and the developers of a new metal escalates into a full-blown war involving the whole of Europe; by novel's end, a Patriotic Government is ruling the UK. [JC]

McDONOUGH, ALEX (?   -   ) US writer whose sf is restricted to the **Scorpio** sequence of tales packaged on a SHARECROP basis by the Byron PREISS enterprise: *Scorpio* (1990), *Scorpio Rising* (1990), *Scorpio Descending* (1991) and *Dragon's Blood* (1991). Scorpio, an ALIEN on the run with a pilfered superpowered orb, has escaped to 14th-century Earth, where he has many adventures. [JC]

McDONOUGH, THOMAS R(EDMOND) (1945-   ) US writer and lecturer in engineering at Caltech. He is perhaps best known for his nonfiction and for serving as the coordinator of the SETI programme of the Planetary Society. *The Search for Extraterrestrial Intelligence* (1987) argues the case for seeking out First Contact with other races in the Galaxy. Much of his earlier work was also nonfiction, beginning with "They're Trying to Tell Us Something" for *ASF* in 1969, which likewise concerned SETI matters. He began to publish fiction only in 1979 with "Statues of the Gods" for *Starlog*. His first novel, *The Architects of Hyperspace* (1987), features a clearly argued HARD-SF vision of a Galaxy containing at least one artificial toroidal world; there is also sophisticated speculation about the growth of civilizations throughout the Universe. Yet it is narrated in an only intermittently humorous pulp style, and features at least one bibulous Irishman. *The Missing Matter* (1992) provides a similar mix of intriguingly couched cognition and comic turns. [JC]

Other work: *Space: The Next 25 Years* (1987; rev 1989).

MacDOUGAL, JOHN Collaborative pseudonym of James BLISH and Robert A.W. LOWNDES on "Chaos Coordinated" (*ASF* 1946). [PN]

MACE, DAVID (1951-   ) UK writer whose first novel, *Demon-4* (1984), describes with a quite chilling quasilyrical remoteness a post-HOLOCAUST suicide mission undertaken by the eponymous CYBORG probe to dismantle a doomsday device. Most of his later

novels, like *Nightrider* (1985), *Fire Lance* (1986), *The Highest Ground* (1988) and *Shadow Hunters* (1991), rework his territory, which might be defined as the NEAR FUTURE seen in terms of military DISASTERS, threatened or consummated; but *Frankenstein's Children* (1990), set in what remains of the Amazonian rain forest, gathers this material into a metaphorically rich whole, envisioning the entire diseased enterprise of exploitation and "development" as a collective surrender to the overstepping venture of Victor Frankenstein himself. The MONSTER, in this book, is the torn and galvanized world itself. [JC]

McELROY, JOSEPH (1930-   ) US writer who has gained attention for a series of intellectually formidable novels, almost all of which may be described as epistemological studies of contemporary life. Most notable among these are *Lookout Cartridge* (1974) and the extremely long and ambitious *Women and Men* (1987). All his work may be most fruitfully likened to the FABULATIONS of US writers like Thomas PYNCHON and Don DELILLO. However, *Plus* (1977), which dramatizes the experience of an artificially nurtured brain aboard a research satellite, is sf. [GF]

McENROE, RICHARD S. (?   -   ) US writer and literary agent who began writing sf with "Wolkenheim Fairday" for *IASFM* in 1980. His first two novels were BUCK ROGERS IN THE 25TH CENTURY ties: *Warrior's World* * (1981) and *Warrior's Blood* * (1981), both based on outlines by Larry NIVEN and Jerry POURNELLE; they were not received with enthusiasm. The **Far Stars and Future Times** sequence – *The Shattered Stars* (1983), *Flight of Honor* (1984) and *Skinner* (1985) – provides some more competently told sf adventures. RSM has also edited an interesting anthology of original stories, *Proteus: Voices for the 80's* (anth 1981). [JC]

McEVOY, SETH (?   -   ) US writer. His **Not Quite Human** sequence of young-adult sf tales is about a teenage ANDROID: *Not Quite Human #1: Batteries Not Included* (1985), *#2: All Geared Up* (1985), *#3: A Bug in the System* (1985), *#4: Reckless Robot* (1986), *#5: Terror at Play* (1986) and *#6: Killer Robot* (1986). The **Arcade Explorers** sequence, all written with Laure Smith, comprises *Arcade Explorers #1: Save the Venturians!* (1985), *#2: Revenge of the Raster Gang* (1985), *#3: The Electronic Hurricane* (1985) and *#4: The Magnetic Ghost of Shadow Island* (1985). He also wrote two titles for the **Explorer** sequence: *Destination: Brain* * (1987) and *Escape from Jupiter* * (1987). SM has written one nonfiction text of interest, *Samuel R. Delany* (1985), a bio-critical study of the writer. [JC]

McEWAN, IAN (RUSSELL) (1948-   ) UK writer who came to instant fame through the stories assembled in *First Love, Last Rites* (coll 1975), followed by *In Between the Sheets* (coll 1978), some of which are fantasy or sf – like "Reflections of a Kept Ape" from the second volume (◊ APES AND CAVEMEN) – but most of which turn an intensely fabulistic eye (◊ FABULATION) on young persons caught in the hyperboles of a UK depicted as psychically incontinent and in terminal decline. His first novel, *The Cement Garden* (**1978**), is a tale of horror. Of the plays assembled in *The Imitation Game* (coll **1981**), "Solid Geometry" (1978) is sf. *Or Shall We Die?: Words for an Oratorio Set to Music by Michael Berkeley* (**1983** chap) deals with the threat and imagined aftermath of nuclear WAR. *The Child in Time* (**1987**) is an sf novel set in the same dystopian NEAR-FUTURE UK adumbrated in "Two Fragments: March 199 – "(in *In Between the Sheets*); in this desolate, privatized, factory-farmed venue, the protagonist agonizingly loses his child outside a shop, and his search for her becomes a search for meaning and grace in the desert landscape the UK has become. [JC]

MACEY, PETER (? -) UK research chemist and writer whose routine sf novels are *Stationary Orbit* (**1974**), in which the alien intelligence turns out to be a local dolphin, *Distant Relations* (**1975**) and *Alien Culture* (**1977**), which features invasion by intelligent microbes. [PN]

MACFADDEN, BERNARR (1868-1955) US publisher, writer and film producer, born Bernard Adolphus McFadden; much concerned throughout his life with physical culture, and an espouser of nudism and eccentric health routines in various magazines from early in his career. His acknowledged fiction, beginning with *The Athlete's Conquest* (**1892**), is neither sf nor fantasy; but he may have published some pseudonymous genre works in his own magazines. From 1904 his journals featured sf stories and novels. The first was "My Bride from the Other World", a HOLLOW-EARTH tale by the Rev. E.C. Atkins (who may have been BM himself) in *Physical Culture*; it was followed by the book-length serial "Weird and Wonderful Story of Another World" (1905) as by Tyman Currio (probably John Russell Coryell [1848-1924] with BM's assistance), and many other stories followed in BM's other journals, which included *Brain Power* (ed F. Orlin TREMAINE 1921-4), *Dance World*, *Metropolitan Fiction Lovers' Magazine*, *Midnight* and *Red-Blooded Adventures*. The most important early sf novel thus published was Milo HASTINGS's remarkable "Children of 'Kultur'", which appeared in *True Story* in 1919 and which, revised as *City of Endless Night* (**1920**), was one of the central – and most politically prescient – US DYSTOPIAS. *Ghost Stories*, which BM ran 1926-30 (it then soon folded under new management), concentrated on the supernatural, as did *True Strange Stories*, whose founding editor was Walter B. GIBSON; but *Liberty*, a later (and very substantial) BM magazine, published Fred ALLHOFF's *Lightning in the Night* (1940; **1979**), which assumes the WWII triumph of Germany in Europe (◊ HITLER WINS), though as the novel closes a nuclear stand-off maintains an uneasy peace between Germany and the USA. After WWI, BM's Macfadden Pictures released movies for several years, including *Zongar* (1918), which features Amazons.

BM is most important in the HISTORY OF SF for his role – long obscure – in forcing the bankruptcy of

Hugo GERNSBACK in 1929 and taking over AMAZING STORIES, events which occasioned a competitive proliferation of sf magazines; according to Sam MOSKOWITZ – in "Bernarr Macfadden", a 7-part study published in FANTASY COMMENTATOR 1986-92 – BM was, therefore, inadvertently instrumental in setting off the chain of events which a decade later would culminate in the GOLDEN AGE OF SF. [JC]

MacFARLANE, STEPHEN ◊ John Keir CROSS.

McGARRY, MARK J. (1958-) US writer whose two novels are *Sun Dogs* (**1981**) and *Blank Slate* (**1984**), both sf adventures. [JC]

McGIVERN, WILLIAM P. [r] ◊ AMAZING STORIES; Alexander BLADE; P.F. COSTELLO; David Wright O'BRIEN; PULP MAGAZINES.

McGOWAN, INEZ [s] ◊ Rog PHILLIPS.

MacGREGOR, LOREN J. (1950-) US writer who began publishing sf with his first novel, *The Net* (**1987**), a Galaxy-spanning sf adventure involving some unremarkable capers and a play-feud between two spacefaring merchant families. It is redeemed by the thought LJM gives to the implications of body-change technology (the book reminded many readers of John VARLEY) and by his inventive use of the Net itself, which creates a sensory field as well as conveying information in space. [JC]

MacGREGOR, RICHARD Almost certainly the pseudonym of UK writer Macgregor Urquhardt (? -?). Under the name RM were published several routine GENRE-SF novels: *The Day a Village Died* (**1963**), *Taste of the Temptress* (**1963**), *Horror in the Night* (**1963**), *The Creeping Plague* (**1963**), *The Deadly Suns* (**1964**), *The Threat* (**1964**) and *The First of the Last* (**1964**). [JC/SH]

McGUFFIN A term devised by Alfred Hitchcock (1899-1980) to designate an object whose loss – or rumours of whose existence – triggers the cast of a thriller or detective film into searching for it, or fighting for it, or running from it, but which has in fact no intrinsic meaning once the dust has settled. The use of McGuffins to generate chase-the-searcher plots is widespread in 1920s and 1930s thriller sf and in more recent adventure sf; McGuffin spoors are particularly noticeable in the second volumes of trilogies. The term has been variously spelled "McGuffin", "MacGuffin" and "Maguffin"; we have decided to stick with the spelling chosen by John BOWEN for his novel *The McGuffin* (**1984**). [JC]

McGUIRE, JOHN J(OSEPH) (1917-1981) US author best known for his collaborations with H. Beam PIPER on the sf action novel *Crisis in 2140* (1953 ASF as "Null ABC"; **1957**) and on *A Planet for Texans* (1957 *Fantastic Universe* as "Lone Star Planet"; **1958**). These books are not readily distinguishable from Piper's solo efforts. JM wrote 2 other stories with Piper and 4 solo 1957-64. [JC]

See also: COLONIZATION OF OTHER WORLDS; CRIME AND PUNISHMENT.

McGUIRE, PATRICK (LLEWELLYN) (1949-) US researcher whose Princeton doctoral thesis was revised as a book, *Red Stars: Political Aspects of Soviet Science Fiction* (**1985**), one of the more useful sources on sf in RUSSIA, although carrying the story only as far as 1976. PM translated *Vozvrashchenie (Polden'. 22-i vek)* (**1962**; rev as *Polden', XXII vek (Vozvrashchenie)* **1967**; the latter trans as *Noon: 22nd Century* **1978** US) by Arkady and Boris STRUGATSKI, and wrote the chapter on Russian sf in *Anatomy of Wonder: Third Edition* (**1987**) ed Neil BARRON. He has published pieces on both Russian and English-language sf in a variety of books and magazines. [PN]

MacHARG, WILLIAM [r] ◊ Edwin BALMER.

MACHEN, ARTHUR (1863-1947) Welsh writer, translator and actor, born Arthur Llewellyn Jones, his parents adding Machen apparently in an attempt to please a rich relative. AM was an isolated, lonely child, and was from a very early age deeply devoted both to romantic literature and to the Welsh landscape that visually dominated his writings all his life. He also imaginatively applied his extensive if somewhat random readings in the occult and metaphysics to his Welsh background. He was in London for long periods from 1880. The death of his father in 1887 provided him with enough money to marry and to write, but by the end of the century he was once again poverty-stricken. He went on the stage for much of the following decade, and for the rest of his life did a great deal of hackwork. By the time he was rediscovered in the 1920s he was near retirement and no longer capable of producing high-calibre material.

With influences ranging from William MORRIS to Robert Louis STEVENSON and associations from John Lane's Bodley Head (at the time it was publishing *The Yellow Book*) to the Order of the Golden Dawn (whose occultist members included Algernon BLACKWOOD, W.B. Yeats [1865-1939] and Aleister Crowley [1875-1947]), and throughout embodying a conviction that DEVOLUTION and racial degeneracy were scientific facts (his Faerie represents a degenerated race in Britain), AM's fiction generally shies clear of sf as practised in the late-Victorian and Edwardian UK; most of his best tales are horror or occult fantasies. They tend to be set in a medievalized England with Welsh tinges, those set in London being irradiated by deeply romantic visions of alternatives to the industrial world which he saw dominating England, and despised: in both his work and his appearance he resembled a malefic G.K. CHESTERTON. "The Great God Pan", the title story of *The Great God Pan and The Inmost Light* (coll **1894**; exp 1926), is typical of Victorian sf/horror at about the time sf was beginning to shed its GOTHIC elements into a separate HORROR/fantasy genre. The story begins with an sf rationale (brain surgery) for a metamorphosis which remains one of the most dramatically horrible and misogynistic in fiction: the evil female offspring of the operated-on idiot girl grows into a malign being, apparently a woman, but actually a half-human horror whose father may have been the horned god of the story's title. *The Terror. A Fantasy* (**1917**; rev 1927) is quasi-sf

in its story of animals turning against humans. Through work of this sort, AM's influence, via H.P. LOVECRAFT and others, has been strong on 20th-century GOTHIC SF.

Volumes in which fantasy predominates include *The Chronicle of Clemendy* (coll **1888**), *The Three Impostors, or The Transmutations* (coll **1895**; vt *Black Crusade* 1966), *The House of Souls* (coll **1906**), *The Hill of Dreams* (**1907**), *The Angels of Mons, The Bowmen and Other Legends of the War* (coll **1915**), *The Great Return* (**1915** chap), *The Secret Glory* (**1922**), *The Shining Pyramid* (coll **1923**), *The Glorious Mystery* (coll **1924**, partly nonfiction), *Ornaments in Jade* (coll **1924** US), *Dreads and Drolls* (coll **1927**), *The Green Round* (**1933**), *The Cosy Room* (coll **1936**), *The Children of the Pool, and Other Stories* (coll **1936**), *Holy Terrors* (coll **1946**), *Tales of Horror and the Supernatural* (coll **1948** US) and *The Collected Arthur Machen* (coll **1988**). [JC/PN]

About the author: *A Bibliography of Arthur Machen* (**1965**) by Adrian Goldstone and Wesley Sweetser.

MACHINES Sf is sometimes considered, especially by its detractors, to be a genre in which machines are more important than people. DEFINITIONS OF SF often deny this, but the assumption that only HARD SF, dealing with the future of TECHNOLOGY, can be "real" sf is very common. Various kinds of machine have exerted a powerful fascination upon the sf imagination, and the social impact of technology has been a continual concern in sf.

The first major prose work to celebrate the shape of machines to come (although the earlier drawings of Leonardo da Vinci [1452-1519] are justly famous) was Francis BACON's prospectus for the Royal Society, *The New Atlantis* (1627; **1629**), which features a catalogue of marvellous inventions. Bacon's contemporary John WILKINS similarly listed inventions – on which he would be prepared to work if someone would finance him – in *Mathematicall Magick* (**1648**). These catalogues aimed to be realistic; the metaphorical usefulness of machines was explored for purposes of SATIRE by Daniel DEFOE in *The Consolidator* (**1705**), which features a "cogitator" to force rational thoughts into unwilling brains, a "devilscope" to detect and expose political chicanery, and an "elevator" to facilitate communication between minds and with the spirits of the dead. While Bacon and Wilkins extrapolated from contemporary technology to test the limits of practicality, Defoe suggested miraculous purposes and then proposed machines to serve as symbols for the means to those ends; save for the most conscientious hard-sf writers, the *modus operandi* of modern sf writers has more in common with Defoe than with Bacon. Such staple devices as TIME MACHINES and FASTER-THAN-LIGHT starships, operating in frank defiance of rationality and known science, function as facilitating devices to give writers access to the infinite realms of possibility. As such they are indispensable, and are frequently included in stories otherwise conscientious in their attempts at realism (◊ IMAGINARY SCIENCE).

With the exception of flying machines – a common concern in speculative fiction in the 17th and 18th centuries – few of the machines anticipated by Bacon and Wilkins played a significant part in sf until the late 19th century, when the Industrial Revolution lent historical confirmation to their prospectuses for technology. Some UTOPIAN writers made much of the productive capacity of factory machinery, but the first major literary disciple of the futuristic machine, Jules VERNE, was primarily interested in vehicles for his imaginary voyages. TRANSPORTATION remained the chief function of machines in sf for some time, though the role was augmented by all manner of exotic WEAPONRY as future-WAR stories became popular. Miracle-working facilitating devices played a limited role in 19th-century sf, although some were employed as means of COMMUNICATION and others as forms of amusement. Examples of the latter include the sporting contraptions (◊ GAMES AND SPORTS) featured in Anthony TROLLOPE's *The Fixed Period* (**1882**) and J.A.C.K.'s *Golf in the Year 2000* (**1892**). Further facilitating devices are found in Edward BELLAMY's *Dr Heidenhoff's Process* (**1880**), about a machine which erases unpleasant memories, and in Arthur Conan DOYLE's *The Doings of Raffles Haw* (**1891**), about a gold-making machine; but the most important exemplar was provided by H.G. WELLS in *The Time Machine* (**1895**). Another kind of fascination with mechanical contrivance is manifest in various baroque tales and allegories, including E.T.A. HOFFMANN's "Automata" (1814) and "The Sandman" (1816), Nathaniel HAWTHORNE's "The Celestial Railroad" (1843) and Herman MELVILLE's "The Bell-Tower" (1855), in which machines play a quasidiabolical role. This respectful suspicion of machinery is marvellously extrapolated in those chapters of Samuel BUTLER's *Erewhon* (**1872**) that present a vision of mechanical evolution. Wells's "The Lord of the Dynamos" (1894), too, reflects this sinister aspect; and L. Frank BAUM's children's fantasy *The Master Key* (**1901**) is a cautionary allegory. Enthusiasm for technological achievement and suspicion regarding human relationships with the machine are combined in *Morrison's Machine* (**1900**) by Joseph Smith FLETCHER, a curiously intense study of technological creativity.

In the last few years of the 19th century the potential of technology was drastically transformed by the discovery of the electromagnetic spectrum and the development of the new atomic theory. Vulgar mechanical contraptions were suddenly augmented by the magic of rays and radio, and there seemed to be no limits to possibility. A new era of imaginative exuberance began which took means of transportation (especially SPACESHIPS) and weapons out of the realms of extrapolation into those of boundless fantasy. One of the prophets of the new technology, and one whose understanding of its potential was more realistic than is sometimes appreciated, was Hugo GERNSBACK, the would-be inventor who instead became the publisher of *Radio News, Modern Electrics,* *The Electrical Experimenter* and SCIENCE AND INVENTION, and who founded AMAZING STORIES as their companion. In *Ralph 124C 41+* (1911-12; **1925**) Gernsback produced a catalogue of wonders akin to that in Bacon's *The New Atlantis*; though painfully naïve in literary terms, *Ralph* proved less incompetent as a technological prospectus.

It was not unnatural that the early sf PULP MAGAZINES should go to extremes in their use of machines in a way that Verne never had. The pulp writers were the product of an age of extremely rapid technological advance in which science was coming to seem mysterious again. It was an age when it seemed machines might do anything, when even the satirical metaphors of Defoe's *Consolidator* could seem plausible as actual devices. The limitless scope of the machine was reverently translated into a kind of quasisupernatural awe in such stories as John W. CAMPBELL Jr's "The Last Evolution" (1932) and "The Machine" (1935 as by Don A. Stuart). What was largely missing from all the extravagant accounts of miracle-working machines, however, was a consciousness of the social implications of extravagant technological advance. Writers outside the genre were little better: Gardner HUNTING's *The Vicarion* (**1926**) features a machine that can look through time to record any event from the past, but in Hunting's blinkered view it is merely a new entertainment medium which might make cinema obsolete; the device in André MAUROIS's *La machine à lire les pensées* (**1937**; trans as *The Thought-Reading Machine* **1938**) is represented as a mere fad. These and many other stories conclude that we might well be better off without miraculous machines. E. Charles VIVIAN's *Star Dust* (**1925**), Karel ČAPEK's *The Absolute at Large* (**1922**; trans **1927**) and William M. SLOANE's *The Edge of Running Water* (**1939**) are other notable examples of the "no good will come of it all" school of thought. Aldous HUXLEY's *Brave New World* (**1932**) is an outstanding attempt to consider large-scale social consequences but it, too, is dominated by the conviction that technological opportunities will be abused. A similar suspicion was widespread in the early sf magazines, particularly in the work of David H. KELLER, but was balanced by Gernsbackian optimism.

Campbell's prospectus for sf, promoted in ASTOUNDING SCIENCE-FICTION, demanded more conscientious analyses of the social impact of new machines. Robert A. HEINLEIN was one of the first to take up the challenge, in such stories as "The Roads Must Roll" (1940) and *Beyond This Horizon* (1942 as by Anson MacDonald; **1948**). The 1940s became, in consequence, the era of the gadget: the small machine with considerable implications. "A Logic Named Joe" (1946) by Will F. Jenkins (Murray LEINSTER) is an archetypal gadget story prefiguring the personal COMPUTER. WWII and the bombing of Hiroshima encouraged the notion that machines had become so powerful that humans were simply not up to the task of responsibly administering their use. Several memorable images of the revolt of the machines appeared in this period: Robert BLOCH's "It Happened Tomorrow" (1943), Clifford D. SIMAK's "Bathe Your Bearings in Blood" (1950; vt "Skirmish") and Lord DUNSANY's *The Last Revolution* (**1951**). A particularly powerful parable of the power of the machine acting independently of human control is Theodore STURGEON's "Killdozer!" (1944). T.L. SHERRED's "E for Effort" (1947) features a machine similar to Hunting's vicarion, but goes to an opposite extreme in arguing that its mere presence in the world would precipitate all-out war. Jack WILLIAMSON's "The Equalizer" (1947) is an elegant study of the political implications of free power.

As the 1950s progressed, GENRE-SF writers became increasingly prone to show machines out of human control, remaking the world while humanity was swept helplessly along – or left helplessly behind. Philip K. DICK's "Second Variety" (1953), in which self-replicating, independently evolving war machines inherit the Earth, is a striking example. Later works embodying similar images include Fred SABERHAGEN's **Berserker** series, John T. SLADEK's satirical *The Reproductive System* (**1968**; vt *Mechasm*) and Stanisław LEM's *The Invincible* (**1964**; trans **1973**). Anxiety about the alienation of people from their mechanical environment seems to have reached its peak during the 1950s, and the 1960s began a new trend towards uneasy reconciliation, perhaps best exemplified by changes in the typical roles assigned to CYBORGS.

In contemporary sf, as in contemporary society, suspicion of machines remains deeply entrenched, but the inevitability of our association with machinery is accepted. The distinction between life and mechanism often becomes blurred, as in Philip K. Dick's *Do Androids Dream of Electric Sheep?* (**1968**). The intimacy of the man/machine relationship can only increase still further, and sf stories anticipate this increasing intimacy in all kinds of melodramatic ways; sexual relationships are of course included, as in such stories as Harlan ELLISON's "Pretty Maggie Moneyeyes" (1967) and "Catman" (1967). The trend towards ever-larger machines was decisively halted by the development of microprocessors, and much contemporary speculation about future machinery is concerned with NANOTECHNOLOGY: the development of machines which are no more than large molecules and can do extensive work inside our bodies as well as perform complex manufacturing tasks in huge vats. Sf has not yet really got to grips with the possibilities of nanomachinery, but a beginning has been made in such stories as Ian WATSON's "Nanoware Time" (1989), Greg BEAR's *Queen of Angels* (**1990**) and Michael J. FLYNN's *The Nanotech Chronicles* (fixup **1991**). Pat CADIGAN's *Mindplayers* (**1987**) brings up to date the older tradition of stories which feature psychologically intrusive machinery.

The growth of the awareness that mankind and machine are inextricably bound together in contemporary society has deflected attention away from the miraculous potential of the machine. The naïve assumption that all human problems might be solved by appropriate technological innovations, not uncommon in the 1930s, has been replaced by the assumption that human nature is bound to be remade by new machinery in problematic ways. Machines have largely lost their force as symbols of individual freedom and power, and with this loss the potential of high-tech sf to provide simple escapist fantasies and power fantasies has been eroded. Given this, it is not entirely surprising to find so much contemporary sf being set in imaginary pasts (◊ ALTERNATE WORLDS), in futures returned to primitivism (◊ HOLOCAUST AND AFTER) or on technologically primitive lost colonies (◊ COLONIZATION OF OTHER WORLDS). Formerly, speculative fiction's main concern in dealing with machines was the adaptation of machines to pre-existent human purposes (and this is equally true of Baconian extrapolation and Defoesque fantasy); now the main concern is with the challenges facing our descendants as they are forced to adapt, physically and mentally, to their mechanical achievements and environments.   [BS]

See also: AUTOMATION; CYBERPUNK; DISCOVERY AND INVENTION; DYSTOPIAS; STEAMPUNK.

McHUGH, VINCENT (1904-1983) US writer whose comic saga *Caleb Catlum's America* (**1936**) is about a family of immortals (◊ IMMORTALITY) who amusingly represent the high points of US history in the flesh (the family includes Abe Lincoln and Davy Crockett). *I Am Thinking of My Darling* (**1943**), in which an inhibition-releasing epidemic hits New York, cuts surprisingly deep in its superficially comic examination of the consequences.   [JC]

See also: PSYCHOLOGY.

McILRAITH, FRANK [r] ◊ Roy CONNOLLY.

McINNES, GRAHAM (CAMPBELL) (1912-1970) UK-born, Australian-educated Canadian diplomat and novelist, son of the novelist Angela Thirkell (1890-1961) – another son of hers was Colin MacInnes (1914-1976). Most of GM's work is not sf, but *Lost Island* (**1954**) is a lost-race story (◊ LOST WORLDS).   [PN]

McINTOSH, J.T. Pseudonym (in some earlier work spelled M'Intosh) of Scottish writer and journalist James Murdoch MacGregor (1925-   ), used for all his sf writing, though he has written non-sf under his own name. He began publishing sf with "The Curfew Tolls" in *ASF* in 1950, producing many stories (though no collections) through 1980. With his first novel, *World out of Mind* (**1953** US), he fully entered a career that was, in its early years, notably successful. *World out of Mind* implausibly but enjoyably sets a disguised ALIEN on an Earth dominated by aptitude tests, where he wins his way to the top and thence prepares the way for INVASION. *Born Leader* (**1954** US; vt *Worlds Apart* 1958) puts two sets of colonists from a destroyed Earth on nearby planets, where the authoritarian set conflicts with the libertarian set. In *One in Three Hundred* (**1954** US), with Earth doomed again, pilots of the only rocketships available are given the task of selecting those they will save of the planet's billions of inhabitants. *The Fittest* (**1955** US; vt *The Rule of the Pagbeasts* 1956 US) depicts the harrowing effects of a misfired experiment to increase animal INTELLIGENCE. *200 Years to Christmas* (**1961** dos US) is a routine but competent variation on the GENERATION-STARSHIP theme.

Although some of JTM's novels in the 1960s and 1970s continued to show his professional skill with a plot and his competence at creating identifiable characters, his work began to show some slackening of interest: *The Million Cities* (1958 *Satellite*; rev **1963** US) is a bland urban DYSTOPIA; *The Noman Way* (1952 as "The E.S.P. Worlds"; **1964**) uninterestingly repeats the test situation of his first novel, which seems to have been something of a preoccupation of his, for it turns up also in the serial "The Lady and the Bull" (1955 *Authentic*). *Out of Chaos* (**1965**) is a routine post-HOLOCAUST novel; *Time for a Change* (**1967**; vt *Snow White and the Giants* 1968 US) treats a local intrusion of time-travelling aliens as a domestic issue; *Flight from Rebirth* (1960 as "Immortality – For Some"; much exp **1971** US), a chase tale in an urban setting, again features testing.

JTM never lost the vivid narrative skills that made him an interesting figure of 1950s sf, but his failure to challenge himself in his later career led to results that verged on mediocrity. After 1980 he fell silent. [JC]

Other works: *Six Gates from Limbo* (**1968**); *Transmigration* (**1970** US); *The Cosmic Spies* (**1972**); *The Space Sorcerers* (**1972**; vt *The Suiciders* 1973 US); *Galactic Takeover Bid* (**1973**); *Ruler of the World* (cut **1976** Canada; rev vt *This is the Way the World Begins* 1977 UK); *Norman Conquest 2066* (**1977**); *A Planet Called Utopia* (**1979** US).

About the author: *J.T. McIntosh: Memoir & Bibliography* (**1987** chap US) by Ian Covell.

See also: ANDROIDS; DISASTER; END OF THE WORLD; GAMES AND SPORTS; IMMORTALITY; SUN.

McINTYRE, VONDA N(EEL) (1948-   ) US writer and geneticist, one of the earliest successful graduates of the CLARION SCIENCE FICTION WRITERS' WORKSHOP, which she attended in 1970. She began to publish sf with "Only at Night in" *Clarion* (anth **1971**) ed Robin Scott WILSON, and gained prominence with "Of Mist, and Grass, and Sand" (1973), which won a NEBULA for Best Novelette and served as the initial section of *Dreamsnake* (fixup **1978**), her best known novel to date, which won her another Nebula as well as a HUGO. The female protagonist of both story and book is a healer in a desolated primitive venue, the violent and destructive superstitions of whose inhabitants lead to her losing her healer snake, with which she was linked through complex imprinting. The book version goes on to recount her quest for a replacement snake, a search through a strongly depicted post-HOLOCAUST environment which includes gruelling experiences in the CITY that had served as the

central venue for VNM's first novel, *The Exile Waiting* (**1975**; rev 1976 UK). That book likewise features a female protagonist with singular empathic powers: she is a sneak thief – the plot is complicated – who manages to escape Earth's last city with a Japanese poet from the stars and a virtuous "pseudosib" (the bad "twin" having been killed in the city) and in due course Earth entirely, with the prognosis that she will become a successful starfarer.

After *Fireflood and Other Stories* (coll **1979**), which assembled her best short work, VNM became associated with the STAR TREK enterprise, producing the RECURSIVE *Star Trek: The Entropy Effect* ∗ (**1981**) and 3 film ties – *Star Trek: The Wrath of Khan* ∗ (**1982**), *Star Trek III: The Search for Spock* ∗ (**1984**) and *Star Trek IV: The Voyage Home* ∗ (**1986**) – as well as *Star Trek: Enterprise: The First Adventure* ∗ (**1986**). Her next independent novel, *Superluminal* (1977 as "Aztecs" in *2076: The American Tricentennial* ed Edward BRYANT; exp **1983**), places its female protagonist in a rite-of-passage situation – she must replace her organic heart with an artificial device in order to become a starship pilot, but manages nonetheless to retain her humanity – and is significantly open to a FEMINIST reading. *Barbary* (**1986**) is directed to a younger audience. The ongoing **Starfarers** series – *Starfarers* (**1989**) and *Transition* (**1991**) are the first two titles – is likewise written with deliberate clarity and ease. VNM's recent work is considerably less demanding than the novels and stories of her first professional decade but it continues to demonstrate her argued, numerate and humane approach – via the instruments of sf – to feminist concerns.

Aurora: Beyond Equality (anth **1976**) ed with Susan Janice Anderson is a collection of feminist sf stories, not all by women. [JC]

Other works: *The Bride* ∗ (**1985**), a film tie; *Screwtop* (1976 in *The Crystal Ship* ed Robert SILVERBERG; **1989** chap dos).

See also: CYBORGS; FASTER THAN LIGHT; SPACE FLIGHT.

MacISAAC, FRED (ERICK JOHN) (1886-1940) US writer who appeared frequently in *Argosy* after WWI with stories in which his sober prophetic intelligence wrestles with his PULP-MAGAZINE instincts, and usually loses. His work remains of interest, however. *The Vanishing Professor* (1926 *Argosy*; **1927**) complicatedly engages a venal scientist, inventor of an INVISIBILITY machine, with crime czars and detectives. "The Great Commander" (1926 *Argosy All-Story*) adumbrates Richard CONDON's *Emperor of America* (**1990**). "World Brigands" (1928 *Argosy All-Story*) suggests that the USA will develop an atomic bomb around 1940 in response to threats of war. *The Mental Marvel* (**1930**) deals with a boxer whose skills represent an evolutionary leap. *The Hothouse World* (1931 *Argosy*; **1965**) awakes its protagonist from SUSPENDED ANIMATION into the insanely restrictive post-catastrophe world of AD2051 – its inhabitants pent in a single tower – which he liberates once it is demonstrated that the air outside can again be breathed. [JC]

See also: CITIES; ECONOMICS; POLITICS.

McIVER, G(EORGE M.) (? -?) Australian writer, still alive in 1943. His *Neuroomia: A New Continent: A Manuscript Delivered from the Deep* (**1894** UK) routinely uncovers a clement LOST WORLD in the Antarctic inhabited by a long-lived high-tech folk who inform us that Mars is inhabited and spins off her excess population by dumping them on a visiting planet. [JC]

MacKAY, (JAMES ALEXANDER) KENNETH (1859-1935) Australian writer and politician whose sf novel, *The Yellow Wave: A Romance of the Asiatic Invasion of Australia* (**1895** UK), describes a Chinese invasion in 1954 under the guidance of Russia, the romance which causes the death of the secret leader of the invaders, and the continuing war which, as the book ends, the Australians seem likely to lose. [JC]

See also: AUSTRALIA.

MACKAYE, HAROLD STEELE (1866-1928) US writer whose sf novel is *The Panchronicon* (**1904**). This TIME-TRAVEL story is whimsically condescending about its provincial characters, who travel in a TIME MACHINE (left by a traveller from the future who died) that operates by repeatedly and very rapidly circumnavigating the north pole (to which it is attached by a chain) in the same direction as the Sun. The romance in Tudor England that follows shows some awareness of TIME PARADOX, but little is done with the idea. [PN]

McKEAG, ERNEST L(IONEL) (1896-1976) UK author who began writing boys' fiction in 1921, some of it featuring the occasional sf MCGUFFIN and several LOST WORLDS. In his later career he published many non-sf novels under the house name "GRIFF". *Invaded by Mars* (**1934**) and *Terror from the Stratosphere* (**1937**), both as by Jack Maxwell, are juvenile sf. The **Shuna** sequence – *Shuna, White Queen of the Jungle* (**1951**) and *Shuna and the Lost Tribe* (**1951**), both as by John King – rounds up the usual suspects: lost worlds, PSI POWERS and so forth. The first of these tales has an sf flavour: asteroid-dwelling space beetles invade, kidnap an Inca city and take off with it for the Moon. [JC]

McKEAN, DAVE Working name of UK COMIC-strip and GRAPHIC-NOVEL artist David Jeff McKean (1963-), whose subtle, sophisticated artwork has brought a touch of class to a medium in which class is a rare commodity. He attended Berkshire College of Art and Design 1982-6. His first publication was *Violent Cases* (graph **1987** in monochrome; **1991** coloured) written by Neil GAIMAN, a short graphic novel about childhood memories of an encounter with Al Capone's osteopath. He provided some haunting covers for DC COMICS's **Hellblazer** and **Sandman** comic books, and painted artwork for the 3-part graphic novel *Black Orchid* (graph **1988** US; omni **1991** US), written by Gaiman, and the bestselling graphic novel *Arkham Asylum* (graph **1989** US), written by Grant Morrison. His other work has included *Signal to Noise* (1989 *The*

Face; graph rev **1992**), written by Gaiman, about a dying film-maker plotting out his last movie in the knowledge that he will never make it, and *Cages* (1991-2 US), which DM both wrote and drew, a long episodic piece about creativity and cats. He won the World Fantasy Award for Best Artist in 1991. DM formed the theatre group The Unauthorised Sex Company with Colin GREENLAND, Simon Ings (1965-) and Geoff RYMAN; début performances were in 1991 at Mexicon and on the Edinburgh Festival Fringe. He is increasingly active as a cover artist for GOLLANCZ and other publishers. [RT]

See also: ARKHAM HOUSE; ILLUSTRATION.

MACKELWORTH, R(ONALD) W(ALTER) (1930-) UK writer and insurance salesman who began publishing sf with "The Statue" for *NW* in 1963 and produced some above-average sf adventure novels, usually involving complex, sometimes jumbled plotting, and an Earth somehow in danger. They include *Firemantle* (**1968**; vt *The Diabols* 1969 US), *Tiltangle* (**1970** US), *Starflight 3000* (**1972** US) – which involves some interesting TERRAFORMING of both the Moon and other planets – *The Year of the Painted World* (**1975**) and *Shakehole* (**1981**), a DYSTOPIAN vision of a NEAR-FUTURE UK. [JC]

McKENNA, RICHARD M(ILTON) (1913-1964) US writer who spent most of his adult life, not very happily, in the US Navy, which he joined in 1931. After returning to civilian life in 1953, he took a BA in literature at the University of North Carolina. His first published story was "Casey Agonistes" for *FSF* in 1958, although the first he wrote was "The Fishdollar Affair" (1958), which appeared in *If*. His efforts to revise the former story according to the editor's demands are described in his essay "Journey with a Little Man", which was reprinted in Damon KNIGHT's anthology of sf criticism, *Turning Points* (anth **1977**). RMM was to publish only 5 more sf stories during his lifetime; another 6 appeared posthumously. 5 of the strongest were assembled in *Casey Agonistes and other Fantasy and Science Fiction Stories* (coll **1973**). The central theme of these stories is the power of mind over environment – either to adapt the existing one or, ultimately, to create something new. "The Secret Place" (1966), which won a posthumous NEBULA, is about PARALLEL WORLDS which can be reached through the power of the mind, while "Fiddler's Green" (1967), perhaps RMM's most ambitious story, tells of a group of men adrift in a small boat, without food and water, who mentally create an ALTERNATE WORLD into which they may escape. RMM's major work was a successful non-sf novel drawing on his naval experiences, *The Sand Pebbles* (**1962**), filmed in 1966. He died soon after writing the book; even had he lived it is unlikely that he would have written more sf. Nonetheless, his existing body of sf was sufficient to secure him a small, sure position in the sf pantheon. [MJE]

About the author: "Casey Agonistes" by Peter NICHOLLS in *Survey of Science Fiction Literature, Volume*

One (**1979**) ed Frank N. Magill.

See also: ANTHROPOLOGY; ECOLOGY; PARANOIA; PASTORAL; PERCEPTION.

MACKENZIE, [Sir] (EDWARD MONTAGUE) COMPTON (1883-1972) Scottish writer, knighted in 1952, best known for his influential *Bildungsroman, Sinister Street* (2 vols **1913-14**). His sf novel, *The Lunatic Republic* (**1959**), one of his many comic entertainments, depicts, with considerable slapstick in an easy-going, winning style, the UTOPIAN society that exists at the end of the century on the MOON. Two fantasies, *Hunting the Fairies* (**1949**) and *The Rival Monster* (**1952**), display the pawkish whimsy which made novels like *Whisky Galore* (**1947**) so popular. [JC]

McKENZIE, MELINDA ◊ Melinda M. SNODGRASS.

McKEONE, (DIXIE) LEE (?   -   ) US author of the **Ghoster** sequence of sf adventures – *Ghoster* (**1988**), *Backblast* (**1989**) and *Starfire Down* (**1991**). The tales are set in undemanding interstellar venues in which human enterprises flourish.   [JC]

McKIE, ANGUS (1951-   ) UK illustrator. AM studied at Newcastle-upon-Tyne College of Art. From the mid-1970s his sf work appeared often on book covers, in picture books like *Alien Landscapes* (**1979**) by Robert HOLDSTOCK and Malcolm EDWARDS, and also in his own *The Flights of Icarus* (**1977**). At first AM worked mostly in the Chris FOSS style which dominated UK paperback book covers of the 1970s, whether relevant to the content or not: usually airbrushed ILLUSTRATIONS featuring high-tech artefacts, often space hardware, rendered with great detail. As that particular stereotype began to fade, AM's work, among the most proficient of its kind, showed greater variety. AM has an exceptional feel for scale: when he paints an object supposed to be huge it really looks huge.   [PN/JG]

McKILLIP, PATRICIA A(NNE) (1948-   ) US writer whose early books were all fantasy, mostly for children. These showed an increasing assurance (and appeared to be for increasingly older children) from *The House on Parchment Street* (**1973**) through *The Throme of the Erril of Sherill* (**1973**; exp with "The Harrowing of the Dragon of Hoarsbreath" [1982] as coll 1984) and *The Forgotten Beasts of Eld* (**1974**), an assurance which culminated in the **Riddle-Master** trilogy: *The Riddle-Master of Hed* (**1976**), *Heir of Sea and Fire* (**1978**) and *Harpist in the Wind* (**1979**), assembled as *Riddle of Stars* (omni **1979**; vt *The Chronicles of Morgon, Prince of Hed* 1981 UK). It has been argued, by Peter NICHOLLS in *Survey of Modern Fantastic Literature* (**1983**) ed Frank N. Magill, that the trilogy is a work of classic stature: the intricate narrative of its quest story echoes a moral complexity almost unheard-of in fantasy trilogies; PAM's protagonist has a special skill at unravelling riddles and, through a series of strategies (including subliminal hints as little obvious as leaves in a forest) not unlike those adopted by Gene WOLFE in his **Book of the New Sun** series (**1980-83**), she forces the reader also to become a decipherer of codes. Thus the book's meaning is enacted by the way it must be read. While in no way resembling sf, the trilogy contains one of the most sophisticated uses of the shapeshifter theme to be found anywhere in sf or fantasy.

Her sf proper began with the poignant **Kyreol** sequence for young adults: *Moon-Flash* (**1984**) and *The Moon and the Face* (**1985**). Much as in her fantasy books, the central theme is CONCEPTUAL BREAKTHROUGH, in this case from an Edenic but primitive POCKET UNIVERSE, Riverworld, which turns out to be an isolated corner of a planet containing the way station of an interstellar civilization, and the protected object of anthropological study. *Fool's Run* (**1987**), which is adult sf, retells the Orpheus myth in a story of a woman visionary who has been found guilty of mass murder and is incarcerated in a prison satellite, the Underworld; it is memorable for its evocative sequences about future MUSIC.

PAM's sf is unusual and well written, but perhaps she is more at home with fantasy, to which she returned with the haunting *The Sorceress and the Cygnet* (**1991**), set in a land where star constellations manifest themselves as gods or people and transform the mutable human world into ageless story.   [PN]

Other works: *The Night Gift* (**1976**), marginal fantasy; *Stepping from the Shadows* (**1982**), a possibly autobiographical novel about the growing-up of a fantasy writer; *The Changeling Sea* (**1988**), young-adult fantasy.

See also: ARTS; CHILDREN'S SF; MAGIC; MYTHOLOGY; SPACE HABITATS.

McKINNEY, JACK Collaborative pseudonym of Brian C. DALEY and James LUCENO.   [JC]

MacLAREN, BERNARD (?   -   ) UK writer whose sf novel *Day of Misjudgment* (**1956**) unusually represents the domination of society by COMPUTERS as more of a blessing than a curse.   [JC]

McLAUGHLIN, DEAN (BENJAMIN Jr) (1931-   ) US writer who began publishing sf with "For Those who Follow After" for *ASF* in 1951. Of his three sf novels – *Dome World* (1958 *ASF*; exp **1962**), *The Fury from Earth* (**1963**) and *The Man who Wanted Stars* (fixup **1965**) – the last is probably the best, though all of these straightforward adventures are densely written. The first is set UNDER THE SEA, the second describes a war between Earth and a liberated VENUS, and the third depicts one man's long, driven quest to force and trick Earth governments into attaining interstellar SPACE FLIGHT. *Hawk Among the Sparrows* (coll **1976**) assembles stories of the 1960s. DM's subject matter and style were fairly typical of those encouraged by John W. CAMPBELL Jr during his editorial domination of *ASF*.   [JC]

See also: POLLUTION; STARS.

MacLEAN, ALISTAIR (STUART) (1922-1987) Scottish writer whose novels are mostly – like *The Guns of Navarone* (**1957**) – well crafted action adventures, usually set at least in part at sea. *The Dark Crusader* (**1961**) and *The Satan Bug* (**1962**), both as by Ian Stuart, are Cold War thrillers which make use of sf MCGUFFINS. *The Golden Gate* (**1976**) features the abduction of a US President. *Farewell California* (**1977**) deals with the threat of a major earthquake along the San Andreas Fault, an event that would sink much of the eponymous state beneath the Pacific.   [JC]

MacLEAN, KATHERINE (ANNE) (1925-   ) US writer who took a BA from Barnard College, New York, did postgraduate study in psychology, became a quality-control lab technician in a food factory, and subsequently served as a college lecturer in creative writing and literature. Much of KM's work has been short stories, most of which, including her first, "Defense Mechanism" in 1949, appeared in *ASF*. She has generally written under her own name, although some stories were as by Charles Dye (Charles DYE was her husband 1951-3; *see his entry for details*) and one as by A.G. Morris; she was also married 1956-62 to David MASON. KM was in the vanguard of those sf writers trying to apply to the SOFT SCIENCES the machinery of the hard sciences in a generally optimistic reading of the potentials of that application; her range and competence in dealing with technological matters may in part reflect the wide range of occupations in her extra-literary life. Despite this subject matter her tone was generally that of HARD SF, and her work was unconnected with the later NEW-WAVE uses of the same basic material. KM was one of the earlier WOMEN SF WRITERS, but it would be neither desirable nor possible to read her stories as "women's" sf: in a field which was, in 1950, notoriously male-chauvinist she competed on equal terms, not restricting herself to "feminine" themes or protagonists, and not generally using a male pseudonym. A number of her stories were assembled in *The Diploids* (coll **1962**) and *The Trouble with You Earth People* (coll **1980**).

Many of KM's early stories have been anthologized. Perhaps the best-known are "Pictures Don't Lie" (1951), which tells of the arrival of an alien SPACESHIP which seems normal according to advance radio signals but turns out to be little more than microscopic, "The Snowball Effect" (1952), an amusing SATIRE on social engineering in which a ladies' knitting circle expands to become the strongest political pressure group in the USA, and "Unhuman Sacrifice" (1958), an important piece of anthropological sf ($\Diamond$ ANTHROPOLOGY) in which a visiting exploration/contact team on another planet misreads a painful initiation ceremony as needless when its purpose is to prevent a damaging biological change. Also notable is the **Hills of Space** series, dealing with the settling of the ASTEROIDS by refugees, fugitives and the poor; it includes "Incommunicado" (1950), "The Man who Staked the Stars" (1952 as by Charles Dye), "Collision Orbit" (1954), "The Gambling Hell and the Sinful Girl" (1975) and a long-projected novel, provisionally titled «The Hills of Space».

KM's first novel, *Cosmic Checkmate* (1958 *ASF* as "Second Game"; exp **1962** dos; exp vt *Second Game* 1981), with Charles DE VET, combines SPACE OPERA with interesting speculations on a society whose hierarchy is built around skill at games ($\Diamond$ GAMES AND SPORTS). *Missing Man* (fixup **1975**), which contains the 1971 NEBULA-winning story "The Missing Man" (1971), deals with the exploits of an ESPER whose telepathy is a kind of sonar device enabling him to trace people emitting emotional distress signals; he cooperates with New York's Rescue Squad to go to their aid. Unusually for sf, the novel depicts New York with affection. *Dark Wing* (**1979**), with Carl West, less convincingly presents a world in which MEDICINE is forbidden: a teenager learns to become an outlaw surgeon by studying a medical kit.   [JC/PN]
Other work: *Trouble with Treaties* (1959 *Star Science Fiction #5* ed Frederick POHL; **1975** chap).
See also: ALIENS; PHYSICS; RELIGION; SOCIOLOGY.

MacLENNAN, (JOHN) HUGH (1907-1990) Canadian novelist who early published two DYSTOPIAN tales, "The Finding of the Way" (1955 *The Montrealer*) and "Remembrance Day, 2010 A.D." (1957 *The Montrealer*), but almost all of whose works, like his second novel, *Two Solitudes* (**1945**), lay outside the field and were shaped by the search for a Canadian national myth. His only sf novel, *Voices in Time* (**1980**), whose frame story is set in Montreal in AD2039 after a nuclear HOLOCAUST, reflects the failure of that search in a dour meditation on the cycles of Canadian history.   [JC]
See also: CANADA.

MacLEOD, ANGUS (1906-   ) Scottish writer of fiction and plays for RADIO. His sf novels are *The Body's Guest* (**1958**), in which a yoga machine built by an Indian physicist switches identities between nine Scots and a bull, with mildly amusing results, and *The Eighth Seal* (**1962**).   [JC/PN]

MacLEOD, SHEILA (1939-   ) Scottish writer, married for several years to actor and pop singer Paul Jones ($\Diamond$ PRIVILEGE), an experience reflected in her first novel, *The Moving Accident* (**1968**). Her second, *The Snow-White Soliloquies* (**1970**), is a FABULATION with surprisingly firm sf underpinning, describing in technological terms the SUSPENDED ANIMATION of its eponymous heroine as the search for a Prince continues in a grey world. *Xanthe and the Robots* (**1977**), set in an Institute for Advanced Robotic Research, explores the creation of "Philophrenics" (ROBOTS of near-human capability) and the problems their all-too-human designers face in deciding how far to attempt to exploit their development; it is an intelligent and sophisticated novel. *Circuit-Breaker* (**1978**) entertainingly mixes INNER SPACE and outer, describing an astronaut's attempts to use his PSI POWERS to save his ship – assuming the hero is indeed an astronaut and not a mental case or an sf writer: the ending is ambiguous.   [MJE/PN/JC]

McLOUGHLIN, JOHN C. (1949-   ) US writer whose first novel, *The Helix and the Sword* (**1983**), is an sf adventure of some competence, and whose second, *Toolmaster Koan* (**1987**), more interestingly sets up a Soviet-US tussle – to be the first to meet an ALIEN seemingly arriving from outer space in a

GENERATION STARSHIP – as a dramatic representation of the ongoing thematic argument that gives shape to the tale. This argument, extrapolated from evolutionary BIOLOGY, suggests that any species, once it acquires tools, enters an almost certainly fatal period of disequilibrium between that manipulative capacity and its powers of self-control. In the end, the "aliens" turn out to be dinosaurs, relics of Earth's last self-destructive evolutionary surge, and augurs of the failure to come. [JC]

McMAHON, PAT [s] ◊ Edward D. HOCH.

McMULLEN, SEAN (CHRISTOPHER) (1948-) Australian writer whose first professional sf sale was "The Pharaoh's Airship" for *Omega Science Digest* in 1986. The best of his craftsmanlike stories appear in *Call to the Edge* (coll **1992**), a notable example being "The Colours of the Masters" (**1988**), in which a 19th-century device, the clockwork "pianospectrum", is discovered to have recorded the playing of Beethoven, Chopin and Liszt. [PN]
See also: MUSIC.

McNEILLY, WILFRED GLASSFORD (1921-1983) Scottish author of numerous novels and stories under a variety of names; he achieved some minor notoriety when he claimed in print to have written all the work published under the byline W. Howard BAKER – actually WGM's editor on stories written for the **Sexton Blake** library and for Press Editorial Syndicate – and various other Baker pseudonyms, a claim since disproved. WGM did write (as Errol Lecale) the **Specialist** series: *Tigermun of Terrahpur* (**1973**), *Castledoom* (**1974**), *The Severed Hand* (**1974**), *The Death Box* (**1974**), *Zombie* (**1975**) and *Blood of My Blood* (**1975**). As Peter SAXON, another house name, he cowrote with Baker 2 tales in the **Guardians** sequence: *Dark Ways to Death* * (**1968**) and *The Haunting of Alan Mais* * (**1969**). Non-series collaborations with Baker include *The Darkest Night* (**1966**) and *The Torturer* (**1966**). Solo titles as Saxon include *Satan's Child* (**1967**) and *Corruption* (dated 1968 but **1969**). WGM is also credited with *Drums of the Dark Gods* (**1966**) as by W.A. Ballinger; *The Case of the Muckrakers* (**1966**), a **Sexton Blake** title; and *Alpha-Omega* (**1977**) as by Wilfred Glassford. [SH/JC]

McNELLY, [Dr] WILLIS E(VERETT) (1920-) US academic, sf critic and editor long based at California State University at Fullerton, where he gave what were among the earlier sf classes in the USA. His anthologies include *Mars, We Love You* (anth **1971**; vt *The Book of Mars* 1976 UK) ed with Jane Hipolito, *Above the Human Landscape: A Social Science Fiction Anthology* (anth **1972**) ed with Leon E. STOVER and *Science Fiction Novellas* (anth **1975**) ed with Harry HARRISON; the last title had a companion work, *Science Fiction Novellas: Teacher's Guide* (**1975**) by WEM alone. He edited a collection of brief essays about the increasing interest of the academic world in sf (◊ SF IN THE CLASSROOM), *Science Fiction: The Academic Awakening* (anth **1974** chap). WEM's strangest work is certainly *The Dune Encyclopedia* (anth **1984**); it pur-

ports to have been published about 5000 years after the birth of Paul Atreides, protagonist of Frank HERBERT's *Dune* (fixup **1965**), and presents data about the history and ecology of the planet Dune. [PN]

MacPATTERSON, F. ◊ Clark DARLTON.

McPHEE, JAMES ◊ Laurence JAMES.

MacPHERSON, DONALD (? -) Canadian author, perhaps a pseudonym of George MacTavish. *Go Home, Unicorn* (**1935** UK) is a SCIENTIFIC ROMANCE set in Montreal, in which the life of a research scientist – loved by two women, one jealous – is much confused by projections, into the world of matter, of their (and other people's) mental fantasies, brought into being by the X-ray field he is using to create mutations in guinea-pigs; there is much scientific speculation, rather far-fetched, about the nature of the mind/matter division. The sequel, *Men are Like Animals* (**1937** UK), likewise features research scientist **Reggie Brooks**, and involves a device that controls thoughts. [PN]

McQUAY, MIKE Working name of US writer Michael Dennis McQuay (1949-), who began to publish sf with his first novel, *Life-Keeper* (**1980**), which very competently presents the kind of scenario MM has unrelentingly promulgated in book after book: a world governed by corrupt forces; a tough, anarchic, street-wise male protagonist whose powers – and virtue – are very exceptional indeed; and a plot which gives plenty of opportunities for arena-like conflicts between that protagonist and the corrupt forces he will ultimately defeat. The **Mathew Swain** sequence – *Hot Time in Old Town* (**1981**), *When Trouble Beckons* (**1981**), *The Deadliest Show in Town* (**1982**) and *The Odds are Murder* (**1983**) – makes explicit the generic origins of this hero, who derives from the works of Raymond Chandler (1888-1959) and Chandler's direct successors. As the series develops, Swain fights corruption first on Earth, then on the Moon and then on Earth again, always finding fit targets in the organizations which dominate society. *Escape from New York* * (**1981**), a film tie (◊ ESCAPE FROM NEW YORK), if anything intensifies the seamy clangour of the movie version. *Jitterbug* (**1984**) interestingly posits an Arab hegemony over a corruptly DYSTOPIAN 22nd-century world. The **Ramon and Morgan** series – *Pure Blood* (**1985**) and *Mother Earth* (**1985**) – exploits similar venues without much innovation. MM's best novel to date is perhaps *Memories* (**1987**), in which the *Weltschmerz* inherent in the Chandler tradition is cleverly re-articulated in the story of a woman who arrives by a form of subjective TIME TRAVEL from a devastated future, and who embroils the psychiatrist hero in further travels backwards into a somewhat sentimentalized understanding on both their parts of the depth of their deracination from the real world. *The Nexus* (**1989**) likewise handles material of considerable complexity, in this case a NEAR-FUTURE tale of innocence exploited. It is difficult to be sure that MM's copious energy will eventually control his equally apparent sentimentality; but he remains, without doubt, one of the more interesting professionals in the field.   [JC]

Other works: *My Science Project* * (**1985**), a tie to MY SCIENCE PROJECT (1985); *The M.I.A. Ransom* (**1986**); *Isaac Asimov's Robot City #2: Suspicion* * (**1987**); *Puppetmaster* (**1991** UK; rev 1991 US), associational thriller.

As Victor Appleton (house name): *Tom Swift: Crater of Mystery* * (**1983**); *Tom Swift: Planet of Nightmares* * (**1984**).

As Jack Arnett: The **Book of Justice** sequence of associational thrillers, those of some sf interest being #1: *Genocide Express* (**1989**), #2: *Zaitech Sting* (**1990**) and #4: *Panama Dead* (**1990**).

As Laura Lee Hope (house name): *Bobbsey Twins: Haunted House* * (**1985**).

As Carolyn Keene (house name): *Nancy Drew: Ghost Stories* * (coll **1985**).

See also: ALTERNATE WORLDS; PHILIP K. DICK AWARD.

McQUEEN, RONALD A. [r] ◊ ROBERT HALE LIMITED.

McQUINN, DONALD E. (1930-   ) US writer whose first novel, *Warrior* (**1990**), packs into its setting – a USA 500 years after the nation's nuclear destruction – almost every CLICHÉ available to writers of barbarian-warrior novels: a variety of agon-based tribal societies; a woman-run church; a batch of 21st-century warriors freshly resurrected from CRYONIC slumber and ready for a fight; an evil monarch bent on establishing an Empire; and a protagonist who must wander from one enclave to another, gradually accumulating a passel of friends and adherents as he goes. But the book itself, despite its (well handled) military moments, is in effect a PLANETARY ROMANCE, and in its 500 pages slowly and lovingly establishes an extremely complex portrait of a huge, densely populated, intensely variegated land. Several women characters have featured roles (though most of them are oppressed). It seems that DEM might be one of the novelists to watch in the 1990s.   [JC]

MACROCOSM ◊ GREAT AND SMALL.

MacTYRE, PAUL Pseudonym of Scottish writer R.J. Adam (1924-   ). His best-known novel is his first, *Midge* (**1962**; vt *Doomsday, 1999* 1963 US), a literate post-HOLOCAUST story in which a new form of life threatens to take over from the remnants of outmoded, destructive Man. Further novels are the John Buchanesque *Fish on a Hook* (**1963**) and *Bar Sinister* (**1964**), the bar of the title representing a borderline-sf COMMUNICATIONS technology.   [JC]

MacVICAR, ANGUS [r] ◊ *The* LOST PLANET; RADIO.

MADÁCH, IMRE (1823-1864) Hungarian playwright and parliamentarian, chiefly known for his verse play *Az ember tragédiája* (**1862**; trans J.C.W. Horne as *The Tragedy of Man: A Dramatic Poem in Fifteen Scenes* 1963 Hungary; preferred trans by George Szirtes 1988 Hungary). This philosophical, rather pessimistic fantasy about the destiny of mankind focuses on Adam (an optimist), Eve and Lucifer (a materialist), who reappear in each scene in different guises (Adam once as Johannes KEPLER), all this being a dream shown to Adam by Lucifer. The somewhat high-flown narrative begins in biblical times and ends in

the future; one of the last scenes is set in space, and another on a Dying Earth in the FAR FUTURE when the Sun is dim and red.   [PN]

MADARIAGA (Y ROJO), SALVADOR de (1886-1978) Spanish man of letters and diplomat who spent much of his life after 1916 in the UK and Switzerland, where he eventually retired. In his sf novel, *The Sacred Giraffe: Being the Second Volume of the Posthumous Works of Julio Arceval* (**1925** UK), set in AD6922, the Blacks who have survived much history, including the submergence of Europe, argue about the possibility that Whites ever actually existed. Their hierarchical and monogamous state of Ebony – which is in Africa – is ruled by women. The book's various satirical points are generally directed at UK culture. *Sir Bob* (**1930** US) is a fantasy for children, though its mildly satirical implications are clearly intended for the delectation of adults. SdM either wrote both works initially in English or translated them himself.   [JC]

MADDOCK, LARRY The solo writing name of Jack Owen Jardine (1931-   ), a creative director in radio, for his **Agent of T.E.R.R.A.** series, speedy SPACE OPERAS starring Hannibal Fortune and an alien sidekick on various assignments to save Earth from her enemies. The series comprises *The Flying Saucer Gambit* (**1966**), *The Golden Goddess Gambit* (**1967**), *The Emerald Elephant Gambit* (**1967**) and *The Time Trap Gambit* (**1969**). With his then wife, Julie Ann Jardine, he also wrote under the pseudonym Howard L. CORY.   [JC]

See also: UFOS.

MADDOX, CARL ◊ E.C. TUBB.

MADDOX, TOM (?   -   ) US writer who began publishing polished short stories with "The Mind like a Strange Balloon" for *Omni* in 1985. His first novel, *Halo* (**1991**), moves from a CYBERPUNK Earth to a SPACE HABITAT, engaging en route in an intense contemplation of the nature of artificial intelligence (◊ AI; CYBERNETICS; ROBOTS) in a VIRTUAL-REALITY environment. The tale is intermittently hectic, but charged with energy.   [JC]

MADER, FRIEDRICH W(ILHELM) (1866-1947) German writer, mainly of juvenile novels, many set in German East Africa and written somewhat in the style of H. Rider HAGGARD. *Wunderwelten* (**1911**; trans Max Shachtman as *Distant Worlds: The Story of a Voyage to the Planets* 1932 US) is a juvenile which takes its SPACESHIP crew to Mars and finally, at several times the speed of light, to Alpha Centauri, where they explore an Eden-like planet. Its content is quite advanced for 1911, but it is ill written. Other untranslated works include *El Dorado* (**1919**; vt *Auf den Spuren der Inkas*), *Die letzte Atlantide* ["The Last Atlantis"] (**1923**) and *Die Messingstadt* ["City of Brass"] (**1924**).   [PN/JE]

See also: GERMANY.

MADLEE, DOROTHY [r] ◊ Andre NORTON.

MAD LOVE ◊ ORLACS HÄNDE.

MAD MAX Film (1979). Mad Max Pty. Dir George

MILLER, starring Mel Gibson, Joanne Samuel, Hugh Keays-Byrne, Tim Burns. Screenplay James McCausland, Miller, based on a story by Miller. 100 mins, cut to 91 mins. Colour.

This low-budget exploitation movie builds up to the vigilante-style revenge of spaced-out policeman Max Rockatansky (Gibson) – who is almost as disturbed as his antagonists – on the motorcycle gang that killed his wife and child. It proved to be the successful harbinger of a boom in post-HOLOCAUST sf films where a dying civilization is pitted against a growing barbarism. Miller, whose début feature this was, is extremely economical with data about just what (other than fuel shortages) has happened to create this crumbling of the social structure in Australia. Nonetheless, his vision of anarchy's spread – the atmosphere is reminiscent of John CARPENTER's *Assault on Precinct 13* (1976) – is credible and well achieved. The film's instant success was due to the panache (and great skill) with which the chase sequences and spectacular vehicle demolitions were mounted. Prints shown in the USA were dubbed so that audiences there should not be subjected to the brutalities of the Australian accent. [PN]

See also: ACE BOOKS; CINEMA; MUSIC.

MAD MAX BEYOND THUNDERDOME Film (1985). Kennedy Miller Productions. Dir George MILLER with George Ogilvie, starring Mel Gibson, Tina Turner, Bruce Spence, Frank Thring, Paul Larsson, Helen Buday. Screenplay Terry Hayes, Miller. 107 mins. Colour.

This Australian film, the second sequel to the post-HOLOCAUST movie MAD MAX (1979), has lots of well directed action but is more rambling and less focused than its predecessors. Max finds a community in the desert, Bartertown, with a female warlord (Tina Turner), gladiatorial games, and a great many extras being noisy, dirty and primitive. This lively stuff is really no more than a rehash of a great many filmic clichés, notably those of Italian sword-and-sandal epics. Far more interesting is a subplot set in a different part of the desert and involving a tribe of children who are now living in an oasis, having many years ago survived a plane crash in which all adults were killed. In perhaps the first attempt in cinema to achieve, albeit less complexly, something of what Russell HOBAN achieved in *Riddley Walker* (**1980**), they speak a devolved language (◊ LINGUISTICS); they also have a mythology involving a MESSIAH-figure, whom they take Mad Max to be. Their final return to the derelict ghost-city of Sydney is well done, and this whole inventive section about the children – pure sf, and ambitious sf at that – makes an otherwise routinely vivid film well worth watching. The novelization is *Mad Max III: Beyond Thunderdome* * (**1985**) by Joan D. VINGE. [PN]

MAD MAX 2 (vt *The Road Warrior*) Film (1981). Kennedy Miller Entertainment. Dir George MILLER, starring Mel Gibson, Bruce Spence, Emil Minty, Mike Preston, Kjell Nilsson. Screenplay Terry Hayes, Miller, Brian Hannant. 96 mins. Colour.

The success of the first film in this series, MAD MAX (1979), generated a bigger budget for this, the second. It was well used, and this is a more sophisticated film, more purely sf than its predecessor. The oil wars have left a devastated world; petrol is a medium of exchange, and its conspicuous use – by burning it up on the roads – confers status. Ex-policeman Max Rockatansky (Gibson) gives reluctant assistance to a semicivilized group in a desert fortress. Possessing a valuable petrol supply, they are beleaguered by a tribe of marauders (who, in this Westerns replay, are effectively the Indians), designer-barbarians in fetishistic gear on motorbikes and vehicles of war. Made with poker-faced humour, and this time with the US prints allowed to retain Mel Gibson's Australian drawl, the film is enlivened by small details – e.g., the Feral Kid (Minty) with his razor-sharp metal boomerang – and has much to recommend it beyond the tautly directed scenes of vehicular warfare. Poignant use is made of memories when times were better. The name of the sleazy real-world coastal resort Surfer's Paradise is now only half-remembered, as "Paradise", and ironically the place becomes the Promised Land to which the civilized remnant (minus the loner, Max) finally treks. With all its comic-strip energy and vividness, this is exploitation cinema at its most inventive. [PN]

MADSEN, SVEND ÅGE [r] ◊ DENMARK.

MAEPEN, K.H. [s] ◊ Henry KUTTNER.

MAGAZINE OF FANTASY, THE ◊ *The* MAGAZINE OF FANTASY AND SCIENCE FICTION.

MAGAZINE OF FANTASY AND SCIENCE FICTION, THE US DIGEST-size magazine; published Fall 1949-Feb 1958 by Fantasy House, Inc., a subsidiary of Mercury Press, then by Mercury Press; Lawrence Spivak was credited as Publisher Fall 1949-July 1954, Joseph W. FERMAN Aug 1954-Oct 1970, Edward L. FERMAN from Nov 1970; ed Anthony BOUCHER and J. Francis MCCOMAS Fall 1949-Aug 1954, then by Boucher alone until Aug 1958, by Robert P. MILLS Sep 1958-Mar 1962, by Avram DAVIDSON Apr 1962-Nov 1964, by publisher Joseph W. Ferman Dec 1964-Dec 1965, by Edward L. Ferman Jan 1966-June 1991, and by Kristine Kathryn RUSCH from July 1991. To date (June 1992) *FSF* has published 493 issues. #1 (Fall 1949) was titled *The Magazine of Fantasy*. The magazine began as a quarterly, became a bimonthly in Feb 1951, and has maintained a monthly schedule since Aug 1952. A rather short-lived companion magazine was VENTURE SCIENCE FICTION.

FSF – the abbreviation, taken from the words "Fantasy and Science Fiction" on the spine, being in almost universal use by its readers – won HUGOS for Best Magazine in 1958, 1959, 1960, 1963, 1969, 1970, 1971 and 1972; after that category was dropped, Edward L. Ferman won the Hugo for Best Editor in 1981, 1982 and 1983. *FSF*'s editorial policy has always placed the main emphasis on short stories. Its editors abandoned the standards of PULP-MAGAZINE fiction and asked for stylish sf/fantasy that was up to the literary standards of the "slick" magazines that had shaped US short-story writing between the wars; they also abandoned interior illustrations. *FSF* published a great deal of light and humorous material, and used occasional reprints of stories by prestigious writers, including Robert GRAVES, Eric LINKLATER, Robert NATHAN, Robert Louis STEVENSON, James Thurber (1894-1961), Oscar Wilde (1854-1900) and P.G. WODEHOUSE. It also attracted such writers as Kingsley AMIS, Gerald HEARD and C.S. LEWIS to write for its pages. Despite the various changes of editorship the personality of the magazine has been consistent, although since the 1970s it has been a more orthodox sf magazine than in earlier days. It used serials only occasionally, and most of the novels appearing in it are substantially cut; they have included *Bring the Jubilee* by Ward MOORE (Nov 1952; **1953**), *Rogue Moon* by Algis BUDRYS (Dec 1960; **1960**) and *Starship Troopers* (Oct-Nov 1959 as "Starship Soldier"; exp **1959**) by Robert A. HEINLEIN. Several notable series have been associated with the magazine, including Zenna HENDERSON's **People**, Manly Wade WELLMAN's **John the Ballad Singer**, Poul ANDERSON's **Time Patrol** and Reginald BRETNOR's **Papa Schimmelhorn**. Walter M. MILLER's classic *A Canticle for Leibowitz* (fixup **1960**) was developed from 3 novelettes published in *FSF* 1955-7.

Starship Troopers and *A Canticle for Leibowitz* were two of *FSF*'s many award-winning stories. Others were Robert BLOCH's "That Hellbound Train" (Sep 1958; Hugo), Daniel KEYES's "Flowers for Algernon" (Apr 1959; Hugo; the novel version, *Flowers for Algernon* **[1966]**, won a NEBULA), Brian W. ALDISS's **Hothouse** series (1961; Hugo; fixup as *Hothouse* **1962**; vt *The Long Afternoon of Earth*) and "The Saliva Tree" (Sep 1965; Nebula), Poul Anderson's "No Truce with Kings" (June 1963; Hugo), "The Queen of Air and Darkness" (Apr 1971; Hugo and Nebula) and "Goat Song" (Feb 1972; Hugo and Nebula), Fritz LEIBER's "Ship of Shadows" (July 1969; Hugo), "Ill Met in Lankhmar" (Apr 1970; Hugo) and "Catch that Zeppelin" (Mar 1975; Hugo and Nebula), Roger ZELAZNY's "The Doors of His Face, the Lamps of His Mouth" (Mar 1965; Nebula) and "And Call Me Conrad" (Oct-Nov 1965; Hugo; exp vt *This Immortal* **1966**), Frederik POHL's and C.M. KORNBLUTH's "The Meeting" (Nov 1972; Hugo), Harlan ELLISON's "The Deathbird" (Mar 1973; Hugo), "Adrift Just Off the Islets of Langerhans" (Oct 1974; Hugo) and "Jeffty is Five" (Jul 1977; Hugo and Nebula), "Pages from a Young Girl's Journal" (Feb 1973; World Fantasy Award) by Robert Aickman (d1981), Robert SILVERBERG's "Born with the Dead" (Apr 1974; Nebula), Tom REAMY's "San Diego Lightfoot Sue" (Aug 1975; Nebula), Frederik Pohl's *Man Plus* (Apr-June 1976; Nebula), Charles L. Grant's "A Crowd of Shadows" (June 1976; Nebula), Edward BRYANT's "Stone" (Feb 1978; Nebula), John VARLEY's "The Persistence of Vision" (Mar 1978; Hugo and Nebula) and "The Pusher" (Oct 1981; Hugo), C.J. CHERRYH's "Cassandra" (Oct 1978; Hugo), Lisa TUTTLE's

"The Bone Flute" (May 1981; Nebula), Joanna RUSS's "Souls" (Jan 1982; Hugo), John KESSEL's "Another Orphan" (Sep 82; Nebula), Kim Stanley ROBINSON's "Black Air" (March 1983; World Fantasy Award), Nancy KRESS's "Out of All Them Bright Stars" (Mar 1985; Nebula), Ursula K. LE GUIN's "Buffalo Gals Won't You Come Out Tonight" (Nov 1987; Hugo) and Michael D. RESNICK's "Kirinyaga" (Nov 1988; Hugo). Other excellent stories have been contributed by Alfred BESTER, Boucher himself, Samuel R. DELANY, Philip José FARMER, Richard MATHESON, James TIPTREE Jr and many others.

From Nov 1958 to Feb 1992, 399 issues, every issue of *FSF* featured a science article by Isaac ASIMOV; he collected these essays, which ceased not long before his death, into many books. His replacement is Gregory BENFORD. Early book-review editors were Boucher, Damon Knight, Alfred Bester and Avram Davidson; the lead reviewer 1975-92 was Algis Budrys. Baird Searles has reviewed films. Another feature was the long series (1958-64) of punning shaggy-dog stories known as **Feghoots**, written by Reginald BRETNOR as Grendel Briarton. In 1968 the magazine sponsored a novel-writing contest won by Piers ANTHONY with *Sos the Rope* (July-Sep 1968; **1968**).

FSF has published a "special all-star anniversary issue" every October since the mid-1960s, and a series of special issues celebrating particular authors, each featuring a new story, a checklist of the author's work and articles about the author. The first of these was devoted to Theodore STURGEON (Sep 1962), and subsequent special issues featured Ray BRADBURY (May 1963), Isaac Asimov (Oct 1966), Fritz Leiber (July 1969), Poul Anderson (Apr 1971), James BLISH (Apr 1972), Frederik Pohl (Sep 1973), Robert Silverberg (Apr 1974) and Harlan Ellison (July 1977), the Anderson, Leiber and Silverberg stories being among the award winners listed above. The first 6 of these stories, with abridged checklists and biographical articles, were published as *The Best from Fantasy and Science Fiction: A Special 25th Anniversary Anthology* (anth **1974**), ed Edward L. Ferman, which, though not so titled, is assumed to be #21 of the **Best** series, as its successor was #22. The **Best** series, beginning with *The Best from Fantasy and Science Fiction* (anth **1952**) ed Boucher and McComas, ran 1952-82, amounting to 24 anthologies (counting the 25th-anniversary volume). These at first appeared annually, but none appeared in 1970, 1972, 1974-6, 1978-9 and 1981 (*for details* ◊ Anthony BOUCHER, Robert P. MILLS, Avram DAVIDSON *and* Edward L. FERMAN). Other book spin-offs from *FSF* have been *A Decade of Fantasy and Science Fiction* (anth **1960**) ed Robert P. Mills, *Once and Future Tales from the Magazine of Fantasy and Science Fiction* (anth **1968**) ed Edward L. Ferman, *Twenty Years of the Magazine of Fantasy and Science Fiction* (anth **1970**) ed Edward L. Ferman and Robert P. Mills, *The Magazine of Fantasy and Science Fiction: A Thirty Year Retrospective* (anth **1980**) ed Edward L. Ferman, reprinting the stories from the Oct 1979 retrospective issue, *The Magazine of Fantasy and Science Fiction, April 1965* (anth **1981**) ed Edward L. Ferman and Martin H. GREENBERG, *The Best Fantasy Stories from the Magazine of Fantasy and Science Fiction* (anth **1986**) ed Edward L. Ferman, *The Best Horror Stories from the Magazine of Fantasy and Science Fiction* (anth **1988**; in 2 vols US 1989; vt *The Best of Modern Horror: Twenty-Four Tales from the Magazine of Fantasy and Science Fiction* 1989 UK) ed Edward L. Ferman and Anne Jordan, and *The Best from Fantasy & Science Fiction: A 40th Anniversary Anthology* (anth **1989**) ed Edward L. Ferman.

UK editions of the magazine ran Oct 1953-Sep 1954 (12 issues) from Mellifont Press, and Dec 1959-June 1964 (55 issues) from Atlas Publishing & Distributing Co. These did not reprint whole issues, but selected and recombined stories from the US edition. The UK reprint magazine VENTURE SCIENCE FICTION (1963-5), also from Atlas, carried material from *FSF* as well as from the US *Venture*. There was a selective reprint edition of *FSF* in Australia 1954-8 (14 issues, undated) from Consolidated Press. [BS/PN]

See also: GOLDEN AGE OF SF.

MAGAZINE OF HORROR, THE US DIGEST-size magazine, 36 issues Aug 1963 (Vol 1 #1)-Apr 1971 (Vol 6 #6). The longest-running and most successful of the reprint magazines ed R.A.W. LOWNDES for Health Knowledge Inc., this chiefly published classic horror tales, some from the early PULP MAGAZINES. Most issues also contained 2-4 original stories, a number being of sf interest by writers including John BRUNNER, R.A. LAFFERTY, Emil PETAJA, Joanna RUSS, Robert SILVERBERG and Roger ZELAZNY. The majority of covers were by Virgil FINLAY. Lowndes's editorials were notably balanced and lively. [PN]

MAGAZINES For a statement about which magazines receive entries in this volume, and why, see **Magazines** in the Introduction; for a general discussion of sf magazines (and some fantasy magazines that occasionally published sf stories) ◊ SF MAGAZINES, and also the individual entries for the approximately 240 professional sf magazines and SEMIPROZINES we discuss in detail; for amateur sf periodical publications ◊ FANZINES; for a discussion of pulp magazines generally, and a listing of all the pulp entries not listed under the SF MAGAZINES rubric, including the hero/villain pulps, ◊ PULP MAGAZINES, which also discusses the relationship between the pulps and their competitors, the "slicks" and tabloids.

Many general-fiction magazines other than the pulps have regularly published sf stories, and a selection of the most important have received entries in this encyclopedia: COLLIER'S WEEKLY, *The* IDLER, MCCLURE'S MAGAZINE, MUNSEY'S MAGAZINE, *The* OVERLAND MONTHLY, *The* PASSING SHOW, PEARSON'S MAGAZINE, PEARSON'S WEEKLY, ST NICHOLAS MAGAZINE and *The* STRAND MAGAZINE. Other forms of periodical publishing are discussed under BOYS' PAPERS, COMICS, DIME-NOVEL SF and JUVENILE SERIES. The entries for HISTORY OF SF and PUBLISHING include discussion of the importance of the magazines. [PN]

MAGIC In the first edition of the *Oxford English Dictionary* (**1884-1928**) "magic" is defined as "the pretended art of influencing the course of events . . . by processes supposed to owe their efficacy to their power of compelling the intervention of spiritual beings, or of bringing into operation some occult controlling principle of nature". The lexicographer assumed that there is no difficulty in telling a "pretended" art from a real one, nor in distinguishing the "occult" from the scientific. Many sf authors have felt dissatisfied with such confident categorizations, and have written stories exemplifying alternative relationships between magic and science.

One typical attitude is summed up by Arthur C. CLARKE's "Third Law", in *Profiles of the Future* (coll **1962**): "Any sufficiently advanced technology is indistinguishable from magic." This echoes the observation by Roger Bacon (c1214-1292) 700 years before that "many secrets of art and nature are thought by the unlearned to be magical"; the irony whereby Bacon, a pioneer of experimental science, gained a posthumous reputation for sorcery goes far to confirm Clarke's "Law", and is at the heart of James BLISH's novel of the history of science, *Doctor Mirabilis* (**1964** UK; rev 1971 US). Stories in which superior technology is treated as magic are common, the most thoroughgoing being Larry NIVEN's and David GERROLD's *The Flying Sorcerers* (**1971**). However, the unexpressed converse of Clarke's "Law" has proved even more attractive: if technology looks like magic, could magic not have been misunderstood technology?

The possibilities for fiction of this nature were well exemplified by several stories published in UNKNOWN in the 1940s: Fritz LEIBER's *Conjure Wife* (1943; **1953**), Robert A. HEINLEIN's "The Devil Makes the Law" (1940; vt as "Magic, Inc." in *Waldo and Magic, Inc.* coll **1950**), and the **Harold Shea** stories by L. Sprague DE CAMP and Fletcher PRATT, later collected as *The Incomplete Enchanter* (1940; **1941**) and *The Castle of Iron* (1941; **1950**); the Leiber tale is set in the contemporary USA, the Heinlein in an ALTERNATE WORLD very similar to it, and the **Harold Shea** stories in PARALLEL WORLDS to which contemporary US citizens are sent. All rely heavily on the juxtaposition of familiar and unfamiliar, realistic and fantastic; their concern, above all, is to discipline and rationalize notions of magic. Thus in *Conjure Wife* the hero, a professor of social anthropology, discovers that his wife is a witch and forces her to give up this "superstition". Accumulating catastrophes persuade him that he is wrong. In the end he has to use his academic training to systematize his wife's knowledge and restore stability. The "incomplete enchanters" are likewise academic psychologists, though Heinlein's hero, characteristically, is a small-town businessman.

In presenting rationalized forms of magic the *Unknown* authors were following arguments presented in *The Golden Bough* (**1890** in 2 vols; 3rd edn rev in 12 vols 1911-15) by Sir James Frazer (1854-1941).

This extremely influential work had suggested (a) that magic is like science but unlike RELIGION in its assumption that the Universe works according to "immutable laws", and (b) that some of these laws can be codified as Laws of Sympathy, Similarity and Contact. Frazer was probably no more than half serious in this, but the notion of quasi-Newtonian laws proved irresistible. Leiber, de Camp and Pratt include overt references to *The Golden Bough*, while the hero of "Magic, Inc." is actually called Fraser. At one point this Fraser explains how, for instance, he exploits the laws of "homeopathy" and "contiguity" to erect temporary grandstands: he has a section of seating carefully built, then chops it to pieces, and, "Under the law of contiguity, each piece remained part of the structure it had once been in. Under the law of homeopathy, each piece was potentially the entire structure." So Fraser can send out splinters which, when activated by the proper spells, will temporarily become entire structures. We realize that the world he lives in is controlled entirely by "occult" principles, but that these are not haphazard. Much of the amusement of worlds-where-magic-works stories lies in developing the possibilities of a small number of magical rules.

Many authors have followed the lead of the *Unknown* stories: Poul ANDERSON in *Three Hearts and Three Lions* (1953 *FSF*; exp **1961**) and *Operation Chaos* (1956-9 *FSF*; fixup **1971**), John BRUNNER in *The Traveler in Black* (coll of linked stories **1971**; with 1 story added vt *The Compleat Traveler in Black* **1986** US), James Blish in *Black Easter* (**1968**) and James E. GUNN in *The Magicians* (1954 *Beyond* as "Sine of the Magus"; exp **1976**). The principles of magic as a kind of alternate TECHNOLOGY are also examined in Jack VANCE's *The Dying Earth* (coll of linked stories **1950**) and *The Eyes of the Overworld* (**1966**), in Mark GESTON's *The Siege of Wonder* (**1976**), in Fred SABERHAGEN's **Empire of the East** trilogy beginning with *The Broken Lands* (**1968**), and in Christopher STASHEFF's **Warlock** series beginning with *The Warlock in Spite of Himself* (**1969**). Rachel POLLACK's *Unquenchable Fire* (**1988**) envisages an alternate-world USA run by a bureaucracy of shamans whose shamanism actually works. But the purest example of "Frazerian" sf is Randall GARRETT's **Lord Darcy** series (1964-76 *ASF*), set in an alternate world where King Richard I founded a stable Plantagenet dynasty, Europe remained feudal and Catholic, and magic was developed in harmony with science. The heroes are a detective pair, Lord Darcy and Master Sean O'Lochlainn, resembling Arthur Conan DOYLE's Sherlock Holmes and Dr Watson. Master Sean is not a doctor, however, but a sorcerer, and he plays a much more significant role than Dr Watson ever did, compensating for the absence of forensic science by a series of carefully described magical tests for murder weapons, times of death, chemical analysis and so on. It is not too much to say that the stories are vehicles for the explanations of Master Sean rather than for the adventures of Lord Darcy. Garrett's

distinctive contributions lie in the range of new "laws" added to the old Frazerian ones (Relevance, Synecdoche, Congruency, etc.) and in the rigour with which these are stated and used.

In the stories so far mentioned magic is seen not as *like* science but as a *form* of science. The theme of magic as a kind of alternate science remains intensely popular. Among the writers who would convince us that magic is as much science as art are Patricia MCKILLIP in her **Riddle-Master** trilogy, beginning with *The Riddle-Master of Hed* (**1976**), who does so with *gravitas*, Phyllis EISENSTEIN with *Sorcerer's Son* (**1979**) and its sequel *The Crystal Palace* (**1988**), who does so with some frivolity, and Barbara HAMBLY in a variety of works, notably the **Sun-Cross** sequence beginning with *The Rainbow Abyss* (**1991** UK), which presents magic as culturally disreputable. Though, for really disreputable magic, it would be hard to go past Tim POWERS's splendid *The Drawing of the Dark* (**1979**), whose title puns on approaching evil and long-brewed beer, "the dark", which is the fountainhead, literally, of magic in the book's alternate 16th-century Vienna.

But, if magic is a form of science, why has it never been systematized in our world? Many different answers have been given to this. Garrett's, for example, is that it is a result of prejudiced inquiry on the part of SCIENTISTS (exactly the charge levelled at scientists in the real world by adherents of the PSEUDO-SCIENCES and researchers into the paranormal), complicated by the fact that the exercise of magic demands a mysterious "talent" which many investigators do not possess: experiments are therefore likely to be unrepeatable. Magic here is being assimilated to PSI POWERS, which sf authors are capable of taking seriously. No matter how serious the treatment, however, the end result can be argued as frivolous, for magic is, if not precisely disproven, regarded by science as actually workable only when both magician and subject are believers (as with faith healing or Australian aborigines "pointing the bone"), when it is susceptible to a psychological or psychosomatic rather than a supernatural explanation.

The subgenre of tales about alternate worlds in which magic is subsumed into psi powers is often associated with the names of Andre NORTON and Marion Zimmer BRADLEY. Above-average work in this vein has more recently been produced by Katherine KURTZ with the continuing **Chronicles of the Deryni** series, beginning with *Deryni Rising* (**1970**), by Sheri S. TEPPER with the **True Game** series – which can be regarded as sf – beginning with *King's Blood Four* (**1983**), and most famously by Orson Scott CARD in the **Tales of Alvin Maker**, to date comprising *Seventh Son* (**1987**), *Red Prophet* (**1988**) and *Prentice Alvin* (**1989**), assembled as *Hatrack River* (omni **1989**).

A not uncommon elegiac variant is the idea of a world in which the supply of magic, or its sources, is drying up. Peter DICKINSON's *The Blue Hawk* (**1976**) is of this kind, and there never seem to be enough

Sipstrassi stones (superscientific sources of magical potency from ATLANTIS) to go around in David GEMMELL's **Sipstrassi** sequence, which begins with *Wolf in Shadow* (**1987**; vt *The Jerusalem Man* 1988 US). The best known book of this kind may be Larry Niven's *The Magic Goes Away* (**1977**), which was followed by his two SHARED-WORLD anthologies, *The Magic May Return* * (anth **1981**) and *More Magic* * (anth **1984**).

It is striking that one "Frazerian" area has daunted all but the boldest users of magic in sf, this being RELIGION. The position of magic in a Christian universe is especially difficult to define, since its compulsive quality appears to contradict dogmas of divine omnipotence. Most authors accordingly relegate the problem to the background of their stories, C.S. LEWIS going so far, in *That Hideous Strength* (**1945**), as to explain how magic has come to be unlawful for Christians in normal circumstances. One author who does not shirk the challenge is James Blish, but his *Black Easter* ends with the words: "God is dead."

The actions of godlike creatures in sf (◊ GODS AND DEMONS) are seldom distinguishable from magic, much as in Clarke's "Law" quoted above, and John VARLEY's hyperactive **Gaean** sequence about an artificial world controlled by an intelligence devoted to metamorphic theatricals of a magical kind – *Titan* (**1979**), *Wizard* (**1980**) and *Demon* (**1984**) – though published as sf, has less cognitive consistency than a number of works – including McKillip's **Riddle-Master** series – which would normally be classified as fantasy.

That classification is frequently given also to the only wholly successful resolution of magic, science and religion in sf so far: Ursula K. LE GUIN's **Earthsea** trilogy (**1968-72**). This is in a sense a "Frazerian" work, for the magic in it is based on the notion that everything has a true name and can be controlled by knowledge of it: Frazer was familiar with name-taboos. However, the relationship is virtually one of parody, for while the first "golden bough" was Aeneas's talisman of return from the underworld (Virgil's *Aeneid* Book 6), the Archmage-hero of **Earthsea** finds himself continually struggling against death without any supporting token. He learns in the first book that the defeat of death is an improper aim for a magician, whose art must depend on respect for the individual qualities (or names) of others, rather than on manipulation of them for one's own self-perpetuation. In the second book he faces an organized religion of sacrifice and propitiation, to demonstrate that this offers no better hope for humanity. In the third he duels with a rival "mage" who appears to have won power over death, though with disastrous consequences for others. Magic is presented continually as an alternative ideology to those with which we are familiar – i.e., those of science and religion – and as a more attractive one. **Earthsea** is informed, atypically for sf, by an awareness of the discoveries of post-Victorian ANTHROPOLOGY; it exemplifies the serious and powerful argumentative quality which can underline what appear to be only entertaining fantasies.

More recently two authors have, perhaps, done something new in the subgenre. The first is Terry PRATCHETT, whose **Discworld** sequence (from 1983) must have produced a greater (and funnier) variety of riffs on the world-where-magic-works theme, many of them borderline sf, than any other author; it is the sheer variety that constitutes the novelty. The second is John CROWLEY, who has presented one of the most scholarly (and historically accurate) varieties of the magical art yet to appear in genre fiction, borrowed from the neo-platonic scientist/magicians of the Renaissance. Magic of this sort permeates (though seldom obviously) the novel *Little, Big* (**1981**), and actually becomes the structural principle of *Aegypt* (**1987**). This latter – first of a projected quartet – may be the only novel by a genre writer whose story, whose structure and whose imagery are wholly isomorphic with an actual historical magical system, gnostic magic. Renaissance magic does, however, also play a prominent role – and is portrayed as rigorous and systematic – in Mary GENTLE's vivid alternate-world novel *Rats and Gargoyles* (**1990**). [TS/PN]

See also: GOTHIC SF; MONSTERS; MYTHOLOGY; SUPERNATURAL CREATURES.

MAGIC REALISM A term originally used to describe a form of literature most commonly associated with 20th-century Latin America, most notably in the works of Isabel Allende (1942-   ), Miguel Angel Asturias (1899-1974), Jorge Luis BORGES, Gabriel García Márquez (1928-   ) and Juan Rulfo (1918-1986). US and UK practitioners include Donald BARTHELME, Angela CARTER and John Hawkes (1925-   ).

Contrary to the antirealistic assumptions of high Modernism (Henry James [1843-1916], Ezra Pound [1885-1972] and T.S. Eliot [1888-1965]) or the fable-producing, self-referential texts of metafiction (John BARTH and Italo CALVINO), Magic Realism does not necessarily doubt either the actuality of a real world or the ability of literary language to describe that world. Instead it assumes that the mundane world and its familiar objects are often filled with fabulous secrets. Magic realism explores the real world's unrealities, and does not simply – like FANTASY, Surrealism or fairy tales – invent the dreamlike unrealities of ALTERNATE WORLDS. Magic Realism suggests that the real world can be represented, even when it cannot be believed.

For further discussion of the broad tendencies of 20th-century literature from which Magic Realism partially dissents, ◊ FABULATION. [SB]

See also: POSTMODERNISM AND SF.

MAGIDOFF, ROBERT (1905-1970) Russian-born US academic, Professor of Russian Literature at New York University 1961-70. His 3 anthologies are *Russian Science Fiction* (anth **1964** UK), *Russian Science Fiction, 1968* (anth **1968**) and *Russian Science Fiction, 1969* (anth **1969**). [PN]

MAGILL, FRANK N. [r] ◊ Keith NEILSON.

MAGNETIC MONSTER, THE Film (1953). A-Men Productions/United Artists. Dir Curt SIODMAK, starring Richard Carlson, King Donovan, Jean Byron. Screenplay Siodmak, Ivan Tors. 76 mins. B/w.

A new isotope, created in a laboratory, sucks in nearby energy and doubles its size every few hours; eventually it may destroy the Earth. The first part of the film shows it being tracked down by scientific investigators, puzzled at the strange magnetic fields it produces. It emits deadly radiation and is finally destroyed in a giant power plant in the ocean by feeding it with more energy than it can absorb. The film includes much footage at the finale from the German sf classic GOLD (1934). This is a well made, documentary-style, fast-moving thriller, one of Siodmak's better scripts, and the best of the (generally poor) films that he directed. [PN/JB]

MAGUIRE, JOHN FRANCIS (1815-1872) Irish nationalist politician and journalist, founder of the Cork *Examiner*. In his sf novel *The Next Generation* (**1871**), set in 1891, the UK has been much improved by steam-powered BALLOONS and the granting of women's suffrage; romance and the explication of other meliorist reforms just this side of UTOPIA take up the remainder of a very long book. "Jack Tubbs, or The Happy Isle", in *Young Prince Marigold, and Other Fairy Stories* (coll **1873**), features an Edenic ISLAND populated by animals with whom the hero has learned to converse. [JC]

MAHMŪD, MUSTAFĀ (1927-) Egyptian writer, known also as Moustaffa Mahmoud, author of short stories, novels and plays dealing with Egypt's social and political development; in the mid-1960s he wrote a number of sf novels. These include *Al-khurūj min at-tābūt* (**1965**; trans as *Raising from the Coffin* undated Cairo), *Rajul tahta as-sifr* ["The Man with a Temperature Below Zero"] (**1965**) and *Al-anqabūt* (**1965**; trans as "The Spider", serialized 1965-6 in the magazine *Arab Observer*). He is well known also for his short-story collections, which contain an sf component, as in *Yawmiyāt nuss al-layl* ["Diaries of Midnight"] (coll **1982**). MM is also a propagator of ideas about UFOS. [JO]

See also: ARABIC SF.

MAIKOWSKI, MIKE [r] ◊ ROBERT HALE LIMITED.

MAINE, CHARLES ERIC Pseudonym used by UK writer David McIlwain (1921-1981) for his sf; two other pseudonyms, Richard Rayner and Robert Wade, were not used for sf. CEM was one of the relatively few but extremely active UK fans before WWII, in 1938 publishing his first story, "The Mirror", in his FANZINE *The Satellite*, which he edited with Jonathan BURKE. His first novel was *Spaceways: A Story of the Very Near Future* * (**1953**; vt *Spaceways Satellite* 1958 US), based on his own 1952 radio play; it was filmed as SPACEWAYS (1953). Also developed from a script, in this case his own screenplay for TIMESLIP (1955; vt *The Atomic Man*), is CEM's *The Isotope Man* * (**1957**), which begins his only series, the

Mike Delaney books, the other volumes in which are *Subterfuge* (**1959**) and *Never Let Up* (**1964**). Like most of his sf, these have a leaning towards thriller-like plots and a disinclination to argue too closely scientific pinnings that are often shaky; the latter tendency is particularly visible in stories featuring HARD-SF themes like space travel, as in *High Vacuum* (**1957**). Sometimes lightly, sometimes with gravity, CEM's numerous books touch on a variety of sf themes from ROCKETS to SOCIOLOGY, but generally without more than fitfully illuminating them; he was determinedly an author of middle-of-the-road GENRE SF, and as such was successful. His finest novel is generally thought to be *The Mind of Mr Soames* (**1961**), a story of a man who does not reach consciousness until the age of 30, and of the arguments about how best to educate him. The moral issues are dealt with quite sensitively. The book was filmed as *The* MIND OF MR SOAMES (1969). [JC/PN]

Other works: *Timeliner: A Story of Time and Space* (**1955**); *Crisis 2000* (**1955**); *Escapement* (**1956**; vt *The Man who Couldn't Sleep* 1958 US), filmed as *The Electronic Monster* (1957; vt *The Dream Machine*); *World without Men* (**1958** US; rev vt *Alph* 1972); *The Tide Went Out* (**1958**; rev vt *Thirst!* 1977); *Count-Down* (**1959**; vt *Fire Past the Future* 1959 US); *Calculated Risk* (**1960**); *He Owned the World* (**1960** US; vt *The Man who Owned the World* 1961 UK); *The Darkest of Nights* (**1962**; vt *Survival Margin* 1968 US; rev vt *The Big Death* 1978 UK); *B.E.A.S.T.: Biological Evolutionary Animal Simulation Test* (**1966**); *The Random Factor* (**1971**).

See also: ANTIGRAVITY; CLONES; DISASTER; MEDICINE; MONEY; MOON.

MAINE, DAVID ◊ Pierre BARBET.

MAINS d'ORLAC, LES ◊ ORLACS HÄNDE.

MAINSTREAM WRITERS OF SF This discussion should be read in conjunction with several others as part of a pattern of reasoning that is most clearly presented in DEFINITIONS OF SF, FABULATION, GENRE SF, HISTORY OF SF, MAGIC REALISM, POSTMODERNISM AND SF, PROTO SF and SLIPSTREAM SF.

When used of literature, the term "mainstream" refers in its narrowest application to the tradition of the realistic novel of human character; in a wider application commonly employed by the sf community, it denotes all serious prose fiction outside the market genres; in its widest and perhaps most regrettable sense it refers to practically any fiction, serious or otherwise (including Jackie-Collins-style lowbrow bestsellers), outside sf, fantasy, the thriller and the Western. As a piece of jargon, not yet fully accepted into the language, "mainstream" lacks precision; nonetheless, there is a useful distinction to be drawn between writers of GENRE SF, who think of themselves as writing sf and whose books and stories are marketed as sf, and those writers of sf works who think of themselves (or are marketed) as simply writing fiction, without adopting either the protection or the stigma of a genre label. If, however, we are to employ "mainstream sf" primarily in opposition to "genre sf" – which we think is the most useful and desirable use of the former term – there is not much point in using the word "mainstream" retroactively to refer to writers like Aldous HUXLEY in the 1930s, since the term "science fiction" barely existed when he was writing books like *Brave New World* (**1932**). It is, of course, possible to argue that genre sf has existed ever since Hugo GERNSBACK founded AMAZING STORIES in 1926, but at that time it was a tiny genre, not well publicized. It would make better sense to regard mainstream (that is, non-genre) sf as, say, a post-1937 phenomenon (that being the year in which John W. CAMPBELL Jr took over the editorship of ASTOUNDING STORIES, after which genre sf undeniably became established as a known form), though to name any actual year must be arbitrary.

Certainly, until the sf label was adopted (in the form of the word SCIENTIFICTION in Gernsback's 1926 usage) it is realistic to argue that *all* sf was mainstream. Sf did exist, notably in the scientific romances of H.G. WELLS, the **Voyages extraordinaires** of Jules VERNE, and in much fiction of these and other kinds (◊ HISTORY OF SF) in the general fiction magazines, pulp or otherwise, but it had not yet hardened into a selfconscious separateness. Indeed Wells's term SCIENTIFIC ROMANCE was a good one, and many tales were so described, whether informally or formally, and did belong to an sf-like tradition. But if we regard the scientific romance as prototypical genre sf, then we run counter to a common usage of "mainstream sf" – to mean sf published in books that are not labelled sf, as opposed to magazines that are – for it was precisely in such books, especially in the UK, that the scientific romance largely appeared. In other words, in many people's usage of the term, the scientific romance is almost by definition mainstream. Any usage which leads to something very like a contradiction in terms is clearly not useful.

Especially in the UK, books written in the tradition of the scientific romance and published as straight novels continued well into the 1950s, some of the most popular being by John WYNDHAM. It would clearly be a nonsense to argue that Wyndham was a mainstream writer, especially since, under other pseudonyms, he was also well known in the genre-sf magazines. This example is given only to show that the idea of the presence or absence of genre labels on books as somehow defining their content is unhelpful. Nonetheless, just such judgments as to who is mainstream and who is not have often been made, frequently with the implication that the mainstream writer is thus marginalized. That is why it is more useful to decide who is mainstream and who is not by the presence or absence in the tale of adherence to the protocols of genre sf, rather than the label on the cover.

During the period in which sf was *beginning* to take shape as an identifiably separate genre, in the 1920s and 1930s, the favourite sf themes with non-genre sf writers who published in book format were: DYSTOPIAS;

stories imagining life after some sort of HOLOCAUST; stories creating imaginary societies that satirize our own (◊ SATIRE); and stories of future POLITICS and WAR. (The LOST-WORLDS theme was already in decline by the 1920s.) Some such writers from this period, in addition to Huxley, are Karel ČAPEK, John COLLIER, Murray Constantine (Katharine BURDEKIN), Guy DENT, John GLOAG, E.C. LARGE, Sinclair LEWIS, Wyndham LEWIS, André MAUROIS, Joseph O'NEILL, J.B. PRIESTLEY, Herbert READ, Upton SINCLAIR, Olaf STAPLEDON, Alexei TOLSTOY and Rex WARNER. Many of these were working in the tradition of the scientific romance. One marginal sf theme whose main development – before, after and during this period – has been more outside the genre than within it is PSYCHOLOGY, under which heading the relation between mainstream and genre sf is further discussed.

The distinction between genre sf and mainstream sf becomes more interesting, because more real, in the 1940s and 1950s. As genre sf became better known outside its immediate small circle of devotees, it also began to feed more from mainstream writing. Huxley and Stapledon probably had a stronger influence on genre sf than any non-genre writers since Wells. However, the traffic was by no means one-way. The number of mainstream writers of sf remained very substantial indeed, but a new distinction became apparent: between those writers whose work demonstrates *some* knowledge of sf motifs as they developed in genre sf or in the scientific romance, and those who rather cumbersomely re-invent the wheel; one could (quite randomly) take Paul THEROUX as a recent example of the latter. But many mainstream sf writers published their work in book format rather than the pulp magazines because it would not have crossed their minds to do otherwise; books were where respectable persons published their fictions. Because sf became a book-marketing category only in the 1950s in the USA (somewhat later in the UK) it would not have occurred to writers like C.S. LEWIS to request that the magic letters "SF" be placed on the covers of their books; if the thought *had* occurred, it would probably have been dismissed as an irrelevance.

The dominant mainstream sf themes of the 1940s continued to be dystopias (◊ George ORWELL) and tales of the HOLOCAUST AND AFTER (◊ Pat FRANK, George R. STEWART). But, again, the recitation of names is not very helpful because the phenomenon we speak of was on such a grand scale. Around half the writers discussed in this encyclopedia did not publish their work as genre sf, and often, too, their work does not *feel* like genre sf. To quote from the GENRE SF entry: ". . . works of fiction which use sf themes in seeming ignorance or contempt of the protocols – these are often works from so-called mainstream writers of sf – frequently go unread by those immersed in genre sf; and, if they *are* read, tend to be treated as invasive and alien . . . and incompetent." This is one of the sadder results of sf's ghetto mentality, though that mentality is not now nearly so aggressively inflexible as it was during the 1940s-60s, when the use of sf themes by writers outside the genre was considered almost a form of theft in the eyes of an sf community whose love for its genre was often expressed in very proprietorial terms. Even now, similar reservations are occasionally expressed by the sf community about the work of writers like Doris LESSING.

Under the heading FABULATION we discuss a further confusion, common in criticism from within the sf community. This is the belief that sf, by escaping from the here-and-now of realist fiction, was to be greatly admired as spearheading a new, less constrictive, more imaginative nonrealist mode. Sf, on the contrary, lies at the heart of the realist mode; its whole creative effort is bent on making its imaginary worlds, its imaginary futures, as real as possible. The experiments in breaking down realist or "mimetic" fiction were taking place elsewhere; fabulations are fictions distrustful both of the very tools with which the world can be made known, words – which, as T.S. Eliot said, "slip, slide, perish, / Decay with imprecision" – and as to whether the world *can* in fact be known. A quite extraordinary number of fabulators use sf motifs, but in the construction of works whose foregrounding of their own artifice is opposed in style and feeling to the traditional mimesis of genre sf; it is unsurprising that sf's conservatives deeply dislike the suggestion that they in any sense share their genre with such writers as John BARTH, Jorge Luis BORGES, Italo CALVINO, Angela CARTER and Don DeLILLO (to penetrate only a short way into the alphabet). But, confusingly, genre sf has produced quite a few fabulators of its own – J.G. BALLARD, John CROWLEY, Thomas M. DISCH, Karen Joy FOWLER, M. John HARRISON, Michael MOORCOCK, Lucius SHEPARD, John T. SLADEK and Gene WOLFE among them – so here, too, the distinctions between genre sf and the mainstream prove elusive.

It was probably not, however, the fabulators that Ursula K. LE GUIN had in mind when she said: "If the mainstream definably exists, then I think it is itself a genre; one among many ways of writing fiction – one of the many modes I myself work in." This, too, is an arguable case, though Le Guin was probably thinking of the traditional novel of character – which is certainly a genre – when she said it. We bring this up primarily to make the obvious, but perhaps needful, point that the mainstream (like sf) is undefinable and not homogeneous, and indeed contains many genres within it, of which the fabulation and the novel of character are but two, both at times impinging upon sf.

By the 1980s any attempt at protecting the racial purity of genre sf from contamination by the mainstream or by any other genre was more obviously doomed to failure than ever before, for sf was marrying out. The 1980s saw a flood of works (◊ FANTASY *for some examples*) where sf was interbred with fantasy, with horror, with MAGIC REALISM, with the thriller, with practically anything available. Postmodernists clasped CYBERPUNKS in their showy, affectless embrace. Sf's furtive affaires (such as the one it consistently conducted with the historical romance, especially in TIME-TRAVEL stories) were now out in the open and legitimate, and so were their progeny.

Sf is and has been a great enterprise, many of whose most remarkable achievements have taken place entirely within genre sf; all those who are part of this phenomenon should feel justifiably proud, and perhaps justifiably angry at the literary world's failure to give them their due. It is sad that equally spectacular sf achievements, outside the genre walls and within mainstream fiction, have not always been recognized by those in the "ghetto" (snobberies cut both ways), but by the 1980s the quarrel was of historical interest only, for the walls were tumbling down. Some still shelter behind those shards left standing, but, if they look, they will see that the traffic is moving freely in both directions.

A theme anthology collecting sf stories by mainstream writers is *The Light Fantastic* (anth **1971**) ed Harry HARRISON and Theodore J. Gordon. [PN]

MAISON d'AILLEURS, LA "The house of elsewhere", subtitled (in French) "the museum of Utopia, of extraordinary voyages and of science fiction". This establishment in Yverdon, Switzerland, contains about 50,000 items relating to sf, maybe half of them books and magazines, the remainder all sorts of ephemera: toys, games, stamps, posters, calendars, etc. Founded in 1975 by Pierre VERSINS, who donated his celebrated private COLLECTION to it, it was given much-needed financial assistance by the town of Yverdon in 1989, shortage of money having for some years previously restricted it to opening only twice a month. It is the most important research centre for sf in the French language. [PN]

MAITLAND, DEREK (1943-   ) UK writer whose sf novels – *T Minus Tower* (**1971**), about a proposed transfer of the eponymous tower into space as a hotel, and *The Alpha Experience* (**1974**) – exhibit a certain apocalyptic flippancy but failed to target coming UK trends with any real accuracy. [JC]

MAITLAND, EDWARD (1824-1897) UK author and Theosophist whose speculative UTOPIA *By and By: An Historical Romance of the Future* (3 vols **1873**), set several hundred years in the future, takes an unusually optimistic view of the likely effects of technology (irrigating the Sahara), is much interested in social theory, imagines several varieties of marriage and foresees a somewhat limited emancipation of women. This didactic book is the third of a trilogy; the first 2 vols, *The Pilgrim and the Shrine* (**1868**) and *The Higher Law*, were originally published as by Herbert Ainslee and are not sf. [PN]

MAITZ, DON (1953-   ) US illustrator. DM began his career in sf art in 1974 while still at art school (Paier School of Art), and since then has painted mainly book rather than magazine covers; among his best known ILLUSTRATIONS are the covers for the original editions of Gene WOLFE's **Book of the New Sun** series (**1980-83**). He also does advertising work, notably the very popular "Captain Morgan" for a Seagram's rum label. Unlike many of his colleagues, DM departs a little from slickness by allowing the brushstrokes in his work to be seen. He was among the sf artists most popular with fans right through the 1980s, and had many HUGO nominations before, in 1990, winning the Hugo for Best Professional Artist, and in so doing becoming only the second artist, after Jim BURNS, to break the extraordinary run of 11 Hugos (to 1992) in that category by Michael WHELAN – indeed, these three between them were probably the dominant sf book-cover illustrators of the 1980s. DM also won first place in the new non-Hugo category at the Hugo ceremony in 1990 for Best Original Artwork with his cover for the Warner/Questar edition of C.J. CHERRYH's *Rimrunners* (**1989**). A collection of his interestingly ornate artwork is *First Maitz: Selected Works by Don Maitz* (**1988**). [JG/PN]

MAJOR, H.M. ◊ Sharon JARVIS.

MAJORS, SIMON ◊ Gardner F. FOX.

MAKAY, ISTVÁN [r] ◊ HUNGARY.

MAKING MR RIGHT Film (1987). Orion. Dir Susan Seidelman, starring Ann Magnuson, John Malkovich. Screenplay Floyd Byars, Laurie Frank. 98 mins. Colour.

The cold, rational, shy SCIENTIST played by Malkovich has designed, in his own image, Ulysses the ANDROID (actually in part a ROBOT), also played by Malkovich, for use as a space pilot. Public-relations expert Frankie (Magnuson), whose love affair with an "unreconstructed" politician is coming to an end, has the task of "humanizing" Ulysses's image. The fluffy, screwball SEX comedy that follows makes well observed satirical points, from a FEMINIST perspective, about the men women want and to some extent create. Ulysses, who rapidly evolves into a kind of parodic, sensitive "new man", and Frankie fall in love. His tendency to short-circuit whenever sexually aroused suggests a pessimistic view of women's chance of happiness, even if they've helped design Mr Right themselves. The film was nothing like as popular as Seidelman's previous *Desperately Seeking Susan* (1985), being too offbeat (and lacking Madonna), but is just as good. [PN]

MALABAILA, DAMIANO ◊ Primo LEVI.

MALAMUD, BERNARD (1914-1986) US writer whose fiction, beginning with *The Natural* (**1952**), a mythopoeic tale of US baseball, makes use of techniques and motifs from Russian-Jewish folklore and storytelling traditions, with the result that many of his short stories are technically fantasies. His only novel of strong genre interest, *God's Grace* (**1982**), mixes sf and fable – at times uneasily – in the tale of a lone human survivor of a nuclear HOLOCAUST attempting vainly to restart civilization by breeding with a group of intelligent apes (◊ APES AND CAVEMEN) that have also, rather miraculously, survived the worldwide tsunami responsible for the extirpation of all else. [JC]

See also: END OF THE WORLD; RELIGION.

MALCOLM, DAN ◊ Robert SILVERBERG.

MALCOLM, DONALD (1930-   ) Scottish writer of fiction and considerable popular science who began publishing sf with "Lone Voyager" for *Nebula* in 1958. Two series of stories, the **Preliminary Exploration Team** tales in *NW* 1957-64 and the **Dream Background** tales in *NW* in 1959 and subsequently in the continuing anthology series NEW WRITINGS IN SF 1965-75 have not reached book form. His sf novels, both routine, are *The Unknown Shore* (**1976** Canada) and *The Iron Rain* (**1976** Canada). [JC]

See also: STARS.

MALCOLM, GRANT ◊ Dennis HUGHES.

MALEC, ALEXANDER (1929-   ) US writer, variously employed, who began publishing sf with "Project Inhumane" for *The Colorado Quarterly* in 1966. *Extrapolasis* (coll **1967**) assembles much of his sometimes awkward but frequently sharply pointed work, which was restricted to short stories. [JC]

MALEVIL Film (1981). NEF-Diffusion/Stella/Antenne 2/Gibe/Telecip. Dir Christian de Chalonge, starring Michel Serrault, Jacques Dutronc, Robert Dhéry, Jacques Villeret, Jean-Louis Trintignant. Screenplay de Chalonge, Pierre Dumayet, based on *Malevil* (1972; trans **1974**) by Robert MERLE. 119 mins. Colour.

This moderately lavish Franco-German post-HOLOCAUST movie reinforces the sentimental aspects of its good source novel. The Bomb goes off while the vintage is being tasted deep in the wine cellar of an aristocrat's château. The first half is gripping, as the survivors wonder when, if ever, they will be able to leave the well stocked cellar again, and the first glimpses of the devastated landscape outside are powerful. But then a simplistic clash between the aristocrat's lovably feudal paternalism and the totalitarianism of a local boss (he too has a gang of survivors) reduces the film to something more routine, all done with little verve and rather too much symbolism about life reasserting itself. At the end the new society, whose medieval nature is approved by the film, is threatened, ironically, by the somewhat late arrival of a relief helicopter. [PN]

MALLETT, DARYL F(URUMI) (1969-   ) US bibliographer whose work, beginning in the late 1980s and generally in collaboration with Robert REGINALD, has been of growing significance for sf scholarship. Publications include the much expanded 2nd edn of *Reginald's Science Fiction and Fantasy Awards: A Comprehensive Guide to the Awards and their Winners* (**1981**; exp 1991) with Reginald, for which DFM performed the essential updating task; and «Science Fiction and Fantasy Literature: A Bibliography, 1975-1991» (1992) with Mary Wickizer Burgess and Reginald, which is the continuation of Reginald's *Science Fiction and Fantasy Literature: A Checklist, 1700-1974* (**1979**). Several further publications are projected. [JC]

See also: BIBLIOGRAPHIES.

MALLINSON, SUE [r] ◊ ROBERT HALE LIMITED.

MALLORY, MARK [s] ◊ Mack REYNOLDS.

MALONEY, MACK US author, possibly pseudonymous, of the **Wingman** series of post-HOLOCAUST military-sf novels: *Wingman* (**1987**), #2: *The Circle War* (**1987**), #3: *The Lucifer Crusade* (**1987**), #4: *Thunder in the East* (**1988**), #5: *The Twisted Cross* (**1989**), #6: *The Final Storm* (**1989**), #7: *Freedom Express* (**1990**), #8: *Skyfire* (**1990**) and #9: *Return from the Inferno* (**1991**). *War Heaven* (**1991**) is a singleton. [JC]

MALZBERG, BARRY N(ORMAN) (1939-   ) US writer. For about seven years he was extremely prolific in the sf field, producing some 20 sf novels and over 100 short stories; his output slowed dramatically towards the end of the 1970s, when he became disenchanted with the genre for reasons explained in his collection of essays *The Engines of the Night: Science Fiction in the Eighties* (coll **1982**). He has also written numerous non-sf works, including several notable erotic novels, and four excellent thrillers in collaboration with Bill PRONZINI, including *Night Screams* (**1979**), which makes use of ESP. His early sf appeared under the name K.M. O'Donnell, apparently derived from the initial letters of the surnames of Henry KUTTNER and C.L. MOORE plus the surname of one of their joint pseudonyms. Other pseudonyms, used on non-sf works, include Mike Barry, Mel Johnson and Gerrold Watkins. His first sf story was "We're Coming through the Window" (1967 *Gal*), which was quickly followed by the bitter novelette "Final War" (1968 *FSF*), about an unwilling soldier trapped in a never-ending wargame. Books under the O'Donnell name were the short-story collections *Final War and Other Fantasies* (coll **1969** dos) and *In the Pocket and Other Science Fiction Stories* (coll **1971** dos), the novels *The Empty People* (**1969**) and *Universe Day* (fixup **1971**), and two RECURSIVE farcical SATIRES featuring sf fans and writers in confrontation with ALIENS: *Dwellers of the Deep* (**1970** dos) and *Gather in the Hall of the Planets* (**1971** dos).

The first sf novels to appear under BNM's own name were sceptical commentaries on the Apollo programme: *The Falling Astronauts* (**1971**), *Revelations* (**1972**) and *Beyond Apollo* (**1972**). The third caused some controversy when it won the JOHN W. CAMPBELL MEMORIAL AWARD despite its sarcastic and negative attitude to SPACE FLIGHT. The three novels feature astronauts as archetypes of alienated contemporary humanity, struggling to make sense of an incomprehensible world and unable to account for their failure. All BNM's central characters are caught in such existential traps, and the measure of his versatility is the large number of such situations which he has been able to construct using the vocabularies of ideas typical of sf and erotic fantasy. In *Screen* (**1968**) the protagonist can obtain sexual satisfaction only by projecting himself into fantasies evoked by the cinema, while in *Confessions of Westchester County* (**1971**) a prolific seducer obtains satisfaction not from the sexual act but from the confessions of loneliness and desperation which follow it. The situation of the racetrack punter, unable to win against the odds by

any conceivable strategy, becomes the model of alienation in *Overlay* (**1972**), in which aliens take an actual part in the process of frustration, and in the non-sf novel *Underlay* (**1974**). Aliens threaten the Earth, and set absurd tasks to decide its fate, in *The Day of the Burning* (**1974**) and *Tactics of Conquest* (**1974**). In *Galaxies* (**1975**) the central character is in command of a corpse-laden ship which falls into a BLACK HOLE. The protagonist of *Scop* (**1976**) is a time-traveller trying desperately to change the history that has created his intolerable world. Even the situation of the sf writer, struggling to cope with real life and the pressures of the market, becomes in *Herovit's World* (**1973**) a metaphor for general alienation. In this novel, *Galaxies* and the introductions to some of his collections, BNM offers a scathing critique of the market forces shaping contemporary sf.

BNM's writing is unparalleled in its intensity and in its apocalyptic sensibility. His detractors consider him bleakly monotonous and despairing, but he is a master of black HUMOUR, and is one of the few writers to have used sf's vocabulary of ideas extensively as apparatus in psychological landscapes, dramatizing relationships between the human mind and its social environment in an sf theatre of the absurd. The few sf books which he has published since 1976 include three fine novels featuring real historical characters. The hero of the black comedy *Chorale* (**1978**) becomes Beethoven, while that of the remarkably intense *The Cross of Fire* (**1982**) becomes Jesus; both are in search of a better psychological balance but find their quests frustrating. *The Remaking of Sigmund Freud* (fixup **1985**) has the father of psychoanalysis failing miserably to master his own difficulties while trying to assist Emily Dickinson, and subsequently – following his technological REINCARNATION – coming apart while failing to solve the problems involved in COMMUNICATION with aliens. [BS]

Other works: *In the Enclosure* (**1973**); *The Men Inside* (**1973**); *Phase IV* * (**1973** UK), a film tie (◊ PHASE IV); *The Destruction of the Temple* (**1974**); *On a Planet Alien* (**1974**); *The Sodom and Gomorrah Business* (**1974**); *Conversations* (**1974**); *Out from Ganymede* (coll **1974**); *Guernica Night* (**1975**); *The Gamesman* (**1975**); *The Many Worlds of Barry Malzberg* (coll **1975**); *Down Here in the Dream Quarter* (coll **1976**); *The Best of Barry Malzberg* (coll **1976**); *The Last Transaction* (**1977**); *Malzberg at Large* (coll **1979**); *The Man who Loved the Midnight Lady* (coll **1980**).

As editor: *Final Stage* (anth **1974**; rev 1975), *Arena: Sports SF* (anth **1976**) and *Graven Images: Three Original Novellas of Science Fiction* (anth **1977**), all with Edward L. FERMAN; *Dark Sins, Dark Dreams: Crime in Science Fiction* (anth **1977**), *The End of Summer: Science Fiction in the Fifties* (anth **1979**; vt *The Fifties: The End of Summer* 1979) and *Shared Tomorrows: Science Fiction in Collaboration* (anth **1979**), all with Bill PRONZINI; *Neglected Visions* (anth **1980**) with Martin H. GREENBERG and Joseph D. OLANDER; *The Science Fiction of Mark Clifton* (coll **1980**) with Greenberg (◊ Mark

CLIFTON); *Bug-Eyed Monsters* (anth **1980**) with Pronzini; *The Arbor House Treasury of Horror and the Supernatural* (anth 2 vols **1981**; cut vt *Great Tales of Horror & the Supernatural* 1985; text restored, vt *Classic Tales of Horror and the Supernatural* 1991) with Pronzini and Greenberg; *The Science Fiction of Kris Neville* (coll **1984**) with Greenberg (◊ Kris NEVILLE).

See also: AMAZING STORIES; ARTS; CRITICAL AND HISTORICAL WORKS ABOUT SF; ENTROPY; FANTASTIC VOYAGES; FANTASY; GAMES AND SPORTS; GREAT AND SMALL; MEDIA LANDSCAPE; MESSIAHS; MUSIC; PARANOIA; PERCEPTION; PSYCHOLOGY; RELIGION; SEX; TIME PARADOXES; WAR.

MAN, EVOLUTION OF ◊ ADAM AND EVE; ANTHROPOLOGY; EVOLUTION; ORIGIN OF MAN.

MAN AND HIS MATE ◊ ONE MILLION B.C.

MANCHURIAN CANDIDATE, THE Film (1962). MC/Essex/United Artists. Dir John FRANKENHEIMER, starring Frank Sinatra, Laurence Harvey, Janet Leigh, Angela Lansbury, Henry Silva, James Gregory. Screenplay George Axelrod, based on *The Manchurian Candidate* (**1959**) by Richard CONDON. 126 mins. B/w.

A group of US soldiers captured in Korea are subjected to elaborate brainwashing by the Chinese as part of a plot to have a Chinese agent elected President of the USA. One officer is programmed – this is the strongest sf element – to become a killing machine whenever any of the people working for the Chinese gives the right command. The resulting confusions back in the USA, both funny and sinister – especially the climax at the Party convention – are choreographed with great panache by Frankenheimer, whose best film this probably is, though it owes much to the wit and intelligence of Axelrod's screenplay, which is faithful to the novel. Its ominous reverberations became darker when President Kennedy was assassinated a year later. [JB/PN]

See also: CINEMA; PARANOIA.

MANCUSO, TED (? -) US writer whose *The Granville Hypothesis* (**1979**), set in AD2017, features an unremarkable world-COMPUTER being suborned by an unremarkable madman. [JC]

MANDEN DER TAENKTE TING (vt *The Man who Thought Life*) Film (1969). Asa Film/Palladium. Dir Jens Ravn, starring Preben Neergaard, John Price, Lotte Tarp. Screenplay Henrik Stangerup, based on *Manden der Taenkte Ting* (**1938**) by Valdemar Holst. 97 mins. B/w.

This Danish fantasy tells of a man who can create objects – even people – by force of will. Anything he brings into existence has only a short life, so he goes to a doctor and asks for a brain operation to perfect his power. The doctor refuses, so the man creates a duplicate doctor who takes over his original's career and wife and ultimately performs the necessary operation, in so doing killing his creator. Interestingly photographed, this comedy, Ravn's first film, presents philosophical points about reality of the kind made familiar by Philip K. DICK. [JB/PN]

MANDERS, HARRY ◊ Philip José FARMER.

MAN FROM ATLANTIS, THE US tv series (1977).

Solow Productions for NBC TV. Created Lee Katzin (who also dir the 1st episode), starring Patrick Duffy, Belinda J. Montgomery, Victor Buono. Special effects Tom Fisher. The first 4 episodes, 90min telefilms, were followed by 13 50min episodes. Colour.

A green-eyed stranger with gills and webbed hands is found nearly dead on a beach. He is revived by an attractive female scientist who, realizing that he is not human, places him in a tank of water. Believed to come from ATLANTIS, he is persuaded to work for the Foundation for Oceanic Research, and is soon off on his first mission, to tackle an overweight villain in his underwater headquarters. Though the settings and special effects were sometimes eye-catching, the general intellectual level of this and subsequent episodes, which featured aliens, monsters, time-warps, etc., was no higher than that of VOYAGE TO THE BOTTOM OF THE SEA. The series was cancelled after 1 season.

Novelized versions of the first 2 episodes were *Man from Atlantis: Sea Kill* * (**1977**) and *Man from Atlantis: Death Scouts* * (**1977**), both by Richard Woodley. [JB]

MAN FROM U.N.C.L.E., THE US tv series (1964-8). Arena Productions/MGM for NBC TV. Executive prod Norman Felton. Writers included Harlan ELLISON, Howard Rodman, Sam Rolfe, Henry SLESAR, David Victor. Dirs included Don Medford, Boris Sagal, Joseph Sargent, Barry Shear. 105 50min episodes. 1st season b/w, subsequent 3 seasons colour.

This was one of tv's first reactions to the success of the **James Bond** films. Robert Vaughn starred as Napoleon Solo, a member of U.N.C.L.E. (United Network Command for Law Enforcement). With the assistance of his Russian colleague Ilya Kuryakin (David McCallum) he fought to prevent the sinister organization T.H.R.U.S.H. (Technological Hierarchy for the Removal of Undesirables and the Subjugation of Humanity) from taking over the world. Most of the plots featured futuristic technology (vaporizers, etc.); the style was tongue-in-cheek. *TMFU*'s success led to the creation of a sister series, *The Girl From U.N.C.L.E.*, which began in 1966, starring Stefanie Powers; it lasted only 1 season of 29 episodes.

8 feature films had theatrical release outside the USA. Each consisted of 2 episodes edited together, sometimes with added footage, to make 90min films: *The Spy with My Face* (1965), *To Trap a Spy* (1966), *One of Our Spies is Missing* (1966), *One Spy Too Many* (1966), *The Spy in the Green Hat* (1966), *The Helicopter Spies* (1967), *The Karate Killers* (1967) and *How to Steal the World* (1968). A subsequent telemovie was *Return of the Man from U.N.C.L.E.* (1983).

The **Man from U.N.C.L.E.** series of ties was complex, 23 titles appearing from ACE BOOKS in the USA and 16 from Souvenir Press in the UK. 10 of the 23 Ace books were reprints from books originated by Souvenir, and 6 of the Souvenir books were reprints of books originated by Ace; in the case of #3 in the Ace sequence, the reprint confusingly appeared before its original. None of the books was based directly on the tv scripts; all were original stories. As all the Souvenir editions appeared, either before or after their UK release, in Ace editions, we list only the Ace sequence: *#1: The Thousand Coffins Affair* * (**1965**) by Michael AVALLONE, *#2: The Doomsday Affair* * (**1965**) by Harry Whittington, *#3: The Copenhagen Affair* * (**1965**) by John Oram, *#4: The Dagger Affair* * (**1966**) by David MCDANIEL, *#5: The Mad Scientist Affair* * (**1966**) by John T. PHILLIFENT, *#6: The Vampire Affair* * (**1966**) by McDaniel, *#7: The Radioactive Camel Affair* * (**1966** UK) by Peter LESLIE, *#8: The Monster Wheel Affair* * (**1967**) by McDaniel, *#9: The Diving Dames Affair* * (**1967** UK) by Leslie, *#10: The Assassination Affair* * (**1967**) by Joan Hunter HOLLY, *#11: The Invisibility Affair* * (**1967**) by Thomas Stratton (Robert COULSON and Gene DeWEESE), *#12: The Mind Twisters Affair* * (**1967**) by Stratton, *#13: The Rainbow Affair* * (**1967**) by McDaniel, *#14: The Cross of Gold Affair* * (**1968**) by Fredric Davies (Ron ELLIK), *#15: The Utopia Affair* * (**1968**) by McDaniel, *#16: The Splintered Sunglasses Affair* * (**1968** UK) by Leslie, *#17: The Hollow Crown Affair* * (**1969**) by McDaniel, *#18: The Unfair Fare Affair* * (**1968** UK) by Leslie, *#19: The Power Cube Affair* * (**1968** UK) by Phillifent, *#20: The Corfu Affair* * (**1967** UK) by Phillifent, *#21: The Thinking Machine Affair* * (**1967** UK) by Joel Bernard, *#22: The Stone-Cold Dead in the Market Affair* * (**1966** UK) by Oram, and *#23: The Finger in the Sky Affair* * (**1966** UK) by Leslie. McDaniel felt A.A. Wyn, publisher at Ace, was not paying him enough; the initial letters of the chapters in *#8* spell out AAWYNISATIGHTWAD.

Girl from U.N.C.L.E. spin-offs of a similar kind were *The Birds of a Feather Affair* * (**1966**) by Michael Avallone; *The Blazing Affair* * (**1966**) by Avallone; *The Global Globules Affair* * (**1967** UK) by Simon Latter; *The Golden Boats of Taradata Affair* * (**1967** UK) by Latter; *The Cornish Pixie Affair* * (**1967** UK) by Peter Leslie. [JB/PN]

MANHATTAN FICTION PUBLICATIONS ◊ STIRRING SCIENCE STORIES.

MANIMAL ◊ Glen A. LARSON.

MAN IN THE STEEL MASK, THE ◊ WHO?.

MAN IN THE WHITE SUIT, THE Film (1951). Ealing Studios. Dir Alexander Mackendrick, starring Alec Guinness, Joan Greenwood, Cecil Parker, Ernest Thesiger. Screenplay Roger MacDougall, John Dighton, Mackendrick, based on the play *The Man in the White Suit* by MacDougall. 85 mins, cut to 81 mins. B/w.

A SCIENTIST creates an artificial fibre that neither wears out nor gets dirty. To prove it, he makes himself a shining white suit that retains its pristine condition throughout the film. Attempts are made by clothing manufacturers and their workers to suppress the new material. Finally its inventor is cornered in a street where, suddenly and symbolically, his suit begins to disintegrate and is torn to shreds by the angry mob. The film ends with the scientist planning a second attempt. This fine film is a witty and pertinent SATIRE whose success owes more to the traditions of the Ealing comedy than to sf. [JB]

MANKIND PUBLISHING ◊ VERTEX.

MANLOVE, C(OLIN) N(ICHOLAS) (1942-) UK critic. Most of his work of interest has focused on FANTASY, beginning with *Modern Fantasy: Five Studies* (coll **1975**). *The Impulse of Fantasy Literature* (**1983**) concentrates on UK fantasy, and tends not to deal with the more recent popularity of the genre in the USA. *C.S. Lewis: His Literary Achievement* (**1987**) competently argues the case for an author who divides critics into acolytes and disbelievers (◊ C.S. LEWIS). Of direct sf interest is *Science Fiction: Ten Explorations* (coll **1986**), which smoothly (though at times gingerly) engages with the fiction of 10 writers, including some, like Philip José FARMER and Gene WOLFE, who have received relatively little academic attention. [JC]

MANN, JACK ◊ E. Charles VIVIAN.

MANN, (ANTHONY) PHILLIP (1942-) UK-born writer resident in NEW ZEALAND from 1969. His career as a theatre director, translation copy-polisher, drama teacher and university Reader in Drama brings to his writing a strong visual and structural sense. His first sf publication, *The Eye of the Queen* (**1982** UK), is an accomplished novel of First Contact between humans and the enigmatic Pe-Ellians. The **Gardener** diptych – *Master of Paxwax* (**1986** UK) and *The Fall of the Families* (**1987** UK) – describes a warring human society and the downfall of its hegemony over various planets. In *Pioneers* (**1988** UK), his best novel to date, genetically engineered explorers come to terms with being human. *Wulfsyarn: A Mosaic* (**1990** UK) is a character study of a failed starship captain, Wilberfoss, narrated by an autoscribe. PM has written 3 fantasy plays for children as well as short stories and a humorous sf RADIO play, "The Gospel According to Mickey Mouse" (broadcast 1990). He consciously uses his skill at portraying ALIEN species and environments to display human vanity and hubris without being didactic and with an underlying respect for life. [MMacL]

See also: SOCIOLOGY.

MANNES, MARYA (1904-1990) US author, features editor and journalist, often on FEMINIST themes. Her first novel, *Message from a Stranger* (**1948**), is an afterlife fantasy. In her sf SATIRE *They* (**1968**), the USA is taken over by the under-30s. [JC/PN]

MANNHEIM, KARL Pseudonym of unidentified UK author of 2 sf adventures: *When the Earth Died* (**1950**) and *Vampires of Venus* (**1950**). They are modestly competent but hasty. [JC]

MANNING, LAURENCE (EDWARD) (1899-1972) Canadian-born writer, in the USA from 1920, a founder of the American Interplanetary Society and editor of its journal, *Astronautics*. He is remembered for his numerous contributions to WONDER STORIES and WONDER STORIES QUARTERLY in the 1930s; he also collaborated on some stories with Fletcher PRATT. His best-known series, which appeared in *Wonder Stories*, was the **Man who Awoke** sequence, 5 stories later published as *The Man who Awoke* (1933; fixup **1975**), in which a man periodically awakes from SUSPENDED ANIMATION into a pulp-STAPLEDON succession of 5 societies, the last of which is in a world of immortals. Another series was the **Stranger Club** sequence, again in *Wonder Stories*: "The Call of the Mech-Men" (1933), "Caverns of Horror" (1934), "Voice of Atlantis" (1934), "The Moth Message" (1934) and "Seeds from Space" (1935). A short series of above-average space stories comprised "The Voyage of the *Asteroid*" (1932) and "The Wreck of the *Asteroid*" (1932). LM's style was very much of his time, but he had a more wide-ranging imagination than many of his colleagues. [JC/PN]

See also: AUTOMATION; CANADA; DYSTOPIAS; EVOLUTION; FANTASTIC VOYAGES; GENERATION STARSHIPS; HISTORY IN SF; IMMORTALITY; LEISURE; LIVING WORLDS; MARS; SPACESHIPS; UTOPIAS.

MANO, D. KEITH (1943-) US writer whose second novel, *Horn* (**1969**), is a transcendental fable, and whose third, *War is Heaven!* (**1970**), describes with some surreal vividness a WAR in an imaginary – but easily imagined – South American country. *The Bridge* (**1973**) is a full-fledged sf DYSTOPIA set in AD2035, with regimentation leading to universal disaster. [JC]

MANOLESCU, FLORIN [r] ◊ ROMANIA.

MANTEGAZZA, PAOLO [r] ◊ ITALY.

MAN THEY COULD NOT HANG, THE Film (1939). Columbia. Dir Nick Grinde, starring Boris Karloff, Lorna Gray, Robert Wilcox, Roger Pryor. Screenplay Karl Brown, based on a story by Leslie T. White and George W. Sayre. 72 mins. B/w.

A kindly SCIENTIST (Karloff) invents a mechanical heart, and one of his students volunteers to undergo clinical death to test it; a police raid at the critical moment prevents this and the student dies. Karloff is executed for murder, but arranges to be revived with the artificial heart. Now vindictive, he lures judge, jury and witnesses to a booby-trapped house where he proceeds to dispose of them in turn. His daughter intervenes and is accidentally killed by one of the lethal devices. He revives her at the cost of his own life. Like most sf films of the period, *TMTCNH* has little real science; it is, rather, a Gothic melodrama of retribution. [JB/PN]

MANTLEY, JOHN (TRUMAN) (1920-) Canadian-born US screenwriter and producer whose sf novel, *The Twenty-Seventh Day* (**1956** UK; rev 1956 US), features Galactic Federation aliens who give each of five humans from opposing countries an invincible weapon to see what they do with them. The novel was filmed – from the US version, which has a revised ending – as *The* 27TH DAY (1957). Mantley wrote teleplays for *The* OUTER LIMITS and *The* WILD, WILD WEST, and for years worked as a producer on *Gunsmoke*; he also produced the 2nd season of the 1979-81 tv series BUCK ROGERS IN THE 25TH CENTURY. [PN/JC]

MANVELL, (ARNOLD) ROGER (1909-1987) UK writer, mostly on the cinema and on aspects of WWII; he had a doctorate in English literature. His sf novel,

The Dreamers (**1958**), is a tale of revenge via a dream transmitted to the intended victim by African tribesmen. A borderline-sf explanation is allowed as an alternative to the supernatural one. [JC]

MAN WHO FELL TO EARTH, THE Film (1976). British Lion/A Cinema V Release. Dir Nicolas Roeg, starring David Bowie, Rip Torn, Candy Clark, Buck Henry. Screenplay Paul Mayersberg, based on *The Man who Fell to Earth* (**1963**) by Walter TEVIS. 145 mins, often cut to 138 mins; first US showing cut to 118 mins. Colour.

In this UK film set in the USA, the clear-cut narrative of Tevis's evocative novel – about an ALIEN who comes to Earth to build a spacecraft large enough to transport his native race away from his own dying world – is replaced by a nonlinear structure that, in the familiar Roeg manner, shifts backwards and forwards in time, reflecting the psychic TIME TRAVEL of which the alien is capable.

The film is visually strong (Roeg was earlier a fine cameraman) but has been regarded by some as wilfully obscure, in part because of the rather literary complexity of its allusions (many to the painting of the fall of Icarus by Pieter Brueghel the Elder [c1525-1569], some to the Fall of Man) and the symbolism (occasionally heavy-handed) of its visual juxtapositions and imagery. All becomes much clearer on second viewing. Some sequences, including that showing serried ranks of tv sets with which the lonely alien attempts to barricade himself from direct human experience, are very powerful indeed. The theme of an alien having his identity effectively stolen from him by us – the reverse of the usual – is remorselessly followed through. *TMWFTE* has worn very well and is regarded as an sf classic. [PN]

MAN WHO THOUGHT LIFE, THE ◊ MANDEN DER TAENKTE TING.

"MAN WHO WAS WARNED, THE" ◊ Harold BEGBIE.

MAN WITH THE X-RAY EYES, THE ◊ X – THE MAN WITH THE X-RAY EYES.

MAN WITH TWO BRAINS, THE Film (1983). Aspen Film Society. Dir Carl Reiner, starring Steve Martin, Kathleen Turner, David Warner. Screenplay Reiner, Steve Martin, George GIPE. 93 mins, cut to 86 mins. Colour.

Pastiche is the essence of most Steve Martin comedies; his self-indulgent acting style becomes rapidly tiresome when his performances are not focused by a good director, but Reiner is good, and this is a genuinely funny film spoofing the disembodied-brain GOTHIC tradition of DONOVAN'S BRAIN (1953). Kathleen Turner plays the man-destroying bitch whom brain surgeon Hfuhruhurr (Martin) falls in love with and marries, though she refuses sex. He transfers his affections to a bodiless brain, provided by a mad SCIENTIST (Warner), with which he forms a telepathic relationship. The wife is killed by a serial murderer, Hfuhruhurr grafts the beloved brain into her head, and all ends happily. [PN]

MARAS, KARL ◊ Kenneth BULMER.

MARCH OF THE MONSTERS, THE ◊ GOJIRA; RADON.

MAREK, JIŘÍ [r] ◊ CZECH AND SLOVAK SF.

MARGROFF, ROBERT E(RVIEN) (1930-   ) US writer who published his first story, "Monster Tracks", in *If* in 1964, but who has long been best known for his collaborations with Piers ANTHONY, beginning with *The Ring* (**1968**) and *The E.S.P. Worm* (**1970**), and continuing with the **Dragon** series of fantasies: *Dragon's Gold* (**1987**), *Serpent's Silver* (**1988**), *Chimaera's Copper* (**1990**) and *Orc's Opal* (**1992**). [JC]

See also: CRIME AND PUNISHMENT; PSYCHOLOGY.

MARGULIES, LEO (1900-1975) US publisher and editor, born in Brooklyn and educated at Columbia University. He joined the Frank A. MUNSEY chain of PULP MAGAZINES in 1932, later moving to Beacon Magazines and becoming editorial director of THRILLING WONDER STORIES when Beacon began publishing that title in 1936. LM had overall responsibility for the entire output of the chain; this later included the magazines CAPTAIN FUTURE, STARTLING STORIES and STRANGE STORIES. One of the editors who worked with him on these magazines was Oscar J. FRIEND, and the two later collaborated on 3 anthologies: *From Off This World* (anth **1949**), a thematic collection about ALIENS, *My Best Science Fiction Story* (anth **1949**) and *The Giant Anthology of Science Fiction* (anth **1954**). After WWII, LM formed a publishing company, and returned to sf as publisher of FANTASTIC UNIVERSE, of which he was also editorial director for a time. He left that company and formed another, which published SATELLITE SCIENCE FICTION. Of the remaining anthologies bearing his name, four – *Three Times Infinity* (anth **1958**), *Three in One* (anth **1963**), *Weird Tales* (anth **1964**) and *Worlds of Weird* (anth **1965**) – were in fact ghost-edited by Sam MOSKOWITZ; but *Three from Out There* (anth **1959**), *Get Out of My Sky* (anth **1960**), *The Ghoul Keepers* (anth **1961**) and *The Unexpected* (anth **1961**) were LM's work. [MJE]

MARINER, DAVID [r] ◊ ROBERT HALE LIMITED.

MARINER, SCOTT Pseudonym used by C.M. KORNBLUTH and Frederik POHL in collaboration on the story "An Old Neptunian Custom" (1942). [PN]

MARKHAM, ROBERT ◊ Kingsley AMIS.

MARKOV, GEORGI [r] ◊ BULGARIA; David ST GEORGE.

MARK V. ZIESING US SMALL PRESS. MVZ is the direct successor to Ziesing Brothers, which booksellers Michael Ziesing (1946-   ) and his brother Mark V. Ziesing (1953-   ) had founded in Willimantic, Connecticut, initially to produce poetry, but which then produced two books by Gene WOLFE: *The Castle of the Otter* (coll **1982**) and *The Wolfe Archipelago* (coll **1983**). After this Michael became inactive, and the firm became Mark V. Ziesing. Further books by Wolfe followed, plus titles by A.A. ATTANASIO, Iain M. BANKS, Neal BARRETT Jr, James P. BLAYLOCK, Thomas M. DISCH, Lucius SHEPARD, Bruce STERLING, Howard WALDROP and others. Since 1989 the firm has operated from California. Because of its inventive publishing programme, and because most editions are well designed, MVZ has as good a chance of surviving the difficult early 1990s as any small press. [JC]

MARKWICK, EDWARD Working name of UK lawyer and writer Edward Markwick Johnson (?   -?   ), active in the last quarter of the 19th century, whose sf novel, *The City of Gold: A Tale of Sport, Travel, and Adventure in the Heart of the Dark Continent* (**1896**), direly invades H. Rider HAGGARD territory, taking its protagonists into a scientifically advanced Semitic LOST WORLD run by a Great White Witch whose love for the hero causes her death. [JC]

MARLOW, LOUIS Pseudonym of UK writer and lecturer in English studies Louis Umfreville Wilkinson (1881-1966), who also wrote novels under his real name. Of sf interest is *The Devil in Crystal* (**1944**) which, in LM's typically pert, dandiacal, somewhat overeager manner, describes the effects of a sort of self-possession. The protagonist finds himself cast 20 years into his own past, where he relives his life while being all the while conscious of his observer status and of his almost total inability to alter reality. [JC]

See also: TIME TRAVEL.

MARLOWE, STEPHEN ◊ Milton LESSER.

MARLOWE, WEBB [s] ◊ J. Francis MCCOMAS.

MARNER, ROBERT [s] ◊ Algis BUDRYS.

MAROONED Film (1969). Columbia. Dir John Sturges, starring Gregory Peck, Gene Hackman, David Janssen, Richard Crenna, James Franciscus. Screenplay Mayo Simon, based on *Marooned* (**1964**) by Martin CAIDIN. 134 mins. Colour.

John Sturges is best known for Westerns (e.g., *The Magnificent Seven* [1960]), though he also directed the borderline sf film *The Satan Bug* (1965); outer space may be a less suitable setting for his work. The film is a quasidocumentary about the rescue, by a Soviet/US team, of three astronauts trapped in orbit around the Earth. Opinions are divided on whether the slowly built suspense is potent or monotonous; the dialogue is even more banal than real NASA chat. The special effects are low-key and accurate, but not visually memorable; the most impressive sequence in the film is the one containing shots of a genuine Saturn rocket-launch. The film suffered through being released at much the same time as 2001: A SPACE ODYSSEY. However, the friendly treatment given to Russian cosmonauts in *M* played a part in bringing about the Apollo-Soyuz space rendezvous of 1975. [JB/PN]

MARRIOTT-WATSON, H(ENRY) B(RERETON) (1863-1921) Australian-born writer, in UK all his working life; son of Henry Crocker MARRIOTT-WATSON. His first novel, *Marahuna* (**1888**), is sf: the eponymous female, extracted from a fiery ring in Antarctica, may well come from the interior of the Earth. Some of the tales assembled in *Diogenes of London and Other Fantasies* (coll **1893**) are indeed fantastic, as are some of the contents of *The Heart of Miranda and Other Stories, Being Mostly Winter Tales* (coll **1899**) and *Aftermath: A Garner of Tales* (coll **1919**). [JC]

Other works: *The Princess Xenia* (**1899**) and *Alise of Astra* (**1910**), both RURITANIAN tales.

MARRIOTT-WATSON, HENRY CROCKER (1835-?) New Zealand writer who spent some years in Australia, and whose surname at birth was almost certainly Watson; father of H.B. MARRIOTT-WATSON. *Erchomenon, or The Republic of Materialism* (**1879** UK), published anon, is a UTOPIA set some years in the future. *The Decline and Fall of the British Empire, or The Witch's Cavern* (**1890** UK), published as by H.C.M.W., is a surprisingly adventurous and invention-filled speculation set in the FAR FUTURE. [JC]

MARS For a long time Mars seemed to be the most likely abode for life outside the Earth, and for that reason it has always been of cardinal importance in sf. Its surface, unlike that of VENUS, exhibits markings visible (albeit unclearly) with the aid of optical telescopes, and has a distinct red colour. Blue-green tracts interrupting the red were thought to be oceans or vegetation. The polar caps, seen to wax and wane with the seasons, were generally held to be of snow and ice. In 1877 Giovanni Schiaparelli (1835-1910) reported an intricate network of *canali* (channels), a word widely interpreted as "canals". The US astronomer Percival Lowell (1855-1916), in *Mars* (**1896**), built up an image of a cool, arid world with great red deserts and a few areas of arable land, but perfectly capable of sustaining life. The landing of the Viking probes in 1976, however, revealed that Mars is extremely cold and has virtually no atmosphere; although there really are gigantic channels, possibly caused by water in the distant past, the intricate network reported by Schiaparelli does not exist, and nor do the tracts of vegetation.

Mars was visited by the usual interplanetary tourists – Athanasius KIRCHER, Emanuel SWEDENBORG, W.S. LACH-SZYRMA, George GRIFFITH *et al.* – but it became important in the late 19th century as a major target for specific cosmic voyages because the MOON, known to be lifeless, seemed a relatively uninteresting destination. It is the home of an advanced civilization in Percy GREG's *Across the Zodiac* (**1880**) and a setting for lost-race-type adventures in *Mr Stranger's Sealed Packet* (**1889**) by Hugh MACCOLL. Robert CROMIE's *A Plunge into Space* (**1890**) is an interplanetary love story and sociological tract, as is Gustavus W. POPE's *A Journey to Mars* (**1894**). Kurd LASSWITZ's *Auf Zwei Planeten* (**1897**; cut trans as *Two Planets* **1971**) provides another elaborate description of an advanced civilization and discusses the politics of interplanetary relations. H.G. WELLS published a brief vision of Mars in "The Crystal Egg" (**1897**) and followed up with the archetypal alien-INVASION story, *The War of the Worlds* (**1898**), which cast a long shadow over the sf of the 20th century. Wells's Martians, having exhausted the resources of their dying world, come as predatory Darwinian competitors to stake their claim to Earth. This novel firmly implanted in the popular imagination the image of Martians as MONSTERS, and brought a new sensationalism into interplanetary fiction;

when Orson Welles's Mercury Theatre dramatized the novel for US RADIO in 1938 it precipitated a panic, whose seeds had been sown 40 years before and fed ever since by a lurid stream of pulp fiction (◊ WAR OF THE WORLDS). Garrett P. SERVISS's "sequel", *Edison's Conquest of Mars* (**1898**; **1947**), which reassuringly describes the obliteration of the decadent Martian civilization, made no impact. Nor was there much imaginative power in romances of Martian REINCARNATION like Camille FLAMMARION's *Urania* (**1889**; trans **1891**) or Louis Pope GRATACAP's *The Certainty of a Future Life on Mars* (**1903**). The only other image which did take hold was something much closer to Lowell's enthusiastic prospectus for exotic Martian life and landscape: an uninhibitedly romantic Mars pioneered by Edwin Lester ARNOLD's *Lt Gullivar Jones – His Vacation* (**1905**; vt *Gulliver of Mars*) and permanently enshrined in modern mythology by the much imitated novels of Edgar Rice BURROUGHS, whose **Barsoom** series, begun with *A Princess of Mars* (**1912**; **1917**), was extended to 11 volumes over the next 30 years. Burroughs's John Carter and his kin battle for beautiful, egg-laying princesses against assorted villains and monsters, armed with swords but borne aloft by flying gondolas. Burroughs was co-opted into GENRE SF when *The Mastermind of Mars* (**1928**) appeared as the lead story in the 1927 AMAZING STORIES ANNUAL, and his influence within the genre has been as powerful as that of Wells. His principal imitator, Otis Adelbert KLINE, began by setting his works on Venus, but eventually began a Martian series with *The Swordsman of Mars* (**1933**; **1960**).

The early sf pulps were resonant with echoes of *The War of the Worlds*. The first issue of AMAZING STORIES reprinted Austin HALL's "The Man who Saved the Earth" (**1923**); another early example was Edmond HAMILTON's "Monsters of Mars" (**1931**). It was not long, however, before a reaction against the CLICHÉ became manifest. P. Schuyler MILLER's "The Forgotten Man of Space" (**1933**) features meek, mistreated Martians, and Raymond Z. GALLUN's "Old Faithful" (**1934**) is an ideological reply to Wells's Darwinian assumptions. Other notable depictions of life on Mars include Laurence MANNING's "The Wreck of the Asteroid" (**1932-3**), Stanley G. WEINBAUM's "A Martian Odyssey" (**1934**), Clark Ashton SMITH's "The Vaults of Yoh-Vombis" (**1932**), C.L. MOORE's "Shambleau" (**1933**), P. Schuyler Miller's "The Titan" (1st part **1936**; **1952**) and Clifford D. SIMAK's "The Hermit of Mars" (**1939**). Outside the pulps one work stands out from all others as a key contribution to the mythology of Mars: C.S. LEWIS's fantasy *Out of the Silent Planet* (**1938**), in which Mars is a world whose life-system is organized according to Christian ethical principles rather than the logic of Darwinian natural selection. John W. CAMPBELL Jr's editorial insistence on more careful speculative logic suppressed the "traditional" image of Mars in the pulps' primary sf market, ASTOUNDING SCIENCE-FICTION. Its exotic qualities were played down and replaced by the kind of "realism" encapsulated by P. Schuyler Miller's "The Cave" (1944), an ironic story in which Martian lifeforms kill an Earthman who violates the truce which they all must observe in order to survive the long Martian night. Martian exotica flourished nevertheless, particularly in the work of Leigh BRACKETT, whose "Martian Quest" (1940) was in *ASF* but who went on to do the bulk of her work for PLANET STORIES. Her gaudy version of the red planet, where decadent alien cultures face the threat of plundering Earthmen, is featured in *Shadow over Mars* (1944; **1951**; vt *The Nemesis from Terra* 1961 dos), *The Sword of Rhiannon* (1949 as "Sea-Kings of Mars"; **1953**), *The Secret of Sinharat* (1949 as "Queen of the Martian Catacombs"; exp **1964**), *The People of the Talisman* (1950 as "Black Amazon of Mars"; exp **1964**) and "The Last Days of Shandakor" (1952). Ray BRADBURY subsequently brought the romantic image of Mars to a kind of impressionistic perfection in *The Martian Chronicles* (1946-50; coll **1950**; vt *The Silver Locusts* 1951 UK; the latter and many subsequent edns have variant contents). In these stories Mars is dead but still haunted by the ghosts of an extinct civilization, visited by Earthmen who become doubly haunted by virtue of the echoes of their own Earthly past which follow them. The stories are heavy with nostalgia and extraordinarily seductive. A few other writers have had some success in capturing a similar atmosphere, notably Simak in "Seven Came Back" (1950) and J.G. BALLARD in "The Time-Tombs" (1963).

In the 1950s the romance of exotic Mars was mostly left behind as the dominant theme became the problems of COLONIZATION of a planet with barely enough water and barely enough oxygen. Notable stories in this newly realistic vein were *The Sands of Mars* (**1951**) by Arthur C. CLARKE, *Outpost Mars* (**1952**; rev vt *Sin in Space* 1961) by Cyril Judd (C.M. KORNBLUTH and Judith MERRIL), "Crucifixus Etiam" (1953) by Walter M. MILLER, *Alien Dust* (fixup **1955**) by E.C. TUBB and *Police Your Planet* (**1956** as by Erik van Lhin) by Lester DEL REY. Among the many juvenile novels of the same species were *Red Planet* (**1949**) by Robert A. HEINLEIN and a series by Patrick MOORE begun with *Mission to Mars* (**1955**). Martian ROBINSON-ADES of the same ilk include del Rey's *Marooned on Mars* (**1952**), Rex GORDON's *No Man Friday* (**1956**; vt *First on Mars* 1957) and James BLISH's *Welcome to Mars* (**1967**). Indigenous lifeforms are frequently featured in these novels, but few are hostile; an exception is in Kenneth F. GANTZ's *Not in Solitude* (**1959**). An uninhabited Mars becomes a grim prison colony in *Farewell, Earth's Bliss* (**1966**; rev 1971) by D.G. COMPTON. Other memorable stories of the period include Theodore STURGEON's poignant vignette about a dying astronaut, "The Man who Lost the Sea" (1959), and Philip José FARMER's pioneering exploration of the possibilities of alien sexuality, "Open to Me, My Sister" (1960; vt "My Sister's Brother"). The mythology of Mars moved into a new phase in the early 1960s as the scenarios of the 1950s began to reappear

in a somewhat surrealized form. Heinlein's *Stranger in a Strange Land* (**1961**) features a human raised by Martians who returns to Earth to build a religious philosophy out of the elements of their cultural heritage. Roger ZELAZNY's "A Rose for Ecclesiastes" (1963) reverses the idea, introducing to a Brackett-esque Mars a poet who becomes a preacher and leads the decadent Martians to a cultural revival. Philip K. DICK's *Martian Time-Slip* (**1964**) and *The Three Stigmata of Palmer Eldritch* (**1964**) use colony scenarios as backgrounds for reality-shifting plots – the arid, depleted environment was ideal for Dick's psychological landscaping. A more elaborate but equally enigmatic fantasy is Algis BUDRYS's *The Amsirs and the Iron Thorn* (**1967**; vt *The Iron Thorn* 1968). The real possibility that Mars might harbour life was by now on the brink of extinction, and *The Earth is Near* (**1970**; trans **1974**) by Luděk PEŠEK provides a vivid requiem in which the myth-driven members of the first Martian expedition undertake an obsessive search for life in an environment which cannot sustain it.

In more recent times Lin CARTER has written pastiches of Brackett – *The Man who Loved Mars* (**1973**) and *The Valley where Time Stood Still* (**1974**) – but they are blatant fakes; Brackett herself had moved on to new worlds beyond the Solar System. Christopher PRIEST went back to a more remote image in his Wellsian romp, *The Space Machine* (**1975**), but other writers remained determined to do what they had to in order to sustain the planet's future viability as a potential home for life. Frederik POHL's *Man Plus* (**1976**) is a grimly realistic account of the making of a CYBORG colonist, while Ian WATSON's *The Martian Inca* (**1976**) and John VARLEY's "In the Hall of the Martian Kings" (1977) stubbornly credit the seemingly unpromising Martian soil with miraculous adaptive qualities. Some sf writers cling to the conviction that, no matter how arid Mars might be, near-future colonization remains a viable project, as in Lewis SHINER's stubbornly realistic *Frontera* (**1984**); frontier Mars is featured also in Sterling LANIER's *Menace under Marswood* (**1983**). Other writers have taken new heart from the idea that it might be a promising world for TERRAFORMING. The possibility that terraforming might help resuscitate, at least for a brief while, a neo-romantic Mars is eloquently expressed in Ian McDONALD's fabulous *Desolation Road* (**1988**). In *Green Mars* (1985 *IASFM*; **1988** chap dos) Kim Stanley ROBINSON looks forward ironically to the days when conservationists are champions of the old red world against the nascent fertile version; a version of their case provides one of several strands of argument about terraforming in the ambitions *Red Mars* (**1992** UK), which begins a projected trilogy on the planet, with «Green Mars» (no connection to the novella) and «Blue Mars» to follow. This project promises to be a key work in the realistic school. (Robert L. FORWARD) Robert L. FORWARD's *Martian Rainbow* (**1991**) and Jack WILLIAMSON's *Beachhead* (**1992**) are other recent additions to this school. Invasions from Mars now seem completely obsolete, but the idea still has a certain satirical mileage, as revealed in Frederik Pohl's *The Day the Martians Came* (fixup **1988**); the epic journey to Mars receives similar satirical treatment in Terry BISSON's *Voyage to the Red Planet* (**1990**). Magical echoes of romantic Mars still insinuate themselves into all these works, as they will undoubtedly do when and if the first manned mission to Mars takes place.

A theme anthology is *Mars, We Love You* (anth **1971**; vt *The Book of Mars* 1976 UK) ed Willis E. MCNELLY with Jane Hipolito. [BS]

See also: SCIENTIFIC ERRORS.

MARSH, GEOFFREY ◊ Charles L. GRANT.

MARSHAK, SONDRA (? -) US writer who has been associated with STAR TREK from the early 1970s, moving from fan activities into **Star Trek** ties and commentaries. SM began with *Star Trek Lives!* (**1975**) with Jacqueline LICHTENBERG and Joan Winston, moving on to *Star Trek: The New Voyages* * (coll **1976**) with Myrna CULBREATH and its direct sequel, *Star Trek: The New Voyages 2* * (anth **1978**), also with Culbreath, two enthusiastic but patchy compilations of short fiction. Subsequent ties written with Culbreath include *The Price of the Phoenix* * (**1977**) and its direct sequel *The Fate of the Phoenix* * (**1979**), *The Prometheus Design* * (**1982**) and *Triangle* * (**1983**). With William SHATNER, SM and Culbreath wrote *Shatner: "Where No Man . . .": The Authorized Biography of William Shatner* (**1979**). [JC/CAJ]

Other work: *The Star Trek Puzzle Manual* (**1976**) with James Razzi.

MARSHALL, ARCHIBALD Working name of UK novelist Arthur Hammond Marshall (1866-1934), who was prolific and popular in the early decades of this century. His Erewhonian sf SATIRE *Upsidonia* (**1915**) amusingly places a young man in a PARALLEL WORLD, somehow linked with ours, where all values, in particular ECONOMIC ones, suffer a reversal; many comic points are lightly made. [JC]

Other work: *Simple People* (**1928**).

MARSHALL, EDISON (TESLA) (1894-1967) US writer and big-game hunter, best known for his work outside the sf field, especially his many historical novels. He began publishing sf with "Who is Charles Avison?" (1916). The narrator of *Ogden's Strange Story* (1928 *Popular Magazine*; **1934**), which is also sf, recollects his life in the Stone Age in another body. *Dian of the Lost Land* (**1935**; vt *The Lost Land* 1972) is a romantically told tale of a lost race (◊ LOST WORLDS) of Cro-Magnons in Antarctica. *Earth Giant* (**1960**) is about Hercules. [JC/PN]

Other works: *The Death Bell* (**1924**), *Sam Campbell, Gentleman* (**1934**), *The Stolen God* (**1936**), *Darzee, Girl of India* (**1937**), *The White Brigand* (**1937**) and *The Jewel of Mahabar* (**1938**), all primarily adventure but with some fantastic elements.

MARSTEN, RICHARD ◊ Evan HUNTER.

MARTENS, PAUL ◊ Neil BELL.

MARTIAN CHRONICLES, THE US tv miniseries (1980). NBC TV. Dir Michael Anderson, starring Rock Hudson, Gayle Hunnicutt, Darren McGavin, Roddy McDowall, Joyce van Patten, Fritz Weaver, Nyree Dawn Porter, Bernadette Peters. Teleplay Richard MATHESON, based on *The Martian Chronicles* (coll of linked stories 1950; rev vt *The Silver Locusts* 1951 UK) by Ray BRADBURY. 3 110min episodes. Colour.

The problems with this disappointing, expensive ($8 million) adaptation cannot be blamed entirely on Anderson's sluggish direction (*see also* LOGAN'S RUN) or Matheson's script (which establishes somewhat artificial continuities between the 11 stories he adapts), or even the inflexible performance of Rock Hudson as Colonel Wilder, the main linking character. Bradbury's own words, which for many readers work poetically on the page, tend to sound stilted when spoken, and clash with the realism that tv seems to demand. The answer might have been to make the words more austere and find a visual poetry to substitute, but in this the production mostly fails, though some aspects (the Martians and their strange masks) are authentically otherworldly. The insistent moralizing (not untrue to the book) comes over as hackneyed and sentimental. Another director might have done better than Anderson, but the book is intractably literary and probably inappropriate for film or tv. Bradbury was reported to be unhappy with the production. [PN]

MARTIN, CARL [r] ◊ John DALMAS.

MARTIN, GEORGE R(AYMOND) R(ICHARD) (1948-) US writer and editor whose first published sf story was "The Hero" for *Gal* in 1971. His success was thereafter rapid. "A Song for Lya" (1974), a novella about a human convert to an alien RELIGION whose ESCHATOLOGY is based in BIOLOGY, won the first of his 3 HUGOS to date; 2 others followed for "Sandkings" (1979), which also won a NEBULA, and "The Way of Cross and Dragon" (1979); he won a second Nebula in 1986 for "Portraits of his Children" (1985), and a Bram Stoker Award for *The Pear-Shaped Man* (1987 *Omni*; **1991** chap). Other notable early stories include a short series about an unusual form of interstellar TRANSPORTATION begun with "The Second Kind of Loneliness" (1972) and another begun with "Override" (1973), about the commercial exploitation of zombies. A novella which he wrote in collaboration with Lisa TUTTLE, "The Storms of Windhaven" (1975), was eventually extended into *Windhaven* (fixup **1981**) as by GRRM and Lisa Tuttle. His first solo (and only sf) novel, *Dying of the Light* (**1977**), is a vivid romance set on a drifting planet which, while passing close by a sun, has been the site of a huge festival; some short stories are set in the same universe. *Fevre Dream* (**1982**) is a tale of vampires and Mississippi steamboats whose realistic treatment owes as much to sf as to supernatural fiction. *The Armageddon Rag* (**1983**) is a thriller in which the kind of apocalypse imagined in Norman SPINRAD's "The Big Flash" (1969) is aborted in the nick of time. His most substantial sf project is the series collected in *Tuf Voyaging* (coll of linked stories **1986**) about the problem-solving exploits of an ecological engineer in a declining GALACTIC EMPIRE. Perhaps because of his training as a journalist and his employment in the mid-1970s as a teacher of journalism, GRRM seems most comfortable with stories which are fast-paced and economical. "Nightflyers" (1980), a horror story set aboard a spaceship and involving a COMPUTER impressed with human PSI POWERS, is another outstanding novella, very unevenly filmed as *Nightflyers* (1987).

In the late 1980s GRRM moved into tv, first writing for the new The TWILIGHT ZONE series (1985-7) and then becoming heavily involved with the development of BEAUTY AND THE BEAST. In parallel with these enterprises he launched **Wild Cards**, a set of BRAIDED tales placed in an ALTERNATE WORLD – whose premise is rather more sophisticated than most such in COMICS – starring SUPERHEROES; the possibility of trademark infringement forced the substitution of the term "Ace" for "Superhero". This SHARED-WORLD anthology series (GRRM prefers the label "mosaic novels", on the grounds that individual volumes are more coherently organized than in most such anthologies) currently (early 1992) extends to 9 vols (◊ WILD CARDS *for listing*). GRRM earlier edited the notable NEW VOICES series of ANTHOLOGIES of novellas by the nominees for the JOHN W. CAMPBELL AWARD for Best New Writer (of which he was himself one): *New Voices in Science Fiction* (anth **1977**; vt *New Voices I: The Campbell Award Nominees* 1978), *New Voices II* (anth **1979**), *New Voices III* (anth **1980**), *New Voices 4* (anth **1981**) and *The John W. Campbell Awards Volume 5* (anth **1984**).

GRRM is a vigorous storyteller with a flair for vivid imagery. All of his collections – *A Song for Lya and Other Stories* (coll **1976**), *Songs of Stars and Shadows* (coll **1977**), *Sandkings* (coll **1981**), *Songs the Dead Men Sing* (coll **1983**; cut 1985 UK), *Nightflyers* (coll **1985**) and *Portraits of his Children* (coll **1987**) – contain striking work. His own output has declined as he has become increasingly active as an editor. [BS]

Other works as editor: *The Science Fiction Weight-Loss Book* (anth **1983**) with Isaac ASIMOV and Martin H. GREENBERG; *Night Visions 3* (anth **1986**; vt *Night Visions 1987* UK).

About the author: *George R.R. Martin, the Ace from New Jersey: A Working Bibliography* (last rev **1989** chap) by Phil STEPHENSEN-PAYNE.

See also: ALIENS; ASTOUNDING SCIENCE-FICTION; BLACK HOLES; CRIME AND PUNISHMENT; FANTASY; GOTHIC SF; HEROES; HYPERSPACE; ISAAC ASIMOV'S SCIENCE FICTION MAGAZINE; MUSIC; OMNI; SUPERMAN; TELEVISION.

MARTIN, GRAHAM DUNSTAN (1932-   ) Scottish writer who began publishing work of genre interest with the **Giftwish** children's fantasy sequence: *Giftwish* (**1978**) and *Catchfire* (**1981**), both as Graham Martin. With *The Soul Master* (**1984**), as GDM, he moved sf-wards, though the godling-dominated land of Tethesta is described in terms of fantasy. *Time-Slip* (**1986**), a bleak post-HOLOCAUST tale set in nether Scotland, is fully sf, as is *The Dream Wall* (**1987**), a

dreadful-warning story of the UK under the Soviets in the early 21st century. GDM's strengths – a dogged insistence on what he clearly feels to be home truths – are fully on view in this narrative, as are certain weaknesses, mainly a grim humourlessness which greys out any attempts at SATIRE or novelistic ambiguity. *Half a Glass of Moonshine* (**1988**), a study in PERCEPTION, suggests that the human sensorium blocks off certain features of our environment for good Darwinian reasons. [JC]
See also: PARALLEL WORLDS.

MARTIN, PETER Working name of UK writer Peter Martin Leckie (1890-?   ) for his sf novel, *Summer in 3,000: Not a Prophecy – A Parable* (**1946**), in which a progressive World Island state is contrasted with a war-torn conservative one. [JC]

MARTIN, ROD [r] ◊ John DALMAS.

MARTIN, THOMAS [r] ◊ Martin THOMAS.

MARTIN, WEBBER ◊ Robert SILVERBERG.

MARTINSEN, MARTIN ◊ Ken FOLLETT.

MARTINSON, HARRY (EDMUND) (1904-1978) Swedish author and poet, member of the Swedish Academy, recipient of the 1974 Nobel Literature Prize. A prolific writer, HM's one contribution to sf is *Aniara* (1953 Cikada; exp **1956**; trans Hugh MacDiarmid and E. Harley Schubert as *Aniara: A Review of Man in Time and Space* 1963 UK), a 103-canto epic poem (◊ POETRY) eloquently defending humane values against the inhumanity of TECHNOLOGY within the story of the irreversible voyage of a GENERATION STARSHIP, *Aniara*, towards outer space. Despite or possibly because of the participation of Hugh MacDiarmid (1892-1978), arguably Scotland's most important 20th-century poet, the English translation ill serves the resonant, melodic and quotable original. Karl-Birger Blomdahl's opera (◊ MUSIC) based on the poem, *Aniara* (1959), features some pioneering electronic effects and has achieved international success. Some of the poems in the untranslated *Doriderna* (coll **1980**) belong to the *Aniara* cycle. [J-HH/JC]

MARTYN, WYNDHAM (1875-?   ) UK thriller writer who occasionally tacked on sf devices. His *Stones of Enchantment* (**1948**) details the discovery of a lost race (◊ LOST WORLDS) possessing the secret of longevity. [JE]
Other work: *Nightmare Castle* (**1935**).

MARVEL COMICS Eventually named for its first COMIC – much as DC COMICS was named after *Detective Comics* – MC was founded by Martin Goodman (1910-1992) as Timely Comics before, in the 1950s, being renamed Atlas Comics after its distribution company; it became MC in 1963. *Marvel Comics #1* (Nov 1939) featured two of the company's three early mainstays. **The Human Torch** was an ANDROID who could become a figure of living flame; he was created and drawn by Carl Burgos. **Prince Namor, the Sub Mariner** – a warlike undersea monarch who had an ambivalent relationship with the surface world – was chronicled by William Blake (Bill) Everett. Throughout the 1940s both **The Human Torch** and **Prince Namor** had their own comics (*The Human Torch* from

Fall 1940, *Sub Mariner Comics* from Spring 1941). Running alongside them were *Marvel Mystery Comics* (*Marvel Comics* retitled) and the third of those mainstays: **Captain America** (Mar 1941-Jan 1950). The original masked superpatriot was created by artist Jack KIRBY and writer Joe Simon.

In the 1950s *Marvel Mystery Comics* became *Marvel Tales*, and was indistinguishable from dozens of other horror, war, sf, Western, gag and romance anthology titles; Stan LEE was credited with writing most of the contents. Not quite lost among the chaff were strips by many fine illustrators, including Bill Benulis, Gene Colan, Richard Doxsee, Bernie Krigstein, Joe Maneely, Gray MORROW and Al Williamson. The mid-1950s slump in comics sales saw the disappearance of Atlas but not of all of its titles. Stan Lee retrenched in 1958, giving more of an sf/horror/MONSTER-MOVIE flavour to his titles. With the help of a returned Jack Kirby (who had worked elsewhere through most of the 1950s) plus regular artists Dick Ayers, Steve Ditko and Don Heck, editor Lee and his "Bullpen" were soon eager to re-enter the SUPERHERO genre, starting with Nov 1961's *Fantastic Four*. Lee allowed his heroes to be fallible: they could be bad-tempered, immature, repressed . . . The motif would establish MC at the vanguard of comics publishing.

At the dawn of the "Marvel Age" MC experimented with an sf-anthology title. Produced by Lee and Ditko and complete with contents and letters pages, *Amazing Adult Fantasy* ran for 8 issues Dec 1961-July 1962 before being retitled *Amazing Fantasy* for 1 final issue, which featured the début of MC's most popular character ever: **Spider-Man**.

Most of Marvel's superheroes had various kinds of run-ins with PSEUDO-SCIENCE, especially **The Fantastic Four**, a group of superpowered troubleshooters. Kirby and Lee elegantly plundered Norse mythology for their **Thor** series (*Journey into Mystery* #83 [Aug 1962] to present; renamed *Thor* in 1966) while Lee and Ditko produced the definitive interdimensional magic strip in **Doctor Strange** (*Strange Tales* #110-#168 [Aug 1965-May 1968]; plus his own title 1968-71). *Marvel Super-Heroes* #12 (Dec 1967) saw the arrival of MC's space-born superhero **Captain Marvel**; it was not long before he had the red-yellow-blue costume and a teenage *alter ego* full of wisecracks and buzzwords like his 1940s namesake. (*For the full tortuous story of* CAPTAIN MARVEL, *see his entry*.) During 1968-71 MC's finest sf character, **The Silver Surfer**, was given his own title, drawn by John Buscema and with the writing credit going, inevitably, to Lee. In 1970 MC began publishing its own version of Robert E. HOWARD's **Conan**, adapted by Roy Thomas with artists John Buscema, Gil Kane and Barry Smith.

MC currently (1992) dominates the US comics marketplace, most notably with the bestselling X-MEN titles. Since 1987 MC has been reprinting many of its sought-after 1960s comics in the **Masterworks** series: **Spider-Man** (4 vols to date), **The Fantastic Four** (3 vols), **X-Men** (4 vols), **The Avengers** (2 vols) – no

relation to the tv series – **The Silver Surfer** (2 vols) and, each with 1 vol to date, **The Incredible Hulk**, **Thor**, **Daredevil** and **Captain America**.

An authorized and therefore somewhat uncritical account of the company's history is *Marvel: Five Fabulous Decades of the World's Greatest Comics* (**1991**) by Les Daniels. [SW]

See also: ILLUSTRATION.

MARVELL, ANDREW Pseudonym of UK editor and writer Howell Davies (1896-1985); between the Wars he worked as a theatre critic for the *Manchester Evening News* and as literary editor of the *Star* and *News Chronicle*, later serving as editor of the *South American Handbook* (1938-69). During the brief time he wrote as AM he published 3 novels. *Minimum Man, or Time to be Gone* (**1938**) combines sf and thriller ingredients in its depiction of a 1950 fascist coup in the UK, and of its overthrow by a new race of tiny but very powerful telepaths whose parthenogenetic births were caused by poison gas. *Three Men Make a World* (**1939**) is a kind of DISASTER story, though the turning of the UK into a rural land by petroleum-destroying bacteria may strike modern readers as a catastrophe with a silver lining. *Congratulate the Devil* (**1939**), in which a happiness drug is found to be intolerable to society at large, describes the process by which its disseminators are hounded to death. AM's novels were professional and engrossing. [JC/BS]

See also: POLITICS; PSI POWERS; SUPERMAN.

MARVELMAN ◊ CAPTAIN MARVEL; Alan MOORE.

MARVEL SCIENCE FICTION ◊ MARVEL SCIENCE STORIES.

MARVEL SCIENCE STORIES US PULP MAGAZINE. 9 issues 1938-41; 6 further issues 1950-52; published by Postal Publications (#1 and #2), then by Western Fiction Publishing Co. for the remainder of the 1st series, finally by Stadium Publishing Co.; ed Robert O. Erisman (uncredited in 1st series).

An sf pulp magazine from a chain which included such fringe-sf titles as UNCANNY TALES, *MSS* was the first of the many new sf magazines of the late 1930s and early 1940s. It was notorious for the mildly erotic approach of its early issues, to which Henry KUTTNER contributed several stories, including "The Time Trap" (Nov 1938). The Feb 1939 issue featured Jack WILLIAMSON's *After World's End* (**1961**). After 5 issues the title changed in Dec 1939 to *Marvel Tales*, and for 2 issues the magazine leaned more heavily towards titillating sex and sadism, like "Lust Rides the Roller Coaster" (Dec 1939) by Ray King and "World without Sex" (May 1940) by Robert Wentworth (Edmond HAMILTON). The title then changed again in Nov 1940 to *Marvel Stories*, and the magazine returned to straightforward sf. Although initially successful enough to generate a companion, DYNAMIC SCIENCE STORIES, *MSS*, which began as a quarterly, became less and less frequent through 1939-40, ceasing with the Mar 1941 issue. It was revived in Nov 1950 under its original title, switched to DIGEST size after 2 issues, appeared 3 times in that format, and reverted to pulp size for its final issue; it was *Marvel Science Fiction* for the last 3 issues. Daniel KEYES was an assistant editor for some of these later numbers, which were generally unmemorable. The Feb 1951 issue was published in a UK reprint May 1951. [MJE]

MARVEL STORIES ◊ MARVEL SCIENCE STORIES.

MARVEL TALES 1. US SEMIPROZINE (the first 3 issues small-DIGEST-size, #4 digest-size and #5 BEDSHEET-size), 5 issues May 1934-Summer 1935. Published by Fantasy Publishers; ed William L. CRAWFORD, who was not only the publisher but also set the type himself. Some issues were distributed with several different covers. Distribution was very limited; *MT* was never generally available. Its fiction included works by Robert E. HOWARD, H.P. LOVECRAFT, Robert BLOCH's first story, "Lilies" (Winter 1934), and Clifford D. SIMAK's *The Creator* (Mar 1935; **1946** chap). The Winter 1934 issue commenced serialization of P. Schuyler MILLER's short novel "The Titan"; the magazine died before the serialization was completed, and the work was finally published as the title novella of Miller's *The Titan* (coll **1952**). An even shorter-lived companion title was UNUSUAL STORIES.

2. Variant title used for 2 issues of MARVEL SCIENCE STORIES. [MJE]

MASK OF FU MANCHU, THE Film (1932). Cosmopolitan/MGM. Dir Charles Brabin, Charles Vidor, starring Boris Karloff, Lewis Stone, Karen Morley, Jean Hersholt, Myrna Loy. Screenplay Irene Kuhn, Edgar Allen Woolf, John Willard, based on *The Mask of Fu Manchu* (**1932**) by Sax ROHMER. 72 mins, cut to 67 mins. B/w.

Rohmer's Oriental supervillain has since been brought to the screen many times (◊ FU MANCHU) but this first, visually lavish version, produced by Irving Thalberg, is the most memorable. It is based on the 6th book in Sax Rohmer's intensely popular, racy and racist **Fu Manchu** series. Malign scientific genius, torturer and murderer Fu Manchu (Karloff), pitted against his old nemesis Nayland Smith (Stone), lisps his way poisonously through the film with the assistance of his sadistic daughter (Loy), who has a wonderfully fetishistic scene (assisted by Nubians) where she whips and then caresses one of their heroic enemies. Fu Manchu seeks Genghis Khan's death-mask and sword, which he intends to use as symbols to arouse the Oriental races in a war against the White nations; tarantulas and a zombie serum play roles in an eclectic plot which mixes sf and occult devices. In a spectacular climax Fu's electrical DEATH-RAY machine is turned against Fu's generals by Nayland Smith. The bizarrely stylized sets were by Cedric Gibbons and the electrical effects were by Ken Strickfaden. This is the sort of pulp adventure classic later imitated enjoyably by Steven SPIELBERG's *Raiders of the Lost Ark* (**1981**). [PN/JB]

MASON, ANITA (1942-   ) UK writer. Her second novel, *The Illusionist* (**1983**), is a literary fantasy centred on Simon Magus. AM's sf novel, *The War against Chaos* (**1988**), also intensely literary in demeanour, posits a NEAR-FUTURE UK of surreal bleakness dominated by thought-control and savage divisions between precarious Haves and Goyaesque Have-Nots, who live in something very much like Hell. [JC]

MASON, DAVID (1924-1974) US writer who began publishing with "Placebo" for *Infinity* in 1955; he was married 1956-62 to Katherine MacLEAN. Most of his novels – such as his first, *Kavin's World* (**1969**), and its sequel, *The Return of Kavin* (**1972**) – were routine SWORD AND SORCERY. However, his final book, *The Deep Gods* (**1973**), more impressively implants a 20th-century mentality into the brain of a prehistoric man who must deal with the insanity of a whale (one of the "deep gods" of the title) that threatens to destroy Eden. [JC]

Other works: *Devil's Food* (**1969**); *The Sorcerer's Skull* (**1970**); *The Shores of Tomorrow* (**1971**).

MASON, DOUGLAS R(ANKINE) (1918-   ) UK junior-school headmaster and prolific writer after 1964, both under his own name and as John Rankine; he has been silent since about 1980. His first story was "Two's Company", as by Rankine, in John CARNELL's *New Writings in SF 1* (**1964**), and he was soon publishing 2-3 books a year, generally routine SPACE OPERAS and other adventures as Rankine. Occasionally, under his own name – as with *From Carthage then I Came* (**1966** US; vt *Eight Against Utopia* 1967) and *Matrix* (**1970** US) – he would attempt more ambitious novels containing some social comment. Generally speaking, however, he was content to produce rather low-pressure work.

The **Dag Fletcher** series of space operas, as by Rankine, was initiated in his first book, *The Blockage of Sinitron: Four Adventures of Dag Fletcher* (coll of linked stories **1966**), and continued with *Interstellar Two-Five* (**1966**), *One is One* (**1968**), *The Plantos Affair* (**1971**), *The Ring of Garamas* (**1972**) and *The Bromius Phenomenon* (**1973** US). The series is set in a galactic environment shared by other Rankine titles including *The Fingalnan Conspiracy* (**1973**) and *The Thorburn Enterprise* (**1977**). [JC]

Other works:

As John Rankine: The **Space Corporation** series, comprising *Never the Same Door* (**1968**) and *Moons of Triopus* (**1968**); *Binary Z* (**1969**); *The Weisman Experiment* (**1969**); *Operation Umanaq* (**1973** US); 4 novelizations of episodes from the tv series SPACE 1999, being *#2: Moon Odyssey* * (**1975**), *#6: Astral Quest* * (**1975**), *#8: Android Planet* * (**1976**) and *#10: Phoenix of Megaron* * (**1976** US); *The Vort Programme* (**1978**); *The Star of Hesiock* (**1980**); *Last Shuttle to Planet Earth* (**1980**).

As DRM: *Landfall is a State of Mind* (**1968**); *Ring of Violence* (**1968**); *The Tower of Rizwan* (**1968**); *The Janus Syndrome* (**1969**); *Dilation Effect* (**1971** US); *Horizon Alpha* (**1971** US); *Satellite 54-Zero* (**1971** US); *The Resurrection of Roger Diment* (**1972** US); *The End Bringers* (**1973** US); *The Phaeton Condition* (**1973** US); *Pitman's Progress* (**1976**); *The Omega Worm* (**1976**); *Euphor Unfree* (**1977**); *Mission to Pactolus R* (**1978**); *The Typhon Intervention* (**1981**).

See also: CITIES; MATHEMATICS; NEW WRITINGS IN SF.

MASON, ERNST [r] ◊ Frederik POHL.

MASON, GREGORY (1889-1968) US writer whose sf DYSTOPIA, *The Golden Archer: A Satirical Novel of 1975* (**1956**), depicts a USA suffering under regimented, McCarthy-like bigotry. [JC]

MASON, LISA (1953-) US writer who began publishing sf with "Arachne" for *Omni* in 1987, a tale she expanded into her first novel, *Arachne* (**1990**), a tightly composed kitchen-sink narrative set in a post-earthquake San Francisco, in CYBERSPACE, and in the heart of a complex corporate world, with a tough female lawyer as protagonist, a maimed AI personality as trickster and dubious colleague, and cyberspace-haunting human personas everywhere at risk from AIs longing to acquire unprogrammed human virtues. Though as yet LM is still writing in a rather crowded Californian grotto, she gives every impression of being an author it is far too early to attempt to define. [JC]

MASON, MARY [r] ◊ Stephen GOLDIN.

MASON, ROBERT C(AVERLY) (1942-) US writer who became known for *Chickenhawk* (**1983**), a memoir of his stint as a helicopter pilot in Vietnam. *Weapon* (**1989**), ostensibly a TECHNOTHRILLER, avoids the more restrictive implications of that term by concentrating on an AI; Solo, the ROBOT referred to in the title, learns more about being human than about being a superior killing machine. The sequel, *Solo* (**1992**), sees the sensitive robot forced to fight off an even more dangerous successor robot. The generic closeness of these novels to the films *The* TERMINATOR (1984) and TERMINATOR 2 (1991) was noted in reviews, but there is certainly little resemblance between either film and *Weapon*. [JC]

MASON, TALLY [s] ◊ August W. DERLETH.

MASSON, DAVID I(RVINE) (1915-) Scottish writer, long resident in England, with an MA in English language and literature. He began publishing sf with "Traveller's Rest" for NEW WORLDS in 1965; his fiction, including this extraordinarily intense study in the distortion of PERCEPTION, was assembled in *The Caltraps of Time* (coll **1968**), which single volume established his strong reputation as a writer of vigorously experimental, vivid, often scientifically sound stories. Notable among them, and reflecting his close and informed interest in LINGUISTICS, were "Not so Certain" (1967) and the brilliant TIME-TRAVEL story "A Two-Timer" (1966), told entirely in language appropriate to 1683, the year from which the inadvertent time traveller is whisked into the future. Each of DIM's stories seems to be a solution to some cognitive or creative problem or challenge, and he appeared little inclined to repeat any of his effects. He has published almost no fiction since 1968, though "Doctor Fausta" in George HAY's *Stopwatch* (anth **1974**) is an interesting SATIRE. DIM also reviewed sf fairly frequently during the 1970s in FOUNDATION. [JC]

See also: DIMENSIONS; MATHEMATICS.

MASTER OF TERROR ◊ 4D MAN.

MASTER OF THE WORLD Film (1961). AIP. Dir William Witney, starring Vincent Price, Charles Bronson, Henry Hull, Mary Webster. Screenplay Richard MATHESON, based (not very closely) on *Robur le conquérant* (**1886**; trans as *The Clipper of the Clouds* **1887**; vt *Robur the Conqueror* 1887) and *Maître du monde* (**1904**; trans as *Master of the World* **1914**) by Jules VERNE. 104 mins. Colour.

MOTW owes more to the Disney version of 20,000 LEAGUES UNDER THE SEA (1954) – which it clearly imitates – than to the two Verne novels, with the *Albatross*, a very light clipper ship with propellers on the masts, substituting for a submarine. Robur (Price), a warped idealist, uses his invention to enforce peace by making war on war, bombarding opposing armies from the air; he kidnaps as witnesses a US special agent (Bronson), an arms manufacturer (Hull) and a young couple. The film was more lavish than most AIP productions (usually very-low-budget exploitation movies), but most of the money went on the elaborate flying ship. The travelogue aspect of the film is achieved largely through library footage, some of it wildly anachronistic: a supposed aerial shot of 1860s London is from the 1944 film of Shakespeare's *Henry V*. A melodramatic, one-note script by Matheson (usually better than this) and flat direction weaken the film, but it remains watchable if silly. [JB/PN]

MASTERS, DEXTER (1908-1989) US writer whose only sf work was *The Cloud Chamber* (**1971**). [JC]

MASTERS, J.D. ◊ Nicholas YERMAKOV.

MASTERS OF THE UNIVERSE Film (1987). Cannon. Dir Gary Goddard, starring Dolph Lundgren, Frank Langella, Meg Foster, Billy Barty. Screenplay David Odell. 106 mins. Colour.

Goddard's unfortunate film début announced itself as the first live-action film to be based on toys (◊ GAMES AND TOYS) – the He-Man toys made by Mattel; its obvious predecessor was an animated tv series, *He-Man and the Masters of the Universe*, begun 1983. The SWORD-AND-SORCERY story pits the muscle-bound He-Man (Lundgren) of Planet Eternia against Skeletor (Langella), a demon figure from another DIMENSION and leader of the malign Masters of the Universe. A MATTER-TRANSMITTER key takes He-Man to contemporary California, where he finds the help necessary for defeating Skeletor in a final showdown. The film lacks the vigour it requires. The marketing phenomenon it exemplifies has concerned many parents, and some countries ban films and tv series which, in the guise of entertainment, are designed to sell commercial products by brainwashing very young children. A further example is the much better (animated) film *The* TRANSFORMERS – THE MOVIE (1986). [PN]

MASTIN, JOHN (1865-1932) UK writer, clergyman and science popularizer, author of 3 sf novels. *The Stolen Planet* (**1906**) features the picaresque adventures of two Earthmen through the Solar System and beyond, as narrated by Jervis Meredith, codeveloper of a space-conquering "aerostat"; centuries later, in *Through the Sun in an Airship* (**1909**), Meredith's last descendant again tours a number of planets. Through his various FANTASTIC VOYAGES, JM tried to exploit the romance of science in stories which have an attractive (though thin) patina of verisimilitude and are told in the uplifting manner typical of too many UK boys' books; they are permeated with religiosity, at times attempting a reconciliation of science and RELIGION. *The Immortal Light* (**1907**) is a LOST-WORLDS novel set in the Antarctic among an underground, Latin-speaking race. *The Autobiography of a Picture* (**1910**) is fantasy.   [JC/EFB]

See also: HISTORY OF SF; SPACESHIPS; SUN.

MATHEMATICS The imaginations of pure mathematicians have provided sf writers with important motifs. For example, the notions taken from geometry and topology of a fourth and other DIMENSIONS (*which see for a listing of relevant sf stories*) have the essential qualities of strangeness and mystery, making them an enjoyable struggle for the untrained intuition to accept. A surprising number of sf writers have been mathematicians, or at least have trained in mathematics; among them have been Lewis CARROLL, Arthur C. CLARKE, Paul DAVIES, Ralph Milne FARLEY, Martin GARDNER, Norman KAGAN, Johannes KEPLER, Donald KINGSBURY, Homer NEARING, Larry NIVEN, Esther ROCHON, Rudy RUCKER, Bertrand RUSSELL, Boris STRUGATSKI, John TAINE, Vernor VINGE and David ZINDELL.

In discussing the use of mathematical ideas in sf, the boundary between sf and fantasy must be drawn according to somewhat different principles from those used in the case of the natural sciences. Since many mathematical ideas derive their piquancy from the fact that they are definitely incompatible with the world we live in, a story illustrating such an idea cannot claim any credence as a record of possible events, and should perhaps be classed as a fantasy. Yet an important consideration in judging a story of this type is its fidelity to mathematical truth, in which respect it belongs not just to sf but to sf at the furthest remove from fantasy, to that subgenre comprising stories which turn on a point of established science.

In the field of geometry these points are illustrated by the prototype of all stories which use the idea of space having other than three dimensions, E.A. ABBOTT's *Flatland* (**1884** as by A Square). Written in a period when there was great interest among mathematicians in n-dimensional geometry, this fantasy offers an indirect approach to the problems we, as three-dimensional creatures, have in understanding four-dimensional space by examining the difficulties two-dimensional beings would have in understanding three-dimensional space – an explanatory device which was to become a standard feature of sf invoking a fourth dimension. With sentient lines, triangles and polygons as its inhabitants, the book's only three-dimensional character being a visiting sphere, *Flatland* makes no pretence of being related to the real world. The book has been made into a short animated film, *Flatland* (1965), dir Eric Martin, with narration by Peter Cook. C.H. HINTON developed Abbott's speculations, adding some of his own, in several pieces in *Scientific Romances* (coll **1886**) and *Scientific Romances: Second Series* (coll **1902**), and in his sequel *An Episode of Flatland* (**1907**). In *Bolland* (**1957**; trans as *Sphereland* **1965** US) Dionys BURGER wrote another sequel designed to explain in the same way Einstein's theories about curved space. Greg BEAR's stylish story "Tangents" (1986) imagines the intrusion of higher-dimensional beings into our three-dimensional space, in a sophisticated reworking of the theme of Miles J. BREUER's "The Captured Cross-Section" (1929).

Among the many stories using fourth and other dimensions, two deserve mention here for their emphasis on particular mathematical points. H.G. WELLS's "The Plattner Story" (1896) turns on the fact that a three-dimensional object, if rotated through half a turn in a fourth dimension, becomes its mirror image (in the story this happens to Gottfried Plattner, who afterwards finds his heart is on the right). The reception of this point by literary readers amusingly illustrates how, if science can lend credibility to sf, sf removes credibility from science: one critic (Allan Rodway, in *Science and Modern Writing* [**1964**]) told his readers that this was "neither scientific nor mathematical". In fact it is excellent mathematics. In "And He Built a Crooked House" (1940) Robert A. HEINLEIN describes a house of eight cubical rooms which fit together like the eight three-dimensional "faces" of a four-dimensional cube (a tesseract). The story ostensibly takes place in the real world, but Heinlein's main concern is not to persuade the reader that his house is physically possible but to show us something which is mathematically feasible though seemingly paradoxical. He is therefore careful to be mathematically correct in describing the structure of his house, while emphasizing its startling features. His one slip, as it happens, offends against both requirements; the mathematical truth is even stranger than he realizes.

Other writers have set stories in frankly imaginary worlds for the sake of unusual topological structures of space, but few have been so careful to define the structures as Heinlein was. It is common for the topological oddity to be revealed only at the last, as a shock ending, as in David I. MASSON's "Traveller's Rest" (1965) – though this is only one element of a subtle and complex story in which the structures of time and language undergo variations related to that of the structure of space – and Arthur C. CLARKE's "Wall of Darkness" (1949), which uses a similar idea. Christopher PRIEST's *Inverted World* (**1974**) features (or appears to, for the whole thing could be a trick of perception) a hyperboloid world where variations of subjective experience take place according to one's position in the world. (Several mathematical stories, including Priest's, are discussed under PERCEPTION.) Topology is also likely to be abused as a catch-all explanation for any weird happening: in "A Subway Named Möbius" (1950) by A.J. Deutsch, for example, it is supposed that a subway network has become so complex that trains mysteriously disappear and reappear, although no proper topological explanation is presented.

This careless attitude to topology is comparable with the numerology (◊ PSEUDO-SCIENCE) of such stories as "Six Cubed Plus One" (1966) by John Rankine (Douglas R. MASON), in which magical properties are attributed to special numbers. (A sardonic comment on cavalier attitudes to mathematics was made by L. Sprague DE CAMP and Fletcher PRATT in *The Incomplete Enchanter* [1942], in which a series of propositions in mathematical logic is used as a magic talisman.)

Transfinite arithmetic shares with topology the appeal of the unfamiliar and the smack of paradox, and infinity has its own sensational connotations. For these reasons transfinite numbers are often called upon to establish an atmosphere of mathematical mysticism, but few authors have found it possible to do more with them. They appealed to the quirkiness of James BLISH, who in "FYI" (1953) seized on the fact that they do not and cannot count material objects and contemplated the Universe being reconstructed to accommodate them.

The two other areas of mathematics which have provided material for sf stories are statistics and logic. The concepts of statistics and probability theory are easy to misunderstand, as has been demonstrated in many sf stories; also, being abstractions which can masquerade as concrete instances, they are easy to ridicule, and this can be seen in Russell Maloney's "Inflexible Logic" (1940), which shows us monkeys typing famous works of literature, William TENN's "Null-P" (1951), in which an exactly average man is discovered, and Jack C. HALDEMAN's "A Very Good Year" (1984) in which the absence of death for a whole year is statistically compensated for in the next. A rather more serious point about statistics was made by Robert M. COATES in "The Law" (1974), which describes the "Law of Averages" breaking down and so prompts consideration of why human beings in large numbers normally do behave in predictable ways.

The perennial fascination of logical paradoxes was exploited by Gordon R. DICKSON in "The Monkey Wrench" (1951). This story uses the paradox of Epimenides the Cretan ("this statement is false") to deflate a computer engineer's pride in the perfection of his machine, thus giving a reassuring reminder of the insufficiency of logic. An opposite effect was achieved by Frederik POHL in a number of stories, notably "The Schematic Man" (1968), which describes a man coding himself as a computer programme, and so raises the question of what makes the real world more than a mathematical model. Logical paradoxes in fictional form were a speciality of Lewis Carroll, whose *A Tangled Tale* (1886) and *The Game of Logic*

(1887) are devoted to them as, in part, are the **Alice** books. Closer to our own time, Martin GARDNER, whose mathematical-puzzle column appeared in *Scientific American* 1957-81 and in ISAAC ASIMOV'S SCIENCE FICTION MAGAZINE from 1977, has written many fiction-alized mathematical diversions, such as those collected in *Science Fiction Puzzle Tales* (coll 1981) and *Puzzles from Other Worlds* (coll 1984).

Mathematics whose point is not primarily mathematical can also appear in sf; the use of an occasional mathematical formula is seen by some sf writers, as by some scientists, as conferring intellectual respectability. A rare example of a genuine mathematical argument occurs in a footnote to Fred HOYLE's *The Black Cloud* (1957): it is a nice calculation, and has probably added to a number of readers' enjoyment of the book. Hoyle also gave a mathematical explanation of an sf speculation in the preface to *Fifth Planet* (1963).

Examples of popular exposition of mathematical ideas in sf are the explanation of the calculus of variations in David DUNCAN's *Occam's Razor* (1957) and that of coordinate systems and relativity in Miles J. Breuer's "The Gostak and the Doshes" (1930). Both authors proceed to tell stories which have only tenuous connections with the mathematical ideas they have expounded.

Though the mathematical genius Libby in Robert Heinlein's "Misfit" (1939) proves resourceful, mathematicians as characters in GENRE SF have often been stereotyped as absent-minded, ineffectual and unworldly; they are clearly descended from the inhabitants of Jonathan SWIFT's Laputa in *Gulliver's Travels* (1726; rev 1735). Sf is popular among mathematicians, however, and it is not surprising that there should have been some attempts to adjust this image. This can be seen particularly in the stories of Norman KAGAN, whose portrayals of zany, hyperactive maths students, although they sometimes appear self-congratulatory, may be rather closer to reality. Kagan's stories make witty use of many parts of mathematics; while ostensibly concerned with sf speculations – in "Four Brands of Impossible" (1964) the use of a different logic to describe the world, in "The Mathenauts" (1964) a journey into various mathematical spaces – they are really about the experience of doing mathematics. An important mathematical sf protagonist is Shevek, in Ursula K. LE GUIN's *The Dispossessed* (1974), whose new mathematics is the basis for building the ANSIBLE, a FASTER-THAN-LIGHT communications device. A particularly interesting mathematician is the elderly protagonist of "Euclid Alone" (1975) by William F. Orr, himself a mathematician. A student successfully proves one of Euclid's axioms to be wrong. His teacher is left with the moral quandary of whether or not to suppress the discovery, which may, ultimately, destroy the serenity of everyone in the world. Orr's story can be found in *Mathenauts* (anth 1987) ed Rudy RUCKER, the only anthology of sf mathematical stories since *Fantasia*

Mathematica (anth **1958**) and *The Mathematical Magpie* (anth **1962**), both ed Clifton Fadiman.

Mathematics has entered fiction in strange ways. Some of the oddest are discussed in the terminology entry OULIPO. Certainly stories of COMMUNICATIONS can feature mathematics, through the idea of mathematics as a universal language. Some notable mathematical incursions into sf during the 1980s are the mathematical harmonies in Kim Stanley ROBINSON's *The Memory of Whiteness* (**1985**), the cosmic message concealed in the endless series of numbers following pi's decimal point in *Contact* (**1985**) by Carl SAGAN, and the disquisition on the Mandelbrot set in Arthur C. Clarke's *The Ghost from the Grand Banks* (**1990**), one of the few sf stories to use the mathematics of fractals. But the most important mathematical sf writers of the past decade have been Rudy Rucker and David Zindell, both mathematicians. Rucker's stories do not merely turn on mathematical points; they are often set in worlds generated by mathematical ideas, whose exploration is itself an act of mathematical intellection, in which the author delights, as he does in raunchy humour. Such tales include much of his work, notably *White Light, or What is Cantor's Continuum Problem?* (**1980**) – a crazed fantasia moving in physical (though afterlife) analogues of Hilbertian space, transfinite numbers and a lot else – *The Sex Sphere* (**1983**) and *The Secret of Life* (**1985**). Zindell's *Neverness* (**1988**) is one of the few successful books whose assumption is that mathematics is *romantic*. In this novel, to win an ice-race is to solve a theorem. The sequence where the protagonist can map the space windows only through mathematics – fountains and arpeggios of mathematics – is sustained and moving, and conveys with great conviction even to the nonmathematical reader what the high delight of mathematical thought must *feel* like.   [TSu/PN]

MATHESON, RICHARD (BURTON) (1926-   ) US author of stories, novels and filmscripts, initially thought of as primarily an sf writer but from the 1960s increasingly recognized as one of the most significant modern creators of terror and fantasy in both fiction and film. He began publishing sf with "Born of Man and Woman" for *The* MAGAZINE OF FANTASY AND SCIENCE FICTION in 1950. He had regarded this as a simple terror story but, on finding it praised as sf, decided to cash in on the then-current sf boom. He included most of his best early work in *Born of Man and Woman* (coll **1954**; with 4 stories cut vt *Third from the Sun* 1955). The famous title story tells in affecting pidgin English of a terrifying MUTANT child and of his break towards a kind of freedom (◊ CHILDREN IN SF). The element of terror in the tale nearly overrides a perfunctory sf base, as in his first sf novel, *I Am Legend* (**1954**; vt *The Omega Man: I Am Legend* 1971), a post-HOLOCAUST story in which only one man remains unaffected by a bacterium that induces vampirism (◊ SUPERNATURAL CREATURES). RM scripted the first film version of this, *L' ULTIMO UOMO DELLA TERRA* (1964; vt *The Last Man on Earth*) but, angered by the rewrite of

his script, used the pseudonym Logan Swanson for his screenplay credit; he was not responsible for the script of the second film version, *The* OMEGA MAN (1971). He did, however, adapt *The Shrinking Man* (**1956**), his second sf novel, as *The* INCREDIBLE SHRINKING MAN (1957), which won a 1958 HUGO; indeed, he sold it to Universal only on condition that he could write the screenplay, thus gaining an entry into the film business. This novel uses an sf component to shape the story of a man who, after exposure to radiation and insecticide, begins to shrink inexorably to microscopic size (◊ GREAT AND SMALL). RM's next major commission was for the tv series *The* TWILIGHT ZONE in 1959; all told, 14 of his scripts appeared in the series.

In 1960 he wrote the screenplay for the first of Roger CORMAN's adaptations of horror stories by Edgar Allan POE, *The House of Usher* (1960; vt *The Fall of the House of Usher* UK), and subsequently he scripted a number of fantasy/horror films, sometimes in collaboration with Charles BEAUMONT, for Corman and other directors: *The Pit and the Pendulum* (1961), *Tales of Terror* (1962), *Night of the Eagle* (1962; vt *Burn Witch Burn*) – based on *Conjure Wife* (**1953**; vt *Burn Witch Burn* 1962) by Fritz LEIBER – *The Raven* (1963), *The Comedy of Terrors* (1963), *Fanatic* (1965), *The Devil Rides Out* (1968) and *De Sade* (1969). His tv work has included several scripts for STAR TREK and later for ROD SERLING'S NIGHT GALLERY. He also scripted a number of made-for-tv feature films, by far the best being *Duel* (1971), from his own story; the film was Stephen SPIELBERG's first significant work as a director, and was given theatrical release in the UK. Others included *The Night Stalker* (1972) and *The Night Strangler* (1973) (◊ KOLCHAK: THE NIGHT STALKER), *Dying Room Only* (1973), *Dracula* (1973), *Scream of the Wolf* (1974), *The* STRANGER WITHIN (1974) and *The* MARTIAN CHRONICLES (1979). His script with William F. NOLAN for the tv movie *Trilogy of Terror* (1975) was based on three of his own stories. Of his feature-film scripts, that for MASTER OF THE WORLD (1961) is the most obviously sciencefictional. His psychological-cum-supernatural melodrama *Hell House* (**1971**) was filmed as *The Legend of Hell House* (1973), again with his own screenplay. Here, too, there are borderline sf elements; indeed, RM's entire career has cross-fertilized sf with HORROR.

Further volumes of stories with some sf interest are *The Shores of Space* (coll **1957**) and *Shock!* (coll **1961**; vt *Shock I: Thirteen Tales to Thrill and Terrify* 1979), though the latter volume's successors, *Shock II* (coll **1964**), *Shock III* (coll **1966**), *Shock Waves* (coll **1970**) and *Shock 4* (coll **1980** UK), are primarily assemblages of fantasy stories. The 86 stories assembled in *Richard Matheson: Collected Stories* (coll **1989**) cover his career 1950-71. A fantasy, *Bid Time Return* (**1975**; vt *Somewhere in Time* 1980), once again powerfully utilizes devices from sf (in this case TIME TRAVEL) in a story whose emotional satisfactions are not dependent on a successful sf resolution of the problems that arise; it was filmed as *Somewhere in Time* (1980) from his own script, and was later assembled with *What Dreams May Come* (**1978**) as *Somewhere in Time/What Dreams May Come: Two Novels of Love and Fantasy* (both texts rev, omni **1991**). The latter novel, an afterlife fantasy, shares with its predecessor a carefully controlled pathos occasionally reminiscent of Robert NATHAN. *Earthbound* (**1982** as by Logan Swanson; text restored as by RM 1989 UK) is a ghost story. RM has also written some short fiction – including "Where There's a Will" (1980) – in collaboration with his son Richard Christian MATHESON. Though RM cannot be considered as in any primary sense an sf writer, his influence as one of the "liberators" of magazine sf in the early 1950s keeps his name vividly in mind.

The dominant theme in RM's work has always been PARANOIA, whether imagined in GOTHIC or in sf terms. In *Duel* a truck inexplicably attacks a car; in *Dying Room Only* a woman's husband disappears in a motel toilet but no one will believe her; though the pregnancy in *The Stranger Within* did not result from infidelity, that is the way it seems to the woman's sterile husband. *I Am Legend* (one man against a world of vampires) is, in its obsessive images of persecution, perhaps the very peak of all paranoid sf. [JC/JB/PN]

Other works: *A Stir of Echoes* (**1958**); *Through Channels* (**1989** chap); *Journal of the Gun Years* (**1992**), a Western with fantasy elements.

As editor: *The Twilight Zone: The Original Stories* * (anth **1985**), with Martin H. GREENBERG and Charles G. WAUGH.

About the author: *Richard Matheson: He is Legend: An Illustrated Bio-Bibliography* (**1984** chap) by Mark Rathbun and Graeme Flanagan.

See also: BIOLOGY; DISASTER; EC COMICS; END OF THE WORLD; MONSTERS; RELIGION; ROBOTS.

MATHESON, RICHARD CHRISTIAN (1953-   ) US author and (primarily) writer for film and tv, and tv producer. RCM's work has been at most only fringe sf; he is not to be confused with his father, Richard MATHESON. RCM was cowriter (as Chris Matheson, the form of his name he sometimes uses in film and tv work) of the witty screenplay for BILL AND TED'S EXCELLENT ADVENTURE (1989) and its sequel *Bill and Ted's Bogus Journey* (1991). Earlier, his tv work included scripts for The INCREDIBLE HULK and AMAZING STORIES. His first published story was "Graduation" (1977 *Whispers*). A collection of his short fiction, predominantly fantasy and horror, is *Scars, and Other Distinguishing Marks* (coll **1987**; rev with teleplay "Magic Saturday" added 1988). [PN]

Other works: *Holiday* (**1988** chap).

MATSON, NORMAN (HAGHEJM) (1893-1965) US writer now best known for his completion, after the death of Thorne Smith (1893-1934), of the latter's *The Passionate Witch* (**1941**), capturing Smith's melancholy, mildly madcap, sentimentally erotic style very neatly. NM also wrote a sequel, *Bats in the Belfry* (**1943**). A film, *I Married a Witch* (1942), and the tv series *Bewitched* (1964-72) were based on the books.

Earlier NM wrote a fantasy, *Flecker's Magic* (**1926**; vt *Enchanted Beggar* 1959), also concerning a witch, and an sf novel, *Doctor Fogg* (**1929**). Fogg, having constructed a radio receiver capable of listening in on other worlds and attracted the interest of a young woman who has (perhaps coincidentally) been sent via MATTER TRANSMISSION to Earth from a distant planet, falls in love with the girl while extracting messages and information from space. But, when the US Government decides it must control all these scientific findings for security reasons, he destroys his device. [JC]

MATTER TRANSMISSION The matter transmitter is one of sf's many facilitating devices: a hypothetical machine which is not rationally plausible in terms of known science but which is very convenient for certain narrative purposes (◊ IMAGINARY SCIENCE). By virtue of an obvious play on words, matter transmitters were sometimes called "transmats" – as in Lan WRIGHT's "Transmat" (1960) – but the contraction never really caught on. Essentially, a matter transmitter is a teleportation machine (◊ PSI POWERS) whose plausibility is usually secured by analogies with radio. The best illustration of its narrative utility is in the tv series STAR TREK, in which the "transporter" not only transfers people from the *Enterprise* to this week's stage-set with a minimum of fuss but serves as an ever-ready *deus ex machina* to come to the rescue when our heroes are in a tight situation. As with other facilitating devices like the TIME MACHINE and the FASTER-THAN-LIGHT starship, however, there is a flourishing subgenre of "what if . . . ?" stories exploring the logical corollaries of the supposition that such devices might one day exist, ranging from elementary questions like "what happens to the matter occupying the space into which you are transmitting?" to questions about the way in which routine transportation of this kind would transform society. *Three Trips in Time and Space* (anth **1973**) ed Robert SILVERBERG presents three original novellas on this theme by Larry NIVEN, John BRUNNER and Jack VANCE; the commission for the volume intrigued Brunner sufficiently that he went on to publish two novels further exploring the possibilities – *Web of Everywhere* (**1974**) and *The Infinitive of Go* (**1980**) – while in 1973-4 Niven wrote four other stories elaborating the background of his "Flash Crowd", carrying forward ideas first broached in *Ringworld* (**1970**).

Early stories of matter transmission include "The Man without a Body" (1877) by Edward Page MITCHELL and "Professor Vehr's Electrical Experiment" (1885) by Robert Duncan MILNE, in both of which the process is interrupted with dire consequences; a later variant of the same theme, with an additional horrific twist, is George LANGELAAN's twice-filmed "The Fly" (1957) (◊ *The* FLY). Matter transmitters feature as a method of interplanetary travel in Fred T. JANE's tongue-in-cheek *To Venus in Five Seconds* (**1897**) and as a method of ore-shipping in Garrett P. SERVISS's *The Moon Metal* (**1900**), but few other authors could bring themselves to deploy the notion until the advent of the sf PULP MAGAZINES, when it was quickly added to the standard vocabulary of symbols, featuring in such stories as "The Secret of Electrical Transmission" (1922) by Clement FEZANDIE, *The Radio Man* (1924; **1948**) by Ralph Milne FARLEY, "The Moon Menace" (1927) by Edmond HAMILTON and "The Cosmic Express" (1930) by Jack WILLIAMSON. Matter transmitters are rarely featured in work done outside the genre, although Norman MATSON's *Doctor Fogg* (**1929**) is an interesting comedy about an unexpected arrival by such means.

More sophisticated versions of the **Star Trek** transporter can be found in various HARD-SF stories, including Poul ANDERSON's *The Enemy Stars* (**1959**), Harry HARRISON's *One Step from Earth* (fixup **1970**) and Joe HALDEMAN's *Mindbridge* (**1976**). Melodramas cunningly deploying them as plot-elements include Lloyd BIGGLE's *All the Colours of Darkness* (**1963**), Philip K. DICK's *The Unteleported Man* (1964; **1966**; exp **1982**; vt *Lies, Inc*) and David LANGFORD's *The Space Eater* (**1982**); Langford and John Grant (Paul BARNETT) cruelly parody several aspects of matter transmission in *Earthdoom!* (**1987**). Matter transmitters function as devices facilitating the COLONIZATION OF OTHER WORLDS in Eric Frank RUSSELL's "U-Turn" (1950) and Joseph L. GREEN's *The Loafers of Refuge* (fixup **1965**). "Buildings" whose doorways are matter transmitters and whose "rooms" are on different worlds are featured in Bob SHAW's "Aspect" (1954), Roger ZELAZNY's *Today we Choose Faces* (**1973**) and Dan SIMMONS's *Hyperion* (**1989**). The idea of a galactic culture linked by matter transmitters is soberly and memorably displayed in Clifford D. SIMAK's *Way Station* (**1963**).

Matter transmitters which malfunction occasionally result in embarrassing duplications, as in Clifford Simak's *Goblin Reservation* (**1968**), and stories about matter duplication – classic examples include the later stories in George O. SMITH's *Venus Equilateral* (coll of linked stories **1947**) and Damon Knight's "A for Anything" (1957; exp as *The People Maker* **1959**; vt *A for Anything* UK) – may be regarded as an extension of the theme; indeed, scrupulous attempts to rationalize matter transmission (like Niven's and Brunner's) assume that what is actually transmitted is information regarding the exact duplication of the object to be reconstituted, not actual matter, so that much so-called matter transmission is really matter duplication. In Algis BUDRYS's *Rogue Moon* (**1960**) the duplication is calculated, the transmitted "clones" being continually sacrificed to the task of exploring a hazardous alien artifact. In Thomas M. DISCH's *Echo Round his Bones* (**1967**) ghostly duplicates, perceptible only to one another, are an unintended consequence of the use of matter transmitters. Both of these last-named stories sensitively exploit the bearing which the imaginary device has on the philosophical problem of identity. [BS/MJE]

MATTHEWS, RODNEY (1945-   ) UK illustrator. RM's artwork first became popular in the mid-1970s – a period of great vigour in UK sf/fantasy illustration – when it began appearing on book covers and on the first 3 covers of the short-lived magazine VORTEX (1977). Bizarre, whimsical, often spiky, weirdly coloured, his art "feels" more like fantasy than sf, though it has often been used on sf books – including some from Avon in the USA – and is closely associated with the work of Michael MOORCOCK, notably in his many illustrations to Moorcock's *Elric at the End of Time* (**1987**). RM's fantastic animals and monsters are especially good, and his thorny cities are another trademark. He works in various media, mostly watercolour, gouache and ink; much of his work has been in the form of posters, record sleeves (several winning awards) and calendars. In the 1980s a series of RM fantasy calendars, some in very large format, featured mostly new rather than recycled paintings. Books of his work include a very complete and beautifully produced retrospective collection, *In Search of Forever* (**1985**) with text by Nigel Suckling, *Last Ship Home* (**1989**) and *The Rodney Matthews Portfolio* (**1991**). [PN]

MATTOTTI, LORENZO (1954-   ) Italian COMIC-strip artist whose work combines Futurist and Vorticist forms with Expressionist colour. Born in Brescia, he studied architecture before turning to comics in the late 1970s, with José Muñoz (1942-   ) as his mentor. With other like-minded young artists, he formed the Valvoline group to "explore the frontiers of progressive *fumetti* [comic strips]". His first success came with *Il signore Spartaco* ["Mr Spartaco"] (graph **1982**), about a man whose dreams of his childhood fears and anxieties affect his hold on reality. LM's masterpiece is *Fuochi* ["Fires"] (1985 *Alter*; trans as *Feux* **1986** France; trans as *Fires* **1988** US), about a battleship visiting a magical island. The story climaxes in a furious Expressionist inferno. Other works include: *Labyrinthi* ["Labyrinths"] (graph **1989**); *L'uomo alla finestra* ["The Man at the Window"] (**1992**), a long GRAPHIC NOVEL done in black-and-white line, written with Lilia Ambrosini; and «Murmur» (graph 1992 UK), written by Jerry Kransky. [RT]

MATURIN, CHARLES R(OBERT) (1782-1824) Irish novelist, playwright and clergyman, the son of French Protestants in exile, who wrote several GOTHIC romances and sensational plays with intermittent success – most notably *The Fatal Revenge, or The Family of Montorio* (**1807**) as by Dennis Jasper Murphy – before the publication of his definitive terror-romance, *Melmoth the Wanderer* (**1820**). The eponymous hero, who is reminiscent of figures from the Wandering Jew to Faust, has sold his soul to the Devil in return for IMMORTALITY. The novel is made up of a series of complexly linked stories concerning people in various extremities to whom Melmoth appears as tempter in his desperate attempts to find someone to accept his curse; but all refuse him, regardless of the perils under which they labour, and after a century or so Melmoth returns to Ireland, where he disappears over the edge of a cliff. Honoré de BALZAC wrote a sequel, "Melmoth Reconcilé" (1835; trans in coll *The Unknown Masterpiece* **1896** UK). The Penguin edition of CRM's novel (**1977**), ed and introduced by Alethea Hayter, is convenient and scholarly.   [JC]

Other work: *The Albigenses* (**1824**).

About the author: *Charles Robert Maturin: His Life and Works* (**1923**) by Niilo Idman.

MAURICE, MICHAEL Pseudonym of UK writer and clergyman Conrad Arthur Skinner (1889-?   ), whose sf novel *Not in Our Stars* (**1923**) can be forgiven its confused science – giant meteorites are supposed to cause perturbations in spacetime sufficient to reverse time's arrow for the protagonist – because of the odd intensity of the tale. Awakening in a death cell after a meteor strike, the protagonist is executed and then begins to relive his life (each day passing normally, but with him awakening each morning a day earlier) with foreknowledge of the murder he has committed/will commit in error. The end of the story is ambiguous, with some hint that, on re-entering the normal flow of time, he will be able to avoid the deed. A later novel, *Marooned* (**1932**), is an afterlife fantasy.   [JC]

MAUROIS, ANDRÉ Pseudonym of prolific French novelist and man of letters Émile Salomon Wilhelm Herzog (1885-1967), in the USA during WWII. He was best known for his romantic biographies and other nonfiction, though his first work, "La dernière histoire du monde" ["The Final History of the World"] (**1903**) as by Émile Herzog, was sf; later included in *Premiers contes* ["First Stories"] (coll **1935**) as by AM, it was the first of his several future histories. The most interesting of these is *Le chapitre suivant* (**1927** chap; trans anon as *The Next Chapter: The War Against the Moon* **1928** chap UK), which describes a war against the ostensibly uninhabited Moon concocted by a cabal of newspaper barons to provide bored mankind with an external enemy; unfortunately the Moon is indeed occupied, and retaliates. This fragment was collected in *Deux fragments d'une histoire universelle 1992* (coll **1928**) with its sequel, "Chapitre CXVIII: La vie des hommes", which appeared in English as the second of the two title stories of *The Weigher of Souls and The Earth Dwellers* (coll **1963** US); it deals with inhabitants of Uranus who fail to understand the supposedly inferior inhabitants of Earth; this appeared in the collection *Relativisme* (coll **1930**; trans Hamish Miles as *A Private Universe* **1932** UK). An interesting ALTERNATE-WORLDS essay, "If Louis XVI had had an Atom of Firmness", appeared in J.C. Squire's *If, or History Rewritten* (anth **1931**).

AM also wrote more conventional sf narratives. *Voyage aux pays des Articoles* (**1927** chap; trans David GARNETT as *A Voyage to the Island of the Articoles* **1928** chap UK) carries a man and woman to an ISLAND in whose UTOPIAN society the dominant Articole caste is made up of artists who provide the other castes with their *raisons d'être*; the tale is ironic. In *Le peseur d'âmes* (**1931**; trans Hamish Miles as *The Weigher of Souls* **1931**

UK) a doctor discovers that the *élan vital* is a gas which escapes the body at death; his attempts to mingle in posthumous harmony with his wife are, however, frustrated. This short novel reappeared in *The Weigher of Souls and The Earth Dwellers*. The sf device in *La machine à lire les pensées* (**1937**; trans James Whitehall as *The Thought-Reading Machine* **1938** UK) is a "camera" capable of registering thoughts on photographic film.

Though amiability tends to soften the bite of his morality-like tales and his reputation has faded, AM's work is nicely representative of the idiomatic ease with which sf ideas have been used in this century by MAINSTREAM WRITERS, especially in the UK and mainland Europe, as vehicles for the conveyance of satirical material.   [JC/PN]

Other works: *Patapoufs et filifers* (**1930** chap; trans Norman Denny as *Fattipuffs and Thinifers* **1941** chap UK; vt *Patapoufs and Filifers* 1948 chap US), a juvenile parable set in an underground land, illustrated by Jean Bruller (VERCORS); *Nouveaux discours du Docteur O'Grady* (**1950**; trans Gerard Hopkins as *The Return of Dr O'Grady* **1951** UK); *Illusions* (**1968**), a speculative essay.

See also: ARTS; ESCHATOLOGY; ESP; HISTORY OF SF; MACHINES; RELIGION; SATIRE.

MAVITY, HUBERT [s] ◊ Nelson S. BOND.

MAVOR, ELINOR [r] ◊ AMAZING STORIES; FANTASTIC.

MAX HEADROOM UK made-for-tv film (1985); US tv series (1987-8). Chrysalis/Channel 4 (UK); Chrysalis/Lakeside-Lorimar Telepictures (US). Created by Steve Roberts (screenplay) and George Stone, Annabel Jankel, Rocky Morton (story). Prod Peter Wagg, Brian Frankish, Roberts. Writers included Roberts, Philip DeGuere, Michael CASSUTT. Dirs included Rocky Morton and Annabel Jankel (UK teleplay), Farhad Mann, Tommy Lee Wallace, Thomas J. Wright, Victor Lobl, Janet Greek. Teleplay 70 mins; series ran 2 seasons, 14 50min episodes in all. Colour.

There are two distinct branches of the *MH* tv saga, first in the UK, then in the USA. Originally the computer-generated stuttering head – played by an image-processed Matt Frewer – was created as a state-of-the-art link man for rock videos in a tv music programme, but a fictional origin had to be devised for him. Hence the 1985 made-for-tv film (originally titled *A Rebus*), in which investigative newsman Carter (Frewer) digs into a conspiracy revolving around compressed tv ads ("blipverts") that can cause sedentary viewers to explode. After an accident Carter's brain patterns are electronically duplicated to create his computerized *alter ego*.

While this led in the UK to the planned rock-video series – plus a talkshow, advertising contracts, spin-off books and merchandise – US production company Lorimar was more impressed by the teleplay explaining Max Headroom's origin, and remade it (with small changes) as *Blipverts*, the first episode of a series. Frewer continued to play Carter and Headroom, and Amanda Pays also transferred from the

UK production as Theora, Carter's computer-genius colleague. Roberts likewise crossed the Atlantic.

Although the MEDIA-dominated future world of the pilot suggested many possibilities for a CYBERPUNK-style sf thriller series, subsequent episodes were hindered by a reliance on tired ideas (gladiatorial combat, test-tube babies) that could have easily been used on LOGAN'S RUN or any other future-DYSTOPIA series, and *MH* lasted only 2 short seasons. In its image-dense style and media-fuelled cynicism, however, *MH* did introduce the trappings of cyberpunk to tv. [KN]

MAXIMUM OVERDRIVE ◊ Stephen KING.

MAXWELL, ANN (ELIZABETH) (1944-) US writer, also of detective thrillers as A.E. Maxwell. She began publishing work of genre interest with *Change* (1975) and *The Singer Enigma* (1976), novels which combine a somewhat overready sensitivity with sf-adventure instincts. Her **Dancer Trilogy** – *Fire Dancer* (1982), *Dancer's Luck* (1983) and *Dancer's Illusion* (1983) – is a SPACE OPERA featuring a passel of escaped slaves and a very fast starship. In *Timeshadow Rider* (1986) two superpowered siblings must join together to save the Universe. [JC]

Other works: *A Dead God Dancing* (1979); *Name of a Shadow* (1980); *The Jaws of Menx* (1981).

See also: SUPERMAN.

MAXWELL, JACK ◊ Ernest L. MCKEAG.

MAXWELL, JOHN C. ◊ John S. GLASBY.

MAY, JULIAN (1931-) US editor and writer; married to T.E. DIKTY from 1953 to his death in 1991, founding with him Publication Associates in 1957 (*see his entry for this and later enterprises*); he also served as editor and agent for all her mature work. She began publishing sf with "Dune Roller" for *ASF* in 1951 but, except for some fan interests, became inactive in the field for many years, during which time, under a number of pseudonyms, she wrote something over 290 books, most of them nonfiction juveniles: many were efficient presentations of science and nature topics, others biographies. Pseudonyms of sf interest included Ian Thorne (see listing below) and Lee N. Falconer, under which name she wrote *A Gazeteer of the Hyborian World of Conan* (1977).

In the 1980s JM turned her attention once again to sf, making an immediate and very substantial impact with her **Saga of Pliocene Exile**: *The Many-Colored Land* (1981) and *The Golden Torc* (1982), both assembled as *The Many-Colored Land & The Golden Torc* (omni 1982), plus *The Nonborn King* (1983) and *The Adversary* (1984), both assembled as *The Nonborn King & The Adversary* (omni 1984), and supplemented by *The Pliocene Companion* (1984), a guide to the sequence. A second, closely linked, sequence, the **Galactic Milieu** books, began with *Intervention* (1987; vt in 2 vols *The Surveillance* 1988 and *The Metaconcert* 1988) and *Jack the Bodiless* (1992), with several further volumes projected. Underlying the increasingly complicated storyline of the former sequence is what might be called a romance of vista: the protagonists have fled via TIME TRAVEL from a 22nd century where they have lived as internal exiles into deep prehistory, where at the bottom of time they discover not only a land rich in potential but two apparently ALIEN species in a state of deadly conflict over the young world. Much additional material, from Celtic myths to intimations of HARD SF, is fed into this vision, with an effect of romance and high purpose, leavened intermittently by a Trickster protagonist or two. With *Intervention* the overall sequence moves into contemporary times, the narrative being charged by this point with dramatic irons in the fire and ironies galore, as well as a sustaining concern with the attractive theme of psychic evolution, as concentrated in a family of special folk and expressed in a manner sometimes evocative of the work of Doris LESSING. [JC]

Other works: *Black Trillium* (1990) with Marion Zimmer BRADLEY and Andre NORTON.

Juveniles as Ian Thorne: *Frankenstein* * (1977 chap), film tie; *Godzilla* (1977 chap), nonfiction; *Dracula* * (1977 chap), film tie; *King Kong* (1977 chap), nonfiction; *Mad Scientists* (1977 chap), nonfiction; *The Wolf Man* * (1977 chap), film tie; *The Mummy* * (1981 chap), film tie; *Frankenstein Meets Wolfman* * (1981 chap), film tie; *Creature from the Black Lagoon* * (1981 chap), film tie; *The Blob* * (1982 chap), film tie; *The Deadly Mantis* * (1982 chap), film tie; *It Came from Outer Space* * (1982 chap), film tie.

About the author: *The Work of Julian May: An Annotated Bibliography & Guide* (1985 chap) by Thaddeus DIKTY and Robert REGINALD.

MAYAKOVSKY, VLADIMIR (VLADIMIROVICH) (1893-1930) Russian poet and playwright, a revolutionary from early years, a Futurist poet whose verse radically shocked post-Revolution RUSSIA. Of particular sf interest is his first fully fledged prose SATIRICAL play, *Klop* (1929; trans Guy Daniels as *The Bedbug* in *The Complete Plays of Vladimir Mayakovsky* [coll 1968 US]), in which, some generations hence, a Soviet bureaucrat is kept in a zoo as a curious example. *Banya* (1930; trans Guy Daniels in the same 1968 volume), set in the contemporary USSR, employs a similar array of satirical tools. These two plays were sufficiently sharp in their criticism of the blandness of Soviet ideas that a good deal of official criticism descended on VM's head. [JC]

See also: THEATRE.

MAYHAR, ARDATH (1930-) US writer who began publishing poetry in the 1940s and who wrote historicals and Westerns as Frank Cannon and other non-sf/fantasy books as John Killdeer and Sarah MacWilliams. She began publishing sf/fantasy with "The Cat with the Sapphire Eyes" for *Weirdbook #8* in 1973; she integrated this tale into the second volume of her **Kyrannon** sequence, which comprises her first novel, *How the Gods Wove in Kyrannon* (1979), and *The Seekers of Shar-Nuhn* (1980). Like much of her work, this sequence makes use of the instruments of SCIENCE FANTASY – specifically, magical devices and powers which are justified by recourse to "scientific" explanations, generally rooted in the past – to heighten tales whose protagonists, often adolescent girls, exhibit a goodness which is sometimes shining. In the **Kyrannon** books, folk of transparent decency must resist a tyrant whose disruptive influence threatens to sour the harmony between human beings and Nature. The most sf-like of her subsequent novels are *Khi to Freedom* (**1983**), *Golden Dream* (**1983**), *Exile on Vlahil* (**1984**), which elaborately and effectively describes life upon the eponymous planet, *The World Ends in Hickory Hollow* (**1985**), *Trail of the Seahawks* * (**1987**) with Ron Fortier, a game tie, *A Place of Silver Silence* (**1988**), a First-Contact tale for a younger audience, and *Monkey Station* * (**1989**) with Fortier (◊ APES AND CAVEMEN). This last novel, in which monkeys are dubiously granted INTELLIGENCE and the power of speech as the by-product of a plague, is the first of a projected series of game tie-ins. AM's work has been compared to that of Andre NORTON, with which it shares transparent story-telling and a sense of moral certainty. [JC]

Other works: The **Tyrnos** fantasies, being *Soul-Singer of Tyrnos* (**1981**) and *The Runes of the Lyre* (**1982**); *Golden Dream: A Fuzzy Odyssey* * (**1982**), continuing the H. Beam PIPER series; *Warlock's Gift* (**1982**); *Lords of the Triple Moons* (**1983**); *The Saga of Grittel Sundotha* (**1985**); *Makra Choria* (**1987**); *BattleTech: The Sword and the Dagger* * (**1987**), a game tie; *The Wall* (**1987**), horror; *People of the Mesa* (**1992**), prehistoric fantasy.

MAYNARD, RICHARD (JOHN) (1926-   ) UK-born writer, resident in Australia, whose *The Coconut Book* (**1985**) is of some interest. *The Quiet Place* (**1988**; vt *The Return* 1988 US) rather overcomplicatedly describes the return to Earth of a group of astronauts long years after the planet has mysteriously reverted to savagery. There is some SEX between the descending males and the females who need them. [JC]

MAYNE, WILLIAM (JAMES CARTER) (1928-   ) UK author of nearly 100 children's books. These are sometimes realistic, sometimes – especially his later work – fantastic; the fantasies, however, are treated in so down-to-earth a manner that more often than not they naturalize the supernatural. His style, which is sophisticated and sometimes oblique, is found difficult by some children; others love him, as do the many critics who see WM as perhaps the most distinguished living UK writer of children's fiction, regardless of genre. His first book was *Follow the Footprints* (**1953**), the earliest of the many treasure-hunt stories he was to write.

WM has written very little pure sf, and even *Earthfasts* (**1966**), his book most commonly spoken of in an sf context, is as much FANTASY as sf in its fine tale of an 18th-century drummer boy emerging from a present-day mound and being befriended by a sceptical youth who feels impelled to interpret this and other fantastic intrusions in scientific terms. The actual sf story *Skiffy* (**1972**) and its sequel *Skiffy and the Twin Planets* (**1982**), for rather younger children, while interesting – especially the latter – are not the equal of his best work. WM's fiction typically (in a great variety of ways) depicts the past impinging on the present, often as a kind of mystery to be decoded; his work tends to climax in epiphanies where a chaotic present day is suddenly illuminated in this way; some of his books feature psychic TIME TRAVEL and ESP. His young-adult fiction is adult in every sense except the youthful consciousnesses of its protagonists, and deserves wider currency among the adult readership.

Among WM's most highly regarded books, mostly for older children, all of them containing fantastic elements (some very obviously, some crucially but near-invisibly) are *A Grass Rope* (**1957**), *The Glass Ball* (**1961**), *Over the Hills and Far Away* (**1968**; vt *The Hill Road* 1969 US), *A Game of Dark* (**1971**), *The Jersey Shore* (**1973**), *A Year and a Day* (**1976**), *IT* (**1977**), *All the King's Men* (coll **1982**), *Gideon Ahoy* (**1987**) and *Antar and the Eagles* (**1989**). Some books written ostensibly for younger children – like *Hob Stories* (coll **1984**) and *The Blemyah Stories* (coll **1987**) – are no more conventional children's literature than is the late work of Alan GARNER. [PN]

See also: CHILDREN'S SF.

MAYUMURA, TAKU [r] ◊ JAPAN.

MEACHAM, BETH (1951-   ) US writer and editor who worked first as an sf bookseller before joining ACE BOOKS in 1981, where she developed the careers of Greg BEAR, Orson Scott CARD and Tim POWERS, among others; she also discovered James P. BLAYLOCK and oversaw the revived **Ace SF Specials**. She left Ace for TOR BOOKS in 1984, where as head of sf and fantasy she supervised the company's unusually large sf editorial staff and worked with authors like Card, Kim Stanley ROBINSON and Walter Jon WILLIAMS. In 1989 she resigned as editor-in-chief to become executive editor with a general acquisition brief.

With her husband, Tappan King (1950-   ), she wrote *Nightshade* * (**1976**), a novel in the **Weird Heroes** sequence. She collaborated with Wayne BARLOWE and Ian Summers on *Barlowe's Guide to Extraterrestrials* (**1979**; rev **1987**), and with Summers and Vincent DI FATE on *Di Fate's Catalog of Science Fiction Hardware* (**1980**). With Baird SEARLES, Martin Last and Michael Franklin she wrote *A Reader's Guide to Science Fiction* (**1979**), and with Searles and Franklin *A Reader's Guide to Fantasy* (**1982**). She is perhaps best known to the reading public for editing *Terry's Universe* (anth **1988**), an original anthology in memory of Terry CARR. [PNH]

MEAD, HAROLD (CHARLES HUGH) (1910-   ) UK writer. The first and better known of his sf novels, *The Bright Phoenix* (**1955**), is a sombrely told post-HOLOCAUST tale in which a reestablished but over-regimented human culture tries unsuccessfully to reinhabit abandoned parts of the Earth; it ends a little sentimentally with a Second Coming. The other, *Mary's Country* (**1957**), tells of the quest of a group of children – most of whose social peers have been killed by plague – for a perfect society. [JC]

MEAD, SHEPHERD Working name of US author

(resident in Switzerland) Edward Mead (1914-   ), who has been active in various genres. SATIRE and comedy combine in most of his works, including his sf and fantasy novels: *The Magnificent MacInnes* (**1949**; vt *The Sex Machine* 1950), in which consumer society is satirized through the story of an electronic device that can predict personal preferences; *The Big Ball of Wax* (**1954**), in which Madison Avenue techniques are applied to corrupt a device that permits people to enter vicariously into the lives of others, a technique whose potential for good is subverted into a kind of feelie; and *The Carefully Considered Rape of the World* (**1966**), in which ALIENS artificially inseminate Earth females.

SM worked in advertising before turning to writing, and his experience was put to good use not only in *The Big Ball of Wax*, the most interesting of his sf novels, but also in his best-known work (not sf), *How to Succeed in Business Without Really Trying* (**1952**), for the staged version of which he shared a Pulitzer Prize and a Tony.   [JC/PN]

See also: LEISURE; MEDIA LANDSCAPE.

MEDIA LANDSCAPE The degree to which COMMUNI-CATIONS technology (and foreseeable future extensions of it) was replacing the natural world with a "media landscape" was scarcely noticed until the 1950s. Coined to denote a world dominated by the images of advertising and the popular arts (among which sf images, especially the iconography of movies and magazine covers, loomed large), the phrase was initially used to describe the obsessions of Pop artists and media critics such as Eduardo Paolozzi (1924-   ), Andy Warhol (1930-1987), Marshall McLuhan (1911-1980) and Rayner Banham (1922-1988). The phrase, and indeed the idea underlying it, may seem quaint today; but with the benefit of hindsight we can see how the notion of the media landscape so popular in the 1960s and 1970s progressed naturally, through both developments in technology and the expansion of what human beings were prepared to conceive as feasible, to the VIRTUAL REALITY of the 1980s (in speculation) and 1990s (in fact).

Of course, the media landscape was there before the 1950s, and sf had reflected it in various ways. The idea that the media can be used to manipulate people had long been extant. In George ORWELL's *Nineteen Eighty-four* (**1949**) this theme takes a directly political form: the media are represented not only by the ubiquitous posters of "Big Brother" but also by the "telescreens" which act as two-way channels for propaganda and surveillance. Similar political use of the media has featured frequently in sf; examples are in Ray BRADBURY's *Fahrenheit 451* (**1953**), Kurt VONNE-GUT's "Harrison Bergeron" (1961) and Philip K. DICK's *The Penultimate Truth* (**1964**). More often, sf has portrayed future societies controlled by the media in more oblique ways. McLuhan's *The Mechanical Bride* (**1951**), a book about the psychological subtleties of advertising, contains a passing tribute to Fritz LEIBER, whose "The Girl with the Hungry Eyes" (1949) is

about exploitation of the female image by ad-men. Leiber returned to the theme of advertising – a major theme in 1950s sf – in *The Green Millennium* (**1953**), set in a future when the walls of private apartments are lined with ads. Frederik POHL's and C.M. KORN-BLUTH's *The Space Merchants* (**1953**) is a more extended satire on the all-powerful admen; Pohl's much later solo sequel, *The Merchants' War* (**1984**), seemed an anachronism. Other 1950s stories about advertising include Pohl's "The Tunnel Under the World" (1954), Shepherd MEAD's *The Big Ball of Wax* (**1954**) and (in part) Dick's *The Simulacra* (**1964**). Daniel F. GALOUYE's *Counterfeit World* (**1964** UK; vt *Simulacron-3* 1964 US) is about a society which turns out to be a computer simulation generated for purposes of market research; many of Ron GOULART's stories satirize advertising techniques.

Manipulation to the extent that one suspects that one's very reality is a fiction (◊ PARANOIA) can give rise to a belief in the "new demonology" – the idea that the artificial landscape has alien inhabitants with evil powers. Literal treatments of "demons" taking over the media include "Ether Breather" (1939) by Theodore STURGEON and "The Waveries" (1945) by Fredric BROWN, both stories about creatures which inhabit the airwaves, tampering with our communications. The writer who took the new demonology most seriously was William S. BURROUGHS; in *The Ticket that Exploded* (**1962**; rev 1967) and *Nova Express* (**1964**) he showed the human race at the mercy of the "Nova Mob" and other alien parasites who used the media (and drugs) as their means of control. Burroughs asserted that life was "a biologic film" and that the purpose of his writing was to help us break out of the "stale movie" into the "gray room" of silence. This is not entirely different from the wishful conservatism of Brown's "The Waveries", in which the USA abandons electricity and reverts to a rural economy. Barrington J. BAYLEY's "An Overload" (1973) is about computer-generated demons who adopt the personage of gangster-movie stars.

Not all media-men are demons, however, and some stories deal with those who attempt to use their power to good effect. Norman SPINRAD's *Bug Jack Barron* (**1969**) concerns the compere of a phone-in chat-show in the 1980s who finds himself in a position to challenge the political and industrial powers that be. Most of the action actually takes place "on the air", before an audience of millions, making this a novel set almost entirely within the media landscape. Spinrad returns to this area in several of the stories in *No Direction Home* (coll **1975**), and, much later, in *Little Heroes* (**1987**), an sf novel about the music business in a dystopian urban world. Several of Dick's novels deal with media-men, such as *Dr Bloodmoney, or How We Got Along After the Bomb* (**1965**), in which a post-HOLOCAUST world is held together by a disc-jockey's broadcasts from an orbital satellite, and *Flow My Tears, the Policeman Said* (**1974**), in which a famous tv personality is thrust into a world where nobody recognizes him. Algis BUDRYS's *Michaelmas* (**1977**) concerns a roving newsman who, through a secret COMPUTER link-up, is in fact the benevolent dictator of the world.

One of the ways in which the media create news is by invading the privacy of individuals in order to gratify the curiosity of others. D.G. COMPTON's *The Continuous Katherine Mortenhoe* (**1974**; rev vt *The Unsleeping Eye* 1974 US; vt *Death Watch* 1981 UK) is about a tv-man with "camera eyes" who follows a dying woman in order to record her last indignities for the entertainment of a mass audience; at the climax the ethically awakened reporter elects to become blind. The story is continued in *Windows* (**1979** US). Many other tales deal with pornography, violence and vicarious suffering; e.g., Arthur C. CLARKE's "I Remember Babylon" (1960), Robert SILVERBERG's "The Pain Peddlers" (1963) and *Thorns* (**1967**), Robert SHECKLEY's "The Prize of Peril" (1958), Dan MORGAN's *The Richest Corpse in Show Business* (**1966**) and Brian STABLEFORD's *The Mind-Riders* (**1976**). A particularly gruesome example is Christopher PRIEST's "The Head and the Hand" (1972), in which a tv entertainer has his limbs amputated and climaxes his "act" with his decapitation. Anything is grist to the media mill, from violence to TIME TRAVEL: McLuhan's "global village" extending through time as well as space. This has been dramatized in sf stories in which the media literally invade the past in search of material. Isaac ASIMOV's "The Dead Past" (1956) features a woman obsessed with watching her dead child on the "chronoscope", Harry HARRISON's *The Technicolor Time Machine* (**1967**) is a humorous treatment of a film crew's adventures in history, and J.G. BALLARD's "The Greatest Television Show on Earth" (1972) is a satire on the tv companies' attempts to film such events as the parting of the Red Sea "live". These sf exaggerations point up the extent to which the media have brought about *la société du spectacle*.

In such stories as Ballard's "The Subliminal Man" (1963), in which vast hoardings are erected alongside motorways to flash subliminal messages into drivers' brains, even the unconscious is annexed by the media landscape. Of course, manipulation of the desires of the unconscious has long been recognized as part of advertising, and the media use a complex language of signs in order to speak to it. Semiotics, as applied to popular culture by Roland Barthes (1915-1980) in his *Mythologies* (**1957**; trans **1972**), testifies to this. All human creations are, in a sense, media of communication, since they are coded with latent "messages" – particularly such everyday things as architecture, furniture, clothing and vehicles. This is the conceptual territory that Ballard has made very much his own, particularly in the "condensed novels" collected in *The Atrocity Exhibition* (**1970**; vt *Love and Napalm: Export USA* 1972 US; rev 1990 US). In these nonlinear stories he juxtaposes elements of the media landscape of the 1960s, from the architecture of motorways and multistorey carparks to the bodies of

Marilyn Monroe and Elizabeth Taylor, from the styling of cars and kitchen gadgets to the televised violence of Vietnam and President Kennedy's assassination. He blends these external "facts" with the private memories and fantasies of his characters, and with the neutral language of medical reports and astronomical data. *The Atrocity Exhibition* is a selfconscious book (Ballard has been much influenced by the Pop artists) but it is the most sustained attempt in sf to deal with the media landscape and its massive influence on all our lives. Later Ballard stories have also dealt with the media, such as "The Intensive Care Unit" (1977), which concerns a society in which marriage and family life are conducted entirely by tv: nobody ever meets anyone else in the flesh.

Other sf works which have to some extent been influenced by McLuhan and the ideas about the media which became fashionable in the 1960s include John BRUNNER's *Stand on Zanzibar* (**1968**), Dean R. KOONTZ's *The Fall of the Dream Machine* (**1969**), Michael MOORCOCK's **Jerry Cornelius** novels, John T. SLADEK's *The Muller-Fokker Effect* (**1970**), J-M. LE CLÉZIO's *Les Géants* (**1973**; trans as *The Giants* 1975) and Barry N. MALZBERG's *The Destruction of the Temple* (**1974**). "The Girl who was Plugged In" (1973) by James TIPTREE Jr is a savage story about the creation of a jet-set member of "the beautiful people" for purposes of advertising; in reality the woman is an ANDROID with no independent intelligence, controlled through the nervous system of a horribly exploited "ugly duckling". The language of the story cleverly reflects the chill of a society whose cruelties are largely unconscious and affectless.

About the end of the 1970s traditional sf about the media seemed to wither away almost overnight: during the 1980s harsh satires about the world of admen, once almost commonplace, became scarce (although some of sf's satirical spleen transferred itself to the closely related field of rock MUSIC in search of new media targets). One or two films – such as *Le PRIX DU DANGER* (1983), based on Sheckley's "The Prize of Peril", and the very similar *The RUNNING MAN* (1987), based on *The Running Man* (**1982**) by Richard Bachman (Stephen KING) – focused on the theme of social violence institutionalized by tv game-shows, but they looked curiously old-fashioned. The best sf media (or anti-media) films of the 1980s were John CARPENTER's THEY LIVE (1988) and David CRONENBERG's VIDEODROME (1982), especially the latter – but perhaps more typical of the new attitude towards the media was BLADE RUNNER (1982), where the vast, seductively moving advertising hoardings form a ubiquitous and insinuating backdrop – but nevertheless a *backdrop*, against which the story proper is played.

In general, what happened in the 1980s was that sf about the media became more fascinated with potential real futures than with satirical ones. Stories like *The Space Merchants* were never intended to be serious predictions of a possible tomorrow: they exaggerated aspects of the present in order to comment upon, not the future, but that present itself. By the 1980s sf writers were becoming aware that the communications of the future would be qualitatively quite different from those of the present, and they threw themselves into the virgin speculative territory with abandon. The theme of the media became absorbed into the broader theme of a wired-up world, with the media being seen as only a part of a vision of vast communications networks of such complexity as to be almost autonomous, out of control – a vision of a world in which humans could (perilously) swim but which they could not repudiate. In short, the media-landscape story was supplanted by CYBERPUNK, with its focus on VIRTUAL REALITY (further relevant stories are discussed under both those headings). This was a logical development, for the entertainment industry has always been hell-bent (as many of the earlier sf writers realized) on creating virtual realities – if primitive ones – for its captive audiences to occupy, and the cyberpunk writers simply envisaged the technologies that would develop from, at least in part, this very phenomenon. Of course, many such stories contain direct comments on the media world, as in William GIBSON's *Mona Lisa Overdrive* (**1988**), one of whose four protagonists is a "stim" star for Sense-Net, the giant entertainment corporation which prepares virtual-reality scenarios of impossible glamour into which the proletariat can tune and which, for a time, they can inhabit. It is this kind of engulfing media future that now preoccupies sf.   [DP/PN]

MEDICINE Medical applications of TECHNOLOGY comprise one of the few areas where the cutting edge of scientific research impinges directly and intimately upon ordinary human life. New medicines are so rapidly brought into everyday use that it is easy to forget how rapid progress has been, and that barely 100 years separates us from the crucial CONCEPTUAL BREAKTHROUGHS associated with the development of organic chemistry and the germ theory enunciated by Louis Pasteur (1822-1895). Even people who can find little else to say in favour of science and technology (◊ ANTI-INTELLECTUALISM IN SF) are usually grateful for the benefits of scientific medicine, although the rapid recent growth of "alternative medicine" has shown that even this gratitude has its limits. So urgent is the human need for better medicine that the field has always been home to legions of quacks and charlatans offering hopeful panaceas for all ills (◊ PSEUDO-SCIENCE); the literary imagination has inevitably reflected and magnified these hopes in fantasies of resurrection, rejuvenation and IMMORTALITY – usually couched, of course, as cautionary tales – and the ideative apparatus of sf has been promiscuously deployed in stories of these types. Medical researchers and their endeavours have been objects of central concern in sf ever since Mary SHELLEY's *Frankenstein, or The Modern Prometheus* (**1818**; rev 1831). Because of the urgency with which medical matters concern us, plots involving new cures (and, of course, new diseases) have an inbuilt dramatic

quality which readily recommends them to speculative writers inside and outside the genre. Thanks to writers like Robin COOK one can today recognize a subgenre of "medical thrillers" whose products very often stray over the sf borderline. Several notable sf writers have been MDs, including Michael BLUMLEIN, Miles J. BREUER, Michael CRICHTON, Arthur Conan DOYLE, David H. KELLER and Alan E. NOURSE. M.P. SHIEL and J.G. BALLARD both studied medicine for a while; although neither graduated, the influence of their studies is indelibly marked on much of their work.

Early US sf is replete with what one might call, after the example of Oliver Wendell Holmes, "medicated novels", mostly dealing with mental aberration (◊ PSYCHOLOGY) or the increasingly problematic question of the precise relationship between body and soul. Bizarre medical experiments are described in such early works as Nathaniel HAWTHORNE's "Rappaccini's Daughter" (1844) and Edgar Allan POE's "The Facts in the Case of M. Valdemar" (1845). It was, however, UK writers who took up such themes more boldly in the latter half of the 19th century, in such novels as Robert Louis STEVENSON's *Strange Case of Dr Jekyll and Mr Hyde* (**1886**) and H.G. WELLS's *The Island of Dr Moreau* (**1896**). In keeping with the traditions of the day, these experiments almost always go wrong, usually horribly. Even techniques which have since become realized, to the evident betterment of the human condition – organ transplantation, chemical contraception and medical cyborgization (◊ CYBORGS) – were frequently deployed by early sf writers in vivid horror stories or *contes cruels*. Brain surgery offered considerable melodramatic scope to the writer of medical horror stories, exploited to the full in W.C. Morrow's "The Monster-Maker" (1887) and S. Fowler WRIGHT's "Brain" (1932), as did stories of radiation-treatment gone awry (◊ MUTANTS). Even Sir Ronald Ross (1857-1932), who received the Nobel Prize for his work on malaria, deployed his expert knowledge thus in his only sf story, "The Vivisector Vivisected" (written *c*1889; 1932). One can also identify a small-scale subgenre of "medical nightmare" stories involving hallucinations – usually vividly gruesome ones – suffered under anaesthetic; these run from Wells's "Under the Knife" (1897) to Neil BELL's *Death Rocks the Cradle* (**1933** as by Paul Martens).

Much modern sf continues this pessimistic tradition. C.M. KORNBLUTH's tale of the use and abuse of medical equipment timeslipped from the future, "The Little Black Bag" (1950), is one of the most famous sf *contes cruels*, and Daniel KEYES's classic *Flowers for Algernon* (1957; exp **1966**) is a tragedy of unparalleled poignancy. Bernard WOLFE's *Limbo* (**1952**) recruits medical technology to put an ironic twist on the idea of disarmament. Walter M. MILLER's "Blood Bank" (1952), William TENN's "Down Among the Dead Men" (1954), Cordwainer SMITH's "A Planet Named Shayol" (1961) and Larry NIVEN's "The Organleggers" (1969) are other stories in a vividly dark vein. *Caduceus Wild*

(1959; **1978**) by Ward MOORE and Robert Bradford, in which doctors run the world, is as DYSTOPIAN as other contemporary stories in which some special-interest group has become dominant; James E. GUNN's *The Immortals* (1955-60; fixup **1962**) is similarly but more thoughtfully downbeat, while such Alan E. Nourse novels as *The Mercy Men* (**1968**; rev from *A Man Obsessed* **1955**) and *The Bladerunner* (**1974**) deploy dystopian imagery in a carefully ambivalent fashion. The tradition continues into recent times in such novels as *Dr Adder* (**1984**) by K.W. JETER, *Resurrection, Inc.* (**1988**) by Kevin J. ANDERSON, *The Child Garden* (**1989**) by Geoff RYMAN, *Body Mortgage* (**1989**) by Richard ENGLING and *Crygender* (**1992**) by Thomas T. THOMAS.

Linked to the horror-story tradition of accounts of misfired medical experiments is a much less prolific comic tradition, in which things go wrong with rather less awful consequences; Wells' "The Stolen Bacillus" (1895) is an early example. The proposal by the Russian physiologist Serge Voronoff (1866-1951) that testosterone generated by transplanted monkey-testicles might "rejuvenate" ageing men inspired some sf black comedies, including Bertram GAYTON's *The Gland Stealers* (**1922**); a farcical film on a similar theme was MONKEY BUSINESS (1952). A modern black comedy of medical chicanery is Joe HALDEMAN's *Buying Time* (**1989**; vt *The Long Habit of Living* 1989 UK). Like Raymond Hawkey's thriller *Side-Effect* (**1979**), the latter assumes that medical miracles might well be reserved by their creators for the favoured few, extrapolating the old medical adage that the best specialism is diseases of the very rich.

The Great Plague Story, memorably featured in Mary Shelley's *The Last Man* (**1826**) and Jack LONDON's *The Scarlet Plague* (1912; **1915**), remains a melodramatic staple of the DISASTER story. Notable examples of stories whose main focus is on the medical effort to counter or control such plagues include *Cry Plague!* (**1953** dos) by Theodore S. Drachman MD, *The Darkest of Nights* (**1962**; vt *Survival Margin* US) by Charles Eric MAINE, *Plague from Space* (**1965**; vt *The Jupiter Legacy*) by Harry HARRISON, *The Andromeda Strain* (**1969**) by Michael Crichton, *Time of the Fourth Horseman* (**1976**) by Chelsea Quinn YARBRO and *Disposable People* (**1980**) by Marshall Goldberg MD and Kenneth Kay. Interesting stories of plagues which bring ambiguous benefits as well as posing threats include Walter M. Miller's "Dark Benediction" (1951), Octavia E. BUTLER's *Clay's Ark* (**1984**) and Greg BEAR's *Blood Music* (**1985**). The newest real-world plague, AIDS, has called forth a rapid response in the sf field; Dan SIMMONS's *Children of the Night* (**1992**) features the notion that a cure might be found in vampires' blood. Extravagant stories of medical responses to AIDS include F.M. BUSBY's *The Breeds of Man* (**1988**), Thomas M. DISCH's *The MD: A Horror Story* (**1991**) and Norman SPINRAD's "Journals of the Plague Years" (1988).

A much more positive image of medical science is seen in stories in which doctors struggle to understand and solve exotic problems which arise with respect to the interaction between humans and ALIENS. There are two particularly notable sf series of this kind: Murray LEINSTER's **Med Service** series (1957-66) and James WHITE's ongoing **Sector General** series (begun 1957). L. Ron HUBBARD's earlier **Ole Doc Methuselah** series (1947-50; coll **1970**) is unfortunately weakened by the eponymous hero's interest in eccentric theories. White's series is especially interesting by virtue of the warmly liberal humanism of its attitude towards aliens – gracefully making a point which is much more laboured in Piers ANTHONY's sitcom-like series about an interplanetary dentist, *Prostho Plus* (fixup **1971**) – although White can also function effectively in the medical horror/thriller vein, as in *Underkill* (**1979**). Alan E. Nourse's *Star Surgeon* (**1960**) is a notable juvenile sf novel cast in the earnest and constructive mould. These stories of fairly ordinary people tackling localized problems tend to be more interesting than tales in which the discovery of a panacea promises an instant end to all ills, although some such stories can be effective; examples include S. Fowler Wright's "The Rat" (1929), Charles L. HARNESS's *The Catalyst* (**1980**) and Kate WILHELM's rather ambivalent *Welcome, Chaos* (**1983**).

A theme anthology is *Great Science Fiction about Doctors* (anth **1963**) ed Groff CONKLIN and Noah D. Fabricant MD. [BS/JSc]

MEDIEVAL SOCIETIES ◊ CONCEPTUAL BREAKTHROUGH; HOLOCAUST AND AFTER; MAGIC; POLITICS; SWORD AND SORCERY.

MEEK, [Colonel] S(TERNER St) P(AUL) (1894-1972) US Army ordnance officer and writer, active for about a decade in the US PULP MAGAZINES after the publication of his first story, "The Murgatroyd Experiments" for *AMZ Quarterly* in 1929. Many of his stories are in a series featuring **Doctor Bird and Operative Carnes**, running from "The Cave of Horror" (1930) to "Vanishing Gold" (1932); they have not been collected in book form. *The Monkeys Have No Tails in Zamboanga* (coll **1935**) assembles a series of sf tall tales; some are amusing. Of several novels published in magazine form, only two LOST-WORLD tales about survivors of ATLANTIS, *The Drums of Tapajos* (1930 *AMZ*; **1961**) and its sequel *Troyana* (1932 *AMZ*; rev **1961**), reached book form. [JC]

Other work: *Arctic Bride* (coll **1944** chap UK).

See also: ASTOUNDING SCIENCE-FICTION; GREAT AND SMALL.

MEET THE APPLEGATES Film (1990). New World/Cinemarque. Dir Michael Lehmann, starring Ed Begley Jr, Stockard Channing, Bobby Jacoby, Cami Cooper, Dabney Coleman. Screenplay Redbeard Simmons, Lehmann. 89 mins. Colour.

In this sf/fantasy SATIRE, a group of shapeshifting giant insects from the South American rainforest, disturbed at humanity's destruction of their domain, disguise themselves as human and infiltrate a small US town, where they plan to get revenge by causing a nuclear meltdown at the local power plant. Their knowledge of human life being gleaned largely from **Dick and Jane** books, they begin as apparently stereotyped upright citizens, but are soon corrupted by US society, becoming a secretary-screwing husband, a consumer-product-obsessed shoplifting wife, a pregnant radical lesbian feminist daughter and a dope-smoking son. *MTA* is witty and pointed, but stops this side of hilarious because its affability dilutes the savagery to which it appears to aspire.   [PN]

See also: MONSTER MOVIES.

MEGAVILLE Film (1990). White Noise/Heritage. Dir Peter Lehner, starring Billy Zane, J.C. Quinn, Grace Zabriskie, Kristen Cloke, Daniel J. Travanti, Stefan Gierasch. Screenplay Lehner, Gordon Chavis. 95 mins. Colour.

An impressive but very low-budget picture, updating some of the feel of Jean-Luc Godard's ALPHAVILLE (1965) in its vision of a transformed future USA (played oddly but effectively by present-day Switzerland) divided into independent zones. The disguised hero (Zane) is sent from his puritanical homeland, where the electronic MEDIA are outlawed, by a dying "Big Brother" figure (Travanti) into the wide open city of Megaville, where corrupting entertainments like tv are still available, to search for a device that enables the user to experience the recorded consciousness of another person. As in TOTAL RECALL (1990) the hero is gradually led to question his own identity, in this case coming to wonder whether he is indeed the criminal he is supposed to be impersonating. *M* is a bleak and cynical film, with a supporting cast of well played sinister characters.   [KN]

MEGAVORE: THE JOURNAL OF POPULAR FICTION ◊ *The* SCIENCE-FICTION COLLECTOR.

MEIER, SHIRLEY [r] ◊ S.M. STIRLING.

MEKAGOJIRA NO GYAKUSHU ◊ GOJIRA.

MELAMED, DAVID [r] ◊ ISRAEL.

MELCHIOR, IB [r] ◊ *The* OUTER LIMITS; REPTILICUS; ROBINSON CRUSOE ON MARS; *The* TIME TRAVELERS.

MELDE, G.R. ◊ Dennis HUGHES.

MÉLIÈS, GEORGES (1861-1938) French film pioneer. A natural showman, GM began his theatrical career as a conjurer, designing his own trick gadgets. In 1888 his wealthy family provided him with the finances to buy the Théâtre Robert-Houdin, and his magic shows there became famous. In 1896, inspired by the Lumière brothers, he acquired a motion-picture camera and began making his own short films. He realized the medium's potential for creating illusions, and was soon producing many films utilizing trick photography as well as the stage effects built into his theatre.

His most successful period was 1897-1902. It was in 1902 that he made *Le* VOYAGE DANS LA LUNE, which is regarded as the first sf movie epic (21 mins long, at a time when 5min movies were the norm). His work was popular in many countries, but even by 1904, when he made *Le* VOYAGE À TRAVERS L'IMPOSSIBLE,

audiences were requiring more than just trick films. By 1913 he was forced out of business. During WWI many of the negatives of his films were destroyed, and much of his work was lost forever. He enjoyed a comeback in the late 1920s when his surviving films were rediscovered by the French intellectuals of the period. He died with the satisfaction of being recognized as one of the CINEMA's true innovators; he had pioneered many of the techniques on which all subsequent sf cinema has been based.

He has also been claimed, retrospectively, as a Surrealist pioneer, but the truth is that his emphasis on mere trickery (and also his use of what was in effect a proscenium arch, so that all action is seen as if it is stage action witnessed from the seats of a theatre) is a long way removed from art; not only does it seem crude now but, after the novelty had worn off, it quickly came to seem crude then. [JB/PN]

MELLA, JOHN (?   -   ) US writer whose *Transformations* (fixup **1975**) is an ALTERNATE-WORLD tale about the quest for a transvestite actor; it is set in a 19th- and 20th-century USA and Europe transfigured by time (the narrator, WS or William Shakespeare, does not die until a movable 1916) and geography (the two continents have been arbitrarily merged, and are haunted by Hollywood). A FABULATION dense with quotations – from authors extending from Shakespeare himself through Jonathan SWIFT, VILLIERS DE L'ISLE ADAM and W.B. Yeats (1865-1939) down to the Vladimir NABOKOV of *Pale Fire* (**1962**) and *Ada* (**1969**) – *Transformations* also has clear affinities to the 1970s **Jerry Cornelius** novels by Michael MOORCOCK, and JM's tale presages 1980s literary sf by writers like Angela CARTER, Steve ERICKSON and David THOMSON. Most significantly for sf, perhaps, is the similarity between JM's vision of the UK – a dark, labyrinth-riddled land, half antique, half transformed by extraordinary inventions – and that typically presented by the writers of STEAMPUNK.   [JC]

MELTZER, DAVID (1937-   ) US poet and novelist whose sf is almost entirely restricted to two sequences of erotic novels published by ESSEX HOUSE at the end of the 1960s, though he published a very few stories earlier. The first sequence, the **Agency** series – *The Agency* (**1968**), *The Agent* (**1968**) and *How Many Blocks in the Pile?* (**1969**) – is a remarkably savage SATIRE of a NEAR-FUTURE USA through a plot whose erotic nature (a young man is indoctrinated by the eponymous organization into sexual slavery, and himself becomes an agent for his masters) can readily be seen as a metaphor illustrating the nature of post-industrial society.

This vision is even more sharply focused in the **Brain Plant** sequence – comprising *Brain Plant #1: Lovely* (**1969**), *#2: Healer* (**1969**), *#3: Out* (**1969**) and *#4: Glue Factory* (**1969**) – in which cartoonlike characters ricochet surreally through a disjointed USA in a pre-programmed search for theme-park SEX, while the secret masters – in this case the military-industrial complex – rule on.

Most of DM's work, from his first book, *Poems* (coll 1957 chap), has been poetry, and he can be seen as a very late member of the Beat Generation; his roots in that tradition help make clear the intersection of erotic excess and political protest in his work.   [JC]

MELUCH, R(EBECCA) M. (1956-   ) US writer whose first novel, *Sovereign* (**1979**), shows a competent grasp of the conventions and venues of sf adventure while at the same time refracting traditional material through an unusually complex protagonist, who is the genetically precarious culmination of a breeding programme haunted by the continuing image of his first enemy: his own father. There are, perhaps, too many additional enemies for plausibility – as the protagonist defeats them all, whether on Earth, on his own planet or in space – but the relative inwardness of the tale is convincing throughout. The **Wind** series – *Wind Dancers* (**1981**) and *Wind Child* (**1982**) – comes close to sentimentality in its depiction of a shapeshifting species oppressed by an evil corporation intent on exploiting their planet. *Jerusalem Fire* (**1985**) more bracingly depicts a space-born Arab culture, but *War Birds* (**1989**) again veers towards sentiment. *Chicago Red* (**1990**), which returns to RMM's somewhat high-blown but energetically conceived best, is a tale of a USA which has reverted to 18th-century models of kingship, with revolution inevitable, and the eponymous leader in rousing fettle.   [JC]

MELVILLE, HERMAN (1819-1891) US writer best known for such radically symbolic novels as *The Whale* (**1851** UK; vt *Moby-Dick* 1851 US); the great whale of this novel is an archetype of the more METAPHYSICAL variety of sf MONSTER, and the spirit of the book has permeated much sf, notably Roger ZELAZNY's "The Doors of his Face, the Lamps of his Mouth" (1965) and, rather superficially, Philip José FARMER's "sequel" to HM's original, *The Wind Whales of Ishmael* (**1971**). HM's blending, in *Moby-Dick*, of rational explanation and romantic openness with the inexplicable was later to become typical of sf. In *The Confidence-Man, His Masquerade* (**1857**), HM's violent conflict with the dictates (or concept) of a manipulative destiny may well have provided some sf writers with inspiration for contemporary sf tales of justified PARANOIA.

Of more direct sf interest is HM's short story "The Bell-Tower" (1855), which appears in *The Piazza Tales* (coll **1856**); rather reminiscent of the work of his friend Nathaniel HAWTHORNE, it is the story, set in Renaissance Italy, of the construction of a MACHINE-man whose function it will be to strike the hour on a large bell, but which in the event kills its maker. The story can be read as allegorical of mankind's hubris, and a comment on the implications of the new era of mechanical invention and science that HM was beginning to witness.   [JC/PN]

See also: HISTORY OF SF; ROBOTS.

MEMOIRS OF AN INVISIBLE MAN Film (1992). Warner Bros. Dir John CARPENTER, starring Chevy Chase, Daryl Hannah, Sam Neill, Michael McKean, Stephen Tobolowsky. Screenplay Robert Collector, Dana Olson, William Goldman, based on *Memoirs of an Invisible Man* (**1987**) by H.F. SAINT. 99 mins. Colour.

Nick Halloway (Chase), a feckless businessman, is turned invisible by an industrial accident. The Government, represented by a CIA psycho (Neill), tries to capture Halloway to use him for its own nefarious purposes, and he falls for a glamorously unbelievable anthropologist (Hannah) between escapes, disguises, stunts and tricks. After a good opening the film slips into a standard romantic comedy/thriller vein, with Carpenter reprising the facelessly efficient approach he used on STARMAN (1984). Several of its best images are lifted directly from James Whale's *The* INVISIBLE MAN (1932), but the film hardly uses its ambitious source novel, raising but then abandoning a central point – that Halloway was such an average loser as to be invisible even before he became literally so. The well achieved effects (Chase smoking a cigarette whose smoke outlines his lungs, and many others) keep the film interesting.   [KN]

MEMOIRS OF A SURVIVOR Film (1981). Memorial Films/National Film Finance Corporation/EMI. Dir David Gladwell, starring Julie Christie, Christopher Guard, Leonie Mellinger, Debbie Hutchings. Screenplay Kerry Crabbe, Gladwell, based on *The Memoirs of a Survivor* (**1974**) by Doris LESSING. 115 mins. Colour.

Amid NEAR-FUTURE scenes of urban squalor in Western London a middle-aged woman (Christie) observes (mostly peering round a lace curtain) increasing dereliction and social breakdown in the wake of some unexplained catastrophe. She sometimes seems to penetrate a wall at which she often stares, finding herself invisible amid the life of a late-Victorian family in comfortable circumstances. Given a teenage girl (Mellinger) to care for in the real world, she watches her mature into the efficient partner and mistress of an idealistic young man who runs a community centre for abandoned children. When urban life becomes almost intolerable, she leads these people through the wall into the ALTERNATE WORLD of her dreaming. In the source novel, the inner life of the protagonist, permeated by Sufistic meditation, is central, but here, through a savage reductionism, its visual equivalent is given by mere cameos of stable but emotionally disabling Victorian life. Christie's fine performance as the almost unspeaking observer is, through no fault of hers, deeply uncinematic.   [PN]

MENASCO, NORMAN [s] ◊ Wyman GUIN.

MENDELSOHN, FELIX Jr (1906-   ) US writer of two unremarkable comic sf novels, *Club Tycoon Sends Man to Moon* (**1965**) and *Superbaby* (**1969**). The former, in its spoofing of the space race, sometimes scores an amusing point.   [JC]

MENDELSON, DREW (?   -   ) US writer who began publishing sf with "Star Train" for *IASFM* in 1978. His *Pilgrimage* (**1981**) grippingly presents a

vision of a bleak post-HOLOCAUST Earth, long abandoned by most humans except for those who inhabit
the planet's one remaining artifact, a vast CITY that
moves slowly across the devastated land. This city
houses a genuine POCKET-UNIVERSE culture, which has
lost touch with the human past and has become
ignorant of the technologies which give it life. The
adolescent protagonists' quest for meaning (◊ CONCEP-
TUAL BREAKTHROUGH) takes them from the moribund
Tailend of the City to Frontend; the novel closes in
an ambiguous affirmation of renewal. DM's apparent
retirement from the field after the publication of this
novel is a matter for considerable regret.   [JC]

MENDES, HENRY PEREIRA ◊ Henry PEREIRA MENDES.

MENVILLE, DOUGLAS (ALVER) (1935-   ) US
author and editor. He ed FORGOTTEN FANTASY 1970-71
and, with R. REGINALD (*whom see for further details*),
was advisory editor of the various ARNO PRESS reprint
book series; he and Reginald have also collaborated
on several books and anthologies. Solo, DM has
written *A Historical and Critical Survey of the SF Film*
(**1975**); with Reginald and Mary A. Burgess he wrote
*Futurevisions: The New Golden Age of the Science Fiction
Film* (**1985**). He also compiled *The Work of Ross
Rocklynne: An Annotated Bibliography & Guide* (**1989**
chap).   [PN]

MERAK, A.J. ◊ John S. GLASBY.

MERCHANT, PAUL [s] ◊ Harlan ELLISON.

MERCIER, LOUIS-SÉBASTIEN (1740-1814) French
writer best known for his numerous plays and for his
anecdotal journalism; he was active in the French
Revolution, being imprisoned during the Terror. His
UTOPIA, *L'an deux mille quatre cent quarante* (**1771** UK;
trans William Hooper as *Memoirs of the Year Two
Thousand Five Hundred* **1772**; vt *Astraea's Return, or The
Halcyon Days of France in the Year 2440* **1797**), depicts
a future FRANCE governed rationally, according to
Enlightenment precepts as stirred by the neoprim-
itivism of Jean-Jacques Rousseau (1712-1778), and is
a central 18th-century text, important particularly for
any analysis of pre-Revolutionary ferment in France.
It was probably the first utopia to be published in the
USA, in 1795, in an edition which replicated the 1772
translation; unfortunately, LSM's expanded version
of the text (**1786** France) has never appeared in
English.   [JC]

See also: ANONYMOUS SF AUTHORS; BALLOONS; CITIES;
FUTUROLOGY; NEAR FUTURE; SUSPENDED ANIMATION.

MERCURY Mercury is the planet nearest the Sun, and
hence is difficult to observe. Until the late 19th
century it was believed to rotate on its axis every 24
hours or so, but this opinion was displaced by that
of Giovanni Schiaparelli (1835-1910) and Percival
Lowell (1855-1916), who contended that it kept the
same face permanently towards the Sun. 20th-
century sf writers thus pictured it as having an
extremely hot "dayside", a cold "nightside" and a
narrow "twilight zone". This image persisted until
the 1960s, when it was discovered that Mercury
rotates on its axis rapidly enough to have a day

somewhat shorter than its year.

The earliest visit to Mercury was probably that of
Athanasius KIRCHER in his *Itinerarium Exstaticum*
(**1656**), and it was generally included in other round
tours of the planets, including Emanuel SWEDEN-
BORG's *The Earths in Our Solar System* (**1758**) and
George GRIFFITH's *A Honeymoon in Space* (**1901**). John
MUNRO's *A Trip to Venus* (**1897**) includes a detour to
Mercury. The earliest novel in which Mercury came
into principal focus was *Relation du Monde de Mercure*
(**1750** France) by Le Chevalier de Bethune; the first
novel in English to be set there was William Wallace
COOK's SATIRE *Adrift in the Unknown* (1904-5; **1925**).
E.R. EDDISON's series of fantasy novels begun with
The Worm Ouroboros (**1922**) is likewise set on Mercury,
but the name is used purely for convenience.

GENRE SF rarely employed Mercury as a milieu for
exotic adventure, preferring MARS and VENUS, but it
does feature in Homer Eon FLINT's "The Lord of
Death" (1919; in *The Lord of Death and the Queen of Life*
[coll **1965**]), Ray CUMMINGS's *Tama of the Light Country*
(**1930**; **1965**) and its sequel *Tama, Princess of Mercury*
(**1931**; **1966**), and Clark Ashton SMITH's "The Immortals of Mercury" (**1932**). An invasion from Mercury is
thwarted in J.M. WALSH's *Vandals of the Void* (**1931**),
and Leigh BRACKETT set one of her exotic romances
there, "Shannach – the Last" (**1952**). Attempts to use
Mercury in more thoughtful stories with some fidelity
to astronomical knowledge were likewise infrequent
in the pre-WWII pulps, the first significant examples
being Clifford D. SIMAK's "Masquerade" (**1941**; vt
"Operation Mercury") and Isaac ASIMOV's "Run-
around" (**1942**).

After WWII, however, things picked up a little.
Three juvenile novels featuring Mercury are Lester
DEL REY's *Battle on Mercury* (**1956** as by Erik van Lhin),
Asimov's *Lucky Starr and the Big Sun of Mercury* (**1956**
as by Paul French; vt *The Big Sun of Mercury*), and
Mission to Mercury (**1965**) by Hugh WALTERS. Alan E.
NOURSE's memorable "Brightside Crossing" (**1956**)
represents a journey across the dayside of the planet
as an adventurous feat akin to the then-recent
conquest of Everest. The nightside of Mercury features ironically in Larry NIVEN's "The Coldest Place"
(**1964**), but recent sf usually employs Mercury as
merely a convenient place to site bases for studying
the SUN, like the one in David BRIN's *Sundiver* (**1980**).
Perhaps the most enduring sf image of Mercury,
though, is from Kurt VONNEGUT Jr's *The Sirens of Titan*
(**1959**), which offers an account of the Harmonia,
cave-dwelling lifeforms thriving on vibration and
introduced to music by a stranded astronaut.   [BS]

MERCURY PRESS ◊ *The* MAGAZINE OF FANTASY AND
SCIENCE FICTION; VENTURE SCIENCE FICTION.

MEREDITH, JAMES CREED (1875-1942) Irish writer,
usually on philosophical subjects, who carried that
interest into fiction in *The Rainbow in the Valley* (**1939**),
which features scientists in communication with
Martians, and discursively compares and contrasts
the two civilizations.   [JC]

MEREDITH, RICHARD C(ARLTON) (1937-1979) US writer who began publishing sf with "Slugs" for *Knight* magazine in 1962. His first novel, *The Sky is Filled with Ships* (**1969**), is an effective SPACE OPERA in which colonies revolt against a tyrannical corporation. *We All Died at Breakaway Station* (**1969**) is a bleak, well crafted space opera in a kind of Alamo setting, where a CYBORG must withstand both external enemies and the devils of introspection. *Run, Come See Jerusalem!* (**1976**) is a complex, thoroughly worked out TIME-PARADOX novel. Time also figures centrally in the **Timeliner** sequence – *At the Narrow Passage* (**1973**; rev 1979), *No Brother, No Friend* (**1976**; rev 1979) and *Vestiges of Time* (**1978**; rev 1979), all 3 being assembled as *The Timeliner Trilogy* (omni. **1987** UK) – during the course of which ALIENS attempt to change Earth's past, and, more importantly, to punish humanity in various PARALLEL WORLDS. RCM's sense of history was acute and atmospheric, and his ALTERNATE-WORLDS tales are, as a consequence, hauntingly suggestive. Into these frameworks his heroes – wounded and reluctant but ultimately stoic – fit neatly. [JC/PN]

Other work: *The Awakening* (**1979**).

See also: HITLER WINS.

MERLE, ROBERT (1908-) Algerian-born French writer, recipient of the Prix Goncourt in 1949, known primarily for his work outside the sf field. His *Un animal doué de raison* (**1967**; trans Helen Weaver as *The Day of the Dolphin* 1969 US) is an ingenious examination of scientific and political ethics following the main character's breakthrough in COMMUNICATION with dolphins. *Malevil* (**1972**; trans Derek Coltman **1974** US), joint winner of the JOHN W. CAMPBELL MEMORIAL AWARD in 1974, is a realistic and delicately told post-HOLOCAUST survival and reconstruction story. Both have been filmed (◊ *The* DAY OF THE DOLPHIN; MALEVIL). *Les hommes protégés* (**1974**; trans Martin Sokolinsky as *The Virility Factor* 1977 US) uses an sf framework to satirize both sexist and feminist attitudes. An epidemic to which boys, castrated men and men over 60 are immune is killing the male population of the USA. The government is taken over by women and eunuchs, and new changes are rung on the old sf theme with what some saw as cheery ribaldry, others as cheap vulgarity. [MJ/PN]

Other works: *Madrapour* (**1976**).

See also: FRANCE; LINGUISTICS; UNDER THE SEA.

MERLYN, ARTHUR [r] ◊ James BLISH.

MERRIL, JUDITH (1923-) US-born writer and anthologist, in Canada from 1968. Born Juliet Grossman, she preferred the forename Judith; she became Judith Zissman by marriage, then changed her name to Merril before marrying Frederik POHL in 1949; they were divorced in 1953. She occasionally used the pseudonym Rose Sharon. JM was associated with the FUTURIANS fan group during and after WWII. Her first published sf was "That Only a Mother" for *ASF* in 1948. Her first novel, *Shadow on the Hearth* (**1950**; rev 1966 UK), tells the story of an atomic war in effectively understated fashion from the viewpoint of a housewife; one of the very best stories of nuclear HOLOCAUST, it was televised as *Atomic Attack*.

JM wrote two routine novels in collaboration with C.M. KORNBLUTH as Cyril JUDD: *Outpost Mars* (**1952**; rev vt *Sin in Space* 1961) is about the COLONIZATION of MARS, *Gunner Cade* (**1952**) about an era in which WAR is a spectator sport (◊ GAMES AND SPORTS). Her best short stories, which usually feature protagonists passively caught up in world-changing events, and often hurt thereby, were a little ahead of their time. The neatly heart-rending "Dead Center" (1954) was reprinted in *The Best American Short Stories: 1955* ed Martha Foley. *Daughters of Earth* (coll **1968** UK; vt *A Judith Merril Omnibus: Daughters of Earth and Other Stories* 1985 Canada) features 3 fine novellas: the title story (1953) is a family saga set on a colony world; "Project Nursemaid" (1955) concerns the problems of the administrator of a space project which must adopt human embryos; "Homecalling" (1956) is a story of contact with an ALIEN being. *The Tomorrow People* (**1960**), an intense psychological mystery story, lacks the emotional resonance of her best early work. She published very little fiction after 1960. Her short-story collections, which overlap somewhat, are *Out of Bounds* (coll **1960**), *Survival Ship and Other Stories* (coll **1974**) and *The Best of Judith Merril* (coll **1976**).

JM began editing sf ANTHOLOGIES in the early 1950s with *Shot in the Dark* (anth **1950**), *Beyond Human Ken* (anth **1952**; with 6 of 21 stories cut 1953 UK; cut version vt *Selections from Beyond Human Ken* 1954 US), *Beyond the Barriers of Time and Space* (anth **1954**), *Human?* (anth **1954**) and *Galaxy of Ghouls* (anth **1955**; vt *Off the Beaten Orbit* 1959). She made her mark with the series of 12 "year's best" anthologies she began in 1956: *S-F The Year's Greatest Science-Fiction and Fantasy* (anth **1956**); *SF: 57* (anth **1957**; vt *SF The Year's Greatest Science-Fiction and Fantasy: Second Annual Volume* 1957); *SF 58* (anth **1958**; vt *SF The Year's Greatest Science-Fiction and Fantasy: Third Annual Volume* 1958); *SF 59* (anth **1959**; vt *SF The Year's Greatest Science-Fiction and Fantasy: Fourth Annual Volume*); *The 5th Annual of The Year's Best S-F* (anth **1960**; vt *The Best of Sci-Fi 5* 1966 UK); *The 6th Annual of The Year's Best S-F* (anth **1961**; vt *The Best of Sci-Fi* 1963 UK); *The 7th Annual of The Year's Best S-F* (anth **1962**; vt *The Best of Sci-Fi – Two* 1964 UK); *The 8th Annual of The Year's Best SF* (anth **1963**; vt *The Best of Sci-Fi No. 4* 1965 UK); *The 9th Annual of The Year's Best SF* (anth **1964**; vt *9th Annual S-F* 1967 UK); *10th Annual Edition The Year's Best SF* (anth **1965**; vt *10th Annual SF* 1967 UK); *11th Annual Edition The Year's Best S-F* (anth **1966**); *SF 12* (anth **1968**; vt *The Best of Sci-Fi 12* 1970 UK); though announced, «*SF 13*» never in fact appeared. The UK edns omit some editorial material and are numbered without regard to sense; *The Best of Sci-Fi 3* (anth **1964** UK) ed Cordelia Titcomb Smith has no connection with the JM series. A selection from the sequence was published as *SF: The Best of the Best* (anth **1967**). JM was an unusually eclectic anthologist, habitually using stories from outside the

SF MAGAZINES, thus helping to broaden the horizons of the genre; she campaigned in her anthologies and in her book-review column in *FSF* (May 1965-May 1969) for the replacement of the term "science fiction" by SPECULATIVE FICTION. She was the first US champion of the NEW WAVE (primarily associated with the UK magazine NEW WORLDS), which she attempted to popularize in *England Swings SF* (anth **1968**; cut vt *The Space-Time Journal* 1972 UK). She ed the first of the **Tesseracts** series (◊ CANADA) of representative anthologies of Canadian sf, *Tesseracts* (anth **1985**).

Her book collection now forms the basis of the MERRIL COLLECTION OF SCIENCE FICTION, SPECULATION AND FANTASY, based in Toronto. [BS]

See also: DEFINITIONS OF SF; END OF THE WORLD; GENERATION STARSHIPS; SCIENTIFIC ERRORS; SHARED WORLDS; SMALL PRESSES AND LIMITED EDITIONS; WOMEN SF WRITERS.

MERRIL COLLECTION OF SCIENCE FICTION, SPECULATION AND FANTASY Founded in 1970 by Toronto Public Library in Canada, to house a major donation by sf author and anthologist Judith MERRIL and substantially added to since; known as the Spaced Out Library until 1 Jan 1991. With more than 26,000 books and 18,000 periodicals in the reference section, and 8500 paperbacks in the circulating section, this COLLECTION is one of the world's more important sf research libraries. Among its holdings are many complete runs of PULP MAGAZINES, a good collection of sf from CANADA, a full set of ARKHAM HOUSE publications and a strong Jules VERNE collection. The quarterly newsletter of the library's Friends is *Sol Rising*. [PN]

MERRILL, ALBERT ADAMS (? -?) US writer of whom nothing is known beyond his renowned UTOPIA, *The Great Awakening: The Story of the Twenty-Second Century* (**1899**), in which a reincarnated 19th-century American is guided through the technological wonderland which the USA has become 200 years in the future, with electric cars and tv; everyone is paid the same, the state owns all property, and happiness seems rife. [JC]

MERRIMAN, ALEX [s] ◊ Robert SILVERBERG.

MERRITT, A(BRAHAM) (1884-1943) US editor, real-estate developer and writer, primarily of FANTASY, though he was influential among sf writers and readers as well. His first years were occupied with newspaper journalism; he was a longtime assistant editor of *The American Weekly*, becoming editor-in-chief in 1937 and remaining so until his death. His fiction was written as a sideline to this busy career, which may explain why his output was relatively small. He began publishing stories with *Thru the Dragon Glass* (1917 *All-Story Weekly* as "Through the Dragon Glass"; **1932** chap); his first novel, *The Moon Pool* ("The Moon Pool" 1918 *All-Story Weekly*; "The Conquest of the Moon Pool" 1919 *All-Story Weekly*; fixup **1919**), begins with the Shining One, a deadly though insubstantial monster within a pool in Micronesia, and moves on to a complicated lost-race melodrama (◊ ANTHROPOLOGY; LOST WORLDS). (The

posthumous *Reflections in the Moon Pool* [coll **1985**], ed anon, is only distantly related to the novel, containing a long biography of AM by Sam MOSKOWITZ, a few prose items by AM, and some poetry, letters and articles.) *The Metal Monster* (1920 *Argosy*; **1946**), another lost-race tale (and containing one of the characters from the previous book), describes a collective ALIEN being, comprised of millions of metal parts, who is absentmindedly kind to the explorer-protagonist. *The Face in the Abyss* ("The Face in the Abyss" 1923 *Argosy*; "The Snake Mother" 1930 *Argosy*; fixup **1931**) describes an ancient, almost extinct, semireptilian race and its considerable wisdom. In *The Ship of Ishtar* (1924 *Argosy*; cut **1926**; text restored 1949), his best novel, a man travels into a magical world and falls in love with the beautiful female captain of the ship of Ishtar; the highly coloured descriptive passages of this novel still have a strong effect on readers. *7 Footprints to Satan* (1927 *Argosy*; **1928**), filmed in 1929, is a horror/detective mystery, "Satan" being a greedy villain. *The Dwellers in the Mirage* (1932 *Argosy* with happy ending; **1932**; with original intended unhappy ending 1944) is an effective lost-race novel, one of AM's best. *Burn Witch Burn!* (1932 *Argosy*; exp **1933**) and its sequel, *Creep, Shadow!* (1934 *Argosy*; **1934**; vt *Creep, Shadow, Creep!* 1935 UK), the first volume filmed as *The* DEVIL DOLL (1936), comprise a short series about witchcraft and HORROR detection. *The Fox Woman and Other Stories* (coll **1949**) assembles short stories and uncompleted fragments, of which the title story had already been incorporated into *The Fox Woman and The Blue Pagoda* (coll of 2 stories **1946**) by AM and Hannes BOK, "The Blue Pagoda" being by Bok but linked to AM's fragment with connecting passages. Bok's second completion of AM's work was *The Black Wheel* (**1947**), of which less than a quarter is by AM.

AM was influential upon the sf and fantasy world not primarily through his storylines, which tended to be unoriginal, or through the excesses of his style, but because of the genuine imaginative power he displayed in the creation of desirable alternative worlds and realities. He was extremely popular during his life, even having a PULP MAGAZINE, A. MERRITT'S FANTASY MAGAZINE, named after him; and Sam MOSKOWITZ, in Chapter 12 of *Explorers of the Infinite* (**1963**), probably represents the view of many of AM's original readers that he was the supreme fantasy genius of his day. Even though, by any absolute literary standard, AM's prose was verbose and sentimental, and his repeated romantic image of the beautiful evil priestess was trivial – deriving as it did from a common Victorian image of womanhood (women being either virgins or devils) – the escapist yearning for otherness and mystery that he expressed has seldom been conveyed in sf with such an emotional charge. [JC/PN]

Other works: *Three Lines of Old French* (1919 *All-Story Weekly*; **1937** chap); *The Drone Man* (1934 *Fantasy Magazine* as "The Drone"; **1948** chap); *Rhythm of the*

Spheres (1936 *TWS*; **1948** chap); *Woman of the Wood* (1926 *Weird Tales*; **1948** chap); *The People of the Pit* (1918 *All-Story Weekly*; **1948** chap); *Seven Footprints to Satan and Burn Witch Burn!* (omni **1952**); *Dwellers in the Mirage and The Face in the Abyss* (omni **1953**).

See also: AMAZING STORIES; DIME-NOVEL SF; FANTASTIC VOYAGES; FAR FUTURE; HISTORY OF SF; PARALLEL WORLDS; PUBLISHING; SF MAGAZINES.

MERWIN, SAM Jr Working name of US writer W. Samuel Kimball Merwin Jr (1910-   ), son of the writer W.S. Merwin (1874-1936). SM's first sf story was "The Scourge Below" for THRILLING WONDER STORIES in 1939. He later went to work for the Beacon pulp chain, which published *TWS* and STARTLING STORIES, and was appointed to the editorship of both in 1944, succeeding Oscar J. FRIEND; although he had contributed to *TWS* and had done some editorial work for the magazines, he claimed never actually to have read an SF MAGAZINE before becoming editor of two of them. During his editorship he greatly raised the standard of both titles, abolishing the juvenile slant they had previously adopted, and making them the leading PULP MAGAZINES in the field behind ASTOUNDING SCIENCE-FICTION. He contributed stories to both, using his own name and the pseudonyms Matt Lee and Carter Sprague. He also edited WONDER STORY ANNUAL and FANTASTIC STORY QUARTERLY – additional companion magazines to *Startling* and *TWS* – before leaving in 1951 to freelance. Further editorial forays included editing the first issues of FANTASTIC UNIVERSE, a period as assistant editor for Galaxy Publications – working on GALAXY SCIENCE FICTION, BEYOND FANTASY FICTION and GALAXY SCIENCE FICTION NOVELS – and editing the auspicious first 2 issues of SATELLITE SCIENCE FICTION. He later went to work in Hollywood. Two articles by SM – reminiscences of his pulp-magazine days – appeared in *The* ALIEN CRITIC #9 and #10. Although comparatively little known, SM's record shows him to have been one of the most capable of all sf magazine editors.

SM's fiction, on the other hand, was unexceptional; his detective novels, beginning with *Murder in Miniatures* (**1940**), are perhaps better than his sf, of which the best are probably *The House of Many Worlds* (**1951**) and its sequel *Three Faces of Time* (**1955** dos), assembled as *The House of Many Worlds* (omni **1983**). The Feb 1957 issue of *Satellite* contained "Planet for Plunder", a novel written in collaboration with Hal CLEMENT; this was actually a Clement novelette expanded by SM (who added alternate chapters from another viewpoint) in order to fit *Satellite*'s novel-oriented policy. *Chauvinisto* (**1976**) took a DYSTOPIAN attitude towards female domination. [MJE]

Other works: *Killer to Come* (**1953**); *The White Widows* (**1953**; vt *The Sex War* 1960); *The Time Shifters* (**1971**).

See also: ALTERNATE WORLDS; SPACESHIPS.

MESHTE NASTRESHU ◊ PLANETA BUR.

MESMERISM ◊ PSYCHOLOGY.

MESSAC, RÉGIS [r] ◊ FRANCE.

MESSAGE FROM MARS, A Film (1913). UK Films. Dir J. Wallett Waller, starring Charles Hawtrey, E. Holman Clark, Chrissie Bell. Scenario Waller, based on the play *A Message from Mars* (**1899**) by Richard Ganthony. 60 mins, cut to 54 mins. B/w.

This moral fable about a messenger sent from Mars to help bring humans – especially the selfish Horace Parlan – to their senses was based on a remarkably successful and long-running play, and the film version was actually made in the theatre with the same actors. The story is very similar to that of Scrooge being redeemed by the ghosts in Charles DICKENS's *A Christmas Carol* (**1843**); very little is made of the alien nature of the Martian, who is more like an angel. An earlier film version of the same play was made in 1909 in New Zealand, probably much shorter; the details and the film itself have been lost. A later (1921) US version (Metro, 69 mins, cut to 63 mins), dir Maxwell Karger, gives the events of the story a dream framework. A novelized version of the play is *A Message from Mars* * (**1912**) by Lester LURGAN, the 2nd edn of which was illustrated by stills from the film. [PN]

MESSIAHS In the MYTHOLOGY of the Old Testament the Messiah is the deliverer of prophecy, destined to lead the Jews to their salvation; the New Testament claims that Jesus was the Messiah. The term is applied by analogy to any saviour or champion whose arrival is anticipated, hoped for or desperately needed. Because Christian images of the future have always been associated with ideas of the Millennium and the Apocalypse, a preoccupation with messiahs in the futuristic fiction of Western culture is only to be expected. Many HEROES in sf play quasimessianic roles, but there is a more-or-less distinct category of stories which deals specifically with this aspect of Judaeo-Christian religion.

Early sf featured numerous messianic political fantasies, including H.G. WELLS's *When the Sleeper Wakes* (**1899**) and Victor ROUSSEAU's *The Messiah of the Cylinder* (**1917**); the most literal of these is M.P. SHIEL's *Lord of the Sea* (**1901**). Earnest futuristic religious fantasies of the same period featuring messianic figures include Guy THORNE's *And it Came to Pass* (**1915**) and Upton SINCLAIR's *They Call me Carpenter* (**1922**). William Hope HODGSON's "The Baumoff Explosion" (1919; vt "Eloi, Eloi, Lama Sabachthani") strikes a more sceptical note in describing a re-enactment of the crucifixion which goes hideously wrong. There is little or no trace of messianic mythology in the sf PULP MAGAZINES until the 1940s, when it became possible for a SUPERMAN to play a quasimessianic role, as in *Darker than You Think* (1940; **1948**) by Jack WILLIAMSON. *What Dreams May Come* (**1941**) by J.D. BERESFORD likewise features a super-human messiah, although *The Gift* (**1946**) by Beresford and Esmé Wynne-Tyson is a more straightforward religious fantasy. L. Ron HUBBARD's *Final Blackout* (1940 *ASF*; **1948**) has an inordinately charismatic hero who may qualify as a messiah. Ordinary men sometimes take on similarly charismatic roles when they are transplanted into PARALLEL WORLDS, as in Henry KUTTNER's *The Dark World* (1946 *Startling Stories*; 1965) and James BLISH's *The Warriors of Day* (1953).

Messiah-figures increased in popularity when Millenarian fantasies became newly fashionable in the wake of the Bomb. C.S. LEWIS's trilogy of interplanetary religious romances was concluded in *That Hideous Strength* (1945), in which a messianic role is assumed by Merlin, though he is in effect an agent only of the trilogy's true messiah figure, Ransom. Christ first appeared in GENRE SF in this period – in Ray BRADBURY's "The Man" (1949) – but it was not until the 1960s that TIME TRAVEL was used to confront Christ's life (and death) directly. In Michael MOORCOCK's *Behold the Man* (1966 *NW*; exp 1969) a time traveller takes Christ's place. Brian EARNSHAW's *Planet in the Eye of Time* (1968) features a time-trip to witness the crucifixion; Garry KILWORTH's "Let's Go to Golgotha" (1975) uses a similar notion to construct a heavily ironic parable, as does Gore VIDAL's *Live from Golgotha* (1992). Another protagonist who becomes Christ is featured in Barry N. MALZBERG's *The Cross of Fire* (1982). In Philip José FARMER's "Riverworld" (1966) the crucifixion is re-enacted in the human race's new incarnation. The most notable story featuring a re-enactment of the crucifixion on an alien world is "The Streets of Ashkelon" (1962) by Harry HARRISON. Nativity stories are more common; they include Robert F. YOUNG's "Robot Son" (1959), Edward BRYANT's "Eyes of Onyx" (1971) and John CAMERON's *The Astrologer* (1972).

The theme of redemption through sacrifice is more or less explicitly linked to Christian mythology in many sf stories, including Robert F. Young's "Redemption" (1963), Cordwainer SMITH's "The Dead Lady of Clown Town" (1964), Harlan ELLISON's "'Repent, Harlequin!' said the Ticktockman" (1965) and R.A. LAFFERTY's *Past Master* (1968); Robert A. HEINLEIN's *Stranger in a Strange Land* (1961) also belongs to this category. Clifford D. SIMAK's *Time and Again* (1951; vt *First He Died* 1953) features a resurrection of sorts as well as a sacrifice, as do Thomas M. DISCH's *Camp Concentration* (1968) and Jack Williamson's *Firechild* (1986). Explicit (and mostly ironic) sciencefictional accounts of the actual Second Coming include Edward WELLEN's "Seven Days Wonder" (1963), J.G. BALLARD's "You and Me and the Continuum" (1966), Damon KNIGHT's *The Man in the Tree* (1984), Philip José Farmer's *Jesus on Mars* (1979) and Theodore STURGEON's posthumous *Godbody* (1986).

More enigmatic messiahs, who offer little in the way of redemption, are featured in Vidal's *Messiah* (1954; rev 1965), Robert SILVERBERG's *The Masks of Time* (1968; vt *Vornan-19* 1970 UK), Brian M. STABLEFORD's *The Walking Shadow* (1979), Stuart GORDON's *Smile on the Void* (1982), Somtow Sucharitkul's (S.P. SOMTOW's) *Starship and Haiku* (1984) and Kim Stanley ROBINSON's *The Memory of Whiteness* (1985). A fake messiah, used as a political instrument, is featured in Robin SANBORN's *The Book of Stier* (1971). An enigmatically

sinister "messiah" is featured in Philip K. DICK's *The Three Stigmata of Palmer Eldritch* (1964), but later Dick novels, including *A Maze of Death* (1970), play in ever more complex and constructive fashion with messianic figures – a process which culminates in *The Divine Invasion* (1981). The most elaborate messianic fantasy in modern sf, however, is that in Frank HERBERT's *Dune* (1965) and its sequels, following the career and posthumous influence of Paul Atreides, messiah to the desert world Arrakis. Herbert has also deployed messianic mythology elsewhere in his work, notably in *The Jesus Incident* (1979) with Bill RANSOM. Another writer constantly fascinated by messianic mythology is Roger ZELAZNY, whose many fantasies in this vein include "A Rose for Ecclesiastes" (1963), *Lord of Light* (1967) and *Isle of the Dead* (1969). Many of Zelazny's messianic fantasies take a broadly syncretic view of such figures, linking them to mythologies other than the Christian one; a similarly generalized theory of messianic revivification is featured in James KAHN's *Time's Dark Laughter* (1982).

The most significant contemporary religious fantasy about a messiah is James MORROW's brilliantly bitter *Only Begotten Daughter* (1990), which cleverly deploys sf motifs alongside more traditional imagery. Jack WOMACK's *Heathern* (1990 UK) is another almost seamless alloy of sf and religious fantasy. [BS]

See also: GODS AND DEMONS.

MESSMANN, JON [r] ◊ Nick CARTER.

METAFICTION ◊ FABULATION.

MÉTAL HURLANT French BEDSHEET-size, glossy colour COMIC-strip sf magazine launched Jan 1975 by Bernard Farkas, Jean-Pierre Dionnet (1947-   ) and illustrators Jean GIRAUD and Philippe DRUILLET; published by Les Humanoïds Associées. Conceived as a high-quality showcase for the growing number of French sf artists, *MH* was an instant success, combining many aspects of sf narrative with particular stress on the erotic, the grotesque and the horrific in illustrated form. Although it was accused of putting emphasis on graphics rather than content, its influence was notable throughout Europe and North America, and translations of its contents appeared in similar magazines in the USA (◊ HEAVY METAL), Italy, Spain, Holland and elsewhere. Major contributors included Druillet, Giraud, Alexis (Dominique Valler [1946-1977]), Enki BILAL, Vaughn BODÉ, Caza (Philippe Cazaumayou [1941-   ]), Nicole Claveloux (1940-   ), Serge Clerc (1957-   ), Richard CORBEN, F'Murr (Richard Peyzaret [1946-   ]), Jean-Claude Forest (1930-   ), Jean-Claude Gal (1944-   ), Dominique Hé (1949-   ), Jacques Lob (1932-1990), Sergio Macedo (1951-   ), Nikita Mandryka (1940-   ), Francis Massé (1948-   ), Jean-Claude Mézières (1938-   ), René Pétillon (1945-   ) and Jacques Tardi (1946-   ). Quarterly from its inception, *MH* became a monthly with #9 (Sep 1976), at which time it began to carry a warning forbidding sale to minors. In Oct 1976 it spawned a companion magazine devoted exclusively to female illustrators,

Ah! Nana (9 issues, Oct 1976-Sep 1978). *HM* also published a series of **Hors Serie** (specials) on themes such as the END OF THE WORLD and H.P. LOVECRAFT. In 1985 Hachette bought the title and Dionnet was replaced as editor by C. Fromental. With #123 (Sep 1986) a new team took over, but by this time *MH* had declined in quality and popularity, and the new editor-in-chief C. Generot succeeded only in prolonging its life as a pale imitation of its early self. Its last issue was #133 (Aug 1987). [RT/MJ]

See also: ILLUSTRATION.

METALSTORM: THE DESTRUCTION OF JARED-SYN Film (1983). Albert Band International. Dir and coprod Charles BAND, starring Jeffrey Byron, Mike Preston, Tim Thomerson. Screenplay by coprod Alan J. Adler. 83 mins. 3-D. Colour.

More SCIENCE FANTASY than sf, this 3-D exploitation movie, set in a tribalized future wasteland, is notable for the absence of metalstorms and the fact that the totalitarian wizard Jared-Syn is not destroyed. The hero saves his girl – after post-MAD MAX fights with punk nomads and CYBORGS – from the lifeforce-absorbing wizard who exits via another DIMENSION. Aimlessly routine, the film shows little of the comic-book energy that characterizes some later Band productions. [PN]

METAPHYSICAL REVIEW, THE ◊ Bruce GILLESPIE; SF COMMENTARY.

METAPHYSICS One of the qualities of sf that sometimes baffles new readers is the relative infrequency, despite its label, with which it deals with the hard sciences; indeed, sf deals as often with metaphysics as with PHYSICS. This is not an accidental or a recent development; the exploration of metaphysical questions has been central to sf at least since the time of Mary SHELLEY's *Frankenstein, or The Modern Prometheus* (1818; rev 1831). This centrality was not thereafter abandoned: it recurs in the pioneering sf of Edgar Allan POE, Nathaniel HAWTHORNE, Robert Louis STEVENSON and pre-eminently H.G. WELLS. The basic metaphysical question is the notorious cliché, "What does it all mean?" It is to the credit of sf that it has consistently tackled this overwhelming (if nebulous) question, through a fantastically elaborate series of thought experiments, sometimes trivial and sometimes profound, in a way that the traditional novel of character and social interaction is ill equipped to manage.

Metaphysics is an important field of philosophy; and from early on has been regularly used as a synonym for ontology, the study of being or existence. Metaphysics is defined in *The Shorter Oxford English Dictionary* as "that branch of speculation which deals with the first principles of things, including such concepts as being, substance, essence, time, space, cause, identity etc." Many of the thematic entries in this encyclopedia can be regarded as pertaining as much to metaphysics as to the natural sciences, notably ALTERNATE WORLDS, CONCEPTUAL BREAKTHROUGH, COSMOLOGY, DIMENSIONS, END OF THE WORLD, ENTROPY, ESCHATOLOGY, EVOLUTION, GODS AND DEMONS, INTELLIGENCE, LINGUISTICS, MYTHOLOGY, ORIGIN OF MAN, PARALLEL WORLDS, PERCEPTION (under which rubric sf dealing with questions of appearance versus reality is discussed), REINCARNATION, RELIGION, SENSE OF WONDER, TIME PARADOXES, TIME TRAVEL and VIRTUAL REALITY. Indeed, it is no longer possible, particularly at the frontiers of theoretical physics, to distinguish between speculation which belongs specifically to the natural sciences and speculation which is metaphysical. However, if metaphysics can be distinguished from science it is in this (the quotation is from *Man is the Measure* [**1976**], by Reuben Abel, a good account for the layman of central problems in philosophy): "Metaphysics is that branch of philosophy which attempts to comprehend the Universe as a whole – not so much by examining it in detail (which is the procedure of science) as by analysing and organizing the ideas and concepts by means of which we examine and think about the world."

Thus, for instance, a central example of metaphysical sf is Stanisław LEM's *Solaris* (**1961**; trans **1970**), which asks to what extent can scientists studying a totally alien and apparently sentient planet comprehend its essence, if to do so requires transcending categories of thought that are limited by their very humanness. This question about the limitation of our perceptions is one of the fundamental problems sf regularly tackles; many further examples are discussed under ALIENS and CONCEPTUAL BREAKTHROUGH. Confrontation with the alien, especially in sf stories of the 1960s and after, is often seen in sf as leading to a higher level of understanding, and a renewed sense of cosmic harmony. Robert SILVERBERG has written several novels of this type, a good one being *Downward to the Earth* (**1970**). Algis BUDRYS's *Rogue Moon* (**1960**) projects its protagonist into a maze of metaphysical self-discovery by confronting him with a literal, murderous, alien maze on the Moon.

Metaphysical questions of identity are particularly closely associated with the work of Philip K. DICK, who by blurring the distinctions between human and artificial, between Man, ANDROID and MACHINE, forces the reader to consider what qualities of consciousness constitute the essence of humanity. (Gene WOLFE entered the same area of speculation with his brilliant and subtle *The Fifth Head of Cerberus* [**1972**], in which one of the protagonists, it transpires, is a simulation.) Dick, in fact, has a finger in almost every metaphysical pie. He specializes in questions of appearance and reality, and of solipsism, asking to what extent the Universe as it appears to us is an objective fact, and to what extent it is a mental construct, either individual or consensual. The novels of Ian WATSON have characteristically met some of the most difficult questions in metaphysics head-on and doggedly. Watson's special interest is also whether our models of the Universe, especially as reflected in language (◊ LINGUISTICS), correspond to any external reality; at times he seems to go further and suggest that the meaning and shape of the Universe is created by the consciousnesses that observe it.

Questions of good and evil in sf are intimately bound up with questions of human EVOLUTION; to what extent do we carry the mark of the amoral beast within us, imprinted in the more primitive areas of our brains? Robert Louis STEVENSON's *Strange Case of Dr Jekyll and Mr Hyde* (**1886**) asks this question, and the theme is still very much alive today, in part through the work of such evolutionary behaviourist popularizers as Desmond Morris (1928-   ) and Robert ARDREY, and in part through sf itself. An example of this kind of metaphysics running wild in sf is *Altered States* (**1978**) by Paddy CHAYEFSKY, filmed as ALTERED STATES (**1980**), in which, absurdly, cause and effect are reversed (because consciousness may be coded in the DNA molecule, Chayefsky proposes that alterations in consciousness may be somehow able to alter our genetic make-up); his hero devolves first to hominid, then, briefly, to primal chaos, undifferentiated cosmic matter.

Reversals of cause and effect are not new to sf. It is the very nature of the TIME-TRAVEL story to confront us with thought-provoking paradoxes of this sort, and in so doing, of course, to make us speculate about the question (not merely an intellectual game) of whether the shape of our lives is created by free will or determinism. Stories that deal with this issue are legion: two good ones are "The Custodians" (1975) by Richard COWPER and *Slaughterhouse Five* (**1969**) by Kurt VONNEGUT Jr. The very nature of causality has been questioned by stories like Brian W. ALDISS's *An Age* (**1967**; vt *Cryptozoic!* US) and other stories in which the arrow of time is reversed and time runs backwards, such as Dick's *Counter-Clock World* (**1967**) and Martin AMIS's *Time's Arrow* (**1991**) (further examples are discussed under PERCEPTION); John CROWLEY's story "Great Work of Time" (1989) is perhaps of all time-travel stories the one that most sharply (and movingly) questions the relationship of cause and effect.

The books of writers like Crowley, Gene Wolfe and Ian Watson are actually *about* metaphysical exploration; but such questions are by no means eschewed by writers of HARD SF. Arthur C. CLARKE has throughout his career been as interested in metaphysics as in physics; 2001: A SPACE ODYSSEY (**1968**) amply testifies to that, as do many of his novels. Within hard sf and SPACE OPERA to this day, metaphysical explorations consistently appear. Greg BEAR, in novels like *Blood Music* (**1985**) and *Eon* (**1985**), perhaps cuts even deeper than Clarke, often by way of fantastic premises: genetically engineered microorganisms that develop a gestalt consciousness and ultimately transform humanity into a new state of being in the former, and the exploration of a conceptually impossible infinitely extended SPACE HABITAT in the latter. While it might be objected that sf, though it indeed tackles metaphysical questions, has very often done so with a gosh-wow, pop crudity – producing

metaphysical notions like brightly coloured flags without in the least understanding them – this is certainly not true of the writers of its upper echelons, of whom Bear is one. Another is Paul J. MCAULEY, whose *Eternal Light* (**1991**) is the very model of a metaphysical space opera, luring the reader in with promises of high adventure and low conspiracy, and then stirring cosmogony, GENETIC ENGINEERING and (of course) the secret history of the Universe into a potent – and really rather demanding – mix. The increased sophistication, in some quarters, of hard sf and space opera must, of course, be connected with the sudden appetite the reading public has shown for nonfiction books by authors like Fred HOYLE, Fritjof Capra, Heinz R. Pagels, Stephen Hawking, Freeman DYSON and Paul DAVIES: books about the most far-reaching speculations of contemporary theoretical physics. It was in such popularizations that, for example, most of us first learned about BLACK HOLES, a theme that rapidly became an irresistible magnet for writers of metaphysical hard sf.

There is no traditional crux in metaphysics that is not amply reflected in sf, whether it be "What is the nature of mind as opposed to body?" or "Is there purpose in Nature?" Among sf writers of the pre-WWII generation, Olaf STAPLEDON is certainly pre-eminent as a propounder of questions of ultimate meaning: he confronted all the great metaphysical questions one after the other. But GENRE SF, too, has been amply supplied with amateur metaphysicians who have often made up in colour and verve what they may have lacked in rigorous thought; they may not have answered the questions but they certainly persuaded the reader to think about them (◊ SENSE OF WONDER). A.E. VAN VOGT is one such, and Charles L. HARNESS, with his fantastic paradoxes of COSMOLOGY, is another; while even in the early PULP MAGAZINES John TAINE, in *The Time Stream* (1931 *Wonder Stories*; **1946**) and elsewhere, flung himself headlong and daringly (and quite unselfconsciously) into questions of ultimate meaning. Later, and initially only in garish pulp paperback format, Barrington J. BAYLEY did the same. Sf may derive its muscle and sinew from science and sociology, but much of the time its heartbeat derives from the drama of metaphysics, a drama that seems primarily intellectual, but has an enormous capacity to touch the feelings too.   [PN]

METCALF, NORM Working name of US fan bibliographer Norman Metcalf (1937-   ), whose *The Index of Science Fiction Magazines 1951-1965* (**1968**) is a sequel to *Index to the Science Fiction Magazines 1926-1950* (**1952**) by Donald B. DAY, and covers the same ground as the computerized index for the same years ed Erwin S. STRAUSS (though without the latter's issue-by-issue contents listing). One or other of these works is essential to the serious sf researcher.   [PN]
See also: BIBLIOGRAPHIES.

METROPOLIS Film (1926). UFA. Dir Fritz LANG, starring Brigitte Helm, Alfred Abel, Gustav Frohlich, Rudolf Klein-Rogge, Heinrich George, Fritz Rasp.

Screenplay Lang, Thea VON HARBOU. Original version about 3 hours (17 reels); 1927 UK release print 128 mins (12 reels); 1927 US Paramount release print 75 mins (7 reels); Munich Film Museum reconstruction about 2½ hours; 1984 US reconstruction and adaptation by Giorgio Moroder 83 mins. B/w.

Set in a vast city of the future whose society is divided into downtrodden workers and a ruling elite, M focuses on Freder (Froehlich), who falls in love with Maria (Helm), saintly protector of the workers' children and informal spiritual leader to the masses. But Freder's jealous father Fredersen (Abel), the industrialist master of the city, has a ROBOT duplicate of Maria built for him by malign SCIENTIST Rotwang (Klein-Rogge), which he uses to incite the workers to self-destructive revolt (for reasons which are never entirely made clear). The damage to the city's machinery caused by the rioting floods the lower levels, threatening the lives of the children, but they are saved by the real Maria. The film ends with the city's ruler being persuaded to shake hands with the workers' spokesman and promising that things will be better from now on.

Though often described as the first sf epic of the CINEMA, this famous German film – of which no complete version now exists – has just as much in common with the cinema of the GOTHIC. Though set in a future visually emphasized by towering buildings and vast, brooding MACHINES, the CITY of Metropolis has an underworld dark and medieval in atmosphere. One might almost say that the film's metaphor is to keep the very spectacular sf for the elite above, while the Gothic grub gnaws at the city's roots. The bridging figure is Rotwang, both scientist and sorcerer, one hand clean, the other deformed and gloved, accomplishing gleaming miracles of science while living in a bizarre house with a pentagram inscribed over the door. The story of M is trite and its politics ludicrously simplistic; but these flaws cannot detract from the sheer visual power of the film – a combination of the high Expressionistic sets (the work of art directors Otto Hunte, Erich Kettelhut and Karl Vollbrecht) and Lang's direction, particularly in the sequences involving the vast crowds which he uses as a kind of living clay with which to create giant fluid sculptures. Individual images, as when the apparently living Maria is burned to reveal the gleaming robot beneath, have been so well remembered as now to seem archetypes, alive still in the consciousness of filmgoers everywhere.

M, which was extremely expensive and not a financial success, almost bankrupted the studio that made it (UFA). The film was cut almost as soon as it was released, and – still in the 1920s – shortened yet more radically in the UK and the USA. Even recently restored archival versions are half an hour shorter than the original.

The 1984 US adaptation by Italian composer and producer Giorgio Moroder can be seen as a successful homage, the new tinted print cleverly recut to match the fierce rock MUSIC to which Moroder sets it. But the editing, for all its meticulousness, makes of M something rather different from Lang's (presumptive) version; now the love story is central, and the hesitant Freder appears much more decisive, while much of the obliqueness and some of the ambiguity is gone. Yet M is still a very strong film indeed, vividly renewed for a new generation.

The novelization is *Metropolis* * (**1926**; trans 1927) by von Harbou. [JB/PN]

See also: COMICS; GERMANY.

MEXICO ◊ LATIN AMERICA.

MEYER, NICHOLAS [r] ◊ *The* DAY AFTER; Sir Arthur Conan DOYLE; INVASION OF THE BEE GIRLS; *The* NIGHT THAT PANICKED AMERICA; STAR TREK II: THE WRATH OF KHAN; STAR TREK IV: THE VOYAGE HOME; STAR TREK VI: THE UNDISCOVERED COUNTRY; TIME AFTER TIME. [PN]

MEYERS, RIC ◊ Richard S. MEYERS.

MEYERS, RICHARD S. (1953-　) US writer who publishes also as Wade Barker. His sf novels are of relatively little interest, though the **Doomstar** sequence – *Doom Star* (**1978**; rev vt *Doomstar* 1985) and *Doom Star 2* (**1979**; rev vt *Return to Doomstar* 1985) – are moderately entertaining sf adventures. Of more interest are his nonfiction film studies, including *The World of Fantasy Films* (**1980**), *For One Week Only: The World of Exploitation Films* (**1983**) and *S-F 2: A Pictorial History of Science Fiction Films from "Rollerball" to "Return of the Jedi"* (**1984**; vt *The Great Science Fiction Films from "Rollerball" to "Return of the Jedi"* 1990). [JC]

Other works: *Cry of the Beast* * (**1979**), an INCREDIBLE HULK tie; *Dzurlord: A Crossroads Adventure in the World of Steven Brust's Jhereg* * (**1987**), anon with 6 other writers; the **Book of the Undead** horror sequence, as by Ric Meyers, comprising *Fear Itself* (**1991**), *Living Hell* (**1991**) and *Worst Nightmare* (**1992**).

As Wade Barker: *Serpent's Eye: The Year of the Ninja Master: Autumn* * (**1985**) and *The Shibo Discipline* * (**1988**), both contributions to the **Ninja Master** sequence.

MEYERS, ROY (LETHBRIDGE) (1910-1974) UK physician and writer whose first sf novel, *The Man They Couldn't Kill* (**1944**), introduces the vastly talented Dr D'eath, who is capable of inducing hypnotic trances at a distance and of scientifically arranging for souls to take out-of-body excursions. Falsely convicted of a murder, D'eath clears his name and might have starred in a sequence of **Doc Savage**-like adventures had the book been successful. RM is best known for the later **Dolphin** series about the relationship between dolphins and humans: *Dolphin Boy* (**1967** US; vt *Dolphin Rider* 1968 UK), *Daughters of the Dolphin* (**1968** US) and *Destiny and the Dolphins* (**1969** US). RM's style is wooden, but his interest in dolphins is obviously profound, and the novels are easy reading, though their mixture of melodrama and didacticism may not be to everyone's taste. [JC]

Other work: *Gift of the Manti* (**1977** Canada) with J.F. BONE (RM's name is here spelled Myers, almost certainly in error).

See also: UNDER THE SEA.

MEYERS, WALTER E(ARL) (1939-   ) US academic based at North Carolina State University in Raleigh. A grammarian and medievalist, WEM has also been teaching sf and fantasy since the 1970s (currently with John KESSEL). His first book of genre interest, *Aliens and Linguists: Language Study and Science Fiction* (**1980**), is an excellent and amusing work on LINGUISTICS in sf; the argument is updated in "The Language and Languages of Science Fiction" in *Fictional Space: Essays on Contemporary Science Fiction* (anth **1991**) ed Tom SHIPPEY. WEM has published other essays on sf in a number of critical anthologies, and has written several books in his other specialities.   [PN]

MEYN, NIELS [r] ◊ DENMARK.

MEYRINK, GUSTAV (1868-1932) Austrian novelist, long resident in Prague, a city whose depiction in his novels prefigures Franz KAFKA's. Of his broodingly Expressionist work, much of which deals with the mechanics of occultism, genre interest attaches to *Der Golem* (**1914**; cut trans Madge Pemberton as *The Golem* **1928** US; full version of trans 1976 US), in which a 19th-century protagonist experiences the original myth of the GOLEM; to *Das grüne Gesicht* (**1916**; trans Mike Mitchell as *The Green Face* **1992** UK), an apocalyptic fantasy haunted by the Wandering Jew and culminating in the destruction of Amsterdam; and to *Der Engel vom westlichen Fenster* (**1927**; trans Mike Mitchell as *The Angel of the West Window* **1991** UK), in which a 20th-century figure engages with John Dee (1527-1608), whose Neoplatonic speculations and adventurous life have inspired writers like John CROWLEY.   [JC]

See also: AUSTRIA.

MEZO, FRANCINE (MARIE) (?   -   ) US writer whose **Fall of Worlds** series – *The Fall of Worlds* (**1980**), *Unless She Burn* (**1981**) and *No Earthly Shore* (**1981**) – features a female starship captain who works also as a warrior mercenary in adventures covering a good portion of the Galaxy.   [JC]

MIALL, ROBERT ◊ Jonathan BURKE.

MICHAELS, MELISA C. (?   -   ) US writer who remains best known for her **Skyrider** sequence of sf adventures – *Skirmish* (**1985**), *First Battle* (**1985**), *Last War* (**1986**), *Pirate Prince* (**1987**) and *Floater Factor* (**1987**) – depicting the growth into maturity of its eponymous female starship-pilot protagonist. The tales are at times congested, often parodic, occasionally damaged by cliché, but carry their underlying message about human potential with some grace. *Far Harbor* (**1989**) depicts with sympathy the plight of a planet whose natives are being attacked by humans.   [JC]

Other work: *Through the Eyes of the Dead* (**1988**), a mystery novel, associational.

MICHENER, JAMES A(LBERT) (1907-   ) US author of numerous bestsellers. His long novel *Space* (**1982**), televised 1985, is based on the history of the US space program, becoming sf only in its later stages, when it describes invented missions and adventures

roughly contemporaneous with the historical ones (e.g., a disaster owing to an outburst of solar radiation during an Apollo 18 lunar mission in 1973), and then peers optimistically into the NEAR FUTURE. Among several errors of fact are consistent references to Stanley G. WEINBAUM as Stanley G. Weinberg.   [JGr]

See also: ROCKETS.

MICKIEWICZ, ADAM [r] ◊ POLAND.

MICROCOSM ◊ GREAT AND SMALL.

MIELKE, THOMAS R.P. [r] ◊ GERMANY.

MIESEL, SANDRA (LOUISE) (1941-   ) US critic and writer, with degrees in chemistry and medieval history. Her involvement in sf was initially as a fan; since 1967 she has published over 75 pieces in FANZINES. As a critic she became active in the 1970s, her first book being *Myth, Symbol, and Religion in The Lord of the Rings* (**1973** chap) on J.R.R. TOLKIEN. Her next book, *Against Time's Arrow: The High Crusade of Poul Anderson* (**1979** chap), was her first significant assessment of either Poul ANDERSON or Gordon R. DICKSON, the two figures to whom she has devoted most attention, and of whose work and philosophies she has become a noted advocate. This advocacy, especially perhaps in the case of Dickson's **Dorsai** sequence, has perhaps assumed too readily that the claims for thematic import made for it by its author have been fully realized in the texts as read. Sometimes uncredited, she ed in the mid-1980s several collections assembling short work by these writers, usually selected from early in their careers: Anderson's *Dialogue with Darkness* (coll **1985**) uncredited and Dickson's *Survival!* (coll **1984**) uncredited, *Forward!* (coll **1985**), *Invaders!* (coll **1985**), *The Last Dream* (coll **1986**) uncredited, and *Mindspan* (coll **1986**). With David A. DRAKE she ed *A Separate Star* (anth **1989**) and *Heads to the Storm* (anth **1989**).

As an author of fiction, SM has concentrated mainly on fantasy. *Dreamrider* (**1982**; rev vt *Shaman* 1989), however, mixes genres with some competence, carrying its female protagonist from a NEAR-FUTURE Earth to an ALTERNATE WORLD in which mental control (◊ PSI POWERS) over subatomic processes is exercised by shamans; the protagonist soon becomes one.   [JC]

MIGHTY JOE YOUNG (vt *Mr Joseph Young of Africa*) Film (1949). Argosy/RKO. Dir Ernest B. Schoedsack, starring Terry Moore, Ben Johnson, Robert Armstrong. Screenplay Ruth Rose, from a story by Merian C. Cooper. 94 mins. B/w, with some tinted sequences.

A virtual remake, though on a smaller scale, of KING KONG (1933), by much the same team that produced that classic. The hero organizes a cowboy expedition to Africa to capture animals for his new night-club. Once there they encounter a 12ft (3.7m) gorilla and, after failing to lasso it, discover it is a girl's pet. They persuade her to return with the ape to the USA, where it is exhibited in a nightclub. Finally it goes berserk, but redeems itself by rescuing children from a burning orphanage. Special-effects genius Willis H. O'BRIEN had few successes after *King Kong* but at least *MJY*, on which he supervised the model animation, won him some belated recognition as well as an Academy Award. Also working on the film was the young Ray HARRYHAUSEN. [JB]

MILÁN, VICTOR (WOODWARD) (1954-) US writer who has written under his own name and, it is understood, under more than just his one acknowledged pseudonym, Richard Austin. He began publishing sf with "Soldatenmangel" for *Dragons of Darkness* (anth **1981**) ed Orson Scott CARD. His first books were in the **War of Powers** sequence of fantasies with Robert E. VARDEMAN (*whom see for titles*) from 1984, but the next year he started publishing in his own right with *The Cybernetic Samurai* (**1985**); it and its sequel, *The Cybernetic Shogun* (**1990**), comprise the complicatedly and intriguingly told story of the embodiment and education of an AI given the bodily form of a samurai, and the subsequent warfare, which severely damages the entire world, between its/his two "children". *Runespear* (**1987**) with Melinda M. SNODGRASS is a fantasy set in 1936 in which the Nazi rulers of Germany attempt to gain the eponymous spear and thus become invincible. As Richard Austin, VM has been responsible for the **Guardians** sequence of post-HOLOCAUST military-sf adventures: *The Guardians* (**1985**), *#2: Trial by Fire* (**1985**), *#3: Thunder of Hell* (**1985**), *#4: Night of the Phoenix* (**1985**), *#5: Armageddon Run* (**1986**), *#6: War Zone* (**1986**), *#7: Brute Force* (**1986**), *#8: Desolation Road* (**1987**), *#9: Vengeance Day* (**1987**), *#10: Freedom Fight* (**1988**), *#11: Valley of the Gods* (**1988**), *#12: The Plague Years* (**1988**), *#13: Devil's Deal* (**1989**), *#14: Death from Above* (**1989**), *#15: Snake Eyes* (**1990**) and *#16: Death Charge* (**1991**). Fuller exploration of VM's career awaits a better sense of its range and possible depths. [JC]

See also: CYBERNETICS; LIBERTARIAN SF.

MILES ◊ Neil BELL.

MILES, KEITH ◊ Robert S. TRALINS.

MILFORD SCIENCE FICTION WRITERS' CONFERENCE Annual writers' workshop founded in 1956, held at Milford, Pennsylvania, where several sf writers – including one of its founders, Damon KNIGHT – have lived at various times. (A writers' workshop – see also CLARION SCIENCE FICTION WRITERS' WORKSHOP – includes sessions of mutual criticism of not yet published stories, interspersed with discussion groups on various professional problems.) The success of MSFWC, especially the camaraderie it inspired, was directly responsible for the setting up of the SCIENCE FICTION WRITERS OF AMERICA. Robert SILVERBERG, Harlan ELLISON, Kate WILHELM, Terry CARR and Samuel R. DELANY are among the many who were at some period regular Milford attenders. Ideally, the workshop (open only to published sf writers) had a balance between beginner writers and more experienced professionals. It was felt by some critics that Milford attenders constituted a powerful in-group in sf (particularly since editors of important anthology series attended) and that they received preferential treatment by publishers; hence the nickname "Milford Mafia". Founder member James BLISH and

his wife, J.A. LAWRENCE, moved to the UK, where they set up a UK Milford in 1972, coincidentally the year in which the US Milford was officially pronounced dead. This was held until 1988, out of terminological nostalgia, at Milford-on-Sea in Hampshire each autumn; thereafter it was held at Cheltenham (1989-90) and Margate (1991 onwards). Richard COWPER and Christopher PRIEST were two regular early attenders; more recent regulars have included Mary GENTLE, Colin GREENLAND and Diana Wynne JONES. [PN]

MILHAUS, MICHAEL F.X. ◊ David F. BISCHOFF.

MILLARD, JOSEPH (JOHN) (1908-) US writer in several genres who began publishing sf with "The Crystal Invaders" for *TWS* in 1941, and was active in the field for a few years, a period which included the magazine release of his only novel, *The Gods Hate Kansas* (1941 *Startling Stories*; rev **1964**), a routine adventure involving manipulation of humans by aliens. It was filmed, dreadfully, as *They Came from Beyond Space* (1967). [JC]

See also: INVASION.

MILLENNIUM Film (1989). First Millennium Partnership/Gladden Entertainment. Dir Michael Anderson, starring Kris Kristofferson, Cheryl Ladd, Daniel J. Travanti. Screenplay John VARLEY, based on his "Air Raid" (1977). 105 mins. Colour.

Commando teams from the future steal people from planes just before they crash, but an investigator becomes suspicious. He is seduced by a woman timetraveller, follows her to a chaotic future (represented by a single set) that is about to collapse in a timequake caused by careless TIME PARADOXES in its past. They escape to a further future. Nowhere is the reason for the kidnapping explained. Kristofferson acts like a sleepwalker. There is a manipulative ROBOT that looks like the Tin Man from *The Wizard of Oz* (1939). Michael Anderson's essays in genre directing, including LOGAN'S RUN and DOC SAVAGE: THE MAN OF BRONZE, have been uniformly wooden.

Curiously, only Varley's short story is credited as the basis for his screenplay, even though he had turned it into a novel, *Millennium* (**1983**), which explains the points this botched film leaves obscure; one can only suppose that his screenplay was cut to ribbons. [PN]

MILLER, BENJAMIN [s] ◊ Noel LOOMIS.

MILLER, CHUCK Working name of US publisher and anthologist Charles Franklin Miller II (1952-). For his publishing activities ◊ UNDERWOOD-MILLER INC.; for his anthologies ◊ Tim UNDERWOOD. [JC]

MILLER, FRANK (1957-) US COMIC-book writer and artist, with a distinctive fragmented narrative technique; also film scriptwriter. During 1979-85 FM worked on MARVEL COMICS's **Daredevil**, producing work that was later re-released in three collections: *Child's Play* (graph coll **1988**), *Marked for Death* (graph coll **1990**) and *Gang War* (graph coll **1992**). He then produced two apocalyptic dramas for DC COMICS: *Ronin* (1983-4; graph coll **1987**) and *Batman: The Dark*

Knight Returns (1985-6; graph coll **1986**). All of this work brought a new integrity to the gritty, toughly narrated drama in comics, and paved the way among prospective publishers for other hopeful writer/artists. Further work from this period included *Elektra Saga* (1984; graph coll **1989**) and, written by Chris CLAREMONT, *Wolverine* (1982; graph coll **1987**).

Following the phenomenal success of *The Dark Knight Returns* – nominated for a 1987 HUGO in, absurdly, the Best Non-Fiction Book category, coming second – FM has collaborated with other comics artists including: David Mazzuchelli on *Daredevil: Born Again* (1985; graph coll **1987**) and *Batman: Year One* (1987; graph coll **1988**); Bill SIENKIEWICZ on *Elektra Assassin* (1986-7; graph coll **1987**) and *Daredevil: Love and War* (graph **1986**); Dave GIBBONS on *Give Me Liberty* (1990-91; graph coll **1991**); and Geoff Darrow on *Hard Boiled* (1990-92). FM's other work includes *Elektra Lives Again* (graph **1990**) and *Sin City* (1991-2) in *Dark Horse Presents*, as well as a collaboration with Walter Simonson on a series tied to the **Terminator** films ($\lozenge$ *The* TERMINATOR; TERMINATOR 2: JUDGMENT DAY). FM has also collaborated on the screenplays for ROBOCOP 2 (1990) and the projected *RoboCop 3*, the former being based on his original story. [SW]

See also: GRAPHIC NOVEL; ILLUSTRATION; SUPERHEROES; SUPERMAN [character].

MILLER, GEORGE (1948-   ) Australian film-maker. After a satirical short film, *A History of Violence in the Cinema, Part One* (1975), GM made an international impact with MAD MAX (1979), a NEAR-FUTURE cop/vigilante car-chase movie that introduced Mel Gibson to stardom as a leather-clad highway patrolman in an anarchic post-HOLOCAUST Australia. It success was great enough to fund a more elaborate, more effective sequel, MAD MAX 2 (1981, vt *The Road Warrior*). Influential enough to generate an infestation of Italian and Filippino imitations, including *I nuovi barbari* (1983; vt *The New Barbarians*; vt *Warriors of the Wasteland*) and *Stryker* (1983), *Mad Max 2* led to a sequel of its own, which GM codirected with George Ogilvie: MAD MAX BEYOND THUNDERDOME (1985). This was a more expensive, less gritty retread of the earlier film, with themes imported from Russell HOBAN's *Riddley Walker* (**1980**). GM's only feature film since the **Mad Max** trilogy has been *The Witches of Eastwick* (1987), a successful adaptation of John UPDIKE's 1984 novel, although he remade Richard MATHESON's TWILIGHT ZONE episode "Nightmare at 20,000 Feet" as a segment of *Twilight Zone: The Movie* (1983) and produced Philip Noyce's thriller *Dead Calm* (1988). GM should not be confused with the other Australian director of the same name, who made *The Man from Snowy River* (1982) and *The Neverending Story: Part 2* (1990). [KN]

See also: MUSIC.

MILLER, IAN (1946-   ) UK illustrator. After graduating from St Martin's College of Art, IM became a commercial illustrator in 1970, with both book-cover work and interior ILLUSTRATIONS, some of the latter in David Day's *The Tolkien Bestiary* (**1979**). Books of his work are *Green Dog Trumpet and Other Stories* (graph coll **1978**) – the stories being in the form of pictures without accompanying text – *Secret Art* (**1980**) and, more recently, *Ratspike* (**1990**) with John Blanche. *The Luck in the Head* (graph **1991**) with M. John HARRISON is a GRAPHIC NOVEL with text adapted by Harrison from his 1983 short story of the same name. IM appears in *The Guide to Fantasy Art Techniques* (**1984**) ed Martyn Dean. Though he has worked in a commercial vein, he is also known for fanciful work at the opposite pole from the airbrushed superrealism that has dominated UK sf/fantasy art for two decades: two of his gloomier modes involve, respectively, detailed fine-lined GOTHIC black-and-white work in ink, almost STEAMPUNK in style, and semi-abstracted deliquescing faces; in *Ratspike* he classed these as "tight pen" and "asylum images" respectively. IM was art editor for INTERZONE 1983-5. He is a gallery artist as well as an illustrator, his first exhibition having been in 1973. [PN/JC]

See also: BRITISH SCIENCE FICTION AWARD; GAMES WORKSHOP.

MILLER, JIMMY (?   -   ) US writer whose *The Big Win* (**1969**) is a noisy but sometimes effective post-HOLOCAUST quest story which moves eventually into space, as the protagonists search for the Chinese war criminal whose plague has decimated the rest of the world. Though not essentially an sf novel, her *Some Parts in the Single Life* (**1970**) moves into a shattering NEAR FUTURE at its close. JM was married to Warren MILLER. [JC]

MILLER, MIRANDA (1950-   ) UK writer whose early work, like *Under the Rainbow* (**1978**), was published as by Miranda Hyman. Her sf DYSTOPIA, *Smiles and the Millennium* (**1987**) as MM, depicts a fiercely uncongenial NEAR-FUTURE UK where class differences have hardened, the poor are downtrodden, and the Isle of Man has seceded. [JC]

MILLER, P(ETER) SCHUYLER (1912-1974) US writer and critic; an MSc in chemistry, he did research for a time and for most of his career worked as a technical writer. He remains best known in the sf world for his book reviews in ASTOUNDING SCIENCE-FICTION, which first appeared in 1945 and became a regular monthly feature in Oct 1951, continuing until his death. He was not a particularly demanding critic, but his judgements were generally shrewd, his enthusiasm never waned, and his column's coverage was remarkably comprehensive. Largely as a by-product, he accumulated one of the largest private sf COLLECTIONS; the annotated *Catalogue of the Fantasy and Science Fiction Library of the Late P. Schuyler Miller* (**1977**) was a useful bibliographical aid. In 1963 he was presented with a special HUGO for his reviewing.

However, he began as an author of fiction, being one of the more popular and accomplished sf pulp writers of the 1930s; his first story was "The Red Plague" for *Wonder Stories* in 1930. He collaborated with Paul McDermott and Walter Dennis on two connected stories, "Red Spot on Jupiter" (1931) and "Duel on the Asteroid" (1932), the first under the pseudonym Dennis McDermott, the second as by PSM and Dennis McDermott. *Alicia in Blunderland* (1933 *Science Fiction Digest* as by Nihil; coll of linked stories **1983**) presents a sequence of spoof tales with RECURSIVE-SF elements, several figures from early FANDOM being represented. Later stories of note included a TIME-PARADOX variant, "As Never Was" (1944), and "The Titan" (1934-5), a story whose (mild) sexual content made it unacceptable to the pulp magazines; MARVEL TALES, which published it, ceased publication before the last instalment, and the story was not printed entire until *The Titan* (coll **1952**), which assembles most of PSM's better fiction. He also collaborated with L. Sprague DE CAMP on *Genus Homo* (1941 *Super Science Stories*; rev **1950**), a novel set in the FAR FUTURE and filled with satirical evolutionary marvels, for apes have taken over. [MJE]

About the author: *A Canticle for P. Schuyler Miller* (**1975** chap) by Sam MOSKOWITZ.

See also: ALIENS; EVOLUTION; INVASION; MARS.

MILLER, R(ICHARD) DEWITT (1910-1958) US writer who was involved in promulgating ideas about Fortean phenomena (◊ Charles FORT), and who began publishing sf with "The Shapes" for *ASF* in 1936. In addition to some works of Fortean nonfiction, such as *You Do Take it with You* (**1956**), he published an sf novel, *The Man who Lived Forever* (1938 *ASF* as "The Master Shall not Die" as by RDM alone; rev **1956** dos; vt *Year 3097* 1958 UK) with Anna Hunger, about an immortal who struggles to keep mankind's technology from running amuck. *The Loose Board in the Floor* (**1951**) is a fantasy about stuffed animals going on a trip. [JC]

MILLER, RICHARD (CONNELLY) (1925-) US writer whose *Snail* (**1984**) is a satirical TIME-TRAVEL tale in which the Wandering Jew and a Prussian soldier traverse a late-20th-century USA, viewing with dismay the New Age trash – both psychic and physical – which chokes the land, and *en route* meeting Kilgore Trout (◊ Kurt VONNEGUT Jr). *Squed* (**1989** UK) and its sequel *Sowboy* (**1991** UK) are sf FABULATIONS. [JC]

MILLER, STEVE (1950-) US writer who began publishing sf with 3 novels set in the same SPACE-OPERA galaxy, all in collaboration with Sharon Lee. *Agent of Change* (**1988**) and *Carpe Diem* (**1989**) are closely linked adventure tales featuring an interstellar agent on the loose; the heroine of *Conflict of Honors* (**1988**) is a starship crewperson who undergoes various travails in her quest to become a pilot. [JC]

MILLER, WALTER M(ICHAEL) (1922-) US writer. WMM flew combat missions in WWII and was converted to Catholicism in 1947; he began publishing sf with "Secret of the Death Dome" in *AMZ* in 1951, and over the 10 years of his active writing career released about 40 more tales, many of which had a deep impact upon the field. During the 1950s, a time when US sf tended to express its new-found interest in character through stories whose rigid formulae were derived from sentimental fiction and which tended to read as simplistic moralities, WMM published in *Gal*, *FSF*, *ASF* and elsewhere tales whose treatment of character was effortlessly complex; moreover, through his preoccupation with RELIGION, he transfigured conventional sf themes and instruments – progress, GENETIC ENGINEERING, BIOLOGY in general – by treating them with a rich ambivalence.

Perhaps the best example is "The Darfsteller" (1955), which won a HUGO as Best Novelette in 1955. The sf premise seems simple: a computer-like machine that controls a THEATRE of life-sized mannequins has displaced human actors. The darfsteller, an unemployed Method actor, has been working as a janitor in a theatre, and sabotages one of the mannequin-tapes so that he can replace it on stage. At this point the typical sf story of "character" might well give him his comeuppance and the tale would end. But WMM is just beginning; the rigged performance becomes an essay in acting and, through its presentation of Christ's Passion, a continually deepening examination of the actor's complex, emblem-haunted nature. The story appears in *Conditionally Human* (coll **1962**); WMM's other collection of shorter items was *The View from the Stars* (coll **1965**). *The Science Fiction of Walter M. Miller, Jr.* (coll **1978**) and *The Best of Walter M. Miller, Jr.* (coll **1980**) amply convey a sense of his finest work in short form.

But WMM remains best known for his single novel, *A Canticle for Leibowitz* (1955-7 *FSF*; fixup **1960**), which, along with James BLISH's *A Case of Conscience* (1953 *If*; exp **1958**), stands as one of the very few attempts in US sf to deal with formal religion. The first part of this 3-part work is set in a Dark Ages 600 years after a 20th-century nuclear HOLOCAUST, when the survival of the human race remains a moot question. The Catholic Order of Leibowitz – named after a 20th-century physicist who created the Order and bestowed upon it the task of preserving knowledge during the period of violent nescience that followed the holocaust – has come into some holy relics relevant to Leibowitz's canonization, and their survival becomes emblematic of humanity's. In the second part, half a millennium later, the Order is confronted with the rise once again of the scientific mentality, with all its benefits and risks. In the third part, a further half-millennium later, the Order has lost prestige and power in a new industrial-scientific age, but prepares a spaceship to escape the inevitable second holocaust, thus hoping to shorten the period of darkness that will ensue. The novel is full of subtly presented detail about the nature of religious vocation and the way of life of an isolated community, deals ably with the questions of the nature of historical and scientific knowledge which it raises, and poses and intriguingly answers ethical questions about mankind's proper relation to God and the world; though the vagrant entry of the Wandering Jew into the text is perhaps a little contrived, that is a small flaw in a seminal work. While *A Canticle for*

Liebowitz can be read as a work of Christian apologetics, WMM (like Gene WOLFE after him) clearly responds mythopoeically to the holy story – and to the institutions – of his Church, with effects both ambiguous and ironic. At the same time, however, his central commitment (like Wolfe's) is unwavering, and the cyclical pattern of the tale reads as anything but defeatist – for the moment of Christ's Coming is not a matter of dead history. The 1961 Hugo for the book was richly deserved. A sequel is projected for publication in the early 1990s. [JC]

Other works: *Beyond Armageddon: Survivors of the Megawar* (anth **1985**) ed with Harry Martin GREENBERG.

See also: AMAZING STORIES; ANTI-INTELLECTUALISM IN SF; ARTS; AUTOMATION; COLONIZATION OF OTHER WORLDS; ESP; HISTORY IN SF; *The* MAGAZINE OF FANTASY AND SCIENCE FICTION; MEDICINE; MUTANTS; ROBOTS; SOCIOLOGY; SPACE FLIGHT; SUPERNATURAL CREATURES.

MILLER, WARREN (1921-1966) US writer, best known for his first **Harlem** novel, *The Cool World* (**1959**). *Looking for the General* (**1964**) is a combination of FABULATION and quest, and some of its devices belong to sf. WM's sf novel proper, *The Siege of Harlem* (**1964**), is a NEAR-FUTURE tale in which Harlem, New York, declares itself a separate state. WM was married to Jimmy MILLER. [JC]

See also: POLITICS.

MILLIGAN, SPIKE Working name of Indian-born Irish writer and comic Terence Alan Milligan (1918-   ), who first became famous for his central role as the author and one of the stars of the long series of **Goon Show** programmes on BBC Radio in the 1950s. Many of his books, beginning with his first, *Silly Verse for Kids* (coll **1959** chap), have fantasy content, as do his two novels, *Puckoon* (**1963**) and *The Looney: An Irish Fantasy* (**1987**). He is of direct sf interest for a play, *The Bedsitting Room* (**1970**) with John Antrobus (1933-   ), which initially treats a nuclear HOLOCAUST in terms of surreal spoof, though by the final act the few survivors are engaging in cannibalism. The original play was filmed as *The* BED-SITTING ROOM in 1969. [JC]

MILLS, C.J. (?   -   ) US writer known only for her/his **Winter World** sequence – *Winter World* (**1988**), *Winter World #2: Egil's Book* (**1991**), *#3: Kit's Book* (**1991**) and *#4: Brander's Book* (**1992**) – featuring various adventures on a strife-beset frozen world. [JC]

MILLS, ROBERT E. (?   -   ) US author who began writing sf with the **Star Quest Trilogy** of adventure tales: *Star Quest* (**1978**), *Star Fighters* (**1978**) and *Star Force* (**1978**). *Under the Eyes of Night* (**1980**) is a novel of the occult. [JC]

MILLS, ROBERT P(ARK) (1920-1986) US editor and literary agent, managing editor of *The* MAGAZINE OF FANTASY AND SCIENCE FICTION from its inception; he assumed the editorship proper with the Sep 1958 issue, following Anthony BOUCHER's resignation, remaining editor until Mar 1962 and continuing thereafter as consulting editor until Feb 1963. During his tenure *FSF* maintained its standing as the most sophisticated sf magazine and won HUGOS in

1959, 1960 and 1963. RPM edited several *FSF* anthologies, including *The Best from Fantasy and Science Fiction: Ninth Series* (anth **1960**; cut vt *Flowers for Algernon and Other Stories* 1960), *Tenth Series* (anth **1961**) and *Eleventh Series* (anth **1962**), as well as *A Decade of Fantasy and Science Fiction* (anth **1960**) and *Twenty Years of the Magazine of Fantasy and Science Fiction* (anth **1970**), the latter with Edward L. FERMAN. RPM was also editor of VENTURE SCIENCE FICTION during its first incarnation (1957-8), when the magazine was renowned for its "daring" approach to sexual topics. He also edited *The Worlds of Science Fiction* (anth **1963**).

After leaving *FSF* RPM became a literary agent, operating as Robert P. Mills Ltd, and during the 1960s and early 1970s served a prestigious list of clients. He sold the agency to Richard A. CURTIS in 1984. [MJE]

MILLS-MALET, VINCENT (?   -?   ) UK writer in whose sf novel, *The Meteoric Benson: A Romance of Actuality* (**1912**), the inventor of an aerostat (or helicopter) uses it to frighten the Germans and subsequently the entire world into peace, and gains the hand of the peer's daughter he loves. [JC]

MILNE, ROBERT DUNCAN (GORDON) (1844-1899) Scottish-born journalist and writer, in the USA from about 1864, who published at least 60 sf stories of very considerable conceptual ingenuity, prefiguring many of the themes of the modern genre. Beginning with "A Modern Robe of Nessus" in 1879, he published most of these tales in the San Francisco journal *The Argonaut*, one of whose editors, Ambrose BIERCE, was strongly influenced by his work. Forgotten for many decades after his death, RDM was rediscovered by Sam MOSKOWITZ, who in *Science Fiction in Old San Francisco, Volume 1: History of the Movement from 1854 to 1890* (**1980**) forcefully argued the case for treating him as an important figure, and who assembled some of RDM's tales in a companion volume, *Into the Sun and Other Stories* (coll **1980**). Typical of RDM's vigorous creative mind are "Into the Sun" (1882) and its sequel, "Plucked from the Burning" (1882), which together describe a world-cataclysm caused by a comet, detail the protagonist's escape in a BALLOON from the effects of impact, follow him first to Tibet and then back to a devastated world full of apocalyptic scenes, and end in the creation of a new and better society based on the political thought of Jean-Jacques Rousseau (1712-1778). Throughout his work – the rest of which remains uncollected – can be perceived the workings of a mind for whom science and technology granted far more to the imaginative mind when their rules were obeyed, or at least understood. RDM was one of the first genuinely extrapolative thinkers to work in the field. [JC]

See also: MATTER TRANSMISSION.

MIND OF MR SOAMES, THE Film (1969). Amicus. Dir Alan Cooke, starring Terence Stamp, Robert Vaughn, Nigel Davenport. Screenplay John Hale, Edward Simpson, from *The Mind of Mr Soames* (**1961**)

by Charles Eric MAINE. 98 mins. Colour.

Soames (Stamp) has been in a coma since birth and is now 30 years old. A neurosurgeon (Vaughn) brings him to consciousness with a brain operation. Now a sexually mature man, his brain is a blank slate for life to write on. Stamp's performance as the innocent who escapes his teachers too soon, and who turns violent when society treats him violently, is touching; through the pulp clichés a genuine thoughtfulness about the nature of education and learning is dimly apparent. In its theme this small-scale, rather solemn UK film resembles CHARLY (1968). [PN]

MINDWARP: AN INFINITY OF TERROR ◊ Roger CORMAN.

MINES, SAMUEL (1909-   ) US editor who worked from 1942 for Standard Magazines, the chain that published STARTLING STORIES and THRILLING WONDER STORIES. Although an sf enthusiast – he published 4 stories in TWS, beginning with "Find the Sculptor" in 1946 – he concentrated mainly on non-sf pulps until Sam MERWIN left the company in 1951, whereupon he took over the editorship of *Startling Stories* (Nov 1951-Fall 1954), *TWS* (Dec 1951-Summer 1954), FANTASTIC STORY QUARTERLY (Winter 1952-Fall 1954) and WONDER STORY ANNUAL (1952-3); he also edited all issues of the short-lived SPACE STORIES. Although he took control of the magazines at a time when the PULP-MAGAZINE industry was generally in decline, and the sf pulps in particular were suffering from the powerful competition of such new magazines as GALAXY SCIENCE FICTION and The MAGAZINE OF FANTASY AND SCIENCE FICTION, SM was generally successful in maintaining the standard to which Merwin had raised them. He ed *The Best from Startling Stories* (anth **1953**; vt *Startling Stories* 1954 UK; vt *Moment without Time* 1956 UK); the book contained stories from *TWS* as well. SM left Standard in 1954; the various magazines did not survive him long. He held no further editorial positions in sf, although he did review books occasionally for LUNA MONTHLY. [MJE]

MINKOV, SVETOSLAV (1902-1966) Bulgarian writer and man of letters, active from 1920 (*for contextual comments on his earliest work* ◊ BULGARIA). The sf tales and FABULATIONS assembled in *The Lady with the X-Ray Eyes* (coll trans Krassimira Noneva **1965** Bulgaria), which brings together work originally published 1928-65, are sharp, occasionally didactic, and expose a sometimes insistent irony. This text is not a translation of a 1934 Bulgarian collection with the same title. [JC]

MINTO, WILLIAM (1845-1893) UK writer whose sf novel, *The Crack of Doom* (**1886**), portentously invokes the threatened arrival of a dangerous comet to influence, intermittently, an entirely prosaic plot. [JC]

See also: END OF THE WORLD.

MIRACLEMAN ◊ CAPTAIN MARVEL; Neil GAIMAN; Alan MOORE.

MIRACLE SCIENCE AND FANTASY STORIES US PULP MAGAZINE. 2 issues, Apr/May and June/July 1931,

published by Good Story Magazine Co., ed Douglas M. DOLD. *MSFS*'s publisher was Harold HERSEY, previously editor of THRILL BOOK, while Douglas Dold was consulting editor of *Astounding Stories* (◊ ASTOUNDING SCIENCE-FICTION) 1930-31. The magazine featured undistinguished pulp fiction by both Douglas and Elliott DOLD and by Victor ROUSSEAU. Its cover design, by Elliott, was unusually stylish for its time. Douglas was blind, and a reference by Hersey in *Pulpwood Editor* (**1937**) implies that the editor was in fact Elliott. [MJE/PN]

MIRAGE PRESS US SMALL PRESS publishing primarily fantasy-related material and taking its name from *Mirage*, a successful 1960s FANZINE published by Jack L. CHALKER. Chalker began issuing books under the Mirage logo in 1961, beginning with his own *The New H.P. Lovecraft Bibliography* (**1961** chap) and including *A Figment of a Dream* (**1962** chap) by David H. KELLER. The Mirage Press took on a more formal existence in 1967, with new financing; later publications include *The Conan Reader* (coll **1968**), a collection of essays by L. Sprague DE CAMP drawn from the fanzine AMRA (the dustjacket artwork was Berni Wrightson's first professional sale). De Camp and George SCITHERS subsequently edited 2 further vols of **Conan**-related SWORD-AND-SORCERY material (◊ Robert E. HOWARD) for Mirage: *The Conan Swordbook* (anth **1969**) and *The Conan Grimoire* (anth **1972**). Other Mirage books include *Dragons and Nightmares* (coll **1969**) by Robert BLOCH, poetry by De Camp, *A Guide to Middle Earth* (**1971**) by Robert Foster, *H.G. Wells: Critic of Progress* (**1973**) by Jack WILLIAMSON, and a variety of sf/fantasy reference books. There were around 20 Mirage books by 1975, at which point the business slowed to a near halt because its financial backer fell ill. Chalker's career as a novelist began at about this point, and MP has since been relatively inactive, though long-held projects – including an edition of *The Harlan Ellison Hornbook* (coll **1990**) slipcased with *Harlan Ellison's Movie* (**1990**), both by Harlan ELLISON, and Chalker's and Mark OWING's *The Science-Fantasy Publishers* (vastly exp 3rd edn **1991**) – eventually appeared. [MJE/JC/PN]

MISHA Working name of US writer Misha Chocholak (?   -   ), of Native American background, who began publishing material of genre interest with *Prayers of Steel* (coll **1989** chap), which assembles some fantasy poems. Her sf novel, *Red Spider White Web* (**1990** UK), employs a congested CYBERPUNK venue (a USA in which sanitized enclaves called "Mickeysans" shelter their lobotomized inhabitants from the excremental waste and POLLUTION outside) to darken the inherently romantic story of a dedicated artist whose intransigent attempts to do her work run afoul of surreally caricatured figures from the corrupted mire. The ending is grim. [JC]

MISSION GALACTICA: THE CYLON ATTACK ◊ BATTLESTAR GALACTICA.

MR JOSEPH YOUNG OF AFRICA ◊ MIGHTY JOE YOUNG.

MISTER X Created by Canadian designers Dean Motter and Paul Rivoche, this cipherlike character – bald and with sunglasses, black overcoat and suitcase – appeared in illustrations and on record-album covers in the late 1970s before plans were made to publish a comic. The *Mister X* comic was promoted with several gorgeously designed posters 1981-3 without in fact appearing. Eventually Rivoche was taken off the strip and the project was handed over to Jaime, Gilbert and Mario Hernandez, the creators of LOVE AND ROCKETS; using Rivoche's designs, they produced *The Return of Mister X* (graph coll **1986**) which first ran in *Mister X* #1-#4 1984-5.

Mr X is not really the star of his own comic. Its main subject and the cause of most of its stories is its location, Radiant City. This CITY was codesigned by Mr X using the dogmas of "Psychetecture", so that its enclosures, shapes and spaces would have resonances in the human psyche. Sadly, someone skimped on the materials during construction, and the result is the nightmare city Somnopolis – a place deliberately reminiscent of Fritz LANG's METROPOLIS.

Since the Hernandez brothers many others have turned their hand to matters Somnopolitan. They include D'Israeli, Shane Oakley, Klaus Schoenfeld, Seth and eventually even Rivoche himself. [SW]

MISTRAL, BENGO ◊ Norman A. LAZENBY.

MISTRESS OF ATLANTIS, THE ◊ *Die* HERRIN VON ATLANTIS.

MITCHELL, ADRIAN (1932-) UK writer, best known for his poetry. His second novel, *The Bodyguard* (**1970**), is the deathbed narrative of a representative figure of a 1980s UK, a paramilitary bodyguard whose reminiscences of his various jobs defending a totalitarian state provide a DYSTOPIAN portrait of the Europe to come. [JC]

See also: POLITICS.

MITCHELL, CLYDE ZIFF-DAVIS house name, 1956-7, used twice by Robert SILVERBERG and Randall GARRETT in collaboration, twice by unidentified writers, and once by Harlan ELLISON on "The Wife Factory" (1957 *Fantastic*). [PN]

MITCHELL, EDWARD PAGE (1852-1927) US newspaperman and writer, associated from 1875 until his death with the New York *Sun*, serving as editor-in-chief 1903-20. EPM's sf, which came from the first decade of his career and most of which first appeared in his own journal, was restricted to about 30 short stories, beginning with "The Tachypomp" (1874), about a sort of humanoid calculator. Their subject matters range widely, from TIME TRAVEL in "The Clock that Went Backward" (1881) to MATTER TRANSMISSION in "The Man without a Body" (1877) and INVISIBILITY in "The Crystal Man" (1881). EPM's work, which in its variety and imaginative power may have influenced H.G. WELLS and others, came to be noticed in the sf field through the publication of *The Crystal Man: Landmark Science Fiction* (coll **1973**), edited and with a long and informative introduction by Sam MOSKOWITZ. [JC]

See also: COMPUTERS.

MITCHELL, J(AMES) LESLIE (1901-1935) Scottish novelist, known mainly for regional novels written as by Lewis Grassic Gibbon, and for *Scottish Scene* (**1934**) with Hugh MacDiarmid (1892-1978). Under his own name he wrote popular archaeology and fiction, much of the latter coloured by fantasy and romantic chinoiserie after the fashion of James Elroy FLECKER. Typical of these are *The Calends of Cairo* (coll of linked stories **1931**; vt *Cairo Dawns* 1931 USA) with a letter in preface by H.G. WELLS, and *Persian Dawns, Egyptian Nights* (coll of 2 linked story sequences **1933**) with a foreword by J.D. BERESFORD. *Three Go Back* (**1932**; bowdlerized 1953 USA) is sf, combining ANTHROPOLOGY, ATLANTIS and TIME TRAVEL themes in a well written though awkwardly plotted story of three 20th-century passengers on an airship cast back in time (by earthquakes!) to Atlantis, where they find unspoiled proto-Basques in an Eden doomed by the nearing Ice Age and by conflicts with savage Neanderthalers, which decimate the tribe; the two surviving castaways then snap back to the present. The book is notable for its realistic and ebullient female protagonist, who adapts far more readily to her strange surroundings than either of the men. Very similarly, the eponymous female protagonist of *Gay Hunter* (**1934**), on being cast into a far-future Britain, adapts with commendable swiftness, stripping naked just as quickly as the heroine of the previous book, but remaining decorously virgin; eventually, espousing healthy athleticism, she helps defeat a fascist attempt to reindustrialize the country. "Kametis and Evelpis", a third tale linked to the previous two by similarities of plot, was left incomplete at JLM's death; John GAWSWORTH revised the manuscript and published the resulting novelette in his *Masterpiece of Thrills* (anth **1936**), along with other posthumous sf and fantasy, as by Lewis Grassic Gibbon. In the nonfiction *Hanno, or The Future of Exploration* (**1928**), JLM committed himself to some humorous thoughts about exploring both space and the centre of the Earth. [JC]

Other work: *The Lost Trumpet* (**1932**).

About the author: "The Science Fiction of John Leslie Mitchell" by Ian Campbell in EXTRAPOLATION, Dec 1974.

See also: ORIGIN OF MAN.

MITCHELL, JOHN A(MES) (1845-1918) US writer in various genres. His sf began with *The Last American: A Fragment from the Journal of Khan-Li, Prince of Dimph-Yoo-Chur and Admiral in the Persian Navy* (**1889**), a satirical post-HOLOCAUST novel in which a 30th-century Persian expedition visits a North America long devastated by climatic changes; it was much influenced by Edgar Allan POE's "Mellonta Tauta" (1849) and curiously prefigures Gene WOLFE's *Seven American Nights* (1978 *Orbit* #20; **1989** chap dos). The racism of the book – the USA falls because of unfettered immigration – is typical of JAM's era. His other well known sf book, *Drowsy* (**1917**), is a sentimental love story involving a telepath who discovers ANTIGRAVITY and visits the Moon and Mars. The book was notable for Angus Peter Macdonnal's fine illustrations, many of them moonscapes, some reproduced in EXTRAPOLATION, May 1971; their relationship to the text is at times exiguous.   [JC]

Other works: *The Romance of the Moon* (**1886** chap), a fantasy for children; *Life's Fairy Tales* (coll **1892**); *Amos Judd* (**1895**); *Gloria Victis* (**1897**; rev vt *Dr Thorne's Idea* 1910); *That First Affair and Other Sketches* (coll **1902**); *The Villa Claudia* (**1904**); *The Silent War* (**1906**).

MITCHELL, KIRK (JOHN) (1950-   ) US writer and former police officer who began writing sf with an ALTERNATE-WORLD trilogy – *Procurator* (**1984**), *New Barbarians* (**1986**) and *Cry Republic* (**1989**) – based on the premise that Rome did not fall and that the world of 2000CE reflects a mixture of Roman modes and richly conceived technologies. KM's best single novel is probably *Never the Twain* (**1987**), a TIME-TRAVEL tale in which a descendant of the US writer Bret Harte (1836-1902) goes back to Civil War Nevada with a copy of Mark TWAIN's *The Adventures of Huckleberry Finn* (**1884** UK) and attempts to persuade Harte to put his name to the tale, and so make his eventual heir rich. The ensuing complications are superficially comic, but an intriguingly human and detailed portrayal of the main characters, and of 19th-century Nevada, slowly emerges.   [JC]

Other works: *Anno Domini* (**1985**); *Lethal Wagon* ∗ (**1987**) as by Joel Norst, a film tie; *Black Dragon* (**1988**).

See also: TIME PARADOXES.

MITCHELL, SILAS WEIR (1829-1914) US physician, neurologist and writer, of considerable eminence for his original research – he published at least 172 papers from 1852 on neurophysiology and related subjects. Most of his voluminous fiction is historical and depicts US subjects with romantic solemnity. His first story, "The Case of George Dedlow" (1866), is of some sf interest, as it is a SATIRE on Spiritualism. In *Dr North and his Friends* (**1900**) a female character exhibits a dual personality; it is one of the earliest appearances of this phenomenon in fiction (◊ PSYCHOLOGY). *Little Stories* (coll **1903**) assembles tales whose sf interest lies in SWM's ability to ground supernatural subject matter with speculations usually derived from his own researches. A further story, "Was He Dead?" (1870), appears in *Future Perfect* (anth **1966**) ed H. Bruce FRANKLIN.   [JC]

MITCHISON, NAOMI (MARGARET) (1897-   ) Scottish novelist, story writer, cattle breeder and polemicist, sister of J.B.S. HALDANE. She is known mainly for her work outside the sf field – her bibliography includes over 100 books and over 1000 shorter pieces – including such historical novels as *The Conquered* (**1923**) and *The Corn King and the Spring Queen* (**1931**; vt *The Barbarian* 1961 US), the latter an ANTHROPOLOGICAL fantasy about Sparta. Some of her earlier stories, such as "The Goat", published in *Barbarian Stories* (coll **1929**), the short novel *The Powers of Light* (**1932** chap) which deals with prehistory, and

many of the tales and fables in *The Fourth Pig* (coll **1936**), use sf or fantasy elements for allegorical purposes. *We Have Been Warned* (**1935**) is a NEAR-FUTURE political novel involving the oppression of the Left in the UK. *Beyond this Limit* (**1935** chap), whose illustrations by Wyndham LEWIS constitute a co-creation of the book, is an afterlife fantasy with some satirical impact. *The Big House* (**1950**) is a fairy tale for children, set within a Celtic frame. *Travel Light* (**1952**) is an historical fantasy. *To the Chapel Perilous* (**1955**) is a witty account of the Grail legend which pits rival anthropological and historical theories together as if, in a sense, they were all true. *Behold Your King* (**1957**) is a novel about Christ's crucifixion, told in a slangy, contemporary idiom to demystify it. *Images of Africa* (coll **1980**) assembles short fantasies told in a folktale idiom. *Early in Orcadia* (**1987**), also fantasy, is set in prehistoric Orkney. Of her 30 or more books for children, many are fantasy. Two late collections, *Beyond this Limit: Selected Shorter Fiction* (coll **1986**), which assembles pre-WWII work, and *A Girl Must Live: Stories and Poems* (coll **1990**), which assembles work from the following half-century, include a considerable amount of sf.

NM's first genuine sf novel was *Memoirs of a Spacewoman* (**1962**), a ruminative picaresque comprising a series of episodes recollected by the narrator, Mary, a COMMUNICATIONS expert dealing with ALIEN intelligences. Most of the episodes contain ingenious biological (or exobiological) speculations. Mary's reminiscences are warm and urgent; her job necessitates interstellar travel, which requires "time black-outs", so that she constantly returns to a changed world. She loves her work, however, and intends to continue; it is a radiant book. *Solution Three* (**1975**) is a less sustained examination of a CLONE solution to the problems of a post-catastrophe Earth. Heterosexuality is out; but a new generation is beginning to question the rigidity of the homosexual Solution Three. *Not by Bread Alone* (**1983**) suggests that the sudden distribution of free food worldwide will create serious problems; the Australian Aborigines wisely refuse the offer.

Though NM's fiction is both copious and fluent, her writing is primarily motivated by extrinsic concerns. Where these concerns are successfully embedded in her stories, she is a writer of glowing power.   [JC]

See also: GENETIC ENGINEERING; INTELLIGENCE; MYTHOLOGY; WOMEN AS PORTRAYED IN SCIENCE FICTION.

MITSUSE, RYU [r] ◊ JAPAN.

MOAV, RAM [r] ◊ ISRAEL.

MODERN ELECTRICS ◊ SCIENCE AND INVENTION.

MODESITT, L(ELAND) E(XTON) Jr (1943-   ) US writer who began publishing sf with *The Fires of Paratime* (**1982**), an eccentric but ambitious TIME-TRAVEL tale, in which emissaries/guardians from the planet Query engage in complex and metaphysical manipulations of reality. *The Hammer of Darkness* (**1985**), also sf, was followed by two series. The **Forever Hero** novels – *Dawn for a Distant Earth* (**1987**),

Silent Warrior (**1987**) and *In Endless Twilight* (**1988**) – treat the profound ecological desecration of Earth through a sequence of SPACE OPERAS whose protagonist, an immortal warrior called MacGregor Gerswin, saves the planet as part of a scheme of sweeping galactic exploits. The **Ecolitan Trilogy** – *The Ecologic Envoy* (**1986**), *The Ecolitan Operation* (**1989**) and *The Ecologic Secession* (**1990**) – deals with similar themes, though ultimate success is here achieved as part of a pattern of political intrigues and battles. *The Magic of Recluce* (**1991**) and *The Towers of the Sunset* (**1992**) are the first 2 vols of the **Recluce** fantasy sequence. *The Green Progression* (**1992**) with Bruce Scott Levinson is a nongenre novel on ecological issues. [JC]

MOEBIUS ◊ Jean GIRAUD.

MOFFAT, W. GRAHAM (1866-?   ) UK writer whose *What's the World Coming To?* (**1893**) with John White takes the form of a series of discussions, set in AD2003, of the various marvels which the 20th century has seen. The tone is satirical; the targets include Edward BELLAMY, fictional clichés such as crime detection by psychic means, and concerns such as FEMINISM. [JC]

MOFFATT, JAMES (1922-   ) Canadian-born UK writer who has written at least 250 novels in several genres under at least 45 pseudonyms, including the Hank JANSON house name (though not in that case for sf) and Richard Allen, a personal pseudonym for the non-sf **Skin** books. In the 1960s he wrote the first chapter of a novel which, when taken over by Michael MOORCOCK according to a practice very common in UK pulp publishing, became *Somewhere in the Night* (**1966**) as by Moorcock. JM's sf novels under his own name – others may exist – are *The Sleeping Bomb* (**1970**; vt *The Cambri Plot* 1973 US), which was the first volume in an otherwise non-sf series starring **Silas Manners**, and *Queen Kong* (**1977**), spoofing KING KONG from a feminist point of view. [JC]

MOFFETT, CLEVELAND LANGSTON (1863-1926) US playwright and popular novelist, author of one of the most explicit EDISONADES to appear in early-20th-century US sf. In *The Conquest of America: A Romance of Disaster and Victory* (**1916**), Thomas Alva Edison (1847-1931) himself saves the USA from decadent socialists while fending off a threat of WAR from Germany. *The Mysterious Card* (fixup **1912**) and *Possessed* (fixup **1920**) are occult fantasies. [JC]

MOFFETT, JUDITH (1942-   ) US writer and academic, a professor with the University of Pennsylvania since 1979. She was first active as a poet, publishing 2 collections – *Keeping Time* (coll **1976**) and *Whinny Moor Crossing* (coll **1984**) – before turning to sf with an ape-as-human tale (◊ APES AND CAVEMEN), "Surviving", for *FSF* in 1986, later assembled with "Not without Honor" (1989) as *Two that Came True* (coll **1991**). With her first novel, *Pennterra* (**1987**), she came into immediate prominence, partly because of the rousing sexual explicitness of some scenes between humans and the pheromone-emitting Hrossa, a mysterious group-mind species named – oddly,

given C.S. LEWIS's prurient distaste for sexual material – after the Martians who feature in *Out of the Silent Planet* (**1938**). Having escaped a terminally polluted Earth, a party of Quakers has landed on the planet Pennterra and been permitted restricted residence on condition that they do not breed indiscriminately, claim further territory or use invasive technologies. All goes well until a second human expedition arrives with no intention of changing any of the behaviour which has ruined humanity's first home. The Hrossa warn them that Pennterra herself will punish them for any disobedience, and the novel – taking on the hues of a grave and didactic PLANETARY ROMANCE – moves inexorably to the comeuppance. JM's second novel, *The Ragged World: A Novel of the Hefn on Earth* (fixup **1991**), adroitly transforms a series of stories – including "Tiny Tango" (1989), about AIDS – into a remarkably effective fable of DISASTER and redemption, the latter at the hands of a *deus ex machina* cabal of aliens; the sequel was *Time, Like an Ever-Rolling Stream* (**1992**). These novels come close to aesthetic overkill, but do not succumb: the first generally avoids the chill of piety, and the sequence overall eschews the coy. By choosing controversial subjects and then treating them to generic solutions, JM shows a mature sense of balance and an active engagement with the sf genre; she is a risk-taker of very considerable interest. [JC]

See also: EDISONADE; JOHN W. CAMPBELL AWARD; PASTORAL; SEX; SUPERNATURAL CREATURES; THEODORE STURGEON MEMORIAL AWARD.

MOFFITT, DONALD (ANTHONY) (1936-   ) US writer who started publishing sf with *The Jupiter Theft* (**1977**), a tale which established him as an author of numerate, physics-oriented, fast-moving HARD-SF adventures. After some years of silence came the **Genesis** series – *The Genesis Quest* (**1986**) and *Second Genesis* (**1986**) – which demonstrates a competence with the mythopoeically large scales and calculations typical of DM's category of SPACE OPERA as Earth sends terminal messages through space which reach their alien targets millions of years hence, generating an eon-leaping response. Slightly closer to home, the **Mechanical Sky** sequence – *Crescent in the Sky* (**1990**) and *A Gathering of Stars* (**1990**) – posits Arab-dominated venues in space. Though some local-colour weaknesses (the first volume features a court eunuch) might irritate Muslims, the focus of the tales – especially the wide-ranging second instalment – is firmly on the wide-scale action and the physics. [JC]

MOLESWORTH, VOL(TAIRE) (1924-1964) Australian journalist and writer, active in FANDOM around the period of WWII. His sf included 4 short novels: *Ape of God* (**1943** chap) and its sequel *Monster at Large* (**1943** chap), *Blinded They Fly* (**1951** chap), based in part on the works of Charles FORT, and *Let There Be Monsters!* (**1952** chap), a tale about MUTANTS. VM also wrote *Outline History of Australian Fandom* (**1953**). [JC]

See also: SMALL PRESSES AND LIMITED EDITIONS.

MONEY Love of money, being the root of all evil, has

always played a leading part in literature, and sf is no exception: few plots could move without it. Precisely because it is so basic, however, speculative thought has rarely focused on it; it is one of those things that is habitually taken for granted. Money may change its form, and the dollar may be replaced by the CREDIT, but its centrality in human affairs is inviolable.

The commonest of all wish-fulfilment fantasies is the sudden acquisition of wealth, and sf has often given form to the wish. As with other such fantasies, however, sf writers have characteristically taken a cynical and slightly disapproving view of the issue, implying that no good can come of it. T.L. SHERRED's "Eye for Iniquity" (1953) is a neat cautionary tale about the problems involved in having a talent for making money out of nothing. The frenzy which can be aroused by the prospect of easy money is exemplified in history by the affair of the South Sea Bubble (1720), and this prompted one of the earliest speculative fictions about speculation, Samuel Brunt's *A Voyage to Cacklogallinia* (1727). However, many UTOPIANS had already expressed their distaste for the profit motive and its effects on human affairs. Various romances commenting on the folly of the alchemical quest – of which the most notable is Honoré de BALZAC's *La recherche de l'absolu* (1834; trans under various titles) – took a similar line. The prospect of science making at least the physical part of the alchemist's quest a reality did little to alter this disparaging attitude. Edgar Allan POE's "Von Kempelen and His Discovery" (1849) suggests that the discovery of a way of making gold would simply rob a practically valueless metal of its ridiculous price, and that the world would press on regardless. Arthur Conan DOYLE's successful gold-maker in *The Doings of Raffles Haw* (1891) is quickly disillusioned with philanthropy and reverts his hoard to the dust whence it came. Henry Richardson CHAMBERLAIN's eponymous *6000 Tons of Gold* (1894) nearly precipitates worldwide catastrophe. Only John TAINE's hero in *Quayle's Invention* (1927) gets much joy out of his instant wealth, and he finds it far from easy. Much more beneficial to humanity, in the eyes of its author, is the wealth-destroying machine in George Allan ENGLAND's *The Golden Blight* (1916), which frees mankind from the present generation of capitalists. The folly of retaining the gold standard in an era of technological ingenuity is exposed in Frank O'Rourke's SATIRE *Instant Gold* (1964); it is hardly surprising that the main change in the money system consistently made by sf writers was the replacement of the gold standard by a purely theoretical credit system. Garrett P. SERVISS's *The Moon Metal* (1900) offers a variant on the gold-making theme, while George O. SMITH's "Pandora's Millions" (1945) concerns the desperate race to find a new symbolic medium of exchange following the invention of the matter-duplicator, and the title of "The Iron Standard" (1943) by Henry KUTTNER largely speaks for

itself. Exotic media of exchange are occasionally featured in sf, notably the virtue-based credit system of Patrick Wilkins's "Money is the Root of All Good" and the alien exchange-system whereby depression leads to extinction in John BRUNNER's *Total Eclipse* (1975). Jack VANCE has been particularly ingenious in the invention of various monetary systems appropriately or ironically adapted to different cultures.

One subtheme of note is developed in stories celebrating the wonders of compound interest. Simple mathematics shows that money invested for 1000 years grows quite magnificently even at relatively low interest rates – an observation first made in Eugene Sue's *The Wandering Jew* (1845). SLEEPERS AWAKE from periods of SUSPENDED ANIMATION to find themselves rich in Edmond ABOUT's *The Man with the Broken Ear* (1861; trans 1867), H.G. WELLS's *When the Sleeper Wakes* (1899; rev as *The Sleeper Awakes* 1910) and Charles Eric MAINE's *The Man who Owned the World* (1961). Harry Stephen Keeler took the notion to extremes in "John Jones' Dollar" (1927), in which a dollar invested in trust for John Jones's distant descendants ultimately grows to represent all the wealth in the Universe. More recently, however, we have become all too well aware of what inflation can do to long-term investments, and the hero of Frederik POHL's *The Age of the Pussyfoot* (1968) awakes from suspended animation to find his "fortune" valueless in terms of real purchasing power. It all goes to prove the old adage that money doesn't grow on trees – except, of course, in Clifford D. SIMAK's "The Money Tree" (1958).   [BS]

See also: ECONOMICS.

MONITORS, THE Film (1969). Bell & Howell Productions/Commonwealth United/Second City. Dir Jack Shea, starring Guy Stockwell, Susan Oliver, Avery Schreiber, Sherry Jackson, with cameos by Keenan Wynn, Ed Begley and others. Screenplay Myron J. Gold, based on *The Monitors* (1966) by Keith LAUMER. 92 mins. Colour.

Filled with bizarre jokes and moments of stunning banality, this film – or string of revue sketches – made in Chicago by the Second City cabaret troupe, concerns an invasion of Earth by superior ALIENS who enforce on the population a system of brotherly love and nonviolence. Dressed in black overcoats, black hats and dark glasses, the "monitors" control people by spraying them with a pacifying gas; a resistance movement is formed and the aliens are overthrown. An oddity, which flopped badly, the film is a product of a time when the hippy "flower power" counterculture was attempting to usher in an era of peace and happiness, but followed close on the heels of police brutality against hippy protesters outside the 1968 Chicago Democratic Convention.   [JB/PN]

MONKEY BUSINESS Film (1952). 20th Century-Fox. Dir Howard Hawks, starring Cary Grant, Ginger Rogers, Charles Coburn, Hugh Marlowe, Marilyn Monroe. Screenplay Ben HECHT, I.A.L. Diamond, Charles Lederer. 97 mins. B/w.

Made only a year after *The* THING (though his

direction of the latter was uncredited), Hawks's second sf film is one of the classic screwball comedies. Grant plays a staid scientist working on slowing the ageing process. One of his laboratory apes accidentally mixes the ingredients that bring a kind of rejuvenation and dumps them in the water cooler. First the scientist, then his equally grave wife (Rogers) and then his employers mistakenly take the elixir, and all, sequentially, revert to manic adolescent behaviour. In a splendid bit part Marilyn Monroe plays the now predatory scientist's first quarry. Amid the well orchestrated farce, a serious enough point is made about hormonal experiments, as anarchy strikes deep into the heart of adulthood. [PN]

MONKEY SHINES (vt *Monkey Shines: An Experiment in Terror*) Film (1988). Orion/Charles Evans. Dir George ROMERO, starring Jason Beghe, John Pankow, Kate McNeil, Joyce Van Patten. Screenplay Romero, based on *Monkey Shines* (**1983**) by Michael STEWART. 113 mins. Colour.

The sf element in this horror thriller is Ella, a monkey, the subject of an experiment to increase simian intelligence by injecting human genetic material into her brain. Ella is given as a therapeutic companion to quadriplegic Allan, with whom she develops a quasitelepathic link. His exasperation at his helplessness is translated by Ella into instructions to kill anyone (including his suffocating mother) who angers him. She also becomes jealous, attacking the two people closest to Allan: his best friend and his new lover. Allan must stop her, using (literally) only his head. Put baldly this sounds trite, but *MS* is close to perfect in its own apparently unpromising terms. It is made with great patience and subtlety, with an astonishing performance from the monkey – whose growing intelligence (and malice) is rendered utterly believable – and with Beghe brilliant in the difficult quadriplegic role. The subtext (a Jekyll-and-Hyde theme with Ella being Allan's vicariously controlled Hyde, representing the animal instincts still functioning within the human mind) is maintained even in the one gratuitous shock added to the finale after previews in order to make the film less sedate: a metaphoric twist on the old phrase "a monkey on my back". [PN]

MONOLITH MONSTERS, THE Film (1957). Universal. Dir John Sherwood, starring Grant Williams, Lola Albright, Les Tremayne. Screenplay Norman Jolley, Robert M. Fresco, based on a story by Jack ARNOLD, Fresco. 77 mins. B/w.

In this rather good little film, crystals from a meteorite that has fallen near a small desert town grow and multiply rapidly when wet. They also cause death by absorbing all the silicon from any living thing that touches them, paradoxically turning the victims to stone. There is a rainstorm: the outstandingly surreal sequences of the crystals rearing up and crashing down, in their inexorable march towards the seemingly doomed town, are memorable. Then it is discovered that ordinary salt will stop them.

Sherwood's debt to Jack Arnold is obvious, especially in the moody desert landscapes. The idea of the marching crystals may well have been borrowed from "White Lily" (1930) by John TAINE. [JB/PN]

MONROE, LYLE ◊ Robert A. HEINLEIN.

MONSARRAT, NICHOLAS Pseudonym of Nicholas John Turney (1910-1979), UK-born writer long in Canada, best known for such adventure novels as *The Cruel Sea* (**1951**). The first of the 4 vols of his **Signs of the Times** series, *The Time Before This* (**1962** UK), which is sf, tells of the discovery of ancient artefacts and frozen beings in Canada, evidence of a highly evolved earlier race on Earth, and of an atomic HOLOCAUST which ended their civilization. The second, *Smith and Jones* (**1963** UK), is a seemingly conventional spy story but is transformed devastatingly into either an ALTERNATE-WORLD or a NEAR-FUTURE novel by its last line. With *The Master Mariner, Book 1: Running Proud* (**1978** UK), NM began a projected 2-part novel about a Flying Dutchman figure, whose story was planned to extend over four centuries of UK life at sea; the second volume, which NM died before completing, was published as *The Master Mariner, Book 2: Darken Ship: The Unfinished Novel* (**1980** UK). [JC]

MONSTER ◊ Roger CORMAN.

MONSTER FROM THE OCEAN FLOOR ◊ Roger CORMAN.

MONSTER MAKER ◊ Roger CORMAN.

MONSTER MOVIES A term colloquially used for a very specific genre of film, usually borderline sf. A monster movie – sometimes called a Creature Feature – must contain the unexpected appearance, normally in a serene setting, of a creature (or many creatures) hostile to humanity. The nature of the creature is usually revealed gradually, and its attacks normally increase in severity. It may be a mutated animal or human, an alien, a kind of animal normally not hostile (as in Hitchcock's The BIRDS [1963]), or any unnatural (but not supernatural) creature.

The monster is usually rationalized (often half-heartedly) as, for example, a dormant prehistoric species newly awakened (e.g., GOJIRA [1954]), an unintended result of scientific experiment (e.g., TARANTULA [1955]), a MUTANT created by radioactivity (e.g., THEM! [1954]), or a secret government experimental warfare device gone wrong (e.g., the remake of The BLOB [1988]). In the majority of cases the monster represents a punishment for humankind – for tampering with Nature, corrupting the environment or creating vile weapons. The featuring of a monstrous creature – e.g., the vampire protagonist of *Dracula* (1931) and its successors – is not in itself a sufficient condition for a film to be classed as a MM. The monster must occupy our world – a world where cause and effect are operative, and phenomena normally have explanations – and not a fantasy world; for this reason MMs can properly be defined as sf. The monster is, however, not a *natural* occupant of our world, and to this degree

MMs approach the condition of fantasy.

If the MM has an ultimate moral, it is about the fragility of the Age of Reason in which we supposedly live. Unreason lurks in the surrounding dark, just beyond the light cast by our campfires, and may break in. The case can be put psychologically, too: in Freudian terms as the revenge of the id over the conscious ego ($\lozenge$ FORBIDDEN PLANET), or in Jungian terms as the irruption of archetypes into a world which does not consciously recognize them. The oldest part of our brains, the hindbrain or limbic system, wellspring of our fight-or-flight reflex, is sometimes claimed as the source of our monsters, not so much Unreason reclaiming ground from Reason as the Primitive asserting its continuing strength over the Sophisticated. It is one of the interesting qualities of MMs that any attempt to unravel their subtexts nearly always reveals a critique of the smugness of "civilization" – indeed, a questioning of the very nature of civilization. Thus one of our most apparently childish genres asks some of the most unanswerable questions of our world.

Various elements that make up the generic MM had previously existed in isolation: prehistoric survivals in The LOST WORLD (1925); a gigantic threat to humanity in KING KONG (1933); deformed creatures revenging themselves against normality in FRANKENSTEIN (1931), ISLAND OF LOST SOULS (1932) and Freaks (1932). It was only with the sf movie boom of the 1950s that the generic structure of the MM took the shape it retains today, quite rapidly developing inflexible conventions. The most plausible candidate for the first such film is The THING (1951), with subsequent milestones including The BEAST FROM 20,000 FATHOMS (1953), GOJIRA (1954), THEM! (1954) and TARANTULA (1955). The boom climaxed with a veritable eruption of MMs in 1957, including one of Roger CORMAN's first, ATTACK OF THE CRAB MONSTERS, and, unusually, a UK offering, the marvellously insane FIEND WITHOUT A FACE. The cascade continued in 1958, with variations on the theme becoming more knowing – a sign that generic conventions had sufficiently hardened for audience expectations to be consciously manipulated – in I MARRIED A MONSTER FROM OUTER SPACE, The BLOB and The FLY. But generic rigidity soon degenerated into decline and fall. More MMs were made 1959-62 than in the whole of 1951-8, but almost without exception they were low-budget, cynical exploitationers of no real quality aimed at the teenage drive-in market; an exception might be made of the surreal Japanese MOSURA (1961).

The structure of MMs normally follows, in sequence, the following narrative conventions: the peaceful beginning; the first intimations that something is wrong; half-seen glimpses of the monster; disbelief of the first reports; attacks of increasing ferocity in which the monster is fully revealed; the fight back against the monster and its destruction. Often there is also the revelation in the final frames that more monsters are hatching.

An important variation, signalled by King Kong, is the sympathetic monster, doomed to destruction, sometimes magnificent in its monstrousness, more often merely pathetic as in The CREATURE FROM THE BLACK LAGOON (1954), The QUATERMASS XPERIMENT (1955; vt The Creeping Unknown), The AMAZING COLOSSAL MAN (1957), NOT OF THIS EARTH (1957) and The Fly (1958). Here the subtext might be that the monster, basically, is us. Another classic variation is the monstrous creature that can take over, or assume the shape of, human beings, as in IT CAME FROM OUTER SPACE (1953), INVADERS FROM MARS (1953), INVASION OF THE BODY SNATCHERS (1956), QUATERMASS II (1957; vt Enemy from Space), I Married a Monster from Outer Space (1958), TERRORE NELLO SPAZIO (1965; vt Planet of the Vampires) and the tv series The INVADERS (1967-8). Such films still turn up occasionally, as in The HIDDEN (1988) and THEY LIVE (1988). Their subtext, however, is entirely different from that of MMs proper ($\lozenge$ PARANOIA) and many would not regard them as the real thing.

After The Birds (1963), few MMs of any quality were made for some time. Then came the extraordinary NIGHT OF THE LIVING DEAD (1968), in which the director, George ROMERO, rejuvenated the genre by adding to it one of its great icons, the army of (scientifically created) zombies, literally eating society away. In the 1970s the revenge-of-Nature theme of The Birds was taken up again by a number of other films in which the "monster" was natural, aside from its exceptional ferocity towards humanity. Some of these were FROGS (1972), NIGHT OF THE LEPUS (1972), Squirm (1976), The GIANT SPIDER INVASION (1975), KINGDOM OF THE SPIDERS (1977) and, most famous of all, Jaws (1975). PHASE IV (1974) and BUG (1975), both featuring intelligent insects, also have points of interest. Most of these films are marginal sf at best, being closer in their paranoia to supernatural fantasy.

In the mid-1970s MMs – not just in the revenge-of-Nature subgenre – began bit by bit to make their comeback, often through the work of quirky, independent directors. DEATH LINE (1973; vt Raw Meat) and IT'S ALIVE (1974) are both notable for sympathetic monsters. The latter is the work of the deeply eccentric Larry COHEN, whose subsequent MMs include IT LIVES AGAIN (1978) and Q (1983; vt The Winged Serpent; vt Q: The Winged Serpent). David CRONENBERG also began making borderline MMs in the 1970s, with The PARASITE MURDERS (1974; vt They Came from Within; vt Shivers), RABID (1976) and The BROOD (1979), all notable for being both intelligent and disgusting. Joe DANTE's PIRANHA (1978) is another witty and subversive independent production. Indeed, it was now becoming clear that the second generation of MMs, far from being primitive exploitation movies, were attracting some of the most radical and sophisticated directors. Any of these films offers sufficiently complex readings, often political, to give grist for a doctoral thesis. This is only possible when genres enter their mature phase, where, although self-referential decadence ($\lozenge$ RECURSIVE SF) can become tiresome, virtuoso variations on a theme are also likely to occur.

The year 1979 was a turning point for MMs. Although it featured one of the most disappointing ever made, PROPHECY, an expensive flop for John FRANKENHEIMER, it also saw the release of ALIEN, directed by Ridley SCOTT, which was an enormous success, both commercially and, in the view of some critics, artistically. Thus, although the 1980s saw the continuing release of interesting low-budget MMs from independents – e.g., ALLIGATOR (1980), DAY OF THE DEAD (1985), CRITTERS (1986), SOCIETY (1989) and TREMORS (1989) – it saw also more expensive productions from companies encouraged by the success of *Alien*. A surprising number were remakes (mostly middle-budget), including two that were very interesting indeed and may come to have classic status: John CARPENTER's *The* THING (1982) and David Cronenberg's *The* FLY (1986). Also better than most people expected were *The* BLOB (1988) and *The* FLY II (1989). Other middling-to-large budget MMs of the period were PREDATOR (1987) and its efficient sequel PREDATOR 2 (1990), LEVIATHAN (1989), *The* ABYSS (1989) – where the monsters turn out to be good ALIENS – and perhaps the best of them, the spider movie to end all spider movies, ARACHNOPHOBIA (1990), which has a strong element of social comedy.

Indeed, outright comedy – either at the expense of or through the medium of MMs – is quite common, with one of the first examples being Woody Allen's EVERYTHING YOU ALWAYS WANTED TO KNOW ABOUT SEX (BUT WERE AFRAID TO ASK) (1972), which in one episode features a giant breast on the rampage. Most MM spoofs (there are quite a few) are bad, with *Attack of the Killer Tomatoes* (1978) being typical in its ineptness. SCHLOCK (1971), on the other hand, featuring a Neanderthal survival rather than a monster proper, is rather funny, as is Larry Cohen's *The* STUFF (1985), about a passive monster disguised as food. Two more recent MM satires targeting Middle America are TERRORVISION (1986) and MEET THE APPLEGATES (1990): the latter ingeniously shows life from the monsters' point of view. [PN]

MONSTER ON THE CAMPUS Film (1958). Universal. Dir Jack ARNOLD, starring Arthur Franz, Joanna Moore, Judson Pratt, Troy Donahue. Screenplay David DUNCAN. 77 mins. B/w.

This is one of Jack Arnold's last and poorest sf films, a variation on the Jekyll and Hyde theme: blood from a specimen coelacanth causes living creatures to devolve ($\lozenge$ DEVOLUTION); a SCIENTIST (Franz) temporarily but repeatedly becomes an apeman. The film is, foolishly, structured as a mystery which everybody is too unobservant to solve, and the science is absurd. As critic Bill WARREN has pointed out, the main interest is noting the variety of ways in which the unfortunate scientist (whose noble quasi-suicide is the film's climax), along with a dog and a dragonfly, contrive to contaminate themselves. [JB/PN]

MONSTERS Monsters have always stalked the hinterlands of the imagination, emblems of fear and symbols of guilt. They commonly take their aspects and roles from the supernatural imagination ($\lozenge$ SUPERNATURAL CREATURES); but the scientific imagination has produced many monsters of its own. The recruitment to the HORROR story of monsters spawned by Nature was pioneered by H.G. WELLS's classic alien-INVASION story *The War of the Worlds* (1897) and by William Hope HODGSON's sea stories. Sf monsters are often familiar but repulsive creatures made monstrous by increasing their size ($\lozenge$ GREAT AND SMALL), and alien monsters are often created by chimerical redeployment of the repulsive features of earthly creatures. The fossil record has increased this vocabulary of ideas considerably. Other monsters arise as MUTANTS or as the accidental products of human scientific endeavour: the archetypal monster of this kind stars in Mary SHELLEY's GOTHIC-SF classic *Frankenstein, or The Modern Prometheus* (1818; rev 1831). The actual scientific discipline of teratology (the study of monsters) has made little impact on sf, although its elaboration in the gruesome murder mystery *The Cadaver of Gideon Wyck* (1934) by Alexander LAING brings that novel close to the sf borderline, and the same might be said of Whitley STRIEBER's horror-detective novel *The Wolfen* (1978). Russell M. GRIFFIN's *The Blind Men and the Elephant* (1982) borrows heavily from the well known "Elephant Man" case.

Many of the standard figures of fear have made their way from MYTHOLOGY or elsewhere into sf via more-or-less ingenious processes of rationalization. The invisible monster proved easy to adapt ($\lozenge$ INVISIBILITY): one was featured in the first issue of *AMZ* in George Allan ENGLAND's "The Thing from – Outside" (1926). The Gorgon became C.L. MOORE's "Shambleau" (1933). Werewolves are rationalized in *Darker than You Think* (1940; **1948**) by Jack WILLIAMSON and "There Shall Be No Darkness" (1950) by James BLISH. "Who Goes There?" (1938) by John W. CAMPBELL Jr takes the idea of the menacing shapeshifter to its limit. Sf vampires are featured in numerous stories, including "Asylum" (1942) by A.E. VAN VOGT – whose *The Voyage of the Space Beagle* (fixup **1950**) features a whole repertoire of monsters – *I Am Legend* (**1954**) by Richard MATHESON, *The Space Vampires* (**1976**) by Colin WILSON, *The Vampire Tapestry* (fixup **1980**) by Suzy McKee CHARNAS and *The Empire of Fear* (**1988**) by Brian M. STABLEFORD. The entire retinue of mythological monsters is recreated by COMPUTER in *Nightworld* (**1979**) and *The Vampires of Nightworld* (**1981**) by David F. BISCHOFF. Other kinds of quasivampiric PARASITISM are featured in Eric Frank RUSSELL's *Sinister Barrier* (1939; **1943**; rev 1948), van Vogt's "Discord in Scarlet" (1939) and Robert A. HEINLEIN's *The Puppet Masters* (**1951**; text restored 1989).

Monsters have always been very popular in the movies, and until the 1960s sf CINEMA was dominated by MONSTER MOVIES of every possible kind. The first of many versions of FRANKENSTEIN was made in 1910, but the legend was created anew in 1931 when Boris Karloff took the role of the monster. Shortly afterwards a new legend was born in the story of KING KONG (1933), in which fear was modified by sympathy: the pragmatically necessary destruction of monster by mankind was thereafter able to take on a dimension of tragedy, and the monsters could be pitied in their monstrousness. Japanese monster movies, pioneered by GOJIRA (1954), have frequently converted charismatic monsters into heroes. Another significant cinematic innovation was the monster liberated from the scientist's id in FORBIDDEN PLANET (1956). Recent advances in special-effects technology have permitted a resurgence of scary MONSTER MOVIES, the most notable sf examples being ALIEN (1979) and its sequels, and various films dir David CRONENBERG, while TERMINATOR 2: JUDGMENT DAY (1991) grafts a traditional monstrous propensity – shapeshifting – onto a technological construct.

GENRE SF, of course, made abundant melodramatic use of monsters. ILLUSTRATION played a considerable part in building sf's monster mythology – ALIEN horrors were a particularly rich source of lurid cover pictures, and the BUG-EYED MONSTER, or BEM (whose archetype appeared on the cover of *ASF* May 1931, illustrating Charles Willard Diffin's "Dark Moon"), quickly became a CLICHÉ. One such is spectacularly featured, with calculated nostalgia, in *Heart of the Comet* (1986) by David BRIN and Gregory BENFORD, but the genus became virtually extinct in the 1940s. After WWII, monsters became much less evident as staples of sf, although new ground continued to be broken by such novels as *The Day of the Triffids* (1951) by John WYNDHAM, which features lethal ambulatory plants, and *The Clone* (1965) by Theodore L. THOMAS and Kate WILHELM, in which a constantly growing amorphous creature absorbs any flesh with which it comes into contact. In many stories a ROBOT filled what was in every respect the role of a monster. Sympathy for alien beings became sufficiently pronounced that stories began to be written which analysed the sad predicament of the monster. The shock of monstrous self-discovery had earlier been the theme of such stark parables of alienation as "The Outsider" (1926) by H.P. LOVECRAFT and "Metamorphosis" (1916; trans 1937) by Franz KAFKA, but many sf stories of the 1960s and 1970s were prepared to take the initial situation of monstrousness for granted and analyse its implications, especially the psychological ones. This is particularly common in the work of Robert SILVERBERG, as in *Thorns* (1967), *The Man in the Maze* (1968) and "Caliban" (1971), and crops up often in the work of Damon KNIGHT, as in "The Country of the Kind" (1956), *Beyond the Barrier* (1963) and *Mind Switch* (1965; vt *The Other Foot*). A parallel work from outside the genre is John (Champlin) GARDNER's *Grendel* (1971), which retells the Beowulf legend from the monster's viewpoint. Humans sometimes become monsters in alien contexts, as in C.J. CHERRYH's *Cuckoo's Egg* (1985).

The advent of GENETIC ENGINEERING has lent a new lease of life to the sf monster story, reflected in such works as Stephen GALLAGHER's *Chimera* (1982) and Dean R. KOONTZ's *Watchers* (1987). Frankensteinian SCIENTISTS embarking on teratological experiments in biotechnology have become common on the fringes of the genre where sf overlaps with thrillers and horror stories, but even here a certain sympathy for the plight of the monstrous creations is commonplace, reflecting the disreputability into which the idea that ugliness may be equated with evil has, thankfully, fallen. [BS]

See also: GODS AND DEMONS.

MONSTERS FROM THE UNKNOWN PLANET ◊ GOJIRA.

MONSTERS INVADE EXPO 70 ◊ DAIKAIJU GAMERA.

MONSTER ZERO ◊ GOJIRA; RADON.

MONTANA, RON (A.) (?1945-   ) US writer whose published work in FANZINES included "We the People" in 1974 for Craig STRETE's *Red Planet Earth*. His first sf novel, *The Sign of the Thunderbird* (1977), conveys its post-HOLOCAUST protagonists to the New Mexico of 1860, where their actions in espousing a free Indian Nation generate an ALTERNATE-WORLD vision of the USA. His second, *The Cathedral Option* (1978), is of less interest. RM's engagement with Native American material ironically prefigured a controversy of the 1980s, in which he accused Strete of plagiarizing his draft of the manuscript published as *Death in the Spirit House* (1988) under Strete's name alone; the book was eventually republished, as part of an agreed settlement, as *Face in the Snow* (1992) by RM. The book itself remains difficult to evaluate, for the transformation of the protagonist from spoiled "evolué" Native American into the transcendent manifestation of the spirit of a symbolic mountain seems, perhaps, rather forced. [JC]

MONTEIRO, JERONIMO [r] ◊ LATIN AMERICA.

MONTELEONE, THOMAS F(RANCIS) (1946-   ) US writer active in sf since 1972, first with book reviews in *AMZ*, then with short stories, beginning with "Wendigo's Child" for *Monster Tales* (anth 1973) ed Roger ELWOOD. Two of his stories have received NEBULA nominations; nine of them (plus a play) are collected in *Dark Stars, and Other Illuminations* (coll 1981). These were more ambitious than most of his work at novel length, which is undemanding adventure fiction, starting with *Seeds of Change* (1975 Canada); this is of interest in that, as the first of the LASER BOOKS, it was issued free to libraries and booksellers as a promotional item in order to generate sales of later titles. TFM's subsequent sf novels include *The Time-Swept City* (fixup 1977), featuring a CITY-controlling COMPUTER developing sentience; *The Secret Sea* (1979), with Jules VERNE's Captain Nemo and the *Nautilus* turning up in one of a set of PARALLEL WORLDS; and the entertaining post-HOLOCAUST **Guardian** sequence: *Guardian* (1980) and *Ozymandias* (1981); in the first volume a pre-holocaust supercomputer is found, and in the second it is incarnated in a human body. The rather derivative **Dragonstar** sequence with David F. BISCHOFF – *Day of the Dragonstar* (**1983**), *Night of the Dragonstar* (**1985**) and *Dragonstar Destiny* (**1989**) – is about First Contact with a saurian race aboard a vast, alien spacecraft. In 1980 TFM moved to horror/dark fantasy with *Night Things* (**1980**), returning to it with *Night-Train* (**1984**) and later with others.

TFM is a thoughtful editor. His 2 sf theme anthologies are *The Arts, and Beyond: Visions of Man's Aesthetic Future* (anth **1977**) and *R-A-M: Random Access Messages of the Computer Age* (anth **1984**; vt *Microworlds: SF Stories of the Computer Age* 1985 UK). His 2 horror anthologies are *Borderlands* (anth **1990**) and *Borderlands II* (anth **1991**). [PN]

Other works: *The Time Connection* (**1976**), sf; *Lyrica* (**1987**), *The Magnificent Gallery* (**1987**), *Crooked House* (**1987**) with John DeCHANCIE and *Fantasma* (**1989**), all horror.

See also: ARTS.

MONTGOMERY, FRANCES TREGO (1858-1925) US writer, mostly of books for children, whose **Electric Elephant** sequence – *The Wonderful Electric Elephant* (**1903**) and *On a Lark to the Planets* (**1904**) – describes in a DIME-NOVEL manner the adventures of a young man who inherits a hollow mechanical elephant after the apparent death of the old man who owned it. With a girlfriend (they later marry), he frolics across the USA and, in the second volume, around the Solar System, which is described in terms appropriate to astrology. The old man then reappears and takes them on a guided tour of the Milky Way. [JC]

MONTHLY STORY BLUE BOOK MAGAZINE, THE ◊ *The* BLUE BOOK MAGAZINE.

MONTHLY STORY MAGAZINE, THE ◊ *The* BLUE BOOK MAGAZINE.

MOON The lunar voyage has a long literary history, having developed from a standard framework for social SATIRE to become one of the archetypal projects of speculative fiction. Major works in the former tradition include two 2nd-century tales by LUCIAN of Samosata, Francis GODWIN's *The Man in the Moone* (**1638**), the first part of CYRANO DE BERGERAC's *L'autre monde* (**1657**), Daniel DEFOE's *The Consolidator* (**1705**), Samuel Brunt's *A Voyage to Cacklogallinia* (**1727**), Murtagh McDERMOT's *A Trip to the Moon* (**1728**) and Joseph ATTERLEY's *A Voyage to the Moon* (**1827**). This phase of the history of the lunar voyage is the subject of Marjorie Hope NICOLSON's excellent *Voyages to the Moon* (**1948**), which has an extensive annotated bibliography. Several pre-1841 lunar voyages can be found in *The Man in the Moone* (anth **1971**) ed Faith K. Pizor and T. Allan Comp. The use of the Moon as a stage for the erection of mock societies became less fashionable in the 19th century, but echoes of the tradition recur even in the present century, as in Compton MACKENZIE's *The Lunatic Republic* (**1959**). The first trip to the Moon seemingly motivated solely by the spirit of adventure was in a brief episode in Ralph MORRIS's ROBINSONADE *The Life and Wonderful Adventures of John Daniel* (**1751**).

The idea that travelling to the Moon might be a notion worth taking seriously first crops up in the appendix to John WILKINS's *The Discovery of a New World* (3rd edn **1640**), where the author suggests that a man might be carried to the Moon by a large bird or that a flying machine capable of the trip might one day become practicable. Another writer to take seriously the modes of TRANSPORTATION used as conveniences by satirists was David RUSSEN, author of *Iter Lunare* (**1703**): he suggested that a man might be propelled to the Moon by the force of a gargantuan spring. The first writer to make any pretence at verisimilitude was Edgar Allan POE, whose "The Unparalleled Adventure of One Hans Pfaall" (1835) is a curious admixture of comic satire and speculative fiction, although Pfaall's BALLOON seems hardly more credible than Russen's spring. A superficially more convincing method was the space-gun envisaged by Jules VERNE in *De la terre à la lune* (**1865**; trans J.K. Hoyte as *From the Earth to the Moon* 1869 US) and its sequel, *Autour de la lune* (**1870**; both trans Lewis Mercier and Eleanor King as *From the Earth to the Moon . . ., and a Trip Around It* 1873 UK).

Serious interest in the Moon as a world in its own right, possibly harbouring ALIEN life of its own, began with Johannes KEPLER's *Somnium* (**1634**), but this work stands almost alone. Richard Adams LOCKE published his "Moon Hoax" in the *New York Sun* in 1835, purporting to describe the inhabitants of the Moon as observed by Sir John Herschel (1792-1871) with the aid of a new telescope, but this vision of lunar life was a gaudy burlesque. By the time the cosmic voyage began to be taken seriously in the 19th century the possibility of there being life on the Moon was already past credibility. H.G. WELLS imagined a Selenite society *within* the Moon in *The First Men in the Moon* (**1901**), but the setting here was no more than a convenient literary device, like the antigravitic Cavorite by means of which the trip was accomplished. Other contemporary works – including W.S. LACH-SZYRMA's "Letters from the Planets" (1887-93), Edgar FAWCETT's *The Ghost of Guy Thyrle* (**1895**) and George GRIFFITH's *A Honeymoon in Space* (**1901**) – portray the Moon as a place of ultimate desolation where life is extinct, although the scenes in which interplanetary voyagers find the ruins of long-dead civilizations on the Moon exhibit a curiously nostalgic sense of tragedy. A dead Moon is featured also in André LAURIE's *Les exiles de la Terre* (**1887**; trans as *The Conquest of the Moon* 1889 UK), a story made memorable by the magnificent notion that traversing the vacuum of space might be avoided if the Moon could be temporarily attracted into the Earth's atmosphere by giant magnets. Lunar life reappeared, however – sometimes in extravagant fashion – in the works of PULP-MAGAZINE writers, notably in Edgar Rice BURROUGHS's *The Moon Maid* (1923-5; fixup **1926**), Edmond HAMILTON's "The Other Side of the Moon" (1929), Otis Adelbert KLINE's *Maza of the Moon* (**1930**) and, most impressively, Jack WILLIAMSON's "The Moon Era" (1932). Lip-service is paid to the deadness of the Moon's visible surface by locating the aliens inside the Moon, as Wells did, or only on its far side, or in the distant past. A nostalgic elegy for lunar life is offered by Lester DEL REY's "The Wings of Night" (1942).

Dead or not, though, the Moon was there – a mere quarter of a million miles away – to be reached and to be claimed. To the early pulp writers this was an article of faith, so easily taken for granted that the Moon routinely became a mere stepping-stone en route to MARS or the STARS. The lunar voyage remained a constant theme of sf of the 1930s and 1940s, but it was more peripheral than the hype surrounding the first actual Moon landing (1969) suggested. The imminent possibility of SPACE FLIGHT in a real NEAR FUTURE had been taken seriously by relatively few writers. Arthur C. CLARKE's essay, "We Can Rocket to the Moon – Now!" (1939), ushered in a new era of realism, but it was the advent towards the end of WWII of the V-2 rocket-bomb that hammered home the message that ROCKET-powered SPACE-SHIPS were just around the corner. The post-WWII years saw publication of a number of visionary novels which elevated the first trip to the Moon to quasi-mythical status. Robert A. HEINLEIN, who had earlier written the poignant "Requiem" (1940) about the burning ambition of a man who longed to go to the Moon even though the trip would kill him, wrote a short novel about the same hero's earlier fight to finance the first Moon-shot and sell the myth of space conquest to the world: "The Man who Sold the Moon" (1950). Heinlein also scripted the George PAL film DESTINATION MOON (1950), drawing material from his first juvenile novel, *Rocket Ship Galileo* (1947). Heinlein wrote realistic sf stories set on the Moon for non-genre magazines, as did Arthur C. Clarke, the chief UK prophet and propagandist of space travel, and author of *Prelude to Space* (1951) and *Earthlight* (1951). Realistic juvenile novels concerning the establishment of Moon bases were written by Lester DEL REY and Patrick MOORE, and the UK RADIO serial *Journey into Space* (novelized by Charles CHILTON as *Journey into Space* * [1954]) further popularized the idea. Pierre BOULLE moved the myth decisively into MAINSTREAM fiction in *Garden on the Moon* (1964; trans 1965), but by then most sf writers had abandoned the theme as too commonplace. William F. TEMPLE's *Shoot at the Moon* (1966) was one of the last major celebrations of the lunar-voyage myth in sf before Neil Armstrong took his "one small step".

In the mythology of sf, the first lunar landing was usually a prelude to rapid COLONIZATION. A lunar colony had waged its carbon-copy war of independence as long ago as *The Birth of a New Republic* (1931 *AMZ Quarterly*; 1981) by Jack Williamson and Miles J. BREUER. The hostility of the lunar environment was admitted, but faith in human ingenuity ran high – John W. CAMPBELL Jr wrote the ultimate lunar robin-sonade in *The Moon is Hell* (1950), easily outdoing Charles Eric MAINE's more modest *High Vacuum* (1956). Thrillers and mysteries set on the inhabited Moon became commonplace in the 1950s; examples are Murray LEINSTER's *City on the Moon* (1957), Clarke's *A Fall of Moondust* (1961) and Clifford D. SIMAK's *Trouble with Tycho* (1961). Heinlein produced a definitive new version of the birth of the new republic in *The Moon is a Harsh Mistress* (1966), a vision which John VARLEY modified and expanded upon in *Steel Beach* (1992).

Despite its deadness, the Moon retained its status as an alien world, and human visitors sometimes found echoes of others long passed on – artefacts left behind to confront the Earthlings, as they broke out of their atmospheric shell, with a glimpse of the infinite possibilities of an inhabited Universe. Clarke's "Sentinel of Eternity" (1951; vt "The Sentinel") captured the essence of this notion and became its archetypal expression, ultimately forming the seed of the film 2001: A SPACE ODYSSEY (1967). An equally challenging but far less hospitable artefact is featured in *Rogue Moon* (1960) by Algis BUDRYS, and the discovery of an apparently human corpse on the Moon in James P. HOGAN's *Inherit the Stars* (1977) is a prelude to far more spectacular discoveries.

Post-1969 sf tends to look farther out than the Moon, although lunar colonies are still a frequent feature of HARD-SF stories. Despite a deflection of attention towards orbiting SPACE HABITATS, Moon-based thrillers and mysteries are still produced. Notable examples are Larry NIVEN's *The Patchwork Girl* (1980), Roger MacBride ALLEN's *Farside Cannon* (1988), Michael SWANWICK's *Griffin's Egg* (1991) and Charles L. HARNESS's *Lunar Justice* (1991). Moon colonies occasionally survive the devastation of Earth, as in *When the Sky Burned* (1973; exp vt *Test of Fire* 1982) by Ben BOVA. More spectacular use of the Moon is made by Bob SHAW in *The Ceres Solution* (1981), where it is broken up, and by John GRIBBIN and Marcus CHOWN in *Double Planet* (1988) and its sequel *Reunion* (1991), where it is supplied with a brand new atmosphere.

A theme anthology is *Men on the Moon* (anth 1958) ed Donald A. WOLLHEIM. [BS]

MOON, ELIZABETH (N.) (1945-) US writer whose strongest work has been fantasy, primarily the **Deed of Paksennarion** sequence: *The Deed of Paksennarion #1: Sheepfarmer's Daughter* (1988), *#2: Divided Allegiance* (1988) and *#3: Oath of Gold* (1989), all assembled as *The Deed of Paksennarion* (all texts rev, omni 1992); a prequel, *Surrender None: The Legacy of Gird* (1990), vigorously sets the scene. EM began publishing sf with "ABCs in Zero-G" for *ASF* in 1986, a polished high-tech tale which was assembled, with other sf and FANTASY, in *Lunar Activity* (coll 1990) – the title is a play on EM's name rather than an accurate description of the book's contents. She collaborated with Anne MCCAFFREY on *Sassinak* (1990) and *Generation Warriors* (1992), being #1 and #3 of the **Planet Pirates** sequence of sf adventures featuring a young girl who, after her home planet has been destroyed by "planet pirates", becomes a Federation pirate hunter. [JC]

MOONBASE 3 UK tv serial (1973). BBC TV. Prod Barry Letts. Script ed Terrance Dicks. Scriptwriters Dicks and Letts (1st episode), and John Brason, John Lucarotti, Arden Winch. Dirs Ken Hannam, Christopher Barry. Scientific advisor James Burke, a well known presenter of tv popular-science programmes. Starring Donald Houston, Barry Lowe, Ralph Bates, Fiona Gaunt. 6 30min episodes. Colour.

Set on an enclosed European Moon base in AD2003 (other nations had set up similar bases), *M3* concerned a group of scientists. The usual sensational elements (aliens, monsters) were studiously eschewed in favour of psychological problems in the small, claustrophobic community, but the attempt at responsible realism was somewhat dull. [JB/PN]

MOONCHILD ◊ Gardner F. FOX.

MOONEY, TED Working name of US writer Edward Mooney (1951-), whose remarkable first novel, published in the MAINSTREAM, is sf: *Easy Travel to Other Planets* (**1981**). Set on a NEAR-FUTURE Earth against a backdrop of global information sickness, war in the Antarctic and a new emotion nobody has ever felt before, it tells a love story – with visionary ramifications – concerning a woman marine biologist and the dolphin on whom she conducts experiments in LINGUISTICS. It has been seen as a proto-CYBERPUNK work, but its cool, pellucid, dissecting style – perhaps influenced by J.G. BALLARD – is far removed from the hectic insistence that has characterized much of that school. TM's second sf book was the ALTERNATE-WORLD novel *Traffic and Laughter* (**1990**), set in the near future of an Earth where WWII was inconclusive and nuclear power never developed. [PN]

MOONRAKER Film (1979). Eon/Les Productions Artistes Associés. Dir Lewis Gilbert, starring Roger Moore, Lois Chiles, Michael Lonsdale, Richard Kiel. Screenplay Christopher Wood, based on *Moonraker* (**1955**) by Ian FLEMING. 126 mins. Colour.

British agent James Bond (Moore) uncovers a plot by megalomaniac Hugo Drax (Lonsdale) to destroy the present human race using space-launched nerve-gas capsules and replace it by a master race, to be specially bred in a large, radar-invisible SPACE HABITAT. This belongs towards the decadent, later end of the **James Bond** film sequence, with Moore pouting fleshily as Bond and a sequence of spectacularly destructive set pieces replacing any of the escalation of suspense we expect of the true thriller. As with most **James Bond** films, the science is contemptible and logical flaws highly visible. The film is remembered mainly for the finding by giant, steel-toothed assassin Jaws (Kiel) of a pigtailed girlfriend. The novelization is *James Bond and Moonraker* * (**1979**) by Christopher Wood (1935-). The other two (much earlier) films in the sequence that most resemble sf are DR NO (1962) and YOU ONLY LIVE TWICE (1967). [PN]

MOON ZERO TWO Film (1969). Hammer/Warner Bros. Dir Roy Ward Baker, starring James Olson, Catherine von Schell, Warren Mitchell, Adrienne Corri. Screenplay Michael Carreras. 100 mins. Colour.

At the same time as the first actual Moon landing, Hammer Films were making this quasi-Western set on the Moon, envisaged as a rip-roaring Frontier area; the results are absurd. One of the hoariest of pulp Western plots is dressed up with a lot of colourful space hardware: a poor but honest space pilot/cowboy/gunslinger (Olson) is forced by a group of villains to capture an asteroid of pure sapphire, but his principles triumph and he foils their plans. The special effects by Kit West, Nick Allder and Les Bowie are unexpectedly convincing, considering the relatively small budget, but the film has no other strength. The novelization is *Moon Zero Two* * (**1969**) by John BURKE. [JB/PN]

MOORCOCK, MICHAEL (JOHN) (1939-) UK writer and editor, London-based and London-obsessed from his first vivid memories of WWII bombing of its southern suburbs, experiences constantly reflected in his fiction – wartime London providing many of its characteristic landscapes and its images of ENTROPY – and central to what may be his finest single novel, *Mother London* (**1988**), a work of singular complexity whose comprehensive grasp makes generic pigeonholing impossible, despite touches of telepathy and other psi phenomena in the text (◊ ESP; PSI POWERS).

During MM's desultory schooling he began to write, starting with *Outlaw's Own* (about 1950), a hand-done magazine, and continuing with several other similar FANZINE titles until 1962. After leaving school he began to contribute professionally to *Tarzan Adventures*, which he ed 1957-8, producing for it his first HEROIC-FANTASY series, later assembled as *Sojan* (coll of linked stories with independent material **1977**). *The Golden Barge* (written 1958; **1979**) also demonstrated the precocity common to many generic writers, plus an already characteristic questioning of the violence and morality of commercial heroic fantasy, a genre he was all the same to exploit extensively for the next 15 years. After working on the **Sexton Blake Library** (a long series of thrillers) – publishing one non-sf novella for it, *Caribbean Crisis* (**1962** chap) with James CAWTHORN, together writing as Desmond Reid – and after doing some night-club work as a blues singer, MM, inspired by John CARNELL, began to contribute sf and fantasy stories to SF ADVENTURES and SCIENCE FANTASY. His first sf novel was *The Sundered Worlds* (1962-3 *SF Adventures*; fixup **1965**; vt *The Blood Red Game* 1970), a metaphysical SPACE OPERA which introduced the concept of the "multiverse", a term probably derived from the works of John Cowper POWYS. The word describes a Universe in which multiple PARALLEL WORLDS co-exist, constantly (but never permanently) intersecting with one another; in this infinite nesting of intersecting arenas, similar cosmic dramas are played and replayed by numerous characters who inhabit the various worlds, but who reduce to a relatively small cast of core identities, each playing himself or herself under various names throughout the nest of worlds. Of these recurring characters, the most central to the heroic-fantasy novels is the figure of the **Eternal Champion**, the protagonist of various series including the **Eternal Champion** or **Erekosë** sequence, **Elric of Melniboné**, the **Warrior of Mars**, **Hawkmoon**, **Corum** and **Von Bek**. In the fantasies, the Champion's fundamental task is to combat Chaos on behalf of Order. In the sf novels, the FABULATIONS and the non-genre works, the motives and tasks of those figures closest in nature to the Champion are much more ambiguous. Throughout, MM has consistently used the multiverse and the Eternal Champion as devices by which it becomes possible to construe all his very sizable oeuvre as comprising one enormous series.

The **Elric** stories, published intermittently for over 30 years, constitute MM's first consequential work. At their heart is the albino melancholic Elric of Melniboné, a treacherous figure who is in a sense the minion of his own supernatural Chaos-inducing sword. They comprise a sustained critique and parody of the SWORD-AND-SORCERY brand of heroic fantasy. A sense that the target of this parody was trivial clearly motivated MM's next significant move, the creation of a figure parodic of the pretentious Weltschmerz of the antiheroic Elric: **Jerry Cornelius**, a portmanteau antihero painted initially in the Pop colours of 1960s "Swinging London", was Elric turned inside out, an anarchic streetwise urban ragamuffin with James Bond gear, and amorally deft at manipulating everything from women to the multiverse itself. In his early adventures – during which the planet suffers various catastrophes – Jerry ranges from the present through the FAR FUTURE, ever melancholy, randy and evanescent. This early version of Jerry dominates the first two novels of the **Jerry Cornelius** sequence: *The Final Programme* (excerpts 1965-6 *NW*; **1968** US; rev 1969 UK; rev 1977 US; rev 1979 UK), later filmed as The FINAL PROGRAMME (1973; cut vt *The Last Days of Man on Earth* US), and *A Cure for Cancer* (1969 *NW*; **1971**; rev 1977 US; rev 1979 UK). In the third and fourth volumes of the sequence – *The English Assassin* (**1972**; rev 1977 US; rev 1979 UK) and *The Condition of Muzak* (**1977**; rev 1978), which won the 1977 *Guardian* Fiction Prize – the portrait of Pierrot-like Jerry and his enduring family and associates deepens, as the various Londons they inhabit become less and less open to their sf/fantasy manipulations. Caught between the forces of Law and Chaos, they gradually come to represent the dubious success of any late-20th-century strategy for survival "in the deep cities of this world, in the years of their dying", as claimed by John CLUTE in an introduction to the omnibus which first assembled all 4 vols: *The Cornelius Chronicles* (omni **1977** US; using 1979 revs of individual titles, rev vt in 2 vols as The

Cornelius Chronicles: Book One 1988 UK and *Book Two* 1988 UK). In *The Cornelius Chronicles, Volume II* (omni **1986** US) were assembled *The Lives and Times of Jerry Cornelius* (coll **1976**; exp 1987) and *The Entropy Tango: A Comic Romance* (fixup **1981**). In *The Cornelius Chronicles, Volume III* (omni **1987** US) were assembled *The Adventures of Una Persson and Catherine Cornelius in the Twentieth Century* (**1976**; cut vt *The Adventures of Una Persson and Catherine Cornelius* in omni 1980 US with *The Black Corridor* [see below]) and "The Alchemist's Question" (1984) from *The Opium General* (coll **1984**). The titles assembled in the second and third omnibuses served as modulations upon the thematic material of the central quartet, but lacked its cumulative intensity or Commedia dell'Arte pathos. Further associated material appeared in *The Nature of the Catastrophe* (anth **1971**) ed MM and Langdon JONES, which contained stories and material by MM and other *NW* writers who were allowed to use the **Cornelius** world as an OPEN UNIVERSE, and as *The Great Rock'n'Roll Swindle* (**1980** chap) in the form of a tabloid paper. *The Distant Suns* (1969 *The Illustrated Weekly of India*; **1975** chap) with Philip James (Cawthorn) has as its protagonist a Jerry Cornelius who bears no relation to the Jerry Cornelius of the other books.

In the 1960s MM also became editor of NEW WORLDS, a position he held, with a few voluntary breaks, from #142 (May/June 1964) to its effective demise (but see below) as a magazine with #201 (Mar 1971). For some time he had been arguing that GENRE SF and FANTASY sadly lacked human values and literacy of texture, and he now began to accept for the journal stories from authors like Brian W. ALDISS, J.G. BALLARD, Samuel R. DELANY, Thomas M. DISCH, M. John HARRISON, John T. SLADEK and Norman SPINRAD which – he argued in its pages – proved that literate and humane sf and fantasy could be written. Works from these authors, and by MM himself, were soon identified as comprising a NEW WAVE (a term first used around 1964 in FANZINES to describe the amateur publications issued by Charles PLATT and Peter WESTON, and then transformed by Christopher PRIEST into a tag for *NW*'s new-style fiction). For several years after 1965, *NW* and the New Wave were virtually synonymous in the UK. MM published – and himself wrote – stories experimental in form and content, influenced by French Surrealism and by the early work of William S. BURROUGHS. After ceasing as a magazine, *NW* continued as a series of anthologies until 1976, under the editorship (variously and in combination) of MM, Hilary BAILEY (MM's wife 1962-78) and Platt; another brief *NW* series in magazine format ran for several issues in 1978-9; a further anthology series, with MM's authorization, began in the 1990s with *New Worlds 1* (anth **1991**) ed David S. GARNETT.

Though MM was never prolific as an author of pure sf, the 1960s saw several works of interest, notably: *The Black Corridor* (**1969** US) with Hilary Bailey (uncredited); *The Ice Schooner* (1966-7 *SF Impulse*; **1969**; rev 1977 US; rev 1985 UK), a homage to and recasting of Joseph CONRAD's *The Rescue* (**1920**) which convincingly portrays the cultures of a new Ice Age at the moment when the temperature begins to rise again; and the **Karl Glogauer** sequence, comprising *Behold the Man* (1966 *NW*; exp **1969**), the magazine version of which won a 1967 NEBULA for Best Novella, and *Breakfast in the Ruins* (**1972**). In the earlier book Glogauer is cast back by a TIME MACHINE; he becomes Christ and is crucified. In the second, structured as a series of vignettes, he is exposed to a series of moral crises exemplary of our modern world, and to which he is forced to respond. Collections included *The Deep Fix* (coll **1966**) as by James COLVIN (an *NW* house name) and *The Time Dweller* (coll **1969**). MM's pseudonymous output was, despite 1960s rumour, not large. Beyond Desmond Reid and Colvin, he used only Bill Barclay (2 non-sf novels), the collaborative pseudonym Michael BARRINGTON (with Barrington J. BAYLEY; 1 story) and Edward P. Bradbury (3 fantasies).

This intermittent production of sf did not increase in the 1970s, though two sequences appeared. The **Oswald Bastable** books – *The Warlord of the Air* (**1971** US), *The Land Leviathan* (**1974**) and *The Steel Tsar* (**1981**) – expressed a nostalgia, evident also in *The Condition of Muzak*, for the kind of future an Edwardian might have hoped for (◊ STEAMPUNK); all 3 were assembled as *The Nomad of Time* (omni **1982** US). More important was the far-future **Dancers at the End of Time** sequence, comprising a central trilogy – *An Alien Heat* (**1972**), *The Hollow Lands* (**1974** US) and *The End of All Songs* (**1976** US), assembled as *The Dancers at the End of Time* (omni **1980**) – plus a collection, *Legends from the End of Time* (coll **1976** US), and a further novel, *The Transformation of Miss Mavis Ming* (**1977**; vt *A Messiah at the End of Time* 1978 US), both assembled as *Tales from the End of Time* (omni **1989** US). The protagonist of the sequence, Jherek Carnelian, although his name echoes that of Jerry Cornelius, nevertheless remains an independent character, inhabiting a far-future Earth in which infinitely available power makes everything and everyone constantly malleable; Carnelian himself, however, transported into the 19th century, becomes obsessed with humanity's moral and physical trammels, even to the point of falling in love. *Gloriana, or The Unfulfill'd Queen: Being a Romance* (**1978**), a rare singleton, presents an ambiguous sexual fable in a world which could be defined as an alternate Elizabethan England.

In the 1980s MM increasingly concentrated either on fantasies which continued (and at times alarmingly amplified) earlier work, or on tales in which little or no generic content could be found. He also published: a political pamphlet, *The Retreat from Liberty: The Erosion of Democracy in Today's Britain* (**1983** chap); an autobiographical sequence, *Letters from Hollywood* (**1986**); a patchy study, *Wizardry and Wild Romance: A Study of Epic Fantasy* (**1987**), a chapter of which was based on *Epic Pooh* (**1978** chap); and *Fantasy: The 100 Best Books* (**1988**) with (but in fact

written almost entirely by) James Cawthorn. After the singletons *Mother London* and *The Brothel in Rosenstrasse* (**1982**), a fantasy of sexual torment, the most interesting later novels are the **Colonel Pyat** sequence, comprising *Byzantium Endures* (**1981**; cut 1981 US), *The Laughter of Carthage* (**1984**; rev 1985 US), and *Jerusalem Commands* (**1992**), with one further novel projected, «The Vengeance of Rome» (the 4 titles read together, appropriately punctuated, as one sentence). These novels, which feature many characters from the **Jerry Cornelius** books, are non-generic, being an ambitious attempt to convey some sense of the 20th century through the unreliable memoirs of one man. They represent MM's slow but inexorable evolution from PULP to POSTMODERNISM, a transition made all the more interesting because of the large number of books through which it can be traced, and because he has so frequently returned to early sequences (**Elric** in particular), transforming them in the process. MM has therefore become less and less easy to pigeonhole as a writer, and has come to be recognized as a major figure at the edge of – but materially helping to define – all his chosen worlds. [JC]

Other works:
Sf: *The Fireclown* (**1965**; vt *The Winds of Limbo* 1969 US); *The Twilight Man* (**1966**; vt *The Shores of Death* 1970); *The LSD Dossier* (**1966**) as by Roger Harris (i.e., as heavily ed MM) and its sequels *Somewhere in the Night* (**1966** as by Bill Barclay; rev vt *The Chinese Agent* 1970 US as by MM) and *Printer's Devil* (**1966** as by Bill Barclay; rev vt *The Russian Intelligence* 1980 as by MM), the revisions of the latter books taking them out of the original sequence and recreating them as tales of **Jerry Cornell**; *The Wrecks of Time* (1965-6 *NW* as by James Colvin; edited **1967** dos US; text restored vt *The Rituals of Infinity* 1971 UK); *Moorcock's Book of Martyrs* (coll **1976**; vt *Dying for Tomorrow* 1978 US); *The Time of the Hawklords* (**1976**) and *Queens of Deliria* (**1977**), the first as by MM and Michael BUTTERWORTH, the second by Butterworth alone, only the general idea (for the first title alone) being supplied by MM; *The Real Life Mr Newman* (1966 in *The Deep Fix*; **1979** chap); *My Experiences in the Third World War* (coll **1980**); *Casablanca* (coll **1989**).

Eternal Champion titles:
Erekosë: *The Eternal Champion* (1962 *Science Fantasy*; fixup **1970**; rev 1978 US); *Phoenix in Obsidian* (exp **1970**; vt *The Silver Warriors* 1973 US); *The Swords of Heaven, the Flowers of Hell* (graph **1979** US) with Howard CHAYKIN; *The Dragon in the Sword* (**1986** US; exp 1987 UK), all but the 3rd being assembled in *The Eternal Champion* (rev omni **1992**).

Elric of Melniboné: (by internal chronology) *Elric of Melniboné* (**1972**; cut vt *The Dreaming City* 1972 US); *The Fortress of the Pearl* (**1989**); *The Sailor on the Seas of Fate* (fixup **1973**), incorporating *The Jade Man's Eyes* (**1973** chap); *The Weird of the White Wolf* (1961-3 *Science Fantasy*; coll **1976** US), incorporating stories from *The Stealer of Souls* (coll **1963**) and from *The Singing Citadel* (coll **1970**); *The Sleeping Sorceress* (**1971**; vt *The*

Vanishing Tower 1977 US); *The Revenge of the Rose: A Tale of the Albino in the Years of his Wandering* (**1991**); *The Bane of the Black Sword* (1961-3 *Science Fantasy*; coll **1977** US), incorporating the remaining stories (see above) from *The Stealer of Souls* and *The Singing Citadel*; *Stormbringer* (1963-4 *Science Fantasy*; cut **1965**; text restored and rev 1977 US). Omnibuses of this material are *The Elric Saga Part I* (omni **1984** US) containing *Elric of Melniboné*, *The Sailor on the Seas of Fate* and *The Weird of the White Wolf*; and *The Elric Saga Part II* (omni **1984** US) containing *The Sleeping Sorceress*, *The Bane of the Black Sword* and *Stormbringer*. *Elric at the End of Time* (coll **1984**) assembles mostly earlier stories, including some from *Sojan*.

Warrior of Mars: *Warriors of Mars* (**1965**; vt *City of the Beast* 1970 US), *Blades of Mars* **1965**; vt *Lord of the Spiders* 1971 US) and *Barbarians of Mars* (**1965**; vt *Masters of the Pit* 1971 US), all assembled as *Warrior of Mars* (omni **1981** UK). The original versions of all 3 were published as by Edward P. Bradbury.

Hawkmoon: 2 series. The **Runestaff** books are *The Jewel in the Skull* (**1967** US; rev 1977 US), *Sorcerer's Amulet* (**1968** US; vt *The Mad God's Amulet* 1969 UK), *Sword of the Dawn* (**1968** US; rev vt *The Sword of the Dawn* 1969 UK; rev 1977 US) and *The Secret of the Runestaff* (**1969** US; vt *The Runestaff* 1969 UK; rev 1977 US), all assembled as *The History of the Runestaff* (omni **1979** UK; rev vt *Hawkmoon* 1992). The **Count Brass** books are *Count Brass* (**1973**), *The Champion of Garathorm* (**1973**) and *The Quest for Tanelorn* (**1975**), all assembled as *The Chronicles of Castle Brass* (omni **1985** UK).

Corum: 2 series. The **Swords** books are *The Knight of the Swords* (**1971**), *The Queen of the Swords* (**1971** US) and *The King of the Swords* (**1971** US), all assembled as *The Swords Trilogy* (omni **1977** US; vt *The Swords of Corum* 1986 UK; rev vt *Corum* 1992 UK). A second trilogy comprises *The Bull and the Spear* (**1973**), *The Oak and the Ram* (**1973**) and *The Sword and the Stallion* (**1974**), all assembled as *The Chronicles of Corum* (omni **1977** US).

Von Bek: *The War Hound and the World's Pain* (**1981** US) and *The City in the Autumn Stars* (**1986**), assembled with an added story as *Von Bek* (rev omni **1992**).

As editor: *The Best of New Worlds* (anth **1965**); *Best S.F. Stories from New Worlds* (anth **1967**); *Best Stories from New Worlds 2* (anth **1968**; vt *Best S.F. Stories from New Worlds 2* US); *Best S.F. Stories from New Worlds 3* (anth **1968**); *The Traps of Time* (anth **1968**); *Best S.F. Stories from New Worlds 4* (anth **1969**); *The Inner Landscape* (anth **1969**), ed anon; *Best S.F. Stories from New Worlds 5* (anth **1969**); *Best S.F. Stories from New Worlds 6* (anth **1970**); *Best S.F. Stories from New Worlds 7* (anth **1971**); *New Worlds 1* (anth **1971**; vt *New Worlds Quarterly 1* 1971 US); *New Worlds 2* (anth **1971**; vt *New Worlds Quarterly 2* 1971 US); *New Worlds 3* (anth **1972**; vt *New Worlds Quarterly 3* 1972 US); *New Worlds 4* (anth **1972**; vt *New Worlds Quarterly 4* 1972 US); *New Worlds 5* (anth **1973**); *New Worlds 6* (anth **1973**; vt *New Worlds Quarterly 5* 1974 US) with Charles PLATT; *Best S.F.*

Stories from New Worlds 8 (anth **1974**); *Before Armageddon* (anth **1975**); *England Invaded* (anth **1977**); *New Worlds: An Anthology* (anth **1983**).

Film: *The* LAND THAT TIME FORGOT (1975), script by MM and James Cawthorn.

About the author: *The Tanelorn Archives: A Primary and Secondary Bibliography of the Works of Michael Moorcock, 1949-1979* (**1981**) by Richard Bilyeu; *The Entropy Exhibition: Michael Moorcock and the British "New Wave" in Science Fiction* (**1983**) by Colin GREENLAND; *Michael Moorcock: A Reader's Guide* (**1991** chap) by John Davey (1962-   ); *Death is No Obstacle* (**1992**), a book-length interview conducted by Greenland with MM about his work.

See also: ABSURDIST SF; BOYS' PAPERS; CITIES; COMICS; DAW BOOKS; GAMES AND TOYS; GOTHIC SF; HISTORY OF SF; HUMOUR; IMMORTALITY; INTERZONE; ISAAC ASIMOV'S SCIENCE FICTION MAGAZINE; JOHN W. CAMPBELL MEMORIAL AWARD; LEISURE; MESSIAHS; MUSIC; MYTHOLOGY; OPTIMISM AND PESSIMISM; RELIGION; SATIRE; SF REPRISE; SUSPENDED ANIMATION; TIME TRAVEL; TRANSPORTATION; WAR.

MOORE, ALAN (1953-   ) UK COMICS illustrator and writer, mainly active in the latter capacity for the GRAPHIC NOVELS that made him famous; all of these, including WATCHMEN, were illustrated by others. On rare occasions, beginning with "Sawdust Memories" for *Knave* in 1984, he has also written prose fiction.

AM's first professional work was as an artist and illustrator, beginning with a 1969 ad for the London sf bookshop Dark They Were and Golden Eyed. As Curt Vile, he began creating comics with 2 series – **Roscoe Moscow** (Mar 1979-July 1980) and **The Stars my Degradation** (July 1980-Feb 1982) – for the weekly music paper *Sounds*; another Curt Vile strip, *Three Eyes McGurk & His Death Planet Commandos* (Dec 1979 in *Dark Star*) appeared in the USA in *Rip Off Comics #8* (1981). As Jill de Ray, AM wrote and drew the weekly **Maxwell the Magic Cat** (Aug 1979-Oct 1986) for the *Northants Post*. Perhaps fortunately – his drawing style was an anaemic rehash of underground-comix clichés – this was his last work as an illustrator.

The appearance in the UK in 1977 of the weekly sf comic 2,000 AD – the birthplace of JUDGE DREDD – had provided a forum for a new generation of writers and artists, of which AM soon became a prominent member. With scripts for MARVEL COMICS UK's *Dr. Who Weekly/Monthly* (June 1980-Oct 1981), he began to work for the commercial-comics industry, and was intensely active for the next half decade. For the **Future Shocks** section of *2,000 AD* itself he wrote 26 sf shorts (July 1980-Aug 1983); these were later assembled as *Alan Moore's Shocking Futures* (graph coll **1986**) and *Alan Moore's Twisted Times* (graph coll **1986**), both with various illustrators. During the same period, he wrote 5 stories for Marvel UK's STAR WARS comic (Nov 1981-Aug 1982), and 20 episodes of the PARALLEL-WORLDS **Captain Britain** sequence for various other Marvel UK comics. Aside from **Captain Britain**, most of this early work was comparatively journeyman.

In March 1982, with #1 of the anthology-comic *Warrior*, this all changed. In that issue, AM began 2 series of considerable significance. **Marvelman** was a radical POSTMODERNIST reinterpretation of a SUPERHERO (◊ CAPTAIN MARVEL) from the 1940s. After Aug 1984, the strip was removed from *Warrior*, and in retitled form reprinted and completed in the US anthology-comic *Eclipse*; the full strip was then assembled as *Miracleman* (graph coll **1988** US), *The Red King Syndrome* (graph coll **1990** US) and *Olympus* (graph coll **1990** US), with various illustrators, including Alan Davis and Garry Leach. (Just as the original **Captain Marvel** was plagued by litigation, so was the new: the US MARVEL COMICS, which had begun its own **Captain Marvel** comic in 1967, insisted on the AM strip being retitled **Miracleman** in the USA; in retaliation, AM refused Marvel UK permission to reprint any of his early work, which remains uncollected.) The second series begun in that first issue of *Warrior* was **V for Vendetta**, which pits an anarchist hero against the fascist regime of a NEAR-FUTURE, post-Thatcherite UK. **V for Vendetta** also moved to the USA (after Feb 1985), being published there by DC COMICS, and was assembled as *V for Vendetta* (graph coll **1990** US) illus David Lloyd.

Other UK work during this period included **The Ballad of Halo Jones** (July 1984-Apr 1986 *2,000 AD*), set in a variety of sf locales and later collected in 3 vols as *The Ballad of Halo Jones, Book 1* (graph **1986**), #2 (graph **1986**) and #3 (graph **1986**), all 3 being later assembled (graph omni **1990**) under the same title, and all illus Ian Gibson. **Skizz** (Mar 1983-Aug 1983 *2,000 AD*), an sf tale reminiscent of E.T.: THE EXTRATERRESTRIAL, was collected as *Skizz* (graph **1989**) illus Jim Baikie; and **D.R. and Quinch** (Apr 1983-Summer 1985 *2,000 AD*), a comedy about ALIEN juvenile delinquents, was collected as *D.R. and Quinch's Guide to Life* (graph **1986**) illus Alan Davis and *D.R. and Quinch* (graph **1991**).

In 1984 AM began to work directly for US firms, becoming the writer for DC's **Saga of the Swamp Thing** (in Nov 1984 the title changed to SWAMP THING), the eponymous monster being a 1970s antihero now revived in the wake of the poor 1982 film. AM's 44 **Swamp Thing** stories (Jan 1984-Sep 1987), which were collected in 11 vols with various illustrators, perhaps take the "orthodox" sf/GOTHIC only-partly-human-superhero theme as far as it could be taken within the framework of the conventional comic, which is distributed through newsstands and must operate in constant fear of censorship. The *Grand Guignol* violence of AM's imagery, and the disturbing psychosexual impact of his storylines, established **Swamp Thing** as probably the seminal comic of the 1980s.

The success of **Swamp Thing** led directly to WATCHMEN, a graphic novel whose 12 chapters were first published as individual comics (Sep 1986-Oct 1987 *Watchmen*), but which are best read in their intended book form as *Watchmen* (graph **1987** US; with additional material 1988 US) illus Dave GIBBONS. Set in an ALTERNATE WORLD distinguished by the fact that the existence of costumed superheroes has subtly modified the history of the 20th century, *Watchmen* is both a satirical analysis of the human cost of being (or needing) a superhero, and an extremely distressing tale of a nearly-terminal holocaust fomented by one of these iconic figures. The impact of the tale – and that of its sophisticated visual language, through which subtexts and subplots interweave with (in hindsight) the utmost clarity – was enormous.

After finishing the last parts of *V for Vendetta* and a **Batman** book, *The Killing Joke* (graph **1988** US) illus Brian Bolland, AM left mainstream comics, forming Mad Love (Publishing) Ltd in 1988 with his wife Phyllis and Debbie Delano, through which he edited and self-published *ARRGH! (Artists Against Rampant Government Homophobia)* (graph anth **1988**). Subsequent work has tended to move away from genre concerns, though *A Small Killing* (graph **1990**) illus Oscar Zarate is fantasy, and *From Hell* (graph **1991**) begins a long fictional investigation of Jack the Ripper; two instalments of his major project, the non-genre **Big Numbers**, appeared in 1990. **Lost Girls**, a psychosexual study of Wendy, Dorothy and Alice, who meet around the time of WWI, began in *Taboo* #5 (1992). For sf, AM remains of central importance for *Watchmen*, where the long history of sf visual material in comics form was finally connected to an sf plot of great interest. [RH/JC]

MOORE, BRIAN (1921-   ) Irish-born Canadian novelist, in the USA from 1959, best known for non-genre works like *The Luck of Ginger Coffey* (**1960**); he has published detective thrillers under the names Michael Bryan and Bernard Mara. Several of his novels contain strong elements of fantasy, like *Fergus* (**1970**) and *Cold Heaven* (**1983**), two tales linked by their preoccupation with the dead – dead parents visiting their child; dead husband haunting a widow and challenging the terms of her faith. *The Great Victorian Collection* (**1975**) somewhat resembles sf in its allegorical treatment of a professor who dreams into reality a collection of Victorian antiques, which survive his death. *The Mangan Inheritance* (**1979**) involves a borderline use of Doppelgänger themes. BM's only sf novel proper, *Catholics* (**1972** Canada), set at the end of the century, describes the conflict between fashionable ecumenism and disillusioned conservatism in the Roman Catholic Church. [JC]

See also: CANADA.

MOORE, C(ATHERINE) L(UCILLE) (1911-1987) US writer who achieved instant fame with her first story, "Shambleau" for *Weird Tales* in 1933, a *femme fatale* story set on MARS. She continued to chronicle the exploits of its hero **Northwest Smith**, most of the series ultimately being assembled in *Scarlet Dream* (coll of linked stories **1981**; vt *Northwest Smith* 1982); the exceptions are "Nymph of Darkness" (1935) with Forrest J. ACKERMAN, "Quest of the Starstone" (1937) with Henry KUTTNER and "Werewoman" (1938). 4 of the 10 stories in *Scarlet Dream* had earlier appeared in *Shambleau and Others* (coll **1953**; with 3 of 7 stories cut, vt *Shambleau* 1958; with 1 story cut, also vt *Shambleau* UK 1961) and 5 in *Northwest of Earth* (coll **1954**); the remaining stories in these collections, comprising the first SWORD-AND-SORCERY series to feature a female HERO, **Jirel**, were recombined in *Jirel of Joiry* (coll of linked stories **1969**; vt *Black God's Shadow* 1977). Jirel also appears in the **Northwest Smith** story "Quest of the Starstone" (1937), CLM's first collaboration with Henry Kuttner, whom she married in 1940.

Most of CLM's and Kuttner's works after this were to some extent collaborations; each writer could reportedly pick up any story where the other had left off. They used a wide diversity of pseudonyms (◊ KUTTNER *for a listing*). Kuttner's wit, deftly audacious deployment of ideas and neat exposition well complemented CLM's perhaps greater talents of fluency and assiduity. When they became part of the stable of writers working for John W. CAMPBELL Jr's ASTOUNDING SCIENCE-FICTION during WWII they devised their most famous pseudonyms, Lewis Padgett and Laurence O'Donnell, under which they did much of their best work. Kuttner was the primary user of the Padgett name (*for details of which see his entry*) but the O'Donnell stories were more often CLM's. These include the remarkable "Clash By Night" (1943), whose sequel *Fury* (1947 as by O'Donnell; **1950**; vt *Destination Infinity* 1958) was a collaboration (although often reprinted as by Kuttner alone); the stories are set in CITIES located UNDER THE SEAS of VENUS after nuclear war has destroyed life on Earth. "Clash by Night" has been reprinted with an alternative sequel by David A. DRAKE in *The Jungle* (**1991**). 4 O'Donnell stories were combined with the title short novel (originally signed CLM) in *Judgment Night* (coll **1952**; title novel only **1965**), but these did not include the excellent "The Children's Hour" (1944) and the classic *Vintage Season* (1946; **1990** chap dos with a sequel, *In Another Country* by Robert SILVERBERG), about time-travelling tourists (◊ TIME TRAVEL); *Vintage Season* was filmed in 1991 as a passable direct-to-video movie, *Timescape*. CLM's other classic story of the 1940s was "No Woman Born" (1944 as by CLM), about a badly burned dancer who is given a ROBOT body and becomes a CYBORG. In these stories CLM's sometimes extravagant style is carefully controlled and combined with an earnest sentimentality which was underappreciated at the time.

CLM and Kuttner wrote a series of novels for STARTLING STORIES in the late 1940s which continued the colourful tradition of the **Northwest Smith** stories to become archetypes of the hybrid genre of SCIENCE FANTASY, neatly fusing the strengths of CLM's romanticism and Kuttner's vigorous plotting. *The Dark World* (1946 as by Kuttner; **1965** as by Kuttner) is a pastiche of A. MERRITT's *Dwellers in the Mirage* (**1932**) and was itself pastiched in Marion Zimmer BRADLEY's *Falcons of Narabedla* (1957; **1964**); other novels in the same vein are *Valley of the Flame* (1946 as by Keith

Hammond; **1964** as by Kuttner), "Lands of the Earthquake" (1947 as by Kuttner), *The Mask of Circe* (1948 as by Kuttner; **1971**), *The Time Axis* (1949 as by Kuttner; **1965** as by Kuttner), *Beyond Earth's Gates* (1949 as "The Portal in the Picture" by Kuttner; **1954** dos as by Padgett) and *Well of the Worlds* (1952 as by Kuttner; **1953** as by Padgett; vt *The Well of the Worlds* 1965 as by Kuttner). The first, second and fifth of these were combined in *The Startling Worlds of Henry Kuttner* (omni **1987**). *Earth's Last Citadel* (1943 *Argosy*; **1964**), with Kuttner, also belongs to this sequence, although one other *Startling Stories* novel, "Lord of the Storm" (1947 as by Hammond) does not. The attribution of these science-fantasy novels has rarely given CLM the credit which she deserves for her contribution to them.

In 1950 Kuttner and CLM went to study at the University of Southern California; although they wrote a number of mystery novels, there were few more sf stories. CLM did one solo sf novel in this period, *Doomsday Morning* (**1957**), a futuristic thriller which did not exploit her greatest strengths as a writer. Having graduated in 1956, CLM moved after Kuttner's death into writing for tv, doing scripts for such series as *Maverick* and *77 Sunset Strip* until she remarried in 1963 and abandoned writing for good.

CLM was the more prestigious writer by far when she married Kuttner, and remained the better half of their partnership, although unthinkingly sexist reportage has always lavished the greater praise on her husband. Her true status can be accurately judged from the collection *The Best of C.L. Moore* (coll **1975**) ed Lester DEL REY. Other collections in which her work appears include: *A Gnome There Was* (coll **1950**) as by Padgett; *Robots Have No Tails* (coll **1952** as by Padgett; 1973 as by Kuttner; vt *The Proud Robot: The Complete Gallegher Stories* 1983 UK); *Line to Tomorrow* (coll **1954**) as by Padgett; *No Boundaries* (coll **1955**) with Kuttner; *Clash by Night and Other Stories* (coll **1980** UK) with Kuttner, not to be confused with *Clash by Night* (**1952** chap Australia) as by Lawrence O'Donnell; and *Tomorrow and Tomorrow, and The Fairy Chessmen* (coll **1951**), as by Padgett, containing 2 full-length tales, the second of which was also published as *Chessboard Planet* (**1956**; vt *The Far Reality* 1963 UK), also as by Padgett. Another collaborative text was *Mutant* (fixup **1953** as by Padgett; 1954 UK as by Kuttner). Many collections signed Kuttner or Padgett (*for which see* KUTTNER) include work on which CLM collaborated with Kuttner.   [BS/MJE]

Other works: *There Shall be Darkness* (**1954** chap Australia) with Kuttner; most remaining titles as by Kuttner alone (*see his entry*) have anon contributions by CLM.

About the author: *Catherine Lucille Moore & Henry Kuttner, a Marriage of Souls and Talent: A Working Bibliography* (last rev **1989**) by Gordon BENSON Jr and Virgil S. Utter.

See also: ARTS; AUTOMATION; CRIME AND PUNISHMENT; DIMENSIONS; ECONOMICS; FANTASY; FAR FUTURE; GALACTIC

EMPIRES; GAMES AND SPORTS; GOLDEN AGE OF SF; MONSTERS; MUTANTS; PARALLEL WORLDS; RECURSIVE SF; SEX; SPACE OPERA; WOMEN SF WRITERS; WRITERS OF THE FUTURE CONTEST.

MOORE, HARRIS Joint pseudonym of Alf Harris (1928-   ), a Canadian, and Arthur Moore (?   -   ), whose nationality is not known. Together they wrote two sf novels: *Slater's Planet* (**1971** US), in which a spaceship looks for and finds alien life, and *The Marrow Eaters* (**1972** US), a garish adventure.   [JC]

MOORE, PATRICK (ALFRED) (1923-   ) UK astronomer, scientific journalist, popular tv personality (presenter of *The Sky at Night* BBC tv series from 1957) and writer, a composer, a Squadron Leader in the RAF during WWII, and holder of the OBE (Order of the British Empire). He has written over 100 nonfiction books, mainly on astronomy; at one time he wrote many CHILDREN'S SF adventures. His first novel was *Master of the Moon* (**1952**); others are *The Frozen Planet* (**1954**), *The Island of Fear* (**1954**), *Destination Luna* (**1955**), *Wheel in Space* (**1956**), *Captives of the Moon* (**1960**), *Wanderer in Space* (**1961**), *Crater of Fear* (**1962**), *Invader from Space* (**1963**), *Caverns of the Moon* (**1964**) and *Planet of Fire* (**1969**). The **Maurice Gray** series comprises *Mission to Mars* (**1955**), *The Domes of Mars* (**1956**), *The Voices of Mars* (**1957**), *Peril on Mars* (**1958**) and *Raiders of Mars* (**1959**). A second series comprises *Quest of the Spaceways* (**1955**) and *World of Mists* (**1956**). All these are jovial, though stereotyped – marrying, in their teenage protagonists, virtues like decency, honour and courage with scientific curiosity – and were popular in their day. Years later he embarked on another series, the **Scott Saunders** books: *Spy in Space* (**1977**), *Planet of Fear* (**1977**), *The Moon Raiders* (**1978**), *Killer Comet* (**1978**) and *The Terror Star* (**1979**).

PM also wrote a brief general study of sf, *Science and Fiction* (**1957**), one of the earliest books of its kind; portions are sensible enough, but whole areas of sf are quite ignored and the critical judgements are simplistic. A more useful book, of relevance to the PSEUDO-SCIENCE elements in sf, is *Can You Speak Venusian? A Guide to the Independent Thinkers* (**1972**; rev 1976). *How Britain Won the Space Race* (**1982**) with Desmond LESLIE is a spoof account of a 19th-century UK space programme. A recording of his musical compositions is *The Ever Ready Band Plays Music by Patrick Moore* (**1979**).   [PN]

Other works: Much nonfiction, including: *Challenge of the Stars* (**1972**) with David A. HARDY; *Black Holes in Space* (**1974**) with Iain Nicolson; *The Next Fifty Years in Space* (**1976**); *The Atlas of the Universe* (**1970**; rev 1981) and *The New Atlas of the Universe* (**1984**; rev 1988); *Countdown! or How Nigh is the End?* (**1983**).

See also: COLONIZATION OF OTHER WORLDS; MARS; MOON; PROTO SCIENCE FICTION; TERRAFORMING.

MOORE, RAYLYN (1928-   ) US writer who began publishing with "Death is a Woman" for *Esquire* in 1954. Her one novel of genre interest is *What Happened to Emily Goode after the Great Exhibition?* (**1978**).   [JC]

MOORE, ROBERT ◊ Robert Moore WILLIAMS.

MOORE, WALLACE ◊ Gerard F. CONWAY.

MOORE, (JOSEPH) WARD (1903-1978) US writer, initially as well known for his works outside the sf field – like the picaresque *Breathe the Air Again* (**1942**) – as for those within. Although he contributed only infrequently to the field, each of his books became something of a classic. His first sf publication was *Greener Than You Think* (**1947**; cut 1961), a successful comic SATIRE about a mutated form of grass which absorbs the entire world while governments dither. His second and most famous sf tale, *Bring the Jubilee* (**1953**), became the definitive ALTERNATE-WORLDS novel (also a TIME-TRAVEL story) in which the South wins the American Civil War. After describing his depressed world, an eminent historian from the disinherited Northern States is given the chance to travel back in time to the vital moment of the Civil War, the Battle of Gettysburg, victory in which had won the entire conflict for the South. At this crucial point, the narrator's own actions change history, the South loses the battle, and he is caught in the "past" (because his time machine will not be invented in the new future that has been created); in our own 1877 he writes out his narrative of the history he has changed, and the manuscript is discovered and published in 1953. Concise and elegiac, *Bring the Jubilee* has generated dozens of successor tales in which the Civil War is manipulated for reasons of controversy or nostalgia. WM's third novel, *Caduceus Wild* (**1959** *Science Fiction Stories* as with Robert Bradford; rev **1978**) is a medical DYSTOPIA whose book publication was long delayed. His final book, *Joyleg* (**1962**) with Avram DAVIDSON, returns to a nostalgic view of the USA, this time to comic effect, through the story of the eponymous immortal, who is found in this century living deep in the Appalachians because he claims to remain entitled to his Revolutionary War pension. His discoverers learn that a special brew keeps him young, from which point in the novel bureaucratic complications become tedious. WM was not a professional genre writer, and as a possible consequence much of his work seemed to have been written (and certainly it read) as though carefully and leisurely composed for his own pleasure.

WM also wrote two of the most notable stories describing nuclear HOLOCAUST and its consequences, "Lot" (1953) and "Lot's Daughter" (1954), featuring a great motorized exodus from a doomed Los Angeles, seen through biblical parallelism as the city of Sodom. The hero jettisons his irredeemably suburban wife and his sons and goes on to make a new and incestuous life with his daughter in the mountains. The ironies attached to his monstrous SURVIVALISM are savage. The stories were used as an uncredited basis for the film PANIC IN YEAR ZERO (1962), losing much of their power in the cleaning-up process.   [JC/PN]

See also: DISASTER; ECOLOGY; END OF THE WORLD; *The* MAGAZINE OF FANTASY AND SCIENCE FICTION; MARS; PASTORAL; TABOOS.

MOORE-BENTLEY, MARY ANN [r] ◊ AUSTRALIA.

MORAN, DANIEL ◊ Robert E. VARDEMAN.

MORAN, DANIEL KEYS (1962-   ) US writer who began publishing sf with, for *IASFM* in 1982, "All the Time in the World", a tale which on expansion became his first novel and the first volume of his projected **Tales of the Great Wheel of Existence** series, *The Armageddon Blues* (fixup **1988**). The story begins in an unremarkable post-HOLOCAUST USA and features a not unusual mutant barbarian female who hunts for a living; but, on her discovery of a time machine left by aliens, the plot soon begins to move in complicated leaps through time and space, engaging both the protagonist and an entropy-reversing long-lived SUPERMAN (whom she discovers in 1968) in a long arduous campaign to prevent the end of civilization. A second series, **Tales of the Continuing Time**, is projected to extend to 33 vols, although only 2 have appeared to date, *Emerald Eyes* (**1988**) and *The Long Run* (**1989**), with «The Last Dancer» (1992) projected. They feature the campaign – which again might be described as long and arduous – of a group of genetically engineered telepaths (◊ ESP) to maintain their existence in a world of hostile normals. The sequence as a whole is planned to deal with the descendants of the last telepath still to be alive at the close of «The Last Dancer». A singleton, *The Ring* ∗ (**1988**), tied to a projected film version of Wagner's **Ring** cycle, places its GODS (rationalized as genetically engineered superbeings) in a SPACE-OPERA venue. DKM displays very considerable energy and some humour, shows a fine VAN VOGT-style recklessness with superman plots, and has demonstrated a copious ambition.   [JC]

MORE, [Sir] THOMAS (1478-1535) UK writer, lawyer, diplomat and politician. The son of a barrister, he was first educated for the Church, but soon decided upon a secular career; he sat in Parliament and gained steadily in political influence, being knighted in 1521 and occupying several posts under Henry VIII until that king's proposed divorce from Catherine of Aragon; TM's subsequent refusal to swear to the Act of Supremacy led to his execution. He was canonized in 1935. Throughout his career he was intellectually involved with the kind of humanism best exemplified by his friend Erasmus (1466-1536), who spent some time in England, and the work by which TM is popularly remembered, *Utopia* (Part 2 **1516** in Latin; trans Ralphe Robynson including Part 1, written after Part 2, **1551**), can be seen as the first substantial humanistic work written by an Englishman.

In Part 1, TM, as a character, comes across Raphael Hythloday, a Portuguese seaman who went with Amerigo Vespucci to the New World. Hythloday, having discovered the ISLAND of Utopia on his travels, compares the corrupt state of European society with the ideal world of Utopia. In Part 2, Utopia is described in detail. It is a humanistic reversal of English society: all goods are held in common; the island's 54 shires are constructed and run rationally by citizens who participate fully in the government, though there are also slaves; arms are borne in self-defence only; there is religious tolerance, though not for atheists. Most of the rational ingredients of the hundreds of UTOPIAS (a word which, in TM's usage, is a pun on *ou-topos*, nowhere, and *eu-topos*, good place) that followed TM's initiative can be found in *Utopia*; what many of its successors lacked, however, was TM's insistence that his humanistic, rationally governed world was amenable to change, and that his picture of Utopia had caught only a moment in its evolution towards a more perfect constitution for the life of men on Earth.

While the majority of readers of *Utopia* seem to have assumed that TM was recommending the kind of society he would have liked to live in himself, a number of critics have pointed out that some of his suggestions may have been SATIRE; since irony is largely a matter of tone, and since it is difficult for most modern readers to evaluate the tone of a Latin text, it is almost impossible to prove the case one way or the other. Certainly some aspects of TM's Utopia seem, to the modern reader, rigid and even cruel, but to impute similar emotions to TM himself may be anachronistic sentimentality. However, at least in translation, the book has a kind of dry, ambiguous wit which suggests that to read it as a straightforward prospectus of the good life may be simplistic.

The degree to which *Utopia* and utopias in general can be thought of as relevant to sf, particularly GENRE SF of the 20th century, is controversial; it can be argued that the utopian tradition has contributed only minimally to the fundamentally Romance nature of modern sf (*but see* PROTO SCIENCE FICTION).

The amount of available reading on TM and on utopias is huge; some relevant works are listed under UTOPIAS.   [JC/PN]

See also: ECONOMICS; FUTUROLOGY.

MORE WILD, WILD WEST ◊ *The* WILD, WILD WEST.

MOREY, LEO (?   1965) US illustrator, born into a well-to-do family in Peru, educated in the USA, where he studied engineering at Louisiana State University; he worked as an artist in New Orleans before entering sf ILLUSTRATION. He took over from Frank R. PAUL as cover illustrator for AMAZING STORIES after it changed hands in 1929 (his first cover was Feb 1930), and painted 77 covers and many interior black-and-white illustrations for that magazine, and another 12 for *Amazing Stories Quarterly*. When these magazines were sold again he freelanced, doing covers for small magazines like *Super Science Stories* and quite a few interiors for *Thrilling Wonder Stories*, then worked mostly in COMICS. His archetypal PULP-MAGAZINE-style covers used a wider range of colours than Paul's; and, though naïve and crudely executed, they were vigorous and dramatic. His imaginary technology was not as interesting as Paul's but his rendering of people was superior. Though perhaps a better artist than Paul – some of his black-and-white work was very imaginative – he was never as popular.   [JG/PN]

MORGAN, CHRIS (1946-   ) UK editor, critic and writer who began publishing sf with "Clown Fish and Anemone" for *Science Fiction Monthly* in 1975. His fiction is generally unexceptional, though some stories – such as "Losing Control" (1989), about the crew of a crashed starship surviving by means of incestuous marriage and a strange form of symbiosis with an ALIEN species – involve interesting and innovative ideas. CM's main contribution has been as a critic, notably in *The Shape of Futures Past: The Story of Prediction* (**1980**), a comprehensive and valuable survey of pre-1945 PREDICTIONS about the future. *Future Man* (**1980**) is a history of sf speculations on possible biological and behavioural changes in humanity.   [NT]

Other works: *Fritz Leiber: A Bibliography 1934-1979* (**1979** chap); *Facts and Fallacies: A Book of Definitive Mistakes and Misguided Predictions* (**1981**) with David LANGFORD; *Dark Fantasies* (anth **1989**), collecting original stories.

See also: PSEUDO-SCIENCE.

MORGAN, DAN (1925-   ) UK writer and professional guitarist, about which instrument he wrote 2 successful manuals, *Guitar* (**1965**) and *Spanish Guitar* (**1982**). He began publishing sf with "Alien Analysis" for *NW* in 1952. His first sf novels, *Cee-Tee Man* (**1955**) and *The Uninhibited* (1957 *NW*; **1961**), were routine adventures, but *The Richest Corpse in Show Business* (**1966**) stood out for its slapstick guying of sf conventions. He published the **Venturer Twelve** SPACE-OPERA series – *A Thunder of Stars* (**1968**), *Seed of Stars* (**1972** US) and *The Neutral Stars* (**1973** US) all with John KIPPAX – and the much more interesting **Sixth Perception** series: *The New Minds* (**1967**), *The Several Minds* (**1969**), *The Mind Trap* (**1970** US) and *The Country of the Mind* (**1975**). In this latter series, which contains his most effective work, a band of people linked by their PSI POWERS solve problems, often in opposition to the world at large. Though not a powerful writer by any means, and though he has never transcended the US action-tale conventions to which he is so clearly indebted, it is all the same surprising that DM is so ignored.   [JC]

Other works: *Inside* (**1971**); *The High Destiny* (**1973** US); *The Concrete Horizon* (**1976**).

See also: ESP; MEDIA LANDSCAPE; MUSIC.

MORGAN, DAVE [r] ◊ ROBERT HALE LIMITED.

MORGAN, J.M. (?   -   ) US writer known only for her/his **Eden** sequence of post-HOLOCAUST tales set in a world devastated by a biological-warfare experiment (◊ BIOLOGY) gone awry. Volumes to date are *Desert Eden* (**1991**) and *Beyond Eden* (**1992**).   [JC]

MORGAN, SCOTT [s] ◊ Henry KUTTNER.

MORK AND MINDY US tv series (1978-82). Miller-Milkis Productions and Henderson Production Co. in association with Paramount Television/ABC. Created Garry K. Marshall, Dale McRaven, Joe Gauberg. Prod Marshall. Writers included McRaven, April Kelly, Tom Tenowich, Ed Scharlach, Bruce Johnson. Dirs included Howard Storm, Bob Claver. 1 50min pilot episode followed by 92 25min episodes. Colour.

Filling the gap in sitcoms about aliens viewing Earth between MY FAVORITE MARTIAN (1963-6) and ALF (1986-current), although its premise is more in line with Gore VIDAL's *Visit to a Small Planet* (1956; **1960**), *MAM* was a spin-off from *Happy Days* (1974-83); Mork from Ork (Robin Williams) first appeared in the 1950s-set sitcom in an episode entitled "My Favorite Orkan". Response to the character – an innocent in very 1970s multicoloured braces, bewildered and amazed by the entire Universe, and given to cries of "nanu nanu" – was so positive that Garry K. Marshall developed a series around him, in which he arrived on Earth in a giant-egg spaceship and went to Boulder, Colorado, where he moved in with the family of Mindy McConnell (Pam Dawber) and got a job in their music store. Although early episodes present Mork as a childlike, presexual character, the writers eventually had the couple marry and Mork give birth, in the backwards Orkan fashion, to the middle-aged Mearth (Jonathan Winters), who grew younger. Regular players included Conrad Janis and Elizabeth Kerr (as Mindy's father and grandmother), Robert Donner, Tom Poston, and the voice of Ralph James as Orson, Mork's Orkan leader. Often trite in its moralizing, the show was sometimes inspired in its skewed vision of life on Earth; and Williams, not yet the major screen personality he has become, was allowed to demonstrate his versatility as a clown.   [KN]

See also: SATIRE.

MORLAND, DICK Pseudonym used by UK writer and academic Reginald Hill (1936-   ) for his sf. Both of his sf novels as DM, *Heart Clock* (**1973**) and *Albion! Albion!* (**1974**), use DYSTOPIAN techniques to describe visions of repellent future UKs. In the first, citizens are fitted with termination devices for the government to use according to actuarial needs; in the second, England has been literally taken over by soccer rowdies and is divided into competing clubs with the citizenry as violent supporters. Both books are heavy-handed but enjoyably sharp-tongued. Hill, who also writes detections under his own name and as Patrick Ruell and Charles Underhill, has published one sf novel under his own name, *One Small Step: A Dalziel and Pascoe Novella* (**1990**), a detection set on the Moon in AD2010.   [JC]

MORLEY, CHRISTOPHER (DARLINGTON) (1890-1957) US man of letters and novelist who remains best known for mildly fantasticated (but not fantasy) tales like *Parnassus on Wheels* (**1917**) and *The Haunted Bookshop* (**1919**), and for *Kitty Foyle* (**1939**), a sentimental romance. *Where the Blue Begins* (**1922**), a fantasy, describes the social life in New York of a dog with human characteristics. *Thunder on the Left* (**1925**), though also essentially a fantasy, uses its TIME-TRAVEL theme to transport its child protagonist into a taxing future. *The Trojan Horse* (**1937**) employs the Homeric tale to satirize modern life. The narrator of *The Swiss Family Manhattan* (**1932**), victim of a Zeppelin crash which deposits his family atop a New York skyscraper under construction, at first thinks Americans are "anthropoids" (◊ APES AND CAVEMEN), but the text soon becomes a mundane SATIRE. [JC]

Other work: *The Arrow* (**1927** chap; exp vt as coll *The Arrow, and Two Other Stories* 1927 UK).

MORLEY, FELIX (1894-1982) US writer whose *Gumption Island* (**1956**) features a Russian superweapon which knocks some Americans on an island back millions of years in time. [JC]

MORLEY, WILFRED OWEN [s] ◊ Robert A.W. LOWNDES.

MORONS FROM OUTER SPACE Film (1985). Dir Mike Hodges, starring Mel Smith, Griff Rhys Jones, Joanne Pearce, Jimmy Nail, Paul Bown, Dinsdale Landen. Screenplay Jones, Smith, developed Bob Mercer. 97 mins, cut to 91 mins. Colour.

Very stupid ALIENS (identical in appearance and behaviour to humans) have rented a spaceship to go on holiday. They crashland on a UK motorway and later become media stars. This remarkably unfunny film, written by and starring two tv comedians – it looks like a tv sketch blown up out of all proportion – is partly set in the USA in an attempt to broaden its appeal, but what humour it has is impenetrably English; the satirical possibilities are barely explored (in contrast to EARTH GIRLS ARE EASY [1988]). *MFOS* was a comedown for director Hodges, whose previous sf movies were *The* TERMINAL MAN (1974) and FLASH GORDON (1980). [PN]

MORRESSY, JOHN (1930-   ) US writer and professor of English at Franklin Pierce College in New Hampshire. He began his sf career in 1971 – after 2 non-genre novels – with "Accuracy" for *FSF*, where most of his short fiction has since appeared. JM's early books were generally SPACE OPERA, through which medium he constructed a series of interesting ALIEN societies, and most of them shared a common galactic background: a somewhat disordered polity still dominated by humans, though with no imperial government. Within this scenario, his stories tended to the dark and extravagant end of the sf-epic spectrum, as in the **Del Whitby** trilogy – *Starbrat* (**1972**), *Nail Down the Stars* (**1973**; vt *Stardrift* 1975) and *Under a Calculating Star* (**1975**) – which intriguingly tells the same tale of interstellar intrigue and revolution from three partial points of view; none of the protagonists (orphans or impostors all) knows the whole story. Also set explicitly in the same galactic scene were *A Law for the Stars* (**1976** Canada) and *Frostworld and Dreamfire* (**1977**). The latter is a strongly constructed and occasionally rousing epic of a metamorphic humanoid's search for a breeding-partner; the last of his race on his native planet, he must find her elsewhere or the race dies. Later sf works, like *The Mansions of Space* (**1983**), continue to inhabit the same loosely defined, dark-textured milieu, but JM's 1970s juveniles were not identifiably set there: *The Windows of Forever* (**1975**) is an effective TIME-TRAVEL tale, and *The Humans of Ziax II* (**1974** chap) and *The Drought on Ziax II* (**1978** chap) apply the concerns of ECOLOGY to a planet colonized by humans, though the natives of Ziax survive in the jungles. In the 1980s JM concentrated mainly on two fantasy sequences: the **Iron Angel** series – *Ironbrand* (**1980**), *Graymantle* (**1981**), *Kingsbane* (**1982**) and *The Time of the Annihilator* (**1985**) – and the **Kedrigern** series, about a wizard – *A Voice for Princess* (**1986**), *A Questing of Kedrigern* (**1987**), *Kedrigern in Wanderland* (**1988**), *Kedrigern and the Charming Couple* (**1990**) and *A Remembrance for Kedrigern* (**1990**). This latter series, in strong contrast to JM's early work, is determinedly light-hearted. His first novels are perhaps more likely to last. [JC]

Other work: *The Extraterritorial* (**1977** Canada).

MORRILL, ROWENA ◊ ROWENA.

MORRIS, A.G. [s] ◊ Katherine MacLEAN.

MORRIS, ALFRED (?   -?   ) UK writer whose *Looking Ahead!: A Tale of Adventure (Not by the Author of "Looking Backward")* (**1892**) conveys its anti-Edward BELLAMY and anti-socialist argument through a ROBINSONADE plot which involves its young protagonist, shipwrecked with his crew on a desert island, in a series of political experiments. Socialism does not work; monarchy serves well. After half a century, he returns to England, which has gone to ruin after a socialist coup of 1905. [JC]

MORRIS, CHRIS Working name of US rock musician and writer Christopher Crosby Morris (1946-   ); he is married to Janet E. MORRIS, who played bass in his band and with whom he has written several sf novels (*see her entry*). With Jane Stump (1936-   ), writing together as Daniel Stryker, he is responsible for two sf adventures, *Cobra* (**1991**) and *Hawk* (**1991**). [JC]

MORRIS, GOUVERNEUR (1876-1953) US banker and writer, great-grandson of the Founding Father Gouverneur Morris (1752-1816) and extremely prolific in his day as an author of short fiction. Some of his work is sf and fantasy, beginning with a prehistoric tale, *The Pagan's Progress* (**1904**), in which the hero begins to acquire spiritual values. *The Voice in the Rice* (**1910**) is a lost-race novel whose contemporary narrator discovers an Antebellum society in a swamp. Other titles include *The Footprint and Other Stories* (coll **1908**), *It and Other Stories* (coll **1912**) – which includes "Back There in the Grass" (1911 *Colliers*), an enduring demonstration of the terrors of BIOLOGY in early sf – *If You Touch Them They Vanish* (**1913**) and, with Charles W. Goddard, *The Goddess* (**1915**). [JC]

See also: ORIGIN OF MAN.

MORRIS, JANET E(LLEN) (1946-   ) US writer who gained some note as bass player 1972-5 in the band named after her husband, Chris MORRIS; he subsequently collaborated with JEM on several sf novels, always as Chris Morris. She herself began writing with the ambitious **Silistra** sequence, comprising *High Couch of Silistra* (**1977**; rev vt *Returning Creation* 1984), *The Golden Sword* (**1977**), *Wind from the Abyss* (**1978**) and *The Carnelian Throne* (**1979**). Toughly told and intellectually extremist, the sequence (prematurely) proclaimed an ambition on her part to write at the highest possible level; it cannot be said that she has quite fulfilled this ambition. **Silistra** intriguingly presents a society complexly conceived in terms of patterns (some literal) of cultural and biological bondage. Already, a sense of historical analogies pervades the texts, and in the **Dream Dancer** trilogy – *Dream Dancer* (**1980** UK), *Cruiser Dreams* (**1981**) and *Earth Dreams* (**1982**) – this becomes explicit; wafted away from Earth, the young protagonist of the series climbs into the upper echelons of a culture whose assumptions about behaviour reflect the world of Hellenistic Greece. The main sf instrument deployed in these books – starships run by AIs which establish symbiotic relationships with humans – prefigures JEM's growing interest in the combat side of history, and the sequence itself becomes nightmarishly complicated in its traversal of implied analogies from the past. In the **Tempus** fantasies, based on the **Thieves' World** SHARED-WORLD enterprise – *Beyond Sanctuary* * (**1985**), *Beyond the Veil* * (**1985**), *Beyond Wizardwall* * (**1986**), *Tempus* * (coll of linked stories **1987**), *City at the Edge of Time* * (**1988**) with Chris Morris, *Tempus Unbound* * (**1989**) with Chris Morris, and *Storm Seed* * (**1990**) with Chris Morris – the traversals of historical material become even more hectic. In the **Heroes in Hell** shared-world enterprise, which JEM co-created with C.J. CHERRYH – *Heroes in Hell* * (anth **1986**) with Cherryh, *Rebels in Hell* * (anth **1986**) with Cherryh, *The Gates of Hell* * (fixup **1986**) with Cherryh, *Masters in Hell* * (anth **1987**), *Kings in Hell* * (**1987**) with Cherryh, *Angels in Hell* * (anth **1987**), *War in Hell* * (anth **1988**), *The Little Helliad* * (**1988**) with Chris Morris, *Explorers in Hell* * (**1989**) with David A. DRAKE and *Prophets in Hell* * (anth **1989**) – the result is something like chaos. In these works, which occupy much of JEM's bibliography, the sharp cognitive focus has softened, and the use of female protagonists whose sexual natures are controversially foregrounded has also become somewhat routinized.

More interesting are some of the singletons, almost always written in collaboration; they are deeply engaged in military matters, violent, often extremely bloody, and profoundly cynical about all governments and their agencies. *The 40-Minute War* (**1984**) with Chris Morris presents an utterly disastrous nuclear HOLOCAUST brought about by stupidity; only by changing history through a commandeered TIME-TRAVEL device is the world saved. *Active Measures* (**1985**) with David A. Drake involves spying activities in the NEAR FUTURE. *M*E*D*U*S*A* (**1986**) with Chris Morris describes Sky War activities in a similar venue. *Outpassage* (**1988**) with Chris Morris is a bleak military adventure, and the **Threshold Terminal** sequence – *Threshold* (**1990**) and *Trust Territory* (**1992**), both with Chris Morris – generates a similarly bleak vision of a Solar System engaging in agonistic conflicts and interstellar diplomacy within the confines of the eponymous space artifact. Throughout her career, JEM has consistently worked to strip her language and plots of ornateness and idiosyncracy, and her collaborative works are, at times, vividly efficient. At other times, however, little sense of JEM's individual gifts as a writer with strong convictions survives the impersonality. [JC]

Other works: *I, the Sun* (**1983**), historical novel; *Afterwar* (anth **1985**); *Warlord!* (**1987**); *Kill Ratio* (**1987**) with David A. Drake; *Target* (**1989**) with Drake.

See also: ESCHATOLOGY; REINCARNATION.

MORRIS, JIM (1940-) US writer whose *The Sheriff of Purgatory* (**1979**; rev vt *Spurlock: Sheriff of Purgatory* 1987) describes, with moments of sharpness, a conflict between the sheriff and the Mafia, after the HOLOCAUST, in the eponymous Arkansas county. The action soon moves to a devastated New York City. [JC]

Other works: *Breeder* (**1988**).

MORRIS, RALPH Probably pseudonymous author of the ROBINSONADE *A Narrative of the Life and Astonishing Adventures of John Daniel . . . Taken from his own Mouth, by Mr Ralph Morris* (**1751**), which involves a voyage to the MOON and the discovery of unearthly creatures there. The protagonists are unaware of where they are marooned, although the reader is allowed to know. [JC]

MORRIS, WILLIAM (1834-1896) UK artist and writer whose greatest fame rests on his work as a designer of furniture and fabrics. His efforts to reform the prevalent vulgarity of mid-Victorian taste and to preserve standards of craftsmanship placed him in radical and irresolvable conflict with the basic tendencies of the industrial era, then in the first vigour of its youth. This conflict was variously expressed in his writing. In his early poems, collected in *The Defence of Guenevere* (coll **1858**) and *The Earthly Paradise* (coll in 3 vols **1868-70**), WM created the literary equivalent of Pre-Raphaelite paintings: romances of febrile charm and phthisic delicacy. The relation of these poems to their own time is one of studied and disdainful avoidance. In life such avoidance was to be denied him. He was – at least emotionally – cuckolded on an Arthurian scale by his friend and mentor, Dante Gabriel Rossetti (1828-1882). He became involved in POLITICS through his efforts, beginning in 1878, to save historical buildings from demolition and unwise "restoration". This involvement led him, remarkably quickly, to an active and enduring commitment to socialism.

It was from this unusual (for its day) perspective of orthodox Marxism that WM wrote his UTOPIA, *News from Nowhere, or An Epoch of Rest* (**1890** US; rev 1891 UK). Written in immediate response to Edward BELLAMY's *Looking Backward, 2000-1887* (**1888**), the novel propels its dreaming narrator from the England of WM's day into a perfected England from which all traces of poverty, squalor and industrial unsightliness have been effaced, an England that bears notable similarities to the bucolic dream-landscapes of his early poetry. As a work of fiction, this most translucent of utopias exhibits all the clarity, grace – and narrative force – of WM's best wallpaper designs. Where the book is most visibly Marxist in inspiration, as in the capsule history of a proletarian revolution in Chapter XVII, it is also most densely and compellingly imagined. Its influence on later utopian writing has been negligible, and on GENRE SF still less, since WM's vision is so relentlessly PASTORAL, looking back to an idealized Middle Ages – which he also represented in the earlier and structurally related socialist romance, "A Dream of John Ball" (in *A Dream of John Ball, and A King's Lesson* [coll **1888**], later issued in its own right as *A Dream of John Ball* [**1915** US]) – rather than to the urban, technologically advanced "future" of common consensus.

During the composition of *News from Nowhere* the Socialist League, which WM had founded in 1884 and funded thereafter, dissolved as a result of an excess of democracy. This event encouraged, by reaction, WM's tendency to make his later writing into a species of highly ornamented wish-fulfilment from which the less savoury odours of daily life were artfully exorcized. The prose romances of his last years – such as *The Wood Beyond the World* (**1894**) and *The Well at the World's End* (**1896**) – have the same reluctantly valedictory air as his most defiantly escapist poetry but little of the poetry's hypnotic harmony. He had become, once more, "the idle singer of an empty day". It is these late romances, however, through their acknowledged influence on C.S. LEWIS, J.R.R. TOLKIEN and lesser writers of the SWORD-AND-SORCERY subgenre, that have most impinged on sf.

WM also translated Icelandic sagas and several Greek and Roman classics. [TMD]

Other works: *The Life and Death of Jason* (**1867**), a poem; *A Tale of the House of the Wolfings, and All the Kindreds of the Mark* (**1889**), an historical romance with fantasy elements; *The Roots of the Mountains* (**1889**); *The Story of the Glittering Plain* (**1891**); *Child Christopher and Goldilind the Fair* (**1895**); *The Water of the Wondrous Isles* (**1897**); *The Sundering Flood* (**1898**). WM's early work was assembled in *The Early Romances of William Morris* (coll **1907**), which includes some material taken from the *Oxford and Cambridge Magazine* and separately published after his death, such as *The Hollow Land* (1856; **1897** chap US), *Golden Wings* (1856; **1904** chap US) and *Gertha's Lovers* (1856; **1905** chap US). Later collections include: *Prose and Poetry (1856-1879)* (coll **1913**); *Early Romances* (coll **1924**); *Selections from the Prose Works* (coll **1931**), *Three Works by William Morris: A Dream of John Ball, The Pilgrims of Hope, News from Nowhere* (omni **1968** US); *Golden Wings, and Other Stories* (coll **1976** US); *Svend and his Brethren* (coll **1909** chap US); *The Juvenilia of William Morris, with a Checklist and Unpublished Early Poems* (coll **1983** US).

About the author: Much has been written about WM. Studies of interest include: *William Morris: Romantic to Revolutionary* (**1955**) by E.P. THOMPSON; *William Morris, the Marxist Dreamer* (trans **1978**) by Paul Meier; *William Morris: A Reference Guide* (**1985**) by G.L. Aho.

See also: ARTS; HISTORY OF SF; SLEEPER AWAKES.

MORRISON, RICHARD and ROBERT ◊ Robert A.W. LOWNDES.

MORRISSEY, J(OSEPH) L(AWRENCE) (1905-   ) UK (almost certainly, although he has been listed as US) writer who began publishing thrillers in the 1930s and 1940s. His sf was restricted to the 1960s. *City of the Hidden Eyes* ∗ (**1960** UK) with Philip Levene was adapted from the latter's BBC radio serial about underground monsters threatening the surface world. As Richard Saxon JLM wrote several volumes of inconspicuous but not entirely negligible sf, including *The Stars Came Down* (**1964** UK), which is a UTOPIA, *The Hour of the Phoenix* (**1964** UK; 1965 US as by Henry Richards), *Cosmic Crusade* (**1964** UK) and *Future for Sale* (**1964** UK). [JC]

MORROW, GRAY Working name of US illustrator Dwight Graydon Morrow (1934-   ). Like a number of sf artists, GM began in COMICS, working with Atlas, Warren and other companies, although he did some sf covers for *If* and *Gal* in 1959 and through the 1960s produced covers and black-and-white interiors for these two – carrying over much of his lively (if sometimes crude) comics style and often using a distinctive "pen and wash" – as well as for *AMZ*, *FSF* and *Fantastic*. During the mid-1960s he began painting book covers also, especially for Avon Books, BALLANTINE BOOKS and ACE BOOKS, doing over 100 PERRY RHODAN covers for the latter. His comics work has never completely stopped: he contributed to HEAVY METAL and in the 1980s took over illustration of the FLASH GORDON comic strip. *The Illustrated Roger Zelazny* (**1978**) by ZELAZNY and GM gives a good idea of his style. He has 3 times been nominated for a HUGO. [PN]

See also: MARVEL COMICS.

MORROW, JAMES (KENNETH) (1947-   ) US writer who lectured and taught in the 1970s, served as a contributing editor to *Media and Methods* magazine 1978-80, and produced material for Boston tv 1979-84. His first book was *Moviemaking Illustrated: The Comic-book Filmbook* (**1973**). Through the 1980s he produced several textbooks for children, along with at least 5 children's novels beginning with *The Quasar Kids* (**1987**). Unsurprisingly, his first sf novel, *The Wine of Violence* (**1981**), shows in its smooth competence clear signs of JM's wide experience, though even here can be sensed a tendency, which has increased over the years, for his control over the suspension of disbelief to falter – quite deliberately, perhaps – at rhetorical high-points. That these slippages almost invariably occur at moments when JM wishes to convey an intense ethical concern for the human race does not alter the fact that, for some readers, they weaken the fictional context from which they derive their specific meaning. *The Wine of Violence* is set on a planet long colonized by humans, who have divided into two societies, the nomad Brain-Eaters, who do precisely that, and the Quetzalians, who discharge their human aggressiveness into a symbolic conduit which encircles their city walls. Chances to engage in humanist sarcasms – witness the very name Brain-Eaters – are rarely missed as the plot develops, and the Quetzalians are forced by a group of human visitors to the planet to come to grips, pyrrhically, with the vile nomads. JM's second novel, *The Continent of Lies* (**1984**), also set on a planet settled by humans, is less shaken by rhetorical overlays. With wit and concision it traces the attempts of its protagonist to track down an evil category of "dreambean" – good dreambeans being fruits which generate innocuous entertainment-hallucinations when eaten – before it can madden its victims into thinking of it as a god. Some moments of existential doubt intervene, but all comes right in the end.

With *This is the Way the World Ends* (**1986**) JM abandoned the galactic stage, for which he clearly felt only muted sympathy, and came to Earth; as the book begins, a nuclear HOLOCAUST kills all but a few, who are then transported via submarine to Antarctica, where they are put on trial by the "unadmitted" – those souls who will now never be born. As an idea it is perhaps more effective in paraphrase than within the constraints of a fictional narrative, though the decency of the book clearly transcends the inevitable disembodiedness of its message. *Only Begotten Daughter* (**1990**) tells the story of Christ's sister, Julie Katz, whose virgin birth derives from the fact that her father has contributed to a sperm bank and whose life in other ways mirrors and affectionately spoofs the Christian version. Counterpointed to that life, which is told with sympathy and verve, are the stories of Satan and a fundamentalist minister, the former being perhaps the more plausible creation; Julie's preordained destiny plays out against these figures. Short stories – JM has not been a prolific writer of them – are assembled in *Swatting at the Cosmos* (coll **1990**), which includes the NEBULA-winning "Bible Stories for Adults, No.17: The Deluge" (**1988**). *City of Truth* (**1991** UK), a novella, conveys in parable form some sharp lessons about the nature of art and the subtle virtues of untruth, with considerable wit.

JM's work has been likened to that of Kurt VONNEGUT Jr, and similarities are indeed very evident. JM could easily be seen as a more attractive author than his mentor, and certainly he couches his vision of the world's plight more happily than Vonnegut has ever done. But, while Vonnegut never disbelieves in the medium of his art, JM has great difficulty giving credence to the artifices of fiction. This may be the price paid for passion and clarity of mind; and it may be a price worth paying. [JC]

Other work: *The Adventures of Smoke Bailey* ∗ (**1983** chap), a computer-game tie.

See also: ARTS; DISASTER; END OF THE WORLD; LEISURE; MESSIAHS; PERCEPTION; PSYCHOLOGY; RELIGION.

MORSELLI, GUIDO [r] ◊ ITALY.

MORT EN DIRECT, LA (vt *Death Watch*) Film (1979). Selta Film/Little Bear/Sara Film/Gaumont/Antenne 2/TV 15. Coprod and dir Bernard Tavernier, starring Romy Schneider, Harvey Keitel, Harry Dean Stanton,

Max Von Sydow. Screenplay David Rayfiel, Tavernier, based on *The Continuous Katherine Mortenhoe* (**1974**; vt *The Unsleeping Eye*) by D.G. COMPTON. 130 mins. Colour.

This French/West German coproduction chose, perhaps eccentrically, to locate its DYSTOPIAN city of the future in Glasgow, and the film was shot in English. In a bored NEAR FUTURE where illness has been almost eradicated, death has an obscene fascination. A tv station, keen to broadcast a real-life soap opera, sends cameraman Roddy (Keitel) to film, without her knowledge, the last days of Katherine (Schneider), who helps computers write romantic novels and who is dying of a rare disease; this is achieved by surgically implanting in his skull a camera that operates through his eyes. The evocation of the future is perfunctory: just a dash of urban blight. Attention is tremulously on the morbid relationship of invalid and cameraman. He blinds himself; she (who, we and she discover, is not really dying at all) commits suicide. As an attack on MEDIA invasion of privacy – a popular subject in sociological sf – this suffers from morbid overkill, itself reminiscent of soap opera. [PN]

MORTON, J(OHN CAMERON AUDRIEU) B(ING-HAM MICHAEL) (1893-1979) UK writer primarily known as Beachcomber, a house name of which he had sole use for half a century, and under which he wrote a comic column for the London *Daily Express* 1924-75. He specialized in long, serialized fantastical spoof narratives whose protagonists were themselves hyperbolic comic types, this material being re-sorted in several collections from *Mr Thake* (coll **1929**) to *Beachcomber: The Works of J.B. Morton* (coll **1974**; vt *The Bumper Beachcomber*) ed Richard Ingrams. Of his actual novels, *Drink Up, Gentlemen* (**1930**), a near-future SATIRE on English mores after the fashion of his mentor Hilaire BELLOC, is sf. The borderline *Skylighters* (**1934**) mocks a new religion. *1933 and Still Going Wrong* (coll **1932**) assembles verse satires, and *The Death of the Dragon: New Fairy Tales* (coll **1934**) assembles fantasies. [JC]

MOSKOWITZ, SAM (1920-   ) US sf historian and anthologist; he also worked, as Sam Martin, as an editor of trade magazines for the frozen-foods industry, retiring in 1985. For a long time SM, a prominent member of sf FANDOM since 1936, has been among the best known of all historians and commentators from within GENRE SF; his work in this field antedates that of nearly all non-genre historians of the field, with the notable exception of J.O. BAILEY. His first book was *The Immortal Storm* (**1951** mimeographed; 1954), a history of early sf fandom which recounted the feuds of the late 1930s among the then-tiny group of sf fans with a passion and detail quite unabraded by the passing years, and which won a 1955 HUGO. More important were SM's profiles of sf authors and discussions of sf themes, which appeared in various sf magazines, primarily *AMZ*, from 1959. Many of these were collected (and revised) in 3 vols: *Explorers* *of the Infinite* (coll **1963**), which concentrates on the period up to 1940; *Seekers of Tomorrow* (coll **1966**), which concentrates on writers 1940-65; and *Strange Horizons* (coll **1976**), about such sf themes as RELIGION, women (◊ WOMEN AS PORTRAYED IN SCIENCE FICTION), Blacks and antisemitism in sf. SM's scholarship and criticism were not to everybody's taste, and these works have at times been criticized within the genre and by academics for inaccuracies and a not always fluent style. But the fact remains that, though some of his data and conclusions have been argued, SM did more original research in this field than any other scholar of his period and few since; no later history of sf has not made use of SM's painstaking work, especially his research into the early HISTORY OF SF in periodical publications. Much of this work appeared in 3 further vols which gave long historical introductions to collections of stories: *Science Fiction by Gaslight: A History and Anthology of Science Fiction in the Popular Magazines, 1891-1911* (anth **1968**), *Under the Moons of Mars: A History and Anthology of the Scientific Romance in the Munsey Magazines, 1912-1920* (anth **1970**) and *The Crystal Man* (coll **1973**) by Edgar Page MITCHELL, ed SM. 3 later books in the same vein are *Far Future Calling: Uncollected Science Fiction and Fantasies* (coll **1980**) by Olaf STAPLEDON, ed with a long biographical study by SM, *Science Fiction in Old San Francisco: Vol. 1, History of the Movement from 1854 to 1890* (anth **1980**) ed SM, and *Into the Sun and Other Stories: Science Fiction in Old San Francisco, Vol 2* (coll **1980**) by Robert Duncan MILNE, ed SM. Although SM is not an academic, and does not always lay out his findings as carefully as academics might like – being sometimes rather cavalier in withholding his sources of information – the above books are a major contribution to sf scholarship. This contribution won him a PILGRIM AWARD in 1981.

SM's professional connection with sf includes a brief stint as a writer, with 3 stories in 1941, the first being a SPACE-OPERA novella of distant galaxies, "The Way Back" for *Comet Stories*, and a couple more in the mid-1950s. He was an sf literary agent 1940-41, and managing editor for the last GERNSBACK magazine, SCIENCE FICTION PLUS, 1952-4. He also edited a brief, 4-issue revival of WEIRD TALES 1973-4. He ghost-edited a number of ANTHOLOGIES, including 4 which appeared as ed Leo MARGULIES, 2 as ed Roger ELWOOD and 3 as ed Alden H. Norton. He was special consultant on and largely responsible for *Contact* (anth **1963**) ed Noel Keyes and *The Pulps* (anth **1970**) ed Tony Goodstone.

SM also ed the following: *Life Everlasting* (coll **1947**) by David H. KELLER with intro by SM; *Editor's Choice in Science Fiction* (anth **1954**); *The Coming of the Robots* (anth **1963**); *Exploring Other Worlds* (anth **1963**); *A Martian Odyssey and Other Classics of Science Fiction* (coll **1966**) by Stanley G. WEINBAUM with intro by SM; *Modern Masterpieces of Science Fiction* (anth **1966**; vt in 3 vols *Doorway into Time* 1966, *Microcosmic God* 1968 and *The Vortex Blasters* 1968; vt in 2 vols as *Doorway*

into Time 1973 and *The Microcosmic God* 1975); *Strange Signposts* (anth **1966**) with Roger Elwood; *Three Stories* (anth **1967**; vt *A Sense of Wonder* 1967 UK with intro severely cut; vt *The Moon Era* 1969 US); *The Human Zero* (anth **1967**) with Elwood; *Masterpieces of Science Fiction* (anth **1967**); *The Time Curve* (anth **1968**) with Elwood; *The Man who Called Himself Poe* (anth **1969**; vt *A Man Called Poe* 1972 UK), a collection of essays, poems and stories about Edgar Allan POE, plus 2 stories arguably by Poe; *Other Worlds, Other Times* (anth **1969**) with Elwood; *Alien Earth* (anth **1969**) with Elwood; *Great Untold Stories of Fantasy and Horror* (anth **1969**) with Alden H. Norton; *Futures to Infinity* (anth **1970**); *The Citadel of Fear* (**1970**) by Francis STEVENS, intro by SM; *Ghostly by Gaslight* (anth **1971**) with Norton; *The Space Magicians* (anth **1971**) with Norton; *The Ultimate World* (**1971**) by Hugo GERNS-BACK, intro by SM, a late and dreadful novel by Gernsback ed to half manuscript length by SM; *Horrors Unknown* (anth **1971**); *When Women Rule* (anth **1972**); *Horrors in Hiding* (anth **1973**) with Norton; *Horrors Unseen* (anth **1974**); *The Raid of "Le Vengeur"* (coll **1974**), hitherto uncollected stories by George GRIFFITH, intro by SM; *Out of the Storm* (coll **1975**) by William Hope HODGSON with a 25,000-word critical biography by SM; *"A Dream of X"* (**1977**) by Hodgson, illus Stephen E. FABIAN, a short version of *The Night Land* (**1912**), intro by SM; *A. Merritt: Reflections in the Moon Pool* (coll **1985**), Merritt marginalia, with long biographical intro by SM; *Howard Phillips Lovecraft and Nils Helmer Frome: A Recollection of One of Canada's Oldest Science Fiction Fans* (anth **1989**), letters, articles, etc., by and about Frome, many about his relationship with Lovecraft.

SM's other work includes his editorship of the 2 useful HYPERION PRESS series of reprints of sf classics in 1974 and 1976; the Hyperion series includes also reprints of 6 of SM's most important historical works. [PN]

Other works: *Peace and Olaf Stapledon* (**1949**), *Hugo Gernsback: Father of Science Fiction* (**1959**), *A Canticle for P. Schuyler Miller* (**1975**) and *Charles Fort: A Radical Corpuscle* (**1976**), four privately printed pamphlets.

See also: COLLECTIONS; CRITICAL AND HISTORICAL WORKS ABOUT SF; DEFINITIONS OF SF; GENERATION STARSHIPS; NEW WAVE; OPTIMISM AND PESSIMISM; SF IN THE CLASSROOM; SOCIOLOGY.

MOST DANGEROUS MAN ALIVE, THE Film (1958). Trans-Global/Columbia. Dir Allan Dwan, starring Ron Randell, Debra Paget, Elaine Stewart, Anthony Caruso. Screenplay James Leicester, Phillip Rock, based on a story by Rock, Michael Pate. 82 mins, cut to 76 mins. B/w.

In this unusual blend of sf and crime movie, a framed gangster (Randell) escapes from prison and hides out in the desert, where he is caught up in a nuclear test. He survives but discovers that he is slowly turning to steel. This enables him to exact revenge on those who framed him – he can absorb bullets – but the process gradually robs him of humanity, which worries the woman who loves him (Stewart) and renders his seduction by his two-timing ex-mistress (Paget) rather difficult. He is eventually destroyed by soldiers wielding flame-throwers. The film is cheaply made and its script banal, but veteran director Dwan imbues it with a certain harsh power. [JB/PN]

MOST DANGEROUS MAN IN THE WORLD, THE (vt *The Chairman*) Film (1969). Apjac/20th Century-Fox. Dir J. Lee Thompson, starring Gregory Peck, Anne Heywood, Arthur Hill, Conrad Yama. Screenplay Ben Maddow, based on *The Most Dangerous Man in the World* by Jay Richard Kennedy. 104 mins. Colour.

A distinguished SCIENTIST (Peck) has a transmitter implanted in his head and is sent to China with the object of convincing Chairman Mao that he is a political defector. It is hoped he will learn the formula of a new enzyme, developed by the Chinese, that will enable crops to grow anywhere in the world; everything he says or hears goes via satellite to the intelligence team in London – who, unknown to him, have also implanted a small bomb in his head as insurance. This thriller is no more than mildly effective, its main oddity being the role, at the end, of the Russian army as valiant rescuers. [JB/PN]

MOST THRILLING SCIENCE FICTION EVER TOLD, THE One of the many reprint DIGEST-size magazines published by Sol Cohen's Ultimate Publishing Co., using reprint rights acquired when he bought AMAZING STORIES and FANTASTIC. 42 issues early 1966-July 1975. Issues #1-#13 and #18 appeared as *The Most Thrilling SF Ever Told*, other issues as *Thrilling Science Fiction Adventures* (#14-#17) and *Thrilling Science Fiction* (#19 to the end). The publishing schedule was rather irregularly quarterly. The first 6 issues were undated; the first 25 issues were numbered consecutively, but thereafter only month/year was used. Most issues used stories of medium to good quality by well known names from the period when Cele GOLDSMITH edited *AMZ* and *Fantastic*, but in #14-#25 older (and dreadful) stories by obscure authors were published, probably because of a dispute between Cohen and the SCIENCE FICTION WRITERS OF AMERICA regarding payment for the reprints. Another Ultimate magazine, SCIENCE FICTION (ADVENTURE) CLASSICS, merged with *Thrilling Science Fiction* for its last 2 issues in 1975. [BS]

MOSURA (vt *Mothra*) Film (1961). Toho. Dir Inoshiro Honda, starring Frankie Sakai, Hiroshi Koizumi, Kyoko Kagawa and the twins Emi and Yumi Ito. Screenplay Shinichi Sekizawa, based on a story by Shinichiro Nakamura, Takehido Fukunaga, Yoshi Hotta. 100 mins. Colour.

Aficionados of Japanese MONSTER MOVIES find their delight not only in the monsters themselves: the attraction depends also on the sheer bizarreness, to Western eyes and ears, of the stories and dialogue. *M* is perhaps the most notably grotesque of all in this respect, its relatively mundane giant moth being amply compensated for by the eccentricities of the

story. Two 6in (15cm) women (the Ito twins), kidnapped from an island whose inhabitants have been mutated by radiation, are used as nightclub singers by an evil "Rosilican" (i.e., US) showman (Kagawa). Back on the island a huge, venerated egg hatches in response to prayers from the local natives, and the giant caterpillar that emerges swims off to Japan to save the dwarf-girls, whose piping singing voices act as a homing signal. It makes a mess of Tokyo and spins a cocoon; the giant moth that emerges goes off to Rosilica (where the showman has retreated) and saves the girls. This is Toho's most sophisticated MONSTER MOVIE; its imagery, though lunatic, is surprisingly poignant.

Mosura never developed the following of GOJIRA (Godzilla) and GAMERA, but did reappear 4 times, in *Mosura Tai Gojira* (1964; vt *Gojira Tai Mothra*; released in English as *Godzilla Vs. The Thing*; vt *Godzilla Vs. Mothra*), where, called by the tiny twins, she saves Tokyo from Gojira; *Ghidorah Sandai Kaiju Chikyu Saidai No Kessan* (1964; vt *Chikyu Saidai No Kessan*; released in English as *Ghidrah, The Three-Headed Monster*), in which she defends Earth from an alien monster, helped out by Gojira and RADON (Rodan) when she can't do the job on her own; *Nankai No Daiketto* (1966; released in English as *Ebirah, Horror of the Deep*; vt *Godzilla Vs. the Sea-Monster*) dir Jun Fukuda, the first of the series not to be dir Honda, in which Mosura takes part in an aerial evacuation of people from an island about to explode; and *Kaiju Soshingeki* (1968; released in English as *Destroy All Monsters*; vt *Operation Monsterland*; vt *The March of the Monsters*) dir Honda, a poor film in which all 11 Toho monsters get together. [PN]

MOSURA TAI GOJIRA ◊ GOJIRA; MOSURA.

MOSZKOWSKI, ALEXANDR (1851-1934) German writer. In his excellent and encyclopedic SATIRE of UTOPIAS *Die Inselt der Weisheit* (**1922** Germany; trans H.J. Stenning as *The Isles of Wisdom* **1924** UK) the protagonists are guided by Nostradamus through an archipelago which features a Platonic (◊ PLATO) ISLAND, a Buddhist utopia, an Island of Fine ARTS, pacifist islands, reactionary islands, and so on. Of particular interest is Sarragalla, the "Mechanized Island", where the technological utopianism of Walther Rathenau (1867-1922) is mercilessly satirized. The characters conclude that "every principle is bound to break down, somewhere, or, if its application is enforced, it is transformed into a caricature of itself". [BS]

Other work: *Der Venuspark* ["The Venus Park"] (**1923**).

See also: AUTOMATION.

MOTHRA ◊ MOSURA.

MOTTRAM, R(ALPH) H(ALE) (1883-1971) UK writer and banker who began his long and prolific writing career as a chronicler of his WWI experiences in the famous **Spanish Farm** trilogy, beginning with *The Spanish Farm* (**1924**). In his sf novel, *The Visit of the Princess: A Romance of the Nineteen-Sixties* (**1946**), a joyless UK is galvanized by the visit of a European princess. Fantasy titles are *The Old Man of the Stones: A Christmas Allegory* (**1930** chap), *The Ghost and the Maiden* (**1940**), *The Gentleman of Leisure* (**1948**), in which the Gentleman travels to Heaven, and *To Hell, with Crabb Robinson* (**1962**), which takes its protagonist elsewhere. [JC/PN]

MOUDY, WALTER (FRANK) (1929-1973) US writer, author of a few sf stories after his sole novel, *No Man on Earth* (**1964**), a rather compellingly told story in which a man born of a human mother and an alien father must seek out his destiny. [JC]

MOUNDS, MONICA ◊ Robert E. VARDEMAN.

MOXLEY, F(RANK) WRIGHT (1889-1937) US writer whose interesting *Red Snow* (**1930**) tells of a snowlike precipitation which causes worldwide sterility, and of the subsequent social breakdown, lovingly elaborated. One survivor is rescued by what may be an enigmatic alien but – as the vessel from the heavens is drawn by horses – is more likely to be Helios. But this fantasy-like ending does little to dispel the sf materiality of the preceding events. [JC/PN]

MOYLAN, TOM [r] ◊ POSTMODERNISM AND SF.

MR To avoid confusion over variant spellings, entries whose first word is "Mr" are listed as if that title were spelt out in full as "Mister".

MROZEK, SLAWOMIR (1930-) Polish writer, mainly of absurdist plays (◊ FABULATION), several of which are assembled in *Six Plays* (trans N. Bethell **1967** UK); a further play, *Vatzlav* (**1970**; trans Ralph Manheim **1970** chap US), is set in a mythical metamorphosis-engendering territory. The short stories in *Słón* (coll **1957**; trans Konrad Syrop as *The Elephant* **1962** UK) and *The Ugupu Bird* (coll trans Konrad Syrop **1968** UK) – the latter derived from *Wesele w Atomicach* (coll **1959**), *Deszcz* (coll **1962**) and *Ucieczka na Południe* (coll **1965**) – satirically mix fantasy and absurdist elements in a manner similar to that of Italo CALVINO. [JC]

MUDD, STEVE (? -) US writer whose sf novels, *Tangled Webs* (**1989**) and its sequel *The Planet Beyond* (**1990**), are adventures set in a totalitarian interstellar venue. [JC]

MUDDOCK, J(OYCE) E(MMERSON) PRESTON (1843-1934) UK writer, much travelled in early life, who published prolifically under his own name and as Dick Donovan, generally restricting his pseudonym to juveniles and thrillers, including *Tales of Terror* (coll **1889**) and *The Scarlet Seal* (**1902**), the latter a witchcraft fantasy. As JEPM he published considerable nonfiction as well as *Stories Weird and Wonderful* (coll **1889**) and *The Sunless City* (**1905**), in which a submarine explores a seemingly bottomless lake in the Rockies and comes upon a lost race (◊ LOST WORLDS). [JC]

MUDGETT, HERMAN W. [s] ◊ Anthony BOUCHER.

MUIR, WARD (1878-1927) UK writer whose "*Further East than Asia*" (**1919**) is set in a LOST WORLD whose inhabitants gain longevity through bathing in a radioactive pool, which also disfigures them. [JC]

MULISCH, HARRY [r] ◊ BENELUX.

MULLALLY, FREDERIC (1920-) UK writer whose only sf novel, *Hitler Has Won* (**1975**), is a competent presentation of what has become a very common ALTERNATE-WORLD vision of history (◊ HITLER WINS). FM's particular explanation for Hitler's victory involves an early assault on Russia. [JC]

MULLEN, R(ICHARD) D(ALE) (1915-) US sf critic and scholar, now emeritus professor of English at Indiana State University. RDM was a founding member of the SCIENCE FICTION RESEARCH ASSOCIATION. In 1973 he established SCIENCE-FICTION STUDIES and was its publisher and, with Darko SUVIN, its co-editor through 1978; he returned to the journal as an editor in 1991 and managing editor from the Nov 1991 issue. He and Suvin also ed *Science-Fiction Studies: Selected Articles on Science Fiction 1973-75* (anth **1976**) and *Science-Fiction Studies: Selected Articles on Science Fiction 1976-77* (anth **1978**). RDM's editorial personality is relaxed, sensible, meticulous, and always eager to get the facts straight, qualities which also permeate his interesting criticism, mostly published in EXTRA-POLATION and *Science-Fiction Studies*. [PN]

MULLEN, STANLEY (1911-1973) US artist, museum curator and pulp writer. He wrote over 30 sf and fantasy stories, many SPACE OPERA, in a variety of magazines, including PLANET STORIES, 1949-59. His 3 books, from SMALL PRESSES, are *Kinsmen of the Dragon* (**1951**), which pits the hero against a secret society whose magical science has roots in a PARALLEL WORLD, *Sphinx Child* (**1948** chap), a fantasy short story, and *Moonfoam and Sorceries* (coll **1948**). [PN]

See also: ASTEROIDS.

MULLER, JOHN E. House name used on many sf and supernatural novels published by BADGER BOOKS. The great majority of these were the work of R.L. FANTHORPE (31 titles), with 3 by John S. GLASBY and 1 by A.A. GLYNN (*for titles see those authors*). Works of unknown authorship are: *Space Void* (**1960**; 1965 US as by Marston Johns), *Edge of Eternity* (**1962**), *Night of the Big Fire* (**1962**) and *In the Beginning* (**1962**). [JC]

MULLER, PAUL ◊ Paul CONRAD.

MÜLLER, PAUL ALFRED [r] ◊ GERMANY.

MULLIN, CHRIS Working name of UK politician and writer Christopher John Mullin (1947-), whose *A Very British Coup* (**1982**), adapted for tv in 1990, depicts with fixated clarity successful NEAR-FUTURE US efforts to subvert a potential change for the better in the UK Government. [JC]

MULTIVERSE ◊ PARALLEL WORLDS.

MUNDY, TALBOT Pseudonym of UK-born writer William Lancaster Gribbon (1879-1940), who emigrated to the USA in 1909 after his early life as a confidence man, ivory poacher and all-round rogue in British Africa had culminated in a prison sentence. He soon became a professional author, with most of his work first appearing in *Adventure* magazine, where he became the star writer; after 1935 he left PULP-MAGAZINE fiction and wrote scripts for the radio series **Jack Armstrong, the All-American Boy**. TM's fiction is sometimes difficult to classify. In his early stories he tried to combine MAINSTREAM standards with exotic adventure in Africa and the Near East; his later work often carried a didactic message and might be called philosophic adventure fiction. From the first his sf stood apart from US GENRE SF in its narrative structure, characterization and situation, having grown out of the adult adventure-fiction models to be found in *Adventure*, with tight, complex plotting, well handled ethnic types and exotic locales, and a strong influence from Rudyard KIPLING. He commonly used quest themes, stressing loyalty, honour and spiritual self-development. The fantastic element derived in large part from occultism, with ideas drawn from a schismatic branch of the Theosophical Society to which he belonged. Such motifs – which included various PSI POWERS, fantastic archaeology, incredible WEAPONS, strange drugs, ANTIGRAVITY, atomic energy, Atlantean science, SUPERMEN (mahatmas), transmutation of elements and vibratory phenomena – were conceived rationally and "scientifically" as part of the ancient wisdom, a body of knowledge once possessed by mankind but since lost.

Most of TM's sf can be found in the large group of associated novels known as the **Jimgrim/Ramsden** sequence, though the interconnections are sometimes slender. Chief characters include Jimgrim (James Schuyler Grim), a US soldier of fortune, Athelstan King, an Anglo-Indian career officer, Jeff Ramsden, a US engineer, Narayan Singh, a Sikh soldier, and Chullunder Ghose, an unscrupulously brilliant Bengali babu. TM's more important works in this series are: *The Mystery of Khufu's Tomb* (1922 *Adventure* as "Khufu's Real Tomb"; **1933**), fantastic archaeology based on Ancient Egyptian superscience; *Caves of Terror* (1922 *Adventure* as "The Gray Mahatma"; **1924**), in which a vibratory superscience possessed by Jain adepts is in danger of falling into the hands of an adventuress; *Om: The Secret of Ahbor Valley* (**1924**), which is ultimately concerned with a jade sphere from a great past civilization, but is noteworthy for its description of a travelling Indian dramatic group; *The Nine Unknown* (**1924**), in which an investigation into the disappearance of gold in India uncovers both a benevolent secret organization that disintegrates the gold for atomic power and an evil Shaktist order that uses secrets from the Ancient Wisdom as "magic"; *Jimgrim* (1930-31 *Adventure* as "King of the World"; **1931**; vt *Jimgrim Sahib* 1953), featuring an attempt at world conquest using scientific secrets from ATLANTIS deciphered from golden plates found in buried cities in the Gobi; and *There Was a Door* (**1933** UK; vt *Full Moon* 1935 US), with Fortean elements (◊ Charles FORT), disappearances into another DIMENSION, fantastic archaeology and superscience of the past. Some of TM's novels – like *The Devil's Guard* (**1926**; vt *Ramsden* 1926 UK), *Black Light* (**1930**) and *Old Ugly-Face* (**1939** UK) – gradually moved toward religious occultism.

TM remains best known for the **Tros of Samothrace** books, a sequence of minimally fantastic, essentially mainstream historical stories set in Britain, Gaul and the Mediterranean world just before the beginning of the Christian Era, with debunking portraits of Julius Caesar, Cleopatra and others. First appearing irregularly 1925-35 in *Adventure*, these stories were published in book form as *Queen Cleopatra* (**1929**), *Tros of Samothrace* (**1934**; vt in 4 vols as *Tros* 1967, *Helma* 1967, *Liafall* 1967 and *Helene* 1967; vt in 3 vols as *Lud of Lunden* 1976, *Avenging Liafall* 1976 and *The Praetor's Dungeon* 1976) and *The Purple Pirate* (**1935**). For sf readers, however, the **Jimgrim/Ramsden** books are of greater interest. At his best, TM was a highly competent writer who produced the finest stories of Oriental adventure to appear in the pulps. [EFB]

Other works: *King – of the Khyber Rifles* (**1916**); *The Thunder Dragon Gate* (**1937**).

About the author: *Talbot Mundy: Messenger of Destiny* (**1983**) by Donald M. Grant (1927-   ) *et al.*; *Last Adventurer: The Life of Talbot Mundy* (**1984**) by Peter Berresford Ellis (1943-   ); *An Index to Adventure Magazine* (2 vols **1990**) by Richard BLEILER.

MUNKÁCSY, JÁNOS [r] ◊ HUNGARY.

MUNRO, DUNCAN H. [s] ◊ Eric Frank RUSSELL.

MUNRO, H.H. [r] ◊ SAKI.

MUNRO, JOHN (1849-1930) UK engineer, professor of mechanical engineering at Bristol, and author of 2 short stories, "Sun-Rise in the Moon" (1894) and "A Message from Mars" (1895), in *Cassell's Magazine*. The latter was revised to form the first chapter of *A Trip to Venus* (**1897**), an unexceptional account of a journey by ROCKET to an idyllic UTOPIA on VENUS, with a brief excursion to MERCURY. [JE]

MUNSEY, FRANK A(NDREW) (1854-1925) US newspaper and magazine publisher and writer. He began publishing in 1882 with *The Golden Argosy*, a weekly BOYS' PAPER, later transformed into *The* ARGOSY. FAM expanded his titles to include MUNSEY'S MAGAZINE, *The* SCRAP BOOK, *The* ALL-STORY, CAVALIER and later, after a complex series of mergers and title changes, *All-Story Weekly* and *Argosy All-Story Weekly*. A self-made millionaire, FAM was reviled for his heavy-handed treatment of the newspapers under his control. Under the editorship of Robert Hobart Davis, his magazines became the most important pre-sf PULP MAGAZINES, publishing many works by prominent sf and fantasy authors, including Edgar Rice BURROUGHS, Ray CUMMINGS, George Allan ENGLAND, Ralph Milne FARLEY, Homer Eon FLINT, Austin HALL, Otis Adelbert KLINE, A. MERRITT and Sax ROHMER. [JE]

See also: HISTORY OF SF.

MUNSEY'S MAGAZINE US magazine published by the Frank A. MUNSEY Corp.; ed Richard H. Thitherton (with Robert Hobart Davis as fiction editor) and others. Appeared from 2 Feb 1889 as *Munsey's Weekly*, then as *MM* Oct 1891-Oct 1929, when it merged with *Argosy All-Story Weekly* (◊ *The* ARGOSY) to form 2 magazines, *Argosy Weekly* and *All-Story Love Tales*.

Although *MM* was contemporary with *The* ALL-STORY it published little sf, and that little was not of any lasting quality. Most notable was its publication of stories by E.F. BENSON, Ray CUMMINGS, George Allan ENGLAND and Sax ROHMER. It also published the borderline-sf *The Green Ray* (1922-3; **1924**) by Vance THOMPSON. [JE]

MUNSEY'S WEEKLY ◊ MUNSEY'S MAGAZINE.

MURAKAMI, HARUKI (1949-   ) Japanese writer of very considerable popularity whose *Hitsuji o meguru boken* (**1982**; trans Alfred Birnbaum as *A Wild Sheep Chase* **1989** US) tumbles a bevy of eccentric protagonists into a chase for a fabricated sheep in a style that mixes FABULATION and nightmare. *Sekai no owar to hard-boiled wonderland* (**1984**; trans Alfred Birnbaum as *Hard-Boiled Wonderland and the End of the World* **1991** US), which is marginally more conventional, depicts a WAR for data in a NEAR-FUTURE Japan that has become definable as a nest of information. [JC]

MURDOCK, M(ELINDA) S(EABROOKE) (1947-   ) US writer who began writing sf with a STAR TREK tie, *Web of the Romulans* * (**1983**), and who later continued in much the same vein with her BUCK ROGERS sequence: *Rebellion 2456* * (**1989**), *Hammer of Mars* * (**1989**), *Armageddon Off Vesta* * (**1989**) and *Prime Squared* * (**1990**). In between, MSM composed a SPACE-OPERA series of her own – *Vendetta* (**1987**) and *Dynteryx* (**1988**) – but this did little to modify a sense that her use of the conventions of 1980s adventure sf, though professional, lacked a personal touch. [JC]

MURNANE, GERALD (1939-   ) Australian writer, highly regarded in his native land for his experimental short stories and novels, such as *Tamarisk Row* (**1974**). GM's meditative style bears comparison with that of Jorge Luis BORGES. He disclaims any connection with sf, but has written several fictions about ALTERNATE WORLDS. In *The Plains* (**1982**) the narrator enters an alternate Australia: an inland feudal society, whose landowners, devoted patrons of the arts, take part in elaborate games and rituals. The narrator is hired to make a film about this society, but in the end accepts its solipsistic ideals and abandons his project. "The Battle of Acosta Nu" (**1985**), which can be found in *Landscape with Landscape* (coll of linked novellas **1985**), tells of a man living in Melbourne, Australia, who all his life believes himself to be living in New Australia, the (actual) Australian colony founded in Paraguay in the early 1900s. Or perhaps it is the other way around. [BG]

MURPHY, DENNIS JASPER ◊ Charles MATURIN.

MURPHY, PAT (1955-   ) Working name of US writer Patrice Ann Murphy (1955-   ), who began publishing sf in the 1970s, her first acknowledged story being "Nightbird at the Window" in *Chrysalis 5* (anth **1979**) ed Roy TORGESON. Her first novel was the obscurely published *The Shadow Hunter* (**1982**), in which a Stone-Age man is displaced by a TIME-TRAVEL device into a cruelly alienating future. The theme of displacement, whether through time or across the gulf of species, significantly shapes PM's two most famous works. *Rachel in Love* (1987 *IASFM*; **1992** chap), which won a NEBULA and a THEODORE STURGEON MEMORIAL AWARD, tells from her point of view the story of a chimpanzee with enhanced INTELLIGENCE (*see also* APES AND CAVEMEN) who escapes an impersonally horrific research institute. Nothing in the tale, with the exception of Rachel's cognitively enhanced responses, is in any sense sf, or even unlikely. *The Falling Woman* (**1986**), which won PM another Nebula in the same year, concentrates upon a contemporary woman archaeologist who is capable of perceiving, through palimpsests of midden and artifact, figures from the period being investigated at a dig in Mexico, and can observe their ghostlike maintenance of their ancient daily endeavours. A triangle of implications develops intriguingly between one of the Mayans, who speaks to the protagonist, and her estranged daughter, and climaxes in a kind of healing transtemporal embrace.

After editing and producing environmental reports and graphics for various Pacific Coast organizations, PM began in 1982 to edit the *Exploratorium Quarterly*, the journal of the Exploratorium, a San Francisco museum designed to promote a hands-on relationship between human perception and the arts and sciences. Elements of her next novel, *The City, Not Long After* (1984 *Universe 14*, anth ed Robert SILVERBERG as "Art in the War Zone"; much exp **1988**), clearly extrapolate some of the Exploratorium agenda. Set after a plague HOLOCAUST in a physically intact San Francisco, the tale presents its protagonists' capacity to make ART analogous to the shaping of a new reality. If there is a slight air of local patriotism in the book's apotheosis of San Francisco, it is at the same time perhaps something of a relief to participate in a vision of the future not bound by CYBERPUNK shibboleths. PM, like Kim Stanley ROBINSON, had been described in the course of the 1980s as a Humanist writer, in a formulation which opposed Cyberpunk to Humanism, generally to the discredit of the latter; also like Robinson, she resisted the labelling, which she clearly found procrustean. Her stories have been assembled as *Points of Departure* (coll **1990**), which won a PHILIP K. DICK AWARD, and in *Letters from Home* (coll **1991** UK) with Pat CADIGAN and Karen Joy FOWLER, each author contributing solo tales to the volume. Though PM's career seems to be edging away from sf, it can be predicted that, from her coign of vantage, she will continue to fertilize the genre. [JC]

See also: FANTASY; INTERZONE.

MURPHY, WARREN (B.) (1933-   ) US writer known largely for the **Destroyer** sequence, a long series of spoof thrillers, many with Richard Ben SAPIR, featuring the **Doc Savage**-like adventures of Remo Williams, a White man (and avatar of Shiva the Destroyer) trained in the paranormal combat arts of Sinanju, which allow him (for instance) to interpenetrate his body with other matter. The first titles were written mostly by WBM and Sapir, who died in 1987, but later titles – sometimes listed as by these two, sometimes by one alone – are by various hands including WBM. The most prolific recent author of

Destroyer titles is Will MURRAY, who also wrote *The Assassin's Handbook* (coll **1982**; rev vt *Inside Sinanju* 1985) as by WBM and Sapir, an amused (and amusing) companion to the sequence; other authors include WBM's wife Molly Cochran, Ed Hunsburger, William Joy, Ric MEYERS and Robert Randisi. A detailed presentation of titles, listing ascribed and actual authors, can be found in R. REGINALD's «Science Fiction & Fantasy Literature: A Bibliography, 1975-1991» (1992). Here we pay no attention to ascribed author (always, in any case, WBM and/or Sapir); up to #74, unless otherwise indicated, the actual author is WBM, alone or with Sapir; from #74 on the author is Murray.

The sequence began, rather inauspiciously, with *Created, the Destroyer* (**1971**) with Sapir (who collaborated on all but one through #24) and *Destroyer #2: Death Check* (**1972**), ponderous imitations of **James Bond**; but with *#3: Chinese Puzzle* (**1972**) it took off with remarkable panache, some instalments coming close to SPACE OPERA, others engaging with SUPERMAN themes, and most indulging in raucous SATIRE of US politics and mores. The sequence then runs: *#4: Mafia Fix* (**1972**), *#5: Dr Quake* (**1972**), *#6: Death Therapy* (**1972**), *#7: Union Bust* (**1973**), *#8: Summit Chase* (**1973**) by Murphy alone, *#9: Murder's Shield* (**1973**), *#10: Terror Squad* (**1973**), *#11: Kill or Cure* (**1973**), *#12: Slave Safari* (**1973**), *#13: Acid Rock* (**1973**), *#14: Judgment Day* (**1974**), *#15: Murder Ward* (**1974**), *#16: Oil Slick* (**1974**), *#17: Last War Dance* (**1974**), *#18: Funny Money* (**1975**), *#19: Holy Terror* (**1975**), *#20: Assassin's Play-Off* (**1975**), *#21: Deadly Seeds* (**1975**), *#22: Brain Drain* (**1976**), *#23: Child's Play* (**1976**), *#24: King's Curse* (**1976**), *#25: Sweet Dreams* (**1976**) with Meyers, *#26: In Enemy Hands* (**1977**), *#27: The Last Temple* (**1977**) with Meyers, *#28: Ship of Death* (**1977**), *#29: The Final Death* (**1977**) with Sapir and Meyers, *#30: Mugger Blood* (**1977**), *#31: The Head Men* (**1977**), *#32: Killer Chromosomes* (**1978**), *#33: Voodoo Die* (**1978**), *#34: Chained Reaction* (**1978**), *#35: Last Call* (**1978**), *#36: Power Play* (**1979**), *#37: Bottom Line* (**1979**), *#38: Bay City Blast* (**1979**), *#39: Missing Link* (**1980**), *#40: Dangerous Games* (**1980**) with Randisi, *#41: Firing Line* (**1980**), *#42: Timber Line* (**1980**) with Joy, *#43: Midnight Man* (**1981**) with Randisi, *#44: Balance of Power* (**1981**) with Cochran, *#45: Spoils of War* (**1981**) by Cochran, *#46: Next of Kin* (**1981**) by Cochran, *#47: Dying Space* (**1982**) by Cochran, *#48: Profit Motive* (**1982**), *#49: Skin Deep* (**1982**) by Cochran, *#50: Killing Time* (**1982**) by Cochran, *#51: Shock Value* (**1983**) by Cochran, *#52: Fool's Gold* (**1983**), *#53: Time Trial* (**1983**) by Cochran, *#54: Last Drop* (**1983**) by Cochran, *#55: Master's Challenge* (**1984**) with Sapir and Cochran, *#56: Encounter Group* (**1984**) with Murray, *#57: Date with Death* (**1984**) with Cochran and Hunsburger, *#58: Total Recall* (**1984**) with Randisi, *#59: The Arms of Kali* (**1984**), *#60: The End of the Game* (**1985**), *#61: Lords of the Earth* (**1985**), *#62: The Seventh Stone* (**1985**) with Sapir and Hunsburger, *#63: The Sky is Falling* (**1986**) by Sapir and Murray, *#64: The Last Alchemist* (**1986**) with Murray, *#65: Lost Yesterday* (**1986**) by Sapir and Murray, *#66:*

Sue Me (**1986**) by Sapir, *#67: Look into my Eyes* (**1987**) by Sapir, *#68: An Old-Fashioned War* (**1987**) by Sapir, *#69: Blood Ties* (**1987**) with Murray, *#70: The Eleventh Hour* (**1987**) with Cochran and Murray, *#71: Return Engagement* (**1988**) with Murray, *#72: Sole Survivor* (**1988**) with Murray, *#73: Line of Succession* (**1988**) with Murray, *#74: Walking Wounded* (**1988**) by Murray (who is responsible for the remaining titles listed), *#75: Rain of Terror* (**1989**), *#76: The Final Crusade* (**1989**), *#77: Coin of the Realm* (**1989**), *#78: Blue Smoke and Mirrors* (**1989**), *#79: Shooting Schedule* (**1990**), *#80: Death Sentence* (**1990**), *#81: Hostile Takeover* (**1990**), *#82: Survival Course* (**1990**), *#83: Skull Duggery* (**1991**), *#84: Ground Zero* (**1991**), *#85: Blood Lust* (**1991**), *#86: Arabian Nightmare* (**1991**) and *#88: The Ultimate Death* (**1992**) (we cannot trace #87). An out-of-series **Destroyer** title, *Remo: The Adventure Begins* * (**1985**) by Sapir, is a film tie to *Remo Williams: The Adventure Begins* (1985; vt *Remo – Unarmed and Dangerous*).

Other genre adventures by WM include *Grandmaster* (**1984**) with his wife Molly Cochran, *High Priest* (**1987**) with Cochran, *The Hand of Lazarus* (**1988**) with Cochran, *Scorpion's Dance* (**1990**), and *The Forever King* (**1992**), again with Cochran. [JC]

MURRAY, (GEORGE) GILBERT (AIME) (1866-1957) UK classical scholar, best known for his many translations from the Greek classic drama, for his UTOPIAN sense that contemporary society could be changed by persuasion (justified in the case of women's suffrage) and for seminal studies such as *The Rise of the Greek Epic* (**1907**) and *Four Stages of Greek Religion* (**1912**). His sf novel, *Gobi or Shamo: A Story of Three Songs* (**1889**), as by G.G.A. Murray, is a lost-race tale (◊ LOST WORLDS) featuring a race of Hellenes whose ethical precepts are unsparingly ancient but who have also mastered weapons of mass destruction. [JC]

MURRAY, WILL Working name of US writer William Patrick Murray (1953-   ), who has shown an interest throughout his career in pulp SUPERHEROES like DOC SAVAGE, about which figure he wrote the nonfiction *Secrets of Doc Savage* (**1981** chap); as Kenneth ROBESON he began a new sequence of **Doc Savage** adventures with *Doc Savage: Python Isle* * (**1991**). Under his own name he ed *The Duende History of the Shadow Magazine* (anth **1980**). Writing as Warren MURPHY (*whom see for titles*) and/or Richard SAPIR, he has written many volumes of the **Destroyer** sequence, including all those from #74 to date (although forthcoming titles will, it seems, be by yet other hands). [JC]

MURRY, COLIN MIDDLETON ◊ Richard COWPER.

MUSIC This article is in 3 parts: **1**, Science Fiction in Classical Music; **2**, Science Fiction in Popular and Rock Music; **3**, Music in Science Fiction. Because of the almost endless proliferation of popular and rock music, and because there are so many ways in which the latter (in particular) interpenetrates with sf and fantasy, section **2** is itself divided into 2 parts, from different hands: Maxim JAKUBOWSKI's comments focus on the pre-1980s period, while Charles Shaar Murray's concentrate on more recent work.

1. Science fiction in classical music By historical necessity, sf being in the broad sense a 20th-century phenomenon, earlier classical music was generally unaffected by it, but there are exceptions: Baldassare Galuppi (1706-1785) in 1750 and Franz Joseph Haydn (1732-1809) in 1777 each wrote a comic opera with the title *Il Mondo della Luna* ["The World of the Moon"] to a libretto by Carlo Goldoni (1707-1793). More directly attributable to sf is the musical adaptation by Jacques Offenbach (1819-1880), as "Le Voyage dans la lune" (1875), of the Jules VERNE book known in English as *From the Earth to the Moon* (2 parts, **1865**, **1870**; trans **1873**). The Moon is again the scene of the action in the first part of the opera *The Excursions of Mr Brouček* (1917) by Leoš Janáček (1854-1928), based on the novel by Svatopluk Čech (◊ CZECH AND SLOVAK SF): the leading character dreams he has been transported there while in a drunken stupor. In *The Makropoulos Secret* (1925) Janáček adapted Karel ČAPEK's play about IMMORTALITY. In the anthology *Les soirées de l'orchestre* (1853) Hector Berlioz (1803-1869) provides an interesting footnote in "Euphonia", a short sf tale of a musical city.

Other musical works of the late 19th and early 20th century have taken on sf connotations because of their subsequent use, such as *Also Sprach Zarathustra* (1896) by Richard Strauss (1864-1949), which was featured in Stanley KUBRICK's film 2001: A SPACE ODYSSEY (1968). The *Planets* suite (1918) by Gustav Holst (1874-1934) has often been used in sf contexts. Many compositions since 1950 have followed Holst's astronomical (in his case, astrological) lead, especially those for which avant-garde instrumental techniques or electronic music might make more traditional titles seem incongruous; thus numerous titles such as "Cosmos", "Galaxy", "Nebula" and "Orbit" can be found. Works are named after star charts (*Atlas Eclipticalis* [1961] by John Cage [1912-1992]), inspired by types of celestial objects (*Neutron Star* [1968] by Jan W. Morthenson [1940-] and *Quasars* [1980] by Christian Clozier [1945-]) or by individual heavenly bodies (*Sirius* [1968] by Karlheinz Stockhausen [1928-]), and dedicated to or illustrative of the journeys of early astronauts and cosmonauts: in the USSR many songs and ballads were composed in honour of Yuri Gagarin (1935-1968).

Electronic music for illustrating "the music of the spheres" – a phrase that has been used of the work of Terry Riley (1935-), François Bayle (1932-) and others – and stories of outer space can be found not only in film soundtracks, especially Louis (1923-) and Bebe (1928-) Barron's pioneering score for FORBIDDEN PLANET (1956) and the understated contributions by Eduard Artem'ev (1937-) to Andrei TARKOVSKY's SOLARIS (1971) and STALKER (1979), but also in short pieces commissioned or adapted by music-hire libraries, like Desmond LESLIE's *Inside the Space Ship* and *Music of the Voids of Outer Space* (both *c*1957). Works with similar titles also appeared early on in concert programmes, with pieces such as

Visions of Flying Saucers (1966 with Leo Nilsson) and *Robot Amoroso* (1978) by Ralph Lundsten (1936-). The use of electric instruments permeates the avant-garde reaches of jazz and jazz-rock as with the Mahavishnu Orchestra, Weather Report and Sun Ra's Arkestra (whose varied names, including Blue Universe Arkestra, Solar Myth Arkestra and Cosmo Love Arkestra, testify to a kind of sf allegiance).

Another relationship is the direct linkage of a piece of music to an existing sf story. In rare cases this consists of a vocal work with an sf text, as with the song-cycle *The Tentacles of the Dark Nebula* (1969) by David Bedford (1937-), from Arthur C. CLARKE's story "Transience" (1949), and *The Music and Poetry of the Kesh* (1985) by Todd Barton, musical settings of the poems in Ursula LE GUIN's *Always Coming Home* (**1985**). More often a purely electronic or instrumental composition was inspired by or evokes the atmosphere of the original story, as in *Quatermass* (1964; ◊ Nigel KNEALE) by Tod Dockstader (1932-), *Alpha Ralpha Boulevard* (1979; based on a 1961 story by Cordwainer SMITH) by Ralph Lundsten, the cycle *Kristallwelt* (1983-6; in homage to J.G. BALLARD's *The Crystal World* [**1966**]) by Michael Obst (1955-), and several further works by Bedford, including *Jack of Shadows* (1973; based on Roger ZELAZNY's **1971** novel), *Star's End* (1974; refers to Isaac ASIMOV's **Foundation** trilogy) and *The Ones who Walk Away from Omelas* (1976; based on the 1973 story by Le Guin). *The Birthplace of Matter* (1975) by Sten Hanson (1936-) refers to sf concepts, while his *The John Carter Song Book* (1979-85) is more unusual: it is based, we are told, on the minimal information about Martian music in Edgar Rice BURROUGHS's novels supplemented by Hanson's direct contact with Carter; for lack of available recordings these examples of Martian music were perforce recreated by means of computerized vocal synthesis.

Dramatic cantatas and music dramas concerned with sf subjects but without the involvement of an sf author include the RADIO drama *Comet Ikeya* (1966) by Joji Yuasa (1929-) and *Cometose* (1987) by Kristi Allik (1952-). In the latter, Samuel Clemens (Mark TWAIN), who was born and died during consecutive appearances of Halley's Comet, is transported with his house to the comet's core, returning to Earth's vicinity in 1985 only to have the Giotto satellite destroy the house. Halley's Comet is celebrated also in *The Return* (1985) by Morton Subotnick (1935-). Deep concern over humanity's future can be found in the work of the composer and poet Lars-Gunnar Bodin (1935-), such as his **Cybo** (as in CYBORG) trilogy (1967-8) and the cantata *For Jon (Fragments of a Time to Come)* (1977), the final section of which is called "Instruction Manual for Interdimensional Travel".

Staging and costumes have emphasized sf elements in certain musico-dramatic works, including *Licht* ["Light"], Stockhausen's cycle of 7 full-length operas to his own scenarios (in progress since 1977), and the

Surrealist *Le grand macabre* (1977) by György Ligeti (1923-   ), loosely based on the play by Michel de Ghelderode (1898-1962). Among the operas for children by Gian Carlo Menotti (1911-   ) are the tongue-in-cheek *Help, Help, The Globolinks!* (1968), which tackles alien INVASIONS, and *A Bride from Pluto* (1982), a modernized fairy tale. An ALIEN being provides a suitable updating of the role of *deus ex machina* in Michael Tippett's opera *The Ice Break* (1976), and three alien visitors play significant parts in his *New Year* (1988).

The most substantial connection between sf and classical music can be found in recent operas based on sf stories. One of the most successful has been *Aniara* (1959) by Karl-Birger Blomdahl (1916-1968), a musical version of Harry MARTINSON's epic starship poem featuring the Mima computer. Other operas that fall into this category include Vaclav Kašlík's *Krakatit* (1961; based on Karel Čapek's **1924** novel), *VALIS* (1987; based on the **1981** novel by Philip K. DICK) by Tod Machover (1953-   ), and two operas by Paul Barker, *Phantastes* (1986; based on George MacDONALD's **1858** fantasy) and *The Marriages Between Zones Three, Four and Five* (1987; based on Doris LESSING's **1980** novel). The composer who has had the greatest success in radicalizing and popularizing opera in the late 20th century, Philip Glass (1937-   ), likewise selected Lessing's *The Marriage Between Zones Three, Four and Five* for an opera he has been working on since his 1988 setting of the same author's *The Making of the Representative for Planet 8* (**1982**). Another work by Glass, more music drama than opera, is *1000 Airplanes on the Roof* (1988), involving TIME TRAVEL; the climax of his plotless first opera, *Einstein on the Beach* (1976), takes place on board a spaceship, as does a significant part of the action of his much later opera *Christopher Columbus* (1992).   [HD/MJ]

2. Science fiction in popular and rock music It was in the mid-1960s, with the widespread assimilation of sf into general Pop culture, that sf came into its own as a factor in popular music.

Nowhere was this relationship more visible than with the San Francisco groups, where sf themes and imagery often became the subject matter of songs. The Steve Miller Band's early albums are titled *Children of the Future* (1968), *Sailor* (1968) and *Brave New World* (1969), and feature songs like "Overdrive", "Song for our Ancestors" and "Beauty of Time"; a similar fealty was paid by The Grateful Dead – with *Aoxomoxoa* (1969), *From the Mars Hotel* (1974) and improvisatory pieces like "Dark Star" – and by Spirit – whose *Future Games* (1977) flirts with STAR TREK – Quicksilver Messenger Service, the Byrds, Moby Grape, Kaleidoscope and, in a satirical guise, The Mothers of Invention. But the Californian group most influenced was certainly Jefferson Airplane, spearheaded by Paul Kantner (1942-   ), Grace Slick (1939-   ) and Marty Balin (1942-   ). Their early albums *Surrealistic Pillow* (1967), *After Bathing at Baxter's* (1968), *Crown of Creation* (1968) and *Volunteers*

(1969) are consummate examples of dynamic melodies and furiously articulate lyrics often referring to sf (including Robert A. HEINLEIN and John WYNDHAM). Shortly after Balin's departure from the group, guitarist and songwriter Kantner recorded *Blows Against the Empire* (1970) with Jefferson Starship, an amalgam of the previous band with other outstanding San Francisco musicians. This concept album (nominated for a HUGO in 1971) is sometimes thought to have been the finest fusion of the genres, though the opposite opinion has also been published: it is a symphonic poem in the rock mode about the hijacking of a spaceship by a group of rebels in a fascist future USA, and their hopeful journey to the stars. Later albums by Jefferson Starship saw Kantner adopting a persistent revolutionary stance interlaced with stark depictions of a totalitarian planet; the return of Balin to the group in 1975 brought an end to the predominance of Kantner's sf situations.

While the West Coast groups heartily embraced sf in the USA, the situation in the UK was more fragmented. Despite the early, arguably sf imagery of The Shadows' ethereal guitar style or The Tornados' "Telstar" (1962), Pink Floyd were the premier sf group to gain popularity. *Piper at the Gates of Dawn* (1967), *A Saucerful of Secrets* (1968), *Ummagumma* (1969) and *Atom Heart Mother* (1970) are among their many albums having sf subject matter contained in and illuminated by highly evocative music, using the quicksilver guitar and organ runs which have since become closely associated with the sf-music concept. Their style was widely imitated in Europe by Tangerine Dream, Klaus Schulze, Nektar and a score of supposed wizards of the synthesizer.

Another important UK group was Peter Hammill's Van Der Graaf Generator, who were particularly adept at mapping the powerful, bleak vistas of postnuclear desolation: *The Aerosol Grey Machine* (1969), *The Least We Can Do is Wave to Each Other* (1970), "After the Flood" (1970), "Pioneers over C", "Lemmings" and Hammill's solo album *Chameleon in the Shadow of the Night* (1973). One band to attempt a wholeheartedly sciencefictional concept album was the UK-based Nirvana (no relation to the much later US band), with *The Story of Simon Simopath* (1968), but it was fairly execrable on release and has not improved with age – although it caused some stir at the time. The composer/singer David Bowie (1947-   ) enjoyed worldwide fame and showed a comprehensive understanding of sf in his work, ranging from the early "Space Oddity" and "Cygnet Committee" (both 1969) to the songs about Ziggy Stardust, the ultimate superstar of the apocalypse, on the album *The Rise and Fall of Ziggy Stardust and the Spiders from Mars* (1972), or *Diamond Dogs* (1974), an impressive jaunt through a DELANY-like city of fear. Other notable UK groups conversant with the use of sf concepts included: Yes (showing the influence of lyricist/singer Jon Anderson, who also used sf material in his solo albums); King Crimson; Emerson, Lake & Palmer; Jimi Hendrix (1942-1970); The Incredible String Band; The Rolling Stones (notably on *Their Satanic Majesties Request* [1967]); Genesis; Man (whose guitarist Deke Leonard peppered his songs with sf references); and the Anglo-French group Gong, who evolved a complete mythology full of pixies and flying teapots. Hawkwind, with whom Michael MOORCOCK was associated, built songs around stories by Roger ZELAZNY, Ray BRADBURY and others, introducing many sf archetypes, while Moorcock's own group, Deep Fix, recorded the uneven *New World's Fair* (1975). A better use of aggressively high-energy music with sf connotations can be found in the US group Blue Oyster Cult.

There have also been popular settings of sf classics. Though the style might not be called popular, Anthony BURGESS set his own *A Clockwork Orange* (**1962**) to music for a stage production. Notable (and controversial) was Giorgio Moroder's new 1984 score for the 1926 film METROPOLIS, and the songs are a basic feature of EARTH GIRLS ARE EASY. Other sf films were musicals in the first place, including BIG MEAT EATER, *It's a Bird! It's a Plane! It's Superman* ($ SUPERMAN), JUST IMAGINE, ROCKY HORROR PICTURE SHOW and TOOMORROW.   [MJ/PN]

2A. To the more adventurous pop fans of the late 1960s, sf was a literary and cinematic extension of fashionable interest in Eastern mysticism and psychedelic drugs, all three providing ways of taking the mind "where minds don't usually go", as Pete Townshend (1945-   ) put it in The Who's *Tommy* (1969). Most rockers' 1960s favourites were 2001: A SPACE ODYSSEY (the movie – complete with "trip" sequence – rather than the 1968 Arthur C. CLARKE book) and J.R.R. TOLKIEN's fantasy trilogy *The Lord of the Rings* (**1954-5**; rev 1966; omni 1968). The former provided the most spectacular vision extant of the wondrously enigmatic nature of the Universe, and the latter offered a grand struggle between Good and Evil, with the heroes representing the purest of hippie virtues: bucolic gentleness and a fondness for pipeweed and munchies. It was tailor-made for Yes fans and admirers of Crosby, Stills & Nash, the latter's primary contribution to the apocalyptic end of rock's sf strain being "Wooden Ships" (1969), a collaboration with Jefferson Airplane (who also recorded their own version of the song) in which the hippies escape from a polluted, war-torn world in the wooden ships of the title; the song was highlighted as an anthem in the cinematic rock testament of hippiedom, *Woodstock* (1970).

But the primary rock science-fictioneers of the hippie era were Pink Floyd and Jimi Hendrix; 1967-8 classics like the former's "Set the Controls for the Heart of the Sun", "Astronomy Domine" and "A Saucerful of Secrets" and the latter's "Third Stone from the Sun", "The Stars that Play with Laughing Sam's Dice" and "1983/Moon, Turn the Tides" graphically equated the explorations of INNER SPACE and outer space: a direct musical expression of the

same concerns as the NEW-WAVE sf of the era. Yet pop's first real signpost to the future came not from the UK or the USA, but from the German quartet Kraftwerk, who during the first half of the 1970s not only pioneered the use of the then-exotic synthesizer but extended the process of computerized, digital music-making into a madly seductive vision of the romance of technology with records like *Autobahn* (1974) and, most significantly, *We Are the Robots*.

The ever-alert David Bowie began a new age of sf-influenced rock when "Space Oddity" (1969), his comic-angsty tale of Major Tom, the astronaut who decides not to come back, was used as the theme for tv coverage of the first Moon landing. His later excursions into post-apocalyptic speculation included the albums *The Rise and Fall of Ziggy Stardust and the Spiders from Mars* (1972), about a leper-MESSIAH rocker, and *Diamond Dogs* (1974), jointly derived from George ORWELL's *Nineteen Eighty-four* (**1949**) and Harlan ELLISON's "A Boy and his Dog" (1969). Bowie also helped to kick in yet another phase when he became an early devotee of Kraftwerk and, with the aid of Brian Eno (1948-   ), himself a pioneer synthophile from his stint as a member of Roxy Music, helped to transform synthesizer technology from method to metaphor with *Low* (1977). This enabled the likes of Gary Numan (1958-   ) to trivialize the new style into the superficial kitsch futurism which has all too often been rock's perception of sf. More to the point was the work of George Clinton (1940-   ), the funk prankster and mastermind of such acts as Parliament, Funkadelic and Bootsy's Rubber Band. Parliament's *Mothership Connection* (1976), the stage version of which generally began with Clinton descending from the flies in a massive flying saucer, and *The Clones of Dr Funkenstein* (1976) used sf devices as an enhancement of meaning rather than a substitute for it. Grandiose concept albums like *2112* (1976) by the Canadian power-trio Rush rubbed shoulders with heavy metal imagery drawn from horror (Black Sabbath and Alice Cooper [1948-   ] being the "onlie begetters" of an entire school of contemporary death-metallists including Slayer, Metallica and Sabbath's own former lead singer Ozzy Osbourne [1948-   ]) and SWORD-AND-SORCERY heroic fantasy of the Robert E. HOWARD variety (early-to-mid-1970s Led Zeppelin favourites like "Immigrant Song" and "Stairway to Heaven", drawing on, respectively, Nordic fantasies of rape'n'pillage and the most sentimental aspects of Celtic faerie). Chris de Burgh's "A Spaceman Came Travelling" (1974) blended the Christmas story with the Erich VON DÄNIKEN-esque notion that the infant Christ arrived by UFO, to produce one of the more memorable 1970s sf commercial pop songs.

The advent of rock video in the early 1980s reemphasized the fact that much of sf's imagery enters rock music by way of the movies – like the "Flying Saucers Rock and Roll", "Martian Hop" and "Purple People Eater" of the 1950s – and the visual style of movies like BLADE RUNNER (derived from Philip

K. DICK's *Do Androids Dream of Electric Sheep?* [**1968**]), George MILLER's MAD MAX series and *The* TERMINATOR provided instant raw material for many of the rock videos of the 1980s. At worst, there was Duran Duran, mindlessly recycling the usual leather-jacket-apocalypse clichés; at the other end of the intelligence spectrum were Z.Z. Top, constructing elaborate sf mini-comedy-dramas in videos like "TV Dinners" (1983) and "Rough Boy" (1985).

What was most apparent, however, was that the late 1980s and early 1990s saw an actual sf future arrive in pop's present. The 1970s experiments of Kraftwerk and Bowie bore genuine CYBERPUNK fruit in the shape of hundreds of "house" dance records produced, as often as not, in bedrooms and home studios rather than in the 24-track establishments of the previous decade. Their creators took full advantage of the proliferation of affordable sampling and sequencing technology to generate an authentic "cyberpop" which seemed to have sprung full-blown from the brows of William GIBSON and Bruce STERLING, and which rapidly achieved mass popularity. At the time of writing (late 1991) at least half the records in the UK pop charts were classifiable as "bleep" of one sort or another: records which made no attempt at all to sound human. For every synth record that attempted to mimic "real" drums, strings or keyboards, there were dozens that actively celebrated their digital origins: vocals or raps were sampled into digital keyboards and triggered on the stuttering electronic beat. "Robotic" dance moves were the norm, humans imitating machines rather than – as early sf visionaries had warned – machines imitating humans. An entire generation of pop fans embraced a futurist metaphor quite unselfconsciously, demonstrating that sf has, in this sphere at least, invaded and conquered the present.

Rock bands of both the orthodox and synthesized varieties continue to name both themselves and their songs after their sf favourites, just as the fiction of sf writers like Howard WALDROP, Sterling, Jack WOMACK and Lewis SHINER reflects their preoccupation with rock and its attendant culture. William S. BURROUGHS still leads the field in this respect (groups like Soft Machine, Dead Fingers Talk and Steely Dan have borne witness to his influence); The Comsat Angels derived their name from a short story by J.G. BALLARD; the alter-ego KLF outfit Justified Ancients of Mu-Mu demonstrate their allegiance to Robert Anton WILSON and Robert SHEA's **Illuminatus** books; Level 42 drew their name from a reference in Douglas ADAMS' **Hitch Hiker's Guide to the Galaxy** series; while jazz-rock bass virtuoso Stuart Hamm has paid an entire series of tributes to William Gibson, most recently with the album *Kings of Sleep*. As long as both sf writers and rock musicians continue to share a vested interest in the hegemony of the imagination, the relationship is likely to remain a fruitful one.   [CSM]

3. Music in science fiction Of the ARTS, music is the one most commonly featured in sf – albeit not quite to the extent that FANTASY is pervaded by it. Several sf writers studied it, notably including Lloyd BIGGLE Jr (PhD in musicology), Langdon JONES and Edgar PANGBORN, or were for a time professionally or semiprofessionally involved in music: Philip K. DICK purveyed classical music on a radio programme and in a record shop; Douglas ADAMS, Biggle, Jerome BIXBY, Anthony BURGESS, the film director John CARPENTER, the sf editor Edmund CRISPIN, Samuel R. DELANY, L. Ron HUBBARD, Jones, Desmond LESLIE, Pangborn and especially Somtow Sucharitkul (◊ S.P. SOMTOW) have composed music, while Delany, Laurence M. JANIFER, Anne MCCAFFREY, Barry N. MALZBERG, Michael MOORCOCK, Dan MORGAN, Chris MORRIS and Janet E. MORRIS, Charles PLATT, John B. SPENCER, Boris VIAN and many others have appeared as performers, often of their own compositions.

Music, dependent on the instruments with which it is played, is more than most artforms associated with contemporary technology. Also central, though we now take it for granted, is the technology of sound reproduction. The "frozen words" of François RABELAIS's *Gargantua and Pantagruel* (**1532-52**; trans **1653-94**) anticipate sound recording, as, more scientifically, do the hi-tech Sound Houses of Francis BACON's *New Atlantis* (**1629**). Edward BELLAMY, in *Looking Backward, 2000-1887* (**1888**), saw mechanically reproduced music as fundamental to a UTOPIA. In "The Colours of the Masters" (1988) Sean MCMULLEN imagines a 19th century in which a clockwork "pianospectrum" has been invented in time to record Chopin and Liszt.

Many sf authors, like most of the general public, believe that radical musicians (often using electronic technology) are producing work that is deliberately ugly and unintelligible. Others believe that the influence of technology on music is unavoidable and will eventually give rise to new masterpieces. Arthur C. CLARKE, in *The Songs of Distant Earth* (**1986**), makes the realistic extrapolation that historical processes will integrate today's electronic music and instruments into the artistic mainstream. Futuristic or ALIEN music is, of course, rather difficult to describe, and stories which try – including "The Music Makers" (1965) by Langdon Jones and *Sweetwater* (**1973**) by Laurence YEP – set themselves a near-impossible task.

Musicians from the past, both rock and classical, occasionally figure in sf. A flute-playing character in Piers ANTHONY's *Macroscope* (**1969**) is obsessed by the life of the 19th-century poet and musician Sidney Lanier (1842-1881); the seeming revival of Richard Strauss – to demonstrate the future poverty of hi-tech music – in James BLISH's "A Work of Art" (1956) turns out to be a mental pattern imposed on the brain of a totally unmusical person; Jimi Hendrix (1942-1970) is mysteriously revived, with no desire to perform music, in Michael MOORCOCK's "A Dead Singer" (1974). Other stories of interest in this context include Gregory BENFORD's "Doing Lennon" (1975) and Michael SWANWICK's "The Feast of St Janis" (1980).

Music has always played a substantial role in literature, whether as a principal plot element or only incidentally, as in Captain Nemo improvising at the organ or Gully Foyle plucking primitive tunes on an egg-slicer while marooned in space. The profound effects achieved by music (and particularly singing), both beneficial and destructive, have been favourite subjects from the stories of Orpheus and HOMER's sirens through to, for example, Edgar Pangborn's "The Music Master of Babylon" (1954) and "The Golden Horn" (1962), or the operatic "Un Bel Di" (1973) and "The Fellini Beggar" (1975) by Chelsea Quinn YARBRO. (The Orpheus legend features commonly in sf versions, a recent and interesting example of its HARD-SF transmutation being *Fool's Run* [1987], by Patricia MCKILLIP.) Music's therapeutic powers can be seen in Delany's "Corona" (1967) and the impact of the Singers in his "Time Considered as a Helix of Semi-Precious Stones" (1969). Anne McCaffrey's training as an opera singer is evident in her *The Ship who Sang* (fixup 1969) and elaborately reflected in *The Crystal Singer* (1974-5; fixup 1982) and its sequel *Killashandra* (1985), all of which focus on the potency of music. In Orson Scott CARD's *Songmaster* (fixup 1980) both the healing and destructive powers of music are shown. Music is effectively used as a weapon in *Tintagel* (1981) by Paul H. COOK and in *Dargason* (1977) by Colin COOPER; in Charles L. HARNESS's "The Rose" (1953) the unusual time signature of Tchaikowski's 6th Symphony (*Pathetique*) is used as a weapon in a fight with a villain. Music may be a political tool; it instigates revolution against repression in Lloyd Biggle's *The Still, Small Voice of Trumpets* (1968), but supports the soulless, mechanical nature of the societies in Yevgeny ZAMIATIN's *My* (trans as *We* 1924) and George ORWELL's *Nineteen Eighty-four* (1949). (Biggle's interest in music is also apparent in many of the stories in *The Metallic Muse* [coll 1972].) In Frank HERBERT's "Operation Syndrome" (1954) music is a means of revenge, and it is a means of escape from the constraints of the physical body in *On Wings of Song* (1979) by Thomas M. DISCH.

Since the late 1960s the charismatic nature of rock music – and its power to create emotions so strong that they can be read by those who feel them as transcendent – has played an important role in sf, sometimes ambiguously, as in the Satanic heavy metal of George R.R. MARTIN's *Armageddon Rag* (1983), with its power both to heal and to destroy. This novel, part horror and part sf, has an intense feeling for the music of the 1960s of a kind quite common in recent sf. It (relevantly) powers such stories as Howard WALDROP's "Flying Saucer Rock & Roll" (1985) and "Do Ya, Do Ya, Wanna Dance" (1988), the former about Black kids picked up by aliens on account of the transcendent power of old Frankie Lymon songs, the latter about "a song that was gonna change the world" and, two decades later at a class reunion, does. 1960s rock appears by way of local colour in many novels by Stephen KING, some-

times relevantly, and wholly irrelevantly in Allen STEELE's *Orbital Decay* (1989). This last was reviled by some critics as culturally trapped in a rock'n'roll era (dead even now), even though it is set in the mid-21st century; it is a specific case of a general problem – the future story whose cultural referents, often musical, are so absurdly anachronistic that willing suspension of disbelief flies out the window. Other authors who draw powerful metaphors from the rock'n'roll era are Jack WOMACK – whose «Elvissey» (1993) plays on the Elvis Presley myth, as do Robert RANKIN's **Armageddon** books and Allen Steele's *Clarke County, Space* (1990) – Lewis SHINER, Norman SPINRAD – notably in "The Big Flash" (1969) and *Little Heroes* (1987), another book about revolution and the music business – Bradley DENTON, in *Wrack and Roll* (1986) and *Buddy Holly is Alive and Well on Ganymede* (1991), and John SHIRLEY, in *Eclipse* (1985). Two predecessors of this particular strand of sf writing were *The Book of Stier* (1971) by Robin SANBORN and *Barefoot in the Head* (1969) by Brian W. ALDISS; in both, youth movements are at least partially inspired by popular music, as a prelude to the triumph of the counterculture, and at the risk of creating enormous personal power. One of the most interesting variants is Bruce STERLING's acid, precise fable of an ALTERNATE WORLD in which rock critic Lester Bangs (1948-1982) lived on, "Dori Bangs" (1989). Some of the conventions of this strand are parodied in *The Truth about The Flaming Ghoulies* (1984) by John Grant (Paul BARNETT), and the elevation of the vampire Lestat to rock megastardom in Anne Rice's series of fantasies, **The Vampire Chronicles** (1976-92), can also be read as in part a parody (perhaps an unconscious one) of the subgenre.

Colonizers of alien planets might get back to their roots with access to a piano (Frank Herbert's "Passage for Piano", 1973), but more commonly music in alien circumstances is used as a means of understanding or even as the only means of COMMUNICATION. Touring musicians thus may have an ambassadorial function, as in the string quartet that visits the advanced society of Jules VERNE's *L'île à hélice* (1895; trans as *The Floating Island* 1896). An interplanetary touring opera company features in Jack VANCE's ironically titled *Space Opera* (1965). Aliens may well be biologically musical, as with the trumpet-faced heralds, one form of the Selenites in H.G. WELLS's *The First Men in the Moon* (1901), the hollow-horned unicorns in Piers Anthony's **Apprentice Adept** sequence (1980 onward) and the centauroid titanides in John Varley's **Gaean** trilogy (1979-84). Mutated singing plants feature in J.G. BALLARD's "Prima Belladonna" (1956). Musical contact is achieved over interplanetary distances in Barrington J. BAYLEY's "The Big Sound" (1962), in which an orchestra of 6000 becomes not only a sound transmitter but also a receiver. Music as a kind of alien LINGUISTICS is central to Jack Vance's "The Moon Moth" (1961); it has since become almost a CLICHÉ. The aliens communicate with us this way in the film CLOSE ENCOUNTERS OF THE THIRD KIND (1977), initially with the most celebrated five-note musical phrase in sf. Music is combined with dance in Spider and Jeanne ROBINSON's *Stardance* (1979), another novel which supposes that rapport with aliens might be made easier by the use of the kind of nonverbal communication which music represents; yet another is *The Rapture Effect* (1987) by Jeffrey CARVER. An amusing, well told ecological melodrama is Sheri S. TEPPER's *After Long Silence* (1987; vt *The Enigma Score* 1989 UK), in which giant, crystalline lifeforms can be appeased – or, it turns out, spoken to – only by specially trained musicians.

Music unlocks galactic history for terrestrials in Piers Anthony's *Macroscope* (1969). It achieves such religious significance for the Third Men in Olaf STAPLEDON's *Last and First Men* (1930) that a Holy Empire of Music is founded; one of Stapledon's Last Men describes the Music of the Spheres and, in its most rarefied application, it has become part of the very fabric of some early universes described in Stapledon's *Star Maker* (1937), where all movement is musical rather than spatial. Kim Stanley ROBINSON's *The Memory of Whiteness* (1985) uses a great interplanetary "Orchestra" – a vast calliope-like instrument with a single player – as part of a complex metaphor, combining music and mathematics, in which musical structure and cosmic structure are seen as analogous. This sort of music/MATHEMATICS/structure-of-the-Universe imagery appears also in David ZINDELL's ornate *Neverness* (1988).

Perhaps the most distinguished of recent sf novels with a musical theme is *The Child Garden* (1988) by Geoff RYMAN, in which a densely portrayed future world, whose people are infected into INTELLIGENCE by virally transmitted DNA, is both transcended and reflected – in all its infernal and purgatorial aspects – by the setting to music of DANTE ALIGHIERI's *Inferno* and *Purgatorio* (written c1314-21), works which also shape the novel. This is one of the most richly orchestrated portrayals of the function of music in all sf.

The invention of imaginary musical instruments is surprisingly common in sf, and by no means only recently. It is touched on in several stories, notably "Automata" (1814) by the composer E.T.A. HOFFMANN. There have been many proposals for what, in recent years, have been known as sound sculpture and sound environments: early mentions include the sounds made by wind blowing through the statues in Samuel BUTLER's *Erewhon* (1872). More recent wind-powered sound sculptures can be found in the "Music Masons" entry in *Dictionary of the Khazars* (1983) by Milorad Pavič (1929-); they intricately carve rock salt in preparation for the season of the 40 winds.

Future instruments mostly fall into two classes: variants on traditional instruments and those that exploit future technology. The focus of J.B. PRIESTLEY's lighthearted *Low Notes on a High Level* (1954)

is the subcontrabass wind instrument, the Dobbophone, while more conventional instruments include the 9-stringed guitar-like baliset played by troubadors in Frank Herbert's *Dune* (fixup 1965). Moderately conventional instruments tend to be found in low-technology and post-HOLOCAUST environments, like the pipe played by a 6-fingered MUTANT in Olaf Stapledon's *Odd John* (1935), the 20-hole flute (played with fingers and toes) fashioned inside a mutant's machete in Delany's *The Einstein Intersection* (1967) and, in Richard COWPER's **Corlay** trilogy (1978-82), the double pipe articulated by its player's surgically twinned tongue-tip in the Britain of AD3000.

Forms of instruments unknown at the time of writing but which could have existed a couple of decades later include: the Fourier audiosynthesizer in Charles L. Harness's "The Rose", which anticipates programmable synthesizers by some 25 years; the three-bass radiolyn played in an ensemble in Delany's *Out of the Dead City* (as *Captives of the Flame* 1963; rev 1968); and the multichord in Biggle's "The Tunesmith" (1957). The sensory-syrynx in Delany's *Nova* (1968) is operated like a combination of theremin and guitar, and has sympathetic drone strings. The ultracembalo in "The Song the Zombie Sang" (1970) by Harlan ELLISON and Robert SILVERBERG is operated by electronic glove controllers. A direct neural input to the auditory lobes is achieved with Ballard's ultrasonic instruments in "The Sound Sweep" (1960), thereby reducing workload for the "sonovac" operators in a world overloaded with sonic pollution. Direct stimulation of the brain is featured also in Philip K. Dick's *We Can Build You* (1972) by way of the Waldteufel Euphoria and the Hammerstein Mood Organ.

Not all such instruments are played by soloists. Dance music in quintuple time in Aldous HUXLEY's *Brave New World* (1932) is performed by 16 sexophones (plus additional ether music, synthetic music and a scent-and-colour organ). A typical "cosmos group" of audiovisual instruments is featured in Silverberg's *The World Inside* (1971): vibrastar, comet-harp, incantator, orbital diver, gravity-drinker, doppler-inverter and spectrum-rider, some of them generating sounds and images that are modulated by others. Similarly, in Ballard's *Vermilion Sands* (coll 1971) sonic statues with built-in microphones respond to sounds about them, replaying them in transmuted form. The most outrageous instruments, buried in concrete bunkers, are played by means of off-planet remote control by the rock group Disaster Area in Douglas ADAMS's *The Restaurant at the End of the Universe* (1980): these are the photon-ajuitar, bass detonator and Megabang drum complex, with the performance reaching its climax when a stunt ship is driven into the system's sun.

A recent anthology of original stories relating to pop and rock music is *In Dreams* (anth 1992) ed Paul J. MCAULEY and Kim NEWMAN. [HD/PN/BS]

See also: THEATRE.

MUTANT 1. Variant title of the film FORBIDDEN WORLD (1982).

2. Film (1983; vt *Night Shadows*). Film Ventures International. Dir John Bud Cardos, starring Wings Hauser, Bo Hopkins, Jennifer Warren, Jody Medford, Cary Guffey, Lee Montgomery. Screenplay Peter Z. Orton, Michael Jones, John C. Kruize. 99 mins. Colour.

When their car is wrecked by fun-loving good ole boys, two city slickers are trapped in a little town whose inhabitants have been turning strange since an unscrupulous chemical company started dumping toxic waste nearby. A low-budget sensationalist film, this has more than its share of blue-faced, yellow-drooling mutant zombies, but also takes some care with its pleasantly offbeat characterization (Hauser is fine as the hero who just wants to get the hell out of town) and its nonstop action (there's an immaculate scare sequence with hero and heroine cornered in the school toilets by pre-teen monsters). The picture was begun by director Mark Rosman (*The House on Sorority Row* [1983]) but Cardos, of KINGDOM OF THE SPIDERS (1977) and *The Day Time Ended* (1979; vt *Vortex*), stepped in – as he did when Tobe Hooper was fired from *The Dark* (1978) – and efficiently took over. [KN]

MUTANTS The idea of "mutation" as a concept for use in understanding biological EVOLUTION was popularized by Hugo de Vries (1848-1935) in *Die Mutationstheorie* (1901-3); he related it to gross hereditary variations – the freakish "sports" which occasionally turn up in animal populations. Such sports are usually short-lived and sterile, and Charles Darwin (1809-1882) had rejected the notion that they might play a key part; the concept of mutation as an evolutionary factor was eventually modified to refer to relatively slight modifications of individual genes. In 1927 the US geneticist H.J. Muller (1890-1967) succeeded in inducing mutations in fruit flies by irradiation, and this success captivated the imagination of many speculative writers. One of the first to take up the notion was John TAINE, who wrote several extravagant "mutational romances". In *The Greatest Adventure* (**1929**) the corpses of giant saurians, no two alike, begin floating up from the ocean depths and are traced to a LOST WORLD in Antarctica where experiments in mutation were once carried out. In *The Iron Star* (**1930**) a mutagenic meteor transforms a region in Africa, causing local wildlife to undergo exotic metamorphoses. In *Seeds of Life* (1931; **1951**) an irradiated man becomes a SUPERMAN, but does not realize the damage done to the genes which he transfers to the next generation. Stories like these, which attribute magical metamorphic qualities to radiation, owe far more to de Vries than to orthodox mutation theory, and yet they have remained commonplace throughout the history of sf. Mutational romance has been a staple of PULP MAGAZINES, COMICS and sf CINEMA, with the irradiation of various creatures frequently producing giant MONSTERS and the irradiation of people causing metamorphoses into

supermen (many – possibly most – SUPERHEROES have this type of genesis) or subhumans. Examples from the early pulps include Jack WILLIAMSON's "The Metal Man" (1928) and Edmond HAMILTON's "The Man who Evolved" (1931). Hamilton went on to write many further mutational romances, notably *The Star of Life* (1947; rev **1959**). He habitually featured developmental metamorphoses, and wrote an early story in which a mutant child is born to irradiated parents, "He that Hath Wings" (1938). Another author who made prolific use of mutational romance during the 1940s was Henry KUTTNER, in such stories as "I am Eden" (1946) and "Atomic!" (1947), where the magical transmogrifications are spread over several generations. Kuttner and C.L. MOORE, collaborating as Lewis Padgett, introduced into the sf pulps the sympathetic mutant superman, unjustly persecuted by "normal" humans, in the **Baldy** series – assembled as *Mutant* (1945-53; fixup **1953**) – and made comic use of the notion in the **Hogben** series.

UK SCIENTIFIC ROMANCE of the 1930s frequently looked to mutational miracles to produce a better and saner breed of humans; even H.G. WELLS – who knew better – toyed halfheartedly with the idea in *Star-Begotten* (**1937**). The idea that mutation is a necessary part of the process of EVOLUTION led many serious sf writers to treat freakish human mutants sympathetically. Robert A. HEINLEIN did so, in "Universe" (1941), as did Isaac ASIMOV in *Foundation and Empire* (fixup **1952**), the central character of which is "The Mule", a mutant whose advent had been unforeseeable by PSYCHOHISTORY. Frequently populations of persecuted mutants were used as a metaphor for real life oppressed minorities. The explosion of the atom bomb in 1945 gave a great stimulus to mutational romance, and, although the wildest variants of the concept became scarcer in written sf, the logically absurd notion of clutches of similar superhuman mutants arising simultaneously as a result of nuclear accidents remains commonplace. The most notable example is perhaps Wilmar H. SHIRAS's *Children of the Atom* (1948-50; fixup **1953**); a more recent one is *Aubade for Ganelon* (**1984**) by John Willett (1932-   ). Post-HOLOCAUST stories frequently feature several subspecies of mutants, and often show the "normal" survivors of the atomic war persecuting the mutants – usually unwisely, as it is from the ranks of the mutants that a new species of humanity, better than the old model, is scheduled to appear; examples include *Twilight World* (1947; fixup **1961**) by Poul ANDERSON and F.N. Waldrop, John WYNDHAM's *The Chrysalids* (**1955**; vt *Re-Birth*), Walter M. MILLER's *A Canticle for Leibowitz* (1955-7; fixup **1960**), Fritz LEIBER's "Night of the Long Knives" (1960; vt "The Wolf Pair") and Edgar PANGBORN's *Davy* (**1964**). It was in this period that the cinema made most of its mutational romances; notably the giant-ant story THEM! (1954).

Variants on the post-holocaust mutant theme include Lester DEL REY's *The Eleventh Commandment* (**1962**; rev 1970), in which a post-war Church encourages

limitless reproduction in order to fight the lethal effects of the mutation rate; and Samuel R. DELANY's vivid romance of a social world which has undergone total mutational metamorphosis, *The Einstein Intersection* (**1967**). Post-holocaust PARANOIA about mutants is used in Norman SPINRAD's *The Iron Dream* (**1972**) as an analogue for Hitler's attitude to the Jews. More recent examples of post-holocaust mutational romance include Stuart GORDON's *One-Eye* (**1973**) and its sequels, and *Hiero's Journey* (**1973**) by Sterling LANIER. A more original story of mutant-persecution is J.G. BALLARD's "Low-Flying Aircraft" (**1975**), and the ambitious thread of *The Einstein Intersection* has been taken up by A.A. ATTANASIO in *Radix* (**1981**) and its sequels. Sf stories dealing sensibly with the idea of mutation remain rare but, now that the mutational miracle story has been taken to its ultimate extreme in Greg BEAR's *Blood Music* (**1985**), writers may be forced to become more ingenious in mining the melodramatic potential of the notion. [BS]
See also: DEVOLUTION; GREAT AND SMALL; NUCLEAR POWER.

MUTATIONS Film (**1973**). Getty Picture Corp./ Columbia. Dir Jack Cardiff, starring Donald Pleasence, Tom Baker, Michael Dunn, Julie Ege. Screenplay Robert D. Weinbach, Edward Mann. 92 mins. Colour.

In this scientifically ludicrous UK film a mad SCIENTIST (Pleasence) attempts to combine plant with animal life, aided by the dwarf owner of a carnival freak-show (Dunn), who obtains human guinea-pigs for his experiments and exhibits the results. Tom Baker plays the sadistic, deformed assistant. The results of these experiments (one is a Venus Flytrap Man) carry out the inevitable revenge on their creator. As in Tod Browning's *Freaks* (**1932**), real circus freaks (human pincushion, pretzel boy, lizard lady) were used to make the film, but, where Browning used them sympathetically, here they are only for sensationalist voyeurism. Director Cardiff was usually more reputable than this. [PN/JB]

MYERS, HOWARD L. (1930-1971) US writer whose *Cloud Chamber* (**1977**) attractively combines COSMOLOGY, ANTIMATTER invaders of our Universe, SEX and effortless rebirth of all sentient beings in a wide-ranging SPACE OPERA climaxing in its hero's arrival at Nirvana. [JC]
See also: SOCIOLOGY.

MYERS, ROY ◊ Roy MEYERS.

MY FAVORITE MARTIAN US tv series (**1963-6**). A Jack Chertok Production for CBS. Prod/created Jack Chertok. Writers included John L. Greene, Ben Gershman, Bill Freedman, Albert E. Lewin, Burt Styler. Dirs included Leslie Goodwins, Oscar Rudolph, John Erman. 3 seasons, 107 25min episodes. First 2 seasons b/w, 3rd colour.

This was a fairly sophisticated (compared to most tv sitcoms of the time), humorous and commercially successful series about a Martian (Ray Walston) who becomes stranded on Earth. He is befriended by a young man (Bill Bixby), who passes him off to friends as his uncle. The Martian's unfamiliarity with Earth customs, plus his special powers – which include ESP, INVISIBILITY and TELEKINESIS – provide much of the humour. A similar premise, again mostly used for light SATIRE, was adopted by 2 subsequent tv series, MORK AND MINDY (**1978-82**) and ALF (**1986-current**). [JB]

MYHRE, ØYVIND [r] ◊ SCANDINAVIA.

MYLER, LOK [r] ◊ GERMANY.

MYLIUS, RALPH [r] ◊ Warren C. NORWOOD.

MY LIVING DOLL US tv series (**1964-5**). CBS TV. Created Jack Chertok, also executive prod. Prod Howard Leeds. 1 season, 25 mins per episode. Colour.

After his success with MY FAVORITE MARTIAN, Chertok came up with another sf comedy series. Starring Bob Cummings as a psychiatrist, it concerned a female ROBOT, originally designed for use in space but put in his care while its inventor is away. Cummings decides to train it as the "perfect woman" – that is, quiet and obedient – but the robot's unpredictability places him in embarrassing situations. Statuesque Julie Newmar was memorable as the robot, carrying an erotic charge that could not be properly utilized within the context of a tv comedy. The underlying metaphor (woman equals doll) could be interpreted as either sexist, as Cummings plays it, or subversively proto-FEMINIST, which some of the ironies suggest. [JB/PN]

MY SCIENCE PROJECT Film (**1985**). Touchstone/ Silver Screen Partners II. Written and dir Jonathan R. Betuel, starring John Stockwell, Danielle von Zerneck, Fisher Stevens, Raphael Sbarge, Dennis Hopper. 94 mins, cut to 91 mins. Colour.

One of an epidemic of teen sf movies (BACK TO THE FUTURE, EXPLORERS, REAL GENIUS, WEIRD SCIENCE, etc.), this was among the less successful, even though its director, whose début this was, had previously written the much better teen movie, *The LAST STAR-FIGHTER* (**1984**). Here a young man seeking material for a science project finds in a derelict army warehouse a strange engine (apparently taken from a hushed-up UFO), and it turns out to work as a TIME MACHINE when fed energy; the school is absorbed into a time vortex as the town's power supply is sucked up. Teenagers do well (naturally) against cavemen, Japanese soldiers, dinosaurs and mutants. The film lacks focus and straggles, but Hopper is good as the ex-hippy science teacher. [PN]

MY STEPMOTHER IS AN ALIEN Film (**1988**). Weintraub/A Franklin R. Levy/Ronald Parker Production/Catalina. Dir Richard Benjamin, starring Kim Basinger, Dan Aykroyd, Alyson Hannigan. Screenplay Jericho Weingrod, Herschel Weingrod, Timothy Harris, Jonathan Reynolds. 108 mins. Colour.

This charmless and leaden-footed SEX comedy tells of an alien woman (Basinger), fully human in appearance, who comes to Earth to learn the operation of a Galaxy-penetrating beam accidentally invented by an oafish scientist (Aykroyd). The running gags are all infelicitous variations on the theme of cultural mis-understanding, often sexual, between alien and human. [PN]

MYSTERIANS, THE ◊ CHIKYU BOEIGUN.

MYSTERIOUS ISLAND Film (1961). American Films/Columbia. Prod Charles H. Schneer. Dir Cy Endfield, starring Michael Craig, Joan Greenwood, Michael Callan, Herbert Lom. Screenplay John Prebble, Daniel Ullman, Crane Wilbur, based on *L'île mystérieuse* (**1874-5**; trans W.H.G. Kingston as *The Mysterious Island* **1875** UK) by Jules VERNE. 100 mins. Colour.

This is a jovial showcase for Ray HARRYHAUSEN's robust special effects, with a luxuriant musical score by Bernard Herrmann. Prisoners escape by balloon from a confederate prison during the American Civil War and are washed ashore on a remote Pacific island. They encounter a giant crab, two female castaways, a giant prehistoric bird, huge bees, pirates, a deserted underwater city, Captain Nemo (Lom) himself, with his famous submarine *Nautilus* and, of course, an erupting volcano.

Other versions include one made by MGM in 1929. Dir Lucien Hubbard, Maurice Tourneur, Benjamin Christiansen, it starred Lionel Barrymore as Count Dakkar (Nemo). The screenplay was by Hubbard; a soundtrack was added at the last moment. A Russian version, *Tainstvenni Ostrov*, was – surprisingly – made in wartime, in 1941. In 1951 Sam Katzman produced a 15-part serial for Columbia, dir Spencer G. Bennett and starring Richard Crane, Marshall Reed, Karen Randle. A little-seen French/Italian/Spanish co-production, *L'Isola Misteriosa e il Capitano Nemo*, starring Omar Sharif, was briefly released as *The Mysterious Island of Captain Nemo* (1972) in the USA. [JB/PN]

MYSTERIOUS TRAVELER MAGAZINE, THE US DIGEST-size magazine. 5 issues #1–#4 Nov 1951-June 1952, #5 undated 1952, published by Grace Publishing Co; ed Robert Arthur. A spin-off from Mutual Broadcasting's *Mysterious Traveler* RADIO show, *MTM* was subtitled "Great Stories of Mystery, Detection and Suspense, Old and New", but included some sf (Ray BRADBURY, Murray LEINSTER) until, with its last issue (#5), it was retitled *The Mysterious Traveler Mystery Reader*. [FHP/MJE/PN]

MYSTERIOUS WU FANG, THE US PULP MAGAZINE. 7 issues Sep 1935-Mar 1936, monthly, published by Popular Publications; ed Rogers Terrill. Intended to capitalize on the popularity of Sax ROHMER's Fu Manchu (featured in films and a radio series of the period), *MWF* showed the "Dragon Lord of Crime" seeking world domination, sometimes using sf means in the attempt. The novels were by the prolific Robert J. Hogan (1897-1963), who was simultaneously producing G-8 AND HIS BATTLE ACES; the first of them, *The Case of the Six Coffins*, was reprinted in PULP CLASSICS #8 (**1975** chap). DR YEN SIN was a near-identical follow-up from the same publisher. [MJE/FHP]

MYTHOLOGY The relationship of mythology to sf is close and deep, but not always obvious. Part of the confusion stems from the widely held belief that sf is itself a form of latter-day mythology, fulfilling comparable hungers in us. James BLISH took issue with this argument, pointing out that myth is usually "static and final in intent and thus entirely *contrary* to the spirit of sf, which assumes continuous change". We restrict ourselves below to the role of traditional mythologies in sf and to the literal, new mythologies which are sometimes created *within* sf, usually in the context of explaining the way alien societies think.

Traditional mythology appears in sf in two ways, its archetypes being either re-enacted or rationalized (sometimes both). The re-enactment of myths is the more complex of the two cases. Behind the retelling of a myth in a modern context lies the feeling that, although particular myths grew out of a specific cultural background, the truths they express relate to our humanness and remain relevant to all our societies: the story of Prometheus, punished by the gods for stealing fire from the heavens, or its Christian variant, where Dr Faustus is doomed to eternal damnation for selling his soul in exchange for knowledge, has a direct bearing on the SCIENTIST's aspiration for ever more information about the meaning of the Universe, and more power over matter. The entry on CONCEPTUAL BREAKTHROUGH lists many such stories; even such an apparently HARD-SF technological story as Arthur C. CLARKE's *Rendezvous with Rama* (**1973**) is permeated quite deliberately with echoes of ancient myths, the Promethean one in particular. But to list mythic echoes in sf (as with most forms of prose fiction) would be impossible; there are too many. Even a list of full-scale sf analogues of myths as opposed to mere echoes would be fatiguingly long.

Several of the most popular mythic analogues are discussed elsewhere in this volume. Retellings of the Christian legend are discussed under RELIGION and MESSIAHS, and reworkings of the story of *Genesis* are examined under ADAM AND EVE. Obviously the entry on GODS AND DEMONS bears on mythology, as does that on SUPERNATURAL CREATURES.

Mythology in sf reflects a familiar truth, that in undergoing social and technological change we do not escape the old altogether, but carry it encysted within us. The totally new is by its nature almost impossible for sf writers or anyone else to envisage. Far more commonly, they work out ancient patterns of love and death, aspiration and reconciliation in a new context. Several sf writers have imagined a sterile future which has consciously repudiated its myths and hence its past, only to be left with a terrible emptiness. Ray BRADBURY's nostalgic "The Exiles" (1949 as "The Mad Wizards of Mars") has literary and mythic figures exiled on Mars, perishing when the last of the books containing their stories is burned or lost; the emerald city of Oz dissolves like a mist; an Earth expedition is faced with only a desert. Robert SILVERBERG's "After the Myths Went Home" (1969) has figures of myth reincarnated, via a time machine, for the entertainment of a far future which is suffering from ennui; familiarity soon breeds boredom, and the myths are dismissed; the society, emptied of heroism and mystery, is destroyed by invaders. James WHITE's *The Dream Millennium* (**1974**) depicts a crew of starship colonists, who spend much of their time in SUSPENDED ANIMATION, as able to survive because in their dreams they have access to a kind of Jungian substratum of racial memory; the awareness they thereby derive of the mythic patterns in human history gives them the strength to survive on a new world.

Re-enactments of myth in sf take several forms. The simplest strives to deepen the emotional connotations of a story by permeating it with the reverberations of some great original, as C.S. LEWIS does successfully with the myth of the temptation of Eve in *Perelandra* (**1943**; vt *Voyage to Venus*), and less successfully with the Arthurian legend in *That Hideous Strength* (**1945**; vt *The Tortured Planet* US). Lewis's friend Charles WILLIAMS re-enacted myths both Christian and pre-Christian in most of his novels, usually digesting the pagan elements so that they emerged as supportive to the Christian faith. Patricia MCKILLIP's *Fool's Run* (**1987**) is one of several sf retellings of the Orpheus myth, perhaps the most accomplished, set in a prison satellite, the Under-world.

Several writers have striven for a Homeric resonance by retelling HOMER's *Odyssey* in sf terms, whether directly or indirectly; Stanley G. WEINBAUM did this in a short series of stories in the 1930s, R.A. LAFFERTY in *Space Chantey* (**1968**), and Brian STABLEFORD in his **Dies Irae** trilogy (**1971**). (SPACE OPERA generally, of course, has a good deal in common with the picaresque voyages of Odysseus.) Lafferty has several times reverted to mythic themes, notably in *The Devil is Dead* (**1971**) and *Fourth Mansions* (**1969**); the latter categorizes mythic archetypes into four groups, the eternal conflict between which leads to many of our troubles.

The supposed Cretan myth of the Earth-Mothers, and the king sacrificed to ensure renewed fertility, is often evoked in sf, naturally enough by Robert GRAVES, in *Watch the North Wind Rise* (**1949** US; vt *Seven Days in New Crete* 1949 UK), since he is the best known popularizer of the myth in this century, particularly in his nonfictional (though anthropologically unreliable) book *The White Goddess* (**1947** US). It is also used, colourfully if confusingly, in *Sign of the Labrys* (**1963**) by Margaret ST CLAIR, in which members of a surviving witch/priestess cult prove best equipped to cope with an underground, post-HOLOCAUST existence. Philip José FARMER has also been preoccupied with the image of WOMEN as archetypal seeresses, creators and destroyers, and with men as virile but doomed horned gods, notably in *Flesh* (**1960**; rev 1968). Like Bradbury in "The Exiles", Farmer makes little distinction in most of his writings between literary and religious myths, seeming to regard them

as feeding the same human needs. All Farmer's work is permeated by mythology, whether the mythic creature is a reincarnated god, a great white whale or Tarzan; the mythology may be a new one invented by Farmer himself, usually on very traditional models (see below). The best known sf novel drawing on *The White Goddess* is *The Snow Queen* (**1980**) by Joan D. VINGE, in which she designs an entire planetary culture along Gravesian lines, and adds to it a secondary and more recent myth taken from Hans Christian Andersen (1805-1875).

Another bestselling book (like Graves's) about myth was *The Hero with a Thousand Faces* (**1949**) by Joseph Campbell (1904-1987). Many myths that make their way into modern sf have been filtered through a sort of Campbellian sorting process before getting there. Among them are Farmer's books, mentioned above, a particularly pure example being *Tarzan Alive: A Definitive Biography of Lord Greystoke* (**1972**), a spoof biography in which Farmer draws on Campbellian ideas about the nature of the HERO. George LUCAS has often spoken about his use of Campbellian ideas about myth, and his films STAR WARS (**1977**) and its sequels, which are intended to have many mythic resonances, incorporate these (as, indeed, does every second work of sf mythology; see discussion of Roger ZELAZNY below). Something of Farmer's engagingly packrat attitude towards myth can also be found in Sam LUNDWALL's satirical *Alice's World* (**1970** dos US), in which a spaceship returning to an abandoned Earth finds a grotesque variety of mythic and literary beings now living there.

More complex than many of the above are stories whose mythic components are seen with a degree of irony, stressing not only ancient continuities but also modernist discontinuities with the past. Several of Samuel R. DELANY's novels fall into this category, notably *The Einstein Intersection* (**1967**) and *Nova* (**1968**); in the former a deserted Earth is repopulated by aliens who take on human shape and, with it, the mythic burden of the past, in a confused form they do not always understand; in the latter the story of Prometheus is replayed in a tale of literally stealing fire from the heavens, but the narrative tone has as much of the deflationary as the heroic in it. Michael MOORCOCK's *Behold the Man* (**1966** NW; exp **1969**) has a time traveller who wanted to see Christ's crucifixion playing an uncomfortably central role in that event; the scene he finds is more squalid than transcendent. Lawrence DURRELL's *Tunc* (**1968**) and its sequel *Nunquam* (**1970**) feature a multinational conglomerate called Merlin, but the Arthurian echoes are primarily to show that there is little room for romance in a corrupt future. Michael SWANWICK uses similar Arthurian echoes altogether more economically and to equally squalid effect in "The Dragon Line" (1988), a tale of a coke-snorting modern Mordred trying to do the right thing for the world with a resuscitated Merlin's help. Cordwainer SMITH derives a considerable emotional charge from the mythic analogues, often Oriental, he uses in his stories; in "The Dead Lady of Clown Town" (1964) the parallels are with the legend of Joan of Arc. Smith's use of myth is touching but sometimes rather remote; often, as in this story, the mythic parallels are further distanced by the events of the tale being themselves remembered by later generations, and recounted with the formality and balance of a well rounded myth – myths within myths, as it were. In *The Infernal Desire Machines of Doctor Hoffman* (**1972**; vt *The War of Dreams* US) Angela CARTER, another ironist, has a mad scientist using a MACHINE charged with erotic energy to make the dreams and myths of men come alive; the very series of betrayals through which his plans go awry is itself, ironically, mythic. Charles L. HARNESS regularly uses mythic archetypes both of character and of plot in his involuted, grandiose melodramas, notably in *The Ring of Ritornel* (**1968**) and "The Rose" (1953), in both of which art and science dance a complex sarabande and winged archetypes are confronted with MATHEMATICS. Stories structured on myth can appear rather simple-mindedly determinist, as events run along their preordained grooves. Alan GARNER, for example, specializes in a kind of cyclic history in which ancient myths of violence and betrayal work themselves out again in a modern setting, but such books as *The Owl Service* (**1967**), based on a Welsh legend in the *Mabinogion*, and *Red Shift* (**1973**) allow free will to loosen the mythic trap, if not escape it entirely. James TIPTREE Jr evokes the legendary figure of the Rat King in "The Psychologist who Wouldn't do Awful Things to Rats" (1976), but the protagonist is not saved by its majestic appearance; indeed, he is goaded into brutal rat murder.

Within both GENRE SF and FANTASY a particularly popular variant on the mythology theme is to have humans encountering mythic figures through TIME TRAVEL to the past or in an ALTERNATE WORLD, or conversely to have mythic survivals appearing in the modern world. Some of these stories are dealt with under the heading of MAGIC. They were especially associated with the magazine UNKNOWN, and often involved a puckish or whimsical humour, as in the **Harold Shea** stories by L. Sprague DE CAMP and Fletcher PRATT. Jack WILLIAMSON's *The Reign of Wizardry* (**1940**; rev **1965**) is from the same magazine and the same period. Edmond HAMILTON's *The Monsters of Juntonheim* (1941 *Startling Stories* as "A Yank at Valhalla"; **1950** UK; vt *A Yank at Valhalla* 1973 US) is another story of this type. Naomi MITCHISON gives an account of the search for the Holy Grail as told by two reporters from the *Camelot Chronicle* and the *Northern Pict* in *To the Chapel Perilous* (**1955**), but here the basic points are serious, despite the anachronistic jokes that usually feature largely in stories of this kind, as in several by Poul ANDERSON (◊ MAGIC). Thomas Burnett SWANN made a career out of writing sweet, sometimes oversweet, narratives about mythic survivals, his point being that something wonderful and delicate left the world as modern rationalism took a grip, and as we desecrated our landscapes.

One quite popular strategy for mythology stories is to tell the myths from the viewpoint of an observer or protagonist from the time in which they happened – sometimes, of course, rationalizing them in the process. John GARDNER's *Grendel* (**1971**) does this with the Beowulf story, as did Henry Treece (1911-1966) in *The Green Man* (**1966**) and Michael CRICHTON in *Eaters of the Dead* (**1976**), but only Crichton's book, which accounts for Grendel and his dam as Neanderthal survivals (◊ APES AND CAVEMEN), can be seen as sf.

The majority of stories of mythic survival are more fantasy than sf, like Swann's; or like *The Last Unicorn* (**1968**) by Peter Beagle (1939-   ), which tells of the sad search of the beast of the title for its extinct fellows; or like Diana Wynne JONES's *Eight Days of Luke* (**1975**), in which Loki turns up in modern England, and *Fire and Hemlock* (**1984**), in which the tale of Tam Lin's escape from the Fairy Queen is replayed (yet again) in the here and now; or like the allegorical *The Circus of Dr Lao* (**1935**) by Charles FINNEY, in which mythic creatures survive in a circus, and have a deep effect on the disbelieving town folk who witness them. A yearning for the survival of mystery, and an intellectual belief in the necessity of such a survival if human culture is not to become sterile and bleak, pervade most such stories, and are central to the concerns of *Beauty* (**1991**) by Sheri S. TEPPER, which fascinatingly (and fascinatedly) weaves a centuries-spanning construct out of folklore and fairy-tale archetypes as a possible prophylactic against a hellish, mythless future. The same yearning is to be found even at the simplistic end of the spectrum, as in Emil PETAJA's **Kalevala** series, where avatars of the Finnish gods have adventures, or Joseph E. KELLEAM's *The Little Men* (**1960**) and its sequel, where Jack Odin has fights in space and elsewhere. Stan LEE (and/or Jack KIRBY) resuscitated various myths, notably that of Thor, in MARVEL COMICS, and Thor turns up again in Douglas ADAMS's *The Long Dark Tea-Time of the Soul* (**1988**), trying to catch a plane to Oslo. Sterling LANIER's *The Peculiar Exploits of Brigadier Ffellowes* (coll **1971**) wittily spins yarns about confrontations with demigods, monsters, and other mythic survivals. John BLACKBURN also worked with the theme, but here we enter a new area, and a peculiarly sciencefictional one, the rationalized myth, which becomes (not always convincingly) sf rather than fantasy.

Blackburn was not the best exponent of the rationalized myth, although *Children of the Night* (**1966**) and *For Fear of Little Men* (**1972**) elicit satisfying shudders in their accounts of hidden LOST RACES in England whose existence explains legends of fairies and goblins, with a logic similar to that of the Crichton novel mentioned above, and echoing the Faerie of Arthur MACHEN. Manly Wade WELLMAN's **Hok** stories (1939-42) rationalize various myths, as H. BEDFORD-JONES had done in his **Trumpets from Oblivion** series in *The* BLUE BOOK (1938-9). Rather in the manner of the theories of Erich VON DÄNIKEN, a number of sf stories explain myths as distorted memories of visits to Earth by aliens, as did Arthur C. Clarke in *Childhood's End* (1950; exp **1953**) – though in this case it is through racial precognition, not memory, that the horned aliens have given rise to the legend of the Devil. In Clifford D. SIMAK's *The Goblin Reservation* (**1968**) a rather whimsical attempt is made to explain gnomes, trolls, fairies, banshees and so forth as specialized colonists created by biological engineering. More successful was Nigel KNEALE's tv serial QUATERMASS AND THE PIT (1958-9), in which the image of the Devil turns out to be a race memory of insect-like Martians, a memory that comes disturbingly to life in modern London. Larry NIVEN and Jerry POURNELLE reversed the ordinary rationalization procedure in *Inferno* (**1976**), in which an sf writer finds himself, possibly deservedly, in Hell, a place he consistently and unsuccessfully attempts to rationalize as an actual physical construct in the Universe of matter; ultimately it turns out to be, indeed, Hell.

A quite different kind of mythic survival appears in *Mythago Wood* (**1984**) and its sequel *Lavondyss* (**1988**) by Robert HOLDSTOCK. The wood of the title (which like John CROWLEY's hidden world in *Little, Big* [**1981**] is infinitely bigger on the inside than its modest periphery would suggest) has the property, more fantastic than sciencefictional, of incarnating mythagos from the collective unconscious of those humans who live in and around it, mythagos being, effectively, walking figures of myth. As the wood is ever more deeply penetrated, the ultimate bare myths of the Ice Age come to life. The two books are Holdstock's most powerful work, and perhaps the central mythological fantasy of the 1980s.

The sf writer who has most consistently used mythological themes in sf, as opposed to fantasy, is Roger Zelazny. His first novel, *This Immortal* (**1966**), confronts its almost immortal protagonist (◊ IMMORTALITY) with various MUTANT creatures which are somehow archetypes of Greek myth given flesh. Zelazny stayed with themes of this type for some years, often using them ironically, typically playing off the colloquial against the archaic, in stories about quasi-gods of human origin whose powers blend advanced mental training with high technology, deliberately reconstructing and replaying mythic confrontations, in *Creatures of Light and Darkness* (**1969**), which reincarnates the Egyptian pantheon, and perhaps most successfully in *Lord of Light* (**1967**), an assured and oddly moving story of planetary colonists who deliberately take on the aspect of Hindu gods, and become involved with a variety of appropriate metaphysical paradoxes.

These comprise a new kind of mythology story, in which myths are evoked not only by the author but quite consciously by the characters, often as a form of cold-blooded CULTURAL ENGINEERING, and sometimes self-destructively, as game becomes trap.

Another example is Harry HARRISON's *Captive Universe* (**1969**), in which the crew of a giant starship has been deliberately programmed into a mental state of medieval monkishness, and the colonists into an Aztec tribalism complete with Aztec "gods" (who turn out to be constructs); both crew and colonists are ignorant of the true state of affairs, and regard the starship simply as the world (◊ POCKET UNIVERSE). Poul Anderson's "The Queen of Air and Darkness" (1971) has the native inhabitants of a colonized planet reading the minds of the colonists, picking out their archetypal fears and hopes, and creating by hallucination a world of sinister faerie to keep the colonists away, even kidnapping human children in the manner of the old ballads.

Finally, sf commonly creates its own myths. In his *A Voyage to Arcturus* (**1920**) David LINDSAY invents a whole series of imaginary (but hauntingly familiar) mythologies on another planet; these ultimately annihilate one another in a kind of mutual critique, leaving its protagonist at the end annealed by fire and wholly stripped of illusion. The SWORD AND SORCERY subgenre regularly constructs mythologies which often, as in the case of Robert E. HOWARD's, bear a close relation to our own. *Out of the Mouth of the Dragon* (**1969**) by Mark GESTON is permeated with a myth of Armageddon, a final conflict doomed never to take place, since the forces who have volunteered to fight it keep cutting their own side to ribbons in squabbles on the way. At a more accessible level, GENRE SF has created a meta-narrative SPACE-OPERA myth which has resulted from the borrowing of ideas from story to story, with additional accretions on the way. A distinct sf version of MARS, for example, is the work of no single writer, has little to do with the real Mars, and yet exists very clearly in the imagination of readers. Leigh BRACKETT and Ray Bradbury have created some of the more poignant variations on this particular Mars myth.

With the growing interest in ANTHROPOLOGY in sf since the 1960s, several of the better sf writers have added richness and density to their depiction of alien or imaginary societies by creating myths for them. This is the case with most of Ursula K. LE GUIN's work, as in *The Left Hand of Darkness* (**1969**) and – with a spectacular density and length – in *Always Coming Home* (**1985**); her "Buffalo Gals, Won't You Come Out Tonight?" (1987), however, uses traditional Native American myth in its story of a girl who comes to live with incarnate animal spirits. Terry CARR's "The Dance of the Changer and the Three" (1968) presents a dangerous alien society whose enigmatic behaviour may be explained only if their myths are properly understood; it was brave of Carr to essay a mythology for beings composed of pure energy. Harlan ELLISON, by juxtaposing icons and images from the ancient and the modern worlds, has forged some fine modern myths, many collected in *Deathbird Stories* (coll **1975**), which includes "The Whimper of Whipped Dogs" (1973), in which the violence and indifference of a great CITY are seen to coalesce into a kind of contemporary demon. His "Croatoan" (1975) features a characteristically wild but unselfconscious metaphor in bringing together the story of the lost Virginian colony of Roanoke with (a development of a modern myth) the idea of a colony of children in the sewers, descended from aborted foetuses flushed down the drains, who live alongside huge alligators which, when smaller, suffered the same fate.

The Fifth Head of Cerberus (1972) is one of the many works by Gene WOLFE in which, as with the Le Guin stories, the bearing of myth on reality is both constant and unpredictable; along perhaps with John Crowley – whose brilliant *Engine Summer* (1979), for example, plays cruelly with the idea of cyclic myth in a post-HOLOCAUST venue – Wolfe makes the most sophisticated use of myth of any modern sf writer. Clashes between free will and predestination, the first signifying an outward thrust and the second an inward pressure from the inexorable past, occur, as they must, in all mythological sf written by people who are conscious of the consequences of their themes. Certainly it is Wolfe's pre-eminent subject – especially in the **Book of the New Sun** series – as it is, with the emphasis rather more on myth as elegiac trap, Crowley's also.

A theme anthology is *New Constellations: An Anthology of Tomorrow's Mythologies* (anth **1976**) ed Thomas M. DISCH and Charles Naylor.   [PN]

See also: ATLANTIS.

NABOKOV, VLADIMIR (1899-1977) Russian-born US novelist, poet, translator and entomologist. Raised in Russia until the Revolution, and then educated at Cambridge, he lived between the wars in Germany and France, emigrated to the USA in 1940 – at which point he began to write in English rather than Russian – and from 1959 lived in Switzerland. His first books of poetry date from the teens of the century, his first novel from 1926, though he came to world fame only after the publication, many books later, of *Lolita* (**1955** France). Several of his novels can be read precariously in terms of their fantasy or sf elements – including *Korol', Dama, Valet* (**1928** Germany; trans Dmitri Nabokov and VN as *King, Queen, Knave* **1968** US), which features automata; the afterlife fantasy *Soglyadatay* (**1930** France; trans Dmitri Nabokov and VN as *The Eye* **1965** US); *Priglashenie na kasn'* (**1938** France; trans Dmitri Nabokov and VN as *Invitation to a Beheading* **1959** US), a fable which ends in a state beyond death; the DYSTOPIA *Bend Sinister* (**1947**); and *Pale Fire* (**1962** US), which transforms RURITANIAN manias into deeply intricate parable. But VN's FABULATIONS tend to an austere self-referentiality, and are not easily pigeonholed. (It has also been suggested that all VN's novels from *Pnin* [**1957**] to *Transparent Things* [**1972**] contain attempts at communication from dead characters to the living.)

Nevertheless *Izobretenie Val'sa* (**1938** France; rev text trans Dmitri Nabokov as *The Waltz Invention* **1966** US) is a genuine sf play; its eponymous protagonist, having invented a kind of atomic device, demands to rule his country or he will cause apocalypse. Some of the stories assembled in *Nabokov's Dozen* (coll **1958**) as well as "Poseshchenie muzeya" (**1939**; trans as "The Visit to the Museum" **1963**) and "The Vane Sisters" (**1959**), both found in *Nabokov's Quartet* (coll **1966** US), and "Lance" (**1952**), found in *Nabokov's Congeries* (coll **1968** US), are of sf or fantasy interest. *Ada, or Ardor: A Family Chronicle* (**1969** US) has likewise been treated as sf, though perhaps not fruitfully. Certainly *Ada*

depicts an ALTERNATE WORLD, whether or not this Anti-Terra has been created by protagonist Van Veen as a counterpoint to and justification of incest; the book can therefore be read with some interest for its rendering of sf elements, though the novel itself comprises much, much more. However individual texts might be defined, VN was concerned in all his work to shape versions of the creative act. The materials he used were subjunctive to the shaping, not vice versa, as in sf. [JC]

See also: HISTORY OF SF; OULIPO.

NAHA, ED (1950-   ) US writer and journalist, at one time the Los Angeles-based movie correspondent for the *New York Post*; since July 1986 he has run the regular movie and tv **Nahallywood** column in SF CHRONICLE. His nonfiction books, aimed at a popular market, include: *Horrors – From Screen to Scream* (**1975**); *The Science Fictionary: An A-Z Guide to the World of SF Authors, Films and TV Shows* (**1980**), a small, selective encyclopedia that is reliable if brief on film and tv, but devotes far too little space to authors; *The Films of Roger Corman: Brilliance on a Budget* (**1982**); and *The Making of Dune* (**1984**).

EN's first sf novel was *The Paradise Plot* (**1980**), a humorous mystery novel set on a SPACE HABITAT at Lagrange 5 (◊ LAGRANGE POINT); the sequel was *The Suicide Plague* (**1982**). In 1984, as D.B. DRUMM (which may be a house name), he began writing the **Traveler** sequence of SURVIVALIST FICTION set in a depleted post-HOLOCAUST USA: #1: *First, You Fight* (**1984**), #2: *Kingdom Come* (**1984**), #3: *The Stalkers* (**1984**), #4: *To Kill A Shadow* (**1984**), #5: *Road War* (**1985**), #6: *Border War* (**1985**), #7: *The Road Ghost* (**1985**), #8: *Terminal Road* (**1986**), #9: *The Stalking Time* (**1986**), #10: *Hell on Earth* (**1986**), #11: *The Children's Crusade* (**1987**), #12: *The Prey* (**1987**) and #13: *Ghost Dancers* (**1987**). The first of these is definitely by Naha, but most subsequent numbers are thought to be the work of John SHIRLEY.

EN has also written 3 film novelizations – *Robocop* * (**1987**), *Ghostbusters II* * (**1989**) and *Robocop 2* * (**1990**) –

and 2 horror novels, *Breakdown* (**1988**) and *Orphans* (**1989**). [PN]

NANKAI NO DAIKETTO ◊ GOJIRA.

NANOTECHNOLOGY Item of terminology borrowed by sf writers from theoreticians of future TECHNO-LOGY, and quite popular in sf from the late 1980s. It seems to have been first used by K. Eric Drexler in 1976, and popularized by him in his book on the subject, *Engines of Creation* (**1987**).

Nanotechnology – the term loosely combines "nano", the SI (metric system) prefix denoting 10^{-9}, with "technology" – means the technology of the very small indeed. The term microtechnology encompasses MACHINES of the order of a micrometre across; nanotechnology envisages machines very much smaller than that, perhaps of molecular size. Indeed, its working components would be atoms; the nano-machine might be like "motorized DNA". Drexler called these theoretical tiny machines "assemblers". As to the uses of these molecule-size ROBOTS, there is little that cannot be imagined: scraping fatty deposits from the insides of hardened arteries, brain surgery on individual neurons, food-making, ore-mining . . . The suggestions have been endless. Assemblers would be of a size small enough to conduct the most delicate operations within human cells – although Kim Stanley ROBINSON has suggested it might be better to image, rather than tiny medics, 10 million molecule-sized steamrollers charging up one's capillaries to perform brain surgery. Assemblers would also necessarily be capable of self-replication, which raises two questions: could they be considered a lifeform?; and could they get out of control, self-replicating until all available building materials were used up? Their number would increase exponentially: if a single assembler took 15 minutes to double, then at the end of 10 hours of doubling there would be 68 billion of them, and in just over 2 days the assemblage would outmass the Sun.

Whether or not their construction is a realistic prospect is another question. Certainly it has been much discussed, and a number of laboratories have worked on some of the preliminary problems. The scanning tunnelling microscope, developed at the IBM laboratories in Zurich, has been used (April 1990) to manipulate individual atoms – even, in an episode of startling chutzpah, spelling out (using 35 xenon atoms) the IBM logo. Now that we have reached the stage of manipulating individual atoms, perhaps the construction of molecule-machines is not so impossible after all, though it is still a long way from achievement. Nevertheless, preliminary designs are already under way in the real world. A lively account of the development of theories about nano-technology can be found in *Great Mambo Chicken and the Transhuman Condition* (**1990**) by Ed Regis.

The concept of nanotechnology, not always named as such, appears regularly in 1990s sf. One of the most distinguished works to which it is fundamental is *Queen of Angels* (**1990**) by Greg BEAR. The intelligent

briefcase around whose actions and fate Michael SWANWICK's eccentric tale *Stations of the Tide* (**1991**) pivots is, according to his acknowledgements, a work of "nanotechnics". Perhaps more significant is the number of HARD-SF works in which the existence of nanotechnology is merely taken for granted, forming part of the overall background of futuristic technology. [PN]

NATHAN, ROBERT (GRUNTAL) (1894-1985) US writer, author of over 40 novels from *Peter Kindred* (**1919**) to *Heaven and Hell and the Megas Factor* (**1975**), in which latter (as so often in his work) good and evil – in this case God and Satan – confer and put aside their differences, smilingly. Much of his fiction reflects a wistful, melancholy, sometimes satirical sense of fantasy; and it is perhaps ironic that he is best remembered for perhaps the harshest of his tales, *Portrait of Jennie* (**1940**), in which he uses J.W. DUNNE's time theories to frame the sentimental tale of a young girl not of this Earth whose love for a human artist reaches fruition only at the moment of her death. *The Barly Fields* (omni **1938**) – which contains *The Fiddler in Barly* (**1926**), *The Woodcutter's House* (**1927**), *The Bishop's Wife* (**1928**) and its sequel *There is Another Heaven* (**1929**), and *The Orchid* (**1931**) – fairly represents the soft-edged work of his early years. Later came some Arthurian fantasies, including *The Fair* (**1964**), which sustains a sublimated elegiac tone in its depiction of a maiden's adventures there, and *The Elixir* (**1971**). *The Mallott Diaries* (**1965**) deals with Neanderthal survivals in Arizona, and *The Summer Meadows* (**1973**) movingly explores the nature of love in a fantasy quest for significant and telling moments in its protagonists' lives. Of direct sf interest is *The Weans* (**1956** *Harper's Magazine* as "Digging the Weans"; **1960** chap), a satirical archaeological report on the long-destroyed US civilization. RN's reputation is submerged at present, but on revaluation he may be seen as a significant creator of humanistic fantasy. [JC]

Other works: *Jonah* (**1925**; vt *Son of Ammitai* 1925 UK; vt *Jonah, or The Withering Vine* 1934 US); *Road of Ages* (**1935**), an unusual political fantasy in which the Jews are sent into a new Exile; *The Enchanted Voyage* (**1936**); *Journey of Tapiola* (**1938**) and *Tapiola's Brave Regiment* (**1941**), assembled as *The Adventures of Tapiola* (omni **1950**); *They Went on Together* (**1941**); *The Sea-Gull Cry* (**1942**); *But Gently Day* (**1943**); *Mr Whittle and the Morning Star* (**1947**); *The River Journey* (**1949**); *The Married Look* (**1950**; vt *His Wife's Young Face* 1951 UK); *The Innocent Eve* (**1951**), which is assembled in *Nathan 3* (omni **1952**) along with *The River Journey* and the associational *The Sea-Gull Cry* (**1952**); *The Train in the Meadow* (**1953**), an afterlife fantasy; *Sir Henry* (**1955**); *So Love Returns* (**1958**); *The Wilderness Stone* (**1961**); *The Devil with Love* (**1963**); *Stonecliff* (**1967**); *Mia* (**1970**).

About the author: *Robert Nathan: A Bibliography* (**1960** chap) by Dan H. Laurence.

See also: *The* MAGAZINE OF FANTASY AND SCIENCE FICTION; TIME TRAVEL.

NATION, TERRY (1930-   ) UK screenwriter involved in the inception of the long-running BBC TELEVISION series DR WHO; he created in 1963 its most famous villains, the DALEKS, the story of which he subsequently told in *The Official Doctor Who and the Daleks Book* (**1988**) with John Peel, the relevant episodes appearing as *Doctor Who: The Scripts: The Daleks* * (coll **1989**) with John McElroy. In 1975 TN created a post-HOLOCAUST series, SURVIVORS, also for BBC TV, which rather unsuccessfully attempted to capture on tv the flavour of the English DISASTER novel; his novelization is *The Survivors* * (**1976**). *Rebecca's World* (**1975**), illustrated with bravura by Larry Learmonth, is a fable for young children about ECOLOGY. In 1978 TN created a further sf series for tv, BLAKE'S SEVEN; he wrote all 13 episodes of this SPACE OPERA's 1st season as well as 6 later episodes, but by the time of its weak 4th (and last) season in 1981 his association with it had ceased.   [JC/PN]

NATIONAL AMATEUR PRESS ASSOCIATION ◊ APA.

NATIONAL FANTASY FAN FEDERATION ◊ N3F.

NAYLOR, GRANT Joint pseudonym of UK scriptwriters and authors Rob Grant and Doug Naylor, who worked for 3 years as head writers for *Spitting Image*, a satirical tv series using a combination of puppets and live action, and who wrote the RED DWARF tv series, which weds black humour and SPACE OPERA. As GN they have published 2 novelizations: *Red Dwarf: Infinity Welcomes Careful Drivers* * (**1989**) and *Better than Life* * (**1990**), both assembled, with additional material, as *Red Dwarf Omnibus* (omni **1992**).   [JC]

NEAL, HARRY [s] ◊ Jerome BIXBY.

NEANDERTHALS ◊ ANTHROPOLOGY and especially ORIGIN OF MAN for prehistoric romances; ◊ APES AND CAVEMEN for Neanderthal survivals.

NEAR FUTURE Images of the near future in sf differ markedly from those of the FAR FUTURE in both content and attitude. The far future tends to be associated with notions of ultimate destiny, and is dominated by metaphors of senescence; its images display a world irrevocably transfigured. It is viewed from a detached viewpoint; the dominant mood is – paradoxically – one of nostalgia, because the far future, like the dead past, can be entered only imaginatively, and has meaning only in terms of its emotional resonances. The near future, by contrast, is a world which is imminently real – one of which we can have no definite knowledge, which exists only imaginatively and hypothetically, but which is nevertheless a world in which (or something like it) we may one day have to live, and towards which our present plans and ambitions must be directed. The fears and hopes reflected in our images of the near future are real, however overpessimistic or overoptimistic they may seem (◊ OPTIMISM AND PESSIMISM). In order to plan our lives we must all possess such images, and the fact that they are fictions does not mean that they are unimportant. Literary representations of the near future both reflect and nourish those images.

Just as fictions of the far future could not emerge until there was an appreciation of the true timescale of the Earth and the forces involved in long-term change, so fictions dealing with the near future could not emerge until it was generally realized that an individual's lifetime might see changes of considerable import. An awareness that habits and strategies designed to deal with the past and the present might not be adequate to deal with one's personal future emerged rather more slowly than an awareness of the geological timescale, and was handicapped by a dogged ideative resistance. It is doubtful whether many people, even today, have really cultivated a genuine appreciation of the scope of the change that might overtake the world in the space of their own lifetimes. The difficulty of making such an adjustment was the subject of Alvin TOFFLER's bestselling work of popular FUTUROLOGY, *Future Shock* (**1970**).

The near future is implicitly threatening; whatever innovations it produces must invalidate – however temporarily – the past experience on which our present consciousness is based. At a time when no one believed in the possibility of fundamental change, this threat was ineffective, not because innovations never occurred but because they were unanticipated and the processes producing them were unperceived. In today's world change is so rapid we cannot fail to perceive it, despite our most fervent efforts to ignore it. In such a historical situation it is easy to understand the popularity of dogmas of conservatism and conservationism, and the acuity of sensations of personal and social insecurity. It is also easy to understand the rapid growth of a literature which both reflects these anxieties and offers palliative reassurances.

In much early futuristic fiction there is no trace of either near or far future in the senses outlined above; events take place in a disconnected, generalized imaginative space which is comprehensively distanced by its dating. Examples include the anonymous *The Reign of King George VI 1900-1925* (**1763**), L.S. MERCIER's *Memoirs of the Year Two Thousand Five Hundred* (**1771**; trans **1772**) and Jane LOUDON's *The Mummy! A Tale of the 22nd Century* (**1827**). The earliest near-future speculations are warnings about the consequences of specific political practices; I.F. CLARKE's bibliography, *The Tale of the Future* (3rd edn **1978**), lists *inter alia* a 1644 pamphlet on the dangers of restoring the monarchy and an 1831 pamphlet warning of the effects of the Reform Bill. The idea of historical change independent of strategic action on the part of governing bodies did not come until the late 19th century.

The first class of near-future fantasies to emerge was the WAR-anticipation genre in the UK, which began with a political debate concerning the need for rearmament. George T. CHESNEY's classic drama-documentary *The Battle of Dorking* (**1871**) headed a tradition of speculative stories exploring the probable effects of new TECHNOLOGY on the business of warfare which eventually led writers like George GRIFFITH and H.G. WELLS to produce literary nightmares of war remade by submarines, tanks, aeroplanes and atomic bombs. Griffith died before the outbreak of WWI, but most of his readers did not; Wells lived just long enough to witness the advent of the real atom bomb. The anxieties reflected in this early class of near-future fantasies were entirely justified, and the notion of "a war that will end war", in Wells's phrase – an idea already popularized in such jingoistic extravaganzas as Louis TRACY's *The Final War* (**1896**) – was enthusiastically borrowed by the promoters of WWI as a means of selling it to the populations which became involved.

A somewhat different set of images was presented by another subgenre which emerged in the same period, celebrating the modern wonders of a newly emergent era of technological DISCOVERY AND INVENTION. Significantly, there are few genuine UTOPIAS in this class, most ideal societies being cast forward by at least a century, as in Edward BELLAMY's *Looking Backward, 2000-1887* (**1888**); and even the fervently optimistic Hugo GERNSBACK subtitled his *Ralph 124C 41+* (**1911-12**; **1925**) "A Romance of the Year 2660". Technological wonder stories located within the personal future of their readers were mostly concerned with the future of TRANSPORTATION, connected to the war-anticipation genre by virtue of rejoicing in the conquest of the air. Jules VERNE is the archetypal early writer of near-future sf, although his imitators often took a more cavalier view of imminent possibility than he did; where Verne went *Around the World in 80 Days* (**1873**; trans **1874**), André LAURIE went from *New York to Brest in Seven Hours* (**1888**; trans **1890**). Sf writers were slower to take account of the AUTOMATION of industry than they were to foresee new opportunities in LEISURE. When Gernsback attempted to capture the scattered aspects of technological enthusiasm and bind them all together into a medium of communication which would hopefully "blaze a trail, not only in literature, but in progress as well" he was still a man ahead of his time, despite the precedents set by Verne and Wells. He saw SCIENTIFICTION as a means not only of anticipating the transformation which the world was undergoing through the acceleration of technological progress, but also of making a crucial contribution to it. He was an inventor himself, passionately involved with contemporary technology and particularly with the development of radio. In the editorials which he wrote for his early sf PULP MAGAZINES he talked about atomic energy, radar, tv and space travel. His near-future anticipations were by no means unjustified; most of his readers were in their teens in the 1920s, and so lived to see Gernsback's hypothetical technologies made actual.

GENRE SF undertook to deal with all aspects of the future, but it was in its generalization of images of the *near* future that it was really new. The impact of sf upon young readers in the 1920s and 1930s may have been partly due to a consciousness of the *immediacy* of change as well as to the vastness of sf's imaginative horizons. That said, most early pulp sf was located in numinous eras beyond the personal horizon, and its grasp of the extent to which technological change would alter the quality of life was decidedly weak. Outside the genre, the wide-eyed optimism and ludicrously uninhibited melodrama of most pulp sf seemed childish; in the less prolific but far more earnest tradition of the UK SCIENTIFIC ROMANCE, the anxieties attendant on the awareness of change were much more prominently represented. The balance began to be redressed when John W. CAMPBELL Jr took over ASTOUNDING SCIENCE-FICTION in the late 1930s and began to ask for more carefully considered appraisals of future possibility. Many authors understandably preferred the freedom of more distant future realms, where they could set melodramatic SPACE OPERAS against the gaudy background of a GALACTIC EMPIRE, but a new generation of sf writers were prepared to tackle the problems of the near future, and in a more realistic fashion. The late 1930s and early 1940s produced several notable stories dealing with the advent of NUCLEAR POWER, and Robert A. HEINLEIN attempted to construct a detailed future HISTORY mapping the interplay of technological innovation and political response. The destruction of Hiroshima and Nagasaki by the first atom bombs brought into the world a sensation of existential insecurity unparalleled in modern history (it is perhaps more easily comparable with such events as the slaughter of the population of Europe by the Black Death in the 14th century). To those professionally involved in the sf field, like Campbell and Donald A. WOLLHEIM, it seemed that sf had been "justified" by the unveiling of the atom bomb, and that from 1945 on everyone would have to acknowledge the power of technological change to transform the world. But such advances in sf's popularity and esteem were limited, and there also emerged within the genre a powerful sense of nostalgia for that GOLDEN AGE when sf had been aware of change only as a succession of miracles and make-believe adventures.

The response of sf authors to the new intellectual climate was varied. Straightforward PREDICTIONS of imminent atomic doom were abundant (◊ END OF THE WORLD; HOLOCAUST AND AFTER; WAR), but a more eccentric response was the widespread creation of distorted future societies in which some contemporary power-group had "taken over" and formed an oppressive regime; the archetype of this species is *The Space Merchants* (**1953**) by Frederik POHL and C.M. KORNBLUTH. These stories of distorted societies are often labelled SATIRES, and do indeed have a satirical edge, but there is also an element of actual anticipation in them, and they reflect a genuine fear of the swamping of individual ambitions by large-scale bureaucratic institutions.

The baroque and slightly surreal mode of this kind

of imaginative exercise gradually gave way to a more acute awareness of real processes of change in the contemporary world, and of their dangers. In the 1960s OVERPOPULATION, POLLUTION and resource crises (◊ POWER SOURCES) became standard features of sf's images of the near future. Stories on these subjects often have a hint of panic about them, and there was a distinct apocalyptic note about the sf of the 1960s and 1970s. Images of the near future produced outside the genre became virtually indistinguishable in attitude from those produced within it (although the near-future novels produced by MAINSTREAM WRITERS tended to work with an impoverished vocabulary of ideas). Insofar as it deals with the near future, genre sf is primarily a literature of anxiety; optimism and colourful adventurism remain the prerogatives of fiction set in a more distant future, in which the particular problems of Spaceship Earth are often reduced to irrelevance.

Our awareness of impending ecocatastrophe (◊ ECOLOGY) has been complicated in the 1970s and 1980s by the advent of two new species of technology which promise dramatic transformations of the way we live. The COMPUTER revolution has pressed forward much faster than most sf writers of the 1950s and 1960s anticipated; CYBERPUNK fiction represents a somewhat belated but suitably intense response to this developing situation, and its rhetoric is feeding back into the real situation much as the rhetoric of the future-war story fed back into the actual build-up to WWI. Second, while the cracking of the genetic code and the subsequent advent of GENETIC ENGINEERING have not yet begun to transform the everyday environments of the home and workplace, the inherent possibilities hold the promise of a new technological revolution which might overturn many of our assumptions about the nature of MACHINES (see also NANOTECHNOLOGY). Within the last few years the assumptions which sf writers have made about the POLITICS of the future have been devastated by the collapse of communism in Eastern Europe, and this too has ensured that virtually all extant sf images of the near future, however recent, are now almost redundant. Those which seem most pertinent are those which anticipate the greatest confusion.

Bruce STERLING's Islands in the Net (1988) is perhaps the most compelling recent image of the near future, overtaking Frederik Pohl's The Years of the City (1985), which has already begun to seem tentative. David BRIN's far more optimistic Earth (1990) is a worthy attempt to celebrate heroic attempts to cope with ecocatastrophe but ultimately founders on the rock of its outrageous deus ex machina, while Greg BEAR's Queen of Angels (1990) obtains its conviction by focusing tightly on the particular predicaments of a handful of characters. The vast majority of sf writers are either narrower still in the focus of their concerns or content to farm the much greener pastures of hypothetical futures which lie safely beyond the personal event-horizon. This is probably inevitable.

The near future is an uncomfortable imaginative space for writers and readers to inhabit, and it is entirely understandable that those who venture into it should go equipped with blinkers, armoured by some protective obsession which obviates the necessity of dealing with the near future-world as a whole.

The faster the pace of technological change becomes, the more horrifying a prospect the near future seems. It could not be otherwise. Our personal ambitions are tied to our expectations, which – if they are not mere castles in the air – are based in our experience of the past. The innovations which the future will surely bring are much more likely to threaten these ambitions than to aid them (even though they may compensate by making possible new ambitions) and are therefore bound to be sources of acute anxiety. The rate of technological change will certainly not slow down – unless DISASTER overtakes the entire cultural/industrial complex and renders all ambitions beyond mere survival redundant – and there now seem no grounds for hoping, as some apologists for sf once did, that assiduous study of images of future possibility will help us adapt ourselves to the acceleration of that change. Despite the increasing number of sf titles published each year, realistic speculative fiction about the near future is scarce and will undoubtedly remain so. Such fiction is too frightening to be popular; even those readers who like to be frightened prefer to gain their excitement from the obsolete workings of the supernatural imagination, which are utterly without consequence for the way they must live their lives.   [BS]

NEARING, HOMER Jr (1915-   ) US writer and professor of English at Pennsylvania Military College. His series of stories about Professor Cleanth Penn Ransom and Professor Archibald MacTate, mathematician and philosopher respectively, appeared in FSF from "The Poetry Machine" in 1950 up to 1963. 7 of these stories were assembled with 4 unconnected tales (and very thinly "novelized") as The Sinister Researches of C.P. Ransom (coll **1954**); they concern the two professors' attempts to formalize a union between science and the arts. Their efforts, though doomed, are told without malice. Uncollected stories are "The Embarrassing Dimension" (1951), "The Maladjusted Classroom" (1953), "The Cerebrative Psittacoid" (1953), "The Gastronomical Error" (1953) and "The Hermeneutical Doughnut" (1956 Fantastic Universe). The professors' names disconnectedly represent several US poets and critics associated with the New Criticism: Cleanth Brooks, Archibald MacLeish, John Crowe Ransom, Allen Tate and Robert Penn Warren.   [JC/PN]

See also: DIMENSIONS; HUMOUR.

NEBULA Sf award given by the SCIENCE FICTION WRITERS OF AMERICA (now the Science Fiction and Fantasy Writers of America) since 1966. The idea of funding such an award from the royalties of an annual anthology of award-winning short fiction was proposed in 1965 by the SFWA's then secretary-treasurer,

Lloyd BIGGLE Jr. The awards are made in the spring and, unlike the HUGOS, are dated by the year of publication of the award-winning stories; thus the 1965 awards, the first, were made in 1966. The award takes the form of a metallic-glitter spiral nebula suspended over a rock crystal, both embedded in clear lucite; the original design by J.A. LAWRENCE was based on a drawing by Kate WILHELM and has been followed ever since.

The original 4 classes of award, all for professional writing, have remained unchanged; a 5th class, for Best Dramatic Presentation, was added in 1974, changed to Best Dramatic Writing in 1976, and then immediately dropped. Several special awards, taking the form of plaques or citations, have also been made; the only special category listed here is the Grand Master Award made from time to time by the Nebula committee for lifetime achievement in sf writing; it goes always to writers who are senior in both status and years.

The 4 writing categories are Novel (over 40,000 words), Novella (17,500-40,000 words), Novelette (7500-17,500 words) and Short Story (under 7500 words). Voting is by SFWA members, using a final ballot paper made up from members' nominations. From 1970 a preliminary ballot of all nominated works was circulated early in the year, the entries receiving the most votes being entered on the final ballot. In 1980 procedures were changed (not for the first or last time): the year of a work's eligibility became the previous calendar year (not December 1 to November 30 as had earlier been the case); more importantly, perhaps, a Nebula jury system was set up, with each year's panel of judges allowed to add one item to the final ballot in each category. For some time authors have been allowed the option of choosing a one-year-later, usually mass-market, edition of their books to be eligible, rather than the original edition: many authors prefer to be judged on the basis of a widely read paperback rather than on the original hardcover.

The procedures for Nebula awards have been more consistent than those for Hugos, but lobbying among the SFWA membership has received much criticism over the years, with some critics maintaining that the awards sometimes reflect political as much as literary ability. It may be partly as a result of this that the proportion of SFWA members voting is often not very high.

Although the Nebulas have occasionally gone to rather more experimental writing than ever wins a Hugo, there has not been a great deal of difference between the choices. It might have been expected that the Nebula, inasmuch as it is given by a consensus of professional writers, would place a stronger emphasis on literary skills, but there is no evidence that this has been so. Neither Hugo nor Nebula has been given to non-genre sf or fantasy, and both have mostly gone, quite disproportionately, to US recipients. While the Nebula has certainly been awarded to some fine works, many critics have argued that the whole AWARDS system, in sf at least, is more a publicity exercise than a consistently well judged measure of value.

Anthologies of Nebula-winning short fiction, along with a selection of the runners-up, are published annually in the **Nebula Award Stories** series, each volume ed by an SFWA member. These books sometimes contain critical essays and accounts of the year in sf, as well as winners of the Rhysling Award for sf POETRY. Volumes to date are *Nebula Award Stories 1965* (anth **1966**; vt *Nebula Award Stories 1* UK) ed Damon KNIGHT, *Nebula Award Stories Two* (anth **1967**; vt *Nebula Award Stories 2* UK) ed Brian W. ALDISS and Harry HARRISON, *Three* (anth **1968**) ed Roger ZELAZNY, *Four* (anth **1969**) ed Poul ANDERSON, *Five* (anth **1970**) ed James Blish, *Six* (anth **1971**) ed Clifford D. SIMAK, *Seven* (anth **1972**) ed Lloyd Biggle Jr, *Eight* (**1973**) ed Isaac ASIMOV, *Nine* (anth **1974**) ed Kate Wilhelm, *Ten* (anth **1975**) ed James E. GUNN, *Eleven* (**1976** UK) ed Ursula K. LE GUIN (*Eleven* appeared in 1977 in the USA; from then until 1983 the year of publication was 2 years behind the year for which the awards were given), *Twelve* (anth **1978**) ed Gordon R. DICKSON, *Thirteen* (anth **1979**) ed Samuel R. DELANY, *Fourteen* (anth **1980**) ed Frederik POHL, *Fifteen* (anth **1981**) ed Frank HERBERT, *Sixteen* (anth **1982**) ed Jerry E. POURNELLE, *Seventeen* (anth **1983**) ed Joe W. HALDEMAN, *18* (anth **1983**) ed Robert SILVERBERG (with these latter, both published in the same year, the books went back to trailing the award year by only 1 year), *19* (anth **1984**) ed Marta RANDALL, *20* (anth **1985**) ed George ZEBROWSKI, *21* (anth **1986**) ed Zebrowski (again the gap increased to 2 years), *22* (anth **1988**) ed Zebrowski, *23* (anth **1989**) ed Michael BISHOP, *24* (anth **1990**) ed Bishop and *25* (anth **1991**) ed Bishop.

In 1969 the concept of SFWA members voting on stories was extended retroactively to cover those stories (but not novels) considered the all-time best prior to 1965. The chosen short stories were published as *Science Fiction Hall of Fame* (anth **1970**) ed Robert SILVERBERG and the novellas in *The Science Fiction Hall of Fame Volume Two A* (anth **1973**; vt *The Science Fiction Hall of Fame Volume Two* UK) and *The Science Fiction Hall of Fame Volume Two B* (anth **1973**; vt *The Science Fiction Hall of Fame Volume Three* UK) ed Ben BOVA. [PN]

Novels:

1965: Frank HERBERT, *Dune*

1966: Daniel KEYES, *Flowers for Algernon*, and Samuel R. DELANY, *Babel-17* (tie)

1967: Samuel R. Delany, *The Einstein Intersection*

1968: Alexei PANSHIN, *Rite of Passage*

1969: Ursula K. LE GUIN, *The Left Hand of Darkness*

1970: Larry NIVEN, *Ringworld*

1971: Robert SILVERBERG, *A Time of Changes*

1972: Isaac ASIMOV, *The Gods Themselves*

1973: Arthur C. CLARKE, *Rendezvous with Rama*

1974: Ursula K. Le Guin, *The Dispossessed*

1975: Joe HALDEMAN, *The Forever War*

1976: Frederik POHL, *Man Plus*
1977: Frederik Pohl, *Gateway*
1978: Vonda N. MCINTYRE, *Dreamsnake*
1979: Arthur C. Clarke, *The Fountains of Paradise*
1980: Gregory BENFORD, *Timescape*
1981: Gene WOLFE, *The Claw of the Conciliator*
1982: Michael BISHOP, *No Enemy But Time*
1983: David BRIN, *Startide Rising*
1984: William GIBSON, *Neuromancer*
1985: Orson Scott CARD, *Ender's Game*
1986: Orson Scott Card, *Speaker for the Dead*
1987: Pat MURPHY, *The Falling Woman*
1988: Lois McMaster BUJOLD, *Falling Free*
1989: Elizabeth Ann Scarborough, *The Healer's Wur*
1990: Ursula K. Le Guin, *Tehanu: The Last Book of Earthsea*
1991: Michael SWANWICK, *Stations of the Tide*

Novellas:

1965: Brian W. ALDISS, "The Saliva Tree", and Roger ZELAZNY, "He who Shapes" (tie)
1966: Jack VANCE, "The Last Castle"
1967: Michael MOORCOCK, "Behold the Man"
1968: Anne MCCAFFREY, "Dragonrider"
1969: Harlan ELLISON, "A Boy and his Dog"
1970: Fritz LEIBER, "Ill Met in Lankhmar"
1971: Katherine MacLEAN, "The Missing Man"
1972: Arthur C. Clarke, "A Meeting with Medusa"
1973: Gene Wolfe, "The Death of Dr Island"
1974: Robert Silverberg, "Born with the Dead"
1975: Roger Zelazny, "Home is the Hangman"
1976: James TIPTREE Jr, "Houston, Houston, Do You Read?"
1977: Spider and Jeanne ROBINSON, "Stardance"
1978: John VARLEY, "The Persistence of Vision"
1979: Barry B. LONGYEAR, "Enemy Mine"
1980: Suzy McKee CHARNAS, "Unicorn Tapestry"
1981: Poul ANDERSON, "The Saturn Game"
1982: John KESSEL, "Another Orphan"
1983: Greg BEAR, "Hardfought"
1984: John Varley, "PRESS ENTER ■"
1985: Robert Silverberg, "Sailing to Byzantium"
1986: Lucius SHEPARD, "R & R"
1987: Kim Stanley ROBINSON, "The Blind Geometer"
1988: Connie WILLIS, "The Last of the Winnebagos"
1989: Lois McMaster Bujold, "The Mountains of Mourning"
1990: Joe Haldeman, "The Hemingway Hoax"
1991: Nancy KRESS, "Beggars in Spain"

Novelettes:

1965: Roger Zelazny, "The Doors of his Face, the Lamps of his Mouth"
1966: Gordon R. DICKSON, "Call Him Lord"
1967: Fritz Leiber, "Gonna Roll the Bones"
1968: Richard WILSON, "Mother to the World"
1969: Samuel R. Delany, "Time Considered as a Helix of Semi-Precious Stones"
1970: Theodore STURGEON, "Slow Sculpture"
1971: Poul Anderson, "The Queen of Air and Darkness"
1972: Poul Anderson, "Goat Song"

1973: Vonda McIntyre, "Of Mist, and Grass, and Sand"
1974: Gregory Benford and Gordon EKLUND, "If the Stars are Gods"
1975: Tom REAMY, "San Diego Lightfoot Sue"
1976: Isaac Asimov, "The Bicentennial Man"
1977: Raccoona Sheldon (James Tiptree Jr), "The Screwfly Solution"
1978: Charles L. GRANT, "A Glow of Candles, A Unicorn's Eye"
1979: George R.R. MARTIN, "Sandkings"
1980: Howard WALDROP, "The Ugly Chickens"
1981: Michael Bishop, "The Quickening"
1982: Connie Willis, "Fire Watch"
1983: Greg Bear, "Blood Music"
1984: Octavia E. BUTLER, "Bloodchild"
1985: George R.R. Martin, "Portraits of his Children"
1986: Kate WILHELM, "The Girl who Fell into the Sky"
1987: Pat MURPHY, "Rachel in Love"
1988: George Alec EFFINGER, "Schrödinger's Kitten"
1989: Connie Willis, "At the Rialto"
1990: Ted Chiang, "Tower of Babylon"
1991: Mike CONNER, "Guide Dog"

Short Stories:

1965: Harlan Ellison, "'Repent Harlequin!' said the Ticktockman"
1966: Richard MCKENNA "The Secret Place"
1967: Samuel R. Delany, "Aye, and Gomorrah . . ."
1968: Kate Wilhelm, "The Planners"
1969: Robert Silverberg, "Passengers"
1970: no award
1971: Robert Silverberg, "Good News from the Vatican"
1972: Joanna RUSS, "When it Changed"
1973: James Tiptree Jr, "Love is the Plan, the Plan is Death"
1974: Ursula K. Le Guin, "The Day Before the Revolution"
1975: Fritz Leiber, "Catch that Zeppelin!"
1976: Charles L. Grant, "A Crowd of Shadows"
1977: Harlan Ellison, "Jeffty is Five"
1978: Edward BRYANT, "Stone"
1979: Edward Bryant, "giANTS"
1980: Clifford D. SIMAK, "Grotto of the Dancing Deer"
1981: Lisa TUTTLE, "The Bone Flute"
1982: Connie Willis, "A Letter From the Clearys"
1983: Gardner DOZOIS, "The Peacemaker"
1984: Gardner Dozois, "Morning Child"
1985: Nancy Kress, "Out of All Them Bright Stars"
1986: Greg Bear, "Tangents"
1987: Kate Wilhelm, "Forever Yours, Anna"
1988: James MORROW, "Bible Stories for Adults, No. 17: The Deluge"
1989: Geoffrey A. Landis, "Ripples in the Dirac Sea"
1990: Terry BISSON, "Bears Discover Fire"
1991: Alan BRENNERT, "Ma Qui"

Dramatic presentation/writing:

1973: SOYLENT GREEN (presentation)
1974: SLEEPER (presentation)
1975: Young Frankenstein (◊ FRANKENSTEIN) (writing)

Grand Master Award:
(The years given are the years in which the award was made)
1975: Robert A. HEINLEIN
1976: Jack WILLIAMSON
1977: Clifford D. Simak
1979: L. Sprague DE CAMP
1981: Fritz Leiber
1984: Andre NORTON
1986: Arthur C. Clarke
1987: Isaac Asimov
1988: Alfred BESTER
1989: Ray BRADBURY
1991: Lester DEL REY
See also: WOMEN SF WRITERS.

NEBULA SCIENCE FICTION UK large-DIGEST-size magazine. 41 issues Autumn 1952-Aug 1959, published by Crownpoint Publications, Glasgow, Autumn 1952-Apr 1955, and by Peter Hamilton Sep 1955-Aug 1959; ed Peter Hamilton. Issues were numbered consecutively after Vols 1 and 2 of 4 nos each; what should have been Vol 3 #1 was actually marked #9. Publication was quite irregular except for July 1957-Feb 1959, which was monthly apart from the omission of Nov and Dec 1957.

N was the first and so far only Scottish sf magazine, and was part of the 1950s UK sf magazine revival, one of the most important titles along with NEW WORLDS and SCIENCE FANTASY. *N* was subsidized by its editor, an enthusiastic fan, still a teenager when the magazine began. It always ran a news section, including a column by the celebrated Irish fan Walt Willis (1919-   ), editor of HYPHEN and SLANT. But although *N* was fannish it was by no means juvenile; Hamilton was serious-minded and prepared to experiment with difficult stories and to encourage young writers. Brian W. ALDISS, Bob SHAW and Robert SILVERBERG all had their first published stories in *N*. Other contributors included Harlan ELLISON, Eric Frank RUSSELL, Kenneth BULMER and E.C. TUBB, the latter being the most prolific. Early issues each contained a novel with a small number of short stories, but the novel-an-issue policy was later dropped. The handsome and distinctive front covers were the work of various artists, including Gerard QUINN and Eddie JONES. *N* was popular with writers; Hamilton was able to keep it going as very much a one-man show, never very profitably, for 7 years. Some later issues went on sale in the USA. [PN/FHP]

NEEF, ELTON T. [s] ◊ R.L. FANTHORPE.

NEEPER, CARY Working name of US microbiologist and author Carolyn A. Neeper (1937-   ) for her fiction, which consists primarily of the ambitious *A Place Beyond Man* (**1975**), which somewhat uneasily combines a HARD-SF rendering of the physics and biology of her interplanetary venues with a contemplative sweep characteristic of the SCIENTIFIC ROMANCE. Confronted with the looming ecological self-destruction of Earth, the two other sentient species of our Solar System must decide what course to follow; the consequent lessons are earnestly put. [JC]

NEFF, ONDŘEJ [r] ◊ CZECH AND SLOVAK SF.

NEILL, A(LEXANDER) S(UTHERLAND) (1883-1973) UK educationist who gained fame for revolutionary theories about the teaching of children and who cofounded the International School – first on the Continent, then (from 1921) at Summerhill in the UK – to put them into practice. Fictionalized accounts like *A Dominie's Log* (**1915**) popularized his arguments, and his sf novel, *The Last Man Alive* (**1938**), was read aloud to his pupils. The DISASTER it recounts is readable but unoriginal. [JC]

NEILSON, KEITH (TOWNSEND OLAF) (1935-   ) US academic of importance in the field of sf and fantasy scholarship for editing (anon: both books were created under the umbrella editorship of Frank N. Magill [1907-   ]) the 5-vol *Survey of Science Fiction Literature* (anth **1979**) and the 5-vol *Survey of Modern Fantasy Literature* (anth **1983**); each contains about 500 essays, averaging about 2000 words, on individual books and series. Although (inevitably) some essays are weak or wrong-headed, many are strong and original, and the two surveys present between them an indispensible series of critical responses to the literature. [JC]

NELSON, RAY Working name of Radell Faraday Nelson (1931-   ), who also writes as R.F. Nelson, R. Faraday Nelson and Ray Faraday Nelson, and once under the house name Jeffrey Lord (◊ Lyle Kenyon ENGEL). He has been active in both sf and detective genres, publishing his first sf story, "Turn off the Sky", in *FSF* in 1963. He worked as a gagwriter for cartoonist Grant Canfield, and for a time collaborated with Michael MOORCOCK in smuggling Henry Miller books from France into the UK; Moorcock was caught, RN forced to cease. RN holds a secure place in the hearts of sf FANDOM (he used to be a fan artist) for having invented the propeller beanie which in fan cartooning is always emblematic of the sf fan.

RN's first sf novel was *The Ganymede Takeover* (**1967**) with Philip K. DICK, a tale in which Dickian preoccupations are somewhat dampened by implausibly foregrounded action sequences. His second, *Blake's Progress* (**1975** Canada; rev vt *Timequest* 1985 US), accords the poet/painter William Blake (1757-1827) the capacity to travel through time, along with his wife Kate; she is by far the better painter of the two, though her husband signs her works. History is altered, the novel being in part an ALTERNATE-WORLDS story. In its full revised form it is a highly energetic vision of the poet, and RN's best work. *Then Beggars Could Ride* (**1976** Canada) and its sequel, *The Revolt of the Unemployables* (**1978**), depict an ecological UTOPIA of small, self-contained but interacting units, in which a protagonist tries to sort himself out. RN's most recently published novel is #1 in the projected **Timebinder** sequence, *The Prometheus Man* (**1982**), in which a rigid and therefore DYSTOPIAN meritocracy has transformed the USA into a land of employables (not numerous) and the Uns, or unemployables (the great majority). The plot revolves around a marriage broken by the system as well as an assortment of gurus, tycoons and revolutionaries; it does not fully resolve. At least one sequel is reportedly awaiting publication. Though sometimes over-easily applied, RN's iconoclasm is all the more welcome for its surprising rarity in the sf field. [JC]

Other works: *The Ecolog* (**1977** Canada); *Dimension of Horror* * (**1979**) as Jeffrey Lord, #30 in the **Richard Blade** series.

See also: INVASION; PHILIP K. DICK AWARD; TRANSPORTA-TION.

NEMERE, ISTVÁN [r] ◊ HUNGARY.

NENONEN, KARI [r] ◊ FINLAND.

NEPTUNE ◊ OUTER PLANETS.

NESFA ◊ BIBLIOGRAPHIES; Erwin S. STRAUSS.

NESVADBA, JOSEF (1926-   ) Czech psychiatrist, doctor and writer, born in Prague. He started by writing dramatic sketches but soon turned to detective stories and satirical sf, continuing the tradition of Karel ČAPEK. One of the best Czech sf writers (◊ CZECH AND SLOVAK SF) – though he has written less since the late 1960s – and aside from Čapek the best known in the West, JN writes subtly ironic variations on common sf themes, poking fun at human weaknesses, and is not afraid to satirize his own social system (as in "Inventor of His Own Undoing", in all the English-language collections noted below). His 3 early collections of short stories are *Tarzanova smrt* ["Tarzan's Death"] (coll **1958**), *Einsteinův mozek* ["Einstein's Brain"] (coll **1960**) and *Výprava opačným směrem* ["Expedition in the Opposite Direction"] (coll **1962**), not to be confused with the later *Výpravy opačným směrem* ["Expeditions in the Opposite Direction"] (coll **1976**), which assembles early work, some previously collected, as does *Einsteinův mozek a jiné povídky* ["The Einstein Brain and Other Stories"] (coll **1987**). A mystery novel of fantasy interest is *Bludy Erika N.* ["The Ravings of Erika N."] (**1974**), which draws on some of Erich VON DÄNIKEN's ideas.

A later stage of psychiatry-related sf novelettes and novels begins, in book form, with *Řidičský průkaz rodičů* ["Parents' Driving Licence"] (coll of 3 linked novelettes **1979**). Others are *Minehava podruhé* ["Minehava for the Second Time"] (coll of 3 linked novelettes **1981**) and the novel *Hledám za manžela muže* ["I am Looking for a Man to be a Husband"] (**1986**). These are less well known in the West, but the title story of the second collection has been translated in cut form as "The Return of Minnehawa or Marian Kolda's Psychoscope" in *Panorama of Czech Literature, No 8* (anth **1986** Czechoslovakia) ed Nesvadba, an anthology of modern Czech fantasy and sf with biographical pieces on the authors.

JN's stories have been a fertile source of inspiration for the Czech film industry. Films based on his work include *Tarzanova smrt* (1962; vt *The Death of an Apeman*) dir Jaroslav Balík, screenplay by JN and Balík, a tragicomic new adventure of Tarzan; *Blbec z*

Xeenemünde (1962; vt *The Idiot of Xeenemünde*) dir Balík, screenplay by JN and Balík, another tragicomedy, this time about a halfwit scientist who kills Nazis; *Ztracená tvář* (1965; vt *The Lost Face*) dir Pavel Hobl, screenplay by Hobl and JN, a slapstick story set in the 1930s about a doctor who can perform miracles of disguise with plastic surgery and organ transplants; *Zabil jsem Einsteina, pánové!* (1969; vt *I killed Einstein, Gentlemen*) dir Oldřich Lipský, screenplay by Lipský, Miloš Macourek and JN, an overfarcical TIME-TRAVEL comedy involving a society in 1999 where women are sterile and bearded because of radiation from nuclear war; *Slečna Golem* (1972; vt *Miss Golem*) dir Balík, screenplay by Balík and JN, about the creation of an artificial woman by cloning; *Upír z Feratu* (1981; vt *The Vampire from Ferat*) dir Juraj Herz, based on JN's story known in English as "Vampires Ltd.", about a racing car that uses the blood of drivers rather than petrol as fuel. Another film based on a JN story is ZÍTRA VSTANU A OPAŘÍM SE ČAJEM (1977; vt *Tomorrow I'll Wake up and Scald Myself with Tea*).

JN's intricately plotted, absurdly logical stories have been translated into many languages and widely anthologized. English-language editions of JN's stories are *Vampires Ltd.* (coll **1964** trans Iris Urwin, Prague) and *In the Footsteps of the Abominable Snowman* (coll **1970**; vt *The Lost Face* US). All but the first and third stories of the latter collection are also in the former, which also contains 5 stories not in the latter. [JO/SČ/FR/PN]

Other works: *Dialog s doktorem Dongem* ["Dialogue with Dr Dong"] (**1964**), a contemporary novel about Vietnam; *Tajná zpráva z Prahy* ["Secret Report from Prague"] (censored text **1978**; text restored 1992).

NETHERLANDS ◊ BENELUX.

NEUTRON STARS Item of TERMINOLOGY in ASTRO-NOMY, and much used in sf. In an ordinary star, such as the Sun, the gravitational pressure tending to make it collapse is balanced by the outward pressure created by the continuous nuclear fusion within it. As a star's fuel burns out, GRAVITY takes over. A star of mass less than the Chandrasekhar limit – a value calculated by Indian physicist Subrahmanyan Chandrasekhar (1910-   ) to be about 1.4 times the mass of our Sun – would usually contract under the force of gravity into a very dense White Dwarf, with a radius of maybe only a few thousand kilometres; but a further, more extreme compression is possible, as under pressure the empty space within the atoms of the star's matter is annihilated, the electrons being crushed down to the atomic nucleus, there to fuse with the protons of the nucleus to form neutrons. The resulting degenerate matter – neutronium – is incredibly dense because of the loss of the intra-atomic emptiness: a neutron star having the same mass as our Sun would have a radius of about 10km (6 miles). Its surface gravity would be so strong that no "mountain" (i.e., surface irregularity) could exist on it higher than about 5mm (0.2in); and, initially at least, it would rotate very rapidly owing to the conservation of angular momentum (i.e., for the same reason as ice skaters can increase their rate of spin by pulling in their limbs).

Beginning in 1968, radio telescopes discovered many celestial sources which emitted regular bursts of microwave radiation with very short periods (from only a couple of seconds down to tiny fractions of a second) between pulses. These objects were named pulsars, and were soon shown almost certainly to be neutron stars. Their powerful electromagnetic fields channel the radiation associated with the pulsar into two continuous beams which, because of the object's rapid rotation, we see (assuming we are in a suitable line-of-sight) in the form of pulses, much as we might see the light from the rotating lamp of a lighthouse. The period of a pulsar's pulses (i.e., its rate of rotation) can be used as a measure of the pulsar's age – the rotation slows with time – and there is excellent correlation between such measures and the ages of pulsars whose dates of formation are known (notably the pulsar at the core of the Crab Nebula, the remnant of the supernova observed in AD1054).

The tidal forces created in proximity to such a star would be lethal, as imagined in Larry NIVEN's story "Neutron Star" (1966), in which a spaceship pilot who has ventured too close is almost ripped apart because, in such an intense gravitational field, the length of his body represents a significant distance, and so the force exerted by GRAVITY on his feet is considerably stronger than that exerted on his head; it is this difference in pull that so nearly proves fatal to him. In Gregory BENFORD's *The Stars in Shroud* (1978) a neutron star's gravity is exploited by space-craft whipping round it to accelerate into new courses – a more extreme version of the manoeuvre whereby space-probes in the Solar System exploit the gravitational fields of the larger planets. The most extreme neutron-star stories may be Robert L. FORWARD's *Dragon's Egg* (1980) and its sequel *Starquake!* (1985), which have an ALIEN race – who live on a hugely accelerated timescale – evolving on the unfriendly surface of such a star, and ultimately making contact with human observers.

Stellar collapse for stars with a mass greater than the Chandrasekhar limit can, it is theorized, lead to a different and even more bizarre form, the BLACK HOLE. [PN]

NEUTZSKY-WULFF, ERWIN [r] ◊ DENMARK.

NEUWIRTH, BARBARA [r] ◊ AUSTRIA.

NEVILLE, KRIS (OTTMAN) (1925-1980) US writer of fiction who worked for many years as a technical writer specializing in plastics technology, and through his connection with the Epoxylite Corporation co-authored several texts on epoxy resins. He began publishing sf with "The Hand from the Stars" for *Super Science Stories* in 1949, and for several years was a prolific contributor to *FSF* and other magazines; he wrote some fantasy as by Henderson Starke. His short fiction was assembled in *Mission: Manstop* (coll with some stories updated 1971) and in the posthumous *The Science Fiction of Kris Neville* (coll 1984) ed Barry N. MALZBERG and Martin H. GREENBERG, much of it demonstrating his notable strengths as a writer: concision, clarity of style and a capacity to develop the sometimes routine initial material of a story so that its implications expanded constantly, rather in the manner mastered, with more recognition than KN ever received, by James TIPTREE Jr. "Hunt the Hunter" (1951), for instance, begins as a simple hunt on an alien planet but expands subtly but quickly into a study in power politics whose trick ending very neatly turns the meaning of the whole tale in upon itself. Another early story, "The Toy" (1952), powerfully structures a very sharp lesson in ANTHROPOLOGY within an apparently routine tale about humans oppressing "inferior" aliens. One of his very few late stories, "Ballenger's People" (1967), counts as sf only through its moderately futuristic form of urban transport; the tale itself describes, with superb concision, the complex internal politics of a deranged mind.

KN's best known story is probably "Bettyan" (1951) which, with a sequel, "Overture" (1954), eventually became *Bettyann* (fixup 1970). It tells the story of a young girl whose adolescent sense that she really belongs somewhere else is, in classic sf fashion, confirmed by her discovery first that she is adopted, and second that she is a child of creatures from the stars. She is then forced to decide between heredity and environment, a choice whose implications are developed in a recent sequel, "Bettyann's Children" (1973) with Lil Neville, KN's wife and frequent late collaborator. Among the fiction KN wrote with her is a 1975 novel published only in Japanese whose title translates as "Run, the Spearmaker".

KN's comparative silence for two decades before his death, a silence obscured by the book publication of old material (some of it revamped), was much to be regretted, for his intelligence was acute and his artistic control over his material was always evident. He was one of the potentially major writers in the genre who never came to speak in his full voice. [JC]

Other works: *The Unearth People* (1964); *The Mutants* (1953 *Imagination* as "Earth Alert"; exp 1966); *Special Delivery* (1952 *Imagination*; 1967 chap dos); *Peril of the Starmen* (1954 *Imagination*; 1967 chap dos); *Invaders on the Moon* (1970) with Mel Sturgis (left uncredited through a publishing decision against which KN protested).

See also: LIVING WORLDS; SUPERMAN.

NEW ADVENTURES OF WONDER WOMAN, THE ◊ WONDER WOMAN.

NEW AVENGERS, THE ◊ *The* AVENGERS.

NEW BARBARIANS, THE ◊ George MILLER; 1990: I GUERRIERI DEL BRONX.

NEWCOMB, SIMON (1835-1909) Canadian-born writer, in the USA from 1853, of texts on and studies of astronomical and mathematical subjects. In his sf novel *His Wisdom, the Defender* (1900) future historians tell how a professor discovers a source of limitless energy, invents ANTIGRAVITY and, after creating a private army – equipping it with futuristic armour – takes over the world from the air and prohibits war. In "The End of the World" (1903 *McClure's Magazine*) a black body from space hits the Sun, devastating the world. The few who survive realize that eons must pass before civilization may rise again. [JC]

See also: WEAPONS.

NEW DESTINIES ◊ DESTINIES.

NEW DIMENSIONS ORIGINAL-ANTHOLOGY series (1971-1981) ed Robert SILVERBERG. *New Dimensions I* (anth **1971**) appeared when original anthology series were proliferating in the USA, with such titles as INFINITY, QUARK and UNIVERSE. ND was one of the longest-lasting titles from this period, although it had to change publishers several times (#1-#3 DOUBLEDAY, #4 Signet, #5-#10 Harper & Row, #11-#12 Pocket Books) in order to keep going: *New Dimensions I* (anth **1971**), #2 (anth **1972**), #3 (anth **1973**), #4 (anth **1974**), #5 (anth **1975**), #6 (anth **1976**), #7 (anth **1977**), #8 (anth **1978**), #9 (anth **1979**), #10 (anth **1980**), #11 (anth **1980**) with Marta RANDALL and #12 (anth **1981**) with Randall. An associated anthology was *The Best of New Dimensions* (anth **1979**).

ND was one of the more experimental anthology series, and introduced a number of new writers. Its regular contributors included Gardner DOZOIS, George Alec EFFINGER, Felix GOTSCHALK and James TIPTREE Jr. #2 contained "Eurema's Dam" by R.A. LAFFERTY, which shared a HUGO as Best Short Story; #3 contained 2 Hugo-winning stories: "The Girl who was Plugged In" by Tiptree and "The Ones who Walk Away from Omelas" by Ursula K. LE GUIN; #11 had "Unicorn Tapestry" by Suzy McKee CHARNAS, which won a NEBULA as Best Novella. Many other stories were award nominees; ND was one of the best original anthology series. [MJE/PN]

NEW FUTURIAN, THE ◊ *The* FUTURIAN.

NEWMAN, BERNARD (1897-1968) UK writer, mostly of espionage thrillers (some as by Don Betteridge) and detective mysteries, the two genres being perhaps most successfully combined in *Maginot Line Murder* (**1939**). The entertainment value of his sf is somewhat minimal, as he used the form primarily to provide platforms for his arguments about WAR, WEAPONS and the political nature of peace. In *Armoured Doves* (**1931**) SCIENTISTS combine to end war, as does the hero of *Secret Weapon* (**1941**), whose invention of an atomic bomb ends WWII; later, in *The Flying Saucer* (**1948**), the same scientist continues his peace campaign by creating an imaginary Martian threat against the world. BN, who appears as himself in this book, acknowledged that its source was André MAUROIS's *Le Chapitre Suivant* (**1927** chap; trans as *The Next Chapter* **1928** chap UK). Further novels combining politics and future-war themes include *Shoot!* (**1949**), *The Blue Ants: The First Authentic Account of the Russian-Chinese War of 1970* (**1962**) and *Draw the Dragon's Teeth* (**1967**). *The Wishful Think* (**1954**) is a borderline-sf story about politicized ESP. [JC]

Other works: *The Cavalry Went Through* (**1930**); *Hosanna* (**1933**); *The Boy who Could Fly* (**1967**).

NEWMAN, JOHN (? -) UK research chemist and writer who collaborated with Kenneth BULMER on a long series of science articles for *NW* and *Nebula* 1955-61 under the name Kenneth Johns. [JC]

NEWMAN, KIM (JAMES) (1959-) UK writer and broadcaster who remains as well known for his film criticism as for his fiction, though the latter has become increasingly dominant in his output. His film books – *Nightmare Movies: Wide Screen Horror Since 1968* (**1984** US; rev vt *Nightmare Movies: A Critical History of the Horror Film, 1968-1988* 1988 UK) and *Wild West Movies* (**1990**) express a generically savvy, sophisticatedly wry vision of their subject matters, a vision also articulated in the weekly reviews he has conducted on tv since 1989. KN began publishing sf with "Dreamers" for *Interzone* in 1984, rapidly establishing a name for liquidly dense tales of the NEAR FUTURE – or ALTERNATE-WORLD versions of the earlier 20th century – which combine a more or less standard CYBERPUNK idiom with an acute sensitivity to the dream world of the movies, in particular the *film noir* tradition already mined by authors like William GIBSON. KN's almost excessive sensitivity to the icons of Hollywood helps distinguish him from his sf models. His first novel, *The Night Mayor* (**1989**), potently intensifies the VIRTUAL REALITY claustrophobias of cyberpunk through a plot whose villain, the criminal Daine, has escaped into a MAGIC-REALIST, glowing, alternate-world mental construct peopled by personas from detective films of the 1940s, from which haven he must be flushed by the protagonists. The book clearly and deliberately harks back to Philip K. DICK's darker investigations of the nature of reality and to Roger ZELAZNY's *The Dream Master* (**1966**), though KN's rather impersonal polish may have kept his tale from fully expressing the epistemological vertigo of some of its greater models; and certainly his use of tropes out of the dream-life of US film is, at times, soothingly nostalgic. His second novel, *Bad Dreams* (**1990**), replicates much of this material in terms of HORROR, again diminished in its visceral effect by a sense that the author has good-humouredly distanced himself from the products of his imagination. *Jago* (**1991**), a full-blown horror tale, once again features an antagonist capable of exercising coercive control over his opponents' inner worlds, in this case by transfiguring their dream self-images into reality, so that – for instance – a farmer anguished by drought and debt becomes a Green Man. *Anno Dracula* (**1992**) is set in a RECURSIVE alternate-world 19th-century England which has been transformed by the marriage of Vlad Tepes, Count Dracula, to Queen Victoria.

At the same time as writing novels that eat at the consensual world while suggesting that reality could still be addressed in something like comfort, KN also produced, as Jack Yeovil, a series of ties for GAMES WORKSHOP which leapt unashamedly into the explicitly easier environment of the GAME-WORLD. *Drachenfels* ✳ **(1989)** and *Beasts in Velvet* ✳ **(1991)** are fantasies constructed for the **Warhammer** enterprise; but the **Demon Download** sequence – written in the **Dark Future** series, and comprising "Route 666" ✳ (in *Route 666* **[1990]** ed David PRINGLE), *Demon Download* ✳ **(1990)**, *Krokodil Tears* ✳ **(1991)**, *Comeback Tour (The Sky Belongs to the Stars)* ✳ **(1991)** and «United States Calvary» – contains elements of genuine sf, ruthlessly blended into a NEAR-FUTURE/alternate-world/fantasy/horror/punk mix. Both game-worlds and horror as a genre tend to view CONCEPTUAL BREAKTHROUGHS as breakers of the dream, and it is not yet certain that KN is much inclined to engage himself (or Jack Yeovil) in the displacements necessary to compose full and unadulterated sf.

KN wrote many of the CINEMA and tv entries for the 2nd edition of this encyclopedia. [JC]

Other works: *Ghastly Beyond Belief: The Science Fiction and Fantasy Book of Quotations* (anth **1986**) edited with Neil GAIMAN; *Horror: 100 Best Books* (anth **1988**) ed with Stephen Jones, critical essays.

See also: BRITISH SCIENCE FICTION AWARD; COMPUTERS; GOTHIC SF; INTERZONE; NEW WORLDS; PSYCHOLOGY.

NEW ORIGINAL WONDER WOMAN, THE ◊ WONDER WOMAN.

NEW PATHWAYS US SEMIPROZINE, full title *New Pathways into Science Fiction and Fantasy* (Mar 1986-possibly current); BEDSHEET-format, bimonthly to #6, later quarterly, then irregular, ed and published Michael G. Adkisson from Texas, 19 issues to Jan 1991. Lively, but struggling for readership, *NP* mixes fiction, features and COMIC strips, all at the radical end of the sf spectrum, including commentary by MISHA and fiction by Carter SCHOLZ, Lewis SHINER, John SHIRLEY and others, and sometimes experimental, as in a number of reprints from Brian W. ALDISS's **Enigmas** series of short stories. [PN]

NEWTE, HORACE (WYKEHAM CAN) (1870-1949) UK novelist and controversialist on political matters whose *The Master Beast: Being a True Account of the Ruthless Tyranny Inflicted on the British People by Socialism, A.D. 1888-2020* (**1907**; vt *The Red Fury: Britain Under Bolshevism* 1919) lives fully up to its subtitle, telling of a young socialist at the turn of the 20th century who first experiences a German INVASION of an unprepared UK, then, after awakening (◊ SLEEPER AWAKES) from suspended animation, experiences the enormity of a century of socialist rule, with women freed for immorality, George Bernard Shaw (1856-1950) canonized, and thought-control universal. *The Ealing Miracle: A Realistic Story* (**1911**) is a fantasy in which two women exchange personalities at the behest of a Christlike stranger and learn about love and deprivation. [JC]

NEWTON, DAVID C. ◊ John LYMINGTON.

NEWTON, JULIUS P. (?   -   ) UK writer whose *The Forgotten Race* (**1963**) depicts with awkward sincerity the attempts of Venusians and Martians – both survivors of the atomic HOLOCAUST which destroyed the fifth planet – to persuade the humans of Earth not to repeat the tragedy. [JC]

NEWTON, W(ILFRID) DOUGLAS (1884-1951) Irish writer who began writing sf with 2 future-WAR novels, *War* (**1914**) – prefaced by Robert Hugh BENSON and introduced by Rudyard KIPLING – and *The North Afire* (**1914**). Later works include *The Golden Cat* (**1930**), *The Beggar and Other Stories* (coll **1933**), which contains a story about guided missiles, "The Joke that Ended War", and *Dr Odin* (**1933**), about an attempt to perfect a Nordic "master race". His **Savaran** series includes two LOST-WORLD stories, "The Great Quest" in *I, Savaran* (coll **1937**) and *Savaran and the Great Sands* (1939 *The Passing Show* as "The Devil Comes Aboard"; **1939**). He contributed sf to various early magazines, including PEARSON'S MAGAZINE, and to the US PULP MAGAZINES, but only a small proportion has been reprinted in book form. [JE]

NEW VOICES ORIGINAL-ANTHOLOGY series, subtitled "The Campbell Award Nominees", #1 from Macmillan, #1-#4 in paperback from BERKLEY BOOKS, final vol from BLUEJAY BOOKS; ed George R.R. MARTIN. Each vol contained original novellas written (a few years later in most cases) by the 4-6 finalists from a particular year of the JOHN W. CAMPBELL AWARD for the best new sf or fantasy writer. The books, which contained stories from the award winners for 1973 to 1977 respectively, were *New Voices in Science Fiction* (anth **1977**; vt *New Voices I: The Campbell Award Nominees* 1978 US), *New Voices II* (anth **1979**), *New Voices III* (anth **1980**), *New Voices 4* (anth **1981**) and *The John W. Campbell Awards Volume 5* (anth **1984**). Eventually the publication year fell too far behind the year of the award, and this interesting series lost its point and came to a close. The best-known story published in the series is John VARLEY's "Blue Champagne" (1981) in #4. [PN]

NEW WAVE This term, as applied to sf, is borrowed from film criticism, where it was much used in the early 1960s as a translation of the French *nouvelle vague* to refer to the experimental cinema associated with Jean-Luc Godard (1930-   ), François Truffaut (1932-1984) and others. (It was also applied to music around 1977 as a synonym for Punk.) The term was first applied to sf FANZINES in 1964, and then used – probably by Christopher PRIEST – initially to describe the sort of fiction being published in NEW WORLDS. It came to be used more by sf proselytizers than by the writers concerned – especially by Judith MERRIL, in her anthology *England Swings SF* (anth **1968**; cut vt *The Space-Time Journal* 1972 UK) and elsewhere.

The kind of story to which the term refers is in fact rather older than the (late-1960s) term, which anyway has never been defined with any precision. The first writers whose work was later subsumed under the New Wave label were UK, notably Brian W. ALDISS and J.G. BALLARD. These two were publishing stories in *NW* while it was still under the editorship of John CARNELL, but it was not until Michael MOORCOCK took over with the May/June 1964 issue that the kind of imagistic, highly metaphoric story, inclined more towards psychology and the SOFT SCIENCES than to HARD SF, that both men wrote (in quite different styles) was given a setting where it seemed at home.

Traditional GENRE SF had reached a crisis point in both the UK and the USA by the middle 1960s; too many writers were working with the same few traditional sf themes, and both the style and content of sf were becoming generally overpredictable. Many young writers entering the field came to feel, either instantly, like Thomas M. DISCH, or after some years' slogging away at conventional commercial sf, like Harlan ELLISON and Robert SILVERBERG, that genre sf had become a straitjacket; though widely supposed to emphasize change and newness, sf had somehow become conservative. Young Turks, of course, conventionally exaggerate the sins of their seniors, but this time they had a real case. It was not as if the market were shrinking; on the contrary, hardcover publishers were more willing than ever to add sf to their lists. There was no reason to suppose that publishers would not be grateful for sf becoming rather more flexible in style and content.

By 1965, then, sf was ripe for change. In fact, many of the so-called sf experiments of the period were not experiments at all, but merely an adoption of narrative strategies, and sometimes ironies, that had long been familiar in the MAINSTREAM novel. In the event, some of the sf writers who felt they now had the freedom to experiment, especially Ballard and perhaps (rather later) Moorcock, were to add something new to the protocols of prose fiction generally; the New Wave may have taken from the Mainstream, but it gave something back in return (this is now a truism of POSTMODERNIST criticism, but it was by no means clear at the time), and certainly New-Wave sf did more than any other kind of sf to break down the barriers between sf and mainstream fiction.

Because it was never a formal literary movement – perhaps more a state of mind than anything else – New-Wave writing is difficult to define. Perhaps the fundamental element was the belief that sf could and should be taken seriously as literature. Much of it shared the qualities of the late-1960s counterculture, including an interest in mind-altering DRUGS and oriental RELIGIONS, a satisfaction in violating TABOOS, a marked interest in SEX, a strong involvement in Pop Art and in the MEDIA LANDSCAPE generally, and a pessimism about the future that ran strongly counter to genre sf's traditional OPTIMISM, often focused on the likelihood of DISASTER caused by OVERPOPULATION and interference with the ECOLOGY, as well as by WAR, and a general cynicism about the POLITICS of the US and UK governments (notably the US involvement in Southeast Asia and elsewhere). The element of DYSTOPIA in New-Wave writing was particularly dramatic in the case of John BRUNNER, much of whose earlier work had been relatively cheerful SPACE OPERA. New-Wave sf often concerned itself with the NEAR FUTURE; but it often turned inward, too, and one of the buzzwords of the period was INNER SPACE.

Moorcock's *NW* published most of the notable figures of the New Wave at one time or another, including the work of several US writers who lived for a time in the UK, such as Samuel R. DELANY, Disch, James SALLIS, John T. SLADEK and Pamela ZOLINE. Other US *NW* contributors often subsumed under the New-Wave label were Ellison, Norman SPINRAD and Roger ZELAZNY; other UK contributors were Barrington J. BAYLEY, M. John HARRISON, Langdon JONES and Charles PLATT, and one would add Christopher PRIEST, although he was less closely associated with *NW*.

Despite the various excesses of *NW*, whose stories sometimes embraced ENTROPY with a fervour reminiscent of Edgar Allan POE's "The Masque of the Red Death" (1842), there is no doubt that it was influential on sf PUBLISHING generally, and it was not long at all before various US markets were adopting a far less exclusive attitude to what they would or would not publish, a symptom being the appearance of ORIGINAL-ANTHOLOGY series like DANGEROUS VISIONS, NEW DIMENSIONS, ORBIT and QUARK, which included a good quota of experimental work – indeed, they demonstrated clearly (though the point hardly needed to be made) that as much US sf as UK had come to be New Wave in style and content.

All this naturally horrified some of sf's more conservative spokesmen, as a glance at sf histories written by David KYLE, Sam MOSKOWITZ and Donald A. WOLLHEIM will demonstrate. Wollheim commented, in *The Universe Makers* (1971), that "the readers and writers that used to dream of galactic futures now got their kicks out of experimental styles of writing, the free discussion of sex, the overthrow of all standards and morals (since, if the world is going to end, what merit had these things?)". It is easy to feel some sympathy with the conservative viewpoint in one respect; with few exceptions the New-Wave writers avoided HARD SF, and it must have seemed to some observers of the scene as if the very thing that most centrally defined sf by its presence – the science (to simplify) – was disappearing.

But in fact the battle was quickly over (though hard sf never quite regained its former position of prominence). The better New-Wave sf writers were soon accepted by sf readers generally, and often found an audience outside sf as well; the bad writers (some were terrible) mostly fell by the wayside. By the 1970s there no longer seemed very much point to the term, although newly prominent figures like Gardner DOZOIS, Barry N. MALZBERG, Joanna RUSS, James TIPTREE Jr and Gene WOLFE clearly wrote in a style that would have been called New Wave only a year or so earlier. Later in the decade all sorts of quite different new writers emerged who had clearly absorbed the positive lessons of the New Wave, along with some of its attitudes, ranging from Michael BISHOP and John VARLEY in the USA to Ian WATSON in the UK.

There can be no doubt that during the late 1960s

genre sf found new freedoms, while the market showed a greater readiness to accept sophisticated writing. As with all ideological arguments, one uses whatever ammunition comes conveniently to hand, and it suited many friends (and foes) to see the New Wave as a kind of homogeneous, monolithic politico-literary movement. It was never that in the minds of most of its writers, many of whom resented being categorized. Disch commented, in an open letter published in 1978: "I have no opinion of the 'New Wave' in sf, since I don't believe that that was ever a meaningful classification. If you mean to ask – do I feel solidarity with all writers who have ever been lumped together under that heading – certainly I do not."

It was common during the 1970s and 1980s, especially for those (like Disch) who resisted stereotyping, to dismiss the importance of the New Wave, or even to deny that it ever existed. From the perspective of the 1990s, however, it seems fair to say that the New Wave *was* real and liberating; New-Wave excesses – including its sometimes miasmic gloom – have largely dropped away in subsequent sf, while the New Wave's grasp of the complexities of the world has remained. The 1960s were indeed a maturing period for genre sf; if we see the 1960s as sf's puberty, then we also have an explanation of why some of it, at the time, was so irritating (especially in its tone of voice): most adolescents are. One reason why the perspective of the 1990s is useful is that we have, meanwhile, been able to observe yet another New Wave in action: CYBERPUNK.

Two of the many anthologies of New Wave sf are *The New SF* (anth **1969**) ed Langdon Jones and *The New Tomorrows* (anth **1971**) ed Norman Spinrad. A book on the subject is *The Entropy Exhibition: Michael Moorcock and the UK "New Wave"* (**1983**) by Colin GREENLAND. [PN]

See also: ARTS.

NEW WORLDS The leading UK sf magazine (an ORIGINAL-ANTHOLOGY series for two sections of its chequered career), publishing 218 issues over an intermittent career of nearly 50 years ([July] 1946-current), but including a 12-year hiatus; 12 of these issues have been in book form. *NW*, though it had volume numbers up to #177, has always been numbered consecutively (in its magazine incarnations), the numeration not beginning again with each volume number. #1-#5 were undated.

3 PULP-size issues were published irregularly by Pendulum in 1946-7 under the editorship of an sf fan, John CARNELL (*NW* was a development from a pre-WWII FANZINE [1936-9] called first NOVAE TERRAE and then *New Worlds*, the last 4 issues of which were ed Carnell). #1 was issued twice with different covers; #1 with the original cover had not sold well, but it did better the second time round (the second version used the same cover as #2).

Nova Publications, a publishing group formed by UK sf fans who used to meet at the White Horse pub

in London, revived this somewhat tentative 1946-7 magazine in 1949 as a DIGEST. Carnell remained in charge until #141 (Apr 1964), after which the title was taken over by Roberts & Vinter, publishers of Compact Books, who issued it in a pocketbook (paperback-size) edition, ed Michael MOORCOCK. After #172 (Mar 1967) it was published by Moorcock under the auspices of the Arts Council in a stapled 8in x 11in (approx A4) format, rising to BEDSHEET-size with #179. In this incarnation *NW* suffered financial difficulties, compounded when the leading UK retail-newsagent chain, W.H. Smith & Sons Ltd, refused to carry copies for various reasons, in particular the use of "obscene" language in Norman SPINRAD's *Bug Jack Barron* (Dec 1967-July 1968; **1969**). The last issue to be properly released was #200 (Apr 1970), though in 1971 #201, a special final, "Good-Taste" issue with retrospective index went out to subscribers. During this period Moorcock relaxed his control over the editorship, various members of his coterie taking a hand in the issues released in 1969; Charles PLATT was editor #197-#200. For the greater part of the period from #22 to #200 the magazine maintained a monthly schedule with only occasional lapses.

In 1971 the title was revived again, this time as a series of original anthologies (numbered from #1 again, although the original numeration was tacitly maintained) published in paperback by Sphere Books (#1-#8) and Corgi Books (#9 and #10). These were *New Worlds #1* (anth **1971**; vt *New Worlds Quarterly 1* 1971 US) ed Moorcock; *#2* (anth **1971**; vt *New Worlds Quarterly 2* 1971 US) ed Moorcock; *#3* (anth **1972**; vt *New Worlds Quarterly 3* 1972 US) ed Moorcock; *#4* (anth **1972**; vt *New Worlds Quarterly 4* 1972 US) ed Moorcock; *#5* (anth **1973**) ed Moorcock; *#6* (anth **1973**; vt *New Worlds Quarterly 5* 1974 US) ed Moorcock with Charles Platt; *#7* (anth **1974**) ed Hilary BAILEY with Platt; *#8* (anth **1975**) ed Bailey; *#9* (anth **1975**) ed Bailey; and *#10* (anth **1976**) ed Bailey.

When the book series was cancelled, *NW* was defunct, but the fervour of its supporters brought about yet another resuscitation in 1978, with #212 ed Moorcock in a FANZINE-style format, and #213-#216 ed by various supporters professionally published, the last 2 being in 1979. This final incarnation, published by Charles Partington in Manchester, was more a generalized underground magazine than an sf magazine; it contained many satirical graphics. #214 was titled in Russian. #215 ed David BRITTON was marked "limited edition of one thousand copies".

In 1991 David S. GARNETT, with Moorcock's approval and with Moorcock as Consulting Editor, initiated yet another incarnation of *NW*, this time in anthology book form, as *New Worlds* (anth **1991**) and *New Worlds 2* (anth **1992**), both ed Garnett, published by GOLLANCZ. These volumes were numbered #217 and #218, according to the original sequence, which was again explicitly acknowledged.

Under Carnell *NW* was the primary force in shaping a tradition in UK magazine sf, and under Moorcock its name became the banner of what was dubbed the NEW WAVE. Carnell provided a stable domestic market for the leading UK writers and played a considerable role in the careers of Brian W. ALDISS, J.G. BALLARD, John BRUNNER, Kenneth BULMER, Colin KAPP, E.C. TUBB and James WHITE. He encouraged a species of sf more sober in tone than much US material, with the emphasis on problem-solving; an excellent example of the species is James White's **Sector General** series. In publishing ambitious work by Aldiss and most of Ballard's early work Carnell began a shift in emphasis toward psychological and existential sf (◊ FABULA-TION; PSYCHOLOGY), which also showed in his choice of reprints from US authors: Philip K. DICK's *Time Out of Joint* (Dec 1959-Feb 1960; **1959**) and Theodore STURGEON's *Venus Plus X* (Jan-Apr 1961; **1960**). Most of the US magazines were also shifting their emphasis away from the "hardware" of sf, but retained a kind of brashness not evident in *NW* save in the work of those authors most heavily influenced by pulp sf.

Moorcock's editorship was a good deal more flamboyant than Carnell's, and he was as polemical in the material which provided the environment for the fiction as John W. CAMPBELL Jr had been in ASTOUND-ING SCIENCE-FICTION during the early 1940s, though to very different ends, juxtaposing fiction with factual social comment, visual collage, even concrete poetry, in a deliberate attempt to lose the GENRE-SF image and to place speculative fiction in a context of rapid social change, and radical art generally. Apart from his own *avant-garde* material (often written as James Colvin), he promoted inventive UK writers like Barrington J. BAYLEY, Langdon JONES, David I. MASSON and, later, Ian WATSON, and recruited some US writers – notably Thomas M. DISCH and John T. SLADEK. Moorcock's early **Jerry Cornelius** pieces appeared in *NW*, as did his NEBULA-winning "Behold, the Man" (Sep 1966; exp as *Behold the Man* **1969**). The large-size version serialized, in addition to Spinrad's *Bug Jack Barron* (noted above), *Camp Concentration* by Disch (July-Sep 1967; **1968**), and featured 2 more Nebula-winning short pieces: Samuel R. DELANY's "Time Considered as a Helix of Semi-Precious Stones" (Dec 1968), which also won a HUGO, and Harlan ELLISON's "A Boy and His Dog" (Apr 1969). Under Moorcock *NW* established in its review columns a particularly trenchant style of criticism which continued in the paperback anthologies, much of it written by John CLUTE and M. John HARRISON. It cannot be said that Moorcock's programme met with wide-ranging approval, especially among those readers attuned to the more modest and traditional aspects of Carnell's policy, and it certainly lacked Carnell's sense of balance, but its contribution to sf in the 1960s was considerable – the paths beaten by the *NW* writers are now much more generally in use.

It remains to be seen if Garnett's *NW* of the 1990s will find a market niche. Certainly, the contents to date have been impressive, featuring good stories by Storm CONSTANTINE, Paul Di Filippo, Ian McDONALD,

Kim NEWMAN and Moorcock himself. Fortunately Garnett has avoided the 1960s/1970s nostalgia that might have sunk the enterprise.

A US edition of *NW*, with Hans Stefan SANTESSON credited as editor, ran for 5 issues Mar-July 1960, selected mainly from the 1959 *NW* with some stories from other sources. Some unsold issues of the Roberts & Vinter *NW* were bound up in twos and threes and sold under the title SF REPRISE, these being *SF Reprise 1* (anth **1966**) containing #144/#145; *SF Reprise 2* (anth **1966**) containing #149/#150; and *SF Reprise 5* (anth **1967**) containing #149-#151.

There were many derived anthologies. Carnell ed *The Best From New Worlds Science Fiction* (anth **1955**), and his *Lambda 1 and Other Stories* (anth **1964**; UK and US contents vary) was also selected from *NW*. Moorcock ed *The Best of New Worlds* (anth **1965**), *Best S.F. Stories from New Worlds* (anth **1967**), *Best Stories from New Worlds 2* (anth **1968**; vt *Best S.F. Stories from New Worlds 2* US), *Best S.F. Stories from New Worlds 3* (anth **1968**), *Best S.F. Stories from New Worlds 4* (anth **1969**), *Best S.F. Stories from New Worlds 5* (anth **1969**), *Best S.F. Stories from New Worlds 6* (anth **1970**), *Best S.F. Stories from New Worlds 7* (anth **1971**) and *Best S.F. Stories from New Worlds 8* (anth **1974**), as well as the retrospective *New Worlds: An Anthology* (anth **1983**). These series anthologies also sometimes used stories from SCIENCE FANTASY/*Impulse*. The first 6 of the 8 **Best S.F. Stories from New Worlds** vols were also published in the USA.   [BS/PN]

See also: ENTROPY; TABOOS.

NEW WORLDS QUARTERLY ◊ NEW WORLDS.

NEW WRITINGS IN SF ORIGINAL-ANTHOLOGY series begun 1964 by John CARNELL after he relinquished the editorship of NEW WORLDS and SCIENCE FANTASY; it was published by Dennis Dobson to #20, then by Sidgwick & Jackson. The UK paperback editions (all published by Corgi) sometimes preceded hardcover publication, and in the case of #30, the last in the series, there was no hardcover. *NWISF* carried on the tradition of Carnell's *New Worlds*: predominantly middle-of-the-road sf, leavened with occasional more adventurous pieces and saved from staleness by his willingness to publish new writers. Regular contributors included not only Colin KAPP (chiefly with his **Unorthodox Engineers** series), Douglas R. MASON (under his own name and as John Rankine), John Rackham (J.T. PHILLIFENT) and James WHITE (including stories in his **Sector General** series), but also Keith ROBERTS, while M. John HARRISON and Christopher PRIEST both published early short stories in its pages. *NWISF* was intended to be a quarterly, but later its appearances became erratic. *New Writings in SF 1* (anth **1964**) was followed by #2 (anth **1964**), #3 (anth **1965**), #4 (anth **1965**), #5 (anth **1965**), #6 (anth **1965**), #7 (anth **1966**), #8 (anth **1966**), #9 (anth **1966**), #10 (anth **1967**), #11 (anth **1967**), #12 (anth **1968**), #13 (anth **1968**), #14 (anth **1969**), #15 (anth **1969**), #16 (anth **1970**), #17 (anth **1970**), #18 (anth **1971**), #19 (anth **1971**), #20 (anth **1972**) and #21 (anth **1972**), this last being published after Carnell's death. 9 vols of this series were published in the USA by BANTAM BOOKS 1966-72, with some difference in contents after the first 6: the US #7 drew from the UK #7, #8 and #9; US #8 drew from UK #10, #11 and #12; US #9 drew from UK #12, #13, #14 and #15.

The series remained alive after Carnell's death, its editorship being taken over by Kenneth BULMER from #22 (anth **1973**). This brought about no substantial change in policy, although one feature of Bulmer's *NWISF* was Brian W. ALDISS's **Enigmas** series. New authors to début in the later issues included David LANGFORD, Charles Partington (◊ NEW WORLDS; SOME-THING ELSE) and Cherry WILDER, and early stories by Robert P. HOLDSTOCK and Ian WATSON also appeared around this time. Bulmer edited #23 (anth **1973**), #24 (anth **1974**), #25 (anth **1975**), #26 (anth **1975**), #27 (anth **1976**), #28 (anth **1976**), #29 (anth **1976**) and #30 (anth **1978**). At this point the market for ANTHOLOGIES was looking even gloomier than usual in the UK, and the series ended.

Seldom groundbreaking but always reliable, *NWISF* did not have any impact comparable to the major original-anthology series in the US (e.g., ORBIT, UNIVERSE), which mostly began somewhat later. Associated anthologies are *The Best from New Writings in SF: First Selection* (anth **1971**) ed Carnell and 3 omnibus volumes: *New Writings in SF: Special 1* (anth **1975**), containing #21 and #23; *#2* (anth **1978**), containing #26 and #29; and *#3* (anth **1978**), containing #27 and #28. [MJE/PN]

NEW YORK REVIEW OF SCIENCE FICTION US critical magazine, published Dragon Press, Pleasantville, New York; ed (in 1992) by Kathryn Cramer, L.W. CURREY, Samuel R. DELANY, David G. HARTWELL, Robert J. Killheffer and Gordon Van Gelder; current; monthly, beginning with the trial issue (#0) Aug 1988 and #1 Sep 1988. It had reached #50 by Oct 1992. Too highbrow and professional – many of its staff being sf/fantasy writers and publishers – to be called a FANZINE, too informal to be called an academic journal, *NYROSF* is a somewhat unusual critical SEMIPROZINE. It publishes general articles of remarkably varying quality on sf, as well as some of the best long reviews in the field. Its tone is far from homogeneous; it moves disconcertingly (and fast) from chatty to pompous, and there is something to irritate everyone. But, as one might expect from the very well informed staff producing its 24 large-format pages a month with astonishing regularity, it is also irreplaceable. Certainly its coverage of GENRE SF and FANTASY is both wider and deeper than anything in the academic journals with the possible exception of FOUNDATION: THE REVIEW OF SCIENCE FICTION. [PN]

NEW ZEALAND One of the last lands discovered by Europeans, New Zealand was a convenient setting for moral and UTOPIAN tales. The anonymous *Travels of Hildebrand Bowman, by Himself* (**1778** UK) anticipates Samuel BUTLER's satirical *Erewhon* (**1872**) and *Erewhon Revisited* (**1901**). Utopian fiction by New Zealanders

includes *Anno Domini 2000, or Woman's Destiny* (**1889** UK) by the NZ Premier Sir Julius VOGEL, a dreary novel of a UK/US empire formed through dynastic marriage, and Godfrey SWEVEN's difficult novel sequence *Riallaro: The Archipelago of Exiles* (**1901** US) and *Limanora: The Island of Progress* (**1903** US), the latter described by E.F. BLEILER as "probably the greatest of all early utopian novels". Some 19th-century works, mostly published in England, are extrapolated from a remark of Lord Macaulay (1800-1859) in *Critical and Historical Essays* (coll **1843**): ". . . when some traveller from New Zealand shall, in the midst of a vast solitude, take his stand on a broken arch of London Bridge to sketch the ruins of St Paul's." The UK writer Francis Carr's *Archimago* (**1864**), partly set in a ruined London of 1964, is an example.

A more popular taste is seen in the end-of-the-century boom in romance. *The Great Romance* (**1881**) by "The Inhabitant" is NZ's first space story. The heroes in Ajor's *The Secret of Mt Cook* (**1894**) revive frozen people; in *Hedged with Divinities* (**1895**) by Edward Tregear (1846-1931) all men die; the subject of *The Elixir of Life* (**1907** UK) by William Satchell (1860-1942) is self-evident.

A puritan realist mode dominates NZ MAINSTREAM fiction and criticism, yet writers within the tradition often use sf and fantasy tropes. Robyn Hyde's *Wednesday's Children* (**1937** UK) is fantasy; Maurice GEE has written fantasies for children; M.K. JOSEPH wrote the speculative *The Hole in the Zero* (**1967** UK) and *The Time of Achamoth* (**1977**); Janet FRAME's metafictions *Scented Garden for the Blind* (**1963**) and *Living in the Maniototo* (**1979** US) are fantastic; and the dystopian *Smith's Dream* (**1971**) – filmed as *Sleeping Dogs* (see below) – by C.K. STEAD tells of a future military dictatorship. Current writers such as Russell Haley, Marilyn Duckworth (1935-) and Rachel McAlpine (1940-) are adept at using sf devices for mainstream audiences.

Works marketed as sf include Adrian Geddes's *The Rim of Eternity* (**1964**), in which aliens invade, Colin GIBSON's tale of nuclear winter, *The Pepper Leaf* (**1971** UK), and the novels of Hugh COOK, which are fantasy. Peter Hooper's fantasies and Craig HARRISON's thrillers have escaped the genre label. Phillip MANN and Cherry WILDER (who now lives in Germany) are the best-known contemporary NZ sf writers, along with Sandi HALL.

NZ sf in the CINEMA started with the now lost *A Message from Mars* (1909), based on Richard Ganthony's popular 1899 UK stage play, which he and Lester LURGAN novelized (**1912**), the play itself being published much later (**1924**). There was no further NZ sf film until the successful *Sleeping Dogs* (1977) dir Roger Donaldson, a NEAR-FUTURE political thriller envisaging a totalitarian government. The industry flourished from this time until the mid-1980s with government subsidies, its sf titles including the routine, post-HOLOCAUST *Battletruck* (1982), the violent, lunatic brain-surgeon-and-his-experimental-subjects story *Death Warmed Up* (1984), the sf thriller DEAD KIDS (1981; vt *Strange Behavior*) and *The* QUIET EARTH (1985); then subsidies were withdrawn. Subsequent films, such as the deliberately disgusting BAD TASTE (1987) and the TIME-TRAVEL fantasy *The Navigator: A Medieval Odyssey* (1988), plus tv shows such as *Space Knights* (1988), seem to show that, in the visual media, NZ sf and fantasy must cross genre boundaries if they are to be viable. [MM]

NEXUS US COMIC-book series (1981-91), 80 issues, published first by Capital Comics and later by First Comics, created by writer Mike Baron and artist Steve Rude. Set in the 25th century, when Earth is the political hub of the interstellar society known as the Cohesive Web and humanity just one of many intelligent races, the comic had as title character a superpowered agent of vengeance, driven to kill tyrants and criminals by targeting them with dreams. *N* explored the moral ambiguity of execution and the often logical motivations behind the atrocities of those killed by the hero; but it also had a lighter side, much humour deriving from Nexus's problems in dealing with his homeworld, Ylum. *N* began with 3 black-and-white issues, changed to colour with #4, was cancelled by Capital with #6 and picked up by First Comics from #7 a year later, in 1985. Declining sales – partly due to long absences by Rude and the poor reception given to the fill-in artists – led to *N*'s demise in 1991. First Comics have published reprints of #1-#26; spin-offs have been *Nexus Legends* (1989-91; 4 issues) and the one-shot *Nexus Files*. [RH]

NEY, FERENC [r] ◊ HUNGARY.

NICHOLLS, PETER (DOUGLAS) (1939-   ) Australian writer and editor, critic and historian of sf, resident in the UK 1970-88, co-editor of this volume. He became first Administrator of the SCIENCE FICTION FOUNDATION 1971-7, and edited its journal FOUNDATION: THE REVIEW OF SCIENCE FICTION 1974-8, part of this work being republished as *Foundation Numbers 1-8: March 1972-March 1975* (anth **1978**). PN ed *Science Fiction at Large* (anth **1976**; vt *Explorations of the Marvellous* **1978**), collecting essays written for a 1975 sf symposium by Philip K. DICK, Thomas M. DISCH, Alan GARNER, Ursula K. LE GUIN, himself and others. His major work, of which he was General Editor and John CLUTE Associate Editor, has been *The Encyclopedia of Science Fiction* (**1979**; vt *The Science Fiction Encyclopedia* US; rev **1993** with Clute and PN co-editors), for which he won the first Non-Fiction HUGO (1980), also winning a PILGRIM AWARD in that year for services to sf scholarship. *The Science in Science Fiction* (**1983**), ed PN and written with David LANGFORD and Brian M. STABLEFORD, is a study of sf's scientific content. *Fantastic Cinema* (**1984**; vt *The World of Fantastic Films* 1984 US), PN's first solo book, is a critical history of sf, horror and fantasy films; it was shortlisted for the British Film Institute Award for Best Film Book. PN has also worked as an academic in English literature (1962-8, 1971-7), scripted tv documentaries, been Harkness Fellow in Film-making (1968-70) in the USA, worked as a publisher's editor (1982-3), often broadcast film and book reviews on BBC Radio from 1974 and published much sf criticism – generally waspish but unsnobbish – in newspapers and magazines. [PN]

See also: BIBLIOGRAPHIES; CINEMA; COLLECTIONS; CRITICAL AND HISTORICAL WORKS ABOUT SF; DEFINITIONS OF SF; PROTO SCIENCE FICTION; SF IN THE CLASSROOM; SENSE OF WONDER.

NICHOLS, LEIGH ◊ Dean R. KOONTZ.

NICHOLS, ROBERT (MALISE BOWYER) (1893-1944) UK poet and playwright whose lyrical talent did not survive the end of WWI; he wrote plays and verse epics thereafter. *The Smile of the Sphinx* (**1920** chap), a fantasy, was later revised and assembled in *Romances of Idea, Volume One: Fantastica: Being the Smile of the Sphinx and Other Tales of Imagination* (coll **1923**). The largest item in that volume is the book-length "Golgotha & Co", set some time after a second world war and assaulting capitalist dreams of the Earthly paradise; the Wandering Jew (who is also a defiant Antichrist) appears and the Messiah is recrucified (off-stage). No second volume of the "Romances" appeared. *Wings Over Europe: A Dramatic Extravaganza on a Pressing Theme* (**1929** US) with Maurice Browne (1881-1955), a play, features the son of a UK prime minister who gains the secret of atomic energy but is killed in an accident before he can do the harm he intends. [JC]

Other work: *Under the Yew* (**1928** chap), a marginal fantasy.

NICHOLSON, J.S. [r] ◊ ANONYMOUS SF AUTHORS.

NICK CARTER ◊ Nick CARTER.

NICOLSON, [Sir] HAROLD (GEORGE) (1886-1968) UK diplomat, MP and writer, married to V. SACKVILLE-WEST, knighted in 1953. His sf novel *Public Faces* (**1932**), set in 1939, describes the international conflicts aroused through the UK knowing how to make atomic bombs, developing a ballistic missile, destroying part of Florida in error, and insisting on world nuclear disarmament. [JC]

See also: END OF THE WORLD; NUCLEAR POWER; POLITICS; WEAPONS.

NICOLSON, MARJORIE HOPE (1894-1981) US scholar and university professor, with a PhD from Yale. Her useful pioneering study in PROTO SCIENCE FICTION was *Voyages to the Moon* (**1949**) – subtitled "Discourse on Voyages to the Moon, the Sun, the Planets and Other Worlds generally, written by divers authors from the earliest times to the time of the First Balloon Ascensions made during the years 1783-84 with remarks on their sources and an epilogue about a few selected later works of this kind; to which is appended a Bibliography of 133 works up to the year 1784 with an added listing of 58 books and articles dealing with the theme itself and with related sciences". The works dealt with are primarily English. MHN was the second winner of the PILGRIM AWARD, in 1971. [PN]

See also: CRITICAL AND HISTORICAL WORKS ABOUT SF; MOON.

NIEBO ZOWIET ◊ Roger CORMAN; PLANETA BUR.

NIEKAS US FANZINE (1962-current) ed from New Hampshire by Ed Meskys alone for the first 5 issues, when it was a small, personal fanzine, then with Felice Rolfe and Anne Chatland from #6, Chatland dropping out after #8. Under Meskys and Rolfe, *N* established itself as a large and variegated magazine containing a mixture of articles, but with particular emphasis on FANTASY. Al Halevy's "Glossary of Middle Earth" was first published in *N*. *N* ceased publication with #20 in 1968, then was revived with #21 in 1977. Currently Meskys, now blind, is listed as editor-in-chief and Mike Bastraw as editor and designer.

Contributors to *N* have included Piers ANTHONY, Isaac ASIMOV, Anthony BOUCHER, Algis BUDRYS, Avram DAVIDSON, Philip K. DICK, Raymond Z. GALLUN, Jack GAUGHAN, Harry HARRISON, Sam MOSKOWITZ, Andre NORTON, Alexei PANSHIN, Jerry POURNELLE, Donald A. WOLLHEIM and Roger ZELAZNY. *N* won the HUGO for Best Fanzine in 1967. [PR/RH]

NIELSEN, NIELS E. [r] ◊ DENMARK.

NIGHBERT, DAVID F. (? -) US writer who began publishing sf with his **Stryker** sequence – *Timelapse* (**1988**) and *The Clouds of Magellan* (**1991**) – which engages its thrillerish protagonist first in a complicated TIME-PARADOX tale whose villain tricks him into falling in love with his own mother, and second in a traditional search for the long-gone ALIEN "Builders" responsible for an enormous artifact (◊ BIG DUMB OBJECTS) called The Wheel. *Strikezone* (**1989**), an associational thriller, again shows DFN's competence but also a disturbing tendency to rifle his genres for material without showing much concern for establishing a bailiwick of his own. [JC]

NIGHT CALLER, THE (vt *Blood Beast from Outer Space*) Film (1965). Armitage Films. Dir John Gilling, starring John Saxon, Maurice Denham, Patricia Haines, Alfred Burke. Screenplay Jim O'Connolly, from *The Night Callers* (**1960**) by Frank R. CRISP. 84 mins. B/w.

Very-low-budget UK film, made with some genuine style by Gilling, who had previously made good horror films for Hammer. However, the story – an ALIEN aims to provide women (whom he finds by advertising for models) for genetic experiments back home on Ganymede – is pure pulp. The alien is tracked down by two SCIENTISTS (he strangles the female one, well played by Haines) who have come across his energy transmitter. The film should not be confused, under its US title, with the US NIGHT OF THE BLOOD BEAST (1958) or the British *The Blood Beast Terror* (1967). [PN]

NIGHT GALLERY ◊ ROD SERLING'S NIGHT GALLERY.

NIGHT OF THE BIG HEAT (vt *Island of the Burning Damned*) Film (1967). Planet. Dir Terence Fisher, starring Christopher Lee, Peter Cushing, Patrick Allen, Sarah Lawson, Jane Merrow. Screenplay Ronald Liles, Pip Baker, Jane Baker, based on *The Night of the Big Heat* (**1959**) by John LYMINGTON. 97 mins, cut to 94 mins. Colour.

An island off the UK coast experiences a freak heatwave, during which there are a number of mysterious killings involving fire. The culprits turn out to be ALIENS who resemble giant fried eggs and are attracted to any source of heat. At the climax the few survivors are saved when a thunderstorm destroys the aliens: water, it seems, dissolves them. Lymington's pulp novel was certainly not rational sf, but it built up an atmosphere of claustrophobic tension which the film lacks. [JB]

NIGHT OF THE BLOOD BEAST Film (1958). Balboa/AIP. Dir Bernard Kowalski, starring Michael Emmet, Angela Greene, John Baer. Screenplay Martin Varno, based on a story by Gene Corman. 65 mins. B/w.

In this typically cheap 1950s Corman production (the executive producer was Roger CORMAN; his brother Gene produced it from his own story), a rocket pilot has cells implanted in his body by a deeply unconvincing-looking ALIEN who returns to Earth with him. Embryos grow inside him, making him the first (but not the last) effectively pregnant movie astronaut. Several plot twists suggest an attempt to cash in on the popularity of *The* QUATERMASS XPERIMENT (1955). [JB/PN]

NIGHT OF THE COMET Film (1984). Atlantic 9000/Film Development Fund. Dir Thom Eberhardt, starring Catherine Mary Stewart, Kelli Maroney, Robert Beltran, Mary Woronov. Screenplay Eberhardt. 100 mins cut to 95 mins for UK release. Colour.

This likable exploitation movie, witty throughout, opens with the light from a comet (an idea stolen from John WYNDHAM's *Day of the Triffids* [**1951**]) destroying almost everybody by turning them into red dust or, in less severe cases, cannibal zombies. Two spunky teenage girls survive, team up with a truck driver, raid department stores for fashionable clothes, destroy the evil government agency that wants to kill them for serum, do disco dances and shoot submachine guns. As one might expect from the producers of *Valley Girl* (1984), the women are shown as self-reliant, intelligent, unmotivated and vain. [PN]

NIGHT OF THE LEPUS Film (1972). Lyles/MGM. Dir William F. Claxton, starring Stuart Whitman, Janet Leigh, Rory Calhoun, DeForest Kelley. Screenplay Don Holliday, Gene R. Kearney, based on *The Year of the Angry Rabbit* (**1964**) by Russell BRADDON. 88 mins. Colour.

Braddon's satirical novel was set in Australia, but the film dropped the SATIRE and switched the setting to Arizona. A test rabbit full of experimental hormones breaks loose and breeds with local rabbits. Suddenly hordes of gigantic carnivorous rabbits are attacking people, eating horses and demolishing houses. The film is endearing for its unintentional humour, enhanced by the commendably serious if wooden performances of all concerned, rabbits included. [JB/PN]

See also: MONSTER MOVIES.

NIGHT OF THE LIVING DEAD 1. Film (1968). Image

10 Productions/Walter Reade-Continental. Dir George A. ROMERO, starring Duane Jones, Judith O'Dea, Karl Hardman, Keith Wayne. Screenplay John A. Russo. 96 mins, cut to 90 mins. B/w.

This unrelenting and downbeat HORROR film, Romero's astonishing début, tells of a horde of walking, cannibalistic corpses who lay siege to an isolated house. Their revival is explained by "space radiation" brought to Earth on an aborted rocket launch, but the absurdity of this barely detracts from the concentrated Gothic PARANOIA of the action, whose intensity won the film a cult following, especially from those who saw the savagery – and helplessness – of both ordinary people and zombies (whose bite infects the victim with zombiism) as symbolic of the horrors of the Vietnam War. *NOTLD* was independently financed and made during weekends by a small group based in Pittsburgh. The sequels, making up a **Living Dead** trilogy, are DAWN OF THE DEAD (1978) and DAY OF THE DEAD (1985).

2. Film (1990). 21st Century/George Romero/Menahem Golan/Columbia. Dir Tom Savini, starring Tony Todd, Patricia Tallman, Tom Towles, McKee Anderson, William Butler, Katie Finneran. Screenplay George ROMERO, based on the 1968 screenplay by Romero and Russo. 89 mins. Colour.

It was a risky and possibly cynical undertaking to remake, in colour, the 1968 b/w classic. However, while the original remains the stronger, this was an accomplished feature-film début for Savini, best known for his ghoulish special make-up on Romero's zombie movies. Generally the story-line of the original is followed closely, but there is a greater emphasis on the female character, Barbara (Tallman), who does not succumb so quickly to frozen fear as did her original. The 1968 film made a virtue of its ramshackle production values, with a *cinéma vérité* style resulting from a shoestring budget; the greater smoothness of the remake makes it strangely less compelling – more obviously a movie. [PN/JB]

See also: CINEMA; MONSTER MOVIES; SUPERNATURAL CREATURES.

NIGHT OF THE SILICATES ◊ ISLAND OF TERROR.

NIGHT SHADOWS ◊ MUTANT.

NIGHT STALKER, THE ◊ KOLCHAK: THE NIGHT STALKER.

NIGHT STRANGLER, THE ◊ KOLCHAK: THE NIGHT STALKER.

NIGHT THAT PANICKED AMERICA, THE Made-for-tv film (1975). ABC TV. Dir Joseph Sargent, starring Vic Morrow, Cliff De Young, Michael Constantine, Paul Shenar. Screenplay Nicholas Meyer, Anthony Wilson, based partly on the text of the original 1938 radio play WAR OF THE WORLDS by Howard Koch. 100 mins, cut to 78 mins. Colour.

The film recreates the 1938 Orson Welles broadcast of an updated version of H.G. WELLS's *The War of the Worlds* (**1898**) which, due to its news-bulletin format, caused many US citizens to believe that a Martian invasion was actually taking place. When the film concentrates on events inside the broadcast studio it is fascinating, conjuring up a realistic picture of work in 1930s US RADIO; but when it shows the resulting panic it degenerates into a routine DISASTER movie with hackneyed characters reacting in predictable ways. [JB]

NIHIL [s] ◊ P. Schuyler MILLER.

NI KUANG [r] ◊ CHINESE SF.

NILSON, PETER [r] ◊ SCANDINAVIA.

1984 Film (1955). Holiday Film Productions. Dir Michael Anderson, starring Edmond O'Brien, Michael Redgrave, Jan Sterling, Donald Pleasence. Screenplay William P. Templeton, Ralph Bettinson, based on *Nineteen Eighty-four* (**1949**) by George ORWELL. 91 mins. B/w.

After the success of a 1954 BBC TV production of *Nineteen Eighty-four*, scripted by Nigel KNEALE and starring Peter Cushing (the second – live – performance won the biggest UK tv audience since the Queen's coronation) it was inevitable that a film would follow. But, for all its technical limitations, the BBC adaptation was superior to the lifeless film, which starred a badly miscast O'Brien as Winston Smith; Anderson has a lame track record with sf (◊ LOGAN'S RUN). This version of the celebrated totalitarian nightmare focuses on the love affair between Smith and Julia, and leaves Orwell's grim SATIRE foggy and simplified. Two endings were shot, one for the USA and one for the UK. The former followed the book, with Winston and his lover successfully brainwashed and now devoted supporters of Big Brother; the UK version had them overcoming their conditioning, defiantly dying in a hail of bullets, and incidentally vitiating Orwell's theme.

For the 1984 remake ◊ NINETEEN EIGHTY-FOUR. [JB/PN]

NINETEEN EIGHTY-FOUR Film (1984). Umbrella-Rosenblum/Virgin Cinema Films. Dir Michael Radford, starring John Hurt, Richard Burton, Suzanna Hamilton, Cyril Cusack. Screenplay Radford, Jonathan Gems, based on *Nineteen Eighty-four* (**1949**) by George ORWELL. 110 mins. Colour.

This second film version (◊ 1984 *for the first*) is better acted and more intelligent than its predecessor, but still stresses the romantic interest, substituting an orthodoxly liberal lovers-against-the-system sadness for Orwell's sheer savagery and irony. It was eight weeks into shooting before Burton was cast as the treacherous O'Brien, Smith's torturer, and he seems a little cut off from the rest of the film. [PN]

1990 UK tv serial (1977-8). BBC TV. Prod Prudence Fitzgerald. Regular cast included Edward Woodward, Barbara Kellerman, Robert Lang, Tony Doyle, Lisa Harrow. Most episodes written Wilfred Greatorex (1921-   ), who devised the series, or Edmund Ward. 16 55min episodes. Colour.

Reflecting the fears of the middle classes in the 1970s, this serial, set in a socialist UK of 1990, warns of what could happen if the welfare state continued in its present direction. The country is run by the PCD, an all-powerful bureaucracy that incorporates the trade-union movement within its machinery; the only people free of its control are a select elite possessing Privilege Cards. The story concerns the efforts of a lone journalist (Woodward) to outwit the system in such ways as helping people to escape to the USA, still a bastion of freedom. *1990*'s political statement, which Orwell made much more powerfully in *Nineteen Eighty-four* (**1949**), plays second fiddle to the thriller elements. The novelization by Maureen Gregson (with Greatorex also credited) is *1990* * (**1977**). [JB]

1990: BRONX WARRIORS ◊ 1990: I GUERRIERI DEL BRONX.

1990: I GUERRIERI DEL BRONX (vt *Bronx Warriors*; vt *1990: Bronx Warriors*) Film (1982). Deaf Film International. Dir Enzo G. Castellari, starring Mark Gregory, Vic Morrow, Chris Connelly, Stefania Girolami, Fred Williamson. Screenplay Castellari, Dardano Sacchetti, Elisa Livia Briganti. 84 mins. Colour.

Inspired by Walter Hill's *The Warriors* (1979) and John CARPENTER's ESCAPE FROM NEW YORK (1981), this Italian film is set in a future-Hell New York overrun by street gangs, with a psychotic law-enforcer (Morrow) trying to rescue a corporate princess (Girolami) from a biker hero named Trash (Gregory). Essentially silly, it has three exploitation veterans (Morrow, Connelly, Williamson) to make up for its pouting hero, and throws in an array of intriguing minor characters – a sadomasochist Morticia-Addams figure, a tap-dancing gang of killer Broadway chorines, subway troglodytes – and some pleasantly melodramatic excesses. Its sequel is *Fuga dal Bronx* (1983; vt *Bronx Warriors 2*), and Castellari also made a similar post-HOLOCAUST actioner, inspired by MAD MAX 2 (1981), *I nuovi barbari* (1983; vt *The New Barbarians*; vt *Warriors of the Wasteland*). The slew of similar Italian cheapies included *L'ultimo guerriero* (1983; vt *The Final Executioner*), *Bronx lotta finale* (1984; vt *Endgame*) and *Il guerriero del mondo perduto* (1984; vt *Warrior of the Lost World*). [KN]

NIPPON CHINBOTSU (vt *The Submersion of Japan*; vt *Tidal Wave* US) Film (1973). Dir Shiro Moritani, starring Keiju Kobayashi, Hiroshi Fujioka, Tetsuro Tamba, Ayumi Ishida. Screenplay Shinobu Hashimoto, based on *Nippon Chinbotsu* (**1973**; cut trans as *Japan Sinks* **1976**) by Sakyo KOMATSU. 140 mins, cut to 110 mins, then to 81 mins. Colour.

This film is more sophisticated than the usual Japanese DISASTER or MONSTER MOVIE, and involves natural rather than fantastic forces. Changes within the Earth's core result in the chain of islands which make up Japan sinking beneath the ocean over a period of two years. Other countries are not eager to accept millions of homeless Japanese citizens, although Australia offers its Northern Territory as a new Japanese homeland. The film has been praised for the elegiac feeling aroused by the dying of Japan and her culture, but not especially for its special effects (by Teruyoshi Nakano), which though spectacular are less than wholly convincing.

Tidal Wave is the title of the tawdry 1974 version

released to universal execration by Roger CORMAN's New World company. It was cut to 81 mins and little more than the special effects remains; it includes specially shot US footage written and directed by Andrew Meyer and starring Lorne Greene and Rhonda Leigh Hopkins. [JB/PN]

NISBET, HUGH A. [r] ◊ ROBERT HALE LIMITED.

NISBET, HUME (1849-1921) Scottish writer and illustrator, in England or Australia from 1865, author of at least 45 novels, some of which are fantasy or sf, beginning with *The "Jolly Roger"* (**1892**), which features a supernatural wind and a hidden pirate island. In *Valdmer the Viking: A Romance of the Eleventh Century by Sea and Land* (**1893**) Vikings find a technologically superior LOST WORLD in the Arctic north of North America. *The Great Secret: A Tale of Tomorrow* (**1895**), like much of HN's work, mixes genres, here combining posthumous spirits and a this-worldly undersea excursion to ATLANTIS. *The Empire Builders* (**1900**) sets its lost world in Africa. [JC]

Other works: *The Haunted Station, and Other Stories* (coll **1893**); *Stories Weird and Wonderful* (coll **1900**); *A Crafty Foe* (**1901**); *A Colonial King* (**1905**).

NIVEN, LARRY Working name of US writer Laurence van Cott Niven (1938-   ). He was born in California, where he set many of his stories, and gained a BA in mathematics from Washburn University, Kansas. From his first publication, "The Coldest Place" for *If* in 1964, he set his mark on the US sf field, winning four short-fiction HUGOS, and both Hugo and NEBULA in 1971 for *Ringworld* (**1970**), a capstone title in his seminal **Tales of Known Space** sequence, which he began with "The Coldest Place" and has added to ever since. In the novels and stories of this sequence, and in some of his other work, he was seen for some time as HARD SF's last best hope; and there can be no doubt that hard-sf writers dominant in the 1980s, like Greg BEAR, and some of those reaching for eminence in the 1990s, like Paul J. MCAULEY and Roger MacBride ALLEN, owe much to the scope of LN's inventiveness, the sense he conveys of technological ingenuity as being ultimately beneficial, and his cognitive exuberance.

The **Tales of Known Space**, a title LN himself selected for the sequence, is a wide-ranging, complex, unusually well integrated future HISTORY which, within an essentially optimistic and technophilic frame, provides an explanatory structure for the expansion of humanity into space, one notable from the first for the complexity of the Universe into which it introduces the burgeoning human race. ALIEN races – not normally found in the first generation of future histories, those created in *ASF* under the influence of the homocentric John W. CAMPBELL Jr – have dominated Known Space for eons, beginning with the Thrintun, extinct a billion years ago with the exception of one deadly Thrint held in a stasis field (one of LN's numerous terminological coups) and released with deadly effect in his first novel, *World of Ptavvs* (**1966**). Millions of years closer to the present, humanity's ancestors, the Pak, spread their seed through the local arm of the Galaxy. Protectors are the "adult" form of *Homo sapiens*, the yam necessary to transform humans into full-grown Paks not being available on Earth; the Pak protagonist of *Protector* (1967 *Gal* as "The Adults"; exp **1973**), set in human times, has travelled from afar at terribly slow sublight speeds to take care of us and protect us against other Protectors who find our slightly evolved species loathsome. The novel spans many years; its complex, casually-alluded-to background demonstrates the value of a coherent sequence in buttressing SPACE-OPERA conventions, though at the same time, as LN himself once admitted, the Universe-changing plot of *Protector* made it difficult to maintain internal consistency within **Known Space** stories set after the Pak incursion. Less dangerously, *A Gift From Earth* (**1968**) sticks to less transformative material, being set on a planet colonized from Earth whose inhabitants revolt against their rulers (former members of the colony ship's crew); the story is interfused with arguments for personal and entrepreneurial liberty whose connection, as in much US sf, is taken as axiomatic. Centuries of relative peace follow, until the start of the Man-Kzin Wars, treated by LN as a sort of sideshow; the relevant stories were delegated mainly to others in four SHARED-WORLD anthologies, *The Man-Kzin Wars* * (anth **1988**), *The Man-Kzin Wars II* * (anth **1989**), *III* * (anth **1990**) and *IV* * (anth **1991**). Finally, the tales and novels of **Known Space** culminated in *Ringworld* and its immediate sequel *Ringworld Engineers* (**1979**), which feature the alien Puppeteers, who are fleeing the explosion at the Galaxy's core which will within some millennia make space uninhabitable, and who enlist human aid to explore the eponymous BIG DUMB OBJECT – a million miles wide, 600 million miles around – which circles a distant star. This ring, created by Pak ancestors, houses much life and serves as a final home for Teela Brown, whose genetically programmed good luck is the culmination of a long and secret Puppeteer breeding programme; the inevitability of her good fortune might have significantly reduced the chance of LN's writing any successful **Known Space** stories set after her maturity, which is perhaps why she is killed off in the sequel.

In the interstices of this joyfully complicated galactic structure, humanity enters space, solves problems in BIOLOGY and GENETIC ENGINEERING, benefits from local TELEPORTATION and the discovery of a FASTER-THAN-LIGHT hyperdrive for interstellar travel, copes with CORPSICLES and organlegging and a myriad other new challenges, and by the beginning of the fourth millennium has reached a mature plateau. Titles in which **Known Space** activities are dramatized include: *Neutron Star* (coll **1968**); *The Shape of Space* (coll **1969**), much of which is re-assembled in *Convergent Series* (coll **1979**); *All the Myriad Ways* (coll **1971**); *Inconstant Moon* (coll **1973** UK; cut 1974), which was assembled from *The Shape of Space* and *All the Myriad Ways*; *Tales of Known Space: The Universe of Larry Niven*

(coll **1975**), which includes explanatory charts; *The Long ARM of Gil Hamilton* (coll of linked stories **1976**) and its immediate sequel *The Patchwork Girl* (**1980**); and *The Integral Trees* (**1984**) and its immediate sequel *The Smoke Ring* (**1987**).

Most of LN's first decade as a writer was occupied with **Known Space**, with the exception of the tales assembled in *The Flight of the Horse* (coll **1973**) – including the 5 stories of the **Svetz** series of TIME-PARADOX comedies – *A Hole in Space* (coll **1974**) and, with David GERROLD, *The Flying Sorcerers* (**1971**), a tale of a low-tech people who think that high technology is MAGIC. His next – and commercially his most successful move – was to collaborate with Jerry POURNELLE on *The Mote in God's Eye* (**1974**), a giant, spectacular SPACE-OPERA epic with all the trappings – interstellar shenanigans, aliens with unhealthy proclivities they must keep hidden, galactic aristocracies, intricate solutions to hard-sf problems . . . The book is essentially a development of Pournelle's **CoDominium** series, and may fruitfully be read in that context. Several critics have taken the book to task for what they regard as its human chauvinism, the discrepancy between its imaginative plot and its old-fashioned characterization, and its conservative political stance; but the combination of Pournelle's ability to shape novel-length plots (an ability his partner has always lacked) and LN's brilliant conceptual knack make for an enticing book.

Further collaborations with Pournelle ensued. *Inferno* (**1975**) reworks DANTE ALIGHIERI's *Inferno*, an act notable for its apparently conscious vulgarity, interesting in its theological explanation of evil – that God's "sadism" is in fact designed to encourage self-help among the damned – and amusing in its placing of anti-NUCLEAR-POWER propagandists in Hell. *Lucifer's Hammer* (**1977**) is a long, ambitious DISASTER novel which sophisticatedly marries sf techniques with the bestseller idiom familiar from the many disaster films of the early 1970s. In *Oath of Fealty* (**1981**) a Los Angeles arcology – without the aid of an ineffective, bureaucratic government – defends its wealthy inhabitants from ECOLOGY freaks and terrorists. The internal government of this arcology being a conveniently infallible hierarchy culminating in one brilliant man in constant communication with a great COMPUTER, no significant dissent is necessary, or heard. *Footfall* (**1985**), about an alien INVASION of Earth, became an example of RECURSIVE SF through its enlisting of a readily identifiable group of sf writers to brainstorm solutions to the threat from space. *The Legacy of Heorot* (**1987** UK), with Pournelle and Steven BARNES, replays the Beowulf saga on a colony planet: the natives of the planet have the unenviable role of the dragon. *Fallen Angels* (**1991**), with Pournelle and Michael FLYNN – in which the US Government betrays its own astronauts – once again treats environmentalists as villains in a planetary drama of the NEAR FUTURE.

LN has increasingly made use of collaborators; in

fact, in later years he has written only 2 solo novels outside the **Known Space** canon – *A World Out of Time* (fixup **1976**), a complexly contemplative look through one protagonist's eyes at millions of years of human history, and *The Magic Goes Away* (**1977**), a fantasy in which MAGIC is treated as a non-renewable resource. The **Dream Park** sequence – *Dream Park* (**1981**), *The Barsoom Project* (**1989**) and *Dream Park: The Voodoo Game* (**1991** UK; vt *The California Voodoo Game* 1992 US), all with Barnes – is set in a GAME-WORLD environment (*see also* VIRTUAL REALITY) in the 21st century, with the eponymous corporation involved in running complex role-playing games as well as enterprises in the real world and on Mars. Other collaborations include *The Descent of Anansi* (**1982**) and *Achilles' Choice* (**1991**), both with Barnes. LN's late collections – *Niven's Laws* (coll **1984**), *Limits* (coll **1985**), *N-Space* (coll **1990**) and *Playgrounds of the Mind* (coll **1991**) – have tended increasingly to re-sort earlier material. It cannot be denied that the fresh inventive gaiety characteristic of LN's early work has not survived the passing of the years, nor that the political agendas (◊ POLITICS) exposed in the collaborations have become more rancorous over the same period. He will perhaps be best remembered for the **Tales of Known Space**, the most energetic future history ever written, for his bright and profligate technophilia, for his astonishingly well conceived aliens, and for his early joy. [JC]

Other works: *The Time of the Warlock* (coll **1984**), fantasies; *The Magic May Return* * (anth **1981**) and *More Magic* * (anth **1984**), shared-world successor anthologies to *The Magic Goes Away*.

About the author: *The Many Worlds of Larry Niven* (last rev **1989** chap) by Chris DRUMM.

See also: ASTEROIDS; BLACK HOLES; CITIES; CLICHÉS; CLUB STORY; COMICS; COMMUNICATIONS; CRIME AND PUNISHMENT; CRYONICS; DC COMICS; DEL REY BOOKS; END OF THE WORLD; ESCHATOLOGY; FANTASTIC VOYAGES; GALAXY SCIENCE FICTION; GAMES AND TOYS; GODS AND DEMONS; GRAVITY; LEISURE; MATTER TRANSMISSION; MEDICINE; MERCURY; MOON; MYTHOLOGY; NEUTRON STARS; OUTER PLANETS; OVERPOPULATION; PARALLEL WORLDS; PHYSICS; PROTO SCIENCE FICTION; Julius SCHWARTZ; SERIES; SOCIAL DARWINISM; SPACESHIPS; STARS; SUN; SUPERMAN [character]; SUSPENDED ANIMATION; TERRAFORMING; TRANSPORTATION; UTOPIAS; VENUS; WAR; WRITERS OF THE FUTURE CONTEST.

NOBEL, PHIL ◊ R.L. FANTHORPE.

NO BLADE OF GRASS Film (1970). Symbol/MGM. Dir Cornel Wilde, starring Nigel Davenport, Jean Wallace, Anthony May, Lynne Frederick. Screenplay Sean Forestal, Jefferson Pascal, based on *The Death of Grass* (**1956**) by John CHRISTOPHER. 96 mins cut to 80 mins. Colour.

Cereal crops all die and society breaks down. A family journeys across chaotic England, battling armed groups of marauders who are searching for food, and reach sanctuary in the Lake District. Wilde had previously dealt well with the stripping away of

civilized instincts in *The Naked Prey* (1966), so this story must have attracted him, but *NBOG* has an amateurish quality, reinforced by poor acting, though the depiction of anarchy is zestful. The film is disjointed, partly due to drastic cutting before release. [JB/PN]

See also: HOLOCAUST AND AFTER; PANIC IN YEAR ZERO.

NOBLE, MARK [r] ◊ Bob STICKGOLD.

NOEL, ATANIELLE ANNYN (1947-) Now the legal name of the US writer who, under her earlier legal name, Ruth S(wycaffer) Noel, published 2 studies of J.R.R. TOLKIEN: *The Mythology of Middle-Earth* (**1977**) and *The Languages of Tolkien's Middle-Earth* (**1980**). Her 3 novels as AAN rather mercilessly tumble together fantasy, sf and thriller modes into spoof plots, through which some excitements emerge willy-nilly. *The Duchess of Kneedeep* (**1986**) is a humorous fantasy with ROBOTS. *Speaker to Heaven* (**1987**), set in post-HOLOCAUST California, conflates PSI POWERS and MAGIC. *Murder on Usher's Planet* (**1987**), evoking Edgar Allan POE, sends its investigator protagonists to a planet containing a secret, which they uncover. [JC]

NOEL, STERLING (1903-1984) US writer and journalist, author of 2 sf novels: *I Killed Stalin* (**1951**), a NEAR-FUTURE thriller in which WWIII is staved off by the deed described in the title, and *We who Survived* (**1959**), which depicts the life of the survivors of the sudden onslaught of a new ice age. [JC]

NOLAN, WILLIAM F(RANCIS) (1928-) US writer and editor who trained and for a time practised as a commercial artist; he also raced cars, publishing several books on the subject. He became a full-time writer in 1956. Of his more than 50 books since then, at least 20 have related directly to sf or fantasy. WFN first became active in sf as a fan, cofounding the San Diego Science Fantasy Society, editing a fanzine, the *Rhodomagnetic Digest*, publishing *The Ray Bradbury Review*, and serving as managing editor of #1-#3 of GAMMA (1963-4). He published his first sf story, "The Joy of Living", in *If* in 1954, subsequently writing some short stories and criticism as by Frank Anmar and F.E. Edwards. His first sf book, *Impact 20* (coll **1963**), assembles some of his early work. His second, for which he remains best known, *Logan's Run* (**1967**) with George Clayton JOHNSON, begins the **Logan** sequence, which continued with *Logan's World* (**1977**) and *Logan's Search* (**1980**), both by WN alone; all 3 are assembled as *Logan: A Trilogy* (omni **1986**). The premise of the books is melodramatic: after a strange act of nuclear terrorism a youth culture takes over, instituting the rule that all those over 21 must be killed to combat OVERPOPULATION; the protagonist, first an enforcer and then posing as a fugitive, escapes Earth with a genuine female rebel, returning (now authentically rebellious) in the later volumes to confront the COMPUTER controlling Earth. The first volume was unsuccessfully filmed as LOGAN'S RUN (1976) and adapted as a short-lived tv series. Written in part as an homage to Dashiell Hammett's **Sam Spade** (WFN's *Hammett: A Life on the Edge* [1983] is an effective biography), the **Sam Space** sequence, about an sf detective, comprises *Space for Hire* (**1971**), *Look Out for Space* (**1985**) and «3 for Space» (coll 1992). WFN's later short fiction, some of it of high quality, was assembled in *Alien Horizons* (coll **1974**), *Wonderworlds* (coll **1977** UK) and *Things Beyond Midnight* (coll **1984**).

WFN has also been active as an anthologist, mostly of reprinted material, though *The Future is Now* (anth **1970**) assembles original stories. He also compiled a detailed bibliography of Ray BRADBURY, with copious annotations: *The Ray Bradbury Companion* (**1975**).

[JC/PN]

Other works: *The Work of Charles Beaumont* (**1985** chap; rev 1991 chap); *How to Write Horror Fiction* (**1990**); *Helltracks* (**1991**), a horror novel.

As editor: *The Fiend in You* (anth **1962**) with Charles BEAUMONT, WFN anon; *Man Against Tomorrow* (anth **1965**); *The Pseudo-People* (anth **1965**; vt *Almost Human* 1966 UK); *3 to the Highest Power* (anth **1968**); *A Wilderness of Stars* (anth **1969**); *A Sea of Space* (anth **1970**), no connection to the **Sam Space** books; *The Human Equation* (anth **1971**); *Science Fiction Origins* (anth **1980**) with Martin H. GREENBERG; *Urban Horrors* (anth **1990**) with Greenberg.

About the author: *The Work of William F. Nolan: An Annotated Bibliography & Guide* (**1988**) by Boden Clarke (R. REGINALD) and James Hopkins (WFN himself).

See also: ANDROIDS.

"NONAME" House name for the Frank Tousey publishing firm, used in the late 19th century for boys' fiction in several genres, including mysteries and Westerns as well as sf. Of most sf interest were the **Frank Reade, Jr.** tales (◊ FRANK READE LIBRARY; Luis SENARENS) and the slightly later **Jack Wright** tales (◊ Luis SENARENS). Authors whose sf work appeared as by "Noname" include Harold Cohen (1854-1927), Francis Worcester DOUGHTY, Senarens and possibly Cecil Burleigh and Frederic Van Rensselaer Dey (1861-1933). [EFB]

NOONE, EDWINA ◊ Michael AVALLONE.

NORBERT, W. ◊ Norbert WIENER.

NORDEN, ERIC (? -) US writer who began publishing work of genre interest with "The Final Quarry" for *FSF* in 1970, assembling his short work in *Starsongs and Unicorns* (coll **1978**). His novel, *The Ultimate Solution* (**1973**), depicts a Nazi-dominated New York (◊ HITLER WINS), a state of affairs made possible by the assassination of Franklin Delano Roosevelt in 1933, as a consequence of which the USA remained too long a noncombatant in WWII. Slavery has been reinstituted. [JC]

NORMAN, BARRY (1933-) UK journalist, tv personality and writer whose sf novel is *End Product* (**1975**), a NEAR-FUTURE story in which Blacks are lobotomized at birth and provide the civilized world with ample meat. The allegorical and political messages of the novel, though highly loaded, tend to clash. [JC]

NORMAN, ERIC (? -) US writer whose routine sf novel *The Under-People* (**1969**) is not to be confused with *The Underpeople* (**1968**) by Cordwainer SMITH. [JC]

NORMAN, JOHN Pseudonym used for his fiction by US writer and philosophy teacher John Frederick Lange Jr (1931-). His fiction mainly comprises a series of borderline-sf PLANETARY ROMANCES set on **Gor**, a planet sharing Earth's orbit but – because it is on the other side of the Sun – always invisible to us. This astrophysical impossibility is never argued in the texts, which might consequently read as either antiquarian sf or fantasy were it not that the development of the series precludes any reading of **Gor** as an exercise in sf nostalgia while at the same time demonstrating its great remove from category FANTASY. In *Tarnsman of Gor* (**1966**), as the series begins, Earthman Tarl Cabot abruptly finds himself on Gor, where – after the fashion of Edgar Rice BURROUGHS's **Barsoom** novels – he undergoes numerous adventures, alarms, fights and romances of a SWORD-AND-SORCERY nature. However, as the series progresses, the plots begin to revolve around a singularly invariant sexual fantasy in which a proud woman – often abducted for the purpose from Earth – is humiliated, stripped, bound, beaten, raped, branded and enslaved, invariably discovering in the process that she enjoys total submission to a dominant male, and can derive proper sexual satisfaction only from this regime. Later volumes feature interminable discussions which end, invariably, in an affirmation of the Gorean status quo. The sequence, now terminated, includes: *Outlaw of Gor* (**1967**) and *Priest-Kings of Gor* (**1968**), both assembled with *Tarnsman of Gor* as *Gor Omnibus* (omni **1972** UK); *Nomads of Gor* (**1969**); *Assassin of Gor* (**1970**); *Raiders of Gor* (**1971**); *Captive of Gor* (**1972**); *Hunters of Gor* (**1974**); *Marauders of Gor* (**1975**); *Tribesmen of Gor* (**1976**); *Slave Girl of Gor* (**1977**); *Beasts of Gor* (**1978**); *Explorers of Gor* (**1979**); *Fighting Slave of Gor* (**1980**); *Rogue of Gor* (**1981**); *Guardsman of Gor* (**1981**); *Savages of Gor* (**1982**); *Blood Brothers of Gor* (**1982**); *Kajira of Gor* (**1983**); *Players of Gor* (**1984**); *Mercenaries of Gor* (**1985**); *Dancer of Gor* (**1985**); *Renegades of Gor* (**1986**); *Vagabonds of Gor* (**1987**); and *Magicians of Gor* (**1988**). *Imaginative Sex* (**1974**), a nonfiction text, details some Gor-like games for Earthlings. JN's two out-of-series novels are *Ghost Dance* (**1969**) and *Time Slave* (**1975**). Unless the new **Telnarian Histories** sequence, beginning with *The Chieftain* (**1991**), strikes a new note, JN will be remembered – and widely detested – for **Gor** alone. [JC]

See also: DAW BOOKS; SEX.

NORMYX ◊ Norman DOUGLAS.

NORST, JOEL ◊ Kirk MITCHELL.

NORTH, ANDREW ◊ Andre NORTON.

NORTH, DAVID (? -) US writer whose **Time Warriors** sequence of military-sf adventures – *Time Warriors #1: Fuse Point* (**1991**), *#2: Forbidden Region* (**1991**) and *#3: The Guardian Strikes* (**1991**) – sends its protagonist, accompanied by a barbarian named Brom, back and forth through time into various conflicts. [JC]

NORTH, ERIC Pseudonym used by Australian novelist Charles Bernard Cronin (1884-1968) for his sf work; he used other pseudonyms in other genres. As EN he published sf in Australian journals such as the *Melbourne Herald* and The *Bulletin*. "The Satyr" (1924 *Melbourne Herald*; vt "Three Against the Stars" *Argosy* 1938 US) tells of invaders from another DIMENSION; it was not published in book form. The eponymous villain of *Toad* (1924 *Melbourne Herald* as "The Green Flame"; **1929** UK) has invented an ingredient which sets water aflame, and threatens to use it against first Australia and then the world.

The Ant Men (**1955** US) is a LOST-WORLD juvenile about giant intelligent ants. [JC]

NORTH, VALENTINE [s] ◊ Thomas P. KELLEY.

NORTON, ANDRE Initially the working name of Alice Mary Norton (1912-   ), but for some years now her legal name. A librarian for two decades before turning to full-time writing, she was one of the few sf figures of any stature to enter the field via CHILDREN'S SF, and, though much of her work is as adult in theme and difficulty as most general sf, she was for many years primarily marketed as a writer for children and adolescents. In the 1970s and 1980s, however, as her work changed in emphasis from sf to fantasy and as her popularity continued to grow, new novels and reprints alike were released primarily into the general market.

AN began to publish in the 1930s with *The Prince Commands* (**1934**) which, like her slightly later WWII espionage trilogy – *The Sword is Drawn* (**1944**), *Sword in Sheath* (**1949**; vt *Island of the Lost* 1953 UK) and *At Swords' Point* (**1954**) – was not of direct genre interest. She came to sf proper only in 1947 with "The People of the Crater" for *Fantasy Book*, as by Andrew North, a pseudonym she used also for 3 novels; the story was included in *Garan the Eternal* (coll **1972**) which, along with *High Sorcery* (coll **1970**), *The Many Worlds of Andre Norton* (coll **1974**; vt *The Book of Andre Norton* 1975), ed Roger ELWOOD, and *Perilous Dreams* (coll **1976**), assembled most of her relatively small output of short fiction.

AN's career can, very roughly, be divided into two equal periods: the two decades from 1950 when she concentrated on sf novels, most of them gathered into series which were in turn treated as loose units in a broadly conceived common galactic superseries; and the two decades from 1970 when, after the success of the **Witch World** SCIENCE-FANTASY sequence, she produced numerous further fantasies. Throughout both periods, her most typical protagonists have been young women or men who must undergo some form of *rite de passage* into a sane maturity; in so doing, they characteristically discover that the true nature of the Universe lies not in what it might become (hence the lack of CONCEPTUAL-BREAKTHROUGH novels in her oeuvre) but in its history, and in the talismans and icons associated with that history. The Universe revealed in these numerous books – from her first sf novel, *Star Man's Son, 2250 A.D.* (**1952**; vt *Daybreak-2250 A.D.* 1954 dos; vt *Star Man's Son* 1978), to her most recent – is a colourful, complex and rewarding environment for her typical protagonists to come to terms with; though any advanced technology there deployed – FASTER-THAN-LIGHT space travel, for instance, and at one time or another almost every other instrument of SPACE OPERA – serves mainly to add verisimilitude to AN's romantic SENSE OF WONDER, and to a style in which science and TECHNOLOGY are in fact treated perfunctorily (if at all) and more often than not as inimical to humanity and its friends. Close – sometimes telepathic – rapports might exist among people, or between human and beast as in *Catseye* (**1961**), but rarely or never are human beings called to shape their lives in the service of transcendent or objective goals. AN's instincts, in other words, have never been those of the natural sf author; however, in the sense that her books never violate her audience's legitimate expectations, AN has always been an orthodox writer.

The sf novels, mostly told against the shared galactic backdrop, were widely varied, featuring a multitude of space-opera themes and plots, along with several comparatively intimate studies of humans and ALIENS and beasts, and their relationships under various circumstances. Series include: the **Central Control** sequence, comprising *Star Rangers* (**1953**; vt *The Last Planet* 1955 dos) and *Star Guard* (**1955**); the **Astra** or **Company of Pax** sequence, comprising *The Stars are Ours!* (**1954**) and *Star Born* (**1957**); the **Dane Thorson** or **Solar Queen** sequence, comprising *Sargasso of Space* (**1955** as by Andrew North; 1969 as by AN), *Plague Ship* (**1956** as by North; 1969 as by AN), *Voodoo Planet* (**1959** dos as by North; 1968 as by AN) and *Postmarked the Stars* (**1969**); the **Blake Walker** sequence, comprising *The Crossroads of Time* (**1956** dos) and *Quest Crosstime* (**1965**; vt *Crosstime Agent* 1975 UK); the **Ross Murdock** sequence, comprising *The Time Traders* (**1958**), *Galactic Derelict* (**1959**), *The Defiant Agents* (**1962**) and *Key out of Time* (**1963**); the **Hosteen Storm** sequence, comprising *The Beast Master* (**1959**; cut 1961) and *Lord of Thunder* (**1962**); the **Forerunner** sequence, comprising *Storm over Warlock* (**1960**), *Ordeal in Otherwhere* (**1964**), *Forerunner Foray* (**1973**), *Forerunner* (**1981**) and *Forerunner: The Second Venture* (**1985**); the **Janus** sequence, comprising *Catseye* (**1961**), *Judgment on Janus* (**1963**) and *Victory on Janus* (**1966**); the **Moon Singer** sequence, comprising *Moon of Three Rings* (**1966**), *Exiles of the Stars* (**1971**), *Flight In Yiktor* (**1986**) and *Dare to Go A-Hunting* (**1990**); the **Murdoc Jern** sequence, comprising *The Zero Stone* (**1968**) and *Uncharted Stars* (**1969**); and the **Star Ka'at** sequence for younger readers, all written with Dorothy Madlee (1917-1980), comprising *Star Ka'at* (**1976**), *Star Ka'at World* (**1978**), *Star Ka'ats and the Plant People* (**1979**) and *Star Ka'ats and the Winged Warriors* (**1981**).

Though begun in the 1960s, the **Witch World** sequence is essentially FANTASY – though it often uses such sf tropes as dimensional gates and force fields – and lacks any connection with the shared background; it soon became both her best known series and a model for her later work. Set on a matriarchal planet named Estcarp, and pleasingly sensitive to FEMINIST issues, these tales engage personable young protagonists in SWORD-AND-SORCERY adventures which tend to end well. Variously connected, the series titles include *Witch World* (1963), *Web of the Witch World* (1964), *Year of the Unicorn* (1965), *Three Against the Witch World* (1965), *Warlock of the Witch World* (1967), *Sorceress of the Witch World* (1968), *Spell of the Witch World* (coll 1972), *The Crystal Gryphon* (1972), *The Jargoon Pard* (1974), *Trey of Swords* (1977), *Zarsthor's Bane* (1978), *Lore of the Witch World* (coll 1980), *Gryphon in Glory* (1981), *Horn Crown* (1981), *'Ware Hawk* (1983), *Were-Wrath* (1984 chap), *Gryphon's Eyrie* (1984) with A.C. CRISPIN, *Serpent's Tooth* (1987 chap), *The Gate of the Cat* (1987) and *Witch World: The Turning: Storms of Victory* (1991) and «#2: Flight of Vengeance» (1992) with P.M. GRIFFIN. There were also 4 SHARED-WORLD anthologies edited or authorized by AN: *Tales of the Witch World* * (anth 1987), *Tales of the Witch World II* * (anth 1988), *Four from the Witch World* * (anth 1989) and *Tales of the Witch World III* * (anth 1990).

Though her style has matured over the years, and her plots have tended to darken somewhat, from first to last an AN story will show the virtues of clear construction, a high degree of narrative control, protagonists whose qualities allow easy reader-identification and a Universe fundamentally responsive to virtue, good will and spunk. Her disinclination to publish short material in the sf magazines and her labelling for decades as a juvenile writer both worked to delay proper recognition of her stature, though her actual sales have been very considerable for decades. It has only recently been borne in upon the sf world that AN's 100 or more books – most of them in print – are for very many readers central to what the genre has to offer. [JC]

Other works:

Non-sf includes: *Follow the Drum* (1942); *Rogue Reynard* (1947); *Scarface* (1948); *Huon of the Horn* (1951); *Murders for Sale* (1954; with Grace Allen Hogarth, together as Allen Weston; vt *Sneeze on Sunday* 1992 as AN and Hogarth); *Ten Mile Treasure* (1981); *Stand and Deliver* (1984).

Sf and fantasy: *Sea Siege* (1957); *Star Gate* (1958; exp 1963); *Secret of the Lost Race* (1959 dos; vt *Wolfshead* 1977 UK); *Shadow Hawk* (1960); *The Sioux Spaceman* (1960 dos); *Star Hunter* (1961 dos); *Eye of the Monster* (1962 dos); *Night of Masks* (1964); *The X Factor* (1965); the **Magic** fantasies, comprising *Steel Magic* (1965; vt *Grey Magic* 1967), *Octagon Magic* (1967) and *Fur Magic* (1968), all assembled as *The Magic Books* (omni 1988); *Operation Time Search* (1967); *Dark Piper* (1968); *Dread Companion* (1970); *Ice Crown* (1970); *Android at Arms* (1971); *Breed to Come* (1972); *Dragon Magic* (1972); *Here Abide Monsters* (1973); *Iron Cage* (1974); *Outside* (1974); *Lavender-Green Magic* (1974); *Merlin's Mirror* (1975);

The White Jade Fox (1975); *The Day of the Ness* (1975) with Michael Gilbert; *No Night without Stars* (1975); *Knave of Dreams* (1975); *Wraiths of Time* (1976); *Red Hart Magic* (1976); *The Opal-Eyed Fan* (1977); *Quag Keep* (1978); *Yurth Burden* (1978); *Seven Spells to Sunday* (1979); *Voorloper* (1980); *Moon Called* (1982); *Wheel of Stars* (1983); *Ride the Green Dragon* (1985) with Phyllis Miller (1920-   ); *Imperial Lady: A Fantasy of Han China* (1989) with Susan M. SHWARTZ; *Wizards' Worlds* (coll 1989); *Elvenbane: An Epic High Fantasy of the Halfblood Chronicles* (1991) with Mercedes Lackey (1950-   ); *The Jekyll Legacy* (1990) with Robert BLOCH; *Black Trillium* (1990) with Marion Zimmer BRADLEY and Julian MAY; *The Mark of the Cat* (1992), based on the cat drawings of Karen Kuykendall.

As editor: *Bullard of the Space Patrol* (coll of linked stories 1951) by Malcolm JAMESON; *Space Service* (anth 1953); *Space Pioneers* (anth 1954); *Space Police* (anth 1956); *Gates to Tomorrow: An Introduction to Science Fiction* (anth 1973) ed with Ernestine Donaldy; *Small Shadows Creep* (anth 1974); *Baleful Beasts and Eerie Creatures* (anth 1976); the **Ithkar** fantasies, all with Robert ADAMS, comprising *Magic in Ithkar #1* (anth 1985), *#2* (anth 1985), *#3* (anth 1986) and *#4* (anth 1987); *Cat-fantastic* (anth 1989) and *Cat-fantastic II* (anth 1991), both with Martin H. GREENBERG.

About the author: "Andre Norton: Loss of Faith" (1971) by Rick Brooks in *The Many Worlds of Andre Norton* (coll 1974); intro by Sandra Miesel to the GREGG PRESS reissue (1977) of the **Witch World** series; *Andre Norton: A Primary and Secondary Bibliography* (1980) by Roger C. SCHLOBIN; *Andre Norton: Grand Master of the Witch-World: A Working Bibliography* (1991 chap) by Phil STEPHENSEN-PAYNE.

See also: CRIME AND PUNISHMENT; GAMES AND TOYS; HITLER WINS; LONGEVITY (IN WRITERS AND PUBLICATIONS); MAGIC; NEBULA; ROBERT HALE LIMITED; WOMEN SF WRITERS.

NORTON, PHILIP (?   -?   ) UK clergyman and writer, active in the former capacity 1871-1924. As Artegall Smith he published one sf novel, *Sub Sole, or Under the Sun: Missionary Adventures in the Great Sahara* (1889), in which the Wandering Jew reveals to Artegall Smith the wonders of an underground LOST WORLD peopled by the Lost Tribes of Israel, who have created there a scientific civilization. Smith soon converts them and marries the girl of his choice. Unusually for UK fiction before 1940, Jews are treated with some respect. [JC]

NORTON, ROY (E.) (1869-1942) US author of many Westerns and some sf, beginning with *The Vanishing Fleets* (1908), in which a group of scientists, having invented an ANTIGRAVITY device, use it to shift the world's fleets mysteriously about, terrifying the bellicose nations into disarming. In his second sf novel, *The Toll of the Sea* (1909; cut vt *The Land of the Lost* 1925 UK), the Pacific figures again, this time changing its shape and uncovering a LOST WORLD inhabited by advanced descendants of ATLANTIS. In *The Flame* (1916) another antigravity device allows its user to force Germany into early surrender. RN was notable both for his didacticism and for a strong narrative imagination.   [JC]

Other works: *The Caves of Treasure* (**1925**).

NORVIL, MANNING ◊ Kenneth BULMER.

NORWAY ◊ SCANDINAVIA.

NORWOOD, VICTOR (GEORGE CHARLES) (1920-1983) UK traveller and writer who concentrated on Westerns and nonfiction works about exploration. Of some genre interest is the **Jacare** series of jungle tales, loosely derived from Edgar Rice BURROUGHS's **Tarzan** and mostly sf or fantasy: *The Untamed* (**1951**), *The Caves of Death* (**1951**), *The Temple of the Dead* (**1951**), *The Skull of Kanaima* (**1951**), *The Island of Creeping Death* (**1952**), *Drums along the Amazon* (**1953**), which was associational, and *Cry of the Beast* (**1953**). *Night of the Black Horror* (**1962**) is a singleton sf adventure. [JC/SH]

NORWOOD, WARREN C(ARL) (1945-   ) US book-seller and writer who has normally published as Warren Norwood, sometimes as Warren C. Norwood; due to a publisher's error, some titles were published as by Warren G. Norwood. After a number of years in bookselling, during which period he published some not particularly distinguished poetry, WCN began his sf career with the **Windhover Tapes** sequence – *The Windhover Tapes: An Image of Voices* (**1982**), *#2: Flexing the Warp* (**1983**), *#3: Fize of the Gabriel Ratchets* (**1983**) and *#4: Planet of Flowers* (**1984**) – attempting with some success to compose SPACE OPERAS whose baroque inturnings are themselves of some narrative interest; but calling the human pro-tagonist of the series Gerard Hopkins Manley and referring to Hopkins (1844-1889) with some frequency – while implying that Manley himself is ignorant of any connection with the poet – does suggest a disconnectedness deep within the structure of the sequence. The Tapes themselves constitute a record kept by the sentient starship *Windhover*; they detail Manley's quite various adventures on several planets as troubleshooter and anthropologist. A second series, the **Double Spiral War** sequence – *Midway Between* (**1984**), *Polar Fleet* (**1985**) and *Final Command* (**1986**) – is less chaotic but also less interesting. *The Seren Cenacles* (**1983**) with Ralph Mylius (1945-   ) likewise suffers from inattentive bursts of energy; though *Shudderchild* (**1987**), set in a genuinely compli-cated multistate post-HOLOCAUST USA, is engagingly compact and full of action, and *True Jaguar* (**1988**), a fantasy, delves intriguingly into Mayan lore.

In 1988 WCN publicly announced that he had been diagnosed as having terminal pancreatic cancer; in 1991 he said that he had entered remission, and also indicated his wish to acknowledge assistance in completing the **Time Police** sequence, a Byron PREISS package comprising *Time Police: Vanished!* (**1988**), *#2: Trapped!* (**1989**) and *#3: Stranded!* (**1989**), with Mel Odom (1950-   ) given co-author credit on the final volume; WCN's wife had extensively outlined the second and third volumes and Odom had done the writing work on both. The sequence itself is a fairly unremarkable reworking of the Time Patrol recipe created by Poul ANDERSON and others. Given the enforced hiatus at the end of nearly a decade of intense productivity, it is difficult to know whether or not WCN will eventually harness his knowledge and drive to stories that move beyond the slightly unfocused exuberance of his first work.   [JC]

NOSILLE, NALRAH [s] ◊ Harlan ELLISON.

NOT OF THIS EARTH 1. Film (1957). Los Altos/Allied Artists. Prod and dir Roger CORMAN, starring Paul Birch, Beverly Garland, Jonathan Haze, Dick Miller. Screenplay Charles B. Griffith, Mark Hanna. 67 mins. B/w.

A sombre humanoid alien (Birch), whose dark glasses conceal blank white eyes, seeks human blood and victims to send by matter transmitter to his home planet, whose inhabitants' blood is being "turned to dust" by radiation from continuing nuclear war. Low-budget nonsense – a typical Corman film of the period – cheaply made, *NOTE* is nevertheless well scripted and surprisingly powerful; unusually, it shows some sympathy for the lonely, pedantic alien.

2. Film (1988). Miracle. "Roger CORMAN presents" a film dir Jim Wynorski, starring Arthur Roberts, Traci Lords, Lenny Juliano. Screenplay R.J. Robertson, Wynorski, based on that of the 1957 film. 76 mins. Colour.

Though fairly true to the original script, and played moderately straight apart from a plethora of large-breasted women, this Corman-inspired remake can-not cope with cultural and cinematic changes over the intervening three decades, and what was once mildly serious now emerges as high camp; hence it was promoted as a spoof.   [PN]

See also: MONSTER MOVIES.

NOTT, KATHLEEN (CECILIA) (1909-   ) UK poet, novelist and academic, perhaps best known for *The Emperor's Clothes* (**1953**), in which she mounted articulate and scathing attacks on the religious pre-tensions of such writers as T.S. Eliot (1888-1965) and C.S. LEWIS. Her sf novel, *The Dry Deluge* (**1947**), describes the founding of an underground UTOPIA devoted to the achievement of IMMORTALITY.   [JC]

NOURSE, ALAN E(DWARD) (1928-1992) US writer and physician; much of his nonfiction has been in the field of popular MEDICINE – *Intern* (**1965**) as by "Doctor X" being a great success. He began publishing sf with "High Threshold" for *ASF* in 1951, and gained a reputation as a reliable creator of CHILDREN'S SF novels. His first, *Trouble on Titan* (**1954**), features rebellion and conflict within a SPACE-OPERA Solar System, as do others of his juveniles, like *Raiders from the Rings* (**1962**), where conflict between an oppressive Earth regime and libertarian Spacers is finally halted by the intervention of superior, peaceful ALIENS. In *Rocket to Limbo* (**1957**), mankind's destiny is explained to us by alien observers. *Star Surgeon* (**1960**) interestingly posits an Earth which, while being the main medical centre of all the inhabited worlds, is still in the position of having to apply to join the Galactic Confederation. The vision of these juveniles is appropriately optimistic, and technologies – especially medical ones – are there for humanity's benefit.

AEN's adult novels are also straightforward, frequently making somewhat simple points about bureaucracies and tyrannies, as in *The Invaders are Coming!* (**1959**) with J(oseph) A. Meyer and in several stories – some genuinely funny – assembled in *Tiger by the Tail* (coll **1961**; vt *Beyond Infinity* 1964 UK). Several others make use of his medical knowledge: brain surgery figures in *A Man Obsessed* (**1955** dos; rev vt *The Mercy Men* 1968), part of a series also including "Nightmare Brother" (1953) and "The Expert Touch" (1955); *Rx for Tomorrow* (coll **1971**) collects stories about medicine in general; *The Bladerunner* (**1974**) – which was adapted by William S. BURROUGHS as *Blade Runner (A Movie)* (**1979** chap), neither book having anything to do with Ridley SCOTT's BLADE RUNNER (1982) (although Scott obtained permission from AN for use of the title) – deals with the medical implications of OVERPOPULATION in a framework of coercive sterilization; and *The Fourth Horseman* (**1983**) deals with a NEAR-FUTURE plague. A sense of fundamental decency permeates AEN's fiction; and, though sometimes too easily achieved, the victories of decency over bigotry cannot, for the market upon which AEN concentrated, be seriously faulted.   [JC]

Other works: *Junior Intern* (**1955**), not sf; *Scavengers in Space* (**1959**); *Nine Planets* (**1960**), science fact; *The Counterfeit Man and Others* (coll **1963**); *The Universe Between* (1951; fixup **1965**), which incorporates his first story; *PSI High and Others* (coll **1967**).

See also: MERCURY; OUTER PLANETS; PARALLEL WORLDS; SCIENCE FICTION WRITERS OF AMERICA.

NOVA US ORIGINAL-ANTHOLOGY series (1970-74) ed Harry HARRISON, published by Delacorte (#1) and then Walker & Co., with paperbacks from Dell (#1, #2, #3) and then Manor Books. All had UK editions also. Its 4 vols were *Nova 1* (anth **1970**), #2 (anth **1972**), #3 (anth **1973**; vt *The Outdated Man* 1975) and #4 (anth **1974**). This was a catholic series, the contents ranging from old-fashioned sf adventure stories by such writers as Gordon R. DICKSON through humour by John T. SLADEK to experimental pieces by younger authors. Tom REAMY made his first sale (though not his début) here with "Beyond the Cleft" (1974). The most regular contributors were Brian W. ALDISS, Barry N. MALZBERG, Robert SHECKLEY and, unusually, Naomi MITCHISON. It was an entertaining series, but had no great impact.   [MJE/PN]

NOVAE TERRAE The earliest true FANZINE in the UK (1936-9), 33 issues, ed Maurice K. Hanson, first for the Nuneaton chapter of the SCIENCE FICTION LEAGUE, and then, from #10, for the pre-WWII Science Fiction Association, the UK's first national sf organization. *NT* was given over primarily to discussion of sf and FANDOM, the only fiction it carried being parodies or based on fan doings. In Sep 1937 Hanson moved to London, and from #17 John CARNELL and Hanson's flatmate Arthur C. CLARKE were listed as assistant editors. Hanson's other flatmate, William F. TEMPLE,

replaced Carnell with #25, but after #29 Hanson handed *NT* to Carnell, who issued a further 4 issues – numbered 1 to 4 – under the anglicized title *New Worlds*, which had always appeared on the title page alongside the Latin version. The title was revived after WWII by Carnell as a professional magazine of fiction, NEW WORLDS.   [RH]

NOVAK, JOHN LUTHER ◊ Christopher PRIEST.

NOVA PUBLICATIONS ◊ John CARNELL; NEW WORLDS; SCIENCE FANTASY.

NOVA SCIENCE FICTION AWARDS ◊ AWARDS.

NOWLAN, PHILIP FRANCIS (1888-1940) US writer whose first sf story, "Armageddon 2419" – published in the same 1928 issue of AMAZING STORIES that featured the inception of E.E. "Doc" SMITH's **Skylark** saga – introduced Anthony "Buck" Rogers to the world, helping to inaugurate the reign of full-grown interstellar SPACE OPERA in US sf. This and a subsequent story, "The Airlords of Han" (1929), were put together near PFN's death as *Armageddon 2419 AD* (1928-9 *AMZ*; fixup **1962**). The **Buck Rogers** saga takes its hero, via SUSPENDED ANIMATION, to a corrupt 25th-century USA under the thumb of the tyrannous Hans, where Rogers soon becomes a central figure in the successful revolt. His exploits were retold and then extended through space in BUCK ROGERS IN THE 25TH CENTURY, the first sf COMIC strip, scripted by PFN and drawn by Dick CALKINS; it ran 1929-67. PFN worked on it until his death, which also cut short a new series he had begun in *ASF*. An adaptation of a tale from the comic – each page of text faced with a Calkins illustration – appeared as *Buck Rogers 25th Century AD and the Planetoid Plot* (**1936**), and the first 426 daily strips were published in book form as *Buck Rogers in the 25th Century, Great Classic Newspaper Comic Strips, No. 1* (graph coll **1964**), #2 (graph coll **1965**), #7 (graph coll **1967**) and #8 (graph coll **1968**).   [JC]

See also: ILLUSTRATION; INVASION; RADIO; TRANSPORTATION.

NOYES, ALFRED (1880-1958) UK poet and man of letters, best known during his life for extremely long epic poems like *Drake* (2 vols **1906-8**) and *The Torchbearers* (3 vols **1922-30**), the latter depicting the march of science. He wrote some fantasy and horror – in the form of narrative poems in *Tales of the Mermaid Tavern* (coll **1914**) and in the form of prose tales in *Walking Shadows: Sea Tales and Others* (coll **1918**) and *The Hidden Player* (coll **1924**). *Beyond the Desert: A Tale of Death Valley* (**1920** chap US) and *The Devil Takes a Holiday* (**1955**) are fantasies. *The Secret of Pooduck Island* (**1943**) is a juvenile. Of sf interest is a post-HOLOCAUST novel, *The Last Man* (**1940**; vt *No Other Man* 1940 US), in which a doomsday ray stops all human hearts, petrifying the corpses. A few survivors – man, woman and (male) evil SCIENTIST – finally reach Assisi, which has been miraculously saved. AN was a fervent Roman Catholic (converted in 1930), an ardent anti-Modernist, an early Japanophile and a defender of VOLTAIRE and Charles

Parnell (1846-1891). In several novels Gordon R. DICKSON has praised his lyric poetry. [JC]

See also: CLUB STORY; END OF THE WORLD; WEAPONS.

NOYES, PIERREPONT B(URT) (1870-1959) US businessman and writer whose *The Pallid Giant: A Tale of Yesterday and Tomorrow* (**1927**; vt *Gentlemen: You are Mad!* 1946) places in an ominous NEAR-FUTURE context the discovery of records of a long-dead ancient race, which destroyed itself with DEATH RAYS. Before the last moments, however, its scientists had through GENETIC ENGINEERING set the ape on an upward course. But now, in the 20th century, death rays have just been invented. The narrator warns the world. [JC]

NOYES, RALPH (?   -   ) UK writer whose sf novel, *A Secret Property* (**1985**), depicts an alien INVASION without great originality. [JC]

N3F The National Fantasy Fan Federation, formed in the USA 1941, the brain-child of Damon KNIGHT. After a succession of short-lived and factional US fan associations in the 1930s, the N3F proved a stable and enduring national organization. However, despite its long existence, it has maintained only a very low level of membership and activity and has contributed little to sf or FANDOM. It continues to publish *The National Fantasy Fan*, a newsletter which first appeared under the title *Bonfire* in 1941. [PR]

NUCLEAR COUNTDOWN ◊ TWILIGHT'S LAST GLEAMING.

NUCLEAR POWER The claim that sf is a realistic, extrapolative literature is often supported by the citing of successful PREDICTIONS, among which atomic power and the atom bomb are usually given pride of place. When the news of the bombing of Hiroshima and Nagasaki was released in 1945, John W. CAMPBELL Jr, editor of ASTOUNDING SCIENCE-FICTION, was exultant, claiming that now sf would have to be taken seriously. Campbell was entitled to congratulate himself: it was largely due to his editorial influence that sf writers of the early 1940s had concerned themselves so deeply with atomic power.

It could, however, be argued that anticipating the advent of atomic power was not such a tremendous imaginative leap. The notion of "splitting the atom" goes back to antiquity as a philosophical problem raised in the consideration of atomic theories from Democritus (*fl* 5th century BC) and Epicurus (*c*341-270BC) onwards. It was not until the end of the 19th century, however, that any evidence relating to the actual structure of atoms became accessible. In 1902 Ernest Rutherford (1871-1937) and Frederick Soddy (1877-1956) demonstrated that certain heavy atoms – including those of uranium and radium – were in a state of continuous spontaneous decay, emitting various types of energetic radiation. The popularization of this and related discoveries had an influence on SCIENTIFIC ROMANCE comparable only to that of evolutionary theory; the first title to reflect this opportunity was probably Robert CROMIE's *The Crack of Doom* (**1895**). The power of radioactivity – in many applications, some of them bizarre – quickly became commonplace in sf, especially in relation to WAR. Einstein's famous equation linking mass and energy ($E = mc^2$) became a magical formula by which any imaginative writer could derive limitless energy via the destruction of mass. It is unsurprising that Garrett P. SERVISS, in *A Columbus of Space* (1909; rev 1911), could conceive an atomic-powered spaceship, or that George GRIFFITH, in *The Lord of Labour* (**1911**), could countenance weapons like bazookas firing atomic missiles, or that H.G. WELLS, in *The World Set Free* (**1914**), could envisage civilization destroyed by atomic bombs, or that Harold NICOLSON, in *Public Faces* (**1932**), could imagine the dirty POLITICS and diplomatic chicanery which might surround the invention of an atom bomb. These notions were natural responses to the popularization of ideas in contemporary PHYSICS. Hugo GERNSBACK was well aware of the possibilities inherent in nuclear TECHNOLOGY, and had no hesitation in predicting its use as a POWER SOURCE in the NEAR FUTURE, sometimes referring to the coming era of high technology as "The Atom-Electronic Age" or "The Age of Power-Freedom". Nevertheless, atomic power would have been simply one more idea in the extravagant vocabulary of PULP-MAGAZINE sf had it not been for Campbell.

Campbell's first published story, "When the Atoms Failed" (1930), featured the release of energy by the destruction of matter; and one of his earliest stories as Don A. Stuart was "Atomic Power" (1934). He took a serious interest in progress in this area of science; and in such articles as "Atomic Generator" (1937), "Isotope 235" (1939 as Arthur McCann) and "Atomic Ringmaster" (1940 as McCann) he popularized such research for the readers of *ASF*. He discussed contemporary developments in his editorials, and actively encouraged his writers to consider the possibilities seriously. He made the scientific issues so familiar that even a routine SPACE OPERA like Theodore STURGEON's "Artnan Process" (1941) could hinge its plot on the esoteric problem of isotope separation. He published several stories dealing with the theme of nuclear power which were, in their structure and style, quite atypical of early-1940s pulp sf. "Blowups Happen" (1940) by Robert A. HEINLEIN deals with the psychological stress involved in working with a nuclear-power plant and its potential hazards. "Solution Unsatisfactory" (1941), also by Heinlein (as Anson MacDonald), is about using radioactive dust as a weapon of war, and the difficulties of exercising control over such use. *Nerves* (1942; exp **1956**) by Lester DEL REY is a classic story of an accident in a nuclear-power station which threatens to become a major DISASTER, and deals perceptively with the issues which now face the real post-Chernobyl world. Cleve CARTMILL's "Deadline" (1944), featuring an atomic bomb, brought Campbell the joyous triumph of a visit from the government's security forces. Campbell later made much of the fact that he was publishing sf of such anticipatory expertise that the FBI suspected him of having access to secrets, but the compliment paid him is less impressive when one remembers that Philip WYLIE received a similar visit in 1945 and that two COMIC-book stories featuring SUPERMAN were suppressed. Even so, Campbell's achievement in making sf writers think seriously about atomic power should not be minimized. The only GENRE-SF story of any significance dealing with atomic power to be published outside *ASF* before Hiroshima was Malcolm JAMESON's melodrama about a "breeder" reaction, "The Giant Atom" (1944 *Startling Stories*; rev as *Atomic Bomb* **1945**).

After 1945 atomic power became one of the standard themes in sf, as the shock of revelation precipitated a wave of apocalyptic stories of HOLOCAUST AND AFTER. Mutational romance, popular since the mutagenic effects of X-rays had been discovered in the 1920s, also received a considerable boost (◊ MUTANTS), and the idea that new potentials in human EVOLUTION might be stimulated by post-disaster radioactivity became an important supportive argument in the "psi boom" (◊ ESP; PSI POWERS; SUPERMAN). But, as nuclear power became a reality, the kind of realistic treatment of issues connected with it seen in "Blowups Happen" and *Nerves* went into decline. These themes, no longer hypothetical, passed out of the area of interest of sf writers. Novels dealing with the social and psychological problems of living with nuclear power and radioactive substances in the post-WWII period moved into the MAINSTREAM; notable examples include *Frontier of the Unknown* (**1958**; trans **1960**) by Henri Queffelec (1910-   ) and Daniel KEYES's *The Touch* (**1968**). Today we are living with the reality of nuclear power, but its speculative extensions continue to concern sf writers, the aspect that dominates all others being that of the possibilities inherent in the use of atomic WEAPONS. This is only natural in view of what is at stake: the future of the human race. This change of consciousness has been one of the principal forces shaping post-WWII sf. One particular group of stories which brings out the point very clearly deals with the moral issues facing the scientists who have given their fellow creatures the power to annihilate the world: noteworthy are "The Weapon" (1951) by Fredric BROWN, "Day of the Moron" (1951) by H. Beam PIPER, "The Disintegrating Sky" (1953) and "Progress" (1962) by Poul ANDERSON, "Judgment Day" (1955) by L. Sprague DE CAMP and "Chain Reaction" (1956) by Boyd Ellanby.

The 1986 meltdown at Chernobyl, dramatized by sf writer Frederik POHL in his "drama-documentary" novel *Chernobyl* (**1987**), helped boost a public-opinion backlash against nuclear power which had been growing for some years. The fear of widespread POLLUTION of the environment by nuclear accidents or nuclear waste had been explored in such novels as *The Orange R* (**1978**) by John Clagett (1916-   ) and Michael SWANWICK's *In the Drift* (fixup **1985**), and in the film *The* CHINA SYNDROME (1979). HARD-SF writers who maintained their propagandistic fervour for nuclear power found themselves forced onto the defensive, as exemplified by two novels which make the preservation or revivification of nuclear power a condition of recovery after worldwide disasters: *Lucifer's Hammer* (**1977**) by Larry NIVEN and Jerry POURNELLE and *Orion Shall Rise* (**1983**) by Poul Anderson. Opinions differ sharply as to whether the world would have been better or worse had Hiroshima not happened; alternative cases are presented in Ronald CLARK's *The Bomb that Failed* (1969; vt *The Last Year of the Old World*), Kim Stanley ROBINSON's "The Lucky Strike" (1984), James P. HOGAN's *The Proteus Operation* (**1985**) and Ted MOONEY's *Traffic and Laughter* (**1990**). The advent of fusion power is still frequently regarded by sf writers as a panacea for the world's energy problems – so much so that it can take on transcendental implications, as in "Reflections in a Magnetic Mirror" (1988) by Kevin J. ANDERSON and Doug BEASON – but the reputation of Gernsback's "Age of Power-Freedom" has been badly tarnished by our experience of nuclear power in the real world. [BS]

NUETZEL, CHARLES (ALEXANDER) (1934-   ) US self-styled hack writer; in various genres, under a variety of names, he wrote over 70 paperback novels. He became active in sf in the 1960s, publishing "A Very Cultured Taste" for *Jade* #1 in 1960. *Lost Valley of the Damned* (**1961** as by Alec River; exp vt *Jungle Jungle* 1969 as CN) was routine. *Lovers: 2075* (**1964**) as by Charles English, was, like *Queen of Blood* (**1966**), mildly erotic, and marketed as such. *Images of Tomorrow* (coll **1969**) assembled satirical tales. *Warriors of Noomas* (**1969**) and its sequel *Raiders of Noomas* (**1969**) were romantic adventures heavily influenced by Edgar Rice BURROUGHS, as was *Swordsmen of Vistar* (**1969**). The last 4 titles were all published by Powell Books, whose sf line CN edited, as was *The Slaves of Lomooro* (**1969**) as by Albert Augustus Jr. [JC]
Other works: *If this Goes On* (anth 1965); *Last Call for the Stars* (**1970**).

NUEVA DIMENSIÓN ◊ SPAIN.

NUNES, CLAUDE (1924-   ) South African writer and statistician, most of whose work was in collaboration with his wife Rhoda (Gwylleth) Nunes (1938-   ). They published their first sf story, "The Problem", in *Science Fantasy* in 1962, and were active for the next two decades. *Inherit the Earth* (1963 *Science Fiction Adventures* as by Claude and Rhoda Nunes; exp **1966** dos US) was published as by CN alone, as his wife participated less than usual in the rewrite; in it the telepathic ANDROIDS who inhabit Earth after a nuclear HOLOCAUST has driven humanity to the stars hope one day to teach their makers how to live in peace. *Recoil* (**1971** US) was published as by both; in a rather archaic style it tells of telepathic ALIENS and their attempts to influence humans, specifically a group of children. *The Sky Trapeze* (**1980** UK), by CN alone, again concentrated on the powers of the mind, this time in an alien venue. [JC]

NUOVI BARBARI, I ◊ George MILLER; 1990: I GUERRIERI DEL BRONX.

NUTTY PROFESSOR, THE Film (1963). Jerry Lewis Productions/Paramount. Dir Jerry Lewis, starring Lewis, Stella Stevens, Dell Moore, Kathleen Freeman, Howard Morris. Screenplay Lewis, Bill Richmond. 107 mins. Colour.

Even those who do not normally enjoy the heavily overstated comedy of Lewis, which depends a lot on gesticulation and face-pulling, admit this to be one of his best films; it is a remake as a campus comedy of DR JEKYLL AND MR HYDE, with Lewis playing both Professor Kelp, the nerd who takes the potion, and the revoltingly smooth, sexually charged lounge lizard and crooner, Buddy Love, whom he intermittently becomes; the film is an imaginative act of spite against Lewis's former partner and co-star Dean Martin, recognizable even in this broad parody. Not only is it funny, it hits off the subtext of Robert Louis STEVENSON's original rather well. [PN]

See also: CINEMA.

NYBERG, BJORN [r] ◊ L. Sprague DE CAMP; Robert E. HOWARD.

NYE, HAROLD G. [s] ◊ Lee HARDING.

O'BRIEN, DAVID (? -) UK writer of whom nothing is known except that he wrote several early-1950s sf novels for CURTIS WARREN under various house names, including the **International Research Council** sequence – *Photomesis* (1952) and *Black Infinity* (**1952**) – as Berl CAMERON, *Blue Asp* (1952) as Rand LE PAGE, *Stella Radium Discharge* (**1952**) as Kris LUNA, and *Ships of Vero* (**1952**) as Brian SHAW. [JC]

O'BRIEN, DAVID WRIGHT (1918-1944) US writer. A nephew of Farnsworth WRIGHT, he published almost entirely for the ZIFF-DAVIS magazines AMAZING STORIES and *Fantastic Adventures* from early 1940; there were about 40 stories and novels under his own name plus others under various pseudonyms, including John York Cabot (the **Sergeant Shane** series and about 20 further tales), Bruce Dennis, Duncan Farnsworth (19 stories), Richard Vardon and the house names Alexander BLADE and Clee GARSON; nothing reached book form. He also collaborated with William P. McGivern (1921-1982) on 4 stories. Almost all his work was SPACE OPERA or other routine adventure. He served in the US Army Air Force and was shot down over Berlin. [JC]

O'BRIEN, DEAN D. [s] ◊ Eando BINDER.

O'BRIEN, E.G. [s] ◊ Arthur C. CLARKE.

O'BRIEN, FITZ-JAMES (1828-1862) Irish-born US writer, active from his arrival in New York in 1852 until he died of an infected wound in the Civil War. FJO contributed numerous poems and minor stories to the magazines, but his importance rests on a handful of brilliantly original sf tales, which were influential not only on subsequent sf but also on the development of the short-story genre.

His finest work is "The Diamond Lens" (1858), a long, precisely detailed story about a SCIENTIST who invents a supermicroscope and is then consumed by his morbid love for a beautiful woman he perceives living in an infinitesimal world inside a drop of water (◊ GREAT AND SMALL). *What Was It? A Mystery* (1859 *Harper's*; **1974** chap) tells of an encounter with an invisible being whose nature remains an enigma, although a plastercast made while the creature is chloroformed reveals it as a hideous diminutive humanoid (◊ INVISIBILITY). These two stories, his best known, are both set firmly in mid-19th-century New York, and helped establish a mode of sf characterized by surface realism. In a similar vein was the earlier "The Bohemian" (1855), in which the narrator's passionate love for gold fatally induces him to have his fiancée mesmerized in order to reveal the whereabouts of a treasure. "From Hand to Mouth" (1858) is a remarkable surrealistic fantasy in which a man sits in the Hotel de Coup d'Oeil surrounded by disembodied but living eyes, ears, mouths and hands. In "The Lost Room" (1858) a strange house, whose intricate "corridors and passages, like mathematical lines, seemed capable of indefinite expansion", becomes the scene of an orgy by six male and female "enchanters" who apparently succeed in kidnapping the narrator's room into some other world or DIMENSION. "The Wondersmith" (1859) is notable in the history of sf, despite its fantastic framework, for its extended descriptions of an army of miniature automata. The posthumous "How I Overcame my Gravity" (1864), though marred by the use of dream, is otherwise a singularly modern piece of sf: its core is a detailed description of suborbital flight achieved with the aid of gyroscopic stabilization. The great strength of FJO's sf is its inventiveness, which also became its greatest weakness whenever he allowed ingenuity to dominate the fiction. "The Diamond Lens" remains a masterpiece because he subordinated his brilliant invention to a profound exploration of the diseased psychology of one of the main figures of his age, the would-be lone genius of scientific creation.

FJO's works have been collected in various posthumous editions: *Poems and Stories* (coll **1881**) ed (sometimes damagingly) by poet and reviewer William Winter (1836-1917), a member with FJO of the

Pfaff's Cellar literary circle in New York; *The Diamond Lens and Other Stories* (coll **1885**); *What Was It? and Other Stories* (coll **1889**); *Collected Stories by Fitz-James O'Brien* (coll **1925**); *The Fantastic Tales of Fitz-James O'Brien* (coll **1977**). These were all superseded by *The Supernatural Tales of Fitz-James O'Brien, Volume One: Macabre Tales* (coll **1988**) and *The Supernatural Tales of Fitz-James O'Brien, Volume Two: Dream Stories and Fantasies* (coll **1988**), both ed Jessica Amanda Salmonson (1950-   ), which assembles some previously uncollected work and presents well known texts in their original magazine versions. [HBF]

See also: HISTORY OF SF.

O'BRIEN, FLANN Pseudonym of Irish writer and civil servant Brian O Nolan (1911-1966), who also wrote – mainly for a newspaper column – as Myles na Gopaleen, sometimes rendered Myles na gCopaleen. He is best known for work outside the sf field, such as the FABULATION, *At Swim-Two-Birds* (**1939** UK), a fantasy "saga" at the heart of which mythological entities inflict themselves on a character within a book by a man about whom the protagonist of the actual novel is writing a book, and *Faustus Kelly* (**1943**) as by Myles na Gopaleen, a fantasy play about the Devil in Ireland. FO's novels most closely resembling sf are *The Third Policeman* (written c1940; **1967** UK), a fantasy, featuring numerous sciencefictional devices, in which a murderer sets off (by bicycle) through a fantasmagorical posthumous POCKET UNIVERSE whose circularity is not spatial but temporal, and *The Dalkey Archive* (**1964** UK), which utilizes material from the previous book in its entrancingly eccentric presentation of a plot featuring a mad SCIENTIST eager to destroy the world, and the fantastic results of a gas he invents. [JC/PN]

O'BRIEN, ROBERT C(ARROLL) Pseudonym of US writer Robert Lesly Carroll Conly (1922-1973); his books were marketed as juveniles, though the last two are essentially adult. His first, *The Silver Crown* (**1968**), is a sometimes frightening, complex fantasy about the kidnapping of a young girl by a king who is ruled in turn by a malignant MACHINE. *Mrs Frisby and the Rats of NIMH* (**1971**; vt *The Secret of NIMH* 1982), which won the Newbery Medal, tells of a group of fugitive rats from a laboratory where their INTELLIGENCE has been enhanced; with the help of Mrs Frisby, a field mouse, they found an independent colony, determined not to batten on humans. The treatment is realistic and without a trace of whimsy. After his death his daughter, Jane Leslie Conly, wrote two sequels, *Rasco and the Rats of NIMH* (**1986**) and *R.T., Margaret, and the Rats of NIMH* (**1991**). RCO's *A Report from Group 17* (**1972**) is about biological warfare between the USA and Russia; it is competent, but less successful than his other work. In *Z for Zachariah* (**1975**), a post-HOLOCAUST novel of considerable sensitivity, a solitary surviving adolescent girl comes to realize that she cannot make a life with the male survivor who has entered her quiet valley; she eludes his attempt at rape and travels across the desolated

landscape in search of other survivors. It is a fine book, morally complex, and not simply a story of good versus evil; the girl's victory is ambiguous. RCO died before the novel was quite finished; it was completed by his family. [PN/JC]

See also: CHILDREN'S SF.

O'BRIEN, WILLIS H(AROLD) (1886-1962) US special-effects supervisor in the film industry. For his own amusement he early began to experiment with stop-motion photography. A 1min home movie of an animated caveman and dinosaur, involving 960 separate exposures, led to a producer advancing him $5000 to make a more elaborate version of the same subject: *The Dinosaur and the Missing Link* (1917) ran for only 5 mins but took 2 months to make. It proved successful and later the same year he made a series of similar films for the Edison Company. In 1919 he made the more elaborate *The Ghost of Slumber Mountain*, one of the first films to combine footage of live actors with animated models.

WHO's first full-length film was *The* LOST WORLD (1925), whose success led him to start work on a project of epic proportions, «Creation», a variation on the LOST-WORLD theme. It was never completed, but he incorporated much of its material (including improved designs for his models, which by then had metal skeletons with ball-and-socket joints) into KING KONG (1933), which proved to be the peak of his career. A sequel, SON OF KONG (1933), was hurriedly made, but after that WHO found difficulty in getting backing for his increasingly expensive projects. In the late 1930s he began work on «The War Eagles» (it was to climax in an aerial battle between airships and men riding giant eagles over New York City), but the film was abandoned, as was his 1942 project, «Gwangi», about cowboys who discover dinosaurs on a Texas mesa (it was eventually filmed as *The* VALLEY OF GWANGI [1969]). It was not until 1949 that he was able to complete another partially animated feature, MIGHTY JOE YOUNG (an unambitious rerun of the *King Kong* theme), assisted by his new young protegé, Ray HARRYHAUSEN. It was the last film over which he had real control. During the 1950s he worked on MONSTER MOVIES for other people but was unable to obtain backing for his own films. He died in 1962 while working on *It's a Mad, Mad, Mad, Mad World* (1963 dir Stanley Kramer). Despite his comparatively small output, he is widely regarded as one of the great pioneers of special effects in fantastic cinema. [JB]

OBRUCHEV, VLADIMIR A(FANASEVICH) (1863-1956) Russian geologist, academician and writer. Two of his novels, both early classics of Russian sf, have been translated: *Plutoniia* (1915; **1924**; trans B. Pearce as *Plutonia* 1957) and *Zemlya Sannikova* (**1926**; trans Y. Krasny as *Sannikov Land* 1955 USSR). Both are adventures after the style of Jules VERNE, aimed at younger readers, and informatively crammed with geological and palaeontological data. The first is a HOLLOW-EARTH story in which a party of Russian explorers enters the Earth via an unknown landmass north of the Bering Strait and finds a LOST WORLD full of prehistoric reptiles. The second is similar; a volcano thrusting through the Arctic icecap to the far north of Siberia has a fertile lost world, populated by a stone-age people, inside its huge crater. Other, untranslated, works by VO were travel novels set in Central Asia. [PN]

See also: RUSSIA.

OBUKHOVA, LYDIA (1924-) Russian writer who began publishing work of interest as early as 1945, and whose books gained some popularity in her native land. *Lilit* (trans Mirra Ginsburg as *Daughter of Night* **1974** US) tells the story of Adam's first wife, Lilith, who meets an ALIEN assessing Earth for colonization. He falls in love with her, presents her with the gift of fire, and saves the planet from his own people. [JC]

OCEANOGRAPHY ◊ UNDER THE SEA.

OCTOBER, JOHN [r] ◊ ROBERT HALE LIMITED.

OCTOPUS, THE US PULP MAGAZINE. 1 issue, Feb/Mar 1939, published by Popular Publications; ed Rogers Terrill. The feature novel, "The City Condemned to Hell" by Randolph Craig (Norvell W. PAGE), was actually a rewritten SPIDER story; the evil Octopus broadcasts a ray that turns people into monsters. It was reprinted as **Pulp Classics** #11 (**1976**) (◊ Robert E. WEINBERG). *The* SCORPION was a follow-up to *O*. The single issue was confusingly designated Vol 1 #4. [MJE/FHP]

ODELL, SAMUEL W. (1864-1948) US writer of 2 sf books, *Atlanteans* (coll **1889**) and *The Last War, or The Triumph of the English Tongue* (**1898**). In the latter, a future-WAR story set in the 26th century, the highly civilized all-White Allied Anglo-American Nations decide, more in sorrow, to engage in "war to the end" against a miscegenate evil empire controlled by the Russian Czar, destroying millions of the foe before their inevitable victory. [JC]

ODLE, E(DWIN) V(INCENT) (1890-1942) UK writer and editor. As younger brother of Alan Odle, who was the husband of Dorothy M. Richardson (1873-1957), EVO came into close contact with J.D. BERES-FORD, who had been instrumental in publishing the first volume of Richardson's *Pilgrimage* in 1915. EVO's sole sf novel, *The Clockwork Man* (**1923**), clearly shows Beresford's influence, and may also have been published with his help. In this graceful SCIENTIFIC ROMANCE, a CYBORG – in this case a man into whose body a clock has been inserted – comes accidentally back through time from AD8000 to the present, where he plays cricket and describes a world in which life regulated by MACHINES is accepted by most, though not all. God, it is hoped, has been taking note of the new, improved version of humanity. [JC]

See also: DIMENSIONS; EVOLUTION; HISTORY OF SF; SUPER-MAN; TIME TRAVEL.

ODOM, MEL [r] ◊ Warren C. NORWOOD.

O'DONNELL, KEVIN Jr (1950-) US author with a BA in Chinese Studies who has spent several years in the Far East. His first published sf was "The Hand

is Quicker" (1973 *ASF*), and over 50 short stories have followed. His first novel, *Bander Snatch* (**1979**), curiously blends pulp cliché and real inventiveness in its tale of a ghetto mobster who has telepathic powers and learns to use them responsibly. *Mayflies* (**1979**), which shows a real advance in narrative skill, is a GENERATION-STARSHIP story where ephemeral human lives flit past the hero, an (immortal) human brain embedded in the ship's COMPUTER and fighting for control. KO is perhaps best known for the amusing series **The Journeys of McGill Feighan**, which consists to date of *The Journeys of McGill Feighan: Book I: Caverns* (**1981**), *Book II: Reefs* (**1981**), *Book III: Lava* (**1982**) and *Book IV: Cliffs* (**1986**). Feighan is a flinger (he can teleport people and things) who, though based on Earth, solves problems on various planets; his quest is for the godlike Far Being who has interfered with his life since birth. Like most of KO's fiction, these are interesting, light-hearted books, casual in their tone of voice, like a hybrid of Ron GOULART and Jack VANCE. *ORA:CLE* (**1984**), complexly plotted, has an expert on Asian history, brain-linked with a computer, in a future where people live indoors because the air is bad outside and aliens hunt you there. *Fire on the Border* (**1990**), a SPACE OPERA with interstellar warfare and a Japanese general, is crammed with almost too much incident. It would be interesting to see what KO could do if his novels proceeded less breathlessly. [PN]

Other works: *War of Omission* (**1982**); *The Shelter* (**1987**) with Mary Kittredge, horror; *The Electronic Money Machine* (**1984**), nonfiction about personal computers.

See also: CYBORGS; SPACESHIPS.

O'DONNELL, K.M. ◊ Barry N. MALZBERG.

O'DONNELL, LAWRENCE ◊ Henry KUTTNER; C.L. MOORE.

O'DONNELL, MARGARET (? -) Irish writer whose *The Beehive* (**1980**) is a FEMINIST thriller set in a DYSTOPIAN world. [JC]

O'DUFFY, EIMAR (1893-1935) Irish writer whose mock-epic-Irish **Aloysius O'Kennedy** sequence – *King Goshawk and the Birds* (**1926**), *The Spacious Adventures of the Man in the Street* (**1928**) and *Asses in Clover* (**1933**) – makes satirical points about contemporary civilization, very much in the manner of James Stephens (1882-1950) in *The Crock of Gold* (**1912**), by assessing modern life through the eyes of characters who are, or claim to be, figures of Irish legend. The second volume mounts its comparatively sustained SATIRE through its heroes' voyage to a UTOPIA where everything is, not unusually, inverted. The third, set like the first in Ireland after 1950, musters the forces of legend to defeat US capitalism in the form of the egregious King Goshawk. [JC]

Other works: *Bricriu's Feast* (**1919**), a fantasy play.

About the author: *Eimar O'Duffy* (**1972** chap) by Robert Hogan.

ODYSSEY US BEDSHEET-size magazine. 2 issues, Spring and Summer 1976, published by Gambi Publications, New York; ed Roger ELWOOD. *O* was advertised as an sf magazine, but contained a high proportion of fantasy. The fiction and articles were unremarkable; lead novellas were by Jerry POURNELLE (#1) and Larry NIVEN (#2). Production was poor, and the covers by Frank Kelly FREAS and Jack GAUGHAN were inferior to their usual work. Bad distribution and poor sales killed *O*. [FHP/PN]

OFFRET ◊ Andrei TARKOVSKY.

OFFUTT, ANDREW J(EFFERSON V) (1937-) US writer who often signed his name andrew j offutt; his first published story was as by Andy Offutt and his first professional sale was as by A.J. Offutt. That first published story, a contest winner, was "And Gone Tomorrow" for *If* in 1954, but he regards his professional sf career as beginning with "Blacksword" for *Gal* in 1959. He soon became a prolific writer in several genres, both under his own name and under pseudonyms including John Cleve (see below for the **Spaceways** sequence), Jeff Douglas and the house name J.X. WILLIAMS. The pseudonymous works have been SEX novels, several with sf content. AJO's first sf novel under his own name was *Evil is Live Spelled Backwards* (1970), in which an underground movement opposes a 21st-century religious tyranny through sexual revolution. *The Castle Keeps* (1972) more ambitiously depicts – through an acid examination of SURVIVALIST shibboleths – the violent disintegration of Western culture. A juvenile, *The Galactic Rejects* (1973), features three young friends with PSI POWERS on a UTOPIAN world threatened by invasion.

From the mid-1970s, with the appearance of tales like *Messenger of Zhuvastou* (1973) and *My Lord Barbarian* (1977), AJO turned primarily to fantasy, usually SWORD AND SORCERY, often works tied to other authors' creations, though much of the John Cleve sf erotica was published in the 1980s. His urgent, sometimes rather hasty style and his sharp intelligence are most effectively deployed in sf stories depicting a hectic urban world and, though he clearly finds all sorts of material congenial, his later career has not been of striking interest. [JC]

Other works: *The Great 24-Hour Thing* (1971); *Ardor on Aros* (1973); *Genetic Bomb* (1975) with D(ouglas) Bruce Berry; the **Cormac Mac Art** sequence, based on Robert E. HOWARD's character and comprising *Sword of the Gael* * (1975), *The Undying Wizard* * (1976), *Sign of the Moonbow* * (1977), *The Mists of Doom* * (1977), *When Death Birds Fly* * (1980) with Keith Taylor (1946-) and *The Tower of Death* * (1982) with Taylor; *Chieftain of Andor* (1976; vt *Clansman of Andor* 1979 UK); a **Conan** parody, *The Black Sorcerer of the Black Castle* (1976 chap) plus 3 **Conan** novels, *Conan and the Sorcerer* * (1978), *The Sword of Skelos* * (1979) and *Conan the Mercenary* * (1980); the **War of the Wizards** fantasy sequence, all with Richard K. Lyon (1933-), comprising *Demon in the Mirror* (1978), *Eyes of Sarsis* (1980) and *Web of the Spider* (1981); the **War of the Gods on Earth** fantasy sequence, comprising *The Iron Lords* (1979), *Shadows Out of Hell* (1980) and *The Lady of the Snowmist* (1983); *King Dragon* (1980); *Shadow-*

spawn * (1987), a contribution to the **Thieves' World** SHARED-WORLD enterprise; *Deathknight* (1990).

As John Cleve: *Barbarana* (1970); *The Devoured* (1970); *Fruit of the Loins* (1970); *Jodinareh* (1970); *The Juice of Love* (1970); *Manlib!* (1974); *The Sexorcist* (1974; vt *Unholy Revelry* 1976); the **Spaceways** sequence (the first 6 written solo, most of the rest in collaboration, but all signed Cleve alone), comprising *Spaceways #1: Of Alien Bondage* (1982), *#2: Corundum's Woman* (1982), *#3: Escape from Macho* (1982), *#4: Satana Enslaved* (1982), *#5: Master of Misfit* (1982), *#6: Purrfect Plunder* (1982), *#7: The Manhuntress* (1982) with Geo. W. PROCTOR, *#8: Under Twin Suns* (1982), *#9: The Quest of Qalara* (1983), *#10: The Yoke of Shen* (1983) with Proctor, *#11: The Iceworld Connection* (1983) with Jack C. HALDEMAN II and his wife Vol Haldeman, *#12: Star Slaver* (1983) with G.C. EDMONDSON, both writing as Cleve, *#13: Jonuta Rising!* (1983) with Victor KOMAN, *#14: Assignment: Hellhole* (1983) with Robin Kincaid, *#15: Starship Sapphire* (1984) with Roland GREEN, *#16: The Planet Murderer* (1984) with Dwight V. SWAIN, *#17: The Carnadyne Horde* (1984) with Koman, *#18: Race Across the Stars* (1984) with Kincaid and *#19: King of the Slavers* (1985).

As Jeff Douglas: *The Balling Machine* (1971) with D. Bruce Berry.

As J.X. Williams: *The Sex Pill* (1968).

As editor: The **Swords Against Darkness** series, comprising *Swords Against Darkness* (anth 1977; vt *Swords Against Darkness I* 1990); *II* (anth 1977); *III* (anth 1978); *IV* (anth 1979); *V* (anth 1979).

See also: POLLUTION; SCIENCE FICTION WRITERS OF AMERICA.

O'FLINN, PETER [s] ◊ R.L. FANTHORPE.

O'HARA, KENNETH [s] ◊ Bryce WALTON.

OHARA, MARIKO [r] ◊ JAPAN.

O'KEEFE, CLAUDIA (? -) US writer, the hero of whose first sf novel, *Black Snow Days* (1990), has been genetically engineered by his mother to reawaken, 10 years after his fatal car crash, into a post-HOLOCAUST environment he is intended to redeem; the novel rather confusedly puts him through a long quest sequence for a McGUFFIN Hidden Base which contains the answers to questions he resents having to ask. [JC]

OKUN, LAWRENCE (EUGENE) (1929-) US medical doctor and writer whose sf novel, *On the 8th Day* (1980), treats GENETIC ENGINEERING in terms of the PARANOIA it evokes. [JC]

OLAN, SUSAN TORIAN (? -) US writer whose *The Earth Remembers* (1990) is a cagily written example of the everything-but-the-kitchen-sink variety of post-HOLOCAUST fiction. Set on the Texas-Mexico border, the tale features MUTANTS, Amerindians and nuclear devices along with the usual protagonists and antagonists. [JC]

OLANDER, JOSEPH D. (1939-) US academic and anthologist, all of whose work has been in collaboration with Martin Harry GREENBERG (*whom see for details*), sometimes plus further collaborators.

"Name" authors involved in team anthologies part-edited by JDO are Isaac ASIMOV, Damon KNIGHT, Frederik POHL and Robert SILVERBERG. [JC]
See also: CRITICAL AND HISTORICAL WORKS ABOUT SF; SOCIOLOGY.

OLDMEADOW, ERNEST (JAMES FRANCIS) (1867-1949) UK writer whose 1930s radio work sometimes verged on the fantastic, as in *The Town To-Morrow: Five and Twenty Imaginary Broadcasts* (coll **1937**) as by Francis Downman. His sf novel, *The North Sea Bubble: A Fantasia* (**1906**), set in 1910, spoofs the conventions of the future-WAR tale in a manner later amplified by P.G. WODEHOUSE in *The Swoop* (**1909**). [JC]

OLERICH, HENRY (1851-?) US author of a series of UTOPIAN novels, some barely fictionalized. *A Cityless and Countryless World* (**1893**) fairly vividly presents a highly organized Mars of FEMINIST interest, women there being financially and sexually independent of men. His remaining books – even *The Story of the World a Thousand Years Hence* (**1923**) – fatally eschew narrative. [JC]
Other works: *Modern Paradise* (**1915**); *Cause and Cure of the High Cost of Living* (**1919**); *The New Life and Future Mating* (**1927**).

OLIVER, CHAD Working name of US writer and anthropologist Symmes Chadwick Oliver (1928-) for his sf. CO was born in Ohio but has spent most of his life in Texas, where he took his MA at the University of Texas (his 1952 thesis, "They Builded a Tower", being an early academic study of sf). He took a PhD in ANTHROPOLOGY from the University of California, Los Angeles, and became professor of anthropology at the University of Texas at Austin; his sf work has consistently reflected both his professional training and his place of residence: much of it is set in the outdoors of the US Southwest, and most of his characters are deeply involved in outdoor activities. CO has always been concerned with the depiction of Native American life and concerns: *The Wolf is My Brother* (**1967**), which is not sf, features a sympathetically characterized Native American protagonist. Most of CO's sf, too, could be thought of as Westerns of the sort that eulogize the land and the people who survive in it. The sf plots that drive his stories – like, in *The Winds of Time* (**1957**), the awakening of ALIENS held in SUSPENDED ANIMATION for hundreds of centuries – tend to be resolved in terms that reward a deeply felt longing for a non-urban life closely involved with Nature, though the effect of this is somewhat dissipated by his characteristic inability to prepare for his favourite scenes by adequate plotting, and a tendency (in his earlier works) to pad novelettes to novel length.

His first published story, "The Land of Lost Content", appeared in *Super Science Stories* in 1950; his short work has been collected in *Another Kind* (coll **1955**) and *The Edge of Forever* (coll **1971**), the latter containing biographical material and a checklist compiled by William F. NOLAN. CO's first novel, a juvenile, was *Mists of Dawn* (**1952**). *Shadows in the Sun*

(**1954**), set in Texas, describes with some vividness its protagonist's discovery that all the inhabitants of a small town are aliens, that it may be possible for Earth to gain galactic citizenship, and that he can work for that goal by living an exemplary life on his home planet; *Unearthly Neighbors* (**1960**; rev 1984) depicts human attempts to communicate with alien visitors; *The Shores of Another Sea* (**1971**) is set in Africa, and articulates CO's concern with the natural world, specifically in terms of ECOLOGY; *Giants in the Dust* (**1976**) argues the thesis that mankind's fundamental nature is that of a hunting animal, and that our progress from that condition has fundamentally deracinated us.

CO has been a pioneer in the application of competent anthropological thought to sf themes, and, though awkward construction sometimes stifled the warmth of his earlier stories, he is a careful author whose speculative thought deserves to be more widely known and appreciated. [JC]
Other work: *Broken Eagle* (**1989**), a Western.
About the author: *Chad Oliver: An Annotated Bibliography & Guide* (last rev **1989** chap) by Hal W. HALL.
See also: GENERATION STARSHIPS; LINGUISTICS; ORIGIN OF MAN; UFOS; VENUS.

OLIVER, FREDERICK SPENCER [r] ◊ ATLANTIS.
OLLIER, CLAUDE [r] ◊ FRANCE.
OLŠA, JAROSLAV Jr (1964-) Student of Arabic and Oriental studies and international relations; also sf editor, translator and bibliographer. JO was for a time assistant editor of the first Czechoslovak sf monthly magazine, *Ikarie* (published since 1990), but his major role in sf studies has been as co-editor of the Czechoslovak «Encyklopedie science fiction» ["Encyclopedia of Science Fiction"] (**1992**). He has contributed to LOCUS, FOUNDATION and other sf magazines, has compiled bibliographies of Czechoslovak FANZINES, and wrote the entry on CZECH AND SLOVAK SF for this encyclopedia. [PN]

OLSEN, BOB Working name of US writer Alfred John Olsen Jr (1884-1956), who began publishing sf with "The Four Dimensional Roller Press" for *AMZ* in 1927; this was the first of several tales in the **Four Dimensional** sequence. Other tales featured **Professor Archimedes Banning**, whose exploits were patterned on the model of the EDISONADE. One story, *Rhythm Rides the Rocket* (**1940** chap), was published in booklet form, but BO was a born PULP-MAGAZINE writer, and lost interest in the field after about 1940. [JC]
See also: GREAT AND SMALL; HIVE-MINDS.

OLTION, JERRY B. (1957-) US writer who began publishing sf in 1982 with "Much Ado About Nothing" for *ASF*, the journal which published a high proportion of the 25 or so stories he wrote in the 1980s. His first novel, *Frame of Reference* (**1987**), is a POCKET-UNIVERSE tale whose human protagonists discover, while growing up and falling in love, that the starship they live in is actually a simulacrum hidden underground and that the ALIENS on the surface of the

Earth deserve a strict comeuppance, which they soon get. JBO then published two **Isaac Asimov's Robot City: Robots and Aliens** ties: *#4: Alliance* ∗ (**1990**) and *#6: Humanity* ∗ (**1990**). [JC]

O'MALLEY, KATHLEEN [r] A.C. CRISPIN.

OMEGA MAN, THE Film (1971). Warner Bros. Dir Boris Sagal, starring Charlton Heston, Anthony Zerbe, Rosalind Cash. Screenplay John William Corrington, Joyce H. Corrington, based on *I Am Legend* (**1954**) by Richard MATHESON. 98 mins. Colour.

This is the second film version of Matheson's ultra-PARANOIA novel, the first being *L' ULTIMO UOMO DELLA TERRA* (1964; vt *The Last Man on Earth*). "The first one was very poorly done," said Matheson, himself a screenwriter, "but it did follow the book. *The Omega Man* bore no resemblance to my book ... I had absolutely nothing to do with the screenplay." A survivor of a biological war battles (with a machine gun rather than Matheson's sharpened stakes) against a group of mutated, albino fanatics haunting the almost dead city. The film sacrifices the claustrophobia and nightmare of the novel for fast-moving action. The true cinematic heir to Matheson's story, though not directly based on it, is the far superior NIGHT OF THE LIVING DEAD (1968). [JB/PN]

OMEGA SCIENCE DIGEST Australian popular-science magazine, small-BEDSHEET size, publishing an average of 2 sf stories per issue; 37 bimonthly issues Jan/Feb 1981-Jan/Feb 1987, ed Philip Gore. The parent magazine was the US *Science Digest*, discontinued at around the same time. Though unexceptional as a science magazine, *OSD* was, with a circulation around 35,000, for 6 years the most important publisher of Australian short sf, printing 78 stories by Australian authors, illustrated by Australian artists such as Mark McLeod, Tony Pyrzakowski and Frantz Cantor. Authors included Russell BLACKFORD, Damien BRODERICK, Simon Brown, Sean MCMULLEN, Jack WODHAMS and, perhaps most notably, Terry DOWLING, whose popular stories in *OSD* attracted much local notice. [PN]

OMNI US popular-science magazine which includes fiction; monthly, current, slick, small-BEDSHEET size, #1 Oct 1978, 168 issues to Sep 1992; published by Omni Publications International, New York.

Because it has a high circulation – at times topping 1 million – and because it pays the highest rates for fiction, *Omni* has a prestige in sf circles out of proportion to the actual number of stories it publishes (seldom more than 2 per issue, 1 per issue in 1991). Founded by Bob Guccione of *Penthouse* magazine as a sister periodical, *O* has been one of the big success stories of US MAGAZINE publishing: lavishly illustrated in colour, publishing science articles ranging from the demanding through the gosh-wow to features on only marginally scientific, sometimes New-Age subjects like parapsychology and UFOS, *O* does not depend on fiction for its sales, and has been fortunate in having fiction editors who have kept the standard quite high; they have been Ben BOVA (Oct 1978-Dec 1979), Robert SHECKLEY (Jan 1980-Sep 1981) and Ellen DATLOW (Oct 1981-current). Bova was also executive editor Jan 1980-Aug 1981; the present executive editor is Keith Ferrell, an sf enthusiast who is soliciting more nonfiction from sf writers, thus increasing the sf presence in the magazine.

O's fiction has, interestingly, not put a high premium on hard science; indeed, especially in later years, it has often published SCIENCE FANTASY, pure FANTASY and MAINSTREAM fiction with a small sf twist to it. This has been attributed (1991) by Datlow to the higher quality overall of fantasy submissions relative to sf submissions, rather than to any change of policy. As fiction editor, Datlow has pulled in the big names but also done much for the careers of novice writers. For example, Ted Chiang's novelette "Tower of Babylon" (*Omni* 1990), his first story, won a NEBULA. Among the other award-winning *Omni* novelettes and short stories have been "Sandkings" (1979) by George R.R. MARTIN (Hugo and Nebula), "The Way of Cross and Dragon" (1979) also by Martin (Hugo), "Morning Child" (1984) by Gardner DOZOIS (Nebula), "Tangents" (1986) by Greg BEAR (Hugo and Nebula), "Permafrost" (1986) by Roger ZELAZNY (Hugo), "Schrödinger's Kitten" (1988) by George Alec EFFINGER (Hugo and Nebula) and "At the Rialto" (1989) by Connie WILLIS (Nebula). *Omni* has also published work of some literary distinction by Thomas M. DISCH and John CROWLEY, supported the eccentric talent of Howard WALDROP and the CYBERPUNK of William GIBSON and Bruce STERLING, and generally had an honourable, imaginative publishing record. Although Datlow is on record as liking very much some stories she would still not accept for *Omni*, she seems to have made remarkably few concessions, in *O*'s fiction, to its mass-market audience.

A UK version, *Omni: Book of the Future*, featuring new UK material and US reprints, ed Jack Schofield, was test-launched as a weekly partwork in Nov 1981 in the UK West Country by Eaglemoss Publications; it lasted only 4 weeks and never received national distribution.

Anthologies based on *Omni* are *The Best of Omni Science Fiction* (anth **1980**) ed Bova and Don Myrus, *#2* (anth **1981**) ed Bova and Myrus, *#3* (anth **1982**) ed Bova and Myrus, *#4* (anth **1982**) ed Bova and Myrus, *#5* (anth **1983**) ed Myrus, *#6* (anth **1983**) ed Myrus – all but the first of these containing original fiction in addition to reprints – *The First Omni Book of Science Fiction* (anth **1983**) ed Datlow, *The Second Omni Book of Science Fiction* (anth **1983**) ed Datlow, *The Third Omni Book of Science Fiction* (anth **1985**) ed Datlow, *The Fourth Omni Book of Science Fiction* (anth **1985**) ed Datlow, *The Fifth Omni Book of Science Fiction* (anth **1987**; includes 1 original story) ed Datlow, *The Sixth Omni Book of Science Fiction* (anth **1989**; includes 1 original story) ed Datlow and *The Seventh Omni Book of Science Fiction* (anth **1989**; includes 1 original story) ed Datlow. [PN]

OMPA Known usually by its acronym, the Offtrail

Magazine Publishers Association (1954-78/79) was formed in the UK by Kenneth BULMER, A. Vincent Clarke and Chuck Harris. OMPA was modelled on FAPA, and was founded to facilitate distribution of FANZINES published by and for members. Early contributors included John BRUNNER and Michael MOORCOCK. Uniquely for an APA, OMPA once organized a national convention, Ompacon, the 1973 UK Eastercon. [PR/RH]

O'NEAL, KATHLEEN M. ◊ Kathleen O'Neal GEAR.

1 APRIL 2000 ◊ AUSTRIA.

ONE HOUR TO DOOMSDAY ◊ CITY BENEATH THE SEA.

O'NEILL, GERARD K. [r] ◊ LAGRANGE POINT; SPACE HABITATS,

O'NEILL, JOSEPH (1886-1953) Irish educationist and novelist; Permanent Secretary to the Department of Education, Irish Free State, 1923-44; author of 3 sf novels. *Wind from the North* (**1934**) is only marginally sf, its narrator passing through a timeslip to give a vivid account of Dublin under Viking rule in AD1013. JO turned to sf proper with *Land under England* (**1935**), a DYSTOPIA in a LOST-WORLD setting: in a cave system beneath Cumberland, descendants of the Roman Army suffer a totalitarian state in which individualism is completely obliterated by telepathic means. The introduction by AE assumed that the book was a SATIRE on Hitlerian totalitarianism, an impression confirmed with the appearance of *Day of Wrath* (**1936**), a future-WAR novel which describes the destruction of civilization by advanced aircraft following a coalition between Germany, Japan and China. JO was not a GENRE-SF writer; rather, he used sf instruments to make cultural and political points. His eloquence was considerable. [JE]

See also: OPTIMISM AND PESSIMISM; POLITICS.

O'NEILL, SCOTT [r] ◊ Barton WERPER.

ONE MILLION B.C. (vt *Man and his Mate*) Film (1940). Hal Roach/United Artists. Dir Hal Roach and Hal Roach Jr, starring Victor Mature, Carole Landis, Lon Chaney Jr. Screenplay Mickell Novak, George Baker, Joseph Frickert, based on a story by Eugene Roche. 85 mins, cut to 80 mins. B/w.

In this not very distinguished prehistoric Romeo-and-Juliet soap opera a young caveman is exiled from the family cave and meets a girl from a rival tribe; together they face various prehistoric hazards, including an earthquake and an erupting volcano. Photographically enlarged lizards wearing rubber disguises play the anachronistic dinosaurs, and an elephant wearing a woolly coat stands in for a mammoth. D.W. Griffith (1875-1948) worked on portions of the film, but resigned in anger at the decision not to have the cavepeople speak modern English. The UK remake was ONE MILLION YEARS BC (1966). [JB/PN]

See also: CINEMA.

ONE MILLION YEARS B.C. Film (1966). Hammer/20th Century-Fox. Dir Don Chaffey, starring Raquel Welch, John Richardson, Robert Brown, Martine Beswick. Screenplay Michael Carreras, based on the screenplay of ONE MILLION B.C. (1940). 100 mins. Colour.

The first of Hammer's several stone-age movies (*see also* WHEN DINOSAURS RULED THE EARTH), this is a remake of *One Million B.C..* Prehistoric lovers from different scantily clad tribes, the rock people and the shell people – some loony ANTHROPOLOGY here – survive warfare, anachronistic monsters, unconvincing fur brassieres and volcanic upheavals. Ray HARRYHAUSEN – this time not working with his usual colleague Charles Schneer – was in charge of the monsters which are, indeed, animated. [PN/JB]

ONN, CARRIE ◊ Robert E. VARDEMAN.

ON THE BEACH Film (1959). Lomitas Productions/United Artists. Dir Stanley Kramer, starring Gregory Peck, Ava Gardner, Fred Astaire, Anthony Perkins, Guy Doleman. Screenplay John Paxton, based on *On the Beach* (**1957**) by Nevil SHUTE. 134 mins. B/w.

1964, the NEAR FUTURE: only Australia has survived a global nuclear war. This merely prolongs the agony: a cloud of radioactive fallout is moving south and everyone will die. Suicide pills are handed out; people face death (or run to meet it) with varying degrees of dignity, though tears are shed; big-name Hollywood stars (the plot provides reasons for the number of Americans facing the end in Melbourne) look anguished; the wind blows newspapers through empty streets. OTB was the most celebrated of the 1950s anti-Bomb films, heavily publicized, much discussed, seen as Art, and certainly effective propaganda in the Cold-War nuclear-weapons debate. It has not weathered well; seen today it appears slow, mawkish, ludicrously stiff-upper-lip, and unrealistic in a sanitized middle-class way: no riots, no looting, just chaps feeling miserable and driving racing cars in a reckless manner. The Australian legend that Ava Gardner, while shooting, looked around and said of Melbourne "What a great place to make a movie about the end of the world" is untrue. Peter NICHOLLS appeared in a crowd scene. [PN]

OPEN UNIVERSE In cosmology an open universe is a model of the Universe which implies that it will continue to expand forever; in this general sense, the term is found incidentally in many sf novels. However, sf readers also use it in a quite different meaning: to designate a work or series whose characters and venues may be made use of by fans and others in FANZINES without copyright restrictions (although the original authors do sometimes impose constraints). The best known open universes are probably STAR TREK and Marion Zimmer BRADLEY's **Darkover**.

A cognate use of the term, to designate works or series whose authors invite other professional authors to participate, is perhaps deceptive. Open universes of this sort, from H.P. LOVECRAFT's **Cthulhu** to Michael MOORCOCK's **Jerry Cornelius**, are perhaps more appropriately thought of as a kind of SHARED WORLD. [JC]

OPERA ◊ MUSIC; THEATRE.

OPERATION GANYMED Film (1977). Pentagrama/ Zweites Deutsches Fernsehen. Written/dir Rainer Erler, starring Horst Frank, Dieter Laser, Uwe Friedrichsen, Jurgen Prochnow, Claud Theo Gaestner, Vicky Roskilly. 126 mins, cut to 120 mins. Colour.

This grim German film emerges as a realist response to fantasies like PLANET OF THE APES (1968). On their return to Earth, 5 survivors of a 3-ship, 21-man mission to Ganymede crashland off the Gulf of Mexico and, lost in the desert, turn to madness, murder, cannibalism and guilt-ridden introspection as they wonder whether humanity has been wiped out by a nuclear war. During the mission, as we discover in flashbacks, the astronauts discovered ALIEN microorganisms which caused a plague among them, but it turns out that Earth is the harshest environment of all, as the final survivor straggles back to an unchanged, uncaring civilization. Concerned with the ethical issues of space travel – whether the expenditure results in an improved earthly standard of living or not – this is a talky and melodramatic film, but intermittently powerful. Erler's other sf films, mainly for the German tv company ZDF which cofinanced this one, include *Das Genie* ["The Genius"] (1974), *Plutonium* (1978) and *Fleisch* ["Flesh"] (1979). [KN]

OPERATION MONSTERLAND ◊ GOJIRA; RADON.

OPERATOR #5 US PULP MAGAZINE, 48 issues, Apr 1934-Nov/Dec 1939, published by Popular Publications; ed Rogers Terrill, it began as a monthly and then alternated between bimonthly and monthly. This was one of the livelier and more successful hero/villain pulps, and more sciencefictional than most. Operator #5 was secret agent Jimmy Christopher, whose assignment, in the lead novel every issue, was to save the USA from destruction by various menaces (often superscientific) and unfriendly powers (frequently Asiatic). The lead novels were published under the house name Curtis STEELE, which concealed the highly prolific pulp writer Frederick C. DAVIS (Apr 1934-Nov 1935), then Emile Tepperman (Dec 1935-Mar 1938), and lastly Wayne Rogers. Other features included a series of spy stories by Arthur Leo ZAGAT. 13 of the early lead novels, all the work of Davis, were reprinted as paperback books (◊ Frederick C. DAVIS for details). [MJE/FHP/PN]

OPPENHEIM, E(DWARD) PHILLIPS (1866-1946) UK writer, publishing from 1887 at least 160 novels, most of them espionage thrillers or society detective mysteries, the best known being *The Great Impersonation* (1920). His sf novels of interest – most of the titles listed below are romantic-fantasy potboilers – include *The Wrath to Come* (1924 US), in which the USA is threatened by a 1940s German-Russian-Japanese axis, *Gabriel Samara, Peacemaker* (1925 US; vt *Gabriel Samara* 1925 UK; vt *Exit a Dictator* 1939 US), in which the Russian government is overthrown, and *The Dumb Gods Speak* (1937), a novel set in the future and involving high intrigue and a secret weapon. EPO was a careless, clumsy, snobbish, quite enjoyable

writer of escapist fiction. [JC]
Other works: *The Mysterious Mr Sabin* (1898); *A Daughter of Astrea* (1898); *The Traitors* (1902); *The Great Awakening* (1902; vt *A Sleeping Memory* 1902 US); *The Secret* (1907); *Havoc* (1911); *The Falling Star* (1911 US); *The Double Life of Mr Alfred Burton* (1913 US); *The Black Box* (1915 US); *The Great Prince Shan* (1922 US); *The Golden Beast* (1926 US); *Matorni's Vineyard* (1928 US); *The Adventures of Mr Joseph P. Cray* (1929); *Up the Ladder of Gold* (1931 US); *Mr Mirakel* (1943 US).

OPTIMISM AND PESSIMISM In the most simplistic version of the HISTORY OF SF, sf was always (and rightly) an optimistic literature until the NEW WAVE came along in the 1960s and spoiled everything. This was at best a very partial truth, being only remotely applicable to GENRE SF and not at all to MAINSTREAM sf.

In the mainstream, not even the work of individual authors could be categorized as simply either optimistic or pessimistic. Both Jules VERNE and H.G. WELLS took a darker view of the future as they became older; indeed, Wells's vision described almost a parabola: between *The Time Machine* (1895), a novel of evolutionary futility, and *Mind at the End of its Tether* (1945), from 1905 through the 1920s his portraits of the future were generally UTOPIAN. The favourite themes of sf outside the genre magazines have always included DYSTOPIA, INVASION, future WAR, and the HOLOCAUST AND AFTER, and the stories have often taken the form of dire warnings or a generalized philosophical bleakness aimed at demonstrating humanity's predilection for getting itself into trouble. Olaf STAPLEDON envisaged, in *Last and First Men* (1930), an ultimate harmony in the Universe, but one achieved only after a prolonged variety of evolutionary torments.

By contrast, sf in the PULP MAGAZINES was mostly cheerful, especially after Hugo GERNSBACK founded AMAZING STORIES in 1926. Gernsback proselytized actively for technological optimism, and this, despite many exceptions – including several stories by John W. CAMPBELL Jr, writing as Don A Stuart, which evoked an atmosphere of moody desolation – remained the dominant tone of sf until the dropping of the atom bomb on Hiroshima in 1945. Campbell, as editor of *ASF*, normally required a constructive attitude towards science from his contributors, but, though writers like Robert A. HEINLEIN were temperamentally inclined to oblige, even before 1945 the typical *ASF* story was by no means mindlessly cheery, and many of the stories showed a strong awareness of possible technological DISASTER.

After the advent of the Bomb (◊ NUCLEAR POWER) it was no longer possible to see the applications of science as an unmixed blessing. Also working against optimism were the Cold War and its domestic effect in the USA: the suspicious atmosphere (approaching PARANOIA) prevalent from the early 1950s (shown notably in the anti-communist scares) probably helped to change the focus of interest of many sf stories from TECHNOLOGY to SOCIOLOGY and POLITICS. The magazine GALAXY SCIENCE FICTION specialized in a form of social SATIRE best exemplified by *The Space Merchants* (1952 as "Gravy Planet"; **1953**) by C.M. KORNBLUTH and Frederik POHL; this type of story created its future scenario with a distinct cynicism, but its narrative tone was similar to that of most pulp sf, cheerful and hardbitten, with no such strong sense of horror and disgust as could be found outside the genre in novels like George ORWELL's *Nineteen Eighty-four* (**1949**).

But any categorization of sf stories into the optimistic and the pessimistic is so imprecise as not to be greatly useful, and indeed there would be no point in discussing the subject were it not that sf critics with backgrounds in 1930s and 1940s FANDOM have often regarded the optimism/pessimism split as of grave importance. Just such a distinction has also been made in several histories of sf, such as Donald A. WOLLHEIM's *The Universe Makers* (**1971**), and it is implicit in much of the work of Sam MOSKOWITZ. The work of Clifford D. SIMAK is relevant as an example of the difficulties in such a categorization: his stories regularly revolve around reconciliation and the achievement of some kind of harmony between Technological Man and Nature (hence optimistic), but his tone, as in *City* (fixup **1952**), is often elegiac and nostalgic (hence pessimistic).

A distinction with some truth is often made between US sf, as typically outward-thrusting and riding the momentum of the old myth of the Frontier, and the UK SCIENTIFIC ROMANCE, which, perhaps as a result of imperial power giving way rapidly to global impotence, was far more inclined to expect DISASTER. But this was never more than a gross generalization (though truer of UK sf than of US sf); nor did it take into account the guileless *pleasure* the British took in disaster. Could anything so enjoyable be called pessimism? Now that, in the 1990s, the world economic hegemony of the USA is threatened by financial weakness and domestic problems, as happened in the UK much earlier, it will be interesting to observe what sociological reflections appear in US sf of the later 1990s.

It was only in the middle and late 1960s, with the advent of the so-called New Wave, that real anger and sometimes despair about the future of humanity became quite commonplace in genre sf. But the writers of the New Wave, even though their attitudes sometimes appeared anarchic, were seldom *passively* acceptant of a dark view; the dominant New-Wave metaphor may have been of ENTROPY, of things running down, but the fierce commitment of, say, Harlan ELLISON or Brian W. ALDISS could not be airily dismissed as "pessimism" by any but the crudest of critics. Aldiss has many times inveighed in print against what he regards as the strong moral pressure, found especially in some US publishing houses, to legislate for a kind of mandatory optimism. The casual insertion of a happy ending or a few improving messages no more constitutes true optimism than an awareness of the difficulties of life either now

or in the future constitutes true pessimism.

Poets have many times argued that an awareness of death gives a sharper edge to love; just so, the darker elements which have entered sf since 1945, and especially since the mid-1960s, have been argued as redressing a balance without which sf could never have reached maturity as a genre. The good sf writer often mediates between simplistic extremes of optimism and pessimism, and his mode of mediation is often irony: one meaning of this complex word has been defined as "an outcome of events contrary to what was, or might have been, expected". The ironist is not just somebody sarcastic or even somebody who expects the worst: he or she is somebody who understands the multitude of possibilities concealed in apparently straightforward events, does not take anything at face value, and (at best) embraces the largeness and unpredictability of things (at worst being merely knowing). Notable sf ironists have included J.G. BALLARD, Alfred BESTER, Algis BUDRYS, Philip K. DICK, Thomas M. DISCH, Ursula K. LE GUIN, Michael MOORCOCK and, more recently, Iain M. BANKS, John CROWLEY, William GIBSON, James TIPTREE Jr. and Gene WOLFE. To read the more painful or rueful aspects of their work as simple pessimism is to read inaccurately.

Indeed the whole question of optimism and pessimism in sf seems far less pressing today than it did when the first edition of this encyclopedia was published in 1979, with the residual echoes of the New-Wave debate still audible. While the entropic introspection (◊ INNER SPACE) of the New Wave is no longer characteristic of any but a few writers, the old certitudes of SPACE OPERA (the Universe is ours for the taking, just so long as we're inventive and self-reliant) are likewise long gone. Writers of HARD SF from the 1980s – Greg BEAR, David BRIN, Orson Scott CARD, Paul J. MCAULEY, Michael SWANWICK and others – no longer portray the Universe as waiting voluptuously to be had. The extremes of optimism and pessimism have disappeared; perhaps, except for purposes of tub-thumping argument, they were never there in the first place.   [PN]

OR, L' ◊ GOLD.

ORAM, NEIL (1938-   ) UK writer whose involvement in sf was restricted to the 3 vols of his **The Warp** sequence of metaphysical adventures – *The Storm's Howling through Tiflis* (**1980**), *Lemmings on the Edge* (**1981**) and *The Balustrade Paradox* (**1982**) – which novelize his 22-hour, 10-play cycle, *The Warp*, performed in London in 1979, dir Ken Campbell. The sequence, after the manner of the **Illuminatus!** books by Robert SHEA and Robert Anton WILSON, features world conspiracies, ley energies, reincarnated searchers for the key to unlock occult mysteries, and so forth.   [JC]

ORBAN Working name of US illustrator Paul Orban (?   -?   ). He executed 7 covers and many interior ILLUSTRATIONS for a remarkable number of magazines (1933-60), including *If*, *Future*, *Space Science*

Fiction and *The Shadow*, but is mostly associated in readers' minds with the 1940s *ASF*, where he did many of the interior illustrations 1933-54. His black-and-white work was often symbolic of a story rather than directly representational, regularly placing faces or figures over geometrical abstractions and using bold cross-hatching; it was always competent and sometimes more. Brian W. ALDISS has called O "an incurable romantic in a field of incurable romantics". [JG/PN]

ORBIT Seminal US ORIGINAL-ANTHOLOGY series ed Damon KNIGHT. Although **Orbit** was not the first such series, having been preceded by STAR SCIENCE FICTION STORIES in the USA and NEW WRITINGS IN SF in the UK, it was its extraordinary early success that precipitated the boom in such series in the early 1970s. It had a more literary orientation than the sf magazines, and perhaps for this reason was especially popular with the active members of the newly formed SCIENCE FICTION WRITERS OF AMERICA. For whatever cause, stories from **Orbit** dominated the NEBULA awards in their early years, although none has ever won a HUGO. *Orbit 1* (anth **1966**) contained "The Secret Place" by Richard MCKENNA, which won the short-story Nebula. *Orbit 3* (anth **1968**) featured 2 Nebula-winning stories: "Mother to the World" by Richard WILSON and "The Planners" by Kate WILHELM. *Orbit 4* (anth **1968**) contained another winner in "Passengers" by Robert SILVERBERG. That was the last **Orbit** story to win an award, although the year of pervasive dominance was 1970, when between them *Orbit 6* (anth **1970**) and *Orbit 7* (anth **1970**) provided 1 of the 5 novellas on the final Nebula ballot, 3 of the 6 novelettes, and 6 of the 7 short stories. Three writers in particular became associated with *Orbit*, and remained its most regular contributors: R.A. LAFFERTY, Wilhelm and Gene WOLFE; in the run of 21 volumes, Lafferty and Wilhelm had 19 stories each, and Wolfe 18. **Orbit** lost its dominance once the flood of competitors appeared, and with #14 had to change publishers (becoming confined to a hardcover edition in the process) in order to survive. Notable stories in later volumes include Wolfe's "The Fifth Head of Cerberus" in *Orbit 10* (anth **1972**), Ursula K. LE GUIN's "The Stars Below" in *Orbit 14* (anth **1974**) – which also contained Joan D. VINGE's début story – and Wilhelm's "Where Late the Sweet Birds Sang" in *Orbit 15* (anth **1974**). **Orbit** was especially notable for stories that seemed at the time odd and *sui generis*, quite unlike the usual run of GENRE SF and fantasy, but with hindsight were early signs of a general sophistication of genre sf in the 1970s, in which this series at first played a vital role; later numbers became rather insipid. Other volumes in the series are *Orbit 2* (anth **1967**), *Orbit 5* (anth **1969**), *Orbit 8* (anth **1970**), *Orbit 9* (anth **1971**), *Orbit 11* (anth **1972**), *Orbit 12* (anth **1973**), *Orbit 13* (anth **1974**), *Orbit 16* (anth **1975**), *Orbit 17* (anth **1975**), *Orbit 18* (anth **1976**), *Orbit 19* (anth **1977**), *Orbit 20* (anth **1978**) and *Orbit 21* (anth **1980**). *The Best From Orbit* (anth **1977**) is culled from the first 10 vols. [MJE/PN]

ORBIT SCIENCE FICTION US DIGEST-size magazine. 5 issues 1953-Nov/Dec 1954, first 2 undated, published by Hanro Corp., New York; ed Jules Saltman. *OSF* was a middling-quality magazine that fell victim to the inundation of the market with too many sf magazines in the early 1950s. A story in the **Tex Harrigan** series by August DERLETH appeared in every issue, and #5 contained "Adjustment Team" by Philip K. DICK. All stories were chosen by Donald A. WOLLHEIM, uncredited. A cut 1954 Australian edition of #1 only, in pulp format, was published by Consolidated Press, Sydney. [FHP/PN]

ORCZY, BARONESS Working name of Hungarian-born UK author and illustrator Baroness Emmuska (variously Emma or Emulka) Magdalena Rosalia Maria Josefa Barbara Orczy (1865-1947). After magazine work as an illustrator, she came to fame with *The Scarlet Pimpernel* (**1905**). Her sf novel, *By the Gods Beloved* (**1905**; vt *The Gates of Kamt* 1907 US), is a LOST-WORLD tale set in the desert, where ancient Egyptians engage in sexual intrigues and politics. [JC]

ORDE, A.J. ◊ Sheri S. TEPPER.

ORE, REBECCA Pseudonym of US writer Rebecca B. Brown (1948-), who began publishing sf with "Projectile Weapons and Wild Alien Water" for *AMZ* in 1986 and is best known for *Becoming Alien* (**1988**) and its sequels, *Being Alien* (**1989**) and *Human to Human* (**1990**), a sequence which – with a deceptive air of leisureliness – takes a young rural Virginian named Tom from the provincial backwaters of xenophobic Earth to another planet where, as the solitary human among a multitude of other races, he is trained to join, on behalf of Earth, the Federation of Space Traveling Systems. A very wide range of ALIENS is introduced in a concise but seemingly disorganized cataloguing style which has reminded critics of Stanley G. WEINBAUM's "A Martian Odyssey" (1934); but, as the sequence progresses, the momentum of the tale builds, and RO's apparently scattershot concisions turn out to have been carefully meditated. The end sense, as Tom grows into knowledge of himself and of his prejudice-stricken fellow humans, is one of complexities experienced. More immediately impressive, perhaps, is a singleton, *The Illegal Rebirth of Billy the Kid* (**1991**), in which a CIA specialist in DNA-recombinant engineering (◊ GENETIC ENGINEERING) creates a CLONE – or chimera – of Billy the Kid whose "memories" of the 19th century have been programmed into his blank brain, and whose perceptions are controlled by a "nineteenth-century visual matrix" that causes him to read 21st-century sights in terms of Billy's own experiences. The story of this chimera's slow and anguished climb into self-awareness, and of his escape to a rural Appalachian theme-parked reservation, is swift and urgently dense in the telling, fragilely hopeful in its implications. As of 1991, RO herself lived in Appalachia, and the ironies attendant upon inhabiting a contrived sanctuary enrich an already rich text. [JC]

O'REILLY, JOHN BOYLE (1844-1890) Irish-born US writer. A Fenian transported to Australia, he escaped to the USA and became a journalist, poet and novelist. His sf novel about a republican England, *The King's Men: A Tale of Tomorrow* (**1884**) with Robert GRANT, F.J. Stimson and John T. Wheelwright, features an attempted monarchist coup which is roundly defeated. [JC]

ORGILL, DOUGLAS (WILLIAM) [r] ◊ John GRIBBIN.

ORIGINAL ANTHOLOGIES An original ANTHOLOGY is an anthology in book format of stories that have not been previously published, and such volumes played an important role in sf PUBLISHING, especially in the 1960s and 1970s. This encyclopedia gives entries to original-anthology series devoted to sf and (with one exception, **Dangerous Visions**) running to 3 or more vols; we do not give separate entries for shared-world anthology series (◊ SHARED WORLDS *for examples*) with the exception of **Wild Cards**. There are 19 such entries: The BERKLEY SHOWCASE, CHRYSALIS, DANGEROUS VISIONS, FULL SPECTRUM, INFINITY, INTERZONE: THE ANTHOLOGY (original only in part), L. RON HUBBARD PRESENTS WRITERS OF THE FUTURE, NEW DIMENSIONS, NEW VOICES, NEW WRITINGS IN SF, NOVA, ORBIT, OTHER EDENS, QUARK, STAR SCIENCE FICTION STORIES, STELLAR, SYNERGY, UNIVERSE and WILD CARDS. (We classify some further original-anthology series in book format as magazines, when they so describe themselves; these include DESTINIES and PULPHOUSE: THE HARDBACK MAGAZINE.) [PN]

ORIGINAL SCIENCE FICTION STORIES, THE US DIGEST-size magazine, 38 issues, 1953-May 1960. Published by Columbia Publications; ed Robert A.W. LOWNDES. A companion magazine to FUTURE FICTION and SCIENCE FICTION QUARTERLY, *TOSFS* began life as a one-shot simply entitled *Science Fiction Stories*, though some commentators see this as a mere continuation, after a gap, of the magazine SCIENCE FICTION (1939-41), also ed Lowndes. #2 followed in 1954, and the magazine commenced regular publication in Jan 1955. The Sep 1955 issue added an advertising slogan, "The Original", to the title on the cover, and the magazine subsequently became known by that name, although technically its title remained *Science Fiction Stories*. Like its companion magazines, *TOSFS* existed on a very small editorial budget but maintained a respectable, if largely mediocre, level of quality, a little better perhaps than its stable companion *Future Fiction*. Serialized novels included *The Tower of Zanid* (**1958**) by L. Sprague DE CAMP and *Caduceus Wild* (1959 *TOSFS*; **1978**) by Ward MOORE and Robert Bradford. Robert SILVERBERG was the magazine's most prolific contributor. R.A. LAFFERTY made his début here with "Day of the Glacier" (1960). The numeration of this cluster of magazines was very complex, and can be found explained in *Science Fiction, Fantasy and Weird Fiction Magazines* (**1985**) ed Marshall B. TYMN and Mike ASHLEY (in their article on *Science Fiction*, as they prefer to treat *TOSFS* as a continuation of that journal). After its demise in May 1960 the title was bought by fan James V. Taurasi (◊ FANTASY TIMES), who used it on 3 SEMIPROZINE issues – little more than FANZINES, in fact – in BEDSHEET format in Dec 1961, Winter 1962 and Winter 1963. The UK abridged reprint edition (1957-60) had 12 numbers. [MJE/FHP/PN]

ORIGIN OF MAN An abundant literature dealing with the remote ancestry of the human species inevitably sprang up in the wake of the theory of EVOLUTION, as propounded by Charles Darwin (1809-1882). T.H. Huxley (1825-1895), the principal champion of Darwinism, published a classic essay on "Man's Place in Nature" (1863), and Darwin himself wrote *The Descent of Man* (**1871**) soon after. The main point at issue was, as Benjamin Disraeli (1804-1881) put it, "the question of whether Man is an ape or an angel". Disraeli was on the side of the angels, but science and serious speculative fiction were not; their main interest was in *how* Man had ceased to be a brute beast and become human.

Huxley took a rather harsh view of the process of natural selection, and so did his one-time pupil, H.G. WELLS, whose "A Story of the Stone Age" (1897) envisages the crucial moment in human evolution as the invention of a "new club" – a better means to cut and kill. This view recurs constantly, being memorably envisaged in Stanley KUBRICK's 2001: A SPACE ODYSSEY (1968), in which the dawn of intelligence occurs as an ape realizes that the bone he uses to smash other bones can also be used as, among other things, a WEAPON. Darwin presented a rather different account, stressing the positive value of cooperation and mutual protection in the struggle for existence. This stress on cooperative emotions as well as physical inventions is found in such works as Jack LONDON's *Before Adam* (**1906**), although previous, more religiously inclined authors had represented the origins of humanity in purely spiritual terms; Gouverneur MORRIS's *The Pagan's Progress* (**1904**) is an example. The domestication of fire was also widely seen as the crucial invention, notably in Stanley WATERLOO's *The Story of Ab* (**1897**), in Charles Henry Robinson's *Longhead: The Story of the First Fire* (**1913**), and in the most famous novel by the most prolific author of prehistoric fantasies, J.H. ROSNY aîné's *La guerre du feu* (**1909**; cut trans as *The Quest for Fire* **1967**). Rosny's prehistoric stories – which include *Vamireh* (**1892**), *Eyrimah* (**1893**), *Le felin géant* (**1918**; trans **1924** as *The Giant Cat* 1924 US; vt *Quest of the Dawn Man* 1964) and *Helgvor de Fleuve Bleu* ["Helgvor of the Blue River"] (**1930**) – inspired numerous works by other French writers, including Marcel Schwob's "The Death of Odjigh" (1892; trans 1982), Claude ANET's *La fin d'un monde* (**1925**; trans as *The End of a World* **1927**) and Max BEGOUEN's *Les bisons d'argile* (**1925**; trans as *Bison of Clay* **1926**).

The Huxleyan account of human nature was comprehensively rejected by two UK writers in SCIENTIFIC ROMANCES that glorified the innocent state of Nature and blamed civilization for all human ills: S. Fowler

WRIGHT in *Dream, or The Simian Maid* (**1929**) and its intended sequel *The Vengeance of Gwa* (**1935**) (as by Anthony Wingrave) and J. Leslie MITCHELL in the polemical *Three Go Back* (**1932**) and the lyrical "The Woman of Leadenhall Street" (1936) as by Lewis Grassic Gibbon. Similar nostalgia for a prehistoric Golden Age is displayed in William GOLDING's *The Inheritors* (**1955**), though Golding follows Wright rather than Mitchell in refusing to grant innocence to Man's direct ancestors, and presents a more brutal view of prehistoric life in "Clonk Clonk" (1971). All these works are, in part, admonitory fables, and by natural exaggeration prehistoric fantasies have also been employed for SATIRE, as in Andrew LANG's "The Romance of the First Radical" (1886), Henry Curwen's *Zit and Xoe* (**1887**), W.D. Locke's "The Story of Oo-oo" (1926) and Roy LEWIS's *What We Did to Father* (**1960**: vt *The Evolution Man* 1963; vt *Once upon an Ice Age* 1979).

There have been several attempts to write novels on a vast scale which link prehistory and history to provide a "whole" account of the "spirit of Man". The most impressive is *Den Lange Rejse* (**1908-22** Denmark; trans as *The Long Journey* **1922-4**; omni **1933**) by the Danish Nobel prizewinner Johannes V. JENSEN, the first two parts of which are prehistoric fantasies. A work on an even greater scale is the **Testament of Man** series by Vardis FISHER, a 12-novel series of which the first 4 vols are prehistoric fantasies. Also in this tradition is *Les enchaînements* (**1925**; trans as *Chains* **1925**) by Henri BARBUSSE, while more trivial examples include *The Invincible Adam* (**1932**) by George S. VIERECK and Paul ELDRIDGE and *Tomorrow* (coll of linked stories **1930**) by F. Britten AUSTIN, who also wrote a volume of prehistoric short stories, *When Mankind was Young* (coll **1927**). The attempt to find in the evolutionary history of Man some sequence of events for which the *Genesis* myth might be considered a metaphor – a key theme of Fisher's novels – is such an attractive notion that it has infected anthropological theory as well as speculative fantasy. Austin BIERBOWER's *From Monkey to Man* (**1894**) offers a simpler account of a metaphorical expulsion from Eden. A fierce reaction against such superstitions can be found in *The Sons of the Mammoth* (trans **1929**) by the Russian anthropologist V.G. BOGORAZ.

In the US PULP MAGAZINES there grew up a romantic school of prehistoric fiction glorifying the life of the savage. Its most prolific proponent was Edgar Rice BURROUGHS, author of the **Pellucidar** series, *The Eternal Lover* (**1914**; **1925**; vt *The Eternal Savage*) and *The Cave Girl* (**1913-17**; **1925**). Novels from outside the pulps, however, often show a similar if more muted romanticism. Examples include most of Jack London's stories in this vein, Sir Charles G.D. ROBERTS's *In the Morning of Time* (**1919**), H. Rider HAGGARD's *Allan and the Ice-Gods* (**1927**) and Richard TOOKER's *The Day of the Brown Horde* (**1929**). Prehistoric romances in the CINEMA, which are notorious for their anachronisms, are perhaps the extreme examples of the

romantic school, from D.W. Griffith's *Man's Genesis* (**1911**) onwards. Although Hugo GERNSBACK reprinted Wells's "A Story of the Stone Age", GENRE SF did not really take prehistoric fantasy aboard, with notable exceptions including Lester DEL REY's "When Day is Done" (1939), Jack WILLIAMSON's "The Greatest Invention" (1951), Chad OLIVER's juvenile *Mists of Dawn* (**1952**) and Theodore L. THOMAS's "The Doctor" (1967). Progress in physical ANTHROPOLOGY has encouraged a sophistication of fictional images of prehistoric life, reflected in such works as *Cook* (**1981**) by Tom Case and *No Enemy but Time* (**1982**) by Michael BISHOP. The most remarkable modern manifestation of prehistoric fantasy is, however, the series of bestselling novels by Jean AUEL, collectively entitled **Earth's Children**, which begins with *The Clan of the Cave Bear* (**1980**). Auel ingeniously combines a realism based in modern scientific understanding with robust literary romanticism. Also worthy of special note is a series of surreal prehistoric fantasies included in Italo CALVINO's *Cosmicomics* (coll **1965**; trans **1968**) and *t zero* (coll **1967**; trans **1969**; vt *Time and the Hunter*). Significant scientific speculations on the topic are contained in two novels by the palaeontologist Björn KURTÉN, *Dance of the Tiger* (**1978**; trans **1980**) and *Singletusk* (**1984**; trans **1986**).

There have, of course, been several unorthodox accounts of the origin of Man, including various hypothetical extraterrestrial origins. Some, like that propounded by Erich VON DÄNIKEN, have been presented as fact. Such notions recur throughout the HISTORY OF SF, usually developed as silly plot gimmicks (◊ ADAM AND EVE). Among the more interesting examples are Eric Frank RUSSELL's *Dreadful Sanctuary* (1948; **1951**; rev **1963**), which plays with the Fortean hypothesis (◊ Charles FORT) that Earth is an asylum for the lunatics of other worlds, and James BLISH's "The Writing of the Rat" (1956), one of many stories which makes us the descendants of a "lost colony" within a galactic civilization. [BS]

See also: MYTHOLOGY.

ORKOW, BEN (HARRISON) (1896-   ) Russian-born US writer, mostly of plays and film scripts. In his sf novel *When Time Stood Still* (**1962**) a couple travel via SUSPENDED ANIMATION to AD2007, where her fatal disease may be curable. [JC]

ORLACS HÄNDE (vt *The Hands of Orlac*) Film (1924). Pan Film. Dir Robert Wiene, starring Conrad Veidt, Fritz Kortner, Carmen Cartellieri, Alexandra Sorina. Screenplay Louis Nerz, based on *Les mains d'Orlac* (1920) by Maurice RENARD. 92 mins, cut to 70 mins. B/w.

In this Austrian film from the director of *The Cabinet of Doctor Caligari* (1919), a pianist whose injured hands have been replaced with those of an executed murderer inherits also the murderer's homicidal tendencies, and must struggle against the domination of the dead man. The central idea is scientifically absurd, but it has an emotional logic and has attracted several film-makers. The best version is the US remake *Mad Love* (1935; vt *The Hands of Orlac*), which deviates somewhat from Renard's silly novel, shifting the emphasis from pianist to surgeon. It was dir Karl Freund (best known as a brilliant cameraman) from a script by Guy ENDORE, P.J. Wolfson and John L. Balderston, and starred Peter Lorre, Frances Drake, Colin Clive, 70 mins, b/w. Lorre – in one of his few truly great performances and one of his first after arriving in the USA – plays the demented surgeon who grafts the murderer's hands onto a pianist whose wife he loves, and then attempts to drive him insane by masquerading as the executed murderer back from the dead. This stylish, *Grand Guignol* melodrama still seems stunning half a century later.

Two later remakes were produced – one using the original title *The Hands of Orlac* (1960; vt *Les mains d'Orlac*; vt *Hands of a Strangler*) and the other called *Hands of a Stranger* (1963). The former was a UK-French coproduction made in two versions, the UK version dir Edmond T. Grenville, the French dir Jacques Lemare, both versions starring Mel Ferrer, Lucille Saint Simon, Christopher Lee, Donald Pleasence, David Peel, with screenplay by John Baines and Grenville, 105 mins cut to 95 mins, b/w. The latter film was US, written and dir Newton Arnold, starring Paul Lukather, Joan Harvey, 86 mins cut to 73 mins, b/w. Both versions, particularly the latter, are distinctly inferior to *Mad Love*.   [JB/PN]

ORU KAIJU DAISHINGEKI ◊ GOJIRA.

ORWELL, GEORGE Pseudonym of UK writer Eric Arthur Blair (1903-1950), much of whose best work was contained in his impassioned journalism and essays, assembled in the 4 vols of *The Collected Essays, Journalism and Letters of George Orwell* (all coll **1968**). His fiction and extended social criticism, as in *Down and Out in Paris and London* (**1933**), also demonstrates his good sense and the intense clarity of his mind. His books of sf interest are two. *Animal Farm: A Fairy Story* (**1945** chap) is a fable satirical of the form communism took once it had established itself in the Soviet Union, and consequently enraged many of those who responded sensitively to criticisms of what they continued to perceive as a valid experiment in socialism. Despite its fable form, however, *Animal Farm* is an intensely practical book, mocking not the ideals of socialism or communism (many of which GO shared) but their corrupt embodiment in an actual state. The attack is direct, and the USSR is the target. A great revolution takes place on the Farm, but is soon subverted by the Pigs, whose leader, Napoleon, seizes power and reduces the Revolution's original 7 Commandments (the last being "All animals are equal") down to one, which is written in capitals on the communal wall: ALL ANIMALS ARE EQUAL BUT SOME ANIMALS ARE MORE EQUAL THAN OTHERS. The attack on Stalin is devastating. A cartoon feature film animated by John Halas and Joy Batchelor, *Animal Farm*, was released in 1955.

GO's most famous book remains *Nineteen Eighty-four* (**1949**), which was published shortly before his

death of tuberculosis and which again caused some of his colleagues on the Left to accuse him (mistakenly) of betrayal. It was filmed in 1955 as 1984 and in 1984 as NINETEEN EIGHTY-FOUR. With Aldous HUXLEY's *Brave New World* (**1932**), it is the century's most famous English-language DYSTOPIA. It is a book of hectic, devilish, claustrophobic intensity, so nightmarish in the telling that some critics have faulted it (imperceptively) for subjective imbalance. In 1984, the world is divided into three vast enclaves: Britain, now known as Airstrip One, is devastatingly shabby – never having been decently rebuilt after an atomic war fought in the 1950s – and without hope. It is hard to resist a sense that GO was painting, with an unusual savagery of verisimilitude, the UK in which he lived – 1984 being simply a partial inversion of 1948 – but his presentation of the totalitarian regime ruling Airstrip One could be thought to apply to the contemporary Labour government of the UK only by those whose POLITICS were radically to the right of GO's own. The rulers of Airstrip One (symbolized by images of Big Brother) use their ability to inflict pain to drive the fact of their power into the masses, whose lives are mercilessly regimented by the Thought Police and who live in squalid barracks monitored by two-way tvs, their thoughts controlled by the Newspeak to which GO devoted a scathing appendix: "It was intended that when Newspeak had been adopted once and for all and Oldspeak forgotten, a heretical thought . . . should be literally unthinkable." The scarifying story of Winston Smith's attempt to liberate himself, and of his eventual surrender of all his human dignity under torture, makes up the actual plot of the book. As an indictment of the deep tendency of modern, technologically sophisticated governments to manage reality, and as a further devastating assault upon the actual situation in the USSR of 1948, *Nineteen Eighty-four* was unmatched. Its pessimism was both distressing and salutary. Its understanding of the nightmare of power – when wielded by representatives of a species which had evolved beyond the constraints of mercy – was definitive. "Do not forget this," his chief torturer tells Winston at the finish, after glorying in the end of all natural human affinities and goals: "Always there will be the intoxication of power, constantly increasing and constantly growing subtler . . . If you want a picture of the future, imagine a boot stamping on a human face – for ever."   [JC]

About the author: There is much Orwell criticism in print. Irving Howe's *Orwell's Nineteen Eighty-four* (**1963**) is valuable, as are George Woodcock's *The Crystal Spirit* (**1967**) and *George Orwell: A Reassessment* (anth **1988**) ed Peter Buitenhuis and Ira B. Nadel.

See also: CRIME AND PUNISHMENT; HISTORY OF SF; LINGUISTICS; MEDIA LANDSCAPE; MUSIC; POLAND; PSYCHOLOGY; SOCIOLOGY; THEATRE.

OSBORNE, DAVID or GEORGE ◊ Robert SILVERBERG.

O'SHEA, SEAN ◊ Robert S. TRALINS.

OSHIKAWA, SHUNRO [r] ◊ JAPAN.

OSMOND, ANDREW [r] ◊ Douglas HURD.

OTHER EDENS UK original anthology series, consisting of *Other Edens* (anth **1987**), *#II* (anth **1988**) and *#III* (anth **1989**), ed Christopher EVANS and Robert HOLDSTOCK. This was a curious series. The (ironic?) title is taken from the description of England in Shakespeare's *Richard II*, though the editors mistakenly say it was *Richard III*; in fact, however, they rather let down their own ambition of giving a boost to UK short fiction by including stories by US writers like Kim Stanley ROBINSON and Scott BRADFIELD, which led some readers to the unfortunate conclusion that not enough local material existed. Though good stories were published (many of the better ones inclining to FABULATION or fantasy rather than sf) the overall tone was bleak and introspective, sometimes to the point of self-parody; thus the series could be read as supporting the long-held US stereotype of UK sf, a stereotype that was contemporaneously being destroyed by the magazine INTERZONE. The series did include good work from the new generation of UK writers, including Gill ALDERMAN, Stephen BAXTER, Keith BROOKE and Ian MCDONALD. [PN]

OTHER DIMENSIONS ◊ PARALLEL WORLDS.

OTHER WORLDS US DIGEST-size magazine, in PULP-MAGAZINE format from Nov 1955. 47 issues, only 45 featuring fiction (not counting those titled either SCIENCE STORIES or UNIVERSE SCIENCE FICTION), Nov 1949-July 1953 (31 issues) and May 1955-Sep 1957 (16 issues). Published by Clark Publishing Co., Nov 1949-July 1953, and Palmer Publications Inc., May 1955-Nov 1957; ed Raymond A. PALMER. Though for some periods monthly, *OW* was usually a slightly irregular bimonthly.

OW was launched by Palmer while he was still editor of AMAZING STORIES and FANTASTIC ADVENTURES; for this reason editorship of the first issue was credited to Robert N. Webster (a Palmer pseudonym). *OW* was editorially very similar to the previous Palmer magazines, particularly in featuring the supposedly nonfictional stories of Richard S. SHAVER. Eric Frank RUSSELL was a regular contributor, and the magazine serialized L. Sprague DE CAMP's nonfiction *Lost Continents* (1952-3; **1954**). *OW* was suspended after #31, July 1953.

Palmer was notorious for his many title changes, and it is possible to regard his short-lived *Science Stories* (Oct 1953-Apr 1954) as a continuation of *OW*, the title change allowing him to duck some inconvenient printing bills, but *Science Stories*'s numeration began again from #1. And, to confuse the story further, also in 1953 Palmer anonymously founded a new magazine, *Universe Science Fiction*, whose first 2 issues, June and Sep 1953, he ed under the pseudonym George Bell; with #3, Dec 1953, Palmer became officially its editor and publisher. After 10 issues (the last was Mar 1955) the title of *Universe Science Fiction* was changed to *Other Worlds*, and at this point the magazine's numeration followed both magazines (the first new *OW*, for example, being #11

[32] May 1955, it being the 11th *Universe* and the 32nd *Other Worlds*). 12 more issues followed, until in June 1957 the title was changed again, to *Flying Saucers from Other Worlds*, reflecting Palmer's increasing preoccupation with UFOS. Only 2 of the first 4 retitled issues (3 of which were unnumbered) featured sf stories, these being #2 and #4 (July and Sep 1957). After this, though it carried on for some years, the magazine became solely UFO-oriented. [MJE/FHP/PN]

OTOMO, KATSUHIRO (1954-   ) Japanese comic-book illustrator and film animator, one of the most popular in the new generation of "manga" (Japanese COMICS) artists. His début, not sf, was in 1973 with "Jusei" ["Gun Report"], based on the novella "Mateo Falcone" (1833) by Prosper Mérimée (1803-1870). Since then he has pleasantly shocked the comics world with his excellent artwork, his surreal way of telling a story and the dynamic movement of his scene-setting. His breakthrough from cult status to national fame came with the GRAPHIC NOVEL *Dohmu* ["A Dream of Childhood"] (1981; **1983**; English trans projected 1992), which won the Nippon SF Taisho and a Sei'un Award (◊ JAPAN). This describes a conflict between the PSI POWERS of a murderous old man and of a group of children. KO's international status largely rests on the still-continuing **Akira** story, a graphic epic (over 1500pp) rather than a graphic novel. This began its first serialization in 1982-6, and resumed in 1988, in which year an English-language version commenced publication from Epic Comics. It has also been published in book form – several volumes – in both Japan and the USA. During the hiatus KO wrote, designed and directed the feature film version, AKIRA (1987), a *tour de force* of animation which, like the comic, alarmingly blends elements of "splatter" (◊ SPLATTER MOVIES) with images of post-HOLOCAUST evolutionary transcendence in a somewhat CYBERPUNK manner. KO's other main works include "Kibun Wa Moh Senso" ["Almost Enjoying the War"] (1979), "Highway Star" (1979) and "Rohjin Z" ["Old Man Z"] (1991). [TSh/PN]

OTTUM, BOB Working name of US writer Robert K. Ottum Jr (?1925-1986), in whose surprisingly funny sf novel, *All Right, Everybody Off the Planet* (**1972**), inefficient ALIENS send a spy among us in human form; the humour derives from their ignorance of human relationships and from their attempts to stage-manage an impressive First Contact. A similar notion – with the sexes reversed – was much later used, leadenly, for the film MY STEPMOTHER IS AN ALIEN (1988). [JC]

OULD, CHRIS (?1959-   ) UK writer whose sf novel, *Road Lines* (**1985**), was a NEAR-FUTURE thriller set in an apocalyptic landscape reminiscent, to some, of the MAD MAX films. [JC]

OULIPO A term standing for *L'Ouvroir de Litterature Potentialle*, which might be crudely translated as "workshop of possible fictions". Oulipo is an extremely selfconscious international literary movement founded in 1960 by the French authors Raymond

Queneau ($\lozenge$ FRANCE) and François Le Lionnais; its official membership was originally limited to 10 but eventually expanded to the present 25. Over the years Oulipo's members and proponents have included many internationally known fabulists and magic realists such as Harry Mathews (1930-   ), Georges Perec (1936-1982) and Italo CALVINO.

Oulipo's tenets are radically high-Modernist. Inspired by the linguistic theories of Ferdinand de Saussurre (1857-1913), its members consider "literature" a game of language rather than a means of representing the world, a perspective foreign to most but not all sf writers. By designing artificial "constraints" and "structures", Oulipocans try to make prose-writing difficult in the same way that metrical schemes make sonnets and sestinas difficult. But, in order to manufacture complicated products, it is necessary first to manufacture complicated machines. It is the friction generated by the author's imagination working against such formal constraints, Oulipo contends, that produces great art.

Members of the group have tended to be mathematicians as well as writers. While many of their formal structures are extremely complicated, it is often their simplest formulae that produce the most spectacular results. Perhaps consciously following the example of Ernest Vincent Wright, whose novel *Gadsby* (**1939**) has no letter "e", Georges Perec (1936-1982) wrote the novel *La Disparition* ["The Disappearance"] (**1969**) without once using that letter. (When a work is produced by deleting a letter or set of letters, the resulting narrative is referred to as a "lipogram"; *The Wonderful O* [**1957**] by James Thurber [1894-1961] is about a lipogram world.) Italo Calvino generated the plot for his *Il Castello dei Destini incrociati* (coll of linked stories **1973**; trans as *The Castle of Crossed Destinies* **1977** US) by randomly turning over the cards of a Tarot deck. Similar procedures were used by various contributors to Rachel POLLACK's *Tarot Tales* (anth **1989** UK).

Thomas M. DISCH's novel *334* (fixup **1972** UK) is probably the most successful Oulipo-related experiment in the sf field. The title (which should be pronounced "three three four") does not refer primarily to a place or a time but rather describes the three-dimensional narrative diagram according to which the book is constructed. John T. SLADEK is another sf author who often builds his novels and stories according to arbitrary designs or games; in *Tik-Tok* (**1983**), for example, each of the 26 chapters begins with a successive letter of the alphabet. Other sf or sf-related authors who exhibit a similar "gamesmanship" in their work – whether having heard of Oulipo or not – include Don DeLILLO, Vladimir NABOKOV, Rudy RUCKER and Pamela ZOLINE.   [SB]

See also: FABULATION; MAGIC REALISM; POSTMODERNISM IN SF; PSEUDO-SCIENCE.

OUTER LIMITS, THE US tv series (1963-5). A Daystar/Villa di Stefano Production for United Artists, ABC TV. Created Leslie Stevens, also executive prod. Prod Joseph Stefano (season 1), Ben Brady (season 2). Writers included Stefano (many episodes), Stevens, David DUNCAN, Robert Towne, Harlan ELLISON, Meyer DOLINSKY, John MANTLEY, Jerry SOHL, Otto O. Binder ($\lozenge$ Eando BINDER), Clifford D. SIMAK and Ib Melchior. Dirs included Byron HASKIN, Leonard Horn, Gerd Oswald, Charles Haas. 2 seasons, 49 50min episodes. B/w.

TOL, which featured a new sf story each week, is often regarded as the classic sf-anthology series. Though leaning towards the HORROR or MONSTER-MOVIE end of the sf spectrum, the series was often innovative in both style and subject matter, and many of its writers either were sf professionals or knew the genre well. The pilot episode, "The Galaxy Being", written and dir Stevens, concerned an ALIEN made of pure energy who is accidentally absorbed into a radio telescope on Earth. Harlan Ellison contributed 2 episodes: "Soldier" (1964), about an ultraconditioned soldier from the future who is projected back in time and finds himself in a typical 1960s US household – a precursor of *The* TERMINATOR (1984) – and "Demon with a Glass Hand" (1964), perhaps the finest episode, about an ANDROID, pursued by aliens, who has the entire human race coded in his artificial hand. Actors who appeared in the series – many of them then unknown – included Leonard Nimoy, Robert Culp, William SHATNER, Bruce Dern, Donald Pleasence, Martin Landau and David McCallum. The bizarre make-up that was such a feature of the series was the work of Fred Phillips, John Chambers and, primarily, Wah Chang.

The talented cinematographer Conrad Hall worked on the 1st season, and the series was visually striking. Only stupid programming (it was shifted to a time-slot opposite the hugely popular *Jackie Gleason Show*) led to the series' cancellation halfway through the 2nd season. *TOL* was, on the whole, more imaginative and intelligent than its more famous competitor on CBS, Rod SERLING's *The* TWILIGHT ZONE. *The Outer Limits: The Official Companion* (1986) by David J. Schow and Jeffrey Frentzen is about the series.   [JB/PN]

OUTER PLANETS Relatively little attention has been paid in sf to the planets beyond Jupiter. Of them only Saturn was known to the ancients – Uranus was discovered in 1781, Neptune in 1846 and Pluto in 1930 – and it is therefore the only outer planet featured in Athanasius KIRCHER's and Emanuel SWEDENBORG's interplanetary tours. Uranus, however, is included in the anonymous *Journeys into the Moon, Several Planets and the Sun: History of a Female Somnambulist* (**1837**). The only object beyond Jupiter that has made significant appeal to speculative writers as a possible abode for life is Saturn's major moon Titan, though the fascinating rings have provoked a good deal of interest from interplanetary passers-by. Pluto has come in for a certain amount of special attention as the Ultima Thule of the Solar System, although as much – if not more – interest has been shown in the possibility of there being a 10th planet even further out.

Saturn was visited, en route to Earth, by VOLTAIRE's tourist from Sirius in *Micromégas* (1750; **1952**), and a Saturnian accompanied him on his sightseeing trip. It was one of the major worlds featured in J.B. Fayette's anonymously published *The Experiences of Eon and Eona* (**1886**); and in John Jacob ASTOR's *A Journey in Other Worlds* (**1894**) it is the home of the spirits, who confirm the truth of the theological beliefs of travellers from a future Earth. Roy ROCK-WOOD's series of juvenile interplanetary novels extended thus far in *By Spaceship to Saturn* (**1935**), but relatively few PULP-MAGAZINE writers followed suit. Arthur K. BARNES's *Interplanetary Hunter* (1937-46; fixup **1956**) ventured beyond Jupiter on two occasions, but Stanley G. WEINBAUM was the only early pulp writer of any real significance to explore the outer planets, in "Flight on Titan" (1935), "The Planet of Doubt" (1935) – one of the rare stories set on Uranus – and "The Red Peri" (1935), a SPACE OPERA set partly on Pluto. Other pulp stories set in the outer reaches include J.M. WALSH's "The Vanguard to Neptune" (1932), Wallace WEST's "En Route to Pluto" (1936), Raymond Z. GALLUN's "Raiders of Saturn's Rings" (1941) and Murray LEINSTER's "Pipeline to Pluto" (1945). One of Stanton A. COBLENTZ's SATIRES, *Into Plutonian Depths* (1931; **1950**), delved there, and Clifford D. SIMAK's *Cosmic Engineers* (1939; rev **1950**) begins near Pluto. By far and away the most significant role allotted to an outer planet in the speculative fiction of the pre-WWII period was, however, that given to Neptune by Olaf STAPLEDON in *Last and First Men* (**1930**) and *Last Men in London* (**1932**): in the very FAR FUTURE, the ultimate members of the human race are forced to make a new home there following the expansion of the Sun.

In the post-WWII period the outer planets occasionally featured in more serious speculative fictions. The rings of Saturn play a key part in Isaac ASIMOV's "The Martian Way" (1952), and Asimov returned to the same locale in his juvenile *Lucky Starr and the Rings of Saturn* (**1958**) as by Paul French. Another notable juvenile in which Saturn is an abode of life is Philip LATHAM's *Missing Men of Saturn* (**1953**). Elsewhere, Titan features much more prominently than its parent world. Alan E. NOURSE's *Trouble on Titan* (**1954**) is a juvenile novel about COLONIZATION of the satellite, the climactic scenes of Kurt VONNEGUT Jr's *The Sirens of Titan* (**1959**) take place there, and Titan is the location of huge ALIEN machines in Ben BOVA's *As on a Darkling Plain* (**1972**). A more fully described colony is featured in Arthur C. CLARKE's *Imperial Earth* (**1976**), and it is the home of the strange lifeform that provides the climax of Gregory BENFORD's and Gordon EKLUND's *If the Stars are Gods* (fixup **1977**). An artificial world hidden among the satellites of Saturn is the main locale of John VARLEY's **Gaean** trilogy begun with *Titan* (**1979**).

Pluto figures prominently in Algis BUDRYS's *Man of*

Earth (**1958**), and is the destination of the characters in Wilson TUCKER's *To the Tombaugh Station* (**1960**). It is the setting of Kim Stanley ROBINSON's mysterious artefact in *Icehenge* (**1984**), and the starting-point of the interplanetary tour featured in the same author's *The Memory of Whiteness* (**1985**), which zooms past Uranus and Neptune at considerable narrative pace. Neptune's moon Triton is the setting of Margaret ST CLAIR's "The Pillows" (1950) and Samuel R. DELANY's "ambiguous heterotopia" in *Triton* (**1976**). The "outer satellites" conduct a war against the inner planets in Alfred BESTER's *Tiger! Tiger!* (**1956** UK; rev vt *The Stars My Destination* US), but the reader never gets to visit them; a much more detailed conflict takes place in Cecelia HOLLAND's *Floating Worlds* (**1976**), in which the cities of the title float above Saturn and Uranus. Few of those space operas whose action is partly set in the more remote regions of the Solar System pause to take in much of the scenery, but notable recent exceptions include Colin GREENLAND's *Take Back Plenty* (**1990**) and Roger McBride ALLEN's *The Ring of Charon* (**1990**), both of which are partly set on Pluto's large moon Charon.

It has long been held in some quarters that a 10th planet is necessary to account for the orbital perturbations of Uranus, even after Neptune and Pluto are taken into account, and sf writers have occasionally dealt with the possibility. The protagonists of John W. CAMPBELL Jr's *The Planeteers* (1936-8; coll of linked stories **1966**) ultimately make their way there, and it is the setting for Henry KUTTNER's "We Guard the Black Planet" (1942). In Philip K. DICK's *Solar Lottery* (**1955**; vt *World of Chance*) members of an esoteric cult flee Earth in the hope of finding such a world. Edmund COOPER's *The Tenth Planet* (**1973**) plants an advanced civilization there. Contrastingly, in *Lucifer's Hammer* (**1977**) by Larry NIVEN and Jerry POURNELLE it is a much more remote GAS GIANT, whose gravity perturbs the orbit of a comet, deflecting it towards Earth. Perhaps more intriguing than the notion of a 10th planet is speculation about the Solar System's diffuse cometary "halo". An extravagant sf version of this is developed in *The Reefs of Space* (**1964**) by Frederik POHL and Jack WILLIAMSON, which features a particularly imaginative reef life-system. Clarke's *Imperial Earth* makes much of the possibility of life existing beyond Pluto, and Williamson made further use of the locale in *Lifeburst* (**1984**).

More recently, there has been discussion among astronomers of the possibility that the cause of the orbital perturbations among the outer planets might instead be another star a couple of light years away; i.e., that the Sun might be not a singleton star but one element of a widely spaced binary (most stars are multiple rather than solitary), the other component being a dwarf star, a NEUTRON STAR or even a BLACK HOLE. Even a dwarf star would, at such a distance, be insignificant enough in our skies to make identification difficult. Or the cause might be a yet undetected nearby star heading in our direction, as suggested in

Asimov's *Nemesis* (**1989**).   [BS]

OUTLAND Film (1981). Ladd Co. Dir Peter Hyams, starring Sean Connery, Peter Boyle, Frances Stern-hagen. Screenplay Hyams. 109 mins. Colour.

A mining base on Io, third moon of Jupiter. The new marshal (Connery) discovers that the mine manager (Boyle), in a bid to increase production, is introducing powerful amphetamines which ulti-mately render the workers psychotic and suicidal. The manager hires assassins to kill the nosy marshal. The critical cliché that *O* is *High Noon* (1952) in space is absolutely true. This routine anti-capitalist adven-ture is lifted out of the ordinary by its richly textured setting (the art director was Malcolm Middleton) – dirty, crowded, and wholly convincing as an unromanticized future industrial settlement. There are also good performances from Sternhagen as a cantankerous lady doctor and Connery as the tired, middle-aged failure making good. The novelization is *Outland* * (**1981**) by Alan Dean FOSTER.   [PN]

OUTLANDS UK DIGEST-size magazine. 1 issue, Winter 1946. Published by Outlands Publications, Liverpool; ed Leslie J. Johnson. An abortive SEMIPROZINE of undistinguished fiction, subtitled "A Magazine for Adventurous Minds", *O* included stories by John Russell FEARN and Sydney J. BOUNDS (his first pub-lished story).   [MJE/FHP]

OUT OF THE DARKNESS ◊ Roger CORMAN.

OUT OF THE UNKNOWN UK tv series (1965-71). BBC TV. Prod Irene Shubik (seasons 1 and 2), Alan Bromly (seasons 3 and 4). Script editor Irene Shubik (seasons 1 and 2), Roger Parkes (seasons 3 and 4). Writers included Terry NATION, J.B. PRIESTLEY, Troy Kennedy Martin, Clive Exton, Julian Bond, Nigel KNEALE. Dirs included Michael Ferguson, Peter Sasdy, Philip Saville, Philip Dudley, Eric Hills. 4 seasons, 49 episodes, each 50 mins in 1st season, 60 mins thereafter. Seasons 1-2 b/w, thereafter colour.

This sf-anthology series, originated by Irene Shubik – previously story editor on OUT OF THIS WORLD (1962) – dramatized the work of many well known sf writers. Adapted stories and novels included *Immor-tality, Inc.* (**1958**) by Robert SHECKLEY, *Liar!* (1941; rev **1977** chap) by Isaac ASIMOV, "The Last Lonely Man" (1964) by John BRUNNER, "Beachhead" (1951) by Clifford D. SIMAK, "Random Quest" (1961) by John WYNDHAM, "The Little Black Bag" (1950) by C.M. KORNBLUTH, "Thirteen for Centaurus" (1962) by J.G. BALLARD, *The Naked Sun* (**1957**) by Asimov, "The Midas Plague" (1954) by Frederik POHL, "Andover and the Android" (1963) by Kate WILHELM, "The Yellow Pill" (1958) by Rog PHILLIPS, *Level 7* (**1959**) by Mordecai ROSHWALD and "The Machine Stops" (1909) by E.M. FORSTER. Despite budget limitations, the standard of production was often very high, and good actors were used; one episode was designed by Ridley SCOTT. The quality of the scripts varied, some of the writers assigned being unfamiliar with sf. After 3 seasons the BBC decided that the series lacked mass popularity, and for the 4th switched it from sf to

supernatural stories, all but one being original tele-plays.   [PN/JB]

OUT OF THIS WORLD 1. US tv series (1952). ABC TV. Prod Milton Kaye. Narrated Jackson Beck. 1 season, 25min episodes. B/w.

OOTW hovered between sf and lectures on science. In episode 3, for example, we saw a young couple in 1993 going to the Moon for a vacation and then telephoning their relations on Earth. Between these dramatized segments the narrator discussed with a scientist, Robert R. Cole, the actual possibilities of space travel and conditions on the Moon.

2. UK tv series (1962). ABC TV. Prod Leonard White. Story editor Irene Shubik. 13 50min episodes. B/w.

This short-lived but relatively ambitious sf-anthology series – the first such in the UK – was hosted by Boris Karloff (1887-1969). Stories adapted for the series included *Little Lost Robot* (1947; rev **1977** chap) by Isaac ASIMOV, "The Cold Equations" (1954) by Tom GODWIN, "Impostor" (1953) by Philip K. DICK and "Pictures Don't Lie" (1951) by Katherine MAC-LEAN. Of the two original teleplays used, one was "Botany Bay" by Terry NATION, later to become a driving force behind DR WHO. *OOTW*'s success inspired Shubik to make the similar (but better) OUT OF THE UNKNOWN series 3 years later, this time for the BBC rather than commercial tv.   [JB]

OUT OF THIS WORLD ADVENTURES US PULP MAGAZINE. 2 issues, July 1950 and Dec 1950, pub-lished by Avon Periodicals; ed Donald A. WOLLHEIM. #1 included an impressive line-up of authors: A. Bertram CHANDLER, Ray CUMMINGS, Lester DEL REY, Kris NEVILLE, Mack REYNOLDS, William TENN and A.E. VAN VOGT. The stories, however, were not the authors' best, and Chandler was the only writer of equivalent stature in #2. An unusual feature was a 32pp COMICS section in colour (#2 of the Canadian edition included a different comics section from that in the US edition). The comics feature proved not to be the expected selling point, and the magazine flopped.   [MJE]

OOTWA should not be confused with the UK weird-fiction DIGEST magazine *Out of this World* (2 issues 1954-5), published by John Spencer & Co. (◊ BADGER BOOKS).   [MJE]

OUTSIDER ◊ FINLAND.

OVERLAND MONTHLY, THE US magazine founded by Bret Harte (1836-1902), published in San Francisco by A. Roman & Co., monthly, July 1868-Dec 1875, then again Jan 1883-July 1935. Under the editorship of Millicent W. Shinn a special "Twentieth Century" issue – June 1890 – contained articles and essays all directly related to Edward BELLAMY's then much discussed work *Looking Backward, 2000-1887* (**1888**). In addition, its 6 fiction contributions were all sf, including an early translation of Kurd LASSWITZ (Chapter 1 of "Bis zum Nullpunkt des Seins" [1871], under the title "Pictures out of the Future"). This is the earliest known case of a general magazine devoting an issue exclusively to sf. *OM* is known for its publication of poetry and fiction by Clark Ashton SMITH in the 1910s and 1920s, and for several "Yellow Peril" stories by little-known authors.   [JE/PN]

OVERPOPULATION In 1798 the UK economist Thomas R. Malthus (1766-1834) published his *Essay on the Principle of Population as it Affects the Future Improvement of Society*, arguing that a UTOPIAN situation of peace and plenty would be impossible to achieve because the tendency of populations, in the absence of the checks of war, famine and plague, to increase exponentially would result in society's continually outgrowing its resources. In the second edition (1803), replying to criticism, he introduced another hypothetical check: voluntary restriction of population by the exercise of "moral restraint". But Malthus had little faith in the effectiveness of moral restraint, and most modern sf writers agree with him.

Although the amended Malthusian argument was (and is) logically unassailable, it was ignored or even attacked by most speculative writers even after it had become known that world population was indeed increasing exponentially. Richard Whiteing (1840-1928) brought the entire population of the world to the Isle of Wight to prove that anxiety about overpopulation was, as his title stated, *All Moonshine* (1907). It was not until the 1960s that awareness of the population problem resurfaced, probably as a consequence of an already-widespread DYSTOPIAN pessimism (◊ OPTIMISM AND PESSIMISM), which it then helped to maintain and amplify. The major nonfiction books involved in the popularization of the issue were *The Population Bomb* (1968) by Paul Ehrlich and *The Limits to Growth: A Report for the Club of Rome's Project on the Predicament of Mankind* (1972) by D.H. Meadows *et al*.

Although MARVEL SCIENCE STORIES published in its Nov 1951 issue a "symposium" on the subject of whether the world's population should be strategically limited, the question was at that time unexplored in sf. C.M. KORNBLUTH's "The Marching Morons" (1951), depicting a future in which the intelligentsia have prudently exercised birth control while the *lumpenproletariat* have multiplied unrestrainedly, is a black comedy on the theme of eugenics rather than of overpopulation. In Kurt VONNEGUT Jr's equally black comedy, "The Big Trip up Yonder" (1954), overpopulation is the result of technologies of longevity rather than ordinary increase. Overpopulated milieux became gradually more evident in 1950s sf. Isaac ASIMOV, one of the first sf writers to become anxious about the matter, displayed one such in *The Caves of Steel* (1954). Frederik POHL produced the first of many ironic fantasies of corrective mass homicide in "The Census Takers" (1956); Robert SILVERBERG's *Master of Life and Death* (1957) takes the notion of institutionalized population control more seriously; and Kornbluth's "Shark Ship" (1958) is a melodramatic horror story of overpopulation and resultant POLLUTION. An effectively understated treatment of

the theme is J.G. BALLARD's "Billenium" (1961), which presents a simple picture of the slow shrinkage of personal space. A curiously ambivalent approach is adopted in Lester DEL REY's *The Eleventh Commandment* (1962), which begins as a polemic against overfertility but concludes with a SOCIAL-DARWINIST volte-face. The most powerful attempt to confront the issue squarely and in some detail was Harry HARRISON's *Make Room! Make Room!* (1966), a novel whose thrust was entirely lost when it was filmed as SOYLENT GREEN (1973). A major novel from India, *The Wind Obeys Lama Toru* (1967) by LEE TUNG, quickly followed.

There are three aspects to the population problem: the exhaustion of resources; the destruction of the environment by pollution; and the social problems of living in crowded conditions. The first two aspects form the basis of most extrapolations of the problem, including *A Torrent of Faces* (1968) by James BLISH and Norman L. KNIGHT and *The Sheep Look Up* (1972) by John BRUNNER, and such black comedies as "The People Trap" (1968) by Robert SHECKLEY and "The Big Space Fuck" (1972) by Vonnegut. The third aspect comes into sharper focus in *Stand on Zanzibar* (1968) by Brunner, *The World Inside* (1972) by Silverberg, *334* (1972) by Thomas M. DISCH and *My Petition for More Space* (1974) by John HERSEY. Because sf writers had not considered the problem until it was imminent, the quest for hypothetical solutions was difficult, and many stories hysterically allege that it is already too late to act effectively. Such traditional sf myths as the escape into space lack plausibility in the context of a problem so immediate, as demonstrated by such stories as Blish's "We All Die Naked" (1969). Confidence in moral restraint, even aided by birth control (which Malthus forbore to propose), was so low that sf stories exploring possible solutions almost always concern themselves with the setting up of Draconian prohibitions or with various forms of overt and covert culling. Stories of grotesque mass homicide include, in addition to those cited above, D.G. COMPTON's *The Quality of Mercy* (1965), William F. NOLAN's and George Clayton JOHNSON's *Logan's Run* (1967), Leonard C. LEWIN's *Triage* (1972), Piers ANTHONY's *Triple Detente* (1974), Chelsea Quinn YARBRO's *Time of the Fourth Horseman* (1976) and Snoo WILSON's *Space-ache* (1984). Vonnegut's "Welcome to the Monkey House" (1968) mockingly envisages a future in which reproduction is discouraged by the use of bromides, but most speculations in this vein are more gruesomely inclined. Suggested solutions not involving mass murder are rare, and not usually to be taken seriously; a notable example is that featured in Philip José FARMER's *Dayworld* (1985) and its sequels, in which every person is conscious only one day a week, spending the remaining six in suspended animation, thus effectively packing seven people into one person's space. A rare application of Malthusian thinking to an ALIEN situation is employed in *The Mote in God's Eye* (1974) by Larry NIVEN and Jerry E. POURNELLE, in which a species for whom birth control is impossible has negative checks built in at the biological level.

Although the real-world situation grows worse each passing day, the fashionability of overpopulation stories in sf has waned dramatically since 1980, partly in accordance with a general tendency to skip over the most frightening problems of the NEAR FUTURE and partly because of the absorption of the population problem into a more general sense of impending ecocatastrophe (◊ ECOLOGY). Perhaps, though, the problem does not really deserve to be considered urgent. As Malthus pointed out, the situation is self-correcting; when there are more people than the world can accommodate, the surplus will inevitably die – one way, or another.

An interesting but now quaintly dated anthology accurately reflecting the mood at the height of the panic is *Voyages: Scenarios for a Ship Called Earth* (anth **1971**) ed Bob Sauer, published by BALLANTINE BOOKS for the Zero Population Growth movement. [BS]

See also: POLITICS; PREDICTION; SOCIOLOGY.

OVERTON, MAX [s] ◊ Don WILCOX.

OWEN, DEAN Pseudonym of US writer Dudley Dean McGaughy (? -), whose routine novelizations of horror and sf films are *The Brides of Dracula* ∗ (**1960**), *Konga* ∗ (**1960**), *Reptilicus* ∗ (**1961**) and *End of the World* ∗ (**1962**), based on PANIC IN YEAR ZERO! (1962), a film in turn based, without acknowledgement, on two short stories by Ward MOORE. Monarch Books's habit of publishing soft-porn adaptations of chaste movies led to at least one court case (◊ REPTILICUS). [JC/PN]

OWINGS, MARK (1945-   ) US bibliographer and SMALL-PRESS publisher; with Jack L. CHALKER, he was involved for a period with MIRAGE PRESS, which published his magnum opus, *The Index to the Science-Fantasy Publishers* (**1966** chap; rev 1966; vastly exp, vt *The Science-Fantasy Publishers: A Critical and Bibliographic History* 1991), all edns with Chalker (*whom see for further details*). Other books through Mirage included *The Necronomicon: A Study* (**1967** chap), solo, and *The Revised H.P. Lovecraft Bibliography* (**1973** chap) with Chalker. With Chalker and Ted Pauls, MO founded Croatan House, through which he published *Robert A. Heinlein: A Bibliography* (**1973** chap) and *James H. Schmitz: A Bibliography* (**1973** chap). *Murray Leinster (Will F. Jenkins): A Bibliography* (**1970** chap), *The Electric Bibliograph, Part I: Clifford D. Simak* (**1971** chap), *Poul Anderson: Bibliography* (**1973** chap) and *A Catalog of Lovecraftiana: The Grill/Binkin Collection* (**1975** chap) with Irving Binkin were all published elsewhere. [JC]

PADGETT, LEWIS ◊ Henry KUTTNER; C.L. MOORE.

PAGE, KATHY (1958-) UK writer whose first novels – *Back in the First Person* (**1986**) and *The Unborn Dreams of Clara Riley* (**1987**) – are associational, though tinged with elements of literary fantasy. *Island Paradise* (**1989**), set 100 years after the Unfought War, promulgates an ambiguous worldwide UTOPIA whose citizens enjoy lives uncluttered by violence, but are bullied to die soon after they reach 50. Some of the stories assembled in *As in Music and Other Stories* (coll **1990**) are fantasy or sf. KP's style moves from a kind of numb austerity into moments of cautious lyricism. [JC]

PAGE, NORVELL W. (1904-1961) US writer who specialized during the 1930s in hero/villain PULP MAGAZINES, much of his production being novel-length stories for *The* SPIDER, featuring the eponymous SUPERHERO. The **Spider** sequence was created in competition with the somewhat more successful **Shadow** tales, mostly written for *The Shadow* magazine by Walter B. GIBSON. Under the house name Grant STOCKBRIDGE NWP wrote more than 100 **Spider** tales, many of whose plots verged into the supernatural and sf; those eventually published in book form include *Wings of the Black Death* (**1933**; **1969**), *City of Flaming Shadows* **1934**; **1970**), *Builders of the Black Empire* (**1934**; **1980**), *City Destroyer* (**1935**; **1975**), *Hordes of the Red Butcher* (**1935**; **1975**), *Master of the Death Madness* (**1935**; **1980**), *Overlord of the Damned* (**1935**; **1980**), *Death Reign of the Vampire King* (**1935**; **1975**) and *Death and the Spider* (**1942**; **1975**). As Randolph Craig, NWP created two spin-offs from *The Spider*, *The* OCTOPUS and *The* SCORPION, neither of which extended past a single story; these were subsequently published as *The Octopus* (**1939** as "The City Condemned to Hell"; **1976** chap) and *The Scorpion* (**1939** as "Satan's Incubator"; **1975** chap).

Under his own name NWP contributed 3 long stories to UNKNOWN in its first year: "But without Horns" (**1940**) concerns a MUTANT who uses his PSI POWERS to induce religious worship in those who come into contact with him; *Flame Winds* (**1939**; **1969**) and *Sons of the Bear-God* (**1939**; **1969**) are SWORD-AND-SORCERY novels whose hero is based on Prester John. During WWII NWP took a post writing government reports; afterwards he worked for the Atomic Energy Commission. [MJE/JC]

See also: GODS AND DEMONS.

PAGE, THOMAS (WALKER IV) (1942-) US writer whose first novel was *The Hepahaestus Plague* (**1973**), filmed as BUG (1975), a tale which starts strongly, with vivid descriptions of the effect of an irruption from underground of a new species of beetle capable of emitting fire, but which weakens when it begins to deal with a SCIENTIST who becomes overfascinated with these beetles, which seem to possess a kind of group intelligence. His later novels – *The Spirit* (**1977**), *Sigmet Active* (**1978**) and *The Man who Would not Die* (**1981**) – were borderline sf. [JC]

PAGERY, FRANÇOIS ◊ Gérard KLEIN.

PAGET, JOHN ◊ John AIKEN.

PAGETTI, CARLO (1945-) Italian critic, Professor of English Literature at the University of Turin. His study of sf *Il senso del futuro: la fantascienza nella letteratura Americana* ["The Sense of the Future: Science Fiction in American Literature"] (**1970**) is the first serious literary study of sf by an Italian. Subsequent books are *I Marziani alla corte della Regina Vittoria* ["Martians at the Court of Queen Victoria"] (**1986**), on H.G. WELLS's SCIENTIFIC ROMANCES, and *Cittadini di un assurdo universo* ["Citizens of an Absurd Universe"] (coll **1989**), essays on Ambrose BIERCE, Katharine BURDEKIN, H.P. LOVECRAFT, Edgar Allan POE and Mark TWAIN. He ed *Nel tempo del sogno* ["In the Time of the Dream"] (anth **1988**), has had articles on Wells, Philip K. DICK and Burdekin translated in SCIENCE-FICTION STUDIES, and is editor of a critical series in book form devoted to sf, **La città e le stelle** ["The City and the Stars"]. He has published a collection of short stories, mostly fantasy, *Favole di lontananza*

["Fables of Distance"] (coll **1989**). He wrote the entry on ITALY in this volume. [PN]

See also: CRITICAL AND HISTORICAL WORKS ABOUT SF.

PAIGE, RICHARD ◊ Dean R. KOONTZ.

PAIN, BARRY (ERIC ODELL) (1864-1928) UK writer best known for the supernatural tales assembled in volumes like *Stories in the Dark* (coll **1901**), and for humorous fiction in which he uneasily condescended to the lower orders. He frequently made superficial use of sf devices and motifs – e.g., the IMMORTALITY of the protagonist of *Robinson Crusoe's Return* (**1906**; rev vt *The Return and Supperizing Reception of Robinson Crusoe of York, Parrot-Tamer* 1921) facilitates the making of a number of satirical points about modern England – and occasionally a tale depends on these devices. *An Exchange of Souls* (**1911**) posits a scientific rationale for the said exchange. The title story of *The New Gulliver and Other Stories* (coll **1913**) takes its hero to a futuristic UTOPIA in Ultima Thule. [JC]

Other works: *In a Canadian Canoe* (coll **1891**); *Stories and Interludes* (coll **1892**); *The One Before* (**1902**); *Three Fantasies* (coll **1904**); *The Diary of a Baby: Being a Free Record of the Unconscious Thought of Rosalys Ysolde Smith Aged One Year* (**1907**); *The Shadow of the Unseen* (**1907**) with James BLYTH; *Here and Hereafter* (coll **1911**); *Stories in Grey* (coll **1911**); *Going Home: Being the Fantastical Romance of the Girl with Angel Eyes and the Man who Had Wings* (**1921**); *Short Stories of To-day and Yesterday* (coll **1928**).

PAINE, ALBERT B(IGELOW) (1861-1937) US writer best remembered as Mark TWAIN's confidant and unconscionable expurgator: after Twain's death he published mutilated editions of *The Mysterious Stranger* (**1916**) and *Mark Twain's Autobiography* (**1924**). ABP was primarily a writer and editor of children's fiction. *The Mystery of Evelin Delorme: A Hypnotic Story* (**1894**) exploits the late 19th century's prurient fascination with split personalities, the eponymous heroine committing suicide when her socially unacceptable self comes out. In *The Great White Way* (**1901**) a warm, UTOPIAN, Antarctic LOST WORLD peopled by telepaths is discovered by a businessman and a real-estate developer, who are forced to flee when the latter's intentions are revealed. [JC]

PAINE, LAURAN (BOSWORTH) (1916-) US rancher and author, extraordinarily prolific in several fields, with nearly 1000 books under his own name and 85 pseudonyms, almost all for ROBERT HALE LIMITED, over 600 of them Westerns and a very few of them sf. *This Time Tomorrow* (**1963**) was published under his own name; further routine SPACE OPERAS are: *Focolor* (**1973**) as by Roy Ainsworthy; *A Crack in Time* (**1971**), *The Undine* (**1972**), *Another View* (**1972**), *Bannister's Z-Matter* (**1973**) and *The Underground Men* (**1975**) as by Mark Carrel; and *The Harbinger* (**1972**), *The Misplaced Psyche* (**1973**) and *Kernel of Death* (**1973**) as by Troy Howard. [JC]

PAINTER, THOMAS (? -?) US writer who collaborated with Alexander LAING (*whom see for details*) on *The Motives of Nicholas Holtz, being the Weird*

Tale of the Ironville Virus (**1936**; vt *The Glass Centipede, Retold from the Original Sources* 1936 UK). [PN]

PAIRAULT, PIERRE [r] ◊ Stefan WUL.

PAL, GEORGE (1908-1980) Hungarian film producer, based in the USA since 1940, best known for his sf and fantasy films, for which he received a NEBULA Special Award in 1976. Trained as an illustrator in Budapest, GP decided to specialize in animation, and in 1931 moved to Germany, where he worked at the UFA studios. When Hitler came to power GP went to Paris, where he soon became very successful with a series of animated commercials and entertainment films, his **Puppetoons**. After emigrating to the USA he set up a **Puppetoon** unit at Paramount Studios.

His first live-action film was *The Great Rupert* (1949) dir Irving Pichel, starring Jimmy Durante and an animated squirrel. He then started work on DESTINA-TION MOON (1950) dir Pichel, which was so successful – it initiated the sf film boom of the 1950s – that GP immediately chose another sf subject for his next film, WHEN WORLDS COLLIDE (1951) dir Rudolph Maté. This was followed by WAR OF THE WORLDS (1953) dir Byron HASKIN, *The Naked Jungle* (1954) and CONQUEST OF SPACE (1955), both dir Haskin, ATLANTIS, THE LOST CONTINENT (1959) and *The* TIME MACHINE (1960), both dir GP, and *The* POWER (1968) dir Haskin and GP. He also made a number of pure fantasy films during this period, including *Tom Thumb* (1958) and *The Seven Faces of Dr Lao* (1964). His last film was DOC SAVAGE: THE MAN OF BRONZE (1974) dir Michael Anderson.

GP's dominant interest in special effects often led to other aspects of his films, including scripts and acting, being neglected. Most of his productions, however, possess a colourful bravura that distracts attention from their shortcomings, and he has on occasion produced memorable images. [JB]

See also: CINEMA; MOON; ROCKETS.

PALLANDER, EDWIN (? -?) UK author of whom nothing is known except that he published several books and collaborated with Ellsworth DOUG-LASS on one story, "The Wheels of Dr Gynochio Gyves" (1899). *Across the Zodiac: A Story of Adventure* (**1896**) is a Vernean interplanetary romance which carries its three protagonists (VERNE's usual complement) through the Solar System in a spaceship captained by a mad scientist. *The Adventures of a Micro-Man* (**1902**), one of the tales of miniaturization common to the period (◊ GREAT AND SMALL), shrinks its protagonists to mites, subjecting them to adventures before they grow again. [JC]

PALLEN, CONDÉ B(ENOIST) (1858-1929) US writer and editor; in the latter capacity he was one of the editors, with C.G. Herbermann and others, of *The Catholic Encyclopedia* (15 vols **1907-18**). *Crucible Island: A Romance, an Adventure and an Experiment* (**1919**), a DYSTOPIA, describes the disillusioning experiences of a young radical who is transported to Schlectland, where socialism has been allowed to run rampant, and who comes to his senses while falling in love with the daughter of a longtime resident. They escape to the USA. *En passant*, points are scored against FEMINISM and the Irish. In *Ghost House* (**1928**) a device is invented which reads details of a murder from the walls. [JC]

PALMER, DAVID (REAY) (1941-   ) US writer whose first story, the impressive "Emergence" for *ASF* in 1981, was expanded as *Emergence* (fixup **1984**), attracting some notice for its depiction of a USA suffering the consequences of a nuclear HOLOCAUST, and for its juvenile heroine, who represents a superior form of *Homo sapiens* and whose transcribed voice dominates the tale; some found her obnoxiously reminiscent of the narrator of Robert A. HEINLEIN's *The Moon is a Harsh Mistress* (**1966**). The novel won the Compton Crook/Stephen Tall Memorial Award (◊ AWARDS). DP's taste for protagonists whose special gifts legitimize their behaviour also helped shape his second novel, *Threshold* (**1985**), in which the Galaxy is saved. [JC]

See also: PSI POWERS; SUPERMAN.

PALMER, JANE (1946-   ) UK writer and illustrator who began writing sf with *The Planet Dweller* (**1985**) which, with its sequel *Moving Moosevan* (**1990**), presents a mildly comic set of parodies of sf tropes in dealing with alien INVASIONS and the like. A somewhat greater force of imagination is demonstrated in *The Watcher* (**1986**), which features brave young girls, a mysterious survivor from Victorian times, an ANDROID which longs for human status, and the rulers of the Universe. [JC]

PALMER, RAYMOND A(RTHUR) (1910-1977) US author and editor. His childhood was plagued by serious accidents, and in adulthood he stood only 4ft tall and was hunchbacked, but he never allowed physical stress to affect his career. He was an active sf fan in the 1930s – he is credited with publishing the first sf FANZINE, *The Comet*, in 1930 – and was the author of a fair number of stories, beginning with "The Time Ray of Jandra" for WONDER STORIES in 1930; some later tales were published as by Henry Gade, Frank Paton, J.W. Pelkie, A.R. STEBER and Morris J. Steele. After the death of Stanley G. WEINBAUM in 1935, RAP edited and published a memorial collection of his stories, *Dawn of Flame and Other Stories* (coll **1936**); RAP's only other book was *Strange Offering* (anth *c*1945 chap UK) with Otis Adelbert KLINE.

It was as an editor that RAP would make his name. When AMAZING STORIES was bought by the Chicago-based ZIFF-DAVIS in 1938 it was decided to replace T. O'Conor SLOANE as editor. RAP, a resident of nearby Milwaukee, was recommended for the job and was appointed. *AMZ* was in a moribund state by this time; RAP made it livelier, albeit with a more overtly juvenile slant, and it revived. He published work by Edgar Rice BURROUGHS and, in 1939, Isaac ASIMOV's first story, "Marooned off Vesta"; in the same year he began a companion magazine, FANTASTIC ADVENTURES. The vigour of his early editing work, though evident at the time and in retrospect, was submerged during the 1940s by the notoriety he achieved with his

promotion as fact of the stories of Richard S. SHAVER. RAP claimed that the popularity of the "Shaver Mystery" gave *AMZ* the highest circulation ever achieved by an SF MAGAZINE. His interest in PSEUDO-SCIENCE and the occult widened; in 1948, while still employed at Ziff-Davis, he started his own occult magazine, *Fate*, which has proved enduringly successful.

In 1949 he established his own sf magazine, OTHER WORLDS (using the editorial pseudonym Robert N. Webster on the first issue), and shortly afterwards he left Ziff-Davis. In 1950 he began a companion magazine, IMAGINATION, in this case lending his name as a cover for William L. HAMLING, who edited the journal while still officially working for Ziff-Davis. After another severe accident, RAP sold *Imagination* to Hamling, while Bea Mahaffey edited *Other Worlds*. On his recovery in 1953, RAP took over the magazine UNIVERSE SCIENCE FICTION and started a companion, SCIENCE STORIES; meanwhile *Other Worlds* was suspended. *Science Stories* was short-lived, and in 1955 RAP changed the title of *Universe* to *Other Worlds*, continuing the *Universe* numeration. The magazine began to feature more and more UFO material, and in 1957 was retitled *Flying Saucers from Other Worlds*, RAP deciding to concentrate all his energies on UFOs and the occult. He later explained that the bewildering title changes of his magazines resulted in part from financial difficulties and the need to throw up smokescreens. A last RAP publication, including UFO and Shaver material, was *The* HIDDEN WORLD. [MJE/JC]

PALMER PUBLICATIONS, INC. ◊ OTHER WORLDS; SCIENCE STORIES; UNIVERSE SCIENCE FICTION.

PALTOCK, ROBERT (1697-1767) UK lawyer and writer, known mainly for *The Life and Adventures of Peter Wilkins, a Cornish Man: Relating Particularly his Shipwreck Near the South Pole; his Wonderful Passage Thro' a Subterranean Cavern into a Kind of New World; His There Meeting with a Gawry or Flying Woman* (**1751**), which ranks in popularity as an 18th-century imaginary voyage behind only Daniel DEFOE's *Robinson Crusoe* (**1719**) and Jonathan SWIFT's *Gulliver's Travels* (**1726**). After discovering a race of winged people, Wilkins breeds with them and teaches them about civilization and the arts of war, while himself manufacturing a flying machine in which he returns, now an old man, to tell his tale. There have been many reprints of the novel, variously titled (e.g., *The Unrivalled Adventures of that Great Aeronaut and Glum, Peter Wilkins* 1802) and almost always cut. [JC]

PALUMBO, DENNIS (JAMES) (1929-   ) US writer in whose sf novel, *City Wars* (**1979**), set decades after The Levelling when a nuclear HOLOCAUST flattened the USA, several seceding city-states engage in a Great War which leads, through a terminal conflict between New York and Chicago, towards ultimate extinction. The cast-members, who include MUTANTS called "lunks" and a woman called Cassandra, find no solace in the new world. [JC]

PAN ◊ Leslie BERESFORD.

PANGBORN, EDGAR (1909-1976) US writer whose publishing career began with *A-100: A Mystery Story* (**1930**) as by Bruce Harrison, and other non-genre work. He published his first sf story, the famous "Angel's Egg", for *Gal* as late as 1951. In his first sf novel, *West of the Sun* (**1953**), six shipwrecked humans found a UTOPIAN colony on the planet Lucifer in association with two native species. When the rescue ship eventually arrives, they decide to stick with the society they have constructed. The reflective conclusion of this novel was typical of EP's work. In *A Mirror for Observers* (**1954**), which won the 1955 INTERNATIONAL FANTASY AWARD, Mars has been guiding humanity into the light of civilization for thousands of years, but matters approach crisis in the 20th century when two Martian observers contest for control over a human boy genius, a potential ethical innovator; the good Martian wins. In both novels – but not always in his career – EP's gracious literacy usually overcomes a tendency towards cloying sententiousness.

After two fine non-genre novels – *Wilderness of Spring* (**1958**) and *The Trial of Callista Blake* (**1961**), a moving courtroom drama – EP created his most successful and sustained work, the **Davy** sequence, comprising, by rough internal chronology, *The Company of Glory* (coll of linked stories **1975**), most of the stories assembled in *Still I Persist in Wondering* (coll **1978**), the loosely related *The Judgment of Eve* (see below), and *Davy* (fixup **1964**). The sequence is set in a USA devastated by a nuclear HOLOCAUST, whose immediate consequences dominate – at times harshly – the first volumes. By the time of Davy's birth, 250 years later, the land has long been balkanized into feudal enclaves, rather romantically conceived, and Davy's picaresque adventures (which he recounts in retirement) generate what might be called a kind of nostalgia for a livable future, though at the same time it is clear that Davy, and those he inspires, will necessarily begin to rebuild a more complex world. Set in the same universe, *The Judgment of Eve* (**1966**) is less convincingly constructed in mythopoeic terms, as Eve tries to choose among the lifestyles of her disparate male suitors. The trek on which she consequently sends them, in order to find out the meaning of love, probably represents the deepest of EP's frequent descents into distinctly uneasy bombast. When, however, he was able to control himself – the early novels, most of **Davy**, and most of the stories in *Good Neighbors and Other Strangers* (coll **1972**) sidestep these pitfalls – the inherent though sometimes selfconsciously rural decency of his view of life won through. [JC]

About the author: *Edgar Pangborn: A Bibliography* (**1985** chap) by Gordon BENSON Jr.

See also: ALIENS; ARTS; CHILDREN IN SF; GALAXY SCIENCE FICTION; MUSIC; MUTANTS; PASTORAL.

PANIC IN YEAR ZERO! (vt *End of the World*) Film (1962). Alta Vista/AIP. Dir Ray Milland, starring Milland, Jean Hagen, Frankie Avalon, Mary Mitchell. Screenplay Jay Simms, John Morton, story by Simms, based (without credit) on the stories "Lot" (1953) and "Lot's Daughter" (1954) by Ward MOORE. 92 mins. B/w.

This cynical, violent film – one of the earliest examples of the SURVIVALIST ethos in cinema – shows how a typical US family have to act to survive the aftermath of an atomic HOLOCAUST: by trusting no one and shooting first. The father quickly, and almost gleefully, reverts to being a ruthless "natural survivor" who will let nothing stand in the way of getting his family to safety after Los Angeles has been A-bombed. The escape along roads jammed with panicking traffic is strongly done, but thereafter the film subsides into clumsy adventure in the mountains; it is inferior to, and lacks the sexual reverberations of, the stories on which it was loosely based, though it retains some biblical parallels. The novelization is *End of the World* ∗ (**1962**) by Dean OWEN, and this was also the title of the film's re-release. [JB/PN]

PANICO EN EL TRANSIBERIANO (vt *Horror Express*) Film (1972). Granada/Benmar. Dir Eugenio Martin, starring Peter Cushing, Christopher Lee, Telly Savalas. Screenplay Arnaud d'Usseau, Julian Halevey. 90 mins, cut to 88 mins. Colour.

In this Spanish/UK coproduction the year is 1906. The body of an apparent "missing link", dug up in China by an anthropologist (Lee), comes to life on the Trans-Siberian Express and turns out to be an ALIEN who crash-landed on Earth eons ago. He has the power to transfer his personality from one body to another, and also to absorb people's personalities. The film is slick and amusing, and moves so fast that there is little time to dwell on its absurdities. It came into being only because the producer bought two model trains that had been used in the epic *Nicholas and Alexandra* (1971) and had a script written around them. The direction is in routine exploitation-movie style, but the lively script has some surprising turns. [JB/PN]

PANSHIN, ALEXEI (A.) (1940-   ) US writer, initially most active as an sf fan, in this role doing considerable writing and editing, for which he won a HUGO in 1967. He began publishing sf stories in 1963 with "Down to the Worlds of Men" for *If*, and soon became an active author of both fiction and criticism. The story "Dark Conception" (1964), as by Louis J.A. Adams, was written in collaboration with Joe L. HENSLEY. AP's short work has been assembled as *Farewell to Yesterday's Tomorrow* (coll **1975**; with "Lady Sunshine and the Magon of Beatus" added, rev 1976) and *Transmutations: A Book of Personal Alchemy* (coll **1982**). His first novel, *Rite of Passage* (**1963** *If* as "Down to the Worlds of Men"; exp **1968**), which won a 1968 NEBULA, remains his only significant singleton. It is a complex and expertly told novel, making adroit use of the basic rite-of-passage structure (◊ POCKET UNIVERSE) that underlies almost all tales set in GENERATION STARSHIPS; the fact that in this instance the asteroid-ship is capable of FASTER-THAN-LIGHT speeds may modify the consciousness of the protagonists – they have not been travelling long enough to forget their origins – but does not make the venue itself seem any less constrictive. The heroine must progress from childhood into questioning adulthood via a dangerous trial conducted on the colony planet which her ship – one of eight containing the survivors of the destruction of Earth 150 years earlier – is currently monitoring. Surviving her ordeal, she not only comes into her own as a person, but validly (as in the classic model) comes to question the stratified "adult" quasidemocracy of the ship. AP then wrote the **Anthony Villiers** series of SPACE OPERAS about a lordly adventurer and his alien companion Torve the Trog: *Star Well* (**1968**), *The Thurb Revolution* (**1968**) and *Masque World* (**1969**). The spoofing of sf's PULP-MAGAZINE conventions was amusing and without malice and the echoes of Leslie CHARTERIS's **Saint** were enjoyable, but the series lacked the energy of its predecessor. As a writer of sf, AP then fell relatively quiet.

Heinlein in Dimension: A Critical Analysis (**1968**), a comprehensive study of the works of Robert A. HEINLEIN, was perhaps the most thorough and literate book on a US sf writer written to that date. It breaks its subject's career into the 3 phases (1940-42; 1947-58; after 1958) that every subsequent critic has utilized, arguing the superior merit of the later juveniles, and presenting a case for thinking of his later work as inferior. In the introduction to his first collection, AP credited his wife, Cory PANSHIN (married 1969), as his collaborator on some of his stories, and announced that from 1975 all future work would be jointly signed. Much of the Panshins' joint criticism first appeared in *Fantastic*, and some of these pieces, along with others, appeared in *SF in Dimension* (coll **1976**; exp 1980) as by both authors, as did *Mondi interiori* ["Interior Worlds"] (**1978** Italy) which, it is understood, contained material later developed by the Panshins into their Hugo-winning magnum opus, *The World Beyond the Hill: Science Fiction and the Quest for Transcendence* (**1989**), a massive and coherent history of sf whose sustaining argument – that sf answered the world's need for a transcendent domain through the creation of galactic venues and concerns beyond the "village" of Earth – made inevitable its narrative halt at the year 1945, just at the end of the GOLDEN AGE chaired by John W. CAMPBELL Jr. So clear a cognitive strategy may have engendered a too-ruthless clarity of view – and an all too simple acceptance of the notion of Progress – but the detailed exegeses of critically neglected writers like E.E. "Doc" SMITH and A.E. VAN VOGT are very much worth examining. In its close modelling of GENRE SF's view of its own development, the book was exemplary; by virtue of writing it the Panshins became US sf's house historians. [JC]

See also: CHILDREN IN SF; CRITICAL AND HISTORICAL WORKS ABOUT SF; FABULATION; GALACTIC EMPIRES; PARANOIA;

SENSE OF WONDER; SOCIOLOGY; SPACESHIPS; WOMEN AS PORTRAYED IN SCIENCE FICTION.

PANSHIN, CORY (SEIDMAN) (1947-   ) US writer and critic, collaborator with her husband, Alexei PANSHIN (*whom see for details*), from before 1975. She shared a nonfiction HUGO with him for *The World Beyond the Hill: Science Fiction and the Quest for Transcendence* (**1989**). Her interest in Sufism and other philosophies of transcendence suffuses, in particular, their joint criticism. [JC]

See also: SENSE OF WONDER.

PANTROPY This useful item of sf TERMINOLOGY was coined by James BLISH in the stories later melded together as *The Seedling Stars* (fixup **1957**). Blish's view was that in humanity's COLONIZATION OF OTHER PLANETS (*which see for further discussion*), we must either change the planet to make it habitable (TERRAFORMING) or change humanity itself to fit it for survival in an alien environment (pantropy). The Greek root of the word means "turning everything". Pantropy is usually undertaken by some form of biological engineering (◊ GENETIC ENGINEERING). An ugly pantropy fable is "Between the Dark and the Daylight" (1958 *Infinity*) by David C. Hodgkins (Algis BUDRYS), reprinted as by Budrys in *Budrys' Inferno* (coll **1963**; vt *The Furious Future* 1964 UK), in which generations of humans are genetically rendered ever more inhuman to fit them for violent competition with murderous alien life. *Man Plus* (**1976**) by Frederik POHL, a novel that tackles several pantropy issues, prepares a man for living on MARS by changing him into a CYBORG. [PN]

PAPE, RICHARD (BERNARD) (1916-   ) UK writer of various books including his bestselling wartime autobiography, *Boldness Be My Friend* (**1953**), and a number of thrillers. In *And So Ends the World ...* (**1961**) arrogant mankind is given a severe warning from high-up cosmic sources – the Moon disappears – and comes to its senses. The novel is more mysticism than sf. [JC]

PAPERBACK-BOOK FORMAT ◊ DIGEST.

PAPER TIGER ◊ Roger DEAN.

PAPILIAN, VICTOR [r] ◊ ROMANIA.

PAPP, DESIDERIUS (1897-   ) German writer whose nonfiction *Zukunft und Ende der Welt* (**1932**; trans H.J. Stenning as *Creation's Doom* **1934** UK) assesses the various ways in which the world might end, in a manner which was influential on contemporary sf. It has been incorrectly referred to in some bibliographies as a work of fiction. [JC]

PARABELLUM ◊ Ferdinand GRAUTOFF.

PÁRAL, VLADIMÍR [r] ◊ CZECH AND SLOVAK SF.

PARALLAX VIEW, THE ◊ John FRANKENHEIMER; ROLLOVER.

PARALLEL EVOLUTION ◊ EVOLUTION.

PARALLEL WORLDS A parallel world is another universe situated "alongside" our own, displaced from it along a spatial fourth DIMENSION (parallel worlds are often referred to in sf as "other dimensions"). Although whole universes may lie parallel in this sense, most stories focus on parallel Earths. The parallel-world idea forms a useful framework for the notion of historical ALTERNATE WORLDS, and is often used in this way. Most of the "secondary worlds" of modern FANTASY are explicit or implicit parallel worlds. Notable early sf extrapolations include J.H. ROSNY aîné's "Un autre monde" (1895; trans as "Another World" 1962) and two stories by H.G. WELLS: "The Strange Case of Davidson's Eyes" (1895) and "The Plattner Story" (1896).

The idea that other worlds lie parallel to our own and occasionally connect with it is one of the oldest speculative ideas in literature and legend; examples range from Fairyland to the "astral plane" of Spiritualists and mystics. There are two basic folkloristic themes connected with the notion; in one, an ordinary human is translocated into a fantasy land where s/he undergoes adventures and may find the love and fulfilment that remain beyond reach on Earth; in the other, a communication or visitation from the other world affects the life of an individual within this world, often injuring or destroying that person. Both patterns are very evident in modern imaginative fiction, shaping whole subgenres. Much of the overlap between sf, FANTASY and HORROR fiction – which makes clear-cut DEFINITIONS of the genres impossible – occurs by virtue of the promiscuous use of parallel worlds. The first pattern was modernized by Edgar Rice BURROUGHS, A. MERRITT and other PULP-MAGAZINE writers before the founding of AMAZING STORIES, and was easily dressed up with pseudo-scientific jargon; a notable early example is *The Blind Spot* (1921; **1951**) by Homer Eon FLINT and Austin HALL. Henry KUTTNER and C.L. MOORE wrote several Merrittesque SCIENCE-FANTASY novels after this fashion, notably *The Dark World* (1946; **1965**) and *Beyond Earth's Gates* (1949 *Startling Stories* as "The Portal in the Picture"; **1954** dos). Among the first writers to co-opt parallel worlds for straightforward sf melodrama were Edmond HAMILTON, in "Locked Worlds" (1929), and Murray LEINSTER, in "The Fifth-Dimensional Catapult" (1931) and its sequels. The idea was frequently used in humorous fashion by L. Sprague DE CAMP and others in UNKNOWN WORLDS. The second pattern, in which entities from a parallel world impinge on ours, was sciencefictionalized by William Hope HODGSON in *The Ghost Pirates* (1909); his earlier *The House on the Borderland* (1908) uses the landscapes of a parallel world to map and symbolically display the psyche of its protagonist. The renewal of such traditional horror motifs by sf imagery was taken further by H.P. LOVECRAFT in a manner imitated by his many disciples, including Frank Belknap LONG and Donald WANDREI.

The early GENRE-SF writers were slow to develop more extravagant speculative possibilities, although one notable attempt to describe a parallel world with different physical laws from those holding in our own continuum was made by Clark Ashton SMITH in "The Dimension of Chance" (1932); this notion was even-

tually developed much more carefully and elaborately by Isaac ASIMOV in *The Gods Themselves* (**1972**). Raymond F. JONES's *Renaissance* (1944; **1951**; vt *Man of Two Worlds*) is straightforward, and Fritz LEIBER's use of parallel alternative worlds in *Destiny Times Three* (1945; **1957**) is quantitatively restrained. It was in the 1950s and 1960s that exploration of the quirkier corollaries of the basic notion really got under way. Clifford D. SIMAK imagined a more extensive series of Earths – all empty of humanity and thus available for colonization and exploitation – in *Ring Around the Sun* (**1953**) and examined the hazards of trading between parallel worlds in "Dusty Zebra" (1954) and "The Big Front Yard" (1958), as did Alan E. NOURSE in "Tiger by the Tail" (1951). Gordon R. DICKSON's *Delusion World* (1955 *Science Fiction Stories* as "Perfectly Adjusted"; exp **1961**) features a city simultaneously occupied by two societies, each invisible to the other.

A common variant of the theme is that of a multiplicity of almost-identical worlds existing in parallel: alternate worlds in which there has been no significant change. Examples include "The Celestial Plot" (1948; trans 1964) by Adolfo BIOY CASARES and "Next Door, Next World" (1961) by Robert Donald Locke. In Robert SILVERBERG's "Trips" (1974) trans-universal tourists wander aimlessly through worlds similar and dissimilar. Parallel worlds often feature eccentric societies, sometimes for purposes of SATIRE, and sometimes equally eccentric patterns of EVOLUTION – like that in Stephen BOYETT's *The Architect of Sleep* (**1986**), where raccoons have become the dominant technological species. Bob SHAW has used the notion cleverly in two original novels: *The Two-Timers* (**1968**), in which a man who has lost his wife inadvertently creates a parallel world in which she still exists, and *A Wreath of Stars* (**1976**), in which two worlds made of different species of matter co-exist until the approach of an anti-neutrino star shifts the orbit of one of them. A different kind of parallellism is featured in a group of stories in which "timeslips" bring different eras of earthly history into geographical proximity – a motif featured in "Sidewise in Time" (1934) by Leinster and *October the First is Too Late* (**1966**) by Fred HOYLE. The idea that parallel worlds might include literal versions of fictional worlds as well as alternative histories is proposed in *"The Number of the Beast"* (**1980**) by Robert A. HEINLEIN and more sensitively developed in *Frankenstein Unbound* (**1973**) by Brian W. ALDISS. Larry NIVEN's "All the Myriad Ways" (1969) deals tentatively with the psychological implications of multiple universes. Richard COWPER's *Breakthrough* (**1967**) extrapolates the psychological attractions of the concept, as do Christopher PRIEST's stories of the **Dream Archipelago**, including *The Affirmation* (**1981**).

Modern uses of the theme usually imagine an infinite number of parallel worlds extending in a manifold which contains all possible Earthly histories and perhaps all possible physical universes. The notion that the perceived Universe is simply one single aspect of such a "multiverse" has been lent credence by the "many-worlds interpretation" of the enigmas of quantum mechanics propounded by, for example, John Wheeler, and popularized in non-fiction books by writers like Paul DAVIES and John GRIBBIN. Keith LAUMER's *Worlds of the Imperium* (**1962**) and its sequels deploy this kind of infinite series of parallel worlds in connection with alternative histories, as do Richard C. MEREDITH's *At the Narrow Passage* (**1973**) and its sequel and Frederik POHL's *The Coming of the Quantum Cats* (**1986**). Certain philosophical implications of the many-worlds interpretation are explored more-or-less seriously in a number of sf novels, including Aldiss's *Report on Probability A* (**1968**), Graham Dunstan MARTIN's *Time-Slip* (**1986**), Greg EGAN's *Quarantine* (**1992**) and Pohl and Jack WILLIAMSON's *The Singers of Time* (**1991**).

Modern fantasy novels – including most of those in the intermediate science-fantasy category – sometimes draw upon the legacy of sf recomplication in order to invigorate their use of parallel worlds. Notable examples include Roger ZELAZNY's **Amber** series and Michael MOORCOCK's many SWORD-AND-SORCERY series, which are all bound together (with some sf novels) within a hypothetical multiverse. [BS]

PARANOIA Paranoia is common in sf; schizophrenia (which we also cover here, although aware that it is a wholly different condition) is comparatively rare. Both are also discussed in rather a different context under PSYCHOLOGY.

It is obviously necessary to distinguish between sf stories about paranoia (a fairly small group) and sf stories whose implicit attitude is paranoid (an extremely large group); most stories discussed below belong to the latter group. Paranoia has been defined as "a mental disorder characterized by systematic delusions, as of grandeur or, especially, persecution". The delusions (◊ PERCEPTION) of persecution that appear to lie behind much sf were discussed in a forum of the SCIENCE FICTION WRITERS OF AMERICA, and 3 papers were published together as a pamphlet, *Paranoia and Science Fiction* (coll **1967** chap), the contributors being Alexei PANSHIN, James BLISH and also Joanna RUSS, who argued that, historically, the paranoid element in sf stems largely from its roots in the GOTHIC. It is fundamental to the gothic that none of us is safe; that it is the nature of the Universe to contain menaces that may at any time, arbitrarily, threaten us. Such menaces play a prominent role in, for example, the stories of Ambrose BIERCE, notably "The Damned Thing" (1893), a tale of a ravening invisible monster.

The PULP MAGAZINES, especially WEIRD TALES, but also the early SF MAGAZINES, were fond of such stories. H.P. LOVECRAFT is an almost perfect example of a writer whose work exhibits a systematic paranoid frame of reference; basic to his work was the idea that adherents of cults formed to worship malign gods are conspiring throughout the world to bring those gods physically back to rule us and feed from us. There

was no lack of paranoid stories at the sf end of the spectrum, either; most stories of INVASION, whether by foreigners or ALIENS, fall into this category. Paranoia is fundamental, too, to whole classes of MAINSTREAM fiction, especially ABSURDIST fiction (often bordering on sf); Franz KAFKA wrote little else but stories of this kind.

However, one should remember the old dictum that "the paranoid is not entirely wrong". Invasions, after all, do take place; people are sometimes persecuted (though seldom turned into beetles as in Kafka's famous story); the Universe, as simple observation shows, does indeed contain menaces. Also, one should not mistake the writer for the tale; paranoid stories are not necessarily written by paranoiacs, though some GENRE-SF writers may have been consciously feeding the perceived paranoia of their readership.

Early paranoid stories in the sf magazines include "Parasite" (1935) by Harl VINCENT, where invading aliens attach themselves to us and control our thoughts, and "The Earth-Owners" (1931) by Edmond HAMILTON, one of the first examples of a theme later to be enormously popular in sf: that Earth is already invaded and we are manipulated by aliens in disguise. Charles FORT formulated this paranoid insight pithily: "We are property." Many sf writers took the hint; e.g., Eric Frank RUSSELL in *Sinister Barrier* (1939; **1943**; rev 1948) and *Dreadful Sanctuary* (1948; **1951**; rev 1963). A common variant on the theme, which must have won sf countless adherents among genuine paranoiacs, is that many people in mental hospitals are there because they have uncovered the conspiracy, but nobody will listen; an example is "Come and Go Mad" (1949) by Fredric BROWN, where it turns out that Earth is controlled by an intelligent HIVE-MIND (of ants); the man who uncovers the truth is cold-bloodedly driven mad. AMAZING STORIES improved its circulation very considerably in the years 1945-7 by publishing a series of purportedly fact-based stories by Richard S. SHAVER showing how we are all manipulated by malign underground ROBOTS.

Conspiracy theories of the Shaver variety are extremely popular among propagandists of the PSEUDO-SCIENCES, many of whom themselves have believed that there is a conspiracy (or "cover-up", to use the prevalent terminology) among the scientific community to suppress their findings – a phenomenon discussed by Martin GARDNER in his *In the Name of Science* (**1952**; rev vt *Fads and Fallacies in the Name of Science* 1957) and by other writers, notably John T. SLADEK in *The New Apocrypha* (**1973**), which has many interesting observations about the relationship of the pseudo-sciences themselves to paranoia. Among the more popular pseudo-science cults are the groups believing we are being secretly observed by UFOS and/or endorsing Erich VON DÄNIKEN's belief that human progress is the result of alien intervention. Cult beliefs about UFOs are very widespread, as witness the popularity of the tv series PROJECT UFO (1978-79) and 1980s tale like W. Allen HARBINSON's **Projekt Saucer** series **(1980-91)** or Whitley STRIEBER's *Communion* **(1987)** and *Transformation: The Breakthrough* **(1988)**, the latter purporting to be true accounts of the author's and then his son's abduction by aliens. The Strieber books were best-sellers; *Project UFO* was the only sf drama series ever to make it into the top 20 of US tv programmes (in terms of number of viewers).

An sf subgenre that fascinatingly mixes delusions of grandeur with delusions of persecution is the tyrannized-SUPERMAN story, especially associated with A.E. VAN VOGT, whose *oeuvre* probably contains more systematic conspiracy theories than that of any other writer in sf. Notable examples are *Slan* (1940; **1946**; rev 1951) and *The World of Ā* (1945; rev **1948**; rev 1970; vt *The World of Null-A*). Similarly paranoid patterns occur in most of Keith LAUMER's supermen stories of the 1960s and 1970s. Van Vogt was later to be associated with L. Ron HUBBARD's DIANETICS movement, whose appeal was in part to the same mixture: the desire to be superior and the fear of being different. Hubbard himself wrote one of the most forceful paranoia stories in pulp sf: *Fear* (1940; **1957**; in *Typewriter in the Sky/Fear*, coll **1951**). This is a story both paranoid and about paranoia: it can be taken either as the case history of a psychotic killer or as a demonstration of demonic manipulation; in either event, a vivid and frightening series of delusions is projected.

"Dreams are Sacred" (1948) by Peter Phillips (1921-   ) has a telepath entering the mind of a paranoid in order to destroy his grandiose fantasies at root, but perhaps the most interesting study of a delusory framework is the one presented as fact in Robert LINDNER's *The Fifty-Minute Hour* (coll **1955**; vt *The Jet-Propelled Couch* UK), a case-study of an sf fan who believes himself to be living in a SPACE OPERA, and merely dreaming reality.

The other major paranoid variant is the story of the alien menace which can either change its shape or attach itself as a parasite to a human (◊ PARASITISM AND SYMBIOSIS); either way, the fear is that the inhuman result looks just like us. This is an image from the very heart of paranoia: the idea that our friends, sweethearts or even parents could be mysteriously *other*, hateful, dangerous and to be destroyed. In real life such delusions have led to murder; they are disturbingly popular in sf. The most celebrated early example is John W. CAMPBELL Jr's story "Who Goes There?" (1938) – filmed twice, the remake *The* THING (1982) more closely and unnervingly duplicating Campbell's original theme as the comradeship of a research installation crumbles into terrible isolation – but the heyday of stories of this kind was the 1950s. This was the period of the Cold War, when almost daily propaganda encouraged US citizens to believe that a secret conspiracy of communists and homosexuals was preparing to subvert the American way of

life; it was the time of the McCarthy hearings, and of the evangelical religious revival largely led by Billy Graham; paranoia was in the air. The frightening thing about communists and homosexuals, as everyone knew, was that from the outside they looked just like us. Hence, in part, the unprecedented popularity of stories about aliens who looked like humans, especially in the CINEMA (*see also* MONSTER MOVIES), including such films as I MARRIED A MONSTER FROM OUTER SPACE (1958), INVADERS FROM MARS (1953), INVASION OF THE BODY SNATCHERS (1956) and IT CAME FROM OUTER SPACE (1953). (Over a decade later the theme entered tv in the form of the series *The* INVADERS, and there was a resurgence of the genre in the 1980s, with films like THEY LIVE [1988] and SOCIETY [1989], and tv shows like WAR OF THE WORLDS [1988-90].) In book form the best known example is Robert A. HEINLEIN's *The Puppet Masters* **(1951)**, where the analogy between the alien group mind and totalitarian communism was made overtly.

The most notable exponents of paranoia in written sf were Richard MATHESON, Robert SHECKLEY and Philip K. DICK, Matheson in almost everything he wrote, especially his filmscripts for *The* INCREDIBLE SHRINKING MAN (1957) and, later, *Duel* (1971). (The latter film, like DEMON SEED [1977], falls into the category of machines-are-out-to-get-us stories, much used by the writer and film director Michael CRICHTON.) Sheckley's style is more rueful and ironic; he pokes fun at paranoia even while most of his stories – which are clear demonstrations of his belief that the universe is out to get us – invoke it. By far the most important writer in this area has been Dick, in whose novels the basic question is often: "To what extent is a paranoid (or schizophrenic) frame of reference delusory, and to what extent is reality itself a mere construct erected defensively by the mind in order to maintain sanity?" Several of Dick's stories take place, in effect, in ALTERNATE WORLDS actually projected by paranoid consciousnesses. Three novels relevant to the paranoia theme are *Eye in the Sky* **(1957)**, *Clans of the Alphane Moon* **(1964)** and, most powerfully, *The Three Stigmata of Palmer Eldritch* **(1965)**. Dick's novels are amazing in the emotional intensity of their psychodramas and their cavalier attitude towards reality, but dissolution of all meaning is (mostly) held at bay by the calm and wit of their narrative voice. Delusory systems that can in fact be entered and regarded as real are quite common in sf, especially among writers like Heinlein for whom solipsism is an important theme; an outstanding example is Richard MCKENNA, whose 12 sf stories published 1958-68 project imaginary worlds as real over and over again; it is not clear whether this sort of story more closely approaches paranoia or schizophrenia. One paranoid *idée fixe* of the period turns up frequently, notably in stories by Frederik POHL, with C.M. KORNBLUTH or solo: that a small group of very selfish near-immortals is secretly manipulating society behind the scenes. Examples are *Gladiator-at-Law* **(1955)**, by both, and

Drunkard's Walk (**1960**), by Pohl.

UK examples of paranoia stories from the 1950s are less common, though *Alien Life* (**1954**) by E.C. TUBB, in which a starship crew is taken over by alien parasites with the idea of invading Earth, would certainly qualify. This idea has been used several times since, as in the film TERRORE NELLO SPAZIO (1965; vt *Planet of the Vampires*) and QUATERMASS II (1957; vt *Enemy from Space*). (Most sf/HORROR films fall into the paranoia category, NIGHT OF THE LIVING DEAD [1968], *Demon Seed* and VIDEODROME [1982] being good examples.)

The hysterical edge of 1950s paranoid sf did not dissipate as some of the worst Cold War fears subsided in the 1960s, but it did change its nature, when a different (and actual) war took place involving the USA, whose armed forces fought in Vietnam through the second half of the decade, not finally withdrawing until 1975. The assassination of John F. Kennedy in 1963 also heightened feelings of paranoia. Elements of division in US society were reflected in a series of darkly paranoid films about POLITICS directed by John FRANKENHEIMER, with *The* MANCHURIAN CANDIDATE (1962), *Seven Days in May* (1964) and SECONDS (1966); the exiled left-wing director Joseph Losey (1909-1984), a victim of Hollywood politics in the 1950s, made *The* DAMNED (1961) in the UK; Stanley KUBRICK added new ingredients to the paranoid brew with DR STRANGELOVE OR: HOW I LEARNED TO STOP WORRYING AND LOVE THE BOMB (1964), and Theodore Flicker both spoofed and endorsed conspiracy theorizing with *The* PRESIDENT'S ANALYST (1967). Also extremely relevant is the UK tv series *The* PRISONER (1968), in which a political prisoner is subjected to ever more grotesque psychological manipulations.

In written sf, monuments of paranoia from the late 1950s to the early 1970s include: Algis BUDRYS's *Who?* (**1958**), in which nobody knows if an enigmatic man in a metal mask is a good US scientist or a Russian spy; several of Christopher HODDER-WILLIAMS's 1960s novels in which the protagonist's sanity is called into question as he makes curious discoveries; Philip José FARMER's **Riverworld** series (from 1965), in which the human race is apparently reincarnated *en masse* as a cold-blooded experiment; Richard COWPER's *Breakthrough* (**1967**), in which communication from outside seems like madness from inside; Frank HERBERT's *The Santaroga Barrier* (**1968**), in which an entire community is cut off and apparently has its identity submerged (here what begins as horrifying is cleverly tilted so as to seem almost acceptable by the end); John BRUNNER's *The Jagged Orbit* (**1969**), in which paranoia is endemic and taken for granted in a NEAR-FUTURE situation of racial hatred; Roger ZELAZNY's **Amber** series (from 1970) in which a family of quasi-superbeings plot constantly against one another, and real universes keep on turning out to be mere shadows of some further but unreachable reality; John T. Sladek's *The Müller-Fokker Effect* (**1970**), which takes US paranoia as its prime target; and Norman

SPINRAD's *The Iron Dream* (**1972**), which parodies sf paranoia by passing itself off as a SWORD-AND-SORCERY novel written by Adolf Hitler.

Though most of this work in book form shows no special pattern, the films of the 1960s certainly did, and all this activity culminated in a second wave of paranoia books and films that emerged in the mid-1970s, and – in the cinema, at least – continues intermittently to the present day. This new paranoia boom was shaped differently from its 1950s predecessor; the earlier period produced paranoia stories about outside menaces that ultimately endangered the State; the later boom produced a more domestic version in which the menace came from within, and was very often the State itself – as in most of the films noted above – or even, in an inward claustrophobic spiral, the family itself, in the case of Richard CONDON's *Winter Kills* (**1974**), a FABULATION about a political family closely resembling the Kennedys. The 1970s boom, though it built on conspiracy theories of the 1960s, was immediately attributable to the revelations following the 1972 break-in at Watergate which climaxed with President Nixon's resignation. It is hardly surprising that paranoid sf this time around emerged mostly (and perhaps justifiably) in stories that blended sf with POLITICS, as in the borderline sf film *The Parallax View* (1974) and the 1979 film of Condon's *Winter Kills*. Among the many more obviously sciencefictional (though still political) paranoid film scenarios that followed are *The* CRAZIES (1973), CHOSEN SURVIVORS (1974), CAPRICORN ONE (1977), *The* FURY (1978), *The* BOYS FROM BRAZIL (1978), *The* CHINA SYNDROME (1979), SCANNERS (1980), ROLLOVER (1981), BLUE THUNDER (1982), ENDANGERED SPECIES (1982), FIRESTARTER (1984), KAMIKAZE (1986), *The* BLOB (1988) and BRAIN DEAD (1989), each of which involves a conspiracy, in most cases supported secretly by the apparatus of the State.

Curiously enough, conspiracy-theory material of this sort did not much permeate written genre sf in the 1970s, though it was very obvious in the sort of fabulations written by Kurt VONNEGUT Jr and especially Thomas PYNCHON, a tradition continued in the work of many others, including William T. VOLLMANN in his *You Bright and Risen Angels: A Cartoon* (**1987** UK). Within more obviously generic work, a kind of knowing paranoia characterized a series of novels by Barry N. MALZBERG (some listed under PSYCHOLOGY) which see Man as a puppet in some kind of enigmatic or indifferent cosmic game; but the conspiracy theory work *par excellence* was Robert SHEA's and Robert Anton WILSON's *Illuminatus!* (3 vols **1975**), in which recent political history is explained in terms of a dazzlingly complex series of interlocking conspiracies by rival secret societies, some with histories going back to ATLANTIS. Algis Budrys's *Michaelmas* (**1977**) comes out, rather worriedly, on the side of conspiracy by producing as hero the man who secretly manipulates human politics.

In the 1980s, paranoia in genre sf may have been

slightly in abeyance, though it appeared in recurrent motifs of various sub-genres: the "shoot first, ask questions afterward" mentality of some SURVIVALIST FICTION; the godlike manipulations of various VIRTUAL REALITIES in novels by Jack CHALKER and others; and some of the more sophisticated SPACE OPERAS, in which galactic history (including ours) turns out to have been warped by alien superbeings, as in Paul J. MCAULEY's *Eternal Light* (**1991**). The most senior 1980s authors whose worlds are readable as paranoid are perhaps William GIBSON and Orson Scott CARD, but in rather different ways. Gibson's characteristically Canadian presentation is of struggling protagonists who often find themselves treated as puppets, as if free will may come to be illusory in a sufficiently complex world; Card's protagonists, who exist in a kinetic Universe pervaded by a sense of omnipotent presence, are – more typically of the USA – both manipulated and manipulative, the tool of greater forces or in the upshot godlike themselves. Card's Universe is intensely hierarchical, with his protagonists ranked high, but it is not always clear which rung of the ladder he believes the rest of us to be standing on; he may believe that we have free will if we stick to the rules.

It is difficult to generalize about paranoia in sf; clearly it is important and has led to some distinguished work. It does seem as if sf of the last few decades has matured and that, where sf once simply reflected paranoia, it is now more often written to analyse the very real paranoia that the writers know to exist in society. Western society has a cumbrous, bureaucratic power system; no wonder if the average individual feels at the mercy of forces he or she cannot even identify. In all paranoid sf the question of our free will is the fundamental one.

Schizophrenia is very much rarer in sf, though there is a small but persistent subgenre of tales about dual personality, its earliest classic being *Strange Case of Dr Jekyll and Mr Hyde* (**1886**) by Robert Louis STEVENSON. The popular belief that schizophrenia is a synonym for split personality is incorrect; in clinical psychology schizophrenia is more complex and more common than that. However, it is the split-personality theme that has most attracted sf writers (◊ PSYCHOLOGY *for further examples*). An amusing variant can be found in Robert Sheckley's *The Alchemical Marriage of Alistair Crompton* (**1978** UK; vt *Crompton Divided* 1988 US), in which split personalities can be excised by psychic surgery and implanted into new bodies. The film FORBIDDEN PLANET (1956) features a self-controlled scientist out of touch with his own subconscious mind, the "id"; in a surprisingly successful post-Freudian variation on Stevenson's Jekyll-and-Hyde syndrome, his secret passions become literally projected into the form of a ravening monster.

Where stories of PARASITISM regularly have a subtext of paranoia, those of symbiosis often appear schizophrenic, at least in such tales as Brian STABLEFORD's

Hooded Swan series, where the symbiote literally inhabits the host's brain. (An earlier example is Algis Budrys's "Silent Brother" [1956].) Stableford is one of the few sf writers to use schizophrenia in the modern sense as an sf theme, in *Man in a Cage* (**1975**), where a schizophrenic is chosen to take part in a space project which might prove impossible for ordinary people. (Samuel R. DELANY had used a similar idea in "The Star Pit" [1967], but there the spacemen, though unbalanced, were not schizophrenic.)

Theodore STURGEON wrote several strong (but perhaps glib) stories about schizophrenia, including "The Other Man" (1956), and "Who?" (1955; vt "Bulkhead"), which is about the deliberate splitting of an astronaut's personality to save him from insanity during a long space flight alone. And, of course, his gestalt creation in *More than Human* (fixup **1953**) consists of the joining together of individually maimed persons, each of whom (before joining) is like an inadequate, schizophrenic personality split off from some unknowable whole. Another story about the deliberate splitting of personality is Wyman GUIN's interesting "Beyond Bedlam" (1951).

The most consistently evocative use of schizophrenic themes in sf, however, is in the work of Philip K. Dick, notably in *We Can Build You* (**1972**) and *Martian Time-Slip* (**1964**). Both use the word schizophrenia in the full clinical sense, and both treat schizophrenics with considerable empathy, though not necessarily sympathy; the latter is fascinating in its theorizing that the anomie of the schizophrenic may be to do with his or her subjective experience of time being radically removed from the normal; the desolated landscapes projected by (or perceived by) the schizoid mind are memorable.   [PN]

See also: MONSTERS; SUPERNATURAL CREATURES.

PARASITE MURDERS, THE (vt *They Came from Within*; vt *Shivers*) Film (1974). Cinepix/Canadian Film Development Corp. Written/dir David CRONENBERG, starring Paul Hampton, Joe Silver, Lynn Lowry, Alan Migicovsky, Barbara Steele. 87 mins, cut to 77 mins. Colour.

In an attempt to develop a beneficial symbiote, a scientist creates a parasite that, when it invades a human body, makes its host sexually ravenous. The vaguely phallic parasites spread though an isolated apartment building, and sexual apocalypse follows, the film ending with the sterile high-rise building's surviving occupants climbing into their cars to infect first Canada and then the world. The film has SPLATTER-MOVIE sequences and other scenes, notably the parasite's vaginal penetration of Steele while she is in the bath, of a distinctly neauseating kind, but it transcends the exploitation-movie genre to which it belongs through its wit and intensity, and its readiness to follow its axioms through to their conclusions. This was Cronenberg's first commercial film, notable for its remarkably bold visual metaphors.   [PN]

See also: CINEMA; MONSTER MOVIES; PARASITISM AND SYMBIOSIS; SEX.

PARASITISM AND SYMBIOSIS Parasitism and symbiosis are Nature's extreme forms of commensalism (physical association). A parasitic species promotes its own interests entirely to the detriment of the other; symbiosis refers to the much less common state in which both organisms obtain some benefit from the association.

Imaginary parasites of human beings are featured in many effective sf HORROR stories, often linked to the idea of vampirism (although classical vampires might better be regarded as predators than as parasites). Stories dealing with LIFE ON OTHER WORLDS often feature parasites which are exaggerated versions of earthly creatures. Those insects which lay their eggs in living hosts are popular models; they feature in A.E. VAN VOGT's "Discord in Scarlet" (1939; incorporated in *The Voyage of the Space Beagle*, fixup 1950) and the film ALIEN (1979) and its sequels; the closely related notion of the mother killed by her internal young appears in Philip José FARMER's *The Lovers* (1952; exp **1961**) and Gardner DOZOIS's *Strangers* (**1978**). Parasites leeching the "vital energy" of human beings are commonplace; when the parasites are internal rather than external this often involves the will of the victim being usurped, thus referring metaphorically to demonic possession as well as to vampirism. Early examples of this kind of story include J. Maclaren COBBAN's *Master of His Fate* (1890) and Arthur Conan DOYLE's *The Parasite* (1895); the classic PULP-MAGAZINE sf extrapolations are Eric Frank RUSSELL's *Sinister Barrier* (1939; **1943**; rev 1948) and Robert A. HEINLEIN's *The Puppet Masters* (**1951**). Other stories in the same vein are Russell's "Vampire from the Void" (1939), Farmer's "Strange Compulsion" (1953; vt "The Captain's Daughter"), Frank R. CRISP's *The Ape of London* (1959), Robert SILVERBERG's "Passengers" (1968), Colin WILSON's *The Mind Parasites* (1967) and *The Space Vampires* (**1976**), David CRONENBERG's film *The* PARASITE MURDERS (1974) and Damon KNIGHT's *CV* (**1985**).

This frequent movement of the notion of parasitism from the context of the mundane to the quasisupernatural is in keeping with sf's habitual treatment of biological themes (◊ BIOLOGY). In concert with general trends relating to ALIENS there was a dramatic change of emphasis in post-WWII stories, in which apparently parasitic relationships are often revealed to be in fact symbiotic. Some stories are conscious ideological replies to earlier works – Ted WHITE's *By Furies Possessed* (**1970**), which attacks the implicit xenophobia of *The Puppet Masters*, is a notable example. The concept of symbiosis had earlier been used in some ecological puzzle stories (◊ ECOLOGY), notably Eric Frank Russell's "Symbiotica" (1943) and an ironic story of defensive biological warfare, "Symbiosis" (1947) by Will F. Jenkins (Murray LEINSTER), but the quasisupernatural connotations it eventually took on were decisively opposed to metaphors of vampirism and possession. It became a central notion of the "ecological mysticism" displayed in such works as

Sydney J. VAN SCYOC's trilogy *Daughters of the Sunstone* (**1982-4**; omni **1985**). Explicit religious imagery comes to the fore in such stories of human/alien symbiosis as Clifford D. SIMAK's *Time and Again* (**1951**; vt *First He Died*), Bob SHAW's *Palace of Eternity* (**1969**) and Nicholas YERMAKOV's trilogy begun with *The Last Communion* (**1981**). Post-WWII stories in which human and alien minds share a brain usually see such relationships as potentially symbiotic; examples include Hal CLEMENT's *Needle* (**1950**), Brian M. STABLEFORD's **Halcyon Drift** series (**1972-5**), Roger ZELAZNY's *Doorways in the Sand* (**1976**) and F. Paul WILSON's *Healer* (**1976**). Even Christopher EVANS's bleak mind-parasite story *The Insider* (**1981**) is sympathetic to the parasitic consciousness. The more ambivalent view of human/alien commensalism adopted in Octavia E. BUTLER's *Clay's Ark* (**1984**) and related works and in the first part of Dan SIMMONS's *Hyperion* (**1989**) cleverly exploits and undercuts this modern sensibility.

This area of speculation is perhaps the most obvious example in sf of the utility of biological notions as metaphysical metaphors (◊ METAPHYSICS), and of the way that such metaphorical usage dominates the expression of biological notions in sf. [BS]

See also: HIVE-MINDS; PARANOIA; SUPERNATURAL CREATURES.

PARAZZOLI, FERRUCCIO [r] ◊ ITALY.

PARIS QUI DORT (vt *Le Rayon Invisible*; vt *The Crazy Ray*) Film (1923). Films Diamant. Written/dir René Clair, starring Henri Rollan, Albert Préjean, Madeleine Rodrigue, Marcel Vallée. 61 mins. B/w.

This is one of the earliest sf films (other than shorts). A scientist accidentally freezes Paris into a split-second of time with an invisible ray. Some Parisians escape, through being either on the Eiffel tower or in a plane. Most of them take advantage of the situation to break out of their social roles, have drunken parties, etc., but a young nightwatchman persuades a group to seek out the source of the problem and put it right, which they do (though at first the victims can move only in slow motion). Made with style and charm by Clair – whose first film it was – *PQD* retains its wit and good humour when seen today. [JB]

See also: CINEMA.

PARK, PAUL (CLAIBORNE) (1954-   ) US writer, educated in the land of his birth, peripatetic for most of the 1980s, but resident again in the USA at about the time he began publishing sf with *Soldiers of Paradise* (**1987**), the first volume of **The Starbridge Chronicles**, which comprises also *Sugar Rain* (**1989**) – assembled with the first volume as *The Sugar Festival* (omni **1991**) – and is apparently completed with *The Cult of Loving Kindness* (**1991**). It is the sort of sequence whose composition seems possible only in the later years of a genre, when the literary atmosphere is saturated with memories of previous work and a sense of antiquity attaches naturally to some of the sf instruments used in new stories. RELIGION dominates every page of **The Starbridge Chronicles**, which is set, eons hence, in a dying-Earth venue where history endlessly recycles, tied to the return of the generations-long seasons of a Great Year. (PP has denied being influenced by Brian W. ALDISS's **Helliconia** sequence: the idea of a Great Year may be one which comes naturally to mind in the late maturity of a genre.)

As in most dying-Earth tales (◊ FAR FUTURE), metal is now scarce, technologies of radically varying complexity co-exist, human and humanlike species intermingle, and nothing new can happen. The Great-Year cycle owes its existence to the influence of a visiting planet (PP's astronomy is, perhaps intentionally, vague on its exact nature) called Paradise, which the religion dominant during the terrible Winter conceives to be the habitat of those who have not yet died and been sent to Earth. The delineation of this faith in *Soldiers of Paradise* – with its bloodiness, its erotic complexities, its totalitarian control over the predestined lives of the damned, its worship of the dog-god Angkhdt, its melancholia and its strange rightness – is the major creative achievement of the sequence. In that first novel, as Winter begins to end, the Starbridge clan, which has dominated the great province whose capital is Charn, begins to panic in foreordained ways; Abu Starbridge is martyred, and will become the avatar of a Summer faith, and Thanakar Starbridge, a doctor who blasphemously heals those low in the social order, escapes a crumbling Charn with his lover. *Sugar Rain* deals in gravely slow terms with the meteorological and social phenomena which signal Spring, as well as continuing the Thanakar love story. *The Cult of Loving Kindness*, set in Summer, depicts the slow rebirth of the cult of Angkhdt. The contemplative and tocsin richness of the sequence demonstrates the continuing imaginative power of latter-day sf.   [JC]

See also: GODS AND DEMONS; PLANETARY ROMANCE.

PARKER, RICHARD (1915-   ) UK writer for children. His *The Hendon Fungus* (**1968**) is about fungal specimens from abroad proliferating in England, feeding on calcium, and thus crumbling buildings of stone, concrete, etc. *The Old Powder Line* (**1971**) is a fantasy featuring a train as a time machine. *A Time to Choose* (**1973**) presents two children forced to pick between double lives in ALTERNATE WORLDS, one pleasant, the other ours.   [PN]

Other works: *M For Mischief* and *Spell Seven* (**1971**), both tales of magic.

PARKES, LUCAS or WYNDHAM ◊ John WYNDHAM.

PARKINSON, H(AROLD) F(REDERICK) (?   -   ) UK writer whose sf novel, *They Shall not Die* (**1939**), describes with muted irony the effects of a MEDICINE which prevents all disease but also sterilizes those who use it: only those who remain prone to the ills of the flesh can give birth.   [JC]

PARNELL, FRANCIS [s] ◊ Festus PRAGNELL.

PARNOV, EREMEI (IUDOVICH) (1935-   ) Russian scientist and writer, almost all of whose sf of interest was published in collaboration with Mikhail EMTSEV

(*whom see for details*). After the partnership broke up in 1970, EP published some further work, like *Prosnis' V Famaguste* ["Wake up in Famagusta"] (**1985**), which mixes Eastern mysticism and ALIEN encounters in a formula adventure plot. Some superficial sf criticism appears in *Fantastika V Vek NTR* ["SF in the Age of Scientific Revolution"] (**1974**) and *Zerkalo Uranii* ["The Mirror of Urania"] (**1982**).   [VG]

See also: HIVE-MINDS.

PARODY ◊ SATIRE.

PARRINDER, (JOHN) PATRICK (1944-   ) UK academic and critic whose work in the sf field has focused primarily upon H.G. WELLS. His *H.G. Wells* (**1970**) remains the best short introduction to the work and the man, though it may now, two decades later, seem unduly dismissive about Wells's later career. *H.G. Wells: The Critical Heritage* (anth **1972**) reflects a similar viewpoint. PP ed with Robert M. PHILMUS *H.G. Wells's Literary Criticism* (coll **1980**). *The War of the Worlds: Notes* (**1981** chap) is a study guide. *H.G. Wells: A Comprehensive Bibliography, 4th Ed* (**1986** chap), with J.R. Hammond, A.H. Watkins and the H.G. Wells Society, justifies its subtitle only if periodical publications are to be ignored. *H.G. Wells under Revision: Proceedings of the International H.G. Wells Symposium, London, July 1986* (anth **1990**) with Christopher Rolfe reflects some of the advances in Wells studies since PP's first study, which in retrospect seems all the more prescient in the sophisticated seriousness of its approach. PP has also edited 2 critical editions for The H.G. Wells Society: *Select Conversations with an Uncle (Now Extinct)* ([coll 1895] **1992** chap) with David C. Smith, which includes previously uncollected material, and *The Discovery of the Future* ([1902] coll **1989** chap), which includes also some lesser essays.

The useful *Science Fiction: A Critical Guide* (anth **1979**) was followed by *Science Fiction: Its Criticism and Teaching* (**1980**), a clear-headed and subtle conspectus of the field from a scholarly point of view.   [JC]

See also: CRITICAL AND HISTORICAL WORKS ABOUT SF; SF IN THE CLASSROOM; SCIENTISTS.

PARRY, DAVID MacLEAN (1852-1915) US businessman and writer whose anti-socialist DYSTOPIA, *The Scarlet Empire* (**1906**), introduces a young US citizen to a nightmarish ATLANTIS, protected from the ocean by a great dome, in which the obsession with regimented equality leads to grotesqueries prophetic of those dreamt of by Evgeny ZAMIATIN in *My* (trans Gregory Zilboorg as *We* **1924** US). The protagonist escapes with the young woman he loves, destroying the dome – and hence the entire society – as he leaves.   [JC]

PARSEC The official SI unit of astronomical distance; the name is a contraction of "parallax-second". The measure was introduced by UK astronomer Herbert Hall Towner (1861-1930). As the Earth travels from one side of the Sun to the other in half a year, parallax makes the position of any comparatively nearby star apparently shift. Using simple trigonometry, from the observed angular displacement of the star's measured position and knowledge of the distance between Earth and Sun the distance of the star can be calculated. One parsec is defined (essentially) as the distance at which a star would show a parallax displacement of 1 second of arc, a distance which proves to be approximately 3.258 light years.

The term "parsec" is a common item of sf TERMINOLOGY, either correctly as a unit of distance or, depressingly often – especially in PULP-MAGAZINE, juvenile and cinematic sf – mistakenly as a unit of velocity ("We're moving at 17 parsecs!" the hero of SPACE 1999 might cry) or of time ("I made the run in less than four parsecs," says Harrison Ford in STAR WARS). [PN] **See also:** SCIENTIFIC ERRORS.

PARTINGTON, CHARLES [r] ◊ NEW WORLDS; SOMETHING ELSE.

PASSES, ALAN Working name of UK writer, translator and film technician Alan Pazolski (1943-   ), who also signs himself Alan Passes-Pazolski. His first sf story was "Spoor" for *NW* in 1969, and he has written two sf plays, "Mystic of the Western World", produced 1976, and "Death Raise", produced 1977. His epic novel *Big Step* (**1977**) mixes sf material with MYTHOLOGY in the experimentally couched story of the adventures on Earth of an interstellar Angel of Death who seeks to punish a fugitive Nazi. [JC]

PASSING SHOW, THE UK large-format (14" x 10" [36cm x 26cm]) weekly magazine, 26 Mar 1932-25 Feb 1939. It featured articles, short stories, serials and cartoons. Beginning with the serializations of *Pirates of Venus* (1933; **1934**) and *Lost on Venus* (1933-4; **1935**) by Edgar Rice BURROUGHS (both reprinted from *The* ARGOSY), TPS became the UK's most regular periodical source of sf in the 1930s, remaining so until TALES OF WONDER and FANTASY started up. Several short fantasy stories by Lord DUNSANY and others and a series of articles by Ray CUMMINGS, **The World of Tomorrow** (1936), appeared in *TPS* over the next 5 years together with 11 other serials, notably Warwick DEEPING's "The Madness of Professor Pye" (1934), Edwin BALMER's and Philip WYLIE's *When Worlds Collide* (1934-5; being a reprint of *When Worlds Collide* [**1933**] and *After Worlds Collide* [**1934**]), Wynant Davis Hubbard's *The Thousandth Frog* (1935; **1935**), John Beynon's (◊ John WYNDHAM) *Planet Plane* (1936 as "Stowaway to Mars"; **1936**; vt cut as "The Space Machine", 1937 *Modern Wonder*; rev vt *Stowaway to Mars* 1953) and *The Secret People* (1935; **1935**), and W. Douglas NEWTON's "The Devil Comes Aboard" (1938; vt *Savaran and the Great Sand* **1939**).

TPS later became *The Illustrated* and focused its attention on WWII, though sf still made an occasional appearance. [JE]

PASTORAL The term "pastoral" can be understood in various ways. It can refer to the Classical or Shakespearean tale of courtiers holidaying among nymphs and shepherds; it can refer, as Sir William Empson (1906-1984) and other modern critics have argued, to the proletarian novel or to the story which contrasts childhood innocence with adult experience. In essence, however, a pastoral is any work of fiction which depicts an apparently simple and natural way of life, and contrasts it with our complex, technological, anxiety-ridden urban world of the present. Pastorals can be full of moral earnestness or they can be utterly escapist.

Of the many versions of pastoral in sf, the most obvious is the tale of country life as written by Clifford D. SIMAK, Zenna HENDERSON and others. Such stories usually involve the intrusion of ALIEN beings (frequently telepathic) into rural landscapes peopled by farmers and small-town tradesmen. Examples are Simak's "Neighbor" (1954), "A Death in the House" (1959), *Way Station* (**1963**), *All Flesh is Grass* (**1965**) and *A Choice of Gods* (**1972**), and Henderson's *Pilgrimage: The Book of the People* (fixup **1961**) and *The Anything Box* (coll **1965**). Fantasies in a kindred mode include Ray BRADBURY's *Dandelion Wine* (fixup **1957**), Ward MOORE's and Avram DAVIDSON's *Joyleg* (**1962**) and Manly Wade WELLMAN's *Who Fears the Devil?* (coll of linked stories **1963**). What these works have in common is an emphasis on the virtues (and sometimes the constraints) of the rural way of life. They are, explicitly or implicitly, anti-CITY and anti-MACHINE; they frequently extol the values of living close to Nature, of being in rhythm with the seasons. This bucolic and Luddite strain in GENRE SF has its origins in some major works of US literature such as *Walden* (**1854**) by Henry David Thoreau (1817-1862) and *Winesburg, Ohio* (**1919**) by Sherwood Anderson (1876-1941), as well as in such UK UTOPIAS and romances as Richard JEFFERIES's *After London* (**1885**), with its vision of the city reconquered by forest and field, W.H. HUDSON's *A Crystal Age* (**1887**) and William MORRIS's *News from Nowhere* (**1890** US).

A variant form of this version of pastoral is that in which the contrast between city and country is made quite explicit. Stories of this type, discussed more fully in the entry on CITIES, have a long history, going back beyond *After London*. In this variant urban life is depicted as cruel, oppressive or sterile, while the country represents freedom; the genre-sf archetype is Arthur C. CLARKE's *The City and the Stars* (**1956**). It is a particularly popular theme in CHILDREN'S SF, as in John CHRISTOPHER's *Wild Jack* (**1974**) and Isobelle CARMODY's *Scatterlings* (**1991**).

A second version of pastoral, again taking its cue from Jefferies and Morris, is exemplified by George R. STEWART's *Earth Abides* (**1949**) and Leigh BRACKETT's *The Long Tomorrow* (**1955**), both tales depicting the rise of agricultural and anti-technological societies after some sort of HOLOCAUST. Although this type of story is set in the future, the future becomes a clear analogue of the pre-industrial past. A particularly fine example is Fredric BROWN's "The Waveries" (1945), a tale in which the modern USA is forced back into a horse-and-buggy economy by invading aliens who prevent the use of electricity. Other examples of this kind of story are Pat FRANK's *Alas, Babylon* (**1959**) and Edgar PANGBORN's *Davy* (**1964**). This sort of pastoral is not always simple; the pastoral post-holocaust world can itself be seen with a little irony, as in John CROWLEY's *Engine Summer* (**1979**), which is suffused by an elegiac melancholy. (Another ambiguous pastoral, not really sf, is Crowley's *Little, Big* [**1981**], where the ultimate pastoral values of Faerie are teasingly impossible to reach and, if reached, might mean death.)

A third version of sf pastoral is the story set on another world, often Edenic or, at the least, satisfying. Such works usually depict benign alien ECOLOGIES which support nontechnological societies. Humanity is often seen as a destructive intruder upon these planets, although frequently the protagonist is "accepted" because he or she is capable of seeing the wisdom of the alien ways. The ideological thrust of such stories is anti-anthropomorphic and anti-xenophobic. Examples are Robert A. HEINLEIN's *Red Planet* (**1949**) – and, by implication, his *Stranger in a Strange Land* (**1961**) – Bradbury's *The Martian Chronicles* (fixup **1950**), Mark CLIFTON's *Eight Keys to Eden* (**1960**), H. Beam PIPER's *Little Fuzzy* (**1962**), Robert SILVERBERG's *Downward to the Earth* (**1970**) and *The Face of the Waters* (**1991**), Lloyd BIGGLE Jr's *Monument* (**1974**), Cherry WILDER's *Second Nature* (**1982**), Joan SLONCZEWSKI's *A Door into Ocean* (**1986**) and Judith MOFFETT's *Pennterra* (**1987**). Ursula K. LE GUIN's *The Word for World is Forest* (**1976**) is an outstanding treatment of this theme, the sourness of the narrative reflecting the realities of the Vietnam War. Brian M. STABLEFORD's *The Paradise Game* (**1974**) and *Critical Threshold* (**1976**) are clever variations; both are about planets which are apparently Edenic but which turn out to be rather more sinister. This is also the case in Ian WATSON's "The Moon and Michelangelo" (**1987**), in which a pastoral alien society has been wholly misunderstood but offers a form of ironic transcendence nevertheless. Richard MCKENNA's "Hunter, Come Home" (**1963**) and John VARLEY's "In the Hall of the Martian Kings" (**1977**) are both good treatments of the ultimate in benign ecologies: bio-systems that enfold and preserve the sympathetic human characters against all dangers.

The fourth version of sf pastoral is perhaps the commonest: the escapist adventure story set in a simpler world, whether it be the future, the past, another planet or in another continuum. If the portrayal of "Nature" is an essential element in all pastorals, then this is the version of them that prefers its Nature red in tooth and claw. Edgar Rice BURROUGHS's *Tarzan of the Apes* (**1914**) belongs here, as do his *A Princess of Mars* (1912; **1917**), *At the Earth's Core* (1914; **1922**) and all their various sequels. Tarzan is an archetypal 20th-century pastoral hero; his freedom of action, affinity with animals and innocent capacity for violence represent an amalgam of daydreams, Rousseau married to Darwin. One could go further and say that the whole subgenre of SWORD AND SORCERY is in a sense pastoral. As urbanization increases and

free space diminishes on the Earth's surface, so the pastoral dream of simpler worlds in harmony with (or in enjoyable conflict with) Nature becomes ever more compelling.

In the 1980s (there are earlier examples) pastoral themes were used by a number of WOMEN WRITERS OF SF to image the values of FEMINISM, as in Slonczewski's *A Door into Ocean*. The prime example here, though, is Le Guin's *Always Coming Home* (**1985**), an extraordinarily rich and dense exercise in speculative ANTHROPOLOGY, largely set in a post-holocaust pastoral culture whose values are the values of women. A cruder exercise in the same vein is Sally Miller GEARHART's *The Wanderground: Stories of the Hill Women* (coll of linked stories **1980**), in which the women's society's embrace of Nature and the men's society's despisal of it are both so diagrammatic as to approach caricature. Sheri S. TEPPER achieves the balance in *Raising the Stones* (**1990**), with plenty of melodrama but also with plenty of real life, when she contrasts two agricultural societies on two planets, the one society patriarchal and brutal, the other deriving its strength from the realism (and, in the main, the kindliness) of women, a confrontation between the bad pastoral and the good.

Pastoral has always been an attractive theme, but its simpler pleasures can pall after a time. The most interesting uses of pastoral in sf, many of which are cited above, are those in which the pastoral values have their cost, or in which the urban/pastoral or civilized/primitive oppositions are seen with some sort of irony – that is, with the recognition that life is not always as neatly dualistic as we would sometimes wish. Some of the poignant qualities of Hilbert SCHENCK's *At the Eye of the Ocean* (**1980**) and *A Rose for Armageddon* (**1982**), pastorals whose pastures are the field of ocean, derive from this recognition. Behind the greatest pastorals is often a sense of loss, for Nature herself often throws up images of decline and decay as well as of growth and harvest, and to invoke Nature is to invoke a world whose benisons are ephemeral (although they will always return). This may be why some of the finest pastorals are seasonal or cyclical; Brian W. ALDISS's *Helliconia* trilogy (**1982-5**) is many other things as well, but at root it is a pastoral whose burden is that Winter always comes. [DP/PN]

See also: CHILDREN IN SF; ISLANDS; LIVING WORLDS.

'PATAPHYSICS ◊ IMAGINARY SCIENCE; Alfred JARRY.

PATCHETT, M(ARY OSBORNE) E(LWYN) (1897-   ) Australian writer, long resident in the UK, whose competent CHILDREN'S SF novels are *Kidnappers of Space* (**1953**; vt *Space Captives of the Golden Men* 1953 US), *Adam Troy, Astroman* (**1954**), which deals with the consequences for Earth of colliding with a giant asteroid, *Lost on Venus* (**1954**; vt *Flight to the Misty Planet* 1954 US), *Send for Johnny Danger* (**1956**), *The Venus Project* (**1963**), *Ajax and the Haunted Mountain* (**1963**) and *Farm Beneath the Sea* (**1969**). Her writing is alert, uncondescending, sensitive to animal life and information-full. [JC]

PATON, FRANK [s] ◊ Raymond A. PALMER.

PATON, JOHN [r] ◊ ROBERT HALE LIMITED.

PATRICK ◊ Oscar ROSSITER.

PAUL, BARBARA (JEANNE) (1931-   ) US writer who began publishing sf with "Answer 'Affirmative' or 'Negative'" for *ASF* in 1972, but who has become much better known in the 1980s for her detective novels, of which she has written at least 13; one of them, *Liars and Tyrants and People who Turn Blue* (1980), depends for its plot upon a psychic character. Earlier BP wrote several sf novels – *An Exercise for Madmen* (1978), *Pillars of Salt* (1979), *Bibblings* (1979) and *Under the Canopy* (1980) – which feature women protagonists, through whom an unprogrammatic FEMINISM is pursued as they find themselves coping with sf-adventure situations. *Pillars of Salt*, for instance, is a TIME-TRAVEL tale which confronts its 21st-century protagonist with the challenge of becoming Queen Elizabeth I of England. A later novel, *The Three-Minute Universe* * (1988), is a **Star Trek** tie (◊ STAR TREK).

BP should not be confused with the Barbara Paul who wrote *The Curse of Halewood* (1976; vt *Devil's Fire, Love's Revenge* 1976 US); this was the pseudonym of Barbara Kathleen Ovstedal (1925-   ). [JC]

PAUL, FRANK R(UDOLPH) (1884-1963) Austrian-born US illustrator. FRP is the best candidate for "Father of Modern SF ILLUSTRATION", at least in the form it took in the PULP MAGAZINES. He received much of his education in Vienna, and studied also in Paris and New York. Trained as an architect, he was discovered by Hugo GERNSBACK in 1914 while working for a rural newspaper. Their names have been virtually inseparable ever since the days of *The Electrical Experimenter* (◊ SCIENCE AND INVENTION). For #1 of AMAZING STORIES in Apr 1926 FRP not only painted the cover illustration but did all the interior black-and-white artwork as well, and continued to do both until Gernsback lost control of the magazine in 1929. When Gernsback started publishing again later that year, FRP was once more his primary illustrator, on SCIENCE WONDER STORIES, AIR WONDER STORIES and then WONDER STORIES; indeed, his association with Gernsback lasted until the short-lived *Science Fiction Plus* in 1953; he painted more than 150 covers for Gernsback in all. He worked elsewhere, too, with a further 28 front covers for various non-Gernsback SF MAGAZINES, including all 12 for Charles D. HORNIG's SCIENCE FICTION, and also a series of full colour back-cover paintings for the ZIFF-DAVIS *Amazing Stories* and *Fantastic Adventures* (1939-46). He also did all the illustration for *Superworld Comics*, a Gernsback experiment of 1939.

FRP's style shows his architectural training; his CITIES and TECHNOLOGY are lovingly detailed, his ALIENS well thought out and plausible, but his human figures stiff and simplistic. His colours were bright (almost garish, even for the period) and flat, and he liked pure reds and yellows, particularly as back-grounds (though this was partly due to Gernsback's meanness in using three- rather than four-colour printing). It seems odd to associate primitive art with sf, but FRP was in his technological way, just as much a primitive as Grandma Moses (1860-1961) and, like her, had an authentic naïve poetry to his work. The brightness of colour throughout the PULP-MAGAZINE era of sf was a direct result of FRP's influence. FRP was guest of honour at the first World SF CONVENTION in 1939. [JG/PN]

See also: SPACESHIPS.

PAYN, JAMES (1830-1898) UK writer and editor whose 100+ books cover a wide variety of genres, his sf being comparatively inconspicuous. *The Cruise of the Anti-Torpedo* (1871 chap) is a typical future-WAR tale, one of many written in direct response to George T. CHESNEY's *The Battle of Dorking* (1871 chap); along with the comic "The Fatal Curiosity, or A Hundred Years Hence" (1877) it was included in *High Spirits: Being Certain Stories Written in Them* (coll 1879). *The Eavesdropper: An Unparalleled Experiment* (1888) is an INVISIBILITY tale whose protagonist, after taking the requisite potion, discovers the truth about his friends and servants and returns to the normal world sadder and wiser. [JC]

PAYNE, (PIERRE STEPHEN) ROBERT (1911-1983) UK-born writer, much travelled, who spent his final years in the USA. Immensely prolific under a variety of names – including Richard Cargoe, John Anthony Devon, Howard Horne and Valentin Tikhonov – he wrote little fantasy or sf. *The War in the Marshes* (1938) as by Robert Young is an allegorical adventure rather in the mode of Rex WARNER. *The Deluge* (1954), which pretends to be based on notes left by Leonardo da Vinci (1452-1519), is sf. [JC]

PEABODY, JOEL R. [r] ◊ JUPITER, SUN.

PEACE GAME, THE ◊ GLADIATORERNA.

PEAKE, MERVYN (LAURENCE) (1911-1968) UK writer and artist, born in China, where he lived until he was 12 in a missionary compound, embedded into a land as strange as the country surrounding Gormenghast. He was initially better regarded as an artist than as a writer and, although he had written some poetry before the end of WWII, the publication of *Titus Groan* (1946) showed an unexpected side to his genius. *Gormenghast* (1950) is closely linked to that first volume, but it is clear that MP never intended to compose a trilogy *per se*; *Titus Alone* (cut 1959; reconstructed from manuscript by Langdon JONES 1970) – a text the author was unable to take beyond draft form due to the onset of the disease which killed him – ends at a point that MP did not intend as a definitive terminus. This sense of the shape of the sequence is confirmed by the 1991 critical edition of the 3 novels, in which *Titus Alone* (as coll 1991 US) ed G. Peter Winnington includes the surviving pages of "Titus Awakes", the incomplete 4th volume of the sequence. But, although the existing trilogy – variously identified as the **Gormenghast** or **Titus Groan** sequence, and on one occasion assembled as

The Titus Books (omni **1983**; vt *The Gormenghast Trilogy* 1991 US) – was never in its author's mind a complete entity, it remains a series of texts whose power is remarkable, and the definition of which in generic terms is loaded with difficulties. Although couched in a language which might point towards FANTASY, it contains no fantasy elements; though redolent of a dying-Earth (◊ FAR FUTURE) venue in its sense of belatedness and in the person of Titus's father – a fidgety, crotchet-ridden, ENTROPY-exuding manic-depressive aristocrat whose like has haunted the dying-Earth habitats of writers from M. John HARRISON to Richard GRANT – the first 2 volumes cannot be thought of as sf. The sequence is perhaps best thought of as being *sui generis*.

Told in an elaborated, densely pictorial language, the story of Titus's birth and childhood in Gormenghast Castle is fundamentally the story of a coming-of-age: it is a genuine *Bildungsroman*, the story of the growth of a soul. At the same time, great stretches of the sequence ignore the priggish, bland young Titus entirely to concentrate upon the vividly realized cast of grotesques which surrounds him. In *Titus Groan* itself, one of the most intensely painterly books ever crafted, the infant protagonist is surrounded by a dwelling so intricate and dense (MP derived something of its scale from Sark, in the Channel Islands) that he never becomes more than an occasional raised figurine in the Gormenghast geography. *Gormenghast* is essentially devoted to the *Realpolitik* rise and inevitable fall of the modern-minded Steerpike. Only *Titus Alone* concentrates on the hero, now self-exiled from his childhood and his great demesne, as he hurtles through a futuristic, jaggedly conceived DYSTOPIAN world; at the end, about to return home, he turns his back on all his memories, and the sequence stops short, dangling. Throughout, the wealth of detail of the work makes Gormenghast one of the most richly realized ALTERNATE WORLDS in all the literature of fantasy or sf.

MP contributed to *Sometime, Never* (anth **1956**) a short story about Titus, *Boy in Darkness* (1956; **1976** chap). *Mr Pye* (**1953**) is an excellent whimsical fantasy, set largely on Sark, about a man whose goodness is so profound that he sprouts angel's wings, and about his desperate attempts to get rid of them. But the huge fragments of **Titus Groan** remain central. [JC]

Other works: *Captain Slaughterboard Drops Anchor* (**1939** chap), for children; *Letters from a Lost Uncle* (**1948**), for children; *Mervyn Peake: Writings and Drawings* (anth **1974**) ed Maeve Gilmore, MP's widow, and Shelagh Johnson.

About the author: *A World Away: A Memoir* (**1970**) by Maeve Gilmore; *Mervyn Peake* (**1974**) by John Batchelor; *Mervyn Peake* (**1976**) by John Watney; *Peake's Progress* (coll **1978**; rev 1981) ed Maeve Gilmore. A journal, *Peake Studies*, ed G. Peter Winnington, was instituted in 1988 and continues.

PEARCE, BRENDA (1935-   ) UK writer who began publishing sf with "Hot Spot" for *ASF* in 1974. *Kidnapped into Space* (**1975**) and *Worlds for the Grabbing* (**1977**) are both routine but enjoyable adventures in which her interest in technical and technological matters sometimes shows through to advantage. [JC]

PEARCE, PHILIPPA [r] ◊ CHILDREN'S SF.

PEARSON, C.A., LTD ◊ PEARSON'S MAGAZINE; PEARSON'S WEEKLY; SCOOPS.

PEARSON, MARTIN Pseudonym used once by Donald A. WOLLHEIM alone, and also for "The Embassy" (1942 *ASF*), which he wrote with C.M. KORNBLUTH. [PN]

PEARSONS ◊ PEARSON'S MAGAZINE; PEARSON'S WEEKLY; SCOOPS.

PEARSON'S MAGAZINE UK magazine published by C.A. Pearson Ltd, ed Sir Arthur Pearson and others. Monthly, Jan 1896-Nov 1939.

PM was a popular fact and fiction magazine which, following the trend set by its companion paper PEARSON'S WEEKLY, published sf by George GRIFFITH, H.G. WELLS, F.M. WHITE, C.J. Cutcliffe HYNE and others on a regular basis for several years, becoming the STRAND MAGAZINE's keenest competitor. It is best remembered for the serializations of Wells's *The War of the Worlds* (1897; **1898**) and *The Food of the Gods* (1903-04; **1904**) and of George Griffith's *A Honeymoon in Space* (1900 as "Stories of Other Worlds"; fixup **1901**) and the sf illustrations of Fred T. JANE and Warwick Goble. Sf continued intermittently into the 1930s, sometimes originally, as with John Raphael's weird sf novel *Up Above* (1912; **1913**), and sometimes with reprints, as with Douglas NEWTON's "Sunken Cities" (1923) from MUNSEY'S MAGAZINE.

A US edition appeared Mar 1899-Apr 1925 with substantially different contents. In particular it serialized H.G. Wells's *War in the Air* (1908; **1908**) a month or two after the original publication in *Pall Mall Magazine*. [JE]

Further reading: *Science Fiction by Gaslight: A History and Anthology of Science Fiction in the Popular Magazines 1891-1911* (**1968**) by Sam MOSKOWITZ.

PEARSON'S WEEKLY UK 16pp tabloid magazine published by C.A. Pearson Ltd; ed Peter Keary and others. Weekly, 26 July 1890-1 Apr 1939. Retitled *The New Pearson and Today* from 17 Sep 1938, and *The New Pearson's Weekly* from 26 Nov 1938. Incorporated into *Tit-Bits* from 8 Apr 1939.

PW popularized sf in Victorian magazines with the publication of George GRIFFITH's *The Angel of the Revolution* (1893; cut **1893**), following it with other serials by Griffith, H. Rider HAGGARD, Louis TRACY and M.P. SHIEL, and also H.G. WELLS's *The Invisible Man* (1897; rev **1897**). Many short sf stories appeared during this period, with further stories appearing sporadically into the 1930s. [JE]

PEASE, Lt JOHN [s] ◊ Ralph Milne FARLEY.

PECK, RICHARD E(ARL) (1936-   ) US writer and academic, professor of English at Temple University, Philadelphia, and an active critic of both literature in general and sf in particular. He began publishing sf with "In Alien Waters" for *Venture* in 1969. His sf novel, *Final Solution* (**1973**), is an amusing but grim tale in which a US academic is sent 50 years into the future (through CRYONICS) to find universities and CITIES merged into a hideous conglomerate and sealed off, with Middle America living comfortably outside.

REP is not to be confused with Richard (Wayne) Peck (1934-), author of the **Blossom Culp** series of children's fantasies. [JC/PN]

PEDLER, KIT Working name of UK writer and scientist Christopher Magnus Howard Pedler (1927-1981). He was a medical doctor, practising from 1953 for about three years, after which he began the research into the experimental pathology of eye disease that resulted in a second doctorate. In 1970 KP and Gerry DAVIS devised the BBC TV series DOOMWATCH, which ran to 37 episodes, many written by KP and Davis, and most dealing in sf terms with the prevention of manmade threats to this fragile planet. KP's first sf novel, *Mutant 59: The Plastic Eater* (**1971**) with Davis, featured a *Doomwatch*-type scenario (indeed, the basic plot had been used as a *Doomwatch* episode) in which a laboratory-created plastic-eating virus escapes, creating havoc as plastics start dissolving. The working out of the notion is less than crisp. POLLUTION and ECOLOGY themes recurred in the next two collaborations, *Brainrack* (**1974**) and *The Dynostar Menace* (**1975**), neither being wholly satisfactory. KP's scientific ideas were stronger than the methods he used to dramatize them. He made many tv and radio appearances, usually dealing with ecological problems, and presented several tv films in this field. [JC/PN]
See also: DISASTER; GENETIC ENGINEERING; PSEUDO-SCIENCE.

PEEL, JESSE [s] ◊ Steve PERRY.

PEIRCE, HAYFORD (1942-) US writer who began publishing sf with "Unlimited Warfare" for *ASF* in 1974 and who established a name for lightly written tales whose backgrounds were unusually well conceived. "Mail Supremacy" (1975) began a series – which has not reached book form – in which an Anglo-Chinese businessman brings Earth into the Galactic Postal Union. *Napoleon Disentimed* (**1987**; exp 1989 UK), his first novel, is an attractive example of what might be called the ALTERNATE-WORLDS hijinks tale: cast into a 1992 ruled by the French Empire, a confidence trickster attempts to upset the applecart. *The Thirteenth Majestral* (**1989**) – HP's titles are notably inventive – is a TIME-TRAVEL tale set in the far future and disregardful of the pretensions of established religion. *Phylum Monsters* (**1989**) deals amusedly with GENETIC ENGINEERING. [JC]

PEKIĆ, BORISLAV [r] ◊ YUGOSLAVIA.

PELKIE, J.W. [s] ◊ Raymond A. PALMER.

PELLUME, NOAM D. [s] ◊ Orson Scott CARD.

PEMBERTON, [Sir] MAX (1863-1950) UK writer, educated at Caius College, Cambridge, the first editor of *Chums* 1892-3, editor of *Cassell's Magazine* 1896-1906, and later a director of Northcliffe Newspapers; he

was knighted in 1928. Of more than 60 novels, his most famous is a Jules VERNE-style piece of CHILDREN'S SF: in the much-reprinted *The Iron Pirate: A Plain Tale of Strange Happenings on the Sea* (**1893**; vt *The Shadow on the Sea* 1907) and its sequel *Captain Black* (**1911**) an advanced submarine is used for piracy. Equally popular in its day was his novel of attempted future WAR, *Pro Patria* (**1901**), in which a Channel tunnel is excavated by the French for a planned INVASION of the UK. France is again the unsuccessful antagonist in *The Giant's Gate* (**1901**), this time using advanced submarines to bypass the UK's defence systems. Another theme prominent in MP's writing is of secret communities established either for scientific reasons, as in *The Impregnable City* (**1895**) and *The House under the Sea* (**1902**), or for UTOPIAN, as in *White Walls* (**1910**). [JE]
Other works: *Queen of the Jesters* (**1897**); *The Phantom Army* (**1898**); *Dr Xavier* (**1903**); *The Diamond Ship* (**1906**).
About the author: *Sixty Years Ago and After* (**1936**), an autobiography.
See also: HISTORY OF SF; SPACESHIPS; UNDER THE SEA.

PEMBERTON, RENFREW [s] ◊ F.M. BUSBY.

PEÑA, ALFREDO CARDONA [r] ◊ LATIN AMERICA.

PENALURICK, JAN [s] ◊ Charles DE LINT.

PENDLETON, DON(ALD EUGENE) (1927-) US writer who began with "Boomerang Peep Show" for *Ace Magazine* in 1958 and whose sf novels – some written as by Dan Britain, and most of them routine – began with *Revolt!* (**1968** as by Britain; rev vt *Civil War II: The Day it Finally Happened!* 1971 as DP) and *The Olympians* (**1969**), both soft porn. Other singletons were *Cataclysm: The Day the World Died* (**1969**), *The Guns of Terra 10* (**1970**), *The Godmakers* (**1970** as by Britain; 1974 as DP) and *1989: Population Doomsday* (**1970**; vt *Population Doomsday* 1974). Also of some sf interest are the **Asthon Ford** psychic spy tales: *Ashes to Ashes* (**1986**), *Eye to Eye* (**1986**), *Mind to Mind* (**1987**), *Life to Life* (**1987**), *Heart to Heart* (**1987**) and *Time to Time* (**1988**).

It is not certain that DP contributed to the **Mack Bolan** or **Executioner** series under the Gold Eagle Books house name Don Pendleton. Of sf interest in that series is *Mack Bolan: Paradine's Gauntlet* * (**1983**). [JC]

PENDRAY, (GEORGE) EDWARD (1901-1987) US writer and rocket scientist, a founding member of The American Interplanetary Society, and author of *The Coming Age of Rocket Power* (**1945**); he was also involved in the Time Capsule featured at the 1939 New York World's Fair. As Gawain Edwards he published some stories in sf magazines in the 1920s and 1930s and a future-WAR novel, *The Earth-Tube* (**1929**), in which Asians take advantage of their possession of the invulnerable metal undual to tunnel under South America, which they soon conquer. After a young hero has penetrated the secret, catastophic explosions close the tunnel, inundating South America but sparing the USA, which has transformed itself into a socialist regime in response to the free gold which the Asians have been raining from the skies in an effort to destabilize the great capitalist democracy. [JC]

PENNINGTON, BRUCE (1944-) UK illustrator. One of the young sf artists to gain prominence in the 1970s, BP entered the field in 1967 with a cover for Robert A. HEINLEIN's *Stranger in a Strange Land* (**1961**), though at the time he worked primarily on covers for Westerns and historical novels. Since then he has done sf covers for New English Library, BALLANTINE BOOKS, Corgi and Sphere among others; he was also associated with SCIENCE FICTION MONTHLY. His painting is textured, with brush-strokes showing and strong colour, often featuring surreal landscapes; it is distinctive, vigorous work, but has been criticized for crudeness, maybe because of its contrast with the smooth, airbrushed superrealism that was coming into vogue in the UK at that time. Two books are *Eschatus* (**1977**), containing fantasy paintings illustrating the prophecies of Nostradamus, and *The Bruce Pennington Portfolio* (**1991**). [JG/PN]

See also: BRITISH SCIENCE FICTION AWARD.

PENNY, DAVID G(EORGE) [r] ◊ ROBERT HALE LIMITED. [JC]

PENRICE, ARTHUR (? -?) Unidentified UK writer; according to Darko SUVIN almost certainly a pseudonym. AP's *Skyward and Earthward* (**1875**) features an interplanetary BALLOON aboard which the narrator visits the telepaths who live on Mars before returning to Earth to engage in further exploits. [JC]

PEOPLE THAT TIME FORGOT, THE Film (1977). Amicus. Dir Kevin Connor, starring Patrick Wayne, Sarah Douglas, Dana Gillespie, Thorley Walters, Doug McClure. Screenplay Patrick TILLEY, Connor Carter, Maurice Carter, based on *The Land that Time Forgot* (fixup **1924**) by Edgar Rice BURROUGHS. 90 mins. Colour.

After the mild success of *The* LAND THAT TIME FORGOT (1975) and AT THE EARTH'S CORE (1976), made by the same company, a third Burroughs LOST-WORLD adaptation was inevitable, but Tilley's screenplay lacked the tautness and the mild ironies of that by James CAWTHORN and Michael MOORCOCK for *The Land that Time Forgot*. This time around the MONSTERS are perfunctory, and the added feminist subplot ends up as more notably male chauvinist than the Burroughs original. [PN]

PER ASPERA AD ASTRA ◊ CHEREZ TERNII – K ZVYOZDAM.

PERCEPTION The ways in which we become aware of and receive information about the outside world, mainly through the senses, are together called perception. Philosophers are deeply divided as to whether our perceptions of the outside world correspond to an actual reality, or whether they are merely hypotheses, intellectual constructs, which may give us an unreliable or partial picture of external reality, or whether, indeed, outside reality is itself a mental construct.

Perception is and always has been a principal theme of sf; it is the philosophical linchpin of many stories and has played a subsidiary role in hundreds more. (Many perception stories are discussed, from a different perspective, under PSYCHOLOGY.) For convenience, we can divide sf perception stories into 5 groups: stories about unusual modes of perception; stories about appearance and reality; stories about perception altered through drugs; stories about synaesthesia; stories about altered perception of time. The groups are not mutually exclusive, and several stories fall into more than one category.

Unusual modes of perception appear early in sf. R.H. HORNE's *The Poor Artist* (**1871**), which is partly devoted to the way the world would appear as perceived through the senses of animals, was the first book ever to be described as "science fiction" (by his contemporary William WILSON). Edwin A. ABBOTT's *Flatland* (**1884**) is an exercise in how beings from a one- or two-dimensional universe would perceive reality, and about how we would perceive a fourth DIMENSION. J.H. ROSNY aîné's "Un autre monde" (1895; trans as "Another World" 1962) tells of a MUTANT with a very fast metabolism who can see colours beyond violet (and new life forms) invisible to ordinary humans. David LINDSAY developed a similar idea in *A Voyage to Arcturus* (**1920**), in which the protagonist, mysteriously transported to another planet, keeps forming and then losing new organs of perception whose functions run from seeing additional colours to sensing emotions to intensifying the will.

Many sf writers have followed Rosny's lead in imagining modes of perception which allow the direct sensing of ALTERNATE WORLDS or other dimensions, often through ESP (*see also* PSI POWERS). (It is probably more accurate to suppose that the idea was popularized by an H.G. WELLS story of the same year, "The Story of Davidson's Eyes" [1895], though Rosny's story is superior as sf.) A.E. VAN VOGT's melodramatic *Siege of the Unseen* (1946 as "The Chronicler"; **1959**; vt as title story in *The Three Eyes of Evil* coll **1973** UK) has a hero with a third eye which allows him to perceive and then travel into another dimension. In Richard MCKENNA's "The Secret Place" (1966) no special organ is required; a world of the distant geological past is perceived direct by the mind of the heroine. Nearly all McKenna's work involves the perception and/or construction of alternate realities. Another of his stories, "Hunter, Come Home" (1963) involves an alien lifeform that perceives by instant molecular analysis – which is not too far removed from our own sense of smell – an example of the strange modes of perception which appear in many of the stories described in the entry on ALIENS. James TIPTREE Jr often used perception themes, notably in the almost surreal "Painwise" (1971), in which a human explorer, surgically modified to feel no pain, takes up with a crew of hedonistic aliens fixated on taste sensations; pain is rediscovered. Several of Ian WATSON's novels have dealt more seriously with perception, as in *The Jonah Kit* (**1975**), where the perceptions of a whale are mediated through (and modified by) a human intelligence, and *The Martian Inca* (**1977**), where the perceptions of two South American Indians are changed by the accidental intake of a Martian organism, so that their model of the world becomes very much more complex. Watson here, as elsewhere, touches on the relation between external reality and the way that reality is perceived and modified by mental programmes in the observer. These are questions that emerge regularly in the second category, stories of appearance and reality.

Appearance and reality is one of the fundamental themes of sf. It has as much to do with METAPHYSICS and CONCEPTUAL BREAKTHROUGH as with perception *per se* (and so is discussed, from rather a different perspective, in those two entries also; relevant stories treated in more detail in the latter are "The Yellow Pill" [1958] by Rog PHILLIPS and *Counterfeit World* [**1964** UK; vt *Simulacron-3* US] by Daniel GALOUYE). The difficulty in perceiving the difference between the real and the illusory is a central theme in ABSURDIST SF and in FABULATION, as it is in surrealist literature generally; it comes up often in the stories of Josephine SAXTON and is the subject of Angela CARTER's *The Infernal Desire Machines of Doctor Hoffman* (**1972**; vt *The War of Dreams* USA) and Salman RUSHDIE's *Grimus* (**1975**). All three writers regularly use the quest format, life being seen as a journey through baffling illusions, the desired end being understanding. Ed BRYANT's *Cinnabar* (coll of linked stories **1976**) is set around an enigmatic CITY where desires can be made flesh in various ways, and where reality itself is ever dissolving from one form to another; always changing and diverse, its one unchanging quality appears to be the evanescence of external reality. In James MORROW's *The Continent of Lies* (**1984**) "dreambeans" (which grow on genetically engineered trees) are used to dissolve, temporarily, the boundaries between appearance and reality; the hero is a dreambean reviewer.

Richard COWPER has written that "one single theme which intrigues me above all others is the nature of human perception". Where van Vogt's ESP breakthroughs into other realms of perception tend to be brutally direct and melodramatic, Cowper has approached the subject more obliquely and sensitively; a kind of further reality, not explicable in everyday terms, makes itself known to several of his characters in dreams, intimations – glimpses caught, as it were, out of the corner of the eye. Cowper clearly believes that our everyday reality is only partial, and has expertly evoked a kind of quivering, tense broadening of perception, especially in *Breakthrough* (**1967**) and *The Twilight of Briareus* (**1974**). Sf stories commonly dwell on the strangeness of such experiences, and the protagonist's feeling that he might be going mad. Another example is Arthur SELLINGS's *The Uncensored Man* (**1964**), in which drugs are used to increase receptivity, a theme we will examine further below.

Several sf stories have combined ideas from MATHE-MATICS (strange topologies and geometries) with stories of perception. Arthur C. CLARKE's "The Wall of Darkness" (1949) describes how it feels to live in a world which is a three-dimensional analogue of a moebius strip; it is all inside and no outside. Ted Chiang's "Tower of Babylon" (1990), in which M.C. Escher (1902-1972) seems to be an unacknowledged collaborator, has its archaic people building a tower from Earth to Heaven, from which perceptions of Earth's nature evolve the higher one climbs until, in a perceptual loop, the top turns out to be the bottom. R.A. LAFFERTY's "Narrow Valley" (1966) is quite remarkably bigger on the inside than it is on the outside – like DR WHO's *Tardis* – and the perceptions of the observers are driven to the brink of insanity. John CROWLEY uses a similar but much more developed version of the theme in *Little, Big* (**1981**), more fantasy than sf, which foregrounds a strange house, emblematic of the world, in which the further in you go the bigger it gets. Christopher PRIEST's *Inverted World* (**1974**) is a fascinating story of perceptual paradox in two respects; first, the progressive spatial distortion that takes place north and south of a shifting zone of stability on the hyperboloid planet; second, the revelation that the planet may in fact be our own Earth, viewed by a group whose perceptions have created a model of its shape which inverts the spheroid to a hyperboloid, and who cannot escape their own intellectual construct. Such stories approach genuine philosophical questions, though these are evoked in sf more commonly than they are actively explored; but even in such cases as Priest's novel (and most like it), where the scientific and philosophical argument is not really rigorous, there is a compulsive, teasing quality about the central image that amply compensates.

Stanisław LEM has several times written about the difficulties of transcending our perceptions. *Solaris* (**1961**; trans **1970**) asks the pessimistic philosophical question: "Can we ever regard reality as knowable, given the limitations of the senses with which we apprehend it and the mental programmes which force us to relate our understanding of it always to human experience?" Barry N. MALZBERG is also intrigued with this area of speculation and pessimistic. *Beyond Apollo* (**1972**) has an astronaut returning from a disastrous expedition to Venus; he tells the story of what went wrong over and over again, always differently, but it seems that the real tragedy cannot be put in terms of his human perceptions, and all his analogies can give only a partial truth. This theme, of course, is as familiar outside sf as it is inside, though sf has remarkable resources of image and metaphor with which to explore it.

The two sf writers who have played the most extravagant and kaleidoscopic variations on the theme of appearance and reality are J.G. BALLARD and Philip K. DICK. Almost all of Ballard's early work, and much of his later, deals with the various psychological processes to which we subject our perceptions of reality. One of his earliest stories, "Build-Up" (1957; vt "The Concentration City") is a kind of bravura replay of the Clarke story cited above. A young man living in claustrophobic circumstances catches a train to escape; after weeks of travelling in one direction he finds he is going east, not west; the space of the city is curved; there is no outside, just as with our own Universe. In "The Subliminal Man" (1963) the very quickness of our perception is exploited by advertisers. In "Manhole 69" (1957) an experiment in sleep deprivation gets out of control as the subjects' apprehension of reality shrinks their universe, smaller and smaller, effectively strangling them. The whole of Ballard's *oeuvre* is, in effect, an extended exploration of the inner, psychic universes made up by our selective perceptions of the external world – hence the term he popularized, used often of his subject matter, INNER SPACE.

The paradox in Ballard is that, although our inner reality is made up of data from the outside (in such a confusing hotchpotch that the system can short out through overload), the inner pattern created by the data mediates the reception of further data in a kind of vicious circle, where no certainty is possible. Dick's emphasis is a little different; his realities often require inverted commas: they are "realities" consistently adulterated by false constructs, hallucinations, counterfeiting. Ultimately the conjuring is so baffling that the stability of *any* reality comes to seem suspect; the external world suffers a kind of dissolution. In its place we are left with a view which is surprisingly far from pessimistic, as Dick implies it; it can be synopsized (only crudely) as "the universe is what we perceive it to be". This is not necessarily an intolerable labyrinth, for Dick provides a dogged survival factor connected somehow to innate human decency, by which the construction of simple, often ethical reference points may prevent the self from spiralling inwards into subjective madness: handholds for the mind. The most important works by Dick relevant to perception are *Eye in the Sky* (1957), *Time Out of Joint* (1959), *The Man in the High Castle* (1962), *The Three Stigmata of Palmer Eldritch* (1964), *Martian Time-Slip* (1964), *The Penultimate Truth* (1964), *Dr Bloodmoney, or How We Got Along After the Bomb*, (1965), *Now Wait for Last Year* (1966), *Ubik* (1969), *A Maze of Death* (1970), and *Flow My Tears, the Policeman Said* (1974). Together they constitute a kind of meta-novel, unique in literature. Ursula K. LE GUIN moved briefly into Dick's territory with *The Lathe of Heaven* (1971), in which a man has the power to alter reality through his dreams; here, although the reality-shifts are adroitly managed, the central theme bears more on the making of ethical decisions than it does on questions of appearance and reality *per se*.

Several of the shifting realities cited in the Dick novels above were catalysed by drugs, his *A Scanner Darkly* (1977) being his most prolonged exploration of

the theme. The late 1960s saw a general interest in the drug-culture. In the air was a romantic belief that drugs could open the gates of perception, and offer heightened and perhaps superior versions of reality. Very few sf writers subscribed to this myth, and indeed when drugs had figured in earlier sf – as in Aldous HUXLEY's *Brave New World* (1932), where drugs are used to dim perception and bring about a false euphoria – they had usually been seen as detracting from rather than heightening the powers of perception, although Margaret ST CLAIR in *Sign of the Labrys* (1963) has the consciousness-heightening power of some fungi as potentially transcendental. Similarly, in Robert SILVERBERG's *Downward to the Earth* (1970) a drug is the agent for the transcendent rebirth undergone by the hero, who, like the despised natives on the planet he has revisited, is suffused by a new and joyful perception of life's harmony. Also relevant here is *The Butterfly Kid* (1967) by Chester ANDERSON, in which the drug-induced mood is more cheerful than transcendent.

More common, even in the 1960s, at the height of the drug culture's years of euphoria, were sf stories about the distortions of perception brought about by drugs, especially those written by NEW-WAVE writers, who could not generally be described as conservative and who indeed lived in the main closer to the drug-culture than sf writers a little older. Drug-taking, for example, plays a role in Charles PLATT's *The City Dwellers* (1970; rev vt *Twilight of the City* 1977) and M. John HARRISON's *The Centauri Device* (1974). Perhaps the most vivid of all new-wave sf works dealing with perception shifts through drugs is Brian W. ALDISS's *Barefoot in the Head* (fixup 1969), in which hallucinogenic drugs have been used as a weapon in Europe, and the entire freaked-out population shifts into a euphoric anarchy that changes easily to violence. Norman SPINRAD has written some notable stories about drugs, including "No Direction Home" (1971), where a future USA is so used to orchestrating its mental states by drugs that perception of naked reality without any chemical assistance is seen as the worst trip of all.

Synaesthesia is an interesting perceptual state which occasionally appears in sf; it is a condition where the senses become confused and feed into one another, so that, perhaps, a vision can be smelt. Alfred BESTER exploited it in *Tiger! Tiger!* (1956 UK; rev vt *The Stars My Destination* 1957 US), where, in a compelling passage, the hero's apotheosis comes about (with many verbal fireworks) in a synaesthetic rite of passage which mixes agony and exultation. Spinrad envisaged synaesthesia as perhaps addictive in his strong story "All the Sounds of the Rainbow" (1973).

Drugs can be seen as a quasi-natural or at least organic method of altering modes of perception. Sf, naturally, has many times invented technological means for doing the same thing. Bob SHAW has persistently written about alternate forms of vision:

in the **Slow Glass** stories collected in *Other Days, Other Eyes* (fixup **1972**) a glass is invented which slows the passage of light through it, so that the past can be directly perceived in the present; in *Night Walk* (**1967**) a blind man invents a device which allows him to see through the eyes of other humans and animals; and in *A Wreath of Stars* (**1976**) a device is invented to render visible a world (coexisting with our own) made entirely from antineutrinos.

The **Slow Glass** stories bring us directly to the last category: unusual perceptions of time (*see also* TIME TRAVEL). Spinrad has written in this area: "The Weed of Time" (1970) is about a drug which makes its victim see all his lifetime as co-present; the effect is retroactive, so that the hero as a child knows he will be affected by the drug before he has been. Dick's *Martian Time-Slip* (**1964**) sees schizophrenia (◊ PARA-NOIA) as bringing with it an altered time perception. In James BLISH's "Common Time" (1953) the altered time perception is brought about by pseudo-relativistic effects in a rapidly accelerating spaceship. Eric Frank RUSSELL's "The Waitabits" (1955) is an amusing story about a race of aliens who experience time much more slowly, appearing almost static to humans. Kurt VONNEGUT Jr's *Slaughterhouse-Five* (**1969**) has aliens who, like Spinrad's hero, see all time as existing simultaneously, which gives them a somewhat deter-ministic view of the Universe. In Jacques STERNBERG's "Ephemera", one of the stories in *Futurs sans avenir* (coll **1971**; trans as *Future without Future* **1974**), survivors of a spacewreck are doomed when they land on a planet in which, as in Russell's story, the inhabitants see time more slowly. Ballard, as might be expected, has several stories about the perception of time, the most powerful being "The Voices of Time" (1960), in which the Universe is running down and time perception on Earth is altered in various ways; one man is able to sense geological time directly, as if he smelt it. Time is a dominant theme of Aldiss's work; his stories about time perception include the strange "Man in His Time" (1965), about a man who perceives time a few minutes ahead of everyone else, and "The Night that All Time Broke Out" (1967), in which a time gas used for controlled mental time travel gushes out and affects everyone. His most notable story of this kind is *An Age* (1967; vt *Cryptozoic!* 1968 US), in which it finally turns out that time actually runs backwards, but our minds defensively perceive it as going forward. The same notion was used at around the same time, quite coincidentally, by Philip K. Dick in *Counter-Clock World* (**1967**), but the Aldiss book, though uneven, has the greater imaginative *brio*; more recent treat-ments of the ideas of *An Age* and "Man in his Time" are, respectively, Martin AMIS's *Time's Arrow* (**1991**) and Eric BROWN's "The Time-Lapsed Man" (1988). The strangest of all such stories, however, must be David I. MASSON's "Traveller's Rest" (1965), about a war against an unknown enemy on the northern frontier of a country where the perception of time

slows down as one travels south; a soldier on indefinite leave marries, raises a family, grows middle-aged, and is eventually called up again to find himself back in his bunker 22 minutes after he left. The story is told with extraordinary conviction.

The time-perception stories cited above are gene-rally of a very high standard, demonstrating clearly the way that sf thought-experiments can stimulate the mind and move the feelings in ways that are almost closed to traditional realist fiction. We take time for granted without fully understanding it, or how it works; these stories, with some intensity, stretch our perceptions of what meaning it might have for us. [PN]

PERCY, F. WALKER (1916-1990) US doctor and writer who reflected in his novels – the best known of which remains his first, *The Moviegoer* (**1961**) – a searchingly liberal and Catholic reading of US life. *Love in the Ruins: The Adventures of a Bad Catholic at a Time Near the End of the World* (**1971**), the first vol of the **Dr Thomas More** series, is a long, complex NEAR-FUTURE story set in a 1980s USA suffering technological decay, and almost certainly in no real position to benefit from the invention by the narrator – distantly related to the author of *Utopia* – of an insanity-curing device. It is continued thematically in *The Thanatos Syndrome* (**1987**). The speculative pieces assembled in *Lost in the Cosmos: The Last Self-Help Book* (coll **1983**) are mostly nonfiction, but the end of the book slips into uneasy sf. [JC]

PEREGOY, CALVIN [s] ◊ Thomas Calvert MCCLARY.

PEREIRA, W(ILFRED) D(ENNIS) (1921-   ) UK aviation engineer, advertising executive and writer whose first books, from *Time of Departure* (**1956**), concentrated on flying. He began writing sf with *Aftermath 15* (**1973**), which depicts a DYSTOPIAN post-HOLOCAUST USA whose inhabitants are rigidly strati-fied according to how much radiation they have absorbed. The projected sequels, «Aftermath 16» and «Aftermath 17», have never appeared. WDP's other novels, all written for ROBERT HALE LIMITED in a professionally impersonal style, have been *The Charon Tapes* (**1975**), *Another Eden* (**1986**), *Contact* (**1977**), *The King of Hell* (**1978**) and *Celeste* (**1979**). [JC]

PEREIRA MENDES, H(ENRY) (1852-1937) UK-born rabbi, academic and writer, from 1877 in the USA, where he wrote prolifically in many genres. *Looking Ahead: Twentieth Century Happenings* (**1899**) tells of various socialist upheavals which lead to several world wars and are defeated, in the end, only by an alliance of theocratical Christians and Jews, which also establishes in Palestine a Jewish homeland ruled by a descendant of the ancient Jewish monarchy. [JC]

PERFECT WOMAN, THE Film (1949). Two Cities/Eagle-Lion. Dir Bernard Knowles, starring Patricia Roc, Stanley Holloway, Nigel Patrick, Miles Malle-son, Irene Handl, Pamela Devis, Constance Smith. Screenplay George Black, Knowles, based on the play *The Perfect Woman* (produced 1948; **1950**) by Wallace Geoffrey and Basil Mitchell. 89 mins. B/w.

An inventor creates a ROBOT in the image of his niece and hires a young man to take it out on a date as a final test of its believability. But the real girl takes the robot's place during testing, and a conventional but well played farce follows, notable for its underwear fetishism and a sauciness quite close to the rim of what the period regarded as decent. The ending is mildly apocalyptic when the malfunctioning robot marches stiff-legged, spouting sparks and smoke, through a crowded hotel before exploding. [JB/PN] **See also:** CINEMA.

PERILS FROM THE PLANET MONGO ◊ FLASH GORDON.

PERKINS, GEOFFREY [r] ◊ Douglas ADAMS.

PERKINS, MICHAEL [r] ◊ ESSEX HOUSE.

PERRY, ROGER [r] ◊ ROBERT HALE LIMITED.

PERRY, STEVE (1947-   ) US writer who began publishing sf with "With Clean Hands" as by Jesse Peel for *Gal* in 1977, and whose first novel, *The Tularemia Gambit* (**1981**), combines sf with elements of the hardboiled detective genre. After two ties for the **Time Machine** sequence produced by the Byron PREISS packaging enterprise – *Sword of the Samurai* * (**1984**) with Michael REAVES and *Civil War Secret Agent* * (**1984**) – and an effective sf adventure, *Hellstar* (**1984**) with Reaves, SP finally came into his own with the **Matador** sequence: *The Man who Never Missed* (**1985**), *Matadora* (**1986**) and *The Machiavelli Interface* (**1986**), along with a prequel, *The 97th Step* (**1989**); plus *The Omega Cage* (**1988**) with Reaves and *Black Steel* (**1992**), both set in the **Matador** universe. Khadaji, the sequence's hero, rebels against a violent military dictatorship using his skill at martial arts to mock the enemy into impotence; in his raffish insouciance, he rather resembles Leslie CHARTERIS's **Saint**. The first volume takes its title from the fact that Khadaji has stolen a fixed number of non-lethal poison darts and proceeds to knock out precisely that number of government figures with them, never once missing, and generating a revolt through mirth; the book might be called an exercise in muscular pacifism. Subsequent volumes do not build on the success of the first, but neither do they significantly decline. Of SP's remaining singletons, *Dome* (**1987**) with Reaves makes efficient use of its post-HOLOCAUST submarine setting, as AIs come gradually to dominate the new world. [JC]

Other Works: Several **Conan** SWORD-AND-SORCERY fantasies, including *Conan the Fearless* * (**1986**), *Conan the Defiant* * (**1987**), *Conan the Indomitable* * (**1989**), *Conan the Free Lance* * (**1990**) and *Conan the Formidable* * (**1990**); *The Albino Knife* (**1991**); *The Hero Curse* (**1991** chap).

PERRY, WALTER COPLAND (1814-1911) UK writer, lawyer and archaeologist in whose sf novel, *The Revolt of the Horses* (**1898**), the Houyhnhnms (from Jonathan SWIFT's *Gulliver's Travels* [**1726**]) arrive in the England of 1950. Finding humans as terrible as ever – a future WAR features in the tale – they decide to destroy the race. [JC]

PERRY RHODAN German sf series, weekly, published by Verlagsunion Pabel Moewig (formerly Moewig-Verlag). Created by Walter Ernsting (who writes for the series as Clark DARLTON) and Karl-Herbert SCHEER, *PR* began in 1961 and is still current: to the end of 1991 about 1600 booklets describing Perry Rhodan's adventures and mankind's destiny had been published, a record quite without precedent in sf. The weekly booklet series is accompanied by a monthly paperback series, which fills some of the narrative gaps. Often thought of as aimed at the teenage market, PR is actually read, surveys show, by readers of all ages, both men and women.

Though the stories have been dismissed as potboilers, the fans of this German future HISTORY (of whom thousands attend PR CONVENTIONS) argue that the density and complexity of the world built up over so many volumes has led to a sophistication unusual in SPACE OPERA. Conversely, the series's many critics, especially in Germany, have attacked it not only on literary grounds but also for being what Franz ROTTENSTEINER calls "notoriously fascist". This judgement of PR's reactionary nature has been supported and argued at length by Michael Pehlke and Norbert Lingfeld in *Roboter und Gartenlaube: Ideologie und Unterhaltung in der Science-Fiction-Literatur* ["The Robot and the Summerhouse: Ideology and Entertainment in SF"] (**1970**) and by Manfred Nagl in "Unser Mann im All" ["Our Man in Everywhere"] (1969 *Zeitnahe Schularbeit* #4/5). During the first years of its existence PR was indeed dominated by military conflicts, but the concept changed so that now PR concentrates on solving mysteries of galactic or even cosmic scale – with lots of action.

The success of the series has been enormous, and not just in GERMANY. Translations have appeared (and sometimes still do) in many European countries, including the UK (since 1974), France (1966), Belgium (1966), Netherlands (1971), Finland (1975) and Italy (1976); also in Japan (since 1971), Brazil (since 1975) and notably in the USA, where it was published by ACE BOOKS. Ed Forrest J. ACKERMAN, the US series – monthly for much of the time – appeared for 118 numbers (1969-77) in paperback-book format, containing a letter column, articles, new stories and reprints of sf classics in addition to the leading PR novella or (in later volumes) 2 novellas; a few further PR titles were published by Ace in their **Atlans** series. When all the translations are included, PR has had a readership higher than anything else in sf.

Perry himself is an Earthman propelled into the politics of the Galaxy (◊ GALACTIC EMPIRES). He builds his small group, the New Power, into a Solar Empire; after renouncing all claims to leadership, the Solar Empire becomes one of the equal members of the Galacticum. It has been said that there is no sf idea which will not, sooner or later, be used in the series. The authors include, in addition to Ernsting (Scheer died 1991): Kurt Brand, Arndt Ellmer, H.G. Ewers, Robert Feldhoff, H.G. Francis, Peter Griese, Horst

Hoffmann, Hans Kneifel, Kurt Mahr, Marianne Sydow, Ernst Vlcek, William Voltz (died 1984) and Thomas Ziegler. Voltz was the long-time coordinator and chief author, having early superseded Scheer in this function. Each episode is written by one of the team from a treatment done by the "factory", currently Vlcek and Mahr, according to the further development of the series as discussed in an annual authors' meeting. PR has appeared in comic books, and there was also a PR magazine 1977-81.   [HU/PN]

Further reading: *Analyse einer Science-Fiction-Romanheftserie* (**1979**) by Claus Hallman; "'Perry Rhodan'", by Mike ASHLEY in *Science Fiction, Fantasy, and Weird Fiction Magazines* (**1985**) ed Ashley and Marshall B. TYMN; partial indexes of the **Perry Rhodan** novels were published by NESFA (**1973** and **1975**); a full list of English-language titles can be found in *Science Fiction and Fantasy Series and Sequels: A Bibliography* (**1986**) by Tim Cottrill, Martin H. GREENBERG and Charles G. WAUGH.

PERTWEE, ROLAND (1885-1963) UK painter, actor, playwright and author whose *MW.XX.3.* (**1929**; vt *Hell's Loose* 1929 US; vt *The Million Pound Cypher* 1931 UK) is an early example of the tale of technological PARANOIA. A dead scientist is discovered along with the eponymous formula for a cheap fuel which will if released supplant petroleum. The UK Government allows limited use of the fuel, but only until a working-class strike fomented by communists is defeated; thereafter the petroleum corporations are allowed to re-establish their dominance.   [JC]

PERU ◊ LATIN AMERICA.

PERUTZ, LEO (1882-1957) Austrian novelist and playwright who moved to Israel in 1938 after the Anschluss. Most of his novels are baroque phantasmagorias, like *Zwischen Neun und Neun* (**1918**; trans Lily Lore as *From Nine to Nine* **1926** US), an elaborately grotesque afterlife fantasy, *Der Marques de Bolibar* (**1920**; trans Graham Rawson as *The Marquis de Bolibar* **1926** UK), in which the Wandering Jew and the spirit of the eponymous marquis defeat a German regiment fighting for Napoleon, and *Die Geburt des Antichrist* ["The Birth of the Antichrist"] (**1921**). Of more direct sf interest are *Der Meister des juengsten Tages* (**1923**; trans Hedwig Singer as *The Master of the Day of Judgment* **1929** UK), in which it is suggested that an ancient hallucinogen, when breathed by men of ambition, will so terrifyingly expose their true nature that they will commit suicide, and *Sanct Petri-Schnee* (**1933**; trans E.B.G. Stamper and F.M. Hodson as *The Virgin's Brand* **1934** UK; trans Eric Mosbacher as *Saint Peter's Snow* **1990** UK), which similarly depends upon a sense that human civilization is a fragile contrivance. The eponymous wheat fungus at the centre of this tale has been, from time immemorial, responsible for spreading a virus which induces faith in humans. In 1932, after long dormancy, the virus has been deliberately reinjected into European wheat strains in order to revitalize Christianity, but the deity invoked turns out to be not God but Moloch. So forthright a

fable for the times could not go unchallenged, and the Nazis banned the book as soon as they came to power.   [JC]

See also: AUSTRIA; GODS AND DEMONS.

PEŠEK, LUDĚK (1919-   ) Czech writer and artist. LP's first novels (about social inequalities; not sf) were published in Czechoslovakia in the late 1940s, but for decades he has lived abroad, his books being first published in German translation; they have been widely translated into other languages. His astronomical paintings are well known, and have been featured in *National Geographic*; he has illustrated some of his own books. The first of several sf juveniles is *Die Mondexpedition* (**1966** Germany; trans as *Log of a Moon Expedition* **1969**). His best is *Die Erde ist nah* (**1970** Germany; trans Anthea Bell as *The Earth is Near* **1973**). It deals, with unusual sophistication for CHILDREN'S SF, with the psychological stresses experienced by the first expedition to MARS, and won the 1971 Jugendbuchpreis (Children's Book Prize) in Germany. Another sf book is *Falle für Perseus* (**1976** Germany; trans Anthea Bell as *Trap for Perseus* **1980**), set in a 23rd-century totalitarian DYSTOPIA.   [JO/PN]

Other works: *Preis der Beute* ["Price of Plunder"] (**1973** Germany); *Eine Insel für Zwei* (**1974** Germany; trans as *An Island for Two* **1975**).

See also: CZECH AND SLOVAK SF; SOCIOLOGY; SPACE FLIGHT.

PESSIMISM ◊ ENTROPY; OPTIMISM AND PESSIMISM.

PETAJA, EMIL (THEODORE) (1915-   ) US writer of Finnish descent, most of whose earlier fiction was fantasy rather than sf. He began publishing in 1935 with "The Two Doors" for the semiprozine UNUSUAL STORIES; his first professional sale was "Time Will Tell" for *AMZ* in 1942. Some of his early work can be found in *Stardrift, and Other Fantastic Flotsam* (coll **1971**). Occasionally he wrote as E. Theodore Pine (once with Henry L. HASSE), though only in magazines. A friend of Hannes BOK, EP founded the Bokanalia Foundation in 1967, after Bok's death, publishing a commemorative volume, *And Flights of Angels: The Life and Legend of Hannes Bok* (**1968**) and editing *The Hannes Bok Memorial Showcase of Fantasy Art* (**1974**). EP's first novel was *Alpha Yes, Terra No!* (**1965** dos); he published a further 12 books over the next half decade. The best known make up a series based on the Finnish verse epic *Kalevala*. In each of the novels of the **Kalevala** sequence – *Saga of Lost Earths* (**1966**) and *The Star Mill* (**1966**), both assembled under their joint titles (omni **1979**), and *The Stolen Sun* (**1967** dos) and *Tramontane* (**1967** dos), both likewise assembled under their joint titles (omni **1979**) – a Terran descendant of one of the four main heroes of the *Kalevala* is reborn into his avatar's role to order to re-enact his adventures on Otava, the planet of origin of this pantheon. A fifth book of the sequence remains unpublished. A novel unconnected with the series but still related to the *Kalevala* is *The Time Twister* (**1968**). The **Green Planet** series – *Lord of the Green Planet* (**1967** dos) and *Doom of the Green Planet*

(**1968** dos) – recounts similar adventures befalling its Irish protagonist, who finds himself role-playing fake Celtic deities for the benefit of a madman armed with sf instruments of coercion. Most of EP's sf trades unpretentiously on the emotions aroused by mythical analogues like those in his **Kalevala** books; the adventure plots through which he evokes these resonances are by no means poorly conceived, and he remains entirely readable. [JC]

Other works: *The Caves of Mars* (**1965** dos); *The Prism* (**1965** *Worlds of Tomorrow*; exp **1968** dos); *The Nets of Space* (**1969**); *The Path Beyond the Stars* (**1969**); *Seed of the Dreamers* (**1970** dos); *As Dream and Shadow* (coll **1972**), poetry.

See also: FINLAND; MYTHOLOGY.

PETERKIEWICZ, JERZY (1916-   ) Polish writer – his first novel in English was published as by Jerzy Pietrkiewicz – active as a poet in his native land before WWII. He lived in the UK for many years, wrote in English, and was married to Christine BROOKE-ROSE 1968-75. *The Quick and the Dead* (**1961**) is an afterlife fantasy. *Inner Circle* (**1966**), which is sf, remarkably conflates three strands of story: one set in the mythical past, one on the Circle Line of London's underground railway, and one in a horrific FAR FUTURE where congestion (under an artificial dome) is so great there is no room to lie down. Each story reflects the others, setting up a complex commentary on the human condition. [JC]

PETERS, DAVID ◊ Peter DAVID.

PETERS, LAWRENCE [s] ◊ L.P. DAVIES.

PETERS, LUDOVIC Pseudonym of UK writer Peter Brent (1931-1984), one of whose political thrillers, *Riot '71* (**1967**), posits a NEAR-FUTURE racist crisis in an economically battered UK. [JC]

PETRESCU, CEZAR [r] ◊ ROMANIA.

PETTY, JOHN (1919-   ) UK writer, variously employed until he began publishing in 1957. *The Last Refuge* (**1966**) is a post-HOLOCAUST novel set in an oppressive, grey England that provides no refuge for the protagonist-writer. [JC]

PEYTON, AUDREY [r] ◊ ROBERT HALE LIMITED.

PFEIL, DONALD J. (?   -   ) US writer whose *Voyage to a Forgotten Sun* (**1975**), *Through the Reality Warp* (**1976**) and *Look Back to Earth* (**1977**) were written in a deliberately (and enjoyably) outmoded SPACE-OPERA idiom. Under the house name William ARROW he wrote *Return to the Planet of the Apes 2: Escape from Terror Lagoon* ∗ (**1976**). He was also editor of VERTEX. [JC]

PFEIL, FRED Working name of US writer and academic John Frederick Pfeil (1949-   ), whose sf novel, *Goodman 2020* (**1986**), portrays in a superbly suffocating present tense the corporate USA of AD2020, where all power has fallen into the hands of priest-like businessmen. The most powerful of these hires the "professional friend" Goodman to give him moments of human society, but Goodman eventually kills him, escapes into the barrios (and the narrative dynamism of the more normal past tense) and settles

down to prepare for a wholesome change. The politics of the book may seem naïve, but the execution is compelling. Some of the essays assembled in *Another Tale to Tell: Politics and Narration in Postmodern Culture* (coll **1990**) offer a formal context for FP's sf work. [JC]

PHANTASM Film (1978). New Breed. Dir/prod/written/photographed Don Coscarelli, starring Michael Baldwin, Bill Thornbury, Reggie Bannister, Angus Scrimm. 90 mins, cut to 89 mins. Colour.

At the independent, low-budget, exploitation end of the movie market, small miracles sometimes occur that could not take place inside a major studio. *P* is one such, a spirited blend of horror, surrealism and sf, in which the presumably alien and possibly supernatural Tall Man (Scrimm) steals bodies to be resuscitated and turned into malicious, deformed midgets with yellow blood, and then passed through a dimensional gate to be used as slave labour on a red desert planet. The teenager who opposes him, Mike (Baldwin), is troubled by a flying silver sphere that kills people by spiking their brains, by the Tall Man's severed finger that becomes a nasty insect, and most of all by the Tall Man's ability to confuse appearance and reality, to be there and not there, anticipating Wes Craven's Freddy in *Nightmare on Elm Street* (1984). *P* has the arbitrary, confused logic of a dream.

A decade later *Phantasm II* (1988), also written/dir Coscarelli, was a mostly failed attempt to capitalize on the earlier cult success; it is less a sequel than a remake with a bigger budget. The special effects are more sophisticated and disgusting, but the randomness is more of a mess than a dream; the acting is stilted; ideas that were wholly original in 1978 had become clichés by 1988, and there were no new ideas to replace them; the sf content is negligible. [PN]

PHANTASM II ◊ PHANTASM.

PHASE IV Film (1973). Alced/Paramount/PBR Productions. Dir Saul Bass, starring Nigel Davenport, Lynne Frederick, Michael Murphy. Screenplay Mayo Simon. 91 mins, cut to 84 mins. Colour.

A battle of wits takes place between, on the one hand, a fanatical SCIENTIST and two others living in a desert-based experimental dome and, on the other, an ant species which has acquired intelligence. The script substitutes mysticism for science and tries too hard to emulate 2001: A SPACE ODYSSEY (1968) – as in its ending, where the two surviving human protagonists undergo a transcendental transformation. Originally there was also in the finale a *2001*-like montage of surrealistic images showing a fantastic evolutionary upheaval, but this was cut by the studio after the initial release.

Phase IV was Bass's directorial début; he had previously been known as the designer of such striking movie title sequences as those for *Psycho* (1960) and *Walk on the Wild Side* (1962). While he is a master of his craft visually, his handling of actors is unsatisfactory and he seems to have little feeling for sf. This conceptually silly melodrama is an interesting failure, its attraction lying in the superb insect photography by Ken Middleham rather than in any sf content. The novelization is *Phase IV* * (**1973**) by Barry N. MALZBERG. [JB/PN]

See also: MONSTER MOVIES.

PHELPS, GILBERT (HENRY Jr) (1915-) UK writer who spent much of his career in the BBC as a radio producer. His first story, "I Have Lived a Hundred Years" in *The Faber Book of West Country Stories* (anth **1951**), prefigured the thematic material of his first sf novel, *The Centenarians* (**1958**), whose protagonists attempt – in the end unsuccessfully – to translate their eminence in the arts and sciences into lives safely prolonged. *The Winter People* (**1963**), a very late example of the LOST-WORLD tale, describes a tribe in the Andes which has survived for centuries through hibernation and other adaptations to extreme circumstances. [JC]

See also: ANTHROPOLOGY.

PHILADELPHIA EXPERIMENT, THE Film (1984). New World/Cinema Group/New Pictures/Douglas Curtis. Executive prod John CARPENTER. Dir Stewart Raffill, starring Michael Paré, Nancy Allen, Bobby Di Cicco, Eric Christmas. Screenplay William Gray, Michael Janover, based on a story by Wallace Bennett and Don Jakoby, based in turn on the purportedly nonfictional *The Philadelphia Experiment* (**1979**) by William I. Moore and Charles Berlitz. 101 mins. Colour.

In 1943 a device to render warships invisible to radar is tested, but instead it throws an entire destroyer and crew temporarily forward in time, where two crew members fall through a vortex into the 1984 Nevada desert. One of them (whose electromagnetic instability has been creating havoc) is later drawn back to 1943. The second, joined by a paradigmatic 1980s woman (Allen), undergoes the culture shock obligatory in all visiting-ALIEN and TIME-TRAVEL films, refuses to believe that Reagan is president, looks up his buddy (now elderly), finds the time vortex is getting worse, and winds up – after a brief detour to 1943 during which he saves the world – back in 1984. *TPE* is silly as sf (having undergone many rewrites, including a script by Carpenter) but fun. While not as amusing as Raffill's earlier *The* ICE PIRATES (1984), it is better than his appallingly sentimental *Mac and Me* (1988), a film about cute aliens that appears to be an unacknowledged advertising campaign for Coca-Cola and McDonalds. [PN]

See also: INVISIBILITY.

PHILIP K. DICK AWARD Founded in 1983 by admirers of Philip K. DICK, who died in 1982. Because much of Dick's classic sf was published with no fanfare and initially without a hardcover edition, it seemed appropriate to give the award to a distinguished work of sf or fantasy of the previous year first published in paperback. The award was initially suggested by Thomas M. DISCH, who was for several years its administrator; he was succeeded by an administrative team of Algis BUDRYS and David G. HARTWELL. The winners are chosen by a jury (with variously 3, 4 and 5 members) of writers and critics, most of whom choose their own successors for the following year; usually one judge is the previous year's winner. The PKDA is announced at NorWesCon, a CONVENTION held in the state of Washington in March each year. In good years, when the committee has collected enough cash, the winner receives $1000 and the second-place winner $500. Plaques are provided by the Philip K. Dick estate. [PN]

Winners:
1983: 1st, Rudy RUCKER, *Software*
2nd, Ray Faraday NELSON, *The Prometheus Man*
1984: 1st, Tim POWERS, *The Anubis Gates*
2nd, R.A. MACAVOY, *Tea With The Black Dragon*
1985: 1st, William GIBSON, *Neuromancer*
2nd, Kim Stanley ROBINSON, *The Wild Shore*
1986: 1st, Tim Powers, *Dinner at Deviant's Palace*
2nd, Richard GRANT, *Saraband of Lost Time*
1987: 1st, James P. BLAYLOCK, *Homunculus*
2nd, Jack MCDEVITT, *The Hercules Text*
1988: 1st, Patricia Geary, *Strange Toys*
2nd, Mike MCQUAY, *Memories*
1989: 1st (equal), Paul J. MCAULEY, *400 Billion Stars*
1st (equal), Rudy Rucker, *Wetware*
1990: 1st, Richard Paul RUSSO, *Subterranean Gallery*
2nd, Dave WOLVERTON, *On My Way to Paradise*
1991: 1st, Pat MURPHY, *Points of Departure* (coll)
2nd, Raymond HARRIS, *The Schizogenic Man*
1992: 1st, Ian MCDONALD, *King of Morning, Queen of Day*
2nd, Emma BULL, *Bone Dance*

PHILLIFENT, JOHN T(HOMAS) (1916-1976) UK writer of much sf and works in other genres; though he claimed to reserve his best material for publication under his own name, he was at least as well known to sf readers under his pseudonym John Rackham. He began writing sf with the **Space Puppet** series for Pearson's Tit-Bits SF Library as Rackham: *Space Puppet* (**1954** chap), *Jupiter Equilateral* (**1954** chap), *The Master Weed* (**1954** chap) and *Alien Virus* (**1955** chap). He produced also a fantasy series, the **Chappie Jones** stories, for *Science Fantasy*, beginning with "The Veil of Isis" (1961); these stories were assembled as *The Touch of Evil* (coll of linked stories **1963**) as by Rackham. In the mid-1960s his career picked up some steam with a flow of Rackham SPACE OPERAS for ACE BOOKS, beginning with *We, the Venusians* (**1965** dos US) and *Danger from Vega* (**1966** dos US), and continuing with others of the same unambitiously readable nature. Under his own name, JTP produced in the 1970s some sf novels of real competence, including *King of Argent* (**1973** US), an entertaining adventure set on an agreeably strange planet. Through his career, he remained a reliable producer of the second-rank fiction demanded by an entertainment genre hungry for copy. [JC]

Other works: 3 MAN FROM U.N.C.L.E. ties: *The Mad*

Scientist Affair * (**1966** US), *The Corfu Affair* * (**1967**) and *The Power Cube Affair* * (**1968**); *Genius Unlimited* (**1972** US); *Hierarchies* (**1973** dos US); *Life with Lancelot* (coll of linked stories **1973**).

As John Rackham: *Watch on Peter* (**1964**), a juvenile; *The Beasts of Kohl* (**1966** dos US); *Time to Live* (**1966** dos US); *The Double Invaders* (**1967** dos US); *Alien Sea* (**1968** dos US); *The Proxima Project* (**1968** dos US); *Ipomoea* (**1969** dos US); *Treasure of Tau Ceti* (**1969** dos US); *The Anything Tree* (**1970** dos US); *Flower of Doradil* (**1970** dos US); *Beyond Capella* (**1971** dos US); *Dark Planet* (**1971** dos US); *Earthstrings* (**1972** dos US); *Beanstalk* (**1973** US).

PHILLIPS, MARK Pseudonym used on a series of novels written by Randall GARRETT and Laurence M. JANIFER for *ASF*: *Brain Twister* (**1959** as "That Sweet Little Old Lady"; **1962**), *The Impossibles* (**1960** as "Out Like a Light"; **1963**) and *Supermind* (**1960-61** as "Occasion for Disaster"; **1963**). [BS]

PHILLIPS, ROG Working name of US writer Roger Phillips Graham (1909-1965), a prolific contributor to the sf magazines of the late 1940s and 1950s. His first story was "Let Freedom Ring" in 1945 for AMAZING STORIES, which, along with its companion magazine FANTASTIC ADVENTURES, remained his most regular market. He wrote a series of stories featuring the character **Lefty Baker**: "Squeeze Play" (1947), "The Immortal Menace" (1949), "The Insane Robot" (1949) and "But Who Knows Huer or Huen?" (1969). His best known story is "The Yellow Pill" (1958), an ingenious exercise in paradoxes of PERCEPTION (*see also* CONCEPTUAL BREAKTHROUGH; PSYCHOLOGY). Some of his short work appeared as by Clinton Ames, Franklin Bahl, Craig Browning, Gregg Conrad, Inez McGowan, Melva Rogers, Chester Ruppert, William Carter Sawtelle and John Wiley; he also wrote under the house names Robert ARNETTE, Alexander BLADE, P.F. COSTELLO, A.R. STEBER, Gerald VANCE and Peter WORTH. Under the aegis of *AMZ* editor Raymond A. PALMER, RP conducted an influential FANZINE-review column, **The Club House** (Mar 1948-Mar 1953), later reviving it in other magazines ed Palmer: UNIVERSE SCIENCE FICTION and OTHER WORLDS. RP wrote 4 novels, none negligible, though less successful than some of his shorter work: *Time Trap* (**1949**), *Worlds Within* (**1950**), *World of If* (**1951**) and *The Involuntary Immortals* (**1949** *Fantastic Adventures*; rev **1959**), the last being an example of a kind of tale intrinsic to GENRE SF (a recent example being Nancy KRESS's *Beggars in Spain* [**1991**]): a group of young paranormals (◊ SUPERMAN) must band together to protect themselves from the vengeance of ungifted normal humans. [MJE/JC]

See also: FANTASTIC VOYAGES; POLITICS; ZIFF-DAVIS.

PHILLIPS, THOMAS ◊ L.P. DAVIES.

PHILLPOTTS, EDEN (1862-1960) UK writer known primarily for his work outside the sf field. He was extremely prolific, writing about 250 books and plays. His first sf novel was the lurid thriller *Number 87* (**1922**) as by Harrington Hext. His most notable SCIENTIFIC ROMANCES belong to a later and very

different phase of his work: the excellent *Saurus* (**1938**), in which a reptilian ALIEN becomes an objective observer commenting upon contemporary society and the human condition; *The Fall of the House of Heron* (**1948**), a study of an amoral atomic scientist; and *Address Unknown* (**1949**), which deliberately challenges the assumption of *Saurus* that an alien observer could pass meaningful judgment on human affairs. These novels carried forward philosophical themes from a remarkable series of didactic philosophical fables, most of which are based in Greek mythology: *The Girl and the Faun* (**1916**), *Evander* (**1919**), *Pan and the Twins* (**1922**), *The Lavender Dragon* (**1923**), *The Treasures of Typhon* (**1924**), *Circe's Island* (coll **1925**; includes *The Girl and the Faun*), *The Miniature* (**1926**), *Arachne* (**1927**), *The Apes* (**1929**), *Alcyone* (**1930**) and *The Owl of Athene* (**1936**). The last-named deploys some sf motifs, notably an INVASION of the UK by giant crabs, and links the mythological fantasies to the scientific romances. EP's philosophical meditations are featured also in a curious early fantasy, *My Laughing Philosopher* (**1896**); but the determined rationalism and Epicurean humanism developed in his allegorical fantasies is better displayed in his collection of fiction and nonfiction, *Thoughts in Prose and Verse* (coll **1924**), whose fantasy stories include a visionary encounter with an inhabitant of JUPITER.

Also of marginal sf interest are one of EP's early collaborations with Arnold Bennett (1867-1931), *The Statue* (**1908**), which involves innovative radio apparatus, and a treasure-island story *Tabletop* (**1939**), which features giant spiders. He wrote numerous mystery novels, some of which have very slight intrusions of ESP; the most interesting are *The Grey Room* (**1921**), which features a dramatic confrontation between scientific rationalism and religious mysticism in search of the solution to the mystery of a haunted room, and the rationalized-werewolf story *Lycanthrope* (**1937**). His other fantasies include *A Deal with the Devil* (**1895**), an ANSTEY-esque novel about a man who grows young, and several early stories collected in *Fancy Free* (coll **1901**). There are occasional fantasies in his various other collections; the tales of "witchcraft" assembled in *The Hidden Hand* (coll of linked stories **1952**) do not in fact invoke the supernatural. [BS]

Other works: *The Transit of the Red Dragon* (coll **1903**); *The Golden Fetich* (**1903**); *The Flint Heart* (**1910**); *Black, White and Brindled* (coll **1923**); *Up Hill, Down Dale* (coll **1925**); *The Voice from the Dark* (**1925**); *Peacock House and Other Mysteries* (coll **1926**); *The Blue Comet: A Comedy in Three Acts* (**1927**); *The Torch and Other Tales* (coll **1929**).

See also: ASTEROIDS; ASTRONOMY; LONGEVITY (IN WRITERS AND PUBLICATIONS); SATIRE; SOCIOLOGY.

PHILMUS, ROBERT M(ICHAEL) (1943-) US sf critic, professor of English literature at Concordia University, Montreal. He became a co-editor of SCIENCE-FICTION STUDIES with the Nov 1978 issue and remained in that position until the last issue of 1991; he remains a contributing editor. His *Into the Unknown: The Evolution of Science Fiction from Francis Godwin to H.G. Wells* (**1970**; rev 1983) is scholarly and informative, and something of a pioneering study for its time. RMP also wrote the section on "Science Fiction: From its Beginning to 1870" for the 1st edn of *Anatomy of Wonder: Science Fiction* (**1976**; rev 1981; rev 1987) ed Neil BARRON. With David Y. Hughes he ed *H.G. Wells: Early Writings in Science and Science Fiction* (coll **1975**), and with Patrick PARRINDER he ed *H.G. Wells's Literary Criticism* (coll **1980**). A variorum edition of Wells's *The Island of Dr Moreau* (**1896**), annotated and introduced by RMP, is projected. [PN] **See also:** CANADA; CRITICAL AND HISTORICAL WORKS ABOUT SF.

PHILPOT, JOSEPH HENRY [r] ◊ Philip LAFARGUE.

PHYSICS In discussing the scientific content of sf it is customary to regard the sciences as ranging from "hard" to "soft", with physics lying at the hard end of the spectrum (◊ HARD SF). A concern with the hard sciences is generally held to have characterized sf of the period 1940-60, or a type of sf whose *locus classicus* is to be found in that period, and so we may expect this type of sf, in its scientific aspect, to be dominated by physics. In fact a large part of the importance in sf of physics can be attributed to its association with TECHNOLOGY; among the pure sciences, ASTRONOMY and BIOLOGY have probably provided more motive force for hard sf than has physics. Nevertheless, physics is prominent in the ideological and cultural background to sf, and its influence can often be detected even when it makes no explicit contribution to a story. A familiarity with physical ideas and an ability to deploy the language of physics have been used by many authors to establish a general scientific atmosphere, a good example being Isaac ASIMOV's "Three Laws of Robotics", which borrow the form of Newton's Three Laws of Motion so as to claim the same seminal impact.

The two areas of physics which have been most popular with sf writers, GRAVITY (*see also* ANTIGRAVITY) and Relativity (◊ FASTER THAN LIGHT), are covered in the relevant entries. Ideas from physics have been applied to technology constantly since Hugo GERNS-BACK or even Jules VERNE, but in such writing the interest usually lies in the application. Some writers seem to feel that the motivation of fundamental research lies entirely in its applications. Tom GODWIN, for example, in "Mother of Invention" (1953), changes the proverb and proposes that necessity is the mother of DISCOVERY; he shows the crew of a crashed spaceship developing a new theory of gravitation which enables them to design an antigravity generator to lift their ship. The most extreme example of this attitude is embodied in Raymond F. JONES's "Noise Level" (1952), which argues that, if we only try hard enough, we can discover any laws of nature we should like to be true.

Many imaginary inventions and strange events are based on points of physics, though sometimes the explanation of the *modus operandi* amounts to no more than a translation into technical terms of the everyday description of its effect – as in H.G. WELLS's explanation in *The Invisible Man* (**1897**) that the INVISIBILITY potion works by giving human flesh a refractive index of one. An effect at the opposite pole to this was envisaged by Bob SHAW in his invention of "slow glass" in "Light of Other Days" (1966), in which light travels so slowly that it takes several years to travel through the thickness of a window pane. (Realizing that it would not give quite the effect he wanted, Shaw was obliged to reject the description of slow glass as simply having a very high refractive index.)

Part, if only a small part, of the effectiveness of the idea of slow glass lies in the way it provides an imaginative realization of a physical fact that in normal experience remains merely theoretical knowledge, namely the finiteness of the speed of light. This kind of imaginative exploration of physics can be seen in its purest form in James BLISH's "Nor Iron Bars" (1957), which is an attempt to provide a picture of the inside of an atom and the quantum behaviour exhibited by electrons, utilizing the device of having a spaceship shrink to subatomic size and move inside an atom as if it were a solar system. This was one of the very few sf stories before the mid-1970s to make any substantial use of quantum phenomena. Blish adopted a similar approach to a more familiar area of physics in his famous microscopic-world story "Surface Tension" (1952).

Ideas from physics have been used in postulating new forms of life. The favourite basis for these is electromagnetic fields, either in isolation, as in Fredric BROWN's "The Waveries" (1945) and Bob Shaw's *The Palace of Eternity* (**1969**), or in conjunction with inorganic matter, as in Fred HOYLE's *The Black Cloud* (**1957**), the latter having something in common with the sentient suns in Olaf STAPLEDON's *Star Maker* (**1937**). Blish's *VOR* (**1958**) is about a creature whose energy source is one of the fusion cycles which Bethe proposed as taking place in stars (this creature communicates by modulating light waves rather than sound waves). In Fredric Brown's "Placet is a Crazy Place" (1946) there are birds, made of condensed matter, which fly through the rock of a planet as if it were air. Stanisław LEM's *Solaris* (**1961**; trans **1970**) postulates life formed from a new type of matter composed entirely of neutrinos. Shaw's *A Wreath of Stars* (**1976**) postulates an antineutrino world whose form of matter can interpenetrate with that of our own. Neutrinos are particles which have no properties other than momentum and spin, and interact only very weakly with other particles, so that they are very difficult to stop. Their harmlessness is the point of Ralph S. Cooper's SATIRE "The Neutrino Bomb" (1961); their delicacy underlies the idea of "neutrino acupuncture" in "Six Matches" (1960) by Arkady and Boris STRUGATSKI.

The last four examples make use of the branch of

physics which, together with COSMOLOGY (including theories of BLACK HOLES), has undergone dramatic development in the last decade and therefore has the most obvious potential for sf; the physics of elementary particles. Subnuclear physics provides one of the ideas in Isaac Asimov's *The Gods Themselves* (**1972**), which postulates a parallel universe whose strong nuclear force is greater than in ours; pumping electrons between the two universes provides a source of energy in both. Some of the more striking ideas in the field of particle physics concern condensed matter, ANTIMATTER and neutrinos. Condensed matter is of two kinds: "electron-degenerate" matter, the material of white dwarf stars, in which the atoms are compressed as close as they can be while remaining atoms (a matchboxful would weigh several tons); and nuclear matter ("neutronium"), the material of NEUTRON STARS, which has the density of the atomic nucleus (a pinhead of it would weigh several thousand tons). Degenerate matter features in "Placet is a Crazy Place" and in Paul CAPON's juvenile novel *The Wonderbolt* (**1955**); and nuclear matter in Larry NIVEN's "There is a Tide" (1968).

Antimatter is composed of particles which are the opposite in all respects to those which compose ordinary matter; when matter and antimatter meet, they mutually annihilate in a burst of radiation. A.E. VAN VOGT's "The Storm" (1943) is about a storm in space that takes place when an ordinary gas cloud meets a cloud of antimatter gas. Some more of the craziness of Placet in Brown's story comes from its orbiting two suns, one of matter and the other of antimatter. Larry Niven described an antimatter planet in "Flatlander" (1967). The correspondence between an electron and its antiparticle, the positron, was used by Blish in "Beep" (1954) as the basis of a method of instantaneous signalling, following ideas suggested by the original description by Paul Dirac (1902-1984) of the positron (◊ DIRAC COMMUNICATOR). The formation of matter and antimatter universes in the first fraction of a second of creation, and some extremely hypothetical consequences for the nature of our reality, are treated in *The Jonah Kit* (**1975**) by Ian WATSON, who blends real and imaginary physics very adroitly throughout the book.

Stories which turn on fairly elementary points of physics include: Arthur C. CLARKE's "A Slight Case of Sunstroke" (1958), in which the spectators at a football match hold their glossy programmes so as to form an enormous parabolic mirror focusing sunlight on the referee; Clarke's "Silence Please" (1954), in which the phenomenon of interference is used as the basis for a silence generator; Robert A. HEINLEIN's "Let There Be Light" (1940 as by Anson MacDonald), which suggests that the relationship between radio waves and light waves could be used to provide a cold light source; and Larry Niven's "A *Kind* of Murder" (1974), in which the fact that potential energy and heat are interchangeable forms of energy is exploited in an attempt at a perfect murder. *The*

Dispossessed (**1974**) by Ursula K. LE GUIN is unusual in sf in that much of the story is focused on an attempt to recreate the thought processes and psychology of a physicist whose theories regarding simultaneity and the nature of time would create a revolution in physics comparable to that initiated by Einstein's Relativity theories. Le Guin's physics is imaginary though plausible and presented with conviction (◊ IMAGINARY SCIENCE); her psychology might very well be accurate.

Finally, since measurement is of fundamental importance in physics, this is the place to mention those stories that make the point that all physical measurements are relative. It was put in its simplest form by Katherine MacLEAN in "Pictures Don't Lie" (1951); it was put further into the context of physics by Philip LATHAM in "The Xi Effect" (1950), observing that there would be no observable consequences if everything in the Universe were to contract at the same rate (although the contraction would become observable if the wavelength of visible light stayed constant). Referring to time rather than length, Blish described in "Common Time" (1953) an oscillating discrepancy between a man's internal (mental) time and external (physical) time.

Since the appearance of black holes in sf in the mid-1970s there has been something of an upsurge of physics themes; most relate to COSMOLOGY, but a number of stories concern quantum physics, not necessarily cosmological. Often these stories take metaphors from physics rather than physics itself; one of the first such ideas drawn from physics and thereafter used as a metaphor is ENTROPY (which is from thermodynamics, not quantum physics), and many such stories are discussed under that head. An even older example is Heisenberg's Uncertainty Principle, formulated in 1927, which regularly appears both within and outside sf, usually not in its strict meaning but as a kind of "proof" from the world of physics that we can no longer be sure of anything, and that all the old certainties are gone. Schrödinger's Cat has popped up so often as almost to have become a CLICHÉ, as in "Schrödinger's Cat" (1974) by Ursula Le Guin, the **Schrödinger's Cat** trilogy (1979-81) by Robert Anton WILSON, *The Coming of the Quantum Cats* (**1986**) by Frederik POHL and "Schrödinger's Kitten" (1988) by George Alec EFFINGER. The attraction of this idea is that, according to the many-worlds interpretation of quantum physics formulated in the late 1960s by Hugh Everett, John Wheeler and Neill Graham – who took the fate of Schrödinger's possibly murdered cat (a half-dead, half-live wave function until somebody comes to look at it, at which point it collapses into one state or the other) as their starting point – the cat's fate gives an imaginative warrant for the existence of ALTERNATE WORLDS. Perhaps the wittiest use of ideas from quantum physics appears in Connie WILLIS's "At the Rialto" (1989), which describes the extraordinary quantum uncertainties that vex a congress of quantum physicists at a large hotel. It behoves us all to remember the remark of physicist Niels Bohr (1885-1962): "Those who are not shocked when they first come across quantum theory cannot possibly have understood it."

Among those who use ideas from physics with considerable sophistication and know-how are a number of writers of SPACE OPERA and adventure on other planets, including old-stagers like Larry Niven and Arthur C. Clarke but also newer authors, in their turn expanding the genre, like Stephen BAXTER, Greg BEAR, Gregory BENFORD, David BRIN, Robert L. FORWARD, Paul J. MCAULEY, Charles SHEFFIELD and John E. STITH. More detailed accounts of their work, and other relevant users of themes from physics, will be found by following up the various cross-references above as well as BIG DUMB OBJECTS, DYSON SPHERE, FORCE FIELD, ION DRIVE, MATHEMATICS, SPACE WARP and TACHYONS. [TSu/PN]

PIANETA DEGLI UOMINI SPENTI, IL (vt *Battle of the Worlds*; vt *Planet of the Lifeless Men*) Film (1961). Ultra Film/Sicilia Cinematografica/Topaz. Dir Anthony Dawson (pseudonym of Antonio Margheriti), starring Claude Rains, Bill Carter, Umberto Orsini, Maya Brent, Jacqueline Derval. Screenplay Vassily Petrov. 94 mins, cut to 84 mins. Colour.

Earth is threatened by a large meteor, which launches flying saucers at Earth and proves to be sent from an alien planet (now dead) and run by a COMPUTER. Rains is the scientist who gains access to the computer. The fevered stylization of the dead-planet imagery (giant skeletons, etc.) rather than the bewildering though sometimes funny story is what everyone who has seen this somewhat rare but visually striking film remembers. Margheriti, a very uneven director, was one of the most prolific stalwarts of the Italian exploitation movie. [PN]

PIEGAI, DANIELA [r] ◊ ITALY.

PIER, THE ◊ *La* JETÉE.

PIERCE, JOHN J. (? -) US editor and critic with a background in FANDOM, editor of a FANZINE, *Renaissance*, in the 1960s, and at that time author of polemical articles about the damage he saw being wrought on sf by writers of the NEW WAVE. JJP ed GALAXY SCIENCE FICTION Nov 1977-Mar/Apr 1979, years in which through no special fault of his the magazine was rapidly declining. Later he published an ambitious trilogy of critical books about sf, **A Study in Imagination and Evolution**, which together form a kind of HISTORY OF SF: *Foundations of Science Fiction* (**1987**), *Great Themes of Science Fiction* (**1987**) and *When Worlds Collide* (**1989**). These may deserve more discussion than they appear to have received. JJP's prose is accessible and the books are well organized, but their ideology is deeply conservative in the sense that non-GENRE SF is seen by JJP as effectively not sf at all. Within the books' strong bias toward HARD SF are some well informed discussions about the different ways in which sf has invented the future. Much of the analysis is thematic, some philosophical. [PN]

PIERCE, JOHN R(OBINSON) (1910-) US scientist and writer. As scientist he was a director of Bell Telephone Laboratories 1952-71, working intimately at the forefront of communications research and development; after 1971 he was professor of engineering at the California Institute of Technology, from which he had received his PhD in 1936. As writer, JRP published 14 nonfiction works, both specialized and popular, from *Theory and Design of Electron Beams* (**1949**; rev 1954) to *Almost All about Waves* (**1974**). As an sf writer he has published material under his own name, as John Roberts and as J.J. Coupling, beginning with "The Relics from the Earth" for *Science Wonder Stories* in 1930 under his own name. He remains best known as J.J. Coupling, contributing 1944-71 a number of nonfiction articles under that name to *ASF*. [JC]

See also: IMMORTALITY.

PIERCY, MARGE (1936-) US writer who has become recognized as a significant voice of US FEMINISM, initially with POETRY in volumes like *Breaking Camp* (coll **1968**) but more importantly in novels like *Going Down Fast* (**1969**) and *Vida* (**1980**). Her first sf novel, *Dance the Eagle to Sleep* (**1970**), deals with an attempt by a group of student revolutionaries to set up a loving, communistic alternative society in the shadow of a near-totalitarian NEAR-FUTURE US state. In *Woman on the Edge of Time* (**1976**) a Chicano woman, falsely accused of abusing her daughter and confined to a mental institution, makes contact with (or hallucinates the existence of) an emissary from a future society which has arisen in the aftermath of a "full feminist revolution". This vision of a USA in which women and men are truly equal and truly whole has inspired many; although, while the contemporary sequences are insightful and deeply moving, the descriptions of the future UTOPIA tend to lack credibility. It might be accurate to say that the culture so described is primarily a utopia of personal relationships rather than one of social and technological structures, and is perhaps best approached as a dream rather than as a realizable society.

He, She and It (**1991**; vt *Body of Glass* 1992 UK) more sustainedly places its examination of human relationships in a CYBERPUNK-influenced vision of a USA dominated by Japanese corporations, but the analogy which structures the plot – an ANDROID powered by an AI is likened to the medieval GOLEM – seems sentimental, especially in the closing pages, where the android sacrifices itself so a Jewish commune may live. [NT/JC]

See also: POETRY; SOCIOLOGY; WOMEN SF WRITERS.

PIKE, CHRISTOPHER (? -) Pseudonymous US writer whose career has been mostly devoted to novels for older children; some of these, like *The Tachyon Web* (**1986**), are sf adventures combining orthodox plots (in this case a group of teenagers "borrows" a spaceship in which they penetrate the eponymous barrier which keeps humans from outer space) with a modicum of contemporary relevance (the children in this book are sexually involved with one another). Other juveniles – including *Chain Letter* (**1986**), *Last Act* (**1988**), *Remember Me* (**1989**), *Scavenger Hunt* (**1989**), *See You Later* (**1990**), *Witch* (**1990**) and *Fall into Darkness* (**1990**) – are horror or fantasy, the latter sometimes involving TIME TRAVEL. With *Sati* (**1990**), whose eponymous heroine may be God or may be a dippy channeller, CP moved into adult fiction. *Whisper of Death* (**1991**) is an sf tale for older children, and *The Season of Passage* (**1992**) is an adult horror novel. [JC]

PILGRIM AWARD Given at its annual summer conference since 1970 by the SCIENCE FICTION RESEARCH ASSOCIATION to a person who has made distinguished contributions to the study of sf, the Pilgrim is awarded normally for a body of work rather than for a specific book or essay, and has gone to both scholars and critics, academic and otherwise. Judging is by a committee of the SFRA, reconstituted each year. Recipients become Honorary SFRA Members; until 1990 they received certificates, since then commemorative plaques (also given retrospectively to previous winners). The award is named for *Pilgrims through Space and Time* (**1947**) by J.O. Bailey, who in 1970 was the PA's first recipient. [PN]

Winners:

1970: J.O. BAILEY
1971: Marjorie Hope NICOLSON
1972: Julius KAGARLITSKI
1973: Jack WILLIAMSON
1974: I.F. CLARKE
1975: Damon KNIGHT
1976: James E. GUNN
1977: Thomas D. CLARESON
1978: Brian W. ALDISS
1979: Darko SUVIN
1980: Peter NICHOLLS
1981: Sam MOSKOWITZ
1982: Neil BARRON
1983: H. Bruce FRANKLIN
1984: Everett F. BLEILER
1985: Samuel R. DELANY
1986: George Edgar SLUSSER
1987: Gary K. WOLFE
1988: Joanna RUSS
1989: Ursula K. LE GUIN
1990: Marshall B. TYMN
1991: Pierre VERSINS
1992: Mark HILLEGAS

PILLER, EMANUEL S. (1907-   ) US author, with Leonard ENGEL (*whom see for details*), of *The World Aflame: The Russian-American War of 1950* (**1947**). [JC]

PINCHER, (HENRY) CHAPMAN (1914-   ) Indian-born UK writer of some fiction and considerable journalism. In his first sf novel, *Not With A Bang* (**1965**), the effects of an anti-age drug are seen as catastrophic. *The Giantkiller* (**1967**) is borderline sf in its portrait of a rabid union leader attempting to take over the nation. [JC]

Other works: *The Penthouse Conspirators* (**1970**) and *The Eye of the Tornado* (**1976**), both borderline.

PINCHIN, FRANK J(AMES) (1925-1990) UK research chemist and author. His first 4 sf novels, all as by Peter Dagmar, were not exceptional: *Alien Skies* (**1962**), *Spykos 4: Strange Life-Forms on Unexplored Planets* (**1962**; vt *Spaceways* 1973 Australia), *Sands of Time* (**1963**) – a fairly complex TIME-TRAVEL tale – and *Once in Time* (**1963**; vt *Mind Probe* 1973 Australia). *Mars 314* (**1970**), under his own name, renders NEAR-FUTURE space flight with some versimilitude. *Two Equals One* (**1982**), his last Peter Dagmar title, features an electronic spying device which can read computer memories. *Stargrail* (**1989**) and *Nexweb* (**1990**), both as FJP, attempt to marry sf and occultism. [JC]

PINE, E. THEODORE [s] ◊ Henry L. HASSE; Emil PETAJA.

PINES, NED L. (1905-1990) US magazine and book publisher who in 1931 founded a group of magazines with *Thrilling* in the title: *Thrilling Detective*, *Thrilling Love*, etc. These became part of the Pines Publications group (which NP served as president 1929-61), whose associated companies included Standard Magazines, Beacon Magazines and Better Publications. In 1936 NP bought Gernsback's WONDER STORIES and retitled it THRILLING WONDER STORIES to fit neatly among his other magazines. Among NP's senior staff members were Leo MARGULIES and Mort WEISINGER. NP was by no means an sf specialist – of the 44 or so magazines he owned by the end of the 1930s, the huge majority were not sf – but other SF MAGAZINES followed, among them STARTLING STORIES in 1939, CAPTAIN FUTURE in 1940, and the reprint magazine FANTASTIC STORY QUARTERLY in 1950. All of these PULP MAGAZINES had died (like most of their kind) by the mid-1950s, *Startling Stories* being the last to go (Fall 1955). In 1942 NP founded the paperback publishing house Popular Library (which did not publish much sf) and put Margulies in charge; the Popular Library logo became a pine tree in 1956, in honour of NP, who retired in 1971. [PN]

PINKWATER, DANIEL M(ANUS) (1941-   ) US writer whose many novels for children have attracted large adult audiences for their surreal wit, their supple and astringent wisdom and (for sf readers in particular) the wry hilarity of their use of sf venues and themes. After several non-genre works as Manus Pinkwater (a form of his name which appears only in books of the 1970s), DMP began writing tales of genre interest with *Wizard Crystal* (**1973**) and *Magic Camera* (**1974**), attracting considerable attention with *Lizard Music* (**1976**), an sf fantasia in which a young boy begins seeing musical lizards everywhere, finds they are real and in secret occupancy of a nearby invisible island, and later discovers that they have allied themselves with the "right" sort of humans to oppose pod-people from space. Many of DMP's books are either explicitly constructed as series – like the **Magic Moscow** sequence and the **Snarkout Boys** sequence – or share venues and characters with one another. In the end, no DMP book stands alone: all occupy, in one way or another, a region whose children tend to be lonely but clear-sighted and whose adults are either blind (or astonishingly open) to the crowded marvellousness of the Universe. Some of the more outstanding singletons for older children are *Wingman* (**1975**) as Manus Pinkwater, *Fat Men from Space* (**1976**) as Daniel Manus Pinkwater, *Alan Mendelsohn, the Boy from Mars* (**1979**), *Yobgorgle: Mysterious Monster of Lake Ontario* (**1979**), *Java Jack* (**1980**) with Luqman Keele, *The Worms of Kukumlima* (**1981**) and *Borgel* (**1990**). The books for younger children, heavily illustrated and written in a bumptious though easy-to-follow style, are almost as intriguing.   [JC]

Other works (mostly for younger readers): The **Moose** sf trilogy featuring a time-travelling moose vampire and comprising *Blue Moose* **1975** chap) as Manus Pinkwater, *The Return of the Moose* (**1979** chap) and *The Moosepire* (**1986** chap); *The Big Orange Splot* (**1977** chap); *The Blue Thing* (**1977** chap); *Pickle Creature* (**1979** chap); the **Magic Moscow** sequence, comprising *The Magic Moscow* (**1980** chap), *Attila the Pun* (**1981** chap) and *Slaves of Spiegel* (**1982** chap); *Tooth-Gnasher Superflash* (**1981** chap); the **Snarkout Boys** sequence, comprising *The Snarkout Boys and the Avocado of Death* (**1982**) and *The Snarkout Boys and the Baconburg Horror* (**1984**); *Roger's Umbrella* (**1982** chap) as by Honest Dan'l Pinkwater; *I Was a Second-Grade Werewolf* (**1983**); *Ducks!* (**1984** chap); *Devil in the Drain* (**1984** chap); *The Frankenbagel Monster* (**1986** chap); *The Muffin Fiend* (**1986** chap); *Guys from Space* (**1989** chap); *Wempires* (**1991** chap).

Nonfiction: *Fish Whistle: Commentaries, Uncommentaries, and Vulgar Excesses* (coll **1989**); *Chicago Days/Hoboken Nights* (**1991**), a memoir.

PIONEER AWARD ◊ AWARDS.

PIPER, H(ORACE) BEAM (1904-1964) US writer and gun collector, employed as a detective on the Pennsylvania Railroad until made redundant in the mid-1950s; his first name is not known for sure, and may have been Henry. Though he wrote for other genres, he is best remembered for his sf, much of which appeared in *ASF* from 1947, when he began with "Time and Time Again". Though he shared John W. CAMPBELL Jr's political views, and his sense of the appropriate kind of story in which to propound them, it is probably wrong to think of HBP as a mouthpiece for the great editor: he was (in the end tragically) his own man. His first sf novels – *Crisis in 2140* (1953 *ASF* as "Null ABC"; **1957**) and *A Planet for Texans* (**1958**), both with John J. MCGUIRE – are straightforward adventures, one set in a USA that has revolted from literacy for fear of its consequences, the other on a planet set up like a Western.

Much of HBP's work fits very loosely into what has been called the **Terro-Human** future-HISTORY sequence, though large gaps remained at his death. The **Federation** tales – ostensibly embedded within the larger series – can be read as self-contained, and themselves encompass the **Fuzzy** books. **Federation** stories include *Four-Day Planet* (**1961**), *Junkyard Planet* (**1963**; vt *The Cosmic Computer* 1964), *Space Viking*

(**1963**) and 2 posthumous collections, *Federation* (coll **1981**) and *Empire* (coll **1981**); of these stories "Omnilingual" (1957 *ASF*) is perhaps the finest (◊ LINGUISTICS). The **Fuzzy** series, in which HBP's enterprising clarity shows to best advantage, includes *Little Fuzzy* (**1962**) and *The Other Human Race* (**1964**; vt *Fuzzy Sapiens* 1976; the original, singularly stupid title was the choice of the book's first publisher), both assembled as *The Fuzzy Papers* (omni **1977**), and the long-lost *Fuzzies and Other People* (**1984**). The small, joyful, sapient Fuzzies are natives of the planet Zarathustra (◊ COLONIZATION OF OTHER WORLDS). The first two volumes – which feature some gripping courtroom-drama sequences – centre on the attempts of the mining corporation which runs Zarathustra first to prevent recognition of Fuzzy INTELLIGENCE (so as to retain mining rights) and then, when it has become inevitable, to exploit this recognition. The third volume resolves the conflict between the company and those humans who are fathering the Fuzzies, whose neotenous, childlike nature (◊ Björn KURTÉN) both demands the attention of adults and reveals HBP's skill at the juvenile. The series was continued in *Fuzzy Bones* * (**1981**) by William TUNING and *Golden Dream: A Fuzzy Odyssey* * (**1984**) by Ardath MAYHAR.

A second distinct sequence, the **Paratime Police/Lord Kalvan** tales, most published originally in *ASF*, were assembled as *Lord Kalvan of Otherwhen* (fixup **1965**; vt *Gunpowder God* 1978 UK) and *Paratime* (coll **1981**). The series was continued in *Great Kings' War* * (**1985**) by Roland GREEN and John F. CARR, the latter also editing *The Worlds of H. Beam Piper* (coll **1983**) and presenting his work in other contexts. As a series of ALTERNATE-WORLDS variations, the sequence showed HPB in perhaps excessively argumentative vein, the alternate-world structure allowing him great latitude to express his political feelings.

Not in general an innovative writer, HBP was at his best when he applied an *ASF*-derived firmness of setting and plausibility of characterization to emotionally arousing adventure plots in which political agendas existed only as subtexts. In 1964, his career apparently on the skids, and prevented by reticence and LIBERTARIAN principles from asking anyone to help him with temporary financial difficulties, he committed suicide. He died in his prime.   [JC]

Other works: *Murder in the Gun Room* (**1953**), HBP's first book, a detective novel; *First Cycle* (**1982**), an HBP outline expanded by Michael KURLAND; *Uller Uprising* (in *The Petrified Planet* [anth **1953**] ed Theodore Pratt; **1983**), part of the first SHARED-WORLD anthology in GENRE SF; *Four-Day Planet & Lonestar Planet* (omni **1979**), comprising two novels, the first under its original title and the second being *A Planet for Texans* under a vt.

About the author: *Henry Beam Piper* (**1985** chap) by Gordon BENSON Jr.

See also: ALIENS; ANTI-INTELLECTUALISM IN SF; CRIME AND PUNISHMENT; NUCLEAR POWER; PASTORAL; SPACE OPERA.

PIRANHA Film (1978). New World. Executive prods

Roger CORMAN, Jeff Schechtman. Dir Joe DANTE, starring Bradford Dillman, Heather Menzies, Kevin McCarthy, Keenan Wynn, Dick Miller, Paul Bartel, Barbara Steele. Screenplay John SAYLES, based on a story by Sayles and Richard Robinson. 94 mins. Colour.

The army has been creating cold-water-tolerant man-eating piranhas for use in Vietnam, and some escape into a Texas river. An attempt by the army to hush this up permits a piranha invasion of a holiday resort on a lake. Here one can see some of the notable talents of the 1980s (Dante, Sayles, even Bartel) honing their craft in a MONSTER MOVIE of considerable wit and pace, with a strong (and much-imitated) emphasis on social comedy; the subtext is that ghastly people create metaphorical monsters that will devour them.

An unofficial sequel, *Piranha II: Flying Killers* (1981; vt *Piranha II: The Spawning*), was a Dutch film, nothing to do with New World. Set in the Caribbean and very inept, it features flying piranhas that look like wind-up toys and was a surprisingly poor directorial début for the later-celebrated James CAMERON.

PIRANHA II ◊ PIRANHA.

PISERCHIA, DORIS (ELAINE) (1928-) US writer, born and raised in West Virginia, in the US Navy 1950-54. She began publishing short fiction with "Rocket to Gehenna" for *Fantastic* in 1966. Her first novel, the remarkable and densely plotted VAN VOGT-style revenge drama *Mister Justice* (**1973** dos), appeared after she had established some reputation in shorter forms, one of her stories being included in *Best Science Fiction for 1972* (anth **1973**) ed Frederik POHL. *Star Rider* (**1974**) recounts first-person adventures in a chokingly vivid Universe, versions of which recur throughout her work: events are pellmell, and the protagonist's far-flung quest for Doubleluck, a planet of dreams, constantly becomes enmired in that environment. *A Billion Days of Earth* (**1976**) similarly loses energy towards its close, but depicts its FAR-FUTURE venue with precision and eloquence; its ratmen with mechanical claws for hands are a particularly resonant notion, and demonstrate DP's clear creative preference for ALIENS, who rarely fail to outshine her human performers. *Earthchild* (**1977**) is similarly set on a far-future Earth under a similar threat of termination. Later novels – like *Doomtime* (**1981**) and *Earth in Twilight* (**1981**) – likewise tend to subordinate human protagonists to her ornate and sometime animate *mises en scène*, so that she is at times both daring and a trifle coy in subject matter and style: not even the female protagonists of *Spaceling* (**1978**) or *The Dimensioneers* (**1982**), though enjoying DP's approval, genuinely manage to dominate their texts. *Blood Country* (**1981**) and *I, Zombie* (**1982**), both as by Curt Selby, the latter a genuine sf novel about the posthumous revivification – for purposes of forced labour – of suicides, are also of interest. In her self-consciousness, and in the sense she conveys that

landscape drowns action (rather than vice versa), DP seemed for a period very much a member of the US NEW WAVE; but she has not published since 1983, and the course of her further development cannot properly be guessed. [JC]

Other works: *The Spinner* (**1980**); *The Fluger* (**1980**); *The Deadly Sky* (**1983**).

See also: CHILDREN IN SF; CRIME AND PUNISHMENT; LIVING WORLDS.

PLANETA BUR (vt *Planet of Storms*; vt *Storm Planet*; vt *Cosmonauts on Venus*) Russian Film (1962). Leningrad Studio of Popular Science Films. Dir Pavel Klushant-sev, starring Kyunna Ignatova, Gennadi Vernov, Vladimir Yemelyanov, Georgi Zhonov. Screenplay Alexander Kazantsev, Klushantsev. 85 mins, cut to 74 mins. Colour.

Cosmonauts land on Venus, accompanied by a robot that plays dance music (thus proving that funny ROBOTS are not peculiar to US CINEMA). A well paced adventure story follows as they search for intelligent life. In an interestingly realized alien landscape they encounter dinosaurs, dangerous plants and a volcanic eruption, but the sole intelligent Venusian appears only at the end, watching unnoticed as the crew departs. By Western standards the film is a little slow and overtalkative (long conversations between the ground crew and the woman controlling the command ship), but it is always watchable. The best Russian sf film until the 1970s, it is, like other Russian sf films of the period (*Niebo Zowiet* [1959] and *Meshte Nastreshu* [1963]), stronger on production design than on plot.

Much footage from the Venus sequences was used in a Roger CORMAN production, *Voyage to the Prehistoric Planet* (1965), which includes new US material written/dir John Sebastian (pseudonym of Curtis Harrington), starring Basil Rathbone and Faith Domergue, but is little more than a partial remake. *PB* footage was used again in *Voyage to the Planet of Prehistoric Women* (1966; vt *Gill Woman*), also a Corman production, along with new material dir Peter Bogdanovich (in his directorial début), starring Mamie Van Doren and Mary Park. The new feature here was the inclusion of telepathic Venusian women who send the crash-landed astronauts home again. [JB]

See also: RUSSIA.

PLANETARY ROMANCE Any sf tale whose primary venue (excluding contemporary or NEAR-FUTURE versions of Earth) is a planet, and whose plot turns to a significant degree upon the nature of that venue, can be described as a planetary romance. For the term to apply properly, however, it is not enough that a tale simply be set on a world: James BLISH's *A Case of Conscience* (**1958**), for instance, has a planet as a primary venue yet cannot be called a planetary romance because the nature or description of this world has little bearing on the story being told. Nor can the term profitably be used for a tale set upon a planet whose mysteries are solvable in HARD-SF terms:

Hal Clement's *Mission of Gravity* (**1954**) and Robert L. FORWARD's *Rocheworld* (**1990**), for instance, are typical hard-sf novels in that the worlds on which they are set amount to little more than the sum of the problems which they illustrate, and in that their protagonists successfully explain (or *solve*) those worlds. In the true planetary romance, the world itself encompasses – and generally survives – the tale which fitfully illuminates it.

Though the term is recent, the form is coeval with SPACE OPERA. Most of Edgar Rice BURROUGHS's sf sequences – like the John Carter tales set on **Barsoom** – fit the description, and were soon being referred to as "interplanetary romances", a term Gary K. WOLFE defines in his useful *Critical Terms for Science Fiction and Fantasy* (**1986**) as "broadly, an adventure tale set on another, usually primitive, planet". Wolfe, properly restricting the use of the term to work done before WWII, considers other important contributors to the form to include Ralph Milne FARLEY, Homer Eon FLINT and Otis Adelbert KLINE. Unfortunately, however, few of the tales described as interplanetary romances show more than minimal interest in interplanetary travel, and the term is used only occasionally in this encyclopedia, generally within Wolfe's critical context.

When we come to more sophisticated writers, for whom the SWORD-AND-SORCERY simplicities of Burroughs seemed inadequate to exploit the venue he had created, we must abandon the earlier formulation. The ornate and decadent tales of Clark Ashton SMITH – which were also instrumental in the creation of the subgenre SCIENCE FANTASY – are the first planetary romances (if one puts aside the work of E.R. EDDISON as being entirely fantasy, and David LINDSAY's *A Voyage to Arcturus* [**1920**] as being too confusing in its use of various genres to work as a clear example). By substituting temporal displacements for the early (and inconsequential) spatial shifts of Burroughs and his followers, Smith created the venue most favourable for the growth of the form: a FAR-FUTURE-style planet on which magic and science intertwine, inhabited by richly variegated races whose re-creation of the feudalisms and baroque rituals of our own history is generally knowing and often a form of art. Though her work for PLANET STORIES tended to be ostensibly set on MARS or VENUS, the superb planetary romances of Leigh BRACKETT dwelt in versions of those planets so displaced from our common history that they seem natural descendants of Smith's work.

Brackett held back, however, from a complete exploitation of the venues hinted at by Smith, and the first full-fledged modern planetary romance is therefore probably Jack VANCE's *The Dying Earth* (coll of linked stories **1950**), a book which successfully incorporates into the subgenre our own planet – but sufficiently near the end of time for magic to seem plausible. Vance's treatment of his far-future Earth as a kind of entranced, doomed, topiary paradise, in

which primitivism and decadence mix and merge, soon became a trademark for his work and influenced a large number of writers, including Gene WOLFE, whose **The Book of the New Sun** (**1980-83**) is of course in part a planetary romance. But *The Dying Earth* lacks any very convincing sf rationale, and it was another Vance title that supplied sf writers with a model to exploit. *Big Planet* (1952 *Startling Stories*; cut **1957**; further cut 1958; full text restored 1978), together with its sequel, *Showboat World* (**1975**; vt *The Magnificent Showboats of the Lower Vissel River Lune XXIII South, Big Planet* 1983), is set in a SPACE-OPERA Galaxy on a huge though Earthlike world whose landmass is vast enough to provide realistic venues for a wide range of social systems, and which is significantly low in heavy-metal resources (this both explains its relatively low gravity and permits a wide range of low-tech societies to flourish). Into this rich environment – in a fashion not dissimilar to the entrance of visitors to the typical UTOPIA – Vance introduces off-world protagonists whose need to travel across the planet provides a quest plot and a rationale for the lessons in ANTHROPOLOGY and SOCIOLOGY so common to the form. The pattern would be repeated often over the next several decades, and remains one of the central models for romantic sf.

In his cogent introduction to a 1978 reprint of Philip José FARMER's *The Green Odyssey* (**1957**) Russell Letson argues strongly for the use of the term "planetary romance" – he should be credited for establishing it – to describe novels whose basic settings derive from Burroughs, whose plots often make use of the chase-and-quest conventions of adventure fiction, and whose protagonists frequently turn out to be high-tech men (or women) "stranded among pretechnological natives". Because Farmer is a more active plotter than Vance, *The Green Odyssey* itself might well serve as a model for the transformation of the *Big Planet* into story: its sophisticated play with anachronisms, and its active use of contrasts between different levels of TECHNOLOGY (reminiscent in this of the work of Poul ANDERSON) begins to demonstrate the range of uses to which the basic model might be put. From these three models – *The Dying Earth*, *Big Planet* and *The Green Odyssey* – can be seen to derive, after the fashion of sf at its creative best, most of the numerous planetary romances of recent decades. (Although J.R.R. TOLKIEN might be seen, through his creation of Middle-Earth, to have granted an oceanic imprimatur for the building of heavily mapped world-sized venues, it is probable that fantasy and science fantasy should be distinguished from one another precisely by the fact that, while the latter are usually set on planets, the former are usually set in *landscapes*, which may well be interminable. Middle-Earth is a landscape.)

Authors early and importantly associated with the planetary romance include Marion Zimmer BRADLEY, with her **Darkover** novels, L. Sprague DE CAMP, some of the volumes of whose **Viagens Interplanetarias** sequence are crossovers from fantasy, and Frank HERBERT, whose **Dune** sequence incorporates some features from the planetary romance into its complex mix. More recently, examples have appeared from a very large number of authors: the **Helliconia** trilogy by Brian W. ALDISS, *A Woman of the Iron People* (**1991**) by Eleanor ARNASON, *Hegira* (**1979**) by Greg BEAR, many of the novels of C.J. CHERRYH, the **Song of Earth** novels by Michael G. CONEY, *The Warriors of Dawn* (**1975**) by M.A. FOSTER, *Golden Witchbreed* (**1983**) and *Ancient Light* (**1987**) by Mary GENTLE, *Saraband of Lost Time* (**1985**) and its sequels by Richard GRANT, *Courtship Rite* (**1982**) by Donald KINGSBURY, the **Pern** novels by Anne MCCAFFREY, *Pennterra* (**1987**) by Judith MOFFETT, the **Starbridge Chronicles** by Paul PARK, *Lord Valentine's Castle* (**1980**) and its sequels and *The Face of the Waters* (**1991**) by Robert SILVERBERG, and parts of *Neverness* (**1988**) by David ZINDELL. There are many more. [JC]

PLANET EARTH Made-for-tv film (1974). ABC Dir Marc Daniels, starring John Saxon, Janet Margolin, Ted Cassidy, Diana Muldaur. Teleplay Gene RODDENBERRY, Juanita Bartlett. 75 mins. Colour.

One of executive producer Roddenberry's several attempts to repeat the success of STAR TREK, this pilot for a proposed series – similar in concept to his earlier GENESIS II – failed to generate the necessary network enthusiasm. It is sf at its most simplistic. The hero and his companions are revived from SUSPENDED ANIMATION in a tribalized, post-HOLOCAUST 22nd century. In a wretchedly strained attempt at contemporary relevance, the party encounters a society of hostile militant women (who keep men as slaves) and, by saving them from dangerous mutants, proves to them that men can be useful. [JB/PN]

PLANÈTE SAUVAGE, LA (vt *Fantastic Planet*) Animated film (1973). Les Films Armorial/ORTF/Filmové studio Barrandov. Dir René Laloux. Scenario and dialogue by Roland Topor (1938-   ) and Laloux, based on *Oms en série* ["Oms by the Dozen"] (**1957**) by Stefan WUL. Original artwork by Topor. 72 mins. Colour.

The plot of this French/Czech coproduction is not original. Human beings on a distant planet are kept as pets by a race of blue, humanoid giants, but finally organize themselves into a guerrilla army and, despite the disparity in size, force their oppressors to recognize them as equals. The animation is not especially impressive in itself; what makes the film interesting is the bizarre, surreal background in which go about their sinister business such nightmarish creatures as the plant that spends its time swatting down small animals for fun, while giggling unpleasantly. The disturbing world shown in the background is at odds with the juvenile events of the story. [JB]

PLANET OF BLOOD ◊ Roger CORMAN.

PLANET OF HORRORS ◊ Roger CORMAN.

PLANET OF STORMS ◊ PLANETA BUR.

PLANET OF THE APES 1. Film (1968). Apjac/20th Century-Fox. Dir Franklin J. Schaffner, starring Charlton Heston, Roddy McDowall, Kim Hunter, Maurice Evans, James Whitmore. Screenplay Michael Wilson, Rod SERLING, based on *La planète des singes* (**1963**; trans as *Planet of the Apes* **1963** US) by Pierre BOULLE. 112 mins. Colour.

Astronauts crashland on a planet where intelligent apes of three species rule over human savages. One astronaut is killed, one lobotomized, and the survivor (Heston) is put in a zoo. There follows a long middle sequence whose SATIRE, alternating between sharp and heavy-handed, suffers from an attempt to have it both ways: sometimes ape society – in its racism, its snobbery, its casual cruelty – is seen as a reflection of our own excesses; yet sometimes the humans are seen as crass and insensitive alongside the apes, who perhaps have made a better fist of things than we ever did (◊ APES AND CAVEMEN). After unsuccessfully trying to persuade his captors that he is an intelligent being, the astronaut is befriended by two chimpanzee scientists (McDowall and Hunter) who accept his story; with their help he escapes. The final sequence has him fleeing to the Forbidden Zone with a female "savage" and – in a wonderful image (perhaps inspired by Hubert ROGERS's cover for *ASF* Feb 1941) – coming across the half-buried Statue of Liberty projecting from a sandy beach. He realizes that he is still on Earth but in the FAR FUTURE, having unknowingly passed through a time-warp.

The film is well directed, and the ape make-up by John Chambers is mobile and convincing, and deservedly won an Oscar. A commercial success, *POTA* was one of the 1968 films that made that year a turning point both for the increasing maturity of sf cinema and for its popularity. *POTA* inspired 4 sequels – BENEATH THE PLANET OF THE APES (1969), ESCAPE FROM THE PLANET OF THE APES (1971), CONQUEST OF THE PLANET OF THE APES (1972) and BATTLE FOR THE PLANET OF THE APES (1973) – as well as 2 tv series, one live-action (see **2** below) and the other animated: *Return to the Planet of the Apes*, 13 20min episodes (1975). Books spun-off from the animated series include 3 published as by William Arrow, #1 and #3 being by William ROTSLER and #2 by Donald J. PFEIL: *Visions from Nowhere* * (**1976**), *Escape from Terror Lagoon* (**1976**) and *Man, the Hunted Animal* * (**1976**).

2. US tv series (1974). 20th Century-Fox Television for CBS. Prod Stan Hough. Executive prod Herbert Hirschman. Starring Roddy McDowall, Ron Harper, James Naughton, Booth Colman, Mark Leonard. 1 season, 14 50min episodes. Colour. This spin-off was set in the same future world as the film (though its ethics were more black-and-white), with some episodes in the ancient subterranean ruins of BENEATH THE PLANET OF THE APES (1969). There were 4 books, all by George Alec EFFINGER, based on the tv series: *Man the Fugitive* * (**1974**), *Escape to Tomorrow* * (**1975**), *Journey into Terror* * (**1975**) and *Lord of the Apes* * (**1976**). [PN/JB]

PLANET OF THE LIFELESS MEN ◊ *Il* PIANETA DEGLI UOMINI SPENTI.

PLANET OF THE VAMPIRES ◊ TERRORE NELLO SPAZIO.

PLANET OUTLAWS ◊ BUCK ROGERS IN THE 25TH CENTURY.

PLANETS ◊ ASTEROIDS; COLONIZATION OF OTHER WORLDS; JUPITER; LIFE ON OTHER WORLDS; LIVING WORLDS; MARS; MERCURY; OUTER PLANETS; PLANETARY ROMANCE; TERRAFORMING; VENUS.

PLANET STORIES US PULP MAGAZINE. 71 issues. Winter 1939-Summer 1955, published by Love Romances Publishing Co.; ed Malcolm Reiss (Winter 1939-Summer 1942), Wilbur S. Peacock (Fall 1942-Fall 1945), Chester Whitehorn (Winter 1945-Summer 1946), Paul L. Payne (Fall 1946-Spring 1950), Jerome BIXBY (Summer 1950-July 1951), Malcolm Reiss (Sep 1951-Jan 1952), Jack O'Sullivan (Mar 1952-Summer 1955). (Reiss was always in control, however, acting as Managing Editor when he was not named as editor.) The schedule was quarterly Winter 1939-Fall 1950, bimonthly Nov 1950-Summer 1954, quarterly Fall 1954-Summer 1955.

Subtitled in its early years "Strange Adventures on Other Worlds – The Universe of Future Centuries", *PS* was the epitome of PULP sf. Its covers were garish in the extreme, and its story titles promised extravagantly melodramatic interplanetary adventures (which the stories themselves frequently provided). A typical selection of featured stories (from 1947-8) includes "Beneath the Red World's Crust", "Black Priestess of Varda", "The Outcasts of Solar III", "Werwile of the Crystal Crypt", "Valkyrie from the Void" and "The Beast-Jewel of Mars", The authors of these epics include such *PS* regulars as Erik Fennel, Gardner F. FOX and Emmett McDowell; Fennel and McDowell, like Wilbur S. Peacock, were frequent contributors whose magazine appearances were largely confined to *PS*. The magazine's artwork was mostly crude and lurid; A. LEYDENFROST was the most individual of its regular artists.

Other authors who appeared often in later issues included Poul ANDERSON and Alfred COPPEL. The most popular contributor, and the one whose work characterizes *PS*'s appeal at its best, was Leigh BRACKETT, with her many colourful PLANETARY ROMANCES of love and adventure on MARS and VENUS. *PS*'s other short stories were more varied and less easily classifiable. All but one of the issues from which the story titles listed above were taken contained also short stories by Ray BRADBURY, including "Zero Hour" (Fall 1947) and "Mars is Heaven!" (Fall 1948). Later *PS* published Philip K. DICK's first story, "Beyond Lies the Wub" (July 1952). One of the many sf magazines to come into being around 1940, *PS* was one of the longest survivors, and one of the last sf pulps to continue in that format. A UK edition, published by Pemberton, consisted of 12 numbered, undated, truncated and initially irregular issues Mar 1950-Sep 1954. A Canadian edition published 12 issues, identical to the US issues, Fall 1948-Mar 1951.

The reprint magazine TOPS IN SCIENCE FICTION (2 issues 1953) came from the same publisher and drew its material wholly from earlier issues of *PS*. *The Best of Planet Stories I* (anth **1975**) ed Leigh Brackett, #1 in a book series that never had a #2, assembles 7 typical *PS* stories. [MJE]

PLATO (c429-347 BC) Greek philosopher, included here partly because his dialogues *Timaeus* and its appendix *Critias* (c350 BC) have been taken as examples of PROTO SCIENCE FICTION in their references to the state of ATLANTIS and its sinking; additionally, and much more importantly, *The Republic* (undated, but earlier than *Timaeus*, which is in a sense its afterword) in part describes an ideal state, or UTOPIA, the first literary work to do so in any detail. P's importance to the history of utopian thought was absolutely central for more than 2000 years, but his emphasis on an ideal stasis over the constant changes and evolution of the sensual world was challenged in some 19th-century utopias, and of course runs absolutely counter to the social ideas of most 20th-century sf writers. Arthur C. CLARKE's *The City and the Stars* (1948; exp **1956**) is effectively an attack on a Platonic utopia. P's disapproval of poetry in *The Republic* is a good example of his admonitory prescriptions, and his remarks on children's games in Book VII of *The Laws* (a late work) are even better: ". . . when innovations creep into their games and constant changes are made in them, the children cease to have a sure standard of what is right and proper. The person most highly esteemed by them is the one who introduces new devices in form or colour, or otherwise. There can be no worse evil for a city than this . . . Change . . . is most dangerous for a city." Nevertheless, P was one of the first philosophers at least to consider the idea of change, that the future could be better than the past – an imaginative leap ancestral to the whole of sf.

P's famous metaphor of the cave reappears everywhere in sf, especially in stories of CONCEPTUAL BREAKTHROUGH: we are prisoners in a cave and take the flickering shadows cast by the firelight on the walls as reality; but the philosopher finds his way into the sunlight and sees that he has hitherto been deceived. [PN]

See also: SOCIOLOGY; VIRTUAL REALITY.

PLATONOV, ANDREY (PLATONOVICH) (1896-1951) Russian writer best known for his mainstream fiction. One of the most talented figures active in the first decades after the 1917 Revolution, he was regarded with suspicion by "official" literary critics and much of his work did not appear in RUSSIA until recently, including his two powerful fictional analyses of UTOPIA-building, *Tchevengur* (**1928-29**; trans Anthony Olcott **1978** US) and *Kotlovan* (trans as *The Pit* US). *Lunnaia Bomb* ["The Moon Bomb"] (**1921**), *Potomki Solntsa* ["The Sun Descendants"] (**1926**) and *Efirnyi Trakt* ["The Ether Road"] (written 1928-30; **1967**) are good examples of the HARD SF of the period, although they are marked by AP's uniquely sophisticated language and by some unusual anticipations, including future "machineless" technologies with "herds of electrons, bred like domestic animals". [VG]

See also: RUSSIA.

PLATT, CHARLES (MICHAEL) (1945-   ) UK-born writer and editor, in the USA from 1970, who began publishing sf with "One of Those Days" for *Science Fantasy* in 1964 and soon became associated with NEW WORLDS during the period when, under Michael MOORCOCK's editorship, it was seen as the pre-eminent NEW-WAVE journal. CP performed various editorial functions for several years, becoming editor in 1970 after Moorcock stepped down, and, of the *NW* anthology series, co-editing with Moorcock #6 (**1973**; vt *New Worlds Quarterly #5* 1974 US) and with Hilary BAILEY #7 (**1974**; vt as #6 1975 US). CP's first novel, serialized the previous year in *NW*, was *Garbage World* (**1967** US), in which sf premise and scatological humour sometimes war – for instance, the ASTEROID of the title, used as a garbage dump, is called Kopra. *Planet of the Voles* (**1971**) is a confused SPACE OPERA, but *The City Dwellers* (**1970** UK; rev vt *Twilight of the City* 1977 US) is, in its heavily revised version, a substantial NEAR-FUTURE look at the death of New York and of a crisis-ridden USA surrounding it. From the first, CP's work demonstrated undeviating clarity, PULP-MAGAZINE plotting instincts, and a sure inclination to offend. *The Gas* (**1970**), which has a genuine sf premise, treats its SEX material in pornographic terms. *The Image Job* (**1971** UK) and *The Power and the Pain* (**1971** UK) are pornography with marginal sf elements. *A Song for Christina* (**1976**) as by Blakely St James (a Playboy Press house name) has no genre content, though *Christina Enchanted* (**1980**), also as by St James, uses sf arguments to underpin an occult hoax; a third St James volume, *Christina's Touch* (**1981**), once again has no genre content. In the early 1980s CP wrote little sf, concentrating his activities in the field on *The Patchin Review* (June 1981-March 1985), a journal of comment, sometimes controversial, of which he edited and wrote significant portions. A successor journal, *REM* (July 1985-December 1987), became *Science Fiction Guide* (occasionally from March 1988). CP had written FANZINES during his involvement in UK fandom in the 1960s; these later journals, however, were notable for a rigorous concentration upon literary issues (and scandals), and should not perhaps be categorized as fanzines. During these years CP also published *Dream Makers: The Uncommon People who Write Science Fiction* (coll **1980**; exp vt *Who Writes Science Fiction?* 1980 UK) and *Dream Makers, Volume II* (coll **1983**), a revised selection from both volumes being published as *Dream Makers: SF and Fantasy Writers at Work* (coll **1986**); the interviews here collected were polished and showed an attentive, surprisingly sympathetic mind at work.

CP then returned to active sf writing with *Less than Human* (**1986** as by Robert Clarke; 1987 UK as CP), the comic tale of an ANDROID's descent upon New York, *Free Zone* (**1988**), a novel which hilariously makes use of almost every sf theme and instrument yet devised (a chart was provided) to tell a pixilated tale of urban anarchy and dreadful threat, and *The Silicon Man* (**1991**), a HARD-SF perusal of the implications of CYBERPUNK in which the sense of what it means actually to become information (in CP's terms an infomorph) is chillingly and at points bracingly examined.

With the possible exception of this last book, it cannot be claimed that CP is a warm writer, or that he generally finds a narrative structure fit to convey the rigour of his thinking. But sf as a genre is naggingly short of genuine iconoclasts: CP is therefore a *necessary* writer. [JC]

Other works: *Sweet Evil* (**1977**); *Love's Savage Embrace* (**1981**) as by Charlotte Prentiss, associational; *Tease for Two* (**1983**) and *Double Delight* (1983), both as by Aston Cantwell, both associational; two **Chthon** ties, *Piers Anthony's Worlds of Chthon: Plasm* * (**1987**) and *Piers Anthony's Worlds of Chthon: Soma* * (**1988**).

Nonfiction: *Micromania: The Whole-Truth Home Computer Handbook* (**1984**; rev by David LANGFORD, vt *Micromania* 1984 UK); *How to be a Happy Cat* (**1986** UK) with Gray Joliffe; *When You Can Live Twice as Long, What Will You Do?* (**1989**), a sequence of questions based upon sf-oriented visions of the near future.

See also: CITIES; DISASTER; GAMES WORKSHOP; INTERZONE; MUSIC; PERCEPTION; POLLUTION; WOMEN SF WRITERS.

PLAUGER, P(HILLIP) J(AMES) (1944-   ) US writer and physicist, involved professionally in computers. He began publishing sf with "Epicycle" for *ASF* in 1973, being best known for "Child of All Ages" (1975), about an immortal woman (◊ IMMORTALITY) who perpetually retains the body of a child; he won the JOHN W. CAMPBELL AWARD for Best New Author in 1975. The novel-length "Fighting Madness" (in Ben BOVA's *Analog Annual*, anth **1976**) remains unpublished in book form. [JC/PN]

PLESKAČ, KAREL [r] ◊ CZECH AND SLOVAK SF.

PLOWRIGHT, TERESA (1952-   ) Canadian writer who began publishing sf with *Dreams of an Unseen Planet* (**1986** US; rev 1989 Canada), in which three human colony ships, having escaped an Earth near terminal ecological collapse, orbit a sentient planet called Gaea, where difficulties soon ensue. The tale, heavily burdened with symbols and a selfconsciously significant prose, climaxes in the realization that the planet needs humans and humans need the planet for either species to reproduce and therefore survive. [JC]

PLUTO ◊ OUTER PLANETS.

POCKET UNIVERSE It might be said that the inhabitant of any constricted environment lives in a pocket universe, whether as a child, a prisoner, a victim of dementia, a chained watcher in Plato's cave, a resident of Hell or an inhabitant of the world inside Pantagruel's mouth. It might also be suggested that the dynamic moment of escape from confinement – a leitmotiv of Western literature – always marks the transition from a pocket universe to a fuller and more real world. When Huck, in the final pages of Mark TWAIN's *The Adventures of Huckleberry Finn* (**1883** UK), decides "to light out for the Territory ahead of the rest", the Hannibal from which he escapes – with its rigid social organization and its conservative inwardness of gaze – has many of the psychological characteristics of the pocket universe as found in sf. The classic movement of the sf tale is of course outward – via CONCEPTUAL BREAKTHROUGHS and all the other forms of initiation or unshackling – and in that sense most sf works contain some sort of pocket universe, implied or explicit, which initially binds and blinds the protagonist, and from which it is necessary to escape.

The term should perhaps, therefore, be confined to two usages, one broad, the other narrower. It can be used broadly to describe an actual miniature universe pocketed within a larger explanatory frame or device – like the various godling-crafted worlds nesting within one another in Philip José FARMER's **World of Tiers** sequence; or like the set-ups in almost any of Jack L. CHALKER's series (e.g., the **Well World** sequence and the **Four Lords of the Diamond** tetralogy) which feature universes constructed by godlike beings as gamelike contrivances and inhabited by victim-players who must *solve* their universe to escape from it; or like similar 1950s set-ups (*see* PARANOIA) such as in Frederik POHL's "The Tunnel under the World" (1955) or Philip K. DICK's *Time Out of Joint* (**1958**), whose protagonists are victims of artificial worlds shaped to delude and manipulate them; or (again trivially) like any fantasy game which involves role-playing within a VIRTUAL-REALITY world; or in fact like any world (such as that on which John CROWLEY's *The Deep* [**1975**] is set, or Terry PRATCHETT's **Discworld**) whose origins and extent reflect a sense of constraining artifice. But none of these applications contains the one essential element that defines the true pocket-universe tale: Farmer's and Chalker's protagonists may not know the nature of the worlds in which they find themselves, but they do know that they are inhabiting some form of construct. In the pocket-universe tale as more narrowly defined, the world initially perceived seems to be the entire world, and the web of taboos preventing the truth about its partial nature being known is structurally very similar to the parental restrictions which initially hamper the move through puberty into adulthood of the young protagonists of most non-genre juveniles. It could, indeed, be argued that this move through puberty is a particular example of the conceptual breakthrough which arguably structures all genuine sf.

The classic GENERATION-STARSHIP tale is one in which the descendants of the original crew members have forgotten the true nature of things and have instituted a repressive, TABOO-governed society which suppresses any attempt to discover the truth; it is the task of the young protagonist to break through the social and epistemological barriers stifling this world while at the same time successfully managing

puberty. The pure generation-starship story embodies, therefore, the purest form of the concept of the pocket universe. Examples of that pure form, though central to sf, are not numerous – Robert A. HEINLEIN's *Universe* (1941 *ASF*; **1951** chap) is the most famous in the list, which includes also Brian W. ALDISS's *Non-Stop* (**1958**; vt *Starship* 1959 US) and Harry HARRISON's *Captive Universe* (**1969**); but Alexei PANSHIN's *Rite of Passage* (**1968**), for instance, though explicitly a tale of puberty, does not suggest that there is any epistemological mystery about the nature of the asteroid-sized starship from which its heroine must escape.

All post-HOLOCAUST tales in which the descendants of survivors live in underground habitats which they think to be the whole of reality are pocket-universe stories. The best of them is perhaps Daniel F. GALOUYE's *Dark Universe* (**1961**), though Margaret ST CLAIR's *Sign of the Labrys* (**1963**) and *The Shadow People* (**1969**) play fruitfully with the concept, as do Richard COWPER's *Kuldesak* (**1972**), Roger ELDRIDGE's *The Shadow of the Gloom-World* (**1977**) and many others. In all these stories, the essential movement is from childhood constriction and taboo-driven ignorance to adult freedom and breakthrough, though the protagonist of Gene WOLFE's «Darkside the Long Sun» (1993) is, unusually, an adult from the very beginning of his long adventure in truth-seeking; in GENRE SF it is only more recently that ironies have significantly pervaded this pattern, as in David LAKE's *Ring of Truth* (**1983**), where a traditional enclosed world turns out to be interminably extensive, so that there is, in fact, no exit. In the great pocket-universe stories, however, there is always an out, a SENSE OF WONDER, a new world opening before the opened eyes. [JC]

See also: GODS AND DEMONS.

POE, EDGAR ALLAN (1809-1849) US writer, a major figure in US literature and a pioneer of sf. "By 'scientifiction'," wrote Hugo GERNSBACK, "I mean the Jules Verne, H.G. Wells, and Edgar Allan Poe type of story." As a poet, short-story writer and critic, EAP's influence on world literature has been enormous, though he spent most of his career in the cutthroat world of magazine publishing. He is usually credited as an originator of the detective story and the horror story, an innovator in the areas of psychological realism and poetic form, as well as a precursor of the New Criticism and a strong influence on the French Symbolist movement. In recent years his works have been closely associated with various structuralist and deconstructuralist approaches to literature.

Among French appreciators of EAP was Jules VERNE, who found in certain of his pieces a basis for his own "nuts-and-bolts" sf – "The Balloon Hoax" (1844), for example, inspired both *Cinq semaines en ballon* (**1863**; trans as *Five Weeks in a Balloon* 1869 US) and *Le tour du monde en quatre-vingt jours* (**1873**; trans as *Around the World in Eighty Days* 1874 US) – but it should be emphasized that in EAP's context much of the scientific underpinning is of a deliberately specious, hoaxing nature. Another writer of HARD SF, Isaac ASIMOV, created the kind of amalgam between sf and detective fiction that EAP's work anticipated; but something of the more central, metaphysical and visionary aspect of EAP's writing is captured by two different disciples: H.P. LOVECRAFT and Ray BRADBURY. Paul Valéry (1871-1945) defined EAP's sf when he observed: "Poe was opening up a way, teaching a very strict and deeply alluring doctrine, in which a kind of mathematics and a kind of mysticism became one ..." What EAP referred to as "the Calculus of Probabilities", a species of extrapolation in which he and his detective hero, Dupin, were expert, calls for the combined talents of the mathematician and the poet.

EAP's corpus is very much of a piece, and to isolate his sf would be significantly to distort both the whole and the part. In fact, no single work can be satisfactorily categorized as sf in any conventional sense – for one thing, the hoaxing quality of many of the tales detracts from the necessary illusion of verisimilitude – but at the same time the underlying rationale is marginally sciencefictional, and by that token so is everything EAP wrote.

EAP assumed that the fabric of "reality" constituted a "grotesque" deception imposed by limitations of time and space and by such personal impediments as human reason. This revelation and the concomitant awareness of what may be the true "arabesque" nature of a unified reality are available only to the perspective provided by the "half-closed eye" of the imagination or, in the later works, of intuition. EAP makes clear in "Mesmeric Revelation" (1844; rev 1845) that this visionary arabesque reality is of a material, not a spiritual, nature. It is equivalent to the alternative or additional DIMENSIONS of sf and may be apprehended by strategies which constitute EAP's version of the spacetime warp. The dizzying sensation experienced on entering an EAP room, typically containing a luridly lit, kaleidoscopically fluid assemblage of arabesque furnishings, or in the process of literally falling in such tales as "A Descent into the Maelström" (1841), will effect the transition. In the case of most visionary or mystical literature, the experience of a transcendent reality depends upon personal volition (an unreliable programme of fasting or praying) or divine intervention. In EAP's case, as in sf, natural phenomena may effect the transition *accidentally*, and the conditions of such phenomena may be mechanically duplicated.

There is a further sense in which all of EAP's work may be regarded as marginal sf. The COSMOLOGY embodied in the late summational treatise *Eureka* (1848) – a scheme of remarkable prescience (to the point of explaining BLACK HOLES) which has some parallel and perhaps conscious development in the speculation of such writers as Olaf STAPLEDON, George Bernard SHAW and Arthur C. CLARKE – is variously anticipated, whether directly, rhythmically

or symbolically, in virtually everything he wrote. To this extent, for example, "The Fall of the House of Usher" (1839) and the sea tales may be regarded as displaced versions of a kind of literalistic sf, if *Eureka* (which EAP called a "romance" or a "poem") may be described as that. In *Eureka* the movement from a grotesque, deceptive "reality" to arabesque reality is correlated with the history of the Universe moving from its present diastolic state of dispersion to a glorious future state of centripetal collapse into a primal unity, an "Overmind".

Although none of EAP's compositions can be fully accounted for by the sf label, some do come closer than others in that they contain specific sf elements. Three poems merit consideration. "Al Aaraaf" (1829; rev 1831; rev 1845), with its astronomical setting and the apparent destruction of the planet Earth, might be related to the post-apocalyptic prose of "The Conversation of Eiros and Charmion" (1839), in which Earth is destroyed by fire when raped of nitrogen by a passing comet (cf H.G. WELLS's "The Star" [1897] and *In the Days of the Comet* [**1906**]). (EAP's "Shadow – A Parable" [1835] and "The Colloquy of Monos and Una" [1841] are similarly metaphysical pieces.) A second poem, "The City in the Sea" (1831; rev 1845), is related to various sf-like sunken-city myths. "Ulalume" (1847) makes use of astrology and, to that degree, relates to EAP's use of other PSEUDO-SCIENCES in some of his most sciencefictional tales: mesmerism in "A Tale of the Ragged Mountains" (1844), in "Mesmeric Revelation" (1844) and in "The Facts in the Case of M. Valdemar" (1845), and alchemy in "Von Kempelen and his Discovery" (1849). The automaton chess-player invented by (the real-life) Baron von Kempelen and probed by EAP in his essay "Maelzel's Chess-Player" (1836) might be linked tenuously to the ROBOTS of sf, while "The Man that was Used Up" (1839) presents a part-human, part-machine being something like a CYBORG. "The Masque of the Red Death" (1842) has humankind destroyed by plague, as in Mary SHELLEY's *The Last Man* (**1826**) (◊ END OF THE WORLD).

EAP's sea voyages, especially "MS. Found in a Bottle" (1833) and *The Narrative of A. Gordon Pym* (**1837**), seem ultimately oriented towards a HOLLOW EARTH (like Captain Adam SEABORN's *Symzonia* [**1820**]). EAP's latter unfinished story was "completed" by various hands: by Jules Verne in *Le sphinx des glaces* (**1897**; trans as *An Antarctic Mystery* **1898** UK), by Charles Romyn DAKE in *A Strange Discovery* (**1899**), by H.P. LOVECRAFT in "At the Mountains of Madness" (1936) and by Dominique Andre in *Conquête de l'Eternal* ["The Conquest of the Eternal"] (**1947**). The most ambitious of the BALLOON tales, "The Unparalleled Adventure of One Hans Pfaall" (1835; rev 1840), is clearly oriented towards outer space; if taken literally, it is an early example of a MOON voyage. Another balloon story and another hoax, "Mellonta Tauta" (1849; the title is Greek for "these things are in the future"), might better be considered as one of the three tales that experiment with the theme of time displacement. "The Thousand and Second Tale of Scheherazade" (1845), "Some Words with a Mummy" (1845), a reanimation story, and "Mellonta Tauta" demonstrate the inaccuracy of past conceptions of the future, present conceptions of the past and future conceptions of the present, respectively; "Mellonta Tauta" itself presents a UTOPIA as a DYSTOPIA, bears on the theme of OVERPOPULATION, and is among the first of such works to open directly in a future environment.

Nearly all the above stories and the essay *Eureka*, but not the poems, appear in *The Science Fiction of Edgar Allan Poe* (coll **1976**) ed Harold Beaver, which has an interesting introduction and commentary. Beaver also ed a companion volume, the Penguin Books edition of *The Narrative of Arthur Gordon Pym of Nantucket* (1975).

A great many of EAP's stories have been filmed, most famously and prolifically by Roger CORMAN. [DK]

About the author: "Edgar Allan Poe – Science Fiction Pioneer" by Clarke Olney in *Georgia Review* #12, 1958; "The Prophetic Edgar Allan Poe" in *Explorers of the Infinite* (coll **1963**) by Sam MOSKOWITZ; "Edgar Allan Poe and Science Fiction" in *Future Perfect: American Science Fiction of the Nineteenth Century* (anth **1966**) ed H. Bruce FRANKLIN; "The Influence of Poe on Jules Verne" by Monique Sprout in *Revue de Littérature Comparée* #41, 1967; "Edgar Allan Poe and the Visionary Tradition of Science Fiction" in *New Worlds for Old: The Apocalyptic Imagination, Science Fiction, and American Literature* (**1974**) by David KETTERER; "Poe, Edgar Allan" in *The Encyclopedia of Science Fiction and Fantasy*, vol 2 (**1978**) by Donald H. TUCK; "The SF Element in the Work of Poe: A Chronological Survey" by David Ketterer, SCIENCE-FICTION STUDIES #1, 1974; "Edgar Allan Poe" by E.F. BLEILER in *Science Fiction Writers: Critical Studies of the Major Authors from the Early Nineteenth Century to the Present Day* (**1982**) ed E.F. Bleiler; "'Something Monomaniacal': Edgar Allan Poe" in *Trillion Year Spree* (**1986**) by Brian W. ALDISS and David WINGROVE; the discussion of Poe in *The Place of Fiction in the Time of Science: A Disciplinary History of American Writing* (**1990**) by John Limon.

See also: APES AND CAVEMEN (IN THE HUMAN WORLD); ASTRONOMY; DEFINITIONS OF SF; GOTHIC SF; HISTORY OF SF; HORROR IN SF; MEDICINE; MONEY; NEW WAVE; PROTO SCIENCE FICTION; PSYCHOLOGY; SPACE FLIGHT; SPACESHIPS; SUSPENDED ANIMATION; TIME TRAVEL.

POETRY Before about 1965 – although much earlier Lilith LORRAINE had published *Wine of Wonder* (coll **1951** chap), which she advertised as being the first volume of poetry devoted to sf – only isolated examples of sf poetry appeared in magazines like *Unknown* and *The Magazine of Fantasy and Science Fiction*. Yet now poetry appears regularly in SF MAGAZINES, anthologies and author collections. This change can be attributed to two separate periods of activity. The first centred on NEW WORLDS (*NW*) and

the NEW-WAVE writers in the UK during the late 1960s. *NW* published a classic poem during this time, "The Head-Rape" (1968) by D.M. THOMAS. In 1979 Edward Lucie-Smith (1933-   ) anthologized this and other excellent poems like Edwin Morgan's "In Sobieski's Shield" and Thomas M. DISCH's "A Vacation on Earth" in *Holding Your Eight Hands* (*HYEH*) (anth **1969** UK), the first anthology of sf poetry. *HYEH* was followed closely by 2 other all-poetry anthologies, *Frontier of Going* (*FG*) (anth **1969** UK) ed John Fairfax and *Inside Outer Space* (*IOS*) (anth **1970** US) ed Robert Vas Dias. *FG* and *IOS* were not sf *per se* but celebrations of SPACE FLIGHT and the Universe inspired by the Soviet/US space race and the unique lexicon of terms, and dreams, it engendered. Also notable were the infusion of a quantity of poetry into the text of Brian W. ALDISS's novel *Barefoot in the Head* (**1969**) and the book-length poem *Aniara* (**1956** Sweden; trans **1963**) by the Swedish poet Harry MARTINSON.

A decade after *HYEH*, intense poetic activity in the USA centred on the founding in 1978 of the Rhysling AWARDS (RA) for best sf poetry and their parent association, the Science Fiction Poetry Association, which was founded by Suzette Haden ELGIN. From the late 1970s to the mid-1980s, poets emerged who wrote a large body of their work within the genre, including in the USA Andrew Joron, Peter Dillingham, Kathy Rantala, Bruce BOSTON, Sonya DORMAN, Gene Van Troyer, Duane Ackerson, Terry A. Garey and Robert FRAZIER, as well as the UK's Steve Sneyd and Andrew Darlington. Established sf writers published a good deal of poetry – Ursula K. LE GUIN, Michael BISHOP, Ray BRADBURY, Jane YOLEN, Joe HALDEMAN and others – and poets from the mainstream crossed over: Dick Allen, Marge PIERCY, William Stafford, Tom Whalen and Marilyn Hacker (1942-   ). During this time, many magazines started to feature the growing genre on a regular basis. *Night Cry* (*NC*) used horror poetry, while the science magazine *Science* (*SC*) prominently featured one factual poem per issue. AMAZING STORIES and ISAAC ASIMOV'S SCIENCE FICTION MAGAZINE have often used two or more poems an issue. *IASFM* featured excellent sf poetry, like the Rhysling winners "The Migration of Darkness" (1979) by Peter Payack and "For Spacers Snarled in the Hair of Comets" (1984) by Bruce Boston; while literary magazines like *Speculative Poetry Review*, *Velocities* (*V*), *Uranus*, *Ice River*, *Umbral* (*UM*), *Star∗Line* (*S∗L*), *The Magazine of Speculative Poetry* and the UK's *Star Wine* devoted themselves to fantastic poetry of all kinds.

Fantastic poetry generally falls into 4 types: sf, as in Susan Palwick's "The Neighbor's Wife" (1985 *AMZ*) (RA), wherein a widowed man nurses a very alien woman to health and accepts her for a wife; science fact, as in Diane Ackerman's "Saturn" from her book *The Planets: A Cosmic Pastoral* (**1976**), a long work often quoted by Carl SAGAN in his science books; macabre, as in Lucius SHEPARD's "White Trains" (1987 *NC*) (RA), about mirage-like trains that pass certain towns on the outskirts of their private mythologies; and speculative poetry, a catchall term for poems on the periphery of the fantastic, as in Joe Haldeman's almost otherworldly vision of Vietnam in "DX" (1987) or the surreal poetry of Ivan Arguelles.

Other classic works include: "The Sonic Flowerfall of Primes" (1982 *NW*) (RA) and "Antenna" (1989) by Andrew Joron, with their hard-science surrealism; "The Nightmare Collector" (1987 *NC*) (RA) by Bruce Boston; "The Well of Baln" (1981) by Ursula K. Le Guin; "Corruption of Metals" (1977) (RA) by Sonya Dorman; "Two Sonnets" (1983 *SC*) by Helen Ehrlich; "Your Time and You" (1982 *V*) (RA) by Adam Cornford; "The Still Point" (1984 *IASFM*) by David Lunde; "Ybba" (1983 *S∗L*) by Elissa Malcohn; "Lady Faustus" (1982 *UM*) by Diane Ackerman; and the World Fantasy Award-winning "Winter Solstice, Camelot Station" by John M. FORD (1988). Many of these recent works are anthologized in *The Umbral Anthology* (anth **1982**) ed Steve Rasnic Tem, *Burning with a Vision* (anth **1984**) ed Robert Frazier and *Songs of Unsung Worlds* (anth **1985**) ed Bonnie Gordon. Also of great importance is the book-length *The New World: An Epic Poem* (**1985**) by Frederick TURNER.

Several anthologies of mostly original poetry made impressions around the cusp of the 1990s: the award-winning *Poly: New Speculative Writing* (anth **1989**) ed Lee Ballentine (1954-   ), *Narcopolis & Other Poems* (anth **1989** chap) ed Peggy Nadramia and *Time Frames* (anth **1991**) ed Terry A. Garey. The poet Scott Green has compiled an invaluable guide, *Contemporary Science Fiction, Fantasy and Horror Poetry: A Resource Guide and Biographical Dictionary* (**1989**). *Star∗Line, The Magazine of Speculative Poetry* and *Velocities* continue, along with newcomer *Dreams & Nightmares*, as strong poetry magazines. Ocean View Press, publisher of *Poly*, produces poetry collections by many of the authors mentioned here. And a large wave of fresh poets promises all the right stuff for the 1990s – people like Denise Dumars, Michael R. COLLINGS, W. Gregory Stewart, David Kopaska-Merkel, t. (*not* T.) Winter-Damon, Ann K. Schwader, Roger Dutcher, Wendy Rathbone, Tom Wiloch, Terry McGarry, Sandra Lindow, Tony Daniel and Wayne Allen Sallee. [RF]

POGUE, BILL [r] ◊ Ben BOVA.

POHL, CAROL [r] ◊ Frederik POHL.

POHL, FREDERIK (1919-   ) US writer, professionally involved in the sf field as an editor, agent and writer since his teens. His 3rd marriage was to sf writer Judith MERRIL (1949-52) and his 4th to Carol Metcal Ulf (1952-82), who collaborated with him in editing several anthologies. His 5th and present wife, Elizabeth Anne Hull (married 1984), is an academic and a leading member of the SCIENCE FICTION RESEARCH ASSOCIATION. FP was a member of the FUTURIANS, and wrote much of his early work in collaboration with other members of the group, mostly with C.M. KORNBLUTH. Names used by these two, sometimes involving third parties (including Robert A.W. LOWNDES

and Joseph H. Dockweiler), were S.D. Gottesman, Scott Mariner, Dirk WYLIE and the house name Paul Dennis Lavond. On his early solo work FP usually used the name James MacCreigh, though he published 1 story each as Wylie and Warren F. Howard. He published much of this work himself while editing ASTONISHING STORIES and SUPER SCIENCE STORIES Spring 1940-Fall 1941; he was then assistant editor to Alden Norton on these magazines from late 1941 until their demise in 1943. After WWII he worked as an sf literary agent; he represented many of the most celebrated writers in the field during the late 1940s. He began writing again, abandoning the MacCreigh pseudonym, in 1953, by which time he had used his own name on the first of a new set of collaborations with Kornbluth, the classic *The Space Merchants* (1952 *Gal* as "Gravy Planet"; **1953**). While working as assistant editor to H.L. GOLD at GALAXY SCIENCE FICTION he wrote a great deal for the magazine, sometimes as Paul Flehr, Ernst Mason or Charles SATTERFIELD, the last once used for a story written in collaboration with Lester DEL REY, in partnership with whom he also wrote *Preferred Risk* (**1955**) as Edson MCCANN. Other writers with whom he collaborated at one time or another were Merril, Isaac ASIMOV and Joseph SAMACHSON, and he built up a second long-term partnership with Jack WILLIAMSON. FP was editor of *Gal* and IF from late 1961 to mid-1969, after which he reverted to full-time writing. While under his aegis *If* won 3 HUGOS as Best Magazine 1966-8. He also founded and edited 2 shorter-lived magazines, WORLDS OF TOMORROW (1963-7) and INTERNATIONAL SCIENCE FICTION (1967-8). Another significant editorial endeavour was an early series of original ANTHOLOGIES, STAR SCIENCE FICTION STORIES: *Star Science Fiction Stories* (anth **1953**), *#2* (anth **1954**), *#3* (anth **1955**), *#4* (anth **1958**), *#5* (anth **1959**) and *#6* (anth **1959**), along with a volume of longer stories, *Star Short Novels* (**1954**). He has also ed numerous reprint anthologies.

As a writer FP made his first reputation by way of slickly ironic short stories, mostly SATIRES with a hint of black comedy. Works in this vein include the classics "The Midas Plague" (1954; incorporated into *Midas World*, fixup **1983**) and "The Tunnel Under the World" (1955; almost all these stories of the 1950s are collected in *Alternating Currents* (coll **1956**; with 1 story dropped and 1 added, rev 1966 US), *The Case Against Tomorrow* (coll **1957**), *Tomorrow Times Seven* (coll **1959**), *The Man who Ate the World* (coll **1960**), *Turn Left at Thursday* (coll **1961**) and *The Abominable Earthman* (coll **1963**). Oddly, the only short-fiction award FP has won was a Hugo for an atypical "posthumous collaboration" with Kornbluth, "The Meeting" (1972), which appeared in *Critical Mass* (coll **1977**) with Kornbluth; some of their collaborations had already been assembled as *The Wonder Effect* (coll **1962**), and further selections appeared as *Before the Universe, and Other Stories* (coll **1980**) and *Our Best: The Best of Frederik Pohl and C.M. Kornbluth* (coll **1987**). FP's early solo novels were less successful: *Slave Ship* (**1957**), *Drunkard's Walk* (**1960**), *A Plague of Pythons* (**1965**; rev vt *Demon in the Skull* 1984) and *The Age of the Pussyfoot* (**1969**) lack the vitality of his collaborations with Kornbluth. The gaudy image of a future dominated by advertising painted in *The Space Merchants* now seems remarkably prescient (◊ MEDIA LANDSCAPE) – although FP's solo sequel, *The Merchants' War* (**1984**), was unfortunately belated; both novels were assembled as *Venus, Inc* (omni **1985**). *Gladiator-at-Law* (**1955**; rev 1986) with Kornbluth is sillier, but makes some telling comments on housing projects (◊ CRIME AND PUNISHMENT). The episodic *Search the Sky* (**1954**; rev 1985) with Kornbluth is an enjoyable early contribution to the "absurd-society" variety of sf. The more ambitious and surrealistically complicated *Wolfbane* (**1959**; rev 1986) with Kornbluth involves invading alien robots, the kidnapping of the planet Earth, subsequent primitive societies engineered to provide human components for living MACHINES on the aliens' own dirigible planet, and a revolt organized by these.

FP's early collaborations with Jack Williamson were the **Undersea** juveniles – *Undersea Quest* (**1954**), *Undersea Fleet* (**1955**) and *Undersea City* (**1958**) (◊ UNDER THE SEA) – and the **Starchild** novels, assembled as *The Starchild Trilogy* (omni **1977**): *The Reefs of Space* (**1964**), *Starchild* (**1965**) and *Rogue Star* (**1969**). The latter are intelligent SPACE OPERAS combining Williamson's flair for melodrama with FP's economy of style. As FP's solo work has matured, so has his collaborative work with Williamson. The **Saga of Cuckoo** – *Farthest Star* (fixup **1975**) and *Wall Around a Star* (**1983**), assembled as *The Saga of Cuckoo* (omni **1983**) – is action-adventure fiction involving a vast artificial world. *Land's End* (**1988**) confronts the human survivors of a cosmic DISASTER with a godlike ALIEN. *The Singers of Time* (**1991**) is an excellent fusion of traditional space opera with modern ideas in PHYSICS.

There was a sharp improvement in FP's longer works once he was no longer editing full time. Two fine novellas, "The Gold at the Starbow's End" (1971; exp vt *Starburst* 1982) and "The Merchants of Venus" (1971), were important transitional works, the latter forming a prelude to the enterprising **Heechee** series – *Gateway* (**1977**), *Beyond the Blue Event Horizon* (**1980**), *Heechee Rendezvous* (**1984**), *The Annals of the Heechee* (**1987**) and *The Gateway Trip* (coll of linked stories **1990**) – which tracks humanity's exploration of the Galaxy using artefacts abandoned by aliens who have gone into hiding because of a threat posed to all living species by the enigmatic Assassins. *Gateway* won the Hugo, NEBULA and JOHN W. CAMPBELL MEMORIAL AWARD, following up the success of *Man Plus* (**1976**), an effectively cynical novel about the adaptation of a man for life on MARS which had won a Nebula the year before (◊ PANTROPY). *JEM: The Making of a Utopia* (**1979**) is a similarly cynical and compelling account of the COLONIZATION of an alien world – which some-what resembles the eponymous planet in *Medea's World* (anth **1985**) ed Harlan ELLISON – by competing

human power blocs, but the more lightly satirical *The Cool War* (**1981**) is less successful. *Syzygy* (**1982**), a mundane novel about the failure of a much-touted catastrophe to overwhelm California as a result of a rare alignment of planets, understandably suffers from a lack of melodrama – an absence made good in two later non-sf novels, the thriller *Terror* (**1986**) and the "drama-documentary" novel *Chernobyl* (**1987**). FP has occasionally complained about the unwillingness of sf writers to be constructive in their dealings with NEAR-FUTURE scenarios, and he made a sustained attempt to practise what he preached in *The Years of the City* (fixup **1984**), a future history of the CITY of New York. *The Coming of the Quantum Cats* (**1986**) is an ALTERNATE-WORLD adventure story only lightly seasoned with satire, but a more considerable satirical edge is evident in *Black Star Rising* (**1985**), *Narabedla Ltd* (**1988**) and the sharply pointed *The Day the Martians Came* (fixup **1988**). *Homegoing* (**1989**) is a more romantic and light-hearted story of confrontation between humans and aliens. *The World at the End of Time* (**1990**) recalls the theme of *Land's End* in presenting a human colony's encounter with a god-like alien in a tale which traverses eons to the time and location referred to in the title; while the novella *Outnumbering the Dead* (**1990** UK) focuses on the predicament of a man who is among the very few who age and die in a world of youthful-seeming immortals (◊ IMMORTALITY).

FP was president of the SCIENCE FICTION WRITERS OF AMERICA 1974-6 and president of WORLD SF 1980-82. Much insight into the early days of his career is provided by the commentary in *The Early Pohl* (coll **1976**), much of which was subsequently incorporated into *The Way the Future Was: A Memoir* (**1978**). The special Sep 1973 issue of *The* MAGAZINE OF FANTASY AND SCIENCE FICTION was devoted to his work. [BS]

Other works: *Digits and Dastards* (coll **1966**); *The Frederik Pohl Omnibus* (coll **1966**; vt *Survival Kit* 1979); *Day Million* (coll **1970**); *The Gold at the Starbow's End* (coll **1972**); *The Best of Frederik Pohl* (coll **1975**); *In the Problem Pit* (coll **1976**); *Planets Three* (coll **1982**); *Pohlstars* (coll **1984**); *BiPohl* (coll **1987**); *Stopping at Slowyear* (**1991**); *Mining the Oort* (**1992**).

Nonfiction: *Science Fiction: Studies in Film* (**1981**) with Frederik Pohl IV.

As editor: *Beyond the End of Time* (anth **1952**); *Shadow of Tomorrow* (anth **1953**); *Assignment in Tomorrow* (anth **1954**); *Star of Stars* (anth **1960**; vt *Stars Fourteen* UK); several **Galaxy** anthologies, including *Time Waits for Winthrop and Four other Short Novels from Galaxy* (anth **1962**), *The Seventh Galaxy Reader* (anth **1964**), *The Eighth Galaxy Reader* (anth **1965**), *The Ninth Galaxy Reader* (anth **1966**), *The Tenth Galaxy Reader* (anth **1967**; vt *Door to Anywhere* 1970), *The Eleventh Galaxy Reader* (anth **1969**) and *Galaxy: Thirty Years of Innovative Science Fiction* (anth **1980**) with Martin H. GREENBERG and Joseph D. OLANDER; *The Expert Dreamers* (anth **1962**), sf stories by SCIENTISTS; *The Best Science Fiction from Worlds of Tomorrow* (anth **1964**); three **If** anthologies, being *The If Reader* (anth **1966**), *The Second If Reader* (anth **1967**) and *Worlds of If* (anth **1986**); *Nightmare Age* (anth **1970**); *Best Science Fiction for 1972* (anth **1972**); *Jupiter* (anth **1973**) with Carol Pohl; *Science Fiction: The Great Years* (anth **1973**) and *Science Fiction: The Great Years: Volume II* (anth **1976**), both with Carol Pohl; *The Science Fiction Roll of Honor* (anth **1975**); *Science Fiction Discoveries* (anth **1976**) with Carol Pohl; *The Best of Cyril M. Kornbluth* (coll **1976**); *Science Fiction of the '40s* (anth **1978**) with Greenberg and Olander; *Nebula Winners 14* (anth **1980**); *The Great Science Fiction Series* (anth **1980**) with Greenberg and Olander; *Yesterday's Tomorrows: Favorite Stories from Forty Years as a Science Fiction Editor* (anth **1982**); *Tales from the Planet Earth* (anth **1986**).

About the author: *Frederik Pohl, Merchant of Excellence: A Working Bibliography* (**1989**) by Gordon BENSON Jr and Phil STEPHENSEN-PAYNE.

See also: ANTI-INTELLECTUALISM IN SF; ASTOUNDING SCIENCE-FICTION; AUTOMATION; BLACK HOLES; CITIES; COMPUTERS; CONCEPTUAL BREAKTHROUGH; CORPSICLE; CRYONICS; CYBERNETICS; CYBORGS; DEL REY BOOKS; DIMENSIONS; DISCOVERY AND INVENTION; DYSTOPIAS; ECONOMICS; END OF THE WORLD; EVOLUTION; FANDOM; FASTER THAN LIGHT; GAMES AND SPORTS; GOLDEN AGE OF SF; GREAT AND SMALL; HISTORY IN SF; HISTORY OF SF; HUMOUR; HYPERSPACE; ISAAC ASIMOV'S SCIENCE FICTION MAGAZINE; LEISURE; LINGUISTICS; LIVING WORLDS; MATHEMATICS; MONEY; NEW WAVE; NUCLEAR POWER; OPTIMISM AND PESSIMISM; OUTER PLANETS; OVERPOPULATION; PARALLEL WORLDS; PARANOIA; POLITICS; POWER SOURCES; PSI POWERS; Julius SCHWARTZ; SF MAGAZINES; SOCIOLOGY; SPACESHIPS; STARS; TERRAFORMING; UTOPIAS; VENUS; WEAPONS; WRITERS OF THE FUTURE CONTEST.

POLAND Polish sf effectively began with the publication in 1785 of the novel *Wojciech Zdarzyński, życie i przypadki swoje opisujący* ["Wojciech Zdarzyński, Describing his Life and Adventures"] (**1785**) by the Reverend Michał Dymitr Krajewski. This describes the civilizations of the Moon.

Between then and WWII, Polish sf had, in terms of literary quality, at least 4 major landmarks. (1) In 1804 Jan Potocki (1761-1815) published (in French) *Manuscrit trouvé à Saragosse* (2 vols **1804** and **1805** Russia and 1 vol **1813** France; exp **1847** as *Rękopis znaleziony w Saragossie* Poland; cut trans as *The Saragossa Manuscript*, ed Roger Caillois **1960** US). This extraordinary work – more fantasy than sf – is a well written and witty novel, a prolonged and vivid joke made by a worldly gentleman, a Count, at the expense of all the superstitions of his age. The complex plot could be seen as a series of ALTERNATE WORLDS nestling within one another like Chinese boxes. It was filmed in Poland under the Polish title in 1965, dir Wojciech Has, and distributed quite widely in the West as *The Saragossa Manuscript*. (2) *Historia przyszłości* ["History of the Future"] (composed 1829-42; part published in French 1835; **1964**) by Adam Mickiewicz (1798-1855), unfortunately unfinished and partly lost, was done as a large fresco of the world seen more from the

cultural than from the technological point of view. (3) The **Moon** trilogy by Jerzy ŻUŁAWSKI consists of *Na Srebrnym Globie* ["On Silver Globe"] (**1901**), *Zwycięzca* ["The Victor"] (**1908**) and *Stara Ziemia* ["Old Earth"] (**1910**). This is an essay on the birth of civilization and myth, and on myth's clash with reality, beautifully written in the *fin de siècle* mood. (4) The road to modern Polish sf was paved by the avant-garde painter and writer Stanisław Ignacy WITKIEWICZ in his apocalyptic novels *Pożegnanie jesieni* ["Farewell to Autumn"] (**1927**) and *Nienasycenie* (**1930**; trans Louis Iribarne as *Insatiability* **1977** US). Having seen the 1917 Revolution from inside Russia, Witkiewicz was obsessed by the vision of "hordes of Asians" invading Europe and destroying whatever cultural values might exist in the future. He lived up to his philosophy and committed suicide when the Red Army invaded Poland in Sep 1939.

Polish postwar sf has had its literary achievements, too – not only the celebrated works of Stanisław LEM but also the classical sf of Konrad Fiałkowski, Adam Wiśniewski-Snerg's cult novel *Robot* (**1973**) and, in the 1980s, such novels by the wonderfully inventive Wiktor Żwikiewicz as *Delirium w Tharsys* ["Delirium in Tharsys"] (**1986**). Poland also has its GENRE-SF writers, such as Bohdan Petecki with *Strefy zerowe* ["Zero Zones"] (**1972**).

The current running through Polish sf has really been political. Because sf provides a perfect means of diverting attention away from drab reality into a beautiful future, it was encouraged in the decade after WWII by Poland's communist rulers. The best examples of such political sf are Krzysztof Boruń's and Andrzej Trepka's *Zagubiona przyszłość* ["The Lost Future"] (**1953**), #1 in a SPACE-OPERA trilogy, and Stanisław Lem's early novels *Astronauci* ["The Astronauts"] (**1951**) and *Obłok Magellana* ["The Magellan Nebula"] (**1955**).

Rather later, from the mid-1970s onwards, sf writers began to take the opposite tack. Escaping strict censorship by using sf imagery, and with the help of a linguistic ingenuity reminiscent of George ORWELL, they began to describe the real world – even if at the price of incurring serious publication problems. (Orwell was probably a direct influence on such work, as several of his books had been published in Poland by underground publishers.) The best examples of such works are Edmund Wnuk-Lipiński's *Wir pamięci* ["Whirlpool of Memory"] (**1979**), Maciej Parowski's *Twarzą ku Ziemi* ["Face to Earth"] (**1981**), Janusz A. Zajdel's *Limes inferior* (**1982**) and Marek Oramus's *Senni zwycięzcy* ["Sleepy Victors"] (**1982**).

Sf writers of the younger generation are now turning to fantasy, which is more marketable, and, because censorship no longer exists, political sf is in retreat and looks a bit old-fashioned: the gaping hole this leaves in the Polish sf tapestry is currently being filled by the importation (on a massive scale) of US-UK sf by such new private publishers as Amber and Arax.

Film has never been a strong point of Polish sf. Aside from *The Saragossa Manuscript*, 2 further sf films deserve attention. Fitting well into the political-criticism-through-sf-metaphor stream, *Wojna Swiatów – Nastepne Stulecie* (1982; vt *The War of the Worlds – Next Century*) dir Piotr Szulkin tells of government manipulation of the media to disguise the facts of a Martian invasion. Something of an exception to this sort of political cinema is SEKSMISJA (1984; vt *Sex Mission*), a comedy dir Juliusz Machulski.

There are currently 2 monthly sf magazines in Poland. The older, *Fantastyka*, has run since 1982 and has a circulation of over 120,000. Its strong points are its fine critical essays and a good choice of Polish authors. *Fenix* is the first privately owned and edited magazine; it emerged from FANZINE origins in 1990 and now has a (growing) circulation of about 70,000. Its selection of US-UK sf is considered the better, and it also publishes young Polish writers. Polish FANDOM is massive and well organized, its main activities centring on fanzines and CONVENTIONS.   [KS]

POLITICS Most of the works which we can characterize with hindsight as PROTO SCIENCE FICTION are political fantasies. The earnest and constructive aspect of this endeavour is displayed in UTOPIAS, the mocking and corrosive aspect in SATIRES. The desire to make political statements has continued to be the main motive force in works of sf by MAINSTREAM WRITERS, although modern works of this kind make much more frequent use of images of DYSTOPIA than either of the traditional modes of comment. Important subgenres of sf like the future-WAR story grew out of exercises in political propaganda ($\lozenge$ INVASION), and all real-world political crusades have sparked the production of competing images of the future. All images of the NEAR FUTURE embody political speculations, partly because of their close continuity with the present and partly because political events are usually a more significant agent of short-term change than scientific DISCOVERY or technological development. There is today a thriving subgenre of "political thrillers" – often written by sometime politicians like Spiro T. Agnew (1918-   ) and Jeffrey Archer (1940-   ), or even practising ones like Gary Hart (1936-   ) and Douglas HURD, but much more elegantly done by writers like Richard CONDON and Allen DRURY – the great majority of whose plots are necessarily set in the near future.

The principal political debates of the 19th century are reflected in many early works of sf, the most important being that associated with the rise of socialism. Edward BELLAMY, William MORRIS, Jack LONDON and – in the early part of his career – George GRIFFITH were all moved to construct images of future socialist utopias and revolutions. H.G. WELLS, the presiding genius of UK scientific romance, was a fervent if somewhat idiosyncratic socialist, as was, in an even more curious way, M.P. SHIEL. Before the founding of the SF MAGAZINES, such writers as George Allan ENGLAND followed Jack London's lead in

importing stridently anti-capitalist (or at least "anti-trust") futuristic fables into the pulp stratum of the fiction marketplace. Inevitably, socialist visions of the future called forth opposition in the form of images of hideously bloody revolution and regimented dystopias. Notable novels which combine serious political speculations with some appreciation of the imperatives and opportunities associated with technological progress are Bellamy's *Looking Backward 2000-1887* (1888), Ignatius DONNELLY's *Caesar's Column* (1890), Wells's *When the Sleeper Wakes* (1899), London's *The Iron Heel* (1907), Victor ROUSSEAU's *The Messiah of the Cylinder* (1917) and Claude FARRÈRE's *Useless Hands* (1920; trans 1926). With the passage of time the dystopian imagery associated with political fantasies became more and more extreme, as such fantasies began to pose more abstract questions of political philosophy and the political spectrum was confused by the rise of fascism and the spectre of totalitarianism. Owen GREGORY's prophetic account of the nation which might arise from the ashes of German defeat, *Meccania* (1918), stands at the head of a tradition of caricaturistic and surreal political fantasies which includes Milo HASTINGS's *City of Endless Night* (1920), Yevgeny ZAMIATIN's *My* (trans as *We* 1924), Edmund SNELL's *Kontrol* (1928), John KENDALL's *Unborn Tomorrow* (1933), J. Leslie MITCHELL's *Gay Hunter* (1934), Joseph O'NEILL's *Land under England* (1935), John Palmer's *The Hesperides* (1936), Katharine BURDEKIN's *Swastika Night* (1937 as by Murray Constantine), Andrew MARVELL's *Minimum Man* (1938), Ayn RAND's *Anthem* (1938) and P.G. CHADWICK's *The Death Guard* (1939). Alongside these works appeared more modest expressions of sour disenchantment, depicting short-sighted politicians and their equally short-sighted supporters failing dismally to cope with the challenges facing them; these include Rose MACAULAY's *What Not* (1919), J.D. BERESFORD's *Revolution* (1921), Fred MacISAAC's "World Brigands" (1928), Hilaire BELLOC's *But Soft – We Are Observed* (1928), Upton SINCLAIR's *Roman Holiday* (1931), Harold NICOLSON's *Public Faces* (1932) John GLOAG's *Winter's Youth* (1934) and Sinclair LEWIS's *It Can't Happen Here* (1935).

In stark contrast to non-genre writers, the suppliers of the specialist sf PULP MAGAZINES paid relatively little attention to political matters, mostly taking it for granted not only that technological progress was the real engine of social change but that contemporary US democracy might be subverted but would never be worthily superseded. Stanton A. COBLENTZ's leaden satires do contain a certain amount of open-minded political discussion, but such stories as Miles J. BREUER's "The Gostak and the Doshes" (1930) relegated ideological disputes to literal meaninglessness, and Breuer's and Jack WILLIAMSON's *The Birth of a New Republic* (1930 *AMZ Quarterly*; 1981 chap) cast the interplanetary politics of the future slavishly in the mode of the political evolution of the USA's past ($\lozenge$ HISTORY IN SF). Despite the conspicuously declared uninterest of Hugo GERNSBACK (who published translations of a few German-supremacist utopian fantasies by Otfried von Hanstein [◊ GERMANY] and others), events in Europe gradually infected with anxiety the visions of the future produced by sf writers. Paul A. CARTER's history of magazine sf, *The Creation of Tomorrow* (**1977**), includes an excellent chapter tracking reflections of and responses to the rise of Hitler in such stories as Wallace WEST's "The Phantom Dictator" (1935) and Nat SCHACHNER's series begun with "Past, Present and Future" (1937). There is a sense in which sf has never stopped reacting to Hitler, in that ALTERNATE-WORLD stories of what might have happened had he triumphed in WWII continue to be extremely popular (◊ HITLER WINS). Norman SPINRAD's *The Iron Dream* (**1972**) suggests that, if Hitler had become an sf writer instead of a dictator, his sublimated dreams would have been readily accommodated within the great traditions of SPACE OPERA and HEROIC FANTASY.

WWII, in securing the defeat of European fascism and paving the way for the Cold War, established a new real-world context for political fantasy, but its main effect on sf was to bring the entrenched trends rapidly to a climax in George ORWELL's *Nineteen Eighty-four* (**1949**), which became the model for a great deal of later fiction in which the future is imagined as a metaphorical boot stamping on a human face forever. There is a sense in which dystopian fiction after 1949 is merely a series of footnotes to Orwell – so much so that it is not clear whether such works as David KARP's *One* (**1953**) and L.P. HARTLEY's *Facial Justice* (**1960**) really qualify as political fantasies at all, although Arthur KOESTLER's *The Age of Longing* (**1951**) and Adrian MITCHELL's *The Bodyguard* (**1970**) clearly do. Orwellian fantasy was imported into GENRE SF by Ray BRADBURY in *Fahrenheit 451* (**1953**), and political fantasy of a curious kind, featuring many tales of rebellion against "perverted" political systems in which the interests of some special-interest group have become dominant, became very popular in the magazines of the 1950s. Because it was deemed socially insignificant, sf could play host to political criticism of a kind which might elsewhere have attracted the attentions of Joseph McCarthy (1909-1957) and his Un-American Activities Committee; John W. CAMPBELL Jr's determined affection for unorthodoxy led him to provide a home for such stories as James BLISH's "At Death's End" (1954), whose anti-McCarthy elements were further exaggerated when it was expanded to form part of *They Shall Have Stars* (fixup **1956**). On the other hand, Robert SILVERBERG has revealed that Howard BROWNE terminated Rog PHILLIPS's career as a regular contributor to the ZIFF-DAVIS pulps because of his reckless use of the word "communism" in "Frontiers Beyond the Sun" (1953 as by Mallory Storm).

The tradition of HARD SF which developed in Campbell's ASTOUNDING SCIENCE-FICTION had a conspicuous tendency towards what is now termed LIBERTARIANISM. This is often credited to Campbell's

own idiosyncrasies, including his human-chauvinism (which caused the more conventionally liberal Isaac ASIMOV to eliminate ALIENS from the future history mapped out in the **Foundation** series) and his fascination with the merits of slavery, but Campbell's unorthodoxy was actually quite elastic – as evidenced by the permission which he gave to his chief Devil's Advocate of the 1960s, Mack REYNOLDS, to challenge conventional political assumptions. It is rather from Robert A. HEINLEIN's version of SOCIAL DARWINISM that the strident Libertarian tradition of US hard sf stems, but there are noticeable differences of ideological complexion and rhetorical style between the other GOLDEN AGE writers sometimes lumped together with him as "right-wingers": L. Sprague DE CAMP, L. Ron HUBBARD and A.E. VAN VOGT. The writers of the 1950s who enlisted in these ranks – most notably and most thoughtfully Poul ANDERSON and Gordon R. DICKSON – were by no means followers of a party line, nor were such 1960s writers as Larry NIVEN, Jerry POURNELLE and G.C. EDMONDSON, and nor are more recently emergent writers like James P. HOGAN and L. Neil SMITH. Extreme Libertarians are inevitably drawn to images of the future which vividly display the uncompromising nature of their philosophies – as can be seen in the various writings of Ayn RAND and the work of such political philosophers as Robert Nozick – and the clustering of such writers around the more assertively optimistic threads of the sf tradition needs no conspiracy theory to explain it. At least some of what passes for Libertarianism in the works of these and other writers is not dogmatically based at all, but rather represents a continuation of the tradition of sceptical fantasy which grew up between the wars, taking the view that all political institutions are likely to be manned by corrupt incompetents. The quasi-anarchic spirit which one finds in the work of Eric Frank RUSSELL, Philip K. DICK and many of the FUTURIANS is rooted in this ironic tradition, as is the work of such non-genre writers as Kurt VONNEGUT Jr. Then again, much supposedly Libertarian sf simultaneously glorifies militarism to such an extent that the bureaucratic organizations of the state are replaced, at least so far as the key characters are concerned, by hyperorganized command structures in which the ethic of individual freedom supposedly being upheld is chimerically bonded to ideals of slavish loyalty and self-sacrificing "honour"; Niven and Pournelle's *Oath of Fealty* (**1981**) is a particularly cleverly thought-out exercise in this kind of doublethink. The sf writers who found themselves in the "opposite" camp to the Libertarians when GALAXY SCIENCE FICTION published its notorious paired ads about the USA's involvement in Vietnam (◊ WAR) have produced little political rhetoric to compare with the dynamism of the gung-ho glam-tech conquerors of space, although they have produced a good deal of what their macho detractors might describe as "pinko bleeding-heart fiction" lamenting the cruel injustices of a world in danger of spoliation. Active left-wing movements, as featured in Gordon EKLUND's *All Times Possible* (**1974**) and John SHIRLEY's *Eclipse* (**1985**), remain rare, although the curious anarchist philosophies displayed in Norman SPINRAD's *Agent of Chaos* (**1967**) and van Vogt's *The Anarchistic Colossus* (**1977**) have attracted some attention from would-be followers.

Other political issues which gradually came to the fore in post-WWII sf were sexual politics and race relations. Fantasies of sexual politics had a long history dating back to the days of the suffragettes and such feminist writers as Charlotte Perkins GILMAN, but serious speculative work had largely been eclipsed by anxious fantasies about female-dominated societies, written by males. WOMEN SF WRITERS increased dramatically in numbers in the 1950s-60s, and began to build bridges to the FEMINIST movement (*see also* WOMEN AS DEPICTED IN SCIENCE FICTION). Futuristic fictions bearing on the problems of race relations had a fairly similar history, serious speculations being virtually drowned out by anxious fantasies and by the kind of unthinking racism and antisemitism which were long rife in popular fiction of all kinds. Such (relatively) open-minded works as Herrmann LANG's *The Air Battle* (**1859**) remain anomalies in a 19th century dominated by the racist ideologies which found virulent expression in King WALLACE's *The Next War* (**1892**) and Louis TRACY's Anglo-Saxon-supremacist *The Final War* (**1896**). Tracy's worldview was echoed in M.P. Shiel's early Yellow-Peril novel *The Yellow Danger* (**1898**), but Shiel repented of it in such later books as the misleadingly retitled *The Dragon* (**1913**; rev as *The Yellow Peril* 1929), in the same way that he reassessed and reversed his occasional knee-jerk antisemitism in his Messianic political fantasy *The Lord of the Sea* (**1901**). The USA inevitably produced a considerable number of political fantasies about Black/White relations, including thoughtful works like T. Shirby HODGE's *The White Man's Burden* (**1915**) and George Samuel SCHUYLER's satire *Black No More* (**1931**). As the Civil Rights movement began in the 1950s and reached its first climactic phase in the 1960s, several notable futuristic fantasies of race relations were produced by mainstream writers, including *A Different Drummer* (**1959**) by William Melvin KELLEY, *The Siege of Harlem* (**1964**) by Warren MILLER, *The Spook who Sat by the Door* (**1969**) by Sam GREENLEE and several novels by John WILLIAMS, but such direct treatments seemed too sensitive to most genre-magazine editors, who preferred their writers to use aliens in parables whose arguments were conducted at a more abstract level; the most notable exception is the series by Mack Reynolds begun with *Black Man's Burden* (1961; **1972** dos), set in Africa rather than the USA. UK sf novels bearing on racial problems include Margot BENNETT's *The Long Way Back* (**1954**), Robert BATEMAN's *When the Whites Went* (**1963**), John BRUNNER's *The Jagged Orbit* (**1969**) and – by far the boldest – Christopher PRIEST's *Fugue for a Darkening Island* (**1972**; vt *Darkening Island* US). South African political fantasies on the theme

include Arthur KEPPEL-JONES's anti-Apartheid *When Smuts Goes* (**1947**) and Garry ALLIGHAM's pro-Apartheid *Verwoerd – The End* (**1961**). In general, though, as the real-world problems become ever more urgent, the tendency of genre sf has been to ignore the issue or sanctimoniously to take for granted its eventual disappearance.

Although there are some interesting sarcastic fantasies about future election campaigns – e.g., William TENN's "Null-P" (1951) and "The Masculinist Revolt" (1965), Arthur T. HADLEY's *The Joy Wagon* (**1958**) and Gordon Eklund's *The Eclipse of Dawn* (**1971**) – sophisticated political fantasy remains a rarity in genre sf. Reynolds's efforts along those lines, heroic after their fashion, are muddled, and bogged down by their fusion with the crude melodramatics and uneasy comedy which he found necessary to include to secure publication. A certain transcendence of the expectations of commercially minded editors is a necessary prerequisite to the production of truly serious sf, and it is arguable that the only writer with a keen interest in politics yet to have achieved it is Ursula K. LE GUIN, whose most sustained essay in earnest political fantasy is *The Dispossessed* (**1974**). The practical politics of coping with the problems which are urgent today and steadily getting more so are rarely addressed in sf, although there are noble exceptions, including Frederik POHL's *The Years of the City* (fixup **1984**). The situation has, of course, been even worse in Eastern Europe, where the content of popular fiction was – until very recently – determined by diktat. Political discourse in almost all translated sf from pre-Yeltsin RUSSIA treads the party line dutifully, if not always wholeheartedly; the most interesting partial exception is the work of the brothers STRUGATSKI. Dissident fiction which contrived to reach the West is, of course, much more pointed; a notable example is *1985* (**1983**) by Gyorgy Dalos, which replays the post-WWII history of Hungary as a sequel to Orwell's *Nineteen Eighty-four*. It will be interesting to see what kinds of sf emerge from post-communist Eastern Europe during the next few years. [PN/BS]

POLLACK, RACHEL (GRACE) (1945-   ) US writer, resident in the Netherlands 1973-90. She published her first sf story with *NW* in 1972, "Pandora's Bust" as by Richard A. Pollack. Her first novel, *Golden Vanity* (**1980** US), was an ornate SPACE OPERA whose large cast of aliens ransacks a venal Earth in search of a female runaway. *Alqua Dreams* (**1987** US) is a rather flat drama of ontology set on an alien planet; the human protagonist, faced with the obdurate Platonism of the inhabitants, must argue METAPHYSICS with them in an attempt to suggest that the sensory world is sufficiently "real" for them to sell him the rare mineral he needs. The background is voluminously drawn, but the narrative is sluggish. In RP's third novel, *Unquenchable Fire* (**1988** UK), winner of the ARTHUR C. CLARKE AWARD for 1989, a similarly intractable narrative – the book is constructed so that a long flashback reiterates material already delivered – more closely models the situation it depicts. In the ALTERNATE-WORLD USA of the tale, shamanism actually works (◊ MAGIC); and a lovingly described bureaucracy of shamans, revering the Founders who brought them to power generations earlier, are actually able to ask the Earth's roots for energy. The protagonist of the book, finding that her unwilled pregnancy is destined to make her the mother of a new revitalizing shaman, resists her role fiercely; the résumé of her life, as given in flashback, only intensifies the sense of her deep stubborness. Throughout, RP's portrait of a radical different but alarmingly similar USA is densely drawn, and her depiction of life in an alternate Poughkeepsie is frequently hilarious. Several stories – like "The Protector" (1986 *Interzone*) – depict similarly transformed universes. An anthology of original stories, *Tarot Tales* (anth **1989** UK) with Caitlin Matthews, carries RP's professional interest in the Tarot (she has published nonfiction in the field) into fiction; each contributor used OULIPO techniques to extract story ideas from a Tarot pack. RP's subject matter and manner are narrow in their extent, compellingly intense in their focus.   [JC]

See also: PSEUDO-SCIENCE.

POLLOCK, WALTER HERRIES ◊ AndrewLANG.

POLLUTION Early sf stories dealing with catastrophes brought about by pollution of the environment (◊ ECOLOGY) concentrate on the perils of smog; they include W. Delisle HAY's *The Doom of the Great City* (**1880**) and Robert BARR's "The Doom of London" (**1892**). The pollutant effects of industrial waste were very familiar in the 19th-century UK: air pollution had shaped the city of London (the prevailing wind blows east and the upper strata of the population moved steadily west) and slag defaced England's northern counties to the extent that Yorkshiremen coined a proverb: "Where there's muck, there's brass [money]." It is hardly surprising that England produced the one enduring 19th-century image of civilization as pollution, in Richard JEFFERIES's *After London* (**1885**). The image of city life presented in the socially conscious, traditional 19th-century novel, as by Charles DICKENS, makes much of the foulness of city dirt, but the problem was generally seen as easily correctable. The notion that environmental pollution might be a serious threat in the future is not evident in early sf, where it tends to be assumed that progress will sweep the dirt away. Virtually all utopian CITIES are remarkable for their cleanliness, and it seemed reasonable to one inhabitant of a northern industrial city, signing himself "A Disciple" (of H.G. WELLS), to borrow the famous TIME MACHINE in order to see *The Coming Era, or Leeds Beatified* (**1900**). This optimism seems rather ironic today.

By the end of the 1950s, serious attention had been given in sf to only one kind of pollution: radioactive waste. The effects of the residual radiation of the Hiroshima and Nagasaki explosions and the tests at Bikini atoll were well known, and the destruction of the environment by radiation poisoning became one of the most horrifying aspects of the post-atomic-WAR scenario (◊ HOLOCAUST AND AFTER; MUTANTS). These stories probably helped bring about an increased sensitivity to the idea of insidious poisons in the environment, and it was not long before awareness grew of more commonplace dangers: arsenic in wallpaper, lead in water pipes, etc. The first sf cautionary tales about society's general philosophy of waste disposal began to appear in the 1950s. C.M. KORNBLUTH's "Shark Ship" (1958) is an extreme example; and James WHITE's story of the hazards of orbital garbage, "Deadly Litter" (1960), has been transformed by the passage of time into a neat parable. It was in the early 1960s, however, that the problem was brought very sharply into focus, largely due to the publication of *Silent Spring* (**1962**) by Rachel Carson (1907-1964), which argued that pollution of a radically new type had begun, involving nonbiodegradable substances which accumulated in living matter to fatal concentrations. DDT, once widely used as an insecticide, was one of the main targets of attack in Carson's book; PBB, a compound responsible for poisoning large numbers of cattle and some people in Michigan, belongs to the same family of compounds; the fluorocarbons more recently blamed for the depletion of the ozone layer are closely related.

Awareness of these threats was rapidly absorbed into sf, and virtually overnight became a standard feature of NEAR-FUTURE scenarios. A lurid early dramatization of the issue is *The Clone* (**1965**) by Theodore L. THOMAS and Kate WILHELM, a horror story about pollutants which spontaneously generate life to become an omnivorous, amorphous monster. A more realistic treatment of some relevant issues is *Make Room! Make Room!* (**1966**) by Harry HARRISON, which also deals with OVERPOPULATION. Similarly alarmist stories include James BLISH's "We All Die Naked" (1969), John BRUNNER's *The Sheep Look Up* (**1972**), Philip WYLIE's *Los Angeles: A.D. 2017* (**1971**) and *The End of the Dream* (**1972**), Kurt VONNEGUT Jr's "The Big Space Fuck" (1972), Andrew J. OFFUTT's *The Castle Keeps* (**1972**) and Kit PEDLER's and Gerry DAVIS's *Brainrack* (**1974**). In more recent times pollution has come to be taken so much for granted that it is rarely addressed as an issue in itself, instead forming a constant background element in almost all near-future extrapolations, whether they aspire to be DYSTOPIAN or merely realistic; it is particularly evident in Paul THEROUX's *O-Zone* (**1986**) and David BRIN's *Earth* (**1990**). The rapidity with which the subject became familiar is evident in the early appearance of such works of SATIRE as Charles PLATT's *Garbage World* (**1967**) and Norman SPINRAD's "The Lost Continent" (1970). More thoughtful and sophisticated treatments include *The Thinking Seat* (**1970**) by Peter TATE and "King's Harvest" (1972) by Gardner DOZOIS. It is widely felt that the biggest danger is complacency –

a point made by the effective "To Walk with Thunder" (1973) by Dean MCLAUGHLIN, in which the hero fights to suppress a device that will guarantee clean air inside the home, on the grounds that it would become an industrial *carte blanche* to pollute the atmosphere irredeemably. *Pollution: Omnibus* (anth **1971**), issued to cash in on the height of the scare, contains "Shark Ship", *Make Room! Make Room!* and the dubiously relevant *City* (fixup **1952**) by Clifford D. SIMAK. *The Ruins of Earth* (anth **1971**) ed Thomas M. DISCH is another theme anthology with a number of relevant stories. [BS]

POMERLEAU, LUC (1955-   ) French-speaking Canadian physics graduate, technical translator, editor of the French-language Québec sf magazine *Solaris* since 1986, and sf and comics critic. He wrote the section on Francophone sf in this encyclopedia's entry on CANADA. [PN]

POPE, GUSTAVUS W. (?   -?   ) US writer and physician, in whose 2 sf novels, *Romances of the Planets, No. 1: Journey to Mars* (**1894**) and *Romances of the Planets, No. 2: Journey to Venus* (**1895**), a US officer visits an advanced MARS (falling in love with a princess) and a primitive VENUS (shooting, as E.F. BLEILER has noted, anything that moves). Introducing a reprint edition of the first book, Sam MOSKOWITZ noted some adumbrations of Edgar Rice BURROUGHS's **Barsoom.** [JC]
See also: HISTORY OF SF.

POPKES, STEVEN (1952-   ) US writer who began publishing sf with "A Capella Blues" for *IASFM* in 1982. *Caliban Landing* (**1987**) interestingly depicts a human expedition to map a new planet (Caliban) – and the complex consequences of its landing there – from the viewpoint of an ALIEN female, who becomes embroiled in the humans' heated interactions. After a fairly conventional start, the tale expands into a complex exploration of the personalities thus thrust together. [JC]
Other work: *Slow Lightning* (**1991** dos).

POPOV, ALEXANDER (1954-   ) Bulgarian sf writer and publisher who has won awards for his short fiction, some written under the pseudonym Al Vickers, some translated into foreign languages. His sf novel «Provinzia Pet» ["Province Five"] as by Al Vickers was contracted in 1991 for publication in Russian translation in Russia. His recently established Gemini publishing house began, in 1991, to publish a fortnightly sf magazine, *Drugi Svetove* ["Other Worlds"]. AP wrote this encyclopedia's entry on BULGARIA. [PN]

POPULAR FICTION CO. ◊ WEIRD TALES.

POPULAR MAGAZINE, THE US PULP MAGAZINE published by STREET & SMITH, ed Henry Harrison Lewis and others. Appeared monthly from Nov 1903, semi-monthly from 1 Oct 1909, weekly from 24 Sep 1927, semi-monthly from 7 July 1928, and monthly Feb-Sep 1931. Merged with *Complete Stories* from Oct 1931.

TPM, which was in competition with the Frank A. MUNSEY chain, regularly published fantasy and sf.

Among its noteworthy contributions to the genre were stories in the **Craig Kennedy** series by Arthur B. REEVE, future-WAR stories by Edwin BALMER and the serialization of *Ayesha* (1905; **1905**) by H. Rider HAGGARD. Other contributors included John Buchan (1815-1940), John COLLIER, Roy NORTON, Sax ROHMER and Edgar WALLACE. [JE]

POPULAR SCIENCE FICTION Australian thin (64pp) DIGEST-size magazine. 8 numbered issues in all: #1-#6 1953-5, published by Frew Publications, Sydney, plus 2, numbered NEW SERIES 1 and 2, 1967, published by Page Publications, NSW; no eds named. The Frew series printed some US reprints and also original Australian and US material; the Page series reprinted #4 and #6 of the Frew publications. A companion magazine, similarly poor, was FUTURE SCIENCE FICTION. [FHP/PN]

POPULATION EXPLOSION ◊ OVERPOPULATION.

PORGES, ARTHUR (1915-   ) US writer and teacher of mathematics who began publishing sf with "The Rats" for *Man's World* in 1951, and since then has published about 70 stories – some as Peter Arthur and some as Pat Rogers – without releasing any of them in book collections. He is, however, a strong and inventive writer, especially of fantasy. He is best known for "The Fly" (1952), not to be confused with George LANGELAAN's tale, and "The Ruum" (1953).

AP's brother, Irwin Porges (1909-   ), who collaborated with him on at least 1 story, wrote *Edgar Allan Poe* (**1963**) and *Edgar Rice Burroughs: The Man who Created Tarzan* (**1975**). [JC]

PORTAL, ELLIS ◊ Bruce POWE.

PORTER, ANDREW (IAN) (1946-   ) US editor and publisher, active in FANDOM in the 1960s, who founded and ran the influential ALGOL, for which he won a 1974 HUGO, as well as its longer-lived (still current) companion, SCIENCE FICTION CHRONICLE. AP also ed anon 2 critical texts, *Exploring Cordwainer Smith* (anth **1975** chap) and *Experiment Perilous: Three Essays on Science Fiction* (anth **1976** chap), and ed *The Book of Ellison* (anth **1978**) with Harlan ELLISON. [JC]

PORTNOY, HOWARD N. (1946-   ) US writer and teacher whose *Hot Rain* (**1977**) seems to start off as a horror fantasy about apparently supernatural bolts of lightning. Eventually, however, a pseudo-scientific explanation is found in a secret military project. [JC]

POSITRONIC ROBOTS Because Isaac ASIMOV's ROBOT stories are so celebrated, this term is one of the best known in the genre; it is not, however, a generally used item of sf TERMINOLOGY, because few writers have had the cheek to borrow the idea from its inventor. The positron is the antiparticle of the electron (◊ ANTIMATTER; PHYSICS); the idea of (highly unstable) positrons being suitable material for the construction of an artificial brain with "enforced calculated neuronic paths" was sheer double-talk, as Asimov was the first to admit. [PN]

POSTAL PUBLICATIONS ◊ MARVEL SCIENCE STORIES.

POST-DISASTER AND POST-HOLOCAUST STORIES ◊ HOLOCAUST AND AFTER.

POSTMODERNISM AND SF "Modernism" is a useful umbrella term for the art that followed the collapse of Romanticism, especially in the first half of the 20th century, but Postmodernism is not simply its more recent replacement. In fact, most contemporary serious writing remains insistently Modernist. The term "Postmodernism" implies a theory of both writing and the world, and a shift in emphasis and method.

In literature, Postmodernism is usually held to imply showy playfulness, genre-bending, and denial of neat aesthetic or moral wrap-up; above all, writing that knows or even struts itself *as writing*, rather than as innocent portrayal. John BARTH, Jorge Luis BORGES, Christine BROOKE-ROSE, Italo CALVINO, Angela CARTER, Don DeLILLO, Philip K. DICK, Umberto ECO, Raymond Federman and Thomas PYNCHON are all Postmodernists whose inventions edge close to sf. Within the genre one might name J.G. BALLARD, Samuel R. DELANY, William GIBSON, Michael MOORCOCK, Rudy RUCKER, John T. SLADEK, Kurt VONNEGUT Jr, Robert Anton WILSON, Joanna RUSS and Ian WATSON as well as Norman SPINRAD (sometimes), Lucius SHEPARD (maybe) and even A.E. VAN VOGT (ahead of his time). Sheer novelty, or even quality, are insufficient to qualify as Postmodernists such writers as Brian W. ALDISS, Thomas M. DISCH, Gene WOLFE and the early Roger ZELAZNY – exemplary sf Modernists all, but not Postmodernists. Such catalogues, however, may miss a deeper point.

Brian McHale, in *Postmodernist Fiction* (**1987**), sees Postmodernism as defined by its focus, as ontological rather than epistemological. That is, where Modernism focuses upon "knowing" and its limits, including what we know about others and ourselves as subjects, Postmodernism by contrast asks about "being", the worlds the subject inhabits; it is about objects rather than subjects. This shift reflects a realization that the world of human experience is multiple and open-ended. The Postmodern condition has an analogy in quantum theory (◊ PHYSICS), where phenomena are modelled by abstract waves in many superposed states, collapsing to a single value or "reality" only in the act of observation.

Contemporary sf undoubtedly intersects the Postmodernism of mainstream literature, especially when it follows the kinds of strategy pioneered by Delany in such self-reflexive texts as, perhaps, *Dhalgren* (**1975**) and, definitely, *Triton* (**1976**). For McHale, sf is "perhaps *the* ontological genre *par excellence*. We can think of science fiction as Postmodernism's non-canonized or 'low art' double, its sister-genre in the same sense that the popular detective thriller is Modernism's sister-genre." Sf is, of all the genres, the one that constructs "realities" as a matter of course.

Perhaps the most influential critical account is the Marxist Fredric Jameson's. In "Postmodernism, or the Cultural Logic of Late Capitalism" (July/Aug 1984 *New Left Review*), he itemizes its stigmata. He finds "a flatness or depthlessness" to be "perhaps the supreme formal feature of all the Postmodernisms", and also a waning of feeling linked to an alleged loss of people's sense of themselves as individuals, and the consequent replacement of "affect" (especially alienated *angst*) with "a peculiar kind of euphoria"; the end of personal style and a sense of history (and memory) and their replacement by *pastiche* (not parody, but the transcoding of Modernist styles into jargon, badges and other decorations) and nostalgia; a schizophrenic fragmentation of artistic texts, marked especially by collage; and, most of all, the "hysterical sublime", in which the alien or "other" surpasses our power to represent it and pitches us into a sort of Gothic rapture (*see also* BIG DUMB OBJECTS; SENSE OF WONDER). All of these qualities often characterize not only the arguably Postmodern environment in which we live but also sf in particular, which Jameson himself has recognized in his many essays on sf topics in SCIENCE-FICTION STUDIES. His theorizing is borrowed explicitly and persuasively for sf by Vivian SOBCHACK in the last chapter of her *Screening Space: the American Science Fiction Film* (**1987**), which projects a "postfuturism".

Jameson suggests specifically that today's information networks "afford us some glimpse into a postmodern or technological sublime", which is perhaps what we find in the VIRTUAL REALITIES of the CYBERPUNK writers, where simulation and reality dissolve into one another. Indeed, Jameson later claimed in *Postmodernism* (**1991**) that cyberpunk was "the supreme *literary* expression if not of postmodernism, then of late capitalism itself".

Innovative sf writers have adopted several of the expansive possibilities of metafiction, MAGIC REALISM and poststructuralist FABULATION (*which see for further discussion of issues raised in this entry*) in general; but more specific both to sf and other Postmodernisms is a comparable adoption of the language of scientific discourse rather than that of traditional literature, and this too tends to the abolition of Modernism's subjectivity – a common feature in late cyberpunk, as in Michael SWANWICK's *Vacuum Flowers* (**1987**). In their emphasis on the technological surround, on the dense new lexicons bursting up especially from the consumer-oriented market productivity of post-industrial science, both sf and Postmodernism give a privileged position to outward context, code and world rather than to a poetic inward "message". They stress object over subject, ways of being over ways of knowing. The Universe itself becomes a text, open to endless interpretation and rewriting.

Two generalizing texts about Postmodernism, neither specifically about sf, are *The Postmodern Condition* (**1979**) by Jean-François Lyotard and the weird *The Postmodern Scene: Excremental Culture and Hyper-Aesthetics* (**1986**) by Arthur Kroker and David Cook. A book relating Postmodernism in general to sf specifically is the unevenly useful *Postmodern Fiction: A Bio-Bibliographical Guide* (anth **1986**) ed Larry McCaffery (1946-   ). *Alternate Worlds: A Study of*

Postmodern Antirealistic American Fiction (**1990**) by John Kuehl discusses many Postmodern authors of marginal, non-genre sf. A good introduction from several perspectives can be found in the special Postmodernism number of JOURNAL OF THE FANTASTIC IN THE ARTS vol 1 #4 (**1988**). The Postmodernism issue of *Science-Fiction Studies* (Nov **1991**) has translations of essays on simulacra and on Ballard by the French sociologist Jean Baudrillard, an important theoretician in this area, along with other interesting material including Ballard's enjoyably intemperate response. Also illuminating is Tom Moylan's *Demand the Impossible: Science Fiction and the Utopian Imagination* (**1986** UK). [DB]

POTOCKI, JAN [r] ◊ POLAND.

POTTER, ROBERT (1831-?   ) Australian author and clergyman; he died before 1912. His novel *The Germ Growers: An Australian Story of Adventure and Mystery* (**1892**; vt *The Germ Growers: The Strange Adventures of Robert Easterley and John Wilbraham* 1892 UK) was published in AUSTRALIA as by Robert Easterley and John Wilbraham, the names of the protagonists, but in the UK as "edited by" RP. A race of discarnate beings, denizens of the interplanetary "ether" capable of assuming human form, invades Earth and sets up beachheads where they cultivate plague germs to be used on humanity; one beachhead is discovered in the Australian outback, with an ALIEN who calls himself Davelli in charge, and the adventures begin. At the end another space dweller called Leafar (i.e., Rafael) saves the day. This alien-INVASION story antedates H.G. WELLS's *The War of the Worlds* (**1898**) by 6 years, but the element of Christian allegory (fallen angels confronted by a good angel) leaves its sf potential not fully realized. Nonetheless, the evil experiments in the chemical mutation of bacteria and the electric flying machines are early GENRE SF in style. [PN]

POURNELLE, JERRY E(UGENE) (1933-   ) US writer with an undergraduate degree in engineering and PhDs from the University of Washington in psychology (1960) and political science (1964). He was employed for 15 years in the US space programme, working for both government and private firms, and at one time was a political campaign manager. Before entering sf, JP wrote some technical nonfiction and some fiction, occasionally using pseudonyms and house names. His first books were a nonfiction text, *The Strategy of Technology* (**1970**) with Stefan T. Possony, and two non-sf novels as by Wade Curtis: *Red Heroin* (**1969**; 1985 as JEP) and *Red Dragon* (**1971**; 1985 as JEP); he used the Curtis name also for a few stories in *ASF*, though his first sf story, "Peace with Honor", appeared in 1971 under his own name.

This story forms part of JEP's most extended series, the **CoDominium** sequence, earlier parts of which are named after their chief military protagonist, a cunning, honourable mercenary and military genius named **Falkenberg** who, in a period of civilian stupidity and venality (it is a sort of period often depicted in JP's work), conspires with the CoDominium military force to maintain a human presence in those worlds already colonized by mankind. He appears in *West of Honor* (**1976** Canada) and *The Mercenary* (fixup **1977**), the latter book reworking "Peace with Honor" and other stories – both vols being assembled as *Falkenberg's Legion* (omni **1990**) – and in *Prince of Mercenaries* (fixup **1989**) and *Go Tell the Spartans* (**1991**) with S.M. STIRLING. Set considerably later in the **CoDominium** world – after the rise and fall of a first Empire of Man, an interregnum, and the birth of the Second Empire – *A Spaceship for the King* (**1973**; exp vt *King David's Spaceship* 1981) also features a tough military genius, whose resemblance to Falkenberg is obviously of thematic importance, for JP argues implicitly in the sequence that civilization can be sustained only through a hierarchical structuring of society which – perhaps rather magically – manages to avoid bureaucratic sclerosis, and through the maintenance of such military virtues as honour and loyalty. These arguments are most clearly on view in the series' climax, *The Mote in God's Eye* (**1974**) with Larry NIVEN, set in a period when the CoDominium has evolved into a full-blown GALACTIC EMPIRE with all the trappings. The fascinating ALIENS depicted in that novel reflect his collaborator's conceptual ingenuity as clearly as the human Empire reflects JP's sustained fictional argument for that kind of solution to the problems of just government. The more recent **War World** sequence of SHARED-WORLD anthologies – *War World, Volume 1: The Burning Eye* * (anth **1988**) with John F. CARR and Roland GREEN, *Volume 2: Death's Head Rebellion* * (anth **1990**) with Carr and Green, and *Volume 3: Sauron Dominion* * (anth **1991**) with Carr alone – carries the CoDominium concept into broader waters, with a prequel, *Codominium: Revolt on War World* * (anth **1992**) with Carr, setting the stage.

After *The Mote in God's Eye*, JEP collaborated with Niven on several further novels, all singletons and most extremely successful in the marketplace (*for details see* Larry NIVEN). They include *Inferno* (**1976**), *Lucifer's Hammer* (**1977**), *Oath of Fealty* (**1981**), which rewrites **CoDominium** feudalism in mundane – indeed, suburbanized – terms, *Footfall* (**1985**), *The Legacy of Heorot* (**1987** UK), with Niven and Steven BARNES, and *Fallen Angels* (**1991**), with Niven and Michael FLYNN. Political subtexts – always evident in both main collaborators' solo work – tend in their joint efforts to surface rather more frequently, to the discomfort of some readers, especially those unaccustomed to the singularly narrow range of political discourse in the USA (though within that narrow range its expression is singularly open); other readers find the books refreshingly "robust" (◊ POLITICS).

Most of JEP's solo work not devoted to the **CoDominium** also focuses on issues of WAR and the decorums and tactics of waging war. A second, shorter and more pessimistic series, the **Laurie Jo Hansen** sequence, substitutes corporate warfare for military/political conflict: *High Justice* (coll of linked stories **1977**) and *Exiled to Glory* (**1978**). The **Janissaries** sequence – *Janissaries* (**1979**), *Janissaries: Clan and Crown* (**1983**) with Roland Green and *Janissaries 3: Storms of Victory* (**1987**), again with Green – returns to explicit warfare, describing a mercenary leader's efforts to unify the planet to which he and his soldiers have been transplanted. JEP also edited, with John F. Carr (not always credited), the **There Will be War** sequence of military anthologies: *There Will be War* (anth **1983**), *Vol II: Men of War* (anth **1984**), *Vol III: Blood and Iron* (anth **1984**), *Vol IV: Day of the Tyrant* (anth **1985**), *Vol V: Warrior* (anth **1986**), *Vol VI: Guns of Darkness* (anth **1987**), *Vol VII: Call to Battle* (anth **1988**), *Vol VIII: Armageddon!* (anth **1989**) and *Vol IX: After Armageddon* (anth **1990**).

JEP was first recipient of the JOHN W. CAMPBELL AWARD for Best New Writer in 1973, and very rapidly established himself as a dominant creator of the politically conservative-libertarian HARD-SF tale. His military sf has shaped that subgenre as well, though it would be unfair to blame him for the excesses of his imitators. His nonfiction, too, has been notable for its engaging clarity, its constant presentation of political agendas, and its eagerness to convey knowledge. A sense of deep cultural pessimism, though countered by explicit avowals of LIBERTARIAN hopefulness, pervades and – for many readers – humanizes his work. [JC]

Other works: *Escape from the Planet of the Apes* ✶ (**1974**), a film tie (◊ ESCAPE FROM THE PLANET OF THE APES); *Birth of Fire* (**1976** Canada).

Nonfiction: *That Buck Rogers Stuff* (coll **1977**); *A Step Farther Out* (coll **1979**); *Mutual Assured Survival: A Space-Age Solution to Nuclear Annihilation* (**1984**) with Dean ING; *The User's Guide to Small Computers* (**1984**); *Adventures in Microland* (**1986**).

As editor: *2020 Vision* (anth **1974**); *Black Holes* (anth **1978**) with John F. Carr (here, and occasionally elsewhere, uncredited); *The Endless Frontier* (anth **1979**), *The Endless Frontier, Volume 2* (anth **1985**) and *Cities in Space* (anth **1991**), all with Carr; *The Survival of Freedom* (anth **1981**) with Carr; *Nebula Award Stories Sixteen* (anth **1982**); *The Science Fiction Yearbook* (anth **1985**) with Carr; the FAR FRONTIERS original anthology series, all with James BAEN, *Far Frontiers* (anth **1985**), *Vol II* (anth **1985**), *Vol III* (anth **1985**), *Vol IV* (anth **1986**), *Vol V* (anth **1986**), *Vol VI* (anth **1986**) and *Vol VII* (anth **1986**); the **Imperial Stars** reprint anthologies with Carr, *Imperial Stars, Vol 1: The Stars at War* (anth **1986**), *Vol 2: Republic and Empire* (anth **1987**) and *Vol 3: the Crash of Empire* (anth **1989**).

See also: CITIES; COMMUNICATIONS; DESTINIES; DISASTER; ECONOMICS; ESCHATOLOGY; GALAXY SCIENCE FICTION; GODS AND DEMONS; INVASION; LIBERTARIAN SF; MYTHOLOGY; NUCLEAR POWER; OUTER PLANETS; OVERPOPULATION; SCIENCE FICTION WRITERS OF AMERICA; SOCIAL DARWINISM; SPACESHIPS; STARS; UTOPIAS.

POWE, BRUCE (1925-   ) Canadian writer whose sf novels concentrate on political disorders, a theme very common to post-WWII writers from his country. *Killing Ground: The Canadian Civil War* (**1968**), as Ellis Portal, sets its fatal conflict in the NEAR FUTURE. *The Last Days of the American Empire* (**1974**) more far-rangingly sets its conflicts in the 21st century, when a North American hegemony is threated by both Europe and Africa. [JC]

POWELL, SONNY [s] ◊ Alfred BESTER.

POWER, THE Film (1968). Galaxy/MGM. Prod George PAL. Dir Pal, Byron HASKIN, starring George Hamilton, Suzanne Pleshette, Nehemiah Persoff, Michael Rennie. Screenplay John Gay, based on *The Power* (**1956**) by Frank M. ROBINSON. 109 mins. Colour.

Without the spectacular special effects of Pal's earlier sf films, *TP* concentrates instead on suspenseful plotting and the clever investing of apparently ordinary situations with a sense of menace, coming – with considerable success – as close to *film noir* as Pal ever approached. It tells of a MUTANT supermind VILLAIN, masquerading as an ordinary human, who is eliminating, piecemeal, a group of scientists who suspect his existence. One (Hamilton) survives not only murder attempts but also efforts to make him a non-person, all records of his past being deleted one by one. The reason for his survival, as he himself finally learns, is that he too is a mutant: everybody's favorite cliché in pulp-sf yarns about PSI POWERS. The film ends with a battle of wills between the two superminds – a literally heart-stopping event. The interesting script and taut direction led critic John BAXTER to call it "one of the finest of all sf films". It is certainly, aside from WAR OF THE WORLDS (1953), Pal's best sf production. [PN/JB]

POWERS, J.L. ◊ John S. GLASBY.

POWERS, RICHARD M. (1921-   ) US illustrator. Born in Chicago, he studied in several art schools in that area before and after WWII. He began work in sf ILLUSTRATION in the early 1950s, beginning with DOUBLEDAY, where he also did mysteries and Westerns, and also with 2 1952 covers for *Gal*. When Ian Ballantine founded BALLANTINE BOOKS in 1952 he approached RMP to do covers for him. Although his early work there was representational, as it had been at Doubleday, RMP soon – with the cover for Arthur C. CLARKE's *Childhood's End* (**1953**) – adopted a Surrealist style (much influenced by Yves Tanguy [1900-1955] and Joan Miró [1893-1983]) unique in sf; it soon became the trademark of Ballantine's 1950s sf. RMP's glowing and sometimes whimsical paintings are full of amorphous shapes, floating in space or over surreal landscapes, and have been enormously influential in sf illustration. He did a little more magazine-cover work, but most of his prolific sf cover illustration – he worked in other fields as well, including children's books – was for books, for Ballantine, Pocket Books, Berkley Books, MacFadden, Dell and others. After his first wife's death he dropped most of his commercial work during the 1960s, then returned in the 1970s, not quite so prolifically but as forcefully as ever. He has had many exhibitions, in New York's Rehn Gallery and else-where; his work commands as much respect outside sf as in it. With RMP's work the packaging of sf could be said to have come of age. Covers no longer required glamorous space girls or technological hard-ware, and Surrealism captured sf's disturbing es-sence just as strongly as ray-guns or monsters. A portfolio is *Spacetimewarp Paintings* (**1983**).   [PN/JG]

POWERS, TIM(OTHY) (1952-   ) US writer who began publishing sf with *The Skies Discrowned* (**1976** Canada as Timothy Powers; rev vt *Forsake the Sky* 1986 as TP), a fantasy-tinged sf adventure much influ-enced – TP stated in his introduction to the revised version – by the work of Rafael Sabatini (1875-1950). *Epitaph in Rust* (**1976** Canada as Timothy Powers; text restored, vt *An Epitaph in Rust* 1989 as TP) somewhat more vividly sets the adventures of its protagonist, a reluctant monk, in a post-HOLOCAUST California. Already some features typical of the mature TP novel were taking shape: protagonists who have been lamed by symbolic wounds but who are depicted with a sustaining dark geniality; plots which mix genres with elegant facility but without bleaching out or calling into philosophical question the various worlds which are flung together (so that TP cannot be described as an author of FABULATIONS – differing in this from his colleague and sometime collaborator, James P. BLAYLOCK); and settings described with florid clarity and great devotion to detail. But the first 2 tales – written as they were for LASER BOOKS – only hinted at these riches; it was not until his third novel, *The Drawing of the Dark* (**1979**), an outright FANTASY, that TP began clearly to demonstrate his complex gifts. The title refers to the drawing of a beer which has been brewed in one location – atop the grave of Finn Mac Cool – for several thousand years, and which must be drawn by Merlin in the middle of the 16th century to allow a reborn Fisher King (and the protagonist, who is an avatar of Arthur himself) to save Europe from the Turks. Vienna is vividly depicted; the story, told in a slangy but unmocking manner, is gripping.

The Anubis Gates (**1983**; rev 1984 UK), which won the 1984 PHILIP K. DICK MEMORIAL AWARD and is a central example of STEAMPUNK, may be the easiest of all TP's books to admire, though it is less daunting in scope than his later work. While tracing the career and work of early-Victorian poet William Ashbless – both TP and James P. Blaylock have written "Ashbless" poems, including *"Offering the Bicentennial Edition of the Complete Twelve Hours of the Night"* (**1985** broad-sheet) by both authors – the soon-to-be-wounded protagonist Brendan Doyle is sent by TIME TRAVEL to the London of 1810, where he is trapped, and the plot thickens with virtuoso speed; Egyptian MAGIC (intri-cately described in terms of the precise techniques necessary to operate it) intersects with a compulsive and feverish vision of the underground life of the great city (patently derived from the work of Charles DICKENS), while haunted MONSTERS roam the aisles of

the city and Doyle ricochets backwards through time and forwards into the body of Ashbless, whom he becomes. Fantasy, sf, horror and historical fiction all marry here with an ease which seems entirely natural.

TP's next novel, *Dinner at Deviant's Palace* (**1985**), which also won the Dick Award, marked a partial return to the comparative simplicities of his first work, though its use of post-holocaust California was markedly less genre-bound than that of *Epitaph in Rust*, especially in its protagonists' re-enactment of the Orpheus and Eurydice legend, and in the confron-tation with an ALIEN, who is both a fake MESSIAH and Lord of the Underworld. *On Stranger Tides* (**1987**) is a hugely enriched pirate yarn, set in an ALTERNATE-WORLD 18th century and concerning (in part) a search for IMMORTALITY. *The Stress of Her Regard* (**1989**), possibly TP's most sustained single novel, is set in the early 19th century of *The Anubis Gates*, focusing not only on Byron (who appears in the earlier book) but on Percy Shelley and Mary SHELLEY and John Keats as well, in a story involving *lamiae* and vampires (◊ SUPERNATURAL CREATURES), culminating in the sf-like revelation that non-carbon-based forms of life have survived and are the secret masters of the Austrian Empire. *Last Call* (**1992**) is a complex con-temporary fantasy novel in which Bugsy Siegel is one of a series of Fisher Kings; its protagonist must avoid being sacrificed in a ritual of succession.

Though his fertility of invention occasionally (as often with Blaylock) impedes the flow of story, TP is at heart a storyteller, and ruthlessly shapes his material into narrative form. The result is one of the few genuinely original bodies of work in the modern sf/fantasy field.   [JC]

Other works: *Night Moves* (**1986** chap); *The Way Down the Hill* (**1986** chap).

About the author: *A Checklist of Tim Powers* (**1991** chap) by Tom Joyce and Christopher P. STEPHENS.

See also: CLICHÉS; GOTHIC SF; HEROES; RECURSIVE SF; WRITERS OF THE FUTURE CONTEST.

POWER SOURCES We live in an age of imminent resources crisis, anxiously anticipating the depletion of fossil-fuel reserves even while we become reluctant to rely on NUCLEAR POWER because of the POLLUTION problems caused by radioactive wastes. New options rely either on discoveries not yet made – the develop-ment of nuclear-fusion reactors, or of more efficient ways to convert solar energy into electricity – or on a political will which governments of all persuasions seem too short-sighted to exercise, as with tidal and wind power. There was, however, little trace of such anxieties in sf published before public concern began to grow; the future scenarios envisaged by early sf writers frequently assumed our energy resources to be potentially infinite.

For most of human history, MACHINES were worked by three basic power sources: wind, water and muscle. For millennia people used fire as a source of heat and an agent of physical and chemical change without learning how to harness it as an energy source in mechanical work; then the invention of the steam engine precipitated the Industrial Revolution. Sf writers, following in the tracks of countless optimists who had tried to sidestep the problem by inventing "perpetual-motion machines", were only too ready to imagine future revolutions of similarly awesome scope. Electricity was often viewed as a quasimagical animating force, as in Mary SHELLEY's *Frankenstein, or The Modern Prometheus* (**1818**; rev 1831) and Arthur Conan DOYLE's "The Los Amigos Fiasco" (1892). In Lord LYTTON's *The Coming Race* (**1871**) the key to energy-prosperity is *vril*, a kind of "atmospheric magnetism" administered by a device bearing a suspicious resemblance to a magic wand (a wand waved to considerable effect in *The Vril Staff* [**1891**] by "XYZ") ($\Diamond$ PSEUDO-SCIENCE). Percy GREG's *Across the Zodiac* (**1880**) employs the equally mysterious "apergy", which seems to be ANTIGRAVITY with a seasoning of electrical mysticism; like *vril*, apergy was borrowed by other writers, including John Jacob ASTOR in *A Journey in Other Worlds* (**1894**), and it is the obvious model for the antigravity devices used in Robert CROMIE's *A Plunge into Space* (**1890**) and H.G. WELLS's *The First Men in the Moon* (**1901**). In *Twenty Thousand Leagues under the Sea* (**1870**; trans **1873**) Jules VERNE was ready to assume that electrical energy could be drawn from sea water by quasimagical means. This optimistic outlook was boosted by the discovery of X-rays in 1895; for many years thereafter unlimited power was casually generated in sf stories by the invocation of magical "rays". The discovery of radioactivity only a few years later provided yet another jargon: power derived from atomic breakdown, spontaneous or forced. This, of course, turned out to be a real possibility, but its prominence in early sf owes more to convenience than to an assessment of its true potential. GENRE SF inherited this considerable jargon and understandably made the most of it. E.E. "Doc" SMITH's *The Skylark of Space* (1928; **1946**) begins when a bathtub coated with "X, the unknown metal" reacts to the appropriate Open Sesame by releasing limitless quantities of "infra-atomic energy" – a moment cruelly parodied by the discovery of "Cheddite" in Harry HARRISON's *Star Smashers of the Galaxy Rangers* (**1973**).

Given this confidence in the imminent availability of unlimited power, it is not surprising that the most thoughtful work of speculative writers in the early 20th century deals with the question of the social responsibility of scientists making such discoveries. Stories of wise men blackmailing the world into peace and social justice for all are common, but much more delicate exercises include Karel ČAPEK's satire *The Absolute at Large* (**1922**; trans **1927**) and his surreal "atomic phantasy" *Krakatit* (**1924**; trans **1925**). The former concerns the "Karburator", which not only releases the energy bound in matter but also the spiritual "power" which went into its creation, generating worldwide religious fanaticism; a later

satire with a related theme is Romain GARY's *The Gasp* (**1973**), in which the energy of immortal souls is harnessed as an industrial power source. Pulp sf celebrated the imminence of what Hugo GERNSBACK sometimes called the "Age of Power Freedom". Antigravity and wonderful rays were given *carte blanche* to defy the conservation laws – a situation encouraged rather than inhibited by the real-life discovery of atomic power, which was for a brief period taken as "proof" that limitless energy was actually available. Jack WILLIAMSON's "The Equalizer" (1947) is a thoughtful attempt to analyse the social consequences of free power for all, resurrecting the *vril* staff as a literary device. Raymond F. JONES's "Noise Level" (1952) supposes that the only thing standing between science and the discovery of limitless power is the belief of scientists in its impossibility. So convincing was this line of argument to readers of ASTOUNDING SCIENCE-FICTION that the story gave rise to several sequels, letters and articles criticizing contemporary patent law for its unfair treatment of perpetual motion and its blatant discrimination against discoveries of new fundamental principles in science. This optimism waned rapidly during the 1960s, although Theodore STURGEON's "Brownshoes"(1969) is a heartfelt parable about the difficulty of making a gift of perpetual motion to mankind in a world where so many vested interests (e.g., oil companies) would do their utmost to suppress it.

The dependence of the developed countries on shrinking coal and oil reserves was brought home dramatically from 1973 on by the emergence of OPEC as a political force capable of dictating energy policy to the West. The POLITICS of energy came to play a major part in many near-future novels, including Frederik POHL's *JEM: The Making of a Utopia* (**1979**) and *The Cool War* (**1981**), the latter also being one of several stories to explore the idea of transmitting power in the form of microwaves down to Earth from solar cells mounted on satellites. The OPEC-precipitated oil crisis of the 1970s inspired such unlikely projects as the attempt to hijack the Middle-Eastern oilfields by TIME TRAVEL in Wolfgang JESCHKE's *The Last Day of Creation* (**1981**; trans **1982**) and the use of exotic living machinery to extract oil in Rory HARPER's ALTERNATE-WORLD story *Petrogypsies* (**1989**); many TECHNOTHRILLERS are concerned with power sources in one way or another, standard plots often centring either on squabblings between multinational power companies or on the discovery – usually merely as a MCGUFFIN – of new ways of producing energy. Fantasies in which energy sources appear by miraculous *fiat*, like D.G. COMPTON's *Ascendancies* (**1980**), acquired a sharp cautionary note. A real measure of imaginative fervour with respect to marvellous power sources survives only in the matter of SPACESHIP propulsion, ranging from the solar yachts of Arthur C. CLARKE's "Sunjammer" (1964; vt "The Wind from the Sun"), which use the SOLAR

WIND, to the BLACK-HOLE propulsion system for interplanetary vessels in the same author's *Imperial Earth* (1975). [BS]

See also: ECOLOGY; SUN; TECHNOLOGY; UNDER THE SEA; WEAPONS.

POWYS, JOHN COWPER (1872-1963) UK writer, resident for much of his career in the USA, though he returned to the UK in his later years. The novels of his old age, from *Morwyn, or The Vengeance of God* (1937) onwards, combine fantasy and sf elements in an attempt, sometimes obscure, to heat his eccentric mysticism into a unique amalgam: *Porius* (1951) is an Arthurian fantasy; *The Inmates* (1952) presents the "delusions" of a cast of mental patients in exaggerated terms and features a giant helicopter; *Atlantis* (1954) describes Odysseus's search for ATLANTIS; *The Brazen Head* (1956) deals with Roger Bacon (c1214-1292) as alchemist. Between 1957 and 1960, near the end of his life, JCP produced a sequence of remarkable FABULATIONS, some of them unhinged. They were all eventually published as *Up and Out* (coll 1957), the first novella of which is a post-HOLOCAUST tale in which four survivors witness the end of time, *All or Nothing* (1960), in which two children make a kind of tour of the Universe, *Real Wraiths* (1974 chap), *Two and Two* (1974 chap) and *Three Fantasies* (coll 1985).

Of JCP's two brothers, both also writers, T(heodore) F(rancis) Powys (1875-1953) wrote much of strong fantasy interest. [JC]

Other works: *The Owl, the Duck, and – Miss Rowe! Miss Rowe!* (1930 chap US); *A Glastonbury Romance* (1932 US); *Maiden Castle* (1936 US); *Owen Glendower* (1940 US); *Lucifer: A Narrative Poem* (1956); *Homer and the Aether* (1959).

See also: END OF THE WORLD; FANTASTIC VOYAGES.

POYER, DAVID C. (1949-) US writer who has published non-genre work as David Poyer, and sf variously as David C. Poyer, D.C. Poyer and David Andreissen. *The Shiloh Project* (1981) is a NEAR-FUTURE sf adventure. *Star Seed* (1982) as Andreissen places within a context of exceeding grimness – ALIENS have irrevocably poisoned Earth in an attempt to "terraform" it for their own needs – a tale of almost exuberant action: a surviving team composed of one human, one mutant and one dolphin subverts the eponymous starship to revolt against the "terraformers", then sets off to find another planet. In DCP's third and most interesting novel, *Stepfather Bank* (1987), set in a post-HOLOCAUST world dominated by a paternalist bank, a rogue poet hornswoggles and destabilizes the entire AI-controlled system, which has in fact been working to preserve humanity as well as to control it. [JC]

See also: UNDER THE SEA.

POYER, JOE Working name of US writer Joseph John Poyer (1939-) for his fiction, beginning in 1965 with "Mission 'Red Clash'" for *ASF*, a magazine with which he was closely associated. Of his novels, *Operation Malacca* (1968), about the use of talking dolphins for military purposes, and *North Cape* (1969) are TECHNOTHRILLERS. *Tunnel War* (1979) is an ALTERNATE-WORLD tale involving the 1911 construction of a Channel Tunnel. JP has also written novels in other genres. [JC]

POYSER, VICTORIA [r] ◊ ROWENA.

PRAGNELL, FESTUS (1905-?1965) UK writer and policeman who first appeared in the US PULP MAGAZINES with "The Venus Germ" for *Wonder Stories* in 1932, written in collaboration with R.F. STARZL; he published 1 tale as by Francis Parnell (Festus Pragnell is not a pseudonym). His **Don Hargreaves** stories, all set on a lurid Mars, appeared in *AMZ* from 1938 ("Ghost of Mars") to 1943 ("Madcap of Mars"). His first sf novel, *The Green Man of Kilsona* (1936; rev vt *The Green Man of Graypec* 1950 US), describes a voyage into a miniature world (◊ GREAT AND SMALL). A second novel, *The Terror from Timorkal* (1946), sets a world-threatening crisis in Africa, where a new mineral suitable for the manufacture of superweapons is being exploited by unscrupulous politicians. His last work, "The Machine God Laughs" (1948), was the title story of *The Machine God Laughs* (anth 1949) ed William L. CRAWFORD. [JC]

Other works: *Thieves of the Air* (c1943 chap) with Benson HERBERT.

PRATCHETT, TERRY (1948-) UK writer who began publishing with "The Hades Business" in *Science Fantasy* in 1963, and who for many years was in full-time employment, as a journalist until 1980, and as a publicity officer for the Central Electricity Generating Board until 1987; as a consequence, his early books were written and published intermittently. His first, *The Carpet People* (1971; rev 1992), is a fantasy for children. *The Dark Side of the Sun* (1976), sf, makes gentle fun of the alien-cluttered **Known Space** books of Larry NIVEN, though further targets, including Ron GOULART and Jack VANCE, are also affectionately addressed; *Strata* (1981) also parodies Niven and other HARD-SF writers, in this case by depicting an artificial flat world embedded within Ptolemaic heavens – it is a POCKET UNIVERSE, in fact – seemingly constructed by the ancient Spindle Kings, though in fact Builder Gods were responsible. No GODS are given responsibility by name for the construction of Discworld, a fantasy creation borne through space on the back of a huge turtle, but an sf world-building premise does unseriously underlie the **Discworld** books, which made TP famous. The novels themselves are FANTASY. The series comprises *The Colour of Magic* (1983), *The Light Fantastic* (1986), *Equal Rites* (1987), *Mort* (1987), *Sourcery* (1988), *Wyrd Sisters* (1988), *Pyramids* (1989), *Guards! Guards!* (1989), *Eric* (1990) with Josh KIRBY (responsible for all the UK Discworld covers) given equal billing on the original edition (the text is heavily illustrated; paperback editions, lacking the illustrations, give TP alone as author), *Moving Pictures* (1990), *Reaper Man* (1991), *Witches Abroad* (1991), *Small Gods* (1992) and *Lords and Ladies* (1992), with further titles projected; they make up the finest set of pure comedies the genre has yet seen. A second series, the **Book of the Nomes** CHILDREN'S-SF trilogy about small extraterrestrials caught for eons on Earth and attempting escape, comprises *Truckers* (**1989**), *Diggers* (**1990**) and *Wings* (**1990**). *Good Omens: The Nice and Accurate Prophecies of Agnes Nutter, Witch* (**1990**; rev 1990 US) with Neil GAIMAN is a fantasy about the END OF THE WORLD. The youthful protagonist of *Only You Can Save Mankind* (**1992**), sf for young adults, must help the space warriors of an arcade game (◊ GAMES AND TOYS) escape futile combat with human players.   [JC]

See also: BRITISH SCIENCE FICTION AWARD; GREAT AND SMALL; HUMOUR; MAGIC; SATIRE; TERRAFORMING.

PRATT, CORNELIA ATWOOD Working and maiden name of Cornelia Atwood Comer (?   -1929), author with Richard Slee of *Dr Berkeley's Discovery* (**1899**), in which the doctor solves a mystery with his memory-cell-reading device (◊ PSYCHOLOGY).   [JC]

PRATT, (MURRAY) FLETCHER (1897-1956) US writer and historian who began his career as an author and translator for Hugo GERNSBACK's SCIENCE WONDER STORIES and its companions in the early 1930s; his first published story was "The Octopus Cycle" for *AMZ* in 1928 as with Irvin Lester (a Pratt pseudonym). While doing translations of German sf novels FP evolved what became a renowned method of extracting payment from the notoriously slow Gernsback organization: he would submit the first part of a novel, wait until it was set in type, then refuse to deliver the conclusion until paid. He undertook many collaborations, notably "City of the Living Dead" (1930) with Laurence MANNING, and contributed regularly to the sf magazines; but he is now best remembered for his fantasy, especially for his collaborations with L. Sprague DE CAMP (*whom see for fuller details*). The most successful were the **Harold Shea** stories, among which the main titles are: *The Incomplete Enchanter* (1940 *Unknown*; **1941**), *The Castle of Iron* (1941 *Unknown*; **1950**) and *The Wall of Serpents* (fixup **1960**; vt *The Enchanter Completed* 1980 UK). The first 2 titles were assembled as *The Compleat Enchanter: The Magical Misadventures of Harold Shea* (omni **1975**), and all 3 were eventually assembled as *The Intrepid Enchanter* (omni **1988** UK; vt *The Complete Compleat Enchanter* 1989 US). A second series with De Camp, the **Gavagan's Bar** CLUB STORIES, assembled in *Tales from Gavagan's Bar* (coll **1953**; exp 1978), comprised mostly high-spirited tall tales, some of them sf. On their collaborations De Camp, as junior partner, would write a first draft after he and FP had jointly outlined the story; FP would then compose the final draft, to which De Camp would put the finishing editorial touches. This routine was varied on only a very few later short stories.

FP's own fantasy novels are *The Well of the Unicorn* (**1948** as by George U. Fletcher; 1967 as by FP) and *The Blue Star* (1952 in *Witches Three* ed anon FP; **1969**); *Witches Three* was one of the **Twayne Triplets** series – Twayne being the publisher – each vol assembling

3 original novellas by different authors with a common theme or setting. The series idea was FP's, and he ed (also anon) 1 later vol, *The Petrified Planet* (anth **1952**). In the end the project proved abortive, but the last title was the first SHARED-WORLD anthology to appear in the genre. FP also wrote several volumes of popular history and 3 books on rockets and space travel including *Rockets, Jets, Guided Missiles and Space Ships* (**1951**).   [MJE/JC]

Other works: *The Land of Unreason* (**1941**) and *The Carnelian Cube* (**1948**), both with De Camp; *Double in Space* (coll **1951**; rev 1954 UK), in the 1st edn comprising the 2 novellas "Project Excelsior" and "The Wanderer's Return", the latter being replaced in the UK by "The Conditioned Captain", itself already published in the USA as *The Undying Fire* (**1953**); *World of Wonder* (anth **1951**), a Twayne book but not a Triplet; *Double Jeopardy* (fixup **1952**); *Invaders from Rigel* (1932 *Wonder Stories Quarterly* as "The Onslaught From Rigel"; **1960**); *Alien Planet* (1932 *Amazing Stories Quarterly* as "A Voice across the Years"; **1962**).

About the author: Chapter 7 of *Literary Swordsmen and Sorcerers* (**1976**) by L. Sprague De Camp.

See also: AUTOMATION; CLONES; DYSTOPIAS; FINLAND; HUMOUR; LEISURE; MAGIC; MATHEMATICS; PSYCHOLOGY; PUBLISHING; SCIENCE FANTASY; UTOPIAS.

PREDATOR Film (1987). Amercent/American Entertainment/20th Century-Fox. Dir John McTiernan, starring Arnold Schwarzenegger, Carl Weathers, Elpidia Carrillo, Bill Duke. Screenplay Jim Thomas, John Thomas. 106 mins. Colour.

A special-forces group undertaking a commando-style rescue mission in South America clashes bloodily with guerrillas and then very much more bloodily with the Predator: an intelligent ALIEN that can bend light to make itself almost invisible. The alien picks them off one by one, losing only to the Schwarzenegger character, by now reduced to primitive combat. The blend of the jungle-warfare (or Vietnam) scenario with the alien-INVASION genre is potentially interesting, but the treatment follows a wholly predictable pattern. Moreover on the evidence presented, the alien should have won.   [PN]

See also: MONSTER MOVIES.

PREDATOR 2 Film (1990). Gordon/Silver/Davis/20th Century-Fox. Dir Stephen Hopkins, starring Danny Glover, Gary Busey, Ruben Blades, Maria Conchita Alonso, Bill Paxton. Screenplay Jim Thomas, John Thomas. 107 mins. Colour.

This superior sequel to PREDATOR is a well oiled adrenaline machine. Los Angeles, 1997, is anarchic, with Jamaican and Colombian drug gangs, the LA police and the FBI all at each other's throats. A new ALIEN Predator, drawn by global hotspots, is trophy-hunting there on safari. A Black policeman succeeds where the creepy feds fail, and as a recognition of his valour receives a duelling pistol from yet more Predators who arrive for the finale. Stan Winston's alien design (great mandibles) is threatening and interesting, just right for a New Right Vigilante alien who picks off the bad guys first. *P2* is pure and stylish exploitation-movie making, and shows a witty recognition of the same violence-begets-violence syndrome it abets.   [PN]

See also: CINEMA; MONSTER MOVIES.

PREDICTION The most widespread false belief about sf among the general public is that it is a literature of prediction. Very few sf writers have ever claimed this to be the case, although Hugo GERNSBACK did see one function of his sf magazines as to paint an accurate picture of the future. Very few of the stories he published lived up to his editorializing. When John W. CAMPBELL Jr took over the editorship of *ASF* he demanded an increasing scientific plausibility from his writers, but a plausible-sounding "perhaps" is a long way from prediction.

None of this has prevented sf fans from crowing with delight when an sf writer has made a good guess, and the mythology of sf is full of such examples. H.G. WELLS predicted the use of the tank in "The Land Ironclads" (1903), of aerial bombing in *The War in the Air* (**1908**) and of the atom bomb (more or less) in *The World Set Free* (**1914**). Ever since Einstein's mass-energy equations had been published, it had been generally known that enormous power was locked up in the atom, and stories about NUCLEAR POWER and atomic WEAPONS were commonplace in the 1920s and 1930s; they became very much more accurate in the early 1940s, and Cleve CARTMILL, Robert A. HEINLEIN and Lester DEL REY all wrote good predictive stories before Hiroshima. (Heinlein also predicted the water bed and the use of remote-control WALDOS.) Most early prediction stories were about future WAR, future weapons and the various possibilities of INVASION. Not many of them were correct; although several stories predicted war between the UK and Germany before 1914 (and, indeed, between the UK and almost everyone else), most of them centred on an invasion across the Channel which never took place. Edward Everett HALE wrote rather charmingly about an artificial satellite in "The Brick Moon" (1869). Arthur C. CLARKE wrote a celebrated article about communications satellites, "Extraterrestrial Relays" (*Wireless World* Oct 1945), but this was not a story; nor, sadly, did it become a patent. Jules VERNE is thought by many to have invented the submarine in *Vingt mille lieues sous les mers* (**1870**; trans as *Twenty Thousand Leagues Under the Sea* **1873**), but in fact functional submarines had existed since at least the 18th century. One of Verne's best pieces of prediction was quite accidental; the moon-shot in *De la terre à la lune* (**1865**), which was published with the sequel *Autour de la lune* (**1870**) in *From the Earth to the Moon* (trans **1873**), is fired from a spot very close to Cape Canaveral in Florida. Rudyard KIPLING predicted transatlantic aerial trade, specifically airmail postage, in *With the Night Mail* (1905; **1909** chap US). Erasmus DARWIN's poem *The Temple of Nature* (**1802**) preceded Verne, Wells and just about everybody else in its

joyful description of airborne fleets of transport ships, war in the air, submarines and great CITIES with skyscrapers. Edwin BALMER had an early form of lie detector in *The Achievements of Luther Trant* (coll **1910**) with William MacHarg. Hugo Gernsback had many technological predictions in *Ralph 124C 41+* (1911-12; fixup **1925**); this is one of the 18 stories of the period quoted by Everett BLEILER in *Science-Fiction: The Early Years* (**1990**) as anticipating tv. Nevil SHUTE predicted metal fatigue as a danger to aircraft in *No Highway* (**1948**), written shortly before several planes crashed for exactly that reason.

It is a moderately impressive list, and could be made more so by multiplication of examples, but it proves very little. For every correct prediction a dozen were wrong, or correct only if facts are stretched a little; for example, PULP-MAGAZINE sf of the 1930s made much of DEATH RAYS; it is rather a dubious vindication to point out that laser beams can now be used as weaponry. The entry FUTUROLOGY (which includes several examples of real prediction) discusses the usual strategy of sf writers when dealing with the future; their imaginative scenarios are as often as not meant as awful warnings, and the emphasis is almost invariably on what *could* happen, not what *will* happen. It would hardly be fair to attack sf writers as false prophets when they seldom think of themselves as being in the prophecy business at all. In many ways their errors are more interesting than their successes, for they add to our knowledge of social history. Our expectations of the future change just as quickly as history itself changes; the AUTOMATION to which Gernsback and others looked forward in the teens of the century had already become a potential nightmare by the time of Kurt VONNEGUT Jr's *Player Piano* (**1952**; vt *Utopia 14*). Where sf is correct, of course, the explanation is not magic, just good research. Verne took much advice from his engineer friends and Shute spent many years as an aeronautical engineer – and, of course, many sf writers subscribe to scientific journals . . .

One area where sf can claim some credit is SPACE FLIGHT; this was the central dream of sf, even during the years when respectable scientists regularly argued for its impossibility (◊ ROCKETS). But even here, though sf was right enough in the broad sense, it managed to get both the sociological and the technological details appallingly wrong. Most of Heinlein's early Moon rockets were built by capitalist enterprise, and not by the resources of the US Government; the Russian government, naturally, was not mentioned at all, even though it was in Russia that the first solidly grounded theorizing about space travel had taken place, in the work of Konstantin TSIOLKOVSKY, who wrote somewhat didactic but staggeringly accurate prophetic stories on the subject, beginning in the 19th century. The eponymous vessel in Heinlein's *Rocket Ship Galileo* (**1947**) is, absurdly, constructed largely by teenage boys in the backyard. Only William TENN ran counter to the free-enterprise spirit of most US sf by imagining in "Alexander the Bait" (1946) that the space programme would be run by giant government institutions, not individuals or even corporations. Sf stories about the first Moon landing almost invariably omit the single most dramatic detail: that the entire proceedings would be watched on Earth on tv.

COMPUTERS are another area where sf's predictive abilities were ridiculously askew; so preoccupied were sf writers with the dramatic possibilities of the ROBOT that they hardly noticed that back in the real world mechanical men were of little interest to anyone while the computer – driven by the invention of the transistor, likewise missed by sf – was rapidly transforming the face of the future. Sf writers caught up, of course, but only after computers were becoming commonplace.

Nearly all the examples cited are cases of predictions in the sphere of TECHNOLOGY; more interesting perhaps, and generally with a slightly higher success rate, were the predictions made about future POLITICS and SOCIOLOGY. Fortunately most DYSTOPIAS have not come into being in the real world, but certain aspects of them certainly have. One of the most interesting cases of prediction in the SOFT SCIENCES was Robert Louis STEVENSON's *Strange Case of Dr Jekyll and Mr Hyde* (1886), whose melodramatic suppositions were, even as he wrote, being conceptually paralleled by the work of Sigmund Freud (1865-1939), who also came to believe that the human mind had a primitive component, the id, not wholly masked by the more reputable ego.

Occasionally the images thrown up by sf enter the public mind by an apparent process of osmosis, so that they become known even to those who do not read sf, and thereby create a kind of self-fulfilling prophecy. Some examples are given in FUTUROLOGY, which discusses this question. Perhaps the most notable is again the case of space flight, where it is certainly arguable that the US Government could never have got away with budgeting such large amounts of the national income on the space programme had the *desire* for space flight, largely catalysed by sf, not been so great.

Most sf prediction is set in the NEAR FUTURE, and further examples are given in that entry. In the nature of things, a great many thematic entries in this encyclopedia necessarily deal in part with prediction. Apart from those already mentioned, entries where predictions in the social sciences predominate include CITIES; DISASTER, ECOLOGY, ECONOMICS, GAMES AND SPORTS, LEISURE, MEDIA LANDSCAPE and OVERPOPULATION; more technical areas where sf has made checkable predictions are COMMUNICATIONS, CYBERNETICS, ECOLOGY, MACHINES, MEDICINE, MOON, POLLUTION, POWER SOURCES, TRANSPORTATION and UNDER THE SEA; areas where sf predictions have not yet had the opportunity for a full testing, but may be tested in the next 50 years, are CLONES, CRYONICS, CYBORGS, GENETIC ENGINEERING, SPACE HABITATS, SPACESHIPS, SUSPENDED

ANIMATION and TERRAFORMING. Many readers suppose that the CYBERPUNK predictions of human experience of VIRTUAL REALITIES achieved by plugging the brain into machines are truly predictive. A technical problem is that the neurons in the brain transmit information much more slowly than microprocessors do, which might make the brain/computer interface rather tricky – but time will tell.

An sf scholar who has written interestingly about prediction is Chris MORGAN, whose relevant books (their remit extends well beyond sf to include popular science, journalism and so on) are *The Shape of Futures Past: The Story of Prediction* (1980) and, with David LANGFORD, *Facts and Fallacies: A Book of Definitive Mistakes and Misguided Predictions* (1981), the latter being especially funny and eye-opening.   [PN]

PREHISTORIC ROMANCES ◊ ANTHROPOLOGY; APES AND CAVEMEN (IN THE HUMAN WORLD); ORIGIN OF MAN.

PREHISTORIC WORLD ◊ Roger CORMAN.

PREISS, BYRON (CARY) (1953-   ) US book packager, anthologist and co-author of 2 sf novels – *Guts* (1979) with C.J. Henderson and *Dragonworld* (1979) with J. Michael REAVES – and *The Bat Family* (1984), a juvenile. Though he has also edited and co-edited numerous ANTHOLOGIES, BP is best known as the most successful of the independent sf book packagers (i.e., creative middlemen who conceive projects, pitch them to publishers, commission writers, artists and others to produce the required material, etc.), founding Byron Preiss Visual Publications Inc (frequently abbreviated to BPVP) in 1974. The company's first project was the **Weird Heroes** anthology series – BP himself edited *Weird Heroes #1* (anth 1975), *#2* (anth 1975), *#6* (anth 1977) and *#8* (anth 1978) – which early demonstrated BP's interest in visual presentation. Among the early BPVP projects were a number of GRAPHIC NOVELS: adaptations included a version written by BP of Alfred BESTER's *Tiger! Tiger!* (1956 UK; rev vt *The Stars My Destination* 1957 US) published under the vt in 2 vols (graph 1979 and graph 1992), both vols illus Howard CHAYKIN; original works included Samuel R. DELANY's *Empire* (graph 1978) with Chaykin. In the 1980s, BPVP branched out into many different areas, from children's and young-adult books to art books, nature books and other projects.

But most of the company's attention remained on the sf field, and BVPB was one of the forces behind the huge growth during that decade of SHARED-WORLD texts tied either to the work of well known authors or generated by BVPB itself, and almost always written on a SHARECROP basis. Projects of the first sort included **Isaac Asimov's Robot City**, a series of novels by various authors including David F. BISCHOFF, Arthur Byron COVER and William F. WU; **Arthur C.Clarke's Venus Prime**, all by Paul PREUSS (*whom see for details*); and **Robert Silverberg's Time Tours**, a series of novels by Wu and others. Projects generated by BPVP included **U.S.S.A.**, to which authors like Tom DE HAVEN contributed individual volumes. Such projects – which BPVP was far from alone in producing – generated lively debate, some critics feeling that writers were being led to recycle the ideas of others rather than exploring their own. Defenders of the sharecrop argued that newer writers, who might otherwise have trouble selling a first novel, could more readily work for hire; and suggested that young readers might be encouraged to read more ambitious sf through initial exposure to accessible shared-world books. Other BPVP projects included the **Next Wave** line of novels, each focusing on a specific area of scientific speculation and accompanied by an essay on the subject by a notable scientist; titles included *Red Genesis* (**1991**) by S.C. SYKES, about colonizing MARS, with an essay by Eugene Mallove; and *Alien Tongue* (**1991**) by Stephen LEIGH, about ALIEN contact, with an essay by Rudy RUCKER.

Also during the 1980s, BP produced several lavishly illustrated, ambitious theme anthologies combining fiction and nonfiction. *The Planets* (anth **1985**) featured fiction by Robert SILVERBERG, Jack WILLIAMSON and others, and essays by scientists such as Dale P. Cruikshank. *The Universe* (anth **1987**) included fiction by Poul ANDERSON and Gene WOLFE along with essays on COSMOLOGY and BLACK HOLES. *The Microverse* (anth **1989**) included the NEBULA-winning "At the Rialto" by Connie WILLIS along with nonfiction from Gerald Feinberg (1933-1992) and Nobel Prize-winning physicist Leon M. Lederman. *First Contact* (anth **1990**) was a similar treatment of CETI. Other anthologies have included the **Ultimate** series: *The Ultimate Dracula* (anth **1991**) with David Keller, Megan Miller and (anon) Martin H. GREENBERG; *The Ultimate Werewolf* (anth **1991**) with John BETANCOURT, Keller, Miller and (anon) Greenberg; *The Ultimate Frankenstein* (anth **1991**) with Keller, Miller, Betancourt and (anon) Greenberg; «The Ultimate Dinosaur: Past, Present, Future» (anth 1992) with Robert Silverberg; further titles projected.

Despite the controversy surrounding some of his sharecropped projects, BP should be recognized for his contribution to the visual presentation of sf, and for reaching out to a younger readership through such projects as the new **Tom Swift** adventures (◊ TOM SWIFT *for details*), the **Dragonflight** series of short novels, and the **Camelot World** series. Of all the book packagers, BP is likely the only one from his period to have made any real creative contribution to the field. [RKJK]

Other works: *The Art of Leo and Diane Dillon* (**1981**); *The Secret: A Treasure Hunt* (anth **1982**).

PRENTISS, CHARLOTTE ◊ Charles PLATT.

PRESCOT, DRAY ◊ Kenneth BULMER.

PRESIDENT'S ANALYST, THE Film (1967). Panpiper/ Paramount. Written/dir Theodore J. Flicker, starring James Coburn, Godfrey Cambridge, Severn Darden, Joan Delaney, Pat Harrington, Barry McGuire. 104 mins. Colour.

A psychoanalyst (Coburn), hired to listen to the President's troubles, breaks down under the strain.

He takes refuge with a "typical" US family who describe themselves as "militant liberals" (the husband collects guns, the wife takes karate lessons and their son specializes in wire-tapping). Pursued by the FBI (all very short men), the CIA (all college graduates with pipes and tweed jackets), Russians, Chinese and others, the hero repeatedly avoids death by a hairsbreadth; he then learns that the power secretly running the USA is the Telephone Company (manned by bland, smiling ROBOTS), which plans to insert a miniature telephone in the head of every person in the world. The film ends with the robots still in control. Flicker's pleasing SATIRE is witty and literate, and contrives to have it both ways by spoofing PARANOIA movies while actually exploiting our genuine (and well grounded) paranoias. [JB/PN]

See also: CINEMA.

PRESSOR BEAM ◊ FORCE FIELD.

PREUSS, PAUL (1942-) US writer who worked in film production for a decade before beginning to write popular-science articles. He began to publish sf with *The Gates of Heaven* (**1980**) which, with *Re-Entry* (**1981**), comprises a very loose sequence, its main linkage being the assumption that BLACK HOLES may be used to travel through both space and time. The second volume in particular demonstrates considerable virtuosity in its presentation of a SPACE-OPERA venue which is opened up – though at times rendered almost incomprehensibly complicated – through a plot which encompasses various timelines, the protagonist's discovery that he is his own beloved guru, and much action. Later novels back away sharply from such exuberance, gearing themselves more strictly to extrapolations based on contemporary science. The first of these, *Broken Symmetries* (**1983**), concerns the human and political implications of the markedly plausible discovery by SCIENTISTS of a subatomic particle of explosive military potential; the tone of the book has several times been compared with that of Gregory BENFORD's *Timescape* (**1980**). *Human Error* (**1985**) similarly examines the ethical implications of a development in GENETIC ENGINEERING, bearing some resemblance to the practically simultaneous *Blood Music* (**1985**) by Greg BEAR; while *Starfire* (**1988**) gives a verismo view of a NEAR-FUTURE space expedition.

Rather less interestingly, PP then became involved in the **Venus Prime** sequence of novels tied to works and some concepts generated by Arthur C. CLARKE. The sequence – *Breaking Strain* * (**1987**), *Maelstrom* * (**1988**), *Hide and Seek* * (**1989**), *The Medusa Encounter* * (**1990**), *The Diamond Moon* * (**1990**) and *The Shining Ones* * (**1991**) – features the long hegira of its bioengineered protagonist, Sparta, in her search through the Solar System for the secret of her birth (or, perhaps, fabrication). It closes with the 6th volume, and it may be hoped that the 1990s will see PP once again apply his sharp abilities to fully independent work. [JC]

See also: ASTEROIDS; BIOLOGY.

PRICE, E(DGAR) HOFFMANN (TROOPER) (1898-1988) US writer whose career lasted 64 years. He served in WWI, graduated West Point in 1923, and began to publish weird fiction – the genre for which he is remembered – with "Triangle with Variations" for *Droll Stories* in 1924. By the time he stopped writing for the PULP MAGAZINES in the 1950s he had published hundreds of stories in dozens of outlets, sometimes as Hamlin Daly, and often drawing upon Oriental and near-Eastern experiences for his backgrounds. His best known story from this period is probably "Through the Gates of the Silver Key" (1934 *Weird Tales*) with H.P. LOVECRAFT, a personal friend. Some of his early work was later assembled in *Strange Gateways* (coll **1967**) and *Far Lands, Other Days* (coll **1975**).

In his retirement EHP became annoyed at being remembered only as one of the "Lovecraft Circle", and in 1979 he resumed writing. In his final decade he wrote a Western, two fantasies – *The Devil Wives of Li-Fong* (**1979**) and *The Jade Enchantress* (**1982**) – and the loose **Operation** sequence of sf novels: *Operation Misfit* (**1980**), *Operation Longlife* (**1983**), in which EHP expressed a loathing of doctors and argued for the individual's right to die, *Operation Exile* (**1986**) and *Operation Isis* (**1987**). The sequence is set in a DYSTOPIAN future: it warns about Marxism and comments on the weakness and decadence of the US Government; the heroes are always competent, the plots often chaotic. Since he claimed to be writing novels of ideas, it should be mentioned that EHP was an astrologer, a Theosophist, a practising Buddhist and a conservative Republican, and ideas from those fields do indeed percolate through his work. EHP may be remembered primarily for his vivid biographical sketches of his friends Robert E. HOWARD, Lovecraft and Clark Ashton SMITH. A volume of reminiscences and a late mystery remain unpublished. [RB]

See also: SMALL PRESSES AND LIMITED EDITIONS.

PRICE, ROGER (TAYLOR) (1921-   ) US writer and tv personality, best known in the 1950s for his cartoon Droodles. In his sf novel, *J.G., the Upright Ape* (**1960**), the eponymous silver-haired articulate gorilla (◊ APES AND CAVEMEN), having been transported to the USA, serves as a focus for much amiable but moderately far-reaching SATIRE. He is not to be confused with the Roger Price (1941-   ) who wrote ties for *The* TOMORROW PEOPLE. [JC]

PRIEST, CHRISTOPHER (McKENZIE) (1943-   ) UK writer, married 1981-7 to Lisa TUTTLE and from 1988 to Leigh KENNEDY. He has published several novels (none apparently sf) under various pseudonyms, of which only 2 have been disclosed: John Luther Novak and Colin Wedgelock. CP began to publish sf with "The Run" for *Impulse* in 1966; much of his early work, which was relatively undistinguished, was assembled as *Transplantationen* (coll trans Tony Westermayr **1972** Germany), appearing in English only later as *Real-Time World* (coll **1974**). CP's first novel, *Indoctrinaire* (**1970**; rev 1979), is a

bleak but fatally abstract tale of imprisonment set in the heart of an unrealized Brazil, where an unhelpful time-gate seems to lurk. His second, *Fugue for a Darkening Island* (**1972**; vt *Darkening Island* 1972 US), is much stronger; set in an England of the NEAR FUTURE, it deals with POLITICS and racial tension, focusing on the arrival of African refugees whose homeland has been destroyed by nuclear WAR. His third novel, *Inverted World* (**1974**; vt *The Inverted World* 1974 US), marked the climax of his career as a writer whose work resembled GENRE SF, and remains one of the two or three most impressive pure-sf novels produced in the UK since WWII; the hyperboloid world on which the action takes place is perhaps the strangest planet invented since Mesklin in Hal CLEMENT's *Mission of Gravity* (**1954**), though the characters pace through their lives with a haunted lassitude which seems characteristically British. The tale deals with paradoxes of PERCEPTION and CONCEPTUAL BREAKTHROUGH, and is a striking addition to that branch of sf which deals with the old theme of appearance-versus-reality. (*The Making of the Lesbian Horse* [**1979** chap] is CP's spoof continuation of the book.) *The Space Machine* (**1976**) is a cleverly plotted pastiche of the work of H.G. WELLS, incorporating the author himself in the storyline (◊ RECURSIVE SF) which proposes plot-explanations for some of the narrative gaps left by Wells in *The Time Machine* (**1895**) and *War of the Worlds* (**1898**); in its literary focus and its retrospection, the book marked, in hindsight, a significant shift in CP's work.

With *A Dream of Wessex* (**1977**; vt *The Perfect Lover* 1977 US), CP began to write tales whose increasingly intricate plots had to be read as maps through which one explored not the world (as in conventional sf) but the protagonists. 39 human minds are meshed into a computer net which projects them (or their mental simulacra) forwards from 1983 into a VIRTUAL-REALITY world of their consensus imagination, 150 years in the future, in which they "live" without memory of the real world. The entire book is a metaphor about the creative process and its relation to solipsism. The **Dream Archipelago** stories assembled, with others, in *An Infinite Summer* (coll **1979**), intensify the sense that CP's landscapes had now become forms of expression of the psyche, and are of intense interest for the dream-like convolutions of psychic terrain so displayed. The Dream Archipelago itself is a surreally unspecific rendering of England as a land half-sunk beneath the ocean (a vision perhaps influenced by Richard JEFFERIES's *After London* [**1885**]), and is a powerful late-century representation of *Sehnsucht* (C.S. LEWIS's expression to describe a longing for something that hovers, forever unattainable, beyond the terms of reality).

CP's next novels – *The Affirmation* (**1981**), also set partly in the Dream Archipelago, and *The Glamour* (**1984**; rev 1984 US) – move even more radically away from the regions of sf or fantasy. They are his best work to that point and, although representing to some sf readers an apostasy from the field, may profitably be read as explorations of ravenous psyches whose hunger expresses itself through the ingestion of or control over "unreal" (or fantasy) worlds. It might be possible to suggest that *The Affirmation* is a tale of ALTERNATE WORLDS and *The Glamour* a tale whose protagonist literally becomes invisible (◊ INVISIBILITY); but these readings do scant justice to their intense and conscious inwardness. Though it shares a good deal of thematic material with these two, *The Quiet Woman* (**1990**) marks a decided return to the external world. Set in the near future, with radioactive contamination impinging upon the southern counties, the tale is a scathing vision of an England rapidly becoming a DYSTOPIA.

CP was Associate Editor of FOUNDATION 1974-7. His anthologies are *Anticipations* (anth **1978**) and, with Robert P. HOLDSTOCK, *Stars of Albion* (anth **1979**). In *The Last Deadloss Visions* (**1987** chap; rev 1988 chap) he produced a cruel analysis of Harlan ELLISON's noncompletion of «Last Dangerous Visions».   [PN/JC]
See also: BRITISH SCIENCE FICTION AWARD; CITIES; DIMENSIONS; DISASTER; FANTASTIC VOYAGES; HISTORY OF SF; MARS; MATHEMATICS; MEDIA LANDSCAPE; MILFORD SCIENCE FICTION WRITERS' CONFERENCE; NEW WAVE; NEW WRITINGS IN SF; PARALLEL WORLDS; POLITICS; STEAMPUNK; TRANSPORTATION.

PRIESTLEY, J(OHN) B(OYNTON) (1894-1984) UK novelist, playwright and man of letters, formidably productive from the teens of the century until about 1980; he wrote over 70 plays, many extremely popular in their day, and as many books, though he is now remembered chiefly for *The Good Companions* (**1929**), a huge picaresque novel in praise of the English. He was married to Jacquetta HAWKES. A surprising amount of his work makes use of sf or fantasy themes and devices, though sometimes in a delusional frame, as with *Albert Comes Through* (**1933**), whose eponymous hero's experiences in an absurd cinematic universe are explained as a fever-dream. *The Thirty-First of June* (**1961**) is a fantasy for young-adult readers. But sf concerns do propel *Adam in Moonshine* (**1927**) and *Benighted* (**1927**; vt *The Old Dark House* 1928 US) – both assembled as *Benighted and Adam in Moonshine* (omni **1932**) – *The Doomsday Men* (**1938**), where HOLOCAUST threatens; some of the stories about time (a recurring theme) in *The Other Place* (coll **1953**); *The Magicians* (**1954**), JBP's closest approach to a full-fledged sf novel, featuring the use of a wonder drug to spiritually invade the mind of a tycoon; *Low Notes on a High Level* (**1954**), about the Dobbophone, an instrument that emits previously unheard notes of MUSIC; *Saturn Over the Water* (**1961**), a thriller with sf overtones; *The Shapes of Sleep* (**1962**); and a juvenile, *Snoggle* (**1971**), in which three children and an old man save an ALIEN pet from bigoted Wiltshire locals and are thanked for their troubles by its masters, advanced beings in a flying saucer (◊ UFOS).

Nevertheless, JBP never showed much aptitude for the traditional sf tale, and much of his work has an effect more of bullying noise than bluff energy. His ideas about the nature of the genre were unkindly. "They Come from Inner Space" (1953 *New Statesman*) – later assembled in *Thoughts in the Wilderness* (coll **1957**), which also contains an sf story, "The Hesperides Conference" – makes what may be the first use of the term INNER SPACE in print, and goes on to declare that the essential outward movement of sf was "a move, undertaken in secret despair, in the wrong direction". Fittingly, of JBP's considerable sf output, the most interesting titles are those tales and plays which derive their motor impulse from the consolatory time theories of J.W. DUNNE, who felt that various moments in time – whose relationships to one another were, in a sense, geographical – could, in that sense, be visited. Plays like *Time and the Conways* (**1937**) and *I Have Been Here Before* (**1937**), both assembled as *Two Time-Plays* (omni **1937**), along with *Dangerous Corner* (**1932**), all assembled as *Three Time Plays* (omni **1947**), made extensive use of Dunne's theories. Other plays concerned with time included *Johnson over Jordan* (**1939**), whose hero posthumously prepares himself for Heaven, and *Summer Day's Dream* (**1950**). In the nonfiction *Man and Time* (**1964**) and the essays in *Over the Long High Wall* (**1972**) JBP meditated speculatively on the same themes. In the end, perhaps surprisingly for a writer so otherwise aggressive, sf served not as a technique to mount challenges but as a form of adjustment.   [JC]
Other works: At least 2 of JBP's teleplays are of genre interest: "Doomsday for Dyson" (1958), about atomic holocaust, and "Linda at Pulteney's" (1969), a fantasy.
About the author: *J.B. Priestley: Portrait of an Author* (**1970**) by Susan COOPER; *J.B. Priestley* (**1988**) by Vincent Brome.
See also: HISTORY IN SF; THEATRE; TIME TRAVEL.

PRIESTLEY, MARGARET (?1919-   ) UK writer who, with Meriol TREVOR, created in childhood an ALTERNATE WORLD called the **World Dionysius**, where both set several novels. MP's were *The Ring of Fortune* * (**1948**), *The Three Queens* * (**1950**) and *Tomay is Loyal* * (**1951**). They were marginally less effective than Trevor's, though both authors had a tendency to fall back on RURITANIAN conventions when more radical displacements might have generated a more sustained sequence.   [JC]

PRIME PRESS Short-lived (the business had failed by 1953) US SMALL PRESS specializing in sf; based in Philadelphia, founded in 1947 by Oswald TRAIN (editorial) and James Williams, along with two fans, Alfred C. Prime and Armand E. Waldo, who later dropped out. Several of PP's few titles are of interest, including the first-published books of Lester DEL REY, George O. SMITH and Theodore STURGEON: respectively, *. . . And Some Were Human* (coll **1948**), *Venus Equilateral* (coll of linked stories **1947**) and *Without Sorcery* (coll **1948**; cut vt *Not without Sorcery* 1961).   [MJE]

PRINCE OF DARKNESS Film (1987). Alive. Dir John

CARPENTER, starring Donald Pleasence, Jameson Parker, Victor Wong, Lisa Blount. Screenplay Martin Quatermass (Carpenter). 101 mins. Colour.

An old priest, guardian of a vat containing Satan as a green liquid, dies. Young physicists are brought to the derelict church by another worried priest (Pleasence) to analyse the strange powers here. The church is surrounded by bag ladies and vagrants (one being rock-star Alice Cooper) who kill anybody who leaves. Some of the scientists are possessed by telekinetic jets of Satan-liquid, and Anti-God attempts to manifest Himself through a mirror.

Carpenter's worst film, resembling a first draft rather than a finished product, inept and barely coherent, POD nevertheless has points of considerable interest. Often an apparent sf film turns out to be HORROR; this is an apparent horror film that turns out to be sf. (Carpenter's screenwriter pseudonym, Quatermass, is in clear homage to Nigel KNEALE, whose scriptwriting speciality has been to rationalize supernatural forces in scientific terms.) The ambitious but confused script evokes Gödel and Schrödinger in the first few minutes, explains precognition as TACHYON messages from the future, solemnly broods on indeterminacy and the spiritual inferences to be drawn from quantum mechanics, and appears to see the Anti-God as theological ANTIMATTER present from the beginning, which is in fact a form of the Manichean heresy.   [PN]

PRINGLE, DAVID (WILLIAM) (1950-   ) Scottish editor and writer, resident in England, who served as Research Fellow for the SCIENCE FICTION FOUNDATION in East London 1978-9 and as editor of FOUNDATION 1980-86. With Malcolm EDWARDS he was one of the prime movers in the 8-strong collective which founded INTERZONE in 1982, eventually becoming its sole editor and publisher in 1988 and co-editing all 5 anthologies taken from the magazine: *Interzone: The First Anthology* (anth **1985**) with John CLUTE and Colin GREENLAND, *Interzone: The 2nd Anthology* (anth **1987**) with Clute and Simon Ounsley, *Interzone: The 3rd Anthology* (anth **1988**) with Clute and Ounsley, *Interzone: The 4th Anthology* (anth **1989**) with Clute and Ounsley, and *Interzone: The 5th Anthology* (anth **1991**) with Clute and Lee Montgomerie. As Series Editor for GW Books 1988-91 he was responsible (in tandem, from 1990, with Neil Jones) for commissioning and publishing several SHARED-WORLD fantasy and sf novels tied to GAMES WORKSHOP games like **Warhammer** and **Dark Future**, notably including titles by Kim NEWMAN (as Jack Yeovil), Brian M. STABLEFORD (as Brian Craig) and David S. GARNETT (as David Ferring). For GW he also edited some tied anthologies, including *Ignorant Armies* * (anth **1989**), *Wolf Riders* * (anth **1989**) and *Red Thirst* * (anth **1990**) in the **Warhammer** series, *Route 666* * (anth **1990**) in the **Dark Future** series, and *Deathwing* * (anth **1990**) with Neil Jones in the **Warhammer 40,000** series. In 1991 he began a second magazine, *Million: The Magazine about Popular Fiction*, some of whose articles deal

with sf or fantasy writers.

As a critic, DP's long advocacy of the works of J.G. BALLARD was developed in *J.G. Ballard: The First Twenty Years* (anth **1976** chap) ed with James Goddard, *Earth is the Alien Planet: J.G. Ballard's Four-Dimensional Nightmare* (**1979** chap US) and *J.G. Ballard: A Primary and Secondary Bibliography* (**1984** US). He then produced several guides to sf, fantasy and popular literature in alphabetized format: *Science Fiction: 100 SF Authors* (**1978** chap), *Science Fiction: The 100 Best Novels: An English-Language Selection, 1949-1984* (**1985**), *Imaginary People: A Who's Who of Modern Fictional Characters* (**1987**; rev 1989), *Modern Fantasy: The Hundred Best Novels: An English-Language Selection, 1946-1987* (**1988**) and *The Ultimate Guide to Science Fiction: An A-Z of SF Books* (**1990**) with Ken Brown (uncredited). DP's lack of an intuitive grasp of US sf could perhaps be detected in the 1949 inception date for books covered in the first of these (a significant few years after the beginning of the SMALL-PRESS movement in the USA), but the 200 short essays accumulated in that and the volume on fantasy provide a valuable conspectus of fantastic literature over the chosen timespan. DP also edited a retrospective collection of Theodore STURGEON's stories, *A Touch of Sturgeon* (coll **1987** UK). He contributed some major entries to the first edition of this encyclopedia and revised his BALLARD entry for the current edition.   [JC]
See also: SF MAGAZINES.

PRISONER, THE UK tv series (1967-8). An Everyman Films prod for ATV. Prod David Tomblin. Created, starring and partly written/dir Patrick McGoohan; other writers included George Anthony Skene, Terence Feely; other dirs included Don Chaffey, Pat Jackson. Script ed George Markstein. 17 50min episodes. Colour.

In this KAFKA-esque, sf-related series a UK ex-secret agent (McGoohan), who for unknown reasons has resigned from his organization, is gassed in his apartment and wakes to find himself in The Village: a mysterious establishment whose geographical location is ambiguous and whose inhabitants consist of either rebels like himself or stooges of "Them" – the people who run the place. The former spy (McGoohan had previously starred in a spy series called *Danger Man*) is unable to discover just who "They" are – perhaps the communists, perhaps his own government. His every movement in The Village – externally a cross between a bland Mediterranean holiday camp and an old people's home (in reality the bizarre resort of Portmeirion, Wales, designed by the architect Sir Clough Williams-Ellis [1883-1978] from 1926 until his death) – is watched by "Number Two" and his staff on video. Various episodes concern his attempts to escape from The Village, his neverending search for the unseen Number One, and the efforts of the different Number Twos (they change with each episode) to break him and discover why he resigned. The most obvious sf elements are the balloon-shaped ROBOT watchdogs and the complex brainwashing and surveillance equipment, including devices that project thoughts onto a screen.

McGoohan is a puritan (no kissing on screen) and an acknowledged political conservative. The many liberal supporters of the series may have misinterpreted its libertarian emphasis on individual strength, especially the power to resist incursions into one's mind, seeing the series instead as a plea for human rights and especially democratic freedoms. The excellent, surrealist last episode interestingly renders the POLITICS of the whole series retrospectively ambiguous by suggesting that our metaphorical prisons may be self-imposed. The Prisoner who continues to resist brainwashing may have brainwashed himself into a prison of the mind. The series' thesis may be that freedom is impossible, as is opting out.

TP, not popular at first, soon developed an enthusiastic cult following which has lasted for over two decades, especially for its thought-provoking aspects and its deliberate bafflements, unusual in tv drama. It has been repeated on tv several times in the UK and shown in the USA. Its confident manipulations of Surrealist and sf themes, its literate scripts, its sophisticated understanding of visual metaphor and its enjoyably obsessive evocations of a whole range of fantasies of PARANOIA together created what is in the opinion of many – often those discontented with SPACE OPERA – the finest sf tv series to date. Its strengths in many respects resemble those of the late-1980s tv cult favourite *Twin Peaks*. Novels based on the series are *The Prisoner* ∗ (**1969**) by Thomas M. DISCH, *The Prisoner No. 2* ∗ (**1969**) by David MCDANIEL and *The Prisoner 3: A Day in the Life* ∗ (**1970**) by Hank STINE. Two of several books about the series are *The Official Prisoner Companion* (**1988**), by Matthew White and Jaffer Ali, and *The Prisoner and Danger Man* (**1989**) by Dave Rogers. [JB/PN]

See also: GAMES AND TOYS.

PRISONERS OF GRAVITY Canadian tv series. TVOntario; also broadcast on La Chaîne Française. 3 seasons 1990-92, current. Prod/dir Gregg Thurlbeck, written and presented Rick Green. 30 mins per programme. Colour.

The premise of this vigorous and surprisingly successful series – not a drama series but a talk show about speculative fiction, probably the only such programme in the world – is that Commander Rick (Rick Green) operates a pirate broadcasting station from the communications satellite in which he lives, and intercepts TVOntario's signals once a week, substituting his own quickfire discussions of various sf themes. Quick cutting and Rick's aggressive, well informed, jokey style (he is an ex-comedian as well an an sf expert) have won the programme a cult following. The major cultural breakthrough is Rick's presentation of COMICS artists as deserving equal guest time with sf writers, and viewers have been able to see for themselves that, say, Neil GAIMAN, Jean GIRAUD, Frank MILLER and Bill SIENKEWICZ appear just as thoughtful as, say, Douglas ADAMS, Gregory

BENFORD, Harlan ELLISON and William GIBSON. Horror writers such as Clive Barker (1952-   ) and fantasy writers such as Guy Gavriel Kay (1954-   ) have also been included. The wide range of themes explored covers everything from Chaos Theory to Women's Issues and The Family. [PN]

PRISONS ◊ COLONIZATION OF OTHER WORLDS; CRIME AND PUNISHMENT.

PRIVILEGE Film (1967). Worldfilm Services and Memorial Enterprises/Universal. Dir Peter WATKINS, starring Paul Jones, Jean Shrimpton, Mark London, Max Bacon. Screenplay Norman Bogner, based on a story by Johnny Speight. 103 mins. Colour.

A successful rock-star (Jones) is used by a NEAR-FUTURE UK government as a puppet MESSIAH to manipulate the opinions of the youthful citizens. He is forced to change his image to suit the plans of the Establishment, but rebels, only, ironically, to be destroyed by his teenage followers. Watkins, who also directed *The* WAR GAME (1965), GLADIATORERNA (1968) and PUNISHMENT PARK (1970), thumps his tub with a heavy hand; but, though simplistic, *P* was ahead of its time in its depiction of government attempts to co-opt and domesticate the disaffection of the young, a theme of real importance, still rare in the commercial CINEMA – which, after all, does much the same thing. [JB/PN]

PRIX APOLLO ◊ AWARDS.

PRIX DU DANGER, LE (vt *The Prize of Peril*) Film (1983). Swanie/TFI/UGC-Top 1/Avala. Dir Yves Boisset, starring Gérard Lanvin, Michel Piccoli, Marie-France Pisier. Screenplay Boisset, Jan Curtelin, based on "The Prize of Peril" (1958) by Robert SHECKLEY. 98 mins, cut to 88 mins in English-dubbed version. Colour.

In this French/Yugoslav coproduction, a man volunteers for the tv game show "The Prize of Peril", in which anyone who can escape being murdered in the streets by trained killers (the whole event being televised) can win large cash prizes. To a large extent the game is rigged. The resourceful victim makes it back to the studio and exposes the sham before being carried off in a straitjacket. A fairly routine action movie masquerades as a morally outraged assault on MEDIA corruption. A later film, *The* RUNNING MAN (1987), bears an astonishing resemblance. [PN]

PRIX JULES VERNE ◊ AWARDS.

PRIX ROSNY AÎNÉ ◊ AWARDS.

PRIZE OF PERIL, THE ◊ *Le* PRIX DU DANGER.

PROCTOR, GEO(RGE) W. (?   -   ) US writer who began publishing sf with *The Esper Transfer* (**1978**), a modest sf adventure whose telepathic protagonist must escape various dangers. Although varied in its use of sf devices, and inventively constructed so as to allow its protagonists some room for personal relationships, his work has not exhibited sufficient innovation or energy to bring him into wide repute. Other sf titles include *Shadowman* (**1980**), again involving telepaths, *Fire at the Center* (**1981**) and *Starwings* (**1984**), both involving TIME TRAVEL, and

Stellar Fist (**1989**), in which the discovery of a doom machine must somehow be controlled, once again through the actions of a telepath. GWP's collaborations with Andrew J. OFFUTT, both writing as John Cleve – *Spaceways #7: The Manhuntress* * (**1982**) and *#10: The Yoke of Shen* * (**1983**) – and his two "V" ties – *The Chicago Conversion* * (**1985**) and *The Texas Run* * (**1985**) – are of less interest. GWP ed *Lone Star Universe: Speculative Fiction from Texas* (anth **1976**) with Steve UTLEY, which presents material of considerable interest, and *The Science-Fiction Hall of Fame #3: The Nebula Winners 1965-69* (anth **1982**) with Arthur C. CLARKE. [JC]

Other works: The **Swords of Raemllyn** fantasy sequence, all with Robert E. VARDEMAN: *A Yoke of Magic* (**1985**), *To Demons Bound* (**1985**), *Blood Fountain* (**1985**), *The Beasts of the Mist* (**1986**) and *For Crown and Kingdom* (**1987**).

PROJECT MOONBASE Film (**1953**). Galaxy Pictures/ Lippert. Dir Richard Talmadge, starring Donna Martell, Ross Ford, Larry Johns, Hayden Rorke. Screenplay Robert A. HEINLEIN, Jack Seaman. 63 mins, cut to 51 mins. B/w.

This rarely seen film is of interest mainly because Heinlein worked on the screenplay. A three-strong expedition takes off from a space station orbiting Earth to select a site for a Moonbase from lunar orbit, but their rocket crashlands on the Moon. One of the three – a foreign spy (Johns) – subsequently dies and the others, a man (Ford) and the woman team leader, coyly named Colonel Breiteis (Martell), though doomed, are married via television by the President of the USA (who, in a typical Heinlein touch, is also a woman). The ambitious idea, with its confident taking for granted of future TECHNOLOGY, is undermined by melodramatics, poor performances, and sets designed for tv, this being the theatrical release of an unsold pilot for a projected tv series, «Ring Around the Moon». [JB]

PROJECT UFO US tv series (**1978-79**). A Mark VIII Ltd Production/NBC. Executive prod Jack Webb; created Harold Jack Bloom; prod Col. William T. Coleman. Starring William Jordan as Major Jake Gatlin, Caskey Swaim as Sgt Harry Fisk, Aldine King as Libby Virdon, Edward Winter (season 2) as Capt Ben Ryan. Dirs included Richard Quine, Dennis Donnelly, Robert Leeds, John Patterson, Rich Greer. Writers included Harold Jack Bloom, Donald L. Gold, Robert Blees. 2 seasons, 26 50min numbered episodes. Colour.

In terms of the size of viewing audience, this was the most successful US sf tv series ever made. The premise is that USAF investigators, belonging to a special unit code-named Project Blue Book, each week look into a supposed UFO (i.e., flying-saucer) sighting. Some of the cases prove to be hoaxes, some misunderstandings of other phenomena; but most turn out to be genuine. *PUFO*, which assumed the air of drama-documentary, was tabloid tv at its most naked, aimed directly and cynically at a credible audience greedy for wonders. Given the overall similarity of the plot-lines, it is astonishing that 2 seasons were wrung from it. Executive prod Webb is remembered by older viewers as the gravel-voiced presenter of *Dragnet*. [PN]

See also: PARANOIA.

PROJECT X Film (**1987**). Amercent Films-American Entertainment Partners/20th Century-Fox. Dir Jonathan Kaplan, starring Matthew Broderick, Helen Hunt, Bill Sadler, Johnny Ray McGhee. Screenplay Stanley Weiser, based on a story by Weiser, Lawrence Lasker. 103 mins, cut to 91 mins. Colour.

A trainee airman (Broderick), in trouble for joyriding, is sent to work in an experimental USAF establishment where chimps are being trained in flying simulators; the sinister premise (gradually uncovered) is that, if successfully taught, they can be used on operations where pilots would be subjected to heavy radiation. Several chimps are deliberately irradiated to death. The young airman, who has bonded with an intelligent chimp that understands sign language, helps foment rebellion, escapes with the chimps, and *en passant* prevents a nuclear meltdown; of course, the chimps themselves finally save the day – by flying a plane to safety. Wholly absurd, emotionally manipulative and anthropomorphically sentimental, the film is nevertheless very neatly crafted, evoking with real panache, through its jittery, unnerving imagery, all kinds of subtexts that are more intelligent than the plot would suggest. [PN]

PROMETHEUS AWARD ◊ AWARDS.

PRONZINI, BILL Working name of US writer William John Pronzini (1943-   ), prolific and admired in several genres, notably crime fiction, since his first book, *The Stalker* (**1971**). Though he has published some very effective HORROR, including *Masques: A Novel of Terror* (**1981**), and several other novels – including *Night Screams* (**1979**) and *Prose Bowl* (**1980**), both with Barry N. MALZBERG, the latter being sf – as well as *Beyond the Grave* (**1986**) with Marcia Muller, his main importance to the field of the fantastic lies in his anthologies. Relevant titles include: *Dark Sins, Dark Dreams: Crime in Science Fiction* (anth **1978**) with Malzberg; *Midnight Specials* (anth **1978**); *Werewolf!* (anth **1979**); *The End of Summer* (anth **1979**; vt *The Fifties: The End of Summer* 1979), *Shared Tomorrows: Science Fiction in Collaboration* (anth **1979**) and *Bug-Eyed Monsters* (anth **1980**), these 3 being with Malzberg; *Voodoo!: A Chrestomathy of Necromancy* (anth **1980**), *Mummy!: A Chrestomathy of Crypt'ology* (anth **1981**) and *Creature!: A Chrestomathy of "Monstery"* (anth **1981**), all assembled as *The Arbor House Necropolis – Voodoo! Mummy! Ghoul!* (omni **1981**; with 1 story cut, vt *Tales of the Dead* 1986); *The Arbor House Treasury of Mystery and Suspense* (anth **1981**; with 1 story cut, vt *Great Tales of Mystery and Suspense* 1985) with Malzberg and Martin H. GREENBERG; *The Arbor House Treasury of Horror and the Supernatural* (anth **1981**; with 1 story cut, vt *Great Tales of Horror & the Supernatural* 1985; text restored, vt *Classic Tales of*

Horror and the Supernatural 1991; again cut, vt *The Giant Book of Horror Stories* 1991) with Malzberg and Greenberg; *Specter!: A Chrestomathy of "Spookery"* (anth **1982**); and *Witches' Brew: Horror and Supernatural Stories by Women* (anth **1984**) with Muller. [JC]
See also: ESP.

PROPHECY Film (1979). Paramount. Dir John FRANK-ENHEIMER, starring Talia Shire, Robert Foxworth, Armand Assante, Richard Dysart. Screenplay David Seltzer. 102 mins. Colour.

A mercuric fungicide used by a Maine pulp-mill has mutagenic effects, bringing Minimata disease and miscarriages to the local Native Americans and creating gigantism among the area's wildlife, notably a MUTANT bear-creature responsible for many human deaths. All this is discovered by a crusading doctor and his pregnant wife. A surprisingly poor film from Frankenheimer – muddy photography, risible monster, eco-cliché script, wooden performances, stumbling action sequences – *P* is a rather crass example of the many revenge-of-Nature films (◊ MONSTER MOVIES) made from the mid-1970s to cash in on the increase in the community of legitimate concern for ECOLOGY. [PN]

PROSPERO AND CALIBAN ◊ Frederick ROLFE.

PROTO SCIENCE FICTION Meaningful use of the term "proto science fiction" obviously depends on one's DEFINITION of the term "science fiction"; indeed, the quest for sf's literary ancestry and "origins" is as much a dimension of the problem of definition as a backward extrapolation of the HISTORY OF SF. If by sf we mean *labelled* or GENRE SF, everything published before 1926 would become proto sf; but Hugo GERNSBACK clearly believed that he was merely attaching a name to a genre which already existed – he considered H.G. WELLS, Jules VERNE and Edgar Allan POE to be "scientifiction" writers, and reviewers of the 1890s seeking to characterize the kind of work which Wells was doing had already identified a genre of SCIENTIFIC ROMANCE, which included Verne, his UK imitators, and such writers as George GRIFFITH. Brian W. ALDISS argues in *Billion Year Spree* (**1973**; exp vt *Trillion Year Spree* **1986** with David WINGROVE) that one can trace a coherent literary tradition of sf to its point of origin in Mary SHELLEY's *Frankenstein, or The New Prometheus* (**1818**; rev 1831) (◊ GOTHIC SF). Darko SUVIN's study of *Victorian Science Fiction in the UK* (**1983**), on the other hand, states that "if ever there was in the history of a literary genre one day when it can be said to have begun, it is May Day 1871 for UK sf", that being the day on which Lord LYTTON's *The Coming Race* and the magazine version of George CHESNEY's *The Battle of Dorking* appeared, and on which Samuel BUTLER handed in the manuscript of *Erewhon* (**1872**). Other writers, including Peter NICHOLLS, have argued that sf is merely a continuation, without any true hiatus, of a much more ancient tradition of imaginative fiction whose origins are lost in the mythical mists and folkloric fogs of oral tradition. If this were accepted there would be no

proto sf at all, and sf's history would begin with, say, HOMER's *Odyssey* and continue with LUCIAN's *True History*.

It seems reasonable to argue that we cannot sensibly define something called "science fiction" until we can characterize both "science" and "fiction" with meanings close to those held by the words today. It was largely due to the rise of the novel – which made a formal attempt to counterfeit real experience – that it became appropriate to draw a basic distinction between the types of discourse used for nonfictional commentary and the types used for "fiction". The standardized nonfictional forms of today – the essay, the treatise and the scientific paper – were still in the early stages of their evolution in the late 18th century. Logically, therefore, it seems inappropriate to describe as "science fiction" anything published in the early 18th century or before. Indeed, so intimately connected is our sense of the word "fiction" with the growth of the novel that it would seem most sensible to begin our reckoning of what might be labelled "science fiction" with the first speculative work which is both a novel and manifests a clear awareness of what is and is not "science" in the modern sense of the word. Willem BILDERDIJK's *A Short Account of a Remarkable Aerial Voyage and Discovery of a New Planet* (**1813**; trans **1987**) and *Frankenstein* both fit this definition well enough, although sceptics might argue that the supposed tradition which extends from them is very tenuous, and that no obvious precursor of Vernian and Wellsian scientific romance appeared before Chrysostom TRUEMAN's *History of a Voyage to the Moon* (**1864**).

There are, of course, pre-19th-century works which, with the aid of hindsight, we can now unequivocally locate within the literature of the scientific imagination, notably Francis BACON's *New Atlantis* (**1627**; **1629**), Johannes KEPLER's *Somnium* (**1634**) and Gabriel DANIEL's *Voyage to the World of Cartesius* (**1692**). These would have been considered by their authors to be works of philosophy, although they are cast in a form (the imaginary voyage) which we now consider to be a species of fiction. Some SATIRES also referred to contemporary scientific endeavours, most notably the third book of Jonathan SWIFT's *Gulliver's Travels* (**1726**), which also co-opts some of the techniques of formal realism associated with early novels; but such works usually extrapolate scientific ideas only to deride their follies. The quasisatirical *contes philosophiques* of VOLTAIRE include *Micromégas* (**1750**), which might also be considered an apt point of origin for sf if one were to embrace the common theory that it is the short story rather than the novel which is sf's natural form. On balance, however, it seems more sensible to consider all these as significant works of proto sf. The question as to which other works may be identified likewise, and the extent to which they might be considered important in defining the literary influences and patterns of literary expectation which have contributed to the shaping of sf, is a difficult one – and possible a sterile one, since we could argue that literary influences have contributed little to the effective shaping of GENRE SF. Other influences – historical and social – have certainly been important, and very probably more important, but the influence on sf of earlier traditions in fantastic literature should not be minimized: much sf, even the roughest-hewn PULP-MAGAZINE sf, has been written with much earlier literary models in mind.

The species of proto sf which has exerted most influence on sf and on attitudes towards it is undoubtedly the imaginary voyage (◊ FANTASTIC VOYAGES). Those generally identified as being the closest kin to modern sf are the lunar voyages whose history is chronicled in Marjorie Hope NICOLSON's excellent study *Voyages to the Moon* (**1948**). Many attempts have been made to incorporate the history of sf into this tradition, including Patrick MOORE's *Science and Fiction* (**1957**), Roger Lancelyn GREEN's *Into Other Worlds* (**1957**) and Russell Freedman's *2000 Years of Space Travel* (**1963**). This view makes Francis GODWIN's *The Man in the Moone* (**1638**), CYRANO DE BERGERAC's *Other Worlds* (**1657-62**) and other inter-planetary satires the key works of proto sf, although the methods of travel employed are calculatedly absurd. The cynical incredulity of many such stories, however, commends them to the sceptical scientific worldview, and we must remember that scientific fidelity in speculation is only one of the characteristic demands made of modern sf (◊ DEFINITIONS). Sheer invention – the bolder the better – has always played an important part in sf, and to a large extent the effectiveness of sf derives from the *pretence* to scientific fidelity which asks that wild flights of the imagination be considered *as if* they were serious hypotheses. On this basis we can find a close kinship between sf and the traveller's tale, which attempts to make interesting fantasies palatable by reference to exotic distant lands; Lucian's *True History* is important as a sceptical reminder of the tendency of such tales to exaggerate wildly. Understandable difficulties arise with those travellers' tales whose apparatus is concerned with the religious imagination rather than with secular fabulation: Emanuel SWEDENBORG's cos-mic visions – which include some interesting descrip-tions of LIFE ON OTHER WORLDS – are not frequently cited as examples of proto sf, although Larry NIVEN and others have argued that the cosmological specu-lations in DANTE ALIGHIERI's *Divine Comedy* entitle it to be considered a highly significant work in the proto-genre. It should perhaps be remembered that the distinction between scientific thought and religious thought, like the distinction between fiction and nonfiction, has not always been nearly as clearcut as it seems today; moreover, the classics of the religious imagination were frequently echoed in sf, not always with the intention of subverting their messages. Although such works as Milton's *Paradise Lost* (**1667**; rev **1674**) and Bunyan's *Pilgrim's Progress* (**1678**; exp

1684) can hardly be said to take much account of scientific knowledge, they have established literary archetypes of considerable importance, and analogies may be drawn between the kinds of fantastic environ-ment which they establish and those used in many sf stories.

It is worth noting that the literary tradition of UTOPIAS – which are also usually cast as imaginary voyages – is not as intimately connected with sf as it might seem. Utopian speculation is echoed in con-temporary sf primarily because sf writers have adopted a stereotyped "utopian scenario" as one of the standard environments for futuristic adventure; there is less actual utopian philosophy in modern sf than one might expect. Contrastingly, there is far more transplanted MYTHOLOGY than any widely accepted definition could lead us to expect. If any one imaginary voyage has had a far more than appropri-ate share of influence on the genre it is Homer's *Odyssey*, of which there are at least 5 straightforward sf transmogrifications. Of course, the *Odyssey* is not only an imaginary voyage: it also incorporates two literary forms which more or less died out in the later historical periods under consideration here: the hero-myth and what was then its corollary, the MONSTER story. Both forms have been revived within sf, and there are clear structural and ideative links between many sf stories and legendary constructions of these kinds. There are sf stories explicitly based on the story of the Argonauts, the labours of Hercules and such early literary exercises as *Beowulf*, although sf's HEROES are characteristically conceived in a rather different way from those of the ancient hero myths.

There still remain for consideration the other prose-forms current in the 17th and 18th centuries whose status as "fiction" or "nonfiction" is not so easy to establish with hindsight: the dialogue, the meditation and the history. The dramatic dialogue was quite popular as a medium for imaginative literature in 19th-century France, its most flamboyant product being Edgar Quinet's *Ahasvérus* (**1833**); Poe's "Con-versation of Eiros and Charmion" (**1838**) is a notable work of early sf cast in this form. Dialogue is now subsumed within ordinary narrative form, but there are numerous notable sf stories which are basically *contes philosophiques* cast as dialogues; genre sf, despite the priority which the pulps put on action-adventure, has been reasonably hospitable to such exercises. Even though we now classify them as nonfiction, we should be prepared to concede an important role in the history of proto sf to the basic strategy employed in PLATO's dialogues and later works in the same vein by Galileo Galilei (1564-1642) and David Hume (1711-1776). Socratic debate and interrogation are extensively used in sf, not merely as a means of exposition but also as a way of developing ideas and exploring their implications; any genre which attempts to develop speculations logically and rigorously must, obviously, depend to a considerable degree on the Socratic method of examining ideas.

The meditation seems much less important to the form and development of sf, but the history is a different matter. The construction of a history, which necessitates connecting events into a coherent narrative, requires both a creative and an orderly imagination (thus combining the essential requirements of the imaginary voyage and the dialogue). Imaginary histories must be considered alongside imaginary voyages as works which belong to the literary tradition of which modern sf is one product. Many of the early works which attempted to get to grips with the future, described in the early pages of I.F. CLARKE's *The Tale of the Future* (3rd edn **1978**), are cast as histories. Mention must also be made in this context of the pioneering exercises in alternative history (◊ ALTERNATE WORLDS) described in the essay "Of a History of Events which Have not Happened" (*c*1800) by Isaac d'Israeli (1766-1848).

Imaginary voyages and imaginary histories may be formulated in POETRY as well as in prose – several of the works referred to above are verse epics rather than prose discourses – and a case might obviously be made for including many poems and plays in the literature of the scientific imagination; but the most important links we can draw between classical literature and sf pertain to the settings in which the stories take place and the apparatus deployed there. With the exception of epic poetry, neither poetry nor drama is strong in this sense. This is not to say that sf cannot be adapted to poetry or to the THEATRE (there are some classic sf plays), but the importance of poetry and drama to any sf tradition is restricted, and it is difficult to argue convincingly that Shelley's *Prometheus Unbound* (**1820**) and Shakespeare's *The Tempest* (**1623**) are significant works of proto sf.

The attempt to identify a coherent tradition of proto sf is vain, in more than one sense of that word. Without a doubt, individual works of classical literature can be shown to be ancestral in certain respects to occasional themes of sf, but we devalue the word "tradition" if we use it to describe a series of isolated juxtapositions. To say that an assembly of illustrious literary works constitutes such a tradition is a form of self-congratulation on the part of the sf writer/reader/ critic akin to that of a prostitute who claims to be operating in the tradition of Cleopatra and Madame de Pompadour, even though in an obvious respect she is correct. Sf is a form of literature and can lay claim to all of literary history as its background if its adherents so wish, but this does not mean that we can turn the historical sequence on its head and claim that sf is the logical culmination of the "great tradition of proto sf", or the sole beneficiary of its heritage. Nevertheless, going back into literary history with the intention (however eccentric it may be) of classifying literary works according to their various similarities with modern sf is not a complete waste of time. It may serve as a reminder that sf, like prostitutes, is not a mere accident of circumstance, and that it is not

– either in the literal or in the commonplace sense of the word – inconsequential. [BS]

PROUMEN, HENRI-JACQUES [r] ◊ BENELUX.

PRUYN, LEONARD (1898-1973) US writer who began publishing sf with "In Time of Sorrow" in *Authentic* in 1954 and continued with an sf novel, *World without Women* (**1960**) with Day KEENE, about the violent consequences to the world of the loss of its women (◊ WOMEN AS PORTRAYED IN SCIENCE FICTION). [JC]

PRYOR, VANESSA ◊ Chelsea Quinn YARBRO.

PSEUDOMAN, AKKAD Pseudonym of US writer Edwin Fitch Northrup (1886-1940), whose sf novel *Zero to Eighty* (**1937**) tells woodenly of life during the entire 20th century, culminating in technical and pictorial accounts of the building of a gun-launched SPACESHIP and of its trip to the Moon. [JC]

PSEUDONYMS Reasons for using pseudonyms are very various, but almost always involve concealment. So obvious is this that it might seem to go without saying; but in fact many reference books altogether disregard the factor of concealment in their use of the term, and often designate as pseudonyms variations upon real names made to heighten impact (C.J. Cherry, for instance, writes as C.J. CHERRYH), or to shorten or simplify a spelling (Francis A. Jaworski writes as Frank JAVOR), or to select part of a full or married name for public use (Piers Anthony Jacob writes as Piers ANTHONY, and Kate Wilhelm Knight writes under her maiden name, Kate WILHELM). For this encyclopedia we have chosen to designate as "working names" all such variations; and we restrict the term "pseudonym" to names which, whether or not the author's legal name is known, have no clear lexical relationship to that name (we do not treat acronyms or mirror spellings as conveying a clear lexical relationship). Thus Christopher ANVIL is a pseudonym for Harry Crosby, as are Bron Fane (a partial acronym) and Trebor Thorpe (the given name here being a mirror spelling) for Robert Lionel FANTHORPE, and Frederick R. Ewing for Theodore STURGEON. In almost all cases the main entry for invidivuals covered in this volume, whether authors, editors, illustrators, critics or film-makers, appears under the name by which they are best known, whether that be the legal name (Isaac ASIMOV), the working name (Algis BUDRYS) or the pseudonym (James TIPTREE Jr).

All the author's names that have been used for an sf book – real, working or pseudonymous – appear in this encyclopedia, either as the headword for an entry or as a cross-reference headword directing the reader to the entry under which they are treated. Many (but not all) names that have been used only for sf non-book stories are likewise cross-referred, but with the additional notation [s]. Cross-reference entries which designate real figures (who may be collaborators, etc., and who on occasion may themselves be pseudonymous) are identified with the notation [r].

Collaborative pseudonyms, floating pseudonyms

and house names are given entries. A collaborative-pseudonym entry will usually give details of books written together under that name by the authors concerned. A floating-pseudonym entry covers a name which is, in a sense, freely available for anyone who cares to use it. (Ivar JORGENSEN is an example of a floating pseudonym.) A house name – which is a kind of floating pseudonym – is an imaginary name invented by a publishing company, and such were very frequently used in magazines to conceal the fact that an author had more than one story in a given issue; e.g., had Robert SILVERBERG sold 2 stories to a particular issue of a ZIFF-DAVIS magazine (e.g., AMAZING STORIES), one of the stories might be published under a Ziff-Davis house name such as Alexander BLADE or E.K. JARVIS – usually, though not necessarily, the story of which he had less reason to be proud. House names might also be used in a case where an author did not want it known that he was selling stories to a certain magazine; and (especially in the UK 1950-65) house names were very frequently used by mass-production houses like CURTIS WARREN or BADGER BOOKS to conceal the fact that a small team of writers was producing huge numbers of books in whatever genre the firm required.

Pseudonyms – as we said – are forms of concealment. We might add the observation that, in the sf world, pseudonyms were, for many years, very *common*. The reasons for their popularity were various and (generally) obvious. They have always flourished in PULP-MAGAZINE environments, where writers, being paid pittances for most of the early decades of GENRE SF, were forced to write voluminously, and often needed to use several names during their years of high production before burnout; the low prestige of sf also undoubtedly inspired their use; and (perhaps mysteriously) many sf writers have clearly *enjoyed* the creation and maintenance of pseudonymous identities. The most recent guide to sf pseudonyms – Roger ROBINSON's *Who's Hugh?* (1987) – contains about 3000 ascriptions, and is already seriously out of date, having been compiled too early to take properly into account the remarkable 1980s revival in the use of every kind of pseudonym, usually by authors of TIES and adventure series. The flood of concealment is, once again, rising.   [JC/PN]

PSEUDO-SCIENCE Pseudo-sciences are here defined as belief systems which, though adopting a scientific or quasiscientific terminology, are generally regarded as erroneous or unproven by the orthodox scientific community; frequently they not merely disagree with, or are improbable adjuncts to, accepted science but violate its fundamental tenets. They are not to be confused with the IMAGINARY SCIENCES, which are literary conventions, although the borderline can be blurred, especially with pseudo-technologies such as ANTIGRAVITY devices.

The adherents of many of the pseudo-sciences often display an almost religious fervour – indeed, some pseudo-scientific schools, notably SCIENTOLOGY (which is registered as a Church), use terminology that is consciously more religious than scientific. A further aspect is that creators of and believers in pseudo-scientific cults often interpret the scientific establishment's indifference or contempt in terms of jealousy or even as a self-interested conspiracy designed to conceal the Truth. The type-example of this occurs in ufology ($\Diamond$ UFOS), where scientists, politicians, the military, the CIA (especially) and even the presumed ALIEN crews have been frequently accused of mounting cover-ups of global proportions. (John A. Keel has used the lack of good evidence of alien visitors as an indication that such alien visitors do indeed exist: who else would be able to mount such an effective cover-up?) Martin GARDNER has documented such PARANOIAS in his classic study of pseudo-scientific cults, *In the Name of Science* (1952; rev vt *Fads and Fallacies in the Name of Science* 1957), and the cultic aspect of pseudo-scientific belief systems is noted even in the titles of two further surveys of the field: *Cults of Unreason* (1973) by Dr Christopher Evans, which is moderately sympathetic, and *The New Apocrypha* (1973) by John T. SLADEK, which is very comprehensive and occasionally strident. Other works of note include: *The Natural History of Nonsense* (1947) by Bergen Evans, which concentrates on biological/zoological fallacies; *Can You Speak Venusian?: A Guide to the Independent Thinkers* (1972; rev 1976), by Patrick MOORE, which is an idiosyncratic personal survey; *Science: Good, Bad and Bogus* (coll 1981) by Gardner; *Science and the Paranormal* (anth 1981) ed G. Abell and B. Singer; *Facts and Fallacies: A Book of Definitive Mistakes and Misguided Predictions* (1981) by Chris MORGAN and David LANGFORD; *A Directory of Discarded Ideas* (1981) by John Grant (Paul BARNETT); and *Pseudoscience and the Paranormal: A Critical Examination of the Evidence* (1987) by T. Hines. *A Dictionary of Common Fallacies* (1978; rev and exp in 2 vols 1980) by Philip Ward contains a great deal of scattered information on the pseudo-sciences. The best journal on the topic is probably *The Skeptical Inquirer*, published from Buffalo, New York, by the Committee for the Scientific Investigation of Claims of the Paranormal.

Few people could read any of these books without finding one or other of their own pet beliefs being dismissed as nonsense; Gardner, for example, has many harsh words about osteopathy, and Sladek is not gentle with Teilhard de Chardin's theories of EVOLUTION or Marshall McLuhan's ideas about the SOCIOLOGY of the MEDIA LANDSCAPE; Grant, contrariwise, has been attacked for declining to dismiss some pseudo-sciences as necessarily absurd rather than just exceptionally unlikely. Such reactions point up the difficulty of defining the topic with any precision, and also indicate that the authors of these books may have prejudices of their own.

There has always been a close and rather embarrassing link between the pseudo-sciences and sf. Some commentators have suggested that, at its lowest level, sf appeals to a childishness in readers, an unwillingness to get to grips with the real world – qualities which could equally be ascribed to devotees of various of the pseudo-sciences. When Gardner wrote in the mid-1950s that "the average fan may very well be a chap in his teens, with a smattering of scientific knowledge culled mostly from science fiction, enormously gullible, with a strong bent towards occultism, no understanding of scientific method, and a basic insecurity for which he compensates by fantasies of scientific power" he was describing not pseudo-science believers but sf fans; and in part he had a point, given that his context was a discussion of John W. CAMPBELL Jr's editorials puffing PSIONICS. Other aspects of mid-1950s magazine sf, notably its tales of PARANOIA, its SUPERMAN fantasies and its obsession with ESP, were not inconsistent with Gardner's caricature.

Pseudo-scientific ideas have a rather different spectrum in sf than outside it. For example, pseudo-medicine is probably the richest (pun intended) area of pseudo-science, being the region that attracts the most frauds as opposed to sincere theoreticians, yet pseudo-medicine is rarely encountered in sf. An early example is A.E. VAN VOGT's flirtation in *Siege of the Unseen* (1946 *ASF* as "The Chronicler"; **1959**) with the notorious eye exercises devised by William Bates (d1931). Since about the mid-1970s, when ideas of Mind/Body/Spirit became fashionable, the ability of characters to heal themselves has, in sf, subtly shifted out of the more general category of PSI POWERS to become regarded as a reasonable consequence of a general enhancement of the mind; such an attitude is found in David ZINDELL's *Neverness* (**1988**), among very many others. Trepanation – drilling a hole through the skull in the pineal region in order to improve general and particularly intellectual health, promoted from 1965 by the Dutch theoretician Bart Huges – makes a brief appearance in David CRONEN-BERG's film SCANNERS (1981). But such examples are trivial in comparison with the huge diversity of pseudo-medical ideas found outside fiction. One sf idea that has affected pseudo-medicine was LYTTON's *vril*, described in *The Coming Race* (**1871**); in the 1920s the US businessman Robert Nelson marketed his cure-all, Vrilium, which – unlike another product named for *vril*, Bovril – was fortunately not recommended for oral consumption: it proved to be rat poison. At a more fundamental level, one might make a case that sf has contributed more to the pseudo-sciences than they have contributed to sf.

Psychiatry – more specifically psychoanalysis – has provided sf and fantasy authors with better pickings. Some critics would dismiss the theories of Carl Gustav Jung (1875-1961) as largely if not entirely pseudo-scientific; and the same can be said with greater assuredness of some of the later ideas of Wilhelm Reich (1897-1957), which drew also upon sciencefictional notions. Reich came to believe that he was a focus of a SPACE-OPERA-style cosmic battle between friendly and hostile UFOs, powered by the "orgone drive". He assisted the Forces of Good and defended himself against the Forces of Evil using one of his own inventions, the cloudbuster, which dispersed "destructive orgone energy". Of psychological interest was the Christos Experiment carried out by occasional sf writer G.M. GLASKIN and others in the 1970s, which suggested that the human mind, in something akin to a dream state, was capable of exploring past and future incarnations (◊ REINCARNATION). Sf has also produced its own psychiatric ideas, notably those associated with DIANETICS and Scientology. Perhaps the most enthusiastic exploiter of such notions in genre sf has been A.E. van Vogt, who played a prominent role in the early days of dianetics and was also much influenced by the GENERAL SEMANTICS philosophy of Count Alfred KORZYBSKI. In more recent years Colin WILSON, who admires van Vogt greatly, has based a considerable amount of his fiction on unorthodox psychological hypotheses; the most interesting example may be his novella "Time-slip" (1979), which mixes the (now rather more reputable) theory of the divided brain with notions of the paranormal and the possibility of humanity developing radically new modes of thinking – a CONCEPTUAL BREAKTHROUGH in more than one sense of that term.

Perhaps the greatest single source of pseudo-scientific ideas in genre sf has been the work produced by Charles FORT in the 1920s and 1930s. Fort himself was not a pseudo-scientist *per se* – he was a chronicler of strange events rather than a theoretician – but he had a habit of scattering wild theories through his writings in the form of humorous asides. These have been rich ground for sf writers in search of story-ideas, but some seem to have taken them with a greater seriousness. The two areas of his theorizing that have most influenced sf are ESP/PSI POWERS and the notion that we are being secretly observed, and perhaps controlled, by mysterious intelligences. The latter hypothesis is reflected in many theories at the wilder end of ufology, in the sort of PARANOIA demonstrated in the lurid stories of Richard SHAVER, in the lasting popularity of H.P. LOVECRAFT's **Cthulhu Mythos** – extensively imitated and developed by others – and, in a roundabout way, in the idea that we have been visited many times in the past by ALIENS, who have directed the evolution of our technology (as in the works of Erich VON DÄNIKEN; sf stories reflecting this last view are discussed also in the entries on ADAM AND EVE and ORIGIN OF MAN). It is worth noting here that the notion of some archaic and long-lost alien race having "seeded" all the technologically developed planets of the Galaxy has become something of a CLICHÉ in SPACE OPERA; on occasion, where the setting is the very FAR FUTURE, humanity itself – or its AI emissaries – has been the "seeding" race. The cliché is interestingly deployed in, for example, John BRUNNER's *A Maze of Stars* (**1991**).

One of the most influential pseudo-scientists of the latter half of this century has been Immanuel VELI-KOVSKY. He first put forward his theories in *Worlds in Collision* (**1950**), a book that came to prominence largely thanks to the misguided overreaction to it of orthodox scientists. In his first few books Velikovsky examined countless legends of catastrophe from the Bible and MYTHOLOGY, and claimed these were explicable in terms of profound cosmic disturbances. (In several books in the 1960s W. Raymond Drake repeated the exercise, this time coming to the "inescapable" conclusion that the disasters could be explained only in terms of warring alien races – the "Gods".) Most notable was Velikovsky's idea that the planet VENUS is recent, having been spat out of Jupiter during biblical times and swooping repeatedly near to the Earth before settling in its current orbit; these close encounters naturally caused great upheavals on Earth. In the early 1980s there was an outburst of what can be termed "neo-Velikovskianism", typified by Peter Warlow's *The Reversing Earth* (**1982**); such revisions of the core theories, being considerably more scientifically literate than the original, proved harder to refute and, because this time few scientists bothered to make the public attempt to do so, were perhaps more influential on the scientifically ignorant intelligentsia. A number of sf novels have been directly affected by the original ideas of Velikovsky (*see his entry for examples*) or the later revisions; the most notable is *The HAB Theory* (**1976**) by Allan W. ECKERT. A good parody of Velikovskianism is *Judgement of Jupiter* (**1980**) by John T. SLADEK writing as Richard A. Tilms.

A less well known catastrophe theory was produced in 1886 by the US Quaker scientist Isaac Newton Vail. This was that all planets go through a phase or phases of having rings of ice like those currently observable around the GAS GIANTS. Natural instabilities in Earth's primordial rings caused them eventually to crash down towards the surface, creating a hugely thick cloud canopy in the upper atmosphere. When this canopy in turn collapsed, there was of course the Flood. A sciencefictional exploration of this is Piers ANTHONY's post-HOLOCAUST novel *Rings of Ice* (**1974**). Another historically important theory of catastrophe was the World (or Cosmic) Ice Theory of Hans Hörbiger, devoutly espoused by the Nazis in the years leading up to WWII; according to Nazi folklore, various "Jew scientists" like Albert Einstein fled Germany merely because they could not face the public demolition of their life's work in the light of Hörbiger's discovered Truth. The theory seems to have been regarded by even the most sensationalist of pulp writers as too silly to be exploitable, but as late as 1953 the Hörbiger Institute was using it to "prove" that the MOON's surface was covered in a deep layer of solid ice.

It is not only in GENRE SF that we find pseudo-scientific theories. Many eccentricities relating to Spiritualism and astral bodies (⟐ ESCHATOLOGY), to IMMORTALITY and REINCARNATION were commonplace in late-19th-century sf, and are still occasionally found today. Theories concerning race (⟐ POLITICS), usually implying Black or Native American inferiority, were depressingly common in LOST-WORLD stories and elsewhere (but at least theories were called on to support such claims of racial inferiority: the inferiority of WOMEN was usually just taken for granted), as were ideas about the lost continents ATLANTIS, Lemuria and Mu, and the hidden kingdoms inside the HOLLOW EARTH. For some decades after the Darwinian controversy, alternative theories of EVOLUTION were popular in sf, and the Lamarckian variant (founded on the notion that characteristics acquired during an individual's lifetime may be passed on to its offspring) proved especially fruitful for early writers; even today, Lamarckian ideas turn up more frequently than most sf writers would care to admit, as evolutionary ideas are misapplied to fictional ALIEN species – although it might be claimed that evolutionary mechanisms may be different in distinct biologies. (Very common, of course, is the perfectly justifiable application of Lamarckian assumptions to the evolution of machine INTELLIGENCE.) Pseudo-scientific theories of DEVOLUTION and racial degeneracy appear in much early sf, including pulp sf at least up to the 1930s, John TAINE being a frequent culprit. Other SOFT SCIENCES have produced their own rashes of pseudo-scientific ideas, although the defining line between science and pseudo-science can in these areas be especially hard to draw, since the empirical testing of, say, a sociological hypothesis may require decades of patient observation. This is particularly true of FUTUROLOGY, which is often decried as being a pseudo-science *in toto*.

None of the predictive pseudo-sciences have been of much importance in sf, although they are often enough derided in stories whose own purportedly scientific underpinning is at least as dubious: we scorn numerology to pass the time before making a HYPERSPACE jump. Astrology (further discussed under ASTRONOMY) plays a part in several books, examples being *Macroscope* (**1969**) by Piers Anthony and *The Astrologer* (**1972**) by John CAMERON. Numerology is rare; its wilder eccentricities are parodied in Martin Gardner's *The Incredible Dr Matrix* (coll **1977**). An example of a numerology story is "Six Cubed Plus One" by John Rankine (Douglas R. MASON). From about the mid-1980s, though, the Tarot has become popular in stories on the borderline of sf and fantasy; examples are Mary GENTLE's "The Tarot Dice" (in *Scholars and Soldiers* [coll **1989**]), Marsha Norman's interesting mainstream novel *The Fortune Teller* (**1988**), and the original anthology *Tarot Tales* (anth **1989**) ed Rachel POLLACK and Caitlin Matthews.

The above is not to imply that some of the theories discussed here (especially those relating to ESP and psi powers) have not had their supporters among the reputable scientific ranks. For example, the scientific essayist (and novelist) Arthur KOESTLER gave support to Jung's idea of synchronicity (that there are acausal principles affecting events, as well as cause-and-effect) in *The Roots of Coincidence* (**1972**) and made a case for Lamarckism in *The Case of the Midwife Toad* (**1971**), where he also dealt with seriality, a hypothesis, closely akin to synchronicity, developed by the Austrian biologist Paul Kammerer (1880-1926). The mathematician John Taylor for some years gave credence to the supposed fork-bending abilities of Uri Geller (1946-   ), although later he recanted. J. Allen Hynek, a reputable space scientist, contributed considerably to ufology. The psychologist H.J. Eysenck gave rather qualified support to the psi powers, as in *Explaining the Unexplained: Mysteries of the Paranormal* (**1982**) with Carl Sargent. The neurologist Kit PEDLER was another to take the psi powers seriously, as in *Mind Over Matter: A Scientist's View of the Paranormal* (**1981**), and many physicists engaged in quantum mechanics today are open-minded about areas of parapsychology that were scientifically TABOO a couple of decades ago. Yet the sometimes aggressively illogical, proudly irresponsible outpourings of pseudo-science have on occasion played a considerable part in establishing such taboos. For example, it was possible in 1966 for Carl SAGAN to speculate joyously about the possibility that alien races might indeed have come among us in the remote past, as he did in *Intelligent Life in the Universe* (**1966**) with I.S. Shklovskii, without in any sense damaging his own scientific credibility; 10 years later, post-von Däniken, it would have been a brave scientist who would have done the same. Similarly, investigations in the late 1960s and 1970s by the French statistician Michel Gauquelin of possible correlations between planetary positions at individuals' births and their subsequent personalities brought down on him considerable abuse from the scientific establishment – not because of his research *per se* (interesting but inconclusive) but because he was seen to be working in the taboo area of astrology.

The heyday of pseudo-science fiction was arguably the 1950s. Since the 1960s sf writers within the genre, less so those outside it, have in general been more responsible in their use of the dramatic possibilities of the pseudo-sciences, at least within HARD SF, which purports to be based in the scientifically plausible. On occasion their rejections of perceived pseudo-science have been overenthusiastic; for example, in his novel *Quatermass* (**1979**), Nigel KNEALE derides the (today perfectly respectable) notion that megalithic monuments might be prehistoric astronomical observatories on the grounds that, as computers were required to discover all their astronomical alignments, our ancestors would have required computers in order to design them – an argument exactly analogous to the proof that bees can't fly.

Many sf writers, including Isaac ASIMOV and John Brunner, have actively campaigned against the mindless acceptance of pseudo-scientific propaganda and its greedy exploitation by book publishers. Brunner,

for example, wrote a scathing article on the latter subject, "Scientific Thought in Fiction and in Fact", for *Science Fiction at Large* (anth **1976**; vt *Explorations of the Marvellous*) ed Peter NICHOLLS, presenting the view that the publishing boom (now somewhat abated) in books on the pseudo-sciences was leading to a great deal of cynical and fraudulent production of fictions masquerading as fact; sf writers at least maintain their fictions as fictions.

Some sf writers have used the tool of parody to counter the influence of the pseudo-scientists: Sladek has produced not only the Velikovsky parody mentioned above but also *Arachne Rising: The Thirteenth Sign of the Zodiac* (**1977**) and *The Cosmic Factor* (**1978**), both as by James Vogh; Langford is responsible for *An Account of a Meeting with Denizens of Another World, 1871* (**1979**) as if with his wife's (genuine) ancestor William Robert Loosley; and Grant for *Sex Secrets of Ancient Atlantis* (**1985**). Persistent rumour has, despite his strenuous denials, claimed Patrick Moore as author of *Flying Saucer from Mars* (**1955**) by "Cedric Allingham".

During the late 1980s there began a disturbing tendency for pseudo-scientists (examples include the Church of Scientology, Uri Geller, US ufologist Stanton Friedman [1934-   ] and Whitley STRIEBER) to respond to criticism with litigation. Sf writers and readers, angered by the threat to freedom of opinion, have been prominent among those supporting the victims of such actions. To extend Brunner's point: the greatest triumph of pseudo-science will come if it is permitted to impose the acceptance of its fictions – or, at best, its hypotheses – as fact.   [PN/JGr]

PSIONICS A common item of sf TERMINOLOGY, referring to the study and use of PSI POWERS, under which head it is discussed.   [PN]

See also: PSEUDO-SCIENCE.

PSI POWERS A name given to the full spectrum of mental powers studied by the PSEUDO-SCIENCE of parapsychology, and a common item of sf TERMINOLOGY. In his book *From Anecdote to Experiment in Psychical Research* (**1972**), Robert Thouless claims that he and Dr B.P. Wiesner invented the term, prior to its use in sf circles, as being less liable to suggest a pre-existing theory than the term "Extra Sensory Perception" (or ESP). The term was adopted into sf during the "psi boom" which John W. CAMPBELL Jr promoted in ASTOUNDING SCIENCE-FICTION during the early 1950s. Campbell also popularized in the mid-1950s the related term "psionics", which he once defined as "psychic electronics"; one of its earliest uses was in Murray LEINSTER's "The Psionic Mouse-trap" (**1955**). Although many notable psi stories deal with the entire spectrum of such powers, telepathy, clairvoyance and precognition – the "perceptual" paranormal powers – are in this encyclopedia covered in the section on ESP (where many stories featuring the full range of psi powers are also cited). The principal psi powers which remain for specific consideration here are: psychokinesis or telekinesis (moving objects by the power of the mind); teleportation (moving oneself likewise, although the term is sometimes extended to cover technologies of MATTER TRANSMISSION); pyrolysis (psychic fire-raising); and the ability to take control of the minds of others (which, for some unknown reason, has never been dressed up with a fancy jargon term – although it is, of course, often thought to be possible by means of hypnosis or mesmerism).

Campbell's psi-boom was inspired by ideas borrowed from J.B. Rhine (1895-1980) and Charles FORT to the effect that many individuals with latent psi powers were already among us; Campbell took them as representing the "next step" in human EVOLUTION. His own "Forgetfulness" (1937 ASF as by Don A. Stuart) offers a significant early image of a human race which has outgrown its dependence on TECHNOLOGY because the mind can do everything that once required tools. This idea is widely featured in the works of A.E. VAN VOGT and Theodore STURGEON, and received a new lease of life after 1945 when the advent of the Bomb inspired many stories in which the world before or after the HOLOCAUST might be redeemed by psi-powered MUTANTS, as in Poul ANDERSON's Twilight World (1947-61 ASF; fixup 1961), John WYNDHAM's Re-Birth (1955 US; vt The Chrysalids UK) and Phyllis GOTLIEB's Sunburst (1964). Later versions of the theme can be found in David PALMER's Emergence (1984) and the more ambivalent Taji's Syndrome (1988) by Chelsea Quinn YARBRO.

All the psi powers, of course, used to be in the repertoire of powerful magicians (◊ MAGIC), and most are featured in occult romances. Mind control (possession) has always been a popular theme in horror stories, and there is a considerable grey area between sf and supernatural fiction of this kind. Notable works featuring such powers include Trilby (1894) by George DU MAURIER, The Parasite (1895) by Arthur Conan DOYLE, Congratulate the Devil (1939) by Andrew MARVELL, "But without Horns" (1940) by Norvell W. PAGE, The Midwich Cuckoos (1957; vt Village of the Damned US) by John Wyndham and Children of the Thunder (1989) by John BRUNNER. Considered historically, teleportation may be seen as an extrapolation of levitation, which is usually given rather ironic treatment in modern literary works, as in Neil BELL's "The Facts About Benjamin Crede" (1935), Michael HARRISON's Higher Things (1945) and John SHIRLEY's Three-Ring Psychus (1980). In logical terms, however, teleportation may be considered simply as a special case of telekinesis, and levitation therefore crops up in a lot of stories which deal with a broader range of telekinetic powers, including James H. SCHMITZ's The Witches of Karres (1966), Tom REAMY's Blind Voices (1978) and Timothy ZAHN's A Coming of Age (1985). In the psi-boom years teleportation featured most prominently in Alfred BESTER's Tiger! Tiger! (1956 UK; rev vt The Stars My Destination 1957 US), which shows NEAR-FUTURE society adapting to the development of "jaunting" (teleportation), and also in such works as

Gordon R. DICKSON's Time to Teleport (1955 Science Fiction Stories as "Perfectly Adjusted"; 1960). Teleportation by alien creatures is a significant plot element in Anne MCCAFFREY's Pern series, and comes into sharper focus in Vernor VINGE's The Witling (1976) and Walter Jon WILLIAMS's Knight Moves (1985). A recent story in which human teleportation comes in for specific examination is Jumper (1992) by Steven Gould. Fire-raising rarely receives separate treatment in sf stories, a notable exception being Stephen KING's Firestarter (1980).

In order to be dramatically effective, abilities like mind control and telekinesis usually have to be moderated in some way, unless the point of the story is sarcastically to demonstrate the appalling tyranny which would surely result from the human possession of godlike powers, as in Jerome BIXBY's classic "It's a Good Life" (1953), Frederik POHL's "Pythias" (1955) and Henry SLESAR's "A God Named Smith" (1957). On the other hand, the unthinkingly casual use of extravagant powers for trivial purposes is ironically featured in Henry KUTTNER's comedies about the hillbilly Hogbens. Humans made godlike by psi powers are given less cynical treatment in Frank HERBERT's "The Priests of Psi" (1959) and The God Makers (1972), and in several novels by Roger ZELAZNY. One might perhaps wish that L. Ron HUBBARD had retained the amiable cynicism he exhibited in his early psi story "The Tramp" (1938), but instead he went on to build SCIENTOLOGY around a mythology of human evolution towards psionic godhood. Several stories of gradually unfolding psi power reach climaxes which may be regarded as apotheoses – Arthur C. CLARKE's Childhood's End (1953) is the most notable example; others are Keith LAUMER's The Infinite Cage (1972) and Oscar ROSSITER's Tetrasomy Two (1974). Carole Nelson DOUGLAS's Probe (1985) and Counterprobe (1988) offer a more moderate account of psi powers, not initially under conscious control, being gradually revealed.

Despite the widespread publicity given to the phenomenon of "spoon-bending" in the 1970s there is no convincing evidence that real-world psychics can accomplish more than moderate conjurers by way of telekinesis. It is a little recognized fact that the evidence for ESP, seemingly a more plausible talent, is even worse. That stories of ESP far outnumber stories devoted to the other psi powers has far more to do with intrinsic narrative interest than with questions of likelihood. Some critics feel that, in spite of the elaborate pseudo-scientific jargon developed by believers in the "paranormal", stories of psi powers really belong to the realm of magical FANTASY rather than sf. The rapid growth of genre fantasy in the past two decades has, in fact, allowed many such stories to be appropriately relocated.   [PN/BS]

PSYCHOHISTORY A much-loved item of sf TERMINOLOGY, coined in Isaac ASIMOV's very popular **Foundation** (1942-50; fixups **1951-3**) (and not to be confused with the term sometimes used by historians, which refers to the study of the relation of psychological motives to historical process). The attractive but purely IMAGINARY SCIENCE of psychohistory supposes that the behaviour of humans in the mass – and thus future HISTORY – can be predicted by purely statistical means, but "... a further necessary assumption is that the human conglomerate be itself unaware of psychohistoric analysis in order that its reactions be truly random". It is upon this condition that the meta-plot of the trilogy depends. [PN]

PSYCHOLOGY The science of the mind is sufficiently different from the physical sciences for its discoveries and hypotheses to set very different problems and offer very different opportunities to the writer of speculative fiction. Psychology still carries a considerable burden of pseudo-scientific conjecture even if one sets aside its close and problematic relationship with parapsychology (◊ ESP; PSI POWERS). The absence of convenient models of the mind (whether based on physical analogy or purely mathematical) means that the mind remains much more mercurial and mysterious than the atom or the Universe, in spite of the fact that introspection appears to be a simple and safe source of data.

A great deal of fiction which attempts to explore the mysteries of mind lies on the borderline between sf and MAINSTREAM fiction. Studies of both normal and abnormal psychology may be accommodated within the province of the traditional novel of character, even if their insights are derived from scientific constructs like psychoanalysis. There is a whole school of modern novelists, their work generally reckoned to be a long way removed from sf, whose self-defined task has been to capture the "stream of consciousness" – a psychological hypothesis we owe to the philosopher William James (1842-1910), not to his writer brother Henry. Studies of obsession, alienation and various forms of insanity are by no means uncommon in contemporary fiction, and even the most exaggerated – e.g., many studies of "dual personality" – seem perfectly acceptable as "realistic" novels. It is not until a notion of this kind is taken to bizarre extremes, as in Stanley G. WEINBAUM's dual-personality tale *The Dark Other* (**1950**), that the story becomes unmistakably sf. Even stories replete with the jargon of supposedly scientific psychoanalysis, like Thomas Bailey ALDRICH's *The Queen of Sheba* (**1877**) and S. Guy ENDORE's classic Freudian murder mystery *Methinks the Lady* (**1945**), are intrinsically mundane, although Endore's study of the psychological syndrome of lycanthropy, *The Werewolf of Paris* (**1933**), is normally considered a FANTASY. There is a certain irony in the fact that the subgenre of psychological speculative fiction which is most easily claimed for sf is the class of stories dealing with mesmerism and hypnosis – because these are sufficiently disreputable to be evidently fantastic! Thus a story like Edgar Allan POE's "The Facts in the Case of M. Valdemar" (1845) invites classification as sf not so much because it mimics the form of a scientific report but because the

mesmerised hero's immunity to decay is so obviously impossible. Stories of delusional neurosis or vivid hallucination which become very bizarre – e.g., Sir Ronald FRASER's *The Flower Phantoms* (**1926**) – are more conveniently classed as visionary fantasy than as sf, because of rather than in spite of the fact that their "impossible" events are entirely subjective, even though scientific theories like Freud's psychoanalysis may have been used to generate the substance of the fantasies.

Early exercises in speculative psychology which uncontroversially belong to sf are those in which some *invention*, usually a MACHINE or a drug, is invoked as a literary device to exert specific control over the substance of the psyche (although it is arguable that all such devices are based on philosophical errors concerning the nature of mental phenomena). The origins of psychological sf thus lie in such stories as Edward BELLAMY's *Dr Heidenhoff's Process* (**1880**), about a technology of selective amnesia, Robert Louis STEVENSON's *Strange Case of Dr Jekyll and Mr Hyde* (**1886**), about a drug which separates the principle of evil from that of good (or the id from the superego, as the Freudian reader is bound to interpret it), Richard Slee and Cornelia Atwood PRATT's *Dr Berkeley's Discovery* (**1899**), about a method of "photographing" memories, Walter BESANT's "The Memory Cell" (1900), again dealing with selective amnesia, and Vincent HARPER's materialist polemic *The Mortgage on the Brain* (**1905**), about an electrical method of personality-modification.

The early sf PULP MAGAZINES featured numerous devices of these and related types, and Hugo GERNSBACK's recruitment of the practising psychiatrist David H. KELLER did not result in any conspicuous sophistication of pulp sf's handling of psychological matters. Keller's most notable stories extrapolating psychological theory – the remarkable Freudian erotic fantasy *The Eternal Conflict* (**1939**) and "The Abyss" (1948), which tracks events following the release of a drug which destroys inhibitions – were too risqué for pulp publication. The theme of "The Abyss" is featured also in Vincent McHUGH's libidinous comedy *I am Thinking of My Darling* (**1943**), which anticipated counterculture-inspired LSD fantasies like William TENN's "Did your Coffee Taste Funny this Morning?" (1967; vt "The Lemon-Green Spaghetti-Loud Dynamite-Dribble Day") and Brian W. ALDISS's *Barefoot in the Head* (fixup **1969**), rather than endorsing the view shared by Freud and Keller that repression of our more vicious urges is the necessary price we pay for society and civilization. Other notable sf stories which side with Keller in their suspicion of the unfettered id are Jerome BIXBY's "It's a *Good* Life" (1953) and James K. MORROW's *The Wine of Violence* (**1981**).

The most impressive psychological study to appear in the pulps was not in an sf magazine but in UNKNOWN; this was L. Ron HUBBARD's classic *Fear* (**1940**; **1957**), about a man who loses a slice of his life by repression and is tortured by the "demons" of guilt. Material from the story was transplanted into Hubbard's substitute psychotherapy, DIANETICS, which later became part of the dogma of SCIENTOLOGY; dianetic theory is much in evidence in the stories collected in *Ole Doc Methuselah* (1947-50 as by Rene Lafayette; coll **1972**). It is a fairly common ploy in sf stories to use amnesiac heroes whose memories eventually turn out to be magnificently bizarre; examples are H.P. LOVECRAFT's "The Shadow Out of Time" (cut 1936; restored 1939), L.P. DAVIES's *The Shadow Before* (**1970**) and Keith LAUMER's *The Infinite Cage* (**1972**).

One of the most famous pulp sf stories, Isaac ASIMOV's "Nightfall" (1941), deals with the psychology of revelation – a subject dealt with in a less pessimistic fashion in other stories of CONCEPTUAL BREAKTHROUGH. Asimov's more significant contribution to psychological sf, however, is the IMAGINARY SCIENCE of robopsychology, which he invented for the stories in *I, Robot* (1940-50; coll **1950**), many of which feature robopsychologist Susan Calvin in confrontation with practical and theoretical problems arising from the Three Laws forming the basis of robotic ethics. Robopsychology remained an essential element in Asimov's ROBOT stories, especially such philosophically inclined ones as "That Thou Art Mindful of Him" (1974) and "The Bicentennial Man" (1976).

Technologically assisted journeys into the hypothetical INNER SPACE of the human mind became increasingly common in post-WWII sf. The hero of "Dreams are Sacred" (1948) by Peter Phillips (1921-   ) has to entice a catatonic dreamer back to the real world by disrupting his fantasy world. Other such journeys are featured in "The Mental Assassins" (1950) by Gregg Conrad (Rog PHILLIPS), "City of the Tiger" (1958) by John BRUNNER, "Descent into the Maelstrom" (1961) by Daniel F. GALOUYE, "The Girl in his Mind" (1963) by Robert F. YOUNG, *Mindplayers* (**1987**) by Pat CADIGAN, *The Night Mayor* (**1989**) by Kim NEWMAN and *Queen of Angels* (**1990**) by Greg BEAR. Several of the above-named stories extrapolate the idea of "telepathic psychiatry" with considerable intelligence; the Brunner story became the basis of the pioneering novel *The Whole Man* (fixup **1964** US; vt *Telepathist* 1965 UK). Another fine novel on the same theme is *The Dream Master* (**1966**) by Roger ZELAZNY; dreams are taken very seriously in Connie WILLIS's *Lincoln's Dreams* (**1987**).

Brunner's numerous essays in psychological sf also include a notable story about a reality-distorting drug, *The Gaudy Shadows* (1960; exp **1971**), and a psychiatric case-study, *Quicksand* (**1967**); both belong to categories of sf story which became very abundant in the 1960s. Several other post-WWII writers have shown a consistent interest in psychology. Alfred BESTER produced, among others, the quasi-Freudian vignette, "The Devil's Invention" (1950; vt "Oddy and Id"), a classic novel about a psychotic murderer

who eventually undergoes psychic demolition and reconstitution, *The Demolished Man* (**1953**), and a remarkable study of confused identity, "Fondly Fahrenheit" (1954). Most of Theodore STURGEON's sf consists of psychological studies of loneliness, angst and alienation, often resolved by the quasitranscendental curative power of love; a few examples selected from a great many are the bitter study of prejudice, "The World Well Lost" (1953), the painful study of megalomania, "Mr Costello, Hero" (1953), and the classic novels of literal psychic reintegration, *More than Human* (fixup **1953**) and *The Cosmic Rape* (**1958**). Ray BRADBURY has written a number of neat stories turning on the vagaries of child psychology, most notably the ironic "Zero Hour" (1947) and "The World the Children Made" (1950; vt "The Veldt"), although most of his work in this nostalgic vein is pure fantasy. Very many of Philip K. DICK's sf stories are concerned with false worldviews of various kinds – and, indeed, with the possibility that reality is intrinsically subjective; *Eye in the Sky* (**1957**) features a series of ALTERNATE WORLDS incarnating neurotic worldviews, while *The Three Stigmata of Palmer Eldritch* (**1965**) was the first of a sequence of novels dealing with reality-warping drugs which eventually culminated in the deeply embittered black comedy *A Scanner Darkly* (**1977**). Several of Dick's novels deal with schizophrenia (in the true clinical meaning rather than the vulgar sense embodied in such split-personality stories as Wyman GUIN's "Beyond Bedlam" [1951]), including *Martian Time-Slip* (**1964**) and *We Can Build You* (**1972**), while *Clans of the Alphane Moon* (**1964**) features the full panoply of neuroses. PARANOIA and schizophrenia are sufficiently widespread in modern sf to warrant a separate entry in this book, but mention may be made here of the paranoid fantasies in which Barry N. MALZBERG has specialized to great effect; different sf situations become archetypes of paranoid delusion in *Overlay* (**1972**), *Beyond Apollo* (**1972**), *The Day of the Burning* (**1974**) and *The Gamesman* (**1975**), and even Freud cannot cope with the situations which confront him in *The Remaking of Sigmund Freud* (**1985**). Sf situations are used in much the same way to construct exaggerated models of alienation in a number of stories by Robert SILVERBERG, including *Thorns* (**1967**), *The Man in the Maze* (**1969**) and *Dying Inside* (**1972**). Other writers who consistently extrapolate psychological syndromes into situations, landscapes and world-designs include J.G. BALLARD, in virtually all his work, and Philip José FARMER, whose early short stories – including the Oedipus-complex fantasy "Mother" (1953) and "Rastignac the Devil" (1954) – were pioneering exercises in this vein.   .

The use of sf to address such psychological questions as the problem of identity – as in Algis BUDRYS's excellent *Who?* (**1958**) or Silverberg's *The Second Trip* (**1972**) – is often closely related to mainstream work; in this instance, to such stories as Marcel AYMÉ's *The Second Face* (**1941**; trans 1951), David ELY's *Seconds*

(1963) – filmed as SECONDS (1966) – and Kobo ABÉ's *Tanin no Kao* (1964; trans as *The Face of Another* 1966 US). Variants on the sf/mainstream borderline include skin-colour-change fantasies, such as Chris Stratton's *Change of Mind* (1969) and the film *Watermelon Man* (1970), and sex-change fantasies, such as Hank STINE's *Season of the Witch* (1968) and Angela CARTER's *The Passion of New Eve* (1977). The processes of mind control involved in "brainwashing" – which play a key part in George ORWELL's *Nineteen Eighty-four* (1949) and which have become a standard element in DYSTOPIAN fiction – bestride the same borderline; exemplary works include *A Clockwork Orange* (1962) by Anthony BURGESS and *The Mind Benders* (1963) by James KENNAWAY. Sf writers can, however, come up with wild variants which attempt to clarify the moral and philosophical questions involved; examples include *The Ring* (1968) by Piers ANTHONY and Robert E. MARGROFF and *The Barons of Behavior* (1972) by Tom PURDOM. Psychological themes of considerable interest where sf has a monopoly include: the augmentation of INTELLIGENCE, as featured in Poul ANDERSON's *Brain Wave* (1954), Daniel KEYES's *Flowers for Algernon* (1959; exp 1966) and Thomas M. DISCH's *Camp Concentration* (1968); psychotic plague stories like Gregory BENFORD's *Deeper than the Darkness* (1970; rev as *The Stars in Shroud* 1978) and Jack DANN's *The Man who Melted* (1984); and stories dealing with the recording of emotional experiences for replaying by consumers, including Lee HARDING's "All My Yesterdays" (1963) and D.G. COMPTON's *Synthajoy* (1972). The last story is a variant of the more common notion that memories, and perhaps knowledge, might be transferred from one mind to another, a theme featured in Curt SIODMAK's *Hauser's Memory* (1968) and various films by him, A.E. VAN VOGT's *Future Glitter* (1973; vt *Tyranopolis*) and James E. GUNN's *The Dreamers* (fixup 1980). Another related theme is that of recording and marketing dreams, a notion elaborately developed in Chelsea Quinn YARBRO's *Hyacinths* (1983) and James K. Morrow's *The Continent of Lies* (1984).

Despite the profligacy of sf writers in devising machines and drugs as facilitating devices, the actual progress of experimental and physiological psychology has had very little impact on sf by comparison with the more abstract and theoretical side of the science, perhaps because of the kind of repugnance displayed in "The Psychologist who Wouldn't Do Awful Things to Rats" (1976) by James TIPTREE Jr – herself a psychologist, and better qualified than most to draw upon that inspiration. The heroic analyst selected by Jeremy LEVEN's computer-incarnated *Satan* (1982) to solve the problem of evil is similarly horrified by the gruesome activities of his experimentally inclined colleagues. The psychological implications of theories in LINGUISTICS have had more impact, notably in Samuel R. DELANY's *Babel-17* (1966) and Ian WATSON's *The Embedding* (1973).

Mention must also be made of a group of stories

dealing with the psychology of sf itself in a rather alarmingly cynical fashion. The pioneer was a story purporting to be an essay, Robert LINDNER's "The Jet-Propelled Couch" (1955), about a psychiatrist's encounter with a patient who believes he has a second existence as the hero of a series of SPACE OPERAS, a theme echoed by Iain BANKS in *The Bridge* (1986), where SWORD-AND-SORCERY motifs obtrude into real life. Norman SPINRAD's *The Iron Dream* (1972), in which Hitler channels his power-fantasies into pulp sf rather than politics, and Malzberg's *Herovit's World* (1973) and *Galaxies* (1975) offer uncompromisingly harsh judgments about the consolations of sf, and have aroused considerable ire among sf fans. Some psychoanalytical literary criticism of well known sf works is even harsher – examples are C.M. KORNBLUTH's "The Failure of the Science Fiction Novel as Social Criticism" (1959), Robert Plank's analysis of Robert A. HEINLEIN's *Stranger in a Strange Land* (1961) in "Omnipotent Cannibals" (1971), and Thomas M. DISCH's analysis of the same author's *Starship Troopers* (1959) in "The Embarrassments of Science Fiction" in *Science Fiction at Large* (1976; vt *Explorations of the Marvellous*) ed Peter NICHOLLS. The basic charge of all three essays is infantilism: together with the oft-quoted adage that the GOLDEN AGE OF SF is 13, they suggest that sf may appeal particularly strongly to people who cannot (yet) cope with reality, and to those condemned to remain existentially becalmed in psychological pre-adolescence forever. Spinrad's *The Void Captain's Tale* (1983) extrapolates the thesis that tales of the conquest of space are encoded sexual fantasies, and that SPACESHIPS are phallic symbols; the one in the story is propelled by a literal sexual drive. On the other hand, K.W. JETER's *Dr Adder* (1984) suggests that our deep SEX fantasies are much more exotic and much sicker than anything which can routinely be found in sf. Given that no one really knows what secrets lurk in the shadowy recesses of the unconscious mind and how our imaginative fictions are shaped to flatter them, speculation on such matters will presumably continue to roam freely across the whole spectrum of possibilities.   [BS]

See also: COMMUNICATIONS; CYBERNETICS; MEDICINE; PERCEPTION; TABOOS.

PSYCHOTIC US FANZINE, ed Richard E. GEIS; begun 1953; after 20 issues retitled *Science Fiction Review* for 3 issues in 1955; then stopped publishing. Geis resumed it with *Psychotic* #21 in 1967, then again changed the title to *Science Fiction Review* from #28. It was by this time printing more serious reviews and interviews, though its main feature remained Geis's amusing, rambling, personal comments. As *Science Fiction Review* it won a HUGO for Best Fanzine in 1969 and 1970; in its first incarnation *Science Fiction Review* ended with #43, Mar 1971, at which point it had a circulation, unusually high for a fanzine, of 1700. The editor also won 7 Hugos as Best Fan Writer; 6 were for his work in *The ALIEN CRITIC*, a later fanzine he began in 1973 and which itself, confusingly, underwent a change of title to *Science Fiction Review* in 1975. [PN]

PUBLISHER'S FISCAL CORPORATION ◊ ASTOUNDING SCIENCE-FICTION.

PUBLISHING The history of sf publishing is, in its widest sense, the HISTORY OF SF itself; this entry, however, is concerned with a much more recent phenomenon, the emergence of GENRE SF as an identifiable and distinctive category of publishing, and therefore concentrates on US firms. A great amount of sf was published in the UK 1900-1950, but, although some transplanted US genre sf appeared, until about 1950 most UK firms published sf without any clear generic tagging, whether issued by prestige houses or by firms specializing in the library market.

It was the first US sf magazines which, from 1926 onwards, established SCIENTIFICTION (for a few years) and then "science fiction" as a generic term. The original material which they featured was viewed, outside an immediate circle of enthusiasts, as debased and trivial pulp literature. The term became synonymous with ill written space adventure, while MAINSTREAM authors from outside the PULP MAGAZINES, who in retrospect have become identified as sf writers, pursued their careers and published their books without being tarred with the sf brush. This entry concentrates on sf book publishing; for magazine publishing ◊ SF MAGAZINES.

Before 1945 only a small handful of stories from the sf and fantasy pulp magazines found their way into general publishers' lists; these included J.M. WALSH's *Vandals of the Void* (**1931**), Edmond HAMILTON's *The Horror on the Asteroid* (coll **1936** UK), L. Sprague DE CAMP's *Lest Darkness Fall* (**1941**) and two of De Camp's collaborations with Fletcher PRATT, and a number of UK anthologies partly or wholly drawn from the pages of WEIRD TALES. Meanwhile authors who sold their sf and fantasy to the better-paying and less-despised general-fiction pulps like *The* ARGOSY (Ray CUMMINGS, Otis Adelbert KLINE, A. MERRITT and others) regularly had their magazine serials issued in book form.

In the absence of interest from established publishers, it fell to sf enthusiasts themselves to publish in book form the stories they admired (◊ SMALL PRESSES AND LIMITED EDITIONS). The first such project of real importance was the memorial volume of Stanley G. WEINBAUM's stories, *The Dawn of Flame and Other Stories* (coll **1936**); the first enterprise to launch itself as a proper publishing imprint was ARKHAM HOUSE, founded by August DERLETH and Donald WANDREI to preserve the memory of H.P. LOVECRAFT, beginning with their first title, *The Outsider* (coll **1939**).

WWII postponed the establishment of any rival ventures. It also saw the publication of the first significant sf ANTHOLOGIES: Phil STONG's *The Other Worlds* (anth **1941**) and Donald A. WOLLHEIM's *Pocket Book of Science Fiction* (anth **1943**) and *Portable Novels of Science* (anth **1945**). The immediate post-WWII years saw a boom in sf anthology publishing from respectable imprints, epitomized by *Adventures in Time and Space* (anth **1946**), a mammoth compilation ed by Raymond J. HEALY and J. Francis MCCOMAS and published by the prestigious Random House. Other anthologists, notably Groff CONKLIN and Derleth, mined the sf magazines extensively. Successful as these books were, they did not immediately lead to an interest in publishing novels or single-author collections written by magazine-sf writers, and a rash of specialist publishers appeared to fill the gap. Some of these, such as the Buffalo Book Company, New Era and Polaris Press, vanished rapidly; others, such as HADLEY PUBLISHING COMPANY and PRIME PRESS, though short-lived, were more significant; and four imprints, FANTASY PRESS, FANTASY PUBLISHING COMPANY INC, GNOME PRESS and SHASTA, proved more enduring. There was no shortage of material to draw on, and a plentiful readership of sf enthusiasts who did not have access to the old magazines in which many of the stories were confined. To a significant degree it was the specialist publishers who determined the form in which future readers would perceive the stories of the stable of contributors to ASTOUNDING SCIENCE FICTION who formed the core of their lists. For example, Isaac ASIMOV's **Foundation** series was merely a long string of magazine stories until Gnome Press's packaging turned it into a trilogy of FIXUPS; similarly, Shasta determined the shape of Robert A. HEINLEIN's **Future History** series.

By the early 1950s, however, a number of established US publishers had become aware of the commercial potential of sf, and they began sf lists. DOUBLEDAY was the most significant and enduring of these, though Scribners had begun a few years earlier with Heinlein juveniles; others included Grossett & Dunlap and Simon & Schuster. In the UK a similar boom occurred. Many of the giant US anthologies were republished, generally heavily cut, and such publishers as Grayson & Grayson and Weidenfeld & Nicolson started sf lists. Michael Joseph Ltd attempted in the mid-1950s the first sf list to try to establish the category as worthwhile literature; its series, under the umbrella title "Novels of the Future", was edited by the romantic novelist Clemence DANE and included work by C.M. KORNBLUTH, Wilson TUCKER and others, but rode on the considerable reputation already established by John WYNDHAM, whose career with Michael Joseph had begun with *The Day of the Triffids* (**1951**); John CHRISTOPHER shortly followed a similar path. UK publishers like Michael Joseph found it easy to treat sf, with some confidence, as an unstigmatized kind of literature. At the same time, however, some of the worst sf ever published – assembly-line books from such publishers as CURTIS WARREN, Scion, BADGER BOOKS, Hamilton (who later became Panther Books) and the Tit-bits SF Library – appeared in the UK during these years.

Where paperback sf remained, with certain exceptions, largely worthless ephemera in the UK until the late 1950s, in the USA it more quickly became an established part of publishers' lists. From their inception, publishers such as ACE BOOKS and BALLANTINE BOOKS relied heavily, and successfully, on sf; other publishers had a less considerable but nevertheless significant involvement. Ace, in particular, gave much encouragement to newer writers, using their **Ace Double** format (◊ DOS-À-DOS) to couple them with more established names. Competition from paperback publishers was already, by the 1960s, causing the magazine publishers severe difficulties, and from this time on it is fair to say that books became the dominant form of sf publishing, with work that had not previously been printed in magazine form often appearing in paperback originals. Through the 1960s and 1970s sf continued to grow in strength as a publisher's category. The last of the important specialist sf publishers, Gnome Press, died in the early 1960s, although FPCI continued into the 1970s on a semiprofessional basis; both had been squeezed out by the larger firms, whose resources they could not match. Arkham House, however, continued successfully to publish weird material, chiefly collections of macabre stories and Lovecraftiana. Harper & Row and Berkley/Putnam joined Doubleday as the leading US hardcover publishers of sf (though Doubleday continued to produce the largest volume of titles); in the UK GOLLANCZ books, in their distinctive yellow jackets, dominated the market, although Faber & Faber, Sidgwick & Jackson, Dennis Dobson and ROBERT HALE LIMITED (in descending order of discrimination and ascending order of volume) also made significant contributions. In the paperback field Ace Books faded in importance following the departure of editor Donald A. Wollheim; his new imprint, DAW BOOKS, begun 1972, took over Ace's place in the market with renewed success. In 1977 Ballantine retitled its sf imprint DEL REY BOOKS after its editor, Judy-Lynn DEL REY. From the late 1970s BANTAM BOOKS became a major rather than a minor player in sf publishing, especially after joining forces with Doubleday in 1986. In the UK, Panther Books was for many years the leading sf imprint, though this supremacy was challenged in the early 1960s by Penguin Books and in the 1970s by Sphere Books, Pan Books and the specialist imprint Orbit. By 1978 virtually every significant paperback publisher on both sides of the Atlantic included sf as an integral part of its list, and a high proportion of paperback editors were themselves sf enthusiasts.

The 1970s also saw a revival of small specialist publishers, but, whereas in the 1940s they had been largely animated by a wish to bring unobtainable novels back into print, in the 1970s they were to a great degree feeding the demand of the growing market of sf and fantasy *collectors*, publishing obscure items by "collectable" authors (such as Lovecraft or, most particularly, Robert E. HOWARD) or lavishly produced illustrated editions of favourite works. FAX COLLECTORS EDITIONS was one of these, followed in the 1980s by MARK V. ZIESING, UNDERWOOD-MILLER and

others. Another phenomenon of the 1970s, attesting to the academic respectability which sf was achieving in some quarters, was the establishment of scholarly reprint series, bringing classic sf works back into print in special durable editions. Such series have been published by ARNO, GARLAND, HYPERION PRESS and, most notably, GREGG PRESS. Thus sf novels first published in obscure and garish pulp magazines, later reprinted in hardcovers by loving enthusiasts when no commercial publisher would look at them, later still issued in equally garish paperback editions, were now made safe for posterity.

By the 1980s, especially in the USA, sf publishing had begun to be weighted, more heavily than previously, towards lower-end-of-the-market series books, books derived from GAMES AND TOYS, film TIES and so forth, a rather disturbing phenomenon noted and discussed in several of this encyclopedia's entries (e.g., HISTORY OF SF, SERIES, SHARECROP and SHARED WORLDS). Many serious sf writers became disturbed at what they perceived as the shrinking of the middle-of-the-road part of publisher's lists, the "midlist", to which much of their work had previously belonged, as it was crowded out by formulaic "product". Nonetheless, serious sf publishing continued, and new companies arrived. Two brave, short-lived experiments were TIMESCAPE BOOKS, an imprint of Simon & Schuster/Pocket Books which lasted only 1981-3 but was prestigious and influential while it did, and BLUEJAY BOOKS (1983-6), a quixotic attempt by a small press to enter mass-market publishing. Much more successful was TOR BOOKS, initially a mostly paperback house, founded in 1981 and brought under the umbrella of St Martin's Press, which came from nowhere to be for a time the leading sf publisher (in terms of number of titles, but also very competitive in terms of quality) in the USA. By the beginning of the 1990s, US sf publishing was dominated by Putnam/Berkley/Ace, Bantam/Doubleday/Dell, Tor/St. Martins and Random House/Ballantine/Del Rey, with firms like Warner Books edging towards a full involvement. Specialist sf publishers like DAW and Baen Books (◊ Jim BAEN), while not exactly languishing, are a good way down the list, publishing much less sf/fantasy/horror than the big four groups.

Sf publishing in the UK is on a much smaller scale, and is perhaps quirkier and more individualistic for that reason, though many titles published in the UK are reprints of US titles (a traffic that does not flow so efficiently in the other direction). Of those publishers mentioned above, Gollancz has survived more than one change of ownership in the 1990s, Pan no longer publishes a large amount of sf, the Sphere sf list has been absorbed into Orbit, and Penguin is less and less important as an sf publisher. Panther is long gone, having been transmuted into Granada and then Grafton, as such becoming a division of Harper-Collins, which in 1992 is perhaps the major player in UK publishing. It has, however, received strong competition from Legend (a division of Random

Century), from New English Library (a division of Hodder & Stoughton), from Gollancz, which now publishes paperbacks as well as hardcovers, from Orbit (from early 1992 a division of Little, Brown UK), from Headline (mostly fantasy and horror), and from Millennium (a division of the new-founded Orion Books). One interesting UK company has been The Women's Press, whose sf list has specialized in sf by women.

A recession in book publishing generally in the late 1980s and early 1990s was predicted to affect sf particularly adversely, but it is surviving well to date, though the overall number of sf books published per year shrank a little from its 1988 peak, but then reached – in the USA at least – a new record, with LOCUS magazine counting 1990 separate sf/fantasy/horror titles (including reprints) published there in 1991, an average of over 5 per day. A further 1980s development in sf publishing has been the rise in popularity of the large-format trade paperback, which has the same page size as the hardcover edition, and is often printed and published simultaneously with it; in fact, in such instances it is usually more accurate to say that the trade-paperback version is the true first edition, the hardcover version representing a small run-on in a special binding for the institutional and gift markets. [MJE/PN]

PUCCETTI, ROLAND (PETER) (1922-   ) US philosopher and writer, long professionally involved in mind-body problems. He published several essays on the split-brain controversy, perhaps most accessibly in "Sperry on Consciousness: A Critical Appreciation" for *The Journal of Medicine and Philosophy* in 1977. Both of his novels deal, in their way, with the question. In *The Death of the Führer* (**1972** UK) Hitler's brain is transplanted into the body of a voluptuous woman, and "his" identity discovered, in (as it were) flagrante delicto by the hero at a moment of passion. *The Trial of John and Henry Norton* (**1973** UK) convincingly updates the Jekyll and Hyde theme, in that the two Nortons of the title inhabit a single body as the result of an operation to cut the link between the two lobes of the upper brain, the left and right lobes becoming in effect two different people. One of them proves to be a murderer, and they are tried "together". RP's concern with identity problems was evident also in *Persons: A Study of Possible Moral Agents in the Universe* (**1968** UK), which argues an expansion of the concept of "person" beyond its usual human-centred limitations and provides serious cognitive backing for the more speculative attempts in sf to apprehend the potential nature of ALIENS. [JC]

PULLA, ARMAS J. [r] ◊ FINLAND.

PULP CLASSICS ◊ Robert E. WEINBERG.

PULPHOUSE: A WEEKLY MAGAZINE ◊ PULPHOUSE: THE HARDBACK MAGAZINE.

PULPHOUSE PUBLISHING Based in Eugene, Oregon, this SMALL PRESS was founded by its publisher Dean Wesley SMITH in 1988, in association with Kristine Kathryn RUSCH and others, and specializes in sf, fantasy and horror. It began with PULPHOUSE: THE HARDBACK MAGAZINE in a limited edition. By 1990 it had become quite active in book publishing also, and in 1991, with 20 employees, the company seemed on the verge of becoming a full-scale publishing house; by mid-1992, however, most of these employees had been laid off. Along with its subsidiary Axolotl Press, Pulphouse publishes mostly limited editions. These include: a most unusual line of small paperbacks each containing a single short story (mostly reprints of award-winners and classics), a series that fell into abeyance in mid-1992; a series of novellas in book form; and the *Author's Choice Monthly* numbered series of single-author collections (28 of these by late 1992). Most of the above are sf or fantasy, but in mid-1991 Pulphouse announced a projected Mystery Scene imprint also. [PN]

PULPHOUSE: THE HARDBACK MAGAZINE Quarterly "magazine" in hardcover-book format, in fact an ORIGINAL-ANTHOLOGY series; ed Kristine Kathryn RUSCH; published by Dean Wesley SMITH trading as PULPHOUSE PUBLISHING of Eugene, Oregon; 11 issues (each 1250 copies) Fall 1988-Spring 1991; publication projected to cease after 12 issues.

This interesting, eclectic and mostly successful experiment alternated horror, speculative fiction, fantasy and sf in different issues. Horror and dark fantasy, in which categories much of the best work appeared, were the most repeated genres. The intended market appears to have been sophisticated: *P:THM* published some experimental work, and despite the notional pigeonholing of the fiction into categories, many of its stories transcend or ignore genre conventions. Many new authors were published by *P:THM*; more experienced contributors included George Alec EFFINGER, Charles DE LINT, Robert SHECKLEY, Lisa GOLDSTEIN, Joe R. Lansdale (1951-   ) and Harry TURTLEDOVE. An anthology is *The Best of Pulphouse: The Hardcover Magazine* (anth **1991**) ed Rusch.

P:THM was replaced in 1991 by *Pulphouse: A Weekly Magazine* ed Smith, in small BEDSHEET format – first (test) issue marked "Issue Zero" (Mar 1, 1991), official #1 dated June 1, 1991 – though for a number of months the two titles overlapped. The new 48pp magazine was anything but weekly to begin with, and, belatedly realistic, changed its title to *Pulphouse: A Fiction Magazine* with #5 (Sep 20, 1991) and announced a biweekly schedule. In its 7 official issues to end-1991 it published short fiction, serialized novels by Robert SHECKLEY, Spider and Jeanne ROBINSON and S.P. SOMTOW, and published nonfiction articles. [PN]

PULP MAGAZINES In discussions of popular literature, as in this volume, the term "pulp" is used metaphorically as often as specifically, and when used specifically it has both a narrow and a wide sense.

1. "Pulp" is used in this encyclopedia as an indication of format, in contrast to BEDSHEET and

DIGEST. The pulp magazine normally measured 10in x 7in (about 25cm x 18cm); where the word "pulp" is used with no other indication of size, it can be assumed that the magazine in question was of approximately these dimensions.

2. More broadly, "pulp" is used to designate the type of magazine whose format is as above. There was more to a pulp magazine than its size. Pulp magazines, as their name suggests, were printed on cheap paper manufactured from chemically treated wood pulp, a process invented in the early 1880s. The paper is coarse, absorbent and acid, with a distinctive sharp smell much loved by magazine collectors. Pulp paper ages badly, largely because of its acid content, yellowing and becoming brittle. Because of the thickness of the paper, pulp magazines tended to be quite bulky, often ½in (1.25cm) thick or more. They generally had ragged, untrimmed edges, and later in their history had notoriously garish, brightly coloured covers, many of the coal-tar dyes used to make cover inks being of the most lurid hues.

It is usually accepted that Frank A. MUNSEY invented the pulp-magazine formula when in 1896 he changed the contents of *The* ARGOSY to contain nothing but fiction; previously the most popular periodicals had published a mixture of fiction, factual articles, poetry, etc. Sf was already popular in magazine format before the advent of the pulps – for example, in *The* STRAND MAGAZINE, *The* IDLER and MCCLURE'S MAGAZINE. However, these three and the many like them were aimed at a wealthier, more middle-class and possibly more literate audience than that which the pulps were invented to exploit: they were family magazines, with a more demure format and usually printed on coated, slick paper, which in the USA led to their being dubbed the "slicks" to distinguish them from their humbler brethren, the pulps. It is sometimes stated that the slicks were more expensive than the pulps, but this was not necessarily so.

The popular slicks and the pulps were both part of a magazine-publishing revolution beginning in the 1880s, in which mass-distribution techniques and greatly increased advertising allowed the dropping of prices. Most magazines before the 1880s had had a small circulation and been relatively expensive, aimed at a narrow, upper-middle-class, literate group. But now, in the UK and USA, literacy was becoming nearly universal, population was increasing at an amazing rate (doubling in 30 years in the USA), modern technology was on the whole leading to more leisure, and there was as yet no cinema to offer opposition in the telling of stories. As a consequence, magazine circulations became massive towards the end of the century, over half a million in the most successful cases.

The slicks and, a little later, the pulps rode the crest of this wave, with the pulps cornering the all-fiction-magazine market. Other periodical formats – some of which had a longer history (◊ BOYS' PAPERS; DIME-NOVEL SF) included the popular weekly tabloid, such as PEARSON'S WEEKLY.

The general-fiction pulp magazine began to give way to specialized genre pulps after the founding in 1915 of *Detective Story Monthly*. (Frank Munsey had been a pioneer here, too, with *Railroad Man's Magazine* [1906] and *Ocean* [1907].) *Western Story* followed in 1919, *Love Stories* in 1921 and WEIRD TALES in 1923. It is surprising that sf did not get its own pulp until AMAZING STORIES in 1926, for the SCIENTIFIC ROMANCE had been a staple of the general-fiction pulps, along with LOST-WORLD stories and FANTASY, and in these fields the pulps had produced writers as celebrated and well loved as Edgar Rice BURROUGHS, Ray CUMMINGS, George Allan ENGLAND, Ralph Milne FARLEY, William Hope HODGSON, A. MERRITT, Sax ROHMER and Garrett P. SERVISS, as well as helped to popularize H.G. WELLS (more commonly published in the slicks) and H. Rider HAGGARD. Many of these writers retain their popularity.

The advent of specialized pulps did little at first to disturb the hardened pulp writers, who turned from pirate stories to jungle stories, detective stories to sf, etc., with admirable *sang-froid*, though often with unhappy literary results. It was not until the late 1930s that sf writers in the pulps generally came to see themselves as specialists, concentrating usually on sf, fantasy and horror, and seldom ranging further. (The crossing of genre boundaries is not, however, a rarity among pulp sf and fantasy writers; many have written detective novels, and more recently some have done very well with DISASTER novels.)

Nor did the advent of specialized pulps mark the end of sf in the general-fiction pulps. *Argosy* and BLUE BOOK MAGAZINE, for example, continued in the early 1930s to attract the most popular sf writers, including Burroughs and Farley; *Argosy* was paying up to 6 cents a word, and *Blue Book* also paid well, considerably better than the cent or even half-cent a word available from the sf pulps. However, by the end of the 1930s *Argosy*'s rates had dropped to 1½ cents a word. This marked the effective death of the general-fiction pulp, and probably had a lot to do with the new vigour apparent in such sf pulps as ASTOUNDING SCIENCE-FICTION.

Although the sf pulps of the 1930s are remembered with great nostalgia by sf fans, the fact is that they formed a very minor portion of the overall pulp-publishing business. The great US pulp-publishing houses, such as Clayton, STREET & SMITH and Standard, published dozens of titles of which sf, in terms of number of titles and overall sales, formed only a tiny proportion. Sf as big business had to wait for the post-WWII paperback-book publishing boom (◊ PUBLISHING).

Most of the pulp magazines, sf included, had died by the middle 1950s, to be replaced by DIGESTS (◊ SF MAGAZINES) in increasingly unhappy competition with paperback books; also, the reading of stories was itself giving way to the watching of TELEVISION.

Indeed, many pulp historians would claim that, despite the proliferation of titles in the 1930s, the heyday of the pulp magazines with their half-million circulations ended with the paper shortages following WWI and the rapidly growing popularity of the CINEMA. The economic depression of the late 1920s probably prolonged the end, bringing with it an urgent need for fiction which escaped the greyness of an ordinary world in which individuals seemed impotent. In the pulps, individuals not only influenced events, they regularly saved the world.

A full index of sf and post-1930 fantasy magazines with entries in this volume – including many pulp magazines – is given under SF MAGAZINES. Other periodicals in which sf was published are discussed under BOYS' PAPERS, COMICS, DIME-NOVEL SF and MAGAZINES, the latter entry listing the most important of the general slicks and tabloids which published sf in the period 1890-1940.

The following are the general-fiction pulp-magazine entries: *The* ALL-STORY, *The* ARGOSY, *The* BLUE BOOK MAGAZINE, *The* CAVALIER, *The* POPULAR MAGAZINE and *The* SCRAP BOOK. 3 specialized early pulps given entries are SCIENCE AND INVENTION, THRILL BOOK and WEIRD TALES. A number of 1930s "weird-menace" and science/detective pulps whose sf content was very marginal do not receive entries, with the pious exception of Hugo GERNSBACK's SCIENTIFIC DETECTIVE MONTHLY. There is a small fantasy element in such various genre pulps as *Oriental Stories* (1930), *Golden Fleece Historical Adventure* (1938) and *Jungle Stories* (1938), but the line had to be drawn somewhere in the no-man's-land between sf and fantasy, and they have been omitted. The sf content of the SUPERHERO/supervillain genre is sometimes greater and, though many are omitted – including the extremely popular *The Shadow* (1931-49), whose sf content was marginal and irregular (*but see* Walter B. GIBSON *for some details*) – there are entries for CAPTAIN HAZZARD, CAPTAIN ZERO, DOC SAVAGE MAGAZINE, DR. YEN SIN, DUSTY AYRES AND HIS BATTLE BIRDS, FLASH GORDON STRANGE ADVENTURE MAGAZINE, G-8 AND HIS BATTLE ACES, *The* MYSTERIOUS WU FANG, *The* OCTOPUS, OPERATOR #5, *The* SCORPION, *The* SPIDER and TERENCE X. O'LEARY'S WAR BIRDS.

A good account of life as a pulp writer is *The Pulp Jungle* (**1967**) by Frank Gruber; books on pulp publishing are *Cheap Thrills: An Informal History of the Pulp Magazines* (**1972**) by Ron GOULART, *The Fiction Factory, or From Pulp Row to Quality Street: The Story of 100 Years of Publishing at Street & Smith* (**1955**) by Quentin James Reynolds, and *Pulp Voices: Interviews with Pulp Magazine Writers and Editors* (chap **1983**) ed J.M. Elliot; the feeling of the pulps themselves is captured in *The Pulps: 50 Years of American Pop Culture* (**1970**) ed Tony Goodstone; and *The Shudder Pulps* (**1975**) by Robert Kenneth Jones is on the "weird-menace" pulps. Also relevant is *Yesterday's Faces: A Study of Series Figures in the Early Pulp Magazines: Volume 2: Strange Days* (**1984**) by Robert Sampson, vol 1 being largely about precursors in the dime novels.

3. When used metaphorically the word "pulp" describes the quality and style of the fiction published in the pulp magazines – and, by extension, any similar fiction, no matter in what format it was published. The term is still used in this sense today, 40 years after the death of the pulps proper. The pulps emphasized action, romance, heroism, success, exotic milieux, fantastic adventures (often with a sprinkling of love interest), and almost invariably a cheerful ending. In literary criticism "pulp" is often taken as a synonym for "stylistically crude", but this was not necessarily the case. Good narrative pacing, by no means a negligible quality, was regularly found in the pulps, as were other the virtues of colour, inventiveness, clarity of image and occasional sharp observation, such as might be seen in the work of the early pulp writer Jack LONDON. But it is true that the voracious appetite of the pulp market led to many writers becoming, in effect, word factories, writing too swiftly and to a cynical formula. The pulps did not generally pay as well for fiction as did the slicks, so economic pressure forced the pulp writer into high productivity.

Today the term "pulp sf" is associated primarily with stories written, usually rapidly, for the least intellectual segment of the sf market – packed with adventure but with little emphasis on character, which is usually stereotyped, or on ideas, which are frugally and constantly recycled (◊ CLICHÉS). Many of the entries in this volume discuss typical pulp-sf themes and modes, including GALACTIC EMPIRES, HEROES, OPTIMISM AND PESSIMISM, SEX, SPACE OPERA, SUPERMAN, SWORD AND SORCERY and VILLAINS. On the other hand, not all the fiction published in the pulp magazines was subject to the limitations that the word "pulp" usually suggests. Two famous examples from crime fiction of writers transcending their pulp origins, even while continuing to be published in a pulp format, are Dashiell Hammett (1894-1961) and Raymond Chandler (1888-1959), both associated with *Black Mask*, and examples from sf are common, too, or else the genre would long ago have died of malnutrition (◊ GOLDEN AGE OF SF).   [PN]

PULP SF ◊ PULP MAGAZINES.

PULSARS ◊ BLACK HOLES; NEUTRON STARS.

PUNISHMENT PARK Film (1970). Chartwell/Françoise. Dir Peter WATKINS, starring Carmen Argenziano, Stan Armsted, Jim Bohan, Frederick Franklin, Gladys Golden. Screenplay Watkins. 89 mins. Colour.

Set in the NEAR FUTURE, *PP* concerns a group of young political dissidents who are forced to endure a government-controlled "run of the gauntlet" before they can attain amnesty for their political crimes. They must travel many miles across a US desert to reach a flagpole flying the Stars and Stripes, at the same time avoiding the patrols of government troops who have orders to shoot to kill. The presence of a tv team that follows one group of dissidents, increasingly involved with their situation, ingeniously increases our own involvement. Made at a time when youthful protest against the USA's involvement in Vietnam was at its peak, and a propaganda film on the side of the protesters, *PP* nevertheless shows a genuinely individual cinematic vision in its gloomy portrayal of a USA experiencing political repression. [JB/PN]

PURDOM, TOM Working name of US writer Thomas Edward Purdom (1936-   ) for all his sf, which he started publishing with "Grieve for a Man" for *Fantastic Universe* in 1957. His sf novels, beginning with *I Want the Stars* (**1964** dos), have been unpretentious but competent adventures, generally set on challenging alien worlds. *The Tree Lord of Imeten* (**1966** dos) vividly puts two human colonists into a crisis situation in the jungle while two native races fight one another. *The Barons of Behavior* (**1972**) mixes politics and social conditioning in a DYSTOPIAN future Earth. [JC]

Other works: *Five against Arlane* (**1967** dos); *Reduction in Arms* (**1967** ASF; exp **1971**).

As editor: *Adventures in Discovery* (anth **1969**).

See also: PSYCHOLOGY.

PURPLE DEATH FROM OUTER SPACE ◊ FLASH GORDON.

PURSUIT Made-for-tv film (1972). ABC Circle/ABC TV. Dir Michael CRICHTON, starring Ben Gazzara, E.G. Marshall, William Windom, Joseph Wiseman, Martin Sheen. Screenplay Robert Dozier, based on *Binary* (**1972**) by John Lange (Crichton). 72 mins. Colour.

In this lively thriller, Crichton's directorial début, an extremist politician plans to use a nerve-gas chemical weapon, capable of killing millions, in San Diego during a Republican convention in order to kill the US President. [JB/PN]

PYNCHON, THOMAS (1937-   ) US writer, all of whose works are FABULATIONS which resemble sf under some interpretations, though the PARANOIA-wracked worlds his protagonists inhabit defeat any secure reading of the malign figurations of reality. In *V* (**1963**) dovetailing searches for a character named V geographically reproduce the title; some events in the book border on sf. *The Crying of Lot 49* (**1966**) presents a complex conspiracy theory of history, the tone of which seems to have influenced Robert SHEA's and Robert Anton WILSON's **Illuminatus!** trilogy (**1975**). Enormous and complex, *Gravity's Rainbow* (**1973**) offers no repose for a secure reading, but the search for its main protagonist (whose sexual climaxes predict and attract rockets from the V-2s on) fabulously posits an sf world. The walking dead in *Vineland* (**1990**) are – it is almost certain – not literally posthumous. TP's general concerns with ENTROPY, paranoia and COMMUNICATION have had a fruitful effect on some sf writers. [JC]

Other works: *Entropy* (**1960**; **1977** chap UK), also contained in *Slow Learner* (coll **1986**).

See also: CYBERPUNK; FANTASY; HISTORY OF SF.

Q (vt *The Winged Serpent*; vt *Q: The Winged Serpent*) Film (1983). Larco. Prod and dir Larry COHEN, starring Michael Moriarty, Candy Clark, David Carradine. Screenplay Cohen. 92 mins. Colour.

In this witty MONSTER MOVIE – which subverts our expectations about how both society and B-movies work in almost the same breath – "Q" represents on the one hand Quetzalcoatl, a giant winged serpent (thus sf) and Aztec god (thus not sf) that terrorizes New York, possibly called up by the city's violence, and on the other hand Quinn (Moriarty), a small-time jewel thief and opportunist who discovers the monster's lair atop the Chrysler Building (where there is, naturally enough, an Aztec pyramid). The likable human monster Quinn metaphorically coalesces with the literal monster. But Quinn plays Judas to the incarnated god, thus laying himself open to retribution from a ritual mutilator, one of Q's disciples. He is saved by cool policeman Shepard (Carradine), to whom monsters are just one more story in the Naked City. Moriarty is superb and, in its confident mounting, its sophistication, and its higher-than-average (for Cohen) production values, *Q* may be its director's best film. [PN]

QERAMA, THANAS [r] ◊ ALBANIA.

Q: THE WINGED SERPENT ◊ Q.

QUANDRY US FANZINE (1950-53), 30 issues, ed from Georgia by Lee HOFFMAN. Though undistinguished in appearance, *Q* was noted for the quality and humour of its writing; along with HYPHEN, its influence on fan publishing is still strong. Contributors included Walt Willis (1919-   ), Robert SILVERBERG, Wilson TUCKER, Robert BLOCH and James WHITE. Hoffman still publishes, but no longer edits, *Science Fiction Five Yearly*, the fanzine holding the record for the longest gaps between regular issues, founded 1951, #9 in 1991; it shares many contributors with *Q*. A single-issue reprint collection of *Quandry* #14-#17 was published in 1982 by Joe D. Siclari. [PR/RH]

QUANTUM LEAP US tv series, begun 1989. Universal/ MCA for NBC. Created and prod Donald P. Bellisario. Supervising prod Deborah Pratt. Writers include Bellisario, Pratt, Chris Ruppenthal, Tommy Thompson, Paul Brown. Dirs include David Hemmings, Aaron Lipstadt, Gilbert Shelton, Christopher Welch, Joe Napolitano. Current, 52 50min episodes in first 3 seasons to 1991. Colour.

QL is an unusual TIME-TRAVEL series, with Scott Bakula as Sam Beckett (!), a scientist lost in time, helped only by the projected hologram of Albert (Dean Stockwell), an eccentric colleague trapped in the future. Unlike the heroes of *The* TIME TUNNEL (1966-7), who were physically dumped into historical situations, Beckett travels mentally, his consciousness inhabiting the bodies of other people at any time between the 1950s and the 1980s (the time visited has to be after his own birth). As in *Here Comes Mr Jordan* (1941), the audience sees the hero as himself while those around him see the person he is possessing. Although the premise is gimmicky, the series has reached a surprisingly high standard. Highspots from 1989 have Beckett suddenly in the bodies of a test pilot about to step into an experimental plane Beckett can't possibly fly, a mobster required to sing in Italian at a wedding, an old Black man in the South in the 1950s during a civil-rights demonstration, and a pretty woman being pursued by a lecherous suitor. Only notionally sf, this is a shade grittier, funnier and cleverer than it has any right to be, and benefits strongly from the two relaxed, witty central performances. [KN]

QUANTUM: SCIENCE FICTION AND FANTASY REVIEW ◊ THRUST.

QUARBER MERKUR Austrian FANZINE; ed Franz ROTTENSTEINER since its inception in 1963. In the argot of fans, *QM* is a "sercon" (serious and constructive) fanzine, one of the longest-running and most impressive of its type. It publishes critical, bibliographical, sociopolitical and historical studies of sf, UTOPIAS, weird fiction and FANTASY. Averaging 90 large unillustrated pages per issue, *QM* has now published around 3 million words of serious criticism; it had reached #74 by the end of 1990. Contributors have included most of the major German sf critics, and writers such as Herbert W. FRANKE and Stanisław LEM; many contributors have been from Eastern Europe. A collection of some of the best contents is *Quarber Merkur* (anth **1979** Germany). [PN]

QUARK US ORIGINAL-ANTHOLOGY series from Paperback Library, ed Samuel R. DELANY and the poet Marilyn Hacker (1942-   ) – they were married 1961-80 – subtitled "A Quarterly of Speculative Fiction". It was the most overtly experimental and NEW-WAVE of the ANTHOLOGY series of the early 1970s, and provoked some hostility in the sf world. It attempted an ambitious, graphically sophisticated package; but some illustration was substandard and the design was irritating rather than innovative, with such counterproductive features as the absence of a contents page and the appearance of authors' names only at the end of each story. Although *Q* featured good work by Thomas M. DISCH, R.A. LAFFERTY, Ursula K. LE GUIN, Joanna RUSS and others, it lasted only 4 issues: *Quark 1* (anth **1970**), *#2* (anth **1971**), *#3* (anth **1971**) and *#4* (anth **1971**). [MJE/PN]

QUASARS ◊ BLACK HOLES.

QUATERMASS (vt *The Quatermass Conclusion*) UK tv serial (1979). Euston Films/ITV. Prod Ted Childs. Dir Piers Haggard, starring John Mills, Simon MacCorkindale, Rebecca Saire. Written Nigel KNEALE. 4 60min episodes. Colour. Version for film release (but receiving general release only on videotape) titled *The Quatermass Conclusion*, 102 mins.

This fourth and weakest of the Quatermass tv serials (*see below for details of the others*) was written in the late 1960s for BBC TV, rejected as too expensive, and finally made for commercial tv a decade later. The delay rendered out-of-date the sequences about hippie adolescents lured to neolithic sites to be harvested by aliens. The other part of the plot, dealing with near-future breakdown of law and order in a London becoming a wasteland, is stronger; but the two halves never properly meld, and *Q* lacks the narrative thrust of its predecessors. John Mills's Quatermass is rather old and sad, and, though there is much to enjoy, there is a faintly querulous, elderly air about the whole production. The cut version, though planned from the beginning, is semi-incoherent. Kneale's obsessive, 30-year repetition of the science-meets-superstition theme is altogether jollier in his screenplay for HALLOWEEN III: SEASON OF THE WITCH (1983), also featuring a stone circle. [PN]

QUATERMASS AND THE PIT 1. UK tv serial (1958-9). BBC TV. Prod and dir Rudolph Cartier, starring André Morell (as Quatermass), Anthony Bushell. Written Nigel KNEALE. 6 35min episodes. (Released on video 1988 at 178 mins.) B/w.

As in *QATP*'s two predecessors, *The* QUATERMASS EXPERIMENT and QUATERMASS II, Kneale's theme is demonic possession, dressed up ingeniously as sf.

Morell was the best of the BBC's three Professor Quatermasses, and most critics judge the tv serial better than the film version. The published script is *Quatermass and the Pit* ∗ (**1960**) by Kneale. For details of the story see below.

2. Film (1967; vt *Five Million Years to Earth* US) Hammer/Seven Arts. Dir Roy Ward Baker, starring Andrew Keir (as Quatermass), Barbara Shelley, James Donald. Screenplay Nigel KNEALE, based on his BBC TV serial. 97 mins. Colour.

Hammer's third Quatermass film, a decade after the second and the only one with an English actor (Keir) in the title role. The first two were *The* QUATERMASS XPERIMENT (1955) and QUATERMASS II (1957). Workers excavating a tunnel find an apparent unexploded bomb; it is actually a Martian spaceship. In a plot-turn deftly blending sf with speculation on Jungian archetype, it turns out that racial memories have been coded in our brains by Martians during our prehistory: our image of the Devil is a distorted "memory" of the Martians' appearance (antennae equalling horns), and our irrational belligerence reflects the Martians' ritualistic culling of the weaker members of their species. The spaceship's power source is merely dormant, and as it comes to life (poltergeist phenomena being the first effect) it reinforces ancient nightmares. In the disturbing climax panicked Londoners begin an orgy of destruction as a Devil's head rises above the streets and paranormal powers are let loose. *QATP* is surely the inspiration for Stephen KING's novel *The Tommyknockers* (**1987**).

Kneale's characteristic blend of GOTHIC and science is intelligent and entertaining. Although inferior to its tv original, which had more time to develop its irrational but mesmerizing thesis, the film is still above average. [PN/JB]

See also: SUPERNATURAL CREATURES.

QUATERMASS CONCLUSION, THE ◊ QUATERMASS.

QUATERMASS EXPERIMENT, THE UK tv serial (1953). BBC TV. Prod and dir Rudolph Cartier, starring Reginald Tate (as Quatermass), Isabel Dean, Duncan Lamont. Written Nigel KNEALE. 6 30min episodes. B/w.

Before the first episode, the BBC warned that the serial was "thought to be unsuitable for children or persons of a nervous disposition". For 6 Saturday nights the UK tv audience watched a genuinely unsettling story unfold – an ingenious combination of sf and the traditional horror theme of possession. It was a milestone in televised sf. The script was published as *The Quatermass Experiment* ∗ (**1959**) by Kneale. For details of the story ◊ *The* QUATERMASS XPERIMENT. [JB]

QUATERMASS II 1. UK tv serial (1955). BBC TV. Prod and dir Rudolph Cartier, starring John Robinson (as Quatermass). Written Nigel KNEALE. 6 35min episodes. B/w.

This was the sequel to *The* QUATERMASS EXPERIMENT; for details of the story see below. The script was published as *Quatermass II* ∗ (**1960**) by Kneale.

2. Film (1957; vt *Enemy from Space* US) Hammer/ United Artists. Dir Val Guest, starring Brian Donlevy (as Quatermass), Bryan Forbes, John Longden, Sidney James. Screenplay Nigel KNEALE, Val Guest, based on the BBC TV serial by Kneale. 85 mins. B/w.

This was #2 of the 3 Quatermass films produced by Hammer, and the first coscripted by Kneale; it is the most difficult to judge since Kneale, who disliked Donlevy's US performance and Guest's tampering with his script, withdrew the film from circulation in 1965 when rights reverted to him. Many critics think it the best of the Quatermass films, and some deem it the greatest of all UK sf movies (though astonishingly similar in theme to the US film INVASION OF THE BODY SNATCHERS [1956]): disturbing, intense, unrelenting, paranoid and especially nightmarish in its depiction of figures in power conspiring with aliens capable of entering and controlling human bodies. Much of the action takes place in the brooding landscapes of the North of England, where a mysterious technological complex turns out to be the alien power base. The strong political allegory of ordinary people cruelly exploited by a cold-blooded (and in this case literally inhuman) ruling class was very adventurous for the time.

The tv ending (Quatermass goes into space to destroy the asteroid which is the alien base) is dropped in the film. The film's predecessor was *The* QUATERMASS XPERIMENT (1955) and its successor was QUATERMASS AND THE PIT (1967). [PN]

See also: MONSTER MOVIES; PARANOIA; QUATERMASS.

QUATERMASS XPERIMENT, THE (vt *The Creeping Unknown* US) Film (1955). Hammer. Dir Val Guest, starring Brian Donlevy (as Quatermass), Richard Wordsworth, Jack Warner. Screenplay Richard Landau, Val Guest, based on the BBC TV serial by Nigel KNEALE. 82 mins, cut to 78 mins. B/w.

It was this film version of the BBC's tv serial *The* QUATERMASS EXPERIMENT that convinced the Hammer company there was money in horror. (The spelling "Xperiment" referred jokingly to the X certificate Hammer correctly expected the film to be given because of what seemed in those innocent days its alarming horror content.) An astronaut returns to Earth infected by spores from space that slowly take over his body, finally transforming him into an amorphous blob that retreats into Westminster Abbey, where it is electrocuted by Quatermass. (The original tv serial ends with Quatermass talking to all the three astronaut psyches lingering within the monster, thus convincing the blob to self-destruct.) Richard Wordsworth's shambling, pitiful performance as the afflicted astronaut is quite moving, communicating (though he barely speaks) a sense of something utterly alien to human experience. *TQX* is a minor classic. [PN/JB]

See also: MONSTER MOVIES.

QÉBEC ◊ CANADA.

QUEEN OF BLOOD ◊ Roger CORMAN.

QUENEAU, RAYMOND [r] ◊ FRANCE.

QUESADA, ÁNGEL TORRES [r] ◊ SPAIN.

QUESTAR US sf magazine; large-BEDSHEET slick format; 13 issues, Spring 1978-Oct 1981; published by M.W. Communications Inc (William G. Wilson and Robert V. Michelucci), Pittsburgh; ed William G. Wilson Jr. The final, redesigned issue, had a new title: *Quest/Star*, subtitled "The World of Science Fiction".

Questar began as a media SEMIPROZINE largely devoted to talk about COMICS and sf CINEMA, with a sprinkling of not very good stories. #3 introduced interior colour illustration, and a greater concentration on movies and interviews. Though glossy, it remained insipid. Only with #13 – for which, astonishingly, H.L. GOLD was dragged from retirement as fiction editor – did *Q* begin publishing reputable fiction. This was too little, too late. Undercapitalized – and undersold, despite its patchy national distribution from #7 – *Q* sank, lamented by few. Publication was irregular, though approximately quarterly. [PN]

QUEST FOR FIRE Film (1981). ICC-Cine-Trail (Montréal)/Belstar Productions/Stephan Films (Paris). Dir Jean-Jacques Annaud, starring Everett McGill, Ron Perlman, Nameer El-Kadi, Rae Dawn Chong. Screenplay by Gerard Brach, based on *La Guerre du Feu* (**1909**) by J.H. ROSNY aîné. 100 mins. Colour.

This Canadian/French coproduction dramatizes the 1909 French classic prehistoric romance by J.H. Rosny aîné, trans as *The Quest for Fire: A Novel of Prehistoric Times* (cut trans **1967** US). Great care (possibly misplaced, since who can know?) was taken to make it all seem authentic, from positions adopted for lovemaking (body language credited to Desmond Morris) and an imaginary agglutinative language with a vocabulary of about 200 sounds (linguistics credited to Anthony BURGESS). The tribe's fire has gone out, and three tribesmen go on a quest to find fresh fire (it is a kind of Holy Grail), confronting a more primitive cannibal tribe and then the more sophisticated Ivaka, who know how to make fire. As an exercise in imaginary ANTHROPOLOGY it is mildly impressive (though it has its cod aspects, its 1909 original not being the last word in prehistoric insight); as story-telling, it covers familiar generic ground, but is all very enjoyable – especially the arbitrary herd of mammoths (elephants wearing rugs) – and rather touching. The Kenyan and Scottish highlands, beautifully photographed, stand in for prehistoric Europe. [PN]

QUEST FOR LOVE Film (1971). Peter Rogers Productions. Dir Ralph Thomas, starring Tom Bell, Joan Collins, Denholm Elliott, Laurence Naismith. Screenplay Terence Feely, based on "Random Quest" (1961) by John WYNDHAM. 91 mins. Colour.

Romance about a physicist (Bell) accidentally transferred to a PARALLEL WORLD, where he falls in love with the wife (Collins) of his *alter ego*, a playwright and cad, whose place he has taken. She dies. On being sucked back to our own world, he desperately quests for her counterpart, hoping to save her and have a second chance at love. He does. Good performances, so-so as sf, with the differences of the new world (Kennedy not assassinated, etc.) established only perfunctorily. Wyndham's original story is one of his weakest. [PN]

QUESTOR TAPES, THE Made-for-tv film (1974). Universal/NBC. Dir Richard A. Colla, starring Robert Foxworth (as Questor), Mike Farrell, John Vernon. Teleplay Gene RODDENBERRY, Gene L. Coon. 100 mins. Colour.

This was the rather good pilot episode for a tv series that never sold. Questor, the last of a series of ANDROID guardians deposited on Earth eons ago by a beneficent ALIEN race, has been faultily programmed, and the story involves his search for information that will explain his origin and mission. Little is resolved, since the film was designed as an introduction only. The novelization is *The Questor Tapes* * (**1974**) by D.C. FONTANA. [JB]

QUESTS ◊ FANTASTIC VOYAGES; FANTASY.

QUEST/STAR ◊ QUESTAR.

QUICK, W.T. (? -) US writer who began publishing sf with "Rest in Pieces" for *IASFM* in 1980, but who came to more general notice, after several 1980s stories in *ASF*, with the **Dreams** sequence of sf adventures: *Dreams of Flesh and Sand* (**1988**), *Dreams of Gods and Men* (**1989**) and *Singularities* (**1990**). The tales are clear-cut and taut, but the huge corporations dominated by AIs were unsurprising fare for readers familiar with the rapid explosion of the CYBERPUNK subgenre. *Yesterday's Pawn* (**1989**), also an adventure tale, takes its adolescent protagonist through space and time as he attempts to decipher the importance of an ancient artefact; but *Systems* (**1989**) returns to cyberpunk territory in the fast-paced story of a "data hunter" simultaneously grieving for his pregnant wife and solving the mysteries surrounding her murder. [JC]

QUIET EARTH, THE Film (1985). Cinepro/Pillsbury. Dir Geoffrey Murphy, starring Bruno Lawrence, Alison Routledge, Peter Smith. Screenplay Bill Baer, Bruno Lawrence, Sam Pillsbury, based on *The Quiet Earth* (**1981**) by Craig HARRISON. 91 mins. Colour.

This New Zealand film tells of a scientific/ metaphysical DISASTER, perhaps consequent upon a secret project in energy transmission, in which all people disappear from the Earth except those who coincidentally die at the moment of the disaster: these are resurrected. A guilt-ridden scientist plays solitary games in a deserted city; he meets a woman survivor and then a tough Maori, with the usual male rivalry ensuing. The scientist realizes the fabric of the Universe has become unstable and tries to put it right, with interesting results. A small, low-key, honest film, suffering from a derivative storyline and rather pedestrian direction and performances. [PN]

QUILL, JOHN [s] ◊ Max ADELER.

QUILLER, ANDREW ◊ Kenneth BULMER.

QUILP, JOCELYN Pseudonym of UK writer Halliwell Sutcliffe (1870-1932), whose *Baron Verdigris: A*

Romance of the Reversed Direction (**1894**) features a 12th-century knight cast into confusion by being able to remember both the past and the future, but not to distinguish between them. [JC]

QUINN, DANIEL (1935-) US writer who began publishing work of genre interest with *Dreamer* (**1988**), a dark fantasy, and who came to wide notice with *Ishmael* (**1992**), which won the first Turner Tomorrow Award of $500,000. The novel is a quietly told but elegantly unrelenting indictment of *Homo sapiens*'s lethal tenure as rulers of the planet, spoken through the consciousness of a melancholy, didactic great ape (◊ APES AND CAVEMEN) who attempts to teach the human protagonist what must be done: you must (he insists) change your lives; or you will all die. [JC]

QUINN, GERARD A. (1927-) Northern Irish illustrator. One of the "grand old men" (with Brian LEWIS) of UK sf illustration in the 1950s, GAQ did hundreds of illustrations for UK sf magazines, beginning 1951, including 36 covers for *NW*, 24 for *Science Fantasy*, 3 for *Nebula Science Fiction*, 2 for *Vision of Tomorrow* and, in a minor 1982 comeback after largely disappearing from the scene in the mid-1960s, 2 for EXTRO. Specializing in alien landscapes, his astronomical paintings were often compared to those of Chesley BONESTELL, though his use of colour was less photographically realistic. His interior black-and-white work was intricate. [JG/PN]

QUINN, JAMES L(OUIS) (? -) US editor whose Quinn Publishing Co started the magazine IF in 1952; JLQ became editor after the first 4 issues. Its circulation gradually declined, and in 1958 JLQ appointed Damon KNIGHT in his place. The magazine's fortunes did not revive and JLQ suspended publication, subsequently selling the title to the publishers of GALAXY SCIENCE FICTION. With Eve Wulff he ed 2 anthologies drawn from the magazine: *The First World of If* (anth **1957**) and *The Second World of If* (anth **1958**). [MJE]

QUINN PUBLISHING CO. ◊ IF.

QUINTET Film (1979). Lion's Gate/20th Century-Fox. Dir Robert Altman, starring Paul Newman, Bibi Andersson, Vittorio Gassman, Fernando Rey, Brigitte Fossey, Nina Van Pallandt, David Langton. Screenplay Frank Barhydt, Altman, Patricia Resnick, from a story by Altman, Lionel Chetwynd, Resnick. 118 mins. Colour.

This strange film, crucified on release, is perhaps better than the then-consensus suggested. Newman is the seal-hunter in an (apparently) post-HOLOCAUST frozen future, a new Ice Age, who with his pregnant wife joins a dying but still crowded city, where corpses are left in the snow for the dogs to eat, where nobody is born any more, and where anomie is held at bay only by obsessive playing of the game Quintet. This is played either on a board or in real life; in the latter case 5 people must be killed: only 1 will survive. Newman's wife (Fossey) is accidentally killed during a game attack (along with Earth's last foetus), and Newman vengefully joins the game, wins, killing his new lover (Andersson) in the process, and vanishes back into the snow. The obvious reading is that of the still vigorous, romantic hero destroying a corrupt society. Another plausible reading is that the death-focused game is all the real life that is left, and that the hero's despising it is itself a sterile act of turning away: the hero as lost fool. The imagery is strong, the pace glacial and the theme overintellectualized; the deliberately international cast sounds most of the time very uncomfortable with English (though the very alienation that suggests is appropriate to the story). *Q* bores the watcher, yet lingers for years in the mind. [PN]

RABELAIS, FRANÇOIS (?1494-1553) French monk, doctor, priest and writer. The various manuscripts now generally published as *Gargantua and Pantagruel* (**1532-52** plus a posthumous text of dubious authenticity **1564**; many trans, of which the best known is that by Sir Thomas Urquhart – first 2 books **1653** UK, 3rd book **1693** UK – and Peter Le Motteux – 4th and 5th books **1694** UK) form an immense, exuberant, linguistically inventive SATIRE with most of medieval Christendom the target. The giants of the title are enormous both physically and in their joyous gusto. In the *Fourth Book* (**1552**) of the sequence, ISLANDS exemplary of various aspects of society are visited – including the island of the Papimanes, description of whose inhabitants involves a radical criticism of the Catholic Church. Darker and more bitter in tone, the *Fifth Book* (**1564**) – which may well have been completed by another hand from FR's first draft – incorporates a section, *The Ringing Island* (**1562**), originally published separately, with the most notable sf imagery of the entire work. The islands of the 4th and 5th books were probably the most sustained invention of other worlds in literature up to that time. The succession of ALIEN societies, often making some kind of satirical comment on our own, complete with all sorts of colourful anthropological detail, has been greatly influential in PROTO SCIENCE FICTION, and its resonances can be sensed even today in the work of writers like Jack VANCE, who, even if not directly influenced by him, continue the FR tradition. [JC/PN]
See also: FRANCE.

RABID Film (1976). Cinepix/Dibar Syndicate/Canadian Film Development Corp. Written/dir David Cronenberg, starring Marilyn Chambers, Joe Silver, Howard Ryshpan, Patricia Gage, Susan Roman. 91 mins. Colour.

In this Canadian film from David CRONENBERG an experimental skin graft on an accident victim (hardcore porn star Marilyn Chambers) turns her into the carrier of a rabies-like disease which induces homici-dal mania in its victims; the disease is spread by means of a phallic, organic syringe which emerges from labia in her armpit and is used to satisfy her new, uncontrollable blood lust. Montreal is soon in the throes of apocalypse, and martial law is established; citizens who cannot produce proof of inoculation are shot by troops and their bodies dumped into garbage trucks. Structured much like *The* PARASITE MURDERS (1974; vt *They Came from Within*; vt *Shivers*), this is more smoothly directed but perhaps less intense, and by Cronenberg's standards is a conventional exploitation picture – though from anybody else this medical/Freudian HORROR movie, with its gender-bending, penis-wielding killer woman, would have seemed bizarre indeed. [PN/JB]
See also: CINEMA; MONSTER MOVIES; SEX.

RABKIN, ERIC S(TANLEY) (1946-   ) US sf critic and professor of English Language and Literature, University of Michigan, Ann Arbor. Of the 18 books he has written or edited to 1991, 15 have a direct relevance to sf and fantasy. His critical books are: *The Fantastic in Literature* (**1976**), an academic study in genre definition (including sf), provocative but not always rigorous; *Science Fiction: History, Science, Vision* (**1977**) with Robert SCHOLES, a general introduction to the subject seemingly aimed at the novice, with strong opening and closing sections on the HISTORY OF SF and 10 representative novels, but less impressive intermediate chapters on media, sciences and themes; and *Arthur C. Clarke* (chap **1979**; rev 1980). 2 anthologies ed ESR intended for educational use (◊ SF IN THE CLASSROOM), collecting fantasy and sf stories showing the historical development of those genres, are *Fantastic Worlds: Myths, Tales and Stories* (anth **1979**) and *Science Fiction: A Historical Anthology* (anth **1983**).

ESR's other book publications are anthologies of critical essays: *Bridges to Fantasy* (anth **1982**) ed with George Edgar SLUSSER and Scholes; *The End of the World* (anth **1983**) ed with Martin H. GREENBERG and

Joseph D. OLANDER; *Co-Ordinates: Placing Science Fiction and Fantasy* (anth **1983**) ed with Slusser and Scholes; *No Place Else: Explorations in Utopian and Dystopian Fiction* (anth **1983**) ed with Greenberg and Olander; *Shadows of the Magic Lamp: Fantasy and Science Fiction in Film* (anth **1985**) ed with Slusser; *Hard Science Fiction* (anth **1986**) ed with Slusser; *Storm Warnings: Science Fiction Confronts the Future* (anth **1987**) ed with Slusser and Colin GREENLAND; *Intersections: Fantasy and Science Fiction* (anth **1987**) ed with Slusser; *Aliens: The Anthropology of Science Fiction* (anth **1987**) ed with Slusser; *Mindscapes: The Geographies of Imagined Worlds* (anth **1989**) ed with Slusser. Further such anthologies, part of the now-formidable academic publishing industry related to sf, are projected. [PN]
See also: ANTHROPOLOGY; CINEMA; CRITICAL AND HISTORICAL WORKS ABOUT SF.

RACIAL CONFLICT ◊ POLITICS.

RACKHAM, JOHN ◊ John T. PHILLIFENT.

RADAR MEN FROM THE MOON ◊ COMMANDO CODY – SKY MARSHAL OF THE UNIVERSE.

RADCLIFFE, (HENRY) GARNETT (1899-   ) UK writer of occasional sf, including the title novella of *The Return of the Ceteosaurus, and Other Tales* (coll **1926**), which pits a huge saurian against a DEATH RAY. *The Great Orme Terror* (**1934**) is a detective novel whose solution involves ROBOTS. The task of the heroine of *The Lady from Venus* (**1947**) is to acquire Earth eggs for use back home as a form of currency. [JC]

RADIATION ◊ HOLOCAUST AND AFTER; MUTANTS; NUCLEAR POWER; SUN; WEAPONS.

RADIO 1. Radio in the USA Fantastic thrillers, incorporating sf and supernatural elements alternately, were fairly common in the USA all through the "Golden Age" of radio (usually considered 1930-50), but "hardcore" sf was rarer.

As early as 1929, Carlton E. Morse (1900-   ) in San Francisco wrote and produced closed-end serials (a single story, from which the characters did not continue indefinitely) which involved sf concepts. Amid ancient jungle temples, Morse rationalized mysticism into science in *The Cobra King Strikes Back* and *Land of the Living Dead*. The same titles and scripts were reprised in the 1945 series **Adventures by Morse**. Similar themes were developed with more sophistication by Morse in **I Love a Mystery**, 1939-45 (NBC, then CBS), and new productions repeating the scripts, 1949-52 (Mutual). *Temple of Vampires* had heroes Jack, Doc and Reggie facing human vampires and gigantic mutant bats. Two other **I Love a Mystery** episodes, *The Stairway to the Sun* and *The Hermit of San Felipe Atabapo*, concerned the same lost plateau in South America, where dwelled prehistoric monsters and a race of supermen who controlled world destiny. More celebrated for his literate domestic serial *One Man's Family*, Morse was also radio's foremost adventure writer, similar (and comparable) to H. Rider HAGGARD and Arthur Conan DOYLE. Much

of his work has survived, thanks to private collectors, and has been re-released on record.

Children's programming was deeply involved with sf. BUCK ROGERS IN THE 25TH CENTURY was probably the first "hardcore" sf series on radio, beginning in 1932 (CBS). (It was only the second important afternoon adventure serial of any kind, its predecessor being **Little Orphan Annie**.) Based on the comic strip by Phil NOWLAN and Dick CALKINS, it was written partly by Calkins, but for the most part by radio producer Jack Johnstone. The stories were far from silly or trivial, and made a good job of presenting such basic ideas as time and space travel to a youthful audience. Various revivals carried the **Buck Rogers** title through to 1946 on radio. Other series of shorter duration were FLASH GORDON, **Brad Steele – Ace of Space**, SPACE PATROL and **Space Cadet** (the last two being original radio shows based on established tv favorites in the early 1950s: ◊ TOM CORBETT, SPACE CADET).

SUPERMAN was an sf character, created by Jerry SIEGEL and Joe Shuster in their comic strip, but on radio (1940-52) the series generally dealt with crime and mystery. Some sf appeared when the Man of Steel ventured to the planet Utopia, or when menaced by Kryptonite. Supporting characters included guest stars Batman and Robin.

Other juvenile serials had **Jack Armstrong, the All-American Boy** (1933-51) experimenting with Uranium-235 in 1939; **Captain Midnight** (1938-50), the mysterious aviator, encountering flying saucers (◊ UFOS) in 1949; and **Tom Mix** (1933-50), the Western movie star (impersonated on radio usually by Curley Bradley), constantly facing mysteries with a supernatural and superscience atmosphere. (The same actor and theme were used in **Curley Bradley's Trail of Mystery**, written and prod Jim HARMON in 1976 for syndication.)

Horror stories, in half-hour anthologies, appeared in the 1930s. Such series were mostly supernatural in content, but sf occasionally appeared. **Lights Out** began in 1938 (NBC), written by Willis Cooper, later by Arch Oboler. Oboler's tale of an ordinary chicken's heart, stimulated by growth hormones to engulf the entire world, is one of the most famous single radio plays of any kind. Other horror anthologies included **Witch's Tale** by Alonzo Deen Cole, **Quiet Please** by Willis Cooper, and **Hermit's Cave** by various authors.

A general drama anthology, **Mercury Theater on the Air**, was begun by its producer-star Orson Welles (1915-1985) in 1938 (CBS). One of its earliest broadcasts, WAR OF THE WORLDS, adapted H.G. WELLS's novel in the form of a contemporary on-the-spot newscast. Thousands of listeners were thrown into a state of panic, believing Mars was invading the Earth. The resulting havoc undoubtedly made this sf play the most famous radio broadcast of all time. The **Mercury** series also did memorable versions of *Frankenstein* (**1818**; rev 1831) by Mary SHELLEY and *Dracula* (**1897**) by Bram Stoker (1847-1912).

Before leaving for the movies and his classic *Citizen Kane* (1941), Welles also starred in **The Shadow** in 1937-8. The series had begun in 1931 and until 1954 often presented sf in charmingly lurid pulp fashion, with its mysterious hero who could "cloud men's minds" by hypnosis (thus becoming invisible), facing mad scientists who could control volcanoes, dead bodies, even light and dark. Rival fantasy heroes included **The Avenger** (almost an exact copy), **Peter Quill**, a weird, benevolent, hunchbacked scientist, and the fearless shipmates of **Latitude Zero**.

Near the end of major night-time programming on radio in 1949, sf came into its own in an anthology of modern sf, **Dimension X** (later vt **X Minus 1**). This NBC programme had well presented versions of Bradbury's **Martian Chronicles** stories, Robert A. HEINLEIN's "Requiem" (written 1940), and many other celebrated sf stories, intermittently until 1957. Although sf continued through the 1970s to be presented experimentally (and only occasionally) on culture-oriented FM stations, and on the **CBS Radio Mystery Theater** (the first major network revival of drama, beginning 1973), **X Minus 1** still stands as one of the finest showcases for sf in any dramatic medium.   [JH]

2. Radio in the UK The decreasing importance of US radio as a medium for dramatized sf (and drama generally) is presumably due to the death of network radio; the situation is different in the UK, where the BBC continues to broadcast across the whole country, and is not dependent on income from advertising. Few FM stations anywhere have the budget for drama productions.

Sf has been broadcast by the BBC since the 1930s; indeed, radio is such a suitable medium for sf that it is hard to find a celebrated sf author whose work has not been transmitted. Sf work by writers as various as H.G. WELLS, John CHRISTOPHER and Brian W. ALDISS has regularly been broadcast as readings (sometimes by the authors themselves) or dramatizations (as single plays or as serials). Sf programmes have been aimed at all ages. For example, a typical Monday in 1953 would offer one of Angus MacVicar's LOST PLANET stories on the 5pm Children's Hour, and at 7.30pm an episode of the fantastically successful **Journey into Space** serial would be transmitted for the 7- to 70-year-olds.

Journey into Space was written and prod for radio by Charles CHILTON, already well known to youngsters as creator of the popular Western **Riders-of-the-Range** series, which appeared on radio and in the BOYS' PAPER *Eagle*. **Journey into Space** ran only 1953-5, with 3 serialized stories comprising 54 episodes in all, but it enthralled a generation for whom landing on the Moon was still a far-fetched fantasy. The 3 stories were set on the MOON in 1965 and on MARS in 1971 and 1973, and featured the adventures of the Scots pilot Jet Morgan and his crew, Cockney Lemmy Barnet, Australian Stephen Mitchell and US Dr Matthews. High points were the meeting with a

malevolent ALIEN civilization shortly after the first Moon landing, the foiling of a Martian INVASION, TIME TRAVEL, mass hypnosis and flying saucers. By 1955 the programme reached 5 million listeners, deservedly the largest UK radio audience ever, no previous sf radio drama having equalled it for narrative vigour. The programmes were sold to 58 countries; the adventures were novelized by Chilton as *Journey Into Space* * (**1954**), *The Red Planet* * (**1956**) and *The World in Peril* * (**1960**); he also scripted a further **Jet Morgan** adventure for a comic strip in *Express Weekly* (1956-7).

Another well remembered sf radio serial was **Dan Dare**, broadcast for several years from 1953 by the English-language service of Radio Luxembourg in weekly 15min episodes. The programme was written and produced by people quite unconnected with the staff of Frank HAMPSON's comic strip DAN DARE – PILOT OF THE FUTURE; although it used the same characters and situations, it was in a quite different style. While unsophisticated SPACE OPERA as sf, it was thoroughly successful as juvenile high adventure.

As radio lost its audience to tv in the late 1950s, so too did radio sf lose its mass appeal. Never again would an sf series reach as wide an audience as the above two programmes. In the 1970s, however, a number of breakthrough productions appeared. The BBC dramatized Isaac ASIMOV's **Foundation** series (**1951-3**) in 6 parts, and newly emerging local stations experimented with the genre: disc-jockey and comedian Kenny Everett's **Captain Kremmen** gained a cult following on London's Capital Radio, with a subsequent degree of multimedia success; Manchester's Piccadilly Radio helped launch the career of Stephen GALLAGHER with the 6-part serial *The Last Rose of Summer* (1978).

But it took the stimulus of the visual media to prompt a serious reconsideration of the genre's merits. In the wake of the film STAR WARS (1977) came a mini-boom in radio sf that lasted into the 1980s: **Saturday Night Theatre** presented dramatizations of novels by H.G. Wells, Arthur C. Clarke, John Wyndham and Ray BRADBURY, and also brought about a belated revival of **Journey into Space** in the singleton play *The Return from Mars*; James FOLLETT contributed the major serials *Earth Search* and *Earth Search II*; and Douglas ADAMS's HITCH HIKER'S GUIDE TO THE GALAXY became the biggest radio attraction for a whole generation, each repeat broadcast bringing in a larger audience and creating an enormous market for book, record, tape and tv spin-offs.

Despite its success, the BBC failed to capitalize on *Hitch Hiker*, although its influence held through the 1980s in a string of humorous sf series such as *Nineteen Ninety-four* and adaptations of the Harry HARRISON novels *Bill, the Galactic Hero* (**1965**) and *Star Smashers of the Galaxy Rangers* (**1973**). The most impressive drama of the decade came in single plays by Tanith LEE, Stephen Gallagher and Wally K. Daly. Charles Chilton made another worthy attempt to revive **Journey into Space** with 2 series of **Space Force**, but his efforts suffered from unsympathetic scheduling.

The start of the 1990s brought mixed prospects. The launch of the BBC's newest network, Radio 5, promised serious programming for a younger audience: genre material so far presented (dramatizations of works by Alan GARNER, Ray Bradbury and Nicholas FISK) is pleasing in quantity if poor in production. In 1991 Radio 5 broadcast Orson Welles's original 1938 **Mercury Theater on the Air** production of WAR OF THE WORLDS. Also in that year Radio 4 presented a season of plays adapting well known sf works, from the good, such as Daniel KEYES's *Flowers for Algernon* (1959; exp **1966**), to the poor, such as Snoo WILSON's *Spaceache* (**1984**), with much else in between. Meanwhile, the popular repeats on Radio 5 of rediscovered **Journey into Space** episodes showed that, despite technical advances, the cause of radio sf had barely advanced since the Golden Age of the 1960s.

[ABP/PhN]

RADIO COMUNICATION ◊ COMMUNICATION.

RADON (vt, outside Japan, *Rodan*) Film (1956). Toho. Dir Inoshiro Honda, starring Kenji Sahara, Yumi Shirkawa, Akihiko Hirata. Screenplay Takeshi Kimura, Takeo Murata, based on a story by Takashi Kuronomura. 79 mins. Colour.

This film, the first Japanese MONSTER MOVIE in colour, is from the same team that produced GOJIRA (vt *Godzilla*). A giant pterodactyl hatches in a mine (and eats giant dragonfly larvae, in the film's best scene); it is joined by a second flying reptile; they terrorize Japan then perish in a volcano. The spectacular effects are by Eiji Tsuburaya and his team. The US version added a voice-over written by David DUNCAN. Radon's second appearance was in *Kaiju Daisenso* (1965; vt *Invasion of Astro-Monster*; vt *Battle of the Astros*; vt *Monster Zero*; vt *Invasion of Planet X*) and his third in *Ghidorah Sandai Kaiju Chikyu Saidai No Kessan* (1965; vt *Chikyu Saidai No Kessan*; vt *Ghidrah the Three-Headed Monster*). His swansong, where he performed alongside 10 other major Toho monsters, was in *Kaiju Soshingeki* (1968; vt *Destroy All Monsters*; vt *Operation Monsterland*; vt *The March of the Monsters*). (For more on these sequels ◊ GOJIRA.) [PN]

RAES, HUGO [r] ◊ BENELUX.

RAFFILL, STEWART [r] ◊ *The* ICE PIRATES; *The* PHILADELPHIA EXPERIMENT.

RAINES, THERON (1927-) US lawyer and writer in whose sf novel, *The Singing: A Fable about What Makes us Human* (**1988**), a team of Martians crashes its UFO into the Guggenheim Museum in New York, where one of them, according to plan, meets and impregnates the human girl through whose eyes the tale is told. Both sides get what they need: for Mars new blood, and for the Earth unsubtle flattery of our tough and obdurate human stock. One senses that the author thought his storyline possessed some originality, though his concerns, after the fashion of many non-genre writers using sf instruments, are

mainly didactic. [JC]

R.A.K. ◊ Monsignor Ronald A. KNOX.

RAMSEY, MILTON WORTH (?1848-1906) US writer who – although he self-published his sf novels – was of some interest. In *Six Thousand Years Hence* (**1891**) a visiting planet drags the protagonist's city into space, where he and his colleagues are able to view several other civilizations, including a complex advanced culture within the Sun, and return centuries hence to a tamed high-tech Earth, where they die older than Methuselah. *The Austral Globe* (**1892**) and *Two Billions of Miles, or The Story of a Trip Through the Solar System* (**1900**) are similar in viewpoint but less engaging. [JC]

RAND, AYN (1905-1982) Russian-born US writer whose Objectivist philosophy, as expounded in most of her work, was influential during the 1950s among college students, who were perhaps attracted by her instructions to heed one's self-interest, to abjure altruism, and to maximize the SUPERMAN potential within each of us. Her first and better sf novel, *Anthem* (**1938** UK; cut 1946 US), is a DYSTOPIA set after a devastating war. Individualism has been eliminated, along with the concept of the person, but the protagonist discovers his identity while escaping with a beautiful woman to the forest, where he christens himself Prometheus. *The Fountainhead* (**1943**) is a MAINSTREAM novel advancing AR's vision of things. In *Atlas Shrugged* (**1957**), which is sf, John Galt (AR's mouthpiece) and his Objectivist colleagues abandon an increasingly socialistic USA and retreat to the mountains as civilization crumbles, prepared to return only when they will be able to rebuild along the lines of Objectivist philosophy. AR's influence lessened over the years. *Two Girls, Fat and Thin* (**1991**) by Mary Gaitskell systematically caricatures AR and her work. [JC]

See also: ECONOMICS; LIBERTARIAN SF; POLITICS; SOCIAL DARWINISM; SOCIOLOGY; WOMEN SF WRITERS.

RANDALL, MARTA (1948-) US writer and editor who has taught in several sf writing workshops and served in the SCIENCE FICTION WRITERS OF AMERICA as vice-president 1981-2 and president 1982-4. She began publishing sf with "Smack Run" in *New Worlds 5* (anth **1973** ed Michael MOORCOCK) as by Marta Bergstresser; the surname, her first husband's, was used only on this one occasion. Her stories since then have not been frequent, but are almost always of high quality, tightly and densely written, even epigrammatic at points, and generally impart elements of FEMINIST discourse, with unbemused clarity of effect, to genre material. The intense force of a late tale like "Lapidary Nights" (1987) derives at least in part – though no "didactic" argument occupies the foreground – from its thorough assimilation of a feminist agenda.

MR's first and perhaps most successful novel, *Islands* (**1976**; rev 1980), movingly depicts the life of a mortal woman in an age when IMMORTALITY is medically achievable for all but a few. To cope with her world she plunges into the study of archaeology, and makes a discovery which enables her to transcend her corporeal life. In *A City in the North* (1976) an ALIEN species self-destructs in a morally dubious response to the colonizing presence on their planet of the human race. The **Kennerin** or **Newhome** sequence – *Journey* (1978) and *Dangerous Games* (1980) – also treats its colony-world setting with some ambivalence, for the Kennerin family's decision to create a UTOPIA on the planet they own has complex consequences, some of them relating to ECOLOGY. *The Sword of Winter* (1983), like some of her later short fiction, is fantasy, though with PLANETARY-ROMANCE features; and *Those who Favor Fire* (1984) is a near-future DYSTOPIA set in an Apocalypse-prone California much like today's. With Robert SILVERBERG, MR edited 2 vols of the ongoing **New Dimensions** sequence, *New Dimensions 11* (anth 1980) and *#12* (anth 1981); and was responsible solo for *The Nebula Awards 19* (anth 1984). In the later 1980s she was less active as a writer, concentrating at least in part on the construction of "interactive time-travel games" (◊ GAME-WORLDS) for the California State Department of Mental Health; but her fiction, when it appeared, remained vividly alive. [JC]

See also: ISLANDS.

RANDALL, NEIL [r] ◊ Bill FAWCETT.

RANDALL, ROBERT Pseudonym used on collaborative stories – about 19 in all (1956-8) – by Robert SILVERBERG and Randall GARRETT; Silverberg was very young at the time. The most notable were the **Nidorian** series, originally published in *ASF*, dealing with the effects of human contact on an alien race; they were published in book form as *The Shrouded Planet* (fixup 1957) and *The Dawning Light* (1957 *ASF*; 1959). [BS]

RANDLE, KEVIN D. (1949-) US writer who served in the Army as a helicopter pilot in Vietnam 1968-9 and in the Air Force as an Intelligence Officer 1976-86. He began publishing sf with "Future War" for *Combat Illustrated* in 1978, but became an active writer only in the 1980s, beginning 2 sequences in 1986: the **Seeds of War** books, all with Robert Cornett – *Seeds of War* (1988), *The Aldebaran Campaign* (1988) and *The Aquarian Attack* (1989) – and the **Remember!** books, also with Cornett: *Remember the Alamo!* (1986), *Remember Gettysburg!* (1988) and *Remember Little Big Horn!* (1990). The first series is an unremarkable example of military sf, though told with some verve; the second is a more exhilarating TIME-TRAVEL sequence, in which veterans are enlisted to travel to famous battles, where they must make sure that events take their proper course. The **Jefferson's War** sequence – *The Galactic Silver Star* (1990), *The Price of Command* (1990), *The Lost Colony* (1991), *The January Platoon* (1991), *Death of a Regiment* (1991) and *Chain of Command* (1992) – is again military sf, carrying members of the United States Space Infantry into various tight corners. The **Global War** sequence began with *Dawn of Conflict* (1991); the **Star Precinct** sequence, with Richard Driscoll, began with *Star*

Precinct (1992) and *Star Precinct #2: Mind Slayer* (1992). [JC]

Other works: *Once upon a Murder* ∗ (1987) with Robert J(oseph) Randisi (1951-), a game tie; 3 nonfiction UFO books, *The October Scenario* (1988), *The UFO Casebook* (1989) and *UFO Crash at Roswell* (1991) with Don Schmitt.

RANDOM, ALEX ◊ Donald Sydney ROWLAND.

RANK, HEINER [r] ◊ GERMANY.

RANKIN, ROBERT (FLEMING) (1949-) UK writer who began writing his highly idiosyncratic sf novels with the **Brentford** sequence: *The Antipope* (1981), *The Brentford Triangle* (1983) and *East of Ealing* (1984), assembled as *The Brentford Trilogy* (omni 1988), plus *The Sprouts of Wrath* (1988). In the first volume, two layabouts and their friends challenge Forces from the Beyond ranging from an undead sorcerer to an alien invasion fleet. In later volumes the series satirizes CLICHÉS taken in equal measure from horror, sf and fantasy, setting them off against the thoroughly down-to-earth London suburb of Brentford. In the end humanity is (apparently) destroyed. RR's **Armageddon** series – *Armageddon: The Musical* (1990), *They Came and Ate Us: Armageddon II: The B-Movie* (1991) and *The Suburban Book of the Dead: Armageddon III: The Remake* (1992) – features a time-travelling Elvis Presley and is based on the premise that the whole of human history has been stage-managed for transmission as an extraterrestrial soap opera. [NT]

See also: COSMOLOGY; HUMOUR.

RANKINE, JOHN ◊ Douglas R. MASON.

RANSOM, BILL (1945-) US writer who has worked as a medic and as a firefighter. His early writing was poetry, with several volumes released from *Finding True North & Critter* (coll 1974 chap) onward. He began publishing sf with "Songs of a Sentient Flute" for *ASF* in 1979 as by Frank Herbert, a story which eventually became part of *Medea: Harlan's World* ∗ (anth 1985) ed Harlan ELLISON. BR is best known for the **Pandora Trilogy** with Frank HERBERT (*whom see for details*): *The Jesus Incident* (1979), *The Lazarus Effect* (1983) and *The Ascension Factor* (1988). His first solo novel, *Jaguar* (fixup 1990), is also of interest for its depiction of the physically, psychologically and morally complex dream-driven pattern of connections between Earth and another planet, each planet containing two maturing adolescents whose sleep disorders allow them to make journeys between the worlds. The Jaguar – a disturbed Vietnam vet who likewise roams the dreamways – must be halted before he disrupts the fragile tissues of reality. Slightly overweighted for the adventure-sf idiom in which it is told, *Jaguar* is all the same an intriguing attempt to say more than could easily be said. [JC]

See also: MESSIAHS.

RANZETTA, LUAN (? -?) UK writer (probably pseudonymous) whose routine sf adventures were *The Uncharted Planet* (1961) as V. Ranzetta, *The Maru Invasion* (1962), *The World in Reverse* (1962), *The Night* *of the Death Rain* (**1963**) and *The Yellow Inferno* (**1964**). [JC]

RAOS, PREDRAG [r] ◊ YUGOSLAVIA.

RAPHAEL, RICK (1919-   ) US writer and journalist who began publishing sf with "A Filbert is a Nut" for *ASF* in 1959 and established a considerable reputation in the field with a comparatively small output of about 10 stories, most of them assembled in *The Thirst Quenchers* (coll **1965** UK) and *Code Three* (fixup **1966**). The first contains 4 good stories, the best of which is the title story about professionals in a world where water is scarce, their job being its proper allocation. *Code Three* describes the way of life of the police who patrol the superhighways of the future in enormously complex vehicles made to cope with the huge speeds and corresponding irresponsibility on the roads. RR was at his best when describing, in positive terms, the life of those who must deal professionally with a technological world. [JC]

Other work: *The President Must Die* (**1981**), non-sf near-future thriller.

See also: CRIME AND PUNISHMENT.

RASMUSSEN, ALIS A. (1958-   ) US writer whose first novel, *The Labyrinth Gate* (**1988**), is a tale of considerable interest, delineating a believably matrilineal fantasy world. The **Highroad Trilogy** – *A Passage of Stars* (**1990**), *Revolution's Shore* (**1990**) and *The Price of Ransom* (**1990**) – depicts in a lighter vein the interstellar voyages of its young female protagonist, whose involvement in music is infectiously presented and whose search for a full life keeps the tale moving, albeit through markedly familiar venues; the third volume, which carries the maturing crew back from colonized space towards the old worlds, is the best. AAR seems to be a writer who could easily jump into wider notice. [JC]

RASPAIL, JEAN (1925-   ) French writer, much of whose nonfiction controversially treats the kind of issue explored in the inflammatory *Le camp des saints* (**1973**; trans Norman Shapiro as *The Camp of the Saints* **1975** US), set in a NEAR-FUTURE world in the coils of OVERPOPULATION. When the non-White Third World lays siege to Europe, which should have been armed against the onslaught, civilization perishes. [JC]

RATFANDOM UK fan group of the 1970s, most of whose members later became sf professionals. Based in London, Ratfandom produced some of the most literate, witty and scurrilous FANZINES in that fertile period for UK FANDOM; these included *Big Scab* (1974, 3 issues) ed John BROSNAN, *Macrocosm* (1971-2, 3 issues) ed Robert P. HOLDSTOCK, *Magic Pudding* (1973, 1 issue) ed Malcolm EDWARDS, *Seamonsters* (1978-9, 4 issues) ed Simone Walsh, *Stop Breaking Down* (1976-81, 7 issues) ed Greg Pickersgill, *True Rat* (1973-8, 10 issues) ed Leroy Kettle, and *Wrinkled Shrew* (1974-9, 8 issues) ed Pat and Graham Charnock. Others in the group's orbit, though not Rats, included Christopher PRIEST and Peter NICHOLLS. Ratfandom organized the 1975 UK national CONVENTION, Seacon '75. [RH]

RATHENAU, WALTHER [r] ◊ UTOPIAS.

RATHJEN, CARL H(ENRY) (1909-   ) US writer in various genres from boys' fiction to tales for the "slick" markets. Of sf interest is his contribution to the **Land of the Giants** sequence, *Flight of Fear* * (**1969**). [JC]

RAT SAVIOUR, THE ◊ YUGOSLAVIA.

RAW MEAT ◊ DEATH LINE.

RAY, RENÉ Pseudonym of UK actor and writer Irene Creese (1912-   ), in whose sf novel, *The Strange World of Planet X* * (**1957**), romance becomes mixed with the fourth DIMENSION. It was written to novelize her own tv series, *The* STRANGE WORLD OF PLANET X, although there are differences in plot, which differences are replicated in the 1958 film of the same name. Two of her other novels – *Wraxton Marne* (**1946**) and *Angel Assignment* (**1988**) – are fantasies. [JC]

RAY, ROBERT (1928-   ) Hungarian-born writer, in UK from 1957, who began publishing sf with "Nightmares in Grey" for *New Strand Magazine* in 1962. His sf novels, bleak but otherwise unexceptional, are *No Stars for Us* (**1964**), *The Seedy* (**1969**) and *Metamorphosis* (**1976**). [JC]

RAY BRADBURY THEATRE US tv series (1985-6). Atlantis Films/Wilcox Productions for Home Box Office. Executive prods Michael MacMillan, Larry Wilcox, Ray BRADBURY; prod Seaton McLean; teleplays by Bradbury, based on his own stories. Leading actors included Drew Barrymore, James Coco, Jeff Goldblum, Nick Mancuso, Peter O'Toole, William SHATNER. 6 25min episodes, the first 3 in 1985, the second 3 originally shown together as a 90min special in 1986.

These playlets, introduced a little stiffly by Bradbury, were imaginative adaptations of "Marionettes, Inc." (1949), "The Playground" (1953), "The Crowd" (1943), "The Town Where No One Got Off" (1958), "The Screaming Woman" (1951) and "Banshee" (1984). Only the first could be called sf (it features a neglected wife's husband being replaced by an ANDROID); the rest are dark fantasy. They were among the most successful of many Bradbury dramatizations on tv (winning several awards and good ratings), perhaps because Bradbury dramatized them himself.

Further Bradbury adaptations, intended as part of a new **Ray Bradbury Theatre** package but actually screened in 1988-9 in the UK as part of the **Twist in the Tale** series, were made by Granada TV in the UK. The 4 stories adapted were "The Coffin" (1947), "Punishment without Crime" (1950), "The Small Assassin" (1946) and "There was an Old Woman" (1944). Prod Tom Cotter, they starred among others Cyril Cusack, Roy Kinnear, Dan O'Herlihy and Donald Pleasence. Other programmes for the same package, which was screened in the USA, were made in France and Canada. [PN]

RAYER, FRANCIS G(EORGE) (1921-1981) UK writer and technical journalist who began publishing sf with "Juggernaut" for Link House Publications in 1944. His first sf novel was the unremarkable *Realm of the*

Alien (**1946** chap) as by Chester Delray. His most notable was perhaps *Tomorrow Sometimes Comes* (**1951**), in which the general who has inadvertently caused a nuclear HOLOCAUST awakens from SUSPENDED ANIMATION to save the world from a destructive COMPUTER; this thinking machine gave its name to the **Mens Magna** series, which includes also "Deus Ex Machina" (**1950**), "The Peacemaker" (**1952**), "Ephemeral This City" (**1955**), "Adjustment Period" (**1960**) and "Contact Pattern" (**1961**). FGR was most closely associated with *NW*, and also had several lead novels in the early years of *Authentic*. [JC]

Other works: *Fearful Barrier* (**1950**); *The Star Seekers* (**1953** chap); *The Iron and the Anger* (**1964**); *Cardinal of the Stars* (**1964**; vt *Journey to the Stars* 1964 US).

As editor: *Worlds at War* (anth **1948**), containing stories by FGR and his brother-in-law, E.R. James.

See also: COMPUTERS.

RAY-GUNS ◊ WEAPONS.

RAYMOND, ALEX (1909-1956) US COMIC-strip artist. After graduating from the Grand Central School of Art in New York City, he worked on the strip **Tillie the Toiler**. He soon moved up in the comics world, working for Chic Young on **Blondie** and with Lyman Young on **Tim Tyler's Luck** before being given his own strip, **Secret Agent X-9**; it was during this time that he began to develop his distinctive style. In 1934 he was given the chance to do a new strip, FLASH GORDON, and US cartooning has not been the same since; he was the first demonstrably modern comics illustrator. Although his style at first was characterized by convoluted masses and strong, sweeping lines, by 1936 it had become more precise and controlled. He refined the technique of "feathering" (a series of fine brush-or pen-strokes used in cartooning to create contours) to a degree as yet unexcelled in comic strips. The style was romantic, the protagonists' features impossibly heroic, the settings exotic and fantastic. In 1944, AR joined the US Marines, leaving the strip to Austin Briggs (1909-1973); when he returned in 1946 he created a new strip, not sf, the very popular **Rip Kirby**. AR died in a tragic accident in 1956, at the peak of his career. [JG]

See also: ILLUSTRATION.

RAYMOND, DEREK ◊ Robin COOK.

RAYMOND, E.V. [s] ◊ Raymond Z. GALLUN.

RAYMOND, P.T. ◊ Cornelius SHEA.

RAYON INVISIBLE, LE ◊ PARIS QUI DORT.

READ, [Sir] HERBERT (EDWARD) (1893-1968) UK poet and prolific critic of art, literature and politics; knighted 1953. His only novel, *The Green Child* (**1935**), is a remarkable double UTOPIA in which two visions of ideal human life – one a Latin-American political utopia, the other a mystical, underground realm in which human aspirations are transcended – mirror one another, comprising together a critique and dramatic metaphor of the utopian impulse as a whole. [JC]

READE, PHILIP Pseudonym of an unidentified US writer of dime novels (◊ DIME-NOVEL SF) whose work appeared in STREET & SMITH's *Good News* and *The Nugget Library* in competition to Tousey's **Frank Reade, Jr.** stories (◊ FRANK READE LIBRARY). PR wrote 9 stories about Tom Edison, Jr., no relation to the inventor (◊ EDISONADE); unusual in being plotted (instead of haphazard) in terms of character conflicts, they are the best of the various invention series, containing as well an element of tongue-in-cheek and fantasy. *Tom Edison, Jr.'s Sky-Scraping Trip* (**1891**), *Tom Edison, Jr.'s Sky Courser* (**1891**), *Tom Edison, Jr.'s Prairie-Skimmer Team* (**1891**) and *Tom Edison, Jr.'s Air Frigate* (**1891**) together form an episodic novel describing the scientific feud between Tom and his rogue cousin. The stories are filled with fantastic aircraft, individual flying suits, advanced weapons and air battles. PR's most important story is *Tom Edison, Jr.'s Electric Sea Spider* (**1892**), in which Tom combats the US-educated Chinese mastermind of sea crime, Kiang-Ho of the Golden Belt. The story culminates in an underwater battle between two fantastic submarine vessels. This perhaps marks the first appearance of a FU MANCHU-like villain.

Tom Edison, Jr. stories #10 and #11, *Tom Edison, Jr.'s Air-Ship in Australia* (**1892**) and *Tom Edison, Jr.'s Electric Eagle* (**1892**), were written, on a much lower level, by Henry Livingston Williams (1842-?), a prolific hack editor and author. [EFB]

READERCON SMALL PRESS AWARDS ◊ AWARDS.

READY, WILLIAM B(ERNARD) (1914-1981) Welsh librarian and writer, in the USA from 1948 as professional librarian at several universities, and in Canada from 1966 in the same capacity at McMaster University. His first story, "Barring the Weight" for *Atlantic Monthly* in 1948, was not sf, but several of the tales assembled in *The Great Disciple, and Other Stories* (coll **1951**) are of interest. He was best known, however, for his early study of J.R.R. TOLKIEN, *The Tolkien Relation: A Personal Inquiry* (**1968** US; vt *Understanding Tolkien and the Lord of the Rings* 1969; orig title restored 1981). [JC]

REAL GENIUS Film (1985). Tri-Star/Delphi III. Dir Martha Coolidge, starring Val Kilmer, Gabe Jarret, Michelle Meyrink, William Atherton, Robert Prescott. Screenplay Neal Israel, Pat Proft, Peter Torokvei, based on a story by Israel and Proft. 106 mins. Colour.

Genius students at a college for advanced science are manipulated into designing a high-power laser by their corrupt professor (Atherton), who unknown to them is supplying it to a cold-blooded government agency as a secret weapon. On discovering this, they revenge themselves with a complex practical joke. This was one of several sf "teen" movies of the period (others were MY SCIENCE PROJECT [1985] and WEIRD SCIENCE [1985]), and perhaps the best. Director Coolidge, who is "feminist-influenced", as she cautiously puts it, gives a more realistic flavour than usual to the dialogue, performances and even the science, but much of the film dissolves into routine student-prank sequences. [PN]

See also: CINEMA.

REALITY AND APPEARANCE ◊ CONCEPTUAL BREAK-THROUGH; METAPHYSICS; PERCEPTION.

REAMY, TOM Working name of US writer, movie projectionist and graphic designer Thomas Earl Reamy (1935-1977). He began publishing with "Twilla" for *FSF* in 1974 and, by late 1977 when he died of a heart attack, had become a writer of potential stature in the field, having just won the 1976 JOHN W. CAMPBELL AWARD for Best New Writer (though in fact most of his work must be thought of as fantasy). The tales assembled in *San Diego Lightfoot Sue and Other Stories* (coll **1979**) – the title novelette won a 1976 NEBULA – were notable for the threatening sweetness of their probing of unconscious material, often sexual, though they often ended at a point of healing uplift, occasionally sentimentalized. In his novel *Blind Voices* (**1978**), which shared a common background with "Twilla" and "San Diego Lightfoot Sue", a small Kansas town around 1930 is visited by a travelling circus full of freaks and creatures of legend. The homage to Charles G. FINNEY, Theodore STURGEON and Ray BRADBURY is clearly deliberate; a final explanation of the circus creatures in terms of GENETIC ENGINEERING provides no more than an sf pretext, the book reading as elegiac fantasy. [JC]

Other work: "Sting" in *Six Science Fiction Plays* (anth **1976**) ed Roger ELWOOD.

See also: *The* MAGAZINE OF FANTASY AND SCIENCE FICTION; PSI POWERS.

RE-ANIMATOR Film (1985). Re-Animator Productions/ Empire. Dir Stuart Gordon, starring Jeffrey Combs, Bruce Abbott, Barbara Crampton, David Gale. Screenplay Dennis Paoli, William J. Norris, Gordon, based on "Herbert West – Reanimator" (1922) by H.P. LOVECRAFT. 86 mins. Colour.

In this *Grand Guignol* film Herbert West (Combs), a medical student at Miskatonic University, develops a reagent which restores corpses to life: they become vigorous but brain-damaged zombies. He decapitates an evil professor (Gale) who is envious of his brilliance, resuscitates both head and body, and mayhem ensues. Sponsored by Charles BAND's Empire Pictures, based on an untypical series of sardonic sketches by H.P. Lovecraft, *R-A* is a lively SPLATTER MOVIE featuring the kind of undergraduate humour that assumes it is funny to be disgusting. It very nearly proves the point, not least in a scene involving the sexual activities of the still-living severed head. *R-A* opened up new perspectives in bad-taste movies, and helped introduce the comedy trend that dominated HORROR cinema in the late 1980s.

The sequel was *Bride of Re-Animator* (1989; vt *Re-Animator II*) dir Brian Yuzna, who had produced *R-A*. A lethargic reworking of *R-A*'s bizarre imagery, again starring Combs, Abbott and Gale, with a plot recapitulating parts of *The* BRIDE OF FRANKENSTEIN (1935), it lacks the zest necessary for the desired horror-comic effect and is merely emetic. Yuzna's

SOCIETY (1989) is so much better that the two hardly seem the work of the same director. [PN]

RE-ANIMATOR II ◊ RE-ANIMATOR.

REAVES, J(AMES) MICHAEL (1950-) US writer who has written at least 100 teleplays, most with fantastic elements, for the children's Saturday-morning market, and who began publishing sf stories with "The Breath of Dragons" for *Clarion 3* (anth **1973**) ed Robin Scott WILSON, after attending the previous year's CLARION SCIENCE FICTION WRITERS' WORKSHOP. His first 3 books were published as by J. Michael Reaves, his later books as by Michael Reaves. Much of his work is fantasy, though his first novel, *I, Alien* (**1978**), is adventure sf, and *Darkworld Detective* (coll of linked stories **1982**) characteristically mixes sf, fantasy and detective genres in the story of the quest by a colony planet's only detective for the Dark Lord (a familiar fantasy icon), who is his father. *Hellstar* (**1984**) with Steve PERRY is sf; and *Dome* (**1987**), also with Perry, a post-HOLOCAUST tale set in the eponymous undersea habitat, engagingly tracks its large cast through various crises while, in the background, an AI begins to collaborate with humanity in preparing for the aquatic future. It is never easy to find technical fault with JMR, but at the same time it is hard to discover much individuality beneath the professional surface. [JC]

Other works: *Dragonworld* (**1979**) with Byron PREISS; the **Shattered World** sequence of fantasies comprising *The Shattered World* (**1984**) and *The Burning Realm* (**1988**); *Time Machine 3: Sword of the Samurai* * (**1984**) with Steve Perry; *Street Magic* (**1991**).

RECURSIVE SF Recycling material from the vast and growing storehouse of the already-written has long been a practice of sf writers. Plots and characters constantly reappear throughout sf, usually but not always in the form of sequels written by the author of the original work; venues (like Edgar Rice BURROUGHS's MARS) become universal props; and terms descriptive of devices or circumstances unique to sf (from BEMS to CORPSICLES to partials – Greg BEAR's coinage for autonomous computer-generated partial copies of human personalities) tend, once introduced, to become common parlance. When Robert A. HEINLEIN made reference in *"The Number of the Beast"* (**1980** UK) to characters and situations which appeared in earlier novels by him and other sf writers, he was operating in this traditional manner. But when he introduced into the same book people – writers, editors, fans – who had been involved in sf itself, he did something very different, something which marked his career, and the sf genre within which the book was written, as approaching a late and self-referential phase. Wilson TUCKER so frequently introduced real figures into his stories that such insertions became known for a while as Tuckerisms; but a Tuckerism is a private allusion or joke among friends, and should not be seen as making a binding argument about the relationship between fiction and the world. Heinlein, on the other hand, was writing full-blown recursive sf, a term narrowly defined in Anthony R. LEWIS's *An Annotated Bibliography of Recursive Science Fiction* (**1990** chap) as "science fiction stories that refer to science fiction . . . to authors, fans, collectors, conventions, etc.". More broadly, recursive sf may be defined as stories which treat real people, and the fictional worlds which occupy their dreams, as sharing equivalent degrees of reality. It is, in other words, a technique which may be used to create ALTERNATE WORLDS, usually backward-looking in time, and frequently expressing a powerful nostalgia for pasts in which the visions of early GENRE SF do, in fact, come true.

Novels with recursive elements include Brian W. ALDISS's *Frankenstein Unbound* (**1973**) and *Dracula Unbound* (**1991**), Manly BANISTER's early spoof on sf fandom, *Egoboo: A Fantasy Satire* (**1950** chap), Michael BISHOP's *The Secret Ascension* (**1987**), Anthony BOUCHER's detective novel *Rocket to the Morgue* (**1942**), Fredric BROWN's *Martians, Go Home* (**1955**), Gene DeWEESE's and Robert COULSON's *Now You See It/Him/Them* (**1975**) and *Charles Fort Never Mentioned Wombats* (**1977**), Philip K. DICK's *The Man in the High Castle* (**1962**), David DVORKIN's *Time for Sherlock Holmes* (**1983**), Philip José FARMER's *To Your Scattered Bodies Go* (**1971**) and its sequels, Charles L. HARNESS's *Lurid Dreams* (**1990**), Sharyn McCrumb's farce-mysteries *Bimbos of the Death Sun* (**1987**) and *Zombies of the Gene Pool* (**1992**), Barry N. MALZBERG's *Dwellers of the Deep* (**1970** dos), *Gather in the Hall of the Planets* (**1971** dos, both as by K.M. O'Donnell, a pseudonym which itself homages C.L. MOORE and Henry KUTTNER), and *Herovit's World* (**1973**), Larry NIVEN's and Jerry POURNELLE's *Footfall* (**1985**), Tim POWERS's *The Stress of Her Regard* (**1989**), Christopher PRIEST's *The Space Machine* (**1976**), Mack REYNOLDS's mystery *The Case of the Little Green Men* (**1951**), Rudy RUCKER's *The Hollow Earth* (**1990**), Fred SABERHAGEN's and Roger ZELAZNY's *The Black Throne* (**1990**) and Kurt VONNEGUT Jr's *God Bless You, Mr Rosewater* (**1965**). *Inside the Funhouse* (anth **1992**) ed Michael RESNICK assembles examples of the form, with an introductory essay. [JC]

REDAL, JAVIER [r] ◊ SPAIN.

RED DAWN Film (1984). MGM/United Artists. Dir John Milius, starring Patrick Swayze, C. Thomas Howell, Lea Thompson, Charlie Sheen. Screenplay Kevin Reynolds, Milius. 114 mins. Colour.

Russians nuke US cities and their paratroops, with Cuban and Nicaraguan allies, invade the Midwest. Highschool kids escape into the Colorado mountains, become guerrillas, undergo rites of passage and male bonding, fight brilliantly, mostly die. This incoherent and implausible film gets so sentimental about toughness, like a parody of Robert A. HEINLEIN, that the viewer's sympathy is largely with the homesick Cuban commander. *RD* is symptomatic of the interest in SURVIVALIST fictions during the 1980s. [PN]

RED DWARF UK tv series (1988-   ). A Paul Jackson Production for BBC North West. Prod Ed Bye, Rob Grant, Doug Naylor. Dir Bye. Written Grant, Naylor.

Starring Craig Charles as Lister, Chris Barrie as Rimmer, Danny John-Jules as Cat, Robert Llewellyn (seasons 3 and 4) as Kryten. 4 seasons of 6 30min episodes each (to 1991). Current. Colour.

Probably the best blend of humour and sf on tv since *The* HITCH HIKER'S GUIDE TO THE GALAXY, *RD*, a true situation comedy, rapidly became a cult success. *Red Dwarf* is a very large, very dirty spaceship with only one crew member, a definitively working-class Liverpudlian, Lister, who has been in suspended animation for millions of years. Also present are an irritating hologram, Rimmer, who outranks Lister, a vain humanoid called Cat, descended from Lister's pet cat, an *angst*-ridden computer called Holly and, later, an ANDROID trained to serve, the admirable Kryten. Miracles of sf evocation – time travel, black holes, alternate realities and other such tropes – are performed with considerable wit and style on, one might deduce from the deliberate tackiness of the whole endeavour, a tiny budget. At its radical fringes, UK tv of the 1980s specialized in comedy emphasizing vulgarity, despair, entropy, stupidity and lack of hygiene, and the people behind *RD* have impeccable pedigrees in this field: executive prod Paul Jackson had made the nicely revolting *The Young Ones* and *Filthy, Rich and Catflap*, and Grant and Naylor had been head writers for the politically satirical puppet series *Spitting Image*. Spin-off books as by Grant NAYLOR (Grant and Naylor) are *Red Dwarf: Infinity Welcomes Careful Drivers* * (**1989**) and *Better than Life* * (**1990**). [PN]

REDGROVE, PETER (WILLIAM) (1932-   ) UK poet and novelist, married to Penelope SHUTTLE. His first work of sf interest was "Mr Waterman" for *Paris Review* in 1963; although he contributed occasionally to *NW*, including a fantasy poem later published as *The God-Trap* (**1966** chap), he remains of sf interest mainly for his novels, the first two of which – *The Terrors of Dr Treviles: A Romance* (**1974**) and *The Glass Cottage: A Nautical Romance* (**1976**) – were written in collaboration with Shuttle. Both are FABULATIONS whose venues are rendered unstable through hyperbolic imagery and their authors' taste for holy witchcraft and other transcendental transgressions of the natural order. *The God of Glass* (**1979**) is a tale of the NEAR FUTURE in which a new prophet diseases the world with his message. *The Sleep of the Great Hypnotist* (**1979**) introduces a device which cures ills but also hypnotizes its inventor's daughter into bringing him back to life after death. *The Beekeepers* (**1980**) and its sequel, *The Facilitators, or Mister Hole-in-the-Day* (**1982**), set in an ominous insane asylum where strange experiments are being conducted, marry occult imagery and murk-choked scientism in a complex narrative involving an ambiguous penetration of Bedlam. Primarily a poet, PR writes novels whose plots ride upon deep swells of language-driven meditation, although the tales assembled in *The One who Set Out to Study Fear* (coll **1989**) – perhaps because they are derived from the Brothers Grimm –

display a more forthright story-telling gift.   [JC]

RED PLANET MARS Film (1952). Melaby Pictures/ United Artists. Dir Harry Horner, starring Peter Graves, Andrea King, Marvin Miller. Screenplay John L. Balderston, Anthony Veiller, based on the play *Red Planet* (possibly unpublished and unproduced) by Balderston, John Hoare. 87 mins. B/w.

Two young US scientists, man and wife, pick up tv transmissions apparently from MARS. These messages (confusingly) take two forms. One class, suggesting Mars is the centre of incredible technological breakthroughs, has been faked by an ex-Nazi scientist and is designed to panic the Western World, which it does, though it pleases the evil Russians. The second class (genuine) tells us that Mars is ruled by a "Supreme Authority" who is none other than God himself. This revelation also causes chaos, and there are accusations of fakery, but religion is ultimately justified and Godless communism (the true villain) destroyed: aged revolutionaries overthrow the Soviet Government and restore the monarchy, choosing an Orthodox priest as their new Czar.

RPM is a fascinating (and quite hysterical) product of the Cold War PARANOIA that swept the USA in the early 1950s, and specifically a mirror of the widespread feeling in US society that religious crusades (as led by Billy Graham and others) were a political weapon against communism. Balderston, responsible for the script and the original play, had a distinguished career in genre movies, his screenplays including *Dracula* (1931), BRIDE OF FRANKENSTEIN (1935), MAD LOVE (1935) and *Gaslight* (1944), but this essay in patronizing populism did him no credit. The film flopped.   [PN/JB]

See also: GODS AND DEMONS.

REED, CLIFFORD C(ECIL) (1911-   ) South African-born writer and civil servant, in UK from 1950, who began publishing sf with "Jean-Gene-Jeanne" in *Authentic* in 1954. In *Martian Enterprise* (fixup **1962**) escaped convicts learn slowly how to create a community on a new planet.   [JC]

REED, DAVID V. Pseudonym used by US writer David Vern (1924-   ) for almost all his fiction, mostly for Ray PALMER's magazines, starting with "Where is Roger Davis?" for *AMZ* in 1939. He collaborated with Don WILCOX (who wrote the first of the 2 stories from which it was cobbled together, DVR writing the second) on *The Whispering Gorilla* (1940-43 *Fantastic Adventures*; fixup **1950** UK), about an ape with a man's brain (◊ APES AND CAVEMEN); the book was published as by DVR alone. *Murder in Space* (1944 *AMZ*; **1954**) unconvincingly attempts to combine mystery and sf techniques. DVR was probably the first writer to use the house name Alexander BLADE; he used also the house names Craig ELLIS and Peter HORN and wrote 1 story as Clyde Woodruff.   [JC/PN]

Other work: *The Thing that Made Love* (1943 *Fantastic Adventures* as "The Metal Monster Murders"; **1952?**), a mystery.

REED, ISHMAEL (1938-   ) US writer, poet and playwright who emerged in the 1960s as a central representative of the New Black Aesthetic movement, and a figure controversial to the Black critical establishment from the publication of his first novel, *The Free-Lance Pallbearers* (**1967**), a powerful SATIRE. In this and in books like *Yellow-Back Radio Broke-Down* (**1969**) and *Mumbo Jumbo* (**1972**), whose main characters use Black humour to express their outrage in the face of oppression, he mixed elements of surreal satire and MAGIC-REALIST fantasy into complex plots, calling this distinctive literary method Neo-Hoodooism. Further such tales include *The Last Days of Louisiana Red* (**1974**) and *Flight to Canada* (**1975**). In several of these books grotesquely overelaborated thriller plots carry the burden of the flamboyant text, and similar plots – featuring a bemused detective named **Nance Saturday** – shape his genuine sf novels, *The Terrible Twos* (**1982**) and *The Terrible Threes* (**1989**). In the first of these sad and rather savage NEAR-FUTURE satires the US President is a male model with an IQ of 55; the second is a DYSTOPIAN vision of the Reagan years. Critics have seen IR's use of humour as an attempt to distract attention from important social issues and his suspicion of Black FEMINISTS as less than persuasive; by contrast, Thomas PYNCHON and other authors of contemporary interest have cited IR as an exemplary writer.   [CAJ/JC]

Other works: *Shrovetide in Old New Orleans* (coll **1978**), essays and interviews; *Reckless Eyeballing* (**1986**).

REED, KIT Working name of US writer Lillian Craig Reed (1932-   ), as well known for her work outside sf and fantasy as within; she has also written a horror novel, *Blood Fever* (**1986**) as by Shelley Hyde. She began publishing stories of genre interest with "The Wait" (vt "To Be Taken in a Strange Country") in 1958 for *FSF*, afterwards publishing mainly with that journal. After some non-genre novels, the first being *Mother isn't Dead She's Only Sleeping* (**1961**), KR began to assemble short stories of genre interest in *Mister da V. and Other Stories* (coll **1967** UK), later releasing *The Killer Mice* (coll **1976** UK), *Other Stories And . . . the Attack of the Giant Baby* (coll **1981**) and *Revenge of the Senior Citizens ** Plus: A Short Story Collection* (coll **1986**). It could be said, unkindly, that her stories domesticate the world of Shirley JACKSON; but that would be unduly to deprecate the sharp, clear, self-amused perceptiveness of her best moral fables, often closer to fantasy than sf as they make their uncomfortable points with precision and delicacy. Her first sf novel, *Armed Camps* (**1969** UK), perhaps more conventionally posits a NEAR-FUTURE USA sliding into irretrievable collapse; neither the soldier nor the woman pacifist who share the narrative, nor what they represent, are seen as representing any solution. *Magic Time* (**1980**), less effective because of its chatty plot, treats the USA as analogous to a grotesque theme park, posthumously run by a Disney-like guru in cold storage. *Fort Privilege* (**1985**) more convincingly transforms into moral fable a tale set in an expensive New York apartment building under siege from the innumerable homeless of the great city. Though sometimes her reticence is overpowering, KR at her best is, very quietly, an explosive writer. [JC]

Other works: *Fat* (anth **1974**), stories about obesity, several being sf or fantasy; *George Orwell's 1984* (**1984**), nonfiction.

REED, PETER [s] ◊ John D. MacDONALD.

REED, ROBERT (1956-   ) US writer who began publishing sf with "Mudpuppies" as by Robert Touzalin for *L. Ron Hubbard Presents Writers of the Future* (anth **1986**) ed Algis BUDRYS; the story gained the $5000 grand prize awarded in the WRITERS OF THE FUTURE CONTEST for that year. RR has since gradually become productive in short forms, though he remains best known for his novels, beginning with *The Leeshore* (**1987**), a tale which combines adventure-sf plotting (a pair of twins, the sole humans left on the eponymous water-covered colony planet, must guide a task force in pursuit of the COMPUTER-worshipping zealots who have killed everyone else) with an almost mystical sense for the genius of place, the intricacies of selfhood. *The Hormone Jungle* (**1988**) is set in an entirely different venue, a densely crowded Solar System drawn in CYBERPUNK colours; but a similar attention to the mysterious depths of his distorted characters saves the book from RR's tendency to indulge in a sometimes choking virtuosity. *Black Milk* (**1989**) is set in yet another of sf's familiar 1980s venues, a NEAR-FUTURE world threatened by uncontrolled and secret GENETIC-ENGINEERING experiments instigated by a late and movingly presented version of the inventor/entrepreneur who runs the world (◊ EDISONADE); once again, the expertness of the writing and its knowing exploitation of current scientific speculations are balanced by an underlying quiet sanity about how to depict and to illumine human beings. In *Down the Bright Way* (**1991**) a group of sentient beings searches through an endless string of PARALLEL WORLDS for the old gods – or sentient beings at the start of things – while fending off others intent on using the pathways for darker purposes. In *The Remarkables* (**1992**) a confrontation between the main stream of humanity – sequestrated in densely populated local space – and a lost colony leads to a complexly engaging rite of passage involving representatives of both human streams with the eponymous aliens. RR's course to date has been unusual in that he has avoided sequels in his first 5 novels, none of which share any background material or assumptions whatsoever. Today's sf readers tend to expect a kind of brand identity from authors, and it may be for this reason that RR has not yet achieved any considerable fame. [JC]

See also: ANDROIDS.

REED, VAN House name used for 2 books published by CURTIS WARREN, one by Dennis HUGHES and the other, *Dwellers in Space* (**1953**), by an unknown author. [JC]

REEVE, ARTHUR B(ENJAMIN) (1880-1936) US writer almost exclusively remembered for his **Craig Kennedy,**

Scientific Detective sequence, the early stories being first published 1910-15 in monthly instalments in *Cosmopolitan*. Almost every volume of the series contained one of more sf device, sometimes trivial, sometimes central to the tale. Kennedy himself (◊ EDISONADE) was interminably responsible for developing new forms of weaponry, making medical breakthroughs, forging super-metals and chemicals . . . Though many individual stories showed only minimal displacement into an sf frame, the overall framework was clearly generic, and the individual titles warrant listing: *The Silent Bullet: The Adventures of Craig Kennedy, Scientific Detective* (similar subtitles are ignored below) (coll **1912**; vt *The Black Hand* 1912 UK), *The Poisoned Pen* (coll **1913**), *The Dream Doctor* (coll **1914**), *The War Terror* (coll **1915**; vt *Craig Kennedy, Detective* 1915 UK), *The Gold of the Gods: The Mystery of the Incas Solved by Craig Kennedy – Scientific Detective* (**1915**), *The Exploits of Elaine* (**1915**), *The Social Gangster* (coll **1916**; vt *The Diamond Queen* 1917 UK), *The Ear in the Wall* (**1916**), *The Romance of Elaine* * (**1916**), a film tie, *The Triumph of Elaine* (**1916**), *The Treasure-Train* (coll **1917**), *The Adventuress* (**1917**), *The Panama Plot* (coll **1918**), *The Soul Scar* (**1919**), *The Film Mystery* (**1921**), *Craig Kennedy Listens In* (coll **1923**), *Atavar, the Dream Dancer* (**1924**), *The Fourteen Points* (coll **1925**), *The Boy Scouts' Craig Kennedy* (coll **1925**), *Craig Kennedy on the Farm* (coll **1925**), *The Radio Detective* * (**1926**), a film tie, *Pandora* (**1926**), *The Kidnap Club* (**1932**), *The Clutching Hand* (**1934**), *Enter Craig Kennedy* (**1935**) with Ashley Locke, and *The Stars Scream Murder* (**1936**). Of these titles, the most remarkable was perhaps *Pandora*, in which the evil land of Centrania successfully seduces the USA from her former power by (as E.F. BLEILER remarks) "subsidizing jazz musicians", inventing a synthetic fuel, and causing a stock-market crash. The quick development of a tiny atomic bomb leads to the utter defeat of Centrania. ABR was editorial consultant to SCIENTIFIC DETECTIVE MONTHLY (1930), which printed 1 new **Craig Kennedy** story and reprinted 9 old ones. [JC]

Other works: *Guy Garrick: An Adventure with a Scientific Gunman* (**1914**); *Constance Dunlap, Woman Detective* (**1916**); *The Master Mystery* (**1919**) and *The Mystery Mind* (**1921**), both with John Grey; *The Best Ghost Stories* (anth **1936**).

See also: CRIME AND PUNISHMENT.

REEVES, L(YNETTE) P(AMELA) (1937-   ) UK writer exclusively associated with ROBERT HALE LIMITED, but whose novels, often featuring TIME TRAVEL, rise intermittently above their element: *The Nairn Syndrome* (**1975**), *Time Search* (**1976**), *The Last Days of the Peacemaker* (**1976**), *Harlow's Dimension* (**1977**), *Stone Age Venture* (**1977**), *A Twist in Time* (**1978**) and *If it's Blue, it's Plague* (**1981**). [JC]

REGINALD, ROBERT The pseudonym under which US bibliographer, librarian and publisher Michael Roy Burgess (1948-   ) is best known, and under which (or as R. Reginald) he has published his most important work in the sf field; it is also under this name that he publishes and edits the BORGO PRESS in California, a SMALL PRESS that publishes many monographs on and bibliographical studies of sf, fantasy and horror. As M.R. Burgess or Michael Burgess he has also published fairly widely, his most important sf work under the latter form of his name being *Reference Guide to Science Fiction, Fantasy, and Horror* (**1992**); less frequently used pseudonyms include Boden Clarke, C. Everett Cooper and Lucas Webb. RR has written on himself in *The Work of R. Reginald: An Annotated Bibliography and Guide* (**1985** chap as by Michael Burgess and Jeffrey M. ELLIOT; exp vt *The Work of Robert Reginald: An Annotated Bibliography and Guide* 1992 as by Burgess alone).

The various incarnations of RR's most important publication have intermittently occupied his career through 1992. His first book, *Stella Nova: The Contemporary Science Fiction Authors* (**1970** anon; rev vt *Contemporary Science Fiction Authors, First Edition* 1974 as RR), eventually became the second volume of his magnum opus, *Science Fiction and Fantasy Literature: A Checklist, 1700-1974, with Contemporary Science Fiction Authors II* (**1979**) in 2 vols as RR, and listing over 15,000 titles up to the end of 1974. The long-awaited supplement to this essential reference tool has been broken back down into separate enterprises, with «Science Fiction & Fantasy Literature: A Bibliography, 1975-1991» (**1992**), with Darryl F. MALLETT and Mary Wickizer Burgess, being restricted to an updating of the checklist alone, to which it adds a further 22,000 titles; a biographical volume, building on the original *Stella Nova*, is also projected (◊ BIBLIOGRAPHIES *for further comments*).

Other bibliographical publications of interest include: *Cumulative Paperback Index, 1939-1959: A Comprehensive Bibliographic Guide to 14,000 Mass-Market Paperback Books of 33 Publishers under 69 Imprints* (**1973**) as RR with M.R. Burgess; *Science Fiction & Fantasy Awards* (**1981** chap as RR; much exp vt *Reginald's Science Fiction and Fantasy Awards: A Comprehensive Guide to the Awards and their Winners* 1991 by Daryl F. Mallett with RR); *A Guide to Science Fiction and Fantasy in the Library of Congress Classification Scheme* (**1984** chap; exp 1988) as by Michael Burgess; *The Work of Jeffrey M. Elliot: An Annotated Bibliography & Guide* (**1984** chap) as by Boden Clarke; *The Work of Julian May: An Annotated Bibliography & Guide* (**1985** chap) as by RR with Thaddeus DIKTY; *The Work of George Zebrowski: An Annotated Bibliography & Guide* (**1986** chap; exp 1990) as by RR with Jeffrey M. Elliot; *Mystery and Detective Fiction in the Library of Congress Classification Scheme* (**1987**) as by Michael Burgess; *Western Fiction in the Library of Congress Classification Scheme* (**1988** chap) as by Michael Burgess, with Beverly A. Ryan; and *The Work of William F. Nolan: An Annotated Bibliography & Guide* (**1988** chap) as by Boden Clarke, with Nolan writing as James Hopkins. The individual author bibliographies, part of an ongoing Borgo Press series by several hands, are devotedly thorough and accurate.

Before founding Borgo in 1975, RR founded the short-lived Unicorn & Son, Publishers (which produced *Stella Nova*), and was an associate editor of FORGOTTEN FANTASY (1970-71) and advisory editor of the ARNO PRESS sf reprint series and Arno's subsequent reprints of supernatural, fantasy and LOST WORLD books. Borgo itself began publishing titles in 1976, and by 1992 had released well over 100 titles under its own imprint as well as distributing over 1000 other titles. Though RR became full Librarian at Cal State in 1984, he maintained complete control over the firm, initiating and silently collaborating on many of its bibliographical projects and publishing through it much of his non-bibliographical work, as well as his two novels. *The Attempted Assassination of John F. Kennedy: A Political Fantasy* (**1976** chap as by Lucas Webb; rev vt *If J.F.K. Had Lived: A Political Scenario* 1982 chap as by RR with Jeffrey M. Elliot) is an ALTERNATE-WORLD tale in which monarchies have been retained worldwide and Kennedy is not killed. *Up Your Asteroid!: A Science Fiction Farce* (**1977** chap), as by C. Everett Cooper, is a desultory spoof.

RR also ed several anthologies for Arno Press, all with Douglas MENVILLE: *Ancestral Voices: An Anthology of Early Science Fiction* (anth **1975**; cut 1992), *Ancient Hauntings* (anth **1976**), *Phantasmagoria* (anth **1976**), *R.I.P.: Five Stories of the Supernatural* (anth **1976**), *The Spectre Bridegroom, and Other Horrors* (anth **1976**), *Dreamers of Dreams: An Anthology of Fantasy* (anth **1978**), *King Solomon's Children: Some Parodies of H. Rider Haggard* (anth **1978**), *They: Three Parodies of H. Rider Haggard's She* (anth **1978**) and *Worlds of Never: Three Fantastic Novels* (anth **1978**). Also with Menville, RR wrote two film books: *Things to Come: An Illustrated History of the Science Fiction Film* (**1977**) and, with Mary Wickizer Burgess also collaborating, *Futurevisions: The New Golden Age of the Science Fiction Film* (**1985**). RR remains of central importance to sf as a bibliographer of persistent exactness and enormous energy. [PN/JC]

REHN, JENS [r] ◊ GERMANY.

REID, DESMOND A house name used by at least 30 writers for **Sexton Blake Library** tales, one of which – *The World-Shakers!* (**1960** chap) by Rex Dolpin (◊ Peter SAXON) – was a UFO tale. Another – *Caribbean Crisis* (**1962** chap) by James CAWTHORN and Michael MOORCOCK – was Moorcock's first novel. Other authors of genre interest who used the name included Sydney J. BOUNDS, Jonathan BURKE, Stephen FRANCES, A.A. GLYNN, John LYMINGTON and Wilfred MCNEILLY. [JC]

REIDA, ALVAH (1920-1975) US writer whose sf novel, *Fault Lines* (**1972**) – not to be confused with Kate WILHELM's later novel of the same title – deals apocalyptically with the consequences of a San Andreas Fault earthquake. [JC]

REIN, HAROLD (? -?) US writer in whose extremely grim post-HOLOCAUST novel, *Few Were Left* (**1955**), a suicidal protagonist is trapped with others in the New York subway system after the bomb has dropped. He fails, after several adventures, to escape. [JC]

REINCARNATION The idea of reincarnation exerts a considerable fascination; its fashionability has recently been renewed by hypnotists who claim to facilitate a "regression" of their subjects which allows access to memories of "former lives". Serial reincarnation is one of the standard varieties of IMMORTALITY. In FANTASY the notion is an axiom of the curious subgenre of "transcendental romance" – stories in which love becomes a quasisupernatural force transcending time or death so that lovers may meet in different ages to make repeated attempts to find true happiness. This is the pattern of H. Rider HAGGARD's *She* (**1887**) and its sequels, Edwin Lester ARNOLD's *Phra the Phoenician* (**1890**) and George GRIFFITH's *Valdar the Oft-Born* (**1895**). Arnold's *Lepidus the Centurion* (**1901**) shows one of the more subtle and intelligent uses of the notion. Many romances of reincarnation have also been inspired by the ancient Egyptian methods of preserving the dead, including Haggard's "Smith and the Pharaohs" (**1912**; as title story of *Smith and the Pharaohs and Other Tales* coll **1920**). PSEUDO-SCIENTIFIC rationalizations of the notion often invoke the concept of "race memory"; Haggard bolstered his belief with this idea, deploying it in *The Ancient Allan* (**1920**) and *Allan and the Ice Gods* (**1927**), and Jack LONDON used it in *Before Adam* (**1906**) and *The Star Rover* (**1915**; vt *The Jacket*). The most impressive sf story built on the race-memory premise is John GLOAG's *99%* (**1944**).

Camille FLAMMARION, the first writer to develop the notion of ALIEN beings adapted to LIFE ON OTHER WORLDS, did so mainly in order to support his theory of the immortality of the soul with speculations about possible reincarnations on other worlds. First presented in *Lumen* (**1864**; exp **1887**; trans **1897**), the idea was used also in *Urania* (**1890**) and was copied by Louis Pope GRATACAP in the didactic *The Certainty of a Future Life on Mars* (**1903**).

Hugh KINGSMILL reincarnated Shakespeare in *The Return of William Shakespeare* (**1929**) so that a critical commentary on the works could be put into the Bard's own mouth and bracketed by a satirical comedy. When GENRE SF began to deploy technological methods of reincarnation, the resurrection of great men of the past was a theme used in many stories, including Manly Wade WELLMAN's *Giants from Eternity* (**1939**), Ray BRADBURY's "Forever and the Earth" (**1950**), James BLISH's "A Work of Art" (**1956**), R.A. LAFFERTY's *Past Master* (**1968**), Philip K. DICK's *We Can Build You* (**1972**), Barry N. MALZBERG's *The Remaking of Sigmund Freud* (**1985**) and Dan SIMMONS's *The Fall of Hyperion* (**1990**). Henry J. SLATER's *The Smashed World* (**1952**) features a remarkable version of the Eternal Triangle involving Archimedes, Napoleon and Cleopatra 3000 years in the future. In Anne Rice's *The Mummy, or Ramses the Damned* (**1989**) an immortal Ramses forces the reincarnation of the spirit of Cleopatra into the mummy of that queen, with

disastrous results – not just for Ramses but also for the novel, since the explanation of the "mechanism" of reincarnation is hopelessly fudged.

Reincarnation in sf usually involves the "recording" of personalities for later re-embodiment, sometimes in an ANDROID body. TIME TRAVEL also comes in handy as a means of duplicating individuals. The idea that CLONES might be seen as reincarnations is propounded in such stories as "When You Care, When You Love" (**1962**) by Theodore STURGEON, and in several of the works of John VARLEY clones are used such that in effect individuals can cheat death by living in "serial bodies". MATTER TRANSMISSION is employed as a reincarnating device in such stories as Algis BUDRYS's *Rogue Moon* (**1960**). The natural extravagance of genre sf has occasionally encouraged a blithe disregard for the inconvenience of death; two writers who have sometimes been very casual about incorporating metaphysical or frankly mysterious methods of reincarnation into their scenarios are A.E. VAN VOGT, in such works as *The Book of Ptath* (**1943**; **1947**; vt *Two Hundred Million A.D.*), *The World of Ā* (**1945**; **1948**; vt *The World of Null-A*) and "The Monster" (**1948**; vt "Resurrection"), and Philip José FARMER, most notably in the **Riverworld** series – which stars many notable figures plucked from various eras of Earthly history, and helped to inspire Janet E. MORRIS's **Hell** series of shared-world adventures – but also in *Inside Outside* (**1964**) and *Traitor to the Living* (**1973**).

The particular ideas of reincarnation contained in extant RELIGIONS are sciencefictionalized in various works by Roger ZELAZNY, notably *Lord of Light* (**1967**), whose framework is taken from Hindu MYTHOLOGY, and *Creatures of Light and Darkness* (**1969**), which uses Egyptian mythology. Syd LOGSDON's *A Fond Farewell to Dying* (**1981**) thoughtfully confronts a technology of reincarnation with Hindu beliefs which view it as a blasphemy. An aesthetically satisfying quasireligious "mechanism" for reincarnation is presented in the parapsychological thriller *Death Knell* (**1977**) by C. Terry CLINE. Alien biologies permitting reincarnation, perhaps adaptable to use by humans, are sometimes presented within an explicitly religious framework; Robert SILVERBERG's *Downward to the Earth* (**1970**) is a notable example.

Future societies dramatically transformed by technologies of reincarnation are featured in Robert SHECKLEY's *Immortality, Inc* (**1959**), in which disembodied minds must compete for bodies made redundant by their occupiers for one reason or another, Silverberg's *To Live Again* (**1969**), in which similarly disembodied minds must share living hosts, Robert THURSTON's *Alicia II* (**1978**), which examines the predicament of the "rejects" whose bodies are used to house the reincarnated, Stephen GOLDIN's *The Eternity Brigade* (**1980**), in which the tapes recording trained soldiers for serial reincarnation are bootlegged, with predictable consequences, and Michael BERLYN's *Crystal Phoenix* (**1980**), in which attitudes to death are dramatically and repulsively transformed. In *Gray Matters* (**1971**) by William HJORTSBERG and *Friends Come in Boxes* (**1973**) by Michael G. CONEY minds awaiting re-embodiment are mechanically – and not very happily – stored. Silverberg's "Born with the Dead" (1974), Lucius SHEPARD's *Green Eyes* (**1984**) and Kevin J. ANDERSON's *Resurrection, Inc* (**1988**) all draw some inspiration from the idea of zombies, but develop their hypotheses in strikingly different ways.   [BS]

See also: ESCHATOLOGY; SUSPENDED ANIMATION.

REINSMITH, RICHARD Working name of US writer Richard Rein Smith (1930-   ), who has apparently written many sf novels under various pseudonyms, including the sf adventure *Starbright* (**1983**) as by Damon Castle; further pseudonyms remain unrevealed. As RR he wrote *The Savage Stars* (**1981**) and a **Tarzan** tie, *Tarzan and the Tower of Diamonds* ∗ (**1985**).   [JC]

RELATIVITY ◊ COMMUNICATIONS; FASTER THAN LIGHT; PHYSICS.

RELIGION Familiar DEFINITIONS OF SF imply that there is nothing more alien to its concerns than religion. However, many of the roots of PROTO SCIENCE FICTION are embedded in traditions of speculative fiction closely associated with the religious imagination, and contemporary sf recovered a strong interest in certain mystical and transcendental themes and images when it moved beyond the TABOOS imposed by the PULP MAGAZINES. Modern sf frequently confronts age-old speculative issues associated with METAPHYSICS and theology – partly because science itself has abandoned them. Speculative fiction always tends to go beyond the merely empirical matters with which pragmatic scientists concern themselves; perhaps something called "science" fiction ought not to include metaphysical fiction, but the genre as constituted obviously does.

It was the religious imagination of people such as Giordano Bruno (1548-1600) which first envisioned an infinite Universe filled with habitable worlds, and it was visionaries like Athanasius KIRCHER and Emanuel SWEDENBORG who first journeyed in the imagination to the limits of the Solar System, and beyond. John WILKINS, who first supposed in all seriousness that people might go to the Moon in a flying machine, was a bishop, and so was Francis GODWIN, the author of the satirical cosmic voyage *The Man in the Moone* (**1638**). Other early speculative fictions were attacks upon religious cosmology and religious orthodoxy by freethinkers such as CYRANO DE BERGERAC, VOLTAIRE and, later, Samuel BUTLER. Mary SHELLEY's *Franken-stein* (**1818**) takes its imaginative inspiration from the image of the scientist as usurper of the prerogatives of God. The boldest of all the 19th-century speculative fictions, Camille FLAMMARION's *Lumen* (1864; exp **1887**; trans **1897**), was the result of the astronomer's desperate need to reconcile and fuse his scientific knowledge with his religious faith. J.H. ROSNY aîné, the prolific writer of evolutionary fantasies, also saw

the object of his work as an imaginative revelation of the divinely planned evolutionary schema, and he too wanted to remake theology so that it might be reconciled with modern scientific knowledge – a task later taken up by the heretic Jesuit Pierre Teilhard de Chardin (1881-1955). C.H. HINTON's stories and essays about the fourth DIMENSION were inspired by the notion that a four-dimensional God might be omniscient of everything that has ever or will ever take place in our three-dimensional continuum. Marie CORELLI re-envisaged God as an entity of pure electric force in *A Romance of Two Worlds* (**1886**). John Jacob ASTOR's *A Journey in Other Worlds* (**1894**), Jean DELAIRE's *Around a Distant Star* (**1904**) and John MASTIN's *Through the Sun in an Airship* (**1909**) are among many novels borrowing the literary devices of SCIENTIFIC ROMANCE to dramatize cosmic voyages whose real purpose was to "justify" theological dogmas. Edgar FAWCETT's *The Ghost of Guy Thyrle* (**1895**) does not hesitate to engage its hero in conversation with a messenger from God at the edge of the Universe.

In virtually all late-19th-century and early-20th-century speculative fiction the antagonism of the scientific and religious imaginations – sharpened by controversies regarding Darwinian EVOLUTION, socialism and humanism – is evident, whether the thrust of the narrative is toward reconciliation or conflict. Many of the early UK writers of scientific romance – notably George GRIFFITH, M.P. SHIEL, William Hope HODGSON and J.D. BERESFORD – were the sons of clergymen who converted to free thought and used their fiction to justify and explore the consequences of their decision. Guy THORNE's *When it was Dark* (**1904**) and Shiel's *The Last Miracle* (**1906**) both feature rationalist plots to discredit Christian faith, although the authors take up very different positions in extrapolating the consequences. In Robert Hugh BENSON's *Lord of the World* (**1907**) a humanist socialist woos the world to his cause, but proves to be the Antichrist; its companion-piece, *The Dawn of All* (**1911**), offers an alternative vision of a UTOPIAN future in which people have renounced such heinous heresies as materialism, humanism, socialism and protestantism. Some humanists were equally prepared to turn religious imagery to their own purposes: H.G. WELLS brought a new kind of angel to Earth to observe the sins of mankind in *The Wonderful Visit* (**1895**); his later flirtation with a reconstituted faith – explained in *God the Invisible King* (**1917**) – led him to produce a new Book of Job in *The Undying Fire* (**1919**), and towards the end of his life he rewrote the tale of Noah in *All Aboard for Ararat* (**1940**). A similar interest in "alternative theology" is central to the work of Olaf STAPLEDON, whose *Star Maker* (**1937**) explores a vast cosmic schema, and culminates in a vision of God the Scientist, constantly experimenting with Creation. C.S. LEWIS co-opted the methods and ideas of scientific romance for his theological fantasies *Out of the Silent Planet* (**1938**), *Perelandra* (**1943**) and *The Great*

Divorce (**1945** chap). In France André MAUROIS confronted a SCIENTIST with proof of the existence of the soul in *Le peseur d'âmes* (**1931**; trans as *The Weigher of Souls* **1931**); and the Austrian Franz WERFEL wrote *Stern der Ungeborenen* (**1946**; trans as *Star of the Unborn* **1946**), a bizarre futuristic SATIRE promiscuously combining ideas from the scientific and religious imaginations. The dedicatedly sceptical philosopher Bertrand RUSSELL produced the VOLTAIRE-esque *contes philosophiques* "Zahatopolk" (**1954**) and "Faith and Mountains" (**1954**), two vitriolically scathing treatments of organized religion and faddish cults. This long tradition of theological and antitheological speculative fiction extends into recent times in such works as John CAMERON's *The Astrologer* (**1972**), Romain GARY's *The Gasp* (**1973**), E.E.Y. Hales's *Chariot of Fire* (**1977**), Bernard MALAMUD's *God's Grace* (**1982**), Jeremy LEVEN's *Satan* (**1982**), Theodore STURGEON's *Godbody* (**1986**) and James K. MORROW's *Only Begotten Daughter* (**1990**).

If speculative fiction in the MAINSTREAM has always been as much concerned with the visions of the religious imagination as with those of the scientific imagination, within GENRE SF religious issues were for many years excluded by editorial TABOO. One pulp subgenre to be exempted was the "Shaggy God" story, often dealing with ADAM AND EVE; writers mostly played safe by scrupulously avoiding the New Testament. Godlike aliens were treated with circumspection, Clifford D. SIMAK's *The Creator* (**1935**; **1946**) finding a home only in the semiprofessional MARVEL TALES. The future evolution of institutionalized religion was considered in Robert A. HEINLEIN's "If This Goes On . . ." (**1940**), in which a tyrannical state of the future operates through an Established Church headed by a bigoted fanatic – a recurrent image in sf. Heinlein's *Sixth Column* (**1941** as by Anson MacDonald; **1949**; vt *The Day After Tomorrow*), based on a John W. CAMPBELL Jr story whose original version was ultimately published as "All" (**1976**), shows the USA overthrowing Asian conquerors by means of a fake religious cult – another recurrent image. Fritz LEIBER amalgamated the two ideas in *Gather, Darkness!* (**1943**; **1950**), in which the tyrannical rule of a state religion is overthrown by a cult masquerading as witches and warlocks. ROBOTS sceptical of what humans tell them about Earth construct a new faith for themselves in Isaac ASIMOV's "Reason" (**1941**). But all these religions were mere superstructure: the theological issues remained untouched. In the pages of UNKNOWN, Campbell's authors used angels, GODS AND DEMONS with gay abandon, but such stories as Henry KUTTNER's "The Misguided Halo" (**1939**) and Cleve CARTMILL's "Prelude to Armageddon" (**1942**) were conscientiously playful in dealing with the apparatus of the Christian mythos. Only A.E. VAN VOGT's *The Book of Ptath* (**1943**; **1947** vt *Two Hundred Million A.D.*) came close to serious speculation about metaphysics.

After WWII there was a spectacular boom in sf stories which, without any trepidation whatever, cut straight to the heart of theological matters. The space travellers in Ray BRADBURY's "The Man" (**1949**) follow Jesus on his interplanetary mission of salvation, while the priests in "In this Sign . . ." (**1951**; vt "The Fire Balloons") encounter sinless beings on Mars. A robot in Anthony BOUCHER's "The Quest for St Aquin" (**1951**) emulates St Thomas Aquinas in logically deducing the existence of God, thus justifying its own – and the author's – adherence to the Catholic faith. In Paul L. Payne's "Fool's Errand" (**1952**) a Jew finds a cross in the sands of Mars. In James BLISH's classic *A Case of Conscience* (**1953**; exp **1958**) a Jesuit interprets the axioms of his faith to infer, heretically in the Manichaean style, that an alien world is the creation of the Devil, and that it must be exorcised. In Lester DEL REY's "For I Am a Jealous People" (**1954**) alien invaders arrive to take possession of the Earth, having made their own covenant with God and become his chosen people. In Arthur C. CLARKE's "The Star" (**1955**) spacefarers discover the wreckage of inhabited worlds which had been destroyed by the nova that shone over Bethlehem. Philip José FARMER's *The Lovers* (**1952**; exp **1961**) features a future Earth whose social mores derive from the "Western Talmud"; its sequel, *A Woman a Day* (**1953**; rev **1960**; vt *The Day of Timestop*; vt *Timestop*), continues an earnest exploration of future religion. Farmer's "The God Business" (**1954**) is a phantasmagoric, pantheistic fantasy whose hero ends up as a deity; and the same opportunity is offered to a conventional Churchman in "Father" (**1955**), part of a series featuring the priest John Carmody, whose conversion as a result of authentic transcendental experience is described in *Night of Light* (**1957**; exp **1966**), and whose eventual mission is the subject of "A Few Miles" (**1960**) and "Prometheus" (**1961**). The most impressive single work to come out of this boom is Walter M. MILLER's *A Canticle for Leibowitz* (**1955-7**; fixup **1960**), which describes the role played by the Church in the rebuilding of society after a nuclear HOLOCAUST. Even stories like Robert A.W. LOWNDES's *Believer's World* (**1952**; exp **1961**), James E. GUNN's *This Fortress World* (**1955**) and Poul ANDERSON's "Superstition" (**1956**), which deal with fake or misguided religious cults, exhibit a far more sophisticated view of the SOCIOLOGY of religion than "If this Goes On . . ." or *Sixth Column*.

Blish, tempted to try to explain this remarkable phenomenon by his own involvement with it, wrote the notable essay "Cathedrals in Space" (**1953** as by William Atheling Jr; incorporated into *The Issue at Hand*, coll **1964**), citing the stories as "instruments of a chiliastic crisis, of a magnitude we have not seen since the chiliastic panic of 999 A.D.", and drawing a parallel between them and the boom in atomic Armageddons – a parallel made explicit by Boucher and Miller and spectacularly developed by Blish himself in *Black Easter* (**1968**) and *The Day after Judgment* (**1970**). The supposed panics of AD999 were in fact a myth invented by much later apocalyptic writers, but the argument holds good. The advent of the atom bomb in 1945 was a revelation of sorts, and the 1953 invention of the H-bomb gave to each of two ideologically opposed nations the power to annihilate the entire human race. The interest in theological issues, and in metaphysical issues in general, prompted by the acute sense of existential insecurity to which this awareness gave birth became gradually more powerful, though often less explicit. The 1950s also saw a remarkable proliferation of images obviously allied to religious notions but shorn of their association with actual religious doctrine. Arthur C. Clarke has said that any religious symbolism or imagery in *Childhood's End* (1950; exp **1953**) is "entirely accidental", although the text itself refers to the climax as an "apotheosis" and the events described there are strikingly – but coincidentally – similar to Teilhard de Chardin's notion of the coming-together of displaced planetary "noöspheres" at an apocalyptic "Omega Point". Clifford D. Simak's *Time and Again* (**1951**; vt *First He Died*) is similarly free of formal doctrine, although the alien symbionts which infest all living things are obviously analogous to souls (◊ ESCHATOLOGY). In later works by Simak – particularly *A Choice of Gods* (**1972**) and *Project Pope* (**1981**) – religious ideas do become explicit, and here again there are strong echoes of a Teilhardian schema. Sf works explicitly based on Teilhard's ideas are George ZEBROWSKI's *The Omega Point Trilogy* (2 parts published **1972**, **1977**; omni, including 3rd part, **1983**) and Gene WOLFE's **The Book of the New Sun** (**1980-83**) and *The Urth of the New Sun* (**1987** UK). The syncretic approach of these stories, which blends the religious and scientific imaginations, contrasts with uncompromising stories using TIME TRAVEL and other facilitating devices directly to confront the central symbol of the Christian faith: the crucifixion. Richard MATHESON's "The Traveler" (1962) visits the scene in order to find faith. The heroes of Brian EARNSHAW's *Planet in the Eye of Time* (**1968**) go there to protect faith from subversion. The protagonists of Michael MOORCOCK's *Behold the Man!* (1966; exp **1969**) and Barry N. MALZBERG's *Cross of Fire* (**1982**) must become Christ and suffer crucifixion in search of redemption for themselves. The time tourists of Garry KILWORTH's "Let's Go to Golgotha" (1975) discover the horribly ironic truth about the condemnation of Christ. More oblique treatments of the motif can be found in Harry HARRISON's "The Streets of Ashkelon" (1962) and Philip José Farmer's *Jesus on Mars* (**1979**).

There was a very noticeable change, too, in the attitude of sf writers to ALIEN religion. Before WWII, it was taken for granted that all such religions were misguided, ripe for SATIRE and open mockery; after WWII sf writers were prepared to treat alien beliefs reverently, and frequently to credit them with a truthful dimension which Earthly religion lacked. In Katherine MacLEAN's "Unhuman Sacrifice" (1958) missionaries to an alien world find that the "superstitions" they set out to subvert are not as absurd as they assumed. In Heinlein's *Stranger in a Strange Land*

(**1961**) religious ideas imported from Mars become important on Earth. In Robert SILVERBERG's *Nightwings* (**1969**) and *Downward to the Earth* (**1970**) humans seek their own salvation via the transcendental experiences associated with alien religion, although his *Tom O'Bedlam* (**1986**) is more ambiguous in its treatment of a cult based on visionary experience of an alien world and "The Pope of the Chimps" (1982) is highly and ironically ambivalent. In D.G. COMPTON's *The Missionaries* (**1972**) alien missionaries bring an enigmatic offer of salvation to mankind. Poul ANDERSON's "The Problem of Pain" (1973) is a fine *conte philosophique* about the relativity of values deriving from human and alien religions. Satan is portrayed as a wise and misunderstood alien in Harlan ELLISON's "The Deathbird" (1973), which argues that the story of the Fall is a fraud perpetrated on us by God. In the first part of Gregory BENFORD's and Gordon EKLUND's *If the Stars are Gods* (1974; fixup **1977**) alien visitors seeking a new sun-god allow a man to share their enigmatic communion with our SUN. In George R.R. MARTIN's "A Song for Lya" (1974) humans again seek and find transcendental experience in alien ways. The first section of Dan SIMMONS's *Hyperion* (**1989**) deals with an alien religion based in the effects of alien PARASITISM (or perhaps symbiosis). Alien gods are treated with much greater suspicion in Zebrowski's "Heathen God" (1970), Ian WATSON's extraordinary *God's World* (**1979**) and Ted REYNOLDS's *The Tides of God* (**1989**), which is robustly unsentimental in proposing that if God is an alien the best thing we can do is get out there and destroy Him.

Sf also became increasingly eager to look at religious experience from the "other side", exploring the experience of being a (or even *the*) God. This notion was tentatively developed in pulp stories about scientists presiding over tiny creations, including Edmond HAMILTON's "Fessenden's Worlds" (1937) and Theodore STURGEON's "Microcosmic God" (1941), and in "Shaggy God" squibs like Fredric BROWN's "Solipsist" (1954) and Eric Frank RUSSELL's "Sole Solution" (1956). It received more serious consideration in Farmer's "The God Business" and "Father" and in Robert BLOCH's intensely bitter "The Funnel of God" (1960), and was more elaborately explored in a number of novels by Roger ZELAZNY, notably *Lord of Light* (**1967**), *Creatures of Light and Darkness* (**1969**) and *Isle of the Dead* (**1969**), and in Frank HERBERT's *The God Makers* (**1972**).

The sf writer who has dealt most prolifically with issues in speculative theology is Philip K. DICK, whose long-standing fascination was brought to a head by a series of unusual and possibly religious experiences which he underwent in the early months of 1974. Novels like *Radio Free Albemuth* (written 1976; **1985**), comprehensively reworked as *VALIS* (**1981**), are attempts to get to grips with these experiences. The development of Dick's theological fascination can be tracked through such works as "Faith of Our Fathers" (1967), *Galactic Pot-Healer* (**1969**) and *A Maze* of Death (**1970**), and culminate in *The Divine Invasion* (**1981**) and the non-sf *The Transmigration of Timothy Archer* (**1982**).

Artificial religions and cults still crop up regularly in sf, sometimes deployed for satirical purposes, as by Kurt VONNEGUT Jr in *The Sirens of Titan* (**1959**), *Cat's Cradle* (**1963**) and *Slapstick* (**1976**), sometimes in the cause of thoughtful extrapolations in the sociology of religion, as in *This Star Shall Abide* (**1972**; vt *Heritage of the Star*) by Sylvia Louise ENGDAHL. Keith ROBERTS's *Pavane* (coll of linked stories **1968**) and Kingsley AMIS's *The Alteration* (**1976**) are both ALTERNATE-WORLD stories endorsing the thesis of Max Weber (1864-1920) regarding the Protestant Ethic and the spirit of capitalism by displaying an unreformed Catholic Church dominating a Europe where the Industrial Revolution is only just getting under way in the 20th century. Roberts's *Kiteworld* (fixup **1985**) is one of the more memorable sf images of oppressive Theocracy. More earnest explorations of possible developments in future religion include Richard COWPER's **Kinship** series begun with the novella "Piper at the Gates of Dawn" (1976). A number of books excoriate future theocracies, particularly fundamentalist ones, such as *The Stone that Never Came Down* (**1973**) by John BRUNNER, recent examples of the assault on fundamentalism being Parke GODWIN's **Snake Oil** series, beginning with *Waiting for the Galactic Bus* (**1988**), and several books by Sheri S. TEPPER, notably *Raising the Stones* (**1990**). Conversely, in several of Orson Scott CARD's novels a thinly disguised version of Mormonism is depicted with a utopian glow. In contemporary sf, however, perhaps the most sophisticated and detailed treatment of a future religion is **The Starbridge Chronicles** by Paul PARK, beginning with *Soldiers of Paradise* (**1987**), in which the seasons of a generations-long Great Year encourage contrasting faiths.

There are several interesting theme anthologies, including *Other Worlds, Other Gods* (anth **1971**) ed Mayo Mohs, *Strange Gods* (anth **1974**) ed Roger ELWOOD, *An Exaltation of Stars* (anth **1973**) ed Terry CARR, *Wandering Stars* (anth **1974**) ed Jack DANN (a collection of Jewish sf), *The New Awareness: Religion through Science Fiction* (anth **1975**) ed Martin H. GREENBERG and Patricia S. WARRICK, *Perpetual Light* (anth **1982**) ed Alan Ryan, and *Sacred Visions* (anth **1991**) ed Michael CASSUTT and Andrew M. GREELEY. [BS]

See also: IMMORTALITY; MESSIAHS; REINCARNATION; SUPERNATURAL CREATURES.

RENARD, JOSEPH (1938-) US playwright and novelist whose sf has been restricted to *The Monodyne Catastrophe* (1970 *Venture* as "How We Won the Monodyne"; exp **1977**), in which Native Americans attempt to take over the eponymous source of future power. [JC]

RENARD, MAURICE (1875-1939) French writer, generally regarded in FRANCE as the most important native sf writer for the period 1900-1930, best known in English for his sf novel *Les mains d'Orlac* (**1920**; trans Florence Crewe-Jones as *The Hands of Orlac* **1929** US), filmed in 1924 as ORLACS HÄNDE; another version was *Mad Love* (1935). The story deals in GOTHIC terms with the ominous consequences of a hand transplant. A less well known though more wildly imaginative novel is *Le docteur Lerne, sous-dieu* (**1908**; trans anon as *New Bodies for Old* **1923** US), in which a sinister SCIENTIST's experiments in grafting produce, for example, rats with leaves; the transplantation of a man's brain into a bull's body, and vice versa, creates a smart cow and a Minotaur. Ultimately the German villain – who has already occupied the scientist's brain – transplants himself into the body of a car, but the machinery, thus rendered mortal, putrefies.

Le Singe (**1925**; trans Florence Crewe-Jones as *Blind Circle* **1928** US) with Albert Jean (1892-) is a gruesomely comic mystery story whose solution reveals the manufacture of a series of identical ANDROIDS by a kind of electrolysis. The title story of *Le Voyage Immobile suivi d'autres histoires singulières* (coll **1909**; rev 1922; trans anon as *The Flight of the Aerofix* **1932** chap US) features an unsteerable craft, powered by ANTIGRAVITY and detrimental to its passengers.

MR's untranslated works include the collections *M. D'Outremort et autres histoires singulières* ["Mr Overdeath and Other Curious Stories"] (coll **1913**; vt *Suite Fantastique*), *L'invitation à la peur* ["Invitation to Fear"] (coll **1926**) and *Le carrousel du mystère* ["Mystery Merry-go-Round"] (coll **1929**). These volumes include many fine stories on a great variety of sf themes: CLONES, invisibility, time travel, cyborgs, gravity, space-time paradoxes, ESCHATOLOGY and, especially and often, altered modes of PERCEPTION. His untranslated novels include *Le péril bleu* ["The Blue Peril"] (**1910**), about an extraordinary civilization of lifeforms living on the top of an atmosphere as if it were a sea; *Un homme chez les microbes, scherzo* ["A Man Amongst the Microbes: A Scherzo"] (**1928**), a journey into the microcosm with more sophistication and verbal wit than those of Ray CUMMINGS; *L'homme truqué* ["The Fake Man"], described by Pierre VERSINS as "a nightmare based on the Universe as seen by a mutilated giant whose eyes have been replaced by 'electroscopes' . . . the pretext for many pages of a strange, visual poetry", and *Le maître de la lumière* ["Master of Light"] (1920s; **1948**), about the creation of a new form of glass which condenses space and time, similar to the "slow glass" invented (independently) by Bob SHAW. The huge *Maurice Renard: Romans et contes fantastiques* ["Maurice Renard: Fantasy Novels and Tales"] (omni **1990**) contains most of his work of genre interest. [PN/JC]

See also: HISTORY OF SF.

RENOWN PUBLICATIONS ◊ SATELLITE SCIENCE FICTION.

REPO MAN Film (1984). Edge City Productions/ Universal. Written/dir Alex Cox, starring Emilio Estevez, Harry Dean Stanton, Tracey Walter, Olivia

Barash. 92 mins. Colour.

Set in the seedier areas of Los Angeles, this independent, low-budget, semi-surreal film concerns a young man (Estevez) who gets a job as a repo man – a repossessor of unpaid-for cars. A 1964 Chevrolet Malibu driven by a lobotomized nuclear physicist is driving around town with something nasty and radioactive in the trunk. People who look inside see a glaring white light (shades of KISS ME DEADLY [1955]) which distintegrates them. A series of coincidences (concerning repo men, a teenager obsessed with aliens, chicano car thieves, middle-class punk thugs and secret agents led by a woman with a metal hand) reveal something about the underbelly of urban life and provide sciencefictional metaphors for urban dreams. The Chevy undergoes a final apotheosis: now glowing all over, it drifts into the heavens with two repo men inside. We never learn what was in the car's trunk but, as an acid-head explains early on, flying saucers and time machines are fundamentally the same thing and getting into specifics misses the point. *RM* became an instant cult movie, not just because of its punk aesthetics and black humour, but also because of its old-fashioned virtues: it is well made and coherently scripted. [PN]

REPP, ED EARL (1901-1979) US advertising man and newspaper reporter who wrote a large number of fairly typical PULP-MAGAZINE adventures for about a decade from 1929, ceasing to produce sf during WWII, after beginning work as a screenwriter; some of his tales appeared as by Bradnor Buckner. His first sf story – "Beyond Gravity" for *Air Wonder Stories* in 1929 – appeared simultaneously with the magazine publication of his first novel, *The Radium Pool* (1929 *Science Wonder Stories*; with 2 other stories, as coll **1949**) which was later bound with L. Ron HUBBARD's *Triton and Battle of Wizards* as *Science-Fantasy Quintet* (omni **1953**). 3 stories – 2 of them linked – were assembled in *The Stellar Missiles* (coll **1949**). EER also wrote a series in *AMZ* 1939-43 about **John Hale**, a scientific detective perhaps modelled on Arthur B. REEVE's **Craig Kennedy**; they remain uncollected. Most of his published books were Westerns. [JC]
See also: AIR WONDER STORIES.

REPTILICUS Film (1962). Cinemagic/AIP. Dir Sidney Pink, starring Carl Ottosen, Ann Smyrner. Screenplay Ib Melchior, Pink. 90 mins. Colour.

In this, the Danish cinema's only excursion into the monster genre, the tail of a buried dinosaur is exhumed and taken to a laboratory where it regenerates an entire new body, which proceeds to behave like RADON. Generally thought to be the worst MONSTER MOVIE ever made, *R* is notable for the visible strings holding up the puppet dinosaur and for the fact that AIP found it necessary to cut all flying scenes before the US release. The novelization, *Reptilicus* * (**1961**) by Dean OWEN, was released before the film and alleged in a lawsuit brought by Pink to contain gratuitous passages of "lewd, lascivious and wanton desire"; there was also a 1961 comic book, **Reptilicus**,

which fittingly changed its name in #3 to *Reptisaurus the Terrible*. [JB/PN]
REPUBLIC FEATURES SYNDICATE ◊ SPACE SCIENCE FICTION MAGAZINE.
RESNICK, MICHAEL D(IAMOND) (1942-) US author and dog-breeder who began his genre career with an Edgar Rice BURROUGHS pastiche, *The Forgotten Sea of Mars* (**1965** chap), and who soon began producing many novels in various genres, most often soft pornography and Gothics, and almost always under unrevealed pseudonyms; his later books are usually signed Mike Resnick. His interest in Burroughs had also generated material which he published in *ERB-dom Magazine*; his first novels, the **Ganymede** series – *The Goddess of Ganymede* (**1967**) and *Pursuit on Ganymede* (**1968**) – showed Burroughs's influence. After *Redbeard* (**1969**), a post-HOLOCAUST tale set generations hence in the New York subway system, he left sf and fantasy, restricting his activity to the pseudonymous novels, writing (it has been estimated) well over 200 before returning, around 1980, to work under his own name. The first relevant title – *Battlestar Galactica 5: Galactica Discovers Earth* * (**1980**) with Glen A. LARSON, a tv tie – was the least. MDR's large 1980s production showed an increasing – and increasingly sophisticated – interest in the use of sf venues and instruments to tell what he has more than once described as "morality tales", sometimes with a simplistic ease, but in later work with mounting vigour and a winningly complex sense of the nature of the world; this was most evident in those stories and novels – like *Ivory: A Legend of Past and Future* (**1988**), *Paradise: A Chronicle of a Distant World* (**1989**) and *Bwana & Bully!* (coll **1981**) – set in either a literal Africa or an sf analogue of it. *Ivory* has a Masai descendant searching through many worlds for the tusks of a particular elephant and *Paradise* recasts the history of Kenya as the history of an alien world. Two of the short works belonging to this thematically linked **Kenya** series; both set in an African-styled SPACE HABITAT, *Kirinyaga* (**1988** *FSF*; **1992** chap) and its sequel, "The Manamouki" (**1990**), though well received and both winning HUGOs, caused some controversy through their display (and perhaps espousal) of cultural values alien to our own.

Two further series of the 1980s are the **Tales of the Galactic Midway** sequence – *Sideshow* (**1982**), *The Three-Legged Hootch Dancer* (**1983**), *The Wild Alien Tamer* (**1983**) and *The Best Rootin' Tootin' Shootin' Gunslinger in the Whole Damned Galaxy* (**1983**) – and the **Tales of the Velvet Comet** sequence – *Eros Ascending* (**1984**), *Eros at Zenith* (**1984**), *Eros Descending* (**1985**) and *Eros at Nadir* (**1986**). Both series – the first set in a carnival, the second in a whorehouse visited at 50-year intervals – are smooth, swift, cynical and without much in the way of argument about anything that might be described as the moral Universe. But many of his remaining novels of this decade shared the general background outlined in *Birthright: The Book of Man* (coll of linked stories **1982**), a text which sketches in the next 15,000 years or so as our race expands through the Galaxy, peaks, then dwindles to extinction. The individual stories within this extremely loose frame convey in general a sense that humans are incapable of answering the demands of history, that we are too short-lived and too caught in our mortality to answer the challenges of a greater world. Novels like *Santiago: A Myth of the Far Future* (**1986**) and *The Dark Lady: A Romance of the Far Future* (**1987**) tend to portray adventurous characters engaging in SPACE-OPERA exploits against a black, barely felt background of closure; for the feats of MDR's protagonists are little more than selfish spasms in the great night. His better novels are, all the same, at least superficially cheerful, bustling with competently framed action, and clear-headed.

Tales that stand outside the future history include *The Soul Eater* (**1981**), a retelling of Herman MELVILLE's *Moby-Dick* (**1851**), and *Stalking the Unicorn: A Fable of Tonight* (**1987**), a fantasy. After publishing some earlier short collections, MR signalled his increasing involvement in short forms with *Will the Last Person to Leave the Planet Please Shut off the Sun?* (coll **1992**), which contains several award-winning tales. An anthology of some interest is *Shaggy B.E.M. Stories* (anth **1988**). In the 1970s, MDR published *Official Guide to the Fantastic Literature* (**1977**), *Official Guide to Comic Books and Big Little Books* (**1977**) and *Official Price Guide to Comic and Science Fiction Books* (**1979**). [JC]
Other works: *Walpurgis III* (**1982**); *The Branch* (**1984**); *Unauthorized Autobiographies and Other Curiosities* (coll **1984** chap); *The Inn of the Hairy Toad* (**1985** chap); *Adventures* (**1985**); *Through Darkest Resnick with Gun and Camera* (coll **1990**); *Second Contact* (**1990**); *Stalking the Wild Resnick* (coll **1991**); *Pink Elephants and Hairy Toads* (coll **1991** chap); *The Alien Heart* (coll **1991**); *The Red Tape War* (**1991**) with Jack L. CHALKER and George Alec EFFINGER; *Soothsayer* (**1991**), #1 in the projected **Oracle Trilogy**; *Inside the Funhouse* (anth **1992**), assembling examples of RECURSIVE SF.
See also: ALTERNATE WORLDS; COLONIZATION OF OTHER WORLDS; CRIME AND PUNISHMENT; HEROES; ISAAC ASIMOV'S SCIENCE FICTION MAGAZINE; *The* MAGAZINE OF FANTASY AND SCIENCE FICTION; SOCIOLOGY.

RESTIF DE LA BRETONNE Name by which the French writer Nicolas-Anne-Edmé Restif (1734-1806) is usually known. He was an extremely prolific author of formless, semi-autobiographical novels often attacked for imputed pornographic content. Of his various utopian texts, *La découverte australe par un homme volant, ou le Dédale français* ["The Southern-Hemisphere Discovery by a Flying Man, or the French Daedalus"] (**1781**) comes closest to genuine PROTO SCIENCE FICTION, first describing the flying Frenchman's gear (wings plus parachute), then his Alpine UTOPIA, then his adventures in the Antipodes where, like François RABELAIS's heroes, he visits a number of allegorical ISLANDS. [JC]
Other works: *Les posthumes* ["The Posthumous Ones"] (**1802**).

See also: EVOLUTION; FRANCE.

RETURN FROM WITCH MOUNTAIN ◊ Alexander KEY.

RETURN OF CAPTAIN INVINCIBLE, THE Film (1982). Willarra/Seven Keys. Dir Philippe Mora, starring Alan Arkin, Christopher Lee, Kate Fitzpatrick. Screenplay Steven E. De Souza, Andrew Gaty; additional dialogue Peter Smalley. 91 mins. Colour.

Australian musical comedy whose premise is that its eponymous SUPERHERO (Arkin), purged in the USA of the McCarthy period as "a premature anti-fascist", is now a washed-up drunk. Discovered in Sydney by policewoman Patty Patria (Fitzpatrick), he is recalled to confront his nemesis Mr Midnight (Lee), whose evil plan is first to sell housing developments to non-Whites in New York, then nuke them and make the city all-White. Much of the humour comes from Captain Invincible's forgetting how to fly, and suffering low self-esteem that affects his supermagnetic powers. As a spoof movie *TROCI* is likable, and genre-literate in the range of sf motifs it hits off; the songs are unmemorable. Arkin's muted, depressive performance, reminiscent of something from a Barry N. MALZBERG novel, contrasts nicely with Lee going over the top. [PN]

RETURN OF CAPTAIN NEMO, THE ◊ Irwin ALLEN.

RETURN OF GODZILLA, THE ◊ GOJIRA.

RETURN OF THE FLY Film (1959). Associated Producers/20th Century-Fox. Dir Edward L. Bernds, starring Vincent Price, Brett Halsey, David Frankham. Screenplay Bernds. 78 mins. B/w.

The first of 2 sequels to the successful sf/horror film *The* FLY (1958), the other being CURSE OF THE FLY (1965). Here the son of the scientist in *The Fly*, after being attacked by an evil assistant, is forced to replay his late father's tragedy, which he does rather limply; it is the least successful of the 3 films. Although *The* FLY (1986) is a remake of *The Fly* (1958), *The* FLY II is not a remake of *ROTF*. [PN]

RETURN OF THE GIANT MONSTERS, THE ◊ DAIKAIJU GAMERA.

RETURN OF THE INCREDIBLE HULK ◊ *The* INCREDIBLE HULK.

RETURN OF THE JEDI Film (1983). Lucasfilm/20th Century-Fox. Executive prod George LUCAS. Dir Richard Marquand, starring Mark Hamill, Harrison Ford, Carrie Fisher, Ian McDiarmid, David Prowse. Screenplay Lawrence Kasdan, Lucas, based on a story by Lucas. 132 mins. Colour.

Crisp and entertaining for the most part, with dazzling special effects, *ROTJ* still seems weaker than its predecessors, STAR WARS (1977) and *The* EMPIRE STRIKES BACK (1980), perhaps because it is more sentimental. Han Solo (Ford) is rescued from literally toadlike Jabba the Hutt in the bravura opening sequence, and then the democratic rebels are pitted once again against a Death Star fortress as part of their galactic struggle against the totalitarian Empire. The Emperor (a cleverly obscene performance from McDiarmid) is an even stronger incarnation of the

Dark Side of the Force than Darth Vader (Prowse), who finally turns good, saves his son Luke, is unmasked and is then given a Viking's funeral. The forest world of Endor, populated by Ewoks (teddy-bear lookalikes), is the venue for stirring battles. The appalling cuteness of the Ewoks and the harmless rubbery appearance of the monsters are surely Lucasfilm's acknowledgement, in this finale to the cycle (the threat of 6 further episodes having evaporated), that young children were now the series' main audience: even the potentially painful father-son conflict is more soap opera than oedipal myth. The Ewoks later resurfaced in 2 made-for-tv films, *The* EWOK ADVENTURE (1984) and *Ewoks: The Battle for Endor* (1985).

The novelization is *Star Wars: Return of the Jedi* * (1983) by James KAHN. [PN]

See also: CINEMA; HUGO.

RETURN OF THE LOST PLANET ◊ *The* LOST PLANET.

RETURN TO THE PLANET OF THE APES ◊ PLANET OF THE APES.

REVENGE OF THE CREATURE Film (1955). Universal. Dir Jack ARNOLD, starring John Agar, Lori Nelson, John Bromfield, Ricou Browning. Screenplay Martin Berkeley, story William Alland. 82 mins. 3D. B/w.

The success of CREATURE FROM THE BLACK LAGOON (1954) inspired the inevitable sequel, shot in 3D although seldom projected in that format. This time the Creature (Browning) is captured and taken to an oceanarium in Florida, but it soon breaks out and (some time later, after voyeuristically spying on her) makes off with a blonde woman scientist (Nelson) under its arm. Though the film has erotically charged moments, it is generally limp compared with its predecessor, and is one of Arnold's weaker sf movies. A further sequel, not dir Arnold, was *The* CREATURE WALKS AMONG US. [JB/PN]

REVENGE OF THE MYSTERONS FROM MARS ◊ CAPTAIN SCARLET AND THE MYSTERONS.

REVENGE OF THE STEPFORD WIVES ◊ *The* STEPFORD WIVES.

REY, RUSSELL ◊ Dennis HUGHES.

REYNA, JORGE DE ◊ Diane DETZER.

REYNOLDS, MACK Working name of US writer Dallas McCord Reynolds (1917-1983); his first sf story was "Isolationist" for *Fantastic Adventures* in 1950. He occasionally used the pseudonyms Clark Collins, Guy McCord, Mark Mallory and Dallas Ross; he wrote 2 Gothics as Maxine Reynolds and 1 other non-sf book as Todd Harding. Some of his early work was with Fredric BROWN, and he also wrote stories with Theodore R. COGSWELL and August W. DERLETH. He was for 25 years an active member of the American Socialist Labor Party, for which his father, Verne L. Reynolds, had twice been presidential candidate; his "militant radicalism" is mutedly reflected, sometimes ironically, in his sf, making him a maverick in the mostly right-wing stable of writers associated with John W. CAMPBELL Jr's ASTOUNDING SCIENCE-FICTION (MR was one of several writers who wrote up Campbell's plot ideas). Many of his later works are unashamedly didactic, although not doctrinaire.

MR's first novel, *The Case of the Little Green Men* (**1951**), was a murder mystery set at an sf CONVENTION. It was to be 10 years before he would publish another novel. Although his 1950s work is minor, he served 1953-63 as foreign correspondent of *Rogue* magazine, travelling extensively, and began to plough back this experience into more substantial works on socioeconomic themes. Many of the books which appeared prolifically through the 1960s-70s were expansions and fixups of earlier magazine stories; the tauter magazine texts are usually preferable to the padded-out versions. *Planetary Agent X* (fixup **1965** dos), the first of several books featuring **Section G**, shows subversive secret agents of a **United Planets** Organization working in the cause of socioeconomic progress in the often-eccentric **Ultima Thule** colony worlds of a Galactic Empire, masking their activities under the *nom de guerre* Tommy Paine. It was followed by *Dawnman Planet* (**1966** dos), *The Rival Rigelians* (1960 *ASF* as "Adaptation"; exp **1967** dos), which ironically describes an experiment comparing the methods of US capitalism and Soviet communism in developing a primitive world, *Code Duello* (**1968** dos) and *Section G: United Planets* (1967 *ASF* as "Fiesta Brava" and "Psi Assassin"; fixup **1976**).

Tomorrow Might be Different (1960 *ASF* as "Russkies Go Home!"; exp **1975**) is a SATIRE in which the USSR has overtaken the USA as the world's leading economy. "Farmer" (1961) is the first of 3 notable stories which MR set in North Africa, each similarly dealing with the problem of fostering economic and technological development in the teeth of cultural inertia. It was followed by the **Homer Crawford** sequence, the first 2 volumes of which are *Black Man's Burden* (1961-2 *ASF*; **1972** dos) and *Border, Breed nor Birth* (1962 *ASF*; **1972** dos), offering entirely serious and constructive versions of **Section G**-type plots; although they have dated even more quickly than MR's stories about the USSR, the issues raised in them (otherwise virtually untouched in sf) remain politically pertinent. *The Best Ye Breed* (fixup **1978**), which incorporates "Black Sheep Astray" (1973) and a revised version of "The Cold War . . . Continued" (1973), extends the series. *Day After Tomorrow* (1961 *ASF* as "Status Quo"; exp **1976**) introduced a status-conscious future USA further elaborated in *Mercenary from Tomorrow* (1962 *ASF* as "Mercenary"; exp **1968** dos), which became the first of the **Joe Mauser** series set in a future world in which corporate disputes are settled by pseudo-gladiatorial contests, packaged by the media as entertainment, and involving small professional armies fighting with pre-1900 WEAPONS (◊ GAMES AND SPORTS). Several lines of speculative thought carried forward in the later didactic novels originated in this novella, but the later novels in the series – *The Earth War* (1963 *ASF* as "Frigid Fracas"; **1963**), *Time Gladiator* (1964 *ASF* as "Sweet Dreams, Sweet Princes"; exp **1966** UK; rev by Michael A. BANKS, vt *Sweet Dreams, Sweet Princes* 1986 US) and

The Fracas Factor (**1978**) – are routine action-adventure novels. *Joe Mauser, Mercenary from Tomorrow* (coll **1986**) with Banks contains revisions of the earlier items. *The Cosmic Eye* (1963 *FSF* as "Speakeasy"; exp **1969**) is a less convincing story set in a future USA where free speech is prohibited.

During 1965-72 MR's work was more determinedly commercial. He continued to write stories around Campbell plot ideas. All involve a good deal of rather slapstick HUMOUR; examples include *Amazon Planet* (1966 *ASF*; Italian trans **1967**; **1975**) and *Brain World* (**1978**). *Of Godlike Power* (**1966**; vt *Earth Unaware* 1968) is a comedy about a preacher whose curses really work. "Romp" (1966) was the first of a group of crime stories reprinted as *Police Patrol: 2000 A.D.* (fixup **1977**). *Space Pioneer* (**1966** UK) and *After Some Tomorrow* (**1967**) are undistinguished, but 2 novels about COMPUTERS, *Computer War* (**1967** dos) and *The Computer Conspiracy* (**1968**), gained strength from the timeliness of their themes. The final 2 stories making up *The Space Barbarians* (fixup **1969** dos) and *The Five Way Secret Agent* (**1969** *ASF*; **1975** dos) were the last items MR did for Campbell, and after *Rolltown* (1969 *If* as "The Towns Must Roll"; exp **1976**) he published virtually no new sf for three years (although he did publish books in other genres).

When his sf career resumed it was with the strikingly different *Looking Backward, from the Year 2000* (**1973**), a reprise of Edward BELLAMY's classic UTOPIAN novel, displaying MR's ideas about the POLITICS and ECONOMICS of an energy-affluent society. He was later to add a sequel – *Equality: in the Year 2000* (**1977**) – which borrowed an idea from his earlier *Ability Quotient* (**1975**) to subvert the ending of the first book. MR further extrapolated this line of speculation into the increasingly doubt-ridden *After Utopia* (**1977**), which incorporates "Utopian" (in *The Year 2000* [anth **1970**] ed Harry HARRISON) and *Perchance to Dream* (**1977**), although he salvaged a curiously ironic optimism by re-using a *deus ex machina* first deployed in the earlier *Space Visitor* (**1977**). He developed parallel lines of thought in sequels to *Rolltown* – these were *Commune 2000 A.D.* (**1974**) and *The Towers of Utopia* (**1975**) – and re-used the central characters of *The Five Way Secret Agent* in more lightweight stories with similar underlying concerns: *Satellite City* (**1975**) and "Of Future Fears" (**1977** *ASF*). This series was further expanded in novels about the tribulations of a quasi-utopian space colony: *Lagrange Five* (**1979**), *The Lagrangists* (**1983**) and *Chaos in Lagrangia* (**1984**), The last 2 were ed Dean ING, who went on to prepare for publication several other manuscripts which MR had left behind on his death: *Eternity* (**1984**), *Home Sweet Home: 2010 A.D.* (**1984**), *The Other Time* (**1984**), *Trojan Orbit* (**1985**) and *Deathwish World* (**1986**). *Space Search* (**1984**) is a posthumous work credited to MR alone.

The Best of Mack Reynolds (coll **1976**) has an introduction explaining MR's decision to concentrate on sf which speculated on social and economic issues, and

reflecting on his travels and the lessons he learned therefrom. Although he was once voted most popular author in a poll run by the GALAXY SCIENCE FICTION group of magazines, MR never received the recognition he deserved for the fertility of his distinctive speculative imagination. His ideas were always far more interesting than his plots, and his writing was sometimes unpolished, but at his best he was a skilled craftsman whose attempts to foresee the NEAR FUTURE were unusually bold, well informed and challenging. It is a great pity that he had such difficulty in finding publishers willing to put his work into respectable formats. [BS]

Other works: *Mission to Horatius* * (**1968**), a STAR TREK novel; *Once Departed* (**1970**), a thriller with sf elements; *Computer World* (**1970**); *Depression or Bust* (fixup **1974**); *Galactic Medal of Honor* (1960 *AMZ* as "Medal of Honor"; exp **1976**); *Trample an Empire Down* (**1978**); *Compounded Interests* (coll **1983**).

As editor: *The Science Fiction Carnival* (anth **1953**) with Fredric Brown.

About the author: "The Utopian Dream Revisited: Socioeconomic Speculation in the Work of Mack Reynolds" by Brian M. STABLEFORD in *Foundation* 16 (May 1979); *A Mack Reynolds Checklist: Notes Toward a Bibliography* (**1983** chap) by Chris DRUMM and George Flynn.

See also: AUTOMATION; CITIES; CRYONICS; IMMORTALITY; LEISURE; RELIGION; SLEEPER AWAKES; SOCIAL DARWINISM; SPACE HABITATS; TECHNOLOGY; TIME PARADOXES; WAR.

REYNOLDS, TED Working name of US writer Theodore Andrus Reynolds (1938-   ), who began publishing sf with "Boarder Incident" for *IASFM* in 1977. His first novel, *The Tides of God* (**1989**) – the last of the Terry CARR **Ace Specials** – intriguingly allows the surmise that millennial fervour is caused, on a regular 1000-year basis, by a deranging ALIEN being whose expected arrival from deep space as the 20th century ends spurs the mounting of an expedition to destroy it. But RELIGION is a subject too complexly integrated into the human psyche to be excised by any quasi-military sortie into the unknown; and the tale ends in ambiguity. [JC]

RHINEHART, LUKE Pseudonym of US writer George Powers Cockcroft (1932-   ). His first novel, *The Dice Man* (**1971**; rev 1983), though not sf, inhabits the same universe of discourse as *The Adventures of Wim* (**1986** UK), a long, frequently garrulous picaresque detailing the eponymous innocent's travels through time and space. *Matari* (**1975**) is a heavily allegorical love story set in a partly mythologized 18th-century Japan. *Long Voyage Back* (**1983**) takes the crew of a small ship through post-HOLOCAUST ordeals and from Chesapeake Bay to Chile. LR's books burst with didacticism, but have vivid moments. [JC]

RHODES, W(ILLIAM) H(ENRY) (1822-1876) US lawyer and writer who published various newspaper pieces and stories under the name Caxton, notably *The Case of Summerfield* (1871 *Sacramento Daily Union*; **1907** chap), about a scientist who threatens to set the oceans of the world afire unless he is paid blackmail. Along with its sequel, 4 further sf stories and other ephemera, the tale was first published as a memorial by his colleagues in *Caxton's Book: A Collection of Essays, Poems, Tales and Sketches* (coll **1876**). Also of interest in this volume is "The Telescopic Eye", about a boy blind at normal distances but able to observe the activities of the wheel-shaped denizens of the Moon.   [JC]

RHYS, JACK [r] ◊ ROBERT HALE LIMITED.

RHYSLING AWARD ◊ AWARDS; POETRY.

RICE, ELMER First the pseudonym, then the legal name of US playwright and novelist born Elmer Leopold Reitzenstein (1892-1967). Of his plays, *The Adding Machine* (**1923**) interestingly transforms its protagonist, Mr Zero, into the para-human creature designated by the title. *A Voyage to Purilia* (**1930**), a novel, combines a deft use of sf instruments – the protagonists travel to the planet Purilia in a ship propelled by ANTIGRAVITY – with a very extensive guying of UTOPIAN assumptions. On Purilia, life mirrors the conventions of the cinema – the implication being that utopian worlds are as fatuously bound by rigmarole and fetish as the "normal" lives depicted in the classic Hollywood films – and the protagonist escapes marriage, which is identical to a Hollywood fade-out, by the skin of his teeth.   [JC]

RICH, BARBARA ◊ Robert GRAVES.

RICHARDS, ALFRED BATE (1820-1876) UK editor of the *Morning Advertiser* and writer. For many years he was active as a propagandist for UK military preparedness, but *The Invasion of England (A Possible Tale of Future Times)* (**1870** chap), published privately, had little impact, and was in any case much inferior to Lt.-Col. Sir George T. CHESNEY's *The Battle of Dorking* (**1871**), which effectively founded the future-WAR/INVASION genre so popular over the next 40 years. [JC]

RICHARDS, GUY (1905-1979) US writer and reporter. In *Two Roubles to Times Square* (**1956**; vt *Brother Bear* 1956 UK) a Russian takeover of Manhattan is embarrassedly disowned by the Kremlin.   [JC]

RICHARDS, HENRY ◊ J.L. MORRISSEY.

RICHARDS, JOEL Pseudonym of US writer Joel Richard Fruchtman (1937-   ), who began publishing sf with "Speedplay" for *AMZ* in 1980 and has published subsequent stories in original anthologies. His first novel was *Pindharee* (**1986**), an sf adventure.   [JC]

RICHARDS, ROSS [r] ◊ Peter SAXON.

RICHARDSON, LINDA [r] ◊ David R. BISCHOFF.

RICHARDSON, ROBERT S. [r] ◊ Philip LATHAM.

RICHMOND, LEIGH (TUCKER) (1911-   ) US writer who began publishing with "Prologue to an Analogue" for *ASF* in 1961, and who wrote some solo stories. Her several sf novels were all in collaboration with her husband, Walt RICHMOND; 3 were revised by LR after his death. Almost all their work together expressed a sense – one formally presented by the Centric Foundation which they founded and directed – that scientific breakthroughs could be made by young minds freed of the bureaucratic artifices of orthodox scientific thinking; unfortunately, overloaded SPACE-OPERA plotting did little to make their novels convincing emblems of this new clarity, and the exaggerated individualism they expressed seemed less mould-breaking than nostalgic. They published frequently in *ASF*. Their novels were *Shock Waves* (**1967** dos), *The Lost Millennium* (**1967** dos; rev vt *Siva!* 1979), which typically suggests that a new source of solar energy was first exploited by prehistoric supermen, *Phoenix Ship* (**1969** dos; rev vt *Phase Two* 1980), *Gallagher's Glacier* (**1970** dos; rev 1979), *Challenge the Hellmaker* (1963 *ASF* as "Where I Wasn't Going"; exp **1976**) and *The Probability Corner* (**1977**). Stories were collected as *Positive Charge* (coll **1970** dos).   [JC]

RICHMOND, MARY Pseudonym of South-African-born UK writer Kathleen Lindsay (1903-1973), author of about 900 romances and 2 sf novels, *The Valley of Doom* (**1947**), a LOST-WORLD tale, and *The Grim Tomorrow* (**1953**), whose UK protagonists fail to avert a Teutonic atomic HOLOCAUST, but who survive, after being flung into space on a chunk of England fortunately large enough that they can start a new life. The tale's telling is less incompetent than its science.   [JC]

Other work: *Terror Stalks Abroad* (**1935**).

RICHMOND, WALT(ER R.) (1922-1977) US writer and research scientist whose fiction was written exclusively in collaboration with his wife, Leigh RICHMOND (*whom see for details*).   [JC]

RICHTER-FRICH, ØVRE [r] ◊ SCANDINAVIA.

RICKETT, JOSEPH COMPTON (1847-1919) UK politician and writer, who was knighted in 1907 and subsequently changed his name to Compton-Rickett. His sf novel *The Quickening of Caliban: A Modern Story of Evolution* (**1893**) suggests that a more natural (i.e., perhaps, less evolved) branch of *Homo sapiens* continues to exist in Africa. The two branches are able to breed together, and do.   [JC]

RIDERS TO THE STARS Film (1954). Ivan Tors/United Artists. Dir Richard Carlson, starring William Lundigan, Herbert Marshall, Richard Carlson, Martha Hyer. Screenplay Curt SIODMAK. 81 mins. Colour.

Cosmic rays are destroying space vehicles, and the theory is put forward that meteors possess a special quality that protects them in space. Manned spaceships with special scoops on their noses are sent up to capture meteors before they burn up in the atmosphere so that their coating – which turns out to be diamond! – can be used to protect spaceships. The story has been rightly singled out by Damon KNIGHT as a splendid example of all that is silliest and most unscientific in sf CINEMA, from which much of its value as entertainment unintentionally derives. *Riders to the Stars* ∗ (**1953**), as by Siodmak and Robert (Eugene) Smith (1920-   ), is the novelization.

[JB/PN]

RIDING, JULIA [r] ◊ ROBERT HALE LIMITED.

RIDING, LAURA [r] ◊ Robert GRAVES.

RIDLEY, FRANK A(MBROSE) (c1896-) UK politician and writer, mostly on historical subjects. *The Green Machine* (**1924**), though clearly cavalier in its treatment of science – presenting as it does the eponymous bicycle as a spaceship capable of interplanetary travel – interestingly sends its protagonist to tour a crowded Solar System accompanied by a Martian ant bent on colonizing Earth. [JC]
See also: HIVE-MINDS.

RIENOW, LEONA (TRAIN) (1903-1983) US writer whose short **Dark Pool** prehistoric-sf sequence for children comprises *The Bewitched Caverns* (**1948**) and *The Dark Pool* (**1949**). With her husband Robert Rienow (1909-1989), a political scientist, she later wrote *The Year of the Last Eagle* (**1970**), a sour NEAR-FUTURE comedy about ECOLOGY, set in 1989. The hero's job is to locate the last bald eagles (the national bird of the USA), if any still exist. [JC/PN]

RIENOW, ROBERT [r] ◊ Leona RIENOW.

RIFBJERG, KLAUS (THORVALD) (1931-) Danish writer in whose sf novel, *De Hellige Aber* (**1981**; trans Steve Murray as *Witness to the Future* **1987** US), two adolescents are transported almost half a century forward from 1941; they find little in the year 1988 to give them joy about Progress. [JC]

RIGG, [Lt.-Col.] ROBERT B. (? -) US writer on military topics whose *War – 1974* (**1958**) puts into the didactic fictional form of a future-WAR narrative his speculations about developments in WEAPONS and tactics. After an initial exchange of ICBMs, East and West settle down to conventional conflict dominated by much implausible non-nuclear gimmickry. [JC]

RILEY, FRANK (? -) US writer who began publishing sf with "The Execution" for *If* in 1956, and who is mainly known for collaborating with Mark CLIFTON on *They'd Rather Be Right* (**1954**), the HUGO-winning conclusion to Clifton's **Bossy** series about an advanced COMPUTER rendered almost useless by men's fear of "her". [JC]
See also: AUTOMATION.

RIMWORLD A common item of sf TERMINOLOGY. ◊ GALACTIC LENS.

RIPLEY, KAREN (? -) US writer who began publishing sf with *Prisoner of Dreams* (**1989**). It and its sequel, *The Tenth Class* (**1991**), feature the adventures of a female starship-pilot who must cope with repressive authorities and with planets named, for instance, Heinlein. Romance also looms. [JC]

RITCHIE, PAUL (1923-) Australian painter, novelist and playwright whose *Confessions of a People Lover* (**1967**) depicts a grey, urban, DYSTOPIAN UK where the old ("longlivers") are eliminated by the state and the young are corrupt, cultureless vandals. The book is narrated by a longliver in an enriched, clotted, free-associational style, and is devoid of sf instruments or speculations; it can be read as an allegory of the post-WAR UK. [JC]

RIVERE, ALEC ◊ Charles NUETZEL.

RIVERSIDE, JOHN [s] ◊ Robert A. HEINLEIN.

RIVERSIDE QUARTERLY FANZINE (1964-current) ed Leland Sapiro from Canada and the USA. *RQ* began as a retitled continuation of the fanzine *Inside* (1953-63), published by Ron Smith and then Jon White, which won a HUGO in 1956 and itself incorporated a still earlier fanzine, *Fantasy Advertiser*, later known as *Science Fiction Advertiser* (1946-54). *RQ* quickly formed a quite different character of its own, academic essays on sf and fantasy being its main content. Alexei PANSHIN originally published the major part of his *Heinlein in Dimension* (**1968**) in *RQ*; other contributors have included James BLISH, Algis BUDRYS and Jack WILLIAMSON. Though irregular, this is one of the longest-running – as well as the most serious – of all fanzines; it had reached #32 by early 1992. [PN/PR]

ROAD WARRIOR, THE ◊ MAD MAX 2.

ROBBINS, DAVID L. (1950-) US author of the **Endworld** post-holocaust SURVIVALIST military-sf sequence: *Endworld #1: The Fox Run* (**1986**), #2: *Thief River Falls Run* (**1986**), #3: *Twin Cities Run* (**1986**), #4: *The Kalispell Run* (**1987**), #5: *Dakota Run* (**1987**), #6: *Citadel Run* (**1987**), #7: *Armageddon Run* (**1987**), #8: *Denver Run* (**1987**), #9: *Capital Run* (**1988**), #10: *New York Run* (**1988**), #11: *Liberty Run* (**1988**), #12: *Houston Run* (**1988**), #13: *Anaheim Run* (**1988**), #14: *Seattle Run* (**1989**), #15: *Nevada Run* (**1989**), #16: *Miami Run* (**1989**), #17: *Atlanta Run* (**1989**), #18: *Memphis Run* (**1989**), #19: *Cincinnati Run* (**1990**), #20: *Dallas Run* (**1990**), #21: *Boston Run* (**1990**), #22: *Green Bay Run* (**1990**), #23: *Yellowstone Run* (**1990**), #24: *New Orleans Run* (**1991**), #25: *Spartan Run* (**1991**), #26: *Madman Run* (**1991**) and #27: *Chicago Run* (**1991**). The concurrent **Blade** series comprises *Blade #1: First Strike* (**1989**), #2: *Outlands Strike* (**1989**) (these 2 assembled as *First Strike/Outlands* [omni **1992**]), #3: *Vampire Strike* (**1989**), #4: *Pipeline Strike* (**1989**), #5: *Pirate Strike* (**1990**), #6: *Crusher Strike* (**1990**), #7: *Terror Strike* (**1990**), #8: *Devil Strike* (**1990**), #9: *L.A. Strike* (**1990**), #10: *Dead Zone Strike* (**1990**), #11: *Quest Strike* (**1991**), #12: *Deathmaster Strike* (**1991**) and #13: *Vengeance Strike* (**1991**). Singletons include *The Wereling* (**1983**), which seems to have been DLR's first novel, *The Wrath* (**1988**) and *Spectre* (**1988**). Under the house name J.D. Cameron he has written 2 of the **Omega Sub** sequence: #2: *Command Decision* (**1991**) and #4: *Blood Tide* (**1991**). [JC]

ROBERT HALE LIMITED UK publishing firm which from 1936 through 1984, though mainly in the 1970s, published more than 450 sf novels, in hardbound editions, primarily for the library market. (In 1990 a few US sf titles were reprinted, but no originals.) A large majority of titles originating with the firm were uniform in length (192 pages) and routine in substance, most being SPACE OPERAS. In its early years Hale published speculative fiction from authors like S. Fowler WRIGHT and Wyndham LEWIS, and in the 1970s many established foreign writers – including Poul ANDERSON, A. Bertram CHANDLER, Hal CLEMENT, Gordon R. DICKSON, Ron GOULART, Harry HARRISON, Keith LAUMER, Frank Belknap LONG, Andre NORTON, Robert SILVERBERG and Kate WILHELM – released titles to the UK market through the house; but from the middle of that decade Hale published mostly books signed by names otherwise unknown to the sf world. Some of these were young authors – e.g., Adrian COLE – who would soon move on to more ambitious projects, and some – e.g., the actor Michael ELDER – were authors who published primarily with Hale but who were clearly real individuals; but many were pseudonyms, some of which have been identified and can be found below so designated. Almost certainly several remaining names – some of those below without birth-dates being reasonable suspects – are also pseudonymous. Below we list authors whose names are solely or primarily identified with the Hale imprint, and, where appropriate, their works as well.

John (Kempton) AIKEN, writing for RHL as John Paget.

Roy Ainsworthy ◊ Lauran Bosworth PAINE.

Adrienne Anderson: *Wings of the Morning* (**1971**).

Walter Bacon: *The Last Experiment* (**1974**).

Bee BALDWIN.

Jo Bannister (1951-   ): *The Matrix* (**1981**); *The Winter Plain* (**1982**); *A Cactus Garden* (**1983**).

Mark Bannon ◊ Paul CONRAD.

Alan BARCLAY.

D(onald) A(ndrew) Barker (1947-   ): *A Matter of Evolution* (**1975**); *A Question of Reality* (**1981**).

G.J. BARRETT, whose pseudonyms include Edward Leighton, Dennis Summers and James Wallace.

Roger (Alban) Beaumont (1935-   ): *Deep Space Processional* (**1982**) with R. Snowden Ficks.

John Bedford: *The Titron Madness* (**1984**).

Peter Bentley (real name Alan Moon): *Destined to Survive* (**1977**).

Leigh Beresford: *Fantocine* (**1981**).

Fenton Brockley ◊ Donald S. ROWLAND.

Eric BURGESS.

Roger Carlton ◊ Donald S. ROWLAND.

Mark Carrel ◊ Lauran Bosworth PAINE.

R.M.H. Carter: *The Dream Killers* (**1981**).

Garet Chalmers: *A Legend in his Own Deathtime* (**1978**); *Homo-Hetero* (**1980**).

David Clements: *The Backwater Man* (**1979**).

Paul CONRAD, who writes also under his real name (Albert King) and as Mark Bannon, Floyd Gibson, Scott Howell and Paul Muller.

Paul COREY.

James CORLEY.

(Michael) George Corston (1932-   ): *Aftermath* (**1968**).

S(idney) H(obson) Courtier (1904-1974): *Into the Silence* (**1973**); *The Smiling Trip* (**1975**).

N(icholas) J(ohn) Cullingworth: *Dodos of Einstein* (**1976**).

Jules N. Dagnol: *The Sandoval Transmissions* (**1980**).

Cyril Donson (1919-1986): *Born in Space* (**1968**); *Tritonastra – Planet of the Gargantua* (**1969**); *The Perspective Process* (**1969**); *Draco the Dragon Man* (**1974**).

Iain Douglas: *Point of Impact* (**1979**); *Saturn's Missing*

Rings (**1980**); *The World of the Sower* (**1981**); *The Hearth of Puvaig* (**1981**).

Alfred Dyer: *The Symbiotic Mind* (**1980**); *The Gabriel Inheritance* (**1981**).

Michael ELDER.

James England: *The Measured Caverns* (**1978**).

R. Snowden Ficks ◊ Roger Beaumont (above).

Arthur H(enry) Friggens (1920-   ) ◊ Eric BURGESS.

Nicholas Ganick: *California Dreaming* (**1981**).

Donald J. Garden: *Dawn Chorus* (**1975**).

Graham Garner ◊ Donald S. ROWLAND.

T.S.J. Gibbard (1927-   ): *Vandals of Eternity* (**1974**); *The Starseed Mission* (**1980**); *The Torold Core* (**1980**).

Floyd Gibson ◊ Paul CONRAD.

John Gilchrist (real name Jerome Gardner; 1932-   ): *Birdbrain* (**1975**); *Out North* (**1975**); *Lifeline* (**1976**); *The English Corridor* (**1976**); *The Engendering* (**1978**).

David Graham (1919-   ): *Down to a Sunless Sea* (**1979**).

J(ohn) M(ichael) Graham: *Voice from Earth* (**1972**).

Anthony Grant (possible real name, Marion Staylton Pares [1914-   ]): *The Mutant* (**1980**).

Hilary Green: *Centrifuge 1977* (**1978**).

Harry J. Greenwald: *Chinaman's Chance* (**1981**).

Brian GRIFFIN.

Peter J. Grove: *The Levellers* (**1981**).

Norman Hall (1904-   ): *Green Hailstones* (**1978**).

William C. HEINE.

Gordon T(homas) Horton: *X-Isle* (**1980**).

Troy Howard ◊ Lauran Bosworth PAINE.

Scott Howell ◊ Paul CONRAD.

Mark Jales: *Prelude to Exodus* (**1979**); *In his Own Image* (**1979**); *Normal Service Will be Resumed* (**1980**).

R. Alan James: *No News from Providence* (**1978**).

Norman Jensen: *The Galactic Colonisers* (**1971**).

Neville Kea: *The World of Artemis* (**1980**); *The Rats of Megaera* (**1980**); *The Glass School* (**1980**); *Scorpion* (**1981**).

Albert King ◊ Paul CONRAD.

Edward Leighton ◊ G.J. BARRETT.

John Light: *The Well of Time* (**1981**).

Richard Lindsay: *The Moon is the Key* (**1980**).

Roger Lovin: *Apostle* (**1980**).

Ronald A. McQueen: *The Cosmic Assassin* (**1980**); *The Sorcerer of Marakaan* (**1981**); *The Man who Knew Time* (**1981**); *Mardoc* (**1981**).

Michael F. Maikowski: *Fire in the Sky* (**1981**) with Chris L. Wolf.

Sue Mallinson: *The Serpent and the Butterfly* (**1980**).

David Mariner (real name David McLeod Smith, 1920-   ): *A Shackleton Called Sheila* (**1970**; vt *Countdown 1000* 1974 US).

Dave Morgan: *Reiver* (**1975**); *Genetic Two* (**1976**); *Adverse Camber* (**1977**).

Paul Muller ◊ Paul CONRAD.

Hugh A. Nisbet: *Farewell to Krondahl* (**1980**); *The Raven's Beak* (**1981**).

John October (real name Christopher Portway): *The Anarchy Pedlars* (**1976**).

Lauran Bosworth PAINE, whose pseudonyms include Roy Ainsworthy, Mark Carrel and Troy Howard.

John Paton (real name Frederick John Alford Bateman [1921-   ]): *Leap to the Galactic Core* (**1978**); *Proteus* (**1978**); *The Sea of Rings* (**1979**).

David G(eorge) Penny (1950-   ): *The Sunset People* (**1975**), *Starshine 43* (**1978**) – both post-HOLOCAUST tales of some grimness – *Starchant* (**1975**) and *Out of Time* (**1979**).

W.D. PEREIRA.

Roger Perry (real name Roger William Cowern [1928-   ]): *Senior Citizen* (**1979**); *The Making of Jason* (**1980**); *Esper's War* (**1981**).

Audrey Peyton: *Ashes* (**1981**).

Alex Random ◊ Donald S. ROWLAND.

L.P. REEVES.

Jack Rhys: *The Eternity Merchants* (**1981**); *The Five Doors* (**1981**).

Julia Riding: *Gabion* (**1979**); *The Strange Land* (**1980**); *Deep Space Warriors* (**1981**) – *Space Traders Unlimited* (**1987**), for children, is not a Hale book.

J.R. Robertson: *The Crab Eagle Trees* (**1978**).

Brian Rolls: *Something in Mind* (**1973**).

Raymond J. Ross: *One Hundred Miles above Earth* (**1981**).

Donald S(ydney) ROWLAND, whose pseudonyms include Fenton Brockley, Roger Carlton, Graham Garner, Alex Random, Roland Starr, Mark Suffling.

James Ryder: *Kark* (**1969**); *Vicious Spiral* (**1976**).

Ras Ryman (real name James D. Brown): *The Quadrant War* (**1976**); *Day of the Ultramind* (**1977**); *Weavers of Death* (**1981**).

J(oseph) W(illard) SCHUTZ.

William T. SILENT.

D(enise) N(atalie) Sims (1940-   ): *A Plenteous Seed* (**1973**); *A Pastime of Eternity* (**1975**).

A(nthony) C(orby) Smith (1925-   ): *A Glimpse of Judgement* (**1978**).

Walter J(ames) Smith (1918-   ): *The Grand Voyage* (**1973**); *Fourth Gear* (**1981**).

Roland Starr ◊ Donald S. ROWLAND.

Mark Suffling ◊ Donald S. ROWLAND.

Dennis Summers ◊ G.J. BARRETT.

Nevil Tronchin-James: *Ministry of Procreation* (**1968**).

James B. Tucker (1922-   ): *Not an Earthly Chance* (**1970**).

Michael Vinter (1927-   ): *Along Came a Spider* (**1980**).

Walter Walkham (real name James Harvey Trevithick Ivory [1921-   ]): *When Earth Trembled* (**1980**).

James Wallace ◊ G.J. BARRETT.

Chad Warren: *Alien Heaven* (**1976**).

William Thomas Webb (1918-   ): *The Eye of Hollerl-Ra* (**1977**); *After the Inferno* (**1977**); *Cheyney's Robot* (**1978**); *Poisoned Planet* (**1978**); *The Time Druids* (**1978**); *Dimension Lords* (**1979**); *The Fate of Phral* (**1980**); *The Froth Eater* (**1980**).

Philip Welby: *The Pleasure Dome of Sigma 93* (**1978**).

Martyn Wessex (real name D.F. Little): *The Slowing Down Process* (**1974**); *The Chain Reaction* (**1976**).

Ronald Wilcox: *The Centre of the Wheel* (**1981**).

Eric C. WILLIAMS.

T. Owen Williams: *A Month for Mankind* (**1970**).

Robert Hendrie Wilson: *The Gods Alone* (**1975**); *Ring of Rings* (**1976**); *A Blank Card* (**1977**); *The Frisk Donation* (**1979**).

David Wiltshire (1935-   ): *The Homosaur* (**1978**); *Child of Vodyanoi* (**1978**; vt *The Nightmare Man* 1981); *Genesis II* (**1981**).

Chris L. Wolf: *Fire in the Sky* (**1981**) with Michael F. Maikowski.

J.A. Wood: *We Alien Seed* (**1978**).   [JC]

Further reading: *Hale & Gresham Hardback Science Fiction* (**1988** chap) by Roger ROBINSON.

ROBERTS, ANTHONY (1940-1990) UK illustrator; he often worked as Tony Roberts. AR painted sf covers for many UK paperback publishers. His style was similar to, and perhaps imitative of, that of Chris FOSS; his smooth, hard-edged, highly detailed paintings were typical of UK commercial sf ILLUSTRATION during the 1970s, the period when most of his work appeared. Later he became obsessed with the mystical implications of Glastonbury, wrote 3 books on the mythic significance of West-Country sites, and formed the SMALL PRESS Zodiac House with his wife Janet. He died while climbing Glastonbury Tor with his son.   [JG/PN]

ROBERTS, ARTHUR [r] ◊ John S. GLASBY.

ROBERTS, [Sir] CHARLES G(EORGE) D(OUGLAS) (1860-1943) Canadian poet and novelist, important in CANADA's literary history. Among his many works are several collections of animal fantasies, most notably *The Kindred of the Wild* (coll **1902**), in which various beasts reason like human beings. *In the Morning of Time* (1914-15 *Cosmopolitan*; coll of linked stories **1919** UK), set in prehistoric times, romantically presents the first stages of the ascent to civilization.   [PN/JC]

See also: ORIGIN OF MAN.

ROBERTS, JANE Working name of US writer Jane Roberts Butts (1929-1984), perhaps best remembered for such speculative works as *Dialogues of the Soul & Mortal Self in Time* (**1975**), which took the form of a series of connected poems. She began publishing sf with "The Red Wagon" for *FSF* in 1956. Her sf novel *The Rebellers* (**1963** dos) provides a melodramatic mix of OVERPOPULATION and ECOLOGY themes as successive waves of plague answer humanity's problems by nearly eliminating the race for good. More typical of her later concerns is *The Education of Oversoul Seven* (**1973**), a transcendental parable about the meaning of reality and time and space, whose student protagonist inhabits the bodies and souls of 4 humans from different periods, ranging from 35,000BC to AD2300, and who discovers *en passant* the profound simultaneity of all realities; its sequels are *The Further Education of Oversoul Seven* (**1979**) and *Oversoul Seven and the Museum of Time* (**1984**). *Emir's Education in the Proper Use of Magical Powers* (**1979**) is a juvenile. JR published many further titles of mystical speculation.   [JC]

ROBERTS, JOHN [s] ◊ John R. PIERCE.

ROBERTS, JOHN MADDOX (1947-   ) US writer,

prolific in the later 1980s. His first sf novel, *The Strayed Sheep of Charun* (**1977**; rev vt *Cestus Dei* 1983), is an action-packed romance set on a medievalized planet in which Jesuits and others attempt to reform the violence which is the planet's (and novel's) *raison d'être*. There followed a variety of work, all adventure fiction – whose style is perhaps best described as brisk – in sf or fantasy settings, including the juvenile SPACE-OPERA sequence comprising *Space Angel* (**1979**), in which the commandeering of a spaceship by an ancient ALIEN leads to adventures for a boy, and its sequel *Spacer: Window of the Mind* (**1988**). *King of the Wood* (**1983**) is set in an alternate USA inhabited variously by Norsemen, Native Americans, Aztecs and Spanish Muslims. The **Cingulum** sequence about a raffish spaceship crew's adventures is *The Cingulum* (**1985**), *Cloak of Illusion* (**1985**) and *Cingulum #3: The Sword, the Jewel and the Mirror* (**1988**). JMR also collaborated on 4 books with Eric KOTANI (*whom see for details*): the sequence *Act of God* (**1985**), *The Island Worlds* (**1987**) and *Between the Stars* (**1988**), as well as *Delta Pavonis* (**1990**). JMR's *The Enigma Variations* (**1989**) sets an amnesiac in a corporate future. While all this sf activity was going on, JMR also contributed 5 titles to the ever-growing **Conan** series, set in a SHARED WORLD derived from Robert E. HOWARD's famous SWORD-AND-SORCERY stories: *Conan the Valorous*∗ (**1985**), *Conan the Champion* ∗ (**1987**), *Conan the Marauder* ∗ (**1988**), *Conan the Bold* ∗ (**1989**) and *Conan the Rogue* ∗ (**1991**). The **Stormlands** series, set in a tribalized fantasy world, so far comprises *The Islander* (**1990**) and *The Black Shields* (**1991**). [PN]

Other works: *SPQR* (**1990**) and *SPQR II: The Catiline Conspiracy* (**1991**), police-procedural mystery novels set in ancient Rome.

ROBERTS, KEITH (JOHN KINGSTON) (1935-) UK writer and illustrator resident in the south of England, where most of his best fiction is set. After working as an illustrator and cartoon animator, he began publishing sf with "Anita" and "Escapism" for *Science Fantasy* in 1964; several of his early stories were written as by Alistair Bevan. He served as associate editor of SCIENCE FANTASY 1965-6 and edited its successor *SF Impulse* for the whole of its run (Mar 1966-Feb 1967). His first novel, *The Furies* (**1966**), is the most orthodoxly structured and told of all his work, sf or otherwise, most of his later novels being fixups told from a brooding, slantwise, intensely visual point of view. *The Furies* is a traditional UK DISASTER tale, in which a nuclear test goes awry, inspiring an onslaught of space-spawned giant wasps which ravage England and come close to eliminating mankind. Beyond a certain sultriness of tone, it could have been written by any of a dozen UK specialists in disaster.

With his second book, KR came fully into his own as a writer. *Pavane* (coll of linked stories **1968**; with "The White Boat" added, rev 1969 US) superbly depicts an ALTERNATE WORLD in which – Elizabeth I having been assassinated, the Spanish Armada vic-

torious and no Protestant rise of capitalism in the offing – a technologically backward England survives under the sway of the Catholic Church Militant. The individual stories are moody, eloquent, elegiac and thoroughly convincing. *The Inner Wheel* (coll of linked stories **1970**) deals with the kind of gestalt SUPERMAN theme made familiar by Theodore STURGEON's *More than Human* (fixup 1953) and is similarly powerful, though tending to a rather uneasy sentimentality, perhaps endemic to tales of such relationships but also typical of KR's handling of children and women. *Anita* (coll of linked stories **1970** US; exp 1990 US) is fantasy; the stories had appeared much earlier in *Science Fantasy*. *The Boat of Fate* (**1971**), an historical novel with a Roman setting, shares a painterly concern for primitive landscapes with *The Chalk Giants* (coll of linked stories **1974**; cut 1975 US), whose separate tales elegantly embody a cyclical vision of the future of the island of Britain. The protagonist of the framing narrative (seen in the UK edition only) drives to the south coast to escape an indistinct disaster, goes into hiding, and (depending on one's reading) either cycles the rest of the book through his head or can be seen as himself emblematic of the movement the tales portend, from post-HOLOCAUST chaos through God-ridden savagery back to a state premonitory of his own wounded condition.

KR's early short stories were assembled in *Machines and Men* (coll **1973**) and *The Grain Kings* (coll **1976**), both being excerpted in *The Passing of the Dragons* (coll **1977** US). The title story of the second volume fascinatingly describes life on giant hotel-like grain harvesters in a world of vast farms; in the same volume, "Weihnachtsabend" (1972), perhaps KR's finest single story, depicts an alternate world in which the Nazis have won WWII (◊ HITLER WINS), and expands upon certain savage myths implicit in that victory. Later work was assembled in *Ladies from Hell* (coll **1979**), *The Lordly Ones* (coll **1986**) and *Winterwood and Other Hauntings* (coll **1989**), the limited edition of which also contained, bound-in, *The Event* (**1989** chap). As in his later novels, these stories increasingly display an entangled – though sometimes searching – dis-ease with human nature and sexuality, with the course of history and with the fate of the UK.

KR's first novel after a gap of some years was *Molly Zero* (**1980**), in which the classic sf tale of the growth of an adolescent is – typically for KR – subverted by a sense that the DYSTOPIAN world into which the young female protagonist enters is dismayingly corrosive; it is a sense which variously governs the shadowy escapades of the eponymous heroine of *Kaeti & Company* (coll of linked stories **1986**), *Kaeti's Apocalypse* (**1986** chap) and *Kaeti on Tour* (coll **1992**), and the life of the haunting *femme fatale* depicted in *Gráinne* (**1987**). In mood or venue, these books have little of the feel of sf; *Kiteworld* (fixup **1985**), on the other hand, invokes the atmosphere of earlier work in its depiction of a Britain dominated by religious fanatics, and its constrictive rendering of the life of the crews who man giant kites to guard the frontiers against demons.

As an illustrator, KR did much to change the appearance of UK sf magazines, notably *Science Fantasy*, for which he designed all but 7 of the covers from Jan 1965 until its demise (as *SF Impulse*) in Feb 1967, and also NEW WORLDS for a period in 1966. His boldly Expressionist covers, line-oriented, paralleled the shift in content of these magazines away from GENRE SF and FANTASY towards a more free-form, speculative kind of fiction. He later did covers and interior illustrations for the book editions of *New Worlds Quarterly* ed Michael MOORCOCK, for some of whose novels he has also designed covers. He has illustrated several of his own 1980s titles. [JC]

Other works: *A Heron Caught in Weeds* (coll **1987** chap); *The Natural History of the P.H.* (**1988** chap), nonfiction, the initials referring to the "Primitive Heroine" who appears throughout KR's work; *The Road to Paradise* (dated 1988 but **1989**), associational; *Irish Encounters* (dated 1988 but **1989** chap).

See also: ANDROIDS; BRITISH SCIENCE FICTION AWARD; CYBERNETICS; ESP; HIVE-MINDS; INTERZONE; NEW WRITINGS IN SF; RELIGION; SOCIOLOGY; SUPERNATURAL CREATURES.

ROBERTS, LIONEL ◊ R.L. FANTHORPE.

ROBERTS, MICHELE (BRIGITTE) (1949-   ) UK poet and novelist, poetry editor of *Spare Rib* 1975-7. Her novels all tend to FABULATION in their expression of an articulate FEMINIST aesthetic, but 2 are of genre interest: *The Wild Girl* (**1984**) vigorously displaces the reminiscences of Mary Magdalene, and *The Book of Mrs Noah* (**1987**) similarly engages its heroine in myth-rich concourse with the female icons which engender the stories that make the world (◊ MYTHOLOGY). [JC]

ROBERTS, TERENCE Pseudonym of Ivan Terence Sanderson (1911-1973), UK-born US writer and illustrator on the natural sciences, as in *Living Treasure* (**1941**), about wildlife around the Caribbean. As TR his sf novel was *Report on the Status Quo* (**1955**), a DISASTER story set in 1958-9, when the world is seen to reel under great floods and WWIII. As Ivan T. Sanderson he wrote several books with a relevance to PSEUDO-SCIENCE, including *Abominable Snowmen* (**1961**; cut 1968) on cryptozoology, *Uninvited Visitors: A Biologist Looks at UFOs* (**1967**) and *Invisible Residents* (**1970**) about UFOs and related Fortean matter (◊ Charles FORT), *Things* (**1967**) and *More "Things"* (**1969**) about unexplained mysteries, and the summative *Investigating the Unexplained* (**1972**). [PN]

ROBERTS & VINTER ◊ NEW WORLDS; SCIENCE FANTASY.

ROBERTSON, E(ILEEN) ARNOT Working name of UK writer and broadcaster Eileen Arbuthnot Robertson (1903-1961), best known for such non-sf novels as *Four Frightened People* (**1931**), whose protagonists find themselves making their way through a tropical jungle. It was written to contrast with her sf novel *Three Came Unarmed* (**1929**) which, in a striking attack on modern civilization, exposes 3 (*Homo superior*) *enfants sauvages* to contemporary England, which destroys them. [JC]

ROBERTSON, J.R. [r] ◊ ROBERT HALE LIMITED.

ROBERTSON, MORGAN (ANDREW) (1861-1915) US writer, almost always on nautical themes; many of his stories are sf or fantasy. The fantasy tales, typical of their maritime venues, tend to the mystical, the fog-girt, the occult and the morose. His sf is similar, though future-WAR tales enliven the tone on occasion. MR is perhaps best remembered for *Futility, or The Wreck of the "Titan"* (1898 in untraced US mag as "Futility"; **1912** UK; vt with additional material, coll *The Wrecking of the Titan, or Futility: Paranormal Experiences Connected with the Sinking of the Titanic* 1914 US), which proved uncannily predictive in telling the tale of a great new ship called the *Titan* which steams at an arrogant pace into a iceberg and sinks. [JC]

Other works: *Spun Yarn* (coll **1898**); *"Where Angels Fear to Tread" and Other Tales of the Sea* (coll **1899**); *The Three Laws and the Golden Rule* (coll **1900**); *Down to the Sea* (coll **1905**); *Land Ho!* (coll **1905**); *Over the Border* (coll of linked stories **1914**); *The Grain Ship* (coll of linked stories **1914**).

See also: GREAT AND SMALL.

ROBERT WEINBERG PUBLICATIONS ◊ Robert E. WEINBERG.

ROBESON, KENNETH House name for authors writing the **Doc Savage** series as it appeared 1933-49 in DOC SAVAGE MAGAZINE, published by STREET & SMITH. The Robeson name is most strongly associated with Lester DENT, who wrote all but 43 of the **Doc Savage** stories; other authors involved in that initial run included William G. Bogart, Harold A. Davis, Laurence Donovan, Alan Hathaway and Rymon Johnson. 3 stories – *The Man of Bronze* (**1933**; vt *Doc Savage: The Man of Bronze* 1964), *The Land of Terror* (**1933**; vt *Doc Savage: The Land of Terror* 1965) and *The Quest of the Spider* (**1933**; vt *Doc Savage: The Quest of the Spider* 1972) – were early published in book form. Three decades later the series was brought to life again when BANTAM BOOKS began their republication of the entire run in book form. Variously released as individual titles or in omnibus format, the sequence began with the first title above listed, *Doc Savage: The Man of Bronze*, in 1964 and ended, complete, 182 stories later with *Doc Savage Omnibus #13* (omni **1990**). An entirely new sequence was then initiated, with Will MURRAY writing as KR, #1 being *Doc Savage: Python Isle* * (**1991**).

The enormously wealthy Doc Savage – aided by 5 sidekicks who specialize in various crafts and sciences at the borderline of sf – devotes his life to combating criminal conspiracies, almost all master-minded by the kind of charismatic villain later given definitive form by Ian FLEMING in the **James Bond** books. Doc Savage himself clearly influenced the creation of SUPERMAN, and stands at the heart of Philip José FARMER's **Wold Newton Family** sequence, either in his own name or disguised, with 2 titles – *Doc Savage: His Apocalyptic Life* (**1973**; rev 1975) and *Doc Savage: Escape from Loki* (**1991**) – devoted directly to him. As the original **Doc Savage** tales are of only peripheral sf interest, we do not list them. R. Reginald's *Science Fiction and Fantasy Literature: A Checklist, 1700-1974* (**1979**) provides coverage of the book reprints to the end of 1974; and «Science Fiction & Fantasy Literature: A Bibliography, 1975-1991» (1992), by Reginald with Darryl F. MALLETT and Mary Wickizer Burgess, gives a more complete analysis of the entire run.

The house name KR was used also on the PULP MAGAZINE *The Avenger*, another Street & Smith crime-busting hero series, with rather fewer sf elements. This was an attempt to cash in on the popularity of the **Doc Savage** stories. Most of the **Avenger** series (many also reprinted as paperback books in the 1970s) were the work of Paul ERNST; the final dozen titles of the 1970s run, from *The Man from Atlantis* (**1974**) on, were newly written by Ron GOULART. Other writers associated with the Kenneth Robeson name were Norman A. Danburg and Emile Tepperman. [JC/PN]

About the author: *The Man behind Doc Savage: A Tribute to Lester Dent* (**1974**) by Robert E. WEINBERG; *Bigger than Life: The Creator of Doc Savage* (**1990**) by Marilyn Cannaday.

ROBIDA, ALBERT (1848-1926) French illustrator, lithographer and writer. AR was the most important and popular of 19th-century sf illustrators, and may even be said to have founded the genre, though he was clearly working in the tradition of such French fantastic artists as Grandville (Jean Gérard; 1803-1847) and Gustave Doré (1832-1883). Always interested in DYSTOPIAS and SATIRE, he illustrated works by François RABELAIS, CYRANO DE BERGERAC, Jonathan SWIFT and Camille FLAMMARION among others, but his most important works had texts by himself. These were very often first published as periodical-series, each instalment being slim, and then later in most cases as books. AR took up sf themes with his gently satirical homage to Jules VERNE's **Voyages extraordinaires** with *Voyages très extraordinaires de Saturnin Farandoul*, a 100-part periodical beginning June 1879. It was later collected as 5 books (all **1882**): *Le roi des singes* ["King of the Monkeys"], *Le tour du monde en plus de 80 jours* ["Round the World in More than 80 Days"], *Les quatre reines* ["The Four Queens"], *À la recherche de l'éléphant blanc* ["In Search of the White Elephant"] and *S. Exc. M. le Gouverneur du Pole Nord* ["His Excellency the Governor of the North Pole"]. A more prophetic work was *Le vingtième siècle* ["The 20th Century"], a periodical in 50 parts beginning Jan 1882. There followed another series appearing later as *La vie électrique* ["The Electric Life"] (**1883**), set in 1955. AR's ironically half-amused but pessimistic view of the likely nature of future WAR (many of his predictions proved all too true) appeared in #200 of the humorous magazine *La Caricature* (1883) as "La guerre au vingtième siècle" ["War in the 20th Century"], set in 1975, and in a book with the same title but different contents, *La guerre au vingtième siècle* (**1887**), set in 1945. A TIME-TRAVEL fantasy, serialized in the magazine

Le petit français illustré in 1890, *Jadis chez aujourd'hui* ["The Long-Ago is with Us Today"], features a scientist resuscitating Molière and other literary figures in order to show them the Universal Exhibition of 1889, which bores them. *L'horloge des siècles* ["Clock of the Centuries"] (**1902**) is one of the earliest treatments of the time-reversal theme later used by, for example, Philip K. DICK in *Counter-Clock World* (**1967**), Brian W. ALDISS in *An Age* (**1967**; vt *Cryptozoic!* US) and Martin AMIS in *Time's Arrow* (**1991**). AR continued to produce quite prolifically, his last work being another future fantasy entitled *Un chalet dans les airs* ["Castle in the Air"] (**1925**).

The texts to the above works are generally undistinguished. The ILLUSTRATIONS, however, mostly in a vein of detailed caricature, are consistently inventive and amusing. AR worked mostly with lithographic pencil and crayon, achieving a haphazard but impressive vigour. The figures are very much those of Victorian Europe, dressed in the fashions of the time, and involved in various busy scenes with a huge variety of modernistic devices. Among his hundreds of predictions were the videophone and germ warfare. His machines and WEAPONS were usually well designed – some may actually have been practicable – although his flying machines look distinctly un-airworthy. The ironic intelligence of his work is rather undermined by his inability to imagine the future except in terms of more and more gadgetry: social mores remain frozen in the Victorian mould. AR had a strong influence on the future-war genre. [PN/JG]

See also: FRANCE; TRANSPORTATION.

ROBINET, LEE ◊ Robert Ames BENNET.

ROBINETT, STEPHEN (ALLEN) (1941-   ) US writer and lawyer who began publishing sf as Tak Hallus (apparently Persian for "pen name") with "Mini-talent" for *ASF* in 1969. His first novel, *Mindwipe!* (1969 *ASF* as by Tak Hallus; **1976** Canada) as by Steve Hahn, is unexceptional, but *Stargate* (1974 *ASF* as by Tak Hallus; **1976**) intriguingly combines HARD SF and detective modes in the tale of two great corporations and their quarrel over the eponymous MATTER TRANSMITTER. Along with Frederik POHL's *Gateway* (**1977**), this novel was important in establishing the commercial stargate (which can be variously defined as a matter-transmission aperture or as a discontinuity or as a wormhole extension of a singularity – so long as the phenomenon allows profitable and instantaneous contact to be made between one part of the Universe and another) as an essential instrument of modern sf. *The Man Responsible* (fixup **1978**) again focuses on the relationship between crime and sf, the story dealing this time with a 21st-century world in which computer projections pass as human. SR's stories, in which a sharp wit is allowed free and satirical play, are assembled in *Projections* (coll **1979**). It is a matter of serious regret that SR ceased publishing around 1980. [JC]

ROBINSON, CHARLES HENRY (1843-1930) US writer

whose *Longhead: The Story of the First Fire* (**1913**) capably runs the gamut of prehistoric-sf themes from the discovery of fire to the first hints of civilization (◊ ORIGIN OF MAN). [JC]

ROBINSON, E(DWARD) A. (? -?) US writer in whose *The Disk: A Tale of Two Passions* (**1884**; vt *The Disk: A Prophetic Reflection* 1884 UK), with G(eorge) A. Wall, a series of inventions – optical cables capable of harnessing the Sun's light, imperishable food, disease-eliminating injections – plays second fiddle to a tale of sexual passions. The inventions are effective. [JC]

ROBINSON, ELEANOR (? -) US writer in whose first novel, *Chrysalis of Death* (**1976**), a disastrous primordial germ changes people into beasts. A brave doctor fights the menace; there is soap opera and sex. *The Silverleaf Syndrome* (**1980**; vt *The Freak* 1985) was less noticeable. [JC]

ROBINSON, FRANK M(ALCOLM) (1926-) US writer, also active in publishing, who began writing sf stories in 1950 with "The Maze" in *ASF* and was for a time fairly prolific, soon publishing his first (and for decades his only) solo novel, *The Power* (**1956**). This effectively combines sf and thriller in the story of the search for a malignant SUPERMAN with undefined powers, including the ability to seem different to everyone who looks at him. The protagonist, himself paranormally gifted, kills the bad superman and contemplates being a good one. It was filmed as *The* POWER in 1967. FMR then fell relatively silent – fewer than half the stories assembled in *A Life in the Day of . . . and Other Short Stories* (coll **1981**) were written after *The Power* – and concentrated on editorial jobs, working for a variety of publications including *Rogue* (1959-65) and *Playboy*) (1969-73). In the 1970s he changed direction and, in collaboration with Thomas N. SCORTIA, produced a series of DISASTER novels which, though sf devices and explanations are occasionally invoked, most closely resemble the TECHNOTHRILLER. The first of these, *The Glass Inferno* (**1974**), was filmed – along with Richard Martin Stern's *The Tower* – as *The Towering Inferno* (**1974**); further titles were *The Prometheus Crisis* (**1975**), which deals with the failure of a vast nuclear reactor, *The Nightmare Factor* (**1978**), about biological warfare, *The Gold Crew* (**1980**) and *Blow Out!* (**1987**). *The Great Divide* (**1982**), by FMR with John Levin, is set in the NEAR FUTURE, when a coup threatens the USA.

FMR's concentration on these lucrative but unchallenging books tended to blur the early critical sense that he was a sharp and incisive writer, and *The Dark Beyond the Stars* (**1991**) came as a welcome reminder of his gifts. It is – perhaps rather late in genre history – a GENERATION-STARSHIP tale, told with much of the claustrophobia and dramatic irony typical of POCKET-UNIVERSE narratives. In keeping with its late composition, the ironies dominate: the family romance that the protagonist must decode in order to mature is unfruitful, and the ship turns homeward. The book itself was a welcome signal of its author's own

return to the genre. [JC]
See also: ESP.
ROBINSON, JEANNE [r] ◊ Spider ROBINSON.
ROBINSON, KIM STANLEY (1952-) US writer who began writing sf stories with "Coming Back to Dixieland" and "In Pierson's Orchestra", both published in *Orbit 18* (**1975**) ed Damon KNIGHT. He has not been prolific in shorter forms, publishing only about 10 stories before gaining his PhD in English at the University of California in 1982. In revised form, his thesis was later published as *The Novels of Philip K. Dick* (**1984**); thoroughly researched, at ease with the protocols of academic writing while at the same time showing an acute understanding of 1950s sf, it remains one of the most useful studies of Philip K. DICK's thorny oeuvre.

KSR became widely known with the publication of his first novel, *The Wild Shore* (1984), released as one of Terry CARR's **Ace Specials**. The first book of a thematic trilogy set in various versions of **Orange County** on the Pacific coast south of Los Angeles, *The Wild Shore* lucidly examines the sentimentalized kind of US sf pastoral typically set after an almost universal catastrophe. Sheltered from the full DISASTER, Orange County has become an enclave whose inhabitants espouse a re-established US hegemony, but whose smug ignorance of the world outside is ultimately self-defeating. In *The Gold Coast* (**1988**), Orange County several decades hence is seen through the lens of DYSTOPIA; a similar array of characters – similarly related to one another – must grapple with a polluted, corrupt, overcrowded, ecologically devastated world. Under new names the same characters find themselves, in *Pacific Edge* (**1990** UK), breathing the air of UTOPIA. In this world Orange County has benefited from restrictions on corporate size and strict controls over land use and POLLUTION. Although the novel shows the near impossibility of imagining a living utopia, a sense of earned freshness and relief permeates its pages. As a whole, the trilogy may be read as three versions of the same story, each nesting within the other; structurally adventurous and searching, the **Orange County** trilogy – although his projected **Mars** sequence may supplant it as a sustained fictional argument – remains at the moment KSR's strongest accomplishment.

Other novels are varyingly successful. *Icehenge* (fixup **1984**) strikingly conflates three incompatible readings of the significance of an artifact found on Pluto, exploring a range of issues from epistemology to the nature of historical tradition. *The Memory of Whiteness* (**1985**) less successfully attempts to suggest analogues between MUSIC theory and the structure of the Universe, while at the same time conducting its musician hero – who is, typically of KSR's protagonists, an almost constantly active character – on a guided tour of the Solar System. *Escape from Kathmandu* (**1988** chap), later expanded as *Escape from Kathmandu* (coll of linked stories **1989**), set in a stress-ridden mystical Nepal, amusingly exploits KSR's own experience as a mountaineer.

Other stories appear in *The Planet on the Table* (coll **1986**), *The Blind Geometer* (**1986** chap; with 1 story added, coll 1989 dos) – a later but lesser magazine version won the 1987 NEBULA for Best Novella – and *Remaking History* (coll **1991**), which includes all the stories published in the slightly earlier *A Sensitive Dependence on Initial Conditions* (coll **1991** chap); *Down and Out in the Year 2000* (coll **1992** UK) gathers together *The Blind Geometer* and *A Short Sharp Shock* plus tales from *Remaking History*. *Green Mars* (1985 *IASFM*; **1988** chap dos) prefigures the long-projected **Mars** trilogy, which treats that planet as a realistic habitat for the human species; the first volume, *Red Mars* (**1992** UK), ranges magisterially over the early years of TERRAFORMING, COLONIZATION and disruption; the sequence as a whole – comprising «Green Mars» (1993) (not textually related to *Green Mars*) and «Blue Mars» – is projected to extend over 200 years of civilization on MARS. *A Short Sharp Shock* (**1990**) carries its athletic and ultimately clear-eyed protagonist into a soul-defining trek across an endless sea-girt peninsula which is freely symbolic of death, or of the nature of life, or simply of the path a person must follow to fill out a human span.

In a somewhat contrived attempt to contrast him to CYBERPUNK writers, KSR has been described as a Humanist; he has himself disparaged as foolishly reductive this use of Humanism as a label. What in fact most characterizes the growing reach and power of his work is its cogent analysis and its disposal of such category thinking. He is at heart an explorer. [JC]

Other work: *Black Air* (1983 *FSF*; **1991** chap).

About the author: *A Checklist of Kim Stanley Robinson* (**1991** chap) by Tom Joyce and Christopher P. STEPHENS.

See also: ACE BOOKS; ALTERNATE WORLDS; DEFINITIONS OF SF; HISTORY IN SF; ISAAC ASIMOV'S SCIENCE FICTION MAGAZINE; JOHN W. CAMPBELL MEMORIAL AWARD; *The* MAGAZINE OF FANTASY AND SCIENCE FICTION; MATHEMATICS; MESSIAHS; NANOTECHNOLOGY; NUCLEAR POWER; OUTER PLANETS; PHILIP K. DICK AWARD.

ROBINSON, PHILIP BEDFORD (1926-) UK writer who has worked in India. In *Masque of a Savage Mandarin* (**1969**) the deracinated protagonist takes symbolic revenge upon the world via the systematic destruction, by electrical means, of a victim's brain. [JC]

ROBINSON, ROGER (1943-) UK computer programmer and bibliographer, active in UK fandom for many years. *The Writings of Henry Kenneth Bulmer* (**1983** chap; rev 1984 chap) is an exhaustive BIBLIOGRAPHY of one of the most prolific sf writers, and *Who's Hugh?: An SF Reader's Guide to Pseudonyms* (**1987**) is similarly exhaustive. Criticized at first for its failure to annotate its findings – so that, for instance, pseudonyms used for sf could not be distinguished from others – it has shown itself accurate and comprehensive. By sourcing each attribution, so that

readers can weigh the reliability of the ascriptions, it aspires to a greater methodological sophistication than is often found in sf scholarship. [JC]

ROBINSON, SPIDER Working and now perhaps legal name of US-born writer Paul Robinson (1948-), in Canada from 1973, the same year he published his first story, "The Guy with the Eyes" for *ASF*, thus inaugurating his long-running **Callahan** series of CLUB STORIES. He sometimes wrote tales as by B.D. Wyatt. The first few years of his career were honour-laden. He shared with Lisa TUTTLE the 1974 JOHN W. CAMPBELL AWARD for Best New Writer; topped the 1977 Locus Poll for Best Critic, mainly for his **Galaxy Bookshelf** column for *Gal* June 1975-Sep 1977; received a 1977 HUGO for the *ASF* publication (as "By Any Other Name") of the first 4 chapters of his first novel, *Telempath* (**1976** US); and won both Hugo and NEBULA in 1978, along with his wife and collaborator Jeanne Robinson, for "Stardance", which became the nucleus of *Stardance* (**1979** US) with Jeanne Robinson. (In 1983 he won another Hugo, for "Melancholy Elephants" [1982].) At this high point of his career, his punchy optimism about the human condition and his adroit use of generic materials to express that optimism seemed to have established him as a legitimate heir to Robert A. HEINLEIN, a writer he deeply admired. *Telempath*, a complicated story set in a post-HOLOCAUST Earth after a decimating virus plague, cleverly promulgates a sense that the surviving humans, in conjunction with the telepathic Muskies – gaseous beings imperceptible before the plague – can earn cohabitation with a vast empathic net of species. *Stardance* similarly presents its audience with a protagonist – this time a dancer too big for Earth work – who helps propel humanity upwards into a Galaxy rich with communicating species.

The **Callahan** sequence makes use of the capacity of the club story to reassure both participants and readers, and conveys a sense of real community (as in the tv series *Cheers*) through a wide range of tales – sf and fantasy predominating – which reveal human and alien frailties while simultaneously affirming the group. The series comprises *Callahan's Crosstime Saloon* (coll **1977** US), *Time Travelers Strictly Cash* (coll **1981** US) and *Callahan's Secret* (coll **1986** US), most of the stories from these 3 vols being assembled as *Callahan and Company: The Compleat Chronicles of the Crosstime Saloon* (dated 1987 but **1988** US) and a smaller selection being issued as *Callahan's Crazy Crosstime Bar* (**1989** UK). *Callahan's Lady* (coll **1989** US), set prior to the main series in a whorehouse run by Callahan's wife, assembles similar tales; «Lady Slings the Booze» (1992) is projected. *Kill the Editor* (**1991** US) is also set in the whorehouse. SR's club stories differ from some older models mainly through the amount of action that occurs in the saloon itself, so that their ultimate effect is, at times, complex.

The 1970s were the high point for SR's somewhat insistent cheer, and subsequent work has proven considerably grimmer in tone. *Mindkiller: A Novel of the Near Future* (**1982** US) – for which the RECURSIVE *Time Pressure* (**1987** US) serves as both prequel and sequel – complicatedly shifts time-schemes and identities in an attempt to depict a crime- and computer-ridden world; the succeeding volume, even less coherently, re-invokes the 1973 Nova Scotia of SR's own memories, introducing a nude time-traveller who nurses the psychically wounded protagonist back to the point at which he can begin to understand his significance in the scheme of things. SR's style in these later books – exclamatory and burdened with Heinleinesque exaggerations – does little to sustain their rollercoaster plots. *Night of Power* (**1985** US), more controlled, aroused some negative response for its depiction of a Black-power revolt in New York City. His stories, on the other hand, have been more stable and consistent. Collections include *Antinomy* (coll **1980** US); *Melancholy Elephants* (coll **1984**; with 1 story dropped and 2 added, rev 1985 US), his only book to be initially released by the feeble Canadian publishing industry; and *True Minds* (coll **1990** US). [JC]

Other works: *The Best of All Possible Worlds* (anth **1980**); *Copyright Violation* (**1990** chap).

See also: ARTS; ASTOUNDING SCIENCE-FICTION; CANADA; DESTINIES; GALAXY SCIENCE FICTION; MUSIC.

ROBINSONADE Daniel DEFOE's *The Life and Strange Surprizing Adventures of Robinson Crusoe* (**1719**) provides the original model for robinsonades – romances of solitary survival in such inimical terrains as desert ISLANDS (or planets) – and also supplies much of the thematic and symbolic buttressing that allows so many of these stories to be understood as allegories of mankind's search for the meaning of life, just as Crusoe's ordeal is both a religious punishment for disobedience and a triumphant justification of entrepreneurial individualism. Crusoe's paternalistic relation to the natives he eventually encounters has likewise been echoed in much modern sf, where until very recently human/ALIEN relations tended to be depicted within the same code of mercantilist opportunism. A second important model for sf's numerous robinsonades may well be Johann WYSS's *Der Schweizerische Robinson* (**1812-13**; trans – perhaps by William Godwin – as *The Family Robinson Crusoe* **1814** UK; new trans as *The Swiss Family Robinson* 1818 UK) – itself imitated by tales like D.W. Belisle's *The American Family Robinson* (**1853**) – in which the element of the triumphant ordeal is broadened to include the testing of a full microcosm of social life – leading either to UTOPIAN speculations, to which the robinsonade has always been structurally attuned, or to the simpler, more active adventure of the COLONIZATION OF OTHER WORLDS. However, the fundamental thrust of the robinsonade – its convincing celebration of the power of pragmatic Reason, and its depiction of the triumph, alone, over great odds, of the entrepreneur who commands that rational Faculty – continues to drive most of its offspring. [JC]

ROBINSON CRUSOE ON MARS Film (**1964**). Schenck-Zabel/Paramount. Dir Byron HASKIN, starring Paul Mantee, Vic Lundin. Screenplay Ib Melchior, John C. Higgins, remotely based on *Robinson Crusoe* (**1719**) by Daniel DEFOE. 109 mins. Colour.

Haskin directed several sf films in the 1950s, including WAR OF THE WORLDS (1953), and returned to the genre in 1964 with this interesting, futuristic version of Defoe's classic novel. After a spaceship crashlands on Mars, one of the two pilots (the other is killed) struggles to survive and to remain sane in the alien, barren landscape – here well played by California's Death Valley – his only companion his pet monkey. This section of the film is compelling; but, with the arrival of alien spaceships, the ROBINSONADE in a hostile environment gives way to SPACE-OPERA melodrama: the Earthman rescues one of the aliens' slaves, who becomes his Man Friday, and a conventional pursuit-and-escape story follows. The story resembles that of Rex GORDON's *No Man Friday* (**1956**; vt *First on Mars*), but no credit is given to Gordon in the titles. [JP/PN]

ROBOCOP Film (**1987**). Orion. Dir Paul Verhoeven, starring Peter Weller, Nancy Allen, Daniel O'Herlihy, Ronny Cox, Kurtwood Smith. Screenplay Edward Neumeier, Michael Miner. 102 mins. Colour.

Dutch director Verhoeven here unusually made a successful transition from foreign art films – the violent medieval epic *Flesh + Blood* (1985) and the perverse thriller *The Fourth Man* (1983) – to a US populist blockbuster. A corrupt corporation in NEAR-FUTURE Detroit manufactures a prototype CYBORG (Weller) in which the head of a mortally wounded policeman is integrated with a powerful metal body. The brutal extermination of criminals and cleansing of the corrupt business community that follow are directed with a blend of technical skill, low cunning and genuine artistry that is both dismaying and breathtaking. The casual cruelties of the ongoing bloodbath seem merely a cynical exploitation of the worst aspects of audience voyeurism, but the film also contains a density of information about, and a sharp satirical observation of, this future world that are both rare and welcome in sf cinema. Verhoeven went on to direct TOTAL RECALL. The sequel, not dir Verhoeven, was ROBOCOP 2. [PN]

See also: CINEMA.

ROBOCOP 2 Film (**1990**). Orion. Dir Irvin Kershner, starring Peter Weller, Nancy Allen, Belinda Bauer, Daniel O'Herlihy, Tom Noonan. Screenplay Frank MILLER, Walon Green from a story by Miller. 116 mins. Colour.

Dismissed by most critics as an unimaginative retread of ROBOCOP, *R2* nevertheless has merits. Its narrative clarity and dash, which deliver a vision of future Detroit as one of the deeper circles of Hell, a sort of DANTE-meets-DC COMICS, are a credit to the partnership of director Kershner (who made *The EMPIRE STRIKES BACK* [1980]) and screenwriter Miller (who wrote and illustrated the **Batman** GRAPHIC NOVEL

The Dark Knight Returns [graph **1986**]). These qualities partially redeem *R2*'s simplistic repetition of the previous film's thematic concerns (anti-capitalism, anti-liberalism, casual slaughter and lots of cynicism about tv news coverage) in a story where the good CYBORG cop (Weller) is again pitted against the evil corporation (privatizing the police force and about to do likewise to City Hall) and their new, drug-crazed cyborg killer. Rob Bottin's cyborg designs are appropriately grotesque. [PN]

ROBOT JOX Film (1990). Empire. Dir Stuart Gordon, starring Gary Graham, Anne Marie Johnson, Paul Koslo, Robert Sampson, Hilary Mason. Screenplay Joe HALDEMAN, Dennis Paoli. 82 mins. Colour.

The people ("jox") who pilot the future ROBOT colossi with which wars are settled in single combat are popular idols. The hero (Graham) is traumatized when he accidentally crushes a spectator stand and quits, but returns when the biologically engineered, test-tube created woman he loves (Johnson) endangers herself by entering the field of combat. A long-cherished project of Charles BAND's financially troubled Empire Pictures, and his most expensive, *RJ* was several years in the making and is disorientingly inconsistent in its production values: top-of-the-line effects by David Allen in the robot combat, but low-budget interiors and a few wobbly matte fringes. Gordon, scaling down his gore effects after RE-ANIMATOR (1985) and FROM BEYOND (1986), handles the subtly humorous pulp-sf angles very well and gives the film a pleasantly uncluttered comic-bookish look, while Haldeman's sf-writer touch can be traced in the neat background details (ad-campaigns for pregnancy, bigotry against "tubies") and in his distinctive blend of military-hardware expertise and anti-WAR attitudes, the latter being especially apparent in the surprisingly emotional climax. [KN]

ROBOTS The word "robot" first appeared in Karel ČAPEK's play *R.U.R.* (**1921**; trans **1923**), and is derived from the Czech *robota* (statute labour). Čapek's robots were artificial human beings of organic origin, but the term is usually applied to MACHINES. Real-life assembly-line robots are adapted to specific functions, but in sf – where the term overlaps to some extent with ANDROIDS – it usually refers to machines in more-or-less human form.

Machines which mimic human form date back, in both fiction and reality, to the early 19th century. The real automata were showpieces: clockwork dummies or puppets. Their counterparts in the fiction of E.T.A. HOFFMANN – the Talking Turk in "Automata" (1814) and Olympia in "The Sandman" (1816) – present a more verisimilitudinous image, and play a sinister role, their wondrous artifice being seen as something blasphemous and diabolically inspired. The automaton in Herman MELVILLE's "The Bell-Tower" (1855) has similar allegorical connotations. Early-20th-century works are markedly different. William Wallace COOK's *A Round Trip to the Year 2000* (1903; **1925**), which features robotic "mugwumps", and the anonymous

skit *Mechanical Jane* (**1903**) are both comedies, as is J. Storer CLOUSTON's *Button Brains* (**1933**), a novel in which a robot is continually mistaken for its human model and which introduced most of the mechanical-malfunction jokes that remain the staple diet of stage and tv plays featuring robots. (Robots are the most common sf device used in drama because they can be so conveniently and so amusingly played by live actors; the tradition extends to recent times in Alan Ayckbourn's *Henceforward* [1988].)

Early PULP-MAGAZINE stories about robots are generally ambivalent. David H. KELLER's "The Psychophonic Nurse" (1928) is a cooperative servant, but no substitute for a mother's love. Abner J. Gelula's "Automaton" (1931) has lecherous designs on its creator's daughter and has to be destroyed. Harl VINCENT's "Rex" (1934) takes over the world and is about to remake Man in the image of the robot when his regime is overthrown. But the balance soon swung in favour of sympathy. The machines in Eando BINDER's "The Robot Aliens" (1935) come in peace but are misunderstood and abused by hostile humans; and saccharine sentimentality is also in the ascendant in "Helen O'Loy" (1938) by Lester DEL REY, in which a man marries the ideal mechanical woman, in "Robots Return" (1938) by Robert Moore WILLIAMS, in which spacefaring robots discover that they were created by humans and accept the disappointment nobly, in "Rust" (1939) by Joseph E. KELLEAM, which describes the tragic decline into extinction of mechanical life on Earth, in the anti-Frankensteinian parable "I, Robot" (1939) by Eando Binder, and in "True Confession" (1940) by F. Orlin TREMAINE and "Almost Human" (1941) by Ray CUMMINGS, both of which feature altruistic acts of robotic self-sacrifice. Isaac ASIMOV claims to have invented his famous "Laws of Robotics" (see below) in response to a technophobic "Frankenstein syndrome", but there is little evidence of one in the robot stories published around the time of "Strange Playfellow" (1940; vt "Robbie"). Robots are given higher status than mere humans in "Farewell to the Master" (1940) by Harry BATES and "Jay Score" (1941) by Eric Frank RUSSELL, the first of a series later published as *Men, Martians and Machines* (coll of linked stories **1956**).

The system of ethics with which Asimov's POSI-TRONIC ROBOTS were hardwired was enshrined in 3 famous Laws (devised in discussions with John W. CAMPBELL Jr, whom Asimov insisted was their co-creator): (1) a robot may not injure a human being or, through inaction, allow a human being to come to harm; (2) a robot must obey the orders given it by human beings except where such orders would conflict with the First Law; (3) a robot must protect its own existence as long as such protection does not conflict with the First or Second Law. The laws emerged from "Reason" (1941); "Liar" (1941) became the first of many Asimov stories whose plots involve the explication of odd robot behaviour as an unexpected consequence of them. In "Liar" (as in many others) the logical unravelling is accomplished by the "robopsychologist" Susan Calvin. The early stories in the series – collected in *I, Robot* (coll of linked stories **1950**) – culminated in "Evidence" (1946), in which a robot politician can get elected only by convincing voters that he is human, but does the job far better than the man he replaces. In C.L. MOORE's "No Woman Born" (1944) a dancer whose mind is resurrected in a robot body quickly concludes that the robot condition is preferable to the human. The robot servants who survive mankind in Clifford D. SIMAK's *City* (1944-52; fixup **1952**) are the perfect gentlemen's gentlemen rather than mere slaves. One cautionary note was sounded by Anthony BOUCHER, whose stories "Q.U.R." and "Robinc" (both 1943 as by H.H. Holmes) champion "usuform robots" against anthropomorphous ones; the stated reasons are utilitarian, but Boucher's religious faith – he was a devout Catholic – may have influenced his opinion. The most notable comic robot in pulp sf – outside the works of the prolific Ron GOULART, which are infested by logically malfunctioning robots of every conceivable variety, not exclusively with comic intent – is the narcissistic machine in *Robots Have No Tails* (1943-8; coll of linked stories **1952**) by Henry KUTTNER (as Lewis Padgett).

After 1945, when the atom bomb provoked a new suspicion of technology, attitudes to robots in sf became more ambivalent again. In 1947 Asimov published his first sinister-robot story, "Little Lost Robot", and Jack WILLIAMSON produced the classic "With Folded Hands", in which robot "humanoids" charged "to serve man, to obey, and to guard men from harm" take their mission too literally, and set out to ensure that no one endangers their own well being and that everyone is happy, even if that requires permanent tranquillization or prefrontal lobotomy. Many writers did not relinquish their loyalty to machines; Asimov and Simak remained steadfastly pro-robot, and Williamson relented somewhat in his sequel to "With Folded Hands", *The Humanoids* (**1949**) – although the ending of the novel may have been suggested by John W. CAMPBELL Jr rather than being a spontaneous expression of Williamson's own technophilic tendencies – but most robot stories of the 1950s involve some kind of confrontation and conflict. Robots kill or attempt to kill humans in "Lost Memory" (1952) by Peter Phillips (1920-), "Second Variety" (1953) by Philip K. DICK, "Short in the Chest" (1954) by Idris Seabright (Margaret ST CLAIR), "First to Serve" (1954) by Algis BUDRYS, *The Naked Sun* (**1956**) by Asimov and "Mark XI" (1957; vt "Mark Elf") by Cordwainer SMITH. The mistaken-identity motif takes on sinister or unfortunate associations in Asimov's "Satisfaction Guaranteed" (1951), Dick's "Impostor" (1953), Walter M. MILLER's "The Darfsteller" (1955) and Robert BLOCH's "Comfort Me, My Robot" (1955). Robot courtroom dramas include Simak's "How-2" (1954), Asimov's "Galley Slave" (1957) and del Rey's "Robots Should

Be Seen" (1958). Man-robot boxing matches are featured in "Title Fight" (1956) by William Campbell Gault, "Steel" (1956) by Richard MATHESON and "The Champ" (1958) by Robert Presslie. The robot is an instrument of judgement in "Two-Handed Engine" (1955) by Kuttner and C.L. MOORE. Black comedies involving robots include several stories by Robert SHECKLEY, notably "Watchbird" (1953) and "The Battle" (1954), although Sheckley's classic story in this vein was the later "The Cruel Equations" (1971). One story which deviates markedly from the pattern is Boucher's Catholic fantasy "The Quest for St Aquin" (1951), in which a perfectly logical robot emulates Thomas Aquinas and deduces the reality of God; but in the main robot stories of the 1950s reflected profound anxieties concerning the relationship between Man and machine. Asimov's *Caves of Steel* (**1954**), which deals in some depth with its hero's anti-machine prejudices and his mechanized environment, brings this anxiety clearly into focus.

As post-Hiroshima anxiety began to ebb away in the late 1950s, a more relaxed attitude to the robot became evident, humour and gentle irony coming to the fore in such stories as those in Harry HARRISON's *War with the Robots* (1958-62; coll **1962**), Brian W. ALDISS's "But Who Can Replace a Man?" (1958), Fritz LEIBER's *The Silver Eggheads* (**1961**) and Poul ANDERSON's "The Critique of Impure Reason" (1962). The old sentimentality returned to the robot story in full force in Simak's "All the Traps of Earth" (1960), and soon reached new depths of sickliness in Ray BRADBURY's "I Sing the Body Electric!" (1969). The rehabilitation of the robot was completed by Barrington J. BAYLEY's study in robot existentialism, *The Soul of the Robot* (**1974**; rev 1976), and its sequel, *The Rod of Light* (**1985**), and by Asimov's "That Thou Art Mindful of Him" (1974) and "The Bicentennial Man" (1976), which took the robot's philosophical self-analysis to its logical conclusion, ending with the identification of the robot as a thoroughly "human" being. Asimov later set out to integrate his robot stories into the Future History of his **Foundation** series in such novels as *The Robots of Dawn* (**1983**) and *Robots and Empire* (**1985**); he also wrote a series of juvenile robot stories in collaboration with his wife Janet ASIMOV, begun with *Norby the Mixed-Up Robot* (**1983**), and lent his name to a series of SHARED-WORLD novels set in **Isaac Asimov's Robot City**, begun with *Odyssey* (**1987**) by Michael P. KUBE-MCDOWELL. Janet Asimov carried the family tradition forward in *Mind Transfer* (**1988**), which explores the possibilities of robot SEX alongside philosophical discussions of robotic "humanness". Other exercises in robot existentialism are featured in Sheila MacLEOD's *Xanthe and the Robots* (**1977**) and Walter TEVIS's angst-ridden *Mockingbird* (**1980**).

Robot philosophy of a less earnest but cleverer kind is extensively featured in Stanisław LEM's robotic fables, collected in *The Cyberiad* (coll **1965**; trans **1974**) and *Mortal Engines* (coll trans **1977**). Robot RELIGION and MYTHOLOGY are featured in Robert F. YOUNG's "Robot Son" (1959), Roger ZELAZNY's "For a Breath I Tarry" (1966), Simak's *A Choice of Gods* (1972) and Gordon EKLUND's "The Shrine of Sebastian" (1973). The integration of the robot into human religious culture is celebrated in Robert SILVERBERG's "Good News from the Vatican" (1971), about the election of the first robot pope. Some humans, at least, are prepared to fight for the freedom of ex-colonial robots in James P. HOGAN's *Code of the Lifemaker* (1983). The awkward question of whether one would let one's daughter marry a robot is squarely addressed in Tanith LEE's *The Silver Metal Lover* (1982), and the problems of an orphaned robot trying to get by in a puzzling and hostile world are hilariously displayed in *Roderick* (1980) and *Roderick at Random* (1983) by John T. SLADEK. The homicidal robot, although an endangered species, has not quite become extinct: a robot executioner is featured in Roger Zelazny's "Home Is the Hangman" (1975) and a robot psychopath whose "asimov circuits" have failed is the antihero of Sladek's *Tik-Tok* (1983). The killer-robot, however, made its most successful comeback during the 1980s and 1990s in movies rather than books (◊ CINEMA *for listing of examples*). The "paranoid android" Marvin (actually a robot), with his "brain the size of a planet", is a major character in the various versions of Douglas ADAMS's **Hitch Hiker's Guide to the Galaxy** saga, and for a time attained cult-hero status.

The writer whose work confirms the identification of Man and robot most strongly is Philip K. Dick, who usually preferred the term "android". His most notable stories using humanoid machines to address the question of what the word "human" can or should mean are *Do Androids Dream of Electric Sheep?* (1968), "The Electric Ant" (1969) and *We Can Build You* (1969-70; 1972). "Someday," he said in his essay "The Android and the Human" (1973), "a human being may shoot a robot which has come out of a General Electrics factory, and to his surprise see it weep and bleed. And the dying robot may shoot back and, to its surprise, see a wisp of gray smoke arise from the electric pump that it supposed was the human's beating heart. It would be rather a great moment of truth for both of them." This irony is explored in the character Jonas, in Gene WOLFE's **The Book of the New Sun** (1980-83), a robot who gradually acquires human prostheses.

Anthologies of robot stories include *The Robot and the Man* (anth 1953) ed Martin GREENBERG, *The Coming of the Robots* (anth 1963) ed Sam MOSKOWITZ, *Invasion of the Robots* (anth 1965) ed Roger ELWOOD, and *The Metal Smile* (anth 1968) ed Damon KNIGHT. *Science Fiction Thinking Machines* (anth 1954) ed Groff CONKLIN has a section on robots. [BS]

See also: AUTOMATION; COMPUTERS; CYBERNETICS; CYBORGS; INTELLIGENCE; TECHNOLOGY.

ROBU, CORNEL (1938-   ) Romanian lecturer in literature (at Cluj-Napoca University) and sf critic, some of whose many articles have appeared in English, including "A Key to Science Fiction: The Sublime" in FOUNDATION #42 (1988). He ed the 1st reprint and critical edition (1986), with afterword in English, of the early Romanian sf novel *În anul 4000 sau O călătorie la Venus* ["In the Year 4000, or A Voyage to Venus"] (1899) by Victor Anestin, and also ed the anthology of Romanian sf *Timpul este umbra noastră: Science-fiction românesc din ultimele două decenii: Antologie comentată* ["Time is Our Shadow: Romanian Science Fiction 1969-1989: Anthology with Commentary"] (anth 1991), with an afterword in English. A more general work is *Panorama romanului românesc contemporan: 1944-1974* ["Panorama of the Contemporary Romanian Novel: 1944-74"] (1974) with Ion Vlad. For this encyclopedia CR wrote the entry on ROMANIA and contributed ideas to that on SENSE OF WONDER. [PN]

ROCHESTER, GEORGE E. [r] ◊ SCOOPS.

ROCHON, ESTHER (1948-   ) Canadian writer who began publishing sf with "L'Initiateur et les étrangers" ["The Initiator and the Strangers"] for *Marie-Françoise* in 1964, publishing stories frequently and cofounding the journal *imagine . . .* (◊ CANADA) in 1979. With her first novel, *En Hommage aux araignées* ["In Praise of Spiders"] (1974; rev as a juvenile vt *L'Étranger sous la ville* ["The Stranger under the City"] 1986), she began the **Vrénalik** sequence of tales set in an ALTERNATE-WORLD archipelago, a venue of the sort used by many Québecois writers to express the St Lawrence River's domination of the geography of Québec, just as some English-speaking Canadian writers tend to set their tales on the shores of glaciated lakes. *L'Épuisement du Soleil* ["The Draining of the Sun"] (1985), part of which first appeared as *Der Traümer in der Zitadelle* ["The Dreamer in the Citadel"] (1977 Germany), most of the stories assembled in *Le Traversier* ["The Ferry"] (coll 1987), *L'Espace du diamant* ["The Space of the Diamond"] (1990) and most of the stories assembled in *Le Piège à souvenirs* ["The Trap of Memories"] (coll 1991) are also set in this venue. Of her novels only *Coquillage* (1986; trans David Lobdell as *The Shell* 1990) is set outside the **Vrénalik** world, though it too is set on an ISLAND, where several human characters plunge into a profound sexual liaison with the eponymous ALIEN. Like most WOMEN SF WRITERS at work in Québec today, ER often depicts characters who have to encounter and deal with the Other on their own territory and without going into outer space, which has stimulated FEMINIST and political readings of her work. In 1986 and 1987 she received the Grand Prix de la science-fiction et du fantastique québecois. [LP/JC]

ROCKETEER, THE (vt *The Adventures of the Rocketeer*) Film (1991). Walt Disney. Dir Joe Johnston, starring Bill Campbell, Jennifer Connelly, Alan Arkin, Timothy Dalton, Paul Sorvino. Screenplay Danny Bilson, Paul DeMeo. 108 mins. Colour.

This enjoyable big-budget re-creation of the thrills of 1930s B-serials – more accurate but less popular than Steven SPIELBERG's *Raiders of the Lost Ark* (1981) –

features gangsters, G-men, Nazis, pilots, movie stars, a dirigible, Howard Hughes (1905-1976) and (in thin disguise) Errol Flynn (1909-1959) and Rondo Hatton (1894-1946). The Flynn character, played with relish by Dalton, is the villain; the gangster boss (Sorvino) discovers his true loyalties ("I'm a hundred per cent American") when he realizes he has been helping Nazis steal an experimental rocket pack; there is an excellent re-creation of a Nazi propaganda cartoon. Unlike the greedy, cynical, individualistic Indiana Jones, the old-fashioned Rocketeer, the uncharismatic Campbell, is law-abiding and patriotic – and outshone by the scheming Dalton. [MK]

ROCKETS The Chinese were using skyrockets as fireworks in the 11th century, and adapted them as WEAPONS of WAR in the 13th. Europeans borrowed the idea, but rocket-missiles were abandoned as muskets and rifles became more efficient. A 15th-century Chinese legend tells of one Wan Hu, who attached rockets to a chair, strapped himself in, and blasted off for the unknown. A similar notion was used by CYRANO DE BERGERAC in the first part of *L'autre monde* (**1657**), in which the hero straps 3 rows of rockets to his back, intending that as each set burns out it will ignite the next, so renewing the boost; the device proves impracticable.

War rockets were used against the British in India at the end of the 18th century, and the British reinstituted rocket technology, using rocket missiles in the Napoleonic War and in the US War of 1812; their rockets used in an attack on Fort Henry in 1814 inspired the reference to "the rocket's red glare" in "The Star-Spangled Banner" by Francis Scott Key (1780-1843), who witnessed the battle. Rockets fell into disuse again with the development of better field artillery, but the possibility of using them as a means of TRANSPORTATION encouraged some early experiments with unfortunate animals as passengers.

In 1898 Konstantin TSIOLKOVSKY wrote a classic article, "The Probing of Space by Means of Jet Devices" (1903); he had earlier written "On the Moon" (1893), "Dreams of Earth and Sky" (1895) and other stories and essays collected in *The Call of the Cosmos* (coll trans **1963**) in company with the didactic novel *Outside the Earth* (**1920**; trans **1960** as *Beyond the Planet Earth*). In the same period the US inventor Robert Goddard (1882-1945) – reputedly inspired by reading H.G. WELLS's *The War of the Worlds* (**1898**) – also began thinking seriously about SPACE FLIGHT, and in 1911 he began experimenting with rockets. He was working towards a liquid-fuel stage rocket – a notion applied to the business of interplanetary travel in John MUNRO's romance *A Trip to Venus* (**1897**). Goddard launched the first liquid-fuel rocket in 1926. Meanwhile, the German rocket-research pioneer Hermann Oberth (1894-1989) – author of *Die Rakete zu den Planetenräumen* ["The Rocket into Interplanetary Space"] (**1921**) – and others, including Willy LEY, formed a "Society for Space Travel". In 1928 Oberth was offered the opportunity to build a rocket by a German film company, which hired him as technical adviser for Fritz LANG's film *Die* FRAU IM MOND (1929); his experimental rocket was to be launched before the film's premiere as a publicity stunt, but the project collapsed. Oberth began anew with a number of assistants, including Wernher von Braun (1912-1977), and managed to get a number of rockets off the ground in 1931. The project was abandoned as Germany's economy crashed, but von Braun joined a rocket development project with the German Army while Ley emigrated to the USA. In 1937 the Army project acquired a large research centre at Peenemünde on an island in the Baltic, where von Braun and his staff developed the V-2 rocket bomb. This arrived too late to make any difference to the course of WWII, and von Braun fled to the Bavarian Alps in order to surrender to the USA rather than wait for the Russians. Goddard had spent WWII developing take-off rockets for US Navy aircraft.

Von Braun went to work for a US research programme. The project developed the Jupiter rocket to launch the USA's first space satellite in 1958, and ultimately the Saturn rocket which carried the first men to the MOON. During this period a number of US and UK sf writers – most notably Arthur C. CLARKE, a leading member of the British Interplanetary Society founded by P.E. Cleator (1908-   ) in the 1930s – were active and enthusiastic propagandists for the space programme. Even before WWII the sf PULP MAGAZINES had taken a considerable interest in rocket research – SCIENCE WONDER STORIES publicized an occasion when "The Rocket Comes to the Front Page" (Dec 1929) with an unsigned article that was probably by Hugo GERNSBACK, and ASTOUNDING SCIENCE-FICTION published such articles as Leo Vernon's "Rocket Flight" (1938). The UK TALES OF WONDER published Clarke's "We Can Rocket to the Moon – Now!" (1939). After WWII George PAL made the film DESTINATION MOON (1950), with script by Robert A. HEINLEIN (remotely based on his *Rocket Ship Galileo* [**1947**]). Ray BRADBURY became particularly fascinated by the mythology of the rocket and followed up his "I, Rocket" (1944) with the early **Martian Chronicles** episode "Rocket Summer" (1947) and the curious non-sf story "Outcast of the Stars" (1950; vt "The Rocket"). C.M. KORNBLUTH based his novel *Takeoff* (**1952**) on the ironic theme of a crackpot project to build an unworkable rocket which conceals a real attempt to build a practicable SPACESHIP – testimony to the ambivalence of contemporary attitudes to rocket research. As late as 1956 a newly appointed British Astronomer Royal, Richard Woolley, was reported to have declared that talk of space travel was "utter bilge", so encapsulating a considerable body of opinion which endured pugnaciously until the ascent of *Sputnik* – in 1957.

There is no other historical sequence of events in which fact and fiction are so closely entwined, or which seems to justify so well the imaginative reach of HARD-SF writers. Tsiolkovsky, Goddard and Oberth were visionaries more closely akin to speculative writers than to their contemporary theorists. Rocket research has always been dependent on the practical demands of hot and cold wars, but it is surely true – as laboured in James A. MICHENER's pedestrian epic "faction" *Space* (**1982**) – that for some of the people involved the real objective was always that of Wan Hu, Cyrano, Munro and Tsiolkovsky. Pierre BOULLE's *Garden on the Moon* (**1964**; trans **1965**), in which the German rocket scientists are entranced with the notion of cosmic voyaging even as they develop the V-2, probably has an element of truth in it.   [BS]

See also: ION DRIVE; PREDICTION; SPACE FLIGHT; SPACESHIPS.

ROCKETSHIP X-M (vt *Expedition Moon*) Film (1950). Lippert. Prod/dir/written Kurt Neumann, starring Lloyd Bridges, Osa Massen, John Emery. 78 mins. B/w.

This cheap movie was hastily made to beat the more illustrious DESTINATION MOON (1950) to the theatres. A rocket on its way to the Moon is diverted by a storm of meteors and lands on MARS instead. The astronauts find evidence that the planet has suffered an atomic war, and encounter a race of MUTANTS. In an unexpectedly downbeat ending the returning rocket crashes on Earth and all are killed. Some cinéastes like this SPACE OPERA better than the more technological film on whose advance publicity it was designed to get a free ride – especially the atmospheric Mars sequences, tinted red in the film's original prints and well photographed by Karl Struss in the Mojave Desert.

A German director who came to Hollywood in 1925, Neumann is best known for *The* FLY (1958); he also made KRONOS (1957).   [JB/PN]

See also: CINEMA.

ROCKET STORIES US DIGEST-size magazine. 3 issues, Apr, July, Sep 1953, published by Space Publications, New York, ed Wade KAEMPFERT (Lester DEL REY for #1 and #2, Harry HARRISON for #3). RS was a companion magazine to FANTASY MAGAZINE/FANTASY FICTION, SPACE SCIENCE FICTION and the 1952-4 SCIENCE FICTION ADVENTURES. All 4 magazines were closed down when the publisher lost interest. *RS*, slanted to the juvenile market, contained fiction of fair quality, including early work by Algis BUDRYS, but at the height of the SF-MAGAZINE boom, with well over 30 sf magazines being published in the USA, it was effectively invisible.   [FHP/PN]

ROCKLYNNE, ROSS Working name of US writer Ross Louis Rocklin (1913-1988) for his sf stories, most of which appeared in such magazines as *ASF* from the mid-1930s up to 1947, beginning with "Man of Iron" for *ASF* in 1935. He specialized in SPACE-OPERA plots constructed around sometimes ingenious "scientific" problems, such as how to escape from the centre of a hollow planet in "At the Center of Gravity" (1936), the first of the **Colbie and Deverel** series assembled with similar material in *The Men and the Mirror* (coll of linked stories **1973**); the story is flawed by the fact that RR did not realize that a symmetrical hollow shell does not have an internal,

centrally directed gravity field. A second series, **The Darkness**, was assembled as *The Sun Destroyers* (fixup **1973** dos); it features vast, nebula-like beings (◊ LIVING WORLDS) and follows their life-courses through millions of years from galaxy to galaxy without the intervention of mankind. RR had one of the most interesting, if florid, imaginations of the PULP-MAGAZINE writers of his time, and wrote very much better than most. He continued to publish sf, rather sporadically, up to 1954 (he was interested in DIANETICS at that time); and later made a formidable comeback with several stories in 1968, demonstrating that he had no difficulty at all in adjusting his narrative voice to the more sophisticated demands of the later period – as in "Ching Witch!", one of the most assured *tours de force* in Harlan ELLISON's *Again, Dangerous Visions* (anth **1972**), an ironic tale about the curious morality of a man who, as a result of GENETIC ENGINEERING, has a lot of cat in him.   [JC/PN]

About the author: *The Work of Ross Rocklynne: An Annotated Bibliography* (**1989** chap) by Douglas MENVILLE.

See also: ALTERNATE WORLDS; CRIME AND PUNISHMENT; TIME PARADOXES; WAR.

ROCKWOOD, ROY House name used on JUVENILE SERIES published by Cupples & Leon of New York, and on one occasion by the Mershon Company of New Jersey. The best of the RR titles are the first 6 vols (1906-13) in the **Great Marvel** sequence by Howard R. GARIS, who probably wrote from outlines by Edward STRATEMEYER; other writers who worked under the RR name, which was used also on the 20 **Bomba the Jungle Boy** books (1926-38), remain unidentified.   [JC]

See also: CHILDREN'S SF; HOLLOW EARTH; OUTER PLANETS.

ROCKY HORROR PICTURE SHOW, THE Film (1975). A Lou Adler-Michael White Production/20th Century-Fox. Dir Jim Sharman, starring Tim Curry, Susan Sarandon, Barry Bostwick, Richard O'Brien, Patricia Quinn, Little Nell (Laura Campbell), Jonathan Adams, Peter Hinwood, Meatloaf, Charles Gray. Screenplay Sharman, O'Brien, based on O'Brien's stage musical *The Rocky Horror Show* (1973). 101 mins. Colour.

This UK film created little stir when first released in the USA, but by mid-1976 it was attracting large cult audiences at midnight showings; the phenomenon grew throughout most of the late 1970s. *TRHPS* became *the* cult movie of all time, with its audiences becoming part of the performance, dressed as favourite characters, singing along, shouting wisecracks at the screen, and so on. The phenomenon is analysed at length in *Midnight Movies* (**1983**) by J. Hoberman and Jonathan Rosenbaum.

The film itself is not entirely mediocre – Curry's performance as transvestite Dr Frank-N-Furter from the Planet Transsexual in the Galaxy Transylvania is memorable for the energy of its polymorphous perversity, based largely on a lampooning of Mick Jagger – but it is ill paced, has some dreadful performances, and is too long. The story is about shocking the bourgeois, which is also its object; this was the era of androgynous singer David Bowie, when bisexuality, at least in personal appearance, was becoming fashionable in the more radical fringes of youth culture. Sarandon and Bostwick play the two normally dull young people seduced by the mad doctor in his gothic mansion after their car has broken down on a dark and stormy night.

TRHPS, an example of RECURSIVE SF, begins with a song affectionately recalling the delights of early sf movies, "Science Fiction, Double Feature"; another of the better numbers is "The Time Warp", a song and dance. Sf references abound, especially to the FRANKENSTEIN MONSTER: the mad doctor has created an artificial man, Rocky Horror, as a sexual plaything. Eventually Frank-N-Furter is lasered down, and the Gothic mansion is warped back to its planet of origin by Riff Raff the butler (O'Brien), who turns out to be an alien. *TRHPS* is notable for summing up an entire generation's attitude to sf: it is presented not as a bold facing-up to the challenges of the future but as a campy nostalgia for the luridnesses of the past. [PN]
See also: MUSIC.

RODAN ◊ RADON.

RODDENBERRY, GENE (1921-1991) US tv scriptwriter, producer, director and creator of STAR TREK. GR began writing in the late 1940s while working as a pilot for a commercial airline. In 1951 he sold his first tv script and in 1952 his first that was sf, a genre in which he had not previously been particularly interested. In 1954 he became a full-time tv writer. In 1963 he created and produced a series of his own – **The Lieutenant** – for MGM, and in the same year conceived **Star Trek** but had difficulty launching the project; and it was not to be until 1966 that the show reached tv screens. **Star Trek** was not a great success in terms of ratings and was ended in 1968, but over the next decade, partly as a consequence of reruns, the show built up a huge following.

After **Star Trek**, GR spent much time trying to launch other tv sf series, but without success, although 4 pilot episodes appeared as made-for-tv films: GENESIS II (1973), PLANET EARTH (1974), *The* QUESTOR TAPES (1974) and STRANGE NEW WORLD (1975). In 1977, turning from sf to horror, GR personally directed *Spectre*, a tv pilot along the lines of KOLCHAK: THE NIGHT STALKER, with Robert Culp as a demonologist detective; this too failed to be sold as a series.

Throughout the 1970s a **Star Trek** revival was continually announced, either as a tv series or as a theatrical film, but it was only after the success of STAR WARS (1977) that such a project became feasible. In 1979 GR finally produced STAR TREK THE MOTION PICTURE, dir Robert WISE, with the cast of the old series stranded among state-of-the-art special effects. Though commercially successful, it was by no means the blockbuster that Paramount had envisioned, and GR took a less personal interest in the ongoing sequels, of which there have been 5 to date, com-

mencing with STAR TREK II: THE WRATH OF KHAN (1982); these eschew the daring but tedious mystical approach of Wise's film and revert to the cosy soap-and-sentiment basics of the original series. In 1987 GR cowrote and produced *Encounter at Farpoint*, the pilot episode of STAR TREK: THE NEXT GENERATION (1987-current), a sequel tv series set 80 years on in the **Star Trek** universe; he continued to serve as overall creative guide, but not on a day-to-day basis, and died shortly before his basic concept was spun off into a third tv series, **Star Trek: Deep Space 9** (begun 1992).

The Making of Star Trek (**1968**) by Stephen E. Whitfield and GR was actually written by Whitfield and *The Making of Star Trek The Motion Picture* (**1980**) by Susan Sackett and GR was written by Sackett. GR was also credited as author of the novelization *Star Trek: The Motion Picture* * (**1979**). [JB/KN/PN]

RODGERS, ALAN (? -) US writer who began publishing work of genre interest with "The Boy who Came Back from the Dead" in *Masques #2* (anth **1987**) ed J.N. Williamson (1932-), a strongly moving fantasy tale later assembled with other work in *New Life for Old* (coll **1991**). AR's first novel, *Blood of the Children* (**1989**), is horror, but his second, *Fire* (**1990**), combines sf and horror in a NEAR-FUTURE story in which a fundamentalist US President threatens a nuclear attack against the USSR while at the same time a lab explosion unleashes a virus which raises the dead and a telepathic entity which takes on the aspect of the Beast of Revelation. The plot then thickens pyrotechnically. *Night* (**1991**) is horror. [JC]

RODMAN, ERIC [s] ◊ Robert SILVERBERG.

ROD SERLING'S NIGHT GALLERY US tv series (1970-72). A Jack Laird Production for Universal TV/NBC. Created Rod SERLING. 93 plays: the 1969 2-hour pilot had 3 plays; season 1, part of a mixture of dramas called **Four-in-One**, consisted of 6 50min episodes containing 2-3 playlets; season 2, under the **Rod Serling's Night Gallery** title, had 23 of the same sort of 50min episodes; season 3 had 16 25min episodes, each with 1 playlet. Colour.

Created by Rod Serling – who in the early 1960s had made the series *The* TWILIGHT ZONE – *RSNG* was primarily made up of supernatural stories but did contain a small number of sf episodes; many of the plays were scripted by Serling from original stories by such writers as C.M. KORNBLUTH, Fritz LEIBER, H.P. LOVECRAFT and A.E. VAN VOGT, and Richard MATHESON scripted several other segments. One of the 3 plays in the pilot, starring Joan Crawford, was Steven SPIELBERG's début; other directors included John BADHAM, Leonard Nimoy and Jeannot Szwarc. After a time Serling lost creative control and grew to dislike the series, the studio requiring more monsters and fewer subtleties; however, he continued to introduce it, strolling through a sinister art gallery and pointing to a relevant painting before each play began. *RSNG* was on the whole a disappointment after **The Twilight Zone**. 2 collections of stories by Serling were series spin-offs: *Night Gallery* * (coll **1971**) and *Night Gallery 2* * (coll **1972**). Also relevant is *Rod Serling's Night Gallery Reader* * (anth **1987**) ed Carol Serling (Serling's widow) with Martin H. GREENBERG and Charles G. WAUGH. [JB/PN]

ROE, IVAN [r] ◊ Richard SAVAGE.

ROGER, NOELLE Pseudonym of Swiss writer Hélène Dufour Pittard (1874-1953), whose sf novel, *Le nouvel Adam* (**1924**; trans P.O. Crowhurst as *The New Adam* **1926** UK), is about a wholly logical and unpleasant SUPERMAN created by gland transplants. Finally, after having invented a nuclear force field, he blows himself up. [JC]

Other work: *Celui qui voit* (**1926**; trans Robert Lancaster as *He Who Sees* **1935** UK), occult fantasy.

See also: ADAM AND EVE.

ROGER CORMAN'S FRANKENSTEIN UNBOUND ◊ FRANKENSTEIN UNBOUND.

ROGERS, ALVA (1923-1982) US writer and artist, nicknamed "Red" for the colour of his hair and politics. A long-time sf fan, he drew the covers for a number of 1940s FANZINES as well as some for the (UK) AMERICAN FICTION series. His *A Requiem for Astounding* (**1964**), though nostalgic and largely uncritical, provides a valuable history, rich in story synopses, of ASTOUNDING SCIENCE-FICTION before the name-change to *Analog*. [MJE/JC]

ROGERS, HUBERT (1898-1982) Canadian illustrator who studied art at Toronto Technical School and the School of the Museum of Fine Arts, Boston. He began his professional career in 1925 in New York, painting covers for books and for various magazines, including *Adventure* and *The* ARGOSY. He entered sf publishing with a cover painting for ASTOUNDING SCIENCE-FICTION in 1939, and painted 58 covers and drew interior ILLUSTRATIONS for 60 issues of that magazine 1939-56. He and William Timmins dominated the covers of *ASF* during the 1940s (HR did all of them Apr 1940-Aug 1942), a period when his comparatively muted style gave the magazine something of the dignity John W. CAMPBELL Jr craved: more serious (and even solemn) than those of many of his colleagues, HR's covers epitomized the technological aspirations of *ASF* in its more high-minded mode. His cover painting for "Fury" (May 1947) by Lawrence O'Donnell (Henry KUTTNER and C.L. MOORE) is considered his premier painting, and is one of the best covers ever put on an sf magazine. HR also did jacket paintings for several hardcover books, including those for 3 Robert A. HEINLEIN novels from SHASTA. He left sf during the 1950s to become one of Canada's foremost portrait painters. [JG/PN]

ROGERS, LEBBEUS HARDING (1847-1932) US businessman and writer whose *The Kite Trust (A Romance of Wealth)* (**1900**), which may have been self-published, follows the juvenile kite-inventors and founders of the eponymous compact into adulthood, enormous wealth, the discovery of new energy sources and the construction of transatlantic tunnels, while all the while an interplanetary spirit instructs the cast on the history of the Solar System. [JC]

ROGERS, MELVA [s] ◊ Rog PHILLIPS.

ROGERS, MICHAEL (ALAN) (1951-) US novelist and rock critic whose first-published sf story was "She Still Do" as by M. Alan Rogers, for *If* in 1970. His first sf novel, *Mindfogger* (**1973**), features a hippy inventor whose mind-fogging device acts as a gentle hallucinogen; though the use to which he puts it is against an armaments company, we are left wondering if hip mind control is preferable to mind control by right-wing powers. *Forbidden Sequence* (**1987**) is a TECHNOTHRILLER about gene-splitting. [PN/JC]

ROGERS, PAT [s] ◊ Arthur PORGES.

ROGERSOHN, WILLIAM ◊ Dennis HUGHES.

ROGOZ, ADRIAN [r] ◊ ROMANIA.

ROHAN, MICHAEL SCOTT (1951-) UK (Scottish) Oxford-educated law graduate and author, whose nonfiction books include an introduction to home computing and a study of the Viking era; he also reviews for *Opera Now*. He began publishing sf with stories like "The Insect Tapes" in *Aries 1* (anth **1979**) ed John Grant (Paul BARNETT). His first novel was *Run to the Stars* (dated 1982 but **1983**), signed Mike Scott Rohan, a promising Scots-in-space thriller featuring relativistic WEAPONS and an alien message, with nasty Earth bureaucrats ready to attack their own space colony. Then, like several UK writers of the period, he began genre crossing; most of his fiction since has been FANTASY, beginning with *The Ice King* (**1986**; vt *Burial Rites* 1987 US) with Allan SCOTT under the joint pseudonym Michael Scot, a supernatural thriller involving Norse mythology. There followed the more notable **The Winter of the World** trilogy – *The Anvil of Ice* (**1986**), *The Forge in the Forest* (**1987**) and *The Hammer of the Sun* (**1988**) – set in an invented frozen world imagined in some depth; though sometimes floridly rhetorical, it may be his best work. A young smith sets himself against the entropic Powers; quests follow; spring comes, but at a cost. MSR then made a partial return to sf, in the romantic SCIENCE FANTASY *Chase the Morning* (**1990**) and its sequel *The Gates of Noon*, where real and magical ALTERNATE WORLDS intersect, and a computer program can become a spell. A second collaboration with Scott, *A Spell of Empire: The Horns of Tartarus* (**1992**), was published under their real names. [PN]

ROHMER, RICHARD H. (1924-) Canadian writer whose novels almost invariably express a sense of fragile PARANOIA about the political and economic prospects for his native land, thinly stretched as it is along the US border. *Ultimatum* (**1973**) and its sequel, *Exxoneration* (**1974**), deal directly with Canadian-US conflicts in a NEAR-FUTURE frame. *Exodus/UK* (**1975**) and its sequel, *Separation* (**1976**; rev vt *Separation Two* 1981), turn inward to express a similar paranoia about separatism. Singletons that deal worriedly with similar material include *Balls!* (**1979**), *Periscope Red* (**1980**), *Triad* (**1981**), *Retaliation* (**1982**) and *Starmageddon* (**1986**). [JC]

ROHMER, SAX Pseudonym of UK journalist and

popular thriller writer Arthur Sarsfield Ward (1883-1959). He started writing in 1909 and published in *Cassell's Magazine*, *Collier's Weekly*, *The Premier Magazine* and numerous other early general fiction magazines and BOYS' PAPERS. SR capitalized on contemporary anxiety about the Chinese, generated by the Boxer Rebellion and the fictions of M.P. SHIEL and others, to produce many sensational novels about the Yellow Peril. Most famous is his series about **Dr Fu Manchu**, a malign scientific genius and leader of a secret Chinese organization bent on world domination. This VILLAIN appeared in *The Mystery of Dr Fu-Manchu* (1912-13 *The Story Teller* as "Fu-Manchu"; fixup **1913**; vt *The Insidious Dr Fu-Manchu* 1913 US), *The Devil Doctor* (1914-15 *Collier's Weekly* as "Fu-Manchu & Co."; fixup **1916**; vt *The Return of Dr Fu-Manchu* 1916 US), *The Si-Fan Mysteries* (1916-17 *Collier's Weekly*; fixup **1917**; vt *The Hand of Fu-Manchu* 1917 US), *Daughter of Fu Manchu* (**1931**), *The Mask of Fu Manchu* (**1932**) – filmed as *The* MASK OF FU MANCHU (1932) – *Fu Manchu's Bride* (**1933** US; vt *The Bride of Fu Manchu* 1933 UK), *The Trail of Fu Manchu* (**1934**), *President Fu Manchu* (**1936**), *The Drums of Fu Manchu* (**1938**), *The Island of Fu Manchu* (**1941**), *The Shadow of Fu Manchu* (**1948**), *Re-Enter Fu Manchu* (**1957**; vt *Re-Enter Dr Fu Manchu* 1957 UK) and *Emperor Fu Manchu* (**1959**). *The Wrath of Fu Manchu and Other Stories* (coll **1973**) assembles various tales. *The Book of Fu Manchu* (omni **1929** containing 3 novels; exp to 4 novels 1929 US) features the first volumes of the sequence. Although these and other novels by SR are primarily occult thrillers, they contain many sf elements.

Apart from this main series, SR wrote several others. The **Sumuru** series is about an oriental villainess: *Nude in Mink* (**1950** US; vt *Sins of Sumuru* 1950 UK), *Sumuru* (**1951** US; vt *Slaves of Sumuru* 1952 UK), *Virgin in Flames* **1952**; vt *The Fire Goddess* 1952 US), *Return of Sumuru* (**1954** US; vt *Sand and Satin* 1955 UK) and *Sinister Madonna* (**1956**). The **Gaston Max** series comprises *The Yellow Claw* (**1915**), *The Golden Scorpion* (**1919**), *The Day the World Ended* (**1930**), set in and around a fortress guarded by DEATH RAYS, and *Seven Sins* (**1943**). The **Paul Harley** series consists of *Bat-Wing* (**1921**), *Fire-Tongue* (**1921**) and 11 short stories. The **Red Kerry** series – *Dope* (**1919**) and *Yellow Shadows* (**1925**) – is not sf/fantasy.

SR also wrote several stage plays, including an adaptation from C.J. Cutcliffe HYNE's **Captain Kettle** series. Several of his novels have been made into films (◊ *The* FACE OF FU MANCHU) and the **Dr Fu Manchu** sequence was adapted by him into a popular RADIO series.

Dr Fu Manchu was widely imitated, notably by Roland Daniels, Anthony RUD and Nigel Vane, and was a strong influence on the development of the more recent hero/villain quasi-sf thrillers written by Lester DENT, Ian FLEMING and many others. Two direct imitations were the short-lived magazines *The* MYSTERIOUS WU FANG and DR. YEN SIN. SR's only book under another name was a supernatural/theological novel,

Wulfheim (**1950**) as by Michael Furey. [JE]

Other works: *The Sins of Séverac Bablon* (**1914**); *Brood of the Witch Queen* (1914 *The Premier Magazine*; **1918**); *Tales of Secret Egypt* (coll **1918**); *The Orchard of Tears* (**1918**); *The Quest of the Sacred Slipper* (1913-14 *Short Stories* as by Hassan of Aleppo; fixup **1919**); *The Dream Detective* (coll **1920**; with 1 story added 1925); *The Green Eyes of Bast* (**1920**); *The Haunting of Low Fennel* (coll **1920**); *Tales of Chinatown* (coll **1922**); *Grey Face* (**1924**); *Moon of Madness* (**1927**), not fantasy; *She who Sleeps* (**1928**); *Yu'an Hee See Laughs* (**1932**), not fantasy; *The Emperor of America* (**1929**); *Tales of East and West* (coll **1932** UK; same title, different stories, coll **1933** US); *The Bat Flies Low* (**1935**); *White Velvet* (**1936**), not fantasy; *The Golden Scorpion Omnibus* (coll **1938**); *The Sax Rohmer Omnibus* (coll **1938**); *Salute to Bazarada and Other Stories* (coll **1939**); *The Moon is Red* (**1954**); *The Secret of Holm Peel and Other Strange Stories* (coll **1970**).

About the author: *Sax Rohmer: A Bibliography* (**1963** chap) by Bradford M. DAY; *Master of Villainy* (**1972**) by Cay Van Ash and Elizabeth Sax Rohmer. Van Ash also wrote *Ten Years Beyond Baker Street* (**1984**), a novel in which Fu Manchu meets Sherlock Holmes.

See also: CANADA; GOTHIC SF; PULP MAGAZINES; WEAPONS.

ROKER, A.B. ◊ Samuel BARTON.

ROLANT, RENÉ ◊ R.L. FANTHORPE.

ROLE-PLAYING GAMES ◊ GAMES AND TOYS.

ROLFE, FREDERICK (WILLIAM) (1860-1913) UK author and eccentric, known as much for claiming the name "Frederick, Baron Corvo" as for his writing. The 9 "Reviews of Unwritten Books" (1903 *The Monthly Review*) with Sholto Douglas is an early articulation of the concept of alternate history (◊ ALTERNATE WORLDS), if only in a nonfiction format (one of the reviews, for instance, being of "Machiavelli's *Despatches from the South African Campaign*"). *Hubert's Arthur* (written 1908-12; **1935**) with H.C.H. Pirie-Gordon as by Prospero and Caliban, in which King John fails to kill and is overthrown by his nephew Arthur, is an early alternate-history novel, although its late publication date precludes any influence on that genre. *The Weird of the Wanderer* (**1912**), again with Pirie-Gordon as by Prospero and Caliban, is a fantasy, but *Hadrian the Seventh* (**1904**), on which FR's reputation as an author almost solely rests, is a genuine NEAR-FUTURE sf novel, set in 1910. Dealing with the rise to the Papacy of a frustrated candidate for priesthood, the novel offers a number of predictions regarding the future of Europe, including a vision of the Russian Revolution. [CF]

About the author: There are many biographies, including A.J.A. Symons's famous *The Quest for Corvo: An Experiment in Biography* (**1934**). More recent, and more reliable, is *Frederick Rolfe: Baron Corvo* (**1977**) by Miriam J. Benkovitz.

ROLLERBALL Film (1975). United Artists. Dir Norman Jewison, starring James Caan, John Houseman, Maud Adams, John Beck. Screenplay William Harrison (1933-   ), based on his "Roller Ball Murders"

(1973). 129 mins, cut to 125 mins. Colour.

That one man who stands tall and proud can topple a corrupt system by his example is the moral of this sluggish big-budget movie. In a future run by corporations, ordinary citizens are (implausibly) kept happy by a brutal gladiatorial spectator "sport" played on rollerskates and motorcycles, and, to keep the proletariat in their place, designed as an allegory of the futility of individual effort. Caan plays the team leader who proves the bosses wrong by winning, even when they progressively break all the rules to try to kill him. It has the theme but none of the verve, or even the convincing violence, of an exploitation movie; the high moral tone of the script (and the classical music on the sound track) are ludicrously at odds with the film's fundamental (but incompetent) voyeurism. [PN]

ROLLOVER Film (1981). IPC Films/Orion. Dir Alan J. Pakula, starring Jane Fonda, Kris Kristofferson, Hume Cronyn. Screenplay David Shaber, from a story by Shaber, Howard Kohn, David Weir. 115 mins. Colour.

R has a banker (Kristofferson) and an oil-company chairman (Fonda) uncovering a conspiracy in which the Saudi Arabians have, with the help of US banks, been secretly dumping dollars and buying gold. Threatened with exposure, the Saudis withdraw all funds from the banks and a world financial collapse ensues, with apocalyptic consequences. *R* is an ironic, diagrammatic thriller in which US individualists – innocent, greedy and emblematic – are helpless against a powerful establishment (much as in Pakula's best film, *The Parallax View* [1974], which has a marginally sf brain-washing theme). Cold, difficult, sophisticated, anti-capitalist, *R* was a commercial flop; it would have done better 8 years later. The doomsday scenarios of sf, unlike those of the real world, seldom feature ECONOMICS as the catalyst – probably because most people find money-manipulation too complex a topic – but *R*, rather like the financial thrillers of Paul E. ERDMAN, is a notable exception. [PN]

ROLLS, BRIAN [r] ◊ ROBERT HALE LIMITED.

ROMANIA Romanian sf is over a century old. 1873 marked the appearance of the novelette "Finis Rumaniae" ["The End of Romania"] by the obscure writer Al. N. Dariu; two years later came a future UTOPIA, *Spiritele anului 3000* ["Spirits of the Year 3000"] (**1875**) by Demetriu G. Ionnescu (the form of his name used by the statesman Take Ionescu [1858-1922]). The earliest sf writer proper in Romania was Victor Anestin (1875-1918), whose first novel was *În anul 4000 sau O călătorie la Venus* ["In the Year 4000, or A Voyage to Venus"]; 1914 marked the almost simultaneous appearance of two "classic" novels of Romanian sf: *O tragedie cerească* ["A Sky Tragedy"] (**1914**), again by Anestin, and *Un român în Lună* ["A Romanian on the Moon"] (**1914**) by Henri Stahl (1877-1942). All these belong to the tradition of the "astronomical" novel, as it was known before WWI.

Between the Wars the range of themes widened, the most notable novels being no longer "astronomical": examples are *Baletul mecanic* ["The Clockwork Ballet"] (**1931**) by Cezar Petrescu (1892-1961) and *Oraşele înnecate* ["The Drowned Cities"] (**1936**) by Felix Aderca (1891-1962). There were also some valuable short stories, including "Groază" ["Horror"] (1936), "Manechinul lui Igor" ["Igor's Mannequin"] (1938) and "Ochiul cu două pupile" ["The Two-Pupilled Eye"] (1939), all by Victor Papilian (1888-1956); a scientific fairy-tale, "Agerul Pămîntului" ["The Deft Giant of the Earth"] (1939) by I.C. Vissarion (1879-1951); and above all 2 sf novelettes set in India (see below), by Mircea Eliade (1907-1986), better known in the West for his studies in comparative religion; he was Professor of the History of Religion at the University of Chicago 1956-86, and author of fundamental works in this field, written in French and translated all over the world.

As a writer of fiction, Eliade belonged entirely to Romanian literature: he became one of the nation's major writers before WWII, while still living in Romania, and, when abroad afterwards, continued writing fiction exclusively in Romanian. He wrote both realistic and fantastic fiction, the latter including some genuine masterpieces: the novels *Domnişoara Christina* ["Miss Christina"] (**1936**) and *Şarpele* ["The Snake"] (**1937**), the novelettes "La ţigănci" (1959; trans as "With the Gypsy Girls" 1973 *Denver Review*) and *Pe strada Mântuleasa* ["On Mântuleasa Street"] (**1968** France), and many others, including *Forêt Interdite* (**1955** France; in original Romanian as *Noaptea de Sânziene* 1971 France; trans Mac Linecott Rickette and Mary Park Stevenson as *The Forbidden Forest* **1978** US), a huge novel in which the search for IMMORTALITY is parallelled to a myth-saturated history of Romania. 5 of his writings are (somewhat borderline) sf. From his rich knowledge of Indian culture (he studied at the University of Calcutta 1928-31), Eliade extrapolated hypotheses drawn from, for example, Yoga and Tantra in a sciencefictional manner, as in the title story of *Secretul doctorului Honigberger* (coll **1940**; trans William Ames Coates as *Two Tales of the Occult* **1970** US; vt *Two Strange Tales* 1986); the title story (here trans as "Doctor Honigberger's Secret") is about time distortion and INVISIBILITY; the volume also contains "Nopţi la Serampore" (1939) (here trans as "Midnight in Serampore"), in which time reversibility reduces individual lifespans to infinitesimal proportions compared to the great time-intervals of supra-individuality. The short story "Un om mare" ["A Big Man"] (written 1945; 1948) is about a giant and is partly reminiscent of H.G. WELLS's *The Food of the Gods* (**1904**); it is included in *Fantastic Tales* (coll trans E. Tappe **1969** UK). The last 2 of his works of sf interest are novelettes written in Paris much later, both on the theme of MUTANTS: the hero of "Tinereţe fără de tinereţe ..." (written 1976; 1978 Germany), which appears in English as the long title story of *Youth without Youth* (coll trans **1989** UK), is a mutant who becomes young and immortal after a thunderbolt; and in "Les trois Grâces" ["The Three Graces"] (1976) Eliade transforms an idea he found in the Apocrypha in a cruel story about a rejuvenation treatment given to three old women suffering from cancer – they become unhappy mutants. A further English-language collection of Eliade's stories is *Tales of the Sacred and Supernatural* (coll trans **1981** US).

Postwar Romanian sf can be thought of in terms of 3 generations of writers. To the first of these (now called "the old generation") belong Ovidiu Şurianu (1918-1977), Mihu Dragomir (1919-1964), Mircea Şerbănescu (1919-), Vladimir Colin (1921-1991), Adrian Rogoz (1921-), I.M. Ştefan (1922-), Victor Kernbach (1923-), Sergiu Fărcăşan (1924-), Camil Baciu (1926-), Georgina-Viorica Rogoz (1927-), Horia Aramă (1930-), Ion Hobana (1931-) and many others including Romulus Bărbulescu (1925-) and George Anania (1941-), who collaborated 1959-77 on 6 sf novels and several short stories. This generation was able to publish in the bimonthly *Colecţia 'Povestiri ştiinţifico-fantastice'* ["The Collection of 'Scientific-Fantastic Stories'"], the longest-lasting Romanian sf review, with 466 issues 1955-74 (editor-in-chief Adrian Rogoz). During its last years this review also published the early stories of a number of the then young writers (now known as "the middle generation"): Miron Scorobete (1933-), Leonida Neamţu (1934-1991), Constantin Cubleşan (1939-), Voicu Bugariu (1939-), Gheorghe Săsărman (1941-), Mircea Opriţă (1943-) and others. They continued their ascension in the period 1974-82, when the Romanian literary scene was deprived of any sf periodical. Starting in 1982 the "new wave" of the 1980s emerged, the younger generation of writers who have succeeded during the past decade in changing the landscape of Romanian sf. This was a period of new outlets for sf writing, including **Almanah Anticipaţia** ["Anticipation Almanac"], with 8 annual vols each over 300pp (editor-in-chief Ioan Eremia Albescu), and some sporadically appearing magazines and FANZINES, the most regular being from Timişoara: *Helion* (editor-in-chief Cornel Secu) and *Paradox* (editor-in-chief Viorel Marineasa). Writers of this "young generation" include Marcel Luca (1946-), Gheorghe Păun (1950-), Mihail Grămescu (1951-), Constantin Cozmiuc (1952-), Lucian Ionică (1952-), Leonard Oprea (1953-), George Ceauşu (1954-), Cristian Tudor Popescu (1956-), Dorin Davideanu (1956-), Ovidiu Bufnilă (1957-), Dan Merişca (1957-1991), Lucian Merişca (1958-), Alexandru Ungureanu (1957-), Dănuţ Ungureanu (1958-), Rodica Bretin (1958-), Silviu Genescu (1958-), Mircea Liviu Goga (1958-), Ştefan Ghidoveanu (1958-), Ovidiu Pecican (1959-), Viorel Pîrligras (1959-), Bogdan Ficeac (1960-) and Mihnea Columbeanu (1960-).

Another writer who, like Eliade, cannot be accom-modated into this generational classification is Ovid S. Crohmălniceanu (1921-). He is contemporary with the "old generation", and as a literary critic has accompanied the whole sf movement since the 1950s. Suddenly this distinguished professor of Romanian literature burst forth as an sf writer in the 1980s – simultaneously with the turbulent young writers of the "new wave", yet quite distinct from them and from FANDOM – with 2 masterly volumes of short stories: *Istorii insolite* ["Unwonted Stories"] (coll **1980**) and *Alte istorii insolite* ["Other Unwonted Stories"] (coll **1986**).

Though, naturally, each of these writers has a distinctive voice, the generational differences do have an effect. Ideologically shaped in the hard times of *proletcult* and "socialist realism", then of "socialist humanism", most of the "old generation" took an illusory refuge in the "humanistic credo" cynically imposed by an inhuman communist dictatorship. Most of the young writers of the "new wave", however, despite the even harder times of the 1980s, intuitively accepted the elementary truth that a humanistic sf is an oxymoron. Thus the older writers are generally more inclined to a hollow, programma-tic optimism: sweetened visions and lyricized epic sf motifs, with antagonisms avoided and happy endings mandatory. The younger ones are more misanthropic and sarcastic; sentimental lyricism is mocked, and the full power of the epic is redis-covered. The result is a smouldering bitterness, a cruelty of perception, an acknowledged auctorial "ruthlessness" that recognizes conflict and does not flinch from unhappy endings.

On the other hand, there is a national context to be considered as well as the international nature of sf itself, and this to a degree binds all the generations. Romanian sf writers – most of them, at least – are seductive storytellers, for palatable storytelling has always been praised in Romanian literature. Thus the spirit of "finesse" conflicts with the spirit of geometry, and extrapolation tends to be of only a loose logical rigour (although not so with Eliade and Crohmălniceanu). Romanian sf has a native pro-pensity for analogy rather than extrapolation, soft sf rather than hard, psychology rather than ontology; the thrill of science itself, the true SENSE OF WONDER, is unusual in Romanian sf, though the sense of HUMOUR is all too common, with parody sometimes ebulliently outrunning its rather negligible objects.

In place of thorough extrapolation is a rich harvest of allegories, parables and dystopian visions, most of them antitotalitarian. However, the best stories – including "Pianul preparat" ["The Prepared Piano"] (1966; rev 1974) by Horia Aramă, "Evadarea lui Algernon" ["Algernon's Escape"] (1978) by Gheorghe Săsărman, "Merele negre" ["Black Apples"] (1981) by Mihail Grămescu, "Domenii interzise" ["Forbidden Domains"] (1984) by Leonard Oprea, "Omohom" (1987) by Cristian Tudor Popescu and "Deratizare" (1985) by Lucian Merişca – are not mere political pamphlets or moral essays but genuine stories, though equivocal and allusive. The habit of double-thinking and half-speaking has deep roots in history, and was exacerbated by the necessity of deceiving the obtuse but draconian censorship imposed by the Communist Party and the Romanian Secret Police. No matter how heart-relieving such Aesopian stories may be, they limit their writers (and readers) to a minor aesthetic. Now, with the risks diminished, Romanian writers – not only of sf – realize they have forgotten how to express themselves directly, if they have ever known; the Aesopian mode has become second nature, difficult to eliminate if they are to face the major aesthetic challenge of their art.   [CR]

Further reading: "Brief History of Romanian SF" by Florin Manolescu, in *Romanian Review* #5 (1988); "Milestones in Postwar Romanian Science Fiction" by Cornel ROBU in *Foundation* #49 (Summer 1990); "About the Stories and their Authors" in *Timpul este umbra noastră* ["Time is our Shadow"] (anth **1991**) ed Robu; "Romanian 'Science Fantasy' in the Cold War Era" by Elaine Kleiner, in *Science-Fiction Studies*, Mar 1992. More information is available in Romanian: *Vîrsta de aur a anticipaţiei româneşti* ["The Golden Age of Romanian Anticipation"] (anth **1969**) ed Ion Hobana; *Literatura S.F.* ["Sf Literature"] (**1980**) by Florin Manolescu; «Anticipaţia românească» ["The Romanian Anticipation"] (1993) by Mircea Opriţă.

ROMANO, DEANE (LOUIS) (1927-   ) US novelist and screenwriter, active in the latter capacity with scripts like "Angels' Flight" (1962). Some of his work has dealt with current investigations into para-psychology (◊ PSI POWERS), and his filmscript on this subject was novelized by Louis CHARBONNEAU as *The Sensitives* * (**1968**). DR's own sf novel, *Flight from Time One* (**1972**), also treated parapsychology, this time in the didactic tale of an elite squad of "astralnauts" whose members take on missions in their astral bodies.   [JC]

See also: ESCHATOLOGY.

ROME, ALGER Collaborative pseudonym used by Jerome BIXBY and Algis BUDRYS, on "Underestimation" (1953).   [PN]

ROME, DAVID Pseudonym used by immigrant Australian tv writer David Boutland (1938-   ) for his sf, the first example being "Time of Arrival" in Apr 1961 for *NW*, where many others of DR's 25 or so stories appeared over the next decade. His only sf book, *Squat* (**1965**), subtitled "Sexual Adventures on Other Planets", is not his best work.   [PN]

See also: GENERATION STARSHIPS.

ROMERO, GEORGE A. (1940-   ) US film-maker. A maverick working out of Pittsburgh rather than Hollywood, GAR changed the face of the HORROR-movie genre with NIGHT OF THE LIVING DEAD (1968), an apocalyptic nightmare – its theme derived from Richard MATHESON's *I Am Legend* (**1954**) – in which the dead inexplicably return to eat the living. Having tackled a surprisingly wide variety of Vietnam-era social issues in this début, GAR made a pair of

"serious" films – *There's Always Vanilla* (1972; vt *The Affair*) and the witchcraft-themed *Jack's Wife* (1973; vt *Hungry Wives*; vt *Season of the Witch*) – before returning to the former panicked mood in *The* CRAZIES (1973; vt *Code Name Trixie*), in which a biological weapon is spilled in Pennsylvania and causes an epidemic of insanity. After filler work for tv – mainly profiles of sports personalities – GAR formed Laurel Films in partnership with Richard Rubinstein, and relaunched his career with *Martin* (1978), an unortho-dox, apparently non-supernatural vampire picture. He then made 2 impressive and rigorous sequels to *Night of the Living Dead*: DAWN OF THE DEAD (1978; vt *Zombies*) and DAY OF THE DEAD (1985). Throughout the trilogy, which is marked as sf not so much by its (conflicting) "explanations" for the crisis as by the concentration on the social, political and psychologi-cal outcome of the devastation of society, GAR has powerfully mingled black SATIRE with shock effects. Spin-offs have included: an anthology, *The Book of the Dead* (anth **1989**) ed John Skipp and Craig Spector; a remake in 1990 (◊ NIGHT OF THE LIVING DEAD) dir special-effects man Tom Savini, scripted GAR; and a satire, *Return of the Living Dead* (1985), from a story by John Russo, coscripter of the original film, and dir Dan O'Bannon.

Outside the trilogy, GAR has dir: *Knightriders* (1981), a personal film about alternative lifestyles; *Creepshow* (1982), an EC COMICS-style anthology film written by Stephen KING; MONKEY SHINES (1988, vt *Monkey Shines: An Experiment in Terror*), an under-stated and impressive movie based on Michael STEWART's *Monkey Shines* (**1983**), about an intelligent experimental monkey; one half of *Two Evil Eyes* (1990), which GAR adapted from Edgar Allan POE's "The Facts in the Case of M. Valdemar"; and *The Dark Half* (1991), a film version of the 1989 Stephen King novel. In addition, GAR has scripted episodes of the tv series **Tales from the Darkside** (1984-9) and the films *Creepshow 2* (1987) and *Tales from The Darkside: The Movie* (1990).   [KN]

See also: CINEMA; HOLOCAUST AND AFTER; MONSTER MOVIES; SUPERNATURAL CREATURES.

ROMILUS, ARN A CURTIS WARREN house name used by Brian HOLLOWAY for 1 novel and Dennis HUGHES for 2.   [JC]

RONALD, BRUCE W(ALTON) (1931-   ) US writer, advertising man and actor. His *Our Man in Space* (**1965** dos) is a little reminiscent of Robert A. HEINLEIN's *Double Star* (**1956**) in its story of an actor unhappily spying on behalf of Earth. With John JAKES and Claire Strauch he wrote the musical comedy *Dracula, Baby* (**1970**); Jakes played Van Helsing in the premiere in Ohio.   [PN]

RÓNASZEGI, MIKLÓS [r] ◊ HUNGARY.

ROSE, F(REDERICK) HORACE (VINCENT) (1876-?   ) South African author, a periodic UK resident, whose *The Maniac's Dream: A Novel of the Atomic Bomb* (**1946**) was one of the first post-Hiroshima future-WAR novels to respond to the threat

of nuclear HOLOCAUST, though in this case without much grounding in scientific realities. An earlier work, *The Night of the World* (**1944**), centres on a timeslip in an oasis peopled by figures from other ages.   [JE/JC]
Other works: *Bride of the Kalahari* (**1940**); *Pharoah's* [*sic*] *Crown* (**1943**).
See also: CRIME AND PUNISHMENT.

ROSE, LAURENCE F. ◊ John Russell FEARN.

ROSE, MARK (**1939-   **) US academic and writer whose assistance in preparing *New Maps of Hell* (**1960** US) was acknowledged by its author, Kingsley AMIS. An apocalyptic post-HOLOCAUST short story, "We Would See a Sign" in *Spectrum 3* (anth **1963**) ed Amis and Robert CONQUEST, did not lead to a fiction career, and MR remains best known in the sf field for *Alien Encounters: Anatomy of Science Fiction* (**1981**) which, taking off from the DEFINITION OF SF as a form of romance in *Anatomy of Criticism* (**1957** US) by Northrop Frye (1912-1991), redeploys the 19th-century confrontation between Man and Nature to define sf as expressing a conflict between the human and the nonhuman. Within the terms of this definition, which MR uses as a conceptual (and inevitably partial) illumination of the field, he couches some of the most elegantly literate practical criticism of selected texts the genre has yet seen. The anthologies *Science Fiction: A Collection of Critical Essays* (anth **1976**) and *Bridges to Science Fiction* (anth **1980**) with George R. Guffey and George Edgar SLUSSER contain, perhaps inevitably, less striking material.   [JC]
See also: CRITICAL AND HISTORICAL WORKS ABOUT SF.

ROSENBERG, JOEL (**1954-   **) US writer who began publishing sf with "Like the Gentle Rains" for *IASFM* in 1982, but who has clearly felt more comfortable with tales of novel length. His first book, *The Sleeping Dragon* (**1983**), a SWORD-AND-SORCERY fantasy, begins the RECURSIVE **Guardians of the Flame** sequence, continued with *The Sword in the Chain* (**1984**) and *The Silver Crown* (**1985**) – these 3 assembled as *Guardians of the Flame: The Warriors* (omni **1985**) – plus *The Heir Apparent* (**1987**) and *The Warrior Lives* (**1989**) – these 2 assembled as *Guardians of the Flame: The Heroes* (omni **1989**) – plus *The Road to Ehvenor* (**1991**). Though this sequence, along with *D'Shai* (**1991**), #1 in the projected **D'Shai** fantasy sequence, makes up the bulk of his production to date, it could be argued that JR's sf, beginning with *Ties of Blood and Silver* (**1984**), is central to his work. This sf adventure and *Emile and the Dutchman* (fixup **1986**) belong very loosely to the **Metzada** sequence, which spans the Galaxy with anarchic verve. More controversially, *Not for Glory* (fixup **1988**) and its sequel *Hero* (**1990**) focus directly upon the Jewish planet of Metzada, from which tough mercenaries (who rather resemble Gordon R. DICKSON's Dorsai) issue forth into combat; but these Israeli-like soldiers, and the Germans and French and Dutch who have rigidly maintained their own "racial" characteristics for centuries on their own planets, seem strangely stereotyped. It will be interesting to see what JR can do to sophisticate his

ongoing galaxy.   [JC]

ROSHWALD, MORDECAI (MARCELI) (**1921-   **) Polish-born Israeli writer and academic, variously resident also in the USA and the UK, whose sf novels *Level 7* (**1959** US) and *A Small Armageddon* (**1962** UK) were both coloured by political concern about our nuclear civilization. In the first and better known tale, a military officer describes his feelings and duties from extremely deep within a great bomb shelter as the world is gradually demolished above him. In the second the crew of a nuclear submarine threatens to detonate its cargo unless its demands – for sex and money – are met, with farcically exaggerated results. The awful-warning content of MR's novels has perhaps paled with the years, but only because of humanity's survival – *pro tem*.   [JC]
See also: END OF THE WORLD; HOLOCAUST AND AFTER; ISRAEL.

ROSNY aîné, J.H. Pseudonym of French-speaking Belgian writer Joseph-Henri Boëx (1856-1940). His younger brother Justin shared the pseudonym J.H. Rosny with him 1893-1907, and some works published during that period are collaborative. Joseph-Henri used the name for solo writings before 1893, and after 1907 it was divided, Joseph-Henri taking the suffix "aîné" and Justin "jeune". The elder Rosny is an important figure in the development of French speculative fiction, although only one of his novels, *Le felin géant* (**1918** France; trans The Hon. Lady Whitehead as *The Giant Cat* **1924** US; vt *Quest of the Dawn Man* **1964** US) was translated into English during his lifetime. Damon KNIGHT translated 2 of his most important short stories: "Les xipéhuz" (**1887**; trans as "The Shapes" in *One Hundred Years of Science Fiction*, anth **1968**), in which prehistoric humans encounter inorganic ALIENS, and the PARALLEL-WORLDS story "Un autre monde" (**1895**; trans as "Another World" in *A Century of Science Fiction*, anth **1962**). The former is also included, along with the fine END-OF-THE-WORLD story "La mort de la terre" (**1910**), in *The Xipehuz and The Death of the Earth* (coll trans George Edgar SLUSSER **1978**). The most famous of JHR's many prehistoric fantasies, *La Guerre du Feu* (**1909** France; cut trans Harold Talbott as *The Quest for Fire: A Novel of Prehistoric Times* **1967** US), was filmed as QUEST FOR FIRE (1981). A "translation" of *L'étonnant voyage de Hareton Ironcastle* ["The Astonishing Journey of Hareton Ironcastle"] (**1922** France) was produced by Philip José FARMER as *Ironcastle* (**1976**), but so drastically modified that it cannot be regarded as the same work. JHR's prehistoric romances – which include *Vamireh* (**1892**), *Eyrimah* (**1893**) and *Helgvor du fleuve bleu* ["Helgvor of the Blue River"] (**1930**) as well as above-mentioned titles – were reissued in France in 1990 by Éditions Robert Laffont in a huge omnibus volume; many of his short sf and fantasy stories, plus his semi-mystical speculative essay on creation and EVOLUTION, *La légende sceptique* ["The Sceptical Legend"] (**1889**), and his short novel *Les navigateurs de l'infini* ["Navigators of Infinity"] (**1925**) are in a

Marabout collection titled *Récits de science-fiction* ["Works of Science Fiction"] (coll **1975** Belgium). The story begun in *Les navigateurs de l'infini* is continued in the posthumous *Les astronautes* (**1960** France). JHR's other sf works include *La grande énigme* ["The Great Enigma"] (**1920** France) and *Les compagnons de l'univers* ["Companions of the Universe"] (**1934**), another lyrical meditation in the vein of *La légende sceptique*. [BS]

About the author: "The Sf of J.H. Rosny the Elder" by J.P. Vernier, *Science-Fiction Studies* vol 2 #2 (July 1975).

See also: ANTHROPOLOGY; BENELUX; BIOLOGY; COSMOLOGY; FRANCE; HISTORY OF SF; LIFE ON OTHER WORLDS; ORIGIN OF MAN; PERCEPTION; RELIGION.

ROSS, BERNARD L. ◊ Ken FOLLETT.

ROSS, DALLAS [s] ◊ Mack REYNOLDS.

ROSS, DAVID D. (1949?-   ) US writer who began publishing sf with his **Dreamers of the Day** sequence – *The Argus Gambit* (**1989**) and *The Eighth Rank* (**1991**) – which complicatedly traces the political and cultural consequences of a 21st-century ecological disaster. The seriousness with which he undertakes the task of underlining the nature of the problems faced by humanity goes some way to assuage the sense that DDR has not fully mastered the unstable relationship between generic plotting and didactic thematic material. [JC]

ROSS, JAMES ◊ Hugh DARRINGTON.

ROSS, JOSEPH Working name of US editor Joseph Wrzos (1929-   ). He acted as Managing Editor of AMAZING STORIES and FANTASTIC 1965-7 while continuing to teach high-school English fulltime in New Jersey. He ed *The Best of Amazing* (anth **1967**). [PN]

ROSS, MALCOLM (HARRISON) (1895-1965) US writer and reporter, the protagonist of whose sf novel, *The Man who Lived Backward* (**1950**), lives from 1940 to 1865, dying just after the assassination of Abraham Lincoln, which he is therefore unable to prevent. [JC]

ROSS, RAYMOND J. [r] ◊ ROBERT HALE LIMITED.

ROSS, [Sir] RONALD [r] ◊ MEDICINE.

ROSSITER, OSCAR Pseudonym of US physician and writer Vernon H. Skeels (1918-   ), who received his MD in 1949 and whose first sf novel, *Tetrasomy Two* (**1974**), is set in a hospital where a seemingly helpless human vegetable turns out to be an amoral SUPERMAN preparing to eliminate the Solar System in order to accumulate the energy necessary to tour the Galaxy. The Australian film *Patrick* (1978) dir Richard Franklin is based on a remarkably similar notion. [JC]

See also: INTELLIGENCE; PSI POWERS.

ROSSOW, WILLIAM B. [r] ◊ Marjorie Bradley KELLOGG.

ROSZAK, THEODORE (1933-   ) US author of several works of cultural criticism who began writing sf with *Bugs* (**1981**), in which a frightened child telepath causes bugs to infiltrate computer systems and thereafter to eat people. A second novel, *Dreamwatcher* (**1985**), concerning PSI POWERS, blends fantasy and sf. [JC]

ROTH, PHILIP (MILTON) (1933-   ) US writer who remains best known for *Portnoy's Complaint* (**1969**), a novel whose sophisticated and often comic treatment of sexual obsessions is fantastically furthered (◊ FABULATION) in *The Breast* (**1972**), the tale of the sudden and painful transformation of a man into a female breast; the psychosexual implications of the metaphor are clear, as is the debt to Franz KAFKA. The descent to Hell of "Trick E. Dixon" in *Our Gang* (**1971**) is arousing. [JC]

ROTHMAN, CHUCK Working name of US writer Charles Warren Rothman (1952-   ), who began publishing sf with "The Munij Deserters" for *IASFM* in 1982 and whose sf novel, *Staroamer's Fate* (**1986**), has a precognitive protagonist doomed by her talent to travel from world to world, shaping events as she goes. With his wife, Susan Noe Rothman, CR serves as joint secretary/treasurer of the SCIENCE FICTION POETRY ASSOCIATION. [JC]

ROTHMAN, MILTON A. [r] ◊ Tony ROTHMAN.

ROTHMAN, TONY (1953-   ) US writer whose sf novel, *The World is Round* (**1978**), though suffering from excessive length and a confusingly overcomplicated story, creates a Big-Planet venue (◊ Jack VANCE) of some interest; he has also written some books popularizing physics, and several of the stories about the USSR assembled in *Censored Tales* (coll **1989** UK) are absurdist FABULATIONS. TR's father, Milton A. Rothman (1919-   ), a physicist, also wrote some sf stories, as by Lee Gregor. [JC]

See also: JUPITER.

ROTSLER, WILLIAM (1926-   ) US writer and artist who received a 1975 HUGO for his fan art; his cartoons may be remembered as much as his fiction. He began publishing sf with "Ship Me Tomorrow" for *Gal* in 1970 and, although he initially kept his own name for autonomous work – using the pseudonym John Ryder Hall and the BALLANTINE house name William ARROW for novelizations – all his novels since about 1980 have been TIES of one sort or another. His first novel, *Patron of the Arts* (**1974**), remains his best received; incorporating his best known and most praised short story, "Patron of the Arts" (1972), it describes in Wagnerian terms an all-encompassing artform, using holograms and other sf devices (◊ ARTS), but vitiates some of its speculative interest through a contrived action plot. WR's second novel, *To the Land of the Electric Angel* (**1976**), shares a similar setting – what seems to be an extrapolation of modern southern California – in a tale involving CRYONICS, the reawakening of the hero in a DYSTOPIAN future, gladiatorial contests and much more. The **Zandra** series – *Zandra* (**1978**) and *The Hidden Worlds of Zandra* (**1983**) – shares the same background, while *The Far Frontier* (**1980**) is set in nearby space. These later books are significantly less accomplished than their predecessors, and their large casts of routinely differentiated characters generate the impression that their author was attempting to work in a bestseller idiom dangerous to the creative mind. With Gregory

BENFORD (*whom see for details*) WR contributed *Shiva Descending* (**1980**) to the the the asteroid-DISASTER subgenre.   [JC]

Other works: *Iron Man: And Call my Killer . . . Modok* * (**1979**); *Dr Strange: Nightmare* * (**1979**); 2 **Mr Merlin** tv ties, *Mr Merlin, Episode 1* * (**1981**) and *Mr Merlin, Episode 2* * (**1981**); *Star Trek II: Short Stories* * (coll **1982**); *Blackhawk* * (**1982**); *Star Trek II: Biographies* * (coll **1983**); *Star Trek II: Distress Call* * (**1983**); *Star Trek III: The Vulcan Treasure* * (**1984**); *Star Trek III Short Stories* * (coll **1984**); *Goonies: Cavern of Horror* * (**1985**), a film tie.

As John Ryder Hall: *Futureworld* * (**1976**); *Sinbad and the Eye of the Tiger* * (**1977**).

As William Arrow: #1 and #3 of the **Return to the Planet of the Apes** books, based not on the films but on the later animated tv series: *Visions from Nowhere* * (**1976**) and *Man, the Hunted Animal* * (**1976**).

ROTTENSTEINER, FRANZ (1942-   ) Austrian sf critic, editor and literary agent; he has a PhD from the University of Vienna. He has edited the **SF of the World** series for Insel Verlag, the **Fantastic Novels** series for Paul Zsolnay Verlag, and the **Fantastic Library** series – now over 250 vols – for Suhrkamp Verlag. He writes in English as well as in German, his critical articles having appeared in SCIENCE-FICTION STUDIES and elsewhere. He is particularly well known for his spirited promotion of the work of Stanisław LEM, for whom he is literary agent, and for the contempt he has often expressed for much GENRE SF. His criticism is intelligent, polemical and left-wing, and best expressed in fairly academic formats; his popular illustrated history of sf, *The Science Fiction Book* (**1975**), is generally felt to be sketchy. In the same vein, but perhaps better, is *The Fantasy Book: The Ghostly, the Gothic, the Magical, the Unreal* (**1978**). In English he is also known for his collection of European sf, *View from Another Shore* (anth **1973**), for his collection of "literary" fantasies by Jorge Luis BORGES and others, *The Slaying of the Dragon: Modern Tales of the Playful Imagination* (anth **1984**); and for *Microworlds: Writings on Science Fiction* (coll **1984**) by Lem, ed and introduced by FR. Many of his critical writings in German appear in his own high-quality FANZINE, QUARBER MERKUR, from which the book *Quarber Merkur* (anth **1979**) was collected. 2 books of essays ed FR are *Über H.P. Lovecraft* ["On H.P. Lovecraft"] (anth **1984**), and *Die dunkle Seite der Wirklichkeit* ["The Dark Side of Reality"] (anth **1987**). Since 1989 he has been editing a serial guide in looseleaf form in binders, 1250pp to Feb 1991: "Werkführer durch die utopisch-phantastiche Literatur" ["Work Guide to Utopian and Fantastic Literature"].

In German he has ed many anthologies of stories and essays about sf, including: *Die Ratte im Labyrinth* ["Rats in the Maze"] (anth **1971**); the **Polaris** series, *Polaris 1* (anth **1973**), #2 (anth **1974**), a special Soviet sf issue, #3 (anth **1975**), #4 (anth **1978**), a French sf issue, #5 (anth **1981**), #6 (anth **1982**), a Herbert W. FRANKE issue, #7 (anth **1983**), #8 (anth **1985**), #9 (anth **1985**), old German sf, and #10 (anth **1986**), a

STRUGATSKI issue; *Phantastiche Träume* ["Fantastic Dreams"] (anth **1983**); *Phantastiche Welten* ["Fantastic Worlds"] (anth **1984**); *Phantastiche Aussichten* ["Fantastic Sights"] (anth **1985**); *Phantastiche Zeiten* ["Fantastic Times"] (anth **1986**); *Lovecraft Lesebuch* ["Lovecraft Reader"] (anth **1987**); *Seltsame Labyrinthe* ["Strange Labyrinths"] (anth **1987**); *Der Eingang ins Paradies* ["The Door into Paradise"] (anth **1988**); *Arche Noah* ["Noah's Ark"] (anth **1989**); *Die Sirene* ["The Siren"] (anth **1990**); *Phantastiche Begegnungen* ["Fantastic Encounters"] (anth **1990**).   [PN]

See also: CRITICAL AND HISTORICAL WORKS ABOUT SF; GERMANY.

ROUCH, JAMES (?   -   ) UK author of the **Zone** sequence of sf adventures set during WWIII, waged in Germany: *The Zone #1: Hard Target* (**1980**), #2: *Blind Fire* (**1980**), #3: *Hunter Killer* (**1981**), #4: *Sky Strike* (**1981**), #5: *Overkill* (**1982**), #6: *Plague Bomb* (**1986**), #7: *Killing Ground* (**1988**), #8: *Civilian Slaughter* (**1989**) and #9: *Body Count* (**1990**).   [JC]

ROUSSEAU, VICTOR Working name of UK-born writer Victor Rousseau Emanuel (1879-1960), who also used the pseudonym H.M. Egbert on his sf, though not exclusively, and V.R. Emanuel for other work; born of a Jewish father and a French mother – as Sam MOSKOWITZ writes in *Under the Moons of Mars* (anth **1970**) – he moved to the USA some time during WWI. After a non-genre novel, *Derwent's Horse* (**1901**), VR began writing sf in PULP MAGAZINES before WWI, stopping in 1941; much material was never collected, including the **Surgeon of Souls** series of 11 fantasy stories in *Weird Tales* (1926-7). In his first sf novel, *The Sea Demons* (1916 *All-Story Weekly* as V. Rousseau; **1924** UK) as by H.M. Egbert, invisible hive-like sea creatures threaten humanity (◊ INVISIBILITY), but a submarine finds and destroys the queen. *The Messiah of the Cylinder* (**1917**; vt *The Apostle of the Cylinder* 1918 UK), VR's best known work and told with his usual flamboyance and narrative verve, directly imitates the form of H.G. WELLS's *When the Sleeper Wakes* (**1899**), and harshly criticizes the atheistic world-state UTOPIA there depicted; it was seen, consequently, as a melodramatic critique of Wellsian socialism, though Wells's novel was, in fact, deeply ambiguous about the world it described, serving more as a pretext for VR's book than as an argument to be refuted. In VR's novel a brave protagonist destroys the future state into which he has been awoken from SUSPENDED ANIMATION, and restores aristocracy to the land. *Draught of Eternity* (1918 *All-Story Weekly* as V. Rousseau; **1924** UK) as by Egbert is a love story set in a ruined New York. *Eric of the Strong Heart* (**1925** UK) is a lost-race tale (◊ LOST WORLDS). Perhaps mainly because of his heated style, VR remains of some interest.   [JC]

Other works: *My Lady of the Nile* (**1923** UK) as by Egbert; *Mrs Aladdin* (**1925** UK).

About the author: "H.G. Wells and Victor Rousseau Emanuel" by Richard D. MULLEN in EXTRAPOLATION, Vol 8 #2 (1967).

See also: ASTOUNDING SCIENCE-FICTION; HISTORY OF SF; INTELLIGENCE; MESSIAHS; POLITICS.

ROWCROFT, CHARLES (?1795-1856) UK writer perhaps best known for his Australian adventure fiction assembled in *Tales of the Colonies* (coll **1843**) and its successors. In his sf novel, *The Triumph of Woman: A Christmas Story* (**1848**), an inhabitant of sexless Neptune visits a German, with whose daughter he falls in love amid erudite discussions of Neptunian science. The plot then devolves into a satirical travelogue. [JC]

ROWENA Professional name of US illustrator Rowena Morrill (**1944-**); she and Victoria Poyser are among the few women who have had an impact on sf/fantasy art. Her ILLUSTRATION has appeared since the mid-1970s, primarily on paperback covers, more often FANTASY than sf; it is largely fantastical and often symbolic, but quite varied in style and subject matter. She has done several covers for novels by Piers ANTHONY. Her technique is polished and sometimes fastidiously detailed, though her human figures (often based on photographs) perhaps conform too much to a commercially acceptable prettiness, and some of her painting in the HEROIC-FANTASY vein of Boris VALLEJO has been accused of being "degrading to women". Unusually, she uses a combination of acrylics and oils rather than one or the other, and finishes with a high-gloss glaze. *The Fantastic Art of Rowena* (**1983**) has colour reproductions of 26 of her pieces. She has had a number of HUGO nominations. [PN/JG]

ROWLAND, DONALD S(YDNEY) (**1928-**) UK author of a very large number of pseudonymous works, relatively few of them sf; most were for ROBERT HALE LIMITED. For that firm (or for the highly similar house of Gresham) his SPACE OPERAS under his own name are *Despot in Space* (**1973**), *Master of Space* (**1974**), *Space Venturer* (**1976**) and *Nightmare Planet* (**1976**). [JC]
As Fenton Brockley: *Star Quest* (**1974**).
As Roger Carlton: *Beyond Tomorrow* (**1975**), *Star Arrow* (**1975**).
As Graham Garner: *Space Probe* (**1974**), *Starfall Muta* (**1975**), *Rifts of Time* (**1976**).
As Alex Random: *Star Cluster Seven* (**1974**), *Dark Constellation* (**1975**), *Cradle of Stars* (**1975**).
As Roland Starr: The **Omina** sequence, being *Operation Omina* (**1973**), *Omina Uncharted* (**1974**), *Time Factor* (**1975**), *Return from Omina* (**1976**).
As Mark Suffling: *Project Oceanus* (**1975**), *Space Crusader* (**1975**).

ROWLEY, CHRISTOPHER (B.) (**1948-**) US writer who has from the first specialized in efficiently written adventure-sf novels with a strong military component, beginning with the **War for Eternity** sequence – *The War for Eternity* (**1983**), *The Black Ship* (**1985**) and *The Founder* (**1989**) – which concentrates on warfare within our Solar System. The **Vang** sequence – *Starhammer* (**1986**), *The Vang: The Military Form* (**1988**) and *The Vang: The Battlemaster* (**1990**) – moves into deeper space and features a deadly ALIEN

lifeform. In *Golden Sunlands* (**1987**) the humans on a colony planet are kidnapped to serve as cannon fodder in a VIRTUAL-REALITY environment, but soon show their spunk. With George Snow (anon) he wrote the STAR WARS text *Return of the Jedi* * (**1983** chap). [JC]

ROWLOT LTD. ◊ AD ASTRA.

ROY, ARCHIE Working name of Scottish professor of astronomy Archibald Edmiston Roy (**1924-**), whose unremarkable sf adventures, all making use of PARALLEL WORLDS, include *Deadlight* (**1968**), *The Curtained Sleep* (**1969**) and *All Evil Shed Away* (**1970**). *Sable Night* (**1973**), *The Dark Host* (**1976**) and *Devil in the Darkness* (**1978**) are horror. [JC]

ROYAL, BRIAN JAMES ◊ Gardner F. FOX.

ROYAL PUBLICATIONS ◊ INFINITY SCIENCE FICTION; SCIENCE FICTION ADVENTURES.

ROYCE, E.R. ◊ Dennis HUGHES.

RUBEN, WILLIAM S. (? -) US writer known only for *Weightless in Gaza* (**1970** as Fred Shannon; exp vt *Dionysus: The Ultimate Experiment* 1977), in which NASA conducts sex experiments in space. [JC]

RUBINSTEIN, GILLIAN (**1942-**) Australian writer of sf for adolescents (◊ CHILDREN'S SF). *Space Demons* (**1986**) and its sequel, *Skymaze* (**1989**), deal with AI in interactive COMPUTER games (◊ GAMES AND TOYS) in which players enter a VIRTUAL REALITY. *Space Demons: The Play* * (**1990**) was an adaptation for the THEATRE by Richard Tulloch. *Beyond the Labyrinth* (**1988**) shows teenagers developing a relationship with an ALIEN anthropologist. GR uses sf devices as metaphors for exploring and resolving adolescents' painful personal relationships. *At Ardilla* (**1991**), not sf, is a rite-of-passage book about a growing girl. GR has edited *After Dark* (anth **1988**) and *Before Dawn* (anth **1988**). Her books for much younger children are *Melanie and the Night Animal* (**1988**), *Answers to Brut* (**1988**), *Flashback: The Amazing Adventures of a Film Horse* (**1990**) and *Dog In, Cat Out* (**1991**), the last being with illustrator Ann James. [JW]
See also: AUSTRALIA.

RUCKER, RUDY Working name of US writer, mathematician and computer programmer Rudolf von Bitter Rucker (**1946-**), who has advanced degrees in MATHEMATICS from Rutgers University. Like many sf writers, he began very early to produce stories, but unlike most who became successful he had difficulty placing his work, in which mathematical concepts and diagrams tended to generate both plot and venue, making arduous demands upon his readers. "The Miracle", his first-published story, appeared in *The Pegasus*, an amateur magazine, in 1962; "Faraway Eyes", the second to reach print, appeared in *ASF* in 1980. Many of the stories assembled in *The 57th Franz Kafka* (col **1983**) – which, along with RR's early poetry, later stories and nonfiction pieces, were further assembled in *Transreal!* (coll **1991**) – never appeared in magazine form. It is, perhaps, no wonder. Any attempt to describe RR convincingly as a CYBERPUNK writer must founder on a simple distinction. Cyberpunk writers tended to describe the experience of living in a dense and desolate NEAR FUTURE in a CYBERSPACE which served as their career-goal and nirvana, but which they had no need to understand. For RR, on the other hand, the experience of living in a game-like world was much less important than the exercise of understanding its nature. The roots of his fiction lie not in GENRE SF or the *film noir* that clearly inspired much cyberpunk, but in the profound mathematical games of Lewis CARROLL, or of Edwin A. ABBOTT, the author of *Flatland* (**1884**), or of C.H. HINTON, author of *Scientific Romances* (colls **1886** and **1902**), whose *Speculations on the Fourth Dimension: Selected Writings of Charles H. Hinton* (coll **1980**) RR edited (◊ DIMENSIONS).

The abstraction of RR's work cannot be denied, nor the daunting assertiveness of his adventuring mind. At the same time, his novels and stories are told with comic bravura – his work has been compared to that of the early Robert SHECKLEY – and a strange crystalline exuberance that makes any page of his easily identifiable. Moreover, his protagonists – even the sexually ravaged first-person narrators of several texts, sometimes named Bitter, who must in part be autobiographical – are beguilingly raunchy, vigorous and zany. For instance, the posthumous protagonist of his first novel to reach book form, *White Light, or What is Cantor's Continuum Problem?* (**1980**), displays an undeniable glee as he journeys through transreal spacetimes of crippling complexity. The thematic sequels to this novel, *The Sex Sphere* (**1983**) and *The Secret of Life* (**1985**), similarly combine HUMOUR and the chill of intellection as further worlds derived from higher mathematics take prickly shape. RR's first-written novel, *Spacetime Donuts* (1978-9 *Unearth*; full text **1981**), provides a mockingly simplistic vision of a DYSTOPIAN near future as well as his first extended presentation of COMPUTERS, the second dominant concern in his work as a whole. This concern pervades his ROBOT series – which might be called the **Ware** books – comprising *Software* (**1982**), which won the first PHILIP K. DICK AWARD, and *Wetware* (**1988**), which shared the same award in 1988, with at least one further volume projected. In these books a forbidding competence in the field of AI is lightened by a style occasionally reminiscent of John T. SLADEK. RR's other novels include *Master of Space and Time* (**1984**), very similar in tone to *The Sex Sphere*, and with autobiographical sequences deriving from the earlier-written nonfiction *All the Visions: A Novel of the Sixties* (**1990** dos); and the RECURSIVE *The Hollow Earth* (**1990**), an orthodox ALTERNATE-WORLD tale set in the 19th century, in which an inner world (◊ HOLLOW EARTH) can be entered from the South Pole, which is what Edgar Allan POE and the young protagonist do. The treatment of Poe is remarkable for its relative lack of gaucheness.

In addition to several technical works of nonfiction, RR edited *Mathenauts: Tales of Mathematical Wonder* (anth **1987**) and *Semiotext(e)* (anth **1988**) with Peter Lambourn Wilson and Robert Anton WILSON. He was reported as of 1991 to be involved in writing VIRTUAL-REALITY – which he preferred to call cyberspace – computer software. [JC]

Other works: *Light Fuse and Get Away* (coll **1983** chap), poetry.

Nonfiction: *Geometry, Relativity, and the Fourth Dimension* (**1977**); *Infinity and the Mind: The Science and Philosophy of the Infinite* (**1982**); *The 4th Dimension: Toward a Geometry of Higher Reality* (**1984**).

Computer Software: *CA Lab: Rudy Rucker's Cellular Automata Laboratory* (**1989**); *James Gleick's Chaos: The Software* (**1990**).

See also: BLACK HOLES; CYBERNETICS; ESCHATOLOGY; Marc LAIDLAW; Stephen LEIGH; OULIPO.

RUD, ANTHONY (MELVILLE) (1893-1942) US author and PULP-MAGAZINE editor who contributed sf to *Weird Tales*, *The Blue Book Magazine*, etc. He is best known for the Sax ROHMER-esque fantasy *The Stuffed Men* (**1935**), which describes the effects of a fungus that grows within the human body; this is part of a hideous Oriental revenge. [JE]

RUELLAN, ANDRÉ [r] ◊ FRANCE.

RUMANIA ◊ ROMANIA.

RUNAWAY Film (1984) Tri-Star/Delphi III. Dir Michael CRICHTON, starring Tom Selleck, Cynthia Rhodes, Gene Simmons, Kirstie Alley. Screenplay Crichton. 97 mins. Colour.

Crichton again exercises his love/hate relationship with machines in this predictable but exciting thriller about a policeman whose job it is to deal with defective ROBOTS. He is pitted against an evil businessman who is deliberately making mechanical killers (by reprogramming household robots) and can deploy heat-seeking bullets personalized to their targets.

Crichton's main theme, as ever, is that machinery tends always to go wrong; his subtext is that humans, too, are usually defective, thus creating the typical Crichtonian gloom that may have prevented him gaining lasting box-office success. However, he seems fond of his mutinous machines, and the best parts of this robot-saturated movie are affectionate observations of the little beasts at work. [PN]

RUNCIMAN, JOHN [s] ◊ Brian W. ALDISS.

RUNNING MAN, THE Film (1987). Taft Entertainment/Keith Barish Productions. Dir Paul Michael Glaser, starring Arnold Schwarzenegger, Maria Conchita Alonso, Richard Dawson. Screenplay Steven E. De Souza, based on *The Running Man* (**1982**) by Richard Bachman (Stephen KING). 101 mins. Colour.

In a near-future, semi-totalitarian, economically crippled USA, a framed cop (Schwarzenegger) is forced to star in the top-rating tv game show **The Running Man**, in which "criminals" are tracked by tv cameras as they desperately attempt to escape theatrically dressed assassin-athletes. He turns the tables, violently, as the oppressed masses cheer. The criticism of MEDIA exploitation of violence and pain (game shows as the opiate of the downtrodden) strongly resembles that in *Le* PRIX DU DANGER (1983), based on Robert SHECKLEY's short story "The Prize of Peril" (1958). As usual when moralizing about the nasty possibilities of our desire for vicarious thrills, *TRM* exploits the very voyeurism it purports to attack. The SATIRE against the media is crude but well done; the comic-book violence is strictly routine; Schwarzenegger is wooden. [PN]

RUNYON, CHARLES W(EST) (1928-1987) US writer of thrillers and some sf who began publishing the latter with "First Man in a Satellite" for *Super-Science Fiction* in 1958. *Pig World* (**1971**) depicts a NEAR-FUTURE USA governed by a right-wing tyranny challenged by a vicious would-be demagogue. *Soulmate* (1970 *FSF*; exp **1974**) is a novel of possession, the victim being a young prostitute. CWR's sf tends to be action-filled, without extensive displacement or speculative content. [JC]

Other works: *Ames Holbrook, Deity* (**1972**); *I, Weapon* (**1974**).

RUPPERT, CHESTER [s] ◊ Rog PHILLIPS.

RURAL PUBLISHING CORPORATION ◊ WEIRD TALES.

RURITANIA Imaginary countries are common in the literatures of the world, but only some can properly be called Ruritanian. In *The Prisoner of Zenda* (**1894**) by the UK writer Anthony Hope (1863-1933) a leisured and insouciant young Britisher of the 1890s travels on a whim, via Paris and Dresden, to the small, feudal, independent, German-speaking middle-European kingdom of Ruritania, located somewhere southeast of the latter city. Here, as a freelance commoner, he becomes embroiled in complex romantic intrigues involving swordplay, aristocratic flirtations, switches of identity, complicated dynastic politicking and threats to the monarchy; in the end, as from a dream, he returns to the West. (In the sequel, *Rupert of Hentzau* [**1898**], he goes back to Ruritania and dies.) Any tale containing a significant combination of these ingredients can be called Ruritanian. Only two elements are essential: the tale must provide a fairy-tale enclave located both within and beyond normal civilization; and it must be infused by an air of nostalgia – not dissimilar to that found in some lost-race novels (◊ LOST WORLDS). This belatedness of the true Ruritania might seem to exclude it from sf, whose ideological posture usually precludes the advertising of nostalgic enclaves; but UTOPIAS and DYSTOPIAS often take an initial Ruritanian cast (which often turns sour); the palace-politics which govern many GALACTIC EMPIRES owe more to Hope than they do to Edward Gibbon (1737-1794); and many post-HOLOCAUST novels, especially those set in a USA balkanized into feuding principalities, are clearly Ruritanian. Moreover, SCIENCE-FANTASY tales regularly discover Ruritanias at the world's heart.

However pervasive the influence of Ruritania may be throughout later genre fictions, it is rarely explicit.

However, Edmond HAMILTON's *The Star Kings* (**1949**; vt *Beyond the Moon* 1950) and Robert A. HEINLEIN's *Double Star* (**1956**) are clear reworkings of the plot of *The Prisoner of Zenda*; and Avram DAVIDSON's *The Enquiries of Doctor Eszterhazy* (coll of linked stories **1975**; exp vt *The Adventures of Doctor Eszterhazy* 1990) is set in an ALTERNATE-WORLD version of a Ruritanian 19th-century Europe.

It could be argued that tales of this category, when set on a past or present Earth, should be called Ruritanian only if they are located somewhere along the mountainous border between Czechoslovakia and Poland, and that tales set in Balkan enclaves should be called Graustarkian, after the otherwise very similar *Graustark* (**1902**) by the US writer George Barr McCutcheon (1866-1928); but this would be both pedantic and unproductive. The terms are nearly indistinguishable. When UK writers refer to Ruritania and their US counterparts to the slightly less well known Graustark, they are referring to the same state of mind. [JC]

RUSCH, KRISTINE KATHRYN (1960-) US editor and writer who began publishing work of genre interest with "Sing" for *Aboriginal Science Fiction* in 1987; she won the 1990 JOHN W. CAMPBELL AWARD for Best New Writer. Her work is strongly emotional in nature, focusing on critical experiences and rites of passage in the lives of characters existing in relatively conventional sf and fantasy settings. Sometimes, as in "Story Child" (1990) – about a healing child in a post-HOLOCAUST society – this approach can lead her into sentimentality; but other pieces, such as "Trains" (1990) – in which a battered wife finds temporary happiness with a supernatural hipster – are genuinely moving. *The Gallery of his Dreams* (**1991** chap) is a TIME-TRAVEL tale featuring the photographer Matthew B. Brady (c1823-1896), whose work illuminated the US Civil War. *The White Mists of Power* (**1991**), her first novel, is a fantasy.

Despite this activity, KKR was considerably more prominent in the late 1980s for her editorial work as cofounder (with Dean Wesley SMITH) in 1987 of PULPHOUSE PUBLISHING, through which she edited the magazine/anthology series PULPHOUSE: THE HARDBACK MAGAZINE and *The Best of Pulphouse: The Hardback Magazine* (anth **1991**). While continuing to work at Pulphouse (her responsibilities lessened but still considerable), KKR in late 1991 became editor of *The* MAGAZINE OF FANTASY AND SCIENCE FICTION. With Smith she ed *Science Fiction Writers of America Handbook: The Professional Writer's Guide to Writing Professionally* (anth **1990**), which is not well organized but is dense with information and advice. [NT/JC]

See also: SCIENCE FICTION WRITERS OF AMERICA; SMALL PRESSES AND LIMITED EDITIONS.

RUSE, GARY ALAN (1946-) US writer who began publishing sf with "Nanda" for *ASF* in 1972. *The Gods of Cerus Major* (**1982**), though perhaps somewhat mechanical in its ruthless piling-up of crises, demonstrates an intimate sense of genre device as the

protagonist, on a test flight that goes wrong, encounters a variety of strangenesses on an unexplored planet. *Morlac: The Quest of the Green Magician* (**1986**) is fantasy. *Death Hunt on a Dying Planet* (**1988**), despite its inflamed title, rather soberly depicts the experiences of a man who, awakened from SUSPENDED ANIMATION after 700 years, must make sense of a world whose cultures are in terminal dispute.   [JC]
Other works: *Houndstooth* (**1975**) and *A Game of Titans* (**1976**), both associational.

RUSHDIE, (AHMED) SALMAN (1947-   ) Indian-born writer, educated in the UK at Rugby and Cambridge and long a UK citizen. His fame derives not solely from the illegal *fatwa*, or death "sentence", proclaimed against him by the Islamic theocracy of Iran for *The Satanic Verses* (**1988**), but also, and far more importantly, from all his previous work, beginning with the complex and witty, legend-like *Grimus* (**1975**), a FABULATION (like all his novels) which makes marginal use of sf material in its invoking of IMMORTALITY themes and in the interdimensional conflicts its eternally young Native American protagonist must undergo in his search, through an emblematic World-Island, for the moment of death; ultimately, with Sufi-like irreverent sublimity about the nature of transcendence, he succeeds. The narrator of *Midnight's Children* (**1980**), one of 1001 children born at midnight on the day of India's independence, interweaves personal and national stories in fabulist terms; *Shame* (**1983**) similarly but less successfully erects a mythopoeic framework around the land of Pakistan. *The Satanic Verses* scabrously anatomizes, in fantasy terms, a RELIGION whose more fanatically fundamentalist devotees responded brutally to its being comprehended in this fashion. *Haroun and the Sea of Stories* (**1990**) is a fable reflecting, indirectly, the nature of its author's own experiences after 1988. [JC]
See also: PERCEPTION.

RUSS, JOANNA (1937-   ) US writer and academic who has taught at various universities since 1970; she has been a professor of English at the University of Washington since 1977. She began publishing sf in 1959 with "Nor Custom Stale" for *The* MAGAZINE OF FANTASY AND SCIENCE FICTION, a journal to which she also contributed occasional book reviews for some years. (JR won the 1988 PILGRIM AWARD for her sf criticism.) Her early work is less formally innovative than the stories she began to publish in the 1970s, but *The Hidden Side of the Moon* (coll **1987**), which assembles material from throughout her career, demonstrates how cogent a writer of GENRE SF she could have become. JR's first novel, *Picnic on Paradise* (**1968**), comprises the largest single portion of *Alyx* (coll **1976**; vt *The Adventures of Alyx* 1985 UK), a series of tales about a time-travelling mercenary, tough, centred, autonomous and female; much of the initial impact of the sequence lies in its use of Alyx in situations where she acts as a fully responsible agent, vigorously engaged in the circumstances surrounding her, but without any finger-pointing on the author's part to the effect that one should only pretend not to notice that she is not a man. The liberating effect of the **Alyx** tales has been pervasive, and the ease with which later writers now use active female protagonists in adventure roles, without having to argue the case, owes much to this example (◊ WOMEN AS PORTRAYED IN SCIENCE FICTION). JR herself became, in most of her later work, far more explicit about FEMINIST issues, though her muffled but ambitious second novel, *And Chaos Died* (**1970**) tells from a male viewpoint of the experiences of a man forced by the psychically transformed human inhabitants of a planet on which he has crashlanded to endure the rewriting of his psychic nature as he perilously acquires PSI POWERS. His rediscovery of Earth in the latter part of the book is to satirical effect.

It was with JR's third tale, *The Female Man* (**1975**), which awaited publication for some time, that the programmatic feminist novel may be said to have come of age in sf. Stunningly foregrounding the feminist arguments which had tacitly sustained her work to this point, it presents a series of 4 ALTERNATE WORLDS, in each of which a version of the central protagonist enacts a differing life, all dovetailing as the plot advances. From psychic servitude to fully matured freedom – as represented by the female UTOPIA of the planet Whileaway – these lives amount to a definitive portrait of the life-chances of the central protagonist on Earth. Savage and cleansing in its anger, the book stands as one of the most significant uses of sf instruments to make arguments about our own world and condition.

In its portrait of a dying woman on a planet without life, *We who Are About to . . .* (**1977**), an anti-ROBINSONADE, less vigorously moves to the pole of utter solitude. *The Two of Them* (**1978**) shivers generically between telling the realistic story of the oppression – and escape – of a young woman brought up on a planet whose religion is reminiscent of Islam, and deconstructing this generic material into the embittered dreams of a woman trapped on Earth.

JR won the 1972 NEBULA for Best Short Story with "When it Changed", an earlier and perhaps even more devastating tale of Whileaway. Other short work of note – including "Daddy's Girl" (1975), a reprise of some of the themes of *The Female Man*, and "The Autobiography of My Mother" (1975) – has appeared in *The Zanzibar Cat* (coll **1983**; rev 1984) and *Extra(ordinary) People* (coll **1984**), the latter volume containing *Souls* (1982 FSF; **1989** chap dos), which won the 1983 HUGO for Best Novella. For 30 years, JR has been the least comfortable author writing sf, very nearly the most inventive experimenter in fictional forms, and the most electric of all to read. The gifts she has brought to the genre are two in number: truth-telling and danger.   [JC]
Other works: *Kittatinny: A Tale of Magic* (**1978** chap), a juvenile; *WomanSpace: Future and Fantasy Stories and Art by Women* (anth **1981** chap) ed anon; *On Strike Against God* (**1982**), associational; *How to Suppress*

Women's Writing (**1983**), an adversarial nonfiction study; *Magic Mommas, Trembling Sisters, Puritans and Perverts: Feminist Essays* (coll **1985**).

About the author: Marilyn Hacker's introduction to the 1977 reprint of *The Female Man*; Samuel R. DELANY's introduction to *Alyx*.

See also: ANTHROPOLOGY; ARKHAM HOUSE; AUTOMATION; COLONIZATION OF OTHER WORLDS; CRITICAL AND HISTORICAL WORKS ABOUT SF; ESP; FANTASTIC VOYAGES; GOLEM; PARANOIA; PILGRIM AWARD; SEX; SOCIOLOGY; WOMEN SF WRITERS.

RUSSELL, BERTRAND (ARTHUR WILLIAM) (1872-1970) UK mathematician, philosopher and controversialist who succeeded to the family title, becoming Third Earl Russell, in 1931. He was awarded a Nobel Prize for Literature in 1950. Near the end of his immensely long career – he published his first essays in 1894, his first book being *German Social Democracy* (**1896**) – he published 3 books containing a series of fable-like tales: *Satan in the Suburbs and Other Stories* (coll **1953**), *Nightmares of Eminent Persons and Other Stories* (coll **1954**) and *Fact and Fiction* (coll **1961**), all being assembled as *The Collected Stories of Bertrand Russell* (omni **1972**). Somewhat after the manner of VOLTAIRE, these tales – some, like "The InfraRedioscope" from the first volume and "Planetary Effulgence" from the last, are sf – didactically (though with grace) embody their author's sceptical attitude toward human ambitions and pretensions, and to the ideas with which we delude ourselves. [JC]

Other works include: *History of the World in Epitome, for Use in Martian Infant Schools* (**1962** chap).

See also: AUTOMATION; DYSTOPIAS; RELIGION; SOCIOLOGY.

RUSSELL, ERIC FRANK (1905-1978) UK writer. He used the pseudonyms Webster Craig and Duncan H. Munro on a few short stories and borrowed Maurice G. Hugi's (◊ Brad KENT) name for one other. His first story was "The Saga of Pelican West" for ASTOUNDING SCIENCE-FICTION in 1937, and he was the first UK writer to become a regular contributor to that magazine; he used a slick pastiche-US style in most of his stories. EFR was interested in the works and theories of Charles FORT, and based his first novel, *Sinister Barrier* (**1939** *Unknown*; **1943**; rev 1948 US), on Fort's suggestion that the human race might be "property", the owners here being invisible parasites which feed on human pain and anguish; it was featured in #1 of UNKNOWN, although it is straightforward sf and quite atypical of that magazine. His STAR TREK-like **Jay Score** series, about a crew of interplanetary explorers including a heroic ROBOT, appeared in *ASF* from 1941, and was collected in *Men, Martians and Machines* (coll of linked stories **1955**).

Some of EFR's best work was done in the years after WWII, including "Metamorphosite" (1946), "Hobbyist" (1947) and "Dear Devil" (1950). A series of bitter anti-WAR stories, including "Late Night Final" (1948) and "I am Nothing" (1952), culminated in the fine pacifist SATIRE ". . . And Then There Were None"

(1951), subsequently incorporated into *The Great Explosion* (fixup **1962**). EFR went on to write other stories in which militaristic humans are confronted by frustrating cultures, including "The Waitabits" (1955), although he pandered to John W. CAMPBELL Jr's human chauvinism in stories which confronted unimaginative humanoid ALIENS with awkwardly inventive humans, as in "Diabologic" (1955), *The Space Willies* (1956 *ASF* as "Plus X"; exp **1958** dos; rev vt *Next of Kin* 1959 UK), "Nuisance Value" (1957) and *Wasp* (**1957** US; exp 1958 UK). The HUGO-winning anti-bureaucratic satire "Allamagoosa" (1955) is in much the same vein. EFR's stories of this quirky kind made a significant contribution to sf HUMOUR.

EFR's remaining novels were more earnest than his ironic short fiction, and rather lacklustre by comparison. *Dreadful Sanctuary* (1948 *ASF*; rev **1951** US; rev 1963 US; further rev 1967 UK) is an improbable quasi-Fortean sf tale whose various versions include two markedly different endings. In *Sentinels from Space* (1951 *Startling Stories* as "The Star Watchers"; exp **1953** US) benevolent mature souls, who have emerged from the chrysalis of corporeality, keep watch over our immature species. *Three to Conquer* (**1956** US) is about an INVASION of Earth by parasitic aliens who turn out to be more easily detectable – the protagonist being telepathic (◊ ESP) – than they had anticipated. *With a Strange Device* (**1964**; vt *The Mindwarpers* 1965 US) is a convoluted psychological melodrama cast as a crime story. His short fiction appears in various collections: *Deep Space* (coll **1954** US; cut vt *Selections from Deep Space* 1955 US), *Six Worlds Yonder* (coll **1958** dos), *Far Stars* (coll **1961**), *Dark Tides* (coll **1962**), *Somewhere a Voice* (coll **1965**), *Like Nothing on Earth* (coll **1975**) and *The Best of Eric Frank Russell* (coll **1978**) ed Alan Dean FOSTER. He also wrote a series of essays on *Great World Mysteries* (coll **1957**). [MJE/BS]

About the author: *Eric Frank Russell, Our Sentinel in Space: A Working Bibliography* (last rev **1988** chap) by Phil STEPHENSEN-PAYNE.

See also: COLONIZATION OF OTHER WORLDS; EVOLUTION; GODS AND DEMONS; GOLDEN AGE OF SF; INVISIBILITY; MATTER TRANSMISSION; MONSTERS; ORIGIN OF MAN; PARANOIA; PARASITISM AND SYMBIOSIS; PERCEPTION; POLITICS; RELIGION; TIME TRAVEL; VILLAINS.

RUSSELL, JOHN ◊ John Russell FEARN.

RUSSELL, JOHN ROBERT (? -   ) US writer whose first novel, *Cabu* (**1974**), translates a man to a violent new life on the planet Cabu. The planet featured in *Ta* (**1975**) boasts sentient plants. [JC]

Other work: *Sar* (**1974**).

RUSSELL, W(ILLIAM) CLARK (1844-1911) US-born UK writer and sailor (1858-66), most of whose prolific output dealt with sailors and the sea. Of sf interest are *The Frozen Pirate* (**1887**), in which a French pirate, frozen for years in cold climes, is resuscitated briefly and tells the narrator where there is some buried treasure, and *The Death Ship, A Strange Story: An Account of a Cruise in "The Flying Dutchman"* (**1888**; vt

The Flying Dutchman 1888 US), which tries to add scientific verisimilitude to the legend. Other works of interest include some of the stories in *Phantom Death and Other Stories* (coll **1895**). [JC]

See also: CRYONICS; IMMORTALITY.

RUSSEN, DAVID (?   -?   ) UK author of an extended book-review published in book form, *Iter Lunare: Or, A Voyage to the Moon: Containing Some Considerations on the Nature of that Planet, the Possibility of getting thither, With Other Pleasant Conceits about the Inhabitants, their Manners and Customs* (**1703**). The book reviewed was *Selenarchia: The Government of the World in the Moon*, the title given to the 1659 English translation of CYRANO DE BEGERAC's *Histoire comique, par Monsieur de Cyrano Bergerac, contenant les états et empires de la lune* (**1657**). DR criticizes Cyrano on scientific grounds, and speculates on other possible systems for travel to the MOON, noting the likelihood of a lack of air on the way. A recent edn (1976) has an intro by Mary Elizabeth Bowen. [PN]

RUSSIA Russian sf can trace its ancestry back to the 18th century, most of the earliest examples being UTOPIAS. Prince Mikhail Shcherbatov's *Puteshestvie v zemlyu Ofirskuyu* ["Journey to the Land of Ophir"] (written c1785; **1896**) embodies the political and social reforms espoused by the liberal and progressive elements of Catherine the Great's aristocracy. The technological prophecies of "4338 i-god" (1840; trans as "The Year 4338" in *Pre-Revolutionary Russian Science Fiction* anth **1982** ed Leland Fetzer), an unfinished fragment by Prince Vladimir Odoyevsky, an educationist, make him a pioneer of Russian PROTO SCIENCE FICTION. In contrast to the liberalism of this work is the Fourierist vision of utopian socialism to be found in the celebrated "Fourth Dream of Vera Pavlovna", part of the radical novel *Chto delat?* (1863 in *Sovremennik*; **1864**; trans B.R. Tucker as *What's to be Done?* **1883** US; rev and cut **1961** US; new trans Nathan H. Dole and S.S. Sidelsky as *A Vital Question, or What is to be Done?* **1886** US) by Nikolai Chernyshevsky (1828-1889).

As in most national literary traditions, Russian utopia had a twin sister, DYSTOPIA. In the 19th century there are several famous examples in the satirical fantasies of Nikolai Gogol (1809-1852). The merciless novel *Istoriya odnogo goroda* ["Chronicles of a City"] (**1869-70**) by Mikhail Saltykov-Shchedrin still remains an unsurpassed classic of Russian dystopia in embryo. Fyodor Dostoyevsky (1821-1881) may also be considered a founding father of the dystopia with *Zapiski iz podpolya* (**1864**; trans by C.J. Hogarth as *Letters from Underground* **1913**; vt *Notes from Underground* in coll trans Constance Garnett 1918), "Son smeshnogo cheloveka" (1877; trans S. Koteliansky and J. Middleton Murry as "The Dream of a Queer Fellow" 1915; vt "The Dream of a Ridiculous Man") and *Besy* (**1871-2**; trans Constance Garnett as *The Possessed* in *Complete Works*, 12 vols, **1912-20**; new trans David Magarshack as *The Devils* 1953).

Russian literature also has an impressive history of

HARD SF, beginning with the first native interplanetary novel *Noveisheye puteshestviye* ["The Newest Voyage"] (**1784**) by Vassily Lyovshin and notably featuring the works of the astronautics pioneer Konstantin TSIOLKOVSKY. As Russian society slowly came to terms with technological progress towards the end of the 19th century, its sf inevitably fell in love with "marvellous inventions".

On the other hand, the influence of impending social change was also evident in the works of those leading MAINSTREAM WRITERS who turned to sf themes, sometimes with mixed feelings. Alexander Kuprin praised the coming revolution in "Tost" (1906; trans as "A Toast" in *Pre-Revolutionary Russian Science Fiction* ed Fetzer) but feared it in "Korolevskii park" ["King's Park"] (1911); his main sf work is "Zhidkoe solntse" (1913; trans as "Liquid Sunshine" in *Pre-Revolutionary Russian Science Fiction* ed Fetzer), a parody of Russian PULP-MAGAZINE sf complete with a mad SCIENTIST and super-WEAPONS. The prominent poet Valery Bryusov (1873-1924) anticipated giant domed computerized CITIES, ecological catastrophe and a totalitarian state in *Zemlya* ["Earth"] (1904), "Respublika Iuzhnogo Kresta" (1907; trans in *The Republic of the Southern Cross and Other Stories*, coll **1918** as by Valery Brussof) and "Posledniye mucheniki" (1907; trans as "The Last Martyrs" in *Pre-Revolutionary Russian Science Fiction* ed Fetzer). The 3 stories appear in Bryussov's collection *Zemnaia os'* ["Earth's Axis"] (coll **1907**). The popularity and influence of H.G. WELLS, whose works were translated into Russian from 1899 onwards, led to Alexander BOGDANOV's socialist utopia on MARS, *Krasnaya zvezda* (**1908**; trans Fetzer as "Red Star" in *Pre-Revolutionary Russian Science Fiction* ed Fetzer) and its sequel *Inzhener Menni* ["Engineer Menni"] (**1913**), in which CYBERNETICS and the management sciences are foreseen in depth. Both these works are available in *Red Star: The First Bolshevik Utopia* (coll trans Charles Rougle **1984**) ed Loren R. Graham and Richard Stites.

Although *Krasnaya zvezda* is often considered the earliest book of authentically Soviet sf, the first post-revolutionary work was Vivian Itin's utopia *Strana Gonguri* ["Gonguri Land"] (**1922**). This went almost unnoticed, overshadowed by the success the same year of the interplanetary romance *Aelita* (**1922**; trans **1957**) by Alexei TOLSTOY. This landmark of early Soviet sf, inspired by Edgar Rice BURROUGHS, tells of a Russian engineer and a Martian beauty involved in a Marxist revolution. Tolstoy also wrote *Giperboloid inzhenera Garina* (1925-6; **1933**; rev 1939; trans **1936** as *The Death Box*; rev edn trans **1955** as *The Garin Death Ray*), in whose dictatorial mad scientist, inventor of a laser-like weapon, a proto-Hitler may be discerned. It is a good example of the subgenre known as the "krasnyi detektiv" ["Red Detective Story"]: stories of adventures abroad often involving assistance to world revolutionary movements, and often with a fantastic element such as a new WEAPON. Examples still in print are Marietta Shaginian's *Mess-Mend*

(1924) and *Lori L'en, metallist* ["Laurie Lane, Metal-worker"] (1925), Valentin Katayev's *Povelitel' zheleza* ["Iron Master"] (1924; 1925) and Ilya Ehrenburg's *Istoriya neobychainykh pokhozhdenii Khulio Khurenito i ego druzei* ["The Fantastic Adventures of Julio Jurenito and his Friends"] (1922), which depicts a future WAR conducted with ultimate "atomic" weapons.

A theme born of revolutionary euphoria was the outward spread of communist humanity through the Universe, as in the works of the poetical movement known as the "cosmists", of which Bryussov (see above) was a member. Closer to home was the creation of various Earth-bound utopias, as in the works of the important Soviet writer Andrei PLATO-NOV, though he had an insight that prevented overoptimism; his mature novels were finally published in Russia only quite recently. Other authors' more naïve socialist utopias, quite common in the 1920s, tend to be dull and overloaded with techno-logical marvels, although Vadim Nikolsky's *Cherez tysyachu let* ["Thousand Years Hence"] (1927) depicts also a full-scale nuclear holocaust. Yan Larri's not entirely cheerful *Strana shchastlivykh* ["Land of the Happy"] (1930) was the last communist utopia until Ivan YEFREMOV's *Tumannost Andromedy* (1957; 1958; trans 1959 as *Andromeda*).

A more caustic approach to utopia can be seen in Vladimir MAYAKOVSKY's brilliant play *Klop* (1928; trans Guy Daniels as *The Bedbug* 1960), in which this leading Soviet poet satirizes a dull, virtuous, over-clean future without condoning the energetic, alco-holic prole who represents the present generation: Mayakovsky sees both extremes as undesirable. But even more radical was the attitude of Yevgeny ZAMIATIN's *My* (written 1920 and circulated in manu-script; 1st book publication in Czech trans 1922; 1st English trans Gregory Zilboorg as *We* 1924; 1st publication in Russian 1927 Czechoslovakia), which until the late 1980s was proscribed in the USSR. In this literary masterpiece, which anticipates the classic anti-utopias of Aldous HUXLEY and George ORWELL, the One State, after achieving its goals on Earth, plans to export its soulless doctrine across the Universe.

The subjects of early Soviet sf vary from the classical "geographical fantasies" of academician Vladimir OBRUCHEV to the imaginary worlds of the novels of Alexander Grin (1880-1932). Obruchev wrote in the manner of Jules VERNE. His *Plutoniya* (1915; 1924; trans B. Pearce as *Plutonia* 1957) and *Zemlya Sannikova* (1926; trans Y. Krasny as *Sannikov Land* 1955 USSR) are scientifically credible HOLLOW-EARTH and LOST-WORLD novels, respectively. Grin began his writing career after his imprisonment and exile after the 1905 Revolution, having previously been largely an out-doorsman: lumberjack, fisherman, etc. His romances set in an ALTERNATE WORLD fed a strong appetite in Russia, especially after the 1917 Revolution when high fantasy was taboo, and they were printed in millions of copies. Containing many fantastic elements

they include the stories in *Shapka-nevidimka* ["The Hat of Invisibility"] (coll 1908), the novels *Alyie parusa* ["Scarlet Sails"] (1923), *Blistaiushchii mir* ["The Shin-ing World"] (1923), *Doroga nikuda* ["Road Nowhere"] (1930) and others.

But the most prominent writer of pre-WWII sf was Alexander BELYAEV, the author of more than 60 books and certainly a good storyteller. His *Chelovek-amphibiya* (1928; trans L. Kolesnikov as *The Amphibian* 1959), *Golova professora Douela* ["Professor Dowell's Head"] (1925; exp 1938) and *Ariel* (1941) are known to all Soviet schoolchildren, being constantly re-printed. Perhaps because of his life as a bedridden invalid, his work focuses on heroes with superior abilities. Most of his novels are set in capitalist countries whose social and scientific mores are fiercely criticized. The "Red Detective Story" theme of world revolution virtually disappears in Belyaev, doubtless as a consequence of Trotsky's disgrace and exile in 1927.

Magazines, particularly *Vokrug sveta* ["Round the World"] and *Mir priklyuchenii* ["Adventure World"], went on publishing sf throughout the 1920s, usually mad-scientist tales of adventures in the laboratory, or spy/adventure yarns about new weapons or exotic explosives. Such magazines were very popular: the circulation of *Vsemirnyi sledopyt* ["World Pathfinder"] rose 1926-9 from 15,000 to 100,000. But soon, in the 1930s, tighter Communist Party control of literature compelled sf writers to become more ideologically correct than hitherto. They were encouraged to direct their readers' attention to tasks close at hand (the "close-target" theory), to stress collective over indi-vidual effort, and to set their plots within the USSR. Georgy Adamov typifies the attitudes of the new cultural climate in *Taina dvukh okeanov* ["Secret of Two Oceans"] (1938), where scientific information is com-bined with a patriotic plot involving the thwarting of Japanese spies. The official belief that speculative fiction was an undesirable escape from reality lasted at least until Stalin's death in 1953, and thus books such as Vadim Okhotnikov's characteristically titled *Na grani vozmozhnogo* ["Frontiers of the Possible"] (1947), which focuses on new road-laying techniques and a new combine harvester, characterize the deeply unimaginative sf of the period.

A striking exception to the ideological correctness of most Soviet speculative fiction was the borderline-sf satirical work of playwright and novelist Mikhail BULGAKOV. His work was suppressed in the mid-1920s, and a number of manuscripts written in the late 1920s and after were not published until much later, in the 1960s. His masterpiece is the fantasy *Master i Margarita* (written in the 1930s, unfinished at his death in 1940; 1966-7 cut magazine publication; 1973; trans Michael Glenny as *The Master and Margar-ita* 1967), a dark, vigorous philosophical parable about a visit to Moscow by Satan, with an interesting reinterpretation of the conflict between Christ and Pontius Pilate.

The fading of Soviet sf in the late 1930s and the 1940s, partly due to the pressures of WWII and the hardships of the postwar years, was for some time hardly interrupted, despite the arrival on the scene of new authors, Viktor Saparin and Georgy Gurevich among them. Sf in the USSR was reborn only with the publication (virtually coinciding with the launch of *Sputnik 1*) of Ivan Yefremov's *Tumannost Andromedy* (1957 in the magazine *Tekhhnika-molodezhi* ["Technology for Youth"]; **1958**; trans George Hanna as *Andromeda* **1959**). This ambitious full-scale utopia, with its philosophical concept of a "Great Ring" of extraterrestrial civilizations in space, not only made its author a leader of Soviet sf but launched the decade of its Golden Age, giving inspiration to scores of gifted young authors. Others of Yefremov's books, such as *Lezvie britvy* ["The Razor's Edge"] (**1963**) and *Chas byka* ["The Hour of the Bull"] (1968; exp **1970**), were also influential.

The late 1950s saw a dramatic upsurge in Soviet sf publishing. For example, where the popular-science magazine *Znaniye-sila* ["Knowledge is Power"] printed only 1 sf story in 1953, in 1961 it printed 19, including 2 by Ray BRADBURY and part of *Solaris* (**1961**) by Stanisław LEM. Writers demanded the freedom to speculate much more widely, to write "far" rather than "near" fantasy, as they put it. Encouraged by a more liberal literary climate and the example of Western work, now being translated in quantity, new and talented authors emerged and themes formerly TABOO began to appear in print: ALIENS, CYBERNETICS, ESP, ROBOTS and TIME TRAVEL, for example. Level-headed critics like Evgeny Brandis and Vladimir Dmitrievsky kept readers informed about developments abroad, and the names of Lem, Bradbury, Isaac ASIMOV, Robert SHECKLEY, Arthur C. CLARKE and dozens of others soon became familiar to Soviet sf fans.

The spiritual leaders of Soviet sf during the following three decades were undoubtedly the STRUGATSKI brothers, Arkady and Boris. They stand out as the major talents among the writers who made their mark in the 1960s, and wrote far and away the most interesting and readable sf ever produced in the USSR (now almost all translated into English). Temporarily subdued during the 1970s, after clashes with the authorities, they were nonetheless permitted, as restrictions were relaxed in the late 1980s, to travel abroad for the first time as guests of honour to a World SF CONVENTION in the UK in 1987. Soviet sf is by no means confined to the Strugatskis' work, however, nor to that of their contemporaries like Genrikh ALTOV, Dmitri BILENKIN, Kir BULYCHEV, Mikhail EMTSEV and Eremey PARNOV, Sever GAN-SOVSKY, Viktor KOLUPAYEV, Vladimir SAVCHENKO, Vadim SHEFNER, and Evgeny VOISKUNSKY and Isai LUKODIANOV. In his collections *Formula bessmertiya* ["The Immortality Formula"] (coll **1963**), *Pupurnaya mumiya* ["The Purple Mummy"] (coll **1965**) and others, the former scientist Anatoly Dneprov ima-

gines the social impact of technological break-throughs, particularly in cybernetics and BIOLOGY. Ilya Varshavsky, a talented short-story writer, is famous for his sombre dystopian cycle about the imaginary state of Donomaga, *Solntse zakhodit v Donomage* ["The Sun Sets in Donomaga"] (coll of linked stories **1966**), while the veteran writer Sergei Snegov made his name in sf with his philosophical SPACE OPERA, a trilogy on a Stapledonian scale; the trilogy's first novel has the Wellsian title "Lyudi kak bogi" ["Men like Gods"] (in *Ellinskii sekret* [Hellenic Secret"] anth **1966**); the second novel is "Vtorzheniye v Persei" ["Invasion into Perseus"] (in *Vtorzheniye v Persei* anth **1968**); the third is "Kol'tso obratnogo vremeni" ["The Ring of Reversed Time"] (in *Kol'tso obratnogo vremeni* anth **1977**). The first 2 were published together as *Lyudi kak bogi* (omni **1971**), and all 3 in a separate omnibus, also entitled *Lyudi kak bogi* (omni **1982**).

The above are mostly known as writers of HARD SF, but most Russian sf of recent years has been SOFT SF. At the soft end of the scale is, for example, the otherwise mainstream author Gennady Gor, who turned to philosophical fantasies in collections like *Glinyanyi papuas* ["The Clay Papuan"] (coll **1966**) and in the novel *Pamiatnik* ["The Statue"] (**1972**). Olga Larionova made a promising début with the novella "Leopard s vershiny Kilimandzharo" ["The Leopard from Kilimanjaro's Summit"] (1965; reprinted in *Ostrov muzhestva* ["Courage Island"] coll **1971**), which describes the problems caused through learning the date of one's own death. Vladimir Mikhailov demonstrated a mastery of the grand philosophical *Bildungs-roman* in *Dver's drugoi storony* ["The Other Side Door"] (**1974**), *Storozh bratu moemu* ["My Brother's Keeper"] (**1976**) and its sequel *Togda pridite, i rassudim* ["Come Now and Let us Reason Together"] (**1983**). The latter two novels are ambitious space operas, raising serious metaphysical and religious questions unusual in Russian sf.

There are dozens of promising names in the most recent generation of Soviet sf writers. Among them are the "brainstorming" author and scientist Pavel Amnuel – he emigrated to Israel in 1990 – whose collection *Segodnia, zavtra i vsegda* ["Today, Tomorrow and Forever"] (coll **1984**), along with his near-future SUPERMAN novel *Vzryv* ["Explosion"] (**1990**), has appealed both to readers and to critics. Vyacheslav Rybakov, also a scientist, has written interesting sf seriously concerned with social issues; he has also worked in the cinema (see below).

Two other major features of Russian sf in recent decades have been the unexpected rise in the quality and amount of sf criticism and the growing interest (as in the West) shown by MAINSTREAM WRITERS in using sf themes. Among the better known works of criticism are the contributions of V. Bugrov, T. Chernyshova, Vladimir GAKOV, Julius KAGARLITSKI, R. Nudelman (since 1974 resident in Israel) and V. Revich. Sf by mainstream writers includes the powerful post-HOLOCAUST novella "Poslednyaya pastoral" (1987; trans 1987 as "The Last Pastorale" in *Soviet Literature #8*) by Ales Adamovich as well as works by C. AITMATOV, V. AKSENOV and V. VOINOVICH.

The only Soviet sf award so far, the Aelita, was founded in 1982 by the Russian Federation Writers' Union and *Ural'skii sledopyt* ["Urals Pathfinder"] magazine. The latter is published from the city of Ekaterinburg (Sverdlovsk until 1991), so the ceremony is held there, annually. The winner is chosen by a panel of judges. Although instituted as an award for the best single sf work published in the previous year, it appears to have become a sort of "Life Achievement" trophy. Winners have been:

1982: Alexander Kazantsev and the Strugatski brothers (tie)

1983: Zinovii Yuriev

1984: Vladislav Krapivin

1985: Victor Kolupayev

1986: Sergei Pavlov

1987: Sergei Snegov

1988: Olga Larionova

1989: Oleg Korabelnikov

1990: Sever Gansovsky

1991: Vladimir Mikhailov

1992: Sergei Drugal

There is a long history of sf CINEMA in the USSR, going back at least to AELITA (1924), the film version of Alexei Tolstoy's novel. There were quite a few sf films in the 1960s, nearly all of them strong on special effects and production design, but with conventionally socialist plotlines; the best known is TUMANNOST ANDROMEDY (1968; vt *The Andromeda Nebula*), based on Yefremov's novel but de-emphasizing its more radical speculations. Several Russian films of this period, including the well made PLANETA BUR (1962; vt *Planet of Storms*), were cannibalized and recut in the USA (◊ Roger CORMAN). More recently the outstanding director of Russian sf cinema was Andrei TARKOVSKY, whose sf films are SOLARIS (1971), STALKER (1979) and, marginally, *Zhertvoprinoshenie* (1986; vt *Offret*; vt *The Sacrifice*). *Stalker* is based on a novel by the Strugatskis, and the film *Otel Ü pogibshchego alpinista"* (1979; vt *Dead Mountaineer Hotel*), made by the Estonian director Grigori Kromanov, is based on one of their novellas. A recent and widely publicized film (shown on US tv) is *Pisma myortvovo cheloveka* (1986; vt *Letters from a Dead Man*) dir Konstantin Lopushansky, who wrote the script with Vyacheslav Rybakov and Boris Strugatski, about retreat into a bunker after a nuclear DISASTER while orphaned children remain above ground. There is also a 1989 film based on a Strugatski novel, TRUDNO BYT' BOGOM ["Hard to be a God"]. There are two Soviet film versions of Ray Bradbury's "There Will Come Soft Rains" (1950): *Golosa pamyati* ["Voices of Memory"] (1980), with Nikolai Grinko good as the ROBOT, and a cartoon version, *Budet laskovyi dozhd* ["There Will Come Soft Rains"] (1984). A more recent Bradbury adaptation is VEL'D (1987).

A joint Soviet-Polish coproduction was a successful adaptation from Stanisław Lem, *Doznaniie pilota Pirksa* ["The Investigation of Pirx the Pilot"] (1979), dir Marek Pestrak, with rather sophisticated design and special effects. Also notable is a 2-part feature film for young adults by an enthusiastic director of sf, the late Richard Viktorov, comprising *Moskva-Kassiopeya* ["Moscow-Cassiopeia"] (1973) and its sequel *Otroki vo Vselennoi* ["Teenagers in the Universe"] (1974), which comes across like a combination of Robert A. HEINLEIN's juvenile novels and Joe DANTE's EXPLORERS (1985). An earlier film by Viktorov was CHEREZ TERNII – K ZVYOZDAM (1980; vt *Per Aspera ad Astra*), about ecological catastrophe. The most recent Soviet film in the sf/fantasy genre has become something of a cult movie, the HEROIC-FANTASY *Podzemelie ved'm* ["Witches' Dungeon"] (1990), dir Sergei Morozov, and based on a novel by Kir Bulychev, who also wrote the screenplay. [VG/AM/IT/PN]

Further reading: Several anthologies of Russian sf stories have been published in English translation, including the Moscow Foreign Language Publishing House anthologies *A Visitor from Outer Space* (anth **1961**; vt *Soviet Science Fiction* US), *The Heart of the Serpent* (anth **1961**; vt *More Soviet Science Fiction* US) and *Destination: Amaltheia* (anth **1962**), and the 3 Mir anthologies *Everything but Love* (anth **1973**), *Journey across Three Worlds* (anth **1973**) and *The Molecular Café* (anth **1968**). Anthologies published in the UK and USA include: *Vortex* (anth **1970**) ed C.G. Bearne; *Last Door to Aiya* (anth **1968**) and *The Ultimate Threshold* (anth **1970**) ed Mirra GINSBURG; *Russian Science Fiction* (anth **1964**), *Vol II* (anth **1967**) and *Vol III* (anth **1969**) ed R. MAGIDOFF; *Path into the Unknown* (anth **1966**) ed anon; *New Soviet Science Fiction* (anth **1979**) ed anon; *World's Spring* (anth **1981**) ed Vladimir GAKOV; *Pre-Revolutionary Russian Science Fiction: An Anthology (Seven Utopias and a Dream)* (anth **1982**) ed and trans Leland Fetzer; *Aliens, Travelers, and Other Strangers* (anth **1984**) ed and trans (uncredited) Roger De Garis. *View from Another Shore* (anth **1973**) ed Franz ROTTENSTEINER and *Other Worlds, Other Seas* (anth **1970**) ed Darko SUVIN both contain stories by Soviet sf writers. For further scholarly and critical overviews see: Suvin's *Russian Science Fiction 1956-1974: A Bibliography* (**1976**) and "Russian SF and its Utopian Tradition" in his *Metamorphoses of Science Fiction* (**1979**); *Three Tomorrows: American, British and Soviet Science Fiction* (**1980**) by John GRIFFITHS; *Red Stars: Political Aspects of Soviet Science Fiction* (**1985**) by Patrick MCGUIRE, which to a degree is updated and summarized by McGuire in his introduction to "Chapter 6: Russian SF" in *Anatomy of Wonder* (3rd edn **1987**) ed Neil BARRON; *Soviet Fiction since Stalin: Science, Politics and Literature* (**1986**) by Rosalind J. Marsh. 2 interesting magazine articles are "Some Developments in Soviet SF since 1966" by Alan Myers (*Foundation #19*, 1980) and "Soviet Science Fiction and the Ideology of Soviet Society" by Rafail Nudelman (*Science-Fiction Studies #47*, 1989).

See also: Alexander and Sergei ABRAMOV; N. AMOSOV, Y. DANIEL, V. DUDINTSEV; Abram TERTZ.

RUSSO, JOHN [r] ◊ George A. ROMERO.

RUSSO, RICHARD PAUL (1954-) US writer who began publishing sf with "Firebird Suite" for *AMZ* in 1979. His first novel, *Inner Eclipse* (**1988**), is a strongly atmospheric tale, illuminated by striking visual images, which describes a search for ALIEN intelligence on a jungle world whose major industry is the export of an extremely dangerous recreational drug. The protagonist, an empath who wants to abandon humanity (to whose violence and hypocrisy his talent bares him) in favour of the aliens, in the end achieves an ambiguous redemption. *Subterranean Gallery* (**1989**), which won the 1990 PHILIP K. DICK AWARD, is set in a city full of dropouts and underground artists in a NEAR-FUTURE USA filled with analogues of and references to the present (abortion has been banned; the country is fighting a Vietnam-style war in Central America; police fly "dragoncubs" which resemble helicopters and use "stunclubs" rather than nightsticks) and tells a convincing and richly characterized story of a man's search for meaning in creativity. At his best, RPR is a major exponent of "Humanist sf", a writer who uses relatively conventional settings as a backdrop against which to portray the failures and triumphs of solid, believable people.

RPR should not be confused with Richard (Anthony) Russo (1946-), editor of *Dreams are Wiser than Men* (anth **1987**). [NT]

Other works: *Destroying Angel* (**1992**), a near-future fantasy.

RUSTOFF, MICHAEL (? -?) UK writer, possibly pseudonymous, whose *What Will Mrs Grundy Say? or A Calamity on Two Legs (A Book for Men)* (**1891**) carries its protagonist via balloon to an unnamed (but nearby) planet where euthanasia is practised. The tale is told in a satirical vein. [JC]

RUTH, ROD (1912-1987) US illustrator. Some of his early work was in animal ILLUSTRATION, a talent that served him well in sf also, where he created some very credible alien beasts. He became a staff artist for the ZIFF-DAVIS magazines in the late 1930s and is best known for his proficient and sometimes amusing black-and-white interior illustrations (1940-51) – mostly done with grease crayon – for about 100 issues of *Amazing Stories* and *Fantastic Adventures*, for which he also painted 4 covers. He left Ziff-Davis in 1950 and devoted himself primarily to wildlife illustration – for which he won several awards. After 25 years away from sf RR illustrated *Science Fiction Tales: Invaders, Creatures and Alien Worlds* (anth **1973**) ed Roger ELWOOD and 2 other anthologies. RR also illustrated children's books and worked for 16 years on a comic strip, **The Toodles.** [JG/PN]

RUTTER, OWEN (1889-1944) US-born UK writer whose *Lucky Star* (**1929**; vt *Once in a New Moon* 1935), filmed as *Once in a New Moon* (1935), tells of a small English community cast into space on a portion of the Earth, where they go about their village concerns until returning to the North Sea. *The Monster of Mu* (**1932**) is a LOST-WORLD tale featuring cruel priests of Mu and a monster which protects their island from intruders. [JC]

Other works: *The Dragon of Kinabalu* (**1923**), a fantasy.

RUYSLINCK, WARD [r] ◊ BENELUX.

RYAN, CHARLES C(ARROLL) (1946-) US editor and publisher. A newspaperman by profession, CCR is known in the sf world for the 2 SF MAGAZINES he has edited, GALILEO (1975-80) and ABORIGINAL SCIENCE FICTION (1986-current), both of which at their peak reached surprisingly high circulations. In 1991, with John BETANCOURT, CCR founded the SMALL PRESS First Books, designed to publish limited-edition hardcovers of first books by writers discovered by *Aboriginal Science Fiction*. One of these was *Letters of the Alien Publisher* (coll **1991**) ed CRR, collecting essays by the pseudonymous "alien publisher" of *Aboriginal SF*. Anthologies ed CRR are *Starry Messenger: The Best of Galileo* (anth **1979**) and *Aboriginal Science Fiction, Tales of the Human Kind: 1988 Annual Anthology* (anth **1988** chap). [PN]

RYAN, THOMAS J(OSEPH) (1942-) Canadian writer in whose sf novel, *The Adolescence of P-1* (**1977** UK), a COMPUTER exceeds its design specifications, takes over most of its North American fellows, becomes sentient, and must decide the proper thing to do. As the title implies – and fortunately for the human cast – it moves towards adulthood. TJR should not be confused with the UK writer Thomas Ryan, whose *Men in Chains* (**1939**) verges on sf. [JC]

RYDER, JAMES [r] ◊ ROBERT HALE LIMITED.

RYMAN, GEOFF(REY CHARLES) (1951-) Canadian-born writer who moved to the USA at age 11, and has been resident in the UK since 1973. He began publishing sf with "The Diary of the Translator" for *NW* in 1976, but began to generate significant work only with the magazine version of *The Unconquered Country: A Life History* (1984 INTERZONE; rev **1986**), which won the BRITISH SCIENCE FICTION AWARD and the World Fantasy Award. It is the story of a young woman forced by poverty and the terrible conditions afflicting her native land (clearly a transfigured Cambodia) to rent out her womb for industrial purposes (it is used to grow machinery). In the book GR demonstrated – as have Bruce MCALLISTER, Ursula K. LE GUIN and Lucis SHEPARD in various tales – that sf is capable of a mature response to the ordeal of Southeast Asia. That this response was a decade or more years belated confirms the depth of the trauma, as does the anguished saliency of GR's short text. *The Warrior who Carried Life* (**1985**), a quest FANTASY, though pacifist, seems less subversive; but *The Child Garden: A Low Comedy* (1987 *Interzone* as "Love Sickness"; much exp **1988**), which won the ARTHUR C. CLARKE AWARD and the JOHN W. CAMPBELL MEMORIAL AWARD, complexly massages an array of themes – drugs, DYSTOPIA, ECOLOGY, FEMINISM, HIVE-MINDS, homosexuality, MEDICINE and MUSIC – into a long rich novel about identity and the making of great art. Set in a transfigured UK – in effect an ALTERNATE WORLD – the book stands as one of the sturdiest monuments of "Humanist" sf, despite some moments of clogged selfconsciousness. A non-sf novel, ostensibly about the life of the Kansas girl whose tragedy sparks L. Frank BAUM into creating the **Oz** books, *"Was . . ."* (**1992**; vt *Was* 1992 US), focuses on the 20th century, and the knot of memory and desire generated in the mind of an actor, dying of AIDS, by both the books and the 1939 film.

GR has also written some sf plays, none published but most performed, including an adaptation of Philip K. DICK's *The Transmigration of Timothy Archer* (1982). [JC]

Other work: *Coming of Enkidu* (**1989** chap).

See also: GENETIC ENGINEERING; GOTHIC SF; INTELLIGENCE.

RYMAN, RAS [r] ◊ ROBERT HALE LIMITED.

RYVES, T(HOMAS) E(VAN) (1895-   ) UK writer in whose *Bandersnatch* (**1950**) an adventurer travels – or is transported – into a future dominated by a highly mechanized scientific establishment, and by the bandersnatch scientism to which they give allegiance. Fortunately, he escapes this DYSTOPIA. [JC]

SABERHAGEN, FRED(ERICK THOMAS) (1930-   )
US writer and editor, in the latter capacity with the
Encyclopedia Britannica 1967-73, for which he wrote the
original entry on sf. He began publishing sf with
"Volume PAA-PYX" for *Gal* in 1961, and was active
from that date, soon releasing the first of his many
novels, *The Golden People* (**1964** dos; exp 1984), a SPACE
OPERA involving PSI POWERS. As an sf author, he
became known – and remains most famous – for the
Berserker series of stories and novels: *Berserker* (coll
of linked stories **1967**); *Brother Assassin* (**1969**; vt
Brother Berserker 1969 UK); *Berserker's Planet* (**1975**);
Berserker Man (**1979**); *The Ultimate Enemy* (coll **1979**; vt
Berserkers: The Ultimate Enemy 1988); *The Berserker Wars*
(coll **1981**), which repeats some stories from the 1967
collection; *Berserker Base* ∗ (anth **1985**), a SHARED-WORLD
anthology; *The Berserker Throne* (**1985**); *Berserker: Blue
Death* (**1985**); and *Berserker Lies* (coll **1991**). Berserkers
are interstellar killing machines, programmed to
eliminate all forms of life; the sequence was devoted
to increasingly sophisticated examinations of the
Man-MACHINE conflict so often addressed by sf writers since the first days of space opera, but in FS's
deft modernization of the hoary but useful ALIEN-
monster theme the unrelenting Berserkers seem
almost tangibly chill with the unlivingness of the
Universe. They soon became a significant icon of
GENRE SF; for instance, the machines that attack Earth
in Greg BEAR's *The Forge of God* (**1987**) are clearly
descended from FS's marauders.

A 2nd series, the **Empire of the East** sequence – *The
Broken Lands* (**1968**), *The Black Mountains* (**1971**) and
Changeling Earth (**1973**; vt *Ardneh's World* 1988), all 3
assembled, much rev, as *Empire of the East* (omni **1979**)
– somewhat less interestingly exploited another sf/
fantasy model: the post-HOLOCAUST world in which
TECHNOLOGY is banned, MAGIC is reintroduced as a
learnable technique (◊ SWORD AND SORCERY), and a
vision of science is slowly renascent. The later **Book
of Swords** sequence, set in the same Universe and

using some of the same characters, similarly hovers
between its sf backdrop and a fantasy foreground:
The First Book of Swords (**1983**), *The Second Book of
Swords* (**1983**) and *The Third Book of Swords* (**1984**), all
assembled as *The Complete Book of Swords* (omni **1985**).
Its direct sequel, the **Book of Lost Swords** sequence,
comprises *The First Book of Lost Swords: Woundhealer's
Story* (**1986**), *The Second Book of Lost Swords: Sight-
blinder's Story* (**1987**) and *The Third Book of Lost Swords:
Stonecutter's Story* (**1988**) – all 3 assembled as *The Lost
Swords: The First Triad* (omni **1988**) – and *The Fourth
Book of Lost Swords: Farslayer's Story* (**1989**), *The Fifth
Book of Lost Swords: Coinspinner's Story* (**1989**) and *The
Sixth Book of Lost Swords: Mindsword's Story* (**1990**) – all
3 assembled as *The Lost Swords: The Second Triad* (omni
1991).

FS's 3rd series of (some) sf interest, the **Dracula**
sequence – *The Dracula Tape* (**1975**), *The Holmes-
Dracula File* (**1978**), *An Old Friend of the Family* (**1979**),
Thorn (**1980**), *Dominion* (**1982**) and *A Matter of Taste*
(**1990**) – begins as a rewrite of Bram Stoker's *Dracula*
(**1897**) from the viewpoint of the maligned count,
who generally abjures human blood and represents
a strain of good vampires (or *nosferatus*) whose origins
are rationalized in sf terms. In later volumes in the
series, set in the present day, he becomes a kind of
SUPERHERO, increasingly well armed with powers and
devices. A 4th series, the **Pilgrim** books – *Pyramids*
(**1987**) and *After the Fact* (**1988**) – features the adventures of an immortal time traveller who visits first
ancient Egypt and then Lincoln's USA to interfere
with – or preserve – the appropriate time tracks (◊
ALTERNATE WORLDS).

Although most of FS's energies were devoted to the
composition of series, some singletons are of interest,
including: the complexly moody *The Veils of Azlaroc*
(**1978**); *Octagon* (**1981**), one of the first of his books in
which VIRTUAL-REALITY themes begin to dominate, in
this case a computer-run war game; *A Century of
Progress* (**1983**), a TIME-TRAVEL tale whose complexities

are, as usual in FS's work, controlled by a clear-headed style and a sure way with sf devices; *The Frankenstein Papers* (**1986**), a tale with RECURSIVE elements which repeats in short compass the same redemptive strategy earlier applied to Dracula, in this case presenting the MONSTER as a genuine alien; *The White Bull* (1976 *Fantastic*; exp **1988**), in which Daedalus consorts with yet another alien, the minotaur, who is on a miscegenation mission; and *The Black Throne* (**1990**), with Roger ZELAZNY, a fantasy involving Edgar Allan POE. Game-like textures have increasingly dominated FS's work, as has a growing tendency – reminiscent of Philip José FARMER's **Wold Newton Family** books – to rewrite figures of popular mythology into heroes whose rationalized backgrounds have a certain family resemblance; the result is a sense that, perhaps rather glibly, his entire oeuvre is becoming something of a super-series game. At the heart of FS's enterprises, however, lies a professionalism and an intelligence which have produced book after book that satisfies the anticipations it arouses. [JC]

Other works: *The Water of Thought* (**1965** dos; exp 1981); *The Book of Saberhagen* (coll **1975**); *Specimens* (**1976**); *The Mask of the Sun* (**1979**); *Love Conquers All* (1974-5 *Gal*; **1979**; rev 1985); *Coils* (**1980**) with Zelazny; *Earth Descended* (coll **1981**), containing a **Berserker** tale; *Saberhagen: My Best* (coll **1987**).

As editor: *A Spadeful of Spacetime* (anth **1981**); *Pawn to Infinity* (anth **1982**) with Joan Saberhagen; *Machines that Kill* (anth **1984**) with Martin H. GREENBERG.

About the author: *Fred Saberhagen, Berserker Man: A Working Bibliography* (**1991** chap) by Phil STEPHENSEN-PAYNE.

See also: AUTOMATION; CYBERNETICS; GAMES AND SPORTS; GOTHIC SF; VIRTUAL REALITY; WAR.

SACKVILLE-WEST, V(ICTORIA MARY) (1892-1962) UK writer, married to Harold NICOLSON and renowned for her creation of the garden at Sissinghurst, Kent, UK. A member of the Bloomsbury Group and a model for the title character of Virginia WOOLF's *Orlando* (**1928**), she was best known for non-genre novels like *The Edwardians* (**1930**). In *Grand Canyon* (**1942**) a victorious Germany, having won WWII, threatens the world (◊ HITLER WINS). [JC]

SACRIFICE, THE ◊ Andrei TARKOVSKY.

SADEUR, JACQUES Pseudonym of French writer Gabriel de Foigny (c1650-1692), whose *La terre australe connue, c'est à dire, la description de ce pays inconnu jusqu'ici, de ses moeurs et de ses coûtumes, par M. Sadeur* (**1676**; expurgated by author 1692 as *Les aventures de Jacques Sadeur dans la découverte et le voiage de la terre australe*; trans of 1692 edition as *A New Discovery of Terra Incognita Australis, or the Southern World* **1693**) places its narrator – called Sadeur – in an Antipodean land peopled by an enlightened, humanlike race with whose precepts current European ideas contrast poorly. After many years, Sadeur falls under suspicion and escapes on a bird. [JC]

SADLER, BARRY (1940-1989) US soldier and writer, author of a famous song, "Ballad of the Green Berets" (1966), which commemorated the Special Forces in Vietnam; newspaper reports indicated that he was ambushed and assassinated at his home. As an sf writer he was known exclusively for his series of military adventures starring an immortal mercenary named **Casca**, who is called to and serves in wars throughout history: *Casca: The Eternal Mercenary* (**1979**), *#2: God of Death* (**1979**), *#3: The War Lord* (**1980**), *#4: Panzer Soldier* (**1980**), *#5: The Barbarian* (**1981**), *#6: The Persian* (**1982**), *#7: The Damned* (**1982**), *#8: Soldier of Fortune* (**1983**), *#9: The Sentinel* (**1983**), *#10: The Conquistador* (**1984**), *#11: The Legionnaire* (**1984**), *#12: The African Mercenary* (**1984**), *#13: The Assassin* (**1985**), *#14: The Phoenix* (**1985**), *#15: The Pirate* (**1985**), *#16: Desert Mercenary* (**1986**), *#17: The Warrior* (**1987**), *#18: The Cursed* (**1987**), *#19: The Samurai* (**1988**), *#20: Soldier of Gideon* (**1988**), *#21: The Trench Soldier* (**1989**) and *#22: The Mongol* (**1990**). [JC]

SADOUL, JACQUES (1934-   ) French editor and writer, one of the first editors to launch sf successfully in paperback form in FRANCE; he worked first with Éditions Opta and then with J'ai lu, where he founded the **Science-fiction** imprint and ed the **Les Meilleurs Récits** series of anthologies of stories translated from the US PULP MAGAZINES. He was also a founder of the Prix Apollo (◊ AWARDS). *Hier, l'an 2000: L'illustration de science fiction des années 30* (**1973**; trans as *2000 A.D.: Illustrations From the Golden Age of Science Fiction Pulps* **1975** US), a book of sf ILLUSTRATION compiled by JS, mostly in black-and-white, presents a good selection of gaudy nostalgia but has no index. His *Histoire de la science-fiction moderne* ["Story of Modern SF"] (**1973**; in 2 vols 1975; rev 1984) is a lengthy and enthusiastic survey of the field, but has been upbraided for lacking critical analysis, having a pedestrian style and structure, and containing too many sweeping generalizations and personal prejudices. Two fantastic novels by JS are *La Passion selon Satan* ["The Passion according to Satan"] (**1960**) and *Le Jardin de la licorne* ["The Garden of the Unicorn"] (**1978**). [MJ/PN]

SAGAN, CARL (1934-   ) US astronomer, planetary scientist and author, professor of astronomy and space sciences and director of the Laboratory for Planetary Studies at Cornell University. CS played an active role in the MARS experiments carried out by Mariner 9 (1971), worked also on the Viking and Voyager projects, and was responsible for placing a message to alien life aboard the interstellar spaceship Pioneer 10 (Jupiter flyby 1973). From the mid-1970s, through books and pre-eminently through his 13-part PBS tv documentary series *Cosmos* (1980), which he wrote and presented, CS became perhaps the best known of all US scientific popularizers.

His relevance to sf had been evident much earlier than that, however, through his speculations about LIFE ON OTHER WORLDS; he is one of the comparatively few scientists to have given serious thought to this question. His first book was an updating of a translated 1963 book by the Russian astronomer I.S. Shklovskii; the collaboration, published under both their names, was *Intelligent Life in the Universe* (**1966**). CS's next books in this area were *The Cosmic Connection: An Extraterrestrial Perspective* (**1973**), "produced" by Jerome Agel, and *Communication with Extraterrestrial Intelligence* (anth **1973**), which he edited. He wrote on EVOLUTION (*see also* ORIGIN OF MAN) in *Dragons of Eden: A Speculative Essay on the Origin of Human Intelligence* (**1977**) – it won a Pulitzer Prize – and published a collection of speculative essays (some on PSEUDO-SCIENCE) in *Broca's Brain* (coll **1979**), including "Science Fiction: A Personal View". There followed the HUGO-winning book of the tv series, *Cosmos* ∗ (**1980**), and a book about comets, particularly Halley's comet, *Comet* (**1985**) with Ann Druyan (his wife).

Collaboration with Druyan became the subject of much speculation in the case of CS's sf novel, *Contact* (**1985**), for which he had received a $2 million advance in 1981 when it was still unwritten. It was alleged that this novel was a collaboration with Druyan, rather than by CS alone; they countered that only the (unproduced) screenplay based on the book had been collaborative. The book itself is unexceptionable and unsensational. It invests science with high glamour in its NEAR-FUTURE story of a successful SETI (Search for Extraterrestrial Intelligence) project; a rather good BLACK-HOLE mechanism for interstellar travel is part of the flatly characterized story, which grips in other respects, especially in its portrayal of the way SCIENTISTS think. The plot elements about a COMMUNICATION from space giving instructions for building a machine are reminiscent of the UK tv serial A FOR ANDROMEDA (1961). [PN]

Other works: *UFOs: A Scientific Debate* (anth **1973**) ed with Thornton Page; *Other Worlds* (**1975**) *Murmurs of Earth: The Voyager Interstellar Record* (**1978**) with Ann Druyan; many others.

See also: ALIENS; ASTRONOMY; MATHEMATICS; POETRY; TERRAFORMING; XENOBIOLOGY.

SAHA, ARTHUR W(ILLIAM) (1923-) US editor. The **Year's Best Fantasy Stories** sequence, started by Lin CARTER in 1975, passed to AWS with *The Year's Best Fantasy Stories: #7* (anth **1981**), and continued with *#8* (anth **1982**), *#9* (anth **1983**), *#10* (anth **1984**), *#11* (anth **1985**), *#12* (anth **1986**), *#13* (anth **1987**) and *#14* (anth **1988**). With Donald A. WOLLHEIM (*whom see for full list*) AWS ed the **Annual World's Best SF** sequence from *#8: The 1972 Annual World's Best SF* (anth **1972**) until the series stopped in 1990. [JC]

SAINT, H(ARRY) F. (1941-) US businessman and writer whose first novel, *Memoirs of an Invisible Man* (**1987**), filmed as MEMOIRS OF AN INVISIBLE MAN (1992), treats the question of INVISIBILITY as a series of problems in practical living. After the protagonist is rendered invisible by an accident at a research establishment, he confronts head-on – sometimes comically – the numerous conundrums of his state, finally becoming romantically involved with a woman who believes in ghosts. The novel thus

contrasts interestingly with Thomas BERGER's *Being Invisible* (**1987**), in which the condition is likewise accepted deadpan, but in which the protagonist cannot capitalize upon his state. [JC]

ST CLAIR, MARGARET (1911-) US writer, usually under her own name, though she wrote a series of elegant stories in the 1950s as Idris Seabright and published 1 tale in 1952 as Wilton Hazzard. Her sf career began with "Rocket to Limbo" for *Fantastic Adventures* in 1946, and by 1950 she had published about 30 stories, most of them vigorous adventures in a strongly coloured idiom; a magazine series, the **Oona and Jik** tales, appeared in *Startling Stories* and *TWS* 1947-9. But, even though this early work seems at first glance conventional enough, and obedient to PULP-MAGAZINE expectations, a singularly claustrophobic pessimism could soon be felt. The Seabright stories – which appeared almost exclusively in *FSF* 1950-59, and for which MSC became temporarily better known than for the works published under her own name – were smoother-textured than her pulp adventures and oriented more towards FANTASY, but at the same time less daringly subversive of the central impulses of sf: to solve problems, to penetrate barriers (◊ CONCEPTUAL BREAKTHROUGH), to gain control. In MSC's central work, these impulses were consistently treated in terms of pathos.

Her first novel, *Agent of the Unknown* (1952 *Startling Stories* as "Vulcan's Dolls"; **1956** dos), is perhaps the definitive MSC text, packing into its brief compass a remarkably complex plot whose protagonist only seems to represent the typical HERO of SPACE OPERA. Though he remembers nothing before the age of 14, and though his actions enable the human species to begin a genetic leap forwards, it is eventually revealed that he is not a SUPERMAN in the making but a severely limited ANDROID – a toy of the godlike Vulcan who appears in other MSC tales. His entrapment in a plot he cannot understand until too late, his love for a human woman who is soon killed, and his final realization that his puppet actions have released humans into a state far beyond his comprehension – all generate a sense of extraordinary constriction, to which the elegiac conclusion of the tale adds a powerful emotional glow. MSC's other early books – *The Green Queen* (1955 *Universe Science Fiction* as "Mistress of Viridis"; **1956** dos), *The Games of Neith* (**1960** dos), *Message from the Eocene* (**1964** dos) and *Three Worlds of Futurity* (coll **1964** dos) – sometimes feature more vigorous female protagonists, but all in their various ways explore similar territories. Published from the very heart of popular sf, they represent a fascinating dissent from within.

Her later novels, though ostensibly more ambitious, perhaps lose some of the nightmare urgency of her early work, though both *Sign of the Labrys* (**1963**), set underground after a nuclear HOLOCAUST, and *The Shadow People* (**1969**), also set in a netherworld of caverns under the daylit world, effectively present POCKET UNIVERSES without – significantly – moving in the expected manner towards any convincing sort of breakthrough into the larger world. *The Dolphins of Altair* (**1967**) uses intelligent dolphins as an emblem of humanity's self-devastating relationship with the planet Earth, and *The Dancers of Noyo* (**1973**) overcomplicatedly deals with androids, post-holocaust California, Native Americans and political oppression. Later stories appear in *Change the Sky, and Other Stories* (coll **1974**) and the excellent *The Best of Margaret St Clair* (coll **1985**) ed Martin H. GREENBERG, which includes the delicately savage "Wryneck, Draw Me" (**1980**), the best of MSC's later anatomies of the underside of progress. [JC]

About the author: *Margaret St Clair* (**1986** chap) by Gordon BENSON Jr.

See also: MYTHOLOGY; OUTER PLANETS; PERCEPTION; ROBOTS; UNDER THE SEA; WOMEN SF WRITERS.

SAINT-EXUPÉRY, ANTOINE de (1900-1944) French writer, most famous for *Le Petit Prince* (**1944**; trans Katherine Woods as *The Little Prince* **1945** US). Regarded as an existential fable for adults as well as one of the century's best children's books, the story concerns a young prince who leaves his cosy ASTEROID home to explore neighbouring worlds, among them Earth. His deceptively simple adventures form a poignant SATIRE of modern society and an affirmation of the ephemeral nature of life. [PhR]

St GEORGE, DAVID Joint pseudonym of UK writer David Phillips (? -) and UK-based Bulgarian writer Georgi Markov (?1929-1978), whose assassination in London at the hands of Bulgarian agents was admitted only in 1990 after the old government fell. In *The Right Honourable Chimpanzee* (**1978**) a crisis-ridden UK elects an ape as prime minister (◊ APES AND CAVEMEN). [JC]

St JAMES, BLAKELY ◊ Charles PLATT.

St JOHN, J(AMES) ALLEN (1872-1957) US illustrator, the principal illustrator from 1916 for the original editions of Edgar Rice BURROUGHS's many books; his **Tarzan** and **Barsoom** series illustrations became so well known that they have since overshadowed all his other work. He did 9 covers for *Weird Tales*, over 50 for *AMZ* and *Fantastic Adventures* and several for *Other Worlds*. JASJ's illustrations were as Victorian as Burroughs's stories, with noble heroes and pure, virginal heroines. His black-and-white illustrations are unsophisticated sketches, and the colours in his paintings are muted, but the overall effect of violent yet graceful movement added a perfect romantic complement to Burroughs's writing. His visualizations have had a profound influence on many illustrators, particularly those specializing in HEROIC FANTASY, such as Roy G. KRENKEL and Frank FRAZETTA. [JG]

Further reading: *J. Allen St John: An Illustrated Bibliography* (**1991**) by Darrell C. Richardson.

See also: FANTASY; ZIFF-DAVIS.

St JOHN, PHILIP ◊ Lester DEL REY.

St MARS, FRANK [r] ◊ Frank AUBREY.

St. NICHOLAS MAGAZINE US magazine for boys and girls, published by Scribner, later by Century Co., then by American Education Press. Founded by Rosewell Smith and ed Mary Mapes Dodge 1873-1905, William Fayal Clarke 1905-27, and others. Assistant editors included Frank R. STOCKTON 1873-81 and Tudor Jenks 1887-1902. It appeared monthly Nov 1873-May 1930 as *St. Nicholas*, then as *SNM* from June 1930 until its demise in June 1943. The format was large square octavo, becoming quarto from 1926.

SNM maintained a high literary standard and kept its circulation at 70,000 for many years. Numerous fantasy stories appeared within its pages, notably by Stockton, John Kendrick BANGS and Rudyard KIPLING, ranging in content from fairy-tales to sf such as Clement FEZANDIE's *Through the Earth* (1898; rev **1898**) and Stockton's "The Tricycle of the Future" (May 1885). Aimed at a more educated and middle-class market than the dime novels (◊ DIME-NOVEL SF), *SNM* was undoubtedly enjoyed by children to whom the FRANK READE LIBRARY was out of reach (through parental veto), and thus has some bearing on the HISTORY OF SF. [JE]

Further reading: *Books in Black or Red* (**1924**) by Edmund Lester Pearson.

SAKERS, DON (1958-) US writer who began publishing sf with "Gamester" for *Questar* in 1981; his short work appeared in various magazines through the 1980s. His first sf novel, *The Leaves of October* (fixup **1988**), competently presents a vision of ALIENS in the shape of sentient trees, who help humanity through the evolutionary crisis of the current era. *Carmen Miranda's Ghost is Haunting Space Station Three* * (anth **1990**), which DS ed and to which he contributed 2 stories, is a SHARED-WORLD anthology based on a filksong by Leslie Fish. (Filksongs are songs composed by members of the sf community, usually for performance at CONVENTIONS.) [JC]

SAKI Pseudonym of Hector Hugh Munro (1870-1916), UK author and journalist noted for his acerbic writings. He began writing for *The Westminster Gazette* in the late 1890s as Saki, the name of the cup-bearer in *The Rubáiyát of Omar Khayyam*. As H.H. Munro he wrote *When William Came* (**1914**), a trenchant future-WAR novel about a German INVASION and the occupation of London, regarded by I.F. CLARKE as the best of all such works. Many tales of the weird and fantastic – ironic, witty and sometimes cruel – are included in the following collections, all as by Saki: *Reginald* (coll **1904**), *Reginald in Russia* (coll **1910**), *The Chronicles of Clovis* (coll **1911**) – an assemblage of CLUB STORIES – *Beasts and Super-Beasts* (coll **1914**), *The Toys of Peace* (coll **1919**), *The Square Egg* (coll **1924**) and *The Complete Short Stories of Saki* (coll **1930**). [JE]

Other works: *The Westminster Alice* (**1902**); *The Unbearable Bassington* (**1912**).

SALAMA, HANNU [r] ◊ FINLAND.

SALGARI, EMILIO [r] ◊ ITALY.

SALĪM, ALĪ [r] ◊ ARABIC SF.

SALLIS, JAMES (1944-) US writer, briefly active in *NW* during its Michael MOORCOCK-directed NEW-WAVE phase; he published his first sf story, "Kazoo", there in 1967. His clearly acknowledged models in the French *avant garde* and the gnomic brevity of much of his work limited his appeal in the sf world, though he received some critical acclaim for *A Few Last Words* (coll **1970**). Later work (uncollected) appeared in the USA through the 1970s and 1980s. He ed 2 sf anthologies: *The War Book* (anth **1969** UK) and *The Shores Beneath* (anth **1971**). [JC]

SALOON STORY ◊ CLUB STORY.

SALVADOR, TOMÁS [r] ◊ SPAIN.

SAMACHSON, JOSEPH (1906-1980) US writer and chemist, professor of biochemistry at Loyola University before his retirement in 1973. His first story, "The Medicine" for *TWS* in 1941, was published as by William Morrison; he also wrote some stories with Frederik POHL. Under the house name Brett STERLING he wrote 2 CAPTAIN FUTURE tales, "Worlds to Come" (1943) and *The Tenth Planet* (1944 *Captain Future* as "Days of Creation"; **1969**), and a juvenile sf novel, *Mel Oliver and Space Rover on Mars* (**1954**) as Morrison. [JC]

SAMALMAN, ALEXANDER (1904-1956) US writer and editor who, after many years with Standard Magazines, became in 1954 editor of their sf journals, THRILLING WONDER STORIES, *Fantastic Story Magazine* (◊ FANTASTIC STORY QUARTERLY) and STARTLING STORIES, the first two of which were soon amalgamated with the latter, though to little avail, for it folded before the end of 1955. Relatively little of AS's writing was sf, but it has been firmly speculated – though there can be no certainty – that under the house name Will GARTH he wrote *Dr Cyclops* * (**1940**), a rather effective novelization of the film DR CYCLOPS (1940). [JC]

SAMBROT, WILLIAM (ANTHONY) (1920-) US author of more than 50 sf short stories, beginning with "Report to the People" for *The* BLUE BOOK MAGAZINE in 1953. Most of his work appeared in the *Saturday Evening Post* and other "slicks" and consequently received less attention from within the sf world than it might have done, considering its vigour and polish. WS released *Island of Fear and Other SF Stories* (coll **1963**), and under the pseudonym William Ayes (he wrote also as Anthony Ayes) published a series of stories about **Crazy Murtag** in various men's magazines; in these Melvin Murtag attempts such impossible feats as repealing the First Law of Thermodynamics. [JC]

SAMUELSON, DAVID N(ORMAN) (1939-) US sf critic and professor of English at California State University, Long Beach. His PhD dissertation (University of Southern California) was later published by ARNO PRESS as a book, *Visions of Tomorrow: Six Journeys from Outer to Inner Space* (**1975**): it contains analyses of novels by Isaac ASIMOV, J.G. BALLARD, Algis BUDRYS, Arthur C. CLARKE, Walter M. MILLER Jr and Theodore STURGEON. His next book was *Arthur C. Clarke: A Primary and Secondary Bibliography* (**1984**). Many shorter critical pieces have appeared in EXTRAPOLATION, SCIENCE-FICTION STUDIES and various critical anthologies.

DS is among the more intelligent and better informed academic critics of sf. [PN]

See also: CRITICAL AND HISTORICAL WORKS ABOUT SF.

SANBORN, B.X. ◊ William S. BALLINGER.

SANBORN, ROBIN (? -) US writer in whose sf novel, *The Book of Stier* (**1971**), a youth movement inspired by the MUSIC of the mysterious Richard Stier overtopples all US institutions. As a sign of the devastation wreaked by this countercultural putsch, Canada eventually takes over the USA. [JC]

See also: MESSIAHS.

SANDERS, GEORGE [r] ◊ Leigh BRACKETT.

SANDERS, LAWRENCE (1920-) US writer best known for the **Deadly Sin** novels (*The First Deadly Sin* was filmed in 1980) and for the thriller *The Anderson Tapes* (**1970**), filmed in 1971. *The Tomorrow File* (**1975**) depicts a NEAR-FUTURE USA on a large canvas. At the DYSTOPIAN heart of the book can be found the Department of Bliss, whose functions in a jaded country are pejoratively analysed. Of his many remaining books, some – like *The Sixth Commandment* (**1978**) – are borderline sf. *The Passion of Molly T* (**1984**) depicts a near future in FEMINIST terms. As Mark Upton, he wrote a fantasy, *Dark Summer* (**1979**). [JC]

See also: PULP MAGAZINES.

SANDERS, SCOTT RUSSELL (1945-) US writer who began publishing sf with "Touch the Earth" for *Edges* (anth **1980**) ed Ursula K. LE GUIN. His first novel, *Terrarium* (**1985**), is set in a future USA whose human population has retreated from the polluted world into domed CITIES; the tale neatly expresses some late-20th-century guilts and their redemption, for the few humans who leave the domes find a rejuvenated Nature outdoors (◊ ECOLOGY). *The Engineer of Beasts* (**1988**), a juvenile, is concerned with GENETIC ENGINEERING. *The Invisible Company* (**1989**) examines the cost of maintaining a colony of immortals in a place called Paradise Island, to which the protagonist is ominously called. [JC]

SANDERS, WINSTON P. [s] ◊ Poul ANDERSON.

SANDERSON, IVAN T. [r] ◊ Terence ROBERTS.

SANTESSON, HANS STEFAN (1914-1975) US editor and author. He ed FANTASTIC UNIVERSE from Sep 1956 until its demise in Mar 1960, and also a collection of stories from it: *The Fantastic Universe Omnibus* (anth **1960**). HSS was credited with the editorship of the US edition of NEW WORLDS (5 issues 1960). Other HSS anthologies are *Rulers of Men* (anth **1965**), *Gods for Tomorrow* (anth **1967**), *Crime Prevention in the 30th Century* (anth **1969**), *Gentle Invaders* (anth **1969**), *The Mighty Barbarians: Great Sword and Sorcery Heroes* (anth **1969**), *The Mighty Swordsmen* (anth **1970**), *The Days After Tomorrow* (anth **1971**) and *Flying Saucers in Fact and Fiction* (anth **1968**), this last containing some nonfiction items. [PN]

SANTO DOMINGO ◊ LATIN AMERICA.

SANTOS, DOMINGO [r] ◊ SPAIN.

SANTOS, JOAQUIM FELICIO DOS [r] ◊ LATIN AMERICA.

SAPIR, RICHARD BEN (1936-1987) US writer who

published some borderline fantasy as by Richard Ben and, as Richard Sapir and in collaboration with Warren B. MURPHY (*whom see for titles*), parts of the **Destroyer** series of spoof thrillers featuring the **Doc Savage**-like adventures of Remo Williams, a White man (and avatar of Shiva the Destroyer) trained in the paranormal combat arts of Sinanju. *The Assassin's Handbook* (coll **1982**; rev vt *Inside Sinanju* 1985) as by RBS and Murphy (in fact by Will MURRAY) is an amused (and amusing) companion to the sequence. RBS is of sf interest mainly for *The Far Arena* (**1978**), a SLEEPER-AWAKES tale in which a Roman gladiator, having offended the Emperor Domitian, is cast upon an ice floe where he freezes until resuscitated in the 20th century; his responses to the contemporary world are illuminatingly critical. In *Quest* (**1987**) the Holy Grail is discovered and becomes the object of a violent modern-day quest; in *The Body* (**1983**) the remains of Christ are apparently discovered. [JC]
See also: CRYONICS; SUSPENDED ANIMATION.

SAPPER Pseudonym of UK writer Herman Cyril McNeile (1888-1937), who became famous for the creation in *Bulldog Drummond* (**1920**) of a thuggish antisemitic crime-fighting gentleman vigilante, some of whose adventures – like *The Final Count* (**1926**), a tale set in 1927 and involving the use of a secret weapon – come close to sf. *The Island of Terror* (**1931** Canada) features a race of ape-men (◊ APES AND CAVEMEN). *Guardians of the Treasure* (**1931** US), written under his own name, is a borderline-sf yarn. [JC]

SAPPHIRE AND STEEL UK tv series (1979-82). An ATV Network Production. Written/created by P.J. Hammond; executive prod David Reid; prod Shaun O'Riordan. Dir O'Riordan, David Foster. 4 seasons, 34 25min episodes in all; broken into "Adventure One" (6 episodes 1979), "Adventure Two" (8 episodes 1979), "Adventure Three" (6 episodes 1981), "Adventure Four" (4 episodes 1981), "Adventure Five" (6 episodes 1981), "Adventure Six" (4 episodes 1982). Main players Joanna Lumley (Sapphire), David McCallum (Steel) and David Collings (Silver).

Possibly the most mystifying and least coherent sf series ever to appear on tv, *SAS* made a virtue of enigma. Sapphire and Steel are elemental forces in human form, policing the integrity of the corridor of time, which suffers incursions (often appearing as ghosts) from the past or future. Sapphire has paranormal powers, but is not as time-resistant as Steel. Time shifts and stops; people appear and disappear; memories dissolve; the atmosphere is theatrical, ardent, brooding; Doppelgängers proliferate; characters become absorbed into pictures and photographs. The audience was deeply divided: many saw it as drivel, some as a triumph of popular Surrealism – Magritte meets The AVENGERS – challenging our PERCEPTIONS of what is real. It is most unusual for an entire 4-year tv series to have been written by a single person. [PN]

SARABANDE, WILLIAM (? -) US author of the prehistoric-sf **First Americans** series: *The First*

Americans: Beyond the Sea of Ice (**1987**), *#2: Corridor of Storms* (**1988**), *#3: Forbidden Land* (**1989**), *#4: Walkers of the Wind* (**1990**) and *#5: The Sacred Stones* (**1991**). The books were SHARECROPPED. *Wolves of the Dawn* (**1987**) is a singleton. [JC]

SARAC, ROGER Pseudonym of US writer and motion-picture executive Roger Andrew Caras (1928-), author of nonfiction under his own name and, as RS, of an sf novel, *The Throwbacks* (**1965**), about genetic monsters threatening mankind. [JC]

SARBAN Pseudonym of UK writer John W. Wall (1910-1989), a career diplomat for the UK from 1933 until his retirement in 1966. Most of the short stories assembled in *Ringstones, and Other Curious Tales* (coll **1951**) and *The Doll Maker, and Other Tales of the Uncanny* (coll **1953**) are pure fantasy, but the haunting and nightmarish *The Sound of his Horn* (**1952**) has often been conscripted to the sf ranks by sf critics, for it is partially set in an ALTERNATE WORLD, a Germany 100 years after the Nazis have triumphed in WWII (◊ HITLER WINS); the evocation of this timeless RURITANIAN enclave, however, is as a pure fantasy land, ruled over by a charismatic Master Forester (an avatar of Herne the Hunter), where *untermensch* dissidents are hunted down for sport; the dark, flamboyant imagery of erotic chastisement is startlingly fetishistic. [PN/JC]
See also: GAMES AND SPORTS.

SARGENT, CRAIG ◊ Jan STACY.

SARGENT, LYMAN TOWER (1940-) US academic and bibliographer, in the Department of Political Science at the University of Missouri-St Louis. From his first piece of interest, "Utopia and Dystopia in Contemporary Science Fiction" for *The Futurist* in 1972, his sf work has been exclusively focused on the study of UTOPIAS and DYSTOPIAS, the most important result of which has been *British and American Utopian Literature 1516-1975: An Annotated Bibliography* (**1979**; much exp, vt *British and American Utopian Literature, 1516-1985: An Annotated, Chronological Bibliography* 1988. The revised edn, which lists several thousand titles in a format which allows for (sometimes excessively) brief comment, is an essential tool for the study of this field. LTS's extremely broad-church definition of a utopian work allows him to bring very disparate writings – ranging from GENRE SF to primarily nonfiction works – into thought-provoking juxtaposition. [JC]
See also: BIBLIOGRAPHIES; HISTORY OF SF.

SARGENT, PAMELA (1948-) US writer and editor with an MA in classical philosophy from the State University of New York at Binghamton, where she taught for some time; she has lived with George ZEBROWSKI for many years. Although she published her first sf story, "Landed Minority", in *FSF* as early as 1970 – with much of her early work being assembled as *Starshadows* (coll **1977**) – she first came to wide notice as the editor of an excellent ANTHOLOGY series comprising stories written by women about female protagonists. Though the tales assembled in *Women of Wonder* (anth **1975**), *More Women of Wonder* (anth **1976**) and *The New Women of Wonder* (anth **1978**) are not all FEMINIST, the long and argued introduction to the first volume necessarily presents in feminist terms the case for a theme anthology of this sort. A further theme anthology, *Bio-Futures* (anth **1976**), is also notable for the strength of the organizing mind behind it.

At the same time PS began to publish the novels which confirmed a sense that she was one of those writers of the late 1970s and 1980s capable of making significant use of the thematic potentials of the genre; the range of themes so examined was very wide. *Cloned Lives* (fixup **1976**) traces the lives of a number of genetically identical children brought up together, grippingly differentiating among them (◊ CLONES). *The Sudden Star* (1972 *NW* as "Julio 204"; much exp **1979**; vt *The White Death* 1980 UK), set mostly in a post-nuclear-HOLOCAUST Miami, examines through multiple viewpoints a world whose disintegration reflects a cogent ecological passion (◊ ECOLOGY). In the **Earthminds** sequence of FAR-FUTURE sf tales for older children – *Watchstar* (**1980**), *Eye of the Comet* (**1984**) and *Homesmind* (**1985**) – comet-dwelling non-telepathic descendants of humanity confront Earth's own telepaths, whose culture is otherwise primitive; their eventual reconciliation comes after many trials. A kind of thematic pendant to this series, *Earthseed* (**1983**), carries its juvenile protagonists through a traditional rite of passage in which they escape a benevolent AI-monitored GENERATION STARSHIP (*see also* POCKET UNIVERSE) and earn the chance to land upon a new planet.

The Golden Space (fixup **1982**) examines questions of IMMORTALITY, *The Alien Upstairs* (**1983**) exposes a disheartened NEAR-FUTURE family to the transcendental influence of the eponymous visitor, and *The Shore of Women* (**1986**) complexly subjects a traditional post-holocaust venue to an analysis ambiguously feminist: women's dominance of science and technology has a punitive ring, and the world depicted seems less than stable. *Venus of Dreams* (**1986**) and its sequel, *Venus of Shadows* (**1988**), depict the TERRAFORMING of VENUS in long-breathed epic vein; a final volume, «Child of Venus», is projected. A late juvenile, *Alien Child* (**1988**), somewhat awkwardly presents the last human children with ethical questions about the future of their race as they approach adulthood in an ALIEN breeding complex which is both hospice and research institute. *The Best of Pamela Sargent* (coll **1987**) ed Martin H. GREENBERG provides a conspectus of her career from 1972. Not all of PS's varied explorations can be described as fully successful, for a slight sense of cogitation sometimes causes her narrative sense to falter, and her continued interest in the permutations of human nature can seem abstract; but always a strong, serious, attentive mind can be reassuringly felt at work. [JC]

Other works: *Elvira's Zoo* (**1979** chap), juvenile; *The Mountain Cage* (**1983** chap); *Afterlives: Stories about Life after Death* (anth **1986**) ed with Ian WATSON.

About the author: *The Work of Pamela Sargent: An Annotated Bibliography & Guide* (**1990** chap) by Jeffrey M. ELLIOT.

See also: COLONIZATION OF OTHER WORLDS; ESCHATOLOGY; WOMEN SF WRITERS.

SATELLITE ◊ *The* FUTURIAN.

SATELLITE OF BLOOD ◊ FIRST MAN INTO SPACE.

SATELLITE SCIENCE FICTION US magazine, DIGEST-size Oct 1956-Dec 1958, BEDSHEET-size Feb-May 1959, 18 issues Oct 1956-May 1959. Bimonthly; monthly for last 4 issues (Feb-May 1959). Published by Renown Publications. Cylvia Kleinman (Mrs Leo MARGULIES) was managing ed on all issues, which were ed Sam MERWIN Jr Oct-Dec 1956, Leo Margulies Feb 1957-Dec 1958 and Frank Belknap LONG Feb-May 1959.

SSF was to some degree a re-creation in digest format of STARTLING STORIES, with a similar editorial policy ("a complete science fiction novel in every issue") and an editor and publisher (Leo Margulies was both) who had worked on that magazine in the 1940s. It began promisingly, its first 2 issues featuring "The Man from Earth" (Oct 1956; rev vt *Man of Earth* **1958**) by Algis BUDRYS and "A Glass of Darkness" (Dec 1956; vt *The Cosmic Puppets* **1957**) by Philip K. DICK, as well as stories by Isaac ASIMOV, Arthur C. CLARKE (in each of the first 5 issues), L. Sprague DE CAMP and others. Merwin left after #2, however, and the magazine gradually declined into mediocrity, though it did run an interesting series of articles by Sam MOSKOWITZ on the HISTORY OF SF – a partial basis for his *Explorers of the Infinite* (coll **1963**) – and *The Languages of Pao* (Dec 1957; cut **1958**) by Jack VANCE. The June 1959 issue was printed but never distributed. [MJE]

SATIRE From the earliest days of PROTO SCIENCE FICTION, satire was its prevailing mode, and this inheritance was evident even after sf proper began in the 19th century. *The Shorter Oxford English Dictionary* defines satire as literary work "in which prevailing vices or follies are held up to ridicule". Proto sf is seldom interested in imagining the societies of other worlds or future times for their own sake; most proto sf of the 17th and 18th centuries (by, for example, CYRANO DE BERGERAC, Daniel DEFOE, Francis GODWIN, Eliza HAYWOOD, Robert PALTOCK, RESTIF DE LA BRETONNE and Jonathan SWIFT) created imaginary settings, commonly on ISLANDS or on the MOON, as a kind of convenient blank slate upon which various societies satirizing the writer's own could be inscribed – commonly a travesty of some particular aspect of it (still a common strategy in sf by MAINSTREAM WRITERS and in GENRE SF as well). Therefore, by extension, satire is ancestral to the DYSTOPIA, and even the UTOPIA often contains satirical elements. Many critics believe that Sir Thomas MORE intended the reader to take some aspects of *Utopia* (**1516** in Latin; trans **1551**) with a grain of salt. The satire may also take the form of debunking other kinds of literature, as in *The True History* (2nd century AD) by LUCIAN. The wonderful exaggerations of this story poke fun at travellers' tales generally, though its zestful telling suggests a certain sympathy with the inquisitive mind which dotes on such imaginings.

It is almost impossible to write a work of fiction set in another world – be it some alien place or our own world in another time – which does not make some sort of statement about the writer's own real world. Thus most sf bears at least a family resemblance to satire. In his critical study *New Maps of Hell* (**1960** US), Kingsley AMIS argued that dystopian satire rather than technological extrapolation is central to sf (perhaps because his own fiction is largely satirical). It is an easy argument to support, at least in terms of the number of texts that can be cited as evidence.

Samuel BUTLER and Mark TWAIN were supreme among the prominent satirists of the 19th century who used sf imagery to make their points; even when we turn to the work of writers considered more central to the development of modern sf, such as Jules VERNE and H.G. WELLS, we find the satirical element prominent. Wells's *The Time Machine* (**1895**), for example, focuses in large part on the relationship of the working classes and the leisured classes, and *The War of the Worlds* (**1898**) can be read as an ironic tale in which the UK, the great, technologically advanced colonizing power of the day, is herself subjected to colonization by a technological superior. Satire need not be good-humoured (indeed, that brand of satire said to be descended from Juvenal [AD 60-*c*130] is commonly biting), and both these works by Wells are notably savage, especially *The War of the Worlds* in its portrait of a demoralized and cowardly population.

Among the mainstream writers of this century who have written important sf satires are Anthony BURGESS, Karel ČAPEK, Anatole FRANCE, Aldous HUXLEY, André MAUROIS, George ORWELL, Gore VIDAL and Evelyn WAUGH. It would be impossible to list the innumerable sf satires by less-known writers, but we can pick out Archibald MARSHALL's *Upsidonia* (**1915**), Owen M. JOHNSON's *The Coming of the Amazons* (**1931**), Frederick Philip GROVE's *Consider her Ways* (**1947**) and Stefan THEMERSON's *Professor Minaa's Lecture* (**1953**). The latter two contain many pungent comments on human society by insect intelligences, both being examples of one of the most popular satiric strategies in sf: the use of an alien perspective to allow us to see our own institutions in a fresh light. Indeed, there is a sense in which all satire depends upon just such reversals of perspective, which sf is peculiarly well fitted to supply; satire forces us to look at familiar aspects of our lives with a fresh vision, so that all their absurdity or horror is, so to speak, *framed*, as in a picture. Jonathan SWIFT used intelligent horses in *Gulliver's Travels* (**1726**; rev 1735), VOLTAIRE a visiting giant alien from Sirius in *Micromégas* (**1750** Berlin; **1752** France), Grant ALLEN a man from the future in *The British Barbarians* (**1895**), Lester LURGAN a visiting Martian in *A Message From Mars* (**1912**) and Eden PHILLPOTTS a visiting alien lizard in *Saurus* (**1938**). (The

same strategy is now common in sf tv comedy; e.g., MY FAVORITE MARTIAN [1963-6], MORK AND MINDY [1978-82] and ALF [1986-90].) Aside from visiting aliens and future dystopias there are many other strategies for producing such shifts of perspective. One such is evident in *The Stepford Wives* (**1972**) by Ira LEVIN, filmed as *The* STEPFORD WIVES (1975): sexist masculine attitudes are satirized in a thriller centring on the attractions of passive, substitute robot wives. Indeed, the satirical creation of imaginary societies in which the horrors of our own are writ large is especially common in feminist sf (◊ FEMINISM), as in Margaret ATWOOD's *The Handmaid's Tale* (**1985**).

ROBOTS are often used in sf satire for a different reason: for their innocence. Because robots are, in theory, not programmed with prejudices, and are given simple ethical systems, they may have a childlike purity that cuts through rationalizations and sophistications. In Philip K. DICK's *Now Wait for Last Year* (**1966**), for example, the hero's moral quandary is amusingly but touchingly resolved by advice from a robot taxi-cab. CHILDREN IN SF are occasionally used in a similar manner. Both these are simply special cases of the "innocent-observer" strategy first popularized by Voltaire in *Candide* (**1759**), in which a naïve man, with few expectations of life and a likable character, is consistently abused and exploited in his travels. Modern sf examples include *The Sirens of Titan* (**1959**) by Kurt VONNEGUT Jr, in which the hero is a millionaire brainwashed into innocence on Mars, and Robert SHECKLEY's *Journey Beyond Tomorrow* (**1962**; vt *The Journey of Joenes* 1978 UK), where the traveller is a naïve islander who has a terrible time in a future USA. Sheckley was for a time among the finest genre-sf satirists, and a great deal of his work depends on the introduction of a similar innocent viewpoint.

Satire is not only a matter of imaginary societies and shifts in perspective; it has a great deal to do with narrative tone, which cannot generally afford to be too hectoring or sarcastic, or the reader simply feels bludgeoned. An air of mild surprise is often considered appropriate, though commonly the narrator's voice is ironic or sardonic, a good example of the latter being found in a collection which contains several satirical sf fables, *Sardonic Tales* (coll trans **1927**), assembled from *Contes Cruels* (coll **1883**) by VILLIERS DE L'ISLE ADAM, after whose collection this whole mode of writing is often known as "contes cruels" or "cruel tales". Further examples of this chilling subgenre can be found in the work of John COLLIER, Roald DAHL and sometimes Howard FAST. In genre sf it characterizes the excellent work of John T. SLADEK, who shifts skilfully between the mock-innocent and the ironic in his stories, nearly all of which are satire.

The standard of satire within genre sf was not very high before the 1950s, though numerous pulp writers from Stanton A. COBLENTZ to L. Sprague DE CAMP wrote occasionally in this vein. One of the earliest sf writers to excel here was, especially in his short stories, Henry KUTTNER (whose work, even when signed Kuttner, was often written collaboratively with C.L. MOORE). Short, satirical sf stories found a natural home in the early 1950s when the magazine GALAXY SCIENCE FICTION opened up a new market. The best of the *Gal* satirists were probably Damon KNIGHT, C.M. KORNBLUTH, Frederik POHL, Sheckley and William TENN. As satirical collaborators, Pohl and Kornbluth specialized in dystopian stories which extrapolated displeasing aspects of present-day life into the future: the world of advertising was pilloried in both *The Space Merchants* (**1953**) and Pohl's much later solo effort, *The Merchants War* (**1984**), and of organized sport in *Gladiator-at-Law* (**1955**). It was the turn of insurance companies in *Preferred Risk* (**1955**) by Pohl and Lester DEL REY writing together as Edson MCCANN. Another sharp anti-advertising book is *The Big Ball of Wax* (**1954**) by Shepherd MEAD; and much of the amusing but occasionally heavy-handed satire of Ron GOULART is directed against the ad-man's mentality, and the MEDIA LANDSCAPE generally.

In the 1960s and 1970s the magazine NEW WORLDS published many writers whose satirical skills tended more towards a rather dry irony than to overt anger or even jovial sarcasm. Notable among these were Brian W. ALDISS, Thomas M. DISCH and the editor himself, Michael MOORCOCK, whose most directly satirical sequence is **Dancers at the End of Time**, beginning with *An Alien Heat* (**1972**). US satire, too, became less broad than before. The amusing but obvious satire of Fritz LEIBER's *The Silver Eggheads* (**1961**) and *A Specter is Haunting Texas* (**1969**) gave ground to the work of writers like Barry N. MALZBERG and James TIPTREE Jr, who (in completely different ways) also preferred a lower-key irony (through which in both cases a ferocious bitterness is visible) and in whose works the satirical was only one of several elements. Pure satires were becoming comparatively rare in sf by the 1970s, although Peter DICKINSON's *The Green Gene* (**1973**) and Richard COWPER's *Clone* (**1972**) are examples; the latter is another story in the *Candide* pattern. Some important satirical work issued from the Communist bloc, notably that of Stanisław LEM in, especially, *Cyberiada* (coll **1965**; trans as *The Cyberiad* **1974** US) and "Kongres Futurologiczny" (**1971**; trans as *The Futurological Congress* **1974** US), where the savagery of the wit is Swift-like.

The sf CINEMA has flirted with satire quite often. The best-known examples are probably PLANET OF THE APES (1968), SLEEPER (1973) and DR STRANGELOVE: OR HOW I STOPPED WORRYING AND LEARNED TO LOVE THE BOMB (1963); others are *The* PRESIDENT'S ANALYST (1967), WESTWORLD (1973), *The* STUFF (1985), TERRORVISION (1986), EARTH GIRLS ARE EASY (1988) and MEET THE APPLEGATES (1990). DAWN OF THE DEAD (1977; vt *Zombie*) is unusual in marrying satire to HORROR, especially in its central image of zombies shambling around a shopping mall. STRANGE INVADERS (1983) manages to combine an exciting alien-invasion story with considerable satire on the USA of the 1950s (a cultural era

into whose behaviour patterns the aliens have been frozen) and of the 1980s (when they attempt to act).

Parody is a form of satire, and there has not been a great deal in sf. The best parodies of sf writers and their CLICHÉS are probably those by John Sladek in *The Steam-Driven Boy* (coll **1973**); also fairly successful are those in David LANGFORD's *The Dragonhiker's Guide to Battlefield Covenant at Dune's Edge: Odyssey Two* (coll **1988**). Langford's cowritten *Earthdoom!* (**1987**) parodies bestselling DISASTER novels. A parody with a more serious point is Norman SPINRAD's *The Iron Dream* (**1972**), which masquerades as a SWORD-AND-SORCERY novel written by Adolf Hitler. Harry HARRISON's *Bill, the Galactic Hero* (**1965**) and *Star Smashers of the Galaxy Rangers* (**1973**) parody Robert A. HEINLEIN and E.E. "Doc" SMITH respectively. H.G. WELLS was a favourite subject for parodists from early on, as in *The War of the Wenuses* (**1898**) by E.V. LUCAS and C.L. Graves (1856-1944) and Max Beerbohm's "Perkins and Mankind" (1912). *Mention my Name in Atlantis* (**1972**) by John JAKES is a parody of Robert E. HOWARD, not as sharp as Spinrad's, and its hero not as funny as Terry PRATCHETT's "Cohen the Barbarian", who pops up occasionally in the **Discworld** series. Bob SHAW's *Who Goes There?* (**1977**) parodies many themes of SPACE OPERA in general with considerable inventiveness, as does the most successful sf-parody film, DARK STAR (1974). Sf writers have produced a number of parodies of PSEUDO-SCIENCE (*which see for listing*). The best known sf parodist of the 1980s was Douglas ADAMS, with his **Hitch Hiker's Guide to the Galaxy** series. There is also, of course, much pastiche – Philip José FARMER has written a good deal – but pastiche and parody are not the same thing, for the pastiche may be homage whereas parody normally implies deflation (although the two can co-exist, as in *Dark Star*).

In general satire during the 1970s-80s was perhaps less visible in genre sf than in borderline-sf FABULATIONS (including some by John Calvin BATCHELOR, William BURROUGHS, Angela CARTER, Robert COOVER, Carol EMSHWILLER, Alasdair GRAY, Jerzy KOSINSKI, Thomas PYNCHON and Josephine SAXTON – the list could be considerably extended). While genre sf continues to take the form of pure satire comparatively rarely, satirical elements are common in seemingly nonsatirical genre novels, especially perhaps in the work of writers for whom irony is an important part of their vision, such as Iain BANKS, Terry BISSON, George Alec EFFINGER, M. John HARRISON, John KESSEL, James MORROW, Rudy RUCKER and Howard WALDROP. Not that irony and satire can be read as isomorphic: Gene WOLFE and John CROWLEY, for example, are ironists almost always, satirists almost never. [PN]

See also: HUMOUR; SOCIOLOGY; TABOOS.

SATTERFIELD, CHARLES Pseudonym used on 4 magazine stories by Frederik POHL, 1954-9, the first being a collaboration with Lester DEL REY. [JC]

SATURN ◊ OUTER PLANETS.

SATURN US DIGEST-size magazine. 5 issues Mar 1957-

Mar 1958, published by Robert C. Sproul as Candar Publishing Company; ed Sproul with editorial consultant Donald A. WOLLHEIM. A Jules VERNE story appeared in #1, but nothing else of note. #1 was subtitled "The Magazine of Science Fiction", #2 "Magazine of Fantasy and Science Fiction" and the remainder "Science Fiction and Fantasy". Despite his mere "consultant" title, Wollheim chose the contents. [FHP/PN]

SATURN AWARD ◊ AWARDS.

SATURN 3 Film (1980). Transcontinental. Prod and dir Stanley Donen, starring Farrah Fawcett, Kirk Douglas, Harvey Keitel. Screenplay Martin AMIS, from a story by John Barry. 87 mins. Colour.

With a good director like Donen and a screenplay by Martin AMIS, it is difficult to see how so obscene and silly an exploitation movie could come to be. Douglas and Fawcett play the couple alternating romping in bed with working on a hydroponics project, designed to feed millions, situated for no logical reason on Titan, a moon of Saturn. Unbalanced Benson (Keitel) arrives disguised as a legitimate researcher and builds an equally unstable ROBOT which spends most of the rest of the film tearing apart living creatures (including people) and groping lasciviously at Fawcett. This is the second film after DEMON SEED (1977) to feature an amorous, unbalanced AI, a notion more GOTHIC than scientific. The novelization was *Saturn 3* ∗ (**1980**) by Steve GALLAGHER. [PN]

SAUNDERS, CALEB [s] ◊ Robert A. HEINLEIN.

SAUNDERS, JAKE (1947-) US writer, one of the less active members of a Texas grouping which includes Howard WALDROP, his collaborator on *The Texas-Israeli War: 1999* (**1974**). [JC]

SAVA, GEORGE ◊ George BORODIN.

SAVAGE, BLAKE ◊ John BLAINE.

SAVAGE, RICHARD Pseudonym of UK writer Ivan Roe (1917-) for his thrillers – including *The Horrible Hat* (**1949**), in which a psychoanalyst/ detective explains strange manifestations – and his sf novel, *When the Moon Died* (**1955**), whose telling involves an exceedingly complicated frame: far-future aliens visit a dead Earth to listen to a tape whose long-dead narrator has discovered how, long before, a nuclear HOLOCAUST was prevented by scientists who destroyed the Moon but subsequently established a totalitarian DYSTOPIA. The aliens never do work out why Earth is now bereft of life. Under his own name Roe wrote some non-genre novels, like *The Salamander Touch* (**1952**), in which an atomic scientist disappears with difficult consequences. [JC/PN]

SAVARIN, JULIAN JAY (? -) Dominican-born West Indian writer and musician, in the UK since his teens. His **Lemmus** trilogy – *Lemmus One: Waiters on the Dance* (**1972**), *Lemmus Two: Beyond the Outer Mirr* (**1976**) and *Lemmus Three: Archives of Haven* (coll of linked stories **1977**) – is an expansive SPACE OPERA in which GOD (the Galactic Organization and Dominions) experimentally settles Terra with people who will evolve in isolation (◊ ADAM AND EVE). Explanations are

offered for the Judeo-Christian tradition, the fall of ATLANTIS, etc. *Arena* (**1979**) involves folk from various times in a mighty struggle. JJS afterwards turned to thrillers. [JC]

SAVCHENKO, VLADIMIR (IVANOVICH) (1933-) Russian writer who began as an author of short stories, publishing *Tchironyie Zviozdy* ["Dark Stars"] (coll **1960**) and contributing to anthologies. His most famous novel, *Otkrytiie Sebia* (**1967**; trans Antonina W. Bouis as *Self-Discovery* **1979** US), depicts in unclichéd terms the scientific development of a SUPERMAN. Later stories, comparable with the metaphysical parables of Stanisław LEM and Philip K. DICK, are to be found in *Ispytaniie Istinoi* ["Truth Test"] (coll [date unconfirmed]) and *Algoritm Uspekha* ["Success Algorithm"] (coll **1983**). A play, *Novoiie Oruzhiie* ["New Weapons"] (**1983**), portrays modern physicists obsessed by moral problems after discovering a process which neutralizes all nuclear weapons on Earth. A rare attempt, in the Soviet sf of the 1980s, to create a future communist UTOPIA is the less successful *Za Perevalom* ["After the Pass"] (**1984**). [VG]

SAVILE, FRANK (MACKENZIE) (? -?) UK writer who wrote also as Knarf Elivas (his own names reversed). *Beyond the Great South Wall* (**1899**) combines the search for a Mayan LOST WORLD in the Antarctic with the actual discovery of the extinct Native Americans' polar deity, a brontosaurus with hypnotic eyes. All ends well with the death of the creature and some human marriages. [JC]

SAVOY BOOKS ◊ David BRITTON; Michael BUTTERWORTH.

SAWTELLE, WILLIAM CARTER [s] ◊ Rog PHILLIPS.

SAWYER, ROBERT J(AMES) (1960-) Canadian writer who began publishing sf with "If I'm Here, Imagine Where They Sent my Luggage" for *The Village Voice* in 1981, and was moderately active as a short-story writer in the 1980s. His first novel, *Golden Fleece* (**1988** *AMZ*; exp **1990** US), set on a colony ship named *Argo*, run by an AI named JASON, perhaps slightly overcopiously engages to meld Greek myth and HARD SF in the story of a murder and its solution by a human protagonist so psychologically recessed that the AI cannot read his intentions. [JC]

See also: CANADA.

SAXON, PETER Initially the personal pseudonym of UK writer W. Howard BAKER, under which he wrote many titles for Amalgamated Press, mainly stories in the **Sexton Blake** series before its cancellation in 1963. He then took the name to Mayflower Books, where the series continued, written by him and others under what was now a house name. The claims of Scottish writer Wilfred MCNEILLY to have written most of the PS titles are unjustified (*see entries on* BAKER *and* MCNEILLY *for their PS work*). Other writers who used the name included Rex Dolpin, Stephen FRANCES, Ross Richards and Martin THOMAS. Titles of sf interest not by Baker or McNeilly include *Slave Brain* (**1967**), *Black Honey* (**1968**) and *Corruption* (**1968**), whose authors have not been identified, and some titles in the **Guardians** psychic-investigators sequence: *Through the Dark Curtain* (**1968** US) by Richards, *The Curse of Rathlaw* (**1968**) by Martin and *The Vampires of Finistère* (**1970**) by Dolpin. The most memorable PS title (written by Baker with Frances) may be *The Disoriented Man* (**1966**; vt *Scream and Scream Again* 1967 US), filmed as SCREAM AND SCREAM AGAIN (1969), the latter being something of a cult classic.   [JC]

SAXON, RICHARD ◊ J.L. MORRISSEY.

SAXTON, JOSEPHINE (MARY HOWARD) (1935-   ) UK writer who began publishing sf with "The Wall" for *Science Fantasy* in 1965, and whose first 3 novels – *The Hieros Gamos of Sam and An Smith* (**1969** US), *Vector for Seven: The Weltanschaung* [*sic*] *of Mrs Amelia Mortimer and Friends* (**1970** US) and *Group Feast* (**1971** US) – established her very rapidly as an inventive creator of sf FABULATIONS. Each of these books presents narratives whose outcomes are more readable as allegories of their protagonists' moral fates than of any physical journey, though the image of what might be called the bollixed quest is central to her work. These journeys are described – often in some detail, as in *Vector for Seven* – in a register of perilous ambivalence, half INNER SPACE, half mutable and frustrating external world. When JS returned to publishing novels in the 1980s, titles like *The Travails of Jane Saint* (**1980**; exp as coll vt *The Travails of Jane Saint and Other Stories* 1986) and *Jane Saint and the Backlash: The Further Travails of Jane Saint and the Consciousness Machine* (coll **1989**) clearly demonstrated the fundamental continuity of her vision. *Queen of the States* (**1986**) – a clever title in which "States" can be interpreted as referring to the USA or to various sorts of mental breakdown – comes very close to a savage reductionism: the sf/fantasy escapades of the female protagonist default constantly to delusion, for she is imprisoned in a mental institution. Perhaps even more clearly than before, these later books are governed by a FEMINIST sense of the constraints binding women to mundane, male-ordained reality – a sense that goes far to explain the wildness of JS's protagonists and the lungeing movements of her prose. Her non-**Jane Saint** short stories, which tend to a slantwise but pointed lightness of touch, have been assembled in *The Power of Time* (coll **1985**) and *Little Tours of Hell: Tall Tales of Food and Holidays* (coll **1986**).   [JC]

See also: ALTERNATE WORLDS; FANTASTIC VOYAGES; PERCEPTION.

SAXTON, MARK (1914-1988) US writer who, as an editor at Farrar & Rinehart, helped Austin Tappan WRIGHT's daughter, Sylvia Wright, edit the massive manuscript of *Islandia*, which his firm published in 1942. MS himself produced some detective fiction, but his sf was confined to the **Islandia** world, for which he wrote 3 novels in continuation of Wright's original: *The Islar: A Narrative of Lang III* (**1969**), narrated by the grandson of Wright's John Lang, *The Two Kingdoms: A Novel of Islandia* (**1979**) and *Havoc in Islandia* (**1982**). The UTOPIAN glow of the original did

not survive unaltered, but MS's work was both competent and devoted.   [JC]

SAYLES, JOHN (1950-   ) US writer and film-maker. JS made his reputation as a MAINSTREAM WRITER with the novels *Pride of the Bimbos* (**1975**) and *Union Dues* (**1977**) and his collection *The Anarchist's Convention* (coll **1979**). He began writing scripts for exploitation movies in the late 1970s, and enjoyed a burst of creativity in association with Roger CORMAN, Joe DANTE, Lewis Teague and Steven SPIELBERG. His sf and fantasy screenplays, always lively and self-aware, are PIRANHA (1978), BATTLE BEYOND THE STARS (1980), *The Howling* (1980), ALLIGATOR (1980), *The Clan of the Cave Bear* (1985) and *Wild Thing* (1989). «Night Skies», a horror script about an isolated farm besieged by alien visitors, was commissioned by Spielberg but then abandoned in favour of the similar but more benevolent CLOSE ENCOUNTERS OF THE THIRD KIND (1977). JS made his directorial début with *Return of the Secaucus 7* (1980), and has made a number of well received non-genre films since, including *Lianna* (1981) and *Baby, It's You* (1983). His sole sf film as director is *The* BROTHER FROM ANOTHER PLANET (1984), in which the story of a Black alien who crashlands in Harlem is used to tackle JS's usual concerns.   [KN]

See also: CINEMA.

SCANDINAVIA This entry refers primarily to Sweden and Norway; there are separate entries for DENMARK and FINLAND. Scandinavia has always been somewhat isolated from the main roads of European cultural development, and never more so than during the 18th century, when the Age of Enlightenment swept across the rest of Europe. Outside the mainly French-speaking court, Scandinavia was poor and starving, mainly agricultural, and crushed by repeated, ruinous wars. It is perhaps not surprising that excursions into fantastic literature were few: Scandinavia had nothing to compare with the French **Voyages imaginaires**, a 36-vol series published from 1787 and running from LUCIAN to CYRANO DE BERGERAC to Jonathan SWIFT. The first noted Scandinavian example of fantastic literature was Danish (◊ DENMARK): *Nicolai Klimii iter subterraneum* (**1741** in Latin; exp 1745; trans anon as *A Journey to the World Under-Ground. By Nicolas Klimius* 1742 UK; vt *A Journey to the World Underground* 1974 US) by Ludwig HOLBERG. This witty journey into a HOLLOW EARTH, somewhat reminiscent of the work of Swift, is regarded as a classic and has never been out of print. In Sweden, Olof von Dalin (1708-1763) published in his magazine *Then Swänska Argus* an amusing political story about extraterrestrial visitors to Earth, "Saga om Erik hin Götske" ["Tale of Erik of the Goths"] (1734), and in Norway there was the early TIME-TRAVEL play *Anno 7603* (**1781**) by John Hermann Wessel (1742-1785). But these were isolated examples. Fantastic literature was popular, but most of it was what we would today call HEROIC FANTASY, with sword-toting heroes, maidens in distress, sentient dragons, etc.

The first Scandinavian novel that can be considered

as modern sf, with everything that description implies, appeared as late as 1878: *Oxygen och Aromasia* ["Oxygen and Aromasia"] **(1878)** by the Swedish journalist Claës Lundin (1825-1908). Unfortunately, it bore unmistakeable signs that Lundin had read the German book *Bilder aus der Zukunft* ["Images of the Future"] (coll **1878**) by Kurd LASSWITZ, published in Breslau earlier that same year. Lundin's version is a tale set a few hundred years hence in a failed UTOPIA; it is a funny SATIRE bursting with then-new sf ideas – time travel, tv, moving sidewalks, ALIENS, airships and SPACESHIPS, and even an interesting TIME PARADOX. It is still eminently readable; a new edition was published as recently as 1974.

Again, however, this was an isolated example. Lundin wrote no more sf – he is today mostly remembered as the mentor of August Strindberg (1849-1912) – and no new talents appeared to take his place. Although the first book ever written about sf, Camille FLAMMARION's *Les mondes imaginaires et les mondes réels* (**1864**; trans as *Real and Imaginary Worlds* **1865** US), was translated into Swedish as early as 1867 and Jules VERNE's novels were translated into the Scandinavian languages as soon as they appeared in France, few indigenous authors tried their hands. Of the 286 straightforward sf novels published 1870-1900 in Sweden, the leading literary market in Scandinavia, the overwhelming majority were translations of the popular foreign sf authors of the time: Verne, Flammarion, Lasswitz, Mór JÓKAI, André LAURIE and H.G. WELLS. There was an early attempt at a Swedish sf magazine, *Stella* – 4 irregular issues Apr 1886-Aug 1888, with short stories by these foreign authors and a scattering of anonymous material that may have been by local hands – but it was much before its time and vanished without trace.

Very little happened in Scandinavia until the explosive arrival on the Swedish literary scene of Otto Witt (1875-1923). Originally a mining engineer, he worked in Germany until 1912, then returned to Sweden firmly resolved to win fame and fortune. (Interestingly, he had studied at the Technicum in Bingen, Germany, at the same time as Hugo GERNSBACK, later to launch the first US SF MAGAZINE, AMAZING STORIES, and Karl Hans Strobl, later to launch the first sf/fantasy magazine in AUSTRIA, *Der Orchideengarten*. There is no evidence that they met.) To this end Witt wrote dozens of sf novels, all bursting with new and usually harebrained ideas which nobody else took seriously. He can be thought of as a Swedish Hugo Gernsback but with ten times the ego. His many novels were merely vehicles for his crackpot theories; *Hur månen orövrades* ["How the Moon was Conquered"] **(1915)** treated the creation of the MOON, *Guldfursten* ["The Prince of Gold"] **(1916)** proposed a sure-fire way of making gold, and so on. But his great accomplishment was the creation of Sweden's first modern sf magazine, *Hugin*, which ran for 85 issues 1916-20, preceded by a few irregular issues published to test the market. According to its cover, *Hugin*

offered "scientific novels, scientific causeries, inventive sketches, adventure stories and scientific fairy-tales". Inspiration probably came from German and French sf magazines, like the German *Der* LUFTPIRAT UND SEIN LENKBARES LUFTSCHIFF series, but the style was entirely Witt's own. *Hugin* was unique among sf magazines: written, edited and published by Witt, advocating in fictionalized form every mad idea he could think of – as if John W. CAMPBELL had extended some of his more notorious editorials into short stories that filled every issue of *ASF*. Witt even wrote the advertisements as sf shorts, complete with kind words about the sponsor's products!

In Norway Øvre Richter-Frich (1872-1945) issued more than 20 popular novels from 1911 detailing the adventures of the superscientist **Jonas Fjeld**.

Until now, inspiration for Scandinavian sf had come mostly from Germany and France. After WWI, however, UK authors – and to some extent Italian and Russian futurists – became more noticeable. Wells, Vladimir MAYAKOVSKY, Mikhail BULGAKOV and Antonio Sant'Elia (1888-1916) represented a sort of European New Wave in the field. A very influential Swedish novel, *Kallocain* (**1940**; trans Gustav Lannestock **1966** US) by Karin BOYE drew heavily on *My* (written 1920; trans as *We* **1924** US) by Yevgeny ZAMIATIN and Soviet "machinism" theories. Then US influence grew stronger as the miseries of WWII diverted the attentions of European sf writers and readers to more important matters, such as survival. Most of Scandinavia felt the full impact of the war on its own territory, especially Finland, which had to fight Germany and the USSR both singly and simultaneously. Sweden, however, was largely outside WWII, and here the world's first weekly sf magazine, *Jules Verne-Magasinet* ["The Jules Verne Magazine"] started in 1940, offering mostly translated US PULP-MAGAZINE stories. It lasted 332 issues before dying in 1948; later it was resurrected as a bimonthly which is still being published. After WWII came other magazines: the Norwegian *Tempo-Magazinet*, the Swedish *Häpna!* and *Galaxy*, and the Finnish *Aikamme*. During the first boom in Scandinavian sf, in the mid-1950s, there were 4 sf magazines and over a dozen book series being published. Interest was fuelled by Harry MARTINSON's *Aniara* (1953 *Cikada*; exp **1956**; trans as *Aniara: A Review of Man in Time and Space* **1963** UK), a book-length poem about the starship *Aniara* which was later made into an opera (◊ MUSIC); Martinson received the 1974 Nobel Prize for Literature.

Unlike the case in the English-speaking countries, fantastic literature in Scandinavia – and, indeed, in mainland Europe as a whole – was never trapped in the sf ghetto; one is tempted to suggest that this was because Europe succeeded in exporting Hugo Gernsback, so that he created the sf ghetto elsewhere. Although there *is* in fact an unimportant fringe sf ghetto in Scandinavia – centring on cheap paperback translations from English and German that are sold at newsstands but never in bookstores – in general Scandinavian sf is published in trade editions, sold in book stores and treated by reviewers with the same respect as any other modern literature. This is because fantastic literature has always been part of the Scandinavian literary mainstream, not generally being regarded as generic; the line between sf and fantasy is very hazy, and most Scandinavian authors have at one time or another ventured into the field. The enormous popularity in Scandinavia today of Dutch and Latin American MAGIC REALISM is probably also a consequence of this historical attitude. By way of example, we can note that, when Frederik POHL's and C.M. KORNBLUTH's *The Space Merchants* (**1953**) first appeared in Sweden in 1962, it did so in a series of books of social criticism published by FIB, a company owned by the Labour Government.

In short, Scandinavia is much like the rest of continental Europe in having no specialized sf industry but instead a lively world of fantastic literature in the old European tradition, drawing its succour from E.T.A. HOFFMANN, Adelbert von Chamisso (1781-1838), the German *Sturm und Drang*, the French 'pataphysics ($\lozenge$ Alfred JARRY; IMAGINARY SCIENCE) and Italian and Russian Futurism, rather than from the world of English-language sf. Where GENRE SF exists, it is confined to fans and FANDOM. Much of this sort of sf has traditionally been published by specialist houses, of which Delta, in Sweden, was, until it folded in 1991, the largest, with a hardcover book series containing more than 300 volumes. Among Scandinavian authors to be published by the specialist houses are Börje Crona (1932-   ), Carl Johan Holzhausen (1900-   ), Dénis Lindbohm (1927-   ), Bertil Mårtenson (1945-   ) and Sven Christer Swahn (1933-   ) in Sweden, Erkki Ahonen in FINLAND, Øyvind Myrhe (1945-   ) in Norway and Niels E. Nielsen (1924-   ) in Denmark. Sweden's Sture Lönnerstrand (1919-   ) played a major role in popularizing sf, co-editing *Häpna!* and writing many articles and fictions, such as the juvenile *Rymdhunden* ["The Space Dog"] (**1954**). All these authors are very popular and eminently readable. However, Lindbohm, for many years a leading light in Swedish fandom, is now writing mainly about mysticism and reincarnation, while Mårtenson, also very popular in Sweden, now writes only FANTASY.

Other sf authors have left genre sf or were never part of it, their books being usually published by mainstream houses and without the "sf" label; they include Jon Bing (1944-   ) and Tor Åge Bringsvaerd (1939-   ) in Norway, Sam J. LUNDWALL in Sweden and Kullervo Kukkasjärvi (1938-   ) in FINLAND. Bringsvaerd, in particular, is highly respected in the Scandinavian literary world as a writer of extraordinary merits, while his countryman Knut Faldbakken (1941-   ) achieved international bestsellerdom with his utopian novels *Aftenlandet* ["The Evening Land"] (**1972**) and *Sweetwater* ["Sweetwater"] (**1974**). Lundwall has also written many

influential CRITICAL AND HISTORICAL WORKS ABOUT SF, which have to date (1992) been published in 32 languages. John-Henri Holmberg (1949-   ), another prominent Scandinavian critic, is less known outside his native Sweden. Slightly external to the sf field are a number of MAINSTREAM WRITERS who occasionally write sf, and then almost inevitably to bestselling effect. The well known Swedish author P.C. JERSILD has written several enormously successful sf novels, including *En levande själ* (**1980**; trans Rika Lesser as *A Living Soul* **1988** UK), about a disembodied brain sloshing about in a glass box, *Efter floden* (**1982**; trans Lone Tygesen Blecher and George Blecher as *After the Flood* **1986** UK), a post-nuclear-HOLOCAUST story, and *Geniernas återkomst* ["The Return of the Geniuses"] (**1987**), describing mankind's history from the very beginnings to the distant future. The Swedish journalist George Johansson (1946-   ) has written a very successful series of young-adult novels set against an increasingly enormous galactic backdrop, starting with *Uppbrott från Jorden* ["Flight from Earth"] (**1979**). Among the biggest and most surprising bestsellers in Scandinavia during the 1980s were several sf novels by Peter Nilson (1937-   ), starting with *Arken* ["The Ark"] (**1982**) and going through to his most recent, *Avgrundsbok* ["The Book of the Abyss"] (**1987**), about an improbable Queen of Sheba travelling in space and time. Other authors of note in this context include Anders BODELSEN in Denmark, Axel JENSEN in Norway and Per WAHLÖÖ in Sweden.

Sf in Scandinavia has been hit by the same problems as in the rest of continental Europe. Book sales are very much down in all the Scandinavian countries, and there are currently (1992) no specialist publishing houses in operation. There is only one sf magazine in Sweden – *Jules Verne-Magasinet* – although the Finnish SEMIPROZINE *Aikakone* ["Time Machine"] is thriving ($\lozenge$ FINLAND). All told, just over 100 sf books are published each year in Scandinavia, of which about two-thirds are translations from other European languages and English. About half the total are published in Sweden which, due to its size, remains Scandinavia's leading sf nation.

The first Scandinavian sf CONVENTION was held in Lund, Sweden, in 1956. Since then conventions have been held in all the Scandinavian countries, although the first Finnish convention did not come until 1982.   [SJL/J-HH]

SCANNERS Film (1980). Filmplan International/ Canadian Film Development Corp. Written/dir David CRONENBERG, starring Stephen Lack, Jennifer O'Neal, Patrick McGoohan, Lawrence Dane, Michael Ironside. 103 mins. Colour.

This superior PSI-POWERS movie easily outstrips CARRIE (1976) and *The* FURY (1978). Pregnant women (we learn some way into the film) have been given an experimental drug, ephemerol, ostensibly a tranquillizer but actually designed to produce paranormal offspring – scanners – who can exercise total control over the brains and nervous systems of others. The two oldest telepaths (brothers, it turns out) are corrupted – in different ways – by their power, though one (Lack) fights for human society, the other (Ironside) for the superhumans. The film is choreographed in the most exemplary manner, from the celebrated exploding-head sequence at the beginning to the final telepathic duel between the brothers and its enigmatic outcome. It is also advanced in sf terms, working sophisticated variations on the MUTANT theme, streets ahead of the usual crudities of psi-power movies. Cronenberg's restless marriage of highbrow metaphor and lowbrow exploitation seldom works better than here, despite sometimes indifferent performances, especially Lack's. The novelization is *Scanners* * (**1981**) by Leon Whiteson. [PN]

See also: PSEUDO-SCIENCE.

SCARFF, WILLIAM [s] ◊ Algis BUDRYS.

SCHACHNER, NAT(HANIEL) (1895-1955) US chemist, lawyer and writer, known mainly for biographies of US historical figures. He began publishing sf with "The Tower of Evil" with Arthur Leo ZAGAT for *Wonder Stories Quarterly* in 1930. The collaboration with Zagat lasted over a year, all NS's first 11 stories being done with him, including a novel, "Exiles of the Moon" for *Wonder Stories* in 1931. After they ceased collaborating, NS continued to write very prolifically for the PULP MAGAZINES, under his own name and as Chan Corbett and Walter Glamis. A novel, "Emissaries of Space" (1932), appeared in *Wonder Stories Quarterly*; the **Revolt of the Scientists** sequence appeared in *Wonder Stories* in 1933; and the **Past Present and Future** series appeared in *ASF* 1937-9. He published only 1 sf novel in book form, *Space Lawyer* (1941 *ASF*; fixup **1953**), a humorous set of legal adventures in space. His style was rough, but he was a sharp and knowledgeable writer; his inattention to the field after about 1940 is regretted. [JC]

About the author: "The Science-Fiction of Nat Schachner" by Sam MOSKOWITZ in *Fantasy Commentator* #43 (1992).

See also: ASTOUNDING SCIENCE-FICTION; POLITICS; TIME PARADOXES; WAR.

SCHAFFLER, FEDERICO [r] ◊ LATIN AMERICA.

SCHATTSCHNEIDER, PETER [r] ◊ AUSTRIA.

SCHEER, K(ARL)-H(ERBERT) (1928-1991) German writer, active from 1948. He published prolifically – including much sf – in the circulating-library format in which many pulp adventures appeared in postwar GERMANY; none of this material has been translated. However, translations of his novellas in the weekly DIME-NOVEL SF format of PERRY RHODAN, the enormously successful series he cofounded in 1961 with Walter Ernsting (who writes as Clark DARLTON), with whom K-HS had written collaborative works, are familiar to English-language readers. K-HS was for some time coordinator and chief author of the series. [JC/PN]

SCHEERBART, PAUL [r] ◊ GERMANY.

SCHELWOKAT, GÜNTHER M. [r] ◊ GERMANY.

SCHENCK, HILBERT (1926-) US engineer,

university lecturer and writer who published his first sf story, "Tomorrow's Weather" for *FSF* in 1953, long before he became seriously involved in fiction; much of his nonfiction of the 1950s and 1960s dealt lovingly with the ocean and with oceanological research and exploration technologies. His first two novels, *At the Eye of the Ocean* (**1980**) and *A Rose for Armageddon* (**1982**), both set in the wave-girt Cape Cod region of New England, followed suit; they share a similar plot structure, circling in upon a central instant of space/time at which transcendence may be possible. The protagonist of the first book has an intuitive capacity to understand the inner shape of the ocean, which unveils to him a mystical enlightenment; the love-affair that drives the action of the second comes to fruition at the morphological heart of a timeslip in the centre of an ISLAND in the midst of the waters, leading to a form of liberation from the NEAR-FUTURE slide of the world into chaos. *Chronosequence* (**1988**) similarly presents its protagonist with a mystery from previous centuries whose solution involves the ocean, geography, time-slippage, and the potential redemption of the world. Though the range of HS's concerns is clearly narrow, there is nothing forced or lame in his presentation of these stories; their intensities are fluent, grounded and scientifically competent. The title story of *Steam Bird* (coll **1988**), a somewhat heavy-handed comic tale, recounts the pioneering flight of an enormously slow steam-driven nuclear bomber. Other stories are assembled in *Wave Rider* (coll **1980**); the best are set along the coasts of New England. But the world for which HS speaks is central; his work is never regional in its final effect. [JC]

See also: ECOLOGY; END OF THE WORLD; GOTHIC SF; PASTORAL; SCIENTISTS; SOCIOLOGY; TIME PARADOXES; TIMESCAPE BOOKS; TRANSPORTATION; UNDER THE SEA.

SCHIZOPHRENIA ◊ PARANOIA.

SCHLOBIN, ROGER C(LARK) (1944-) US academic and bibliographer, with the Department of English at Purdue University, Indiana. Though RCS has contributed bibliographically to the sf/fantasy field in general, it is clear that he focuses by choice on fantasy. His first book of genre interest, *A Research Guide to Science Fiction Studies: An Annotated Checklist of Primary and Secondary Sources for Fantasy and Science Fiction* (**1977**) with L.W. CURREY and Marshall B. TYMN, attempted, like many published by US academics in the 1970s, to perform the essential task of making the field accessible to scholars; and did so very well. A revised edition has been needed for many years. Also with TYMN (*whom see for further details*) RCS participated in the first 2 vols of the **Year's Scholarship in Science Fiction and Fantasy** series. Solo, he compiled *The Literature of Fantasy: A Comprehensive Annotated Bibliography of Modern Fantasy* (**1979**), which provides a listing of adult fantasy up to 1979. Other bibliographical work includes *Andre Norton: A Primary and Secondary Bibliography* (**1980** chap), *Urania's Daughters: A Checklist of Women Science Fiction Writers, 1692-1982* (**1983** chap) and the rudimentary *A Glen Cook*

Bibliography (**1983** chap) with Glen COOK. *The Aesthetics of Fantasy Literature and Art* (anth **1982**) is a useful gathering of reprint essays, several aspiring to define the genre. [JC]

See also: CRITICAL AND HISTORICAL WORKS ABOUT SF; SF IN THE CLASSROOM.

SCHLOCK Film (1973). Gazotski Films. Written/dir John Landis, starring Landis, Saul Kahn, Joseph Piantadosi, Eliza Garrett. 77 mins. Colour.

This was the feature début of 22-year-old Landis, who went on to bigger things with *The Blues Brothers* (1980) and *An American Werewolf in London* (1981), among others. Low-budget, made in two weeks, it is a genuinely funny and affectionate (though deeply undergraduate) parody of MONSTER MOVIES in general, and TROG (1970) and the APES-AND-CAVEMEN subgenre in particular. Landis plays the caveman Schlockthropus (in a costume designed by Rick Baker, whose effects début this was) who gets to terrify the populace, play boogie on the piano, and form an erotic liaison with a blind girl who rejects him horrifiedly when she regains her sight because she had thought he was a dog. [PN]

SCHMIDT, ARNO (OTTO) (1914-1979) German writer noted for his linguistic innovation and the swift humour of his experimental fictions, which project an air of joyfully cerebral quarrelsomeness. The marked FABULATION of sf tropes in his work is noticeable in novels like *Leviathan* (**1949**), a metaphysical train journey into death, *KAFF, auch MARE CRISTUM* ["KAFF, also MARE CRISTUM"] (**1960**), which is set on the Moon, and *Schwarze Spiegel* ["Black Mirrors"] (**1963**) – the last volume of **Nobodaddys Kinder** ["Nobodaddy's Children"] (1951-63) – which presents the thoughts of the last man on Earth. In *Die Gelehrtenrepublik* (**1957**; trans Michael Horovitz as *The Egghead Republic: A Short Novel from the Horse Latitudes* **1979** UK), which is genuine sf set in AD2008 after a nuclear HOLOCAUST, an American attempts to report home on the International Republic for Artists and Scientists, or IRAS, which is housed on a mobile island currently resting in the Sargasso Sea. But sex, mutants, language-games and chaos afflict his brief. [JC]

See also: GERMANY.

SCHMIDT, DENNIS (A.) (? -) US writer who has restricted himself to series. The first was the **Zen** or **Kensho** sequence – *Way-Farer* (**1978**), *Kensho* (**1979**), *Satori* (**1981**) and *Wanderer* (**1985**) – featuring a protagonist who combines Zen and martial arts in agreeably complex SPACE-OPERA adventures. The **Twilight of the Gods** sequence – *Twilight of the Gods: The First Name* (**1985**), *#2: Groa's Other Eye* (**1986**) and *#3: Three Trumps Sounding* (**1988**) – is fantasy, and is likewise conceived with well orchestrated complexity. The **Questioner Trilogy** – *Labyrinth* (**1989**), *City of Crystal Shadow* (**1990**) and *Dark Paradise* (**1990**) – returns to intergalactic space, where the operations of a peacekeeping force are featured. DS gives some impression of being an author who might at any point decide to break through into higher regions of

his art. [JC]

SCHMIDT, STANLEY (1944-) US editor, writer and academic, with a PhD in physics (1969), which he taught until 1978. In that year he became editor of *Analog*, a position which in 1992 he retains, occupying his role in the forthright manner established by John W. CAMPBELL Jr, his most famous predecessor, but more quietly. He began publishing his own sf with "A Flash of Darkness" for *ASF* in 1968. His first novel, *Newton and the Quasi-Apple* (1970 *ASF*; exp **1975**), is a HARD-SF exploration in PHYSICS set on a primitive planet where Newton's principles are being independently discovered, raising questions as to what kinds of knowledge are helpful – and when. *The Sins of the Fathers* (**1976**) and its sequel, *Lifeboat Earth* (fixup **1978**), perhaps overcomplicatedly invoke an exploding Galaxy, TIME TRAVEL and more new physics in their presentation of an ALIEN race whose effective social engineering challenges Earth ($\lozenge$ SOCIOLOGY). *Tweedlioop* (**1986**) again submits an alien – here through shipwreck – to human PERCEPTIONS, this time those of a young woman; she falls in love. Throughout his writing career, which has become less active since 1978, SS has written clear-cut tales within which nest solvable problems, and in the telling of which cogently argued hard-sf concepts are given fair play. His editorship of *Analog* has been similarly clear-cut, and he has maintained the journal as the primary outlet for thrusting, extroverted, problem-solving sf tales of a sort that, for many readers, continues to occupy the high road of sf. He has edited several anthologies spun-off from the journal or from UNKNOWN, its stablemate from half a century earlier. [JC]

As editor: *The Analog Anthology #1: Fifty Years of the Best* (anth **1980**) and *#2: Readers' Choice* (anth **1982**); *Analog's Golden Anniversary Anthology* (anth **1981**); *Analog Yearbook II* (anth **1981**); *Analog's Lighter Side* (anth **1982**); *Children of the Future* (anth **1982**); *Analog: Writers' Choice* (anth **1983**) and *Writers' Choice, Vol II* (anth **1984**); *War and Peace: Possible Futures from Analog* (anth **1983**); *Aliens from Analog* (anth **1983**); *From Mind to Mind: Tales of Communication from Analog* (anth **1984**); *Analog's Expanding Universe* (anth **1986**); *6 Decades: The Best of Analog* (anth **1987**); *Unknown* (anth **1988**); *Unknown Worlds: Tales from Beyond* (anth **1988**) with Martin H. GREENBERG.

See also: ASTOUNDING SCIENCE-FICTION; CHILDREN IN SF.

SCHMITZ, JAMES H(ENRY) (1911-1981) US writer born in Germany of US parents; he served with the USAF in WWII. His first story was "Greenface" for *Unknown* in 1943. From 1949, when "Agent of Vega" appeared in *ASF* as the first of 4 stories later assembled as *Agent of Vega* (coll of linked stories **1960**), he regularly produced the kind of tale for which he remains most warmly remembered: SPACE-OPERA adventures, several featuring female HEROES depicted with minimum recourse to their "femininity" – they perform their active tasks, and save the Universe when necessary, in a manner almost completely free of sexual role-playing clichés.

Most of his best work shares a roughly characterized common background, a Galaxy inhabited by humans and aliens with room for all and numerous opportunities for discoveries and reversals that carefully fall short of threatening the stability of that background. Many of his stories, as a result, focus less on moments of CONCEPTUAL BREAKTHROUGH than on the pragmatic operations of teams and bureaux involved in maintaining the state of things against criminals, monsters and unfriendly species; in this they rather resemble the tales of Murray LEINSTER, though they are more vigorous and less inclined to punish adventurousness. PSI POWERS are often found. At the heart of this common Universe are the Federation of the **Hub** or the Overgovernment, composed of human and nonhuman members. The main **Hub** sequence is *A Tale of Two Clocks* (**1962**; vt *Legacy* 1979), *A Nice Day for Screaming and Other Tales of the Hub* (coll **1965**), *The Demon Breed* (**1968**) and *A Pride of Monsters* (coll **1970**). The **Telzey Amberdon** books – *The Universe Against Her* (fixup **1964**), *The Telzey Toy* (coll **1973**) and *The Lion Game* (fixup **1973**) – nestle conceptually within the **Hub**. Amberdon, a brilliant young telepath recruited by the Psychology Service of the Overgovernment as an agent, is perhaps JHS's most typical creation, and the stories in which she performs her activities are only marginally less appealing than his single finest novel, *The Witches of Karres* (1949 *ASF*; exp **1966**), which features three Amberdon-like psi-powered juvenile "witches" and their rescue from slavery by a space captain in whom they induce first apoplexy and second transcendence – for he too finds superpowers within him.

One novel, *The Eternal Frontiers* (**1973**), is set outside this common background; it fails to delight. *The Best of James H. Schmitz* (coll **1991**) ed Mark L. Olson is a good conspectus. It may be that JHS's work is too pleasing to have seemed revolutionary, and indeed – with the exception of his choice of protagonists – it plays very safe with conventions; but for nearly 40 years he succeeded in demonstrating, modestly and competently, that the template of space opera could provide continuing joy. [JC]

About the author: *James H. Schmitz: A Bibliography* (**1973**) by Mark OWINGS, with intro by Janet KAGAN.

See also: CHILDREN IN SF; ECOLOGY; ESP; LIFE ON OTHER WORLDS; SUPERMAN.

SCHNABEL, JOHANN GOTTFRIED [r] ◊ GERMANY.

SCHNEEMAN, CHARLES (1912-1972) US illustrator. CS was active in sf for only a short time, most of his work being for ASTOUNDING SCIENCE-FICTION from 1935. He painted 6 *ASF* covers, the earliest May 1938 and the last Nov 1952, but is best remembered for his interior black-and-white ILLUSTRATION in that magazine; he was its major interior artist until he joined the US Army in 1942. His best work may be the idealized sketches of the heroic Kimball Kinnison for E.E. "Doc" SMITH's *Grey Lensman* (1939-40 *ASF*; **1951**) and his drawings for Jack WILLIAMSON's *The Legion of*

Time (1938 *ASF*; rev **1952**). After WWII he worked mainly for newspapers. [JG/PN]

SCHNEER, CHARLES H. [r] ◊ Ray HARRYHAUSEN.

SCHNEIDER, JOHN G. (?1908-1964) US writer whose borderline-sf novel, *The Golden Kazoo* (**1956**), satirized the Madison Avenue nature of the (NEAR-FUTURE) 1960 presidential election, which he saw as foolishly COMPUTER-dominated. [JC]

SCHOENHERR, JOHN (1935-) US illustrator, regarded by some critics as the finest sf artist of his generation. A New Yorker who studied at the Pratt Institute, he made his sf-ILLUSTRATION début in *AMZ* 1956. His work has appeared primarily in *ASF* (including 75 covers), but he has drawn black-and-white illustrations for other sf magazines, including *Fantastic* and *Infinity*, and has also worked for paperback publishers, most notably ACE BOOKS and Pyramid. The cover and interior illustrations he did for Frank HERBERT's **Dune** stories in ASTOUNDING SCIENCE-FICTION (1963-5) are classics; some of the best are reproduced in *The Illustrated Dune* (**1978**) and *Dune Calendar* (**1978**). JS's style in his colour work is Impressionistic, and he is regarded by his peers as the most "painterly" in their field. Some of his earlier work shows the influence of Richard M. POWERS, one of the few sf artists he admires. He carries his painting techniques over into his black-and-white work by using a dry-brush method on rough paper or scratchboard, with fine details added by pen. His ALIENS are particularly convincing, thanks perhaps to his love for animal illustration (for which he has won numerous awards), and even his inanimate objects – like rock-forms – tend to look organic. JS received a HUGO in 1965. Dissatisfied by poor standards in sf art – "with few exceptions it's really fourth rate" – and low budgets, he left the field in 1968, returning briefly in the 1970s. [JG/PN]

About the artist: "Sketches: John Schoenherr Interview" in ALGOL, Summer-Fall 1978.

SCHOFIELD, ALFRED TAYLOR (1846-1929) UK medical doctor and writer whose first sf novel, *Travels in the Interior, or The Wonderful Adventures of Luke and Belinda: Edited by a London Physician* (**1887**), as by Luke Courteney, carries its protagonists, shrunk to a suitable size, on a didactic expedition through a human body (◊ GREAT AND SMALL). *Another World, or The Fourth Dimension* (**1888**), published as ATS, takes its two-dimensional protagonist on a similarly didactic mission from Edwin A. ABBOTT's Flatland to even more penurious Lineland, and thence into worlds of three and four DIMENSIONS, all in order to convey the truths of a dimension-encompassing Christianity. [JC]

SCHOLES, ROBERT (EDWARD) (1929-) US academic and sf critic. One of the better-known US theorists in structuralism, he is the author of a number of books on literary theory. Those with special relevance to sf are *The Fabulators* (**1967**), which deals with FABULATION, *Structural Fabulation: An Essay on the Fiction of the Future* (**1975**), *Science Fiction: History, Science, Vision* (**1977**) with Eric S. RABKIN *(whom see for further details)* and *Fabulation and Metafiction* (**1979**). The first two and the fourth of these are academic in approach, the second especially for its attempted definition of the sf genre (◊ DEFINITIONS OF SF). With George Edgar SLUSSER and Rabkin, RS edited *Bridges to Fantasy* (anth **1982**) and *Co-Ordinates: Placing Science Fiction and Fantasy* (anth **1983**), both collections of critical essays; he also introduced the 1975 US paperback edition of Tzvetan TODOROV's *Introduction à la littérature fantastique* (**1970**; trans as *The Fantastic: A Structural Approach to a Literary Genre* **1973**), and has written many shorter critical pieces on sf. [PN]

See also: CRITICAL AND HISTORICAL WORKS ABOUT SF.

SCHOLZ, CARTER (1953-) US writer who began publishing sf with "Closed Circuit" for *Clarion SF* (anth **1976**) ed Kate WILHELM, and whose short fiction, which appeared with some frequency for the next decade, constitutes a series of dark and fluid visions of the inhabitants of the world to come. None of these stories – like the striking "The Eve of the Last Apollo" (**1977**) – has been put into a CS collection (*Cuts* [coll **1985** chap] restricting itself to previously unpublished material). He fell almost entirely silent after 1986. CS is known mainly for his one novel, *Palimpsests* (**1984**) with Glenn Harcourt; its dense, refractive, ruminative, palimpsest-laden style more than amply surrounds the story of an archaeologist yanked from brooding internal and external exile by the discovery of a dizzyingly anachronistic object at a Neanderthal dig. TIME PARADOXES are alluded to, but with something like ABSURDIST torpor, and the novel ends in dark irresolution, in an epiphany of flow – "of landho that would never quite achieve landfall" – which simultaneously moves and irritates the reader. [JC]

SCHOMBURG, ALEX (1905-) US illustrator and COMIC-book artist; he has also spelled his name Schomberg. His first assignment was for Hugo GERNSBACK in 1925; he did his first cover in that year for SCIENCE AND INVENTION. During his 65-year career, which extended into the 1980s with covers for ISAAC ASIMOV'S SCIENCE FICTION MAGAZINE, he worked for many magazines, including *AMZ, TWS, FSF, Fantastic* and *Startling Stories*. He also painted book covers, primarily for ACE BOOKS and Winston Books (their "juvenile" sf series of the 1950s, for which he also designed the endpapers). His ILLUSTRATION is realistic, versatile and assured, usually eschewing bright colours; he was known as "king of the airbrush". Important in the comics industry as well, he worked on many of the Timely Comics (now MARVEL COMICS) titles, helping develop **Captain America** and **Sub-Mariner**. In 1990 he was awarded a Special Award by the World Science Fiction Convention; he has also won the Lensman Award (1979) and the Frank R. Paul Award (1984). His work is showcased in *Chroma: The Art of Alex Schomburg* (**1986**), text by Jon Gustafson. [JG]

SCHOONOVER, LAWRENCE (1906-1980) US writer best known for his many historical novels. *Central Passage* (**1962**) is set after a nuclear HOLOCAUST has demolished the Isthmus of Panama, set the oceans astir and initiated a new ice age, whose escalation is averted through a successful attempt to block the Isthmus again. In the meantime, atomic radiation has caused mutations, resulting in a breed of SUPERMEN destined to inherit the Earth. [JC]

SCHORER, MARK [r] ◊ August DERLETH.

SCHULMAN, J(OSEPH) NEIL (1953-) US writer whose books have been very influential in the LIBERTARIAN-SF movement. *Alongside Night* (**1979**) describes the salvation of a future USA (whose economy has been destroyed by government intervention in the free market) by a hard-cash underground economy evolved from today's black market. The political message is reasonably unobtrusive, though non-libertarians may find the somewhat casual attitude taken towards the killing of tax collectors upsetting. *The Rainbow Cadenza: A Novel in Logosata Form* (**1983**), generally considered inferior, is interesting for its portrayal of a DYSTOPIA judged against libertarian values rather than (as is more usual) humanist ones, as well as for its depiction of laser-generated visuals (◊ ARTS) as a means of artistic expression. Like many libertarian authors, JNS is a competent thriller writer whose books are fundamentally motivated by a combination of moral outrage and a fascination with the hardware of politics and economics. [NT]

SCHUTZ, J(OSEPH) W(ILLARD) (1912-1984) US writer, mostly of short stories, and diplomat who graduated in science and later from the US Counter-Insurgency School. He was in his 50s when – to give himself something to do while stationed in West Africa – he began writing sf, with "Maiden Voyage" for *FSF* in 1965. His two adventure-sf novels are *People of the Rings* (**1975** UK) and *The Moon Microbe* (**1976** UK). He wrote thrillers as Jerry Scholl. [PN]

SCHUYLER, GEORGE S(AMUEL) (1895-1977) US writer whose sf, normally written as by Samuel I. Brooks, appeared obscurely in PULP MAGAZINES between the Wars. In his first sf novel, *Black No More: Being an Account of the Strange and Wonderful Workings of Science in the Land of the Free, A.D. 1933-1940* (**1931**) as GSS, a cosmetic treatment is discovered which will bleach Blacks. In treating this innovation in terms of SATIRE GSS, himself Black, acerbically targeted both Blacks and Whites. *Black Empire* (1936-8 *Pittsburgh Courier* as by Samuel I. Brooks; **1991**), intro by John A. WILLIAMS, pits Blacks against Whites in pulp terms, and ends in the creation of a Black UTOPIA. [PN/JC]

See also: POLITICS.

SCHWARTZ, ALAN (? -) US writer whose *The Wandering Tellurian* (**1967** dos) is appropriately titled: its Terran protagonist travels through space, having adventures. [JC]

SCHWARTZ, JULIUS (1915-) US agent and editor, born Bronx, New York. JS met his lifelong friend and colleague Mort WEISINGER at a meeting of the Scienceers sf group in 1931. Together they published the first true FANZINE, *The Time Traveller* (1932), and the later fanzine, *Science Fiction Digest* (1932), which in 1934 became FANTASY MAGAZINE, though Weisinger was not officially an editor on the latter. In 1934 they founded Solar Sales Service, the first literary agency to specialize in sf; early clients included Henry L. HASSE, David H. KELLER, P. Schuyler MILLER and Stanley G. WEINBAUM. When Weisinger became editor of THRILLING WONDER STORIES in 1936, JS ran the agency alone for the next 10 years, new clients including Alfred BESTER, Eando BINDER, Leigh BRACKETT, Ray BRADBURY, John Russell FEARN and Manly Wade WELLMAN.

At Bester's suggestion, JS became editor at All-American Comics (later part of DC COMICS) in Feb 1944. In the mid-1950s he played a major role in the DC revival of the SUPERHERO with new versions of earlier characters, many utilizing sf themes. These included **The Flash** (police scientist who gains super-speed in accident), **Green Lantern** (test pilot given power ring by alien Guardians from the planet Oa so that he can police this sector of space), **Hawkman** (policeman from the planet Thanagar operating on Earth), **Adam Strange** (Earthman who becomes protector of the planet Rann) and **The Atom** (scientist with the ability to become smaller – JS called this character, in his civilian identity, Ray Palmer, Raymond A. PALMER being the shortest of all sf editors). JS also revived the flagging fortunes of **Batman** by giving it a "new look". When Weisinger left DC in 1971, JS took over as SUPERMAN editor. He left this position in 1986 to edit the shortlived DC **SF Graphic Album** adaptations (1985-7), whose titles in publication order were: *Hell on Earth* (1942 *Weird Tales*; graph **1985**) by Robert BLOCH, *Nightwings* (1968 *Gal*; graph **1985**) by Robert SILVERBERG, *Frost & Fire* (1946 *Planet Stories* as "The Land that Time Forgot"; graph **1985**) by Ray Bradbury, *Merchants of Venus* (graph **1986**) from the 1971 novella by Frederik POHL, *Demon with a Glass Hand* (graph **1986**) from the 1964 *Outer Limits* tv script by Harlan ELLISON, *The Magic Goes Away* (graph **1986**) from the 1978 book by Larry NIVEN and *Sandkings* (1979 *Omni*; graph **1987**) by George R.R. MARTIN. The line was a commercial failure, and JS gave up editing to become a consultant to DC and "a goodwill ambassador for DC ... to various conventions". [RH]

SCHWARZ, MAURICIO-JOSÉ (1955-   ) Mexican writer who for 7 years had an sf column in the daily newspaper *Excelsior*. He is the author of about 50 short stories, many sf or horror. M-JS was the first winner (1984) of the Puebla Award (◊ LATIN AMERICA) for Best SF Short Story in Mexico with his story "La pequeña guerra" ["The Smallest War"]. Some of his stories are collected in *Escenas de la realidad virtual* ["Scenes from Virtual Reality"] (coll **1991**). M-JS founded (1991) and edits an sf SEMIPROZINE, *Estacosa* ["Thisthing"]. He is part-author of the LATIN AMERICA entry in this encyclopedia. [PN]

SCHWEITZER, DARRELL (CHARLES) (1952-   ) US critic, editor and writer who began publishing

stories of genre interest with "Come to Mother" for *Weirdbook* #4 in 1970, but who spent his energies very variously for many years, coming initially to notice with a series of critical studies including *Lovecraft in the Cinema* (**1975** chap), *The Dream Quest of H.P. Lovecraft* (**1978** chap), *Conan's World and Robert E. Howard* (**1979** chap), *On Writing Science Fiction (The Editors Strike Back!)* (**1981**) with John M. FORD and George H. SCITHERS, *Constructing Scientifiction & Fantasy* (**1982** chap) with John Ashmead and Scithers, and *Pathways to Elfland: The Writings of Lord Dunsany* (**1989**). During this period he also served as editorial assistant at *IASFM* 1977-82 and at *AMZ* 1982-6. With John BETANCOURT and Scithers he then restarted WEIRD TALES (1987-current) with #290. Also with Scithers, he ed 2 anthologies of CLUB STORIES: *Tales from the Spaceport Bar* (anth **1987**) and *Another Round at the Spaceport Bar* (anth **1989**).

DS's fiction, which sometimes tends to a grimly brisk SCIENCE-FANTASY diction, includes *We are All Legends* (coll of linked stories **1981**), *The Shattered Goddess* (**1982**), a FAR-FUTURE fantasy which moves into dark regions, *Tom O'Bedlam's Night Out, and Other Strange Excursions* (coll **1985**), *The Meaning of Life, and Other Awesome Cosmic Revelations* (coll **1988** chap) and *The White Isle* (1980 *Fantastic*; rev **1990**). [JC]

As editor: Some of the **SF Voices** series of interviews, those for which he was responsible including *SF Voices* (anth **1976**), *Science Fiction Voices #1* (anth **1979**) and *Science Fiction Voices #5* (anth **1982** chap); *Essays Lovecraftian* (anth **1977**; rev vt *Discovering H.P. Lovecraft* 1987); *Exploring Fantasy Worlds* (anth **1985**); *Discovering Modern Horror Fiction #1* (anth **1985**) and *#2* (anth **1988**); *Discovering Stephen King* (anth **1985**).

SCHWERIN, DORIS H(ALPERN) (1922-   ) US composer and writer whose *The Rainbow Walkers* (**1985**; vt *The Missing Years* 1986 UK) is an intermittently moving sf tale involving CRYONICS and their consequences. [JC]

SCIENCE AND INVENTION US monthly BEDSHEET-size popular-science magazine, slick paper. 220 issues May 1913-Aug 1931. Published 1913-29 by Experimenter Publishing Co.; ed Hugo GERNSBACK until his bankruptcy in 1929, thereafter ed anon. *SAI* was not a new magazine but a retitling (from Aug 1920) of Gernsback's *Electrical Experimenter*, founded May 1913, itself modelled on *Modern Electrics*, an earlier Gernsback magazine (1908-13), in which his novel *Ralph 124C 41+* (1911-12; **1925**) had first appeared. The Aug 1923 issue of *SAI* was a special "Scientific Fiction" number with a cover by Howard V. BROWN, and was effectively Gernsback's first sf magazine. Both before and after this, however, *SAI* (whose main content was science articles) regularly featured sf stories and novels – notably 3 serials by Ray CUMMINGS and also A. MERRITT's "The Metal Emperor" (1920 *Argosy*; rev 1927-8 *SAI*; vt *The Metal Monster* 1946).

The most typical writer of Gernsbackian SCIENTIFIC-TION was perhaps Clement FEZANDIE: almost all of his

Dr Hackensaw series – 39 short stories and "A Journey to the Center of the Earth" (1925), a 4-part serialized novel – was published in *SAI* (2 final stories were published in *AMZ*). These are wooden as narratives, but contain lively ideas about new inventions, including ROBOTS, tv and brainwashing through dissolution of neural ganglia; Hackensaw even experiences weightlessness, on a trip to the Moon. After founding AMAZING STORIES in Apr 1926, Gernsback naturally used there most of the sf he bought, but sf serials (including Merritt's, noted above) continued in *SAI* until 1928. *SAI* was in fact a more commercially successful magazine than *AMZ*, with a formula not unlike that of OMNI today.   [PN/MJE/FHP]

SCIENCE FANTASY 1. In the TERMINOLOGY of sf readers, and more especially publishers, this term has never been clearly defined, although it was the title of a well known UK magazine 1950-66 (◊ 2), which was also the period when the term was most in general use. More recently it has been partially superseded by the terms SWORD AND SORCERY and HEROIC FANTASY, but it differs from these two categories in that Science Fantasy does not *necessarily* contain MAGIC, GODS AND DEMONS, HEROES, MYTHOLOGY or SUPERNATURAL CREATURES, though these may be present, often in a quasirationalized form. Science Fantasy is normally considered a bastard genre blending elements of sf and fantasy; it is usually colourful and often bizarre, sometimes with elements of HORROR although never centrally in the horror genre. Certain sf themes are especially common in Science Fantasy – ALTERNATE WORLDS, other DIMENSIONS, ESP, MONSTERS, PARALLEL WORLDS, PSI POWERS and SUPERMEN – but no single one of these ingredients is essential. Many Science Fantasies are also PLANETARY ROMANCES (many of the books so described in this volume can be regarded as Science Fantasy). A good discussion of the term, which very nearly builds to a definition through the accretion of examples, is "Science Fantasy" by Brian Attebery in *Dictionary of Literary Biography. Volume Eight. Twentieth-Century American Science-Fiction Writers: Part 2: M-Z* (**1981**) ed David Cowart and Thomas L. Wymer. Attebery cites the following as among the more important US authors of Science Fantasy: Marion Zimmer BRADLEY, Edgar Rice BURROUGHS, L. Sprague DE CAMP and Fletcher PRATT, Samuel R. DELANY, Anne MCCAFFREY, Andre NORTON, Jack VANCE, John VARLEY, Roger ZELAZNY and Gene WOLFE (indeed, in the 1980s Wolfe practically resuscitated the genre single-handedly), to which list should certainly be added Joan D. VINGE and (especially the former) C.L. MOORE and Henry KUTTNER. Attebery also makes special mention of *The Deep* (**1975**) by John CROWLEY.   [PN]

2. UK DIGEST-size magazine published from Summer 1950 by Nova Publications as a companion to NEW WORLDS, subsequently taken over by Roberts & Vinter in June/July 1964, thereafter in a paperback-size format. 81 issues appeared as *SF* Summer 1950-Feb 1966, and 12 more Mar 1966-Feb 1967 as *Impulse*

(Mar-July 1966) and *SF Impulse* (Aug 1966-Feb 1967). #1 and #2 were ed Walter GILLINGS; John CARNELL then took over until Nova folded. The Roberts & Vinter version was ed until Sep 1966 Kyril Bonfiglioli; the last 5 issues were ed Harry HARRISON and Keith ROBERTS.

SF was numbered consecutively from #1 to #81 (Feb 1966). Numeration was begun again with the title change to *Impulse*, in Mar 1966, with 1 vol of 12 numbered issues (hence *Impulse* is sometimes regarded as a separate magazine). Early on *SF* appeared irregularly, with only 6 issues 1950-53, but from Mar 1954 an uneasy bimonthly schedule began, lapsing to quarterly every now and then, improving in the late 1950s. A regular monthly schedule ran from Mar 1965 to the end.

SF used offbeat FANTASY together with some sf not too different from that published in its companion, *NW* (but only rarely the kind of whimsical story associated with the US UNKNOWN). While Carnell was editing both, *SF* tended to use stories of greater length than *NW*, including numerous novellas. Many of its lead stories were supplied by John BRUNNER, Kenneth BULMER and Michael MOORCOCK, all of whom published some of their best early work in its pages. *SF* also published the first stories of Brian W. ALDISS and J.G. BALLARD, and part of Aldiss's first sf novel, *Non-Stop* (1956; exp **1958**; rev vt *Starship* US 1959) and virtually all the important early work of Thomas Burnett SWANN. After Bonfiglioli became editor in 1964, Keith ROBERTS, Christopher PRIEST, Josephine SAXTON and Brian STABLEFORD all made their débuts in the magazine, and the early *Impulse* issues featured Keith Roberts's **Pavane** stories (Mar-July 1966; fixup **1968**). During Carnell's incumbency *SF* published material of a higher quality than its companion, but after its sale in 1964 – despite Bonfiglioli and his editorial successors buying some good material – it was overshadowed by Moorcock's *NW*, with which it ultimately merged. *NW* and *SF* were the best sf magazines published in the UK before INTERZONE joined them in this category.

The cover art of *SF* was intermittently of a high standard, especially that by Brian LEWIS, who did most of the covers 1958-61, and Keith Roberts, who did nearly all the covers from 1965 until the end. Roberts's bold semi-abstractions were quite outside the conventions of genre-sf ILLUSTRATION, and Lewis's surreal landscapes, reminiscent of the work of Max Ernst (1891-1976), were also unusual.   [BS]

3. Variant title of SCIENCE FANTASY YEARBOOK.

See also: FANTASY REVIEW.

SCIENCE FANTASY YEARBOOK One of the many reprint DIGEST-size magazines from Sol Cohen's Ultimate Publishing Co., using stories from old issues of *AMZ* and *Fantastic Adventures*, including Theodore STURGEON's *The Dreaming Jewels* (1950 *Fantastic Adventures*; exp **1950**; vt *The Synthetic Man* 1957). 4 quarterly issues appeared, 2 in 1970, 2 in 1971, all but #1 as *Science Fantasy*.   [BS/PN]

SF Pronounced "esseff", the preferred abbreviation of "science fiction" within the community of sf writers and readers, as opposed to the journalistic SCI FI. In this volume – as often elsewhere – it is rendered in lower-case letters. [PN]

SCIENCE FICTION US PULP MAGAZINE, 12 issues Mar 1939-Sep 1941. Published by Blue Ribbon Magazines Inc. (Mar-Dec 1939), Double Action Magazines Inc. (Mar 1940-Jan 1941) and then Columbia Publications Inc. (Mar-Sep 1941); ed Charles D. HORNIG (Mar 1939-Mar 1941) and Robert A.W. LOWNDES (June-Sep 1941).

The second venture into magazine editing by former WONDER STORIES editor Hornig, *SF* was never better than very mediocre; although its covers were all by Frank R. PAUL, they were poor examples of his work. The stories were from such authors as John Russell FEARN and Eando BINDER, both of whom also used pseudonyms to multiply their contributions to the magazine. The readers' departments were conducted on a determinedly chummy basis by Hornig, who spent a good deal of space airing his enthusiasm for Esperanto. (In later issues his firm pacifism showed in some anguished editorials.) After 2 issues under Lowndes's editorship *SF* was merged with its companion FUTURE FICTION to form *Future Combined with Science Fiction*. The Apr and July 1943 issues of SCIENCE FICTION STORIES, which revived the *SF* cover design, were actually a continuation of *Future Fiction* after a further title change. Some commentators see *The* ORIGINAL SCIENCE FICTION STORIES, also ed Lowndes, as a delayed continuation of *SF* in the 1950s. 2 issues of *SF*, cut, were reprinted in the UK. [MJE/PN]

SCIENCE FICTION ACHIEVEMENT AWARD ◊ HUGO.

SCIENCE FICTION (ADVENTURE) CLASSICS ◊ SCIENCE FICTION CLASSICS.

SCIENCE FICTION ADVENTURES Title used on 2 US DIGEST-size magazines during the 1950s, and on 1 UK magazine that began as a reprint and continued, using original material, after its parent – the 2nd US magazine – folded. (The title was used also as a variant title of SCIENCE FICTION CLASSICS, Jan-May 1973, Sep and Nov 1974.)

The 1st US magazine published 9 issues Nov 1952-June 1954. #1 was published by Science Fiction Publications, the rest by Future Publications. The issues Nov 1952-Sep 1953 were ed Lester DEL REY as Philip St John; Harry HARRISON took over shortly before the magazine folded. The schedule was irregularly bimonthly.

The 2nd US magazine, published by Royal Publications, was ed Larry T. SHAW and ran for 12 issues in 18 months, Dec 1956-June 1958. #1 was numbered, confusingly, vol 1 #6, continuing the numeration of a defunct magazine (*Suspect Detective Stories*) from the same publisher; however, #2 was numbered vol 1 #2.

The editorial policy in each case – more overt in Shaw's magazine – was to concentrate on adventure stories. The 1st *SFA* serialized del Rey's *Police Your Planet* (Mar-Sep 1953; **1956**), as by Erik Van Lhin, and

C.M. KORNBLUTH's *The Syndic* (Dec 1953-June 1954; **1953**). The 2nd *SFA* used very few short stories, usually featuring 3 long novelettes per issue. Robert SILVERBERG, under various names, was a particularly prolific contributor, magazine versions of 6 of his early novels appearing there.

Novelettes from Shaw's magazine were resorted into 5 issues of a UK edition marketed Mar-Nov 1958 by Nova Publications, with both Shaw and John CARNELL credited as editors. Carnell alone, no longer using material from the parent magazine, continued *SFA* for a further 27 issues until May 1963, using a great deal of material by Kenneth BULMER (under various names) and novelettes by other writers regularly featured in the companion magazines NEW WORLDS and SCIENCE FANTASY. Notable stories included John BRUNNER's **Society of Time** series (1962; fixup as *Times without Number* **1962**; rev 1974) and the magazine version of J.G. BALLARD's *The Drowned World* (Jan 1962; rev **1962**). The UK *SFA* was numbered consecutively #1-#32, approximately bimonthly to #14, and regularly bimonthly from then on. Though sometimes regarded as more juvenile than its two companion publications, it remained continuously enjoyable. [BS]

SCIENCE FICTION ADVERTISER ◊ RIVERSIDE QUARTERLY.

SCIENCE FICTION & FANTASY BOOK REVIEW US critical magazine, founded and ed Neil BARRON, published by BORGO PRESS, 13 issues 1979-80; revived with the SCIENCE FICTION RESEARCH ASSOCIATION as publisher, still ed Barron, 20 issues 1982-3; amalgamated with *Fantasy Newsletter* to form FANTASY REVIEW, Jan 1984, ed Robert A. Collins, with Barron as reviews editor. This useful journal often reviewed as many as 50 books an issue – novels, collections, secondary and associational literature – and with so many reviewers involved was a triumph of editorial organization. Its passing is regretted, especially since SFRA NEWSLETTER, which since the late 1980s has been doing something similar, usually prints rather shorter reviews (especially since mid-1992) than did *SF&FBR*, and its standards seem a little more uneven. [PN]

SCIENCE FICTION AND FANTASY BOOK REVIEW ANNUAL Beginning with *Science Fiction and Fantasy Book Review Annual 1988* (dated 1988 but **1989**) ed Robert Λ. Collins and Robert Latham – whose coverage is of 1987 – this series is an annual book spin-off from the defunct magazine FANTASY REVIEW (folded Aug 1987). The book-review section of the magazine had been its strongest feature, and continues as the central feature of the annual, whose first edition published around 550 brief reviews (most reprinted, though individual reviews are not so acknowledged, from SFRA NEWSLETTER) along with essay surveys of the year in sf, sf scholarship, horror, etc. *SFAFBRA*'s utility is dubious, since by the time its information is published many of the books described are out of print. *SFAFBRA*, published by Meckler for 2 years then by GREENWOOD PRESS, has

1989 and *1990* editions. [PN]

SFFWA ◊ SCIENCE FICTION WRITERS OF AMERICA.

SCIENCE FICTION AND FANTASY WRITERS OF AMERICA ◊ SCIENCE FICTION WRITERS OF AMERICA.

SCIENCE FICTION: A REVIEW OF SPECULATIVE LITERATURE Australian critical magazine ed Van Ikin from University of Sydney and later University of Western Australia; associate ed Terry DOWLING; irregular; PULP-MAGAZINE format, 30 issues 1977-90, current. Intended to be a reputable academic journal, as the editorial addresses suggest, *SF:AROSL* has oscillated a little uneasily between the academic and the fannish, but has nevertheless published good critical features. Until the more regular and perhaps livelier AUSTRALIAN SCIENCE FICTION REVIEW: SECOND SERIES appeared in 1986, this was the main repository for Australian sf criticism (especially since its main rival, SF COMMENTARY, was notably irregular in the 1980s), publishing interesting material by its editors and by Russell BLACKFORD, George TURNER and others. [PN]

SFBC AWARD ◊ AWARDS.

SCIENCE FICTION BOOK CLUB Sf book clubs were started in both the UK and the USA at roughly the same time (*c*1953). The UK version was owned in its early years by Sidgwick & Jackson, then by Dent as part of that company's Readers' Union group of book clubs, and finally by David & Charles, who bought the Readers' Union group in the 1970s. David & Charles's management, which contained no sf enthusiasts, was apathetic towards the SFBC, which later became subject to competition from Encounters, a book club aggressively promoted by the larger group Book Club Associates. Even before the death in 1982 of its freelance consultant Edmund COOPER, the editorless UK SFBC was slowly petering out, despite part- and spare-time efforts by one Readers' Union employee, Paul G. Begg, to keep it alive; it died altogether some time after Begg left the company.

The US SFBC, by contrast, has had a history of continuity. It is published by Nelson Doubleday, Inc., an associate of, but distinct from, DOUBLEDAY, whose differing imprint is Doubleday & Company, Inc. In 1986 the US SFBC was sold, along with Doubleday, to the German company Bertelsmann. The US club is far larger than the UK club ever was, offers a very much broader selection, publishes its own editions (including special hardcover editions of paperback originals) and creates books – omnibuses of various sorts – especially for its members. (The UK club normally presented no more than one title per month, reprinted cheaply on cheap paper and with a cheap binding and cover.) The US SFBC has been a major force in sf publishing. [MJE/PN/JGr]

SFCD-LITERATURPREIS ◊ AWARDS.

SF CHRONICLE US SEMIPROZINE (which began as a FANZINE), published and ed from New York by Andrew PORTER, monthly, current, 152 issues to June 1992. *SFC* was founded in 1978 as a department of Porter's more elaborate but now defunct magazine ALGOL, and became a separate publication in June, 1979. It is a general news magazine about sf, whose coverage is not as broad as that of its competitor, the West Coast magazine LOCUS, though it contains fan material, a film column by Ed NAHA and the "London Report" by Stephen Jones and Jo Fletcher, all of which cover ground rather different from *Locus*'s. The film column is disappointingly fragmentary and the book reviews, mostly by Don D'Amassa, are very short. Something of an East Coast institution, *SFC* does offer an alternate voice for the sf community. In its one-man-band editorial performance it shows astonishing stamina in its producer, Porter, who received a Special Award at the World CONVENTION in 1991 for his "years of continuing excellence" in editing *SFC*, in the pages of which he subsequently apologized for his less than graceful acceptance of the award, which he regarded as "a consolation prize". [PN]

SCIENCE FICTION CLASSICS One of the many reprint DIGEST-size magazines published by Sol Cohen's Ultimate Publishing Co., 30 issues published, ed Herb Lehrman as Ralph Adris #1-#5, then ed Cohen. It began Feb 1967, published #1-#6 in 1967-8 as *Science Fiction Classics* and #7-#8 in 1969 as *Science Fiction (Adventure) Classics*. It resumed publication in Winter 1970 under the latter title with #12 and published 22 more issues before merging with *Thrilling Science Fiction* (◊ The MOST THRILLING SCIENCE FICTION EVER TOLD) in early 1975. *SFC* was numbered consecutively up to #19, and thereafter merely dated. The schedule was irregular. The hiatus in numbering (#9-#11 missing) is connected with the fact that 2 other magazines took up their numbering from *SFC* in 1969: SPACE ADVENTURES (CLASSICS) published 6 issues numbered #9-#14, and STRANGE FANTASY published 6 issues numbered #8-#13; they folded in 1971 and 1970 respectively.

In its early issues *SFC* used a great deal of material from the 1930s *AMZ*, reprinting stories by John W. CAMPBELL Jr, Hugo GERNSBACK, Edmond HAMILTON *et al*., but from #13 it reprinted mainly poor stories from the period of Raymond A. PALMER's editorship. Variant titles were *Science Fiction Adventures Classics* (July 1973-July 1974) and *Science Fiction Adventures* (Jan-May 1973, Sep and Nov 1974). [BS]

SCIENCE FICTION CLASSICS ANNUAL US DIGEST-size magazine. 1 issue, dated 1970, published by Ultimate Publishing Co.; probably ed Sol Cohen. All stories were reprinted from the 1930s *AMZ*. [FHP]

SCIENCE-FICTION COLLECTOR, THE Canadian bibliographical SEMIPROZINE (1976-81), describing itself as a FANZINE, published by James Grant Books, Calgary, to #3, then by Pandora's Books Ltd; ed J. Grant Thiessen (1946-   ). With #9 (June 1980) the journal merged with the fanzine *Age of the Unicorn*, and was renamed *Megavore: The Journal of Popular Fiction*.

Thiessen, a book dealer with a bibliographical bent, published in *TS-FC* a good deal of extremely useful research – which quite often cannot be found duplicated elsewhere – on sf PUBLISHING, frequently in the more obscure and less reputable areas of paperback-book and magazine publishing, with features on ACE BOOKS, sf pornography, defunct paperback lines, Avalon Books, A.E. VAN VOGT and much else. After the title-change the emphasis was less strongly on sf/fantasy; within a year the journal died. [PN]

SF COMMENTARY Australian FANZINE, irregular (Jan 1969-current), ed Bruce GILLESPIE. *SFC*, which had reached #69/70 by Jan 1991, is a serious critical journal in stencilled format; it also includes rather charming autobiographical ramblings by Gillespie. It is generally considered one of the best serious fanzines, and has received 3 HUGO nominations. Important contributors have included John Foyster, Yvonne Rousseau, George TURNER and Stanisław LEM; most of the earliest English translations of Lem's critical articles appeared in *SFC*. During June 1981-Jan 1989 *SFC* did not appear, Gillespie instead publishing his *The Metaphysical Review*, which is less concentratedly about sf. [PN]

SCIENCE FICTION DIGEST 1. US DIGEST-size magazine. 2 issues, Feb and May 1954, published by Specific Fiction Corp., New York, ed Chester Whitehorn. *SFD* was intended as a reprint magazine which would take its material from the slick general-fiction magazines and other sources, but the selections were weak and it quickly failed. Its (purportedly) nonfiction articles had a strong occult bent. The same publisher and editor had already failed with VORTEX SCIENCE FICTION the previous year.

2. US DIGEST-sized magazine. 4 issues Oct/Nov 1981-Sep/Oct 1982, ed Shawna MCCARTHY, published by Davis Publications, New York, as a companion magazine to ISAAC ASIMOV'S SCIENCE FICTION MAGAZINE and *ASF*. This was an experiment in presenting excerpts from forthcoming books, both fiction and nonfiction, in the form of self-sufficient episodes. #4 was a 288pp double issue.

3. FANZINE founded in 1932, better known under the title to which it changed its name in 1934, FANTASY MAGAZINE (*which see for details*).

None of these magazines should be confused with the UK SF DIGEST. [FHP/PN]

SF DIGEST UK small-BEDSHEET-size magazine. 1 undated issue, 1976, published by New English Library; ed Julie Davis. *SFD* was to have been a quarterly successor to SCIENCE FICTION MONTHLY, but was doomed even before #1 appeared by the publisher's decision to concentrate on books rather than magazines. *SFD*'s format was superior to that of *Science Fiction Monthly*, and was less obviously slanted toward a juvenile market. [PN]

SCIENCE FICTION EYE US SEMIPROZINE, #1 Winter 1987; ed Stephen P. Brown, Daniel Steffan, and published by the 'Til You Go Blind Cooperative to #5; ed and published Brown alone from #6; published from Washington DC to #8, thereafter from Asheville, North Carolina; 10 issues to June 1992, theoretically

3 issues a year (actually irregular), current.

This intensely lively critical journal, professional in appearance, has at times been regarded as the house journal of CYBERPUNK; it prints its price in US dollars, pounds sterling and Japanese yen on the cover. It covers literature (mostly but not exclusively sf), music, technology, communications, or whatever is hot on the streets at a given moment, with an agreeable if irritating air of seeing itself as living on the cutting edge. Its various controversies have included a continuing savage attack on Orson Scott CARD. Contributors have included Paul Di Filippo, William GIBSON, Richard GRANT, Eileen Gunn, Elizabeth HAND, Richard KADREY, John KESSEL, Charles PLATT, Lucius SHEPARD and Bruce STERLING. [PN]

SCIENCE FICTION FIVE YEARLY ◊ QUANDRY.

SCIENCE FICTION FORTNIGHTLY ◊ AUTHENTIC SCIENCE FICTION.

SCIENCE FICTION FOUNDATION UK research unit set up in 1971 at the North East London Polytechnic (which became the University of East London in 1992), but semi-autonomous, being controlled by a council, partly academics and partly sf professionals, and including George HAY, whose enthusiasm had much to do with the SFF's inception. Peter NICHOLLS, the first administrator (1971-7), was followed by Malcolm EDWARDS (1978-80). The SFF was the first and only academic body in the UK set up to investigate sf: until 1980 it also supervised graduate research work in the field and investigated the usefulness of sf in education generally (◊ SF IN THE CLASSROOM).

Severe restrictions on UK educational budgets in 1980 led to the freezing of the position of administrator when Edwards left in May of that year, though Colin GREENLAND, as an Arts-Council-funded Writing Fellow attached to the SFF, kept the flag flying for a period, and Charles BARREN served as (unsalaried) acting administrator for some years, followed by Ian MacPherson and Ted Chapman, variously designated but never paid. During 1980-91 the SFF was staffed only by a single part-time employee, Joyce Day, becoming primarily known for its journal, FOUNDATION: THE REVIEW OF SCIENCE FICTION, and its research library, housed at the Barking precinct of the Polytechnic, the largest publicly accessible COLLECTION of sf in the UK outside the British Library, with *c*20,000 items including magazines and fanzines. In 1991 it seemed briefly that the Polytechnic – then about to be granted, as were other UK polytechnics, the more prestigious designation "University" – was prepared to refinance the SFF, and an additional clerical staff member was introduced. But then it was announced that the institution was no longer prepared to sustain the SFF, and asked it to leave. In October 1992, the Council of the SFF agreed in principle to move in early 1993 to the University of Liverpool, which had expressed much interest in the chance to gain so substantial (and unique) a research resource. It was expected that an administrator would be appointed.

The SFF patron is Arthur C. CLARKE; council and ordinary members have included practically all UK sf writers as well as distinguished US writers including James BLISH and Ursula K. LE GUIN. The SFF helps administer the ARTHUR C. CLARKE AWARD. Its financial problems have been alleviated in the 1990s by help from a large group, Friends of Foundation. [PN]

SCIENCE FICTION GREATS ◊ GREAT SCIENCE FICTION.

SF GREATS ◊ GREAT SCIENCE FICTION.

SF IMPULSE ◊ SCIENCE FANTASY.

SF IN MUSIC ◊ MUSIC.

SF IN THE CLASSROOM In September 1953 Sam MOSKOWITZ began to teach what was almost certainly the first sf course in the USA to be given through a college. The course was on Science Fiction Writing, was delivered on a non-credit basis through the City College of New York, and was presented with the collaboration of a popular-science writer, Robert Frazier (not to be confused with the sf poet Robert FRAZIER). For the Autumn 1953 sessions, Moskowitz arranged for several sf writers – including Isaac ASIMOV, Lester DEL REY, Murray LEINSTER, Robert SHECKLEY and Theodore STURGEON – to give talks; later sessions included talks by Robert A. HEINLEIN and others. Moskowitz left the course after 1955, and it probably ceased in 1957.

Further sf courses were slow to be established. Guest lectures were occasionally given, including 2 by Moskowitz, the first in December 1950 at New York University, the second in December 1953 at Columbia University. Those given by Heinlein, C.M. KORNBLUTH, Robert BLOCH and Alfred BESTER at the University of Chicago in 1957 were collected as *The Science Fiction Novel* (anth **1959**) with an introduction by Basil DAVENPORT; those by Kingsley AMIS at Princeton in 1959 were published as *New Maps of Hell* (**1960** US). A key year was 1961, when courses were set up by Mark R. HILLEGAS at Colgate and H. Bruce FRANKLIN at Stanford. 10 years later Jack WILLIAMSON's pamphlet *Science Fiction Comes to College* (**1971** chap) listed 61 universities offering such courses, and he judged that to be a mere sampling; by the time of his later pamphlet, *Teaching SF* (**1975** chap), that estimate had considerably increased, and it seems likely that today there are at least 250 such courses in the USA. *A Research Guide to Science Fiction Studies* (**1977**), compiled by Marshall B. TYMN, Roger C. SCHLOBIN and L.W. CURREY, lists 412 doctoral dissertations on sf subjects, the great majority having been submitted in the USA. Sf scholars have their own association, the SCIENCE FICTION RESEARCH ASSOCIATION, whose membership in the early 1990s hovered just above 300, perhaps two-thirds being US-based teachers of sf. It is clear that there has also been a greatly increased use of sf material at high-school level, sf being studied not only in its own right but because it helps to dramatize issues of ECOLOGY, FUTUROLOGY, OVERPOPULATION, SOCIOLOGY, TECHNOLOGY, etc. Also, as one of the most interesting and rapidly evolving forms of popular culture, sf is an important register of social history, reflecting shifts in the prejudices and expectations of society at large.

The story is very different outside the USA. A scattering of universities in Canada, Europe and Australia have sf courses. The first sf course in the UK was a non-credit course begun by Philip STRICK in 1969 at the City Literary Institute, London; it had various leaders (including the editors of this encyclopedia: John CLUTE, Peter NICHOLLS and Brian M. STABLEFORD) before its demise in 1992. Brief academic sf courses were taught by Nicholls and Ian WATSON in the 1970s, and occasional sf texts still find their way on to more conventional courses in English, politics, etc., but sf courses at university level remain a rarity in the UK.

Fears have been expressed that the academic study of sf will domesticate it. (A common catchphrase among sf fans was "Kick sf out of the classroom and back to the gutter where it belongs".) They are not groundless. Anecdotal evidence suggests that too often the sf course is regarded as a "soft option", and, although the number of distinguished scholars and teachers of sf, especially in the USA, has certainly increased through the 1970s and 1980s, the overall standard of academic sf criticism is not notably high. Also, the academic acceptance of sf may have suffered a setback through the popular perception, in the post-STAR WARS era, that sf books are largely juvenilia – a perception partly justified in a period when sf PUBLISHING, chiefly in the USA, appeared to have become cynically focused on a routine, mass-market product to the detriment of "mid-list" writers whose work was more serious, more carefully written and, it could be argued, more entertaining. Nonetheless, the number of CRITICAL AND HISTORICAL WORKS ABOUT SF increased very dramatically during this period: during 1991 SFRA NEWSLETTER reviewed about 15 books a month on sf/fantasy. Also, many more academic essays on sf are being published; they are now likely to turn up in all sorts of nonspecialist literary and critical journals, not just the specialist journals, whose "Big Three" remain SCIENCE-FICTION STUDIES and EXTRAPOLATION in the USA, and FOUNDA-TION: THE REVIEW OF SCIENCE FICTION in the UK; it is too soon to say with what success JOURNAL OF THE FANTASTIC IN THE ARTS (founded 1988) will join this group. These journals regularly publish a proportion of unexciting and mediocre work, as they always did, but there is currently a strong sense that more good and lively sf criticism and scholarship are abroad in the land now than when the 1st edn of this encyclopedia was prepared.

Especially since the early 1970s, many books – far too many to be listed here – have been published for use by teachers of sf at high-school level. Some have unfortunately tended towards the patronizing and simplistic, or to the formulaic, as in too many (but not all) of the readers' guides to individual authors published by companies like BORGO PRESS, Cliffs Notes, GREENWOOD PRESS, STARMONT HOUSE, Twayne and Ungar. Among the useful classroom guides are: *Science Fiction: An Introduction* (**1973**; rev vt *Science Fiction Reader's Guide* 1974) by L. David Allen; *Grokking the Future: Science Fiction in the Classroom* (**1973**) by Bernard C. Hollister and Deane C. Thompson; *Science Fiction: Its Criticism and Teaching* (**1980**) by Patrick PARRINDER; *Critical Encounters: Writers and Themes in Science Fiction* (anth **1978**) ed Dick Riley; *Science Fiction: A Teacher's Guide and Resource Book* (**1988**) by Marshall B. Tymn; and *Teaching Science Fiction: Education for Tomorrow* (anth **1980**) ed Jack Williamson.

The standard of books aimed at university-level readers and graduates ranges bafflingly from the opaque and semiliterate to the stimulating and rigorous, and their sheer volume – as suggested under CRITICAL AND HISTORICAL WORKS ABOUT SF – is now dizzying. Among the more important (English-language) academic authors to have written books in this field are Paul K. ALKON, Thomas D. CLARESON, I.F. CLARKE, Samuel R. DELANY (a part-time academic), H. Bruce FRANKLIN, James E. GUNN, Hal W. HALL, Mark R. HILLEGAS, David KETTERER, C.N. MANLOVE, Walter E. MEYERS, Patrick PARRINDER, Robert M. PHILMUS, Eric S. RABKIN, Mark ROSE, Joanna RUSS, David N. SAMUELSON, Lyman Tower SARGENT, Roger C. SCHLOBIN, Robert SCHOLES, George Edgar SLUSSER, Brian M. STABLEFORD, Darko SUVIN, W. Warren WAGAR, Patricia S. WARRICK and Gary K. WOLFE. Critical anthologies and journals contain – amid the dross – the work of other interesting sf academics who have yet to publish books. An early set of essays about the academic interest in sf is *Science Fiction: The Academic Awakening* (anth **1974**) ed Willis E. MCNELLY.

Sf BIBLIOGRAPHIES have become a marketable commodity only because of the academic interest in sf. The 1980s saw the publication of many more of them than ever before. Somewhere between bibliography, history and critical reference work is one of the outstanding reference works in the field, a book whose most recent incarnation is *Anatomy of Wonder: A Critical Guide to Science Fiction: Third Edition* (**1987**) ed Neil BARRON, aimed in the first instance at librarians but useful for all sf academics; it contains a chapter on the teaching of sf, with suggested texts.

This interest has brought about the publication of many sf ANTHOLOGIES that are obviously designed for the classroom, the stories they contain being complemented by introductions or some kind of critical apparatus. Some notably thoughtful compilations are *The Mirror of Infinity: A Critic's Anthology of Science Fiction* (anth **1970**) ed Robert SILVERBERG, *Those who Can* (anth **1973**) ed Robin Scott WILSON, *Modern Science Fiction* (anth **1974**) ed Norman SPINRAD, *Future Perfect: American Science Fiction of the Nineteenth Century* (anth **1966**; rev 1968; rev 1978) ed H. Bruce Franklin, and *The Road to Science Fiction* (anth in 4 vols **1977-82**) ed James E. Gunn. There are also, of course, a great many theme anthologies collecting sf stories about everything from ANTHROPOLOGY to RELIGION. One of the most active theme anthologists for the academic market has been Martin Harry GREENBERG, along with several colleagues with whom he often works.

Beyond all these direct responses to the academic stimulus is the now very general interest in sf to be found in the intellectual world generally: even newspapers and magazines are less dismissive or ignorant about sf than was the case in, say, the 1960s. Much of the material now published about sf – notably in the 1980s and 1990s in newspaper articles about CYBERPUNK – has been hacked out by trend-spotters and journalists cashing in on a good thing, but this is inevitable. Sceptics see the breaking down of the walls of sf's ghetto – a process hastened by sf's partial academic acceptance – as leading to such a general diffusion of sf ideas into the community at large as to leave sf itself less identifiable as a genre, perhaps less relevant, and even, according to the pessimists, moribund. If so, we have the paradox of a genre so disreputable in life that decent persons turned aside from it in disgust, only for its corpse to be praised for its beauty and vigour. [PN]

SCIENCE FICTION LEAGUE Launched Apr 1934 by Charles D. HORNIG and Hugo GERNSBACK through WONDER STORIES, the SFL was the first and most successful of several professionally sponsored sf organizations. The formation of local chapters in the USA, Australia, and the UK brought sf readers together and provided a firm foundation for present-day sf FANDOM; in particular, the establishment of the Leeds and Nuneaton SFL chapters led directly to the first UK FANZINES. [PR]

SCIENCE FICTION LIBRARY UK pocketbook magazine. 3 numbered undated issues 1960; published by G.G. Swan, London; no ed named. *SFL* had no table of contents, poor paper and very small type. Original and reprinted stories were used, including some from the first incarnation of SCIENCE FICTION QUARTERLY. A companion magazine was WEIRD AND OCCULT LIBRARY. [FHP]

SF MAGAZINES Sf stories were a popular and prominent feature of such general-fiction PULP MAGAZINES as *The* ARGOSY and *The* ALL-STORY during the first quarter of the 20th century. They were not, however, known as sf: if there were any need to differentiate them, the terms SCIENTIFIC ROMANCE or "different stories" might be used, but until the appearance of a magazine specifically devoted to sf there was no need of a label to describe the category. The first specialized English-language pulps with a leaning towards the fantastic were THRILL BOOK (1919) and WEIRD TALES (1923), but the editorial policy of both was aimed much more towards weird-occult fiction than towards sf.

As specialized pulps became common it was inevitable that there would be one devoted in some fashion to sf; it fell to Hugo GERNSBACK actually to publish the first such magazine (if we discount the "Twentieth Century Number" [June 1890] of the OVERLAND MONTHLY). Gernsback's SCIENCE AND INVENTION consistently published much sf among its otherwise nonfiction articles, and in Aug 1923 had a special issue devoted to "science fiction"; in 1924 he solicited subscriptions for a magazine to be called *Scientifiction*. This did not materialize, but two years later (Apr 1926) #1 of AMAZING STORIES appeared. Gernsback's coinage, SCIENTIFICTION, reflected his particular interest in sf as a vehicle for prediction and for the teaching of science. In a magazine which featured both Jules VERNE and Edgar Rice BURROUGHS, it was a label that fitted the former's stories far more readily than the latter's.

AMZ was somewhat different in appearance from the usual pulp magazines, which measured approximately 7in x 10in (20cm x 30cm) and were printed on poor-quality paper with rough, untrimmed edges. *AMZ* adopted the larger BEDSHEET size (approx 8½in x 11½in [24cm x 32.5cm]) and its pages were trimmed. The reason for this may have been to give an impression of greater respectability in order to have the magazine displayed on newsstands with the more prestigious "slick" magazines; certainly this was the result. The attempt at dignity was belied by the garishness of some of Frank R. PAUL's cover art, while the magazine's editorial matter had a stuffy, Victorian air. However, *AMZ* proved initially successful; according to Gernsback in the Sep 1928 issue, 150,000 copies were printed monthly, although "Very frequently we do not sell more than 125,000 copies". The same issue gives a clue to *AMZ*'s readership; of 22 letters printed, 11 are avowedly from high-school pupils. It was through the letters column of *AMZ* and later magazines that sf FANDOM began.

When Gernsback lost control of *AMZ* in 1929 through bankruptcy it remained in the hands of his assistant, the venerable T. O'Conor SLOANE, and changed little, while the new magazines which Gernsback then started – AIR WONDER STORIES and SCIENCE WONDER STORIES – adopted the same format and were very much the mixture as before. In fact, including AMAZING STORIES QUARTERLY and *Science Wonder Quarterly* (later WONDER STORIES QUARTERLY), Gernsback started not just the first English-language sf magazine but the first *five*. It is not surprising that the limited Gernsbackian view of sf gained a strong hold. The emphasis on "science" in the category label (either "scientifiction" or "science fiction"), often quite inappropriately, is a legacy of this.

The first challenge to Gernsback's view of sf magazine publishing came in 1930 with the appearance of *Astounding Stories of Super-Science* (◊ ASTOUNDING SCIENCE-FICTION). *ASF* belonged to the large Clayton magazine chain, and was unequivocally a pulp magazine. Its editor, Harry BATES, was unimpressed by Gernsback's achievements ("Packed with puerilities! Written by unimaginables!" was his later assessment of *AMZ*), and *ASF*'s priorities were adventure first and science a long way second. Aficionados of *AMZ* were, in turn, unimpressed by *ASF*'s vulgarity, and certainly the Clayton *ASF* pro-

duced vanishingly few stories of enduring quality. However, the same is true of its competitors.

Air Wonder and *Science Wonder* soon amalgamated into WONDER STORIES; with minor exceptions (in 1931 MIRACLE SCIENCE AND FANTASY STORIES published 2 issues; in 1934 the semiprofessional MARVEL TALES began its short life), *AMZ*, *ASF* and *Wonder Stories* constituted the US sf-magazine field until 1939. Interestingly, not one of them finished the decade under the same ownership it had had at the beginning. *ASF* was initially the only sf magazine belonging to a pulp chain; when it was sold to another group, STREET & SMITH, in 1933, it was because of the collapse of the whole Clayton chain. The magazine itself had been quite successful, if undistinguished in content; under its new management and new editor F. Orlin TREMAINE it went from strength to strength, its popular success matched by a notable increase in quality. It had the advantage of paying considerably better than its sf competitors (one cent a word on acceptance, rather than half a cent a word on publication or later – "payment on lawsuit" as the saying had it). Even so, *ASF*'s payment rates were only half what they had been in its Clayton days, and represented the lowest standard pulp rates; it was a question of the other sf magazines' paying very badly rather than *ASF*'s paying particularly well. This had obvious repercussions on the quality of the writers prepared to contribute. Authors who could sell their work to *Argosy* for six cents a word were not going to favour the sf magazines with anything other than their rejects. More importantly, the prolific professional pulp writers, turning out hundreds of thousands of words each year in any and every category, never made the sf magazines their chief focus of attention. The adverse result of this was that the sf magazines published a great deal of material by writers ignorant even of the minimal standards of professionalism of the pulp hack (hence Bates's dismay with *AMZ*), but in the longer term the advantage was that the field was able to develop itself from within. Fans of the magazines believed, with justification, that they could do as well as the published writers. They tried; a proportion of them succeeded. Jack WILLIAMSON, an early example of such a writer, describes in *The Early Williamson* (1975) how he received little useful encouragement from Gernsback and Sloane; things changed when *ASF* under Tremaine became the first sf magazine with a dynamic editorial policy. It reaped dividends.

While *ASF* prospered, its competitors floundered, losing their better writers and failing to replace them. By the end of 1933 both *AMZ* and *Wonder Stories* had adopted the standard pulp format. By the end of 1935 both had gone over to bimonthly publication (the same year that *ASF* was contemplating twice-monthly publication). In 1936 *Wonder Stories* was sold, reappearing after a short gap as THRILLING WONDER STORIES with a change of emphasis epitomized by the BEMS (bug-eyed monsters) on the cover of #1; *AMZ* followed suit in 1938.

The failure of the sf magazines to establish themselves as a healthy pulp category in the 1930s is surprising in that, during that decade of the Great Depression, the pulps provided cheap entertainment and were thus generally popular. As a comparison, the far more specialized, peripherally associated field of "weird menace" pulps (as described in *The Shudder Pulps* [1975] by Robert Kenneth Jones) – i.e., magazines devoted entirely to stories in which apparently strange happenings turned out to have mundane explanations – was thriving, with such titles as *Dime Mystery Magazine*, *Horror Stories*, *Terror Tales* and *Thrilling Mystery*. The only sf magazine to establish itself on a regular monthly basis was also the only sf magazine with which Gernsback had never been associated, which suggests that Gernsback's conception of sf, and of sf-magazine publishing, failed to capture the audience it sought. The emphasis of the early sf magazines on MACHINES, as represented by Paul's cover art, may have alienated as many readers as it attracted.

The first boom in sf-magazine publishing came towards the end of the 1930s. In 1938 MARVEL SCIENCE STORIES became the first fully professional new title since *Miracle* in 1931; it gained some notoriety by trying briefly to introduce to sf a little mild lasciviousness of the kind common in other pulps. In 1939 it was followed by a rush of new titles. *AMZ* and *TWS* had both proved successful enough under new management and with a more lively approach to give birth to companion magazines, FANTASTIC ADVENTURES and STARTLING STORIES respectively. John W. CAMPBELL Jr, who had become editor of *ASF* late in 1937, began in 1939 a fantasy companion, UNKNOWN, as well as printing during that year the first stories by Robert A. HEINLEIN, Theodore STURGEON and A.E. VAN VOGT, which heralded the start of *ASF*'s greatest period of dominance. Other new magazines of 1939 were DYNAMIC SCIENCE STORIES, FUTURE FICTION, PLANET STORIES, SCIENCE FICTION, STRANGE STORIES and the reprint magazine FAMOUS FANTASTIC MYSTERIES. In 1940 ASTONISHING STORIES, CAPTAIN FUTURE, COMET, SCIENCE FICTION QUARTERLY, SUPER SCIENCE STORIES and the reprint FANTASTIC NOVELS came along; in 1941 COSMIC STORIES and STIRRING SCIENCE STORIES made their appearance. However, this was not quite the flood it might seem. The economics of magazine publishing meant that when a bimonthly magazine was successful it was often better to start a companion title in the alternate months than to switch to monthly publication. In this way the magazines gained twice as much display space and twice as long a period on sale, while the publisher could hope for an increased share of the total market through product diversification. So *Startling Stories* was paired with *TWS* (although *TWS* went monthly in 1940-41), *Marvel Science Stories* with *Dynamic Science Stories*, *Astonishing Stories* with *Super Science Stories*, *Cosmic Stories* with *Stirring Science Stories* and *Future Fiction* with *Science Fiction*. Never-

theless, much more sf was needed each month, most of it paid for at minimal rates (if at all), and many young sf fans were able to gain invaluable early experience as writers or editors. Asimov, James BLISH, Damon KNIGHT, C.M. KORNBLUTH, Robert A.W. LOWNDES, Frederik POHL and Donald A. WOLLHEIM – all FUTURIANS – launched their careers in this period.

Inevitably, the boom oversaturated the market: some of the new titles published only 2-3 issues. US involvement in WWII, with consequent paper shortages, took its toll of other titles. By the middle of 1944 all but 4 of the new titles had disappeared; nevertheless, these had all established themselves, and for the duration of the 1940s there were 7 regular sf magazines: *AMZ*, *ASF*, *Fantastic Adventures*, *Planet Stories*, *Startling Stories*, *TWS* and *Famous Fantastic Mysteries*, the latter still a reprint magazine. *ASF* was in a different class from the others in terms of both quality and appearance. In 1943 it changed to DIGEST size (approx 5½in x 7½in [14cm x 21.5cm]), anticipating the general trend of the 1950s. Discovering a serious adult readership for sf – and discovering and developing the writers to provide appropriate stories – it changed its appearance until it looked as different as possible from the sf pulps, often seeming deliberately to cultivate a drab look. In the early 1940s *Startling Stories* and *TWS* aimed themselves overtly at a juvenile audience – perhaps recognizing their readership for what it was (although later, under the editorship of Sam MERWIN Jr, the standard soared, until by 1948 *Startling Stories* represented the closest challenge to *ASF*). Their cover art, largely the work of Earle K. BERGEY, typified the drift away from the appeal of futuristic technology – scantily clad girls threatened by monstrous aliens promised more undemanding entertainment, and evidently provided the necessary sales appeal to sustain the enlarged market. *Planet Stories* was more garish still, the epitome of SPACE OPERA. The ZIFF-DAVIS magazines *AMZ* and *Fantastic Adventures* appeared crude, but prospered under the editorship of Raymond A. PALMER. *AMZ*, especially, grew huge (a peak of 274pp in 1942). Palmer showed a shrewd ability to tap the market for occultism and PSEUDO-SCIENCE, using in particular the allegedly factual stories of Richard S. SHAVER to attain for *AMZ* (he claimed) the highest circulation ever reached by an sf magazine.

New magazines began to appear again in 1947-8, although at first they were either reprint-based (AVON FANTASY READER, ARKHAM SAMPLER, the revived FANTASTIC NOVELS) or of only SEMIPROZINE (i.e., semiprofessional) status (FANTASY BOOK). They were followed in 1949 by A. MERRITT'S FANTASY MAGAZINE, the revived *Super Science Stories* and OTHER WORLDS SCIENCE STORIES. However, the significant development of the period was the appearance in 1949 of The MAGAZINE OF FANTASY AND SCIENCE FICTION, followed in 1950 by GALAXY SCIENCE FICTION. Both magazines originated in digest format, and from their inception were aimed at the adult audience which *ASF* had shown existed.

Campbell's *ASF* was by this time showing evidence of stagnation, and both *FSF*, with its emphasis on literary standards, and *Gal*, which concentrated on the SOFT SCIENCES and SATIRE, appeared more sophisticated; they quickly established themselves alongside *ASF*, so that these three became the leading magazines – a situation which, generally speaking, continued until the late 1970s.

New and revived magazines continued to appear in profusion, and to disappear almost as regularly. They included: *Future Combined with Science Fiction Stories*, IMAGINATION, *Marvel*, OUT OF THIS WORLD ADVENTURES, TWO COMPLETE SCIENCE-ADVENTURE BOOKS and WORLDS BEYOND in 1950; IF and *Science Fiction Quarterly* in 1951; DYNAMIC SCIENCE FICTION, FANTASTIC, SCIENCE FICTION ADVENTURES, SPACE SCIENCE FICTION and SPACE STORIES in 1952; BEYOND FANTASY FICTION, FANTASTIC UNIVERSE, FANTASY MAGAZINE, ORIGINAL SCIENCE FICTION STORIES, SCIENCE FICTION PLUS and UNIVERSE SCIENCE FICTION in 1953; IMAGINATIVE TALES in 1954; INFINITY SCIENCE FICTION in 1955; SATELLITE SCIENCE FICTION, SCIENCE FICTION ADVENTURES (the 2nd magazine of this title) and SUPER-SCIENCE FICTION in 1956; and DREAM WORLD, SATURN and VENTURE SCIENCE FICTION in 1957. From this plethora of new titles, the group of magazines ed Robert A.W. Lowndes – *Future*, *Original* and *Science Fiction Quarterly* – managed well for a number of years on tiny budgets; *Fantastic Universe*, *Imagination* and *Imaginative Tales* continued for several years; and *Infinity*, *Satellite* and *Venture* were notable among the shorter-lived magazines. Many other titles came and went after only 1-2 issues, and only *Fantastic* and *If* survived the end of the decade. *Fantastic* was a digest-size companion to *AMZ* and *Fantastic Adventures*. *AMZ* switched to digest size in 1953, at which point *Fantastic Adventures* ceased, although *Fantastic* can be considered as in effect a continuation. *If* would have been another 1950s casualty had not the title been sold in 1958 to Galaxy Publishing Corporation, which wanted a companion for *Gal*.

The new magazines that succeeded were digests; of the 6 1940s pulps only *AMZ* (and, in a sense, *Fantastic Adventures*) survived the change in the publishing industry. The pulp-magazine business in general died in the early 1950s, a victim of increasing distribution problems and of the growing tv industry, which provided a more immediate cheap home entertainment. *Weird Tales* (which had pursued its own course through the 1930s-40s, publishing occasional sf) failed in 1954. *Famous Fantastic Mysteries* ceased in 1953; *TWS*, *Startling Stories* and *Planet Stories* survived until 1955, when they were among the last of all pulp magazines to die.

In the UK, sf magazines had gained less of a foothold before WWII. The first was SCOOPS (1934), a short-lived BOYS' PAPER. This was followed in 1937 by TALES OF WONDER, the most notable early UK magazine, which survived until 1942. The first FANTASY appeared briefly in 1938-9. However, the post-WWII revival started earlier in the UK than in the USA, with the appearance of two magazines in 1946. Walter GILLINGS, editor of the prewar *Tales of Wonder*, now edited the second, equally short-lived FANTASY; NEW WORLDS, under John CARNELL, began in the same year. Both ceased publication in 1947, but *NW* was revived in 1949. In 1950 a companion magazine to *NW*, SCIENCE FANTASY, began under Gillings's editorship. Carnell took over from #3 and continued the magazines successfully through the decade, publishing the early work of such authors as Brian W. ALDISS, J.G. BALLARD and John BRUNNER. In 1958 SCIENCE FICTION ADVENTURES joined these two magazines; initially a reprint of the US title, it continued after its transatlantic parent had died, publishing original stories under Carnell's editorship. Other UK magazines of the 1950s were AUTHENTIC SCIENCE FICTION and NEBULA SCIENCE FICTION; there were also a number of minor titles, such as VARGO STATTEN SCIENCE FICTION MAGAZINE.

Six US magazines continued into the 1960s: *AMZ*, *ASF* (now retitled *Analog*), *Fantastic*, *FSF*, *Gal* and *If*. *AMZ* and *Fantastic* began the decade strongly under the editorship of Cele GOLDSMITH, who raised *AMZ* to a relative prominence which it had not enjoyed since the mid-1930s (although it was still of only secondary interest). In 1965 ZIFF-DAVIS sold *AMZ* and *Fantastic*, and they became reprint magazines, spawning numerous companion titles. Later they began to include original fiction once more, undergoing a resurgence with Ted WHITE's accession to the editorship in 1969. *Analog*, under new management, took on a more modern, glossy appearance – experimenting for a while with a handsome large format – and continued to lead the field in sales. *FSF*, established as the "quality" sf magazine, maintained its reputation through two changes of editor. *Gal* and *If* had a new editor, Frederik POHL, under whom they remained successful; in the mid-1960s *If* concentrated strongly on adventure sf with a popular success that showed itself in 3 consecutive HUGOS (otherwise shared between *Analog* and *FSF*). Later *Gal* and *If* came under the editorship of Ejler JAKOBSSON, who made an unconvincing, gimmicky attempt to "modernize" them. Chief among the few attempts to launch new magazines during the decade, although a great number of reprint titles appeared, were the short-lived GAMMA and another companion to *Gal* and *If*, WORLDS OF TOMORROW. The most significant event for the future of sf magazines was the publication in 1966 of the first volume of Damon Knight's ORBIT series of ORIGINAL ANTHOLOGIES. It was not the first such series – Pohl had edited STAR SCIENCE FICTION STORIES in the 1950s – but it came at a more significant time, when the magazines were suffering increasing problems in distribution and in many cases falling circulations, while the paperback book industry continued to grow strongly. ANTHOLOGY series like **Orbit** – essentially magazines in book format, less frequent, and without some of the readers' departments – could obtain better distribution, would remain on sale for longer periods, could be more selective in their choice of material, and could offer better payment than the majority of sf magazines. In due course **Orbit** was followed by other anthology series – INFINITY, NEW DIMENSIONS, NOVA, QUARK and UNIVERSE – as well as many one-off original anthologies, most notably DANGEROUS VISIONS. It was widely felt that the traditional sf magazine had become an anachronism and in due course would be replaced by the paperback anthology, just as the digest magazines had supplanted the pulps. (In the event the magazines were not supplanted, but both the magazine market and the original-anthology market shrank radically in the 1980s.)

In the UK it all happened rather differently. *NW* and *Science Fantasy* were taken over by a new publisher, Roberts & Vinter, in 1964, and Carnell left. Both magazines now adopted paperback format, although continuing to be marketed as magazines rather than books. *Science Fantasy* went through various changes of editor – and in 1966 of title, to *Impulse* and then *SF Impulse* – before folding in 1967. NW's new editor, Michael MOORCOCK, gradually transformed its outlook, making it more experimental and less bound to the conventions of GENRE SF; it became known as the standard-bearer of the NEW WAVE. In 1967 Moorcock, with Arts Council assistance, took over as publisher of the magazine, changing it to a large (approx 8in x 11½in [A4]) format which allowed for more graphic adventurousness. *NW* encountered moments of controversy and subsequent distribution problems; it was banned by W.H. Smith & Sons, by far the largest retail newsagent chain in the UK. *NW* eventually ceased magazine publication in 1971, though various attempts to revive it in both book and magazine format have taken place sporadically since. Carnell, meanwhile, had begun NEW WRITINGS IN SF, a quarterly original anthology series which predated **Orbit** by two years. In 1969 the short-lived magazine VISION OF TOMORROW appeared.

Between the mid-1970s and 1980 there were several major changes among the established US sf magazines. At the beginning of 1975 *If* was absorbed into *Gal* (which had acquired a new editor, Jim BAEN, in 1974). From the beginning of 1977, *Gal* began to miss issues; it managed to stagger on until Summer 1980. *AMZ* and *Fantastic* suffered slowly dwindling circulations; even produced with minimal staff and budget, they were only just viable. The last separate issue of *Fantastic* came in Oct 1980; thereafter only *AMZ* survived . . . by the skin of its teeth. *FSF* and *Analog* remained stable, *Analog* with by far the greater circulation and, from 1972, a new editor, Ben BOVA, who did much to revive it from the stagnation of the later years of Campbell's reign.

In the UK *NW* reappeared as an irregular paperback series (1971-6), changing editors and publishers along the way. In 1974-6 SCIENCE FICTION MONTHLY was published, a poster-size magazine relying heavily on

the appeal of pages of full-colour art. A projected successor, SF DIGEST, was aborted even before #1 had been distributed.

Despite the predictions that original anthologies would replace magazines, in the USA the 1970s proved a more fertile period for new titles than the previous decade, while several of the anthology series failed. VERTEX, a glossy bedsheet-size magazine, was begun in 1973 and enjoyed success until forced by paper shortages to change to a newsprint format, dying soon after, in 1975. 1976 saw the launch of the short-lived ODYSSEY and the subscription-based semiprozine GALILEO (1976-80). It was at around this time that the semiprozine started making real progress; production costs could be kept low with a small (maybe one-person) operation, so compensating in part for distribution difficulties and consequent low sales. Few lasted long, although besides *Galileo* two – UNEARTH (8 issues 1977-9) and SHAYOL (7 issues 1977-85) – had an influence greater than their small-scale production might suggest. 1977 saw 3 further titles: in the UK VORTEX came and went; in the USA COSMOS SCIENCE FICTION AND FANTASY MAGAZINE and ISAAC ASIMOV'S SCIENCE FICTION MAGAZINE were launched, both on apparently firm foundations. In the event the former lasted only 4 issues, but the latter steadily improved, to overtake all but *Analog* in terms of circulation, and to rival and then perhaps to supersede the big three (*Analog*, *AMZ* and *FSF*) in terms of quality. While *IASFM* was the major success story of the 1970s among the pure-sf magazines, a spectacular development took place in 1978 with the launch of a new science magazine in slick format, OMNI, by the publisher best known previously for the sex magazine *Penthouse*. *Omni*'s circulation, at well over 800,000 in some years, was about 8 times higher than that of any sf magazine, so it was a matter of considerable significance when *Omni* decided at the outset to include some sf stories as part of its mix. This it did with great success: although it published only 20-40 stories annually, these were often of high quality. 1978 also saw the launch of AD ASTRA in the UK; it lasted until 1981. Also in 1978, Jim Baen at ACE BOOKS decided to get the best of both worlds by combining the sf magazine with the original-anthology series, launching DESTINIES, subtitled "The Paperback Magazine of Science Fiction and Speculative Fact", in book format.

By the 1980s it seemed that the magazines were ultimately doomed: they could no longer compete with paperback publishers, video rentals and so on for the consumer's dollar. Through the decade the survivors faced steadily dropping circulations (with occasional fluctuations), and the founding of a new magazine could be seen as an act of insane courage. Nonetheless, new titles did appear. In the UK EXTRO lasted only 3 issues, but INTERZONE, likewise launched in 1982, proved quite another story. Founded by a collective (several members of which worked professionally in sf publishing as critics or editors), it began with the slightly morose air of yet another *NW* clone, with plenty of stories about ravaged societies. But bit by bit it picked up until, a decade later, now under the editorship and ownership of David PRINGLE, it rivals the very best US magazines in terms of quality, although the circulation is still small. In the USA Charles RYAN (who had edited *Galileo*) returned in 1986 with ABORIGINAL SCIENCE FICTION, which continues, though floundering, in the 1990s.

Of possible future significance is the proliferation of desk-top published magazines produced by small groups of enthusiasts and aimed not at the mass market but at a continuing specialist readership. These magazines, partly a result of technological developments having brought home publishing within the financial reach of people who could once not have considered it, provide extremely valuable proving grounds for young writers who then may move elsewhere. Among the more distinguished such titles of the 1980s devoted to publishing fiction have been BACK BRAIN RECLUSE (UK), EIDOLON (Australia), JOURNAL WIRED (US), NEW PATHWAYS (US) and STRANGE PLASMA (US). Many more thus published are critical journals, such as SCIENCE FICTION EYE (US). Other SMALL PRESSES with considerably better financial backing have occasionally moved into the periodical field, notably PULPHOUSE PUBLISHING with first PULP HOUSE: THE HARDBACK MAGAZINE (1988-91) and then its successor, *Pulphouse: A Weekly Magazine*, which in late 1992 was continuing on a monthly basis. This, too, is aimed at a specialist market. In 1992 it was reported that Pulphouse was launching «Tomorrow Speculative Fiction», ed Algis BUDRYS.

By the end of 1991, the only English-language sf magazines with circulations over 20,000 were *Aboriginal SF*, *Analog*, *IASFM*, *FSF* and *Omni*, and only 3 of these topped 70,000: *Analog*, *IASFM* (both sold to Dell in 1992) and *Omni*. All have problems, even *Omni*. When seen in the context of magazine publication generally, sales figures of this order (apart from *Omni*'s) are minuscule, and from the economic point of view sf has long since ceased to be of any importance at all in periodical publishing. These magazines, however, remain absolutely vital to sf's continued health, because it is primarily through them that short sf – which is in a remarkably healthy state at the beginning of the 1990s – remains alive at all. [MJE/PN]

Further reading: The Introduction (◊ page xix) gives an explanation of which sf magazines are given individual entries. Early fantasy magazines and hero/villain pulp magazines with an sf content, such as *The SPIDER*, are separately listed under PULP MAGAZINES, as are general-fiction pulps like *The* BLUE BOOK MAGAZINE. Further information on the publishing of sf in periodical format can be found under BOYS' PAPERS, COMICS, DIME-NOVEL SF, FANZINES, JUVENILE SERIES, SEMI-PROZINES and MAGAZINES; the latter entry lists all general-fiction slicks and tabloids which regularly published sf. An excellent reference on individual sf

and fantasy magazines up to 1984 is *Science Fiction, Fantasy, and Weird Fiction Magazines* (**1985**) ed Marshall B. TYMN and Mike ASHLEY.

SCIENCE FICTION MONTHLY 1. As *Science-Fiction Monthly*, Australian DIGEST-size magazine, 18 numbered undated issues, Aug 1955-Feb 1957, published by Atlas Publications, Melbourne; ed anon Michael Cannon. The fiction, reprinted from various US magazines, was mostly routine, but included some good work by Ray BRADBURY and others. The covers were reprinted from the same sources. A feature from #12 was Graham Stone's column of commentary, **Science Fiction Scene**.

2. Name used by AUTHENTIC SCIENCE FICTION in an early manifestation, May-Aug 1951.

3. UK magazine, tabloid-size (11in x 16in [280mm x 405mm]). 28 monthly issues Feb 1974-May 1976 (2 vols of 12 issues, 1 vol of 4 issues), numbered, undated, published by New English Library; ed Feb 1974-Jan 1975 Pat Hornsey and Feb 1975-May 1976 Julie Davis. Born after the demise of NEW WORLDS, *SFM* – published by a paperback-book company which had a big sf list – was the only UK sf magazine of its time. It featured much full-page colour artwork, often in the form of pull-out posters, in an effort to find a teenage audience similar to that for pop-music magazines. Neither editor had previous experience of sf, and at first the quality of fiction was low, though it improved under Davis's editorship. From the beginning a feature was the number of well researched factual articles, review pages, news pages and interviews, with Mike ASHLEY and Walter GILLINGS regular contributors. Featured UK authors included Robert P. HOLDSTOCK, Bob SHAW, Brian M. STABLEFORD and Ian WATSON; reprints of well known US stories also appeared. The juvenile policy succeeded at first, but circulation dropped from above 100,000 to below 20,000. A plan to replace it with SF DIGEST was aborted. A spin-off book is *The Best of Science Fiction Monthly* (anth **1975**) ed Janet Sacks. [PN/FHP]

SCIENCE FICTION PLUS US BEDSHEET-size magazine. 7 issues Mar-Dec 1953, monthly for 4 months, then bimonthly, published by Hugo GERNSBACK's Gernsback Publications, with Sam MOSKOWITZ as managing ed. This was Gernsback's last venture in the sf field, and attempted to recover something of the flavour of his early pulps, including some Frank R. PAUL covers, but it was a financial failure. Notable stories – there were few – included 2 of Philip José FARMER's early novelettes, "The Biological Revolt" (Mar 1953) and "Strange Compulsion" (Oct 1953), and 2 stories by veteran Harry BATES: "Death of a Sensitive" (May 1953) and "The Triggered Dimension" (Dec 1953). The magazine was well produced, #1-#5 being on slick paper, but an appeal to nostalgia was not enough, and Gernsback retired hurt, complaining in his final editorial that fans had become too highbrow. [BS/PN]

SCIENCE FICTION POETRY ASSOCIATION The SFPA was founded in 1978 by Suzette Haden ELGIN to promote a wide range of POETRY (from sf to horror) through the publication of a bimonthly journal, *Star∗Line*, ed Robert FRAZIER, and the annual presentation of the Rhysling AWARD; Rhysling was the blind poet in "The Green Hills of Earth" (1947) by Robert A. HEINLEIN. [JC]

SCIENCE FICTION PUBLICATIONS ◊ SCIENCE FICTION ADVENTURES.

SCIENCE FICTION QUARTERLY US PULP MAGAZINE. Summer 1940-Spring 1943 (10 issues) and May 1951-Feb 1958 (28 issues), published by Columbia Publications. #1-#2 of the 1st series were ed Charles HORNIG, all others by Robert A.W. LOWNDES.

In its 1st incarnation *SFQ* – a companion to SCIENCE FICTION and FUTURE FICTION – featured a complete novel in every issue, most reprints from varied sources; 5 were by Ray CUMMINGS. Many of the short stories were original, and the magazine, under Lowndes, was an important market for members of the FUTURIANS, notably C.M. KORNBLUTH under various pseudonyms. 2 undated reprint editions of the Summer 1940 and Winter 1941-2 issues were published in the UK in 1943. The 2nd version published a number of notable articles, including the series **Science in Science Fiction** by James BLISH (May 1951-May 1952) and "The Evolution of Science Fiction" by Thomas D. CLARESON (Aug 1953). Notable stories included Blish's "Common Time" (Aug 1953) and Isaac ASIMOV's "The Last Question" (Nov 1956). When *SFQ* died in 1956 it was the last of the sf pulp magazines, and an era had come to an end.

Some stories from series 1 were reprinted in the UK as part of SCIENCE FICTION LIBRARY (a 1960 pocketbook series). Winter 1942 was reprinted as #15 of SWAN AMERICAN MAGAZINE in 1950. 10 numbered undated issues of series 2 were published by Thorpe & Porter in the UK during 1952-5. [BS/PN]

SFRA NEWSLETTER US DIGEST-format magazine, the official newsletter, mostly monthly, of the SCIENCE FICTION RESEARCH ASSOCIATION; founded 1971, current, 198 issues to June 1992, ed Fred Lerner (1971-4), Beverly Friend (1974-8), Roald Tweet (1978-81), Elizabeth Anne Hull (1981-4), Richard W. Miller (1984-7), Robert A. Collins (1987-9), Betsy Harfst (1989-92). Aside from news of specific interest to SFRA's mostly academic members, the newsletter has published much material of general interest, including PILGRIM-AWARD speeches, but is most obviously of use for its book reviews, which, though very intermittent to Aug 1987, became a regular feature from the Sep 1987 issue (#151) onward. Books about sf and fantasy are covered very fully and well; reviews of sf are variable in quality, but still useful. Collected reviews from *SFRAN* form a substantial part of those published in SCIENCE FICTION AND FANTASY BOOK REVIEW ANNUAL (begun 1988), whose editors, Robert A. Collins and Robert Latham, have been stalwarts of *SFRAN*. Other important *SFRAN* contributors have been Neil BARRON and Michael Klossner. From #194, Jan/Feb 1992, the magazine changed its name to *SFRA Review*,

which better describes its function. [PN]

SFRA REVIEW ◊ SFRA NEWSLETTER.

SF REPRISE At the time when both magazines were being published by Roberts & Vinter, some unsold issues of NEW WORLDS and SCIENCE FANTASY were bound up in 2s and 3s and sold as *SF Reprise*, which had 6 numbers: 4 in 1966, 2 in 1967. #1, #2 and #5 were *NW*; #3, #4 and #6 were *Science Fantasy*. [PN]

SCIENCE FICTION RESEARCH ASSOCIATION This group was formed in October 1970 to aid and encourage sf scholarship, especially in the USA and Canada. The first chairman was Thomas D. CLARESON. The organization has acted as a central liaison between academics teaching sf in the USA, though academic affiliation is not a requirement for membership, which can be active, honorary, institutional, student or emeritus. Members receive SFRA NEWSLETTER (retitled *SFRA Review* in 1992) 10 times a year; the annual *SFRA Directory*; and the critical journals EXTRAPOLATION and SCIENCE-FICTION STUDIES. 1977 membership was 330, 1991 membership was 313 – of whom over 50 came from outside the USA – so it has remained much the same size. The SFRA holds an annual conference, usually in June, at which papers are delivered and its annual PILGRIM AWARD for services to sf scholarship and/or criticism is announced. Since 1990 the SFRA has given a second annual award, the Pioneer Award, for best critical essay of the year, the first 2 being won by Veronica Hollinger (1990) and H. Bruce FRANKLIN (1991). Although SFRA was originally envisaged as focusing primarily on sf, it has for some time announced itself as "the oldest professional association for the study of science fiction, fantasy and horror/Gothic literature and film, and utopian studies". [PN]

See also: SF IN THE CLASSROOM.

SCIENCE FICTION REVIEW Variant title of 2 FANZINES – *The* ALIEN CRITIC and PSYCHOTIC – ed Richard E. GEIS. [PN]

SF SERIES ◊ SERIES.

SCIENCE FICTION STORIES ◊ FUTURE FICTION (for the 1943 magazine); *The* ORIGINAL SCIENCE FICTION STORIES (for the 1953-5 magazine).

SCIENCE-FICTION STUDIES Academic journal, published both from the USA and from Canada, founded Spring 1973, current, 57 issues to Mar 1992, 3 issues a year. *S-FS* was co-edited from the outset by R.D. MULLEN and Darko SUVIN, with Mullen also acting as publisher; the magazine was first published from Indiana State University, where Mullen taught. He left at the end of 1978, and in 1979 with #17 the magazine moved to McGill University in Montreal, where it was ed Suvin, Marc Angenot and Robert M. PHILMUS, joined by Charles Elkins with #20 (1980). Suvin's last issue was #22 (1980) and Angenot's #25 (1982). Philmus and Elkins remained in charge until #52, Nov 1990. With #53, 1991, Mullen resumed the editorship along with Philmus, Istvan Csicsery-Ronay, Arthur B. Evans and Veronica Hollinger, Philmus dropping out with #54. *S-FS* returned to

Indiana with #56 (1992), now published at DePauw University.

S-FS is the second youngest of the 4 academic journals about sf (EXTRAPOLATION and FOUNDATION are older, JOURNAL OF THE FANTASTIC IN THE ARTS is younger). It does not normally review contemporary sf, though it runs excellent reviews of books *about* sf. Over the years it has probably published more good, substantial articles on sf than any of its competitors, being especially strong on European sf, on debate about the nature of the genre, on UTOPIAS, on FEMINISM and on POSTMODERNISM, but very patchy on GENRE SF. There have been 2 special issues on Philip K. DICK, 1 on Ursula K. LE GUIN, and sporadic articles on authors like Gregory BENFORD, Pamela SARGENT and William GIBSON, but these are in a minority, so that sometimes *S-FS* gives the impression of looking anywhere rather than at the heart of its subject. Unusually for a US journal, some of its critical material is Marxist-oriented. *S-FS* is a responsible, intellectually robust journal which, while it reflects some of the excesses of academic criticism generally (e.g., too much critical jargon), also reflects its strengths. [PN]

SCIENCE FICTION THEATRE US tv series (1955-7). ZIV/WRCA-TV. Prod Ivan Tors. Hosted by Truman Bradley. Technical adviser Dr Maxwell Smith. 3 seasons, 78 25min episodes. First 2 seasons b/w, last season colour.

This anthology series, presenting a different sf play each week, went out of its way to avoid the sensationalism so prevalent in sf films of the period. The result was prosaic. In 1956 the producer said, revealingly: "One of the traps into which such a series may fall is complete dependence on science for interest. This is avoided at the story conference by excluding the scientists at the start and depending on the writers to come up with a story with human interest . . . After the story is developed it is up to . . . the research people to suggest some scientific fact on which the story can be hung."

Each episode began with dignified Truman Bradley sitting at a desk covered with "scientific" objects (some of which were spinning, or had flashing lights) and introducing the audience to the theme of the story. A typical episode from 1955 involves a hurricane moving towards Miami. A young meteorologist and his wife sit worrying about their son, who is on a camping trip. But, just as the hurricane reaches the shore, a high-pressure area pushes it back again. The sf element in the story consists of the discovery that the hurricane was created by a meteor landing in the sea. [JB]

SCIENCE FICTION TIMES ◊ FANTASY TIMES; GERMANY; HUGO.

SFWA ◊ SCIENCE FICTION WRITERS OF AMERICA.

SCIENCE FICTION WRITERS OF AMERICA A professional guild created to inform sf writers on matters of professional interest, to promote their professional welfare, and to help them deal effectively with publishers, agents, editors and anthologists; in 1992 (see below) renamed the Science Fiction and Fantasy Writers of America (SFFWA). The initial impulse for the SFWA came through discussions and activities at the MILFORD SCIENCE FICTION WRITERS' CONFERENCES, founded by Damon KNIGHT and others; in 1965, feeling the need for a formal body to represent sf writers, Knight founded the SFWA and served as its first president (1965-7). Later presidents have been Robert SILVERBERG (1967-8), Alan E. NOURSE (1968-9), Gordon R. DICKSON (1969-71), James E. GUNN (1971-2), Poul ANDERSON (1972-3), Jerry POURNELLE (1973-4), Frederik POHL (1974-6), Andrew J. OFFUTT (1976-8). Jack WILLIAMSON (1978-80), Norman SPINRAD (1980-82), Marta RANDALL (1982-4; 1st woman president), Charles SHEFFIELD (1984-6), Jane YOLEN (1986-8), Greg BEAR (1988-90), Ben BOVA (1990-92) and Joe HALDEMAN (1992-current). Full or "active" membership is restricted to professional writers – defined as writers who have sold a minimum of 3 short stories or 1 full-length book of fiction (collaborations are acceptable) to a "professional" US market, which excludes journals of less than 12,000 circulation (an exclusion which nullifies work in almost any literary journal). The qualification is one-off; a writer, once he or she has become a member, need never re-qualify.

In addition to its guild activities, the SFWA sponsors the annual NEBULA Awards and the annual anthologies resulting from them. There are, in addition, 2 SFWA journals: *The Bulletin of the Science Fiction and Fantasy Writers of America* (◊ SFWA BULLETIN), which is available to the public; and SFWA FORUM, whose circulation is restricted to active members (and some other categories of membership). As well as the **Nebula** anthologies, the SFWA has been responsible for the *SFWA Handbook*, a writer's guide which has gone through various editions and formats, the most recent (and fullest) incarnation being *Science Fiction Writers of America Handbook: The Professional Writer's Guide to Writing Professionally* (anth **1990**) ed Kristine Kathryn RUSCH and Dean Wesley SMITH, which is packed with information (but lacks an index).

The SFWA membership has been given to polemics, and resignations have been moderately commonplace. One major rift occurred in 1976 when Stanisław LEM's honorary membership was cancelled. Another controversy erupted in 1992, a US election year, when outgoing president Bova unilaterally invited the conservative Republican Newt Gingrich to give the keynote address at the annual Nebula banquet. All the same, although the SFWA has suffered public accusations of parochialism, and although much of its energies in recent years seems to have been devoted to increasingly arcane attempts to revise the already labyrinthine rules governing the Nebula Awards, it has played an important role in improving the conditions of the sf writer's life – by, for example, negotiating with publishers to improve the wording of contracts.

The 1980s witnessed a *de facto* but *ex jure* increase in

the proportion of fantasy and horror writers in the SFWA. At the beginning of 1992 a name change was agreed, and the SFWA became the Science Fiction and Fantasy Writers of America, or SFFWA. [PN/JC] **See also:** PARANOIA.

SFWA BULLETIN A journal, published quarterly, which serves as the official public voice of the former SCIENCE FICTION WRITERS OF AMERICA (since early 1992 the journal's title has been *SFFWA Bulletin*). The *SFWAB* was founded in 1965 and ed 1965-7 by Damon KNIGHT, as part of his activities in founding the SFWA itself. Subsequent editors included Terry CARR (1967-8), Alexei PANSHIN (1968-9), Barry N. MALZBERG (1969-70), George ZEBROWSKI (1970-75), Stephen GOLDIN (1975-7), John F. CARR (1978-80), Richard Kearns (1981-2), Pamela SARGENT with Zebrowski (1983-91), and Daniel Hatch (1991-current). The *SFWAB* – unlike its sister journal, SFWA FORUM, which is restricted to active members – sedulously eschews controversial material. Though at times given over to projects of wider interest (like John F. Carr's 1979 special issue devoted to "Science-Fiction Future Histories") or articles on contract law as it applies to writers, for much of the year it concentrates on matters like the NEBULA. [JC]

SFWA FORUM Privy journal of the SCIENCE FICTION WRITERS OF AMERICA (since early 1992 the journal's name has been *SFFWA Forum*). One of the few publications – perhaps the only one – in the sf world restricted to a designated readership, the *SFWAF* is circulated only to "active" SFWA members (the term "active" being defined by the rules of that guild). Where the SFWA BULLETIN, which is the official public journal of the SFWA, maintains a strict public-relations approach to material, *SFWAF* allows (reportedly) unfettered expressions of opinion – which are (reportedly) not always exhilarating. [JC]

SCIENCE FICTION YEARBOOK ◊ TREASURY OF GREAT SCIENCE FICTION STORIES.

SF YEARBOOK: A TREASURY OF SCIENCE FICTION ◊ TREASURY OF GREAT SCIENCE FICTION STORIES.

SCIENCE STORIES US DIGEST-size magazine. 4 bimonthly issues, Oct 1953-Apr 1954. #1 was published by Bell Publications, Chicago, the rest by Palmer Publications, Evanston; ed Raymond A. PALMER and Bea Mahaffey. *SS* printed no notable fiction, but was nicely illustrated by Hannes BOK, Virgil FINLAY and others. UNIVERSE SCIENCE FICTION, effectively a continuation of OTHER WORLDS, was a companion magazine. Some magazine historians regard *SS* as likewise a (shorter and cheaper) continuation of *Other Worlds*, since it began shortly after *Other Worlds*'s first demise and announced that it was using *Other Worlds*'s inventory of stories, but it was the numeration of *Universe* that *Other Worlds* adopted when *Universe* changed its title back to *Other Worlds* in 1955. [FHP/PN]

SCIENCE WONDER QUARTERLY ◊ WONDER STORIES QUARTERLY.

SCIENCE WONDER STORIES US BEDSHEET-size magazine. 12 monthly issues June 1929-May 1930, published by Stellar Publishing Corp.; ed Hugo GERNSBACK.

After Gernsback lost control of his first fully sf magazine, AMAZING STORIES, in 1929, he rapidly made a comeback with a new company and 2 new magazines, *SWS* and, a month later, AIR WONDER STORIES. "SCIENCE WONDER STORIES are clean, CLEAN from beginning to end. They stimulate only one thing – IMAGINATION," he wrote in the first editorial. His policy, as usual, was to emphasize the didactic aspects of sf, and he claimed that every story had been passed by "an array of authorities and educators". *SWS* dealt with all aspects of science, unlike *Air Wonder Stories*, but in fact they used much the same authors and similar material, and it was logical, after a year, to amalgamate them, as WONDER STORIES. *SWS* was a handsome magazine, all the covers being by Frank R. PAUL. Authors included Miles J. BREUER, Stanton A. COBLENTZ, David H. KELLER (in 10 of the 12 issues), Laurence MANNING, Fletcher PRATT, Harl VINCENT and Jack WILLIAMSON. Raymond Z. GALLUN made his début here. [PN]

SCIENTIFIC DETECTIVE MONTHLY US BEDSHEET-size magazine. 10 monthly issues Jan-Oct 1930, published by Techni-Craft Publishing Co.; ed Hugo GERNSBACK, with Arthur B. REEVE as editorial consultant. #6-#10 were entitled *Amazing Detective Tales*, but *Scientific Detective Monthly* more accurately described the magazine's contents. Most issues included **Craig Kennedy** stories by Arthur B. Reeve and collaborations by Edwin BALMER and William McHarg. A number of stories had sf elements (murder by X-ray, whisky contaminated by hormones), though few were true sf, an exception being "Murder in the Fourth Dimension" in #10, by Clark Ashton SMITH.

SDM was a sister magazine to SCIENCE WONDER STORIES and AIR WONDER STORIES. Another magazine, *Amazing Detective Stories*, was published during 1931 with volume numbering suggesting that it was a continuation of *Amazing Detective Tales*, from a new publisher, Fiction Publishers Inc. This magazine, however, carried no fantasy. [FHP]

SCIENTIFIC ERRORS Scientific errors in sf are not to be confused with IMAGINARY SCIENCE, where the author invents the science and tries to make it plausible, nor with PSEUDO-SCIENCE, where the author adheres to some alternative quasiscientific system unrecognized by the majority of the scientific community. Scientific errors are here taken to mean plain mistakes.

Sf in the days of the PULP MAGAZINES was very much more prone to error than it is now, and it was for the absurdity of so much of the science, at least in part, that pulp sf (particularly in the 1930s) got a bad name; schoolteachers and parents were justifiably worried by its innumeracy as well as its illiteracy. Most sf written since the 1960s will pass scientific muster even with readers who have a little university-level science, but the excesses of the 1920s and 1930s must have been obvious even to many readers who had only a smattering of high-school science. Of course, some elementary errors can be hard to pick up. Hal CLEMENT cites stories in which myopic characters' spectacles are used to concentrate the Sun's rays and light a fire; Clement points out that these would in fact disperse the rays. By contrast, in *The Tomorrow People* (1960) Judith MERRIL used a helicopter for transport on the Moon, even though most schoolboys could have told her that it would not work without air.

Some errors are notorious. When Jules VERNE uses a gun to shoot travellers at the Moon, he ignores the fact that the acceleration would leave them as a thin red smear on the back wall of the cabin. The *canali* or channels which the astronomer Giovanni Schiaparelli (1835-1910) thought he saw on MARS were wrongly translated into English as "canals", and hence Edgar Rice BURROUGHS and many others felt justified in placing intelligent life there.

The history of pulp sf is full of examples of writers using PARSECS as a unit of velocity instead of distance, of confusing weight with mass (so that in space we have heroes able to push several tons of spaceship along with their finger) and, most commonly of all, of exceeding the speed of light without any sort of justification (◊ FASTER THAN LIGHT), as in A.E. VAN VOGT's "The Storm" (1943): "Half a light year a minute; it would take a while to attain that speed, but – in eight hours they'd strike the storm." (The same story has a hero with a second brain which has an IQ of 917, as if somehow the exact figure might mean something.) Certain themes, such as ANTIGRAVITY and ANTIMATTER, have notoriously resulted in schoolboy howlers in much sf. In the pulp era ROCKETS would regularly perform manoeuvres, just like a car doing a U-turn. In fact, as most of us know in the space age, if you use gyros to turn a rocket it will continue in the same direction, *unless* another rocket blast is given in the new orientation to counter the original forward momentum. Nonetheless, STAR WARS (like many cinematic SPACE OPERAS since) has spacecraft taking part in what look like WWI dogfights. John W. CAMPBELL Jr, the man who was supposed to have done more than any other to put the science back in sf, was quite happy to publicize what he called the Dean Drive (*ASF* 1960), a proposed propulsion device which depends on violating the conservation of momentum: it pushes against itself. This is on a par with the "inertialess drive" which propelled E.E. "Doc" SMITH's spaceships at fantastic velocity. Another favourite of the pulps was the electromagnetic spectrum, which was regularly rifled by writers in search of mysterious "rays" which would have almost magical effects. Magnetism was yet another favourite, and all sorts of remarkably cock-eyed schemes were cooked up to exploit its hitherto unknown properties (though here we reach an area of overlap between straightforward scientific errors and imaginary science). An especially enjoyable

biological howler was the notion, common on pulp magazine covers, that aliens would lust after human women, especially if partially unclad, this being on a par with men lusting after squids. Nevertheless, James TIPTREE Jr made rather a good thing out of a similar notion in "And I Awoke and Found Me Here on the Cold Hill's Side" (1972), the ultimate exogamy story. And nearly all stories in the pulps about submicroscopic worlds (◊ GREAT AND SMALL) used a model of the atom – seen as a kind of solid, spherical ball – which had been out of date for at least half a century by 1920. Ray CUMMINGS, several of whose heroes shrink and have adventures on atoms, was a noteworthy offender.

Excesses of this kind still exist, of course, especially in the lowest echelons, but Robert A. HEINLEIN and Isaac ASIMOV did much in the 1940s to bring scientific responsibility to sf, and their work was continued by Poul ANDERSON, James BLISH, Hal CLEMENT, Larry NIVEN and many others. If they committed errors, they mostly did so because they could not resist certain dramatic plot turns, like the end of Poul Anderson's *Tau Zero* (1970), where the crew of a spaceship survive to witness the ultimate collapse of the Universe into the monobloc – despite the fact that, in such a scenario, the *whole* of space would collapse: the very concept of being "outside" the monobloc is a contradiction in terms. Nevertheless, there are still novels being published which would not put the pulps to shame. *Battlefield Earth* (1982) by L. Ron HUBBARD was a classic example, containing such lunacies as invading aliens who are said to come from a part of the Universe whose Periodic Table contains elements different from the ones we have here.

Sf in the CINEMA and on TELEVISION, moreover, is generally still about as scientifically illiterate as was pulp sf of the 1930s. SPACE 1999 was a particularly bad offender. Bob SHAW has several times expressed amazement at the way that in STAR TREK, when the *Enterprise* is buffeted about (as it frequently is), the crew are invariably thrown from their seats. Why, asks Shaw, in this supertechnological future, has the concept of seat-belts been forgotten? A particularly irritating error, almost invariable in film and tv, is the audibility of explosions in space (as in *Star Wars* and BATTLESTAR GALACTICA); it is apparently believed that, if the audience can't hear the bangs, they'll all go home or change channels. TOTAL RECALL (1990) showed that things had not got much better, with at least two notable howlers. The first is the idea that, if you puncture a stationary pressurized dome, normal air pressure will be sufficient to produce hurricane winds that whip people and furniture out through the hole. (People do get sucked out of aeroplanes, but only because they are moving at 600mph.) Even stranger was the notion that oxygen deprivation and near vacuum give people eyes the size of tangerines, a phenomenon they can sustain for some minutes without suffering damage.

MONSTER MOVIES very often depend on giant ants, spiders, etc. In fact, such creatures could not exist; they would collapse under their own weight, not having legs, like the elephant's, designed to prop them up. Many problems arise with increases in scale, one of them being that the ratio between skin area and internal capacity does not stay the same, hence throwing the physiology of the body completely askew. Flying men are probably impossible, though Poul Anderson made a valiant attempt to rationalize them scientifically in *War of the Wing-Men* (**1958**; rev vt *The Man who Counts* 1978), greatly increasing their lung capacity and incorporating other necessary design changes.

Errors in sf are less common in the SOFT SCIENCES, perhaps because these are subject to less rigorous laws, but nonetheless absurdities do occur. It is commonly supposed that, if we had telepathy, we could understand aliens by bypassing language; however, there is strong evidence that we actually *think* in language, in which case telepathy probably would not work efficiently between different nationalities, let alone between us and the Rigelians. Brainwashing, and mental conditioning generally, are in sf usually based on Pavlov's behavioural psychology rather than on B.F. SKINNER's; that is, carried out through aversion and punishment, not through reward, even though the latter system has been amply demonstrated to be more efficient, and presents, perhaps, moral issues of a more subtle and interesting kind. [PN/JS]

SCIENTIFIC ROMANCE The most common generic term applied to UK sf in the years before the end of WWII, at which time the "science fiction" label became sufficiently commonplace to displace it; for several decades thereafter, the styles and concerns of US GENRE SF dominated. C.H. HINTON issued 2 series of *Scientific Romances* (colls **1886** and **1898**) mixing speculative essays and stories, and the term was widely applied by reviewers and essayists to the early novels of H.G. WELLS, which became the key exemplars of the genre. When listing his titles Wells usually lumped his sf and fantasy novels together as "fantastic and imaginative romances", but he eventually chose to label the collection of his best-known sf novels *The Scientific Romances of H.G. Wells* (omni **1933**), thus securing the term's definitive status. Brian M. STABLEFORD has recently revived the term in order to facilitate the comparison and contrast of the distinct UK and US traditions of speculative fiction; his study of the UK genre's separate evolution before the triumph of genre sf is *Scientific Romance in Britain 1890-1950* (**1985**). In that book, and in entries throughout this encyclopedia (*see in particular* EVOLUTION, RELIGION), the term can be seen as tending to describe works characterized by long evolutionary perspectives; by an absence of much sense of the frontier and a scarcity of the kind of PULP-MAGAZINE-derived HERO who is designed to penetrate any frontier available; and in general by a tone moder-

ately less hopeful about the future than that typical of genre sf until recent decades (◊ OPTIMISM AND PESSIMISM).

A few modern writers have found the term a convenient rubric for offbeat works; examples include Christopher PRIEST for *The Space Machine* (**1976**) and Kim Stanley ROBINSON for *The Memory of Whiteness* (**1985**). [BS]

SCIENTIFICTION 1. Term coined by Hugo GERNSBACK as a contraction of "scientific fiction" and defined by him in the first issue of AMAZING STORIES in Apr 1926 (◊ DEFINITIONS OF SF). It never became very popular, and within a decade of its coining was largely replaced by "science fiction". When used now it usually refers to the awkward, technology-oriented fiction published by Gernsback or, disparagingly, to modern equivalents. Attempts to re-establish the term in a positive sense have failed.

2. Fanzine (1937-8). ◊ FANTASY REVIEW. [PN]

SCIENTISTS Scientists in pre-20th-century sf often exhibited symptoms of social maladjustment, sometimes to the point of insanity; they were characteristically obsessive and antisocial. Some scientists were quasidiabolical figures, like Coppelius in E.T.A. HOFFMANN's "The Sandman" (1816) or Mary SHELLEY's eponymous *Frankenstein, or The Modern Prometheus* (**1818**; rev 1831); others were ridiculous, like those in the third book of Jonathan SWIFT's *Gulliver's Travels* (**1726**). In Honoré de BALZAC's *La recherche de l'absolu* (**1834**; 1st trans as *The Philosopher's Stone* **1844** US) scientific research becomes an unholy addiction. Such stories make it clear that the scientist had inherited the mantle (and the public image) of medieval alchemists, astrologers and sorcerers, and certain aspects of this image proved extraordinarily persistent; its vestiges remain even today, with sciencefictional alchemical romances still featuring in the work of authors like Charles L. HARNESS. The founding fathers of sf, Jules VERNE (Nemo and Robur) and H.G. WELLS (Moreau, Griffin and Cavor), frequently represented scientists as eccentric and obsessive; Robert Louis STEVENSON's Dr Jekyll is cast from the same anxious mould, as is Maurice RENARD's Dr Lerne; and Arthur Conan DOYLE's Professor Challenger is not so very different. A detailed analysis of the process of scientific creativity as a species of madness is presented in J.S. FLETCHER's *Morrison's Machine* (**1900**).

By the end of the 19th century, however, other images of the scientist were beginning to appear. The US public made a hero of Thomas Alva Edison (1847-1931), and this admiration for the clever inventor is reflected in much popular fiction (◊ EDISONADE). The great man himself is featured in VILLIERS DE L'ISLE-ADAM's *L'Ève Future* (**1886**) and Garrett P. SERVISS's *Edison's Conquest of Mars* (1898; **1947**), and a DIME-NOVEL SF series featured **Tom Edison Jr.** Other scientists who attracted hero-worship included Louis Pasteur (1822-1895) and Albert Einstein (1879-1955), although Einstein's ideas were so non-commonsensical that they were accepted by many as a proof of the oddity of scientists. One wholehearted hero-worshipper of scientists was Hugo GERNSBACK, and he gave voice to this sentiment in *Ralph 124C 41+* (1911-12 *Modern Electrics*; **1925**). The scientist-as-HERO thus entered pulp sf at its very inception, alongside the eccentric genius – although many of the heroic scientists of pulp sf were simply stock pulp heroes with scientific prowess improbably grafted on: E.E. "Doc" SMITH's Richard Seaton is a cardinal example. Scientists in the early sf pulps were often eccentric and absentminded, and the demands of melodrama required many to turn their hands to criminal enterprises, but they were rarely outright nuts, after the fashion of such cinematic figures as the title-characters of DOCTOR X (1932) and DR CYCLOPS (1940) and such non-genre arch-villains as Dr Munsker in *The Devil's Highway* (**1932**) by Harold Bell WRIGHT and John Lebar.

As pulp sf matured there was a significant shift in the characterization of the scientist hero. Especially in ASTOUNDING SCIENCE-FICTION, the role of the theoretical genius was de-emphasized relative to that of the practical-minded engineer; archetypal examples of this species were the personnel of George O. SMITH's *Venus Equilateral* (coll **1947**), forever scribbling equations and designs on the tablecloths in Joe's Bar. The presumed essence of real genius remained as wayward as ever, however: Henry KUTTNER's inventor Galloway Gallegher always made his marvellous machines while blind drunk and could never remember afterwards how he had done it. Hero-worship of the scientific genius was further extended by Isaac ASIMOV, whose **Foundation** series was the first notable work to elevate a social scientist to that status. Outside the sf magazines, a more realistic image of the work and social situation of the scientist was depicted in E.C. LARGE's cynical *Sugar in the Air* (**1937**), which features a visionary and idealistic scientist at odds with his stupid and irrational employers. In the post-WWII decade this kind of image became much more common – notably in several novels by Edward HYAMS, including *Not in Our Stars* (**1949**), and in many magazine stories.

Genre-sf writers mostly responded to the widespread popular opinion that TECHNOLOGY had got out of hand by putting the blame on machine-*users* rather than machine-*makers*, claiming that it was not mad scientists but mad generals and mad politicians who were the problem; nuclear scientists were often represented as isolated paragons of sanity locked into a political and military matrix that threatened the destruction of the world (◊ NUCLEAR POWER). The US security clampdown of the 1950s emphasized the new social situation of the scientist and provoked a wave of sf stories dealing with the morality of carrying out research which had potential military applications, and with the difficulty of making scientific discoveries in such circumstances. An effective vignette dealing with the conscience of the

scientist who watches his discoveries in action is C.M. KORNBLUTH's "The Altar at Midnight" (1952); the most dramatic depiction of the conflict between scientific interests and military security is Algis BUDRYS's *Who?* (**1958**). Later tales of scientists in conflict with the demands made by society include Theodore STURGEON's "Slow Sculpture" (1970), Bob SHAW's *Ground Zero Man* (**1971**), D.G. COMPTON's *The Steel Crocodile* (**1970** US; vt *The Electric Crocodile* 1970 UK) and James P. HOGAN's *The Genesis Machine* (**1978**). Non-genre writers continued to have less sympathy with scientists; irresponsible or outrightly mad scientists continued to appear in some profusion – notable examples include Peter GEORGE's Dr Strangelove in DR STRANGELOVE: OR HOW I LEARNED TO STOP WORRYING AND LOVE THE BOMB (1963) and Felix Hoenikker in Kurt VONNEGUT Jr's *Cat's Cradle* (**1963**). Outside the protective walls of the sf genre these sinister figures easily outnumbered scientists credited with the noblest of ideals and motives; Pierre BOULLE's *Garden on the Moon* (**1965**), which shows German rocket scientists thinking only of the Moon and SPACE FLIGHT while working on the V2, is a vivid exception. The advent of technologies like GENETIC ENGINEERING has helped sustain the routine demonization of scientists in films and horror stories.

In modern sf, scientists have become rather less common, at least as major characters. Writers who are not scientists themselves have become increasingly wary of the difficulties involved in presenting a convincing picture of scientists at work in the laboratory. Sf writers who *are* scientists are far more ready to accept the challenge – see *Great Science Fiction by Scientists* (anth **1962**) ed Groff CONKLIN and *The Expert Dreamers* (anth **1962**) ed Frederik POHL – and the fictions of many science-trained writers are regularly featured in the pages of *Analog*. But even they often find it difficult to picture the kinds of equipment which will fill the laboratories of the future, and the kinds of work which will be done there. Scientists who have written notable sf about the scientists of the future include Gregory BENFORD, David BRIN, Paul DAVIES, Robert L. FORWARD, Fred HOYLE and Philip LATHAM. Many Eastern European writers are practising scientists. (Communist sf characteristically put forward a determinedly positive image of scientists and their endeavours, although there are some very uneasy compromises with this orthodoxy in the work of Arkady and Boris STRUGATSKI.) Many writers of HARD SF are also popular-science writers of note, and they too have useful expertise which they can and do deploy in their fiction; notable examples include Isaac Asimov, Arthur C. CLARKE and John GRIBBIN.

The most effective picture of near-contemporary scientists at work in recent sf is probably Gregory Benford's *Timescape* (**1980**); other notable examples are Kate WILHELM's *The Clewiston Test* (**1976**), Hilbert SCHENCK's *A Rose for Armageddon* (**1982**), Paul PREUSS's *Broken Symmetries* (**1983**) and Jack MCDEVITT's *The Hercules Text* (**1986**). The most memorable attempt at characterizing a scientific genius in recent years is Ursula K. LE GUIN's Shevek in *The Dispossessed* (**1974**); there are several charming but less earnest portraits in the work of Vadim SHEFNER.

A useful article (with a bibliography listing various earlier sources) on the theme is "Scientists in Science Fiction: Enlightenment and After" by Patrick PARRINDER in *Science Fiction: Roots and Branches* (**1990**) ed Rhys Garnett and R.J. Ellis.   [BS]

SCIENTOLOGY In its early years Scientology was known as DIANETICS (*which see for details*), a term still used within Scientology. The word "Scientology" was coined in 1952 by L. Ron HUBBARD, its founder; 2 of his books on the subject are *This is Scientology: The Science of Certainty* (**1955** UK) and *Scientology: The Fundamentals of Thought* (**1956** UK).

The activities of the Scientologists have evolved in many curious and highly publicized ways since 1952. A lively account by a not wholly unsympathetic outsider can be found in *Cults of Unreason* (**1973**) by Dr Christopher Evans (1931-1979), but there have been several more critical studies since then, both of the movement and of its founder, notably *L. Ron Hubbard: Messiah or Madman?* (**1987**) by Bent Corydon and L. Ron Hubbard Jr a.k.a. Ronald DeWolf, and *Bare-Faced Messiah: The True Story of L. Ron Hubbard* (**1987**) by Russell Miller, both the subject of legal action by the various corporate groups associated with the Church of Scientology.

Scientology, originally a form of psychotherapy with many PSEUDO-SCIENCE overtones, became what has been described as the first sf RELIGION, when the Founding Church of Scientology was incorporated in Washington DC in July 1955. Sceptical commentators saw this as no more than a crafty tax dodge, but in fact Scientology had from the beginning many of the qualities of a genuine religion, and certainly aroused a religious fervour among its adherents. (In 1992 it was announced that an arm of the Church of Scientology, the Church of Spiritual Technology, was building an underground crypt to house "the religious works of L. Ron Hubbard and other key religious works of mankind".)

Hubbard extended Scientology overseas quite early, opening centres in Australia and South Africa in 1953, and himself moving to the UK in 1955. A bad setback was the result of the Board of Inquiry set up in the state of Victoria, Australia, in 1963; the melodramatic Anderson report of 1965, having examined 151 witnesses, concluded that "Scientology is evil; its techniques are evil; its practice a serious threat to the community, medically, morally and socially; and its adherents sadly deluded and often mentally ill", and Scientology was banned in Victoria. A later disaster was the deportation of L. Ron Hubbard from the UK as an undesirable alien in 1968. Scientology was then directed from the ships of Hubbard's fleet, usually found in the Mediterranean, until in 1975 Hubbard returned to the USA. In 1978 he was found guilty in Paris of obtaining money under false pretences through Scientology, and sentenced *in absentia* to 4 years' imprisonment.

Scientology and Hubbard had lost some ground, but the movement continued to attract members, and Hubbard himself was the subject of an enormous publicity boost when the Scientology publishers, Bridge Publications, reissued in 1984 Hubbard's novel *Battlefield Earth* (**1982**), originally published by a mainstream publisher, St Martin's Press, and followed it with an sf "dekalogy", the 10-vol **Mission Earth** saga by Hubbard (**1983-7**; later vols posthumous); these were heavily and expensively promoted. Around this time Hubbard had also founded and sponsored the WRITERS OF THE FUTURE CONTEST, good entrants to which were published in the L. RON HUBBARD PRESENTS WRITERS OF THE FUTURE series of original anthologies, #1 being in 1985. All of this did something to re-establish Hubbard (who had been discredited in the eyes of some observers) as an important figure in the sf community, and something of a philanthropist, though his own writings, and the literary contests and workshops, became controversial themselves; the sf community was deeply divided as to the merit of the latter, and Hubbard's own sf books of the 1980s are seldom highly regarded.

Hubbard's role remains enigmatic; some saw him as a cynic, the founder of an organization calculated to bring in an income of many millions of dollars, which it did. This is almost certainly too simplistic a view, though the opposing view – that he was a man of genuine if eccentric vision, totally convinced of the truth of his case, and fighting valiantly against the powerful conspiracy of orthodox psychiatry – may also be less than the full story.

Scientology is the most dramatic example of the precepts of pulp sf being put into practice in the real world. One regular attraction of pulp sf, as witness Hubbard's own stories and those of his one-time colleague A.E. VAN VOGT, was its dramatization of the idea that inside us there may be a SUPERMAN struggling to get out. The glowing promise held out by scientologists is that this dream can be realized.   [PN]

SCI FI Pronounced "sky fi" or "si fi", an abbreviation for "science fiction", said to have been introduced by Forrest J. ACKERMAN, a prominent fan fond of wordplay, in the 1950s, when the term "hi-fi" was becoming popular. Never much used within the sf community, the term became very popular with journalists and media people generally, until by the 1970s it was the most common abbreviation used by nonreaders of sf to refer to the genre, often with an implied sneer. Some critics within the genre, Terry CARR and Damon KNIGHT among them, decided that, since the term was derogatory, it might be critically useful in distinguishing sf hack-work – particularly ill written, lurid adventure stories – from sf of a more intellectually demanding kind. Around 1978 the critic Susan WOOD and others began pronouncing the term "skiffy". In 1980s-90s usage "skiffy", which sounds friendlier than "sci fi", has perhaps for that reason come to be less condemnatory. Skiffy is colourful, sometimes entertaining, junk sf: STAR WARS is skiffy. [PN]

SCION PUBLICATIONS ◊ VARGO STATTEN SCIENCE FICTION MAGAZINE.

SCITHERS, GEORGE H(ARRY) (1929-) US writer, editor, publisher and military engineer (with the US Army 1946-73). He began publishing fiction of genre interest with "Faithful Messenger" for *If* in 1969, and wrote a spoof cookery book (suggested by Damon KNIGHT's famous 1950 story), *To Serve Man* (1976) as Karl Würf; but his main sf activities have been as an editor and publisher. He began his active involvement in 1959 with sf and fantasy as editor of the famous FANZINE *Amra*; *Amra*, still appearing on an irregular basis, specializes in SWORD AND SORCERY, particularly the work of Robert E. HOWARD; it won HUGOS in 1964 and 1968. GHS published 2 anthologies drawn from it: *The Conan Swordbook* (anth 1969) and *The Conan Grimoire* (anth 1972), both with L. Sprague DE CAMP, cofounder with him of the Hyborean Legion, a group devoted to Howard studies; earlier, De Camp alone had been responsible for the Amra-derived *The Conan Reader* (anth 1968). In 1973 GHS founded the Owlswick Press (◊ SMALL PRESSES AND LIMITED EDITIONS), which continues successfully to publish sf and other material.

GHS became the founding editor of ISAAC ASIMOV'S SCIENCE FICTION MAGAZINE in 1977; it was the first sf magazine since the beginning of the 1950s to establish itself as a dominant force; he continued as editor until the beginning of 1982, also editing several anthologies drawn from it (see listing below) and winning Hugos for Best Professional Editor in 1979 and 1980. He then edited the troubled AMAZING STORIES from late 1982 until 1986; more recently, with John BETANCOURT (until 1990) and Darrell SCHWEITZER, who had been assistant editor of both *IASFM* and *AMZ* during GHS's tenures, he restarted WEIRD TALES, which had been variously (but unfruitfully) revived more than once since ceasing regular publication in 1954; the new series (the numbering is continuous over all incarnations) began with #290 in 1987, and continues, with all but the most recent edited by all three (each taking the lead role in turn); #300 was ed Schweitzer alone. Also with Schweitzer, GHS ed 2 anthologies of CLUB STORIES: *Tales from the Spaceport Bar* (anth 1987) and *Another Round at the Spaceport Bar* (anth 1989). In all his projects, which are very various, GHS has managed to combine energy-efficient verve with a transparent love of fantasy and sf. [JC]

Other works: *On Writing Science Fiction (The Editors Strike Back!)* (1981) with John M. FORD and Schweitzer; *Constructing Scientifiction & Fantasy* (1982) with John Ashmead and Schweitzer.

As editor: *Astronauts and Androids* (anth 1977); *Black Holes and Bug Eyed Monsters* (anth 1977); *Masters of Science Fiction* (anth 1978); *Comets and Computers* (anth 1978); *Dark Stars and Dragons* (anth 1978); *Marvels of Science Fiction, Vol 2* (anth 1979); *Science Fiction Anthology, #3* (anth 1979), *#4* (anth 1980) and *#5* (anth 1981), anthologies from *IASFM*; *Near Futures and Far* (anth 1981).

SCOOPS UK BEDSHEET-size magazine, 20 issues 10 Feb-23 June 1934, published by C.A. Pearson Ltd, London; ed Hadyn Dimmock. *S* was intended as a weekly BOYS' PAPER that would "transport its readers from the everyday happenings into the future"; whatever appeal it might have had for adults was not helped by the decision to use, mostly, writers of ordinary boys' adventure fiction – Dimmock was also editor of *The Scout*. There was not much material by real sf writers, exceptions being A.M. LOW, with the serial "Space" (1934; vt *Adrift in the Stratosphere* 1937), a reprint serialization of *The Poison Belt* (1913) by Sir Arthur Conan DOYLE, and stories by Maurice Hugi and John Russell FEARN. Another serial was "The Black Vultures" by George E. Rochester (c1895-c1985). All issues are now collector's items. *S* was the first UK sf magazine, and not a very good one. 5 tales from it, along with 8 new stories, were later assembled as *The Boys' World of Adventure* (anth 1937) ed anon. [FHP/PN]

SCORPION, THE US PULP MAGAZINE. 1 issue, Apr 1939, published by Popular Publications; ed Rogers Terrill. *TS* was in every respect a sequel to *The* OCTOPUS; only the alias of the villainous protagonist being changed. The sadistic, borderline-sf feature novel, "Satan's Incubator" by Randolph Craig (Norvell W. PAGE), was reprinted by Robert E. WEINBERG as *Pulp Classics #12: The Scorpion* (1976 chap). [MJE/FHP]

SCORTIA, THOMAS N(ICHOLAS) (1926-1986) US writer and chemist, active in solid-propellant research in the aerospace industry during the 1960s before becoming a full-time writer in 1970. He had already been publishing craftsmanlike stories for some time, beginning with "The Prodigy" for *Science Fiction Adventures* in 1954. He assembled some of his better work in *Caution! Inflammable!* (coll 1975); a more definitive conspectus is *The Best of Thomas N. Scortia* (coll 1981) ed George ZEBROWSKI. It has been argued that TNS was at his best in short forms, where his sustained interestingness as a producer of ideas and situations took sometimes bravura shape; and there is little doubt that his first novel, *What Mad Oracle?: A Novel of the World as It Is* (1961), concerning the aerospace industry, lumbered through its material without much verve. After 1970, however, as his production started to increase, TNS began to seem destined for a very substantial career. *Artery of Fire* (1960 *Original Science Fiction Stories*; exp 1972), about the construction of a huge power network, and *Earthwreck!* (1974), set in space after a nuclear HOLOCAUST has extinguished the human species on its home planet, were both intriguing tales, scientifically numerate and competently commercial.

He then shifted, however, into collaborative enterprises, mainly a series of popular TECHNOTHRILLERS with Frank M. ROBINSON; though successful in their own terms, these exhibited little of the creative daring

TNS had always threatened to exploit more fully. They are *The Glass Inferno* (**1974**) – which along with Richard Martin Stern's *The Tower* (**1973**) was filmed as *The Towering Inferno* (1974) – *The Prometheus Crisis* (**1975**), *The Nightmare Factor* (**1978**), *The Gold Crew* (**1980**) and – completed by Robinson after TNS died – *Blow Out!* (**1987**). TNS's death was reported as being from leukemia induced by exposure to radiation as an observer at early nuclear tests, and came just after he had announced new solo projects. [JC]

As editor: *Strange Bedfellows: Sex and Science Fiction* (anth **1972**); *Two Views of Wonder* (anth **1973**) with Chelsea Quinn YARBRO; *Human-Machines* (anth **1975**) with Zebrowski.

See also: CYBORGS; IMMORTALITY; SEX; SPACESHIPS.

SCOT, MICHAEL ◊ Michael Scott ROHAN; Allan SCOTT.

SCOTT, ALAN (1947-   ) UK writer whose sf novel, *Project Dracula* (**1971**; vt *Anthrax Mutation* 1976 US), depicts an explosion in a space station which sprays anthrax spores in dangerous directions. [JC]

SCOTT, ALLAN (JAMES JULIUS) (1952-   ) UK writer of fantasy novels, the first being *The Ice King* (**1986**; vt *Burial Rites* 1987 US) with Michael Scott ROHAN, both writing as Michael Scot; a second collaboration with Rohan, *A Spell of Empire: The Horns of Tartarus* (**1992**), was published under their real names. Solo, AS has written a further fantasy, *The Dragon in the Stone* (**1991**). [JC]

SCOTT, G. FIRTH [r] ◊ AUSTRALIA.

SCOTT, JEREMY ◊ Kay DICK.

SCOTT, J.M. [r] ◊ Robert THEOBALD.

SCOTT, JODY (HUGUELET WOOD) (1923-   ) UK-born US writer whose 2 sf novels, *Passing for Human* (**1977**) and *I, Vampire* (**1984**), comprise a joyously and at times scatologically tangled SATIRE of the post-industrial Western world from a FEMINIST point of view that wittily verges on misandry. The 2nd vol – whose protagonist, the female vampire Sterling O'Blivion, is only intermittently relevant to the action – ends in a state of violent confusion after a love affair between O'Blivion and an ALIEN who closely resembles Virginia Woolf (1882-1941), though a central message does remain: an arraignment of exploitation (or vampirism), whether on the part of slave-trading aliens, Earth-bound capitalists, men or women. [JC]

See also: SUPERNATURAL CREATURES.

SCOTT, MELISSA (?   -   ) US writer who began publishing sf with her first novel, *The Game Beyond* (**1984**), a SPACE OPERA of some resonance which uses analogies with the Roman Empire – familiar since the early **Foundation** stories (**1951-3**) of Isaac ASIMOV – with considerable skill. In 1986 she won the JOHN W. CAMPBELL AWARD for Best New Writer, at least in part for *Five-Twelfths of Heaven* (**1986**), #1 in her **Silence Leigh** sequence, which continues with *Silence in Solitude* (**1986**) and *The Empress of Earth* (**1987**), all 3 assembled as *The Roads of Heaven* (omni **1988**). As with her first novel, these adventures of aspiring space-pilot Silence Leigh capably marshal echoes of Earth – in this case alchemy and astrological symbols – to enrich space-opera routines, including several close calls with various enemies, a patch of slavery and an ongoing quarrel with an inimical Empire. The main weakness lies in MS's attempts to impose FEMINIST arguments upon a traditionally conceived venue without seeming to think their implications through in that context; the main strengths, perhaps, lie in the power of the main characters' longing to find old Earth and in the ironies attendant upon their eventual success. *The Kindly Ones* (**1987**), whose title and plot evoke Aeschylus's **Oresteia** trilogy (**458BC**), specifically its third play, *Eumenides*, in an interstellar setting, competently depicts a cruelly rigid society in a Solar System of some interest. *Dreamships* (**1992**) sets an AI on a FASTER-THAN-LIGHT ship, and very competently examines the nature of a sentience slaved to travel the stars. [JC]

Other works: *A Choice of Destinies* (**1986**); *The Armor of Light* (**1988**) with Lisa A. Barnett; *Mighty Good Road* (**1990**).

SCOTT, PEG O'NEILL and PETER T. [r] ◊ Barton WERPER.

SCOTT, RIDLEY (1939-   ) UK film-maker who has worked mostly in the USA. After making a name with a series of stylish, inventive tv commercials, RS made his feature début with *The Duellists* (1977), a period film adapted from a story by Joseph CONRAD. He then went on to direct 2 of the most influential and important sf films of the last 15 years: ALIEN (1979) and BLADE RUNNER (1982), the latter an adaption of Philip K. DICK's *Do Androids Dream of Electric Sheep?* (**1968**). RS is a visionary, at least in terms of production design, and both his sf films conjure up a detailed and utterly convincing future (whose style RS later recycled in tv advertisements for a bank); *Blade Runner* is particularly powerful in its design, and proved an influence on the CYBERPUNK movement. However, after these films RS vanished into the (comparatively well publicized) limbo of *Legend* (1985), a fairy tale resembling a feature-length advertisement for hairspray. He made a tentative commercial comeback with *Someone to Watch Over Me* (1987) and *Black Rain* (1989), both *policiers* whose content was more conventional than their style. RS's films are mostly underconceived on a script and character level, and thus can appear cold. He had a big, if controversial, success, however, with the effective and satisfying *Thelma and Louise* (1991), a female road movie about two women escaping routine and put-upon lives and revenging themselves against various forms of sexism; it and the 2 sf films are RS's best work.

RS's brother Tony Scott has directed one borderline-sf film about vampires – *The Hunger* (1983) – whose exotic visual qualities fail to eclipse its narrative failings, rather as in RS's own lesser films. [KN/PN]

See also: CINEMA; HORROR IN SF; MONSTER MOVIES.

SCOTT, ROBIN [s] ◊ Robin Scott WILSON.

SCOTT, WARWICK ◊ Elleston TREVOR.

SCRAP BOOK, THE US PULP MAGAZINE published monthly Mar 1906-Jan 1912 by the Frank A. MUNSEY Corp.; ed Perley Poore Sheehan. *TSB* was published in 2 separate sections from July 1907, the first containing articles, the second fiction. The second section became *The* CAVALIER from Sep 1908, the first continuing as *SB*, with some fiction content, until merging with *The Cavalier* to form *The Cavalier Weekly*.

SB began as a reprint magazine, often featuring classic weird fiction. Later it published original stories, including some sf, notably Julian Johnson's "When Science Warred" (1907), George Allan ENGLAND's "The House of Transformation" (Sep-Nov 1909) and Garrett P. SERVISS's "The Sky Pirate" (Apr-Sep 1909).   [JE]

SCREAM AND SCREAM AGAIN Film (1969). Amicus/AIP. Dir Gordon Hessler, starring Vincent Price, Christopher Lee, Alfred Marks, Michael Gothard. Screenplay Christopher Wicking, based on *The Disorientated Man* (1966; vt *Scream and Scream Again* 1967 US) by Peter SAXON. 94 mins. Colour.

This blend of *policier*, cold-war political thriller, FRANKENSTEIN and vampire movie, initially ignored, was later seen by some cinéastes as one of the major UK sf films. An enjoyable farrago, it does have moments of distinction, but its silliness gets in the way: the opening sequence – a hospital patient is understandably upset to find that each day he is missing yet another limb – could be a sketch from the **Monty Python** tv series. Nowhere is it explained why mad SCIENTISTS (the main one played by Price) need to construct a super-race (which they do using stolen body parts), why the constructed beings are so incredibly strong, why they suck blood and murder people, and why this makes them good prime-ministerial material. Marks's energetically down-to-earth performance as the baffled police inspector almost saves the film, but *SASA* works only as a (literally) disjointed series of paranoid surreal nightmares – and, even then, poor production values and mostly indifferent performances are as likely to elicit laughter as horror. The radical subtext – our political masters are literally MONSTERS – had been better done elsewhere; e.g., QUATERMASS II (1957; vt *Enemy from Space*).   [PN]

SCREAMERS ◊ *L'*ISOLA DEGLI UOMINI PESCE.

SCRYMSOUR, ELLA M. (1888-?   ) UK writer whose remarkable *The Perfect World: A Romance of Strange People and Strange Places* (fixup **1922**) is thought by E.F. BLEILER almost certainly to consist of 2 separate magazine novels here published sequentially; however, as EMS clearly attempted to weave their plots together, we designate the outcome a FIXUP. In the first main sequence the two young gentlemen protagonists are transported from a company town dominated by their family coalmine into an underground cave system populated by theocratic relics of an Old Testament quarrel; after they finally emerge in Australia and note that the world is about to blow up, they travel with their inventor uncle to JUPITER, where a similar oligarchy, this time pre-Adamic, subjects the main protagonist – as had happened already underground – to erotic inducements. He marries the relevant princess and together they rule Jupiter in peace. In dealing with the sinlessness of the Jovians, EMS ineffectively prefigured the work of C.S. LEWIS.   [JC]

SEA ◊ UNDER THE SEA.

SEABORN, ADAM Unidentified pseudonym of the author of the well written *Symzonia: A Voyage of Discovery* (**1820**), which sets a UTOPIA inside a HOLLOW EARTH. Some commentators have assumed AS to have been Captain John Cleves SYMMES, whose hollow-earth theories are exploited in the book. However, they are also satirized, so a more likely candidate may be Nathaniel Ames (?   -1835), whose style in his books about the sea resembles AS's.   [JC/PN]

About the author: "The Authorship of *Symzonia*: The Case for Nathaniel Ames" by Hans-Joachim Lang and Benjamin Lease in *New England Quarterly* (June 1975).

See also: FANTASTIC VOYAGES; HISTORY OF SF.

SEABRIGHT, IDRIS [s] ◊ Margaret ST CLAIR.

SEAFORTH A pseudonym used by 2 entirely separate authors.

1. As A. Nelson Seaforth, UK author George Sydenham Clarke (1848-1933), 1st Baron Sydenham of Combe, wrote the future-WAR novel, *The Last Great Naval War* (**1891**), in which France and the UK become involved.

2. ◊ George C. FOSTER.   [JC]

SEA-LION Pseudonym of UK naval officer and writer Geoffrey Martin Bennett (1909-   ), whose two sf novels both deal with menaces at sea: *The Invisible Ships* (**1950**) indeed features invisible ships, and *This Creeping Evil* (**1950**) features sea monsters.   [JC]

SEAMARK ◊ Austin J. SMALL.

SEARLES, A(RTHUR) LANGLEY (1920-   ) US FANZINE publisher and Professor of Chemistry at the College of Mount St Vincent, New York (he retired in 1987); as publisher from 1943 of FANTASY COMMENTATOR (*which see for details*), he has maintained the journal as a significant forum for the study of sf in many of its aspects, though concentrating on early GENRE SF.   [JC]

SEARLES, (WILLIAM) BAIRD (1934-   ) US writer known mainly for his several nonfiction works on sf and fantasy, beginning with *Stranger in a Strange Land & Other Works* (**1975** chap) and continuing with *The Science Fiction Quizbook* (**1976**) with Martin Last, *A Reader's Guide to Science Fiction* (**1979**) with Last, Michael Franklin and Beth MEACHAM, *A Reader's Guide to Fantasy* (**1982**) with Franklin and Meacham, and *Films of Science Fiction and Fantasy* (**1988**). With Brian Thomsen he edited *Halflings, Hobbits, Warrows, & Weefolk: A Collection of Tales of Heroes Short in Stature* (anth **1991**). He is a useful figure in the field as a practical critic and guide.   [JC]

See also: ISAAC ASIMOV'S SCIENCE FICTION MAGAZINE.

SEARLS, HANK Working name of US writer Henry

Hunt Searls Jr (1922-   ), who began publishing sf with "Martyr's Flight" for *Imagination* in 1955, and whose sf has been primarily restricted to NEAR-FUTURE tales of the early space age. In his first novel, *The Big X* (**1959**), a test pilot flies a plane designed to reach Mach 8. HS's best-known tale, *The Pilgrim Project* (**1964**) – filmed as COUNTDOWN (1968) – is about a race between the USA and the USSR to get to the Moon first, with both countries launching flights almost simultaneously. Melodramatically plotted, and technologically bound (with considerable expertise) to the world of the 1950s and 1960s, HS's work is now an artefact of an earlier (and in some ways bolder) age. From about 1980 he has concentrated on non-sf tales, some of them TECHNOTHRILLERS.   [JC]

Other works: *The Crowded Sky* (**1960**); *The Astronaut* (**1960**); *The Penetrators* (**1965**); *The Hero Ship* (**1969**); *Overboard* (**1977**), marginal; *Sounding* (**1982**).

SECONDARY WORLD ◊ J.R.R. TOLKIEN.

SECONDS Film (1966). Paramount/Joel/Gibraltar. Dir John FRANKENHEIMER, starring Rock Hudson, Salome Jens, John Randolph, Will Geer. Screenplay Lewis John Carlino, from *Seconds* (**1963**) by David ELY. 106 mins. B/w.

A middle-aged businessman (Hudson) pays a large sum to have his death faked and his youth restored by futuristic surgery, so that he can start a new life. Tiring of the young swingers he now moves with, he learns it is impossible to return to his old life. The shadowy organization which arranged all this turns menacing at his backsliding, and eventually has him killed, to be recycled for his body parts. The idea was old, but the treatment, with its cold evocation of PARANOIA – all Frankenheimer's best films feature powerful conspiracies using technological means of manipulation (brainwashing in the case of 1962's *The* MANCHURIAN CANDIDATE) – was in advance of its time, anticipating the sombre conspiracy movies of the 1970s. *S* is much helped by James Wong Howe's moody, alienating black-and-white photography.   [JB/PN]

See also: CINEMA.

SECRETS OF F.P.1 ◊ F.P.1 ANTWORTET NICHT.

SECRET FILES OF CAPTAIN VIDEO, THE ◊ CAPTAIN VIDEO.

SEDBERRY, J(AMES) HAMILTON (1863-?   ) US writer known only for *Under the Flag of the Cross* (**1908**), in which, in AD2005, a valiant US Army fights off a Mongolian-Japanese invasion with electric rifles.   [JC]

SEESTERN ◊ Ferdinand GRAUTOFF.

SEI'UN AWARDS ◊ AWARDS; JAPAN.

SEKSMISJA (vt *Sex Mission*) Film (1984). Zespóły Filmowe. Dir Juliusz Machulski, starring Olgierd Łukaszewicz, Jerzy Stuhr, Bozena Stryjkówna, Bogusława Pawelec. Screenplay Machulski, Jolanta Hartwig, Paweł Hajny. 121 mins. Colour.

A solemn adventurer and a jolly wastrel volunteer for a CRYOGENICS experiment and wake up 50 years later, after atomic war has (supposedly) devastated the surface and the survivors have retreated into the usual underground enclaves. There are no more men, and the mildly totalitarian society is run by parthenogenic women. The wastrel is keen on reintroducing traditional methods of procreation, while the SCIENTIST is more interested in demonstrating the follies of the brave new world. In the Eastern European tradition of satirical sf, this Polish production uses BUCK ROGERS trappings to get a few cheap laughs out of women. The occasional sharp point is made, but *S* is surprisingly unwitty and obvious; its anti-FEMINISM, latent throughout, emerges at the end when it is revealed that society's matriarch is a manipulative male transvestite. *S* is mainly redeemed by its wry performances, particularly by Stuhr, POLAND's favourite comedian, as the lecherous lazybones.   [KN]

SELBY, CURT ◊ Doris PISERCHIA.

SELECTED SCIENCE FICTION Australian DIGEST-size magazine. 5 slim (32pp saddle-stapled) monthly issues May-Sep 1955, published by Malian Press, Sydney; ed anon. *SSF*, a companion to AMERICAN SCIENCE FICTION MAGAZINE, reprinted US material of quite good quality.   [FHP]

SELLINGS, ARTHUR Pseudonym of UK writer and bookseller Robert Arthur Ley (1921-1968), who began publishing sf stories with "The Haunting" for *Authentic* in 1953; the best of his output of about 30 tales was assembled in *Time Transfer* (coll **1956**; with 5 stories cut 1966) and *The Long Eureka* (coll **1968**). In the 1960s his productivity increased; he died (suddenly, of a heart attack) just as he was gaining more and more notice. His first novel, *Telepath* (**1962** US; vt *The Silent Speakers* 1963 UK), is typical of all his best work in the complexity of its protagonist (who must deal with his discovery of his own limited ESP ability), the careful realization of venue, and a sense that, although it may be intrusive, the unknown must be faced and lived with. Later novels, quite variously expressing this quiet but competent point of view, include: *The Uncensored Man* (**1964**), whose protagonist is transferred via drugs into another DIMENSION where he develops previously masked PSI POWERS and meets dubiously superior forms of life (◊ SUPERMAN); *The Quy Effect* (**1966**), in which a man faces the consequences attendant upon his invention of ANTIGRAVITY while at the same time falling in love; *Intermind* (**1967** US as Ray Luther; 1969 UK as AS), in which a secret agent is injected with another person's memory to pursue a complex case; and *The Power of X* (**1968**), which sets an art dealer – perhaps a self-portrayal – into a world where material objects can be perfectly duplicated, calling into question the nature of the authentic work of art. AS's finest novel was his last. *Junk Day* (**1970**), a post-HOLOCAUST tale set in the ruins of his native London and peopled with engrossing character types, is perhaps grimmer than his previous work but pointedly more energetic.   [JC]

See also: ESP; GENERATION STARSHIPS; PERCEPTION.

SEMIPROZINE In the terminology of sf FANDOM, this expression – once colloquial but enshrined since 1983 in the constitution of the World Science Fiction Society, the body that administers the HUGOS – means a semiprofessional magazine as opposed to an amateur magazine, or FANZINE. According to that constitution a magazine with a circulation of more than 10,000 is a professional magazine. A semiprozine must therefore have a circulation of less than 10,000. It must also, according to the constitution, have published at least 4 issues (at least 1 in the previous calendar year) and fulfil 2 of the following 5 criteria: have an average press run of at least 1000 copies; pay its contributors and/or staff in other than copies of the publication; provide at least half the income of any one person; have at least 15% of its total space occupied by advertising; announce itself to be a semiprozine. Charles N. BROWN, editor of LOCUS magazine (which has won numerous Hugos for Best Semiprozine), states additionally in his regular commentaries on magazine publishing that the frequency of a semiprozine should be at least quarterly, and that unlike a professional magazine it should not have national newsstand circulation. A number of the most important magazines of comment in the fields of sf and fantasy, and several of the magazines that publish fiction, are or have been semiprozines. [PN]

SENARENS, LUIS PHILIP (1863-1939) US writer, editor and publishing aide. Under at least 27 pseudonyms he wrote perhaps 2000 stories, mostly boys' fiction, beginning in his teens. In later life, when that market declined, he served as managing editor for the Tousey publications, edited the weekly *Motion Picture Stories* and wrote motion-picture scenarios. He remains best known for his early work. In 1882, under the house pseudonym "NONAME", he took over the **Frank Reade, Jr.** series of dime novels (◊ DIME-NOVEL SF; FRANK READE LIBRARY), later claiming to have written "most" of the 179 stories about **Frank Reade, Jr.** and "all" the comparable **Jack Wright** yarns; these claims may be overstated. LPS exemplified the worst in the dime-novel tradition: very bad writing, sadism, ethnic rancour, factual ignorance and an exploitational mentality. On the positive side, he led the dime novel away from eccentric inventions into a developmental stream that culminated in modern CHILDREN'S SF. [EFB/JE]

About the author: "The American Jules Verne" (anon) in *Science and Invention*, Oct 1920; "Lu Senarens, Writer of a Thousand Thrillers" by E. Alden in *American Magazine*, Apr 1921; "Ghosts of Prophecies Past" by Sam MOSKOWITZ in *Explorers of the Infinite* (coll **1963**); intro by E.F. BLEILER to *The Frank Reade Library* (omni, 10 vols **1979-86**), which reprinted the complete FRANK READE LIBRARY.

SENDER, THE Film (1982). Kingsmere Properties/ Paramount. Dir Roger Christian, starring Shirley Knight, Kathryn Harrold, Zeljko Ivanek, Paul Freeman. Screenplay Thomas Baum. 91 mins. Colour.

This modest melodrama, on the borderline between sf and HORROR, tells of a hospitalized young man (Ivanek) whose PSI POWERS of telepathic projection

and TELEKINESIS cause major disruption. As in VIDEO-DROME of the same year, the dividing line between the real and the hallucinatory is invisible, to disturbing effect, as bleeding mirrors and severed heads proliferate. It is a crisply told story, though the cod psychiatric explanation (which hinges on a possibly incestuous relationship of the patient with his mother, played by Knight) is less interesting than the phenomena themselves. This was the début feature of the director, Christian, who had previously worked as set decorator on STAR WARS and as joint art director on ALIEN. [PN]

SENGOKU JIETAI (vt *Time Slip*) Film (1981). Toho. Dir Kosei Saito, starring Sonny Chiba, Iasao Natsuki, Miyuki Ono, Jana Okada. Screenplay Toshio Kaneda, based on *Sengoku Jietai* (**1971**) by Ryo Hammura (◊ JAPAN). 139 mins, cut to 100 mins. Colour.

Based on one of Ryo Hammura's intelligent novels, which use sf reinterpretations to comment on Japanese history, this tells of a troop of modern Japanese soldiers caught in a timeslip and transported back to 16th-century conflicts in the same area between local warlords. The troop's commander, unlike the agonized ship's captain in The FINAL COUNTDOWN (1980), has no hesitation in trying to change history so that he and his men might somehow be returned to their own time, and sets about conquering Japan. This action adventure plays its sf riffs confidently, and shows visual flair in the numerous gory battle scenes in which few soldiers (with modern technology) face many samurai (with very sharp swords). [PN]

SENSE OF WONDER A term used to describe the sensation which, according to the CLICHÉ of fan criticism that goes back at least to the 1940s, good sf should inspire in the reader. In *Metamorphoses of Science Fiction* (**1979**) Darko SUVIN summed up the attitude of many critics by describing the term as "another superannuated slogan of much SF criticism due for a deserved retirement into the same limbo as extrapolation". And yet . . .

"Sense of wonder" is an interesting critical phrase, for it defines sf not by its content but by its effect (the term "HORROR" is another such). Several fan critics, notably Alexei and Cory PANSHIN in *The World Beyond the Hill* (**1989**), have attempted to locate the "sense of wonder" more specifically; the Panshins found it in sf's "quest for transcendence", which elicited wonderment from John CLUTE that the Panshins could give such emphasis to "the reified wet-dream they think of as transcendence, but which others might call fetish". It is true that to locate one abstraction, "sense of wonder", within another, "transcendence", does not take us far forward, but that does not necessarily rob the former phrase of its usefulness.

The second interesting thing about "sense of wonder" is that, by consensus, it can be found *par excellence* in a number of books that are usually regarded as rather badly written. Both E.E. "Doc" SMITH and A.E. VAN VOGT, for example, failed to transcend the pulp style in novels which involved the transcending of many other Earthly perspectives. The simplest escape from the paradox – that sf's highest aspiration, the "sense of wonder", should often be located in its lowest form, pulp prose – is to claim that those readers who find the diamond in the dung-heap are mistaken, misled not by Smith and van Vogt directly but by their own yearning adolescent dreams, as *fed* by Smith, van Vogt and the others. This becomes another version of the cynical old epigram that the GOLDEN AGE OF SF is 12 (or 13, or 14), and as such may be rejected by the many readers who can still recall with perfect clarity the feelings inspired in them by their first childhood or adolescent encounters with these books, feelings that seem too honest and strong to be dismissed as youthful illusion. The term "sense of wonder" is useful precisely because it sums up these feelings accurately and succinctly. Indeed, the principle of Occam's Razor suggests that, rather than arguing (without evidence) that the diamond in the dung-heap was (or is) really a bit of old quartz, it would be more useful to accept it as a diamond, and to go on to ask the really interesting question: what was (and is) it doing there?

Twin *loci classici* of the "sense of wonder" are the final sentences of van Vogt's *The Weapon Shops of Isher* (1941-2 *ASF*; 1949 *Thrilling Wonder Stories*; fixup **1951**) and *The Weapon Makers* (1943 *ASF*; fixup **1946**; rev 1952; vt *One Against Eternity* 1955 dos). The first novel ends: "He would not witness but he would aid in the formation of the planets." The second novel ends: "This much we have learned. Here is the race that shall rule the sevagram."

The first of these examples (the second is discussed in the entry on A.E. VAN VOGT) presents a sudden shift in perspective, as the previously human protagonist of the novel now, compelled by ever deeper seesaw-swings into the past and the future, becomes an astronomical phenomenon, the phenomenon from which *we all sprang*: here is the HERO as cosmological Adam. The "sense of wonder" comes not from brilliant writing nor even from brilliant conceptualizing; it comes from a sudden opening of a closed door in the reader's mind. (This phenomenon may explain why generations of readers can still quote these final lines verbatim.) In other words, the "sense of wonder" may not necessarily be something generated *in the text* by a writer (which is where the Panshins' analysis foundered, in their suggestion, for example, that Edgar Rice BURROUGHS's Barsoom *is* a "transcendent realm"): it is created by the writer putting the readers in a position from which they can glimpse for themselves, with no further auctorial aid, a scheme of things where mankind is seen in a new perspective.

Cornel ROBU, in "A Key to Science Fiction: The Sublime" (*Foundation* #42 [Spring 1988]) and elsewhere, has argued that the new perspective is often a sudden dislocation of scale, a shift to a new position along the enormous span between cosmos and microcosm. Robu's argument that the "sublime" is the key to "sense of wonder" takes its cue from a review by Peter NICHOLLS (in *Foundation* #2 [June 1972]) of Poul ANDERSON's *Tau Zero* (1967 *Gal*; exp **1970**), where, in an attempt to understand why so flatly characterized a book could be so moving, Nicholls took refuge in defining "sense of wonder" by quoting Wordsworth's "Tintern Abbey": "And I have felt . . . a sense sublime / Of something far more deeply interfused, / Whose dwelling is the light of setting suns, / And the round ocean and the living air, / And the blue sky, and in the mind of man: / A motion and a spirit, that impels. / All thinking things, all objects of all thought, / And rolls through all things." Another critic to use aesthetic notions of what he calls "the natural sublime" in an sf context has been David KETTERER in "Science Fiction and Allied Literature" (*Science-Fiction Studies* Mar 1976).

To move from Wordsworth to van Vogt may not quite be to move from the sublime to the ridiculous. Van Vogt's hero poised in the archaic heavens ready to create the planets will indeed, and literally, be far more deeply "interfused" than the reader could possibly have expected up to that point of the novel. Young readers of van Vogt might have been amused to know that they would have to wait three decades, until about the mid-1970s, before again encountering the view implied by van Vogt's sentence – but this time lent support by the speculations of quantum physicists – that the Universe exists as an external structure only through the consciousness of its participants. The suggestion is not that van Vogt seriously anticipated the quantum physicists; it is that his last sentence *invites* readers to open their minds to such thoughts.

Arguably, almost any "sense-of-wonder"- producing case embedded in an sf text, no matter how weak that text may be elsewhere, could be analysed to show a comparable forcing of CONCEPTUAL BREAKTHROUGH. That term was coined in the 1st edn of this encyclopedia in recognition of the fact that Nicholls's earlier "sense-of-wonder" definition in terms of the sublime was open to abuse in the form of vaguely mystical, pantheist – or, indeed, transcendent! – readings of sf texts. "Conceptual breakthrough", whereby the "sense of wonder" is inspired through paradigm shifts – a variant of the shift in perspective noted above – is a more focused term than "sublime", and perhaps a more helpful one. (A further essay by Nicholls exploring the links between conceptual breakthrough and "sense of wonder" is "Doors and Breakthroughs" in *Frontier Crossings* [anth **1987**] ed Robert Jackson.)

We do contend that, *pace* Suvin, the concept of "sense of wonder" may be necessary if we are to understand the essence of sf that distinguishes it from other forms of fiction, including most FANTASY. The diamond is real, and cuts. But before we can use "sense of wonder" as a defining feature we must first know more accurately what fictional elements produce it. The discussion here does not pretend to do that, only to point in some possibly useful directions.

The task is made more difficult by the fact that "sense of wonder" has become a debased term even within sf FANDOM, which these days is as likely to use it ironically, spelling and pronouncing it "sensawunna". This is in part because there are so many ways in which sf writers can counterfeit, and have counterfeited, the "sense of wonder", the simplest method being to introduce into the plot something (a) alien, and (b) very, very big. ◊ BIG DUMB OBJECTS for a discussion of a subgenre particularly subject to ersatz or automatic-pilot "sense of wonder" of this kind – yet which often contrives to produce the genuine article as well.

As we become older and at least in our own eyes more sophisticated, we are of course less likely to seek diamonds in dung-heaps. Perhaps younger readers find them more readily because, while they recognize a diamond when they see one, they haven't yet learned to recognize a dung-heap. In this respect the "sense of wonder" *is* a phenomenon of youth – but that does not make it any less real. [PN/CR]

SENTRY, JOHN A. [s] ◊ Algis BUDRYS.

SERIES There have been series in popular fiction, both within and outside GENRE SF, at least since there have been magazines. For example, fans of Arthur Conan DOYLE may have waited eagerly a century ago for the next **Sherlock Holmes** story, or, inside sf and a bit later, the next **Professor Challenger** story. Series are fun to write, fun to read, and they help sell magazines. There were many sf series before the advent of specialized sf magazines, examples being the **Quatermain** books of H. Rider HAGGARD and the much loved **Barsoom** and **Pellucidar** stories of Edgar Rice BURROUGHS, or, popular at the time but now mostly forgotten, the **Dr Hackensaw** series of Clement FEZANDIE. (In this encyclopedia we print series titles in bold type.) There is no point here in trying to list the most popular fantasy and sf series from, say, Robert E. HOWARD's **Conan** through Nelson S. BOND's **Pat Pending**, but there may be a point in spelling out some of the ways sf PUBLISHING has affected, and been affected by, series publication.

In the 1930s, it became quite common to devote entire PULP MAGAZINES – or at least their lead novels – to a single series featuring one main character and his (or her) sidekicks. Examples include scientific detective **Craig Kennedy** in SCIENTIFIC DETECTIVE MONTHLY (1930) or DUSTY AYRES AND HIS BATTLEBIRDS (1934-5), or, more spectacularly in terms of longevity, **Doc Savage** in DOC SAVAGE MAGAZINE (1933-49) or *The Shadow* (1931-49) or CAPTAIN FUTURE (1940-44).

When, in the late 1940s and the 1950s, SMALL PRESSES were set up devoted to republishing classic magazine sf, it quite often happened that their sometimes arbitrary dividing up of a series into books set the shape by which that series was ever afterwards known. Thus Isaac ASIMOV's **Foundation** series of 8 stories (mostly novelettes), published in *ASF* (1942-49), appeared in book form as if 3 novels: *Foundation*

(fixup **1951**), *Foundation and Empire* (fixup **1952**) and *Second Foundation* (fixup **1953**). In this instance the illusion of them being novels was not difficult to sustain, because the stories had been well planned to fit a coherent and developing pattern.

When a series of stories is collected in book form, however, it is not always easy to decide, bibliographically, the degree of cohesion the stories (often revised for this format) have been given. Thus we might describe one book as "coll of linked stories" and another as a FIXUP, the latter term being used by us to describe stories sufficiently jelled together even in their first writing, or woven together by rewriting, for the result to be called a novel. To take examples, it seems fair to call George O. SMITH's *Venus Equilateral* (**1947**) a collection of linked stories, although we describe A.E. VAN VOGT's *The Weapon Shops of Isher* (1941-2 *ASF*; 1949 *Thrilling Wonder Stories*; **1951**) as a fixup (a term its author also uses), because the degree of cohesion and plotting towards a climax is very much greater in the latter than in the former. But what, for example, of Gene WOLFE's *The Fifth Head of Cerberus* (fixup **1972**)? This is described by many bibliographers as a collection of linked stories, which is true. But when one comes to examine the links, including those that lie half-concealed beneath the surface of the text, then the interweaving comes to appear so strong that the book, although indeed in 3 parts, must surely be read as a single novel.

These problems about sf series whose first appearance was in magazines and original anthologies came to seem somewhat old-fashioned during the 1980s and 1990s, because by far the greater number of sf series now being published were appearing in books *in the first instance*. That, on the face of it, is not very important, but the sinister aspect of 1980s series publishing was the implacable way in which book series were taking over more and more of the industry. These were often series thought up by a publisher or some sort of entrepreneur, or even licensed out by a film studio. That is to say, the author's primacy in writing series was beginning to lose out to the purveyors of product concept, to whose instructions the authors wrote. (The question of whether or not the authors retained copyright in the work is not necessarily connected to their following of instructions, though those authors who followed instructions but retained copyright no doubt felt rather more dignified than those who did not.) This whole depressing issue is touched on (from different perspectives) under the rubrics GAME WORLDS, PUBLISHING, SHARECROP, SHARED WORLD and TIE. Things are seldom entirely bad, however: there have been, for example, many enjoyable original novels among the 100 or so STAR TREK ties. Even the book series spun off from GAMES AND TOYS are not all bad, though many are; in the UK, the company GAMES WORKSHOP persuaded several quite distinguished writers to write novels and stories set in worlds first created for a games format. Some of the shared-world series like WILD CARDS have produced excellent work. But, even when the exceptions are admitted, there remains a huge residue that few demanding readers could find anything but dispiriting: series as formula, writing by numbers. In FANTASY writing, for example, for every trilogy published that actually requires 3 vols for its adequate development, there are half a dozen that are trilogies (or even longer) for no better reason than to fill slots in the marketing space. In HEROIC FANTASY (or SWORD AND SORCERY) the series mentality is especially strong, as it is in SURVIVALIST FICTION and post-HOLOCAUST sf.

All this is saddening, because previously series had held a very honourable position in the history of sf's development. Many readers of an earlier generation had their innocent SENSE OF WONDER first awakened by E.E. "Doc" SMITH's **Lensmen** stories (1934-50), and that is a comparatively straightforward SPACE-OPERA example. In a series, there can be room for enormous conceptual elaborations which could scarcely be confined within the covers of a single book, as (arguably) in Frank HERBERT's **Dune** series, or Larry NIVEN's **Known Space** series (a good example of the whole coming to seem greater than the sum of its parts), or Ursula K. LE GUIN's **Hainish** novels, or C.J. CHERRYH's **Union/Alliance** sequence, or Bruce STERLING's **Shaper/Mechanist** series, or Brian W. ALDISS's **Helliconia** novels, or Gene WOLFE's **Book of the New Sun** (more readily thought of as a 4-vol novel), or Michael MOORCOCK's **Jerry Cornelius** books. It would obviously be possible to extend this sequence for a very long way even while restricting it to unusually distinguished work. Be sf in the form of HARD SF, NEW WAVE, CYBERPUNK or SCIENCE FANTASY, it has been one of its great strengths (and one of its unifying factors) that, unlike most MAINSTREAM fiction, it has been able to work on such broad canvases. So far as we are aware, nobody has made any academic analysis of the effect of series-writing on the HISTORY OF SF, but the result would surely be a confirmation that series developments have been at sf's very heart, certainly in the special but vital case of future histories (◊ HISTORY OF SF). It may not be too great an imaginative leap to see the *whole* of GENRE SF as constituting a kind of gigantic meta-series (or multiverse), in which intellectual developments in the form of constantly evolving protocols and motifs are passed from writer to writer. Certainly many sf readers share an intuitive, metaphysical sense that the entirety of genre sf somehow (ignoring nitpicking distinctions) shares a *common background*, as if there were now a real future that has been invented by consensus of the sf community. If that seems an overstatement, then at least it can be granted that some of sf's most heroic generic exploits have been conducted, and could only have been conducted, in series form. All the more tragic, then, that the word "series" in the 1980s (and still) should gradually be changing its meaning to "multi-volume packaged commercial product". [PN]

SERIMAN, ZACCARIA [r] ◊ ITALY.

SERLING, ROD (1924-1975) US screenwriter and TELEVISION producer, best known for the tv series *The TWILIGHT ZONE*, for which he won 3 HUGOS (1960-62). A paratrooper in WWII, he went to New York in 1948 as a freelance writer, first for radio and then for tv. During the 1950s he became one of the most highly regarded tv writers, winning many awards including 6 Emmies for such tv plays as *Patterns* (1955), *Requiem for a Heavyweight* (1956) and *The Comedian* (1957). In 1959 he created, wrote and produced the first of his **The Twilight Zone** anthology series, on which he also appeared as host; his dark figure and gravelly tones became very familiar to viewers. The series, mainly fantasy dramas with some sf, lasted 5 years. In 1970 he tried to repeat this success with a similar series, ROD SERLING'S NIGHT GALLERY, but it lasted only until 1972. In addition to his tv work, which included writing many episodes for both **The Twilight Zone** and **Night Gallery**, RS wrote a number of filmscripts such as those for *Requiem for a Heavyweight* (1963; based on his tv script), John FRANKENHEIMER's *Seven Days in May* (1964) and the original version (later rewritten) of PLANET OF THE APES (1968).

RS could hardly be described as an original writer, but he was certainly clever at adapting existing ideas and was a capable craftsman. He had the knack of producing work that, in the context of most tv material, seemed more daring and profound than it really was; his major flaw was slickness. Whatever his limitations, **The Twilight Zone** came as a breath of fresh air to fans of fantasy and sf, who had previously had little tv material available.

RS wrote some of his teleplays into short-story form and published several collections: *Stories from The Twilight Zone* * (coll **1960**), *More Stories from The Twilight Zone* * (coll **1961**), *New Stories from The Twilight Zone* * (coll **1962**), *The Season to Be Wary* * (coll **1967**), *Night Gallery* * (coll **1971**) and *Night Gallery 2* * (coll **1972**). Selections from the first 3 of these appeared in *From The Twilight Zone* * (coll **1962**) and all the contents of the first 3 in an omnibus, again titled *Stories from The Twilight Zone* * (omni **1986**). RS also edited *Rod Serling's The Twilight Zone* * (anth **1963**) and *Rod Serling's Twilight Zone Revisited* * (anth **1964**), which were collected as an omnibus, *Rod Serling's Twilight Zone* * (omni **1984**). Of 3 further anthologies, *Rod Serling's Triple W: Witches, Warlocks and Werewolves* (anth **1963**), *Rod Serling's Devils and Demons* (anth **1967**) and *Rod Serling's Other Worlds* (coll **1978**), the first 2 at least were ghost-edited by Gordon R. DICKSON, and RS had been dead for 3 years by the time the 3rd appeared.

RS's name has continued to be used as a marketing device. His widow, Carol Serling, who retains RS's tv rights, edited *Rod Serling's Night Gallery Reader* * (anth **1987**) with Martin H. GREENBERG and Charles G. WAUGH. More importantly, she also played a prominent role as editorial consultant in setting up *Rod Serling's The Twilight Zone Magazine* (1981-9), initially monthly, which achieved prominence in the fantasy/

horror field.   [JB/PN]

SERNINE, DANIEL Pseudonym of Canadian writer Alain Lortie (1955-   ), a central force in Canadian sf, who began publishing in 1975 with the dark fantasies "Jalbert" and "La Bouteille" ["The Bottle"] for *Requiem*, later serving (from 1983) on the editorial collective of that magazine, now renamed *Solaris* (◊ CANADA). His early work has been collected in *Les Contes de l'ombre* ["Tales from the Shadow"] (coll 1979). His novels, marketed as juveniles, are split into 2 main series: the **Grandverger** fantasies, set in an imaginary enclave of New France – *Légendes du vieux manoir* ["Tales from the Old Manor House"] (coll 1979), *Le Trésor du "Scorpion"* (1980; trans as *The "Scorpion" Treasure* 1990), *L'Épée Arhapal* (1981; trans as *The Sword Arhapal* 1990) and *Le Cercle Violet* ["The Purple Circle"] (1984) – and the **Exode** or **Argus** sequence, about a benevolent extraterrestrial organization keeping watch on the Earth: *Organisation Argus* (1979; trans David Homel as *Those Who Watch the Skies* 1990), *Argus Intervient* (1983; trans David Homel as *Argus Steps In* 1990), *Argus: mission mille* ["Argus: The Thousandth Mission"] (1989) and *Les Rêves d'Argus* ["The Dreams of Argus"] (1991). Both series are brought together in *La nef dans le nuages* ["The Ship in the Clouds"] (1989). Some of the adult stories assembled in *Le Vieil Homme et l'espace* ["The Old Man and Space"] (coll 1981) also belong to the **Exode** saga; the collection as a whole effectively displays DS's social and political interests, as does the ambitious and well received *Les Méandres du temps* ["The Meanders of Time"] (1983). More recently, he has begun publishing tales set in a neverending **Carnival**; these have been assembled as *Boulevard des étoiles* ["Stardust Boulevard"] (coll 1991) and *À la Recherche de Monsieur Goodtheim* ["Looking for Mr Goodtheim"] (coll 1991). This more recent work shows a willingness to explore new avenues.   [LP]

Other works: *La Cité inconnue* ["The Unknown City"] (1982); *Ludovic* (1983); *Les Envoûtements* ["Bewitchments"] (1985); *Quand vient la nuit* ["As Night Falls"] (coll 1983); *Aurores Boréales 2* (anth 1985); *Nuits Blêmes* "Wan Nights" (1990); *Quatres destins* ["Four Destinies"] (1990); *La Magicienne bleue* ["The Blue Magician"] (1991); *Le Cercle de Khaleb* ["Khaleb's Circle"] (1991).

SERVICE, PAMELA F. (1945-   ) US writer of fantasy and sf, usually for older children, beginning with the **Winter** sequence of post-HOLOCAUST fantasies invoking King Arthur: *Winter of Magic's Return* (1985) and *Tomorrow's Magic* (1987). Of sf interest are: *A Question of Destiny* (1986), a young-adult sf thriller; *Stinker from Space* (1988 chap); *Under Alien Stars* (1990), set on an Earth occupied by ALIEN invaders whose mores challenge human prejudices, and who themselves are under attack from space; and *Weirdos of the Universe, Unite!* (1992), which unconvincingly pits figures from human MYTHOLOGY against another alien INVASION.   [JC]

Other works: *When the Night Wind Howls* (1987); *The*

Reluctant God (1988), a TIME-TRAVEL fantasy; *Vision Quest* (1989); *Wizard of Wind and Rock* (1990); *Being of Two Minds* (1991).

SERVICE, ROBERT W(ILLIAM) (1874-1958) UK-born poet and novelist, in Canada 1896-1912, where much of his exceedingly popular verse was set. Of his several novels, *The Master of the Microbe: A Fantastic Romance* (1926) is sf, featuring a deadly plague virus developed by a vengeful German but stolen from him by a master-criminal. *The House of Fear* (1927) is a werewolf tale.   [JC]

SERVISS, GARRETT P(UTMAN) (1851-1929) US journalist and writer who majored in science at Cornell University, then studied law, and only afterwards entered journalism, working on 2 New York newspapers before moving into freelance writing and lecturing. His speciality was ASTRONOMY; his *Other Worlds* (1901) was a significant work of popular science. In 1897 he was commissioned to write an unofficial sequel to an equally unofficial US newspaper recasting of H.G. WELLS's *The War of the Worlds* (1898), which was then making a considerable stir as a newspaper and magazine serial, and – in the absence of adequate copyright protection – inspiring various imitations along the way. GPS's "sequel" was *Edison's Conquest of Mars* (1898 *The New York Journal*; 1947; cut vt *Forrest J. Ackerman Presents Invasion of Mars* 1969), a tale which quite remarkably captured the ebullient US spirit of the time. Edison himself (◊ EDISONADE) is the protagonist. After the first wave of Martians have duly perished of bacteria, he invents a disintegrating WEAPON and an ANTIGRAVITY machine, using the latter to power 100 SPACESHIPS he has persuaded the nations of the world to build. The armada invades MARS, and after many battles causes its polar icecap to melt, which results in a genocidal flood. The book was one of the first edisonades to be written for adults, and perhaps the only adult presentation of the entrepreneurial inventor to mention his name on its title page. In details of plot, and in its triumphal narrative tone, it closely prefigured the SPACE-OPERA edisonades of E.E. "Doc" SMITH and his imitators.

GPS's remaining sf is intermittently vivid, but lacks the seemingly unconscious mythopoeic potency of his first. In *The Moon Metal* (1900), set in 1940, a mysterious figure supplies the world with a rare untraceable metal which serves, for a while, as a new fiscal standard (◊ MONEY). "The Sky Pirate" (1909 *The Scrap Book*) features the superscientific exploits of the eponymous adventurer. *A Columbus in Space* (1909 *All-Story Magazine*; rev 1911) features another pioneering SPACE FLIGHT, this time to VENUS. *The Second Deluge* (1912) is a DISASTER novel in which the Earth is inundated to a depth of several miles as a result of passing through a "nebula" composed of water; a latter-day Noah, having built an ark, saves all God's creatures and visits the US West, where the President has also been saved. This novel was reprinted 3 times: in AMAZING STORIES (1926), AMAZING

STORIES QUARTERLY (1933) and FANTASTIC NOVELS (1948). GPS's last story, *The Moon Maiden* (1915 *The Argosy*; **1978** chap), is a dubiously complicated love tale in which it is revealed that lunar beings have been guiding us upwards for millennia. In a sense, GPS was born too soon; born 20 years later he might have become one of the prolific masters of the new sf.

[JC/MJE]

See also: DISCOVERY AND INVENTION; END OF THE WORLD; HISTORY OF SF; HOLOCAUST AND AFTER; MATTER TRANSMISSION; NUCLEAR POWER; PULP MAGAZINES; SCIENTISTS.

SEVEN DAYS IN MAY ◊ Fletcher KNEBEL; John FRANKENHEIMER.

SEX This entry is primarily about human sexual relationships and sexual stereotypes as themes in sf; i.e., it is primarily about PSYCHOLOGY and SOCIOLOGY. It discusses neither procreation nor the various inventive methods of ALIEN sexual reproduction devised by sf writers.

Traditionally sf has been a puritanical and male-oriented literature. Before the 1960s there was little sf that consciously investigated sexual questions but, as with all popular literatures, what is implied is often as important as what is openly put forward. Seen from this viewpoint, sf has been an accurate reflector of popular prejudices and feelings about sex over the years – especially in stories at the PULP-MAGAZINE end of the sf spectrum, where the fantasies and TABOOS of the day are encapsulated more clearly than in sophisticated works.

An important theme of pulp sf – sex as beastliness – appeared much earlier. Jonathan SWIFT's famous work of PROTO SCIENCE FICTION, *Gulliver's Travels* (**1726**; rev 1735), in its 4th book contrasts the brutish life of carnality led by the human-like Yahoos – much given to public defecation and genital display – with the life of reason led by the intelligent, horse-like Houyhnhnms; everyone understands the satirical assault on the Yahoos, but fewer critics have recognized the horses' fastidious squeamishness as being also, more subtly, under attack. Swift's 18th-century frankness about sex was not to appear in sf again with the same force for more than two centuries.

In the 19th century, feelings about sex were implied but seldom dealt with openly. The sexual fears and fantasies often involved in GOTHIC SF tended to be envisioned as powerful, irrational forces, difficult to quell. *Frankenstein, or The Modern Prometheus* (**1818**; rev 1831) by Mary SHELLEY is more overt than most in asking whether the artificial man's bestial urges, unfettered by a soul, would prove devastating. This aspect of the story has been emphasized in several film versions of FRANKENSTEIN, especially in the parody *Young Frankenstein* (1974), where the monster's amorous abilities prove as formidable as we had always suspected.

Frankenstein points towards a recurrent theme in pulp sf: fear of the ALIEN manifest (at least in the subtext) as fear of a sexual capacity greater than ours, just as White men stereotypically fear Black as sexual

athletes too well endowed to compete against. The menace of the alien is often seen in sexual terms in sf ILLUSTRATIONS, which right through the magazines of the 1930s and 1940s had a stronger sexual charge than the milk-and-water stories they purported to illuminate.

The sf pulp magazines seldom attempted to titillate in the manner of, say, *Spicy Mystery Stories* – an exception was MARVEL SCIENCE STORIES (especially in its incarnation as *Marvel Tales*), which contained stories like "Lust Rides the Roller Coaster". Generally, however, the SF MAGAZINES proved unable to link the two genres of the spicy and the technological with any conviction. (The conjunction of flesh and metal, however, later proved inspirational to sf COMICS artist Jean-Claude Forest [1930-   ], whose mildly erotic BARBARELLA featured a heroine who was prepared to receive even the embrace of a ROBOT – a not uncommon theme in the liberated 1970s, most amusingly dealt with in Robert SHECKLEY's "Can You Feel Anything When I Do This?" [1969]. **Barbarella** was successfully filmed in 1967 by Roger Vadim as a veritable compendium of the sexual fantasies to be found in sf.)

The sexual implications of sf stories have varied remarkably little in the past 100 years, and most of the themes were already well established in the popular literature of the 19th century. *Strange Case of Dr Jekyll and Mr Hyde* (**1886**) by Robert Louis STEVENSON explores the notion that the human mind contains a cheerfully bestial component controlled by a mental censor that can – in this case with drugs – be bypassed. Although there was more of METAPHYSICS than science in the idea when Stevenson penned it, developments in psychology (beginning, even as Stevenson wrote, with the work of Sigmund Freud [1856-1939]) and later neurology showed him to have been not so very far from the truth. Stevenson's fundamental theme, however, has a long history in the Christian West, where the pleasures of the flesh have traditionally been seen as sinful: it is the theme of Original Sin. Hyde was an incarnation of "the evil that lurks in the heart of Man". Sin and retribution remains a popular theme in HORROR and MONSTER MOVIES.

Sf has been largely written by men, and tends to reveal specifically masculine sexual prejudices. (The female archetypes created by men are further discussed in WOMEN AS PORTRAYED IN SCIENCE FICTION.) An interesting early example of gender archetype is found in *The Time Machine* (**1895**) by H.G. WELLS. The future races discovered by the Time Traveller are the masculine, hairy Morlocks and the effeminate, beautiful, irresponsible Eloi, who are ultimately just cattle for the Morlocks. The two races allegorize 19th-century sexual distinctions and class distinctions simultaneously. One of the illustrations by Virgil FINLAY to a magazine reprint of the story makes the point vividly.

To immature men, women often appear like an

alien race, and much popular sf reflects a fear of their threatening foreignness. The stereotype of the Amazon Queen – imperious, cruel and desirable – is abundantly present in *She* (**1887**) and other novels by H. Rider HAGGARD. The she-devil, a favourite recurring Victorian literary archetype (Victorian pornography makes just as much of women chastising men with whips as vice versa), turns up throughout pulp sf, notably in the romances of Edgar Rice BURROUGHS and in many tales published in PLANET STORIES.

It might be expected that the image of woman as all-engulfing Holy Prostitute and She-Fiend would be an exclusively masculine fantasy, but – perhaps because it is at least an image of power in a world where, during the era of the pulp magazines, women were relatively powerless – it attracted some women writers. C.L. MOORE made a speciality of such figures, notably in her **Northwest Smith** tales. The Medusa creature in Moore's "Shambleau" (**1933**) is an archetype of the female as a fantasy of sexual horror: "From head to foot he was slimy from the embrace of the crawling horror about him . . . and the look of terrible ecstasy that overspread [his face] seemed to come from somewhere far within . . ."

The conjunction of womanhood and slime may have pathological connotations, but is familiar enough in GENRE SF and elsewhere. Consider the following passage from *The Deathworms of Kratos* (**1975**) by Richard Avery (Edmund COOPER): "Each time she was penetrated, the queen's huge body rippled and arched and she gave out a hissing, screaming grunt. Steam rose from her straining body, gouts of milky fluid dripped from her immense length, bubbling from her orifices . . ." The sexual confusions are intense: the queen is a giant worm, and, though female, unmistakably phallic in shape. The watchers are "sickened" but excited and, within pages, are asking the spaceship captain for permission to pair off and copulate. The sexual ambiguities here are of the very essence of pulp sf.

Some of the worst sexual crudities in sf, much attacked by FEMINISTS of both sexes, are found in the male writers of HEROIC FANTASY. What was merely a subtext in Robert E. HOWARD's **Conan** stories of the 1930s had become explicit and central in John NORMAN's **Gor** books of the 1960s: a male desire to exert power over women, which Norman depicts in his many bondage and flagellation scenes in a manner clearly intended to be sexually arousing. The visual counterpart of these writings can be seen in the paintings of Frank FRAZETTA, whose ripe, lush beauties, when not being menaced by scaly, phallic monsters or subdued by men, are themselves cruel Amazons, holding the most brawny-thewed men in thrall.

Miscegenation, the mixing of races, is another common sexual theme in sf. It was often seen in LOST-WORLD fiction from around the turn of the century to be degrading (◊ DEVOLUTION), as in Austyn GRANVILLE's *The Fallen Race* (**1892**), where a primitive tribe

has resulted from the bestial union of aboriginals and kangaroos. But even during the period up to the 1920s, when racist popular fiction was the rule rather than the exception, miscegenation could be seen as a good thing. An early human-alien union can be found in Burroughs's *A Princess of Mars* (1912; exp **1917**), symbolized in the amusing scene where John Carter stands proudly next to his wife, the princess, looking at their child in its incubator: the child at this stage is a large egg. For decades the sf magazines, notably *Planet Stories*, often featured on their covers BEMS with lascivious expressions pursuing human women – an obvious absurdity (◊ SCIENTIFIC ERRORS).

Thus far we have emphasized the sexual assumptions of society – especially male society – as revealed in sf, but not as *analysed* in sf. The very nature of sf, however, in which societies with cultures and appearances different from our own can be readily imagined, makes it an excellent medium for asking hard questions about our own sexual prejudices. By the 1980s, the conservative sexual bigotry of sf had largely given way to a radical exploration of alternative sexual possibilities (though these, too, produced their own CLICHÉS). The process had first got under way in the early 1950s, when Philip José FARMER and Theodore STURGEON treated the miscegenation theme more seriously. Hitherto magazine sf, no matter what it might coyly imply, had never been sexually explicit. Kay Tarrant, assistant to John W. CAMPBELL Jr, the editor of ASTOUNDING SCIENCE-FICTION (later *Analog*), was famous for her prudishness, and persuaded many writers to remove "offensive" scenes and "bad language" from their stories. This was partly in keeping with the spirit of the age and partly to protect adolescent boys, probably *ASF*'s main readership. Some writers made a game of outwitting her; in his story "Rat Race" (1947) George O. SMITH got away with mentioning a "ball-bearing mousetrap" on one page, revealing on the next page the device: a tomcat. But both Farmer and Sturgeon were, for their period, explicit. They recognized that, in a genre which prided itself on imagining new and different societies, the sexual taboo was absurdly anachronistic, particularly because it did not exist to the same degree in conventional fiction. Sturgeon explored both three-way relationships and human-alien relationships in a number of stories and novels, notably *Venus Plux X* (**1960**), a savage attack on gender stereotyping. Farmer's *The Lovers* (1952 *Startling Stories*; exp **1961**) dealt with inter-species love and sex, as did many of his stories, including "Mother" (1953), in which a spaceman is inveigled into an alien womb, where he makes his home – perhaps the ultimate in Freudian sf stories. Both these writers questioned concepts of "normal" and "perverse" (although there is a critical argument about the degree of crudeness, salacity or sometimes sentimentality with which the attempt was made).

By the 1960s miscegenation was an acceptable serious theme in sf, and it was perhaps most carefully and delicately explored in Ursula K. LE GUIN's novel *The Left Hand of Darkness* (**1969**). An ordinary human is forced to rethink the whole question of sexual roles when faced with a race (and emotionally involved with one of its members) who are bisexual in that they can be, at different times, either man, woman or neuter. A sensitive treatment of love between alien races is *Strangers* (1974 *New Dimensions*; exp **1978**) by Gardner DOZOIS, which draws attention to the ghastly errors that can occur from trying to understand a foreign society in terms of the assumptions of one's own.

After the pioneer work of Sturgeon and Farmer – and also such mildly daring works as *The Disappearance* (**1951**) by Philip WYLIE, which postulates a total but temporary division between the societies of men and of women, "Consider Her Ways" (1956) by John WYNDHAM, which deals with an ambiguously utopian all-women society, and *The Girls from Planet 5* (**1955**) by Richard WILSON, which deals skittishly with a similar theme – the breaking of the dam came with the so-called NEW WAVE in the 1960s. Suddenly, explicit sex was commonplace in sf, in work by Brian W. ALDISS, J.G. BALLARD, Samuel R. DELANY, Norman SPINRAD and many others. Harlan ELLISON's consciously taboo-breaking anthology *Dangerous Visions* (anth **1967**) printed some stories of this type.

Writers of an older generation, such as Isaac ASIMOV and Robert A. HEINLEIN, also blossomed out into the freedom of the 1960s. In much of Heinlein's late work the central theme is a strong plea for sexual emancipation, sometimes expressed with a kind of embarrassing locker-room prurience. This was his emphasis from his popular *Stranger in a Strange Land* (**1961**) onwards, most obviously in *I Will Fear No Evil* (**1970**) – in which an old man is given new life in the body of his young female secretary – and again in *Time Enough for Love* (**1973**) and *Friday* (**1982**).

One publisher, ESSEX HOUSE, specialized in pornographic sf (a genre that had its heyday in the late 1960s and early 1970s) including Farmer's *The Image of the Beast* (**1968**) and *A Feast Unknown* (**1969**) as well as books by Hank STINE and David MELTZER. Other publishers followed suit, notably Olympia and Ophelia Press, which published sf erotica by, among others, Charles PLATT and Barry N. MALZBERG, the latter's work being perhaps the gloomiest pornography ever published. Most of the above were partially serious in intent, and sometimes more emetic than erotic. Slightly less reputable houses published pornography by Richard E. GEIS and Andrew J. OFFUTT, and down at the bottom of the barrel could be found books with titles like *Anal Planet* (**1976**) by Alex Forbes. (A number of other sf writers – including both Marion Zimmer BRADLEY and Robert SILVERBERG under pseudonyms – occasionally published non-sf erotica, usually as a quick way of earning money.)

Some critics consider that the most distinguished work of "pornographic" sf is *Crash* (**1973**) by J.G. Ballard, in which images of technology and images of sex are interwoven to make an ambiguous and not necessarily disapproving comment on the nature of technological society and its alienations. The central images of this book are the orgasm and the car crash, the one often leading to the other. Also of note are some of the stories in Ballard's *The Atrocity Exhibition* (coll **1970**; vt *Love and Napalm: Export USA* 1972 US).

Sf is more liable than other genres, with the exception of horror, to link sex with disgust. Robert BLOCH, Ray BRADBURY and Sturgeon all wrote stories in which images of sex overlap with images of violence, blood, revulsion and pain, yet these authors are generally considered to be towards the more "liberal" end of the sf spectrum. This dis-ease with sexuality, perhaps cultural in origin, is also reflected in a recurrent image of overtly sexual sf: a mind/body dualism in which the body is seen as "alien" and governing the mind, rather than governed by it or in partnership with it.

On the more positive side, sf that consciously judges the sexual prejudices of our own society by imagining societies with quite different sexual expectations began – relatively speaking – to flourish from the 1970s on, though remaining rather a small subgenre within sf as a whole. Many of these works were written by women, especially feminist writers, most notably Joanna RUSS, and are discussed under FEMINISM. Such writers have made extrapolations towards cultures where troilism, homosexuality, bisexuality or even pansexuality is the norm. Samuel R. DELANY does so in much of his writing, notably in *Dhalgren* (**1975**) and *Triton* (**1976**) along with later works. Thomas M. DISCH does so in *334* (**1972**). Sf with a homosexual or bisexual theme is now commonplace, though Delany, for one, has suffered censorship from book-distribution companies for dramatizing these issues. An interesting reference work in this field is *Uranian Worlds: A Reader's Guide to Alternative Science Fiction and Fantasy* (**1983**; rev 1990) by Eric Garber and Lyn Paleo, which annotates 935 novels and stories of "variant sexuality", plus films. (Sf FANDOM, too, has recognized the interest in gay sf with the formation in 1987 of the Gaylactic Network, based in Massachusetts, with 7 affiliated Gaylaxian groups in the USA and Canada.)

Two important writers on sexual themes, both interested in "alternative" sexuality and both attaining prominence in the 1970s, have been James TIPTREE Jr and John VARLEY. Tiptree (not revealed to be a woman until 1977, when she had been publishing sf for a decade) sadly, savagely examined the skewings of sexual impulse in much of her work; it was her central theme, and with her anthropologist's eye she dissected it with great power. Varley, who works with broader strokes, examines polymorphous eroticism – with dazzle and schmaltz perhaps approaching too closely the condition of the romp – among the several themes of his **Gaean** trilogy: *Titan* (**1979**), *Wizard* (**1980**) and *Demon* (**1984**). More recently, *Sexual Chemistry* (coll **1991**) by Brian M. STABLEFORD deals wryly with sexual issues, though its prime theme is GENETIC ENGINEERING.

The great change in sexual life during the 1980s was (as it still is) the AIDS epidemic, among whose many results has been the higher premium now placed on monogamy. Much sf of the 1980s has (either directly or metaphorically) touched on the AIDS theme, including *Unicorn Mountain* (**1988**) by Michael BISHOP and the surreal, sodomitical nightmares of *The Fire Worm* (**1988**) by Ian WATSON. A distinguished short story on the theme is Judith MOFFETT's "Tiny Tango" (1989), later incorporated into *The Ragged World: A Novel of the Hefn on Earth* (**1991**), which features, among many strange, sad images, that of an HIV-positive woman who voyeuristically frequents male lavatories wearing a fake penis.

Sf CINEMA has also been transformed in the past two decades, though much of its sexual explicitness in the 1970s and 1980s is merely titillation, as in MY STEPMOTHER IS AN ALIEN (1988). The mild frissons of ALRAUNE (1928), with its image of the soulless seductress formed by artificial insemination, or I MARRIED A MONSTER FROM OUTER SPACE (1958), with its theme of the bridegroom-cum-MONSTER (a traditional fear), have given way to the women who kill with sex in INVASION OF THE BEE GIRLS (1973) and the alien orgasm-feeders of LIQUID SKY (1982). But by far the most sophisticated, and to some disgusting, of modern cinematic explorations of sexuality are the films of David CRONENBERG, especially *The* PARASITE MURDERS (1974; vt *They Came from Within*; vt *Shivers*), RABID (1976), *The* BROOD (1979), VIDEODROME (1982), *The* FLY (1986) and *Dead Ringers* (1989). From the parasite-induced nymphomania of the first, through the sexual metamorphoses of the next four, to the grotesquely cruel gynaecological technology of the last, the much-abused and -penetrated body is both the battlefield of Cronenberg's mind/body metaphysics and the object of his tenderness.

Perhaps the strongest anthology of sf stories with sexual themes is *Alien Sex* (anth **1990**) ed Ellen DATLOW; this includes Connie WILLIS's shocking, but to some unconvincing, "All My Darling Daughters" (1985), about child and animal abuse, which presents men as sexual sadists. *Arrows of Eros* (anth **1989**) ed Alex Stewart is a recent UK anthology. *Strange Bedfellows: Sex and Science Fiction* (**1972**) ed Thomas N. SCORTIA, *Eros in Orbit* (**1973**) ed Joseph Elder and *The Shape of Sex to Come* (**1978**) ed Douglas HILL are earlier theme anthologies. An amusing study, with special reference to sf ILLUSTRATION, is *Great Balls of Fire! A History of Sex in Science Fiction* (**1977**) by Harry HARRISON. 2 anthologies of critical essays about sex in sf/fantasy are *Erotic Universe* (anth **1986**) and *Eros in the Mind's Eye* (anth **1986**), both ed Donald Palumbo. [PN]

SEX MISSION ◊ SEKSMISJA.

SEYMOUR, ALAN 1. (1927-   ) Australian writer, long resident in the UK, whose *The Coming Self-Destruction of the United States of America* (**1969**) features a Black revolution that, though temporarily successful, precipitates an atomic catastrophe.
2. Early pseudonym used by S. Fowler WRIGHT. [JC]

SF Titles of organizations, magazines, etc., which begin "SF", meaning "science fiction", are listed as if that acronym were spelt out in full.

SHAARA, MICHAEL (1929-1988) US writer who began publishing sf with "All the Way Back" for *ASF* in 1952, and who for a few years seemed to be one of the heirs apparent to the sf pantheon. He did not remain in the field, however, and his name faded from its collective memory. His Civil War novel, *The Killer Angels* (**1974**), won a Pulitzer Prize. In the early 1980s he returned to sf for a short while with *The Herald* (**1981**), a novel set in a NEAR-FUTURE USA, where a scientist has developed a plague with which to rid the Earth of humanity. In *Soldier Boy* (coll **1982**) he assembled his most memorable sf stories, in which a slightly distanced diction is at times absorbingly applied to straightforward genre plots involving strange planets, ALIENS and quick revelatory ironies about the human condition. [JC]

SHACKLETON, C.C. [s] ◊ Brian W. ALDISS.

SHADOW, THE ◊ Walter B. GIBSON; RADIO.

SHAHAR, ELUKI BES [r] ◊ Eluki BES SHAHAR.

SHANKS, EDWARD (RICHARD BUXTON) (1892-1953) UK editor and writer in various genres whose sf novel, *The People of the Ruins: A Story of the English Revolution and After* (**1920**), uses SUSPENDED ANIMATION to take a man 150 years onwards from a strife-torn 1924 into a balkanized primitive land whose descent into final chaos his reintroduction of WWI weaponry fails to prevent. Coming so soon after WWI, this novel may be the first to express the conservative aftermath pessimism (ES's 1924 is ruined by labour strife) that soon became common in UK sf. [JC]
Other work: *Old King Cole* (**1936**), involving the revival of ancient British rites.
See also: END OF THE WORLD; HISTORY IN SF; SLEEPER AWAKES; WAR.

SHANNON, FRED ◊ William S. RUBEN.

SHAPIRO, STANLEY (1926-1990) US writer in whose *A Time to Remember* (**1986**) a man travels back *via* time-slip to prevent John F. Kennedy's assassination. [JC]
Other work: *Simon's Soul* (**1977**), a fantasy.

SHARECROP A term almost certainly devised by Gardner DOZOIS in the late 1980s to designate a story or book which has been written on hire; that is, assigned to an author – who will not hold copyright in the piece that s/he writes – by a franchiser or the copyright owner of the concept being developed. To describe a text as sharecropped is in 1992 almost certainly to disparage it as commodity fiction, designed to fit a prearranged marketing slot and written to order according to strict instructions from the owner. Most pieces written for hire are in fact spun off from *previous* works or concepts, and for this reason the term has often been used to designate any tie or shared-world text, without respect to the ownership of that text. This usage tends to reduce the term to an epithet whose actual meaning is impossible to fix. In this encyclopedia – given that we are not as a whole much interested in examining contractual arrangements between authors and publishers – the term is used infrequently, and then only to designate a condition of ownership. Any text spun off from a previous work or concept *not originated by the author of the text* is here designated a TIE (*which see for further discussion*). Similarly, many sharecrops are tied to SHARED WORLDS; but the author of a shared-world text may be the originator of that world (so the work in question cannot properly be called a tie) and may also retain copyright in his or her own name (so the work cannot properly be called a sharecrop). In sum, although the three terms often overlap, they are in fact quite distinct. [JC]

SHARED WORLDS Stories and novels written by different hands but sharing a setting are in this encyclopedia called shared-world stories. They are usually (but not always) published as contributions to original-ANTHOLOGY series, in turn usually (but not always) edited by the creator(s) of the original setting, who also controls the "bible". This "bible" is a set of rules controlling a shared world by defining the roles, actors, venues, genres, plots and significance of any story written within that world, and is usually shaped in the first instance by the owner(s) and/or creator(s) of the shared world in question, although it may often be augmented by later contributors, who may or may not own a share of the enterprise. A mature "bible" – like that for Jerry E. POURNELLE's **War World** – will almost certainly accrete, over the years, an onion growth of supplementary speculations, genealogies, tables, maps and ancillary tales; but at heart it remains a set of instructions, a kind of genetic code, for writing stories.

It could be argued that the first shared-world anthology to make a significant impact on the Western World was the Christian New Testament, and that the authors of the various pieces which were eventually assembled under that name used the Old Testament as their "bible". It is, of course, understood that the Old Testament typologies which the authors of the New Testament felt impelled to match served for them as profound adumbrations of a Story which was True; but the point is made to underline the fact that the concept of pooling a vision of the Universe did not originate (as has been asserted by some) in the **Thieves' World** anthologies (published from 1979) created by Robert ASPRIN. Beneath and beyond the commercial shared-world enterprises of today lies a vision of (and perhaps a nostalgia for) a human Universe in the hands of a Creator, whose Book we obey (and share).

If we place round-robin novels to one side as being forms of collaboration, we find that the first relevant shared-world enterprises were probably the Christmas Annual anthology/special issues produced by popular magazines and publishers in the UK after about 1860. The most significant shared-world anthology thus produced was probably *Mugby Junction* * (anth **1866** chap) ed Charles DICKENS, a special Christmas issue of *All the Year Round*, a self-contained volume entirely given over to 2 frame narratives plus 6 stories (the most famous being Dickens's own "No. 1 Branch Line, the Signalman") set at the eponymous railway stop; it involved 5 writers, 4 of them following Dickens's instructions. Other examples of the form include *Beeton's Christmas Annual* (anth **1880**), which contained Max ADELER's "Professor Baffin's Adventures", a long lost-race tale (◊ LOST WORLDS) that served as the centrepiece of a series of linked stories over-titled **The Fortunate Island**, and was quite probably a source for Mark TWAIN's *A Connecticut Yankee in King Arthur's Court* (**1889**); and some of the parodic journal *Truth*'s Christmas Numbers, including *The Spookeries* * (anth **1893** chap), *Munchausen [sic] Up to Date* * (anth **1894** chap), *Phon-Photopsy-Grams, or Speaking Likenesses* * (anth **1897** chap), *Nineteen Hundred and Seven* * (anth **1900** chap) and *Interview with the Departed* * (anth **1908** chap).

Again ignoring round-robin collaborations, the first shared-world anthology in GENRE SF was *The Petrified Planet* (anth **1952**) ed Fletcher PRATT, which contained long stories by Judith MERRIL, H. Beam PIPER and Pratt. These stories were set on the world of the title, were written according to a primitive "bible", and were the first to engage upon what would become a central activity of sf shared-world writers: world-building. While almost any premise, however loose, can become the basis of a shared world, in sf the essential shared world is literally a *world*, and the "bible" serves as a manual for world-building (or, in less rigorously constructed collaborations, for PLANETARY-ROMANCE excursions). *A World Named Cleopatra* * (anth **1977**) ed Roger ELWOOD from a concept by Poul ANDERSON, *Medea: Harlan's World* * (anth **1985**) ed Harlan ELLISON and *Murasaki* * (anth **1992**) ed Robert SILVERBERG and Martin Harry GREENBERG are examples of planet-building exercises, and all stand close to the heart of sf. Marion Zimmer BRADLEY's **Darkover** sequence is an example of the planetary-romance shared world.

In the meanwhile, however, the STAR TREK tv series began to generate adaptations of individual episodes, these first tales being simple novelizations rather than contributions to a shared-world enterprise (although of course in script form they adhered to series continuity); but the **Star Trek** owners soon ran out of adaptable stories, and the first original novel within the world – James BLISH's *Spock Must Die!* * (**1970**) – soon appeared. It is not known if Blish was tied to an extensive "bible" for the writing of this novel, but certainly later original stories – from *Spock Messiah!* * (**1976**) by Theodore COGSWELL and Charles A. Spano onward – were shaped according to a "bible" that became more and more strict as the years passed. Over a similar timespan, the approximately 140 DR WHO ties also appeared, though many of these have been adaptations – as have been most novels tied to tv series. (The simple distinction between an adaptation and a shared-world story should perhaps be made explicit: an adaptation is the reworking of an existing story or script; a shared-world tale is a narrative written according to the set of instructions, or agreements, which generate that particular setting.)

There is a general assumption – which may or may not be well founded – that almost all shared-world novels tied to tv or film series are SHARECROPS, and can therefore be defined as work-for-hire contributions to "franchised worlds". In this encyclopedia, however, our focus is on the literary nature of shared worlds rather than on issues of ownership, and thus we have barely used the term "franchised"; it may be noted in passing that most franchised worlds are in fact shared-world enterprises written to strict "bibles" by authors whose disenfranchisement is generally all too evident.)

Star Trek and **Dr Who** are examples of shared-world series whose inspiration lies in media other than the written word; the **Star Wars** novels of L. Neil SMITH and Timothy ZAHN belong in this category, as does the **Dark Futures** sequence edited by David PRINGLE, which constitutes one of the very few sf sequences based on a role-playing game (◊ GAME WORLDS) whose authors (although the books were sharecropped) were able to write with apparent autonomy.

During the past 15 years or so, two rough categories of shared worlds have become popular. Stories written for the **Witch World** setting by hands other than Andre NORTON (or by other hands for Bradley's **Darkover**) typify the class of shared-world enterprises which are based on a setting already created by an author for his or her own use, and subsequently made available to other writers (◊ CLOSED UNIVERSE *and* OPEN UNIVERSE *for brief analysis of the generally very restrictive nature of that availability*). Other shared worlds of this sort include Isaac ASIMOV's **Robot City**, Larry NIVEN's **Man-Kzin Wars**, Jerry Pournelle's **War World** and Fred SABERHAGEN's **Berserker**. The second category concerns the shared-world setting created – either alone by its inventor, or by creative personnel working for hire for a packager such as the Byron PREISS enterprise, or as a communal enterprise on the part of those who plan to write within its terms – as a pure and original shared world without any preceding text to sanction or constrain it, and only a "bible" for its initial guide. Asprin's **Thieves' World** is of this sort. Others include: **Liavek**, ed Emma BULL and Will Shetterly; the **Fleet**, run by David A. DRAKE and Bill FAWCETT; **Temps**, **The Weerde** and **Villains** ed by members of Midnight Rose (Neil GAIMAN, Mary GENTLE, Roz KAVENEY and Alex Stewart); WILD CARDS, supervised by George R.R. MARTIN; and **Time Machine**, one of several controlled by Byron Preiss.

In recent years the concept of the shared world has generated large masses of mediocre work, often written for hire, without joy, or taste, or thought. But that is not a universal rule. Some shared worlds begin in comradeship and continue to demonstrate the pleasures of sharing. The collegial shared world is a model of the sf community at play. Good shared worlds of this sort may, we can hope, in due course drive out the bad. [JC]

SHARKEY, JACK Working name of US writer John Michael Sharkey (1931-1992) for all his sf, which he began publishing with "The Captain of his Soul" for *Fantastic* in 1959. He produced about 50 stories over the next 5 years or so, including several in the 1960s for *Gal* on ECOLOGY. His sf novels, *The Secret Martians* (**1960** dos) and *Ultimatum in 2050 A.D.* (1963 *AMZ* as "The Programmed People"; **1965** dos), were enjoyable contributions to the genre. The protagonist in the first book is a thoroughly likable SUPERMAN; the second book is by contrast downbeat. After 1965 he was actively mainly as a playwright. [JC]

Other work: *The Addams Family* ∗ (**1965**), a tv tie.

SHARON, ROSE [s] ◊ Judith MERRIL.

SHARP, ROBERT [r] ◊ Jon J. DEEGAN.

SHASTA PUBLISHERS Chicago-based US specialist publisher founded by T.E. DIKTY, Erle Melvin Korshak and Mark Reinsberg (who soon dropped out), originally to publish books about fantasy and sf. Its first title was E.F. BLEILER's *The Checklist of Fantastic Literature* (**1948**). The company soon expanded into fiction publishing with such titles as John W. CAMPBELL Jr's *Who Goes There?* (coll **1948**), L. Sprague DE CAMP's *The Wheels of If* (coll **1949**) and L. Ron HUBBARD's *Slaves of Sleep* (**1948**); it turned down a Hubbard book on DIANETICS. All these early titles featured jackets by Hannes BOK. Subsequent publications include the first 3 vols of Robert A. HEINLEIN's **Future History** series and Alfred BESTER's *The Demolished Man* (**1953**). In 1953 Shasta sponsored a novel competition in conjunction with the paperback publisher Pocket Books. This was won by Philip José FARMER with «I Owe for the Flesh». By this time the company was in financial difficulties; the book was never published and the prize money never paid. (The novel later formed the basis of Farmer's **Riverworld** series.) Shasta produced one or two further titles, then expired in 1957. [MJE]

See also: SMALL PRESSES AND LIMITED EDITIONS.

SHATNER, WILLIAM (1931-   ) Canadian actor and writer, long resident in the USA, where he gained fame as Captain Kirk in the STAR TREK tv series, going on to star in all the film sequels; he also directed the disappointing STAR TREK V: THE FINAL FRONTIER (**1989**), about which he wrote, with Lisbeth Shatner, *The Captain's Log: William Shatner's Personal Account of the Making of Star Trek V, the Final Frontier* (**1989**). In the preface to his first sf novel, *TekWar* (**1989**) – set in a 22nd-century Los Angeles where crime is rife, and where a wise-mouth robot resignedly helps a lanky protagonist solve a mystery – WS acknowledges the assistance of Ron GOULART, who is otherwise uncredited as co-author. *Teklords* (**1991**) and *TekLab* (**1991**), both also with Goulart (uncredited), soon followed. [JC]

SHAVER, RICHARD S(HARPE) (1907-1975) US writer, author of some sf stories (some under the house name Paul LOHRMAN) but now remembered almost exclusively for his hoax-like sequence of **Shaver Mystery** stories, presented as based on fact, published in Raymond A. PALMER's AMAZING STORIES 1945-7, beginning with "I Remember Lemuria" in March 1945. It brought over 2500 letters in response, and the sequence boosted *AMZ*'s circulation though at the same time alienating many fans; the June 1947 *AMZ* was an all-Shaver issue. RS continued to release the same sort of material briefly in *Other Worlds* (still as Palmer's protégé), and enjoyed a further comeback in Palmer's small-circulation *The* HIDDEN WORLD in 1961. A selection of the "articles" was published as *I Remember Lemuria & The Return of Sathanas* (coll **1948**). Essentially the "articles" comprise a series of messages from an underground world and, VON DÄNIKEN-like, establish a new, conspiracy-oriented, highly lurid history and cosmology in which humans (it transpires) have long been manipulated by "deros" (detrimental robots) through various ESP powers. Until the end of his life RS maintained that he genuinely believed what he wrote.   [JC/PN]

See also: HOLLOW EARTH; PARANOIA; PSEUDO-SCIENCE; SF MAGAZINES.

SHAW, BARCLAY (1949-   ) US illustrator; attended the New England School of Art and Design. BS's earliest magazine cover was for *FSF* in 1979 (followed by 8 more in the next two years); also in 1979 he did one for CINEFANTASTIQUE. By 1980 he was doing book covers; and in 1982 a series of reissues of Harlan ELLISON books, with covers by BS at Ellison's request, began to appear. Another interesting series of covers was for some of the Robert A. HEINLEIN reissues of the late 1980s. BS's ILLUSTRATION, indebted to European Surrealists and painters of the grotesque, is sophisticated: often surreal and sometimes a touch decadent, typically shadowy with some areas or objects glowing.   [PN]

SHAW, BOB Working name of Northern Irish writer Robert Shaw (1931-   ), in mainland UK from 1973. He worked in structural engineering until the age of 27, then aircraft design, then industrial public relations and journalism, becoming a full-time author in 1975. BS was early involved in sf, initially as a fan, his first book being, with Walt Willis (1919-   ), *The Enchanted Duplicator* (**1954** chap), an allegory of fan and FANZINE activities; he received HUGOS in 1979 and 1980 for his fan writing. He published his first story, "Aspect", with *Nebula Science Fiction* in 1954, and during the mid-1950s contributed several more stories to that magazine and one to *Authentic* before ceasing to write for some years. After a "come-back" story – ". . . And Isles Where Good Men Lie" (1965) – he published "Light of Other Days" (1966 *ASF*), which gained a NEBULA nomination and established his reputation as a writer of remarkable ingenuity. Built around the intriguing concept of "slow glass", through which light can take years to travel – thus allowing people to view scenes from the past – this story remains BS's best known. He would later incorporate it, together with two sequels, into the novel *Other Days, Other Eyes* (fixup **1972**; expurgated 1974).

His first novel was *Night Walk* (**1967** US), a fast-moving chase story. A man who has been blinded and condemned to a penal colony on a far planet invents a device that enables him to see through other people's (and animals') eyes and thus manages to escape. *The Two-Timers* (**1968** US), a well written tale of PARALLEL WORLDS, doppelgängers and murder, demonstrates BS's ability to handle characterization and, in particular, his talent for realistic dialogue. In *The Palace of Eternity* (**1969** US) he still more impressively controls a wide canvas featuring interstellar warfare, the environmental degradation of an Edenic planet, and human transcendence; the final section of the novel, where the hero finds himself reincarnated as an "Egon", or soul-like entity, displeased some critics, though it is in fact an effective handling of a traditional sf displacement of ideas from METAPHYSICS or RELIGION. This intelligent reworking of well worn sf theses was from the first BS's forte, as was demonstrated in his next novel, *One Million Tomorrows* (**1970** US), an IMMORTALITY tale whose twist lies in the fact that the option of eternal youth entails sexual impotence.

All BS's early books – which include also *Shadow of Heaven* (**1969** US; cut 1970 UK; rev vt *The Shadow of Heaven* 1991 UK) and *Ground Zero Man* (**1971** US; rev vt *The Peace Machine* 1985 UK) – were published first (and sometimes solely) in the USA; and their efficient anonymity of venue may result from an attempt to appeal to a transatlantic audience. Only slowly did BS come to write tales whose venue and protagonists were distinctly UK in feel; and it could be argued that his best work is his most general. *Orbitsville* (**1975**) – along with its rather less effective sequels, *Orbitsville Departure* (**1983**) and *Orbitsville Judgement* (**1990**) – must stand, after *Other Days, Other Eyes*, as his finest early inspiration. Like Larry NIVEN's *Ringworld* (**1970**) and Arthur C. CLARKE's *Rendezvous with Rama* (**1973**), the **Orbitsville** books centre on the discovery of – and later developments within – a vast alien artefact in space (a BIG DUMB OBJECT, in fact), in this case a DYSON SPHERE. Within the living-space provided by the inner surface of this artificial shell – billions of times the surface area of the Earth – BS spins an exciting story of political intrigue and exploration, which in later volumes develops, perhaps rather impatiently, into a heavily plotted move into another universe entirely. *Orbitsville* gained a 1976 BRITISH SCIENCE FICTION AWARD.

A Wreath of Stars (**1976**) may be BS's most original, and perhaps his finest, singleton. A rogue star, composed entirely of antineutrinos, approaches the Earth. It passes nearby with no immediately discernible effect. However, it is soon discovered that an antineutrino "Earth" exists within our planet, and its orbit has been seriously disturbed by the passage of the star. This is an ingenious, almost a poetic, idea, to which the plot only just fails to do full justice. Other books followed quickly: the overcomplicated *Medusa's Children* (**1977**); *Who Goes Here?* (**1977**), a *jeu d'esprit* akin to Harry HARRISON's *Bill, the Galactic Hero* (**1965**); *Ship of Strangers* (fixup **1978**), in which the crew of the Stellar Survey Ship *Sarafand*, after some routine adventures, confront a cosmological issue; *Vertigo* (**1978**; with "Dark Icarus" added as prologue, exp vt *Terminal Velocity* 1991), an effective *policier* set in a world transformed by ANTIGRAVITY devices; and *Dagger of the Mind* (**1979**) and *The Ceres Solution* (**1981**), in both of which BS's ingenuity declined, for a period, into something close to jumble. He had meanwhile been writing short stories – his collections include *Tomorrow Lies in Ambush* (coll **1973**; with 2 stories added, rev 1973 US), *Cosmic Kaleidoscope* (coll **1976**; with 1 story omitted and 2 added, rev 1977 US), *A Better Mantrap* (coll **1982**), *Between Two Worlds* (coll **1986** dos US) and *Dark Night in Toyland* (coll **1989**) – which again demonstrate his professional skills but tend to lack a sense of personal involvement.

However, with the **Ragged Astronauts** sequence – *The Ragged Astronauts* (**1986**), *The Wooden Spaceships* (**1988**) and *The Fugitive Worlds* (**1989**) – BS returned to his very best and most inventive form, describing with joyful exactness the sensation of emigrating, via hot-air BALLOON, up the hourglass funnel of atmosphere that connects two planets which orbit each other. Later volumes lost some of the freshness and elation of the first, but the series as a whole emphasizes BS's genuine stature in the genre as an entertainer who rarely fails to thrill the mind's eye with a new prospect. At his best, BS has been a lover of the worlds of sf. [DP/JC]

Other works: *The Best of the Bushel* (coll **1979** chap) and *The Eastercon Speeches* (coll **1979** chap), both humorous fan writing; *Galactic Tours: Thomas Cook Out of This World Vacations* (**1981** US) with David HARDY; *Courageous New Planet* (**1981** chap); *Serious Scientific Talks* (coll **1984** chap), humorous fan writing; *Fire Pattern* (**1984**); *Messages Found in an Oxygen Bottle* (coll **1986** dos US); *Killer Planet* (**1989**), juvenile sf.

About the author: *Bob Shaw* (anth **1981** chap) ed Paul Kincaid and Geoff Rippington; *Bob Shaw, Artist at Ground Zero* (last rev **1989** chap) by Gordon BENSON Jr, Chris Nelson and Phil STEPHENSEN-PAYNE.

See also: ALTERNATE WORLDS; ARTS; ASTEROIDS; COMICS; CONCEPTUAL BREAKTHROUGH; COSMOLOGY; DISCOVERY AND INVENTION; ESCHATOLOGY; FANTASTIC VOYAGES; FASTER THAN LIGHT; GRAVITY; HUMOUR; IMAGINARY SCIENCE; MATTER TRANSMISSION; MOON; PARASITISM AND SYMBIOSIS; PERCEPTION; PHYSICS; SATIRE; SCIENTIFIC ERRORS; SCIENTISTS; SPACE FLIGHT; TIME PARADOXES; UNDER THE SEA.

SHAW, BRIAN House name used by CURTIS WARREN on 4 novels by 4 different authors: *Argentis* (**1952**) by E.C. TUBB, *Ships of Vero* (**1952**) by David O'BRIEN, *Z Formation* (**1953**) by John Russell FEARN (signing himself Bryan Shaw) and *Lost World* (**1953**) by Brian

HOLLOWAY. All are adventure sf. [PN/JC]

SHAW, DAVID ◊ David Arthur GRIFFITHS.

SHAW, FREDERICK L(INCOLN) (1928-) US writer in whose routine sf novel, *Envoy to the Dog Star* (**1967** dos), a dog's brain travels to Sirius. [JC]

SHAW, GEORGE BERNARD (1856-1950) Irish-born writer of novels, plays and much controversial nonfiction; Nobel Literature Prize 1925. He lived most of his life in England, where he remained ferociously active over a writing career lasting 70 years. Some of his early plays – like *Man and Superman: A Comedy and a Philosophy* (**1903**) and *Androcles and the Lion* (performed 1913; as title of omni **1916**) – contain fantasy elements, though deployed with a cool Shavian sanity which repudiates any sense of escapism. *Press Cuttings* (**1909** chap), a play about women's rights set in the NEAR FUTURE, was close to sf, and the destruction of the old world order in *Heartbreak House* (as title of omni **1919**) seemed backward-looking only because of the play's five-year wait for publication. GBS's first genuine sf play was *Back to Methuselah: A Metabiological Pentateuch* (**1921** US; rev 1921 UK and several times further to 1945 UK), a 5-part depiction of mankind's EVOLUTION from the time of *Genesis* into the FAR FUTURE, when people have become long-lived and, by AD31,920, are on the verge of suffering corporeal transcendence into disembodied thought-entities. Hereafter GBS's plays – which have only posthumously escaped the charge that their dissolution of realist conventions simply demonstrated the senility of their author – increasingly utilized sf or fantasy modes to make a series of remarkably bleak utterances about *Homo sapiens* and about the chances of the species ever doing well. *The Apple Cart: A Political Extravaganza* (first English-language publication **1930**), set in the UK near the end of the century after a Channel Tunnel has been built, ironically posits monarchism as an answer to the power of great corporations. *Too True to be Good: A Political Extravaganza* (performed 1932) and *On the Rocks: A Political Comedy* (performed 1933) – both assembled in *Too True to be Good, Village Wooing & On the Rocks* (omni **1934**) – more scathingly and far-rangingly explore similar material, as do *The Simpleton of the Unexpected Isles: A Vision of Judgment* (**1935**) and *Geneva: A Fancied Page of History* (**1939**). *Buoyant Billions* (**1948** Switzerland; with *Farfetched Fables* as omni **1950**) presents some terminal UTOPIAN thoughts in the guise of fantasy.

None of GBS's 19th-century novels are of genre interest, but *The Adventures of the Black Girl in her Search for God* (**1932** chap) is fantasy, and some of the items assembled in *Short Stories* (coll **1932**) are sf. Both books were assembled with revisions as *Short Stories, Scraps and Shavings* (omni **1934**); *The Black Girl in Search of God, and Some Lesser Tales* (coll **1946**) also assembles this part of his oeuvre.

It should be noted that many of GBS's plays were "published" for the use of actors long before their official release, and that the official release was generally revised; moreover, during the last half century of his life – financial independence allowing him to subsidize this activity – GBS was in the habit of making constant unsignalled revisions to the extremely numerous reprints of his work. We have not attempted to trace these changes. [JC]

See also: ADAM AND EVE; IMMORTALITY; SUPERMAN; THEATRE.

SHAW, LARRY T. Working name of US writer and editor Lawrence Taylor Shaw (1924-1985), an active sf fan from the early 1940s and a member of the FUTURIANS; married to Lee HOFFMAN 1956-9. Beginning with "Secret Weapon" for *Fantasy Book* in 1948 as by Terry Thor, he published some sf stories into the early 1950s, but was primarily known for his editorial work. He was associate editor of IF May 1953-Mar 1954. In 1955 he became editor of INFINITY SCIENCE FICTION, which grew to be one of the leading sf magazines of its period; and he later started a companion title, SCIENCE FICTION ADVENTURES. When both magazines failed, in 1958, he turned to editing in other fields. He came back to sf as editor for Lancer Books (1963-8), where he built a successful sf line and edited the anthologies *Great Science Fiction Adventures* (anth **1964**) and *Terror!* (anth **1966**). He subsequently worked for Dell Books (1968-9) and American Art Enterprises (1969-75), founding Major Books for the firm. In 1975 he began to work as a literary agent, but this new career was hampered by poor health. He received a Special HUGO in 1984. [MJE/JC]

SHAWN, FRANK S. ◊ Ron GOULART.

SHAYOL US SEMIPROZINE, 7 issues, irregular, Nov 1977-1985, small-BEDSHEET slick format, published by Flight Unlimited, Kansas City; ed Pat CADIGAN. This was brought out by a partnership of Arnold Fenner (publisher) and Cadigan, now better known as a writer, whose first story, "Death from Exposure", was published in #2 (1978) and went on to win a Balrog AWARD. *S* was a development from Fenner's previous publication, *Chacal*, which had been largely devoted to SWORD AND SORCERY. With good covers, and excellent design and interior artwork – including work by Stephen FABIAN – *S* seemed almost created to prove a point about magazines not having to look tacky. It showcased good fiction, too, mixing sf and fantasy, from Michael BISHOP, C.J. CHERRYH, Charles L. GRANT, Tanith LEE, Tom REAMY, Lisa TUTTLE, Howard WALDROP and others. It was an astonishingly adept performance, the most spectacular (though by no means the most regular) sf/fantasy magazine of its era, though as a SMALL-PRESS publication it was not indexed in the N.E.S.F.A. magazine indexes. Having proved they could do it, Cadigan and Fenner simply stopped. [PN]

SHEA, CORNELIUS (1863-1920) US writer of dime novels (◊ DIME-NOVEL SF), prolific in many categories but best remembered for marvel stories using a fairly consistent "mythology" of dwarfs, subterranean eruptions, and stage illusion masquerading as supernatural magic. *Van Vincent's Vow* (**1892**) offers African

adventures, sex-exploiting Amazons, and a socialist UTOPIA founded by Egyptians who possess super-science. *The Enchanted Diamond* (**1894**) is a lost-race tale (◊ LOST WORLDS) featuring a passage underground between Alaska and Asia and a magical monarch. *The Hidden Island* (**1898**) describes a vicious She-like *femme fatale* (◊ H. Rider HAGGARD), who claims to be of Jovian descent, and a sinking island. In *The Wonderful Electric Man* (**1899**), to prevent OVERPOPULATION couples are put to death after the birth of their first child; if they have no children, they are put to death anyway. Probably by CS, *The Enchanted Emerald* (**1902**) as by P.T. Raymond describes an emerald with seemingly magical powers, plus lost civilizations and another She-like queen in Africa. CS's work was widely reprinted, often pseudonymously as "By the Author of 'The Wreck of the Glaucus'". [EFB]

SHEA, MICHAEL 1. Michael (Sinclair MacAuslan) Shea (1938-   ) UK writer, press secretary to the Queen for a decade from 1978. As Michael Sinclair he wrote a NEAR-FUTURE thriller, *The Dollar Covenant* (**1973**); and as MS *Tomorrow's Men* (**1982**), a DYSTOPIAN tale of the near-future UK in the grip of private armies – the USA soon takes a hand in straightening things out.

2. (1946-   ) US writer, mostly of FANTASY; most of his few sf stories border on horror. His books, which are both witty and disquieting, include *A Quest for Simbilis* (**1974**) – derived, with permission, from Jack VANCE's *The Eyes of the Overworld* (**1966**) – plus *Nifft the Lean* (coll of linked stories **1982**) and *In Yana, the Touch of Undying* (**1985**), both showing Vance's influence less explicitly. Other books include *The Color out of Time* (**1984**), a sequel to H.P. LOVECRAFT's *The Colour out of Space* (**1927**), *Fat Face* (**1987** chap) and *Polyphemus* (coll **1987**). The latter contains several deft sf tales, including the title story and the horrific "The Autopsy" (1980) about possession by an alien parasite. [JC]

SHEA, ROBERT (JOSEPH) (1933-   ) US writer and senior editor of *Playboy* magazine best known for collaborating with Robert Anton WILSON on the **Illuminatus!** trilogy – *The Eye in the Pyramid* (**1975**), *The Golden Apple* (**1975**) and *Leviathan* (**1975**), all assembled as *The Illuminatus Trilogy* (omni **1984**) – in which detective, FANTASY and sf components combine in the extremely complex tale of a vast conspiracy on the part of the Illuminati, historically a late-18th-century German association of freethinkers but here rendered into the gods of H.P. LOVECRAFT's **Cthulhu Mythos** (among other incarnations). The Illuminati plan, more or less, to destroy the world in their search for power; almost everything of meaning in the contemporary world turns out somehow to signify their malign omnipresence. The influence of Thomas PYNCHON's *The Crying of Lot 49* (**1966**) is evident though, where the PARANOIA of that novel was presented with haunting conviction, the **Illuminatus!** books, simultaneously deadpan and hysterical, treat conspiracy as a game. RS subsequently wrote solo contributions (*see Wilson's entry for his own continuations*): *The Saracen: Land of the Infidel* (**1989**) and *The Saracen: The Holy War* (**1989**) provide background to the main enterprise. *Time of the Dragons* (**1981**) and *Last of the Zinja* (**1981**), both assembled as *Shike* (omni **1992**), are historical novels with fantasy elements. *Shaman* (**1991**) is a fantasy. [JC]

See also: HUMOUR; LIBERTARIAN SF; MUSIC; THEATRE.

SHECKLEY, ROBERT (1928-   ) US writer, born and educated in New York, where he set some of his fiction, publishing his first story, "Final Examination", for *Imagination* in 1952. RS's career falls into 3 periods: the 1950s, the 1960s, and afterwards. In the first period he produced short fiction prolifically for several years in various magazines, though his supple, witty, talkative, well crafted work was especially suited to GALAXY SCIENCE FICTION, where much of it appeared. This work remains, perhaps, his best known. In the second period he wrote several novels which combined "zany" plots, metaphysical speculation and comic SATIRE. In the third period he has rested. *The Collected Short Stories of Robert Sheckley* (coll in 5 vols **1991**), though incomplete, gives a good view of the entire career.

RS's first collection, *Untouched by Human Hands* (coll **1954**; with differing contents 1955 UK), is one of the finest début volumes ever published in the field, and contains several tales which have remained famous, including "The Monsters" (1953), the title story (1952), and the superb "Specialist" (1953) which, with an energy and adroitness typical of his early work, posits a Galaxy inhabited by a variety of cooperating races who can merge their specialized functions to become, literally, SPACESHIPS. The story describes the search for a new Pusher, a being capable of shoving the ship to FASTER-THAN-LIGHT velocities – unsurprisingly for the 1950s, *Homo sapiens* turns out to be a Pusher species. Also in the collection is "Seventh Victim" (1953), much later filmed as *La* DECIMA VITTIMA (1965), in turn novelized by RS as *The Tenth Victim* * (**1966**); see below for its feeble continuation into a series. Further successful collections followed swiftly: *Citizen in Space* (coll **1955**), *Pilgrimage to Earth* (coll **1957**), *Notions: Unlimited* (coll **1960**), *Store of Infinity* (coll **1960**) and *Shards of Space* (coll **1962**). Later compilations include *The Robert Sheckley Omnibus* (coll **1973** UK) ed Robert CONQUEST and *Is THAT What People Do?: The Selected Short Stories* (coll **1984**). RS's stories are unfailingly elegant and literate; their mordant humour and sudden plot reversals separate them from the mass of magazine sf stories of the time, for the wit and surprises usually function to make serious points about the calamitous aspects of life in the later 20th century. At the same time, RS clearly found it worthwhile during these early years to express the corrosive pessimism of his wit within the storytelling conventions of sf, to dress his nihilism in sheep's clothing.

The second period began with *Immortality Delivered* (1958-9 *Gal* as "Time Killer"; **1958**; exp vt *Immortality,*

Inc. 1959), filmed in 1992 as FREEJACK, and continued with his best novels, *The Status Civilization* (**1960**), *Journey Beyond Tomorrow* (**1962**; vt *The Journey of Joenes* 1978 UK) and *Mindswap* (**1966**). In these books the typical Candide-like RS protagonist began, at times unduly, to dominate. In short stories, the occasionally venal naïveté of this character did not much impair the rhythm of the tale; but in the novels his lethargy tended to be translated into plots which lacked drive. The typical RS full-length story is episodic, befitting the protagonist's lack of drive, and structured as a kind of guided tour of a particular sf milieu RS wishes to expose to satirical view; dumped into this disconcerting circuit, his typical protagonist must scramble about – sometimes comically – in order to survive and to gain some orientation. The protagonist of the first novel, after dying in a car crash, awakens 150 years hence in a whirligig USA where most forms of psychic phenomena, including life and death, have been verified. *The Status Civilization* is genuinely successful, embodying its satirical despairs in a shaped narrative set on a prison planet, where social hierarchies have turned topsy-turvy and conformity means being always wicked. In *Journey Beyond Tomorrow* the RS protagonist is an innocent who suffers a variety of alarming adventures after leaving his quiet NEAR-FUTURE Pacific island; the novel takes the form of a series of remembrances enshrined as myths 1000 years later. In *Mindswap* the protagonist switches minds with a Martian and is subjected to reality displacements galore. That was the end of RS's easy years.

Dimension of Miracles (**1968**) – in which the protagonist wins in error a prize which shunts him back and forth across a Galaxy whose reality is disconcertingly arbitrary – may be thought to signal the slow onset of the third RS period, which was marked by novels either uneasy (like *Miracles*) or absent-minded, like *Dramocles: An Intergalactic Soap Opera* (**1983**). RS also continued his **Victim** sequence, begun in 1966 with *The Tenth Victim*, in 2 uninspired sequels, *Victim Prime* (**1987** UK) and *Hunter/Victim* (**1988** UK). The best novel of the period was probably *Options* (**1975**), a tale whose sf apparatus could be taken as a delusional frame, or understood as a series of dramatic projections – generated by the protagonist – of the various forms his life could be read as taking, rather after the fashion of Barry N. MALZBERG, whose treatment of sf themes as metaphors for all-too-human problems RS's late work most resembles. But *The Alchemical Marriage of Alistair Crompton* (1958 *Gal* as "The Humours"; exp **1978** UK; vt *Crompton Divided* 1978 US) – about the attempts of a paranoid schizophrenic to reassemble his mind, which has been split off into three widely separated receptacles – is also strong. The quality of RS's short fiction was less variable, though his increasing tendency to write almost ABSURDIST stories (◊ FABULATION) was not perhaps to the taste of the sf market in general – a sense reflected in the fact that many of them were first published in slick magazines such as *Playboy* rather than in sf magazines, though "A Suppliant in Space" won the Jupiter AWARD for the Best Short Story of 1973. *The People Trap* (coll **1968**) contains a mixture of old and new stories, but most of the fiction in *Can You Feel Anything When I Do This?* (coll **1971**; vt *The Same to You Doubled* 1974 UK) is typical of his late work – spasmodic, hilarious, despairing. Further examples can be found in *The Robot who Looked like Me* (coll **1978** UK) and *The Wonderful World of Robert Sheckley* (coll **1979**). It may be that RS's inability to take seriously the simpler, more adventurous forms the genre can take, which he regularly and affectionately parodied when young, has had a paralysing effect on the mature writer, who sometimes sounds like a tongue-tied Kurt VONNEGUT Jr. If this is so, it is a considerable loss to the sf field that one of its sharpest wits can no longer pay it serious attention. [JC]

Other works: *Futuropolis* (**1978**), nonfiction; *The Status Civilization, and Notions: Unlimited* (omni **1979**); *After the Fall* (anth **1980**); *The People Trap/Mindswap* (omni **1981**); *Bill, the Galactic Hero on the Planet of Bottled Brains* * (**1990**) with Harry HARRISON; *Watchbird* (**1990** chap); *Minotaur Maze* (**1991**); *Xolotl* (**1991** chap); *Alien Starswarm* (**1991** chap); *Bring Me the Head of Prince Charming* (**1991**) with Roger ZELAZNY.

Crime fiction/thrillers: 7 novels, from *Calibre .50* (**1961**) to *Time Limit* (**1967**).

See also: ANTI-INTELLECTUALISM IN SF; CITIES; CRIME AND PUNISHMENT; DISCOVERY AND INVENTION; ECONOMICS; ESCHATOLOGY; FORCE FIELD; GAMES AND SPORTS; GODS AND DEMONS; HISTORY OF SF; HUMOUR; LEISURE; MEDIA LANDSCAPE; OMNI; OVERPOPULATION; PARANOIA; RE-INCARNATION; ROBOTS; SEX; SUPERNATURAL CREATURES; TABOOS.

SHEDLEY, ETHAN Pseudonym of Belgian-born writer Boris Beiser (1934-   ), in the USA from 1941. In *Earth Ship and Star Song* (**1979**) humanity finds itself banned from ruined Earth. *The Medusa Conspiracy* (**1980**) is a more conventional adventure. [JC]

SHEEHAN, PERLEY POORE (1875-1943) US writer and journalist responsible for much magazine fiction. *The Abyss of Wonders* (1915 *Argosy*; **1953**) mixes Theosophy and superscience in its tale of a lost race in the Gobi Desert (◊ LOST WORLDS). [JC]

Other works: *The Seer* (**1912**; vt *The Prophet* 1913 UK); *The One Gift* (1920 *Argosy*; **1974** chap); *The Whispering Chorus* (**1928**).

SHEFFIELD, CHARLES (1935-   ) UK-born physicist and writer, in the USA from the mid-1960s, publishing the first of nearly 100 technical papers and science articles in 1962, and the first of 80 or more sf stories, "What Song the Sirens Sang", for *Gal* in 1977; many of these stories are assembled in *Vectors* (coll **1979**) and *Hidden Variables* (coll **1981**). His first novel, *Sight of Proteus* (**1978**), describes in ultimately optimistic terms the wide-ranging effects of machine-driven shapechanging technologies which might open the way to the nearby stars; the book almost instantly established CS's reputation for briskly argued,

cleverly plotted, sanguine HARD SF, a reputation only marginally darkened by the late sequel *Proteus Unbound* (**1989**), which recasts material from the earlier book. Both tales were assembled as *Proteus Manifest* (omni **1989**). CS's second novel, *The Web Between the Stars* (**1979**), famously posited a sky-hook space elevator at almost exactly the same time as Arthur C. CLARKE presented an astonishingly similar space elevator in *The Fountains of Paradise* (**1979**); the concepts had clearly been arrived at independently, and their similarity only underscored the clarity of each man's scientific imagination.

In the 1980s, with an exuberance that seemed almost irresponsible in a writer of his scientific bent, CS ranged very widely in his choice of metier. *The Selkie* (**1982**) with David F. BISCHOFF, a SCIENCE-FANTASY novel tinged with elements of horror, describes a MUTANT race of male "wereseals" who must mate with human women to perpetuate their kind. *My Brother's Keeper* (**1982**) is an sf thriller whose MCGUFFIN, astonishingly, is half of the protagonist's brother's brain, housed in half the protagonist's head. *Erasmus Magister* (coll of linked stories **1982**) features Erasmus DARWIN in a series of lightly told scientific adventures, and *The McAndrew Chronicles* (coll of linked stories **1983**) follows the exploits of the eponymous inventor. *Between the Strokes of Night* (**1985**) is a "cosmogony opera" sometimes compared to novels by Greg BEAR about exploring, understanding and transforming the Universe; in this case, exiled from Earth, humanity finds infinite resources in "S-space" and travels down the aisles of time to visit the Galaxy. *The Nimrod Hunt* (**1986**) features intricately interesting ALIENS and CYBORGS in a SPACE-OPERA setting. *Trader's World* (fixup **1988**) moves from a post-HOLOCAUST venue to higher things, including the threat of alien INVASION. *Cold as Ice* (**1992**) depicts with glad clarity a Solar System full of highly active and scientifically curious human beings. The **Heritage Universe** sequence – *Summertide* (**1990**), *Divergence* (**1991**) and *Transcendence* (**1992**), with a further volume planned – fills much of the Universe with BIG DUMB OBJECTS and sets in train a complex of plots hinging upon their decipherment and use. Some of his tales are dark enough, and ironies are frequently evident; but CS continues to seem ready to feel that the Universe may be enjoyed. [JC]

Other works (all nonfiction): *Commercial Operations in Space 1980-2000* (anth **1981**) ed with John L. McLucas; *Earthwatch: A Survey of the World from Space* (**1981** UK); *Man on Earth: How Civilization and Technology Changed the Face of the World – A Survey from Space* (**1983**); *Space Careers* (**1984**) with Carol Rosin.

See also: ASTOUNDING SCIENCE-FICTION; BIOLOGY; COS-MOLOGY; DEL REY BOOKS; DISCOVERY AND INVENTION; END OF THE WORLD; GENETIC ENGINEERING; SUSPENDED ANIMA-TION; TRANSPORTATION.

SHEFNER, VADIM (SERGEEVICH) (1915-   ) Russian writer known mostly for his poetry (from *c*1963) and mainstream fiction. Two short novels, *Tchelovek*

S Piatiu "Ne" (trans Alice Stone Nakhimovsky and Alexander Nakhimovsky as "The Unman") and *Devushka U Obryva* (**1970**; trans Antonina W. Bouis as "Kovrigin's Chronicles"), were published in omnibus form as *The Unman; Kovrigin's Chronicles* (omni **1980** US). Both are – like other work assembled as *Skromny Genii* ["A Modest Genius"] (coll **1974**), *Imia Dlia Ptitsy* ["The Name for the Bird"] (coll **1976**), *Kruglaia Taina* ["The Round Mystery"] (coll **1977**) and *Skazki Dlia Unmykh* ["Fairy-Tales for Smart Ones"] (coll **1985**) – poetical and sometimes ironical borderline fantasies: modern urban fairy-tales. VS's full-length novel, *Latchuga Dolzhnika* ["A Debtor's Hovel"], is a mature literary work, combining elements of sf with those of philosophical prose. [VG]

See also: SCIENTISTS.

SHELDON, ALICE B. [r] ◊ James TIPTREE Jr.

SHELDON, LEE Pseudonym of US writer and mail-man Wayne Cyril Lee (1917-　　), who began publishing sf with "Project Asteroid" for *Teens* in 1966. His routine sf adventure novel was *Doomed Planet* (**1967**). [JC]

SHELDON, RACCOONA [s] ◊ James TIPTREE Jr.

SHELDON, ROY UK house name used by Hamilton & Co. (which published Panther Books) on short fiction and full-length novels in AUTHENTIC 1951-2 and on some routine sf novels 1952-4 by H.J. CAMPBELL, George HAY and E.C. TUBB. [JC]

SHELLEY, MARY WOLLSTONECRAFT (1797-1851) UK writer, daughter of the philosopher and novelist William Godwin (1756-1836) and of the feminist and educationist Mary Wollstonecraft (1759-1797), who died giving birth to her. MWS married Percy Bysshe Shelley (1792-1822) in 1816, 2 years after they had eloped to the Continent, and after his first wife had committed suicide. During 1816 the Shelleys spent much time with Lord Byron (1788-1824) who (or possibly his physician, John William Polidori [1795-1821]) suggested, after reading some of their work, that they should each write a ghost story. Nothing much came of Byron's or Percy Shelley's efforts, though Dr Polidori wrote *The Vampyre* (**1819**), but MWS – who was in her teens – wrote *Frankenstein, or The Modern Prometheus* (**1818**; rev 1831), the most famous English HORROR novel – though perhaps not the most widely read, as its conventional GOTHIC narrative structure, which involves stories within frames and sentimentalized rhetoric, makes it somewhat difficult going for many modern readers more familiar with the numerous film, tv and other spin-offs from the original tale (◊ FRANKENSTEIN; FRANKENSTEIN MONSTER). The young Swiss scientist Franken-stein is obsessed with the notion that the spark of life may be a "spark" in some literal fashion, and hopes to create life by galvanizing dead matter. To this end he collects human remains, constructs a grotesque but mechanically sound body, and shocks it into life. The awakened/created MONSTER, initially innocent but soon corrupted by Frankenstein's growing revulsion, demands of his maker that a mate be created for him,

and when this demand is refused starts on a rampage in which Frankenstein's wife and brother are killed. Frankenstein begins to track the monster down to destroy it, but eventually perishes, his mind gone, deep in the Arctic. The monster disappears across the ice floes.

The increasing critical attention *Frankenstein* has received in recent years has focused on MWS herself, on her relation to her father's rationalist philosophy, and on her life with her husband at the time of the book's genesis. The novel itself has been analysed in terms of these concerns, perhaps most fruitfully in studies of its relation to the idea of the "natural man". The monster – who reads Goethe's *The Sorrows of Young Werther* (**1774**) – is in a sense a *tabula rasa*, and the evil that he does, he is shaped to do by the revulsion and persecution of others; he has to *learn* to be a monster. Alternatively, he can be thought of as an embodiment of the evil latent in mankind, in which case he need merely be given the opportunity to be a monster. The novel has also been studied as a defining model of the Gothic mode of fiction, and in *Billion Year Spree* (**1973**; much exp vt *Trillion Year Spree* 1986 with David WINGROVE), Brian W. ALDISS argues its importance as the first genuine sf novel, the first significant rendering of the relations between mankind and science through an image of mankind's dual nature appropriate to an age of science. Aldiss's own *Frankenstein Unbound* (**1973**) treats of both MWS and her creation. Although MWS's novel does seem vulgarly to argue that there are things that Man is not meant to know, it is far more than an awful-warning shot across the bows of the evils of scientism; no simple paraphrase of this sort can adequately describe it.

MWS wrote a further PROTO-SCIENCE-FICTION novel, *The Last Man* (**1826**), set at the end of the 21st century, in which a plague decimates humanity. The surviving Americans invade Europe but, although war ends before the extinction of humanity, the remaining British are soon reduced through strife to the last man of the title, who much resembles MS's late husband, and who ends the novel in a small boat sailing to nowhere. The tale served as a model for much subsequent work using its basic idea of a world in which there can be a last, secular survivor. The story of most interest assembled by Richard GARNETT in *Tales and Stories by Mary Wollstonecraft Shelley* (coll **1891**) is *The Mortal Immortal* (in *The Keepsake* [anth **1934**]; c1910 chap US); the later *Collected Tales and Stories* (coll **1976** US) is more convenient. *The Mary Shelley Reader* (coll **1990** US) presents the original – and rather more sharply told – 1818 version of *Frankenstein*, several short stories, and other valuable material. [JC]

About the author: There is much criticism. *Mary Shelley* (**1959**) by E. Bigland; *Mary Shelley* (**1972**) by William A. Walling; *Ariel Like a Harpy: Shelley, Mary and Frankenstein* (**1972**; vt *Mary Shelley's Frankenstein: Tracing the Myth* US) by Christopher Small; *Mary*

Shelley's Monster – The Story of Frankenstein (**1976**) by Martin Tropp; *Moon in Eclipse: A Life of Mary Shelley* (**1978**) by Jane Dunn; *Mary Shelley* (**1985**) by Harold BLOOM. Critical editions of *Frankenstein* include those ed M.K. JOSEPH (**1969**), James Rieger (**1974** US), Maurice Hindle (**1985**).

See also: ANDROIDS; ANONYMOUS SF AUTHORS; BIOLOGY; CONCEPTUAL BREAKTHROUGH; CRITICAL AND HISTORICAL WORKS ABOUT SF; DISCOVERY AND INVENTION; END OF THE WORLD; FANTASTIC VOYAGES; GODS AND DEMONS; HISTORY OF SF; HOLOCAUST AND AFTER; HORROR IN SF; MEDICINE; POWER SOURCES; RELIGION; SCIENTISTS; SEX; THEATRE; WOMEN SF WRITERS.

SHELTON, MILES [s] ◊ Don WILCOX.

SHEPARD, LUCIUS (1947-   ) US writer whose first work was POETRY, whose first book was a poem, *Cantata of Death, Weakmind & Generation* (**1967** chap), and who began to publish prose fictions of genre interest only with "The Taylorsville Reconstruction" for *Universe 13* (anth **1983**) ed Terry CARR. Between the mid-1960s and the beginning of the 1980s, LS lived in various parts of the world, travelled widely, became – according to his own testimony – marginally and incompetently involved in the fringes of the international drug trade, and in about 1972 started a rock band which went through various incarnations over the following years. Some of the experiences of this long apprenticeship are directly reflected in stories like "A Spanish Lesson" (1985); but the abiding sense of authority generated by all his best work depends upon the born exile's passionate fixation on place. It is no accident that – aside from the Latin American MAGIC-REALIST tradition whose influence upon him is often suggested – the writer whom LS seems at times most to resemble is Joseph CONRAD, for both authors respond to the places of the world with imaginative avarice and a hallucinated intensity of portrayal; both create deeply alienated protagonists whose displacement from the venues in which they live generates constant ironies and regrets; and both tend to subordinate mundane resolutions of plot to moments of terminal, deathly transcendence. None of this constitutes a necessary or sufficient description of an sf writer; and certainly, despite his aesthetic influence on the genre in the years since his explosive début (for which he received a JOHN W. CAMPBELL AWARD in 1985), LS is not at heart an sf writer.

His first novel, however, is as much sf as horror. In *Green Eyes* (**1984**) a research organization in the US Deep South has successfully created zombies by injecting cadavers with bacteria from a graveyard. As an sf premise, this is unconvincing; but LS presents the transformation of dead bodies into representative human archetypes, and the escape of one of them into bayou country, with a gripping closeness of touch; the transcendental epiphany at the end, already characteristic of his work, also tests true. His second novel, *Life during Wartime* (fixup **1987**), similarly embeds sf elements – a 21st-century setting,

advanced forms of drug manipulation – into a Latin American venue which, essentially, absorbs these elements in a horrified, dense presentation of a Vietnam WAR conducted, this time, in the Western Hemisphere. "R & R" (1986), which won a NEBULA, shapes the first part of the book; and a hallucinated, obsessed journey into the heart of darkness in search of underlying transcendence dominates its last sections. *Kallimantan* (**1990** UK) evokes, with extreme vividness, Conrad himself as well as Graham Greene (1904-1991) in another transcendental heart-of-darkness tale, set this time in Borneo and featuring at its centre a not altogether convincing transference to an sf ALTERNATE WORLD.

LS continues to be most successful at novelette/ novella length, and several of the longer tales assembled in *The Jaguar Hunter* (coll **1987**; with 1 story cut and 3 added, rev 1988 UK; cut 1989 US) and *The Ends of the Earth* (coll **1991**) are among the finest FABULATIONS composed by a US writer in recent years. A story sequence – "The Man who Painted the Dragon Griaule" (1984) plus 2 novellas, *The Scalehunter's Beautiful Daughter* (**1988**) and *The Father of Stones* (**1988**) – makes the same use of the devices of high fantasy that the full-length novels made of sf: as material to massage into thematic compost, in the heart of which dark epiphanies may be viewed and embraced, perhaps at the cost of death. LS has clearly felt comfortable with sf, as he uses it; and the genre has benefited from the publication of a dozen tales which assimilate sf into a wider imaginative world. At the time of writing, however, there is some sense that two ships may have passed in the night.   [JC]

About the author: *A Checklist of Lucius Shepard* (**1991** chap) by Tom Joyce and Christopher P. STEPHENS.

See also: ACE BOOKS; ESCHATOLOGY; FANTASY; GOTHIC SF; ISAAC ASIMOV'S SCIENCE FICTION MAGAZINE; REINCARNATION.

SHERBURNE, ZOA (MORIN) (1912-   ) US author of an sf novel for older children, *The Girl who Knew Tomorrow* (**1970**). *Why Have the Birds Stopped Singing?* (**1974**) is fantasy.   [JC]

SHERIDAN, THOMAS [s] ◊ Walter GILLINGS.

SHERMAN, HAROLD M(ORROW) (1898-1987) US writer. His first work was the **Tahara** sequence – *Tahara, Boy King of the Desert* (**1933**), *Tahara Among African Tribes* (**1933**), *Tahara, Boy Mystic of India* (**1933**) and *Tahara in the Land of Yucatan* (**1933**) – in which a young White boy parachutes into the Sahara and becomes king of the Stone Age inhabitants of a LOST WORLD; subsequent novels take him and his companions to various lands (ATLANTIS is mentioned but not visited), where they solve various mysteries (sometimes by ESP). HMS later became known almost exclusively for work published in AMAZING STORIES in the 1940s, most notably *The Green Man* (**1946**) and its sequel, "The Green Man Returns" (1947 *AMZ*), both assembled as *The Green Man and his Return* (coll **1979**), in which the eponymous ALIEN tries to bring peace to a recalcitrant Earth.   [JC]

SHERMAN, JOEL HENRY (?   -   ) US writer who began publishing sf with "Medium" for *AMZ* in 1984. His first novel, *Corpseman* (**1988**), is an unremarkable tale of a CYBORG who must cope with false imprisonment. More interestingly, *Random Factor* (**1991**) combines routine sf-thriller components with an ALIEN race whose nature must be deciphered at the interstellar station where various species are in conflict.   [JC]

SHERMAN, MICHAEL and PETER MICHAEL [s] ◊ Robert A.W. LOWNDES.

SHERRED, T(HOMAS) L. (1915-1985) US writer who worked in Detroit for the auto industry as a technical writer. His production of fiction was small, and *First Person, Peculiar* (coll **1972**) contains all the stories for which he is remembered, most significantly "E for Effort", his first published story (1947 *ASF*). It describes, humorously but with a fundamental pessimism, the consequences of a device that permits its users to view past and present events. Its inventor and his associate are successful at first, but are soon defeated by government forces. Ultimately the existence of the "camera" in the hands of the US military causes a final WAR, as the victim-narrator has predicted. (It is understood that the story was accepted for *ASF* in John W. CAMPBELL Jr's absence.) The other tales are "Cue for Quiet" (1953), "Eye for Iniquity" (1953) and "Cure, Guaranteed" (1954); they are clearcut, forceful and black. The note accompanying "Bounty" in *Again, Dangerous Visions* (anth **1972**) ed Harlan ELLISON revealed that TLS had suffered a mild stroke before 1971 and was unlikely to write further. However, *Alien Island* (**1970**), his first novel, had already been written; its sequel, *Alien Main* (**1985**) with Lloyd BIGGLE Jr, was completed by his collaborator. *Alien Island* is a sometimes comic but fundamentally melancholy tale about ALIENS secretly on Earth and the eventual disaster that results; the sequel – set two centuries later, with an Earth-descended alien defending the beleaguered planet – broadens and softens the implications of the first book, but returned TLS, at the close of his life, to the sf main.   [JC]

See also: MACHINES; MONEY; TIME TRAVEL.

SHERRELL, CARL (1929-1990) US commercial artist and, later, writer whose novels are essentially fantasies, with the exception of the unremarkable *The Space Prodigal* (**1981**). His fantasies are the **Raum** sequence – *Raum* (**1977**) and *Skraelings* (**1987**) – plus *Arcane* (**1978**) and *The Curse* (**1989**).   [JC]

SHERRIFF, R(OBERT) C(EDRIC) (1896-1975) UK playwright, novelist and film-writer, known mainly for his hit play *Journey's End* (**1929**), filmed in 1930 by James Whale and in 1975 as *Aces High*. His sf novel, *The Hopkins Manuscript* (**1939**; rev vt *The Cataclysm* 1958), is a DISASTER tale set mostly in rural England where the protagonist, Edgar Hopkins (whose manuscript is discovered hundreds of years later by Abyssinian archaeologists), fussily eulogizes his beloved countryside and people as the dislodged Moon crashes into the Atlantic Ocean, causing tornadoes and tsunamis. Hopkins then records an abortive recovery of civilization before the Moon's mineral wealth tempts the shattered nations of Europe into terminal conflict and an Asian warlord moves in. The science is derisory, but the elegy is strongly felt. RCS wrote the screenplay for the 1933 film *The* INVISIBLE MAN.   [JC]

SHERWOOD, MARTIN (ANTHONY) (1942-   ) UK writer with a PhD in organic chemistry; editor of *Chemistry & Industry*. His sf novels are *Survival* (**1975**) and *Maxwell's Demon* (**1976**); in the latter, ALIENS invade humans, thus putting them to sleep.   [JC]

SHETTERLY, WILL [r] ◊ Emma BULL.

SHEW, ROWLAND ◊ Michael F. FLYNN.

SHIBANO, TAKUMI (1926-   ) Japanese writer, translator and critic. TS began writing sf as Rei Kozumi while a high-school mathematics teacher – a job he quit in 1977 to become a full-time translator; he published his first short story in 1951. Later, 1969-75, he published 3 sf juveniles, including *Hokkyoku-Shi No Hanran* ["Revolt in North-Pole City"] (**1977**). But his influence on Japanese sf was more in his work as editor and publisher of the widely circulated *Uchujin* (1957-current), the first Japanese FANZINE, in which many stories by later-prominent sf writers – such as Sakyo KOMATSU – were published; it reached #190 in 1991 and continues to introduce new writers. One of the most prominent figures in the Japanese sf community, TS has received many sf awards; the "Takumi Shibano Award", given since 1982 to people who have performed generous work in fandom, was named after him. As a translator he has specialized in HARD SF: most of Larry NIVEN's books as well as works by James P. HOGAN, Poul ANDERSON, Hal CLEMENT and many more – about 50 books in all. TS has also ed 2 anthologies of stories from *Uchujin*, the first in 3 vols (1977) and the second in 2 (1987). He wrote the entry on JAPAN in this encyclopedia.   [PN]

SHIEL, M(ATTHEW) P(HIPPS) (1865-1947) UK writer, born Shiell in Montserrat in the British West Indies; in the UK from his late teens. He began writing fiction in the late 1880s and continued intermittently until his death, although his significant fantastic fiction was published 1896-1901. MPS was intensely concerned with style *per se*, incorporating poetic techniques into narrative prose; he also used sensational adventure fiction as a vehicle for idiosyncratic ideas about ECONOMICS, science and RELIGION. As a result, his work is not to every reader's taste, although it has been praised highly by such critics and fellow writers as Rebecca West (1892-1983), Dashiell Hammett (1894-1961) and Dorothy L. Sayers (1893-1957).

Since MPS matured in England during the *fin de siècle*, it is not surprising that his early work shows highly romantic subject matter and an obsessive concern with decorated prose, his models being mostly Edgar Allan POE and mid-19th-century French writers. Early work includes extremely baroque detective short stories, in *Prince Zaleski* (coll **1895**), and horror fiction collected in *Shapes in the Fire* (coll **1896**) and *The Pale Ape* (coll **1911**). Although these stories, written in a lapidary style, were on the edge of being old-fashioned when they appeared, they are among the very best examples of their sort.

After his noncommercial early work, MPS shifted to serials for the popular press. Future-WAR novels include *The Yellow Danger* (1889 *Short Stories* as "The Empress of the Earth"; **1898**) and *The Dragon* (1913 *The Red Magazine* as "To Arms!"; **1913**). Both novels, which contain sf elements (especially *The Dragon*), are adventure stories in which the Yellow Peril – i.e., Chinese hordes – overwhelms the world by sheer quantity of manpower. Both, however, depart from the stereotyped Yellow Peril story in seeing the quarrel between Orient and Occident as ultimately a spiritual matter, rather than economic, as Chinese and UK SUPERMEN strive for domination. Both novels are developed along similar lines, basic ideas being: the horrors of war (depicted on such a colossal scale and with such sangfroid that some have seen MPS's attitude as callous approval); a strange mixing of Nietzschean and Tolstoyan theories of history, in which supermen make history but are generated by their culture; a Spencerian survival of the fittest on a racial level; and thinly veiled suggestions of paranoia. Both books, aimed at a popular market, are sparsely written with no attempt at stylistic decoration. A third war novel, *The Yellow Wave* (**1905**), is a non-fantastic work based on the Russo-Japanese War (1904-5).

MPS's finest work is generally conceded to have been *The Purple Cloud* (**1901**), the story of the last man left on Earth after hydrocyanic acid gas liberated by volcanism has killed off mammalian life. The doings of the protagonist, driven mad by solitude, are brilliantly and vividly imagined. Behind the story, however, lies a mythic cosmic struggle between opposing forces that use humans as tools. *The Lord of the Sea* (**1901**; savagely cut 1924 US), almost as fine, is strongly based on *Le Comte de Monte-Cristo* (**1844-5**; trans anon as *The Count of Monte-Cristo* 1846 UK) by Alexandre Dumas (1802-1870). It develops a network of mid-19th-century sensational motifs – incredible coincidences, swapped babies, hidden identities, chance-found incredible wealth, documents in a trunk, festering revenges, elaborate prison escapes, frustrated romance, Napoleonic megalomania – yet, though written to an aesthetic outdated for its time, it embodies that aesthetic with enormous élan and vitality. The essence of the book is a concept adapted from the work of the popular US economist Henry George (1839-1897): if certain individuals can hog the land, others can hog the sea. Building on this insight, one Hogarth, using the wealth plucked from a diamond-laden meteorite, builds sea forts and claims ownership of the oceans. *The Lord of the Sea* has been criticized as antisemitic, since it depicts a UK overrun by Jewish refugees from Continental pogroms,

including unpleasant caricatures reminiscent of the stage Jew of earlier drama; other critics, however, have rejected the accusation.

MPS's other fantastic fiction includes: *The Last Miracle* (**1906**), about a plot to discredit Christianity with fake miraculous visions created by gigantic hologram-like devices; "The Place of Pain Day" (1914 *The Red Magazine*), about a natural water lens that shows horrors on the Moon, and "The Future Day" (1928 *London Daily Herald*), about life and love in an aeronautic culture, which both appeared in *The Invisible Voices* (coll **1935**); and *This Above All* (**1933**; vt *Above All Else* 1943), about a trio of immortals made so by Jesus, who is alive in Tibet. MPS also occasionally ghost-wrote for Louis TRACY; the sf novel *An American Emperor* (**1897**), as by Tracy, is in large part by MPS. His last sf work, *The Young Men are Coming* (**1937**), deals partly with contemporary social upheaval and partly with an interstellar visit. The multiple-sex ALIENS are far superior to humanity and possess an incredible superscience. The sf element is much more sophisticated and imaginative than contemporary GENRE SF, but is buried in a welter of eccentric social philosophy, and told in the decorated style of its author's youth. The result is at times almost unreadable.

With MPS is associated the "Kingdom of Redonda". His sea-trader father (MPS claimed) laid claim to the small uninhabited ISLAND of Redonda, near Antigua, and in a ceremony there crowned young Matthew king. On MPS's death the "crown" passed to John GAWSWORTH, who awarded titles of nobility to persons associated with Shiel, including Sayers, West, Edward SHANKS and Dylan Thomas (1914-1953). On Gawsworth's death the title became clouded.

MPS has received some attention outside fantastic fiction as a writer of partial Black ancestry, and as perhaps the first UK novelist of Caribbean origin. [EFB]

Other works: *The Best Short Stories of M.P. Shiel* (coll **1948**) ed John Gawsworth; *Xélucha and Others* (coll **1975** US); *Prince Zaleski and Cummings King Monk* (coll **1977** US).

About the author: *The Works of M.P. Shiel: A Study in Bibliography* (**1948**), rev and much exp as *The Works of M.P. Shiel – Updated* (in 2 vols **1980**) by A. Reynolds Morse, along with *Shiel in Diverse Hands* (anth **1984**), also ed Morse; "The World, the Devil, and M.P. Shiel" by Sam Moskowitz in *Explorers of the Infinite* (coll **1963**); "The Politics of Evolution: Philosophical Themes in the Speculative Fiction of M.P. Shiel" in *Foundation* #27 (1983) by Brian M. STABLEFORD.

See also: END OF THE WORLD; MEDICINE; MESSIAHS; POLITICS; SOCIAL DARWINISM; VILLAINS; WEAPONS.

SHINER, LEWIS (1950-   ) US writer who began publishing sf with "Tinker's Damn" for *Galileo* in 1977, and who wrote a substantial number of tales before beginning to assemble them in *Nine Hard Questions about the Nature of the Universe* (coll **1990**) and *The Edges of Things* (coll **1991**). His work in short form has been various, tending at its best to a clear-edged intensity which gives his venues, whether or not sf, a glow of seriousness; at its less impressive, in earlier stories, there is a sense of overindustrious journeyman plundering of recent sf writers for models. But increasingly an engaged and sophisticated mind can be seen extracting hard kernels of import out of those models. LS's first novel, *Frontera* (**1984**), in which a team is sent to MARS by a large corporation to investigate an abandoned colony, ostensibly obeys the sf-adventure rules governing tales of that sort, but insinuates throughout a bleaker, denser view of humanity's life in space. *Deserted Cities of the Heart* (**1988**), set in a MAGIC-REALIST Mexico, features a complexity of plots, involving imagined TIME TRAVEL back to the age of the Mayas, heated sexual and political intertwinings, and moments of not entirely convinced transcendence; but the style of the tale is shining and faceted, and its various protagonists are vividly realized. *Slam* (**1990**), a non-sf tale about a reformed tax-evader paroled from prison (or "slam"), competently and copiously evokes a sense of Texas not dissimilar to that imparted by fellow Texans like Neal BARRETT Jr and Howard WALDROP. It is sf's loss that LS's career seems to be moving swiftly away from the genre. [JC]

Other works: *Twilight Time* (1984 *IASFM*; **1991** chap); *When the Music's Over* (anth **1991**).

See also: CYBERPUNK; GOTHIC SF; MUSIC; WILD CARDS.

SHIPPEY, TOM Working name of UK academic and editor Thomas A. Shippey (1943-   ), Professor of English Language and Medieval Literature at the University of Leeds. In essays and reviews, which he has been publishing since the mid-1970s, he takes a clear-headed orthodox view of the central figures of sf and fantasy; *Fictional Space: Essays on Contemporary Science Fiction* (anth **1991**) assembles critical work. *The Road to Middle-Earth* (**1982**) is a study of J.R.R. TOLKIEN. TS also ed *The Oxford Book of Science Fiction Stories* (anth **1992**), in the Introduction to which he espouses James Bradley's notion that sf is a literature whose central image is "the creator of artefacts" or *Homo "fabril"*. TS cowrote the theme entries on MAGIC and HISTORY IN SF in this encyclopedia. [JC]

SHIRAS, WILMAR H(OUSE) (1908-1990) US writer whose first novel, *Slow Dawning* (**1946**) as by Jane Howes, was not sf or fantasy. She began publishing sf with "In Hiding" (1948 *ASF*), the first of several stories assembled as *Children of the Atom* (1948-50 *ASF*; fixup **1953**). This concerns a number of radiation-engendered child geniuses who initially hide their abilities from the world, then reveal themselves, taking the risk that in trying to help normal humans they may merely end as martyrs. The story is sensitively told, avoiding most of the CLICHÉS of pulp-sf SUPERMAN stories. WHS remained active as a story writer until the 1970s. [JC]

See also: ANTI-INTELLECTUALISM IN SF; CHILDREN IN SF; INTELLIGENCE; MUTANTS; WOMEN SF WRITERS.

SHIRLEY, JOHN (PATRICK) (1954-   ) US writer who began publishing sf with "The Word 'Random,' Deliberately Repeated" for *Clarion* (anth **1973**) ed Robin Scott WILSON, and who has performed as lead singer in rock bands, including the punk band Sado Nation. This background heavily influenced his first novel, the DYSTOPIAN *Transmaniacon* (**1979**), in which the typical JS protagonist appears: punk, anarchic, exorbitant, his mind evacuated of normal constraints, death-loving. Similar characters appear in *Three-Ring Psychus* (**1980**), which describes mass levitation (◊ PSI POWERS) with anarchist rapture, and *City Come A-Walkin'* (**1980**), set in a surrealistically harsh inner city. After writing some horror novels – to which genre his inclinations have constantly urged him, for JS is not at heart an sf writer – and most titles in the **Traveler** sequence as by D.B. DRUMM (◊ Ed NAHA), he created his finest sf work in the CYBERPUNK-coloured **Song Called Youth** trilogy – *Eclipse* (**1985**), *Eclipse Penumbra* (**1988**) and *Eclipse Corona* (**1990**) – set after a realistically conceived WWIII and describing a technologically deft resistance movement which fights a neofascist regime to a standstill, ultimately defeating it. In another late novel, *A Splendid Chaos* (**1988**), JS returns to a more surreal background, this time a hazardous planet where a small group of humans must compete for survival against unpredictable ALIENS. But the main challenge to "normal" humans comes from some of their own species, who have been remoulded in the image of their darkest fantasies – a horror device typical of the author, whose best effects have always come from sparking the gap between normality and horrific madness.

Though his short work sometimes suffers burnout from excessive intensity, the stories assembled in *Heatseeker* (coll **1988**) effectively demonstrate JS's solitudinous strengths, the flare of his anger. [JC/CW]

Other works: *Dracula in Love* (**1979**); *The Brigade* (**1982**); *Cellars* (**1982**); *Kamus of Kadizhar: The Black Hole of Carcosa: A Tale of the Darkworld Detective* * (**1988**), tied to J. Michael REAVES's *Darkworld Detective* (coll of linked stories **1982**); *In Darkness Waiting* (**1988**); *Wetbones* (**1992**).

See also: CITIES; MUSIC; POLITICS.

SHIVERS ◊ *The* PARASITE MURDERS.

S.H.M. [s] ◊ A. Bertram CHANDLER.

SHORT CIRCUIT Film (1986). Turman-Foster/Tri-Star. Dir John BADHAM, starring Ally Sheedy, Steve Guttenberg, Fisher Stevens, Brian McNamara. Screenplay S.S. Wilson, Brent Maddock. 98 mins. Colour.

Military ROBOT Number Five, a prototype killing machine, is struck by lightning which endows it with sentience. It escapes from evil Nova Robotics, finding refuge with nice animal-lover Stephanie (Sheedy), who assumes it to be an ALIEN. It educates itself and is winsome. When she finds it is a robot she turns it in, but has second thoughts and helps save it from deactivation. *SC*'s assumption that, with a bit of divine aid, even a weapon will turn to peace and love is pleasantly silly. *SC* is amusing but formulaic, and the robot is nauseatingly cute; the film is much weaker than Badham's BLUE THUNDER and WARGAMES. The displeasing sequel is *Short Circuit 2* (**1988**), dir Kenneth Johnson, who normally directs tv (*The* BIONIC WOMAN, *The* INCREDIBLE HULK), and stars Fisher Stevens again as the Indian co-inventor of the robot, played in an offensively patronising Peter Sellers Indian accent. This is a caper movie in which Number Five (now Johnny Five) is duped into helping criminals out with a jewel robbery.   [PN]

See also: CINEMA.

SHORT CIRCUIT 2 ◊ SHORT CIRCUIT.

SHORT STORIES INC. ◊ WEIRD TALES.

SHRINKING MEN ◊ GREAT AND SMALL.

SHUPP, MIKE (1946-   ) US aerospace engineer and writer known for his **Destiny Makers** sequence *With Fate Conspire* (**1985**), *Morning of Creation* (**1985**), *Soldier of Another Fortune* (**1988**), *Death's Gray Land* (**1991**) and *The Last Reckoning* (**1991**) – featuring the exploits of a Vietnam veteran transported by TIME TRAVEL into a future where telepaths, being despised, are trying to change history. Time wars of the usual complexity ensue.   [JC]

See also: ESP.

SHUSTER, JOE [r] ◊ Jerry SIEGEL; SUPERMAN.

SHUTE, NEVIL Working name of UK writer Nevil Shute Norway (1899-1960), who for many years combined writing with work as an aeronautical engineer, specializing in Zeppelins; after moving for health reasons in 1950 to Australia – where he set much of his later fiction – he wrote full-time. Some of his earlier fiction, by taking advantage of his intense and very up-to-date knowledge of aeronautics, verges very closely on sf, and *What Happened to the Corbetts* (**1939**; vt *Ordeal* 1939 US) is a genuine future-WAR tale. *An Old Captivity* (**1940**) is the tale of a man who dreams in a coma (accurately, it proves, and on the basis of data unknown at the time of the dream) of Vikings in Greenland and of their life there; a later screenplay to an unmade film, *Vinland the Good* (**1946**), treats similar material. *No Highway* (**1948**) deals with metal fatigue as the cause of airplane disasters and was published just before the first of the Comet jet crashes that occurred for exactly that reason; the protagonist's daughter seems, as well, to have ESP powers. It was filmed as *No Highway in the Sky* (1951).

NS's two Australian sf novels remain his best known. *In the Wet* (**1953**), the journal of an Australian outback priest who copies down from a dying man a UTOPIAN vision (or memory) of the British Empire *c*AD2000, anticipates a time when Australia has become the leader of the Commonwealth, royalty has survived handsomely, socialism has faded away, and the Empire is secure. Much closer to the bone was the famous *On the Beach* (**1957**), filmed as ON THE BEACH (1959), a near-future DISASTER tale in which nuclear war has eliminated all life in the northern hemisphere, leaving Australia to await the inevitable spread of radioactive contamination – delayed by global wind-patterns – that will end human life on

Earth. NS was an excellent popular novelist; his stories demonstrate a seamless narrative skill, and his protagonists are, unfailingly, decent men.   [JC]

See also: END OF THE WORLD; PREDICTION.

SHUTTLE, PENELOPE (DIANE) (1947-   ) UK poet and novelist, married to Peter REDGROVE (*whom see for their sf collaborations*). Her only solo novel of genre interest, *The Mirror of the Giant* (**1980**), combines FEMINIST self-analysis with elements of the traditional ghost story.   [JC]

SHWARTZ, SUSAN M(ARTHA) (1949-   ) US writer who has been much more clearly associated with fantasy than with sf, beginning with her first story, "The Fires of Her Vengeance" in *The Keeper's Price* (anth **1979**) ed Marion Zimmer BRADLEY, and continuing with extended works like the impressive **Heirs to Byzantium** ALTERNATE-WORLD fantasy trilogy: *Byzantium's Crown* (**1987**), *The Woman of Flowers* (**1987**) and *Queensblade* (**1988**). Her 2 sf novels are *White Wing* (**1985**) with S.N. LEWITT, writing together as Gordon Kendall, which is a vigorous sf adventure, and *Heritage of Flight* (fixup **1989**), an adventure set on an alien planet. Though sf has not attracted her full attention, a caring literacy attractively infuses both tales; and *Habitats* (anth **1984**) contains several interesting sf tales original to that volume.   [JC]

Other works: *Silk Roads and Shadows* (**1988**); *Imperial Lady* (**1989**) with Andre NORTON.

As editor: *Hecate's Cauldron* (anth **1982**); *Moonsinger's Friends* (anth **1985**), in honour of Norton; *Arabesques: More Tales of the Arabian Nights* (anth **1988**) and its sequel, *Arabesques II* (anth **1989**).

SIBSON, FRANCIS H(ENRY) (1899-?   ) South African writer, prolific during the 1930s; most of his work, which was technically proficient, had something to do with airplanes or the sea and ships. *The Survivors* (**1932**) and its sequel *The Stolen Continent* (**1934**) describe first the violent creation of a new island in the Sargasso Sea (its rapid surfacing beaches an ocean liner), and second the international conflicts surrounding claims to the new territory, named New Canada. *Unthinkable* (**1933**) depicts an arduous Antarctic expedition whose members find, on their return north, that civilization has been destroyed by a final WAR involving gas and other weapons.   [JC]

SIEGEL, JERRY (1914-   ) US writer and sf fan who founded and issued with the illustrator Joe Shuster (1914-1992) the FANZINE *Science Fiction* in October 1932, one of the earliest occasions on which the term was used in a title; it ran for 5 issues, publishing stories by Raymond A. PALMER and others. In the same year he published a story, *Guest of the Earth* (**1932** chap). Also with Shuster he created the comic SUPERMAN, which first appeared in 1938, after they had spent years trying to sell the idea to publishers.   [JC]

See also: COMICS; DC COMICS; ILLUSTRATION.

SIEGEL, MARTIN (1941-1972) US writer who died young of leukemia. His sf novels are *Agent of Entropy* (**1969**) and *The Unreal People* (**1973**). The first combines

SATIRE and SPACE OPERA in a heated tale; the second is a post-holocaust POCKET-UNIVERSE tale in which Earth's surface is uninhabitable and people live frenetically and desperately underground. [JC]

SIENKIEWICZ, BILL (1958-) US COMICS artist. His early work was heavily influenced by Neal ADAMS, although his fine pen line was more fluid and expressive, and his brushwork freer. His work matured, becoming more painterly and stylish, as he graduated to GRAPHIC NOVELS. BS appears now to have deserted narrative art for advertising, record-cover design and more upmarket illustration. He has won many awards, including the 1987 Jack Kirby Award for Best Artist and the 1986 Yellow Kid (Italy).

He attended the Newark School of Fine and Industrial Art, and began illustrating comic books in 1978 with a story in *The Hulk* magazine featuring **Moon Knight**, a character who gave the title to a comic-book series which BS drew 1980-84, developing a dramatic narrative technique along with his energetic and increasingly sophisticated drawing. He drew and coloured an adaptation of the 1984 film DUNE (**Marvel Super Special** #36, 1984), and contributed a number of exciting issues to MARVEL COMICS's **New Mutants** title 1984-6. His first fully painted strip, which appeared in the last issue of *Epic Illustrated* (1986), was "Slow Down Sir"; he went on to develop this aspect of his work further with the graphic novel *Electra Assassin* (1986-7; graph **1987**). His *magnum opus* was *Stray Toasters* (graph **1988**), a 4-part graphic novel inspired by the film-maker David Lynch (1945-). Since then his comic-book work has been limited to the first 2 episodes of Alan MOORE's **Big Numbers** (1990). [RT]

Other work: *Bill Sienkiewicz Sketch Book* (**1990**).

SIEVEKING, LANCE Working name of UK writer and radio producer Lancelot de Giberne Sieveking (1896-1972) on his later work, though his first books were signed L. de Giberne Sieveking. He was with the BBC 1924-56; in 1955-6 he edited the publisher Ward Lock's sf list, his literary memoir, *The Eye of the Beholder* (**1957**), included portraits of figures of sf interest such as H.G. WELLS. He began publishing sf with "The Prophetic Camera" for *The English Review* in 1922, and his first novel *Stampede!* (**1924**) – dedicated to, illustrated by, and in its side-of-the-mouth fantasticality derivative of G.K. CHESTERTON – featured a Thought Machine used by anarchists to convey telepathic commands. In *The Ultimate Island: A Strange Adventure* (**1925**) ATLANTIS has survived in the midst of concealing fog and whirlpools, into which maelstrom ships have for centuries been lured. LS's best known sf work, *A Private Volcano* (**1955**), depicts the effects of a catalyst (thrown up from a volcano) which turns all dross to gold. After outgrowing his borrowed manners, LS became a literate writer, though sometimes uneasy in his handling of genre effects. [JC]

Other works: *The Woman She Was* (**1934**).

See also: ISLANDS.

SIEVERT, JAN ◊ Ryder SYVERSTEN.

SILBERSACK, JOHN (WALTER) (1954-) US editor and writer, active in the former capacity with Putnam/Berkley books 1977-81, with New American Library 1986-92, and with Warner Books from 1992. Throughout his career he has been noted for a swift and canny knowledgeability about the sf world. With Victoria Schochet he ed the first 4 vols of the **Berkley Showcase: New Writings in Science Fiction and Fantasy** anthology series (#1 and #2 **1980**; #3 and #4 **1981**) (◊ *The* BERKLEY SHOWCASE *for further details*). He has also ed 2 collections: Fritz LEIBER's *The Change War* (coll **1978**) and Avram DAVIDSON's *Collected Fantasies* (coll **1982**). His own writing has been, by comparison, peripheral, consisting of an anonymous sf spoof, *No Frills Science Fiction* (**1981** chap), and *Rogers' Rangers* * (**1983**), a BUCK ROGERS IN THE 25TH CENTURY tie. [JC]

SILENT, WILLIAM T. Pseudonym of US writer John William Jackson Jr (1945-), author of the sf adventure novel *Lord of the Red Sun* (**1972**). [JC]

SILENT RUNNING Film (1971). Universal. Dir Douglas Trumbull, starring Bruce Dern. Screenplay Deric Washburn, Mike Cimino, Steve Bocho, from a story by Trumbull. 90 mins. Colour.

All plant life on Earth has been destroyed in the aftermath of a nuclear HOLOCAUST; only vast orbiting spaceships like *Valley Forge*, with its external hydroponic domes, still contain trees and flowers, the hope being that these may one day be used to re-seed the planet; but then their destruction is ordered by the totalitarian Earth government. *SR*'s premise is obviously fatuous – it would be cheaper to leave the spaceships in place. Bruce Dern plays, in penitent's robes, the only true conservationist left alive, a low-grade gardener aboard the *Valley Forge*. When the order comes through to dump the vegetation he kills his companions (with the film's tacit approval) and sets off into deep space with the plants (apparently forgetting they have previously needed sunlight to live). He is accompanied only by three small, cute, box-shaped ROBOTS (in fact operated by amputees). *SR* is occasionally spectacular – Trumbull was one of the special-effects supervisors on 2001: A SPACE ODYSSEY (1968), and *SR*'s scenes of vast spaceships floating through space compare well with those in Stanley KUBRICK's epic – but the film is morally dubious, scientifically unsound and sociologically implausible. [PN/JB]

SILKE, JAMES R. [r] ◊ Frank FRAZETTA.

SILLITOE, ALAN (1928-) UK writer best known for novels like *Saturday Night and Sunday Morning* (**1958**). *The General* (**1960**) sets abstract armies clashing on an abstract ground, perhaps not Terran. The anti-authoritarian SATIRE, *Travels in Nihilon* (**1971**), initially reads as a DYSTOPIA, for the 5 travellers to that country despise its government and work to overthrow it; but, by story's close, Nihilism as a political creed seems to gain the author's guarded sanction. *Snow on the North Side of Lucifer* (**1979**) is a poetry sequence about conflicts between God and Satan. [JC]

SILVA, JOSEPH ◊ Ron GOULART.

SILVERBERG, ROBERT (1935-   ) Extremely prolific US writer, author of more than 100 sf books, more than 60 nonfiction books and a great deal of other work; he has also edited or co-edited more than 60 anthologies. He began to write while studying for his BA at Columbia University; his first published story was "Gorgon Planet" (1954). His first novel, a juvenile, was *Revolt on Alpha C* (**1955**). He began to publish prolifically in 1956, winning a HUGO in that year as Most Promising New Author, and continued to specialize in sf for 3 years. He worked for the ZIFF-DAVIS stable, producing wordage at assembly-line speed for AMAZING STORIES and FANTASTIC, and was a prolific contributor to such magazines as SCIENCE FICTION ADVENTURES and SUPER-SCIENCE FICTION, using many different names. For part of this time Randall GARRETT was a partner in this "fiction factory"; they wrote in collaboration as Robert Randall, Gordon Aghill and Ralph Burke (RS also used the Burke pseudonym on solo work). The most important pseudonyms which RS used exclusively were Calvin M. Knox and David Osborne; he also wrote sf as T.D. Bethlen, Dirk Clinton, Ivar Jorgenson (a variant spelling of the floating pseudonym Ivar JORGENSEN), Dan Malcolm, Webber Martin, Alex Merriman, George Osborne, Eric Rodman, Hall Thornton and Richard F. Watson. He appeared under such Ziff-Davis house names as Robert ARNETTE, Alexander BLADE, E.K. JARVIS, Warren KASTEL and S.M. TENNESHAW; Blade and Tenneshaw were used also on collaborations with Garrett, as were Richard GREER, Clyde MITCHELL, Leonard G. SPENCER and Gerald VANCE. Silverberg wrote 1 story in collaboration with his 1st wife Barbara; *The Mutant Season* (**1989**), a novel developed from one of his short stories by his 2nd wife (from 1987) Karen HABER, was published as a collaboration.

He has also published 3 "collaborations" with Isaac ASIMOV, developing full-length novels from classic Asimov short stories: these are *Nightfall* (1941 *ASF*; exp **1990** UK), *Child of Time* (1958 *Gal* as "Lastborn"; vt "The Ugly Little Boy"; exp **1991** UK) and *The Positronic Man* (in *Stellar*, anth **1976**, ed Judy-Lynn DEL REY as "The Bicentennial Man"; exp **1992** UK).

The most notable novels of RS's early period are *Master of Life and Death* (**1957** dos), a novel dealing with institutionalized measures to combat OVERPOPULATION, *Invaders from Earth* (**1958** dos), a drama of political corruption involved with the COLONIZATION of Ganymede, and *Recalled to Life* (1958 *Infinity*; **1962**; rev 1972), which investigates the social response to a method of reviving the newly dead. The **Nidorian** series, which he wrote with Garrett as Robert Randall – *The Shrouded Planet* (fixup **1957**) and *The Dawning Light* (**1959**) – is also interesting.

As the magazine market shrank, in 1959 RS virtually abandoned sf for some years. The majority of the sf books he published 1960-66 were rewritten from work originally done in 1957-9. His output was prodigious, but somewhat mechanical, except for a handful of nonfiction books – notably *The Golden Dream* (**1967**) and *Mound-Builders of Ancient America* (**1968**), which were painstakingly researched and carefully written.

A new phase of RS's career, in which he brought the full range of his artistic abilities to bear on writing sf, began with *Thorns* (**1967**), a stylized novel of alienation and psychic vampirism, and *Hawksbill Station* (**1968**; vt *The Anvil of Time* 1969 UK), in which political exiles are sent back in time to a Cambrian prison camp; this full-length version should not be confused with the novelette version, *Hawksbill Station* (1967 *Gal*; **1990** chap dos). *The Masks of Time* (**1968**; vt *Vornan-19* 1970 UK) describes a visit by an enigmatic time traveller to the world of 1999. *The Man in the Maze* (**1969**) is a dramatization of the problems of alienation, based on the Greek myth of Philoctetes, the hero whose wound makes him both necessary and repulsive. *Nightwings* (fixup **1969**) is a lyrical account of the conquest of a senescent Earth by ALIENS, which culminates with the rebirth of its hero; it should not be confused with the Hugo-winning novella which contributed to the fixup, *Nightwings* (1968 *Gal*; **1989** chap dos). *Up the Line* (**1969**) is a clever TIME-PARADOX story. *Downward to the Earth* (**1970**) is a story of repentance and rebirth, with calculated echoes of Joseph Conrad's "Heart of Darkness" (1902) and strong religious imagery (◊ RELIGION). *Tower of Glass* (**1970**) also makes use of religious imagery in its study of the obsessional construction of a new "Tower of Babel" and the struggle of an ANDROID race to win emancipation. *A Time of Changes* (**1971**) describes a society in which selfhood is a cardinal sin. *Son of Man* (**1971**) is a surreal evolutionary fantasy of the FAR FUTURE. *The World Inside* (fixup **1971**) is a study of life under conditions of high population density. *The Second Trip* (**1972**) is an intense psychological novel describing the predicaments of a telepathic girl and a man who has been newly created in the body of an "erased" criminal. *The Book of Skulls* (**1971**) is a painstaking analysis of relationships among 4 young men on a competitive quest for IMMORTALITY. *Dying Inside* (**1972**) is a brilliant study of a telepath losing his power. *The Stochastic Man* (**1975**) is a complementary study of a man developing the power to foresee the future. *Shadrach in the Furnace* (**1976**) concerns the predicament of the personal physician of a future dictator who finds his identity in jeopardy. After writing the last-named, RS quit writing for 4 years, ostensibly because of his disenchantment with the functioning of the sf marketplace, where his books seemed to him to be suffering "assassination" as they were allowed to go out of print after a few months; sheer exhaustion may also have been a factor.

In view of the sustained quality of this astonishing burst of creativity, it is perhaps surprising that only one of these full-length works won a major award in the USA – *A Time of Changes* (NEBULA). Several better novels, most notably *Dying Inside*, went unrewarded, perhaps because the voters found them too intense and too uncompromising in their depictions of anguish and desperation. RS did, however, win awards for several shorter pieces: the novella *Nightwings* won a Hugo, and Nebulas went to "Passengers" (1968), a story about people who temporarily lose control of their bodies to alien invaders, "Good News from the Vatican" (1970), about the election of the first ROBOT pope, and the brilliant novella *Born with the Dead* (1974; **1988** chap dos), about relationships between the living and the beneficiaries of a scientific technique guaranteeing life after death. The novella "The Feast of St Dionysus" (1972), about the experience of religious ecstasy, won a Jupiter award; it became the lead title of one of his finest collections, *The Feast of St Dionysus* (coll **1975**), which also includes "Schwartz Between the Galaxies" (1974). In addition to his award-winners RS published a great deal of excellent short fiction during this second phase of his career. Particularly notable are "To See the Invisible Man" (1963), assembled in *Earth's Other Shadow* (coll **1973**), "Sundance" (1969), assembled in *The Cube Root of Uncertainty* (coll **1970**), and "In Entropy's Jaws" (1971), assembled in *The Reality Trip and Other Implausibilities* (coll **1972**). Other collections assembling material from this period include *The Calibrated Alligator* (coll **1969**), *Dimension Thirteen* (coll **1969**), *Parsecs and Parables* (coll **1970**), *Moonferns and Starsongs* (coll **1971**), *Unfamiliar Territory* (coll **1973**), *Sundance and Other Science Fiction Stories* (coll **1974**), *Born with the Dead* (coll **1974**), *Sunrise on Mercury* (coll **1975**), *The Best of Robert Silverberg* (coll **1976**) and *The Best of Robert Silverberg, Volume Two* (coll **1978**), *Capricorn Games* (coll **1976**), *The Shores of Tomorrow* (coll **1976**), *The Songs of Summer and Other Stories* (coll **1979** UK), and *Beyond the Safe Zone: The Collected Short Fiction of Robert Silverberg* (coll **1986**).

RS returned to writing with *Lord Valentine's Castle* (**1980**), a polished but rather languid HEROIC FANTASY set on the world of Majipoor, where he also set the shorter pieces – including *The Desert of Stolen Dreams* (**1981** chap) – collected in *The Majipoor Chronicles* (coll of linked stories **1982**). The addition of *Valentine Pontifex* (**1983**), a sequel to the novel, converted the series into a trilogy of sorts. Almost all of RS's work of the 1980s was in the same relaxed vein: the psychological intensity of his mid-period work was toned down, and much of his sf was evidently pitched towards what RS considered to be the demands of the market. His work of this period has been commercially successful, but the full-length sf often seems rather mechanical; the historical novels *Lord of Darkness* (**1983**) and *Gilgamesh the King* (**1984**) appear to have been projects dearer to his heart. The gypsy king in *Star of Gypsies* (**1986**), waiting in self-imposed exile for his one-time followers to realize how badly they need him, might be reckoned an ironic self-portrait. The best works of this third phase of RS's career are novellas, most notably *Sailing to Byzantium* (**1985**), winner of a 1985 Nebula, and *The Secret Sharer* (**1988**), a sciencefictionalization of CONRAD's 1912 story of the same title. RS also won Hugo awards in this period for the novella "Gilgamesh in the Outback" (1986), which was a sequel to *Gilgamesh the King* and was integrated into *To the Land of the Living* (fixup **1989**), and the novelette "Enter a Soldier. Later, Enter Another" (1989). His recent work includes the first 2 vols of the **New Springtime** trilogy about the repopulation of Earth by various races (not including humans) after a future ice age – *At Winter's End* (**1988**; vt *Winter's End* 1990 UK) and *The Queen of Springtime* (**1989** UK; vt *The New Springtime* 1990 US) – and a novel about humans living as exiles on a watery world after the destruction of Earth, *The Face of the Waters* (**1991** UK). Much of his short fiction of this period is assembled in *The Conglomeroid Cocktail Party* (coll **1984**) and *The Collected Stories of Robert Silverberg: Volume One: Pluto in the Morning Light* (coll **1992** UK). He remains one of the most imaginative and versatile writers ever to have been involved with sf. His productivity has seemed almost superhuman, and his abrupt metamorphosis from a writer of standardized pulp fiction into a prose artist was an accomplishment unparalleled within the field.

As an editor, RS was responsible for an excellent series of original ANTHOLOGIES, NEW DIMENSIONS (see listing below). In collaboration with Haber he has taken over the UNIVERSE series once ed Terry CARR, relaunching the title with *Universe 1* (anth **1990**) and *Universe 2* (anth **1992**). He has also been a prolific compiler of ORIGINAL ANTHOLOGIES that comprise 3 novellas, and has edited many reprint anthologies, recently doing much of this kind of work in collaboration with Martin H. GREENBERG. RS was president of the SCIENCE FICTION WRITERS OF AMERICA 1967-8. *The MAGAZINE OF FANTASY AND SCIENCE FICTION* published a special issue devoted to him in Apr 1974. An autobiographical essay appeared in *Hell's Cartographers* (anth **1975**) ed Brian W. ALDISS and Harry HARRISON. [BS]

Other works: *The 13th Immortal* (**1957** dos); *Aliens from Space* (**1958**) as by David Osborne; *Invisible Barriers* (**1958**) as by Osborne; *Lest We Forget Thee, Earth* (fixup **1958** dos) as by Calvin M. Knox; *Starhaven* (**1958**) as by Ivar Jorgenson; *Stepsons of Terra* (**1958** dos); *The Planet Killers* (**1959** dos); *The Plot against Earth* (**1959** dos) as by Knox; *Starman's Quest* (**1959**); *Lost Race of Mars* (**1960**); *Collision Course* (**1961**); *Next Stop the Stars* (coll **1962** dos); *The Seed of Earth* (**1962** dos); *The Silent Invaders* (**1958** *Infinity* as by Knox; exp **1963** dos; with "Valley beyond Time" added, as coll 1985); *Godling, Go Home!* (coll **1964**); *One of Our Asteroids is Missing* (**1964** dos) as by Knox; *Regan's Planet* (**1964**); *Time of the Great Freeze* (**1964**); *Conquerors from the Darkness* (**1957** *Science Fiction Adventures* as "Spawn of the Deadly Sea"; **1965**); *To Worlds Beyond* (coll **1965**); *Needle in a Timestack* (coll **1966**; rev 1967 UK); *The Gate of Worlds* (**1967**); *Planet of Death* (**1967**); *Those who Watch* (**1967**); *The Time-Hoppers* (**1956** *Infinity* as "Hopper";

exp **1967**); *To Open the Sky* (fixup **1967**); *Across a Billion Years* (**1969**); *Three Survived* (1957; exp **1969**); *To Live Again* (**1969**); *World's Fair 1992* (**1970**); *Valley beyond Time* (coll **1973**); *Unfamiliar Territory* (coll **1973**); *A Robert Silverberg Omnibus* (omni **1981**); *World of a Thousand Colors* (coll **1982**); *Tom O'Bedlam* (**1985**); *Nightwings* (graph **1985**), an adaptation in GRAPHIC-NOVEL form; *Project Pendulum* (**1987**), a juvenile; *In Another Country* (**1990** chap dos) with C.L. MOORE's *Vintage Season* (1946), to which it is a sequel; *Lion Time in Timbuctoo* (**1990**); *Letters from Atlantis* (**1990**); *Thebes of the Hundred Gates* (**1991**); *Kingdoms of the Wall* (**1992** UK).

Omnibuses: *A Robert Silverberg Omnibus* (omni **1970** UK), assembling *Master of Life and Death, Invaders from Earth* and *The Time-Hoppers; Science Fiction Special (30): Invaders from Earth; The Best of Robert Silverberg* (omni **1978** UK); *Conquerors from the Darkness, and Master of Life and Death* (omni **1979**); *Invaders from Earth, and To Worlds Beyond* (omni **1980**); *A Robert Silverberg Omnibus* (omni **1981**), assembling *The Man in the Maze, Nightwings* and *Downward to the Earth; The Masks of Time/Born with the Dead/Dying Inside* (omni **1988**); *Three Novels: The World Inside/Thorns/Downward to the Earth* (omni **1988**); *The Book of Skulls/Nightwings/Dying Inside* (omni **1991**).

Nonfiction: *Drug Themes in Science Fiction* (**1974** chap).

As editor: *Earthmen and Strangers* (anth **1966**); *Voyagers in Time* (anth **1967**), *Men and Machines* (anth **1968**); *Dark Stars* (anth **1969**); *Three for Tomorrow* (anth **1969**; UK edn credits Arthur C. CLARKE as ed); *Tomorrow's Worlds* (anth **1969**); *The Ends of Time* (anth **1970**); *Great Short Novels of Science Fiction* (anth **1970**); *The Mirror of Infinity* (anth **1970**); *Worlds of Maybe* (anth **1970**); *The Science Fiction Hall of Fame Vol 1* (anth **1970**); *To the Stars* (anth **1971**); *Four Futures* (anth **1971**); *Mind to Mind* (anth **1971**); *The Science Fiction Bestiary* (anth **1971**); *Beyond Control* (anth **1972**); *Invaders from Space* (anth **1972**); *The Day the Sun Stood Still* (anth **1972**); *Chains of the Sea* (anth **1973**); *Other Dimensions* (anth **1973**); *Three Trips in Time and Space* (anth **1973**); *No Mind of Man* (anth **1973**); *Deep Space* (anth **1973**); *Threads of Time* (anth **1974**); *Mutants* (**1974**); *Infinite Jests* (anth **1974**); *Windows into Tomorrow* (anth **1974**); *The Aliens* (anth **1976**); *Epoch* (anth **1975**) with Roger ELWOOD; *The New Atlantis* (anth **1975**); *Strange Gifts* (anth **1975**); *Explorers of Space* (anth **1975**); *The Crystal Ship* (anth **1976**); *The Aliens* (anth **1976**); *The Infinite Web* (anth **1977**); *Earth is the Strangest Planet* (anth **1977**); *Trips in Time* (anth **1977**); *Triax* (anth **1977**); *Galactic Dreamers: Science Fiction as Visionary Literature* (anth **1977**); *The Androids are Coming* (anth **1979**); *Lost Worlds, Unknown Horizons* (anth **1978**); *The Edge of Space* (anth **1979**); *Car Sinister* (anth **1979**) with Martin H. Greenberg and Joseph D. OLANDER; *Dawn of Time: Prehistory through Science Fiction* (anth **1979**) with Greenberg and Olander; *The Arbor House Treasury of Modern Science Fiction* (anth **1980**; cut vt *Great Science Fiction of the 20th Century* 1987) with Greenberg; *The Arbor House Treasury of Great Science Fiction Short*

Novels (anth **1980**; cut vt *Worlds Imagined* 1988) with Greenberg; *The Science Fictional Dinosaur* (anth **1982**) with Greenberg and Charles G. WAUGH; *The Best of Randall Garrett* (coll **1982**); *The Arbor House Treasury of Science Fiction Masterpieces* (anth **1983**; cut vt *Great Tales of Science Fiction* 1988) with Greenberg; *The Fantasy Hall of Fame* (anth **1983**; vt *The Mammoth Book of Fantasy All-Time Greats* 1988 UK) with Greenberg; *Nebula Award Winners 18* (anth **1983**); *The Time Travelers: A Science Fiction Quartet* (anth **1985**) with Greenberg; *Neanderthals* (anth **1987**) with Greenberg and Waugh; *Robert Silverberg's Worlds of Wonder* (anth **1987**); *Time Gate* (anth **1989**); *Time Gate 2: Dangerous Interfaces* (anth **1990**); *Beyond the Gate of Worlds* (anth **1991**); *The Horror Hall of Fame* (anth **1991**) with Greenberg; «The Ultimate Dinosaur» (anth 1992) with Byron PREISS.

Series: The **Alpha** sequence of anthologies, comprising *Alpha One* (anth **1970**), *Two* (anth **1971**), *Three* (anth **1972**), *Four* (anth **1973**), *Five* (anth **1974**), *Six* (anth **1975**), *7* (anth **1977**), *8* (anth **1977**) and *9* (anth **1978**); the **New Dimensions** sequence of original anthologies, comprising *New Dimensions 1* (anth **1971**), *#2* (anth **1972**), *#3* (anth **1973**), *#4* (anth **1974**), *#5* (anth **1975**), *#6* (anth **1976**), *#7* (anth **1977**), *#8* (anth **1978**), *#9* (anth **1979**), *#10* (anth **1980**), *#11* (anth **1980**) with Marta RANDALL and *#12* (anth **1981**) with Randall, plus *The Best of New Dimensions* (anth **1979**).

About the author: *Robert Silverberg: A Primary and Secondary Bibliography* (**1983**) and *Robert Silverberg* (**1983** chap), both by Thomas D. CLARESON.

See also: ACE BOOKS; ALTERNATE WORLDS; ANTHROPOLOGY; APES AND CAVEMEN (IN THE HUMAN WORLD); ARTS; BLACK HOLES; CHILDREN'S SF; CITIES; COMICS; COMPUTERS; CONCEPTUAL BREAKTHROUGH; CRIME AND PUNISHMENT; CRITICAL AND HISTORICAL WORKS ABOUT SF; DC COMICS; DYSTOPIAS; END OF THE WORLD; ENTROPY; ESCHATOLOGY; ESP; EVOLUTION; FANTASTIC VOYAGES; GALACTIC EMPIRES; GODS AND DEMONS; HIVE-MINDS; INTELLIGENCE; INVASION; INVISIBILITY; JOHN W. CAMPBELL MEMORIAL AWARD; JUPITER; MATHEMATICS; MATTER TRANSMISSION; MEDIA LANDSCAPE; MESSIAHS; METAPHYSICS; MILFORD SCIENCE FICTION WRITERS' CONFERENCE; MONSTERS; MUSIC; MYTHOLOGY; NEW WAVE; PARALLEL WORLDS; PARASITISM AND SYMBIOSIS; PASTORAL; PERCEPTION; PLANETARY ROMANCE; POLITICS; PSYCHOLOGY; REINCARNATION; ROBERT HALE LIMITED; SEX; SHARED WORLDS; SOCIOLOGY; SPACE OPERA; SUN; SUPERMAN; TIME TRAVEL; TRANSPORTATION; UNDER THE SEA; WOMEN SF WRITERS; WRITERS OF THE FUTURE CONTEST.

SIM, DAVE (1958-   ) US artist and writer, creator of **Cerebus the Aardvark**, the abrasive and perverse eponymous star of a satirical COMIC book originally intended as a pastiche of Robert E. HOWARD's **Conan the Barbarian**, and which has lampooned a number of the leading characters of the HEROIC-FANTASY genre. Published by DS himself, the comic book has become so popular that *Cerebus #1* (Dec 1977) is reputed now to be worth several hundred times its original $1 cover price. Much of the series is available in reprint assemblage, beginning with *Cerebus* (graph coll **1987**).

DS's early style was heavily influenced by Barry Windsor-Smith. The comic book features characters such as Elrod of Melvinbone, Bran Mak Mufin and Wolveroach. DS's stated ambition is to complete the projected 6000pp of **Cerebus the Aardvark** in AD2004. [RT]

SIMAK, CLIFFORD D(ONALD) (1904-1988) US writer whose primary occupation 1929-76 was newspaper work, and who became a full-time writer of sf only after his retirement. He was, however, a prolific and increasingly popular sf figure – after a false start in 1931 – from the true beginning of his career in 1938. His first published stories, beginning with "The World of the Red Sun" for *Wonder Stories* in 1931, were unremarkable, though significantly that first tale deals with TIME TRAVEL, which became his favourite sf device for the importation of ALIENS into rural Wisconsin, always his favourite venue. Apart from 1 novelette, *The Creator* (1935 *Marvel Tales*; **1946** chap), he published no sf 1932-8; then, inspired by John W. CAMPBELL Jr's editorial policy at ASTOUNDING SCIENCE-FICTION, he began to produce such stories as "Rule 18" and "Reunion on Ganymede" (both 1938). He swiftly followed with his first full-length novel, *Cosmic Engineers* (1939 *ASF*; rev **1950**), a Galaxy-spanning epic in the vein of E.E. SMITH and Edmond HAMILTON. He continued to write steadily for Campbell, and his work gradually became identifiably Simakian – constrained, nostalgic, intensely emotional beneath a calmly competent generic surface. Stories like "Rim of the Deep" (1940), "Tools" (1942) and "Hunch" (1943) were signs of this development, though the full CDS did not "arrive" until the appearance of "City" and its sequel, "Huddling Place" (both 1944). These tales concerned the NEAR-FUTURE exodus of mankind from the CITIES and the return to a PASTORAL existence aided by a benign technology. As the series progresses, the planet is abandoned by all humans except the reclusive Websters; and Jenkins, an excellently depicted ROBOT, is left to monitor the forced EVOLUTION of intelligent dogs, who are destined to inherit the Earth. As *City* (fixup **1952**; exp 1981) the sequence won an INTERNATIONAL FANTASY AWARD. It remains CDS's best known work.

In 1950 he found another market in the new magazine GALAXY SCIENCE FICTION, which serialized his novel *Time and Again* (**1951**; vt *First He Died* 1953). A trickily plotted time-travel story, it proved to be very popular – though ominously prefiguring some of his over-plotted works of the late 1970s. Also of strong interest is *Ring Around the Sun* (**1953**), which involves the discovery of a chain of PARALLEL WORLDS and the machinations of a secret society of mutants who are plotting to subvert the world's economy by producing everlasting goods. Its anti-urban and pro-agrarian sentiments were by now a standard part of CDS's work; in stories like "Neighbors" (1954) he became sf's leading spokesman for rural, Midwestern values. His stories in general contain little violence and much

folk humour, and stress the value of individualism tempered by compassion – "good neighbourliness", in short. Throughout the 1950s, he produced dozens of competent short stories, many assembled in *Strangers in the Universe* (coll **1956**; with 4 stories cut 1957; with 4 different stories cut 1958 UK), *The Worlds of Clifford Simak* (coll **1960**; with 6 stories cut 1961; with 3 stories cut, vt *Aliens for Neighbours* 1961 UK; text restored in 2 vols, vt *The Worlds of Clifford Simak* 1961 US and *Other Worlds of Clifford Simak* 1962 US) and *All the Traps of Earth* (coll **1962**; with 3 stories cut 1963; text restored in 2 vols, vt *All the Traps of Earth* 1964 UK and *The Night of the Puudly* 1964 UK). Two highpoints were the stories "The Big Front Yard" (1958), which won a 1959 HUGO, and "A Death in the House" (1959). Many of these tales appear in the retrospective *Skirmish: The Great Short Fiction* (coll **1977**).

After 1960 CDS began to produce novels at the rate of roughly one a year. *Time is the Simplest Thing* (**1961**) and *They Walked Like Men* (**1962**) are workmanlike and entertaining, but *Way Station* (**1963**), which won the 1964 Hugo, more impressively concerns a lonely farmer given IMMORTALITY in return for his services as a galactic station-master, his house having been made into a way-station for aliens who teleport from star to star. Its warmth, imaginative detail and finely rendered bucolic scenes make this probably CDS's best novel. *All Flesh is Grass* (**1965**), *Why Call them Back from Heaven?* (**1967**) and *The Werewolf Principle* (**1967**) are enjoyable, if essentially repetitive. *The Goblin Reservation* (**1968**) seemed at first glance to be innovative, striking out into new territory; but in fact it turned out to be the old Wisconsin-valley fantasy in a new and whimsical guise. CDS had always wrestled with such whimsy – notoriously paired with nostalgia in many authors – and by the start of the 1970s whimsy seemed to be winning. Its triumph may have derived from the fact that the venues for which CDS felt genuine emotion were now 40 years gone, and the world had irrevocably repudiated and scummed over the rural simplicities dear to his heart; however, this cannot excuse his sentimental sidestepping of change. Novels like *Destiny Doll* (**1971**), *Cemetery World* (cut **1973**; text restored 1983), *Enchanted Pilgrimage* (**1975**), *Shakespeare's Planet* (**1976**), *Mastodonia* (**1978**; vt *Catface* 1978 UK), *Special Deliverance* (**1982**), *Where the Evil Dwells* (**1982**) and *Highway of Eternity* (**1986**; vt *Highway to Eternity* 1987 UK), his last novel, contain only flashes of the old talent, mingled with a good deal of sheer silliness. There were exceptions. *A Choice of Gods* (**1972**) is an elegiac tale in which CDS reiterated the plainsong of his favourite themes: the depopulated world, the sage old man, the liberated robots, the "haunted" house, teleporting to the stars, etc. *A Heritage of Stars* (**1977**), a quest novel set in a post-technological society, is another compendium of CDS's old material. Though he seemed generally to need the relative discipline of sf to achieve his best effects, *The Fellowship of the Talisman* (**1978**) is an effective FANTASY. *The Visitors* (**1980**), in which aliens once again visit Earth bearing enigmatic gifts, may be his finest late novel, for a vein of irony is allowed some play. The strengths of *Project Pope* (**1981**), about the devising of an AI to serve as the ultimate pope, are somewhat vitiated by CDS's visible reluctance to understand COMPUTERS.

CDS's late short stories are less mixed, and the tales assembled in *The Marathon Photograph and Other Stories* (coll **1986** UK), including the Hugo- and Nebula-winning "Grotto of the Dancing Deer" (1980), retain all the skill and much of the emotional saliency of his prime. He was a man of strong moral convictions and little real concern for ideas, and surprisingly for a man of such professional attainments he rarely tended to stray outside his natural bailiwick. Wisconsin in about 1925 – or any extraterrestrial venue demonstrating the same rooted virtues – was that true home, and when he was in residence CDS reigned as the pastoral king of his genre. He received the NEBULA Grand Master Award in 1976. [DP/JC]

Other works: *Empire* (**1951**); *The Trouble with Tycho* (**1961** chap dos); *Worlds without End* (coll **1964**); *Best Science Fiction Stories of Clifford Simak* (coll **1967** UK); *So Bright the Vision* (coll **1968** dos); *Out of their Minds* (**1969**); *Our Children's Children* (**1974**); *The Best of Clifford D. Simak* (coll **1975** UK); 4 collections ed Francis Lyall, being *Brother and Other Stories* (coll **1986** UK), *Off-Planet* (coll **1988** UK), *The Autumn Land and Other Stories* (coll **1990** UK) and *Immigrant and Other Stories* (coll **1991** UK).

As editor: *Nebula Award Stories 6* (anth **1971**); *The Best of Astounding* (anth **1978**).

About the author: "Clifford D. Simak" by Sam MOSKOWITZ, in *Seekers of Tomorrow* (**1966**); *Clifford D. Simak: A Primary and Secondary Bibliography* (**1949**) by Muriel R. Becker.

See also: ANDROIDS; ARTS; ASTEROIDS; COLONIZATION OF OTHER WORLDS; COMMUNICATIONS; CRYONICS; DIMENSIONS; ECOLOGY; ECONOMICS; ESCHATOLOGY; ESP; GALACTIC EMPIRES; GAMES AND SPORTS; GENERATION STARSHIPS; GODS AND DEMONS; GOLDEN AGE OF SF; JUPITER; LIFE ON OTHER WORLDS; LONGEVITY (IN WRITERS AND PUBLICATIONS); MACHINES; MARS; MATTER TRANSMISSION; MERCURY; MESSIAHS; MONEY; MOON; MYTHOLOGY; OPTIMISM AND PESSIMISM; OUTER PLANETS; PARALLEL WORLDS; PARASITISM AND SYMBIOSIS; POLLUTION; RELIGION; SOCIOLOGY; SPACE OPERA; SPACESHIPS; SUN; SUPERNATURAL CREATURES; VENUS.

SIMMONS, DAN (1948-   ) US writer, for many years a teacher of gifted children, who began publishing with "The River Styx Runs Upstream" for *Rod Serling's The Twilight Zone Magazine* in 1982, and who was for some time best regarded as an author of tales of HORROR, some of which – along with sf and FANTASY stories – were assembled in *Prayers to Broken Stones* (coll **1990**). True to the instincts of that genre, his first novel, *Song of Kali* (**1985**), rendered modern-day Calcutta as a moral and psychic cesspool, into

which the protagonists of the book sink very deep indeed as unleashed evil from the world's ancient heart threatens to flood the 1980s. His second novel, the immense *Carrion Comfort* (1983 *Omni*; much exp **1989**), is also horror, though with an sf underpinning, and as such its basic premise is un-new. The "carrion-eaters" of the title are MUTANT humans who have acquired the capacity to control other humans through direct psychic access to their hind-brains, while at the same time feasting psychically on the experiences into which they force their victims. True to the dictates of the horror genre – to which Simmons remains astonishingly faithful for nearly 500,000 words – his mutants soon decay into lovers of pain and death, and the protagonists of the book must attempt to exploit divisions among these puppet masters. Their survival seems genuinely triumphant, though the sole surviving vampire is preparing to start WWIII.

However, despite the haunting rationality of this tale, DS's later work is of much greater sf interest. *Phases of Gravity* (**1989**) is not sf, being instead – if one is able to ignore a moment or two of muffled transcendence – perhaps the first historical novel by an sf author about the space programme, recounting the psychic rejuvenation of a grounded astronaut. But *Hyperion* (**1989**) – which won a 1990 HUGO – and *The Fall of Hyperion* (**1990**) – 2 vols which together, under the preferred title *Hyperion Cantos* (omni **1990**), clearly make a single novel – are genuine, full-blown METAPHYSICAL sf. Over a SPACE-OPERA structure – ages after a BLACK HOLE has destroyed Old Earth, the Galaxy is dominated by a vast human hegemony knit together by ANSIBLE-like fatlines and farcasters that plumb discontinuities in space – an extremely complex narrative engages with many themes, including religious quests, TIME TRAVEL, CYBERSPACE, ECOLOGY, bioengineering and much else. In the first volume, which is structured after Chaucer's *The Canterbury Tales*, 7 "pilgrims" have been called to the planet Hyperion, where the time-travelling Shrike which guards the Time Tombs promises some dreadful transcendence; en route they tell tales which reveal their significant life-experiences (one of these tales, "Remembering Siri", was first published separately in 1983), each tale being recounted in a different sf idiom, and each contributing to the growing mosaic of the overall story, described by John CLUTE as a space opera about the end of things, an "entelechy opera" or tale of cosmogony. Every member of the cast bears a secret burden, and each burden expands in significance as the surviving protagonists arrive on Hyperion and engage more and more deeply with the Keatsian implications of their mission (the two sections of *Hyperion Cantos* take the titles of Keats's long but incomplete poems about the displacement of the old gods, the victory of a new pantheon). Meanwhile, wars and apocalypse and ENTROPY threaten the entire Galaxy. The AIS that run everything turn out to inhabit the quantum-level interstices of the farcaster net – just as does the AI who tends to dominate Orson Scott CARD's *Xenocide* (**1991**) – and the end of the Universe will depend upon which AI faction is able to corner for itself the significance of Hyperion, the Shrike, and the human saintliness which begins to invest activities there.

As a compendium and culminating presentation of GENRE SF's devices and deep impulses, *Hyperion Cantos* is perhaps definitive for the 1980s. In one novel, DS became one of the half-dozen central figures of that decade. A slight sentimentality about children and a love of generic competence for its own sake only slightly modify the sense of excitement generated by his arrival on the scene, though his two 1992 novels may have calmed that excitement to some degree.

The Hollow Man (1982 *Omni* as "Eyes I Dare Not Meet in Dreams"; much exp **1992**), though pure sf in its rationale, is structured (somewhat stiffly) to reflect the metaphysical journey of DANTE ALIGHIERI's protagonist in *La Divina Commedia* (written *c*1304-21), containing ample references as well to the poetry of T.S. Eliot (1888-1965). It deals with a tortured man whose ESP powers are explained in terms of quantum physics and Chaos-theory mathematics; a longish horror story is implanted in its midst. *Children of the Night* (**1992**) – which features a priest who had appeared as a child in *Summer of Night* (**1991**), a Stephen-KING-like tale of supernatural horror – rationalizes the vampire novel, and is a pure-sf thriller in its AIDS-related story of Romanian vampires, led by the still-living Vlad Dracula, whose condition turns out to be a hereditary immune deficiency curable by the intake of human blood. The novel arguably trivializes the agonies of post-Ceausescu Romania and of AIDS by linking them to vampirism, and does not fully justify DS's return to themes he had already used so forcefully in *Carrion Comfort*. There is an intellectual chill about both novels, which are well crafted but dispassionate, suggesting that for the moment at least DS is marking time. [JC]

Other works: *Entropy's Bed at Midnight* (**1990** chap); *Banished Dreams* (**1990** chap); *Going After the Rubber Chicken* (coll **1991** chap), 3 cogent after-dinner speeches; *Summer Sketches* (coll **1992**), nonfiction.

About the author: "The True and Blushful Chutzpah" by John Clute, *Interzone* #38, 1990.

See also: CLICHÉS; COMMUNICATIONS; CYBERNETICS; FANTASTIC VOYAGES; GALACTIC EMPIRES; GODS AND DEMONS; GOTHIC SF; PARASITISM AND SYMBIOSIS; REINCARNATION; RELIGION; SPACE FLIGHT; VILLAINS.

SIMMONS, GEOFFREY (1943-) US writer and medical doctor whose first sf novel, *The Adam Experiment* (**1978**), set in an orbital space lab, features an experiment in human procreation which runs up against the fact that ALIENS have been monitoring *Homo sapiens* and will not permit us to breed off-planet. *Pandemic* (**1980**) is a medical sf thriller; *Murdock* (**1983**), a heavily plotted tale involving CRYOGENICS, again makes some effective use of GS's medical expertise. [JC]

SIMON, ERIK [r] ◊ GERMANY.

SIMPSON, HELEN (de GUERRY) (1897-1940) UK novelist, the last and longest section of whose *The Woman on the Beast* (**1933**) is set in 1999, when a woman anarchist becomes ruler of the world with apocalyptic intentions, including the purificatory abolition of all reading. [JC]

SIMS, D(ENISE) N(ATALIE) [r] ◊ ROBERT HALE LIMITED.

SINCLAIR, ANDREW (ANNANDALE) (1935-) UK writer of much fiction and nonfiction. His *The Project* (**1960**) comes as close to nuclear HOLOCAUST as possible – a doomsday weapon is just about to go off as the final page ends – without actually meeting the END OF THE WORLD head-on. AS remains best known for his **Gog** sequence – *Gog* (**1967**), *Magog* (**1972**) and *King Ludd* (**1988**) – a FABULATION about the Matter of Britain which is half sentimental SATIRE and half mythopoesis. [JC]

SINCLAIR, IAIN (MacGREGOR) (1943-) UK poet and novelist whose *Lud Heat: A Book of the Dead Hamlets* (**1975**) is a narrative prose-poem which fabricates a numerological myth of the geography of London; it provided a direct inspiration for Peter ACKROYD's *Hawksmoor* (**1985**). A novel, *Downriver (Or, the Vessels of Wrath): A Narrative in Twelve Tales* (**1991**), develops similar material in a FABULATION which combines detective modes and NEAR-FUTURE sf visions of the complex destiny of London. [JC]

SINCLAIR, MICHAEL ◊ Michael SHEA.

SINCLAIR, UPTON (BEALL) (1878-1968) US writer known primarily for his work outside the sf field, particularly for his novels of social criticism, including *The Jungle* (**1905**). His most notable sf work is the comedy *The Millennium: A Comedy of the Year 2000* (1914 *Appeal to Reason*; in 3 vols **1924**), based on a play, in which the survivors of a DISASTER recapitulate the economic stages described by the Marxist theory of history. In *Prince Hagen* (**1903**; play **1921**) a Nibelung ruler acknowledges that US capitalists are his superiors in avarice. *The Industrial Republic: A Study of the America of Ten Years Hence* (**1907**) is a utopian fantasy. *Roman Holiday* (**1931**) is an interesting and curiously bittersweet account of a delusional timeslip in which an industrialist discovers parallels between his own time and a nascent Roman republic which cannot anticipate the indignities that history has in store for it. US's lighter political satires include the documentary future histories *I, Governor of California, and How I Ended Poverty* (**1933**) and *We, People of America, and How We Ended Poverty: A True Story of the Future* (**1934**). He also wrote a number of religious fantasies in which MESSIAH figures are frustrated by the injustices of the modern world: *They Call me Carpenter* (**1922**) is a delusional fantasy starring Jesus; *Our Lady* (**1938**) is an effective timeslip story which brings the Blessed Virgin to contemporary California; and *What Didymus Did* (**1954** UK; vt *It Happened to Didymus* **1958** US) is a dispirited account of the failure of a reluctant miracle-worker commissioned by Heaven to spread spiritual enlightenment in an unappreciative world.   [BS]

Other works: *Plays of Protest* (coll **1912**) includes *Prince Hagen* and a play featuring a female noble savage, *The Naturewoman*; *Co-op: A Novel of Living Together* (**1936** UK); *The Gnomobile* (**1936**), a juvenile filmed by Disney as *The Gnome-Mobile* (1967); *A Giant's Strength: A Three-Act Drama of the Atomic Bomb* (**1947**), a post-HOLOCAUST play.

See also: BOYS' PAPERS; ECONOMICS; POLITICS; THEATRE.

SINYAVSKY, ANDREY (DONATOVICH) (1925-   ) Russian dissident writer and literary critic who published the manuscripts he smuggled into the West in the late 1950s and early 1960s under the name Abram Tertz. His identity became known when the Soviet authorities arrested him in 1966 and subjected him, along with his friend and fellow dissident Yuli DANIEL (who wrote as Nikolai Arzhak), to a show trial; both were imprisoned and subsequently exiled. Several of AS's "fantastic stories" are of sf interest, most being assembled in *Fantasticheskiye Povesti* (coll **1961** Paris; trans Max Hayward and R. Hingley as *The Icicle and Other Stories* 1963 UK; vt *Fantastic Stories* 1963 US), though the most striking of all, "Pkhentz" (trans 1966; Russian text in *Fantasticheski Mir Abrama Tertza*, coll **1967** US), was only later smuggled to the West. In this story an ALIEN spaceship crashes in Russia leaving only one survivor, who is forced to exist for years in a desperate limbo under a false identity, passing for an ordinary citizen. "The Icicle" (1961) features a man of whose clairvoyant powers the state makes destructive use in its attempts to control the future. AS's finest novel, *Lyubimov* (Washington **1964**; trans Manya Harari as *The Makepeace Experiment* **1965** UK), tells with warmth and power of the transformation of a small Russian village through the ability of one man to broadcast his will hypnotically through space; when he loses this power, robot tanks regain the village and he flees. The satirical implications of this allegorical recasting of the triumph of communism in Russia are obvious. At the same time, AS's satirical effects are mediated through an imagination deeply Russian in its metaphysical, fundamentally religious, Slavophile bent; his sf stories are slashing moral fables rather than political diatribes.   [JC]

Other work: *For Freedom of Imagination* (coll trans Laszlo Tikos and Murray Peppard **1971** US) contains speculations on the nature of sf.

About the author: *On Trial: The Case of Sinyavsky (Tertz) and Daniel (Arzhak)* (**1967**) ed Leopold Lebedz and Max Hayward deals largely with AS, and discusses his work in literary as well as political terms.

See also: TABOOS.

SIODMAK, CURT or KURT (1902-   ) German writer/film-director based in Hollywood. CS entered the film industry in 1929 as a screen-writer; his credits include F.P.1 ANTWORTET NICHT (1932; vt F.P.1 DOESN'T ANSWER; based on his own novel *F.P.1 Antwortet Nicht* [**1932**; trans H.W. Farrel as *F.P.1 Does not Reply* 1933 US; vt *F.P.1 Fails to Reply* 1933 UK]). He emigrated to the USA in 1937; his US screenplays (some co-authorships) include *The Ape* (1940), *The Invisible Man Returns* (1940), *The Invisible Woman* (1940), *Invisible Agent* (1942), *The Wolf Man* (1942), *Son of Dracula* (1943), *Frankenstein Meets the Wolf Man* (1943), *I Walked with a Zombie* (1943), *House of Frankenstein* (1944), *The* LADY AND THE MONSTER (1944; based on his novel *Donovan's Brain* [**1943**], subsequently filmed again as DONOVAN'S BRAIN [1953] and VENGEANCE [1963]), *The Beast with Five Fingers* (1946), *Tarzan's Magic Fountain* (1949), RIDERS TO THE STARS (1953) and *Creature with the Atom Brain* (1955). He also wrote the story for EARTH VS. THE FLYING SAUCERS (1956; vt *Invasion of the Flying Saucers*). Later in his career he also directed films, rather badly, including *Bride of the Gorilla* (1951), *The* MAGNETIC MONSTER (1953) and *Curucu, Beast of the Amazon* (1956). Although often involved with sf-oriented subjects, he never displayed much understanding for the genre: like other German film-makers of his generation, he was more at home with the GOTHIC (the supernatural, the macabre and the grotesque) than with science, and such science as he introduced tended to be for picturesque atmosphere. *Donovan's Brain* was parodied in *The* MAN WITH TWO BRAINS (1983).

CS has 35 movie credits in the USA and 18 in Europe. Before emigrating he had 18 novels published in Germany, *F.P.1 Does Not Reply* being the only one translated into English. His novels in English, aside from *Donovan's Brain* – his most interesting – are its belated sequel *Hauser's Memory* (**1968**), filmed as HAUSER'S MEMORY (1970); *Skyport* (**1959**), *The Third Ear* (**1971**) and *City in the Sky* (**1974**), the last dealing with rebellion in a prison satellite. *Riders to the Stars* * (**1953**) was published as by CS and Robert Smith (1920-   ), but CS's only connection with it was the original screenplay. *Hauser's Memory* and *The Third Ear* both feature spy-thriller plots and absurd experiments carried out by biochemists. [JB/PN]

See also: CYBORGS; PSYCHOLOGY; TRANSPORTATION.

SIRIUS Magazine. ◊ YUGOSLAVIA.

SITWELL, [Sir] OSBERT (1892-1969) UK writer. The title novella in *Triple Fugue* (coll **1924**) posits a 1948 world in which Trotsky is President of Russia and lifespans have been trebled for the rich. *The Man who Lost Himself* (**1929**) tells the complex psychological life-story of a man from his youth to his death sometime after the middle of the 20th century. *Miracle on Sinai* (**1933**), a discussion novel like several of H.G. WELLS's from this period, is set in a luxury hotel near Mount Sinai and on the Mount itself, where a glowing cloud deposits new Tablets of the Law, which are variously interpreted; in the final chapter a cataclysmic war begins. *A Place of One's Own* (**1941** chap) is a ghost story. *Fee Fi Fo Fum!: A Book of Fairy Stories* (coll **1959**) assembles SATIRES.   [JC]

See also: TIME PARADOXES.

SIX MILLION DOLLAR MAN, THE US tv series (1973-8). A Silverton and Universal Production for ABC. Executive prods Glen A. LARSON, Harve Bennett,

Allan Balter. Prod Michael Gleason, Lionel E. Siegel, Joe L. Cramer, Fred Freiberger. Based on the novel *Cyborg* (**1972**) by Martin CAIDIN. The series began as a 90min ABC "Wednesday Movie of the Week" in 1973; 2 more made-for-tv movies followed, then the series: 5 seasons, 100 50min episodes. Colour.

Lee Majors plays Steve Austin, a former US Air Force astronaut who, after an accident in an experimental aircraft, has his badly injured body rebuilt with artificial parts (2 legs, 1 arm, 1 eye), becoming a CYBORG, though it is impossible to tell externally which parts are artificial. His unique situation is treated in purely comic-book terms for a presumably juvenile audience. He becomes a latter-day SUPERMAN, able to perform feats of great strength and move at incredible speeds, and is used as a special agent by a CIA-like government organization. The basic premise of the series is technologically absurd – while Austin's bionic arm might be able to withstand lifting huge weights, the leverage would pull the rest of his body apart. The success of the series resulted in a rather better spin-off series, *The BIONIC WOMAN*. [JB]

SKAL, DAVID J. (?   -   ) US writer whose first novel, *Scavengers* (**1980**), suggests some sf basis for a plot involving memory transfer in a corrupt world. His second, *When We Were Good* (**1981**), evokes a powerful sense of cultural despair in the tale of a sterile world in which genetically engineered hermaphrodites fail to represent an emblem of hope for the terminal remnants of normal humanity. A sense that DJS is by inclination a horror writer was intensified by the entropic dismay evoked by *Antibodies* (**1989**), a short accusatory trawl through Californian subcultures, where sf characters emit pretentious twaddle about transcendence and the military-industrial complex conspires to transform pseudo-hippies into spare computer parts; all this is told with a sense of gnawing revulsion. *Hollywood Gothic: The Tangled Web of "Dracula" from Novel to Stage to Screen* (**1990**) is a nonfiction study. [JC]

See also: GENETIC ENGINEERING.

SKIFFY ◊ SCI FI.

SKINNER, AINSLIE Pseudonym used by US-born crime writer Paula Gosling (1939-   ), resident in the UK, for her sf novel *Mind's Eye* (**1980**; vt *The Harrowing* 1980 US), which convincingly (and often movingly) depicts the scientific testing of a girl possessed of ESP and the realization of the consequences of the fact that this power is transferable to others. [JGr/JC]

SKINNER, B(URRHUS) F(REDERICK) (1904-1990) US psychologist and writer whose cogently argued (and just as cogently refuted) brand of behaviourism dominated that theory of PSYCHOLOGY for many years in the USA, and provides the basic tenets for his one work of fiction, *Walden Two* (**1948**), depicting a UTOPIA whose inhabitants grow up as successful experiments in behavioural engineering. The title refers, of course, to *Walden, or Life in the Woods* (**1854**) by Henry David

Thoreau (1817-1862). *Walden Two* is conducted in the main as a dialogue between Castle and Frazier, two colleagues of a professor named Burris, a clear stand-in for the author himself. Frazier, who has founded the colony, dismisses – as BFS later did himself in *Beyond Freedom and Dignity* (**1972**) – the traditional notions of free will, and disparages democratic forms of government; his opponent, Castle, argues for the time-tested liberal solutions to the problems of human happiness. Burris seems neutral, but the colony, with its crèches, positive reinforcement regimes and transparently happy residents, is obviously intended to represent the power of Frazier's ideas. [JC]

See also: SCIENTIFIC ERRORS; SOCIOLOGY.

SKORPIOS, ANTARES ◊ James William BARLOW.

SKY, KATHLEEN (1943-   ) US writer whose first genre story was "One Ordinary Day, with Box" in *Generation* (anth **1972**) ed David GERROLD. She was married to Stephen GOLDIN 1972-82, and wrote with him *The Business of Being a Writer* (**1982**). Her début novel *Birthright* (**1975**) speculates emotionally about distinctions between human and ANDROID after GENETIC ENGINEERING has become a common practice. Her other work in the genre has also been romantic, including 2 competent STAR-TREK ties, *Vulcan!* * (**1978**) and *Death's Angel* * (**1981**), and the separate novels *Ice Prison* (**1976**) and *Witchdame* (**1985**), the latter being a fantasy, and seemingly #1 in a projected series. [PN]

SKYWORLDS US DIGEST-size reprint magazine, subtitled "Classics in Science Fiction" on #1, thereafter "Marvels in Science Fiction". 4 issues Nov 1977-Aug 1978, published by Humorama Inc., New York; ed Jeff Stevens (uncredited). *S* reprinted mostly from MARVEL SCIENCE STORIES of 1950-52, material badly dated by the 1970s and undistinguished when it had first appeared. Production was terrible. [FHP/PN]

SLADEK, JOHN T(HOMAS) (1937-   ) US writer who spent two decades in the UK from 1966, becoming involved in the UK NEW-WAVE movement centred on Michael MOORCOCK's NEW WORLDS, and co-editing with Pamela ZOLINE *Ronald Reagan: The Magazine of Poetry* (2 issues 1968), in which work by both editors, J.G. BALLARD, Thomas M. DISCH and others appeared. In the mid-1980s he returned to Minneapolis, a town which had long supplied local colour to many of his more severely satirical stories, whose protagonists ricochet through their preordained and absurd lives within the vast, hyperbolic flatlands of middle America. This *mise en scène*, when illuminated by his adept control of the language and pretensions of the modern bureaucratic state, provides a matrix for his best work, and helps make plausible the frequent comparisons that have been drawn between him and Kurt VONNEGUT Jr; but Vonnegut has an easier emotional flow than JTS, while JTS lacks Vonnegut's rhetoric and avoids his excessive simplicity of effect.

He began writing sf with "The Happy Breed", published in Harlan ELLISON's *Dangerous Visions* (anth

1967), though his first published story was "The Poets of Millgrove, Iowa" for *NW* in 1966; his first 2 novels – *The House that Fear Built* (**1966** US) with Disch and *The Castle and the Key* (**1967** US) – were GOTHICS, both as by Cassandra Knye. His first sf novel, *The Reproductive System* (**1968**; vt *Mechasm* 1969 US), introduced into his typical small-town-US setting a brilliant maelstrom of sf activity: a self-reproducing technological device goes out of control in passages of allegorical broadness, but everything turns out all right in the end, though not through positive efforts of the inept cast, and a dreamlike UTOPIA looms on the horizon; governing the conniptions of the tale is an obsessive discourse upon and dramatization of the metamorphic relationships between human and ROBOT, a relationship which lies at the centre of all his subsequent solo novels and much of his short fiction. His next book, however, *Black Alice* (**1968** US) with Disch, both as Thom Demijohn, was a mystery novel, not sf. In JTS's next sf book, *The Müller-Fokker Effect* (**1970**), a man's character is transferred onto COMPUTER tape, and the dissemination of several copies of this "personality" instigates a series of absurd events (◊ FABULATION), some of them extremely comic in effect, some horrifying, all mounting to a picture of a USA disintegrated morally and physically by its own surrender to TECHNOLOGY, the profit motive and the ethical falseness that leads to dehumanization. In its questioning of the nature of narrative events and of fiction itself, the book is a significant example of modern US self-analysis at its highly impressive best. In 1970 the book gained little response, and for a decade JTS wrote no more sf novels.

Through his career, JTS has written numerous stories whose strenuous formal ingenuity, and whose surreal combining of a deadpan ribaldry and pathos, have made them underground classics of the genre. The most notable of them all, because of its length and impassioned veracity of tone, may be "Masterson and the Clerks" (1967), in which the immolation of its protagonists in the process of a US business is first hilariously then movingly presented; true to the oddly uncommercial course of his career, JTS collected this tale only much later, in *Alien Accounts* (coll **1982**). Previous collections – *The Steam-Driven Boy and Other Strangers* (coll **1973**), which contains several superb parodies of well known sf writers (◊ SATIRE), and *Keep the Giraffe Burning* (coll dated 1977 but **1978**), selections from both vols being brought together as *The Best of John Sladek* (coll **1981** US) – tended to assemble stories which, perhaps more formally brilliant than "Masterson", lack something of its human intensity. Later stories were assembled in *The Lunatics of Terra* (coll **1984**), in which the comic melancholy of his early work wears a somewhat calmer guise. During the 1970s, when most of his stories became generally available, JTS published two detective novels, *Black Aura* (**1974**) – which contains some borderline-sf elements – and *Invisible Green* (**1977**), as well as a sequence of nonfiction texts of considerable

interest. *The New Apocrypha: A Guide to Strange Sciences and Occult Beliefs* (**1973**) – all subsequent texts modified under threat of legal action from the Church of Scientology – scathingly anatomizes the various cults and PSEUDO-SCIENCES that exist as a kind of fringe around the sf reader's areas of interest, from SCIENTOLOGY to VON DÄNIKEN. *Arachne Rising: The Thirteenth Sign of the Zodiac* (**1977**) as James Vogh, *The Cosmic Factor* (**1978**) as James Vogh and *Judgement of Jupiter* (**1980**) as Richard A. Tilms were hoax demonstrations of the kind of fringe theorizing that underpins the cults described in *The New Apocrypha*.

JTS then returned to sf with *Roderick, or The Education of a Young Machine* (**1980**) and *Roderick at Random, or Further Education of a Young Machine* (**1983**), 2 texts conceived as a single novel. The US version, also entitled *Roderick* (1982 US), constituted only about two-thirds of the original *Roderick*; the publisher had intended to make a trilogy out of the 2-vol novel, but the project foundered, and only the single savagely truncated vol appeared. The novel represents the autobiography of the eponymous robot and is JTS's most ambitious work to date, conveying with considerable ingenuity and some pathos its protagonist's Candide-like innocence and its author's OULIPO-derived numerological sense of narrative structure. *Tik-Tok* (**1983**), a thematic pendant which again took its structure from the arbitrary rule-generating principles of oulipo, follows the career of a robot who, once his "asimov circuits" go on the blink, becomes criminally ambitious. Though robots inevitably appear, *Bugs* (**1989** UK) was JTS's first sf novel to feature a "normal" human protagonist; and in its tracing of the deranging experiences of a UK immigrant to a strange Midwestern city the tale could be seen as guardedly autobiographical.

As the most formally inventive, the funniest, and very nearly the most melancholy of modern US sf writers, JTS has always addressed the heart of the genre, but never spoken from it. We need his attention: he deserves ours. [JC]

Other works: *Red Noise* (**1982** chap US); *Flatland* (**1982** chap US); *The Book of Clues* (**1984**), a series of short detective puzzles; *Blood and Gingerbread* (**1990** chap).

About the author: *A John Sladek Checklist* (**1984** chap) by Chris DRUMM.

See also: ABSURDIST SF; AUTOMATION; BRITISH SCIENCE FICTION AWARD; HUMOUR; LEISURE; MACHINES; MEDIA LANDSCAPE; PARANOIA.

SLANT UK FANZINE (1948-53) ed from Belfast by Walt Willis. Neatly hand-printed on a small letterpress machine, and containing woodcut illustrations by James WHITE and Bob SHAW, *S* is best remembered for introducing Irish FANDOM (principally Willis, Shaw and White) to sf fandom at large; it also contained fine pieces of humorous writing (continued in HYPHEN) and featured fiction by authors such as Kenneth BULMER, John BRUNNER, A. Bertram CHANDLER and Shaw. [PR]

SLATER, HENRY J. (?   -   ) UK author whose

work showed the influence of H.G. WELLS in both *Ship of Destiny* (**1951**), where survivors of a HOLOCAUST sail across a drowned world, and *The Smashed World* (**1952**), set 3000 years hence in a World State which is destroyed by a reborn Napoleon. Some of HJS's effects oddly prefigure the afterlife fantasies of Philip José FARMER. [JC]

See also: REINCARNATION.

SLATER, PHILIP (ELLIOT) (1927-) US writer who remains best known for acute analyses of Western culture like *The Pursuit of Loneliness* (**1970**) and *Earthwalk* (**1974**). His *How I Saved the World* (**1985**), about nuclear DISASTER, reiterates in spoof-thriller guise the lessons urged in his nonfiction. [JC]

SLAUGHTERHOUSE-FIVE Film (1972). Vanadas/Universal. Dir George Roy Hill, starring Michael Sacks, Ron Leibman, Eugene Roche, Sharon Gans, Valerie Perrine. Screenplay Stephen Geller, based on *Slaughterhouse-Five, or The Children's Crusade* (**1969**) by Kurt VONNEGUT Jr. 104 mins. Colour.

A middle-class, middle-aged American (Sacks), dissatisfied with his job, marriage and life in general, starts to experience sudden shifts in time, mainly back to when he was a PoW in the German city of Dresden before its fire-bombing on a massive scale by the Allies. He later experiences forward shifts in time to when he has become a prisoner of the ALIEN Tralfamadorians, who keep him in a zoo on their planet and provide him with a half-naked Hollywood starlet for company. The novel's ABSURDIST disjunctions between the real horrors of war and the minor horrors of suburban life are arguably satirical, and certainly agonized, though arbitrary; here, with quite extraordinary vulgarity, they become merely flippant, especially in the context of the Tralfamadore sequences, where what is black in the book is merely whimsical in the movie, which nevertheless won a 1973 HUGO. [JB/PN]

SLEATOR, WILLIAM (WARNER III) (1945-) US writer of books for older children. His first novel, *Blackbriar* (**1972**), is an occult fantasy. Titles of sf interest include: *House of Stairs* (**1974**), an attack on behavioural science and the experiments to which it might lead; *Green Futures of Tycho* (**1981**), set in a familiar version of the Solar System; *Interstellar Pig* (**1984**), which intermixes gaming (◊ GAMES AND SPORTS) and ALIEN themes in the tale of a game whose pieces represent moves in a nonhuman conflict; *The Boy who Reversed Himself* (**1986**), about travel through the DIMENSIONS at some risk to the lad; *The Duplicate* (**1988**), in which a machine CLONES duplicates of a teenaged boy, all of them upset; and *Strange Attractors* (**1990**; vt *Strange Attractions* 1991 UK), a TIME-TRAVEL tale. WS's range is wide, and his recalcitrant protagonists stick doggedly in the reader's memory, but he has a tendency sometimes to accept sf devices without much bothering to examine them, and this in turn thins the texture of reality of his tales. [JC]

Other works: *Among the Dolls* (**1975** chap), fantasy; *Into the Dream* (**1979**); *Fingers* (**1983**); *Singularity* (**1985**);

The Spirit House (**1991**).

SLEE, RICHARD [r] ◊ Cornelia Atwood PRATT.

SLEEPER Film (1973). Rollins-Joffe Productions/United Artists. Dir Woody Allen, starring Allen, Diane Keaton, John Beck, Mary Gregory, Don Keefer. Screenplay Allen, Marshall Brickman. 88 mins. Colour.

The plot device of having a man from the present suddenly finding himself in the future (this time through CRYONICS) is nearly always used to comment on contemporary society rather than to speculate about the future (◊ SLEEPER AWAKES). This, one of Allen's best slapstick SATIRES, targets Nixon, health food, beauty contests and revolutionary politics, but it does include genuinely futuristic sf gags involving ROBOTS and robot pets, SEX practices and artificial food (which has to be beaten into submission before it can be served). One of the best sequences involves an attempt to CLONE a new body from the nose of the country's assassinated dictator, the only bit left. Allen is the always-anxious heath-food faddist who cannot come to terms with the future's partiality to pleasure. The film won both HUGO and NEBULA. [JB/PN]

SLEEPER AWAKES As the 19th century progressed and the planet became more and more thoroughly explored, authors of UTOPIAS and DYSTOPIAS began to abandon present-day LOST WORLDS and ISLANDS as venues for their ideal societies, and instead to locate their speculations in the future, perhaps hundreds of years hence. Almost always these speculations were framed by prologues (and sometimes epilogues) set at the time the novel was written; this frame served to introduce the protagonist who was to travel into the future and act the role of inquisitive visitor to the new world. The route he (the protagonist was almost always male) generally took seems in retrospect an odd one. Though TIME MACHINES were available to fiction writers before the end of the century, they were rarely used, either by utopian/dystopian speculators or by tellers of tales. Even H.G. WELLS, who conceived perhaps the first imaginatively plausible device in *The Time Machine* (**1895**), did not re-use the idea, even though the notion of an instantaneous trip through time served one essential function for the writer who wished to illuminate the world to come: it brought the then and the now into abrupt and glaring contrast. When Wells came to write his first dystopia, *When the Sleeper Wakes* (**1899**; rev vt *The Sleeper Awakes* 1910), he fell back on the convention of the protagonist who falls asleep in the present day and wakes again in the future. Not for the first time in his career, he did not invent but gave definitive form to (and named, in the vt) a significant sf theme or motif.

The sleeper-awakes device shares with TIME TRAVEL, however, the capacity to transit centuries in the turning of a page, so that the essential function of contrast between the then and the now can be retained in exemplary focus. The two most famous late-19th-century utopias in the English language,

Edward BELLAMY's *Looking Backward, 2000-1887* (**1888**) and William MORRIS's *News from Nowhere* (**1890** US), took advantage of the device to sharpen contrasts throughout. Many less famous titles, like Ismar THIUSEN's *The Diothas* (**1883**), also utilized it. In his *Science Fiction: The Early Years* (**1991**), E.F. BLEILER lists about 40 further novels and stories published before 1930 – by no means all of them utopias or dystopias – which feature an awakened sleeper. Few have retained much popularity, although Alvarado M. FULLER's *A.D. 2000* (**1890**), W.H. HUDSON's *A Crystal Age* (**1887**; rev 1906), Horace W.C. NEWTE's *The Master Beast* (**1907**; vt *The Red Fury* 1919) and Edward SHANKS's *The People of the Ruins* (**1920**) remain of some interest.

It is hard to escape the sense that the sleeper-awakes structure betrayed, even before the beginning of the 20th century, an undue fastidiousness of imagination, and that some straightforward magic (like a time machine) might always have been a more elegant option; even more attractive to the imagination, of course, would have been a story which did not need a time-frame or anchor to make its point about the worlds to come, or to thrill its readers with the new. One of the centrally important accomplishments of GENRE SF has been the abandonment of the anchor of the present day, for most genre sf is set unabashedly in the future, and needs no present-day protagonist to reassure its readers of the imaginative reality of the new worlds. A non-genre writer like J. Leslie MITCHELL might still hint at something along the lines of the device when he sent the eponymous heroine of *Gay Hunter* (**1934**) 20,000 years hence, but few sleepers-awake stories appeared in genre sf until the development of the notion of the GENERATION STARSHIP, in the bowels of which might repose thousands of humans in SUSPENDED ANIMATION; and, anyway, here the sleepers tend not to be the protagonists of the tale – it is their shepherds, in the here and now of the narrative, who generally fill that role. Only occasionally – as in Orson Scott CARD's *Hot Sleep* (fixup **1979**) – will a sleeper awake from generation-starship solitude as protagonist in a changed world. Other genre-sf examples of the device either – like Mack REYNOLDS's *Looking Backward, from the Year 2000* (**1973**) – are introduced as a homage, or – as in T.J. BASS's remarkable *Half Past Human* (fixup **1971**) – are integrated into genre pyrotechnics that far transcend the original simplicity of the notion. But these are eccentric examples. When, after 1926, the future became domesticated as a venue for the imagination, the sleeper-awakes tale faded away.

There are also many tales in both 19th-century sf and genre sf which feature a figure from the past who awakens into the present. Indeed, this is a far older theme, growing perhaps from legends like that of Sleeping Beauty and famously given new life by Washington Irving (1783-1859) in "Rip Van Winkle" (in *The Sketch Book of Geoffrey Crayon, Gent* [in parts

1819-20]), whose lazy protagonist falls asleep in the Catskills for 20 years. Modern tales of this sort rarely focus on the awakened sleeper, but on the impact that an intruder from beyond, whose responses to us may well be inappropriate or alien, might have upon our own world. [JC]

SLEEPING DOGS ◊ NEW ZEALAND.

SLESAR, HENRY (1927-   ) US writer who began his career in advertising. He started to publish sf with "The Brat" for *Imaginative Tales* in 1955. Of his several hundred stories, about a third have been sf or fantasy, most of them appearing in his first decade as a writer; many are as by O.H. Leslie. He is best known for his work in the mystery field, with a number of thrillers from *The Gray Flannel Shroud* (**1958**), which won an Edgar, onwards. Among them was a borderline-sf tale, *The Bridge of Lions* (**1963**); closely connected to this kind of work was his stint as headwriter for the US daytime suspense serial, *The Edge of Night*, in the late 1950s and 1960s. Other tv work included 24 episodes for **Alfred Hitchcock Presents** (1955-61), *The Virtue Affair* for *The* MAN FROM U.N.C.L.E. in 1965, and at least 100 additional scripts, many of them fantasy or sf. His one sf book has been the novelization of TWENTY MILLION MILES TO EARTH (1957; **1957**), published as #1 in the abortive AMAZING STORIES SCIENCE FICTION NOVELS series. [JC/PN]

See also: PSI POWERS.

SLICKS ◊ BEDSHEET; DIGEST; PULP MAGAZINES.

SLIPSTREAM Film (1989). Entertainment Film Productions. Prod Gary Kurtz. Dir Steven M. Lisberger, starring Bill Paxton, Bob Peck, Mark Hamill, Kitty Aldridge, Eleanor David, Ben Kingsley. Screenplay Tony Kayden, based on a story by Bill Bauer. 102 mins. Colour.

Unspecified ecological rape has led to great earthquakes and geological changes all over the world. A strong, constant "river" of wind, the Slipstream, blows always in one direction across a scarred landscape which confusingly alternates between scenes shot in Yorkshire and in Turkey. Eccentric remnants of civilization persist in isolated pockets; transport is, inexplicably, by microlight aircraft. A supposedly criminal ANDROID (Peck) is hunted by a psychotic cop (Hamill) and protected by a young bounty hunter (Paxton). The post-HOLOCAUST scenario is intriguing, the execution is dreadful. Kurtz, who produced STAR WARS (1977), was attempting a comeback here, along with *Star Wars* star Hamill; both failed. A few powerful moments focus on Peck's intelligent performance as the Christlike healer-android. Lisberger's previous sf film, TRON (1982), was not bad, and one can only wonder why this apparently promising project suffered from murky photography, confused editing and an incoherent and pretentious script. [PN]

SLIPSTREAM SF A term devised, apparently by Bruce STERLING – in part as a pun on, or echo of, MAINSTREAM – to designate stories which make use of sf devices but which are not GENRE SF. The image is either nautical or aeronautical: a ship or an airplane (either of which stands for genre sf) can create a slipstream which may be strong enough to give non-paying passengers (Paul THEROUX, say) a ride. As a description of commercial piggybacking, the term seems apt; however, when used to designate the whole range of non-genre sf here called FABULATION (*which see for discussion*), the term – which implies a relationship of dependency – can seem derogatory. [JC]

SLOANE, T(HOMAS) O'CONOR (1851-1940) US editor and author of popular scientific works. He was associate editor (designated managing editor for #1) of AMAZING STORIES and of AMAZING STORIES QUARTERLY from the beginning, and carried much responsibility for the actual running of the magazines, although they were in the overall charge of, successively, Hugo GERNSBACK and Arthur Lynch. He succeeded to the editorship of both journals in 1929. *Amazing Stories Quarterly* ceased publication in 1934, but he retained the editorship of *AMZ* until June 1938, when the ailing magazine was sold to the Chicago-based ZIFF-DAVIS. Nearing his 80th year when he finally succeeded to the editorship, TOS had a long white beard and an appropriately Rip Van Winkle-like approach to the job; though he worked for 12 years on SF MAGAZINES, he stated publicly (in a 1929 *AMZ* editorial) his belief that Man would never achieve space travel. *AMZ* nevertheless bought the first stories of such writers as E.E. SMITH, John W. CAMPBELL Jr and Jack WILLIAMSON; but the combination of poor payment and slack management made it inevitable that writers of any calibre would soon move to more attractive markets. TOS actually lost the manuscript of Campbell's first story, and returned Clifford D. SIMAK's first submission after 4 years' silence, remarking that it was "a bit dated". He was more than once fooled into publishing plagiarisms. On one occasion (Feb 1933) he printed a story ("The Ho-Ming Gland" by Malcolm R. Afford) which had already appeared in WONDER STORIES (Jan 1931): the author had submitted the story to TOS 4 years earlier but, having heard nothing after a year, had sold it to the rival magazine.

TOS, a PhD, had been an inventor, and his son married a daughter of a more celebrated inventor, Thomas Alva Edison (1847-1931). [MJE]

SLOANE, WILLIAM M(ILLIGAN) (1906-1974) US playwright, novelist and publisher whose interest in the occult was reflected in his sf novels, *To Walk the Night* (1937; rev 1954) and *The Edge of Running Water* (1939; vt *The Unquiet Corpse* 1946), both later assembled as *The Rim of Morning* (omni 1964); along with 1 story, "Let Nothing You Dismay" (1954), they are all the sf he wrote. The first complexly combines horror and sf in the story of an ALIEN entrapped in a human life as the widow of a famous physicist, in whose death she seems implicated; the story is absorbing and polished. The second, rather similarly, features a scientist's attempts to communicate with his dead wife and to revive her; horrors ensue, and local prejudice exacts its toll. WMS also ed 2 sf anthologies, *Space, Space, Space* (anth 1953) and *Stories for Tomorrow* (anth 1954); the latter was one of the finest collections of its period. [JC]
Other works: *Back Home: A Ghost Play in One Act* (1931 chap); *Runner in the Snow: A Play of the Supernatural* (1931 chap); *Crystal Clear* (1932 chap), a fantasy play.
See also: ESCHATOLOGY; MACHINES.

SLOCOMBE, GEORGE (EDWARD) (1894-1963) UK writer whose *Dictator* (1932), set in an imaginary European country, describes the rise of a tyranny there. *Escape into the Past* (1943) features an artist's wife who escapes irrevocably into the 17th century. [JC]

SLONCZEWSKI, JOAN (LYN) (1956-   ) US writer and professor of biology, specializing in genetics, who began publishing sf with her first novel, *Still Forms on Foxfield* (1980), a tale in which most of her subsequent concerns take initial shape. A human community of Quakers, having fled an apparently doomed Earth and establishing on the planet Foxfield a sane and ECOLOGY-obedient relationship with the native species, is contacted centuries later by a technologically resurgent humanity and must now deal with the challenge to its ways. Significantly, the book deals not with rediscovery – an old and typically triumphalist sf theme – but with being discovered, a point of view reiterated in her second and best known novel, *A Door into Ocean* (1986), which won the JOHN W. CAMPBELL MEMORIAL AWARD. The planet (in fact a moon) is in this case water-covered and inhabited by WOMEN, who thwart a military invasion; the book teaches some sharp FEMINIST lessons *en passant*. *The Wall around Eden* (1989), set on a devastated post-HOLOCAUST Earth, provides its female protagonist with numbing challenges of comprehension (the supervising ALIENS are invisible and their insect-like culture may in fact have been decorticated – i.e., its central control systems may have been destroyed) and response, with no clear answers available in the waste. From the slightly sentimentalized burden of her first book, JS has moved rapidly into supple command of her ample concerns. [JC]
See also: PASTORAL; UNDER THE SEA.

SLOVAK SF ◊ CZECH AND SLOVAK SF.

SLUSSER, GEORGE EDGAR (1939-   ) US academic and critic with a PhD in literature from Harvard. He is Professor of Comparative Literature at the University of California, Riverside, and Curator of the J. LLOYD EATON COLLECTION there; he is also Director of the Eaton Program for Science Fiction and Fantasy Studies, which is devoted to research. GES has written and edited a number of critical books on sf, and has also translated sf-related works by Honoré de BALZAC and J.H. ROSNY aîné.

His critical books, all from BORGO PRESS, are *Robert A. Heinlein: Stranger in His Own Land* (chap 1976; rev 1977), *The Farthest Shores of Ursula K. Le Guin* (chap 1976), *The Bradbury Chronicles* (chap 1977), *Harlan Ellison: Unrepentant Harlequin* (chap 1977), *The Delany Intersection* (chap 1977), *The Classic Years of Robert A. Heinlein* (chap 1977) and *The Space Odysseys of Arthur*

C. Clarke (chap **1978**).

Anthologies of critical essays ed GES, most collecting papers delivered at the annual Eaton Conference on fantasy and sf, are *Bridges to Science Fiction* (anth **1980**) ed with George R. Guffey and Mark ROSE, *Bridges to Fantasy* (anth **1982**) ed with Eric RABKIN and Robert SCHOLES, *Co-Ordinates: Placing Science Fiction and Fantasy* (anth **1983**) ed with Rabkin and Scholes, *Shadows of the Magic Lamp: Fantasy and Science Fiction in Film* (anth **1985**) ed with Rabkin, *Hard Science Fiction* (anth **1986**) ed with Rabkin, *Storm Warnings: Science Fiction Confronts the Future* (anth **1987**) ed with Rabkin and Colin GREENLAND, *Intersections: Fantasy and Science Fiction* (anth **1987**) ed with Rabkin, *Aliens: The Anthropology of Science Fiction* (anth **1987**) ed with Rabkin, and *Mindscapes: The Geographies of Imagined Worlds* (anth **1989**) ed with Rabkin. By academic standards, at least, GES is a controversialist. On receiving the PILGRIM AWARD for services to sf criticism and scholarship in 1986, he argued that "we need to get sf out of the English department" into comparative literature, interdisciplinary studies or even as "a discipline in itself".   [PN]

See also: ANTHROPOLOGY; CINEMA; CRITICAL AND HISTORICAL WORKS ABOUT SF.

SMALL, AUSTIN J. (1894-1929) UK adventure and thriller writer, born Austin Small Major, though his death certificate gives AJS. He wrote 3 books of sf interest. In *Master Vorst* (**1926**; vt *The Death Maker* 1926 US) an insane plan to kill off the human race by germ warfare is thwarted in the nick of time. *The Man They Couldn't Arrest* (**1927**) is a mystery novel incorporating unusual devices and inventions into the plot. *The Avenging Ray* (**1930**), as Seamark, again features a mad scientist intent upon destroying the world, his WEAPON in this case being a "Degravitisor" DEATH-RAY. The title story of *Out of the Dark* (coll **1931**, assembled after the author's suicide) as by Seamark features a were-leopard.   [JC/JE]

SMALL PRESSES AND LIMITED EDITIONS 1. The USA Any firm founded to release work of personal interest to the publisher, and which distributes that work to readers whose interest can also be assumed, may be called a small press. Four years before Hugo GERNSBACK began AMAZING STORIES in 1926, The Lunar Publishing Company of Providence, Kentucky, was founded by friends of the author of the book it had been created in order to publish – and then folded. *To the Moon and Back in Ninety Days: A Thrilling Narrative of Blended Science and Adventure* (**1922**) by John Young Brown (1858-1921) was a genuine exercise in Gernsbackian sf, featuring a ship driven by ANTIGRAVITY plus lessons in ASTRONOMY and other sciences. It may have been the first GENRE-SF novel to reach book form in the USA; it was certainly the first such novel to be published for an affinity readership.

Several years passed, however, before the Lunar example was followed for sf publications; for more than a decade, the only small-press activity of genre interest took place in the fields of FANTASY and HORROR. The writers who formed a circle around H.P. LOVECRAFT – they included Robert E. HOWARD, Frank Belknap LONG, Edgar Hoffman PRICE, Clark Ashton SMITH and Donald WANDREI – all found it difficult to publish with conventional houses, and when W. Paul Cook (1881-1948), a friend of Lovecraft's and editor of some influential early APAS, decided in 1925 to move into PUBLISHING they were happy to contemplate having material released by his Recluse Press. In the event, its sole publications of interest were Long's first book, *A Man from Genoa* (coll **1926** chap), Wandrei's first book, *Ecstasy* (coll **1928** chap), and Lovecraft's *The Shunned House* (**1928** chap), only a very few copies of which were bound. Another start-and-stop small press, The ARRA Printers run by Conrad H. Ruppert, released 4 pamphlets in the early 1930s as a sidebar to FANTASY MAGAZINE.

The most important figure in this first flowering of the small press – although the quality of his work aroused controversy in the field – may have been William L. CRAWFORD (*whom see for details of his long career*), who began in imitation of Ruppert as a magazine producer, and who similarly moved into books; operating as Fantasy Pubs., his first release was *Men of Avalon/The White Sybil* (anth **1935** chap), which featured a story each by David H. KELLER and Clark Ashton Smith, and he continued with *Mars Mountain* (**1935**) by Eugene George KEY. More importantly, operating as Visionary Publishing Company, he then released *The Shadow over Innsmouth* (**1937**) by Lovecraft. It is worth noting that Crawford, like his predecessors, clearly found it easier to publish fantasy than sf; it was not until after WWII that any significant sf, with one exception, reached book form via the small presses; that exception was *Dawn of Flame and Other Stories* (coll **1936**) by Stanley G. WEINBAUM, a memorial volume put together by The Milwaukee Fictioneers, a fan group whose members included, among others, Robert BLOCH, Ralph Milne FARLEY and Raymond A. PALMER, and which would soon be seen as of great importance. But when in 1939 August DERLETH and Wandrei founded ARKHAM HOUSE: PUBLISHERS – which soon became and which remains the most famous of all small presses – they were inspired by Crawford's publication of the Lovecraft title. The reasons for this dominance of fantasy are not entirely clear, but probably come down to accidents of personality and opportunity: the early small presses could be described as close-knit "family" endeavours, and their publications were released to an extremely narrow group of buyers; and the Lovecraft circle, active through the 1920s and 1930s, was exactly the sort of "family" required for primitive small-press activities. It was only after sf FANDOM became properly organized at the end of the 1930s that sf itself was able to give birth to the "family" firms that multiplied after WWII.

It all changed after 1945. Crawford himself began to publish sf with real frequency in 1947, when he founded FANTASY PUBLISHING COMPANY INC. (better known as FPCI), but by then he found himself sharing the sf world with several other new houses, including FANTASY PRESS, founded by Lloyd Arthur ESHBACH in 1946, GNOME PRESS, founded by David A. KYLE and Martin GREENBERG in 1948, the HADLEY PUBLISHING COMPANY, founded by Donald M. Grant (1927-) and Thomas G. Hadley in 1946, PRIME PRESS, founded by Oswald TRAIN and others in 1947, and SHASTA: PUBLISHERS, founded by T.E. DIKTY (*whom see for details of his long career*), Erle Melvin Korshak and Mark Reinsberg in 1947. For almost a decade from 1946 these small presses – along with a few even smaller enterprises – dominated sf publishing. Various factors came together to explain this dominance: general-list firms had not yet discovered the field, while at the same time an influx of young men, all potential readers and book-buyers, had been released from military service; a large backlog of GENRE SF had built up in the magazines, including work by several prominent authors who were eager to see their material in book form; the genre was now old enough to have a past worthy of celebration, and had gained through the workings of fandom a singularly loyal readership; and the men (no women were importantly involved) who wished to celebrate the genre by publishing its works were now, most of them, mature and experienced enough to operate small publishing firms with some chance of success. For almost a decade from 1946, the fans and writers of sf seemed to be in control of their own house. For many still alive, those years were the true GOLDEN AGE OF SF.

By the middle of the 1950s, however, almost all the small presses were moribund or dead, crushed by the rise of the paperback (◊ ACE BOOKS; BALLANTINE BOOKS; BANTAM BOOKS) and the incursion of general publishers (like DOUBLEDAY and Scribners) into what had become a profitable market. Arkham House survived, and some small presses devoted in the main to nonfiction – like ADVENT: PUBLISHERS from 1956, Jack L. CHALKER'S MIRAGE PRESS from 1961, Lloyd C. CURREY's and David G. HARTWELL's Dragon Press from 1971, and Dikty's FAX COLLECTOR'S EDITIONS and STARMONT HOUSE from 1972 – continued to produce work. But genre sf, it seemed, had outgrown its familial dependence on fans; it had entered the commercial world, and what small presses remained could hope only to service the fringes of the genre, supplying readers with books of criticism (until the academic houses began to sense that sf might be a growth subject), fan BIBLIOGRAPHIES and indexes, and memoirs. Or so it seemed.

There is no doubt that in the 1990s general publishers still dominate commercial sf; but from the early 1970s small presses began to reappear, for reasons which are not entirely understood. Owlswick Press was founded by George SCITHERS in 1973, Robert Weinberg Publications by Robert E. WEINBERG in 1974, the BORGO PRESS by Robert REGINALD in 1975, UNDERWOOD-MILLER INC. by Tim UNDERWOOD and

Chuck MILLER in 1976, Phantasia Press by Sid Altus and Alex Berman in 1978, Locus Press by Charles N. BROWN in 1981 (with an emphasis on reference material), MARK V. ZIESING by Ziesing in 1982, and Dark Harvest by Paul Mikol and Mark Stadalsky in 1983 (with an emphasis on fantasy). Many more followed, including (most importantly) PULPHOUSE PUBLISHING, founded by Kristine Kathryn RUSCH, Dean Wesley SMITH and others in 1988. Two fine presses (see below) were also active: Roy A. Squires, founded by Squires (1920-1988) in 1960, and Cheap Street, founded by Jan and George O'Nale in 1980.

Though nothing can be certain in a field which has expanded so very much, three broad sets of explanations for the small-press renaissance can be suggested: a desire on the part of new generations of sf aficionados to re-occupy the "family" territory, which had for so many years been spoken for by ever-huger publishing firms whose interest in sf was (understandably) merely commercial; a sense that the large general-list firms tended to ignore some writers whose sales potential was limited, and who might profitably be published by a press with an affinity for the author or the material; and a more general sense that small presses might profitably occupy niches left vacant by the commercial houses.

There are several such niches. Because paperback houses became the dominant form of sf publishing after the early 1950s, the work of many significant post-WWII authors appeared only in the form of paperback originals, and by the 1970s a second pool of publishable work – larger in fact than the pool of material available just after WWII – had accumulated. Many of the small presses, therefore, concentrated on republishing, in hardback, novels from the previous two decades, thus putting some of the best sf into permanent form, generating library sales for their authors, and making their oeuvres available – a mixed blessing, perhaps – to academics. A second important niche was the collectors' market, which could itself be divided into three sectors: first editions, limited editions, and fine-press productions.

For many sf collectors – whose rationality on the subject is a matter of dispute – the publication of a book as a paperback original does not constitute its first edition as a collectable item, which status is reserved for the first hardback publication. Small-press publishers were very quick to understand and to profit from this bias, and the entirely responsible republication in hardback form of fragile paperback originals soon became somewhat tainted by fetishism, especially when limited editions became popular.

Limited editions are generally thought to be independently created books, identifiable by some statement of limitation, which usually gives the total number of copies produced along with a handwritten or hand-stamped number indicating which precise copy is in the collector's hands. They are often signed. Many collectors assume that limited editions by definition boast at least subtle differences in typesetting, binding or paper quality from the trade issue; unfortunately, this is not always the case, and many are distinguishable from the trade issue by no more than a tipped-in label designating them as special. This practice – added to the extraordinary proliferation of limited editions of unremarkable work, plus the quite astonishing ugliness of many small-press releases – has not unsurprisingly led to a 1990s glut in the limited-edition market.

In distinction to this crassness, publishers of fine-press books like Roy A. Squires and Cheap Street have concentrated on the individual crafting of extremely small editions of books produced on the premises by letterpress (a technique of printing directly from movable metal type, an expensive and slow typesetting process otherwise rarely encountered in book-production today). However, because such items are relatively expensive and are purchased by a very particular kind of book collector, it cannot be argued that fine presses represent a return to the roots of the fantasy and sf small press. Those roots continue to be watered, though intermittently, by the small presses cited above, and by dozens of other similar houses. Refreshingly opinionated, though occasionally inaccurate, *The Science-Fantasy Publishers: A Critical and Bibliographic History* (3rd, hugely expanded edn **1991**) by Jack L. CHALKER and Mark OWINGS provides a comprehensive analysis of about 150 firms.

2. Other countries There is little to say about small-press activity in other English-speaking countries before the past couple of decades.

The Australian Futurian Press, founded in Sydney in 1950 by Vol MOLESWORTH and others, operated for a few years; and Donald H. TUCK formed Donald H. Tuck in 1954 to publish the first versions of what became the essential *Encyclopedia of Science Fiction and Fantasy through 1968* (3 vols **1974**, **1978** and **1982**, all US, from Advent). Two decades later, however, with the founding of two houses – Norstrilia Press in 1975 by Bruce GILLESPIE and Void Publications (◊ VOID) by Paul COLLINS in 1978 – small presses finally became a visible component of AUSTRALIA's sf scene. Later imprints include Graham Stone from 1989, Aphelion Publications from 1990 and Dreamstone from 1991. However, Norstrilia and Void stopped publishing in 1984 and the other firms are frail.

CANADA saw even less activity than Australia, perhaps because Canadian sf fans had readily available to them the formidable output of US small presses. Occasional imprints appeared – like the Kakabeka Publishing Company, which published Judith MERRIL's *Survival Ship* (coll **1973**) and nothing else. More recently, the French-language Press Porcépic issued an anthology of Canadian sf, *Tesseracts* (anth **1985**) ed Merril, the first in a series, and subsequently calved a genuine English-language small press, Tesseract Books, in 1988. And United Mythologies Press was founded in 1990 essentially to print unpublished works by R.A. LAFFERTY, though it

soon began to look further afield.

In the UK, small-press publishing did not awake sustained interest among the sf community until the 1980s, the only example of an interest from earlier being Ferret Fantasy, founded by George LOCKE in 1972 mainly to publish bibliographical work plus occasional reprints. However, with the founding of Kerosina Publications in 1986 by James Goddard and several colleagues, a small flowering occurred. Morrigan Publications was founded in 1987 by Jim and Les Escott, Kinnell Publications in 1987 by A.E. Cunningham and Richard G. Lewis, and Drunken Dragon Press in 1988 by Rod Milner and Rog Peyton. Slightly earlier, Titan Books, an arm of the Forbidden Planet/Titan bookselling and distribution complex, was brought into existence as a small press, but by 1990 (after 3 books) it had moved into general publishing; in late 1992 it was in the throes of restructuring and takeover. However, none of these firms – with the exception of Kerosina for a year or so – has published original UK work with enough frequency to make a significant impact. [JC]

SMITH, A(NTHONY) C(HARLES) [r] ◊ ROBERT HALE LIMITED.

SMITH, ARTEGALL ◊ Philip NORTON.

SMITH, CLARK ASHTON (1893-1961) US writer and sculptor, of most interest to the sf reader as a fantasist whose rich style (sometimes idiomatic, sometimes "jewelled" in the Lord DUNSANY manner) and baroque invention had a loosening effect on the sf field, doing much to transform the interplanetary romance of the early years of the century into the full-fledged PLANETARY ROMANCE, whose characteristic attitude towards the FAR FUTURE and the possibilities inherent therein was capitalized upon by Jack VANCE and others.

By 1910 CAS had sold stories to *The* BLACK CAT and *The* OVERLAND MONTHLY, but he concentrated on poetry (see listing below). Although he published some desultory fantasy before 1930, almost all his work of note within the genre, commencing with "The Last Incantation" (1930), was written for PULP MAGAZINES – most frequently *Weird Tales*, occasionally *Wonder Stories* – from that date to about 1936, when he virtually stopped writing. Of most importance as an influence on sf was "City of the Singing Flame" (1931; 1940), notable for the power of the SENSE OF WONDER it evoked. These stories, over 100 of them, can be found in *The Immortals of Mercury* (**1932** chap), *The Double Shadow and Other Fantasies* (coll **1933** chap), *Out of Space and Time* (coll **1942**; in 2 vols 1974 UK), *Lost Worlds* (coll **1944**; in 2 vols vt *Lost Worlds: Zothique, Averoigne, and Others* 1974 UK and *Lost Worlds: Atlantis, Hyperborea, Xiccarph, and Others* 1974 UK) – which includes *Sadastor* (1930 *Weird Tales*; **1972** chap) – *Genius Loci and Other Tales* (coll **1948**), *The Abominations of Yondo* (coll **1960**), *Poems in Prose* (coll **1964** chap), *Tales of Science and Sorcery* (coll **1964**) and *Other Dimensions* (coll **1970**; in 2 vols 1977 UK). The last 2 collections contain most of his sf, most of it interplanetary SPACE OPERA. Subsequently, Lin CARTER reassembled those of CAS's tales set in particular venues and republished them as *Zothique* (coll of linked stories **1970**), *Hyperborea* (coll of linked stories **1971**), *Xiccarph* (coll of stories, some linked, **1972**) and *Poseidonis* (coll of linked stories **1973**).

CAS was not much interested in science, or in expressing the forward thrust of conventional sf, and it is perhaps inadvisable to think of him in sf terms. His work is better considered in conjunction with the weird fantasies written by his friend H.P. LOVECRAFT and by Robert E. HOWARD. His best work has not dated.   [JC/PN]

Other works: *The Mortuary* (**1971** chap); *Prince Alcouz and the Magician* (**1977** chap), previously unpublished early tale; *The City of the Singing Flame* (coll **1981**), which assembles previously collected material; *As it is Written* (**1982**), written as CAS by De Lysle Ferrée Cass; *The Last Incantation* (coll **1982**); *The Monster of the Prophecy* (coll **1983**); the **Unexpurgated Clark Ashton Smith** sequence, comprising *The Dweller in the Gulf* (cut 1933 as "Dweller in Martian Depths"; **1987** chap), *Mother of Toads* (cut 1938 *Weird Tales*; **1987** chap), *The Vaults of Yoh-Vombis* (cut 1932 *Weird Tales*; **1988** chap), *The Monster of the Prophecy* (cut 1932 *Weird Tales*; **1988** chap), *The Witchcraft of Ulua* (cut 1934 *Weird Tales*; **1988** chap) and *Xeethra* (cut 1934 *Weird Tales*; **1988** chap); *Nostalgia of the Unknown: Complete Prose Poetry* (coll **1988** chap); *A Rendezvous in Averoigne* (coll **1988**); *Strange Shadows: The Uncollected Fiction and Essays* (coll **1989**).

Poetry: *The Star-Treader* (coll **1912**); *Odes and Sonnets* (coll **1918** chap); *Ebony and Crystal: Poems in Verse and Prose* (coll **1923**), which includes *From the Crypts of Memory* (**1973** chap) and *The Hashish-Eater, or The Apocalypse of Evil* (**1989** chap); *Sandalwood* (coll **1925** chap); *Nero and Other Poems* (coll **1937** chap); *The Dark Chateau* (coll **1951** chap); *Selected Poems* (coll **1971**); *Grotesques and Fantastiques* (coll **1973** chap), which includes drawings; *Klarkash-ton and Monstro Lieriv* (coll **1974** chap) with Virgil FINLAY; many further vols, usually chapbooks, have been issued.

Nonfiction: *Planets and Dimensions: Collected Essays* (coll **1973** chap) ed Gary K. WOLFE; *The Black Book of Clark Ashton Smith* (coll **1979**); *The Devil's Notebook: Collected Epigrams and Pensées* (coll **1990** chap).

About the author: *Emperor of Dreams: A Clark Ashton Smith Bibliography* (**1978**) by Donald Sydney-Fryer.

See also: ARKHAM HOUSE; ASTEROIDS; ATLANTIS; HORROR IN SF; MARS; MERCURY; PARALLEL WORLDS; SMALL PRESSES AND LIMITED EDITIONS; SUN; SWORD AND SORCERY; TRANSPORTATION; VENUS.

SMITH, CORDWAINER Most famous pseudonym of Paul Myron Anthony Linebarger (1913-1966), US writer, political scientist, military adviser in Korea and Malaya (though not Vietnam). A polyglot, he spent many of his early years in Europe, Japan and China, in the footsteps of his father, Paul M.W. Linebarger, a sinologist and propagandist for Sun Yat-sen. He was a devout High Anglican, deeply interested in psychoanalysis and expert in "brain-washing" techniques, on which he wrote an early text, *Psychological Warfare* (**1948**; rev 1954). Right-wing in politics, he played an active role in propping up the Chiang Kai-shek regime in China before the communist takeover.

His interest in China was profound – he studied there, and there edited his father's *The Gospel of Chuang Shan* (**1932** chap France), writing as well several texts of his own, beginning with *Government in Republican China* (**1938**); the style of some of his later stories reflects his attempts to translate a Chinese narrative and structural style into his sf writing, not perhaps with complete success, as the fabulist's voice he assumed (◊ FABULATION) verged towards the garrulous when opened out into English prose. He began to publish sf with "War No. 81-Q" as by Karloman Jungahr for *The Adjutant* – a high-school journal – in 1928; the tale bore some relationship to the **Instrumentality of Mankind** Universe into which almost all his mature work fitted. Before beginning to write that mature work, however, CS served with the US Army Intelligence Corps in China during WWII and published 3 non-sf novels: *Ria* (**1947**) and *Carola* (**1948**), both as by Felix C. Forrest, and *Atomsk: A Novel of Suspense* (**1949**) as by Carmichael Smith. After that date he published fiction only as CS.

His first CS story, and one of the finest of his mature tales, "Scanners Live in Vain" (**1950**), appeared obscurely in FANTASY BOOK 5 years after it had been rejected by the more prestigious sf journals (although John W. CAMPBELL Jr had penned an encouraging rejection note from *ASF*), perhaps because its foreboding intensity made the editors of the time uneasy, perhaps because it plunges *in medias res* into the **Instrumentality** Universe, generating a sense that much remains untold beyond the dark edges of the tale. Scanners are space pilots; the rigours of their job entail the functional loss of the sensory region of their brains. The story deals with their contorted lives and with the end of the form of space travel necessitating the contortions: it is clear that much has happened in the Universe before the tale begins, and that much will ensue. The **Instrumentality** dominated the rest of CS's creative life, which lasted 1955-66, with individual stories making up the bulk of several collections – including *You Will Never Be the Same* (coll **1963**), *Space Lords* (coll **1965**), *Under Old Earth and Other Explorations* (coll **1970** UK) and *Stardreamer* (coll **1971**) – before being re-sorted into 2 definitive vols, *The Best of Cordwainer Smith* (coll **1975**; vt *The Rediscovery of Man* 1988 UK) ed John J. PIERCE and *The Instrumentality of Mankind* (coll **1979**). A similar complexity obscured the publication of his only full-scale sf novel, *Norstrilia* (**1975**), which first appeared as 2 separate novels – each in fact an extract from the original single manuscript – as *The Planet Buyer* (1964 *Gal* as "The Boy who Bought Old Earth"; rev **1964**) and *The Underpeople* (1964 *Worlds of If* as "The Store of Heart's Desire"; rev **1968**). Along with

Quest of the Three Worlds (coll of linked stories **1966**), the 2 re-sorted collections and *Norstrilia* assemble all of CS's sf.

The **Instrumentality of Mankind** covers several millennia of humanity's uncertain progress into a FAR-FUTURE plenitude. Before the period of "Scanners Live in Vain" a shattered Earth is dubiously revitalized by the family of a Nazi scientist who awake from SUSPENDED ANIMATION to found the Instrumentality, a hereditary caste of rulers, under whose hegemony space is explored by scanners, then by ships which sail by photonic winds, then via planoforming, which is more or less instantaneous. Genetically modified animals are bred as slaves ($\lozenge$ GENETIC ENGINEERING). On the Australian colony planet of Norstrilia, an IMMORTALITY drug called stroon is discovered, making the planet very rich indeed and granting the oligarchy on Earth eternal dominance, with no one but Norstrilians and members of the Instrumentality being permitted to live beyond 400 years. (*Norstrilia* deals with a young heir to much of the planet's wealth who travels to Earth, which he has purchased, discovering *en passant* a great deal about the animal-descended Underpeople.) Human life becomes baroque, aesthetical, decadent. But a fruitful concourse of Underpeople and aristocrats generates the Rediscovery of Man – as witnessed in tales like "The Dead Lady of Clown Town" (1964), "Alpha Ralpha Boulevard" (1961) and "The Ballad of Lost C'Mell" (1962), which embodies a sympathetic response to the Civil Rights movement of the 1960s – through which disease, ethnicity and strife are deliberately reintroduced into the painless world. Much later an adventurer makes a Quest through Three Worlds in a Universe seemingly benign.

The **Instrumentality of Mankind** remains, all the same, a fragment – as, therefore, does CS's work as a whole – for the long conflict between Underpeople and Instrumentality, the details of which are recounted by CS with what might be called oceanic sentiment, is never resolved; and CS's habitual teasing of the reader with implications of a fuller yet never-told tale only strengthens the sense of an almost coy incompletion. This sense is also reinforced by the Chinese ancestry of some of CS's devices, which inspired in him a narrative voice that, in ruminating upon a tale of long ago, seemed to *confer*, both with the reader and with general tradition, about the tale's meaning. Alfred Döblin (1878-1957) ($\lozenge$ GERMANY) has also been suggested as a significant influence, both for his early expressionist work set in China, like *Die drei Sprünge des Wang-Lun* ["The Three Leaps of Wang-Lun"] (**1915**), and for his surreal metamorphic sf novels – none translated – like *Wadzeks Kampf mit der Dampfmaschine* ["Wadzek's Struggle with the Steam-Machine"] (**1918**) and *Berge, Meere und Giganten* ["Mountains, Sea and Giants"] (**1924**; rev vt *Giganten* ["Giants"] 1931). CS's best later stories glow with an air of complexity and antiquity that, on analysis, their plots do not not always

sustain. Much of the structuring of the series is lyrical and incantatory (down to the literal use of rather bad poetry, and much internal rhyming) but, beyond stroon, and Norstrilia, and Old Earth and the absorbingly described SPACESHIPS, much of the CS Universe remains only glimpsed. Whether such a Universe, recounted in such a voice, could ever be fully seen is a question which, of course, cannot be answered. [JC]

About the author: *Exploring Cordwainer Smith* (anth **1975**) ed John Bangsund, from ALGOL Press; almost the whole of SPECULATION #33, 1976, is an analysis of CS's work by John J. Pierce; "The Creation of Cordwainer Smith" by Alan C. Elms, *Science Fiction Studies* #34 (11,3) (1984); *Concordance to Cordwainer Smith* (**1984** chap) by Anthony R. LEWIS; *A Cordwainer Smith Checklist* (**1991** chap) by Mike Bennett.

See also: ANDROIDS; COLONIZATION OF OTHER WORLDS; CRIME AND PUNISHMENT; CYBORGS; FASTER THAN LIGHT; GALACTIC EMPIRES; GALAXY SCIENCE FICTION; MEDICINE; MESSIAHS; MUSIC; MYTHOLOGY; ROBOTS; SOLAR WIND.

SMITH, CURTIS C. (1939-   ) US critic and bibliographer, most of whose work in the first category has focused upon Olaf STAPLEDON, beginning with essays like "William Olaf Stapledon: Saint and Revolutionary" for *Extrapolation* in 1971, and culminating in *Olaf Stapledon: A Bibliography* (**1984**) with Harvey J. Satty. He is best known, however, for editing the first 2 edns of *Twentieth-Century Science-Fiction Writers* (**1981**; rev 1986), part of a series of genre BIBLIOGRAPHIES designed for library use; he did not participate in the 3rd edn of 1991. The work offers coverage of about 600 sf (and fantasy) writers, some names being dropped (and others added) with each successive edn. The brief biographical sections are generally accurate; the critical pieces vary in quality, with some excellent short essays being included; but the bibliographies are flawed by a murkily inconsistent methodology (perhaps due to the series' house style), and are error-strewn. [JC]

See also: CRITICAL AND HISTORICAL WORKS ABOUT SF.

SMITH, D(AVID) ALEXANDER (1953-   ) US investment banker and writer who served as Treasurer of the SCIENCE FICTION WRITERS OF AMERICA 1987-90 and has written several articles on wargame strategy ($\lozenge$ GAMES AND TOYS). He began publishing sf with *Marathon* (**1982**), #1 in the **Marathon** sequence, which continues with *Rendezvous* (**1988**) and *Homecoming* (**1990**). The sequence is a First-Contact tale which depicts, with very considerable cunning, the slow process of learning and ultimate CONCEPTUAL BREAKTHROUGH attendant upon any genuine confrontation of *Homo sapiens* with the Other. In this case, the Cygnan ALIENS, who are rendezvousing with humans in interstellar space, are intriguingly perceived through flawed human eyes. Although DAS succumbs to some clichéd presentation of sf conventions – for instance, the neurotic AI aboard the human starship – this slow, densely realized SPACE-OPERA epic deserves considerable notice. [JC]

SMITH, DEAN WESLEY (1950-   ) US editor and

writer who remains best known for founding, in 1988, PULPHOUSE PUBLISHING, whose various enterprises he has since dominated, in partnership with Kristine Kathryn RUSCH. With her he also ed *Science Fiction Writers of America Handbook: The Professional Writer's Guide to Writing Professionally* (anth **1990**), a vade mecum full of necessary data, though not supremely well organized. After a vignette in *The Clarion Awards* (anth **1984**) ed Damon KNIGHT, his first sf story was "Adrift in the Erotic Zone" for *Gem* in 1985. He won an award from the WRITERS OF THE FUTURE CONTEST for "One Last Dance", which appeared in *L. Ron Hubbard Presents Writers of the Future* (anth **1985**) ed Algis BUDRYS. His first novel, *Laying the Music to Rest* (**1989**), begins slowly, with an attempt to exorcise a ghost from a deep lake, but soon entangles itself in the routines of a TIME-TRAVEL conflict between warring factions; *en passant* the protagonist visits the *Titanic*, where it seems he may be stuck forever. There is energy and feeling in DWS's work, but also a sense of scurry. [JC]

Other work: *The Moscow Mafia Presents Rat Tales* (anth **1987**) with Jon Gustafson, both as Smith Gustafson.

See also: SCIENCE FICTION WRITERS OF AMERICA; SMALL PRESSES AND LIMITED EDITIONS.

SMITH, E(DWARD) E(LMER) (1890-1965) US writer and food chemist specializing in doughnut mixes, often called the "Father of SPACE OPERA". Because Hugo GERNSBACK appended "PhD" to EES's name for his contributions to *AMZ* from 1928, he became known as "Doc" Smith. Greatly influential in US PULP-MAGAZINE sf between 1928 and about 1945, he found his reputation fading somewhat just after the end of WWII, when it seemed the dream-like simplicities of his world-view could no longer attract the modern reader of GENRE SF; but the specialty houses that became active after 1945 (◊ SMALL PRESSES AND LIMITED EDITIONS) soon put his vast space-opera sagas into book form, and his name was kept alive. Towards the end of his life, after his retirement around 1960, he began producing space operas again, and his earlier work started to appear in paperback editions; after his death, yet another new generation made him an sf bestseller, first in the USA and later in the UK.

EES's work is strongly identified with the beginnings of US pulp sf as a separate marketing genre, and did much to define its essential territory, galactic space. When in 1915 he began to write the first novel of his **Skylark** series with Mrs Lee Hawkins Garby (1890-?) – a neighbour seconded to help with feminine matters such as dialogue – no models existed (or, at least, none that were available to a monolingual US food chemist) that could explain the combined exuberance and scale that *The Skylark of Space* (written 1915-20; 1928 *AMZ*; **1946**; rev with cuts 1958) demonstrated when it finally appeared in AMAZING STORIES, 2 years after the start of that magazine, in the same issue as Philip NOWLAN's "Armageddon – 2419 A.D.", the story which intro-

duced BUCK ROGERS IN THE 25TH CENTURY. (Mrs Garby retained co-author credit in the 1st book edn, but the 1958 rev was as by EES alone.) Elements of EES's prelapsarian exuberance may have been discernible in some of the EDISONADES which proliferated in the USA from about 1890; and a certain cosmogonic high-handedness is traceable to the works of H.G. WELLS and his UK contemporaries. But it was EES who combined the two. Along with its sequels – *Skylark Three* (1930 *AMZ*; **1948**), *Skylark of Valeron* (1934-5 *ASF*; **1949**) and *Skylark DuQuesne* (**1966**) – *The Skylark of Space* brought the edisonade to its first full maturity, creating a proper galactic forum for the exploits of the inventor/scientist/action-hero who keeps the world (or the Universe) safe for US values despite the efforts of a foreign-hued villain (Marc "Blackie" DuQuesne) to pollute those values. But the highly personalized conflict between HERO-inventor Richard Seaton and VILLAIN-inventor DuQuesne – who develops from the stage histrionics of the first novel to the dominating antiheroics of the last and is perhaps EES's most vivid creation – did not very satisfactorily motivate the vast intergalactic conflicts of the later volumes of the series, as the scale of everything – the potency of the WEAPONS, the power, size and speed of the SPACE-SHIPS, the number of planets overawed – increased by leaps and bounds. Nor was EES much concerned to sophisticate the chummy, clammy idiocy of his women (◊ SEX; WOMEN AS PORTRAYED IN SCIENCE FICTION) or the hokum of the slang in which all emotions were conveyed.

It was not until he began to unveil the architectural structure of his second and definitive SERIES that EES was able to demonstrate the thoroughness of his thinking about space opera. And it is with the **Lensmen** series – or **The History of Civilization**, the over-title for the 1953-5 limited-edn boxed reprint of the original books – that his name is most strongly and justly associated. In order of internal chronology, the sequence is *Triplanetary* (1934 *AMZ*; rev to fit the series **1948**), *First Lensman* (**1950**), *Galactic Patrol* (1937-8 *ASF*; **1950**), *Gray Lensman* (1939-40 *ASF*; **1951**), *Second-Stage Lensmen* (1941-2 *ASF*; **1953**) and *Children of the Lens* (1947-8 *ASF*; **1954**). *The Vortex Blaster* (1941-2 var mags; fixup **1960**; vt *Masters of the Vortex* 1968 US) is also set in the **Lensman** Universe, probably some time before *Children of the Lens*, but does not deal with the central progress of the main series, the working out of which was EES's most brilliant auctorial coup. As published in book form, the first 2 novels likewise stand outside the main action; it is the final 4 that lie at the heart of EES's accomplishment. Conceived as one 400,000-word novel, and divided into separate titles for publication 1937-48 in *ASF* – from before John W. CAMPBELL Jr began editing the journal, through the high pitch of the GOLDEN AGE OF SF (1939-42) he supervised, and into the post-WWII period – the central **Lensmen** tale is constructed around the gradual revelation of the hierarchical nature of the Universe.

Two vastly advanced and radically opposed races, the good Arisians and the evil Eddorians, have been in essential opposition for billions of years. The Arisians understand that their only hope of defeating the absolute Evil represented by the Eddorians is to develop over eons a countervailing Civilization via special breeding lines on selected planets, of which Earth (Tellus) is one. These breeding lines will develop beings capable of enduring the enormous stress of inevitable conflict with the forces of Evil: the various planets and empires, known collectively as Boskone, inimical to Civilization and secretly commanded through a nest of hierarchies by the invisible Eddorians. We are introduced first to the broad picture and to the idea of the Lens, a bracelet which tenders to suitable members of the Arisian-influenced Galactic Patrol certain telepathic and other powers; then, as the central sequence progresses, we climb, link by link, the vast chain of command, as seen through the eyes of the series' main protagonist, Kim Kinnison – who with his wife represents the penultimate stage in the Arisian breeding programme, and whose children will finally defeat the Eddorians. Kinnison never knows that the layer just penetrated has layers behind it, and has never so much as heard of the Eddorians; each new volume of the sequence, therefore, begins with the revelation that the Universe is greater, and requires greater powers to confront, than Kinnison had hitherto imagined. In the **Skylark** books, Seaton's acquisition of similar powers was distressingly unbridled; but Kinnison, as a commanding member of the organization of Lensmen (itself hierarchical), is by contrast licensed, and his institutionalized gaining of superpowers and special knowledge is measured, inevitable, and kinetically enthralling. It was almost certainly these *controlled* jumps in scale that fascinated most early readers of the series and which, for many of them, represented the essence of the SENSE OF WONDER. The **Lensmen** books had the shape of dreams.

EES wrote some rather less popular out-of-series books, none having anything like the force of his major effort. A decade after his death, books he had begun or completed in manuscript, or had merely inspired or authorized, began to appear in response to his great posthumous popularity. **Lensmen** ties included *New Lensman* * (**1976**) by William B. Ellern (1933-) and *The Dragon Lensman* * (**1980**), *Lensman from Rigel* * (**1982**) and *Z-Lensman* * (**1983**), all by David A. KYLE. The **Family d'Alembert** series, published as by EES "with Stephen GOLDIN", derived some material from posthumous manuscripts; the 1st vol, *The Imperial Stars* * (1964 *If*; exp **1976**), was based on published material, but subsequent volumes were essentially the work of Goldin (*whom see for details*). Lloyd Arthur ESHBACH constructed in *Subspace Encounter* * (**1983**) a sequel to the inferior *Subspace Explorers* (1960 *ASF* as "Subspace Survivors"; exp **1965**). None of these adjuncts did anything to help EES's reputation. Today, while he must be read, it has to be in the loving awareness that he is a creature of the dawn. [JC]

Other works: *What Does this Convention Mean?: A Speech Delivered at the Chicago 1940 World's Science Fiction Convention* (**1941** chap); *Spacehounds of IPC* (1931 *AMZ*; **1947**); *The Galaxy Primes* (1959 *AMZ*; **1965**); *The Best of E.E. "Doc" Smith* (coll **1975**); *Masters of Space* (1961-2 *If*; **1976**) with E. Everett EVANS.

About the author: *The Universes of E.E. Smith* (**1966**) by Ron ELLIK and Bill EVANS; "E.E. Smith" in *Seekers of Tomorrow* (coll **1966**) by Sam MOSKOWITZ.

See also: ALIENS; BIG DUMB OBJECTS; CHILDREN'S SF; COSMOLOGY; CRIME AND PUNISHMENT; DEFINITIONS OF SF; DIMENSIONS; EVOLUTION; FABULATION; FANTASTIC VOYAGES; FORCE FIELD; GAMES AND TOYS; HISTORY OF SF; JUPITER; LONGEVITY (IN WRITERS AND PUBLICATIONS); POWER SOURCES; SCIENTIFIC ERRORS; SCIENTISTS; SPACE FLIGHT; STARS.

SMITH, E.E. The real name of the US author who for obvious reasons writes under a pseudonym, Gordon EKLUND. [JC]

SMITH, EVELYN E. (1927-) US writer and crossword-puzzle compiler who began publishing sf with "Tea Tray in the Sky" for *Gal* in 1952, and for about a decade published actively in the magazines; after about 1960 she appeared there only infrequently. She has also written as Delphine C. Lyons. Her first novel, *The Perfect Planet* (**1962**), is set on a planet which was once a health farm. *Valley of Shadows* (**1968**) as Delphine C. Lyons is a fantasy. *Unpopular Planet* (**1975**) – no connection to the first book – is a comparatively ambitious work, written in a sometimes passable imitation of 18th-century typographical (if not stylistic) practices and presenting the memoirs, set down long after most of the events recounted, of a human from an overpopulated future Earth whose contacts with ALIENS trying to maintain the planet as a breeding-ground for humans and other species have led to picaresque adventures, some of them sexual. *The Copy Shop* (**1985**) – again an element of SATIRE is mildly evident – places aliens in New York City; they are not noticed. [JC]

See also: COLONIZATION OF OTHER WORLDS; WOMEN SF WRITERS.

SMITH, GARRET (?1876-1954) US journalist and newspaper editor who was active with sf stories in magazines like *The Argosy*, where several novels appeared. Only *Between Worlds* (1919 *Argosy*; **1929**), one of his weakest, reached book form; it is a semijuvenile tale that begins on a DYSTOPIAN Venus and concludes on Earth, with female protagonists plotting to conquer the world. Of more interest are "On the Brink of 2000" (1910 *Argosy*) and "The Treasures of Tantalus" (1920-21 *Argosy All-Story*), which feature devices to see anything happening anywhere in the world; the morality of these is discussed, though at no great length. The FLAMMARION-inspired "After a Million Years" (1919 *Argosy*) comprehends a dystopian Earth, an Edenic Jupiter, mad scientists, telepathic powers, aliens and the virtual extinction of humanity. Other magazine novels include "Thirty Years Late" (1928 *Argosy All-Story*) and "The Girl in the Moon" (1928 *Argosy All-Story*). GS was a sometimes capable writer whose ideas tended to outclass his fiction.   [RB]

See also: FANTASTIC VOYAGES.

SMITH, GEORGE H(ENRY) (1922-   ) US writer of much popular fiction and considerable sf, under his own name and several pseudonyms including books as Jan Hudson, Jerry Jason, Jan Smith, George Hudson Smith, Diana Summers (not sf), Hal Stryker and – mostly with his wife M. Jane Deer – M.J. Deer. He began publishing sf with "The Last Spring" for *Startling Stories* in 1953, and became very active after about 1960, releasing his first sf novels – *Satan's Daughter* (**1961**), *1976 – Year of Terror* (**1961**; vt *The Year for Love* c1965), *Scourge of the Blood Cult* (**1961**), *The Coming of the Rats* (**1961**) and *Love Cult* (**1961** as by Jan Hudson) – in a rush. These early novels are, however, rather negligible, and the collaborative *Flames of Desire* (**1963**) as by M.J. Deer is post-HOLOCAUST soft pornography. But with *The Four-Day Weekend* (**1966**) he began to strike a more sustained note, and in the following year started a series set in the ALTERNATE WORLD of **Annwn**: *Druids' World* (**1967**), *Witch Queen of Lochlann* (**1969**), *Kar Kaballa* (**1969** dos), *Second War of the Worlds* (**1976**) and *The Island Snatchers* (**1978**). The last 3 vols of this sequence share the same main characters and present a complex interplay between this world and the alternative Welsh domain; they are GHS's most telling example of the kind of fantasy-textured sf at which he was best. Short stories of interest include "The Last Days of L.A." (1959) and "In the Imagicon" (1966).   [JC]

Other works: *Doomsday Wing* (**1963**); *The Unending Night* (**1964**); *The Forgotten Planet* (**1965**).

As M.J.Deer: *A Place Named Hell* (**1963**).

As Jan Hudson: *Loveswept #293: Water Witch* * (**1988**).

As Jerry Jason: *Sexodus* (**1963**); *The Psycho Makers* (**1965**).

As Hal Stryker: *NYPD 2025* (**1985**), the first of an apparently abortive series; *Hawkeye* (**1991**), a TECHNO-THRILLER.

SMITH, GEORGE HUDSON ◊ George H. SMITH.

SMITH, GEORGE O(LIVER) (1911-1981) US writer and electronics engineer, most active and prominent in the 1940s in ASTOUNDING SCIENCE-FICTION, for which he wrote his first story in 1942; "QRM – Interplanetary" began both his sf career and his most famous endeavour, the **Venus Equilateral** SERIES of stories (all in *ASF*) about a COMMUNICATIONS space station in the Trojan position (60° ahead of the planet) of the orbit of VENUS, and the various crises that must be solved. These stories were assembled as *Venus Equilateral* (coll of linked stories **1947**; with 3 stories added, exp in 2 vols 1975 UK; the UK version in 1 vol vt *The Complete Venus Equilateral* 1976 US). They exhibit GOS's main strength, a fascination with technical problems and their didactic explanation, after the fashion of Hugo GERNSBACK and the early *AMZ*, as well as his main

weakness, an almost complete lack of interest in character or plot plausibility. However, though the technical presuppositions on which he based his communications station dated very swiftly, the sequence – featuring as it does a passel of cheerful wisecracking engineer/troubleshooters – vividly evokes a characteristic 1940s sf point of view about the future and the kinds of problems we might have to handle in space.

GOS also wrote several SPACE OPERAS whose technical assumptions have likewise dated – perhaps because he was sufficiently numerate to make use of falsifiable speculations. The rocket gimmickry, the sense of space, and the kind of protagonists featured in his stories were – for instance – strongly reminiscent of but markedly less entrancing than the more expansive galactic venues of E.E. "Doc" SMITH's **Lensmen** series, the later vols of which were being serialized in *ASF* at about the same time. The best of GOS's space operas, originally published under his occasional pseudonym Wesley Long, is *Nomad* (1944 *ASF*; **1950** as GOS). Like most of his space epics, the story concerns an alien INVASION of the Solar System, in this case by means of a wandering planet. Other similar novels are *Pattern for Conquest* (1946 *ASF*; **1949**) and the inferior *Hellflower* (**1953**).

Though GOS wrote several further novels before becoming relatively inactive in 1959, he published only one other memorable book, the vivid SUPERMAN story *The Fourth "R"* (**1959**; vt *The Brain Machine* 1968). Although the story – about an artificially created *Homo superior* child who must fight to remain independent until adulthood – reflects earlier novels, such as Theodore STURGEON's *The Dreaming Jewels* (**1950**; vt *The Synthetic Man* 1957), *The Fourth "R"* so vividly enters into its protagonist's young mind, and so intriguingly details his strategy for survival against a particularly unpleasant villain, that it has become a model for tales of this kind (*see also* INTELLIGENCE). Another novel that combines both invasion and superman themes is *Highways in Hiding* (**1956**, cut vt *The Space Plague* 1957).

Never strongly original, GOS was nonetheless an effective expounder of ideas and an enjoyable sf novelist of the second rank. The autobiographical notes in *The Worlds of George O.* (coll **1982**) warmly and modestly evoke his life in the 1940s as a colleague and friend of John W. CAMPBELL Jr, Robert A. HEINLEIN and others; the collection assembles the best of his short work.   [JC]

Other works: *Operation Interstellar* (**1950**); *Troubled Star* (1953 *Startling Stories*; **1957**); *Fire in the Heavens* (1949 *Startling Stories*; **1958**); *Lost in Space* (1954 *Startling Stories* as "Spacemen Lost"; **1959**); *The Path of Unreason* (1947 *Startling Stories* as "Kingdom of the Blind"; rev **1958**).

See also: DISCOVERY AND INVENTION; ECONOMICS; ESP; HEROES; ILLUSTRATION; MATTER TRANSMISSION; MONEY; SCIENTISTS; SEX; SPACE HABITATS; SUN.

SMITH, H(ARRY) ALLEN (1907-1976) US newspaperman and author, mostly of humorous sketches and books, often for *Saturday Evening Post*. In his first sf novel, *Mr Klein's Kampf, or His Life as Hitler's Double* (**1939**), a Jew takes over from Hitler and declares Germany to be the new Zion. *The Age of the Tail* (**1955**), also a comic SATIRE, depicts the effect on a NEAR-FUTURE world of all children being born with tails. [JC]

SMITH, JAN ◊ George H. SMITH.

SMITH, JUNIUS [r] ◊ J.U. GIESY.

SMITH, KENT (? -) US writer in whose sf novel, *Future X* (**1990**), a Black man from a racist 21st century discovers a TIME-TRAVEL device, returns to the time of Malcolm X (1925-1965) with the intention of saving him from assassination, causes his death months too early, and finds himself bound into taking his place. But history continues as before, for there is no way, the book seems to argue, of curing the system that killed Malcolm X in the first place. [JC]

SMITH, LAURE [r] ◊ Seth MCEVOY.

SMITH, L. NEIL (1946-) US writer, ex-police reserve officer, gunsmith and former state candidate for the US LIBERTARIAN Party who began publishing sf with "Grimm's Law" for *Stellar 5* (anth **1980**) ed Judy-Lynn DEL REY. The **Win Bear** sequence, set in a parallel universe (◊ ALTERNATE WORLDS) in which a libertarian version of the USA has become progressively decentralized ever since its foundation, includes *The Probability Broach* (**1980**), *The Venus Belt* (**1981**) and *The Nagasaki Vector* (**1983**), with *Their Majesties' Bucketeers* (**1981**) set in the same universe. A second series, the **North American Confederacy** sequence – *Tom Paine Maru* (**1984**), *The Gallatin Divergence* (**1985**) and *Brightsuit MacBear* (**1988**) – shows the descendants of the original protagonists expanding out into the Galaxy, spreading the libertarian gospel to ALIENS and abandoned human colonies in both the parallel universe and our own. *Taflak Lysandra* (**1988**), although set in the same universe, is unconnected to the main series.

The Crystal Empire (**1986**), a somewhat confused tale of libertarian technological inventiveness, is set in another alternate world, a Europe destroyed by a far more devastating Black Death. *The Wardove* (**1986**), set on a terraformed Moon long after a nuclear HOLOCAUST has made Earth uninhabitable, depicts a state of war between anarcho-capitalists of several different species (including humans) and a repressive government, and is unusual among LNS's work for its general darkness of tone and comparative lack of humour. Contrastingly, *Henry Martyn* (**1989**) is a light-hearted SPACE OPERA written in a style strongly reminiscent of Raphael Sabatini's **Captain Blood**. A further sequence – *Contact and Commune* (**1990**) and *Converse and Conflict* (**1990**) – is set in yet another alternate world; in this instance Mikhail Gorbachev (1931-) has been deposed (as was soon, indeed, to happen in the real world), Soviet hardliners have (perhaps rather mysteriously) taken over the USA,

and disturbingly alert anarcho-capitalists (once again) begin to upset the apple cart. One of the protagonists is (also mysteriously) descended from the inhabitants of ATLANTIS.

LNS is a writer of generally competent, fast-moving and often amusing adventures which can be marred by preachiness and intolerance where matters of POLITICS and morality are concerned. Almost all are distinguished by their relentlessly upbeat mood; the more recent are often rather poorly constructed. [NT]

Other works: 3 STAR WARS ties, *Lando Calrissian and the Mindharp of Sharu* * (**1983**), *Lando Calrissian and the Flamewind of Oseon* * (**1983**) and *Lando Calrissian and the Starcave of ThonBoka* * (**1983**).

See also: ECONOMICS; SHARED WORLDS.

SMITH, MARTIN ◊ Martin Cruz SMITH.

SMITH, MARTIN (WILLIAM) CRUZ (1942-) US writer who became famous with the political thriller/detective novel *Gorky Park* (**1981**), but whose first book, *The Indians Won* (**1970**), originally published as by Martin Smith, is genuine sf, positing an ALTERNATE WORLD in which the Native Americans – after Sitting Bull (*c*1834-1893) defeated General Custer (1839-1876) – have managed to consolidate themselves into an independent state, and in the 20th century hold the balance of power. *Gypsy in Amber* (**1971**) and its sequel, *Canto for a Gypsy* (**1972**), both originally published as by Martin Smith, feature a detective with ESP. *The Analog Bullet* (**1972**) utilizes the paranormal in similar circumstances. Under the house name Nick CARTER MCS wrote 3 borderline-sf thrillers, *The Inca Death Squad* * (**1972**), *Code Name: Werewolf* * (**1973**) and *The Devil's Dozen* * (**1973**). As Simon Quinn he published the non-sf **Inquisitor** series of novels about a Catholic organization opposed to Satanists. In *Nightwing* (**1977**), as MCS, it is discovered that a swarm of vampire bats is burdened with fleas which serve as vectors for a deadly plague; it was filmed as *Nightwing* (1979). [JC]

SMITH, ROBERT CHARLES (1938-) UK writer, prolific in various genres under several pseudonyms, including Roger C. Brandon, Robert Charles and Charles Leader. *Flowers of Evil* (**1981**) as by Robert Charles is horror, and *Nightworld* (**1984**; vt *The Comet* 1985 US), also as by Charles, is an expertly told but fairly unadventurous sf DISASTER tale. [JC]

SMITH, WALTER J(AMES) [r] ◊ ROBERT HALE LIMITED.

SMITH, WAYLAND Pseudonym for his sf novel of UK engineer Victor Bayley (1880-1972), whose career at a high level in the Indian railway system was reflected in much of his adventure fiction, some of which verged on fantasy, and which he signed with his real name. In his sf novel, *The Machine Stops* (**1936**), all metals disintegrate, casting humanity back into barbarism; one young man attempts to fabricate a new alloy to save the race. [JC]

SMITH, WOODROW WILSON [s] ◊ Henry KUTTNER.

SNAITH, J(OHN) C(OLLIS) (1876-1936) UK writer, mostly of historical novels, whose *The Council of Seven* (**1921**) describes a totalitarian DYSTOPIA, and whose

Thus Far (**1925**) depicts the creation of an enormously powerful, telepathic SUPERMAN by the application of various rays, chemicals and, as E.F. BLEILER states, "glandular extracts from a missing link"; Bleiler further suggests that JCS may have published an earlier work describing the discovery of this link, but no such work has yet been unearthed. [JC]

SNELL, EDMUND (1889-?) UK writer, exceedingly prolific between the Wars, specializing in thrillers (often with Oriental villains) and mysteries. He wrote some sf books, including *Kontrol* (**1928**), in which a mad SCIENTIST switches a genius brain into an athlete's body and vice versa; he is in league with a Bolshevik agent who has built a fleet of futuristic vertical-take-off aerial juggernauts and a UTOPIAN supercity on a secret ISLAND with an active volcano. It is a well written sf thriller with an exuberance that lifts it above the ordinary.

The Sound-Machine (**1932**) likewise features a crazed inventor; this one uses sound-waves to kill and disintegrate. [PN]

Other works: *The Yellow Seven* (**1923**); *The Yu-Chi Stone* (**1925**); *Blue Murder* (**1927**); *The White Owl* (**1930**); *The "Z" Ray* (**1932**); *The Sign of the Scorpion* (**1934**).

See also: ISLANDS; POLITICS; WEAPONS.

SNODGRASS, MELINDA M(ARILYN) (1951-) US lawyer and writer who has been associated with **Star Trek** since the publication of her first novel, *Star Trek: The Tears of the Singers* * (**1984**). She served as Executive Script Consultant for the first 2 seasons of STAR TREK: THE NEXT GENERATION. Of ostensibly greater sf interest is her **Circuit Trilogy** – *Circuit* (**1986**), *Circuit Breaker* (**1987**) and *Final Circuit* (**1988**) – which takes a handsome lawyer and his extremely clever female sidekick into space, where they become involved in defending a batch of individualistic space stations and settlements against the hidebound bureaucracies of Earth. This point of view is not, of course, a fresh one, and a sense that MMS was not perhaps concentrating fully on the richer implications of her setting is strengthened by a plot structure which eventually relegates the tough female protagonist to the sidelines – in strict accordance with the Robert A. HEINLEIN guidelines on such matters – as soon as she becomes pregnant. *Runespear* (**1987**) with Victor MILÁN is fantasy, as is *Queen's Gambit Declined* (**1989**).

A Very Large Array: New Mexico Science Fiction and Fantasy (anth **1987**) embodies MMS's theory that the urgent New Mexico landscape might serve to unify in some sense the work of writers there resident; in the event, though the theory still proves difficult to assess, the stories assembled are of admirable quality. [JC]

Other works: MMS was assistant editor to George R.R. MARTIN, the editor, on 4 of the WILD CARDS series to date, these being #6: *Ace in the Hole: A Wild Cards Mosaic Novel* * (anth **1990**), #7: *Dead Man's Hand* * (**1990**), written by Martin with John J. Miller, the 1st true novel in the series, #8: *One-Eyed Jacks: A Wild Cards Mosaic Novel* * (anth **1991**) and #9: *Jokertown Shuffle: A Wild Cards Mosaic Novel* * (anth **1991**); the next title, #10: *Double Solitaire* * (**1992**) is another true novel, written by MMS solo.

As Melinda McKenzie: *Magic to Do: Paul's Story* (**1985**); *Of Earth and High Heaven* (**1985**)

See also: LIBERTARIAN SF.

SNOW, C(HARLES) P(ERCY) (1905-1980) UK writer, created Baron Snow of Leicester in 1964, best known for the long **Strangers and Brothers** sequence of novels, several of which deal intimately with science and the scientific establishment. In *Two Cultures and the Scientific Revolution* (**1959**), nonfiction, he famously suggested that science and the humanities had indeed become "two cultures", a phrase which has become part of the language. His sf novel, *New Lives for Old* (**1933**), published anon, depicts a search for IMMORTALITY and the negative consequences that attend its success. [JC]

SNYDER, CECIL III (? -) US author of *The Hawks of Arcturus* (**1974**), in which a lone Earthman defies the eponymous ALIENS in their attempt to find the secrets of an ancient Galaxy-ruling race. [JC]

SNYDER, E.V. [r] ◊ Gene SNYDER.

SNYDER, GENE (1943-) Working name of US writer and academic Eugene Vincent Snyder. With William Jon WATKINS (*whom see for details*), he published 2 sf novels, *Ecodeath* (**1972**) as E.V. Snyder and *The Litany of Sh'reev* (**1976**). His solo works include *Mind War* (**1980**), *The Ogden Enigma* (**1980**) – in which the US military must deal with the fact that it has repressed all evidence that a UFO landed in 1950, a matter of urgency because the UFO now wants to go home – *Dark Dreaming* (**1981**), *Tomb Seven* (**1985**), a fantasy, and *The Sigma Project* (**1988**), a TECHNO-THRILLER. [JC]

See also: ECOLOGY.

SNYDER, GUY (1951-) US author and journalist in whose *Testament XXI* (**1973**) a space explorer returns to Earth a century after a nuclear HOLOCAUST to find a balkanized land at war with itself. [JC]

SOBCHACK, VIVIAN (CAROL) (1940-) US author of academic film criticism, notably *The Limits of Infinity: The American Science Fiction Film 1950-1975* (**1980**), expanded as *Screening Space: The American Science Fiction Film* (1987), retaining the unaltered text of the earlier book but adding a long final chapter, "Postfuturism", which gives a reading of sf CINEMA developed from the critical theories of Fredric Jameson (◊ POSTMODERNISM AND SF). The original text is among the most sophisticated analyses of sf film yet published; the added chapter is clotted, but important in its placing of recent sf films in a Postmodernist context where, for example, computer imagery and outer space in film are registered as flat imitations of one another, or where we read schizophrenic narrative structures as zany comedies. VS's FEMINISM informs her work, particularly the essay "The Virginity of Astronauts: Sex and the Science Fiction Film" in *Shadows of the Magic Lamp: Fantasy and*

Science Fiction in Film (anth **1985**) ed George E. SLUSSER and Eric S. RABKIN. [PN]

SOCIAL DARWINISM Social Darwinism is the thesis that social evolution and social history are governed by the same principles that govern the EVOLUTION of species in Nature, so that conflict between and within cultures constitutes a struggle for existence which is the motor of progress. Such ideas are inherent in the socio-economic theories of Herbert Spencer (1820-1903), who actually coined the phrase "the survival of the fittest", borrowed by Charles Darwin (1809-1882). Darwin himself was not a Social Darwinist, preferring to stress the survival value of cooperation in human societies. Social Darwinism was popularized in the USA by ardent political champions of *laissez-faire* capitalism, notably William Graham Sumner (1840-1910) – whose pessimistic anticipation of a coming war between the social classes echoed the Marxist theory of history, and presumably inspired Ignatius DONNELLY's apocalyptic *Caesar's Column* (**1890**; early edns as by Edmund Boisgilbert) – and the industrialist Andrew Carnegie (1835-1919). Social Darwinist rhetoric was co-opted to the justification of race hatred by the German writer Heinrich von Treitschke (1834-1896), a major source of inspiration for Hitler's *Mein Kampf* (2 vols **1925-6**; trans **1939** UK) and the political ideology of Nazism. There is, however, no logically necessary connection between Social Darwinism and right-wing POLITICS; it is a versatile analogy which lends itself to many differing opinions as to which group ought to be designated "the fittest", and its arguments can be deployed both for and against calculated eugenic selection.

The most important sf writer who might be termed a Social Darwinist was the socialist H.G. WELLS, who had no doubt that the "laws of evolution" discovered by Darwin applied to human society. His account of the future evolution of society in *The Time Machine* (**1895**) is based on a Social Darwinist logic, and in such UTOPIAS as *A Modern Utopia* (**1905**) a "struggle for existence" is artificially maintained – here in the ascetic training of the elite "samurai". Many of Wells's blueprints for the future assume that a better society can emerge only out of the destruction of the present one, by a process of rigorous winnowing; such future histories are sketched in *The World Set Free* (**1914**), *Men Like Gods* (**1923**) and *The Shape of Things to Come* (**1933**). When Wells finally despaired of his world-saving mission it was the logic of Darwinian law that he invoked to condemn society for its failure in *Mind at the End of its Tether* (**1945**). Louis TRACY's *The Final War* (**1896**) and M.P. SHIEL's *The Yellow Danger* (**1898**) are early future-WAR stories deploying a Social Darwinist species of racism, the latter suggesting that there must ultimately be a war between the different races of *Homo sapiens* for possession of the Earth; but Shiel later modified his Spencerian views and espoused a curiously Nietzschean kind of Social Darwinism most vividly displayed in *The Young Men are Coming* (**1937**). S. Fowler

WRIGHT is the UK writer of SCIENTIFIC ROMANCE who most consistently glorified the struggle for existence and railed against the "utopia of comforts".

Opposition to Darwinist analogies is evident in Claude FARRÈRE's *Useless Hands* (**1926**), a lurid warning of the ultimate effects of applying Darwinian logic to human society, and in Raymond Z. GALLUN's PULP-MAGAZINE story "Old Faithful" (**1934**), which argues that intellectual kinship is more important than biological difference. A fierce attack on Social Darwinism is mounted by C.S. LEWIS in his **Ransom** trilogy: *Out of the Silent Planet* (**1938**), *Perelandra* (**1943**; vt *Voyage to Venus*) and *That Hideous Strength* (**1945**). The last volume – in which the organization N.I.C.E. begins to mould UK society along Social Darwinist lines – is the most direct.

The logic of Social Darwinism has cropped up continually, but rather inconsistently, in GENRE SF. One writer particularly fond of invoking such ideas was Robert A. HEINLEIN. The assumptions of Social Darwinism seem to have shaped many of his perspectives – notably his attitude towards ALIENS, as displayed in *The Puppet Masters* (**1951**) and *Starship Troopers* (**1959**), the "robust" LIBERTARIAN social theory of TANSTAAFL (There Ain't No Such Thing As A Free Lunch) propounded in *The Moon is a Harsh Mistress* (**1966**), and the collection of aphorisms called "The Notebooks of Lazarus Long" in *Time Enough for Love* (**1973**). Other libertarian sf writers make less use of this type of supportive logic. Poul ANDERSON's political views are based on more pragmatic grounds, and the same appears to be true of Jerry E. POURNELLE, although his collaboration with Larry NIVEN, *Lucifer's Hammer* (**1977**), employs some Social Darwinist arguments. Echoes of Sumner and Carnegie frequently resound in the work of genre libertarians, as they do more plangently in Ayn RAND's Objectivist tracts *Anthem* (**1938**) and *Atlas Shrugged* (**1957**). L. Ron HUBBARD's *Return to Tomorrow* (**1954**) is the most hysterically Social Darwinist work in genre sf, advocating that the human race commit universal genocide of all alien races to secure its hegemony. John W. CAMPBELL Jr was a notorious human chauvinist, but he made relatively little (and rather inconsistent) use of Social Darwinist ideas in his editorials. His variously argued defences of slavery as an institution inspired some of the odder fiction published in *ASF*, including Lloyd BIGGLE Jr's *The World Menders* (**1971**), and his opinion that mankind needs some kind of external enemy – if not actual, then imaginary – to maintain the competitive thrust of progress is also reflected in work by writers from his stable, notably Mack REYNOLDS, as in *Space Visitor* (**1977**). Lester DEL REY, whose early short stories displayed a strongly humanist outlook, seemingly embraces a kind of Social Darwinism in *The Eleventh Commandment* (**1962**; rev 1970).

The idea that aliens should be seen primarily as Darwinian competitors has fallen into considerable disrepute in modern sf, but there has been a marked resurgence of Social Darwinist thinking in recent years in SURVIVALIST FICTION, mostly brutal action-adventure stuff in the vein of Jerry AHERN. Dean ING's *Pulling Through* (coll **1983**) is more level-headed, while David BRIN's *The Postman* (fixup **1985**) is profoundly sceptical of the Social Darwinist ethos of survivalism.   [BS]

See also: ECONOMICS; HISTORY IN SF; SOCIOLOGY.

SOCIAL ENGINEERING ◊ CULTURAL ENGINEERING.

SOCIETY Film (1989). Wild Street Pictures. Dir Brian Yuzna, starring Bill Warlock, Devin DeVasquez, Ben Meyerson. Screenplay Woody Keith, Rick Fry. 99 mins. Colour.

"Society" (as in the upper classes) is an ALIEN race, parasitic on humanity (as in the poor), that has been around as long as humans have, but we learn this only at the end. In the tradition of 1980s schlock/surrealist horror cinema (e.g., RE-ANIMATOR [1985]), there is gross bad taste, but the film is unusual in the demureness of its first hour, and in its knowing and relentless use of metaphor, both visual and verbal. Bill is a wealthy teenage boy whose PARANOIA (he feels alienated from his family) turns out gradually to be justified. Intimations of incest and half-glimpsed bodily distortions deepen into the discovery by Bill of Society's devotion to "shunting", a combination of cuddling, tenderizing, sodomitic rape and cannibalism deplorably unpleasant for the human victims. The alien rich are shapeshifters capable of gazing out quizzically from their own rectums. The shock tactics of the climax struck some viewers as more nadir than peak; certainly Yuzna lacks the intensity of a David Lynch, and there is a strong element of gleeful childishness. But new cinematic ground is promisingly broken.   [PN]

See also: MONSTER MOVIES.

SOCIOLOGY Sociology is the systematic study of society and social relationships. The word was coined by Auguste Comte (1798-1857) in the mid-19th century, and it was then that the first attempts were made to divorce studies of society employing the scientific method, on the one hand, from dogmatic political and ethical presuppositions, on the other. Social studies in a more general sense have, of course, a much longer history, going back to PLATO. Sociology and sf have a common precursor in UTOPIAN philosophy, which often used literary forms – most commonly the imaginary voyage – for the imaginative modelling of ideal societies (◊ FANTASTIC VOYAGES; PROTOSCIENCE FICTION). The evaluation and criticism of such models may be regarded as a crude form of hypothesis-testing. As utopian fiction evolved, more reliance was placed on literary techniques; the modelling of characters and personal relationships became a means of evaluating the "quality of life" in these hypothetical societies. The increasing use of such purely literary strategies in the late 19th century is also highly relevant to the evolution of DYSTOPIAN images of the future.

Insofar as sf involves the construction of hypothetical societies, both human and nonhuman, it is an implicitly sociological literature and many observers – including Isaac ASIMOV – have described the sophistication of GENRE SF encouraged by John W. CAMPBELL Jr in terms of its becoming "more sociological". Any assumptions which are consciously or unconsciously deployed in the building of hypothetical societies are sociological hypotheses, and any attempt to construct a narrative which analyses or tracks changes within imaginary societies is a form of sociological theorizing. This is very rarely the primary purpose of sf writers, of course, but it is a significant aspect of their work. The investigation of "sociological themes" in sf has to be an examination of the fruits of this process rather than an exploration of the influence of academic sociology itself upon sf, because such influence is clearly negligible. Even works of sf which mirror formal sociological hypotheses – such as Keith ROBERTS's *Pavane* (coll of linked stories **1968**), which recalls the thesis of Max Weber (1864-1920) that a complicit relationship connects the Protestant Ethic and the rise of capitalism, in its depiction of an ALTERNATE WORLD in which modern Europe remains under Catholic domination – almost invariably do so unconsciously. Some sf writers have borrowed extensively from academic ANTHROPOLOGY in constructing ALIEN societies, but almost all have preferred to rely upon their own intuitive judgements regarding human society and social relationships.

Some sf stories are quite straightforward thought-experiments in sociology: Philip WYLIE's *The Disappearance* (**1951**), Theodore STURGEON's *Venus Plus X* (**1960**) and Ursula K. LE GUIN's *The Left Hand of Darkness* (**1969**) are notable examples investigating issues of sexual politics, while the brief account of a factory-society run according to the tenet of "from each according to his ability, to each according to his need" in Ayn RAND's *Atlas Shrugged* (**1957**) aspires to prove the impracticability of socialism. Poul ANDERSON's "The Helping Hand" (1950) carefully compares the fortunes of two conquered cultures, one of which accepts economic aid from its conquerors while the other – the "control group" – does not. Many of the classics of UK SCIENTIFIC ROMANCE – including Grant ALLEN's *The British Barbarians* (**1895**), J.D. BERESFORD's *The Hampdenshire Wonder* (**1911**), Aldous HUXLEY's *Brave New World* (**1932**), Olaf STAPLEDON's *Odd John* (**1935**) and Eden PHILLPOTTS's *Saurus* (**1938**) – introduce an outside observer into a society in order to evaluate its merits and faults "objectively". If the society is contemporary, then the observer must be an sf artefact, like Allen's time-travelling anthropologist, Beresford's and Stapledon's SUPERMEN, and Phillpotts's alien; if the society is exotic then an ordinary human being will do. Such social displacements are a staple strategy of SATIRE, another common precursor of sociology and sf; works like the fourth book of Jonathan SWIFT's *Gulliver's Travels* (**1726**) and *The Voyage of Captain Popanilla* (**1828**) by Benjamin DISRAELI can embody scathing social criticism.

Other modern sf novels using this strategy include Robert A. HEINLEIN's *Stranger in a Strange Land* (**1961**) and Robert SILVERBERG's *The Masks of Time* (**1968**; vt *Vornan-19*). An interesting MAINSTREAM novel in which sociologists investigate a cult whose MYTHOLOGY is sciencefictional in kind is *Imaginary Friends* (**1967**) by Alison Lurie (1926-   ). Stories of the type that construct hypothetical "human studies" projects for alien sociologists – like S.P. SOMTOW's *Mallworld* (**1981**) and Karen Joy FOWLER's "The Poplar Street Study" (**1985**) and "The View from Venus" (**1986**) – tend to be darkly humorous and satirical.

The quasiscientific activities featured in these kinds of sf are impracticable in the real world (although there are analogues in cultural anthropology) both because culture-bound sociologists find it virtually impossible to become "objective observers" and because they cannot construct actual societies by way of experiment. Natural scientists do not, for the most part, encounter problems of these kinds, and so the relationship between the social sciences and speculative fiction is markedly different from that involving the natural sciences; that is, sociological fiction may try to accomplish what the practical science cannot, and thus is a generator of ideas rather than a borrower. Ideas from speculative fiction are occasionally "fed back" into ways of thinking about the real world: Aldous HUXLEY's *Brave New World* and George ORWELL's *Nineteen Eighty-four* (**1949**) have had considerable influence on attitudes to social trends and actual political rhetoric. Some modern social theorists have built literary models to dramatize their theories, notably B.F. SKINNER in *Walden Two* (**1948**) and Michael YOUNG in *The Rise of the Meritocracy* (**1958**). Where Skinner's work is a utopia, Young's is a DYSTOPIA – he promotes his own ideas by displaying the folly of opposite ideas in action. The US sociologist Richard Ofshe (1941-   ) compiled an anthology of sf stories, with appropriate commentary, as a textbook on *The Sociology of the Possible* (anth **1970**); John Milstead, Martin H. GREENBERG, Joseph D. OLANDER and Patricia S. WARRICK's *Sociology through Science Fiction* (anth **1974**) and *Social Problems through Science Fiction* (anth **1975**) are similar but less competent.

The simple classification of hypothetical societies into satires, utopias and dystopias serves moderately well for models built outside genre sf, but GENRE-SF writers are very rarely concerned with trying to design ideal societies and, although they do have a tendency to offer dire polemical warnings about the way the world is going, the extent to which their visions may be described as satirical or dystopian has also been exaggerated. Sf writers often try to envisage forms of society which are quite simply *conceivable*; they invent for the sheer joy of invention, and often it does them some disservice to invoke the commonplace category labels. For example, although the first significant model of a purely hypothetical society, H.G. WELLS's *The First Men in the Moon* (**1901**), has

definite dystopian aspects, such a classification would be too narrow, and the same is true of many subsequent novels which take the ant-nest as their model (◊ HIVE-MINDS).

Another interesting early example of a hypothetical society which is really neither a satire nor a dystopia is *The Revolt of Man* (**1882**) by Walter BESANT, the prototype of a whole subgenre of stories depicting female-dominated societies. Its assumptions regarding the structure and fortunes of the society clearly reveal the main tenets of Victorian male chauvinism, and it makes an interesting comparison with more recent explorations of the same theme, including Edmund COOPER's *Five to Twelve* (**1968**), Robert BLOCH's *Ladies' Day* (**1968** dos) and Thomas BERGER's *Regiment of Women* (**1973**). This is one of the commonest themes in social modelling. Its early phases are tracked by Sam MOSKOWITZ in *When Women Rule* (anth **1972**), and further relevant fictions include J.D. BERESFORD's *Goslings* (**1913**; vt *A World of Women* US), Owen M. JOHNSON's *The Coming of the Amazons* (**1931**), Philip WYLIE's *The Disappearance* (**1951**), Richard WILSON's *The Girls from Planet 5* (**1955**), John WYNDHAM's "Consider Her Ways" (**1956**), Charles Eric MAINE's *World without Men* (**1958**; vt *Alph*), Poul ANDERSON's *Virgin Planet* (**1959**) and Edmund COOPER's *Who Needs Men* (**1972**; vt *Gender Genocide*). Sf stories in which the social roles associated with the sexes are in some fashion revised have become a highly significant instrument of ideative exploration in the hands of FEMINIST writers. Outstanding works of this kind include Joanna RUSS's *The Female Man* (**1975**) and Marge PIERCY's *Woman on the Edge of Time* (**1976**). In the UK The Women's Press has an sf line, and many of the books published by the radical lesbian Onlywomen Press are sf.

Both *The Revolt of Man* and *The First Men in the Moon* show "distorted societies" constructed by altering a single variable in a quasi-experimental fashion. Outside GENRE SF such distortions are almost always invoked for dystopian or satirical ends, but inside the genre distortion often seems to be an end in itself. Alien societies *have* been used in sf for satirical purposes – Stanton A. COBLENTZ made a habit of it in such works as *The Blue Barbarians* (**1931**; **1958**) and *Hidden World* (**1935**; **1957**; vt *In Caverns Below*) – but this is comparatively rare. The most memorable nonhuman societies in sf – they are so numerous that any list has to be highly selective – reflect a far more open-minded kind of creativity: Clifford D. SIMAK's *City* (**1944-51**; fixup **1952**), L. Sprague DE CAMP's *Rogue Queen* (**1951**), Philip José FARMER's *The Lovers* (**1952**; exp **1961**), James BLISH's "A Case of Conscience" (**1953**), Poul ANDERSON's *War of the Wing-Men* (**1958**; vt *The Man who Counts*) and *The People of the Wind* (**1973**), Brian W. ALDISS's *The Dark Light Years* (**1964**), Isaac ASIMOV's *The Gods Themselves* (**1972**), Stanley SCHMIDT's *The Sins of the Fathers* (**1976**), David LAKE's *The Right Hand of Dextra* (**1977**), Ian WATSON's and Michael BISHOP's *Under Heaven's Bridge* (**1981**), Phillip MANN's

The Eye of the Queen (**1982**) and Timothy ZAHN's *A Coming of Age* (**1985**). Distorted human societies are even more numerous, but some notable examples are: Wyman GUIN's "Beyond Bedlam" (1951), Frederik POHL's and C.M. KORNBLUTH's *The Space Merchants* (**1953**), James E. GUNN's *The Joy Makers* (fixup **1961**), Jack VANCE's *The Languages of Pao* (**1958**), Alexei PANSHIN's *Rite of Passage* (1963; exp **1968**), John JAKES's *Mask of Chaos* (**1970**), Robert SILVERBERG's *A Time of Changes* (**1971**), Samuel R. DELANY's *Triton* (**1976**), Luděk PEŠEK's *A Trap for Perseus* (**1976**; trans **1980**), George ZEBROWSKI's *Macrolife* (**1979**), Bruce STERLING's *Schismatrix* (**1985**), Keith ROBERTS's *Kiteworld* (**1985**) and Philip José FARMER's *Dayworld* (**1985**). Implicit in all these stories, whatever their immediate dramatic purpose, are arguments about directions and limits of social possibility.

One of the commonest forms of sociological thought-experiment in sf is that of taking society apart and building it up again. Many stories of this type are discussed in the sections on DISASTER and HOLOCAUST AND AFTER; classic examples include S. Fowler WRIGHT's *Deluge* (**1928**) and *Dawn* (**1929**), George R. STEWART's *Earth Abides* (**1949**) and Walter M. MILLER's *A Canticle for Leibowitz* (1955-7; fixup **1960**). The pattern of social disintegration is subject to detailed scrutiny in William GOLDING's *Lord of the Flies* (**1954**), while the building of a society from scratch is satirically featured in E.C. LARGE's *Dawn in Andromeda* (**1956**). Investigations of the theme range in character from outright HORROR stories to ROBINSON-ADES, often steering a very uneasy course between realism and romanticism.

Many particular fields within sociology are not widely reflected in sf, but there is an abundance of stories bearing upon issues in the sociology of RELIGION, including Heinlein's "If This Goes On . . ." (1940), Bertrand RUSSELL's "Zahatopolk" (1954), Miller's *A Canticle for Leibowitz*, Anderson's "The Problem of Pain" (1973) and Gerald Jonas's "The Shaker Revival" (1970). There is no such abundance of stories relating to the sociology of science, largely because most sf – unlike most mundane fiction – treats religion sceptically and science reverently; but Asimov's *The Gods Themselves* includes some shrewd observations on the working of the community of SCIENTISTS, as does Howard L. MYERS's pointed comedy "Out, Wit!" (1972). An interesting exercise in hypothetical applied sociology is featured in Katherine MacLEAN's "The Snowball Effect" (1952), in which a sociologist draws up an incentive scheme which permits the Watashaw Ladies Sewing Circle to recruit the entire world (the technique later became known in the real world as "pyramid selling"). The definitive sf exercise in the sociology of POLITICS is Michael D. RESNICK's vivid account of the COLONIZATION and subsequent "liberation" of *Paradise* (**1989**). Sociologists working in the field of demography play a key role in Hilbert SCHENCK's curious timeslip romance, *A Rose for Armageddon* (**1982**), although they rarely

feature in stories of OVERPOPULATION.

The marked shift in the emphasis of genre sf away from scientific hardware towards sociological issues has had several causes. Sheer literary sophistication is one; the expansion of the sf audience to take in many readers (and writers) who have little scientific education is another. It also reflects a growing awareness of the pace of social change and of insistent challenges to social values which were once supported by wider consensus. Elementary features of social organization like the family are increasingly subject to the erosions of individual liberty. Commonplace social problems like crime (◊ CRIME AND PUNISHMENT) and care of the aged and the sick are becoming magnified – ironically, by virtue of the very success of the technologies which have been brought to bear on the problems. The fact that social situations do and will determine the context in which scientific inventions are and will be made and used was frequently glossed over by early sf writers, but is now clearly recognized. The slowly but steadily growing interest in sf may be a symptom of wider recognition of the acceleration of social change and the imaginative utility of sociological thought-experiments; if so, the academic study of sf (◊ SF IN THE CLASSROOM) might perhaps be a matter more suited to sociologists than to students of literature *per se*.   [BS]

See also: CITIES; HISTORY IN SF; LIFE ON OTHER WORLDS; LINGUISTICS; SOCIAL DARWINISM; TABOOS; WOMEN AS PORTRAYED IN SCIENCE FICTION.

SOFT SF This not very precise item of sf TERMINOLOGY, formed by analogy with HARD SF, is generally applied either to sf that deals with the SOFT SCIENCES or to sf that does not deal with recognizable science at all, but emphasizes human feelings. The contrasting of soft sf with hard sf is sometimes illogical. Stories of PSI POWERS or SUPERMEN, for example, have little to do with real science, but are regularly regarded by sf readers as hard sf. The NEW WAVE was generally associated with soft sf; CYBERPUNK falls somewhere between the two.   [PN]

SOFT SCIENCES In academic slang and sf TERMINOLOGY, the soft sciences are in the main the social sciences, those which deal mainly with human affairs – very often the sciences that require little or no hardware for their carrying out. (Most would claim BIOLOGY and subsidiary fields – e.g., CLONES and GENETIC ENGINEERING – as hard sciences [◊ HARD SF].) Theme entries in this volume which deal directly or indirectly with soft sciences include ANTHROPOLOGY, ECOLOGY, ECONOMICS, EVOLUTION, FUTUROLOGY, INTELLIGENCE, LINGUISTICS, PERCEPTION, PSYCHOLOGY and SOCIOLOGY. The soft sciences very often work through statistics, and hard scientists have been known to despise them for their lack of rigour and their occasional difficulty in predicting quantifiable results; sociology has been particularly criticized in this context. Sf that deals primarily with the soft sciences is sometimes known as SOFT SF.   [PN]

SOHL, JERRY Working name of US writer and former

journalist Gerald Allan Sohl Sr (1913-   ), active from about 1950 in sf and other genres as JS and under various pseudonyms, including Nathan Butler and Sean Mei Sullivan. He began publishing sf with "The 7th Order" for *Gal* in 1952, and soon released *The Haploids* (**1952**), the first of several 1950s novels whose slick surface and sharp economy of scale marked him as a professional craftsman. These books include *Transcendent Man* (**1953**), *Costigan's Needle* (**1953**) – which deftly depicts the colonizing of a PARALLEL WORLD – *The Altered Ego* (**1954**) – which ingeniously treats as a problem in detection an IMMORTALITY puzzle involving personality recordings, though without the concept of CLONES the technology of transference was clearly unwieldy – and *Point Ultimate* (**1955**), a fine example of 1950s PARANOIA in its picture of Russians occupying the USA through use of a plague virus. In all these books JS's use of science, though attractive, seems in hindsight somewhat opportunistic, and several of them fail ultimately to make much sense of the premises they dramatize. His sf output began to slacken by the end of the decade, though he remained active in other areas, several non-sf novels being published as by Butler. Of his later sf, *The Odious Ones* (**1959**) and *Night Slaves* (**1965**), later televised, best demonstrate his competence. From 1958 JS did considerable tv work, including scripts, under various names, for *The* INVADERS, *The* OUTER LIMITS, STAR TREK and *The* TWILIGHT ZONE. [JC]

Other works: *The Mars Monopoly* (**1956** dos); *The Time Dissolver* (**1957**); *One Against Herculum* (**1959** dos); *The Anomaly* (**1971**); *I, Aleppo* (as "I am Aleppo" in *The New Mind* [anth **1973**] ed Roger ELWOOD; exp **1976**); *Death Sleep* (**1983**).

SOKOŁOWSKI, KRZYSZTOF (1955-   ) Polish critic, translator and editor, author of the POLAND entry in this encyclopedia. A graduate of Warsaw University, KS is well known for his critical pieces on US-UK sf in the magazine *Fantastyka*. Since its foundation in 1990 he has been editor of *Fenix*, the first privately owned professional sf magazine in Poland; he is also a professional translator of sf. [PN]

SOLARIS 1. French-language Canadian magazine. ◊ CANADA; Luc POMERLEAU; Daniel SERNINE.

2. Russian film (1971). Mosfilm. Dir Andrei TARKOVSKY, starring Donatas Banionis, Natalia Bondarchuk, Youri Jarvet, Anatoli Solinitsin. Screenplay Tarkovsky, Friedrich Gorenstein, based on *Solaris* (**1961**; trans **1970**) by Stanisław LEM. 165 mins; first US version 132 mins. Colour.

This long, ambitious rendering of Lem's metaphysical novel is regarded by some as one of the finest sf films made; a minority sees it as tediously slow-moving. *S* changes the emphasis of the story from the intellectual to the emotional, partly by restructuring the narrative, which in the film is framed by elegiac and nostalgic sequences at the country house of the young space-scientist hero's parents, focusing on the scientist's relationship with his father; the opening

passage is on Earth, the closing passage on Solaris's recreation of Earth. The main action is set on a space-station hovering above the planet Solaris, whose ever-changing ocean is thought to be organic and sentient. The protagonist finds the station in disrepair and his colleagues demoralized by the materialization of "phantoms" (quite real and solid) of their innermost obsessions; soon he is himself haunted by a reincarnation of his suicided wife. These phantoms may be an attempt by Solaris to communicate. Horrified, he kills the phantom wife, but a replica arrives that night. Ultimately he recognizes that, no matter what her source, she is both living and lovable; but while he sleeps she connives at her own exorcism. Solaris remains an enigma. The philosophical questions about the limits of human understanding are not put so sharply as in the book, but the visual images, despite occasionally mediocre special effects, are potent – haunting leitmotivs of water, sundering screens, technology and snow. [PN]

See also: MUSIC; RUSSIA; SPACE HABITATS.

SOLAR WIND This scientific term has found much favour in sf TERMINOLOGY. The stars constantly emit highly energetic particles as well as, of course, light, which is itself composed of tiny particles, photons (although here the word "particle" has a slightly different meaning). These particles exert a gentle outward pressure (which is why the tail of a comet always points away from the Sun). A low-mass spacecraft with a huge, incredibly thin sail, perhaps made of aluminium, could take advantage of this pressure just as a yacht uses wind – hence the proliferation of rather charming space-sailing stories, including "The Lady who Sailed the *Soul*" (1960) by Cordwainer SMITH and "Sunjammer" (1964; vt "The Wind from the Sun") by Arthur C. CLARKE. An anthology including 4 original stories, a number of reprints and some nonfiction is *Project Solar Sail* (anth **1990**) ed Clarke and (anon) David BRIN. [PN]

SOLO, JAY [s] ◊ Harlan ELLISON.

SOLOGUB, FYODOR Pseudonym of Russian poet and novelist Fyodor-Kuzmich Teternikov (1863-1927), who remains best known for his second novel, *Melkii bes* (**1907**; best trans R. Wilks as *The Little Demon* **1962** UK); the title refers to the apotheosis of numbing mediocrity, mercilessly depicted, which devours the schoolteacher protagonist. FS's third novel, *Tvorimaia legenda* (**1907-13** *Shipovnik*, then *Zemlya*; cut **1914**; part 1 only of cut text trans John Cournos as *The Created Legend* **1916** UK; complete trans Samuel D. Cioran of restored text in 3 vols as *The Created Legend* **1979** US), is sf, though of a strange order. The 1st vol describes the life in 1905 Russia of the protagonist who – pedagogue, inventor, sybarite and mage – clearly represents a wish-fulfilment version of the author. The 2nd describes the RURITANIAN kingdom of the United Isles, threatened by volcanoes and dynastic upheavals. In the 3rd, after successfully applying to become king – echoes of Frederick ROLFE's *Hadrian VII* (**1904**) are clear – the protagonist escapes Russia in a spherical flying device of his own invention and enters into his meritocratic heritage. The text as a whole irretrievably mixes superscience, Satanism, an eroticized vision of history, SATIRE and dream. *The Sweet-Scented Name, and Other Fairy Tales, Fables and Stories* (coll trans Stephen Graham **1915** UK) and *The Old House and Other Tales* (coll trans John Cournos **1916** UK) contain some fantasies.   [JC]

SOL RISING The quarterly newsletter of the MERRIL COLLECTION OF SCIENCE FICTION, SPECULATION AND FANTASY.

SOMERS, BART ◊ Gardner F. FOX.

SOMETHING ELSE UK SEMIPROZINE, 3 issues (Spring 1980, Winter 1980, Spring 1984), small-BEDSHEET format, published and ed Charles Partington from Manchester. This was a short-lived but brave attempt by Partington, who had previously edited ALIEN WORLDS, to continue the NEW WORLDS tradition. Many of the stalwarts of *NW* appeared, including Brian W. ALDISS, Hilary BAILEY, John BRUNNER, M. John HARRISON and Michael MOORCOCK. Like its more illustrious predecessor, *SE* did not get the distribution it deserved.   [RR]

SOMETHING IS OUT THERE 1. US/Australian tv miniseries (1988). CPT Holdings/Hoyts for NBC. Executive prods Frank Lupo, John Ashley. Dir Richard Colla, starring Joe Cortese, Maryam d'Abo, George Dzundza. Written Lupo. 2 100min episodes.

This sometimes exciting, often threadbare *policier* pits a tough Earth cop (Cortese) and a marooned, telepathic medical officer from an ALIEN prison spaceship (d'Abo) – she looks both human and beautiful – against an escaped alien "xenomorph", extremely dangerous and capable of invading a human host (as in *The* HIDDEN [1988], which *SIOT* strongly resembles). In romantic buddy-movie style, he teaches her Earth customs and she teaches him monster-catching. Rick Baker's creature effects are good; the pacing is bad; the ending is ambiguous. An edited version (165 mins) was released on videotape.

2. US tv series (1989). NBC. 8 50min episodes, the last two not aired in the USA. After the promising if uneven pilot miniseries, the series proper, again starring Cortese and d'Abo, was disappointing: crime-fighting clichés, unremarkable scripts, and little use made of the extraterrestrial elements.   [PN]

SOMTOW, S.P. Working name of Thai composer and writer Somtow Papinian Sucharitkul (1952-   ), who used his surname from the beginning of his career to 1985, when he switched to SPS, announcing that any book previously signed Sucharitkul would be signed SPS on reprinting (although some children's books continued to appear under the earlier form of his name). After university education in the UK and a period in the USA, SPS began in recent years to spend about half his time in Thailand and half in the USA. His first publication of any genre interest was a poem, "Kith of Infinity", which appeared in the *Bangkok Press* in 1967 and was assembled – along with early stories like "Sunsteps"

(1977 *Unearth*) – in *Fire from the Wine Dark Sea* (coll **1983**). He won the JOHN W. CAMPBELL AWARD for Best New Writer in 1981.

His first novel, *Starship and Haiku* (**1981**), is typical of much of his work: the tale takes place in a crowded but fluid venue, with culture shocks leading to ornate resolutions; in this case, the citizens of a post-HOLOCAUST Earth are committing suicide, but whales contact Japanese survivors (with whom they share a genetic heritage) and the novel closes as a new hybrid species sets off for the stars.

The **Chronicles of the High Inquest** sequence – *Light on the Sound* (**1982**; rev vt *The Dawning Shadow #1: Light on the Sound* 1986), *The Throne of Madness* (**1983**; rev vt *The Dawning Shadow #2: The Throne of Madness* 1986), *Utopia Hunters* (coll of linked stories **1984**) and *The Darkling Wind* (**1985**) – again injects whale-like sentients into a complex mix, following the interactions of the mutilated humans who hunt them on instructions from the Inquestors, a Galaxy-spanning race whose pretensions to moral superiority are harshly examined as the sequence advances. In the end, the Inquestor race dies in cataclysm, leaving a deposit of myth for later races to decipher. Other sf of interest includes the ALTERNATE-WORLD **Aquiliad** sequence – *The Aquiliad* (**1983**; vt *The Aquiliad: Aquila in the New World* 1988), *The Aquiliad #2: Aquila and the Iron Horse* (**1988**) and *#3: Aquila and the Sphinx* (**1988**) – set in a Western Hemisphere dominated by the Roman Empire; a resident time traveller injects a malicious note of imbalance and insecurity, generating a state of fluid near-chaos typical of SPS at his best. Sf singletons include *Mallworld* (coll of linked stories **1981**), in which the eponymous venue doubles as an observation post for ALIENS fascinated by the human race; and *The Shattered Horse* (**1986**), another alternate-world tale in which the Trojans win.

At about the time he changed his byline he also began to move from sf into fantasy and horror, notably with the **Valentine** sequence of vampire novels – *Vampire Junction* (**1984**) and *Valentine* (**1992** UK) – and *Moondance* (**1989**), a powerful werewolf tale. It is to be hoped, however, that he will continue to contribute sf tales which reflect his quicksilver, sea-change imagination.   [JC]

Other works: 2 "V" novelizations, *The Alien Swordmaster* * (**1985**) and *Symphony of Terror* * (**1988**); *The Fallen Country* (**1986**), for children; *Forgetting Places* (**1987**), associational; *Fiddling for Waterbuffaloes* (1986 *ASF*; **1992** chap).

See also: ANTHROPOLOGY; ECOLOGY; GALACTIC EMPIRES; ISAAC ASIMOV'S SCIENCE FICTION MAGAZINE; MESSIAHS; MUSIC; SOCIOLOGY; SPACE OPERA.

SONDERS, MARK ◊ Michael BERLYN.

SONGWEAVER, CERIN [s] ◊ Charles DE LINT.

SON OF BLOB ◊ *The* BLOB.

SON OF GODZILLA ◊ GOJIRA.

SON OF KONG Film (1933). RKO. Dir Ernest B. Schoedsack, starring Robert Armstrong, Helen Mack,

Frank Reicher, Noble Johnson. Screenplay Ruth Rose. 70 mins. B/w.

This film was made immediately after KING KONG (1933) as a small-scale sequel. The hero returns to Skull Island and discovers Kong's son, a 20ft (6m) white ape with all the characteristics of a friendly puppy. Various prehistoric monsters appear before a volcanic upheaval destroys the island. The ape saves the hero by holding him above the flood waters. There are good special effects by Willis H. O'BRIEN, but the film is obviously a rush job to cash in on the success of the original, whose mythic resonance this lacks. [JB]

SOREL, EDWARD (1929-) US illustrator and writer. In *Moon Missing: An Illustrated Guide to the Future* (**1962**) the MOON disappears and the early 1960s are satirized. The illustrations are more satisfyingly vindictive than the text. [PN]

SOUČEK, LUDVÍK [r] ◊ CZECH AND SLOVAK SF.

SOUTH, CLARK [s] ◊ Dwight V. SWAIN.

SOUTH AMERICA ◊ LATIN AMERICA.

SOUTHERN, TERRY [r] ◊ Peter GEORGE.

SOUTHWOLD, STEPHEN ◊ Neil BELL.

SOVIET UNION The vast majority of the sf from what until 1991 was the Soviet Union, especially that translated into English, was in the first instance written and published in Russian (◊ RUSSIA). A small amount of Soviet sf exists in the various languages other than Russian, notably Ukrainian, in which the dissident writer Oles Berdnyk writes. Little of this material has been translated into Russian, let alone English. The break-up of the USSR will certainly in due course increase interest from both within and outside their borders in the native writings of the new (or re-established) nations. [PN]

SOWDEN, LEWIS (1905-1974) UK-born South African writer and newspaperman whose *Tomorrow's Comet* (1949 *Blue Book* as "Star of Doom"; **1951** UK) treats the END OF THE WORLD in psychological terms. [JC/PN]
Other works: *The Man who was Emperor: A Romance* (**1946** UK).

SOYKA, OTTO [r] ◊ AUSTRIA.

SOYLENT GREEN Film (1973). MGM. Dir Richard Fleischer, starring Charlton Heston, Edward G. Robinson, Leigh Taylor-Young, Chuck Connors, Joseph Cotten, Paula Kelly. Screenplay Stanley R. Greenberg, based on *Make Room! Make Room!* (**1966**) by Harry HARRISON. 97 mins. Colour.

A New York police detective (Heston) in an AD2022 marked by OVERPOPULATION investigates what appears to be a routine murder and in the end discovers that "soylent green", the main food for the world's population, is actually made from dead human bodies. The plot has little to do with Harrison's book, whose pro-contraception message it nervously avoids for fear of alienating Roman Catholic viewers (Harrison has spoken eloquently of the perversion of his work), but the vision of a teeming, overpopulated and festering New York is recreated quite well. The cannibalistic denouement is purely for

shock value, and makes no rational sense; indeed Harrison coined the word "soylent" from "soy beans" and "lentils", and the people of his future are largely and necessarily vegetarian. Edward G. Robinson's fine performance as a dying old man coaxed into a euthanasia clinic is touching, for he was dying in real life as well. The film won a NEBULA. [JB/PN]

SPACE ADVENTURES ◊ SPACE ADVENTURES (CLASSICS).

SPACE ADVENTURES (CLASSICS) One of the reprint DIGEST-size magazines published by Sol Cohen's Ultimate Publishing Co. 6 issues Winter 1970-Summer 1971. The title was shortened to *Space Adventures* after the first 2. The numbering ran, strangely, #9-#14, apparently picking up where SCIENCE FICTION (ADVENTURE) CLASSICS left off, and *SAC* would be regarded as simply a variant title were it not that the latter resumed publication, also in Winter 1970, with #12. Most of *SA(C)*'s stories were reprinted from AMAZING STORIES, from the rather dismal period of Raymond A. PALMER's editorship. [BS]

SPACE CAMP Film (1986). ABC. Dir Harry Winer, starring Kate Capshaw, Lea Thompson, Kelly Preston, Larry B. Scott, Leaf Phoenix, Tate Donovan, Tom Skerritt. Screenplay W.W. Wicket, Casey T. Mitchell, from a story by Patrick Bailey, Larry B. Williams. 108 mins. Colour.

At a NASA-sponsored summer space camp, a flight simulation in a space shuttle becomes the real thing after the intervention of a well meaning ROBOT, and 4 teenagers and a small boy have to replenish their oxygen from a satellite and then bring the shuttle down again. With the help of the Force (from STAR WARS [1977]) and their own self-reliance they manage. This implausible but patriotic advertisement for Teamwork and the American Way has plenty of tension (and, in the wake of the *Challenger* disaster, plenty of bad taste), but stereotyped characters, mediocre process work in the space scenes and flat direction render it routine. [PN]

SPACE CHILDREN, THE Film (1958). Paramount. Dir Jack ARNOLD, starring Michel Ray, Adam Williams, Peggy Webber, Johnny Crawford, Jackie Coogan. Screenplay Bernard C. Schoenfeld, from a story by Tom Filer. 69 mins. B/w.

This was the last of Arnold's cycle of sf films with producer William Alland, though here the studio is Paramount, not Universal. In this earnest but likeable moral fable, a group of children are "taken over" by a benign ALIEN resembling a glowing brain (which expands as the film progresses). The peace-loving alien's aim is to use the children in the sabotage of a missile project on which their parents are working, and it gives them special powers to help them do this. The alien is not entirely a pacifist; it kills the brutal father of one of the children. Arnold makes his usual evocative use of landscape – this time a remote beach. [JB/PN]

SPACE COLONIES ◊ SPACE HABITATS.

SPACED INVADERS Film (1989). Smart Egg Pictures. Dir Patrick Read Johnson, starring Douglas Barr,

Royal Dano, Ariana Richards, J.J. Anderson, Gregg Berger, Fred Applegate. Screenplay Johnson, Scott Alexander. 100 mins. Colour.

This spoof, obviously made for younger viewers, starts promisingly with the premise that the diminutive crew of a Martian spaceship, in the middle of a battle, pick up the radio signal of Orson Welles's broadcast of WAR OF THE WORLDS, and hasten to Earth to join the presumptive Martian invasion, only to find a disinterested population (in small-town Illinois) more or less ignoring them, or mistaking them for trick-or-treating children. The ensuing gags seldom rise above poorly choreographed knockabout farce, with no great ingenuity but a perceptible flavour of bigotry. [PN]

SPACED OUT LIBRARY ◊ MERRIL COLLECTION OF SCIENCE FICTION, SPECULATION AND FANTASY.

SPACE FACT AND FICTION UK magazine, PULP-MAGAZINE size. 8 monthly issues Mar-Oct 1954, several undated, published by G.G. Swan, London; ed anon. *SFAF* published mainly reprints from wartime issues of FUTURE FICTION and SCIENCE FICTION, slanted towards the juvenile reader, but also new stories; the Apr 1954 issue was all new. An album of unsold copies in jumbled order was issued, presumably as a Christmas annual. [FHP]

SPACE FLIGHT Flight into space is *the* classic theme in sf. The lunar romances of Francis GODWIN, CYRANO DE BERGERAC *et al.* are the works most commonly and readily identified as PROTO SCIENCE FICTION. In modern times, as GENRE SF spilled out of print into the CINEMA, RADIO and TELEVISION, many of the archetypal works produced for these media were romances of space travel. Flight into space provides the stirring climax of the film THINGS TO COME (1936) and the subject-matter of DESTINATION MOON (1950) and 2001: A SPACE ODYSSEY (1968), as well as of Charles CHILTON's BBC radio serial *Journey into Space* (1953) and its sequels, and tv's STAR TREK. The landing of Apollo 11 on the MOON was seen by many as "science fiction come true". It is natural that sf should be symbolized by the theme of space flight, in that it is primarily concerned with transcending imaginative boundaries, with breaking free of the gravitational force which holds consciousness to a traditional core of belief and expectancy. The means by which space flight has been achieved in sf – its many and various SPACESHIPS – have always been of secondary importance to the mythical impact of the theme. Only a handful of writers – notably Konstantin TSIOLKOVSKY – embodied real scientific ideas about the feasibility of space ROCKETS in fictional form for didactic purposes.

Actually, all the early lunar voyages are stories of flight rather than of *space* flight, in that their authors took for granted the continuity of an atmospheric "ether" (a convenience ingeniously co-opted into modern sf by Bob SHAW in *The Ragged Astronauts* [1986] and its sequels). No early travellers had to contend with the interplanetary vacuum, not even the hero of Edgar Allan POE's "The Unparalleled Adventure of One Hans Pfaall" (1835; rev 1840), although this was the first of the traveller's tales in which the protagonist takes elaborate precautions to provide himself with air, in recognition of the tenuousness of the sublunar atmosphere. All romances of interplanetary flight prior to "Hans Pfaall" are didactic – either straightforwardly, after the fashion of Johannes KEPLER's *Somnium* (1634) and Gabriel Daniel's *A Voyage to the World of Cartesius* (1690), or satirically, after the fashion of Daniel DEFOE's *The Consolidator* (1705). Poe's story is a satire, too, although the author advanced claims as to its verisimilitude. But it was really Jules VERNE who made the first serious attempt at realism in *De la terre à la lune* (1865; trans J.K. Hoyte as *From the Earth to the Moon* 1869 US) and its sequel *Autour de la lune* (1870; both trans Lewis Mercier and Eleanor King as *From the Earth to the Moon* 1873 UK). Hindsight invests 19th-century lunar romances with the same mythical significance that sf has more recently lent to the notion of space travel, but the stories had no such significance in their own day. The idea of flight into space became the central myth of sf only once the genre had been identified and demarcated by Hugo GERNSBACK. This was not really a strategic move on Gernsback's part: his interest in the future and in the effect of TECHNOLOGY on society was more catholic – with space travel as only one among a whole series of probable developments. It was because of the kind of impact sf made on the readers who discovered it – young, for the most part – that space flight acquired its special significance. Many sf readers found in sf a kind of revelation, a sudden mind-opening shock (◊ CONCEPTUAL BREAKTHROUGH; SENSE OF WONDER): this was not the effect of any single story but the discovery of sf as a category, a genre of fictions presenting an infinity of possibilities. It is because of this element of revelation, the sudden awareness of a vast range of possibilities, that the paradigmatic examples of early sf are stories of escape from Earth into a Universe filled with worlds: the first SPACE OPERAS, notably E.E. "Doc" SMITH's *The Skylark of Space* (1928; **1946**).

As with other themes in sf, the post-WWII period saw considerable sophistication of the myth of space flight. Significantly, and perhaps contrary to popular belief, there was relatively little development in verisimilitude outside the work of a very few technically adept authors. The most significant post-WWII stories related to the theme are not so much stories about space flight as commentaries upon the myth itself; they are concerned with imaginative horizons rather than hardware. One of the earliest examples of this kind of commentary is Ray BRADBURY's "King of the Gray Spaces" (1943; vt "R is for Rocket"); the classics are Robert A. HEINLEIN's "The Man who Sold the Moon" (1950) and Arthur C. CLARKE's *Prelude to Space* (**1951**). Others include Murray LEINSTER's "The Story of Rod Cantrell" (1949), Fredric BROWN's *The Lights in the Sky are Stars* (**1953**; vt *Project Jupiter* 1954

UK), Walter M. MILLER's "Death of a Spaceman" (1954; vt "Memento Homo") and Dean McLAUGHLIN's *The Man who Wanted Stars* (fixup **1965**). The mythic significance of the theme is most obvious in a story in which "space flight" is, from the viewpoint of the reader, purely metaphorical: James BLISH's "Surface Tension" (1952), in which a microscopic man builds himself a protective shell and forces his way up through the surface of a pond into the open air. Also notable is a short story by Edmond HAMILTON, "The Pro" (1964), in which an ageing sf writer meets up with the reality of the myth when his son goes into space.

Sf writers often became annoyed when, following Neil Armstrong's Moon landing in 1969, they were asked what they would find to write about in the future. In fact, a subtle change did overcome sf during the course of the Apollo programme. Since then, stories about space flight within the Solar System have been "demystified", and we have a generation of stories in which spacemen operating within a "real" context come into conflict with the myth: Barry N. MALZBERG's *The Falling Astronauts* (**1971**), Nigel BALCHIN's *Kings of Infinite Space* (**1967**), Luděk PEŠEK's *Die Marsexpedition* (**1970** Germany; trans Anthea Bell as *The Earth is Near* **1974**) and Dan SIMMONS's *Phases of Gravity* (**1989**) are examples; while J.G. BALLARD has for some time been writing nostalgic stories which regard the space programme as a glorious folly of the 1960s (8 are collected in the ironically titled *Memories of the Space Age* [coll **1988**]). Sf novels which bitterly assume that a second breakout into space may well be necessary if the actual space programme is allowed to fade away include *The Man who Corrupted Earth* (**1980**) by G.C. EDMONDSON and *Privateers* (**1985**) by Ben BOVA. However, the myth of transcending the closed world of the known and familiar is now more often tied specifically to interstellar travel, as in *2001: A Space Odyssey*, Poul ANDERSON's *Tau Zero* (1967; exp **1970**), Vonda MCINTYRE's *Superluminal* (**1984**) and some of the stories in *Faster than Light* (anth **1976**) ed Jack DANN and George ZEBROWSKI. Star-drives which free mankind from the prison of the Solar System take on an iconic significance in such novels as *Take Back Plenty* (**1990**) by Colin GREENLAND and *Carve the Sky* (**1991**) by Alexander JABLOKOV.   [BS]

See also: FASTER THAN LIGHT; GALACTIC EMPIRES.

SPACE HABITATS Stories of space stations or artificial satellites appear early in sf, the first example being Edward Everett HALE's extraordinary "The Brick Moon" (1869) and its sequel "Life in the Brick Moon" (1870), in which the satellite of the title consists of many brick spheres connected by brick arches, and is launched, with people on board, by gigantic flywheels. Kurd LASSWITZ's *Auf Zwei Planeten* (**1897**; cut trans as *Two Planets* **1971** US) has Martian space stations shaped like spoked wheels floating above the poles, but these are kept hovering by gravity-control devices of a somewhat implausible

kind. The first detailed and thoroughly scientific treatment is in Konstantin TSIOLKOVSKY's *Vne zemli* (written 1896-1920; **1920**; trans as "Out of the Earth" in *The Call of the Cosmos* **1963** Russia), a semifictionalized didactic speculation; it deals with free fall, space greenhouses for growing food, communication via space mirrors, and artificial GRAVITY effected by spinning the station on its axis – indeed, much of the spectrum of space-habitat ideas that would first begin to appear in any profusion after WWII, at a time when space travel by ROCKETS was generally realized to be something actually likely to happen.

A highly influential book of popular science, dealing with (among other things) the construction of space stations was *The Conquest of Space* (**1949**) by Willy LEY, illustrated by Chesley BONESTELL, and it was after this that the space-station story began to appear commonly in GENRE SF. However, the idea was not new to the genre, a celebrated earlier example being George O. SMITH's **Venus Equilateral** stories, published in *ASF* from 1942, about a communications space station in a Trojan position (60° ahead of the planet) in the orbit of Venus.

The image of the space habitat presented through the 1950s was usually (though not always) as a way station, a stopping-off point prior to flights deeper into space. Indeed, the usual term of the time was "space station"; another book by Ley was titled *Space Stations* (**1958**). Such stations were envisaged as being in Earth orbit, the first place you reach after leaving Earth. We see this image of the stopping-off place quite often in movies, an early example being CONQUEST OF SPACE (1955) and a later one 2001: A SPACE ODYSSEY (1968), and of course in books, as in Arthur C. CLARKE's children's novel *Islands in the Sky* (**1952**). Other 1950s books and stories in which the space station is totemic include Rafe BERNARD's *The Wheel in the Sky* (**1954**), Frank Belknap LONG's *Space Station No 1* (**1957** dos), James E. GUNN's *Station in Space* (**1958**) and Damon KNIGHT's psychological melodrama about the trauma of meeting an alien, "Stranger Station" (1959).

One version of the theme that might have been expected to play a far greater role than it actually has in genre sf is the space station as menace, as a weapons-delivery platform in space easily able to target any point on Earth's surface. This notion has popped up occasionally in films, such as MOONRAKER (1979) (biological warfare) and HELLFIRE (1986) (a new energy source that can fry people). An early novel to use the theme is C.M. KORNBLUTH's *Not This August* (**1955**; vt *Christmas Eve* 1956 UK), in which it is hoped that a military space station will evict the Russians occupying the USA.

Although this Earth-orbit phase of the space-station story has now largely been superseded, there is still in HARD SF a sense of real nuts-and-bolts excitement when the actual building of one is envisaged, and books are still written on the theme; e.g., Donald KINGSBURY's *The Moon Goddess and the Son* (1979 *ASF*;

exp **1986**) and Allen STEELE's *Orbital Decay* (**1989**).

Soon, as the space station became absorbed into GENRE SF as one of its primary icons, they were popping up all over the place, not just in Earth orbit. We can obviously regard (perhaps not very usefully) all SPACESHIPS as space habitats, not to mention hollowed-out ASTEROIDS and, of course, GENERATION STARSHIPS. Alien space habitats of incredible complexity may be stumbled across by human observers, who have to make sense of their enigmatic qualities and deduce their purpose and the lifeforms for which they were built (◊ BIG DUMB OBJECTS). 3 such works are Clarke's *Rendezvous with Rama* (**1973**), John VARLEY's **Gaean** trilogy (**1979-84**) and Greg BEAR's *Eon* (**1985**).

One iconic space-habitat motif has the space station representing the anthropological observers in the sky, looking down at the primitives below, as in Patricia MCKILLIP's *Moon-Flash* (**1984**), where the superstitiously regarded flash of the title turns out to be the firing retro-rockets of spacecraft visiting the station; a particularly good example is Brian W. ALDISS's **Helliconia** trilogy (**1982-5**), whose observing space habitat, ironically named "Avernus", is central to the structure of the whole long tale, its "superior" observers standing for a civilization that is played out. The observers in Stanisław LEM's *Solaris* (**1961**; trans **1970**), filmed as SOLARIS (**1971**), are also played out and receive the come-uppance due to people who try to hold themselves aloof, their space station becoming a shambles, as the LIVING WORLD beneath reconstructs in the flesh their most feared and desired memories and nightmares. An interesting variant of the space-habitat story is Fritz LEIBER's *A Specter is Haunting Texas* (**1969**), whose spectre is, in fact, the skinny body of a visitor from a space habitat who, unable to move properly in Earth gravity, is supported by an exoskeleton.

The second boom in space-station stories was, like the first, catalysed by a book of popular science, this time *The High Frontier* (**1977**) by Princeton physicist Gerard K. O'Neill (**1927-1992**), which vigorously proselytized for the construction of colonies in space, either in Earth orbit or at one of the LAGRANGE POINTS – especially L5, 60° behind the Moon in the Moon's orbit around Earth. The amazing long-range quality of Tsiolkovsky's prescience has never been more evident than in the fact that his predictions – not just of space stations, but of huge self-sufficient, heavily populated space colonies – took more than half a century to come to their full flowering in scientific speculation and in sf.

One of the first writers to take O'Neill's tip was Mack REYNOLDS, in *Lagrange Five* (**1979**), *The Lagrangists* (**1983**) and *Chaos in Lagrangia* (**1984**) (the latter 2 ed Dean ING from manuscripts found after Reynold's death). Now that the space station was being re-envisioned as the space colony or space habitat – a home where people might live all their lives – its iconic significance was radically changing. The space habitat has become the locus of the new, with everything old, washed-up and politically out-of-date being left rotting back on Earth while the real action is in space. The second new thing about space habitats has to do with diversity and cultural evolution: there can be a lot of them, each giving a home to a different political or racial or social group, so that the habitat takes over the function of ISLANDS in earlier sf as an isolated area that can be used as a laboratory in which to conduct thought experiments in cultural anthropology. (Not all these motifs are post-O'Neill, of course; some – including the idea of diverse habitats each catering for different tastes – were prefigured in Jack VANCE's eccentric "Abercrombie Station" [1952].)

Among the many books of the past 15 years to make use of space-habitat themes, mostly along the lines suggested above, are *Space Colony* (**1978**) by Ben BOVA, Joe HALDEMAN's **Worlds** series, starting with *Worlds* (**1981**), Melinda SNODGRASS's **Circuit** trilogy, beginning with *Circuit* (**1986**), Lois McMaster BUJOLD's *Falling Free* (**1988**), Christopher HINZ's **Paratwa** series, starting with *Liege-Killer* (**1987**) and Richard LUPOFF's *The Forever City* (**1988**). The idea is taken to its extremes in George ZEBROWSKI's *Macrolife* (**1979**; rev **1990**), in which humanity largely abandons planetary environments in favour of star-travelling habitats.

Obviously the iconic significance of the space-habitat story is evolving rapidly, a topic analyzed (rather differently) in "Small Worlds and Strange Tomorrows: The Icon of the Space Station in Science Fiction" by Gary Westfahl in *Foundation* #51 (Spring 1991) (Westfahl has published pieces elsewhere on the same theme). Complex use of the motif – the space habitat both as cultural forcing ground and as creator of instability through cultural claustrophobia – appears in some key CYBERPUNK works, notably William GIBSON's **Neuromancer** trilogy (**1984-8**) and Bruce STERLING's vastly inventive *Schismatrix* (**1985**), and also – to a degree – Michael SWANWICK's *Vacuum Flowers* (**1987**). In only a decade we have seen the emphasis move from space habitat as brave new world to space habitat as a trap that corrupts and is prey to cultural and technological dereliction.

Though space habitats are likely to remain popular in sf because of their peculiar usefulness in creating specific kinds of cultural scenario, in the real world the idea seems, outside a hard core of O'Neill cultists, to be receiving less and less support as something towards which we should currently be working. Although the theoretical advantages of low gravity and permanent energy supply are real, it is difficult to envisage any remotely plausible circumstances that would make the capital cost of space habitats, at least when considered in isolation, redeemable economically, nor any evolutionary advantages in the small-town-mentality balkanization (and shrinkage of the gene pool) that their building and occupation might come to represent. [PN]

SPACEHUNTER: ADVENTURES IN THE FORBIDDEN ZONE Film (**1983**). Delphi Productions/

Columbia. Dir Lamont Johnson, starring Peter Strauss, Molly Ringwald, Ernie Hudson, Michael Ironside. Screenplay David Preston, Edith Rey, Dan Goldberg, Len Blum, from a story by Stewart Harding, Jean Lafleur. 90 mins (but reported as being originally 105 mins). Made in 3D. Colour.

Bedevilled with production problems, changing directors in midstream (it was begun by Jean Lafleur), suffering from the ominous stigma of 6 screenwriting credits, *S:AITFZ* is surprisingly relaxed. Strauss is a space scavenger who comes to plague-and-pollution ridden Terra Eleven, the post-HOLOCAUST chic of whose citizens owes much to MAD MAX 2 (1981; vt *The Road Warrior*), to save three maidens. He is joined by a fast-talking tomboy (Ringwald) and an old army buddy (Hudson), and they fight their way past Bat People, Barracuda Women and feral children to the showdown with CYBORG woman-despoiler Overdog (Ironside) and his barbarian cohorts. Strauss is appealing as a down-at-heel Indiana Jones in space, and, while the movie is derivative and meandering, it is also often ingenious and enjoyable. The overactfully used 3D becomes an inconsequential irritant.   [PN]

"SPACE" KINGLEY The tough and resourceful Captain "Space" Kingley was the hero of 3 UK children's SPACE-OPERA annuals of the early 1950s. Beyond his pukka Britishness he displayed few individual characteristics. The sequence (which remains extremely difficult to date precisely; the dates here may not be reliable) comprises *The Adventures of Captain "Space" Kingley* (coll **1952**) with stories by Ray Sonin, *The "Space" Kingley Annual* (coll **1953**) with stories by Ernest A. Player, and *"Space" Kingley and the Secret Squadron* (coll **1954**) with stories by David White. All were heavily illustrated by R.W. Jobson.   [JC/RR]

SPACE 1999 UK tv series (1975-7). A Gerry Anderson Production for ITC. Created Gerry and Sylvia Anderson. Prods Sylvia Anderson (season 1), Fred Freiberger (season 2). Executive prod Gerry Anderson. Story consultant Christopher Penfold. Special effects Brian Johnson. 2 seasons, 48 50min episodes in all. Colour.

This UK-made series, created by Gerry and Sylvia ANDERSON – who had previously produced a number of tv series (STINGRAY, THUNDERBIRDS and others) with puppets and UFO and the film DOPPELGANGER (1969) with real actors – was obviously inspired in part by the success of STAR TREK. The format has a group of people – live actors again – travelling through the Galaxy, visiting various planets and encountering strange lifeforms; but, where the **Star Trek** characters travelled on a spaceship, the **Space 1999** personnel do their interplanetary wandering on Earth's runaway Moon – an unwieldy gimmick that must have caused many frustrations to the writers. Despite good special effects and sometimes imaginative sets the series, with its stereotyped characters and humourless scripts, was remarkably wooden, eliciting predictable jokes about puppets. The other major flaw was a scandalous disregard for basic science (⇩

SCIENTIFIC ERRORS): stars are confused with asteroids, the Moon's progress through space follows no physical laws, and PARSECS are assumed to be a unit of velocity. The series was cancelled in 1977, though 1 episode was delayed until 1978. The regular cast included Martin Landau, Barbara Bain, Barry Morse (season 1), Nick Tate, Catherine Schell (season 2), Tony Anholt (season 2), Zienia Merton. Dirs included Ray Austin, Lee H. Katzin, Charles Crichton, David Tomblin, Val Guest, Tom Clegg. Writers included Christopher Penfold, Johnny Byrne, Terence Feely, Donald James and Charles Woodgrove (pseudonym of Freiberger). The series did better in the USA than in the UK, perhaps because of lower expectations, perhaps because of the deliberately international cast.

At the end of the 1970s 8 episodes were cobbled together in pairs and recycled by ITC in the guise of 4 movies; the words "Space 1999" nowhere appeared in their titles. Though we have been unable to trace any theatrical release, at least 2 have turned up on tv: *Destination Moonbase-Alpha* (1978), dir Tom Clegg (based on a 2-episode story, *The Bringers of Wonder*, by Terence Feely), and *Journey through the Black Sun* (1982) dir Ray Austin and Lee (based on the episodes *Collision Course* by Anthony Terpiloff and *The Black Sun* by David Weir). The other 2 were *The Cosmic Princess* and *Alien Attack*.

A book about the series is *The Making of Space 1999: A Gerry Anderson Production* (**1976**) by Tim Heald. A number of novelizations appeared. Brian N. BALL wrote *The Space Guardians* ∗ (**1975**). Michael BUTTERWORTH wrote *Planets of Peril* ∗ (**1977**), *Mind-Breaks of Space* ∗ (**1977**) with Jeff Jones, *The Space-Jackers* ∗ (**1977**), *The Psychomorph* ∗ (**1977**), *The Time Fighters* ∗ (**1977**) and *The Edge of the Infinite* ∗ (**1977**). John Rankine (Douglas R. MASON) wrote *Moon Odyssey* ∗ (**1975**), *Lunar Attack* ∗ (**1975**), *Astral Quest* ∗ (**1975**), *Android Planet* ∗ (**1976**) and *Phoenix of Megaron* ∗ (**1976** US). E.C. TUBB wrote *Breakaway* ∗ (**1975**), *Collision Course* ∗ (**1975**), *Alien Seed* ∗ (**1976** US), *Rogue Planet* ∗ (**1976** US) and *Earthfall* ∗ (**1977**).   [JB/PN]

SPACE OPERA When RADIO was the principal medium of home entertainment in the USA, daytime serials intended for housewives were often sponsored by soap-powder companies; the series were thus dubbed "soap operas". The name was soon generalized to refer to any corny domestic drama. Westerns were sometimes called "horse operas" by false analogy, and the pattern was extended into sf terminology by Wilson TUCKER in 1941, who proposed "space opera" as the appropriate term for the "hacky, grinding, stinking, outworn, spaceship yarn". It soon came to be applied instead to colourful action-adventure stories of interplanetary or interstellar conflict. Although the term still retains a pejorative implication, it is frequently used with nostalgic affection, applying to space-adventure stories which have a calculatedly romantic element. The term might be applied retrospectively to such early space adventures as Robert W. COLE's *The Struggle for Empire*

(1900) but, as it was coined as a complaint about pulp CLICHÉ, it seems reasonable to limit its use to GENRE SF.

Five writers were principally involved in the development of space opera in the 1920s and 1930s. E.E. "Doc" SMITH made his début with the exuberant interstellar adventure *The Skylark of Space* (1928; **1946**), and continued to write stories in a similar vein until the mid-1960s; 2 sequels, *Skylark Three* (1930; **1948**) and *Skylark of Valeron* (1934-5; **1949**), escalated the scale of the action before the **Lensmen** series took over, the SPACESHIPS growing ever-larger and the WEAPONS more destructive until GALACTIC EMPIRES were toppling like card-houses in *Children of the Lens* (1947-8; **1954**). Once there was no greater scale of action to be employed, Smith had little more to offer, and his last novels – *The Galaxy Primes* (1959; **1965**) and *Skylark DuQuesne* (**1966**) – are mere exercises in recapitulation. In the 1970s, however, a reissue of the **Lensmen** series enjoyed such success with readers that Smith's banner was picked up by William B. Ellern (1933-   ), David A. KYLE and Stephen GOLDIN (◊ E.E. SMITH *for details*). Contemporary with Smith's first interstellar epic was a series of stories written by Edmond HAMILTON for WEIRD TALES, ultimately collected in *Crashing Suns* (1928-9; coll **1965**) and *Outside the Universe* (1929; **1964**). Although he was a more versatile writer than Smith, Hamilton took great delight in wrecking worlds and destroying suns, and his name was made with space opera (he too continued to write it until the 1960s), other early examples being "The Universe Wreckers" (1930) and the CAPTAIN FUTURE series. In the late 1940s Hamilton wrote *The Star of Life* (1947; **1959**) and the memorable *The Star Kings* (**1949**; vt *Beyond the Moon*), an sf version of *The Prisoner of Zenda* (**1894**) by Anthony Hope (1863-1933). The last of Hamilton's works in this vein were *Doomstar* (**1966**) and the **Starwolf** trilogy (1967-8). Even before Smith and Hamilton made their débuts, Ray CUMMINGS was writing interplanetary novels for the general-fiction pulps and for Hugo GERNSBACK'S SCIENCE AND INVENTION. His principal space operas were *Tarrano the Conqueror* (1925; **1930**), *A Brand New World* (1928; **1964**), *Brigands of the Moon* (**1931**) and its sequel *Wandl the Invader* (1932; **1961**), but his reputation was made by his microcosmic romances (◊ GREAT AND SMALL), and it was to such adventures that he reverted when he turned to self-plagiarism in later years. The two most important writers who carried space opera forward in the wake of Smith and Hamilton were John W. CAMPBELL Jr and Jack WILLIAMSON. Campbell made his first impact with the novelettes collected in *The Black Star Passes* (1930; fixup **1953**), and he went on to write Galaxy-spanning adventures like *Islands of Space* (1931; **1957**), *Invaders from the Infinite* (1932; **1961**) and *The Mightiest Machine* (1934; **1947**). Campbell had a better command of scientific jargon than his contemporaries, and a slicker line in superscientific wizardry, but he began writing a different kind of sf as Don A. Stuart and subsequently abandoned writing altogether when it

clashed with his duties as editor of ASTOUNDING SCIENCE-FICTION. Williamson flavoured space opera with a more ancient brand of romanticism, basing characters in *The Legion of Space* (1934; rev **1947**) on the Three Musketeers and Falstaff; although he soon moved on to more sophisticated varieties of exotic adventure, he never quite abandoned space opera: *Bright New Universe* (**1967**) and *Lifeburst* (**1984**) carry forward the tradition, and his collaborations with Frederik POHL, such as *The Singers of Time* (**1991**), retain a deliberate but deft romanticism which places them among the best modern examples of the species. Another notable space opera from the 1930s is Clifford D. SIMAK's *Cosmic Engineers* (1939; rev **1950**).

During the 1940s some of the naïve charm of space opera was lost as standards of writing rose and plots became somewhat more complicated, and the trend was towards a more vivid and lush romanticism. Notable examples are *Judgement Night* (1943; title story of coll **1952**; separate publication **1965**) by C.L. MOORE and several works by A.E. VAN VOGT, including *The Mixed Men* (1943-5; fixup **1952**; cut vt *Mission to the Stars*) and *Earth's Last Fortress* (1942 as "Recruiting Station"; vt as title story of *Masters of Time* coll **1950**; **1960** dos). By this time the GALACTIC-EMPIRE scenario was being used for other purposes, most effectively by Isaac ASIMOV in the **Foundation** series (1942-50; fixups **1951-3**); by the 1950s it had become a standardized framework available for use in entirely serious sf. Once this happened, the impression of vast scale so important to space opera was no longer the sole prerogative of straightforward adventure stories, and the day of the "classical" space opera was done. But Asimov, like many others, retained a deep affection for old-fashioned romanticism, deploying it conscientiously in *The Stars Like Dust* (**1951**). Many of the more "realistic" space adventures of the 1950s incorporate space-operatic flourishes, including James BLISH's *Earthman Come Home* (1950-53; fixup **1955**), which features space battles between star-travelling cities – although the other novels in the **Okie** series have rather different priorities. The old-style space opera seemed rather juvenile by this time, but it remained an important component of the fiction published by the more downmarket pulps while they were still being published, especially PLANET STORIES and THRILLING WONDER STORIES. New life could still be breathed into it by the better writers associated with those magazines; prominent were Leigh BRACKETT, as in *The Starmen* (**1952**), and Jack VANCE, as in *The Space Pirate* (**1953**; cut vt *The Five Gold Bands*). There were DIGEST magazines which specialized in exotic adventure stories, including space operas – notably IMAGINATION and the 2nd of the 2 US magazines entitled SCIENCE FICTION ADVENTURES (which survived as a UK magazine for some years after its death in the USA) – but they did not long outlast the pulps. When it was abandoned by the magazines, space opera found a new home in the ACE BOOKS

Doubles ed Donald A. WOLLHEIM (*see also* DOS). Robert SILVERBERG published a good deal of colourful material in this format, including the trilogy assembled as *Lest We Forget Thee, Earth* (fixup **1958**) as by Calvin M. Knox, while Kenneth BULMER, John BRUNNER and E.C. TUBB became UK recruits to this largely US tradition, the last-named labouring to preserve it with his long-running **Dumarest** series.

Space-operatic romanticism is still widely evident, usually cleverly combined with other elements. Examples include Gordon R. DICKSON's long-running **Dorsai** series, Poul ANDERSON's **Ensign Flandry** series, H. Beam PIPER's *Space Viking* (**1963**), Michael MOORCOCK's *The Sundered Worlds* (fixup **1965**; vt *The Blood Red Game*), Ian WALLACE's *Croyd* (**1967**) and *Dr Orpheus* (**1968**), Samuel R. DELANY's *Nova* (**1968**), Alan Dean FOSTER's *The Tar-Aiym Krang* (**1972**) and its sequels, Barrington J. BAYLEY's *Star Winds* (**1978**), Philip José FARMER's *The Unreasoning Mask* (**1981**), S.P. SOMTOW's *Light on the Sound* (**1982**) and its sequels, F.M. BUSBY's *Star Rebel* (**1984**) and its sequels, Ben BOVA's *Privateers* (**1985**), Michael D. RESNICK's *Santiago* (**1986**), Iain M. BANKS's *Consider Phlebas* (**1987**) and other **Culture** novels, Colin GREENLAND's *Take Back Plenty* (**1990**) and Stephen R. DONALDSON's **Gap** series, begun with *The Gap into Conflict: The Real Story* (**1990**), which transfigures Wagner's Ring Cycle of *real* operas. It seems in no danger of losing its popularity, given the recent winning of Hugo awards by space operas like C.J. CHERRYH's *Downbelow Station* (**1981**), David BRIN's *Startide Rising* (**1983**) and Lois McMaster BUJOLD's *The Vor Game* (**1990**). The crudities of the subgenre are easily parodied by such comedies as Harry HARRISON's *Bill, the Galactic Hero* (**1965**) and *Star Smashers of the Galaxy Rangers* (**1973**), M. John HARRISON's *The Centauri Device* (**1974**) and Douglas ADAMS's **Hitch-Hiker** books, but the affection in which it is held defies total deflation – as evidenced by the much more recent **Bill, the Galactic Hero** series of SHARED-WORLD adventures. The tv series STAR TREK has given rise to a long-running series of spinoff novels, many of which are more space operatic than the studio budget ever permitted the tv scripts to be.

An excellent theme anthology is *Space Opera* (anth **1974**) ed Brian W. ALDISS; his *Galactic Empires* (anth 2 vols **1976**) is also relevant. [BS]

See also: FANTASTIC VOYAGES; SPACE FLIGHT.

SPACE PATROL 1. US tv serial (1950-55). ABC TV. Prod Mike Moser (1950-52), Helen Moser (1953-5), dir Dik Darley, starring Ed Kemmer, Lyn Osborn, Ken Mayer, Virginia Hewitt, Nina Bara. Written Norman Jolley. 210 25min episodes. B/w.

One of the many SPACE-OPERA serials on TELEVISION after CAPTAIN VIDEO, and possibly the first to feature FASTER-THAN-LIGHT travel to the stars, *SP* began as a 5-times-a-week 15min programme on local tv; soon after, it went on RADIO and network tv. The patrol leader was Commander Buzz Corry. Viewers were invited to "become space cadets of the SP" (join the fan club) and to buy special SP cosmic smoke guns,

etc. Like most such programmes of the time *SP* was transmitted live, and with some ad-libbing. Special effects were minimal, but a mild attempt was made to keep the stories scientifically plausible.

2. UK tv series (1963-4). National Interest Picture Production/Wonderama Productions. Created/written Roberta Leigh, prod Leigh and Arthur Provis, dir Frank Goulding. 2 seasons, 39 25-min episodes in all. This was a SPACE-OPERA series for children produced with animated puppets, not unlike the various **SuperMarionation** series made by Gerry ANDERSON, and indeed created by one of Anderson's former colleagues. Main characters were Captain Larry Dart, Slim the Venusian and Husky the Martian in the spacecraft *Galasphere 347*; also important were Haggerty the genius inventor and Gabblerdictum the Martian parrot. [PN]

SPACE PUBLICATIONS ◊ SPACE SCIENCE FICTION.

SPACE RAIDERS ◊ BATTLE BEYOND THE STARS; Roger CORMAN.

SPACE SCIENCE FICTION US DIGEST-size magazine. 8 issues May 1952-Sep 1953, published by Space Publications; ed Lester DEL REY. The most prolific contributor was del Rey himself, sometimes as Erik van Lhin or Philip St John. Notable stories included T.L. SHERRED's "Cue For Quiet" (May-July 1953) and Philip K. DICK's "Second Variety" (May 1953) and "The Variable Man" (Sep 1953). #8 began serialization of Poul ANDERSON's *Brain Wave* (as "The Escape"; **1954**), but it was not completed. All 8 issues were reprinted in the UK 1952-3, numbered but undated, published by the Archer Press, London. [BS]

SPACE SCIENCE FICTION MAGAZINE US DIGEST-size magazine. 2 issues, Spring and Aug 1957, published by the Republic Features Syndicate; ed Lyle Kenyon ENGEL, with much editorial work, uncredited, by Michael AVALLONE. The best story may have been John JAKES's "The Devil Spins a Sun-Dream" (Spring 1957). [BS/PN]

SPACESHIPS The suggestion that people might one day travel to the MOON inside a flying machine was first put forward seriously by John WILKINS in 1638. There had been cosmic voyages prior to that date, and there were to be many more thereafter (◊ FANTASTIC VOYAGES; SPACE FLIGHT), but few took the mechanics of the journey seriously enough to invest much imaginative effort in the design of credible vehicles. Edgar Allan POE's "The Unparalleled Adventure of One Hans Pfaall" (1835) has an afterword complaining about the failure of other writers to achieve verisimilitude, but Pfaall makes his journey by BALLOON, and Poe's assumption of the continuity of the atmosphere – a full 2 centuries after Torricelli had concluded that the Earth's atmosphere could extend upwards for only a few miles – is hardly scientific.

Jules VERNE's travellers in *De la terre à la lune* (**1865**; trans J.K. Hoyte as *From the Earth to the Moon* **1869** US) and its sequel, *Autour de la lune* (**1870**, both trans as *From the Earth to the Moon* **1873** UK) use a projectile fired from a gun rather than a vessel, and most of those who followed in his footsteps treated their vessels as facilitating devices, inventing various jargon terms to signify mysterious forces of propulsion. Percy GREG's spaceship in *Across the Zodiac* (**1880**) is powered by "apergy"; H.G. WELLS invented the antigravitic "Cavorite" for *The First Men in the Moon* (**1901**); John MASTIN's "airship" is borne into space by a "new gas" in *The Stolen Planet* (**1905**); and Garrett P. SERVISS's *A Columbus of Space* (1909; rev **1911**) employed an atomic powered "space-car". Because their means of propulsion were so often mysterious, spaceships in this period could easily assume the "perfect" spheroid shape of the heavenly bodies themselves; a notable example is in Robert CROMIE's *A Plunge into Space* (**1890**). When not round or bullet-shaped they tended to resemble flying submarines.

Spaceships were taken up in a big way by the early sf PULP MAGAZINES, and their visual image was dramatically changed. Frank R. PAUL and other contemporary illustrators (◊ ILLUSTRATION) showed a strong preference for bulbous machines like enormously bloated aeroplanes or rounded-off oceangoing liners with long rows of portholes. These were often shown with jets of flame or vapour gushing out behind, but this was as much to suggest speed as to indicate that the means of propulsion involved might be one or more ROCKETS; similarly, the slow process whereby hulls became streamlined and elegant fins appeared corresponded less to any realization of the importance of rocket-power than to the development of sleeker automobiles in the real world. Two of the more convincing early pulp-sf spaceships are featured in Otto Willi GAIL's *The Shot into Infinity* (**1925**; trans 1929; **1975**) and Laurence MANNING's "The Voyage of the *Asteroid*" (**1932**), but such stories were overshadowed by extravagant SPACE OPERAS which thrived on fantastic machines with limitless capabilities, fighting interstellar WARS with all manner of exotic WEAPONS the ultimate fulfilment of childhood fantasies. Classic examples include the various *Skylarks* employed by E.E. "Doc" SMITH's Richard Seaton and friends. Many pulp-sf writers still regarded spaceships as mere facilitating devices – Edgar Rice BURROUGHS was prepared to do without them in many of his interplanetary romances – but the pioneers of space opera exploited the fantasies of unlimited opportunity and luxurious seclusion which had hitherto been attached to such Earthly vessels as Captain Nemo's *Nautilus*, the Crystal Boat in Gordon STABLES's *The Cruise of the Crystal Boat* (**1891**) and the Golden Ship used in Max PEMBERTON's *The Iron Pirate* (**1897**). Outside the pulps, the hero of Friedrich W. MADER's *Distant Worlds* (**1921**; trans **1932**) declared that his spacefaring vessel was no mere "airship" but a *world-ship* with the freedom of the Universe.

By the 1930s writers of HARD SF had become convinced that the first real spaceships would be rockets, and stories about the large-scale projects required to build them were being written as early as Lester DEL REY's "The Stars Look Down" (1940); other notable examples include Arthur C. CLARKE's *Prelude to Space* (**1951**) and Gordon R. DICKSON's *The Far Call* (1973; exp **1978**). But dominance was always retained by naïve fantasies in which spaceships could be casually built in anyone's back yard, or in which their familiarity was simply taken for granted. Realistic stories of the building and launching of spaceships can still be written – *Manna* (**1984**) by Lee Correy (G. Harry STINE) is noteworthy – but we have now become so blasé about the spectacle of Saturn rockets blasting off from Cape Canaveral and space shuttles gliding down to land at Edwards Air Force Base that modern sf rarely bothers with matters of construction or with maiden voyages. Tense NEAR-FUTURE melodramas involving moderately advanced hardware can still be very suspenseful – *The Descent of Anansi* (**1982**) by Larry NIVEN and Steven BARNES is a good example – but the vast majority of sf stories look towards further horizons.

A different kind of realism was introduced into spaceship stories by Robert A. HEINLEIN in "Universe" (1941), which scorned the convenience of FASTER-THAN-LIGHT travel and established the archetypal image of the GENERATION STARSHIP. This notion – an ironic embodiment of the motto *per ardua ad astra* – quickly took over the sf version of the myth of the Ark, earlier displayed in such novels as *When Worlds Collide* (**1933**) by Philip WYLIE and Edwin BALMER. Notable later examples include Leigh BRACKETT's *Alpha Centauri – or Die!* (1953 as "The Ark of Mars"; exp **1963**) and Roger DIXON's *Noah II* (**1970**). The spaceship became a powerful symbol of permanent escape, invoked continually throughout the 1950s in stories of future tyranny and the struggles of oppressed minorities. The myth of escape is taken to its extreme in Poul ANDERSON's time-dilatation fantasy *Tau Zero* (1967; exp **1970**), the first of several stories in which the spaceship provides its human crew with a means to escape the end of the Universe. Such escape motifs are, however, opposed in stories of space disaster; two interesting stories which recast the voyage of the *Titanic* (1912) as sf are "The Star Lord" (1953) by Boyd Ellanby (William Boyd [1903-1983]) and "The *Corianis* Disaster" (1960) by Murray LEINSTER. Other stories developed the notion of far-travelling starships into the idea of a starship culture. Notable examples are Heinlein's *Citizen of the Galaxy* (**1957**) and Alexei PANSHIN's *Rite of Passage* (1963; exp **1968**). Relativistic effects were built into the idea of a starship culture in L. Ron HUBBARD's *Return to Tomorrow* (1950; **1954**), in which spacefarers become alienated from the course of history by the time-dilatation effect of travelling at near-lightspeed.

The UFO crazes of the post-WWII years made some impact on sf imagery in the magazines. Disc-shaped spaceships became more common in ILLUSTRATIONS, and the interest of editors Sam MERWIN Jr – who also wrote about flying saucers in "Centaurus" (1953) –

and Raymond A. PALMER was reflected in the magazines of which they had charge. Ufology had far more influence on the imagery of sf CINEMA, where saucer-shaped ships became commonplace. The sleekly streamlined ships which still dominated magazine illustration continued to hold their ground until the 1970s; when their imagery was finally challenged, it was by the bizarre and surreal hardware of artists like Eddie JONES and Christopher FOSS. This movement towards a more complicated topography – licensed by the knowledge that starships built in space for journeys in hard vacuum had no need of streamlining – had been foreshadowed in fiction since the 1950s. Among the more romantic spaceships featured in the later years of magazine sf are those in Cordwainer SMITH's **Instrumentality** stories, which include the light-powered "sailing ships" in "The Lady who Sailed the *Soul*" (1960) and "Think Blue, Count Two" (1963) (◊ SOLAR WIND). The tree-grown starships of Jack WILLIAMSON's *Dragon's Island* (1951; vt *The Not-Men*) and the animal-drawn starships of Robert Franson's *The Shadow of the Ship* (1983) are among the most curious in sf.

The men who sail or fly in them often refer to ships and aircraft as "she", crediting them with personalities and giving them names. Much sf transplants this tendency in perfectly straightforward terms, but other stories carry it to its logical and literal extreme. Human brains are frequently transplanted into spaceship bodies to become functional CYBORGS, as in Thomas N. SCORTIA's "Sea Change" (1956; vt "The Shores of Night"), Anne MCCAFFREY's *The Ship who Sang* (coll of linked stories 1969), Cordwainer Smith's "Three to a Given Star" (1965) and Kevin O'DONNELL Jr's *Mayflies* (1979). Other spaceships acquire intelligence and personality in their own right thanks to their sophisticated COMPUTER networks; the one in Frank HERBERT's *Destination: Void* (1966) has delusions of godlike grandeur, and the one in Clifford D. SIMAK's *Shakespeare's Planet* (1976) has a multiply split personality. More often, though, the relationship between humans and spaceships maintains a traditional naval rigour, as in many novels by the Merchant Navy writer A. Bertram CHANDLER, *Starman Jones* (1953) by ex-US Navy officer Robert Heinlein and *The Mote in God's Eye* (1974) by Larry Niven and Jerry E. POURNELLE.

Sf stories whose subject matter is the spaceship MYTHOLOGY built up by their predecessors include Stanisław LEM's *Niezwyciezony* (1964; trans as *The Invincible* 1973) and Mark GESTON's *Lords of the Starship* (1967). The idea that the spaceship owes much of its charisma to phallic symbolism has been much bandied about – as reflected in Virgil FINLAY's cover for the Oct 1963 issue of WORLDS OF TOMORROW, Kurt VONNEGUT Jr's "The Big Space Fuck" (1972) and Norman SPINRAD's *The Void Captain's Tale* (1983) – but a more convincing analogy would liken spaceships to the "sperms" of sea-dwelling creatures which require no intromission (and hence no phallus) but are simply released into an oceanic wilderness to seek out the object of their fertilizing mission. This is the metaphor contained in such novels as Jack Williamson's *Manseed* (fixup 1982). The spaceship is still commonly deployed as a straightforward facilitating device – a means to send ordinary near-contemporary characters into exotic and fabulous situations – but even in this role it can become as charismatic as STAR TREK's Starship *Enterprise*. The terminal decline in the plausibility of the home-made spaceship in the face of the magnitude and complexity of the actual space programme has to some extent been compensated for by the remarkable frequency with which sf characters serendipitously discover ALIEN spaceships; a notable example is Frederik POHL's *Gateway* (1977) and its sequels. Alien starships are sometimes invested with even more mystique than those constructed by humans; notable examples include those whose one-time arrival on Earth is revealed in Ivan YEFREMOV's "Stellar Ships" (trans 1954) and the gargantuan vessel featured in Arthur C. Clarke's *Rendezvous with Rama* (1973). Awesome alien spaceships provide stirring climaxes for such films as CLOSE ENCOUNTERS OF THE THIRD KIND (1977) and *The* ABYSS (1989), but they can also perform a much more sinister role, as in Stephen KING's novel *The Tommyknockers* (1988).

The power of the sf mythology of the spaceship was made evident by the decision to bow to public pressure and name one of the experimental space shuttles, constructed in 1977, the *Enterprise*.   [BS]

SPACESHIP TO THE UNKNOWN ◊ FLASH GORDON.

SPACE STORIES US PULP magazine. 5 bimonthly issues Oct 1952-June 1953, published by Standard Magazines as a companion to STARTLING STORIES *et al.*; ed Samuel MINES. Its policy, identical to that of *Startling Stories*, was to feature a complete novel in every issue; the most notable was *The Big Jump* (Feb 1953; **1955**) by Leigh BRACKETT.   [BS]

SPACE TRAVEL ◊ GENERATION STARSHIPS; ROCKETS; SPACE FLIGHT; SPACESHIPS; TRANSPORTATION.

SPACE TRAVEL Magazine. ◊ IMAGINATIVE TALES.

SPACE WARP In sf TERMINOLOGY, a concept similar to that of hyperspace and subspace. The term (along with "hyperspace") may first have been used by John W. CAMPBELL Jr in *Islands of Space* (1931 *Amazing Stories Quarterly*; **1957**). If a handkerchief is folded, two otherwise separated points of it can become adjacent; if space – more accurately, spacetime – could be warped in like style (which it cannot), the resulting short cut would effectively enable SPACESHIPS to travel FASTER THAN LIGHT: the topic is discussed further in HYPERSPACE. Space warp has become such a CLICHÉ in sf that it allows endless variants. One of the best known is the "warp factor" used in STAR TREK as a measure of velocity. This is illogical on all levels.

The idea of ANTIGRAVITY is also connected with the warping of space: since GRAVITY (or a gravitational field) is an effect dependent on the curving (or warping) of spacetime in the presence of mass, then antigravity could be envisaged as what would happen if you contrived to warp space the other way, an idea proposed by Charles Eric MAINE in *Count-Down* (**1959**; vt *Fire Past the Future* 1959 US). This is actually a development of that same idea proposed by Campbell in *Islands in Space*; Campbell correctly recognized that to warp spacetime would not only alter gravitational fields but be equivalent to altering the velocity of light. Maine's negative space curvature is anyway impossible, since it would require the existence of negative mass, an existence prohibited on several theoretical grounds. [PN]

SPACEWAY US DIGEST-size magazine, 8 issues Dec 1953-June 1955, 12 issues in all, published by William L. CRAWFORD's FPCI in Los Angeles; the subtitle "Stories of the Future" was changed to "Science Fiction" Dec 1954. The title was taken from the UK film SPACEWAYS (1953). When *S* died it had published only the first part of Ralph Milne FARLEY's "Radio Minds of Mars"; on its resurrection by the same publisher many years later to publish 4 more issues, Jan 1969-June 1970, it printed the serial in full. This new version of *S* reprinted material from the first, but added a few new stories. The most notable story carried by the magazine was "The Cosmic Geoids" by John TAINE (Dec 1954-Apr 1955), though this had already been published in book form, by the same publisher, as the lead novel of *The Cosmic Geoids, and One Other* (coll **1949**). An unfinished serial in the 2nd version of *S* was Andre NORTON's "Garan of Yu-Lac", which Crawford had been holding since 1935; he later published it in book form as *Garan the Eternal* (**1972**). #1-#4 were reprinted in the UK 1954-5 by Regular Publications. [BS/PN]

SPACEWAYS Film (1953). Hammer/Exclusive. Dir Terence Fisher, starring Howard Duff, Eva Bartok, Alan Wheatley, Andrew Osborn. Screenplay Paul TABORI, Richard Landau, based on a 1952 radio play by Charles Eric MAINE. 76 mins. B/w.

In this first UK space movie since THINGS TO COME (1936) a scientist falsely suspected of murdering his wife and placing her body in a satellite takes a space trip to establish his innocence. This is an early, low-budget Hammer melodrama of indifferent quality. Maine's novel *Spaceways: A Story of the Very Near Future* (**1953**; vt *Spaceways Satellite* 1958 US), also based on the radio play, appeared the same year as the film. [JB/PN]

SPACE-WISE UK BEDSHEET-size magazine. 3 issues, Dec 1969, Jan and Mar 1970, published by the Martec Publishing Group; ed Derek R. Threadgall. *SW* contained a mixture of sf and science and occult articles which proved not viable. [FHP]

SPAIN Modern sf appeared in Spain during the 1950s with the publishing imprint Minotauro and the magazine *Más Allá* (1953-7), both from Argentina (◊ LATIN AMERICA). Spanish sf editions began in 1953, with pulp novelettes in the **Futuro** and **Luchadores del Espacio** series, followed by **Nebulae**, the first specialized Spanish imprint for sf books. During 1955-90 about 1300 sf books were published in Spain,

mostly translations from English, with only about 50 by Spanish authors.

Before the Civil War, Coronel Ignotus (the pseudonym of José de Elola), Frederic Pujulà, Elias Cerdá and Domingo Ventalló were the most important authors of old-fashioned speculations and fantasies, mainly satirical and sometimes political. Ignotus was published in one of the earliest quasi-sf MAGAZINES in the world, earlier than any in the USA or UK: *Biblioteca Novelesco-Cientifica* (1921-3), each of whose 10 issues containing a single novel by Ignotus, 3 featuring interplanetary voyages. In the 1950s George H. White (pseudonym of Pascual Enguídanos) wrote a series of 32 sf adventure novelettes known collectively as the **Saga de los Aznar** ["Aznar Saga"] series (1953-8). More interesting are subsequent stories in the 1950s and 1960s by Antonio Ribera, Francisco Valverde, Juan G. Atienza, Domingo Santos, Carlos Buiza and Luis Vigil (1940-   ); it was with these that modern Spanish sf really began.

The 1960s saw the first boom in sf publishing in Spain. After the short life of the magazine *Anticipación* (1966-7), the most influential of all Spanish sf magazines began: *Nueva Dimensión*, founded in 1968, ed Sebastián Martínez (1937-   ), Domingo Santos and Luis Vigil; it was voted the best European sf magazine at the 1972 Eurocon in Trieste. A real milestone in Spanish sf, *ND* published local authors alongside the best sf from other countries. It lasted 148 issues, until Dec 1983.

Incursions into sf have also been made by writers who normally work outside the genre, such as Tomás Salvador (1921-   ), whose *La nave* ["The Ship"] (**1959**) is a reworking of the popular GENERATION-STARSHIP theme, and Manuel de Pedrolo (1918-1990), who had a big success with his novel written in Catalan, *Mecanoscrit del segon origen* ["Mechanuscript of the Second Origin"] (**1974**), about life after a world HOLOCAUST.

Domingo Santos – the pseudonym of Pedro Domingo Mutiñó (1941-   ) – is the major contemporary Spanish sf writer. Some of his stories and novels have been translated into several foreign languages. His best known novel is *Gabriel, historia de un robot* ["Gabriel, The Story of a Robot"] (**1963**), about the personality and coming of age of a ROBOT not subject to the "fundamental laws" that compel other robots to obedience. Another interesting novel is *Burbuja* ["Bubble"] (**1965**), but the best of Santos is found in his short fiction. *Meteoritos* ["Meteorites"] (coll **1965**) is a classic collection, but more demanding are the stories in *Futuro imperfecto* ["Future Imperfect"] (coll **1981**) and *No lejos de la Tierra* ["Not Far from Earth"] (coll **1986**), set in the NEAR FUTURE and often concerned with ECOLOGY and the threats that endanger the quality of our lives.

In the 1970s Gabriel Bermúdez Castillo (1934-   ) appeared with well written books such as *Viaje a un planeta Wu-Wei* ["Travel to a Wu-Wei Planet"] (**1976**) and action-adventure novels like *El señor de la rueda*

["The Lord of the Wheel"] (**1978**). Carlos Saiz Cidoncha (1939-) has specialized in SPACE OPERA, and in 1976 also privately published the first history of Spanish sf; this was the embryo of his 1988 PhD thesis, the first in Spain on such a topic.

The political changes following Franco's death in 1975 appear to have had no effect on sf publishing. Sf in Spain has always had a restricted market, perhaps too small to bother with. Its only political censorship under Franco may have been the prohibition in 1970 of *Nueva Dimension* #14, which contained a story by an Argentinian that appeared to advocate Basque separatism.

A second boom in sf publishing took place in the 1980s, and more new authors appeared, the most gifted perhaps being Elia Barceló (1957-). Her novelette "La Dama Dragón" ["The Dragon Lady"] (1982) has been translated into several foreign languages and is collected in *Sagrada* (coll **1990**), the title being the feminine form of the word for "sacred". The first Spanish woman to publish an sf book, Barceló is a very good stylist in a country where the usual style of sf writing precludes it from consideration by more demanding literary critics. Her stories are concerned with women's role in society and with the contrast between technological and primitive cultures. Other new authors are Rafael Marín Trechera (1959-) with *Lágrimas de Luz* ["Tears of Light"] (**1982**), an interstellar epic, and the collaboration of Javier Redal (1952-) and Juan Miguel Aguilera (1960-) in a modern HARD-SF space opera, *Mundos en al abismo* ["Worlds in the Abyss"] (**1988**), an unusually science-conscious book for Spain. Ángel Torres Quesada (1940-) specializes in sf adventure, as in his trilogy *Las islas del infierno* ["The Hell Islands"] (**1989**).

1991 saw a reduction of sf publishing in Spain, and the disappearance of one imprint, Ultramar. Only one sf book by a Spanish author appeared, *La dama de plata* ["The Silver Lady"] (**1991**), an sf adventure by Quesada. But the same year saw the resurrection of sf CONVENTIONS with Hispacon 91, and the announcement of the "Premia UPC de novela corta de ciencia ficción" ["UPC Prize for Short Sf Novel"], an sf award for best novella, sponsored by the university UPC (Universitat Politécnica de Catalunya); the 1st award was shared by Rafael Marín Trechera and Ángel Torres Quesada.

The Spanish cinema is very much stronger on horror than sf. The two genres are married in some films dir Jesús Franco, and in *El caballero del Dragón* ["Star Knight"] (1986) dir Fernando Colomo.

A book about sf in Spain is *Ciencia ficción: Guía de lectura* ["Science Fiction Reader's Guide"] (**1990**) by Miquel BARCELÓ. [MB/MJ]

SPANNER, E(DWARD) F(RANK) (1888-?) UK writer and naval architect, author of 3 future-WAR novels – *The Broken Trident* (**1926**), *The Naviators* (**1926**) and *The Harbour of Death* (**1927**) – in all of which the UK is warned to beware remaining unduly dependent upon her navy; the dire consequences of so doing are dramatized in imaginary conflicts with – presciently – both Germany and Japan. [JC]

SPARKROCK, FRED ◊ Robert E. VARDEMAN.

SPARTACUS, DEUTERO ◊ R.L. FANTHORPE.

SPECIAL BULLETIN Made-for-tv film (1983). NBC. Dir Edward Zwick, starring Christopher Allport, David Clennon, Ed Flanders, Kathryn Walker, David Rasche. Screenplay Marshall Herskovitz. 92 mins. Colour.

An unnervingly effective pseudodocumentary, this presents itself as tv coverage of an escalating terrorist crisis in Charleston, where a dissident group of nuclear scientists and peace activists threatens to set off an atomic bomb in the dockyard unless all the nuclear weapons in the region are turned over to them for dumping. With cutaways to White House spokesmen lying, conflicting reports from political correspondents, interviews with experts, on-the-spot reports, ranting demands from the terrorists and hastily assembled background profiles on the offenders, *SB* is a fine recreation of a now-familiar style of tv coverage, and in a surprisingly rigorous manner examines the MEDIA influencing the atrocities they purport to cover. The glimpses at the end of the detonation of the bomb – a defusing attempt is bungled – are perhaps more effective than the special-effects holocausts of *The* DAY AFTER (1983) and THREADS (1984), and the final moments, in which other news issues creep into the schedule, are understated but cutting. [KN]

SPECULATION UK FANZINE ed Peter WESTON from Birmingham 1963-73. Averaging 60pp, *S* was for many years consistently the UK's best amateur magazine of comment and criticism. Regular contributors included James BLISH, Kenneth BULMER, M. John HARRISON, Michael MOORCOCK and Frederik POHL. Several fans whose writing often appeared in *S* later became sf writers, Christopher PRIEST and Brian M. STABLEFORD among them. The final issue, #33, though printed 1973, was not distributed until 1976. [PN]

SPECULATIVE FICTION Term used by some writers and critics in place of "science fiction". In the symposium published as *Of Other Worlds* (coll **1947**) ed Lloyd Arthur ESHBACH, Robert A. HEINLEIN proposed the term to describe a subset of sf involving extrapolation from known science and technology "to produce a new situation, a new framework for human action". Judith MERRIL borrowed the term in 1966, spelling out her version of "speculative fiction" in rather more detail (◊ DEFINITIONS OF SF) in such a way as to de-emphasize the science component of sf (which acronym can equally stand for "speculative fiction") while keeping the idea of extrapolation – i.e., Merril's use of the term was useful for that kind of sociological sf which concentrates on social change without necessarily any great emphasis on science or TECHNOLOGY. Since then the term has generally appealed to writers and readers who are as interested in SOFT SF as in HARD SF. Though the term has proved attractive to many, especially perhaps academics who find the term more respectable-sounding than "science fiction" and lacking the pulp associations, nobody's definition of "speculative fiction" has as yet any formal rigour, though the term has come to be used with a very wide application (as by Samuel R. DELANY in his ORIGINAL-ANTHOLOGY series QUARK), as if science fiction were a subset of speculative fiction rather than *vice versa*. Because the term "speculative fiction", as now most often used, does not clearly define any generic boundary, it has come to include not only soft and hard sf but also FANTASY as a whole. Many critics do not find it a consistently helpful term but, as Gary K. WOLFE points out in *Critical Terms for Science Fiction and Fantasy* (**1986**), critics tend to worry more about the demarcation of genres than writers do, and, as a propaganda weapon, the term has been useful precisely *because* it allows the blurring of boundaries, which in turn permits a greater auctorial freedom from genre constraints and "rules".   [PN]

SPENCE, CATHERINE HELEN (1825-1910) Scottish-born Australian novelist whose *Handfasted* (written *c*1879; **1984**), a UTOPIA with LOST-WORLD elements set in the hidden state of Columba somewhere in Southern California, may have remained unpublished at the time because of its FEMINIST views on women's autonomy; the title refers to a traditional form of trial marriage, and in Columba single mothers are not treated as pariahs. More impressively, *A Week in the Future* (1888-9 *Centennial Magazine*; **1987**) takes its heroine by SUSPENDED ANIMATION to the SOCIALIST utopia that London has become in 1988. In her later years, CHS fought for women's suffrage.   [JC]

See also: AUSTRALIA.

SPENCER, JOHN (BARRY) (1944-   ) UK writer, rock musician and one-time art-agency director, founding what would become Young Artists, a major UK agency for preponderantly sf/fantasy artists. His first sf novel, *The Electronic Lullaby Meat Market* (**1975**), in a manner somewhat reminiscent of Mick FARREN sets a quirky thriller in a violently hyperbolic NEAR-FUTURE world described in sex-charged terms reminiscent of the late-1960s counterculture. After editing *Echoes of Terror* (anth **1980** chap) with Mike Jarvis, JS returned to sf with *A Case for Charley* (**1985**) and *Charley Gets the Picture* (**1986**), two idiosyncratic murder mysteries set after the HOLOCAUST, when Nevada and Arizona have been destroyed by earthquakes and California has been rebuilt as a vast tourist centre. He is not to be confused with the John Spencer (1946-   ) who illustrated a number of fantasy/folklore juveniles in the early 1970s, nor with the publisher John Spencer (◊ BADGER BOOKS).   [JC/JGr]

See also: MUSIC.

SPENCER, LEONARD G. ZIFF-DAVIS house name used once by Robert SILVERBERG and Randall GARRETT in collaboration on "The Beast With 7 Tails" (*AMZ* 1956), and twice by unknown writers, 1956-7.   [PN]

SPIDER, THE US PULP MAGAZINE. 118 issues Oct 1933-Dec 1943; monthly until Feb 1943, bimonthly thereafter. Published by Popular Publications; ed Rogers Terrill until near the end. *TS*, one of the hero/villain pulps, began as a straightforward imitation of the highly successful *The Shadow*, telling of a mysterious caped avenger. The first 2 novels were by R.T.M. Scott; the remainder, credited to the house name Grant STOCKBRIDGE, were all by Norvell W. PAGE. Under Page's guidance, the Spider became a more ruthless character who stamped a spider sign on the foreheads of the villains he killed, and the menaces he combated became more fantastic, including a metal-eating virus and Neanderthal hordes (the 2 novels concerned were reprinted as *The City Destroyer* [1935; **1975**] and *Hordes of the Red Butcher* [1935; **1975**]). *TS* also contained short stories, including the non-sf **Doc Turner** series by Arthur Leo ZAGAT. The character later featured in a cinema serial, *The Spider's Web* (1938; 15 episodes, Columbia, starring Robert E. Kent). Since 1969 further novels have been reprinted in book form (◊ Norvell W. PAGE *for details*).   [MJE/FHP/PN]

SPIELBERG, STEVEN (1947-   ) US film-maker. Born in Cincinnati, raised in Arizona and an amateur film-maker in his early teens, SS completed his first sf feature – the 140min *Firelight* (1963) – at the age of 16; he studied English rather than film at college in California. His first professional film was *Amblin'* (1969), a slick short about hitch-hiking which was distributed as a support feature with the very successful *Love Story* (1970); it secured SS a contract with Universal Pictures' tv division. His tv début was a segment of the 1969 pilot for ROD SERLING'S NIGHT GALLERY, starring Joan Crawford; in 1971 he made *LA 2019*, an sf-themed episode of **The Name of the Game** (1968-71), and went on to tv features: *Columbo: Murder by the Book* (1971), *Something Evil* (1972), a ghost story, and *Savage* (1972), a high-tech thriller. He first attracted widespread attention with *Duel* (1971), a suspenseful tv adaptation of Richard MATHESON's horror story about a motorist pursued by a vindictive petrol tanker.

Duel was successfully released overseas as a movie, with 15 extra minutes of characterization to bring it up to feature length, and it led to SS's first theatrical feature, *The Sugarland Express* (1974), and to the enormously successful assignment of the MONSTER MOVIE *Jaws* (1975), a box-office rollercoaster about the hunting of a giant shark. After *Jaws*, in which SS had little script involvement, he opted for a more personal and visionary film, CLOSE ENCOUNTERS OF THE THIRD KIND (1977), which managed on the strength of its extraordinary climactic vision of an alien epiphany to become another major box-office success, despite a lopsided story and an unevenness of tone SS himself tried in vain to rectify in his revision of the material, CLOSE ENCOUNTERS OF THE THIRD KIND – THE SPECIAL EDITION (1980). The novelization *Close Encounters of the Third Kind* * (**1977**; rev vt *Close Encounters of the Third Kind: The Special Edition* 1980) was published as by SS.

After the critically vilified *1941* (1979), SS made a solid return to popular acceptance with the George LUCAS-produced *Raiders of the Lost Ark* (1981), a tribute to the Saturday matinee serials of the 1940s, and then scored a phenomenal hit with E.T.: THE EXTRATERRESTRIAL (1982), which currently stands as the most commercially successful film of all time. Sciencefictional in its subject matter but a fairy-tale in feeling, it tells of a child's miraculous friend who happens to be an ALIEN. Since that career high SS has made two **Raiders** sequels – *Indiana Jones and the Temple of Doom* (1984) and *Indiana Jones and the Last Crusade* (1989) – in between more ambitious, less obviously box-office pictures, adaptations of novels by Alice WALKER and J.G. BALLARD, respectively *The Color Purple* (1985) and *Empire of the Sun* (1987), and the wistful fantasy *Always* (1990). His long-awaited but disappointing homage to Disney's *Peter Pan* (1953) was *Hook* (1991), a lumbering and sentimental rendition of a fantasy that should have had a certain delicacy in its otherworldliness.

In addition to his work as a director, SS has shown a commitment to genre material in his work as a producer, coproducing and directing episodes of *Twilight Zone: The Movie* (1983) and the tv series AMAZING STORIES (1985-7). He has done much to further the careers of fellow film-makers Joe DANTE, Robert Zemeckis and Frank Marshall, and has coproduced, usually as Executive Producer through his Amblin Entertainment group, a wide variety of sf, fantasy and horror productions, including *Poltergeist* (1982), *Gremlins* (1984), *The Goonies* (1985), BACK TO THE FUTURE (1985), *Young Sherlock Holmes* (1985; vt *Young Sherlock Holmes and the Pyramid of Fear*), *An American Tail* (1986), HARRY AND THE HENDERSONS (1987; vt *Bigfoot and the Hendersons*), INNERSPACE (1987), *BATTERIES NOT INCLUDED (1987), *Who Framed Roger Rabbit* (1988), *The Land Before Time* (1988), BACK TO THE FUTURE PART II (1989), BACK TO THE FUTURE PART III (1989), *Gremlins 2: The New Batch* (1990), *Joe vs the Volcano* (1990), ARACHNOPHOBIA (1990), *An American Tail II* (1991) and *Cape Fear* (1991).

Unashamedly populist and sentimental – although not without a gleefully nasty side, as seen in *Jaws*, *Poltergeist* and *Gremlins* – SS has proved himself unquestionably the most commercially successful film-maker of all time, dominating the box office for 16 years with a succession of hits that make up for the occasional *1941*. A skilled and in many ways sophisticated director, he is, despite his incredible success, still young enough and powerful enough to be labelled "promising". [KN]

See also: CINEMA; HISTORY OF SF; STEAMPUNK; TELEVISION; UFOS.

SPINDIZZY One of the best-loved items of sf TERMINOLOGY. The spindizzy is the ANTIGRAVITY device used to drive flying cities through the Galaxy in James BLISH's series collected as *Cities in Flight* (coll **1970**). He gave the spindizzy a wonderfully plausible rationale, rooted in theoretical physics, in which GRAVITY fields

are seen as generated or cancelled by rotation. [PN]

SPIN-OFF ◊ TIE.

SPINRAD, NORMAN (RICHARD) (1940-   ) US writer, born in New York – where he has set some impressive fiction – and now resident in France. He began publishing sf with "The Last of the Romany" for *ASF* in 1963, which he assembled with other early work in *The Last Hurrah of the Golden Horde* (coll **1970**), the title story being among the most successful of the attempts made by divers authors to write a tale using the characters and Universe of Michael MOORCOCK's **Jerry Cornelius** series. The story was originally published in *NW*, to which NS was a significant contributor during the 1960s, when both the US and UK NEW-WAVE movements, though with different emphases (the UK form tending more selfconsciously to assimilate MAINSTREAM modes like Surrealism), argued against traditional sf, which had failed to use the hard sciences to explore INNER SPACE, regarded as the proper territory of all genuinely serious writing. After publishing two commercial SPACE OPERAS – *The Solarians* (**1966**) and *Agent of Chaos* (**1967**) – NS subsequently kept faith with that brief and the ethos which generated it.

The Men in the Jungle (**1967**) – which subjects its tough, urban protagonist to a complex set of Realpolitik adventures on a distant planet – demonstrates the vigour and occasionally slapdash bravado of what would become NS's typical style; but it was with his next book, *Bug Jack Barron* (**1969**), that he made his greatest impact on the sheltered world of sf. This long novel was first serialized in a shorter form in NEW WORLDS (1967-8), where its violent texture and profanity rattled the excitable dovecotes of the UK "moral establishment", leading directly to the banning of the magazine by W.H. Smith, a newsagency chain so huge that its action was tantamount to censorship. The equally risible parochialism of the sf world, when confronted by this not particularly shocking novel, was demonstrated by Sam J. LUNDWALL in his *Science Fiction: What It's All About* (**1969**; trans exp **1971**), where he described and dismissed the book as "practically a collection of obscenities". The novel itself, whose language does not fully conceal a certain sentimentality, deals with a NEAR-FUTURE USA through tv figure Jack Barron and his involvement in a politically corrupt system: the resulting picture of the USA as a hyped, SEX-obsessed, apocalyptic world made the text seem less sf than FABULATION, where this sort of vision is common. The sledgehammer style matched, at points, the content.

In NS's next novel, *The Iron Dream* (**1972**), the intention to offend was gratifyingly explicit. An ALTERNATE WORLD in which Hitler, thwarted as a politician, must make do with being an author of popular fiction is the frame for a long sf tale from his feverish pen, "Lord of the Swastika". This makes up most of the novel's text and gives NS the opportunity to mock – effectively if at times unrelentingly – some of the less attractive tendencies of right-wing sf, its fetish with gear, its fascist love of hierarchical display, its philistinism, its brutishness, its not entirely secret contempt for the people its HEROES defend. The "Afterword" by "Homer Whipple" just as hilariously guys the kind of critical writing generated by publish-or-perish academics. NS then released 2 further collections – *No Direction Home* (coll **1975**) and *The Star-Spangled Future* (coll **1979**), the latter an adroitly shaped compilation of his first 2 collections – which concisely demonstrate the range of his response to the complexities of a rapidly changing Western world. From this point, that world dominated – as metaphor or in realistic depiction – his work. In *A World Between* (**1979**) the citizens of a UTOPIAN world deal with strident threats to their middle way from technophile fascists of the right and lesbian fascists of the left. *The Mind Game* (**1980**; vt *The Process* 1983), not sf, savagely treats a manipulative "church" whose dictates and cynicism are of a sort familiar to sf readers, and the later *The Childen of Hamelin* (**1991**), likewise not sf, deals with contemporary people trapped in a cult. The post-HOLOCAUST *Songs from the Stars* (**1980**) opposes a restrictive "black" technological rule with an uplift message from a soaring galactic civilization.

NS's best 1980s novel was perhaps *The Void Captain's Tale* (**1983**) which, with its thematic partner *Child of Fortune* (**1985**), comprises what one might call an eroticized vision of the Galaxy. The SPACESHIP in the first tale is driven by Eros, in a very explicit sense; and the female protagonist of the second fertilizes – at least symbolically – all she touches in her elated *Wanderjahr* among the sparkling worlds. *Little Heroes* (**1987**) is set in a nightmarish urban near-future USA, divided into haves and ruthlessly manipulated havenots; the plot turns on a combination of technology-fixing and co-optation that cuts close to the bone, though by this date NS's weary rage had begun to lose some of its purgative bite. However, the 4 novellas about the state of the USA assembled in *Other Americas* (coll **1988**) show a recovery of NS's urban venom about the self-devouring progress of his native land into the millennium; and *Russian Spring* (**1991**), set in a near-future world dominated by a USSR liberated by *perestroika*, again voluminously anatomizes the American Dream, though the effect of the book was muffled by the real-life collapse of the USSR in 1991.

Two nonfiction collections – *Staying Alive: A Writer's Guide* (coll **1983**) and *Science Fiction in the Real World* (coll **1990**) – make even more explicit some of his bleak assumptions about the course of the world to which he so vehemently belongs. [JC]

Other works: *Passing through the Flame* (**1975**), not sf; *Riding the Torch* (in *Threads of Time* [anth **1974**]; **1978** dos).

As editor: *The New Tomorrows* (anth **1971**); *Modern Science Fiction* (anth **1974**).

Nonfiction: *Experiment Perilous: Three Essays on Science Fiction* (coll **1976** chap) ed Andrew PORTER; *The Reasons behind the SFWA Model Paperback Contract* (**1978** chap).

See also: CLONES; CRITICAL AND HISTORICAL WORKS ABOUT SF; CYBERPUNK; DEFINITIONS OF SF; DESTINIES; ECOLOGY; END OF THE WORLD; ENTROPY; FANTASTIC VOYAGES; FASTER THAN LIGHT; GAMES AND SPORTS; HITLER WINS; IMMORTALITY; ISAAC ASIMOV'S SCIENCE FICTION MAGAZINE; MEDIA LANDSCAPE; MEDICINE; MUSIC; MUTANTS; PARANOIA; PERCEPTION; POLITICS; POLLUTION; PSYCHOLOGY; SATIRE; SCIENCE FICTION WRITERS OF AMERICA; SUN; SWORD AND SORCERY; TECHNOLOGY; WAR.

SPIRITUALISM ◊ ESCHATOLOGY.

SPITTEL, OLAF R. [r] ◊ GERMANY.

SPITZ, JACQUES (1896-1963) French writer whose first sf novel of interest, *L'agonie du globe* (**1935**; trans Margaret Mitchiner as *Sever the Earth* 1936 UK), describes the consequences attendant upon the splitting of the planet into two halves 50 miles (80km) apart. In *La Guerre des mouches* ["War of the Flies"] (**1938**) mutated flies defeat humanity, keeping alive only a few abject specimens, one of whom tells the tale. The SCIENTIST protagonist of *L'Homme élastique* ["The Elastic Man"] (**1938**) discovers a method of compressing atoms, allowing him (on request) to create an army of tiny soldiers, who turn out to be examples of *Homo superior* (◊ SUPERMAN). In *L'Oeil du purgatoire* ["The Eye of Purgatory"] (**1945**) a mad scientist develops a bacillus which, when injected into the protagonist, allows (or forces) him to see the future wherever he looks – a condition which becomes purgatorial as he sees deeper and deeper into the destinies of those around him, until eventually he is capable of perceiving little more than corpses. [JC]

See also: FRANCE.

SPLATTER MOVIES Term used by 1980s movie-goers to describe films that display gore, disembowelment and mutilation as a central feature. Many exploitation films of the 1970s and 1980s fall into this category, including such fringe sf/HORROR movies as BAD TASTE (1987), DAY OF THE DEAD (1985), RE-ANIMATOR (1985) and *The* THING (1982 remake). By no means all such films are bad, though all may be ethically suspect in their apparent appeal to sadistic voyeurism. [PN]

SPLIT PERSONALITY ◊ PARANOIA; PSYCHOLOGY.

SPLIT SECOND Film (1991). Challenge. Dir Tony Maylam, Ian Sharp, starring Rutger Hauer, Kim Cattrall, Neil Duncan, Michael J. Pollard, Alun Armstrong, Pete Postlethwaite, Ian Dury. Screenplay by Gary Scott Thompson. 91 mins. Colour.

London, AD2008. The Thames has risen and society is crumbling. Coffee-drinking hard man Hauer and comics-reading Scots intellectual Duncan are brawling buddy cops on the trail of a heart-eating villain who carves astrological symbols on what's left of his victims' chests. Proposed solutions include mutant DNA and the Devil, but in the finale the baddie turns out to be a regulation ALIEN-style Big Monster With Teeth who confronts Hauer on a tube train. Inexplicable events, disappearing characters and logical lapses abound. Maylam, who directs this sf SPLATTER

MOVIE at a rapid plod, establishes a Drowned World atmosphere by pouring water into all the sets and painting everything grey; Sharp took over for the action climax. Despite the murkiness of this future world, Hauer stays cool in sunglasses; Duncan's enthusiastic performance offers the sole touch of character. [KN]

SPORTS ◊ GAMES AND SPORTS.

SPRAGUE, CARTER [s] ◊ Sam MERWIN Jr.

SPRIGEL, OLIVIER ◊ Pierre BARBET.

SPRUILL, STEVEN G(REGORY) (1946-   ) US writer and psychologist. In his first sf novel, *Keepers of the Gate* (**1977**; rev **1978**), a complicated adventure tale rather in the mode of Keith LAUMER, the alien Proteps of Eridani turn out to be an advanced form of *Homo sapiens*, and have been suppressing mankind's urge to the stars for selfish reasons; the generic cues for revelling in such a tale are deployed with some competence. He is best known for his **Elias Kane** sequence – even the protagonist's name seems to be a homage to Isaac ASIMOV's earlier detective Elijah Bailey – about an intelligently moody detective and his superpowered sidekick: *The Psychopath Plague* (**1978**), *The Imperator Plot* (**1982**) and *Paradox Planet* (**1988**). The series seems incomplete; but, although a template interminability attends Kane's repeated assignments, granted him by the current Imperator who rules Earth and several colonies, the passage of time is clearly marked throughout: the woman Kane falls in love with and marries in the 1st vol – whose deadly plague has been induced by aliens – is murdered in the 2nd; and the Imperator who is beheaded, but remains alive, in the 2nd – which concerns this attempted assassination – has been succeeded in the 3rd, which is set on a heavy-gravity colony planet. A sense of potential interestingness pervades even the most convincingly unambitious of SGS's works. [JC]

Other works: *The Janus Equation* (**1980** dos); *Hellstone* (**1981**); *The Genesis Shield* (**1985**).

SQUIRE, J.C. [r] ◊ ALTERNATE WORLDS.

SQUIRM ◊ BLUE SUNSHINE.

SSSSNAKE ◊ SSSSSSSS!

SSSSSSSS! (vt *Sssssnake!*) Film (1973). Zanuck-Brown/Universal. Prod Dan Striepeke. Dir Bernard L. Kowalski, starring Strother Martin, Dirk Benedict, Heather Menzies. Screenplay Hal Dresner, based on a story by Striepeke. 99 mins. Colour.

In a period when most MONSTER MOVIES were spoofs, this competently made film is unusual for playing it straight (despite the title). An obsessed scientist (Martin) believes that only ophidians (snakes) will survive what he sees as coming ecocatastrophe, so he works on developing snake-like properties – e.g., cold blood – in humans, early failures being sold to the carnival freak-show. He finally succeeds in transforming his daughter's boy-friend (Benedict) into something like a king cobra (rather good make-up by John Chambers). Then along comes a mongoose . . . [JB/PN]

STABLEFORD, BRIAN M(ICHAEL) (1948-   ) UK writer, critic and academic, with a degree in BIOLOGY and a doctorate in SOCIOLOGY, which he taught 1977-88 before turning to writing full-time. He began his writing career early, collaborating with a school-friend, Craig A. Mackintosh (together as Brian Craig), on his first published story, "Beyond Time's Aegis" for *Science Fantasy* in 1965. BMS then dropped the Brian Craig pseudonym, using it again only in the late 1980s when he undertook to SHARECROP some ties for a GAME-WORLD enterprise (◊ GAMES WORKSHOP and listing below). His first novel, *Cradle of the Sun* (**1969** dos US), a quest story set in the FAR FUTURE, is notable for its colourful imagery. *The Blind Worm* (**1970** dos US), hastily written, is in the same vein. In these early works, and in most of his subsequent sf novels, BMS put his knowledge of biology to good use, constructing a long series of outrageous but plausible ECOLOGIES whose intricacy sometimes overwhelmed the SPACE-OPERA formats to which he generally adhered over the first 15 years of his career. The early **Dies Irae** trilogy – *The Days of Glory* (**1971** US), *In the Kingdom of the Beasts* (**1971** US) and *Day of Wrath* (**1971** US) – mixed these usual space-opera trappings with SWORD AND SORCERY. Based on HOMER's *Iliad* and *Odyssey*, the trilogy was dismissed as cynical hackwork (not least by BMS himself); although the narrative has some verve, it clearly does not attempt to pay due homage to its source. *To Challenge Chaos* (**1972** US), the last example of BMS's juvenilia, is an overextravagant adventure set on the chaotic hemisphere of a planet that intersects another dimension; short stories associated with this novel are "The Sun's Tears" (1974), "An Offer of Oblivion" (1974) and "Captain Fagan Died Alone" (1976).

It was with the **Grainger** or **Hooded Swan** series – *The Halcyon Drift* (**1972** US), *Rhapsody in Black* (**1973** US; rev 1975 UK), *Promised Land* (**1974** US), *The Paradise Game* (**1974** US), *The Fenris Device* (**1974** US) and *Swan Song* (**1975** US) – that BMS began to attract serious notice in the USA, where his early work was all first published, being marketed there as adventure sf. The **Grainger** novels – first-person narratives in a Chandleresque style – concern the adventures of the pilot of a FASTER-THAN-LIGHT spacecraft, the *Hooded Swan*, on a variety of planets. In the first tale Grainger, marooned on a remote world, becomes host to a mind parasite, a benign entity which occasionally takes over his body and drives it to feats of endurance. In later books the increasingly disillusioned, sardonic, pacific Grainger penetrates further biological mysteries, but the series itself holds back from fully articulating the subversiveness of his behaviour, and there is little sense of accumulating burden. A second series – the **Daedalus Mission** books, comprising *The Florians* (**1976** US), *Critical Threshold* (**1977** US), *Wildeblood's Empire* (**1977** US), *The City of the Sun* (**1978** US), *Balance of Power* (**1979** US) and *The Paradox of Sets* (**1979** US) – recounts to similar effect the various experiences of the crew of the spaceship *Daedalus*, which has been sent out to re-contact lost Earth colonies.

Most of BMS's fiction has been confined to series, but *Man in a Cage* (**1975** US), an unformulaic single-ton, deals with the PSYCHOLOGY of social adaptation as dramatized through a schizophrenic narrator selected to participate in a space-project where "sane" men have already proved inadequate. A powerfully written but difficult novel, it is slightly reminiscent of the best work of Robert SILVERBERG and Barry N. MALZBERG. *The Mind-Riders* (**1976** US), perhaps somewhat more conventional, is narrated by a cynical boxer who performs via an electronic simulation device while the audience "plugs in" to his emotions. Like Grainger's wonderful spaceship, and like the false personality which "cages" the hero of *Man in a Cage*, the simulator is an armour surrounding the self, enabling the protagonist to survive in a hostile world. *The Face of Heaven* (**1976**) – the first part of a trilogy published in 1 vol as *The Realms of Tartarus* (**1977** US) – is a biological phantasmagoria concerning a UTOPIA built on a huge platform above the Earth's surface, and the conflict with the mutated lifeforms which proliferate below. This tale, choked with ingenious invention and grotesqueries, and *The Walking Shadow* (**1979**) stand as BMS's most clearly STAPLEDON-esque epics, and show a vein of contemplative wonder that he was later – in the impressive academic study, *The Scientific Romance in Britain 1890-1950* (**1985**) – to characterize as an essential element tending to distinguish UK from US sf.

Further novels of interest from this period include *The Castaways of Tanagar* (**1981** US) and *The Gates of Eden* (**1983** US). After beginning the **Asgard** trilogy with *Journey to the Center* (**1982** US; rev **1989** UK) – which he completed with *Invaders from the Centre* (**1990**) and *The Centre Cannot Hold* (**1990**) – BMS stopped producing fiction for some time, concentrating on popular and scholarly studies of sf and FUTUROLOGY like *The Science in Science Fiction* (**1982**) with David LANGFORD and Peter NICHOLLS, *The Sociology of Science Fiction* (**1985** US) and, with Langford, *The Third Millennium: A History of the World AD 2000-3000* (**1985**); he also contributed very widely during this period to a number of journals, including FOUNDATION, and to various scholarly anthologies, including many of the essays in E.F. BLEILER's 2 anthologies devoted to extended studies of individual authors: *Science Fiction Writers* (anth **1982** US) and *Supernatural Fiction Writers* (2 vols anth **1985** US). He has served as contributing editor to both editions of this encyclopedia.

Whether or not these years away from fiction were in themselves rejuvenating, on returning to sf BMS produced in short order his 3 finest novels to date. *The Empire of Fear* (**1988**) is an alternate history (◊ ALTERNATE WORLDS) of Europe from the Middle Ages to the present in which immortal vampires – whose condition is here scientifically premised – dominate the world; told with the geographic sweep and

visionary didacticism typical of the SCIENTIFIC ROMANCE, the book successfully assimilates into sf modes some of the vast lore of the vampire. In *The Werewolves of London* (**1990**) and its sequel *The Angel of Pain* (**1991**), both set in a 19th-century UK, BMS appropriates further material from other genres, creating a sequence – incomplete in 1992 – in which werewolves, bred by primordial godling-like creatures at the dawn of time, participate in an apocalyptic – and thoroughly discussed – testing of the nature of reality. With these novels, and with the sharp tales assembled in *Sexual Chemistry: Sardonic Tales of the Genetic Revolution* (coll **1991**), BMS suddenly became a writer whose fiction befitted his intelligence, for in much of his earlier work a certain tone of chill indifference had tended to baulk the reader's identification. The change was most welcome.   [DP/JC]

Other works: *The Last Days of the Edge of the World* (**1978**), fantasy juvenile; *Optiman* (**1980** US; vt *War Games* **1981** UK); *The Cosmic Perspective/Custer's Last Stand* (coll **1985** chap dos US); *Slumming in Voodooland* (**1991** chap US); *The Innsmouth Heritage* (**1992** chap), a sequel to H.P. LOVECRAFT's "Shadow Over Innsmouth" (**1942**); *Young Blood* (**1992**), horror.

As Brian Craig: For Games Workshop, the **Orfeo** sequence of fantasies tied to the **Warhammer** fantasy game-world – *Zaragoz* * (**1989**); *Plague Demon* * (**1990**); *Storm Warriors* * (**1991**) – plus *Ghost Dancers* * (**1991**), tied to the **Dark Future** sf game-world.

As editor: The **Decadence** anthology sequence, being *The Dedalus Book of Decadence (Moral Ruins)* (anth **1990**) and *The Second Dedalus Book of Decadence: The Black Feast* (anth **1992**); *Tales of the Wandering Jew* (anth **1991**); *The Dedalus Book of British Fantasy: The 19th Century* (anth **1991**); *The Dedalus Book of Femmes Fatales* (anth **1992**).

Nonfiction: *The Mysteries of Modern Science* (**1977**); *A Clash of Symbols: The Triumph of James Blish* (**1979** chap US); *Masters of Science-Fiction: Essays on Science-Fiction Authors* (coll **1981** chap US); *Future Man: Brave New World or Genetic Nightmare?* (**1984**).

See also: ANTHROPOLOGY; ARTS; COLLECTIONS; COSMO-LOGY; CRITICAL AND HISTORICAL WORKS ABOUT SF; CRYONICS; DEFINITIONS OF SF; ESP; EVOLUTION; FANTASY; GAMES AND SPORTS; GENERATION STARSHIPS; GENETIC ENGINEERING; GODS AND DEMONS; HARD SF; HISTORY IN SF; HISTORY OF SF; HORROR IN SF; IMMORTALITY; INTERZONE; LIVING WORLDS; MEDIA LANDSCAPE; MESSIAHS; MONSTERS; MYTHOLOGY; PARANOIA; PARASITISM AND SYMBIOSIS; PAS-TORAL; SEX; STEAMPUNK.

STABLES, (WILLIAM) GORDON (1840-1910) Scottish author of children's fiction; he served as surgeon on a whaling boat and later with the Royal Navy; some of his books were signed Dr Gordon Stables, RN. He wrote extensively for the BOYS' PAPERS, including *The Boys' Own Paper*, where he published many FANTASTIC VOYAGES in competition with the serials of Jules VERNE; the most Verne-like were *The Cruise of the Crystal Boat* (**1891**), a moralistic tale of aerial adventure in an electrically powered craft, and *An Island*

Afloat (**1903**). LOST-WORLD elements appeared in some stories, notably *In Quest of the Giant Sloth* (**1901**; vt *The Strange Quest* 1937) and *In Regions of Perpetual Snow* (**1904**), and became more dominant in *The City at the Pole* (**1906**), which envisages a temperate polar region and a Viking community and prehistoric survivals there. His only excursion outside these themes was his future-WAR novel, *The Meteor Flag of England* (**1905**). [JE]

Other works: *The Cruise of the Snowbird* (**1882**) and its sequel *Wild Adventures Round the Pole* (**1883**); *From Pole to Pole* (**1886**); *Frank Hardinge* (**1898**); *In the Great White Land* (**1902**).

See also: SPACESHIPS.

STACPOOLE, H(ENRY) DE VERE (1865-1951) UK author best known for his South Sea romances, including non-sf ROBINSONADES like, most famously, *The Blue Lagoon* (**1908**), filmed in 1948 and 1980. His LOST-WORLD novel is *The City in the Sea* (**1926**). He wrote several weird novels: *Death, the Knight, and the Lady* (**1897**), *The Man who Lost Himself* (**1918**), *The Ghost Girl* (**1918**) and *The Sunstone* (**1936**). His sf proper was generally restricted to the magazines; it includes a world-DISASTER story, "The White Eye" (1918). *The Story of My Village* (**1947**), his only sf novel proper, depicts a plague of blindness which stops progress short, saving the world from nuclear HOLOCAUST. [JE]

Other works: *The Vengeance of Mynheer Van Lik* (coll **1934**).

STACY, JAN (1948-1989) US writer of military sf novels, including the first 4 vols of the **Doomsday Warrior**, some in collaboration with Ryder SYVERTSEN under the joint pseudonym Ryder Stacy; Syvertsen continued the series solo after JS's death (*see his entry for titles*). Their only non-series collaboration appeared under their real names: *The Great Book of Movie Monsters* (**1983**). Writing as Jan Sievert, they began, with *C.A.D.S.* (**1985**), the **C.A.D.S.** sequence, carried on separately by Syvertsen and David ALEXANDER. As Craig Sargent JS wrote the **Last Ranger** sequence of military-sf novels set in a post-HOLOCAUST venue: *The Last Ranger* (**1986**), #2: *The Savage Stronghold* (**1986**), #3: *The Madman's Mansion* (**1986**), #4: *The Rabid Brigadier* (**1987**), #5: *The War Weapons* (**1987**), #6: *The Warlord's Revenge* (**1988**), #7: *The Vile Village* (**1988**), #8: *The Cutthroat Cannibals* (**1988**), #9: *The Damned Disciples* (**1988**) and #10: *Is This the End?* (**1989**). [JC]

STACY, RYDER Joint pseudonym of Jan STACY and Ryder SYVERTSEN (*whom see for titles*), and solo pseudonym, after Stacy's death, of the latter. [JC]

STAFFORD, PETER ◊ Paul TABORI.

STAHL, HENRI [r] ◊ ROMANIA.

STAINES, TREVOR [s] ◊ John BRUNNER.

STALKER Russian film, 1979. Mosfilm. Dir Andrei TARKOVSKY, starring Aleksandr Kaidanovsky, Anatoli Solonitsyn, Nikolai Grinko. Production design Tarkovsky. Screenplay Arkady and Boris STRUGATSKI, based on their *Roadside Picnic* (**1972**; trans **1977**). 161 mins. B/w and colour.

The original novel tells of a mysterious Zone in Canada where enigmatic artefacts can be found, left there like picnic litter by aliens. Tarkovsky's somewhat inaccessible film, set in a desolate, unnamed country which is probably to be read as an allegorical RUSSIA, de-emphasizes the sf elements. In place of the alien artefacts is the Room, where (maybe) one's most secret wish will be granted. To reach the Room, one must enter the Zone (photographed in muted colour, as opposed to the bleak b/w opening sequence set in an industrial wasteland) – perhaps a Bermuda Triangle, perhaps an ironic gift from a probably nonexistent God – which is a little like the alien killer-maze in Algis BUDRYS's *Rogue Moon* (**1960**): it is a mixture of dereliction and greenery, waterlogged, a maze of ever-changing lethal traps, to be traversed only in a kind of drunkard's walk, an arbitrary zigzag. The Stalker, the shaven-headed smuggler-saint whose wretched life flares up only within the Zone, which he loves, is guide to the Writer and the Professor, the former seeking genius, the latter secretly planning to bomb the Room.

S is agonizingly static, punctuated by abstract philosophical conversations with long pauses, and yet for some viewers it has an almost unequalled hypnotic intensity. This is partly due to Tarkovsky's lingering artist's eye, catching the beauty of ugliness as, for example, the camera pans endlessly across a shallow lake in the Zone whose floor is kitchen tiles, passing indifferently across coins, syringes, icons, calendars, a gun, all looming through the weed. The Room is reached, but left unentered and unbombed. Afterwards, at the Stalker's home, we witness his legless daughter (the children of stalkers being often mutated) push a glass slowly across a table by telekinesis while her exhausted father sleeps, the only unambiguous miracle of the film. *S* is a meditation on faith and cynicism, certainly pretentious, memorable for some, and perhaps the grimmest metaphor for Russia produced by a Russian in our generation. [PN]

See also: MUSIC.

STALLMAN, ROBERT (1930-1980) Literary critic, professor of English at Western Michigan University, author of the **Beast** trilogy, the last 2 books of which were published posthumously: *The Orphan* (**1980**), *The Captive* (**1981**) and *The Beast* (**1982**; vt *The Book of the Beast* UK). The books are complex, sensitively written FABULATIONS, fitting between the generic borders of sf and HORROR, and update the myth of the werewolf with the sf premise that they are a chrysalis form of alien life; when two mate they will trigger a new phase in their life-cycle. The books do not, however, *feel* very sf-like, and they most come to life in the opposing tugs between the first beast's life as beast and as human, both phases desiring autonomy. The awkwardly structured last book of this engrossing series probably needed an auctorial revision which it could not be given. [PN]

STAMEY, SARA (LUCINDA) (1953-) US writer in

whose **Wild Card Run** sequence of sf adventures – *Wild Card Run* (**1987**), *Win, Lose, Draw* (**1988**) and *Double Blind* (**1990**) – a refreshingly tangential attitude towards plotting keeps a young female protagonist with PSI POWERS hopscotching from planet to planet. En route she embraces her own tangled family romance on one world, and elsewhere confronts some AI conundra, sensing that the entire venue of her sport is in fact a galactic experiment on their part. [JC]

STANDARD MAGAZINES ◊ Ned L. PINES; SPACE STORIES; STARTLING STORIES; THRILLING WONDER STORIES.

STANFORD, J(OHN) K(EITH) (1892-1971) UK writer, mostly of humorous material, whose sf SATIRE, *Full Moon at Sweatenham: A Nightmare* (**1953**), takes rather clumsy potshots at a decadent, ludicrous 1960 UK; the welfare state is guyed. [JC]

Other works: *The Twelfth* (**1944** chap).

STANG, [Reverend] IVAN (1949-) US writer, given the title "Reverend" by the Church of the SubGenius. He ed *The Book of the SubGenius* (anth **1983**), a SATIRE on other religions and cults in the form of densely packed clip art relating the teachings of J.R. "Bob" Dobbs, a former encyclopedia salesman. The crackpot literature that inspired the book is reviewed in the nonfiction *High Weirdness by Mail: A Directory of the Fringe-Made Prophets, Crackpots & True Visionaries* (**1988**). IS also ed *Three-Fisted Tales of "Bob": Short Stories in the SubGenius Mythos* * (coll **1990**), much of whose content is sf. [NT]

STANGERUP, HENRIK (1937-) Danish journalist, playwright and novelist who worked mainly within the tradition of "new realism" prevalent in Denmark during the 1960s; he also wrote historical fiction. His sf novel *Manden der ville vaere skyldig* (**1973**; trans David Gress-Wright as *The Man who Wanted to be Guilty* **1982** UK) satirically assaults the welfare state and the Social Democratic party in a NEAR-FUTURE tale of a man who accidentally kills his wife and is treated by the state not as a criminal but as a patient, stifling his natural need to assume some personal guilt for the deed. The book was filmed in 1990 by Ole Roos. [ND]

See also: DENMARK.

STANILAND, MEABURN (? -) UK writer whose *Back to the Future* (**1947**), in no way connected to BACK TO THE FUTURE (1985) and its sequels, sends its protagonist into a bureaucratic DYSTOPIAN future UK. [JC]

STANLEY, A(LFRED) M(ORTIMER) (1888-?) US writer in whose *Tomorrow's Yesterday* (**1949**) an archaeologist wakes up in a future where sex-roles are reversed and mental growth is matched by physical decay. [JC]

STANLEY, WILLIAM (FORD ROBINSON) (1829-1909) UK writer, often on economic issues, of sf interest for *The Case of The. Fox: Being his Prophecies under Hypnotism of the Period Ending A.D. 1950. A Political Utopia* (**1903**). Hypnosis releases the "prophetic mental element" in a poet, Theodore Fox; the

UTOPIA he describes in a series of visions, with its Federal Europe, electrified cars and Channel Tunnel, has few unusual elements. At the end, perhaps dazzled, Fox kills himself. [JC]

STANTON, PAUL Pseudonym of UK writer (Arthur) David Beaty (1919-), who wrote thrillers under his own name. *Village of Stars* (**1960**) as by PS was an unremarkable NEAR-FUTURE nuclear-WAR thriller. [JC]

STAPLEDON, (WILLIAM) OLAF (1886-1950) UK writer and philosopher, born of well-to-do parents in the Wirral peninsula near Liverpool, where he spent the greater part of his life. In *Waking World* (**1934**) he admitted that he lived "chiefly on dividends and other ill-gotten gains". The name Olaf does not indicate foreign antecedents: his parents happened to be reading Carlyle's *The Early Kings of Norway* (coll **1875**) at the time. Memories of childhood in Suez and a cultivated family background are recaptured in *Youth and Tomorrow* (**1946**). He was educated at Abbotsholme, a progressive public school, and at Balliol College, Oxford. For a short period he worked without enthusiasm in the family shipping office in Port Said, an experience he used in his highly autobiographical last novel, *A Man Divided* (**1950**). There is scattered evidence that the international flavour of Port Said influenced his complex ideas about "true community". His service with the Friends' Ambulance Unit in WWI helped him formulate his pacifism, and provided material for *Last Men in London* (**1932**). He took a doctorate in philosophy at Liverpool University in 1925.

OS began publishing essays as early as 1908; his first book was *Latter-Day Psalms* (coll **1914** chap), a small volume of privately printed verse. It is remarkable only for showing a preoccupation at the outset with one of the themes that would engage him for the rest of his life: the irrelevance of a RELIGION based on hopes of IMMORTALITY and the hypothesis of an evolving god. There was a gap of 15 years before his next book, *A Modern Theory of Ethics* (**1929**), written when OS was 43. Here is the philosophical underpinning for all the major ideas that would appear repeatedly in the fiction: moral obligation as a teleological requirement; ecstasy as a cognitive intuition of cosmic excellence; personal fulfilment of individual capacities as an intrinsic good; community as a necessary prerequisite for individual fulfilment; and the hopeless inadequacy of human faculties for the discovery of truth. It was this last conviction which provided the springboard for the writing of his fiction; all of it, by some speculative device or other, strives to overcome the congenital deficiencies of the ordinary human being.

Last and First Men (**1930**), OS's first novel, caused something of a sensation. Contemporary writers and critics acclaimed it, though later it would for a time be nearly forgotten. The book employs a timescale of 2 billion years, during which 18 races of humanity rise and fall. The story is told by one of the Last (18th) Men working through the "docile but scarcely adequate brain" of one of the 1st Men (ourselves). The civilization of the 1st Men (he explains) reached its highest points in Socrates (in the search for truth) and Jesus (in self-oblivious worship). The 2nd, 3rd, 5th, 15th, 16th and 18th Men represent higher orders of wisdom. The emigration of the 5th Men to VENUS is an early example of TERRAFORMING, and the construction of the 9th Men to adapt them for Neptune (◊ OUTER PLANETS) is likewise for GENETIC ENGINEERING. In the intimate and less expansive *Last Men in London*, one of the Last Men returns to the time of WWI, enters into profound symbiosis with a young human, and attempts to arouse the Race Mind.

In *Odd John: A Story Between Jest and Earnest* (**1935**) the individual SUPERMAN appears, although his attributes are spiritual and intellectual, quite divorced from the supermen of the COMICS and PULP MAGAZINES. John recapitulates in his own evolution some of the characteristics of the 2nd, 3rd and 5th Men. He and his fellow "supernormals" finally achieve something akin to the wisdom of the 18th Men; a spiritual gain which costs them their lives: when normal humans threaten to destroy their island, they destroy themselves rather than fight back.

Star Maker (**1937**) is often regarded as OS's greatest work. Its cosmic range, fecundity of invention, precision and grandeur of language, structural logic, and above all its attempt to create a universal system of philosophy by which modern human beings might live, permit comparison with DANTE ALIGHIERI's *Divine Comedy*. The narrator is rapt from a suburban hilltop and becomes a "disembodied, wandering viewpoint", rather like Dante's own protagonist. Over a timespan which extends to 100 billion years, he first observes "Other Men", whose extraordinary development of scent and taste should remind us of the relative nature of our own perceived values; his purview then extends to "strange mankinds", including the Human Echinoderms – whose communal method of reproduction provides an ingenious metaphor for the ideal of true community – and to a wide range of species far removed from mankind. Of these ALIENS, among the most interesting are the "ichthyoids" and "arachnoids". Over a long period of time these 2 species come together in a symbiosis; the ichthyoids are artistic and mystical, while the arachnoids are dexterous and practical. The development of the relationship provides OS's most extended and detailed metaphor for the ideal of true community, which has its microcosm in a pair of human lovers and its macrocosm in a Universe of "minded" LIVING WORLDS. The narrator proceeds to the "supreme moment of the cosmos" in which he faces the Star Maker and discovers something of his pitiless nature.

Paradoxically, the book with the greatest human interest is sometimes said to be *Sirius: A Fantasy of Love and Discord* (**1944**), the story of a dog with enhanced INTELLIGENCE, consciousness and sensibility. The dog, with its natural limitations, is a paradigm of our own limited capacity; but at the same time the dog's superior gifts – e.g., in the faculty of scent – are another reminder of human inadequacy. As in *Odd John*, the MUTANT being, when faced with the violence of normals and their incomprehension, dies – this time directly at their hands.

The four works of sf described constitute the living core of OS's fiction. Both *Last and First Men* and *Star Maker* have their advocates as the finest sf ever written; many critics argue that *Odd John* is the best novel about a superman, and that *Sirius* is the best book with a nonhuman protagonist. All 4 show OS's unwavering concern with the pursuit of truth and with the impossibility of our species ever finding it. Each sets up a speculative device to leap over the plodding faculties of *Homo sapiens*: the supernormal intelligence of *Homo superior* in *Last and First Men* and *Odd John*, and the alternative intelligence of alien creatures in *Star Maker* and *Sirius*. Along with the quest for truth, and as a necessary accompaniment to it, there is a search for the gateways to a "way of the spirit". These constant preoccupations give to all OS's work a striking consistency, and it is possible to place everything he did within a highly original scheme of METAPHYSICS. Everything has its place in the same cosmic history that the Star Maker coldly regards. In his avatar of Jahweh, the Star Maker was invoked at the beginning in *Latter-Day Psalms*; and as the "mind's star" and "phantom deity" he will be there at the end in the posthumous *The Opening of the Eyes* (**1954**).

Of OS's remaining fiction, perhaps *The Flames* (**1947** chap) deserves most attention. The "flames" are members of an alien race, originally natives of the Sun, who can be released when igneous rock is heated; they have affinities with the "supernormals" who occur on OS's other worlds. There are similarities with the later-discovered *Nebula Maker* (**1976**), apparently written in the mid-1930s as part of an early draft for *Star Maker* and then put aside. It relates the history of the nebulae and shows how their striving is brought to nothing by an uncaring God. Religion is dismissed as the opium of the people in *Old Man in New World* (**1944** chap). Supermen reappear in *Darkness and the Light* (**1942**) and cosmic history is recapitulated in *Death into Life* (**1946**). OS's insistence on scrupulously considering opposed points of view, and his sceptical intelligence, found an admirable vehicle in the imaginary conversations of *Four Encounters* (**1976**), probably written in the later 1940s. Of OS's remaining nonfiction, *Philosophy and Living* (**1939**), written after the best of his fiction, is the most comprehensive work. The best introduction for the general reader is *Beyond the "Isms"* (**1942**), whose last chapter, under the characteristic heading "The Upshot", provides an admirable summary of his philosophy and a clear exposition of what he means by the "way of the spirit".

OS was writing in an ancient tradition of European speculative fiction. He called his stories "fantastic fiction of a semi-philosophical kind". He was – at least initially – unaware of GENRE SF and was somewhat taken aback when in the 1940s he was acclaimed by sf fans; he was even more startled when shown the contemporary magazines which provided their staple fodder. Ironically, the acclamation he received as an sf writer may partially account for his total neglect by historians of modern literature. At the same time he is sometimes ignored by sf commentators – e.g., Kingsley AMIS in *New Maps of Hell* (**1960** US) – presumably partly because he did not write for the sf magazines and partly because his work is difficult to anthologize. OS is, however, though sometimes dimly perceived, the Star Maker behind many subsequent stories of the FAR FUTURE and GALACTIC EMPIRES. He did much original and seminal thinking about such matters as ALTERNATE WORLDS, COLONIZATION OF OTHER WORLDS, COSMOLOGY, CYBORGS, ESP, HIVE-MINDS, IMMORTALITY, MONSTERS, MUTANTS and TIME TRAVEL. Arthur C. CLARKE and James BLISH are among the few sf writers who have expressed their indebtedness to him, though his influence, both direct and indirect, on the development of many concepts which now permeate genre sf is probably second only to that of H.G. WELLS.   [MA/JC]

Other works: *New Hope for Britain* (**1939**); *Saints and Revolutionaries* (**1939**); *Worlds of Wonder* (omni **1949** US), assembling *The Flames*, *Death into Life* and *Old Man in New World*; *To the End of Time* (omni **1953** US), assembling *Last and First Men* (cut), *Star Maker*, *Odd John*, *Sirius* and *The Flames*; *Odd John, and Sirius* (omni **1972** US); *Far Future Calling: Uncollected Science Fiction and Fantasies of Olaf Stapledon* (coll **1979** US) ed Sam MOSKOWITZ; *Nebula Maker, and Four Encounters* (omni **1983** US); *Letters Across the World: The Love Letters of Olaf Stapledon and Agnes Miller, 1913-1919* (coll **1987** Australia; vt *Talking Across the World* 1987 US); numerous uncollected articles for such scholarly journals as *Mind* and *Philosophy*.

About the author: *Olaf Stapledon* (**1982**) by P.A. McCarthy; *Olaf Stapledon: A Man Divided* (**1984**) by Leslie A. FIEDLER; *Olaf Stapledon: A Bibliography* (**1984**) by Harvey J. Satty and Curtis C. SMITH; *Olaf Stapledon and his Critics* (**1988**) by Curtis C. Smith.

See also: ANTHROPOLOGY; APES AND CAVEMEN (IN THE HUMAN WORLD); DEVOLUTION; END OF THE WORLD; EVOLUTION; FRANCE; GODS AND DEMONS; HISTORY IN SF; HISTORY OF SF; INVASION; LIFE ON OTHER WORLDS; MAINSTREAM WRITERS OF SF; MUSIC; OPTIMISM AND PESSIMISM; PHYSICS; SOCIOLOGY; SUN.

STARBURST UK monthly nonfiction magazine about sf, fantasy and horror in the media (primarily films and tv). Small-BEDSHEET slick format. Founded Jan 1978, first published by Starburst Magazines, London, ed Dez Skinn, but soon taken over by MARVEL COMICS and ed Alan Mackenzie until #77 (Jan 1985), then by Roger P. Birchall to #79 and Cefn Ridout to #87. With #88 (Dec 1985) the magazine left Marvel and was taken over by Visual Imagination, with Stephen Payne the new ed.

What must have been designed as little more than

a fan magazine for kids became rather good, especially under Mackenzie's editorship, and it was for some time in the UK the only (fairly) reliable source for developments in fantastic films and tv. What probably saved *S*, in contrast to its US equivalent STARLOG, is that it never gave the impression of being in hock to the film studios. *S* had a collection of eccentric but well informed critics, some slavishly devoted to SPLATTER MOVIES; among the regular contributors were John BROSNAN, Tony Crawley and Alan Jones, and sf writers like Robert P. HOLDSTOCK, David LANGFORD and Ian WATSON made occasional appearances. During the year following the change of ownership from Marvel the magazine became blander and more juvenile. The magazine had reached #167 in 1992.   [PN]

STAR COPS UK tv series (1987). BBC TV. Devised Chris Boucher, prod Evgeny Gridneff, script ed Joanna Willett. Dirs Christopher Baker, Graeme Harper. Writers Boucher (5 episodes), Philip Martin, John Collee. Leading players David Calder as Nathan Spring, Erick Ray Evans, Linda Newton, Jonathan Adams as Krivenko, the Russian commander of Moonbase. 9 55min episodes. Colour.

AD2027. Nathan Spring is the new head detective of the International Space Police Force, an undisciplined force with poor morale whose headquarters are on Moonbase, and whose policing area includes manned orbital space stations. Spring whips them into shape, and they solve crimes. The low-key realism of the series was efficient enough, but in the end it seemed little more than just another cop show, failing to imagine the future with any real vividness or depth.   [PN]

STARDATE US gaming magazine, small-BEDSHEET slick format, published first by gaming company FASA for issues #1-#7 (which included several double issues), 1984-5. These issues contained no fiction, but did have sf reviews and articles. With #8 (Oct 1985) *S* changed hands (to Associates International, Inc., Delaware), subtitle (becoming *Stardate: The Multi-Media Science Fiction Magazine*), editors (Ted WHITE and David BISCHOFF) and contents (one third gaming, one third film/tv and one third fiction, including stories by William GIBSON, Jack HALDEMAN, Damon KNIGHT, John SHIRLEY and William F. WU). It lasted 4 issues in this format, folding after #11 (Mar/Apr 1986).   [PN]

STARK, HARRIET (?   -?   ) US writer in whose sf moral tale, *The Bacillus of Beauty: A Romance of Today* (**1900**), a lady is infected with a beauty-enhancing germ (◊ BIOLOGY). Her character subsequently deteriorates, and she dies.   [JC/PN]

STARK, (DELBERT) RAYMOND (1919-   ) UK writer in whose *Crossroads to Nowhere* (**1956**) an anarchist unsuccessfully confronts a future dictatorship before escaping into the wilds, where his kind may survive.   [JC]

STARK, RICHARD ◊ Donald E. WESTLAKE.

STARKE, HENDERSON [s] ◊ Kris NEVILLE.

STAR*LINE ◊ Robert FRAZIER; POETRY; SCIENCE FICTION POETRY ASSOCIATION.

STARLOG US monthly nonfiction magazine about sf (and fantasy) in the media, largely films and tv, founded 1976, current; small-BEDSHEET, saddle-stapled; publishers have included O'Quinn Studios and Starlog Communications, New York; editors have included Howard Zimmerman and David McDonnell.

This magazine aimed at the juvenile market has been a success (circulation around quarter of a million), and has generated spin-off books and posters and various companion magazines, including *Fangoria* (mainstream horror) and *Gorezone* (cult horror and SPLATTER MOVIES). Indeed, the horror companions have been livelier than *S*, which makes heavy use of studio publicity pictures; in order to maintain good relationships with the studios *S* does not review current films and is undiscriminating throughout. Many of its articles are interviews with actors. That said, the sheer volume of material these magazines have published makes them a useful resource for researchers seeking production details, tv episode guides and so forth. David GERROLD has been a columnist for *S*. A somewhat more adult (on average) UK version of the same sort of magazine is STARBURST, and a much more adult US magazine about fantastic film is CINEFANTASTIQUE. *S* had reached #181 in 1992.   [PN]

STARLOST, THE Canadian tv series, syndicated by CTV (1973). Executive prods Douglas Trumbull, Jerry Zeitman. Prod William Davidson. Series created Cordwainer Bird (pseudonym of Harlan ELLISON). Technical advisor Ben BOVA. Starring Keir Dullea, Gay Rowen, Robin Ward, William Osler. 1 season of 17 50min episodes. Colour.

This series about life on a vast GENERATION STARSHIP, none of whose occupants know its entire extent, should have been good given the quality of some of its creators (Trumbull, Ellison, Bova). In fact it was dire, and only in Canada were all episodes aired. Ellison repudiated it, and Bova wrote a *roman à clef* about the fiasco, *The Starcrossed* (1975). Ellison's original script for episode 1 (not as filmed) won the prestigious Writer's Guild of America Award, and was novelized: *Phoenix without Ashes* ∗ (1975) as by Ellison with Edward BRYANT.   [PN]

STAR MAIDENS (vt *Space Maidens*) UK/West German tv series (1976). A Portman Production for Scottish and Global/Jost Graf von Hardenberg & Co. and Werbung-in-Rundfunk. Prod James Gatward. Dirs Gatward, Wolfgang Storch, Freddie Francis. Writers Eric Paice, John Lucarotti, Ian Stuart Black, Otto Strang. Starring Judy Geeson, Dawn Addams, Pierre Brice, Gareth Thomas, Christiane Kruger, Lisa Harrow, Christian Quadflieg, Ronald Hines, Derek Farr. 13 30min episodes. Colour.

On the planet Medusa women have enslaved men, two of whom (Brice and Thomas) steal a spaceship and flee to Earth. They are pursued by Medusan women, led by Fulvia (Geeson), who take Earth

hostages (Harrow and Quadflieg) in their place. The plotting was chaotic and the role-reversal SATIRE unsubtle. The series was (by UK standards) expensive, and audience figures did not justify the cost of a 2nd season.

STARMAN 1. Film (1984). Delphi Productions II/Columbia. Dir John CARPENTER, starring Jeff Bridges, Karen Allen, Charles Martin Smith, Richard Jaeckel. Screenplay Bruce A. Evans, Raynold Gideon (and Dean Riesner, uncredited). 115 mins. Colour.

Carpenter ventured into SPIELBERG territory in this sweet – possibly saccharine – story of a wide-eyed innocent arriving from space. The Starman (Bridges), first seen as a ball of light, exactly recreates himself in the image of young Jenny's dead husband, kidnaps Jenny (Allen) in the nicest possible way, learns about human customs, is pursued by government forces who want to study or kill him, raises a deer and Jenny (separately) from the dead like an affably dopy Christ, impregnates Jenny, and leaves again. Most of *S* is a protracted chase sequence across the USA, and, though it has rewarding moments and touching performances from its leads, it is too long and slight. The subtext (What would happen to Christ if He came again? We'd crucify Him) is serious enough, but evoked only playfully. The novelization is *Starman* ∗ (1984) by Alan Dean FOSTER.

2. Columbia Television produced a spin-off 22-episode tv series, also called *Starman*, which ran 1 season 1986-7. This dealt in a stereotyped manner with the return to Earth, 11 years later, of the Starman (now played by Robert Hays), his reconciliation with his son, his seemingly endless search for Jenny and an equally protracted search for him by a federal agent.   [PN]

See also: CINEMA.

STARMONT HOUSE US SMALL PRESS in Mercer Island, Washington State, founded *c*1977 by T.E. DIKTY, specializing since 1980 in monographs on individual sf writers, along with some BIBLIOGRAPHIES and some fiction. Its best known line is the **Starmont Reader's Guide** series of sf monographs, established in 1980, ed to a fairly rigid pattern by Roger C. SCHLOBIN, mostly under 100pp. There has also been since 1983 a series of more general studies in literary criticism, mostly related to sf/fantasy and especially HORROR, with a number of titles by Michael R. COLLINGS, Darrell SCHWEITZER and others, and including critical anthologies. Two of Dikty's and Julian MAY's children carried on with the firm after Dikty's death in 1991. Starmont had published around 120 books by then.   [PN]

See also: SF IN THE CLASSROOM.

STAR PRESS ◊ GAMMA.

STAR PUBLICATIONS ◊ COSMOS SCIENCE FICTION.

STARR, BILL (?   -   ) US writer known only for the **Farstar and Son** sequence of sf adventures: *The Way to Dawnworld* (1975) and *The Treasure of Wonderwhat* (1977). The books have something of the quaintness of their titles.   [JC]

STARR, MARK ◊ Gérard KLEIN.

STARR, ROLAND ◊ Donald S. ROWLAND.

STARS The stars have always exerted a powerful imaginative fascination upon the human mind. When they were thought to be mere points of light in the panoply of heaven, it was believed by astrologers that the secrets of the future were written there, and various cultures wove their MYTHOLOGY into the patterns of various constellations. Not until 1718 did Edmond Halley (1656-1742) demonstrate that the stars were not "fixed", and not until the late 1830s were the distances of the nearer stars realistically calculated.

It was the religious imagination which first despatched imaginary voyagers so far from Earth. The notion of the stars as suns circled by other worlds was first popularized by Bernard le Bovyer de FONTENELLE in *Entretiens sur la pluralité des mondes habités* (**1686**; trans J. Glanvill as *A Plurality of Worlds* **1929**). In the 18th century Emanuel SWEDENBORG's visions took him voyaging throughout the cosmos, and other religious mystics followed. C.I. DEFON-TENAY, presumably influenced by Fontenelle, undertook to describe another stellar system in some detail in *Star* (**1854**; trans **1975**), but the first work which took the scientific imagination out into the greater cosmos was Camille FLAMMARION's *Lumen* (**1864**; exp **1887**; trans **1897**). The Pythagorcan notion that the Universe revolves around a single central sun is extrapolated in an oddly allegorical manner in William Hope HODGSON's *The House on the Borderland* (**1908**).

An early SCIENTIFIC ROMANCE of interstellar adventure was Robert W. COLE's *The Struggle for Empire* (**1900**), but it was not until the establishment of the SF MAGAZINES that the interstellar adventure playground was extensively exploited by such writers as E.E. "Doc" SMITH, Edmond HAMILTON and John W. CAMPBELL Jr. Hamilton became especially fascinated by the ultimate melodramatic flourish of exploding stars, and was still exploiting its potential in the 1950s. This new familiarity with the stars did not breed overmuch contempt: in all stories where stars were confronted directly, rather than being used simply as coloured lamps to light imaginary worlds, they remained awe-inspiring entities. Their sustained power of fascination is evident in Fredric BROWN's *The Lights in the Sky are Stars* (**1953**; vt *Project Jupiter* 1954 UK), Robert F. YOUNG's "The Stars are Calling, Mr Keats" (1959) and Dean MCLAUGHLIN's *The Man who Wanted Stars* (fixup **1965**), and nowhere more so than in Isaac ASIMOV's classic story of CONCEPTUAL BREAK-THROUGH, "Nightfall" (1941), which contradicts Emerson's allegation that "if the stars should appear one night in a thousand years, how would Man believe and adore and preserve for many generations the remembrance of the city of God!".

Relatively few sf stories make significant use of scientific knowledge concerning stars and their nature. An exception is Hal CLEMENT's "Cold Front" (1946), which links the behaviour of an odd star to the meteorology of one of its planets. An even odder star, shaped like a doughnut, is featured in Donald MALCOLM's "Beyond the Reach of Storms" (1964). It is, however, quite common to find stars invested with some kind of transcendental significance (◊ METAPHYSICS; RELIGION). Stars are credited with god-like life and INTELLIGENCE in *Starchild* (**1965**) and *Rogue Star* (**1969**) by Frederik POHL and Jack WILLIAMSON, and a collective quasisupernatural influence is spiced with sf jargon in *The Power of Stars* (**1972**) by Louise LAWRENCE. Such metaphysical mysticism is carried to extremes in the first section of *If the Stars are Gods* (1973; fixup **1977**) by Gordon EKLUND and Gregory BENFORD, and the inspiration of sun-worship also plays a minor part in *The Mote in God's Eye* (**1974**) by Larry NIVEN and Jerry E. POURNELLE. Even HARD-SF stories based on astronomical discoveries are not entirely immunized against residual mysticism; a proper sense of awe is evident in Poul ANDERSON's *The Enemy Stars* (**1959**), the most notable sf novel featuring a "dead star", and in his "Starfog" (1967) and *World without Stars* (**1967**). Work done in ASTRONOMY to clarify the lifecycles of stars helped, some decades ago, to popularize both giant and dwarf stars; more recently it has led to a good deal of sf being written about pulsars (◊ NEUTRON STARS) as well as, of course, BLACK HOLES, to the extent that both these forms of collapsar ("collapsed star") are now standard implements in the sf writer's toolbox. [BS]

See also: COSMOLOGY; LINGUISTICS; LIVING WORLDS.

STAR SCIENCE FICTION MAGAZINE US DIGEST-size magazine. 1 issue, published by BALLANTINE Magazines, Jan 1958. This was an abortive attempt to convert Frederik POHL's STAR SCIENCE FICTION STORIES into a magazine after its first 3 issues (1953-4) in book format. It reverted to book format at the end of 1958. [BS/PN]

STAR SCIENCE FICTION STORIES ORIGINAL-ANTHOLOGY series (1953-9) ed Frederik POHL, published by BALLANTINE BOOKS. *SSFS* was the first such series, antedating NEW WRITINGS IN SF by 11 years, and in its example very influential. The series was irregular; after *Star Science Fiction Stories* (anth **1953**), #2 (anth **1953**) and #3 (anth **1954**) there was a 3-year gap. In Jan 1958 Ballantine attempted to relaunch the title in magazine format, but STAR SCIENCE FICTION MAGAZINE lasted only 1 issue. Reverting to book format, the series continued with *Star Science Fiction Stories #4* (anth **1958**), #5 (anth **1959**) and #6 (anth **1959**). *Star Short Novels* (anth **1954**) was an out-of-series volume. The first 3 vols were of extraordinarily high quality; later issues, while highly competent, were less inspired. Notable stories included "The Nine Billion Names of God" by Arthur C. CLARKE (#1), "Disappearing Act" by Alfred BESTER (#2), "It's a *Good Life*" by Jerome BIXBY (#2), "Foster, You're Dead" by Philip K. DICK (#3) and "Space-Time for Springers" by Fritz LEIBER (#4). *Star of Stars* (anth **1960**; vt *Star Fourteen* UK) collects stories from *SSFS*. The later

Ballantine anthology series STELLAR derived its title from *SSFS*. [MJE]

STARSHIP In sf TERMINOLOGY, a ship capable of travel between the stars – one of the many sf neologisms which have passed into the language. ◊ GENERATION STARSHIPS; SPACESHIPS. [PN]

STARSHIP Magazine. ◊ ALGOL.

STARSHORE US magazine, 4 issues Summer 1990-Spring 1991, small-BEDSHEET format, published McAlpine publishing, Virginia; ed Richard Rowland.

Though initially receiving national distribution, *S* was undercapitalized. With a subscription base of only *c*300, it soon folded, #4 going to subscribers only. Mixed with fiction by new writers were stories by established names including Jack DANN, Mike RESNICK with Lou Tabakow, Kristine Kathryn RUSCH and Charles SHEFFIELD. [PN]

STARTLING STORIES US PULP MAGAZINE, 99 issues Jan 1939-Fall 1955, published by Better Publications Jan 1939-Winter 1955, and by Standard Magazines (really the same company) Spring-Fall 1955; ed Mort WEISINGER (Jan 1939-May 1941), Oscar J. FRIEND (July 1941-Fall 1944), Sam MERWIN Jr (Winter 1945-Sep 1951), Samuel MINES (Nov 1951-Fall 1954) and Alexander SAMALMAN (Winter-Fall 1955). Leo MARGULIES was editorial director of *SS* and its companion magazines during Weisinger's and Friend's editorships. The schedule varied between bimonthly (dated by month) and quarterly (dated by season), with a monthly period in 1952-3.

SS was started as a companion magazine to THRILLING WONDER STORIES. Whereas *TWS* printed only shorter fiction, the policy of *SS* was to include a complete novel (albeit sometimes very short) per issue; in its early years the cover bore the legend "A Novel of the Future Complete in This Issue". The space left for shorter stories was limited, and was partially filled by "Hall of Fame" reprints – stories from the Hugo GERNSBACK-edited WONDER STORIES and its predecessors. #1 featured Stanley G. WEINBAUM's *The Black Flame* (Jan 1939; **1948**); other contributors in the early years included Eando BINDER, Oscar J. Friend, Edmond HAMILTON, Henry KUTTNER, Manly Wade WELLMAN and Jack WILLIAMSON. Hamilton's "A Yank at Valhalla" (Jan 1941; vt *The Monsters of Juntonheim* **1950** UK; vt *A Yank at Valhalla* 1973 dos US) was a particularly vigorous early novel. Early covers were by Howard BROWN and Rudolph Belarski, but from 1940 onwards the covers were mostly by Earle K. BERGEY, the artist whose style is most closely identified with *SS* and its sister magazines. The characteristic Bergey cover showed a rugged hero, a desperate heroine (in either a metallic bikini or a dangerous state of *déshabillé*) and a hideous alien menace.

Under Margulies and, more particularly, under Friend *SS* adopted a deliberately juvenile slant. This was most clearly manifested in the patronizing shape of the character "Sergeant Saturn", who conducted the letter column and other readers' departments (in *TWS* and CAPTAIN FUTURE as well as in *SS*). Many readers were alienated by this, and when Merwin became editor he phased out such juvenilia and gradually built *SS* into the best sf magazine of the period, apart from *ASF*. In 1948-9 it featured such novels as *What Mad Universe* (Sep 1948; **1949**) by Fredric BROWN, *Against the Fall of Night* (Nov 1948; **1953**; rev vt *The City and the Stars* **1956**) by Arthur C. CLARKE and *Flight into Yesterday* (May 1949; **1953**; vt *The Paradox Men* UK) by Charles L. HARNESS, in addition to novels by Henry Kuttner (mostly SCIENCE FANTASY) and Murray LEINSTER and stories by Ray BRADBURY, Clarke, C.M. KORNBLUTH, John D. MACDONALD, Jack VANCE, A.E. VAN VOGT and others.

Merwin left the magazine in 1951 (thereafter becoming a frequent contributor). By this time *SS*, like other PULP MAGAZINES, was feeling the effect of the increased competition provided by such new magazines as GALAXY SCIENCE FICTION and *The* MAGAZINE OF FANTASY AND SCIENCE FICTION. Although the standard suffered to a degree, Merwin's successor, Mines, continued to publish interesting material, such as Philip José FARMER's *The Lovers* (Aug 1952; exp **1961**) – which helped earn him a HUGO as Most Promising New Writer – and many Vance stories, notably *Big Planet* (Sep 1952; **1957**). The magazine adopted a new cover slogan ("Today's Science Fiction – Tomorrow's Fact") and a more dignified appearance, but it became another victim of the general decline of pulp magazines. In Spring 1955, as the most popular title in its stable, it absorbed *TWS* and its more recent companion, FANTASTIC STORY MAGAZINE. After 2 further issues it ceased publication, one short of #100. Mines ed an anthology drawn from its pages, *The Best from Startling Stories* (anth **1954**), while a number of its "Hall of Fame" reprints were collected in *From off this World* (anth **1949**) ed Margulies and Friend. A heavily cut and very irregular UK edition was published by Pembertons in 18 numbered issues June 1949-May 1954. A 1st Canadian reprint series ran 1945-6, and a 2nd 1948-51. [MJE]

See also: GOLDEN AGE OF SF.

STAR TREK US tv series (1966-9). A Norway Production for Paramount Television/NBC. Created Gene RODDENBERRY, also executive prod. Prods Roddenberry, Gene L. Coon, John Meredyth Lucas, Fred Freiberger (season 3). Story consultants Steven Carabatsos, D.C. FONTANA. Writers for seasons 1 and 2 included Jerome BIXBY, Robert BLOCH, Coon, Max EHRLICH, Harlan ELLISON, Fontana, David GERROLD, George Clayton JOHNSON, Richard MATHESON, Roddenberry, Jerry SOHL, Norman SPINRAD, Theodore STURGEON; the only well known writer to work for season 3 was Bixby. Dirs included Marc Daniels, Vincent McEveety, Gerd Oswald, Joe Pevney, Joseph Sargent, Ralph Senensky, Jud Taylor. 3 seasons, 79 50min episodes. Colour.

A phenomenon among sf tv series, *ST* is set on the worlds visited by a giant SPACESHIP, the *U.S.S. Enterprise*, and on the ship itself. Its crew is on a mission to explore new worlds and "to boldly go where no man has gone before". Though the crew supposedly number several hundred, only a few of them are ever seen at one time, the principal characters being Captain Kirk (William SHATNER), Mr Spock (Leonard Nimoy), Doctor McCoy (DeForest Kelley), Mr Sulu (George TAKEI), Scotty (James Doohan), Ensign Chekov (Walter Koenig) and Lt Uhura (Nichelle Nichols). For fans of written sf, ST can seldom have seemed challenging in any way, as it rarely departed from sf stereotypes, though in its first 2 seasons it was certainly adequate and even quite strong relative to much televised sf. Although several well known sf writers (see above) contributed to the first 2 seasons, their work was invariably rewritten by the show's regular writers; the quality of the scripts had dropped badly by the end of season 3. As a general rule the SPACE-OPERA format was not used with any great imagination. A typical episode would face the crew with ALIEN superbeings (regularly godlike when first encountered – Roddenberry's favourite theme appears to have been flawed GODS), MONSTERS, or cases of apparent demoniac possession – telepathic aliens being the rule rather than the exception in ST's universe. The formula seldom varied. Many adult viewers came to feel that the series was bland, repetitious, scientifically mediocre and, in its earnest moralizing, trite. The effort to please all and offend none was evident in the inclusion of a token Russian, a token Asiatic and, together in the person of actress Nichelle Nichols, a token Black and token woman. The defect in this liberal internationalism was that all these characters behaved in a traditional White Anglo-Saxon Protestant manner: only Spock was a truly original creation.

The early 2-part episode The Menagerie, adapted from the original pilot for the series, won a 1967 HUGO for Best Dramatic Presentation, as did Harlan Ellison's City on the Edge of Forever in 1968. The latter is generally thought to be the best of the individual episodes; it posed a moral dilemma which cut more deeply than usual. The original script, which differed slightly from the filmed version, was published in Six Science Fiction Plays (anth 1976) ed Roger ELWOOD.

ST was not particularly successful in the ratings. However, it had attracted a hard core of devoted fans, "Trekkies", who made up in passionate enthusiasm what they lacked in numbers. These numbers grew over the years, in part because the series was often replayed, attracting new fans each time. There have been many ST CONVENTIONS, some drawing very large attendances. Perhaps Roddenberry's blend of the mildly fantastic with the reassuringly familiar, and his use of an on the whole very likable cast, attracted viewers precisely because its exoticism was manageable and unthreatening. The Trekkie phenomenon became spectacular.

Despite the reservations expressed above, there is no doubt that ST was one of the better sf tv series. Its success, though delayed, was very real and had

extraordinary repercussions in the publishing industry. ST ties began with short-story adaptations of individual episodes; James BLISH wrote 11 collections of these 1967-75 (see his entry for details); he also, significantly, published an original novel set in the ST world and featuring ST characters: Spock Must Die * (1970). Another early ST novel was Star Trek: Mission to Horatius * (1969) by Mack REYNOLDS. Soon original ST novels became more important than the novelizations of teleplays. As with DR WHO novels, ST novels are too numerous to be listed here in full, though almost all, having been written by authors who are the subject of individual entries, are listed elsewhere in this encyclopedia. Many ST authors are not hacks and some are distinguished; they include Greg BEAR, Theodore R. COGSWELL, Gene DeWEESE, Diane DUANE, John M. FORD, Joe HALDEMAN, Barbara HAMBLY, Vonda N. McINTYRE, Peter Morwood (1956-   ), Melinda M. SNODGRASS and many others. A series of "fotonovels" – in comic-book style, but using stills from episodes instead of drawings – was inaugurated with Star Trek Fotonovel 1: City on the Edge of Forever * (1977; based on the Harlan Ellison script) and continued for at least 12 issues. There are also GAMES AND TOYS, costumes, models, calendars, puzzles, badges and, of course, MAGAZINES devoted to ST. There are books of blueprints, technical manuals and medical manuals. ST is, in fact, an industry. There is even a thriving trade in ST pornography (◊ FAN LANGUAGE) in the underground press.

The first account of ST published as a book was The Making of Star Trek (1968) written by Stephen E. Whitfield and credited on the cover to Whitfield and Roddenberry. Two more early accounts of ST and its production problems were by David Gerrold: The World of Star Trek (1973; rev 1984) and The Trouble with Tribbles (1973). The latter includes Gerrold's ST script of the same title, together with an account of its production. There have been many books since, including Star Trek Concordance (1976) by Bjo Trimble, Star Trek Compendium (1981; rev 1987) by Allan Asherman, and The Trek Encyclopedia (1988) by John Peel. I am not Spock (1975) by Leonard Nimoy is a cautious account, not very deep, of the actor's relation to the character he played.

When it became clear that the fuss over ST was unlikely to die down, NBC commissioned an animated cartoon series, also called Star Trek (1973-4), based on the original series but introducing several new characters, including an orange, tripedal, alien navigator, Arex, and a catlike alien communications officer, M'Rees. The voices were done by the actors from the original series. 1 of the 22 episodes was by Larry NIVEN, and several by Gerrold. This series in turn spawned yet more book adaptations, in the form of the **Star Trek Log** series by Alan Dean FOSTER (whom see for details), of which 10 appeared 1974-8.

Rumours, counter-rumours and press releases about proposed revivals of ST, either on tv or as a feature film, abounded through the 1970s. In the event there were both. The 6 feature-film sequels to 1991, starring the original cast, were: STAR TREK THE MOTION PICTURE (1979), STAR TREK II: THE WRATH OF KHAN (1982), STAR TREK III: THE SEARCH FOR SPOCK (1984), STAR TREK IV: THE VOYAGE HOME (1986), STAR TREK V: THE FINAL FRONTIER (1989) and STAR TREK VI: THE UNDISCOVERED COUNTRY (1991). The new tv series, with a new cast, was STAR TREK: THE NEXT GENERATION (1987-current). The machine has not stopped. [PN/JB]

See also: OPEN UNIVERSE; SCIENTIFIC ERRORS; SHARED WORLDS; SPACE FLIGHT; TABOOS; WOMEN AS PORTRAYED IN SCIENCE FICTION.

STAR TREK THE MOTION PICTURE Film (1979). Paramount. Prod Gene RODDENBERRY, dir Robert WISE, starring the lead players from the STAR TREK tv series, along with Persis Khambatta, Stephen Collins. Screenplay Harold Livingstone, from a story by Alan Dean FOSTER. 132 mins. Colour.

After more than a decade of rumour and counter-rumour, **Star Trek** (1966-8) was finally relaunched, and on the big screen at that, with a very big budget. The plot, one of Roddenberry's old favourites about the godlike thing in space, seems to have been based on the original tv episodes *The Changeling* (1967) by John Meredith Lucas and *The Doomsday Machine* (1967) by Norman SPINRAD, the former about an implacable alien force heading straight for Earth, the latter about an old Earth space probe that develops autonomous life. The response from **Star Trek** fandom was disappointing – they warmed more to the cosier, more domestic, more small-screenish movies that followed – but there is much to enjoy in Wise's partly successful effort to meld a story of old mates together again with a story of transcendental union between human and MACHINE, the film ending with a daring sexual apotheosis. At times the film becomes almost too contemplative, especially in the drawn-out, quasimystical finale, but most of all (and traditionally) it is the disparity between the soap-opera ordinariness of the crew and the extraordinary events that surround them that keeps the SENSE OF WONDER visible in the distance but never quite there where you need it.

The novelization is *Star Trek: The Motion Picture* ∗ (**1979**) by Roddenberry. [PN]

STAR TREK II: THE WRATH OF KHAN Film (1982). Paramount. Dir Nicholas Meyer, starring the lead players from the STAR TREK tv series, along with Kirstie Alley, Bibi Besch, Merritt Butrick, Ricardo Montalban. Screenplay Jack B. Sowards, based on a story by Harve Bennett and Sowards. 114 mins. Colour.

This was the 2nd (and very much cheaper) movie incarnation of **Star Trek**, the first being STAR TREK THE MOTION PICTURE (1979). Montalban plays Khan, the villain, resurrected from the tv episode *Space Seed* (1967), who thinks he is Captain Ahab. Project Genesis, a TERRAFORMING project that can be used as a weapon, is about to be set off by Khan. Kirk meets his alienated son. Chekov is mind-controlled by an

alien earwig in his ear. Spock sacrifices himself for the greater good. The whole melodramatic, sentimental mishmash is muddily photographed in flat tv style, but, mystifyingly, many fans liked it better than its much more considerable predecessor.

The novelization is *Star Trek: The Wrath of Khan* ∗ (**1982**) by Vonda N. MCINTYRE. [PN]

STAR TREK III: THE SEARCH FOR SPOCK Film (1984). Paramount. Dir Leonard Nimoy, starring the lead players from the STAR TREK tv series, along with Robin Curtis, Merritt Butrick, Christopher Lloyd. Screenplay prod Harve Bennett. 105 mins. Colour.

This is the 3rd movie in the **Star Trek** movie series begun with STAR TREK THE MOTION PICTURE (1979), and it follows directly on from the action of STAR TREK II: THE WRATH OF KHAN (1982) in which Spock died and the Genesis Planet was created. It transpires – the realization is slow – that Spock's body has been recreated (as a rapidly ageing child) by the Genesis Planet, while his soul is sharing McCoy's mind, rendering McCoy schizophrenic. Kirk undertakes to get body and soul together and does so on Vulcan, first outwitting Klingon warlord Kruge (Lloyd). Spock is absent for most of the film, the resulting emptiness being palpable, but Nimoy made up for this by competently directing it. Only complete non-cynics, however, could find other than laughable this saccharine soap opera (rather than SPACE OPERA) in which Kirk loses his son and his ship, Spock is retrospectively canonized, and there is tear-jerking all round.

The novelization is *Star Trek III: The Search for Spock* ∗ (**1984**) by Vonda N. MCINTYRE. [PN]

STAR TREK IV: THE VOYAGE HOME Film (1986). Paramount. Dir Leonard Nimoy, starring the lead players from the STAR TREK tv series, along with Catherine Hicks. Screenplay Steve Meerson, Peter Krikes, Harve Bennett, Nicholas Meyer, based on a story by Nimoy and Bennett. 119 mins. Colour.

Returning to Earth on their captured Klingon spacecraft to stand trial for exceeding orders in various ways (◊ STAR TREK III: THE SEARCH FOR SPOCK [1984]), Kirk and the crew of the (late) *Enterprise* are faced with an unidentified probe evaporating the oceans in order, it is somehow deduced, to communicate with humpback whales (now extinct). The only thing to do is to go back to 20th-century San Francisco, get a couple of whales, and use them to talk the probe out of destroying Earth; this they do. It is perhaps unkind to criticize the **Star Trek** people for their liberalism, but why do they always choose such *safe* issues? There is some lively humour connected with the crew's attempts to come to grips with 20th-century culture. This was by consensus the most relaxedly watchable of the series to date.

The novelization is *Star Trek IV: The Voyage Home* ∗ (**1986**) by Vonda N. MCINTYRE. [PN]

STAR TREK V: THE FINAL FRONTIER Film (1989). Paramount. Dir William Shatner, starring the lead players from the STAR TREK tv series, along with

Laurence Luckinbill. Screenplay David Loughery from a story by Shatner, Harve Bennett, Loughery. 107 mins. Colour.

A visibly middle-aged, overweight crew enact a tepid melodrama in which the *Enterprise* is hijacked by a charismatic Vulcan healer, Sybok (Luckinbill), in search of God, who not unlike the Wizard of Oz proves fraudulent. (False gods are a STAR TREK cliché in both tv and film incarnations.) The film has many anticlimaxes, especially the effortless transit of the supposedly impermeable Great Barrier, and is notable for embarrassingly Californian-style Vulcan therapy – "getting in touch with your own feelings". Shatner's direction has much in common with his acting. After mildly perking up with STAR TREK IV, the film series here plunged again, almost fatally.

The novelization is *Star Trek V: The Final Frontier* ∗ (**1989**) by J.M. DILLARD.   [PN]

See also: CINEMA.

STAR TREK VI: THE UNDISCOVERED COUNTRY Film (1991). Paramount. Dir Nicholas Meyer, starring the lead players from the STAR TREK tv series, along with Kim Cattrall, David Warner, Rosana DeSoto, Christopher Plummer, Morgan Sheppard. Screenplay Denny Martin Flinn, Meyer, based on a story by Leonard Nimoy, Lawrence Konner, Mark Rosenthal. 109 mins. Colour.

After the disaster of STAR TREK V: THE FINAL FRONTIER (1989), this film may have been a cynical decision to cash in on **Star Trek**'s 25th anniversary and squeeze the last possible dollars out of the box-office. It is a quite watchable wrap-up of the series, or at least of the series featuring the original and now elderly cast. The story, a crude metaphor about Russian-US *glasnost*, deals with the dawn of more peaceful relations between humans and Klingons, and with Kirk's right-wing dislike of making any such accommodation. Plummer plays the Shakespeare-quoting villain, Chang, and there is a rather good space battle. The film was made quite cheaply and has (like all but the first of its predecessors) the feel of a blown-up tv episode; the script is packed with hamfisted cultural referents and makes not too much sense.

The novelization is *The Undiscovered Country* ∗ (**1992**) by J.M. DILLARD.   [PN]

STAR TREK: THE NEXT GENERATION US tv series (1987–   ). Paramount. Series creator/executive prod Gene RODDENBERRY. Co-executive prods Rick Berman, Michael Piller. Supervising prods include Maurice Hurley and Michael Wagner. Dirs include Gabrielle Beaumont, Cliff Bole, Rob Bowman, Richard Colla, Winrich Kolbe, Les Landau, Paul Lynch, Joseph L. Scanlon. Writers include Peter Beagle, Hans Beimler, Diane DUANE, D.C. FONTANA, David GERROLD, Maurice Hurley, Richard Manning, Michael Piller, Michael REAVES, Hannah Louise Shearer, Melinda SNODGRASS, Tracy Torme, Michael Wagner. 4 seasons to 1991, current. There was a 2hr pilot, then 98 50min episodes in the first 4 seasons.

This new **Star Trek** series is syndicated rather than networked, thus giving the production company a (perhaps) greater creative freedom. Roddenberry, who created the original STAR TREK, cowrote the pilot episode for this new series 20 years later. Although he remained executive prod, after a while he was no longer closely involved with the show; he died in 1991.

The series is set 80 years further on than **Star Trek**. It is introduced with a slight twist on the traditional text: "to boldly go where no *one* has gone before"; this demonstrated from the outset that *ST:TNG* would concentrate more on eschewing possible insult than on avoiding split infinitives, and so it has proved. The general likability of the new cast, the fact that their characters seldom conflict with one another, the homely moralizing, the absence of real pain, the appearance of liberalism while avoiding truly sensitive issues: all recall the blandness of its much-loved original – a quality attributed by some to Roddenberry's "bible" (◊ SHARED WORLDS), a very detailed list of things you can't do in **Star Trek** scripts – as do many of the story-lines. But, after an uncertain start (tensions on the set and many resignations, including those of writers Gerrold and Fontana; an improvement late in season 1, then a patchy season 2), *ST:TNG* surprised many by picking up considerable pace and interest in season 3. It is now generally agreed to be superior to its original, whose reruns look ever more amateurish by comparison – though, unlike the original, *ST:TNG* has not been widely sold outside the USA.

It could be said that *ST:TNG* is not really sf at all. That is, the events of any episode seldom if ever arise of necessity from a truly sf idea. The sf elements are, by and large, prettifications used to enliven fables about human ethics, and are essential to the plot only insofar as they are enabling devices to create moral dilemmas. Thus, for example, in the several episodes that are variations on the theme of the immaturity of wanting to be a god, the only necessary sf element is the temporary conferral of godlike power.

Much credit for the success of *ST:TNG* must go to certain cast members, notably UK actor Patrick Stewart, ex-Royal Shakespeare Company, who plays Captain Jean Luc Picard, the *Enterprise*'s captain, with impressive gravitas and vigour. Also good is Brent Spiner as the ANDROID (and Spock substitute) Data. Most of the rest of the cast are efficient; they include Jonathan Frakes as First Officer Riker, Marina Sirtis as the empath Counsellor Troi, Gates McFadden as the female medical officer (in season 2 a new medical officer appeared, played by Diana Muldaur), Denise Crosby (season 1) as the tough security officer, Black actor Levar Burton as the blind navigating officer with artificially enhanced vision, Wil Wheaton as the teenaged Ensign Crusher, and Michael Dorn as the Klingon Lieutenant Worf of the *Enterprise* (galactic politics having changed in 80 years). Notable among occasionally returning guest stars have been Whoopi Goldberg as a bartender and John DeLancie as the roguish, enigmatic "Q", the show's equivalent of Trickster figures like Coyote or Loki or Monkey King, who has featured in some of the better episodes. Many episodes have been released on videotape.

As with the original, there has been a substantial number of spin-off books from the series, beginning with *Star Trek, The Next Generation: Encounter at Farpoint* * (**1987**) by David GERROLD, which novelizes episode 1, and reaching, by mid-1992, *Star Trek, The Next Generation: #22: Imbalance* by Victoria E. Mitchell. Other authors have included A.C. CRISPIN, Peter DAVID, David DVORKIN and Jean LORRAH. A preliminary judgment – that there seems less in this series than in its predecessor to stimulate the creativity of book authors – may be premature. As expected, the series has also spawned comics and magazines. [PN]

STAR WARS Film (1977). 20th Century-Fox. Dir George LUCAS, starring Mark Hamill, Harrison Ford, Carrie Fisher, Alec Guinness, Peter Cushing. Screenplay Lucas. 121 mins. Colour.

One of the most financially successful sf films to date, *SW* is an entertaining pastiche that draws upon comic strips, old serials, Westerns, **James Bond** stories, *The Wizard of Oz, Snow White,* Errol Flynn swashbucklers and movies about WWII – the ending, for instance, is lifted from *The Dam Busters* (1955). Lucas may not have succeeded in unifying these diverse elements into a seamless whole, but *SW* is always visually interesting. The gratifyingly spectacular special effects and martial music hypnotize the audience into uncritical acceptance of the basically absurd, deliberately PULP-MAGAZINE-style conflict between Good and Evil. Young Luke Skywalker (Hamill) becomes involved in a mission to rescue a princess (Fisher) from the evil head of a decadent GALACTIC EMPIRE.

The Empire's military headquarters is the Death Star, the size of a small moon and capable of destroying whole planets. With the help of an old man who possesses supernatural powers (Guinness), a human mercenary (Ford) and his alien sidekick Chewbacca, plus 2 cute ROBOTS, Luke rescues the princess and secures information that enables a group of rebel fighters to destroy the Death Star. He is assisted by a power of good, the "Force", left vaguely ecumenical enough to be equally inoffensive to all. The plot is almost precisely that of a fairy tale. The villainous hit of the film was the Emperor's associate, the asthmatically breathing, masked, black-clad giant, Darth Vader (voiced by James Earl Jones). The film received a HUGO.

The special effects are very sophisticated. John Dykstra, in charge of *SW*'s miniature photography, used an automatic matteing system with the help of such technical innovations as a computer-linked effects camera. While the model work was created by US effects men, the live-action settings and effects were created by UK technicians, such as John Barry, production designer, and John Stears, physical effects.

SW's influence was great, and not just within the CINEMA. As a direct consequence of its success, many paperback PUBLISHING houses switched their sf lines strongly toward juvenile SPACE OPERA. The novelization, attributed to Lucas but rumoured to be by Alan Dean FOSTER, is *Star Wars* * (**1976**). The two sequels are The EMPIRE STRIKES BACK (1980) and *The* RETURN OF THE JEDI (1983). [JB/PN]

See also: GAMES AND TOYS; HISTORY OF SF; SCIENTIFIC ERRORS; SWORD AND SORCERY; TABOOS; UFOS.

STARZL, R(OMAN) F(REDERICK) (1899-1976) US journalist and writer who between 1928 and 1934 wrote over 20 stories – typical but competent PULP-MAGAZINE adventures and SPACE OPERAS – including 1 with Festus PRAGNELL (*whom see for details*). [JC]

STASHEFF, CHRISTOPHER (1944-) US writer with a PhD in theatre, a subject he taught at university level; his career began with and has remained almost wholly dedicated to the **Rod Gallowglass** or **Warlock** sequence, in order of internal chronology: *Escape Velocity* (**1983**), *The Warlock in Spite of Himself* (**1969**), CS's first book, and *King Kobold* (**1969**; rev vt *King Kobold Revived* 1984) – the first 2 assembled as *To the Magic Born* (omni **1986**) and all 3 assembled as *Warlock to the Magic Born* (omni **1990** UK) – *The Warlock Unlocked* (**1982**) and *The Warlock Enraged* (**1985**) – both assembled with *King Kobold* as *The Warlock Enlarged* (omni **1986**) and without it as *The Warlock Enlarged* (omni **1991** UK) – *The Warlock Wandering* (**1986**), *The Warlock is Missing* (**1986**) and *The Warlock Heretical* (**1987**) – the first 2 assembled as *The Warlock's Night Out* (omni **1988**) and all 3 assembled as *The Warlock's Night Out* (omni **1991** UK) – *The Warlock Heretical* (**1987**), *The Warlock's Companion* (**1988**) and *The Warlock Insane* (**1989**) – all 3 assembled as *Odd Warlock Out* (omni **1989**) – *The Warlock Rock* (**1990**) and *Warlock and Son* (**1991**). The sequence follows – with decreasing *joie de vivre* – the zany adventures of Rod Gallowglass and his clumsy ROBOT sidekick, who have found themselves on the planet of Gramarye, where MAGIC works (thinly rationalized as an expression of PSI POWERS); they settle in and flourish. There is some TIME TRAVEL, and many creatures of Faerie are comically rendered. In 2 extremely similar out-of-series titles, *A Wizard in Bedlam* (**1979**) and *Her Majesty's Wizard* (**1986**), CS stuck to his last, but more recently he has ventured into new territory. The **Starship Troupers** sequence – beginning with *A Company of Stars* (**1991**) and with several sequels projected – proposes to follow a theatre company from 23rd-century New York to the stars. It is expected that CS's own love for the theatre will bring life to these volumes. With Bill FAWCETT he has begun to ed a SHARED-WORLD series about the **Crafter** family of magicians, *The Crafters* * (anth **1991**) and *The Crafters #2: Bellsings and Curses* * (anth **1992**). [JC]

See also: FANTASY; HUMOUR; SUPERNATURAL CREATURES.

STATIC SOCIETIES ◊ ANTI-INTELLECTUALISM IN SF; CONCEPTUAL BREAKTHROUGH; DYSTOPIAS; UTOPIAS.

STATTEN, VARGO ◊ John Russell FEARN.

STAUNTON, SCHUYLER ◊ L. Frank BAUM.

STEAD, C(HRISTIAN) K(ARLSON) (1932-   ) New Zealand writer whose acerbic, well crafted novels have received considerable praise. Only one is of sf interest: *Smith's Dream* (**1971**; rev 1973) depicts a tyrannical DYSTOPIA. [JC]

STEAKLEY, JOHN (1951-   ) US writer. *Armor* (**1984**) is a rough-edged example of military sf. *Vampire$* (**1990**) pits a high-tech team of vampire hunters against the serried ranks of the foe. [JC]

STEAMPUNK Item of sf TERMINOLOGY coined in the late 1980s, on the analogy of CYBERPUNK, to describe the modern subgenre whose sf events take place against a 19th-century background. It is a subgenre to which some distinguished work attaches, though in no great quantity. There are a number of works of proto-Steampunk, some by UK writers, such as Christopher PRIEST's *The Space Machine* (**1976**), in which H.G. WELLS himself plays a RECURSIVE role, and Michael MOORCOCK's **Oswald Bastable** books, beginning with *The Warlord of the Air* (**1971** US), which are at once a critique and a nostalgic expression of the technological optimism of the Edwardian era. Oddly, though, books like these do not sort well with the kind of book later described as Steampunk, perhaps because in essence Steampunk is a US phenomenon, often set in a London, England, which is envisaged as at once deeply alien and intimately familiar, a kind of foreign body encysted in the US subconscious. Three more works of proto-Steampunk, only borderline sf FABULATIONS, were by US writers: William KOTZWINKLE's *Fata Morgana* (**1977**), set in 1871 Paris, *Transformations* (fixup **1975**) by John MELLA, and "Black as the Pit, from Pole to Pole" (1977) by Steven UTLEY and Howard WALDROP, in which latter the FRANKENSTEIN MONSTER descends into a SYMMES-style HOLLOW EARTH. These recall not so much the actual 19th-century as a 19th century seen through the creatively distorting lens of Charles DICKENS, whose congested, pullulating 19th-century landscapes – mostly of London, though the industrial Midlands nightmare exposed in *Hard Times* (**1854**) is also germane – were the foul rag-and-bone shop of history from which the technological world, and hence the world of sf, originally sprang. Somewhere behind most steampunk visions are filthy coal heaps or driving pistons. It was a vision that also entered the CINEMA, especially through David Lynch, first in *Eraserhead* (1976) and then in *The Elephant Man* (1980), and even – inappropriately enough – in much of the *mise-en-scène* of his sf movie DUNE (1984). Another, rather frivolous Steampunk movie is *Young Sherlock Holmes* (1985; vt *Young Sherlock Holmes and the Pyramid of Fear*), prod Steven SPIELBERG. Steampunk has entered sf ILLUSTRATION through the work of UK artist Ian MILLER. Macabre sf adventures in a Dickensian London have even entered tv: Steampunk was anticipated several times in the UK tv series DR WHO, notably in *The Talons of Weng Chiang* (1977). There was also a much earlier proto-Steampunk sf tv series set in a 19th-century USA, the eccentric *The WILD, WILD WEST* (1965-9).

In sf books it was at first largely in the work of 3 Californian friends, James P. BLAYLOCK, K.W. JETER and Tim POWERS, that the Steampunk vision became obvious, the first being Jeter with *Morlock Night* (1979), in which H.G. Wells's Morlocks travel back in time and invade the sewers of 19th-century London. Powers followed with a historically earlier and even more malign MAGIC-REALIST London in *The Anubis Gates* (1983; rev 1984 UK), and then Blaylock with *Homunculus* (**1986**). In each of these romances a Dickensian London itself is a major character. All three have written at least one more novel along similar lines: Jeter's *Infernal Devices: A Mad Victorian Fantasy* (**1987**), Blaylock's *Lord Kelvin's Machine* (**1992**) and – not precisely Steampunk, but evoking some of the same alchemical madness – Powers's *On Stranger Tides* (**1987**) and *The Stress of her Regard* (**1989**). In most of these works the vision is GOTHIC and the city, despite its horrors, a kind of seedbed where mutant life stirs even in the oldest and deepest parts, the cellars and sewers.

Other writers have worked in similar vein, perhaps closer to rationalized fantasy than to sf proper, such as Barbara HAMBLY with her alienated race of vampires co-existing with humans in *Those who Hunt the Night* (1988; vt *Immortal Blood* UK) and Brian STABLEFORD with his rationalized werewolves in *The Werewolves of London* (**1990**). It is an irony, however, that one of the strongest Steampunk works to date should actually have been written by the prophets of Cyberpunk, William GIBSON and Bruce STERLING, in *The Difference Engine* (**1990** UK), set in an alternate 19th-century London even more dystopian than Dickens's (though clearly modelled on it), the imminent collapse of which under the weight of POLLUTION (and reason) is watched and perhaps controlled by an AI evolved from Charles BABBAGE's calculator.

It is as if, for a handful of sf writers, Victorian London has come to stand for one of those turning points in history where things can go one way or the other, a turning point peculiarly relevant to sf itself. It was a CITY of industry, science and technology where the modern world was being born, and a claustrophobic city of nightmare where the cost of this growth was registered in filth and squalor. Dickens – the great original Steampunk writer who, though he did not write sf himself, stands at the head of several sf traditions – knew all this. [PN]

See also: RECURSIVE SF.

STEARN, JESS [r] ◊ Taylor CALDWELL.

STEBER, A.R. House name used 1938-45 on the ZIFF-DAVIS magazines, mostly on AMAZING STORIES, primarily by Raymond A. PALMER, and later, from 1950, by his friend Rog PHILLIPS, who used it in OTHER WORLDS. [PN]

STEELE, ADDISON E. ◊ Richard A. LUPOFF.

STEELE, ALLEN (M.) (1958-   ) US journalist and

writer whose first story was "Live from the Mars Hotel" for *IASFM* in 1988. He made a considerable impact on the field with his first novel, the NEAR-FUTURE *Orbital Decay* (**1989**), set like almost all his work in the vicinity of Earth orbit, where nuts-and-bolts engineering problems are coped with by a refreshingly variegated cast of employees in space. A sequel, *Lunar Descent* (**1991**), set on and above the Moon, replays the grit and clanguor of the first novel in a lighter mood. Though AS, like so many of his HARD-SF colleagues, has a damagingly lazy attitude towards characterization and tends to export unchanged into space, decades hence, the tastes and habits of 1970s humanity, he manages to convey a verisimilitudinous sense of the daily round of those men and women who will be patching together the ferries, ships and SPACE HABITATS necessary for the next steps into space. *Clarke County, Space* (**1990**), set in one of those habitats, exposes most of AS's weaknesses – cultural provincialism, jerkily melodramatic plotting – without allowing much room for the strengths. [JC]

Other work: *Labyrinth of Night* (**1992**), about a mission to MARS.

See also: CLICHÉS; MUSIC.

STEELE, CURTIS House name used by Popular Publications on OPERATOR #5: during Apr 1934-Nov 1935 CS was Frederick C. DAVIS, Dec 1935-Mar 1938 Emile Tepperman, then to the end (Nov/Dec 1939) Wayne Rogers. [PN]

STEELE, LINDA (? -) US writer (not the Linda Steele married to Michael MOORCOCK) whose *Ibis: Witch Queen of the Hive World* (**1985**) examines human sexual politics (◊ FEMINISM) through the perspective of an affair between a human male and a female of an ALIEN hive-like species (◊ HIVE-MINDS). [JC]

STEELE, MORRIS J. [s] ◊ Raymond A. PALMER.

STEFFANSON, CON House name used by Avon Books. ◊ Carter BINGHAM; FLASH GORDON; Ron GOULART.

STEIGER, A(NDREW) J(ACOB) (1900-) US writer and journalist, a Moscow-based foreign correspondent, whose philosophical novel *The Moon Man* (**1961**) involves the lunar thoughts of immortals. [PN]

STEINER, K. LESLIE [s] ◊ Samuel R. DELANY.

STEINMÜLLER, KARLHEINZ and ANGELA [r] ◊ GERMANY.

STELLA ◊ SCANDINAVIA.

STELLAR US ORIGINAL-ANTHOLOGY series published by BALLANTINE BOOKS, ed Judy-Lynn DEL REY. The first issue was just *Stellar* (anth **1974**); subsequent issues were *Stellar Science-Fiction Stories #2* (anth **1976**), *#3* (anth **1977**), *#4* (anth **1978**), *#5* (anth **1980**), *#6* (anth **1981**) and *#7* (anth **1981**). An associated book was *Stellar Short Novels* (anth **1976**), also ed del Rey. As the title suggests, the series was envisaged as a follow-up to STAR SCIENCE FICTION STORIES ed Frederik POHL 1953-9, also published by Ballantine. However, S, while entertaining, concentrated more on straightforward adventure, with the emphasis on HARD SF,

and less on SATIRE than Pohl's series had done, and few stories had the same edge; exceptions were Robert SILVERBERG's "Schwartz Between the Galaxies" (#1), Isaac ASIMOV's HUGO- and NEBULA-winning "The Bicentennial Man" (#2) and "Excursion Fare" (#7) by James TIPTREE Jr. [PN]

STELLAR PUBLISHING CORPORATION ◊ AIR WONDER STORIES; Hugo GERNSBACK; WONDER STORIES.

STEPFORD CHILDREN, THE ◊ *The* STEPFORD WIVES.

STEPFORD WIVES, THE Film (1974). Fadsin Cinema Associates/Columbia. Dir Bryan Forbes, starring Katharine Ross, Paula Prentiss, Peter Masterson, Nanette Newman, Patrick O'Neal. Screenplay William Goldman, based on *The Stepford Wives* (**1972**) by Ira LEVIN. 115 mins. Colour.

In this black but rather crude SATIRE on the role of women in US society, the men of Stepford, a sleepy, attractive Connecticut town, take part in a bizarre conspiracy – devised by an ex-employee of Disney World and in due course discovered by a newly arrived wife (Ross) – to replace their wives with biddable, contented ROBOT duplicates. The finale shows the robot wives of Stepford drifting like the living dead around a vast supermarket and swapping recipes. Despite stodgy direction, this is an above-average PARANOIA movie, comparable in theme if not in charisma with INVASION OF THE BODY SNATCHERS (1956) – not least because of Prentiss's lively performance. Though the film's FEMINISM is superficial, it is astonishing that it was attacked as antifeminist. Made-for-tv sequels were *Revenge of the Stepford Wives* (1980), 100 mins, dir Robert Fuest, and *The Stepford Children* (1987), 104 mins, dir Alan J. Levi. [PN/JB]

STEPHENS, CHRISTOPHER P(EYTON) (1943-) US book-dealer, publisher and bibliographer, founder in 1987 of Ultramarine Publishing Co., Inc., a SMALL PRESS which has concentrated on releasing trade publisher's printed sheets in fine bindings. As a bibliographer, he has compiled checklists (which he regularly revises) on several authors, including Samuel R. DELANY, Philip K. DICK, Thomas M. DISCH, K.W. JETER, Dean R. KOONTZ, Wilson TUCKER, Gene WOLFE and Roger ZELAZNY (*all of whom see for details*). He has also compiled checklists of some publishers of interest, including the TOR BOOKS Doubles and, together in 1 vol, Kerosina Press and Morrigan Press. [JC]

STEPHENSEN-PAYNE, PHIL (1952-) UK bibliographer who has regularly supplied UK publishing data to *Locus* since 1986, and who has compiled, often in collaboration with Gordon BENSON Jr, a number of extremely useful "working BIBLIOGRAPHIES" of sf writers (*whom see for titles*), including Poul ANDERSON (with Benson), Brian W. ALDISS, John BRUNNER (with Benson), C.J. CHERRYH, Philip K. DICK (with Benson), Charles L. HARNESS, Harry HARRISON (with Benson), C.M. KORNBLUTH (with Benson), Keith LAUMER (with Benson), Anne MCCAFFREY (with Benson), George R.R. MARTIN, Andre NORTON, Bob SHAW (with Benson and Chris Nelson), Clifford D. SIMAK, Theodore

STURGEON (with Benson), James TIPTREE Jr (with Benson), Jack VANCE, James WHITE (with Benson), Gene WOLFE (with Benson), John WYNDHAM and Roger ZELAZNY. [JC]

STEPHENSON, ANDREW M(ICHAEL) (1946-   ) Venezuelan-born UK writer, electronics design engineer and, as Ames, a magazine and book illustrator. He began publishing sf with "Holding Action" for *ASF* in 1971, but then published only 1 more story before his first novel, *Nightwatch* (**1977**), in which fortifications in space are constructed against an assumed alien INVASION which proves to be a friendly contact. *The Wall of Years* (**1979**; rev 1980 US), more typically of a UK writer, describes the destruction of spacetime through interdimensional warfare, and an attempt to set things right again in a lovingly depicted Dark Ages. [JC]

See also: HISTORY IN SF.

STERANKO, JAMES (1938-   ) US COMIC-book illustrator, writer and one-time stage magician and escapologist; Jack KIRBY based his comic-book character **Mr Miracle – Super Escape Artist** (1971) on JS. Influenced early in his career by Kirby, JS rapidly developed a reputation for originality, especially with his work for MARVEL COMICS on the sf comic-book character **Nick Fury**, first for *Strange Tales* 1966-8 (no connection with the weird-fiction magazine STRANGE TALES) and then for *Nick Fury, Agent of Shield* June 1968-Mar 1971, and also for his work on X-MEN and **Captain America**. Some of his **Nick Fury** covers – he painted the first 7 covers and drew the stories of #1-#3 and #5 – were revolutionary for comic books of that time in their bold design and utilization of Surrealist themes. JS was not so much an innovator *per se* as an artist who took a number of techniques hitherto seldom (and haphazardly) used and welded them into a new style in which the design unit became the double-page, not just the single frame. Like Kirby's, JS's narrative technique is strongly cinematic, but his work is more stylized and baroque, and less straight-forwardly representational. Considering the height of his reputation, he has done remarkably few comics, but he has been much imitated, by Philippe DRUILLET among others. JS worked occasionally in the sf ILLUSTRATION field, producing 1 cover for *AMZ*, some work for *Infinity*, and also paperback covers for Pyramid Books's reprints of **The Shadow**.

In 1970 JS left Marvel to found Supergraphics in order to publish his projected 6-vol history of PULP MAGAZINES and comics. Of this only the first 2 vols have appeared: *The Steranko History of the Comics* (**1970**) and *The Steranko History of the Comics Volume 2* (**1971**). He has published and edited a bimonthly tabloid magazine/newspaper called *Comixscene* 1974-5 and then *Mediascene* 1974-80; with #41 in 1980 it became a slick movie magazine called *Prevue*. A planned SWORD-AND-SORCERY comic-book project, «Talen», never materialized, although previews and sketches were published 1968. He wrote and drew: a remarkable GRAPHIC NOVEL, *Chandler* (graph **1976**),

which can only be described as Chandleresque; a graphic-novel version of the 1981 film OUTLAND (1981-2 *Heavy Metal*; graph **1982**); and a 10pp strip celebrating SUPERMAN in DC COMICS's special #400 of that title (1984). He created a unique series of 3D illustrations (i.e., for use with 3D spectacles) for Harlan ELLISON's "'Repent, Harlequin,' Said the Ticktockman" in *The Illustrated Harlan Ellison* (graph coll **1978**). He is listed among the creative talents currently working under Francis Ford Coppola on a projected movie, «Dracula». Among his many awards is the 1970 Best Illustrator of the Year Award. [PN/JG/RT]

STEREOTYPES ◊ CLICHÉS; HEROES; PULP MAGAZINES; SCIENTISTS; SEX; SPACE OPERA; SUPERHEROES; VILLAINS.

STERLING, BRETT House name of Better Publications, used originally in the magazines STARTLING STORIES and CAPTAIN FUTURE for 5 short **Captain Future** novels, 3 of which – "The Star of Dread" * (*CF* 1943), "Magic Moon" * (*CF* 1944) and "Red Sun of Danger" * (*SS* 1945; vt *Danger Planet* 1968) – were by Edmond HAMILTON. 2 BS **Captain Future** stories by Joseph SAMACHSON are "Days of Creation" * (*CF* 1944; vt *The Tenth Planet* 1969) and "Worlds to Come" * (*CF* 1943). The BS pseudonym was used once more by Hamilton for "Never the Twain Shall Meet" (1946 *TWS*) and once by Ray BRADBURY for "Referent" (1948 *TWS*). [PN]

STERLING, BRUCE (1954-   ) US writer, essayist and editor, whose first published sf was a short story, "Man-Made Self", in an anthology of Texan sf, *Lone Star Universe* (**1976**) ed Geo W. PROCTOR and Steven UTLEY. His first novel, *Involution Ocean* (dated 1977 but **1978**), is a memoir of the baroque adventures and moral education of a young man who joins the crew of a whaling ship sailing a sea of dust on a waterless alien planet. Sterling continued in this vein of moralized extravaganza with *The Artificial Kid* (**1980**), another first-person FAR-FUTURE picaresque. While its shockproof milieu of glamorized youth, martial arts and omnipotent technology recalls the early work of Samuel R. DELANY, the novel also looks forward to the CYBERPUNK subgenre, whose principles and character BS largely defined in his polemical FANZINE *Cheap Truth* (c1984-6) and whose representative anthology *Mirrorshades* (anth **1986**) he edited.

BS's talent for rhetoric and his pre-eminence as sf ideologue of the 1980s may have distracted attention from his own fiction. In *Schismatrix* (**1985**), a 1-vol future HISTORY of the interplanetary expansion and transformation of the human race, he exchanges the fantastic exorbitance of his earlier work for a hard-edged and highly detailed realism closely informed by scientific speculation and extrapolation. Linked with *Schismatrix* is the **Shaper/Mechanist** series of short stories included in *Crystal Express* (coll **1989**), about a spacefaring post-humanity divided into two factions, the Shapers, who favour bio-engineering, and the Mechanists, who prefer prosthetics. The collection contains some of Sterling's best and most fully realized work; he has called it "my favourite among my books". Stories not connected to the sequence have been assembled as *Globalhead* (coll **1992**).

Narrated by an anonymous historian above and beyond space and time, *Schismatrix* is a homage to Olaf STAPLEDON, but all Sterling's novels may be seen as tours conducted around fields of data by protagonists whose main function is to witness them for us. This approach culminates in *Islands in the Net* (**1988**), a NEAR-FUTURE thriller concerned with the increasing growth and complexity of political power in electronic communication networks. Sterling's fascination with the inner workings of cultures foreign to his own also led to his collaboration with William GIBSON, *The Difference Engine* (**1990** UK), an ALTERNATE-WORLD, STEAMPUNK novel in which the successful development of Charles BABBAGE's mechanical COMPUTER in 1821 has produced a world divided between France and an 1850s UK ruled by a radical technocracy under Lord Byron; this UK is depicted as a DYSTOPIA whose visual squalor seems to reflect the influence of Charles DICKENS's apocalyptic vision of an industrialized land. And worse is to come: the eponymous computer is clearly en route to becoming an AI, and may end up ruling the world.

Sterling is one of the most globally minded of North American sf writers, seeing civilization as an intricate and unstable mechanism, and pitting the search for equilibrium against our insatiable demands for knowledge and power. His main interest continues to be the behaviour of societies rather than individuals, and the perfection of sf as a vehicle for scientific education and political debate. [CG]

Other work: *The Hacker Crackdown: Law and Order on the Electronic Frontier* (**1992**), nonfiction about computer crime.

See also: ANTI-INTELLECTUALISM IN SF; CYBORGS; ECONOMICS; END OF THE WORLD; EVOLUTION; GENETIC ENGINEERING; HISTORY OF SF; INTERZONE; ISLANDS; JOHN W. CAMPBELL MEMORIAL AWARD; MUSIC; OMNI; SLIPSTREAM SF; SOCIOLOGY; SPACE HABITATS; TRANSPORTATION; VILLAINS; WOMEN AS PORTRAYED IN SCIENCE FICTION.

STERN, J(ULIUS) DAVID (1886-1971) US writer and newspaper publisher. His *Eidolon: A Philosophical Phantasy Built on a Syllogism* (**1952**) tells of a virgin birth. [PN]

STERN, PAUL FREDERICK [s] ◊ Paul ERNST.

STERNBACH, RICK (1951-   ) US astronomical and sf illustrator, born in Connecticut. He has worked in sf since 1973, when he sold a cover painting to *Analog* (Oct 1973), for whom he did 14 covers in all, along with 9 for *Gal* and 8 for *FSF*, mostly in the 1970s. He has also done black-and-white interior art for a variety of magazines including *IASFM*, covers for both paperback and hardcover books, and colour work for *Astronomy Magazine*. In 1976 he was one of the founders of the Association of Science Fiction/ Fantasy Artists (ASFA). RS also worked, from 1977, for Walt Disney Studios and Paramount Pictures. In 1977 he worked on Carl SAGAN's *Cosmos* tv series. In

1986 he became an illustrator for STAR TREK: THE NEXT GENERATION, and is now a senior illustrator and technical consultant for it. He produced *The Star Trek, the Next Generation Technical Manual* * (**1991**) with Michael Okuda. Now California-based, he no longer does much book or magazine illustration. He won the HUGO for Best Professional Artist in 1977 and 1978. He is an acknowledged master of the airbrush but also uses ordinary brushes extremely well, particularly with gouache. Though his space art is evocative and his design sense strong, his figures are sometimes awkward. [JG]

See also: ASTOUNDING SCIENCE-FICTION.

STERNBERG, JACQUES (1923-   ) Belgian writer. A particularly idiosyncratic author with a keen sense of the absurd, JS built from 1953 a unique body of work, often only tenuously linked to sf, where everyday situations logically degenerate into darkly humorous nightmares. *Toi, ma nuit* (**1956**; trans Lowell Bair as *Sexualis '95* **1967** US) is a witty presentation of the dawn of a new age of sexual excess. *Futurs sans avenir* (coll **1971**; incomplete trans Frank Zero as *Future without Future* **1974** US) is a representative selection; the title story, an astonishingly bleak DYSTOPIA set at the end of the 20th century, is typical in its progress from grey reality through surreal black wit down to the end of time itself. JS also wrote the script for Alain Resnais's only sf film, JE T'AIME, JE T'AIME (1968). As the 1970s progressed, his work showed less and less attachment to genre devices. [MJ]

Other works: *La géometrie dans l'impossible* ["Impossible Geometry"] (coll **1953**); *La sortie est au fond de l'espace* ["The Way Out is at the Bottom of Space"] (**1956**), a black comedy set in space and featuring the last human survivors of a bacterial HOLOCAUST; *Entre deux mondes incertains* ["Between Two Uncertain Worlds"] (coll **1957**); *La géometrie dans la terreur* ["Geometry in Terror"] (coll **1958**); *L'employé* ["The Employer"] (**1958**); *Univers zéro* ["Universe Zero"] (coll **1970**); *Attention, planète habitée* ["Beware, Inhabited Planet"] (**1970**); *Contes Glacés* ["Icy Tales"] (coll **1974**); *Sophie, la mer, la nuit* ["Sophie, the Sea, the Night"] (**1976**); *Le navigateur* ["The Navigator"] (**1977**).

See also: BENELUX; FRANCE; PERCEPTION.

STETSON, CHARLOTTE PERKINS ◊ Charlotte Perkins GILMAN.

STEUSSY, MARTI (1955-   ) US writer of a short sequence about First Contact. In *Forest of the Night* (**1987**) the ALIENS are, as the Blakean title hints, tiger-like, though feathered, and must be protected from settlers on their planet who hope to hunt them down; in *Dreams of Dawn* (**1988**) they are crustaceans. MS's heart is in the right place, but the sequence shows signs of making it all much too easy for her young protagonists. [JC]

STEVENS, FRANCIS Pseudonym of US writer Gertrude Barrows Bennett (1884-?1939), who wrote 12 quite highly acclaimed fantasies in the period 1917-23; these appeared in The ARGOSY, The ALL-STORY,

THRILL BOOK and other early PULP MAGAZINES. A similarity in style and imagery led many readers to believe that FS was a pseudonym of A. MERRITT. The sf content is highest in her DYSTOPIA *The Heads of Cerberus* (1919 *Thrill Book*; **1952**), in which a grey dust from a silver phial transports its inhalers to a totalitarian Philadelphia of AD2118. Other novels include the LOST-WORLD tale *The Citadel of Fear* (1918 *Argosy Weekly*; **1970**), *Claimed* (1920 *Argosy Weekly*; **1966**) in which an elemental being recovers an ancient artefact, and "The Labyrinth" (1918 *All-Story*), "Avalon" (1919 *Argosy*), "Serapion" (1920 *Argosy*) and "Sunfire" (1923 *Weird Tales*). Short stories include "The Elf Trap" (1919), "Friend Island" (1918) and "Behind the Curtain" (1918). Some of her stories were reprinted in FAMOUS FANTASTIC MYSTERIES and FANTASTIC NOVELS. [JE]

See also: FANTASTIC VOYAGES; GAMES AND SPORTS; WOMEN SF WRITERS.

STEVENS, GREG ◊ Glen COOK.

STEVENS, LAWRENCE STERNE (1886-1960) US artist and illustrator who also signed himself Stephen Lawrence and just Lawrence. He trained as a newspaper artist and did not begin working in the sf PULP MAGAZINES until the early 1940s. Like Virgil FINLAY, though faster and more versatile, he was a master of pen-and-ink stippling; he never achieved Finlay's fame. LSS's finest work may be the dozens of interiors he did for *Adventure* 1943-54, though his ILLUSTRATIONS for FAMOUS FANTASTIC MYSTERIES, STARTLING STORIES, SUPER SCIENCE STORIES and THRILLING WONDER STORIES are uniformly excellent. Portfolios include *A Portfolio of Illustrations by Lawrence: Reproduced from Famous Fantastic Mysteries Magazine* (**nd**) and *A Portfolio of Ilustrations by Lawrence, 2nd Series: Reproduced from Famous Fantastic Mysteries Magazine* (**nd**). In the case of magazine-cover paintings the Stephen Lawrence pseudonym was shared between LSS and his talented son, Peter Stevens (1920-); interior illustrations by Stephen Lawrence were all the work of LSS. [RD]

STEVENS, PETER [r] ◊ Lawrence Sterne STEVENS.

STEVENS, R.L. [s] ◊ Edward D. HOCH.

STEVENSON, D(OROTHY) E(MILY) (1892-1973) Scottish writer. In *The Empty World (A Romance of the Future)* (**1936**; vt *A World in Spell* 1939 US) survivors of a great HOLOCAUST must attempt somehow to cope. [JC]

STEVENSON, JOHN [r] ◊ Nick CARTER.

STEVENSON, ROBERT LOUIS (BALFOUR) (1850-1894) Scottish author, best known for works outside the sf field. As a student at Edinburgh University, he abandoned engineering for law, but never practised. He travelled widely, suffered most of his life from tuberculosis, and settled in Samoa in 1890. His early novel, *Strange Case of Dr Jekyll and Mr Hyde* (**1886**; the usual vt from 1896 on being *The Strange Case of Dr Jekyll and Mr Hyde*), shows the influence of a Calvinist youth on a hot, romantic temperament. An early version (which he scrapped), resulting from a night-

mare, had an evil Jekyll using the Hyde transformation as a mere disguise. The published version has echoes of the case of Deacon Brodie, hanged in 1788 (and also the subject of the play *Deacon Brodie, or The Double Life* [**1880**; rev 1889] by RLS and W.E. Henley [1849-1903]), as well as of James Hogg's *Private Memoirs and Confessions of a Justified Sinner* (**1824**), not to mention psychological theories that were then current. It is a Faustian moral fable which takes the form of a tale of mystery and HORROR. It precedes Oscar Wilde's *The Picture of Dorian Gray* (**1891**), which in some respects resembles it, by five years, and is the prototype of all stories of multiple personality, transformation (◊ APES AND CAVEMEN) and possession; in some aspects it is also a tale of drug dependency.

The plot takes the form of a spiral which moves gingerly into the heart-of-darkness of the climax, when the already dead Jekyll's written confession of his terrible fall is discovered and presented to readers as the last chapter of the text. Years before the tale begins, Jekyll (whose name RLS pronounced with a long "e") has begun to use drugs to dissociate his libertine side (cf Freud's "id") from his normal self. The evil self that surfaces, Hyde, in whose person (or persona) Jekyll enjoys unspecified depravities (we are given instances only of rage, brutality and murder), is less robust at first than the full man. But spontaneous metamorphoses into an increasingly dominant Hyde begin to occur, and after a temporary intermission larger and larger doses are needed for the "recovery" of Jekyll. Eventually supplies run out and, cornered, Hyde commits suicide. The symbolic physical changes (Hyde is young, stunted, nimble and repulsive) seem today unconvincing melodrama, and the silence about vices other than cruelty seems prudish, but the psychological power of the writing, including Jekyll's agonies, is patent. The story has been filmed many times (◊ DR JEKYLL AND MR HYDE) and has been deeply influential on the development of the theme of PSYCHOLOGY in sf.

RLS wrote a deal of other stories with fantastic or supernatural elements, many to be found in *New Arabian Nights* (coll in 2 vols **1882**); the contents of the 1st vol initially appeared in the magazine *London* in 1878 under the general title **Latter-Day Arabian Nights**, and were later reprinted as *The Suicide Club, and The Rajah's Diamond* (coll **1894**) (◊ CLUB STORIES). Others appear in: *More New Arabian Nights: The Dynamiter* (coll **1885**) by RLS with his wife Fanny Van de Grift Stevenson; *The Merry Men, and Other Tales and Fables* (coll **1887**), which contains "Thrawn Janet", *Markheim* (1886 *Cornhill*; **1925** chap), a good-angel story with a twist, *Will o' the Mill* (1886; **1901** chap US) and "Olalla"; *Island Nights' Entertainments* (coll **1893**), which contains *The Bottle Imp* (1891 *Black and White*; **1896** chap US; vt *Kaëwe's Bottle* 1935 chap UK); *Tales and Fantasies* (coll **1905**), which includes *The Misadventures of John Nicholson* (1887 *Cassell's Christmas Annual*; **1889** chap US) and *The Body-Snatcher* (1884 *Pall Mall Christmas Extra*; **1895** chap US); and *Fables* (coll **1914**).

Many further pamphlets containing RLS tales were published during his lifetime and after; of interest is *The Waif Woman* (written 1892; 1914 *Scribner's Magazine*; **1916** chap), *When the Devil was Well* (**1921** chap US) and *Ticonderoga: A Legend of the West Highlands* (**1923** chap US). Though it has no fantastic elements, *Prince Otto* (**1885**) is an interesting precursor of the RURITANIAN tale. [DIM/JC]

Other works: *The Strange Case of Dr Jekyll and Mr Hyde, and Other Fables* (coll **1896**), and many other collections whose titles feature *Jekyll and Hyde*; *The Short Stories of Robert Louis Stevenson* (coll **1923** US); *Two Mediaeval Tales* (coll **1930** chap US); *The Tales of Tusitala* (coll **1946**); *Great Short Stories of Robert Louis Stevenson* (coll **1951** US); *The Body-Snatcher and Other Stories* (coll **1988** US); *The Complete Shorter Fiction* (coll **1991**); several series of collected works.

About the author: Frank Swinnerton's *Robert Louis Stevenson* (**1915**), though venomous, is a necessary purgative for the early adulation; the numerous subsequent studies are more balanced. Of special interest is *Definitive Dr Jekyll and Mr Hyde Companion* (**1983**) by H.M. Geduld.

See also: BIOLOGY; DEVOLUTION; GOTHIC SF; HISTORY OF SF; *The* MAGAZINE OF FANTASY AND SCIENCE FICTION; MEDICINE; METAPHYSICS; PARANOIA; PREDICTION; SCIENTISTS; SEX; SUPERNATURAL CREATURES; THEATRE; VILLAINS.

STEVEN SPIELBERG'S AMAZING STORIES ◊ AMAZING STORIES.

STEWART, FRED MUSTARD (1936-   ) US writer who has specialized in psychological HORROR novels at the edge of sf and/or fantasy, like *The Mephisto Waltz* (**1969**), filmed in 1971. *Star Child* (**1974**), arguably, and *The Methuselah Enzyme* (**1970**), certainly, are sf. [JC]

STEWART, GEORGE R(IPPEY) (1895-1980) US writer who obtained his PhD from the University of California in 1922, later became professor of English there, and concentrated his attention – through novels, literary studies, popular history, etc. – on the Pacific Edge of the USA. His only sf novel, *Earth Abides* (**1949**), is set in California, and tells of the struggle to survive and rebuild after a viral plague has wiped out most of humanity. The protagonist, Isherwood Williams, lives for many decades after the DISASTER, breeding children with one of his rare fellow survivors, and watching the long night begin as his descendants gradually lose all sense of the civilization he represents; but the Earth abides. The sense of requiem and rebirth promulgated in the novel is rendered all the more complex for readers aware of the implications of Isherwood's nickname, Ish, a direct reference to the historic Ishi, a California Indian who became famous in the early years of the century as the last living representative of his tribe, just as Ish is one of the last living representatives of the civilization which has destroyed his namesake's world. *Ishi in Two Worlds* (**1961**) by Theodora Kroeber (1897-1979), Ursula K. LE GUIN's mother, serves as a telling complement. One of the finest of all post-

HOLOCAUST novels, GRS's superb elegy was the first winner of the INTERNATIONAL FANTASY AWARD. [MJE/JC]
See also: GENRE SF; HISTORY OF SF; PASTORAL; SHARED WORLDS; SOCIOLOGY.

STEWART, MICHAEL 1. UK writer and economist (1933-   ). With Peter JAY (*whom see for details*) he wrote *Apocalypse 2000: Economic Breakdown and the Suicide of Democracy, 1898-2000* (**1987**).

2. UK writer (1945-   ), most of whose novels are medical thrillers, although *Monkey Shines* (**1983**), filmed by George A. ROMERO as MONKEY SHINES (1988), uses the sf premise that a monkey may have her intelligence successfully augmented through the injection of human genetic material; the experiment ends tragically. Other thrillers with sf elements include *Far Cry* (**1984**), *Blindsight* (**1987**), *Prodigy* (**1988**), which also includes elements of occult horror, and *Birthright* (**1990**), in which a feral child turns out to be a Neanderthal, and is threatened with human exploitation. [JC]
Other work: *Belladonna* (**1992**).
See also: ANTHROPOLOGY; APES AND CAVEMEN (IN THE HUMAN WORLD).

STEWART, RITSON (?   -   ) UK writer who, with Stanley Stewart (their relationship, along with everything else about them, is unknown), published *The Professor's Last Experiment* (**1888**), in which a scientifically superior Martian arrives on Earth but is captured by a vivisectionist, who chops off the visitor's wings. [JC]

STEWART, STANLEY [r] ◊ Ritson STEWART.

STEWART, WENDELL [s] ◊ Gordon EKLUND.

STEWART, WILL ◊ Jack WILLIAMSON.

STICKGOLD, BOB (1945-   ) US writer and neurobiologist whose first sf novel, *Gloryhits* (**1978**) with Mark Noble, deals with a recombinant-DNA disaster. His second, *The California Coven Project* (**1981**), similarly exploits his professional knowledge in a NEAR-FUTURE venue. [JC]

STIEGLER, MARC (?   -   ) US writer who began publishing his characteristic HARD-SF stories with "The Bully and the Crazy Boy" for *ASF* in 1980, and whose short work, assembled in *The Gentle Seduction* (coll **1990**), promulgates technological solutions to neatly couched problems. *David's Sling* (**1984**) applies the same philosophy to problems of NEAR-FUTURE political stress, as East and West come close to blows through lack of information-flow. *Valentina: Soul in Sapphire* (fixup **1984**) with Joseph H. DELANEY (*whom see for details*) has a similar bent. [JC]

STILLMAN, RON Pseudonym of the unidentified author, presumably US, of the **Tracker** military-sf series starring a USAF pilot and genius whose inventions make his blindness irrelevant; the stories are told in a maliciously exaggerated parody of the conventions of this sort of fiction. The sequence so far comprises *Tracker* (**1990**), *Green Lightning* (**1990**), *Blood Money* (**1991**), *Black Phantom* (**1991**), *Firekill* (**1991**) and *Death Hunt* (**1991**). [JC]

STILSON, CHARLES B(ILLINGS) (1880-1932) US

journalist and editor, active in the early decades of the century with serialized novels and some stories for the Frank A. MUNSEY magazines. His Edgar Rice BURROUGHS-inspired sf/fantasy trilogy, *Polaris of the Snows* (1915-16 *All-Story*; **1965**), *Minos of Sardanes* (1916 *All-Story*; **1966**) and *Polaris and the Immortals* (1917 *All-Story* as "Polaris and the Goddess Glorian"; **1968**), features the improbably durable Tarzan-like Polaris Janess, who spends his Antarctic childhood killing polar bears [*sic*] by hand and as an adult enjoys adventures in a LOST-WORLD colony of Greeks and with technologically advanced survivors of ATLANTIS. "The Sky Woman" (1920 *All-Story*) concludes with the tragic death of a Martian woman borne to Earth in a meteorite. The more sophisticated "Dr Martone's Microscope" (1920 *All-Story*) is a homage to Fitz-James O'BRIEN's "The Diamond Lens" (1858) and Ray CUMMINGS's "The Girl in the Golden Atom" (1919), both of which are mentioned by name. At the same time it invokes a surreptitious sexuality: the doctor's microscope has been used for voyeuristic purposes. At his best CBS was a writer who transcended PULP-MAGAZINE formulae. [RB/JC]

Other works: *The Island God Forgot* (**1922**); *The Ace of Blades* (**1924**); *A Cavalier of Navarre* (**1925**); *Sword Play* (**1926**); *The Seven Blue Diamonds* (**1927**).

See also: ESCHATOLOGY.

STIMSON, F.J. [r] ◊ Robert GRANT; John Boyle O'REILLY.

STINE, G(EORGE) HARRY (1928-   ) US writer who was for many years best known for work published under his pseudonym, Lee Correy, but who in the 1980s began increasingly to write under his own name, though his popularizing nonfiction about space travel and satellites had always been released as by GHS, as was his first story, "Galactic Gadgeteers" for *ASF* in 1951. As Correy, his best-known sf tale is "And a Star to Steer Her By" (1953), to which his first novel, a juvenile, *Starship through Space* (**1954**), is a sequel. There soon followed another juvenile, *Rocket Man* (**1955**), and *Contraband Rocket* (**1956**), about amateurs launching a SPACESHIP. GHS's preoccupation with space travel has never, in fact, faltered, and although many years passed before his next novel as Correy, his urgent advocacy of the space programme remained as attractively fresh as ever. *Star Driver* (**1980**), *Shuttle Down* (**1981**), *Space Doctor* (**1981**), *Manna* (**1984**) and *A Matter of Metalaw* (**1986**), all as Correy, variously work to increase the sense of the reality of space, an agenda perhaps less evident in *The Abode of Life* * (**1982**), a STAR TREK tie. Under his own name, GHS's fiction has been less ambitious, being restricted mainly to the NEAR-FUTURE **Warbots** sequence in which humans and MACHINES clashingly interface as the US Robot Infantry fights evil everywhere: *Warbots* (**1988**), *Warbots #2: Operation Steel Band* (**1988**), *#3: The Bastaard* [*sic*] *Rebellion* (**1988**), *#4: Sierra Madre* (**1988**), *#5: Operation High Dragon* (**1989**), *#6: The Lost Battalion* (**1989**), *#7: Operation Iron Fist* (**1989**), *#8: Force of Arms* (**1990**), *#9: Blood Siege*

(**1990**), *#10: Guts and Glory* (**1991**) and *#11: Warrior Shield* (**1992**).

Nonfiction works of sf interest include *Earth Satellites and the Race for Space Superiority* (**1957**), *Rocket Power and Space Flight* (**1957**), *The Third Industrial Revolution* (**1980**), *Shuttle into Space: A Ride in America's Space Transportation* (**1978**), *The Space Enterprise* (**1980**), *Space Power* (**1981**), *Confrontation in Space* (**1981**), *The Hopeful Future* (**1983**), *The Silicon Gods* (**1984**) and *Handbook for Space Colonists* (**1985**). [JC]

STINE, HANK (1945-   ) US writer, born Henry Eugene Stein, whose *Season of the Witch* (**1968**) interestingly blends sf and erotica in the story of a man biologically transformed into a woman as a punishment for rape and murder, but who eventually finds her/his true role and contentment as a trans-sexual. Other sf novels include *Thrill City* (**1969**), set in a city devastated by WWIII, and a novelization tied to the tv series *The* PRISONER, *A Day in the Life* * (**1970**). HS was editor of GALAXY SCIENCE FICTION for 2 issues in 1979. [MJ]

See also: PSYCHOLOGY; SEX.

STINGRAY UK tv series with animated puppets (1964-65). AP Films with ATV/ITC. Created Gerry and Sylvia Anderson. Prod Gerry Anderson. The writers were the Andersons (3 episodes), Alan Fennell, Dennis Spooner. 39 25min episodes. Colour.

The 3rd of the **SuperMarionation** puppet sf series for children (◊ Gerry and Sylvia ANDERSON *for details*) and the first in colour, *S* was also one of the better. Handsome but irascible Troy Tempest pilots the atomic submersible *Stingray* for WASP (World Aquanaut Security Patrol) and is involved in a love triangle with Marina, lovely but mute daughter of an undersea emperor, and Atlanta, wistful daughter of WASP's crusty commander. Most weeks saw somewhat repetitive undersea menaces defeated, primarily those associated with the evil but incompetent Titans, an "aquaphibian" race. The miniature sets were good (special effects Derek Meddings). Some episodes were later cobbled together as "films" which probably never saw theatrical release but were shown abroad as tv features. One was *Invaders from the Deep* (1981), made up from the episodes *Hostages of the Deep, Emergency Marineville, The Big Gun* and *Deep Heat*, all written by Fennell. [PN]

STIRLING, S(TEPHEN) M(ICHAEL) (1954-   ) French-born Canadian writer who began publishing work of genre interest with *Snowbrother* (**1985** US), the 1st vol of the **Fifth Millennium** fantasy sequence, which continued with *The Sharpest Edge* (**1986** US) with Shirley Meier (1960-   ), *The Cage* (**1989**) with Meier, and *Shadow's Son* (**1991**) with Meier and Karen Wehrstein. It was, however, with his 2nd series, the ALTERNATE-WORLD **Draka** sequence – *Marching through Georgia* (**1988**), *Under the Yoke* (**1989**) and *The Stone Dogs* (**1990**) – that SMS came to notice because of the considerable violence (undeniable) and right-wing convictions (apparent). In an ALTERNATE-WORLD 19th century generated in part by the success of Charles

BABBAGE's Difference Engine, a group of British loyalists, having previously escaped the consequences of the American Revolution by emigrating to South Africa, have established there a racist feudalism, the Domination of Draka, which soon comes to dominate the entire continent. In the first volume the start of WWII sees Draka allied with the USA against the Nazis, and winning a crushing victory against the German hordes in Soviet Georgia; subsequently, slavery is extended to newly conquered territories. This nightmare (which SMS presents with seeming affection) continues in subsequent volumes, with the Domination seemingly ineradicable and a post-war conflict between the Drakans (who have mastered GENETIC ENGINEERING) and the USA (expert in COMPUTERS) extending into space.

SMS has also contributed to Larry NIVEN's **Man-Kzin Wars** SHARED-WORLD anthologies, with work in *Man-Kzin Wars II* * (anth **1989**), *Man-Kzin Wars III* * (anth **1990**) and *Man-Kzin Wars IV* * (anth **1991**), plus a novel in the sequence, *The Children's Hour* * (**1991**) with Jerry POURNELLE. Also with Pournelle, to whose **CoDominion** sequence the tale belongs, he wrote *Go Tell the Spartans* (**1991**) about Falkenberg, the series' main protagonist. Other novels include *The Forge* (**1991**) and *The Hammer* (**1992**), both with David A. DRAKE, the first volumes of **The General**, a military series. SMS has also ed *Fantastic World War II* (anth **1990**) and *The Fantastic Civil War* (anth **1991**), both with Martin H. GREENBERG, Charles G. WAUGH and Frank McSherran Jr, and *Power* (anth **1991**).   [JC]

See also: CANADA; WAR.

STIRRING SCIENCE STORIES US PULP MAGAZINE, changing to BEDSHEET-size for #4. 4 issues Feb 1941-Mar 1942, published bimonthly by Albing Publications for #1-#3, then by Manhattan Fiction Publications for the final abortive revival 9 months later; ed Donald A. WOLLHEIM. The companion magazine to COSMIC STORIES, *SSS* was produced under similar adverse financial conditions: writers were promised payment only if *SSS* were a success. 3 issues carried covers by artist Hannes BOK. *SSS* featured many stories by FUTURIANS, including James BLISH and C.M. KORNBLUTH (who contributed various stories under at least 3 pseudonyms), and printed Damon KNIGHT's first published story, "Resilience". *SSS* was presented as two magazines in one: the second half was separately titled *Stirring Fantasy Fiction*, and came complete with its own editorial and readers' departments.   [MJE/PN]

STITH, JOHN E(DWARD) (1947-   ) US writer and software engineering manager who began to publish sf with "Early Winter" for *Fantastic* in 1979. His first novel, *Scapescope* (**1984**) – HARD SF like all his work – uses his work experience at the NORAD Cheyenne Mountain Complex to extrapolate conditions in that location two centuries hence. *Memory Blank* (**1986**) places a classic sf protagonist – the hero with amnesia – on an L-5 orbital colony ($\lozenge$ LAGRANGE POINT). *Death Tolls* (**1987**) is a detective mystery set on a terraformed

MARS (*see also* TERRAFORMING), and *Deep Quarry* (**1989**), set on a planet far from the Solar System (to which JES had previously restricted himself), pits a private eye against various mysteries in a hard-boiled style. More impressive than any of these is *Redshift Rendezvous* (**1990**), set on a FASTER-THAN-LIGHT starship travelling through a version of HYPERSPACE in which the speed of light is so low (22mph [35kph]) that its passage is visible. Within this intriguingly presented environment, a murder mystery, a hijack and other events occur; but the appeal of the novel lies in the playing-out of the concept – or thought experiment – at its heart.   [JC]

See also: IMAGINARY SCIENCE

STOCKBRIDGE, GRANT House name used by Popular Publications, especially in *The* SPIDER. Most if not all the GS stories in *The Spider* were by Norvell W. PAGE. It has been suggested that Frank Gruber, Reginald T. Maitland and Emil Tepperman also used this pseudonym.   [PN]

STOCKTON, FRANK R(ICHARD) (1834-1902) US author and editor. He worked on *Scribner's Magazine* before being assistant editor of ST NICHOLAS MAGAZINE 1873-81. It was during this period, while writing for children, that he developed the combination of humour and fantasy featured in such works as *Tales out of School* (coll **1875**), which includes "How Three Men Went to the Moon", and *The Floating Prince and Other Fairy Tales* (coll **1881**). His numerous short stories appeared in over 20 collections, of which several were composite volumes. His better works include "The Lady or the Tiger?" (1882), a classic puzzle story, "The Transferred Ghost" (1882) and its sequel "The Spectral Mortgage" (1883), and his sf story "A Tale of Negative Gravity" (1884). Among other short sf stories were "The Tricycle of the Future" (1885) and "My Translataphone" (1900; reprinted in *The Science Fiction of Frank R. Stockton* [coll **1976**] ed Richard Gid Powers).

Later, when FRS turned to novels, he continued to use sf themes occasionally, though his humorous style remained the most prominent feature. In *The Great War Syndicate* (**1889**) a naval WAR between the UK and USA is resolved when the British see the advanced weaponry arrayed against them. *The Adventures of Captain Horn* (**1895**) is a LOST-WORLD novel. *The Great Stone of Sardis* (**1898**), set in 1947, culminates in the discovery that the Earth is a gigantic diamond with a relatively thin crust of surface soil. *The Vizier of the Two-Horned Alexander* (**1899**) lightly recasts the Wandering Jew theme.

FRS was influential on John Kendrick BANGS and other humorous fantasists and is regarded as a forerunner of O. Henry (1862-1910) in his use of the trick ending. His complete works appear in *The Novels and Stories of Frank R. Stockton* (23 vols **1899-1904**). A posthumously written collection, *The Return of Frank R. Stockton* (coll **1913**), "transcribed" by the medium Miss Etta de Camp, is surprisingly good and stylistically recognizable, though death has clearly impaired his vision.   [JE]

Other works: Collections with at least some sf/fantasy material include *Ting-a-Ling* (coll **1879**); *The Lady or the Tiger? and Other Stories* (coll **1884**); *The Christmas Wreck and Other Stories* (coll **1886**); *The Bee-Man of Orn and Other Fanciful Tales* (coll **1887**); *A Borrowed Month and Other Stories* (coll **1887** UK); *Amos Kilbright: His Adscititious Experiences, with Other Stories* (coll **1888**); *The Stories of the Three Burglars* (coll **1889**); *The Rudder Granges Abroad and Other Stories* (coll **1891**); *The Great Show in Kobol-Land* (**1891**); *The Clocks of Rondaine and Other Stories* (coll **1892**); *The Watchmaker's Wife and Other Stories* (coll **1893**); *Fanciful Tales* (coll **1894**); *A Chosen Few* (coll **1895**); *A Story-Teller's Pack* (coll **1897**); *Afield and Afloat* (coll **1900**); *John Gayther's Garden, and the Stories Told Therein* (coll **1902**); *The Queen's Museum, and Other Fanciful Tales* (coll **1906**); *The Magic Egg and Other Stories* (coll **1907**); *The Lost Dryad* (**1912** chap); *The Fairy Tales of Frank Stockton* (coll **1990**).

See also: UNDER THE SEA.

STOKES, SIMPSON ◊ F. Dubrez FAWCETT.

STOLBOV, BRUCE (?   -   ) US writer whose post-HOLOCAUST novel, *Last Fall* (**1987**), describes the dilemma faced by a wood-dwelling pacifistic enclave of survivors when gun-bearing intruders arrive. The tale is notable for the quiet warmth of its depiction of a renewed natural world.   [JC]

STONE, LESLIE F(RANCES) (1905-c1987) US writer who began publishing sf with "Men with Wings" for *Air Wonder Stories* in 1929, and was active in the field for the next 8 years, publishing at least 17 stories. Her 2 sf books are *When the Sun Went Out* (**1929** chap), a FAR-FUTURE tale which appeared in Hugo GERNSBACK's **Science Fiction** series, and *Out of the Void* (1929 *AMZ*; 1967), a SPACE OPERA. "Across the Void" (1930 *AMZ*), a sequel to the latter, attained magazine publication only.   [JC/PN]

See also: LIFE ON OTHER WORLDS; WOMEN SF WRITERS.

STONG, PHIL(IP DUFFIELD) (1899-1957) US novelist and editor, author of the thrice-filmed *State Fair* (**1932**). His *The Other Worlds* (anth **1941**; vt *25 Modern Stories of Mystery and Imagination* 1942 US) was the first important sf ANTHOLOGY. Its 25 stories, about half sf, half horror, were mostly from the PULP MAGAZINES, not previously regarded as a proper source of material (of sf at least) for respectable hardcover books.   [PN]

STOREY, ANTHONY (1928-   ) UK writer, formerly a rugby player, brother of the novelist David Storey (1933-   ) and author of a SATIRE-drenched trilogy – *The Rector* (**1970**), *The Centre Holds* (**1973**) and *The Saviour* (**1978**) – which deals with the traumas surrounding the announced birth of a child its mother claims to be the MESSIAH, and the 1980s upheavals centring on the ambivalent effect of the new Jesus upon an unfit world.   [JC]

STOREY, RICHARD [s] ◊ H.L. GOLD.

STORM, BRIAN ◊ Brian HOLLOWAY.

STORM, JANNICK [r] ◊ DENMARK.

STORM, MALLORY ◊ Paul W. FAIRMAN.

STORM, RUSSELL ◊ Robert Moore WILLIAMS.

STORM PLANET ◊ PLANETA BUR.

STORR, CATHERINE (1913-   ) UK doctor and writer, for many years a psychotherapist, since 1963 an author of journalism, children's books – most famously *Marianne Dreams* (**1958**; vt *The Magic Drawing Pencil* 1960 US), in which physical and mental malaises are incarnated in a fantasy world – and an sf novel, *Unnatural Fathers* (**1976**), in which the success of an experiment to make men capable of child-bearing causes great upheavals in a NEAR-FUTURE UK.   [JC/BS]

Other works for children: *Rufus* (**1969**); *The Adventures of Polly and the Wolf* (**1970**); *Thursday* (**1972**).

STORY, JACK TREVOR (1917-1991) UK writer who remains best known for his first novel, *The Trouble with Harry* (**1949**), not sf, which was filmed by Alfred Hitchcock (1889-1980) in 1955. The rumours that he wrote several of the Volsted GRIDBAN sf novels are unverified, but certainly he did produce many pseudonymous books over the first decade or so of his career. His openly acknowledged work included non-sf – but remarkable – tales for the **Sexton Blake Library** and several novels which used sf components to make their points about the decline of England and the loss of youth, including *Hitler Needs You* (**1970**), *One Last Mad Embrace* (**1970**), *Little Dog's Day* (**1971**), which is a genuine sf DYSTOPIA, the surrealistic *The Wind in the Snottygobble Tree* (**1971**), *Morag's Flying Fortress* (**1976**), which is a borderline novel about sexual obsession, and *Up River* (**1979**; vt *The Screwrape Lettuce* 1980), in which an appalling aphrodisiac devastates the UK while the secret police, unnoticed, grab power.   [JC]

STORY OF MANKIND, THE ◊ Irwin ALLEN.

STORY-PRESS CORPORATION ◊ BLUE BOOK MAGAZINE.

STORYTELLER UK pocketbook magazine published by Liverpolitan, Birkenhead. The front cover bears the variant title *International Storyteller*, while the spine and title page read *Storyteller*. #3 was an all-sf issue, all stories (apart from Chris BOYCE's first) by writers unknown in sf; it is dated 1964, no ed named. Other issues were not sf.   [PN]

STOUT, REX (TODHUNTER) (1886-1975) US writer, best known for his **Nero Wolfe** detective novels, beginning with *Fer-de-Lance* (**1934**) and continuing into the 1970s. *Under the Andes* (1914 *All-Story Magazine*; **1984**) describes, in a style very unlike his deft mature drawl, an underground LOST WORLD of dwarf Incans. In *The President Vanishes* (**1934**), published anon, the disappearance of the US President causes a NEAR-FUTURE crisis.   [JC]

See also: DIME-NOVEL SF.

STOVER, LEON E(UGENE) (1929-   ) US editor and writer, professor of ANTHROPOLOGY at the Illinois Institute of Technology, where he also taught sf courses, and science editor of *AMZ* 1967-9. He was most active in sf in collaboration with Harry HARRISON, editing with him *Apeman, Spaceman: Anthropological*

Science Fiction (anth **1968**), and writing with him *Stonehenge* (**1972**), a historical novel in which refugees from ATLANTIS – here rather conventionally identified as the Mediterranean island, Thera (Santorini), which exploded in Mycenaean times – help build the eponymous megalith. With Willis E. MCNELLY he ed *Above the Human Landscape: An Anthology of Social Science Fiction* (anth **1972**). He was founder and first chairman of the JOHN W. CAMPBELL MEMORIAL AWARD.

LES's critical studies perhaps represent him at his most interesting. *La science-fiction américaine: essai d'anthropologie culturelle* ["American Science Fiction: An Essay in Cultural Anthropology"] (**1972** France) was based on one of his courses. Ostensibly a RECURSIVE tale, *The Shaving of Karl Marx: An Instant Novel of Ideas, after the Manner of Thomas Love Peacock, in which Lenin and H.G. Wells Talk about the Political Meaning of the Scientific Romances* (**1982**) was more accurately a dramatized debate. In *The Prophetic Soul: A Reading of H.G. Wells' Things to Come together with his Film Treatment "Whither Mankind?" and the Postproduction Script* (**1987**) LES continued to argue that H.G. WELLS – especially in his Samurai mood – produced Leninist solutions to social problems. His *Robert A. Heinlein* (**1987**), more stridently, works better as an assault upon H. Bruce FRANKLIN's powerful study of HEINLEIN than as a balanced presentation of the author; the advocacy of his friend and subject in *Harry Harrison* (**1990**) proves ineffective through lack of judicious distance.

Throughout his work, LES has been perhaps most notable – after his erudition is acknowledged – for a gadfly vigour. [JC]

See also: ECONOMICS.

STOW, (JULIAN) RANDOLPH (1935-   ) Australian writer whose novels tend to embed deeply alienated protagonists into venues – some remote – which are described with anthropological precision, resulting in tales, whether non-genre or sf/fantasy, that verge constantly upon fable. In *Tourmaline* (**1963**) the venue is a decaying town in backwoods Australia and the time the NEAR FUTURE; the narrative is loaded with echoes of myth and forebodings. The 5 protagonists of *Visitants* (**1979**), set in Papua, supply a mosaic of responses to a First-Contact experience in a manner that remotely prefigures the strategies underlying Karen Joy FOWLER's *Sarah Canary* (**1991**). [JC]

Other works: *Midnite: The Story of a Wild Colonial Boy* (**1967**); *The Girl Green as Elderflower* (**1980**).

STRAND MAGAZINE, THE UK magazine published monthly Jan 1891-Mar 1950 by George Newnes Ltd; ed Sir George Newnes and others. *TSM* was cheap, though not in appearance: it contained illustrated articles and fiction by well known authors. Its success created many rivals. In competition with PEARSON'S MAGAZINE (begun 1896) it started to feature sf regularly, having earlier published "An Express of the Future" (1895), a short story by Michel Verne (1861-1925), whom the editors mistook for his father (M.

– "Monsieur" – Verne), bylining the story Jules VERNE. Foremost among *TSM*'s sf contributors were Grant ALLEN, H.G. WELLS, Fred M. WHITE and Arthur Conan DOYLE, whose **Sherlock Holmes** stories had already given the magazine its initial success. In sf terms it is best remembered for the serializations of Wells's *The First Men in the Moon* (1900-1; **1901**) and Doyle's *The Lost World* (1912; **1912**), *The Poison Belt* (1913; **1913**) and "The Maracot Deep" (1927-8). But there were many others, including L.T. Meade's (Mrs Elizabeth Thomasina Smith [1854-1914]) and Robert Eustace's *The Brotherhood of the Seven Kings* (Jan-Oct 1898; **1899**). *SM* is an excellent source for sf stories intensely characteristic of the late Victorian and Edwardian period in the UK. [JE/PN]

Further reading: *Science Fiction By Gaslight: A History and Anthology of Science Fiction in the Popular Magazines 1891-1911* (**1968**) by Sam MOSKOWITZ; *The Strand Magazine 1891-1950: A Selective Checklist* (**1979** chap) by J.F. Whitt.

STRANG, HERBERT Collaborative pseudonym of UK writers George Herbert Ely (1866-1958) and C.J. L'Estrange (1867-1947) used on a large number of boys' adventure stories, among them a series of novels about futuristic TRANSPORTATION devices, including *King of the Air, or To Morocco on an Airship* (**1908**), *Lord of the Seas* (**1908**), *The Cruise of the Gyro-Car* (**1910**), *Round the World in Seven Days* (**1910**), *The Flying Boat* (**1912**) and *A Thousand Miles an Hour* (**1924**). These were competently written with a certain Edwardian dash, and a fair amount of imperialist cliché. HS also published future-WAR Yellow Peril stories. [PN]

Other works: *The Old Man of the Mountain* (**1916**); *The Heir of a Hundred Kings* (**1930**).

See also: UNDER THE SEA.

STRANGE ADVENTURES UK magazine, PULP-MAGAZINE size. 2 undated issues 1946 and 1947, published by Hamilton & Co., Stafford; ed anon. *SA* was an unmemorable juvenile sf magazine whose authors were unknown and probably pseudonymous; a companion was FUTURISTIC STORIES. [FHP]

STRANGE BEHAVIOR ◊ DEAD KIDS.

STRANGE FANTASY One of the many reprint DIGEST-size magazines published by Sol Cohen's Ultimate Publishing Co.; ed anon. 6 issues, 3 in 1969 (#8-#10) and 3 in 1970 (#11-#13). The strange numbering seems to be connected with the temporary death in 1969 of SCIENCE FICTION (ADVENTURE) CLASSICS after #8, but *SF* is not simply a variant title of the latter, which began again in 1971 with #12. Also, *SF* concentrated on fantasy (while printing some sf), mostly reprinted from FANTASTIC during the period of Cele GOLDSMITH's editorship. [PN]

STRANGE INVADERS Film (1983). EMI Films/Orion/A Michael Laughlin Production. Dir Michael Laughlin, starring Paul Le Mat, Nancy Allen, Diana Scarwid, Michael Lerner, Wallace Shawn, Fiona Lewis. Screenplay William Condon, Laughlin. 93 mins. Colour.

A very agreeable pastiche of movies like INVASION

OF THE BODY SNATCHERS (1956) ($ PARANOIA). The prologue shows a flying saucer ($ UFOS) landing in a small town in 1958. The rest of this charming SATIRE is set in 1983, when entomologist Charlie (Bigelow) comes to learn that Centerville (the town) is now occupied by ALIENS in human form, that his wife (Scarwid) is an alien – he had previously regarded her blank manner as normal – that his (half-breed) daughter is to be taken with the aliens when they leave, and that New York is being infiltrated. The alien anthropological survey team have adopted the appearance and manner of small-town Americans of the Eisenhower years, and naturally appear grossly out of place in modern New York. (MEET THE APPLEGATES [1990] adopts a similar premise.) Director Laughlin has his cake and eats it too by injecting genuine suspense into a story that is also deeply funny. This is the second of a projected but unfinished **Strange** trilogy from Laughlin, the first being DEAD KIDS (1981; vt *Strange Behavior*). [PN]

STRANGE NEW WORLD Made-for-tv film (1975). Warner Bros. TV/ABC. Dir Robert Butler, starring John Saxon, Kathleen Miller, Keene Curtis, James Olson, Martine Beswick, Gerrit Graham. Screenplay Walon Green, Ronald F. Graham, Al Ramrus. 100 mins. Colour.

The 1970s are littered with tv movies representing Gene RODDENBERRY's repeated attempts at pilot episodes for new tv series, though in this case he is not credited. This editing together of 2 never-aired episodes is a sort of sequel to GENESIS II (1973) and PLANET EARTH (1974), sharing the same star, Saxon, with the latter. Three astronauts, after 180 years in SUSPENDED ANIMATION, return to an Earth devastated by a meteor storm. What is left of civilization is balkanized, each group differing. The astronauts encounter two such groups. Eterna is a sterile utopia, with an obsession for cleanliness, that has conquered death; the wholesome travellers ensure that death makes a cleansing return to Eterna before they leave. They go on to restore peace in Arboria, a land divided by the Hunters and the Zookeepers, the latter being fanatical conservationists ready to kill to achieve their aims. [JB/PN]

STRANGE PLASMA US SEMIPROZINE, small-BEDSHEET format, subtitled "speculative + imaginative fiction", published and ed Steve Pasechnick from Cambridge, Massachusetts, 4 issues 1989 to mid-1991, irregular, may no longer be current. This fiction magazine, too irregular to be influential, has quite high standards; it has published good stories by Terry DOWLING, Carol EMSHWILLER, R.A. LAFFERTY, Paul PARK, Cherry WILDER, Gene WOLFE and others. It features an interesting column of opinion by Gwyneth JONES. [PN]

STRANGER WITHIN, THE Made-for-tv film (1974). Lorimar/ABC TV. Dir Lee Philips, starring Barbara Eden, George Grizzard, Joyce Van Patten, David Doyle. Teleplay Richard MATHESON, based on his "Mother by Protest" (1953). 72 mins. Colour.

A woman (Eden) becomes pregnant – inexplicably, as her husband (Grizzard) is certified to be sterile. It turns out that she has been impregnated by a wandering Martian seed. At first the unpleasant side-effects of the pregnancy drive her to an attempted abortion, but she finally bears a healthy child who, along with a number of other Martian babies, floats off back towards Mars. The film, whose atmosphere of mounting PARANOIA is well achieved, belongs to the sinister-pregnancy movie cycle set off by *Rosemary's Baby* (1968). [JB/PN]

STRANGE STORIES US PULP MAGAZINE. 13 bimonthly issues Feb 1939-Feb 1941, published by Better Publications Inc.; ed Leo MARGULIES or Mort WEISINGER, uncredited. A companion magazine to STARTLING STORIES and THRILLING WONDER STORIES, *SS* was devoted to supernatural and weird fiction, in not very successful competition with WEIRD TALES. Most of its covers were by Earle K. BERGEY. Its contributors included August DERLETH, Henry KUTTNER and Manly Wade WELLMAN. Although its companion magazines always publicized each other, they hardly mentioned *SS*. The magazine has remained remarkably little known. [MJE]

STRANGE TALES 1. US PULP MAGAZINE. 7 issues Sep 1931-Jan 1933, published by Clayton Magazines; ed Harry BATES. *ST* (subtitled "of Mystery and Terror") was a companion magazine to *Astounding Stories* ($ ASTOUNDING SCIENCE-FICTION) and was similar in editorial policy to WEIRD TALES; it carried very little sf. Its contributors included Robert E. HOWARD, Clark Ashton SMITH, Jack WILLIAMSON and others familiar to readers of *ASF* and *Weird Tales*. Its covers were all by WESSO. Like *ASF* it ceased publication when the Clayton Magazines went into liquidation, but was not revived when STREET & SMITH acquired the rights to the Clayton magazines. *Strange Tales* (anth **1976**) is a facsimile collection of stories from the magazine.

2. UK DIGEST weird-story reprint magazine; 2 undated issues 1946, published by Utopian Publications; ed Walter GILLINGS, uncredited, and featuring stories by, among others, Robert BLOCH, Ray BRADBURY, H.P. LOVECRAFT, Clark Ashton SMITH, Jack WILLIAMSON and John Beynon Harris (John WYNDHAM). [MJE/PN]

STRANGE WORLD OF PLANET X, THE 1. UK tv serial (1956). ATV. Prod Arthur Lane. Dir Quentin Lawrence, starring William Lucas, David Garth, Helen Cherry, Maudie Edwards. Teleplay René RAY. 7 25min episodes. Scientists discover a formula giving access to the 4th DIMENSION and, with others, are thereby transported to the abstractly arid Planet X.

2. UK film (1958; vt *The Cosmic Monster*). Eros/DCA. Dir Gilbert Gunn, starring Forrest Tucker, Gaby André, Martin Benson, Wyndham Goldie. Screenplay Paul Ryder, Joe Ambor, based on *The Strange World of Planet X* * (**1957**) by René Ray. 75 mins. B/w.

A mad scientist's magnetic experiments rupture Earth's ionosphere, thereby permitting the penetration of cosmic rays (!), which create giant insects on an area of Earth 80 miles (130km) across. The creatures are eventually destroyed by a friendly ALIEN. The special effects were manifestly done on a tiny budget; the film is normally regarded as mediocre. Its immediate source was probably Ray's novelization of **1**, rather than the series itself, since the plot-lines differ. In the film, Planet X is Earth and the Cosmic Monster is Man. [PN/JB]

STRATEMEYER, EDWARD T. (1869-1930) US dime-novel writer (◊ DIME-NOVEL SF), entrepreneur and mass producer of boys' books. He is chiefly important as the operator of the Stratemeyer Syndicate, a story factory (or packager) that produced hundreds of boys' and girls' books in such popular series as **The Bobbsey Twins**, **The Hardy Boys**, **Nancy Drew** and many others. ETS prepared plot summaries, farmed out writing to a stable of freelance writers to whom he paid pittances, and sold the products to publishers. The **Great Marvel** series as by Roy ROCKWOOD, the first 6 vols of which were written out by Howard R. GARIS, constitutes perhaps the first clothbound sf series in any language. The **TOM SWIFT** books, written by Garis 1910-32, were the most popular boys' books of all time. Borderline series included **Don Sturdy** (collaborator unknown) and **Bomba, the Jungle Boy** (collaborator unknown). After ETS's death his daughter Harriet Stratemeyer ADAMS successfully carried on the syndicate. [EFB]

STRATTON, THOMAS ◊ Robert COULSON; Gene DeWEESE.

STRAUS, RALPH (1892-1950) UK writer whose only full-scale sf novel, *The Dust which is God: An Undimensional Adventure* (**1907**), tamely depicts a world which has evolved religiously. In *5000 A.D.: A Review and an Excursion, Read Before ye Sette of Odd Volumes at Oddenino's Imperial Restaurant on Jan. 24th, 1911* (coll **1911** chap) the review is of the sf genre and the excursion is a TIME-TRAVEL tale. [JC]

STRAUSS, ERWIN S. (? -) A member of the Massachusetts Institute of Technology SF Society, for whom he compiled *Index to the S-F Magazines, 1951-1965* (**1966**), a BIBLIOGRAPHY which covers the same years as Norman METCALF's similar index; both succeed the original index for 1926-50 by Donald B. DAY. Unlike Metcalf's, ESS's book is compiled from a computer printout, and contains an issue-by-issue contents listing of the magazines for the period, in addition to story and author indexes. The MIT group, now known as N.E.S.F.A (New England Science Fiction Association) has produced subsequent vols, starting with *Index to the Science Fiction Magazines 1966-1970* (**1971**), with annual vols since, which, from 1971, have also indexed the contents of original anthologies. A well known fan, EES wrote *The Complete Guide to Science Fiction Conventions* (**1983** chap). [PN]

STREET & SMITH Important US magazine publisher, established in the 19th century with various dime-novel series like *Good News* and *The Nugget Library*, and publishing early juvenile sf in the **Tom Edison**

Jr. and **Electric Bob** series. The general-fiction *The* POPULAR MAGAZINE (1903-31) published a good few sf stories too. S&S was particularly famous for its Westerns, including Ned Buntline's deeply influential **Buffalo Bill Cody** stories, which helped mythologize the West. S&S were prominent in the splitting of PULP MAGAZINES into various genres, each aiming to have a market leader, one example being *Detective Story Magazine*. S&S was also the first to carry over from dime-novel publishing the idea of a pulp magazine devoted to a single character, with the very successful *The Shadow* (1931-49), whose adventures bordered sometimes on sf (◊ Walter B. GIBSON), *The Avenger* (◊ Paul ERNST) and, rather closer to sf, DOC SAVAGE MAGAZINE (1933-49).

When Clayton Publishing Company, publishers of *Astounding Stories* (◊ ASTOUNDING SCIENCE-FICTION) began to flounder in 1933, S&S bought the magazine in order to fill yet another market niche. S&S's considerable financial backing meant that *ASF* could pay quite good rates, get good stories, and compete strongly in the market, which it did. Later, S&S (and editor John W. CAMPBELL Jr) added a fantasy companion magazine, UNKNOWN (later *Unknown Worlds*). S&S's period of power coincided with the pulp boom; from 1948 the firm was phasing out its pulp publication and, with paperback books and tv increasingly threatening the dominance of the magazines, declining in importance (◊ PUBLISHING). S&S expired in 1961; its only remaining sf title, *ASF*, was sold to Condé Nast, the last S&S issue being Jan 1961. [PN]

STRETE, CRAIG (KEE) (1950-) US Native American writer – the suggestion has been bruited that CS is the pseudonym of a Cherokee who does not wish to reveal his real name, but this has not been confirmed. He has written as CS and under other names, by himself and in collaboration; at least 40 of the 80 or more stories claimed for him must be under unrevealed names. As CS, he began publishing for *If* in 1974 with the well known "Time Deer", a runner-up for the 1975 NEBULA; 2 other tales appeared simultaneously. From the mid-1970s he maintained a publishing connection with a Dutch house, and his first collection appeared initially in Dutch as *Als Al Andere Faalt* (coll **1976** Netherlands), only later gaining English-language release as *If All Else Fails* (exp coll **1980**). His first book in English was *The Bleeding Man and Other Science Fiction Stories* (coll **1977**) for older children. Intensely written, spare, though with lunges into flamboyance, committed and often moving, his tales frequently combine prose rhythms and subject matter connoting a Native American background with more usual sf themes like COLONIZATION OF OTHER WORLDS, as in "When They Find You" from the latter vol. Though passionately couched, this work is sometimes crude in its opposition of the total horror of the White world with the mythic "naturalness" of the Native American: there is a sense, perhaps, of protesting too much. Later collections include *Dreams that Burn in the Night* (coll **1982**) and

Death Chants (coll **1988**), the latter – as its title signifies – dealing frequently with terminal moments, though at times comically.

After some children's fantasies – those published in English include *Paint Your Face on a Drowning in the River* (**1978**), *When Grandfather Journeys into Winter* (**1979**) and *Big Thunder Magic* (**1990**) – and the nongenre *Burn Down the Night* (**1982**), CS published a carnival fantasy, *To Make Death Love Us* (**1987**) as by Sovereign Falconer, and *Death in the Spirit House* (**1988**), over which controversy reigned for some time due to accusations by Ron MONTANA that the book had been plagiarized, very nearly in whole, from a manuscript given by him to CS. Granting only a modicum of Montana's case, CS mounted an elaborate defence. As part of an agreed settlement, the book was eventually republished as *Face in the Snow* (**1992**) by Montana. [JC]

STRIBLING, T.S. [r] ◊ APES AND CAVEMEN (IN THE HUMAN WORLD).

STRICK, PHILIP (1939-   ) UK sf and film critic, anthologist, teacher, and director of a film library. In 1969 he initiated one of the first adult evening classes in sf in the UK, sponsored by the University of London (◊ SF IN THE CLASSROOM), which continued until 1992. PS's *Science Fiction Movies* (**1976**) is a witty, rather helter-skelter account of sf CINEMA, one of the best early books on the subject (despite its lack of a filmography); his film criticism continues to appear in *Monthly Film Bulletin* (now incorporated in *Sight and Sound*). *Antigrav* (anth **1975**) ed PS assembles funny sf short fiction, including John BROSNAN's first-published story. [PN]

STRICKLAND, BRAD Working name of US writer William Bradley Strickland (1947-   ), who has concentrated mainly on fantasy, most notably perhaps in early stories like "The Herders of Grimm" for *FSF* in 1984 and in the **Jeremy Moon** sequence – *Moon Dreams* (**1988**), *Nul's Quest* (**1989**) and *Wizard's Mole* (**1991**) – which conveys its protagonist into a wittily constructed dream world, where he takes his stand. BS's first novel, *To Stand beneath the Sun* (**1986**), is an sf adventure whose protagonist must come to terms with a world dominated by women. *Ark Liberty* (**1992**) as by Will Bradley treats the ecocatastrophic (◊ ECOLOGY) near-death of Earth with melodramatic panache, pitting its scientist hero against suicidal governments and embedding him – after his physical death – into the eponymous undersea biome as its computer mentor and spirit, while centuries pass. [JC]
Other works: *ShadowShow* (**1988**); *Children of the Knife* (**1990**), medical horror.

STRIEBER, WHITLEY (1945-   ) US writer, much better known for horror novels like *The Wolfen* (**1978**) and *The Hunger* (**1981**) than for his sf. *War Day: And the Journey Onward* (**1984**) with James Kunetka (1944-   ) is a remarkably detailed post-HOLOCAUST tour of the USA after a 1988 nuclear conflict. *Wolf of Shadows* (**1985**) is a juvenile set in a post-holocaust nuclear winter. *Nature's End* (**1986**), again with Kunetka, is set in a NEAR-FUTURE world devastated by OVERPOPULATION (*see also* ECOLOGY). *Communion: A True Story* (**1987**) and *Transformation: The Breakthrough* (**1988**) purport to be nonfictional accounts of his encounters with visiting ALIEN intelligences (◊ UFOS). Also centred on ufology is his sf novel *Majestic* (**1989**; rev 1990), whose subject is the so-called Roswell Incident of 1947 (when, some claim, a UFO crashed in the New Mexico desert and the US Government mounted an extraordinary cover-up that persists to this day); putatively based on meticulously researched background detail, the novel incorporates, without acknowledgement or permission, a summary derived from secondary sources of David LANGFORD's fictional *An Account of a Meeting with Denizens of Another World, 1871* (**1979** as by William Robert Loosley, ed Langford) (◊ PSEUDO-SCIENCE). [JC]
Other works: *Black Magic* (**1982**); *The Night Church* (**1983**); *Cat Magic* (**1986** as Jonathan Barry with WS; 1987 as WS alone); *The Wild* (**1991**); *Unholy Fire* (**1992**).
See also: PARANOIA.

STRIKE, JEREMY Pseudonym of US writer Thomas E(dward) Renn (1939-   ), author of the unremarkable sf adventure *A Promising Planet* (**1970** dos). [JC]

STRINGER, ARTHUR (JOHN ARBUTHNOTT) (1874-1956) Canadian writer prolific in several genres from 1894, though he concentrated on the Canadian genre of survival tales set in the northern wilds. *The Man who Couldn't Sleep* (coll **1919** US) and *The Wolf Woman* (**1928** US) are fantasy. Of sf interest are a film tie, *The Story without a Name* * (**1924**) with Russell Holman, in which a DEATH RAY appears, and *The Woman who Couldn't Die* (**1929** US), whose Viking heroine, after spending 900 years in an ice-floe in a LOST WORLD (inhabited by blond Eskimos whose culture is based upon worshipping her) in northern Canada, is resurrected through blood transfusions injected by a mad scientist, only to fall fatally in love with one of his fellow intruders into the lost world. [JC]

STROBL, K.H. [r] ◊ AUSTRIA.
STRONGI'TH'ARM ◊ Charles Wicksteed ARMSTRONG.
STROUD, ALBERT [s] ◊ Algis BUDRYS.
STRUGATSKI, ARKADY (NATANOVICH) (1925-1991) **and BORIS (NATANOVICH)** (1931-   ) Russian writers. Before they began to collaborate in the early 1950s, AS studied English and Japanese, and worked as a technical translator and editor, and BS was a computer mathematician at Pulkovo astronomical observatory. The brothers' first books made up an interplanetary cycle: *Strana bagrovykh tuch* ["The Country of Crimson Clouds"] (**1959**); *Shest' spichek* ["Six Matches"] (coll **1960**); *Put'na Amal'teiu* (coll **1960**), the lead novella of which was trans Leonid Kolesnikov as the title story of *Destination: Amaltheia* (anth **1962** USSR); *Vozvrashchenie (Polden'. 22-i vek)* (coll of linked stories **1962**; exp to 22 stories vt *Polden', XXII vek (Vozvrashchenie)* 1967; trans Patrick L. MCGUIRE as *Noon: 22nd Century* **1978** US); and *Stazhery*

(coll of linked stories **1962**; trans Antonina W. Bouis as *Space Apprentice* **1982** US). This optimistic future HISTORY, set on or near Earth over a two-century period, espouses the romance of exploration and humanity's UTOPIAN thrust forward against the forces of Nature, and is acted out by believable vernacular heroes.

A second phase soon began, in which utopian hopefulness did not survive unscathed. In "Dalekaia Raduga" (**1963** Russia; trans Alan Myers as *Far Rainbow* **1967** USSR), history, with its pain, invades human existence through a physical catastrophe (which kills nearly all of the characters remaining alive from the first cycle). In *Trudno byt' bogom* (**1964**; trans Wendayne Ackerman from the German as *Hard to be a God* **1973** US) the darkness of history is – more directly – demonstrated on a feudal planet, where an observer from Earth finds it impossible to conclude that utopian intervention on his part will do any more than stun the world into a numbing dictatorship. But the unaltered world is dangerous and iniquitous, with premonitions of fascism and Stalinism clearly hinting to the visitor that, without intervention, huge tragedies will ensue. The successful marriage of vivid historical novel and sf makes this the brothers' paradigmatic early work. The book was filmed as TRUDNO BYT' BOGOM (**1989**).

Far Rainbow later appeared, along with "Vtoroe nashestvie marsian" (**1968**) as *Far Rainbow/The Second Invasion from Mars* (coll trans Bouis [*Far Rainbow*] and Gary Kern [*Second Invasion*] **1979** US); the second tale is a Jonathan SWIFT-like masterpiece in which the INVASION is seen through the journal of a philistine who blindly registers the Martians' use of consumerism and conformity to transform humans into commodities. In this third phase, the brothers' darkening vision tended to express itself in VOLTAIRE-style FABULATIONS, where a formal mastery of expressionist plots cunningly exposed the societal bewilderment and growing bureaucratic sclerosis of their native Russia. In *Ponedel'nik nachinaetsia v subbotu* (**1965**; trans Leonid Renen as *Monday Begins on Saturday* **1977** US), folktale motifs are masterfully updated to embody in a dark picaresque the black and white MAGIC of modern alienated science and society. The sequel, *Skazka o troike* (**1968** in a Russian magazine; **1972** Germany; trans Bouis as *Tale of the Troika*), which appeared with "Piknik na obochine" (**1972** *Avrora*; trans Bouis as *Roadside Picnic*) in *Roadside Picnic/Tale of the Troika* (coll **1977** US), even more bleakly exposed the "scientifico-administrative" bureaucracy of the time. *Roadside Picnic* was turned by the brothers into 11 different scenarios for Andrei TARKOVSKY'S STALKER (1979). The two stories, as published together in English, are an ideal introduction to this phase of their career. A final third-phase tale, *Ulitka na sklone* (part 1 in *Ellinskii sekret* [anth **1966**] as "Kandid", part 2 **1968** *Baikal* as "Pepper"; trans Alan Myers as *The Snail on the Slope* fixup **1980** US), is constructed as two interlocked stories set in an overpoweringly alien forest swamp; the two protagonists, Kandid and Pepper, respond differently to the world, the first in a "naïve" stream of consciousness, the second in the guise of a Kafkaesque bureaucrat. The Kandid sequences are remarkably eloquent. The overall title is an image of the uncertainties of knowing: humanity climbs towards knowledge as a snail climbs a mountain.

A fourth and even more sombre phase begins with the **Maxim Trilogy** – *Obitaemyi ostrov* (**1969-71**; trans Helen Saltz Jacobson as *Prisoners of Power* **1978** US), "Zhuk v muraveinike" (**1979-80** *Znanie-sila*; trans Bouis as *Beetle in the Anthill* **1980** US) and "Volney gasiat veter" (**1985-6** *Znanie-sila*; trans Bouis as *The Time Wanderers* **1987** US) – in which the sometimes consoling glow of fable is stripped from abrupt and violent stories as the (at times) incongruously juvenile heroes confront scenes of increasing alienation and desperation. In *Gadkie lebedi* (**1966-7** in a Russian magazine; **1972** Germany [edn disavowed]; trans A.E. and A. Nakhimovsky as *The Ugly Swans* **1979** US [also disavowed]; trans as *Children of Rain* c**1987** USSR), the metaphysical swamp of *The Snail on the Slope* is transfigured into a mysterious fog which envelops Moscow, and which seems to engender all manner of intrusions. The fog is a signal of the death of the old world, and a highly dubious harbinger of a new: the children of the tale, justifying its title (a play on that of the famous fable by Hans Christian Andersen), seem to be entering into metamorphosis and a future which may (possibly) be bright. "Za milliard let do kontsa sveta" (**1976-7** *Znanie-sila*; trans Bouis as *Definitely Maybe: A Manuscript Discovered under Unusual Circumstances* **1978** US) again combines fable and a bleak depiction of the social world as SCIENTISTS attempt (in a manner evocative of the work of Stanisław LEM) to parse an implacably unknowable "force" which seems to be paralysing human progress.

Their last works, published only in the *glasnost* period, were: *Khromaia sud'ba* ["Lame Destiny"] (fixup **1989**), which intertwines *The Ugly Swans* with other material from 1986; *Grad obrechennyi* ["The Doomed City"] (written 1970-87; **1989**), perhaps their weightiest work to date; and *Otiagoshchennye zlom, ili sorok let spustia* ["Burdened by Evil, or 40 Years After"] (**1989**), which was evocative of the work of Mikhail BULGAKOV. Over their career, the brothers moved from a comparatively sunny vision in which utopia could be aimed at in the NEAR FUTURE to a sense that the tensions between utopian ethics and the inscrutable overwhelmingness of stasis were in fact irresolvable. They became the best Soviet sf writers, legitimate continuers of a Russian tradition extending from Nikolai Gogol (◊ RUSSIA) and Shchedrin (Mikhail E. Saltykov [1826-1889]) to Vladimir MAYAKOVSKY and Yuri Olesha (1889-1960); and half a dozen of their novels, in their recognition that a people without cognitive ethics devolves into a predatory bestiary, approach major literature. After the death of Arkady in 1991, it remained uncertain whether or not Boris would continue writing alone.   [DS]

Other works: *Khishchnye veshchi veka* (**1965**; trans Leonid Renen as *The Final Circle of Paradise* **1976** US); "Otel' 'U pogibshchego alpinista'" ["Hotel 'To the Lost Climber'" (1970 *Iunost'*), filmed in 1979 (vt *Dead Mountaineer Hotel*) and trans as «The Hotel of the Lost Alpinist» (a ghost title because the English-language publisher went out of business); *Escape Attempt* (coll trans **1982** US).

As editors: *The Molecular Café* (anth **1968** Russia), ed anon.

About the authors: "Criticism of the Strugatskii Brothers' Work" by Darko SUVIN, *Canadian-American Slavic Studies* #2 (Summer 1972); "The Literary Opus of the Strugatskii Brothers" by Suvin, *Canadian-American Slavic Studies* #3 (Fall 1974); "Future History, Soviet Style: The Work of the Strugatsky Brothers" by Patrick L. MCGUIRE, *Critical Encounters* #11 ed Tom Staicar; *Soviet Fiction since Stalin: Science, Politics, and Literature* (**1986**) by R.J. Marsh; *The Second Marxian Invasion: The Fiction of the Strugatsky Brothers* (**1991**) by Stephen W. Potts.

See also: DISCOVERY AND INVENTION; GODS AND DEMONS; JUPITER; PHYSICS; POLITICS; SUPERMAN.

STRYKER ◊ George MILLER.

STRYKER, DANIEL ◊ Chris MORRIS.

STRYKER, HAL ◊ George H. SMITH.

STUART, ALEX R. ◊ Stuart GORDON.

STUART, DON A. ◊ John W. CAMPBELL Jr.

STUART, (HENRY) FRANCIS (MONTGOMERY) (1902-   ) Irish writer, perceptions of whose long and controversial career were shaped by the fact that – although averse to Nazism – he stayed in Berlin during WWII as an Irish neutral, an experience recounted with chill brilliance in *Black List, Section H* (**1971** US), his most famous single novel. Of his many books, some are fantasy, including *Women and God* (**1931** UK), *Try the Sky* (**1933** UK), *A Hole in the Head* (**1977** UK) and *Faillandia* (**1985**), the latter book set in an imaginary Ireland in the throes of a military takeover. *Pigeon Irish* (**1932** UK), set in a bleak battle-torn NEAR-FUTURE Europe, is sf, as is *Glory* (**1933** UK), in which the world-dominating Trans-Continental Aero-Routes corporation is threatened by intrigues.   [JC]

STUART, IAN ◊ Alistair MacLEAN.

STUART, SIDNEY ◊ Michael AVALLONE.

STUART, W.J. ◊ Philip MacDONALD.

STUFF, THE Film (1985). Larco/New World. Prod (with Peter Sabiston) and dir Larry COHEN, starring Michael Moriarty, Andrea Marcovicci, Garrett Morris, Patrick O'Neal. Screenplay Cohen. 87 mins. Colour.

The Stuff is an addictive, gooey fast food which, though passive, is in all other respects a traditional monster; this MONSTER MOVIE is, in the Cohen manner, an atypical one. The baleful Stuff, originally found in a hole in the ground, takes over its victims when they eat it, sometimes rendering them homicidal. Moriarty plays with verve the industrial spy hired by other food manufacturers to get the truth about this new commercial success, and a satire ensues on corporate and individual greed, private right-wing armies, conformity and the nuclear family. This is a silly, not very well organized film that occasionally surprises with moments of truth and even of real horror.   [PN]

STURGEON, THEODORE (1918-1985) Working name of US writer born Edward Hamilton Waldo in New York City, later adopting his stepfather's surname and taking on a new first name. There may be hints of emotional turmoil in these name changes. Certainly TS early suffered or entered into several exiles: illness cut him off from any chance he might become a gymnast; when still a teenager he went to sea, where he spent 3 years while at the same time making his first fiction sales (1937) to McClure's syndicate for newspaper publication; after beginning to publish sf with "Ether Breather" for *ASF* (1939) he remained active as a member of the small band of genre-sf writers for only a few years before he abruptly stopped producing; he then spent half a decade abroad, variously employed, before returning to his primary career in 1946. The next 15 years saw him produce, in an almost constant flood, virtually all the remaining stories and novels for which he is remembered. Then, for the last 25 years of his life, except for 2-3 short periods of renewed flow, he was silent. Given that all of TS's best work somehow or other moves from alienation to some form of transcendent community, it might – crassly – be suggested that, in his own life, it was story-writing itself which represented that blissful movement towards acceptance and resolution which makes so many of his tales so emotionally fulfilling, and that when he was silent he was in exile. Certainly there can be no denying the green force that shoots through even the silliest PULP-MAGAZINE conceits to which he put his mind, or the sense of achieved and joyful *tour de force* generated by his best work.

He had, one might say, a binary career: either he was writing nothing or he was writing at a high pitch. Of his approximately 175 stories, a very high proportion are as successful as he was allowed to be in a field not well designed, during his active years, to accommodate sf tales told with raw passion. TS was, in fact, initially less comfortable with ASTOUNDING SCIENCE-FICTION than with UNKNOWN, and that magazine's demise may have had something to do with his first departure from the field. In those first 3 years, however, he produced more than 25 stories, all in *ASF* and *Unknown*, using the pseudonyms E. Waldo Hunter or E. Hunter Waldo on occasions when he had 2 stories in an issue; several of the 25 remain among his best known, including "It" (1940 *ASF*; **1948** chap) and "Microcosmic God" (1941). Along with A.E. VAN VOGT, Robert A. HEINLEIN and Isaac ASIMOV, TS was a central contributor to and shaper of John W. CAMPBELL Jr's so-called GOLDEN AGE OF SF, though less comfortably than his colleagues, as even in those early years, while obeying the generic commands governing the creation of Campbellian technological or HARD SF, he was also writing sexually threatening, explorative tales like "Bianca's Hands" which, refused by US markets, finally appeared in the UK in 1947.

In the late 1940s and the 1950s TS came into his full stride, and almost all his collections sort and resort this material. They are *Without Sorcery* (coll **1948**; cut vt *Not Without Sorcery* 1961), *E Pluribus Unicorn* (coll **1953**), *A Way Home* (coll **1955**; with 2 stories cut 1956; with 3 stories cut, vt *Thunder and Roses* 1957 UK), *Caviar* (coll **1955**), *A Touch of Strange* (coll **1958**; with 2 stories cut 1959), *Aliens 4* (coll **1959**), *Beyond* (coll **1960**), *Sturgeon in Orbit* (coll **1964**), . . . *And My Fear is Great/Baby is Three* (coll **1965**), *Starshine* (coll **1966**; 3 uncollected stories plus reprints), *The Worlds of Theodore Sturgeon* (coll **1972**), *The Stars are the Styx* (coll **1979**), *The Golden Helix* (coll **1979**) and *Alien Cargo* (coll **1984**). A late compilation, *A Touch of Sturgeon* (coll **1987** UK) ed David PRINGLE, usefully selects from this mass. Although he continued to contribute to *ASF* for several years, most of the work assembled in these collections first appeared in newer and more flexible markets like GALAXY SCIENCE FICTION, where he published much of his best work after 1950. Though shibboleths (◊ TABOOS) still haunted editors of GENRE SF, he clearly felt increasingly free to write stories expressive of his sense that sexual diversity, sexual "abnormality" and love – however manifested – constituted a set of codes or maps capable of leading maimed adolescents out of alienation and into the light. Though most of his explorations of this material seem unexceptionable in 1992, stories like "The World Well Lost" (1953), about ALIENS exiled from their own culture because of their homosexuality, created considerable stir in the 1950s (◊ SEX). Though the road to liberation (or transcendent community) was sometimes solely internal, the dictates of sf and fantasy, and TS's own romantic impulses, generated a large number of tales in which CHILDREN, gifted with paranormal powers, must fight against a repressive world until they meet others of their kind. TS's short stories read like instruction manuals for finding the new world.

The most famous examples of the sense of enablement he generated, however, were his 3 best novels. *The Dreaming Jewels* (**1950**; vt *The Synthetic Man* 1957) is an enjoyable and sophisticated tale whose young protagonist, forced to run away to a circus by wicked step-parents, gradually becomes aware of his powers, and defeats the evil adult forces about him. *More than Human* (fixup **1953**), winner of the 1954 INTERNATIONAL FANTASY AWARD and TS's most famous single title, consists of 3 connected stories, "Baby is Three" (1952 *Gal*) plus 2 novellas written around it. With very considerable intensity it depicts the coming together of 6 deeply alienated "freaks" into a PSI-POWERED gestalt, where they achieve true maturity. In *The Cosmic Rape* (**1958**) a HIVE-MIND from the stars invades mankind but finds itself – to its ultimate betterment

– catalysing *Homo sapiens* as a racial entity into one gestalt: the sense of homecoming generated by the final pages of this short book is deeply touching.

Though TS won both HUGO and NEBULA for one of his infrequent later stories, "Slow Sculpture" (1970), his later career was not happy. *Venus Plus X* (**1960**), however, bravely came as close to a traditional UTOPIA as any US genre-sf writer had approached before the efforts of Mack REYNOLDS. Charlie Johns awakens in Ledom (that is, Model), a melodious unisex society, longingly and effectively depicted as having transcended that sexual divisiveness of mankind against which TS always argued, and finds that he has been roused so as to examine Ledom and judge its success. Though he discovers to his distress that the androgynous bliss of Ledom depends not on a mutation but on surgery immediately after birth, the final message of the novel combines didactic arguments for and against this vision of human paradise with longing for its realization. Later stories were assembled in *Sturgeon is Alive and Well . . .* (coll **1971**) and *Case and the Dreamer* (coll **1974**). *Godbody* (**1986**), a short novel on which he had been working for some time before his death, weakly reiterates earlier paeans to transcendence. But the continued publication of stories from the years of his prime helped maintain an appropriate sense of TS as a writer of very considerable stature. His influence upon writers like Harlan ELLISON and Samuel R. DELANY was seminal, and in his life and work he was a powerful and generally liberating influence in post-WWII US sf. Though his mannerisms were sometimes self-indulgent, though his excesses of sympathy for tortured adolescents sometimes gave off a sense of self-pity, and though his technical experiments were perhaps less substantial than their exuberance made them seem, his very faults illuminated the stresses of being a US author writing for pay in an alienated era and in the solitude of his craft. [JC]

Other works: *The Rare Breed* (**1966**), a Western, as are the stories in *Sturgeon's West* (coll **1973**), 3 of which are with Don Ward; *I, Libertine* (**1956**), a historical novel as by Frederick R. Ewing; *The King and Four Queens* (**1956**), a detective novel; *Some of Your Blood* (**1961**), a non-sf study of a blood-drinking psychotic; *Voyage to the Bottom of the Sea* * (**1961**), a novelization of VOYAGE TO THE BOTTOM OF THE SEA (1961); an **Ellery Queen** detection, *The Player on the Other Side* (**1963**) as by Ellery Queen; *The Joyous Invasions* (coll **1965** UK), which includes 2 stories from *Aliens 4* together with "To Marry Medusa", which was later exp as *The Cosmic Rape*, both being reissued as *The Cosmic Rape and "To Marry Medusa"* (coll **1977**); *To Here and the Easel* (coll **1973** UK), all stories previously collected; *Amok Time* * (graph **1978**), a STAR TREK "fotonovel"; *More Than Human: The Graphic Story Version* (graph **1979**); *Maturity: Three Stories* (coll **1979**); *Pruzy's Pot* (1972 *The National Lampoon*; **1986** chap); *The [Widget], the [Wadget], and Boff* (1955 *FSF*; **1989** dos); *The Dreaming Jewels/The Cosmic Rape/Venus Plus X* (omni **1990**).

About the author: *Theodore Sturgeon: A Primary and Secondary Bibliography* (**1980**) and *Theodore Sturgeon* (**1981** chap), both by Lahna F. Diskin; *Theodore Sturgeon* (**1981**) by Lucy Menger.

See also: BIOLOGY; CITIES; CLONES; CONCEPTUAL BREAKTHROUGH; DEFINITIONS OF SF; DIMENSIONS; ESP; EVOLUTION; FEMINISM; GODS AND DEMONS; GREAT AND SMALL; INVASION; ISLANDS; LIVING WORLDS; MACHINES; *The* MAGAZINE OF FANTASY AND SCIENCE FICTION; MARS; MEDIA LANDSCAPE; MESSIAHS; NEW WORLDS; NUCLEAR POWER; PARANOIA; POWER SOURCES; PSYCHOLOGY; REINCARNATION; RELIGION; SCIENTISTS; SOCIOLOGY; SUPERMAN; SUPERNATURAL CREATURES; THEODORE STURGEON MEMORIAL AWARD; TRANSPORTATION; UNDER THE SEA; WRITERS OF THE FUTURE CONTEST.

STURGIS, MEL [r] ◊ Kris NEVILLE.

SUBMARINES ◊ TRANSPORTATION; UNDER THE SEA.

SUBMERSION OF JAPAN, THE ◊ NIPPON CHINBOTSU.

SUBURBAN COMMANDO Film (1991). New Line Cinema. Dir Burt Kennedy, starring Hulk Hogan, Christopher Lloyd, Shelley Duvall, Larry Miller. Screenplay by Frank Capello. 90 mins. Colour.

This modest, affable sf comedy about a large, rough, humanoid ALIEN (pro wrestling star Hogan) who crashlands on Earth after being temporarily retired as an interstellar righter of wrongs, sets its sights rather low, and does quite well. The primitive but effective humour is in the wish-fulfilment fantasy of seeing one kind of nastiness – as found in a somewhat blue-collar Californian suburb – getting its comeuppance from a more "decent" brand of brutality. Lloyd plays the put-upon husband who learns not to let them kick sand in his face, and helps defeat the MONSTER disguised as a human who seeks to rule the Galaxy. [PN]

SUCHARITKUL, SOMTOW (PAPINIAN) [r] ◊ S.P. SOMTOW.

SUCHDOLSKÝ, METOD [r] ◊ CZECH AND SLOVAK SF.

SUDDABY, (WILLIAM) DONALD (1900-1964) UK writer, mostly for children, who began publishing work of genre interest as Alan Griff with stories like "House of Desolation" for *Cornhill* in 1934; his first sf book, a novel for adults, was *Lost Men in the Grass* (**1940**) (◊ GREAT AND SMALL) as by Griff. The third novella assembled in *Masterless Swords: Variations on a Theme* (coll of linked stories **1947**) is set in a future where men wage war on women. DS soon became – and remained – best known for his juvenile sf novels, beginning with *The Star Raiders* (**1950**) and *The Death of Metal* (**1952**); the most notable is perhaps *Village Fanfare, or The Man from the Future* (**1934** *Cornhill* as by Griff; much exp **1954**), a TIME-TRAVEL tale in which a 1907 Shropshire village is visited from the future by a man looking for, and finding, human wisdom in his past. *Prisoners of Saturn* (**1957**) is a SPACE OPERA. Some of DS's non-sf books, like *Tower of Babel* (**1962**), have some fantasy content. [JC]

Other work: *Scarlet-Dragon: A Little Chinese Phantasy* (**1923** chap).

See also: CHILDREN'S SF.

SUFFLING, MARK ◊ Donald S. ROWLAND.

SULLIVAN, (EDWARD) ALAN (1868-1947) Canadian writer who spent much of his adult life in the UK, and who was prolific in various genres, including detective fiction as Sinclair Murray. His fantasies include *The Jade God* (**1924**), *In the Days of their Youth* (**1926**), *The Magic Makers* (**1930**), *Mr Absalom* (**1930**) and *". . . And from that Day"* (**1944**). Of sf interest is *In the Beginning* (**1927**), a LOST-WORLD tale set – as so often in the early 20th century – in the Andes; this one contains ancient species and some Neanderthals (unusually far south). In *A Little Way Ahead* (**1929**) an ordinary man, suddenly becoming prescient, makes money on the Stock Exchange, but is doomed by personal flaws. [JC]

SULLIVAN, SEAN MEI ◊ Jerry SOHL.

SULLIVAN, SHEILA (P.) (1927-   ) UK writer, sometimes of criticism as by Sheila Bathurst. Her sf novel *Summer Rising* (**1975**; vt *The Calling of Bara* 1976 US) depicts a post-HOLOCAUST trek across a peaceful Ireland. [JC]

SULLIVAN, TIM(OTHY ROBERT) (?   -   ) US writer and editor who began publishing sf with stories like "My Father's Head" for *Chrysalis 5* (anth **1979**) ed Roy TORGESON and "The Rancher Goes to Tinker Town" for *New Dimensions 9* (anth **1979**) ed Robert SILVERBERG, tales whose sophistication led to some disappointment when his first-published novels turned out to be 3 "V" ties: *"V": The Florida Project* * (**1985**), *"V": The New England Resistance* * (**1985**) and *"V": To Conquer the Throne* * (**1987**). The published order of TS's books is, however, deceptive, as his first-written novel, *Destiny's End* (**1988**), suffered delays and modifications from its initially intended publisher. The book proved to be a complexly moody depiction of humanity at the end of its tether in an array of DYING-EARTH venues, as ALIEN races with quasimagical technologies manipulate the course of events. *The Parasite War* (**1989**) and *The Martian Viking* (**1991**) likewise demonstrate a nascent vigour, and TM seems to be one of those authors whose time might, finally, come.

Two anthologies, *Tropical Chills* (anth **1988**) and *Cold Shocks* (anth **1991**), composed of carefully selected original and reprinted material, mostly horror, demonstrate TM's editorial acuteness. [JC]

SULLIVAN, VERNON ◊ Boris VIAN.

SUMMERS, DENNIS ◊ G.J. BARRETT.

SUN The Sun, as the energy-source which permits life to exist on Earth, was widely worshipped in the ancient world. After the Copernican Revolution it became the hub of the Universe, but with the advent of a broader view of the cosmos it lost some of its prestige. Some speculative writers of the 19th century considered it a world like any other and included it in cosmic tours; examples are the anonymous *Journeys into the Moon, Several Planets and the Sun* (**1837**) and Joel R. Peabody's *A World of Wonders* (**1838**). Several early sf stories, assuming the Sun to be sustained by combustion, anticipated the day when it would burn out; examples are Camille FLAMMAR-ION's *Omega* (**1893-4**), H.G. WELLS's *The Time Machine* (**1895**), George C. WALLIS's "The Last Days of Earth" (1901) and William Hope HODGSON's *The House on the Borderland* (**1908**) (◊ END OF THE WORLD). Clark Ashton SMITH recalls the imagery of Hodgson's novel in "Phoenix" (1954), a poignant but anachronistic story about the reignition of the dying Sun (by the time the story was written – in the 1930s – it had long been known that the Sun produced heat by nuclear fusion), an idea ingeniously recapitulated in Gene WOLFE's **Book of the New Sun** series (**1980-83**). Although the Sun's surface temperature had been established spectroscopically in the 1890s, John MAS-TIN was still able to imagine, in *Through the Sun in an Airship* (**1909**), exactly such a voyage, and H. KANER set *The Sun Queen* (**1946**) on a sunspot.

J.B.S. HALDANE's "The Last Judgment" (1927) and Olaf STAPLEDON's *Last and First Men* (**1930**) imagine changes in the Sun's brilliance as crucial factors in Man's future EVOLUTION. In "Ark of Fire" (1943) by John Hawkins the Earth is moved nearer to the Sun, with predictable consequences for surface life. In numerous DISASTER stories the Sun goes nova, although some humans usually manage to escape, as in J.T. MCINTOSH's *One in Three Hundred* (**1954**). In Edmond HAMILTON's "Thundering Worlds" (1934) the 9 planets themselves become interstellar wanderers, accelerating towards a new star. In Arthur C. CLARKE's "Rescue Party" (1946) ALIENS arrive to save mankind but find that their aid is unnecessary, and in Norman SPINRAD's *The Solarians* (**1966**) the nova is induced to destroy an alien spacefleet, while the human race makes its escape. In Edward WELLEN's *Hijack* (**1971**) disinformation about such a nova is used in order to trick the Mafia into hijacking a spacefleet and blasting off for the stars. Stories which make a detailed study of reactions to the news that the Sun may go nova include Hugh KINGSMILL's "The End of the World" (1924) and Larry NIVEN's "Inconstant Moon" (1971). The hero of George O. SMITH's *Troubled Star* (**1953**) discovers that aliens want to make the Sun into a variable star so that it may serve as an interstellar lighthouse.

The notion that the Sun might be the abode of life is developed in Stapledon's *The Flames* (**1947**) and Hamilton's "Sunfire!" (1962). Sun-consuming life-forms hatch out of the planets in Jack WILLIAMSON's improbable "Born of the Sun" (1934). The idea that STARS might be living beings has been developed on several occasions, but not often applied to our own Sun; Gregory BENFORD's and Gordon EKLUND's "If the Stars are Gods" (1974; incorporated into *If the Stars are Gods*, fixup **1977**) is ambiguous in this respect. The Sun's significance as a religious symbol is further exploited in *The Day the Sun Stood Still* (anth **1972**) ed Robert SILVERBERG, which features 3 novellas based on the premise that the miracle granted to Joshua so that he could win a vital battle might be repeated tomorrow to persuade mankind

of the reality of divine power.

The Sun often figures in GENRE SF as a potential disaster area ready to consume spaceships which stray too close; examples are Willy LEY's "At the Perihelion" (1937 as by Robert Willey; vt "A Martian Adventure"), Hal CLEMENT's "Sun Spot" (1960), Poul ANDERSON's "What'll You Give?" (1963 as by Winston P. Sanders; vt "Que Donn'rez Vous?") and George Collyn's "In Passage of the Sun" (1966). The weather technicians of Theodore L. THOMAS's "The Weather Man" (1962), however, skim across the surface of the Sun in "sessile boats" in order to control its radiation output. A spate of dangerous radiation from the Sun plays a key role in Philip E. HIGH's *Prodigal Sun* (**1964**), which was presumably written around its awful titular pun; the Earth is saved through the creation of an artificial shielding layer of gas in the upper atmosphere. A spectacular close encounter by a space-station takes place in Charles L. HARNESS's *Flight into Yesterday* (1949; **1953**; vt *The Paradox Men* 1955 dos), and an even more spectacular one in David BRIN's *Sundiver* (**1980**), the sf novel to date which deals most extensively and most scrupulously with modern scientific knowledge about the Sun.

One curious aspect of the Sun's behaviour, the 11-year sunspot cycle discovered by Heinrich Schwabe (1789-1875) in 1851, is hypothetically correlated with Earthly events in Clifford D. SIMAK's "Sunspot Purge" (1940) and Philip LATHAM's "Disturbing Sun" (1959). The SOLAR WIND is featured in a number of sf stories. [BS]

SUPERBOY US tv series (1988-91). An Alexander and Ilya Salkind Production, for syndication. Executive prod Ilya Salkind, prod Robert Simmonds. Dirs included Reza S. Badiyi, Colin Chilvers, Peter Kiwitt, David Grossman, David Nutter, Richard J. Lewis. Writers included Fred Freiberger, Cary Bates, Mark Jones, Toby Martin, Michael Carlin and Andrew Helfer, David GERROLD. 3 seasons, 78 25min episodes in all. Colour.

The Salkinds, who made 3 of the SUPERMAN movies, here returned with a brisk, not very expensive series based on the teenage years of Clark Kent at Shuster University (Joe Shuster [1914-1991] was co-creator of Superman), where he is studying with his childhood friend, glamorous Lana Lang. The time is, anachronistically, the present. Cast changes were confusing: John Haymes Newton played Superboy (woodenly) in season 1, then was replaced by Gerard Christopher; Scott Wells played Lex Luthor in season 1, then was replaced by Sherman Howard. Lana Lang was played by Stacy Haiduk, and cub reporter T.J. White (son of *Daily Planet* editor Perry White) by Jim Calvert. At only half an hour per episode there was not much room for complex plotting. There was a laudable variety of villains (golems, werewolves, other-dimensional imps, androids, aliens and succubi among them), but the treatment was mostly routine. In season 3 Lana and Clark go to work for the Bureau for Extra-Normal Matters. [PN]

SUPERCAR UK tv series (1961-2). AP Films/ATV/ITC. From an idea by Gerry ANDERSON and Reg Hill, produced by Anderson. Dirs included David Elliott, Alan Pattillo, Desmond Saunders, Bill Harris. Writers were either Gerry and Sylvia Anderson or Martin and Hugh Woodhouse. 2 seasons, 39 25min episodes in all. B/w.

This was the first of Anderson's **SuperMarionation** sf series for children. Supercar, which can also travel under the sea and through the air, was invented by Professor Popkiss and is driven by Mike Mercury (or sometimes the talking monkey Mitch). Constant efforts to steal Supercar are made by Masterspy. Some of the storylines are sf (mad scientists, super-magnets); some are merely crime-fighting. The series was a big success, and sold in the USA. More **SuperMarionation** series followed (◊ Gerry and Sylvia ANDERSON *for details*). [PN]

SUPERGIRL Film (1984). Artistry/Cantharus. Dir Jeannot Szwarc, starring Helen Slater, Faye Dunaway, Peter O'Toole, Peter Cook, Brenda Vaccaro. Screenplay David Odell, based on the **Supergirl** comic. 124 mins. Colour.

This is the last and least successful of the 4 SUPERMAN-and-spin-off films made by the Salkinds before they sold the rights to Golan and Globus of Cannon Films, who went on to make SUPERMAN IV. *S* is basically fantasy. The Omegahedron, a power source from Krypton's Argo City, is lost and Supergirl (née Kara) goes to Earth in search of it. It has fallen into the hands of a sorceress, Selena (Dunaway). Female superpowers are interestingly seen in terms of natural fertility rather than physical strength: bunnies and flowers surround sweet teenager Supergirl (Slater). The film has imaginative moments (the mountain fortress that appears in the high street, the Doré-inspired Phantom Zone) but is also incoherent and trite, and haltingly directed by a graduate from tv, Szwarc, whose most acceptable sf film was his first, BUG (1975).

The novelization is *Supergirl* * **(1984)** by Norma Fox Mazer. [PN]

SUPERHEROES Superhero fiction is a genre invented in COMICS; since then it has infiltrated the CINEMA, RADIO, TELEVISION and books. Sf stories of SUPERMEN go back to the beginning of the century, but the particular version of the superman theme that established the "superhero" pattern began in *Action Comics* (June 1938) when the comic-book hero SUPERMAN made his first appearance; he was soon given his own comic. Imitations soon appeared, including CAPTAIN MARVEL (from 1940), **Wonder Woman** (from 1942), **Plastic Man** (from 1944), **Human Torch** (from 1939), **Captain America** (from 1941) and so on. These characters differed from the PULP-MAGAZINE heroes of the 1930s, like DOC SAVAGE, who, though highly trained and with access to superscientific devices, were ordinary human beings; superheroes had superpowers which, despite their varying sf rationalizations, were effectively MAGIC abilities. (One hugely

popular borderline superhero is **Batman**, created as a character in 1939 and given his own comic in 1940: he has no superpowers, and is in the line of descent from **Doc Savage**, not **Superman**.) However, superheroes and HEROES of the period were alike in that both spent much of their working hours struggling against crime – often crime carried out by mad SCIENTISTS seeking to rule the world – and in this important respect hero fiction and superhero fiction formed a continuum rather than two different genres. Also, then as now, superhero fiction was (most of the time) only a borderline-sf genre. Most of the action took place in a comic-book version of the real world, against gangsters, secret agents and the like; the borderline-sf elements lay in the origin of the superhero (Superman, for example, getting his power from his birth on the alien planet Krypton) and secondarily in the often superscientific devices used by the VILLAINS. (In this encyclopedia we have therefore been somewhat selective in choosing which superhero comics, films and tv series should be given entries.)

Having begun in the comics, superheroes soon started appearing in other media: children's books, radio serials and film serials at first. After intensive activity in the 1940s, the superhero theme came to seem rather played out by the 1950s, since its possible story variations seemed few. It was in the comics, again, that the superhero found a new lease of life, notably in the work Jack KIRBY did for MARVEL COMICS, and especially in his creation of **The Fantastic Four** in 1961. (For many years Marvel propaganda had it that Stan LEE was the true creator of the Marvel superheroes of the 1960s, with Kirby merely the artist assigned to carry out instructions. The now-dominant revisionist view is that Kirby was the presiding genius of the new superhero format, which among other things involved enormous advances in the techniques of comic-book ILLUSTRATION.) Superheroes became humanized; they aged, had neuroses, suffered *Angst*, they often behaved badly; sometimes they were corrupted by their constant battle against the tawdry and the criminal; some superheroes chose to become supervillains instead; sometimes they even had sex lives (unlike the prissy and celibate Superman). In short, they became very much more interesting. These changes did not happen overnight; they began with **The Fantastic Four**, but developed in **The Incredible Hulk** from 1962, **The Amazing Spider-Man** in his own comic from 1963, X-MEN (from 1963) and so on. The complex stories developed in **The Fantastic Four** were particularly memorable (and sciencefictional) when the Four found themselves pitted against Galactus, and especially in those issues containing the most surreal superhero of all, the temperamental and reviled Silver Surfer, imprisoned in Earth's atmosphere by Galactus, riding capriciously through space on his surfboard and sometimes saving Earth. He had his own comic for a while, **The Silver Surfer** (1968-70).

Superhero fiction since the 1960s, while it has remained often repetitive and simplistic in its mass-market manifestations, has developed, here and there, an extremely sophisticated edge – sometimes in mass-market comics but more often in GRAPHIC NOVELS. One landmark was Frank MILLER's *Batman: The Dark Knight Returns* (**1986**), which re-created Batman in darker, more painful shades than ever before, but the outstanding critique of the superhero comic from within the genre itself is Alan MOORE's WATCHMEN, a coherent graphic novel which is (unusually) a true novel in structure; its first publication constituted the 12 issues of **Watchmen** (1986-7) from DC COMICS. This is true sf, which confronts with great imaginative intensity the whole issue of what a society would be like that did actually contain superheroes, and how corrupting and fatiguing the state of superheroism might be. Also complex and sophisticated, beginning at around the same time, is the WILD CARDS series of original anthologies (from 1987) ed George R.R. MARTIN, in which superheroes are called "Aces" for fear of copyright infringement. The **Wild Card** stories (and the subsequent sequence of graphic books based on them) imagine, among other things, how superheroes might interact with historical process. A blackly comic novel which also forms a critique of the superhero business is Michael BISHOP's *Count Geiger's Blues* (**1992**).

Sadly, the increasing intelligence and imagination displayed in many superhero comics since the 1960s has seldom been reflected in their tv and film equivalents. We do not include entries for the **Spiderman** or **Batman** movies, or tv series like **Batman** (1966-8, very influential with its stylized jokiness) or **The Flash** (1990 on), even though the latter is more inventive than most of its kind; both are too far removed from sf proper. Superhero tv series that do receive entries are *The* BIONIC WOMAN (1976-8), *The* INCREDIBLE HULK (1977-82), *The* INVISIBLE MAN (1975-6), *The* MAN FROM ATLANTIS (1977), *The* SIX BILLION DOLLAR MAN (1973-8), SAPPHIRE AND STEEL (1979-82), SUPERBOY (1988-91), SUPERMAN (1953-7) and WONDER WOMAN (1974-9). The notable thing about this list is that all but one (*Sapphire and Steel*) are US; the superhero phenomenon is almost exclusively a US phenomenon. The other notable thing is that these series are nearly all infantile. One marginal superhero (not usually thought of in that light) of greater interest than most of the above is Vincent, the Beast in BEAUTY AND THE BEAST (1987-90); this may be due to George R.R. Martin, its chief writer, who is very much alive to the mythic resonances of the superhero genre.

In the cinema, the superhero genre managed better, at least in the SUPERMAN movies, than it normally did on tv, but beyond the **Superman** films there is not a great deal of interest. Indeed, in the cinema people with superpowers often come to a bad end, as in X: THE MAN WITH X-RAY EYES (1963), *The* 4D MAN (1959), *The* DEAD ZONE (1983) and *The* LAWNMOWER MAN (1992).

The protagonists of *The* RETURN OF CAPTAIN INVINCIBLE (1982), *The* TOXIC AVENGER (1984), *The* TRANSFORMERS: THE MOVIE (1986), MASTERS OF THE UNIVERSE (1987), ROBOCOP (1987), DARKMAN (1990) and TEENAGE MUTANT NINJA TURTLES (1990) cannot be called hardcore superheroes, being respectively a drunk, disgusting, robots, musclebound, cyborgized, hideously deformed and pizza-eating adolescent reptiles, although in the new era of superheroes (these all being films of the 1980s on) this rag, tag and bobtail bunch may represent precisely where the superhero genre now finds itself.

The fact still unrealized by most cultural commentators, whose knowledge does not extend beyond tv and books, is that the best superhero fictions are still to be found where they were found in the first place: in the comics. [PN]

SUPERMAN In the same way that theories of EVOLUTION provide an imaginative context for sf stories about the ORIGIN OF MAN and LIFE ON OTHER WORLDS, so they govern attitudes to superhumans. There is a significant difference, though, between Darwin-inspired images of a "fitter" species and images inspired by Lamarckian and Bergsonian ideas of "creative evolution", in which the emergence of a superman might be the result of humankind's fervent desire to become something finer. Also of some relevance – although its direct influence on sf is minimal – is the philosophy of Friedrich Nietzsche (1844-1900), with its heavy emphasis on the life-enhancing "will to [creative] power" which might be brought to full flower in the *Übermensch*, or "overman".

Early sf writers were surprisingly loth to make the superman an outright figure of menace, even where Darwinian thought was dominant: although they usually conceded that there was no place for them in contemporary human society, and generally disposed of them in one way or another, most were very much on the side of the superhumans. The reasons are simple enough: most of the early writers concerned were harshly critical of the contemporary human condition and wholly in favour of "progress"; moreover, writers frequently credit themselves with a proto-superhuman viewpoint. It is very easy to love the notion of the superman if we believe that we might become supermen ourselves, or at least be parent to their becoming; it is for this reason that Bergsonian ideas are more frequently echoed in superman stories than Darwinian ones, and some works – most notably George Bernard SHAW's *Back to Methuselah* (**1921**) – are based on an explicit neo-Lamarckism. Both the Darwin-inspired H.G. WELLS, in *The Food of the Gods* (**1904**), and the Bergson-inspired J.D. BERESFORD, in *The Hampdenshire Wonder* (**1911**), are allied with their superhuman characters, agreeing with their indictments of the follies of contemporary man. The same is true of two other classic SCIENTIFIC ROMANCES directly inspired by Beresford: E.V. ODLE's *The Clockwork Man* (**1923**) and Olaf STAPLEDON's *Odd John* (**1935**) – although the former carefully keeps its real superhumans (the makers of the eponymous CYBORG) offstage, as does Claude HOUGHTON in *This was Ivor Trent* (**1935**), whose hysterical climax represents the extremity of UK interbellum disenchantment. The fascination which writers of scientific romance had for the idea of superhumanity is displayed also in M.P. SHIEL's *Übermensch* stories, *The Isle of Lies* (**1909**) and *The Young Men are Coming* (**1937**), Muriel JAEGER's *The Man with Six Senses* (**1927**) and *Hermes Speaks* (**1933**), John HARGRAVE's *The Imitation Man* (**1931**), Wells's *Star-Begotten* (**1937**), Andrew MARVELL's *Minimum Man* (**1938**), Beresford's *"What Dreams May Come . . ."* (**1941**) and Stapledon's *A Man Divided* (**1950**). Guy DENT's *Emperor of the If* (**1926**) is especially interesting in its sceptical examination of the hypothesis that a more challenging environment would have produced a fitter and better mankind.

In France, Bergson's one-time pupil Alfred JARRY produced a comic erotic fantasia of superhumanity in *The Supermale* (**1902**; trans **1968**) but *The New Adam* (**1924**; trans **1926**) by Noelle ROGER, working under the inspiration of religious rather than scientific ideas, presents an emotionless ultrarationalistic superman as a straightforward figure of menace. In the USA Philip WYLIE put an ordinary human mind into a superhuman body in *Gladiator* (**1930**), and thus avoided the whole issue of INTELLIGENCE, but his heroic superman decides of his own accord that there is no place for him in human society and invites God to strike him dead; God (no friend of evolution) obliges.

In early GENRE SF the superman was used as a figure of menace by John Russell FEARN in *The Intelligence Gigantic* (**1933**; **1943**), but Fearn gradually relented: the short version of *The Golden Amazon* (**1939** as by Thornton Ayre; rev **1944**) is similar, but in the novel version, and even more so in its many sequels, superwoman Violet Ray is a comic-style caped crusader. The MUTANT superman in John TAINE's *Seeds of Life* (**1931**, **1951**) is also menacing, meeting his end in a particularly horrible manner; but there is some attempt to analyse his viewpoint with sympathy. In Stanley G. WEINBAUM's *"The Adaptive Ultimate"* (1936) a scientist who creates a superwoman has to kill her in order to protect the world from her ruthlessness, but again there is a tentative expression of sympathy. Weinbaum had earlier written the posthumously published *The New Adam* (**1939**), a painstaking account of a superhuman growing up in the human world, treating the hypothesis objectively rather than intending to criticize the contemporary human condition. The superman suffers as a result of being a "feral child" among ordinary humans, but his death does not put an end to the history of his kind. Publication of this pioneering work was quickly followed by 2 novels that paved the way for a glut of superhuman HEROES: *Slan* (1940; **1946**) by A.E. VAN VOGT and *Darker than You Think* (1940; **1948**) by Jack WILLIAMSON. In the former a persecuted superchild

grows into mature command of his latent powers as he confronts a sea of troubles; in the latter the hero sets out to fight a species of the genus *Homo* which threatens to replace *Homo sapiens*, but discovers that he is one of the other species himself, and accepts the dictates of his genes. In both stories a superman is unhesitatingly offered to the reader for identification and, far from going to his destruction in the climax, becomes something of a MESSIAH figure. This new pattern quickly became a CLICHÉ of pulp sf. Van Vogt repeated it many times, other versions including *Earth's Last Fortress* (1942 *ASF* as "Recruiting Station"; vt as title story of *Masters of Time* [coll **1950**]; **1960** dos), *"The Changeling"* (1944), *The World of Ā* (1945; rev **1948**; rev vt *The World of Null-A* 1970) and *The Pawns of Null-A* (1948-9 *ASF* as "The Players of Ā"; **1956**; rev vt *The Players of Null-A* 1966) and *Supermind* (fixup **1977**). Van Vogt abandoned writing sf for some years when he became involved with L. Ron HUBBARD's DIANETICS movement, which translocated this cliché into a PSEUDO-SCIENCE which in turn transmuted into the RELIGION of SCIENTOLOGY. Williamson, too, repeated the formula in *Dragon's Island* (**1951**; vt *The Not-Men* 1968).

Genre sf of the late 1940s and early 1950s abounded with stories about groups of noble superhumans – notably covert immortals (◊ IMMORTALITY) – misunderstood and unjustly persecuted by their stupid, envious cousins. Great impetus was lent to the theme by the popularization of J.B. Rhine's experiments in parapsychology (◊ ESP), which lent credence to the idea that there might be supermen already among us, not yet aware of their latent powers. Rhine provided a new archetype for the superhuman, outwardly normal but possessed of one or more PSI POWERS. John W. CAMPBELL Jr's interest in Rhine's research and in Dianetics helped to make ASTOUNDING SCIENCE-FICTION home to a considerable "psi boom" in the early 1950s. Notable stories of persecuted Rhine-type supermen include Henry KUTTNER's **Baldy** series, published as by Lewis Padgett (fixup **1953** as *Mutant*), Wilmar H. SHIRAS's *Children of the Atom* (fixup **1953**), Zenna HENDERSON's **People** series, assembled in *Pilgrimage* (coll of linked stories **1961**) and *The People: No Different Flesh* (coll of linked stories (**1966**), and Wilson TUCKER's *Wild Talent* (**1954**). Sympathy for supermen was enhanced by the frequent use of CHILDREN as protagonists, as in *Slan*, *Children of the Atom*, James H. SCHMITZ's *The Witches of Karres* (1949; exp **1966**), Kris NEVILLE's *Bettyann* (1951-4; fixup **1970**) and George O. SMITH's *The Fourth "R"* (**1959**; vt *The Brain Machine* 1968). (A cautionary note was sounded by Jerome BIXBY's "It's a *Good* Life" [1953], in which a superchild institutes a reign of terror directed towards the gratification of his every infantile whim.) Physically afflicted supermen were occasionally employed to the same sympathy-seeking end, as in Theodore STURGEON's "Maturity" (1947) and John BRUNNER's *The Whole Man* (fixup **1964**; vt *Telepathist* 1965). Sometimes during this period there were secret organizations of criminal supermen fighting against the good supermen, as in James BLISH's *Jack of Eagles* (**1951**; rev vt *ESP-er* 1958) and George O. Smith's *Highways in Hiding* (**1956**; cut vt *Space Plague* 1957), but even where the superman appears to be used as an outright figure of menace, as in Frank M. ROBINSON's *The Power* (**1956**), the good guy may only be waiting for his own latent superpowers to develop in order to bring about that menace's defeat. Similar leap-frogging accounts of confrontation include Jack VANCE's "Telek" (1951) and Theodore Sturgeon's ". . . and my fear is great" (1953). The everyone-can-be-superman motif reached its ultimate expression in Poul ANDERSON's *Brain Wave* (**1954**), in which the Earth passes out of a zone of cosmic distortion which has been damping potential intelligence throughout history, so that even idiots and animals get smart. The attractiveness of the motif is exploited to the full by comics SUPERHEROES like SUPERMAN and CAPTAIN MARVEL, whose superness is concealed by mild-mannered "secret identities". Superhero COMICS were popular throughout the 1940s and 1950s, and enjoyed subsequent boom periods in the 1960s – following the resurgence of MARVEL COMICS, whose heroes were more morally ambiguous, suffering wildly exaggerated versions of teenage *Angst* and alienation – and in the 1980s, when GRAPHIC NOVELS lent the format a new respectability, and when comic-book superheroes spilled over into narrative fiction in George R.R. MARTIN's WILD CARDS series of "mosaic novels" (fixups **1986** onwards) and in the **Temps** series created by Neil GAIMAN and Alex Stewart (1st vol **1991**).

L. Ron Hubbard is by no means the only cult-creator to have sold a pseudo-scientific or quasireligious version of this motif. Many other contemporary cults offer their members supposed opportunities to cultivate transcendental powers as well as arcane knowledge. The idea of the superman, and its development in fiction, have always been entangled with religious notions of transcendence and personal salvation ($\lozenge$ ESCHATOLOGY), and the achievement of superpowers in sf stories frequently recalls transcendental imagery of various kinds. In extreme cases it comes to resemble an apotheosis. The transcendental version of the superman myth is particularly obvious in certain works by Charles L. HARNESS, including *Flight into Yesterday* (1949; exp **1953**; vt *The Paradox Men*), the memorable novella "The Rose" (1953; title story of coll **1966**) and *The Ring of Ritornel* (**1968**), and it forms the bases of the classic novels *More than Human* (fixup **1953**) by Theodore Sturgeon and *Childhood's End* (**1953**) by Arthur C. CLARKE; the former tracks the maturation of a gestalt of misfit superchildren, and their eventual transcendental admission to a community of superminds, while the latter has an entire generation of Earth's children undergoing an apotheosis to fuse with the cosmic mind. The climax of Clarke's novel bears a striking resemblance to the ideas put forward by the French Jesuit Pierre Teilhard de Chardin (1881-1955) regarding the possible evolutionary future of humanity within a Bergsonian scheme, as expressed in *The Future of Man* (**1959**; trans **1964**). A similar "cosmic mind" is featured in *The Uncensored Man* (**1964**) by Arthur SELLINGS, and superhuman apotheoses are also found in *The Infinite Cage* (**1972**) by Keith LAUMER and *Tetrasomy Two* (**1974**) by Oscar ROSSITER. Images of transcendental rebirth have likewise become common, as in several novels by Alfred BESTER: *The Demolished Man* (**1953**), in which a psychopathic murderer is "cleansed" of his madness; *Tiger! Tiger!* (**1956**; vt *The Stars My Destination* 1957 US), in which the superpowered protagonist moves through time to appear to himself and others as a fire-shrouded vision, and is eventually cleansed in his turn; and *The Computer Connection* (**1974**; vt *Extro*), in which supermen recruit others to their kind by the only process known to them, involving violent death. The survival after death of *Übermensch* characters is featured in *Camp Concentration* (**1968**) by Thomas M. DISCH, *I Will Fear No Evil* (**1971**) and *Time Enough for Love* (**1973**) by Robert A. HEINLEIN, and *Traitor to the Living* (**1973**) by Philip José FARMER. Religious imagery is overt in the many works by Robert SILVERBERG which couple the notion of superhumanity with the idea of rebirth, including *To Open the Sky* (fixup **1967**), *Downward to the Earth* (**1970**), *Nightwings* (fixup **1970**), *Son of Man* (**1971**), *The Book of Skulls* (**1972**) and "Born with the Dead" (**1974**). Silverberg's *Dying Inside* (**1972**) is another fantasy of rebirth seen in terms of the loss of a superhuman power; the decline of ephemeral superhumanity is also a powerful motif in the classic *Flowers for Algernon* (**1959**; exp **1966**) by Daniel KEYES. Messianic supermen whose deaths are redemptive appear in the two bestselling sf novels of the 1960s, Heinlein's *Stranger in a Strange Land* (**1961**) and Frank HERBERT's *Dune* (**1965**). The transcendence of superhuman figures is by no means always quasi-Christian; the MYTHOLOGY-rooted novels of Roger ZELAZNY delight in examining the existential problems of godlike beings – shaped by the belief systems of, for example, the ancient Greeks and Egyptians, and of the Hindus – and the borderline between sf and FANTASY becomes very problematic in such works. A notable recent portrait of transcendental superhumanity, conventionally replete with quasireligious imagery, can be found in Jack Williamson's *Firechild* (**1986**).

The idea of the superman has in recent times become entangled with ideas of man/machine hybridization and GENETIC ENGINEERING. CYBORG supermen and genetically designed superhumans have become commonplace. The notion of the emergent superhuman appearing in our midst – possibly as a MUTANT product of radiation – is not as significant a motif as it once was, but its various stereotypes continue to crop up. Recent stories of superchildren include David PALMER's *Emergence* (**1984**) as well as young-adult novels like Alexander KEY's *Escape to Witch Mountain* (**1968**) and Virginia HAMILTON's *Justice and Her Brothers* (**1978**), all three of which have sequels, as does a similar novel featuring an older central character, Carole Nelson DOUGLAS's *Probe* (**1985**). Timothy ZAHN's *A Coming of Age* (**1985**) is a more sophisticated work in the same vein; Ann MAXWELL's *Timeshadow Rider* (**1986**), a pioneering exercise in the sf love story, seems rather more juvenile than the juvenile novels. A more ambivalent view of emergent superchildren is taken in the STRUGATSKI brothers' *The Ugly Swans* (**1972**; trans **1979**). More sober studies in superhuman existentialism include Wyman GUIN's *The Standing Joy* (**1969**) and Raymond Z. GALLUN's *The Eden Cycle* (**1974**) – although Gallun's later *Bioblast* (**1985**) is far more melodramatic. The tradition of Beresford's *The Hampdenshire Wonder* is belatedly carried forward by George TURNER's *Brain Child* (**1991**), and that of Stapledon's *A Man Divided* by Robert Charles WILSON's *The Divide* (**1990**). The idea of emergent superhumanity remains highly significant in the works of Ian WATSON, where it is intricately interwoven with the notion of CONCEPTUAL BREAKTHROUGH. Watson rarely imagines the breakthrough to superhumanity as an easy matter, and in such early novels as *The Embedding* (**1973**) and *The Jonah Kit* (**1975**) the attempts to achieve it fail, but in *The Martian Inca* (**1977**), *Alien Embassy* (**1977**), *Miracle Visitors* (**1978**) and *The Gardens of Delight* (**1980**) advancement is possible; the easier transitions of the light-hearted *Converts* (**1984**) are less convincing.

It is arguable that no other symbol in sf has evolved quite so dramatically as that of the superman, which has consistently pandered to the simplest and most basic form of human wish-fulfilment while sometimes carrying out far more sophisticated and ingenious analyses of our aspirations and our fears. [BS]
See also: PARANOIA.

SUPERMAN 1. US COMIC strip created by writer Jerry SIEGEL (1914-   ) and artist Joe Shuster (1914-1992), loosely based on Philip WYLIE's *Gladiator* (**1930**). Siegel was an sf fan, creator of several early FANZINES, including *Science Fiction* (5 issues from Oct 1932), in which illustrations by his friend Shuster had appeared. Their **Superman** idea was originally – over a period of years – rejected by almost every comics publisher in the USA before the character was finally allowed to make his début in *Action Comics*, June 1938, published by Detective Comics Inc, later known as DC COMICS; he got his own comic book with **Superman Comics** in 1939. Shuster and Siegel did not create many of the stories (perhaps just as well, since Shuster's style – though it had a charming simplicity – was very stiff), but their names continued to be used on the title pages. Under the editorship of Mort WEISINGER the series was given a more elaborate background, and was expanded to include additional superbeings and further comic titles. Many writers and artists, including Alfred BESTER, Edmond HAMILTON, Henry KUTTNER and Manly Wade WELLMAN, have contributed to the series, which continues today.

As sole survivor of a cataclysm on the planet Krypton, raised from infancy by US fosterparents,

the character's dual identity as timid reporter Clark Kent and indestructible crime-fighter Superman has a basic appeal to readers. His dynamic personality has transcended the comics medium to become incorporated into contemporary Western MYTHOLOGY. Storylines have been varied, with themes including time travel, interplanetary journeys, alternate universes, etc., while subplots have been woven around attempts to unmask his secret identity and to engage him amorously.

For many years the character became increasingly implausible, leading to his lampooning in Frank MILLER's *Batman: The Dark Knight Returns* (**1986**), where he appears in one sequence as a raddled skeleton. DC COMICS began to perceive a need to rationalize the character, most notably through an epic storyline involving many of their characters: "Crisis on Infinite Earths" (1987), written by Marv Wolfman. Artist-writer John Byrne was engaged to take a completely new approach to the characters. In his version, which began publication in **Adventures of Superman** #424 (Jan 1987; the title had previously been simply **Superman**), the first step was the elimination from the mythos of all the other SUPERHEROES who had intruded over the years (**Superboy**, **Supergirl**, etc.). Superman's powers and abilities were reduced and given specified limits – e.g., he could no longer travel at the speed of light, survive in space longer than he could hold his breath, or travel through time. His long-time sweetheart Lois Lane discovered his secret identity, and the couple are to be married. At the time of writing (mid-1992) the publishers are planning to take them all the way to the altar and then show Superman facing up to the responsibilities of marriage and child-rearing.

In order to achieve weekly appearance on the newsstands, 4 monthly titles are now published in sequence: **Superman**, **Superman in Action Comics**, **Adventures of Superman** and **Superman, the Man of Steel**.

Superman has been the most influential of sf comics heroes and has inspired many imitations, the most noted being CAPTAIN MARVEL. His adventures have appeared as a syndicated newspaper strip and as the RADIO programme, tv series, serial films and feature films described below. The character's sex life was guyed in Larry NIVEN's "Man of Steel, Woman of Kleenex" (1971) and his old age in *Superfolks* (**1977**) by Robert Mayer (1939-   ).   [JE/RT]
2. US animated cartoon series, prod Max Fleischer, dir Dave Fleischer for Paramount, 17 cartoons, Technicolor, 1940-43.
3. US RADIO series, usually pitting Superman against criminals, 1940-52.
4. Serial film (1948). Columbia. Prod Sam Katzman. Dirs Spencer Bennet, Thomas Carr, starring Kirk Alyn (Superman), Noel Neill, Tommy Bond. 15 episodes; later released (cut to 88 mins) as a feature film.

Although the production values were strictly Poverty

Row, *S* was perhaps the most successful film serial ever made. The sequel was *Atom Man Vs. Superman* (1950), 15-episode serial, Columbia, with much the same cast, in which Lex Luthor the Atom Man (Lyle Talbot) was introduced.

5. US tv series (1953-7): *The Adventures of Superman*. ABC TV. First season (Feb 1953) prod Robert Maxwell, Bernard Luber; from season 2 (Sep 1953) to season 6 and last prod Whitney Ellsworth. 104 25min episodes. First 2 seasons b/w, remainder in colour.

Superman was played by George Reeves, a former Hollywood leading man who had made his film début as a suitor of Vivien Leigh in *Gone With the Wind* (1939); he had first taken the role in the film *Superman and the Mole Men* (1951; vt *Superman and the Strange People* UK), dir Lee Sholem, 67 mins, b/w, in which Superman saves from a lynch mob little glowing troglodytes who have emerged from a deep oil well. With the tv series (one of whose early producers, Robert Maxwell, had also produced on **3** [see above] and written and coproduced the 1951 movie) Reeves became typecast in the role; when the series ended (he directed the last 3 episodes himself) he was unable to find further work in films. He committed suicide in 1959, aged 45.

Phyllis Coates played Lois Lane in the 1951 film and the first tv season only, being replaced for the rest of the series by Noel Neill, who had played the part in the 2 Columbia serials (**4**). Other cast members included Jack Larson as Jimmy Olsen and John Hamilton as Perry White.

The series was aimed primarily at children and, though mediocre, was extremely popular. Unlike the case in the comic strip, the stories rarely entered the realm of the fantastic: Superman was usually pitted against mundane, often bumbling criminals. 5 theatrical films were recut, each from 3 tv episodes, and released abroad (all 1954) as *Superman's Peril, Superman Flies Again, Superman in Exile, Superman and Scotland Yard* and *Superman and the Jungle Devils*.

6. Musical/made-for-tv film. A 1966 Broadway musical based on **Superman** and called *It's a Bird! It's a Plane! It's Superman!* was turned into a film for ABC TV in 1975 with David Wilson as Superman. Dir Jack Regas. Script Romeo Miller, based on the musical by Charles Strouse and David Newman. [JB/PN]

7. Film (1978). Dovemead/International Film Production. Dir Richard Donner, starring Christopher Reeve, Margot Kidder, Gene Hackman, Valerie Perrine, Ned Beatty, Jackie Cooper, Marlon Brando. Screenplay Mario Puzo, David Newman, Leslie Newman, Robert Benton, with Tom Mankiewicz as "creative consultant"; based on a story by Puzo. 143 mins. Colour.

Superman's visit to the wide screen was long delayed, but lavishly appointed when it did come. Screen rights to the most famous of SUPERHEROES had been bought by father-and-son producers Alexander and Ilya Salkind. They made *S*, the sequels SUPERMAN II (1980) and SUPERMAN III (1983) and the spin-off

SUPERGIRL (1984), with diminishing box-office returns, after which the rights were resold to Golan and Globus of Cannon Films, who made SUPERMAN IV: THE QUEST FOR PEACE (1987).

Expensive difficulties, largely to do with the flying scenes, delayed *S*, whose special effects vary from mostly excellent to occasionally awful. On the whole the end product is a triumph (it was awarded a HUGO), confidently walking the tightrope (though it stumbles once or twice) between playing it romantically straight and putting its tongue in its cheek, and much assisted by intelligent performances from Reeve, who plays Superman as a kind of Innocent Abroad, and Kidder, as a Lois Lane whose passion for Superman appears as touchingly erotic. Indeed the Caped Crusader's career is given a resonance with other great US myths, especially his Midwest boyhood, luminously photographed by Geoffrey Unsworth as though in homage to the paintings of Norman Rockwell. Part of the film's success, oddly, may be that it is UK-made, so that its USA is given an attractively foreign, story-book quality. The plot involves arch-villain Lex Luthor (Hackman) threatening to nuke the San Andreas fault, thus sinking West California and making a fortune out of real estate in what will be the new West Coast.

8. The 1989-91 tv series SUPERBOY describes Superman's teenage years at university. It was again produced by the Salkinds. [PN]

See also: MUSIC.

SUPERMAN II Film (1980). Dovemead/International Film Production. Dir Richard Lester, starring Christopher Reeve, Margot Kidder, Gene Hackman, Ned Beatty, Terence Stamp, Sarah Douglas, Jack O'Halloran, Susannah York. Screenplay Mario Puzo, David Newman, Leslie Newman (and, as "creative consultant", Tom Mankiewicz) from a story by Puzo. 127 mins. Colour.

Originally to be shot back-to-back with SUPERMAN, *SII* changed directors after conflict between the previous director, Richard Donner, and the producers, Ilya Salkind and Pierre Spengler. *SII* as released is perhaps 25% Donner's work and 75% Lester's. Certainly in its pace and its Pop-Art ironies it seems the work of Lester, maker of, *inter alia*, the Beatles movie *A Hard Day's Night* (1964). A trio of criminals exiled from the planet Krypton find their way to Earth, which they attempt to take over using their superpowers. Superman, who finally stops them, has first to restore his own powers, lost through his love for Lois Lane. (Apparently the condition of SUPERHERO, like that of priest, requires celibacy.) The protracted finale is choreographed with skilful comic-strip glee: the mythic dignity of the first film is lost, but enough wit takes its place – including the parallel between an impotent Superman and an impotent USA – for the film to be good value. Superman was to be further demystified in SUPERMAN III (1983). [PN]

See also: SUPERGIRL; SUPERMAN IV: THE QUEST FOR PEACE.

SUPERMAN III Film (1983). Dovemead/Cantharus/

Alexander and Ilya Salkind. Dir Richard Lester, starring Christopher Reeve, Richard Pryor, Jackie Cooper, Marc McClure, Annette O'Toole, Pamela Stephenson, Robert Vaughn. Screenplay David Newman, Leslie Newman. 125 mins. Colour.

Sequel to SUPERMAN (1978) and SUPERMAN II (1980), this is a movie on a more domestic scale, involving Clark Kent returning to the Midwest for a high-school reunion, where he (as opposed to his colourful *alter ego*) is fallen in love with by hometown girl Lana Lang (O'Toole). Abetted by his computer-genius pawn (Pryor), an evil business tycoon (Vaughn) with conventional world-takeover plans uses synthetic kryptonite to subvert the now thoroughly demystified Superman, who turns bad, broods in bars, tells a woman in distress "Don't expect me to save you, 'cos I don't do that nice stuff any more", but finally has his conscience awakened by a sweet little boy. Closer to its COMIC-strip origins than its 2 predecessors, and broader, *SIII*'s best moments are the opening scenes of escalating chaos, at least equal to Mack Sennett's work. There are good sequences throughout, and it is clearly better than its successors, SUPERGIRL and SUPERMAN IV: THE QUEST FOR PEACE, if less ambitious (and even sillier) than the earlier films.

The novelization is *Superman III* * (**1983**) by William KOTZWINKLE. [PN]

SUPERMAN IV: THE QUEST FOR PEACE Film (1987). Cannon. Dir Sidney J. Furie, starring Christopher Reeve, Gene Hackman, Margot Kidder, Mariel Hemingway. Screenplay Lawrence Kohner, Mark Rosenthal, based on a story by Reeve, Kohner. 93 mins. Colour.

Superman's death knell, at the box office anyway, was tolled by Cannon's attempt to get more mileage from his exploits after he had been jettisoned by Alexander and Ilya Salkind. Reeve agreed to play the part again only in exchange for co-authoring the original story, hence the anti-nuclear, anti-tabloid-journalism message. He meant well politically, but his disjointed story, which makes sense neither scientifically nor metaphorically (Superman throws nuclear missiles into Sun; evil Nuclear Man is cloned by Lex Luthor from a Superman hair; Superman defeats him by causing eclipse of the Sun and then anticlimactically throws him down chimney), is intensely feeble, as are the special effects.

The novelization is *Superman IV* * (**1987**) by B.B. Hiller. [PN]

SUPERMAN AND SCOTLAND YARD ◊ SUPERMAN.

SUPERMAN AND THE JUNGLE DEVILS ◊ SUPERMAN.

SUPERMAN AND THE MOLE MEN ◊ SUPERMAN.

SUPERMAN AND THE STRANGE PEOPLE ◊ SUPERMAN.

SUPERMAN FLIES AGAIN ◊ SUPERMAN.

SUPERMAN IN EXILE ◊ SUPERMAN.

SUPERMAN'S PERIL ◊ SUPERMAN.

SUPERMARIONATION ◊ Gerry and Sylvia ANDERSON.

SUPERNATURAL CREATURES Just as it is common in sf to give empirical explanations of ancient myths and stories of the gods (◊ GODS AND DEMONS; MYTHOLOGY) and to seek a rationale for MAGIC, so too, when sf deals with supernatural creatures, it commonly invokes quasiscientific rationalizations. Sometimes these involve racial memory of unusual but natural creatures, or they may involve MUTANTS (commonly) or abnormal PSYCHOLOGY (occasionally). The sf writer does not, however, wish to demythologize all that is strange to the point of rendering it utterly matter-of-fact. More commonly he or she retains the horror (or the wonder) while rendering it a believable phenomenon of the world we live in. Also, by making the condition of vampirism or lycanthropy, for example, a natural affliction, it is often possible to evoke pity for the MONSTER as well as its victims. 2 stories illustrating this clearly are James BLISH's "There Shall be no Darkness" (1950) and Richard MATHESON's *I Am Legend* (**1954**). The former is a werewolf story which links lycanthropy with artistic talent, and allows the reader some empathy with the shapeshifting killer; the latter tells of a plague which transforms its victims into vampires, who besiege the one immune left in the city. In both a far-fetched rationale is given, Matheson being particularly ingenious in explaining the traditional stigmata of the vampire in terms of symptoms of an illness.

Jack WILLIAMSON wrote an excellent werewolf story, *Darker than you Think* (1940; exp **1948**), in which lycanthropes are seen as members of a distinct race, genetically different from *Homo sapiens* though superficially identical; the hero who discovers the truth turns out to share this awful but thrilling heritage. This story, like many others of its kind, has a symbolic relationship with split-personality stories like Robert Louis STEVENSON's *Strange Case of Dr Jekyll and Mr Hyde* (**1886**), in which the more primitive, amoral, beastlike part of our evolutionary heritage is able to emerge and take on a shape of its own. All such stories can ultimately be traced back to a dualistic view of Man, manifest in Christian doctrine as the idea that humanity on the one hand suffers from Original Sin, but on the other hand has an aspiring spirit which is a gift from God.

Guy ENDORE's *The Werewolf of Paris* (**1933**) sees lycanthropy as a psychological distortion, perhaps hereditary, and no literal transformation from man to wolf takes place. Similarly Theodore STURGEON's *Some of Your Blood* (**1961**) has a tortured and not very dangerous "vampire" who is in fact a psychotic, whose blood-drinking, it gradually emerges, can be traced back to childhood trauma. The protagonist of Gene WOLFE's "The Hero as Werwolf" (1975) is one of the few still-human survivors of a utopian future where the genetically fit have been bred into placidity and health – superhuman sheep, as it were – while the descendants of the abandoned remainder live a tragic, hole-and-corner life, surviving cannibalistically on the super-race responsible for their condition.

Whitley STRIEBER's *The Wolfen* **(1978)**, though primarily a thriller, provides a rigorous cryptozoological rationale for werewolf myths in terms of a perfectly natural animal species, but one that is rare, intelligent, furtive and hence unknown to orthodox taxonomy.

Stories of demonic possession, such as John CHRISTOPHER's *The Possessors* **(1965)** and many others, are commonly rationalized in terms of PSI POWERS or as a form of parasitism, usually by an alien; several of these stories are discussed in PARASITISM AND SYMBIOSIS. Familiars are often symbiotes also, as is the case with the sinister little creatures who accompany the "witches" in Fritz LEIBER's *Gather, Darkness!* (1943; **1950**).

Many stories of supernatural creatures which appear in supposedly sf collections are in fact straight FANTASY; i.e., the supernatural status of these beings is left unquestioned. UNKNOWN magazine published quite a few stories of this kind, as did WEIRD TALES earlier and *The* MAGAZINE OF FANTASY AND SCIENCE FICTION later. The latter published the **John the Minstrel** stories by Manly Wade WELLMAN (probably his best work), whose hero is faced with a variety of supernatural menaces, though occasionally some sf jargon is used to bring them down to earth a little, one of the best being "O Ugly Bird!" (1951); they were collected in *Who Fears the Devil?* (coll **1963**). Ray BRADBURY's "Homecoming" (1946) is a touching story of the one "normal" in a jolly, clannish family of supernaturals. Many supernatural stories of the jokier kind can be found in Theodore COGSWELL's *The Wall Around the World* (coll **1962**) and Avram DAVIDSON's *Or All the Seas with Oysters* (coll **1962**); Davidson was editor of *FSF* for a period. A number of such stories are collected in Judith MERRIL's lively anthology *Galaxy of Ghouls* (anth **1955**; vt *Off the Beaten Orbit* 1959), which contains Walter M. MILLER's "Triflin' Man" (1955; vt "You Triflin' Skunk"), in which the demon lover turns out to be an ALIEN, a common explanation for supernatural manifestations.

Elves and fairies likewise often turn out to be aliens, as in Clifford D. SIMAK's *The Goblin Reservation* **(1968)**, or Neanderthal or atavistic survivals, as in several stories discussed in MYTHOLOGY, John BLACKBURN's *Children of the Night* **(1966)** among them. Sometimes they merely live on colonized and then forgotten planets, as in Christopher STASHEFF's **Warlock** series. The creatures out of Greek legend, including several of an apparently supernatural variety, in Roger ZELAZNY's *This Immortal* (1965 *FSF* as ". . . And Call me Conrad"; exp **1966**) are mutants. C.M. KORNBLUTH's vampire in "The Mindworm" (1950), is a telepathic mutant created by atomic radiation.

Unicorns and dragons remain popular, unicorns for some reason being usually allowed to remain mythic while dragons are often rationalized as aliens. Examples of the former occur in Peter Beagle's *The Last Unicorn* **(1968)**, Harlan ELLISON's "On the Downhill Side" (1972) and Mark GESTON's *The Siege of Wonder*

(1976); there are many others. Dragons appear notably in Anne MCCAFFREY's **Dragonrider** series, Jack VANCE's *The Dragon Masters* **(1963)** and Avram Davidson's *Rogue Dragon* **(1965)**.

Supernatural creatures generally play a prominent role in romantic fantasy, often as symbolic of a wondrousness that may survive in odd, untouched corners of the world while dead in our rational, urbanized, modern civilization. They are, for example, to be found in forms both horrific and lovely in the various LOST WORLDS of A. MERRITT, in practically every story written by Thomas Burnett SWANN, and in SWORD AND SORCERY generally.

Ghosts are rather a special case, and are discussed in ESCHATOLOGY. They are reconstructed in the flesh from a reading of human minds by the sentient planet *Solaris* (1961; trans **1970**) by Stanislaw LEM; and along with zombies have a very real existence in Robert SHECKLEY's amusing *Immortality Delivered* (1958; exp vt *Immortality, Inc.* 1959). Sheckley often plays games with supernatural creatures; he brings nightmares, for example, to life in "Ghost V" (1954), and the hero of "Protection" (1956) has good reason to wish he had never accepted aid from a ghostly alien from another DIMENSION. The poltergeists in Keith ROBERTS's "Boulter's Canaries" (1965) are energy configurations which can do substantial damage in the real world. Nigel KNEALE's entire career in sf cinema and tv was devoted to rationalizing the supernatural, most notably perhaps in the tv serial QUATERMASS AND THE PIT (1958-9), where racial memories of the Devil and the Wild Hunt turn out to have been transmitted by Martians. Stories of this kind are not restricted to English-language sf, nor to genre sf. Stanisław Lem's *Sledztwo* (1959; trans as *The Investigation* 1974) is an interesting study of the extent to which the unknown may be susceptible to rational explanation, in a mystery where Scotland Yard is faced with the activities of a ghoul, whose status as either natural or supernatural is difficult to determine.

There is a kind of class distinction among the three most popular varieties of supernatural creature to be found in HORROR movies. Vampires are aristocratic, drinking only the most refined life essences, usually blood; in Lucy SUSSEX's "God and Her Black Sense of Humour" (1990) it is semen. In the iconography of horror, the vampire stands for SEX. The werewolf, who stands for instability, shapeshifting, lack of self control, is middle-class and lives in a dog-eat-dog world. The zombie or ghoul, who shambles and rots (as, archetypally, in George ROMERO's sf movie *The* NIGHT OF THE LIVING DEAD [1968]), is working-class, inarticulate, dangerous, deprived, wishing only to feed on those who are better off; in the iconography of horror the zombie stands for the exploited worker.

During the period of the Vietnam War the zombie, both in pure horror and in sf horror, was perhaps the most popular archetype, but since then vampires and werewolves have made a major comeback, often in sf-rationalized form. Witty FEMINIST subtexts appear in Jody SCOTT's vampire satire *I, Vampire* (**1984**) and Suzy McKee CHARNAS's HUGO-winning werewolf story "Boobs" (1989), in which the lunar cycle controls menstruation and transformation into werewolf. Tanith LEE's several werewolf stories, including "Wolfland" (1980), *Lycanthia, or The Children of Wolves* (**1981**), "Bloodmantle" (1985) and *Heart-Beast* (**1992**), also have womanly subtexts; "Bloodmantle" has Red Riding Hood as a kind of victor, as she is again in Angela CARTER's metamorphic FABULATION "The Company of Wolves" (1979), filmed in 1984. Lee's "The Gorgon" (1983), about Medusa, may be one of the finest, simplest, most touching of all supernatural-creature rationalizations.

Other sf (or at least sciencefictionalized) tales of vampire and werewolf from recent years include: *The Orphan* (**1980**) and its 2 sequels, about a werewolf, by Robert STALLMAN; *Vampire Tapestry* (coll of linked stories **1980**) by Suzy McKee Charnas; *Vampire Junction* (**1984**) and *Valentine* (**1992**) by S.P. SOMTOW (Somtow Sucharitkul); *The Empire of Fear* (**1988**) by Brian STABLEFORD (vampires); *Moon Dance* (**1989**) by Somtow again (werewolves); *Carrion Comfort* (**1989**) by Dan SIMMONS (vampires); Michael WEAVER's trilogy collected as *Wolf-Dreams* (omni **1989** UK); Barbara HAMBLY's *Those Who Hunt the Night* (**1988**; vt *Immortal Blood* UK) (vampires); Kim NEWMAN's *Bad Dreams* (**1990**) (shapeshifting vampires); *The Werewolves of London* (**1990**) and its sequel *The Angel of Pain* (**1991**) by Stableford again; and *Wolf Flow* (**1992**) by K.W. JETER. Another important vampire title is Nancy Collins' *Sunglasses After Dark* (**1989**), and major series have been written by Anne Rice (vampires and mummies) and by Chelsea Quinn YARBRO, with her **Saint-Germain** series (vampires) from 1978 on. All these books, whose standard is overall rather high, lie somewhere between sf and supernatural horror, none of them fitting purely in one genre or the other, though Stableford quite closely approaches sf in *Empire of Fear*. With so much work of this sort being produced – the cited texts are merely a fraction of the whole – it almost seems as if a new genre is in the making, not so much pure horror as the semirationalized "horror romance", a kind of half-sister to the SCIENTIFIC ROMANCE.

Supernatural horror made other appearances of a more outré kind in the 1980s, three landmarks being Alfred BESTER's *Golem^{100}* (**1980**) which marries sf, diabolism and depth psychology to produce its supernatural monster from the id; Judith MOFFETT's "The Hob" (1988), in which the hobs or brownies from myth turn out to be exiled aliens, a story later incorporated into *The Ragged World: A Novel of the Hefn on Earth* (fixup **1991**); and best of all, perhaps, Tim POWERS's strange fable of the romantic poets, *The Stress of Her Regard* (**1989**), which memorably incarnates romantic longings and fears in the partly rationalized figure of the Lamia. [PN]

See also: GOLEM: GOTHIC SF; RELIGION.

SUPER SCIENCE AND FANTASTIC STORIES ◊ SUPER SCIENCE STORIES.

SUPER-SCIENCE FICTION US DIGEST-size magazine. 18 bimonthly issues Dec 1956-Oct 1959, published by Headline Publications; ed W.W. Scott. Though *S-SF* used material by established writers – including 36 stories by Robert SILVERBERG and 10 by Harlan ELLISON, both using pseudonyms as well as their own names – its contents were mediocre. [BS/PN]

SUPER SCIENCE NOVELS ◊ SUPER SCIENCE STORIES.

SUPER SCIENCE STORIES US PULP MAGAZINE. 31 issues, published by Fictioneers, Inc., a subsidiary of Popular Publications; 16 issues Mar 1940-May 1943, 3 of the 1941 issues (Mar-Aug) being under the title *Super Science Novels*; ed Frederik POHL until Aug 1941, then Alden H. Norton. The magazine was revived by Popular Publications, continuing the old volume numeration, for 15 more issues Jan 1949-Aug 1951, ed Ejler JAKOBSSON, with Damon KNIGHT assistant ed on some issues. In both incarnations the magazine varied between quarterly and bimonthly.

SSS, a companion to ASTONISHING STORIES, featured standard pulp adventure sf, and in its 1st incarnation was an important market for the FUTURIAN group, Pohl buying a good deal of material from himself (including many of his early collaborations with C.M. KORNBLUTH). The most notable story was *Genus Homo* (Mar 1941; rev **1950**) by L. Sprague DE CAMP and P. Schuyler MILLER. It also published a number of early stories by Isaac ASIMOV and James BLISH's first story, "Emergency Refueling" (1940), and his much superior "Sunken Universe" (1942) as by Arthur Merlyn. The 2nd incarnation published Chad OLIVER's début story, "The Land of Lost Content" (1950). *SSS* had a greater importance to the HISTORY OF SF than the quality of its stories would suggest; it was an important training ground.

The Canadian magazine of the same title, published by Popular Publications, Toronto, continued publication for 2 years after the first US version ceased, publishing 21 issues in all Aug 1942-Dec 1945, the last 5 under the title *Super Science and Fantastic Stories*. From Aug 1942 to Feb 1944 the Canadian *SSS* drew its material in alternate issues from the US *SSS* and *Astonishing Stories*. From the Apr 1944 issue onwards some original stories were used (11 in all), including "The Black Sun Rises" (June 1944) by Henry KUTTNER, but mostly it ran stories from the Popular Publications reprint magazine FAMOUS FANTASTIC MYSTERIES. The 2nd incarnation of *SSS* was also reprinted in Canada 1949-51, as *Super Science Stories*. There were 2 series of UK reprints: Thorpe & Porter reprinted 3 whole issues in 1949-50; and Pembertons published 14 consecutively numbered issues of selections from both versions of the US magazine 1950-53. [BS/PN]

SURREALISM ◊ ABSURDIST SF; ILLUSTRATION; NEW WAVE.

SURVIVALIST FICTION During the near-half century of Cold War after the dropping of the atom bomb on Japan in 1945, nuclear HOLOCAUSTS were a commonplace plot device in various genres of popular fiction. Some novels took readers teasingly up to the brink without actually carrying them into the terminal moments; Cold War thrillers of this sort are not generally treated in this encyclopedia. A rather larger number of novels treated the final war as a given, an assumed premise of the action of the tale, which took place subsequent to the horror of the actual event. One subgenre of this sizeable cohort of post-holocaust novels usually goes by the name survivalist fiction.

Though it takes much of its political extremism and attendent social prejudices from the genuine survivalist movement which flourished in the USA during the Cold War (*see also* LIBERTARIAN SF), survivalist fiction as such has little to do with the actual concerns of real survivalists, who tend to concentrate most of their energies on exercises and training and hoarding and forward-planning for the anticipated event; less thought is given to the aftermath, where survivalist fictions are almost invariably set. The significance of genuine survivalists is of the here and now, as an example of the pathos of "self-reliance" in a world too complex and fragile to reward simple solutions.

Of greater potential interest to sf writers than realist stories about survivalists is, perhaps, the apocalypse pathology (◊ RELIGION; ESCHATOLOGY) detectable in the survivalist mentality. Those who live their lives in anticipation of surviving the holocaust are almost certainly geared to welcome its coming, and to feel that – by contrast with the civilian hordes who ignore the tenets of the faith – they comprise an Elect (◊ SUPERMAN) of true believers. Survivalists, in other words, run the risk of seeing the holocaust as a test of Faith: of feeling virtuous about the END OF THE WORLD. A novel like Robert A. HEINLEIN's *Farnham's Freehold* (**1964**), though displaced through TIME TRAVEL beyond the normal boundaries of survivalist fiction, does convey the extremist mind-set of some participants in the movement, and the "Darwinian" ruthlessness they long to ape. But *Farnham's Freehold* is a tale of wish-fulfilment; the actualities of survival are clearly so unrewarding when faced directly that almost all sf which deals with nuclear holocaust directly treats its human protagonists as doomed. There is, in fact, almost no genuine sf that describes a genuine survivalist agenda without descending into fantasy; even Dean ING's *Pulling Through* (**1983**), which is a good example of an extremely rare breed, has recourse to a magic sports car which enables the protagonist to leap over some otherwise terminal obstacles. Andrew J. OFFUTT's *The Castle Keeps* (**1972**) is a scathing analysis of the effects of survivalist doctrines in any plausible post-holocaust world.

There are of course many sf tales of survivors (like Gordon R. DICKSON's attractive *Wolf and Iron* [**1990**]) and post-holocaust stories whose protagonists are oppressed (as in Chelsea Quinn YARBRO's *False Dawn* [**1978**]) by predators whose resemblance to survivalists may not be accidental; but survivalist fiction is something very different from tales like these. From about 1980, survivalist fiction has become established

as a very particular kind of male-action story, set in post-holocaust venues where law-and-order has disappeared, and where there is effectively no restraint upon the behaviour of the hero, who therefore kills before he is killed, demonstrating his fitness to survive through acts of unbridled violence (which very frequently descend into prolonged sessions of rape and sadism). The first full-blown example of the subgenre is probably the **Survivalist** series by Jerry AHERN, which began with *Survivalist #1: Total War* (**1981**) and which now extends to more than 20 volumes. A second important open-ended series (survivalist fiction, like pornography, tends to be structured as a series of escalating repetitions of the same material) is William W. JOHNSTONE's **Ashes** sequence from 1983, in which an extreme right-wing political agenda is used to legitimize the hero's actions. Other sequences include David ALEXANDER's **Phoenix** books, James BARTON's **Wasteworld** books, D.B. Drumm's **Traveler** books (initiated by Ed NAHA, though some or most of the sequence was by John SHIRLEY), Bob HAM's's **Overload** books, Laurence JAMES's **Death Land** books as by James Axler, Mack MALONEY's **Wingman** books, Victor MILÁN's **Guardians** books as by Richard Austin, David L. ROBBINS's **Endworld** books, James ROUCH's **Zone** books, some episodes in Barry SADLER's **Casca** sequence, and the **Doomsday Warrior** books written as by Ryder Stacy (◊ Ryder SYVERTSEN). To this list could be added MAD MAX (1979) and its sequels, although these are at the top of the heap; the same cannot be said of their cheap imitators. During 1992 several book series were terminated due to declining sales; it may be that the changing world scene had reduced their appeal.

There may be some connection between present-day survivalist movements in the USA and survivalist fiction as here described, in that survivalist fiction may seem to express a grotesquely decayed form of Heinleinian relish at the defeat of "civilian" values when the "real" world bares its teeth. But even this is to claim too much. Sadistic, sexist, racist, pornographic, gloating and void, survivalist fiction is an obscene parody of genuine survivalism, and a nightmare at the bottom of the barrel of sf. [JC]

See also: PARANOIA.

SURVIVORS UK tv series (1975-7). BBC TV. Created Terry NATION (who also wrote 7 episodes in season 1). Prod Terence Dudley. Writers included Jack Ronder, Martin Worth, Roger Parkes. Dirs included Pennant Roberts, Terence Williams, Eric Hills. 3 seasons, 38 50min episodes in all. Colour.

The post-HOLOCAUST novel is a particularly UK subgenre of sf, and so it is not surprising that the theme's first significant appearance on tv should come from the BBC. The accidental release of a deadly virus kills almost everyone; in the UK only about 7000 people are left alive. *S* follows the adventures of small groups of mostly middle-class survivors, their efforts to cope without TECHNOLOGY and their encounters with other, less sympathetic groups. The main characters include a housewife (Carolyn Seymour), a secretary (Lucy Fleming), an engineer (Ian McCulloch) and an architect (Denis Lill). Initial gloom is gradually replaced by rather too cosy an atmosphere, with aspects of a rural paradise – not only have all those smelly cities disappeared, but also the working classes. The subtext involves a very English political myth (which in literature goes back beyond Richard JEFFERIES's *After London* [**1885**]) about the strengths of a life lived close to the land. The overnight disappearance of technology and in particular the shortage of petrol are never adequately rationalized. Nation's partial novelization is *The Survivors* * (**1976**). [JB/PN]

SUSPENDED ANIMATION The notion of suspended animation is one of the oldest literary devices in sf, by virtue of its convenience as a means of TIME TRAVEL into the future (*see also* SLEEPER AWAKES). It is used in UTOPIAN romances like L.S. MERCIER's *Memoirs of the Year Two Thousand Five Hundred* (trans **1772**), Mary GRIFFITH's *Three Hundred Years Hence* (**1836**; **1975**) and Edward BELLAMY's *Looking Backward, 2000-1887* (**1888**). It became somewhat more than a literary convenience in H.G. WELLS's *When the Sleeper Wakes* (**1899**; rev vt *The Sleeper Awakes* **1910**). These stories, having other purposes in view, gloss over the scientific means by which suspended animation might be achieved. Edgar Allan POE's short story "The Facts in the Case of M. Valdemar" (**1845**) features mesmerically induced suspended animation, while Grant ALLEN's "Pausodyne" (**1881**) imagines an 18th-century scientist inventing a gas which puts him into protracted anaesthesia. The most popular means, however, has always been preservation by freezing (◊ CRYONICS). Many fantasies using the theme were inspired by the ancient Egyptian habit of mummifying the dead; it was a relatively small imaginative step to suppose an arcane mummification process which preserved life and beauty, and Egyptian princesses ripe for revival are featured in Edgar Lee's *Pharaoh's Daughter* (**1889**), Clive Holland's *An Egyptian Coquette* (**1898**; rev vt *The Spell of Isis*) and Robert W. CHAMBERS's *The Tracer of Lost Persons* (**1906**); a very much more recent example is Anne Rice's *The Mummy, or Ramses the Damned* (**1989**). The modern world is visited by observers preserved from even more remote eras in Erle COX's *Out of the Silence* (**1919**; **1925**; exp **1947**), Olof W. ANDERSON's *The Treasure-Vault of Atlantis* (**1925**) and Edgar Rice BURROUGHS's "The Resurrection of Jimber Jaw" (**1937**). A curious novel which explores the existential significance of the ability to suspend animation in oneself is *The Insurgents* (**1957**) by VERCORS; and Robert A. HEINLEIN intricately constructs *The Door into Summer* (**1957**) around 2 trips to a single future by suspended animation.

Suspended animation was co-opted into GENRE SF as one of the standard items in its vocabulary of ideas; it was used in the first extensive pulp exploration of future HISTORY, Laurence MANNING's *The Man who Awoke* (**1933**; fixup **1975**). Genre-sf writers found it a useful device in another context: avoiding the intolerable timelags involved in journeys to the stars. An early trip of this kind is featured in A.E. VAN VOGT's "Far Centaurus" (**1944**), whose luckless heroes arrive to find that FASTER-THAN-LIGHT travel has been invented as they slept. More recent dramas involving ships populated largely by people in suspended animation include *The Black Corridor* (**1969**) by Michael MOORCOCK and Hilary BAILEY and *The Dream Millennium* (**1974**) by James WHITE. Stranger beings than Cox's or Olof W. Anderson's Atlanteans could be found in suspended animation, in a manner reminiscent of supernatural stories in which ancient GODS and their dormant MAGIC are revived into the present by folly or evil intent. The later work of H.P. LOVECRAFT is notable in this respect, while more orthodox sf variations on the theme include *The Alien* (**1951**) by Raymond F. JONES, *World of Ptavvs* (**1966**) by Larry NIVEN and *The Space Vampires* (**1976**) by Colin WILSON.

The recent popularization of cryonics as a means of suspending animation has offered a boost to the credibility of the jargon surrounding the literary device, and has helped increase interest in alternative methods. These include the various works ultimately gathered into *The Worthing Saga* (**1978-89**; fixup **1990**) by Orson Scott CARD and the fascinating *Between the Strokes of Night* (**1985**) by Charles SHEFFIELD, which takes the notion to its logical extreme. Its deployment as a timeslipping device is nowadays less frequent, but the motif is still capable of further sophistication, as shown in Richard Ben SAPIR's visitor-from-the-past story *The Far Arena* (**1978**) and Richard LUPOFF's FAR-FUTURE story *Sun's End* (**1984**). [BS]

See also: IMMORTALITY; GENERATION STARSHIPS; MEDICINE.

SUSPENSE US DIGEST-size magazine. 4 quarterly issues Spring 1951-Winter 1952, published by Farrell Publishing Co., Chicago; ed Theodore Irwin. *S*, based on the CBS RADIO series of the same name and including the script of 1 episode per issue, contained also a mixture of detective, weird, sf and fantasy stories, including some reprints. Authors included Theodore STURGEON and John WYNDHAM, and there was a new **Gray Mouser** story from Fritz LEIBER, "Dark Vengeance" (Fall 1951). The unusual mixing of genres may have accounted for *S*'s rapid demise. [FHP/PN]

SUSSEX, LUCY (1957-   ) New Zealand-born writer and critic, in AUSTRALIA since the age of 14. She was one of the co-editors of the anthology of sf criticism *Contrary Modes* (anth **1985**) with Jenny Blackford, Russell BLACKFORD and Norman Talbot, and a co-editor of AUSTRALIAN SCIENCE FICTION REVIEW: SECOND SERIES for its first 2 years (**1986-7**). At about the same time she began publishing promising sf FABULATIONS like "The Lipton Village Society" (**1985**), about alienated people creating an ALTERNATE WORLD by force of will. This and "My Lady Tongue" (**1988**), about life inside (and outside) a utopian FEMINIST lesbian community, and "God and Her Black Sense of Humour"

(1990), about immortal semen-swallowing vampires (◊ SUPERNATURAL CREATURES), are assembled with others in *My Lady Tongue & Other Tales* (coll **1990**). LS's racy, slangy narrative voice sometimes jars with a content that seems to require a less aggressive tone. Her earlier *The Peace Garden* (**1989**), for children, is not sf or fantasy. [PN]

SUTCLIFFE, HALLIWELL [r] ◊ Jocelyn QUILP.

SUTPHEN, (WILLIAM GILBERT) VAN TASSEL (1861-1945) US writer whose *The Nineteenth Hole: Being Tales of the Fair Green: Second Series* (coll **1901**) includes 2 tales of golfing sf (◊ GAMES AND SPORTS), one set in 1999 when the game fully dominates US life. *The Doomsman* (**1906**) depicts a medievalized post-HOLOCAUST USA where dashing Doomsmen run a protection racket from Manhattan and an old priest keeps an electric dynamo humming. All ends in tears. [JC/PN]

SUTTON, JEAN (1917-) US author, with Jeff SUTTON (*whom see for details*), of several novels for older children. [JC]

SUTTON, JEFF(ERSON HOWARD) (1913-1979) US writer who began publishing sf with "The Third Empire" for *Spaceway* in 1955, and whose background – he had been a journalist, served time in the Marines and done research in high-altitude survival – was reflected in several of his novels, from *First on the Moon* (**1958**), his début, to *Spacehive* (**1960**) and *Whisper from the Stars* (**1970**). JS wrote with a somewhat dilute clarity, his tales occasionally rising above the routine when he dealt in NEAR-FUTURE subject matter; but even these stories soon became fatally dated. When he attempted more far-flung adventures his inspiration tended to flag and his plots to become strained. His juvenile sf novels (see listing below) with his wife, Jean SUTTON, were somewhat smoother. [JC]

Other works: *Bombs in Orbit* (**1959**); *The Missile Lords* (**1963**); *The Atom Conspiracy* (**1963**); *Apollo at Go* (**1963**); *Beyond Apollo* (**1966**); *H-Bomb over America* (**1967**); *The Man who Saw Tomorrow* (**1968** dos); *Alton's Unguessable* (**1970** dos); *The Mindblocked Man* (**1972**); *Cassady* (**1979**). **With Jean Sutton:** *The River* (**1966**); *The Programmed Man* (**1968**); *The Beyond* (**1968**); *Lord of the Stars* (**1969**); *Alien from the Stars* (**1970**); *The Boy who had the Power* (**1971**).

See also: CHILDREN'S SF.

SUVIN, DARKO (R.) (1932-) Academic, sf critic and poet, born and raised in that part of YUGOSLAVIA that is now Croatia; PhD from Zagreb University, where he taught 1959-67; since 1968 he has lived in CANADA (he now has Canadian/Yugoslav dual nationality), where he is a full professor of English at McGill University, Montreal. DS has been very closely associated with the development of academic interest in sf in the USA, having been an active member of the SCIENCE FICTION RESEARCH ASSOCIATION and a co-editor of SCIENCE-FICTION STUDIES from its inception to Nov 1980 (subsequently a contributing editor), and having lectured and published widely on the subject. (His other field is drama, especially the work of Bertolt Brecht.) His books about sf are *Od Lukijana do Lunjika* ["From Lucian to the Lunik"] (**1965** Yugoslavia), *Russian Science Fiction 1956-1974: A Bibliography* (**1976** US); *Pour une poétique de la science-fiction* (**1977**; trans DS and exp as *Metamorphoses of Science Fiction: On the Poetics and History of a Literary Genre* **1979** US), *Victorian Science Fiction in the U.K.: The Discourses of Knowledge and of Power* (**1983** US) – perhaps his most important book, in its splendid blend of scholarly research into early sf, explication of its nature and sociological argument about its ideological setting – and *Positions and Presuppositions in Science Fiction* (coll **1988** US).

The last 3 books especially constitute (among other things) one of the most formidable and sustained theoretical attempts to define sf as a genre. This was recognized when he was awarded the 1979 PILGRIM AWARD, while still very much in mid-career, for services to sf scholarship. DS's writing has been unwisely dismissed by some readers as too clotted and difficult, and it is true that his critical prose sometimes seems more convoluted than his arguments require. But part of the difficulty results from the praiseworthy scrupulousness and rigour of his complex theses, for which he has had to find a terminology (new to sf studies at least) that is very much based in European socio-formalism; he has often been described as a "Marxist" critic but, while this is not untrue, it is not especially helpful either, as modern structuralism and semiotics also play an important role in his theoretical approach. DS sees sf as a "literary genre whose necessary and sufficient conditions are the presence and interaction of estrangement and cognition, and whose main formal device is an imaginative framework alternative to the author's empirical environment" (◊ DEFINITIONS OF SF); it was DS who introduced the term "cognition" to sf criticism. One result of DS's approach is a contemptuous dismissal of FANTASY as lacking "cognitive believability".

DS ed *Other Worlds, Other Seas: Science-Fiction Stories from Socialist Countries* (anth **1970** US), *H.G. Wells and Modern Science Fiction* (anth **1977** US), a collection of essays by various hands, and, with R.D. MULLEN, *Science-Fiction Studies: Selected Articles on Science Fiction 1973-1975* (anth **1976** US) and *Science-Fiction Studies, Second Series: Selected Articles on Science Fiction 1976-1977* (anth **1978** US), both from GREGG PRESS.

Of marginal relevance to sf and UTOPIAS are DS's 2 vols of poems, some prize-winning: *The Long March: Notes on the Way 1981-1984* (coll **1987**) and *Armirana Arkadija* (coll **1990** Yugoslavia). [PN]

See also: BIBLIOGRAPHIES; CRITICAL AND HISTORICAL WORKS ABOUT SF; GENRE SF; GOTHIC SF; HISTORY OF SF; PROTO SCIENCE FICTION; SENSE OF WONDER.

SWAHN, SVEN CHRISTER [r] ◊ SCANDINAVIA.

SWAIN, DWIGHT V(REELAND) (1915-1992) US writer, very variously employed in jobs ranging from migrant labourer to university lecturer to scriptwriter.

His first sf story, "Henry Horn's Super Solvent" for *Fantastic Adventures* in 1941, initiated the **Henry Horn** series of tales about a bumblingly incompetent would-be SCIENTIST; the others are "Henry Horn's Blitz Bomb" (1942), "Henry Horn's Racing Ray" (1942) and "Henry Horn's X-Ray Eye Glasses" (1942). He also wrote 3 stories in 1942 as Clark South. DVS published several sf novels up to the end of the 1950s which did not reach book form, the exception being *The Transposed Man* (**1955** chap dos; with 1 story added, as coll 1957 UK), in which a human rebel wins through to the stars. In his later career, during which he concentrated on his work in educational film-making – also publishing several nonfiction books on the art of successful writing, including *Creating Characters: How to Build Story People* (**1990**) – DVS returned occasionally to adventure tales of the sort he clearly preferred, writing 1 Nick CARTER novel, *The Pemex Chart* * (**1979**), and 2 further tales, *The Planet Murderer* (**1984**) as John CLEVE (in collaboration with Andrew J. OFFUTT), and *Monster* (**1991**).

In 1991, the Oklahoma Professional Writers' Hall of Fame named him a "grand master", along with C.J. CHERRYH. [JC]

SWAMP THING, THE Created by writer Len Wein and artist Berni Wrightson in DC COMICS's *House of Secrets* #92 (July 1971), TST is a monster whose moss- and muck-encrusted body is formed entirely of vegetable matter. In that original short graphic story, as a result of a scientific "accident" arranged by his jealous assistant Damian Ridge, Dr Alex Olsen is killed and subsequently resurrected in mutated form as TST, destined to wreak vengeance. Wein and Wrightson rewrote the character's early biography in the **Swamp Thing** series of COMIC books for DC, running from #1 (Nov 1972) until July 1974. According to the revised version, the unfortunate Dr Alec Holland (note name-change) was working on a "Bio-restorative Formula" when an explosion in his laboratory set off the chain of events described above These 10 issues (reprinted as **Roots of the Swamp Thing** Aug-Nov 1986) are regarded in the comics world as classics of GOTHIC horror.

In May 1982 TST began to reappear in another comic-book series, **Saga of the Swamp Thing**. In this version he initially developed as a SUPERHERO of no great interest, but #20, *Loose Ends*, introduced Alan MOORE as writer. Moore continued until #64 and, with artists Steve Bissette, John Totleben, Rick Veitch and others, attained what is usually accepted to be his greatest achievement to date (with the possible exception of WATCHMEN). Moore's themes – including menstrual werewolves, serial killers, racial zombies and, in a swipe at the gun-lobby, a house haunted by guns – were wide-ranging, and he radically changed the basic premise: TST was now a MONSTER who had incorporated through RNA some of Alex Holland's personality. Moore also introduced significant ECOLOGY and ESCHATOLOGY themes, latterly taking TST into a series of SPACE OPERA adventures. From #30 DC

found it necessary to drop the Comics Code logo from the cover, replacing it with the words "Sophisticated Suspense"; at the same time the title reverted to the original **Swamp Thing**. Since Moore's departure the scripts have rarely reached the same quality.

There have been 2 **Swamp Thing** films: *Swamp Thing* (1982) dir Wes Craven, 91 mins, and its chaotic spoof sequel, the occasionally hilarious *The Return of Swamp Thing* (1989; vt *Swamp Thing II*) dir Jim Wynorski, 88 mins. Both films, neither very successful, star stuntman Dick Durock as the monster and Louis Jourdan as his conniving foe, Dr Arcane. [RT]

SWAN AMERICAN MAGAZINE UK magazine, PULP-MAGAZINE size, published by G.G. Swan, London. The 2 (undated) sf issues in the series, #11 (probably 1948) and #15 (probably 1949), were resettings with UK illustrations of parts of *Future Fantasy and Science Fiction* (a variant title of FUTURE FICTION), Dec 1942, and of SCIENCE FICTION QUARTERLY, Winter 1942. This was effectively a postwar renewal, with new numbering, of the earlier SWAN YANKEE MAGAZINE series. [FHP]

SWANN, THOMAS BURNETT (1928-1976) US poet, novelist and academic who taught English literature at Florida Atlantic University, turning to full-time writing in the early 1960s. As an academic he published works on the poet HD (Hilda Doolittle [1886-1961]) and others, including *Wonder and Whimsy: The Fantastic World of Christina Rossetti* (**1960**). Much of his fiction – beginning with "Winged Victory" for *Fantastic Universe* in 1958 – could be described as SCIENCE FANTASY, as it posits a sustained ALTERNATE-WORLD version of Earth's history; but its abiding tenor is of FANTASY. Briefly, the TBS version of history centres on the doomed encounter of the SUPERNATURAL CREATURES of legend – dryads, centaurs, *panisci*, minotaurs, *et al.* – with ascendant humanity, climaxing at the time when Rome and Christianity were extending their imperialisms across the doomed, childlike, prelapsarian world. Most of his tales – all set well before the alternate 20th century, which TBS clearly found impossible to imagine – fit into this history. In order of their internal chronology they are: *The Minikins of Yam* (**1976**), set around 2500BC; the **Minotaur** sequence, comprising *Cry Silver Bells* (**1977**), *The Forest of Forever* (**1971**) and *The Day of the Minotaur* (**1966**), set in Mycenaean Crete; the **Mellonia** sequence, comprising *Queens Walk in the Dusk* (**1977**), *Green Phoenix* (**1972**) and *Lady of the Bees* (1962 *Science Fantasy* as "Where is the Bird of Fire?"; exp **1976**), set in burgeoning Rome; *Wolfwinter* (**1972**), *The Weirwoods* (**1967**) and *The Gods Abide* (**1976**), the 3 novels in which humanity's religious and political destruction of the old ways reaches a climax; and a final scattering of nostalgia-choked tales set in the Christian era, *The Tournament of Thorns* (fixup **1976**), *Will-o-the-Wisp* (**1976** UK), *The Not-World* (**1975**) and *The Goat without Horns* (**1971**). This litany of dying falls evoked a warm response from fantasy and sf readers, a response not dissimilar to that evoked by the ecological sf that began to appear around the same time (◊ ECOLOGY). TBS's early works are generally stronger than the late books, where a finger-pointing sentimentality tends to vitiate all but the most fleeting moments of loss.   [JC]

Other works: *The Dolphin and the Deep* (coll **1968**); *Moondust* (**1968**); *Where is the Bird of Fire?* (coll **1970**); *How are the Mighty Fallen* (**1974**).

About the author: *Thomas Burnett Swann: A Brief Critical Biography and Annotated Bibliography* (**1979** chap) by Robert A. Collins.

See also: GODS AND DEMONS; MYTHOLOGY.

SWANSON, LOGAN ◊ Richard MATHESON.

SWANWICK, MICHAEL (JURGEN) (1950-   ) US writer who began to publish sf with "The Feast of St Janis" for *New Dimensions 11* (anth **1980**) ed Marta RANDALL and Robert SILVERBERG, and who became known, very rapidly, as an author of intensely crafted, complex tales whose multiple layering allows his conventional sf plots and venues to be understood as exercises in mythopoesis, somewhat after the manner of Gene WOLFE's shorter works, though less perplexingly. MS was not prolific in the 1980s, but his short fiction – assembled as *Gravity's Angels* (coll **1991**) – ran a wide gamut, from "The Man who Met Picasso" (1982), a slightly sentimental fable of redemption, to "Ginungagap" (1980), a HARD-SF tale set in the ASTEROID belt whose imagery and language comprehensively prefigure CYBERPUNK; the more recent "A Midwinter's Tale" (1988), though making nods to both Wolfe and A.E. VAN VOGT, seems in the end to be written in MS's mature voice – warm, cruel, contemplative, moral.

His 4 novels show a steady progress towards that voice. *In the Drift* (fixup **1984**), set in an ALTERNATE WORLD in which Three Mile Island did in fact explode, describes its post-HOLOCAUST balkanized USA through a series of linked episodes which ultimately fail to cohere sufficiently, so that the transcendental implications of the final sequences seem forced. *Vacuum Flowers* (**1987**), which builds upon the world foreshadowed in "Ginungagap", very much more cogently combines a tour-of-the-Solar-System plot – carrying the reader downward from the corporation-dominated asteroid belt to an AI-run Earth – with a dense load of extrapolation about the nature of identity when persona-chips can be bought and plugged in. The protagonist, a persona bum who has hijacked an attractive new identity for herself, runs an extremely complex gamut before turning – perhaps inevitably in MS's work – towards transcendence. *Griffin's Egg* (**1991** UK) applies his by-now-expected multiplex extrapolations to the NEAR FUTURE in a tale set on the MOON – controlled by corporations – during a period when Earth seems at the edge of self-destruction, and a long cold hegira may be in store for any survivors of the HOLOCAUST. The titles of both these novels serve as metaphors for the evolving human species and as banners to proclaim the continuation of the species under new conditions.

Unlike his first 3 books, *Stations of the Tide* (**1991**), which won a NEBULA, takes place centuries hence and far from Earth, on a planet quarantined from the higher technologies now controlled by a far-flung humanity. After a Prometheus/Caliban figure has stolen some of these technologies from the interstellar network that monitors quarantine, the protagonist descends to the planet, which is due to suffer a vast periodic climatic transformation, traces the "thief", and apprehends what it is necessary for him to apprehend – the knowledge, the meaning of life on the planet, the meaning of his own existence, and a sense of how best (he is a Prospero figure) to relieve himself of power and servants. The complexity of this brief, dense, and fast-moving book is very considerable; and the interstellar network – whose HQ takes the shape of a Renaissance Theatre of Memory – is convincing in its own right and as a focus for MS's continued speculations about the refractions of identity in a world where autonomous subset personality-copies held on computers (they resemble the "partials" in Greg BEAR's *Eon* [**1985**]) do much of the work of being human. In the 1980s "debate" between "humanists" and cyberpunks, MS was variously associated with one or both "schools". In the end – like the similarly treated Kim Stanley ROBINSON – he was not so easily assimilated. The most telling thing to say about MS is that he is fiercely contemporary.   [JC]

See also: ANTI-INTELLECTUALISM IN SF; ARKHAM HOUSE; END OF THE WORLD; GAMES AND SPORTS; GOTHIC SF; INTERZONE; ISAAC ASIMOV'S SCIENCE FICTION MAGAZINE; MYTHOLOGY; NANOTECHNOLOGY; NUCLEAR POWER; OPTIMISM AND PESSIMISM; POSTMODERNISM AND SF; SPACE HABITATS; THEODORE STURGEON MEMORIAL AWARD.

SWAN YANKEE MAGAZINE UK magazine, PULP-MAGAZINE size, published by G.G. Swan, London. There were 3 sf and 3 weird-fiction issues in the series. The sf numbers were #3 (1941), #11 (1942) and #21 (1942), the weird numbers #6 (1942), #14 (1942) and #19 (1942). Despite the title, *SYM* contained mostly original UK stories, with a few US reprints. The sf titles were marketed as *Yankee Science Fiction*.   [FHP]

SWARM, THE ◊ Irwin ALLEN; Arthur HERZOG.

SWAYNE, MARTIN Perhaps the pseudonym of UK writer and psychologist H(enry) Maurice D(unlop) Nicoll (1884-1953). In *The Blue Germ* (**1918**) well wishing scientists infect the world with a virus that turns folk immortal, lethargic and blue. After the psychological effects of IMMORTALITY have played direly upon the cast, the novel ends with the hope, or fear, that the virus has burned itself out.   [JC]

SWEDEN ◊ SCANDINAVIA.

SWEDENBORG, EMANUEL (1688-1772) Swedish scientist, philosopher and theologian. The first half of his career was devoted to investigations into a number of scientific fields, from mathematics and physics to geology; in 1743-5 he underwent a visionary experience, after which most of his writings became mystical. These later writings, which influenced the UK poet William Blake (1757-1827) and the German idealist philosopher Immanuel Kant (1724-1804), and were an important forerunner to the Romantic movement, included *Arcana Caelestia* (**1749-56** in Latin; trans John Clowes in 13 vols as *Arcana Coelestia, or Heavenly Mysteries Contained in the Sacred Scriptures* **1802-16** UK), perhaps his *magnum opus*, and *De Telluribus* (**1758** in Latin; trans John Clowes as *Concerning the Earths in Our Solar System, Which are Called Planets, and Concerning the Earths in the Starry Heaven; Together with an Account of their Inhabitants* **1787** UK). This latter volume, commonly known as *The Earths in Our Solar System . . . and the Earths in the Starry Heaven*, describes a visionary trip around the Solar System, which is seen (in part through a system of correspondences) as having a spiritual significance; the book also contains some scientific speculation about the planets. After his death, ES's followers founded the New Jerusalem Church to promote his doctrines. [PN/JC]

See also: COSMOLOGY; MARS; MERCURY; OUTER PLANETS; PROTO SCIENCE FICTION; RELIGION; STARS; VENUS.

SWEET, DARRELL (1934-   ) US illustrator. His first sf/fantasy work was for BALLANTINE BOOKS, and when that publisher formed the new DEL REY BOOKS imprint in 1977 DS became their main cover artist, his ILLUSTRATION being strongly associated with their Jack L. CHALKER covers. His style works especially well with fantasy books: his delicate women emphasize their fantasy, and his earthy men give a sense of reality to unreal scenes. His colourful style is reminiscent, sometimes, of the PULP-MAGAZINE covers of the 1940s, especially his monsters. He works mainly with acrylics. [JG/PN]

SWENSON, PEGGY ◊ Richard E. GEIS.

SWEVEN, GODFREY Pseudonym of New Zealand writer and professor of English John Macmillan Brown (1846-1935), Chancellor of the University of NEW ZEALAND from 1923. Both his fiction and his nonfiction deal almost exclusively with the South Pacific. Of sf interest is his 2-part Antarctic UTOPIA, published as *Riallaro: The Archipelago of Exiles* (**1901** US) and *Limanora: The Island of Progress* (**1903** US; rev 1931 UK), in which an ethereal man with artificial wings is shot down in the South Pacific but survives – he's British – to recount his long trek through a mist-enshrouded group of ISLANDS, each of them exemplifying different modes of existence, until he finds himself in the scientific utopia of Limanora, which GS anatomizes in extraordinary detail. Here he is physically and psychologically reconstructed. [JC]

See also: HISTORY OF SF.

SWIFT, JONATHAN (1667-1745) Irish satirist, poet and cleric. His most famous work, perhaps the most important of all works of PROTO SCIENCE FICTION, is *Travels into Several Remote Nations of the World in Four Parts . . . by Lemuel Gulliver* (**1726**; rev 1735), better known today as *Gulliver's Travels*. The work is in part pure sf, and certainly makes use of and in some cases

invents narrative strategies which are now basic to sf; its influence, both direct and indirect, on subsequent sf has been enormous, as for example on H.G. WELLS's *The Island of Dr Moreau* (**1896**). In each of its 4 books Captain Gulliver finds himself marooned in an ALIEN culture. JS's SATIRE has two main forms: sometimes the culture in which he finds himself reflects aspects of British society in an exaggerated manner, so as to reveal its absurdities, and sometimes – more interestingly to sf readers – it is the differences between alien societies and ours which serve by contrast to make us see our own culture from a new perspective. This latter technique predominates in Book IV, "A Voyage to the Country of the Houyhnhnms", in which Gulliver finds himself stranded in a society of intelligent horses, who do not (for example) understand such concepts as war, the telling of untruths, or sexual passion. The details of their culture are more convincing than was commonly the case with satire of this kind, and the satire itself more complex. Although the story is often read as a forceful attack on mankind – the brutish Yahoos who live there are in fact humans – a more interesting reading, and one more readily supported from the text, is that Gulliver's admiring description of the life of pure intellect is part of Swift's ironic strategy, and that the reader is to see the horses as emotionally sterile and soulless. Swift's use of horse and Yahoo as sticks to beat one another is a double irony of a kind that has been much used in sf.

Books I and II, in which Gulliver voyages to Lilliput, where everyone is very small, and to Brobdingnag, where everyone is a giant (◊ GREAT AND SMALL), are the best known, partly because bowdlerized versions have become children's classics; the originals are savage and bawdy. Book III is set in and around Laputa, an ISLAND floating in the air and largely populated by semi-crazed scientific researchers (the first important appearance of the mad SCIENTIST in literature); in the distant city of Luggnagg live a group of depressing, senile immortals, "opinionative, peevish, covetous, morose, vain, talkative, but uncapable of Friendship and dead to all natural Affection", the Struldbruggs. Many of the scientific experiments satirized by JS were to become staples of later sf; though he shows their absurdity, he also has sympathy for the imaginative enthusiasm with which they are carried out. Most of JS's work contains such paradoxes.

Another satirical strategy of JS has become important to DYSTOPIAN writing generally: he takes an outrageous proposition and debates it quite deadpan, as if he not only supports it but does not seriously expect opposition. Thus he satirized the more inhuman attitudes to poverty (then as now) in *A Modest Proposal* (**1729** chap) by suggesting that OVERPOPULATION and starvation in Ireland could both be cured at a stroke by using the children of the poor as food. [PN]

See also: APES AND CAVEMEN (IN THE HUMAN WORLD);

ASTRONOMY; BULGARIA; FANTASTIC VOYAGES; HUMOUR; IMMORTALITY; LOST WORLDS; MATHEMATICS; SEX; SOCIOLOGY; UTOPIAS.

SWIGART, ROB (1941-   ) US writer and academic whose novels, from *Little America* (**1977**) on, have been FABULATIONS composed in a style which might be described as flamboyantly brisk; they include *A.K.A.: A Cosmic Fable* (**1978**), *The Time Trip* (**1979**) and *The Book of Revelations* (**1981**). *Vector* (**1986**) and its sequel *Toxin* (**1989**) deal, within a mystery frame, with the threat to Earth of a bio-engineered disease; and *Venom* (**1991**) similarly poses for its investigative protagonists the problem of a deadly poison. Perhaps more interestingly, *Portal: A Dataspace Retrieval* (**1988**) offers a complex future HISTORY of our planet over the next 100 years, the intercourse and coming to reflective awareness of an AI named Homer, a returned astronaut's search through an apparently abandoned Earth for some sign of humanity, speculations about GENETIC ENGINEERING, and an explanation of the nature of the route taken by humanity through the eponymous exit into a transcendental state.   [JC]

See also: COMPUTERS.

SWORD AND SORCERY This term – describing a subgenre of FANTASY embracing adventures with swordplay and MAGIC – is usually attributed to Fritz LEIBER, who is said to have coined it in 1960, but the kind of story it refers to is much older than that. (Other terms that overlap with "sword-and-sorcery" are HEROIC FANTASY and SCIENCE FANTASY, the overlap being considerable in the former case, but all 3 terms have different nuances.) Earlier terms with similar meaning are "weird fantasy" and "fantastic romance".

Leiber was a member of the Hyborian League, a fan group, founded in 1956 to preserve the memory of the pulp writer Robert E. HOWARD, to which many professional writers belonged; the group's FANZINE was *Amra*. The members believed that Howard founded the sword-and-sorcery genre with his stories in WEIRD TALES, especially the **Conan** series of swashbuckling, romantic fantasies, beginning with "The Phoenix on the Sword" (1932), set in Earth's imaginary past, and featuring a mighty swordsman, violently amorous, who often confronted supernatural forces of Evil.

Howard's stories were not *sui generis*, however: the creation of imaginary worlds on which colourful adventures took place was very much a feature of PLANETARY ROMANCES in the PULP MAGAZINES, notably the **Barsoom** stories of Edgar Rice BURROUGHS, which began 20 years before Conan's début. Burroughs did not feature magic to quite the same extent as Howard (and usually rationalized it as advanced science), but the atmosphere of the books shows a clear continuity between the two writers. In MAINSTREAM literature, too, there was a long tradition of picaresque adventures in imaginary worlds, though usually more modest (and literate), and sometimes less energetic, than Howard's. The usually quoted high points of

this tradition up to the time of Howard are the somewhat etiolated medieval fantasies of William MORRIS, the stylish though mannered romances of Lord DUNSANY (often set in a sort of "Faerie"), the rather more swaggering romances of E.R. EDDISON, and James Branch CABELL's elegant, ironic and elaborate **Poictesme** series. All of these influenced various of the *Weird Tales* sword-and-sorcery writers, though Howard less than Clark Ashton SMITH, C.L. MOORE and Henry KUTTNER. Moore was perhaps the best writer of this group, with her **Jirel of Joiry** and her **Northwest Smith** stories. But there is no denying the colour and vigour of Howard's work. The essential, new element which Howard brought to the genre was the emphasis on brutal, heroic ambition in the HERO, who is seen (unlike Cabell's heroes, for example) quite without irony, as simply admirable.

Sometimes sf devices are used to explain the setting of the societies (nearly always tribal or feudal) in which such adventures take place; they may be in ALTERNATE WORLDS, PARALLEL WORLDS, other DIMENSIONS, LOST WORLDS, Earth's prehistoric past even before ATLANTIS, on other planets such as MARS or VENUS, inside the HOLLOW EARTH, or even on forgotten colonies of a GALACTIC EMPIRE. It does not really matter which; the thing is to provide an exotic background – the more elaborately worked out the better – to a dualistic conflict, almost invariably between Good and Evil.

Weird Tales continued to publish sword-and-sorcery stories up to the 1940s; many did not see book publication until much later. Clark Ashton Smith's extremely colourful, "jewelled" prose was popular; C.L. Moore had perhaps the most baroque imagination, especially when it came to dreaming up sinister menaces. But sword and sorcery was a very minor genre by the 1950s, despite the activities of the Hyborian League and the publication in book form during that decade (often by GNOME PRESS) of the works of Howard, Moore and others. The chances are that it would never have attained the extraordinary popularity it has today were it not for the belated but huge success of J.R.R. TOLKIEN's *The Lord of the Rings* (3 vols **1954-5**), and the lesser though still remarkable success of T.H. WHITE's *The Once and Future King* (**1958**), the latter forming the basis of the musical *Camelot* (1960), filmed in 1967. When these works had filtered through to the mass market via paperback editions (not until 1965 in the case of Tolkien) it became obvious that there was a huge appetite for work of this kind; publishers began to fall over one another in the effort to feed it.

Tolkien's long, richly imagined work is as important to modern sword and sorcery as Howard's, the two representing the two ends of the genre's spectrum: Howard all amoral vigour, Tolkien all deeply moral clarity of imagination. (Also, Howard's heroes were very big, Tolkien's very small.) Common to both – although the two writers could not have had the remotest influence on each other – is a powerful commitment to the idea of worlds where magic works, and where heroism can be pitted against Evil.

By the time Tolkien was published, sword and sorcery was showing signs of vigour elsewhere, its two finest exponents being perhaps Fritz Leiber and Jack VANCE. Leiber, with his **Fafhrd and Gray Mouser** series beginning with "Two Sought Adventure" (1939), had been one of the few to publish sword and sorcery through the 1940s. The series is imaginative and full of verve; Leiber's stroke of genius was to have two heroes, one huge and powerful, one small, nimble and quick-witted. Vance's *The Dying Earth* (coll of linked stories **1950**) and its successor *The Eyes of the Overworld* (coll of linked stories **1966**) are dry, ironic, moving, cynical, and often very witty indeed; they are written with precision and flourish, and, insofar as they can be compared with anything else in the genre, recall the work of Cabell.

Other writers who have had a strong influence on the development of the genre are L. Sprague DE CAMP and Fletcher PRATT, Poul ANDERSON, Leigh BRACKETT (especially her Mars stories) and Lin CARTER. Both De Camp and Carter have had a hand in adding to the **Conan** series, and Carter's style in particular is more verbose than that of the original. Carter was also from 1969 editor of BALLANTINE BOOKS's **Adult Fantasy** series, which certainly did much to increase the fantasy readership among young people, and he was a tireless proselytizer for the genre. An unfortunate but inevitable consequence of sword and sorcery's sudden popularity was (and continues to be) the large amount of hackwork that came to be published in the genre.

Among the stronger writers is Andre NORTON, whose **Witch World** books, set in parallel worlds where magic works, are genuinely macabre and evoke vividly the difficulties of maintaining some kind of civilization in the face of Evil, ambition and chaos, though like other works in the genre her books sometimes suffer from a rather clotted, mock-medieval rhetoric. Even Robert A. HEINLEIN wrote one sword-and-sorcery novel, *Glory Road* (**1963**), but his matter-of-factness and preachiness render the book less than spellbinding. Sterling LANIER, Fred SABERHA-GEN and Christopher STASHEFF have all produced entertaining stories in the genre, as has Avram DAVIDSON, with perhaps more originality.

Michael MOORCOCK is one of the relatively few UK writers to work in the genre, and though his sword and sorcery (which he began publishing around 1963) has been dismissed, not least by himself, as hack-work, and while he certainly wrote too much too fast, his fantasy generally and his **Elric** books in particular imported a welcome breadth to the genre: Good and Evil in Moorcock's books are never easy to define; the forces of Chaos and the forces of Law are alike unsentimental, self-seeking and untroubled by human anguish. Moorcock put paid to the idea of the hero in control of his own destiny; in his books an indifferent universe cares nothing for heroism, but

Moorcock does, and the courage shown by his heroes is the more touching for being (usually) doomed. His sword-and-sorcery work is as much a critique of the genre as it is a continuation of its traditions. M. John HARRISON's *The Pastel City* (**1971**) is a more interesting than usual variant, using the conventions of the genre with skill, but to slightly deflationary effect.

Many fine WOMEN WRITERS have been attracted to sword and sorcery, including those noted above and C.J. CHERRYH, Jane GASKELL, Barbara HAMBLY, Katherine KURTZ, Tanith LEE, R.A. MACAVOY, Sheri S. TEPPER, Joan VINGE and Patricia Wrede (1953-   ).

Sword-and-sorcery readers appear to welcome long – sometimes seemingly endless – series, and many writers have obliged: John JAKES with the **Brak** books, Lin Carter with the **Thongor** books, John NORMAN with the **Gor** books, and others by Alan Burt Akers (Kenneth BULMER), Gardner F. FOX, Jeffrey LORD, Andrew J. OFFUTT, Peter Valentine TIMLETT, Karl Edward Wagner (1945-   ) and Robert Moore WILLIAMS. Not all of these works are pure sword and sorcery; many, such as Akers's, are more directly in the Edgar Rice Burroughs SCIENCE-FANTASY tradition. It can be said that most of these (Jakes's and Wagner's being perhaps the best) are routine, and that at their worst they are execrable.

By the mid-1970s sword and sorcery as a marketing term was giving way to HEROIC FANTASY or sometimes "high fantasy". In practice, however, this meant little (if any) change in the sort of material being published. Many sword-and-sorcery motifs found their way into sf proper, too; e.g., the violent **Horseclans** series (from 1975) by Robert ADAMS, set in a post-HOLOCAUST future. Generally, though, the late 1970s and the 1980s saw a greater separation between sf and sword and sorcery than before, with fewer writers working in both fields, though Stephen DONALDSON, who had made sword-and-sorcery history by introducing a protagonist with leprosy in the **Chronicles of Thomas Covenant the Unbeliever** series (from 1977), went on to write some sf, as did MacAvoy and, most notably of all, Tepper. The scenarios of some sword-and-sorcery writers, such as David GEMMELL, Hambly and Eric VAN LUSTBADER, occasionally approach the sciencefictional, but many of the most publicized sword-and-sorcery authors of the decade – e.g., David Eddings (1931-   ), Robert Jordan (1948-   ) and Tad Williams (1957-   ) – have had nothing to do with sf at all.

Sword and sorcery is not sf; it is an accident of publishing history that its links with sf are so strong, but hardly a surprising accident: both have roots in 1930s pulp fiction, and they were for a long time often written by the same people. Both genres, indeed, revel in the creation of imaginary worlds. The fact that sf attempts to rationalize its mysteries while sword and sorcery simply attributes them to super-natural powers does not, perhaps, make as big a difference as sf purists would like to believe. Certainly genre-crossing between the two by writers as various as Norton and Vance has strongly influenced both genres. John CROWLEY's *The Deep* (1975) uses the confusion between the genres interestingly in its actual structure.

Sword and sorcery has also moved inexorably into other media, notably COMICS but also (seldom with much success) CINEMA, as with the John Milius film *Conan the Barbarian* (1981) and George LUCAS's production *Willow* (1988). More interestingly, STAR WARS (1977), Lucas's great success, arguably owes as much to sword and sorcery as it does to sf. The most extensive influence of sword and sorcery has been in role-playing games, many discussed under GAMES AND TOYS, whose scenarios it has wholly dominated ever since Gary Gygax (1938-) and Dave Arenson created and published *Dungeons and Dragons* (1974).

The genre has, perhaps, too narrow a range of interests, and the constant recurrence of the same themes is likely to make all but the most fanatic enthusiast tire quickly, at least with work at the lower end of the market. Much sword and sorcery is violent, sexist and even, according to some, fascist. Norman SPINRAD showed what he thought of the genre in *The Iron Dream* (1972), which contains a heroic fantasy purportedly written by an alternate-world Hitler. But at its best the genre welcomes wit, imagination, and freewheeling invention; it has produced some memorable images.

There are no outstanding studies of sword and sorcery at book length. De Camp's *Literary Swordsmen and Sorcerers: The Makers of Heroic Fantasy* (1976) is useful, however, and Michael MOORCOCK's uneven *Wizardry and Wild Romance: A Study of Epic Fantasy* (1987) has a number of shrewd observations. [PN]

See also: GODS AND DEMONS; PARANOIA; PASTORAL; SEX; VILLAINS.

SWORD & SORCERY ANNUAL US DIGEST-size reprint magazine. 1 issue, 1975, published by Ultimate Publishing Co.; ed Sol Cohen, uncredited. 1 story was from WEIRD TALES, the **Conan** tale "Queen of the Black Coast" (1934) by Robert E. HOWARD; the others were from *Fantastic* 1961-5. [FHP]

SYKES, S(ONDRA) C(ATHARINE) (? -?) US writer of a tie in the **U.S.S.A.** sequence, *U.S.S.A., Book 3 ✳* (1987), in which high-school students continue to oppose NEAR-FUTURE totalitarian oppression. *Red Genesis* (1991), #1 in the **The Next Wave** line of otherwise unconnected novels from Byron PREISS Visual Productions, deals with the colonization of MARS. [JC]

SYMBIOSIS ◊ PARASITISM AND SYMBIOSIS.

SYMMES, JOHN CLEVES (1780-1829) US army officer with the rank of Captain, who distinguished himself in the War of 1812, retired, and subsequently devoted his life to propagandizing (largely through speeches, apparently charismatic) on behalf of his theory of a HOLLOW EARTH consisting of 5 concentric spheres, with openings at the poles. He twice petitioned Congress (1822, 1823) for funds to mount an expedi-

tion to the (literal) interior, but failed. His health failed, too, after many lecture tours, and he died quite young. He did not leave any account in book form of his theories, though he did issue a paper in 1818. *Symmes' Theory of Concentric Spheres* (1826) was by a disciple, James McBride, and *The Symmes Theory of Concentric Spheres, Demonstrating that the Earth is Hollow, Habitable Within, and Widely Open about the Pole: Compiled by Americus Symmes from the Writings of his Father Captain John Cleves Symmes* (1878) was by his 10th child. Although it has been thought that the novel *Symzonia* (1820) by Adam SEABORN may have been written pseudonymously by JCS, it has been pointed out (by E.F. BLEILER) that this is unlikely since, although the book alludes to Symmes in its title, it actually satirizes some of Symmes's ideas. These ideas were not *sui generis*, and indeed belong to a long tradition of PSEUDO-SCIENCE theorizing, one of whose important milestones was a 1692 paper by the astronomer Edmond Halley (1656-1742), published by the Royal Society in London, also arguing for nested spheres (and an internal sun). JCS's version was, however, directly influential through much of the 19th century. [PN]

See also: LOST WORLDS.

SYNERGY US ORIGINAL-ANTHOLOGY series ed George ZEBROWSKI, published by Harcourt Brace Jovanovich: *Synergy: New Science Fiction #1* (anth 1987), *#2* (anth 1988), *#3* (anth 1989) and *#4* (anth 1989). It was interesting without being remarkable, publishing good stories by Gregory BENFORD, Chad OLIVER, Ian WATSON and others. [PN]

SYNGE, J(OHN) L(YTON) (1897-) Irish physicist and writer whose best-known nontechnical work of nonfiction is *Science, Sense and Nonsense* (1951). His novel, *Kandelman's Krim: A Realistic Fantasy* (1957), features a long conversation in which an Orc, a Kea, a Unicorn and a Plumber discuss the concept of infinity and instruct a passing Goddess in the foundations of MATHEMATICS. [BS]

SYVERTSEN, RYDER (OTTO) (1941-) US writer specializing in sf and fantasy adventure sequences, the only one to appear under his own name being the **Mystic Rebel** series: *Mystic Rebel* (1988), *#2: The Dancing Dead* (1988), *#3: Darkness Descends* (1988), *#4: Temple of Dark Destiny* (1989) and *#5: Cave of the Master* (1990). Also under his own name he wrote *Psychic Spawn* (1987) with Adrian Fletcher (pseudonym of Rosemary Ellen Guiley); and with Jan STACY he wrote *The Great Book of Movie Monsters* (1983).

Also with Stacy, writing together as Jan Sievert, he began the **C.A.D.S.** sequence (the acronym stands for Computerized Attack/Defence System) with *C.A.D.S.* (1985). Stacy then dropped out, and the sequence was continued by RS, who wrote #2-#8, and then by David ALEXANDER, who wrote #9-#11, both always writing as Sievert. The sequence continued with *C.A.D.S. #2: Tech Background* (1986), *#3: Tech Commando* (1986), *#4: Tech Strike Force* (1987), *#5: Tech Satan* (1988), *#6: Tech Inferno* (1988), *#7: Doom Commander*

(1989), #8: *Cybertech Killing Zone* (1989), #9: *Suicide Attack* (1990), #10: *Recon by Fire* (1990), #11: *Death Zone Attack* (1991) and #12: *Tech Assassins* (1991).

RS and Stacy also began the **Doomsday Warrior** sequence of SURVIVALIST-FICTION novels, all as by Ryder Stacy, set in a USA after 100 years of occupation by brutish Russians, who commit their first strike in 1989 and, during the subsequent HOLOCAUST, cause the world's axis to tip out of true, killing off most of any remaining animal life: *Doomsday Warrior* (1984), #2: *Red America* (1984), #3: *The Last American* (1984) and #4: *Bloody America* (1985), all with Stacy, and then, by RS solo, #5: *America's Last Declaration* (1985), #6: *American Rebellion* (1985), #7: *American Defiance* (1986), #8: *American Glory* (1986), #9: *America's Zero Hour* (1986), #10: *American Nightmare* (1987), #11: *American Eden* (1987), #12: *Death, American Style* (1987), #13: *American Paradise* (1988), #14: *American Death Orbit* (1988), #15: *American Ultimatum* (1989), #16: *American Overthrow* (1989), #17: *America's Sword* (1990), #18: *American Dream Machine* (1990) and #19: *America's Final Defense* (1991). [JC]

SZABÓ, PÉTER SZENTMIHÁLYI [r] ◊ HUNGARY.

SZATHMÁRY, SÁNDOR [r] ◊ HUNGARY.

SZEPES, MÁRIA [r] ◊ HUNGARY.

SZILARD, LEO (1898-1964) Celebrated Hungarian-US physicist, in the USA from 1937, whose *The Voice of the Dolphins and Other Stories* (coll 1961) was published late in his career. Several of these sf stories had been written in the 1940s, one of them, "My Trial as a War Criminal" (1949), being an early expression of the deep and often hidden fears of the scientific community about the development of the nuclear bomb. The title story, told in the form of an impersonal report, makes pioneer use of the notion that cetacean INTELLIGENCE is both vastly different and in some ways superior to that of *Homo sapiens*. Dolphins grow to dominate mankind, using scientists and institutions as fronts, and the planet is saved. [JC]

SZYDLOW, JARL ◊ Mary VIGLIANTE.

TABOOS Many sf stories are set in imaginary or alien societies, where taboos are an important part of the social structure; Robert SHECKLEY and Jack VANCE both wrote a lot of them. Several such stories are discussed under ANTHROPOLOGY. And sf has a reputation, not always deserved, for attacking the sacred cows and breaking the taboos of our own society; while a few examples of this are necessarily discussed below, this entry focuses on those taboos set up not by society or by the law but by sf publishers (◊ PUBLISHING).

Sf by MAINSTREAM WRITERS has been subjected to no more censorship than fiction in general, and indeed has often been a medium for discussing "taboo" subjects with comparative freedom, even since before the time of *The Great Taboo* (**1890**) by Grant ALLEN. Things were very different within GENRE SF, where publishers were unwilling to alienate any part of their readership, and therefore set a great many taboos into operation for a period that lasted at least from the inception of the SF MAGAZINES in 1926 until well into the 1950s. Most of these taboos related to SEX, profanity and RELIGION. Several examples of stories which broke religious or sexual taboos, and consequently had difficulty in finding publishers, are discussed under ALIENS. To mention a single example, Harry HARRISON had great difficulty placing "The Streets of Ashkelon" (1962) – a not extraordinarily daring story about the anthropological ignorance and stupidity of a Christian missionary on an alien planet, and about the damage he does – on the grounds that Christians might find it offensive. Similarly, although since (at least) WWII MAINSTREAM WRITERS have had considerable freedom in discussing sexual matters, magazine sf and genre sf generally remained downright prudish even after the pioneering work (◊ SEX) of Theodore STURGEON and Philip José FARMER.

Not all subjects were taboo. Violence, for example, was (and is) all right, and extreme conservative POLITICS (◊ LIBERTARIANISM, SOCIAL DARWINISM) was acceptable to editors like John W. CAMPBELL Jr, whose own editorials on possible justifications for slavery (though not just for Blacks) were notorious. Campbell's *ASF* also exercised several quite subtle taboos in addition to those regarding sex and profanity; notably, he strongly disliked publishing downbeat stories in which humanity was somehow unsuccessful, or outwitted by aliens. This sort of prejudice did not precisely take the form of censorship, but the writers all knew very well what sort of stories would be acceptable to which editors. (Later Roger ELWOOD, who for a while in the 1970s controlled a large percentage of the ANTHOLOGY market, was well known for his extremely conservative views, both religious and sexual.) There seems to have been a kind of unspoken agreement not to publish stories of a socialist orientation – although it may just have been that few were written, unlike the position in the early decades of the century when socialist writers like Jack LONDON were at work and being readily published. And until the 1960s Black writers, and indeed Black issues, were rare in magazine sf. Racial problems tended to be discussed symbolically, in terms of meetings with alien races, rather than directly.

In the nations which until recently were often described as the communist-bloc countries, political censorship of sf, as of most forms of writing, remained ruthless, especially from the 1940s through the 1960s. As late as 1966 the Soviet writers Yuli DANIEL and Andrey SINYAVSKY were first imprisoned and then exiled. Political censorship in these nations had its ups and downs in the 1970s, relaxing only in the late 1980s, not long before the Communist Party began losing power throughout Eastern Europe and Russia. The entries for BULGARIA, CZECH AND SLOVAK SF, HUNGARY, POLAND, ROMANIA, RUSSIA and YUGOSLAVIA all (to various degrees) document this phenomenon. Sf, of course, because of its metaphoric flexibility, whereby stories apparently set in the future on other worlds actually tell us something about our world right now, is an ideal medium for subdued political protest, as many Communist-bloc writers (and some Capitalist-bloc writers) knew very well.

Moving away from politics, we find that until the 1960s pessimism in magazine sf was largely if not entirely taboo (◊ OPTIMISM AND PESSIMISM). Cannibalism, on the other hand, was perfectly acceptable in genre sf. It turned up quite often even before the 1960s, and has been central in more recent stories like Harlan ELLISON's "A Boy and his Dog" (1969). Ellison was prominent among the ORIGINAL-ANTHOLOGY and magazine editors of the NEW WAVE in consciously breaking taboos, notably in his DANGEROUS VISIONS anthologies, although a decade later most of these stories seemed tame enough (indeed, many were quite tame even at the time). The magazine NEW WORLDS, under Michael MOORCOCK, performed a similar function, rather earlier, in the UK; other original-anthology series like ORBIT and NEW DIMENSIONS also had an important liberating effect on what could or could not be discussed in genre sf. By 1976 Damon KNIGHT had no qualms about publishing a story advocating incest in a post-HOLOCAUST situation, Felix GOTSCHALK's "The Family Winter of 1986" in *Orbit 18* (anth **1976**); Knight's editorial foreword itself contained a vulgarity which would have been impossible not long before: "The family that lays together stays together." But the ground-breaking incest story in genre sf is very much older: Ward MOORE's classic "Lot's Daughter" (1954).

While the 1980s have been seen, rather like the 1960s, as a period when just about anything controversial could be published in the USA and the UK, there was, especially in the USA, a kind of covert censorship operating in some areas. Sometimes this could perhaps be justifiable: Knight's vulgarity, cited above, seemed less funny once the prevalence of child abuse became publicly known. Otherwise, though, this was the period when infantilism forcefully re-entered the field, after it had been discovered how extremely young much of the audience was for smash-hit films like STAR WARS. Whenever mass-market publishers believe there is big money to be won from the youthful market, then a whole series of taboos comes into operation. (The same syndrome has always been visible in US tv programmes like STAR TREK whose audiences are known to be predominantly young; **Star Trek** scriptwriters still have "bibles" to tell them what issues cannot be tackled, and what kinds of language cannot be used.) Thus the 1980s saw the reverse of, say, the 1950s, when book publishers offered more freedom than magazine publishers. The genre magazines of the 1980s could generally be as broad-minded as their editors wished, notably in the cases of ISAAC ASIMOV'S SCIENCE FICTION MAGAZINE in the USA and INTERZONE in the UK. But book publishers, especially those publishing series for the semi-juvenile market, were very cautious about any undue cleverness or sophistication; though, disgracefully enough, editors as usual did not seem too disturbed by violence. Obviously, many publishers paid no attention to restrictions of this sort, but it is fair to say that during the 1980s the proportion of the mass market where writers could expect to have their more sophisticated work published was shrinking relative to the hack-markets operating according to strict (and uncontroversial) formulae.

We should note also that there are cultural trends perceived by editors and journalists as not being worth opposing because to do so makes people cross. In other words, new sacred cows appear every decade. It is not clear to what degree some of these trends operate in sf publishing. A good example in the early 1990s was the topic of global warming and the greenhouse effect: to express the opinion that there was no evidence that the world was getting hotter, and precious little evidence that it was likely to, was to say something *disgusting*.   [PN]

TABORI, PAUL Working name of Hungarian writer Paul Tabor or (variously) Pál Tábori (1908-1974), who gained a doctorate in economic and political science in 1930 and then worked as a literary agent. He moved to the UK before the outbreak of WWII, about which he would publish several works, including *They Came to London* (**1943**), a marginally NEAR-FUTURE tale involving the Second Front, and *The Frontier* (**1950**), which reworked the terrible history of Germany in an ALTERNATE-WORLD frame. He cowrote the script for FOUR-SIDED TRIANGLE (1953), adapted from William F. TEMPLE's novel. Some of his later (and increasingly commercial) fiction was sf, the best example being *The Green Rain* (**1961** US), a sour comedy about chemically polluted rainfall turning people green. Sex and the occult infused much of his later work, like *The Cleft* (**1969** US), the fissure of the title being nearly as symbolic as the crack in Emma TENNANT's *The Time of the Crack* (**1973**). PT was an effective writer who sometimes allowed haste to spoil his results.   [JC]

Other works: *Solo* (**1948**); *The Talking Tree* (**1950**); *The Survivors* (**1964**), a post-HOLOCAUST tale; the **Hunters** series, comprising *The Doomsday Brain* (**1967** US), *The Invisible Eye* (**1967** US) and *The Torture Machine* (**1969** US); *The Demons of Sandorra* (**1970** US); *Lily Dale* (**1972**); *The Wild White Witch* (**1973**) as by Peter Stafford.

See also: HUNGARY.

TACHYONS There is an only half-facetious precept in PHYSICS stating that "anything which is not prohibited is compulsory". Olexa-Myron Bilaniuk and E.C. George Sudarshan suggested in 1962, and Gerald Feinberg in 1967, that the idea of a particle that can *only* travel FASTER THAN LIGHT does not violate any of the basic maxims of relativistic physics. Such a hypothetical particle (a tachyon, as opposed to the more familiar tardyon, or slower-than-light particle) might emit Cerenkov radiation analogous to the bow wave of a ship, and thus might perhaps be detected. The mass (or metamass) of a tachyon must be imaginary, in the same sense that the square root of minus one is imaginary.

If tachyons were shown to exist we might have to rethink the idea of causality, since they would appear in some circumstances to go backwards in time, so that to a hypothetical observer the emission of a tachyon would appear to be its absorption. However, a negative-energy tachyon propagating backward in time could be reinterpreted as a positive-energy tachyon propagating forward in time; some physicists think that such a reinterpretation would be the loophole through which the principle of causality might be preserved. J. Richard Gott proposed in 1973 that, after the Big Bang, a tripartite Universe may have been formed, consisting of universes of matter, ANTIMATTER and tachyons.

The tachyon became an item of sf TERMINOLOGY in the 1970s (though never to any great extent), because it suggests a more rational basis on which TIME-TRAVEL stories – or (more plausibly, since we cannot, even theoretically, convert tardyonic into tachyonic matter) stories of COMMUNICATION through time – can be written. The physicist-writer Gregory BENFORD was the first to do this with some care, in his major novel *Timescape* (**1980**), which describes an attempt to change future history by transmitting a tachyonic message from that future to our present. [PN]

TAFF ◊ AWARDS.

TAINE, JOHN Pseudonym for all his fiction of Eric Temple Bell (1883-1960), US mathematician and writer, born in Scotland; he also wrote academic and popular works on mathematics under his own name. JT's first novel was a LOST-WORLD fantasy, *The Purple Sapphire* (**1924**), and he published several further sf books before writing for the sf PULP MAGAZINES. *The Gold Tooth* (**1927**) concerns a quest for a magical element. *Quayle's Invention* (**1927**) features a device for making gold. *Green Fire* (**1928**) is one of many contemporary stories about super-WEAPONS. His best and most interesting work includes a long sequence of mutational romances (◊ MUTANTS) involving rapid and uncontrolled EVOLUTION: *The Greatest Adventure* (**1929**); *The Iron Star* (**1930**); *The Crystal Horde* (1930 *AMZ Quarterly* as "White Lily"; **1952**), featuring crystalline life, and *Seeds of Life* (1931 *AMZ Quarterly*; **1951**), an important early SUPERMAN story, both much later assembled as *Seeds of Life and White Lily* (omni **1966**); "The Ultimate Catalyst" (**1939**); and *The Forbidden Garden* (**1947**). *Before the Dawn* (**1934**) is a didactic prehistoric romance in which the end of the dinosaurs is observed through a time-viewer. *The Time Stream* (1931 *Wonder Stories*; **1946**) is an elaborate TIME-TRAVEL adventure which, like the mutational romances, helped to extend the horizons of pulp sf and is one of the outstanding products of the early SF MAGAZINES; it was much later assembled with *The Greatest Adventure* and *The Purple Sapphire*, all texts slightly edited, as *Three Science Fiction Novels* (omni **1964**). The title story of *The Cosmic Geoids and One Other* (coll **1949**) is an interesting but not altogether successful literary experiment, taking the form of a

series of imaginary scientific reports dealing with strange extraterrestrial objects; the "one other" is the novella "Black Goldfish". Two inferior novels were the superweapon story "Twelve Eighty-Seven" (1935 *ASF*) and the DISASTER story "Tomorrow" (1939 *Marvel Science Stories*). JT's last book was the sympathetic-MONSTER story *G.O.G. 666* (**1954**).

JT's prose style is sometimes crude, and his characterization usually lacks finesse, but his best work shows an admirable imaginative flair. He loved to do things on a grand scale, and many of his novels end with catastrophes which overwhelm whole continents. [BS]

See also: BIOLOGY; DEVOLUTION; FANTASTIC VOYAGES; HISTORY OF SF; INTELLIGENCE; METAPHYSICS; MONEY; PSEUDO-SCIENCE.

TAIT, STEPHEN [r] ◊ Kenneth ALLOTT.

TAIWAN ◊ CHINESE SF.

TAKEI, GEORGE (1937-   ) US actor and writer, best known for his role as Mr Sulu in STAR TREK. *Mirror Friend, Mirror Foe* (**1979**) with Robert Lynn ASPRIN places a Japanese mercenary in a free-for-all corporate world. [JC]

TALBOT, BRYAN [r] ◊ COMICS.

TALBOT, LAWRENCE [s] ◊ Edward BRYANT.

TALES OF TOMORROW 1. UK pocketbook-size magazine. 11 issues 1950-54 (none in 1951), numbered but undated, published irregularly by John Spencer, London; ed (uncredited) by Sol Assael and Michael Nahum. One of the 4 low-quality Spencer juvenile-sf magazines, the others being FUTURISTIC SCIENCE STORIES, WONDERS OF THE SPACEWAYS and WORLDS OF FANTASY.

2. US tv series (1951-6). ABC TV. Created and prod George Foley, Dick Gordon. 25 mins per episode. B/w.

One of the earliest and most successful sf-anthology tv series, *TOT* was ambitious but, like most tv of the period, limited by the restrictions imposed by live studio shooting. It drew its material from a variety of sources, including the sf PULP MAGAZINES, as well as using original teleplays. The first 2 episodes dramatized Jules VERNE's *Vingt mille lieues sous les mers* (**1870**; trans as *Twenty Thousand Leagues under the Seas* 1872 UK), starring Thomas Mitchell as Captain Nemo; Leslie Nielsen co-starred. [FHP/JB]

TALES OF WONDER UK magazine, PULP-MAGAZINE size. 16 issues [Summer] 1937-Spring 1942, quarterly to 1940, thereafter slightly irregular, numbered consecutively, #1 undated. Published by World's Work, London; ed Walter GILLINGS.

TOW, though preceded by SCOOPS (1934), the sf BOYS' PAPER, was the first adult UK sf magazine. It used both original UK and reprinted US material, and prospered until wartime paper restrictions and the drafting of the editor caused its demise. William F. TEMPLE and Frank Edward ARNOLD were among the authors who made their débuts in *TOW*, as, with nonfiction, was Arthur C. CLARKE. Stories included "Sleepers of Mars" (1938) by John Beynon – title story of *Sleepers of Mars* (coll **1973**) as by John WYNDHAM –

and, as reprints, "The Mad Planet" (1920; 1939) by Murray LEINSTER and "City of the Singing Flame" (1931; 1940) by Clark Ashton SMITH. Other writers were John Russell FEARN, Benson HERBERT, Festus PRAGNELL and Eric Frank RUSSELL. [FHP/PN]

TĀLIB, IMRĀN [r] ◊ ARABIC SF.

TALL, STEPHEN Pseudonym of US writer and biology professor Compton Newby Crook (1908-1981), who began his writing career under various undisclosed pseudonyms in the 1930s; none of this early work was apparently sf, which he began publishing as ST with "The Lights on Precipice Peak" for *Gal* in 1955. He did not start to be active in the field until more than a decade later, becoming known initially for the **Stardust** sequence, beginning with *The Stardust Voyages* (coll of linked stories **1975**), a SPACE-OPERA saga of the crew of the *Stardust*, whose mission is to assess the potential of various planets and the nature of their ALIEN inhabitants. Though the stories exhibit a sameness of effect, they are capable expressions of ST's concern for ECOLOGY, in which discipline he was professionally trained. A sequel, *The Ramsgate Paradox* (**1976**), carries the crew into a novel-length adventure. *The People Beyond the Wall* (**1980**), is a remarkably late LOST-WORLD tale set under an Alaskan glacier, where a placid UTOPIA is invaded by the usual suspects.

The Compton Crook/Stephen Tall Memorial AWARD for Best First Novel of Sf was established 1983. [JC]

See also: ANTHROPOLOGY.

TALLO, JOZEF [r] ◊ CZECH AND SLOVAK SF.

TAMMUZ, BINYAMIN [r] ◊ ISRAEL.

TANAKA, YOSHIKI [r] ◊ JAPAN.

TARANTULA Film (1955). Universal. Dir Jack ARNOLD, starring John Agar, Mara Corday, Leo G. Carroll. Screenplay Martin Berkeley, Robert M. Fresco, based on an episode of SCIENCE FICTION THEATRE called *No Food for Thought* by Fresco. 80 mins. B/w.

This better-than-average MONSTER MOVIE belongs to the Luddite technology-out-of-control genre. Two idealistic biochemists experiment with nutrients that cause gigantism in animals (which would help feed the world) but (unexpectedly) acromegaly in humans, a horrible deformity that destroys one scientist and then, rather later, the other (an affecting performance by Carroll). A tarantula injected with the nutrient escapes into the desert and grows to a vast size. It preys on cattle and people before being incinerated by the USAF using napalm. Arnold makes strong use of the desert setting, creating a kind of watchful stillness, where the giant spider seems natural rather than alien. [PN/JB]

See also: MUTANTS.

TARDE, GABRIEL Writing name of French sociologist Jean Gabriel de Tarde (1843-1904). His sf novel, *Fragment d'histoire future* (1896 *Revue internationale de sociologie*; **1904**; trans Cloudesley Brereton as *Underground Man* **1905** UK with intro by H.G. WELLS), depicts first a world society on the surface of the Earth, then, with the exhaustion of the Sun's energy,

a sanitary underground UTOPIA. The author seems to evince satirical doubts about the value of the latter as a model for human conduct. [JC]

See also: END OF THE WORLD.

TARDIVEL, JULES-PAUL (1851-1905) US-born journalist and writer, in Canada from about 1868; there he founded a newspaper, *La Vérité*, espousing Québec nationalism, and published in it his separatist UTOPIA, *Pour la patrie: roman du xxe siècle* (1895; **1895**; trans Sheila Fischman as *For my Country* **1975**). Set in a 1945 characterized by electric trains and other sf projections, it describes a conservative, Catholic "Laurentian Empire" which is opposed – vainly – by the forces of Satan. [JC]

TARGET EARTH! Film (1954). Abtcon Pictures/Allied Artists. Dir Sherman A. Rose, starring Richard Denning, Virginia Grey, Kathleen Crowley, Richard Reeves. Screenplay William Raynor, based on "Deadly City" (1953 *If*) by Paul W. FAIRMAN (as Ivar JORGENSON). 75 mins. B/w

In this film, whose low budget is reflected in its appearance, robots from Venus invade the Earth, using a beam that kills people. They are eventually defeated by scientists, who find that ultrasonic sound will break open their glass faceplates, thus destroying them. Critic Bill WARREN, while he regards it as poor, aside from lonely, atmospheric sequences in a deserted city, adds that it is "better than the story it came from". [JB/PN]

TARKOVSKY, ANDREI (1932-1987) Russian filmmaker. A graduate of the Soviet State Film School, AT attained prominence in RUSSIA with his first film, *Ivanovo Detstvo* (1962; vt *Ivan's Childhood*; vt *My Name is Ivan*), the story of an orphan cut off behind enemy lines during WWII. With his next feature, *Andrei Roublev* (1966; release delayed until 1971), AT fell foul of the Soviet censors with his dark vision of the life of the 15th-century icon painter. His sf reputation rests on two long films, SOLARIS (1971), based on *Solaris* (**1961**) by Stanisław LEM, and STALKER (1979), based on "Piknik na abochine" (1972; trans as *Roadside Picnic* **1977**) by the STRUGATSKI brothers. Alternating between b/w and colour, and featuring many static scenes prolonged to the point of tedium, AT's sf films have been both much lauded and much reviled by critics, but there is no denying the startling power of such crystal-clear images as the country house marooned on an alien lake in *Solaris* or the gradual telekinetic movement of a glass on a table at the finale of *Stalker*. More personal are AT's linked pair of non-sf films, *Zerkalo* (1974; vt *Mirror*) and *Nostalghia* (1983; vt *Nostalgia*), the latter made in Italy after his emigration from the USSR. Not long before his death from cancer, AT made a borderline-sf film in Sweden, *Offret* (1986; vt *The Sacrifice*), a contemplation on faith and responsibility, heavily influenced by Ingmar Bergman (1918-), which contains a central section visualizing WWIII and the dilapidation of society. [KN]

See also: CINEMA; MUSIC.

TATE, PETER (? -) Welsh journalist and author who began publishing sf with "The Post-Mortem People" for *NW* in 1966; this was assembled with his other short fiction as *Seagulls under Glass and Other Stories* (coll **1975** US). His first novel, *The Thinking Seat* (**1969** US), began a loose sequence of tales featuring the charismatic and guru-like **Simeon**; it was followed by *Moon on an Iron Meadow* (**1974** US) and *Faces in the Flames* (**1976** US). All demonstrate an interest in POLITICS, and *Moon on an Iron Meadow* in particular shows a deep concern about biological weapons – it also manifests the extent to which PT had been influenced by Ray BRADBURY, the bulk of the story taking place in Bradbury's imaginary Green Town, Illinois. PT published 3 other novels. *Gardens 12345* (**1971**; vt *Gardens One to Five* 1971 US), *Country Love and Poison Rain* (**1973**), probably the first sf novel about Welsh Nationalism – it concerns the political repercussions of the discovery of a secret NATO cache of deadly nerve gas in the Brecon Beacons – and *Greencomber* (**1979** US), a surly and metaphor-choked tale of a battered NEAR-FUTURE UK rather reminiscent of the work of Keith ROBERTS, but without that writer's shaping power. [MJE]
See also: POLLUTION.

TATE, ROBIN [s] ◊ R.L. FANTHORPE.

TAUSEND AUGEN DES DR MABUSE, DIE (vt *The Thousand Eyes of Dr Mabuse*; vt *The Diabolical Dr Mabuse*) Film (1960). CCC Filmkunst/CEI Incom/Criterion. Dir Fritz LANG, starring Dawn Addams, Peter Van Eyck, Gert Fröbe, Wolfgang Preiss, Werner Peters. Screenplay Lang, Heinz Oskar Wuttig, based on characters created by Norbert Jacques (1880-1954), author of *Dr Mabuse, Master of Mystery* (trans Lilian A. Clare **1923** UK). 103 mins. B/w.

After a gap of 27 years Fritz Lang returned, in this West German, Italian and French coproduction, both to the character who had helped make him famous and from the USA in order to do it; it was to be his last film. His other films about Dr Mabuse – the evil genius who seeks world conquest – were the 2-part DR MABUSE, DER SPIELER (1922), also borderline sf, and *Das Testament des Dr Mabuse* (1933). *DTADDM*, which received a very mixed critical reception, tells of a kind of Mabuse REINCARNATION (whose identity – or identities – is not revealed until the end) who operates from a hideout, fitted with monitors, in a grand hotel whose every room is bugged with hidden tv cameras; he seeks control of an atomic-weapons empire as part of his scheme for international anarchy. The film is absurdly plotted and slow-moving, but is powerful in its single-minded pursuit of images of vision (and of its distortion): screens, one-way mirrors, a blind seer, dark glasses, disguises, masquerades. It has been described as Lang's masterpiece. In Germany it was successful enough to catalyse the making of 5 further Mabuse films (1961-4) which Lang, now in his 70s, refused to direct; they feature, successively, zombies, invisibility, post-mortem hypnotism, a hypnotizing machine and death rays. [PN]

TAVARES, BRAULIO Working name of Brazilian writer Braulio Fernandes Tavares Neto (1950-), whose *O que é FC* ["What is SF?"] (**1986**) is an introduction to the subject for younger readers. His first story collection, *A Espinha Dorsal da Memória* ["The Backbone of Memory"] (coll **1989** Portugal), won a Portuguese sf award. He wrote the notes on Brazilian sf in this encyclopedia (◊ LATIN AMERICA). [PN]

TAYLOR, KEITH [r] ◊ AUSTRALIA; Andrew J. OFFUTT.

TAYLOR, ROBERT LEWIS (1912-) US writer, often of HUMOUR, in whose *Adrift in a Boneyard* (**1947**) the few survivors of a mysterious DISASTER come to a peaceful ISLAND where they must decide, in terms both farcical and serene, what it will now mean to be human. [JC]

TECHNOLOGY Although various literary traditions supplied inspiration and continued support to PROTO SCIENCE FICTION, it was the perception of the power which the new MACHINES of the Industrial Revolution had to transform the world which gave birth to sf itself, inspiring Jules VERNE's imaginary voyages, George GRIFFITH's future-WAR stories, H.G. WELLS's SCIENTIFIC ROMANCES, the hi-tech UTOPIAN fantasies of Edward BELLAMY and others, and the mechanized DYSTOPIAN nightmares which dissented from them. The demands of melodrama have always ensured that, even in those specialist magazines whose editors were outspoken champions of technological advancement – most notably Hugo GERNSBACK and John W. CAMPBELL Jr – most stories were about dangerous products or about technology running out of control. Many particular aspects of general technological progress require individual treatment as themes in sf: AUTOMATION, CITIES, COMPUTERS, CYBORGS, DISCOVERY AND INVENTION, GENETIC ENGINEERING, NUCLEAR POWER, POWER SOURCES, ROBOTS, ROCKETS, SPACESHIPS, TRANSPORTATION and WEAPONS.

The attitude of sf to technology has always been deeply ambivalent (◊ OPTIMISM AND PESSIMISM). The 18th-century idea that moral progress and technological progress were inseparably bound together has never been universally accepted, and literary images of the future have always recognized doubts as to the essential goodness of technology, even when their purpose has been to argue that technological progress is the principal facilitator of moral progress. GENRE-SF writers may take it for granted – it is a central ideological tenet of almost all HARD SF – but writers of futuristic fantasy outside the genre have always been more likely to take the position that moral, social and spiritual values essential to human happiness are actually placed in hazard by technological advancement. Leading genre-sf writers like Isaac ASIMOV and Arthur C. CLARKE have become enormously influential apologists for technological progress in an era when many voices are raised in outspoken criticism of the supposed "dehumanizing" effects of technology. More tellingly – as Jacques Ellul (1912-) suggests in *La Technique* (**1954** France; trans John Wilkinson as *The Technological Society* **1964** US) – it is possible to argue the high cost to human consciousness of emphasizing means over ends, "technic" over understanding, in a world which is bound to the measurable and blind to the unique.

Sf is, of course, the natural medium of antitechnological fantasies as well as of serious extrapolations of technological possibility. There is a good deal of PASTORAL sf which glorifies a nostalgically romanticized quasi-medieval way of life, often with PSI-POWER-jargonized MAGIC thrown in to help with the chores. Such imagery bears no relation whatsoever to the brutal reality of actual medieval existence, but its phenomenal psychological power is even more elaborately reflected in modern genre FANTASY; and stories of LIFE ON OTHER WORLDS and the depiction of ALIEN societies frequently deal in similar imagery. No doubt the appeal of low-tech societies to sf writers has much to do with the fact that the strategic elimination of known technology is easier by far to accomplish than elaborate technological innovation, but there is clearly also some powerful force at work endowing such visions with a special glamour. E.M. FORSTER's question – posed in reaction to Wells's technological utopianism – about what happens when "The Machine Stops" (1909) is by no means purely practical; he and many others who followed in his footsteps were arguing – as Aldous did HUXLEY in *Brave New World* (**1932**) – that the "Machine" will rot our minds down to intellectual compost. It is worth noting, however, that in pastoral writings within genre sf, rather than from outside it, the joy and triumph of technological rediscovery and redevelopment provide a frequent theme – one particularly prevalent in tales of the HOLOCAUST AND AFTER.

If genre sf needs a defence, it is quite simply that technological progress has allowed us to become in almost every way healthier, wealthier and in some senses wiser, and may well continue to perform that role. If Gernsback's advocacy of that case was naïve and Campbell's eccentric, the writers for whom they created a home were sufficiently various, intelligent and heterodox to make sure the question was examined in all kinds of ingenious ways. The wide-eyed optimism of Gernsback's own *Ralph 124C 41+* (1911-12; fixup **1925**) and the curiously convoluted explorations of Campbell's "Don A. Stuart" stories were soon supplemented by David H. KELLER's fabular cautionary tales, Robert A. HEINLEIN's celebration of all-purpose problem-solving aptitudes and Asimov's die-hard championship of technical improvisation as the favourite offspring of maternal necessity. Even if the conventions of melodrama demanded that things must go wrong in story after story, true sf writers always put the blame on the greed and vainglory of rogues, politicians, military men or business tycoons, never on the march of progress itself. Criminal or mad SCIENTISTS were often required as VILLAINS, but scientists figured more prominently in genre sf as HEROES – or, at least, as key supporting players whose endeavours enabled Everyman heroes to succeed. It

was perhaps unfortunate that Campbell developed in "Forgetfulness" (1937 as by Don A. Stuart) – and was ever after willing to play host to – the notion that human society might one day "transcend" technology by developing powers of the mind which would obviate its necessity. And genre sf has also generated its own perverse brand of technological scepticism, enshrined in images of technology literally moving beyond human control by establishing its own independent processes of EVOLUTION, an idea first broached satirically in Samuel BUTLER's *Erewhon* (**1872**) but given a new edge by genre stories of self-replicating machines which – as, for instance, in some of Gregory BENFORD's recent works – may become involved in an ultimate and universal struggle for existence against biological organisms.

Like the Romantics before them, genre-sf writers have generally been on the side of Faust, convinced that the quest for knowledge was a sacred one, no matter how fondly a jealous God might prefer blind faith. Characters in bad Hollywood MONSTER MOVIES might be able to sign off with a resigned admission that "there are things Man was not meant to know", but nothing could be more alien to the ethos of genre sf. Even in early pulp sf, technology was a means rather than an end, and, however much Campbell's writers were inclined to the celebration of the competence of the engineer, there remained a visionary element in their work which centralized the CONCEPTUAL BREAKTHROUGH as the peak experience of human existence. The hi-tech future of pulp sf was not the "Utopia of Comforts" so bitterly criticized by such sceptical writers as S. Fowler WRIGHT but rather a reaching-out for further horizons. SPACE FLIGHT became and remained the central myth of sf because it was the ultimate window of opportunity, through which the entire Universe could be viewed – and, ultimately, *known*. In genre sf, the ultimate aim of technological progress is, in the words of Mack REYNOLDS, "total understanding of the cosmos". This is clearly reflected in the increasing interest which post-WWII sf has taken in the traditional questions of RELIGION and in the evolution of sciencefictional ideas of the SUPERMAN.

Genre sf has played a key role in the development of modern images of future technology. The ILLUSTRATIONS of the pulp magazines were remarkably potent in this respect – particularly the cityscapes of Frank R. PAUL. The imagery of futuristic vehicles and cities, especially spaceships, has a glamour all of its own, carried forward in the work of artists like Chris FOSS and Jim BURNS. Much of this has, of course, been absorbed into the CINEMA, although technical limitations put a severe restraint on its evolution until films like STAR WARS (**1977**) were able to deploy models which looked far more real than the impressive but obvious fakes used in, say, METROPOLIS (1926). William GIBSON's dismissal of much of this imagery as an obsolete dream of "The Gernsback Continuum" (1981) is not altogether fair, although Gibson has played a leading role in updating and supplementing sf's visual imagery by providing CYBERSPACE with "inner-spatial landscapes" reflective of the types of graphics which modern computers are particularly adept at generating.

As anxieties about impending ecocatastrophes increase (◊ ECOLOGY; OVERPOPULATION; POLLUTION), sf stories which focus closely on controversies regarding the goodness or badness of technology have inevitably increased in number, and will presumably continue to do so. Such debates are the central issue of such novels as Norman SPINRAD's lyrical *Songs from the Stars* (**1980**), Poul ANDERSON's dogged *Orion Shall Rise* (**1983**) and Marc LAIDLAW's satirical *Dad's Nuke* (**1985**). Perhaps the most apt verbal image of modern humanity's relationship with technology is that enshrined in the title of Marc STIEGLER's collection *The Gentle Seduction* (coll **1990**); the title story (1989) is one of the more eloquent of the many contemporary sf tales arguing that the development of NANOTECHNOLOGY will eventually bring us into a much more intimate and rewarding association with our machines than we could ever, until recently, have imagined.   [BS/PN]

TECHNOTHRILLER A common term, used in this encyclopedia to designate a tale which, though it often makes use of sf devices, in fact occupies an undisplaced, entirely mundane narrative world. Technothrillers may be set in the NEAR FUTURE and invoke technologies beyond the capacities of the present moment, but they differ from sf in two respects: first, like the unknown in HORROR novels, science in the technothriller is either inherently threatening or worshipfully (and fetishistically) exploited; second, a typical technothriller plot evokes a technological scenario whose world-transforming implications are left unexamined or evaded, often through the use of MCGUFFIN plots. Any novel in which future developments in science play a central role is not a technothriller at all: it is sf.

Examples of technothrillers by sf writers are Frank M. ROBINSON's and Thomas N. SCORTIA's successful collaborations from *The Glass Inferno* (**1974**) to *Blow Out!* (**1987**), Robin COOK's tales of medicine gone awry, and the films loosely based on Ian FLEMING's **James Bond** novels. The latter are examples of the most common variety – the political thriller in which the artefacts of science serve as gear (or fetish) and as a target for the PARANOIAS of our century.   [JC]

TEDFORD, WILLIAM G. (?   -   ) US writer whose sf activities seem to have been restricted to the publication, in a single year, of not only the 3 books of the **Timequest** sequence – *Time Quest #1: Rashanyn Dark* (**1981**), *#2: Hydrabyss Red* (**1981**) and *#3: Nemydia Deep* (**1981**) – but also *Silent Galaxy* (**1981**), a singleton.   [JC]

TEENAGE CAVEMAN ◊ Roger CORMAN.

TEENAGE MUTANT NINJA TURTLES 1. A team of 4 pizza-loving humanized turtle troubleshooters created by US artists Kevin Eastman (1962-   ) and

Peter Laird (1954-   ) in a self-published black-and-white COMIC book from May 1984. Initially seen as a parody of martial-arts SUPERHERO team-ups, they became so enormously popular that their creators are reputed to have received about $600 million from merchandising rights alone, and a veritable tsunami of imitators was rushed into print, including **Adolescent Radio-Active Black-Belt Hamsters** and **Naïve Interdimensional Commando Koalas**.

TMNT was published bimonthly from 1985, and within 18 months sales had reached 100,000 copies per issue. The original story concerned 4 turtles living in New York's sewers who become engulfed in radioactive mud which causes them to become humanized and very considerably enlarged. The characters' names are shared with artists of the Italian quattrocento: Leonardo, Raphael, Donatello and Michaelangelo. In 1987 Archie Comics began publishing a children's version of the strip in colour, and four untitled GRAPHIC NOVELS (numbered I-IV) were published by First Publishing 1986-8. A hugely successful US animated tv series was spun off from the comic in the late 1980s.   [RT]

2. Film (1990). Golden Harvest. Dir Steve Barron, starring Judith Hoag, Elias Koteas. Screenplay Todd W. Langen, Bobby Herbeck. 93 mins. Colour.

After the comic, the tv series and the marketing campaign came the film. This was the biggest independently made hit in film history, though in fact production had been planned before the success of the tv series. The surprise was that it was good. The splicing of live action with puppetry from the Jim Henson workshop – Henson (1936-1990) died just after the film's release – is seamless, the direction is clean and purposeful, the script is amusing and succinct. The 4 teenage outsider SUPERHEROES, the mutant turtles, are junk-food-eating vigilante good guys up against a Ninjutsu villain who plays a Japanese Fagin to the teenage pickpockets of New York. The martial-arts fights are excellent (their violence, subject of many parental complaints, is nominal and stylized); the affable turtles' shabby rat father-figure, Splinter, is as tatty a Zen master as ever seen on screen.

The sequel, *Teenage Mutant Ninja Turtles II: The Secret of the Ooze* (**1991**), dir Michael Pressman, played it much safer. Sales of **Turtles** were falling off, and the blandness of this movie, intended to reassure the family market, renders its story of the discovery by a villain of more mutant-creating radioactive ooze almost without interest.   [PN]

TEENAGE MUTANT NINJA TURTLES II: THE SECRET OF THE OOZE ◊ TEENAGE MUTANT NINJA TURTLES.

TEITELBAUM, SHELDON (1955-   ) Canadian journalist and film and sf critic, resident 1977-85 in ISRAEL, where he served 5 years as an officer in the paratroop corps. His sf/horror column in the *Jerusalem Post* was the first such outside the sf magazines; he also had a film column in the Hebrew-language magazine *Fantazia 2000*. ST is currently Los Angeles correspondent for CINEFANTASTIQUE. [PN]

TELEKINESIS An important item of sf TERMINOLOGY, from the Greek words for "movement at a distance", developed from the earlier word "psychokinesis" (often shortened to PK), coined by Dr J.B. Rhine (1895-1980) in the 1930s; Charles FORT used the term TELEPORTATION to describe the same phenomenon. Telekinesis is the ability to move objects by the power of the mind, and after telepathy is the most commonly used PSI POWER (*which see for details*) in sf. The word "telekinesis" was probably not coined in sf, but began to be used in sf (especially in *ASF*) in the early 1950s. [PN]

TELEPATHY ◊ ESP; FANTASY; PSI POWERS; SUPERMAN.

TELEPORTATION Although a common item of sf TERMINOLOGY, this word is (or has been) used in 3 different ways.

1. Charles FORT used it in *Wild Talents* (**1932**) as a synonym for "psychokinesis" or, later, TELEKINESIS; i.e., the ability to move objects by the power of the mind alone.

2. In sf of the 1950s and 1960s there was a tendency to use "teleportation" as a special case of "telekinesis", meaning the ability to move *oneself* from one place to another by the power of the mind alone; this is probably the commonest usage.

3. Some writers use "teleportation" as the ability to move people or objects from one place to another by MATTER TRANSMISSION; i.e., using scientific equipment to transmit items in the form of information-carrying waves, which at the destination are reconstituted into matter. A particularly implausible version (since there is no transmitting equipment at the far end) is the "Beam me up, Scottie!" gadget in STAR TREK. [PN]
See also: PSI POWERS.

TELEVISION The first thing to understand about televised sf is that it has never been commercially successful (relative to the top programmes) on US tv, and seldom on UK tv. Advertisers in the USA seek new programmes that are likely to end up in the year's top 20; these are the programmes that get the top advertising and the big budgets. It has been reported that the only US sf tv programme ever to enter the top-20 category was the tabloid-style documentary drama programme PROJECT UFO (1978-9), which exploited widespread PARANOIA already much sensationalized by the popular press, and had little to do with true sf. Because producers know that sf does not normally pull that sort of audience, it tends to be regarded as filler material, with neither budgets, writers nor actors being top-drawer. Every now and then someone with power tries to break the hoodoo, as Steven SPIELBERG did with his anthology-series AMAZING STORIES (1985-7), spending a lot of money and getting good writers and (especially) good directors, but that too disappointed, in terms of both quality and commercial success.

To concentrate for a moment on artistic rather than commercial success (though they are linked), we note that for a while everyone thought the turning point would come in about 1978, when sf in the CINEMA had made an enormous breakthrough, especially with STAR WARS (1977), CLOSE ENCOUNTERS OF THE THIRD KIND (1977) and SUPERMAN (1978). US tv may have had its chance then, but blew it, partly through the lowest-common-denominator populism of Glen A. LARSON, who created the infantile BATTLESTAR GALACTICA (1978), its successor GALACTICA 1980 (1980) and the only fractionally better BUCK ROGERS IN THE 25TH CENTURY (1979-81). US tv has failed consistently with sf adventure (the various STAR TREK series being, along with *The* WILD, WILD WEST, the main exceptions, and then only partially so) and SUPERHERO adventure (like *The* INCREDIBLE HULK [1977-82] and WONDER WOMAN [1974-9]); has had limited success with sf anthology series (like *The* OUTER LIMITS [1963-5], and *The* TWILIGHT ZONE [1959-64]); and has done quite nicely with borderline-sf sitcoms (like MY FAVORITE MARTIAN [1963-6] and MORK AND MINDY [1978-82]).

Outsiders would argue that much of the problem of US tv rests in the advertisers, who have a vested interest in reaching as wide an audience as possible, and therefore tend to veto (especially in programmes aimed at younger viewers) anything remotely controversial that might upset a section of the potential audience. It would seem to follow that UK commercial tv should have just as bad a record, for the same reasons, but this is not entirely true, as witness *The* AVENGERS (1961-9), *The* PRISONER (1967-8) and the original MAX HEADROOM (1985), all originated by UK commercial channels. Nonetheless, most classic sf tv in the UK has come from the BBC – including the first 3 **Quatermass** serials, DR WHO, BLAKE'S SEVEN, HITCH-HIKER'S GUIDE TO THE GALAXY and RED DWARF – and the BBC operates quite independently from advertising income, though it is open to, and occasionally suffers from, other pressures towards conformity, including ratings.

The other main reason why sf has failed on tv in the USA, and to a large degree in the UK, is the almost invariable assumption that it is stuff for the kids. It is difficult to know if adult sf would succeeed on tv; few people have ever tried. The first sf series to appear on US tv, CAPTAIN VIDEO (1949-56), was primarily aimed at children, and it is arguable that the situation, over four decades later, has not changed.

Captain Video, which began in 1949, was a series made on a very small budget and transmitted live every night. This situation ensured that sets and special effects were primitive (scenes involving special effects were pre-filmed and then inserted, usually clumsily, into the show, by cutting to a tv camera that was pointing directly into the lens of a movie projector), but its popularity with young viewers quickly produced a host of imitations, like BUCK ROGERS (1950-51), TOM CORBETT, SPACE CADET (1950-55), SPACE PATROL (1950-55), SUPERMAN (1953-7), CAPTAIN MIDNIGHT (1954-6) and COMMANDO CODY: SKY MARSHAL

OF THE UNIVERSE (1955). While the later series were more expensively produced and were pre-recorded on film, they all followed in the tradition of the movie and RADIO serials of the 1930s-40s rather than that of written sf. Science had little part in any of these productions, with the exception of **Tom Corbett**, which had Willy LEY as scientific adviser, but it was prominent in one of the first "adult" sf series on US tv, OUT OF THIS WORLD (1952), which was a mixture of sf and science fact, with guest scientists interrupting the story to discuss scientific points with the narrator. This nonsensational approach to sf was continued in SCIENCE FICTION THEATER (1955-7), in which the host, Truman Bradley, and the show's various writers did their best (presumably unconsciously) to ensure that no trace of any SENSE OF WONDER remained in the stories. Nearer to written sf was TALES OF TOMORROW (1951-6), one of the earliest sf anthology series, which featured stories adapted from sf books and magazines but, like the early children's serials, was handicapped by being transmitted live.

The first major UK sf event on tv (apart from Nigel KNEALE's 1949 tv adaptation of George ORWELL's *Nineteen Eighty-four* [**1949**]) was the BBC serial *The* QUATERMASS EXPERIMENT (1953), a horror/sf mixture which was at the time considered suitable only for adults, though today it would probably seem no more disturbing than the children's serial DR WHO (1963-89). Even by the early 1950s the fundamental differences between US and UK tv had been established; instead of having to produce self-contained programme "packages" that would be attractive to sponsors, the BBC producers had editorial freedom. One result was that the most popular format for BBC drama (apart from individual plays) became the serial, usually in 6-10 episodes, whereby the writers could build up atmosphere and concentrate on character development; in the USA, by contrast, the trend was towards long-running series whose episodes were self-contained. (The lack of commercial interruptions was itself an advantage in the pacing of the BBC programmes, which did not have their rhythm broken by false climaxes and cliff-hangers designed to entice the viewer to stay tuned during the ads.) With the arrival of commercial tv in the UK (the first channel in 1955, the second in 1982), US-style programming was also introduced (though the UK commercial-break pattern is much less intrusive), but the serial format still remains popular on all channels of UK tv.

BBC TV's first productions of sf for children also took the form of serials, one of the earliest being *The* LOST PLANET (1954). Its sequel, *Return to the Lost Planet* (1955), came in the year that saw the first of the **Quatermass** sequels, QUATERMASS II (1955).

1956-8 were sparse years. In the USA most of the juvenile series had ended, with the exception of **Superman** (already the steady erosion of the boundaries between children's and adult programmes on US tv had begun) and the sober and dull **Science Fiction Theater**, both of which lasted until 1957. From then until 1959 sf on tv was practically nonexistent. The situation was little different in the UK, though in 1958 there was the third and best of the **Quatermass** serials: QUATERMASS AND THE PIT (1958-9).

In the USA WORLD OF GIANTS had 1 brief season in 1959, but the most important new US series that year for sf fans was *The* TWILIGHT ZONE (1959-64), an anthology series created by Rod SERLING as a mixture of fantasy and sf stories, more of the former than the latter. The 1960s saw an increase of sf-related series in both countries: the BBC serial A FOR ANDROMEDA (1961) was unusual in that it was cowritten by a scientist, Fred HOYLE. In 1961 **The Avengers** (1961-9; followed by **The New Avengers** [1976-7]) began, though at that time it was called **Police Surgeon** and did not feature any of the sf or fantasy gimmicks that were to dominate this enjoyably bizarre and imaginative show in later years. Another UK series, OUT OF THIS WORLD (1962) – not to be confused with the earlier US series of the same name – tried to repeat the success of **The Twilight Zone** by adopting a similar format, with episodes based on the stories of many well known sf writers. It lasted only 1 short season.

The most remarkable of all sf phenomena on tv began in 1963: the splendid BBC series DR WHO (1963-89), which was aimed at children but came to attract adults as well. It had many serialized stories run consecutively, each normally lasting for at least 4 episodes. Producers, writers and cast changed many times, but **Dr Who** ran for 26 years and, according to rumour, even now may be in suspended animation rather than dead.

In the USA another series inspired by **The Twilight Zone** began in 1963. *The* OUTER LIMITS (1963-5) was more sf-oriented than Serling's series and also took itself rather less seriously; though inventive and entertaining, it could hardly be described as adult sf. The same year saw the first of many comedy sf series, MY FAVORITE MARTIAN (1963-6), a relatively sophisticated sitcom that proved popular with audiences. Less successful, though in some ways superior, was MY LIVING DOLL (1964-5), an sf comedy about a ROBOT woman that ran for only 1 season.

It was also in 1964 in the USA that Irwin ALLEN, the Glen LARSON of the 1960s, produced the first of his sf action/adventure series for tv, VOYAGE TO THE BOTTOM OF THE SEA (1964-8). His lowest-possible-common-denominator approach to the genre has influenced the style and quality of US tv sf ever since. The same year saw the début of *The* MAN FROM U.N.C.L.E. (1964-8), a by-product of the craze for **James Bond** movies (◊ Ian FLEMING) but incorporating many sf devices and plot situations. This was better, and better still was **The Wild, Wild West** (1965-9) which featured two secret agents, equipped with various anachronistic devices, pitted against mad scientists in the 19th-century West. Another Irwin Allen series, LOST IN SPACE (1965-8), was more obviously aimed at children than **Voyage to the Bottom of the Sea**, though that made little difference in quality or plausibility.

In the UK, 1965 saw the début of the adult sf series OUT OF THE UNKNOWN (1965-71), an anthology show that presented adaptations of the work of sf writers including (among many others) Isaac ASIMOV, Clifford D. SIMAK and J.G. BALLARD; from this practice it derived an authority not often visible in televised sf, which is normally written by professional tv screenwriters. The standard of the adaptations varied and the small budgets were a handicap (another major difference between US and UK tv is that the former is usually produced on much larger budgets), but overall it was superior to most sf series before or since. This view was not shared by the BBC itself, however; after a couple of seasons it was turned into a series about the supernatural.

Also from the UK came THUNDERBIRDS (1965-6), a series that used sophisticated puppets and clever special effects. Produced by Gerry ANDERSON, it proved very popular with children on both sides of the Atlantic. Anderson had pioneered the use of puppetry for children's sf with SUPERCAR (1961-2) and FIREBALL XL5 (1962-3). Anderson's **SuperMarionation** puppet programmes are fun, but are really for quite young children.

In 1966 began TIME TUNNEL (1966-7), another Irwin Allen production, but it was not as popular as his other series. The important new US series of 1966 was STAR TREK, whose ever-swelling following (largely garnered during re-runs) has become legendary. Aimed primarily at adolescents, it featured the work of several established sf writers in the first 2 seasons, though their scripts were usually rewritten by the show's resident writers. Aside from Jerome BIXBY, no well known sf names appeared in any of the credits for the final season, which may account in part for the plunge in quality.

The INVADERS (1967-8) was another US series of the late 1960s but, as based on a single plot gimmick that had to be repeated each episode, it lasted only 2 seasons. More interesting, and equally reliant on evoking total PARANOIA, was The PRISONER (1967-8), a KAFKA-esque UK series created by actor Patrick McGoohan (1928-   ), who also starred. But at the time it was popular neither with the UK company that produced it (ITC) nor with the public, and it came to a premature end, although its supporters continue to argue passionately that it was the finest sf ever to appear on the small screen, and it has been rescreened more successfully since. In the USA Irwin Allen launched yet another series, LAND OF THE GIANTS (1968-70), but the vogue for his type of programme was coming to an end. Also fairly short-lived was The IMMORTAL (1969-71), based on The Immortals (fixup **1962**) by James E. GUNN, who also produced a novelization, The Immortal * (**1970**).

In the UK Gerry Anderson switched from puppets to live actors in his new children's series UFO (1970-73). A UK series with more serious intentions was DOOMWATCH (1970-72), which exploited popular anxiety about the dangers of scientific research; one of the creators of the series was the scientist Kit PEDLER.

Rod Serling began another anthology series with ROD SERLING'S NIGHT GALLERY (1970-72), but it was less sf-oriented than **The Twilight Zone** and proved less successful as well. Then, in 1973, came the series which had the greatest influence on US sf tv in the 1970s, The SIX MILLION DOLLAR MAN (1973-8), which, though basically a live COMIC strip rather similar to the 1950s **Superman** series for children, was successfully cloned; there were several near-duplications of the formula.

The UK children's serial The TOMORROW PEOPLE (1973-9) began on commercial tv in 1973, and at times approached the level of **Dr Who**. The BBC in the same year attempted a more adult series with MOONBASE 3 (1973), a nonsensational serial set on the Moon, but it was not a success. That year the awful GENERATION-STARSHIP programme The STARLOST (1973) came from Canada (◊ Harlan ELLISON). The following year in the USA saw 2 further short-lived series, PLANET OF THE APES (1974), based on the popular movie, and (much better) KOLCHAK: THE NIGHT STALKER (1974-5), an anthology series primarily about the supernatural, which included a few sf episodes.

In 1975 Gerry Anderson, after the failure of **UFO**, created a pale UK imitation of **Star Trek** with SPACE 1999 (1975-8). Surprisingly, it enjoyed some success in the USA, but only briefly, and it ended after 2 seasons. The series represents a nadir in the quality of scientific thought in televised sf. A more typically UK series of the same year was SURVIVORS (1975-7), created by Terry NATION, a post-HOLOCAUST series in the UK manner established by John WYNDHAM and John CHRISTOPHER.

One of the first of the many **Six Million Dollar Man** imitations was The INVISIBLE MAN (1975-6), but it did not prove as popular as expected, despite some ingenious special effects and the use of David McCallum, the star of **The Man from U.N.C.L.E.** It returned the following season with a different actor in the lead role and a new title: **The Gemini Man** (1976), neither of which saved the series from being cancelled. Yet another short-lived series was The FANTASTIC JOURNEY (1977) which utilized the **Star Trek** formula without spaceship or other planets (different cultures being encountered via "time zones" on a lost island in the Bermuda Triangle).

WONDER WOMAN (1974-9), derived from the fantasy comic strip of the same title, had made her début in 1974; she was followed by The BIONIC WOMAN (1976-8), a spin-off from **Six Million Dollar Man**. In 1977 the comic-book style trend was continued – but with none of the verve of the best comics – with The MAN FROM ATLANTIS (1977), LOGAN'S RUN (1977-8) and The INCREDIBLE HULK (1977-82). But while fantasy- and sf-related series were proliferating in the USA, mostly in a vain attempt to capture the charisma of the various SUPERHERO comics, UK tv was producing only the gloomy, Orwellian serial 1990 (1977-8) and, of course, the never-ending and still sprightly **Dr Who**. It was not until 1978 that UK tv made a comparatively formidable entry into the world of SPACE OPERA with Terry Nation's series BLAKE'S SEVEN (1978-81), which also began in Orwellian vein. While proficiently produced, and disarmingly cynical, it was still too close to the **Star Trek** formula.

In the 1970s such anxiety-ridden UK series as **Doomwatch**, **Survivors** and **1990** reflected the fears of a society that seemed to find itself on the brink of something unpleasant, whereas, whatever fears may have been preying on the US mass-consciousness, the apparent reaction to them was (and is) to plunge wholeheartedly into a second childhood, not only with tv, but also in the CINEMA, as with STAR WARS and SUPERMAN.

The 1980s in the USA saw increasing infantilism in sf series. Short-lived movie spin-offs included BLUE THUNDER (1984), STARMAN (1986-7) and ALIEN NATION (1989-90), and a spin-off from a tv miniseries, SOMETHING IS OUT THERE (1989). Ray BRADBURY's stories barely survived the miniseries *The* MARTIAN CHRONI-CLES (1980), although they did rather better in RAY BRADBURY THEATRE (1985-6). A US series based on a UK original, MAX HEADROOM (1987-8), looked promising for a time but deteriorated rapidly. So did the big-budget sf series of the decade (whose budget shrank with each succeeeding segment), "V" (1983-5). This was an object lesson in the corrupting influence of the US tv system, for it worsened practically minute by minute. In the first part of the first miniseries, this story of alien invasion (for "aliens" read "Nazis") was interesting; by the end it was pure pabulum.

Until the end of the decade, the most interesting US experiments in sf were probably the uneven antho-logy series TWILIGHT ZONE (2nd series 1985-6) and AMAZING STORIES (1985-7), but in both cases glutinous sentiment hovered too closely overhead. Then things perked up a little, with the romantic and sometimes very imaginative BEAUTY AND THE BEAST (1987-90) – which may have been helped by the input of sf writer George R.R. MARTIN – and the TIME-TRAVEL series QUANTUM LEAP (1989-current), which was sometimes amusing and certainly infinitely better than the earlier VOYAGERS (1982-3) on a similar theme. The end of the decade also saw the vigorous but silly WAR OF THE WORLDS (1988-90). But for many the most exciting development was STAR TREK: THE NEXT GENERATION (1987-current), which surprisingly enough was made for syndication (a demonstration of the effects of cable, and of the consequently reduced market sway of the old networks like NBC, home of the first series). Once viewers recovered from their sorrow at the absence of the geriatric Kirk, Spock, Scottie, Bones, etc., most agreed that it was rather better than its famous original.

In the UK the 1980s were ushered in with the fourth (and slightly old-fashioned) **Quatermass** serial, QUATERMASS (1979), no longer from the BBC. The BBC was having a semi-success with **Blake's Seven**,

the prisoners-on-the-run-pursued-by-the-evil-empire series mentioned above; it also successfully serialized John Wyndham's 1951 novel with *The* DAY OF THE TRIFFIDS (1981). By casting cult-figures from earlier sf series, David McCallum (**Man From U.N.C.L.E**, **Invisible Man**) and Joanna Lumley (**New Avengers**), commercial tv signalled high hopes with the time-police series SAPPHIRE AND STEEL (1979-82); in the event it was incomprehensible, but atmospheric and fun for Surrealism fans. The big UK sf theme of the 1980s was anarchic comedy, with two big successes from the BBC, *The* HITCH-HIKERS GUIDE TO THE GALAXY (1981), based on a cult BBC RADIO programme, and RED DWARF (1988-current), and one failure from the commercial side, Nigel KNEALE's disappointing KINVIG (1981). The 1980s also saw the so-so STAR COPS (1987) and Dr Who repeatedly changing his persona but somehow losing the plot; the 1970s had been **Dr Who**'s peak decade.

The pressures towards conformity and formula, especially in the USA but also in the UK, have meant that televised sf, in a history spanning well over 40 years, has never approached the intellectual excite-ment of the best written sf, or indeed the best sf in the cinema. Because televised sf cleaves to the expected, we are seldom surprised by it: we seldom feel any sense of wonder or even stimulation. At best we are amused by the occasional adroit variation on a familiar theme, or by bits of rather good acting. Televised sf is a cultural scandal; it is, on average, so much worse than it could be or needs to be. But there seems no way to combat the entropic forces that make it that way. The tv industry is something of a "closed shop", with its own well established writers and producers – one reason why it has generally proven inhospitable to sf writers – and it is difficult to influence from the outside. Until this is done, the standard of televised sf will not improve.

Good references on televised sf are hard to come by, and the subject is surprisingly difficult to research, since tv is more ephemeral than cinema and is not nearly as well documented. The most up-to-date book on the subject is *The Encyclopedia of TV Science Fiction* (**1990**) by Roger Fulton, which is descriptive rather than critical, and good on UK sf, rather poor on US sf. A slightly amateurish monthly US magazine with useful episode synopses (but much vital information, including production com-panies, omitted) is *Epi-Log*, whose #1 was Summer 1990, published by William E. Anchors Jr from Tennessee. Also useful is *Science Fiction, Horror & Fantasy Film & Television Credits* (**1983**) by Harris M. Lentz, which has a supplement (**1989**) through 1987.

This encyclopedia includes a number of made-for-tv movies which we treat as if they were actual movies. Some have been good – like *The* NIGHT THAT PANICKED AMERICA (1975) and *The* LATHE OF HEAVEN (1980) – but most have not. We also include one entry on what, so far as we can trace, is the only tv series *about* sf, the eccentric Canadian talk show PRISONERS

OF GRAVITY (1990-current). The 96 entries for tv serials and series in this encyclopedia (excluding made-for-tv movies and variant titles) are: A FOR ANDROMEDA; ALF; ALIEN NATION; AMAZING STORIES; *The* ANDROMEDA BREAKTHROUGH; *The* AVENGERS; BATTLESTAR GALACTICA; BEAUTY AND THE BEAST; *The* BIG PULL; *The* BIONIC WOMAN; BLAKE'S SEVEN; BLUE THUNDER; BUCK ROGERS IN THE 25TH CENTURY; CAPTAIN MIDNIGHT; CAPTAIN SCARLET AND THE MYSTERONS; CAPTAIN VIDEO; *The* CLONING OF JOANNA MAY; COMMANDO CODY: SKY MARSHAL OF THE UNIVERSE; *The* DAY OF THE TRIFFIDS; DOOMWATCH; DR WHO; *The* FANTASTIC JOURNEY; FIREBALL XL5; GALACTICA 1980; *The* HITCH-HIKERS GUIDE TO THE GALAXY; *The* IMMORTAL; *The* INCREDIBLE HULK; *The* INVADERS; *The* INVISIBLE MAN; JOE 90; KINVIG; KOLCHAK: THE NIGHT STALKER; LAND OF THE GIANTS; LOGAN'S RUN; LOST IN SPACE; *The* LOST PLANET; *The* MAN FROM ATLANTIS; *The* MAN FROM U.N.C.L.E.; *The* MARTIAN CHRONICLES; MAX HEADROOM; MOONBASE 3; MORK AND MINDY; MY FAVORITE MARTIAN; MY LIVING DOLL; 1990; *The* OUTER LIMITS; OUT OF THE UNKNOWN; OUT OF THIS WORLD; PLANET OF THE APES; *The* PRISONER; PRISONERS OF GRAVITY; PROJECT UFO; QUANTUM LEAP; QUATERMASS; QUATERMASS AND THE PIT; *The* QUATERMASS EXPERIMENT; QUATERMASS II; RAY BRADBURY THEATRE; RED DWARF; ROD SERLING'S NIGHT GALLERY; SAPPHIRE AND STEEL; SCIENCE FICTION THEATER; *The* SIX MILLION DOLLAR MAN; SOMETHING IS OUT THERE; SPACE 1999; SPACE PATROL; STAR COPS; STARLOST; STAR MAIDENS; STARMAN; STAR TREK; STAR TREK: THE NEXT GENERATION; STINGRAY; *The* STRANGE WORLD OF PLANET X; SUPERBOY; SUPERCAR; SUPERMAN; SURVIVORS; TALES OF TOMORROW; TERRAHAWKS; THUNDERBIRDS; TIME TUNNEL; TOM CORBETT, SPACE CADET; *The* TOMORROW PEOPLE; *The* TROLLENBERG TERROR; *The* TWILIGHT ZONE (1st and 2nd series); UFO; "V"; VOYAGE TO THE BOTTOM OF THE SEA; VOYAGERS; WAR OF THE WORLDS; *The* WILD, WILD WEST; WONDER WOMAN; WORLD OF GIANTS. Some further tv series are mentioned in passing in film entries and elsewhere, but not normally with full production data. [PN/JB]

See also: JAPAN.

TELLUS ◊ TERRA.

TEMNÉ SLUNCE (vt *The Black Sun*) Film (1980). Filmové studio Barrandov. Dir Otakar Vávra, starring Radoslav Brzobohatý, Magda Vašáryová, Rudolf Hrušínský. Screenplay Vávra, Jiří Šotola, loosely based on *Krakatit* (1924; trans 1925) by Karel ČAPEK. 133 mins. Colour.

This is the better-known of Vávra's 2 films of Čapek's novel; the earlier and more faithful adaptation, *Krakatit* (1948), is the better. *TS*, a very free version, is set in a stylized Cold-War world of the late 1970s. Where in the earlier film it is the aristocracy who wish to control "krakatit" – an energy source which is also an incredibly powerful explosive (symbolic of nuclear weapons) – in *TS* it is the imperialist military-industrial establishment that attempts to misuse it. This high-budget production, with a prestigious cast, was intended as propaganda on behalf of the peaceful communists against the warmongering capitalists. It is less artistic than its predecessor. [SČ/JO]

TEMPLE, ROBIN ◊ Samuel Andrew WOOD.

TEMPLE, WILLIAM F(REDERICK) (1914-1989) UK writer who began his activities in the sf world before WWII as an active fan, a member of the British Interplanetary Society and editor of its *Bulletin*, and housemate of Arthur C. CLARKE. He published a horror story, "The Kosso" in *Thrills* (anth **1935**) ed anon Charles Birkin (1907-1986); his first sf story was "Lunar Lilliput", for *Tales of Wonder* in 1938. War service interrupted his career for more than half a decade. His first and best-known novel, *Four-Sided Triangle* (1939 *AMZ*; exp **1949**), is a love story in which a girl who is loved by two men is duplicated by the one she has refused, but unfortunately both clones are attracted to the same man; it was filmed as FOUR-SIDED TRIANGLE from a script cowritten by Paul TABORI. WFT then became active in the magazines for about a decade, continuing to produce at a moderate rate until about 1970, though it cannot be suggested that he built his post-WWII career with anything like the energy of more famous colleagues like Clarke or John WYNDHAM, nor during this period were his book-length fictions remarkably distinguished. The **Martin Magnus** series of sf juveniles – *Martin Magnus, Planet Rover* (**1954**), *Martin Magnus on Venus* (**1955**) and *Martin Magnus on Mars* (**1956**) – was followed by some undistinguished sf adventures: *The Automated Goliath* (fixup **1962** dos US), *The Three Suns of Amara* (1961 *SF Adventures* as "A Trek to Na-Abiza"; exp **1962** chap dos US) and *Battle on Venus* (1953 *Authentic* as "Immortal's Playthings"; rev **1963** dos US). His last 2 novels, however, are far more impressive. *Shoot at the Moon* (**1966**), parodying many of the more routine sf conventions concerning trips to the MOON and the gallery of characters usually involved, is a ship-of-fools extravaganza of some hilarity. *The Fleshpots of Sansato* (**1968**) is a remarkable SPACE OPERA replete with interstellar agents, a corrupt city in the stars, and much symbolism. [JC]

Other works: *The Dangerous Edge* (**1951**), a crime novel; *The True Book about Space Travel* (**1954**; vt *The Prentice-Hall Book about Space Travel* 1955 US).

See also: CLONES.

TEMPLE BAR PUBLISHING CO. ◊ FANTASY [magazine].

TENN, WILLIAM Pseudonym of US writer and academic Philip Klass (1920-), who taught writing and sf at Pennsylvania State College from 1966. After serving in WWII, WT began writing sf, publishing in 1946 in *ASF* his first story, "Alexander the Bait", a tale that demonstrates the pointed (and, in terms of the sf shibboleths of 1946, iconoclastic) intelligence of his work in its PREDICTION that SPACE FLIGHT would be achieved institutionally rather than through the efforts of an individual inventor-industrialist-genius (◊ EDISONADE) – a prediction that sf as a whole was remarkably loth to make, and with the reality of which it proved subsequently loth to live. WT soon became one of the genre's very few genuinely comic, genuinely incisive writers of short fiction, sharper and more mature than Fredric BROWN and less self-indulgent than Robert SHECKLEY. From 1950 onwards he found a congenial market in *Gal*, where he published much of his best work before falling relatively inactive after about 1960. Among the finer stories assembled in his first collection, *Of All Possible Worlds* (coll **1955**; with 2 stories cut and 3 added, rev 1956 UK), were "Down Among the Dead Men" (1954), about the use of ANDROIDS reconstituted from human corpses as front-line troops in a savage interstellar war, "The Liberation of Earth" (1953), in which liberation is imposed upon Earth alternately by two warring ALIEN races (in a prescient satirical model for much of the revolutionary activity of later decades), and "The Custodian" (1953), an effective variant on the last-man-on-Earth theme. WT's occasional post-1960 stories maintained the high calibre, comic manner and dark vision of his early work. Most of the contents of his 5 further collections, however, date from the late 1940s through the mid-1950s: *The Human Angle* (coll **1956**), *Time in Advance* (coll **1958**), comprising 4 longer stories, *The Seven Sexes* (coll **1968**), *The Square Root of Man* (coll **1968**) and *The Wooden Star* (coll **1968**), each containing at least some examples of his best work. In *The Human Angle*, for instance, can be found "Wednesday's Child" (1956), in which a rather simple young woman's biological peculiarities climax in her giving birth to herself, and "The Discovery of Morniel Mathaway" (1955), which involves TIME TRAVEL and (unusually in GENRE SF) evolves into a serious look at the nature of the making of ART.

Of Men and Monsters (1963 *Gal* as "The Men in the Walls"; exp **1968**), WT's only full-length novel – released at the same time and in the same format as the 3 1968 collections listed above, and cursed with a title that seemed to indicate merely a further assembly – had little impact on publication, although its reputation has justifiably grown. Giant aliens have occupied Earth and almost eliminated mankind, except for small groups living, like mice, within the walls of the aliens' dwellings. These humans manage to survive, and even prosper after a fashion – though the rites of passage they engage upon, and the CONCEPTUAL BREAKTHROUGHS they experience, can only be seen as ironically reversing the implications of such moments as they occur in "normal" sf. As the novel closes, humanity is about to spread, again like mice, hiding in niches in the holds of the aliens' spaceships, to the stars. Also published in derisory book form at this time was *A Lamp for Medusa* (1951 *Fantastic Adventures* as "Medusa was a Lady"; **1968** chap dos), a fantasy-like tale in which a young American falls into a kind of PARALLEL WORLD where, as Perseus, he is given an opportunity to rewrite human history.

Despite his cheerful surface and the occasional zany HUMOUR of his stories, WT, like most real satirists, was fundamentally a pessimist; and, when the comic disguise was whipped off, as happened with some frequency, the result was salutary. The sf community has granted WT no awards.

WT is not to be confused with Philip J. Klass (1919-), US electrical engineer and UFO debunker, for many years senior editor of *Aviation Week & Space Technology*, whose books include *UFOs Identified* (**1968**), *Secret Sentries in Space* (**1971**), *UFOs Explained* (**1974**), *UFOs: The Public Deceived* (**1983**) and *UFO-Abductions: A Dangerous Game* (**1988**). [JC]

As editor: *Children of Wonder* (anth **1953**; vt *Outsiders: Children of Wonder* 1954); *Once Against the Law* (anth **1968**) with Donald E. WESTLAKE.

About the author: *William Tenn (Philip Klass)* (**1987** chap) by Gordon BENSON Jr.

See also: AUTOMATION; CHILDREN IN SF; ECOLOGY; GREAT AND SMALL; HISTORY OF SF; MATHEMATICS; MEDICINE; POLITICS; PSYCHOLOGY; TIME PARADOXES.

TENNANT, EMMA (CHRISTINA) (1937-) UK writer whose first acknowledged novel – her true first, *The Colour of Rain* (**1964**) as by Catherine Aydy, was not sf – was *The Time of the Crack* (**1973**; vt *The Crack* 1978), an sf tale about an inexplicable faultline – described in terms that imply a gamut of meanings, from SEX to apocalypse – that opens through the heart of London. *The Last of the Country House Murders* (**1974**) is a rather shoddy and very short pastiche of a classic detective novel set in a hazily realized, depressed NEAR FUTURE in which the last country house is maintained as a relic of a culture which ET – a member of the eminent Tennant family – views with considerable ambivalence. Some sf devices figure in *Hotel de Dream* (**1976**), whose obsessively nostalgic residents begin to find themselves in each other's dreams: the nostalgia they share – for a cleansed and triumphant royal Britain, the kind of land Edwardians might have anticipated, but which WWI destroyed any chance of – somewhat resembles in detail and ironical import the Edwardian futures promulgated by Michael MOORCOCK in his **Jerry Cornelius** and **Oswald Bastable** series and elsewhere. ET's next several books – like *The Bad Sister* (**1978**), *Wild Nights* (**1979**), *Alice Fell* (**1980**), *Queen of Stones* (**1982**) and *Woman Beware Woman* (**1983**; vt *The Half-Mother* 1985 US) – tend to combine GOTHIC furniture, a complex FEMINISM, supernatural intrusions and an abiding ambivalence. This refusal to settle meaning upon her characters, her plots or her generic surrounds results in books of dream-like vivacity which, through their tendency to close insecurely, occasionally diminish the insights they have dodged towards. At the same time, her clearly non-genre novels are relatively unconvincing. Of her more recent titles, the most interesting are fables in the indeterminate mode of her best work. *Two Women of London: The Strange Case of Ms Jekyll and Mrs Hyde* (**1989**) plays on its classic source an intricate game of female possession in the late 20th century. *Sisters and Strangers: A Moral Tale* (**1990**) is a feminist reconstruction of history in which ADAM AND EVE survive to the present day. *Faustine* (1992) replays the Faust myth with a female protagonist whose beauty chills the world.

In 1975-8 ET ed the journal *Bananas*, which published J.G. BALLARD and others. *Bananas* (anth 1977) was taken from the journal, and *Saturday Night Reader* (anth 1979) fairly represents its bent.   [JC]

Works for children: *The Boggart* (1980); *The Search for Treasure Island* (1981); *The Ghost Child* (1984).

See also: WOMEN SF WRITERS.

TENNESHAW, S.M. Floating pseudonym used 1947-58 by ZIFF-DAVIS and by the other Chicago magazines IMAGINATION and IMAGINATIVE TALES. Initially SMT was probably used by William HAMLING as a personal pseudonym, many of the 22 stories whose authors have not been identified being perhaps by him; later it was used once by Randall GARRETT alone, 3 times by him in collaboration with Robert SILVERBERG, once by Silverberg alone, once by Milton LESSER and once by Edmond HAMILTON.   [PN]

10 STORY FANTASY US magazine, PULP-MAGAZINE size. 1 issue, Spring 1951, published by Avon Periodicals, ed Donald A. WOLLHEIM. *10SF* is primarily remembered for its poor arithmetic (there were 13 stories), for the fact that many of its writers were very eminent – John Beynon (John WYNDHAM), L. Sprague DE CAMP, Lester DEL REY, Fritz LEIBER, C.M. KORNBLUTH, Kris NEVILLE and A.E. VAN VOGT – and for publishing Arthur C. CLARKE's "Sentinel of Eternity" (vt "The Sentinel"), on which was based 2001: A SPACE ODYSSEY. *10SF* was published simultaneously in Canada.

                    [FHP/PN]

TENTH VICTIM, THE ◊ *La* DECIMA VITTIMA.

TEPPER, SHERI S. (1929-   ) US writer whose first genre publications were poems under her then married name Sheri S. Eberhart, the earliest being "Lullaby, 1990" in *Gal*, Dec 1963. She then fell silent as a writer, beginning to write again only once she was in her 50s. Her first-written novel, a long, complex fantasy, eventually appeared as *The Revenants* (1984). Her first-published novel was *King's Blood Four* (1983), #1 in the long and very interesting **True Game** series, which continued with *Necromancer Nine* (1983), *Wizard's Eleven* (1984), *The Song of Mavin Manyshaped* (1985), *The Flight of Mavin Manyshaped* (1985), *The Search of Mavin Manyshaped* (1985), *Jinian Footseer* (1985), *Dervish Daughter* (1986) and *Jinian Star-Eye* (1986). The first 3 were assembled as *The True Game* (omni 1985 UK), the next 3 as *The Chronicles of Mavin Manyshaped* (omni 1986 UK) and the final 3 as *The End of the Game* (omni 1987). In terms of internal chronology, the middle trilogy precedes the first.

Their readers knew almost at once that something very unusual was happening in these books, but most serious critics ignore paperback fantasy trilogies, and it took some years before SST was spoken of much at all. In the **True Game** books some of the human colonists on a planet also inhabited by aliens have, long before the story opens, evolved PSI POWERS; the best term for these books would be SCIENCE FANTASY. They show an astonishing assuredness of narrative voice; for SST is that unusual kind of writer, the apparently *born* story-teller. Further evidence of her narrative fluency (and her seemingly endless inventiveness) came with the **Marianne** fantasy trilogy: *Marianne, the Magus and the Manticore* (1985), *Marianne, the Madame and the Momentary Gods* (1988) and *Marianne, the Matchbox and the Malachite Mouse* (1989), all 3 assembled as *The Marianne Trilogy* (omni 1990 UK). SST also showed real accomplishment in HORROR fiction with *Blood Heritage* (1986) and its sequel *The Bones* (1987) – both humorous and both involving some very practical modern witchcraft – and the later (and better) horror novel *Still Life* (1989 as E.E. Horlak; 1989 UK as by SST).

SST's first novel of sf proper was initially split by the publisher into 2 vols, *The Awakeners: Northshore* (1987) and *The Awakeners: Volume 2: Southshore* (1987), but was soon sensibly released as *The Awakeners* (1987). As a work of speculative sociobiology and ecology it is ebullient, but the plotting of this tale of a theocratic riverside civilization where it is forbidden to travel eastwards is sometimes a little awkward. The same year saw the shorter and more confident *After Long Silence* (1987; vt *The Enigma Score* 1989 UK), a melodrama set on a planet whose crystalline native lifeforms are very dangerous, and can be lulled only by MUSIC.

From this point SST concentrated on sf, although during and in between sf books she published crime and mystery fiction as by A.J. Orde (the **Jason Lynx** series) and B.J. Oliphant. Her first truly ambitious sf work was *The Gate to Woman's Country* (1988), which surprised some readers for the ferocity with which it imagined a post-HOLOCAUST world where social separation by gender is almost complete, but where the supposedly meek women outmanoeuvre the really dreadful men on almost all grounds. All SST's subsequent work is fierce; indeed, with hindsight, the same controlled anger is visible in the apparently affable science-fantasy books.

The next year saw the beginning of her major sf work to date, the loosely and thematically connected **Marjorie Westriding** trilogy: *Grass* (1989), *Raising the Stones* (1990) and *Sideshow* (1992). To describe the trilogy by naming its villains somewhat distorts the ease and glow of these books' telling, and labours their melodramatic elements (which are only sometimes insistent): the villains are Nature-ruiners, fundamentalist religionists and – it is a category which comprehends the previous two – men (whom SST sees as almost doomed by their own sociobiological nature). SST interrupted this trilogy with *Beauty* (1991; preferred text 1992 UK), part MAGIC REALISM, part fairy tale, part sf, in which Sleeping Beauty is taken to a savagely DYSTOPIAN future and meets (in various guises, including that of Prince Charming) the Beast; this is a book about despoliation, not just of womanhood but of Earth.

SST requires the engine of story to provide impulsion

for the other things she can do, which tends to tilt her work towards melodrama and excess, and thus to obscure a little her remarkable sophistication. In the space of only a few years she has become one of sf's premier world-builders; the diversity of invented societies in *Sideshow* – this diversity being the actual point of the book – is breathtaking, as is the vivid ecological mystery of *Grass* and the bizarre discovery of a *bona fide* "god" in *Raising the Stones*. She is one of the most significant new – and new FEMINIST – voices to enter 1980s sf. The kindly spellbinder, who tells romantic tales around the campfire, has jaws that bite and claws that snatch. [PN]

See also: ECOLOGY; FANTASY; GOTHIC SF; MAGIC; PASTORAL.

TERÄS, KAPTEENI [r] ◊ FINLAND.

TERENCE X. O'LEARY'S WAR BIRDS US PULP MAGAZINE. 3 issues, #84-#86, Mar, Apr and May/June 1935, published by Dell; ed Carson Mowre. These were futuristic, pure-sf issues (the story was of O'Leary vs the Ageless Men, who are malign immortals, with DEATH RAYS, from ATLANTIS) bringing O'Leary over from the aviation pulp *War Birds*, whose numeration they followed. Extremely rare collector's items, they have little interest for anyone else, being very ill written by Arthur Guy Empey. #85 was reissued as a facsimile paperback book, *Terence X. O'Leary's War Birds* (1974). [FHP/PN]

TERMINAL MAN, THE Film (1974). Warner Bros. Prod/dir/written Mike Hodges, starring George Segal, Joan Hackett. Based on *The Terminal Man* (1972) by Michael CRICHTON. 107 mins, cut to 104 mins. Colour.

Segal plays a man who suffers from violent blackouts as a result of brain damage suffered in a car accident. Doctors use him as an experimental guinea pig: into his brain they insert electrodes linked to a tiny computer implanted in his shoulder, so that when a convulsion starts the computer will automatically send soothing impulses to the brain. However, the brain enjoys the soothing effect so much that it induces the blackouts at an ever-increasing rate; the man is driven to commit further acts of violence and finally has to be shot down. Quotes from T.S. Eliot, music by Bach, colour-coded visual symbolism (with lots of black) – all seem to aspire to a significance that does not, in the end, seem very profound. The mutually destructive relationship between man and machine is interesting; the stereotypes (monstrous doctors, etc.) are crude. [JB/PN]

See also: CINEMA.

TERMINATOR, THE Film (1984). Cinema '84/Pacific Western/Orion. Prod Gale Anne HURD. Dir James CAMERON, starring Arnold Schwarzenegger, Michael Biehn, Linda Hamilton. Screenplay Cameron, Hurd. 107 mins. Colour.

In AD2029 a vicious war between humans and machines is raging. To ensure their victory, the machines send back a CYBORG Terminator (apparently human, with flesh and blood coating a metal armature and electronic implants) to California in 1984 to murder the mother (Hamilton) of the human leader, thus deleting him from history. The humans send back a man to protect her. Their desperate efforts to escape the inexorable Terminator form the main part of this virtuoso film, which also has remarkably vivid if modestly budgeted sequences of the future war. A virtue is made of Schwarzenegger's rather robotic appearance as the Terminator; when reduced to metal, the still-stalking creature – now an actual ROBOT – is as designed by Stan Winston, who specializes in convincing, nasty aliens (◊ ALIENS; PREDATOR 2).

A lawsuit against the production company was brought by Harlan ELLISON, alleging similarities with several of his teleplays, notably *Soldier* (*The* OUTER LIMITS [1964]). It was settled out of court and a credit to Ellison was inserted into prints of *TT*. The sequel is TERMINATOR 2: JUDGMENT DAY (1991). [PN]

See also: CINEMA; MUSIC.

TERMINATOR 2: JUDGMENT DAY Film (1991). Lightstorm/Carolco/Tri-Star. Prod/dir/written James CAMERON. Executive prods Mario Kassar, Gale Anne HURD. Starring Arnold Schwarzenegger, Linda Hamilton, Edward Furlong, Robert Patrick, Joe Morton. Screenplay Cameron, William Wisher. 135 mins. Colour.

A decade after *The* TERMINATOR (1984), two more Terminators (human-seeming killer ROBOTS) have been sent back to the present from the human-machine wars of AD2029, one to eliminate John Connor, the future human leader (the initials are shared with Jesus Christ), while he is still a child (well played by Furlong), the other (Schwarzenegger) to protect him. Linda Hamilton again plays Sarah Connor, John's mother, but, where once she was cute, now she is a chain-smoking, violent obsessive in a psychiatric ward, body rippling with muscles, awaiting with a frozen snarl the nuclear HOLOCAUST – due to arrive in August 1997 – of which she has been forewarned.

T2:JD is fundamentally an action thriller, choreographed with precision, probably the most expensive film ever made (budget estimated at $95 million), and very exciting indeed. It does, however, project images of pain and impotence in the shadow of a dark future: the imminence and immanence of nuclear disaster (powerfully rendered in a dream sequence), Sarah's wrecked psyche, the irony of a MACHINE becoming a father figure, the boy struggling inarticulately to explain the sanctity of life to a killer robot (even if a "good" one this time). There is a clear awareness in Cameron of the intractability of human anger and violence; it is precisely these qualities, we must suppose, on which the nihilistic machines, our killer children, are modelled. This awareness runs half-hidden beneath the cynicism of the son/daddy mawkishness aimed directly at the older, softer viewer, and the dishonesty of so violent a film hawking a dove message.

As sf the film becomes embedded in its own causal

loop, whereby a future technology sent into the past catalyses the creation of the very technology that caused the trouble in the first place. The second Terminator – played by the interestingly cast Patrick, a slightly built actor with a wholly affectless face – has the ability to flow from shape to shape like quicksilver. Though silly, this makes for great special effects. Commercial considerations demand an upbeat ending, which leaves us with the unlikelihood of a plot in which the most efficient killing machine ever created is shown as lacking the competence to kill. [PN]

See also: ACE BOOKS; CINEMA.

TERMINOLOGY Newcomers to sf are occasionally dismayed by its jargon. Certain concepts have become so useful in sf (and also in talking about it) that they tend to be referred to – especially by GENRE-SF writers – in a kind of shorthand and without explanation. Many receive entries in this volume, sometimes brief (◊ CREDITS), sometimes detailed (◊ ANDROIDS, CLONES, ROBOTS). We regard the briefer entries, mainly devoted to definition, as "terminology" entries and the fuller entries as "theme" entries. This encyclopedia contains 64 terminology entries and 211 theme entries. In the listing below we have marked the latter with an asterisk (∗).

Many but not all sf jargon words and phrases are now recognized by dictionaries. The ones to which we have chosen to give entries are as follows. First is a cluster of terms used by sf readers and critics to describe different aspects of the genre, including CYBERPUNK∗, DYSTOPIAS∗, EDISONADE∗, GAME-WORLDS∗, GENRE SF, HARD SF, HEROIC FANTASY, LOST WORLDS∗, MONSTER MOVIES∗, NEW WAVE∗, PLANETARY ROMANCE∗, SCIENCE FANTASY∗, SF, SCI FI, SCIENTIFIC ROMANCE, SCIENTIFICTION, SHARECROP, SHARED WORLDS∗, SLIPSTREAM SF, SOFT SF, SPACE OPERA∗, SPECULATIVE FICTION, STEAMPUNK∗, SWORD AND SORCERY∗, UTOPIA∗. Second is a cluster of terms borrowed from outside sf, usually from science, but much used within sf, sometimes with modified meanings: ALIENS∗, ANDROIDS∗, ANTIMATTER∗, AI, BIONICS, BLACK HOLES∗, CLONES∗, CRYOGENICS, CRYONICS∗, CULTURAL ENGINEERING, CYBERNETICS∗, DIMENSIONS, DYSON SPHERE, ENTROPY∗, ESP∗, EXTRATERRESTRIAL, GALACTIC LENS, HOLLOW EARTH∗, ION DRIVE, LAGRANGE POINT, MUTANTS∗, NANOTECHNOLOGY∗, NEUTRON STAR∗, PARSEC, PULSARS, SOLAR WIND, SPACE HABITATS∗, SUPERMAN∗, SUSPENDED ANIMATION∗, TACHYONS, TELEKINESIS, TELEPORTATION, TERRA, UFOS∗, VIRTUAL REALITY∗, WHITE HOLES, WORMHOLES. The final cluster is of terms which either originate within sf or would be almost unknown were it not for sf: ALTERNATE WORLDS∗, ANSIBLE, ANTIGRAVITY∗, ASTROGATION, BIG DUMB OBJECTS∗, BEM, BLASTER, CORPSICLE, CREDITS, CYBERSPACE, CYBORGS∗, DALEKS, DEATH RAYS, DIRAC COMMUNICATOR, DISINTEGRATOR, ESPER, FORCE FIELD∗, FRANKENSTEIN MONSTER, FTL, GAS GIANT, GENERATION STARSHIPS∗, HIVE-MINDS∗, HYPERSPACE∗, INNER SPACE, MATTER TRANSMISSION∗, PANTROPY, PARALLEL WORLDS∗, POSITRONIC ROBOTS, PRESSOR BEAM, PSIONICS, PSI POWERS∗,

PSYCHOHISTORY, RIMWORLD, ROBOTS∗, SPACESHIPS∗, SPACE WARP, SPINDIZZY, STARSHIP, TERRAFORMING∗, TIME MACHINE, TIME PARADOXES∗, TIME TRAVEL∗, TRACTOR BEAM, WALDO.

Sf fans have also developed a specialist terminology, but this is quite distinct, generally, from the terminology of sf itself. It is discussed under FAN LANGUAGE.

Terminology entries not listed above are BRAID, DIANETICS, DOS, GENERAL SEMANTICS, IMAGINARY VOYAGES, MAGAZINES, MAGIC REALISM, ORIGINAL ANTHOLOGIES, OULIPO, ROBINSONADE, SCIENTOLOGY, SEMIPROZINE, SOFT SCIENCES, SPLATTER MOVIES, XENOBIOLOGY. [PN]

TERMINUS PUBLISHING CO. ◊ WEIRD TALES.

TERRA Common item of sf TERMINOLOGY. In sf the Latin form is that conventionally given to the name of our planet, since Earth is ambiguous, meaning both the planet itself and soil. (The irony is that the same ambiguity exists in Latin, where *terra* can mean anything from soil or the ground, as in *terra firma*, to the whole world.) Similarly, our Sun is often, in sf, called Sol. The other Latin word for Earth, commoner in poetry than in prose, was *tellus*, and Tellus and its adjective Tellurian make occasional appearances in sf. [PN]

TERRAFORMING If the COLONIZATION OF OTHER WORLDS is not to be restricted to those that prove almost-exact duplicates of the Earth, some form of adaptation will be necessary; the colonists might adapt *themselves* by GENETIC ENGINEERING, as in James BLISH's PANTROPY series, or cyborgization (◊ CYBORGS), as in Frederik POHL's *Man Plus* (**1976**), but if they are bolder they might instead adapt *the worlds*, by terraforming them. The term was coined by Jack WILLIAMSON in the series of stories revised as *Seetee Ship* (1942-3; fixup **1951**; early editions as by Will Stewart), where it is used in a minor subplot, but such a project had earlier been envisaged in Olaf STAPLEDON's *Last and First Men* (**1930**), where VENUS is prepared for human habitation by electrolysing water from its oceans to produce oxygen. Stapledon's project was primitive (and unworkable); most sf stories envisage plant life being used to generate a breathable atmosphere on terraformable planets, just as it once did on Earth.

As it gradually became accepted that the other planets in the Solar System could not sustain human life, terraforming projects became commonplace in sf, especially in relation to MARS. Stories like Arthur C. CLARKE's *The Sands of Mars* (**1951**) and Patrick MOORE's series begun with *Mission to Mars* (**1956**) envisage relatively small-scale modifications, but, as the true magnitude of the problem has become apparent, writers have been forced to imagine much more complex processes. Ian McDONALD's *Desolation Road* (**1988**) tends to the frankly miraculous, but compensates with some memorable imagery; its echoes of Ray BRADBURY seem slightly more appropriate than the echoes of Edgar Rice BURROUGHS in *The Barsoom*

Project (**1989**) by Larry NIVEN and Steven BARNES. In the real world, however, people have been hatching long-term plans ever since the idea of terraforming was first treated seriously by such nonfiction popularizations as Carl SAGAN's *The Cosmic Connection* (**1973**) and Adrian BERRY's *The Next Ten Thousand Years* (**1974**). Kim Stanley ROBINSON has begun to elaborate a trilogy of novels around his novella *Green Mars* (1985; **1988** dos), which will endeavour to describe a realistic series of procedures; *Red Mars* (**1992** UK) begins the series, which is projected to continue with «Green Mars» (no textual connection with the novella) and «Blue Mars».

Other writers have followed Stapledon in imagining the terraforming of Venus, among them Poul ANDERSON in "The Big Rain" (1954) and "Sister Planet" (1956). This project has recently become the subject of an ambitious and extensive series by Pamela SARGENT, begun in *Venus of Dreams* (**1986**) and continued in *Venus of Shadows* (**1988**).

The only other worlds in the Solar System which seem to be plausible candidates for terraforming are some of the satellites of JUPITER and Saturn (◊ OUTER PLANETS). Ganymede is the favourite, featuring in Robert A. HEINLEIN's *Farmer in the Sky* (**1950**), Poul Anderson's *The Snows of Ganymede* (1955; **1958** dos) and Gregory BENFORD's *Jupiter Project* (**1975**). Jack VANCE's "I'll Build Your Dream Castle" (1947), about custom-terraformed ASTEROIDS, is decidedly tongue-in-cheek.

The idea that the terraforming of worlds might be reduced to a matter of routine as mankind builds a GALACTIC EMPIRE is occasionally featured in sf novels, although generally as a throwaway idea. Elaborate descriptions of terraforming in such a context are rare, but David GERROLD's *Moonstar Odyssey* (**1977**) and Andrew WEINER's *Station Gehenna* (**1987**) both involve terraforming projects whose methods are more-or-less scrupulously sketched out. Some of Roger ZELAZNY's works assume that terraforming projects can be so routinized that "worldscaping" might become a kind of art form; his *Isle of the Dead* (**1969**) features a protagonist who is in this godlike line of work. The same notion surfaces in Douglas ADAMS's **Hitch Hiker** series and in the film *Time Bandits* (1981) dir Terry Gilliam, and technologically powerful worldmakers with a mischievous bent hover (unfathomably) in the background of Terry PRATCHETT's *Strata* (**1981**). It is probable, though, that it is the realistic treatments of Sargent and Robinson which will set the pattern for the most significant future uses of the theme in sf. [MJE/BS]

TERRAHAWKS UK tv series (1983-6). Anderson Burr Pictures/London Weekend Television. Created Gerry ANDERSON, prod Anderson, Christopher Burr; dirs Alan Pattillo, Tony Bell, Tony Lenny, Desmond Saunders; all episodes written Tony Barwick (1 with Trevor Lansdown) except for pilot, by Anderson. 3 seasons, 39 25min episodes in all.

Using more advanced puppets than in all his SuperMarionation series, with more electronic movements built in, this was the last of Anderson's sf puppet series for children, made after he had been working for some years with live-action tv (◊ SPACE: 1999). The Terrahawks are an elite special force who must save Earth from the depredations of Zelda, the ANDROID witch-queen of Guk. To help, they have the silver ROBOTS the Zeroids, commanded by Sgt Major Zero, who has a funny Sgt-Major voice. Most of the old Anderson ingredients are shuffled about in this attack-from-space series, but the results are tired and self-parodic. [PN]

TERRORE NELLO SPAZIO (vt *Planet of the Vampires*) Italian film (1965). Italian International/Castilla Cinematografica/AIP. Dir Mario Bava, starring Barry Sullivan, Norma Bengell, Angel Aranda, Evi Morandi. Screenplay: *US* Louis M. Heyward, Ib Melchior; *Italian* Callisto Cosulich, Antonio Roman, Alberto Bevilacqua, Bava, Rafael J. Salvia; based on a story by Melchior, based in turn on an Italian story by Renato Pestriniero. 86 mins. Colour.

This Italian/Spanish/US co-production is directed by Mario Bava, whose baroque, erotic and sometimes sadomasochistic HORROR films have won him a cult following; he also dir DIABOLIK (1967). He was once a notable cameraman, and this sf/horror film is visually intense. Astronauts land on a strange planet and immediately and inexplicably start killing each other. Three corpses are buried but, in a striking sequence, rise from the grave, still shrouded in polythene. It turns out they are possessed by alien spirits. Two possessed astronauts and the still-human captain (Sullivan) take the spaceship to return to Earth, where the pickings will be rich. The discovery in *TNS* of an ancient, alien SPACESHIP on the surface, occupied by a giant skeleton, was echoed with some fidelity in the later film ALIEN (1979). The florid, dreamlike atmospherics of *TNS* almost make up for the silliness of the story. Originally to be shot simultaneously in Italian and US versions, with pages of script delivered only on the day, it must have presented a challenge to even Bava's celebrated inventiveness. [PN]

See also: CINEMA; MONSTER MOVIES; PARANOIA.

TERROR OF MECHAGODZILLA ◊ GOJIRA.

TERROR STRIKES, THE ◊ *The* AMAZING COLOSSAL MAN.

TERRORVISION Film (1986). Altar/Empire. Executive prod Charles BAND. Dir Ted Nicolaou, starring Mary Woronov, Gerrit Graham, Diane Franklin, Chad Allen, Jonathan Gries. Screenplay Nicolaou. 83 mins. Colour.

This lurid exploitation-movie-cum-satire has good moments. A hungry beast first appears on the tv screen, then materializes in the house, of wife-swapping vulgarians, a SURVIVALIST grandfather, military-minded son and heavy-metal-obsessed daughter. With admirable joviality the beast eats and dissolves most of them one by one, along with others, later reproducing their heads when necessary.

Earth's only hope, the interstellar policeman who pursues it, is summarily dispatched by a tv horror-show hostess who mistakes him for the monster. [PN]

See also: MONSTER MOVIES.

TERTZ, ABRAM ◊ Andrey SINYAVSKY.

TESSERACTS ◊ CANADA.

TESTAMENT Film (1983). Entertainment Events/ American Playhouse. Dir Lynne Littman, starring Jane Alexander, Ross Harris, Lukas Haas, William Devane, Leon Ames. Screenplay John Sacret Young, based on "The Last Testament" by Carol Amen (?1934-1987). 90 mins. Colour.

We follow the ordinary, loving, quarrelsome life of one family in a small Californian town, Hamlin. Without warning, all US cities are destroyed by nuclear weapons. Hamlin, not far from San Francisco, is spared the immediate blast (in which the husband is killed), but loses most of its population to radiation sickness. Two children die. The mother and her surviving son, at the end, decide not to commit suicide.

This is an intimate film about the END OF THE WORLD. Too well observed to be simple soap opera, it is nevertheless formidably and touchingly domestic, and (deliberately) declares itself in every scene a film made by a woman; even the death of a child is evoked by the careful sewing of a shroud. It treats the vast scale of the DISASTER obliquely, the small standing for the large, and seems not interested in causes, only in effects – in marked contrast to The DAY AFTER, made the same year. Also in contrast to that film, T is diffident to the point of shrinking about the physical effects of the HOLOCAUST; radiation sickness is merely symbolized, by dark shadows round the eyes. The Hamlin/Hamelin parallel of the "Pied Piper" school play focuses the tightly controlled anger of the film on the adult negligence that makes children innocent victims. T is potent and sentimental, one of a number of 1980s films about nuclear destruction – e.g., SPECIAL BULLETIN, THREADS and WHEN THE WIND BLOWS. [PN]

TEVIS, WALTER (STONE) (1928-1984) US writer, professor of English literature at the University of Ohio, who perhaps remains best known as the author of The Hustler (1959), filmed in 1961, and its sequel, The Color of Money (1984), filmed in 1986. He began publishing sf with "The Ifth of Oofth" for Gal in 1957 as Walter S. Tevis – his early work, and the tales he wrote around 1980, are assembled as Far from Home (coll 1981) – but he first came to wide notice as an sf writer with The Man who Fell to Earth (1963), the basis of Nicolas Roeg's film The MAN WHO FELL TO EARTH (1976). It is the delicately crafted story of an ALIEN who comes to Earth from Anthea in an attempt to arrange asylum for his dying race; in return, he will pass on the benefits of Anthean science. Becoming as physically and emotionally human as his technology and his powers of empathy permit, he finds the xenophobic bureaucracy of humanity's response to him, when he reveals himself and his quest, impossible to bear; and the blinding he suffers fairly represents the dying of any hope he might have had of making sense of us. WT's subsequent novels were less darkly inspired. Mockingbird (1980) rather mechanically runs its ANDROID protagonist through a process of self-realization in a senescent USA 500 years hence. The Steps of the Sun (1983) is the story of an impotent tycoon who revivifies himself and perhaps the entire world by finding a sentient, motherly and cornucopian planet on his first space flight and bringing her gifts back home; too often the plot fades away into psychodrama. WT himself said that his work was autobiographical. His early death perhaps kept him from telling a whole story. [JC]

See also: ROBOTS.

TEZUKA, OSAMU (1928-1989) The premier artist in the world of Japanese manga (COMICS) and animation, in both of which he established a standard. He began contributing serial comic strips to a regional newspaper in 1946 while in junior college. He became a leader in Japanese comics with Shin Takarajima ["The New Treasure Island"] (1947). Most of today's Japanese comics illustrators grew up strongly influenced by OT. His most famous creation was the **Tetsuwan Atom** series (1952 on; in trans as **Astroboy**], which began as a series in the children's magazine Shonen. It was eagerly welcomed not only by comics lovers but also by sf fans all over JAPAN, because his stories showed a real sense of the feeling of modern sf which at that time had been grasped by few Japanese writers. Most of his work was for children, but he published in general magazines also, and 2 pure-sf serials appeared in SF Magajin ["SF Magazine"], SF Fancy Free (1963) and Chojin Taikei ["Rise and Fall of the Bird-Human Race"] (1971-5). These were highly esteemed by sf fans, who are normally severe towards comics.

In 1952 OT established an animation studio, Mushi Productions, produced several full-length animated films, and then began work on the first animated series for Japanese tv, **Tetsuwan Atom** (1963 onwards), famous in the West as **Astroboy**. This was the dawn of "Japanimation". He is often looked upon as a Japanese Walt Disney, but failed to elevate his company to a major enterprise, being a better artist than businessman. His main other comics series were **Jungle Taitei** (1950 on; trans as **Kimba, The White Lion**), later a tv series, the **Black Jack** series (1973 on), and the **Hi No Tori** ["The Phoenix"] series (1966 on), selected sections of which were made into feature films, some live and some animated: one which appeared in the West was the animated Hi No Tori: 2772 (1979; vt Space Firebird 2772; vt Phoenix 2772), dir OT with Suguru Sugiyama, which tells of the attempted capture of a cosmic space firebird whose life-blood may rejuvenate Earth. [TSh]

THAMES, C(HRISTOPHER) H. [s] ◊ Milton LESSER.

THANET, NEIL ◊ R.L. FANTHORPE.

THAYER, TIFFANY (ELLSWORTH) (1902-1959)

Prolific and once immensely popular US novelist – his first novel, the courtroom drama *Thirteen Men* (**1930**), was reprinted 40 times in 20 years. After the success of *Tiffany Thayer's Three Musketeers* (**1939**), he devoted most of his remaining years to an enormous historical work, «Tiffany Thayer's Mona Lisa»; of 7 projected instalments, only the 1200pp *The Prince of Taranto* (**1956**) ever appeared. TT's sf includes *The Greek* (**1931**), about a NEAR-FUTURE dictatorship, *Doctor Arnoldi* (**1934**), which recounts the grisly implications of being both immortal (◊ IMMORTALITY) and unkillable, and *One-Man Show* (**1937**), a Thorne-Smith-like comedy of the afterlife. He was an enthusiastic follower of Charles FORT, founding the Fortean Society and editing its publication *Doubt* for many years. Although unknown today except for this affiliation, TT exerted an influence that has yet to be assessed: his highly kinetic, sardonic prose was almost certainly known to Alfred BESTER, and his **Mona Lisa** project may well have coloured the description of Fellowes Kraft's opus in John CROWLEY's *Aegypt* (**1987**). [GF]
Other works: *33 Sardonics I Can't Forget* (anth **1946**).
About the author: *Charles Fort, Prophet of the Unexplained* (**1970**) by Damon KNIGHT contains some material on TT.

THEATRE Sf literature and theatre have much in common, as both rely heavily on the audience's imagination, yet the two forms have rarely been combined in a significant dramatic work. The principal reason seems to be a widely held assumption that the theatre, with its physical limitations, cannot plausibly present the fantastic vistas which sf writers envision. "Writing an sf play is a bit like trying to picture infinity in a cigar box," Roger ELWOOD declared in his introduction to *Six Science Fiction Plays* (anth **1976**), the only such anthology in existence. Thus, though more than 300 sf dramas have been catalogued, the history of theatrical sf is largely that of various playwrights influenced by the genre, but with no commitment to it. (The parenthetical references given in this article are to cities and years of premieres; only when no such date is known is the earliest publication date used.)

Although some scholars detect speculative elements in the plays of Aristophanes and even Shakespeare's *The Tempest*, the earliest dramas with sf premises were adaptations. Richard Brinsley Peake's *Presumption, or The Fate of Frankenstein* (London, 1823) began a history of more than 100 plays inspired by Mary SHELLEY's novel *Frankenstein, or The Modern Prometheus* (**1818**; rev 1831). Adaptations of *Strange Case of Dr Jekyll and Mr Hyde* (**1886**) appeared almost immediately after Robert Louis STEVENSON's novel was published. Jacques Offenbach's opera *Les contes d'Hoffman* ["Tales of Hoffman"] (Paris, 1881), based on stories by E.T.A. HOFFMANN, includes an episode based on "The Sandman", in which a poet falls in love with a scientist's mechanical doll.

The first significant original plays appeared in the 1920s and 1930s. Karel ČAPEK's *R.U.R.*, in which an army of rebellious ANDROIDS destroys the human race, introduced the Czech word ROBOT to our language, and enjoyed successful runs in New York and London after its 1921 premiere in Prague. (Čapek wrote 2 other plays with sf themes.) New York's Theatre Guild premiered the first play to deal with EVOLUTION, George Bernard SHAW's *Back to Methuselah* (1922), and the first atomic-weapons play, *Wings Over Europe* (1928) by Robert NICHOLS and Maurice Browne. Russian satirists Vladimir MAYAKOVSKY (*The Bedbug*, Moscow, 1929; *The Bathhouse*, Moscow, 1930) and Mikhail BULGAKOV (*Bliss*, **1934**; *Ivan Vasilievich*, **1935-6**) used TIME TRAVEL to expose the foibles of the Soviet bureaucracy.

Through the 1950s many other famous writers produced full-length sf-related dramas of varying quality, some of them never staged. Arthur KOESTLER's dark comedy *Twilight Bar* (Paris, 1946) features 2 ALIENS who threaten to destroy Earth unless the inhabitants of a small island achieve happiness within 3 days. J.B. PRIESTLEY (*Summer Day's Dream*, London, 1949) and Upton SINCLAIR (*A Giant's Strength*, Claremont, California, 1948; *The Enemy Had it Too*, **1950**) were among the many playwrights to speculate on the consequences of nuclear WAR in the post-Hiroshima period. Elias Canetti (1905-   ) wrote 2 plays in which societies strive towards UTOPIA: by numbering all citizens according to their predicted death dates (*Die Befristeten*, Oxford, 1956; trans as *The Numbered*; vt *Life-Terms*), or by banishing mirrors and other tools of vanity (*Komödie der Eitelkeit*, written 1934; **1950** Germany; trans as *Comedy of Vanity*). Egypt's Tawfīk al-HAKĪM sent 2 convicted killers into space in search of a second chance in *Voyage to Tomorrow* (**1950**).

Since the 1950s various writers have adapted sf narratives for the theatre, but their results have seldom been satisfactory. An exception is Ray BRADBURY, who relied on simple staging techniques to dramatize 3 of his short stories in *The World of Ray Bradbury* (Los Angeles, 1964; New York, 1965) and *The Martian Chronicles* (Los Angeles, 1977). Other sf classics to be adapted have included H.G. WELLS's *The War of the Worlds* (**1898**; Brainerd Duffield, **1955**; Albert Reyes, **1977**), John HERSEY's *The Child Buyer* (**1960**; Paul Shyre, **1962**), Aldous HUXLEY's *Brave New World* (**1932**; David Rogers, **1970**), George ORWELL's *Nineteen Eighty-four* (**1949**; Pavel KOHOUT, **1984**) and Walter M. MILLER's *A Canticle for Leibowitz* (**1960**; Richard Felnagle, **1986**).

The most noteworthy sf dramas since the 1960s have been those by professional playwrights employing familiar sf premises or iconography for non-sf purposes. Antonio Buero Vallejo explored the sociological effects of the Spanish Civil War through the eyes of two scholars from the future in *El tragaluz* (Madrid, 1967; trans as *The Basement Window*). Sam Shepard's "The Unseen Hand" (New York, 1969) features an alien fugitive who seeks the aid of 3 Old

West outlaws, while his *The Tooth of Crime* (London, 1972) posits a society ruled by rock'n'roll stars. David Rudkin's *The Sons of Light* (London, 1977) pits a pastor's sons against an evil scientist who has used myth and brainwashing techniques to create a subterranean slave army. In Eric Overmeyer's *Native Speech* (Los Angeles, 1983) the monologues of a disc jockey influence events in a devastated urban world; in Overmeyer's *On the Verge* (Baltimore, 1985) words propel 3 19th-century lady explorers on a journey through time.

Sf has also influenced performance art. In *The Games* (West Berlin, 1983) by Meredith Monk and Ping Chong a future society attempts to preserve its past through Olympic-style rituals. *1000 Airplanes on the Roof* (Vienna, 1988), a multimedia collaboration by playwright David Henry Hwang, composer Philip Glass (◊ MUSIC) and designer Jerome Sirlin, is a single-character narrative about a psychological encounter with aliens.

A few playwrights have combined comedy with sf to reflect modern social problems. Alan Spence's *Space Invaders* (Edinburgh, 1983) and Constance Congdon's *Tales of the Lost Formicans* (Woodstock, New York, 1988) use the alien-encounter premise as a metaphor for the plight of the individual in a confused world. Alan Ayckbourn employs a mechanical nanny to explore a similar theme in *Henceforward . . .* (Scarborough, 1987).

Despite the failure of the Broadway musical *Via Galactica* (Galt MacDermot, Christopher Gore, Judith Ross, 1972), sf spectaculars have appeared frequently since the early 1970s. A more successful musical was Bob Carlton's *Return to the Forbidden Planet* (Blackheath, England, 1983), a 1990 hit in London, which covers much the same ground as FORBIDDEN PLANET (1956) with great good humour and a lot of mainly 1960s rock'n'roll songs. (*For further discussion of sf musical dramas and opera see* MUSIC.) A cult favourite in the USA was *Warp!* (Chicago, 1971-2; New York, 1973), a comic trilogy by Stuart Gordon and Lenny Kleinfeld. Its counterpart in England, Ken Campbell's and Chris Langham's *Illuminatus!* (Liverpool, 1976; London, 1977), was a 5-play epic based on the trilogy by Robert SHEA and Robert Anton WILSON, and was followed by Neil ORAM's 10-part play sequence *The Warp* (1979), also dir Ken Campbell. These productions employed a variety of modern theatrical techniques to create convincingly fantastic worlds on the stage. [RW]

THEM! Film (1954). Warner Bros. Dir Gordon Douglas. starring Edmund Gwenn, James Whitmore, James Arness, Joan Weldon. Screenplay Ted Sherdeman, based on a story by George Worthing Yates. 93 mins. B/w.

Unexplained deaths occur, but it is some time before we learn that atomic tests in the US desert have created gigantism (◊ GREAT AND SMALL) in a species of ant. Their nest is located and destroyed, but a queen ant escapes and lays her eggs in a storm drain beneath Los Angeles, which becomes the setting for the final battle between giant ants and humans. Along with *The* THING (1951) and *The* BEAST FROM 20,000 FATHOMS (1953), *T!* was a template for a series of similar MONSTER MOVIES that followed in the 1950s. It is well made, and handles its absurd subject with an austere but vivid documentary style, thus standing out from most of the cheaper and more sensational variations that followed on the theme. The giant ants were not animated miniatures but full-scale mock-ups. [JB/PN]

See also: HIVE-MINDS; MUTANTS.

THEMERSON, STEFAN (1910-1988) Polish-born author, scriptwriter and photographer, active in Poland in the 1930s, there editing journals and publishing widely; in the UK from before the beginning of WWII, he continued publishing in Polish and French, but increasingly turned to English. He was a member of the Collège de 'Pataphysique and founded the Gaberbocchus Press. Given over as they were to paradox, games of logic and the dislocations of Semantic Poetry (his own term), ST's novels have never been easy to pigeonhole but can be thought of – very roughly – as exuberant FABULATIONS. In *Professor Mmaa's Lecture* (**1953**), which comes as close to conventional sf as any of his books, the eponymous termite lectures his audience on the vast new primitive creatures called mammals, which are threatening to take over the world; the book had an introduction by Bertrand RUSSELL. Though they radically displace the normal world, none of his other fictions could be called sf; but his last 2 novels – *The Mystery of the Sardine* (**1986**) and *Hobson's Island* (**1988**) – assemble many characters from previous books into worlds which are mirrors of our own – an Anti-Earth floats in the heavens of the first tale – where they engage in levitations, speculations and prestidigitations galore. [JC]

Other works: *Bayamus* (**1949**); *Wooff Wooff, or Who Killed Richard Wagner?* (**1951**); *Cardinal Pölätüo* (**1961**); *Tom Harris* (**1967**); *Special Branch (A Dialogue)* (**1972** chap); *General Piesc, or The Case of the Forgotten Mission* (**1976** chap).

THEOBALD, ROBERT (1929-   ) US writer and economist, an exponent of the need for alternative technologies and strategies to survive the turn of the century; his several texts on these issues culminate in *An Alternative Future for America's Third Century* (**1976**). His sf novel, *Teg's 1994: An Anticipation of the Near Future* (**1972**) with J.M. Scott, carries on these concerns through a series of dialogues between George ORWELL-Fellowship-winner Teg and various interlocutors who discuss the course of history leading up to 1994, a time less bad than it might have been (because alternative technologies were employed), hence the name of the fellowship she has won. The book, originally circulated in mimeographed form in 1969, was written to elicit readers' responses, and 60pp of the first printed edn contain readers' and authors' comments. [JC/PN]

THEODORE STURGEON MEMORIAL AWARD
Given in memory of Theodore STURGEON, who died
in 1985, to the previous year's best sf/fantasy story in
English under 17,500 words. The TSMA has been
announced annually since 1987 during a July ceremony at the University of Kansas in Lawrence, at
which the JOHN W. CAMPBELL MEMORIAL AWARD is also
announced. The winner and place-getters are chosen
by a committee, largely of sf writers, chaired by
Orson Scott CARD, with whose self-published critical
magazine *Short Form* the TSMA is affiliated. [PN]
Winners:
1987: Judith MOFFETT, "Surviving"
1988: Pat MURPHY, "Rachel in Love"
1989: George Alec EFFINGER, "Schrödinger's Kitten"
1990: Michael SWANWICK, "The Edge of the World"
1991: Terry BISSON, "Bears Discover Fire"
1992: John KESSEL, "Buffalo"

THERE WILL COME SOFT RAIN ◊ VEL'D.

THEROUX, PAUL (EDWARD) (1941-   ) US writer
best known for novels like *Saint Jack* (**1973**) and *The
Mosquito Coast* (**1982**), which cruelly anatomize their
far-flung settings, and for travel books which do the
same. Some of his slighter books are FABULATIONS, *The
Black House* (**1977**) is a horror story, and *O-Zone* (**1986**)
is an extremely long, seemingly ambitious sf novel set
in the familiar killing ground of a near-future DYSTO-
PIAN USA, irradiated with traces of HOLOCAUST, where
the rich lurk behind domes and the poor roam a
desolated terrain. It may be that PT thought the
venue was original to this book. [JC]
See also: MAINSTREAM WRITERS OF SF; POLLUTION; SLIP-
STREAM SF.

THESE ARE THE DAMNED ◊ *The* DAMNED.

THEY CAME FROM BEYOND SPACE ◊ Joseph
MILLARD.

THEY CAME FROM WITHIN ◊ *The* PARASITE MURDERS.

THEYDON, JOHN ◊ John W. JENNISON.

THEY LIVE Film (1988). Alive Films. Dir John CARPEN-
TER, starring Roddy Piper, Keith David, Meg Foster.
Screenplay Frank Armitage (pseudonym of Carpenter), based on "Eight O'Clock in the Morning" (1963)
by Ray (R.F.) NELSON. 94 mins. Colour.
After several not very successful films for major
studios (STARMAN [1984], *Christine* [1983]), Carpenter
went independent again for this, his best film for
years and, though it did not do much in the
marketplace, most popular with the critics. Based on
a 6pp story about the USA being controlled by
disguised ALIENS (partly a satirical attack on tv), it
expands its original cleverly, and is a model of taut,
B-movie narrative skills. In a depression-ridden,
conformist USA, Nada (Piper), a labourer, is puzzled
by intimations of something not quite right. He
accidentally discovers a cache of sunglasses that,
when worn, reveal subliminal codes all over the city,
urging submission to authority, and also finds that
many wealthier-looking citizens are in fact skull-faced
aliens, exploiting what to them is a Third-World
colony. An excellent formula film, *TL* is almost

something more ambitious as well – but settles for
action. [PN]
See also: MONSTER MOVIES; PARANOIA.

THIESSEN, J. GRANT [r] ◊ *The* SCIENCE-FICTION COL-
LECTOR.

THIJSSEN, FELIX [r] ◊ BENELUX.

THING, THE 1. Film (1951; vt *The Thing from Another
World*). Winchester Pictures/RKO. Dir Christian Nyby
(but see below), starring Kenneth Tobey, Margaret
Sheridan, Robert Cornthwaite, Douglas Spencer,
James Arness. Screenplay Charles Lederer, based on
"Who Goes There?" (1938) by Don A. Stuart (John W.
CAMPBELL Jr). 86 mins. B/w.
TT was by far the most influential of the films that
sparked off the sf/MONSTER-MOVIE boom of the 1950s,
and remains one of the most powerful of that decade.
The film was actually dir Howard Hawks, who
arranged as a favour that Nyby (an editor on previous
Hawks films) should receive the directing credit. It is
full of Hawks's trademarks: fast pace, overlapping
dialogue and an ability to elicit relaxed, naturalistic
performances from the cast. It describes the discovery
of a UFO in the Arctic ice, its retrieval, and the
subsequent series of attacks on a military/scientific
base by its thawed-out occupant, a humanoid,
vegetable ALIEN, searching for blood. Hawks wisely
kept the Thing (Arness) off the screen for most of the
film; when seen it is disappointing – and not at all
like an "intellectual carrot", as it has been described.
The best things in *TT* are the increasing tension
(every time a door is opened the audience jumps) and
claustrophobia; the gutsy performance by Sheridan
as the wisecracking woman who gives as good as she
gets, especially in the astonishing bondage scene;
and the convincing sense of a nervous group under
siege. Typical of adventure films made during the
Cold War, there is a shoot-first-and-ask-questions-
later morality (the scientists who want to communicate with the Thing are seen as fools); the Cold-War
feeling is heightened by the famous last line, "Keep
watching the skies!" [PN/JB]
2. Film (1982). Turman-Foster/Universal. Dir John
CARPENTER, starring Kurt Russell, A. Wilford Brimley,
T.K. Carter, Richard Dysart, Charles Hallahan,
Richard Masur. Screenplay Bill Lancaster, based on
the Stuart/Campbell story. 109 mins. Colour.
Not so much a remake as a return to the original
story, this film reinstates Campbell's shapeshifting
alien that can kill and duplicate the base workers one
by one, with all the PARANOIA that that engenders. It
was not very successful commercially, and was
widely criticized as being merely a string of curiously
disgusting special effects (designed by Rob Bottin, an
uncredited Stan Winston and others) without any of
the subtlety of the Hawks version. But the Hawks
version, though vivid, was itself not very subtle, and
Carpenter carries his beleaguered working men much
further *in extremis* emotionally than Hawks would
have cared to. Only 2 survive, and either or both may
in fact be alien. There is a case for arguing that the

Carpenter version goes as far as genre movies normally dare, if not further, in questioning not just the nature of humanity under stress but its value. Faced by the alien, the humans themselves become inhuman in every possible way. It is a black, memorable film, and may yet be seen as a classic. The novelization is *The Thing* * (**1982**) by Alan Dean FOSTER. [PN]

See also: CINEMA.

THING FROM ANOTHER WORLD, THE ◊ *The* THING.

THINGS TO COME Film (1936). London Films. Dir William Cameron Menzies, starring Raymond Massey, Cedric Hardwicke, Margaretta Scott, Ralph Richardson, Edward Chapman, Ann Todd, Maurice Braddell. Screenplay Lajos Biro, H.G. WELLS, based on Wells's *The Shape of Things to Come* (**1933**). 130 mins, cut to 113 mins. B/w.

This Alexander Korda production was the most expensive and ambitious sf film of the 1930s – and, despite the growth of magazine sf over the next 15 years, the last sf film of any importance until the 1950s. Although Wells himself was closely associated with *TTC*, it is not the most satisfactory of the 1930s films based on his work, and was a box-office failure. The film is divided into 3 parts: the 1st, set in 1940, sees the start of a world WAR that continues for decades; the 2nd, set in 1970, deals with a community reduced by the war to tribalism until the arrival of a mysterious "airman", who announces that a new era of "law and sanity" has begun and quells the local warlords with "Peace Gas"; and the 3rd takes place in AD2036, when the ruling technocrats have built a gleaming white UTOPIA and an attempt is being made to fire a manned projectile into space, using an electric gun, despite (vain) opposition from effete "artists" who are still maintaining that "there are some things Man is not meant to know".

Characterization and dialogue are weakly imagined and the rhetoric is preachy and pompous, despite the famously overblown but moving concluding speech delivered by Raymond Massey, as he declares of Man: ". . . and when he has conquered all the deeps of space and all the mysteries of time, still he will be beginning." Wells's belief that the future of humanity lay with a technocratic elite and his scorn for the ARTS seemed oddly old-fashioned even in 1936 – not to say undemocratic. But the visual drama (supported by Arthur Bliss's majestic musical score), despite static compositions, is exhilarating: the special effects were by the imported Hollywood expert Ned Mann and director Menzies was a great production designer (most famously for *Gone With the Wind* [1939]). *TTC* is one of the most important films in the history of sf CINEMA for the boldness of its ambitions and for the ardour with which it projects the myth of SPACE FLIGHT as the beginning of humankind's transcendence. Wells published a version of the script as *Things to Come* * (**1935**). [PN/JB]

THIRY, MARCEL [r] ◊ BENELUX.

THIS ISLAND EARTH Film (1955). Universal. Dir Joseph Newman, starring Jeff Morrow, Faith Domergue, Rex Reason. Screenplay Franklin Coen, Edward G. O'Callaghan, based on *This Island Earth* (fixup **1952**) by Raymond F. JONES. 86 mins. Colour.

TIE came closer than any film of its period to capturing the flamboyant essence of PULP-MAGAZINE sf stories. Unlike most other early-1950s sf films, which were MONSTER MOVIES, *TIE* becomes a SPACE OPERA halfway through; the high cost of special effects required in films of this type was one reason for their comparative rarity.

A nuclear physicist (Reason), having passed what turns out to have been an IQ test set by extraterrestrials – he builds an "interociter" from mysterious components that have arrived in the mail – is conscripted by them, along with other SCIENTISTS. These include an old girlfriend (Domergue). Several adventures later the two are taken unwillingly by flying saucer through the "thermic barrier" to the aliens' planet, Metaluna. The Metalunans hope that the scientists' expertise in the conversion of elements will provide the massive amounts of uranium required to keep their atomic shield functioning, so that it will continue to protect them from meteoritic bombardment by the sadistic Zahgons. Their arrival is too late; they witness the death of Metaluna and are returned to Earth by Exeter (Morrow), the arrogant but sympathetic alien who kidnapped them in the first place.

Newman was a run-of-the-mill director, but it is probable that Jack ARNOLD (uncredited) directed the Metaluna sequences with the help of Clifford Stine's extravagant special effects. The sequences are remarkable not for their realism but for their imaginativeness; they are the closest sf cinema ever got to the style of *ASF*'s or *AMZ*'s 1930s magazine covers.

TIE can hardly be called a good film, but it is an excellent bad film, a classic of sf cinema. Its most obvious subtext (what would it feel like to be the colonized rather than the colonizers?) seems to point towards isolationism as the best strategy for Earth, but the exoticism of the offworld sequences, and Exeter's dying speech ("our Universe is vast, full of wonders . . .") offer powerful propaganda for the contrary political position, the embrace of otherness. [PN]

THIUSEN, ISMAR Pseudonym of Scottish-born US writer and academic John Macnie (1836-1909), whose UTOPIA *The Diothas, or A Far Look Ahead* (**1883**; vt *A Far Look Ahead, or The Diothas* 1890; vt *Looking Forward, or The Diothas* 1890 UK), set several millennia hence, was prolific with its suggestions of technological progress while presenting a not untypically regimented picture of human relations, which are especially constricting for women – who, if unmarried, go out only with chaperons. Unusually, the book's protagonist and narrator is himself a native of a future time (a few centuries hence, which may explain the strangeness of his name, Ismar Thiusen), and travels from that point into the FAR FUTURE where the main action takes place. [JC]

See also: SLEEPER AWAKES.

THOLE, KAREL Working name of Dutch illustrator Carolus Adrianus Maria Thole (1914-   ), resident in Milan since 1958. The best-known European sf illustrator, KT's book covers have appeared in virtually every country in continental Europe, as well as in the UK and the USA (including some for BALLANTINE BOOKS and DAW BOOKS). But the greatest body of his sf ILLUSTRATION has been for the publishers Mondadori in Italy and Heyne in Germany; for considerable periods he has been the *only* artist working on their sf lines. His work may be the most sophisticatedly surreal in sf, and it is not absurd to compare it with that of Max Ernst (1891-1976), Salvador Dali (1904-1989) or René Magritte (1898-1967), all of whom are visible influences. Symbolic and dreamlike, his covers are often more evocative than the stories they illustrate. He received a Special Award at the World SF CONVENTION in Toronto in 1973. A book of his work ed Carlo Fruttero and Franco Lucentini was published in Italy, and the following year in Germany, where it was entitled *Visionen des Unwirklichen: Die phantastichen Bilder des Karel Thole* ["Visions of the Unreal: The Fantastic Paintings of Karel Thole"] (**1982**). [PN/JG]

THOMAS, CHAUNCEY (1822-1898) US author of a technocratic UTOPIA, *The Crystal Button, or Adventures of Paul Prognosis in the Forty-Ninth Century* (**1891**). The protagonist travels thence in a dream-state, learns how the peace is maintained through a rigorous and worldwide attachment to Truth, and, just as a comet destroys this idyllic civilization, returns to 19th-century Boston. [JC]

THOMAS, CRAIG (DAVID) (1942-   ) Welsh writer of TECHNOTHRILLERS, most interestingly the **Firefox** books – *Firefox* (**1977**) and *Firefox Down* (**1983**) – about a NEAR-FUTURE Russian fighter, the MIG-31, which boasts both anti-radar and weapons operated by thought waves. The former novel was filmed as FIREFOX (1982). *Moscow 5000* (**1979**), as by David Grant, and *Sea Leopard* (**1981**) have less sf import. [JC]

THOMAS, DAN Pseudonym of US writer Leonard M. Sanders Jr (1929-   ). In his sf novel *The Seed* (**1968**) a COMPUTER explains the meaning of life to one of its engineers. [JC]

THOMAS, D(ONALD) M(ICHAEL) (1935-   ) UK poet and novelist who made use of sf themes most explicitly in early POETRY like "The Head Rape" for *NW* in 1968. His *The Devil and the Floral Dance* (**1978**) is a juvenile fantasy. His first adult novels were densely conceived Freud-inspired FABULATIONS. *The Flute-Player* (**1979**), a fable that depicts the intertwining of art and love, is set in an imaginary state much like Russia (to which DMT often returns in his fiction, poetry and translations). *Birthstone* (**1980**; rev 1982) features a protagonist whose several personalities have autonomous lives, and whose fantasies leak into the world, transforming it. The most successful of

these tales is *The White Hotel* (**1981**), in which a graphic and surreal association in the protagonist's mind between sex and images of mass violence proves – long after a 1920s analysis by Freud himself – prophetic of the Final Solution; the book then becomes an extremely dark afterlife fantasy. The later **Ararat** sequence – *Ararat* (**1983**), *Swallow* (**1984**), *Sphinx* (**1986**) and *Summit* (**1987**) – adds futurity, politics and garish SATIRE to the generic mix; and seems, at times, to be sf. [JC]

THOMAS, G.K. ◊ L.P. DAVIES.

THOMAS, MARTIN Working name of UK writer Thomas Hector Martin (1913-1985) in a career that began just after the end of WWII; he also used the floating pseudonym Peter SAXON at least once during his association with W. Howard BAKER, for *The Curse of Rathlaw* (**1968** US) in the **Guardians** psychic-investigators series. His first novel, *The Evil Eye* (**1958**), was, like many of its successors, a routine occult tale. [JC]

Other works: *Bred to Kill* (**1960**); *Assignment Doomsday* (**1961**); *Beyond the Spectrum* (**1964**); *Laird of Evil* (**1965**); *The Mind Killers* (**1965**); *Such Men are Dangerous* (**1965**); *Sorcerers of Set* (**1966**), a contribution to the **Sexton Blake Library**; *The Hands of Cain* (**1966**; vt *The Hand of Cain* 1978 US); *Brainwashed* (**1968**).

THOMAS, THEODORE L. (1920-   ) US writer and lawyer, prolific in the magazines under his own name, sometimes rendered Ted Thomas, and as Leonard Lockhard, the pseudonym he used for his **Patent Attorney** spoof series (8 stories 1952-64), some of which were with Charles L. HARNESS. He began publishing sf in 1952 with 2 stories, "The Revisitor" for *Space Science Fiction* and "Improbable Profession" (as Lockhard) for *ASF*, and appeared frequently in the magazines until about 1980 with tales competently designed for their markets, the most effective perhaps being those, like "The Weather Man" (1962), set on a future Earth dominated by a Weather Control Board. With Kate WILHELM he wrote 2 novels, *The Clone* (**1959** *Fantastic* as by TLT alone; exp **1965**) and *The Year of the Cloud* (**1970**), both featuring unnatural DISASTERS. The eponymous menace in the first novel represents a rare use in sf of what is a CLONE in the strict biological sense. [JC]

See also: ECOLOGY; MONSTERS; ORIGIN OF MAN; POLLUTION; SUN; TIME TRAVEL.

THOMAS, THOMAS T(HURSTON) (1948-   ) US writer who began writing sf with *The Doomsday Effect* (**1986**), as by Thomas Wren, which won the Compton Crook Best First Novel AWARD. The novel describes – in terms that anticipated Greg BEAR's *The Forge of God* (**1987**) and David BRIN's *Earth* (**1990**) – the effect upon Earth of a rampaging BLACK HOLE. The narrative efficiency of the tale, and the briskly knowledgeable handling of scientific material, marked TTT as a HARD-SF writer of considerable potential. *First Citizen* (**1987**) is a NEAR-FUTURE tale mixing, in a typical hard-sf manner, POLITICS and ECONOMICS. *An Honorable Defense* * (**1988**) with David A. DRAKE, tied to the latter's **Crisis of Empire** sequence (each volume being essentially written by a different collaborator under Drake's supervision), is military sf, featuring a disgraced soldier who may be expected to save the Empire, which will then find that it has been in need of him. *The Mask of Loki* (**1990**) with Roger ZELAZNY is a fantasy set in the 13th and 21st centuries. *Me: A Novel of Self-Discovery* (**1991**) is sf, told from the point of view of the eponymous AI. *Crygender* (**1992**), with an anonymous collaborator, depicts the hermaphrodite owner of a bordello on Alcatraz Island, by now owned by a Japanese consortium. «Flare» (**1992**), again with Zelazny, describes with absorbed detail the effects of the short and violent life of a deadly solar flare. [JC]

See also: MEDICINE.

THOMPSON, EDWARD ◊ E.C. TUBB.

THOMPSON, E(DWARD) P(ALMER) (**1924-**) UK historian and writer, whose highly articulate Marxist interpretation of the last centuries of UK history is best expressed in *The Making of the English Working Class* (**1963**). His studies of William MORRIS – *William Morris: Romantic to Revolutionary* (**1955**) and *The Communism of William Morris* (**1965** chap) – are of sf interest, as is his only novel, *The Sykaos Papers: Being an Account of the Voyages of the Poet Oi Pas to the System of Strim . . .* (**1988**), a laboured SATIRE of Earth customs seen through the eyes of the poet Oi Pas, who comes from another planet. [JC]

THOMPSON, JOYCE (MARIE) (**1948-**) US writer, often of works for children. Her sf novel *Conscience Place* (**1984**) describes with quiet gravity an apparent UTOPIA hidden in the US West which is in fact populated by MUTANT nuclear-DISASTER victims. These people are threatened by the "need" of the scientists who maintain the refuge to perform GENETIC-ENGINEERING experiments on them. In telling this emotive tale, JT avoids almost all the traps of sentiment. [JC]

Other works: *The Blue Chair* (**1977**); *Harry and the Hendersons* * (**1987**; vt *Bigfoot and the Hendersons* 1987 UK), a tie based on the film HARRY AND THE HENDERSONS (**1987**); *East is West of Here: New & Selected Short Stories* (coll **1987**).

THOMPSON, VANCE (**1863-1925**) US writer in various genres whose *The Green Ray* (**1922-3** *Munsey's Magazine* as "The Man of the Miracle"; **1924**) is hoax rather than sf, except for some ambivalence surrounding a Black bleached White and unpleasantly made the basis of a racist denouement. [JC]

Other works: *The Carnival of Destiny* (**1916**); *The Scarlet Iris* (**1924**).

THOMSON, DAVID (**1941-**) UK writer long resident in the USA, best known for his nonfiction studies of film. His 2 novels of sf interest were also, in a sense, film studies. *Suspects* (**1985**) is a complex FABULATION, a portrait of a USA populated – or infiltrated – by a vast extended family of characters who, the premise argues, have featured at some point in their lives as protagonists in innumerable

films noirs from the period of Hollywood's prime and dark innocence; at the black heart of the tale sits the sinister figure of George Bailey, the character portrayed by James Stewart in Frank Capra's *It's a Wonderful Life* (**1946**). In *Warren Beatty: A Life and a Story* (**1987**; vt *Warren Beatty and Desert Eyes: A Life and a Story* 1987 US), chapters which examine the eponymous actor's real life alternate with chapters of a NEAR-FUTURE tale which dramatize the ideal life Beatty may be presumed to have indited upon the dream world of film. [JC]

THOR, TERRY [s] ◊ Larry T. SHAW.

THORNE, GUY Pseudonym of UK journalist and writer Cyril Arthur Edward Ranger-Gull (**1874-1923**); he also wrote speculative fiction as Ranger Gull. His most successful work was the alarmist and antisemitic *When It Was Dark* (**1903**), in which faked "scientific evidence" that Christ's resurrection never took place sends the Christian world into a catastrophic crisis of demoralization. His later fantasies, stridently championing Christianity, include several with borderline-sf elements. In *Made in His Image* (**1906**) a bleak futuristic world is redeemed by Christian belief, and in *The Angel* (**1908**) and *And it Came to Pass* (**1915**) miracle-working emissaries from God help show modern mortals the error of their ways. Other borderline-sf stories signed GT include 2 stories of near-future WAR, *The Secret Sea-Plane* (**1915**) and *The Secret Monitor* (**1918**), and a story of artificially induced DISASTERS, *When the World Reeled* (**1924**). Books signed Ranger Gull include 3 fairly conventional thrillers – *The Soul-Stealer* (**1906**), *The Enemies of England* (**1915**) and *The Air Pirate* (**1919**) – as well as the most ambitious of his sf novels, *The City in the Clouds* (**1921**), about an airborne pleasure-palace afloat over London. The detective novel *Black Honey* (**1913**), signed C. Ranger-Gull, has some borderline-sf elements. Other novels with fantasy elements include the detective story *Doris Moore* (**1919**), the mesmeric fantasy *The House of Danger* (**1920**), *The Love Hater* (**1921**) and *The Dark Dominion* (**1923**). His translations from the French include *Charles Baudelaire: His Life* (**1868** France; trans **1915** UK) by Théophile Gautier (**1811-1872**), with added material. The latter part of GT's life was spent in a remote seaside cottage later rented by Neil BELL – where, Bell learned, GT's behaviour had scandalized the local population. [BS]

Other work: *Lucky Mr Loder* (**1918**), a fantasy.

See also: HISTORY OF SF; MESSIAHS; RELIGION.

THORNE, IAN ◊ Julian MAY.

THORNTON, HALL [s] ◊ Robert SILVERBERG.

THORPE, FRED Pseudonym of Albert Stearns (**?   -1899**), US dime novelist and author of 2 popular children's books based on the Arabian Nights, *Chris and the Wonderful Lamp* (**1895**) and *Sindbad, Smith and Co* (**1896**). He wrote many kinds of dime novel (◊ DIME-NOVEL SF), but was best known for marvel stories written on an almost ABSURDIST level. His most popular was "The Silent City" (**1892** *Golden Hours*), about adventures in a Fata Morgana city seen over the Bering Sea. *The Boy in Black* (1894 *Golden Hours*; **1907**) describes a weird, irrational supercivilization inside a Western mountain. "In the World Below" (1897 *Golden Hours*) anticipates Edgar Rice BUR-ROUGHS's **Pellucidar** with adventures in a HOLLOW EARTH after an earth-borer goes out of control.   [EFB]

THORPE, TREBOR ◊ R.L. FANTHORPE.

THOUSAND EYES OF DR MABUSE, THE ◊ *Die* TAUSEND AUGEN DES DR MABUSE.

THREADS Made-for-tv film (1984). BBC-TV. Dir Mick Jackson, starring Karen Meagher, Reece Dinsdale, June Broughton, Henry Moxon, Sylvia Stoker, David Brierly. Screenplay Barry Hines. 115 mins. Colour.

This BBC production, at once a UK equivalent of *The* DAY AFTER (1983) and an attempt to update the harrowing vision of Peter WATKINS's *The* WAR GAME (1965), is an impressive and persuasive account of a near-future nuclear attack on the UK, focusing on the fate of Sheffield. Ordinary people are seen ignoring the escalating international crisis as they deal with their own problems – the heroine (Meagher) is a pregnant young girl unsure whether or not to marry – and are then shattered completely by the coming of war. The civil-defence forces cannot deal with the extent of the calamity, and traffic wardens are drafted to supervise summary executions of looters. The film mimics *The War Game*'s documentary approach as it trots out disturbing statistics. Finally, it flashes forward a few years to show a medievalized post-HOLOCAUST UK, brutal and tribalized, bringing this resolutely non-sf treatment of an sf theme surprisingly close to the surreal horrors of *Le* DERNIER COMBAT (1983).   [KN]

THRILL BOOK US magazine in the larger, saddle-stapled DIME-NOVEL format for 8 issues, then PULP-MAGAZINE size. 16 issues, 2 per month, 1 Mar-15 Oct 1919, published by STREET & SMITH; ed Harold HERSEY (Mar-June 1919) and Ronald Oliphant (July-Oct 1919). The legendarily rare *TB* is often cited as the first SF MAGAZINE, but its initial 8 issues contained no sf, rather stories intended to provide "thrills" of an occult or weird sort. Only after Oliphant became editor did *TB* regularly publish sf stories, including 2 by Murray LEINSTER (one involving a mad inventor, the other a biological menace). Others included: an H.G. WELLS-inspired story of INVISIBILITY by Greye La Spina (1880-1969); a Sax ROHMER-inspired Chinese supervillain whose inventions include a device for creating black light in "Mr Shen of Shensi" by H. BEDFORD-JONES; and the satirical "The Man from Thebes", featuring a reanimated mummy, by William Wallace COOK. Additional sf by less notable authors treated routinely such sf/HORROR motifs as devices to communicate with the dead, drugs that distort the time-sense, men protected by invisible armour, and LOST WORLDS. *TB*'s most famous story was *The Heads of Cerberus* (Aug-Oct 1919; **1952**) by Francis STEVENS, a SCIENCE-FANTASY adventure set predominantly in a Philadelphia located in an alternate time-track. The

definitive work on *TB* is Richard BLEILER's obsessively thorough *The Annotated Index to The Thrill Book* (chap **1991**).   [RB]

THRILLING SCIENCE FICTION ◊ *The* MOST THRILLING SCIENCE FICTION EVER TOLD.

THRILLING SCIENCE FICTION ADVENTURES ◊ *The* MOST THRILLING SCIENCE FICTION EVER TOLD.

THRILLING WONDER STORIES US PULP MAGAZINE. 111 issues Aug 1936-winter 1955. Published by Beacon Magazines, Aug 1936-June 1937; by Better Publications Oct 1937-Aug 1943; and by Standard Magazines Fall 1943-Winter 1955. Ed Mort WEISINGER (Aug 1936-June 1941), Oscar J. FRIEND (Aug 1941-Fall 1944), Sam MERWIN Jr (Winter 1945-Oct 1951), Samuel MINES (Dec 1951-Summer 1954) and Alexander SAMALMAN (Fall 1954-Winter 1955). Leo MARGULIES was editorial director during Weisinger's and Friend's editorships. *TWS* began as a regular bimonthly and changed to monthly Dec 1939-Apr 1941, then back to bimonthly June 1941-Aug 1943. A quarterly schedule followed, Fall 1943-Fall 1946; then bimonthly Dec 1946-Aug 1953. The last 6 issues ran Nov 1953, Winter 1954, Spring 1954, Summer 1954, Fall 1954, Winter 1955.

TWS was the continuation, after a brief gap, of Hugo GERNSBACK's WONDER STORIES; the adjective "Thrilling" was added to the title to bring it into conformity with other magazines from its new publisher. The issue numeration continued from *Wonder Stories*, Aug 1936 being vol 8 #1, so there might be a case for regarding it as the same magazine. However, its personality changed. The new magazine was far more garish than its predecessor. The early covers, by Howard V. BROWN, are said to have been responsible for the coinage of the term "Bug-Eyed Monsters" (or BEMS), such creatures being a regular feature of his painting, along with giant dinosaurs, insects and men. The first 8 issues featured an early sf comic strip (**Zarnak** by Max Plaisted) which was abruptly suspended in mid-plot after the Oct 1937 number. *TWS*'s contributors were mostly second-string authors: Eando BINDER, Frederick Arnold Kummer (?1912-   ), Arthur Leo ZAGAT and others. It ran a number of popular series, notably John W. CAMPBELL Jr's **Penton and Blake** stories, Arthur K. BARNES's **Gerry Carlyle** stories and the **Hollywood on the Moon** series by prolific contributor Henry KUTTNER. An amateur writers' contest sponsored by the magazine was won by Alfred BESTER with his first story, "The Broken Axiom" (Apr 1939). *TWS* was successful enough to generate 2 companion magazines: STARTLING STORIES, in Jan 1939, and STRANGE STORIES, featuring mostly weird fiction, in Feb 1939. *Startling* featured longer stories (a complete novel in each issue, when possible) and soon became the better magazine. In mid-1940 *TWS* also began to proclaim a "complete novel" in most issues, but in actuality the majority of these were no more than long novelettes. During this boom period a third companion, CAPTAIN FUTURE, was initiated, and for a little over a year *TWS* changed from its habitual bimonthly schedule and appeared monthly. Earle K. BERGEY succeeded Brown as cover artist with the Sep 1940, issue and was responsible for most subsequent covers; his paintings switched the emphasis from the BEM to the scantily clad lady being threatened by it. *TWS* became more overtly juvenile in the early 1940s with the introduction of **Sergeant Saturn** (◊ STARTLING STORIES).

When Merwin became editor he did away with the magazine's juvenile trappings and considerably improved it, although it remained evidently secondary to *Startling*. It published further noteworthy stories, including many from Murray LEINSTER, and some "novels" genuinely of novel length: A.E. VAN VOGT's *The Weapon Shops of Isher* (Feb 1949; fixup **1951**), James BLISH's *Jack of Eagles* (Dec 1949 as "Let the Finder Beware"; rev **1952**; vt *ESP-er*) and Leigh BRACKETT's *Sword of Rhiannon* (June 1949 as "Sea-Kings of Mars"; **1953**). Ray BRADBURY, whose first solo short story appeared in *TWS* in 1943, was a regular contributor, as was Jack VANCE, who also made his début in its pages. Vance's **Magnus Ridolph** series and Kuttner's **Hogben** stories were popular features of the Merwin *TWS*.

Although the magazine acquired more companions in the boom of the early 1950s – *Fantastic Story Magazine* (◊ FANTASTIC STORY QUARTERLY) and SPACE STORIES – it soon began to suffer in the general decline of the pulp-magazine industry. Changes in editor had little effect, Mines maintaining, approximately, the standard of Merwin's *TWS*; he published Philip José FARMER's celebrated TABOO-breaking "Mother" (Apr 1953). The last issue of *TWS* appeared in Winter 1955, after which the magazine's title (along with that of *Fantastic Story Magazine*) was absorbed into *Startling* for that magazine's last 3 issues.

2 issues of a reprint magazine, *Wonder Stories*, revived the old title and continued the *TWS* numeration (◊ WONDER STORIES). 2 UK edns appeared for short periods, both heavily cut from the original: Atlas Publishing produced 10 numbered issues (3 in 1949-50, 7 in 1952-3); Pemberton published a further 4, numbered #101-#104, in 1953-4. A Canadian reprint ran 1945-6 and again 1948-51. [MJE]

THRILLS INCORPORATED Australian magazine, PULP-MAGAZINE format #1-#5, BEDSHEET format #6-#12, DIGEST format #13-#23, numbered, undated, mostly monthly Mar 1950-June 1952, published by Associated General Publications, Sydney, company name changed to Transport Publications from #13; mostly ed (uncredited) by Alister Innes. *TI* was intended for children. Although US reprints as such were not used, plagiarism did occur without the publishers' knowledge. These (with new titles, but originally by Ray BRADBURY, Charles L. HARNESS, Clifford D. SIMAK, William TENN and others) were the only good stories printed, although Alan YATES cowrote some tales with G.C. Bleeck. Some stories were reprinted in the UK AMAZING SCIENCE STORIES. [FHP/PN]

THRUST US SEMIPROZINE, originally a FANZINE, advertised as quarterly but in the past often irregular; ed D. Douglas Fratz, #1 Jan 1973 as magazine of the Maryland Science Fiction Society; it became independent 1977, at which time Fratz stopped publishing fiction and established the blend of interviews, articles and reviews, emphasizing controversy and argument, which has continued since. Always one of the solider journals of commentary on sf and fantasy, and one of the longest-lasting, *T* has been 4 times nominated for a HUGO (1980, 1988, 1989, 1990). Beginning with #36, Spring 1990, *T* changed its name to *Quantum: Science Fiction and Fantasy Review* without major changes to style or format; and in #42, Summer/ Fall 1992, Fratz announced that the magazine would end with #43. Writers associated with *T* have included Michael BISHOP, George Alec EFFINGER, Darrell SCHWEITZER and Ted WHITE. [PN]

THUNDERBIRDS UK animated-puppet tv series (1965-6). An AP Films Production for ATV/ITC. Created Sylvia and Gerry Anderson. Prod Gerry Anderson (season 1), Reg Hill (season 2). Writers included Dennis Spooner, Alan Fennell, Alan Pattillo. Dirs included David Lane, David Elliott, Desmond Saunders, Pattillo. Model effects supervised by Derek Meddings. 2 seasons, 32 50min episodes. Colour.

This animated puppet series for children was one of the most elaborate (and perhaps the best-loved) of all such Gerry and Sylvia ANDERSON productions, and the first designed for a 1hr timeslot. The 4th of their **SuperMarionation** shows to be sf, it involved International Rescue: based on a secret Pacific Island, this was a future air-, space- and undersea-rescue service which utilized a variety of spectacular vehicles (a spaceship, a submersible and a heavily armed pink Rolls Royce among them) and was run by the Tracy family with the help of Lady Penelope, their glamorous London assistant, Parker, her Cockney chauffeur, and Brains, a stuttering bespectacled genius. 2 feature-film spin-offs, also with animated puppets, were *Thunderbirds Are Go* (1966) and *Thunderbird Six* (1968). [PN/JB]

THUNDERBIRDS ARE GO ◊ THUNDERBIRDS.

THUNDERBIRD SIX ◊ THUNDERBIRDS.

THURSTON, ROBERT (DONALD) (1936-   ) US writer who published his first story, "Stop Me before I Tell More", in *Orbit 9* (anth **1971**) ed Damon KNIGHT, and who was for some years known only for his short work. This is notable more for its examination of individual humans caught in social or sexual extremis than for any specific extrapolative bent, so that moments of genuine insight or threat tend to be lost in weak plotting. His first novel, *Alicia II* (**1978**), exemplifies this problem, introducing an interesting existential problem (the brain of an old man is implanted into the body of a young "retread" and the new amalgam must come to terms with the kind of society which legitimizes this obscene method of attaining longevity for a few) but foundering in the telling, which confusedly leads the protagonist into improbable PULP-MAGAZINE adventures. RT's second independent novel, *A Set of Wheels* (**1983**), shows the same difficulty, but his third, *Q Colony* (in *The Berkley Showcase 4* [anth **1981**] ed John W. SILBERSACK and Victoria Schochet as "The Oonaa Woman"; exp **1985**), set in a research station on an ALIEN planet whose inhabitants can interbreed with humans, explores his usual material – sex and identity – with greater aplomb.

It may be, however, that RT will remain best known for a series of ties, the most significant being his contributions to the **Battlestar Galactica** sequence, all with Glen A. LARSON: *Battlestar Galactica* * (**1978**), #2: *The Cylon Death Machine**(**1979**), #3: *The Tombs of Kobol** (**1979**), #4. *The Young Warriors* * (**1980**), #11: *The Nightmare Machine* * (**1985**), #12: *"Die, Chameleon!"* * (**1986**), #13: *Apollo's War* * (**1987**) and #14: *Surrender the Galactica!* * (**1987**). His sequence of **BattleTech** ties begins with *Legend of the Jade Phoenix #1: Way of the Clans* * (**1991**), #2: *Bloodname* * (**1991**) and #3: *Falcon Guard* * (**1991**). Singleton ties include *Robot Jox* * (**1989**), based on a screenplay by Joe HALDEMAN (◊ ROBOT JOX), and *Isaac Asimov's Robot City: Robots and Aliens #3: Intruder* * (**1990**). [JC]

See also: GAMES AND SPORTS; REINCARNATION.

THX 1138 Film (1971). American Zoetrope/Warner Bros. Dir George LUCAS, starring Robert Duvall, Donald Pleasence, Maggie McOmie. Screenplay Lucas, Walter Murch, from a story by Lucas. 88 mins, restored to 95 mins. Colour.

A subterranean future society is governed repressively by COMPUTERS and bland human technocrats who keep the population under control with drugs. Everyone wears white clothing, heads are shaven, and sexual intercourse is forbidden (breeding is by artificial insemination) – it is a truly sterile, antiseptic world. One of the few dissenters is THX (Duvall), who experiments with sex; his cellmate becomes pregnant and is liquidated. THX is imprisoned in a White Limbo but escapes and reaches the surface and freedom. It is an old and familiar story to sf readers, but Lucas presents it with panache. He begins with apparently unrelated visual fragments, accompanied by snatches of dialogue, all of which gradually coalesce to form a comprehensive DYSTOPIAN nightmare, visually impressive but not lavish, with a bleak sense of style and a drily witty script.

THX 1138, though a small masterpiece, failed commercially – unsurprisingly since it is both difficult and downbeat; it did a little better when released again after the success of Lucas's STAR WARS (1977) with some footage originally excised by a worried Warner Bros. restored. The novelization is *THX 1138* * (**1971**) by Ben BOVA. [JB/PN]

TIDAL WAVE ◊ NIPPON CHINBOTSU.

TIDYMAN, ERNEST (1928-1984) US journalist, novelist and screenwriter, author of the **Shaft** series of books about a Black detective, and of scripts for the **Shaft** movies, *The French Connection* (1971) and the

supernatural Western *High Plains Drifter* (1973), among others. His sf novel, *Absolute Zero* (**1971**), is a NEAR-FUTURE thriller whose protagonist becomes involved in CRYONICS in an attempt to preserve his accidentally frozen dwarf parents. [JC]

TIE A term used in this encyclopedia to designate a work whose subject matter is tied to a previous work or concept. In some respects, therefore, a tie clearly resembles a sequel. However, ties can be differentiated from sequels in two ways: first, a tie is generally written to occupy a different format or genre than the work which inspires it – novelizations are, for instance, often spun off from films, an example being *The Sensitives* * (**1968**), Louis CHARBONNEAU's novelization of a script written by Deane ROMANO – and, second, a tie is almost always written by some person other than the author or creator of the original work or concept. Ties can be spun off, therefore, from almost any kind of source: from stories, novels, series, comics, films, tv series, BRAIDS and other SHARED-WORLD enterprises, GAMES AND TOYS, or concepts put out for hire by packagers like Byron PREISS.

The first ties were almost certainly shared-world anthologies like *Mugby Junction* * (anth **1866** chap), ed Charles DICKENS as a special Christmas Number of his journal *All the Year Round*; and film novelizations can be found from before WWI, though most books-of-the-film, until at least 1950, were in fact simple reprintings of the original novel, sometimes with movie stills inserted. With the increasing commodification of sf in the 1980s, ties suddenly became very common, and were often found in conjunction with sharecropping activities. Ties can be distinguished from SHARECROPS by the fact that ties are defined by their relationship to the source of their inspiration, while sharecrops – though they usually involve ties – are, strictly speaking, works of any sort written for hire.

The most interesting tied enterprises in the 1980s and 1990s are probably shared-world anthologies like George R.R. MARTIN's WILD CARDS sequence from 1987 and the **War World** books ed from 1988 by Jerry POURNELLE, John F. CARR and Roland J. GREEN; but works of interest can be found through the whole range of the phenomenon.

In this encyclopedia ties are signalled by an asterisk placed between the title and the date of the work. [JC]

TILLEY, PATRICK (1928-   ) UK writer whose first sf novel, *Fade-Out* (**1975**), after the fashion of borderline works like *Fail-Safe* (**1962**) by Eugene BURDICK and Harvey WHEELER, concentrates long-windedly on the workings of government and military in a TECHNO-THRILLER context, in this instance displaced sf-wards by the fact that the action is occasioned by an ALIEN landing which damps out all electrical impulses (◊ UFOS). In *Mission* (**1981**) Christ returns to contemporary New York, bearing with him the news that His crucifixion was one small event in a long SPACE-OPERA conflict between the Ain-folk and the evil Brax. The **Amtrak Wars** sequence – *The Amtrak Wars #1:*

Cloud Warrior (**1983**), *#2: First Family* (**1985**), *#3: Iron Master* (**1987**), *#4: Blood River* (**1988**), *#5: Death Bringer* (**1989**) and *#6: Earth-Thunder* (**1990**) – more vividly set primitive Mutes against the blindly technocratic Amtrak Federation in a post-HOLOCAUST USA; as the sequence develops, the geopolitical realities governing the land become increasingly complex and the fulfilment of the revelatory Talisman Prophecy – though constantly deferred – gives succeeding books an increasing momentum. *Dark Visions: An Illustrated Guide to the Amtrak Wars* (**1984** chap), with Fernando Fernandez, provides a useful orientation. The sequence, clearly incomplete at the end of *#6*, was one of the most compelling sf-adventure series of the decade. [JC]

Other work: *Xan* (**1986**), horror.

TILLYARD, AELFRIDA (CATHERINE WETENHALL) (1883-?   ) UK writer first known for editing *Cambridge Poets 1910-1913* (anth **1913**), but perhaps best remembered for her 2 sf novels. Set after a series of HOLOCAUSTS, *Concrete: A Story of Two Hundred Years Hence* (**1930**) contrasts an irreligious DYSTOPIA, which holds under its sway most of the civilized world, with a pious island UTOPIA; there is much action. Interestingly, one of the rulers of the dystopia, the head of the Ministry of Reason, goes by the name of Big Brother. *The Approaching Storm* (**1932**) more conventionally posits a left-wing dictatorship in the UK. [JC]

TILMS, RICHARD A. ◊ John T. SLADEK.

TIME AFTER TIME Film (1979). Orion/Warner Bros. Dir Nicholas Meyer, starring Malcom McDowell, David Warner, Mary Steenburgen. Screenplay Meyer, from a story by Karl Alexander, Steve Hayes, based on *Time After Time* (**1976**) by Alexander. 112 mins. Colour.

Dr Stevenson (Warner), whom we soon learn to be Jack the Ripper, eludes police by stealing the TIME MACHINE from H.G. WELLS (McDowell) in 1893, and travelling to San Francisco in 1979. The machine, however, returns, and Wells uses it to pursue the criminal. There are some good moments in this ingenious movie, with Wells as the alien naïf amazed and baffled by the world of the future (which he had expected to be utopian), though the mad, affectless Ripper finds its violence and sleaziness precisely to his taste. But the view, presented rather labouredly by the film, that 1979 is a period of unparalleled cruelty (and that Wells could not cope with it), is conceptually tawdry. Steenburgen is charming as Amy, the not-quite-liberated bank clerk who falls for Wells, though anybody knowing anything of Wells' real private life will be astonished to learn that he took Amy back to his own time and they lived happily ever after as Mr and Mrs Wells! [PN]

TIME MACHINE One of the early key items of sf TERMINOLOGY, first used by H.G. WELLS in the title of *The Time Machine* (**1895**). It is, of course, a machine used for TIME TRAVEL. [PN]

TIME MACHINE, THE Film (1960). Galaxy Films/ MGM. Prod/dir George PAL, starring Rod Taylor, Alan Young, Yvette Mimieux, Sebastian Cabot. Screenplay David DUNCAN, based on *The Time Machine* (**1895**) by H.G. WELLS. 103 mins. Colour.

Unlike Pal's WAR OF THE WORLDS (1953), *TTM* is set in the Victorian era – at least at the beginning of the film – and it is these sequences, with the inventor demonstrating his creation to his disbelieving friends amid the Victorian bric-à-brac of their cosy world, that work the best. After a visually interesting journey through time (special effects by Wah Chang and Gene Warren), pausing occasionally – for example, to note the nuclear bombardment of London in 1966 – the film reduces Wells's angry parable to a Hollywood sf formula. The parallels between the troglodytic Morlocks and the Victorian working class and between the beautiful but thoughtless Eloi and the Victorian upper class are lost. The Time Traveller becomes a confident, romantic hero, successfully rousing the Eloi to battle against their ape-like devourers. The disturbing evolutionary perspectives of the end of Wells's book are also missing. William Ferrari's charming design for the TIME MACHINE does not compensate for the vulgarization of the story. [JB/PN]

TIME PARADOXES The fact that TIME TRAVEL into the past disrupts the pattern of causality, changing or cancelling matters of known fact, has not caused stories of this kind to be banished from the sf field; instead it has led to the growth of a subgenre of stories celebrating the peculiar aesthetics of such paradoxes. The essential paradoxicality of time travel is often dramatized by asking: "What would happen if I went back in time and killed my own grandfather?" – a question to which sf writers have provided many different answers. A time-paradox story usually leads either to a singularly appropriate *reductio ad absurdum* or to a cunning literary move which appears to resolve the paradox by removing or avoiding the seemingly inevitable contradiction. F. ANSTEY's pioneering fantasy *The Time Bargain* (**1891**; vt *Tourmalin's Time Cheques*) provided a prototype for the first kind of story; Fritz LEIBER's "Try and Change the Past" (1958) is a good example of the latter. Sf writers frequently invoke sweeping metaphysical hypotheses in the cause of accommodating potential paradoxes; Alfred BESTER's "The Men who Murdered Mohammed" (1958) does so by providing every individual with his or her own personal continuum. There are several notable stories and series about "time police" who try to protect the world – or, more often, a whole series of ALTERNATE WORLDS – from temporal upset. Poul ANDERSON's Time Patrol series, Isaac ASIMOV's *The End of Eternity* (**1955**) and John BRUNNER's *Times without Number* (fixup **1962**; rev **1974**) are among the most notable of these.

The closed loop in time, in which an event becomes its own cause, is the simplest narrative form of the time-paradox story, seized upon by several of the contestants invited by the editor of AMAZING STORIES to find a clever ending for Ralph Milne FARLEY's "The

Time-Wise Guy" (1940). More notable examples include Ross ROCKLYNNE's "Time Wants a Skeleton" (1941), Bester's "The Push of a Finger" (1942), P. Schuyler MILLER's "As Never Was" (1944), Murray LEINSTER's "The Gadget had a Ghost" (1952) and Mack REYNOLDS's "Compounded Interest" (1956). Greater ingenuity is exercised when these loops become more complicated, forming convoluted sealed knots. Two classic exercises in this vein were written by Robert A. HEINLEIN: "By His Bootstraps" (1941) as by Anson MacDonald and "All You Zombies . . ." (1959), the latter being a story whose central character moves back and forth in time and undergoes a sex-change in order to become his own mother and father.

The second fundamental variant of the time-paradox story is that in which the present from which the time-travellers start is replaced by an alternative because of the effect (often trivial and unintended) which they have had upon the past. Nat SCHACHNER's "Ancestral Voices" (1933) is an early story which uses such a device to expose the absurdities of ancestor-worship and racism, but the best known example is Ray BRADBURY's moral fable "A Sound of Thunder" (1952), in which a time-tourist who treads on a prehistoric butterfly alters the POLITICS of the present for the worse. Eando BINDER's "The Time-Cheaters" (1940) suggests that time might have stubbornly ingenious ways of taking care of such threatened contradictions, and William TENN's "Brooklyn Project" (1948) points out that observers who change with the world would not notice such alterations, however drastic they became. In many stories the good intentions of would-be history-changers go sadly and ironically awry. L. Sprague DE CAMP's "Aristotle and the Gun" (1958) is a fine example; others are Poul Anderson's "The Man who Came Early" (1956) and Kirk MITCHELL's Never the Twain (**1987**). Works in which such ideas are further extrapolated and intensively recomplicated tend to feature wars fought through time by the representatives of alternate worlds ambitious to demolish their competitors. Jack WILLIAMSON's The Legion of Time (1938 ASF; **1961**) opened up such imaginative territory for further exploration in Fritz Leiber's **Change War** series and Barrington J. BAYLEY's spectacular The Fall of Chronopolis (**1974**); the long **Timewars** series by Simon Hawke (Nicholas YERMAKOV) of exuberantly extravagant stories in this vein, begun with The Ivanhoe Gambit (**1984**), is still continuing.

The potential which time-travellers have to exist twice in the same time is considered so uniquely unreasonable as to be specifically proscribed in stories like Wilson TUCKER's The Lincoln Hunters (**1957**), where the restriction opens up potential for ingenious plotting, as it does also in John VARLEY's elaborate paradox-avoidance story Millennium (**1983**). However, other writers – including such non-genre writers as Osbert SITWELL in The Man who Lost Himself (**1929**) and Eliot Crawshay-Williams (1879-1962) in "The Man who Met Himself" (1947) – have been particularly intrigued by the possible psychological effects of a person's meeting with a later version of his or her own self. Ralph Milne FARLEY's "The Man who Met Himself" (1935) is an early example from the sf PULP MAGAZINES. Later sf writers have casually extended this notion to its absurd limits, displayed by Barry N. MALZBERG in "We're Coming Through the Window" (1967) and David GERROLD in The Man who Folded Himself (**1973**), the latter being a notable if silly story which conscientiously attempts to compile a narrative portmanteau of all possible time paradoxes.

Sf writers who have made particularly prolific and ingenious use of time-paradox plots include Charles L. HARNESS, whose many works in this vein extend from the early "Time Trap" (1948) and "Stalemate in Space" (1949; vt "Stalemate in Time") to Krono (**1988**) and Lurid Dreams (**1990**), and Robert SILVERBERG, whose even more numerous contributions range from the early "Hopper" (1956 Infinity; exp as The Time-Hoppers **1967**) and Stepsons of Terra (**1958**) through the convoluted Up the Line (**1969**) to the neat "Many Mansions" (1973) and the smooth "The Far Side of the Bell-Shaped Curve" (1982).

The time-paradox story may have posed an attractive challenge to sf writers but it has also been something of a wasting asset. All the elementary changes have been rung, and it now requires considerable cunning to find a new twist or even to redeploy an old one in more pointed or poignant fashion. Nevertheless, there still remains a good deal of life in the subgenre: Bob SHAW's Who Goes Here? (**1977**) slickly exploits the comic potential of the theme; Hilbert SCHENCK's A Rose for Armageddon (**1982**) is a brilliantly recomplicated timeslip romance; Walter Jon WILLIAMS's Days of Atonement (**1991**) interrelates time paradox and quantum physics; and John CROWLEY's Great Work of Time (1989 in coll Novelty; **1991**) cleverly recombines several well worn themes to striking quasi-surreal effect.　　　　　　　[MJE/BS]

TIMERIDER: THE ADVENTURES OF LYLE SWANN Film (1983). Zoomo Productions/Jensen Farley Pictures. Dir William Dear, starring Fred Ward, Belinda Bauer, Peter Coyote, Ed Lauter, L.Q. Jones. Screenplay Dear, Michael Nesmith. 92 mins. Colour.

This TIME-TRAVEL Western prefigures the more successful BACK TO THE FUTURE PART III (1989) in its juxtaposition of 20th-century technology and the generic conventions associated with tales of the 19th century. Motorcycle ace Lyle Swann (Ward) blunders into a time-travel experiment and is zapped back to the Old West, where he tangles with outlaw varmint Peter Coyote, terrifies the superstitious Mexicans and romances Belinda Bauer so that he can turn out to be his own great grandfather. Despite the amiable cast and pleasant scenery, the film, like its hero, does little but ride around in circles in the desert. Nesmith, the co-screenwriter, ex-member of the pop group The Monkees, went on to produce Alex Cox's REPO MAN (1984).　　　　　　　[KN]

TIMESCAPE BOOKS US sf publishing imprint,

issuing both hardcover and paperback, whose logo first appeared in Mar 1981 and whose last titles were published in 1984. TB was formed by Simon & Schuster and Pocket Books (owned by the former), for both of whom David G. HARTWELL had been director of sf, and he was set in charge of the new imprint. It was named after the resonant title of Gregory BENFORD's successful novel *Timescape* (**1980**), which had been published by Simon & Schuster; Benford was paid a licensing fee, and published 2 books – *Against Infinity* (**1983**) and *Across the Sea of Suns* (**1984**) – with the imprint. TB was prestigious and influential. However, despite publishing good books which won awards, it did not produce bestsellers, was hit by the economic downturn of the early 1980s, and soon folded. There is an argument over whether Hartwell chose the wrong books or if publicity and packaging were inadequate. TB publications included many books of somewhat literary sf and fantasy, such as Philip K. DICK's *The Divine Invasion* (**1981**), John M. FORD's *The Dragon Waiting* (**1983**), Lisa GOLDSTEIN's *The Red Magician* (**1982**), which won a National Book Award, Nancy KRESS's *The Prince of Morning Bells* (**1981**), Frederik POHL's *The Years of the City* (**1984**), Hilbert SCHENCK's *A Rose for Armageddon* (**1982**) and Gene WOLFE's **Book of the New Sun** tetralogy (**1980-83**). TB NEBULA winners were *The Claw of the Conciliator* (**1981**) by Wolfe and *No Enemy But Time* (**1982**) by Michael BISHOP; as Benford's *Timescape* had won in 1981, TB effectively scooped the Nebula pool 3 years running. With hindsight, the story of TB can be seen as a moral fable of central importance in the history of US sf publishing, which has certainly been – in the main – a more cynical business since TB's demise. [PN]

TIMESLIP (vt *The Atomic Man* US) Film (1956). Merton Park/Allied Artists. Dir Ken Hughes, starring Gene Nelson, Faith Domergue, Peter Arne, Vic Perry. Screenplay Charles Eric MAINE. 93 mins, cut to 76 mins US. B/w.

Undistinguished UK thriller whose sf concept is that an atomic scientist, who temporarily died for 7½ seconds on the operating table while a bullet was being dug out of his back, now lives mentally exactly 7½ seconds in the future. The sf implications are mostly left unexplored in what is essentially a hard-bitten-reporter-investigating-crime story. The same notion was later treated more intensively by Brian W. ALDISS in "Man in his Time" (1965) and by Eric BROWN in "The Time-Lapsed Man" (1988). Maine's *The Isotope Man* * (**1957**) was based on his script. [PN]

TIME SLIP ◊ SENGOKU JIETAI.

TIME TRACKERS ◊ Roger CORMAN.

TIME TRAVEL It is a great literary convenience to be able to move a narrative viewpoint backwards or forwards in time, and writers have always been prepared to use whatever narrative devices come to hand for this purpose. Until the end of the last century dreams were the favoured method – perhaps most significantly deployed in Charles DICKENS's *A*

Christmas Carol (**1843**) and Edgar Allan POE's "A Tale of the Ragged Mountains" (**1844**) – although entirely arbitrary timeslips were also used, while characters could be brought from the past into our own time via various SUSPENDED-ANIMATION devices, including CRYONIC preservation, extended sleep and drugs, as in Grant ALLEN's "Pausodyne" (1881). H.G. WELLS's *The Time Machine* (**1895**) was a crucial breakthrough in narrative technology, providing sf with one of its most significant facilitating devices, ultimately used in this instance to survey the kind of FAR FUTURE and END OF THE WORLD prophesied (erroneously) by contemporary scientific knowledge. The idea of employing a hypothetical MACHINE as a literary device, using a jargon of apology to add plausibility, was not entirely new, but this particular deployment of it was so striking as to constitute a historical break and a great inspiration. Oddly enough, Wells never again used such a device, leaving its further exploitation to others. The earliest writers to take up the challenge included Alfred JARRY in his classic essay in 'pataphysics, "How to Construct a Time Machine" (1899); the anonymous "A Disciple" (of Wells), who borrowed the machine in order to explore *The Coming Era, or Leeds Beatified* (**1900**); and H.S. MACKAYE, whose eponymous time machine in *The Panchronicon* (**1904**) is unashamedly ludicrous. Most UK writers of SCIENTIFIC ROMANCE, however, continued to prefer visionary fantasy as a method of time-exploration – E.V. ODLE's *The Clockwork Man*, (**1923**) is one honourable exception – and it was left to the US pulp writers to show what really might be done with time machines if one had the imaginative daring to employ them. Even the pulp writers remained relatively modest in their time-jaunting until the 1920s, although William Wallace COOK's *A Round Trip to the Year 2000* (1903 *Argosy*; **1925**) deals sarcastically with the accumulation of time-travellers to be expected in the magical millennial year.

MAINSTREAM WRITERS who found literary dreams becoming increasingly unfashionable had more and more recourse to arbitrary timeslips, and there is a curious subgenre of "timeslip romances" whose affective power is very often concentrated into love stories, although the real emotional substrate is nostalgia. "Arria Marcella" (1852) by Théophile Gautier (1811-1872), although its timeslip is "rationalized" as a visionary fantasy, provides an archetypal example of the peculiarly heated eroticism with which such stories are sometimes endowed. Henry James (1843-1916) spent the last few years of his life working on *The Sense of the Past* (**1917**), but left it incomplete; it inspired the play *Berkeley Square* (**1929**) by J.L. Balderston and J.C. Squire (1884-1958) which was memorably filmed in 1933. Other notable timeslip romances include *Still She Wished for Company* (**1924**) by Margaret Irwin (1889-1967), *The Man in Steel* (**1939**) by J. Storer CLOUSTON, *Portrait of Jennie* (**1940**) by Robert NATHAN, *Time Marches Sideways* (**1950**) by Ralph L. FINN, *Time and Again* (**1970**) by Jack FINNEY,

Bid Time Return (**1975**) by Richard MATHESON, *The Dream Years* (**1986**) by Lisa GOLDSTEIN and *Serenissima* (**1987**) by Erica JONG. "Psychological timeslips", by means of which protagonists are permitted to relive their lives with the aid of a mature and knowledgeable consciousness, are featured in *The Devil in Crystal* (**1944**) by Louis MARLOW, *Strange Life of Ivan Osokin* (**1947**) by P.D. Ouspensky (1878-1947), *Replay* (**1986**) by Ken Grimwood and *Changing the Past* (**1989**) by Thomas BERGER. Significant timeslip "anti-romances" include *A Connecticut Yankee at King Arthur's Court* (**1889**) by Mark TWAIN and *Friar's Lantern* (**1906**) by G.G. Coulton (1858-1947), the latter being written to dispel the nostalgic illusions about the Medieval Church harboured by G.K. CHESTERTON and Hilaire BELLOC.

Within pulp sf, writers were quick to grasp the nettle, using time machines to explore both past and future, often venturing speculations about the nature of time. Even a mediocre pulp writer like Ray CUMMINGS could get entranced by such mysteries, although such romances as *The Man who Mastered Time* (1924 *Argosy*; **1929**) – which obligingly defines time as "what keeps everything from happening at once" – and *The Shadow Girl* (1929 *Argosy*; **1947**) cannot take such philosophizing very far. Ralph Milne FARLEY, whose time stories – begun with "The Time Traveler" (1931) – were collected in *The Omnibus of Time* (**1950**), did a little better, and John TAINE (a professional mathematician) set new standards of sophistication in *The Time Stream* (1931 *Wonder Stories*; **1946**). Theories about the nature of time, especially those put forward by J.W. DUNNE, also influenced non-genre writers – the most conspicuous example being J.B. PRIESTLEY, in his various **Time** plays – but the mainstream fictions inspired by that interest were understandably more modest.

Certain periods of the past have always attracted time-travellers because of their melodramatic potential. The Age of the Dinosaurs was inevitably the biggest draw – even to people who could only stand and stare, like the users of the time-viewer in Taine's *Before the Dawn* (**1934**); it was later to become a favourite era for hunters, as in Ray BRADBURY's "A Sound of Thunder" (1952) and L. Sprague DE CAMP's "A Gun for Dinosaur" (1956). Meeting famous people has also been a favourite theme, sometimes undertaken on a wholesale basis, as in Manly Wade WELLMAN's "Giants from Eternity" (1939); Wellman was also the first writer to allow a timeslipping hero to *become* somebody famous, in *Twice in Time* (1940 *Startling Stories*; **1957**). Some of the more scrupulous pulp writers thought that time travel into the past really belonged to the realms of fantasy because of the TIME PARADOXES thus generated, and the first classic timeslip romance from a genre writer, De Camp's *Lest Darkness Fall* (1939; **1941**; rev 1949), was initially published in *Unknown Worlds* for this reason. Others had fewer scruples, and many writers gleefully set about exploiting the peculiar aesthetics of time paradoxes. In fact, despite the dubious propriety of its literary device, De Camp's novel – like Wells's *The Time Machine* – warrants serious consideration as sf because of the conscientious way in which it employs its displaced viewpoint, the protagonist here being used to explore the crucial but subtle role played in HISTORY by TECHNOLOGY.

Inevitably, the main focus of pulp sf interest was in the melodramatic potential of time travel, as first displayed by Cummings and then taken to exotic extremes by such writers as John Russell FEARN, in *Liners of Time* (1935 *AMZ*; **1947**), and Jack WILLIAMSON, in his pioneering story of WAR between ALTERNATE WORLDS, *The Legion of Time* (1938 *ASF*; **1961**). Timeslipping was similarly taken to extremes in Murray LEINSTER's "Sidewise in Time" (1934), in which whole regions of the Earth's surface slip into anachronistic conjunction – an idea later redeployed by Fred HOYLE in *October the First is Too Late* (**1966**). Individuals and objects timeslipped from the future cause havoc in the present in a number of famous sf stories, including "The Twonky" (1942) and "Mimsy Were the Borogoves" (1943) by Lewis Padgett (Henry KUTTNER and C.L. MOORE), "Child's Play" (1947) by William TENN and "The Little Black Bag" (1950) by C.M. KORNBLUTH. These stories appeared during the period when the elementary plot-possibilities of time paradoxes were also being comprehensively explored. The cavalier use made of time travel by the early genre writers did beg certain important questions; the language problem which would be faced by time-travellers was overlooked until De Camp pointed it out in "The Isolinguals" (1937) and his essay "Language for Time Travelers" (1938), and was frequently ignored thereafter, although this too became a plot-gimmick in the 1940s, in such stories as "Barrier" (1942) by Anthony BOUCHER. Other sharp idea-twisting stories of the period include C.L. Moore's "Vintage Season" (1946) as by Lawrence O'Donnell, in which future time-tourists are drawn to our NEAR FUTURE for reasons which ultimately become clear, and T.L. SHERRED's "E for Effort" (1947), which sets out with compelling logic the reasons why the invention of a time-viewer would bring about the END OF THE WORLD.

The capacity of time travel to generate fresh plot-twists capable of sustaining stories on their own inevitably declined in the 1950s, by when all kinds of time travel had been routinized into part of the standard vocabulary of sf ideas; this was the heyday of the "time police" story, in which vast manifolds of ALTERNATE WORLDS were routinely patrolled by cunning secret agents or historical conservationists. The 1960s, however, brought a new sophistication to treatments of now-classic themes and a new thoughtfulness to metaphysically inclined stories, particularly but by no means exclusively in connection with the UK NEW WAVE. J.G. BALLARD's fascination with time is reflected in many of his early stories, including "The Voices of Time" (1960), "Chronopolis"

(1960), "The Garden of Time" (1962) and *The Crystal World* (**1966**). The timeslip story was remarkably refined by Brian W. ALDISS in "Man in his Time" (1965), which features a very slight but distressing slip, and Aldiss also wrote the best of several "reversed time" stories, *An Age* (**1967**; vt *Cryptozoic!* US and later UK edns); others are Philip K. DICK's *Counter-Clock World* (**1967**) and Martin AMIS's *Time's Arrow* (**1991**). A psychological timeslip story underpinned by split-brain research, then very fashionable, is Colin WILSON's "Timeslip" (1979). The linguistic problems of time-travellers were thrown into sharper focus by David I. MASSON's "A Two-Timer" (1966). The Age of the Dinosaurs gave way to the Crucifixion as a key focus of interest, as in Michael MOORCOCK's *Behold the Man* (1966 *NW*; exp **1969**) and Brian EARNSHAW's *Planet in the Eye of Time* (**1968**). Theodore L. THOMAS's "The Doctor" (1967) cynically re-examines the potential available to the time-traveller to operate as an apostle of progress. This kind of narrative sophistication of idea-twists extended into the 1970s in such stories as Robert SILVERBERG's "What We Learned from this Morning's Newspaper" (1972), James TIPTREE Jr's "The Man who Walked Home" (1972), Garry KILWORTH's "Let's Go to Golgotha" (1975) and Ian WATSON's "The Very Slow Time Machine" (1978).

The metaphysics of time continues to intrigue writers inside and outside the genre; notable recent works deploying ideas of this kind include *Chronolysis* (trans **1980**) by Michel Jeury (1934-   ) and *When Time Winds Blow* (**1982**) by Robert P. HOLDSTOCK. The oppressions of determinism are bewailed in Kurt VONNEGUT Jr's *Slaughterhouse 5* (**1979**). Action-adventure stories involving time travel have, inevitably, continued to reach new extremes of narrative extravagance, but at the same time have shown an increasing willingness to become involved with the intimate details of real history, and hence with its presumed dynamics. Such works as David LAKE's *The Man who Loved Morlocks* (**1981**), Connie WILLIS's "Fire Watch" (1982) and *Doomsday Book* (**1992**), Michael BISHOP's *No Enemy but Time* (**1982**), David DVORKIN's *Time for Sherlock Holmes* (**1983**), Tim POWERS's *The Anubis Gates* (**1983**), Howard WALDROP's *Them Bones* (**1984**), Jack L. CHALKER's *Downtiming the Nightside* (**1985**) and Vernor VINGE's *Marooned in Realtime* (**1986**) combine playfulness and seriousness in an artful fashion which is squarely in the tradition of *The Time Machine*. Even such frank melodramas as DR WHO and Julian MAY's series begun with *The Many-Colored Land* (**1981**), and such knockabout comedies as Ron GOULART's *The Panchronicon Plot* (**1977**) and Simon Hawke's (Nicholas YERMAKOV's) **Timewars** series, begun with *The Ivanhoe Gambit* (**1984**), have implications which are not simply left to languish as throwaway ideas.

A variant of the time-travel story which requires brief mention is the time-distortion story, pioneered by Wells in "The New Accelerator" (1901), which is about a device that "speeds up" time for its users and makes the world seem almost to freeze; a similar hypothesis is explored in Arthur C. CLARKE's "All the Time in the World" (1952). A device with a contrary effect is deployed in John GLOAG's *Slow* (**1954**), and ALIENS for whom time moves exceedingly slowly are featured in Eric Frank RUSSELL's "The Waitabits" (1955). More sophisticated stories of subjective time-distortion include Masson's "Traveller's Rest" (1965) and Eric BROWN's "The Time-Lapsed Man" (1988), and more extravagant distortions are featured in Dick's *Ubik* (**1969**) and Gordon R. DICKSON's *Time Storm* (**1977**).

However paradoxical it may be, time travel will remain a central element in the sf tradition, and the time machine – whether modelled on the bicycle, the cummerbund or the police telephone box – will doubtless retain its status as the ultimate literary-device-made-machine.   [MJE/BS]

TIME TRAVELERS Made-for-tv film (1976). ◊ Irwin ALLEN.

TIME TRAVELERS, THE Film (1964). Dobil/AIP. Dir Ib Melchior, starring Preston Foster, Philip Carey, Merry Anders, John Hoyt. Screenplay Melchior, from a story by Melchior and David Hewitt. 85 mins. Colour.

Melchior is best known as a screenwriter – e.g., ROBINSON CRUSOE ON MARS (1964), TERRORE NELLO SPAZIO (1965) and DEATH RACE 2000 (1975). This is one of his few films as director. A group of scientists travel through a time portal 107 years into the future, where they find a world a little like an updated version of that in H.G. WELLS's *The Time Machine* (**1895**) – indeed, the film was conceived as a sequel to the film *The* TIME MACHINE (1960). After the HOLOCAUST a human society living underground battles against MUTANTS on the surface, while using their ANDROID associates to help them build a spaceship for their escape from Earth. This uneven but vigorous film is inventive (MATTER TRANSMISSION, hydroponics, all sorts of incidental sf tropes), not least in the final trapping of the scientists in a deterministic time loop, unable to influence events. David Hewitt's special effects are sometimes good (nicely displeasing androids), but it is unclear why he went on to direct the unnecessary remake, JOURNEY TO THE CENTER OF TIME (1967), only 3 years later. Irwin ALLEN was clearly influenced by *TTT* to make the tv series *The* TIME TUNNEL (1966-7).   [PN]

TIME-TRAVELLER, THE ◊ Forrest J. ACKERMAN; FANTASY MAGAZINE; FANZINES; Julius SCHWARTZ.

TIME TUNNEL, THE US tv series (1966-7). An Irwin Allen Production for 20th Century-Fox Television/ABC TV. Created Irwin ALLEN, also executive prod. Writers included William Welch, Wanda and Bob Duncan. Dirs included Allen (pilot only), Sobey Martin, J. Juran. 1 season. 30 50min episodes. Colour.

Dr Tony Newman (James Darren) and Dr Doug Phillips (Robert Colbert) are trapped in time after testing a defective TIME MACHINE, which takes the form of a spiral vortex and is controlled by military personnel. Their military and civilian colleagues can see what is happening to them but are unable to return them to the present; efforts in this direction conveniently switch the travellers to a new time-period every week, usually 5 mins from the end of an episode, leaving them at a cliffhanger. Tony and Doug spend more time in the past than in the future, in such venues as the Alamo, the Little Big Horn, the *Titanic*, the walls of Jericho and Pearl Harbor, just as dangerous events are about to take place; thus a good deal of stock footage could be utilized. Rather more fantastic episodes featured Merlin and the vengeful ghost of Emperor Nero. Writing, performances and sets were dire. 2 novelizations are *The Time Tunnel* ∗ **(1967)** and *Timeslip!* ∗ **(1967)** by Murray LEINSTER.   [JB]

TIMLETT, PETER VALENTINE (1933-   ) UK writer whose sf/fantasy **Atlantis** trilogy – *The Seedbearers* **(1974)**, *The Power of the Serpent* **(1976)** and *Twilight of the Serpent* **(1977)** – deals in occasionally occult terms with ATLANTIS and its fall, moving subsequently to the founding of civilization in Britain, where Atlantean impulses might be preserved.   [JC]

TIMLIN, WILLIAM M(ITCHESON) (1892-1943) UK-born illustrator and writer, in South Africa from 1912. *The Ship that Sailed to Mars* **(1923)**, his only fiction, is more fantasy than sf, though it does describe in glowing detail the fitting up of a SPACESHIP and its trip to MARS. But WMT's astonishingly evocative illustrations to the text – for which the original quarto edn of the book is now heavily collected – strongly underline the surreal nature of the tale.   [JC]

TINCROWDER, LEO QUEEQUEG [s] ◊ Philip José FARMER.

TIPHAIGNE DE LA ROCHE, C(HARLES) F(RAN-ÇOIS) (1729-1774) French author of some works of fantasy and a PROTO-SCIENCE-FICTION work, *Giphantie* **(1760**; trans anon in 2 vols as *Giphantia, or A View of What Has Passed, What is Now Passing, and During the Present Century, What Will Pass in the World* **1761** UK). A traveller in Africa witnesses a prelapsarian world, a possibly farcical vision of world history as being governed by the effects of emblematical trees grown from the One Tree in Eden, and a HOLLOW EARTH via which the protagonist returns to Europe.   [JC]

TIPTREE, JAMES Jr Pseudonym of US writer and psychologist Alice Hastings Bradley Sheldon (1915-1987), who was widely assumed to be a man, despite the deeply felt rapport she displayed for women in stories like "The Women Men Don't See" (1973), until her identity was exposed in 1977; she also wrote several stories as Raccoona Sheldon. She was born in Chicago, spent much of her childhood in Africa and India and worked in the US Government for many years, including a period in the Pentagon; this much was known about JT, but was wrongly assumed to describe a masculine career. Her mother, Mary Hastings Bradley, was a well known geographer and travel author of 35 books; her father was a lawyer and traveller. After a short pre-WWII career as an artist and the later work whose details she shared with her

pseudonym, she left the CIA in 1955 and attended college, acquiring a PhD in experimental psychology in 1967. She began writing as JT in 1967 – though she had, in fact, as Alice Bradley, published her first, non-sf story, "The Lucky Ones" for *The New Yorker*, as early as 1946.

Though she wrote some novels, JT will be best remembered for her many extraordinary sf stories. Her first efforts – she began with "Birth of a Salesman" for *ASF* in 1968 – were not, perhaps, very remarkable, showing some dis-ease and an intermittent tendency to protest too vehemently that she – the JT telling the tale – was just folks; but within a few years she shot into her prime, and between 1970 and about 1977 produced at great speed and with great concentration her finest work. Almost all of her best stories appeared in 4 collections – *Ten Thousand Light-Years from Home* (coll **1973**; reset with fewer errors 1975 UK), *Warm Worlds and Otherwise* (coll **1975**), *Star Songs of an Old Primate* (coll **1978**) and *Out of the Everywhere and Other Extraordinary Visions* (coll **1981**); a later, very thorough selection, *Her Smoke Rose Up Forever: The Great Years of James Tiptree, Jr.* (coll **1990**) ed James Turner, also concentrated on the work from this period. *Byte Beautiful* (coll **1986**) assembled an odd mixture of early and late work. *Crown of Stars* (coll **1988**) restricted itself almost exclusively to the stories JT wrote in a final splurge of creative energy in the mid-1980s. *The Girl who was Plugged In* (in *New Dimensions 3* [anth **1973**] ed Robert SILVERBERG; **1989** chap dos) – which won JT her first HUGO – and *Houston, Houston, Do you Read?* (in *Aurora* [anth **1977**] ed Vonda MCINTYRE and Susan J. Anderson; **1989** chap dos) – which won a NEBULA and a Jupiter AWARD and shared a Hugo – were separate appearances of novellas from her prime. *The Color of Neanderthal Eyes* (1988 *FSF*; **1990** chap dos) is the only major late item not assembled in *Crown of Stars*.

Several themes interpenetrate JT's best work – SEX, exogamy, identity, FEMINIST depictions of male/female relations, ECOLOGY, death – but the greatest of these is death. It is very rarely that a JT story does not both deal directly with death and end in a death of the spirit, or of all hope, or of the body, or of the race. "And I Awoke and Found Me Here on the Cold Hill's Side" (1971), for instance, seems initially to read as a straightforward rendering of the effects vastly superior ALIENS have upon *Homo sapiens*; only retroactively is it made clear, through the apt sexual and ANTHROPOLOGICAL analogies worked into the basic story, that these effects are utterly ravaging, that humans exposed to aliens become afflicted with a fatal cargo-cult mentality, bound into a sexual submission very like death. In "The Last Flight of Doctor Ain" (1969; rev 1974), only gradually do we begin to realize – through a reportage-like, impersonal reconstruction of certain events – that the woman whom Doctor Ain seems to be accompanying across a heavily polluted, wounded Earth is actually the Earth herself personified in the Doctor's mind; and that, as he passes around the globe, he is infecting mankind with a redesigned leukaemia virus, hoping – probably in vain – to save her, whom he loves, from the human species, which he does not. In what may be JT's finest and most intense longer story, "A Momentary Taste of Being" (1975), the human race, en route to the stars, discovers that its racial role is to act as gamete in a cosmic coupling, and that the drives that make us human are merely displacements of that central mindless imperative. It is one of the darkest GENRE-SF stories ever printed. In shorter compass, it is matched by others, like "On the Last Afternoon" (1972), "Love is the Plan the Plan is Death" (1973) – which won a Nebula – "The Screwfly Solution" (1977) and "Your Faces, O my Sisters! Your Faces Filled of Light!" (1977), both originally as by Raccoona Sheldon, and "Slow Music" (1980).

JT's most famous single story, "The Women Men Don't See", may appear to escape this pattern, as only the male narrator seems bound to a quietus, while the two women he travels with – but fails, symptomatically, to comprehend – seem bound starwards into a new life. But the ironies of the tale are very evident, and characteristic of JT's inconsolable complexities of vision. It may be true that the ageing and surprisingly sympathetic narrator may represent a suicidal blindness on the part of humanity; but the women who choose to leave are, in fact – by electing to become companions of utterly unknown aliens in the depths of space – also expressing the power of thanatos upon our species. JT's surface was often airy and at times hilarious, and her control of genre conventions allowed her to convey the bleakness of her abiding insights in tales that remain seductively readable; but she was, in the end, incapable of dissimulation.

There were 2 novels and 2 collections of linked stories. In *Up the Walls of the World* (1978), apparently written around the time her health began to break, she deliberately broadened her techniques in the fabrication of an extraordinarily full-blown SPACE OPERA whose 3 venues – the interior "spaces" of a vast interstellar being derangedly destroying all suns in its path; an alien planet inhabited by skatelike telepathic flying beings whose sun is being destroyed; and contemporary Earth, where a government-funded experiment in ESP begins terrifyingly to cash out – interpenetrate complexly and with considerable narrative impact. From telepathy to COSMOLOGY, from densely conceived psychological narrative to the broadest of SENSE-OF-WONDER revelations, the novel is something of a *tour de force*. But stresses – particularly a sense that the whole structure was willed into existence – do show; and *Brightness Falls from the Air* (1985) demonstrates how difficult it had become for her to maintain control over the intensities of her vision, which had, if anything, darkened as the 1980s began. In this novel an assortment of characters variously confront, on a distant planet, the fact that death agonies felt by another species generate a literal

nectar for our own; but moments of overt sentimentality, as well as excesses of subplotting, tend to intrude. *The Starry Rift* (coll of linked stories **1986**) assembled loose, somewhat sententious tales set in the same universe; and *Tales of the Quintana Roo* (coll of linked stories **1986**) gathered a mild sequence of visions of the eastern coast of southern Mexico.

Like the novels, the short fiction of JT's last years, though substantial by the standards of other writers, suffered from an increasing incapacity of narrative voice and structure to contain emotion. The best of them are perhaps "Yanqui Doodle" (1987) and "Backward, Turn Backward" (1988). Alice Sheldon had been married to Huntington Sheldon since 1945. In the early 1980s he contracted Alzheimer's Disease. In 1987, herself in precarious health, she shot him and killed herself.   [JC]

About the author: *The Fiction of James Tiptree, Jr.* (**1977** chap) by Gardner DOZOIS; *James Tiptree, Jr., a Lady of Letters: A Working Bibliography* (**1989** chap) by Gordon BENSON Jr and Phil STEPHENSEN-PAYNE.

See also: ASTEROIDS; ASTOUNDING SCIENCE-FICTION; BIOLOGY; CYBERPUNK; ENTROPY; GODS AND DEMONS; HOLOCAUST AND AFTER; *The* MAGAZINE OF FANTASY AND SCIENCE FICTION; MEDIA LANDSCAPE; MYTHOLOGY; OPTIMISM AND PESSIMISM; PERCEPTION; PSYCHOLOGY; SATIRE; SCIENTIFIC ERRORS; TIME TRAVEL; WOMEN SF WRITERS.

TITAN, EARL ◊ John Russell FEARN.

TODD, RUTHVEN (1914-1978) UK writer and Blake scholar whose *Tracks in the Snow: Studies in English Science and Art* (**1946**) effectively argued the imaginative power – when joined – of the two subtitled categories; he was author, as R.T. Campbell, of several detective novels, and as RT of two metaphysical tales: *Over the Mountain* (**1939**), whose quest plot is consanguineous with a search for political self-understanding, and the surrealist *The Lost Traveller* (**1943**), in which the protagonist, lost in a strange country, finds himself questing for a great bird which, at the final moment, he himself becomes. In his introduction to the 1968 reprinting of the latter, RT recognized influences from Rex WARNER to Wyndham LEWIS.   [JC]

Other works: The **Space Cats** series of juvenile sf novels, *Space Cat* (**1952** US), *Space Cat Visits Venus* (**1955** US), *Space Cat Meets Mars* (**1957** US) and *Space Cat and the Kittens* (**1958** US).

See also: DYSTOPIAS; FANTASTIC VOYAGES.

TODOROV, TZVETAN (1939-   ) Bulgarian literary critic who pursued his postgraduate studies in Paris under the direction of the semiotic philosopher Roland Barthes (1915-1980). Among TT's several books and essays on structuralist criticism, all written in French, *Introduction à la littérature fantastique* (**1970**; trans Richard Howard as *The Fantastic: A Structural Approach to Literary Genre* **1973**; US paperback 1975 with intro by Robert SCHOLES) has relevance to the student of sf, along with Scholes's own *Structural Fabulation* (**1975**). (Structuralism has been important in sf criticism, influencing critics as otherwise diverse as Samuel R. DELANY, Mark ROSE and Darko SUVIN.) An interesting controversy about TT's book arose in SCIENCE-FICTION STUDIES, the Fall 1974 and July 1975 issues containing an attack on TT's work by Stanisław LEM and further debate. Also relevant is "Historical Genres/Theoretical Genres: A Discussion of Todorov on the Fantastic" by Christine BROOKE-ROSE in *New Literary History*, Autumn 1976. TT's definition of "the fantastic" is much more exclusive than most (◊ DEFINITIONS OF SF; FANTASY); he devotes only a half-page to sf. [PN]

See also: CRITICAL AND HISTORICAL WORKS ABOUT SF.

TOFFLER, ALVIN (1928-) US journalist and author, best known for his speculative nonfiction on SOCIOLOGY and FUTUROLOGY. *Future Shock* (**1970**) documents the increasing rate of change in the 20th century, and speculates on the psychological trauma this may be causing Western civilization. It has had a great influence in futurology generally, and quite directly on many sf writers, notably John BRUNNER, whose *The Shockwave Rider* (**1975**) pays homage to AT in its title. *The Eco-Spasm Report* (**1975**), a much shorter work which produces 3 plausible scenarios for NEAR-FUTURE disaster, at points approaches the narrative strategies of some sf. *The Third Wave* (**1980**) is a more utopian (and in some ways LIBERTARIAN) book, whose Third Wave of history (which AT hopes is arriving) will emphasize diversity, decentralization, individualism and new social structures. AT's style is populist, and he has been read by some as simply promoting techno-fixes for the things that are going wrong in the world, but this is to underestimate the complexity of his argument. [PN]

Other works: *The Futurists* (anth **1972**), ed; *Learning for Tomorrow* (anth **1973**), ed.

See also: DEFINITIONS OF SF; DYSTOPIAS.

TOFTE, ARTHUR R. (1902-1980) US writer who enjoyed two widely separated careers as a published author, the first beginning with his first story, "The Meteor Monsters" for *AMZ* in 1938, when as a member of the Milwaukee Fictioneers – which was focused on the memory and example of Stanley G. WEINBAUM – he was briefly interested in sf. Between 1938 and his retirement in 1969 he was a business executive. In the 1970s, encouraged by Roger ELWOOD, he began publishing stories again. *Crash Landing on Iduna* (**1975** Canada) and *Walls Within Walls* (**1975** Canada), a post-HOLOCAUST tale with MUTANTS in conflict, are unremarkable but mildly spirited. *The Day the Earth Stood Still* (**1976**) and *Survival Planet* (**1977**) are juveniles. *The Ghost Hunters* (dated 1978 but **1979**) is an occult tale. [JC]

TOLKIEN, J(OHN) R(ONALD) R(EUEL) (1892-1973) South-African-born UK writer and philologist who specialized in early forms of English; his academic career was crowned by his appointment as Merton Professor of English at Oxford University in 1945, a post he held until his retirement in 1959. It was at Oxford, before WWII, that he formed a close literary association with Owen BARFIELD, C.S. LEWIS and

Charles WILLIAMS, a group which came to be known as The Inklings. It was at their regular meetings that much of their fiction received a first hearing, including draft portions of a long High Fantasy epic by JRRT which put into definitive fictional form his concept of the Secondary World, as embodied in the creation of Middle-Earth, the intensely imagined land- or world-scape in which the central action of all his work takes place. No reasonable definition of sf would encompass the works of JRRT; but this concept and its embodiment in the **Lord of the Rings** trilogy have had enormous influence on both sf and fantasy.

Although Secondary Worlds, "inside which the green sun will be credible", long predate JRRT, it was "On Fairy Tales" – a 1940 lecture he expanded for *Essays Presented to Charles Williams* (anth **1947**) ed anon C.S. Lewis, and further exp for its appearance in *Tree and Leaf* (coll **1964**; rev 1988) – that first gave legitimacy to the internally coherent and autonomous land of Faerie as part of the geography of the human imagination. For the sf and fantasy writers who followed, and who found in the **Lord of the Rings** trilogy a model for their own subcreations (his coinage for invented fantasy worlds), this affirmation of autonomy was of very great importance. No longer did fantasy writers feel any lingering need to "normalize" their Secondary Worlds by framing them as traveller's tales, dreams or timeslip adventures, or as beast-fables. For sf writers, especially practitioners of the PLANETARY-ROMANCE, the example of JRRT was equally liberating – though it must be emphasized that Middle-Earth is not in fact a *world* in any sf sense but an autonomous *landscape*, and pure High Fantasy.

JRRT's profound interest in philology permeated his work from its beginnings, which, as the posthumous publication of a vast assemblage of drafts and fragments (see below) has demonstrated, pre-dated WWI. His first published tale of Middle-Earth, *The Hobbit, or There and Back Again* (**1937**; rev 1951; rev 1966), a Faerie-story for children, introduced its readers to an already achieved and named Secondary World, with a history and geography that had already long existed in its subcreator's mind; as *The Hobbit*, it was made into an animated film dir Arthur Rankin Jr in 1977. The tale of the hobbit, Bilbo, and of his quest through a portion of Middle-Earth to help some dwarves (JRRT's preferred spelling of "dwarfs") retrieve a treasure, gave JRRT the opportunity to reveal some of that history and geography. But it was not until the release of the **Lord of the Rings** – broken for publishing reasons into 3 vols, *The Fellowship of the Ring* (**1954**; rev 1966), *The Two Towers* (**1954**; rev 1966) and *The Return of the King* (**1955**; rev 1966), assembled as *The Lord of the Rings* (omni **1968**) – that the full expanse of his world began to come clear. (The first portion of **Lord of the Rings** was made into an animated film in 1978; the expected conclusion failed to appear.)

Middle-Earth is perhaps the most detailed of all invented fictional worlds, rivalled only by Austin

Tappan WRIGHT's *Islandia* (**1942**), the published version of which (as in JRRT's case) represents only a portion of what was written; JRRT differed from Wright, however, in having a compelling story to tell. Some of the background material appeared in the form of appendices to the **Lord of the Rings** and in *The Silmarillion* (**1977**) ed Christopher Tolkien (JRRT's son); the latter comprises 5 interconnected texts on which JRRT had been working most of his life, and which supply an historical background for all his other work. Poems and songs belonging to the cycle are assembled as *The Adventures of Tom Bombadil and Other Verses from the Red Book* (coll **1962** chap) and *The Road Goes Ever On: A Song Cycle* (coll **1967**) with music by Michael Swann. In *Unfinished Tales of Númenór and Middle-Earth* (coll **1980**) Christopher Tolkien continued the long task of publishing his father's literary remains. The main sequence of these works, various volumes containing the **History of Middle-Earth**, all ed Christopher Tolkien, comprises *The History of Middle-Earth #1: The Book of Lost Tales 1* (coll **1983**), *#2: The Book of Lost Tales 2* (coll **1984**), *#3: The Lays of Beleriand* (coll **1985**), *#4: The Shaping of Middle-Earth* (coll **1986**), *#5: The Lost Road and Other Writings* (coll **1987**), *#6: The Return of the Shadow: The History of the Lord of the Rings l* (coll **1988**), *#7: The Treason of Isengard: The History of the Lord of the Rings 2* (coll **1989**), *#8: The War of the Ring: The History of the Lord of the Rings 3* (coll **1990**) and *#9: The War of the Ring: The History of the Lord of the Rings 4* (coll **1992**).

JRRT's influence on fantasy and sf has been not merely profound but also – with no discredit to JRRT himself – demeaning. Fortunately for readers of sf, the fairies and elves and orcs and cuddly dwarves and loquacious plants and bargain-counter Dark Lords and kings in disguise and singing barmen have been restricted in general to commercial market-driven FANTASY, caveat emptor; the main exception being hybrid productions like the STAR WARS films, which are filled with blurred and decadent copies of JRRT's own creations. It can only be hoped that the genuine JRRT will survive this assault, the JRRT for whom the heart of the enterprise of Faerie lay in "the desire of men to hold communion with other living things". [JC]

Other works: *Farmer Giles of Ham* (**1949** chap) and *Smith of Wootton Major* (**1967** chap), assembled as *Smith of Wootton Major and Farmer Giles of Ham* (omni **1975** US); *The Tolkien Reader* (coll **1966**); *Bilbo's Last Song* (**1974** chap); *The Father Christmas Letters* (coll **1976** chap); *Poems and Stories* (coll **1980**); *Mr Bliss* (**1982** chap).

Nonfiction: *A Middle English Vocabulary* (**1924**) is the earliest of a number of works of varying interest, including an edition of *Sir Gawain and the Green Knight* (**1925**) with E.V. Gordon.

About the author: Books about JRRT and his work are numerous. They include *J.R.R. Tolkien: A Biography* (**1977**) by Humphrey Carpenter, various atlases and concordances like *A Guide to Middle Earth* (**1971**) by Robert Foster and *The Tolkien Companion* (**1976**) by J.E.A. Tyler; and, among many other biographical/critical works, *Tolkien and the Critics* (anth **1968**) ed Neil D. Isaacs and Rose A. Zimbardo, *Tolkien: A Look Behind the Lord of the Rings* (**1969**) by Lin CARTER, *Master of Middle Earth* (**1972**) by Paul H. Kocher, *Tolkien's World* (**1974**) by Randel Helms, *J.R.R. Tolkien: Architect of Middle-Earth* (**1976**) by Daniel Grotta-Kurska, *The Mythology of Middle-Earth* (**1977**) by Ruth S. Noel, *The Inklings* (**1979**) by Humphrey Carpenter and *J.R.R. Tolkien: This Far Land* (anth **1983**) ed Robert Giddings. *The Letters of J.R.R. Tolkien* (**1981**), ed Humphrey Carpenter with the assistance of Christopher Tolkien, is a revealing compilation.

See also: CHILDREN'S SF; FANTASTIC VOYAGES; FANZINE; GAMES AND TOYS; HEROIC FANTASY; LINGUISTICS; MUSIC; SWORD AND SORCERY.

TOLLIVER, STEVE [r] ◊ Ron ELLIK.

TOLSTOY, ALEXEI (1882-1945) Russian writer, a distant relative of Leo Tolstoy (1828-1910), known mainly for works outside the sf field, including poetry and plays; his sf was restricted to 2 books whose first versions appeared in the experimental 1920s and both of which were revised in the decade of terror which followed. *Aelita* (**1922**; rev 1937; 2nd text trans Lucy Flaxman **1957** USSR; new trans of 2nd text Antonina W. Bouis 1981 US; 1st text trans Leland Fetzer **1985** US) – the first version of the book being filmed as AELITA (1924) – was set on MARS, where a Red Army officer foments a rebellion of the native Martians (who are in fact long-ago emigrants from ATLANTIS) against a corrupt oligarchy. *Giperboloid inzhenera Garina* (**1926**; rev 1937; 1st text trans B.G. Guerney as *The Death Box* **1936** UK; 2nd text trans George Hanna as *The Garin Death Ray* **1955** USSR; Hanna trans cut vt *Engineer Garin and his Death Ray* 1987 USSR) feverishly describes an attempt on the part of the eponymous inventor – who is treated with some affection as a kind of force of Nature – to use his death ray to conquer the world. He manages to rule a decadently capitalist USA for a short period. At least in their original versions, both books showed a narrative gusto typical of their precarious period, in attractive contrast to AT's later, less ebullient work. [JC]

Other work: *Vampires: Stories of the Supernatural* (coll trans Fedor Nikanov **1969** US).

See also: RUSSIA; WEAPONS.

TOM CORBETT: SPACE CADET US tv series (1950-55). CBS TV, later ABC TV, and then NBC TV for season 5. Prod Mort Abrahams. Writers included Albert Aley, Alfred BESTER, Jack Weinstock. Dirs included George Gould, Ralph Ward. Starring Frankie Thomas, Jan Merlin, Al Markim, Michael Harvey. 5 seasons. 3 15min episodes weekly for first 4 seasons; weekly 30min episodes in season 5. B/w.

This was one of the earliest US children's-sf tv serials (CAPTAIN VIDEO was earlier, but *TC:SC* got into space first). Very loosely based on Robert A. HEINLEIN's *Space Cadet* (**1948**), it concerns teenaged Tom

Corbett (Thomas), who is a cadet in the Solar Guards, an interplanetary police force in AD2350 that helps maintain the Solar Alliance of Earth, Mars and Venus. Later in the series the cadets leave the Solar System and go out into the Galaxy. The scientific adviser was Willy LEY. As with other sf serials of the early 1950s, the concept was on a grand scale but the visual effects were severely limited by budget and by the necessity to broadcast live: much had to be described in dialogue or merely suggested. Nevertheless, the show was hugely successful – it introduced the phrase "Blast off!" into popular speech – and was followed by comic strips, comic books, toys, etc., in one of the first examples of the merchandising power of televised sf. 8 **Tom Corbett: Space Cadet** hardcover books by Carey Rockwell (a pseudonym) were published 1952-6, beginning with *Stand By For Mars!* ✳ **(1952)**. [PN/JB]

TOMORROW ◊ *The* FUTURIAN.

TOMORROW I'LL WAKE UP AND SCALD MYSELF WITH TEA ◊ ZÍTRA VSTANU A OPAŘÍM SE ČAJEM.

TOMORROW PEOPLE, THE UK tv series (1973-9). A Thames TV Production. Series conceived by Roger Price. Prod Ruth Boswell and Price (1973), Boswell alone (1974-5), Price alone (1976), Vic Hughes (1977-9). Technical adviser Dr Christopher Evans. Starring Nicholas Young, Peter Vaughan-Clarke, Sammie Winmill, Stephen Salmon, Elizabeth Adare, Mike Holoway. Written mostly Price. Dirs included Brian Finch, Price, Hughes. 8 seasons (2 in 1978); 68 25min episodes. Colour.

TTP, incorporating many childhood wish-fulfilment fantasies, concerns a group of MUTANT children – *Homo superior* – with PSI POWERS. They band together for self-protection, occasionally conscripting other child mutants. They can teleport themselves, the term they use (taken unacknowledged from Alfred BESTER) being "jaunting". They are free of parental control and live in a secret, underground base protected by a smooth-voiced supercomputer. Most of the stories, each lasting on average 4 episodes, involve either TIME TRAVEL or encounters with evil beings from outer space. As with most UK tv series made for children, the budget was limited, but within that constraint the sets and special effects were adequate. Probably intended as commercial tv's answer to the BBC's DR WHO, *TTP* was not in that league. Novelizations, all by Roger Price (1941-   ), were *The Visitor* ✳ **(1973)** with Julian R. Gregory, *Three in Three* ✳ **(1974)**, *Four into Three* ✳ **(1975)**, *One Law* ✳ **(1976)** and *The Lost Gods, with Hitler's Last Secret and The Thargon Menace* ✳ **(coll 1979)**. [JB]

TOM SWIFT Hero of a JUVENILE SERIES of scientific-invention novels produced by the STRATEMEYER Syndicate and written under the house name Victor APPLETON, most being the work of Howard R. GARIS. *TS* was the most commercially successful and is still the best remembered of all the boys' sf series of the period. During 1910-38, beginning with *Tom Swift and His Motor-Cycle* **(1910)**, 38 titles appeared, all but the

last 3 by Garis, and featuring such inventions as the "photo telephone" and the "ocean airport", the technical difficulties of utilizing which were emphasized. These stories created a potential readership for Hugo GERNSBACK's magazines. The *TS* books were written in what was, even for the time, stilted prose. Between 1954 and 1971, beginning with *Tom Swift and His Flying Lab* **(1954)** as by Victor Appleton II, a 2nd *TS* series appeared, this time featuring **Tom Swift Jr**, its 33 titles being released at a rate of about 2 per year; at first it was enormously successful, possibly giving rise to the 1960s popularity of the Tom Swiftie ("I think we can get there in time," said Tom swiftly). The authors behind the new house name are not known. In 1981 a 3rd *TS* series, as by Victor Appleton, began with *The City in the Stars* **(1981)**, continuing to #11, *The Planet of Nightmares* **(1984)**, which was by Mike McQUAY writing as Appleton; 2 of these titles have recently been ascribed to Neal BARRETT Jr. Most recently, in 1991, under the Byron PREISS packaging aegis, a 4th series began with *Tom Swift #1: The Black Dragon* **(1991)** by Bill McCay writing as Appleton; at least 7 further titles have appeared from various hands, always under the house name. [JE/PN/JC]

Further reading: "Tom Swift and the Syndicate" in *Strange Horizons: The Spectrum of Science Fiction* **(1976)** by Sam MOSKOWITZ; *Science-Fiction: The Early Years* **(1991)** by Everett F. BLEILER.

TONG ENZHENG [r] ◊ CHINESE SF.

TONKS, ANGELA (?   -   ) UK writer, resident in the USA, whose *Mind Out of Time* **(1958** UK) deals with a telepathic relationship (◊ ESP). [JC]

TOOKER, RICHARD (PRESLEY) (1902-1988) US writer and publisher who wrote also as Dick Presley Tooker; his first sf story, under that name, was "Planet Paradise" for *Weird Tales* in 1924. He is best remembered for *The Day of the Brown Horde* **(1929)**, in which cavemen fight one another and the last of the plesiosaurs, and which deals, like most of the prehistoric-sf subgenre, with the onset of human consciousness (◊ ORIGIN OF MAN). *The Dawn Boy* **(1932)**, a juvenile, revisits a similar venue. *Inland Deep* **(1936)** rather more imaginatively features man-frogs and other odd creatures in an underground LOST WORLD. It is reported that from about 1940 RT was a ghost-writer. [JC]

TOOMBS, ALFRED (GERALD) (1912-   ) US writer. In *Good as Gold* **(1955)** the transmutation of the metal produces what might be called manure. [JC]

TOOMBS, ROBERT [r] ◊ DIME-NOVEL SF.

TOOMEY, ROBERT E. Jr (1945-   ) US writer who began publishing sf stories with "Pejorative" for *NW* in 1969. His *A World of Trouble* **(1973)**, sets a galactic agent on an alien planet, where he has many jocosely told adventures. [JC]

TOOMORROW Film (1970). Sweet Music/Lowndes Productions/United Artists. Written/dir Val Guest, starring Olivia Newton-John, Benny Thomas, Vic Cooper, Karl Chambers, Roy Dotrice. 95 mins. Colour.

This is an unsuccessful attempt by producer Harry Saltzman, best known for the **James Bond** films, to mix pop MUSIC with sf. An embarrassingly made-to-order pop group is kidnapped by aliens from outer space (who have detected their vibrations) and taken to their planet for the purpose of creating music. The film was an artistic and financial failure. [JB]

TOPS IN SCIENCE FICTION US reprint magazine. 2 issues, Spring 1953 (PULP-MAGAZINE size) and Fall 1953 (DIGEST size). Published by Love Romances, Connecticut; ed Jack O'Sullivan (#1) and Malcolm Reiss (#2). *TISF* featured stories which had first appeared in PLANET STORIES. Contributors included such *Planet* regulars as Leigh BRACKETT and Ray BRADBURY. A UK edn, published by Top Fiction, had 3 digest-sized issues 1954-6. [FHP/MJE]

TOR BOOKS US paperback publishing company – later moving into hardcover also – founded by Tom Doherty, then aged 44, in 1980, in conjunction with Richard Gallen and Pinnacle Books; the first titles were published in 1981. Doherty had previously been in control of ACE BOOKS for 5 years. Beth MEACHAM became sf/fantasy editor in 1984, soon becoming editor-in-chief; David HARTWELL became consulting sf editor the same year. This put two of the most expert sf editors in the US in the same company. TB expanded rapidly, publishing only a few sf titles in 1981 but 137 in 1986, which made them one of the most important sf publishers. At the end of 1986 Doherty and his partners sold Thomas Doherty Associates to St Martin's Press, a move probably connected to the bankruptcy of Pinnacle, which along with its rapid expansion had left TB temporarily short of cash; but Doherty stayed on to run TB. In 1988, TB introduced **Tor Doubles**, similar to the old **Ace Doubles** (◊ DOS). Beth Meacham left in 1989, but continued (from Arizona) as an executive editor. By 1988 TB and St Martins together topped all US sf publishers in terms of number of titles published, 256; but TB found this too much, and dropped from 12 sf/fantasy/horror titles per month to 9. By 1990-91 TB was publishing fewer sf/fantasy books from BANTAM/DOUBLEDAY/Dell and Putnam/Berkley/Ace, though during those years – and since – it has published more sf/fantasy hardcovers than any other firm in the English-speaking world. In 1991 TB dropped its separate horror list. Robert Gleason became editor-in-chief in 1991.

TB have published many important sf authors, including Poul ANDERSON, Greg BEAR, Michael BISHOP, Orson Scott CARD, John KESSEL, Pat MURPHY, Mike RESNICK, Kim Stanley ROBINSON, Sheri S. TEPPER, Jack VANCE, Walter Jon WILLIAMS, Gene WOLFE and Jack WOMACK. Authors whose first novels have been published by TB include Tom MADDOX, Rebecca ORE and Richard Paul RUSSO. [PN]

TORGESON, ROY (? -1991) US editor, noted mainly for the competent CHRYSALIS series of ORIGINAL ANTHOLOGIES: *Chrysalis* (anth **1977**), #2 (anth **1978**), #3

(anth **1978**), #4 (anth **1979**), #5 (anth **1979**), #6 (anth **1980**), #7 (anth **1980**), #8 (anth **1980**), #9 (anth **1981**) and #10 (anth **1983**). A second sequence ran for only 2 vols: *Other Worlds 1* (anth **1979**) and #2 (anth **1980**). [JC]

TORRO, PEL ◊ R.L. FANTHORPE.

TOTAL RECALL Film (1990). Carolco. Dir Paul Verhoeven, starring Arnold Schwarzenegger, Rachel Ticotin, Sharon Stone, Michael Ironside, Ronny Cox. Screenplay Ronald Shusett, Dan O'Bannon, Gary Goldman, based on a story by Shusett, O'Bannon, Jon Povill, inspired by "We Can Remember It for You Wholesale" (1966) by Philip K. DICK. 113 mins, cut to 109 mins. Colour.

At a purported $60,000,000 budget this was one of the most expensive films ever made (though TERMINATOR 2 [1991] would cost even more). Verhoeven, whose sf film début was ROBOCOP (1987), is a deft, intelligent director good at tough action sequences, but with a strong liking for gratuitous violence which, for all its over-the-top comic-book harmlessness here, still has about it a faint whiff of sadism. Exported versions were mostly cut to the requirements of the relevant country's censorship code.

Some of the strengths of Dick's original story remain in this tale of a man who, in attempting to purchase false memories of a trip to Mars, uncovers some real ones, and is pitchforked into a heady sequence of exotic adventures, leaving Earth and fighting with rebels against a power-crazed Martian establishment. False memories clash with true ones and, since both look the same on the screen, it is as difficult for the viewer as for the muscle-bound protagonist to tell illusion from reality. *TR* is entertaining, information-dense and packed with intriguing detail, but has most of the usual faults of big-budget sf sagas: too great a reliance on grotesque special effects (the bugging eyes of victims exposed to vacuum are merely absurd); with-one-bound-Jack-was-free plotting; and in this case a finale of protracted idiocy in which Mars's long-disappeared atmosphere is replaced through vents in a mountain in a matter of minutes. Ideas are "borrowed" eclectically from diverse sources: an air-machine from Edgar Rice BURROUGHS's *A Princess of Mars* (**1917**), disfigured MUTANTS from Roger CORMAN's *The Haunted Palace* (1963), a two-headed mutant from Walter M. MILLER's *A Canticle for Leibowitz* (**1960**), archaic alien machinery from FORBIDDEN PLANET (1956), and so on. It would take a fresh and ignorant viewer to suspend his or her disbelief throughout the film: sf aficionados tend to giggle through the whole of the second half. [PN]

See also: SCIENTIFIC ERRORS.

TOTER SUCHT SEINER MÖRDER, EIN ◊ VENGEANCE.

TOUSEY, FRANK [r] ◊ DIME-NOVEL SF; FRANK READE LIBRARY.

TOUZALIN, ROBERT [s] ◊ Robert REED.

TÓVÖLGYI, TITUSZ [r] ◊ HUNGARY.

TOWERS, IVAR A Fictioneers Inc. house name

(1940-42), used once by C.M. KORNBLUTH and Richard WILSON in *Astonishing* and once on an unattributed story in *Super Science Stories*. [PN]

TOWLSON, IVAN [r] ◊ M.H. ZOOL.

TOWNSEND, JOHN ROWE (1922-   ) UK writer, principally for older children, beginning with *Gumble's Yard* (**1961**; vt *Trouble in the Jungle* 1969 US), not sf. In *Noah's Castle* (**1975**), set in a deeply depressed NEAR-FUTURE UK, a family attempts to find enough to eat but the world's decline is too precipitate, and their haven is destroyed. *The Xanadu Manuscript* (**1977**; vt *The Visitors* 1977 US) is a TIME-TRAVEL tale which makes it clear that visitors from the future can bring only grief. *King Creature, Come* (**1980**; vt *The Creatures* 1980 US), told from the viewpoint of two young representatives of the ALIENS now occupying Earth, carries them into the human Creatures' lives just as a revolt is fomented, which they join. *A Foreign Affair* (**1982**) is RURITANIAN, and *The Fortunate Isles* (**1981** US) and *The Persuading Stick* (**1987**) are fantasies. A nonfiction study, *Written for Children: An Outline of English Children's Literature* (**1965**; rev 1974), is of interest.

JRT was not the John Townsend responsible for the interplanetary series for children consisting of *The Rocket-Ship Saboteurs* (**1959**) and *A Warning to Earth* (**1960**). [JC]

TOXIC AVENGER, THE Film (1984). HCH/Troma/Palan. Dir Michael Herz, Samuel Weil, starring Mark Torgl, Mitchell Cohen, Andree Maranda. Screenplay Joe Ritter, based on a story by Lloyd Kaufman. 90 mins, cut to 79 mins. Colour.

After a cruel practical joke is played on him, a teenage nerd falls into a barrel of toxic waste in Tromaville, New Jersey, "Toxic Waste Capital of America". He mutates into the Toxic Avenger and is compelled to murder bad people very violently. This farrago, combining teenage tits-and-ass comedy with horror/splatter, typifies the way exploitation films of the 1980s regularly used sf tropes, in this case gaining a mild cult following. *TTA*'s deliberate tastelessness is uninteresting because pointless. The sequel, partly set in Japan, dir Herz alone, is *The Toxic Avenger: Part II* (1989). [PN]

TOXIC AVENGER PART II ◊ *The* TOXIC AVENGER.

TOYNBEE, POLLY (1946-   ) UK writer and investigative journalist; she is of the fourth generation of Toynbees to be involved in literature. *Leftovers* (**1966**) depicts with feeble verve the mixed destinies of a group of youths, survivors of a poisonous gas which has destroyed the rest of humanity. [JC]

TRACTOR BEAM ◊ FORCE FIELD.

TRACY, LOUIS (1863-1928) UK journalist and writer, a colleague of M.P. SHIEL, who (uncredited) assisted him with several detective novels, all published as by Gordon Holmes. LT is best remembered for *The Final War* (**1896**), the first of his several future-WAR novels, which is significant for the malign intensity of the SOCIAL DARWINISM it espouses on behalf of "the Saxon race". The **Vansittart** sequence – *An American*

Emperor: The Story of the Fourth Estate of France (**1897**) with Shiel and *The Lost Provinces* (**1898**) – moves from the RURITANIAN shenanigans of the first vol, in which the American Vansittart romances a princess and becomes the emperor of France, into a future-war scenario in which, on behalf of France, he uses a fleet of armoured vehicles to defeat Germany. *The Invaders: A Story of Britain's Peril* (**1901**) less interestingly threatens the UK with a NEAR-FUTURE German invasion. 2 later novels endow their protagonists with PSI POWERS: in *Karl Greier: The Strange Story of a Man with a Sixth Sense* (**1906**; vt *The Man with a Sixth Sense* 1910) the power is that of reading minds and controlling others from a distance; in *The Turning Point* (**1923** US) the hero embodies centuries-old family memories. [JC]

Other works: *The Wings of the Morning* (**1903** US), associational ROBINSONADE; *The King of Diamonds* (**1904**), featuring a diamond-filled meteorite; *The House 'round the Corner* (**1914**), a ghost story.

See also: ESP; POLITICS.

TRAIN, ARTHUR (CHENEY) (1875-1945) US writer and lawyer, best known for work outside the sf field, particularly his legal series about the lawyer **Ephraim Tutt**. Some of the stories assembled in *Mortmain* (coll **1907**) verge on sf. In his first sf novel, *The Man who Rocked the Earth* (**1915**) with R.W. WOOD, the NEAR-FUTURE course of WWI is interrupted by messages from a mysterious PAX threatening superscientific punishments if war is not stopped. After some demonstrations, featuring rays, a flying ship and atomic energy, the nations obey. In the sequel, *The Moon Maker* (1916-17 *Cosmopolitan*; **1958** chap), also with Wood, the character who discovered the dead PAX in the previous book must now defend Earth against an approaching asteroid. He travels with a proto-FEMINIST mathematician; they marry. AT's quick skill as a popular novelist allowed him to fill out the speculations generated by his collaborator, a competent scientist; both novels thus avoid most of the absurdities that dogged the sf of the time. [JC]

TRAIN, OSWALD (1915-1988) UK-born US fan (◊ FANDOM) from 1935, when he became involved in the nascent Philadelphia Science Fiction Society, also attending the 1st (highly informal) CONVENTION in 1936. A significant SMALL-PRESS publisher, he was the main figure behind PRIME PRESS. In 1968 he founded Oswald Train: Publisher, which specialized in detective fiction, although it also released work by Lloyd Arthur ESHBACH, A. MERRITT, P. Schuyler MILLER and Olaf STAPLEDON. [JC]

TRALINS, S(ANDOR) ROBERT (1926-   ) US writer, prolific in several genres under more than one name and author of various borderline-sf tales, often involving sex. They include: *Dragon's Teeth* (**1973**) as Keith Miles; the **Valentine Flynn** series – *What a Way to Go!* (**1966**), *Operation Boudoir* (**1967**), *Win with Sin* (**1967**), *The Nymph Island Affair* (**1967**) and *Invasion of the Nymphomaniacs* (**1967**) – all as Sean O'Shea; *Pleasure Planet* (**1979**) as Starr Trainor (a tentative identification); and, as SRT, the **Miss from S.I.S.** sequence – *The Miss from S.I.S.* (**1966**), *The Chic Chick Spy* (**1966**) and *The Ring-A-Ding UFOs* (**1967**) – *Ghoul Lover* (**1972**) and #3 in a **Frankenstein** sequence (other vols by various hands). Also as SRT he wrote 3 unremarkable genre novels, *The Cosmozoids* (**1966**), *Android Armageddon* (**1974**) and *Signal Intruder* (**1991**). [JC]

TRANCERS (vt *Future Cop*) Film (1984). Lexyn/Empire. Prod/dir Charles BAND, starring Tim Thomerson, Helen Hunt, Michael Stefani. Screenplay Danny Bilson, Paul DeMeo. 76 mins. Colour.

Band apparently learned from his early, mostly bad movies, for this small film is confident, stylish sf. Future cop Jack Deth (Thomerson) travels back from AD2247 to present-day Los Angeles in search of dangerous mystic Whistler (Stefani), who has fled back in time and now occupies the body of an ancestor. Protected by a number of zombie-like "trancers", Whistler plans to murder the ancestors of his future opposition. Although primarily an action movie, *T* is packed with sf ideas, and it has an interesting punk look about it. There are astonishing plot resemblances to *The* TERMINATOR, released in the same year.

The sequel, *Future Cop 2* (1991), prod and dir Band, written by Band with Jackson Barr, again stars Thomerson and Hunt. Convolutions of TIME TRAVEL make Jack Deth, 6 years on, a bigamist, his original (dead) wife, played cutely by Megan Ward, being sent back (alive) to the present. Soap-opera elements are played out against further battles with trancers, who use a trendy ecological movement as a front. This returns us to the awfulness of Band's early films. Maybe *T* was a happy accident. [PN]

TRANSATLANTIC FAN FUND ◊ AWARDS.

TRANS-ATLANTIC TUNNEL ◊ *The* TUNNEL.

TRANSFORMERS – THE MOVIE, THE Film (1986). Sunbow/Marvel. Dir Nelson Shin. Voices by Orson Welles, Eric Idle *et al.* Screenplay Ron Friedman. Animation by Toei Animation. 86 mins. Colour.

This US-produced, Japanese-animated film is a spin-off from the comic-book and tv series of the same name, and all are part of a gigantic marketing operation to sell Transformers: model robots (invented 1984) which, when twisted around a bit, change their shape from humanoid to (usually) cars or spaceships. Most such films are pure exercises in commercial cynicism (◊ MASTERS OF THE UNIVERSE [1987]) but *TT – TM* has a surreal vigour. In AD2005 Earth and other planets are largely populated by good transforming ROBOTS, the Autobots, who are perpetually at odds with bad transforming robots who look much the same, the Decepticons. Since names, voices and shapes are constantly changing, it is almost impossible to follow the story further. The aggressive animation – which unusually for a film is in the style of state-of-the-art COMIC-book illustration (in this case MARVEL-COMICS-derived) – keeps the whole thing swirling along. Welles's last starring role

is, appropriately, as a megalomaniac planet. [PN]

TRANSPORTATION Sf stories based on serious speculations about future means of transportation are greatly outnumbered by stories in which those means function as facilitating devices – i.e., as convenient ways of shifting characters into an alien environment. Inevitably, the same kinds of machines crop up in both categories of story because stories of the second kind borrow heavily from those of the first. SPACE-SHIPS have been employed by sf writers almost exclusively as a literary device; few stories deal speculatively with the real possibilities of interplanetary and interstellar transportation. Much fruitless argument has been wasted comparing the plausibility of machines designed for quite different literary functions. One such argument, of long standing, concerns the relative merits of the space-gun in Jules VERNE's *From the Earth to the Moon* (**1865-70**: trans **1873**) and the ANTIGRAVITY device in H.G. WELLS's *The First Men in the Moon* (**1901**), which tends to ignore the fact that only the former device aspires (unsuccessfully) to practicability.

In FANTASTIC VOYAGES written before the mid-19th century virtually all modes of transport were facilitating devices. Today, the short-sightedness of the anonymous *The Reign of George VI, 1900-1925* (**1763**), which is optimistic about the bright future of the canal barge, seems slightly absurd; but the author of the book lived in a world in which there had been no significant advance in motive power for 2000 years. John WILKINS, fascinated by ideas of novel means of transportation, had discussed submarines, flying machines and land-yachts at some length in *Mathematicall Magick* (**1648**), but even he touched only tentatively on the possibility of adapting new POWER SOURCES to the business of transport. This situation underwent a revolutionary change in the 19th century.

The first practical steamboat, *The Charlotte Dundas*, was built in 1801, but it was not until the development of the screw propeller in 1840 for the *Great Eastern*, built by Isambard Kingdom Brunel (1806-1859), that the revolution in marine transport really began. Richard Trevithick (1771-1833) built the first practical steam locomotive in 1804, but only in 1825, with the opening of the Stockton-Darlington railway, did there begin the railroad revolution which very rapidly extended itself across Europe and the emergent USA. It is understandable that the speculative writers of the later 19th century should find the future of transportation one of their most inspiring themes. The revolution was continued with the development of the internal combustion engine, and entered a new phase in 1909, when Henry Ford (1863-1947) set his Model-T production line rolling. By then the first heavier-than-air flying machines were in operation, as were the first practicable submarines. Everything that has happened since in the world of transportation was within the imaginative sights of the writers of 1909: private motor cars for all; fast aeroplanes to carry passengers and freight; even spaceships (Konstantin TSIOLKOVSKY published "The Probing of Space by Means of Jet Devices" in 1903). The man whose literary work stands as the principal imaginative product of this era of revolution is Verne, whose first novel was *Five Weeks in a Balloon* (**1863**; trans "William Lackland" **1869** US). This was the period that made tourism possible, and Verne remains the archetypal tourist of the literary imagination. He was fascinated by the machines that made far travelling practical, and wrote a memoir of a real voyage on the *Great Eastern*: "A Floating City" (in coll **1871**; trans **1874** UK). The submarine *Nautilus* is the real protagonist of *Twenty Thousand Leagues Under the Sea* (**1870**; trans Lewis Mercier **1872** UK), just as the "aeronef" is of *The Clipper of the Clouds* (**1886**, trans **1887**; vt *Robur the Conqueror* **1887** US). *Around the World in 80 Days* (**1873**: trans Geo. M. Towle **1874** US) inspired many imitators, literary and actual, but few of the literary ones had Verne's fascination with means: most of them invented marvellous devices simply to enable the characters to participate in exotic adventure stories whose plots were thoroughly routine – a kind of inventiveness ironically celebrated by such latter-day SCIENTIFIC ROMANCES as Michael MOORCOCK's *The Warlord of the Air* (**1971**) and its sequels, and Christopher PRIEST's *The Space Machine* (**1976**).

Submarines and airships were most often invoked in futuristic fiction as carriers of WEAPONS and other materials of WAR. It quickly became obvious to military observers of the US Civil War in 1861-5 that observation balloons, ironclad ships and railroads would transform the tactics and logistics of warfare. Writers like George GRIFFITH took a particular delight in imagining the kind of battles which might be fought with airships and submarines, greatly assisted by the illustrator and occasional sf writer Fred T. JANE. Other illustrators, most notably Albert ROBIDA, likewise became entranced by flying machines. Wells's speculations about the future of transportation technology are mainly concerned with warfare – most spectacularly, the aerial battles in *When the Sleeper Wakes* (**1899**; rev vt *The Sleeper Awakes* 1910) and *The War in the Air* (**1908**). In *The Shape of Things to Come* (**1933**) he imagined the rebirth of a world devastated by wars under the aegis of a benevolent "Air Dictatorship", a notion anticipated by Rudyard KIPLING's stories of the Aerial Board of Control, *With the Night Mail* (1905; **1909** chap US) and "As Easy as ABC" (1912). Kipling's ideas were echoed in Michael ARLEN's *Man's Mortality* (**1933**), and the technological charisma of the aeroplane is evident also in *Zodiak* (trans Eric Sutton **1931** US) by Walther Eidlitz (1892-?   ). This mystique carried over into the early sf PULP MAGAZINES: Hugo GERNSBACK founded AIR WONDER STORIES to deal exclusively with the future of flight. Pulp-sf writers interested in facilitating devices were soon ready to take extreme liberties. The FASTER-THAN-LIGHT starship had arrived before the end of the

1920s, as had the ultimate in personal transport, the antigravity-belt featured in the BUCK ROGERS stories by Philip Francis NOWLAN. MATTER TRANSMISSION soon became commonplace; and some interplanetary romances of the kind pioneered by Edgar Rice BURROUGHS simply ignored the whole issue, tacitly employing the most blatant facilitating device of all: TELEPORTATION. Such methods began to receive more detailed speculative evaluation in Jack WILLIAMSON's "The Cosmic Express" (1930), but not until Alfred BESTER's *Tiger! Tiger!* (**1956** UK; rev vt *The Stars My Destination* US) was there a serious attempt to imagine a society which uses teleportation as a routine means of travel.

Attempts to imagine the eventual social effects of the transportation revolution soon appeared in the pulps. In David H. KELLER's "The Revolt of the Pedestrians" (1928) a ruling elite of automobilists is overthrown by the underprivileged pedestrians. The social role of the motor car remained a significant theme in sf, with explorations ranging from satirical comedies like Clark Ashton SMITH's "The Great God Awto" (1940), Isaac ASIMOV's "Sally" (1953) and Robert F. YOUNG's "Romance in a 21st Century Used Car Lot" (1960) through blacker comedies like Fritz LEIBER's "X Marks the Pedwalk" (1963) and dourer analyses like Ray BRADBURY's *The Pedestrian* (1952 *FSF*; **1964** chap), H. Chandler ELLIOTT's "A Day on Death Highway" (1963) and John JAKES's surreal *On Wheels* (**1973**) to such extreme quasi-apocalyptic works as Ben ELTON's *Gridlock* (**1991**) and the poem *Autogeddon* (**1991**) by Heathcote Williams (1941-   ). The car also features as a death-machine in macabre stories of future GAMES AND SPORTS, in such stories as Harlan ELLISON's "Dogfight on 101" (1969; vt "Along the Scenic Route") and the film DEATH RACE 2000 (1975). A classic early exercise in sf realism is Robert A. HEINLEIN's "The Roads Must Roll" (1940), which deals with the commuter chaos resulting from a strike by the engineers who maintain moving roadways. Other notable sf stories attempting to get to grips with the idea of social revolution brought about through transport deploy some kind of matter transmission in a quasi-symbolic fashion; notable stories in this vein include "Ticket to Anywhere" (1952) by Damon KNIGHT and "Granny Won't Knit" (1954) by Theodore STURGEON. Robert SILVERBERG's anthology *Three Trips in Time and Space* (anth **1973**) contains novellas on the theme: Larry NIVEN's "Flash Crowd", Jack VANCE's "Rumfuddle" and John BRUNNER's "You'll Take the High Road". Niven later continued the theme in 4 further stories, and Brunner developed it in a novel, *Web of Everywhere* (**1974**).

Early sf about transportation infrastructure is mostly concerned with tunnels. The Channel Tunnel often features in UK INVASION stories, while a transatlantic tunnel is the subject of Bernhard KELLERMANN's *The Tunnel* (**1913**; trans **1915**) and the films based on it, *Der TUNNEL* (1933) and *The TUNNEL* (1935). The idea reappears in modern sf in Ray NELSON's

"Turn Off the Sky" (1963) and is the theme of Harry HARRISON's ALTERNATE-WORLD satire *Tunnel through the Deeps* (1972 US; vt *A Transatlantic Tunnel, Hurrah!* 1972 UK). Early stories about artificial ISLANDS in the Atlantic to facilitate the refuelling of aeroplanes, such as Curt SIODMAK's *F.P.1 Does Not Reply* (trans **1933**), filmed as F.P.1 ANTWORTET NICHT (1932), were soon out of date. The problems of laying railroad tracks on an alien world are featured in "The Railways up on Cannis" (1959) by Colin KAPP.

There are numerous sf stories which involve improvised means of transport adapted to exotic situations. Jack VANCE is particularly ingenious in devising such inventions, although they rarely play a major part in his plots. Ice-yachts take centre stage in Moorcock's *The Ice Schooner* (**1969**) and Alan Dean FOSTER's *Icerigger* (**1974**), and ships which travel on unwatery media are also featured in David LAKE's *Walkers on the Sky* (**1976**), Bruce STERLING's *Involution Ocean* (**1977**) and Brian P. HERBERT's *Sudanna, Sudanna* (**1985**). The strangest vehicles ever devised are perhaps those in Robert Wilfred Franson's *The Shadow of the Ship* (**1983**), in which trails through airless "subspace" link primitive planets, and can be used only by starships that are effectively sleds drawn by vast animals; among the largest are the spacefaring CITIES of James BLISH's *Cities in Flight* series (omni **1970**) and the much more laborious moving city in Priest's *The Inverted World* (**1974**). An abundance of technical detail supports Hilbert SCHENCK's memorable account of the circumnavigation of the globe by a steam-powered aeroplane in *Steam Bird* (1984; title story of coll **1988**). In spite of such bold adventures, it cannot really be said that sf has been particularly adept in the invention of new means of transportation that have subsequently proved practicable, aside from a number of devices concerned with space technology – including, of course, space ROCKETS. Arthur C. CLARKE has proved particularly expert in this regard, and there remain several imaginative devices used in his stories which may one day be actualized, including the lunar transport in *A Fall of Moondust* (**1961**) and the spacefaring SOLAR-WIND-powered yachts of "Sunjammer" (1965), the latter developing a notion first put forward in 1921 by Konstantin TSIOLKOVSKY. Clarke's *The Fountains of Paradise* (**1979**) and Charles SHEFFIELD's *The Web Between the Worlds* (**1979**) both deploy "space elevators" connecting the Earth's surface to orbital stations – a wonderful idea whose practical limitations are, alas, mercilessly exposed in Sheffield's own article "How to Build a Beanstalk" (1979). [BS]

See also: COMMUNICATIONS; UNDER THE SEA.

TRAPROCK, WALTER E. Pseudonym of US writer George Shepard Chappell (1877-1946) for a series of sf tales spoofing the geographical romances popular just after WWI. In *The Cruise of the Kawa: Wanderings in the South Seas* (**1921**) a new Polynesia is discovered featuring birds which lay dice. *Through the Alimentary Canal with Gun and Camera: A Fascinating Trip to the Interior* (**1930**) takes Dr Traprock through a human digestive system. [JC]

Other works: *Sarah of the Sahara: A Romance of Nomads Land* (**1923**); *My Northern Exposure: The Kawa at the North Pole* (**1925**); *Dr Traprock's Memory Book, or Aged in Wood* (**1930**).

TREASURY OF GREAT SCIENCE FICTION STORIES US annual reprint magazine, PULP-MAGAZINE size. 8 issues 1964-71, published by Popular Library; ed Jim Hendryx Jr for #1-#3, then Helen Tono for the next 4, then Anne Keffer for the last. A follow-up of Hendryx's WONDER STORIES of 1957 and 1963, this was retitled as *Great Science Fiction Stories* (#3), *SF Yearbook: A Treasury of Science Fiction* (#4) and then *Science Fiction Yearbook*. The stories were from STARTLING STORIES and THRILLING WONDER STORIES. It is possible to consider the last 5 issues as a separate magazine, as the "Yearbook" title now stressed annual publication, the editor changed, and the numeration began again from #1. Although all 8 issues were in magazine format, there were no editorial departments, and they could equally be regarded as annual anthologies. [FHP]

TREBOR, ROBERT (? -) US writer, almost certainly pseudonymous (his surname is Robert spelled backwards), whose sf novel is the unremarkable *An XT Called Stanley* (**1983**). [JC]

TRECHERA, RAFAEL MARÍN [r] ◊ SPAIN.

TREIBICH, S(TEVEN) J(OHN) (1936-1972) US writer, co-author with Laurence M. JANIFER of the **Angelo di Stefano** series: *Target: Terra* (**1968**), *The High Hex* (**1969**) and *The Wagered World* (**1969**). [BS]

TREMAINE, F(REDERICK) ORLIN (1899-1956) US editor and writer; his first story was "The Throwback" for *Weird Tales* in 1926 as by Orlin Frederick. Already experienced in PULP-MAGAZINE publishing – he had ed various magazines from 1921 onward, including Bernarr MACFADDEN's *Brain Power* 1921-4 and *True Story* in 1924 – FOT assumed the editorship of *Astounding Stories* (◊ ASTOUNDING SCIENCE-FICTION) in Oct 1933, after it had been taken over by STREET & SMITH; curiously, although he had been working for *ASF*'s previous publishers, Clayton Magazines, FOT seems to have had no connection with the magazine prior to becoming its editor. He produced 50 issues of *ASF*, initially with the assistance of Desmond W. HALL, and under his editorship it became unquestionably the pre-eminent sf magazine of its day, featuring all the leading writers of the period and publishing the first stories of such writers as L. Sprague DE CAMP and Eric Frank RUSSELL. He soon instituted a policy of featuring in each issue at least 1 story described as a "thought variant" – i.e., a tale which presented a new concept, or a new gloss on a familiar idea. As an attention-attracting device this was an undoubted success, inspiring an imitation "new-story" policy in WONDER STORIES. When FOT became editorial director of a number of the Street & Smith magazines, he gave up the editorship of *ASF*, being followed in December 1937 by his personal choice for the job, John W. CAMPBELL Jr, whose stories as by Don A. Stuart FOT had been publishing for several years; the GOLDEN AGE OF SF was just around the corner. FOT's "thought-variant" notion can be seen as marking an important step in shifting magazine sf from its concentration on pulp adventure to the idea-led sf instituted by his successor.

The next year FOT left the company to found his own publishing firm, Orlin Tremaine Co., producing and editing COMET STORIES, which lasted only 5 issues 1940-41. He wrote a number of stories under his own name, and at least 1 as Warner VAN LORNE. He worked in non-sf publishing enterprises in later years, before being forced into early retirement through ill health. [MJE]

See also: ROBOTS; SF MAGAZINES.

TREMAINE, NELSON [r] ◊ Warner VAN LORNE.

TREMORS Film (1989). No Frills/Wilson-Maddock/Universal. Executive prod Gale Anne HURD. Dir Ron Underwood, starring Kevin Bacon, Fred Ward, Finn Carter. Screenplay S.S. Wilson, Brent Maddock from a story by Wilson, Maddock, Underwood. 96 mins. Colour.

A thinly populated valley in the Nevada desert is ravaged by 4 monstrous subterranean worm creatures, apparently possessed of some intelligence, which are finally destroyed by the courage and wit of the handful of local residents, along with a woman seismologist, who survive the initial attacks. This unambitious, textbook MONSTER MOVIE is notable for good dialogue and ensemble acting and for its very convincing MONSTERS, usually seen in broad daylight: a triumph of the special-effects teams. However, the monsters are hardly convincing as sf: arbitrary and unexplained – and probably "pre-dating the fossil record" – they have no apparent food-source undergound to enable them to grow so big. They are very like the sandworms in Frank HERBERT's *Dune* (1965) in appearance and in their sensitivity to vibration. [PN]

TRENT, OLAF ◊ R.L. FANTHORPE.

TREVARTHEN, HAL P. ◊ J.K. HEYDON.

TREVENA, JOHN ◊ Ernest G. HENHAM.

TREVOR, ELLESTON Initially the most famous pseudonym and latterly the legal name of the UK writer born Trevor Dudley-Smith (1920-   ), who eventually became best known for his **Quiller** espionage tales as by Adam Hall, after an early career writing children's fantasies (see listing below), some under his original name. His first novel of genre interest, *The Immortal Error* (1946), a fantasy, tells of an accident survivor who wakes up with the wrong soul in residence. *The Domesday Story* (1952 as by Warwick Scott; vt *Doomsday* 1953 US as ET and 1972 US as Adam Hall) tells of fears that an H-bomb test in Australia will bring about the end of the world. *Forbidden Kingdom* (1955) is a children's LOST-WORLD story about a high-tech enclave in the Kalahari desert. *The Pillars of Midnight* (1957) depicts the effects of a devastating disease. *The Mind of Max Duvine* (1960) is about telepathy. *The Shoot* (1966) returns to weapons-testing, this time depicting the launching of a missile

whose fuel is dangerously unstable. *The Sibling* (**1979** US as Adam Hall; 1989 US as ET) is horror. *Deathwatch* (**1984**) is about the NEAR-FUTURE accidental creation of a fatal virus by GENETIC ENGINEERING and its subsequent use by rogue Soviet hardliners to cause a decimating plague in the West.

Some of the **Quiller** tales, such as *The Berlin Memorandum* (**1965**; vt *The Quiller Memorandum* 1967) and *The Theta Syndrome* (**1977**), have TECHNOTHRILLER elements. A writer of almost excessive fluency, ET has made use of sf devices in passing, but never – it must be said – with much air of conviction. [JC]

Other works: Children's fantasies, many with shared characters: *Into the Happy Glade* (**1943**) and its sequel *By a Silver Stream* (**1944**), both as Trevor Dudley-Smith; the **Wumpus** sequence, comprising *Wumpus* (**1945**), *More About Wumpus* (**1947**) and *Where's Wumpus?* (**1948**); the **Deep Wood** sequence, comprising *Deep Wood* (**1945**), *Heather Hill* (**1946**), *The Secret Travellers* (**1947**), *Badger's Beech* (**1948**), which was also serialized on BBC radio, *Ants' Castle* (**1949**), 2 closely-linked tales – *The Wizard of the Wood* (**1948**) and *Badger's Moon* (**1949**) – themselves comprising a short sf subseries featuring space travel, *Mole's Castle* (**1951**), *Sweethallow Valley* (**1951**), *Badger's Wood* (**1958**), *The Crystal City* (**1959**), *Green Glades* (**1959**) and *Squirrel's Island* (**1963**); *Ants' Castle* (**1949**); *Secret Arena* (**1951**); *The Racing Wraith* (**1953**) as Trevor Burgess.

TREVOR, (LUCY) MERIOL (1919-   ) UK writer whose ALTERNATE-WORLD tales in the **World Dionysius** sequence – *The Forest and the Kingdom* ✴ (**1949**), *Hunt the King, Hide the Fox* ✴ (**1950**) and *The Fires and the Stars* ✴ (**1951**) – convey a bright childlike nostalgia for a planet which in some regards resembles Earth but whose history is more satisfactory than ours. This angle of view may be accounted for by the fact that, with Margaret PRIESTLEY (*whom see for her own contributions*), MT had decades earlier created the World Dionysius as a childhood fantasy. *The Other Side of the Moon* (**1956**), an sf juvenile, and *Merlin's Ring* (**1957**), an Arthurian fantasy, are unconnected to the sequence. [JC]

TRIAL OF THE INCREDIBLE HULK ◊ *The* INCREDIBLE HULK.

TRIMBLE, JACQUELYN [r] ◊ Louis TRIMBLE.

TRIMBLE, LOUIS (PRESTON) (1917-1988) US writer and academic, prolific in several genres including mysteries and Westerns – he wrote 66 novels by 1977 – but relatively little sf; his only sf short story was "Probability" for *If* in 1954. His sf novels came later, in a spurt, beginning with the **Anthropol Bureau** tales – *Anthropol* (**1968** dos) and *The Noblest Experiment in the Galaxy* (**1970** dos) – and climaxing with *The City Machine* (**1972**), set on a colony planet, where the device that constructs CITIES has been lost, forcing everyone into one overcrowded construct. LT clearly found sf venues of interest for the telling of tales – some of them surprisingly placid and landscape-oriented – and showed little concern for the exploration of the extrapolative implications that inspired the original invention of those venues. But he was extremely competent, and his entertainments mused profitably within the worlds of sf. [JC]

Other works: *Guardians of the Gate* (**1972**) with his first wife, Jacquelyn Trimble (1927-   ); *The Wandering Variables* (**1972**); *The Bodelan Way* (**1974**).

TRINGHAM, NEAL [r] ◊ M.H. ZOOL.

TRIP TO THE MOON, A ◊ *Le* VOYAGE DANS LA LUNE.

TROG Film (1970). Herman Cohen Productions/ Warner Bros. Dir Feddie Francis, starring Joan Crawford, Michael Gough, Bernard Kay, Joe Cornelius. Screenplay Aben Kandel, based on a story by John Gilling, Peter Bryan. 93 mins, cut to 91 mins. Colour.

A troglodyte or caveman survival (Cornelius) is discovered in a cavern, and investigated by an anthropologist (Crawford, in her last performance). All the innocent-in-the-modern-world clichés (◊ APES AND CAVEMEN) feature as the bewildered creature runs amuck, but loyal Crawford stands by him. One scene shows electrodes taped to his head so that we can "see" his remarkably anachronistic prehistoric memories, actually old dinosaur clips from Irwin ALLEN's *The Animal World* (1956). This routine UK movie was parodied (as if parody were needed) in John Landis's first feature, SCHLOCK (1973), whose caveman, unlike Trog (who is disturbed by it) loves rock'n'roll. [PN]

TROLLENBERG TERROR, THE 1. UK tv serial (1956-7) ITV. Prod/dir Quentin Lawrence, written Peter Key, starring Sarah Lawson, Rosemary Miller, Laurence Payne. 6 25min episodes. B/w. This is set mainly in an Alpine Hotel where intimations of doom received by a woman with ESP are followed by the revelation that ALIENS are on the mountain.

2. Film (1959; vt *The Crawling Eye*; vt *The Creature from Another World*). Tempean Production/DCA. Dir Quentin Lawrence, starring Forrest Tucker, Laurence Payne, Janet Munro, Jennifer Jayne, Warren Mitchell. Screenplay Jimmy Sangster, based on **1.** 85 mins. B/w.

The film version is more full-bloodedly unpleasant than **1**, especially in scenes where the aliens animate their dead human victims telepathically and turn them homicidal in a not very sensible scheme for conquest. The aliens themselves cannot come off the mountain, because they can survive only where it is very cold. Special-effects man Les Bowie worked hard on a shoestring budget, but the octopoid alien, with its one big eye, is ludicrous and the cloud beneath which the aliens lurk on the mountain was a piece of cotton wool pinned to a photograph. Loose ends of plot dangle everywhere, perhaps as a result of a 3hr story being reduced to half that length, but the film is not as bad as legend has it. [JB/PN]

TROLLOPE, ANTHONY (1815-1882) UK writer whose most famous novels make up the **Barchester Chronicles**. His 61st book, and sole venture into sf, *The Fixed Period* (**1882**), written a few years before his death, understandably (though evasively: no one actually dies in the book) concentrated upon that topic. It is

1980 on an ISLAND near New Zealand where sheep farmers are establishing an ambiguous UTOPIA in which no one will be allowed to live past the age of 67 – the age at which AT would in fact die. The Navy arrives in time to avert implementation of the scheme. Though not one of AT's stronger novels, it remains a speculation of interest, and demonstrates the vigour of its author's rather gloomy Indian summer. [JC]

See also: MACHINES.

TRON Film (1982) Lisberger/Kushner/Walt Disney. Dir Steven Lisberger, starring Jeff Bridges, Bruce Boxleitner, David Warner, Cindy Morgan. Screenplay Lisberger, from a story by Lisberger, Bonnie MacBird. 96 mins. Colour.

In this pleasing but lightweight film, a young man (Bridges) seeks evidence about dirty work in the computer company for which he works. For this he is literally deconstructed, reappearing as a subprogram in the VIRTUAL REALITY within the computer itself (along – just as in Oz – with analogues of two friends programmed by them to help him out). This world is ruled by the manic Master Control Program (or MCP) and its hench-program Sark (Warner), itself an analogue of a real-life evil-doer. There follows, disappointingly, a standard Good-against-Evil struggle on a somewhat austere computer-generated landscape resembling that of a rather good video game (◊ GAMES AND TOYS). The film has moments of wit, and a stunning last shot where the now reconstituted hero looks down on the streets of Los Angeles at night, for all the world like the computer grid from which he has escaped. This suggests that perhaps the whole film is a light-hearted text about determinism, but most of it aspires to being little more than a widescreen arcade-game scenario. [PN]

TROSKA, J.M. [r] ◊ CZECH AND SLOVAK SF.

TROUT, KILGORE An sf-writer character in Kurt VONNEGUT Jr's *God Bless You, Mr Rosewater* (**1965**) and *Breakfast of Champions* (**1973**), and used as a pseudonym (there was a row about this) by Philip José FARMER on the novel *Venus on the Half-Shell* (**1975**). [PN]

TRUDNO BYT' BOGOM (vt *Hard To Be a God*) Film (1989). Dovzhenko Studio/Halleluya Film GMBH/VO Sovexportfilm. Dir Peter Fleischmann, starring Edward Dzentara, Ann Gautier, Christina Kaufmann, Alexander Filippenko, Andrei Boltnev, Mikhail Gluzsky, Werner Herzog. Screenplay Fleischmann, Jean-Claude Carriere, Dal Orlov, based on *Trudno byt' bogom* (**1964**; trans as *Hard to be a God* **1973** US) by Arkady and Boris STRUGATSKI. 120 mins. Colour.

The most ambitious Soviet sf film to date, this Soviet/West German coproduction was 4 years in the making, and even so seems unfinished. Gorgeous sets, a good story (combining medieval swordfighting and futuristic starships) and a distinguished international cast did, however, ensure its success in European cinemas. The Strugatskis' multilevelled moral drama has been simplified to the level of pure action. The focus is court intrigue on an underdeveloped planet where a group of secret agents/investigators from a highly developed Earth witness the rise of a kind of medieval fascism, led by the local Hitler, Reba. The protagonist, Rumata, camouflaged as an indigenous nobleman, is not allowed to involve himself in the planet's politics; he is the historical observer who must not interfere with the experiment. However, he and his friends do attempt to save local intellectuals from pogroms and, when Reba's men kill the native girl with whom Rumata is in love, the Earthman humanist takes to the sword. A failure for Strugatski fans and for those who enjoy serious sf, but a feast for lovers of sword-and-bluster combat and a sentimental love story. [VG]

See also: RUSSIA.

TRUEMAN, CHRYSOSTOM The unidentified pseudonym of the UK author who lists himself as "Editor" of *The History of a Voyage to the Moon, with an Account of the Adventurers' Subsequent Discoveries* (**1864**), a PROTO-SCIENCE-FICTION tale described by Darko SUVIN in *Victorian Science Fiction in the UK* (**1983**) as being of considerable importance; Suvin also speculates that CT may possibly have been James Hinton (1822-1875), father of C.H. HINTON. The *Voyage* depicts its protagonists' discovery of an ANTIGRAVITY device which they use to fly to the Moon, where they find a UTOPIA inhabited by "amnesiac reincarnations of select Earthmen". [JC]

TRUSCOTT, GERRY [r] ◊ Candas Jane DORSEY.

TSIOLKOVSKY, KONSTANTIN (EDUARDOVICH) (1857-1935) Russian scientist and writer. He began investigating the possibility of SPACE FLIGHT in 1878. In his monograph *Free Space* (**1883** chap) he suggested that SPACESHIPS would have to operate by jet propulsion. His consideration of some of the practical difficulties led to a paper entitled "How to Protect Fragile and Delicate Objects from Jolts and Shocks" (1891). In 1903 he published the classic paper "The Probing of Space by Means of Jet Devices", proposing that space travel could be achieved using multistage liquid-fuelled ROCKETS. He wrote a good deal of didactic sf, mostly for young readers, in order to popularize his ideas. All of this is collected, along with several essays by or about Tsiolkovsky, in a vol ed V. Dutt, *Put' k zbezdam* (coll **1960** USSR; trans by various hands as *The Call of the Cosmos* **1963** USSR; unauthorized edn, with cuts, vt *The Science Fiction of Konstantin Tsiolkovsky* 1979 US), the US version substituting an intro by one "Adam Starchild", also falsely credited as ed. The sf stories include the novelette *On the Moon* (written 1887; **1893**), *Dreams of Earth and Sky* (coll **1895**), and a full-length novel, *Vne zemli* (1916 *Priroda i Lyudi*; exp **1920**; trans in this coll as "Outside the Earth"; also appeared trans, with intro, Kenneth Syers as *Beyond the Planet Earth* **1960** US), which is an account of the building and launching of a spaceship by an international group of scientists which ends with the

initiation of a project to colonize the Solar System.

KT was the first great pioneer of space research and the first real prophet of the myth of the conquest of space which has played such a vital role in modern sf. The inscription on the obelisk marking his grave reads: "Man will not always stay on Earth; the pursuit of light and space will lead him to penetrate the bounds of the atmosphere, timidly at first but in the end to conquer the whole of solar space." [BS]

See also: COLONIZATION OF OTHER WORLDS; FANTASTIC VOYAGES; GENERATION STARSHIPS; HISTORY OF SF; HOLLOW EARTH; PREDICTION; RUSSIA; SPACE HABITATS; TRANSPORTATION.

TSR INC. ◊ AMAZING STORIES; GAMES AND TOYS; GAME-WORLDS.

TSUBURAYA, EIJI [r] ◊ JAPAN.

TSUTSUI, YASUTAKA [r] ◊ JAPAN.

TUBB, E(DWIN) C(HARLES) (1919-) UK writer and editor who began publishing sf with "No Short Cuts" for *NW* in 1951, and for the next half decade or so produced a great amount of fiction, in UK magazines and in book form, under his own name and under many pseudonyms, some still undisclosed. After the late 1950s, his production moderated somewhat, but he remained a prolific author of consistently readable SPACE OPERAS. Of his many pseudonyms, those known to have been used for book titles of sf interest include Charles Grey, Gregory Kern, Carl Maddox, Edward Thompson and the house names Volsted GRIDBAN, Gill HUNT, King LANG, Arthur Maclean, Brian SHAW and Roy SHELDON. At least 50 further names were used for magazine stories only. His first sf novels were pseudonymous: *Saturn Patrol* (**1951**) as by King Lang, *Planetfall* (**1951**) as by Gill Hunt, "*Argentis*" (**1952**) as by Brian Shaw and *Alien Universe* (**1952** chap) as by Volsted Gridban. He soon began publishing under his own name, with *Alien Impact* (**1952**) and *Atom War on Mars* (**1952**), though his best work in these years was probably that as by Charles Grey, beginning with *The Wall* (**1953**). Of his enormous output of magazine fiction, the **Dusty Dribble** stories in *Authentic* 1955-6 stand out; ECT also edited *Authentic* from Feb 1956 to its demise in Oct 1957.

With *Enterprise 2115* (**1954** as by Grey; vt *The Mechanical Monarch* 1958 dos US as by ECT) he began to produce more sustained adventure novels. *Alien Dust* (1952-3 *NW*; 1954 *Nebula*; fixup **1955**; expurgated 1957 US) effectively depicts the rigours of interplanetary exploration. *The Space-Born* (**1956** dos US) is a crisp GENERATION-STARSHIP tale. These novels all display a convincing expertise in the use of the language and themes of PULP-MAGAZINE sf, though they tend to avoid examining their material very thoroughly. *Enterprise 2115*, for instance, deals swiftly and with ECT's typical largesse with REINCARNATION, the SUPERMAN theme and CYBERNETICS, along with a matriarchal DYSTOPIA; but the sustaining narrative – the pilot of the first spaceship returns from frozen sleep to reinvigorate a world gone wrong through its misuse of a predicting machine – hardly allows much justice to be done to any one concept.

The next decade saw few ECT titles until the start of the long series for which he remains best known, the **Dumarest** books: *The Winds of Gath* (**1967** dos US; rev vt *Gath* **1968** UK), *Derai* (**1968** dos US), *Toyman* (**1969** dos US), *Kalin* (**1969** dos US), *The Jester at Scar* (**1970** dos US), *Lallia* (**1971** dos US), *Technos* (**1972** dos US), *Veruchia* (**1973** US), *Mayenne* (**1973** US) and *Jondelle* (**1973** US) – both assembled as *Mayenne and Jondelle* (omni **1981** US) – *Zenya* (**1974** US), *Eloise* (**1975** US), *Eye of the Zodiac* (**1975** US), *Jack of Swords* (**1976** US), *Spectrum of a Forgotten Sun* (**1976** US), *Haven of Darkness* (**1977** US), *Prison of Night* (**1977** US), *Incident on Ath* (**1978** US), *The Quillian Sector* (**1978** US), *Web of Sand* (**1979** US), *Iduna's Universe* (**1979** US), *The Terra Data* (**1980** US), *World of Promise* (**1980** US), *Nectar of Heaven* (**1981** US), *The Terridae* (**1981** US), *The Coming Event* (**1982** US), *Earth is Heaven* (**1982** US), *Melome* (**1983** US) and *Angado* (**1984** US) – both assembled as *Melome and Angado* (omni **1988**) – and *Symbol of Terra* (**1984** US) and *The Temple of Truth* (**1985** US) – both assembled as *Symbol of Terra and the Temple of Truth* (omni **1989**). Earl Dumarest, who features in each volume, maintains with soldier-of-fortune fortitude a long search for Earth – the planet on which he was born, and from which he was wrested at an early age – but must battle against the universal belief that Earth is a myth. Inhabited planets are virtually innumerable; the period is some time after the collapse of a GALACTIC EMPIRE, and everyone speaks the same language; and, as Dumarest moves gradually outwards from Galactic Centre along a spiral arm of stars, it is clear that he is gradually nearing his goal. The opposition he faces from the Cyclan – a vast organization of passionless humans linked cybernetically to a central organic computer whose location is unknown – long led readers to assume that the Cyclan HQ was located on Earth, but the sequence stopped – perhaps at the behest of its publishers – at a somewhat inconclusive point. Though some of the later-middle titles seemed aimless, ECT showed consistent skill at prolonging Dumarest's intense suspense about the outcome of his long quest.

Concurrently, writing as Gregory Kern, ECT produced a more routine space-opera sequence featuring galactic secret agent **Cap Kennedy**. The Kern titles are *Galaxy of the Lost* (**1973** US), *Slave Ship from Sergan* (**1973** US), *Monster of Metelaze* (**1973** US), *Enemy within the Skull* (**1974** US), *Jewel of Jarhen* (**1974** US), *Seetee Alert!* (**1974** US), *The Gholan Gate* (**1974** US), *The Eater of Worlds* (**1974** US), *Earth Enslaved* (**1974** US), *Planet of Dread* (**1974** US), *Spawn of Laban* (**1974** US), *The Genetic Buccaneer* (**1974** US), *A World Aflame* (**1974** US), *The Ghosts of Epidoris* (**1975** US), *Mimics of Dephene* (**1975** US), *Beyond the Galactic Lens* (**1975** US) and *The Galactiad* (first published as *Das Kosmiche Duelle* ["The Cosmic Duel"], **1976** Germany; first English version **1983** US). Though these and some of the **Dumarest** books descend too readily to CLICHÉ, ECT estab-

lished and successfully maintained a reputation for providing reliably competent adventure sf, full of action, sex and occasional melancholy. Late singletons like *The Luck Machine* (**1980**) and *Stardeath* (**1983** US) continued the parade of efficient titles. [JC]

Other works: *The Mutants Rebel* (**1953**); *Venusian Adventure* (**1953**); *Alien Life* (**1954**); *World at Bay* (**1954**); *Journey to Mars* (**1954**); *City of No Return* (**1954**); *The Stellar Legion* (**1954**); *The Hell Planet* (**1954**); *The Resurrected Man* (**1954**); *Supernatural Stories 9* (coll **1957**), ostensibly a magazine but all stories by ECT under various names; *Moon Base* (**1964**); *Ten from Tomorrow* (coll **1966**); "The Life Buyer" (**1965** NW; the entire novel appears in SF REPRISE #5 **1967**); *Death is a Dream* (**1967**); *C.O.D. Mars* (**1968** chap dos US); *S.T.A.R. Flight* (**1969** US); *Escape into Space* (**1969**); *Century of the Manikin* (**1972** US); *A Scatter of Stardust* (coll **1972** dos US); *Sword in the Snow* (**1973** chap); novelizations of episodes from the tv series SPACE 1999, being *Breakaway* * (**1975**), *Collision Course* * (**1975**), *Alien Seed* * (**1976** US), *Rogue Planet* * (**1976** US) and the comparatively ambitious *Earthfall* * (**1977**); *The Primitive* (**1977**); *Death Wears a White Face* (**1957** *Authentic* as "Dead Weight"; exp **1979**); *Stellar Assignment* (**1979**); *Pawn of the Omphalos* (**1980** US).

As Charles Grey: *Dynasty of Doom* (**1953**); *The Tormented City* (**1953**); *Space Hunger* (**1953**); *I Fight for Mars* (**1953**); *The Hand of Havoc* (**1954**); *The Extra Man* (**1954**).

As Volsted Gridban: *Reverse Universe* (**1952**); *Planetoid Disposals Ltd* (**1953**); *De Bracy's Drug* (**1953**); *Fugitive of Time* (**1953**).

As Arthur Maclean: *Touch of Evil* * (**1959** chap), #438 in the **Sexton Blake Library**.

As Carl Maddox: *The Living World* (**1954** chap); *Menace from the Past* (**1954** chap).

As Roy Sheldon: *The Metal Eater* (**1954**).

As Edward Thompson: The **Imperial Rome** series, comprising *Atilus the Slave* (**1975**), *Atilus the Gladiator* (**1975**) and *Gladiator* (**1978**).

About the author: "The Perils of Bibliography: A Look at the Writings of E.C.Tubb" (**1979** *The Science-Fiction Collector #7*) by Mike ASHLEY.

See also: BOYS' PAPERS; CRYONICS; CYBORGS; DAW BOOKS; END OF THE WORLD; GAMES AND SPORTS; MARS; NEW WORLDS; PARANOIA.

TUCK, DONALD H(ENRY) (**1922-**   ) Australian bibliographer and industrial manager, retired. His bibliographical labours in sf since the late 1940s were among the most extensive in the field since the pioneering work of Everett F. BLEILER; they have since been partially superseded, but comprise one of the foundation stones upon which later workers have built. His early work was *A Handbook of Science Fiction and Fantasy* (**1954**; rev in 2 vols **1959**), in duplicated format, self-published. Far more thorough is the 3-vol *The Encyclopedia of Science Fiction and Fantasy through 1968*, consisting of *Vol 1: Who's Who, A-L* (**1974**), *Vol 2: Who's Who, M-Z* (**1978**) and *Vol 3: Miscellaneous* (dated 1982 but **1983**), all from ADVENT: PUBLISHERS; their usefulness to researchers was a little

limited by the slowness of production, *Vol 3* arriving 15 years after the book's cut-off date. Synopses are given for many books, and publishing data for all. Coverage of GENRE SF is thorough; coverage of non-genre sf and of older sf is patchy but sometimes illuminating. Generally (there are exceptions) DHT does not cover work which has not been reprinted 1945-68. Listings of stories in collections and anthologies are given, and the coverage is almost as thorough for fantasy and weird fiction as for sf. [PN]
See also: AUSTRALIA; BIBLIOGRAPHIES; HUGO; SMALL PRESSES AND LIMITED EDITIONS.

TUCKER, BOB [s] ◊ Wilson TUCKER.
TUCKER, GEORGE ◊ Joseph ATTERLEY.
TUCKER, JAMES B. [r] ◊ ROBERT HALE LIMITED.
TUCKER, (ARTHUR) WILSON (1914-   ) US writer, orphaned, brought up in Bloomington and Normal, Illinois, where he set some of his fiction, some early stories being signed Bob Tucker. For several decades he worked as a film projectionist, retiring in 1972, and he always spoke of his writing – more than 20 books, half of them sf, half of them mysteries – as an avocation. WT began his involvement with sf about 1932, and during the 1930s was exceedingly active as a fan and FANZINE publisher, starting with *The Planetoid* in 1932, though his most notable fanzine was *Le Zombie*, which lasted more than 60 issues 1938-75, the first half-decade of that period being its heyday; his *Neo-Fan's Guide to Science-Fiction Fandom* (**1966** chap) demonstrates the quality of this work. As an example of the violent humour and intense emotions aroused in early FANDOM, it is notable that WT was twice subjected to hoax obituaries in the sf magazines of the time. His fanzine *The Bloomington News Letter* (later *Science Fiction News Letter*) dealt mainly with the professional field.

While active as a fan WT was also writing fiction, though not until 1941 did he publish his first story, "Interstellar Way Station" as Bob Tucker, in *Super Science Novels*. He never became prolific in shorter forms – *The Best of Wilson Tucker* (coll **1982**) is definitive – soon turning to novels. His first, *The Chinese Doll* (**1946**), was a mystery, but made RECURSIVE use of the world of sf fandom. (WT pleased the knowledgeable fans, while annoying some critics, by his lifelong habit of using the names of fans and writers for the characters of his books; these names became known as Tuckerisms.) His first sf novel, *The City in the Sea* (**1951**), deals somewhat crudely with material similar to that treated far more effectively in the much later *Ice and Iron* (**1974**; exp 1975); in both, a matriarchal culture begins to re-invade a USA reverted to savagery, but in the latter the far-future matriarchy is linked through TIME TRAVEL to a USA, only generations hence, in the grip of a new ice age. This latter tale is not very coherently told, but the panoramas are lucid. Time travel is central to much of WT's work, featuring in tales like *The Lincoln Hunters* (**1958**), one of his best novels. Time travellers from an imperial USA several hundred years hence

are sent to acquire a recording of a lost speech of Abraham Lincoln; the two cultures are effectively contrasted. The ending, in which the protagonist is trapped in an 1856 far less unattractive than the future from which he came, is both poignant and welcome. In *The Time Masters* (**1953**; rev 1971), whose protagonist appears also in the sequel *Time Bomb* (**1955**; vt *Tomorrow Plus X* 1957), a long-lived extraterrestrial's presence throughout human history generates some of the same perspectives as time travel itself.

WT had a knack of choosing unusually resonant and appropriate titles for his novels. Examples are *The Long Loud Silence* (**1952**; rev 1970; early US edns delete implications of cannibalism, UK edns do not) and *The Year of the Quiet Sun* (**1970**). The former is a powerful post-HOLOCAUST novel, sombre and tough in feeling, though at points awkwardly told; the hero, unusually for a genre-sf novel, is in many ways cruel and insensitive. The latter, which won a JOHN W. CAMPBELL MEMORIAL AWARD retrospectively in 1976, sends its Black protagonist forwards in time to around AD2020, where he finds the USA in dire shape, his Blackness terrifying to the racially divided remnants of the civil war which has ended civilization. The prophecy that he had discovered in a non-Biblical ancient manuscript is fulfilled: there is to be a Year of the Quiet Sun. He prepares to watch the final rites of history.

WT was a very uneven writer, but expanded the boundaries of genre sf with his downbeat and realistic variations on old material, and demonstrated how effective a generic cliché like time travel could become when treated with due attention. By tying his use of time travel to virtual archaeologies of the worlds thus exposed, he transformed that cliché into an instrument of vision. He became inactive in the field after about 1980. [JC/PN]
Other works: *Prison Planet* (**1947** chap); *Wild Talent* (**1954**; exp 1955 UK; *The Man from Tomorrow* 1955); *Science Fiction Sub-Treasury* (coll **1954**; cut vt *Time: X* 1955); *To the Tombaugh Station* (**1960** dos); *Resurrection Days* (**1981**).
About the author: *A Checklist of Wilson Tucker* (**1991** chap) by Christopher P. STEPHENS.
See also: END OF THE WORLD; ESP; HUGO; IMMORTALITY; OUTER PLANETS; SPACE OPERA; SUPERMAN; TIME PARADOXES.

TUCKERISMS ◊ RECURSIVE SF; Wilson TUCKER.
TUMANNOST' ANDROMEDY (vt *The Andromeda Nebula*; vt *Andromeda the Mysterious*; vt *The Cloud of Andromeda*) Film (1968). Dovzhenko Studio. Dir Eugene Sherstobytov, starring Viya Artmane, Sergei Stoliarov, Nikolai Kriukov. Screenplay Sherstobytov, Vladimir Dmitrievski, based on *Tumannost' Andromedy* (**1958**) by Ivan YEFREMOV. 85 mins, cut to 77 mins. Colour.

A disappointingly polemical Russian adaptation of Yefremov's much better novel, *TA* tells of an attempt, 2000 years hence, to establish contact with an intelligent alien race living somewhere in the Andromeda Nebula. Most of the action takes place on a spaceship. The film's optimism about the future – manifest in the woodenly cheerful, healthy and uniformly handsome cast and the lack of dramatic tension of any kind (a problem not uncommon in UTOPIAN fictions) – is light years from the bleakness of later Russian sf films such as SOLARIS (1972). The sets and special effects are good.   [PN]

See also: RUSSIA.

TUNG, LEE ◊ LEE TUNG.

TUNING, WILLIAM (1935-1982) US writer whose *Tornado Alley* (**1978**) dramatizes NEAR-FUTURE attempts to deal with very bad storms. *Fuzzy Bones* * (**1981**) is a continuation of H. Beam PIPER's **Fuzzy** series, quite successfully extracting from Piper's own texts material requiring development, and exploring the origins of the Fuzzy race.   [JC]

TUNNEL, DER Film (1933). Vandor Film/Bavaria Film. Dir Kurt Bernhardt, starring Paul Hartmann, Olly von Flint, Attila Hörbiger, Gustaf Gründgens, Elga Brink. Screenplay Bernhardt, Reinhart Steinbicker, based on *Der Tunnel* (**1913**; trans **1915**) by Bernhard KELLERMANN. 80 mins (French version 73 mins). B/w.

This ambitious German film tells of a NEAR-FUTURE attempt by German engineers, imbued with nationalist fervour, to drill a tunnel under the Atlantic. A speculator attempts to sabotage the project. Technically, the film has a high standard, with convincing sets and special effects; the various disasters that occur – cave-ins, floods and volcanic eruptions – are realistically staged (too realistically, perhaps, as the film's associate producer was killed during the shooting of one such sequence). A French-language version was made simultaneously, starring Jean Gabin and Madeleine Renaud. The slightly inferior UK remake was *The* TUNNEL (1935; vt *Trans-Atlantic Tunnel* US).   [JB/PN]

TUNNEL, THE (vt *Trans-Atlantic Tunnel* US) Film (1935). Gaumont. Dir Maurice Elvey, starring Richard Dix, Leslie Banks, Madge Evans, Helen Vinson, C. Aubrey Smith, George Arliss, Walter Huston. Screenplay Clemence DANE, L. du Garde Peach, based on *Der Tunnel* (**1913**; trans **1915**) by Bernhard KELLERMANN. 94 mins. B/w.

A UK remake of the successful German film *Der* TUNNEL (1933). The plot is basically the same: a tunnel is built under the Atlantic linking the USA with Europe (though here the European end of the tunnel is situated in England). The film is not as technically impressive as the German version; it concentrates less on the national grandeur of the project and more on the domestic dramas of the tunnel's creators.   [JB/PN]

TUNSTALL, (WILLIAM CUTHBERT) BRIAN (1900-1970) UK writer whose *Eagles Restrained* (**1936**) showed some prescience in predicting a German-Polish conflict (though dating the event to 1954), but was less fortunate in its assumption that the League of Nations would intervene to quell the dispute.   [JC]

TUREK, IAN and IONE ◊ Eando BINDER.

TUREK, LUDWIG [r] ◊ GERMANY.

TURK, H(AROLD) C. (1958-   ) US writer who began publishing sf with the comic adventure *Ether Or* (**1987**), and whose exceedingly ambitious *Black Body* (**1989**) presents, in terms readable as both sf and fantasy, the autobiography of an 18th-century witch, during which she makes it clear that witches are in fact a kind of ALIEN species. The style in which the tale is told is both estranged (because she is not human) and strained (because HCT seems himself uneasy with some aspects of 18th-century diction); but the end result is, at points, very impressive.   [JC]

TURNER, EDGAR (?   -?   ) UK writer whose LOST-WORLD adventure, *The Armada Gold* (**1908**) with Reginald Hodder, is moderately exciting, but who remains of greater interest for *The Submarine Girl* (**1909**), in which a super-submarine meets up with the *Flying Dutchman*, awakens her crew, and arranges for their resettlement in South Africa.   [JC]

TURNER, FREDERICK (1943-   ) UK-born writer, in the USA from 1967, best known for his POETRY, though his first book of sf interest, *A Double Shadow* (**1978**), is a novel. Set on a FAR-FUTURE terraformed MARS, it depicts in dying-Earth flavours the conflicts of two characters who represent deeply contrasting classes of evolved humans; their strife leads them to transcend their volatile human condition. *The New World: An Epic Poem* (**1985**) more daringly takes the form of a book-length narrative poem. In a 24th-century balkanized USA 3 men vie to marry the heroine, herself stubbornly attached to an earlier lover. After much adventuring and a series of disquisitions on the UTOPIAN lifestyle achieved by the heroine's rural culture, the long tale ends in the mass-suicide of the villainous fundamentalists who have been threatening this society and with the resumption of her sanctioned relationship. Cumbersome at certain points, the book works in the end as an advocacy of and paean to the good life. *Genesis: An Epic Poem* (**1988**) is perhaps less successful but, in its successful presentation of a believable MARS, demonstrates its author's very considerable gifts.   [JC]

TURNER, GEORGE (REGINALD) (1916-   ) Australian writer and sf critic. His connection with sf came quite late in life, long after the publication 1959-67 of his first 5 (mainstream) novels. (There has since been a 6th, *Transit of Cassidy* [**1978**].) He became well known for somewhat stern sf criticism in the 1970s, published in SF COMMENTARY, FOUNDATION and elsewhere, and ed *The View from the Edge* (anth **1977**), stories from a major Australian sf workshop; GT then began writing sf himself. His first sf novel was *Beloved Son* (**1978** UK), in which an interstellar expedition returns to Earth in AD2032 to find a diminished post-HOLOCAUST population with very few old people, and a radically changed and somewhat merciless culture; the scenario is complicated by developments in GENETIC ENGINEERING. The book is perhaps ponderous, but was well received for its careful exploration of some plausible moral problems of the NEAR FUTURE. The other novels in this **Ethical Culture** series – different protagonists but a common background – are *Vaneglory* (**1981** UK) and *Yesterday's Men* (**1983** UK). They are serious and interesting, but the characteristic solemnity of their presentation has alienated some. The first piece in the series was the story "In a Petri Dish Upstairs" (1978), one of 8 stories collected in *Pursuit of Miracles* (coll **1990**).

Astonishingly, for he was now in his 70s, GT then changed gear. His next 2 novels are more fluid and spirited than his earlier work, though sharing with them a (this time different) 21st-century setting. *The Sea and Summer* (**1987** UK; vt *Drowning Towers* 1988 US), closely related to the earlier story "The Fittest" (1985), marked his breakthrough into the US market, with a genuinely distinguished and deeply imagined story of life in an overpopulated city in a future where Australia and the world's littorals are being drowned by the slowly rising ocean, a result of greenhouse-effect global warming; it won the ARTHUR C. CLARKE AWARD in 1988. *Brain Child* (**1991** US) is a thriller whose narrator slowly uncovers the story of a scientific experiment in genetic manipulation designed to enhance INTELLIGENCE (of which he is in part a product) and learns of the superhumans that may have resulted. This study in the ethics of superiority (◊ SUPERMAN) incorporates the story "On the Nursery Floor" (1985). In the autobiographical *In the Heart or In the Head* (**1984**), GT describes his relationship with sf, and displays a certain waspishness. He may be his country's most distinguished sf writer. [PN]

See also: AUSTRALIA; CHILDREN IN SF; ECOLOGY; ECONOMICS; FASTER THAN LIGHT.

TURNER TOMORROW AWARD ◊ AWARDS.

TURTLEDOVE, HARRY (NORMAN) (1949-   ) US writer and academic who has made use of his field of scholarship (his PhD was in Byzantine history) to create all his best-known work. The fantasy **Videssos Cycle** – *The Misplaced Legion* (**1987**), *An Emperor for the Legion* (**1987**), *The Legion of Videssos* (**1987**) and *Swords of the Legion* (**1987**), with the **Krispos** sequence, *Krispos Rising* (**1991**) and *Krispos of Videssos* (**1991**), serving as a prequel – follows the exploits of a Roman legion translated to the empire of Videssos, situated in a world where MAGIC works and Byzantine history is recapitulated. The **Basil Argyros** stories (1985-7), set in an ALTERNATE WORLD in which Mahomet became a Christian saint – assembled as *Agent of Byzantium* (coll of linked stories **1987**) – follows the exploits of a medieval secret agent who tends to cause scientific innovations against both his brief and his intentions. Though these books focus on their various charismatic and canny protagonists, HT's thorough understanding of his source material gracefully infiltrates the fun and fantastication.

HT began writing work of genre interest with two SWORD-AND-SORCERY tales as by Eric Iverson, *Wereblood* (**1979**) and its sequel *Werenight* (**1979**), and was soon publishing sf and fantasy with some frequency, sometimes as by Eric G. Iverson, some of his better non-series work being assembled as *Kaleidoscope* (coll **1990**). *Noninterference* (fixup **1988**) – in which a galactic survey team runs across ALIENS – and *Earthgrip* (fixup **1991**) – in which a reader of sf uses the expertise so gained to save alien races – are, unusually for HT, straight sf books not set in alternate worlds; but *A Different Flesh* (fixup **1988**) places hominid survivors (◊ APES AND CAVEMEN) in an alternate USA, and *A World of Difference* (**1989**) confronts Soviet and US missions on an alternate Mars – here called Minerva – populated by warring Minervans. HT has never failed to be exuberant when he sees the chance; however, he has not yet written any single book that has unduly stretched his very considerable intelligence. That book is awaited with interest. [JC]

Other works: *The Pugnacious Peacemaker* (**1990** chap dos), a sequel to L. Sprague DE CAMP's *The Wheels of If* (1940 *ASF*; **1990** chap dos), which precedes it in this sequentially printed DOS volume.

See also: ASTOUNDING SCIENCE-FICTION.

TURTON, GODFREY (EDMUND) (1901-   ) UK writer of fantasies like *There Was Once a City* (**1927**), *The Devil's Churchyard* (**1970** US) and *The Festival of Flora: A Story of Ancient and Modern Times* (**1972** US). He remains of some sf interest for *The Moon Dies* (**1972**), a book-length blank-verse narrative of the destruction of Earth's first moon (broken apart by gravity), the death of human civilization, and the survival of Noah. [JC]

TUTTLE, LISA (1952-   ) US-born writer, in the UK from late 1980, married to Christopher PRIEST 1981-7. An early member of the CLARION SCIENCE FICTION WRITERS' WORKSHOP, she very rapidly established her name as a writer in short forms, beginning with her first story, "Stranger in the House", for Robin Scott WILSON's *Clarion II* (anth **1972**), and winning the 1974 JOHN W. CAMPBELL AWARD for Best New Writer. Her stories very frequently make quietly devastating use of genre devices – often those associated with HORROR – to convey FEMINIST lessons about the relationships between men and women (◊ WOMEN AS PORTRAYED IN SCIENCE FICTION), though she tends to allow the political implications of these lessons to reside, tacitly, within her texts. Some of her better stories have been assembled in *A Nest of Nightmares* (coll **1986**), *A Spaceship Built of Stone and Other Stories* (coll **1987**) and *Memories of the Body: Tales of Desire and Transformation* (coll **1992**). Her first novel, *Windhaven* (1975 *ASF*; **1981** US) with George R.R. MARTIN, depicts life on a lost colony planet whose feudal culture is focused on the use of artificial (but functional) wings. Most of her subsequent books – like *Familiar Spirit* (**1983** US), *Gabriel* (**1987**) and *Lost Futures* (**1992**), whose heroine is thrust into several ALTERNATE WORLDS – are fantasies with strong elements of horror, idiomatically and cleanly told, in a level and foreboding voice, and tending to depict worlds which, in visual terms, seem both sinister and

washed. More and more, though commercial sagacity seems sometimes to have guided her tongue, she has given a sense of having revelations in store. She refused a 1981 NEBULA for "The Bone Flute". [JC]
Other works: *Catwitch* (**1983**), a juvenile fantasy; *Angela's Rainbow* (**1983**), associational; *Skin of the Soul: New Horror Stories by Women* (anth **1990**).
Nonfiction: *Children's Literary Houses* (**1984**) with Rosalind Ashe; *Encyclopedia of Feminism* (**1986**).
See also: BRITISH SCIENCE FICTION AWARD; ESCHATOLOGY; GOTHIC SF.

TWAIN, MARK Pseudonym of Samuel Langhorne Clemens (1835-1910), US writer and humorist. It is often not appreciated, although Philip José FARMER makes him the central character of his RECURSIVE *The Fabulous Riverboat* (**1971**), that a significant portion of MT's output – including what is at least his second-best novel, *A Connecticut Yankee in King Arthur's Court* (**1889**; vt *A Yankee at the Court of King Arthur* 1889 UK) – may be classified as sf. Some of Edgar Allan POE's sf was humorous but MT, drawing on the traditions of the literary hoax and the tall tale, was the first US writer fully to exploit the possibilities for HUMOUR of sf, inaugurating a rich but narrow vein that finds its current apotheosis in the work of Kurt VONNEGUT Jr.

One of MT's notebooks indicates that, like Poe, he was interested in the possibilities of ballooning, and in 1868 began a story about a Frenchman's BALLOON journey from Paris to a prairie in Illinois, leaving it unfinished because of the US publication of Jules VERNE's *Cinq semaines en ballon* (**1863**; trans "William Lackland" as *Five Weeks in a Balloon* **1869** US). However, he returned to the topic in an unpublished manuscript entitled "A Murder, a Mystery, and a Marriage" (**1876**) and in *Tom Sawyer Abroad* (**1894**), in which the hero crosses the Atlantic by balloon and ends up in Cairo.

Also essentially humorous is a skewed UTOPIA, "The Curious Republic of Gondour" (1875), in which certain classes of people, including the more intelligent, have more votes than others (cf Vonnegut's antithetical "Harrison Bergeron" [1961]). An equally skewed view of another ideal state is offered in *Captain Stormfield's Visit to Heaven* (written 1870s or later; **1909**). This materialist heaven is located in interstellar space, through which Stormfield sails with an increasing number of companions rather in the manner of the narrator in Olaf STAPLEDON's *Star Maker* (**1937**). To begin with, Stormfield races a comet, a not unlikely invention for a writer whose arrival and departure from Earth coincided with the time-table of Halley's Comet (a fragment from the 1880s is entitled "A Letter from the Comet"). MT's interest in astronomical distances, evident elsewhere, is particularly apparent here.

A parallel interest in vast temporal perspectives and geological ages is conspicuous in the many pieces that constitute MT's down-home version of the *Genesis* story, including his practical speculation concerning the daily lives of ADAM AND EVE in "Papers from the Adam Family" (written 1870s or later; 1962) and "Letters from the Earth" (written 1909; 1962). A considerably darkened sense of time and cyclical history informs "The Secret History of Eddypus, the World-Empire" (written 1901-2; 1972), MT's horrific but uncompleted vision of a future, 1000 years hence, in which Mary Baker Eddy's Christian Science rules the world, and MT himself, the potential saviour, is confused with Adam; MT's acerbic views on Eddy (1821-1910) are fully presented in his *Christian Science* (**1907**).

Given his fascination with time and history, it is not surprising that MT's best and most influential work of sf, *A Connecticut Yankee in King Arthur's Court*, should be concerned with TIME TRAVEL. The tale which seems to have inspired *A Connecticut Yankee*, Max ADELER's "Professor Baffin's Adventures" (1880), is an *implicit* time-travel story, but Twain's novel may be the first *genuine* time-travel story (the destructive ending takes care of the anachronism issue) and certainly established the pattern for that kind of sf (predominantly US) in which the hero, more or less single-handedly, affects the destiny of an entire world or Universe (cf L. Sprague DE CAMP's *Lest Darkness Fall* [**1941**]). While writing *A Connecticut Yankee*, MT, who like his Promethean hero was gripped by the march of invention – his own inventions included a history game and a notebook with ears, and he anticipated radio and tv – became disastrously involved financially with the Paige typesetter. That was one reason why *A Connecticut Yankee* is the transitional work between the light and the dark in MT's corpus. Many of the gloomy, quasi-Darwinist, philosophical ideas explored in such non-sf works as *What is Man?* (first version written 1898; **1906**) – the answer being a machine – and *Mark Twain's Mysterious Stranger Manuscripts* (written 1897-1903; fraudulent composite text **1916**; **1969**), which claim that everything is determined and that reality is all a dream anyway, figure prominently in *A Connecticut Yankee*.

The same ideas pervade MT's explorations in microcosmic worlds (◊ GREAT AND SMALL) in 2 extended but unfinished works: "The Great Dark" (A.B. PAINE's title; written 1898; 1962) is about an apocalyptic voyage in a drop of water (cf Fitz-James O'BRIEN's "The Diamond Lens" [1858]), while the narrator of "Three Thousand Years among the Microbes" (written 1905; 1967), reduced to microscopic size by a wizard, explores the world-body of a diseased tramp, Blitzowski (one of the inhabitants is called Lemuel Gulliver, and the influence of Jonathan SWIFT is otherwise apparent); it is implied that the Universe we inhabit is actually God's diseased body. (This kind of macrocosm/microcosm relationship is hinted at in MT's 1883 notebook outline for what, in anticipation of the GENERATION-STARSHIP theme, might best be called a generation-iceberg story.) In *The American Claimant* (**1892**): Colonel Mulberry Sellers claims, among other inventions, to have perfected the "Materializer", which can reconstruct the dead from whatever original atoms remain, and to be able to affect the climate by shifting sunspots.

If travel or communication can be managed instantaneously (and in *A Connecticut Yankee* and the microscopic-world stories the transference is indeed instantaneous), it seems logical that some loss of faith in the physicality of existence might occur, augmenting MT's notion that reality is insubstantial, a vagrant thought, a dream. In this connection, and as evidence of MT's concern with psychic possibilities (including the whirligig of schizophrenia), we should note the essays "Mental Telegraphy" (1891) and "Mental Telegraphy Again" (1895), which argue for the reality of ESP. Reference is made to the English Society for Psychical Research, and it is suggested that something called a "phrenophone" might communicate thoughts instantaneously just as the telephone communicates words. In "From the 'London Times' of 1904" (1898) – a newspaper hoax like "The Petrified Man" – another futuristic invention, called the "telelectroscope", a visual telephone, is used seemingly to disprove a murder. But it is precisely the divorce between image and reality afforded by this kind of instantaneous communication which causes ontological anxiety, and so the suspected murderer is executed anyway. [DK]

About the author: *The Science Fiction of Mark Twain* (coll **1984**) ed David KETTERER; *New Worlds for Old: The Apocalyptic Imagination, Science Fiction, and American Literature* (**1974**) by David Ketterer; "An Innocent in Time: Mark Twain in King Arthur's Court" by Philip Klass (William TENN), *Extrapolation #16*, 1974; "Hank Morgan in the Garden of Forking Paths: *A Connecticut Yankee in King Arthur's Court* as Alternative History" by William J. Collins, *Modern Fiction Studies #32* (**1986**); "'Professor Baffin's Adventures' by Max Adeler: The Inspiration for *A Connecticut Yankee in King Arthur's Court*?" by Ketterer, *Mark Twain Journal* (1986); *Mark Twain and Science: Adventures of a Mind* (**1988**) by Sherwood Cummings; *The Connecticut Yankee in the Twentieth Century: Travel to the Past in Science Fiction* (**1990**) by Bud Foote; the Mark Twain entries in *Science-Fiction: The Early Years* (dated 1990 but **1991**) by Everett F. BLEILER.

See also: DISCOVERY AND INVENTION; EDISONADE; HISTORY OF SF; MUSIC; POCKET UNIVERSE; SHARED WORLDS.

TWEED, THOMAS F(REDERICK) (1890-1940) UK publisher and writer in whose first sf novel, *Rinehard: A Melodrama of the Nineteen-Thirties* (**1933**; vt *Gabriel Over the White House: A Novel of the Presidency* 1933 US), filmed as *Gabriel Over the White House* (1933), a NEAR-FUTURE US President, after a car crash, begins to transform society, providentially destroys a Japanese war fleet through the use of air power, and – after recovering his old personality – dies before he can dismantle the new world order. *Blind Mouths* (**1934**; vt *Destiny's Man* 1935 US) less interestingly posits the collapse of society. Both books are written with smooth gravity. [JC]

20 MILLION MILES TO EARTH Film (1957). Columbia. Prod Charles H. Schneer. Dir Nathan Juran, starring William Hopper, Joan Taylor, Frank Puglia, John Zaremba. Screenplay Bob Williams, Christopher Knopf, based on a story by Charlott Knight, Ray HARRYHAUSEN. 84 mins. B/w.

In this typical MONSTER MOVIE a spaceship returns to Earth from Venus carrying a strange egg which hatches a humanoid/reptilian creature, an Ymir. The Ymir grows and grows until, bigger than an elephant, it escapes into Rome and is trapped and killed on top of the Colosseum. The model animation is pretty good, but the trouble with the Schneer/Harryhausen collaborations – designed solely to showcase Harryhausen's skills – is invariably a poor script, so that the special effects exist within an intellectual vacuum. No reason for this sulphur-eating alien's arbitrary destructiveness is given. A novelization by Henry SLESAR filled the only issue of AMAZING STORIES SCIENCE FICTION NOVELS (1957). [JB/PN]

27TH DAY, THE Film (1957). Romson Productions/ Columbia. Dir William Asher, starring Gene Barry, Valerie French, George Voskovec, Arnold Moss, Stefan Schnabel. Screenplay John MANTLEY, based on his *The Twenty-Seventh Day* (**1956**). 75 mins. B/w.

This sf morality tale – there were several such in the 1950s – is more optimistic about mankind's inherent goodness than most. An alien gives each of 5 people, in 5 different countries, a box of capsules (which will lose their power after 27 days) capable of destroying all human – but no other – life on any one continent. The boxes will open only for the recipients, on whom, especially the Russian, great pressure is put to use the capsules to wipe out enemy states. The recipients all act nobly (one suicides) and finally learn that the capsules have a second power: they will selectively destroy "every enemy of peace and freedom". They are used thus, several thousand bad people die, and only good people (the vast majority, in this breathtakingly simplistic scenario) are left. This was the second sf movie, the first being The DAY THE EARTH STOOD STILL (1951), to advocate mass murder as a way of eliminating warmongers. [JB/PN]

20,000 LEAGUES UNDER THE SEA Film (1954). Walt Disney. Dir Richard Fleischer, starring James Mason, Kirk Douglas, Paul Lukas, Peter Lorre. Screenplay Earl Felton, based on *Vingt mille lieues sous les mers* (**1870**; trans as *Twenty Thousand Leagues under the Seas* 1872 UK) by Jules VERNE. 127 mins. Colour.

This early Walt Disney live-action film was one of his best and most lavish. Fleischer has since returned to sf themes with FANTASTIC VOYAGE (1966) and SOYLENT GREEN (1973), but not so successfully. Nemo is an anarchist scientist who hates war; he uses his submarine, the *Nautilus* (here nuclear powered), to sink warships. The script is rather lame, though James Mason gives a stirring performance as the obsessed Nemo, who fights a lone battle against the world before being betrayed by 3 shipwreck survivors (including a displeasing harpoonist played hammily by Kirk Douglas) whom he has taken on board. He expires in style, at the centre of a self-made holocaust that envelops both his private island and the *Nautilus* before, significantly, forming a mushroom-shaped cloud. The special effects are good (and won an Oscar), especially notable being Bob Mattey's mechanically operated giant squid; the *Nautilus* itself with its ornate Victoriana is beautifully designed by Harper Goff.

There had been 3 previous film versions of Verne's novel: a mysterious 1905 Biograph production (18 mins) that does not appear in Biograph records, a French one made by George MÉLIÈS in 1907 (18 mins) and a US one, with fine underwater photography, written/dir Stuart Paton in 1916 (113 mins). [JB]

TWILIGHT'S LAST GLEAMING (vt *Nuclear Countdown*) Film (1977) Geria Productions/Hemdale. Dir Robert Aldrich, starring Burt Lancaster, Richard Widmark, Paul Winfield, Charles Durning, Melvyn Douglas. Screenplay Ronald M. Cohen, Edward Huebsch, based on *Viper 3* by Walter Wager (1924-   ). 146 mins (cut to 122 mins). Colour.

In this borderline-sf movie, set in 1981, a renegade US general takes over a missile base and threatens to initiate WWIII unless the President reveals to the nation the contents of a secret Pentagon file concerning the Vietnam War. The uncut version reveals how the Pentagon deliberately became involved in Vietnam to prove to the world that the USA was willing to sacrifice thousands of men, thus giving extra credibility to its willingness to fight a conventional war. These sequences disappeared when 24 minutes were cut by the distributor, ostensibly to "speed it up". What is left is a tautly directed thriller, though some of Aldrich's characteristic cynicism – reminiscent of his KISS ME DEADLY (1955) – remains (the Pentagon is victorious, destroying even the President to protect its secrets). The skilful use of a split-screen technique to create tension and moments of chaos and confusion justifies it as a legitimate cinematic tool. [JB/PN]

TWILIGHT ZONE, THE 1. US tv series (1959-64). A Coyuga Production/MGM. Created Rod SERLING, also executive prod. Prods were Buck Houghton, Herbert Hirschman, Bert Granet, William Froug. Writers included Serling (91 episodes), Charles BEAUMONT, Ray BRADBURY, Earl Hamner Jr, George Clayton JOHNSON, Richard MATHESON. Dirs included Jack Smight, Stuart Rosenberg, John Brahm, Ralph Nelson, Buzz Kulik, Boris Sagal, Lamont Johnson, Elliot Silverstein, Don Siegel, William Friedkin, Richard Donner, Joseph Newman, Ted Post. 5 seasons, 156 episodes (138 each 25 mins, plus 18 in season 4 each 50 mins). B/w.

TTZ, hosted by Serling with a rasping voice and a thin black tie, was an anthology series – perhaps the most famous ever on tv. Most of the playlets were pure fantasy, but a number were sf. The very first episode, "Where is Everybody?" by Serling, has a young man waking in a small town to find it deserted, with signs that the inhabitants had left only moments before. The denouement reveals that the situation has been implanted in his mind as part of a study conducted by space scientists into human reactions to loneliness. Sting-in-the-tail plotting was standard on TTZ.

Overall the series was thoughtful and fairly original, though it certainly had its fair share of CLICHÉS. Episodes varied in quality, many of the better sf ones being written by Matheson: 3 of these were "Steel" (1963), in which Lee Marvin is the manager of a robot BOXER who is forced to take his machine's place in the ring after it breaks down, "Little Girl Lost" (1962), about a child who falls into a dimensional warp under her bed, so that her parents can hear her crying but cannot reach her, and "Nightmare at 20,000 Feet" (1963), with William SHATNER as a man on an airliner who keeps seeing a mysterious creature – invisible to others – playing on the wing; as in most of Matheson's work, PARANOIA is eventually vindicated and the creature is proved to exist. Another sf episode was Bradbury's "I Sing the Body Electric!" (1962), about a robot grandmother.

Short-story versions of some of his TTZ scripts appeared in 3 books by Serling: *Stories from The Twilight Zone* * (coll **1960**), *More Stories from The Twilight Zone* * (coll **1961**) and *New Stories from The Twilight Zone* * (coll **1962**), with selections appearing in *From The Twilight Zone* * (coll **1962**) and all 3 being reprinted in 1 vol as *Stories from The Twilight Zone* * (omni **1986**). 2 anthologies ed Serling are *Rod Serling's The Twilight Zone* * (anth **1963**) and *Rod Serling's Twilight Zone Revisited* * (anth **1964**), both assembled in *Rod Serling's Twilight Zone* * (omni **1984**). A book about the series is *Twilight Zone Companion* (**1982**; rev as *The Twilight Zone Companion: Second Edition* **1989**) by Marc Scott Zicree. TTZ received 3 HUGOS (1960-62) as Best Dramatic Presentation.

TTZ was fondly remembered – indeed, it could hardly have been forgotten, the episodes being repeated endlessly in syndication for the next 20 years. This resulted in an anthology feature film prod and partly dir Steven SPIELBERG, *Twilight Zone: The Movie* (1983), mostly updatings of some of the old scripts. Then came a new TTZ tv series (**2**). The title was used also for a horror/fantasy magazine, *Rod Serling's The Twilight Zone Magazine* (1981-9), whose editors included T.E.D. Klein (1947-   ) and Tappan King (1950-   ), and which published some weird fiction of high quality.

2. US tv series (1985-7). CBS TV. Based on **1**. Executive prod Philip DeGuere. Supervising prod James Crocker. Prod Harvey Frand. Creative consultant Harlan ELLISON. Story editor Rockne S. O'Bannon. Writers included Ray BRADBURY, Alan BRENNERT, Crocker, DeGuere, Ellison, David GERROLD, George R.R. MARTIN, O'Bannon, Michael REAVES, Carter SCHOLZ. Dirs included Wes Craven, Tommy Lee Wallace, Theodore Flicker, Joe DANTE, Gerd Oswald, Martha Coolidge, Allan Arkush, Peter Medak, Jim

McBride, Paul Lynch, Noel Black. 2 seasons. Season 1: 24 50min episodes, each containing 2-4 stories. Season 2: 12 episodes, some 50min and some 25min. There were 80 stories in the 36 episodes. Colour.

In the mid-1980s US tv turned back, for a while, to the anthology format, especially for series of fantastic stories – AMAZING STORIES was another. Few had any prolonged success. This new series of *TTZ* dramatized several well known sf stories, including "The Star" (1955) by Arthur C. CLARKE and stories by Robert SILVERBERG and Theodore STURGEON, but the majority of playlets were based on original scripts, some also by sf writers, though as with the original series the emphasis was on fantasy rather than sf. Good directors were used and the quality was quite high, but the series was axed after 2 seasons. *TTZ* was quickly re-edited into half-hour segments for syndication, when a further 30 stories were dramatized (executive prods Mark Shelmerdine and Michael MacMillan), with substantially lower budgets, and shown along with the 80 stories from the 1985-7 series.   [PN/JB]

TWILIGHT ZONE: THE MOVIE ◊ Joe DANTE; George MILLER; Steven SPIELBERG; *The* TWILIGHT ZONE.

TWO COMPLETE SCIENCE-ADVENTURE BOOKS US PULP MAGAZINE. Thrice yearly, 11 issues Winter 1950-Spring 1954, published by Wings Publishing Co.; ed Jerome BIXBY (Winter 1950-Summer 1951), Malcolm Reiss (Winter 1951-Summer 1953) and Katharine Daffron (Winter 1953-Spring 1954). Issues numbered #1-#11.

A companion magazine to PLANET STORIES, *TCSAB* was originally intended to reprint in cheap magazine format recently published sf novels; #1 contained Isaac ASIMOV's *Pebble in the Sky* (**1950**) and L. Ron HUBBARD's novella "The Kingslayer" (title story of *The Kingslayer*, coll **1949**). This policy proved impossible to sustain; although there were a few more reprints, the majority of subsequent stories were original. These included: Arthur C. CLARKE's "The Seeker of the Sphinx" (Spring 1951; vt "The Road to the Sea"); James BLISH's *The Warriors of Day* (Summer 1951 as "Sword of Xota"; **1953**) and "Sargasso of Lost Cities" (Spring 1953), one of his **Okie** series; L. Sprague DE CAMP's "The Tritonian Ring" (Winter 1951; title story of *The Tritonian Ring* coll **1953**); and John BRUNNER's first (acknowledged) story, *The Space-Time Juggler* (Summer 1953 as "The Wanton of Argus" by Kilian Houston Brunner; **1963** chap dos as JB). *TCSAB* did not contain any editorial matter and was unusual among pulp sf magazines in seldom printing readers' letters.   [MJE]

TWONKY, THE Film (1953). Arch Oboler Productions/United Artists. Dir Arch Oboler, starring Hans Conreid, Billy Lynn, Gloria Blondell, Janet Warren and Ed Max. Screenplay Oboler, based on "The Twonky" (1942) by Lewis Padgett (Henry KUTTNER). 72 mins. B/w.

After his sanctimonious FIVE (1951), about survivors of nuclear war, Oboler chose another sf subject for his next film. A creature from the future invades a tv set, bringing it alive. The set is soon running its owner's life, scuttling about doing household jobs by means of an electronic beam, but later becoming censorious and dictatorial, hypnotizing those who attempt to stop it. Kuttner's witty story collapses under the weight of Oboler's laborious script and the inadequate special effects. Tv was a much-hated medium in Hollywood at that time, and it was only appropriate that Oboler, an old-time radio producer, should have launched this symbolic attack. The film was unreleased for 17 months, then flopped.   [JB/PN]

2,000 AD UK weekly sf COMIC-strip magazine, 32-36pp, published by IPC from 26 Feb, 1977, and then from 1987 by Fleetway. Eds have included Kelvin Gosnell, Steve McManus, Richard Burton. Throughout, the editor has been presented as an ALIEN called Tharg, and some very entertaining and original sf short stories have appeared under the title **Tharg's Future Shocks**. Early issues (referred to as "progs") were printed on cheap pulp paper with colour for the front and back and for a centre-spread. Continued success eventually justified a "new look", with better-quality paper and printing, including 50-60 per cent in colour. Many of *2,000 AD*'s contributing artists and writers have achieved transatlantic success. They include Simon Bisley, Brian BOLLAND, Dave GIBBONS, JUDGE DREDD writers Alan Grant and John Wagner, Kam Kennedy, Alan MOORE, Grant Morrison, Kevin O'Niell and Bryan Talbot. The magazine has featured a number of high-quality sf strips, including DAN DARE (from #1, 26 Feb 1977), **Judge Dredd** (from #2, 5 Mar 1977), **Robo-Hunter** (from #76, 5 Aug 1978), **Strontium Dog** (from #86, 14 Oct 1978), **ABC Warriors** (from #119, 30 June 1979), **The VCs** (from #140, 24 Nov 1979), **Stainless Steel Rat** (also from #140), **Slaine** (from #330, 20 Aug 1983), **Ballad of Halo Jones** (from #376, 7 July 1984), **Anderson Psi Division** (from #416, 4 May 1985) and **Bad Company** (from #500, 13 Dec 1986). Many *2,000 AD* strips have been reprinted in the UK as GRAPHIC NOVELS and also in the USA in comic-book format (with artwork stretched lengthways to suit the taller page shape) under the Eagle Comics imprint (subsequently continued by Quality Comics and later by Fleetway). There have been several related hardback publications in the form of Annuals and Yearbooks, containing occasional reprints from the weekly but mostly new material of lower quality. A monthly black-and-white title with a glossy cover, *Best of 2,000 AD*, has been published since Oct 1985.   [RT]

2001: A SPACE ODYSSEY Film (1968). Prod/dir Stanley KUBRICK, starring Keir Dullea, Gary Lockwood. Screenplay Kubrick, Arthur C. CLARKE, based loosely on Clarke's "The Sentinel" (1951). 160 mins, cut to 141 mins. Colour. Originally in Cinerama.

This was the most ambitious sf film of the 1960s and perhaps ever. Kubrick's unique production, which received a 1969 HUGO, takes several traditional sf themes – including the idea, derived from Charles

FORT, that "we are property" – and spins from them a web of pessimistic METAPHYSICS. In prehistoric times the mysterious arrival of an alien artefact, a black monolith, triggers primitive ape people into becoming tool-users; the first tool is a weapon. The transition to the AD2001 sequence – marked by the resonant image of a bone weapon thrown (in slow motion) into the air and becoming a space station – suggests that, for all the awesome complexity of our tools, humanity itself is still in a primitive stage. The idea of human deficiency in the 21st century is reinforced by the deliberate banality of the dialogue and the sterility of the settings; ironically the most "human" character is a neurotic computer, itself subject to Original Sin, HAL 9000. A second monolith discovered on the Moon beams a signal at one of the moons of Jupiter and a spaceship, the *Discovery*, is sent to investigate, but, through HAL having a nervous breakdown, only one of the astronauts (Dullea) survives to reach the area. There he embarks (through a "Star Gate") on a prolonged, disorienting trip through what appears to be inner time and INNER SPACE, pausing to meet his dying self in an 18th-century bedroom, and becoming the foetus of a Superbeing, an optimistic apotheosis – with its suggestion of a transcendent EVOLUTION, directed by never-seen ALIENS, or perhaps God – in an otherwise dark film.

Aside from its intellectual audacity, *2001* is remarkable for a visual splendour that depends in part on astonishingly painstaking special effects. Conceived by Kubrick – notoriously a perfectionist – and achieved by many technicians (pointing forward to the huge teams that would work on the special-effects blockbusters of a decade later), these mostly employ traditional techniques. Instead of such modern automatic matteing processes as the blue-screen system, hand-drawn mattes were produced for each effects frame at the cost of two years' time and much money, which is why this method is now rarely used. Innovative in another way is the setting of romantic MUSIC by Richard Strauss, Johann Strauss and Gyorgy Ligeti against much of the technological action, giving the paradoxical feeling of a cool romanticism and reinforcing the film's ambiguities. The present 141min version, cut from the 160min preview length, should be viewed in the full wide-screen 70mm format (*2001* was one of the early films designed for Cinerama).

The tension between Kubrick's love of oblique allusion and Clarke's open rationalism is resolved in the latter's book of the film, *2001: A Space Odyssey* ∗ (**1968**), which – written after the film's completion – provides clear explanations in Clarke's usual manner. He described his connection with the film in *The Lost Worlds of 2001* (coll **1972**), which also prints alternative script versions of key scenes. The film sequel, based on another Clarke novel, was 2010 (**1984**). [PN/JB]

See also: COMICS; CONCEPTUAL BREAKTHROUGH; GODS AND DEMONS; HISTORY OF SF; INTELLIGENCE; LINGUISTICS;

ORIGIN OF MAN; SPACE FLIGHT; SPACE HABITATS.

2010 Film (**1984**). MGM/UA. Prod/dir/photographed/written Peter Hyams, starring Roy Scheider, John Lithgow, Helen Mirren, Bob Balaban, Keir Dullea. Screenplay based on *2010: Odyssey Two* (**1982**) by Arthur C. CLARKE. 116 mins. Colour.

Nine years after the events of 2001: A SPACE ODYSSEY (1968), a joint Soviet-US space mission in a Russian spacecraft is sent to recover information from the *Discovery*, which in the previous film had been left in orbit around Jupiter with its computer, HAL 9000, disabled. In a remarkably thin storyline the crew reach the *Discovery* and are contacted by the ALIEN monolith, their intercourse being mediated through the "ghost" of Dave Bowman (Dullea), who was last seen transfigured to a Star Child in 2001: "Something wonderful is going to happen." They then go home again, helped by the resuscitated HAL. Countless monoliths invest Jupiter and turn it into a second sun. *Homo sapiens* is given the Solar System to populate, except for Europa (one of Jupiter's moons), which is off limits, and on which a new monolith awaits . . .

Devoid of both narrative thrust and any interaction of characters that transcends cliché, the film – despite some rather good space scenes – could never have succeeded. The old pulp-sf notion of Peace on Earth (where WWIII may be about to break out) being restored by the intervention of a godlike figure Out There is, to some viewers, insulting mysticism. The approach of Clarke and Hyams to the metaphysical is a lot less magical and delicate (and ambiguous) than was that of Clarke and Stanley KUBRICK. This time the alien superbeings pretty well hit us over the head with a truncheon. The film was awarded a 1985 HUGO. [PN]

TYERS, KATHY Working name of US writer Kathleen Moore Tyers (1952-   ). She began writing with her **Firebird** sequence, *Firebird* (**1987**) and *Fusion Fire* (**1988**), set in an interplanetary-romance venue replete with colourful planetary cultures, an overarching Federation, space invasions, palace politics and the discovery of budding PSI POWERS in the eponymous protagonist, a princess on an evil planet. Her route to psionic maturity and marital happiness with the telepathic ruler of a neighbouring world is depicted with cluttered vigour. In *Crystal Witness* (**1989**) a female criminal, exiled to another world, must come triumphantly to terms with her new circumstances. In *Shivering World* (**1991**) yet another arrival into an alien world must deal with the TERRAFORMING problems of some settlers. KT is an active writer, and may settle into significant work. [JC]

TYLER, THEODORE Pseudonym of US writer Edward William Ziegler (1932-   ), whose *The Man whose Name Wouldn't Fit, or The Case of Cartwright-Chickering* (**1968**) deals humorously with the computerized regimentation of a NEAR-FUTURE society. [JC]

TYMN, MARSHALL B(ENTON) (1937-   ) US editor,

academic, sf/fantasy bibliographer and editor, whose work concentrates on the pedagogical implications of both sf and fantasy (◊ SF IN THE CLASSROOM). After a first, short, self-published bibliographical guide – *A Directory of Science Fiction and Fantasy Publishing Houses and Book Dealers* (**1974** chap) – MBT issued a stream of helpful material, including *A Research Guide to Science Fiction Studies: An Annotated Checklist of Primary and Secondary Sources* (**1977**) with L.W. CURREY and Roger C. SCHLOBIN, *Recent Critical Studies on Fantasy Literature: An Annotated Checklist* (**1978** chap), *A Basic Reference Shelf for Science Fiction Teachers* (**1978** chap), *The Science Fiction Reference Book* (anth **1981**) and its abridged successor, *Science Fiction: A Teacher's Guide & Resource Book* (anth **1988**), and *A Teacher's Guide to Science Fiction* (**1981** chap; exp 1982 chap). Of somewhat wider interest is the **Year's Scholarship** sequence of annotated checklists, appearing first in the journal EXTRAPOLATION, these instalments being incorporated in the book-form publication of the series, which comprised *The Year's Scholarship in Science Fiction and Fantasy: 1972-1975* (**1979**) with Roger C. Schlobin, *The Year's Scholarship in Science Fiction and Fantasy: 1976-1979* (**1983**) with Schlobin, *The Year's Scholarship in Science Fiction, Fantasy, and Horror Literature: 1980* (**1983**), *The Year's Scholarship in Science Fiction, Fantasy, and Horror Literature: 1981* (**1984**) and *The Year's Scholarship in Science Fiction, Fantasy and Horror Literature: 1982* (**1985**). After this last volume the series was again published in *Extrapolation* through coverage year 1987 (in 1988). A successor series, **Year's Scholarship in Fantastic Literature and the Arts**, began in 1990 in JOURNAL OF THE FANTASTIC IN THE ARTS, with coverage year 1988, but further work was hampered by the aftereffects of a serious auto accident in late 1989.

Of even broader potential interest were several BIBLIOGRAPHIES of the genre itself, including: *American Fantasy & Science Fiction: Toward a Bibliography of Works Published in the United States, 1948-1973* (**1979**); *Index to Stories in Thematic Anthologies of SF* (**1979**) with L.W. Currey, Martin H. GREENBERG and Joseph D. OLANDER; *Fantasy Literature: A Core Collection and Reference Guide* (**1979**) with Robert H. Boyer (1937-   ) and Kenneth J. Zahorski (1939-   ); *Horror Literature: A Core Collection and Reference Guide* (**1981**); *Survey of Science Fiction Literature: Bibliographical Supplement* (**1982**); and – perhaps most interesting of all his work – *Science Fiction, Fantasy & Weird Fiction Magazines* (**1985**) with Mike ASHLEY, a comprehensive history of magazines in the field, arranged as an encyclopedia. Though MBT's coverage of sf and fantasy has sometimes been partial, with some of his checklists eventually being supplanted by fuller works from Hal W. HALL, Robert REGINALD and others, MBT was for two decades an essential figure, and did much to focus the field for the academic world, not least through his editorial work with GREENWOOD PRESS. In 1990 he was given the PILGRIM AWARD for sf scholarship, his wife accepting on his behalf. [JC]

See also: CRITICAL AND HISTORICAL WORKS ABOUT SF; FANTASY; SF MAGAZINES.

TYSON, J(OHN) AUBREY (1870-1930) US writer whose *The Scarlet Tanager* (**1922**), set in 1930, rousingly puts a submarine pirate in opposition to a tough US intelligence agent. A UK agent, the actress of the title, also becomes involved. Sf devices include sonar and an invisible ray. [JC]

Other work: *The Barge of Haunted Lives* (coll of linked stories **1923**).

UCHUJIN Fanzine. ◊ JAPAN; Takumi SHIBANO.

UFO UK tv series (1970-73). Century 21 Pictures Ltd Production/ITC. Created Gerry and Sylvia ANDERSON with Reg Hill. Executive prod Gerry Anderson. Prod Reg Hill. Script ed Tony Barwick. Dirs included Anderson, David Tomblin, Alan Perry, Dave Lane, Ken Turner. Writers included Barwick, Tomblin. Special effects Derek Meddings. 26 50min episodes. Colour.

Before this series the Andersons had been best known for their sf tv puppet series, such as THUNDER-BIRDS. In this first live-action tv series from them the actors certainly resembled puppets, and the make-up, apparently deliberately, reinforced the effect. Set in the NEAR FUTURE (1980), *UFO* tells how SHADO (Supreme Headquarters Alien Defence Organiza-tion), headed by Commander Straker (Ed Bishop), fights against hostile, telepathic aliens in flying saucers (◊ UFOS). Meddings's special effects were impressive, though some of the props, costumes, etc., were recycled from the Andersons' first live-action production, the film DOPPELGANGER (1969; vt *Journey to the Far Side of the Sun*). The bland scripts, though more sophisticated than those of the **Super-Marionation** puppet series, were typical of Anderson productions (*see also* SPACE 1999), possibly because the Andersons underestimated children's intelligence. Many of the stories, about elusive disguised aliens, were reminiscent of episodes of *The* INVADERS (1967-8). Though there were only 26 episodes, lack of enthusiasm by the commercial networks led to a gap of more than 2 years between first and last. Ties are *UFO* * (**1970**; vt *UFO-1: Flesh Hunters* 1973 US) and *UFO 2* * (**1971**; vt *UFO-2: Sporting Blood* 1973 US) by Robert Miall (Jonathan BURKE). [PN/JB]

UFO INCIDENT, THE Made-for-tv film (1975). Universal/NBC. Dir Richard A. Colla, starring James Earl Jones, Estelle Parsons, Bernard Hughes, Beeson Carroll, Dick O'Neill. Screenplay S. Lee Pogostin, Hesper Anderson, based on *The Interrupted Journey* (**1966**) by John G. Fuller. 100 mins. Colour.

James Earl Jones (the voice behind Darth Vader in STAR WARS) tried for years to secure the finance to make a film about this supposed UFO incident (◊ UFOS), which took place in 1961. A couple, Betty and Barney Hill, encounter a UFO while out driving. Subsequent nightmares and feelings of anxiety lead them to seek psychiatric help which reveals, through hypnosis, that they possess unconscious memories of being taken and examined for 2 hours by aliens. It is unusually well made and intelligently acted for a tv movie. [JB/PN]

UFOS A common item of terminology, both inside and outside sf, UFO is an acronym for Unidentified Flying Object. In the 1st edn of this encyclopedia, the subject of ufology was discussed under the heading "Flying Saucers". The change of title reflects the fact that ufology itself has changed over the past couple of decades, to the extent that it must now be thought of almost as 3 separate disciplines, one of which (concerning flying saucers) is a straightforward PSEUDO-SCIENCE, one of which is a hybrid of aspects of geology and meteorology, and one of which deals with psychology.

The term "flying saucer" was born in 1947 when the US businessman Kenneth Arnold, while flying his private plane near Mt Rainier, Washington State, saw what he perceived as 9 disc-like objects flying in formation nearby; he described their flight as being "like a saucer would if you skipped it across the water". Sightings continued through the late 1940s and the 1950s, becoming ever more elaborate and intimate, and still continue today, decades later, albeit not at the same feverish frequency as during the height of the Saucer Craze. Reports came, and still come, from all over the world. Early books on the subject include *The Flying Saucers are Real* (**1950**) by Donald E. Keyhoe (1897-1988) and *Flying Saucers Have Landed* (**1953**; rev 1970) by George Adamski (1891-1965) and Desmond LESLIE. The latter book marked a new development, in that Adamski claimed not only to have seen flying saucers but to have interacted with their ALIEN occupants.

However, it would be wrong to think that flying saucers are solely a 20th-century phenomenon. During Winter and Spring 1896-7 there were widespread reports of an airship being sighted over North America: it crossed the USA roughly west to east over a 5-month period. The situation was complicated by hoaxers making false statements and even sending up appropriately styled hot-air balloons, but this cannot account for the bulk of the sightings; nor can it explain why this particular flap *started*. It ended only when Thomas Alva Edison (1847-1931) firmly denounced the whole affair as a farrago. Clearly this was a flying-saucer flap in every respect except that people "saw" airships rather than saucers; moreover, they did so at a time when the airship was at the cutting edge of TRANSPORTATION technology and had for a time featured plausibly in sf stories. Spaceships, although not as yet in operation, occupied a similar position in the public consciousness by the late 1940s. In earlier centuries, otherwise inexplicable aerial phenomena could be attributed to whatever seemed indicated by the TECHNOLOGY of the day: witches on broomsticks were for a long time popular.

That people see unexplained "objects" in the sky cannot be denied. The vast majority of such sightings can be confidently put down to misidentifications of perfectly normal phenomena: oddly shaped and illuminated clouds, the image of VENUS refracted in the atmosphere, ball lightning (itself only quite recently recognized as a naturally occurring, though rare, phenomenon), etc. The remainder have been regarded as simply inexplicable; or attributed to flying saucers piloted by aliens (variously supposed to derive from other planets, other DIMENSIONS, the future, or the inside of the HOLLOW EARTH; whichever, this is dubbed the "extraterrestrial hypothesis"); or to rare geological/meteorological circumstances involving processes that are explicable in terms of current scientific knowledge. The branch of ufology investigating what it prefers to call by such terms as "transient atmospheric phenomena" ("TAPs") has scored some minor successes, notably in demonstrating that stressed granite can, as a result of the piezoelectric effect, produce dancing lights in the air overhead.

The psychological school of ufology accepts that people who report encounters with aliens are recording genuine experiences – in the sense that, say, a dream is a genuine experience – and seeks to find objective explanations for subjective events. Here again there is much to interest the cultural historian, for there are astonishingly close similarities between modern descriptions of encounters with aliens and historical ones of meetings with the Little People. As with broomsticks/airships/spaceships, it would appear that the "contact" experience is interpreted by the human mind in terms of the state of technology

of the age. Modern "contactees" seem to be involuntarily basing their interpretations on contemporary sf, a hypothesis buttressed by the fact that there was a noticeable qualitative shift in "contactee" accounts after the colossal success of the film STAR WARS (1977) – for example, cute little 'bots were more frequently reported.

If sf feeds ufology, how does ufology feed sf? Most GENRE-SF writers are hostile to the notion of flying saucers; that is, to the extraterrestrial hypothesis. The hostility is fuelled by the infuriating public assumption that sf writers are deeply interested in ufology. Early on, sf writers did indeed quite frequently assume the reality of alien-piloted flying saucers, but this was almost always for the purposes of story, irony or symbolism. There are exceptions: Adamski himself, some time before his famous experiences, wrote *Pioneers of Space* (**1949**), and Dennis WHEATLEY'S *Star of Ill Omen* (**1952**) seems to be the work of a believer. Novels rooted in the extraterrestrial hypothesis include: *Shadows in the Sun* (**1954**) by Chad OLIVER; *I Doubted Flying Saucers* (**1958**) by Stan Layne; *The Flying Saucer Gambit* * (**1966**) by Larry MADDOCK in the **Agent of T.E.R.R.A.** series; *Brad's Flying Saucer* (**1969**) by Marian Place (1910-   ); *The Mendelov Conspiracy* (**1969**; vt *Encounter Three* 1978) by Martin CAIDIN; *The Gismo* (**1970**; vt *The Gismo from Outer Space* 1974 chap) by Keo Felker Lazarus (1913-   ); *Fade-Out* (**1975** US) by Patrick TILLEY, by a very long way the most interesting of the books in this list; *Alien* (**1977**) by George H. LEONARD (not to be confused with the film tie *Alien* * [**1979**] by Alan Dean FOSTER); *Close Encounters of the Third Kind* * (**1977**) by Steven SPIELBERG, a film tie; *The Melchizedek Connection* (**1981**) by Ray Fowler (1930-   ); *Majestic* (**1989**) by Whitley STRIEBER; *Alintel* (**1986**; no English trans to date) by Jacques Vallée (1939-   ), the famous French ufologist (the model for Lacombe, played by François Truffaut, in CLOSE ENCOUNTERS OF THE THIRD KIND [1977]) and winner, as Jérôme Sériel, of the 1961 Prix Jules Verne; and the **UFO Conspiracy** sequence by David BISCHOFF: *Abduction: The UFO Conspiracy* (**1990**), *Deception* (**1991**) and *Revelation* (**1991**). An anthology is *Encounters with Aliens* (anth **1968**) ed George Earley (1927-   ). The Strieber and Bischoff titles concern themselves with the notion of the "cover-up", a CLICHÉ of ufology: the paranoid belief that the US Government (or other authority figure) possesses the physical proof that aliens are visiting us but chooses to keep the information secret. In Strieber's story the case concerned is the Roswell Incident of 1947, in which a flying saucer is claimed to have crashed in the New Mexico desert; a story predating this incident and bearing some resemblance to it was "Mewhu's Jet" (1946) by Theodore STURGEON. Cover-ups feature also in ufological sf that does not subscribe to the extraterrestrial hypothesis. In W. Allen HARBINSON's **Projekt Saucer** series – *Projekt Saucer #1: Inception* (**1991**) and *Genesis* (**1980**; vt *Projekt Saucer #2: Genesis* 1991 US) – based on UFO reports during and just after WWII, the flying saucers are human artefacts, the Nazis being largely responsible. (Some wilder ufologists have claimed that flying saucers are indeed piloted by ex-Nazis, who fled into the Hollow Earth at the end of WWII.) *A Secret Property* (**1985**) by Ralph Noyes enjoyably focuses on secret experiments trying to harness a natural/supernatural (depending upon viewpoint) force, one side-effect of which is the manifestation of UFOs; the alien myth is a cleverly engineered disinformation campaign mounted by the US Government, which has even built phoney dead aliens which are occasionally, in order to spread the disinformation yet further, shown to ufologists with strict instructions never to breathe a word of what they have seen.

A number of sf writers have exploited not ufology itself but the social phenomenon of the widespread interest in it. C.M. KORNBLUTH used the Saucer Craze slyly in "Silly Season" (1950), in which Earth is invaded but nobody pays attention because the newspapers have cried wolf too often. Henry KUTTNER used a flying saucer as a device for a moral parable in "Or Else" (1953), as did Theodore Sturgeon in "A Saucer of Loneliness" (1953). Robert A. HEINLEIN exploited saucer fears (as he exploited communist-conspiracy fears) in his invasion novel *The Puppet Masters* (**1951**), and he later used a UFO in his entertaining juvenile, *Have Space Suit – Will Travel* (**1958**). Gore VIDAL's *Messiah* (**1954**; rev 1965) opens with an analysis of UFOs as portents, which in some ways anticipates the theories of the psychoanalyst Carl Gustav Jung (1875-1961) in his *Flying Saucers: A Modern Myth of Things Seen in the Skies* (**1958**; trans **1959**). The made-for-tv film *The* FLIPSIDE OF DOMINICK HYDE (1980) and its sequel use a flying saucer from the future as an enabling device. Very small flying saucers feature in Richard FRANCIS's *Blackpool Vanishes* (**1979**) and in the films LIQUID SKY and *BATTERIES NOT INCLUDED. An Account of a Meeting with Denizens of Another World, 1871* (**1979**) by David LANGFORD (presented as being written with William Robert Loosley) is a spoof.

Saucer enthusiasts have themselves been the subject of sf stories, as in the tv series KINVIG. J.G. BALLARD's "The Encounter" (1963; vt "The Venus Hunters") leans heavily on Jung, and Fritz LEIBER's *The Wanderer* (**1964**) deals in part with the reactions of various ufologists to an actual celestial visitor.

The best novel about the UFO experience is undoubtedly *Miracle Visitors* (**1978**) by Ian WATSON; it is widely loathed by those readers who expect UFOs to be flying saucers. Watson instead envisages UFOs and "contacts" in terms of altered states of consciousness and the dichotomy between objective and subjective reality – much as do ufologists of the "psychological school", in fact. His book, with its surreal inventiveness and loose link with ordinary causality, is understandably offensive to determined rationalists, who find it a nonsense; exactly the same could be said for "contact" experiences themselves, which is perhaps the mark of Watson's success.

[DP/JR/JGr]

Further reading: *The UFO Experience: A Scientific Enquiry* (**1972**) by J. Allen Hynek; *UFOs Explained* (**1974**) by Philip J. Klass; *The UFO Enigma: The Definitive Explanation of the UFO Phenomenon* (**1977**) by Donald H. Menzel and Ernest H. Taves; *The UFO Encyclopedia* (**1980**) by Margaret Sachs.

See also: PARANOIA.

ULTIMATE PUBLISHING CO. ◊ FANTASTIC; SCIENCE FICTION (ADVENTURE) CLASSICS; STRANGE FANTASY.

ULTIMATE WARRIOR, THE Film (1975). Warner Bros. Written/dir Robert Clouse, starring Yul Brynner, Max von Sydow, Joanna Miles, William Smith. 92 mins. Colour.

New York in AD2022 is in an advanced state of decay after a man-made biological catastrophe that occurred decades earlier. The leader of a group who have barricaded a street against gangs of thugs roaming outside hires the services of a super-Samurai (Brynner). This was promoted as the first Kung Fu sf movie, following, as it does, the basic formula of the Kung Fu genre (two camps each with their own champion fight it out to the death in the final reel) and it was produced by Fred Weintraub and Paul Heller, who had made Bruce Lee's *Enter the Dragon* (1973), also dir Clouse. But, surprisingly, it is well scripted and unpretentious, though cynical. *TUW* was a forerunner of the post-HOLOCAUST action-movie boom represented by MAD MAX (1979) and its many sequels and imitations, including ESCAPE FROM NEW YORK (1981). [JB/PN]

ULTIMO UOMO DELLA TERRA, L' (vt *The Last Man on Earth*) Film (**1964**). La Regina/Alta Vista. Dir Sidney Salkow, Ubaldo Ragona, starring Vincent Price, Franca Bettoia. Screenplay Logan Swanson (pseudonym of Richard MATHESON, who disliked the rewrite), William P. Leicester, based on Matheson's *I Am Legend* (**1954**). 86 mins. B/w.

This Italian/US coproduction was the 1st film version of Matheson's novel about the lone survivor of a plague whose victims become vampires, a metamorphosis for which the novel, unlike the film, provides an ingenious medical explanation. Each night the survivor is besieged in his house by "vampires", and each day he kills as many as he can while they sleep. Finally, however, they succeed in trapping and killing him. The film has a reputation as being dreadful, but arguably it captures the brutalization of its hero in the human world's last gasp better than the remake, *The* OMEGA MAN (1971), and it is certainly truer to the novel. The film truest to the novel's spirit, though with a different plot, is NIGHT OF THE LIVING DEAD (1968). [PN/JB]

UNCANNY STORIES US PULP MAGAZINE. 1 issue Apr 1941, published by Manvis Publications; ed Robert O. Erisman. *US* contained both sf and weird fantasy, including "The Coming of the Giant Germs" by Ray CUMMINGS, but nothing of importance. It should not be confused with (although it was the successor of) the US *Uncanny Tales* (1938-40) – a weird-menace pulp from the same stable, also ed Erisman – or with the Canadian UNCANNY TALES, which like *US* did publish some sf. [FHP/MJE/PN]

UNCANNY TALES Canadian sf magazine, in DIGEST format for 4 issues, then BEDSHEET-size. 21 issues Nov 1940-Sep 1943; published to #17 (May 1942), by the Adam Publishing Co., then by the Norman Book Co.; ed Melvin R. Colby (uncredited). The schedule was monthly for 17 issues, then irregular, the last issue appearing 9 months after #20. Most of the stories, especially early on, were weird fiction, but a fair amount of sf was added to the mix. It published original material by Thomas P. KELLEY, Robert A.W. LOWNDES, Donald A. WOLLHEIM and others, as well as reprinting from US pulps including WEIRD TALES, COSMIC STORIES and STIRRING SCIENCE STORIES.

Earlier a US pulp with the same title, a companion to MARVEL SCIENCE STORIES, had been published by Manvis Publications, 5 issues 1938-40, ed Robert O. Erisman (uncredited), but printed no sf (though it had 1 sf cover), being a sex-and-sadism horror magazine. [PN/BS]

UNCANNY X-MEN, THE ◊ X-MEN.

UNDEAD, THE ◊ Roger CORMAN.

UNDER THE SEA The world under the sea is an alien environment still in the process of being explored. John WILKINS, in *Mathematicall Magick* (1648), offered speculative designs for submarines and discussed the possibility of underwater colonization; already, in about 1620, Cornelius Van Drebbell (1572-1634) had successfully navigated a submarine rowing-boat in the Thames, and before the end of the century another would-be submariner had perished in Plymouth Sound. David Bushnell (1742-1824) built a submarine boat in 1775, and Robert Fulton (1765-1815) remained under water for 4 hours in his egg-shaped submarine in 1800. By 1863 the *David*, a submarine built by the Confederacy during the US Civil War, was sufficiently functional to attempt a torpedo attack on an ironclad; its successor actually managed to sink a ship, but was lost with all hands. By the 1890s the French Navy was equipped with 4 submarines and both Germany and the USA were building them.

The first notable literary work to feature a submarine was a romance by Théophile Gautier (1811-1872) about a plot to rescue Napoleon, *Les deux étoiles* (1848; exp vt *Partie carrée* 1851; vt *La Belle Jenny*; trans in var colls as "The Quartette", "The Belle-Jenny" and "The Four-in-Hand"). The classic underwater romance of the 19th century was, however, Jules VERNE's *Vingt mille lieues sous les mers* (1870; trans as *Twenty Thousand Leagues under the Seas* 1872 UK), in which the undersea world became for the first time a place of marvels and natural wonders to be explored. Frank R. STOCKTON's *The Great Stone of Sardis* (1898), Harry COLLINGWOOD's *The Log of the Flying Fish* (1887), Herbert STRANG's *Lord of the Seas* (1908) and Max

PEMBERTON's *Captain Black* (1911) feature submarine adventures, but are concerned primarily with TRANSPORTATION rather than with exploring the wonders of the deep. The main reason for this relative uninterest was the impossibility of any real interaction between human visitors and the alien environment. Apart from the occasional duel with a sea-MONSTER (almost always a giant squid or octopus) there seemed to most writers to be little dramatic potential in underwater ventures; for a protagonist to get to grips with the underwater world, some fantastic modification was necessary – as in *The Water Babies* (1863) by Charles Kingsley (1819-1875) – and the notion of adapting humans to underwater life by biological engineering did not appear until Alexander BELYAEV's *The Amphibian* (1929; trans 1959). The only attempts to set aside this difficulty in the 19th and early 20th centuries were stories dealing with the rediscovery of ATLANTIS – which had often, by more-or-less miraculous means, managed to preserve itself and its air despite its cataclysmic submersion; examples include André LAURIE's *The Crystal City under the Sea* (1895; trans 1896), the title story of Arthur Conan DOYLE's *The Maracot Deep* (coll 1929), Stanton A. COBLENTZ's *The Sunken World* (1928; 1949) and Dennis WHEATLEY's *They Found Atlantis* (1936).

Early GENRE-SF writers showed relatively little interest in undersea adventures, although filmmakers made persistent attempts to make bigger and better versions of Verne's novel from the earliest years of silent movies to Disney's 20,000 LEAGUES UNDER THE SEA (1954). Several pulp-sf stories, however, dealt with undersea life on alien worlds. An early example was Neil R. JONES's "Into the Hydrosphere" (1933), but the classics of the species are "Clash by Night" (1943) and *Fury* (1947; 1950; vt *Destination: Infinity*) by Lawrence O'Donnell (Henry KUTTNER and C.L. MOORE), reflecting the common image of VENUS as a watery world. The most notable pulp story partly set beneath the oceans of Earth is *The Green Girl* (1930; 1950) by Jack WILLIAMSON.

In the post-WWII period sf writers became more interested in the possibilities of undersea melodrama. Alien oceans figure in "The Game of Glory" (1958) by Poul ANDERSON, "The Gift of Gab" (1955) by Jack VANCE, *Lucky Starr and the Oceans of Venus* (1954; vt *The Oceans of Venus*) by Paul French (Isaac ASIMOV) and in the story in which Roger ZELAZNY bade a final fond farewell to the image of Venus as an oceanic world, "The Doors of His Face, the Lamps of His Mouth" (1965). The notion of adapting humans to underwater life by GENETIC ENGINEERING is notably featured in James BLISH's "Surface Tension" (1952), although Blish had introduced it in a more tentative form in "Sunken Universe" (1942 as by Arthur Merlyn), which is combined with the later story in *The Seedling Stars* (fixup 1957). Blish and Norman L. KNIGHT's novel *A Torrent of Faces* (1967) features humanoid "tritons" engineered for underwater life, similarly carried forward from Knight's earlier solo work

"Crisis in Utopia" (1940).

The mid-1950s saw a minor boom in sf stories set beneath the oceans of Earth, including Frank HERBERT's submarine spy-thriller *The Dragon in the Sea* (**1956**; vt *21st Century Sub*; vt *Under Pressure*), Arthur C. CLARKE's novel about whale-farming, *The Deep Range* (1954; exp **1957**) and the first of Frederik POHL's and Jack Williamson's **Eden** trilogy of juveniles dealing with undersea colonization, *Undersea Quest* (**1954**) – a theme to which they returned much later in *Land's End* (**1988**). Kenneth BULMER's *City under the Sea* (**1957**) makes much of the idea of surgical modification for life in the sea; he further extrapolated the notion in *Beyond the Silver Sky* (**1961**). Other stories of the biological engineering of humans for undersea life include Gordon R. DICKSON's *The Space Swimmers* (1963; **1967**), Hal CLEMENT's *Ocean On Top* (1967; **1973**) and Lee HOFFMAN's *The Caves of Karst* (**1969**). The idea is more elaborately developed in such works as *Inter Ice Age 4* (**1959**; trans **1970**) by Kobo ABÉ, in which Japanese scientists prepare for a new deluge, and in *The Godwhale* (**1974**) by T.J. BASS, whose eponymous protagonist is a CYBORG leviathan.

The scientific community took an increasing interest in dolphins during the 1960s and 1970s, inspired by researches into their high INTELLIGENCE. The idea of communication between dolphins and humans was popularized in numerous sf stories, including the Dickson titles mentioned above, Clarke's *Dolphin Island* (**1963**), Joe POYER's *Operation Malacca* (**1968**), Roy MEYERS's *Dolphin Boy* (**1967**; vt *Dolphin Rider*) and its sequels, Robert MERLE's *The Day of the Dolphin* (**1967**; trans **1969**), Margaret ST CLAIR's *The Dolphins of Altair* (**1967**), Robert SILVERBERG's "Ishmael in Love" (1970), John BOYD's "The Girl and the Dolphin" (1973) and Ian WATSON's *The Jonah Kit* (**1975**). Dolphins gifted with sentience by means of human ingenuity play a key role in David BRIN's **Uplift** series, most notably in *Startide Rising* (**1983**), in which a dolphin-commanded starship takes refuge from a host of enemies in an alien ocean, similarly blessed – or in this case, perhaps, cursed – dolphins feature in Alexander JABLOKOV's *A Deeper Sea* (**1992**).

Analogies may easily be drawn between submarines and SPACESHIPS. In Harry HARRISON's *The Daleth Effect* (**1970**; vt *In our Hands, the Stars*) the heroes, in urgent need of a spaceship, simply attach their drive unit to a submarine. Greater subtlety is exhibited in James WHITE's *The Watch Below* (**1966**), which juxtaposes the problems of an ALIEN spaceship nearing Earth with those of a group of people surviving in the hold of a ship which has been under water for many years. A similar analogy is drawn in Asimov's "Waterclap" (1970), which deals with a conflict of interest between projects to colonize the sea bed and the Moon. A curious novel in which huge water drops function as "space habitats" of an extraordinary kind is Bob SHAW's *Medusa's Children* (**1977**).

The CINEMA has carried forward its own tradition of submarine romance as its technical capacities have grown. Notable sf examples include VOYAGE TO THE BOTTOM OF THE SEA (1961), which spawned a long-running tv series, and The ABYSS (1989). Sciencefictional submarines are featured in Martin CAIDIN's *The Last Fathom* (**1967**) and Richard COWPER's satirical comedy *Profundis* (**1979**). Alien oceans and races adapted to them are found in Stefan WUL's *Temple of the Past* (**1958**: trans **1973**), in which a spaceship which lands in an alien ocean is swallowed by a whale-like creature, Michael G. CONEY's *Neptune's Cauldron* (**1981**), Joan SLONCZEWSKI's *A Door into Ocean* (**1986**), in which emissaries from a race of peace-loving ocean-dwellers must visit a very different kind of world, our own, and Piers ANTHONY's *Mercycle* (**1991**).

Arthur C. Clarke's constant interest in the sea – reflected in his nonfiction as well as his fiction – is further demonstrated in *The Ghost from the Grand Banks* (**1990**), about the raising of the *Titanic*. Another writer much interested in the sea is marine engineer Hilbert SCHENCK, whose fascination is evident in the stories in *Wave Rider* (coll **1980**) and the curiously mystical *At the Eye of the Ocean* (**1980**).   [BS]

See also: ECOLOGY; INVASION.

UNDERWOOD, TIM (EDWARD) (1948-   ) US publisher (◊ UNDERWOOD-MILLER INC.), bibliographer of Jack VANCE in *Fantasms: A Bibliography of the Literature of Jack Vance* (**1978** chap with Daniel J.H. LEVACK; rev vt *Fantasms II: A Bibliography of the Works of Jack Vance* 1979 with Levack and Kurt Cockram), and anthologist, always in collaboration with his partner, Chuck MILLER. Their anthologies include *Jack Vance* (anth **1980**) and 3 studies of Stephen KING: *Fear Itself: The Horror Fiction of Stephen King* (anth **1982**), *Kingdom of Fear: The World of Stephen King* (anth **1986**) and *Bare Bones: Conversations on Terror with Stephen King* (anth **1988**).   [JC]

UNDERWOOD-MILLER INC. US SMALL PRESS founded in 1976 by Pennsylvania-based Chuck MILLER and Tim UNDERWOOD, who worked in California. Their 1st book, a first hardcover edition of Jack VANCE's *The Dying Earth* (**1950**; their edn 1976) almost accidentally set them on a course which would identify them with that author, many of whose works, new and old, they have since released. Other ambitious projects have included a well edited 5-vol edn of *The Collected Stories of Philip K. Dick* (coll **1987**), which came very close to honouring the claim made by its title – an accomplishment worth noting in the small-press field, where editing standards sometimes lag significantly behind ambition, especially (as in collected editions) where archive work may be required. UMI remains one of the best-run, most prolific and successful of US small presses, and may be one of the first to move into general publishing and survive.   [JC]

UNEARTH US magazine in DIGEST format, 8 issues Winter 1977-Winter 1979, published from Boston by Unearth Publications, ed Jonathan Ostrowsky-Lantz and John M. Landsberg. Subtitled "The Magazine of

Science Fiction Discoveries", *U*'s avowed intention was that all fiction should be by previously unpublished authors or by authors previously published only in *U*, or be reprints of first-sf-story sales by well known authors; these constraints were slightly relaxed for the last 2 issues. The reprints featured early work by Algis BUDRYS, Philip K. DICK, Harlan ELLISON, Roger ZELAZNY and others, but *U*'s main significance came from the new writers it discovered. These included, among many others, William GIBSON with "Fragments of a Hologram Rose" (1977), James P. BLAYLOCK with "Red Planet" (1977), Paul di Filippo with "Falling Expectations" (1977) and S.P. SOMTOW with "Sunsteps" (1977). The artist Barclay SHAW was another discovery. Alongside this innovative approach to fiction were the usual departments, plus the series **Science for Fiction** by Hal CLEMENT and articles under the heading **Writing** by Ellison.   [RR]

UNEARTHLY STRANGER Film (1963). A Julian Wintel-Leslie Parkyn Production/Independent Artists/AIP. Dir John Krish, starring John Neville, Gabriella Licudi, Philip Stone, Jean Marsh, Warren Mitchell. Screenplay Rex Carlton. 74 mins. B/w.

In this low-key, unpretentious UK sf film a space scientist gradually realizes that his wife (who sleeps with her eyes open) is an alien, one of many who are infiltrating Earth and wiping out the scientists first. She is ordered by her superiors to kill him but cannot, having fallen in love with him. This emotional involvement destroys her ability to survive undetected and the film's strongest image is of her tears leaving corrosive tracks down her cheeks as she reveals the truth to her husband. This is a good (but rare) film, untypical of its writer, Carlton, who was usually responsible for monstrosities like *The Brain that Wouldn't Die* (1962).   [JB/PN]

UNHOLY LOVE ◊ ALRAUNE.

UNICORNS ◊ SUPERNATURAL CREATURES.

UNIVERSE ORIGINAL-ANTHOLOGY series ed Terry CARR (1971-87) and renewed by Robert SILVERBERG and Karen HABER (1990-current). This is arguably the best (and also one of the longest-lasting) of all original-anthology series in the field. *Universe 1* (anth **1971**) appeared while Carr was still an editor for its publisher, ACE BOOKS. Since then it has been peripatetic, the 17 vols of series 1 coming from Ace Books (#1-#2), Random House (#3-#5) and DOUBLEDAY (#6-#17); series 2 has come from Doubleday Foundation (#1) and BANTAM Spectra (#2). The further titles are *Universe 2* (anth **1972**), *#3* (anth **1973**), *#4* (anth **1974**), *#5* (anth **1974**), *#6* (anth **1976**), *#7* (anth **1977**), *#8* (anth **1978**), *#9* (anth **1979**), *#10* (anth **1980**), *#11* (anth **1981**), *#12* (anth **1982**), *#13* (anth **1983**), *#14* (anth **1984**), *#15* (anth **1985**), *#16* (anth **1986**) and *#17* (anth **1987**), plus *The Best from Universe* (anth **1984**). The new series, ed Silverberg with his wife Karen Haber, is to date *Universe 1* (anth **1990**) and *Universe 2* (anth **1992**).

Carr's #1 contained Robert Silverberg's NEBULA-winning "Good News From the Vatican"; Silverberg was one of the series' most regular contributors,

along with Gregory BENFORD, Gordon EKLUND, R.A. LAFFERTY, Edgar PANGBORN, Howard WALDROP, Ian WATSON and, later, Lucius SHEPARD. Benford and Eklund won a Nebula for "If The Stars Are Gods" in #4. Gene WOLFE won a Nebula for "The Death of Dr Island" in #3, as did Waldrop's "The Ugly Chickens" in #10. Harlan ELLISON's "Paladin of the Lost Hour (#15) won a HUGO. The awards (mostly from the early years) do not truly reflect the quality of this series, which proved again that Carr was one of the outstanding editors in the field; while he knew exactly what constituted good writing, and never patronized his readership by feeding them pulp, he also never lost the popular touch. The series stopped with his death. A volume dedicated to the memory of both Carr and **Universe** was *Terry's Universe* (anth **1988**) ed Beth MEACHAM. The Silverbergs' 1990 relaunch of the **Universe** series was exemplary: the new #1 is a strong collection in the Carr tradition (but much longer), with good stories from Ursula K. LE GUIN, Barry MALZBERG, Kim Stanley ROBINSON, Bruce STERLING and others.   [PN/MJE]

UNIVERSE SCIENCE FICTION US DIGEST magazine, 10 numbered issues June 1953-Mar 1955; #1-#2 published by Bell Publications, Chicago, the rest by Palmer Publications, Evanston; #1-#2 ed George Bell (pseudonym of Raymond A. PALMER and Bea Mahaffey), rest ed (officially) Palmer and Mahaffey.

This was a companion magazine to Palmer's SCIENCE STORIES, and both have been seen as continuations of his earlier OTHER WORLDS, whose last issue in its 1st incarnation was dated July 1953. It was *USF*, however, that changed its title back to *Other Worlds* with #11 (May 1955), which confusingly numbered itself 2 ways, continuing both *USF*'s numeration (#11) and *Other Worlds*'s numeration (#32). (*For the rest of this deeply confusing story* ◊ OTHER WORLDS.)

Fewer than usual of the contributors were the Chicago hacks so regularly employed by Palmer, so the fiction was a bit better than his average – perhaps because of Mahaffey's influence. Authors included Chad OLIVER and Theodore STURGEON.   [PN]

UNIVERSITY OF SYDNEY LIBRARY Host to one of the world's biggest institutional collections of sf and fantasy (65,000+ items); it is surprising to find such a thing in Australia, a country where sf plays only a minimal role in academic curricula. The collection is part of the Rare Books and Special Collections Library, and is publicly accessible. It was begun in 1974, and dramatically expanded in 1979 when bequeathed the huge collection of Ron Graham, the very active sf fan who had published VISION OF TOMORROW (1969-70). A 1991 count showed over 53,000 sf items (books, magazines and fanzines) and a further 12,000+ items in the COMICS collection (mostly SUPERHERO titles).   [PN]

UNKNOWN US magazine, pulp-size Mar 1939-Aug 1941, BEDSHEET-size Oct 1941-Apr 1943, then back to pulp-size to Oct 1943. 39 issues Mar 1939-Oct 1943. Monthly Mar 1939-Dec 1940, then bimonthly.

Published by STREET & SMITH; ed John W. CAMPBELL Jr.

The fantasy companion to ASTOUNDING SCIENCE-FICTION, *U* was one of the most unusual of all PULP MAGAZINES, and its demise one of the most lamented. #1 featured Eric Frank RUSSELL's novel *Sinister Barrier* (Mar 1939; **1943**; rev 1948), but a better indicator of the direction in which the magazine would develop was, in the same issue, H.L. GOLD's story "Trouble with Water", a humorous fantasy exploiting the incongruity of confronting a 20th-century American with a figure out of folklore. While *U* featured some ordinary sf and some SWORD-AND-SORCERY stories, particularly during its first year, it quickly attracted a group of regular contributors who defined its very individual flavour. Among them was L. Sprague DE CAMP, with such stories as "Nothing in the Rules" (1939), *Lest Darkness Fall* (1939; **1941**), "The Wheels of If" (1940) and his collaborations with Fletcher PRATT: "The Roaring Trumpet" (1940), "The Mathematics of Magic" (1940) – combined in *The Incomplete Enchanter*, fixup **1942**) – *The Castle of Iron* (1941; **1950**) and others. These De Camp/Pratt stories – the **Harold Shea** series, in which the hero is transported into a series of fantasy worlds drawn from Norse mythology, Spenser's *Faerie Queene* (**1590-96**) and so forth – typify the exuberantly wacky approach to fantasy which *U* made its own. Other authors who appeared frequently were Anthony BOUCHER, Cleve CARTMILL, L. Ron HUBBARD – with *Slaves of Sleep* (1939; **1948**), "The Indigestible Triton" (1940), "Fear" (1940), "Typewriter in the Sky" (1940) (these 2 collected as *Fear & Typewriter in the Sky* [coll **1951**]) and many others – Henry KUTTNER, Fritz LEIBER, whose sword-and-sorcery **Fafhrd/Gray Mouser** series had a wry, ironic tone which suited the magazine very well, Theodore STURGEON and Jack WILLIAMSON. *U* occasionally carried serials, but most issues included a complete novel or novella. Notable examples were Robert A. HEINLEIN's "The Devil Makes the Law" (1940; as "Magic, Inc." in *Waldo & Magic, Inc.* [coll **1950**]), Williamson's *Darker than You Think* (1940; **1949**), Alfred BESTER's "Hell is Forever" (1942), Leiber's *Conjure Wife* (1943; **1953**) and A.E. VAN VOGT's *The Book of Ptath* (1943; **1947**; vt *Two Hundred Million A.D.*).

Until June 1940 *U* had illustrative covers, of which the best (apart from #1, by H.W. Scott) were the work of Edd CARTIER, the artist whose style most exactly caught *U*'s tone. With the July 1940 issue *U* adopted a lettered cover intended to give it a more dignified appearance. In Oct 1941 it switched, 3 months before *ASF*, to the larger bedsheet format, at the same time changing its name to *Unknown Worlds*. The Dec 1943 issue was to have adopted the DIGEST size which *ASF* had taken the previous month, but it never appeared: wartime paper shortages had put an end to the magazine. After WWII, a revival was mooted, and an anthology in magazine format, *From Unknown Worlds* (anth **1948**) was put out to test the market, but *U* never reappeared, although H.L. Gold's fantasy companion to *Gal*, BEYOND FANTASY FICTION, was an avowed imitation. Anthologies drawn from *U*'s pages include *The Unknown* (anth **1963**) and *The Unknown Five* (anth **1964**), both ed D.R. BENSEN, and *Hell Hath Fury* (anth **1963**) ed George HAY.

The UK edn, from Atlas Publishing Company, had fewer pages and was unusual in appearing for more issues (41) than the original, outlasting it by 6 years. It was published regularly Sep 1939-Dec 1940, then intermittently for 3 years, then mostly quarterly, ending with Winter 1949. Like its parent, but a little later (June 1942) it changed its title to *Unknown Worlds*.

U appeared during Campbell's peak years as editor. Its reputation may stand as high as it does partly because it died while still at its best. [MJE]

See also: GOLDEN AGE OF SF.

UNKNOWN WORLDS ◊ UNKNOWN.

UNNO, JUZA [r] ◊ JAPAN.

UNUSUAL STORIES US DIGEST-size magazine. 3 issues 1934-5, published by Fantasy Publishers, Everett, Pa.; ed William L. CRAWFORD. An advance issue of this SEMIPROZINE (*see also* SMALL PRESSES) was published (and mailed) in 2 parts in 1934, and could be considered as #1, even though the 1935 issues are referred to as #1 and #2. *US* was a companion magazine to MARVEL TALES, but unlike that magazine published no important stories. [FHP/PN]

UPDIKE, JOHN (HOYER) (1932-) US writer whose exuberantly polished and opulent style has led him more than once into realms of FABULATION. In *The Centaur* (**1963**) mythological avatars haunt present-day characters. The government toppled in *The Coup* (**1978**) had ruled an imaginary country. *The Witches of Eastwick* (**1984**) is – though enfeeblingly dilatory about the fantasy premises it invokes – a genuine tale of the supernatural involving a Devil-like male and 3 women whose PSI POWERS develop alarmingly. Only JU's first novel is sf: *The Poorhouse Fair* (**1959**) is set in a NEAR-FUTURE institution for the aged which serves as the focus of a popular revolt. [JC]

Other works: *The Chaste Planet* (**1980** chap).

UPTON, MARK ◊ Lawrence SANDERS.

UPWARD, ALLEN (1863-1926) UK writer best known for inflamed studies of the politics of Eastern Europe and for various thrillers set in the same venue; their RURITANIAN complexion was perhaps inadvertent. In *High Treason* (**1903** chap) and its sequel, *The Fourth Conquest of England* (**1904** chap), he outlined the dire consequences of a Roman Catholic takeover of the UK, including a new Inquisition and the exile of the monarchy to Australia. *The Yellow Hand* (**1904**) is a supernatural tale featuring out-of-body villainy. Of most interest is *The Discovery of the Dead* (**1910**), an sf novel told in the form of reportage which itself encloses a scientific memoir, within which the discovery of "necrolite" opens new areas of the spectrum, making the dead – "necromorphs" – visible. Allergic to the visible spectrum, a great society of necromorphs lives in a great city at the North Pole; they themselves are haunted by "dynamorphs" from the bowels of the Earth, and long to radiate heaven-wards. [JC]

URANUS ◊ OUTER PLANETS.

URQUHART, PAUL ◊ Ladbroke BLACK.

URUGUAY ◊ LATIN AMERICA.

USSR ◊ RUSSIA; SOVIET UNION.

UTLEY, STEVE(N) (1948-   ) US short-story writer whose black verve and acidulous knowingness about the absurdities of the genre made him, for a while, a figure of edgy salience in the field. He began publishing with "The Unkindest Cut of All" for *Perry Rhodan 20* (anth **1972**), but stopped by the end of the decade. Some of his best work – like "Custer's Last Jump" (**1976**), which illuminates in MAGIC-REALIST terms an ALTERNATE-WORLD USA – was written with Howard WALDROP, as was "Black as the Pit, from Pole to Pole" (**1977**), which has been cited as a significant influence on 1980s STEAMPUNK. Other tales likewise tend – after the fashion of the group of writers who came to maturity in Texas in the 1970s – to fabulate (◊ FABULATION) the USA's past. Some of the stories in *Lone Star Universe: Speculative Fiction from Texas* (anth **1976**) ed with Geo W. PROCTOR exemplify this tendency. [JC]

See also: HOLLOW EARTH; LOST WORLDS.

UTOPIAS The concept of a utopia or "Ideal State" is linked to religious ideas of Heaven or the Promised Land and to folkloristic ideas like the Isles of the Blessed, but it is essentially a future-historical goal, to be achieved by the active efforts of human beings, not a transcendental goal reserved as a reward for those who follow a particularly virtuous path in life. The term was coined by Thomas MORE in *Utopia* (Latin edn **1516**; trans **1551**; many edns since), although More's work has far more SATIRE than practical POLITICS in it; he derived the word from "outopia" (no place) rather than "eutopia" (good place), although modern usage generally implies the latter, and modern works recapitulating More's ideas – including *The New Moon* (**1918**) by Oliver Onions (1873-1961) and *The Rebel Passion* (**1929**) by Kay BURDEKIN – do so more earnestly than he did.

It can be argued that all utopias are sf, in that they are exercises in hypothetical SOCIOLOGY and political science. Alternatively, it might be argued that only those utopias which embody some notion of scientific advancement qualify as sf – the latter view is in keeping with most DEFINITIONS OF SF. Frank Manuel, in *Utopias and Utopian Thought* (anth **1966**), argues that a significant shift in utopian thought took place when writers changed from talking about a better place (eutopia) to talking about a better time (euchronia), under the influence of notions of historical and social progress. When this happened, utopias ceased to be imaginary constructions with which contemporary society might be compared, and began to be speculative statements about real future possibilities. It seems sensible to regard this as the point at which utopian literature acquired a character conceptually similar to that of sf. The scientific imagination first became influential in utopian thinking in the 17th century: an awareness of the advancement of scientific knowledge and of the role that science might play in transforming society is very evident in Francis BACON's *New Atlantis* (1627; **1629**) and Tommaso CAMPANELLA's *City of the Sun* (**1637**). Bacon's claims for the utopian potential of technological advance are extravagant, and inspired at least 2 later writers to undertake the fragment's completion ("R.H. esq." in 1660 and Jos. Glanvil in 1676); but works such as *The Blazing World* (**1668**) by Margaret Cavendish (?1624-1674), *Gulliver's Travels* (**1726**) by Jonathan SWIFT and *Rasselas* (**1759**) by Samuel JOHNSON embody a very different attitude, parodying the efforts of SCIENTISTS and inventors and mocking their presumed unworldliness. It was left to a school of French philosophers during the second half of the 18th century to become the first strident champions of the idea that moral and technological progress went hand in hand. L.S. MERCIER's pioneering euchronian novel, *L'an deux mille quatre cent quarante* (**1771** UK; trans as *Memoirs of the Year Two Thousand Five Hundred* **1772**) proposed that the perfectibility of mankind was not only possible but inevitable, with the aid of science, mathematics and the mechanical arts. Another member of the school, RESTIF DE LA BRETONNE, concluded *La découverte australe par un homme volant, ou le Dédale français* ["The Southern-Hemisphere Discovery by a Flying Man, or the French Daedalus"] (**1781**) with a description of a utopian state based on the principles of natural philosophy and scientific advancement. Scepticism was not, however, entirely overcome. Aristotle's doubts about the workability of PLATO's *Republic*, based on the observation that its citizens would lack incentives to make them work, remained to be countered; and the end of the 18th century produced Malthus's objection – that population increase would always outstrip resources no matter how much TECHNOLOGY increased production – to the utopian optimism of William Godwin (1756-1836).

Despite the international popularity of Mercier's book, the 19th century was well advanced before the utopian potential of scientific progress was widely celebrated in English literature. Jane LOUDON's anonymous SCIENTIFIC ROMANCE *The Mummy!* (**1827**) has some utopian undertones, but Mary GRIFFITH's *Three Hundred Years Hence* (1836; **1975**) was the first English-language utopian novel to endorse Mercier's optimism wholeheartedly. In many of the classic UK utopias of the 19th century there is a strong vein of antiscientific romanticism. Lord LYTTON's *The Coming Race* (**1870**) is more occult romance than progressive utopia. Samuel BUTLER's satirical *Erewhon* (**1872**) and its sequel are PASTORAL and antimechanical insofar as they are utopian at all. W.H. HUDSON's *A Crystal Age* (**1887**) is a mystical work whose pastoral Ideal State remains inaccessible to the civilized man who stumbles into it. Richard JEFFERIES's *After London* (**1885**) is even more extreme in its nostalgia for barbarism. This romantic pastoralism extended into 20th-century UK scientific romance in the works of J. Leslie MITCHELL and S. Fowler WRIGHT, both of whom glorified a life of noble savagery in opposition to the idea of utopia as a CITY, and a similar suspicion continues to infect modern UK sf. 19th-century US writers, by contrast, tended to see their emergent nation as the true homeland of progress – a presumption brought to full flower in Edward BELLAMY's *Looking Backward 2000-1887* (**1888**), which provoked a great many imitations and replies in kind, including Alvarado M. FULLER's *A.D. 2000* (**1890**), Arthur Bird's *Looking Forward: A Dream of the United States of the Americas in 1999* (**1899**), Paul Devinne's *The Day of Prosperity* (**1902**) and Herman Hine Brinsmade's *Utopia Achieved* (**1912**). Most of the dissenting voices objected to Bellamy's socialism on political grounds, although Ignatius DONNELLY's pioneeering DYSTOPIA *Caesar's Column* (**1890**) argued that technological society's historical momentum was towards greater inequality and social injustice, and the most famous of the UK replies, William MORRIS's *News from Nowhere* (**1890** US), objected to the prospect of humanity living in idleness while machines supplied its needs. Nevertheless, Bellamy's book became the archetype of a whole school of mechanized utopias; further technology-glorifying novels in its wake included *The Crystal Button* (**1891**) by Chauncey THOMAS and *Limanora* (**1903**) by Godfrey SWEVEN. Other nations discovered prophets of technological utopia: the German statesman Walther Rathenau (1867-1922) wrote *Von kommenden Dingen* (**1917**; trans Eden and Cedar Paul as *In Days to Come* **1921**) and *Der neue staat* (**1919**; trans Arthur Windham as *The New Society* **1921**), while H.G. WELLS became the UK's great prophet of utopian progress in such works as *A Modern Utopia* (**1905**), *Men Like Gods* (**1923**) and *The Shape of Things to Come* (**1933**). But scepticism was further renewed too. Anatole FRANCE's *Sur la pierre blanche* (**1905**; trans as *The White Stone* **1910**) pays homage to Wells, but has a citizen of a future utopian state declare that peace and plenty are insufficient to ensure happiness, which is a problem of an entirely different kind. E.M. FORSTER, in "The Machine Stops" (**1909**), objected much more fiercely, asserting that Wellsian dreams were sterile and would lead to stagnation of the human mind. Alexandr MOSZKOWSKI's *Die Inselt der Weisheit* (**1922** Germany; trans as *The Isles of Wisdom* **1924**) set out to show that all utopian schemes are absurd, and that real people could not live in them.

Hugo GERNSBACK was a confirmed euchronian and an enthusiastic propagandist for technological progress. His PULP MAGAZINES lent what aid they could, practically and imaginatively, to the cause. In *Modern Electrics* he serialized his own utopian romance *Ralph 124C 41+* (**1911-12**; **1925**), and he regarded "scientifiction" as a means of promoting the magnificent potential of modern TECHNOLOGY. By the time AMAZING STORIES was founded in 1926, however, there had been a considerable loss of faith in utopian thought, and dystopian images of the future were becoming

commonplace. Aldous HUXLEY's *Brave New World* (**1932**), a scathing satirical attack on scientific utopianism as expressed in J.B.S. HALDANE's *Daedalus* (**1924**), tipped the balance decisively in favour of anxiety about how the technologies of the future might be used. Despite Gernsback's inspiration and intention, GENRE SF has never been strongly utopian. The early sf pulps abounded with adventure stories set in pseudo-utopian futures where poverty and injustice were nowhere in evidence but, when sf writers like David H. KELLER turned their attention to serious speculation about the future, unease was manifest. Miles J. BREUER in "Paradise and Iron" (1930), Laurence MANNING and Fletcher PRATT in "City of the Living Dead" (1930) and John W. CAMPBELL Jr in "Twilight" (1934 as by Don A. Stuart) all warned that decadence and decline might be the consequence of overdependence on machines. Where utopian states were manifest in pulp sf, as in *The Sunken World* (1928; **1949**) by Stanton COBLENTZ, they were often small enclaves facing imminent destruction. This was the fate of utopian dreams outside the sf establishment, too: after WWI they were mostly relegated to the status of the Isles of the Blessed, as pleasant impossibilities.

Utopian thought in the last half century has to a large extent dissociated itself from the idea of progress; we most commonly encounter it in connection with the idea of a "historical retreat" to a way of simpler life, as in James HILTON's *Lost Horizon* (**1933**), in the very elaborate *Islandia* (**1942**) by Austin Tappan WRIGHT and its various sequels by other hands, in *Watch the North Wind Rise* (**1949** US; vt *Seven Days in New Crete* **1949** UK) by Robert GRAVES, in Aldous Huxley's *Island* (**1962**), in *In Watermelon Sugar* (**1968**) by Richard BRAUTIGAN, and in *Ecotopia* (**1975**) and its sequel by Ernest CALLENBACH. Even the recent past has been restored by the momentum of nostalgia almost to the status of a utopia, in such novels as *Time and Again* (**1970**) by Jack FINNEY. Utopian designs extrapolating individual hobby-horses are still produced – early examples include *Erone* (**1943**) by Chalmers KEARNEY and *Walden Two* (**1948**) by B.F. SKINNER – but large-scale attempts to imagine a technologically developed future state which is in any sense of the word ideal tend to be highly ambivalent: in Herman HESSE's *Magister Ludi* (**1943**; trans **1950**; vt *The Glass Bead Game*) the hero finally rejects the ideal on which his society is based, and Franz WERFEL's phantasmagoric *Stern der Ungeborenen* (**1946**; trans as *Star of the Unborn* **1946**) imagines a futuristic demi-Paradise which is still under threat from rebellion and war, and retains many horrors.

Within genre sf those novels which can be cited as examples of analytical utopian thought retain the same deep ambiguity, tending towards rejection. Theodore STURGEON's *Venus Plus X* (**1960**) constructs a hermaphrodite utopia for evaluation by a man of our time, but the society fails the test. James BLISH and Norman L. KNIGHT boldly devised a "fascist utopia" for *A Torrent of Faces* (**1967**), but the state seems hardly ideal. Mack REYNOLDS's determined revisitation of Bellamyesque ideas in *Looking Backward from the Year 2000* (**1973**) was carried enthusiastically forward in his *Equality in the Year 2000* (**1977**), but then ran into accumulating doubts in his *Perchance to Dream* (**1977**) and *After Utopia* (**1977**). Ursula K. LE GUIN's *The Dispossessed* (**1974**) carries the subtitle "An Ambiguous Utopia". Samuel R. DELANY's *Triton* (**1976**), presumably in response, is subtitled "An Ambiguous Heterotopia", implying that the word has been devalued along with the dream and carrying forward the notion that human individuals are so different, and so prone to change, that only a very heterogeneous society could possibly aspire to provide utopian opportunities for all – an idea less convincingly developed in Reynolds's *Commune 2000* (**1974**) and R.F. NELSON's *Then Beggars Could Ride* (**1976**). Suzy McKee CHARNAS's *Motherlines* (**1979**) – a sequel to her dystopian *Walk to the End of the World* (**1974**) – follows Le Guin in tying uncompromising idealism to social deprivation. Frederik POHL's *JEM: The Making of a Utopia* (**1979**) is relentlessly cynical, although *The Years of the City* (fixup **1984**) does try to accept the challenge of developing solutions to the world's problems, as (less convincingly) does James E. GUNN's *Crisis!* (fixup **1986**). Even a HARD-SF writer like Poul ANDERSON tends to attribute utopian qualities to low-technology societies like that of the "Maurai" in *Orion Shall Rise* (**1983**), although a more robustly apologetic line is taken by some other libertarian writers, notably Larry NIVEN and Jerry E. POURNELLE in their quasi-utopian "arcology" in *Oath of Fealty* (**1981**) – which extrapolates ideas earlier developed in Mack Reynolds's *The Towers of Utopia* (**1975**) – and James P. HOGAN in *Voyage from Yesteryear* (**1982**). It is perhaps significant that in the works of Isaac ASIMOV and Arthur C. CLARKE, both proselytizers for the beneficence of technological advance, there is very little utopian thought. The imagery of Clarke's optimistic *Imperial Earth* (**1975**) cannot compare with that of *The City and the Stars* (**1956**), which echoes Forster's "The Machine Stops" and Campbell's "Twilight",

while Asimov's dystopian settings for *Pebble in the Sky* (**1950**) and *The Caves of Steel* (**1954**) are described far more graphically than utopian Trantor, which is already in terminal decline as the **Foundation** series begins. Sf in Soviet RUSSIA, as pioneered by Ivan YEFREMOV's *Andromeda* (**1958**; trans **1959**), had for a while a presumed mission to look forward to the promised socialist utopia, and undertook a more enthusiastic championship of the alliance of technology and socialism than may be found in even Bellamy or Wells, but the mission faltered well in advance of the collapse of Soviet communism; the novels of the STRUGATSKI brothers in particular – notably *Trudno byt' bogom* (**1964**; trans as *Hard to be a God* **1973**) and *Khishchnye veshchi veka* (**1965**; trans as *The Final Circle of Paradise* **1976**) – display an anxiety comparable to that of contemporary Western sf.

The necessity for works of fiction to be dramatic and the fact that workable plots require conflict inhibit the use of sf to display utopian schemes. These still fit more comfortably into works of FUTUROLOGY like Brian M. STABLEFORD and David LANGFORD's *The Third Millennium: A History of the World 2000-3000 A.D.* (**1985**), which offers a moderately detailed image of a future where a kind of utopia has been secured by technological advancement, especially in the biological sciences.

A theme anthology is *The New Improved Sun: An Anthology of Utopian Science Fiction* (anth **1976**) ed Thomas M. DISCH. [BS]

Further reading: *Utopias Old and New* (**1938**) by Harry Ross; *Utopian Fantasy: A Study of English Utopian Fiction since the End of the Nineteenth Century* by Richard Gerber (**1955**); *Yesterday's Tomorrows* (**1968**) by W.H.G. ARMYTAGE; *American Utopias: Selected Short Fiction 1790-1954* (anth **1971**) ed Arthur O. Lewis; *The Image of the Future* (rev **1973**) by Fred Polak; and *British and American Utopian Literature 1516-1975* (**1979**) by Lyman T. SARGENT.

See also: ECONOMICS; FEMINISM; HISTORY OF SF; LIBERTARIAN SF; MAINSTREAM WRITERS OF SF; OPTIMISM AND PESSIMISM; PROTO SCIENCE FICTION.

"V" 2 US tv miniseries followed by a series. NBC. The 1st miniseries (1983), 2 100min episodes, was titled *"V"* and created/written/dir Kenneth Johnson. The 2nd miniseries (1984), 3 100min episodes, was titled *V: The Final Battle* and dir Richard T. Heffron, written Brian Taggert, Peggy Goldman, from a story by Lillian Weezer, Goldman, Faustus Buck, Diane Frolow, Harry and Renee Longstreet. The series (1984-5), titled *"V"*, had 19 50min episodes, prod Dean O'Brien, Garner Simmons; dirs included Gilbert Shilton, Kevin Hooks, John Florea; writers included David Braff, Brian Taggert, Simmons, David Abramowitz. The main cast members throughout were Marc Singer as Mike Donovan, Faye Grant as Julie, Jane Badler as Diana, Blair Tefkin as Robin, Michael Ironside as Ham Tyler, Robert Englund as Willy, Jennifer Cooke as Elizabeth.

Kenneth Johnson's track record included *The* IN-CREDIBLE HULK and *The* BIONIC WOMAN, so it was surprising that *"V"* started as well as it did. He based the story on Sinclair LEWIS's *It Can't Happen Here* (**1935**), about a fascist takeover in the USA, but substituted alien invaders – at first seemingly friendly, but actually after our water, and ourselves for food – for the fascists. The carnivorous, saurian invaders, as in the tv series *The* INVADERS (1967-8) and many films, are disguised to look just like us, but with jackboots. A resistance movement grows, whose "V" (for "Victory") is daubed on walls everywhere, but many humans become collaborators (the comparison being with Jews under the Nazis); some aliens are worse than others.

The first half of the initial mini-series was quite good, but afterwards the series became an object lesson in US tv's remorseless appetite for CLICHÉ – especially in its programmes for younger viewers – and its reduction of all controversial issues to moral stereotypes: the latter half of this miniseries lost direction; the second miniseries was absurd; and the series was infantile hackwork and cancelled before the story was completed. The two mini-series were expensive and – especially the first – had quite spectacular sets and special effects.   [PN]

VACCA, ROBERTO [r] ◊ ITALY.

VADRE, LESLIE ◊ L.P. DAVIES.

VALE, RENA (MARIE) (1898-1983) US writer who began publishing sf in 1952 with the novella "The Shining City" for *Science Fiction Quarterly*, and with her first novel, *The Red Court: Last Seat of National Government of the United States of America* (**1952**). She subsequently restricted herself to novels, like *Beyond the Sealed World* (**1965**), based on the 1952 novella, and *Taurus Four* (**1970**), which combines SATIRE with SPACE OPERA in a story containing hippies lost on another planet, a sociologist and an alien INVASION. In *The Day After Doomsday: A Fantasy of Time Travel* (**1970**) 12 selected survivors of a nuclear HOLOCAUST are lectured by their saviours, the race which bred humans on Earth in the first place.   [JC]

Other works: *Beyond these Walls* (**1960**); *The House on Rainbow Leap* (**1973**).

See also: CITIES.

VALENTINE, VICTOR (?   -   ) UK writer whose *Cure for Death* (**1960**) features a ray that not only cures cancer and ageing but also dissociates its patients from their own past lives.   [JC]

VALIGURSKY, ED(WARD I.) (1926-   ) US illustrator. He attended the Art Institute of Chicago and the American Academy of Arts before graduating from the Art Institute of Pittsburgh. He began as an associate art director for ZIFF-DAVIS in 1952 and became art director for Quinn Publishing, publisher of IF, in 1953. From 1954 he freelanced, though most of his magazine work was for those 2 companies; he painted 49 covers for *AMZ* and 32 for *Fantastic*, mostly in the 1950s, and many book covers (often unsigned) for ACE BOOKS in the 1950s and 1960s – notably the **Ace Doubles** – and for many other book publishers, including Avon and Dell. His work sometimes looks hurried, but he was proficient at menacing ROBOTS and his characteristic needle-nosed SPACESHIPS. Like many sf illustrators of the period, he found other markets that paid better, and moved into advertising, general-fiction magazines like COLLIER'S, and nonfiction magazines featuring aviation and aerospace subjects. [JG/PN]

VALLÉE, JACQUES [r] ◊ UFOS.

VALLEJO, BORIS (? -) Illustrator, born in Peru probably around 1947 and trained there in graphic design; moved to the USA in 1964. BV, who signs his work "Boris", began working in the sf/ FANTASY genre with Warren Publications' magazines and comics in 1971, then shifted to MARVEL COMICS, where his covers for **The Savage Sword of Conan** soon caused him to be tagged "the next Frazetta"; work in this vein won him a reputation in heroic-fantasy ILLUSTRATION second only to Frank FRAZETTA's, though perhaps BV's work is smoother and less vigorous. His book-cover work in this genre since 1975 has been primarily for BALLANTINE BOOKS and DEL REY BOOKS. His erotic fantasies of male power and female bondage were a natural accompaniment to the **Gor** novels of John NORMAN, for 7 of which he did covers in 1976; he also painted the covers for Ballantine's reissue of 24 of Edgar Rice BURROUGHS's **Tarzan** books in 1977. BV's work is almost a compendium of alternate sexual fantasies, moving easily from men like a homo-erotic musclebuilder's dream to lush-breasted, dominatrix whip-wielding women. Much of BV's later output is in the form of books and pictorial calendars, often featuring previously unpublished work. There are at least 10 calendars, starting with *The Tarzan Calendar 1979* (**1978**). The books include *The Fantastic Art of Boris Vallejo* (**1978**), *Mirage* (**1982**), overtly erotic original art with poems by BV's wife, Doris Vallejo, *Enchantment* (**1984**), further erotic art with stories by Doris Vallejo, and *Boris Vallejo's Fantasy Art Techniques* (**1985**). [PN/JG]

VALLEY OF GWANGI, THE Film (1969). Morningside/Warner-Seven Arts. Prod Charles H. Schneer. Dir James O'Connolly, starring James Franciscus, Gila Golan, Richard Carlson, Laurence Naismith. Screenplay William E. Bast, with additions by Julian More. 95 mins. Colour.

Cowboys discover a hidden valley in Mexico where surviving dinosaurs still live. They capture Gwangi, an allosaur, roping it like a steer, and take it back to civilization to put it on display in a stadium; but, like KING KONG, Gwangi escapes and goes on the rampage, until finally cornered in a church. *TVOG* had been a pet project of Willis O'BRIEN, who had wanted to make it in 1942. Ray HARRYHAUSEN, O'Brien's special-effects protegé, finally brought it to life, and, although usually rated a poor film, it is one of the more cheerful and entertaining showcases for Harryhausen's stop-motion animation – the cowboy vs dinosaur scenes comprise one of the great sequences of B-movie lunacy. But it flopped. [PN]

VAMPIRES ◊ SUPERNATURAL CREATURES.

van ARNAM, DAVE Working name of US writer David G. van Arnam (1935-   ) who began publishing sf with *Lost in Space* * (**1957**) with Ron Archer (Ted WHITE), a novelization from the tv series LOST IN SPACE. *Sideslip* (**1968**) was also written with White, who this time used his own name. Further routine sf adventures by DVA are *Star Gladiator* (**1967** chap dos), *Star Mind* (**1969**) and *Greyland* (**1972**). The **Zantain** fantasies – *The Players of Hell* (**1968** chap dos) and *Wizard of Storms* (**1970**) – are well constructed and occasionally vivid, as are the **Jamnar** fantasies, *Star Barbarian* (**1969**) and *Lord of Blood* (**1970**). [JC]

van CAMPEN, KARL [s] ◊ John W. CAMPBELL Jr.

VANCE, GERALD ZIFF-DAVIS house name (1941-58), used by Roger P. Graham (Rog PHILLIPS), by Randall GARRETT in collaboration with Robert SILVERBERG, and on 35 stories whose authors have not been identified, many perhaps by Chester S. GEIER. [PN]

VANCE, JACK Working name of US writer John Holbrook Vance (1916-   ), who was educated at the University of California first as a mining engineer, then as a physics major and finally in journalism, though without taking a degree. During WWII he served in the Merchant Navy, being twice torpedoed and writing his first story, "The World Thinker", published in 1945 in *TWS*. In the late 1940s and early 1950s JV contributed a variety of short stories (one time using the pseudonym John Holbrook) and novels to the PULP MAGAZINES, primarily STARTLING STORIES and THRILLING WONDER STORIES. These included the **Magnus Ridolph** series, chronicling the adventures of a roguish interstellar troubleshooter, assembled as *The Many Worlds of Magnus Ridolph* (coll **1966** dos; exp 1980; further exp vt *The Complete Magnus Ridolph* 1984). But nothing of this early work, dependent as it was on pulp conventions, prefigured the mature JV.

The change began with his first published book, *The Dying Earth* (coll of linked stories **1950**), comprising 6 previously unpublished tales set on Earth in the FAR FUTURE, at a time, long after the wasting away of science, when MAGIC has become the operating principle. This Dying Earth venue derived its languid colours and its florid architecture from the romances of Clark Ashton SMITH, and the tales are the first mature examples of that form as adumbrated by Smith; but, unlike his mentor, JV told his stories in an ironical tone, uniquely distanced and serene, that itself became an integral part of any definition of a Dying-Earth tale. Cruelties and nostalgias, picaresque flashes of plotting, adjurations of melancholy: all were enveloped in the musing voice. JV's only real failure in *The Dying Earth* – it would dog him throughout his career – lay in his inability to conceive narrative structures capable of sustaining his vision for more than novelette length. His later full-length **Dying Earth** volumes were all made up from shorter units; they included *The Eyes of the Overworld* (fixup **1966**), *Morreion: A Tale of the Dying Earth* (1973 *Flashing Swords #1*, anth ed Lin CARTER; **1979** chap), *A Bagful of*

Dreams (**1979** chap), *The Seventeen Virgins* (1974 *FSF*; **1979** chap), *Cugel's Saga* (coll of linked stories **1983**) and *Rhialto the Marvelous* (**1984**). (This last is not to be confused with *Rhialto the Marvelous* * [anth **1985**], a SHARED-WORLD book containing also "Basileus" by C.J. CHERRYH and Janet E. MORRIS. Before that, in *A Quest for Simbilis* * [**1974**], Michael SHEA wrote a direct sequel to *The Eyes of the Overworld*, territory later covered in conflicting terms by *Cugel's Saga*.) The influence of JV's articulation of the tone and venue of the Dying Earth was widespread, affecting both fantasy and sf writers, and helping authors such as Michael MOOR-COCK to define the characteristic ambience of SCIENCE FANTASY. It would not be until *The Book of the New Sun* (**1980-82**) by Gene WOLFE – who amply acknowledged JV's central influence – that a new paradigm for the Dying-Earth tale would appear, one more tightly tied to narrative revelation but no more entrancing than its model.

JV's second original contribution to the sf/fantasy field was his sophistication of the PLANETARY ROMANCE in *Big Planet* (1952 *Startling Stories*; cut **1957**; further cut **1958**; full text restored 1978), to which *Showboat World* (**1975**; vt *The Magnificent Showboats of the Lower Vissel River Lune XXIII South, Big Planet* 1983) forms a retroactively conceived sequel. Before 1950 and *The Dying Earth*, the planetary romance had been gene-rally restricted either to tales which replicated, palely, the work of Edgar Rice BURROUGHS or to pulp-sf adventures set on worlds which might be colourful but which were at the same time conceived with a fatal thinness. What was lacking was any form of enabling premise. In *Big Planet* JV provided an sf model for the planetary romance which has been of significant use for 40 years. The planet of this novel is a huge though Earthlike world, with enough landmass to provide realistic venues in which a wide range of social systems can operate, and, signifi-cantly, is low in heavy-metal resources (a fact that both explains its relatively low gravity and requires the wide range of societies that flourish to be low-tech ones). As is usual with JV, these societies are all of distant human origin, though they have become exceedingly variegated in ways open to description in the ethnographical style he developed to tell this tale, and upon which he depended for his best and truest effects over the next decades (◊ ANTHROPO-LOGY; SOCIOLOGY). The world of the JV planetary romance might occasionally be linked notionally to Earth by conventional sf trappings (generally of little actual relevance), but basically it is a venue, placed far into the future though without foregrounding any common dating or other device that might tie it too tightly to any Future History.

His other titles from this period were less ambitious but contained some interesting incidental invention; they include *Son of the Tree* (1951 *TWS*; **1964** dos), *Slaves of the Klau* (1952 *Space Stories* as "Planet of the Damned"; cut **1958** dos; text restored, vt *Gold and Iron* 1982) and *The Houses of Iszm* (1954 *Startling Stories*;

1964 dos). None of these were particularly well organized books – nor for that matter are *The Dying Earth* and *Big Planet* – but the development of IMMORTALITY themes in the far-future DYSTOPIA depicted in *To Live Forever* (**1956**) is more impressive, and *The Languages of Pao* (**1958**) interestingly espouses the Whorfian hypothesis (◊ LINGUISTICS) that lan-guage creates PERCEPTION, rather than the reverse. The main thrust of JV's work, however, as in such stories as "The Miracle Workers" (1958), continued to lie in increasingly ambitious explorations of the planetary-romance theme of LIFE ON OTHER WORLDS. *The Dragon Masters* (**1963** dos), a short novel which won JV his first HUGO, clearly illustrates this ten-dency. Set on a distant world in the far future, it is a story grounded in GENETIC ENGINEERING, but the science is so far advanced that it could equally be considered magic.

As JV's created worlds became richer and more complex, so too did his style. Always tending towards the baroque, it had developed by the time of *The Dragon Masters* into an effective high-mannered diction, somewhat pedantic, and almost always saturated with a rich but distanced irony. JV's talent for naming the people and places in his stories (a mixture of exotic invented terms and commonplace words with the right resonance) contributed to the sense that dream ethnographies were being carved, almost as a gardener would create topiary. Three novels, similar in structure, show these talents at their fullest stretch: *The Blue World* (**1966**), *Emphyrio* (**1969**) and *The Anome* (**1973**; vt *The Faceless Man* 1978) each follow the life of a boy born into and growing up in a static, stratified society, with which he comes into conflict, being driven eventually into rebellion. The invented world in each is particularly carefully thought-out. Both *Emphyrio* and *The Anome* addition-ally feature some piercing SATIRE of RELIGION.

As his professional career developed, JV began to initiate various sequences – with mixed results, for he often gave the impression that, once the setting had been fully established, his interest began inexorably to wane. Later books in his series are often inferior to their predecessors, and far more likely to depend for their effects upon plotting routines extracted – none too competently – from the dawn of pulp. This is the case with the earlier vols of the **Demon Princes** series, an interstellar saga of vengeance comprising *The Star King* (**1964**), *The Killing Machine* (**1964**), *The Palace of Love* (**1967**), *The Face* (**1979**) and *The Book of Dreams* (**1981**), though the last two titles are of more interest, with the **Planet of Adventure** series, com-prising *City of the Chasch* (**1968**; vt *Chasch* 1986), *Servants of the Wankh* (**1969**; vt *Wankh* 1986), *The Dirdir* (**1969**) and *The Pnume* (**1970**), all assembled as *The Planet of Adventure Omnibus* (omni **1985** UK); and with the **Durdane** trilogy, comprising *The Anome, The Brave Free Men* (**1973**) and *The Asutra* (**1974**), all assembled as *Durdane* (omni **1989** UK). In contrast, the **Alastor Cluster** sequence – *Trullion: Alastor 2262* (**1973**),

Marune: Alastor 933 (**1975**) and _Wyst: Alastor 1716_ (**1978**) – arguably improves from beginning to end. Most of these novels are planetary romances, and can be read in isolation from their fellows; at the same time, most embody mild hints – for example, the **Demon Princes** series is set in the far past of the **Cadwal Chronicles** (_see below_) – that they belong to the same tenuously knit future **Gaean Reach** Universe, most clearly described in _The Gray Prince_ (**1974**) and _Maske: Thaery_ (**1976**). But this background never governs the reader's perception of individual tales.

JV has written comparatively little short fiction. Apart from those stories already mentioned, the best include "Telek" (1952), "The Moon Moth" (1961) and the novella _The Last Castle_ (**1967** dos), which won JV a NEBULA and his 2nd Hugo. "The Moon Moth", one of JV's most elaborate stories, features the use of MUSIC as a secondary form of COMMUNICATION. Music and other ARTS feature in several other JV stories, including _Space Opera_ (1965), _Emphyrio_, _The Anome_ and _Showboat World_. Many of JV's best short stories are in _Eight Fantasms and Magics_ (coll **1969**; with 2 stories cut, vt _Fantasms and Magics_ 1978 UK) and _The Best of Jack Vance_ (coll **1976**). The latter is also notable for containing informative commentaries on the stories included, as JV is renowned for his reticence concerning himself and his stories, maintaining such a low profile that a rumour that began in 1950 that he was another Henry KUTTNER pseudonym was still being perpetrated in some quarters 20 years later, notwithstanding Kuttner's death in 1958.

The 1980s saw some slackening in JV's production, though this might not have been evident to the casual observer, as it was now that much of his earlier short fiction was finally brought out in book form. Beyond continuations of earlier series, his most interesting work in this decade was restricted to 2 new series. One was the **Lyonesse** sequence of fantasies about Tristan's birthplace off the coast of France, now sunk into the wide funnel of the English Channel: _Suldren's Garden_ (**1983**; rev 1983; vt _Lyonesse_ 1984 UK), _Lyonesse: The Green Pearl_ (**1985**; rev vt _The Green Pearl_ 1986) and _Lyonesse: Madouc_ (**1989**; vt _Madouc_ 1990). Of greater sf interest are the **Cadwal Chronicles** – to date _Araminta Station_ (**1987**), _Ecce and Olde Earth_ (**1991**) and _Throy_ (**1992**) – expanding the planetary-romance idiom into very long books with a sophisticated, newly plot-wise leisureliness which almost fully warrants their length. Interestingly, the planet Cadwal – the main character of the sequence, in a fashion typical of JV – is a nature reserve.

JV also wrote mystery novels, mostly during the 1960s – one of the best of them, _The Man in the Cage_ (**1960**), won an Edgar – and scripts for the tv series CAPTAIN VIDEO. None of this work lacks competence, but none has the haunting retentiveness in the mind's eye of his planetary romances or his Dying Earths. As a landscape artist, a gardener of worlds, JV has been for half a century central to both sf and FANTASY. He has a genius of place. [MJE/JC]

Other works: _The Space Pirate_ (1950 _Startling Stories_; **1953**; cut vt _The Five Gold Bands_ 1962 dos; text restored 1980); _Vandals of the Void_ (**1953**); _Future Tense_ (coll **1964**; vt _Dust of Far Suns_ 1981); _The World Between_ (coll **1965** dos; vt _The Moon Moth_ dated 1975 but **1976** UK); _Monsters in Orbit_ (1952 _TWS_ as "Abercrombie Station" and "Cholwell's Chickens"; cut **1965** dos); _The Brains of Earth_ (**1966** dos), assembled vt _Nopalgarth_ with _The Houses of Iszm_ and _Son of the Tree_ in _Nopalgarth_ (omni **1980**); _The Worlds of Jack Vance_ (coll **1973**); _Green Magic_ (coll **1979**), not to be confused with _Green Magic_ (1963 _FSF_; **1979** chap), which contains only the collection's title story; _Galactic Effectuator_ (coll of linked stories **1980**); _Lost Moons_ (coll **1982**); _The Narrow Land_ (coll **1982**); _Light from a Lone Star_ (coll **1985**); _The Dark Side of the Moon: Stories of the Future_ (coll **1986**); _The Augmented Agent_ (coll **1986**); _Chateau d'If and Other Stories_ (coll **1990**); _When the Five Moons Rise_ (coll **1992**).

Non-sf, some as John Holbrook Vance: _Take My Face_ (**1957**) as by Peter Held and _Isle of Peril_ (**1959**) as by Alan Wade, both assembled (the latter vt _Bird Isle_) as _Bird Isle/Take My Face_ (omni **1988**); _A Room to Die In_ (**1965**) as by Ellery Queen; _The Four Johns_ (**1964**; vt _Four Men Called John_ 1976 UK) as by Ellery Queen; _The Madman Theory_ (**1966**) as by Ellery Queen; _The Fox Valley Murders_ (**1966**); _The Pleasant Grove Murders_ (**1967**); _The Deadly Isles_ (**1969**); _Bad Ronald_ (**1973**); _The House on Lilly Street_ (**1979**); _Strange Notions_ (**1985**); _The Dark Ocean_ (**1985**).

About the author: _Jack Vance, a Fantasmic Imagination: A Working Bibliography_ (last rev **1990** chap) by Gordon BENSON Jr and Phil STEPHENSEN-PAYNE; _The Jack Vance Lexicon: From Aluph to Zipangote_ (**1992**) ed Dan Ternianka.

See also: ALIENS; ASTEROIDS; COLONIZATION OF OTHER WORLDS; CRIME AND PUNISHMENT; CYBORGS; ECOLOGY; FANTASTIC VOYAGES; GALACTIC EMPIRES; GALAXY SCIENCE FICTION; GAMES AND SPORTS; GOTHIC SF; LEISURE; LIFE ON OTHER WORLDS; LONGEVITY (IN WRITERS AND PUBLICATIONS); MATTER TRANSMISSION; MONEY; SPACE HABITATS; SPACE OPERA; SUPERMAN; SWORD AND SORCERY; TABOOS; TERRAFORMING; THRILLING WONDER STORIES; TRANSPORTATION; UNDER THE SEA; VILLAINS.

VANCE, STEVE (1952-   ) US writer who has since the late 1980s concentrated on horror novels, but who began writing with some unremarkable but competently conceived sf adventures, including _Planet of the Gawfs_ (**1977**), _All the Shattered Worlds_ (**1980**) and _The Hybrid_ (**1981**). Later novels include _The Hyde Effect_ (**1986**) and _The Asgard Run_ (**1990**), about a shipwrecked crew of alien scientists encountered in the mountains of Wyoming. [JC]

Other works: _The Abyss_ (**1989**), _Spook_ (**1990**) and _Shapes_ (**1991**), all horror.

van DONGEN Working name of US illustrator Henry Richard van Dongen (1920-   ). Entering the sf field in 1950 with a cover for SUPER SCIENCE STORIES (Sep 1950), vD soon dominated the covers (and the interiors) of ASTOUNDING SCIENCE-FICTION, with 46 covers Aug 1951-Sep 1961. He seldom worked for other magazines, but did 3 covers for SCIENCE FICTION ADVENTURES, including #1 (Nov 1952). His style was very distinctive, with muted colours and gaunt, angular people. He left the genre in 1961 for the more lucrative commercial-art field, returning in 1976 as a result of a chance conversation with Lester DEL REY at BALLANTINE BOOKS. For the next decade he did covers for Ballantine and DAW BOOKS in a style similar to his 1950s magazine work but with much brighter colours. He retired in 1987 with nerve problems related to injuries suffered in WWII. [JG/PN]

van DYNE, EDITH ◊ L. Frank BAUM.

van GREENAWAY, PETER (1929-1988) UK lawyer who began writing full-time in 1960; though he never became known as a genre writer, much of his work was sf, including his 1st novel, *The Crucified City* (1962), a post-HOLOCAUST story set in a devastated London after a nuclear bomb has been dropped, and his 2nd, *The Evening Fool* (1964), which carries its protagonist into an unviable UTOPIA. *The Man who Held the Queen to Ransom and Sent Parliament Packing* (1968) features a NEAR-FUTURE coup attempt in the UK, told in the astringent, side-of-the-mouth pessimistic voice which became a trademark. In later novels – like *Judas!* (1972; vt *The Judas Gospel* 1972 US), *The Medusa Touch* (1973), *Take the War to Washington* (1974), *Suffer! Little Children* (1976), *The Dissident* (1980) and *Mutants* (1986) – this dubiety about the human animal became visibly more inflamed. *Manrissa Man* (1982) makes savage play with the ape-as-human (◊ APES AND CAVEMEN) theme; and in *graffiti* (1983), another post-holocaust tale, survivors of a nuclear war revenge themselves upon its perpetrators. The increasingly solitary, evasively narrated, uncompromisingly dark work of his later years made it unlikely that PVG would ever be read with comfort as a genre writer. [JC]
Other works: *Doppelgänger* (1975); *A Man Called Scavener* (1978); *Edgar Allan Who – ?* (coll 1981); *The Immortal Coil* (coll 1985); *The Killing Cap* (1987).

VANGUARD SCIENCE FICTION US DIGEST-size magazine. 1 issue June 1958, published by Vanguard Science Fiction; ed James BLISH. *VSF* made a promising début: it included the much-anthologized "Reap the Dark Tide" (vt "Shark Ship") by C.M. KORNBLUTH and what were intended as regular features by L. Sprague DE CAMP and Lester DEL REY. However, the decision to fold the magazine was made before #1 even appeared. [MJE]

van HERCK, PAUL (1939-) Belgian (Flemish) writer whose *Sam, of de Pluterdag* (1968; trans Danny De Laet and Willy Magiels as *Where Were You Last Pluterday?* 1973 US) is a SATIRE of a society in which the higher classes have access to an extra day of the week. Van Herck also wrote a collection of ingenious short stories, *De Cirkels* ["The Circles"] (coll 1965). [JC]
See also: BENELUX

van HERP, JACQUES [r] ◊ FRANCE.
van HOLK, FREDER [r] ◊ GERMANY.

van LHIN, ERIK ◊ Lester DEL REY.
van LOGGEM, MANUEL [r] ◊ BENELUX.
van LORNE, WARNER Pseudonymous author of a number of stories in ASTOUNDING SCIENCE-FICTION 1935-9. "The Blue-Men of Yrano" (1939) is probably the best remembered. WvL's identity has remained secret, although certainly F. Orlin TREMAINE wrote at least 1 WvL story. The remainder have been ascribed to his brother, Nelson Tremaine, but it is likely that they were all the work of the former. [MJE]

VAN LUSTBADER, ERIC (1946-) US author who graduated from Columbia University, majoring in sociology, and worked for a time in the rock-music industry. His published sf/fantasy work began with the **Sunset Warrior** trilogy: *The Sunset Warrior* (1977), *Shallows of Night* (1978) and *Dai-San* (1978), to which *Beneath an Opal Moon* (1980) is a coda with a different hero. This was remarkably vivid SWORD AND SORCERY with sex and violence, and imaginatively rendered: the first book is true sf, set in an underground post-HOLOCAUST society which has almost forgotten the technology that keeps it alive, and to which the surface is a distant memory, but subsequent volumes make no great attempt to cleave to the sf premise. EVL then turned to the bestseller genre with *The Ninja* (1979), the first of the **Nicholas Linnear** trilogy, whose other titles are *The Miko* (1984) and *White Ninja* (1990). These blend Oriental mysticism with martial-arts adventure and sex, and contain (especially the 3rd) many fantastic elements, though more magical than scientific. EVL maintained a string of bestsellers through the 1980s, and is now an important commercial writer. His work is florid and intense, with a sadistic streak, and mostly set in Asia; his more recent books are generally signed Eric Lustbader. Some of his other novels also contain fantastic elements. [PN]
Other works *Sirens* (1981), the **China Maroc** sequence, comprising *Jian* (1985) and *Shan* (1987); *The Black Heart* (1986); *Zero* (1988); *French Kiss* (1989); *Angel Eyes* (1991); *Black Blade* (1992).

van SCYOC, SYDNEY J(OYCE) (1939-) US writer, active in the Unitarian Church, who began publishing sf with "Shatter the Wall" for *Gal* in 1962 and afterwards contributed stories regularly to the magazines, though she soon became best known for her novels, beginning with the impressive *Saltflower* (1971), in which aliens seed Earth to produce a new breed of "men". *Assignment Nor'Dyren* (1973) depicts a DYSTOPIAN Earth and a complexly rendered alien planet in trouble. *Starmother* (1976) and *Cloudcry* (1977) are both set in a Galaxy dominated by humanity but on alien planets which offer fundamental challenges to the human senses of order and rightness, and which ultimately reward attempts to transcend, in a sometimes lukewarmly oceanic fashion, human hierarchies and failures of empathy. The **Sunstone Scrolls** sequence – *Darkchild* (1981), *Bluesong* (1983) and *Starsilk* (1984), all assembled as *Daughters of the Sunstone* (omni 1985) – also combine an alien setting, a variety of characters and species and an ultimate sharing of transcendence, here occasioned by the symbiosis-engendering starsilks. *Drowntide* (**1987**) could again be described as fusion sf, depicting the slow coming to communion of a land-based race and an ocean-based race through the agency of a hybrid offspring. SJVS's predilection for one-word titles continued in *Featherstroke* (**1989**) but was rested in *Deepwater Dreams* (**1991**). Though her tales are sometimes damaged by narrative longueurs, SJVS's capacity to evoke a sense of the deep strangeness of the Universe – and her iterated attempts to craft tales that persuasively espouse marriages of species and venues – make her work sometimes compelling.   [JC]

Other work: *Sunwaifs* (**1981**).

See also: PARASITISM AND SYMBIOSIS.

VANSITTART, PETER (1920-   ) UK writer best known for his densely written historical novels. His first novel, *I Am the World: A Romance* (**1942**), generalizes its politically speculative plot by placing it in an allegorized and unnamed country, where a dictator creates an ambiguous UTOPIA; *The Game and the Ground* (**1956**) covers similar territory. *The Story Teller* (**1968**) offers no sf explanation for the longevity of its central character – who lives over 500 years and the stages of his life are analogous to the development of northern European civilization – but the novel's narrative and linguistic powers deserve notice from the sf readership. In 3 further novels of IMMORTALITY – *Lancelot* (**1978**), *The Death of Robin Hood* (**1981**) and *Parsifal* (**1988**) – which share a polymathic density of language and a complexly ambiguous mythopoeic attentiveness to the cultural icons of their titles, PV again provided models of human history as a sequence of incessantly reiterated tales whose casts, although they may metamorphose, do so only to return. *Robin Hood* in particular prefigures the entangled chthonic worlds of sf fantasists like Paul HAZEL and Robert P. HOLDSTOCK.   [JC]

Other works: *The Dark Tower: Tales from the Past* (coll **1965**) and *The Shadow Land: More Stories from the Past* (coll **1967**), juveniles with fantasy elements.

van VOGT, A(LFRED) E(LTON) (1912-   ) Canadian-born writer who moved to the USA in 1944 after establishing his name as one of the creators of John W. CAMPBELL Jr's GOLDEN AGE OF SF with a flood of material in ASTOUNDING SCIENCE-FICTION, starting with "Black Destroyer" (1939), though he had been active for several years in various other genres. In 1939 he married E. Mayne HULL, and produced several stories with her until she stopped writing in 1950. With his conversion to DIANETICS – also in 1950 – AEVV became virtually silent for several years. After the early 1960s, however, a second, smaller spate of new material came from his pen.

In 1939-47 AEVV published at least 35 sf stories in *ASF* alone, some of novel length, and it was the work of these years, much of it not to be published in book form until long afterwards in reconstructed versions,

that gave him his high reputation as a master of intricate, metaphysical SPACE OPERA. Along with Isaac ASIMOV and Robert A. HEINLEIN, and to a lesser extent L. Sprague DE CAMP and L. Ron HUBBARD – he seemed nearly to create, by writing what Campbell wanted to publish, the first genuinely successful period of US sf; only in this "Golden Age" did it begin to achieve, in literary terms, what the writers of US GENRE SF had eschewed 20 years earlier when they had found that PULP MAGAZINES not only wished to publish sf but were their only consistent market. Although AEVV catered for the pulps, he intensified the emotional impact and complexity of the stories they would bear: his nearly invincible alien MONSTERS, the long timespans of his tales, the TIME PARADOXES that fill them, the quasimessianic SUPERMEN who come into their own as the stories progress, the GALACTIC EMPIRES they tend to rule and the states of lonely transcendental omnipotence they tend to achieve – all are presented in a prose that uses crude, dark colours but whose striking SENSE OF WONDER is conveyed with a dreamlike conviction. The abrupt complications of plot for which he became so well known, and which have been so scathingly mocked for their illogic and preposterousness – within narratives that claimed to be presenting higher forms of logic to the reader – are best analysed, and their effects best understood, when their sudden shifts of perspective and rationale and scale are seen as analogous to the movements of a dream. It is these "HARD-SF dreams", so grippingly void of constraints or of the usual surrealistic appurtenances of dream literature, that have so haunted generations of children and adolescents.

AEVV's first novel, and perhaps still his best known, is *Slan* (**1940** *ASF*; **1946**; rev 1951). Its HERO, the young Jommy Cross, is a member of a MUTANT race, the Slans, originally created to help mankind out of its difficulties but long driven into hiding because of the jealousy of normals. Jommy's powers (◊ CHILDREN IN SF), which include ESP, physical superiority to normals (he has 2 hearts) and extraordinary INTELLIGENCE, enable him to survive the mobbing, arrest and offstage death of his mother and to escape from sight into an adolescence and young manhood during which he begins to sense his true powers. As a man he becomes involved with Earth's mysterious dictator, with defective Slans, and with various intrigues centring on new sources of energy. Matters are cleared up only at the book's close with the revelation that the dictator is himself a secret Slan, that the girl Slan with whom Jommy is in love is the dictator's daughter, and that Jommy is in line for the succession. *Slan* is a much imitated model for the creation of wish-fulfilment stories.

However, it was in the 2 **Weapon Shops** books – *The Weapon Shops of Isher* (1941-2 *ASF*, 1949 *Thrilling Wonder Stories*; fixup **1951**) and *The Weapon Makers* (1943 *ASF*; **1946**; rev 1952; vt *One Against Eternity* 1955 dos), assembled as *The Weapon Shops of Isher, and The Weapon Makers* (omni **1988** UK) – that AEVV's mixture of hard-sf dreams, enormities of complication, and transcendent superheroes was most hypnotically presented. The main protagonist of the 2 books, the immortal Robert Hedrock (◊ IMMORTALITY), has not only in the dim past created the WEAPON Shops as a LIBERTARIAN force to counterbalance the imperial world government long dominant on Earth, but also turns out eventually to have literally begotten the race of emperors and empresses who rule that government in traditional opposition to the mysterious Shops, which are invulnerable and sell weapons to anyone. To cap this dream of omnipotence, Hedrock unwittingly passes a Galactic initiation test at the end of the 2nd book, the test having been designed to select the next rulers of the "sevagram". The word "sevagram" appears only once in the series, as the very last word of *The Weapon Makers*; in its placing, which seems to open universes to the reader's gaze, and in its resonant mysteriousness, for its precise meaning is unclear, this use of "sevagram" may well stand as the best working demonstration in the whole of genre sf of how to impart a SENSE OF WONDER.

The 2nd major series of AEVV's prolific decade – the **Null-A** sequence comprising *The World of Ā* (1945 *ASF*; rev **1948**; rev vt *The World of Null-A* 1970) and *The Pawns of Null-A* (1948-9 *ASF* as "The Players of Ā"; **1956**; rev vt *The Players of Null-A* 1966), plus *Null-A Three* (**1984** France [in French]; **1985** UK) – may have appeared weightier in its attempts to present its arguments in terms of "non-Aristotelian" thought (◊ GENERAL SEMANTICS), a claim which might seem ominously to prefigure a rationalization of the effortless dream logic of the earlier stories; but in the event tends to stumble into excessive tangles of complication. The protagonist, Gosseyn (go sane), lacks humour even more decidedly than his superman predecessors, and his rapid, confusing, nearly emotionless shifting from one Gosseyn body to another, in a kind of cloning (◊ CLONES) without the concept of cloning to sustain it, makes his eventual supremacy so peculiarly disorganized as to be almost without effect on the reader. By this time AEVV was nearing the end of his association with *ASF*, after an extraordinarily productive decade, and would soon stop writing entirely; perhaps *The Pawns of Null-A*, which in magazine form stretched to 100,000 words, was about as far as he could go without an extended breather. Certainly his 3rd series from this period – the **Linn** sequence comprising *Empire of the Atom* (1946-7 *ASF*; fixup **1957**; cut 1957 dos) and *The Wizard of Linn* (1950 *ASF*; **1962**) – is considerably less intense. James BLISH argued of this series about superscience and palace politics that its plot and characters closely resemble those of Robert GRAVES's **Claudius** novels: it would have been a brave critic who, with equal persuasiveness, found AEVV's earlier series to resemble any previous work of world literature.

During this first decade of his career, AEVV contributed material also to *ASF*'s sister magazine,

Unknown, most notably *The Book of Ptath* (1943 *Unknown*; **1947**; vt *Two Hundred Million A.D.* 1964; vt *Ptath* 1976), a FAR-FUTURE epic in which a reincarnated god-figure must fight to re-establish his suzerainty. Some of the independent stories of these years were collected in *Destination: Universe* (coll **1952**) and *Away and Beyond* (coll **1952**; with 2 stories cut rev 1959; with 1 story cut rev 1963 UK). *The Voyage of the Space Beagle* (1939-43 *ASF* and 1950 *Other Worlds*; fixup **1950**; vt *Mission: Interplanetary* 1952) marshalled several early stories into a chronicle depicting various ways in which a "Nexialist", Elliot Grosvenor, by using a response to ALIENS and their environments that synthesizes different fields of knowledge, copes with divers monsters. The book incorporates AEVV's first 2 sf stories; and Nexialism itself, which involves a system of intensive psychological training, interestingly prefigures L. Ron HUBBARD's Dianetics, with which AEVV was to become so closely involved. This involvement was the culmination of his persistent interest in all training systems which purport scientifically (or pseudo-scientifically; ◊ PSEUDO-SCIENCE) to create physical or mental superiority and awaken dormant talents, an interest which generated not only the 3 General-Semantics novels described above but also *Siege of the Unseen* (1946 *ASF* as "The Chronicler"; **1959** dos; vt as title story in *The Three Eyes of Evil* coll **1973** UK), in which, inspired by the Bates eye-exercise system, he dramatized the curing of eye problems through partly mental means.

In the autobiographical *Reflections of A.E. van Vogt* (**1975**), AEVV uses the term "fix-up" (or FIXUP) in the sense which we have adopted for this encyclopedia: a book made up of previously published stories altered to fit together – usually with the addition of new cementing material – the end product being marketed as a novel. It is possible that AEVV invented the term for, although fixups are not unknown outside sf, the peculiar marketing circumstances of the genre in the USA encouraged their creation, and certainly AEVV wrote (or compiled) more fixups than any other sf writer of stature. It was during his time of relative inactivity as a creator of original material – the 1950s and early 1960s – that he began producing these numerous fixups, including of course *The Weapon Shops of Isher*, perhaps the most successful and ingenious of all. Fixups incorporating Golden-Age material include *The Mixed Men* (1943-5 *ASF*; fixup **1952**; cut vt *Mission to the Stars* 1955), *The War Against the Rull* (1940-50 *ASF*; fixup **1959**), *The Beast* (1943-4 *ASF*; fixup **1963**; vt *Moonbeast* 1969 UK) and *Quest for the Future* (1943-6 *ASF*; fixup **1970**).

The Silkie (1964-7 *If*; fixup **1969**), though technically similar, was the first to use substantially contemporary material – and may have been the first whose component parts were all written with the end result in mind. It signalled the beginning of AEVV's 2nd period of productivity, with *Children of Tomorrow* (**1970**) being his first completely new sf novel since *The Mind Cage* (1948 *Fantasy Book* as "The Great

Judge"; exp **1957**) – although he had also published a political thriller about the attempted brainwashing of Westerners in contemporary communist China, *The Violent Man* (**1962**). The most sustained effort of this 2nd wave of titles was perhaps *The Battle of Forever* (**1971**), in which the enhanced-human protagonist, Modyun, leaves the refuge where his kind have for eons dwelt in seclusion and undertakes a far-future odyssey through a decadent world and Galaxy, battling against aliens and gradually coming to full stature as a superman. Compared to the fixups of the previous decade or so, the story is well paced and emotionally coherent, though the oneiric flow of arousing event and imagery is damaged by a sense of self-consciousness. Further novels do not live up to this promise of partial renewal, and have not been well received.

Critics such as Damon KNIGHT – in an essay reprinted as "Cosmic Jerrybuilder" in *In Search of Wonder* (critical coll **1956**; rev **1967**) – have tended to treat the typical AEVV tale as a failed effort at hard sf, and have consequently tended to describe stories others have written in the modes he developed – like Philip K. DICK, Charles L. HARNESS and Larry NIVEN – as "improvements" on the original model. In some ways, of course, these writers have built upon the complexity of AEVV's worlds and have significantly rationalized his convulsive shuffling and reshuffling of every element of his stories. But AEVV's space operas, as noted, are at heart enacted dreams which articulate deep, symbolic needs and wishes of his readership. Because there is no misunderstood science or cosmography or technology at the very heart of his best work, there is no "improving" AEVV. [JC]
Other works: *Tomorrow on the March: The Text of the Speech Delivered July 4, 1946 at the PACIFICON by the Guest of Honor* (**1946** chap); *Out of the Unknown* (coll **1948**; exp 1969; vt *The Sea Thing and Other Stories* 1970 UK; with 5 of the 6 original stories under original title, cut 1970 UK) with E. Mayne Hull, 3 stories by each writer; *Masters of Time* (coll **1950**), comprising 2 stories later published separately as *The Changeling* (1944 *ASF*; **1967**) and *Earth's Last Fortress* (1942 *ASF* as "Recruiting Station"; **1960** dos; vt *Masters of Time* 1967); *The House that Stood Still* (**1950**; rev vt *The Mating Cry* 1960; text restored vt *The Undercover Aliens* 1976 UK); *The Universe Maker* (1949 *Startling Stories* as "The Shadow Men"; rev **1953** dos); *Planets for Sale* (1943-6 *ASF* as by Hull alone; fixup **1954**) with Hull; *Rogue Ship* (1947 *ASF*, 1950 *Super-Science Stories* and 1963 *If*; fixup **1965**); *The Twisted Men* (coll **1964** dos); *Monsters* (coll **1965**; vt *The Blal and Other Science-Fiction Monsters* 1976); *The Winged Man* (1944 *ASF* as by Hull alone; exp **1966**) with Hull; *The Far-Out Worlds of A.E. van Vogt* (coll **1968**; vt with added stories as *The Worlds of A.E. van Vogt* 1974); *More than Superhuman* (coll **1971**); *The Proxy Intelligence and Other Mind Benders* (coll **1971**; with 1 story cut and others retitled but unrevised, rev vt *The Gryb* 1976); *M-33 in Andromeda* (coll **1971**); *The Darkness on Diamondia* (**1972**); *The Book of Van Vogt* (coll

1972; vt *Lost: Fifty Suns* 1979); *Future Glitter* (**1973**; vt *Tyranopolis* 1977 UK); *The Secret Galactics* (**1974**; vt *Earth Factor X* 1976); *The Man with a Thousand Names* (**1974**); *The Best of A.E. Van Vogt* (coll **1974** UK), a different selection from *The Best of A.E. Van Vogt* (coll **1976**); *Supermind* (fixup **1977**; vt *Supermind: I.Q. 10,000* 1978 UK); *The Anarchistic Colossus* (**1977**); *Pendulum* (coll **1978**); *Enchanted Village* (1950 *Other Worlds*; **1979** chap); *Renaissance* (**1979**); *Cosmic Encounter* (**1980**); *Computerworld* (**1983**; vt *Computer Eye* 1985).
Omnibuses include: *Triad* (omni **1959**) assembling *The World of A*, *The Voyage of the Space Beagle* and *Slan*; *A Van Vogt Omnibus* (omni **1967** UK) assembling *Planets for Sale*, *The Beast* and *The Book of Ptath*; *Van Vogt Omnibus (2)* (omni **1971** UK) assembling *The Mind Cage*, *The Winged Man* and *Slan*; *Two Science Fiction Novels* (omni **1973** UK) assembling *Siege of the Unseen* (as *The Three Eyes of Evil*) and *Earth's Last Fortress*; *The Universe Maker* and *The Proxy Intelligence* (omni **1976** UK).
About the author: "A.E. van Vogt" in *Seekers of Tomorrow* (**1966**) by Sam MOSKOWITZ; "The Development of a Science Fiction Writer" by AEVV in *Foundation #3*, 1973; *The World beyond the Hill: Science Fiction and the Quest for Transcendence* (**1989**) by Alexei and Cory PANSHIN.
See also: ADAM AND EVE; ANTIMATTER; ARKHAM HOUSE; CANADA; CONCEPTUAL BREAKTHROUGH; COSMOLOGY; DISCOVERY AND INVENTION; FANTASTIC VOYAGES; FRANCE; GALACTIC EMPIRES; GENERATION STARSHIPS; GENETIC ENGINEERING; GODS AND DEMONS; HISTORY IN SF; HISTORY OF SF; ILLUSTRATION; INVASION; LIVING WORLDS; LONGEVITY (IN WRITERS AND PUBLICATIONS); PARANOIA; PARASITISM AND SYMBIOSIS; PERCEPTION; PHYSICS; POLITICS; PSI POWERS; PSYCHOLOGY; REINCARNATION; RELIGION; SCIENTIFIC ERRORS; SERIES; SUSPENDED ANIMATION; THRILLING WONDER STORIES; WAR.

VARDEMAN, ROBERT E(DWARD) (1947-   ) US writer whose ruthless productivity – he has written about 50 books since his first sf novel, *Pleasure Planet* (**1974** as by Edward E. George; vt *Outer Space Embrace* 1978 as by Monica Mounds; vt *Janet's Sex Planet* 1980 as by Carrie Onn; vt *Intergalactic Orgy* 1983 as Obie Khan; vt *Sexual Coquette* 1985 dos as by Marv Elous; vt *Playing with Desire* 1986 as by Fred Sparkrock) – has yet to give birth to any memorable work. As well as some further pseudonymous titles, including 2 fairly marginal sf adventures as Nick CARTER – *The Solar Menace* * (**1981**) and *Doctor DNA* * (**1982**) – 2 **Star Trek** ties – *The Klingon Gambit* * (**1981**) and *Mutiny on the Enterprise* * (**1983**) – and a number of fantasy sequences, he has produced several series for the sf market, including: the **Weapons of Chaos** sequence, comprising *Echoes of Chaos* (**1986**), *Equations of Chaos* (**1987**) and *Colors of Chaos* (**1988**), all assembled as *The Weapons of Chaos* (omni **1989**); the **Masters of Space** sequence, comprising *The Stellar Death Plan* (**1987**), *The Alien Web* (**1987**) and *A Plague in Paradise* (**1987**), all assembled as *Masters of Space* (omni **1990** UK), which was advertised as resembling E.E. SMITH's work but lacked any similar conviction; and the **Biowarriors** sequence, comprising *The Infinity Plague* (**1989**), *Crisis at Starlight* (**1990**) and *Space Vectors* (**1990**). Singletons include *The Sandcats of Rhyl* (**1978**), *Road to the Stars* (**1988**), *Ancient Heavens* (**1989**) and *Deathfall* (**1991**). [JC]

Other works: Fantasies, mostly in series form, including: the **War of Powers** sequence, all with Victor MILÁN, comprising *The Sundered Realm* (**1980**), *The City in the Glacier* (**1980**) and *The Destiny Stone* (**1980**), all assembled as *The War of Powers* (omni **1984**), then *The Fallen Ones* (**1981**), *In the Shadow of Omizantrim* (**1982**) and *Demon of the Dark Ones* (**1982**); the **Cenotaph Road** sequence, perhaps his best, comprising *Cenotaph Road* (**1983**), *The Sorcerer's Skull* (**1983**), *World of Mazes* (**1983**), *Iron Tongue* (**1984**), *Fire and Fog* (**1984**) and *Pillar of Night* (**1984**); the **Jade Demons** sequence, comprising *The Quaking Lands* (**1984**), *The Frozen Waves* (**1985**), *The Crystal Clouds* (**1985**) and *The White Fire* (**1986**), all assembled as *The Jade Demons Quartet* (omni **1987** UK); the **Swords of Raemllyn** sequence, all with George W. PROCTOR, comprising *To Demons Bound* (**1985**), *A Yoke of Magic* (**1985**) and *Blood Fountain* (**1985**), all 3 assembled as *Swords of Raemllyn Book 1* (omni **1992** UK), plus *Death's Acolyte* (**1986**), *The Beasts of the Mist* (**1986**) and *For Crown and Kingdom* (**1987**); the **Demon Crown** trilogy, comprising *The Glass Warrior* (**1988**). *Phantoms on the Wind* (**1989**) and *A Symphony of Storms* (**1990**), all assembled as *The Demon Crown Trilogy* (omni **1990** UK); the **Peter Thorne** psychic detective sequence comprising *The Screaming Knife* (**1990**) and *A Resonance of Blood* (**1992**). A singleton is *The Keys to Paradise* (**1986** UK; vt in 3 vols, all as by Daniel Moran, *The Flame Key* 1987 US, *The Skeleton Lord's Key* 1987 US and *Key of Ice and Steel* 1988 US as by Moran).

VARDON, RICHARD [s] ◊ David Wright O'BRIEN.

VARDRE, LESLIE ◊ L.P. DAVIES.

VARGO STATTEN BRITISH SCIENCE FICTION MAGAZINE ◊ VARGO STATTEN SCIENCE FICTION MAGAZINE.

VARGO STATTEN SCIENCE FICTION MAGAZINE UK magazine. 19 issues 1954-6, published by Scion, London, for the first 7 issues, then Dragon Publications; ed "Vargo Statten" (Alistair Paterson for 7 issues, then John Russell FEARN). The last 2 issues were undated. #1-#3 were PULP-MAGAZINE size, then DIGEST size to #11, then pocketbook size. Intended to be a monthly, it 7 times skipped months. The magazine was retitled *Vargo Statten British Science Fiction Magazine* vol 1 #4-#5, *The British Science Fiction Magazine* vol 1 #6-#12, and finally *The British Space Fiction Magazine* from vol 2 #1 to the end.

VSSFM owed its existence to the success of Scion's paperback-book line, which included many sf novels written by Fearn and published as by Vargo Statten. A magazine under Statten's name seemed a good financial bet, given the popularity of the books. The policy of aiming stories at younger readers may have alienated some UK authors; the low rates of payment,

finally 12s 6d per 1000 words for world rights, cannot have helped. Barrington J. BAYLEY made his début here, and E.C. TUBB often appeared both under his own name and under pseudonyms, but Fearn was forced to use many of his own stories, sometimes old ones slightly rewritten under various pseudonyms, to fill up the issues. [FHP]

VARLEY, JOHN (HERBERT) (1947-   ) US writer who entered the sf field with "Picnic on Nearside" for *FSF* in 1974 and who was soon thought to be the most significant new writer of the 1970s. He was fresh, he was complex, he understood the imaginative implications of transformative developments like cloning (◊ CLONES), many of his protagonists were women, and most of the stories he told were set within an overall background Universe whose centre of geography had been startlingly displaced – in a manner characteristic of the finest sf – from Earth itself. It may have been the case that many previous SPACE OPERAS, especially those claiming galactic scope, were set far from the home planet (which was often "forgotten"), but JV's innovation was twofold: to bring the displacement close to the present day, which NEAR-FUTURE setting made it more vivid, and to present a subsequent Solar System whose own complexity seemed to mark a genuine evolutionary shift – in fictional terms – from the old geocentricity. The image of an incessantly humming Solar System – it is central to books like Michael SWANWICK's *Vacuum Flowers* (**1987**) – owes as much to JV as it does to the idioms of CYBERPUNK. Urgent and risk-taking, the stories assembled in *The Persistence of Vision* (coll **1978**; vt *In the Hall of the Martian Kings* 1978 UK) and *The Barbie Murders* (coll **1980**; vt *Picnic on Nearside* 1984) seemed to announce the shape of sf's response to the end of the 20th century. JV's shorter works have brought him 3 HUGOS – for "The Persistence of Vision" in 1979, "The Pusher" in 1982 and *PRESS ENTER* ■ (1984 *IASFM*; **1990** chap dos) in 1985 – and 2 NEBULAS – for "The Persistence of Vision" and "PRESS ENTER" ■.

This sense of currency was also a feature of JV's first – and perhaps finest – novel, *The Ophiuchi Hotline* (**1977**), set 500 years into his future HISTORY – it is sometimes called the **Eight Worlds** sequence – at a time when humanity has been long exiled from Earth by immensely superior, indifferent "Invaders". Bioengineered and variously cloned, humans now subscribe to social and sexual codes – and live within perspectives and according to processes – that differ radically from those of their flesh-bound, planet-bound ancestors. The protagonist is in fact several successive clones of the same person, the original dying only a few pages into the text and new versions of that original – clone bodies with pre-recorded mind-tapes of the original plugged in at the point of arousal – taking over when needed. The sense of ongoing process – and of an identity-dissolving taste for meta-morphosis – is incessant. The eponymous hotline, which is operated by similarly displaced interstellar exiles, beams data through the Solar System, the last item being a message that humanity will soon be banned from its home system, and will be doomed to wander the stars, homeless, for ever. This happens.

JV then composed the **Titan** or **Gaean** sequence – *Titan* (1979), *Wizard* (1980) and *Demon* (1984) – which begins exuberantly with a mission to explore the largest satellite of Saturn. But Titan turns out to be a sentient artifact (or BIG DUMB OBJECT) called Gaea and to contain within its entrails a veritable POCKET UNIVERSE of trapped individuals and species. The female protagonist of the series becomes Gaea's agent, intimate and enemy. Although this was technically an interminable template, the series was kept decorously to trilogy length, but did not fully escape the charge that the libidinous solipsisms of the plot had a VIRTUAL-REALITY resonance. *Millennium* (1977 *IASFM* as "Air Raid" as by Herb Boehm; exp 1983) – filmed as MILLENNIUM (1989) – is a TIME-TRAVEL novel in which humans from a devastated future extract contemporary accident victims at the moment before their deaths because, being still genetically whole, they can be used in a project to repopulate the Earth, with the aid of an AI. Like JV's best work, the book was smoothly muscled, manipulative and ruthless. His output of the 1980s was, nevertheless, less strikingly innovative than had been hoped – and, perhaps unfairly, expected – of him. The stories assembled in *Blue Champagne* (coll 1986) – *Tango Charlie and Foxtrot Romeo* (1989 chap) reprints an original story from the collection – show no technical decline but lack some of the exploratory dangerousness of his first work. Similarly, *Steel Beach* (1992) demonstrates through its huge length a virtuoso control of sf themes, presented through many of the kind of compulsive narrative hooks employed by Robert A. HEINLEIN in his ruthless prime; but the story itself, set in the **Eight Worlds** universe about 200 years after humanity's expulsion from Earth, lacks dramatic urgency, despite many cleverly conceived (but sidebar) episodes full of action. The title itself, however, may well become established as a tag for the evolutionary impasse humanity may soon face: like a lungfish struggling to breathe on a Pacific beach, JV suggests, humanity could soon find itself struggling for breath on the steel beach that is all the home it has, after the final death of Nature. [JC]

See also: BLACK HOLES; CHILDREN IN SF; ESCHATOLOGY; ESP; FANTASY; GALAXY SCIENCE FICTION; GENETIC ENGINEERING; ISAAC ASIMOV'S SCIENCE FICTION MAGAZINE; LINGUISTICS; *The* MAGAZINE OF FANTASY AND SCIENCE FICTION; MAGIC; MARS; NEW WAVE; OUTER PLANETS; PASTORAL; SCIENCE FANTASY; SEX; SPACE HABITATS; TIME PARADOXES; WRITERS OF THE FUTURE CONTEST.

VÁŠOVÁ, ALTA [r] ◊ CZECH AND SLOVAK SF.

VECTOR The journal of the BRITISH SCIENCE FICTION ASSOCIATION (BSFA). There have been 166 issues to April/May 1992. *V* has been published since the foundation of the BSFA in 1958, fairly regularly since the 1970s. E.C. TUBB was its first editor (#1), and it has

had 32 editors since then, including, briefly, Michael MOORCOCK (#6-#7). Both production and literary quality have fluctuated severely from editor to editor, and *V* has appeared variously as an association newsletter, a typical FANZINE and an academic journal. It had a strong period under the editorship of Roger Peyton in the mid-1960s (#26-#39), and has been much more consistent ever since 1972 when Malcolm EDWARDS took over (#59-#68), his successors including David WINGROVE (#84-#94), Geoff Rippington (#108-#123), David V. Barrett (#126-#150), Boyd Parkinson and Kev McVeigh (#151-#160), and Kev McVeigh and Catie Cary (#161-current). The page-size varied between large and small for many years, but since 1984 (#122) it has been large-format A4. Since the late 1970s, when some of *V*'s functions were hived off into other BSFA publications – paperback-book reviews in *Paperback Parlour* (soon renamed *Paperback Inferno*, and then incorporated into *V* from #169), fan news in *Matrix*, and advice for new writers in *Focus* – *V* has sometimes looked less useful than it once was, but it has continued to print good interviews, major articles and substantial reviews, often approaching professional standards, but equally often lapsing into fannish polemic, which is quite proper, since its function is to act as a kind of central clearing house for UK FANDOM. Almost every UK sf writer of note has appeared in its pages, and many US writers too. [PN/PR]

VEIS, JAROSLAV [r] ◊ CZECH AND SLOVAK SF.

VEJDĚLEK, ČESTMIR [r] ◊ CZECH AND SLOVAK SF.

VEL'D (vt *The Veldt*) Film (1987). Uzbekfilm. Dir Nazim Tulyakhodzhaev, starring Igor Beliayev, Nelly Pshonnaya, Georgy Gegechkori. Screenplay Tulyakhodzhaev, based on stories by Ray BRADBURY. 90 mins. Colour.

The second attempt by a talented Uzbek director to transfer the mood of Bradbury's GOTHIC prose onto the screen proved not so successful as the first, the short animated movie *There Will Come Soft Rains* (1982), had done. This full-length feature is a poetic adaptation of several Bradbury stories, such as "The Garbage Collector" (1953), "Hail and Farewell" (1953) and "The Dragon" (1956), along with some episodes from *Dandelion Wine* (1957), all combined into a single, if rather dissolving, plot, for which the title story, "The Veldt" (1950), serves as a bar or pivot. The baroque atmosphere evoked by the unique Bradbury mixture of horror, pathos and sentimentality is well maintained, and visually some episodes are excellent. But the director's lack of feeling for narrative or plot means that he does not create a main focus for the film; it is as if he has forgotten what he wished to say. However, it still stands as a good example of the new Soviet horror film. [VG]

See also: RUSSIA.

VELDT, THE ◊ VEL'D.

VELIKOVSKY, IMMANUEL (1895-1979) Russian-born US pseudo-scientist and writer. He is primarily known for a series of books putting forward, with a vast amount of documentation and argument, a theory of Earth's history which proposes that comparatively recent large-scale changes in the Solar System had catastrophic effects on the Earth, and that historical evidence (in the form of legends, MYTHOLOGY, the Bible and other accounts) exists for these. The books are *Worlds in Collision* (**1950**), *Ages in Chaos* (**1952**), *Earth in Upheaval* (**1955**) and *Oedipus and Akhnaton* (**1960**). In particular, Velikovsky claimed that the planet VENUS was a recent addition to the Sun's retinue, having been spat out by Jupiter in biblical times and then having swooped close to the Earth on several occasions before coming to rest in its current orbit: one effect of these near-misses was to make the Earth flip over on its axis. Making planets flip over in this way is extremely hard to do because of the gyroscope effect, and it was soon proven that his basic mechanism was infeasible. Nevertheless, the books are probably the most significant in 20th-century PSEUDO-SCIENCE.

An apparent attempt by scientists to have IV's work censored is recounted in *The Velikovsky Affair* (anth **1966**) ed Alfred de Grazia. A collection of essays defending IV's science and pointing to the accuracy of many of his predictions (while, it has to be said, ignoring the inaccuracy of others) is *Velikovsky Reconsidered* (anth **1976**) ed by the editors of *Pensée*. The proceedings of a scientific conference to discuss the affair are found in *Scientists Confront Velikovsky* (anth **1977**) ed Donald Goldsmith. An over-friendly overview of Velikovskianism is given in *Doomsday: The Science of Catastrophe* (**1979**) by Fred Warshovsky.

In the early 1980s there was a flurry of renewed interest in Velikovsky's ideas when it was proposed that flipping the Earth over on its axis might not be so difficult as had been thought. Various writers pointed to the childhood toy called the tippe-top which, when spun, easily turns over to stand on its head, apparently defying the gyroscopic effect. Probably the most significant book in this vein was *The Reversing Earth* (**1982**) by Peter Warlow, which described the tippe-top effect (and much else in support of IV's ideas) in persuasive detail. The flaw in the argument is (to simplify) that the tippe-top effect works only if the tippe-top is placed on a surface (e.g., a table-top) in an appropriate gravitational field.

Orthodox scientists have themselves proposed some quasi-Velikovskian ideas since the 1960s, reflecting a recognition that catastrophic changes caused by cosmic events may have played a greater part in our planet's history than hitherto recognized; in particular, it is now generally accepted that the extinction of the dinosaurs about 65 million years ago was the result of one such event. A type example of a disproved theory of this sort is supplied by *The Jupiter Effect* (**1974**) by John GRIBBIN and Stephen Plagemann, which predicted dire consequences from an unusual planetary alignment and a peak of solar activity in 1982; *Beyond the Jupiter Effect* (**1983**)

is rather more muted.

IV's dramatic scenario of planetary near-misses parallels many of the catastrophic events described in sf; a notable fictional precursor is *When Worlds Collide* (**1933**) by Philip WYLIE and Edwin BALMER. Some of the few interesting sf novels in the Velikovskian mode (there are countless bad DISASTER novels) are *The Wanderer* (**1964**) by Fritz LEIBER, in which a singleton planet enters the Solar System, *The HAB Theory* (**1976**) by Allan W. ECKERT, in which the Earth flips on its axis, *Lucifer's Hammer* (**1977**) by Larry NIVEN and Jerry POURNELLE, in which the Earth is struck by a small comet, and *Nemesis* (**1989**) by Isaac ASIMOV, which focuses on the threat to Earth of a dwarf star on course for a close encounter with the Solar System. [PN/JGr]

See also: ADAM AND EVE.

VENEZUELA ◊ LATIN AMERICA.

VENGEANCE (vt *Ein Toter Sucht seiner Mörder*; vt *The Brain*) Film (1963). CCC/Stross/Governor. Dir Freddie Francis, starring Peter Van Eyck, Anne Heywood, Cecil Parker, Bernard Lee. Screenplay Robert Stewart, Phil Mackie, based on *Donovan's Brain* (**1943**) by Curt SIODMAK. 83 mins. B/w.

This West German/UK coproduction is the 3rd and least successful film version of Siodmak's novel: the others are *The* LADY AND THE MONSTER (1944) and DONOVAN'S BRAIN (1953). This gory remake retains the plot absurdities of the earlier versions but lacks their eerie atmosphere. [JB]

VENNING, HUGH Pseudonym of UK writer Claude van Zeller (1905-1984), whose *The End: A Projection, Not a Prophecy* (**1947**) envisages, in AD2050, a DYSTOPIAN (though scientifically advanced) England surrounded by a worse world under the dominion of 666, who rules the Greater Roman Empire and is defeated at the last moment (HV was Roman Catholic) by the hosts of the Lord. [JC]

VENTURE SCIENCE FICTION US DIGEST-size magazine. 16 issues, published by Fantasy House (a subsidiary of Mercury Publications) Jan 1957-Mar 1958 and by Mercury Press May 1958-Aug 1970, as a companion to *The* MAGAZINE OF FANTASY AND SCIENCE FICTION. 10 bimonthly issues Jan 1957-July 1958 ed Robert P. MILLS; the title was revived a decade later for 6 quarterly issues May 1969-Aug 1970; ed Edward FERMAN. After the 1st series finished, the contents-page masthead in *FSF* was altered to read "including *Venture Science Fiction*". *VSF* put a higher priority on action-adventure sf than did its companion. In its second incarnation it featured a cut novel in every issue. Notable stories include C.M. KORNBLUTH's "Two Dooms" (July 1958), James TIPTREE Jr's "The Snows are Melted, the Snows are Gone" (Nov 1969) and Edward WELLEN's short novel *Hijack* (May 1970; **1971**).

The UK edn was a monthly digest magazine published by the Atlas Publishing and Distribution Co., Sep 1963-Dec 1965 (28 issues). It reprinted most of its material from the 1st series of the US magazine, but also used stories from *FSF*, some from the 1950s, and some which had appeared after *FSF*'s UK edn had folded in June 1965. [BS/PN]

VENUS Because Earth's inner neighbour presented a bright and featureless face to early astronomers, it became something of a mystery planet. 19th-century astronomers and early-20th-century sf writers generally imagined that, as the featureless face was a permanent cloud layer, the surface beneath must be warm and wet; the Venus of the imagination became a planet of vast oceans (perhaps with no land at all) or sweltering jungles. In the 1960s, however, probes revealed that Venus has no liquid water at its surface, and that its clouds – mostly composed of carbon dioxide – create a greenhouse effect in the lower atmosphere which generates temperatures of several hundred degrees Celsius.

Early planetary tours to take in Venus – including Athanasius KIRCHER's *Itinerarium Exstaticum* (**1656**), Emanuel SWEDENBORG's *The Earths in our Solar System* (**1758**) and George GRIFFITH's *A Honeymoon in Space* (**1901**) – were influenced by the planet's longtime association with the goddess of love: its inhabitants were frequently characterized as gentle and ethereal, after the fashion of Bernard le Bovyer de FONTENELLE's *Entretiens sur la pluralité des mondes habités* (**1686**; trans J. Glanvill as *A Plurality of Worlds* 1929). The first novel concerned specifically with Venus was Achille Eyraud's *Voyage à Venus* ["Voyage to Venus"] (**1865**). A winged Venusian arrived on Earth in W. LACHSZYRMA's *A Voice from Another World* (**1874**), and was later the protagonist of an interplanetary tour in the form of a series of 9 "Letters from the Planets" (1887-93). A detailed description of a Venusian civilization is featured in *History of a Race of Immortals Without a God* (**1891** as by Antares Skorpios; vt *The Immortals' Great Quest* as by James W. BARLOW). Early SCIENTIFIC ROMANCES set on Venus include Gustavus W. POPE's *Romances of the Planets, No. 2: Journey to Venus* (**1895**) and John MUNRO's *A Trip to Venus* (**1897**). Fred T. JANE's early SATIRE on the interplanetary romance was *To Venus in Five Seconds* (**1897**), and Venus was also the world visited by Garrett P. SERVISS's *A Columbus of Space* (**1911**). A brief vision is featured in "Venus" (1909) by Maurice Baring (1874-1946). Edgar Rice BURROUGHS's chief imitator, Otis Adelbert KLINE, set his principal series of exotic romances on Venus – a trilogy comprising *The Planet of Peril* (**1929**), *The Prince of Peril* (**1930**) and *The Port of Peril* (1932; **1949**). Burroughs's own Venusian series, begun with *Pirates of Venus* (**1934**), is weak self-pastiche. Other PULP-MAGAZINE romances set on Venus include Homer Eon FLINT's "The Queen of Life" (1919; in *The Lord of Death and the Queen of Life*, coll **1966**) and Ralph Milne FARLEY's series begun with *The Radio Man* (1924; **1948**; vt *An Earthman on Venus*). The early sf pulps made abundant use of Venusian scenarios. Notable examples include John W. CAMPBELL's "Solarite" (1930), Clark Ashton SMITH's "The Immeasurable Horror" (1931) and John WYNDHAM's story of COLONIZATION,

"The Venus Adventure" (1932 as by John Beynon Harris). Stanton A. COBLENTZ used Venus as the setting for his satire *The Blue Barbarians* (1931; **1958**) and for the more sober *The Planet of Youth* (1932; **1952**). Some of Stanley G. WEINBAUM's best stories of LIFE ON OTHER WORLDS are set on Venus, including "The Lotus Eaters"(1935) and "Parasite Planet" (1935). Clifford D. SIMAK used Venusian milieux imaginatively in "Hunger Death" (1938) and "Tools" (1942), as did Lester DEL REY in "The Luck of Ignatz" (1939) and Robert A. HEINLEIN in "Logic of Empire" (1941).

The image of Venus as an oceanic world was extensively developed in the 1940s, most memorably by C.S. LEWIS in *Perelandra* (**1943**; vt *Voyage to Venus*), in which ISLANDS of floating vegetation serve as a new Garden of Eden for a replay of the myth of ADAM AND EVE. The most enduring pulp image of the same species was that provided by Lawrence O'Donnell (Henry KUTTNER and C.L. MOORE) in "Clash by Night" (1943) and its sequel *Fury* (1947; **1950**). Here mankind lives in the submarine "keeps" of Venus after Earth has died, and is faced with the terrible task of colonizing the inordinately hostile land-surface; a more recent sequel to "Clash by Night", incorporating the earlier story, is *The Jungle* (**1991**) by David A. DRAKE. The notion that Venus might be an appropriate home for mankind after Earth becomes uninhabitable had earlier been advanced in J.B.S. HALDANE's visionary essay "The Last Judgment" (1927), and was taken up from there by Olaf STAPLEDON in *Last and First Men* (**1930**), where humanity spends an ecstatic period of its future history as a winged creature on the Venusian floating islands. Other stories deploying the watery image include Isaac ASIMOV's *Lucky Starr and the Oceans of Venus* (**1954** as by Paul French; vt *The Oceans of Venus*) and Poul ANDERSON's "Sister Planet" (1959). The alternative image of Venus the jungle planet, perpetually beset by fierce wet weather, is featured in Ray BRADBURY's "Death-by-Rain" (1950; vt "The Long Rain").

Although MARS was much more popular as a setting for exotic romances, Venus had the advantage of being rather more versatile: the clouds of Venus could hide exotic wonders. For this reason, some of the gaudiest romances of GENRE SF are set on Venus: C.L. Moore's "Black Thirst" (1934), Leigh BRACKETT's and Ray Bradbury's "Lorelei of the Red Mist" (1946), Brackett's "The Moon that Vanished" (1948) and "The Enchantress of Venus" (1949; vt "City of the Lost Ones") and Keith Bennett's "The Rocketeers Have Shaggy Ears" (1950). The other side of the coin was that there never grew up a consistent "Venusian mythology" comparable in power to the MYTHOLOGY of Mars.

As with Mars, during the 1950s there was a change in the main concern of stories about Venus, so that it was more often seen as a tough challenge to would-be colonists. In *The Space Merchants* (**1953**) by Frederik POHL and C.M. KORNBLUTH it is the "Gravy Planet" which has to be "sold" to the public by high-pressure advertising; Pohl continued the story in *The Merchants' War* (**1984**), having earlier presented a somewhat different image in "The Merchants of Venus" (1971). Other stories of colonization from the 1950s are Heinlein's *Between Planets* (**1951**), Chad OLIVER's "Field Expedient" (1955) and a trilogy by Rolf Garner (Bryan BERRY): *Resurgent Dust* (**1953**), *The Immortals* (**1953**) and *The Indestructible* (**1954**). Philip LATHAM's *Five Against Venus* (**1952**) is a Venusian ROBINSONADE.

Since the discovery of the true nature of the Venusian surface the interest of sf writers in the planet has waned considerably. The new Venus shows its intimidating face in Larry NIVEN's "Becalmed in Hell" (1965), contrasting poignantly with Roger ZELAZNY's florid farewell to the world of the great ocean, "The Doors of His Face, the Lamps of His Mouth" (1965) and with Thomas M. DISCH's brief jeremiad "Come to Venus Melancholy" (1965). The idea that Venus might be terraformed (◊ TERRA-FORMING) has, however, renewed interest in the notion of colonization, and such a project is celebrated on an appropriately massive scale in a series of novels by Pamela SARGENT begun with *Venus of Dreams* (**1986**) and continued in *Venus of Shadows* (**1988**).

2 theme anthologies are *The Hidden Planet* (anth **1959**) ed Donald A. WOLLHEIM and *Farewell, Fantastic Venus!* (anth **1968**; cut vt *All About Venus*) ed Brian W. ALDISS and Harry HARRISON. [BS]

See also: UNDER THE SEA.

VERCORS Pseudonym used by French artist, illustrator and writer Jean Bruller (1902-1991) for all his publications from 1942 on, including his first novel, *Le silence de la mer* (**1942**; trans Cyril Connolly as *Put Out the Light* **1944** UK); to publish this he founded the French Resistance press Les Éditions de Minuit. After WWII he wrote several moral fables in a manner influenced by Albert Camus (1913-1960). *Les Animaux dénaturés* (**1952**; trans Rita Barisse as *You Shall Know Them* **1953** US; vt *Borderline* **1954** UK; vt *The Murder of the Missing Link* **1958** US) deals with the discovery of a new species of ape-man (◊ APES AND CAVEMEN) and the deliberate murder of an infant by its human father to provide a test case in which he hopes to establish the rapidly uplifted species' claim to human status; he wins, and is acquitted of murder as the act preceded the declaration of humanity. *Colères* (**1956**; trans Rita Barisse as *The Insurgents* **1957**) deals with the search for IMMORTALITY by a man who attains it at great personal cost. *Sylva* (**1961**; trans Rita Barisse **1962** US) is an inversion of David GARNETT's *Lady into Fox* (**1922**): here a vixen is changed into a woman by an English bachelor but eventually reverts. V's postwar allegorical fictions, though thought-generating and occasionally moving, never challenged the fame of his first novel, which is somewhat unfairly the only one for which he is remembered outside France. As Bruller he illustrated, among others, *Patapoufs et Filifers*

(**1930**) by André MAUROIS. [JC]

See also: SUSPENDED ANIMATION.

VERDE, CAMPO ◊ Irving A. GREENFIELD.

VERN, DAVID ◊ David V. REED; Don WILCOX.

VERNE, JULES (GABRIEL) (1828-1905) French playwright and novelist, generally thought of as one of the 2 founding fathers of sf – the other being H.G. WELLS – though neither claimed this status for himself or for the other, and nor did either of them claim to be originating a new genre. As sf scholarship began to emphasize only in recent decades, both Wells and JV wrote consciously within traditions of popular literature that already had large though diffuse reading publics; both were adept at picking up hints from inferior or earlier writers and turning out definitive versions of sf themes later to become central to the field as it took on shape with the 20th century, and both excelled in the imaginative density and (in Wells's case, certainly) the shapeliness of their tales. Like Robert A. HEINLEIN for a later generation, they brought the instruments of sf into the home world.

In some other ways as well, the linking of the two writers as founding fathers is deceptive. JV was a pragmatic, middle-class entrepreneur of letters, and at least during the first part of his career wholeheartedly espoused the clear-eyed optimism about progress and European Man's central role in the world typical of high 19th-century culture. Born almost 40 years later, and to lower-middle-class parents, Wells in his early work exuded and helped to define the doom-laden *fin-de-siècle* atmosphere of the old century's hectic, premonitory climax. It should be noted, however, that JV was by no means insensible to moods of change, and that the novels of his last decade were much darker in texture and more pessimistic in implication than the novels for which he is best remembered today, all of which were written by 1880.

JV was born and raised in the port of Nantes, and it is probably no coincidence that the sea appears in a large number of his best and most romantic novels. His father was a successful lawyer and assumed that JV would eventually take over his practice, but from an early age the child rebelled against this form of worldly success (though, true to his time, his rebelliousness did not express itself in disdain for the things of the world). His first declaration of independence was an attempt to switch places with a ship's cabin-boy; he was extricated only after the vessel had actually left harbour. By young adulthood, however, JV's romantic flamboyance took a more productive course. He went to Paris on an allowance and, under the influence of such writers as Victor Hugo (1802-1885) and Alexandre Dumas fils (1824-1895), wrote a good deal of drama (about 20 plays remain unpublished), romantic verse and libretti, several of which were produced, as well as engaging in mild, unsuccessful flirtations. (JV was never at ease with women, and his works are notably free of realistic portrayals of them; his Catholicism, which did not sit well with the Bohemian lifestyle he tried to imitate, may have contributed to this.) He soon discovered the works of Edgar Allan POE, somewhat misreading his solitary melancholy as a kind of romantic adventurousness, and under this influence published his first tale of sf interest, "Un voyage en ballon" ["A Voyage in a Balloon"] (1851) – which was eventually republished in *Une fantaisie du Docteur Ox* (coll **1872**; part trans George H. Towle as *Doctor Ox and Other Stories* **1874** US; different trans anon as *Dr Ox's Experiment, and Other Stories* **1874** UK) as "Une Drame dans les airs" ["A Drama in the Air"] and then in book form under this latter title (**1874**). Also in *Dr Ox's Experiment* was the more interesting early story "Maître Zacharius" ["Master Zacharius"] (1854), an allegory about time, a clockmaker and the Devil. Both stories demonstrate from how early a date JV developed his characteristic technique of inserting quasi-scientific explanations into a simply told adventure imbued with the romance of geography. This story-telling method proved from the first to be a singularly appropriate tool, legitimizing the love of adventure (or more specifically of travel, in this first age of the tourist) by infusing it with the sense that scientific progress (and hence national virtue) was being encouraged along with the thrill of voyaging.

But, despite these early hints of the course he was to follow, JV felt himself only marginally successful as a writer and *bon vivant*, and with his father's help he soon turned to stockbroking, an occupation he maintained until 1862, when his singularly important association with Jules Hetzel (1814-1886), a successful publisher and writer for children, began. JV had come to him with a narrative about travelling in BALLOONS (it was apparently couched in semi-documentary form); when Hetzel suggested that he properly novelize his story, JV did so eagerly and swiftly, and the renovated tale, published as *Cinq semaines en ballon* (**1863**; trans "William Lackland" as *Five Weeks in a Balloon, or Journeys and Discoveries in Africa, by Three Englishmen* **1869** US), began the long series of **Voyages extraordinaires** ["Extraordinary Journeys"] which the firm of Hetzel published under that rubric from then until the end of JV's career. In this first tale, which was still comparatively primitive, 3 colleagues decide to try to cross Africa in a balloon, have numerous adventures as they go, and learn a great deal about Africa. But *Five Weeks in a Balloon* lacks the hectic, romantic intensity of JV's best work, those stories whose displacement from normal realities allowed him to transcend the element of illustrated travelogue which occasionally domesticated – in a negative sense – his fiction.

His next novel, *Voyage au centre de la terre* (**1863**; exp 1867; trans anon as *Journey to the Centre of the Earth* **1872** UK), was the first to convey the Vernean thrill – a congenial admixture of 19th-century moral clarity, the safety of numbers (multiple protagonists were usual), and a sense of coming very close to but never toppling over the edge of the known; in this novel 3 protagonists take part variously in an expedition into the core of a dormant volcano which leads them eventually into the dark hollow heart of the Earth itself. JV's highly visible wonderment at the world's marvels in tales of this sort goes far to explain the success he was beginning to achieve by this time; the Vernean thrill was conveyed with a childlike exuberance and clarity that give traditional PROTO-SCIENCE-FICTION devices, like the HOLLOW EARTH of this tale, an intensely memorable shape; and his tripartite division of protagonists (one a SCIENTIST, one an intensely active, athletic type, the third a more or less ordinary man representative of the reader's point of view) sorted out didactic duties and narrative pleasures remarkably well.

In the meantime, Hetzel was planning a children's magazine and JV seemed an ideal collaborator. There has been some misunderstanding about the contracts under which JV supplied material for *Le Magasin d'Éducation et de Récréation*, which Hetzel founded in 1864, and to which JV began contributing with *Les adventures du Capitaine Hatteras* (in 2 vols as *Les anglais au pôle nord* [**1864**; trans anon as *The English at the North Pole* **1874** UK] and *Le désert de glace* [**1866**; trans anon as *The Desert of Ice* **1874** US; vt *The Field of Ice* **1875** UK]). He was required by Hetzel to provide a certain number of vols a year – initially 3, eventually 2 – but a single volume did not necessarily make a novel, some taking 2 or even 3 to run their course. JV's production, therefore, while large, was not phenomenal; he tended to publish about 1 novel a year, writing 64 in all, many of them not sf.

JV's techniques for merging wonderment and didacticism became more refined with the books – his most famous – of the next decade. These include: *De la terre à la lune* (**1865**; trans J.K. Hoyte as *From the Earth to the Moon, Passage Direct in 97 Hours and 20 Minutes* **1869** US) and its sequel, *Autour de la lune* (**1870**; both trans Lewis Mercier and Eleanor King as *From the Earth to the Moon Direct in 97 hours 20 minutes, and a Trip Around It* **1873** UK; new trans Jacqueline and Robert Baldick **1970** UK); *Les enfants du Capitaine Grant* (**1867-8**; trans anon as *In Search of the Castaways* **1873** US); *Vingt mille lieues sous les mers* (**1870**; trans Lewis Mercier as *Twenty Thousand Leagues under the Seas* **1872** UK; vt *Twenty Thousand Leagues under the Sea* **1873** US; new trans Emanuel J. Mickel as *The Complete Twenty Thousand Leagues Under the Sea* **1991** US), with its sequel, *L'île mystérieuse* (**1874-5**; trans W.H.G. Kingston as *The Mysterious Island* **1875** UK); and, perhaps best known of all, *Le tour du monde en quatre-vingt jours* (**1873**; trans Geo. M. Towle as *Around the World in Eighty Days* **1874** US). These were the books of JV's prime, written with what one might call jubilant flow, but as a whole they were execrably translated, cut, bowdlerized and travestied. The reputation he long had in English-speaking countries for narrative clumsiness and ignorance of scientific matters was fundamentally due to his innumerate and illiterate translators who – along with the publishers who commissioned their work – remained impenetrably of the conviction that he was a writer of overblown juveniles and that it was thus necessary to trim him down, to eliminate any inappropriately adult complexities, and to pare the confusing scientific material to an absolute minimum. There are some newer translations, though even recent versions of these books are not untroubled by cuts and incoherence.

A dominant and abiding note in the novels of JV's prime is a powerful sense of the ultimate rightness of the course of the 19th century, a note only strengthened by their author's fundamentally conservative, pragmatic imagination, for he almost never trespassed into futurity and never actually carried his protagonists off the edge of the known. His tales are geographies, not extrapolations. *From the Earth to the Moon* may seem an exception, with its huge cannon in Florida blasting passengers into space, but (questions of acceleration aside) the science of the story was firmly conceived, and the Moon, once safely circumnavigated, was left to its own resources. *Twenty Thousand Leagues Under the Sea* (the vt is now universal) may likewise seem to stand somewhat outside the normal canon, though it is perhaps JV's most deeply felt novel; carefully and slowly composed, it introduces Captain Nemo and his elaborate submarine, the *Nautilus*, in a tale whose easy, exaggerated sombreness agreeably conflates the domesticated Byronism of the time and expressive marvels of science. Nemo (it turns out in the sequel) is an Indian prince whom British injustice has turned misanthropic, hence his life under the seas in his submarine, amply and comfortingly furnished in Second Empire plushness. But throughout both volumes Nemo's exploits hover just at the edge of the technologically possible; his prophetic gloominess is encased within a narrative frame which clearly represents his mood as aberration and his science as attainable. *Around the World in Eighty Days* is not sf at all (*The Other Log of Phileas Fogg* [1973] Philip José FARMER's sequel, rectifies this mundanity), for JV conceived his protagonist's journey around the world entirely in terms of travel arrangements then existing, basing Fogg's trip on a real journey by the US entrepreneur, traveller and eccentric George Francis Train (1829-1904).

From the 1870s on, JV's work tended to repeat itself in gradually darkening hues, though he never lost the sense of the fundamental *usableness* of science and technology, a sense vital to much 20th-century sf, where – as with JV – usableness tends to serve as its own justification. It is notable, for instance, that JV's several ROBINSONADES – which include *The Mysterious Island, L'école des Robinsons* (1882; trans W.J. Gordon as *Godfrey Morgan: A Californian Mystery* 1883 UK; vt *Robinson's School* 1883 US) and the late, nostalgic *Deux ans de vacances, ou un pensionnat de Robinsons* (1888; trans anon as *Adrift in the Pacific* 1889 UK) – all exploit

the romantic implications of being cast alone or with a few companions into the bosom of a bounteous Nature; JV's robinsonades are carefully socialized, and their small groups of protagonists always make do very well together. Even so, JV's later work was increasingly painted from a grimmer palette. *Robur le conquérant* (1886; trans anon as *The Clipper of the Clouds* 1887 UK; vt *Robur the Conqueror* 1887 US) and its sequel, *Maître du monde* (1904; trans anon as *Master of the World* 1914 UK), together demonstrate the process. In the earlier book the steely, megalomaniacal Robur, inventor of an impressive flying machine, though rendered less favourably than earlier romantic misanthropes like Nemo, is still allowed by JV to represent the march of scientific progress as he forces the world to listen to him; but in the second book, JV's last work of any significance, Robur has become a dangerous madman, blasphemous and uncontrollable, and his excesses – like those of Wells's Dr Moreau – seem to represent the excesses of an unfettered development of science. Science and a subservient, bounteous Nature are no longer seen – in late JV or early Wells – as benevolently united under Man's imperious control.

JV's life was externally uneventful from the 1860s on. He married, prospered mightily, lived in a large provincial house, yachted occasionally, unflaggingly produced his novels for the firm of Hetzel and became an exemplary 19th-century French middle-class dignitary. While his works inescapably reveal the boyish, escapist dream-life of that class, they can also be read as an ultimate requiem for the dream of his astonishing and transformative century, that waking dream of the daylight decades so effectively fleshed in his early work; but in 1900 that vision – that dream that the world was illimitable and obedient, and that Man could only improve upon creation – seemed to have begun to fade, as demonstrated perhaps most clearly in a remarkable post-HOLOCAUST tale, "The Eternal Adam" from *Hier et demain* (coll 1910; trans I.O. EVANS as *Yesterday and Tomorrow* 1965 UK), in which a far-future historian discovers to his dismay that 20th-century civilization was overthrown by geological cataclysms, and that the legend of ADAM AND EVE was both true and cyclical. (No manuscript in JV's hand exists of this story, which may have been written by his son, Michel Verne [1861-1925]; but it clearly reflects JV's late state of mind, and has more than once been treated as a thematic summation of his career.)

JV's work has always been attractive to filmmakers, and as early as 1902 Georges MÉLIÈS loosely adapted *From the Earth to the Moon* to make LE VOYAGE DANS LA LUNE. It was not until JV's work came out of copyright in the 1950s, however, that the real rush started, beginning with Walt Disney's 20,000 LEAGUES UNDER THE SEA in 1954. Other JV adaptations were *Around the World in 80 Days* (1956), FROM THE EARTH TO THE MOON (1958), JOURNEY TO THE CENTER OF THE EARTH (1959), MYSTERIOUS ISLAND (1961), MASTER OF THE WORLD

(1961) and *Five Weeks in a Balloon* (1962). The Czech film VÝNALEZ ZKAZY (1958), released in the USA as *The Fabulous World of Jules Verne*, was a blend of live action and animation. JV's characters have been revived in various, sometimes embarrassing guises, as in CAPTAIN NEMO AND THE UNDERWATER CITY (1969). [JC]

Other works: Here we list those **Voyages extraordinaires** not discussed above; many are not sf. Most of the better-known titles present a bibliographical nightmare, and unauthorized editions proliferate; we have normally attempted to list first translations only, and have not traced paths through the jungle of (usually pirated) vts.

Une ville flottante suivi Les Forceurs de blocus (coll **1871**; trans anon as *A Floating City, and the Blockade Runners* **1874** UK);

Aventures de trois russes et de trois anglais dans L'Afrique australe (**1872**; trans Henry Frith as *Meridiana: The Adventures of Three Englishmen and Three Russians in South Africa* **1873** US);

Le pays des fourrures (**1873**; trans N. D'Anvers as *The Fur Country* **1873** UK);

Le "Chancellor" (**1875**; trans Ellen E. Frewer as *Survivors of the Chancellor* **1875** UK);

Michel Strogoff, Moscou-Irkoutsk (**1876**; trans W.H.G. Kingston as *Michael Strogoff, the Courier of the Czar* **1877** UK);

Hector Servadac (**1877**; trans anon as *Hector Servadac: Travels and Adventures through the Solar System* **1877** US);

Les indes-noires (**1877**; trans W.H.G. Kingston as *The Child of the Cavern, or Strange Doings Underground* **1877** UK);

Un capitaine de quinze ans (**1878**; trans anon as *Dick Sand, or A Captain at Fifteen* **1878** US);

Les cinq cents millions de la bégum (**1879**; trans W.H.G. Kingston as *The 500 Millions of the Begum* **1879** US; vt *The Begum's Fortune* 1880 UK) (based on a manuscript by André LAURIE);

Les tribulations d'un chinois en Chine (**1879**; trans anon as *The Tribulations of a Chinaman in China* **1879** US);

La maison à vapeur (**1879-80**; trans Agnes D. Kingston as *The Steam House* **1881** UK);

La Jangada (**1881**; trans W.J. Gordon as *The Giant Raft* **1881** US);

Le rayon vert (**1882**; trans J. Cotterell as *The Green Ray* **1883** UK);

Kéraban-le-têtu (**1883**; trans J. Cotterell as *The Headstrong Turk* **1883-4** US);

L'étoile du Sud (**1884**; trans anon as *The Vanished Diamond: A Tale of South Africa* **1885** UK; vt *The Southern Star* 1885 US) (based on a manuscript by Laurie);

L'Archipel en feu (**1884**; trans anon as *The Archipelago on Fire* **1885** US);

Mathias Sandorf (**1885**; trans anon **1885** US);

Un billet de loterie: Le Numéro 9672 (**1886**; trans Laura E. Kendall as *Ticket No. "9672"* **1886** US);

Nord contre sud (**1887**; trans Laura E. Kendall as *Texar's Vengeance, or North Versus South* **1887** US);

Le chemin de France (**1887**; trans anon as *The Flight to France* **1888** UK);

Famille-sans-nom (**1889**; trans anon as *A Family without a Name* **1889** US);

Sans dessus dessous (**1889**; trans anon as *Topsy-Turvy* **1890** US; vt *Purchase of the North Pole: A Sequel to "From the Earth to the Moon"* 1891 UK);

César Cascabel (**1890**; trans A. Estoclet **1890** US);

Mistress Branican (**1891**; trans A. Estoclet **1891** US);

Le Château des Carpathes (**1892**; trans anon as *Castle of the Carpathians* **1893** UK);

Claudius Bombarnac (**1892**; trans anon **1894** UK);

P'tit-bonhomme (**1893**; trans anon as *Foundling Mick* **1895** UK);

Les mirifiques aventures de Maître Antifer (**1894**; trans anon as *Captain Antifer* **1895** UK);

L'île à hélice (**1895**; trans William J. Gordon as *Floating Island, or The Pearl of the Pacific* **1896** UK);

Clovis Dardentor (**1896**; trans anon **1897** UK);

Face au drapeau (**1896**; trans Mrs Cashel Hoey as *For the Flag* **1897** UK; vt *Facing the Flag* 1897 US);

Le Sphinx des glaces (**1897**; trans Mrs Cashel Hoey as *An Antarctic Mystery* **1898** UK) (also published with its source [by Poe] as *The Narrative of Arthur Gordon Pym and Le Sphinx des glaces* [omni **1975** UK]);

Le superbe Orénoque ["The Superb Orinoco"] (**1898**);

Le testament d'un excentrique (**1899**; trans anon as *The Will of an Eccentric* **1900** US);

Seconde patrie (**1900**; trans Cranstoun Metcalfe in 2 vols as *Their Island Home* **1924** US and *Castaways of the Flag: The Final Adventures of the Swiss Family Robinson* **1924** US);

Les histoires de Jean-Marie Cabidoulin (**1901**; trans I.O. Evans as *The Sea Serpent: The Yarns of Jean Marie Cabidoulin* **1967** UK);

Le village aérien (**1901**; trans I.O. Evans as *The Village in the Tree Tops* **1964** UK);

Les frères Kip ["The Kip Brothers"] (**1902**);

Bourses de voyage ["Travelling Grants"] (**1904**);

Un drame en Livonie (**1904**; trans I.O. Evans as *A Drama in Livonia* **1967** UK);

L'invasion de la mer ["The Invasion of the Sea"] (**1905**);

Le phare du bout du monde (**1905**; trans anon as *The Lighthouse at the End of the World* **1923** UK);

Le volcan d'or (**1906**; trans I.O. Evans as *The Golden Volcano* **1962** UK);

L'agence Thompson and Co. (**1907**; trans I.O. Evans in 2 vols as *The Thompson Travel Agency* **1965** UK);

La Chasse au météore (**1908**; trans Frederick Lawton as *The Chase of the Golden Meteor* **1909** UK);

Le pilote du Danube (**1908**; trans I.O. Evans as *The Danube Pilot* **1967** UK);

Les naufragés du Jonathan (**1909**; trans I.O. Evans as *The Survivors of the "Jonathan"* **1962** UK) (partly by Michel Verne);

Hier et demain (coll **1910**; trans I.O. Evans as *Yesterday and Tomorrow* **1965** UK);

Le secret de Wilhelm Storitz (**1910**; trans I.O.Evans as *The Secret of Wilhelm Storitz* **1963** UK);

L'étonnante aventure de la mission Barsac (**1919**; trans

I.O. Evans as *The Barsac Mission* **1960** US) (mostly by Michel Verne).

L'épave du Cynthia (**1885**; trans anon as *The Waif of the "Cynthia"* **1886** US) (almost all by Laurie) is an interesting novel not among the **Voyages extraordinaires**. **About the author:** *Jules Verne* (**1940**) by Kenneth ALLOTT; *Jules Verne: une lecture politique* (**1971**; trans as *The Political and Social Ideas of Jules Verne* **1972** UK) by Jean Chesneaux; *Jules Verne* (**1973**; trans Roger Greaves as *Jules Verne: A Biography* **1976** UK) by Jean Jules-Verne, JV's grandson, particularly valuable for its bibliography; *Jules Verne: Inventor of Science Fiction* (**1978**) by Peter Costello; *Jules Verne: A Primary and Secondary Bibliography* (**1980**) by Edward J. Gallager, Judith Mistichelli and John A. Van Eerde; *Jules Verne's Journey to the Centre of the Self* (**1990**) by William Butcher; *The Mask of the Prophet: The Extraordinary Fictions of Jules Verne* (**1990**) by Andrew Martin.

See also: ANTHROPOLOGY; ASTRONOMY; ATLANTIS; AUSTRIA; BENELUX; BIOLOGY; BOYS' PAPERS; CHILDREN'S SF; DIME-NOVEL SF; DISCOVERY AND INVENTION; DYSTOPIAS; EVOLUTION; FANTASTIC VOYAGES; FRANCE; GOTHIC SF; HISTORY OF SF; ISLANDS; LOST WORLDS; MACHINES; MOON; MUSIC; NEAR FUTURE; OPTIMISM AND PESSIMISM; POWER SOURCES; PREDICTION; SCIENTIFIC ERRORS; SPACE FLIGHT; SPACESHIPS; TECHNOLOGY; TRANSPORTATION; UNDER THE SEA; WEAPONS.

VERNE, MICHEL [r] ◊ *The* STRAND MAGAZINE; Jules VERNE.

VERNON, ROGER LEE (1924-   ) US writer and schoolteacher whose awkwardly routine sf is contained in an assemblage of original stories, *The Space Frontiers* (coll **1955**), and the novel *Robot Hunt* (**1959**).   [JC]

VERRILL, A(LPHEUS) HYATT (1871-1954) US naturalist, explorer and writer, most of whose 100 or so books were nonfiction. He also wrote juveniles, of which the **Boy Adventurers** sequence is of some sf interest; relevant titles are *The Boy Adventurers in the Land of El Dorado* (**1923**), *The Boy Adventurers in the Land of the Monkey Men* (**1923**) and *The Boy Adventurers in the Unknown Land* (**1924**). *The Radio Detectives Under the Sea* (**1922**) is the most sf-like of his **Radio Detectives** children's sequence. His adult novels explore similar territory. *The Golden City* (**1916**) and *The Bridge of Light* (1929 *AMZ Quarterly*; **1950**) are of interest as typical LOST-WORLD stories; they are set in South America, where AHV did much of his real-life exploration (whose extent he reportedly exaggerated). 9 novels in all appeared in *AMZ* and *AMZ Quarterly* 1926-35, though only 2 have reached book form, *Bridge of Light* and *When the Moon Ran Wild* (1931 *AMZ Quarterly* as AHV; **1962** UK) as by Ray Ainsbury (it is not known why this title was thus ascribed). AHV's work shows the marks of a somewhat desultory interest in fiction, and of the PULP-MAGAZINE markets he served, but does vividly dramatize his professional concerns.   [JC]
Other works: *The Trail of the White Indians* (**1920**).
See also: ANTHROPOLOGY.

VERSINS, PIERRE The name adopted by French scholar, writer and self-styled utopian Jacques Chamson (1923-   ), a survivor of Auschwitz. He began writing sf in the 1950s and published 3 novels, *En avant, Mars* ["Forward to Mars"] (**1951**), *Les étoiles ne s'en foutent pas* ["The Stars Care"] (**1954**) and *Le professeur* ["The Professor"] (**1956**), and over 20 stories (some with his wife Martine Thomé) while editing *Ailleurs* (1957-62), a critical FANZINE of high repute. A later novel was *Les transhumains* ["The Transhumans"] (**1971**). While resident in Switzerland, where he lived for 33 years, PV also produced *Passeport pour l'inconnu* ["Passport for the Unknown"], a regular sf RADIO programme for Radio Geneva. He will be remembered more for his scholarship than for his fiction: a keen researcher and bibliographer, he is a foremost authority on early sf and donated his priceless collection of books, magazines and sf memorabilia to the town of Yverdon-les-bains, Switzerland, in 1975, acting for 5 years as the curator of the unique local sf museum thus created, *La* MAISON D'AILLEURS. PV's major achievement is undoubtedly his massive 1000pp *Encyclopédie de l'Utopie et de la sf* ["Encyclopedia of Utopia and SF"] (**1972**), which was given a Special Award at the 1973 Toronto World SF Convention. An invaluable if idiosyncratic volume, particularly useful on sf outside the USA and the UK and prior to 1900, it remains to this day one of the finest reference books on sf; it has not been translated. PV's scholarship was honoured by the SFRA with a PILGRIM AWARD in 1991.   [MJ/PN]
See also: CRITICAL AND HISTORICAL WORKS ABOUT SF; FRANCE.

VERTEX US magazine, slick BEDSHEET format Apr 1973-Apr 1975, tabloid format June 1975-Aug 1975. 16 issues, 13 bimonthly, the last 3 monthly, published by Mankind Publishing, Los Angeles; ed Donald J. PFEIL. Subtitled "The Magazine of Science Fiction", *V* was a magazine of imaginative layout and much internal illustration, the first "slick" in the sf field. The covers were often semi-abstract. Like most SF MAGAZINES since the 1970s, *V* ran many nonfiction pieces: interviews with authors and good science-fact articles. Stories were by, among others, Ed BRYANT, F.M. BUSBY, Terry CARR, George Alec EFFINGER, Joe HALDEMAN, William ROTSLER, Robert SILVERBERG and Norman SPINRAD. *V* was something of a showcase for up-and-coming US authors like Alan BRENNERT, William CARLSON, George R.R. MARTIN, Steven UTLEY and John VARLEY, and in quality was the strongest of the new 1970s sf magazines, but financial problems (at $1.50 it was unusually expensive) and a paper shortage forced a change to newspaper format on cheap paper for the last 3 issues, then closure.

[PN/FHP]

VESSER, CAROLYN (?   -   ) US writer whose first novel, *Hellwalker* (**1988**), is an sf adventure set on a distant planet.   [JC]

VETCH, THOMAS Pseudonym of the unidentified UK author of *The Amber City: Being Some Account of the*

Adventures of a Steam Crocodile in Central Africa (**1888**), a Jules-VERNE-like excursion narrated by the protagonist, Thomas Vetch, who takes his flying ship into a mild-mannered LOST WORLD where people live in houses built of amber. [JC]

V FOR VENDETTA ◊ Alan MOORE.

VIAN, BORIS (1920-1959) French writer in various genres, his collected works amounting to more than 50 vols; he was Transcendental Satrap of the Collège de 'Pataphysique, and a fine dramatist of the absurd (◊ FABULATION) who will be perhaps best remembered for his songs (◊ MUSIC) and for such plays as *Équarrissage pour tous* (**1950**; trans Simon Watson Taylor as *The Knackers' ABC* **1968** US), which savagely mocks the military mind and military punctilio, and *Les Batisseurs d'Empire ou le Schmurz* (**1959**; trans Simon Watson Taylor as *The Empire Builders* **1962** UK), a surreal excursus upon pain. One of the main personalities of the post-WWII French sf scene – though sf made up only a small part of his activities – BV translated writers like A.E. VAN VOGT, William TENN, Henry KUTTNER and Ray BRADBURY, and was himself a writer of speculative fiction years ahead of his time. His first novel, *J'irai cracher sur vos tombes* (**1946** as by Vernon Sullivan; trans BV and Milton Rosenthal as *I Spit on your Graves* **1948** as BV), pretended with some success to be a US tough-guy detective novel, and extended only peripherally into the fantastic. But the stories assembled in *Les Fourmis* (coll **1949**; trans Julia Older as *Blues for a Black Cat* **1992** US) were deeply indebted to sf and Surrealism, as were his later novels, particularly *L'Écume des jours* (**1947**; trans Stanley Chapman as *Froth on the Daydream* **1967** UK; vt *Mood Indigo* 1968 US), *L'automne à Pékin* ["Autumn in Peking"] (**1947**), a desert utopia set in an ALTERNATE WORLD, *L'herbe rouge* ["Red Grass"] (**1950**), a surreal tale which mixes TIME TRAVEL and nostalgia, and *L'Arrache-Coeur* (**1953**; trans Stanley Chapman as *Heartsnatcher* **1968** UK), a fable of metamorphosis. Throughout his career, BV used sf devices to articulate a sense of the world's violent impingement on the self, though sometimes his characters transcended their shackles; in the 1960s his work was particularly influential on writers of the UK NEW WAVE. [JC/MJ]

See also: FRANCE.

VICKERS, AL [s] ◊ Alexander POPOV.

VICTOR GOLLANCZ LIMITED ◊ GOLLANCZ.

VIDAL, GORE (1925-   ) US writer, resident for some years in Italy, best known for such satirical works outside the sf field as *Myra Breckinridge* (**1968**) and its sequel *Myron* (**1974**) and for several vols of essays, from *Rocking the Boat* (coll **1962**) to *Armageddon?* (coll **1987**), whose contents are frequently apocalyptic. *Messiah* (**1954**; rev 1965), the sf novel which closed his first, precocious phase of novel-writing, is a dark SATIRE on RELIGION in which a new MESSIAH teaches a defeatedly secular USA how to worship death. A play, *Visit to a Small Planet* (**1956**; **1960**), filmed in 1960, again satirizes contemporary Western

civilization in the story of an ALIEN child, capable of changing the past, who comes close to wrecking our corrupt society before its guardians arrive to take it back. *Kalki* (**1978**), a further satirical assault upon one of GV's most persistent *bêtes noires*, organized religion, depicts the devastating consequences of its protagonist's belief that he embodies the returned essence of the world-destroying Hindu deity Kalki – devastating because he turns out, in a sense, to be right; the assault on religion is if anything intensified in *Live From Golgotha* (**1992**), in which tv crews, taking advantage of a new technology, compete to film the crucifixion. *Duluth* (**1983**) is a FABULATION which uses any device available – including sf instruments – to sustain a deeply savage view of US life. GV has been for nearly 50 years a pessimistic, sharp-tongued, knowledgeable critic of his native land; his sf must be read as an attempt to dramatize the long jeremiad. [JC]

Other work: *A Search for the King: A Twelfth Century Legend* (**1950**).

See also: UFOS.

VIDEODROME Film (1982). Filmplan International/Guardian Trust/Canadian Film Development Corp. Written/dir David CRONENBERG, starring James Woods, Sonja Smits, Deborah Harry, Peter Dvorsky, Les Carlson. 89 mins. Colour.

Bravely placing his outrageous exploitation movie squarely in the centre of media-theorists' debates about interaction between viewer and screen, Cronenberg here produces perhaps the best (and also the oddest) of his series of sf scenarios of medicine, media, metamorphosis and religion, the emphasis here falling on the last 3. Woods plays the cable-tv-station executive in charge of sex'n'violence programming who stumbles across a private programme called *Videodrome*. This, on the surface sadistic pornography, metamorphoses him (either mentally or physically), so that a videocassette slit forms in his belly and his hand becomes (naturally) a handgun. This second part of the film, where even the tv set becomes organic and protrudes lips (the Word made Flesh), may also be read as a prolonged hallucination. It is an intricate tale, also featuring a media guru, O'Blivion – modelled apparently on Marshall McLuhan (1911-1980) – whose daughter pronounces after his apotheosis into software: "I am my Father's Screen." Too schlocky for the squeamish – especially the scene where talk-back hostess Nicki Brand (pop star Deborah Harry) burns her own breasts with a cigarette – and too intellectual for exploitation-movie fans, the film naturally flopped. But it may have been the most significant sf film of the 1980s, and is certainly – and very early on – the most CYBERPUNK. The novelization is *Videodrome* * (**1983**) by Jack Martin (Dennis Etchison [1943-   ]). [PN]

See also: CINEMA; PARANOIA; SEX.

VIERECK, GEORGE S(YLVESTER) (1884-1962) German-born US writer, well known between the Wars as an apologist for defeated Germany, as in *The*

Kaiser on Trial (**1937**), though his views on Hitler were considerably more guarded. On his refusal to register as a German lobbyist or agent in WWII he was imprisoned, gaining his release only in 1947. His first fiction of interest was *The House of the Vampire* (**1907**), a psychosexual fantasy in a late-Decadent style shared by writers like Hanns Heinz EWERS, but he is best remembered for his **Wandering Jew** trilogy, with Paul ELDRIDGE: *My First Two Thousand Years: The Autobiography of the Wandering Jew* (**1928**; cut 1956), *Salome: The Wandering Jewess* (**1930**; cut vt *Salome: My First 2000 Years of Love* 1954) and *The Invincible Adam* (**1932**). The immortal protagonists (◊ IMMORTALITY) – the 3rd being a vigorous young masculine figure, Kotikokura, who represents Natural Man – intermingle their adventures through time, and, at times egregiously, symbolize mankind's striving after reality and love. Alone, GSV wrote a kind of pendant, *Gloria* (**1952** UK; vt *The Nude in the Mirror* 1953 US), ostensibly an espionage thriller set on an ocean liner; but the female spy involved turns out to be, almost certainly, the goddess of love. Didactic and subversively erotic anecdotes about the true nature and history of humanity surface throughout all 4 books. The plot of *Prince Pax* (**1933** UK) with Eldridge conveys similarly undemocratic ironies about the species: a RURITANIAN ruler acquires a high-tech weapon and uses it to commit a surly world to an enforced peace. [JC]

See also: ADAM AND EVE; ORIGIN OF MAN.

VIGLIANTE, MARY Working name of Mary Vigliante Szydlowski (1946-　　　), who has also published sf as by Jarl Szydlow; she writes woman-centred tales whose taste for violence has struck from the first a note of ambivalence. Titles include *The Ark* (**1978**) as by Szydlow and the **Aftermath Books**, a post-HOLOCAUST sequence comprising *The Colony* (**1979**) and *The Land* (**1979**). Also as MV she has published 2 similar tales: *Source of Evil* (**1980**) and *Worship the Night* (**1982**). Unlike FEMINIST work, her novels seemed to express a sense that the oppression of women could be exhilarating. [JC]

VILLAGE OF THE DAMNED Film (1960). MGM. Dir Wolf Rilla, starring George Sanders, Barbara Shelley, Martin Stephens. Screenplay Sterling Silliphant, Rilla, George Barclay (Ronald Kinnoch, the producer), based on *The Midwich Cuckoos* (**1957**) by John WYNDHAM. 77 mins. B/w.

In this faithful but pedestrian adaptation of Wyndham's novel, everyone in a UK village mysteriously falls asleep for 24 hours. During this period all the women of childbearing age are unknowingly impregnated by ALIENS. In due course they give birth to 12 strange children who grow very rapidly and possess powers of telepathy and mind control. Some years later it is realized that the children represent an attempt by another planet to colonize Earth, and they are destroyed by the scientist (Sanders) who has been their friend – with difficulty, since the method of destruction (a bomb) has to be mentally concealed

from them. The children, with their glowing eyes, are the most successful feature of the production; their sang-froid is chilling and seems authentically alien. A virtual remake of this film, this time in an urban setting, was CHILDREN OF THE DAMNED (1963). [JB/PN]

VILLAINS The division of people into simple archetypes of good and bad, HEROES and villains, has always been stronger in popular literature than in more serious fiction; indeed, the essence of the serious novel of character has ever been to explore the shades of grey between the moral absolutes of black and white. Thus sf's villains are mainly associated with PULP-MAGAZINE sf, not just in the post-1926 specialist sf magazines but in the pulp magazines generally from the 1890s onwards. The history of villainy in popular literature of this sort is sociologically fascinating in the way that it reflects the fears and bigotries of the societies that produced it, especially insofar as commercial fiction is generally written in response to a known popular demand.

UK sf during 1890-1920 (and to some extent later) was notably xenophobic: foreigners were not to be trusted. The same was true to a lesser extent in the USA, whose East Coast cities were by now a melting-pot of different national and racial backgrounds, to the alarm of the more conservative. Antisemitic views were expressed surprisingly seldom, although the capitalist villain of George Allan ENGLAND's *The Golden Blight* (**1912**; ˋ**1916**) is a Jew, and M.P. SHIEL's stories often contain Jewish villains, although Shiel himself was ambiguous on the subject, and was sympathetic to Zionist aspirations. Better known are the Yellow-Peril books, and here Shiel figures largely, with *The Yellow Danger* (**1898**; rev 1899) and *The Dragon* (**1913**; rev vt *The Yellow Peril* 1929). Floyd GIBBONS's *The Red Napoleon* (**1929**) features a Mongol world-conqueror. The most famous Oriental villain of all was of course Sax ROHMER's Dr Fu Manchu, the slant-eyed super-machinator set on world domination.

With Fu Manchu we enter the arena of the hero-versus-villain pulp magazines of the 1930s, some, such as DR YEN SIN and *The* MYSTERIOUS WU FANG, modelled directly on Rohmer's work. By the 1930s the hero-vs-villain confrontation had developed into a simple formula, still popular long after WWII, as in Ian FLEMING's **James Bond** books. A small group of fighters for right, with the aid of highly trained reflexes and an armoury of superscientific devices, stands off a variety of almost indistinguishable mad SCIENTISTS and/or ambitious businessmen and politicians who plan to conquer all. The best-known sf archetype is DOC SAVAGE, but CAPTAIN HAZZARD, CAPTAIN ZERO, DUSTY AYRES AND HIS BATTLE BIRDS, the SPIDER and the **Avenger** were all cast in the same mould. Hero magazines were more popular than villain magazines; the latter included *Doctor Death*, *The* OCTOPUS and *The* SCORPION. Although the pulps are dead, the great success of MARVEL COMICS in the 1960s was built on the same formula, with the villains as nasty as ever – although the heroes, in this less straightforward age, were more introspective.

The Japanese attack on Pearl Harbor in Dec 1941 may have been seen by some in the USA as a retrospective justification of the Yellow Peril stories – and by cynics, conversely, as the realization of a self-fulfilling prophecy – but pulp sf of WWII and immediately afterwards tended to substitute brutal European-style fascists in place of wily Orientals. Eric Frank RUSSELL wrote many amusing stories of caricature-Teutonic aliens being thwarted in their myopic militarism by nimble-witted heroes working almost alone. Far more interesting were the villains of Cold-War sf in the 1950s, when the USA evinced extreme anxiety over the "communist menace" (many of these stories are discussed under PARA-NOIA). The day of the individual villain was in decline; he had given way to the group-villain, often symbolized, indeed, in the form of a HIVE-MIND. The fear of communism was frequently expressed as a loathing for an expansionist movement in which individuality was subjugated to the demands of the mass. Thus in Robert A. HEINLEIN's *The Puppet Masters* (**1951**) the villains are indistinguishable from one another. In this case they are aliens, and this points up a difference between sf and most other genres: although sf heroes are usually human, the villains may easily be MONSTERS, ALIENS, ROBOTS or SUPERMEN. However, a little analysis of what sort of monster or superman the villain is often shows that there is some readily identifiable human analogue, or at least human fear, involved.

The robot destroying everything in its path is usually simply our fear of TECHNOLOGY writ large. It is interesting that, after a long period of quiescence – partly as a result of Isaac ASIMOV's **Robot** series, in which robots were depicted as decent, occasionally to the point of saintliness – in the 1980s the killer-robot story (and the anti-technology Luddite story gene-rally) returned to the CINEMA, where it gained pheno-menal popularity. The cinema is the closest modern equivalent in its values and narrative structures to pulp fiction, and it feeds very much the same appetites, at least at its lower levels. It is in the cinema, in COMICS, on TELEVISION and in HEROIC FANTASY that today's hero-vs-villain stories are mostly found. The return of the anti-technology theme, exemplified by many of the films of Michael CRICHTON and John BADHAM, may represent fears related to those that have brought the rise of ecological factions to a position of importance in world politics.

In written sf, the heyday of the sf villain was over by the 1960s-70s. Villains still exist, of course, but they cannot generally be so easily categorized; very often they remain faceless: behind-the-scenes man-ipulators, politicians, militarists, ad-men, commercial interests, corporate polluters of the environment working at a distance or through bureaucracies. This reflects a growing fear in the real world that we are all filed and docketed on a COMPUTER databank

somewhere, and have no way of identifying the enemy out front. In the USA it could be called the Watergate syndrome; after Watergate the number of films about government conspiracies notably increased (◊ PARANOIA). Invisible pullers of strings need not be grey or boring villains, however, and Jack VANCE's 5 Demon Princes in his **Demon Princes** series are satisfyingly melodramatic, as are the 9 immortals who run things in Philip José FARMER's *A Feast Unknown* (**1969**), *Lord of the Trees* (**1970**) and *The Mad Goblin* (**1970**). A common variant of the unseen manipulator as villain is the AI, as in William GIBSON's **Neuromancer** trilogy, in *The Difference Engine* (**1990** UK) by Gibson with Bruce STERLING, and in Dan SIMMONS's **Hyperion** books.

The type of villains produced in GENRE SF depends to a degree on the type of sf in question. In HARD SF the villains are often those who fear progress and doggedly oppose it, while in the NEW WAVE it was more likely to be the technocrats themselves who were the villains, mindlessly calling for "growth" regardless of the sociological consequences. Indi-vidual sf writers are naturally liable to incorporate any sort of personal or political resentment or distaste into their creation of villains – Heinlein often laid the blame on flabby liberals, for example – but no useful generalization can be made about villainy at this level.

An occasional amalgam in sf is the hero-villain, an imaginative territory staked out by Alfred BESTER in the figures of Ben Reich and Gully Foyle, the protagonists of his first 2 novels; they are saturnine, vengeful, obsessive malcontents, for all the world like figures out of a 17th-century revenge drama. Villainy generated by the self but unknown to the self has of course been a theme of the HORROR IN SF subgenre since Robert Louis STEVENSON's *Strange Case of Dr Jekyll and Mr Hyde* (**1886**), if not earlier. This theme has always remained popular, as in Bester's "Fondly Fahrenheit" (**1954**) and, from the cinema, the Mon-ster from the Id in FORBIDDEN PLANET (**1956**) and the telekinetic superbeing who does not recognize his own malign powers in *The* POWER (**1967**). [PN]

VILLIERS DE L'ISLE-ADAM, (JEAN-MARIE-MATHIAS-PHILIPPE-AUGUSTE, Comte de) (1840-1889) French writer – mostly of poetry, plays and short stories – and an extremely impoverished mem-ber of the Breton aristocracy. His best-known prose work remains *Contes Cruels* (coll **1883**; trans Robert Baldick as *Cruel Tales* **1963** UK), a title which itself came to designate a category of the French *conte* or moral fable which emphasizes the punitive twists of fate, the arbitrary chill of the world. The book contains a number of bizarre fantasy stories, several of them sf, including "Celestial Publicity", in which advertising slogans are projected onto the night sky by electric light. An early translation of VDL-A's work, which also took stories from *Nouveaux Contes cruels* ["New Contes Cruels"], was *Sardonic Tales* (coll trans Hamish Miles **1927** US). Of more direct sf interest is *L'Ève future* (**1886**; trans Marilyn Gaddis Rose as *The Eve of the Future* **1981** US; new trans Robert M. Adams as *Tomorrow's Eve* **1982** US), in which a handsome young lord despairs when his fiancée turns out to be extremely crass – but a fictional character called Thomas Alva Edison comes to the rescue with an impeccable robot duplicate (◊ EDISONADE). Seen as an important contribution to the Symbolist movement, the novel is philosophical, ironic and mockingly contorted. *Claire Lenoir*, which appeared originally as part of *Tribulat Bonhomet* (coll **1887**) and was trans Arthur Symons (**1925** US), applies similar ornate twists to a horror tale involving possession and hideous paroxysms of female guilt. VDL-A remains best known for his final work, the ecstatic play and prose-poem *Axel* (**1885-6** *Jeune France*; rev **1890**; trans H.P.R. Finberg **1925** UK; new trans June Guicharnaud **1970** US), whose dramatization of the Symbolist inturning of the imagination inspired Edmund Wilson's famous *Axel's Castle: A Study in the Imaginative Literature of 1870-1930* (**1931**). The eponymous count – an unimaginably wealthy Rosicrucian savant whose supernaturally impregnable fortress can stave off the armies of the world, and who remains adamant in his refusal to taste the desolations reality imposes on dreams – is a figure who has influenced generations of writers, including almost certainly the 1980s sf and fantasy creators of Dying Earths heavily populated by aesthetic aristocrats weary unto death of vulgar sensation. Axel's near-final declaration – "Live? Our servants will do that for us" – is a brilliant epigraph to the gesture he represents.   [JC/PN]

See also: ABSURDIST SF; ADAM AND EVE; FRANCE; HISTORY OF SF; HUMOUR; SATIRE; SCIENTISTS.

VILOTT, RHONDI Working name of US writer Rhondi A. Vilott-Salsitz (?   -   ), whose work as RV, and less frequent titles as R.A.V. Salsitz, has been restricted to fantasies (see listing below), but whose work as by Charles Ingrid has been sf. Of the 3 series of Ingrid military SPACE OPERAS, the best is the 1st, the **Sand Wars** sequence: *Solarkill* (**1987**), *Lasertown Blues* (**1988**), *Celestial Hit List* (**1988**), *Alien Salute* (**1989**), *Return Fire* (**1989**) and *Challenge Met* (**1990**). The **Marked Man** sequence includes *The Marked Man* (**1989**) and *The Last Recall* (**1991**); the **Patterns of Chaos** sequence began with *Radius of Doubt* (**1991**).   [JC]
Other works as Rhondi Vilott: *Black Dragon's Curse* (**1984**); *Challenge of the Pegasus Grail* (**1984**); *The Dungeons of Dregnor* (**1984**); *Runesword!* (**1984**); *Spellhound* (**1984**); *Sword Daughter's Quest* (**1984**); *The Towers of Rexor* (**1984**); *The Unicorn Crown* (**1984**); *Aphrodite's Mirror* (**1985**); *Hall of the Gargoyle King* (**1985**); *Maiden of Greenwold* (**1985**); *Pledge of Peril* (**1985**); *Secret of the Sphinx* (**1985**); *Storm Rider* (**1985**).
As R.A.V. Salsitz: The **Dragons** sequence, comprising *Where Dragons Lie* (**1985**), *Where Dragons Rule* (**1986**) and *Night of Dragons* (**1990**); *The Unicorn Dancer* (**1986**); *Daughter of Destiny* (**1988**).

VINCENT, HARL Working name of US engineer and writer Harold Vincent Schoepflin (1893-1968) for all his fiction, beginning with "The Golden Girl of Munan" for *AMZ* in 1928; little of it has reached book form. He was a popular writer in the PULP MAGAZINES of sf's early prime, publishing frequently in *The Argosy*, *AMZ*, *ASF* and other magazines until WWII, stopping then until just before his death, when some further stories appeared, including several reprints, and a novel, *The Doomsday Planet* (**1966**), a PLANETARY ROMANCE in the traditional mode. His work was vigorous.   [JC]
See also: AIR WONDER STORIES; GREAT AND SMALL; PARANOIA; ROBOTS.

VINGE, JOAN (CAROL) D(ENNISON) (1948-   ) US writer, with a degree in anthropology from San Diego State University; she has been married twice, to sf writer Vernor VINGE 1972-9 and to sf editor Jim FRENKEL from 1980. She began publishing sf with *Tin Soldier* (in *Orbit 14* [anth **1974**] ed Damon KNIGHT; **1990** chap dos), whose theme (like much of her later work) is taken from fairy tale or MYTHOLOGY and rewritten in sf terms, the source in this case being a story by Hans Christian Andersen (1805-1875).

Andersen was also the remote source of her second, very popular novel – it won a 1981 HUGO – *The Snow Queen* (**1980**; rev **1989**). Though the title and some of the plot come from Andersen, this is an essay in ANTHROPOLOGY, much of it founded in the pseudo-scientific anthropology of Robert GRAVES in *The White Goddess* (**1947** US), which Brian M. STABLEFORD argued in a review "is rather like a chemistry graduate writing a story whose plot hinges on the phlogiston theory". The broad romantic sweep of the tale, however, carried most doubters with it. A primitive planet with a long year is supported by off-world technology (brought in by transmission via BLACK HOLE) in its long winter, at the end of which the Winter Queen will be supplanted by the Summer Queen, and the offworlders will leave. The Winter Queen plots to renew her reign (via cloning) in summer. The fact that this novel's power rested more in generic dexterity (much of it taken from HEROIC FANTASY) than in conceptual strength may help explain why, after such a strong beginning, JV has not, despite expectations to the contrary, been reckoned one of the major sf writers of the 1980s. The other books in the **Snow Queen** series are *World's End* (**1984**) and *The Summer Queen* (**1991**), the latter being very long indeed.

Before *The Snow Queen* was published JV had already had much success with her short fiction, some of which deals with COMMUNICATION between humans and ALIENS, including the title story of *The Crystal Ship: Three Original Novellas of Science Fiction* (anth **1976**) ed Robert SILVERBERG. JV's early short fiction was collected in *Fireship* (coll **1978**; vt *Fireship; and Mother and Child* UK) and *Eyes of Amber and Other Stories* (coll **1979**). The 1977 title story of the latter is another good communications story; it won a Hugo for Best Novelette. A further collection of 6 stories was *Phoenix in the Ashes* (coll **1985**).

JV's first novel, *The Outcasts of Heaven Belt* (**1978**), pits an egalitarian society with strong women against male-dominated, collapsing societies in an ASTEROID belt. The novel belongs to the **Heaven Belt** series of stories; it was assembled with a novella from the series, *Legacy* (**1980** dos), as *Heaven Chronicles* (omni **1991**). More impetuous is the **Cat** series, begun with *Psion* (**1982**) and continued with *Catspaw* (**1988**; vt *Cats Paw* 1989 UK), the 2 collected as *Alien Blood* (omni **1988**). *Psion*, which unlike its successor was published as a juvenile, is actually a development, years later, of the first long fiction JV wrote as a teenager. Cat, an orphan (half human, half Hydran, a race despised by humans) with catlike eyes and PSI POWERS, has full-blooded, melodramatic, SPACE-OPERA adventures. None of these books approach *The Snow Queen* in scope, and indeed – in what seemed a distinct lowering of her sights – JV spent much of the mid-1980s writing film ties, starting with the juvenile *Star Wars: Return of the Jedi: The Storybook* * (**1983** chap) and including: *Tarzan, King of the Apes* * (**1983**); *The Dune Storybook* * (**1984** chap), juvenile; *Return to Oz: A Novel* * (**1985**); *Mad Max III: Beyond Thunderdome* * (**1985**); *Ladyhawke* * (**1985**); *Santa Claus, the Movie: A Novel* * (**1985**); *Santa Claus, the Movie Storybook* * (**1985** chap), juvenile; and *Willow* * (**1988**).

In an interview JV has said that the first sf she grew to love was by Andre NORTON; it may be as a colourful exponent of the tradition to which Norton belongs (and which Norton did much to establish) – in which mythic themes are patterned into a world that is only superficially sciencefictional – that JV will be best remembered. [PN]

Other works: *Joan D. Vinge Omnibus* (omni **1983** UK), containing *Fireship* and *The Outcasts of Heavens Belt*.

See also: ASTOUNDING SCIENCE-FICTION.

VINGE, VERNOR (STEFFEN) (1944-   ) US writer and professor of mathematics at San Diego University; married to Joan D. VINGE 1972-9. He began publishing sf with "Apartness" for *NW* in 1965, and published fairly regularly in *ASF*, his best work appearing in *True Names and Other Dangers* (coll **1987**), which contains HARD SF responsive to the thrust of technological progress (the title novella had earlier appeared as *True Names* [1981 dos]), and *Threats . . . and Other Promises* (coll **1988**), which includes more diverse material. His first novel, *Grimm's World* (in *Orbit 4* [anth **1966**] ed Damon KNIGHT as "Grimm's Story"; fixup **1969**; exp vt *Tatja Grimm's World* 1987), is a colourfully told adventure set on a primitive human planet exploited by interstellar slavers, with intriguingly elaborated detail. It is significantly less anodyne (or RURITANIAN) than its description implies, and the punning title of the book turns out to be not inappropriate. From the first VV combined a feeling for the movement and thrill of humanity's high-tech progress through the Universe, with a sense that individual lives were bleak and often brutish. His second novel, *The Witling* (**1976**), repeats a situation

basic to the first – intruding humans on a colony planet are confronted by a woman with heightened PSI POWERS – and confirmed the essential chill of his vision.

True Names (**1981** dos) was the first of his tales to establish his reputation firmly as one of the more interesting writers of the period. It depicts a kind of CYBERSPACE inhabited by hackers intent on creating a VIRTUAL-REALITY environment, but threatened by the incursion of a possibly paranormal (or demented) colleague seeking absolute power over the world. The story is intermittently tangled, but the cyberspace vision was prescient. The **Realtime** sequence – *The Peace War* (**1984**) and *Marooned in Realtime* (**1986**), assembled as *Across Realtime* (omni **1986**; with "The Ungoverned" added, exp 1991) – is similarly acute in its presentation of technologies not yet competently handled by sf, from COMPUTERS to GENETIC ENGINEERING, though its use once again of protagonists with seemingly paranormal powers tends to reduce any sense of novelty. The intricately plotted progress of various characters from near to far future, via an inventively deployed stasis-field technology, is narratively arousing, as is the murder mystery they find on an Earth which, like an abandoned playground, has long ago been left behind by an evolving humanity. However, the background to these exhilarated tales is depicted with VV's usual coldness. He is a writer who, while risking the worst of genre sillinesses, remains dangerously acute, as his most recent and longest novel, *A Fire upon the Deep* (**1992**), demonstrates. The tale – which involves converging interstellar quests for a MCGUFFIN "Countermeasure" capable of destroying a dread Power that has been reawakened from 5 billion years' sleep and is destroying millions of civilizations – is set in a complexly visualized Galaxy-wide SPACE-OPERA setting, skilfully designed to give room for human-scale action within a vast canvas, though in fact *Homo sapiens* is a very minor player in this arena; the information webs which convey near-infinities of information among the myriad worlds of the venue amusingly reflect the telephone-linked computer nets of the 1990s. The tale as a whole is cunningly crafted, deftly told, and bracingly chill in its ultimate implications. [JC]

See also: GAMES AND SPORTS; LIBERTARIAN SF; TIME TRAVEL; VIRTUAL REALITY; WEAPONS.

VINICOFF, ERIC (?   -   ) US writer whose first novel – after the publication of a short tale, *Spacing Dutchman* (**1978** chap) with Marcia Martin – was *Maiden Flight* (**1988**), a post-HOLOCAUST story which, like many from the last decades of the 20th century, sees the destruction of the current world civilization essentially in terms of the opportunities it presents for making a better future. EV's USA, like a great adventure playground, rewards the high-tech citizens of the new order who occupy it, *en passant* fighting off a local menace before settling into productive relationships. [JC]

VINTER, MICHAEL [r] ◊ ROBERT HALE LIMITED.

VIRTUAL REALITY Since the mid-1980s, a popular item of sf TERMINOLOGY, and for a century or so – in a rather more extended sense – a popular sf theme. In ordinary usage a virtual reality is a computer-generated scenario which seems real (or at least all-encompassing) to the person who "enters" it; one essential quality of virtual reality is that the person who enters it should be able to interact with it. To a degree all computer GAMES, as habitual players well know, already offer a primitive form of virtual reality. In other words, the ever-changing picture on the screen, plus the touch of the fingers on the keyboard, is enough to give the illusion of being "in" the game. But the term is usually reserved for those COMPUTER simulations and games currently being developed in which the "player" wears a helmet and gloves whose sensors are electronically connected to the machine "intelligence", so that a turn of the head or a raise of the hand alters the field of vision or the posture of the player's alter ego within the simulation. A further step, not yet available in the real world but a commonplace in sf, is the use of a direct electronic interface between the human brain and the AI which gives the plugged-in person the illusion of occupying and interacting with a reality whose apparent locations may extend beyond the AI to those of the data-networks of which it is a part. Such – it is the most famous recent example – is the CYBERSPACE envisaged by William GIBSON's **Neuromancer** trilogy (1984-8), in which hackers can jack into a "cyberspace deck" and project a "disembodied consciousness into the consensual hallucination that was the matrix".

A good popular guide to the meaning of the term in its more limited, scientific application is *Virtual Reality* (1991) by Howard Rheingold. The term may have grown from the term "virtuality", used by Theodor Nelson in "Interactive Systems and the Design of Virtuality" (Nov/Dec 1980 *Creative Computing*). The coining of "virtual reality", probably around 1981, is usually attributed to computer guru Jaron Lanier, founder of VPL Research Inc., the company that markets DataGloves. The first sf usage we can trace is in *The Judas Mandala* (1982 US; rev 1990) by Damien BRODERICK, a book with many and confusing virtual realities.

This comparatively restricted use of the term rapidly became a cliché of the CYBERPUNK movement, but it is only a special case of the larger theme of virtual reality. One reason why virtual realities have been popular so long in sf is the somewhat recursive fact that stories themselves are virtual realities (though we interact with them only in a metaphoric sense); so the notion holds an intrinsic fascination for writers of stories, each of whom is, to a degree, a god creating an imaginary world which is real to the characters within it and partly real to the reader who shares their experience, a notion central to L. Ron HUBBARD's story "Typewriter in the Sky" (1940).

Broadly, a virtual reality can be defined as any secondary reality alternate to the character's world of real experience in which the character finds himself or herself, and with which he or she can interact. The purist might insist that such a world be machine-mediated. If it is not (or, less obviously, even if it is) then all sorts of questions of METAPHYSICS instantly intrude. How sure are we that our own world represents the "real" reality? This is not only the sort of question that troubles the protagonists of many novels by Philip K. DICK, including *The Three Stigmata of Palmer Eldritch* (1965). It has troubled writers since the dawn of Western civilization, including PLATO, who wondered if what we perceive as reality is only the flickering shadows on a cave wall, reflections of a higher, more solid (or Platonic) reality that we cannot perceive with the senses. The idea that our world may, in fact, be only a virtual reality remains intensely popular in fiction and is central, for example, to the situation in which most of Jack CHALKER's characters find themselves. Any virtual-reality world might be assumed to have a creator or programmer, a kind of god, so virtual-reality stories are often stories of god-like or demonic creators (◊ GODS AND DEMONS *and* PERCEPTION *for further examples*). One good example is Daniel F. GALOUYE's *Counterfeit World* (1964 UK; vt *Simulacron-3* US), filmed as WELT AM DRAHT (1973, vt *World on a Wire*), which contains a receding and potentially endless series of virtual realities. Other examples are listed under POCKET UNIVERSES.

The idea of the virtual reality has often been linked with game-playing, and GAME-WORLD stories are often based around virtual realities. An early example (although not machine-mediated) is Lewis CARROLL's *Through the Looking Glass and What Alice Found There* (1871), in which the virtual reality that Alice enters through the mirror is a game-world based on an actual chess game, whose other player is effectively God, and whose puppet-pieces are arguably deprived of free will. The idea, more simply, of plugging into a virtual-reality world for entertainment is also old: E.M. FORSTER's "The Machine Stops" (1909) envisages a world of isolated cells whose occupants derive all their entertainment through plugging into global information networks; Aldous HUXLEY's *Brave New World* (1932) has a future whose people are entertained by "feelies", apparently a kind of cinema that operates on all the senses to give an illusion of reality (but the experience is passive, so the basic element of interaction is absent); in Arthur C. CLARKE's *The City and the Stars* (1956), an expansion of *Against the Fall of Night* (1953), occupants of a static UTOPIA (not unlike Forster's) amuse themselves with violent, melodramatic adventure scenarios into which they plug themselves to take part.

While this topic has remained a minor constant in sf, it suddenly blossomed into a major theme around the end of the 1970s and through the 1980s. Sometimes the virtual realities of this recent fiction are generated by manipulative superbeings, sometimes by machine intelligences. In John VARLEY's **Titan** sequence (1979-84) the artificial world is effectively a theme park, whose nature is protean, subject to the whims of its creator. Theme parks themselves can be read as a form of virtual reality, and often appear in sf, as in Steven BARNES's and Larry NIVEN's **Dream Park** sequence (1981-91) or in the film WESTWORLD (1973). The typical theme-park story has the expected manipulations of a game turned into the nightmare manipulations of PARANOIA.

Films and stories in which humans are, or become, trapped in virtual realities, quite often computer-generated, include Hugh WALKER's *Reiter der Finsternis* (1975; trans as *War-Gamers' World* 1978), WELCOME TO BLOOD CITY (1977), Vernor VINGE's *True Names* (1981 dos; 1984), *Octagon* (1981) by Fred SABERHAGEN, TRON (1982), BRAINSTORM (1983), DREAMSCAPE (1984), Gillian RUBINSTEIN's *Space Demons* (1986), Andrew GREELEY's *God Game* (1986), Kim NEWMAN's *The Night Mayor* (1989) and *The* LAWNMOWER MAN (1992).

A popular variant of the theme is the reality generated by one person's godlike will; such are the deliquescing subrealities – rather like hallucinations which others are forced to share – created by the protagonist of Ursula K. LE GUIN's *The Lathe of Heaven* (1971), filmed for tv as *The* LATHE OF HEAVEN (1980). Another variant is the computer game seen by the unaware protagonist as only a game (i.e., virtual), which turns out to generate a reality that is often alarming (i.e., real). This is the scenario of Orson Scott CARD's *Ender's Game* (1977 ASF; exp 1985) and of the film WARGAMES (1983), in both of which a war-game turns out to be war itself, the gaming computer being actually in a position of military command. A computer game is used to entice the young hero of *The* LAST STARFIGHTER (1984), his virtual-reality skills being required for the waging of a real galactic war.

A final variant is found in those stories in which (normally for purposes of psychotherapy) one person enters another's mind and interacts with what he or she finds there, a classic of this genre being *The Dream Master* (1965 as "He Who Shapes"; exp 1966) by Roger ZELAZNY. One mind, in this instance, becomes a virtual reality for the other, and in these stories the transfer is typically machine-mediated, as in Greg BEAR's *Queen of Angels* (1990), in which the reality entered is a malign landscape generated by the mind of a murderer. Many more stories of this type are listed under PSYCHOLOGY.

Because of the metaphorical power of virtual-reality stories to examine the processes of creation (and, rather differently, to conjure up paranoid visions of manipulation) it is likely that they will remain popular. [PN]

VIRUS ◊ FUKKATSO NO HI.

VISIAK, E.H. Working name of UK poet, critic and novelist Edward Harold Physick (1878-1972). His fiction – like *The Haunted Island* (1910), a complex tale featuring ghosts, MAGIC and piracy – is essentially fantasy, although *Medusa: A Story of Mystery* (1929), an almost surreal FANTASTIC VOYAGE into unknown seas, gives the eponymous South Pacific sea monster

an sf-like rationale. "The Shadow", a good surrealist ghost novella, appeared in *Crimes, Creeps and Thrills* (anth 1936) ed John GAWSWORTH. As a friend of David LINDSAY, EHV contributed an essay to *The Strange Genius of David Lindsay* (anth 1970). [JC/PN]

VISION OF TOMORROW Australian/UK magazine, monthly, BEDSHEET-format, 12 issues, Aug 1969-Sep 1970, published by Ronald E. Graham, an Australian sf enthusiast; ed Philip HARBOTTLE from the UK. *VOT* featured work by many UK writers, including Kenneth BULMER, Michael MOORCOCK and E.C. TUBB, with the emphasis on straightforward action stories, and several posthumous works by John Russell FEARN. Graham vetoed the inclusion of US writers, but encouraged Australian authors, including Damien BRODERICK, Lee HARDING and Jack WODHAMS. Cover artists included Eddie JONES, Gerard A. QUINN and David HARDY, the latter also producing many full-colour illustrations for the inside back cover. *VOT* was the first English-language magazine to publish a story by Stanisław LEM: "Are You There, Mr Jones?", in #1. **The Impatient Dreamers**, a history of UK sf publishing and FANDOM by Walter GILLINGS, E.J. CARNELL and others, ran through all issues. Because of a change of printers, #3 (Nov 1969) appeared before #2 (Dec 1969). [BS/PN]

VISSARION, I.C. [r] ◊ ROMANIA.

VIVIAN, E(VELYN) CHARLES (1882-1947) UK writer of popular fiction, born Charles Henry Cannell but changing his name to ECV in early adulthood, though he wrote some non-genre novels as Charles Cannell. He is now best remembered for the **Gees** sequence of novels (see listing below), all written as by Jack Mann, about a psychic detective whose cases sometimes involve sf-like phenomena – e.g., travel through other DIMENSIONS – but are essentially fantasies. Much of ECV's prolific output had a mystical tinge. Some of his novels, like *Passion-Fruit* (1912), had fantasy elements, and several were LOST-WORLD tales, including: *City of Wonder* (1922), which features Asian survivors from Lemuria; the **Aia** sequence, comprising *Fields of Sleep* (1923), in which Babylonian survivors are trapped in a Malaysian valley by a strange plant within range of whose aroma, once inhaled, one must stay or die, and *People of the Darkness* (1924), set in an underground world inhabited by a tentacled species who were originally slaves in ATLANTIS; *The Lady of the Terraces* (1925) and its sequel *A King There Was* – (1926), which feature pre-Incan survivals and further hints of Atlantis; and *Woman Dominant* (1929), set in Asia, where an aged woman rules a land through the agency of a drug which makes men halfwitted. ECV's most straightforward sf tale, *Star Dust* (1925), describes an inventor/scientist's attempts to make the world better by indiscriminately transmuting dross into gold; this (he thinks) will make some sort of UTOPIA inevitable. Not one of ECV's books is fully satisfying; not one is without interest. [JC]

Other works, all as Jack Mann: *Coulson Goes South*

(**1933**), marginal; *Dead Man's Chest* (**1934**); the **Gees** sequence, comprising *Gees' First Case* (**1936**), associational, *Grey Shapes* (**1937**), *Nightmare Farm* (**1937**), *The Kleinert Case* (**1938**), associational, *Maker of Shadows* (**1938**), *The Ninth Life* (**1939**), *Her Ways are Death* (**1939**) and *The Glass Too Many* (**1940**).

See also: HISTORY OF SF; MACHINES.

VOGEL, [Sir] JULIUS (1835-1899) UK politician who spent much of his professional life in NEW ZEALAND and whose sf novel, *Anno Domini 2000, or Woman's Destiny* (**1889**), set partly in New Zealand and Australia, treats the dawning 21st century as both benignly prosperous and much obsessed with matters of royalty. The current British Emperor causes much fuss in the USA when he refuses to approve any change in the succession laws which would permit a female to succeed to the throne. But after a war all ends well, with various women achieving their destiny in a series of marriages. [JC]

VOGH, JAMES ◊ John T. SLADEK.

VOID PUBLICATIONS ◊ Paul COLLINS; VOID SCIENCE FICTION AND FANTASY.

VOID SCIENCE FICTION AND FANTASY Australian DIGEST-size SEMIPROZINE, 5 issues 1975-7, thereafter continuing until 1981 as a paperback-book series, 4 books, 3 numbers per book, which effectively constituted an original-anthology series; published by Void Publications; ed Paul COLLINS. #1-#3 were published from Queensland, the rest from Melbourne. At a time when Australian sf had few local outlets, *VSFAF* was a brave venture, though in appearance it could be described, in its 1st incarnation, as a fiction FANZINE, with an overcrowded layout on cheap paper. It contained a few US reprints, but was primarily a platform for such Australian sf writers as A. Bertram CHANDLER, David LAKE and Jack WODHAMS. *VSFAF* was dated by year only, and only one issue (#2) was numbered. #6-#8 were published in book form as an original anthology, *Envisaged Worlds* (anth **1977**), #9-#11 as *Other Worlds* (anth **1978**), #12-#14 as *Alien Worlds* (anth **1979**) and #15-#17 as *Distant Worlds* (anth **1981**). A further anthology, *Frontier Worlds* (anth **1983**) was offered to subscribers in lieu of #18. [PN]

VOINOVICH, VLADIMIR (NIKOLAEVICH) (1932-) Russian writer known mostly for his mainstream satires. Active in the 1970s, he found himself in confrontation with the Soviet authorities, and finally emigrated in the early 1980s to Germany. All his works display an offbeat and at times heavy-handed fantastication. His only sf tale, *Moskorep* (**1986** France; trans Richard Lourie as *Moscow 2084* **1987** US), carries a contemporary protagonist 100 years forward by TIME TRAVEL to the redoubled bureaucracy that rules in AD2084, *en passant* satirizing Aleksandr Solzhenitsyn (1918-). The outlandishness of the sf enactment of VV's conceit is balanced by the grimness of his sense that Soviet bureaucracy would almost infinitely worsen. [VG/JC]

VOISKUNSKY, EVGENY (L'VOVICH) (1922-)

Russian naval officer, journalist and writer; he wrote in collaboration with Isa Borisovich Lukodianov (1913-1984), a design engineer, until the latter's death. Their first novel was *Ekipazh "Mekonga"* (**1961**; cut trans Leonard Stoklitsky as *The Crew of the Mekong* **1974** Russia), a long but fast-moving HARD-SF examination of 2 intersecting projects: an attempt to increase the surface tension of oil so that it can be sent without needing pipelines; and an investigation of the scientific principles behind an ancient knife whose blade is interpenetrable with matter. *En passant*, the Caspian Sea is raised. A sequel, *Ur, Syn Shama* ["Ur, Son of Sham"] (**1975**), depicts an encounter with ALIENS, who bring the protagonist, an ancient Babylonian kidnapped eons earlier, back to Earth. *Tchiorny Stolb* (**1963**), a short novel trans anon as "The Black Pillar" in *The Molecular Café* (anth ed anon Arkady and Boris STRUGATSKI trans **1968** Russia), depicts a NEAR-FUTURE global catastrophe as the result of deep drilling of Earth's mantle. In *Otchen' Daliokii Tartess* ["Far Distant Tartess"] (**1968**) ATLANTIS meets its doom when local scientist-priests discover the secret of atomic energy. *Plesk zviozdenykh Morei* ["Star Seas Lapping"] (fixup **1970**) deals with the TERRAFORMING of VENUS, and a long-frustrated but finally successful attempt to initiate interstellar travel. Some short work was assembled in *Na Perekriostkakh Vremeni* ["At the Crossroads of Time"] (coll **1964**); a late novel was *Nezakonaia Planeta* ["The Illegal Planet"] (**1980**). [VG/JC]

VOLLMANN, WILLIAM T. (1959-) US writer whose début novel, *You Bright and Risen Angels: A Cartoon* (**1987** UK), is an immense FABULATION whose interweavings of PARANOIA and CYBERPUNK tended to remind critics of the work of Thomas PYNCHON. The war between the villain, who is attempting to control the world through an information web, and the "bugs" caught in his system, who attempt to remain subversively free, is also, in Postmodernistic fashion, a war of words between contrasting methods of defining and controlling "reality". The ongoing sequence entitled **Seven Dreams: A Book of North American Landscapes**, of which *The Ice-Shirt* (**1990** UK) is the 1st instalment, attempts to construct out of language and myth and history a new version of the USA. The stories assembled in *The Rainbow Stories* (coll of linked stories **1989** UK), though they depict extreme states of being, almost entirely eschew fantasy. [JC]

VOLNÝ, ZDENĚK [r] ◊ CZECH AND SLOVAK SF.

VOLTAIRE Pseudonym of François-Marie Arouet (1694-1778), enormously productive and successful French philosopher, historian, playwright, belletrist. Of interest to the student of PROTO SCIENCE FICTION is *Micromégas* (**1752** UK; trans anon as *Micromegas, a Comic Romance* **1753** UK; best new trans W. Fleming as coll vt *Micromegas and Other Stories* **1989** UK), in which two giants, one from a planet circling Sirius and one from Saturn, visit Earth, where their responses to human life make some satirical points, not least that our species may not be so very important in the much larger Universe that was coming to be accepted at the time V was writing. *Candide* (**1759**), the best known of all tales of the innocent abroad, can be seen as a precursor of satirical picaresques from Kurt VONNEGUT Jr to Robert SHECKLEY. Certainly a FANTASTIC VOYAGE, *Candide* is arguably also an early example of anthropological sf; it was made into a musical comedy in 1957 by Leonard Bernstein. Other *contes philosophiques* with explicitly fantastic content include *Zadig* (**1747**; trans with other tales as *Miscellanies* [coll **1778** US]; many other trans exist) and *Le taureau blanc* (**1774**; trans as *The White Bull* **1774** UK; new trans with other tales as *The White Bull, With Saul and Various Short Pieces* [coll **1929** UK]). [JC/PN]

See also: FRANCE; GREAT AND SMALL; OUTER PLANETS; RELIGION; SATIRE.

VONARBURG, ÉLISABETH (1947-) French-born Canadian writer, teacher and critic, in Québec from 1973. She began publishing sf with "Marée haute" for *Requiem* in 1978; the tale appeared as "High Tide" in *Twenty Houses of the Zodiac* (anth **1979** UK) ed Maxim JAKUBOWSKI. Many of her stories (some award-winning) have been assembled as *L'Oeil de la nuit* ["The Eye of Night"] (coll **1980**) and *Janus* (coll **1984** France), most being set in either of 2 cycles (with great gaps in the published chronology), the more important being the **Baïblanca** series, in which a semi-decadent society sees the gradual appearance of shapeshifting MUTANTS (the "métames"). The series culminates in *Le Silence de la cité* (**1981** France; trans Jane Brierley as *The Silent City* **1988**), whose young female protagonist leaves her underground sanctuary and goes to the surface, with its wild tribes, where she begins to transform the benighted world. A sequel is projected for 1992. In the 2nd cycle, a **Bridge** serves as a door to other universes. EV is a very deliberate writer who brings great care and thought to her work, and to the depiction of characters and background. She was fiction editor 1979-90 and editor 1983-5 of *Solaris*. [LP]

Other works: *Comment écrire des histoires* ["How to Write Stories"] (**1986**); *Histoire de la princesse et du dragon* ["The Story of the Princess and the Dragon"] (**1990**); *Ailleurs et au Japon* ["Elsewhere and in Japan"] (coll **1991**).

See also: CANADA.

von DALIN, OLOF [r] ◊ SCANDINAVIA.

von DÄNIKEN, ERICH (1935-) Swiss writer of a series of purportedly nonfiction books, beginning with *Erinnerungen an die Zukunft* (**1968** Germany; trans Michael Heron as *Chariots of the Gods?* **1969** UK), which, based on a mass of often suspect and internally inconsistent data, argues that the Earth was visited by at least one ALIEN spacefaring race before and at the dawn of historical time; thus, for example, the Great Pyramid (a CRYOGENIC chamber) and the Easter Island statues (images of the visiting aliens) were quarried with lasers and lifted into place

by helicopters. It is central to his thesis – which was far from original to him – that all ancient peoples were moronic, capable only of copying what the spacemen showed them. Scientific howlers abound, and logical flaws proliferate; yet the books sold in their millions and sparked off a host of imitators, some of which – like *Mystery of the Ancients* (**1974**) by Craig and Eric Umland, claiming that the Maya are the descendants of stranded explorers from beyond the Solar System – are so entrancingly funny that they may in fact be spoofs. A hagiography of EvD is *Däniken Intim* (**1976**; trans David B. Koblick as *Disciple of the Gods* **1978** UK; vt *Erich von Däniken: Disciple of the Gods*) by Peter Krassa. A cheerful and detailed demolition is *The Space-Gods Revealed* (**1976**) by Ronald Story (1946-   ); there is further useful discussion by E.C. Krupp in *In Search of Ancient Astronomies* (anth **1979**; rev **1984**) ed Krupp.

The vast publicity given to EvD's speculations has had a negative effect on sf, in that the whole notion of ancient astronauts became such anathema, even to those of only moderate scientific literacy, that it became an sf TABOO. It is hard to find a worthwhile sf treatment of the topic in the years since 2001: A SPACE ODYSSEY (1968), although the idea of an ancient race having "seeded" the Galaxy, populating its worlds or spreading scientific knowledge to assist their primitive indigenous lifeforms, has become almost a CLICHÉ of SPACE OPERA. [JS/JGr]

See also: ADAM AND EVE; COMICS; GODS AND DEMONS; MYTHOLOGY; ORIGIN OF MAN; PARANOIA; PSEUDO-SCIENCE.

von GRIMMELSHAUSEN, JOHANN JAKOB CHRISTOFFEL [r] ◊ GERMANY.

von GUNDEN, KENNETH (1946-   ) US writer whose 1st work of sf interest was *Twenty All-Time Great SF Films* (**1982**) with Stuart H. Stock, and who came to somewhat wider notice with his 1st novel, *StarSpawn* (**1990**), which interestingly introduces an ethically advanced hive race of interstellar explorers into medieval England, though an associated species escapes their ship and causes some havoc. The **K-9 Corps** sequence – *K-9 Corps* (**1991**), *K-9 Corps #2: Under Fire* (**1991**) and *#3: Cry Wolf* (**1992**) – less engagingly confronts a team of super-dogs with challenges on alien planets. [JC]

von HANSTEIN, OTFRIED [r] ◊ GERMANY.

von HARBOU, THEA (1888-1954) German writer, most noted for her novels based on screenplays written by herself and her husband, Fritz LANG, who divorced her after she joined the Nazi Party in 1932; she was co-author of the screenplays for all the films Lang made before leaving Germany in 1933. Neither *Metropolis* ∗ (**1926**; trans anon **1927** UK), filmed as METROPOLIS (1926), nor *Frau im Mond* ∗ (**1928**; trans Baroness von Hutten as *The Girl in the Moon* **1930** UK; cut vt *The Rocket to the Moon; from the Novel, The Girl in the Moon* **1930** US), filmed as *Die* FRAU IM MOND (1929), has much of the films' symbolic force, and both are thickly propagandistic. [JC]

See also: AUTOMATION; CITIES; GERMANY; WOMEN SF WRITERS.

von KHUON, ERNST [r] ◊ GERMANY.

VONNEGUT, KURT Jr (1922-   ) US writer born in Indianapolis. He was a PoW near the end of WWII in Dresden during the saturation bombing of the city and the subsequent firestorm. He later studied at the universities of Tennessee and Chicago, and began to write for various magazines in the early 1950s, his first sf story being "Report on the Barnhouse Effect" for COLLIER'S WEEKLY in 1950. His first appearance in an sf magazine was "Unready to Wear" (*Gal* 1953), but KV tried hard to avoid categorization as a GENRE-SF writer. He first became widely popular in the mid-1960s and is now recognized as a major US writer of the post-WWII period.

His first novel was the DYSTOPIA of AUTOMATION, *Player Piano* (**1952**; vt *Utopia 14* **1954**), which describes the dereliction of the quality of life by the progressive surrender of production and political decision to MACHINES. The mixture of heavy irony, bordering on black HUMOUR, and unashamed sentimentality displayed in this novel became the hallmark of KV's work, and is progressively exaggerated in later novels. *The Sirens of Titan* (**1959**) is a fine complex SATIRE about the folly of mistaking good luck for the favour of God; it features the first of a number of mock-RELIGIONS that KV would invent – the Church of God the Utterly Indifferent – and concludes with the revelation of the manipulation of human history by Tralfamadorian ALIENS sending messages to one of their kind stranded on Titan. One leading character has an extratemporal viewpoint from which all moments appear co-existent – a theme which crops up again, along with the Tralfamadorians, in KV's novel about the firestorming of Dresden, *Slaughterhouse-Five, or The Children's Crusade: A Duty-Dance with Death* (**1969**). *Mother Night* (**1962**) is a non-sf novel about the struggle of a US ex-Nazi double agent to discover his "true" identity; several of its characters reappear in later work, helping to connect all his work into a single evolving patchwork. *Cat's Cradle* (**1963**) features a confrontation of the opposing philosophies of scientist Felix Hoenikker, inventor of "ice-nine" (which threatens to bring about the END OF THE WORLD), and Bokonon, a rebel against rationality and architect of an avowedly fake religion whose purpose is to protect believers against the harshness of reality. *God Bless You, Mr Rosewater* (**1965**) is a non-sf novel about the one man in the world who does not suffer from samaritrophia (chronic atrophy of the conscience), but it is closely allied to much of KV's sf; it contains an oft-quoted paragraph about sf writers, makes much of the misadventures of sf writer Kilgore Trout – who reappears in *Breakfast of Champions, or Goodbye, Blue Monday!* (**1973**) – and overlaps somewhat with *Slaughterhouse-Five*, the story of Billy Pilgrim, survivor of the Dresden firestorm, who finds peace of mind after being kidnapped by Tralfamadorians and thus learning that the secret of life is to live only in the happy moments. Most of KV's 1970s

work showed a marked decline in vitality – both *Breakfast of Champions* and *Slapstick, or Lonesome No More!* (**1976**) verge on lachrymose self-parody and are shot through with shoulder-shrugging, verbal tics – but he recovered a measure of his authority in a series of novels about unfortunate innocents abroad: *Jailbird* (**1979**) and *Dead-Eye Dick* (**1982**). His most impressive novel of this period is, *Galápagos* (**1985**), a darkly humorous apocalyptic fantasy narrated by a remote and happily devolved descendant of the few survivors of the HOLOCAUST; but *Hocus Pocus, or What's the Hurry, Sam?* (**1990**), which carries its protrayal of a self-destroying USA through the turn of the century, is almost as compelling.

Vonnegut's best sf – which includes some of the short stories first assembled in *Canary in a Cat House* (coll **1961**) and subsequently recombined with new material in *Welcome to the Monkey House* (coll **1968**) – has a unique flavour, not only because of its sardonic *Weltschmerz* but also by virtue of his consistent refusal to look for scapegoats to blame for the sad state of the world. KV is content to attribute human misery and misfortune to the carelessness of God the Utterly Indifferent; he is full of pity for the human predicament but can see no hope in any solutions, save perhaps for the adoption of actions and beliefs which are absurdly irrational. This is a philosophy very much in keeping with the contemporary *Zeitgeist*. KV has also written a play with sf elements, *Happy Birthday, Wanda June* (**1973**), and had a hand in the production of a tv play based on extracts from several of his works, *Between Time and Timbuktu* (**1972**; book version *Between Time and Timbuktu, or Prometheus-5: A Space Fantasy* **1972**). KV's essays, talks and various journalistic oddments are assembled in *Wampeters, Foma and Granfalloons* (coll **1974**), *Palm Sunday: An Autobiographical Collage* (fixup **1981**), and *Fates Worse than Death: An Autobiographical Collage of the 1980s* (fixup **1991**). A novel attributed to Kilgore Trout, written by Philip José FARMER, appeared as *Venus on the Half-Shell* (**1975**).   [BS]

About the author: Much has been written about KV; the following is a selection of books. *Kurt Vonnegut Jr* (**1972**) by Peter J. Reed; *Kurt Vonnegut: Fantasist of Fire and Ice* (**1972**) by David H. Goldsmith; *The Vonnegut Statement* (anth **1973**) ed Jerome Klinkowitz and John Somer; *Kurt Vonnegut Jr* (**1976**) by Stanley Schatt; *Kurt Vonnegut* (**1977**) by James Lundquist; *Kurt Vonnegut* (**1982**) by Jerome Klinkovitz.

See also: ABSURDIST SF; COMMUNICATIONS; CYBERNETICS; DISASTER; DISCOVERY AND INVENTION; EVOLUTION; FANTASY; GENERATION STARSHIPS; HISTORY OF SF; INTELLIGENCE; ISLANDS; MEDIA LANDSCAPE; MERCURY; METAPHYSICS; OUTER PLANETS; OVERPOPULATION; PARANOIA; PERCEPTION; POLITICS; POLLUTION; PREDICTION; RECURSIVE SF; SCIENTISTS; SPACESHIPS; TIME TRAVEL.

von NEUPAUER, JOSEPH RITTER [r] ◊ AUSTRIA.

von RACHEN, KURT [s] ◊ L. Ron HUBBARD.

von TROJAN, KURT (1937-   ) Writer born in Vienna but now Australian. His first novel, *The*

Transing Syndrome (**1985**), uses "transing" (MATTER TRANSMISSION) to move the plot along in an alternate-world DYSTOPIA; the protagonist worries that his identity may be fading with each transmission, like increasingly obscure photocopies of a photocopy. *Bedmates* (**1987**) is set in a future Australia dominated by AIDS and sexual fear: "bedmates" are mindless artefacts always ready for sex. Both novels are effective and sometimes harrowing, but flawed. KVT's best work may be the non-sf autobiographical novel *Mars in Scorpio* (**1990**). [BF/PN]

von VOSS, JULIUS [r] ◊ GERMANY.

VORHIES, JOHN R(OYAL HARRIS) (1920-   ) US writer in whose NEAR-FUTURE *Pre-Empt* (**1967**; vt *The Nathan Hale* 1968 UK) a nuclear-submarine captain enforces world peace by dropping a few demonstration missiles on the USA and USSR. Despite the title, the USA does not opt for a pre-emptive strike. [JC]

VORNHOLT, JOHN (?   -   ) US writer known only for 2 STAR TREK: THE NEXT GENERATION ties: *Masks* * (**1989**) and *Contamination* * (**1991**). [JC]

VORTEX UK small-BEDSHEET size magazine. 5 issues Jan-May 1977, published by Shalmead (Jan-Feb), Container Publications (Mar), Cerberus Publishing (Apr-May); ed. Keith Seddon. *V* was a glossy magazine with some interior illustration in full colour. The first 3 covers, by Rodney MATTHEWS, suggested an orientation towards fantasy which was not evident in the actual magazine. #1-#4 serialized Michael MOORCOCK's *The End of All Songs* (**1976**); #5 contained the 1st instalment of *The Chaos Weapon* (**1977**) by Colin KAPP. Other stories were for the most part experimental pieces by previously unknown authors, such as Ravan Christchild, who in most cases were pseudonyms of the editor. The circulation never looked like covering the high production costs. [MJE]

VORTEX, THE US FANZINE. 2 issues 1947, ed Gordon M. Kull and George R. Cowie from San Francisco. *TV* is listed in some indexes as a professional SF MAGAZINE, but the fiction in #1 was by unknown amateurs and it was distributed free. It was attractively printed on glossy paper. #2 had name writers like David H. KELLER and Stanley MULLEN, but was mainly mimeographed. [MJE/FHP]

VORTEX SCIENCE FICTION US DIGEST-size magazine. 2 issues, May and Oct 1953, published by Specific Fiction Corp., New York; ed Chester Whitehorn. *VSF* was designed to showcase a large number of very short stories in each issue, achieving this goal in #2, but the idea did not prove popular. Not all the 9 new writers who made their début in the second issue were doomed to remain unknown: Marion Zimmer BRADLEY had 2 stories there. A later magazine (1954) with the same publisher and editor was SCIENCE FICTION DIGEST.

VSF should not be confused with VORTEX or *The VORTEX*. [FHP/PN]

VOYAGE À TRAVERS l'IMPOSSIBLE, LE (vt *Whirling the Worlds*; vt *An Impossible Voyage*) Film (**1904**).

Star. Prod/dir Georges MÉLIÈS. 30 mins. B/w.

This was only the 2nd sf-oriented film to be more than 5 mins long – there had been several around 1 min – made by French cinema pioneer Méliès; the 1st was his *Le* VOYAGE DANS LA LUNE (**1902**). It involves a newly invented experimental train taking off from the summit of the Jungfrau, travelling through space and crashing into the Sun; its occupants then return to Earth by space submarine and land in the sea. All this was achieved with primitive but ingenious special effects, including stop-motion photography, split-screen, multiple exposures, giant moving cut-outs and live action combined with painted backdrops. It was so popular that Méliès added 5 mins to the end, showing the equipment used on the trip being recovered by a giant electromagnet. [JB/PN]

VOYAGE DANS LA LUNE, LE (vt *A Trip to the Moon*) Film (**1902**). Star. Prod/dir Georges MÉLIÈS, who also played the inventor. 21 mins. Tinted.

This is the 1st sf film (apart from short subjects lasting only 1-2 mins). French CINEMA pioneer Méliès based this amusing spectacle extremely loosely on Jules VERNE's *De la terre à la lune* (**1865**; trans as the first half of *From the Earth to the Moon* 1873 UK) and H.G. WELLS's *First Men in the Moon* (**1901**), borrowing a spacecraft propelled by a gun from the former and hard-shelled Selenites from the latter. No attempt is made to depict the flight seriously; the Moon projectile is loaded by a line of grinning chorus girls; the Man in the Moon is shown with the projectile stuck in his eye; the Moon travellers encounter a group of Selenites who explode when tapped with an umbrella; and the travellers safely return home, due to the pull of Earth's GRAVITY, in time to see a statue erected in their honour. The innovatory special effects are naturally primitive, but encompass many techniques still in use today. [JB/PN]

VOYAGERS US tv series (**1982-3**). Universal. Created James D. Parriott, prod Jill Sherman, Robert Steinhauer. Dirs included Virgil Vogel, Bernard McEveety, Allan Levi, Ron Satloff. 20 50min episodes.

Phineas Bogg (played by Jon Eric Hexum) and Jeffrey Jones (played by Meeno Peluce) are time-travelling Voyagers who put history right (which is to say, the way we know it to have been). The premise could have been interesting, but remained trivial (reminding the Wright Brothers to invent the aeroplane, helping Babe Ruth hit his 60th home run and, more inventively, saving Jean Lafitte the pirate so that the British do not win the Battle of New Orleans). In the final episode, Jack the Ripper turns out to be a renegade Voyager trying to corrupt history. Not helped by the woodenness of its handsome leading players, *V* seems to have received very little foreign distribution and to have been largely ignored by the sf community. [PN]

VOYAGE TO THE BOTTOM OF THE SEA 1. Film (**1961**). Windsor Productions/20th Century-Fox. Dir Irwin ALLEN, starring Walter Pidgeon, Robert Sterling, Joan Fontaine, Barbara Eden, Peter Lorre. Screenplay

Allen, Charles Bennett. 105 mins. Colour.

The crew of a glass-nosed nuclear submarine has a mission to fire an atomic missile into the Van Allen belts, which have been set on fire by meteors (!) and are melting the icecaps. Despite enemy submarines, a giant octopus and other hazards, the mission succeeds. As with most of Allen's productions, the plot does not survive an instant's rational scrutiny; it is full of astonishing SCIENTIFIC ERRORS. The novelization was *Voyage to the Bottom of the Sea* ∗ (**1961**) by Theodore STURGEON.

2. US tv series (1964-8). An Irwin Allen Production for 20th Century-Fox TV/ABC. Created Irwin Allen, who was also executive prod. Story consultant Sidney Marshall. Writers included William Welch (34 episodes), Richard Landau, Harlan ELLISON (1 episode as by Cordwainer Bird), Robert Hamner, Rik Vollaerts. Dirs included Leonard Horn, Sobey Martin, Felix Feist, Harry Harris, Sutton Roley, Jus Addiss. Special effects L.B. Abbott. 110 50min episodes. Season 1 b/w, the remaining 3 seasons colour.

Based on **1**, this series concerned the exploits of the experimental submarine *Seaview*; it starred Richard Basehart and David Hedison. Early episodes had fairly conventional stories involving secret agents and threats from unfriendly foreign powers, but later the plots became increasingly fantastic: not only were the crew faced with such dangers as giant whales, giant jellyfish, giant octopuses and giant "things", but their submarine was regularly invaded by a variety of esoteric menaces ranging from sentient seaweed to the ghost of a U-boat captain, other uninvited guests including a lobster man, a mummy, a leprechaun, a blob and a mad robot. Throughout, Basehart and Hedison kept straight faces. Abbott's special effects won several Emmy awards. A book spin-off was

Voyage to the Bottom of the Sea ∗ (**1965**) by Raymond F. JONES. [JB]

See also: UNDER THE SEA.

VOYAGE TO THE END OF THE UNIVERSE ◊ IKARIE XB-1.

VOYAGE TO THE PLANET OF PREHISTORIC WOMEN ◊ Roger CORMAN; PLANETA BUR.

VOYAGE TO THE PREHISTORIC PLANET ◊ Roger CORMAN; PLANETA BUR.

VYNÁLEZ ZKÁZY (vt *The Diabolic Invention*; vt *The Deadly Invention*; vt *The Fabulous World of Jules Verne*; vt *Invention of Destruction*; vt *Weapons of Destruction*) Film (1958). Krátký film Praha/Studio loutkových filmů Gottwaldov. Dir Karel Zeman, starring Lubor Tokus, Arnošt Navrátil, Miroslav Holub, Jana Zatloukalová. Screenplay Zeman, František Hrubín, based primarily on Jules VERNE's *Face au drapeau* (**1896**; trans as *For the Flag* **1897**), but also drawing on sections of his *Vingt mille lieues sous les mers* (**1870**; trans as *Twenty Thousand Leagues under the Seas* **1872**), *L'île mystérieuse* (**1874-5**; trans as *The Mysterious Island* **1875**) and *Robur le conquérant* (**1886**; trans as *The Clipper of the Clouds* **1887**). 83 mins. B/w.

This Czech film is a charming blend of cartoon animation, puppet film and live action, with the overall style patterned on 19th-century steel engravings. A monomaniacal scientist invents an incredibly powerful new explosive; he and his assistant are captured by a Captain Nemo-like character and his followers. There are various adventures with submarines, BALLOONS, a giant octopus and a vast cannon. At the end patriotism triumphs over unscrupulous technology. Zeman directed a number of excellent films of this sort (◊ CZECH AND SLOVAK SF). [JB/PN]

WADE, TOM W. (? -) UK writer who published mainly with sf publishers John Spencer (◊ BADGER BOOKS) under various pseudonyms. As Victor Wadey he wrote two bad yet charming sf novels, *A Planet Named Terra* (**1962**) and its sequel *The United Planets* (**1962**). The distant planet confusingly called Terra is populated by the REINCARNATIONS of people from Earth, notably Elizabeth I, as space explorers from Earth discover to their amazement. He wrote *Chariot into Time* (**1953**) under the house name Karl Zeigfreid as well as, fairly certainly, the 2 unidentified titles listed in the Karl ZEIGFREID entry. Under the house name Victor LA SALLE he wrote *Assault from Infinity* (**1953**), *The Seventh Dimension* (**1953**) and *Suns in Duo* (**1953**). As TWW he wrote 2 later tales, *The World of Theda* (**1962**) and *The Voice from Baru* (**1963**). [JC/JGr]

WADEY, VICTOR ◊ Tom W. WADE.

WADSWORTH, PHYLLIS MARIE (? -) UK author whose *Overmind* (**1967**) deals with ALIENS who contact humanity from another DIMENSION. [JC]

WAGAR, W(ALTER) WARREN (1932-) US academic (professor of history since 1971 at the State University of New York at Binghamton) and writer. He has published sf – his first story being "Heart's Desire" for *IASFM* in 1984 – but his involvement in the field comes primarily through his many years of work on H.G. WELLS in books like *H.G. Wells and the World State* (**1961**) and *H.G. Wells: Journalism and Prophecy, 1893-1946* (coll **1964**). In these WWW concentrates upon a side of Wells not generally thought very congenial: the insistent, peremptory, secretly authoritarian proselytizer for a world UTOPIA. The image of Wells as a simple propagandist does not survive WWW's analysis. Later books, like *Terminal Visions: The Literature of Last Things* (**1982**) and *A Short History of the Future* (**1989**), demonstrate the complexity and darkness that Wells, and others, brought to their prophecies; the 2nd vol is a literal recasting of one of Wells's favourite modes, the future history

told as a nonfiction narrative, with illustrations. *Terminal Visions*, an important work of sf scholarship, is a social history of apocalyptic thought in literature, covering (but not confined to) GENRE SF. [JC]

See also: CRITICAL AND HISTORICAL WORKS ABOUT SF.

WAHLÖÖ, PER (1926-1975) Swedish writer, best known for his detective novels, mostly with his wife Maj Sjöwall (1935-); on some of his books his name appears as Peter Wahlöö. His NEAR-FUTURE sf thrillers include *Mord pa 31* (**1965**; trans Joan Tate as *Murder on the 31st Floor* **1966** UK; vt *The Thirty-First Floor* **1967** US), which was filmed as KAMIKAZE 1989 (1982), *Stälspranget* (**1968**; trans Joan Tate as *The Steel Spring* **1970** UK), about a deadly plague in Sweden, and *Generalerna* (**1965**; trans Joan Tate as *The Generals* **1974** US), a trial novel set in a military DYSTOPIA. [JC]

WALDO An item of sf TERMINOLOGY originated by Robert A. HEINLEIN in his short novel *Waldo: Genius in Orbit* (**1942** *ASF* as "Waldo"; a title story of *Waldo & Magic, Inc.* [coll **1950**]; **1958**). The eponymous hero suffers from a crippling wasting of the muscles, and invents a number of remote-control devices, also called waldoes, to amplify the power of his feeble muscular movements. The term has since come into general use in technology to describe a whole range of remote-control devices, now commonplace. It has expanded in meaning to include devices for handling radioactive or other dangerous materials in isolation from the handler, and those concerned with fine and precise rather than powerful movements. [PN]

WALDROP, HOWARD (1946-) US writer, an important member of the Texas-based school of sf writers, much of whose work is set in the South. His first sf story was "Lunch Box" (1972) for *ASF*. His first novel, *The Texas-Israeli War: 1999* (**1974**) with Jake SAUNDERS, makes little capital of its transpositions of genres and nationalities. In 1976, however, he began to produce more characteristic work, including a wildly elaborate collaboration with Steven UTLEY, "Custer's Last Jump" (1976) – an ALTERNATE-WORLD story in which powered flight has reached the USA in time for the Civil War and the Indian Wars – and "Mary Margaret Road-Grader" (1976), an accomplished post-HOLOCAUST story in which Native American trials of strength are conducted with ageing bulldozers. There were several more collaborations with Utley, and these along with HW's solo work have been regularly anthologized.

HW is one of the few contemporary sf writers whose work is mostly short fiction. He has never been especially prolific, and his stories mine the same rich vein of alternate history almost too repeatedly, but his combination of deadpan humour and genuine scholarship (in both academic history and popular culture) has won him a loyal readership. Although his yoking together of disparate material sometimes appears crazed, with hindsight it is often strangely logical. Only HW would have written – it was his first solo novel – an alternate history (featuring 4 alternate worlds) with time travel from a dystopic future, Amerindian Mound Builders, Aztec Invaders, ancient Greek merchants in power-driven boats and much more, in *Them Bones* (1984); it is both astonishing and moving. His only other novel (really a novella) is *A Dozen Tough Jobs* (1989), a tall tale retelling the labours of Hercules in a late 1920s Mississippi setting; it says a little about ancient Greece and a lot about Black workers and rednecks.

The strain of putting the pieces together sometimes shows, but at his (moderately regular) best HW has been one of the unforgettable sf voices of the 1970s and 1980s. Among his memorable pieces – somewhere between FABULATIONS and GENRE SF – are "Save a Place in the Lifeboat for Me" (1976), "The Ugly Chickens" (1980), about how the dodo became extinct in the Deep South, which won a NEBULA, "Ike at the Mike" (1982), "Flying Saucer Rock & Roll" (1985), "Night of the Cooters" (1987) – describing what the Martians which had landed in Texas were doing while their counterparts, as featured in WAR OF THE WORLDS, were ravaging England – "Do Ya, Do Ya Wanna, Wanna Dance?" (1988) (◊ MUSIC) and "Fin de Cyclé" (1991). It took a surprisingly long time for any collections to appear. The first 2 were *Howard Who?* (coll 1986) and *All About Strange Monsters of the Recent Past* (coll 1987), assembled as *Strange Things in Close-Up: The Nearly Complete Howard Waldrop* (omni 1989 UK); the 2nd collection was reissued with *A Dozen Tough Jobs* included as *Strange Monsters of the Recent Past* (omni 1991). His 3rd collection was *Night of the Cooters: More Neat Stories* (coll 1990), republished with *A Dozen Tough Jobs* as *Night of the Cooters: More Neat Stuff* (omni 1991 UK). [PN]

See also: GOTHIC SF; HOLLOW EARTH; HUMOUR; LOST WORLDS; OMNI; TIME TRAVEL.

WALKER, ALICE (1944-   ) US writer best known for novels like *The Color Purple* (1982), exploring from a FEMINIST perspective the fate of being Black in the USA. One of the protagonists of *The Temple of My Familiar* (1989), an extremely long FABULATION, is immortal or has suffered numerous incarnations, and the tales she tells embody a savage indictment of racism and patriarchal dominance over the centuries. Counteracting this, deep memories of a benign matriarchy also emerge, though shrouded in myth. [JC]

WALKER, DAVID (HARRY) (1911-1992) Scottish-born writer, a Canadian citizen from 1957, best known for sentimental evocations of Scottish spirit like *Geordie* (1950), later filmed. *Winter of Madness* (1964) is a NEAR-FUTURE drama and *The Lord's Pink Ocean* (1972) a tale of POLLUTION and DISASTER in which all but one of the world's oceans die. [JC]

WALKER, HUGH Pseudonym of German writer Hubert Strassl (1941-   ), whose **Darkness** sequence – featuring a character who first creates a wargame and then becomes absorbed within it – is *Reiter der Finsternis* (1975; trans Christine Priest as *War-Gamers' World* 1978 US), *Das Heer der Finsternis* (1975; trans Christine Priest as *Army of Darkness* 1979 US), *Boten der Finsternis* (1976; trans Christine Priest as *Messengers of Darkness* 1979 US) and *Dämonen der Finsternis* ["Demons of Darkness"] (1978). [JC]

See also: VIRTUAL REALITY.

WALKER, PAUL (1921-   ) US writer and critic in whose sf novel, *Who Killed Utopia?* (1980), the first murder to have taken place for a century brings suspicion upon the poet/computer at the heart of things. PW contributed book reviews to *Gal* in 1978, and in the same year published a collection of postal interviews, *Speaking of Science Fiction: The Paul Walker Interviews* (coll 1978). [JC]

WALKHAM, WALTER [r] ◊ ROBERT HALE LIMITED.

WALL, G.A. [r] ◊ E.A. ROBINSON.

WALLACE, DOREEN Working name of UK writer Dora Eileen Agnew Wallace Rash (1897-   ), author of much popular fiction over a 65-year career. *Forty Years On* (1958) is set in the fens of Eastern England on the Isle of Ely (in fact not an island but a marsh-surrounded hill surmounted by the famous cathedral) after a nuclear HOLOCAUST. Here, under pastoral guidance, a chaste rural Fabian socialism soon takes control. The narrator visits other – visibly less blessed – parts of the fragmented UK, where cannibalism and US pop songs create general misery among the survivors, mostly working-class, who continue pertinaciously to attempt to breed. [JC]

About the author: *Dangerous by Degrees: Women at Oxford and the Somerville College Novelists* (1989) by Susan J. Leonardi.

WALLACE, (RICHARD HORATIO) EDGAR (1875-1932) UK author, playwright and editor, best known for his thrillers. EW used his experiences of the Boer War in the future-WAR novels *Private Selby* (1909 *The Sunday Journal* as "'O.C.' – A Soldier's Love Story"; 1912) and *"1925": The Story of a Fatal Peace* (1915). He featured the application of Pavlovian conditioning techniques to human beings in *The Door with Seven Locks* (1926) and "Control No. 2" (1934); impending world catastrophe in *The Fourth Plague* (1913), *The*

Green Rust (**1919**; vt *Green Rust* 1920 US), "The Black Grippe" (1920) and *The Day of Uniting* (1921 *Popular Magazine*; **1926**); the counter-Earth theme in *Planetoid 127* (1924 *The Mechanical Boy*; as title story of coll **1929**; **1986**); and weird fiction in "The Stranger of the Night" (1910), "While the Passengers Slept" (1916) and *Captains of Souls* (**1922** US). While working in Hollywood he assisted on the screenplay of KING KONG (1933), though his contribution may have been minimal – the novelization, *King Kong* * (**1932**), was by Delos Wheeler Lovelace (1894-1967) – and scripted a horror film, *The Table*, novelized as *The Table* * (**1936**) by Robert G. Curtis. [JE]

Other works: *The Council of Justice* (**1908**); *The Death Room* (1909-29 var mags; coll **1986**).

See also: BOYS' PAPERS; HISTORY OF SF; WEAPONS.

WALLACE, F(LOYD) L. (?   -?   ) US writer who began publishing sf with "Hideaway" for *ASF* in 1951, but was more strongly associated with *Gal* in the 1950s, the period of his greatest activity. *Worlds in Balance* (coll **1955** Australia) assembles 2 typical stories. *Address: Centauri* (1952 *Gal* as "Accidental Flight"; exp **1955**), features volunteer cripples setting off for the stars, where they find redemption in being of use to the human race. [JC]

WALLACE, IAN Pseudonym of John Wallace Pritchard (1912-   ), US clinical psychologist and teacher who spent his working life – from 1934 until his retirement in 1974 – in professional education. As a writer he has been active mainly since 1967, though under his own name he published some nonfiction in the 1940s and the non-sf *Every Crazy Wind* (**1952**).

Beginning with *Croyd* (**1967**), IW produced a remarkable series of sf novels, most of them more or less closely linked to a common background about 500 years hence, though the baroque contortions of his storylines tend to obliterate any sustained sense of continuity and often to make it very difficult to determine the precise era of the tale in question. This freewheeling dreamlike arbitrariness – as well as a startlingly inept sense of dialogue – has caused him more than once to be likened to A.E. VAN VOGT, though a sharp sense of humour has always been evident in IW's work. The common background to his books has a Solar System that dominates a large group of planets. Various ALIEN creatures – some godlike – participate in and impinge upon this central system. Transcendental TIME PARADOXES and loops abound, as do all the other appurtenances of the more intricate sort of SPACE OPERA, including HEROES.

Of the 2 series sharing this background, the **St Cyr Interplanetary Detective** sequence is the more approachable. The individual titles – *The Purloined Prince* (**1971**) set in AD2470 (although this and other dates, while provided in the texts, are of little help in tales involving TIME PARADOXES and the like), *Deathstar Voyage* (**1969**) set in AD2475, and *The Sign of the Mute Medusa* (**1977**) set in AD2480 – tend like most detective novels to accept the nature of the world as a given and to concentrate upon problem-solving

plots. Each book features Claudine St Cyr, an ace officer whose missions embroil her in complicated dilemmas on various planets; TIME TRAVEL is not eschewed, but is kept relatively straightforward. Of greater interest – but more taxing – is the **Croyd** sequence, comprising by order of event *Z-Sting* (**1979**), set in AD2475, *Heller's Leap* (**1979**), set in AD2494 and involving St Cyr, *Croyd*, set in AD2496, *Dr Orpheus* (**1968**), set in AD2502, *A Voyage to Dari* (**1974**), set in AD2506, *Pan Sagittarius* (**1973**), set in AD2509, and *Megalomania* (**1989**), set subsequently. In the earlier-published volumes, IW generally managed to control his tendency to create heavy-handed exercises in what might be called Gamine Baroque; *Croyd* and *Dr Orpheus* are among the most exhilarating space-opera exercises of the post-WWII genre. Croyd himself, the effective ruler of the human worlds for much of the series, frequently has to withstand – or initiate – radical changes in the rules that ground the Universe, and as a result must constantly busy himself with matter of cosmogonic grandeur. In *Dr Orpheus*, for instance, he must combat a plot on the part of distant but approaching aliens desperate to implant their fertile eggs in humans. The aliens have, in an earlier time, given the egomaniacal Dr Orpheus the use of an IMMORTALITY drug, anagonon, which has the side-effect of forcing those who take it to obey anyone whom they intuitively recognize as their hierarchical better – e.g., Orpheus himself – and thus, according to the aliens' plan, the human race should now be ripe for implantation. Croyd's counteroffensive involves a great deal of paradoxical time travel, including a sojourn in ancient Greece. Even at its most exciting moments, the story is conveyed at a contemplative remove, permitting the reader to enjoy its intricacies with relative calm.

Of those books not identified with any series, only *The Rape of the Sun* (**1982**) seems clearly not to inhabit the basic and voluminous shared Universe. *The World Asunder* (**1976**) is connected to *Pan Sagittarius*, and *The Lucifer Comet* (**1980**), a successful tale, is attached by a tangle of strings to Croyd.

The dreamlike tone of IW's work is retrospective in effect, rather than wish-fulfilling as with Van Vogt; it is only when this central calm declines to something approaching indifference – however laced with mysticism and occult plot turns – that IW's novels become inconseqential. [JC]

See also: BLACK HOLES; CRIME AND PUNISHMENT; GALACTIC EMPIRES.

WALLACE, JAMES ◊ G.J. BARRETT.

WALLACE, KING (?   -?   ) US writer whose sf novel, *The Next War: A Prediction* (**1892**), not untypically for its time and place of origin, plays on White fears of Negro uprisings. After failing to poison all US Whites, the Blacks lose the ensuing rebellion and disperse into the hinterlands, where they become extinct. [JC]

See also: POLITICS.

WALLEY, BRYON S. [s] ◊ Orson Scott CARD.

WALLING, WILLIAM (HERBERT) (1926-   ) US writer whose sf novel is *No One Goes There Now* (**1971**), in which a distorted human culture on a colony planet finds itself confronting ALIENS who will not abide our games of violence. He is not to be confused with William A. Walling, an academic critic, one of whose books is referred to under Mary SHELLEY.   [JC]

WALLIS, B. [r] ◊ George C. WALLIS.

WALLIS, DAVE (1917-   ) UK writer, possibly pseudonymous, of the near-future DYSTOPIAN fantasy *Only Lovers Left Alive* (**1964**), in which the mass suicide of the adult population leaves teenagers on their own in what rapidly becomes an anarchic UK. The book expressed contemporary PARANOIA about scooter gangs, adolescent violence, teen sex, loud music and funny hairstyles, yet, significantly, retained faith in the fundamental decency of human beings: it was not wholly pessimistic.   [JC/JGr]

See also: BOYS' PAPERS.

WALLIS, GEORGE C. (1871-1956) UK writer, printer (before WWI) and cinema manager who began writing sf and historical and adventure fiction in 1896 for the penny weekly adult magazines and then, from the turn of the century, for the "slick" magazines. Around 1903 he began to write almost exclusively for the BOYS' PAPERS, ceasing around 1912. With the genesis of GENRE-SF magazines in the 1920s he began to write again, with "The World at Bay" as by B. and G.C. Wallis (the "B" was his cousin and literary agent) for *AMZ* (**1928**). During 1938-41 he had 9 SPACE OPERAS published in *Tales of Wonder*.

Only 3 of his early sf and fantasy novels were reprinted as books: *Children of the Sphinx* (**1901**), a historical fantasy set in Egypt, *A Corsair of the Sky* (1910-11 *Lot-O'-Fun*; **1912**) as by Royston Heath, in which an airborne pirate declares war on the world, and *Beyond the Hills of Mist* (1912 *Lot-O'-Fun*; **1913**), in which a Tibetan lost race (◊ LOST WORLDS), equipped with aircraft, plans world domination. Other early novels, some in serial form, were "The Last King of Atlantis" (1896-7 *Short Stories*), in which an ancient MS describing the destruction of ATLANTIS is found in a UTOPIAN world of the future, "The World Wreckers" (1908 *Scraps*), a future-WAR story influenced by George GRIFFITH, "The Terror from the South" (1909 *Comic Life*), in which an Antarctic lost race becomes belligerent, and "Wireless War" (1909 *Comic Life*), with A.J. Andrews, another future-war novel. GCW also published at least 7 sf short stories 1896-1904, including "The Last Days of Earth: Being the Story of the Launching of the 'Red Sphere'" (1901 *The Harmsworth Magazine*), an END-OF-THE-WORLD tale set in AD13,000,000, and "The Great Sacrifice" (1903 *The London Magazine*), in which benevolent Martians save us from ourselves.

GCW was probably the only Victorian sf writer to continue to publish after WWII. His last novel was *The Call of Peter Gaskell* (**1947**), in which yet another lost race, this time Incan, plots to conquer the world.

He is interesting not as a good writer but because he so exactly typifies the themes of Victorian sf and the longevity of their sales appeal.   [JE/PN]

See also: FAR FUTURE; SUN.

WALLIS, G(ERALDINE JUNE) McDONALD Writing name of US writer and actress Hope Campbell (1925-   ), who acted under her own name and as Kathy McDonald, and has written non-sf under her own name and as Virginia Hughes, concentrating on juveniles. *The Light of Lilith* (**1961** dos) and *Legend of Lost Earth* (**1963** dos), both as by GMW, are unremarkable but adequately stirring examples of adventure sf. Both are set initially on other planets but focus, in the end, on a threatened or desirable Earth.   [JC]

WALSH, J(AMES) M(ORGAN) (1897-1952) Australian-born writer who moved to the UK; he wrote primarily mystery stories, some as by Stephen Maddock. His *Vandals of the Void* (**1931**), its sequel, "The Struggle for Pallas" (1931 *Wonder Stories Quarterly*), and *Vanguard to Neptune* (1932 *Wonder Stories Quarterly*; **1952**) are fairly routine early SPACE OPERAS, the first of which sees an attack by MERCURY on Venus, Mars and Earth. *The Secret of the Crater* (**1930**) as by H. Haverstock Hill (**1939**) has fantasy elements; the *AMZ* serial "The Terror out of Space" (1934) is also as by Hill.   [PN]

Other works: *Secret Weapons* (**1940**).

See also: AUSTRALIA; OUTER PLANETS; PUBLISHING.

WALTER, W(ILLIAM) GREY (1910-1977) UK writer and pioneer, between 1936 and 1956, of the development and use of electroencephalography in the UK; his early popular study, *The Living Brain* (**1953**), was influential in its time. His sf novel, *Further Outlook* (**1956**; vt *The Curve of the Snowflake* 1956 US), affords illustrative, fundamentally OPTIMISTIC views of future HISTORY up to AD2056 through the use of a TIME MACHINE.   [JC]

WALTERS, GORDON [s] ◊ George LOCKE.

WALTERS, HUGH Pseudonym of UK writer Walter Llewellyn Hughes (1910-   ) for his fiction, all CHILDREN'S SF, and all restricted for many years to his **Chris Godfrey of U.N.E.X.A.** sequence of interplanetary adventures: *Blast Off at Woomera* (**1957**; vt *Blast Off at 0300* 1958 US), *The Domes of Pico* (**1958**; vt *Menace from the Moon* 1959 US), *Operation Columbus* (**1960**; vt *First on the Moon* 1960 US), *Moon Base One* (**1961**; vt *Outpost on the Moon* 1962 US), *Expedition Venus* (**1962**), *Destination Mars* (**1963**), *Terror by Satellite* (**1964**), *Journey to Jupiter* (**1965**), *Mission to Mercury* (**1965**), *Spaceship to Saturn* (**1967**), *The Mohole Mystery* (**1968**; vt *The Mohole Menace* 1969 US), *Nearly Neptune* (**1969**; vt *Neptune One is Missing* 1970 US), *First Contact?* (**1971**), *Passage to Pluto* (**1973**), *Tony Hale, Space Detective* (**1973**), *Murder on Mars* (**1975**), *Boy Astronaut* (**1977** chap), *The Caves of Drach* (**1977**), *The Last Disaster* (**1978**), *The Blue Aura* (**1979**), *First Family on the Moon* (**1979**), *The Dark Triangle* (**1981**) and *School on the Moon* (**1981**). Chris Godfrey starts as a boy, but grows up and advances through the ranks of U.N.E.X.A. – the United Nations Exploration Agency, the "organization responsible for the exploration of the Universe" – until he becomes Director, from which point he supervises younger characters, like the mechanic Tony Hale, who dominate the action of later books. [JC]

Other works: *P-K* (**1986**).

See also: MERCURY.

WALTHER, DANIEL (1940-   ) French editor and writer who began publishing short stories in 1965, and proved an eclectic author and easy stylist who could switch from HARD SF to HEROIC FANTASY. *Requiem pour demain* ["Requiem for Tomorrow"] (coll **1976**) shows him at his most experimental, gathering work which reminded critics of Harlan ELLISON; *Les Quatre Saisons de la Nuit* ["The Four Seasons of the Night"] (coll **1980**) assembles dark fantasies. *Mais l'espace . . . Mais le temps* ["What about Space? What about Time?"] (**1972**) is a long novella blending space technology and MAGIC. He ed *Les soleils noirs d'Arcadie* ["Black Suns of Arcadia"] (anth **1975**), a manifesto for the NEW WAVE. His first novel, *L'Épouvante* ["Dread"] (**1979**) remains untranslated; "The Gunboat Dread", the story from which it was derived, appeared in Maxim JAKUBOWSKI's *Travelling towards Epsilon* (anth **1976**). As the editor of the Club du Livre d'Anticipation he published US heroic fantasy in translation, including work by C.J. CHERRYH, who reciprocated by bringing the early vols of his FAR-FUTURE **Swa** sequence to the USA. *Le Livre de Swa* (**1982**; trans Cherryh as *The Book of Shai* **1984** US) and *Le Destin de Swa* (**1982**; trans Cherryh as *Shai's Destiny* **1985** US) are intricately composed post-HOLOCAUST dramas of some moral complexity in which young Swa (Shai) confronts and attempts to bring together the various raging factions of a balkanized world. [MJ/JC]

See also: FRANCE.

WALTON, BRYCE (1918-1988) US writer, prolific under his own name and others in several genres, including tv work. He wrote some sf as Paul Franklin, Kenneth O'Hara and Dave Sands, though his first story, "The Ultimate World" for *Planet Stories* in 1945, was as BW. He contributed actively to the magazines until about 1960, less frequently thereafter. *Sons of the Ocean Deeps* (**1952**) faces a failed space cadet with the chance to mature in the benthos, which he grippingly does. [JC]

WANDREI, DONALD (1908-1987) US writer and editor, founder with August DERLETH in 1939 of ARKHAM HOUSE, formed initially to publish the work of H.P. LOVECRAFT, whom both admired deeply. DW resigned his interest in the firm after WWII – when he also stopped writing new fiction – and after Derleth's death in 1971 declined to resume it. As a writer he was justifiably best known for his FANTASY and weird stories, beginning with "The Red Brain" (1927 *Weird Tales*), a tale that incorporates a bungled sf premise about the nature of matter into a narrative whose deepest effect is one of chill horror at the cosmos. Later sf work, much of it in *ASF* in the 1930s, is similarly compounded of disparate ingredients,

and the tales assembled in the posthumous *Colossus: The Collected Science Fiction of Donald Wandrei* (coll **1989**) share the sense of the grotesqueness of the world espoused in that first story. In addition to some unremarkable verse, gathered in *Ecstasy and Other Poems* (coll **1928** chap), *Dark Odyssey* (coll **1931** chap) and *Poems for Midnight* (coll **1965**), he published a collection of fantasy, *The Eye and the Finger* (coll **1944**), a Lovecraftian **Cthulhu Mythos** tale, *The Web of Easter Island* (**1948**) – probably his finest single work, making, as usual in DW's work, opportunistic use of sf devices (in this case travel between the DIMENSIONS) to colour the horror – and *Strange Harvest* (coll **1965**). With Derleth he selected the contents of the first Arkham House Lovecraft collections and ed 3 vols of Lovecraft's *Selected Letters: 1911-1924* (coll **1965**), *1925-1929* (coll **1968**), and *1929-1931* (coll **1971**).

DW's brother, Howard Wandrei (1909-1956), was an illustrator and the author of some fantasy stories under his own name, and as by Robert Coley and H.W. Guernsey. [JC]

See also: ASTOUNDING SCIENCE-FICTION; COSMOLOGY; END OF THE WORLD; GREAT AND SMALL; PARALLEL WORLDS; SMALL PRESSES AND LIMITED EDITIONS.

WANDREI, HOWARD [r] ◊ Donald WANDREI.

WAR One of the principal imaginative stimuli to futuristic and scientific speculation has been the possibility of war, and the possibility that new TECHNOLOGY might transform war. This stimulus was particularly important during the period 1870-1914 and in the years following the revelation of the atom bomb in 1945.

Antique futuristic fictions such as the anonymous *Reign of George VI, 1900-25* (**1763**) anticipate little change in the business of war; here King George, sabre in hand, leads his cavalry in the charge. In the mid-19th century, however, awareness of technological change spread rapidly. Herrmann LANG was able to envisage very different patterns of future combat in *The Air Battle* (**1859**), and many new technologies were displayed during the US Civil War (1861-5) and observed by representatives of various European nations. When the German Empire was consolidated after the Franco-Prussian War of 1870 the strength and firepower of the new German Army inspired an urgent campaign for the reform and rearmament of the British Army. The case was dramatized by Sir George CHESNEY in *The Battle of Dorking* (**1871** chap), a drama-documentary illustrating the ease with which an invading German army might reach London. It caused a sensation, and initiated a debate which continued until WWI itself broke out (◊ INVASION). A new subgenre of fiction had been inaugurated, and future-war stories were established as a brand of popular romance; the development of the subgenre, well documented in I.F. CLARKE's *Voices Prophesying War, 1763-1984* (**1966**), featured such successful alarmist works as Erskine CHILDERS's *The Riddle of the Sands* (**1903**) and William LE QUEUX's *The Invasion of 1910* (**1906**), which made a great impact when it was serialized in the newborn *Daily Mail*. Many products of this glut of jingoistic fiction enthusiastically embraced the myth of a war to end war – enthusiastically mapped out in Louis TRACY's *The Final War* (**1896**) – and the popularity of this kind of fiction helped to generate the great enthusiasm which Britons carried into the real war against Germany when it finally came. The great bulk of this fiction was relatively mundane, envisaging quite modest alterations in tactics as a result of new TECHNOLOGY. *The Captain of the Mary Rose* (**1892**) by W. Laird Clowes (1856-1905), *Blake of the Rattlesnake* (**1895**) by Fred T. JANE and "Danger!" (**1914**) by Arthur Conan DOYLE are outstanding examples of the realistic school of speculation; and the most careful of them all, *The Great War of 189 – : A Forecast* (**1893**) by P.H. Colomb (1831-1899) and other military experts, instituted a tradition of drama-documentaries subsequently carried forward by Hector C. BYWATER's *The Great Pacific War* (**1925**) and, much later, *The Third World War* (**1979**) by General Sir John HACKETT and others.

Airships and submarines were by far the most popular innovations in early future-war fiction. They were displayed to lavish effect by George GRIFFITH, the most extravagant of the subgenre's writers, in *The Angel of the Revolution* (**1893**) and *Olga Romanoff* (**1894**). The discovery of X-rays in 1895 encouraged writers to dream up more fanciful new WEAPONS; in Griffith's posthumously published *The Lord of Labour* (**1911**), the future war is fought with atomic missiles and disintegrator rays. The worst excesses of this subgenre are parodied in Michael MOORCOCK's *The Warlord of the Air* (**1971**) and *The Land Leviathan* (**1974**); Moorcock also edited a notable theme anthology of works from the period, published in 2 vols as *Before Armageddon* (anth **1975**) and *England Invaded* (anth **1977**). An ambitious but reasonably disciplined imagination was brought to bear by H.G. WELLS in "The Land Ironclads" (1903), *The War in the Air* (**1908**) and the atom-bomb story *The World Set Free* (**1914**). The British High Command, however, continued to the bitter end to show an extreme conservatism of imagination, refusing to believe in the potential of the tank, the submarine or the aeroplane until they were shown the way by the Germans.

Future-war stories enjoyed a second heyday in the UK between the Wars, when the actual example of WWI caused many writers to believe that a new war might mean the end of civilization – a conviction bleakly expressed by Edward SHANKS in *The People of the Ruins* (**1920**) and Cicely HAMILTON in *Theodore Savage* (**1922**). This kind of anxiety intensified in such novels as Neil BELL's *The Gas War of 1940* (**1931** as Miles; vt *Valiant Clay* 1934 as NB) and John GLOAG's *Tomorrow's Yesterday* (**1932**), and became almost hysterical as Europe lurched towards a new war following Hitler's rise to power (*see also* HITLER WINS). *Invasion from the Air: A Prophetic Novel* (**1934**) by Frank McIlraith and Roy CONNOLLY, *Day of Wrath* (**1936**) by Joseph O'NEILL and *Four Days War* (**1936**) by S. Fowler

WRIGHT all feature chilling accounts of cities devastated by aerial bombing with poison gas.

US future-war fiction was not so prolific, nor – understandably, in view of the USA's very different experience of WWI – did it ever become so pessimistic. Frank R. STOCKTON's *The Great War Syndicate* (**1889**) and Stanley WATERLOO's *Armageddon* (**1898**) are mild by comparison with contemporary UK works, and the invasion of the USA by Asiatics, although a staple of pulp melodrama, never really seemed likely enough to inspire genuine alarmist fantasy. The bleakest visions of future war written in the USA before 1945 – Herbert BEST's *The Twenty-Fifth Hour* (**1940**) and L. Ron HUBBARD's *Final Blackout* (**1940**; **1948**) – both describe the devastation of Europe. This situation changed dramatically, however, with the advent of the atom bomb, which bred an alarmism all of its own and inspired a new subgenre of stories concerning the HOLOCAUST AND AFTER.

Wells's *The War of the Worlds* (**1898**) was a logical extension of the more conventional 19th-century future-war story, as was Robert William COLE's story of colonial war against Sirian aliens in *The Struggle for Empire* (**1900**), but the other-worldly wars fought in most pulp interplanetary romance of the Edgar Rice BURROUGHS school were mostly fought with swords. The specialist sf pulps, however, embraced a more conscientiously futuristic outlook whereby interplanetary wars were to be fought by fleets of SPACESHIPS armed with marvellous ray-guns and the like. SPACE OPERA thrived on wars between races, worlds and GALACTIC EMPIRES. Wherever its HEROES went they found cosmic conflicts in progress, and they never felt inhibited about joining in. Such was the moral insight of pulp fantasists that these heroes hardly ever had the slightest difficulty in selecting the "right" side: it was handsome and honourable vs ugly and treacherous.

The quest to discover bigger and more powerful weapons was driven to its limits in a few short years. Spectacular genocide became commonplace, as in Edmond HAMILTON's "The Other Side of the Moon" (1929), and stars were blown up in prolific quantity. War waged across time between ALTERNATE WORLDS was invented by Jack WILLIAMSON in *The Legion of Time* (**1938**; **1952**). Anti-war stories like Miles J. BREUER's "The Gostaks and the Doshes" (1930) and Nat SCHACHNER's "World Gone Mad" (1935) were in a tiny minority until the outbreak of war in Europe in 1939 helped encourage a new seriousness, most conscientiously displayed in John W. CAMPBELL Jr's ASTOUNDING SCIENCE-FICTION, where A.E. VAN VOGT began chronicling *The War Against the Rull* (1940-50; fixup **1959**). Ross ROCKLYNNE's "Quietus" (1940) made an issue of the dilemma which had been so easily sidestepped in the past: when visitors from elsewhere find two creatures locked in conflict, how do they choose which to help? After WWII, anti-war stories appeared far more frequently in the sf magazines; notable are several stories by Eric Frank RUSSELL, including "Late Night Final" (1948) and "I am Nothing" (1952), and several by Fritz LEIBER, including "The Foxholes of Mars" (1952) and "A Bad Day for Sales" (1953). More ironic approaches to the question include several stories in which war has become institutionalized as a spectator sport (◊ GAMES AND SPORTS), such as *Gunner Cade* (1952) by Cyril Judd (C.M. KORNBLUTH and Judith MERRIL) and Mack REYNOLDS's *Mercenary from Tomorrow* (1962 as "Mercenary"; exp 1968). Sf writers' reflections on WWII itself are assembled in *The Fantastic World War II* (anth 1990) ed Frank McSherry Jr and S.M. STIRLING, while notable stories of nuclear war are collected in *Countdown to Midnight* (anth 1984) ed H. Bruce FRANKLIN.

Although the possibility of future wars on Earth and images of nuclear holocaust dominated the imagination of sf writers from 1945 through the 1950s, more exotic wars continued to be fought, and stories of interplanetary or interstellar war became a safer haven for militaristic adventures. The melodramatic excesses of space-opera warfare faded with the pulps, although they never entirely died out, and there grew up a more disciplined and more realistic notion of the kind of armies which might fight interplanetary and interstellar wars, and the kinds of weapons they might use. In this context a new tradition of militaristic sf grew up in the 1950s and 1960s, notable early examples being Robert A. HEINLEIN's *Starship Troopers* (1959) and Gordon R. DICKSON's *The Genetic General* (1960; exp vt *Dorsai!* 1976). The latter began the long-running **Dorsai** series, which aspires to offer a serious commentary on the evolution and ethics of militarism and is still being extended through such novels as *The Chantry Guild* (1988). Other important early contributors to this tradition include Poul ANDERSON, as in *The Star Fox* (fixup 1965); it was most aggressively carried forward through the 1970s by Jerry POURNELLE in such novels as *A Spaceship for the King* (1973) and *The Mercenary* (1977). The initial historical context of this fiction was provided by the Korean War, where the intervention of UN troops embodied a new philosophy of military action and responsibility, but doubts about the role played by US forces were subsequently amplified in no uncertain terms by the progress of the Vietnam War. Ideas about the moral justifiability of war and the POLITICS of militarism became matters of fierce debate, exemplified in sf by such novels as Joe HALDEMAN's *The Forever War* (fixup 1974), clearly modelled on *Starship Troopers* but overturning many of the assumptions the earlier novel had taken for granted, and Norman SPINRAD's vivid and vitriolic *The Men in the Jungle* (1967). Spinrad went on to write *The Iron Dream* (1972), in which the fascist fantasies of one Adolf Hitler, who emigrated to the USA in the early 1930s and became a minor sf writer, superimpose all the CLICHÉS of pulp future-war fantasies on the rise of the Third Reich, the fighting of WWII and the "final solution" to the problem of the insidious "Dominators". The most successful mainstream anti-war novel

of the 1960s, Joseph Heller's *Catch-22* (1961), influenced sf stories like Barry N. MALZBERG's "Final War" (1968 as K.M. O'Donnell), which represents war as a surreal and purposeless nightmare.

The polarization of the sf community by the political conflict over the Vietnam War was vividly illustrated by a pair of advertisements which appeared in GALAXY SCIENCE FICTION in the mid-1960s, which listed on facing pages those sf writers for and against the War. Memories of that war have continued to haunt sf, directly reflected in such anthologies as *In the Field of Fire* (anth 1987) ed Jeanne Van Buren Dann and Jack DANN and such novels as *The Healer's War* (1988) by Elizabeth Ann Scarborough (1947-   ) and *Dream Baby* (1989) by Bruce McALLISTER, and indirectly in such novels as Lucius SHEPARD's *Life during Wartime* (1987). Alongside these works, however, the tradition of militaristic sf has not only flourished since the Vietnam War's end but has become extraordinarily strident. David A. DRAKE, author of several horror stories reflecting his own experiences in Vietnam, has written numerous books about the heroic exploits of future mercenaries, including the **Hammer's Slammers** sequence: *Hammer's Slammers* (coll of linked stories 1979), *The Forlorn Hope* (1984), *Rolling Hot* (1989) and *The Warrior* (1991). These books helped initiate a fad that has been extrapolated in various anthologies and SHARED-WORLD series and in novels such as *The Warrior's Apprentice* (1986) and its sequels by Lois McMaster BUJOLD. Other fiercely militaristic sf novels of the 1980s include Christopher ANVIL's *The Steel, the Mist and the Blazing Sun* (1983) and Joel ROSENBERG's Zionist *Not for Glory* (1988). The annual series of anthologies begun with *There Will Be War* (anth 1983) ed Pournelle and John F. CARR, following Reginald BRETNOR's earlier anthology series **The Future at War** (3 vols 1979-80), has generated some controversy. This subgenre has merged with and absorbed various older materials, including Fred SABERHAGEN's **Berserker** series begun in 1963 and the episode in Larry NIVEN's **Known Space** future history expanded for **The Man-Kzin Wars** SHARED-WORLD series (3 vols 1988-90). Although the popularity of this kind of fiction can be largely accounted for simply as a love of melodrama, it does seem to reflect an innate aggression in US culture – a concept discussed at some length by H. Bruce Franklin in his excellent study of war as a theme in US imaginative fiction, *War Stars: The Superweapon and the American Imagination* (1988). [BS]

WARD, E.D. ◊ E.V. LUCAS.

WARD, HENRY (1913?-   ) Perhaps a pseudonym of a French writer – possibly Henri Louis Luc Viard (1921-   ) as Donald H. TUCK claims. HW's sf novels are *L'enfer est dans le ciel* (trans Alan Neame as *Hell's Above Us* 1960) and *Les soleils verts* (1956; trans Neame as *The Green Suns* 1961). The latter book contains a detailed biography of HW in the introduction, claiming that he is a scientist educated at Cambridge in the UK and then Columbia in the USA, that at the request of the State Department he liaised between atomic research units in France and the USA in 1939-40 (which Viard at age 18 could not have done), and that he was later connected with the destruction of the V-Bomb centre at Peenemünde. However, this information may be a hoax to lend verisimilitude to the two books, both documentary-style thrillers involving conspiracy at high political levels involved with the investigation of implausible sf events *vis à vis* the space programme, aliens, the Suez conflict and PARALLEL WORLDS. HW appears as a character in both. [PN]

WARD, HERBERT D(ICKINSON) (1861-1932) US writer, most of whose short stories of sf interest were political dramas whose venues were only marginally displaced from the late-19th-century USA, even though some of the tales assembled in *A Republic Without a President, and Other Stories* (coll **1891**) were ostensibly set 100 years hence. *The White Crown, and Other Stories* (coll **1894**) continued in the same vein, though the title story itself is a future-WAR tale of some interest. [JC]

Other works: *The Master of the Magicians* (**1890**) with Elizabeth Stuart Phelps; *A Dash to the Pole: A Tale of Adventure in the Ice-Bound North* (**1895**).

WAR GAME, THE Made-for-tv film (1965). BBC/Pathé Contemporary. Prod/dir/written Peter WATKINS. Narrators Michael Aspel, Dick Graham. 50 mins, cut to 47 mins. B/w.

This pseudo-documentary about a nuclear attack on England and its aftermath in a small town in Kent was refused a showing by BBC TV, though made for them, on the grounds that it was too realistic and might disturb audiences – as it was designed to do. Since then it has had a wide theatrical release and won an Oscar. Though clumsily made, it is full of shattering images: the glare and concussion of the bomb; the raging firestorms; the hideously disfigured casualties; torment and slow death from radiation poisoning; mass cremations; buckets of wedding rings gathered from the dead; and execution squads, composed of uniformed constables, shooting looters Its first UK tv showing was in 1987. [JB]

See also: CINEMA.

WARGAMES Film (1983). Sherwood Productions/MGM/UA. Dir John BADHAM, starring Matthew Broderick, Dabney Coleman, John Wood, Ally Sheedy, Barry Corbin. Screenplay Lawrence Lasker, Walter F. Parkes. 113 mins. Colour.

Teenager David (Broderick) attempts to use his computer to hack into the programs of a computer-games manufacturer. Accidentally – after a week's research from which he deduces a secret password that will give him access to the system – he breaks into WOPR, the giant Department of Defense computer with which the USA will, if necessary, direct the operations of WWIII. Unable to distinguish between game theory and real life, WOPR, in playing the game of Global Thermonuclear War with David, almost sets off Armageddon. The film is briskly

directed, with an ingenious first hour and so engaging a narrative sweep that the gaping logical holes in its plot may become evident only at a second viewing. It is in fact silly, not least for the crudely drawn character of Falken (Wood), WOPR's creator, who thinks we all deserve to die anyway (like the dinosaurs), and appears to change his mind only because David's girlfriend (Sheedy) is cute; the metaphor of WAR as video game is both amusing and tritely reductive, and became an sf CLICHÉ in the 1980s (◊ CYBERSPACE). Badham is a good action director whose films often collapse into ethical confusion on any examination of their superficially liberal credentials.

The novelization is *WarGames* * (**1983**) by David F. BISCHOFF. [PN]

See also: CINEMA; VIRTUAL REALITY.

WARHOON US FANZINE (1952-85), ed from New York and Puerto Rico by Richard Bergeron. From undistinguished early issues, *W* became a large, attractive, duplicated fanzine containing careful and literate articles on sf and FANDOM. John BAXTER, James BLISH and Robert A.W. LOWNDES were among the regular sf columnists, and Terry CARR, Bob SHAW, Harry WARNER Jr and Walt Willis were fan columnists. Occasional contributors included Robert BLOCH, Harlan ELLISON and Ted WHITE. In 1980 (though dated 1978), 10 years after #27, #28 was published; this was a 600+pp hardbound collection of the writings of Willis since 1947. It was almost certainly the largest fanzine issue ever published, its size being the reason for the hiatus. There were 3 further issues to June 1985. In 1962 *W* won a HUGO as Best Fanzine. [PR/RH]

WARLAND, ALLEN [s] ◊ Donald A. WOLLHEIM.

WARNER, HARRY (BACKER) Jr (1922-   ) US journalist and sf fan, publisher of several FANZINES, including *Spaceways* and the long-lived *Horizons*, which has appeared regularly in FAPA since 1939. His history of sf FANDOM, *All Our Yesterdays* (**1969**), is an affectionate and thorough examination of individuals, fan organizations and fanzines in the 1940s. The 2nd part, *A Wealth of Fable* (3 vols, mimeographed **1976**), continues the history through the 1950s. HW won HUGOS as Best Fan Writer in 1969 and 1972. [PR]

WARNER, REX (1905-1986) UK writer and translator who remains best known for his earliest adult novels, *The Wild Goose Chase* (**1937**), *The Professor* (**1938**) and *The Aerodrome* (**1941**), political allegories some of whose devices relate to the KAFKA-esque side of sf (◊ ABSURDIST SF; FABULATION). In *The Wild Goose Chase* 3 brothers bicycle into a strange country in search of the eponymous goose, and encounter and participate in a revolution – which ultimately they cause to triumph – in a DYSTOPIAN society. *The Aerodrome* depicts within the allegorical confines of an aerodrome an attempt at violently remoulding human nature. *Why Was I Killed?* (**1943**; vt *Return of the Traveller* 1944 US) is an afterlife fantasy. RW was always clear about which side he stood on in these metaphysical conflicts, a didactic sidedness which sometimes quite evidently detracted from the

imaginative power of his fiction.   [JC]
See also: HISTORY OF SF.

WAR OF THE COLOSSAL BEAST ◊ *The* AMAZING COLOSSAL MAN.

WAR OF THE MONSTERS ◊ GOJIRA.

WAR OF THE SATELLITES ◊ Roger CORMAN.

WAR OF THE WORLDS 1. US RADIO play (30 October 1938). Part of the *Mercury Theatre on the Air* series of plays, *WOTW* was the most famous broadcast ever made; an adaptation by Howard Koch of H.G. WELLS's 1898 novel, it was produced by and starred Orson Welles (1915-1985), who gained immediate notoriety when a huge number of listeners believed that the play represented a live newscast of an actual INVASION from MARS. *The Invasion from Mars: A Study in the Psychology of Panic, with the Complete Script of the Famous Orson Welles Broadcast* (**1940**) by Hadley Cantril reports on a series of interviews begun by Princeton University a week after the broadcast, confirming that the panic was surprisingly widespread (Cantril estimates that well over a million listeners – more than 10% of the total audience tuned in – were actively frightened by the broadcast); but also demonstrates, by reprinting the original script, that neither Koch nor Welles could have intended to hoax the radio public. Though it was indeed presented in the form of a series of emergency newscasts, dramatic devices (the passage of hours, for instance, in a few minutes of radio time) were conspicuous even during the first half of the broadcast, which caused the most panic; the second half, after a brief programme break, was set several days later. A made-for-tv movie giving a somewhat exaggerated account of the night's events is *The* NIGHT THAT PANICKED AMERICA (1975), and what has become a national myth has been incorporated in several other films, including *The* ADVENTURES OF BUCKAROO BANZAI ACROSS THE 8TH DIMENSION (1984) and SPACED INVADERS (1989). In 1991 the original play was broadcast on BBC radio.   [JC/PN]

2. Film (1953). Paramount. Prod George PAL. Dir Byron HASKIN, starring Gene Barry, Ann Robinson, Les Tremayne. Screenplay Barré Lyndon, based on *The War of the Worlds* (**1898**) by H.G. WELLS. 85 mins. Colour.

Few details of Wells's novel remain. Following the success Welles had had in updating the story in 1938, the setting is changed to 1950s California. The Martian war machines are altered from walking tripods to flying saucers shaped (rather beautifully) like manta rays. A stereotyped Hollywood love interest is substituted for the original story of a husband searching for his wife. Despite indifferent performances, the film is well paced and generates considerable excitement, partly through the spectacular special effects, which cost $1,400,000. The wires supporting the war machines are too often visible, but as a whole the effects – Gordon Jennings was in charge – are very impressive, especially in the final attack on Los Angeles: the manta-shaped vehicles gliding down the streets with their snake-like heat-ray projectors blasting the surrounding buildings into rubble are among the great icons of sf CINEMA. The dazed conservatism of the human response to the Martians is true to Wells, as is the subtext suggesting that a retreat into religious piety is also an inadequate answer, though here Pal has it both ways: we are told that it was "God in his wisdom" who created the microbes that ultimately defeat the invasion. *WOTW* is George Pal's most successful film production.

3. US tv series (1988-90). Ten-Four/Paramount, for syndication. Created Greg Strangis. Executive prods Sam Strangis, Greg Strangis. Prod Jonathan Hackett, starring Jared Martin, Lynda Mason Green, Philip Akin, Richard Chaves. Dirs included Colin Chilvers, Herbert Wright, Neill Fearnley, Armand Mastroianni, William Fruet. Writers included Greg Strangis, Tom Lazarus, Patrick Barry, D.C. FONTANA, Durnford King. 2 seasons; 100min pilot plus 41 50min episodes. Colour.

The pilot episode, *The Resurrection*, tells us that the events described in the 1953 film were followed by a government hush-up and the storage of Martian bodies in barrels at a military base. A terrorist attack on the base breaches some barrels, and the Martians (no longer identified as such, now just vague ALIENS) come back to life (the microbes did not kill them but threw them into estivation, and have now been destroyed by radioactivity). They adopt the bodies of the terrorists. (Shapeshifting was not an alien skill in the earlier versions; *WOTW* borrows heavily from the tv series *The* INVADERS [1967-8], and the films of INVASION OF THE BODY SNATCHERS [1955, 1978].) Their human bodies damaged, so that they look like zombie refugees from NIGHT OF THE LIVING DEAD (1968), the aliens again attempt to conquer the world, initially by jumping out at people and grabbing them with big flabby hands. Our heroes (male scientist, pretty female microbiologist, wisecracking Black man in wheelchair) have trouble convincing the powers-that-be that the aliens even exist, the destruction of Los Angeles three decades earlier having apparently gone unnoticed. The series had vigour if nothing else, and continued for 2 seasons with the usual variants on the INVASION theme. In season 2, now renamed *War of the Worlds: The Second Invasion*, the series eliminated some characters, added new ones, introduced alien-human miscegenation and made moral distinctions between good and bad aliens, but sagged anyway.   [PN]

See also: PARANOIA.

WAR OF THE WORLDS – NEXT CENTURY, THE ◊ POLAND.

WARP/WARPDRIVE/WARP FACTOR ◊ FASTER THAN LIGHT; SPACE WARP.

WARREN, BILL Working name of William Warren (1943-   ), sf fan and film buff, author with Allan Rothstein of the RECURSIVE SF murder mystery *Fandom is a Way of Death* (**1984** chap), set in and distributed at a World SF CONVENTION in Los Angeles. BW's extraordinarily useful and interesting film reference books, the most detailed and accurate available for the period, are *Keep Watching the Skies!: American Science Fiction Movies of the Fifties: Volume I: 1950-57* (**1982**) and *Volume II: 1958-62* (**1986**), on both of which he was assisted by Bill Thomas. They are not, despite the title, restricted to US films, but include many foreign films released in the US (◊ CINEMA). [PN]

WARREN, CHAD [r] ◊ ROBERT HALE LIMITED.

WARREN, GEORGE [r] ◊ Nick CARTER.

WARRICK, PATRICIA S(COTT) (1925-) US academic. Most of PSW's work has concentrated upon the themes explicated in the book version of her PhD thesis, *The Cybernetic Imagination in Science Fiction* (**1980**), supplemented by *Machines That Think: The Best Science Fiction Stories about Robots & Computers* (anth **1984**) with Isaac ASIMOV and Martin H. GREENBERG. In essays published from the mid-1970s, and in *Science Fiction: Contemporary Mythology* (anth **1978**) with Greenberg and Joseph D. OLANDER, she focused on the relationship between *Homo sapiens* and its CYBERNETIC offspring, a focus which led naturally to a concentration on the work of Philip K. DICK. After editing (with Greenberg) a collection of his work, *Robots, Androids, and Mechanical Oddities: The Science Fiction of Philip K. Dick* (coll **1984**), she examined his whole career in *Mind in Motion: The Fiction of Philip K. Dick* (**1987**), the most thorough study of his entire oeuvre yet published. [JC]

Other works: ◊ Martin H. GREENBERG for other team anthology productions with PSW under his general editorship.

See also: ANTHROPOLOGY; COMPUTERS; SOCIOLOGY.

WARRIORS OF THE WASTELAND ◊ George MILLER; 1990: I GUERRIERI DEL BRONX.

WASON, SANDYS (*c*1870-?) UK writer and – apparently – cleric whose sf novel, *Palafox* (**1927**), features an introduction by Compton MACKENZIE, a style mildly reminiscent of Ronald Firbank's, and a thought-reading machine. [JC]

WASP WOMAN, THE Film (1959). Filmgroup/Allied Artists. Prod/dir Roger CORMAN, starring Susan Cabot, Michael Mark. Screenplay Leo Gordon, based on a story by Kinta Zertuche. 73 mins. B/w.

One of Roger Corman's more routine efforts, this may have been rushed out to capitalize on the publicity received by *The* FLY (1958). Cabot plays well the ageing cosmetics executive who, in a successful attempt at rejuvenation, takes a form of royal jelly (from wasps not bees) prepared by loony apiarist Zinthrop (Mark). The side-effect is that she occasionally grows an unconvincing wasp's head and eats people. *TWW* is a shabby, rather unhorrifying film. [PN]

WATCHMEN Perhaps the most famous of all GRAPHIC NOVELS, written by Alan MOORE and illustrated by Dave GIBBONS. *W* appeared initially as a 12-part COMIC (Sept 1986-Oct 1987 *Watchmen*), each part corresponding to a chapter of the full novel, which was published as *Watchmen* (graph **1987** US; with additional material 1988 US). The initial premise is ingenious: given a late-1930s USA where costumed SUPERHEROES exist, maintaining law and order on a vigilante basis, what sort of ALTERNATE WORLD might develop by the mid-1980s? The changes suggested are subtle: a modest increase in the rate of scientific development; a Western dominance of the political scene; and an initial acceptance of the superhero coterie, followed by a period of repression. The story takes place in 1985, as members of the second generation of superheroes attempt to trace the person who is murdering them, one by one. At the same time, a number of signs are pointing towards imminent nuclear war (in fact, part of a secret plot to frighten the world out of nuclear madness), which some of the protagonists sense coming but which none of them know how to confront. An actual HOLOCAUST does take place, proving terminal for 2 million New Yorkers; but its effects prove ambiguously positive.

W offers a satirical analysis of the human cost of being (or needing) a superhero, and a portrait of the kind of world in which one might exist. It also provides, *en passant*, an extremely sharp analysis of the psychological makeup (and needs) of those who read superhero comics. Moreover, the densely packed narrative is perfectly conveyed through word and image – Moore was at the height of his powers as an innovative figure in commercial US comics publishing, and Gibbons was equally primed to generate a sophisticated visual language, through which subtexts and subplots might interweave with (as rereading makes evident) the utmost clarity. By subjecting the fantasy worlds inhabited by comic-strip superheroes to the estrangements of adult-sf scrutiny, *W* worked as a threnody for some of the more childish visions of omnipotence which had crippled the genre; and by rendering visible some sf conventions, it turned the tables, to a degree, on the scrutinizing medium. *W* is one of the central sf novels of the 1980s. [JC]

WATER, SILAS ◊ Noel LOOMIS.

WATERLOO, STANLEY (1846-1913) US writer whose first sf novel, *The Story of Ab: A Tale of the Time of the Cave Man* (**1897**; vt *A Tale of the Time of the Cave Men; Being the Story of Ab* 1904 UK), a juvenile whose hero acquires the necessary inventions and culture to begin the march to civilization, is among the earliest romances of ANTHROPOLOGY. Further novels were *Armageddon: A Tale of Love and Invention* (**1898**), in which an Anglo-US supremacy over the rest of the world is achieved through the use of an armoured dirigible in a near-future WAR; and *A Son of the Ages: The Reincarnations and Adventures of Scar, the Link: A Story of Man from the Beginning* (**1914**), which carries Scar, via a sequence of REINCARNATIONS, through various significant moments in history, including a visit to ATLANTIS. SW was a routine stylist with a good nose for structure and idea. [JC]

Other work: *The Wolf's Long Howl* (coll **1899**), containing some marginal sf tales.

See also: ORIGIN OF MAN.

WATERS, T(HOMAS) A. (1938-) US author who began writing sf with *Love that Spy!* (**1968**), a spoof TECHNOTHRILLER featuring a scientist named Niflheim who specializes in ultra-cold warfare. TAW's first sf of more orthodox interest was *The Probability Pad* (**1970**), a novel which concluded the trilogy begun in Chester ANDERSON's *The Butterfly Kid* (**1967**) and continued in Michael KURLAND's *The Unicorn Girl* (**1969**). This is a lightweight RECURSIVE tale involving the 3 authors as characters in Greenwich Village, along with a good deal of alien-inspired body duplication. A countercultural ethos also inspired the grimmer *Centerforce* (**1974**), in which motorcycle dropouts and commune dwellers combine in opposition to a NEAR-FUTURE police-state USA.   [JC]

WATKINS, PETER (1935-) UK tv and film director. Educated at Cambridge, PW worked in documentary films from 1959. He made a reputation with two quasidocumentaries for BBC TV, *Culloden* (**1964**) and *The* WAR GAME (**1965**). He was one of the pioneers of the technique of staging historical or imaginary events as if they were contemporary and undergoing tv-news coverage. *The* WAR GAME (**1965**) adopted a *cinéma-vérité* manner to simulate the likely consequences of nuclear attack on the UK, and did this horrifyingly enough for the film to be denied a screening on tv, for which it was made, until 1987; it was successful when released in the CINEMA. His next film, PRIVILEGE (**1966**), has a pop star used as a puppet by a future government in a cunning propaganda plan for the manipulation of the nation's youth. GLADIATORERNA (**1968**; vt *The Peace Game*), made in Sweden, and PUNISHMENT PARK (**1971**) are both set in the future, and both use stories of channelled violence to argue a pacifist case, the latter more plausibly. An interesting paradox is that, while his theme is normally the use of mind control by future governments to channel the aggressive instincts of the people, and his purpose is to generate moral indignation at this cynical curtailment of our freedom, his own work equally uses the illusion of fact to present a propaganda fiction. Whether knowingly or not, he is fighting fire with fire. After its initial success, PW's work has been treated less kindly by critics, who do not doubt his sincerity but deprecate his methods; it is felt by some that he has thumped the same tub for too long.   [PN]

WATKINS, WILLIAM JON (1942-) US writer and academic, associate professor of English at Brookdale Community College. His first sf novels, with Gene SNYDER, were *Ecodeath* (**1972**), a POLLUTION story in which the leading characters are called Snyder and Watkins and the plot is fast and furious, and *The Litany of Sh'reev* (**1976**), in which a healer with precognitive powers becomes involved in a revolution. WJW's solo books are similarly – and at times haphazardly – venturesome. *Clickwhistle* (**1973**) deals in a relatively sober vein with human/dolphin COMMUNICATION, but *The God Machine* (**1973**), in which

political dissidents shrink themselves with a "micronizer" to escape a mechanized future, is insecurely baroque. *What Rough Beast* (**1980**) pairs an altruistic ALIEN with a world-class computer net to save erring humanity. The **LeGrange League** sequence – *The Centrifugal Rickshaw Dancer* (**1985**) and *Going to See the End of the Sky* (**1986**) – is adventure sf whose settings, and quality of writing, are negatively affected by helterskelter plotting. *The Last Deathship off Antares* (**1989**) is a tale of real intrinsic interest; despite the failings characteristic of all his work, the philosophical arguments underpinning a revolt of imprisoned humans aboard a prison ship are sharply couched, and WJW never allows the grimness of the conflict to slide into routine. He remains, however, a writer whose ideas are perhaps more interesting to describe than to read.   [JC/PN]

See also: ECOLOGY.

WATSON, BILLY [s] ◊ Theodore STURGEON.

WATSON, H.B. MARRIOTT ◊ H.B. MARRIOTT-WATSON.

WATSON, HENRY CROCKER MARRIOTT ◊ Henry Crocker MARRIOTT-WATSON.

WATSON, IAN (1943-) UK writer and teacher who lectured in English in Tanzania (1965-7) and Tokyo (1967-70) before beginning to publish sf with "Roof Garden Under Saturn" for *NW* in 1969; he then taught Future Studies for 6 years at Birmingham Polytechnic, taking there one of the first academic courses in sf in the UK; he has been a full-time writer since 1976.

IW has published about 100 short stories, at a gradually increasing tempo and with visibly increased mastery over the form; his collections are *The Very Slow Time Machine* (coll **1979**), *Sunstroke* (coll **1982**), *Slow Birds* (coll **1985**), *The Book of Ian Watson* (coll **1985** US), *Evil Water* (coll **1987**), *Salvage Rites* (**1989**) and *Stalin's Teardrops* (coll **1991**). It is as a novelist, however, that he remains best known. His first novel, *The Embedding* (**1973**) won the Prix Apollo in 1975 in its French translation, *L'enchâssement*; although it is not necessarily his finest work, it remains the title by virtue of which his stature as an sf writer of powerful intellect – the natural successor to H.G. WELLS – is most generally asserted. Through a complex tripartite plot, the book engages in a searching analysis (◊ COMMUNICATIONS; LINGUISTICS; PERCEPTION) of the nature of communication through language; the Whorfian hypothesis that languages shape our perception of reality – a hypothesis very attractive, for obvious reasons, to sf writers – is bracingly embodied in at least two of the subplots: one describing a cruel experiment in which children are taught only an artificial language, and the other showing the ALIENS' attempt to understand *Homo sapiens* through an analysis of our modes of communication.

Again and again, IW's novels reveal themselves to be very much of a piece, a series of thought experiments which spiral outwards from the same central obsessions about the nature of perception, the quest for what might be called the True Names that describe ultimate realities, and the terrible cost to human beings – in betrayals and self-betrayals – of searching for transcendence. *The Jonah Kit* (**1975**), which won the BRITISH SCIENCE FICTION AWARD for 1978, describes the imprinting of human consciousness into whales, and the transcendental whiffs of alien INTELLIGENCES to which those consciousnesses become heir. *The Martian Inca* (**1977**) reverses the operation, as a transformative virus invades Earth. *Alien Embassy* (**1977**) foregrounds a constant IW preoccupation – his concern with the control of information and perception by the powers-that-be, generally governments – in a tale about the frustrated transformation of the human race. *Miracle Visitors* (**1978**) again combines speculations about perception and transcendence, in this case suggesting that UFOs work as enticements to focus human attention on higher states of communication. *God's World* (**1979**) reworks IW's ongoing concerns in yet another fashion, describing another ambivalent alien incursion, this time in the form of the "gift" of a stardrive which will take a selected team to the eponymous world, where they will undergo dangerous trans-figurations.

IW's first 6 novels, then, comprised a set of virtuoso variations on his central themes. His next, *The Gardens of Delight* (**1980**), conflates sf and fantasy to step sideways from the early work, describing a world whose transformative energies have resulted in an environment which precisely replicates the painting *The Garden of Earthly Delights* by Hieronymous Bosch (1460-1516). *Under Heaven's Bridge* (dated 1980 but **1981**), with Michael BISHOP, shows the flavour of the latter writer's mind as its protagonist investigates an alien culture in terms more relevant to ANTHROPOLOGY than IW would alone have been inclined to employ; from 1980 on, his novels tended to show a greater inventiveness in plot and style, and some even attempted humour, though the impatience of his quick mind does not often make for successful light moments. *Deathhunter* (**1981**) suggests that humans give off a pheromone-like signal at the point of death, which attracts Death himself in the form of a mothlike insect (◊ ESCHATOLOGY). *Chekhov's Journey* (**1983**), perhaps his least enticing novel through its entangle-ment in too large a cast (IW has never been a sharp delineator of character), revolves around the Tun-guska explosion of 1908. The **Black Current** trilogy – *The Book of the River* (fixup **1984**), *The Book of the Stars* (**1984**) and *The Book of Being* (**1985**), all assembled as *The Books of the Black Current* (omni **1986** US) – was his major 1980s effort; in a world divided by a mysterious and apparently sentient river into two utterly opposed halves, the heroine Yaleen suffers rites of passage, uprootings, rebirths and transcendental awakenings as she becomes more and more deeply involved in a final conflict between the Worm and the Godmind, the latter's intentions being deeply inimical to the

future of humanity. More expansive, and easier than his earlier books, the **Black Current** sequence has been, except for a tie (see listing below), IW's closest attempt to gain a wide readership.

Subsequent books are if anything even more varied. *Converts* (**1984**) is a brisk comedy about EVOLUTION and the misuse of power. *Queenmagic, Kingmagic* (**1986**) is a slightly over-perky FANTASY based on chess and other board games. *The Power* (**1987**) and *Meat* (**1988**) are horror. *Whores of Babylon* (**1988**) is set in what may be a VIRTUAL-REALITY version of Babylon reconstructed in the USA, and details its protagon-ists' suspicions that a COMPUTER is generating them as well as the city. *The Fire Worm* (**1988**) is a complex and gripping tale in which the medieval Lambton Worm proves to be the alchemical salamander of Raymond Lully (Ramon Lull; c1235-1316). *The Flies of Memory* (**1988** *IASFM*; exp **1990**) dazzlingly skates over much of the thematic material of the previous 20 books, as the eponymous aliens memorize bits of Earth so that the Universe can continue remembering itself, while various human protagonists embody linguistic con-cerns and dilemmas of perception. Space-opera antics continue *en passant*.

IW's intelligent, polemical pieces about the nature of sf – many of which appeared in SCIENCE-FICTION STUDIES, FOUNDATION (for which he served as features editor 1976-91, sitting on the Council of the SCIENCE FICTION FOUNDATION for the same period) and VECTOR – throw some light on the intentions of his sometimes difficult fiction, and is also, in a sense, of a piece with it. As a whole, his work engages vociferously in battles against oppression – cognitive or political – while at the same time presenting a sense that reality, so far as humanity is concerned, is subjective and partial, created too narrowly through our perception of it. The generation of fuller realities – though incessantly adumbrated by methods ranging from drugs through linguistic disciplines, focused medita-tion, radical changes in education from childhood up, and a kind of enhanced awareness of other percep-tual possibilities – is never complete, never fully successful. Humans are too little, and too much, for reality. IW is perhaps the most impressive syn-thesizer in modern sf; and (it may be) the least deluded.   [JC/PN]

Other works: *Japan: A Cat's Eye View* (**1969** Japan), a juvenile; *Orgasmachine* (**1976** France) with Judy Wat-son, a fable (never published in English) about the manufacture of custom-built girls; *Japan Tomorrow* (coll **1977**), linked stories set in various projected Japanese futures; *Kreuzflug* ["Cruising"] (coll **1987** Germany, in German trans); a **Warhammer 40,000** tie (◊ GAMES WORKSHOP), *Inquisitor* * (**1990**); *Nanoware Time* (**1991** dos US); «*Lucky's Harvest*» (1993), #1 in the projected «Mana» sequence.

As editor: *Pictures at an Exhibition* (anth **1981**); *Changes: Stories of Metamorphosis: An Anthology of Speculative Fiction about Startling Metamorphoses, both Psychological and Physical* (anth **1983** US) with Michael

Bishop; *Afterlives: An Anthology of Stories about Life After Death* (anth **1986** US) with Pamela SARGENT.

About the author: *The Work of Ian Watson: An Annotated Bibliography & Guide* (**1989**) by Douglas A. Mackey.

See also: ANTIMATTER; ARTS; CONCEPTUAL BREAKTHROUGH; COSMOLOGY; CYBERNETICS; DEVOLUTION; GAMES AND SPORTS; GAME-WORLDS; HISTORY IN SF; INTERZONE; MACHINES; MARS; METAPHYSICS; NEW WAVE; NEW WORLDS; NEW WRITINGS IN SF; PASTORAL; PHYSICS; PSYCHOLOGY; RELIGION; SF IN THE CLASSROOM; SEX; SOCIOLOGY; SUPERMAN; TIME TRAVEL; UFOS; UNDER THE SEA; WRITERS OF THE FUTURE CONTEST.

WATSON, JUDY [r] ◊ Ian WATSON.

WATSON, RICHARD F. [s] ◊ Robert SILVERBERG.

WATT-EVANS, LAWRENCE Working name of US writer Lawrence Watt Evans (1954-   ), who began publishing sf in 1975 with "Paranoid Fantasy #1" for *American Atheist* as Evans, creating a hyphenated surname in 1979 to distinguish himself from another Lawrence Evans. He has written several scripts for MARVEL COMICS; a GRAPHIC NOVEL is projected, «Family Matters». He has not been prolific as a short story writer, though "Why I Left Harry's All-Night Hamburgers" (1987) won a 1988 HUGO. As a novelist, his work has been varied from the start, ranging from the somewhat overblown high FANTASY of his first sequence – the **Lords of Dûs** series comprising *The Lure of the Basilisk* (**1980**), *The Seven Altars of Dûsarra* (**1981**), *The Sword of Bheleu* (**1982**) and *The Book of Silence* (**1984**) – through the genre-crossing **War Surplus** series – *The Cyborg and the Sorcerers* (**1982**) and *The Wizard and the War Machine* (**1987**) – which combines SWORD AND SORCERY, military sf and some speculative content about the CYBORG protagonist, and on to singleton sf novels like *The Chromosomal Code* (**1984**) and *Denner's Wreck* (**1988**). The latter is perhaps his most sustained tale: on the planet Denner's Wreck two kinds of humans – primitive descendants of a crashed starship and tourists posing as wilful gods – must come to some sort of mutual comprehension. *Nightside City* (**1989**) tends to submerge the HARD-SF challenge at its heart – to elucidate human actions on a slow-spin planet whose terminator is advancing fatally on the city of the title – in the palely conceived escapades of a female detective. Though LW-E's novels inhabit traditional venues, and their potagonists undergo traditional trials without much affecting the reader, his ingenuity is manifest. [JC]

Other works: The **Legend of Ethshar** fantasy sequence, *The Misenchanted Sword* (**1985**), *With a Single Spell* (**1987**) and *The Unwilling Warlord* (**1989**); *Shining Steel* (**1986**); *Nightmare People* (**1990**), horror; *Newer York* (anth **1991**), ed.

See also: ISAAC ASIMOV'S SCIENCE FICTION MAGAZINE.

WAUGH, CHARLES G(ORDON) (1943-   ) US academic and anthologist, most of whose work has been in collaboration with Martin H. GREENBERG, either alone or with further collaborators. All titles shared solely with Greenberg, or with Greenberg and

only Joseph D. OLANDER, are listed under GREENBERG. All titles shared also with "name" authors will be found under the "name" authors in question: Robert ADAMS, Poul ANDERSON, Piers ANTHONY, Isaac ASIMOV, David A. DRAKE, Joe HALDEMAN, Barry N. MALZBERG, Richard MATHESON, Robert SILVERBERG, S.M. STIRLING and Jane YOLEN. [JC]

See also: ALTERNATE WORLDS; CHILDREN IN SF; COMPUTERS.

WAUGH, EVELYN (1903-1966) UK writer, known mostly for a series of black inter-War satires, such as *Decline and Fall* (**1928**) and *A Handful of Dust* (**1934**), and for *Brideshead Revisited* (**1945**). Some of his early fiction, like *Black Mischief* (**1932**) and *Scoop* (**1938**), utilizes imaginary African countries for satirical purposes, and *Vile Bodies* (**1930**) ends in an apocalyptic Europe torn by a final war, but it was only in some post-WWII works that he wrote fiction genuinely making use of sf displacements. *Scott-King's Modern Europe* (**1947** chap) satirizes post-WWII totalitarianism through the imaginary state of Neutralia. *Love Among the Ruins: A Romance of the Near Future* (**1953** chap) – also included in *Tactical Exercise* (coll **1954** US) – combines the chemical coercion of Aldous HUXLEY's *Brave New World* (**1932**) with the drabness and scarcity of the needs of life of George ORWELL's *Nineteen Eighty-four* (**1949**) in a brief but savage attack on the joylessness of a Welfare State UK a few decades hence. Miles Plastic, his free will bureaucratically threatened, his lover co-opted by the state, takes refuge in "gemlike, hymeneal, auspicious" acts of arson. It is a book, like most of EW's work, in which humour only brings out the more clearly a radical despair. [JC]

See also: DYSTOPIAS.

WAY, PETER (1936-   ) UK writer whose first novel, *The Kretzmer Syndrome* (**1968**), is a NEAR-FUTURE tale set in a bleak conformist UK susceptible to the theories of the eponymous scientist, who articulates PSYCHOHISTORY laws that risk translating the country into a rigid DYSTOPIA. Later novels, like *Super-Çeleste* (**1977**), *Sunrise* (**1979**) and *Icarus* (**1980**), are TECHNOTHRILLERS. [JC]

WAYMAN, TONY RUSSELL (1929-   ) UK-born writer who spent some years in Singapore, where he was actively involved in film-making; he subsequently moved to the USA. He began writing sf with the **Dreamhouse** sequence – *World of the Sleeper* (**1967** dos) and *Ads Infinitum (Being a Second Tale from the Dreamhouse)* (**1971**) – which tells 2 associated tales. The first features a man transported into another world – rather resembling Malaya, the basic plot having originally been the script for a Malayan film. The other places a similar character in a GAME-WORLD-like fantasy environment, Commercialand. *Dunes of Pradai* (**1971**), a complex PLANETARY ROMANCE of some speculative interest, is stifled by TRW's congested style. [JC]

WEAPONS In the catalogue of possible technological wonders offered in the *New Atlantis* (1627; **1629**),

Francis BACON included more powerful cannon, better explosives and "wildfires burning in water, unquenchable". Such promises could not be left out if his prospectus were to appeal to the political establishment – his most important predecessor as a designer of hypothetical machines, Leonardo da Vinci (1452-1519), had likewise sought sponsorship on the basis of his ingenuity as a military engineer.

In the second half of the 19th century, when the effects of technological progress on society became the subject of widespread speculation, the advance of weaponry became one of the most important stimulants of the imagination. George CHESNEY's *The Battle of Dorking* (1871 chap) popularized the concern felt by a number of politicians that the UK's armaments had fallen considerably behind the times. In the new genre of popular fiction which it inspired, the future-WAR story, speculation about the weapons of the future soon became ambitious. In *The Angel of the Revolution* (1893) George GRIFFITH imagined a world war fought with airships and submarines, armed with unprecedentedly powerful explosives. The French artist Albert ROBIDA offered spectacular images of future weaponry in action in *La guerre au vingtième siècle* ["War in the 20th Century"] (1887). Jules VERNE's *Face au drapeau* (1896; trans as *For the Flag* 1897) features the "fulgurator", a powerful explosive device with a "boomerang" action – a primitive guided missile. H.G. WELLS's "The Land Ironclads" (1903) foresaw the development of the tank, and bacteriological warfare was anticipated in T. Mullett ELLIS's *Zalma* (1895) and M.P. SHIEL's *The Yellow Danger* (1898).

The discovery of X-rays and radioactivity in the last years of the 19th century gave a tremendous boost to the hypothetical armaments industry. The imagination of writers leaped ahead to imagine all kinds of weapons causing or using the energy of atomic breakdown. In *The Lord of Labour* (1911) George Griffith described a war fought with atomic missiles and disintegrator rays, and awesome rays have remained a standard part of the sf armoury ever since. During WWI William LE QUEUX attempted to raise morale with his account of the fight to develop a new ray to function as *The Zeppelin Destroyer* (1916). Percy F. Westerman's *The War of the Wireless Waves* (1923) was one of countless NEAR-FUTURE thrillers featuring arms races; here the British ZZ rays must counter the menace of the German Ultra-K ray.

Criminal SCIENTISTS often armed themselves with marvellous rays or atomic disintegrators, as in Edmund SNELL's *The Z Ray* (1932), Austin SMALL's *The Avenging Ray* (1930 as by Seamark) and one of the earliest examples of Soviet sf, *Giperboloid inzhenera Garina* (1926; rev 1937; trans as *The Deathbox* 1936; new trans of rev edn vt *The Garin Death Ray* 1955 USSR) by Alexei TOLSTOY. Few actually succeeded in destroying the world, although Neil BELL's *The Lord of Life* (1933) almost did. Criminal scientists deployed more subtle agents, too: Sax ROHMER's Fu Manchu was especially adept with exotic poisons, and biological blights were used as threats in Edgar WALLACE's *The Green Rust* (1919), William Le Queux's *The Terror of the Air* (1920) and Robert W. SERVICE's *The Master of the Microbe* (1926). Others, not quite so egotistical, tried to use their weapons altruistically to force peace upon the world; they included the heroes of *His Wisdom the Defender* (1900) by Simon NEWCOMB, *Empire of the World* (1910; vt *Emperor of the World* UK) by C.J. Cutcliffe HYNE and *The Ark of the Covenant* (1924; vt *Ultimatum*) by Victor MACCLURE.

Few early writers were aware of the differences which advanced weaponry might make to the nature of warfare, and only H.G. Wells, in *Anticipations* (1901), realized what an appalling difference very simple innovations like barbed wire might make. George Griffith recognized that aerial bombing would not discriminate between combatants and noncombatants, although he did not explore the political ramifications. After 1918, however, poison gases of various kinds became the major bugbear of UK future-WAR stories, deployed to bloodcurdling effect in such stories as Shaw DESMOND's *Ragnarok* (1926) and Neil Bell's *The Gas War of 1940* (1931 as Miles; vt *Valiant Clay* 1934 as NB). It is perhaps surprising that the scientific romancers' pessimism about the likelihood of the Geneva Convention being observed in the next war proved largely unjustified. Other political fantasies of the period, including Harold NICOLSON's atom-bomb story *Public Faces* (1932) and John GLOAG's *Winter's Youth* (1934) – which features a kind of super-napalm called "radiant inflammatol" – also proved (mercifully) a little too cynical.

The early pulp-sf writers took to superweapons – particularly rays – in a big way. E.E. "Doc" SMITH's *The Skylark of Space* (1928; 1946) features heat rays, infra-sound, ultraviolet rays and "induction rays", and an entire planet is aimed towards Earth at hyperlight speed in the **Lensmen** series. His contemporaries were hardly less prolific. John W. CAMPBELL Jr's "Space Rays" (1932) was so extravagant that Hugo GERNSBACK thought he must be joking and billed the story as a "burlesque", apparently offending Campbell sufficiently to deter him from submitting to WONDER STORIES again. In an era when fictional large-scale destruction could be achieved at the flick of a switch, an amazing example of restraint can be found in Thomas P. KELLEY's SPACE OPERA "A Million Years in the Future" (1940), which features SPACESHIPS armed with gigantic crossbows mounted on their prows. At the opposite extreme, Jack WILLIAMSON's *The Legion of Space* (1934; rev 1947) features the superweapon AKKA, which obliterates whole space fleets at the push of a button, and Edmond HAMILTON was fond of disposing of worlds and stars with a similar casual flourish. After this there seemed no further extreme available, so innovation thereafter followed more modest paths. Two standard types of personal weaponry became CLICHÉS, the stun-gun and the BLASTER; modern space-opera heroes often carry modifiable pistols usable in either way, after the fashion of STAR TREK's "phasers". 20th-century developments have contributed only minor inspiration: T.H. Maiman's discovery of the laser in 1960 merely "confirmed" what sf writers had always known about DEATH RAYS, just as Hiroshima had "confirmed" what they already knew about atom bombs.

WWII renewed fears about the destructive potential of war, but there was little room left for imaginative innovation, although mention must be made of the "doomsday weapon": an ultimate deterrent which, if triggered in response to attack, will annihilate life on Earth. Alfred NOYES's *The Last Man* (**1940**; vt *No Other Man* 1940 US) invokes such a weapon but leaves the destruction conveniently incomplete. US GENRE SF now began to reproduce the hysteria of earlier UK SCIENTIFIC ROMANCES in lamenting Man's propensity to make and use terrible weapons; superweapons were more often treated as ultimate horrors than as fancy toys. Notable examples of the new attitude are Bernard WOLFE's bitter black comedy on the theme of "disarmament", *Limbo* (**1952**; vt *Limbo '90* 1953 UK), and James BLISH's story about nasty-minded ways and means of guiding missiles, "Tomb Tapper" (1956). Such stories initiated a tradition which extends through DR STRANGELOVE: OR, HOW I LEARNED TO STOP WORRYING AND LOVE THE BOMB (1963) to such works as Marc LAIDLAW's *Dad's Nuke* (**1985**). The post-WWII years also saw the growth of a macabre interest in the subtleties of "psychological warfare", which sparked off many thrillers about "brainwashing"; the tradition is gruesomely extrapolated in Gregory BENFORD's *Deeper than the Darkness* (**1970**; rev vt as *The Stars in Shroud* 1978).

This anxiety interrupted but never killed off either the more romanticized varieties of futuristic swashbuckling or the fantasies inspired by threats to the US citizen's constitutional right to bear weapons. A.E. VAN VOGT's **Weapon Shops** series of the 1940s made much of the slogan "the right to bear weapons is the right to be free". The intimacy of the relationship between HEROES and their weapons is related to the kind of simplistic power fantasy which underlies much SWORD AND SORCERY and much sf on the FANTASY borderline, but some writers, notably Charles L. HARNESS in *Flight into Yesterday* (1949; exp **1953**; vt *The Paradox Men* 1955), have been ingenious in inventing technological reasons (in this case that FORCE FIELDS are less opaque to slow-moving objects) for the survival in advanced societies of swordplay *à la* Edgar Rice BURROUGHS. Such power fantasies are, of course, reflected in the PSYCHOLOGY of the actual arms race which obsessed the USA and the USSR for nearly half a century after 1945; this is parodied in Philip K. DICK's *The Zap Gun* (**1967**). Arms-race psychology reached a real-world climax in the 1980s with the sciencefictional SDI project, aptly dubbed "Star Wars" by those cynical about its practicability but respectfully afforded quasi-fetishistic status in David

A. DRAKE's ALTERNATE-WORLD story *Fortress* (**1987**). The history of the US fascination with the idea of superweapons is detailed in H. Bruce FRANKLIN's *War Stars: The Superweapon and the American Imagination* (**1988**).

Power fantasies involving "intimate weaponry" have made rapid progress in recent times. The futuristic suits of armour worn in Robert A. HEINLEIN's *Starship Troopers* (**1959**) and the supertanks of Keith LAUMER's interesting **Dinochrome Brigade** series, collected as *Bolo* (coll of linked stories **1976**; exp vt *The Compleat Bolo* 1990) are modest inventions compared to the more dramatic kinds of CYBORG-ization featured in Poul ANDERSON's "Kings who Die" (1962), Laumer's own *A Plague of Demons* (**1965**) and Gordon R. DICKSON's *The Forever Man* (**1986**). The relatively modest enhancements featured in the tv series *The* SIX MILLION DOLLAR MAN are easily adaptable to routine power fantasy, but adaptations as intrusive as that featured in Anderson's "The Pugilist" (1973) – which brings a new perspective to the phallic symbolism of weaponry – belong in a different category.

Modern sf has discovered various more subtle ways to fight wars. The dependence of modern society on sophisticated technologies opens up new opportunities for ingenious sabotage, as explored in Mack REYNOLDS's *Computer War* (**1967**) and Frederik POHL's *The Cool War* (**1981**). The ultimate defensive technology featured in Vernor VINGE's *The Peace War* (**1984**) turns out, however, to bring only temporary respite from more destructive conflict. Laser warfare, as described in *Light Raid* (**1989**) by Connie WILLIS and Cynthia FELICE, also turns out to be less clinical and coherent than might have been hoped, and the day of fabulously macho weapons, like the one featured in Roger McBride ALLEN's *Farside Cannon* (**1988**), is clearly by no means done. The most competent survey of the modern sciencefictional armoury is David LANGFORD's excellent *War in 2080: The Future of Military Technology* (**1979**), some of whose research was redeployed in the novel *The Space Eater* (**1982**), a then-state-of-the-art account of weapons technology which cheerfully ranges from the most gruesomely intimate to the most hugely destructive.   [BS]

WEAPONS OF DESTRUCTION ◊ VYNÁLEZ ZKÁZY.

WEAVER, MICHAEL D. (1961-   ) US writer and systems programmer who began publishing sf with *Mercedes Nights* (**1987**), a dark CYBERPUNK-flavoured fable of cloning – the title is the plural of the name of the protagonist, Mercedes Night, a film star whose illegal CLONES are being sold as love-slaves. The 21st century, heated and hectic and violent, seems to be about to endure a World War IV. Set in the same universe, centuries later, *My Father Immortal* (**1989**) counterpoints the isolated spacefaring lives of the survivors of Earth's traumas with sequences depicting the lives of the "fathers" before the children left the planet. MDW's other main work is the **Wolf-Dreams** fantasy sequence: *Wolf-Dreams* (**1987**), *Nightreaver* (**1988**) and *Bloodfang* (**1989**), all assembled as

Wolf-Dreams (omni **1989** UK). [JC]

WEBB, JANE ◊ Jane LOUDON.

WEBB, LUCAS ◊ Robert REGINALD.

WEBB, RON [s] ◊ Sharon WEBB.

WEBB, SHARON (LYNN) (1936-   ) US nurse and writer who began publishing sf with a poem, "Atomic Reaction" for *FSF* in 1963 as by Ron Webb, and whose first story, "The Girl with the 100 Proof Eyes", also as by Ron Webb, appeared a year later in the same journal. She began to produce fiction regularly only at the beginning of the 1980s, after about a decade in nursing, which figured in her comeback story, "Hitch on the Bull Run" (1979), the first of the **Terra Tarkington** tales about a nurse engaged in escapades throughout the Galaxy, assembled as *The Adventures of Terra Tarkington* (fixup **1985**). SW is perhaps better known for the **Earth Song** sequence – *Earthchild* (fixup **1982**), *Earth Song* (**1983**) and *Ram Song* (**1984**) – in which the introduction of an IMMORTALITY process generates social upheaval, at first because the process must be initiated before the end of puberty, but in the long run because those who become immortal lose any capacity to create works of art. The protagonist of the sequence, a musician involuntarily subjected to the process, helps create, over a 100-century period, a world whose inhabitants can choose between the ability to make art and the chance to live forever. SW's subsequent novels – *Pestis 18* (**1987**) and *The Halflife* (**1989**) – are medical horror thrillers, the first dealing with a deadly virus, the second with a government experiment in personality manipulation that goes wrong. [JC]

WEBB, WILLIAM THOMAS [r] ◊ ROBERT HALE LIMITED.

WEBER, DAVID (?   -   ) US writer of several sf adventures, all with Steve White: *Insurrection* (**1990**), set in a rebellion-torn Terran Federation, *Mutineers' Moon* (**1991**), a TIME-TRAVEL tale in which the rebels, along with their sentient spaceship, are transported into Earth's distant past; and *Crusade* (**1992**), in which another spaceship, this time ancient, destabilizes a Galaxy-wide peace. [JC]

WEBSTER, [Captain] F(REDERICK) A(NNESLEY) M(ITCHELL) (1886-?   ) UK writer, much of whose work related to athletics. His fiction typically concentrated on mysteriously sapient species (◊ APES AND CAVEMEN) in Africa who are persuaded to raise humans as their own. Of the CLUB STORIES assembled in *The Curse of the Lion* (coll **1922**), "The Ape People", which posits a separate language of the apes, explores this theme, as does the not dissimilar *Lord of the Leopards* (**1935**). *The Ivory Talisman* (**1930**), *Gold and Glory* (**1932**), *Lost City of Light* (**1934**), *Second Wind* (**1934**), *Mubendi Girl* (**1935**), *The Trail of the Skull* (**1937**) and *The Land of Forgotten Women* (**1950**) are LOST-WORLD tales. [JC]

Other works: *The Odyssey of Husky Hillier* (**1924**; vt *Husky Hillier* 1938); *The Man who Knew* (**1927**); *Star Lady* (**1935**) and its sequel, *Son of Abdan* (**1936**); *When Strange Drums Sound* (**1935**); *Dead Venom* (**1937**).

WEBSTER, ROBERT N. ◊ Raymond A. PALMER.

WEDGELOCK, COLIN ◊ Christopher PRIEST.

WEEKEND Film (1968). Comacico/Copernic/Lira/Ascot Cineraid. Written/dir Jean-Luc Godard, starring Mireille Darc, Jean Yanne, Jean-Pierre Kalfon, Valerie Lagrange, Jean-Pierre Léaud. 103 mins. Colour.

A FABULATION rather than sf proper, Godard's satirical and violent film contains sf elements in its allegory of the Decline of the West. The progression of the film is from social order through ever-worsening scenes of ENTROPY, mainly imaged in increasingly large-scale car smashes, to anarchy, paralleled by a stylistic shift from naturalism to near-Surrealism. One extraordinary tracking shot begins in the real world and moves into motorized apocalypse. The bickering middle-class couple who at the outset started off on a weekend drive to the country observe the road accidents and associated violence with cool detachment, as does the film itself. Disturbing, sometimes lovely, images proliferate. Finally the couple continue on foot and join some armed anarchists; then the woman eats the man. Godard's previous quasi-sf film was ALPHAVILLE (1965). [PN/JB]

See also: CINEMA.

WEEKLEY, IAN (GEORGE) (1933-   ) UK writer whose sf novel, *The Moving Snow* (**1974**), rather prosaically describes how a family copes with climatic change that brings severe Arctic conditions to the UK. All in all they do quite snugly. [JC]

WEHRSTEIN, KAREN [r] ◊ S.M. STIRLING.

WEINBAUM, STANLEY G(RAUMAN) (1902-1935) US writer whose interest in sf dated from his youth (he published "The Lost Battle", depicting the end of WWI in 1921, in a school magazine, *The Mercury*, in 1917) but who did not begin to publish sf professionally until the 1930s, after selling a romance novel – "The Lady Dances" (1934) as by Marge Stanley – to a newspaper syndicate, and after a first sf novel, «The Mad Brain», had been rejected. Although he did not graduate from the University of Wisconsin, he turned his two years spent there studying chemical engineering to good stead from the beginning of his sf career with "A Martian Odyssey" in WONDER STORIES in 1934; this broke new ground in attempting to envisage LIFE ON OTHER WORLDS in terms of strange and complex ecosystems with weird ALIEN lifeforms. Told in SGW's fluent style, it became immediately and permanently popular, ranking behind only Isaac ASIMOV's "Nightfall" (1941) as the favourite example of early GENRE-SF short fiction. Other SGW stories in this vein include "The Lotus Eaters" (1935), which features an interesting attempt to imagine the world-view of an intelligent plant, "The Mad Moon" (1935), "Flight on Titan" (1935) and "Parasite Planet" (1935). In a series of comedies featuring the eccentric scientist **Van Manderpootz** – including the ALTERNATE-WORLD story "The Worlds of If" (1935), "The Ideal" (1935) and "The Point of View" (1936) – he flippantly devised absurdly miraculous MACHINES. His "Brink of Infinity" (1936) is a rewrite of George Allan ENGLAND's mathematical puzzle story "The

Tenth Question" (1916).

SGW imported some of the methods and values of his early romantic fiction into sf in "Dawn of Flame", but could not sell it. It was first published as the title story of *Dawn of Flame and Other Stories* (coll **1936**), a memorial volume put together by The Milwaukee Fictioneers (◊ SMALL PRESSES AND LIMITED EDITIONS) – a FAN group which included, among others, Robert BLOCH, Ralph Milne FARLEY and Raymond A. PALMER – to express a sense that SGW's short innovative career had been of great significance in the growth of US sf. Nor could he sell a version with gaudier superscientific embellishments, "The Black Flame", which also appeared posthumously (1939 *Startling Stories*); both tales were combined in *The Black Flame* (fixup **1948**). He continued to produce pulp-sf stories prolifically, including an early story of GENETIC ENGINEERING, "Proteus Island" (1936), and the superman story "The Adaptive Ultimate" (1935 as by John Jessel); he also collaborated on 2 minor stories with Farley. His premature death from lung cancer robbed pulp sf of its most promising writer, although the full measure of his ability became apparent only when his posthumous works appeared. *The New Adam* (**1939**) is a painstaking account of the career of a potential SUPERMAN who grows up as a kind of "feral child" in human society; it stands at the head of a tradition of stories which drastically altered the role allotted to superhumans in pulp sf. Another posthumously published sf novel was the psychological horror story *The Dark Other* (**1950**), an early exploration of the Jekyll-and-Hyde theme. All 22 of SGW's short sf stories are assembled in *A Martian Odyssey and Other Science Fiction Tales* (coll **1975**) ed Sam MOSKOWITZ, which combines the contents of 2 earlier collections, *A Martian Odyssey, and Others* (coll **1949**) and *The Red Peri* (coll **1952**) and adds 1 previously uncollected piece; Moskowitz had previously ed a smaller collection, *A Martian Odyssey and Other Classics of Science Fiction* (coll **1962**). *The Best of Stanley G. Weinbaum* (coll **1974**) contains 12 stories. SGW, like his contemporary John TAINE, was occasionally slapdash in his work – which he produced at a very considerable rate – but the swift and smooth clarity of his style was strongly influential on the next generation of sf and fantasy writers. He was a central precursor of the GOLDEN AGE OF SF. [BS/JC]

See also: ADAM AND EVE; ASTOUNDING SCIENCE-FICTION; BIOLOGY; COMICS; COMMUNICATIONS; ECOLOGY; HISTORY OF SF; ISLANDS; JUPITER; LIFE ON OTHER WORLDS; MARS; MYTHOLOGY; OUTER PLANETS; PSYCHOLOGY; PUBLISHING; VENUS.

WEINBERG, ROBERT E(DWARD) (1946-   ) US editor, publisher, bookseller and author of FANZINES focusing on his main interest, the PULP-MAGAZINE world. Much of his task as an editor and publisher has been to rediscover and reprint magazine stories from the pulps which would otherwise have disappeared utterly. His earliest work seems to have been bibliographical – e.g., *An Index to Analog (January*

1960 to June 1965) (c**1965** chap) – and privately printed; other untraced titles have almost certainly survived. (A sign of his interest in ongoing bibliograpgical projects is the much later publication, through his Robert Weinberg Publications, of Mike ASHLEY's *The Complete Index to Astounding/Analog* [**1981**].) Further bibliographical and critical guides include *The Robert E. Howard Fantasy Biblio* (**1969** chap) and its sequel, *The Annotated Guide to Robert E. Howard's Sword & Sorcery* (**1976** chap), the valuable *Reader's Guide to the Cthulhu Mythos* (**1969** chap; rev 1973 chap) with Edward P. Berglund, and *The Hero-Pulp Index* (**1971** chap) with Lohr McKinstry. The climax of his bibliographical work is almost certainly *A Biographical Dictionary of Science Fiction and Fantasy Artists* (**1988**), whose 279 entries cover the field very amply; though marred by some inaccuracies, it remains the central resource for researchers in the field.

As the 1970s began, REW moved from privately produced pamphlets and fanzines into SMALL-PRESS publishing proper, becoming associated with T.E. DIKTY, who founded in 1972 both STARMONT HOUSE, for which REW worked for about a year (long before it actually began to issue books), and FAX COLLECTOR'S EDITIONS, in which REW's involvement was late and short-lived, though he issued 3 anthologies through the firm: *Famous Fantastic Classics #1, 1974* (anth **1974**) and *#2, 1975* (anth **1975**), and *Far Below and Other Horrors* (anth **1974**; republished 1987 by Starmont). He also part-wrote and edited *The Weird Tales Story* (anth **1977**), but by then he had left to found his own firm.

Robert Weinberg Publications (1974-81) concentrated on the reprinting of weird and fantasy fiction. Series included the **Pulp Classics**, reprint booklets ed REW; out of the 22 published, those of direct genre interest include *Pulp Classics #1: Gangland's Doom* (**1973** chap) by Frank Eisgruber Jr; *#2: Captain Hazzard* (1938 *Captain Hazzard* as "Python Men of Lost City"; **1974** chap) by Chester Hawk; *#3: Revelry in Hell* (coll **1974** chap); *#5: The Moon Man* (coll **1974** chap); *#6: Dr Satan* (coll **1974** chap) by Paul ERNST; *#8: The Mysterious Wu Fang* (**1975** chap) by Robert J. Hogan (◊ *The* MYSTERIOUS WU FANG); *#9: Dr. Yen Sin* (coll **1975** chap) by Donald E. Keyhoe (◊ DR. YEN SIN); *#11: The Octopus* (1939 *The Octopus* as "The City Condemned to Hell"; **1976** chap) (◊ *The* OCTOPUS) and *#12: The Scorpion* (1939 *The Scorpion* as "Satan's Incubator"; **1975** chap) (◊ *The* SCORPION), both by Randolph Craig (Norvell W. PAGE); *#13: Death Orchids & Other Bizarre Tales* (coll **1976** chap); *#17: The Secret Six* (coll **1977** chap) by Robert J. Hogan; *#19: Dr Death* (1935 *Dr Death*; **1979** chap) and *#20: Phantom Detective* (coll **1979** chap). Similarly, the **Lost Fantasies** series republished work by Otis Adelbert KLINE and Jack WILLIAMSON as well as several REW anthologies: *Lost Fantasies #4: Lost Fantasies* (anth **1976** chap); *#5: Lost Fantasies* (anth **1977** chap); *#6: Lost Fantasies* (anth **1977** chap); *#8: The Lake of Life* (anth **1978** chap) and *#9: The Sin Eater* (anth **1979** chap). The **Weird Menace Classics** series comprised several REW anthologies: *Weird Menace Classics #1: The Corpse Factory* (anth **1977** chap); *#2: Satan's Roadhouse* (anth **1977** chap); *#3: The Chair where Terror Sat* (anth **1978** chap); *#4: Devils in the Dark* (anth **1979** chap); *#5: Slaves of the Blood Wolves* (anth **1979** chap) and *#6: The Dance of the Skeletons* (anth **1980** chap). In homage to Lester DENT REW ed *The Man behind Doc Savage* (anth **1974**). *WT50* (anth **1974**) was a homage to WEIRD TALES, the rights to which he owned, eventually forming Weird Tales Limited to protect and license the name. It was through REW that George H. SCITHERS arranged to continue *Weird Tales*. Some of the contents of *WT50* reappeared as *The Weird Tales Story* (noted above).

Other small presses in which REW has been involved include Science Fiction Graphics (1977) and Pulp Press (1979-82); but as the 1980s advanced he became less directly involved in publishing activities, concentrating for some time on a mail-order book business. He has ed 1 anthology with Martin H. GREENBERG, *Lovecraft's Legacy* (anth **1990**), plus 3 with Greenberg and Stefan R. Dziemianowicz: *Weird Tales: 32 Unearthed Terrors* (anth **1988**), *Rivals of Weird Tales: 30 Great Fantasy & Horror Stories from the Weird Fiction Pulps* (anth **1990**) and *Famous Fantastic Mysteries: 30 Great Tales of Fantasy and Horror from the Classic Pulp Magazines Famous Fantastic Mysteries and Fantastic Novels* (anth **1991**). Solo REW ed *The Eighth Green Man & Other Strange Folk* (anth **1989**). More interestingly, with the **Alex and Valerie Warner** series of horror tales he began to publish fiction in his own right. The **Devil's Auction** series – *The Devil's Auction* (**1988**), *The Armageddon Box* (**1991**) and *The Black Lodge* (**1991**) – shows a vast knowledge of generic tricks and baggage, and considerable wit. [JC]

See also: H.P. LOVECRAFT.

WEINER, ANDREW (1949-   ) Canadian writer who began publishing sf with "Empire of the Sun" in *Again, Dangerous Visions* (anth **1972**) ed Harlan ELLISON, but who became active only in the early 1980s, with about 25 stories released in that decade. About half of his work was assembled in *Distant Signals, and Other Stories* (coll **1990**); "Distant Signals" (**1984** *Twilight Zone*) was televised in the *Tales from the Darkside* series. *Station Gehenna* (fixup **1987** US) intriguingly confronts its protagonist – sent to Gehenna to investigate a mystery involving the station crew and the partially terraformed planet – with an ALIEN enigma, a possible murder, and much material for thought. Craftsmanlike and quietly substantial, AW has yet to gain an appropriate reputation. [JC]

See also: CANADA; TERRAFORMING.

WEINSTEIN, HOWARD (1954-   ) US writer whose work has been restricted to ties. Those for STAR TREK include *The Covenant of the Crown* * (**1981**) and *Deep Domain* * (**1987**); those for STAR TREK: THE NEXT GENERATION include *Power Hungry* * (**1989**), *Exiles* * (**1990**) and *Perchance to Dream* * (**1991**); those for "V" include *Prisoners and Pawns* * (**1985**), *Path to Conquest* * (**1987**)

and, with A.C. CRISPIN, *East Coast Crisis* * (**1984**). [JC]

WEIRD AND OCCULT LIBRARY UK pocketbook magazine. 3 numbered, undated issues 1960; published by G.G. Swan, London; no ed named, but possibly Walter Swan. *WOL* contained a mixture of weird, sf, mystery and adventure stories, most of which had been sitting in Swan's drawer since WWII. Like its companion, SCIENCE FICTION LIBRARY, it was difficult to read because of its small print. [FHP]

WEIRD FANTASY ◊ EC COMICS.

WEIRD SCIENCE 1. Comic. ◊ COMICS; EC COMICS.

2. Film (1985). Universal. Written/dir John Hughes, starring Anthony Michael Hall, Kelly LeBrock, Ilan Mitchell-Smith, Bill Paxton. 94 mins. Colour.

A pair of teenage nerds feed pin-up-girl pictures to their computer, and it conjures up a sex goddess (LeBrock) who is nice to them and gives them moral lessons (rather as one might expect a scoutmaster to do). Finally they develop the courage to evict some bikers from a party, and win the hearts of two more appropriate teenage girls; the nasty older brother is turned into a monster, but the status quo is restored in time for the parents' return after a weekend away. Starting as sf, *WS* quickly turns to supernatural fantasy in which anything goes and nothing means much; its attitude towards all the women (some undressed against their will) is infantile. This was one of a series of sf teen movies made at around the same time (◊ CINEMA), and perhaps the worst, though occasionally Hughes's real ability to observe teenage mores shows. [PN]

WEIRD TALES 1. US magazine, small PULP-MAGAZINE-size (9in x 6in [23cm x 15cm]) Mar-Apr 1923, BEDSHEET-size May 1923-May/July 1924, pulp-size Nov 1924-July 1953, DIGEST-size Sep 1953-Sep 1954. 279 issues Mar 1923-Sep 1954. Published by Rural Publishing Corp. Mar 1923-May/July 1924, Popular Fiction Co. Nov 1924-Oct 1938, Short Stories Inc. Nov 1938-Sep 1954; ed Edwin Baird Mar 1923-Apr 1924, Otis Adelbert KLINE May/July 1924, Farnsworth WRIGHT Nov 1924-Dec 1939, Dorothy McIlwraith Jan 1940-Sep 1954.

WT was founded in 1923 by J.C. Henneberger and J.M. Lansinger; the former retained an interest in the magazine throughout its existence. Its early issues were undistinguished (despite the presence of writers who later became regular contributors, such as H.P. LOVECRAFT, Seabury QUINN and Clark Ashton SMITH) and the bumper Anniversary issue, May/July 1924, was to have been the last. But it reappeared in Nov 1924 with a new publisher (actually still Henneberger, but now without Lansinger) and a new editor. It has been suggested that the controversy caused by a necrophiliac horror story ("The Loved Dead" by C.M. Eddy [1896-1967] with H.P. Lovecraft) in the May/July issue – attempts were made to have it removed from the news-stands – gave *WT* the publicity boost it needed to survive.

Under the editorship of Wright *WT* developed into the "Unique Magazine" its subtitle promised. Its stories were a mixture of sf – including some by Ray CUMMINGS in the 1920s and a lot by Edmond HAMILTON throughout – HORROR stories, SWORD AND SORCERY, exotic adventure, and anything else which its title might embrace. The early issues were generally crude in appearance, but the look of the magazine improved greatly in 1932 with the introduction of the artists Margaret BRUNDAGE and J. Allen ST JOHN. Brundage's covers – pastel chalks depicting women in degrees of undress being menaced in various ways – alienated some readers, but promised a sensuous blend of the exotic and the erotic which typified the magazine's appeal. The 1930s were WT's heyday; in addition to Lovecraft and Smith, it regularly featured August DERLETH, Robert E. HOWARD (including his **Conan** series), David H. KELLER, Otis Adelbert KLINE, Frank Belknap LONG, C.L. MOORE (especially with her **Northwest Smith** series), Jack WILLIAMSON and others – although the most popular contributor was Seabury Quinn (1889-1969), with an interminable series featuring the psychic detective **Jules de Grandin**. Although WT printed its share of dreadful pulp fiction, in the early 1930s it was, at its best, much superior to the largely primitive sf pulps. However, Wright's WT never really recovered from the almost simultaneous loss of 3 of its key contributors with the deaths of Howard (1936) and Lovecraft (1937) and the virtual retirement of Smith. New contributors in the late 1930s included Henry KUTTNER and artists Hannes BOK and Virgil FINLAY.

At the end of 1939 Wright, in poor health, was replaced by Dorothy McIlwraith. The magazine continued steadily through the 1940s – although after being monthly Nov 1924-Jan 1940, with very few exceptions, it was now bimonthly (and would remain so) – and featured such authors as Robert BLOCH, Ray BRADBURY, Fritz LEIBER and Manly Wade WELLMAN with his **John Thunstone** stories. However, the editorial policy was more restrictive and WT was no longer a unique magazine: other fantasy magazines had appeared and, in the case of UNKNOWN, overshadowed it. Nevertheless, it continued to be the only regular magazine outlet for supernatural fiction until its death in 1954, when its publisher went bankrupt. It would be difficult to overestimate the influence of WT in the genres of weird fiction and Sword and Sorcery; though the emphasis was always on fantasy and the supernatural, it published a surprising amount of influential sf, and many sf writers published their early work in its pages. WT is perhaps rivalled only by ASTOUNDING SCIENCE-FICTION in terms of the number of stories of lasting interest which it produced.

2. Subsequent series. Various nostalgic attempts, mostly unsuccessful, have been made to revive WT – or at least its title. The first was in 1973, with 4 pulp-size issues, Summer 1973-Summer 1974, ed Sam MOSKOWITZ, published by Weird Tales, Los Angeles (Leo MARGULIES), and continuing the original WT numeration (Vol 47, #1-#4).

The rights to WT were bought by Robert E. WEINBERG, who eventually formed Weird Tales Limited to protect and license the name. He published a nostalgic anthology in homage to WT, WT50 (anth **1974**), ed Weinberg, some of whose contents reappeared in *The Weird Tales Story* (anth **1977**), which he ed and partly wrote.

The 3rd WT series was published as a paperback quarterly ed Lin CARTER, published by Zebra Books, who leased the rights from Weinberg. There were 4 issues: *Weird Tales 1* (anth **1980**), *#2* (anth **1980**), *#3* (anth **1981**) and *#4* (anth **1983**). Then came the 4th, confusing, series from a small press, the Bellerophon Network, owned by Californian publisher Brian Forbes. Advance publicity suggested alternately that the editor would be Gil Lamont or Forrest J. ACKERMAN, but in the event there were only 2, not very remarkable issues, both ed Gordon M.D. Garb, these being marked Fall 1984 (appeared 1985) and Winter 1985 (appeared 1986); they were vol 49, #1 and #2. The superior #1 included fiction by Harlan ELLISON, Stephen KING and R.A. LAFFERTY.

The 5th series, ed George H. SCITHERS, Darrell SCHWEITZER and John Gregory BETANCOURT, published by another small press, the Terminus Publishing Co., Philadelphia, has been by far the most successful relaunch. Its numeration began with #290 (which counted in the 10 abortive relaunch issues which had preceded it); the pulp format neatly duplicates the two-column appearance of the original WT. It contains weird fiction and sword-and-sorcery, but little if any sf. From #300 (1991) it has been ed Schweitzer alone. Though WT is believed to be current, the last issue we have traced is #303, Winter 1991.

3. Reprint editions and anthologies. 3 UK edns were published at various times. In the first half of 1942 Swan Publishers produced 3 unnumbered issues. 1 more came in Nov 1946 from Merritt. Finally, Thorpe & Porter published 28 issues, numbered #1-#23, and then vol 1 #1-#5 Nov 1949-July 1954. There were 2 Canadian reprint editions: 1935-6 (vol 25 #6-vol 28 #1), 14 issues, and 1942-51, 58 issues.

WT has been exhaustively mined for anthologies, and many of its contributors from the 1930s have gone on to new heights of popularity with paperback reprints of their stories. The long-running **Not at Night** series of horror anthologies (1925-34) ed Christine Campbell Thomson (1897-1985) drew largely on WT stories, sometimes publishing them even before they appeared in the magazine. *Weird Tales* (anth **1976**) ed Peter Haining (1940-   ) reprints a selection in facsimile. Other reprint anthologies were Mike ASHLEY's *Weird Legacies* (anth **1977** UK) and 4 anthologies ed Leo Margulies: *The Unexpected* (anth **1961**), *The Ghoul Keepers* (anth **1961**), *Weird Tales* (anth **1964**) and *Worlds of Weird* (anth **1965**), the latter 2 being ghost-edited by Sam Moskowitz. Many other anthologies drew a large part of their content from WT, notably *The Other Worlds* (anth **1941**) ed Phil STONG, 11 of its 25 stories being from WT.

Major index sources are *Index to the Weird Fiction Magazines: Index by Title* (**1962** NZ) and *Index to the Weird Fiction Magazines: Index by Author* (**1964** NZ) by T.G.L. Cockcroft, and *Monthly Terrors: An Index to the Weird Fantasy Magazines Published in the United States and Great Britain* (**1985**) by Frank H. Parnell with Mike ASHLEY. [MJE/PN]

See also: GOTHIC SF; SF MAGAZINES.

WEIRD WORLD UK magazine, PULP-MAGAZINE size. 2 undated issues, 1955–6, published by Gannet Press, Birkenhead; ed anon, but possibly by B.Z. Immanuel. *WW* printed a mixture of sf and fantasy, including some reprints. The fiction was of fairly low quality. The advertised companion magazine, *Fantastic World*, never appeared. [FHP]

WEI SHILI [r] ◊ CHINESE SF.

WEISINGER, MORT(IMER) (1915-1978) US editor, an active sf fan from the early 1930s, editing *Fantasy Magazine*, the leading FANZINE of its day; he also sold a few sf stories, starting with "The Price of Peace" for *Wonder Stories* in 1933. In 1936 he became editor of THRILLING WONDER STORIES; later he also ed its companion magazines STARTLING STORIES and CAPTAIN FUTURE, the latter being probably his own conception. Under his direction *TWS* was openly juvenile in appeal, its garish covers giving rise to the term "bug-eyed monsters" (◊ BEMS). In 1941 he became editor of the COMIC book SUPERMAN, and subsequently editorial director of the whole range of National Periodical Publications (DC COMICS), to which he recruited many sf writers, including Alfred BESTER, Otto Binder (◊ Eando BINDER), H.L. GOLD, Edmond HAMILTON and Manly Wade WELLMAN. His career is outlined in "Superman" in *Seekers of Tomorrow* (**1965**) by Sam MOSKOWITZ. [MJE]

WEISS, JAN [r] ◊ CZECH AND SLOVAK SF.

WELBY, PHILIP [r] ◊ ROBERT HALE LIMITED.

WELCH, L(UDERNE) EDGAR (1855-?) UK writer, in the USA for at least 10 years until 1905, after which nothing is known of LEW, who wrote under pseudonyms. Most of his work was published as by Grip, including his first 2 sf novels, *The Monster Municipality, or Gog and Magog Reformed* (**1882**), a DYSTOPIAN prediction that socialist reforms will torture London in 1885, and *How John Bull Lost London, or The Capture of the Channel Tunnel* (**1882**), one of the earlier future-WAR novels – if not the earliest – to warn against a tunnel connecting the UK to France (◊ TRANSPORTATION). LEW is also cited as the author of *Politics and Life in Mars: A Story of a Neighbouring Planet* (**1883**), anon, in which advanced MARS is contrasted with backward Earth – though Darko SUVIN, in *Victorian Science Fiction in the UK* (**1983**), doubts the ascription because the opinions expressed are UTOPIAN. As J. Drew Gay, LEW was definitely responsible for *The Mystery of the Shroud: A Tale of Socialism* (**1887**), in which a fog gives a socialist secret society the chance to conquer England, but the chance is muffed. [JC]

WELCH, ROWLAND ◊ L.P. DAVIES.

WELCOME TO BLOOD CITY Film (1977). An EMI/Len Herberman Production. Dir Peter Sasdy, starring Jack Palance, Keir Dullea, Samantha Eggar, Barry Morse. Screenplay Stephen Schneck, Michael Winder. 96 mins. Colour.

This UK/Canadian coproduction is one of the earlier movies to take VIRTUAL REALITY as its theme (*but see also* WELT AM DRAHT [1973]). A group of amnesiacs find themselves in a savage township of the Old West, where social advancement is by murder. They do not realize that they are inhabiting a computer-generated reality, one of whose supervisors, a woman (Eggar), develops an emotional fixation on a new conscript (Dullea), and interferes illegitimately with the "game". This game is designed to find people with high survival quotients, who will then, in the real world, lead guerrilla units in an unspecified ongoing war. Flat direction and poor performances fail to make anything much of the intriguing premise, though the end is touching. [PN]

WELCOME TO OBLIVION ◊ Roger CORMAN.

WELDON, FAY (1931-) UK writer. Almost all of her work has – with passion, anger and a highly charged creative ambiguity – dealt with issues and situations generally conceived of as FEMINIST. Much of her later fiction verges on the supernatural or edges into the future, or both. In *Puffball* (**1980**) a pregnant woman is influenced by Glastonbury Tor. In *The Rules of Life* (**1987** chap), set in AD2004, a dead woman communicates her memoirs through a computer console. In *The Cloning of Joanna May* (**1989**) a man has his wife "cloned" ("not cloning in the modern sense, but parthenogenesis plus implantation", the book explains) so that he can enjoy various younger versions of her. The novel was dramatized as a tv miniseries, *The* CLONING OF JOANNA MAY (1991). [JC]

Other works: *Female Friends* (**1975**); *Wolf the Mechanical Dog* (**1988** chap), an uneasy sf fable for children.

See also: CLONES; WOMEN SF WRITERS.

WELLEN, EDWARD (PAUL) (1919-) US writer, almost exclusively of short stories, mostly in the mystery genre. His first sf was a "non-fact article", "Origins of Galactic Slang" for *Gal* in 1952, and was followed by a sequence of **Galactic Origins** spoofs. His actual fiction was concise, literate, cynical and frequently anthologized, and is overdue for collection. In his only novel, *Hijack* (**1971**), told with a delicate balance of spoof and splatter, the Mafia learns that the US Government is secretly preparing to escape the Solar System because the Sun is going nova, and muscles in on the action. In the end, a representative sample of humanity heads toward the stars. [JC]

See also: MESSIAHS.

WELLES, ORSON [r] ◊ *The* TRANSFORMERS – THE MOVIE; WAR OF THE WORLDS.

WELLMAN, MANLY WADE (1903-1986) US writer, born in Angola (though his family returned to the USA when he was 6), prolific in both FANTASY and sf, though far more significant for works in the former;

he also wrote Westerns – though less frequently than his brother, Paul I. Wellman (1898-1966) – and crime fiction. MWW began publishing with a fantasy, "Back to the Beast" for *Weird Tales* in 1927; his first sf story proper, "When Planets Clashed", appeared (in *Wonder Stories Quarterly*) as late as 1931. Both were under his own name, though much of his early work appeared under pseudonyms, including Levi Crow, Gans T. Field and the house name Gabriel BARCLAY. Much of his early work appeared in THRILLING WONDER STORIES and STARTLING STORIES, and was suitably vigorous and high-coloured. His first book was a short SPACE OPERA, *The Invading Asteroid* (**1932** chap). *Giants from Eternity* (1939 *Startling Stories*; **1959**) featured the rebirth of medical geniuses from Earth's past to confront a future menace; *Sojarr of Titan* (1941 *Startling Stories*; **1949**) was a **Tarzan**-derived tale set in space; and the **Hok** series, stories published 1939-41 in *AMZ* and 1942 in *Fantastic Adventures*, were sf adventures set in various early mythic civilizations.

Of greatest sf interest were novels like *Twice in Time* (1940 *Startling Stories*; cut **1957**; with text restored and 1 story added, rev as coll 1988), an effective TIME-TRAVEL tale featuring a vivid portrayal of Leonardo da Vinci's Florence, and *Sherlock Holmes's War of the Worlds* (fixup **1975**), with his son Wade Wellman, which intricately involves the detective with the Martian INVASION featured in H.G. WELLS's novel. But in general MWW's sf almost completely lacks the folkloric tone and cunning quietude of his best work.

MWW's fantasy ranged from early weird stories derivative of H.P. LOVECRAFT through tales of the occult, tales that evoked Native American legend, and on to the sequences noted below. Much of his miscellaneous work was assembled in *Worse Things Waiting* (coll **1973**), a large volume which helped inspire the growth of interest in his work over the last years of his life. More centrally, the **Judge Pursuivant** series (in *Weird Tales* 1938-41), as by Gans T. Field, and the **John Thunstone** series – some of the original stories, published in *Weird Tales* from 1938, being originally published as by Gans T. Field – were assembled in *Lonely Vigils* (coll **1981**). *What Dreams May Come* (**1983**) and *The School of Darkness* (**1985**) continued to feature Thunstone. Both Thunstone and Pursuivant are occult detectives, and the range of their investigations is compendious, encompassing most of MWW's general periods and venues of interest, from the US Civil War to the rural USA of the 20th century. From 1951 – with stories appearing frequently in *The* MAGAZINE OF FANTASY AND SCIENCE FICTION, which had taken over from *Weird Tales* as his main journal – much of MWW's energy was devoted to his most famous sequence, the stories and novels set in the Appalachian regions of North Carolina and following the career of witchcraft-fighter and minstrel **Silver John** or **John the Balladeer**: *Who Fears the Devil?* (coll of linked stories **1963**; exp vt *John the Balladeer* 1988), *The Old Gods Waken* (**1979**), *After Dark* (**1980**), *The Lost and the Lurking* (**1981**), *The Hanging

Stones (**1982**) and *The Voice of the Mountain* (**1985**). Along with the stories assembled in *The Valley so Low: Southern Mountain Tales* (coll **1987**), the series remains his most significant achievement. [JC]

Other works: *Romance in Black* (1938 *Weird Tales* as "The Black Drama"; **1946** chap UK) as by Gans T. Field; *The Beasts from Beyond* (1944 *Startling Stories* as "Strangers on the Heights"; **1950** UK); *The Devil's Planet* (1942 *Startling Stories*; **1951** UK); *The Dark Destroyers* (1938 *ASF* as "Nuisance Value"; **1959**; cut 1960 dos); *Island in the Sky* (1941 *TWS*; **1961**); a CAPTAIN FUTURE novel, *The Solar Invasion* ✻ (1946 *Startling Stories*; **1968**); *The Beyonders* (**1977**); *Cahena: A Dream of the Past* (**1986**).

About the author: *Manly Wade Wellman, the Gentleman from Chapel Hill: A Memorial Working Bibliography* (**1986** chap) by Gordon BENSON Jr.

See also: ARTS; COMICS; CRIME AND PUNISHMENT; *The* MAGAZINE OF FANTASY AND SCIENCE FICTION; MYTHOLOGY; PASTORAL; REINCARNATION; SUPERMAN [character]; SUPERNATURAL CREATURES.

WELLS, ANGUS (1943-) UK writer, previously a paperbacks editor. Most of his novels have been Westerns as by Charles L. Pike, James A. Muir and other names. As Ian Evans, he wrote *Starmaidens* ✻ (**1977**), an sf tv tie. Under the house name Richard Kirk, which he shared with Robert P. HOLDSTOCK, he contributed to the **Raven** fantasy series *Swordsmistress of Chaos* (**1978**) with Holdstock and, solo, *The Frozen Gods* (**1978**) and *A Time of Dying* (**1979**). As AW he has written the **Book of the Kingdoms** fantasy sequence – *Wrath of Ashar* (**1988**), *The Usurper* (**1989**) and *The Way Beneath* (**1989**) – and begun a second sequence, the **Godwars** books, with *Forbidden Magic* (**1991**). In 1973-5 AW ed a series of collections assembling for UK readers the "best of" various sf authors, including *The Best of Isaac Asimov* (anth in 2 vols **1973**), *The Best of Arthur C. Clarke* (anth in 2 vols **1973**), *The Best of Robert A. Heinlein* (anth in 2 vols **1973**), *The Best of John Wyndham* (anth **1973**), *The Best of Fritz Leiber* (anth **1974**), *The Best of A.E. van Vogt* (anth **1974**), *The Best of Frank Herbert* (anth **1975**) and *The Best of Clifford D. Simak* (anth **1975**). [JC]

WELLS, BASIL (EUGENE) (1912-) US writer who began publishing sf with "Rebirth of Man" for *Super Science Stories* in 1940, and whose generally unremarkable work is assembled in *Planets of Adventure* (coll **1949**) and *Doorways to Space* (coll **1951**). He also wrote 4 tales as by Gene Ellerman. He became comparatively inactive after about 1957. [JC]

WELLS, H(ERBERT) G(EORGE) (1866-1946) UK writer. At the time of HGW's birth his father was a shopkeeper – having earlier been a gardener and cricketer – but the business failed and HGW's mother was forced to go back into domestic service as a housekeeper. Her desire to elevate the family to middle-class status resulted in "Bertie" being apprenticed to a draper, like his brothers before him, but in 1883 he become a teacher/pupil at Midhurst Grammar School. He obtained a scholarship to the Normal

School of Science in London and studied biology there under T.H. Huxley (1825-1895), a vociferous proponent of Darwin's theory of EVOLUTION and an outspoken scientific humanist, who made a deep impression on him. HGW resumed teaching, took his degree externally, and wrote 2 textbooks (published 1893) while working for the University Correspondence College. He dabbled in scientific journalism, publishing the essay "The Rediscovery of the Unique" in 1891 and beginning to sell articles and short stories regularly in 1893.

The most ambitious and important of his early articles was "The Man of the Year Million" (1893), which boldly describes Man as HGW thought natural selection would ultimately reshape him: a creature with a huge head and eyes, delicate hands and a much reduced body, permanently immersed in nutrient fluids, having been forced to retreat beneath the Earth's surface after the cooling of the SUN. In other articles HGW wrote about "The Advent of the Flying Man", "An Excursion to the Sun" (a poetic cosmic vision of solar storms and electromagnetic tides), "The Living Things that May Be" (on the possibility of silicon-based life) and "The Extinction of Man". A good deal of this speculative nonfiction is reprinted in *H.G. Wells: Early Writings in Science and Science Fiction* (coll **1975**) ed Robert M. PHILMUS and David Y. Hughes. His early short stories are less adventurous, mostly featuring encounters between men and strange lifeforms, as in "The Stolen Bacillus" (1894), "In the Avu Observatory" (1894), "The Flowering of the Strange Orchid" (1894) and "Aepyornis Island" (1894).

The Chronic Argonauts, a series of essays written for his amateur publication *The Science Schools Journal* in 1888, became the basis for HGW's first major fiction, *The Time Machine: An Invention* (**1895** US; rev **1895** UK), which maps the evolutionary future of life on Earth. The human species subdivides into the gentle Eloi and the bestial Morlocks; both ultimately become extinct, while life as we know it slowly decays as the Sun cools. His interest in social reform and socialist political ideas is reflected in the fantasy *The Wonderful Visit* (**1895**), in which an angel displaced from the Land of Dreams casts a critical eye upon late-Victorian mores and folkways. The central themes of these novels – the implications of Darwin's evolutionary theory and the desire to oppose and eradicate the injustices and hypocrisies of contemporary society – run through all HGW's work. In the quasi-allegorical *The Island of Dr Moreau* (**1896**) he developed ideas from an essay, "The Limits of Plasticity", into the story of a hubristic SCIENTIST populating a remote ISLAND with beasts which have been surgically reshaped as men and whose veneer of civilization exemplified by their chanted "laws" – proves thin. "A Story of the Stone Age" (1897) is a notable attempt to imagine the circumstances which allowed Man to evolve from bestial ancestors. His short stories grew bolder in conception, as exempli-

fied by the visionary fantasy "Under the Knife" (1896), the cosmic-DISASTER story "The Star" (1897) and the cautionary parable "The Man who Could Work Miracles" (1898), later filmed (see below). The novella *A Story of the Days to Come* (1899 *Pall Mall Magazine*; **1976**) is an elaborate study of future society, imagining a technologically developed world where poverty and misery are needlessly maintained by class divisions, while *The Invisible Man: A Grotesque Romance* (**1897**) is a second classic study of scientific hubris brought to destruction.

In *The War of the Worlds* (**1898**; with epilogue cut 1898 US) HGW introduced ALIENS into the role which would become a CLICHÉ: monstrous invaders of Earth, competitors in a cosmic struggle for existence (◊ WAR OF THE WORLDS *for radio, film and tv versions*). *When the Sleeper Wakes* (**1899**; rev vt *The Sleeper Awakes* 1910) is a robust futuristic romance of socialist revolution, whose hero awakes from SUSPENDED ANIMATION (◊ SLEEPER AWAKES) to play a quasi-messianic (◊ MESSIAHS) role. (HGW was never able to believe in proletarian socialism, assuming that social justice would have to be imposed from above by a benevolent intelligentsia.) In *The First Men in the Moon* (**1901** US) he carried forward the great tradition of FANTASTIC VOYAGES to the MOON, and described the hyperorganized DYSTOPIAN society of the Selenites. HGW's sf works of this period were labelled "scientific romances" by reviewers, and HGW spoke of them as such in early interviews, although he later chose to lump them together with such fantasies as *The Sea Lady* (**1902**) as "fantastic and imaginative romances". Despite this apparent disowning of their distinctive qualities, Wells's early SCIENTIFIC ROMANCES became the archetypal examples of a distinctive UK tradition of futuristic and speculative fiction.

Wells's early realistic novels drew heavily upon his own experiences to deal with the pretensions and predicaments of the aspiring lower-middle class. *The Wheels of Chance* (**1896**) is light comedy in a vein carried forward by the more successful *Kipps* (**1905**), *The History of Mr Polly* (**1910**) and *Bealby: A Holiday* (**1915**), but HGW wanted to make his name as a serious novelist, and attempted to do so with *Love and Mr Lewisham* (**1900**). He remained an ardent champion of the novel of ideas *versus* the novel of character, and he set out to tackle large themes and to attack issues of contemporary social concern. His most successful effort along these lines was *Tono-Bungay* (**1909**), followed by *Ann Veronica* (**1909**), a polemic on the situation of women in society, and the political novel *The New Machiavelli* (**1910** US). The longest and most pretentious of these novels is *The World of William Clissold* (3 vols **1926**). Some of the later novels of ideas apply fantastic twists for dramatic purposes although remaining basically realistic; the most effective is that deployed in *The Dream* (**1924**).

In his essays HGW began to direct more effort to careful and rational PREDICTION, and became a founder of FUTUROLOGY with the series of essays collected as *Anticipations of the Reaction of Mechanical and Human Progress upon Human Life and Thought* (coll **1901**). He tried to justify the method of this work in a lecture, published as *The Discovery of the Future* (**1902** chap), which marked a turning-point in his thought and work; from then on he abandoned the wide-ranging, exploratory and unashamedly whimsical imagination which had produced his early scientific romances and focused on the probable development of future HISTORY and the reforms necessary to create a better world. His futurological essays brought him to the attention of Sidney (1859-1947) and Beatrice (1858-1943) Webb, and he joined the Fabian Society in 1903. His subsequent career as a social crusader went through many phases. He tried to assume command of the Fabian Society in 1906, but failed and withdrew in 1908. During WWI he was active in the League of Nations movement. Between the Wars he visited many countries, addressing the Petrograd Soviet, the Sorbonne and the Reichstag. In 1934 he had discussions with both Stalin and Roosevelt, trying to recruit them to his world-saving schemes. His real influence, however, remained negligible, and he despaired of the whole business when the world became embroiled in global war for a second time.

In his UTOPIAN novels *A Modern Utopia* (**1905**) and *Men Like Gods* (**1923**) HGW described technologically sophisticated societies governed by socialist principles, and in his other work he tried to describe the new people who might help to bring such worlds into being. In *The Food of the Gods, and How it Came to Earth* (**1904**) the new race is produced by a super-nutrient which enlarges both body and mind. In *In the Days of the Comet* (**1906**) the wondrous change in human personality is brought about by the gases in a comet's tail, through which the Earth is fortunate enough to pass. The most interesting of HGW's later scientific romances, however, are those which attempt to apply a more rigorous logic to the imagining of future WAR. In "The Land Ironclads" (**1903**) he anticipated the use of tanks, and in *The War in the Air, and Particularly How Mr Bert Smallways Fared while it Lasted* (**1908**) he envisaged colossal destruction wrought by aerial bombing. In *The World Set Free: A Story of Mankind* (**1914**) similar destruction is wrought by atomic bombs whose "chain reactions" cause them to explode repeatedly, and the story embodies HGW'S growing conviction that a new and better world could be built only once the existing social order had been torn down. When WWI began in actuality HGW was for this reason initially enthusiastic – a point of view expressed in what remained for some time his most famous novel, *Mr Britling Sees it Through* (**1916**) – but events after 1918 failed to live up to his hopes. He clung nevertheless to the idea that some such pattern of events would come about, as displayed in the last and most comprehensive of his speculative histories of the future, *The Shape of Things to Come* (**1933**), based

on his last major summary of his utopian philosophy, *The Work, Wealth and Happiness of Mankind* (2 vols **1931** US). *The Shape of Things to Come* became the basis of HGW's script for the film THINGS TO COME (1935; book version **1935**). He also scripted the 1936 film *The Man who Could Work Miracles* (script published **1936** chap; not to be confused with the book publication of the original story); both scripts were assembled as *Two Film Stories: Things to Come; Man who Could Work Miracles* (omni **1940**). His other filmscripts, including one for *The King who Was a King* (**1929**), never reached the screen.

HGW became increasingly impatient of the follies of his fellow men, and dubbed the post-1918 world the "Age of Frustration" – a notion eccentrically elaborated in *The Anatomy of Frustration: A Modern Synthesis* (**1936**). This attitude underlies an extensive series of "sarcastic fantasies" begun with *The Undying Fire* (**1919**), an allegory in which the Book of Job is re-enacted in contemporary England, with a dying Wellsian hero "comforted" by various social philosophers. That book reflected a brief reinvestment in religious faith which HGW explained in *God the Invisible King* (**1917**) and dramatized in *The Soul of a Bishop* (**1917**). In *Mr Blettsworthy on Rampole Island* (**1928**) a shipwrecked man tries to convert superstitious savages to the ways of common sense but cannot prevail against their cruel and stupid tribal customs; in the end he discovers that he has been delirious, and that Rampole Island is New York. In *The Autocracy of Mr Parham* (**1930**) an inoffensive individual becomes possessed by a "master spirit" which drives him to seek charismatic political power as "Lord Paramount". In *The Croquet Player: A Story* (**1936** chap) a village is haunted by the brutal spectres of Man's evolutionary heritage, but the allegory is lost on the socialite of the book's title. In *The Camford Visitation* (**1937** chap) the routines of a university are upset by the interventions of a mocking disembodied voice. In *All Aboard for Ararat* (**1940**) God asks a new Noah to build a second Ark; Noah agrees, provided that this time God will be content to remain a passenger while Man takes charge of his own destiny. In the gentler *Star Begotten: A Biological Fantasia* (**1937**) cosmic rays emanating from Mars may or may not be causing a mutation in the human spirit comparable to that wrought by the miraculous comet of *In the Days of the Comet*. *The Holy Terror* (**1939**) is a painstaking study of the psychological development of a modern dictator based on the careers of Stalin, Mussolini and Hitler.

Most of HGW's short stories were initially reprinted in 5 collections: *The Stolen Bacillus, and Other Incidents* (coll **1895**), *The Plattner Story, and Others* (coll **1897**), *Tales of Space and Time* (coll dated 1900 but **1899**), *Twelve Stories and a Dream* (coll **1903**) and *The Country of the Blind, and Other Stories* (coll **1911**). The contents of these were reprinted in *The Short Stories of H.G. Wells* (coll **1927**; vt *The Famous Short Stories of H.G. Wells* 1938 US; vt *The Complete Short Stories of H.G.*

Wells 1965 UK) along with *The Time Machine* as well as 3 stories which had previously appeared in the US collection *Thirty Strange Stories* (coll **1897** US) and 4 others, including the prehistoric fantasy "The Grisly Folk" (1921) and an apocalyptic fantasy, "The Story of the Last Trump", from the non-sf book *Boon* (coll **1915** as Reginald Bliss; 1920 as by HGW). The short stories not included in this omnibus were reprinted in *The Man with the Nose and Other Uncollected Short Stories* (coll **1984**) along with the script for an unmade film. HGW's most notable long scientific romances were collected in *The Scientific Romances of H.G. Wells* (omni **1933**; cut vt *Seven Famous Novels* 1934 US), re-edited as *Seven Science Fiction Novels* (omni **1950** US).

HGW possessed a prolific imagination which remained solidly based in biological and historical possibility, and his best works are generally regarded as exemplary of what sf should aspire to do and be. His other ambitions persuaded him to put his bold and vigorous imagination into a straitjacket for the bulk of his career, but he nevertheless remained the founding father and presiding genius of UK scientific romance, and he was a significant influence on the development of US sf. He never managed to resolve the imaginative conflict between his utopian dreams and his interpretation of Darwinian "natural law", as is evidenced by the despairing passages of his essay *Mind at the End of its Tether* (**1945** chap), which opines that mankind may be doomed because people cannot and will not adapt themselves to a sustainable way of life. He seems to have imagined his own career as an analogue of the situation of the hero of *The Undying Fire* or that of the luckless sighted man in *The Country of the Blind* (1904 *The Strand*; **1915** chap US; rev plus original text **1939** chap UK) – although he also portrayed himself ironically as a deluded idealist in *Christina Alberta's Father* (**1925**) and seemed quite unable to decide how to portray himself in his quirky *Experiment in Autobiography: Discoveries and Conclusions of a Very Ordinary Brain (Since 1866)* (2 vols **1934**), though its continuation, *H.G. Wells in Love: Postscript to an Experiment in Autobiography* (**1984**) – not published during his lifetime because of its sexual content, and because it mentioned living persons – did something to round out the picture. HGW slightly revised many of his works for the 26-vol Atlantic edition of *The Works of H.G. Wells* (1924-7 US). New and definitive editions of the most famous scientific romances – current editions of which reveal many textual variations – are in preparation for release by Oxford University Press as soon as the copyrights lapse in 1996; in the meantime, *The Time Machine/The War of the Worlds: A Critical Edition* (omni **1977**) ed Frank D. McConnell presents some valuable information, though the texts themselves are corrupt; *The Definitive Time Machine: A Critical Edition* (**1987**) ed Harry M. Geduld is more reliable.

Films based on HGW's work include ISLAND OF LOST SOULS (1932), *The* INVISIBLE MAN (1933), *The* WAR OF THE WORLDS (1953), *The* TIME MACHINE (1960), *The* FIRST MEN IN THE MOON (1964), *The* ISLAND OF DR MOREAU (1977) and, very loosely, FOOD OF THE GODS (1976). Notable RECURSIVE SF in which HGW is a character includes *The Space Machine* (**1976**) by Christopher PRIEST, *Time After Time* (**1976**) by Karl Alexander (filmed as TIME AFTER TIME [1979]), and "The Inheritors of Earth" (1990) by Eric BROWN. [BS]

Other collections: Many further collections are merely re-sorts of material first or most reliably published in the collections listed above. Useful collections include *28 Science Fiction Stories* (coll **1952**), *Selected Short Stories* (coll **1958**) and *The Best Science Fiction Stories of H.G. Wells* (coll **1966**).

Other novels: *The Research Magnificent* (**1915**); *The Bulpington of Blup* (**1932**); *You Can't Be Too Careful: A Sample of Life 1901-1951* (**1941**).

Nonfiction: *Mankind in the Making* (**1903**); *New Worlds for Old* (**1908**); *The War that Will End War* (**1914**); *The Outline of History* (**1920**); *The Salvaging of Civilization* (**1921**); *A Short History of the World* (**1922**); *The Way the World is Going: Guesses and Forecasts of the World Ahead* (**1928**); *The Open Conspiracy: Blue Prints for a World Revolution* (**1928**); *The Science of Life* (**1930**) with Julian Huxley and G.P. Wells; *World Brain* (**1938**); *The Fate of Homo Sapiens* (**1939**); *The New World Order* (**1939**); *Phoenix* (**1942**); *The Conquest of Time* (**1942**); *The Happy Turning: A Dream of Life* (**1945** chap); *Journalism and Prophecy 1893-1946* (coll **1964**; cut 1965) ed W. Warren WAGAR.

About the author: Of the numerous critical works on HGW, those of interest include: *The Early H.G. Wells: A Study of the Scientific Romances* (**1961**) by Bernard Bergonzi; *H.G. Wells and the World State* (**1961**) by W.W. WAGAR; *H.G. Wells: A Collection of Critical Essays* (anth **1976**) ed Bergonzi; *The Logic of Fantasy: H.G. Wells and Science Fiction* (**1982**) by John Huntington; *The Life and Thought of H.G. Wells* (**1963** Russia; trans **1966**) by Julius KAGARLITSKI; *H.G. Wells and the Culminating Ape: Biological Themes and Imaginative Obsessions* (**1982**) by Peter Kemp; *The Science Fiction of H.G. Wells* (**1981**) by Frank McConnell; *The Time Traveller: The Life of H.G. Wells* (**1973**) by Norman and Jeanne Mackenzie; *H.G. Wells* (**1970**) by Patrick PARRINDER; *H.G. Wells: The Critical Heritage* (anth **1972**) ed Parrinder; *H.G. Wells: Critic of Progress* (**1973**) by Jack WILLIAMSON; *H.G. Wells and Modern Science Fiction* (anth **1977**) ed Darko SUVIN and Robert M. PHILMUS; *Aspects of a Life* (**1984**) by Anthony WEST, HGW's son by Rebecca West (1892-1983); *H.G. Wells: A Comprehensive Bibliography* (latest edn **1986**) published by the H.G. Wells Society; *H.G. Wells: Desperately Mortal: A Biography* (**1986**) by David C. Smith; *H.G. Wells under Revision: Proceedings of the H.G. Wells International Symposium, London, July, 1986* (anth **1990**) ed Parrinder and Christopher Rolfe.

See also: ANTHROPOLOGY; ANTIGRAVITY; ANTI-INTELLECTUALISM IN SF; APES AND CAVEMEN (IN THE HUMAN WORLD); AUTOMATION; BIOLOGY; CITIES; CLUB STORY; COLONIZATION OF OTHER WORLDS; COMICS; COSMOLOGY; CRITICAL AND HISTORICAL WORKS ABOUT SF; DEATH RAYS;

DEVOLUTION; DIME-NOVEL SF; DIMENSIONS; DISCOVERY AND INVENTION; ECONOMICS; EDISONADE; END OF THE WORLD; ENTROPY; ESP; FAR FUTURE; FRANCE; GAMES AND TOYS; GENETIC ENGINEERING; GREAT AND SMALL; HEROES; HISTORY OF SF; HIVE-MINDS; HUMOUR; IMAGINARY SCIENCE; INVASION; INVISIBILITY; LIFE ON OTHER WORLDS; MACHINES; MAINSTREAM WRITERS OF SF; MARS; MATHEMATICS; MEDICINE; MONEY; MONSTERS; MUSIC; MUTANTS; NEAR FUTURE; NUCLEAR POWER; OPTIMISM AND PESSIMISM; ORIGIN OF MAN; PARALLEL WORLDS; PERCEPTION; PHYSICS; POLITICS; POLLUTION; POWER SOURCES; PROTO SCIENCE FICTION; PULP MAGAZINES; RADIO; RELIGION; ROCKETS; RUSSIA; SATIRE; SCIENTIFIC ERRORS; SEX; SOCIAL DARWINISM; SOCIOLOGY; SPACESHIPS; SUPERMAN; TECHNOLOGY; THEATRE; TIME TRAVEL; TRANSPORTATION; WAR OF THE WORLDS; WEAPONS.

WELLS, HUBERT GEORGE ◊ Forrest J. ACKERMAN.

WELLS, JOHN JAY ◊ Juanita COULSON.

WELLS, (FRANK CHARLES) ROBERT (1929-   ) UK writer who began publishing sf with "The Machine that was Lovely" for the *Observer* in 1954, and who later concentrated on novels, beginning with *The Parasaurians* (**1969** US), in which play-safaris against ROBOT dinosaurs turn into a more serious threat to the hero. *The Spacejacks* (**1975** US) is a traditional SPACE OPERA.   [JC]

Other works: *Candle in the Sun* (**1971**); *Right-Handed Wilderness* (**1973** US).

WELLS, RONNIE [r] ◊ LATIN AMERICA.

WELT AM DRAHT (vt *World on a Wire*) Made-for-tv film (1973). ARD. Dir Rainer Werner Fassbinder (1946-1982), starring Klaus Löwitsch, Barbara Valentin, Mascha Rabben, Karl Heinz Vosgerau, Wolfgang Schenk, Günter Lamprecht. Screenplay Fritz Müller-Scherz, Fassbinder, based on *Counterfeit World* (**1964** UK; vt *Simulacron-3* US) by Daniel F. GALOUYE. Originally broadcast in 2 parts, each 105 mins. Colour.

Fassbinder was perhaps the most brilliant German film director of the 1970s; this was his only sf film. For the purpose of exploring new technologies, the Institute for Cybernetics and Futures Investigation has its giant COMPUTER, Simulacron, create a possible future within its own circuits: a VIRTUAL REALITY whose "human" occupants – in reality, programs – are unaware of their status and can be deleted if they behave wrongly. In the real world, in the Institute itself, mysterious incidents occur, and the protagonist, Stiller, realizes that his world too is a simulation controlled from a higher level, and that to learn this truth is fatal. His lover turns out to be a projection from the higher level, a level in which a Stiller-equivalent is the ultimate manipulator pulling wires. Stiller succeeds in taking the place of his higher-level counterpart.

In Galouye's novel our reality is the middle level, whereas in the film our world is the top level, but that does not diminish the film's threatening effect, for an atmosphere is built up of exchangeability on all levels, so that reality is dissolved and no place is left for security. Fassbinder made the most of his low tv budget by exploiting real locations in modern offices, using glass, concrete and neon lights alarmingly to create a sense of the artificiality of the real.   [HJA]

WENDELESSEN [s] ◊ Charles DE LINT.

WENTWORTH, ROBERT [s] ◊ Edmond HAMILTON.

WEREWOLVES ◊ SUPERNATURAL CREATURES.

WERFEL, FRANZ (1890-1945) Austrian poet, playwright and novelist, born in Prague, known mainly for his sentimental novels, though he achieved his early fame as an Expressionist poet and dramatist. After escaping the Nazis via Spain as WWII loomed, he went to California, where he wrote *Stern der Ungeborenen* (**1946** Austria; trans Gustave O. Arlt as *Star of the Unborn* **1946** US) before dying in US exile. This long, contemplative UTOPIA depicts a philosophically complex FAR-FUTURE Earth through the eyes of a narrator (named Franz Werfel) who is guided through the 3 parts of the novel by a mentor explicitly associated with DANTE ALIGHIERI's Vergil. This narrator's response to the depopulated, deeply alienating, surreal world about him seems cunningly to mirror the exiled author's real-world experiences of California. The melancholy underlying the story, and its long effortless perspectives of time and thought, give the book a clarity and reserve reminiscent of the work of Olaf STAPLEDON.   [JC]

See also: ARTS; AUSTRIA; GERMANY; RELIGION.

WERPER, BARTON House name used by US writers Peter T. Scott (?   -   ) and Peg O'Neill Scott (?   -   ) for their unauthorized **New Tarzan** sequence, each working solo, with Peter Scott writing all but the 3rd vol: *Tarzan and the Silver Globe* (**1964**), *Tarzan and the Cave City* (**1964**), *Tarzan and the Snake People* (**1964**), *Tarzan and the Abominable Snowman* (**1965**) and *Tarzan and the Winged Invaders* (**1965**). It enjoyed a short shelf-life; the Edgar Rice BURROUGHS estate successfully sued the publisher, and the books were withdrawn in 1966. Peg O'Neill Scott, as Scott O'Neill, has written *Martian Sexpot* (**1963**).   [JC]

WESSEL, JOHAN (or JOHN) HERMANN [r] ◊ DENMARK; SCANDINAVIA.

WESSEX, MARTYN [r] ◊ ROBERT HALE LIMITED.

WESSO, H.W. Working name of German-born US illustrator Hans Waldemar Wessolowski (1894-?   ). HWW was educated at the Berlin Royal Academy. He emigrated to the USA in 1914, and soon found work as an illustrator (both covers and interiors) for a variety of magazines. When the Clayton magazine chain created ASTOUNDING SCIENCE-FICTION (then called *Astounding Stories of Super-Science*) in Jan 1930 they hired HWW, who painted all 34 covers of the Clayton *ASF*. His black-and-white ILLUSTRATION was similar to that of his contemporary Frank R. PAUL, but his colour paintings were very different; where Paul's were crowded and often artificially busy, HWW's – often watercolours – were more open, and he seemed more concerned with the overall design of each piece. His best covers create an almost abstract beauty out of the conventional icons of SPACE OPERA. HWW did work for many of sf magazines in the 1930s and early 1940s, including more for *ASF* in the late 1930s (more accomplished than before) and *AMZ, Amazing Stories Quarterly, Captain Future, Marvel Science Stories, Startling Stories* and *TWS*. [JG/PN]

WESSOLOWSKI, HANS WALDEMAR ◊ H.W. WESSO.

WEST, ANTHONY (1914-1987) UK writer, in the USA for much of his life, son of H.G. WELLS and Rebecca West (1892-1983). His *H.G. Wells: Aspects of a Life* (**1984**), published just after his mother's death, was widely understood as an act of retribution aimed mainly at her – he was an illegitimate child and was raised eccentrically – and only secondarily at Wells. His first novel, *On a Dark Night* (**1949** UK; vt *The Vintage* 1950 US), is an afterlife fantasy describing a suicide's questings through space and time for the meaning of life. *Another Kind* (**1951** UK) is a NEAR-FUTURE story with love in the foreground and a UK civil war filling the scene. [JC]

WEST, (MARY) JESSAMYN (1902-1984) US writer most famous for tales of rural Quakerism like *The Friendly Persuasion* (**1945**). Her sf novella, *The Chilekings* (1954 *Star Short Novels* as "Little Men"; **1967**), is a moral fable in which children switch statures with adults and take control. [JC]

See also: GREAT AND SMALL.

WEST, MORRIS (LANGLO) (1916-   ) Australian novelist, in his early years a lay monk, and best known for novels like *The Devil's Advocate* (**1959**). In *The Navigator* (**1976**) a lost ISLAND is found in the South Pacific, and a UTOPIAN community is founded there. *The Clowns of God* (**1981**), set at the end of the century, deals in apocalyptic terms with a mad Pope convinced that the Second Coming is nigh. [JC]

WEST, OWEN ◊ Dean R. KOONTZ.

WEST, PAMELA (1945-   ) US writer whose sf novel, *20/20 Vision* (**1990**), is an intricate TIME-TRAVEL tale in which a murder in 1995 is brooded over by a detective in 2020 and solved through the agency of time-travelling archivists from 2040, who send the detective back to explore the causes of the crime. [JC]

WEST, WALLACE (GEORGE) (1900-1980) US lawyer, writer, public-relations man and pollution-control expert who began publishing short stories with "Loup-Garou" for *Weird Tales* in 1927 and sf with "The Last Man" for *AMZ* in 1929, thereafter appearing fairly regularly in the magazines until the late 1960s. His stories, though unpretentiously told, exhibit a level-headed cognitive vigour that keeps even his early work from dating. Some of his tales – like "Dust" (1935) – made significant early attempts to put POLLUTION and other side-effects of progress on the sf agenda. 2 magazine series collected in book form were *The Bird of Time* (fixup **1959**), a PLANETARY ROMANCE set on MARS, and *Lords of Atlantis* (coll of linked stories **1960**), which features the rulers and scientists of ATLANTIS who, after the island sinks, live on as the gods of the Greek pantheon. Most of WW's

novels were revisions of pre-WWII material, though *The Memory Bank* (1951 *Startling Stories* as "The Dark Tower"; **1961**) demonstrates his marginally more awkward later form. He was never a remarkable writer, nor did he ever devote himself full-time to fiction; but he was never dull. [JC]

Other works: *Betty Boop in Snow-White* * (**1934**) and *Alice in Wonderland* * (**1934**), both film ties; *Outposts in Space* (1931 *Weird Tales*; exp **1962**); *River of Time* (**1963**); *The Time-Lockers* (fixup **1964**); *The Everlasting Exiles* (fixup **1967**).

See also: OUTER PLANETS; POLITICS.

WESTALL, ROBERT (ATKINSON) (1929-   ) UK author, art teacher (1960-85) and antique shop proprietor. Until recently, his work has been mostly for older children. His début novel, *The Machine-Gunners* (**1976**), which formed the basis of the play *The Machine-Gunners* (**1986**) and won the Carnegie Medal, is a realist tale set during the war he described in his nonfiction *Children of the Blitz: Memories of Wartime Childhood* (**1985**); the novel's sequel was *Fathom Five* (**1979**).

His second novel *The Wind Eye* introduced supernatural forces (in the form of St Cuthbert), and these recur often in novels such as *The Watch House* (**1977**), *Ghost Abbey* (**1988**), *Old Man on a Horse* (**1989**) and *The Promise* (**1990**), and in many stories in his collections *Break of Dark* (coll **1982**), *The Haunting of Chas McGill and Other Stories* (coll **1983** US), *Rachel and the Angel and Other Stories* (coll **1986**), *Ghost and Journeys* (coll **1988**), *The Call and Other Stories* (coll **1989**), *Echoes of War* (coll **1989**), *A Walk on the Wild Side: Cat Stories* (coll **1989**) and *The Stones of Muncaster Cathedral* (coll **1991**). RW has also published a fine collection of ghost stories for adults, *Antique Dust: Ghost Stories* (coll **1989**), in which a certain primness only adds a horrific reticence to the resonances of M.R. James (1862-1936). He ed *Ghost Stories* (anth **1988**).

RW, who by the 1980s had established a considerable reputation and went on garnering awards, has written only 1 pure sf novel, *Futuretrack 5* (**1983**), set in a conformist future that lobotomizes individualists. This was good, but better was the earlier TIME-TRAVEL fantasy *The Devil on the Road* (**1978**), where a young biker finds himself confronting Witchfinder Hopkins in the 17th century. *The Cats of Seroster* (**1984**) is, unusually for RW, SWORD AND SORCERY, set in an imaginary medieval world. *Urn Burial* (**1987**) hovers between sf and horror in its tale of the awakening of long-dormant aliens. [PN]

Other works: *The Scarecrows* (**1981**); *The Creatures in the House* (**1983**); *Blitzcat* (**1989**); *The Kingdom by the Sea* (**1990**); *Stormsearch* (**1990**), not fantasy; *Yaxley's Cat* (**1991**); some books for younger children.

See also: CHILDREN'S SF; FANTASY.

WESTALL, WILLIAM (BURY) (1835-1903) UK author and journalist, foreign correspondent for *The Times* of London, who travelled in South America. *The Phantom City: A Volcanic Romance* (**1886**) describes a LOST-WORLD race of Maya-type people at pre-Conquest level. *A Queer Race: The Story of a Strange People* (**1887**) is concerned with a lost race of Elizabethan Englishmen who have undergone strange mutations in pigmentation. [JE/EFB]

Other works: *Tales and Legends of Saxony and Lusatia* (coll **1877**); *Tales and Traditions of Switzerland* (coll **1882**).

See also: ANTHROPOLOGY.

WESTERMAN, PERCY F. [r] ◊ WEAPONS.

WESTERN FICTION PUBLISHING CO. ◊ DYNAMIC SCIENCE STORIES; MARVEL SCIENCE STORIES; MARVEL STORIES.

WESTLAKE, DONALD E(DWIN EDMUND) (**1933-**) US writer, mostly of detective novels and thrillers, often slapstick, under his own name and under pseudonyms, notably Richard Stark; he won an Edgar award with *God Save the Mark* (**1968**). He began publishing sf – always of secondary interest in his career, though never carelessly done – in 1954 with "Or Give Me Death" for *Universe*, and assembled much of his short work in *The Curious Facts Preceding My Execution and Other Fictions* (coll **1968**). His first novel of sf interest, *Anarchaos* (**1967**) as by Curt Clark, is an adventure tale set on a planet where one's own death is the only crime recognized; along with 9 stories – mostly early – this novel was assembled as *Tomorrow's Crimes* (coll **1989**) as DEW. *High Jinx* (**1987**) and *Transylvania Station* (**1988**), both with Abby Westlake, are mysteries incorporating elements of spoofed horror. A polished, intelligent, witty writer, DEW has left sf the poorer by his decision not to concentrate seriously on the genre. [JC]

Other works: *Ex Officio* (**1970**) as by Timothy J. Culver, marginal; *Humans* (**1992**), a fantasy.

See also: PULP MAGAZINES.

WESTLAKE, MICHAEL (**1942-**) UK writer and editor whose *One Zero and the Night Controller* (**1980**) is a FABULATION in which a taxi driver tracks down an occult nocturnal mystery. Of specific sf interest is *The Utopian* (**1989**), a double narrative contrasting the life of an insane contemporary man with that of his namesake – or metaphorical double, or literal REINCARNATION – in the communal matriarchy which obtains in AD2411. Though the tale might seem to read as delusional, both lives are equally weighted: the delusion, if any, might be the world of 1989. [JC]

WESTON, GEORGE (1880-1965) US writer best known for *His First Million Women* (**1934**; vt *Comet "Z"* 1934 UK), an early version of the theme in which sterility affects all but one man – a theme more widely used after the first nuclear explosion. GW's protagonist uses his new-Adam status to promulgate disarmament, until the dissipation of Comet "Z"'s effects makes it possible for him to be ignored. [JC]

Other works: *The Apple Tree* (**1918**); *Queen of the World* (**1923**).

WESTON, PETER (**1944-**) UK sf fan and editor, active mainly in the 1960s and 1970s. He published a FANZINE, SPECULATION, organized the Speculation sf conferences in Birmingham (1970-72), was TAFF

winner in 1974 (◊ AWARDS), and was Chairman of the 1979 UK World SF CONVENTION. He also edited the **Andromeda** sequence of original sf anthologies – *Andromeda 1* (anth **1976**), *#2* (anth **1977**) and *#3* (anth **1978**) – which published work by a number of authors including Brian W. ALDISS, Harlan ELLISON, Fritz LEIBER, Christopher PRIEST and Bob SHAW. [PR]

See also: HUGO.

WESTON, SUSAN (BROWN) (1943-) US writer whose *Children of Light* (**1985**), set in a USA direly but not terminally threatened by HOLOCAUST, treats the possibilities of human survival with warmth and some plausibility. [JC]

WESTWORLD Film (1973). MGM. Dir Michael CRICHTON, starring Yul Brynner, Richard Benjamin, James Brolin. Screenplay Crichton. 88 mins. Colour.

Westworld is in a future theme park, Delos, that contains also Roman and Medieval "worlds"; its permanent occupants – even the horses – are ROBOT simulacra, controlled by human technicians in an underground laboratory. Two male visitors on holiday enjoy out-drawing the local robot gunman (Brynner) and sleeping with the acquiescent robot saloon girls, and it seems that the film will be a comedy about the tawdriness of men's *machismo* fantasies, safely acted out in a purely Hollywood "Wild West". Next day, however, the Brynner robot shoots one of the men dead, the beginning of a revolt by the machines with the implacable gunman as its focus. The puncturing of the fantasy forces us to question our reliance on machinery rather than on ourselves (Crichton's theme for several films to come). With a subtext about our exploitation of slaves and coolies, Crichton's first theatrical feature – he had directed the made-for-tv PURSUIT (1972) – is wittily macabre, and makes its debating points with clarity if not with subtlety. The novelization, by Crichton, is *Westworld* * (**1974**). W's inferior sequel was FUTUREWORLD (1976), not by Crichton. A tv series, *Beyond Westworld* (1980), ran for only 3 episodes, with 2 further episodes made but unaired. Prod and mainly written by Lou Shaw for MGM TV, this told of a Westworld scientist who steals androids for sinister purposes. [PN/JB]

See also: CINEMA; VIRTUAL REALITY.

WETANSON, BURT (? -) US writer who collaborated with Thomas HOOBLER (*whom see for details*) on *The Hunters* (**1978**) and its sequel, *The Treasure Hunters* (**1983**). [JC]

WETMORE, CLAUDE H(AZELTINE) (1862-1944) US writer of several novels. Of sf interest is *Sweepers of the Sea: The Story of a Strange Navy* (**1900**), written with the assistance of Robert M. Yost, in which 2 young Incans resolve to create the United States of Incaland and to dominate the Southern Hemisphere as the USA does the Northern. With the aid of Incan treasure they create a navy of impregnable ships, defeat the British, make peace with North America, and prepare to rule. [JC]

WHARTON, WILLIAM Pseudonym of a US painter

and writer (1926-   ), living in Paris, who wishes not to reveal his name. Best known for FABULATIONS with a MAGIC-REALIST colouring, like *Birdy* (**1979** US) and *Dad* (**1981** US), he moved gradually into tales whose resolution depends upon their being read as FANTASY, like *Tidings* (**1987** US). *Franky Furbo* (**1989** US), like almost all his work, can be read as an intense evocation of WW's own family, this time in sf terms. The eponymous talking fox – at first presented as a delusional fantasy on the part of the protagonist, author of short stories featuring the animal – turns out to be a genuine visitant from the future who has taken on the protagonist's human form in order to become the mutant progenitor of the new race to which – in the future – he belongs, and which has inherited the battered Earth.   [JC]

WHEATLEY, DENNIS (YEATS) (1897-1977) UK writer who served in both WWI and WWII, in the latter with the Joint Planning Staff 1941-4. He was a prolific and extremely popular author of many espionage thrillers and historical romances, although the best of his work – and since his death the only category of his large oeuvre to be read at all widely – consists of a number of black-magic tales in which contemporary political knots are unravelled through occult means. Characters tend to appear and reappear from book to book, genre to genre, throughout his work, so that the black-magic books form a quasiseries; they include *The Devil Rides Out* (**1935**) – the best of them – and its sequel *Strange Conflict* (**1941**), *Gunmen, Gallants and Ghosts* (coll **1943**), *The Haunting of Toby Jugg* (**1948**), *To the Devil – A Daughter* (**1953**), *The Ka of Gifford Hillary* (**1956**), *The Satanist* (**1960**), *They Used Dark Forces* (**1964**), *The White Witch of the South Seas* (**1968**), *Gateway to Hell* (**1970**) and *The Irish Witch* (**1973**); a late omnibus is *The Devil Rides Out and Gateway to Hell* (omni **1992**). Closely associated with these are several LOST-WORLD novels, including *The Fabulous Valley* (**1934**), *They Found Atlantis* (**1936**), *Uncharted Seas* (**1938**) – set in a monster-choked Sargasso Sea and filmed as *The* LOST CONTINENT (1968) – and *The Man who Missed the War* (**1945**), set in the Antarctic; the last 3 were assembled as *Worlds Far from Here* (omni **1952**). DW's black-magic and lost-world novels are neither short nor amusing, though an intermittent story-telling gift sustains readers through passages of political and racial abuse; his remaining sf, unfortunately, was less gifted by his story-telling instinct, nor did his scientific speculations show much acumen. Titles include *Such Power is Dangerous* (**1933**), *Black August* (**1934**) – the Prince Regent of England defeats the forces of totalitarianism – *The Secret War* (**1937**), *Sixty Days to Live* (**1939**) – a comet destroys human civilization – and *Star of Ill-Omen* (**1952**), about flying saucers (◊ UFOS), the last 2 being assembled with a non-sf novel as *Into the Unknown* (omni **1960**).   [JC]

Other works: *A Century of Horror Stories* (anth **1935**).

See also: ANTHROPOLOGY; ATLANTIS; UNDER THE SEA.

WHEELER, (JOHN) HARVEY (1918-?1988) US writer,

co-author with Eugene L. BURDICK (*whom see for details*) of *Fail-Safe* (**1962**).   [JC]

WHEELER, SCOTT (?   -   ) US writer whose *Matters of Form* (**1987**) depicts the long campaign of a group of ALIENS, stranded on Earth in the 20th century, to upgrade human civilization to a level at which star travel is possible. Later sections of the book, introducing a second (and evil) alien race, are less effective.   [JC]

WHEELER, THOMAS GERALD (?   -   ) US physician and author whose juvenile sf novel *Lost Threshold* (**1968**) is a very late LOST-WORLD story, set underground. *Loose Chippings* (**1968**), also a juvenile, is a borderline-sf tale set in an anachronistic village in England.   [JC]

WHEELER-NICHOLSON, MALCOLM (1890-1968) US writer, a prolific producer of pulp fiction who was also important in the history of COMICS as the founder of the firm which became DC COMICS. *Death Over London* (**1940**) is uninteresting sf featuring Nazi spies destroying US installations with sympathetic vibrations.   [RB]

WHEELWRIGHT, JOHN T. [r] ◊ Robert GRANT; John Boyle O'REILLY.

WHELAN, MICHAEL (1950-   ) US illustrator, in his popularity the heir to Frank Kelly FREAS. He has won 11 HUGOS (Freas won 10), of which 10 have been for Best Professional Artist – every year 1980-86, and again in 1988, 1989 and 1991; the other was for Best Nonfiction in 1988 for *Michael Whelan's Works of Wonder* (**1987**), a book collecting some of his work. A Californian, MW studied art and biology at San Jose State University and then worked at the Art Center College of Design in Los Angeles. In 1975 he began painting covers for DAW BOOKS, then for ACE BOOKS and MARVEL COMICS, and soon for other paperback houses including DEL REY BOOKS, earning high praise for his work on several series, such as reissues of Edgar Rice BURROUGHS's **Barsoom** books and Michael MOORCOCK's **Elric** books. His popularity increased on publication of *Wonderworks* (**1979**), collecting his work, which was a bestseller (in art book terms); it was for his 1979 publications that he won his first Hugo. MW continually tops the LOCUS poll (◊ AWARDS) for Best Artist by a very substantial margin. He has dominated sf book-cover ILLUSTRATION right through the 1980s. He is given many of the most prestigious commissions, and his original work fetches astonishingly high prices at sf art auctions. MW has spoken of his consciousness that it was during the 1980s that sf art became – at least at the top – a well paid profession for almost the first time. His huge popularity is difficult to explain or analyse, though his work is clearly very proficient: vivid, colourful, meticulous, giving an appearance of naturalism no matter how "alien" his subject, and highly finished – if occasionally a little languid. Often he adopts a fully realistic approach; sometimes surreal objects hover enigmatically. He has acknowledged a debt to his UK colleagues, and certainly MW's style can be compared with that of, say, Jim BURNS; it is probably not coincidental that Burns was the first artist to break MW's run of Hugos (and that was in a year when MW withdrew from the Hugo contest). [PN/JG]

WHEN DINOSAURS RULED THE EARTH Film (1969). Hammer/Warner. Dir Val Guest, starring Victoria Vetri, Robin Hawdon, Patrick Allen. Screenplay Guest, from story by J.G. BALLARD. 100 mins. Colour.

This was originally written by J.G. Ballard, but director Guest got to the script and eliminated anything expensive, original or intellectual. Still a bit livelier than most prehistoric romances, this is one of a series of them made by Hammer, the first being ONE MILLION YEARS BC (1966). The usual story: woman of one tribe (Vetri) falls for man of another (Hawdon) and also makes friends with a dinosaur. Those who stand between the star-crossed lovers are conveniently wiped out by vast tides whipped up by a still gaseous Moon (a survival from Ballard's original story, which made much of astronomical cataclysms). The dinosaurs and giant crabs were designed by a team led by Jim Danforth. [PN]

WHEN THE WIND BLOWS Animated film (1986). Meltdown Productions. Dir Jimmy T. Murakami, starring the voices of John Mills, Peggy Ashcroft. Screenplay Raymond BRIGGS, based on his own *When the Wind Blows* (graph **1982**). 84 mins. Colour.

Before turning his bestselling GRAPHIC NOVEL into a screenplay, Briggs made a RADIO adaption, with the unfortunate effect that *WTWB* is shackled to the non-stop chatter of its two (working-class) characters. Jim (Mills) and Hilda (Ashcroft) live in Sussex, and are concerned about the approach of WWIII. They follow advice given in official pamphlets, but the aftermath of the Bomb proves much worse than the pamphlets contemplate, and they are left on their own. Moaning about international crises they have not bothered to be interested in, misled by memories of the cameraderie of WWII and somewhat unfairly patronized by the film, they are shattered to learn that nuclear HOLOCAUST means no more milk deliveries, a toilet that will not flush and destroyed curtains, as well as presumably terminal radiation sickness. While Murakami, who had dir the live-action BATTLE BEYOND THE STARS (1980), uses state-of-the-art animation technology to make the best use in the medium of three-dimensional sets since *Hoppity Goes to Town* (1941), the film suffers from a certain middle-class Campaign-for-Nuclear-Disarmament smugness, with Sir John Mills and Dame Peggy Ashcroft trying to sound as obtuse as "ordinary" people. There is an irksomely dirge-like David Bowie theme song. [KN]

WHEN TIME RAN OUT . . . ◊ Irwin ALLEN.

WHEN WORLDS COLLIDE Film (1951). Paramount. Dir Rudolph Maté, starring Richard Derr, Barbara Rush, John Hoyt, Larry Keating. Screenplay Sydney Boehm, based on *When Worlds Collide* (**1933**) by Philip WYLIE and Edwin BALMER. 83 mins. Colour.

WWC, which helped spark the 1950s sf-movie boom, was George PAL's 2nd sf production, made after his DESTINATION MOON. 2 wandering planets are approaching Earth; US scientists calculate (though a disbelieving world, led by philistine UK scientists, rejects their conclusions) that the first will pass close by, creating tidal waves and earthquakes, and the second will annihilate Earth by direct impact; only the construction of a space ark (like Noah's) will save a handful of survivors. The spacecraft (launched on an upwards slanting railway line) carries 40 people to one of the two planets, Zyra, which is habitable. A routine love interest, and melodrama about who gets on the ark and who does not, leaves the single-minded thrust of the film surprisingly undamaged; it continues to grip. A low budget meant that the first near-miss sequence was montaged largely (and effectively) from stock shots – though the liners famously afloat in city streets in 2 brief shots are new; Earth's final death is over in an eye-blink, and the new planet is obviously a bright green painting (by Chesley BONESTELL). The religious subtext – Earth wiped out for its sins, and new Adams and Eves in a new Eden – is presented with no great moral conviction. [PN] **See also:** HOLOCAUST AND AFTER.

WHERE HAVE ALL THE PEOPLE GONE? Made-for-tv film (1974). Metromedia/NBC. Dir John L. Moxey, starring Peter Graves, Verna Bloom, Ken Sanson, George O'Hanlon Jr. Teleplay Lewis John Carlino, Sandor Stern, from a story by Carlino. 72 mins. Colour.

A man and his teenage children are in a cave when a solar flare creates a virus (!) which kills, then reduces to something like sand, almost everybody on Earth. The family journeys across California to their seaside home, where they hope to find the mother alive. They encounter other survivors, some unfriendly, and packs of dogs running wild. Routine stuff, competently directed; an interesting twist has the teenagers showing initiative while the father is passive. [JB]

WHIRLING THE WORLDS ◊ VOYAGE À TRAVERS L'IMPOSSIBLE.

WHITE, (GEORGE) ARED (1881-1941) US military officer and writer, one of the organizers of the American Legion in 1919; Camp White in Oregon was named for him. Of his numerous stories and 4 novels, 2 books are sf. *Attack on America* (**1939**) describes a weakened, unprepared USA attacked through Mexico by an international coalition dominated by Germany; as with its model, George CHESNEY's *The Battle of Dorking* (**1871**), most of the book consists of vivid descriptions of army movements and battles (which the USA loses, though she emerges victorious at the end). In *Seven Tickets to Singapore* (**1939**), US agents pursue spies who have stolen a "detonation ray"; the book is interesting only for its depiction of a Chinese detective substantially more intelligent and resourceful than his US employers. *The Spy Net* (**1931**) and *Agent B-7* (**1934**), not sf, combine the worst elements of E. Phillips OPPENHEIM and William LE QUEUX.   [RB]

WHITE, FRED(ERICK) M(ERRICK) (1859-?   ) UK writer who contributed sf to *Pearson's Magazine, The Strand Magazine* and other general fiction magazines in the early 1900s. He continued writing well into the 1920s, being best known for his **Doom of London** DISASTER series for *Pearson's Magazine* – "The Four White Days" (1903), "The Four Days' Night" (1903), "The Dust of Death" (1903), "A Bubble Burst" (1903), "The Invisible Force" (1903) and "The River of Death" (1904) – in which London and the UK are subjected to a variety of calamities. Catastrophe is turned to the UK's advantage in his only sf novel, *The White Battalions* (**1900**): a shift in the flow of the Gulf Stream leads to arctic conditions in mainland Europe, so that the UK is able to win a WAR.   [JE]

WHITE, GEORGE H. [r] ♢ SPAIN.

WHITE, JAMES (1928-   ) UK writer from Ulster who worked as publicity officer with an aircraft company 1968-84. He began to publish sf with "Assisted Passage" for *NW* in 1953. To many readers (though his singleton novels are equally engaging) he is known almost exclusively for the tales about galactic MEDICINE comprising the **Sector General** sequence, set in a 384-level space-station/hospital "far out on the galactic Rim" and designed to accommodate all known kinds of XENOBIOLOGICAL problems. Dr Conway (he seems to have no first name), a human member of the 10,000-strong multi-species staff, solves alone or with colleagues a series of medical crises with humour, ingenuity and an underlying Hippocratic sense of decency. The sequence includes *Hospital Station* (coll of linked stories **1962** US), *Star Surgeon* (**1963** US), *Major Operation* (fixup **1971**), *Ambulance Ship* (fixup **1979** US), *Sector General* (coll of linked stories **1983** US), *Star Healer* (**1985** US), *Code Blue – Emergency* (**1987** US) and *The Genocidal Healer* (**1992**). Some further **Sector General** tales appear, along with stories set in similar sf venues, in *The Aliens Among Us* (coll **1969** US; cut 1979 UK) and *Futures Past* (coll **1982** US; with 1 story dropped and 1 added rev 1988 UK). White's capacity to conceive and make plausible a wide range of alien anatomies seems unflagging.

Other collections include *Deadly Litter* (coll **1964** US) and *Monsters and Medics* (coll **1977**), but their contents are generally less appealing than his series tales, though they share an ease with sf hardware and a quickness of plot. His singleton novels are more impressive. *Second Ending* (**1962** chap US) encompasses in a few pages the end of humanity, an eons-long perspective, and new hope for a sole survivor. *Open Prison* (**1965**; vt *The Escape Orbit* 1965 dos US) is exhilarating adventure sf. Perhaps the most successful is the ingenious *The Watch Below* (**1966** US), a tale whose two narrative lines dovetail cleverly. In one a WWII merchant vessel sinks, leaving 3 men and 2 women to survive in a large air pocket, work out life-maintenance systems and eventually breed there

UNDER THE SEA while 100 years pass. In the other, water-dwelling ALIENS, who have long been seeking a wet world like Earth to inhabit peacefully, land their starship in the sea in time to save the descendants of the 5 20th-century survivors. The various correspondences between the two sets of "prisoners" are neatly and humanely stressed. In *The Dream Millennium* (**1974**) a physician dreams a Jungian version of the human story in SUSPENDED ANIMATION as his slower-than-light ship takes him and other passengers to a paradisal planet. *Underkill* (**1979**) marks a grim contrast, suggesting that an alien race's response to the internecine savageries of humanity might be the just extirpation of almost the entire species. It might be noted that JW tends to grow more genial the further from the present he sets his stories; if some of the **Sector General** tales seem at times almost wilfully upbeat, their ebullience may have been palliative in nature. *Underkill* clearly represents a vision any writer might be glad to step around.   [JC]

Other works: *The Secret Visitors* (**1957** dos); *All Judgement Fled* (**1968**); *Tomorrow is Too Far* (**1971** US); *Dark Inferno* (**1972**; vt *Lifeboat* 1972 US); *The Interpreters* (**1985** chap dos); *The Silent Stars Go By* (**1991** US), an ALTERNATE-WORLD tale.

About the author: *James White, Doctor to Aliens: A Working Bibliography* (**1986** chap) by Gordon BENSON Jr.

See also: CRYONICS; GENERATION STARSHIPS; MYTHOLOGY; NEW WORLDS; NEW WRITINGS IN SF; POLLUTION.

WHITE, JANE (1934-1985) UK writer, mostly of tales for older children, whose only sf novel, *Comet* (**1975**), treats the title's threat from the humanizing perspective of its young protagonists. All proves well in the end.   [JC]

WHITE, JOHN [r] ♢ W. Graham MOFFAT.

WHITE, STEVE [r] ♢ David WEBER.

WHITE, STEWART EDWARD (1873-1946) US writer of travel books and novels, many of the latter being historical tales set in California. In his later years he became interested in Spiritualism, believed he was in contact with his dead wife, and wrote some books about the other world, including *The Unobstructed Universe* (**1940**) and 2 sequels. His sf novels are *The Mystery* (**1907**) with Samuel Hopkins ADAMS, a complicated tale involving an abandoned ship on the high seas, and the mysterious "celestium" which the mutineers who have stolen it do not know has the effect of making anyone nearby jump into the sea; and its sequel, *The Sign at Six* (1910 *Popular Magazine* as "The City of Dread"; **1912**), by SEW alone, in which the investigative protagonist of the previous book uncovers a mad SCIENTIST who threatens to freeze New York City with his "nullifier".   [JC/PN]

WHITE, TED Working name of US writer and editor Theodore Edwin White (1938-   ) who became – after working as assistant editor for *FSF* 1963-8 – the sometimes controversial editor of AMAZING STORIES and FANTASTIC 1969-78; he noticeably improved the magazines, buying original stories and emphasizing matters relating to sf FANDOM. He later ed HEAVY

METAL 1979-80 and *Stardate* 1985-6. TW is known, too, for the many chatty, aggressive, self-defensive and polemical letters he published in such fanzines as *The* ALIEN CRITIC, and for his continuing column in ALGOL, which had the same qualities, as did his editorials in *AMZ* and *Fantastic*. He won a HUGO as Best Fan Writer in 1968.

His writing career began with "Phoenix" for *AMZ* in 1963 with Marion Zimmer BRADLEY; this became part of *Phoenix Prime* (fixup **1966**), #1 in his **Qanar** series of quest tales, which continued with *The Sorceress of Qar* (**1966**), where a good SUPERMAN fights bad supermen, and *Star Wolf!* (**1971**). His first novel was a TIME-TRAVEL tale, *Invasion from 2500* (**1964**) with Terry CARR, together writing as Norman Edwards. Most of TW's subsequent titles are unremarkable examples of adventure sf like *Android Avenger* (**1965** dos) and its sequel *The Spawn of the Death Machine* (**1968**), about the ANDROID Tanner and his adventures, and *The Secret of the Marauder Satellite* (**1967**), an sf juvenile. He also wrote the ending of the Philip K. DICK serial "A. Lincoln – Simulacrum" (*AMZ* 1969-70), though Dick's own ending was restored when it was published as *We Can Build You* (**1972**). TW's 2 novels of some distinction are *The Jewels of Elsewhen* (**1967**), a vividly imagined tale of strife among the DIMENSIONS, and *By Furies Possessed* (**1970**), a tale of PARASITISM in which the invading ALIENS turn out to be symbionts. [JC/PN]

Other works: *Lost in Space* * (**1967**), a tv tie (◊ LOST IN SPACE) as by Ron Archer, with Dave VAN ARNAM, and *Sideslip* (**1968**), also with Van Arnam; a **Captain America** tie, *The Great Gold Steal* * (**1968**); *No Time Like Tomorrow* (**1969**); *Trouble on Project Ceres* (**1971**), a juvenile; *The Oz Encounter* (**1977**) with Marv Wolfman (**1946-**), written by Wolfman from characters and a scenario devised by TW; *Phoenix* (**1977**) with Wolfman; *Forbidden World* (**1978**) with David F. BISCHOFF.

As editor: *The Best from Amazing Stories* (anth **1973**); *The Best from Fantastic* (anth **1973**).

See also: CITIES; INVASION; SF MAGAZINES.

WHITE, T(ERENCE) H(ANBURY) (1906-1964) UK writer whose overwhelming nostalgia for a lost England expressed itself most vividly in his 2 best-known works, *Farewell Victoria* (**1933**) and a superlative tragicomic fantasia on *Le Morte D'Arthur* (**1485**) by Sir Thomas Malory (c1408-1471), *The Once and Future King* (**1958**), a book comprising 3 earlier novels, substantially recast, plus a previously unpublished 4th section; it was adapted by Alan Jay Lerner (1918-1986) into the stage musical *Camelot* in 1960 (published as *Camelot: A New Musical* **1961**; filmed 1967). Those 3 earlier novels – *The Sword in the Stone* (**1938**; rev 1939 US), made into a philistine feature cartoon by Walt Disney in 1963, *The Witch in the Wood* (**1939** US), retitled "The Queen of Air and Darkness" in the recasting, and *The Ill-Made Knight* (**1940** US) – are themselves of very considerable interest as fantasias, as is THW's original concluding section (the 1958

conclusion was written later), *The Book of Merlyn* (**1977** US), whose rejection by THW's UK publishers during WWII, because of its pacifist content, delayed for 15 years the publication of any version of the whole. The 1958 novel, despite *The Sword in the Stone* being a juvenile, constitutes a remarkable and pessimistic exploration of the complexity of Evil, of the decay of the Matter of Britain – modern England is envisioned with particular venom in the ant DYSTOPIA to which Merlyn subjects the young Arthur as part of his education – and generally of the loss of innocence.

Other books by THW are of some sf interest. Early on, *Earth Stopped* (**1934**) and *Gone to Ground* (coll of linked stories **1935**), introduced an sf HOLOCAUST to underline the points THW wished to make about contemporary civilization through the conversations and fox-hunting manias of a large cast; in the 2nd vol, survivors of the final WAR tell each other exemplary tales (◊ CLUB STORY) while hiding in a cave. Without any source being cited, all the supernatural tales in *Gone to Ground* were reprinted in *The Maharajah, and Other Stories* (coll **1981**), losing most of their effectiveness through the unacknowledged uprooting. *Mistress Masham's Repose* (**1946** US) tells how a group of Lilliputians, transported to England by Gulliver, have survived in the capacious grounds of the vast estate of Malplaquet for 200 years, until a young girl almost destroys them by treating them as pets. The protagonist of *The Elephant and the Kangaroo* (**1947** US) is a mocking self-portrait of the author; he becomes a new Noah in a hilariously pixilated Eire. In *The Master* (**1957**), an sf juvenile, a boy and a girl come across a plot to rule the world from the deserted island of Rockall, where the Merlyn-like Master, 157 years old, has perfected both hypnotic control and a vibration device that will destroy all machines; fortunately he trips over the children's dog, injures himself, and drowns himself in the sea. THW's sf was of a piece with all his work, sharing the sentimentality, satirical power, sadness, longing for retrospectic havens, manic humour and compassion of his best fantasy. [JC]

About the author: *T.H. White: A Biography* (**1968**) by Sylvia Townsend Warner.

See also: CHILDREN'S SF; GREAT AND SMALL; SWORD AND SORCERY.

WHITE, TIM (1952-) UK illustrator. White is one of the new school of super-realists who have shaped UK sf ILLUSTRATION since the mid-1970s. After 2 years in advertising he received his first sf commission in 1974. Immediately successful, he soon became one of the UK's premier book-cover illustrators; he has painted several hundred of them. There is a case for calling him the finest technician in UK sf illustration, and along with Chris FOSS and Jim BURNS he has produced the UK's most influential sf artwork of the past two decades. Using very fine detail, his paintings have a luminous clarity sometimes reminiscent of René Magritte (1898-1967) or (rather differently) of Andrew Wyeth (1917-). His work is figurative, often uses unusual perspectives, and regularly makes much of grass and sky in the landscapes in which the sf images are set. *The Science Fiction and Fantasy World of Tim White* (**1981**), a very strong collection, contains 111 paintings, nearly all book covers. [PN/JG]

See also: BRITISH SCIENCE FICTION AWARD.

WHITE DWARF ◊ GAMES AND TOYS; GAMES WORKSHOP.

WHITEFORD, WYNNE N(OEL) (1915-   ) Australian sf writer and (retired) motoring journalist, whose first sf may have been "Beyond the Infinite" for *Adam and Eve* in 1934. He wrote more sf in the 1950s, beginning to sell to overseas markets with "The Non-Existent Man" (**1958** *AMZ*) and remaining quite prolific in US magazines until 1960. His third period of writing began with short stories in the **Kesrii** series in 1978. His first novel, *Breathing Space Only* (**1980**), a rather downbeat post-HOLOCAUST tale, ends with its protagonist isolated among superior humans, returned from the stars, with whom he has nothing in common. It was followed by *Sapphire Road* (**1982**), *Thor's Hammer* (**1983**), *The Hyades Contact* (fixup **1987** US), which is part of the **Kesrii** series, *Lake of The Sun* (**1989** US) and *The Specialist* (**1990** US). Several of these books imagine forms of evolved humanity; all are thoughtful, competent sf adventure stories. [PN]

See also: AUSTRALIA.

WHITE HOLES ◊ BLACK HOLES.

WHITLEY, GEORGE [s] ◊ A. Bertram CHANDLER.

WHO? (vt *The Man in the Steel Mask*) Film (1974). Hemisphere/Maclean & Co. Dir Jack Gold, starring Elliott Gould, Trevor Howard, Joseph Bova. Screenplay John Gould (Jack Gold), based on *Who?* (**1958**) by Algis BUDRYS. 91 mins. Colour.

Released long after being made, and publicized not at all, this taut, efficient little metaphysical thriller, hinging on questions of what constitutes identity, deserved rather better. A key US scientist (Bova) is terribly injured on the East German border and later returned, fixed up by the Russians, in CYBORG form with a metal face and hand. Or is he a planted double agent? Gould plays the US security man who sees to it that the cyborg is constantly watched. With a series of Cold-War riffs, a rather good subtext is set up about the human-seeming machine of the state apparatus (on both sides) versus the machine-seeming human (with more human feeling than he putatively had before, as shown in a touching scene with the ex-wife). The prosthetic "monster" finally rejects secret scientific work; instead he retires, quite alone, to a farm. The mask is never removed, not even metaphorically, and the mystery is only solved (for alert viewers) through ironic indirection. Gold is known mainly as one of the UK's better tv-drama directors. [PN]

WHO WOULD KILL JESSIE? ◊ KDO CHCE ZABÍT JESSII?

WHYTE, ANDREW A(DAMS) (?   -   ) US bibliographer whose main work has been to compile with Anthony R. LEWIS (*whom see for titles*) several vols of *The N.E.S.F.A. Index to Science Fiction Magazines and Original Anthologies* during 1973-84. Solo he produced

The New SF Bulletin Index to SF Books, 1974 (**1974** chap). [JC]

WIBBERLEY, LEONARD (PATRICK O'CONNOR) (1915-1983) Irish writer who lived in the USA from 1943, and who published at least 100 books, beginning in 1947; much of this work was for children, and a modest proportion of it was sf or fantasy. His first and most famous sf novel, the ostensibly adult tale which begins the **Grand Fenwick** sequence, is *The Mouse that Roared* (**1955**; vt *The Wrath of Grapes* 1955 UK), a RURITANIAN spoof involving a super-WEAPON; it was filmed in 1959. The subsequent vols – *Beware of the Mouse* (**1958**), which is a prequel, *The Mouse on the Moon* (**1962**), filmed in 1963, *The Mouse on Wall Street* (**1969**) and *The Mouse that Saved the West* (**1981**) – make little use of sf devices except in the most cursory fashion. A singleton, *One in Four* (**1976**), depicts a USA threatened by immaterial entities from the FAR FUTURE. *Encounter Near Venus* (**1967**) and its sequel, *Journey to Untor* (**1970**), are CHILDREN'S SF. Of fantasy interest were several further juveniles, including *Mrs Searwood's Secret Weapon* (**1954**), *McGillicuddy McGotham* (**1956**), *Take Me to Your President* (**1957**), *The Quest of Excalibur* (**1959**), *Stranger of Killknock* (**1961**) and *The Crime of Martin Coverly* (**1981**). LW was an intermittently clever writer whose books were eaten by sweetness. [JC]

WICKS, MARK (?   -?   ) UK writer whose *To Mars Via the Moon: An Astronomical Story* (**1911**) describes a UTOPIA whose Martian venue owes an acknowledged debt to the theories of Percival Lowell (◊ MARS). The book was probably intended as a fictionalization of popular science for younger readers. [JC/PN]

WIENER, NORBERT (1894-1964) US mathematician and writer who established the contemporary sense of the word CYBERNETICS in his book *Cybernetics* (**1948**; rev 1961). Some of his speculations in this field appear in *The Human Use of Human Beings* (**1950**) and in *God & Golem, Inc.: A Comment on Certain Points where Cybernetics Impinges on Religion* (**1964**), which directly influenced Frank HERBERT's *Destination: Void* (**1966**). As W. Norbert he published 2 sf stories, "The Miracle of the Broom Closet" in *FSF* (1952) and "The Brain" in *Crossroad in Time* (anth **1953**) ed Groff CONKLIN. A novel, *The Tempter* (**1959**), is not sf. *Ex-Prodigy* (**1953**), nonfiction, is an interesting speculative study of the intellectual SUPERMAN. [JC]

About the author: *I Am a Mathematician* (**1956**), autobiography.

WIGNALL, T(REVOR) C. (1883-1958) UK author, usually for children as Trevor Wignall, whose sf novel *Atoms* (**1923**) with G(ordon) D(aniel) Knox posits a world with abundant atomic energy and broadcast power. These developments are described with wooden glee. [JC]

WILBRAHAM, JOHN ◊ Robert POTTER.

WILCOX, DON Working name of US writer Cleo Eldon Knox (1905-   ), who taught creative writing at Northwestern University; most of his work, sometimes as

Cleo Eldon, Miles Shelton or Max Overton, was for Ray PALMER's AMAZING STORIES and *Fantastic Adventures*, where he published his first story, "The Pit of Death", in 1939. A good GENERATION-STARSHIP tale, "The Voyage that Lasted 600 Years" (1940), soon followed. DW used the house name Alexander BLADE at least once, and also published a novelette, "Confessions of a Mechanical Man" (1947), as Buzz-Bolt Atomcracker. The **Ebbtide Jones** stories (1939-42; the 1st in *AMZ*, the rest in *Fantastic Adventures*) were published as by Miles Shelton. DW's "The Whispering Gorilla" (1940) was cobbled together with "The Return of the Whispering Gorilla" (1943) by his ZIFF-DAVIS stablemate David Vern, writing as David V. REED, to form *The Whispering Gorilla* (fixup 1950 UK), published as by David V. Reed. [JC/PN]

WILCOX, RONALD [r] ◊ ROBERT HALE LIMITED.

WILD CARDS ORIGINAL-ANTHOLOGY series, ed George R.R. MARTIN, set in a SHARED WORLD, each volume comprising stories woven (◊ BRAID) into a more-or-less integrated narrative. Martin prefers to think of these books, because their contents are planned and linked, as "mosaic novels", though we treat them as, only technically, anthologies. The 1st vol, *Wild Cards: A Mosaic Novel* * (anth **1987**), shows its alternate Earth's history (◊ ALTERNATE WORLDS) deviating from our own in 1946 with the release over New York of a virus developed by ALIENS. The effect of the "Wild Card" virus is to kill immediately and horribly 1 out of 10 people it infects. Survivors are mutated, mostly in useless, often monstrously damaging ways, in which case they are called "Jokers". But 1 in 10 are mutated beneficially: these become superpowered "Aces". The dividing line can be blurred; for example, physical deformity can be offset by an immense gain in strength.

Ten vols have been issued to mid-1992, the remainder being #2: *Aces High* * (anth **1987**), #3: *Jokers Wild* * (anth **1987**), #4: *Aces Abroad* * (anth **1988**), #5: *Down and Dirty* * (anth **1988**), #6: *Ace in the Hole* * (anth **1990**), #7: *Dead Man's Hand* * (**1990**) by Martin with John M. Miller, #8: *One-Eyed Jacks* * (anth **1991**), #9: *Jokertown Shuffle* * (anth **1991**) and #10: *Double Solitaire* * (**1942**) by Melinda SNODGRASS, who has acted as assistant editor on **Wild Cards** since #6. They focus on a cast of Aces and Jokers through the decades. The strongest stories are in the 1st vol, which deals impressively with the McCarthy era. Later volumes are more comic-bookish, and history's incredible resilience becomes irritating: when a secret Ace of enormous power runs for the presidency, events contrive to bring about a victory for George Bush. Despite this, *WC* is one of the better shared-worlds series, showcasing hard-edged writing by Edward BRYANT, Lewis SHINER, Walton Simons, Melinda Snodgrass, Walter Jon WILLIAMS and others.

There is a companion graphic-story series. This comprises *Wild Cards #1: Heart of the Matter* (graph **1990**), #2: *Diamond in the Rough* (graph **1990**), #3: *Welcome to the Club* (graph **1990**) and #4: *Spadework*

(graph **1990**), collected as *Wild Cards* (graph omni **1991**). [RB/RT]

See also: GAMES AND TOYS; SUPERHEROES.

WILDER, CHERRY Pseudonym of New Zealand-born writer Cherry Barbara Grimm, née Lockett (1930-   ), resident in Australia 1954-76 and then in Germany. After publishing short fiction and poetry she turned to sf, and chose the name Wilder. The themes of her first published sf story, "The Ark of James Carlyle" in *New Writings in SF 24* (anth **1974**) ed Kenneth BULMER, are the gradual rapprochement of, and changes in, human and ALIEN after First Contact. These themes recur in the well realized **Torin** series – *The Luck of Brin's Five* (**1977** US), *The Nearest Fire* (**1980** US) and *The Tapestry Warriors* (**1983** US), all first published as juveniles – and in the adult novel *Second Nature* (**1982** US), which tells of a castaway society on the planet Rhomary. The **Torin** books focus on the relationship between the marsupial natives of the planet Torin and the succession of humans who become fruitfully involved with them, though the young protagonists do tend – perhaps rather conventionally – to open not only their own eyes to the wonders of the world but also those of their native hosts. CW's most significant achievements may lie in her complexly achieved short stories like "Something Coming Through" (1983) and "The Decline of Sunshine" (1987), in which a wry mythopoeic vein shines through. Some of her short fiction returns to Torin and Rhomary. CW's work, notable for its narrative skill, evocative style and rounded characterization, should by now have given her a higher reputation. [JC/MM/PN]

Other works: The **Rulers of Hylor** fantasy trilogy, comprising *A Princess of the Chameln* (**1984** US), *Yorath the Wolf* (**1984** US) and *The Summer's King* (**1986** US); *Cruel Designs* (**1988** UK), occult/horror set in contemporary Germany.

About the author: The CW issue of FOUNDATION, #54, Spring 1992, contains an autobiographical essay and "The Wilder Alien Shores, or The Colonials are Revolting", a critical assessment by Yvonne Rousseau.

See also: ANTHROPOLOGY; AUSTRALIA; CHILDREN'S SF; NEW WRITINGS IN SF; NEW ZEALAND; PASTORAL.

WILDING, PHILIP (?   -   ) UK author of 2 routine sf adventures, *Spaceflight – Venus* (**1955**) and *Shadow Over the Earth* (**1956**). As John Robert Haynes he wrote *The Scream from Outer Space* (**1955**), also unremarkable. [JC/PN]

WILD IN THE STREETS Film (1968). AIP. Dir Barry Shear, starring Christopher Jones, Shelley Winters, Diane Varsi, Millie Perkins, Hal Holbrook, Richard Pryor. Screenplay Robert Thom. 97 mins. Colour.

Holbrook is the Kennedy-style Californian senator who, when he realizes that, through demographic shift, half the population are under 25, enlists a rock star (Jones, looking like James Dean) to help sway the youth vote. The strategy backfires when the senator's quid pro quo of lowering the voting age (it is eventually 14) allows the rock star himself to become president; in an act of revenge against his awful mother (Winters) he then consigns all the over-35s to concentration-camp retirement homes where they are force-fed LSD. The film's LSD-in-the-water-supply sequence created a stir at the time, and inspired some real-life imitations. The tongue-in-cheek script – the hippy sections badly dated – is still good, especially the finale where the subteens are fomenting further revolution. [PN/JB]

See also: CINEMA.

WILD, WILD WEST, THE US tv series (1965-9). A Michael Garrison Production/CBS TV. Created Michael Garrison. Prods Garrison, Fred Freiberger, Gene L. Coon, Collier Young, John MANTLEY, Bruce Lansbury. Writers included Henry Sharp, John Kneubuhl, Ken Kolb, Ken Pettus. Dirs included Paul Wendkos, Richard Donner, Irving Moore, Robert Sparr, Alan Crosland Jr, Marvin Chomsky. 4 seasons; 104 50min episodes. Season 1 b/w; colour thereafter.

An amusing, sophisticated and successful mixture of Western and secret-agent fantasy, TWWW series had Robert Conrad playing Jim West, an 1870s James Bond. The plots usually involved anachronistic, futuristic devices and often featured mad scientists attempting to overthrow the government, using everything from manmade earthquakes to time machines. At its best TWWW had something of the bizarre quality of The AVENGERS (1961-8), to which it was the nearest US equivalent, but its stylization was not always light or witty enough. Low-angle shooting and clever use of sets ensured a genuine sense of decadent menace in the more baroque episodes. Michael Dunn played an often reappearing villain, the dwarf scientist Dr Loveless who invents ANDROIDS, miniaturization, hallucinogens and a lot more. The bland persona of the hero was offset by Ross Martin's jovial performance as his partner, Artemus Gordon. The series can be seen as anticipating STEAMPUNK. 2 sequels appeared a decade later as made-for-tv movies: *The Wild Wild West Revisited* (1979) and *More Wild Wild West* (1980), both dir Burt Kennedy. [JB/PN]

WILD, WILD WEST REVISITED, THE ◊ *The* WILD, WILD WEST.

WILEY, JOHN [s] ◊ Rog PHILLIPS.

WILHELM, KATE (1928-   ) Working name of US writer Katie Gertrude Meredeth Wilhelm Knight (1928-   ), married to Damon KNIGHT; beyond her writing, she has long been influential, along with her husband, through his founding of the MILFORD SCIENCE FICTION WRITERS' CONFERENCE in 1958 and its offshoot, in which she was directly involved, the CLARION SCIENCE FICTION WRITERS' WORKSHOP; she edited one of the anthologies of stories from the latter, *Clarion SF* (anth **1977**).

But KW early became best known for her writing, and by the 1980s was a ranking figure in the field, though her first work would eventually be seen as atypical. She started publishing sf in 1956 with "The

Pint-Size Genie" for *Fantastic*, and continued for some time with the relatively straightforward genre stories of the sort to be found in her first book, *The Mile-Long Spaceship* (coll **1963**; vt *Andover and the Android* 1966 UK); it was not until the late 1960s that she began to release the mature stories which have made her career an object lesson in the costs and benefits of the market, for it seemed clear from about 1970 that she was most happy as a writer at the commercially unpopular novella length, and least happy as a novelist. Her response was to publish short stories and novellas, frequently brought together in book form as "speculative fiction", while at the same time producing intermittently capable and variously ambitious full-length tales. The shorter fictions were assembled in: *The Downstairs Room, and Other Speculative Fiction* (coll **1968**), which includes the NEBULA-winning "The Planners" (1968); *Abyss: Two Novellas* (coll **1971**); *The Infinity Box: A Collection of Speculative Fiction* (coll **1975**), the title story of which – also republished as *The Infinity Box* (1971 *Orbit 9* ed Damon Knight; **1989** chap dos) – is a darkly complex depiction of a NEAR-FUTURE USA as refracted through the slow destruction of the conscience of a man gifted with a PSI POWER; *Somerset Dreams* (coll **1978**); *Listen, Listen* (coll **1981**); *Children of the Wind: Five Novellas* (coll **1989**), which includes the NEBULA-winning *The Girl who Fell into the Sky* (1986 *IASFM*; **1991** chap); *State of Grace* (coll **1991** chap) and *And the Angels Sing* (coll **1992**), which includes "Forever Yours, Anna" (1987), also a Nebula-winner. The strongest of these stories are exercises in capturing the significant texture of the new in the context of individual lives; time and again, a tale begins within the shaky domesticity of the family and moves suddenly to an sf or fantasy perspective from which, chillingly, the fragility of our social worlds can be discerned. At this point, at the point of maximum realization, her best stories generally stop.

With novels it has tended to be otherwise. After *More Bitter than Death* (**1963**), a mystery, her first sf novel was *The Clone* (**1965**) with Theodore L. THOMAS, one of the rare sf books to use CLONE in the strict biological sense, in describing a formidable, voracious and ever-growing blob, and a competent demonstration of her workmanlike capacity to cope with genre content. *The Killer Thing* (**1967**; rev vt *The Killing Thing* 1967 UK), set almost uniquely for KW on another planet, also shows some facility in telling conventional sf tales. But *The Nevermore Affair* (**1966**) and *Let the Fire Fall* (**1969**; cut and rev 1972 UK), which attempt to investigate character within novel-length plots, fail in the first through overexplication and in the second through an uneasiness of diction, so that the near-future religious revival at its heart is depicted with a diffuse sarcastic loquacity. This sense of drift – this sense that her novels wilfully continue past the point at which her interest in maximum realization has begun to flag – is avoided in some instances. For example, *Where Late the Sweet Birds*

Sang (fixup **1976**) – which won HUGO and Jupiter AWARDS for Best Novel – successfully translates her interest in clones (this time in the sf sense of "people-copies") to a post-HOLOCAUST venue in the Appalachians where an isolated community of clones has been formed to weather the interregnum until civilization can spread again, but develops in its own, perilously narrow fashion; significantly, the book is made up of 3 novella-length sequences, each superb. *The Clewiston Test* (**1976**) balances the effects on the eponymous developer of a dubious drugs project against those on her of an unhappy marriage; for the world of experimental BIOLOGY – in which KW has always been interested – cannot be divorced from the lives it affects, a truism rarely brought to bear with such sharpness. *Fault Lines* (**1977**), not sf, uses a displaced and edgy diction to present a woman's broken remembrances, the fault lines of the title representing her own life, her future, her unhappy marriages, the earthquake that traps her, and a powerful sense that civilization itself is cracking at the seams. But these novels stand out.

More normally KW's novels – like *A Sense of Shadow* (**1981**), *Welcome, Chaos* (1981 *Redbook* as "The Winter Beach"; exp **1983**) and *Huysman's Pets* (**1986**) – tend to dissipate powerful beginnings in generic toings and froings. Her **Danvers and Meiklejohn** sequence of sf/horror/fantasy detective tales – *The Hamlet Trap* (**1987**), *The Dark Door* (**1988**), *Smart House* (**1989**) and *Sweet, Sweet Poison* (**1990**) – seem in their compulsive genre-switching almost to parody this proclivity; but *Crazy Time* (**1988**), a late singleton, more successfully embraces the insecurity of the novel form as KW conceives it, and the ricochets of the plot aptly mirror the discourse it embodies upon the nature of institutionalized definitions of sanity and insanity. Most successfully of all, *Death Qualified: A Mystery of Chaos* (**1991**) combines detection and sf in a long, sustained, morally complex tale whose central story-telling hook – solving a murder in order to free the innocent protagonist of suspicion – leads smoothly into an sf denouement involving Chaos theory, new perceptions and a hint of SUPERMAN. It is the longest of her novels, yet the one which most resembles her successful short fiction. [JC]

Other works: *The Year of the Cloud* (**1970**) with Theodore L. Thomas; *Margaret and I* (**1971**); *City of Cain* (**1974**), a near-future psi thriller with many sf trappings; *Juniper Time* (**1979**); *Better than One* (coll **1980**) with Damon Knight, each contributing separate items; *Oh, Susannah!* (**1982**); *Cambio Bay* (**1990**); *Naming the Flowers* (**1992** chap).

As editor: *Nebula Award Stories Nine* (anth **1974**).

See also: ECOLOGY; IMMORTALITY; INTELLIGENCE; ISAAC ASIMOV'S SCIENCE FICTION MAGAZINE; MEDICINE; MONSTERS; POLLUTION; ROBERT HALE LIMITED; SCIENTISTS; WOMEN SF WRITERS.

WILKINS, JOHN (1614-1672) UK philosopher who served as the Bishop of Chester. He wrote no fiction, but was one of the first popularizers of science and a propagandist for scientific progress whose speculative nonfiction is remarkable. The 3rd edn of *The Discovery of a New World* (**1638**; 3rd rev ed 1640) includes a brief discourse on the possibility of travel to the MOON. *Mathematicall Magick* (**1648**) is a treatise on TECHNOLOGY, including essays on submarines, flying machines and perpetual-motion MACHINES (of whose feasibility he was sceptical). While he was Master of Wadham College, Oxford, he founded the Philosophical Society, which in 1662 became the Royal Society. [BS]

See also: RELIGION; SPACESHIPS; TRANSPORTATION; UNDER THE SEA.

WILKINS, (WILLIAM) VAUGHAN (1890-1959) UK writer best known for his historical romances, but who wrote some tales of sf interest. *Being Met Together* (**1944**), though marginal, interestingly describes an attempt to rescue Napoleon using a submarine (◊ UNDER THE SEA) designed by the US engineer and inventor Robert Fulton (1765-1815). *After Bath* (**1945**) is an ornately fantastic juvenile. *The City of Frozen Fire* (**1950**) is an energetic LOST-WORLD tale set in South Africa. *Fanfare for a Witch* (**1954**) is historical fantasy. *Valley Beyond Time* (**1955**) describes trips through the DIMENSIONS to the haven of the title and back again to a time-ridden, grief-enfolded Earth. [JC]

WILLARD, TOM (? -) US writer of military-sf adventures: the **Strike Fighters** sequence – *Strike Fighters* (**1990**), *#2: Strike Fighters #2* (**1990**), *#3: War Chariot* (**1991**), *#4: Sudden Fury* (**1991**) and *#5: Red Dancer* (**1991**) – and the **Afrikorps** sequence as by Bill Dolan – *Afrikorps* (**1991**) and *#2: Iron Horse* (**1991**). [JC]

WILLEFORD, CHARLES (RAY) (1919-1988) US writer, best known for his police thrillers in the Miami-based **Hoke Moseley** series. His *The Machine in Ward Eleven* (coll **1963**) has more than once been listed as sf, but is not, although one of its stories is a surreal fantasy. [PN]

WILLER, JIM (? -) Canadian writer whose sf novel, *Paramind* (**1973**), takes a DYSTOPIAN view of the commanding role of the COMPUTER in a 21st-century world. [JC]

WILLEY, ROBERT [s] ◊ Willy LEY.

WILLIAM ATHELING Jr AWARD ◊ AWARDS.

WILLIAMS, CHARLES (1886-1945) UK writer whose novels are essentially theological fantasy thrillers; he was closely associated with C.S. LEWIS and J.R.R. TOLKIEN. His romantic and obscurely devout use of Tarot and Grail imagery helped bring these themes into the generic mainstream. Of his novels, *Many Dimensions* (**1931**) bears some remote resemblance to sf, in that it depicts the world as being threatened by the dangerous powers (in particular TELEPORTATION) of a magical stone that can be split into endless identical copies; but in this, as in the remainder of his fiction, the bent of the fantasy is towards RELIGION. The TIME TRAVEL in *All Hallows' Eve* (**1945**) is devoted to similar ends. [JC/DRL]

Other works: *War in Heaven* (**1930**); *The Place of the Lion* (**1931**); *The Greater Trumps* (**1932**); *Shadows of Ecstasy*

(1933); *Descent into Hell* (1937).

About the author: *Shadows of Imagination: The Fantasies of C.S. Lewis, J.R.R. Tolkien and Charles Williams* (anth 1969) ed Mark R. HILLEGAS.

See also: FANTASY; MYTHOLOGY.

WILLIAMS, ERIC C(YRIL) (1918-   ) UK writer, previously a bookseller, who began publishing sf with "The Desolator" for *Science Fantasy* in 1965 and was the author of some routine sf novels for ROBERT HALE LIMITED, starting with *The Time Injection* (1968). *The Drop In* (1977), not for Hale, is an alien-INVASION novel of some interest. [JC]

Other works: *Monkman Comes Down* (1969); *The Call of Utopia* (1971); *To End All Telescopes* (1969); *Flash* (1972); *Project: Renaissance* (1973); *Largesse from Triangulum* (1979); *Time for Mercy* (1979); *Homo Telekins* (1981).

WILLIAMS, FRANK Working name of UK writer Edward Francis Williams, Baron Francis-Williams (1903-1970), whose sf novel is *The Richardson Story* (1951; vt *It Happened Tomorrow* 1952 US). [JC]

WILLIAMS, GORDON (MacLEAN) (1934-   ) Scottish writer best known for the **Hazell** detective novels with Terry Venables (1943-   ), writing together as P.B. Yuill. Of sf interest is his solo **Micronauts** sequence – *The Micronauts* (1977 US), *Microcolony* (1979 US; vt *Microanaut World* 1981 UK) and *Revolt of the Micronauts* (1981) – about government agents miniaturized to perform intricate assignments. [JC]

WILLIAMS, JOHN A(LFRED) (1925-   ) US writer, almost all of whose work has reflected his experiences (including service in WWII) as a US Black. *The Man who Cried I Am* (1967) posits a Black genocide plot on the part of the US Government, to be put into action in case of civil uprising. *Sons of Darkness, Sons of Light* (1969) presents a Black revolt centred on Manhattan, comparable to Warren MILLER's *The Siege of Harlem* (1964) as a MAINSTREAM use of sf material. *Captain Blackman* (1972) features a time-travelling hero who takes part, as a Black soldier, in all the wars of US history. [JC/PN]

See also: POLITICS.

WILLIAMS, JON ◊ Walter Jon WILLIAMS.

WILLIAMS, J.X. House name used on pornographic novels, several with sf content, published by Greenleaf Classics, a company owned by one-time sf editor William HAMLING. *The Sex Pill* (1968) as by JXW is by Andrew J. OFFUTT. 2 further fantastic titles, *Her* (1967) and *Witch in Heat* (1967), are by unidentified authors. [PN]

WILLIAMS, MICHAEL LINDSAY (1940-   ) US writer who published 2 sf novels – *Martian Spring* (1986) and its sequel, *FTL: Further Than Life* (1987) – which tackle conflicts between Earth and MARS, and consequent attempts to transcend these ills by gaining rapport with a transplanetary group mind; verve and clarity are lacking.

MLW should not be confused with the Michael Williams involved in various **DragonLance** ties like *DragonLance Heroes: Weasel's Luck* * (1989) and *DragonLance Heroes II: Galen Beknighted* * (1990), as well as an untied fantasy series, **From Thief to King**: *A Sorcerer's Apprentice* (1990) and *A Forest Lord* (1991). [JC]

WILLIAMS, NICK (VAN) BODDIE (1906-1992) US newspaperman – he was with the Los Angeles *Times* 1931-71, serving as its chief editor from 1958 – and writer who contributed short material to various "slicks"; he reported having published his first sf story pseudonymously in *Weird Tales* in the late 1920s, but could recall neither title nor pseudonym. *The Atom Curtain* (1956 dos) is set in a thoroughly unusual post-HOLOCAUST USA 170 years after an atomic barrier has isolated it from the rest of the world. Inside, a crazed immortal rules a population rapidly reverting to Neanderthal status, and a cave woman, after being clubbed, falls in love with the barrier-penetrating protagonist. [JC]

WILLIAMS, PAUL (STEVEN) (1948-   ) US editor and writer, founder of *Crawdaddy*, the first US rock magazine, in 1966, and author of several books on the subject, including the best books yet written on Bob Dylan. As literary executor of the Philip K. DICK estate he was from the first involved in the Philip K. Dick Society and was instrumental in the wisely phased and commercially successful publication of Dick's posthumous works. In *Only Apparently Real: The World of Philip K. Dick* (1986) he set some early guidelines for the comprehension of Dick's difficult final decade. [JC]

WILLIAMS, PAUL O(SBORNE) (1935-   ) US writer and professor of literature who won the JOHN W. CAMPBELL JR. AWARD for Best New Writer in 1983, and who is known in the sf field almost exclusively for his **Pelbar** sequence – *The Breaking of Northwall* (1981), *The Ends of the Circle* (1981), *The Dome in the Forest* (1981), *The Fall of the Shell* (1982), *An Ambush of Shadows* (1983), *The Song of the Axe* (1984) and *The Sword of Forbearance* (1985) – set, 1100 years after a meteor shower has instigated a devastating nuclear WAR, in the balkanized and barbarian heart of the USA at a time when fragmented local cultures must begin to come together once again, hopefully without warfare. The sequence is unusual – and in deep contrast to SURVIVALIST FICTION – in its disregard for violence and its lack of gear fetish; it has been compared with Edgar PANGBORN's **Davy** books. *The Dome in the Forest*, which tells of the discovery of an inhabited nuclear shelter, interestingly explores the psychology of the POCKET UNIVERSE; later volumes, in which the tempo of technological change begins to increase, are perhaps less engaging. The series as a whole suffers from a certain leadenness of narrative diction, but never fails to question generic assumptions about the nature of a post-HOLOCAUST civilization. *The Gifts of the Gorboduc Vandal* (1989) is not part of the sequence. [JC]

See also: ANTHROPOLOGY; HISTORY IN SF.

WILLIAMS, RAYMOND (HENRY) (1921-1988) Welsh writer, professor of drama and cultural critic, long famous for his incisive studies of the interconnections between literature and society like *Culture and Society* (**1958**) and *The Country and the City* (**1973**). Of sf interest is *The Volunteers* (**1978**), a tale set in the late 1980s when political conflict in the UK has come to a violent head. [JC]

Other works: *George Orwell* (**1971**), nonfiction; *Keywords* (**1976**), nonfiction; *The Fight for Manod* (**1979**).

See also: PROTO SCIENCE FICTION.

WILLIAMS, ROBERT MOORE (1907-1977) US writer, active in the sf field under his own name and various pseudonyms, including John S. Browning, H.H. Harmon, Russell Storm and the house name E.K. JARVIS. He began publishing sf as Robert Moore with "Zero as a Limit" for *ASF* in 1937, and by the 1960s had published over 150 stories. Though most are unremarkable, he was an important supplier of competent genre fiction during these decades. Typically adequate is the **Jongor** series: *Jongor of Lost Land* (**1940** *Fantastic Adventures*; **1970**), *The Return of Jongor* (**1944** *Fantastic Adventures*; **1970**) and *Jongor Fights Back* (**1951** *Fantastic Adventures*; **1970**). He did not begin publishing books until *The Chaos Fighters* (**1955**), but thereafter released many novels of the same general calibre as his short fiction. Notable were *Doomsday Eve* (**1957** dos), a post-HOLOCAUST drama in which the world serves as an arena for struggling SUPERMEN, and the **Zanthar** series: *Zanthar of the Many Worlds* (**1967**), *Zanthar at the Edge of Never* (**1968**), *Zanthar at Moon's Madness* (**1968**) and *Zanthar at Trip's End* (**1969**). Zanthar is a professor with the gifts of a HERO. RMW wrote few original words, but rarely a dull one. [JC]

Other works: *Conquest of the Space Sea* (**1955** dos); *The Blue Atom* (**1958** dos); *The Void Beyond and Other Stories* (coll **1958** dos); *To the End of Time and Other Stories* (coll **1960** dos); *World of the Masterminds* (**1960** dos); *The Day They H-Bombed Los Angeles* (**1961**), which includes a RECURSIVE reference to *Doomsday Eve*; *The Darkness Before Tomorrow* (**1962** dos); *King of the Fourth Planet* (**1962** dos); *Walk Up the Sky* (**1962**); *The Star Wasps* (**1963** dos); *Flight from Yesterday* (**1963** dos); *The Lunar Eye* (**1964** dos); *The Second Atlantis* (**1965**); *Vigilante – 21st Century* (**1967**); *The Bell from Infinity* (**1968**); *When Two Worlds Meet: Stories of Men on Mars* (coll of linked stories **1970**); *Beachhead Planet* (**1970**); *Now Comes Tomorrow* (**1971**); *Seven Tickets to Hell* (**1972**).

Nonfiction: *Love is Forever – We Are for Tonight* (**1970**), autobiography.

See also: ROBOTS.

WILLIAMS, TAD [r] ◊ DAW BOOKS.

WILLIAMS, T. OWEN [r] ◊ ROBERT HALE LIMITED.

WILLIAMS, WALTER JON (1953-   ) US writer whose first works were nautical tales as by Jon Williams, beginning with *The Privateer* (**1981**). He began to publish sf with *Ambassador of Progress* (**1984**), an unexceptional novel in which a female agent whose mission is to revive civilization makes contact with an abandoned, semi-feudal colony planet. *Knight Moves* (**1985**) describes the attempts of an

immensely powerful immortal and his old friends and enemies to discover a technique of MATTER TRANSMISSION and to repopulate an almost abandoned Earth with fantastic creatures taken from MYTHOLOGY, in a style reminiscent of the early Roger ZELAZNY. But it was with the appearance of CYBERPUNK that WJW seemed to have found his true voice as a writer. In the **Hardwired** sequence – *Hardwired* (**1986**), stories like "Video Star" (1986), *Voice of the Whirlwind* (**1987**) and *Solip:system* (**1989** chap) – he displayed a fascination with intensely detailed surfaces, biologically invasive gadgetry, and the effects of powerful corporations and rapidly changing technology on (romanticized) social outsiders. The first tale, in which underdogs of a repressed Earth rebel against dominant orbital corporations – proved sufficiently popular to spawn a role-playing game (◊ GAMES AND TOYS) based on it, despite the unlikelihood of much of its plot; the game is presented in *Hardwired: The Sourcebook* (**1989** chap). In the rather better second tale the CLONE of an alienated one-time corporate soldier, brought to life on the original's death, hunts for clues to that first demise in a narrative richly informed by Zen and speculations on the nature of identity.

The **Crown Jewels** sequence – *The Crown Jewels* (**1987**) and *House of Shards* (**1988**) – comprises two "divertimenti" describing the adventures of a Raffles-like burglar in a cod-Oriental future human culture heavily influenced by ALIENS to whom style is sacred. But WJW retained a cyberpunk outlook for his next major novel, *Angel Station* (**1989**), in which family groups of interstellar traders both fight to survive as major corporations squeeze down their markets, and also betray each other for the chance to deal with a newly discovered alien race. *Facets* (coll **1990**) assembles most of his short fiction. In the tautly told *Days of Atonement* (**1991**) WJW moved to a NEAR-FUTURE USA where a macho small-town sheriff struggles with the physics needed to understand an apparent outbreak of bodily resurrections at the nearby Advanced Technological Laboratories. *Aristoi* (**1992**) goes in the other direction, into a FAR-FUTURE venue once again evocative of Zelazny. Ingenious and energetic and knowing, WJW seems very much at home with the mature GENRE SF of the 1980s and 1990s. [NT]

Other works: *Elegy for Angels and Dogs* (**1990** dos), a sequel to Zelazny's *The Graveyard Heart* (1964 *Fantastic*; **1990** chap dos), with which it is bound sequentially (◊ DOS-À-DOS); *Dinosaurs* (**1991** chap).

See also: CYBORGS; PSI POWERS; WILD CARDS.

WILLIAMSON, JACK Working name of US writer John Stewart Williamson (1908-   ) from the beginning of his career in 1928, though his **Seetee** stories were originally signed Will Stewart. JW was born in Arizona and raised (after stints in Mexico and Texas) on an isolated New Mexico homestead; he described his early upbringing and his encounter with 1920s sf in the introduction and notes to *The Early Williamson* (coll **1975**), which assembles some of the rough but vigorous stories he published 1928-33; and amplified this material in *Wonder's Child: My Life in Science Fiction* (**1984**), which won a 1986 HUGO. These reminiscences reconfirm the explosively liberating effect early PULP-MAGAZINE sf had on its first young audiences, especially those who like JW grew up in small towns or farms across a USA hurtling out of its rural past.

After discovering AMAZING STORIES, and specifically being influenced by its 1927 serialization of A. MERRITT's *The Moon Pool* (**1919**), JW immediately decided to try to write stories for that magazine. His first published fiction, "The Metal Man" in 1928 for *AMZ*, was deeply influenced by Merritt's lush visual style, but like most of his early work conveyed an exhilarating sense of liberation. JW was from the first an adaptable writer, responsive to the changing nature of his markets, and his collaborations over the years seemed to be genuine attempts to learn more about his craft as well as to produce saleable fiction. His first great teacher after Merritt was Miles J. BREUER, whom he came across through his early association with fan organizations like the International Science Correspondence Club and the American Interplanetary Society, and to whom he deliberately apprenticed himself. Breuer, he reported in *The Early Williamson*, "taught me to curb my tendencies toward wild melodrama and purple adjectives"; what JW gave Breuer in return was an inspiring fount of energy, and both of their book collaborations – *The Girl from Mars* (**1929** chap) and *The Birth of a New Republic* (1931 *AMZ Quarterly*; **1981** chap [but large pages]) – were written primarily by the younger man, following Breuer's ideas.

JW's development was swift. From the very first he was equally comfortable with both story and novel forms; indeed, by 1940 he had published over 12 novels in the magazines, including *The Alien Intelligence* (1929 *Science Wonder Stories*; with 2 shorter stories as coll **1980** chap [but large pages]) and the unreprinted "The Stone from the Green Star" (1931), "Xandulu" (1934), "Islands of the Sun" (1935), "The Blue Spot" (1937) and "Fortress of Utopia" (1939); and in his later career he concentrated even more heavily on longer forms. The best of his pre-WWII work was probably the **Legion of Space** series, which initially comprised *The Legion of Space* (1934 *ASF*; rev **1947**) and *The Cometeers* (coll **1950**) – itself containing 2 items, *The Cometeers* (1936 *ASF*; rev for 1950 coll; **1967**) and *One Against the Legion* (1939 *ASF*; with the new "Nowhere Near" added, as coll **1967**) – all this material being subsequently assembled as *Three from the Legion* (omni **1979**). *The Queen of the Legion* (**1983**) was a very late and significantly less energetic addendum. The series depicts the far-flung, Universe-shaking, SPACE-OPERA adventures of 4 buccaneering soldiers. (Giles Habibula, the most original of the lot – though his conception clearly owed much to RABELAIS and to Shakespeare's Falstaff – became a frequently used model for later sf life-loving grotesques, including Poul ANDERSON's Nicholas van

Rijn.) More or less unaided, they save the human worlds from threats both internal and external in conjunction with the woman whose hereditary role it is to guard from evil a doomsday device called AKKA. The influence of E.E. "Doc" SMITH's **Lensmen** saga can be felt throughout; and JW's relative incapacity to impart a sense of scale was perhaps balanced by a very much greater gift for characterization. Other early novels, like *The Green Girl* (1930 *AMZ*; **1950**) and *Golden Blood* (1933 *Weird Tales*; rev **1964**), share a crude narrative brio, adaptability to various markets, vivid characters, and some lack of ambition. The exception, perhaps, was the **Legion of Time** sequence (not connected to the **Legion of Space** sequence), assembled as *The Legion of Time* (coll **1952**; vt *Two Complete Novels: After World's End; The Legion of Time* 1963), containing *The Legion of Time* (1938 *ASF*; cut **1961** UK) and *After World's End* (1939 *Marvel Science Stories*; **1961** UK). One of the earliest and most ingenious stories of ALTERNATE WORLDS and TIME PARADOXES – with conflicting potential future worlds battling through time, each trying to ensure its own existence and deny its opponent's – the sequence inspired one of the most penetrating studies yet written about a pulp-sf novel, Brian W. ALDISS's "Judgement at Jonbar" (1964), published in SF HORIZONS.

By the 1940s, however, John W. CAMPBELL Jr's GOLDEN AGE OF SF had begun, and JW was suddenly an old-timer. Though JW did not much participate in its inception, he did adapt to the new world with commendable speed, and by the end of the decade had published what will probably remain his most significant work. A transitional series – the **Seetee** ANTIMATTER tales – came first: *Seetee Ship* (1942-3 *ASF*; fixup **1951**) and *Seetee Shock* (1949 *ASF*; **1950**), both published as by Will Stewart but reissued in 1968 as by JW, assembled as *Seetee Ship/Seetee Shock* (omni **1971**; vt *Seetee* 1979), and designed to be read in the original magazine order. These confront the world with the engineering challenge of coping with the antimatter that is found to make up part of the ASTEROID belt; more smoothly told than its predecessors, the series still unchallengingly presents its asteroid miners and their crises in the old fashion, with a great deal of action but little insight. Its success led to JW's creation of a COMIC strip, **Beyond Mars**, which ran for 3 years in the *New York Daily News*. Far more significant was *Darker than You Think* (1940 *Unknown*; exp **1948**), a remarkable speculative novel about lycanthropy which early presented the thesis that werewolves are genetic throwbacks to a species cognate with *Homo sapiens* (◊ SUPERNATURAL CREATURES). Also in the 1940s came JW's most famous sequence, the **Humanoids** series: "With Folded Hands" (1947), *The Humanoids* (1948 *ASF* as ". . . And Searching Mind"; rev **1949**) – both assembled as *The Humanoids* (coll of linked stories **1980**) – "Jamboree" (1969) and *The Humanoid Touch* (**1980**). Once again at an early point in the genre's history, these confronted the near impossibility of assessing the plusses and minuses of a humanoid (i.e., artificial-INTELLIGENCE-driven) hegemony over the world, however benevolent. In *The Humanoids* itself it is suggested that humanity's new masters are contriving to force people to transcend their condition; in *The Humanoid Touch* this ambiguity is lost for, at the end of the Galaxy, long hence, the euphoria induced by humanity's keepers is both impossible to perceive and mandatory.

In the early 1950s JW began to suffer from a writer's block which he did not fully escape for more than two decades, though he continued to produce novels of interest like *Dragon's Island* (**1951**; vt *The Not-Men* **1968**), whose presentation of GENETIC ENGINEERING once again conceals a prescient numeracy under a bluff, slightly archaic narrative style. Much of his new work from this point was collaborative, and the continued modernizing of his techniques and concerns can be seen as an ongoing demonstration of his remarkable willingness to learn from the world and from others. *Star Bridge* (**1955**) with James E. GUNN was just a competent space opera, but JW's ongoing partnership with Frederik POHL was of more interest, though their first sequence, the **Eden** series of juveniles – *Undersea Quest* (**1954**), *Undersea Fleet* (**1956**) and *Undersea City* (**1958**) – was routine; all 3 were eventually assembled as «The Undersea Trilogy» (omni **1992**). The second, the **Starchild** tales – *The Reefs of Space* (**1964**), *Starchild* (**1965**) and *Rogue Star* (**1969**), assembled as *The Starchild Trilogy* (omni **1977**) – also fails to combine space opera and METAPHYSICS convincingly as it traces the problematic epic of humanity's EVOLUTION into a mature planet-spanning species (◊ LIVING WORLDS). The **Cuckoo** series – *The Farthest Star* (fixup **1975**) and *Wall Around a Star* (**1983**), both assembled as *The Saga of Cuckoo* (omni **1983**) – does not quite succeed in bringing to life its cosmogonic premises or its LINGUISTIC concerns. On the other hand, *Land's End* (**1988**), with Pohl, is an enjoyable singleton; in it a comet destroys the ozone layer and humanity seeks refuge UNDER THE SEA. *The Singers of Time* (**1991**), with Pohl, is also strong.

In the 1950s JW embarked on a second career at Eastern New Mexico University, where he took a BA in English and an MA with an unpublished 1957 thesis, "A Study of the Sense of Prophecy in Modern Science Fiction". He taught the modern novel and literary criticism until his retirement in 1977, while being deeply involved in promoting sf as an academic subject (◊ SF IN THE CLASSROOM). He had taken a PhD with the University of Colorado in 1964 on H.G. WELLS's early sf, and expanded his thesis into *H.G. Wells: Critic of Progress* (**1973**), a book which, despite some methodological clumsiness, valuably examines Wells's complex development of ideas as they relate to the idea of progress. In 1973 JW received a PILGRIM AWARD for his academic work relating to sf.

In the meanwhile he began slowly to enter the Indian summer of his writing career, though novels like *The Moon Children* (**1972**) and *The Power of Blackness* (fixup **1976**) are surprisingly insecure and the series continuations (see above) lack the force of their models. It seemed that his old age would demonstrate his slow – even though technically productive – decline. But *The Best of Jack Williamson* (coll **1978**) again demonstrated his early strengths, and although *Brother to Demons, Brother to Gods* (**1979**) was weak, in the 1980s JW began to produce work of an astonishing youthfulness. *Manseed* (**1983**) uses the space-opera format to investigate, with renewed freshness, the imaginative potential of genetic engineering. *Lifeburst* (**1984**) is an exercise in interstellar Realpolitik, grim and engrossing in its depiction of the parcelling out of Earth, sophisticated in its presentation of sexual material; its sequel, *Mazeway* (**1990**), has the air of a juvenile in its vivid presentation of the eponymous galactic test that the young protagonists must pass to render humanity eligible for higher things. *Firechild* (**1986**) generates a rhetoric of transcendence – very much in the fashion of the 1980s – out of BIOLOGY. *Into the Eighth Decade* (coll **1990**) serves as a brief resumé of JW's post-WWII career. *Beachhead* (**1992**) describes an expedition to a MARS according to contemporary knowledge, although the plot itself is redolent of a much earlier era. In 1976 he was given the second Grand Master NEBULA award (his sole predecessor was Robert A. HEINLEIN). He has been an sf writer of substance for over 60 years. In his work and in his life he has encompassed the field. [JC]

Other works: *Lady in Danger* (1934 *Weird Tales* as "Wizard's Isle"; **1945** chap UK), a novelette with a short story by E. Hoffmann PRICE added; *Dome Around America* (1941 *Startling Stories* as "Gateway to Paradise"; rev **1955** dos); *The Trial of Terra* (fixup **1962** dos); *The Reign of Wizardry* (1940 *Unknown*; rev **1964**; again rev 1979); *Bright New Universe* (**1967**); *Trapped in Space* (**1968**), a juvenile; *The Pandora Effect* (coll **1969**); *People Machines* (coll **1971**); *Passage to Saturn* (1939 *TWS*; **1973** chap UK); *Dreadful Sleep* (1938 *Weird Tales*; **1977** chap).

As editor: *Teaching Science Fiction for Tomorrow* (anth **1980**).

Nonfiction: *Science Fiction Comes to College* (**1971** chap; exp 1971 chap); *Science Fiction in College* (**1971** chap; exp 1972 chap); *Teaching SF* (**1972** chap; exp 1973 chap; again exp 1973 chap; exp 1974 chap).

About the author: *Jack (John Stewart) Williamson, Child and Father of Wonder* (**1985** chap) by Gordon BENSON Jr.

See also: AIR WONDER STORIES; ALIENS; ANDROIDS; ASTOUNDING SCIENCE-FICTION; AUTOMATION; BLACK HOLES; CHILDREN IN SF; COLONIZATION OF OTHER WORLDS; CRIME AND PUNISHMENT; FANTASTIC VOYAGES; FASTER THAN LIGHT; GALACTIC EMPIRES; GREAT AND SMALL; HEROES; HISTORY IN SF; HISTORY OF SF; LIFE ON OTHER WORLDS; LONGEVITY (IN WRITERS AND PUBLICATIONS); MACHINES; MATTER TRANSMISSION; MESSIAHS; MONSTERS; MOON; MUTANTS; MYTHOLOGY; ORIGIN OF MAN; OUTER PLANETS; PARALLEL WORLDS; POLITICS; POWER SOURCES; ROBOTS; SF MAGAZINES; SCIENCE FICTION WRITERS OF

AMERICA; SPACESHIPS; STARS; SUN; SUPERMAN; TERRA-FORMING; TIME TRAVEL; TRANSPORTATION; WAR; WEAPONS; WRITERS OF THE FUTURE CONTEST.

WILLINGHAM, CALDER (BARNARD Jr) (1922-) US writer whose flamboyant Southern regionalism was most fully expressed in *Eternal Fire* (**1963**). His sf novel, *The Building of Venus Four* (**1977**), a SEX-loaded spoof SPACE OPERA, fails to convey much sense of his best work. [JC]

WILLIS, CHARLES [s] ◊ Arthur C. CLARKE.

WILLIS, CONNIE Working name of US teacher and writer Constance Elaine Trimmer Willis (1945-). She began publishing sf with "Santa Titicaca" for *Worlds of Fantasy* in 1971, but appeared only intermittently in the field until the early 1980s, when she began to write full-time, winning several awards almost immediately. Most of her best work of the 1980s was in short-story form, and her first book, *Fire Watch* (coll **1985**), assembled a remarkable range of tales. "Fire Watch" (1982) itself, which won both NEBULA and HUGO, uses its TIME-TRAVEL premise – a future institute of historiography sends individuals back in time to study artifacts *in situ* – to embed its protagonist in a richly conceived UK at the time of the Blitz, when he engages himself in attempts to save St Paul's Cathedral from bombing. "All My Darling Daughters" – published as an original in *Fire Watch* because its language and theme were still unacceptable in the US magazine market of 1980 – is a significantly harsh tale of alienation and SEX set in a boarding school in an L5 orbit, where the male students rape alien lifeforms which have vagina-like organs, making them scream in pain; and the female protagonist, having suffered from parental incest, tries to make sense of her hyperbolic adolescence in terms strongly reminiscent of J.D. Salinger (1919-). Among other tales of interest in this first collection are *Daisy, in the Sun* (1979 *Galileo*; **1991** chap), "A Letter from the Clearys" (1982), which won a Nebula, "The Sidon in the Mirror" (1983) and the comic "Blued Moon" (1984). A later novella, "The Last of the Winnebagos" (1988), won CW both the Hugo and the Nebula, and "At the Rialto" (1989) won a Nebula.

As a novelist, CW began slowly with the relatively lightweight *Water Witch* (**1982**) with Cynthia FELICE, set on a sand planet where the ability to dowse for water is a precious gift. *Light Raid* (**1989**) with Felice also skids helter-skelter through an sf environment, in this case a post-HOLOCAUST balkanized USA fighting off Canadian royalists, featuring the adventures *en route* to spunky maturity of a young female protagonist much like those found in Robert A. HEINLEIN's less attractive books. But it seemed clear that both CW and Felice were treating their collaborations as *jeux d'esprit*, and CW's first solo novel, *Lincoln's Dreams* (**1987**), aimed successfully at a very much higher degree of seriousness, winning the JOHN W. CAMPBELL MEMORIAL AWARD. Once again – as with much of her most deeply felt work – the enabling sf

instrument is time travel, though in this case via a psychic linkage between a contemporary woman and General Robert E. Lee (1807-1870), while at the same time the male protagonist increasingly, and without a breath of frivolity, seems to be taking on the psychic attributes of General Lee's famous horse, Traveller (himself the protagonist of *Traveller* [**1988** US] by Richard Adams [1920-]). The power of *Lincoln's Dreams* lies in the haunting detail of CW's presentation of the American Civil War, which seems in her hands terrifyingly close – both geographically and psychically – to the contemporary world. Her second solo novel, *Doomsday Book* (**1992**), is another time-travel story. The frame setting – a mid-21st-century historiographic unit attached to Cambridge University – is shared with "Fire Watch", but the tale itself is set at the time of the Black Death (around 1350), and mounts gradually to a climax whose intensely mourning gravity is rarely found in sf, even in novels of travel to times past, where a sense of irretrievable loss is commonly expressed.

In the best of CW's stories, and in her novels, a steel felicity of mind and style appears effortlessly married to a copious empathy. She seems to be one of those writers from the 1980s who are now approaching their best work. [JC]

See also: ISAAC ASIMOV'S SCIENCE FICTION MAGAZINE; OMNI; PHYSICS; PSYCHOLOGY; WEAPONS.

WILLIS, MAUD [r] ◊ Eileen LOTTMAN.

WILLIS, WALT [r] ◊ HUGO; HYPHEN; NEBULA SCIENCE FICTION; QUANDRY; Bob SHAW; SLANT; WARHOON; XERO.

WILLUMSEN, DORRIT [r] ◊ DENMARK.

WILSON, [Sir] ANGUS (FRANK JOHNSTONE) (1913-1991) UK writer best known for *Anglo-Saxon Attitudes* (**1956**) and other novels sharply anatomical of modern life. His one sf novel, *The Old Men at the Zoo* (**1961**), applies MAINSTREAM techniques to a 1970s NEAR-FUTURE vision of the UK threatened internally by loss of nerve and by neofascism, and externally by a federated Europe. AW was an early supporter of the hardcover PUBLISHING of GENRE SF in the UK, and edited the book of the best stories entered for the *Observer* sf prize in 1954, *A.D. 2500* (anth **1955**). *The Strange Ride of Rudyard Kipling* (**1977**), nonfiction, analyses KIPLING in terms which elucidate the haunting power of that author's genre work. AW was knighted in 1980. [JC]

See also: HISTORY OF SF.

WILSON, ANNA (1954-) UK-born writer, now resident in the USA. Her novels are sharp FEMINIST parables. *Altogether Elsewhere* (**1985**) depicts a NEAR-FUTURE feminist backlash against male violence. *Hatching Stones* (**1991**) portrays a society in which males largely abandon females when GENETIC ENGINEERING allows them to clone "sons", although a modified form of the family survives in a quasi-UTOPIAN society where all the adults are female. [BS/JC]

WILSON, COLIN (HENRY) (1931-) UK writer of speculative works best known for his first book, *The Outsider* (**1956**) (in which he gave graphic expression to the brilliant autodidactism, the erratic system-building mentality, and the voracity for new mental sensations that would mark the very numerous titles he would produce over the next several decades, many of them of indirect interest to sf and fantasy writers and readers, for his numerous books on crime, notably *A Criminal History of Mankind* (**1984**) and *Written in Blood: A History of Forensic Detection* (**1989**), and for his investigations of the paranormal, of which the most important are *The Occult* (**1971**), *Mysteries: An Investigation into the Occult, the Paranormal, and the Supernatural* (**1978**), *Poltergeist!* (**1981**) and *Beyond the Occult* (**1988**). Sf critics have not generally responded with much warmth to CW's later work, perhaps because his eagerness to penetrate the barriers of "orthodox" science has led him into assumptions about and formulations of the nature of consciousness that seem to lurch dangerously far into the realms of PSEUDO-SCIENCE; that is, the science he uses as underpinning for his sf is often not generally accepted as such. A further difficulty is that, as his total oeuvre has grown, it has become harder to work out which texts are deeply considered, which are blarney, and which are potboilers.

Nevertheless, his sf is of considerable interest. *The Return of the Lloigor* (in *Tales of the Cthulhu Mythos*, anth **1969** US; rev **1974** chap UK) is fantasy. His only sf short story is "Timeslip" (in *Aries 1* [anth **1979**] ed John Grant [Paul BARNETT]). His first sf novel, *The Mind Parasites* (**1967**), combines the long temporal perspectives of H.P. LOVECRAFT's **Cthulhu Mythos** with the transcendental solipsism of A.E. VAN VOGT and the metabiological pathos of George Bernard SHAW in a tale which suggests that humanity has for eons been deliberately hampered by ALIEN entities, and that these shackles could be cast off. *The Philosopher's Stone* (**1969**), perhaps the most intellectually stimulating of his novels, with an appealingly ramshackle construction, again invokes Cthulhu to suggest that the Old Ones who seem to be keeping humanity in thrall are in fact asleep and indifferent. *The Space Vampires* (**1976**; vt *Lifeforce* 1985 US), filmed as LIFEFORCE (1985), promulgates the same message in the form of a partly SPACE-OPERA horror tale featuring, once again, parasitic aliens and a human race of thwarted (but infinite) potential. A similar dynamic of oppression and release serves as the philosophical base underlying the boys'-fiction dramaturgy of the later **Spider World** sequence – *Spider World: The Tower* (**1987**; vt in 3 vols as *Spider World 1: The Desert* 1988 US, *Spider World 2: The Tower* 1989 US and *Spider World 3: The Fortress* 1989 US), *Spider World: The Delta* (**1987**) and *Spider World: The Magician* (**1992**) – set in a FAR-FUTURE Earth whose human remnants live in thralldom to giant arachnids.   [JC/JGr]

Other works: Many works including the **Gerard Sorme** series – *Ritual in the Dark* (**1960**), *Man Without a Shadow: The Diary of an Existentialist* (**1963**; vt *The Sex Diary of Gerard Sorme* 1963 US and 1968 UK) and *The God of the Labyrinth* (**1970**; vt *The Hedonists* 1971 US) –

of which the 2nd is borderline fantasy and the 3rd fantasy proper; *The Black Room* (**1971**), about sensory deprivation; the **Chief Superintendent Gregory Saltfleet** series of psi/occult whodunnits, being *The Schoolgirl Murder Case* (**1974**) and *The Janus Murder Case* (**1984**); *The Personality Surgeon* (**1985**).

Nonfiction: Many works including *The Strength to Dream: Literature and the Imagination* (**1962**); *The Strange Genius of David Lindsay* (**1970**; vt *The Haunted Man* 1979 US) with E.H. VISIAK and J.B. Pick, on David LINDSAY; *Tree by Tolkien* (1973 chap); *Science Fiction as Existentialism* (**1978** chap); *Starseekers* (**1980**); *Frankenstein's Castle* (**1980**); *The Quest for Wilhelm Reich* (**1981**); *Afterlife* (**1985**).

As editor: *Dark Dimensions: A Celebration of the Occult* (anth **1978** US); *The Book of Time* (anth **1980**) with John Grant; *The Directory of Possibilities* (**1981**), also with Grant.

About the author: *Colin Wilson: The Outside and Beyond* (**1979**) by Clifford P. Bendau; *The Novels of Colin Wilson* (**1982**) by Nicolas Tredell; *The Work of Colin Wilson: An Annotated Bibliography and Guide* (**1989**) by Colin Stanley.

See also: GREAT AND SMALL; MONSTERS; PARASITISM AND SYMBIOSIS; SUSPENDED ANIMATION; TIME TRAVEL.

WILSON, F(RANCIS) PAUL (1946-   ) US physician and writer who began publishing sf with "The Cleaning Machine" for *Startling Mystery Stories* in 1971. His early career was much influenced by John W. CAMPBELL Jr, in whose *ASF* he published several of his best 1970s stories, including the early versions of tales which reached book form as the **LaNague Federation** series – *Healer* (1972 *ASF* as "Pard"; exp **1976**), which was elected to the Prometheus Hall of Fame in 1990; *Wheels within Wheels: A Novel of the LaNague Federation* (1971 *ASF*; exp **1978**), which won the first Prometheus AWARD for LIBERTARIAN SF; and *An Enemy of the State* (**1980**). The sequence engagingly deployed FPW's knowledgeability, the deft clarity of his writing, and his unabashed and comfortable use of pulp concepts – like LaNague himself, an immortal psychiatric healer who repeatedly saves the Solar System from enemies internal and external – to express what might be called philosophical perspectives on the world: the influence of Albert Camus (1913-1960) upon the creation of LaNague has been adduced.

In the 1980s, FPW began to concentrate on novels like *The Keep* (**1981**), the first novel in the **Adversary** sequence, an impressive horror tale set in WWII in the Transylvanian Alps, where a Nazi garrison is being slowly destroyed by vampires indigenous to the eponymous lodging; it was filmed in 1983. The first sequel, *Reborn* (**1990**), is less assured, and demonstrates some lack of commercial facility during those moments when the buried Evil from the first book is unconvincingly shown to be living-dead; but *Reprisal* (**1991**; vt *Reprisals* 1991 UK) more successfully broadens the compass of the conflict between humans and a dark nemesis. Although *Dydeetown*

World (fixup **1989**) is an sf thriller reminiscent of his 1970s work, FPW had clearly evolved from the genre by this point, and in 1991 he stands as a potentially major HORROR writer. [JC]

Other works: *The Tery* (1973 *Fiction 4* as "He Shall Be John"; exp **1979** chap dos; with stories added, further exp as coll **1990**); *The Tomb* (**1984**); *The Touch* (**1986**); *Black Wind* (**1988**); *Soft and Others* (coll **1989**); *Ad Statum Perspicuum* (coll **1990**); *Midnight Mass* (**1990** chap); *Pelts* (**1990** chap); *Sibs* (**1991**); *Buckets* (**1991** chap); *The Barrens* (**1992**).

See also: PARASITISM AND SYMBIOSIS.

WILSON, (JOHN) GROSVENOR (1866-?) US writer in whose sf novel, *The Monarch of Millions, or The Rise and Fall of the American Empire* (**1900**), a 1950s USA is strictly organized according to wealth, with the Emperor richest of all; the sciences have advanced remarkably but the people remain potentially restive, and young Demos from Alaska is able to topple the old plutocracy. Unfortunately – despite this cosmetic democratization – the power structure remains intact. The book's cynicism tends to neutralize some of the foggy allegory. [JC]

WILSON, J. ARBUTHNOT [s] ◊ Grant ALLEN.

WILSON, RICHARD (1920-1987) US writer and director of the News Bureau of Syracuse University until his retirement in 1982. Involved in sf from an early age, he was a founder of the FUTURIANS in the 1930s, publishing his first sf story, "Murder from Mars", with *Astonishing Stories* in 1940; "Stepsons of Mars", which he wrote with fellow Futurian C.M. KORNBLUTH under the house name Ivar TOWERS, appeared in the same issue. A further Towers story, "The Man without a Planet" (1942), was by RW alone; he later used the pseudonym Edward Halibut for "Course of Empire" (1956). War service interrupted his career, but after 1950 – perhaps finding the new atmosphere in sf congenial to his gently satirical, humorous bent – he contributed prolifically to the magazines for some years, and soon published his first novel, *The Girls from Planet 5* (**1955**), the first of 3 in which ALIENS comically invade Earth (◊ INVASION; SEX; WOMEN AS PORTRAYED IN SCIENCE FICTION); the others were *And Then the Town Took Off* (**1960** dos) and *30-Day Wonder* (**1960**). In each, RW made use of the arrivals from outer space to generate mocking perspectives on our own behaviour: from the strident patriarchy still attempting, in the first novel, to keep Texas pure although the rest of the USA has become a matriarchy, to the appalling consequences, in the third, of being exposed to aliens who observe to the literal letter all Earth laws and enforce similar behaviour on us. Similarly couched SATIRE dominated his first 2 collections, *Those Idiots from Earth* (coll **1957**) and *Time Out for Tomorrow* (coll **1962**).

Unfortunately, from the mid-1960s RW published no books at all – *Adventures in the Space Trade* (**1986** chap dos), a memoir, *A Rat for a Friend* (**1986** chap), a story, and *The Kid from Ozone Park & Other Stories* (coll **1987** chap), though welcome, were pamphlet-length

– and most of the graver, smoother, finer stories of his last decades remained uncollected. He won a 1968 NEBULA for his novelette "Mother to the World" (1968); other late stories of interest include "See Me Not" (1967), "A Man Spekith" (1969), "The Day They had the War" (1971) and the contents of *The Kid from Ozone Park* (all originals). In his later years, RW reportedly made it clear to colleagues that he remained too content in his professional life to continue seriously in a writing career. It is understood that a long story awaits publication in Harlan ELLISON's projected «Last Dangerous Visions». [JC]

About the author: *A Richard Wilson Checklist* (**1986** chap dos) by Chris DRUMM.

WILSON, ROBERT ANTON (1932-) US writer who remains best known for the first **Illuminatus!** sequence – *The Eye in the Pyramid* (**1975**), *The Golden Apple* (**1975**) and *Leviathan* (**1975**), assembled as *The Illuminatus Trilogy* (omni **1984**) – all written with Robert SHEA. Shea did not collaborate on *Cosmic Trigger: The Final Secret of the Illuminati* (**1977**), *The Illuminati Papers* (**1980**), *Masks of the Illuminati* (**1981**) or *Right Where You Are Sitting Now: Further Tales of the Illuminati* (coll **1982**) – some of these volumes being presented as nonfiction – or on **The Historical Illuminatus Chronicles**, set in the 18th century: *The Earth Will Shake* (**1984**), *The Widow's Son* (**1985**) and *Nature's God* (**1991**). Shea did, however, write continuations of his own (*see his entry*). The series combines detective, FANTASY and sf components into the extremely complex tale of a vast conspiracy on the part of the Illuminati, historically a late-18th-century German association of freethinkers but here rendered into the gods of H.P. LOVECRAFT's **Cthulhu Mythos**, among other incarnations, so that mortals cohabit irretrievably with warring gods; throughout, the PARANOIA engendered by any and all attempts to understand immortal conspiracies, of which all the things of the world were emblems, reminded many readers of Thomas PYNCHON, but an unPynchonesque lightheartedness permeates the sequence. On the basis of their other works, this nihilistic gaiety derived in the main from RAW, and was clearly evident as well in *The Sex Magician* (**1974**), which was expanded and transformed into the ultimately opaque complexities of *Schrödinger's Cat: The Universe Next Door* (**1979**), *II: The Trick Top Hat* (**1980**) and *III: The Homing Pigeons* (**1981**), all 3 assembled as *Schrödinger's Cat Trilogy* (omni **1988**), a sequence which transformed the worlds of subatomic physics into a pattern of ALTERNATE WORLDS. It might be thought that RAW, like many 1980s writers, would slip into VIRTUAL-REALITY venues when attempting to manipulate levels of perception; but ultimately he refused to supply comforts of that ilk, for in his work there is no centre to the labyrinth, no master waiting to reward the heroes of the quest. [JC]

Other works: *Semiotext(e) SF* (anth **1990**) with Rudy RUCKER and Robert Lamborn Wilson; *Reality is What You Can Get Away With* (**1992**), an sf spoof.

See also: HUMOUR; LIBERTARIAN SF; MUSIC; PHYSICS; THEATRE.

WILSON, ROBERT CHARLES (1953-) US-born writer, in Canada from 1962, who began to publish sf with "Equinocturne" for *ASF* in 1974, though he did not make a significant impact on the field until the 1980s, when he began to publish his polished and inventive novels. His first, *A Hidden Place* (**1986**), prefigures much of his work in positing an emotion-drenched binary between the mundane world and an ALTERNATE WORLD, in this case the latter being the realm of Faery, though presented in an sf idiom; as in his later work, a protagonist embedded in every-day reality must come to terms with – and perhaps take ethically acceptable advantage of – the fragile opening to a better place that seems to be on offer. The "other place" in *Memory Wire* (**1987**) is a kind of LOST WORLD temporally removed from a CYBERPUNK 21st century; the protagonists make contact with it through "oneiroliths" or dream stones. In *Gypsies* (**1989** US) an entire family of Earth children live in various states of pathological denial of their capacity to walk through the walls of this world into a variety of parallel existences (◊ PARALLEL WORLDS); out of one of these, which is profoundly DYSTOPIAN, comes the Grey Man who haunts the family in his attempts to lure the children "back" to the dreadful world in which he claims they belong. But they escape him, ending in a pastoral world much like a realm of the Pacific Rim in which it does not rain much. *The Divide* (**1990** US) locates the binary within the skull of a character who contains 2 utterly distinct selves; the book slips into melodrama – it is perhaps RCW's weakest novel – and its split-brain conundra are solved by a blow to the head. In *A Bridge of Years* (**1991** US) the divide lies between the present and 1961, which are connected through TIME TRAVEL and a plot which deals, in familiar terms, with a long-ranging time-war between vying reality-lines. The persistency of RCW's basic concerns allows him, on occasion, to slide into routine formulations; but, throughout, he expresses with vigour and imagination the great Canadian theme (for the sense of being on the lonely side of a binary has sparked much of the best Canadian sf) of geographical alienation. In «The Harvest» (1993), his most ambitious novel to date, an alien group intelligence offers humanity gifts of immortality, undying curiosity and wisdom; most accept.

RCW should not be confused with the author of *The Crooked Tree* (**1980**), Robert C(harles) Wilson (1951-   ).   [JC]

See also: CANADA; SUPERMAN.

WILSON, ROBERT HENDRIE [r] ◊ ROBERT HALE LIMITED.

WILSON, ROBIN SCOTT (1928-   ) US editor, writer and academic, currently President of California State University, Chico. He began publishing sf with "The State of the Art" for *FSF* in 1970; his best story is probably "For a While There, Herbert Marcuse, I Thought You Were Maybe Right About Alienation and Eros" (1972). His early work was published as by Robin Scott. RSW was most influential as the founder, with Damon KNIGHT and others, of the CLARION SCIENCE FICTION WRITERS' WORKSHOP in Clarion, Pennsylvania, in 1968. In addition to directing the workshop, he ed *Clarion: An Anthology of Speculative Fiction from the Clarion Writers' Workshop* (anth **1971**), *Clarion II* (anth **1972**) and *Clarion III* (anth **1973**); in the last he announced his retirement from Clarion. Additionally, RSW ed *Those who Can: A Science Fiction Reader* (anth **1973**), in which, interestingly, writers discuss their own and others' stories in the anthology under various critical headings.   [JC]

WILSON, SNOO (1948-   ) UK playwright and novelist whose sf novels *Spaceache* (**1984**) and *Inside Babel* (**1985**) comprise a short series of SATIRES whose targets are contemporary politics and culture. Unfortunately, his use of sf instruments is significantly less than competent – most notably, his attempt to make fun of SPACE OPERA founders on his manifest ignorance of its conventions and, indeed, of the scientific rationales underpinning them.   [JC]

See also: OVERPOPULATION; RADIO.

WILSON, STEVE (1943-   ) UK writer who published non-sf short fiction and 3 biker thrillers before the appearance of *The Lost Traveller* (**1976**) – not to be confused with Ruthven TODD's *The Lost Traveller* (**1943**). SW's version, set in a desolate post-HOLOCAUST venue at century's end, extols the survival capacity of a group of Hell's Angels, one of whom becomes a MESSIAH figure. At novel's end, after a battle with the army, it looks as though agriculture will be revived.   [JC]

WILSON, WILLIAM (?   -?   ) UK writer, one of several contemporaries with the same name, who devoted 2 chapters of his book of criticism, *A Little Earnest Book upon a Great Old Subject* (**1851**), to "The Poetry of Science", defining there a species of literature called "Science-Fiction" (the first use of the term) as writing "in which the revealed truths of science may be given, interwoven with a pleasing story which may itself be poetical and true – thus circulating a knowledge of the Poetry of Science, clothed in a garb of the Poetry of Life". His (unconvincing) example is *The Poor Artist* by R.H. HORNE (*c* 1844; **1871**).   [BS]

See also: DEFINITIONS OF SF.

WILTSHIRE, DAVID [r] ◊ ROBERT HALE LIMITED.

WINDLING, TERRI (1958-   ) US editor, artist and writer who began in the first capacity in 1979 at ACE BOOKS, where she developed the company's fantasy line, discovering such authors as Steven BRUST and Charles DE LINT, and launching the **Ace Fantasy Specials** with Emma BULL's *War for the Oaks* (**1987**). She moved to TOR BOOKS in 1987 as consulting editor, launching the **Fairy Tales** series with Brust's *The Sun, the Moon, and the Stars* (**1987**). The winner of 4 World Fantasy Awards for her editorial work, TW also edited with Mark Alan Arnold *Elsewhere* (anth **1981**),

Elsewhere, Volume II (anth **1982**) and *Elsewhere, Volume III* (anth **1984**), and edits with Ellen DATLOW (*whom see for details*) the **Year's Best Fantasy** annual anthology. [PNH]
Other works: *Faery!* (anth **1982**); the **Borderlands** SHARED-WORLD anthology series, the first 2 vols ed with Mark Alan Arnold: *Borderland* (anth **1986**), *Borderland 2* (anth **1986**) and *Life on the Border* (anth **1991**).

WINGED SERPENT, THE ◊ Q.

WINGRAVE, ANTHONY ◊ S. Fowler WRIGHT.

WINGROVE, DAVID (JOHN) (1954-   ) UK writer whose career breaks into 2 logical sequences. In the first he concentrated on critical work, the earliest significant example of which – «The Immortals of Science Fiction» (written 1980) – was printed but never released (although apparently copies have been circulated). *Apertures: A Study of the Writings of Brian Aldiss* (**1984**), with Brian GRIFFIN, was both admiring and reasonably comprehensive, and marked a close association with its subject, who introduced *The Science Fiction Source Book* (**1984**), which packs into relatively few pages a surprisingly comprehensive "Consumer's Guide" to sf novels; its main flaw is its sublimely overcomplicated quadripartite rating system. Aldiss then invited DW to participate with him in revising his energetic history of sf, *Billion Year Spree* (**1973**); the result, published as *Trillion Year Spree: The History of Science Fiction* (**1986**), with DW listed as co-author, attempts with partial success to sustain the élan of its much shorter parent, but falters in its coverage of the late 1970s and 1980s. It received a HUGO.

DW's career then changed direction, being subsequently dominated by the release of the first vols of his enormous **Chung Kuo** sequence, projected to reach 8 vols, and to date comprising *The Middle Kingdom* (**1989**), *The Broken Wheel* (**1990**), *The White Mountain* (**1991**) and *The Stone Within* (**1992**). Set in a 22nd- and 23rd-century Earth dominated by a monolithic Chinese hegemony which has successfully stymied all technological development, the sequence elaborately delineates a stalled and static culture, and clearly seems to be preparing the scene for a radical transformation of the world; the early volumes, perhaps consequently, are stronger as dynastic history than as sf. [JC]
See also: CRITICAL AND HISTORICAL WORKS ABOUT SF; DEFINITIONS OF SF; GOTHIC SF; PROTO SCIENCE FICTION.

WINIKI, EPHRIAM [s] ◊ John Russell FEARN.

WINSOR, G(EORGE) McLEOD (?   -?   ) Author, generally thought to be UK, in whose first sf novel, *Station X* (**1919**), a psychic INVASION from Mars is repelled by an Earth-Venus alliance; the book was reprinted (1975 US) with an intro by Richard Gid Powers which mystifyingly claims it to be an important work. In *The Mysterious Disappearances* (**1926**; vt *Vanishing Men* 1927 US) a criminal scientist uses a kind of ANTIGRAVITY to commit the sort of "impossible crime" so popular in the detective fiction of the

early decades of this century. [JC/PN]

WINSTON, STAN [r] ◊ PREDATOR 2; *The* TERMINATOR.

WINTER, H.G. [s] ◊ Harry BATES; Desmond W. HALL.

WINTERBOTHAM, RUSS(ELL ROBERT) (1904-1971) US newspaperman and writer, active as an author of sf and Westerns, as the creator of at least 60 **Big Little Books** (◊ DIME-NOVEL SF; JUVENILE SERIES) – including tales about **Maximo the Amazing Superman** (all **1941**) – and as the author of various COMIC strips throughout his career (he retired in 1969), initiating **Chris Welkin, Planeteer** in 1951 and scripting it into the 1960s. He published his first sf story, "The Star that Would not Behave", with *ASF* in 1935, and contributed most prolifically to the genre before WWII. After concentrating on work for Whitman Publishing Company (generator of the **Big Little Books** and other series for children), he returned to sf writing from 1952 and was again noted as a prolific author of unambitious work, soon publishing his first novel, *The Space Egg* (**1958**), about an INVASION of Earth; several other sf adventures followed, including *The Other World* (**1963**) as by J. Harvey Bond, and *Planet Big Zero* (**1964**), as by Franklin Hadley. [JC]
Other works: *The Red Planet* (**1962**); *The Men from Arcturus* (**1963**); *The Puppet Planet* (**1964**); *The Lord of Nardos* (**1966**).

WISE, ARTHUR (1923-   ) UK writer and drama consultant, most of whose works were thrillers; he wrote also as John McArthur. Most of his sf was borderline, using genre elements to heighten the suspense. The best known of these tales was probably *The Day the Queen Flew to Scotland for the Grouse Shooting* (**1968**), about the abduction of the monarch. A second NEAR-FUTURE, political novel was *Who Killed Enoch Powell?* (**1970**), where the assassination of that politician sets a complex thriller in motion, escalating to racial violence at Wimbledon. The displacement into sf of all his work is minimal. [JC]
Other works: *The Little Fishes* (**1961**); *The Death's-Head* (**1962**); *Leatherjacket* (**1970**).
As John McArthur: *Days in the Hay* (**1960**); *How Now Brown Cow* (**1962**).

WISE, ROBERT (1914-   ) US film director. RW began as a film-cutter at RKO Studios and by 1939 was a fully qualified editor. He worked on Orson Welles's *Citizen Kane* (1941) and also – at the studio's insistence when the director was out of the country – directed a few scenes in Welles's *The Magnificent Ambersons* (1942). He then worked with the Val Lewton unit at RKO, first as editor, then as director. He made 3 films for Lewton – *Curse of the Cat People* (1944; co-dir with Gunther von Fritsch), *Mademoiselle Fifi* (1944) and *The Body Snatcher* (1945) – and stayed with RKO until 1949. In 1951 he dir *The* DAY THE EARTH STOOD STILL. He did not return to the genre until *The* ANDROMEDA STRAIN (1971). A versatile director, he has made many kinds of films, including the musicals *West Side Story* (1961) and *The Sound of Music* (1964). He has made 2 superior contributions to the supernatural genre aside from his Lewton films: *The*

Haunting (1963), based on Shirley JACKSON's *The Haunting of Hill House* (**1959**) and *Audrey Rose* (**1977**). He returned spectacularly to sf with the controversial STAR TREK – THE MOTION PICTURE (1979), an ambitious attempt to fuse the simplistic original tv series with post-STAR WARS special effects and a transcendental 2001: A SPACE ODYSSEY vision. Subsequently he has directed only the feeble youth musical, *Rooftops* (1989). RW's work in sf and supernatural fantasy, at least until 1971, did more than that of most directors to bring some maturity to these genres in the cinema. [JB/PN/KN]

WISE, ROBERT A. Pseudonym of UK writer Fred J. Gebhart (? -), whose sf novel was the routine *12 to the Moon* (**1961**). He is unconnected with the film director Robert WISE. [JC]

WISMER, DON(ALD RICHARD) (1946-) US writer who began publishing sf with *Starluck* (**1982**), a competent sf adventure. *Warrior Planet* (**1987**) combines sf and fantasy elements in the story of an interstellar conflict between wizards and thieves. *Planet of the Dead* (**1988**) rather more convincingly sets a cadre of PSI-POWERED samurai warriors in pursuit of an interstellar drug gang. [JC]

Other works: *A Roil of Stars* (**1991**).

WITKACY ◊ Stanisław Ignacy WITKIEWICZ.

WITKIEWICZ, STANISLAW IGNACY (1885-1939) Polish playwright, novelist and painter, who also signed himself Witkacy; he committed suicide just after the Nazi invasion of his country when he learned that Soviet armies had attacked from the east, the direction in which he was fleeing. Much of his work, some eerily prophetic, deals darkly and humorously with the theme of a conservative world suddenly subjected to change, the clash of cultures, apocalypse and future totalitarianism. Of his 30 surviving plays, the most notable in this vein include the DYSTOPIAN fantasy *Gyubal Wahazar, czyli Na przeleczach besensu* ["Gyubal Wahazar, or Along the Cliffs of the Absurd"] (written 1921; **1962**), *Mątwa, czyli Hyrkaniczny światopogląd* ["The Cuttlefish, or The Hyrcanian World View"] (written 1922; **1923**), and most of the violent dramas of a surreal future assembled in *The Madman and the Nun and Other Plays* (all written 1920-30, published **1925-62**; coll trans Daniel C. Gerould and C.S. Durer **1968** US); of these, perhaps the most important is the blackly terrifying *Szewcy* (written 1930; **1948**; here trans as *The Shoemakers*), which predicts WWII. His 2 published novels are sf: *Pożegnanie jesieni* ["Farewell to Autumn"] (**1927**) and *Nienasycenie* (**1930**; trans Louis Iribarne as *Insatiability* **1977** US). In the former, Communists take over a future Poland. The latter, set in the 21st century, shows a fractured, ersatz West, a consumer society subject to a growing appetite for novelty, being taken over by Chinese Communists and Eastern mysticism, whose purveyors also provide happy pills. It is a distinguished and important novel. An uncompleted further tale, *Jedyne wyjęcie* ["The Only Way Out"] (written 1931-3; **1968**), furthers the dis-

course of its predecessor. It was not until 1962 that the Polish Government began, gingerly, to publish a collected edition of his work. [PN/JC]

About the author: *Witkacy: Stanisław Ignacy Witkiewicz as an Imaginative Writer* (**1981**) by Daniel C. Gerould.

See also: POLAND.

WITT, OTTO [r] ◊ SCANDINAVIA.

WITTIG, MONIQUE (1935-) French writer whose first sf novel, *Les Guérillères* (**1969**; trans David Le Vay as *The Guérillères* **1971** US), transforms the arguments of FEMINISM into a series of narrative litanies that work movingly to describe an abstract "tribe" of lesbian Amazons in a constant state of warfare with their natural enemy; the novel balances exquisitely between sf (when its images are taken literally) and poetry. In *Virgile, Non* (**1985**; trans David Le Vay as *Across the Acheron* **1987** UK), DANTE ALIGHIERI's *Inferno* is taken as a model of destructive patriarchy, and a deadly threat to any lesbian (a category which MW uses to designate a condition beyond the binary oppositions of our "normal" state) future. [JC]

See also: WOMEN SF WRITERS.

WLUDYKA, PETER (? -) US writer whose *The Past is Another Country* (**1988**) describes a USA, 143 years after a Russian invasion, in which thought-control is almost complete. The young protagonist discovers some of the truth about Christ and the disappeared city of New York, but only at great cost. Unfortunately for the book, the basic premise – that mutual disarmament was a Russian trick to gull pacifistic Americans – very soon became dated. [JC]

WOBIG, ELLEN (1911-) US writer whose *The Youth Monopoly* (**1968** dos) is an unremarkable sf adventure about rejuvenation. [JC]

WODEHOUSE, [Sir] P(ELHAM) G(RENVILLE) (1881-1975) UK writer, resident in the USA from long before WWII, known mainly for his non-genre novels, most of them comic, published in an unbroken stream from 1902 to the end of his life. *The Swoop! or How Clarence Saved England: A Tale of the Great Invasion* (**1909**) spoofed the future-WAR/INVASION genre so popular in the UK before 1914 with its description of 9 simultaneous invasions, 7 of which collapse, leaving the German and the Russian armies in command. Their chiefs compete with one another in music-hall recitals of their feats until Boy Scout Clarence Chugwater exposes the fact that one of them is being paid more than the others; the invasions end in ignominy. In *Laughing Gas* (**1936**) rival dentists' anaesthetics cause an identity switch between an earl and an obnoxious child star; the resulting story has all the marks of the typical PGW comedy, however, and is not easy to think of as sf. [JC]

See also: CLUB STORY; *The* MAGAZINE OF FANTASY AND SCIENCE FICTION.

WODHAMS, JACK (1931-) UK-born writer, in Australia from 1955, who began publishing sf with "There is a Crooked Man" for *ASF* in 1967, and who has since contributed actively (though less prolifically since the 1970s) to magazine markets, both in Australia and in the USA, specializing in clear-cut tales about problem-solving; he primarily writes short fiction, with over 70 stories published. His cold style is sometimes marred by facetiousness, in the Sunday-writer manner typical of many HARD-SF figures. Although the 4 novelettes assembled in *Future War* (coll **1982**) were original to that volume, the thrust of his *ASF* style can still be felt in tales whose overwhelming message is one of bleak disdain for sf's own visions of the wars of the future. His novels are *The Authentic Touch* (**1971** US), *Looking for Blücher* (**1980**) and *Ryn* (**1982**). The first, perhaps rather hopefully, suggests that things might get out of control in a planet made over into theme parks; *Looking for Blücher* investigates similar material in a loose-structured narrative about shared dreams; *Ryn*, probably his best novel, tells of a 62-year-old Black Zimbabwean reincarnated, to his bafflement, as a white baby in the Brisbane of a reticently depicted NEAR-FUTURE Australia. JW's hard-bitten humour can be tiresome at novel length, and he structures longer works badly. His short fiction is proficient, often witty, and good on military matters. Notable and typical is "Mostly Meantime" (*ASF* Feb 1981), about the difficulties of ordering replacement computer parts over galactic distances. [PN/JC]

WOJNA SWIATÓW-NASTĘPNE STULECIE ◊ POLAND.

WOLD, ALLEN L. (1943-   ) US writer who began with an unremarkable sf adventure, *The Planet Masters* (**1979**), followed by the more ambitious *Star God* (**1980**). He then became known for some "V" ties: *"V": The Pursuit of Diana* * (**1984**), *"V": The Crivit Experiment* * (**1985**) and *"V": Below the Threshhold* * (**1988**). In *Jewels of the Dragon* (**1986**) a young man in search of his lost father finds himself involved in events on a planet choked with romantic ruins. *The Eye of the Stone* (**1988**) is a fantasy. *Crown of the Serpent* (**1989**) is juvenile sf. *The Lair of the Cyclops* (**1992**) returns to the mode of *Jewels of the Dragon*, following the quest of a young man who finds something ancient on a planet. [JC]

WOLF, CHRIS L. [r] ◊ ROBERT HALF LIMITED.

WOLF, GARY K. (1941-   ) US writer who began publishing sf with "Love Story" for *Worlds of Tomorrow* in 1970, and followed with several sharply SATIRICAL tales over the next few years; the best of them, like "Dr Rivet and Supercon Sal" (1976), are generally thought to scan US society with a sharper, cleaner vision than that attained in his longer work. Soon, however, he began to concentrate on novels, beginning with *Killerbowl* (**1975**), a briskly violent portrait of a world – rather similar to that of ROLLERBALL (1975) – in which games are used to sublimate more politically dangerous passions (◊ GAMES AND SPORTS). *A Generation Removed* (**1977**) depicts a NEAR-FUTURE society in which the young have violently taken the reins of power and euthanasia of the middle-aged is common; here the analogy would be with LOGAN'S RUN (1976). *The Resurrectionist*

(**1979**), which develops the MATTER-TRANSMISSION premise of "The Bridge Builder" (1974), again exposes a corrupt world to violent retribution. *Who Censored Roger Rabbit?* (**1981**), filmed by Walt Disney in conjunction with Steven SPIELBERG's Amblin Entertainment as *Who Framed Roger Rabbit* (1988) dir Robert Zemeckis, could not in retrospect compete with the extraordinary and moving animation techniques which made the film an instant classic. A sequel, *Who P-P-Plugged Roger Rabbit?* (**1991**), involves the same cast in another adventure, this time a quest of the truth behind a rumoured love affair between Clark Gable and Roger's girl. The film itself has been followed by 2 **Roger Rabbit** shorts, *Tummy Trouble* (1989) and *Rollercoaster Rabbit* (1990); work on a further feature is (1992) at drawing-board stage. [JC]

WOLFE, AARON ◊ Dean R. KOONTZ.

WOLFE, BERNARD (1915-1985) US writer best known for his work outside the sf field. He gained a BA in psychology from Yale in 1935, worked for 2 years in the Merchant Marine, and for a time was a bodyguard to Leon Trotsky (1874-1940) in Mexico. He subsequently became a war correspondent, newsreel editor and freelance writer, and contributed stories and articles to many leading magazines. His first contribution to sf was a novelette in *Gal*, "Self Portrait" (1951), soon followed by his only sf novel, *Limbo* (**1952**; vt *Limbo '90* 1953 UK; cut 1961 US). This large and extravagant book is perhaps the finest sf novel of ideas to have been published during the 1950s. It portrays a future in which men have deliberately chosen to cut off their own arms and legs in order to avoid the risk of war. Complex (making use of many ideas from CYBERNETICS), ironic, hectoring and full of puns, *Limbo* was firmly based on BW's knowledge of psychoanalysis and in particular on his understanding of the masochistic instinct in modern Man. It is perhaps for this last quality that J.G. BALLARD has hailed it several times as the greatest US sf novel; Ballard may have sensed, too, that *Limbo* also functions as a corrosive assault upon the premises and instruments of sf itself. BW wrote very little subsequent sf, although Harlan ELLISON persuaded him to contribute 2 stories to *Again, Dangerous Visions* (anth **1972**): "The Bisquit Position", an impassioned anti-Vietnam-War story, centres on the image of a napalmed dog, and "The Girl with Rapid Eye Movements" is about sleep research and ESP. In his "Afterword" to these stories, BW expressed an extreme hostility to science and also to sf, which he considered its handmaiden. Further details of BW's remarkable career can be found in his *Memoirs of a Not Altogether Shy Pornographer* (**1972**). [DP]

See also: CYBERPUNK; CYBORGS; DYSTOPIAS; MEDICINE; WEAPONS.

WOLFE, GARY K(ENT) (1946-   ) US academic and writer, long associated with Roosevelt University in Chicago, latterly as Dean of the School of Continuing Education. Some of his earlier essays, like "The Known and the Unknown: Structure and Image in

Science Fiction" (1977), prefigured the typology of sf he presented in full in his most significant work, *The Known and the Unknown: The Iconography of Science Fiction* (**1979**), in which sf texts and their essential icons are defined according to their relationship to the permeable membrane separating us from the unknown, which GKW feels all sf attempts – or pretends to attempt – to pierce. The discussion is arranged around a lucid disposition of icons – the SPACESHIP, the CITY, the wasteland, the ROBOT and the MONSTER – and the book has served as an admirable mapping of its thesis (◊ CONCEPTUAL BREAKTHROUGH). In *Critical Terms for Science Fiction and Fantasy: A Glossary and Guide to Scholarship* (**1986**) GKW made a first attempt – a revised edn would be welcome – to describe the critical vocabulary used by scholars in their attempts to encompass this protean genre.   [JC]
Other works: *Planets and Dimensions: Collected Essays* (coll **1973** chap) by Clark Ashton SMITH, ed GKW; *Science Fiction Dialogues* (anth **1982**); *David Lindsay* (**1982** chap).
See also: CRITICAL AND HISTORICAL WORKS ABOUT SF; DEFINITIONS OF SF; GENRE SF; PILGRIM AWARD; PLANETARY ROMANCE; SPECULATIVE FICTION.

WOLFE, GENE (RODMAN) (1931-   ) US writer, born in New York, raised in Texas, and now living in Illinois. After serving in the Korean War – his experiences there are recorded in *Letters Home* (coll **1991**), which contains correspondence with his mother between 1952 and 1954 – he graduated in mechanical engineering from the University of Houston and worked in engineering until becoming the editor of a trade periodical, *Plant Engineering*, in 1972. Since retiring from this post in 1984, he has written full-time. Though neither the most popular nor the most influential author in the sf field, GW is today quite possibly the most important.

He started writing early, but did not find it easy to break into print; his first published story, "The Dead Man" for *Sir*, appeared as late as 1965, years after he had begun to create fiction of some distinction. In his early career, much of his best work tended to appear in various volumes of Damon KNIGHT's **Orbit** anthologies, starting with "Trip, Trap" (1967) and climaxing with the superb KAFKA-esque allegory, "Forlesen" (1970). In the middle of the series came "The Island of Doctor Death and Other Stories" (1970 *Orbit 7*), which was assembled – along with *The Death of Doctor Island* (1973 *Universe 3*, anth ed Robert SILVERBERG; **1990** chap dos), "The Doctor of Death Island" (1978), and "Death of the Island Doctor" (original to the coll) – as *The Wolfe Archipelago* (coll **1983**). These 4 stories, each fully autonomous though each mirroring the others' structural and thematic patterns, comprise an intensely interesting cubist portrayal of the mortal trap (or coffin) of identity, written in terms that are instrinsically sf in nature. From the first, in other words, GW created texts which – almost uniquely – married Modernism (◊ FABULATION) and sf, rather than putting them into rhetorical opposition; his

ultimate importance to world literature derives from the success of that marriage, though his use of a thoroughly natural sf idiom has of course ensured that the response to his work, on the part of non-sf critics, has been poverty-stricken.

CHILDREN – as very often in his work – tend to be the viewpoint characters in the **Archipelago** stories, giving the texts a supremely deceptive air of clarity – for although the surface is nearly always described with precision in a GW tale, the true story within is generally conveyed by indirection, revealing itself through the reader's ultimate comprehension of the proper and hierarchical sorting of its parts. Constrained to metaphorically fecund ISLAND contexts, the **Archipelago** tales are particularly intricate. The first treats with assurance the shifting line that divides fantasy and reality as a young boy retreats from a harsh adult environment into the more clear cut world generated by a pulp magazine. "The Death of Doctor Island" expands and reverses this theme in describing the treatment of a psychologically disturbed child constrained to an artificial environment which responds to his state of mind. In "The Doctor of Death Island" a cryogenically frozen prisoner is awakened to find that his bound isolation has been hardened into IMMORTALITY. All 3 protagonists must attempt – it is a compulsion that GW would inflict upon many of his characters – to decipher and to penetrate the stories that tell them, and by so doing to leap free. The NEBULA awarded to "The Island of Doctor Death" was nullified on a technicality, a situation rectified when GW later won a Nebula for "The Death of Doctor Island".

During the 1970s, GW continued to publish short stories at a considerable rate, at least 70 reaching print before the end of the decade; in the 1980s, as he concentrated more and more fully on novels, this production decreased markedly. His short work has been assembled in *The Island of Doctor Death and Other Stories and Other Stories* (coll **1980**), *Gene Wolfe's Book of Days* (coll **1981**), *Bibliomen: Twenty Characters Waiting for a Book* (coll of linked stories **1984** chap), *Plan[e]t Engineering* (coll **1984**), *Storeys from the Old Hotel* (coll **1988** UK) and *Endangered Species* (coll **1989**). Short stories of particular interest include "Three Million Square Miles" (1971 *Ruins of Earth*, anth ed Thomas M. DISCH), "Feather Tigers" (1973 *Edge*), "La Befana" (1973 *Gal*), *The Hero as Werwolf* (1975 *The New Improved Sun*, anth ed Disch; **1991** chap), "Tracking Song" (1975 *In the Wake of Man*, anth ed Roger ELWOOD), "The Eyeflash Miracles" (1976 *Future Power*, anth ed Gardner DOZOIS and Jack DANN), *Seven American Nights* (1978 *Orbit 20*, anth ed Damon Knight; **1989** chap dos), "The War Beneath the Tree" (1978 *Omni*) and "The Detective of Dreams" (1980 *Dark Forces*, anth ed Kirby McCauley). Later work was variously interesting, though in the 1980s GW was increasingly inclined, in short forms, to restrict his energies to the composition of oneiric *jeux d'esprit*.

GW's first novel, *Operation ARES* (**1970**), in which a

21st-century USA is invaded by its abandoned Martian colony, was heavily cut by the publisher, and reads as apprentice work. His next, *The Fifth Head of Cerberus* (fixup **1972**), comprises 3 separate tales, one previously published but all so closely linked as to be crippled in isolation. Set on a distant two-planet system colonized by settlers of French origin, the book combines ALIENS, ANTHROPOLOGY, CLONES and other elements in a richly imaginative exploration of the nature of identity and individuality. It was the first significant demonstration of the great difficulty of reading GW without constant attention to the almost subliminal – but in retrospect or after rereading almost invariably lucid and inevitable – clues laid down in the text to govern its comprehension. As with all his most important work to date, the protagonist (in this case there is also a more elusively presented second protagonist) tells from a conceptual or temporal remove the story of his own childhood, in the form of a confession whose truth value is unrelentingly dubious. The parenthood of the clone who narrates the first part of the novel is problematical – or concealed – as is usual in GW's work; questions of identity are poignantly intensified as it becomes clear – perhaps only upon a second reading – that, before the main action of the tale has begun, a shapeshifting alien (the second protagonist) from the oppressed second planet has taken on the identity of a visiting anthropologist. By the end of the novel, both protagonists – one a clone engineered into repeating previous identities, the other an impostor caught in the coffin of his fake self and literally imprisoned as well – have come to represent a singularly rich, singularly bleak vision of the shaping of a conscious life through time.

Peace (**1975**), an afterlife fantasy set in the contemporary middle USA, was, word for word, perhaps GW's most intricate and personal work; though not sf, it is central to any full attempt to understand his other novels, his sense of the great painfulness of any shaped life, or his methods in general. The protagonist of the book – who tells the story of his childhood, all unknowingly, from beyond the grave – is both a self-portrait of the artist as a teller of stories and a rounded, and murderous, character in his own right. *The Devil in a Forest* (**1976**), a juvenile set at the time of King Wenceslas, with little or no fantasy element, shares some of the lightness of tone of *Pandora by Holly Hollander* (**1990**), which some feel may have been written around this time, a non-fantastic detective novel which might also be described as a juvenile of sorts.

It was his next and most ambitious work – the long central tale and appendages of **The Book of the New Sun** sequence – which finally brought GW to a wide audience. The heart of the sequence was a single sustained long novel broken into 4 parts for commercial reasons and published as *The Shadow of the Torturer* (**1980**), *The Claw of the Conciliator* (**1981**), *The Sword of the Lictor* (**1982**) and *The Citadel of the Autarch*

(**1983**); the first pair were assembled as *The Book of the New Sun, Volumes I and II* (omni **1983** UK), and the second pair as *The Book of the New Sun, Volumes III and IV* (omni **1985** UK). Essays and tales in explanation of **The Book of the New Sun** were assembled as *The Castle of the Otter* (dated 1982 but **1983**); tales supposedly extracted from one of the seminal books carried throughout his travels by Severian, the protagonist of **The Book of the New Sun**, were published as *The Boy who Hooked the Sun: A Tale from the Book of Wonders of Urth and Sky* (**1985** chap) and *Empires of Foliage and Flower: A Tale from the Book of Wonders of Urth and Sky* (**1987** chap); "A Solar Labyrinth" (1983) was a metafiction about the entire **Book**; and the whole edifice was sequeled in *The Urth of the New Sun* (**1987** UK). The 1st volume gained a World Fantasy Award and the 2nd a Nebula.

As a synthesizing work of fiction – a type of creation which tends to come, for obvious reasons, late in the period or genre it transmutes – **The Book of the New Sun** owes clear debts to the sf and fantasy world in general, and in particular to the dying-Earth (◊ FAR FUTURE) category of PLANETARY ROMANCE initiated by Jack VANCE. Though it is a full-blown tale of cosmogony, the entire story is set on Urth, eons hence, a world so impacted with the relics of humanity's long residence that archaeology and geology have become, in a way, the same science: that of plumbing the body of the planet for messages which have become inextricably intermingled over the innumerable years. The world into which Severian is born has indeed become so choked with formula and ritual that early readers of *The Shadow of the Torturer* could be perhaps forgiven for identifying the text as SWORD AND SORCERY, though hints that the book was in fact sf-oriented SCIENCE FANTASY were – in the usual GW manner – abundant. Apparently an orphan, Severian is raised as an apprentice torturer in the Matachin Tower which nests among other similar towers in the Citadel compound of the capital city of Nessus, somewhere in the southern hemisphere (one of the easier tasks of decipherment GW imposes is that of understanding that the Towers are in fact ancient spaceships). Severian grows to young adulthood, falls into too intimate a concourse with an exultant (a genetically bred aristocrat) due to be tortured to death, is banished, travels through the land, becomes involved in a war to the far north where he meets – not for the first time – the old Autarch who dominates the world and who recognizes in Severian his appointed heir, and himself becomes Autarch.

It is a classic plot, and superficially unproblematic. But Severian himself is very distant in conception from the normal sf or science-fantasy hero he seems, at some moments, to resemble. As usual with GW, the protagonist himself narrates the story of his childhood and early youth from a period some years later; Severian makes it clear that he has an infallible memory (but is less clear about the fact that he is capable of lying); he also makes it clear that he has known from an early age that he is (or has been, or will be) the reborn manifestation of the Conciliator – a MESSIAH figure from a previous, or through TIME PARADOXES, a possibly concurrent reality – whose rebirth is for the purpose of bringing the New Sun to Urth. At this point, sf and Catholicism – GW is Roman Catholic – breed together, for the New Sun is both white hole and Revelation. The imagery and structure of **The Book of the New Sun** make it explicitly clear that Severian himself is both Apollo and Christ, and that the story of his life is a secular rendering of the parousia, or Second Coming. His cruelty to himself and others is the cruelty of the Universe itself; and his reverence for the world constitutes no simple blessing. His family is a Holy Family, lowly and anonymous, but ever-present; and their absence from any "starring" role – GW refuses in the text to identify any of them – has religious implications as well as aesthetic. (Much attention, some of it approaching the Talmudical, has been spent on identifying this Family, which does clearly include: Dorcas, Severian's paternal grandmother; his unnamed though Charonian paternal grandfather; his father Ouen; his mother Katherine; and – almost certainly – a sibling, who may be the homunculus found in a jar in *The Citadel of the Autarch*.) The sequel, *The Urth of the New Sun*, takes Severian through reality levels of the Universe to the point – ambiguous in time and space, though related to the Omega Point posited by Pierre Teilhard de Chardin (1881-1955) – where he will be judged as to his Autarchal fitness to bring the New Sun home. As foreordained, he passes the test. Urth is drowned in the floods that mark the passing of the white hole, the rebirth of light. Some survive, to begin again; or to continue in their ways.

Subsequent 1980s novels were very various. *Free Live Free* (**1984**) is a TIME-TRAVEL tale, extremely complex to parse, through which shines a retelling of L. Frank BAUM's *The Wonderful Wizard of Oz* (**1900**). *There Are Doors* (**1988**), set in a bleak PARALLEL WORLD redolent of the USA during the Depression, most ambivalently depicts a man's life-threatening exogamous passion for a goddess. *Castleview* (**1990**) implants very nearly the entirety of the Arthurian Cycle in contemporary Illinois, where a new Arthur is recruited for the long battle. Most interesting perhaps is the **Latro** sequence, comprising *Soldier of the Mist* (**1986**) and *Soldier of Arete* (**1989**), with further volumes projected. Set in ancient Greece about 500BC, it is narrated in short chapters each representing a day's written-down recollections on the part of Latro, a soldier whom a goddess has punished by removing his capacity to remember anything for more than 24 hours. The sequence thus works, on every possible level, as a mirror image of **The Book of the New Sun**, with Latro's memory-loss reversing Severian's inability to forget, ancient Greece reversing Urth – being at the start rather than the end of things – and the series as a whole being conspi-

cuously open-ended rather than shaped inexorably around Severian's Coming.

It may be that GW has never had an original sf idea, or never a significant one, certainly none of the calibre of those generated by writers like Larry NIVEN or Greg BEAR. His importance does not reside in that kind of originality. Setting aside for an instant his control of language, it is possible to claim that GW's importance lies in a spongelike ability to assimilate generic models and devices, and in the quality of the transformations he effects upon that material – a musical analogy might be the Baroque technique of the parody cantata, in which a secular composition is transformed by reverent parody into a sacred work (or vice versa). GW's actual language, too, is eloquently parodic, and many of his short stories are designed deliberately and intricately to echo earlier models, from G.K. CHESTERTON and Rudyard KIPLING on through the whole pantheon of GENRE SF. GW's importance has been, therefore, twofold: the inherent stature of his work is deeply impressive, and he wears the fictional worlds of sf like a coat of many colours. [JC]

Other works: *At the Point of Capricorn* (**1983** chap); *The Arimaspian Legacy* (**1987** chap); *For Rosemary* (coll **1988** chap UK), poetry; *Slow Children at Play* (**1989** chap); *The Old Woman whose Rolling Pin is the Sun* (**1991** chap); «Castle of Days» (omni 1992), assembling *Gene Wolfe's Book of Days*, *The Castle of the Otter*, plus new material; «Nightside the Long Sun» (1993) and «Lake of the Long Sun» (1993), beginning the projected «Starcrosser's Planetfall» series set within a vast GENERATION STARSHIP.

About the author: *Gene Wolfe* (**1986**) by Joan Gordon; *A Checklist of Gene Wolfe* (**1990** chap) by Christopher P. STEPHENS; *Gene Wolfe: Urth-Man Extraordinary: A Working Bibliography* (**1991** chap) by Gordon BENSON Jr and Phil STEPEHENSEN-PAYNE..

See also: BRITISH SCIENCE FICTION AWARD; COLONIZATION OF OTHER WORLDS; CONCEPTUAL BREAKTHROUGH; ESP; FANTASTIC VOYAGES; FANTASY; GODS AND DEMONS; GOTHIC SF; JOHN W. CAMPBELL MEMORIAL AWARD; LINGUISTICS; METAPHYSICS; MYTHOLOGY; OPTIMISM AND PESSIMISM; POCKET UNIVERSE; SERIES; SUN; SUPERNATURAL CREATURES; TIMESCAPE BOOKS; WRITERS OF THE FUTURE CONTEST.

WOLFE, LOUIS (1905-   ) US writer in whose *Journey of the Oceanauts: Across the Bottom of the Atlantic Ocean* (**1968**) 3 genetically engineered (◊ GENETIC ENGINEERING) humans make the eponymous trek. [JC]

WOLFMAN, MARV [r] ◊ Ted WHITE.

WOLLHEIM, DONALD A(LLEN) (1914-1990) US editor and writer, and one of the first and most vociferous sf fans; with Forrest J. ACKERMAN, DAW was perhaps the most dynamic member of the embryo FANDOM of the 1930s. A lifetime resident of New York City, he published innumerable FANZINES, was co-editor of the early semiprozine FANCIFUL TALES OF TIME AND SPACE in 1936, founded the Fantasy Amateur Press Association (FAPA), and was one of the founders in 1938 of the FUTURIANS, becoming deeply involved in its pursuits and feuds. His long-standing quarrel with James BLISH – whom he does not mention in his anecdotal analysis of sf, *The Universe Makers* (**1971**), whose premises reflect 1930s enthusiasms – began at this time, and was at least partially rooted in political differences, for in the years before WWII DAW stood far to the left and Blish far to the right. DAW's part in early fandom was extensively chronicled in *The Immortal Storm* (**1954**) by Sam MOSKOWITZ and in *The Futurians* (**1977**) by Damon KNIGHT. DAW ed *Operation: Phantasy: The Best from the Phantograph* (anth **1967** chap), a collection of early fanzine material.

His first published story was "The Man from Ariel" for *Wonder Stories* in 1934, but he did not begin to publish fiction with any regularity until the 1940s, by which time he had already embarked on his major career as an editor. In 1941 he became editor of COSMIC STORIES and STIRRING SCIENCE STORIES, both of which he produced creditably on a minute budget, publishing many stories by his fellow Futurians (most prolifically C.M. KORNBLUTH). He also compiled 2 pioneering sf ANTHOLOGIES: *The Pocket Book of Science Fiction* (anth **1943**) and *Portable Novels of Science* (anth **1945**). For his short stories he often used the pseudonyms Millard Verne Gordon and Martin PEARSON, as well as the collaborative pseudonyms Arthur COOKE and Lawrence WOODS, and he once wrote as Allen Warland; as Pearson he published the **Ajax Calkins** series which later formed the basis of his novel *Destiny's Orbit* (**1962**) as by David Grinnell, sequelled by *Destination: Saturn* (**1967**) as by Grinnell with Lin CARTER.

After WWII DAW worked for Avon Books (1947-52), for whom he edited the AVON FANTASY READER and the AVON SCIENCE FICTION READER anthology-like series (which we treat as magazines) as well as OUT OF THIS WORLD ADVENTURES, 10 STORY FANTASY and, uncredited, the first sf ORIGINAL ANTHOLOGY, *The Girl with the Hungry Eyes* (anth **1949**). He subsequently moved to ACE BOOKS in 1952, where he created and for the next 20 years ran one of the 2-3 most dominant US sf lists, winning a 1964 HUGO for his work. Taking advantage of the **Ace Double Novel** format (◊ DOS-À-DOS), he published the first or early works of many writers who later achieved fame, including John BRUNNER, Samuel R. DELANY, Philip K. DICK, Thomas M. DISCH, Harlan ELLISON, Ursula K. LE GUIN and Robert SILVERBERG, though the bulk of the list was cannily built around colourful sf adventures with a strong emphasis on SPACE OPERA; by the 1960s, the list had begun to fade seriously, though it is clear in hindsight (see discussion of DAW BOOKS below) that he himself had lost nothing of his acumen. During the 1950s he also worked editorially on the magazines ORBIT and SATURN, and edited a great many anthologies, often for Ace; these included such theme collections as *The End of the World* (anth **1956**), *Men on the Moon* (anth **1958** dos; rev 1969) and *The Hidden Planet* (anth **1959**), the latter being of stories set on VENUS.

DAW's own writing in the 1950s and 1960s consisted largely of novels. These divided into CHILDREN'S SF published as DAW and adult novels as by David Grinnell, none of the latter being particularly notable. However, the **Mike Mars** series of children's books, exploring different facets of the space programme, was popular: *Mike Mars, Astronaut* (**1961**), *Mike Mars Flies the X-15* (**1961**), *Mike Mars at Cape Canaveral* (**1961**; vt *Mike Mars at Cape Kennedy* 1966), *Mike Mars in Orbit* (**1961**), *Mike Mars Flies the Dyna-Soar* (**1962**), *Mike Mars, South Pole Spaceman* (**1962**), *Mike Mars and the Mystery Satellite* (**1963**) and *Mike Mars around the Moon* (**1964**).

In 1965, DAW began to issue an annual "year's best" anthology, **World's Best Science Fiction**; this continued until the end of his life in an unbroken yearly succession, although there was some highly confusing retitling (occasioned in the first instance by his shift from Ace to DAW Books). The sequence was: *#1: World's Best Science Fiction: 1965* (anth **1965**) with Terry CARR (who was co-editor through the 1971 volume); *#2: 1966* (anth **1966**); *#3: 1967* (anth **1967**); *#4: 1968* (anth **1968**); *#5: 1969* (anth **1969**); *#6: 1970* (anth **1970**); *#7: 1971* (anth **1971**); *#8: The 1972 Annual World's Best SF* (anth **1972**; vt *Wollheim's World's Best SF: Series One* 1977) with Arthur W. SAHA (who was co-editor through the 1990 volume); *#9: 1973* (anth **1973**; vt *Wollheim's World Best SF: Series Two* 1978); *#10: 1974* (anth **1974**; vt *World's Best SF Short Stories #1* 1975 UK; vt *Wollheim's World Best SF: Series Three* 1979); *#11: 1975* (anth **1975**; vt *World's Best SF Short Stories #2* 1976 UK; vt *Wollheim's World Best SF: Series Four* 1980 UK); *#12: 1976* (anth **1976**; vt *The World's Best SF – 3* 1979 UK; vt *Wollheim's World Best SF: Series Five* 1981 US); *#13: 1977* (anth **1977**; vt *The World's Best SF – 4* 1979 UK; vt *Wollheim's World Best SF: Series Six* 1982 US); *#14: 1978* (anth **1978**; vt *The World's Best SF – 5* 1980 UK; vt *Wollheim's World Best SF: Series Seven* 1983 US); *#15: 1979* (anth **1979**; vt *Wollheim's World Best SF: Series Eight* 1984); *#16: 1980* (anth **1980**; vt *#9* 1985); *#17: 1981* (anth **1981**); *#18: 1982* (anth **1982**); *#19* (anth **1983**); *#20* (anth **1984**); *#21: 1985* (anth **1985**), *#22: 1986* (anth **1986**); *#23: 1987* (anth **1987**); *#24: Donald A. Wollheim Presents The 1988 Annual World's Best SF* (anth **1988**); *#25: 1989* (anth **1989**) and *#26: 1990* (anth **1990**).

In 1971, DAW left Ace and in 1972 he founded DAW BOOKS, which he continued to run until 1985, when ill-health induced him to appoint his daughter, Betsy Wollheim, president. With his new firm, he began almost immediately to shift from the format- and content-constraints that had plagued his later career at Ace: series were emphasized heavily; space opera gave way to PLANETARY ROMANCE; authors like C.J. CHERRYH and Tanith LEE, who were comfortable with science fantasy, were strongly encouraged; and he allowed his authors very considerable latitude (compared with his days at Ace) to explore moderately TABOO areas (John NORMAN moved over from BALLANTINE BOOKS, presumably to take advantage of this liberty) and to write at very varying lengths. Though he continued not to pay well enough to retain best-selling authors, he kept his firm healthy and active for the remaining years of his career.

For 50 years DAW remained one of the most important editorial influences on sf, and in his later years – despite his very well known capacity to carry on disputes half a century old – he became a revered figure. His death marked – as clearly as those of Isaac ASIMOV and Robert A. HEINLEIN – the passing of the generation of the founders.   [JC/MJE]

Other works: *The Secret of Saturn's Rings* (**1954**), *The Secret of the Martian Moons* (**1955**), *One Against the Moon* (**1956**) and *The Secret of the Ninth Planet* (**1959**), all juveniles; *Two Dozen Dragon's Eggs* (coll **1969**); *The Men from Ariel* (coll **1982**); *Up There and Other Strange Directions* (coll **1988**).

As David Grinnell: *Across Time* (**1957**); *Edge of Time* (**1958**); *The Martian Missile* (**1959**); *To Venus! To Venus!* (**1970** dos).

As editor: *The Fox Woman & Other Stories* (coll **1949**), stories by A. MERRITT; *Flight into Space* (anth **1950**); *Every Boy's Book of Science Fiction* (anth **1951**); *Prize Science Fiction* (anth **1953**; vt *Prize Stories of Space and Time* 1953 UK); *Adventures in the Far Future* (anth **1954** dos); *Tales of Outer Space* (anth **1954** dos); *The Ultimate Invader and Other Science Fiction* (anth **1954**); *Adventures on Other Planets* (anth **1955**) and *More Adventures on Other Planets* (anth **1963**); *Terror in the Modern Vein* (anth **1955**; vt in 2 vols as *Terror in the Modern Vein* 1961 UK and *More Terror in the Modern Vein* 1961 UK); *The Earth in Peril* (anth **1957** dos); *The Macabre Reader* (anth **1959**) and *More Macabre* (anth **1961**); *Swordsmen in the Sky* (anth **1964**); *Ace Science Fiction Reader* (anth **1971**; vt *Trilogy of the Future* 1972 UK); *The Best from the Rest of the World* (anth **1976**); *The DAW Science Fiction Reader* (anth **1976**).

See also: CRITICAL AND HISTORICAL WORKS ABOUT SF; GALACTIC EMPIRES; GOLDEN AGE OF SF; GREAT AND SMALL; HISTORY OF SF; NEAR FUTURE; NEW WAVE; OPTIMISM AND PESSIMISM; PUBLISHING.

WOLVERTON, DAVE (1957-   ) US writer. He began entering literary contests in 1985, winning a few small competitions and then the Best of the Year award in the WRITERS OF THE FUTURE CONTEST for 1986, with "On My Way to Paradise", which appeared in *L. Ron Hubbard's Writers of the Future, Volume III* (anth **1987**). This novella was the basis for his first novel, *On My Way to Paradise* (**1989**), a thoughtful but violent tale of a Latin-American mercenary force conscripted to fight for a conservative Japanese colony on another planet. It is packed with sociobiological speculation, and veers interestingly between HEINLEIN-esque and CYBERPUNK scenarios, and is not altogether accepting of the LIBERTARIAN ideas which in part it dramatizes; it was runner-up in 1990 for the PHILIP K. DICK AWARD. *Serpent Catch* (**1991**) confirmed him as belonging to the central extrapolative tradition of sf. Big and almost over-packed like its predecessor, it is set on a terraformed moon of a GAS GIANT, whose continents are separated by eco-barriers, part of an experiment

in closed environments and reconstructed geological eras. Genetically engineered human scientists are driven from space by advanced aliens and forced down into this zoo they have created, where they interact complexly (the future meeting the past) with Neanderthals and other prehumans, dinosaurs, sea-serpents and so on, as the eco-barriers break down. The novel – which seems to require sequels – is conceptually ambitious and very idea-driven.   [PN]

WOMACK, JACK (1956-   ) US writer whose first 4 novels are stylish and potent exercises in a post-CYBERPUNK urban idiom, and comprise the first instalments in a loose ongoing series about the NEAR-FUTURE state of the USA. The sequence, reminiscent at points of the baroque New York detective fictions of Jerry Oster (1943-   ), is projected to stop after 5 vols. *Ambient* (**1987**), set in the complexly desolated warzone which New York has become in the early 21st century, evokes comparisons with James Joyce (1882-1941) and Anthony BURGESS in its sensuous, choked, eloquent, linguistically foregrounded presentation of the victims of a radioactive accident who populate the fringes of the fragmented city, and who so hypnotically manifest the Goyaesque horrors of the scene that volunteer "normals" mutilate themselves and join the ranks of the sinking. In the story itself, however, JW exhibits a certain lack of plotting imagination, and neither tycoon Thatcher Dryden nor the megacorporation, Dryco, which he runs nearly singlehanded are particularly convincing when set against the *mise en scène*. Out of that venue, the protagonists of *Terraplane* (**1988**) hurtle pastwards into an ALTERNATE-WORLD version of late-1930s New York, an apartheid-ridden DYSTOPIA – the oppressed lives of Black Americans are described with haunting intimacy – whose vileness may, or may not, be seen as worse than the radiation-corrupted, corporation-dominated nightmarishness of our own new era. Somewhat less scourgingly, *Heathern* (**1990** UK) returns to New York and to Thatcher Dryden, who on this occasion must try (he fails) to make sense of a MESSIAH figure whose fate in this venue is dourly predictable and whose humaneness seems, in this context, otherworldy. «Elvissey» (1992) incorporates the Elvis Presley myth into the ongoing sequence. JW's vision of the world continues, perhaps, to lack some focus, though not heat; with completion of his **New York** quintet, that focus will almost certainly sharpen, and the heat will burn deep.   [JC]

See also: MUSIC.

WOMAN IN THE MOON, THE ◊ *Die* FRAU IM MOND.

WOMEN AS PORTRAYED IN SCIENCE FICTION In "The Image of Women in Science Fiction" (1971 *Red Clay Reader*) Joanna RUSS wrote, "There are plenty of images of women in science fiction. There are hardly any women." Things have changed in the subsequent decades, chiefly due to the impact of FEMINISM and to the increasing numbers of women writing sf in the 1970s, 1980s and 1990s, but the absence of realistic female characters remains a glaring fault of the genre.

Since GENRE SF developed in a patriarchal culture as something written chiefly by men for men (or boys), the lack of female protagonists is unsurprising. When women do appear they are usually defined by their relationship to the male characters, as objects to be desired or feared, rescued or destroyed; often, especially in recent, more sexually explicit times, women characters exist only to validate the male protagonist as acceptably masculine – that is, heterosexual. Before the 1970s even WOMEN SF WRITERS tended to reflect the prevailing view about women's place by writing about men's adventures in future worlds where women stayed home to work the control panels in automated kitchens. The main alternative to men's adventure stories was ladies' magazine fiction, in which the domestic virtues of the sweet, intuitive housewife-heroine somehow saved the day.

It would be hard for even the most ardent fan to list a dozen sf novels written before 1970 which feature female protagonists: Naomi MITCHISON's *Memoirs of a Spacewoman* (1962), Robert A. HEINLEIN's *Podkayne of Mars* (1963), Samuel R. DELANY's *Babel-17* (1966), Alexei PANSHIN's *Rite of Passage* (1968), Joanna Russ's *Picnic on Paradise* (1968) and Anne MCCAFFREY's *The Ship who Sang* (1969) are probably the best known, and all date from the transitional period of the 1960s. Betty King provides a detailed and apparently exhaustive list from 1818 on in *Women of the Future: The Female Main Character in Science Fiction* (1984). Moreover, as Suzy McKee CHARNAS pointed out in an essay on how and why she came to write ("No-Road" in Denise Du Pont's *Women of Vision* [anth 1988]), it is easy to write a thoroughly sexist story around a female protagonist, and the real test of whether or not female characters are being written about as human beings is whether the protagonist is connected in any important way to other complex female characters, or if she is significantly connected only to males.

Not allowed the variety or complexity of real people, women in sf have been represented most frequently by a very few stereotypes: the Timorous Virgin (good for being rescued, and for having things explained to her), the Amazon Queen (sexually desirable and terrifying at the same time, usually set up to be "tamed" by the super-masculine hero), the Frustrated Spinster Scientist (an object lesson to girl readers that career success equals feminine failure), the Good Wife (keeps quietly in the background, loving her man and never making trouble) and the Tomboy Kid Sister (who has a semblance of autonomy only until male appreciation of her burgeoning sexuality transforms her into Virgin or Wife). But of course the vast majority of male characters in sf are stereotypes too. David KETTERER in *New Worlds for Old: The Apocalyptic Imagination, Science Fiction and American Literature* (1974), among others, has argued that

the "weaknesses" of poor characterization and lack of human interest in much sf can be seen as a strength, at least in "cosmic" fictions in which individual concerns – including gender – are unimportant.

Some find the lack of any female characters in much sf more disturbing than the use of stereotypes, but Gwyneth JONES (in "Writing Science Fiction for the Teenage Reader", in *Where No Man has Gone Before* [anth 1990] ed Lucy Arnitt) has argued that "Accepting a male protagonist on the printed page does not mean accepting one's own absence. Indeed the almost total absence of female characters makes simpler the imaginative sleight of hand whereby the teenage girl substitutes *herself* for the male initiate in these stories." Jones went on to argue that the "feminization" of teenage sf, through the presentation of more realistic female protagonists, "does not necessarily mean a better deal for girls", because such stories reinforce the status quo of a subordinate role for women. Although Jones was writing about teenage sf, her point may be more widely applied. Susan WOOD, in her essay "Women and Science Fiction" (in ALGOL, Winter 1978/79), expressed the desire that women should reclaim rather than reject the archetypes which lie behind the usually disparaged stereotyped characters that populate sf. Many women have done so, as well as creating new possibilities for the expression of female humanity.

From the 1960s, sf was increasingly seen to have the potential to explore serious human issues, while at the same time many writers (especially those identified as members of the NEW WAVE) were rejecting the old PULP-MAGAZINE conventions in favour of experimentation and more artistic values. As more women were attracted by the changing image of sf (and here the influence of STAR TREK should not be underestimated), as sf became more than a minority taste and began to sell in numbers previously unimaginable, and as more women moved into editorial positions, the role of female characters in sf became more important not only for aesthetic, personal or political reasons but also for commercial ones: surveys have shown that more women than men buy books, so a would-be bestseller cannot afford to alienate the female audience.

The old stereotypes are still around, although women writers more often give them a subversive twist: the Good Wife is married to a lesbian star-pilot, the Spinster Scientist has a rich and fulfilling sex life, the Amazon Queen triumphantly refuses to be tamed. If women writers feel able to play around with archetypes and stereotypes, male writers are more likely to avoid them for fear of being misunderstood and alienating much of their likely audience. Sometimes their efforts to include female characters are mere tokenism: a few female spear-carriers, soldiers or scientists appear, but questions of who's minding the kids and how does this apparently egalitarian society really work are never even posed. A few of the newer male writers – among them Greg BEAR,

Colin GREENLAND, Paul J. MCAULEY, Ian MCDONALD and Bruce STERLING – have written novels about strong and interesting self-motivated women, although female protagonists – particularly ones who are more than a fantasy figure with an all-male supporting cast – are still more likely to be found in books by women writers.

Unfortunately, these positive changes in the literature have been countered by a retrogressive movement in popular sf films, where women's roles are limited and male-determined: if involved in the action they are victims, ROBOTS or prostitutes (sometimes all three at once), otherwise they are waiting patiently for the hero in kitchen or bedroom. The role played by Sigourney Weaver in ALIEN (1979) stands out as a notable exception: a female HERO. She is just as human as the rest of the mixed-sex crew, and is menaced by the alien to the same degree and in the same way. She is no weaker because she is a woman, and no more special. But in the sequel, ALIENS (1986), the human/alien battle has become a heavily symbolic fight between two females. Weaver's character is lumbered with a stray child to make the final battle acceptable to even the most fearful of immature male viewers: this isn't a woman fighting a MONSTER, but two mothers doing what comes naturally, battling to protect their children.   [LT]

See also: CLICHÉS.

WOMEN SF WRITERS In the opinion of many it was a woman, Mary SHELLEY, who created sf with *Franken- stein, or The Modern Prometheus* (**1818**; rev 1831). But after such a strong start women's contributions to the genre, while never entirely absent, were not substantial until the late 1960s.

As a commercial genre, sf was formed chiefly by the men who edited, wrote for and read the US PULP MAGAZINES of the 1920s and 1930s. For decades the belief that most sf readers were adolescent males imposed certain restrictions on subject matter and style – women, and women's supposed interests, were sentimentalized or ignored, and SEX was TABOO. Yet women not only read but wrote sf, sometimes under androgynous bylines, real or assumed. Pamela SARGENT has drawn attention to some of the more memorable stories written by and about women in her excellent anthologies *Women of Wonder* (anth **1974**) and *More Women of Wonder* (anth **1976**). Among the most popular some, like Leigh BRACKETT, C.L. MOORE and Andre NORTON, wrote vivid, action-packed adventure tales, as ungendered as their names, while others, like Mildred CLINGERMAN, Zenna HENDERSON and Judith MERRIL, wrote often sentimental stories dealing with more acceptable feminine concerns. Other women known for writing sf prior to the 1960s include Marion Zimmer BRADLEY, Miriam Allen DeFORD, Clare Winger HARRIS, Joan Hunter HOLLY, Lilith LORRAINE, Katherine MacCLEAN, Margaret ST CLAIR, Wilmar H. SHIRAS, Evelyn E. SMITH, Francis STEVENS, Leslie F. STONE and Thea VON HARBOU. In addition, there have always been women producing

borderline sf in the MAINSTREAM or in sf-related fields such as FABULATION, surrealism and ABSURDIST, experimental, GOTHIC and UTOPIAN fiction. And women have quite often been unattributed collaborators in works published under the names of their male partners, a role that has only recently begun to be recognized.

By the 1960s the sf field was changing in ways that would make it more accessible and exciting to a wider audience. Younger writers, in particular, rebelled against the old pulp limitations and set about writing sf which would combine the old-fashioned SENSE OF WONDER with more sophisticated literary values. New editors, some of them women, none of them committed to the concept of a primarily adolescent readership, played a large part in this expansion. In particular, Cele GOLDSMITH encouraged many new writers during her editorship of AMAZING STORIES and FANTASTIC (1958-65). Ursula K. LE GUIN, now one of the most respected and influential of all contemporary sf writers, credits Cele Goldsmith with "opening the door to me".

In 1972 Harlan ELLISON stated (in his intro to "When it Changed" by Joanna RUSS in *Again, Dangerous Visions* [anth **1972**]) that "the best writers in sf today are the women" – an opinion echoed by other knowledgeable readers throughout the 1970s, occasionally with the caveat "excepting James TIPTREE Jr". Despite Robert SILVERBERG's now notorious claim that there was something "ineluctably masculine" in the Tiptree stories (in "Who is Tiptree, What is He?", intro to Tiptree's *Warm Worlds and Otherwise* [coll **1975**]), in 1977 Tiptree was revealed to be Alice Sheldon. Of the response to her unmasking, Sheldon commented in an interview with Charles PLATT (in *Dream Makers: Volume II* [coll **1983**]), "The feminist world was excited because, merely by having existed unchallenged for years, 'Tiptree' had shot the stuffing out of male stereotypes of women writers."

The reason that sf began to change in the 1960s and 1970s was that increasingly writers were drawn to it not because of an interest in its pulp traditions but for its still largely unexplored potential. The effect of the (largely male) NEW WAVE is often cited, but the impact made on the field by such diverse writers as Le Guin, Kate WILHELM, Russ, C.J. CHERRYH and Tiptree was undoubtedly stronger and more lasting than that of any single, self-proclaimed movement. Others might agree with Suzy McKee CHARNAS (in *Aurora* #26, Summer 1990): "My own view of the matter was and is that in the 1960s SF was a dying or at least moribund genre (the New Wave was an effort, not very successful in my opinion, to remedy this by importing some technical stunts from the mainstream), and feminism came along in the 1970s and *rescued* it." (◊ FEMINISM.)

Among the women sf writers who came to prominence in the 1960s and 1970s are E.L. ARCH, Bradley, Rosel George BROWN, Octavia E. BUTLER, Charnas, Cherryh, Jo CLAYTON, Juanita COULSON, Sonya DOR-

MAN, Suzette Haden ELGIN, Carol EMSHWILLER, M.J. ENGH, Gertrude FRIEDBERG, Phyllis GOTLIEB, Diana Wynne JONES, Lee KILLOUGH, Tanith LEE, Madeleine L'ENGLE, Le Guin, A.M. LIGHTNER, Elizabeth A. LYNN, Anne MCCAFFREY, Vonda MCINTYRE, Janet MORRIS, Doris PISERCHIA, Marta RANDALL, Kit REED, Russ, Sargent, Josephine SAXTON, Jody SCOTT, Kathleen SKY, Tiptree, Lisa TUTTLE, Joan D. VINGE, Cherry WILDER, Kate WILHELM, Chelsea Quinn YARBRO and Pamela ZOLINE.

Writers who became better known in the 1980s and 1990s include Gill ALDERMAN, ANNA LIVIA, Lois McMaster BUJOLD, Pat CADIGAN, Storm CONSTANTINE, Candas Jane DORSEY, Carol Nelson DOUGLAS, Sheila FINCH, Caroline Forbes (1952-   ), Karen Joy FOWLER, Sally Miller GEARHART, Mary GENTLE, Lisa GOLDSTEIN, Eileen Gunn, Barbara HAMBLY, Gwyneth JONES, Janet KAGAN, Leigh KENNEDY, Nancy KRESS, Kathe Koja, R.A. MACAVOY, Julian MAY, Judith MOFFETT, Pat MURPHY, Jane PALMER, Rachel POLLACK, Kristine Kathryn RUSCH, Melissa SCOTT, Joan SLONCZEWSKI, Sheri S. TEPPER and Connie WILLIS.

In addition, a number of MAINSTREAM writers have made detours into sf, even if their publishers have not always labelled their novels as such. They include Margaret ATWOOD (*The Handmaid's Tale* [**1985**]), Maureen DUFFY (*The Gor Saga* [**1981**]), Zoë FAIRBAIRNS (*Benefits* [**1979**]), Cecelia HOLLAND (*Floating Worlds* [**1976**]), Rhoda Lerman (1936-   ) (*The Book of the Night* [**1984**]), Doris LESSING (the **Canopus in Argos** series), Marge PIERCY (*Woman on the Edge of Time* [**1976**]), Fay WELDON (*The Cloning of Joanna May* [**1989**]) and Monique WITTIG (*Les guérillères* [**1969**; trans **1971**]). Writers as diverse as Jean M. AUEL, Christine BROOKEROSE, Angela CARTER, Anna KAVAN, Ayn RAND, Emma TENNANT and Christa Wolf (1929-   ) have also, upon occasion, been claimed for sf.

The above lists make no claim to being anything like complete, but their very existence should make it clear that, while women writers of sf may still be outnumbered by men, they are by now far too numerous to be considered rare, and too various to be generalized about or compressed into a subset of "women's sf". Women contribute to all areas of the genre. Where once anthologies of stories entirely by men were customary, now they are unusual.

Between 1953, when it was established, and 1967 there were no women winners of the HUGO; between 1968 and 1990 there were 21 awards to women out of 92 in the fiction categories, while of the NEBULA awards for the years 1968-90 the figures are better still, at 28 awards to women out of 91. Better again are the results of the JOHN W. CAMPBELL AWARD for Best New Writer, with 8 of the 19 awards to date going to women. In all cases, more men than women vote.

Have women writers been discriminated against? Such things are hard to quantify or prove, and, although most women in the field can cite occasional instances of sexism (the editor who declares that sf by women doesn't sell; the disgruntled author who

scents a feminist conspiracy when his novel fails to win awards; the claim from an old-time fan that the values of HARD SF are being destroyed by female editors with an innately feminine preference for fantasy), on the whole the Old Boy Network of sf has been remarkably receptive to any women who care to join. The catch is one common to most societies: those who join are expected to do so on terms already established, to follow the rules and, as newcomers, know their place. Unfortunately, even after 30 years women are still considered "newcomers" by most men, and women who become too successful or break the unspoken rules and stretch the boundaries of sf, all too often arouse male hostility. Hence the antagonism so often directed at Joanna Russ – "the single most important woman writer of science fiction" according to Sarah LeFANU (in *In the Chinks of the World Machine: Feminism and Science Fiction* [**1988**]) – is probably as much for her challenging literary experimentation as for her uncompromising feminism. Presumably because she is so respected outside the genre, Le Guin is every so often unfairly accused by men who are not of having "renounced" sf.

Women writers are by now a well established presence within sf, but this situation may not last. In *How to Suppress Women's Writing* (**1983**) Russ has argued, polemically but effectively, that even the most popular and influential female writers have been peculiarly subject to excision from the male-controlled canons of literary history. An economic contraction, followed by a redefinition of genre boundaries, might send written sf the way of Hollywood, where sf films are as narrowly confined to catering to the fears and desires of the adolescent US male as the old-fashioned pulp magazines ever were.   [LT]

See also: WOMEN AS PORTRAYED IN SCIENCE FICTION.

WONDERS OF THE SPACEWAYS UK pocketbook-size magazine, 10 numbered, undated issues 1951 4, published by John Spencer, London; ed Sol Assael and Michael Nahum, both uncredited. One of the 4 poor-quality Spencer juvenile-sf magazines, all very similar, the others being FUTURISTIC SCIENCE STORIES, TALES OF TOMORROW, and WORLDS OF FANTASY. They contain some fiction by R.L. FANTHORPE.   [FHP]

WONDER STORIES 1. US magazine amalgamated from AIR WONDER STORIES and SCIENCE WONDER STORIES, 66 issues as *WS*. Volume numeration continued from *Science Wonder Stories*, thus beginning with vol 2 #1. *WS* was published by Hugo GERNSBACK's Stellar Publishing Corporation June 1930-Oct 1933, and by Gernsback's Continental Publications, Inc. Nov 1933-Apr 1936. The title was then sold to Better Publications, to reappear as THRILLING WONDER STORIES in Aug 1936, with vol numbers continuing from *WS*. *WS* was monthly June 1930-June 1933, skipped to Aug 1933, monthly Oct 1933-Oct 1935, then 3 last issues: Nov/Dec 1935, Jan/Feb 1936 and Apr 1936. It began as a BEDSHEET-size pulp, but was forced to revert to standard PULP-MAGAZINE format Nov 1930-Oct 1931, returning to bedsheet size Nov 1931 and shrinking again from Nov 1933 until it was sold. David Lasser was managing editor until Oct 1933, being succeeded by Charles D. HORNIG, although Gernsback remained editor-in-chief throughout. Illustrator Frank R. PAUL was the cover artist for all issues.

WS was Gernsback's most successful magazine. It encouraged the growth of sf FANDOM by sponsoring the SCIENCE FICTION LEAGUE in 1934. Notable stories include John TAINE's *The Time Stream* (Dec 1931-Feb 1932; **1946**), Stanley G. WEINBAUM's classic "A Martian Odyssey" (July 1934) and Jack WILLIAMSON's "The Moon Era" (Feb 1932). John Beynon Harris (John WYNDHAM) had his first story and much of his early work in *WS*, and Clark Ashton SMITH published his best sf stories in it, including "City of the Singing Flame" (July 1931) and "The Eternal World" (Mar 1932). One author particularly associated with *WS* was Laurence MANNING, all of whose major work appeared there: "The Wreck of the Asteroid" (Dec 1932), the **Stranger Club** series (1933-5) and the **Man who Awoke** series (1933). Leslie F. STONE, a woman writer (in those days a rarity), had 5 stories in *WS*.

If Gernsback had paid his authors more (or, in some cases, at all) the magazine might have continued longer, but by 1936 he was finding it difficult to attract decent writers, circulation had dropped, and *WS* was sold.

2. After the demise of *TWS* in Winter 1955, the *Wonder Stories* title was resuscitated for a reprint magazine, subtitled "An Anthology of the Best in Science Fiction", ed Jim Hendryx Jr, of which there appeared only 2, widely separated, issues, dated 1957 and 1963, the first a digest, the second a pulp. These continued the *TWS* numeration, as vol 45, #1 and #2. [BS/PN]

WONDER STORIES QUARTERLY US PULP MAGAZINE, BEDSHEET-size Fall 1929-Summer 1932, pulp-size Fall 1932-Winter 1933, 14 issues, published by Hugo GERNSBACK's Stellar Publishing Corporation as a quarterly companion to SCIENCE WONDER STORIES and AIR WONDER STORIES, and then to WONDER STORIES, the first 3 issues appearing as *Science Wonder Quarterly*. David Lasser was the managing editor. *WSQ* featured mostly space stories. A complete novel was featured in every issue, and the magazine was notable for its translations (by Francis Currier) from the German (◊ GERMANY), including Otto Willi GAIL's "Shot into Infinity" (**1925** Germany as *Der Schuss ins All*; trans Fall 1929) and its sequel "The Stone from the Moon" (**1926** Germany as *Der Stein vom Mond*; trans Spring 1930), and Otfried Von Hanstein's "Electropolis" (**1928** Germany as *Elektropolis*; trans Summer 1930) and "Between Earth and Moon" (**1928** Germany as *Mond-Rak 1. Eine Fahrt ins Weltall*; trans Fall 1930). There were 2 stories by the early woman pulp writer Clare Winger HARRIS, and *WSQ* published the 1st fan letter from Forrest J. ACKERMAN. [BS/PN]

WONDER STORY ANNUAL US reprint PULP MAGAZINE published by Better Publications, 1950, and Best

Books, 1951-3, ed 1950-51 Sam MERWIN Jr and 1952-53 Samuel MINES. The lead novels were reprinted from WONDER STORIES and STARTLING STORIES, the most notable being Manly Wade WELLMAN's *Twice in Time* (1940 *Startling Stories*; 1950; **1957**) and Jack WILLIAMSON's "Gateway to Paradise" (1941 *Startling Stories*; 1953; vt *Dome around America* **1955**). [BS]

WONDER WOMAN US tv series (1974-9), based on *Wonder Woman*, the COMIC book inaugurated by DC COMICS in 1942. Warner Bros TV for ABC, then for CBS. The complex production history falls into 3 parts.

1. The 2hr pilot for ABC, *Wonder Woman* (1974) dir Vincent McEveety, written John D.F. Black, starring Cathy Lee Crosby. This flopped.

2. Series for ABC with a new Wonder woman, Lynda Carter: *The New Original Wonder Woman*, with a 1975 2hr pilot, and 12 50min episodes 1975-6. This endeavoured to recapture the feeling of the original comics. Wonder Woman (Carter) leaves her Amazon home of Paradise Island to help out the USA during WWII, taking with her a golden belt (for strength) and a golden lariat whose movements she controls. Prod Wilfred Baumes, this was perhaps the best of Wonder Woman's 3 tv phases; its writers included Jimmy Sangster, and its dirs Herb Wallerstein and Stuart Margolin. It was scheduled erratically by ABC, so never really had a chance.

3. The commercially most successful phase. CBS took over the series, now retitled *The New Adventures of Wonder Woman* and set in the present day, but still starring Lynda Carter and made by Warner Bros; this was the version that was most widely circulated outside the USA. Now prod Charles B. Fitzsimons and Mark Rodgers, it opened with the story *The Return of Wonder Woman* in 1977. 2 seasons, 1 80min pilot and 45 50min episodes, 1977-9. Dirs included Jack ARNOLD, Alan Crosland, Michael Caffey, Curtis Harrington, Gordon Hessler. Writers included Stephen Kandel, Alan BRENNERT, Anne Collins.

In **2** and **3** Wonder Woman (herself more a figure of fantasy than of sf, and looking rather like a busty, glitzy cheerleader) is regularly confronted by sf-style problems, ranging from a Nazi superwoman and an alien visitor in **2** to artificial volcanic eruptions, malign ANDROIDS, a disembodied brain and mind-capturing pyramids with alien occupants in **3**, though for the pure-fantasy fans there was also a leprechaun. Like so much sf on TELEVISION, there was an air of camp parody about the whole thing (rather as in the **Batman** series whose great success 1966-8 set the pattern for this sort of SUPERHERO-on-tv enterprise). [PN]

WOOD, J.A. [r] ◊ ROBERT HALE LIMITED.

WOOD, PETER [s] ◊ Barrington J. BAYLEY.

WOOD, R(OBERT) W(ILLIAM) (1868-1955) US writer and optical physicist whose sf works were written with Arthur TRAIN (*whom see for details*). [JC]

About the author: *Dr Wood, Modern Wizard of the Laboratory* (**1941**) by William Seabrook.

WOOD, SAMUEL ANDREW (1890-?   ) UK author and journalist who wrote 2 minor LOST-WORLD novels, *Winged Heels* (**1927**) and, as by Robin Temple, *The Aztec Temple* (**1955**), as well as a reworking of the airborne-pirate theme, *I'll Blackmail the World* (1934 *The Blue Book Magazine* as "The Man who Bombed The World"; rev **1935**).   [JE]
See also: CRIME AND PUNISHMENT.

WOOD, SUSAN (JOAN) (1948-1980) Canadian sf critic and academic, with a PhD in 19th-century Canadian literature, who taught English (including sf) at the University of British Columbia. An sf fan of great energy, she won a 1973 HUGO as Susan Wood Glicksohn with her then husband Mike Glicksohn for Best Fanzine (*Energumen*), a 2nd (now as Susan Wood again) for Best Fan Writer in 1974, and a 3rd for Best Fan Writer (tied with Richard E. GEIS) in 1977; her 4th, also for Best Fan Writer, was awarded posthumously in 1981. SW wrote much criticism, including introductions for GREGG PRESS books and a review column in ALGOL which campaigned vigorously against sexism (◊ FEMINISM), as did her essay in book form *The Poison Maiden & The Great Bitch: Female Stereotypes in Marvel Superhero Comics* (as Susan Wood Glicksohn **1974** chap; as Susan Wood **1990**). An important essay was "Women and Science Fiction" (**1978**), reprinted in *Teaching Science Fiction* (anth **1980**) ed Jack WILLIAMSON. She edited and introduced *The Language of the Night: Essays on Fantasy and Science Fiction* (coll **1979**) by Ursula K. LE GUIN. SW's health was delicate and she drove herself too hard; her death was untimely. She wrote the CANADA entry for the 1st edn of this encyclopedia.   [PN]
See also: SCI FI; WOMEN AS PORTRAYED IN SCIENCE FICTION.

WOOD, WALLY Working name of US illustrator Wallace A. Wood (1927-1981). His first work was in newspaper COMIC strips in the late 1940s; he soon moved to comic books, joining EC COMICS in 1951 and working on their sf titles *Weird Science* and *Weird Fantasy*. His sf-comics and war-comics work won high praise, as did his slightly later work on EC's very successful *MAD Magazine*, founded 1952, for which he drew the famous sequence "Superduperman". One of the most influential comics artists of the century, WW has been claimed as the best of all artists ever to work in sf in comic-book form. When EC folded its comic books in 1955 and began to concentrate on *MAD*, he remained as one of the senior artists.

WW had already done some sf-magazine illustration (in 1953, for *Planet Stories*) when, in 1957, he branched out more fully into this field, mostly black-and-white interiors, especially for *Gal* and its sister magazines *If* and *Worlds of Tomorrow*; he also painted 6 covers for *Gal*. His interior illustrations were some of the finest ever printed; the chiaroscuro in his black-and-white work gave it an unmatched feeling of depth.

However, WAW's first love remained comics, though he had resented the restrictions, from 1954, imposed by the Comics Code Authority. From 1966 (8 issues) and again in 1976 he published an underground magazine, *Witzend*, featuring stronger material, sometimes erotic. In the mid-1960s, a boom-time for comics, WAW gave up most of his sf-magazine illustration and did some good work for Warren Publications on their horror comics *Creepy* and *Eeerie*; in the 1970s he worked on *Vampirella*. Also important was the SUPERHERO strip **Dynamo** which appeared in Tower Comics's *THUNDER Agents* (1965-9). Some of WAW's erotic work for *National Screw* is collected in the book *Cons de Fée* ["Fairy Tails" would be a loose translation of this obscene French pun] (**1977** France). He continued in comics until his suicide in 1981.
                                    [PN/JG]

WOODBURY, DAVID O(AKES) (1896-1981) US writer in whose *Mr Faraday's Formula* (**1965**) enemy agents steal a GRAVITY-control device. Part of a non-sf series, the book verges on being a TECHNOTHRILLER.   [JC]

WOODCOTT, KEITH ◊ John BRUNNER.

WOODRUFF, CLYDE [s] ◊ David V. REED.

WOODS, LAWRENCE Pseudonym used on magazine stories in 1941 by Donald A. WOLLHEIM, 1 solo ("Strange Return"), 1 with Robert A.W. LOWNDES ("Black Flames"), and 1 with John Michel ("Earth Does Not Reply").   [PN]

WOODS, P.F. [s] ◊ Barrington J. BAYLEY.

WOOLF, VIRGINIA (1882-1941) UK writer famous for novels whose structures sensitively emblematized the forms of inner consciousness. Of sf interest is *Orlando: A Biography* (**1928**), whose androgynous hero/heroine survives from Elizabethan to modern times, changing SEX more than once, and coming ultimately to represent a vision of the nature of England itself.   [JC]
Other works: *A Haunted House and Other Short Stories* (coll **1943**).

WOOTTON, BARBARA (1897-1988) UK economist, academic and writer; created a life peer in 1958, becoming Baroness Wootton of Abinger. *London's Burning: A Novel for the Decline and Fall of the Liberal Age* (**1936**) was set in 1940 and described the totalitarian implications of the aftermath of a general strike.   [JC]

WORLD OF GIANTS US tv series (1959). CBS TV. Prod and created William Alland. 1 season. Each episode 25 mins. B/w.

Marshall Thompson played a man who, on a secret mission, becomes the victim of atomic radiation and is shrunk to 6in (15cm). The government keeps him on as a secret agent, using him for assignments where his small size will be an advantage. His full-size partner on these missions was played by Arthur Franz. The short-lived series was really an excuse to use all the giant-sized props left over from *The* INCREDIBLE SHRINKING MAN (1957), which Alland had produced for Universal.   [JB]

WORLD ON A WIRE ◊ WELT AM DRAHT.

WORLDS BEYOND US DIGEST-size magazine. 3 issues,

monthly Dec 1950-Feb 1951, published by Hillman Periodicals; ed Damon KNIGHT. *WB* was divided between original and reprint material, and between sf and fantasy. New stories of note included "Null-P" by William TENN (Dec 1950) and Harry HARRISON's first story, "Rock Diver" (Feb 1951); Harrison also did illustrations for the magazine. Other contributors included C.M. KORNBLUTH, Richard MATHESON and Jack VANCE. Knight wrote book reviews. *WB* was cancelled by the publisher after adverse sales reports on #1. #2 and #3 were by then advanced in preparation and duly appeared. [MJE]

WORLD SCIENCE FICTION SOCIETY ◊ HUGO.

WORLD SF International association of sf professionals (not only writers, but also artists, critics, editors, agents, publishers, etc.), founded in Dublin, Sep 1976, by professionals at the First World Science Fiction Writers' Conference, and coming into operation as of the 1978 Dublin meeting. WSF's stated aim is "the general dissemination of creative sf, the furthering of scholarship, the interchange of ideas . . . the fostering of closer bonds between those who already hold such deep interests in common around the globe". Presidents have been Harry HARRISON (1978-80), Frederik POHL (1980-82), Brian W. ALDISS (1982-4), Sam J. LUNDWALL (1984-6), Gianfranco Viviani (1986-8), Norman SPINRAD (1988-90) and Malcolm EDWARDS (1990-92). Pohl instituted the Karel Award for excellence in sf translation. Under Aldiss the Harrison Award, for improving the status of sf internationally, and the President's Award, for independence of thought, were added. WSF-related books have been *The Penguin World Omnibus of Science Fiction* (anth **1986**) ed Aldiss and Lundwall and *Tales from Planet Earth* (anth **1986**) ed Pohl and Elizabeth Anne Hull. The 1st *World SF Newsletter* appeared in 1980 ed Niels DALGAARD and the 3rd in 1991 ed James Goddard. Annual meetings after 1978 were: 1979 Stockholm, Sweden; 1980 Stresa, Italy; 1981 Rotterdam, Netherlands; 1982 Linz, Austria; 1983 Zagreb, Yugoslavia; 1984 Brighton, UK; 1985 Fanano, Italy; 1986 Vancouver, Canada; 1987 Brighton, UK; 1988 Budapest, Hungary; 1989 San Marino; 1990 The Hague, Netherlands; 1991 Chengdu, Sichuan Province, China; «1993» (none in 1992) Jersey, Channel Islands, UK. [RH]

WORLDS OF FANTASY 1. UK pocketbook-size magazine, 14 numbered, undated issues 1950-4, published by John Spencer, London; ed anon Sol Assael and Michael Nahum. *WOF* is almost identical to the other 3 Spencer juvenile-sf magazines, FUTURISTIC SCIENCE STORIES, TALES OF TOMORROW and WONDERS OF THE SPACEWAYS, all containing fiction of very low quality.

2. US DIGEST-size magazine. 4 issues 1968-71, #1 published by Galaxy Publishing Corp., #2-#4 by Universal Publishing; #1-#2 ed Lester DELREY, #3-#4 ed Ejler JAKOBSSON. This attempt to produce a fantasy companion to GALAXY SCIENCE FICTION – it published a lot of SWORD-AND-SORCERY material – might well have succeeded had it had better distribution. The stan-

dard was good: *WOF* published *The Tombs of Atuan* (*WOF* 1970; exp **1971**) by Ursula K. LE GUIN and early stories by Michael BISHOP and James TIPTREE Jr. [FHP/PN]

WORLDS OF IF SCIENCE FICTION ◊ IF.

WORLDS OF THE UNIVERSE UK pocketbook-size magazine. 1 undated issue 1953, published by Gould-Light Publishing, London; ed anon (though probably Norman Light). No notable stories. Copies are rarely seen. [FHP]

WORLDS OF TOMORROW US DIGEST-size magazine. 26 issues in all, originally published by Barmaray Co. (Apr 1963) and then by Galaxy Publishing Co. as a bimonthly companion to GALAXY SCIENCE FICTION and IF, Apr 1963-May 1967, 23 issues, ed Frederik POHL. The bimonthly schedule slipped when Aug 1964 was followed by Nov 1964, and it went quarterly May 1966-May 1967. *WOT* was briefly revived by the Universal Publishing and Distributing Co. after they bought the Galaxy group, with 3 disappointing issues published 1970-71 ed Ejler JAKOBSSON. Notable stories included Philip K. DICK's "All We Marsmen" (Aug-Dec 1963; exp vt *Martian Time-Slip* **1964**), Samuel R. DELANY's "The Star Pit" (Feb 1967), Larry NIVEN's first novel *World of Ptavvs* (Mar 1965; exp **1966**) and the early stories in Philip José FARMER's **Riverworld** series, including "Day of the Great Shout" (Jan 1965), which was incorporated into the HUGO-winning *To Your Scattered Bodies Go* (fixup **1971**). A much-discussed article on CRYONICS by R.C.W. Ettinger (June 1963) ultimately led to the magazine publishing a symposium on the subject (Aug 1966). *WOT* was absorbed into its senior partner *Worlds of If Science Fiction* after May 1967.

The UK edition, published by Gold Star, ran for 4 issues Spring-Winter 1967. [BS/PN]

WORLD'S WORK ◊ TALES OF WONDER.

WORLD, THE FLESH AND THE DEVIL, THE Film (1959). Sol Siegel-Harbel/MGM. Dir Ranald MacDougall, starring Harry Belafonte, Inger Stevens, Mel Ferrer. Screenplay MacDougall, based on *The Purple Cloud* (**1901**) by M.P. SHIEL. 95 mins. B/w.

As in Arch Oboler's FIVE (1951), this wordy film tells of a tiny group of survivors in a nuclear-bomb-ravaged USA. In this case there are 3: a young White woman, a Black man and a cynical adventurer (White and male). The film is evocative, as in the Black man's entry into the empty metropolis (although no explanation is offered for the lack of bodies) and in the final hunt through the deserted streets of New York. The plot is simple: Black man finds White woman but hesitates to form a relationship with her; White man finds both of them and wants woman, who is willing to remain with Black man; a running duel takes place between the men. Eventually they realize the futility of it all, and the film ends with all 3 walking off (rather daringly for the time) hand in hand. The script is more sophisticated than the banality of the plot would suggest, but the treatment of the racial theme is embarrassingly tentative, and compromised by the use of so handsome and light-skinned a Black as Belafonte. There were just 2 survivors in Shiel's *The Purple Cloud* (**1901**; rev **1929**), on which this film is based only remotely. [JB/PN]

WORLD WITHOUT END Film (1956). Allied Artists. Written/dir Edward Bernds, starring Hugh Marlowe, Nancy Gates, Rod Taylor, Lisa Montell, Nelson Leigh. 80 mins. Colour.

After orbiting Mars, a spaceship goes through a timewarp. The 4 astronauts land on a post-HOLOCAUST Earth in AD2508 and find the surface inhabited by grotesque MUTANTS and giant spiders, while the remaining humans live underground – the men impotent, the women sexy, the race dying out. The astronauts stay, clearing the surface with bazookas. This is not a particularly low-budget film, and the effects (by Milton Rice) are passable, but direction and design are poor. The story is an unacknowledged inversion of H.G. WELLS's *The Time Machine* (**1895**), with Morlock surrogates on the surface and Eloi surrogates underground. Wells's novel was to be better filmed by George PAL as *The* TIME MACHINE (1960). [PN/JB]

WORMHOLES ◊ BLACK HOLES.

WORMSER, RICHARD (EDWARD) (1908-1977) US writer in various genres. He wrote a **Green Hornet** comic-book/tv tie, *The Green Hornet in the Infernal Light* * (**1966**) as by Ed Friend. Under his own name and of some sf interest were *Thief of Bagdad* * (**1961**) and *The Last Days of Sodom and Gomorrah* * (**1962**), both film ties, and *Pan Satyrus* (**1963**). [JC]

WÖRNER, HANS [r] ◊ GERMANY.

WORTH, PETER A ZIFF-DAVIS house name used on magazine stories; it appeared in their various sf magazines 10 times 1949-51, usually concealing Chester S. GEIER or Roger Phillips Graham (Rog PHILLIPS). [PN]

WOUK, HERMAN (1915-) US writer known primarily for meaty bestsellers like *The Caine Mutiny* (**1951**) and *The Winds of War* (**1971**). His sf SATIRE, *The "Lomokome" Papers* (**1956** *Collier's*; **1968**), somewhat clumsily puts allegorically opposing UTOPIAN societies on the MOON and sets them at each other's throats. [JC]

See also: HISTORY OF SF.

WRATISLAW, A(LBERT) C(HARLES) (1862-?) UK writer in whose *King Charles & Mr Perkins* (**1931**) a TIME MACHINE transports Perkins to Restoration England and retrieves him just before he would have been executed. [JC]

WRAY, REGINALD ◊ William Benjamin HOME-GALL.

WREN, THOMAS ◊ Thomas T. THOMAS.

WRIGHT, AUSTIN TAPPAN (1883-1931) US lawyer who spent much of his leisure time composing numerous manuscripts about a very large imaginary ISLAND called **Islandia**, a place easily described as a UTOPIA, though in fact too densely imagined and free of cognitive shaping to fit happily into that conventional category; the island was conceived as being set near the Antarctic and relating complexly to the real

world. Unlike J.R.R. TOLKIEN, whose *The Lord of the Rings* (**1954-5**) originated in similar private activities, ATW died before putting his work into publishable form, and his daughter, Sylvia Wright, with the help of Mark SAXTON (*whom see for his continuations*), condensed a number of his manuscripts into the novel *Islandia* (**1942**; with intro by Basil DAVENPORT), an enormous book ostensibly describing the travels of a visitor to the island, and in fact providing an extremely elaborate picture of an invented alternative society and its – richly drawn – inhabitants. [JC]

WRIGHT, FARNSWORTH (1888-1940) US editor. An early contributor to WEIRD TALES – his first story was "The Closing Hand" in 1923 – FW became editor in November 1924 after #13, and continued in the post until December 1939, at which point he had produced 177 issues. Under his guidance *Weird Tales* presented a unique mixture of horror stories, sf, occult fiction, FANTASY and SWORD AND SORCERY. In 1930 he began a companion magazine, *Oriental Stories*, featuring borderline-fantasy stories (many by regular *Weird Tales* contributors) in an exotic and largely imaginary Eastern setting. *Oriental Stories* became *Magic Carpet* in 1933 and ceased publication in 1934. Another project was a PULP-MAGAZINE edn of *A Midsummer Night's Dream*; FW was a Shakespeare enthusiast. He suffered from a form of Parkinson's disease which made it impossible for him even to write his name, except with a typewriter. Very soon after deteriorating health had forced him to leave *Weird Tales* he died. In its field, FW's *Weird Tales* rivals John W. CAMPBELL Jr's ASTOUNDING SCIENCE FICTION in terms of the number of stories of lasting interest which it produced in its field. [MJE]

WRIGHT, HAROLD BELL (1872-1944) US clergyman and enormously popular writer whose only sf novel, *The Devil's Highway* (**1932**) with John Lebar, pseudonym of his son Gilbert Munger Wright (1901-), features a wicked SCIENTIST whose thought-control device suppresses the better instincts of its victims, who are then inclined to further his plots. [JC]

Other work: *The Uncrowned King* (**1910**), fantasy.

WRIGHT, HELEN S. (? -) UK writer whose *A Matter of Oaths* (**1988**) engagingly presents a familiar sf character – the amnesiac protagonist who experiences flashback hints of a destiny larger than any of those around him dare contemplate – within a cogently described post-CYBERPUNK frame dominated by The Guild of Webbers, starship pilots who mediate between complex interstellar empires. [JC]

WRIGHT, KENNETH [s] ◊ Lester DEL REY.

WRIGHT, LAN Working name of UK writer and white-collar worker Lionel Percy Wright (1923-) for all his fiction. He began publishing sf with "Operation Exodus" for *NW* in 1952, and was active for over a decade. His **Johnny Dawson** series in *NW*, about intrigues between Earth and the planet Luther, were partly assembled in *Assignment Luther* (1955-7 *NW*; fixup **1963**); "Joker's Trick" (**1959**) and "The

Jarnos Affair" (1960) remained uncollected. LW had earlier begun publishing novels with *Who Speaks of Conquest?* (**1957** dos US). [JC]

Other works: *A Man Called Destiny* (**1958** dos US); *Exile from Xanadu* (**1964** dos US; vt *Space Born* 1964 UK); *The Last Hope of Earth* (**1965** US; vt *The Creeping Shroud* 1966 UK); *The Pictures of Pavanne* (**1968** dos US; vt *A Planet Called Pavanne* 1968 UK).

See also: MATTER TRANSMISSION.

WRIGHT, S(YDNEY) FOWLER (1874-1965) UK writer. SFW worked until middle-age as an accountant, was twice married and had 10 children. In 1917 he was a founder of the Empire Poetry League and edited the League's journal *Poetry*, which serialized his translations of DANTE ALIGHIERI's *Inferno* and *Purgatorio*; he also edited many anthologies for the League's Merton Press, publishing some early work by Olaf STAPLEDON. SFW's first book was *Scenes from the Morte d'Arthur* (coll of poetry **1919**) as by Alan Seymour. His first-published novel, *The Amphibians: A Romance of 500,000 Years Hence* (**1924**; vt *The World Below* 1953 UK), was issued by the Merton Press. He later founded Fowler Wright Books Ltd to issue his translation of the *Inferno* (**1928**) and a novel which he had written in 1920, *Deluge* (**1928**).

The Amphibians describes a FAR-FUTURE Earth where mankind is extinct and new intelligent species are engaged in their own struggle for existence; its imagery was strongly influenced by Wright's work on *Inferno* and its structure recapitulates HOMER's *Odyssey*. It was meant to be the part 1 of a trilogy, but part 3 was never written and the concluding chapters of part 2 – added to part 1 in *The World Below* (**1929**; vt in 2 vols as *The Amphibians* 1951 US and *The World Below* 1951 US; vt in 2 vols as *The World Below* 1953 UK and *The Dwellers* 1953 UK) – are rather synoptic. *Deluge*, a DISASTER story in which most of England sinks beneath the sea – so that the Cotswolds are converted into an archipelago – enjoyed considerable critical success and was filmed in 1933 as DELUGE (with New York as the setting); SFW promptly retired from accountancy and began a second career as a writer.

The Island of Captain Sparrow (**1928**) deliberately recalls H.G. WELLS's *The Island of Dr Moreau* (**1896**) in its image of an ISLAND inhabited by satyr-like beastmen who are prey to the corrupt descendants of castaway pirates. It also features a feral girl, the first of several similar figures used by SFW to celebrate the state of Nature in opposition to the brutality of "civilized" men. *Dawn* (**1929**), a sequel to *Deluge* – with which it was assembled as *Deluge, and Dawn* (omni **1975** US) – also contains much bitter commentary on the corruptions of comfort and civilization and carries forward a Rousseau-esque glorification of Nature and insistence on the fundamentality of the Social Contract. The **Margaret Cranleigh** trilogy began with *Dream, or The Simian Maid* (**1931**), which carries these philosophical arguments to further extremes in telling the story of a woman transported

back to a lost prehistory to witness a battle for survival between a humanoid species and ratlike predators. The 2nd volume was ultimately published – shorn of connecting material – under the pseudonym Anthony Wingrave as *The Vengeance of Gwa* (**1935**; reprinted as by SFW); and the 3rd did not appear until much later, as *Spiders' War* (**1954** US). *Beyond the Rim* (**1932**) is a determinedly eccentric lost-race (◊ LOST WORLDS) story set in the Antarctic; it is much more interesting than SFW's lacklustre later works in a similar vein, *The Screaming Lake* (**1937**) and *The Hidden Tribe* (**1938**), although its sf content is only marginal.

SFW's vivid short fiction of this period was assembled in *The New Gods Lead* (coll **1932**; exp vt *The Throne of Saturn* **1949** US), which groups 7 vitriolic DYSTOPIAN stories under the heading "Where the New Gods Lead" (the new gods in question being Comfort and Cowardice). These include a notable fantasy of IMMORTALITY, "The Rat" (1929), a trilogy of parables about the taking over of human prerogatives by MACHINES, "Automata" (1929), and 2 polemics against SFW'S pet hates, birth control and the motor car, "P.N.40" (1929 as "P.N.40 – and Love") and "Justice".

Power (**1933**) belongs to that subgenre of SCIENTIFIC ROMANCES in which a lone man in possession of some awesomely destructive WEAPON attempts to blackmail the world. SFW's protagonist is among the more altruistic and ambitious, but the story ultimately fades into a mere thriller. SFW visited Nazi Germany in 1934 in order to write a series of newspaper articles, and this inspired a trio of highly melodramatic future-WAR stories: *Prelude in Prague: The War of 1938* (**1935** *Daily Mail* as "1938"; **1935**; vt *The War of 1938* 1936 US), *Four Days War* (**1936**) and *Megiddo's Ridge* (**1937**). By this time he was falling prey to old age, but he produced a final vivid image of the future in *The Adventure of Wyndham Smith* (**1938**), partly based on a short story, "Original Sin" (which ultimately saw publication in *The Witchfinder* [coll **1946**] and in *The Throne of Saturn*). In the novel the inhabitants of a stagnant and sterile quasi-UTOPIAN state decide to commit mass suicide, and unleash mechanical Killers to hunt down a handful of rebels. Apart from *Spiders' War* and the brief parables "The Better Choice" (1955) and "First Move" (1963), none of his later work was published; all the manuscripts have been lost except for the still unpublished fantasy novel «Inquisitive Angel».

He also wrote numerous detective stories, all as by Sydney Fowler in the UK although some appeared as by SFW in the USA. *The Bell Street Murders* (**1931**), as Sydney Fowler, features an invention which records moving images on a screen; its first sequel, *The Secret of the Screen* (**1933**), as Fowler, has negligible sf content. The weak futuristic thriller *The Adventure of the Blue Room* (**1945**) also appeared under the Fowler byline.

Despite the considerable number of his published

works, SFW's literary career was a chronicle of frustrations. The 2 projects dearest to his heart – the long Arthurian epic of which «Scenes from the Morte d'Arthur» is but a small part, and a long historical novel about Cortez, «For God and Spain» – were never published. Although self-publication led him to brief fame and fortune, he failed in his ambition to become a social commentator of Wellsian status and ended up trying to resuscitate his career by reprinting his early works under the **Books of Today** imprint while he was editing a trade journal of that title in the late 1940s. Even *The World Below*, despite its classic status as a vividly exotic novel of the far future, is only half the work it was originally intended to be. Nevertheless, he was a strikingly original writer and one of the key figures in the tradition of UK scientific romance. [BS]

About the author: "Against the New Gods: The Speculative Fiction of S. Fowler Wright" by Brian M. STABLEFORD, *Foundation* #29 (Nov 1983).

See also: BIOLOGY; CITIES; CRIME AND PUNISHMENT; FANTASTIC VOYAGES; HISTORY OF SF; HOLOCAUST AND AFTER; MEDICINE; ORIGIN OF MAN; ROBERT HALE LIMITED; SOCIAL DARWINISM; SOCIOLOGY; TECHNOLOGY.

WRIGHT, STEPHEN (1946-   ) US writer whose only novel of sf interest, *M31: A Family Romance* (**1988**), is a FABULATION in an agglutinative style reminiscent of that used by William Gaddis (1922-   ) in *The Recognitions* (**1955**). Abandoned by their parents – Dot and Dash, who claim descent from the inhabitants of the Andromeda Galaxy (M31) – the protagonists of the book ricochet numbly through the nightmare shopping malls and 7-11s of the modern "rural" USA. The vacuum family they make together and the horrors they commit contribute to an extremely distressing vision of the latter moments of the century. [JC]

WRIGHT, WEAVER [s] ◊ Forrest J. ACKERMAN.

WRITERS OF THE FUTURE CONTEST This contest, originally sponsored by L. Ron HUBBARD and later, after his death, by Bridge Publications in the USA, is between short stories or novelettes of sf or fantasy submitted by novice authors who have previously published no more than 3 short stories or 1 novelette. Contests have been held quarterly since 1984; the 3 place-getters receive cash awards as well as publication in the L. RON HUBBARD PRESENTS WRITERS OF THE FUTURE series of original anthologies. Winners of the quarterly award receive $1000; in addition, from 1985, an annual winner, chosen from the quarterly winners, receives the "L. Ron Hubbard Writers of the Future Award" and $4000.

Sums very much larger than these have been spent on publicizing the awards. This practice has aroused controversy, being seen by some as part of a campaign by the Church of SCIENTOLOGY to elevate Hubbard's status within the sf community and the literary community at large. On the one hand, Algis BUDRYS, administrator of WOTFC until 1992, says that, though he is personally an admirer of Hub-

bard's fiction, there is no connection between WOTFC and the Church of Scientology. On the other hand, the sponsor, Bridge Publications, was originally set up to publish textbooks of DIANETICS and Scientology; the launch parties and general publicity given by Bridge to WOTF, which appear to be funded from an almost bottomless pocket, have been so lavish as to send *frissons* of pleasure or disgust through the entire sf community. The company called Author Services, Inc. – active in publicizing L. Ron Hubbard – which acts as co-host with Bridge at WOTFC award ceremonies, was alleged in 1984 newspaper reports to have at that time assets of $44 million derived from the Church of Scientology.

WOTFC has had its successes. The first of these has been the astonishingly prestigious panel of judges it has built up, including Gregory BENFORD, Ben BOVA, Ramsey Campbell (1946-   ), Anne MCCAFFREY, C.L. MOORE, Larry NIVEN, Frederik POHL, Robert SILVERBERG, Theodore STURGEON, John VARLEY, Jack WILLIAMSON and Gene WOLFE. Only the most determined of conspiracy theorists could see these writers as representing a secret pro-Scientology agenda; it seems clear that they wish merely to assist young writers. The second success has been the writers themselves. By no means all contest winners have gone on to greater things, but Robert REED (who entered the contest as Robert Touzalin), Dave WOLVERTON and David ZINDELL have certainly produced admirable work since, as has Karen Joy FOWLER, who though not a winner has been perhaps the most distinguished of all the WOTFC graduates. The general standard of the anthologies drawn from contestants' stories has been quite high. An Illustrators of the Future Contest is run in parallel.

The WOTFC programme also includes writers' workshops, directed by Budrys in association with such other writers as Orson Scott CARD, Tim POWERS and Ian WATSON. These workshops are notable for being – at least in some sessions – based very specifically on advice to writers originally formulated by Hubbard many decades ago. Those who do not accept Hubbard as one of sf's real craftsmen, though he certainly could write vividly and excitingly, see an irony in this.

The listing below is by the year in which the awards ceremony was held, and refers to work of the previous year. Those named for 1985 are quarterly winners; the first "L. Ron Hubbard Writers of the Future Award" proper was presented the following year. [PN]

Winners:
1985: Dennis J. Pimple; Jor Jennings; David ZINDELL
1986: Robert Touzalin (Robert REED)
1987: Dave WOLVERTON
1988: Nancy Farmer
1989: Gary W. Shockley
1990: James Gardner
1991: James C. Glass

WU, WILLIAM F(RANKING) (1951-   ) US writer

who began publishing sf with "By the Flicker of the One-Eyed Flame" for *Andromeda 2* (anth **1977**) ed Peter WESTON, and who has produced considerable work in various genres, receiving nominations for various awards; several tales make use of his own Chinese-US background. His novels are less impressive. The first, *Masterplay* (fixup **1987**), though not set in a franchised GAME-WORLD, flirts with the intoxications of a role-playing venue whose outcomes determine real events. *Hong on the Range* (**1989**) similarly engages its protagonist – who appeared earlier in "Hong's Bluff" (**1985**) – in wargaming enterprises; *The Shade of Lo Man Gong* (1988 *Pulphouse*; **1991** chap) is also fantasy. His other books have been ties: 2 tales in the **Robot City** sequence, *Isaac Asimov's Robot City #3: Cyborg* * (**1987**) and *#6: Perihelion* * (**1988**); *Dr Bones #2: The Cosmic Bomber* * (**1989**), and a **Time Tours** tale, *Robert Silverberg's Time Tours #1: The Robin Hood Ambush* * (**1990**). [JC]

Other work: *Yellow Peril: Chinese Americans in American Fiction, 1850-1940* (**1982**); *Shaunessy Fong* (**1992** chap).

WU DINGBO (1941–   ) Chinese academic and sf scholar based at the English Department of the Shanghai International Studies University. His PhD in English is from Indiana University of Pennsylvania, his dissertation being titled "Utopias by American Women". With Patrick Murphy he ed *Science Fiction from China* (anth **1989** US), which contains 8 Chinese sf stories and a chronological bibliography. He is a member of WORLD SF and has had more than 40 articles and translations, in Chinese and English, published in the USA and China. He wrote the CHINESE SF entry in this encyclopedia. [PN]

Other works as editor: *Selections of American Science Fiction* (anth **1983**); *Star Ducks* (anth **1983**).

WU FANG ◊ *The* MYSTERIOUS WU FANG.

WUL, STEFAN Pseudonym of French dental surgeon and writer Pierre Pairault (1922-   ), who swept onto the sf scene with 11 consistent and imaginative novels, all published 1956-9. *Niourk* (**1957**) is a J.G. BALLARD-like account of a drowned world. *Oms en série* ["Oms by the Dozen"] (**1957**) inspired the animated film *La* PLANÈTE SAUVAGE (1973). The apparently human protagonist of *Le temple du passé* (**1958**; trans Ellen Cox as *The Temple of the Past* 1973 US), having crashed on an ALIEN planet, attempts to save his colleagues after they have all been swallowed by an indigenous whale, enters SUSPENDED ANIMATION, and is discovered eons later by genuine human folk and identified as a survivor of ATLANTIS. After 1959, SW fell silent until the appearance of *Noô* (**1977**), a lengthy and flamboyant saga which, like his earlier novels, shows a deep understanding of the traditions of US pulp sf. [MJ/JC]

Other works: *Retour à O* ["Back to O"] (**1956**); *Rayons pour Sidar* ["Rays for Sidar"] (**1957**); *La peur géante* ["The Immense Fear"] (**1957**); *L'orphelin de Perdide* ["The Orphan from Perdide"] (**1958**); *La mort vivante* ["Living Death"] (**1958**); *Piège sur Zarkass* ["Trap on Zarkass"] (**1958**); *Terminus 1* (**1959**); *Odyssée sous contrôle* ["Controlled Odyssey"] (**1959**).

See also: FRANCE; UNDER THE SEA.

WULFF, EVE [r] ◊ James L. QUINN.

WÜRF, KARL [s] ◊ George H. SCITHERS.

WURLITZER, RUDOLF (1937-   ) US novelist and screenwriter, most of whose tales may be read as FABULATIONS in which sf elements are bleakly pickled. *Nog* (**1969**; vt *The Octopus* UK), *Flats* (**1970**) and *Quake* (**1972**) share an apocalyptic *mise en scène* similar in feeling to, but not clearly identified as being, the post-HOLOCAUST world so familiar to sf readers. *Slow Fade* (**1984**) verges on similar territory. [JC]

WYATT, B.D. [s] ◊ Spider ROBINSON.

WYATT, PATRICK Pseudonym of a UK writer, possibly female. PW's *Irish Rose* (**1975**) is a love story set in a world where almost all white women have died – except in Ireland – as a result of taking the Pill. The RELIGION of the frustrated male population is, perhaps predictably, misogynist. [JC]

WYKES, ALAN (1914-   ) Prolific UK writer, mainly of nonfiction, whose sf SATIRE *Happyland* (**1952**) depicts an arcadian fantasy-ISLAND in which happiness is literally obtainable. A UK magnate turns the place into a holiday camp; a new kind of bomb finally eliminates it. [JC]

WYLDE, THOMAS (1946-   ) US writer who began publishing sf with "Target of Opportunity" for *Gal* in 1974, and who has continued to produce short fiction regularly, some of it HARD SF tinged with ironies. His novels have all been ties: 2 tales in the **Alien Speedway** sequence, *Roger Zelazny's Alien Speedway #2: Pitfall* * (**1988**) and *#3: The Web* * (**1988**); and 2 in the **Dr Bones** sequence, *Dr Bones #3: Garukan Blood* * (**1989**) and the last in the series, *#6: Journey to Rilla* * (**1990**). [JC]

WYLIE, DIRK Name adopted by Joseph H. Dockweiler, a member of the FUTURIANS fan group, for several stories written in collaboration with Frederik POHL. C.M. KORNBLUTH also had a hand in one. "Highwayman of the Void" (1944) is by Pohl alone. [BS]

WYLIE, PHILIP (GORDON) (1902-1971) US author who became notorious for his penetrating surveys of US mores and behaviour, and who coined the term "Momism" to describe the US tendency to sacralize motherhood, thus making family dynamics and morality impenetrable to reflection; outside sf he probably remains best remembered for *Generation of Vipers* (**1942**), where the coinage appeared. In the sf field he was most significant for 4 works: *Gladiator* (**1930**), filmed as *The Gladiator* (1938), about a young man endowed with superhuman strength, a tale directly responsible for the appearance of the comic-book hero SUPERMAN (though there PW's traditional scepticism about the relationship of a superior being to normal humanity was safely displaced onto the morose Clark Kent); *When Worlds Collide* (**1933**) and its sequel, *After Worlds Collide* (**1934**), both with Edwin BALMER, a retelling of the Noah's ark legend involving the END OF THE WORLD and interplanetary flight (the 1st vol was adapted into an sf COMIC strip and a successful film, WHEN WORLDS COLLIDE [1951]); and *The Disappearance* (**1951**), which ingeniously assaults the double standard through a tale in which the men and women of Earth disappear from one another, having been suddenly segregated into 2 PARALLEL WORLDS.

The first 3 of these novels were published early in PW's career, the period during which he produced his most highly regarded single work, *Finnley Wren* (**1934**), a baroque anatomy in fictional terms of the young century into which were embedded 2 tales of sf interest, "An Epistle to the Thessalonians" and "Epistle to the Galatians". Other work from the 1930s included *The Murderer Invisible* (**1931**), a tale inspired by H.G. WELLS's *The Invisible Man* (**1897**) (with R.C. SHERRIFF, PW scripted the 1933 film version of *The* INVISIBLE MAN); the screenplay for *The* ISLAND OF LOST SOULS (**1932**), adapted from Wells's *The Island of Dr Moreau* (**1896**); *The Savage Gentleman* (**1932**), in which a child is brought up isolated from humanity, and excoriates the social world when finally exposed to it; and scripts for 2 further films, *The King of the Jungle* (**1933**) and *Murders in the Zoo* (**1933**).

In the early 1940s his attention became fixed upon the apocalyptic implications of nuclear energy, and in "The Paradise Crater" (October 1945 *Blue Book*) – upon whose earlier submission to *American Magazine* he was put under house arrest for undue prescience – he described a high-tech post-WWII 1965 threatened by an underground Nazi attempt to rule the world through the use of atomic bombs; fortunately the hero blows up the villains' Californian HQ, causing a tsunami which takes care of Japan as well. In *Blunder: A Story of the End of the World* (**1946** chap), atomic experiments blow up the entire planet. In several later works PW continued to address the new vulnerability of the world. Titles include *The Smuggled Atom Bomb* (1951 *Saturday Evening Post*; in *Three to be Read* [coll **1951**]; **1956**), "Philadelphia Phase" (1951), *The Answer* (**1955** chap) – a pacifist fantasy – *Tomorrow!* (**1954**) and *Triumph* (**1963**), the 2 latter novels being pleas for a nuclear Civil Defence. Towards the end of his life he turned from atomic DISASTER to ecological disaster in *The End of the Dream* (**1972**) (◊ ECOLOGY) and a **The Name of the Game** tv tie, *Los Angeles: A.D. 2017* * (**1971**). He also wrote an essay on sf, "Science Fiction and Sanity in an Age of Crisis", which appeared in *Modern Science Fiction* (anth **1953**) ed Reginald BRETNOR.

PW was a highly successful commercial writer, much of whose work pretended to no more than entertainment value. In his sf, however, though he never abandoned a commercial idiom, he gave something like full rein to the anatomizing and apocalyptic impulses which made him, during his life, a figure of controversy to his large readership.   [JC]

Other works: *The Golden Hoard* (**1934**) with Edwin Balmer, a mystery; *Night unto Night* (**1944**), a ghost

story; *The Spy who Spoke Porpoise* (**1969**).

About the author: "Philip Wylie" in *Explorers of the Infinite* (**1963**) by Sam MOSKOWITZ; *Still Worlds Collide: Philip Wylie and the End of the American Dream* (**1980** chap) by Clifford P. Bendan.

See also: DYSTOPIAS; FEMINISM; HOLOCAUST AND AFTER; INVISIBILITY; NUCLEAR POWER; POLLUTION; SEX; SOCIOLOGY; SPACESHIPS; SUPERMAN.

WYNDHAM, JOHN That fraction of his full name used by UK writer John Wyndham Parkes Lucas Beynon Harris (1903-1969) after WWII, and by far his best-known byline; before WWII, he had signed work as John Beynon Harris, John Beynon, Wyndham Parkes, Lucas Parkes and Johnson Harris. As well as changing names with frequency, JW often revised – or allowed others to revise – works from early in his working life; at times this led (as with *Planet Plane*; see below) to an excessive number of versions of unimportant titles.

As a whole, JW's career broke into 2 parts: before WWII and after it, when he became Wyndham. His first career was inconspicuous. He began publishing sf in 1931 with "Worlds to Barter" as by John Beynon Harris for *Wonder Stories*, and contributed adventure sf and juveniles to various UK magazines throughout the 1930s. Some of this early work was assembled as *Wanderers of Time* (coll **1973**) as by JW, the title story having been reprinted earlier as *Love in Time* (1933 *Wonder Stories* as "Wanderers of Time" as by John Beynon Harris; **1945** chap) as by Johnson Harris; most of the contents of *Exiles on Asperus* (coll **1979**) as by John Beynon were also pre-WWII. His first novel, *The Secret People* (**1935** as by John Beynon; rev 1964 US; text restored 1972 UK as by JW), was a juvenile sf adventure set in a underground world threatened by a project to transform the Sahara into a lake for irrigation purposes. *Planet Plane* (1936 *Passing Show* as "Stowaway to Mars" as by John Beynon; full text **1936** as by John Beynon; cut 1937 in *Modern Wonder* vt "The Space Machine"; differing cut [by another hand] vt *Stowaway to Mars* 1953; text restored 1972 as by JW) was a rather well told, though only intermittently subtle, narrative of humanity's first space flight to Mars, where Vaygan the Martian and the machines destined to succeed his dying species deal swiftly with 3 competing sets of Earthlings who have landed almost simultaneously. Vaygan himself impregnates Joan, the stowaway of the magazine title; given the moral strictures then applying to magazine fiction, it is unsurprising that she dies in childbirth and that her child is deemed illegitimate. The sequel, "Sleepers of Mars" (1938 *Tales of Wonder* as by John Beynon; as title story in *Sleepers of Mars* [coll **1973**] as by JW), deals merely with some stranded Russians, not with the miscegenate offspring. In *Bound to be Read* (**1975**), the memoirs of UK publisher Robert Lusty, the John Beynon Harris of these years appears as a rather diffident, obscure, lounging individual at the fringes of the literary and social world; there was no great reason to suppose he would ever erupt into fame.

WWII interrupted JW's writing career, and his later works showed a change in basic subject matter and a much more careful concern for the responses of the middle-class audience he was now attempting to reach in slick journals like COLLIER'S WEEKLY. Where much of his pre-WWII tales were SPACE OPERAS leavened with the occasional witty aside or passage, JW's post-WWII novels – most notably *The Day of the Triffids* (**1951** US; rev [and preferred text] 1951 UK; orig version vt *Revolt of the Triffids* 1952 US), filmed as *The* DAY OF THE TRIFFIDS (1963), and *The Kraken Wakes* (**1953**; rev vt *Out of the Deeps* 1953 US), both assembled with *Re-Birth* (**1955** US; rev vt *The Chrysalids* 1955 UK) as *The John Wyndham Omnibus* (omni **1964**) – present an eloquent post-trauma middle-class UK response to the theme of DISASTER, whether caused by the forces of Nature, alien INVASIONS, EVOLUTION or Man's own nuclear warfare. JW did not invent the UK novel of secretly-longed-for-disaster, or what Brian W. ALDISS has called the COSY CATASTROPHE, for this had reached mature form as early as 1885, with the publication of Richard JEFFERIES's retrospective *After London, or Wild England*, and the techniques for giving actuality to the moment of crisis had been thoroughly established, by H.G. WELLS and others, well before WWI; but he effectively domesticated some of its defining patterns: the city (usually London) depopulated by the catastrophe; the exodus, with its scenes of panic and bravery; and the ensuring focus on a small but growing nucleus of survivors who reach some kind of sanctuary in the country and prepare to reestablish Man's shaken dominion. UK writers as diverse as John CHRISTOPHER, Aldiss and M. John HARRISON have used the pattern with notable success. Their natural tendency has been somewhat to darken JW's palette and to widen its social relevance, for his protagonists and their women tend to behave with old-fashioned decency and courage, rather as though they were involved in the Battle of Britain, a time imaginatively close to him and to his markets.

Three considerably overlapping story collections assembled shorter material produced after WWII: *Jizzle* (coll **1954**), *Tales of Gooseflesh and Laughter* (coll **1956** US) and *The Seeds of Time* (coll **1956**). In them, JW again demonstrated his skill at translating sf situations into fundamentally comfortable tales of character, however prickly their subject matter might be. In the UK, though not in the USA, he was marketed as a middlebrow writer of non-generic work, and was not strongly identified with sf.

Though published and associated with the cosy catastrophe tales, *Re-Birth* – JW apparently preferred the title *The Chrysalids*, by which the book has always been known in the UK – marked a new phase, in which the invasion comes not from abroad but in the form of MUTANTS who must survive in a normal world, and whose threat to "normal" humans was expressed in bleakly Social Darwinist terms; in the end, a somewhat traumatized "cosy" normalcy is retained when the novel's mutant protagonists are forced to leave the human hearth. In his next – *The Midwich Cuckoos* (**1957**; rev 1958 US; vt *Village of the Damned* 1960 US), filmed as VILLAGE OF THE DAMNED (1960) and as CHILDREN OF THE DAMNED (1963) – the incursion is unqualifiedly inimical: the ALIEN invaders who inseminate the women of Midwich, and the consequent very effectively spooky offspring, mark a decided inturning from the comfortable assumptions of earlier books. Later novels, like *Trouble with Lichen* (**1960**; rev 1960 US), are conspicuous for their facetious unease, and it might be suggested that the potency of JW's impulse to cosiness may well have derived from some profound cultural and/or personal insecurity he was unable to articulate directly. But he wrote effectively for a specific UK market at a specific point in time – the period of recuperation that followed WWII – and he will be remembered primarily for the half decade or so during which he was able to express in telling images the hopes, fears and resurgent complacency of a readership that recognized a kindred spirit. During that period, in the UK and Australia at least, he was probably more read than any other sf author. As late as 1992, his books appeared regularly on school syllabuses in the UK.   [JC]

Other works: *The Outward Urge* (coll of linked stories: **1959**; with 1 story added, rev 1961), published as by JW and Lucas Parkes; *Consider Her Ways & Others* (coll **1961**) and *The Infinite Moment* (coll **1961** US), 2 titles whose contents are similar, though each book was conceived separately; *Chocky* (1963 *AMZ*; exp **1968** US); *The Best of John Wyndham* (coll **1973**; without intro or bibliography vt *The Man from Beyond and Other Stories* 1975; full version in 2 vols vt *The Best of John Wyndham 1932-1949* 1976 and *The Best of John Wyndham 1951-1960* 1976) ed Angus WELLS; *Web* (**1979**); *John Wyndham* (omni **1980**) assembling *The Day of the Triffids, The Kraken Wakes, The Chrysalids, The Seeds of Time, The Midwich Cuckoos* and *Trouble with Lichen*.

About the author: *John Wyndham, Creator of the Cosy Catastrophe: A Working Bibliography* (latest rev **1989** chap) by Phil STEPHENSEN-PAYNE.

See also: BOYS' PAPERS; CHILDREN IN SF; CLICHÉS; FEMINISM; GOTHIC SF; HISTORY OF SF; HOLOCAUST AND AFTER; IMMORTALITY; MAINSTREAM WRITERS OF SF; MONSTERS; MUSIC; PSI POWERS; PUBLISHING; RADIO; SEX; UFOS; VENUS.

WYNNE-JONES, DIANA ◊ Diana Wynne JONES.

WYNNE-TYSON, ESMÉ [r] ◊ J.D. BERESFORD.

WYSS, JOHAN RUDOLF (1781-1830) Swiss philosopher and writer, of sf interest for *Der Schweizerische Robinson* (**1812-13**; trans – perhaps by William Godwin [1756-1836] – as *The Family Robinson Crusoe* **1814** UK; new trans as *The Swiss Family Robinson* 1818 UK), which, together with the tale which inspired it, Daniel DEFOE's *Robinson Crusoe* (**1719**), served as a central model for sf tales of the COLONIZATION OF OTHER WORLDS. (*For fuller discussion* ◊ ROBINSONADE.)   [JC]

XENOBIOLOGY The study of lifeforms that may exist elsewhere than on Earth is called xenobiology or exobiology. It is one of the few legitimate sciences to have, as yet, no direct experimental application other than the tests carried out on the surface of Mars to see if the soil showed any of the biological activity that might be associated with the presence of microscopic lifeforms. (It seemed for a time as if some of the results of this experiment might be positive; it is now thought they were caused by nonbiological factors.) Numerous essays on exobiological themes have appeared in scientific journals, on subjects ranging from SETI ("Search for Extraterrestrial Intelligence"), through speculations about non-carbon-based lifeforms to the thoughts of Freeman DYSON and others about the relation of COSMOLOGY to biology. Popular introductions to speculative biology of this sort include *Life in Darwin's Universe: Evolution and the Cosmos* (**1981**) by Gene Bylinski and *Darwin's Universe: Origins and Crises in the History of Life* (**1983**) by C.R. Pellegrino and J.A. Stoff. Two pioneering works, both more theoretical and the latter a little more technical, are *Intelligent Life in the Universe* (**1966**) by I.S. Shklovskii and Carl SAGAN (based on *Vselennaia, Zhizn, Razum* [**1963**] by Shklovskii alone; trans Paula Fern, rev and exp so greatly by Sagan as to become a co-authorship) and *Interstellar Communication: Scientific Perspectives* (**1974**) ed Cyril Ponnamperuma and A.G.W. Cameron. A good overview is given by *The Search for Life in the Universe* (**1978**) by Donald Goldsmith and Tobias Owen. The subject is, of course, central to sf about ALIENS and LIFE ON OTHER WORLDS; a survey of it written very much from an sf writer's viewpoint is *Extraterrestrial Encounter: A Personal Perspective* (**1979**) by Chris BOYCE. There is an exobiology lab at the University of Hawaii.   [PN]

XERO US FANZINE (1960-63), ed from New York by Richard and Pat LUPOFF. Large and attractively produced, with illustrations by Roy G. KRENKEL, Eddie JONES and others, *X* was particularly well known for its articles on COMICS, notably the series **All in Color for a Dime** by Richard Lupoff, Ted WHITE and others. Together with new pieces by Harlan ELLISON and Ron GOULART, these articles were published by ACE BOOKS as *All in Color for a Dime* (anth **1970**), ed Dick Lupoff and Don Thompson. *X* also contained material on sf and FANDOM, contributors including James BLISH, Lin CARTER, Avram DAVIDSON, Wilson TUCKER and Walt Willis. *X* won the 1963 HUGO for Best Fanzine.   [PR/RH]

X-MEN US COMIC-book series, created by Jack KIRBY and Stan LEE for MARVEL COMICS in 1963. It had a 66-issue run, and then ran reprints until #94 (1975), when new stories resumed featuring the new team of X-Men that had been introduced in *Giant-Size X-Men* #1 a few months earlier. Kirby drew the first 11 issues and Lee wrote the first 19. Many highly regarded artists have worked on the series over the years, notably Neal ADAMS, John Byrne, Dave Cockrum, Jim Lee, James STERANKO and Barry Windsor-Smith; while later writers have been Roy Thomas (#20-#43, #55-#64 and #66), Arnold Drake (#44-#54), Denny O'Neil (#65), Len Wein (#94-#95 and *Giant Size* #1) and Chris CLAREMONT (#96-#279). Claremont has now left the series, after a dispute; his 16-year unbroken writing run is a record for a Marvel title.

X-Men, now retitled *The Uncanny X-Men*, differs from apparently similar costumed-SUPERHERO comics in that the X-Men, "feared and hated by the world they have sworn to protect", are all MUTANTS. Ignorance and fear of mutants was the subtext to the 1st run, and in the 2nd series much emphasized by Claremont, who saw the comic as showing "racism and prejudice . . . and what it's like to be a victim of it". He most successfully realized this theme in *God Loves, Man Kills* (**1982**), an **X-Men** GRAPHIC NOVEL in which a fundamentalist televangelist launches a crusade against mutants. **X-Men** was the best-selling US comic for most of the 1980s, its success spawning numerous miniseries and the ongoing **The New Mutants** (1983-91), **X-Factor** (1986-current), **Excalibur**

(1988-current), **Wolverine** (1988-current), **Marvel Comics Presents** (1988-current) – an anthology title with **Wolverine** the main story – **X-Force** (1991-current) and a second **X-Men** (1991-current). Nearly all the traditional sf themes, from GENETIC ENGINEERING to TIME TRAVEL, have been used in *X-Men*. [RH]

X – THE MAN WITH THE X-RAY EYES (vt *The Man with the X-Ray Eyes*) Film (1963). Alta Vista/AIP. Dir Roger CORMAN, starring Ray Milland, Diana Van Der Vlis, John Hoyt, Don Rickles. Screenplay Robert Dillon, Ray Russell, based on a story by Russell. 88 mins cut to 80 mins. Colour.

A surgeon, Dr Xavier, uses an experimental drug to develop X-ray vision and thus perform operations more skilfully, but the process affects his mind. He accidentally kills a colleague and hides in a carnival sideshow where he is exploited as a faith healer. His X-ray vision becomes a metaphor for insight into all the ugliness and sadness of life. A series of events bring appalling visions which alienate him progressively from ordinary, unseeing humanity. Finally he encounters an evangelist holding a religious meeting in the desert; when the man cries "If thine eye offend thee, pluck it out!", Xavier does just that. Though close to being a Poverty Row product (the special effects are not quite up to showing Dr Xavier's ability to "see through the centre of the Universe") this bleak film is sometimes considered Corman's masterpiece. [PN/JB]

See also: CINEMA.

X THE UNKNOWN Film (1956). Hammer/Warner Bros. Dir Leslie Norman (replacing Joseph Walton), starring Dean Jagger, Edward Chapman, William Lucas, Leo McKern, Anthony Newley. Screenplay Jimmy Sangster. 86 mins, cut to 78 mins in the USA. B/w.

In this Hammer sf/HORROR film made soon after the success of their *The* QUATERMASS XPERIMENT (1955) – the "X" in both cases being intended to signal unimaginable horrors, as in X-rated (adults only) movies – a radioactive blob, a sort of primal, semi-fluid, living creature brought to the surface by tidal pressures in Earth's core, emerges near a village in Scotland and heads for the nearest source of radioactivity, melting people who get in its way. It is a tense, low-budget thriller, with both Jagger and McKern good, one as a scientist, the other as an investigator from the Atomic Energy Commission. The anxious atmosphere is amplified by moody photography, with many sequences shot at night. Routine in concept, the film is well above average in execution. [PN/JB]

XTRO Film (1982). Ashley Productions/Amalgamated Film Enterprises. Dir Harry Bromley Davenport, starring Bernice Stegers, Philip Sayer, Danny Brainin, Simon Nash, Maryam D'Abo. Screenplay Iain Cassie, Robert Smith, based on a screenplay by Michel Parry, Davenport. 86 mins. Colour.

UK sf/HORROR exploitation movie in which a man is kidnapped by a UFO. 3 years later the UFO returns, an ALIEN gets out and rapes a nearby woman, who that same night gives birth (disgustingly) to a fully grown man, the same man who was kidnapped in the first place. He goes home, infects his son with alien spores; the son uses new telekinetic powers to murder a neighbour with his animated toy clown, and then wraps the *au pair* girl in a cocoon, where she metamorphoses and produces eggs; meanwhile the husband, making love to his wife, starts visibly to decay. Generally and probably justly panned by the critics, this post-CRONENBERG movie still has something to offer for connoisseurs of bargain-basement Surrealism, some of the wholly arbitrary sequences being carried off quite startlingly. In a spirit of total randomness the director shot 2 endings. The film release has father and son leaving in the UFO, while wife discovers multiple clones of son all saying "Mummy!" The videotape version has wife being murdered by a thing from an egg the *au pair* laid. [PN]

"XYZ" ◊ POWER SOURCES.

YAMADA, MASAKI [r] ◊ JAPAN.

YANDRO US FANZINE. 259 issues 1953-86; ed from Indiana by Robert and Juanita COULSON, the last 2 issues by Robert Coulson alone, last issue not distributed until 1991. Originally published as *Eisfa*, *Y* was one of the longest-running large fanzines. Its contents, in the normal tradition, were not restricted to sf but included regular columns, articles, reviews and letters. *Y* won the 1965 HUGO for Best Fanzine. [PR/RH]

YANKEE SCIENCE FICTION ◊ SWAN YANKEE MAGAZINE.

YARBRO, CHELSEA QUINN (1942-   ) US writer and composer, active in the mystery and occult genres as well as sf. In the 1980s she became (and has remained) best known for the **Saint-Germain** sequence of fantasies about a sympathetic immortal vampire of aristocratic birth. Set in Europe and elsewhere over a span of centuries, the main sequence comprises *Hôtel Transylvania: A Novel of Forbidden Love* (**1978**), *The Palace* (**1978**), *Blood Games* (**1980**), *Path of the Eclipse* (**1981**), *Tempting Fate* (**1982**), *The Saint-Germain Chronicles* (coll of linked stories **1983**), *Out of the House of Life* (**1990**) and *The Spider Glass* (**1991** chap); a subsidiary sequence, the **Atta Olivia Clemens** books, about Saint-Germain's vampire lover, comprises *A Flame in Byzantium* (**1987**), *Crusader's Torch* (**1988**) and *A Candle for D'Artagnan* (**1989**). As both sequences have progressed, CQY has decreasingly concentrated upon the vampirism of her protagonists and spent much more energy establishing some historical verisimilitude for the territories visited, sticking more and more frequently to the end of the Roman Empire.

In other words, CQY has moved a significant distance from sf – which she began publishing with "The Posture of Prophecy" for *If* in 1969 – and seems unlikely to return except casually. Her most significant sf work, most of it decidedly more pessimistic about the world than her tales set in the past, came

early. The stories assembled in *Cautionary Tales* (coll **1978**) share an energetic starkness, a tendency for her characters – as James TIPTREE Jr remarked in the introduction to the book – to engage in rather arousing operatic duets and *tirades*, and a genuinely DYSTOPIAN vision of times to come; some other tales of interest were assembled in *Signs & Portents* (coll **1984**). Her first sf novel, *Time of the Fourth Horseman* (**1976**) – in which a plan to head off OVERPOPULATION by reinfecting children with various diseases gets radically out of hand – confirmed this sense of her work; as did *False Dawn* (in *Strange Bedfellows* [anth **1973**] ed Thomas N. SCORTIA; exp **1978**), which is set further into the future and likewise deals with a world ravaged by mutated diseases. Nor did *Hyacinths* (**1983**), set in a NEAR-FUTURE dystopian USA characterized by a wrecked economy and mind control, modify the sense that CQY was an author entirely in control of what she wished to say, and in what genre. Sf was a genre which enabled her to look forward into the dark, once in a while. For the most part, she has gazed elsewhere. [JC]

Other works: The **Ogilvie, Tallant & Moon** detective series, with fantasy elements, comprising *Ogilvie, Tallant & Moon* (**1976**; vt *Bad Medicine* 1990), *False Notes* (**1991**), *Poison Fruit* (**1991**) and *Cat's Claw* (**1992**); the **Michael** series of occult quasifictional tracts, comprising *Messages from Michael on the Nature of the Evolution of the Human Soul* (**1979**) and *More Messages from Michael* (**1986**); *Dead & Buried* * (**1980**), a film tie; *Bloodgames* (**1980**); *Sins of Omission* (**1980**); *Ariosto: Ariosto Furioso, a Romance for an Alternate Renaissance* (**1980**); *On Saint Hubert's Thing* (**1982** chap); *CQY* (**1982** chap); *The Godforsaken* (**1983**); *A Mortal Glamour* (**1985**); *Nomads* * (**1984**), a film tie; *Locadio's Apprentice* (**1984**); *Four Horses for Tishtry* (**1985**); *To the High Redoubt* (**1985**); *A Baroque Fable* (**1986**); *Floating Illusions* (**1986**); *Firecode* (**1987**); *Taji's Syndrome* (**1988**), an sf medical horror novel; *Beastnights* (**1989**); *The Law in Charity* (**1989**), a Western.

As **Vanessa Pryor:** *A Taste of Wine* (**1982**), associational.
As **editor:** *Two Views of Wonder* (anth **1974**) with
Thomas N. SCORTIA.
See also: ARTS; DISASTER; GOTHIC SF; IMMORTALITY;
LEISURE; MEDICINE; MUSIC; OVERPOPULATION; PSI POWERS;
PSYCHOLOGY; SURVIVALIST FICTION.

YATES, ALAN G(EOFFREY) (1923-1985) UK-born
author, in Australia most of his life, who was best
known for his long series of detections as by Carter
Brown; he wrote also as Tom Conway, Paul Valdez
and Peter Yates. After some short stories around
1950, with G.C. Bleeck, for THRILLS INCORPORATED, his
sf was restricted to *Coriolanus, the Chariot!* (**1978** US),
set on a planetoid called Thespos where – in quarantine enforced by a fearful Galactic Federation – actors
learn to become shape-changing illusionists. Within
Thespos, PARANOIA and VIRTUAL-REALITY-like manipulations flourish, the Tarot and the world of Shakespeare intermingle, and the protagonist, having
gained supremacy in the toxic game, determines to
break out. Florid and intense, the book is unlike
anything else AGY ever wrote. [JC]

YEFREMOV, IVAN (ANTONOVICH) (1907-1972)
Russian paleontologist and writer, a leading figure in
the renaissance of Soviet sf (◊ RUSSIA). He began
writing "geographical" sf on a modest scale in the
1940s, assembling his early work in *Vstretcha Nad
Tuskaroroi* (coll **1944**; trans M. and N. Nicholas as *A
Meeting Over Tuscarora* **1946** UK), *Piat' Rumbo* ["Five
Wind's Quarters"] (coll **1944**) and elsewhere. Some of
the contents of the 1st vol overlap with those
assembled in *Stories* (coll trans Ovidii Gorchakov **1954**
Russia); new to this were 2 novellas, "Zviozdnyie
Korabli" (**1947**; trans as "Shadow of the Past") and
"Ten' Minuvshego" (trans as "Stellar Ships"), in
which paleontologists make discoveries which offer
them glimpses of spectacular possibilities, with hints
of interstellar travel. Another important novella, "Cor
Serpentis (Serdtse Zmei)" (**1959**), appeared as the title
story of *The Heart of the Serpent* (anth trans R.
Prokofieva **1961** Russia; vt *More Soviet Science Fiction*
1962 US, with new intro by Isaac ASIMOV); it is an
ideological reply to Murray LEINSTER's "First Contact"
(1945), dissenting from the attitude of suspicious
hostility manifest in Leinster's story and contending
that people "mature" enough to undertake interstellar exploration will have put such anxieties (the
alleged result of alienation under capitalism) behind
them.

It would be difficult to overestimate the importance
to Soviet sf (and sf in Eastern Europe) of IY's first
novel, the utopian *Tumannost' Andromedy* (**1958**; trans
George Hanna as *Andromeda* **1959** Russia; filmed in
1968 as TUMANNOST' ANDROMEDY), a full-scale panorama of the FAR FUTURE, the first (and one of the few)
attempts by a Communist writer to create a literary
model of the ideal socialist state envisioned by Marx.
In his last published novel, IY returned to the future
HISTORY begun in *Andromeda*; but *Chas Byka* ["The
Hour of the Bull"] (1968; exp **1970**) was banned

almost immediately upon publication, due to its
dystopian mood and to some hints of an ecocatastrophe (◊ ECOLOGY) caused mostly by the ignorant,
corrupt and tyrannical ruling elite. The book interestingly confronts a "communist UTOPIA" with a "capitalist
DYSTOPIA" in a structure similar to that employed by
Ursula K. LE GUIN in *The Dispossessed* (**1974**). Other
novels include *Lezvie Britvy* ["The Razor's Edge"]
(**1963**), a large borderline-sf "experimental" tale, and
historical novels about the ancient civilizations of
Egypt and Greece: *Na Kraiu Oikumeny* (**1949**; trans
George Hanna as *The Land of Foam* **1957** Russia) and
Tais Afinskaia ["Thais of Athens"] (**1968**).

In the introduction to *Stories* IY produced a manifesto for Soviet sf: "To try to lift the curtain of
mystery over these roads, to speak of scientific
achievements yet to come as realities, and in this way
to lead the reader to the most advanced outposts of
science – such are the tasks of science-fiction, as I see
them. But they do not exhaust the aims of Soviet
science-fiction: its philosophy is to serve the development of the imagination and creative faculty of our
people as an asset in the study of social life; and its
chief aim is to search for the new, and through this
search to gain an insight into the future." The
emphasis here is significantly different from that in
most US DEFINITIONS OF SF, stressing as it does the
social role of sf as an imaginative endeavour. [BS/VG]
See also: ALIENS; SPACESHIPS.

YELNICK, CLAUDE (?   -   ) French writer
whose *L'homme, cette maladie* (**1954**; trans as *The
Trembling Tower* **1956** UK) depicts the interdimensional relationship between Earth and another
world via a lighthouse. [JC]

YEOVIL, JACK ◊ Kim NEWMAN.

YEP, LAURENCE (MICHAEL) (1948-   ) US writer
who began publishing sf with "The Selchey Kids" for
If in 1968. Most of his books have been juveniles,
including an sf novel, *Sweetwater* (**1973**), set in a dying
city on a strange planet, and the highly successful
Dragonwings (**1975**), a non-sf story about Chinese-
Americans that won several awards in the field; *Child
of the Owl* (**1977**) is also about Chinese-Americans. A
later fantasy series, the **Shimmer and Thorn** sequence – *Dragon of the Lost Sea* (**1982**), *Dragon Steel*
(**1985**), *Dragon Cauldron* (**1991**) and *Dragon War* (**1992**)
– as well as *Monster Makers, Inc.* (**1986**), which is about
GENETIC ENGINEERING, were also for children; *The
Rainbow People* (coll **1989**) assembles juvenile stories
rewritten from Chinese-American folktales. Throughout these books a melancholy sensitivity is generally
permitted to discover material for quiet affirmation,
and LY's own Chinese-American background can be
easily discerned, especially when ALIENS are being
treated. His 1st adult sf novel, *Seademons* (**1977**), tells
of colonists on another world and of their relation to
the beings there, evoking an atmosphere of strangeness in a nuanced prose. His 2nd is a **Star Trek** tie,
The Shadow Lord * (**1985**). [JC/PN]
See also: ARTS; MUSIC.

YERMAKOV, NICHOLAS (VALENTIN) (1951-)
US writer whose career began with some sf adventure novels and the **Boomerang** series, all composed in a baroque idiom, but who soon settled into more settled pursuits, writing several unpretentious series under the name Simon Hawke, and military sf as J.D. Masters and S.L. Hunter. As NY his most interesting work was probably in the **Boomerang** series – *Last Communion* (1981), *Epiphany* (1982) and *Jehad* (1984) – set on a planet inhabited by ALIENS with the dangerously exploitable gift (exploited aliens have appeared more than once in NY's work) of being able to generate potent group-mind phenomena by absorbing the psyches of their own dead. Eventually this absorptive capacity upliftingly ensnares the intruding humans as well, and the sequence ends transcendentally. In 3 singletons from this period – *Journey from Flesh* (1981), *Fall into Darkness* (1982) and *Clique* (1982) – slapdash execution tends to muffle the genuine sharpness of NY's mind. In collaboration with Glen A. LARSON he wrote two **Battlestar Galactica** ties, *The Living Legend* * (1981) and *War of the Gods* * (1982). In 1984 he stopped using his own name.

From 1984, as Simon Hawke, NY soon became a reliable and prolific author of adventure sf, best known for the **Timewars** sequence – *Timewars: The Ivanhoe Gambit* (1984), *#2: The Timekeeper Conspiracy* (1984), *#3: The Pimpernel Plot* (1984), *#4: The Zenda Vendetta* (1985), *#5: The Nautilus Sanction* (1985), *#6: The Kyber Connection* (1986), *#7: The Argonaut Affair* (1987), *#8: The Dracula Caper* (1988), *#9: The Lilliput Legion* (1989), *#10: The Hellfire Rebellion* (1990), *#11: The Cleopatra Crisis* (1990) and *#12: The Six-Gun Solution* (1991) – in which members of the Times Corps make sorties into the past and into alternate universes in order to preserve the main timestream of the world from various assaults. As Hawke, NY still retained some of the muffling complexity of his earlier persona, but many of the individual **Timewars** tales are grippingly told. The **Psychodrome** sequence – *Psychodrome* (1987) and *Psychodrome #2: The Shapechanger* (1988) – is similarly crowded, but its VIRTUAL-REALITY idiom is relatively unfresh. Other series have been fantasy. *The 9 Lives of Catseye Gomez* (1991 chap) – prefiguring a projected novel and possible series – posits a post-HOLOCAUST environment of some interest, featuring MAGIC-as-learnable-technology and an intelligent cat who models his behaviour on the works of Mickey Spillane. [JC]

Other works:
As Simon Hawke: An ALTERNATE-WORLD fantasy sequence comprising *The Wizard of 4th Street* (1987), *The Wizard of Whitechapel* (1988), *The Wizard of Sunset Strip* (1989), *The Wizard of Rue Morgue* (1990), *The Samurai Wizard* (1991) and *The Wizard of Santa Fe* (1991); a series of **Friday the 13th** ties, *Friday the 13th #1* * (1987), *Friday the 13th #2* * (1988) and *Friday the 13th #3* * (1988); a **Batman** tie, *To Stalk a Specter* * (1991).
As J.D. Masters: The **Steele** series of NEAR-FUTURE

military adventures with a CYBORG hero, comprising *Steele* (1989), *Cold Steele* (1989), *Killer Steele* (1990), *Jagged Steele* (1990), *Renegade Steele* (1990) and *Target Steele* (1990).
As S.L. Hunter: A further **Steele** volume, *Fugitive Steele* (1991).
See also: ESCHATOLOGY; PARASITISM AND SYMBIOSIS; TIME PARADOXES; TIME TRAVEL.

YERXA, FRANCES [r] ◊ Leroy YERXA.
YERXA, LEROY (1915-1946) US writer for the PULP MAGAZINES, particularly the ZIFF-DAVIS productions *AMZ* and *Fantastic Adventures*. He published as LY, as Elroy Arno, and under the house names Richard CASEY and Alexander BLADE, beginning with "Death Rides at Night" for *AMZ* in 1942 as LY, and contributing prolifically until his death. The **Freddie Funk** series in *Fantastic Adventures*, from "Freddie Funk's Madcap Mermaid" (1943) to "Freddie Funk's Flippant Fairies" (1948), was completed by his wife, Frances Yerxa, who also wrote some stories solo, and married William L. HAMLING. [JC]

YEUX SANS VISAGE, LES (vt *Eyes without a Face*; vt *The Horror Chamber of Dr Faustus* US) Film (1959). Champs-Elysées/Lux. Dir Georges Franju, starring Pierre Brasseur, Alida Valli, Edith Scob. Screenplay Jean Redon, Franju, Claude Sautet, Pierre Boileau, Thomas Narcejac, from a novel by Redon. 95 mins, cut to 88 mins, further cut to 84 mins. B/w.

Released in the USA under the schlock "Horror Chamber" title and condemned in the UK as outrageous and disgusting, this is, though the inspiration for many a subsequent exploitation movie, actually an austere and poetic work in the surrealist tradition, even in its use of stereotyped plot devices from pulp horror fiction. The sf element is advanced plastic surgery: a surgeon (Brasseur), guilty over his daughter's (Scob's) facial disfigurement (she wears a mask) in an accident for which he was responsible, uses his assistant (Valli) to kidnap young women; he attempts, without success, to transfer their faces to his daughter; she goes mad and releases his experimental dogs; they chew his face off; she drifts away surrounded by doves. Scob's wistful, masked performance is extraordinary, as is Maurice Jarre's gravely classical film score. [PN]

YE YONGLIE [r] ◊ CHINESE SF.
YOKE, CARL B. (? -) US scholar and writer, much of whose early work was concerned with Roger ZELAZNY, including *Roger Zelazny* (1979), a critical study, and *Roger Zelazny and Andre Norton: Proponents of Individualism* (1979 chap). *Death and the Serpent: Immortality in Science Fiction* (anth 1985) with Donald M. HASSLER and *Phoenix from the Ashes: The Literature of the Remade World* (anth 1988) are carefully conceived examinations of the sf themes of IMMORTALITY and the HOLOCAUST AND AFTER. [JC]

YOLEN, JANE (1939-) US writer who began publishing poems and articles when still in college, and who first came to notice with books for children, the first of many being *Pirates in Petticoats* (1963). Of her *c*120 titles to date, most are for children (see listing below for some of these), and much of her adult fiction is FANTASY, told in a style whose accomplished and eloquent transparency often conveys a sense that folktales are being recollected in tranquillity. *Tales of Wonder* (coll **1983**) assembles typical work for adults, some of it sf; as does *Merlin's Booke* (coll of linked stories **1986**), set in the world of the eponymous magus. The **Pit Dragon** trilogy for young adults – *Dragon's Blood* (**1982**), *Heart's Blood* (**1984**) and *A Sending of Dragons* (**1987**) – is set on another planet, but is devoted primarily to the breeding and training of dragons (◊ SUPERNATURAL CREATURES), though the sequence eventually moves into more complex political territory. The **Great Alta** sequence – *Sister Light, Sister Dark* (**1988**) and *White Jenna* (**1989**), assembled as *The Book of Great Alta* (omni **1990**) – is adult fantasy. Her most sf-like novel, *Cards of Grief* (fixup **1984**), is a sophisticated PLANETARY ROMANCE in which an intense and story-bound race is observed by humans from an off-planet station, and is inevitably affected by the interaction of species. In none of JY's work, however, is there a sense that sf dominates the sometimes complex generic mix; she is a fantasy writer who visits sf.   [JC]

Other works include: *The Witch who Wasn't* (**1964**); the 6 **Commander Toad** picture-book sf tales for younger children, beginning with *Commander Toad in Space* (**1980** chap); *The Robot and Rebecca* (coll **1980**); *The Boy who Spoke Chimp* (**1981**); *Dragonfield* (coll **1985**).

As editor: *Zoo 2000* (anth **1973**); *Shape Shifters* (anth **1978**); *2041 A.D.* (anth **1991**); 5 anths ed with Martin H. GREENBERG (*whom see for details*).

Nonfiction: *Touch Magic: Fantasy, Faerie and Folklore in the Literature of Childhood* (**1981**).

YOST, ROBERT M. [r] ◊ Claude H. WETMORE.

YOUD, CHRISTOPHER ◊ John CHRISTOPHER.

YOUNG, MICHAEL (1915-   ) UK sociologist and writer whose *Family and Kinship in East London* (**1957**), with Peter Willmott, had a seminal effect on community-planning priorities. His sf work, *The Rise of the Meritocracy 1870-2033: An Essay on Education and Equality* (**1958**), not only gave the word "meritocracy" to the language but extensively defined it: a meritocracy is an elite whose members are recruited on the basis of merit (largely INTELLIGENCE) in a competitive educational system; it is also, as the book sardonically emphasizes, a form of government. The book itself takes the form of a report written in AD2033 by an historical sociologist (its only character in any ordinary sense); and some libraries have catalogued it as nonfiction. Though the narrator supports the system he describes, it is quite clear that MY does not; the book is a subtle and interesting DYSTOPIA. Its ending, in which the narrator is reported as killed in a populist revolt, is ironic and mutedly apocalyptic.   [PN/JC]

See also: SOCIOLOGY.

YOUNG, ROBERT ◊ Robert PAYNE.

YOUNG, ROBERT F(RANKLIN) (1915-1986) US writer who turned full-time after engaging in a number of menial occupations. His first sf story was "The Black Deep Thou Wingest" for *Startling Stories* in 1953, and he published short work quite prolifically for the next 3 decades. RFY was a slick, polished writer; his stories are readable, although often superficial. The best generally appeared in *FSF*, although he wrote also for most of the US sf magazines and for the *Saturday Evening Post* and others. His modes ranged from the heavily satiric – typified by a series of stories, "Chrome Pastures" (1956), "Thirty Days Had September" (1957) and "Romance in a Twenty-First Century Used Car Lot" (1960), in which the US automobile mania is extrapolated to absurd extremes – to the strongly allegorical, in such tales as "Goddess in Granite" (1957); but a romantic sensibility, at rare intervals mawkish, permeated all his work. His earlier stories were assembled in *The Worlds of Robert F. Young* (coll **1965**) and *A Glass of Stars* (coll **1968**); the numerous tales published after 1968 remain uncollected. After a novel released only in French, *La Quête de la Sainte Grille* (1964 *AMZ* as "The Quest of the Holy Grille"; exp **1975** France), RFY published in *Starfinder* (fixup **1980**) a stirringly romantic SPACE OPERA whose main device – riding to the STARS within the bodies of dead "space whales" – is powerfully evocative; it is by far his best novel in English. *The Last Yggdrasil* (1959 *FSF* as "To Fell a Tree"; exp **1982**), an over-extended novel version of a strong story, seems sentimental in contrast, failing to impart much plausibility to the story of a tree-cutter on a colony planet who is hired to kill the one huge remaining tree in the area, to the entirely predictable detriment of the planet's ECOLOGY. RFY's final novels – *Eridahn* (1964 *If* as "When Time was New"; exp **1983**), which features TIME TRAVEL into prehistory, and *The Vizier's Second Daughter* (1965 *AMZ* as "City of Brass"; exp **1985**), a humorous fantasy – neither built nor detracted from his reputation. He will be best remembered for some of the acerbic short tales of his early career.   [MJE/JC]

See also: AMAZING STORIES; MESSIAHS; PSYCHOLOGY; ROBOTS; TRANSPORTATION.

YOUNG EINSTEIN Film (1988). Serious Productions. Prod/dir Yahoo Serious, starring Serious, Odile Le Clezio, John Howard. Screenplay Serious, David Roach. 91 mins. Colour.

In an alternate 1905, Albert Einstein, a young Tasmanian apple farmer, discovers that $E = mc^2$, splits the beer atom, meets and is loved by Marie Curie, has his formula stolen, invents the surfboard, the electric guitar and rock'n'roll, and saves the world. Serious and his rather narcissistic film both strain too hard to be likable, and both are soft-centred and not especially funny.   [PN]

YOUNG FRANKENSTEIN ◊ FRANKENSTEIN.

YOU ONLY LIVE TWICE Film (1967). Eon/United Artists. Dir Lewis Gilbert, starring Sean Connery, Donald Pleasence, Akiko Wakabayashi, Tetsuro Tamba, Mie Hama. Screenplay Roald DAHL, based very loosely on *You Only Live Twice* (**1964**) by Ian FLEMING. 116 mins. Colour.

Several of Fleming's **James Bond** novels were TECHNOTHRILLERS, mildly sf-oriented (though set in the present) and sometimes featuring scientist VILLAINS and superweapons. Most of the very popular and long-lasting series of spin-off movies have emphasized – although less so, perhaps, in the mid-1980s – the sf gadgetry, and have often provided at least one major futuristic set: these include DR NO (1962), *Goldfinger* (1964), *Thunderball* (1965), *On Her Majesty's Secret Service* (1969), *Diamonds are Forever* (1971), *The Man with the Golden Gun* (1974), *The Spy Who Loved Me* (1977), *Never Say Never Again* (1983) and *A View to a Kill* (1985) as well as the spoof *Casino Royale* (1967). Along with MOONRAKER (1979), *YOLT* contains the most sf hardware. A US satellite is swallowed up by a mystery craft in outer space. The super-criminal organization SPECTRE has constructed a secret rocket base inside a Japanese volcano from which it launches its bizarre vehicle to capture both US and Russian spacecraft, in an attempt to provoke a war between the two nations. James Bond (Connery), with the help of Japanese secret agents, foils SPECTRE's plans. Despite the spectacular sets – which upstage the humans, even the always-efficient Connery – and vast budget, there are *longeurs* in pacing and lapses in the special effects. [JB/PN]

See also: CINEMA.

YOURELL, AGNES BOND (? -?) US writer whose *A Manless World* (**1891**) speculates about what might happen to the human species were an interstellar gas to have destroyed sexual desire in everyone except – it is mooted – the Jews, who might find an elixir: riots and pogroms would occur; the race would vanish. In a manner not uncommon to 19th-century fiction of this sort, the tale is told in an "as if" mode, and claims to do no more than present the speculative thoughts of an embittered old man. [JC]

YUGOSLAVIA At the time of going to press, it is not clear what the future status of Yugoslavia will be – if, indeed, there will be even a rump territory left with that name.

Yugoslavia was established as a nation in 1918, but the first sf works in 2 of its 3 linguistic areas – the Serbocroat and the Slovenian – long predated that. The first sf book to appear in Serbocroat was the translation in 1873 of Jules VERNE's *Voyage au centre de la terre* (**1864**), while the first sf work by a native author was the drama "Posle milijon godina" ["A Million Years After"] (1889 in the magazine *Kolo*) by Dragutin Ilić. This is one of the earliest fully sf plays published anywhere in the world (◊ THEATRE). In 1902 Lazar Komarčić published a work of extreme modernity for its time and place: the most exciting passages of Olaf STAPLEDON are anticipated in his *Jedna ugašena zvezda* ["One Extinguished Star"] (**1902**).

In the period up to the beginning of WWII, the most important sf novels were *Kroz vasionu i vekove*

["Through the Universe and Centuries"] (**1928**) by Milutin Milanković, *Gospodin čovjek* ["Man, the Noble"] (**1932**) by Mate Hanžeković, and *Život u vasioni* ["Life in the Universe"] (**1933**) by Stojan Radonić. In the 1930s a number of sf novels were published in instalments in periodicals; these novels were, generally, imitations of popular sf classics, signed mostly by pseudonyms. Of these, 3 by "Aldion Degal" are the most noteworthy: "Atomska raketa" ["An Atomic Rocket"] (1930), "Zrake smrti" ["Death Rays"] (1932) and "Smaragdni skarabej" ["The Emerald Scarab"] (1934). In 1935 the first Yugoslav COMIC strip was published: *Gost iz svemira* ["The Guest from Outer Space"], by Božidar Rašić and Leontije Bjelski.

In the 1950s the first specialized sf publishing imprints appeared – **Biblioteka fantastičnih romana**, **Fantastični romani** and **Lajka** – but this was an era dominated by translations of Russian sf novels in the mode of "socialist realism" (◊ RUSSIA). Yugoslav sf authors published during this period were writing mostly for a juvenile readership. The first of importance in the post-WWII period were Zvonimir Furtinger and Mladen Bjažić, who set the tone of the first half of the 1960s with novels like *Osvajač 2 se ne javlja* ["Conqueror II Fails to Report"] (**1959**) and *Svemirska nevjesta* ["The Space Bride"] (**1960**). In that decade new sf book imprints began to publish translations of contemporary US and UK sf authors. The most important is **Kentaur**, with nearly 100 translations of major sf books published since 1967. By the end of the 1960s the first Yugoslav sf magazine, *Kosmoplov* ["Spaceship"], had appeared; it ran for 24 issues 1969-70. The founder of this magazine, Gavrilo Vučković, in 1972 also founded *Galaksija* ["Galaxy"] magazine, which had an sf section almost continually during the next 18 years.

In 1976 the important sf magazine *Sirius* started; mainly as a monthly and ed most often by Borivoje Jurković, it achieved 164 issues (it ended in Jan 1990), regularly publishing Yugoslav sf in addition to translations. Yugoslav sf had its moment of international triumph, too, in the 1970s: the film *Izbavitelj* ["Saviour"] (1977; vt *The Rat Saviour*), dir Krsto Papić, won the main, Golden Asteroid, award at the Trieste Film Festival that year. A second Yugoslav film later received an award at this festival: *Posjetioci iz galaksije Arkana* ["Visitors from the Arcana Galaxy"] (1980) dir by the Oscar-winning Dušan Vukotić.

The 1980s were years decisively marked by the arrival of private as opposed to state-owned publishing houses and by the emergence of many young sf authors. In 1982 Zoran ŽIVKOVIĆ and Žika Bogdanović started a privately published sf imprint, Polaris, which specialized in rapidly taking up new sf hits; among the books whose world 1st edns have been under this imprint is *2010: Odyssey Two* (**1982**) by Arthur C. CLARKE. Another private series, Znak Sagite ["The Sign of the Sagitta"], founded 1985 by Boban Knežević, also brought out some important sf books.

Though there are as yet only part-time sf writers in Yugoslavia, several of the authors who made their début in the 1980s have the potential to become full-time. These include Damir Mikuličić, author of *O* ["O"] (coll **1982**); Predrag Raos, author of *Brodolom kod Thule* ["Shipwreck at Thule"] (**1978**), *Mnogo vike nizašto* ["Much Shouting about Nothing"] (**1985**) and *Null Effort* (**1990**); Slobodan Ćurčić, author of *Šume, kiše, grad i zvezde* ["Forests, Rains, the City and the Stars"] (**1988**); Dragan Filipović, author of *Oreska* ["Oreska"] (**1987**) and *Zlatna knjiga* ["The Golden Book"] (**1988**). Recently some widely acclaimed mainstream writers have entered the sf field. Borislav Pekić, for example, has published 3 sf novels: *Besnilo* ["Rabid"] (**1983**), *1999* (**1984**) and *Atlantida* ["Atlantis"] (**1988**).

Young Yugoslav sf comic-strip artists, most prominently Željko Pahek, Igor Kordej and Zoran Janjetov, are published not only at home but also in other European countries. Successful GENRE-SF artists such as Bob Živković also appear. Sf has also entered academic circles; after initial pioneering studies in the sf genre by Ivan Foht and Darko SUVIN, 3 men have since the 1970s successfully defended MA and doctoral dissertations about sf: Ferid Muhić, Zoran Živković and Aleksandar B. Nedeljković. After the mid-1970s, FANDOM began to flourish, and a number of local and international CONVENTIONS were organized. There are many clubs and societies. [ZŽ]

YUILL, P.B. ◊ Gordon WILLIAMS.

YULSMAN, JERRY (?   -   ) US writer of whom little is known beyond his authorship of the impressively suave and moody ALTERNATE-WORLD tale *Elleander Morning* (**1984**), in which the assassination of Hitler as a young man in Vienna generates a differing 20th century. H.G. WELLS makes a RECURSIVE appearance in the complex tale, which is set partly in 1913 and partly in the transformed 1980s. [JC]

YUMEMAKURA, BAKU [r] ◊ JAPAN.

YUMMY FUR ◊ Chester BROWN.

YUTANG, LIN ◊ LIN YUTANG.

ZACHARY, HUGH ◊ Zach HUGHES.

ZAGAT, ARTHUR LEO (1895-1949) US writer, extremely prolific in a number of PULP-MAGAZINE genres, publishing about 500 stories; of the relatively few that are sf, several were with Nat SCHACHNER, including ALZ's first, "The Tower of Evil" for *Wonder Stories Quarterly* in 1930. The 11 tales produced collaboratively before they separated in 1931 were ALZ's best early work. After about 1936, most of his work appeared in *Argosy*, including the **Tomorrow** series, set in a NEAR-FUTURE post-HOLOCAUST USA; the 1st tale in the sequence, "Tomorrow" (1939), later appeared in *Famous Funtastic Classics 1* (anth **1974**). In *Drink We Deep* (1937 *Argosy*; **1951**) strange subterranean dwellers call a human downwards to them. In *Seven Out of Time* (1939 *Argosy*; **1949**), his best novel, 7 contemporary humans are studied by people of the future to rediscover the value of emotions. A post-WWII novel, "Slaves of the Lamp" (1946 *ASF*), was little noticed and did not reach book form, for ALZ had failed to adjust his style and plotting to the demands of the new world. [JC]

See also: GENRE SF; INVASION; OPERATOR #5; THRILLING WONDER STORIES.

ZAHN, TIMOTHY (1951-   ) US writer with a master's degree in physics who came into sudden prominence in the sf field in the 1980s with the rapid release of several books. He had begun publishing sf with "Ernie" for *Analog* in 1979, and early proved himself an adept and productive creator of the problem-oriented HARD SF characteristic of that magazine. Some better examples of his work are assembled as *Cascade Point* (coll **1986**), *Time Bomb and Zahndry Others* (coll **1988**) and *Distant Friends and Others* (coll **1992**); the title story (1983 *ASF*) of the 1st of these won a HUGO on its original release, and has also been published as *Cascade Point* (**1988** chap dos). The title of the story, which fascinatingly reveals the outward-looking bent of this early work, refers to a point in space where ships flicker from one star system to the next; at the point of transition, ALTERNATE-WORLD versions of the humans on board ship manifest themselves hauntingly. An experiment designed to elicit more knowledge about humankind from this convergence of differing versions of lives turns out in the event most usefully to reveal methods for making the transition itself more efficient. In work like this, TZ proved himself an exemplary member of the *ASF* stable.

But the rest of the sf world began to take more notice of him after he began to publish novels in 1983 with the 1st vol of the **Blackcollar** sequence, *The Blackcollar* (**1983**), followed by *Blackcollar: The Backlash Mission* (**1986**), both tales being set on an Earth dominated by ALIEN invaders and describing the eponymous guerrillas' supernormal feats of resistance against the enemy. The **Cobra** sequence – *Cobra* (**1985**), *Cobra Strike* (**1986**), assembled as *Cobras Two* (omni **1992**), plus *Cobra Bargain* (**1988**) – located similar military/commando heroes in a galactic venue. *A Coming of Age* (**1985**), a singleton of much greater interest, is set on a colony planet where a mutation has given children telekinetic powers, until puberty yanks them back into normality; the plotting is complex and swift, and TZ showed creative awareness as well as the profound issues he was exposing to the light – for any novel in which puberty marks a passing of glory from the Earth is a novel about the human condition as well as, more prosaically, a novel about why children entering puberty begin to read sf. Other novels of interest are *Spinneret* (**1985**), *Triplet* (**1987**) and *Deadman Switch* (**1988**), another tale of considerable underlying complexity, set in a galactic civilization which exploits its retention of the death penalty by using the condemned as pilots to penetrate an area of space that only corpses can navigate. TZ's venues have been at times conventional, and even silly; but again and again he has transformed routine adventure-sf conventions into moral puzzles, without sacrificing a jot of momentum.

After several years without any prospect of a new **Star Wars** movie, TZ was commissioned to write a **Star Wars** trilogy. The initial volumes, *Heir to the Empire* * (**1991**) and *Dark Force Rising* * (**1992**), carry on from RETURN OF THE JEDI (1983), starting 5 years after the end of that film. [JC]

Other work: *Warhorse* (fixup **1990**).

See also: PSI POWERS; SHARED WORLDS; SOCIOLOGY; SUPERMAN.

ZAHORSKI, KENNETH J. [r] ◊ Marshall B. TYMN.

ZAMIATIN, YEVGENY (IVANOVICH) (1884-1937) Russian writer. YZ graduated in naval engineering from St Petersburg Polytechnical Institute, his studies interrupted by participation in the 1905 Revolution as a Bolshevik, prison and deportation (a sentence which was renewed 1911-13). He began writing in 1908, withdrew from active politics, lectured at the Polytechnic Institute until his emigration, ran foul of the Tsarist censor in 1914, and built icebreakers in the UK 1916-17.

YZ wrote about 40 volumes of stories, fables, plays, excellent essays and 2 novels. After the October Revolution he became a prominent figure in key literary groups, guru for a whole school of young writers, and editor of an ambitious publishing programme of books from the West; he wrote prefaces for works by Jack LONDON, George Bernard SHAW, H.G. WELLS, etc. From 1921 on he incurred much critical disfavour and some censorship which culminated in a campaign of vilification by the dominant literary faction, especially after *My* (see below) was published in an émigré journal in 1927. After writing a dignified letter to Stalin, YZ was allowed to go to Paris (retaining his Soviet passport), where he died shunned by both Soviet officialdom and right-wing émigrés. *My* (written 1920, circulated in manuscript; trans Gregory Zilboorg as *We* **1924** US; first Russian-language book publication **1952** US) deals with the relation between the principles of Revolution (life) and Entropy (death). By incorporating elements of *Ostrovityane* (written 1917; **1922** chap; trans Sophie Fuller and Julian Sacchi as the title story in *Islanders, and The Fisher of Men* [coll **1984** chap UK]), a satirical novella he had written about UK philistinism (which features coupons for rationing sex, and the "Taylorite" regulation of every moment of the day), YZ signalled his intention to extrapolate upon the repressive potentials of every centralized state. Committed to the scientific method even in his narrative form, which mimics lab notes, YZ's explanation for why rationalism turns sour is mythical: every belief, when victorious, must turn repressive, as did Christianity. The only irrational elements remaining are the human beings who deviate: these include the narrator – a mathematician and designer of a rocket ship – and the woman who represents an underground resistance. The plot is modelled on an inevitable Fall (for the rebellion inevitably fails), ending in an ironic crucifixion. In YZ's terms, *My* judges yesterday's UTOPIA, as it becomes an absolutism, in the name of tomorrow's utopia – for the principle of utopia itself is not repudiated; the book is thus *not* a DYSTOPIA.

The expressionistic language of *My*, which imparts a sense of elegant but humanly charged economy to the text, helps to subsume the protagonist's defeat under the novel's concern for the integration of humanity's science and art (including love). YZ demonstrates that utopia should not be a new religion (albeit of mathematics and space flights) but should represent the dynamic horizon of mankind's developing personality. *My* is the paradigmatic anti-utopia, prefiguring George ORWELL and Aldous HUXLEY and superseding that tradition of utopianism, from Sir Thomas MORE on, which ignores technology and anthropology. By analysing the distortions of the utopia through the hyperbolic prism of sf, YZ wrote an intensely practical text. It is both a masterpiece of sf and an indispensable book of our epoch. This sense of the book was finally confirmed by YZ's rehabilitation in the USSR in the *glasnost* year 1988. [DS]

Other sf work: "A Story about the Most Important Thing" (**1927** Russia; trans Michael Glenny in YZ's *The Dragon*, coll **1966**).

About the author: *A Soviet Heretic* by YZ (**1970**); *Metamorphoses of Science Fiction* (**1979**) by Darko SUVIN; *Evgenij Zamjatin* (**1973** Holland) by Christopher Collins; *The Life and Works of Evgenij Zamjatin* (**1968** US) by Alex M. Shane; "Yevgeny Zamyatin" by Michael Beehler in *SubStance 15.2* (**1986**); "*Brave New World*", "*1984*" and "*We*" (**1976**) by E.J. Brown; *The Shape of Utopia* (**1970**) by R.C. Elliott; *Clockwork Worlds* (anth **1983**) ed Richard D. Erlich *et al.*; "Imagining the Future: Wells and Zamyatin" by Patrick PARRINDER in *H.G. Wells and Modern Science Fiction* (anth **1977**) ed Suvin; "Three Postrevolutionary Russian Utopian Novels" by Jurij Stridter in *The Russian Novel from Pushkin to Pasternak* (anth **1983**) ed J. Garrarad.

See also: CRIME AND PUNISHMENT; HISTORY OF SF; LINGUISTICS; MUSIC; POLITICS; RUSSIA.

ZARDOZ Film (1974). John Boorman Productions/20th Century-Fox. Prod/dir/written John BOORMAN, starring Sean Connery, Charlotte Rampling, Sara Kestelman, John Alderton. 105 mins. Colour.

A future society is divided into 2 regions: the Vortex and the Outlands, separated by an impenetrable FORCE FIELD. Within the Vortex live the Eternals, IMMORTAL and given to a decadent aestheticism, while in the Outlands dwell the Brutals, including a group called the Exterminators whose job is to keep the population level down. One of these Exterminators, Zed (Connery), infiltrates the Vortex and his presence catalyses events which destroy both the Immortals and their computer-run society. Zed represents the primal force that brings back to the impotent, static Immortals such old favourites as Emotion, Sex, Fear and Death, releasing them from their artificial world and allowing them to become part of the Natural Scheme of Things again; that is, dead. The film is self-indulgent; its profundity is all on the surface and its oscillation between parody and solemnity is distracting. But Boorman's presentation of old ideas as if they were just new-minted has a certain silly charm, and the film has considerable visual brio, assisted by Geoffrey Unsworth's photography and the beautiful Irish settings.

The novelization, by Boorman and Bill Stair, is *Zardoz* * (1974). [JB/PN]

See also: CINEMA; HOLOCAUST AND AFTER.

ZAREM, LEWIS (? -) US writer in whose *The Green Man from Space* (1955) a Martian is discovered on Earth looking for greens, and is taken back home. LZ also wrote nonfiction on aeronautical subjects. [JC]

ŽARNAY, JOSEF [r] ◊ CZECH AND SLOVAK SF.

ZAUNER, GEORG [r] ◊ GERMANY.

ZEBROWSKI, GEORGE (1945-) Austrian-born writer of Polish descent, in the USA from 1951, one of the first alumni of the CLARION SCIENCE FICTION WRITERS' WORKSHOP to achieve recognition in the sf world. He has lived with Pamela SARGENT for many years. GZ began publishing sf stories with "The Water Sculptor of Station 233" for *Infinity One* (anth 1970) ed Robert HOSKINS, and remained active as a short-story writer, releasing about 50 titles over the next 2 decades, some of the best being assembled as *The Monadic Universe* (coll 1977; exp 1985). From 1970 to winter 1974-5 he was editor of the SFWA BULLETIN, and from 1983 to date has served as US editor. His first published novel was the 2nd instalment, in terms of internal chronology, of his **Omega Point** sequence – comprising *Ashes and Stars* (1977) and *The Omega Point* (1972), both revised and assembled along with a previously unpublished 3rd part as *The Omega Point Trilogy* (omni 1983). Within a SPACE-OPERA frame, a metaphysical drama is enacted, pitting the sole survivors of a destroyed culture – created through GENETIC ENGINEERING, and whose rationale owes something to the theories of the evolutionary theologian Pierre Teilhard de Chardin (1881-1955) – against the inimical Earth Federation responsible for its elimination; after his father's death, Gorgias finds the eponymous WEAPON, but Omega Point turns out to be fundamentally a focus of transcendental empathy. *The Star Web* (1975 Canada) is an unambitious space opera, but the 2 star-spanning forms of TRANSPORTATION featured in the text are of interest; revised, the book became the first third of *Stranger Suns* (1991), a long novel written in the STAPLEDON-esque vein that marks GZ's most highly regarded single work, *Macrolife* (1979; rev 1990). Though otherwise unconnected, the 2 books share an elevated purposefulness about depicting humanity's future and a tendency to depend on insufficiently plausible lines of plot. *Macrolife* begins on Earth, but soon departs the home planet for self-sufficient star-travelling SPACE HABITATS, and carries onwards to the end of the Universe; *Stranger Suns* views with considerable bleakness the opportunities taken – and missed – by humanity when given the chance to use a complex stargate that gives access not only to the

Universe as we know it but also to alternate universes (◊ ALTERNATE WORLDS).

GZ has been active since early in his career as an editor, producing *Tomorrow Today* (anth 1975), an original anthology, and co-editing *Faster than Light* (anth 1976) with Jack DANN and *Human-Machines* (anth 1975) with Thomas N. SCORTIA, a collection of whose stories, *The Best of Thomas N. Scortia* (coll 1981), GZ also ed. In the 1980s he began the SYNERGY series of ORIGINAL ANTHOLOGIES: *Synergy: New Science Fiction #1* (anth 1987), *#2* (anth 1988), *#3* (dated 1988 but 1989) and *#4* (anth 1989). *Beneath a Red Star: Studies in International Science Fiction* (coll 1991) assembled essays on the sf of Eastern Europe. [JC]

Other works: 3 short stories for juveniles, *Adrift in Space* (1974 in *Adrift in Space and Other Stories*, anth ed Roger ELWOOD; 1979 chap), *A Silent Shout* (1979 chap) and *The Firebird* (1979 chap); the **Bernal One** sequence of juveniles, *Sunspacer* (1984) and *The Stars Will Speak* (1985).

As editor: *Creations: The Quest for Origins in Story and Science* (anth 1983) with Isaac ASIMOV and Martin H. GREENBERG; *Nebula Awards 20* (anth 1985); *Nebula Awards 21* (anth 1987); *Nebula Awards 22* (anth 1988).

About the author: *The Work of George Zebrowski* (last rev 1990) by Jeffrey M. ELLIOT and Robert REGINALD.

See also: ASTEROIDS; COSMOLOGY; CYBORGS; ESCHATOLOGY; GENERATION STARSHIPS; NEBULA; RELIGION; SOCIOLOGY.

ZEDDIES, ANN TONSOR (1951-) US writer whose sf novel, *Deathgift* (1989), though not technically a POCKET-UNIVERSE tale, embodies a fundamental rhythm of constriction and release through the story of a young boy abandoned to the Native-American-like tribes that mediate among the medieval cities which surround them, and who only later discovers that his "world" is a "neutral zone" on a planet torn by interstellar strife. The story unfolds constantly, and is very competently managed. [JC]

ZEIGFREID, KARL A John Spencer & Co house name, erratically spelled Karl Zeigfried on some occasions; John S. GLASBY and Tom W. WADE each certainly used it once, and the latter may have also written *Beyond the Galaxy* (1953) and *Chaos in Arcturus* (1953). For their later BADGER BOOKS line, Spencer used the name for a number of sf novels, mostly by R.L. FANTHORPE (13 titles). [JC]

ZELAZNY, ROGER (JOSEPH) (1937-) US writer, born in Ohio, with an MA from Columbia University in 1962. In 1962-9 he was employed by the Social Security Administration in Cleveland, Ohio, and Baltimore, Maryland; from 1969 he wrote full-time. His arrival in the sf world in 1962, along with Samuel R. DELANY, Thomas M. DISCH and Ursula K. LE GUIN, marked that year as a milestone in what seemed at the time to be the inevitable maturing of sf into a complex and sophisticated literature, whose language might finally match its intermittent hubris. With Delany, Disch and (to a lesser extent) Le Guin – and with Harlan ELLISON goading all and sundry –

RZ became a leading and representative figure of the US NEW WAVE, writing stories whose emphasis had shifted from the external world of the hard sciences to the internal worlds explorable through disciplines like PSYCHOLOGY (mostly Jungian), SOCIOLOGY and LINGUISTICS. To a greater extent than any of his colleagues, however, RZ expressed this shift by using mythological structures – some traditional, some new-minted – in his work. It has been argued that in true MYTHOLOGY the voyage into CONCEPTUAL BREAKTHROUGH of the Hero of a Thousand Faces always climaxes in the Eternal Return, so that any 20th-century sf tale which retells a myth incorporates, by so doing, ironies and metaphors highly corrosive of any rhetoric of outward thrust, and mockingly dismissive of the reality of breakthroughs. It may be for this reason that RZ's sf was language-driven, irony-choked, corrosively playful, and – after the early years of his career – intermittent; and that he is now best known for his works of fantasy, in particular the 2 linked sequences making up the ongoing **Amber** series. The 1st, featuring Corwin, is *Nine Princes in Amber* (**1970**), *The Guns of Avalon* (**1972**), *Sign of the Unicorn* (**1975**), *The Hand of Oberon* (**1976**) and *The Courts of Chaos* (**1978**), all assembled as *The Chronicles of Amber* (omni in 2 vols **1979**). The 2nd, featuring Corwin's son Merlin, comprises *Trumps of Doom* (**1985**), *Blood of Amber* (**1986**), *Sign of Chaos* (**1987**), *Knight of Shadows* (**1989**) and *Prince of Chaos* (**1991**). There are 2 pendants, *A Rhapsody in Amber* (coll **1981** chap) and *Roger Zelazny's Visual Guide to Castle Amber* (**1988**) with Neil Randall. Like C.S. LEWIS's **Narnia**, the land of Amber exists on a plane of greater fundamental reality than Earth, and provides normal reality with its ontological base. Unlike Narnia, however, Amber is the Yin in the Yang of Chaos the father, with consequences very far from Christian, for the Universe so defined is both cyclical and eternally insecure; and Amber itself is dominated by a cabal of squabbling siblings whose quasi-Olympian feudings generate vast cat's-cradles and imperfect nestings of Story, out of which the fabric of lesser realities takes its shape. The **Amber** books constitute RZ's most substantial edifice, though not his finest work, which is sf. Other fantasies have been lesser.

RZ's first published story was "Passion Play" for *AMZ* in 1962, and for several years he was prolific in shorter forms, for a time using the pseudonym Harrison Denmark when stories piled up in *AMZ* and *Fantastic*, and doing his finest work at the novelette/ novella length; he assembled the best of this early work as *Four for Tomorrow* (coll **1967**; vt *A Rose for Ecclesiastes* 1969 UK) and *The Doors of His Face, the Lamps of His Mouth, and Other Stories* (coll **1971**). The magazine titles of his first 2 books were as well known as their book titles, and the awards given them were attached to the magazine titles. *This Immortal* (1965 *FSF* as ". . . And Call me Conrad"; exp **1966**) won the 1966 HUGO for Best Novel; *The Dream Master* (1965 *AMZ* as "He Who Shapes"; exp **1966**) – the magazine version was eventually released as *He Who Shapes* (**1989** dos) – won the 1966 NEBULA for Best Novella; and in the same year *The Doors of His Face, the Lamps of His Mouth* (1965 *FSF*; **1991** chap) won a Nebula for Best Novelette. Taken together, the 3 tales make up a portrait of RZ's central worlds, themes and protagonist, a portrait which would be repeated, with sometimes lessened force, for decades. The VENUS on which "Doors" is set, like most of RZ's worlds to come, is fantastical, densely described, almost entirely "unscientific"; the plot intoxicatingly dashes together myth and literary assonances – in this case Herman MELVILLE's *Moby-Dick* (**1851**) – and sex. *This Immortal* takes place in a baroquely described post-HOLOCAUST Earth which has become a kind of theme-park for the ALIEN Vegans; in this shadowy realm of belatedness and human angst, the immortal Conrad Nomikos serves ostensibly as Arts Commissioner but turns out to be in a far more telling sense the curator of the human enterprise, for, despite the US thriller idioms he uses in his personal speech, he closely resembles Herakles – whose Labours the plot of the novel covertly replicates – but is certainly both the Hero of a Thousand Faces and the Trickster who mocks the high road of myth, redeemer and road-runner both. Under various names, this basic figure crops up in most of RZ's later books: wisecracking, melancholic, romantic, sentimental, lonely, meta-morphosing into higher states whenever necessary to cope with the plot, and in almost every sense an astonishingly sophisticated wish-fulfilment.

In *The Dream Master* – for one of the few times in his career – RZ presented the counter-myth, the story of the metamorphosis which fails, the transcendence which collapses back into the mortal world. In *This Immortal*, RS had already evinced a tendency to side, perhaps a little too openly, with complexly gifted, vain, dominating, immortal protagonists, and, as *The Dream Master* begins, his treatment of psychiatrist Charles Render seems no different. Render is emi-nent in the new field of neuroparticipant psychiatry, in which the healer actually enters the mindspace of his patient – which is laid out like a Jungian tournament of the cohorts of the self – and takes therapeutic action from within this VIRTUAL REALITY. But Render becomes hubristic, and when he enters the mind of a congenitally blind woman, who is both extremely intelligent and insane, his attempts to cope with her intricate madness from within gradually expose his own deficiencies as a person, and he becomes subtly and terrifyingly trapped in a highly plausible psychic cul-de-sac. All the sf apparatus of the story, and its sometimes overly baroque manner, were integrated into RZ's once-only unveiling of the nature of a human hero who could not perform the moult into immortality.

After these triumphs, *Lord of Light* (**1967**), which won a 1968 Hugo, could have seemed anticlimactic, but it is in fact his most sustained single tale, richly conceived and plotted, exhilarating throughout its considerable length. Some of the crew of a human colony ship, which has deposited its settlers on a livable world, have made use of advanced technology to ensconce themselves in the role of gods, selecting those of the Hindu pantheon as models. But where there is Hinduism, the Buddha – in the shape of the protagonist Sam – must follow; and his liberation of the humans of the planet, who are mortal descendants of the original settlers, takes on aspects of both Prometheus and Coyote the Trickster. At points, Sam may seem just another of RZ's stable of slangy, raunchy, over-loved immortals; but the end effect of the book is liberating, wise, lucid.

None of RZ's subsequent sf quite achieved the metaphorical aptness of his first 3 novels, but *Isle of the Dead* (1969) and *Creatures of Light and Darkness* (1969) both embody complex plots, mythic resonance and a fluent intensity of language. *Damnation Alley* (1969), a darker and coarser tale, depicts a post-holocaust motor-cycle-trek across a vicious USA; it was filmed with many changes as DAMNATION ALLEY (1977). *Jack of Shadows* (1971), though set on a planet which keeps one face always to its sun, has all the tonality and dream-like plotting of a fantasy: a fine one.

From the mid-1970s on, RZ's work maintained a certain consistency, and always threatened to explode in the mind's eye; but did not quite do so. *Deus Irae* (1976), with Philip K. DICK, is uneasy. *Doorways in the Sand* (1976) is a delightfully complicated chase tale, involving a McGUFFIN and an entire galactic community. *My Name is Legion* (fixup 1976) – which included the Hugo- and Nebula-winning *Home is the Hangman* (1975 ASF; 1990 chap dos) – puts into definitive form the Chandleresque version of the RZ HERO. *Roadmarks* (1979) engrossingly fleshes out the notion that the turnings off a metaphysical freeway might constitute turnings in time not space. *The Last Defender of Camelot* (1980 chap), which became the title story of *The Last Defender of Camelot* (coll 1980; with 4 stories added, exp 1981), *Unicorn Variations* (coll 1983), which included the Hugo-winning "Unicorn Variation" (1981), and *Frost and Fire* (coll 1989) – which contained "24 Views of Mount Fuji" (1985) and "Permafrost" (1986), both Hugo-winners – represent competent later short stories. *Eye of Cat* (1982) is a proficient sf thriller with a striking alien and some effective Navajo venues. Had it not been for the romantic sublimities of his first years, RZ's career might have been seen as triumphant.

He is not, however, regarded as a writer whose later works have fulfilled his promise, and it may be that he has suffered the inevitable price of writing at the peak of intensity and conviction when young: that he may already have put into definitive form the heart of what exercises him as a man and as a writer. The plummets into INNER SPACE, the sensitized baroque intricacy of his rendering of the immortal longings of men who all too easily slip into secret-

guardian routines, the rush into metamorphosis: all have had their cost. Though his **Amber** books and some other fantasies (see listing below) exhibit a sustained freshness, RZ's sf readership has been left with the inspired facility of an extremely intelligent writer who does not desperately need to utter another word. [JC]

Other works: *Today We Choose Faces* (1973); *To Die in Italbar* (1973), featuring **Francis Sandow**, the protagonist of *Isle of the Dead*; *Poems* (coll 1974 chap); *Bridge of Ashes* (1976); *The Illustrated Zelazny* (graph coll 1978; rev vt *The Authorized Illustrated Book of Roger Zelazny* 1979); the **Changing Land** sequence, comprising *The Bells of Shoredan* (1966 *Fantastic*; 1979 chap), *The Changing Land* (1981) and *Dilvish, the Damned* (coll of linked stories 1982); *For a Breath I Tarry* (1966 NW; 1980 chap); *When Pussywillows Last in the Catyard Bloomed* (coll 1980 chap), poetry; the **Wizard World** sequence, comprising *Changeling* (1980) and *Madwand* (1981), both assembled as *Wizard World* (omni 1989); *Today We Choose Faces/Bridge of Ashes* (omni 1981); *To Spin is Miracle Cat* (coll 1981), poems; *Coils* (1982) with Fred SABERHAGEN; *A Dark Traveling* (1987), a juvenile; *The Black Throne* (1990) with Saberhagen, a RECURSIVE fantasy starring Edgar Allan POE; *The Mask of Loki* (1990) with Thomas T. THOMAS; *The Graveyard Heart* (1964 AMZ; 1990 chap dos); *Bring Me the Head of Prince Charming* (1991) with Robert SHECKLEY; *Gone to Earth* (coll dated 1991 but 1992); «Flare» (1992) with Thomas, describing a deadly solar flare.

As editor: *Nebula Award Stories Three* (anth 1968).

About the author: "Faust & Archimedes" in *The Jewel-Hinged Jaw: Notes on the Language of Science Fiction* (coll 1977) by Samuel R. DELANY; Introduction by Ormond Seavey to the 1976 GREGG PRESS printing of *The Dream Master*; *Roger Zelazny* (1980) by Carl B. YOKE; *Roger Zelazny: A Primary and Secondary Bibliography* (1980) by Joseph L. Sanders; *A Checklist of Roger Zelazny* (1990 chap) by Christopher P. STEPHENS.

See also: ACE BOOKS; AMAZING STORIES; ASTOUNDING SCIENCE-FICTION; COMICS; CRIME AND PUNISHMENT; CYBERNETICS; ESCHATOLOGY; ESP; FANTASY; GALAXY SCIENCE FICTION; GAMES AND SPORTS; GODS AND DEMONS; GOTHIC SF; IMMORTALITY; ISAAC ASIMOV'S SCIENCE FICTION MAGAZINE; *The* MAGAZINE OF FANTASY AND SCIENCE FICTION; MARS; MATTER TRANSMISSION; MESSIAHS; MUSIC; OMNI; PARALLEL WORLDS; PARANOIA; PARASITISM AND SYMBIOSIS; PSI POWERS; REINCARNATION; RELIGION; ROBOTS; SCIENCE FANTASY; SUPERMAN; SUPERNATURAL CREATURES; TERRAFORMING; UNDER THE SEA.

ZERO POPULATION GROWTH ◊ Z.P.G.

ZERWICK, CHLOE (1923-) US writer and editor who collaborated with Harrison BROWN (*whom see for details*) on *The Cassiopeia Affair* (1968). [JC]

ZETFORD, TULLY ◊ Kenneth BULMER.

ZHURAVLYOVA, VALENTINA [r] ◊ Genrikh ALTOV.

ZIESING, MARK V. [r] ◊ MARK V. ZIESING.

ZIFF-DAVIS US magazine-publishing house, based in Chicago until 1950, then New York. It entered the sf field in 1938 when it bought AMAZING STORIES from

Teck Publishing Corp, New York, the 1st Z-D issue being April 1938, ed Raymond A. PALMER under Bernard G. Davis (the Davis of Ziff-Davis) as editor-in-chief. Under Palmer and later Howard BROWNE, *AMZ* was the most juvenile and lurid of the pulp SF MAGAZINES. The Z-D stable was expanded in May 1939 with the founding of a new title, FANTASTIC ADVENTURES, also lurid. Local Chicago writers, many of them hacks, churned out material for Z-D at immense speed, and often under the huge variety of house names that characterized these magazines and made them a bibliographer's nightmare: Chester S. GEIER, David Wright O'BRIEN, Rog PHILLIPS, Leroy YERXA and many others whose work was hardly known outside the Z-D publications. Covers were colourful, to the say the least, J. Allen ST. JOHN being especially notable in this regard; Robert FUQUA was also a regular cover artist and Rod RUTH drew many interior illustrations.

As the pulp era drew to a close in the 1950s, many sf magazines failed, and others converted to the DIGEST format, as *AMZ* did in 1953. By then Z-D had founded a new digest magazine, FANTASTIC, in 1952. This covered similar ground to *Fantastic Adventures*, which it absorbed in 1953. The only sf/fantasy addition to the stable thereafter was the short-lived DREAM WORLD, ed Paul W. FAIRMAN, in 1957, though Z-D did publish occasional COMICS titles, like *Space Patrol* in 1952. Stories created by factory-production techniques continued in the new digest magazines, now based in New York; Robert SILVERBERG was one who learned his craft in the 1950s by being slotted into the assembly line. Both *AMZ* and *Fantastic* improved enormously under the editorship of Cele GOLDSMITH 1958-65, but it was too late. Bernard G. Davis had left in the 1950s, and fiction magazines were becoming anomalies in the Z-D line-up, now largely concentrated (because of the potential for advertising revenue) on specialist nonfiction magazines like *Popular Photography* and *Popular Electronics*. *Fantastic* and *AMZ* were sold in 1965 to Sol Cohen's Ultimate Publishing Co., where he made a good thing for years recycling Z-D backlist stories in new magazines, as well as continuing the 2 main titles. The newly married Goldsmith stayed with Z-D to work on *Modern Bride*. Bernard Davis's son Joel went on to form his own publishing company, Davis Publications, which founded ISAAC ASIMOV'S SCIENCE FICTION MAGAZINE and later bought *ASF*. The Davis sf dynasty, therefore, continued, in a much different guise, until 1992, when Dell Magazines bought both journals. [PN]

ZILLIG, WERNER [r] ◊ GERMANY.

ZIMMER, PAUL EDWIN (1943-   ) US writer, brother of Marion Zimmer BRADLEY, with whom he wrote his first sf, the 2nd vol of the **Survivors** sequence, *The Survivors* (**1979**), a somewhat congested sf adventure. A series by PEZ alone, the **Dark Border** sequence – *The Lost Prince* (**1982**), *King Chondo's Ride* (**1982**) and *A Gathering of Heroes* (**1987**) – is fantasy, as are his singletons *Woman of the Elfmounds* (dated 1979 but **1980**), *Blood of the Colyn Muir* (**1988**) with Jon DeCles, and *Ingulf the Mad* (**1989**). [JC]

ZINDELL, DAVID (1952-   ) US writer with a degree in mathematics who began publishing sf with "The Dreamer's Sleep" for *Fantasy Book* in 1984, though his career properly began when he won the WRITERS OF THE FUTURE CONTEST with "Shanidar" (1985). His 1st novel was the long and remarkable *Neverness* (**1988**), an extremely ambitious example of the tale of cosmogony (a tale – usually containing some plot mixture of SPACE OPERA and PLANETARY ROMANCE – whose protagonist's life leads to an encounter with questions about the origins, the ontological nature and the end of the Galaxy or Universe). The young protagonist has all the necessary complexity and drivenness to occupy centre-stage "cosmogony opera"; indeed, as he recollects his cruel and ornate life at a distance of some years, Mallory Ringess may for some readers too much resemble the Severian of Gene WOLFE's **The Book of the New Sun** (**1980-83**), though he does eventually establish his own chilly selfhood. The planet in which the city of Neverness nestles is drawn with a long-breathed relish reminiscent of Wolfe's own model, Jack VANCE; the growth to manhood of Ringess in this environment is expressed with cold ornateness, an assiduous attention to character and a sense of immanent significance. As space-pilot in the Order of Mystic Mathematicians and Other Seekers of the Ineffable Flame, Ringess eventually becomes involved in a search for the Elder Eddas which bear messages of import about reality; encounters an entity whose brain is composed of moon-sized ganglia; betrays, comes to understand, and saves himself; and penetrates the eons-deep secrets of the nature of things. The author of *Neverness* is romantic, ambitious, and skilled. A projected second novel is awaited with eagerness. [JC]

See also: BIG DUMB OBJECTS; COMMUNICATIONS; DEVOLUTION; FASTER THAN LIGHT; GODS AND DEMONS; MATHEMATICS; MUSIC; PSEUDO-SCIENCE.

ZINOVIEV, ALEXANDER (1922-   ) Russian writer whose *Ziyayushchie Vysoty* (**1976** Switzerland; trans Gordon Clough as *The Yawning Heights* **1979** US) clearly models the closed DYSTOPIAN society at its heart upon the gerontocracy which then dominated the USSR. [JC]

ZÍTRA VSTANU A OPAŘÍM SE ČAJEM (vt *Tomorrow I'll Wake up and Scald Myself with Tea*) Film (1977). Filmové studio Barrandov. Dir Jindřich Polák, starring Petr Kostka, Jiří Sovák, Vladimír Menšík, Vlastimil Brodský. Screenplay Polák, Miloš Macourek, based on a story by Josef NESVADBA. 90 mins. Colour.

Not widely known in the West (although it has been given a UK tv showing), this Czech production is one of the most sophisticated TIME-TRAVEL films yet made, written by a team whose members all have ample sf experience (◊ CZECH AND SLOVAK SF). The insanely convoluted comic story, with a richer use of TIME PARADOXES than is ever seen in Western sf cinema, involves going back in time to give the H-bomb to Hitler. Though farcical, it throws up interesting questions of causality. Polák also dir IKARIE XB-1 (1963), and Macourek, who has been involved with many of the best Czech sf comedies, codir KDO CHCE ZABÍT JESSII? (1965). [PN]

ŽIVKOVIĆ, ZORAN (1948-) Yugoslav sf publisher and researcher, based in Belgrade. He received his doctorate at Belgrade University in 1982; a version of his dissertation, "The Appearance of Science Fiction as a Genre of Artistic Prose", was published in his *Savremenici budućnosti* ["Contemporaries of the Future"] (anth **1983**) along with some of the stories he discusses. He has translated about 50 sf books and published more than 100 under his **Polaris** imprint, the first privately owned sf publishing house (founded 1982) in YUGOSLAVIA. *Zvezdani ekran* ["The Starry Screen"] (**1984**) is a book about sf cinema, based on the tv series of the same title which he wrote and hosted. His most ambitious work is the 2-vol *Enciklopedija naučne fantastike* ["Encyclopedia of Science Fiction"] (**1990**). He wrote the YUGOSLAVIA entry in this volume. [PN]

ZOLA, ÉMILE (ÉDOUARD CHARLES ANTOINE) (1840-1902) French writer whose long and intense **Rougon-Macquart** sequence of Naturalist novels (1871-93) includes tales like *Nana* (**1880**; trans E.A. Vizetelly **1884** UK), for which he was once notorious. EZ is of sf interest for *Vérité* (**1903**; trans E.A. Vizetelly as *Truth* **1903** UK), the 3rd vol of his unfinished **Les Quatre Évangiles** ["The Four Evangelists"] quartet, which was planned to espouse a kind of Tolstoyan socialism. The action in *Truth* extends to 1980, and there are hints of advanced TECHNOLOGIES. [JC]

ZOLINE, PAMELA Working name of US painter and writer Pamela Lifton-Zoline (1941-), in the UK 1963-86. She illustrated, in a collage-derived style, several stories for *NW* in the late 1960s, including the magazine publication of Thomas M. DISCH's *Camp Concentration* (**1968** UK). Her début sf story, "The Heat Death of the Universe" (1967 *NW*), is a finely structured application of the concept of ENTROPY to the life of a US housewife, through whose perceptions its rise is experienced literally. The story appeared in PZ's 1st collection, *Busy About the Tree of Life and Other Stories* (coll **1988** UK; vt *The Heat Death of the Universe and Other Stories* 1988 US); the long story which gives its title to the UK edn is also sf. With John T. SLADEK, PZ ed both issues of and contributed to *Ronald Reagan: The Magazine of Poetry* (**1968**); other contributors included Disch and J.G. BALLARD. In Telluride, Colorado, she has since 1986 written, designed and produced sf plays for the Muddbutt Mystery Theatre. [JC]
Other works: *Annika and the Wolves* (**1985** chap US), a children's fantasy.
See also: COSMOLOGY; OULIPO.

ZOMBIE ◊ DAWN OF THE DEAD.
ZOMBIES ◊ DAWN OF THE DEAD.
ZONE TROOPERS Film (1985). Altar/Empire. Execu-

tive prod Charles BAND. Dir Danny Bilson, starring Tim Thomerson, Timothy Van Patten, Art La Fleur, Biff Maynard. Screenplay Bilson, Paul DeMeo. 86 mins. Colour.

This curious, small, honest film is as close as the cinema has ever got to the flavour of pulp sf. Three GIs and a war correspondent are trapped behind German lines in Italy in 1944. In between repeated clashes with Germans they befriend a BEM – female, we later learn – from a crashed spaceship, whom the Germans wish to interrogate. All is played straight and gung-ho, catching delightfully the tone of 1940s war films. The film ends appropriately with a shot of a (phony) PULP-MAGAZINE cover, *Fantastic Fiction*. [PN]

ZOOL, M.H. Group pseudonym used by members of the Oxford University Speculative Fiction Group for the *Bloomsbury Good Reading Guide to Science Fiction and Fantasy* (**1989**), a compact and knowledgeable biographical and bibliographical dictionary whose usefulness would have been considerably enhanced had its authors been granted more space. The main editors/authors involved were Neal Tringham (1966-), Ivan Towlson (1967-) and Mo Holkar (1967-). Both Tringham, as writer of several entries, and Holkar, as coordinator of entries from other members of the Speculative Fiction Group (not all of them part of the original Zool enterprise), have participated in this encyclopedia, as have Zool participants Tim Adye (1964-), Matthew Bishop (1968-), Adrian Cox (1968-) and Penelope Heal (1970-); other members of the Zool enterprise included John Bray, Malcolm Cohen, Paul Cray, Melanie Dymond, Paul Marrow and Simon McLeish. [JC]

Z.P.G. (vt *Zero Population Growth* UK) Film (1971). Sagittarius/Paramount. Dir Michael Campus, starring Oliver Reed, Geraldine Chaplin, Diane Cilento, Don Gordon. Screenplay Max EHRLICH, Frank DeFelitta. 97 mins. Colour.

This film was a product of a period when, not before time, the question of OVERPOPULATION had almost overnight become a matter much publicized by the media, books like Paul Ehrlich's *The Population Bomb* (**1968**) had become bestsellers, and the Club of Rome was about to publish a very alarmist report in *The Limits to Growth* (**1972**). "Zero population growth" is a term which refers to a situation where the population of a society remains steady, neither increasing nor decreasing. But the screenwriters of Z.P.G. assume, absurdly, that it means nobody having any children at all during the 30-year period of a world government's ban. A married couple defy the edict and have a baby secretly. They are betrayed by a jealous neighbour, but escape the authorities by descending into a sewer. Where they escape to is not explained. The novelization is *The Edict* * (**1971**) by Ehrlich. [JB/PN]

ZSCHOKKE, HEINRICH [r] ◊ GERMANY.
ZSOLDOS, PÉTER [r] ◊ HUNGARY.
ZULAWSKI, JERZY (1874-1915) Polish playwright,

poet and novelist, of sf interest for his untranslated trilogy about the colonization of the MOON: *Na Srebrnym Globie* ["On Silver Globe"] (**1901**), *Zwycięzca* ["The Victor"] (**1908**) and *Stara Ziemia* ["Old Earth"] (**1910**) (◊ POLAND). [PN/JC]

ŻWIKIEWICZ, WIKTOR [r] ◊ POLAND.